# Chambers Crossword Dictionary

Chambers

CHAMBERS
An imprint of Chambers Harrap Publishers Ltd
338 Euston Road, London, NW1 3BH

*Chambers Harrap Publishers Ltd is an Hachette UK Company*



This second edition published by Chambers Harrap Publishers Ltd 2007
Hardback edition published 2006
Previous edition published 2000



A CIP catalogue record for this book is available from the British Library.

ISBN 978 0550 10341 3



www.chambers.co.uk

Designed and typeset by Chambers Harrap Publishers Ltd
Printed and bound in the UK by Clays Ltd, St Ives plc

# Contributors

*Chambers Editor*
Hazel Norris

*Editors*
Derek Arthur
Ross Beresford

*Consultants*
Derek Arthur
Ross Beresford
Jonathan Crowther
Don Manley
Tim Moorey

*Contributors*
Vicky Aldus
Katie Brooks

*Crossword Essays*
Jonathan Crowther
Don Manley
Tim Moorey

*Data Management*
Patrick Gaherty

*Prepress Controllers*
Nicolas Echallier
Susan Lawrie
Isla MacLean

*Prepress Manager*
Clair Simpson

*Publishing Manager*
Patrick White

*The editors would like to thank the contributors to The Chambers Thesaurus, Chambers Crossword Lists and Chambers Concise Crossword Dictionary, extracts from which have been used in this text.*

# Preface

Solving crosswords is, by all accounts, an enjoyable way of spending one's leisure hours. More than 80 years after crosswords first appeared in the newspapers, and despite the temptations of sudoku and other puzzles, the crossword is still our favourite pastime. Yet so often crossword-solving can become a frustrating experience, accompanied by the gritting of teeth, the tearing-out of hair and the grumpy tossing aside of pens, as the clues prove baffling and the squares remain mockingly empty. *Chambers Crossword Dictionary* is a balm and a help for exactly those moments, providing as it does a wealth of potential solutions to even the thorniest and most apparently impenetrable clues.

That this new edition has undergone something of a quiet revolution will swiftly become apparent to those familiar with its previous incarnation. It has been thoroughly revised and massively expanded, and now includes more than 500,000 possible solutions to quick and cryptic clues, arranged in more than 19,600 entries. The entries comprise not only thesaurus-style synonyms, but also more than 1,200 reference lists of encyclopedic information, from famous pirates to ancient cities, baseball terms to types of grass. A list of the headwords at which these may be found is given on p.xlv.

*Chambers Crossword Dictionary* draws on material from across the authoritative Chambers reference range, and notably contains many thousands of terms from *The Chambers Dictionary*, including many of the archaic, literary and obscure words so beloved of cryptic crossword compilers. This new edition also makes use of the Chambers clue database, a huge and ever-growing record of the way words are actually used in crosswords. You will now find included abbreviations, symbols, codes and typical crossword jargon, such as 'AB' for 'sailor', or 'flower' to mean 'river'.

A new feature is the inclusion of 'indicators' denoting terms that may be used in a cryptic clue to show that a word or words should be reversed, anagrammatized or otherwise manipulated. For those new to cryptic crosswords, or wishing to brush up on their understanding, a new article that explains how indicators are used in cryptic clues may be found on p.xxvi, while lists of words that may be used as indicators are given on p.xxxiii.

Additional insights into the world of cruciverbalism are given in our highly-regarded introductory essays. 'The art of the crossword setter' by Jonathan Crowther offers an insight into the creation of these puzzles, while 'Crossword English' by Don Manley explains the types of clues that might be encountered and offers advice on how to approach the solving of cryptic crosswords. Tim Moorey writes on 'The art of the crossword clue', discussing the qualities that make for a memorable clue and offering examples of the finest clues so far devised.

This new edition of *Chambers Crossword Dictionary* has benefited immeasurably from the thoughtful advice and skilful editing of Ross Beresford and Derek Arthur, respectively a former and current co-editor of *The Listener* crossword in *The Times*. Their expertise is unsurpassed and their contribution throughout the project has been invaluable. We are also grateful to the previous edition's crossword consultants, Jonathan Crowther and Don Manley, and to Tim Moorey who joined the team for this second edition; their authoritative comments have shaped and immensely improved the dictionary. Finally, we would like to thank the many other people who have been involved in the preparation of this book, and also those who contributed to the first edition, notably Una McGovern and the late Catherine Schwarz. However, any errors, infelicities or omissions remain the sole responsibility of the publishers.

We warmly welcome all comments and suggestions from members of the public, which will be considered for incorporation in future editions. These should be sent to The Editor, *Chambers Crossword Dictionary*, Chambers Harrap Publishers Ltd, 7 Hopetoun Crescent, Edinburgh, EH7 4AY.

*The Publishers*
*Edinburgh, 2006*

**Chambers Crossword Consultants**

**Derek Arthur** is the co-editor of the challenging *Listener* crossword, which appears weekly in *The Times*; this series extends the cryptic crossword format, using themes from literature, science, logic and elsewhere.

**Ross Beresford** is a former co-editor of the *Listener* crossword in *The Times*. He is the author of the widely-used 'TEA & Sympathy' crossword software.

**Jonathan Crowther** is better known to cryptic crossword solvers as Azed, having set crosswords for *The Observer* for 35 years. One of the most highly regarded of all setters, he has also compiled puzzles under the pseudonyms Gong and Ozymandias.

**Don Manley** sets crosswords under a variety of pseudonyms (Bradman, Duck, Giovanni, Pasquale and Quixote) for many national newspapers (including *The Times*, *The Guardian*, *The Independent on Sunday*, the *Financial Times* and *The Sunday Telegraph*).

**Tim Moorey** sets crosswords as part of the Mephisto team for *The Sunday Times* and as Owzat elsewhere. He is the crossword editor of *The Week*, gives talks on crosswords and runs regular crossword workshops.

# Introduction

*Chambers Crossword Dictionary* contains more than 500,000 possible solutions to quick and cryptic crossword clues. It draws on *The Chambers Dictionary, The Chambers Thesaurus* and other books in the Chambers reference range; it also uses the Chambers crossword clue database.

It does not contain definitions, parts of speech, usage labels or similar material. To check the exact meaning of a word or phrase, a dictionary such as *The Chambers Dictionary* is recommended.

This Introduction contains the following information:



## Content

Entries in the *Crossword Dictionary* include both single words and phrases. Also included are abbreviations, short forms, acronyms, symbols, codes and the like, for the answers to crossword clues are often built up from these small pieces. Solvers will also find crossword jargon, such as 'tar' under 'sailor' and 'goat' under 'butter'. Anagrams, however, have not been included; so, for example, an entry for 'rotten time' would not list 'emit'.

Consideration has been given to the differing needs of various kinds of crosswords, from concise to advanced cryptics, and nothing has been excluded simply on the grounds of obscurity. Archaic, dialect, literary and uncommon words have been included, as these are often found in a variety of crosswords, not just (although undoubtedly most frequently) in advanced cryptics such as Azed in *The Observer* and *The Listener* in *The Times*. An emphasis has been placed on unusual short words with helpful letter sequences – for example 'tana' under 'police station' – as these often form the 'building blocks' which make up a cryptic solution. Variant spellings listed in *The Chambers Dictionary* have often been included. Where a usage is dubious but technically possible, as with an archaic variant of a synonym where it is unclear whether the variant is also synonymous with the headword, a degree of leniency has been employed.

The content of the *Crossword Dictionary* is broadly international in scope, with words from Australian, New Zealand, American, Anglo-Indian and other varieties of English included. Some common short foreign words sometimes found in crosswords are included too, such as 'mer' under 'sea' or 'ici' under 'here'.

Synonyms which are only loosely associated with the headword have not been included (for example 'twelfth' will not be found at 'grouse'). However, some names are included, as crossword convention allows references to people by first name or surname; for example 'Berlin' with the synonym 'Irving', 'Lincoln' for 'Abe' or 'Milne' for 'AA'. While a smattering of those most commonly found have been included, the list is not exhaustive and there will be others.

There is debate in crossword circles over what constitutes a 'sound' clue, and some crossword setters and editors do not employ particular uses of words or senses which others consider to be permissible. So as to be of maximum use to solvers of crosswords from a variety of sources, terms have been included in this book even if frowned upon by some. However, some usages considered to be especially contentious (usually as a result of word spacing and grammatical links having been ignored) have not been included, such as 'G' for 'Gateshead', 'm' for 'topmast' or 'fats' for 'breakfast'.

No attempt has been made to ensure that entries are 'symmetrical', ie that a synonym found under one headword (for example 'lucky') will also be found under another broadly synonymous entry (for example 'fortunate'). Since it is impossible to anticipate every reference a clue-writer will come up with, there are bound to be gaps. This deficiency can be mitigated by searching under different headwords, and there may be hints to be picked up from what is given. For example, the entry for 'swimmer' lists 'fish' as a synonym, which suggests that looking at the main entry for 'fish' may be helpful; here the intended solution, say 'eel', may be found.

Plural and inflected forms of words have generally not been given. Solvers should remember that if the wording of a cryptic clue suggests that a plural or verb form is required, they may need to pluralize or otherwise inflect a possible solution found in this *Dictionary*. Some abbreviations listed in the *Dictionary* stand for both singular and plural forms of a word (for example 'kg' can be kilogram or kilograms). For parts of cryptic solutions, plural and other forms may not be straightforward; for example, where 'duck' can conventionally be 'O', then 'ducks' in a clue may indicate 'Os' or 'OO'. This may also be encountered with the reference list of collective nouns, as setters may use 'crows', for example, for 'murder'.

This is also true for comparatives and superlatives; if a clue says 'more' or 'most', for example, it may be that an -er or -est ending needs to be added (for example 'more sensible' for 'saner' or 'most stupid' for 'dopiest'). Similarly, solvers should bear in mind that 'not' may be used in a clue to indicate the prefix 'un-' (for example 'not hidden' for 'unconcealed'), that 'again' may be used for the prefix 're-' (for example 'publish again' for 'reissue'), and so on.

Numbers, and terms which include both numbers and letters, have been included in many instances as some – although not all – setters and editors allow the number 1 to be converted to the letter I (as in the Roman numeral). Thus, 'M1' may be rendered as part of a solution as 'MI', and '1st' as 'IST'.

## Word forms

The forms *-ize* and *-ization* are used throughout, but the alternative *-ise* or *-isation* spellings may be needed for the solutions to some crossword clues.

Similarly, the form 'your' is used in place of 'one's' in phrases such as 'put your foot down'. Solvers should remember that 'one's' may be required instead for a crossword solution. In some instances this may be reflected in the indication of word-length given in a clue: for example, 'sure of yourself' would be denoted as (4,2,8), hence listed here under **14**, whereas 'sure of oneself' would be (4,2,7), which would have been **13**.

Italics have not been used, even where conventionally a word or letter is italicized. This may be noted especially in relation to physics terms, for example, under 'Boltzmann constant' the symbol 'k' is given in roman type, whereas in *The Chambers Dictionary* it is italicized as *k*. Similarly, titles of novels and films, names of ships and other similar instances will all be found in roman type.

Where words can be hyphenated (as a noun) or unhyphenated (as a phrasal verb) both forms are usually included in synonym lists (for example 'back-up' and 'back up' at 'second').

## Word length

The words and phrases given in this dictionary contain 15 letters or fewer, reflecting the most commonly used crossword grids. However, where a list represents a closed set, that is, where a list is clearly defined and limited, then all relevant terms have been included regardless of length. For example, all of the US states and all of the plays of Shakespeare have been included, even though some of these are longer than 15 letters in length.

## Organization of entries

Within the dictionary, words have been sorted into over 19,600 one-stop alphabetical entries by meaning or subject category. Entries provide a range of words that are relevant to the headword, in two types of list:

- synonym lists, which present words with similar meanings to the headword
- reference lists, which present encyclopedic information related to the headword, such as people's names, place names and types of item

Some entries include only one type of list, whereas others include a range of synonyms plus one or more reference lists. For example:

**abbey**
**03** Abb **06** abbacy, friary, priory
**07** convent, minster, nunnery
**08** cloister, seminary **09** cathedral, monastery

*Abbeys include:*

**04** Bath, Iona
**05** Cluny, Kelso, Meaux, Roche, Royal
**06** Bolton, Byland, Hexham, Whitby, Woburn
**07** Citeaux, Furness, Melrose, Tintern, Waltham
**08** Buckfast, Crowland, Dryburgh, Fontenay, Fonthill, Holyrood, Jedburgh, Newstead, Rievaulx
**09** Clairvaux, Fountains, Holy Cross, Kirkstall, Nightmare, Sherborne
**10** Malmesbury, Northanger
**11** Westminster

Reference lists always follow thesaurus-style lists.

Within entries, words are grouped firstly by length, that is by the total number of letters in each word or phrase, and then ordered alphabetically within these word-length sections:

**aisle**
**04** lane, path **07** gangway, passage, walkway **08** alleyway, corridor
**10** passageway **12** deambulatory

Alphabetization is strictly by letter, and some stylistic conventions have been disregarded: for example, 'Mc' will be found at 'Mc' rather than mingled with 'Mac'.

No distinction is made between parts of speech, or between homonyms (words spelled the same but with different meanings), as crossword setters play on multiple meanings and possible ambiguity in clues. For example, the entry for 'rebel' lists synonyms for the adjective, verb and noun senses:

**rebel**
◇ *anagram indicator*
**04** defy, riot **06** flinch, mutine, mutiny, oppose, recoil, resist, revolt, rise up, shrink **07** aginner, beatnik, defiant, disobey, dissent, heretic, run riot, shy away **08** agitator, apostate, mutineer, mutinous, pull back, recusant, revolter **09** dissenter, guerrilla, insurgent **10** malcontent, rebellious, schismatic **11** disobedient, turn against **12** malcontented, paramilitary **13** insubordinate, nonconformist, revolutionary **14** freedom fighter **15** insurrectionary

and the entry for 'dock' presents synonyms for what are, in fact, three separate words, one being a type of plant, another meaning a wharf or to land at a wharf and the third meaning to cut short:

**dock**
◇ *tail deletion indicator*
**02** dk **03** bob, cut, pen **04** clip, crop, land, moor, pier, quay, rump **05** basin, berth, jetty, put in, Rumex, tie up, wharf **06** anchor, deduct, detail, lessen, marina, reduce, remove, sorrel **07** bistort, curtail, harbour, shorten **08** boat yard, canaigre, decrease, diminish, patience, quayside, subtract, truncate, withhold **09** grapetree, polygonum **10** drop anchor, tidal basin, waterfront **12** monk's rhubarb, submarine pen **15** fitting-out basin

Synonym lists for idioms and phrasal verbs derived from many of the headwords are also included and are marked by •:

**vouch**
**• vouch for**
**04** back **06** affirm, assert, assure, avouch, uphold, verify **07** certify, confirm, endorse, support, swear to, warrant **08** attest to, speak for **09** answer for, guarantee **10** asseverate

There may be more than one entry in the *Crossword Dictionary* for a word or phrasal verb. For example, 'shake up' appears as a phrasal verb at the entry for 'shake', but there is also an entry for the noun 'shake-up' as a headword in its own right.

Phrases, idioms and phrasal verbs have been located under the key headword contained and so should be found in an appropriate and intuitive place; *The Chambers Dictionary* has been followed in most instances. However, if a term cannot be found in the first place sought, solvers should try under other likely headwords.

## Expressions of ...

Interjections and similar terms related to emotions are often found in cryptic crossword clues and introduced by 'expression of...' or a similar phrase. In this *Dictionary* these are listed under the relevant headword; for example 'expression of hesitation' may require 'um' or 'er', and these can be found under the headword 'hesitation'.

If expressions relating to a particular emotion cannot be found in the first place sought, solvers should look under a likely alternative; for example, if seeking an 'expression of disapprobation' but finding nothing under 'disapprobation', solvers should then try 'disapproval'.

Lists of interjections, cries, shouts and expressions may be found at the following headwords:

| | | | |
|---|---|---|---|
| admiration | disgust | greeting | reproof |
| agreement | dismay | grief | resignation |
| annoyance | dismissal | hesitation | sarcasm |
| appreciation | dissatisfaction | hunting | scepticism |
| approval | distaste | impatience | silence |
| attention | doubt | invocation | stop |
| concession | drinking | joy | stupidity |
| contempt | emotion | misfortune | success |
| defiance | emphasis | pain | support |
| derision | encouragement | pleasure | surprise |
| disagreement | enthusiasm | praise | sympathy |
| disappointment | excitement | protest | triumph |
| disapproval | farewell | puzzlement | warning |
| disbelief | frenzy | realization | weariness |
| discovery | fright | regret | wonder |
| disdain | gratitude | relief | worry |

## Indicators

Terms which are often used as wordplay indicators in cryptic crossword clues are denoted with a diamond icon and the type of indicator – anagram, hidden, reversal, etc – is given:

**adrift**
◇ *anagram indicator*
**04** lost **05** at sea **07** aimless
**08** drifting, goalless, insecure, rootless
**09** off course, unsettled **10** anchorless, unanchored **11** disoriented
**13** directionless, disorientated

Some words can be used as indicators of more than one kind of word play:

**oddly**
◇ *anagram indicator*
◇ *hidden alternately indicator*
**07** weirdly **09** curiously, strangely, unusually **10** abnormally, remarkably
**11** irregularly

Indicators always follow the headword, idiom or phrasal verb. There may be instances in which an idiom or phrasal verb is followed only by an indicator, and not by synonym entries; this is because it was felt helpful to include the term for its usefulness as an indicator, but where it does not have synonyms in the usual way.

Indicators may not always appear in a cryptic clue in the way in which they appear in the *Dictionary,* but rather may be encountered in an inflected form: for example, 'digest' is marked as an anagram indicator, but solvers may be more likely to encounter it in a cryptic clue as 'digested'. While efforts have been made to denote all common indicators, the lists can never be exhaustive.

More information on the use of indicators in cryptic clues can be found on p.xxvi, and lists of words that may be used as indicators are given on p.xxxiii.

## Reference lists

The reference lists have been derived from *Chambers Crossword Lists* and from other authoritative Chambers reference databases. Lists are entered in the *Dictionary* at the appropriate headword; a list of the headwords at which they may be found is given on p.xlv.

The reference lists are not intended to be all-inclusive, but to strike a balance between comprehensiveness and the likelihood of the words and phrases actually occurring as the solutions to crossword clues. For more comprehensive reference lists, *Chambers Crossword Lists* is recommended.

The reference lists include both historical and current information; for example, in the list of actors are not only contemporary figures like Sir Ian McKellen and Robin Williams, but also notable actors from the past like Richard Burbage and Edward Alleyn. Similarly, the lists may contain both real and fictional or legendary items. For example, the list of heroes includes the legendary Robin Hood, the literary D'Artagnan, the historical William Wallace, the cinematic Indiana Jones and the comic strip Superman.

Reference lists have been subdivided to make finding information easier. For example, there is not one list of singers, but separate lists of classical, folk, jazz, opera, pop and other singers.

Some of the reference lists contain additional information in brackets following core information. For example, first names or nicknames are given in brackets following a surname. In such lists, the core term (the unbracketed term) is presented in bold type to make browsing easier:

*Pirates include:*

**03** **Tew** (Thomas)
**04** **Bart** (Jean), **Gunn** (Ben), **Hook** (Captain), **Kidd** (William), **Otto**, **Read** (Mary), **Smee**
**05** **Barth** (Jean), **Bones** (Billy), **Bonny** (Anne), **Bunce** (Jack), **Drake** (Sir Francis), **Every** (Henry), **Ewart** (Nanty), **Flint** (Captain), **Tache** (Edward), **Teach** (Edward)
**06** **Aubery** (Jean-Benoit), **Conrad**, **Jonsen** (Captain), **Morgan** (Sir Henry), **Silver** (Long John), **Thatch** (Edward), **Walker** (William)
**07** **Dampier** (William), **Lafitte** (Jean), **O'Malley** (Grace), **Rackham** (John), **Roberts** (Bartholomew), **Sparrow** (Captain Jack), **Trumpet** (Solomon)
**08** **Altamont** (Frederick), **Black Dog**, **Blackett** (Nancy), **Blackett** (Peggy), **Blind Pew**, **Redbeard**, **Ringrose** (Basil)
**09** **Black Bart**, **Cleveland** (Clement)
**10** **Barbarossa** (Khair-ed-din), **Blackbeard**, **Calico Jack**
**14** **Long John Silver**

Additional bracketed information is not included in the word-length count although it may form part of the solution to some crossword clues. The regnal numbers of individual popes, queens and kings have generally been omitted.

Common generic terms have often been omitted from the names and terms presented in reference lists, to avoid unwieldy and unnecessary repetition. For example, the word 'abbey' has not been included in names in the list of abbeys, and the word 'saw' has been omitted from the list of saws. Users should be aware that these terms may form part of the solution to some crossword clues.

The reference material has been selected to be as wide-ranging in scope as possible. Solvers should note that:

- numbers may be found in solutions in some instances, as numbers may be encountered or referenced in some form in cryptic puzzles. For example, the list of films includes *2001: A Space Odyssey* and *Apollo 13*.

- some items are included under a certain headword on the grounds of usefulness, even if they are not strictly types of the headword. For example, 'Washington DC' is included in the list of US states and 'tomato' is included in the list of vegetables. Similarly, items which are related to the headword may be included; succulents in the list of cacti, for example.
- variant spellings have been included, for example 'topi' and 'topee' in the list of hats.

In some entries without a distinct reference list, both synonyms and reference-list type information may be found intermingled.

## Cross-references

*Chambers Crossword Dictionary* is extensively cross-referenced to make finding solutions easy. There are two forms of cross-reference; those at main headwords directing users elsewhere:

> **lough** *see* **lake**

and those which suggest that additional information may be found at other entries:

> **petrol**
> **03** gas, LRP **05** ethyl, juice, super
> **08** gasolene, gasoline
> *See also* **fuel**

In many of the latter instances, the cross-reference directs solvers to a relevant reference list. It may also direct solvers to a similar but longer entry with additional synonyms, or may make explicit some crossword jargon or other slang; for example, a cross-reference at 'bloomer' to 'flower', or a cross-reference at 'stir' to 'prison'.

# The art of the crossword setter

## *Jonathan Crowther* (Azed of *The Observer*)

I am regularly asked – as often by people who habitually solve crosswords as by those who never do – how I set about compiling a puzzle, and especially what order I do things in. (The other commonly-asked question is how long each puzzle takes me, but I usually hedge when answering this one. A puzzle is best constructed over several sittings, and I have never bothered to calculate accurately the total time involved.) For most normal crosswords there are three distinct stages, each more time-consuming than the last: (i) constructing the grid pattern, (ii) filling this with words and (iii) writing the clues. The three stages demand different skills, and for this reason I often compartmentalize the first two, constructing several grid patterns at a sitting and then filling all of these with words before returning to the first grid to start the lengthier and more creative process of writing the clues. Let us now look at each stage in turn.

### Crossword grids

There is no absolute rule that crosswords should be symmetrical in design, ie with their blocked squares or bars arranged so that they look the same if the grid is turned upside down or if it is given a quarter-turn. The fact is that most are, and this is the widely-accepted norm. It is also aesthetically pleasing, by no means a negligible consideration. Most importantly, the grid design should ensure a range of entries of varying lengths and a fair distribution of unchecked letters (those which belong to only one word, across or down, and are not 'checked' by a word entered in the other direction). In general the number of unchecked letters is greater in a blocked grid than in a barred one. As a rule of thumb (though one that is regularly infringed by puzzles in a number of our national dailies), no more than half the letters of a solution should be unchecked in a blocked grid. In barred grids, like mine in *The Observer*, the solver can expect a more generous quota of cross-checked letters because such puzzles tend to use more rare and unusual words. In both types of puzzle the inclusion of consecutive unchecked letters in answers is considered bad practice and generally frowned on. It is all a question of fairness to the solver.

There is a fundamental difference in standard grid design between British-style and American-style crosswords. British crosswords, with their tradition of cryptic clues and unchecked letters, normally require the solver to solve every clue in order to complete the puzzle. In most American crosswords, whose clues are not cryptic in the British sense, there are proportionally far fewer blocked squares and they are arranged in such a way that *every* letter is cross-checked, so that, in theory at least, it is possible to complete a puzzle by solving only about half its clues.

In practice, setters of most normal blocked grids in daily or Sunday newspapers in both Britain and the US do not have to concern themselves with grid construction. Each paper uses a limited number of basic patterned grids to which the setter is restricted. In an age of ever-greater standardization this is perhaps inevitable, and it reduces the risk of error, but I still regard it as regrettable and am pleased that no such restriction is placed on me. I derive much satisfaction from exploring the many different grid designs possible within the established parameters: grid size (normally 12 × 12 in my case), number of entries (usually 36), a good spread of entry lengths, and a fair number of unchecked letters. My predecessor Derrick Macnutt (the legendary Ximenes) preferred to let his patterns grow, organically as it were, around the words he wanted to include in his puzzles, effectively merging my first two stages of crossword construction into a single process. My own routine is as I have described, since I start with no preconceptions as to the words I want to use, and this only goes to show that there is no universally prescribed method. There are also no Mosaic laws governing the *size* of crosswords. Blocked grids in daily papers are usually 15 × 15, with about 32 answers (16 across and 16 down), but recent years have seen a growth in the number of 'jumbo' puzzles (typically 27 × 27, with 76 answers), presenting new challenges to solvers and setters alike by the inclusion of longer words and multi-word phrases. In a more modest way, the Azed crossword is now sometimes 13 × 11, enabling me to include 13-letter words on a regular basis. More specialized crosswords explore other designs, including circular diagrams with entries arranged circularly and radially, but these will probably remain the exception and the domain of the seriously dedicated solver.

## Word choice

Having completed the grid, or having chosen it from the available range, the setter moves on to fill it with words. There are computer programs which can do this in the twinkling of an eye, though they are limited to the word-lists in the program's memory. The human brain takes much longer but it can select or reject words according to their suitability for cluing and its own real-world knowledge, a crucial factor in the writing of clues. Which words does one choose, and where does one start? I personally start from what seems the natural place, the top left-hand corner of the grid, extending down and across more or less at the same time while keeping a weather eye open for potential problem areas. Anything in the dictionary is fair game, and for me this means *The Chambers Dictionary*. My task is made easier by *Chambers Words* and *Chambers Back-Words for Crosswords*, books which present words alphabetically (or reverse-alphabetically) by length, so that I can see at a glance, say, all the 7-letter words beginning or ending with L. These aids are available to the solver as well as the setter, of course, but I like to think that whereas they are an invaluable tool for the hard-pressed setter, the solver will turn to them only as a last resort. Solving clues should be a contest of minds between setter and solver, not a series of conundrums to be resolved by reference to a published word-list. I also think the setter should be free to include non-dictionary words and phrases, especially topical ones, if these are sufficiently well known. Assessing what is and is not familiar enough to include here is of course a matter of fine judgement. Some newspapers have a policy of not allowing certain taboo words to be used as answers in their crosswords. In these liberated days such bowdlerization strikes me as rather old-fashioned. Crossword setters, like journalists and other writers, should be trusted to know where to draw the line.

The task of filling a grid with words is naturally easier in blocked diagrams than in barred ones, since the number of unchecked letters is significantly greater in blocked diagrams. In both types the setter develops with experience a feel for the 'shape' of words: common letter-clusters, the distribution of consonants and vowels, 'danger' letters (especially at the ends of words), helpful affixes and inflections, and so on. He or she must think ahead to avoid getting boxed into an awkward corner which will involve undoing part of the grid construction, an agonizing waste of time when deadlines are tight. The *Chambers Crossword Completer* is another valuable tool in this context, especially when setting blocked puzzles. This time words are arranged alphabetically by word length according to the alternate letters of each word, first the odd letters (first, third, fifth, etc) and then the even ones (second, fourth, sixth, etc). Special care needs to be taken with shorter words, especially those of four or five letters. There are comparatively few of these in the language (and of these far fewer begin with vowels than with consonants), so most will have been clued many times already. Good setters try to avoid reusing old clues, however proud of them they may be, and they should also not reuse *words* too often. Guarding against this is not easy, and inevitably, there being no copyright in good ideas, similar or identical clues to the same word will recur, but I do make a conscious effort not to repeat myself and think other setters should do likewise. (As a matter of passing interest, there are more different words in the language of eight letters than of any other word length.)

I have already mentioned fair play between setter and solver. This is an important principle in grid construction, just as much as in the writing of clues. Consonants, especially the less common ones, are generally more helpful to the solver as cross-checking letters than vowels are (with obvious exceptions like I or U in final position), and the setter should recognize this. I know that as a solver I feel hard done by if faced by –A–E, one of the most frequent four-letter-word patterns, especially if the setter has made matters worse by giving the word an extra-difficult clue!

## Clues

The writing of the clues for a crossword is the last and much the most important task for the setter, for it is here that one stamps one's character and personal style on the puzzle. Seasoned solvers develop clear preferences for the style of this or that setter, and satisfied solvers usually remain loyal to a particular puzzle (even, sometimes, if they are less than happy with other aspects of the paper in which it appears). I firmly believe that an impersonal style of cluing can be boring, and there is no harm at all in letting one's own interests, sense of humour, even prejudices, emerge through one's clues, provided always that these are fair and accurate. Don Manley in his essay on 'Crossword English' describes in detail the range of different clue types regularly used by setters. As a setter myself, I follow a method which has not changed greatly over the years. I always write clues in the order in which they appear in the puzzle. Taking the more colourful words first means leaving a 'sump' of less interesting ones till last, an encouragement to treat the latter as second-class citizens and produce second-class clues as a result. I write no more than nine or ten clues at a sitting, having found that if I try to do more staleness sets in and pedestrian clues result. The restorative effects of even quite a short break doing other things can be truly remarkable! At the same time it is important to see the puzzle as a whole and to present a reasonable variety of clue types (not too many anagrams, for example) to ensure a balanced fare for the solver. This can be tricky when a word cries out for one particular treatment but that treatment has already been used for other words in the puzzle (or for the same word in an earlier puzzle), but the principle is sound. The aim must be to divert the solver, not to massage the setter's ego, so variety is important.

Some words are much more difficult to clue interestingly than others. Scientific terms come high on my list of unfavourite words, mainly because their meaning is very specific and does not lend itself to the sort of wordplay that is at the heart of cryptic clue-writing. A word with many meanings offers far greater scope for punning and similar red herrings to strew in the solver's path. But whichever word I am cluing I always strive (with varying success, I'm sure) for three key ingredients in a clue: accuracy, economy and wit. Every clue should lead accurately and unmistakably to its solution, saying precisely and grammatically what it means (though it may not always mean what it appears to say – taking advantage of the manifold ambiguities of our language is an essential part of cryptic clue-writing). It should do this in as few words as are consistent with fair play, avoiding all superfluous verbiage or mere padding. And it should if at all possible be enjoyable to solve, leaving successful solvers feeling both satisfied at their success and pleasurably diverted by the experience.

**About the author**
Jonathan Crowther is better known to many cryptic crossword solvers as Azed, having set crosswords for *The Observer* for 35 years. One of the most highly regarded of all setters, he has also set puzzles under the pseudonyms Gong and Ozymandias. His *Book of Azed Crosswords* is published by Chambers.

# Crossword English

## *Don Manley* (crossword setter and author of *Chambers Crossword Manual*)

I am a monoglot, more or less. Although I studied French at school, I can't say I use it much – except when I have to on holiday, and even then it's a sort of pidgin French. But at least I feel I know English, and since (as Bernard Shaw put it) England and America are two countries divided by a common language, maybe one can be a polyglot just by watching television. Or maybe I can be a polyglot just by coming from Devon, where 'thistles' used to be called 'dashels'.

So what has this to do with crosswords? Well, in a sense Crossword English is rather like a foreign language – and it is a language that must be learnt. What may seem odd (if the cross-section of crossword setters I know is anything to go by) is that the polyglots who can speak French and English are not necessarily polyglots in the sense of knowing English and Crossword English. You're more likely to find that a crossword setter is a computer scientist, a physicist or a mathematician than a French teacher these days.

The irritating thing – to anyone who has not yet learnt Crossword English – is that it looks so like Everyday English. For the crossword which offers definitions only, this is perfectly obvious. So if the clue reads 'Cry of an ass (4)' you can write in BRAY straight away. You might have a few alternative answers for 'River (5)', and if you are living in Nottinghamshire you may be disposed to write in TRENT, but when faced with 'River in Paris (5)' you'll know that anything other than SEINE just isn't sane. So for the definition puzzle we're looking at a test of our ability to recognize synonyms or at a quiz with questions that would crop up early on in 'Who Wants To Be A Millionaire?'. This is as far as most people get with solving crosswords – the verbal quiz solved with a little help from reference books: a dictionary, an atlas and possibly an encyclopedia. They know English but not Crossword English.

So what is Crossword English? It is the language of the cryptic crossword, a language which looks like ordinary English but which has its own strange rules of grammar and construction and which has its own vocabulary. Crossword English is a series of mini-statements, mini-pictures, and mini-stories even, but the statements, the pictures, and the stories are each designed to hide a sort of riddle. So a riddle isn't a bad place to start with as an example of a cryptic clue:

> My first is in Cornwall but isn't in Devon
> For my second shun Hell and start looking in Heaven
> My third you may find in this or in that
> My whole is a creature that sits on the mat

Thus in a woeful verse of 39 words we have written a cryptic clue for CAT, and at each stage along the way we are spoon-fed with a letter at a time. It's obviously a puzzle, even if it's a pretty heavy-handed one.

Now look at these little riddles and see what you make of them:

1. Lady I rather fancy (7)
2. There's nothing in Basildon I like (3)
3. Delightful tea with the best china (8)
4. It's best to have cold sheets (5)
5. Delicate proposal (6)

6. The clock's put back? Relax! (5)
7. Company car? (3-6)
8. It could deflect battle spear (11)
9. Writer gathers wood as something that'll burn quickly (8)
10. Marsh plant enthrals artist (6)
11. Defeat brought by bowling gaining wicket – something captain controls? (9)
12. Amuse the French after a short time (6)
13. Did he have spelling lessons? (3,9,10)
14. Who you'd expect to find at gay weddings in the Isles?! (8)
15. Female beheaded in the sultanate (4)
16. Lab in, Tory out would suit him (4,5)
17. Boyfriend tied ribbon from what we hear (4)
18. Rejected young troublemaker longed to be free (8)
19. Fool about fifty, one not altogether bright (6)
20. 014? (6,5)

Here are twenty 'portrayals' – perfectly sensible 'portrayals' in generally understandable English – though 20 looks a bit odd. All of these were written by myself at some stage over the past fifteen years or so, and as I look at them I see not only Crossword English but a certain kind of Englishness. There is romance in 1 and 17 (and perhaps 5); there is an austere and rather snooty middle-Englishness about 2, 3 and 4; a concern with cricket in 11; hints of a threatening world outside modern England in 8 and 15; and so on. There may even be a touch of humour here and there. This is English language and English culture.

There are twenty puzzles to solve, so how are these clues different from those for BRAY and SEINE? The answer is (fairly) simple, though the implications of the answer may be complicated. It is this. In each cryptic clue there will still be a definition but the clue writer will have done one of two things. He (sometimes she – and, to be honest, we could do with more 'shes') will have either wrapped up the definition in 'cryptic language' or will have provided a definition plus some indication of the letters in the answer. Sometimes the crossword setter will have done both. In most cryptic clues there will be what we call a 'definition' followed by what we call a 'subsidiary indication' (sometimes also called 'wordplay'), or a subsidiary indication followed by a definition, or even an indication and a definition rolled into one. The secret in decoding a clue lies in trying to solve the answer from either or both of these components while using any letters that are already filled in.

If that all sounds horrible, it's because I've tried to give you a grammar lesson, and (as we all know) it's really much better to start learning a language by speaking it or writing it. No one ever really taught me 'all that grammar stuff' when I was a fledgling cruciverbalist (someone who 'does' crosswords). I was lucky enough to have a father who taught me how to solve clues when I was barely out of short trousers, and the best way I can explain Crossword English is to take you through the clues one by one.

1. *Lady I rather fancy (7)*
   The word 'fancy' is one of a huge set of **anagram indicators**. It tells us that the letters next to it are to be made 'fancy' or jumbled up. If you jumble up 'I rather' you get HARRIET, a lady. This clue, then is an **anagram**, perhaps the one form of cryptic clue everyone knows.

2. *There's nothing in Basildon I like (3)*
   If you look carefully, you'll see that there is indeed a word meaning nothing in the sequence of letters 'Basildon I like' and it's NIL. This is a **hidden word**.

3. *Delightful tea with the best china (8)*
   If you put a word for 'tea' and add it to a word for 'the best china', you will add 'char' to 'Ming' to form CHARMING, meaning 'delightful'. This is a **charade clue**.

4. *It's best to have cold sheets (5)*
   As it happens, this is another charade, but this time we join an **abbreviation** 'c' to the sheets (= ream) to form CREAM (the best). Abbreviations are common in subsidiary indications.

5. *Delicate proposal (6)*
   This is a **double-definition** clue, so you can look upon one definition as the official 'definition' and the other one as the 'subsidiary indication' – or vice versa. What word means both 'delicate' and 'proposal'? Answer: TENDER.

6. *The clock's put back? Relax! (5)*
   This suggests (quite rightly) that you'll get an extra hour in bed when the clocks go back. But if you put back a 'timer' you will get REMIT, which means 'relax'. This is a **reversal** clue. In down clues you may see the word 'up' suggesting a reversal. And here the definition is at the end.

7. *Company car? (3-6)*
   You may be tempted to think of this as another double-definition clue and look for a word that means both 'company' and 'car'. In fact the setter is inviting you to think of 'two's company, three's none', and so the answer is TWO-SEATER. There is no indication of letters in this clue, but we have noticed that it has a **cryptic definition**.

8. *It could deflect battle spear (11)*
   We're looking for an anagram of 'battle spear' and find it in BREASTPLATE, but we notice that the clue as a whole is a definition. Every word in the clue is serving as a definition and as part of the subsidiary indication. We call this an **&lit.** clue. This particular type is **anag. &lit.**

9. *Writer gathers wood as something that'll burn quickly (8)*
   The word 'gathers' suggests that a word for 'wood' might be inside a writer. Put 'fir' inside 'Wilde' and you'll find WILDFIRE. This is known as a **container-and-contents** clue.

10. *Marsh plant enthrals artist (6)*
    This is another container-and contents clue. This time we have an abbreviation for artist (RA) inside a plant (moss) to give MORASS.

11. *Defeat brought by bowling gaining wicket – something captain controls? (9)*
    If you solve crosswords you'll need to get used to **cricket vocabulary**. In this charade bowling is 'over', wicket is 'w', and something the captain controls is 'helm'. Put the three together to get OVERWHELM (defeat).

12. *Amuse the French after a short time (6)*
    Although we're talking about Crossword English, we do allow a few **foreign words** to creep in, especially definite and indefinite articles of common European languages. In this charade a short time is 'tick' added to 'the French', which in this case is 'le', giving the answer TICKLE (amuse).

13. *Did he have spelling lessons? (3,9,10)*
    The setter is tempting you to think about spelling in the sense of getting the right letters in sequence. In fact you should think about spelling in the sense of magic. The answer is THE SORCERER'S APPRENTICE, another cryptic definition, this one being set in what we call a **misleading context** occasioned by the **double-meaning** of 'spelling'. You'll find many other double meanings including 'flower' which can mean river. One of the delights of learning Crossword English is to work these out for yourself!

14. *Who you'd expect to find at gay weddings in the Isles?! (8)*
    This is an outrageous charade, the answer being 'he brides' (ie HEBRIDES). No one ever seems to have taken offence. Every crossword should have at least one clue with an element of **humour**.

15. *Female beheaded in the sultanate (4)*
    This is a particular type of **subtractive** clue. Take the head letter off 'woman' to give the sultanate OMAN. If you take up cryptic crosswords you will also learn about 'endless' and 'heartless'.

16. *Lab in, Tory out would suit him (4,5)*
    This is another **anag. &lit.** Note that 'out' is a very common anagram indicator. You should be able to see TONY BLAIR quite easily.

17. *Boyfriend tied ribbon from what we hear (4)*
    When you see words like 'we hear' or 'they say' you almost certainly have a **homophone** clue. Here 'tied ribbon' is 'bow' and BEAU is bow 'from what we hear', ie 'beau' and 'bow' are homophones.

18. *Rejected young troublemaker longed to be free (8)*
    This is a **complex** clue in that it consists of the reverse of one word in a charade with another. A rejected troublemaker is 'Ted' backwards ('det') and longed is 'ached', which when attached makes DETACHED. Who ever calls unruly troublemakers 'teddy-boys' or 'teds' these days? Well, we do in crosswords. This is one example of **preserved obsolescence** in an area of language where we still have an extended-play record (EP) and sex appeal is still 'it'.

19. *Fool about fifty, one not altogether bright (6)*
    In this container-and-contents clue we make use of our knowledge of **Roman numerals**. Fifty is 'L' and 'twit' about 'L, I' is TWILIT. And there's a slightly misleading context here, isn't there?

20. *014? (6,5)*
    This last clue is what one might call a **zany** or **improvised** clue – a sort of one-off cryptic definition. It depends on the solver seeing that 014 = 2 x 007. Since 007 is the agent James Bond, the answer must be DOUBLE AGENT.

With these twenty clues we have touched on all of the most important aspects of Crossword English, and maybe I have already been rather too 'English English' for some. What about other Englishes? Well, I'm writing this introduction for a Scottish publisher with a very special dictionary, *The Chambers Dictionary*. This is of course an excellent 'English English' dictionary but it also contains some excellent English words from the past and some highly unusual Scottish words. *Chambers* should be in every self-respecting crossworder's library, but its greatest treasures tend to come into play in the more difficult puzzles where Edmund (Spenser) and Jock (the archetypal Scot) make frequent appearances.

Across the Atlantic, in the USA and Canada, 'American Crossword English' is developing as cryptic puzzles, based on British puzzles, become more popular. British solvers will find one or two unfamiliar abbreviations, maybe, and the contexts will be more American – but the similarities tend to contradict Shaw's assertion mentioned earlier.

It has often been pointed out that English is ideal for the crossword because words split up so agreeably. How convenient that 'astronomer' is an anagram of 'moon-starer' and how nicely 'bestride' splits into 'best ride'. Clearly it would be difficult to imagine Crossword Urdu, and yet cryptic crosswords do exist in Hebrew, Bengali, Welsh and Dutch – and other languages too, I dare say.

It's time for a final word about the 'custodians' of Crossword English and what they are trying to do. The word 'custodian' may suggest conservatism and a grammar rule-book. There's more to it than that, of course, but there is a necessary element of grammar in crosswords which needs to be preserved. There are, after all, limits to what is acceptable in Everyday English, and it is the same in Crossword English.

In our language the strict grammarians call themselves **Ximeneans** after Ximenes, *The Observer* crossword setter who died in 1971. There is no space here for a digression into the grammar over which crossword setters and their editors argue, but there is an ongoing debate about what is acceptable and what is not. Today the tradition of Ximenes is upheld by his successor Azed, who tells us about his approach to crossword setting elsewhere in this book. Many of today's crossword setters have been competitors in Azed's clue-writing competitions, and so it is no surprise that many of the crossword setters in our national dailies are Ximenean – as are their crossword editors. Puzzles will inevitably vary in style and in level of difficulty. Crossword setters are turning Crossword English Language into Crossword English Literature and different 'readers' (solvers) will inevitably have their own favourite 'authors' (setters). But there are rules within which the custodians make sure that Crossword English operates – rules not just of grammar, but rules of taste. Practitioners of this language don't have to be absolutely politically correct, but their language is still that of the polite drawing-room, not that of the gutter. We can gently poke fun at pompous bishops and politicians (though not by name specifically!), and we can make wry comments about modern society, but we aim to entertain and not to give offence.

We want to give pleasure and intellectual challenge. Crossword English began as a sort of 20th-century poetry for all to enjoy. Long may it continue into the 21st century and beyond.

## About the author

Don Manley sets crosswords under a variety of pseudonyms (Bradman, Duck, Quixote, Pasquale and Giovanni) for many national newspapers (including *The Times*, *The Guardian*, *The Independent on Sunday*, the *Financial Times* and *The Sunday Telegraph*). He is the author of the authoritative *Chambers Crossword Manual*.

# The art of the crossword clue

## *Tim Moorey* (Mephisto of *The Sunday Times*)

What is it that makes certain clues stay in the memory when the vast majority are forgotten as soon as their solutions are discovered? I will try to answer the question by identifying characteristics and qualities that setters strive to find and solvers tend to appreciate. Each is illustrated with my choice of clue examples based on over 50 years of crossword solving, and also with choices made by fellow setters from their own past clues and those of other setters. In addition, having had the task of selecting a 'Clue of the Week' for *The Week* magazine since its inception, I regularly have to consider what constitutes a good clue, and my focus there – and here – is on what solvers are likely to have found satisfying. To an increasing extent, it is also based on actual feedback from *The Sunday Times* and *The Week* solvers, following the introduction several years ago of invitations to respond by email.

It is fairly clear which qualities are enjoyed in favoured clues: in a nutshell, short, simple, well-crafted sentences that paint a coherent and believable but misleading picture are well regarded. If these can be supplemented with topicality and wit, so much the better. Technical soundness is taken for granted, albeit that crossword professionals sometimes heatedly debate exactly what is technically sound. Solvers, I think, are unconcerned with this aspect; if a warm glow of recognition on uncovering the answer is obtained, they will value a clue that some professionals (including this one) rate as 'unsound'.

So here are four things I look for in clue selection:

1. **Definition**
   My test is whether the word or words used in the clue could be substituted for the solution in a normal English sentence.

2. **Ease of solving**
   The clue answer should not be immediately apparent; and the penny should drop after not too long an interval of puzzlement.

3. **Clue length**
   Anything over ten words can make for indigestibility, but I wouldn't rule out clues that are slightly longer.

4. **Artificiality in wording**
   There should be no strain evident, and especially no sign that the clue-writer would ideally have preferred to use a different word or words, but was unable to do so in the interest of clueing integrity.

The clues chosen as examples for this essay include what may be regarded as 'classics', that is to say that they are spoken of and quoted still, in most cases despite having appeared some years ago. I also include more recent clues that have featured as 'Clue of the Week'. In most cases, to give readers a better chance of solving, the solutions are fairly common words.

Now for the qualities and characteristics of memorable clues, with illustrations. Hints are given in italics alongside clues, with solutions provided at the end of the essay.

## 1. Short and succinct

Cryptic definition clues fit this category best, albeit that they may have the disadvantage of not conveying a picture. However, their neatness and deviousness appeal. Ideally, there can only be a unique solution to each of these; note that the bracketed number of letters can sometimes rule out possible alternatives, as in the last of the examples.

Art master (8) *Think old English*

Stiff examination (4,6) *Think Latin*

This cylinder is jammed (5,4) *Think food*

A pound of sultanas (8) *Nothing to do with food*

Bar of soap (6,6) *Two of the three words mislead*

Double definitions – where either word could define the answer – can also be mentioned here. Perhaps the two best known are:

Let rip (4) *Ideas associated with a tear mustn't be shed here*

Driving licence (2-5) *Think of driving in the 'pushy' sense*

## 2. Well-crafted, painting a believable picture

If these qualities can be included in a totally misleading sentence, then you may have a fine clue.

Neglectful having left off dicky bow (9) *Dicky and bow mislead*

Seems a hip replacement brings about stress (9) *Anagram*

Licking for Persians is a prolonged exercise (8) *Two definitions; think ancient battles*

Amazon order mailed with shrink wrapping (6-3) *A very tough but wonderful clue for a rare word; shrink = shy*

In autumn, we're piling up the last of the leaves (8) *Partial anagram*

Tumbler, nuts, smoke, rapture! (7-5) *Anagram*

## 3. Topicality

The references in these clues, in order, are: an infamous fatwa issued against an English novelist; a disastrous attempt in 1980 to rescue US hostages from Iran; fears before the 1990 World Cup relating to unruly English soccer fans; and finally the Iraq war.

He's rued his novel (7) *Anagram*

Carter coup tails off in disarray – prepare for war? (8) *Adjusted anagram*

Trouble Italy has looming? (11) *Anagram*

War's started by Bush? Completely! (6) *W is the answer's first letter*

Also topical was this prize-winning effort to celebrate puzzle number 1000 by Ximenes (or X as he was often known) in 1968; C refers to Chambers.

Up to date product of X and C (8) *Think multiplication*

## 4. Wit and humour

Undoubtedly appreciated by the solver, this is probably the category hardest for setters to achieve, and thus most rarely found. The fine first example won a prize in a Ximenes competition in *The Observer* in 1967, when the recently-coined solution word had not yet made it into the dictionary.

Abbreviations not in Chambers but should not be looked up anyway (4-6) *Think feminine clothes*

Silicone valley! (8) *Think feminine*

Roman marbles lost (3,6,6) *Think Latin*

In which three couples get together for sex (5) *Last word is the key*

Odd if no males could be found here (4,2,3) *Anagram*

Variety of *English* pastry – Dane would look down on it! (7) *Anagram*

Stiff collaring's my trade – it shows what can be done by starch (4,8) *Anagram*

## 5. Definition and secondary indications being the same ('& lit.' type clues)

Often considered as the pinnacle of the clue-writer's art, the best of this type have a conciseness of wording and do not reveal their charms too easily.

We'll get excited with Ring seat (10) *Anagram*

No fellow for mixing (4,4) *Anagram*

I rifle tubs at sea (10) *Anagram*

What you might find in Lechtal overlooking lake? (6) *Overlook here means 'ignore'*

What's tea passed round in? (5) *Tea is 'cha'*

Waitress with large bust could model as this (7-4) *Bust here means 'broken'*

Names I must jot endlessly (8) *Must here means 'in a frenzy'*

What grass is (even for a fool) (5) *Substitute one word for another*

By it 'truth' and 'lie' looked alternately interchangeable (6-5) *Anagram*

## 6. Subtlety of language

This type often requires a second, careful reading of a word or words, not necessarily prominent ones.

Lass I love moving upwards you may find well beneath this (3,3) *Down clue*

A chap could attend this celebration but never does (4,5) *Read it again*

Drink causing a problem? What if it is! (9) *An additive clue*

Item Gran arranged family slides in (5,7) *Family is 'clan'*

Shot with craft on course (9) *Golf and poetry cleverly in play*

A murder suspect, one hears (7) *Last two words especially mislead*

Dive made from upturned punts? (7) *A down clue; think Ireland*

## 7. Technical virtuosity

Long anagrams, as in the first two examples, are often quoted by solvers. This shows that work by setters (whether by computer or not) is appreciated. The third example of virtuosity is also one of the most deceptive clues ever published.

Ground with the Arsenal not getting the least bit of sympathy (5,4,4) *Ground, the past tense of grind*

Poetical scene with surprisingly chaste Lord Archer vegetating (3,3,8,12) *Brooke*

Some job at hand? We'll soon see (4,3,5) *Last word misleads*

## 8. Highly original clues not obviously fitting into any category

These typically require a leap of imagination on the part of the solver and maybe raise an especially wide smile when the penny drops. Even though the first two of the following clues are often considered 'unsound', they do get plaudits from solvers.

HIJKLMNO (5) *Chemistry; no direct definition included*

ONMLKJIH (9) *No direct definition included*

I can identify vehicles here (5) *IVR code knowledge needed*

014? (6,5) *Think spooks*

His, for example (9) *Plural answer*

Finally, the clue most suggested by fellow setters, and my own favourite, goes back over 25 years. It was originated by Les May, who won first prize in *The Observer's* Azed competition, and could have been included in several of the other categories. A tough one to crack but solving it for real would be highly satisfying nonetheless.

Bust down reason (9) *Solution splits into three separate words for the purposes of the secondary reading*

## Solutions and (where known) authors

Where the clue originally appeared under a pseudonym, the pseudonym is shown in brackets after the author's real name. Where there is no pseudonym or no name at all, the clue's author is unknown to me, or it may have featured either in clue-writing competitions or in publications such as *The Times* or *The Daily Telegraph* where setters are unnamed (though in three instances where names are known to me, due credit is given below).

1. TEACHEST; POST MORTEM; SWISS ROLL Adrian Bell *The Times*; SERAGLIO Valerie Coleman; ROVER'S RETURN; RENT; GO-AHEAD Norman Goddard;

2. GENUFLECT; EMPHASISE John Halpern (Mudd); MARATHON and SHIELD-MAY Ross Beresford; FAREWELL *anag we're in fall* H S Tribe; POSTURE-MAKER I M Raab;

3. RUSHDIE John Grimshaw; ACCOUTRE Tim Moorey; HOOLIGANISM Malcolm Barley; WHOLLY Michael Curl (Orlando); THOUSAND Sir Jeremy Morse;

4. MINI-SKIRTS M C Raphael; CLEAVAGE Roy Dean *The Times*; NON COMPOS MENTIS; LATIN *three times two is six* Brian Greer; ISLE OF MAN; YAPSTER Paul Henderson; BODY SNATCHER Sir Jeremy Morse;

5. WAGNERITES Derrick Macnutt (Ximenes); LONE WOLF Don Manley (Quixote); FILIBUSTER A N Clark; CHALET John Tozer; CHINA; SWEATER-GIRL Tim Moorey (Mephisto); AMNESIAC Kathleen Bissett; GREEN *een for ass* Richard Morse; DOUBLE-THINK Colin Dexter;

6. OIL RIG Jonathan Crowther (Azed); STAG PARTY; SUPPOSING; MAGIC LANTERN Colin Dexter; ALBATROSS; EARDRUM; NITERIE *Eire tin reversed* Roger Hooper;

7. WHITE HART LANE Richard Palmer (Merlin); THE OLD VICARAGE GRANTCHESTER John Graham (Araucaria); BATH AND WELLS *hidden clue* Brian Greer;

8. WATER; BACKWATER John Grimshaw *The Times*; ITALY; DOUBLE AGENT *007* Don Manley (Quixote); GREETINGS; BRAINWASH *bra in wash* Les May.

### About the author

Tim Moorey sets crosswords as one of the three-strong Mephisto team for *The Sunday Times*, for which he also regularly contributes *The Sunday Times* crossword. He has additionally appeared as Owzat in newspapers such as *The Independent*, *The Sunday Telegraph* and *The Listener* crossword in *The Times*. He is the crossword editor of *The Week* magazine, gives talks on crosswords and runs regular crossword workshops.

# Indicators in cryptic crossword clues

## *Tim Moorey* (Mephisto of *The Sunday Times*)

### Why do crosswords have 'indicators'?

As compared to definition-only crosswords (general knowledge, quick, easy and the like) which have clues offering only one means of arriving at each solution, cryptic crossword clues usually have two. These are a definition and a secondary way, often termed 'wordplay'. This, in effect, acts as a check on the definition, or vice versa if the solver finds the definition elusive. Wordplay relies on 'indicators', of which there are many types. In effect, an indicator shows how the setter has manipulated the solution, in that a whole word (or part) may have been subject to one or more tricks, such as the following:

| | **Type of indicator** |
|---|---|
| Changed into another word by a letter mix | Anagram |
| Split into parts with one part inside another | Containment/Insertion |
| Letter(s) chosen for subtraction | Deletion |
| Concealed inside the rest of the clue | Hidden |
| Considered as spoken, giving a different word | Homophone |
| Linked to other part(s) | Juxtaposition |
| Written backwards (or upwards for a Down clue) | Reversal |
| Letter(s) chosen for manipulation | Selection |

### How are indicators used?

Indicators are designed to signal to solvers:

- which type of wordplay is to be unravelled
- how to adjust a letter or letters within the clue
- how the whole clue sentence fits together

### What are the main types of indicator?

In the clue examples that follow, the indicator is denoted in bold type.

#### 1 Anagram

In nearly all cryptic crosswords solvers are expected to unravel some solutions from a mix of letters, and there is a need for this wordplay to be flagged up. Hence the anagram indicator, of which there are a huge number. Most – but not all – imply some form of movement, lack of order, change, uncertainty or instability (especially in assumed mental or physical state) in their meanings, albeit often in a concealed surface reading. Anagram indicators such as 'ground' being the past tense of 'grind', and 'bananas' and 'potty' with their double meanings, show such concealment.

There are also some indicators that can only be fully justified by well-established convention. For example, the many synonyms of 'drunk' such as 'pickled', 'stoned' and the like are commonly used, it being assumed that cruciverbal tipplers are wobbly rather than flat out! Nor are setters static in their usages: a modern synonym for 'crazy' such as 'out to lunch' makes a highly misleading anagram indicator, as does 'supply' in the second example.

People seen **working** in Basra (5)

The indicator 'working' for this purpose is in the sense of 'being in action' and it signals a letter mix for the solution ARABS.

Monn (Caterers) **supply** beef and grouse (12)

Here the adverb of 'supple' meaning 'pliant' shows that the first two words must be anagrammatized into REMONSTRANCE meaning complaint, or 'beef' and 'grouse'. Note that as well as wordplay there are two definitions here, a practice often found in advanced puzzles such as Azed or Mephisto.

## 2 Containment

A solution may be split such that one part of it can be seen as being 'outside' another, duly shown by the many indicators of this type. Containment and insertion indicators have the same effect.

Opportunity to **go round** one Italian city (5)

'Opportunity' is 'turn', and when that is put outside 'I' for 'one' you get the Italian city TURIN. Here 'to go round' is the indicator and 'one' for '1' for 'I' is a common crossword convention.

Saw dog **wearing** lead (7)

This requires 'Rover' for 'dog' to be placed inside 'lead' – or rather the metal's abbreviation 'Pb' – to give PROVERB, or 'saw'.

Is **trapped in** burning lift (5)

The indicator 'trapped in' signals that 'is' has to be contained by, ie put inside, 'burning' meaning 'hot' for the solution HOIST, which defines 'lift'.

## 3 Insertion

These have the same effect as containment indicators. A solution may be split such that one part is viewed as being 'inside' another.

Disreputable type in favour of **cutting** discount (9)

If you put 'pro', meaning 'in favour of', inside (ie 'cutting') the term 'rebate' meaning 'discount', the solution REPROBATE, a 'disreputable type', appears.

Crumpet may be so to speak **in** bed (8)

Here the well-concealed definition ends at the word 'so'. The wordplay is then 'utter' meaning 'to speak' in 'bed' leading us nicely to BUTTERED. (Note that the 'to' is to be ignored, as is commonly the practice with verbs in wordplay).

## 4 Deletion

These indicators signal the deletion of a letter or letters (as in the first example), or a whole word within a clue (as in the second example).

Applause left **out** in graduation ceremony (7)

'Applause' is 'clapping' and the indicator demands that its L for 'left' be taken out to leave CAPPING, a 'graduation ceremony'.

Surgeon **fails to get** on in this swell (5)

Take 'on' from 'surgeon' to get to SURGE which is the definition for 'swell'.

Note that the word 'in' here in both deletion examples is being used not as an indicator but as common crossword shorthand, in effect for 'leading to ...' or 'coming from ...'.

Other specific deletion indicators are discussed in Ends deletion indicators, Head deletion indicators, Middle deletion indicators and Tail deletion indicators.

## 5 Ends indicators

### 5a Ends selection

The first and last letters of a word within a clue are indicated for addition to some other letters, or to a whole word, in order to form the solution.

> Urges for example, **both sides** in games (4)

The indicator 'both sides' when applied to 'games' gives two letters G and S. Put these together with 'eg', meaning 'for example', and you have EGGS as in to egg or urge someone on.

### 5b Ends deletion

The first and last letters of a word within a clue are indicated for deletion in order to form the solution.

> **Shell** prawn uncooked (3)

'Shell' in the sense of 'separate from the shell or covering' implies removing the first and last letters of 'prawn' to give RAW meaning 'uncooked'.

## 6 Head indicators

There is a common (but not universally applied) convention that Down solutions should be indicated as the word appears in the completed grid. This means that a distinction is sometimes made between Across and Down clues as regards what constitutes 'heads'. For example, head selection indicators such as 'summit' or 'top' are sometimes said to be applicable to Down clues only.

### 6a Head selection

The first letter of a word within a clue is indicated for addition to some other letters or, as below, to a whole word to form the solution.

> **Starter** with pork and mild pickle (6)

Here the indicator 'starter' is applied to 'pork' to give 'P'. Added to 'light' meaning 'mild' this provides the solution PLIGHT, or a 'pickle' – a predicament if you are in one.

### 6b Head deletion

The first letter of a word is indicated for deletion in order to form the solution.

> Colleague in Monte Carlo event **failing to start** (4)

A 'Monte Carlo event' is a 'rally' which 'fails to start', ie it loses its initial letter. This leaves the answer ALLY, meaning 'colleague'.

## 7 Middle indicators

### 7a Middle selection

The middle letter (or letters) of a word within a clue is indicated for addition to some other letters, or to a whole word, in order to form the solution.

> Plastic building toy on **centre** of floor (4)

'On' for 'leg' (as in cricket) plus the middle letter of floor, 'O', makes LEGO, the required toy.

### 7b Middle deletion

The middle letter (or letters) of a word within a clue is indicated for deletion in order to form the solution.

Royal Artillery really **disheartened**? Seldom (6)

The central two letters 'AL' are eliminated from 'really' to give 'RELY', which put after 'RA' (an abbreviation of 'Royal Artillery') gives RARELY, 'seldom'

## 8 Tail indicators

### 8a Tail selection

The last letter (or letters) of a word within a clue is indicated for addition to some other letters, or to a whole word, in order to form the solution.

Dull **back** of road could be a cul-de-sac (4,3)

'Dull' is 'deaden', to which an added 'D' from 'back of road' provides DEAD END, a 'cul-de-sac'.

### 8b Tail selection down

This is similar to that above, but this indicator is for a Down clue only (see Head indicators above for an explanation of this convention). The above Across clue could be adapted as follows, with 'bottom' as the Tail Selection Down indicator.

Dull **bottom** of road could be a cul-de-sac (4,3)

This gives a Down clue with the same solution DEAD END, a 'cul-de-sac'.

### 8c Tail deletion

The last letter (or letters) of a word is indicated for deletion in order to form the solution.

English poet messing around **endlessly** (6)

'Messing around' is 'larking' which becomes (Philip) LARKIN, the poet, when its last letter is taken off.

### 8d Tail deletion down

This is similar to that above, but this indicator is for a Down clue only.

**Baseless** worry for vehicle (3)

If the final letter of 'care' for 'worry' is ignored, CAR, a 'vehicle', comes out as the Down clue answer.

## 9 Hidden

### 9a Hidden

The indicator instructs solvers to look for the solution within the clue sentence, or wholly within one of the clue's words.

**In** Amritsar it's a common habit (4)

Indicated by 'in', the challenge is to uncover a hidden but defined four-letter word. This is SARI – formed from the last three letters of 'Amritsar' and the first letter of 'it's' – a common habit with the final word in its 'dress' sense.

Sensation **concealed by** Chopin, Sand – needlessly (4,3,7)

Not quite so easy to spot, as a result of its misleading punctuation, is the hidden phrase PINS AND NEEDLES, a sensation.

### 9b Hidden alternately

A second form of this indicator applies where every other letter has to be taken to form the solution word. The indicator will not necessarily always signal whether it's the even or odd letters to be used. For example, the indicator 'regularly' may refer to either even or odd letters.

Select **even parts** of strongest gear (4)

The instruction 'select' indicates taking the even letters in 'strongest' to form a word meaning 'gear'. Hence the solution is TOGS.

## 10 Homophone

In this type, the definition when spoken becomes another word which forms the wordplay. Sometimes with careless word placement, setters do not make clear which is the solution and which the homophone, though this may be established from the word-length. It can also be a problem for solvers as to which part of the English-speaking world, with its many differing pronunciations, is deemed to be speaking the homophone.

It's cold in a S American country **reportedly** (6)

'Reportedly' is an indicator that the solver is looking for a word that sounds like another meaning of 'cold'. 'Chile' clearly fits the bill as a homonym of CHILLY, the answer.

Check **on radio** for weather forecast? (4)

If listening to the radio, 'rein' (meaning 'check') would sound like RAIN, the solution.

## 11 Juxtaposition

### 11a Juxtaposition

The indicator shows that the two words or parts of words need to be placed together for the solution.

Endeavour perhaps to be **alongside** learner in a scrap (6)

Morse ('Endeavour', the first name of Inspector Morse in the novels by Colin Dexter) is juxtaposed with 'L' for 'learner' to make 'scrap', a MORSEL.

### 11b Juxtaposition down

This is similar to that above, but this indicator is for a Down clue only (see Head indicators above for an explanation of this convention).

One **above** Bishop given the answer: forgiveness (10)

'A' for 'one' put on top of 'B' for 'bishop' and 'solution' for 'answer' makes ABSOLUTION, meaning 'forgiveness'. Actually there are two juxtaposition indicators here, in that as well as 'above', the word 'given' also shows that some words are to be placed together.

## 12 Reversal

### 12a Reversal

The whole of a solution word can sometimes be reversed to form another different word (or the same word in the case of a palindrome – see below). It's the job of reversal indicators to show this, and sometimes also reversals of only part of a word which is then subject to more wordplay, as in the second example.

Huge flans **all round** – that's the plan (9)

'Huge flans' are 'mega tarts', which when reversed gives STRATAGEM or 'plan'.

Optimistic US president admitting bad **back** (7)

Reversing 'ill' for 'bad' and putting this inside (further wordplay signalled by 'admitting') Bush gives BULLISH, or 'optimistic'.

### 12b Reversal down

Reversal indicators used in Down clues will often be, for example, 'rising' or 'brought up' rather than those used in Across clues implying reversal horizontally such as 'all round' (as above) or as 'backwards' (see Head indicators above for further explanation of this convention). Using this in the preceding example, a Down clue could have been:

Huge flans **served up** – that's the plan (9)

It's 'served up' showing the necessary upwards movement in 'mega tarts' to lead to the same STRATEGEM solution.

### 12c Reversal palindrome

The third type of reversal indicator applies to palindromic solutions, for which there are a small number of indicators.

This note is small **whichever way you look at it** (5)

The indicator signals that the solution is the same as its reversal, in this case MINIM, the 'small note' of the clue.

## Other indicators

In addition to the most important indicators already covered above, there are some others met in cryptic puzzles that can be mentioned briefly. They tend to be self-explanatory.

### Foreign

Many European languages, especially French, can be indicated, usually obviously but occasionally not so, as in this example:

**Nice** girl has time for a piece of beef (6)

The indicator refers to the French city of Nice, where the word for 'girl' would be 'fille'. Put next to 'T' for 'time', you have FILLET, a piece of beef.

### Archaic

Rather than use the mundane 'archaic' or 'obsolete' as indicators, setters find more interesting and misleading ways of expressing words that are no longer in general usage.

Mark **antique** articles rubbish! (2,3)

'M' for 'mark' (as in Germany before the euro), plus 'ye ye' or two archaic definite 'articles' will show as MY EYE, meaning 'rubbish!'

### Dialect

Different regional words and accents may be referred to, especially British ones such as Scottish and Cockney.

The **Yorkshire** beer in fiction (4)

The solution TALE, meaning 'fiction' in the sense of a lie, comes from 'T' for 'the' as supposedly used in 'Yorkshire' plus 'ALE' for 'beer'.

## Repetition

A small number of indicators show, nearly always self-evidently, when letters or words need to be included more than once in a solution.

The Queen **repeatedly** behind grown-up man of affairs (9)

Thus 'grown-up' is 'adult' which when preceding 'ER' (the Queen) twice gives 'ADULTERER', the 'man of affairs' being sought.

## Conclusion

In the foregoing examples there is mostly only one type of indicator used in any one example. However, it is not uncommon in advanced puzzles to find one or more indicators of the same or different type being used in one clue. For example:

Clever wordplay recalled Thomas Mann's last book about love (3,3)

Here the solver is asked to do all the following:

| | **Indicator (and type)** |
|---|---|
| Abbreviate *Thomas* to TOM | none given |
| Take *Mann's last* as N | *last* (tail selection) |
| Abbreviate *book* to B | none given |
| Abbreviate *love* to O | none given |
| Put TOM N B outside O | *about* (containment) |

Amongst other possibilities, this gives TOMNOB.

| | |
|---|---|
| Reverse this to get BONMOT | *recalled* (reversal) |

And finally split it (3,3) to get BONMOT, meaning 'clever wordplay'.

Note that, as is almost always the case, abbreviations have to be identified without the aid of indicators. The clue is perhaps over-complex and you may or not agree that it offers clever wordplay!

### About the author

Tim Moorey sets crosswords as one of the three-strong Mephisto team for *The Sunday Times*, for which he also regularly contributes *The Sunday Times* crossword. He has additionally appeared as Owzat in newspapers such as *The Independent*, *The Sunday Telegraph* and *The Listener* crossword in *The Times*. He is the crossword editor of *The Week* magazine, gives talks on crosswords and runs regular crossword workshops.

# Indicator lists

The following lists show those headwords, phrasal verbs and idioms that are denoted in the *Crossword Dictionary* as being indicators of cryptic crossword clue wordplay.

The lists have been compiled on the basis of those indicators most commonly seen in crosswords. They are not, and never could be, definitive. The lists reflect the way that these words have been used in actual cryptic clues. Appearance in a list does not mean that such a usage is considered acceptable by all crossword setters and editors.

As explained in the Introduction, indicators may not appear in a cryptic clue in the way in which they appear here, but rather may be encountered in an inflected form – for example the anagram indicator 'digest' is more frequently encountered as 'digested' – or as part of a phrase, for example 'not reaching a conclusion' to indicate a tail deletion. As the lists reflect the headwords of the *Crossword Dictionary*, not every form of every indicator is included.

Additionally, there are some indicators which may be encountered in cryptic clues, but which are not denoted in the text or in the following lists. Examples of these include:

| **Type** | **Indicator example** |
| --- | --- |
| Abbreviation to be used | short |
| Colloquial usage | commonly |
| First half, second half of word selected | left half, right half |
| Insertion between letters SS | aboard ship, on board |
| Move first letter to end | brings first to last, runs down |
| Move internal letter to front | puts foremost |
| Not all letters used | not entirely |
| One of two central letters deleted | half-heartedly |
| Only limited wordplay | slightly |
| Only two, three, etc letters selected | two of, three of, etc |
| Plural word loses final S | singular |
| Proportion of letters in a word selected | half, two-thirds |
| Selection of second, third, fourth, etc letter | second, third, fourth, etc |
| Selection of two letters | couple of |
| Single letter instead of double | just one |
| Substitute letters | replace, take instead, change, changing |
| Unusual homophone | drunkard says (*for a homophone that sounds slurred, eg 'mesh' for 'mess'*) |

It should also be noted that as the number of foreign word indicators is potentially unlimited – any person or place might be used – only the most general have been included here. For example, 'article from Paris', 'day in Calais', 'Renoir's here', 'lake in Savoie' or 'of Chirac's' could all indicate that a French word is required (in these instances, 'la' or 'le', 'jour', 'ici', 'lac' and 'de' respectively).

## Anagram indicators

Anagram indicators include:

abandon
abandoned
aberrant
abnormal
abominable
about
abroad
absurd
abuse
abysmal
abysmally
accident
accidentally
acrobatics
acting
action
activate
active
activity
adapt
adaptable
adaptation
adjust
adjustment
administer
adrift
affected
afflicted
afresh
after injury
aggrieved
agile
agitate
agitated
ague
alarm
allocate
allocation
all over the place
alloy
alter
alteration
alternative
alternatively
amazing
amend
amendment
amiss
amok
analyse
analysis
anarchic
anew
angrily
angry
animated
animatedly
anomalous
anomaly
another
anxious
anyhow
anyway
apart
appalling
appallingly
appliance
applied
appointed
appraisal
arch
around
arousal
arouse
arrange
arrangement
array
artefact
artful
artfully
articulate
articulated
askew
assassinate
assassination
assemble
assorted
astonishing
astray
at fault
at random
atrocious
at sea
away
awful
awfully
awkward
awkwardly
awry
bad
badly
baffle
baffling
bake
bamboozle
bananas
bandy
barbaric
barbarous
barge
barking
baroque
bastard
bats
batter
battered
batting
batty
beaten
beat up
become
bedevil
bedlam
befuddle
belabour
belt
bemuse
bemused
bend
bendy
bent
berserk
bespoke
bewildered
biased
bizarre
bizarrely
blast
blasted
blazing
blend
blessed
blight
blotchy
blow up
blue
blunder
blur
blurred
body
bogus
boil
boiled
boiling
boisterous
bomb
boozy
boss
botch
bother
bottle
bouncing
bouncy
brain
break
break up
breeze
brew
brittle
broach
broadcast
broke
broken
broth
bruise
bubbly
buck
buckle
buffeted
building
built
bully
bum
bumble
bumbling
bundle
bungle
burst
bust
bustle
bustling
busy
butcher
Byzantine
calamitous
camouflage
capricious
career
careless
carelessly
carve
carve up
cast
cavort
change
changeable
chaotic
chew
choppy
chop up
churn
circulate
clobber
clumsy
cocktail
cock up
cock-up
code
collapse
collected
collection
combustible
compilation
compile
complex
complicate
complicated
complication
component
compose
composed
composition
compound
compromise
concerned
concoct

condemn
condemnation
condition
confection
confound
confuse
confused
confusing
confusion
constituent
construct
construe
contaminate
contamination
contort
contrive
contrived
conversion
convert
convertible
convoluted
convulse
cook
cooked
cook up
correct
correction
corrupt
could be
could become
crack
cracked
crackers
crackpot
crack up
craft
craftily
crafty
cranky
crash
crazed
crazily
crazy
creation
criminal
crocked
crook
crooked
cross
crude
crudely
cruel
crumble
crumbly
crush
cuckoo
cultivate
cure
curious
curiously
cut
daft
damage
damaged
dance
dash
dashing
dazed
debris
decompose
defective
deficient
defile
deform
deformed
delirious
deliriously
demented
demolish
deplorable
deploy
deranged
desecrate
design
desperate
desperately
destabilize
destroy
destruction
desultory
deterioration
detour
devastate
devastated
develop
deviant
deviate
deviation
devilish
devious
diabolical
dicky
different
differently
digest
dilapidated
dire
direct
disarrange
disarray
disastrous
disband
discomfit
discompose
disconcert
disconcerting
discord
discordant
discover
diseased
disfigure
disgruntled
disguise
disguised
dish
dishevelled
dish out
disintegrate
disintegration
disjointed
dislocate
dislocation
dismantle
disorder
disordered
disorderly
disorganization
disorganize
disorganized
disorientate
disorientated
disorientation
dispel
disperse
dispersion
disport
dispose
disposed
disposition
disrupt
disruption
dissipate
dissipated
dissolute
dissonant
distillation
distort
distorted
distract
distracted
distraught
distribute
distribution
disturb
disturbance
disturbed
disturbing
dither
diverse
divert
diverting
dizzy
do
doctor
doddering
doddery
dodgy
done
dotty
doubtfully
drastic
drawn
dreadful
dreadfully
dress
dressing
dress up
drift
drunk
drunken
dubious
duff
dynamic
easily
easy
eccentric
edit
effervescent
elaborate
elastic
elevated
embarrass
embarrassed
embroil
emend
emendation
emerge
employ
engineer
enigmatic
enliven
entangle
entanglement
entwine
err
errant
erratic
erratically
erring
erroneous
error
erupt
eruption
evolution
evolve
exchange
excite
excited
excruciate
exercise
exotic
explode
explosive
extract
extraordinarily
extraordinary
extravagant
fabricate
fake
fall
false
faltering
fan
fanciful
fancy
fantastic
fashion
fault

faulty
fearful
ferment
fettle
feverish
fickle
find in
finesse
finicky
fishy
fit
fix
fixed
flabbergasted
flail
flake
flaky
flap
flash
flawed
flexible
flighty
flit
floating
flog
flop
floppy
flounder
flourish
flourished
flourishing
flow
fluctuate
fluff
fluid
flurried
flurry
fluster
flutter
fly
fly open
fog
foolish
foolishly
force
forced
foreign
forge
forged
forlorn
form
foul
founder
found in
fracture
frantic
frantically
freak
freak out
free
freely
frenetic
frenetically
frenzy
fresh
freshen
freshly
frightful
frightfully
frilly
frisky
frolic
frolicsome
fuddled
fudge
full
fumble
funnily
funny
furious
fussy
fuzzy
gaffe
gambol
garble
garbled
generate
giddily
giddy
ginger
gnarled
go crazy
gone
go off
grim
groggy
groom
gross
grotesque
ground
hairy
ham
hammer
hammered
hammer out
hamper
haphazard
haphazardly
happy
harass
harassed
harm
hash
hatch
havoc
haywire
hazy
head over heels
heat
hectic
hellish
helter-skelter
hideous
higgledy-piggledy
high
hit
hopeless
hopelessly
horrible
horribly
horrid
horrific
hotchpotch
hurl
hurt
hybrid
idiotic
ill
ill-assorted
ill at ease
ill-bred
ill-treat
imbecile
impair
impaired
imperfect
implicate
implicated
improper
improperly
inaccurate
incapable
in circulation
incorrect
indecent
indiscriminate
inebriated
inept
ingredient
injure
injured
inky
in motion
inordinate
in pieces
insane
insanely
insanity
insecure
intoxicate
intoxicated
intricate
invalid
invention
involve
involved
irregular
irritated
itinerant
jagged
jangle
jar
jaunty
jazz
jerk
jerky
jig
jiggle
jitters
jittery
jockey
jog
jolt
jostle
judder
juggle
jumble
jumbled
jump
junk
kick
kind of
kink
kinky
knead
knock
knock over
knot
knotty
labour
laboured
labyrinthine
lace
lamentable
lark
launder
lawless
lax
layout
lazily
leap
liberal
light
lit
lively
loaded
loony
loose
loosely
lost
lousy
ludicrous
lunatic
mad
madden
maddening
made-up
madly
madness
make
make up
make-up
maladjusted
malformed
malfunction
malleable
maltreat
mangle

manic
manically
manifest
manifestation
manipulate
manipulation
manoeuvre
manufacture
mar
marshal
mash
masquerade
massage
maul
maybe
mayhem
maze
meandering
meddle
medley
melange
mêlée
melt
mental
merry
mess
messy
metamorphose
metamorphosis
mill
mince
mint
misbehave
misbehaviour
mischievous
mischievously
misconduct
misconstrue
misdirect
miserable
miserably
misfit
misguided
mishandle
mishap
misinterpret
mislead
misleading
mismanage
mismanagement
misplace
misprint
misread
misrepresent
misrepresentation
misshapen
misspell
mistake
mistaken
mistakenly
mistreat
misuse
mix
mixed
mixed up
mix in
mixture
mix up
mix-up
mobile
mobilize
model
modification
modify
mongrel
mortal
mould
mouldy
move
movement
moving
muddle
muddled
muddy
muff
mushy
muss
must
musty
mutate
mutation
mutilate
mutilation
mutinous
mysterious
mysteriously
nastily
nasty
naughty
neaten
neglect
neglected
negligence
negligent
negotiate
negotiation
nervous
nervously
new
newly
nobble
nonsensical
not
novel
nuts
obfuscate
oblique
obscure
obstreperous
odd
oddball
oddly
off
off-colour
on
on the rampage
operate
order
orderly
organization
organize
organized
original
ornate
other
otherwise
out
outlandish
out of hand
out of order
out of place
out of sorts
output
outrageous
outré
outside
overthrow
overturn
painfully
panic
paranormal
pastiche
patchy
pathetic
peculiar
peculiarly
peddle
pell-mell
perform
perhaps
perplex
perturb
perturbed
perverse
perversely
perversion
perversity
pervert
perverted
phoney
pickle
pie
piece
plan
plastered
plastic
play
play around with
play with
ply
police
pollute
pollution
poor
poorly
pop
possible
possibly
potential
potentially
potty
prance
precarious
precariously
preparation
prepare
prepared
preposterous
problem
problematic
process
produce
production
promiscuous
protean
provide
pulverize
pummel
punish
puzzle
quaint
quake
queer
questionable
quirky
quiver
raddled
rag
rage
ragged
ramble
rambling
rampage
rampant
ramshackle
random
randomly
rare
rash
rattle
ravage
ravaged
rave
raving
react
reactionary
realign
rearrange
reassemble
rebel
rebellious
rebuild
recast
reckless
recklessly
recollect
recollection
recondition

reconfigure
reconstitute
reconstruct
recover
recreate
recycle
red
redeploy
redevelop
redevelopment
redistribute
redistribution
redraft
re-edit
reel
refashion
refine
refit
reform
reformat
reformation
refurbish
refurbishment
refuse
regenerate
regenerated
regulate
rehash
rejig
relax
relaxed
relay
remake
remarkable
remedy
remodel
render
renegade
renegotiate
renew
renovate
rent
reorder
reorganize
repackage
repair
replace
reposition
represent
representation
reprocess
reproduce
resettle
reshape
reshuffle
resolution
resolve
resort
restless
restoration
restore
re-use
revamp
reveal
revel
review
revise
revolt
revolting
revolution
revolutionary
rework
rewrite
rickety
ridiculous
ridiculously
rifle
rig
rile
riot
riotous
riotously
rip
ripple
rock
rocky
rogue
roll
rollicking
rolling
rot
rotten
rough
roughen
roughly
round
rouse
rove
rub
rubbish
rude
ruffle
ruin
ruined
rum
run
running
runny
run riot
run wild
rupture
rustic
sabotage
sack
sad
sadly
salad
scatter
scatty
scheme
scour
scraggy
scramble
scrappy
scratch
screw
screwy
scruffy
scuffle
sculpt
sculpture
scuttle
seedy
seethe
serve
set
set out
settlement
shake
shaky
sham
shape
shapeless
shatter
shattered
shell
shift
shifty
shimmer
shimmering
shiver
shock
shoddy
shot
shower
show off
shuffle
sick
signal
silliness
silly
sink
sketchy
skip
slack
slapdash
slaughtered
slide
slip
slippery
slipshod
sloppy
slosh
slovenly
slyly
smash
snarl
solution
solve
somehow
sorry
sort
soup
sozzled
spasmodic
spatter
special
specially
speech
spin
splash
splice
spoil
spongy
sport
sporting
spray
spread
spring
sprinkle
spurious
squiffy
squirm
stagger
staggered
staggering
steaming
stew
stir
stirring
storm
stormy
straighten
strange
strangely
stray
stress
structure
struggle
stumble
stupid
stupidly
style
subtle
subtly
suffer
suffering
sunk
supply
surprising
suspect
suspicious
swap
swill
swim
swimming
swing
swinging
swirl
switch
swop
synthetic
tailor
taint
tangle
tangled
tattered
tease

teeter
terrible
terribly
throb
throw
tidy
tight
tipsy
topple
topsy-turvy
torment
torn
tortuous
torture
toss
totter
tour
tragic
train
trammel
transfer
transfigure
transform
transformation
translate
translation
transmute
transport
transported
transpose
trash
travelling
treat
treatment
tremble
trembling
tremulous
trick
tricky
trip
trouble
troubled
troublesome
tumble
tumbledown
tumult
turbulence
turbulent
turmoil
turn
turning
tweak
twiddle
twinkle
twinkling
twirl
twirling
twist
twisted
twitch
type
ugly
unbalanced
uncertain
uncommon
uncommonly
uncomplicated
uncontrolled
unconventional
unco-ordinated
uncouth
undisciplined
undo
undoing
undone
unduly
uneasy
uneven
unexpected
unexpectedly
unfair
unfairly
unfamiliar
unfit
unfortunate
unfortunately
ungainly
unhappily
unhappy
unholy
unkempt
unnatural
unnaturally
unorthodox
unpredictable
unravel
unreliable
unrest
unrestrained
unrestricted
unruly
unscramble
unseemly
unsettle
unsettled
unsound
unstable
unsteady
untidy
untrue
unusual
unusually
unwind
unwise
upset
upsetting
upturn
use
used
useless
vacillate
vacillating
vacillation
vagrant
vague
vaguely
vandalize
variant
variation
varied
variegated
variety
various
vary
vault
versatile
version
vibrate
vigorous
vigorously
vile
violate
violation
violent
violently
volatile
vulnerable
wacky
wag
waggle
wander
wanton
warp
warring
waste
wasted
wave
waver
wavering
way
weave
weird
whip
whip up
whirl
whisk
wicked
wild
wildly
wind
winding
wobble
wobbly
woeful
work
working
worried
worry
wound
wrack
wreck
wreckage
wrestling
wretched
writhe
wrong
wrongly
wrought
yank
yearning
yield
yielding
zany

## Containment indicators

Containment indicators include:

about
absorb
absorbed
accept
accommodate
accommodating
accommodation
acquire
admit
adopt
around
arrest
assimilate
assume
astride
ate
bag
bear
bearing
beset
besiege
bewilder
bite
biting
box
bracket
break up
bring in
bring round
bury
capture
carry

casing
catch
catching
caught
circle
clasp
cleft
clutch
collect
come to grips with
comprehend
comprise
conceal
concealed
consume
consuming
contain
cover
crossing
custody
describe
detectable
drape
draw in
eat
embody
embrace
encapsulate
encircle
enclose
encompass
enfold
engulf
ensnare
entertain
entertaining
enthral
enthralling
envelop
fence
flank
found in
frame
framework
gather
gathering
get around
get hold of
get round
get to grips with
go about
go around
gobble
go round
grab
grasp
grasping
grip
gripping
guard
gulp
hamper
harbour
hedge
herein
hide
hiding
hold
host
house
housing
hug
imbibe
imprison
include
including
incorporate
in possession
introduce
keep
limit
lock up
net
nurse
obstruct
occlude
outside
over
overshadow
pen
pinch
pocket
possess
protect
purse
receive
repress
restrain
restrict
retain
round
sandwich
secure
see around
seize
shelter
snare
squeeze
stow
stuffing
superficial
surround
surrounding
swallow
tackle
take in
trap
trapped
wearing
welcome
without
wrap

## Insertion indicators

Insertion indicators include:

aboard
amid
amidst
among
at heart
between
bisect
block
break
cleave
collected
cut
cutting
devour
divide
don
during
engage in
enter
feed
fill
filling
find in
get into
go into
half
halve
held by
held in
imprisoned
in
infuse
inside
intercept
interception
interrupt
interruption
invest
involve
occupy
part
parting
penetrate
penetrating
pierce
piercing
puncture
seduce
set in
split
tuck in
tuck into
wear
within

## Deletion indicators

Deletion indicators include:

abandon
absent
cut
disappear
disappearance
dismiss
dismissal
disregard
drop
edit
elude
excision
excluding
fail to get
heave
ignore
junk
lack
lacking
leave
left
lose
missing
nearly
no
not
out
regardless

| | | | |
|---|---|---|---|
| sack | scrub | skip | withdraw |
| sacrifice | shed | small | withhold |
| scratch | shun | take off | |

## Ends indicators

Ends selection indicators include:

| | | | |
|---|---|---|---|
| banks | bounds | edge | limit |
| borders of | casing | extreme | side |
| both sides | determination | fringe | |

Ends deletion indicators include:

| | | | |
|---|---|---|---|
| limited | peel | top and tail | wingless |
| limitless | shell | unlimited | |

## Head indicators

Head selection indicators include:

| | | | |
|---|---|---|---|
| at first | front | leader | start |
| beginner | head | leadership | starter |
| beginning | heading | leading | summit |
| capital | initial | minimum | tip |
| extreme | initially | opener | top |
| first | introduction | opening | |
| foremost | lead | primarily | |

Head deletion indicators include:

| | | | |
|---|---|---|---|
| behead | fail to start | leaderless | topless |
| decapitate | headless | limitless | trim |
| deface | head off | tip-off | |

## Middle indicators

Middle selection indicators include:

| | | | |
|---|---|---|---|
| at heart | centre | heartily | middle |
| central | heart | innards | nucleus |

Middle deletion indicators include:

| | | |
|---|---|---|
| disembowel | empty | heartless |
| disheartened | gutless | heartlessly |

## Tail indicators

Tail selection indicators include:

| | | | |
|---|---|---|---|
| at last | endmost | finally | tail |
| at the end of | extreme | finish | terminal |
| back | far end | foundation | ultimate |
| behind | far side | last | ultimately |
| end | final | lastly | |
| ending | finale | rear | |

Tail selection down indicators include:

base of
bottom
south

Tail deletion indicators include:

- abbreviate
- abridged
- abrupt
- almost
- brief
- briefly
- clip
- contract
- curtail
- curtailment
- cut short
- detail
- detailed
- dock
- endless
- endlessly
- immature
- incomplete
- limit
- limitless
- Manx
- most
- nearly
- reduce
- reduction
- short
- shorten
- shortened
- shortly
- trim
- unfinished

Tail deletion down indicators include:

- baseless
- bottom

## Hidden indicators

Hidden indicators include:

- amid
- amidst
- among
- apparent
- belonging to
- bit
- bottle
- central
- characters in
- concealed
- contain
- content
- continuous
- continuously
- cover
- cover up
- deposit
- discover
- embrace
- emerge
- extract
- find in
- found in
- fragment
- from
- held by
- held in
- hidden
- hide
- immerse
- immersed
- in
- include
- in part
- inside
- keep
- lock up
- part
- part of
- piece
- sample
- show
- slice
- some
- stuffing
- within

Hidden alternately indicators include:

- alternate
- even
- evenly
- even parts
- ignore the odds
- odd
- oddly
- odd parts

## Homophone indicators

Homophone indicators include:

- aloud
- announce
- articulate
- articulated
- audible
- aural
- broadcast
- conversation
- conversational
- converse
- ear
- hear
- hearing
- hearsay
- inform
- list
- listen
- listen in
- murmur
- mutter
- narrate
- on radio
- on telephone
- oral
- orally
- pronounce
- pronounced
- read aloud
- report
- reportedly
- said
- say
- saying
- sound
- speak
- speech
- spoken
- state
- told
- utter
- verbal
- vocal

## Juxtaposition indicators

Juxtaposition indicators include:

- abut
- add
- adjacent
- adjoin
- adjoining
- after
- against
- ahead
- also
- alongside
- altogether
- and
- append
- approach
- arrive
- associate
- associated
- at the end of
- before
- behind

beside
by
chase
come first
continuous
continuously
first
follow
following
given
go together
in front
in front of
join
meet
take on
trail
with

Juxtaposition down indicators include:

above
below
beneath
go under
on
over
subordinate
support
supporter
topping
under

## Reversal indicators

Reversal indicators include:

about
all round
around
back
backfire
backing
backslide
backsliding
backtrack
backward
backwards
boomerang
bring back
capsize
come back
contrary
cutback
east
fall
flip
go around
go back
go back on
go round
go west
head over heels
hinge
in retrospect
in return
inversion
invert
keep back
knock back
make a comeback
on the contrary
preposterous
raise
rampant
reactionary
rear
rebellious
recall
recede
recess
recoil
recollect
recurrent
reflect
reflection
regress
reject
repel
retire
retired
retiring
retreat
retrograde
retrogress
retrospective
return
reversal
reverse
reversion
revert
review
revolution
revolutionary
rotate
round
set back
setback
switch
turn
turn back
turned
turning
turnover
volte-face
wheel

Reversal down indicators include:

arise
ascend
ascendant
bring up
climb
come up
elevate
elevated
give rise to
hold up
keel over
mount
over
overturn
put up
raised
rise
rising
send up
serve up
set up
set-up
take up
turn over
turn up
up
uplift
uprising
upset
upside down
upturn
upward
use up

Palindrome indicators include:

back and forth
either way
to and fro
up and down
whichever way you look at it

## Foreign indicators

Foreign word indicators include:

European
foreign
French
in France
local
translate

## Archaic indicators

Archaic indicators include:

antique
old
old-fashioned
once

## Dialect indicators

Dialect indicators include:

| | | | |
|---|---|---|---|
| American | East End | Sandy | US |
| Cockney | local | Scot | Yorkshire |
| Cumbrian | New York | Scottish | |

## Repetition indicators

Repetition indicators include:

| | | | |
|---|---|---|---|
| couple | repeat | repeatedly | twice |
| double | repeated | repetition | |

# Reference lists

Headwords followed by one or more reference list:

abbey
aboriginal
accommodation
acid
activist
actor, actress
administrative
admiral
Africa
African
agriculture
aircraft
airline
airport
alga, algae
alphabet
America
American
American football
amino acid
amphibian
anaesthetic
analgesic
anatomy
anchor
angel
animal
anniversary
ant
antelope
anthropology
antibiotic
antique
antiseptic
ape
apocryphal
apostle
apple
Arab
arch
archaeology
archbishop
archipelago
architect
architecture
armour
army
art
arthropod
artist
Asia
Asian
asteroid
astronaut
astronomer
athlete
athletics
atmosphere
Australia
Australian football
author
aviation
aviator
award

bacteriology
bacterium
badminton
bag
ballet
baseball
basketball
bat
battle
bay
beach
bean
bear
bed
bedclothes
beer
beetle
belief
believer
berry
bet
Bible
bicycle
biochemistry
biography
biology
bird
birth
biscuit
bishop
black
blemish
blue
bomb
bomber
bone
book
bookbinding
boot
border
botany
bottle
boxer
boxing
boy
brain
bread
bridge
bridle
brown
building
bulb
bushranger
business
businessman, businesswoman
butterfly

cactus
cake
calendar
camera
Canada
canal
canonical
cape
captain
car
cardinal
carpet
carriage
cartoon
castle
cat
cathedral
cattle
cave
celebration
cell
cemetery
cereal
ceremony
chair
channel
charity
cheese
chef
chemical
chemist
chemistry
chess
chicken
choreography
Christmas
church
cicada
cigarette
cinema
circle
circus
city
classification
clean
cloak
clock
clothes, clothing
cloud
clown
club
coat
cocktail
coffee
coin
collar
collective
collector
college
colour
comedian
comedy
comet
comic
command
commander
commonwealth
communication
compass
competition
composer
computer
conductor
constellation
container
continent
contraceptive

cook
cookery
cosmetic
cotton
council
country
county
court
cricket
crime
criminal
crop
cross
crossword
crust
crustacean
currency
cutlery
cutter
cyclist

dagger
dairy
dam
dance
dancer
dandy
daughter
day
death
deer
deficiency
delivery
department
desert
despot
dessert
detective
device
diamond
diary
dinosaur
diocese
director
disease
district
divination
doctor
dog
doll
domestic
dress
drink
drug
duck
dwarf
dye
dynasty

ear
eat
economics
economist
educational
eel
Egyptian
electorate
electrical
element
emblem
embroidery
emperor
empire
empress
engine
engineer
entertainer
entertainment
environment
enzyme
equestrian
essayist
Europe
European
execution
exercise
explorer
explosive
eye

fable
fabric
face
fairground
fairy tale
falcon
farm
fashion
fast
fastener, fastening
fate
feminism
fencing
fern
festival
fever
fictional
fictitious
Field Marshal
fighter
figure
film
fireplace
fireworks
firth
fish
fishing
flag
flower
fly
food
fool
football
footballer
footwear
forest
fortification
fossil
Frenchman
fruit
fuel
fungus
fur
furniture
fury

galaxy
gambling
game
garden
gardener
gardening
gas
gauge
gem
genealogy
general
genetics
geography
geology
German
giant
girl
gland
glass
god, goddess
golf
golf club
golfer
government
governor
grace
grass
Greek
green
grey
grouse
gulf
gun
gymnastics

hair
hairdresser
hairstyle
hat
headdress
heart
heraldry
herb
hero
heroine
highwayman
hill
historian
historical
hobby
hockey
holiday
honour
hormone
horse
horseman,
horsewoman
hour
house
household
humour
hybrid
hydrocarbon

ice
ice hockey
ice skating
incarnation
inflammation
insect
insecticide
institute
instrument
insulator
inventor
invertebrate
Ireland
Irish
island

Japanese
jazz
jewellery
journalism
journalist
judge

karate
key
king
knife
knight
knit
knot

laboratory
lace
lake
language
Latin
law
lawyer
leaf
leather
legal
legend
letter
lettuce
lexicographer
libretto
lie
lily

liqueur
literary
literature
lizard
lock
London
lover
luggage

machinery
mammal
mania
Maori
marriage
marshal
marsupial
martial art
massacre
mathematics
meal
measurement
measuring instrument
meat
medical
medicine
metal
meteor
meteorology
Middle East
military
mineral
miser
missile
missionary
mollusc
monarch
monastery
monk
monkey
monster
month
monument
moon
moss
moth
mountain
mountaineering
mouth
murderer
muscle
muse
museum
mushroom
music
musical
musician
musketeer
Muslim
mythical
mythology

name
narcotic
nationality
NATO
navigation
nerve
news
newspaper
New York
New Zealand
Nobel Prize
nobility
non-fiction
note
novel
number
numeral
nurse
nut

observatory
occult
occupation
ocean
office
official
oil
Olympics
OPEC
opera
optical
orange
oratorio
orchestra
orchid
ore
organ
overture

paint
painter
painting
palace
palaeontologist
palm
pantomime
paper
parasite
Paris
park
parliament
parrot
particle
party
passage
pasta
pastry
patriarch
peninsula
people
pepper
pet
pharaoh
philosopher
philosophy
phobia
photographer
photographic
physics
physiology
pianist
picture
pig
pigment
pike
pine
pink
pirate
plague
plain
planet
plant
plastic
play
playwright
plumbing
poem
poet
poetry
poison
poisoning
poker
police
police officer
political
politician
pope
porcelain
port
potato
pottery
poultry
power
prayer
precipitation
premier
president
priest
primate
prime minister
prince
princess
printing
prison
probe
prophet, prophetess
prosody
protein
province
pseudonym
psychiatrist
psychology
public house
publish
punctuation
punishment
purple
puzzle

qualification
queen
quiz

rabbi
rabbit
race
racecourse
racing
radiation
radio
railway
rainbow
rank
rebel
rebellion
recording
red
refine
reformer
regiment
region
reindeer
relative
religion
religious
reptile
republic
resort
restaurant
revolution
revolutionary
rhetorical
rhyme
river
road
rock
rodent
Roman
roof
room
rope
rowing
rubber
rugby
ruler
ruminant
Russia
Russian

sage
sail
sailing
sailor
saint
salad
sale
salt

satellite
satirist
sauce
sausage
saw
Scandinavian
scanner
scarf
school
science
scientific
Scottish
scripture
sculptor
sculpture
sea
seafood
seal
season
seaweed
sect
sedative
sedge
servant
service
Seven against Thebes
Shakespeare
shark
sheep
ship
shipping
shop
shout
shrub
SI
siege
sight
signal
sin
singer
skier
skiing
skin
smell
snake
snow
soap
society
sofa
soldier
son
song
songwriter
sound
soup
spa
space
spaniel
specialist
speech
spider
spirits
sport
sportsperson
spread
spy
square
stadium
stamp
star
state
stationery
stick
storm
strait
study
sugar
suit
surgeon
surgery
swan
sweet
swimming
sword
symbol

table
taste
tax
tea
teacher
team
teeth
television
tennis
tense
tent
term
terrier
theatre
theatrical
theologian
theory
therapy
thief
tie
time
title
tobacco
tool
torture
tower
town
toy
train
transport
travel
treaty
tree
triangle
tribe
trophy
tumour
tunnel
twin
typeface

umbrella
uncle
underground
underwear
union
United Kingdom
United Nations
United States of America
university
utensil
valve
vegetable
vehicle
vein
vermin
vestment
villain
virtue
virus
vitamin
volcano

wall
war
water
waterfall
weapon
weather
weed
welsh
whale
wheel
whisky
white
wind
window
wine
wise
witch
womanizer
wonder
wood
world
worm
worship
wrestling
writer
writing

year
yellow

zodiac
zoology

# A

**a**
**02** an **03** ane, one, per **05** alpha
• **a French**
**02** un **03** une
• **a German**
**03** ein **04** eine

**aardvark**
**07** antbear **08** anteater, earth-hog **09** groundhog

**aback**
• **take aback**
**04** stun **05** shock, upset **06** dismay **07** astound, set back, stagger, startle **08** astonish, bewilder, knock out, surprise **09** dumbfound **10** disconcert **11** flabbergast

**abalone**
**04** paua, pawa

**abandon**
◇ *anagram indicator*
◇ *deletion indicator*
**04** cede, drop, dump, jilt, quit, sink, stop **05** abort, cease, chuck, ditch, forgo, leave, let go, scrap, waive, yield **06** banish, desert, desist, escape, forego, forhow, get out, give up, jack in, maroon, pack in, resign, strand, vacate **07** bail out, forsake, yield to **08** abdicate, evacuate, forswear, jettison, jump ship, part with, renounce, run out on, wildness **09** break away, give way to, sacrifice, stop doing, surrender, walk out on **10** break loose, depart from, go away from, relinquish, resign from **11** discontinue, impetuosity, leave behind, unrestraint **12** be overcome by, break off with, carelessness, dispense with, kick the habit, leave for dead, recklessness, withdraw from **13** break free from, impulsiveness, leave it at that **14** break it off with, give the elbow to, lose yourself in **15** leave high and dry, leave in the lurch, thoughtlessness, uninhibitedness

**abandoned**
◇ *anagram indicator*
**03** mad, old **04** left, wild **05** crazy, empty **06** unused, vacant, wanton, wicked **07** corrupt, disused, forlorn, immoral **08** derelict, deserted, desolate, forsaken, reckless **09** debauched, dissolute, neglected, reprobate **10** profligate, unoccupied **11** uninhibited **12** unrestrained

**abandonment**
**05** drift, loose **07** cession, discard, Dunkirk, jilting, leaving, neglect, waiving **08** ditching, dropping, giving-up, stopping **09** cessation, desertion, forsaking, marooning, sacrifice, scrapping, stranding, surrender **10** abdication, decampment, exposition **11** dereliction, reprobation, resignation **12** renunciation, running out on **13** leaving behind **14** discontinuance, relinquishment **15** discontinuation, resignation from

**abase**
**05** crawl, lower **06** debase, demean, humble, kowtow, malign **07** degrade, mortify, put down **08** belittle, cast down, suck up to **09** disparage, humiliate

**abasement**
**08** crawling, humility **09** demeaning **10** debasement, humbleness **11** humiliation, sucking up to **13** disparagement, mortification

**abash**
**03** cow **05** quell, shame **06** humble **07** astound **08** confound, face down **09** embarrass, humiliate **10** disconcert **14** discountenance

**abashed**
**07** ashamed, floored, humbled **08** confused **09** affronted, mortified, perturbed, shamefast **10** bewildered, confounded, humiliated, nonplussed, remorseful, shamefaced, taken aback **11** discomfited, discomposed, dumbfounded, embarrassed **12** disconcerted **15** discountenanced

**abate**
**04** alay, ease, fade, faik, fall, sink, slow, vail, wane **05** aleye, allay, allow, appal, let up, quell, remit, slake **06** lessen, pacify, rebate, reduce, relent, soothe, weaken **07** assuage, decline, detract, die down, drop off, dwindle, fall off, qualify, relieve, slacken, subside **08** decrease, diminish, mitigate, moderate, peter out, pluck off, taper off **09** alleviate, attenuate

**abatement**
**04** wane **05** let-up, lysis **06** easing, relief **07** decline **08** decrease, lowering **09** allowance, deduction, dwindling, dying-down, lessening, reduction, remission, weakening **10** diminution, mitigation, moderation, palliation, slackening, subsidence **11** alleviation, assuagement, attenuation, dropping-off

**abattoir**
**08** butchery, shambles **14** slaughterhouse

**abbess**
**03** Abb **09** prelatess

**abbey**
**03** Abb **06** abbacy, friary, priory **07** convent, minster, nunnery **08** cloister, seminary **09** cathedral, monastery

*Abbeys include:*

**04** Bath, Iona
**05** Cluny, Kelso, Meaux, Roche, Royal
**06** Bolton, Byland, Hexham, Whitby, Woburn
**07** Citeaux, Furness, Melrose, Tintern, Waltham
**08** Buckfast, Crowland, Dryburgh, Fontenay, Fonthill, Holyrood, Jedburgh, Newstead, Rievaulx
**09** Clairvaux, Fountains, Holy Cross, Kirkstall, Nightmare, Sherborne
**10** Malmesbury, Northanger
**11** Westminster

**abbot**
**03** Abb **07** prelate **11** commendator **13** archimandrite

**abbreviate**
◇ *tail deletion indicator*
**03** cut **04** clip, trim **06** digest, lessen, précis, reduce, shrink **07** abridge, curtail, cut down, shorten **08** abstract, compress, condense, contract, truncate **09** constrict, summarize

**abbreviated**
**03** cut **05** short **07** clipped, compact, reduced, summary **08** abridged **09** condensed, shortened, truncated **10** contracted

**abbreviation**
**05** short **06** digest, précis, résumé **07** acronym, summary **08** abstract, clipping, mnemonic, synopsis **09** reduction, short form **10** initialism, shortening, truncation **11** abridgement, compression, contraction, curtailment **13** shortened form, summarization, truncated form

*See also* **county**; **United States of America**

**abdicate**
**04** cede, quit **05** forgo, shirk, yield **06** abjure, disown, forego, give up, reject, resign, retire **07** abandon, forsake **08** abnegate, renounce, step down **09** repudiate, stand down, surrender **10** relinquish **14** turn your back on **15** give up the throne, wash your hands of

**abdication**
**07** refusal **08** giving-up **09** disowning, rejection, surrender **10** abjuration, abnegation, retirement
**11** abandonment, repudiation, resignation **12** renunciation, standing-down, stepping-down
**14** relinquishment

**abdomen**
**03** maw, tum **04** guts, puku, womb
**05** belly, bingy, heart, pleon, tummy
**06** gaster, middle, paunch, venter
**07** beer gut, insides, midriff, stomach
**08** pot belly **09** beer belly, ventricle
**10** little Mary **11** bread-basket, corporation, opisthosoma

**abdominal**
**02** ab **05** belly **07** coeliac, gastric, ventral **08** visceral **10** intestinal
**11** ventricular

**abduct**
**05** seize **06** kidnap, ravish, snatch
**07** capture **08** carry off, shanghai
**09** lay hold of **10** run off with, spirit away **11** appropriate, make off with, run away with, take by force **12** hold to ransom **13** take as hostage **15** take away by force

**abduction**
**04** rape **06** kidnap **07** capture, seizure
**09** ravishing, seduction, snatching
**10** enlevement, kidnapping
**11** carrying off **15** taking as hostage

**aberrant**
◇ *anagram indicator*
**03** odd **05** rogue **06** quirky
**07** corrupt, deviant **08** abnormal, atypical, freakish, peculiar, straying
**09** anomalous, defective, deviating, different, divergent, eccentric, irregular, wandering **11** incongruous

**aberration**
**05** lapse **06** oddity **07** anomaly, mistake **08** delusion, straying
**09** deviation, oversight, variation, wandering **10** deliration, divergence
**11** abnormality, instability, peculiarity
**12** eccentricity, irregularity
**13** nonconformity

**abet**
**03** aid **04** back, help, spur **05** egg on
**06** assist, back up, incite, second
**07** condone, endorse, promote, succour, support **08** sanction **09** encourage, lend a hand **11** collude with

**abeyance**
**• in abeyance**
**05** on ice **06** on hold **07** disused, dormant, pending, shelved
**09** postponed, suspended **11** hanging fire **12** in suspension **13** no longer in use **14** not in operation

**abhor**
**04** hate, shun **05** spurn **06** detest, loathe, reject **07** despise **08** execrate
**09** abominate, shudder at **10** cannot bear, recoil from, shrink from **11** cannot abide, cannot stand

**abhorrence**
**04** hate **05** odium **06** enmity, hatred, horror, malice **07** disgust **08** aversion, contempt, distaste, loathing
**09** animosity, revulsion **10** execration, repugnance **11** abomination, detestation

**abhorrent**
**05** hated, yucky **06** horrid, odious
**07** hateful, heinous **08** absonant, detested, horrible **09** detesting, execrable, loathsome, obnoxious, offensive, repellent, repugnant, repulsive, revolting **10** abominable, detestable, disgusting, nauseating
**11** distasteful

**abide**
**03** lie, won **04** bear, hack, last, stay, take **05** brook, dwell, stand, thole
**06** accept, endure, live on, remain, reside **07** persist, stomach, survive
**08** continue, tolerate **09** put up with
**• abide by**
**04** obey **05** stand **06** accept, follow, fulfil, hold to, keep to, uphold **07** agree to, observe, respect, stand by
**08** adhere to, carry out, submit to
**09** conform to, discharge **10** comply with, toe the line **11** go along with, go by the book **15** stick to the rules

**abiding**
**04** firm **05** fixed **06** stable **07** chronic, durable, eternal, lasting **08** constant, enduring, immortal, lifelong, long-term, standing, unending **09** continual, immutable, permanent **10** continuous, persistent, persisting, unchanging
**11** continuance, everlasting, long-lasting, long-running **12** unchangeable

**ability**
**04** gift **05** flair, forte, knack, means, power, savvy, skill, touch **06** genius, powers, talent **07** calibre, faculty, knowhow, prowess, the hang
**08** aptitude, capacity, deftness, facility, strength, the knack **09** adeptness, dexterity, endowment, expertise, potential, resources **10** adroitness, capability, competence, competency, motivation, propensity **11** proficiency, savoir-faire, what it takes, wherewithal
**12** potentiality **13** qualification

**ab initio**
**07** at first, firstly **09** initially, primarily
**10** at the start, originally **11** to begin with, to start with **12** from the start
**14** at the beginning

**abject**
**03** low **04** base, mean, vile **05** awful
**06** sordid, woeful **07** debased, forlorn, ignoble, outcast, pitiful, servile, slavish
**08** degraded, hopeless, pathetic, pitiable, shameful, wretched
**09** execrable, miserable, worthless
**10** degenerate, deplorable, despicable, grovelling, submissive
**11** humiliating, ignominious
**12** contemptible, ingratiating
**13** dishonourable

**abjure**
**04** deny, reny **05** renay, reney
**06** disown, eschew, recant, reject
**07** abandon, disavow, forsake, retract
**08** abdicate, abnegate, disclaim, forswear, renege on, renounce
**09** repudiate **10** relinquish
**12** dispense with

**ablaze**
**03** lit **04** alow **05** afire, aglow, alowe, angry, fiery, lit up **06** aflame, alight, ardent, fuming, on fire, raging
**07** aroused, blazing, burning, excited, fervent, flaming, furious, glowing, ignited, intense, lighted, radiant
**08** flashing, frenzied, gleaming, incensed, in flames, luminous
**09** brilliant, sparkling **10** passionate, shimmering, stimulated **11** exhilarated, illuminated, impassioned
**12** enthusiastic, incandescent

**able**
**03** fit **04** deft, fere **05** adept **06** adroit, clever, expert, fitted, gifted, strong, up to it **07** capable, clued up, skilful, skilled **08** all there, masterly, powerful, talented **09** competent, cut out for, dexterous, effective, efficient, ingenious, on the ball, practised, qualified **10** proficient **11** experienced, intelligent **12** accomplished
**• able to**
**05** fit to **06** free to **09** allowed to, capable of **10** prepared to
**11** competent to, qualified to

**able-bodied**
**02** AB **03** fit **04** fine, hale **05** burly, hardy, lusty, sound, stout, tough
**06** hearty, robust, rugged, strong, sturdy **07** healthy, staunch
**08** powerful, stalwart, vigorous
**09** strapping **12** in good health **13** hale and hearty **14** as fit as a fiddle

**ablution**
**05** laver **07** bathing, rinsing, soaking, washing **08** cleaning **09** cleansing, scrubbing, showering

**abnegate**
**04** deny **06** abjure, eschew, give up, refuse, reject **07** abandon, abstain, disavow, forbear **08** forswear, renounce **09** repudiate, surrender
**10** relinquish

**abnegation**
**08** eschewal, giving-up **09** surrender
**10** abjuration, abstinence, self-denial, temperance **11** forbearance, repudiation **12** renunciation **13** self-sacrifice **14** relinquishment

**abnormal**
◇ *anagram indicator*
**03** odd **04** para- **05** outré, queer, weird **07** curious, deviant, erratic, oddball, strange, uncanny, unusual, wayward **08** aberrant, atypical, peculiar, singular, uncommon
**09** anomalous, different, divergent, eccentric, irregular, unnatural
**10** paranormal, unexpected

**11** exceptional **13** extraordinary, funny peculiar, idiosyncratic, preternatural

**abnormality**
**04** flaw **06** oddity **07** anomaly **08** enormity, vitiligo **09** deformity, deviation, exception, palilalia, water-core **10** aberration, difference, divergence **11** atypicality, bizarreness, dysfunction, monstrosity, pathography, peculiarity, singularity, strangeness, unusualness **12** eccentricity, irregularity, malformation, monstruosity, uncommonness **13** unnaturalness

**abnormally**
**09** extremely, unusually **10** especially, remarkably, uncommonly **12** particularly **13** exceptionally **15** extraordinarily, preternaturally

**aboard**
◇ *insertion indicator*
**02** in, on **04** into, onto **07** on board **09** alongside **11** on board ship

**abode**
**02** in **03** inn, pad, won **04** home, seat, stay **05** lodge, whare **06** libken, remain **07** domicil, habitat, mansion, presage **08** domicile, dwelling, lodgings **09** residence, residency **10** habitation **11** inhabitance, inhabitancy **13** dwelling-place

**abolish**
**03** axe, ban, end **04** chop, dump, sink, stop **05** annul, quash, scrap **06** cancel, repeal, revoke **07** blot out, destroy, expunge, nullify, rescind, subvert, vitiate, wipe out **08** abrogate, down with, get rid of, overturn, stamp out, suppress **09** eliminate, eradicate, overthrow, terminate **10** annihilate, do away with, invalidate, obliterate, put an end to **11** discontinue, exterminate

**abolition**
**03** axe **04** chop **06** ending, repeal **07** dumping, voiding **08** chopping, quashing, stopping **09** annulment, overthrow, scrapping, vitiation **10** abrogation, extinction, rescission, revocation, subversion, withdrawal **11** blotting-out, destruction, dissolution, elimination, eradication, extirpation, rescindment, suppression, termination **12** annihilation, cancellation, invalidation, obliteration **13** doing-away with, extermination, nullification

**abomasum**
**04** read

**abominable**
◇ *anagram indicator*
**04** base, foul, vile **06** cursed, horrid, nefast, odious **07** hateful, heinous **08** damnable, dreadful, god-awful, horrible, terrible, wretched **09** abhorrent, appalling, atrocious, execrable, loathsome, nefandous, obnoxious, offensive, repellent, repugnant, repulsive, revolting **10** despicable, detestable, disgusting, nauseating **12** contemptible **13** reprehensible

**abominably**
**07** beastly **08** horribly, odiously, terribly **09** execrably **10** dreadfully **11** appallingly, obnoxiously **12** disgustingly **13** reprehensibly

**abominate**
**04** hate **05** abhor **06** detest, loathe **07** condemn, despise **08** execrate

**abomination**
**04** evil, hate **05** curse, odium **06** hatred, horror, plague **07** disgust, offence, outrage, torment **08** anathema, atrocity, aversion, disgrace, distaste, loathing **09** hostility, revulsion **10** abhorrence, execration, repugnance **11** detestation

**aboriginal**
**05** first, Koori, local, Murri, Nunga **06** Anangu, native, primal **07** ancient, initial **08** earliest, original, primeval **09** primaeval, primitive **10** indigenous **13** autochthonous, tangata whenua

*Aboriginal activists include:*

**04** **Mabo** (Eddie)
**05** **Scott** (Evelyn)
**06** **Dodson** (Mick), **Dodson** (Patrick), **O'Shane** (Pat)
**07** **Bandler** (Faith), **Gilbert** (Kevin), **Pearson** (Noel), **Perkins** (Charles)
**09** **Yunupingu** (Galarrwuy)
**12** **Burnum Burnum**

*Aboriginal tribes include:*

**03** Wik
**04** Tiwi
**05** Bardi, Yanda
**06** Aranda, Dharug
**07** Noongar, Nyungar
**08** Gurindji, Warlpiri
**09** Kuring-gai, Wiradjuri
**10** Bundjalung, Pitta Pitta, Wemba Wemba
**14** Pitjantjatjara

**aborigine**
**03** gin **05** koori, Maori, myall **06** native **08** indigene **11** black-fellow **15** first inhabitant

**abort**
**03** axe, end **04** fail, halt, stop **05** check **06** thwart **07** call off, nullify, suspend **08** cut short, miscarry **09** frustrate, terminate **11** come to an end, discontinue **12** bring to an end **13** pull the plug on

**abortion**
**08** misbirth **09** foeticide **10** aborticide **11** miscarriage, termination

**abortive**
**04** idle, vain **06** barren, failed, futile **07** misborn, sterile, useless **08** bootless, thwarted **09** fruitless **10** unavailing **11** ineffective, ineffectual **12** unproductive, unsuccessful **13** inefficacious

**abound**
**04** flow, teem **05** crowd, swarm, swell **06** be full, thrive **07** bristle **08** brim over, flourish, increase, overflow **09** exuberate, luxuriate **10** be abundant **11** be plentiful, proliferate, superabound

**about**
◇ *anagram indicator*
◇ *containment indicator*
◇ *reversal indicator*
**01** a, c **02** ca, on, re **03** cir **04** circ, near, over **05** anent, circa, close, round **06** almost, approx, around, beside, nearby, nearly **07** all over, close by, close to, nearing, roughly **08** to and fro **09** apropos of, as regards, regarding **10** adjacent to, concerning, encircling, more or less, relating to, throughout **11** approaching, dealing with, referring to, surrounding, within reach **12** encompassing, here and there, with regard to **13** approximately, concerned with, connected with, in the matter of, in the region of, with respect to **14** on the subject of **15** in the vicinity of, with reference to

**• about to**
**06** all but, soon to **07** going to, ready to **08** all set to **11** intending to, preparing to **12** on the point of, on the verge of

**about-turn**
**03** uey **05** U-turn **08** reversal **09** about-face, turnabout, volte-face **10** turnaround **13** enantiodromia

**above**
◇ *juxtaposition down indicator*
**03** sup, sur **04** atop, over, owre, upon **05** aloft, prior, sopra, super-, supra- **06** before, beyond, higher, high up, on high **07** earlier, on top of **08** immune to, overhead, previous, senior to **09** aforesaid, exceeding, foregoing, not open to, preceding **10** exempt from, higher than, in excess of, prevenient, previously, superior to, surpassing **11** above-stated, greater than, not liable to **12** not exposed to **14** above-mentioned, aforementioned

**• above all**
**07** chiefly, firstly, notably **09** most of all, primarily **10** first of all **15** most importantly

**• above yourself**
**04** smug, vain **05** cocky, proud **07** haughty, stuck-up **08** arrogant, boastful, immodest, puffed-up **09** bigheaded, conceited **10** complacent **11** egotistical, toffee-nosed **12** narcissistic, supercilious, vainglorious **13** self-important, self-satisfied, swollen-headed **14** full of yourself

**• as above**
**02** us **07** ut supra

**above-board**
**04** open, true **05** frank, legit **06** candid, dinkum, honest, kosher, square **07** upright **08** straight, truthful **09** guileless, reputable, veracious

10 forthright, honourable, legitimate, on the level 11 trustworthy 13 fair and square 15 straightforward

**abracadabra**
05 spell 09 gibberish, magic word 10 hocus pocus, mumbo-jumbo, open sesame

**abrade**
03 rub 04 stun 05 awake, chafe, erode, grate, graze, grind, rouse, scour, start 06 scrape 07 scratch, wear off 08 wear away, wear down 10 scrape away

**abrasion**
03 cut 05 chafe, graze 06 scrape 07 chafing, erosion, grating, rubbing, scratch 08 abrading, friction, grinding, scouring, scraping 10 scratching 11 excoriation, wearing-away, wearing-down

**abrasive**
04 bort 05 boart, emery, harsh, nasty, rough, sharp 06 biting 07 brusque, caustic, chafing, erodent, erosive, grating, hurtful 08 annoying, grinding, scraping 09 corrosive, sandpaper 10 frictional, glasspaper, irritating, scratching, unpleasant 11 attritional, garnet-paper, ground glass 14 silicon carbide

**abreast**
02 up 03 hep 05 level 06 afront, au fait, well up 07 in touch 08 familiar, informed, up to date 09 au courant, on the ball 10 acquainted, conversant, side by side 11 cheek by jowl 12 in the picture 13 knowledgeable 15 beside each other, next to each other

**abridge**
03 cut, lop 04 clip 05 elide, prune 06 digest, lessen, précis, reduce 07 curtail, cut down, shorten 08 abstract, compress, condense, contract, cut short, decrease, truncate 09 epitomize, summarize, synopsize 10 abbreviate 11 concentrate 12 circumscribe

**abridged**
◇ *tail deletion indicator*
03 abd, abr 05 short 06 potted 07 clipped, cut down, reduced, shorter 08 cut short, digested 10 contracted, summarized 11 abbreviated

**abridgement**
03 abr 06 abrégé, digest, précis, résumé 07 compend, cutting, epitome, outline, pastime, summary 08 abstract, decrease, synopsis 09 reduction 10 compendium, conspectus, diminution, shortening, truncation 11 contraction, curtailment, diminishing, restriction 12 abbreviation, abbreviature, short version 13 concentration

**abroad**
◇ *anagram indicator*
◇ *foreign word indicator*
03 out 04 away 05 about, forth 06 around, astray, widely 07 at large, current 08 offshore, overseas, publicly 10 far and wide 11 circulating, extensively 14 doing your OE, in foreign parts, to foreign parts 15 out of the country
- **go abroad**
08 emigrate

**abrogate**
03 axe, end 04 chop, dump, stop 05 annul, scrap 06 cancel, repeal, revoke 07 abolish, rescind, retract, reverse, vitiate 08 disenact, dissolve 09 disaffirm, repudiate 10 do away with, invalidate 11 countermand

**abrogation**
03 axe 04 chop 06 repeal 07 dumping 08 recision, reversal 09 abolition, annulment, repealing, scrapping, vitiation 10 overruling, rescinding, rescission, revocation 11 dissolution, repudiation, rescindment 12 cancellation, invalidation 14 countermanding, disaffirmation

**abrupt**
◇ *tail deletion indicator*
03 off 04 bold, curt, rude, snap 05 blunt, brisk, gruff, hasty, quick, rapid, rough, sharp, sheer, short, squab, steep, swift, terse 06 direct, snappy, sudden 07 brusque, hurried, instant, offhand, prerupt, uncivil 08 dramatic, impolite, snappish, vertical 09 immediate, startling 10 dismissive, surprising, unexpected, unforeseen, unfriendly 11 declivitous, precipitate, precipitous, unannounced 12 discourteous 13 instantaneous, unceremonious

**abruptly**
04 bang 05 short 06 curtly, rudely 07 bluntly, briskly, gruffly, hastily, offhand, quickly, rapidly, roughly, shortly, swiftly, tersely 08 directly, snappily, suddenly 09 brusquely, hurriedly, instantly 10 impolitely, snappishly 11 immediately 12 dismissively, unexpectedly 13 precipitately 14 discourteously 15 instantaneously, unceremoniously

**abscess**
04 boil, noma, sore 05 ulcer 06 canker 07 gumboil 08 swelling 09 gathering, impostume, infection 10 imposthume, ulceration 12 inflammation

**abscond**
03 fly 04 bolt, flee, quit 05 scram 06 beat it, decamp, escape, run off, vanish 07 do a bunk, make off, run away, scarper, vamoose 08 clear off, clear out, jump bail, run for it 09 disappear, do a runner, skedaddle 12 absquatulate 15 take French leave

**absence**
03 abs 04 lack, need, want 06 dearth 07 default, paucity, skiving, truancy, vacancy, vacuity 08 omission, scarcity 09 privation 10 bunking off, deficiency 11 absenteeism, abstraction, inattention 12 non-existence 13 non-appearance, non-attendance, playing hookey 14 unavailability
- **feel absence**
04 miss

**absent**
◇ *deletion indicator*
01 a 03 abs, MIA, off, out 04 away, AWOL, gone 05 blank 06 dreamy, truant, vacant 07 faraway, lacking, missing, not here, unaware 08 not there 09 elsewhere, miles away, not around, oblivious, unheeding 10 distracted, in absentia, not present 11 daydreaming, inattentive, preoccupied, unavailable 12 absent-minded
- **absent yourself**
04 exit 06 depart, retire 07 back out, retreat 08 slip away, withdraw 13 take your leave

**absentee**
06 no-show, truant 11 non-attender

**absently**
07 blankly 08 dreamily 12 abstractedly 13 inattentively 14 absent-mindedly

**absent-minded**
06 absent, dreamy, musing, scatty 07 faraway, pensive, unaware 08 absorbed, distrait, dreaming, heedless, yonderly 09 distraite, engrossed, forgetful, miles away, oblivious, unheeding, withdrawn 10 abstracted, distracted, unthinking 11 impractical, inattentive, not all there, preoccupied, unconscious 13 somewhere else, wool-gathering 14 dead to the world, scatterbrained

**absent-mindedly**
07 blankly 08 absently 12 abstractedly 13 inattentively

**absolute**
01 A 03 abs, set 04 dead, firm, full, meer, mere, pure, rank, sure, true 05 final, fixed, rigid, sheer, total, utter 06 entire 07 certain, decided, genuine, perfect, settled, supreme, unmixed 08 almighty, complete, decisive, definite, despotic, outright, positive, thorough 09 autarchic, boundless, downright, out-and-out, sovereign, undivided, universal, unlimited 10 autocratic, conclusive, consummate, definitive, exhaustive, high-handed, omnipotent, peremptory, tyrannical 11 autarchical, categorical, dictatorial, established, indubitable, non-variable, unalterable, unambiguous, unequivocal, unmitigated, unqualified 12 totalitarian, unrestrained, unrestricted 13 authoritarian, non-negotiable, unadulterated, unconditional 14 unquestionable

**absolutely**
03 abs, yes 04 bang, dead, just, mere, very 05 fully, quite, truly 06 fairly,

purely, surely, wholly **07** clearly, exactly, finally, for sure, no doubt, plainly, quite so, totally, utterly **08** entirely, of course **09** assuredly, certainly, decidedly, doubtless, genuinely, naturally, obviously, perfectly, precisely, supremely **10** by all means, completely, decisively, definitely, in every way, infallibly, positively, separately, thoroughly, undeniably **11** à toute force, doubtlessly, undoubtedly **12** conclusively, despotically, exhaustively, high-handedly, tyrannically **13** categorically, dictatorially, unambiguously, unequivocally, without a doubt **14** autocratically, in every respect, unquestionably, wholeheartedly **15** unconditionally

**absolution**
**05** mercy **06** pardon, shrift **07** amnesty, freedom, release **09** acquittal, discharge, pardoning, purgation, remission **10** assoilment, letting off, liberation, redemption **11** deliverance, exculpation, exoneration, forgiveness, vindication **12** emancipation **13** justification

**absolve**
**04** free, quit **05** clear, loose, quite, quyte, remit **06** acquit, assoil, excuse, let off, pardon, quight **07** deliver, forgive, justify, release, set free **08** liberate **09** assoilzie, discharge, exculpate, exonerate, vindicate **10** accomplish, emancipate **11** have mercy on

**absorb**
◇ *containment indicator*
**04** fill, hold, soak, sorb, suck, wrap **05** eat up, mop up, use up **06** blot up, devour, digest, draw in, engage, engulf, fill up, imbibe, ingest, occupy, retain, soak up, suck up, take in, take up **07** consume, drink in, engross, enthral, involve, receive **08** sponge up **09** captivate, fascinate, integrate, preoccupy, swallow up **10** assimilate, monopolize, understand **11** incorporate

**absorbed**
◇ *containment indicator*
**04** rapt **07** riveted **08** involved, occupied **09** engrossed **10** captivated, enthralled, fascinated, interested, spellbound **11** preoccupied, taken up with

**absorbent**
**03** abs **04** dope **06** porous, spongy **07** soaking **08** bibulous, blotting, pervious **09** permeable, receptive, resorbent, retentive **10** absorptive, spongiform **12** assimilative, sorbefacient

**absorbing**
**07** amusing **08** gripping, riveting **09** diverting, enjoyable **10** compelling, compulsive, engrossing, intriguing **11** captivating, enthralling, fascinating, interesting **12** entertaining, preoccupying, spellbinding **13** unputdownable

**absorption**
**07** holding, osmosis **08** monopoly, raptness, riveting, taking-in **09** devouring, drawing-in, immersion, ingestion, soaking-up **10** engagement, engrossing, intentness, occupation **11** captivating, consumption, involvement **12** assimilation **13** attentiveness, concentration, preoccupation

**abstain**
**04** fast, pass, quit, shun, stop **05** avoid, forgo, spare **06** cut out, desist, eschew, forego, give up, jack in, refuse, reject, resist **07** decline, forbear, not vote, refrain **08** hold back, renounce, restrain **09** be neutral, do without, go without **11** stop short of **12** deny yourself, refuse to vote **13** sit on the fence

**abstainer**
**02** TT **06** tee-tee, wowser **08** teetotal **09** Rechabite **11** teetotaller **12** water-drinker

**• abstainers**
**02** AA, TT

**abstemious**
**02** TT **05** sober **06** frugal **07** ascetic, austere, sparing **08** moderate, teetotal **09** abstinent, temperate **10** restrained **11** disciplined, self-denying **14** self-abnegating **15** self-disciplined

**abstention**
**08** celibacy **09** not voting **10** neutrality **13** refusal to vote **15** declining to vote

**abstinence**
**04** fast **07** fasting, refusal **08** eschewal, giving-up, sobriety **09** avoidance, frugality, nephalism, restraint **10** abjuration, abstaining, asceticism, continence, continency, declension, desistance, moderation, refraining, self-denial, temperance, water wagon **11** forbearance, self-control, teetotalism **12** going-without, renunciation **13** non-indulgence, self-restraint **14** abstemiousness, self-discipline

*See also* **fast**

**abstinent**
**05** sober **06** frugal **07** ascetic **08** moderate, teetotal **09** continent, temperate **10** abstaining, abstemious, forbearing, restrained **11** self-denying **12** non-indulgent **14** self-controlled, self-restrained **15** self-disciplined

**abstract**
**03** abs, cut, tap **04** deep **06** arcane, detach, digest, précis, remove, résumé, subtle **07** abridge, complex, cut down, draw off, epitome, extract, general, isolate, outline, shorten, subduce, subduct, summary, take out **08** abstruse, academic, compress, condense, discrete, ideative, notional, prescind, profound, separate, syllabus, symbolic, synopsis, take away, withdraw **09** contrived, recondite, summarize **10** abbreviate, compendium, conceptual, conspectus, dissociate, ideational, indefinite **11** abridgement, compression, generalized, non-concrete, suppositive, theoretical, unpractical, unrealistic **12** hypothetical, intellectual, metaphysical, non-realistic **13** philosophical, suppositional **14** recapitulation

**• in the abstract**
**07** on paper **08** in theory **09** generally **10** notionally **11** in abstracto **12** conceptually **13** theoretically **14** hypothetically **15** philosophically

**abstracted**
**06** absent, dreamy, musing, scatty **07** bemused, faraway, pensive, unaware **08** absorbed, dreaming, heedless **09** engrossed, forgetful, miles away, oblivious, unheeding, withdrawn **10** distracted, unthinking **11** impractical, inattentive, inconscient, preoccupied, unconscious **12** absent-minded **13** wool-gathering **14** scatterbrained

**abstractedly**
**07** blankly **08** absently **13** inattentively **14** absent-mindedly

**abstraction**
**04** idea **05** dream **06** entity, notion, revery, theory **07** absence, concept, formula, removal, reverie, theorem, thought **09** isolation **10** absorption, conception, conjecture, dreaminess, extraction, generality, hypothesis, remoteness, separation, withdrawal **11** bemusedness, distraction, inattention, pensiveness **13** preoccupation **14** generalization

**abstruse**
**04** deep, high, long **06** arcane, hidden, subtle **07** complex, cryptic, Delphic, obscure **08** esoteric, hermetic, profound, puzzling **09** enigmatic, exquisite, recherché, recondite **10** hermetical, mysterious, perplexing **11** inscrutable **12** unfathomable

**absurd**
◇ *anagram indicator*
**04** daft **05** crazy, funny, gonzo, inane, silly **06** stupid **07** asinine, comical, foolish, idiotic, Laputan, risible **08** cockeyed, derisory, farcical, humorous, Laputian **09** fantastic, grotesque, illogical, laughable, ludicrous, priceless, senseless, unearthly, untenable **10** irrational, ridiculous **11** harebrained, implausible, incongruous, meaningless, nonsensical, paradoxical **12** preposterous, unreasonable

**absurdity**
**04** joke **05** farce, folly **06** drivel, humour, idiocy **07** charade, inanity, paradox, rubbish, twaddle

**08** claptrap, daftness, malarkey, nonsense, ridicule, solecism, travesty **09** craziness, gibberish, silliness, stupidity **10** balderdash, caricature **11** fatuousness, foolishness, incongruity **12** illogicality **13** irrationality, ludicrousness, senselessness **14** implausibility, ridiculousness **15** meaninglessness

**absurdly**

**07** crazily, funnily, inanely **08** stupidly **09** comically, foolishly, laughably, untenably **10** farcically, humorously **11** idiotically, implausibly, ludicrously, senselessly **12** irrationally, ridiculously, unreasonably **13** fantastically, incongruously, meaninglessly, nonsensically, paradoxically **14** preposterously

**abundance**

**04** bags, glut, load, lots **05** feast, flush, fouth, fowth, heaps, loads, piles, routh, rowth, scads, sonce, sonse, store **06** bounty, excess, masses, oodles, plenty, riches, stacks, wealth **07** bonanza, fortune, lashing, oodlins, pleroma, tallent **08** fullness, lashings, opulence, overflow, plethora, richness **09** affluence, amplitude, fertility, plenitude, profusion **10** exuberance, generosity, lavishness, luxuriance, profligacy **11** copiousness, corn in Egypt, great supply, munificence, prodigality **12** extravagance, milk and honey **13** plentifulness, rack and manger **14** stouth and routh

**abundant**

**04** full, rank, rich **05** ample, hefty, large, thick **06** filled, galore, lavish, strong **07** copious, opulent, profuse, teeming **08** affluent, generous, in plenty, prolific **09** bounteous, bountiful, exuberant, luxuriant, plenteous, plentiful **11** overflowing **12** well-supplied **14** more than enough

**abundantly**

**04** very, well **05** amply, jolly **06** highly, plenty, really **07** acutely, awfully, greatly, utterly **08** severely, terribly **09** copiously, decidedly, extremely, intensely, profusely, unusually **10** completely, dreadfully, remarkably, thoroughly, uncommonly **11** exceedingly, excessively, extensively, exuberantly, frightfully, in abundance, in profusion, plentifully **12** immoderately, inordinately, prolifically, terrifically, unreasonably **13** exceptionally **15** extraordinarily

**abuse**

◇ *anagram indicator*

**03** hit, mud **04** beat, harm, hurt, rail, rape **05** bully, curse, libel, scold, serve, slate, smear, snash, wrong **06** batter, damage, defame, impugn, injure, injury, insult, jawing, malign, misuse, molest, oppugn, pick on, revile, tirade, verbal **07** affront, beating, calumny, censure, cruelty, cursing, exploit, insults, jobbery, miscall, offence, oppress, slag off, slander, swear at, torture, upbraid, violate, vitriol **08** be rude to, bullyrag, chuck off, derision, diatribe, ill-treat, maltreat, misapply, mistreat, reproach, scolding, swearing **09** call names, castigate, contumely, denigrate, disparage, invective, misemploy, swear-word, victimize **10** calumniate, chuck off at, defamation, imposition, oppression, upbraiding, vituperate **11** castigation, clapperclaw, denigration, hurl abuse at, malediction, molestation, mud-slinging, name-calling **12** billingsgate, calumniation, exploitation, ill-treatment, interference, maltreatment, mistreatment, vilification, vituperation **13** disparagement, interfere with, misemployment, sexual assault, treat like dirt **14** harass sexually, misapplication **15** assault sexually, take advantage of

**abusive**

**04** rude **05** cruel **06** bitchy, brutal **07** harmful, hurtful, railing, satiric **08** reviling, scathing, scolding, scornful **09** injurious, insulting, invective, libellous, maligning, offensive, satirical, vilifying **10** censorious, defamatory, derogatory, pejorative, scurrilous, slanderous, upbraiding **11** blasphemous, castigating, denigrating, destructive, disparaging, opprobrious, reproachful **12** calumniating, contumelious, vituperative

**abusively**

**06** rudely **07** cruelly **08** bitchily, brutally **10** revilingly, scathingly, scoldingly, scornfully **11** injuriously, insultingly, offensively **12** calumniously, censoriously, pejoratively, scurrilously, upbraidingly **13** blasphemously, denigratingly, disparagingly, opprobriously, reproachfully **14** contumeliously, vituperatively

**abut**

◇ *juxtaposition indicator*

**04** join, lean **05** touch **06** adjoin, border **07** conjoin, impinge, verge on **08** be next to

**abysmal**

◇ *anagram indicator*

**05** awful, utter **06** dismal **08** complete, dreadful, shocking, terrible **09** appalling, frightful **10** bottomless **11** disgraceful **12** unfathomable

**abysmally**

◇ *anagram indicator*

**07** awfully **08** terribly **10** dreadfully **11** appallingly, frightfully **13** disgracefully

**abyss**

**03** pit **04** gulf, hell, void **05** abysm, chasm, depth, gorge, gulph **06** abrupt, canyon, crater, depths, ravine **07** Avernus, fissure, swallow **08** crevasse, profound, Tartarus **09** barathrum **13** bottomless pit

**acacia**

**03** koa **05** babul, boree, mulga, myall, sally **06** bablah, gidgee, gidjee, mimosa, sallee **07** robinia, shittah **08** brigalow **09** blackwood, doornboom, fever tree, flame-tree **10** locust tree **11** shittah tree **12** golden wattle **13** kangaroo-thorn

**academic**

**03** don **04** acca **05** smart, tutor **06** brainy, fellow, master, pedant **07** bookish, donnish, erudite, learned, scholar, serious, student, teacher, trainer **08** abstract, bookworm, educated, educator, highbrow, lecturer, literary, notional, studious, well-read **09** pedagogue, professor, scholarly **10** conceptual, instructor, irrelevant, ivory-tower, scholastic **11** conjectural, educational, impractical, pedagogical, speculative, theoretical **12** hypothetical, intellectual, man of letters, well-educated **13** instructional, suppositional **14** woman of letters

**academician**

**01** A **02** RA **03** ARA, RSA

**academy**

**01** A **02** RA **03** RAM **04** RADA **05** forty **06** school **07** academe, college **08** immortal, seminary **09** institute **10** university **11** charm school

**acanthus**

**07** ruellia **08** many-root **10** thunbergia **11** bear's-breech, brankursine, shrimp plant

**accede**

**05** admit, agree, bow to **06** accept, assume, attain, come to, concur, give in **07** agree to, consent, inherit, succeed **08** assent to, back down, take over **09** acquiesce, consent to, succeed to **10** comply with

**accelerate**

**05** hurry, speed **06** hasten, open up, spur on, step up **07** advance, forward, further, promote, quicken, speed up **08** antedate, expedite, go faster, step on it **09** festinate, stimulate **10** facilitate **11** drive faster, gather speed, pick up speed, precipitate, put on a spurt **12** gain momentum, step on the gas **14** step on the juice **15** put your foot down

**acceleration**

**01** a, g **07** speed-up **08** momentum **09** hastening, promotion **10** expedition, forwarding, speeding-up, stepping-up **11** advancement, furtherance, stimulation **14** gathering speed, rate of increase

**accent**

**04** beat, dash, tone **05** acute, force, grave, ictus, pitch, pulse, twang **06** brogue, rhythm, stress, timbre, tittle

**07** cadence, diction **08** emphasis, priority **09** diacritic, intensity, pulsation **10** circumflex, importance, inflection, intonation, modulation, prominence **11** enunciation, underlining **12** accentuation, articulation, highlighting
**13** pronunciation **15** diacritical mark

**accentuate**
**06** accent, deepen, show up, stress
**07** point up **08** heighten
**09** emphasize, highlight, intensify, spotlight, underline **10** strengthen, underscore **15** make great play of

**accept**
◇ *containment indicator*
**03** buy, get **04** bear, gain, have, take, wear **05** abide, admit, adopt, allow, bow to, grasp, stand, trust **06** come by, credit, endure, give in, honour, jump at, obtain, pocket, secure, suffer, take on, take up **07** abide by, acquire, agree to, approve, believe, embrace, fall for, let go of, receive, stomach, swallow, welcome, yield to **08** accede to, back down, face up to, say yes to, tolerate
**09** approbate, believe in, consent to, integrate, put up with, recognize, undertake **10** comply with, concur with, not say no to **11** acknowledge, acquiesce in, be certain of, go along with, take on board **12** be resigned to
**13** make the best of, receive warmly
**15** come to terms with

**acceptable**
**01** U **02** OK, on **04** so-so **06** not bad
**07** welcome **08** adequate, all right, moderate, passable, pleasant, pleasing
**09** agreeable, allowable, desirable, tolerable **10** admissible, delightful, gratifying, reasonable **11** appreciated, appropriate, permissible **12** satisfactory, the done thing **15** unexceptionable
• **make acceptable**
**04** sell

**acceptably**
**08** passably, suitably **09** agreeably, desirably, tolerably **10** adequately, moderately, reasonably
**13** appropriately **14** satisfactorily

**acceptance**
**02** OK **03** acc, nod **04** acpt **05** faith, trust **06** assent, belief, buying, taking
**07** bearing, consent, gaining, getting, receipt, welcome **08** adoption, approval, credence, currency, giving-in, securing, taking on, taking-up
**09** accepting, accession, acquiring, admission, agreement, embracing, endurance, obtaining, receiving, tolerance, welcoming **10** admittance, assumption, compliance, facing up to, falling for **11** affirmation, backing-down, concurrence, endorsement, integration, recognition, resignation, undertaking **12** acquiescence, ratification **13** putting up with, taking on board **14** going along with, seal of approval **15** acknowledgement, making the best of, stamp of approval

**accepted**
**01** a **04** taen **05** taken, usual
**06** agreed, common, normal
**07** correct, regular **08** admitted, approved, orthodox, ratified, received, standard **09** confirmed, customary, universal **10** acceptable, authorized, recognized, sanctioned
**11** appropriate, established, traditional
**12** acknowledged, conventional, time-honoured

**access**
**03** key, use **04** door, path, read, road
**05** drive, entry, log on, way in
**06** course, entrée, locate **07** gateway, ingress, passage **08** approach, driveway, entering, entrance, retrieve
**09** admission **10** admittance **12** gain access to, means of entry, right of entry
**13** accessibility **15** means of approach, permission to see

**accessibility**
**11** convenience **12** availability, ease of access **13** attainability, obtainability
**15** approachability, intelligibility

**accessible**
**04** near, open **05** handy, ready
**06** nearby, on hand, patent **07** general
**09** available, get-at-able, reachable
**10** achievable, attainable, come-at-able, convenient, easy to read, obtainable, procurable **11** close at hand, close to hand, within cooee
**12** approachable, easy to follow, intelligible, user-friendly
**14** comprehensible, understandable

**accession**
**04** gain, gift **06** afflux, influx
**08** addition, increase, purchase
**09** affluxion, attaining **10** assumption, possession, succession, taking over
**11** acquisition, inheritance

**accessorize**
**04** trim **05** add to, adorn **06** bedaub, set off **07** augment, bedizen, enhance
**08** contrast, decorate, round off
**10** complement, supplement

**accessory**
**03** aid, hat **04** belt, help **05** add-in, add-on, extra, frill, shoes **06** gloves, helper **07** abettor, adjunct, cathead, fitting, handbag, partner **08** addition, conniver, ornament, trimming
**09** adornment, ancillary, appendage, assistant, associate, attribute, auxiliary, colleague, component, extension, jewellery, secondary **10** accomplice, additional, attachment, complement, decoration, incidental, peripheral, subsidiary, supplement **11** confederate, subordinate **12** appurtenance, contributory, supplemental
**13** embellishment, supplementary

**accident**
◇ *anagram indicator*
**03** cva, hap, RTA **04** blow, fate, luck
**05** crash, fluke, freak, prang, shunt, smash, wreck **06** bingle, chance, hazard, mishap, pile-up, upcast
**07** fortune, smash-up, tragedy
**08** blowdown, calamity, casualty, disaster, fatality, fortuity, good luck
**09** collision, mischance **10** misfortune
**11** coincidence, contingency, contretemps, good fortune, serendipity **12** circumstance, happenstance, misadventure

**accidental**
**04** flat **05** fluky, sharp **06** casual, chance, flukey, random **07** natural, outward **08** aleatory, external
**09** adventive, dividuous, haphazard, uncertain, unplanned, unwitting
**10** contingent, fortuitous, incidental, unexpected, unforeseen, unintended
**11** inadvertent, promiscuous, unlooked-for **12** adventitious, uncalculated **13** serendipitous, unanticipated, unintentional
**14** unpremeditated

**accidentally**
◇ *anagram indicator*
**08** bechance, by chance, randomly
**09** by mistake **10** by accident **11** ex accidenti, haphazardly, unwittingly
**12** fortuitously, incidentally, unexpectedly **13** inadvertently
**14** adventitiously **15** serendipitously, unintentionally

**acclaim**
**04** clap, hail, laud **05** cheer, exalt, extol, toast, voice **06** cheers, eulogy, homage, honour, praise, salute
**07** applaud, commend, fanfare, ovation, tribute, welcome
**08** applause, approval, bouquets, cheering, clapping, eulogium, eulogize, plaudits, shouting
**09** celebrate, extolment, laudation, publicity, rave about **10** exaltation
**11** acclamation, approbation, celebration **12** commendation

**acclaimed**
**05** famed, great, noted **06** famous
**07** admired, eminent, exalted, notable, revered **08** honoured, renowned
**09** legendary, prominent
**10** celebrated **11** illustrious, outstanding **13** distinguished

**acclamation**
**03** rap **04** wrap **05** paean **06** bravos, eulogy, homage, honour, praise
**07** fanfare, ovation, tribute, welcome
**08** applause, approval, cheering, clapping, shouting **09** panegyric
**10** enthusiasm, exaltation, laudations
**11** approbation, celebration
**12** commendation **13** felicitations
**15** congratulations

**acclimatization**
**10** adaptation, adjustment
**11** acclimation, habituation, orientation **13** accommodation, acculturation **14** naturalization
**15** familiarization

**acclimatize**
**04** salt **05** adapt, inure **06** adjust, attune **07** conform **08** accustom

09 acclimate, get used to, habituate 10 naturalize 11 accommodate, acculturate, familiarize 12 find your feet 15 get your bearings

**accolade**
05 award 06 homage, honour, praise 07 dubbing, embrace, tribute 11 recognition, testimonial 12 pat on the back

**accommodate**
◇ *containment indicator*
03 aid, fit 04 help, hold, seat, take 05 adapt, board, house, lodge, put up, serve 06 adjust, assist, attune, bestow, billet, comply, modify, oblige, settle, supply, take in 07 compose, conform, provide, quarter, shelter 08 accustom, cater for, domicile 09 fit in with, habituate, harmonize, reconcile 11 acclimatize, be helpful to, give a hand to, have room for, lend a hand to 12 have space for

**accommodating**
◇ *containment indicator*
04 kind 07 helpful, pliable, willing 08 friendly, obliging 09 agreeable, compliant, indulgent, unselfish 10 hospitable 11 complaisant, considerate, co-operative, sympathetic

**accommodation**
◇ *containment indicator*
04 home 05 abode, board, place, rooms 07 harmony, housing, lodging, quarter, storage 08 dwelling, lodgings, quarters 09 agreement, residence 10 compromise, conformity, settlement 11 negotiation 12 negotiations 13 understanding 14 reconciliation

*Accommodation types include:*

03 inn, pad, pod
04 camp, digs, flat, gaff, gite, tent, yurt
05 b and b, cabin, hotel, house, igloo, lodge, motel, squat, villa
06 bedsit, billet, camper, duplex, flotel, hostel, jack-up, refuge, studio, succah, sukkah
07 caravan, cottage, dockage, floatel, lairage, parador, pension, shelter, taverna
08 barracks, berthage, crashpad, pod hotel, roomette, shipping, stabling, tenement, wharfage
09 apartment, bedsitter, bunkhouse, camper van, dormitory, full board, half board, penthouse, residence, rooming-in, timeshare
10 guardhouse, guest house, labour camp, mobile home
11 bachelor pad, bed and board, youth hostel
12 halfway house, hunting-lodge, room and board, self-catering
13 boarding-house, habitat module
14 loft conversion
15 bed and breakfast, hall of residence, married quarters

*See also* **building**; **house**; **tent**

**accompaniment**
04 vamp 06 backup, patter 07 adjunct, backing, bourdon, descant, support 08 addition, obligato 09 accessory, obbligato, orchestra, side order 10 background, complement, supplement 11 coexistence, concomitant, tracklement

**• provide accompaniment**
04 la-la

**accompanist**
04 comp 11 accompanier 12 backing group 15 instrumentalist

**accompany**
04 back, chum 05 usher 06 assist, attend, convoy, escort, follow, go with, squire, wait on 07 coexist, conduct, consort, partner, support 08 belong to, chaperon, coincide, come with, play with, tag along, wait upon, walk with 09 associate, chaperone, companion, occur with 10 complement, supplement, travel with 11 go along with 12 tag along with 13 associate with, come along with 14 go together with, hang around with

**accomplice**
04 aide, ally, mate 05 shill, stale 06 bonnet, button, helper 07 abettor, fedarie, nobbler, partner 08 approver, complice, copemate, federary, foedarie, henchman, sidekick, swagsman 09 accessory, assistant, associate, colleague, copesmate, federarie 11 confederate, conspirator 12 collaborator, participator, right-hand man 14 right-hand woman

**accomplish**
02 do 06 attain, effect, finish, fulfil, hack it, manage, obtain, wangle 07 achieve, compass, execute, perform, produce, realize 08 bring off, carry out, complete, complish, conclude, engineer 09 discharge, pull it off 10 bring about, consummate, effectuate 15 carry into effect, deliver the goods

**accomplished**
03 ace 04 arch, done, over 05 adept 06 adroit, expert, gifted, savant, wicked 07 learned, savante, skilful, skilled 08 compleat, masterly, polished, talented 09 practised 10 consummate, cultivated, proficient 11 experienced 12 professional

**accomplishment**
03 act, art 04 deed, feat, gift 05 doing, forte, knack, skill 06 stroke, talent, virtue 07 ability, exploit, faculty, finesse, prowess, quality, triumph 08 aptitude, exercise, fruition 09 discharge, effecting, execution, finishing, operation 10 attainment, capability, completion, conclusion, fulfilling, fulfilment, futurition, management, perfection, production 11 achievement, carrying-out, performance, proficiency, realization 12 consummation 13 qualification 14 stroke of genius

**accord**
04 deal, give, jibe, pact, sort, suit 05 agree, allow, chime, endow, grant, match, unity, yield 06 assent, bestow, concur, confer, extend, square, tender, treaty 07 compact, concert, conform, congree, consort, harmony, present 08 contract, sympathy 09 agreement, concordat, congruity, consensus, harmonize, unanimity, vouchsafe 10 accordance, conformity, congruence, convention, correspond, settlement 11 be in harmony, concurrence 13 be in agreement 14 correspondence

**• of your own accord**
06 freely 09 willingly 11 voluntarily

**• with one accord**
09 of one mind 11 unanimously

**accordance**

**• in accordance with**
02 by 05 after, under 10 in line with, obedient to 12 in relation to, in the light of 13 in concert with, in keeping with, in the manner of 14 consistent with, in proportion to 15 in agreement with

**according**
03 acc

**• according to**
03 per 05 after, as per 08 as said by, secundum 10 as stated by, in line with, obedient to 11 as claimed by, depending on 12 in relation to, in the light of 13 in keeping with, in the manner of, on the report of 14 consistent with, in proportion to

**accordingly**
02 so 04 duly, ergo, thus 05 fitly, hence 08 properly, suitably 09 agreeably, as a result, therefore 10 sure enough, thereafter 12 consequently, consistently 13 appropriately, for that reason, in consequence 15 correspondingly

**accost**
04 bord, hail, halt, stop 05 abord, assay, board, boord, borde 06 attack, boorde, detain, molest, nobble, waylay 07 address, solicit 08 approach, confront 09 importune 10 buttonhole

**account**
02 a/c 03 acc, tab 04 acct, bill, deem, hold, sake, tale 05 books, count, story, value 06 assess, behalf, detail, esteem, import, ledger, memoir, moment, reckon, record, regard, report, sketch, view as 07 adjudge, believe, charges, details, history, invoice, journal, version, write up 08 appraise, consider, look upon, regard as, register 09 chronicle, inventory, narration, narrative, portrayal, statement 10 commentary, importance 11 consequence, description, distinction, explanation 12 presentation, significance

**• account for**
04 give, kill 06 defeat, make up, say

why, supply **07** clear up, destroy, explain, justify, provide **08** comprise **09** answer for, eliminate, elucidate, represent, vindicate **10** constitute, illuminate **11** rationalize **14** give reasons for

• **falsify accounts**
**04** cook, rort **12** cook the books

• **give an account of**
**04** tell **06** relate

• **on account of**
**02** o/a **03** for **04** over **05** along **07** because, owing to, through **08** in view of **09** because of **10** by virtue of, in virtue of **11** the reason is **12** for the sake of

• **on no account**
**05** never, no way **12** certainly not **13** not on your life

**accountability**
**09** liability, reporting **10** obligation **11** amenability **13** answerability **14** responsibility

**accountable**
**05** bound **06** liable **07** obliged **08** amenable **09** comptable, comptible, obligated **10** answerable, chargeable, explicable **11** charged with, responsible

**accountant**
**02** CA **03** ACA, acc, CPA **06** bookie **09** bookmaker **11** bean counter

**accoutrements**
**03** kit **04** gear **05** stuff **06** outfit, things **07** clobber **08** fittings, fixtures **09** caparison, equipment, trimmings **10** adornments **11** decorations, furnishings, odds and ends **12** appointments **13** appurtenances, bits and pieces, paraphernalia

**accredit**
**06** depute **07** approve, certify, endorse, license, warrant **09** attribute, authorize, recognize **10** commission **11** certificate

**accredited**
**07** deputed **08** approved, endorsed, licensed, official **09** appointed, certified, qualified **10** authorized, recognized **12** certificated, commissioned

**accretion**
**05** add-on **06** growth **07** build-up **08** addition, increase **09** gathering, increment **10** collecting, cumulation, supplement **12** accumulation, augmentation

**accrue**
**05** amass, mount **07** augment, be added, build up, collect, mount up **08** increase **10** accumulate

**accumulate**
**04** gain, grow, pile, pool **05** amass, hoard, stash, store, tot up **06** accrue, distil, garner, gather, pile up **07** acquire, augment, build up, collect, congest, distill **08** assemble, cumulate, increase, multiply, snowball **09** aggregate, stockpile

**accumulation**
**04** gain, heap, mass, pile **05** hoard, stack, stock, store **06** growth **07** accrual, build-up, reserve **08** assembly, increase **09** accretion, aggregate, gathering, stockpile **10** building-up, collection, cumulation **11** acquisition **12** augmentation **14** conglomeration, multiplication

**accumulative**
**07** growing **08** mounting **09** enlarging **10** increasing **11** multiplying, snowballing

**accuracy**
**05** truth **06** verity **08** fidelity, veracity **09** closeness, exactness, precision **10** exactitude **11** carefulness, correctness **12** authenticity, faithfulness, scrupulosity, truthfulness, veridicality **14** meticulousness

**accurate**
**04** fair, nice, true **05** close, exact, right, sound, valid **06** bang on, dead-on, spot-on, strict **07** correct, factual, literal, perfect, precise **08** faithful, on target, rigorous, truthful, unerring **09** authentic, faultless, on the mark, veracious, veridical, well-aimed **10** meticulous **11** word-for-word, word-perfect **12** well-directed **13** letter-perfect

**accurately**
**05** truly **07** closely, exactly **08** strictly **09** correctly, literally, perfectly, precisely **10** faithfully, rigorously, truthfully, unerringly **11** faultlessly, veraciously, veridically **12** meticulously

**accursed**
**05** blest, hated **06** damned, doomed, goddam, sacred **07** blessed, goddamn, hateful **08** maledict, wretched **09** bewitched, condemned, execrable, goddamned, loathsome **10** abominable, bedevilled, despicable, detestable **13** anathematized

**accusation**
**03** tax **04** bill **05** blame, cause, libel, smear **06** charge, threap, threep **08** citation, delation, gravamen **09** challenge, complaint, invective **10** allegation, imputation, indictment **11** arraignment, crimination, impeachment, inculpation, information, prosecution **12** denunciation **13** incrimination, recrimination

**accuse**
**03** tax **04** book, cite **05** blame, frame, peach **06** allege, appeal, charge, detect, impugn, impute, indict **07** appeach, arraign, asperse, attaint, censure, impeach, reprove **08** confront, denounce **09** attribute, challenge, criminate, implicate, prosecute **10** put on trial **11** incriminate, recriminate **12** bring charges, press charges **13** inform against **14** throw the book at **15** hold responsible, make accusations, make allegations

**accustom**
**03** use **05** adapt, enure, inure, teach **06** adjust, attune **07** conform **08** occasion **09** acclimate, climatize, get used to, habituate **11** acclimatize, accommodate, familiarize **15** get familiar with

**accustomed**
**03** old **04** tame, used, wont **05** fixed, given, usual **06** at home, inured, normal, wonted **07** general, regular, routine **08** everyday, familiar, frequent, habitual, ordinary **09** customary **10** acquainted, habituated, prevailing **11** established, traditional **12** acclimatized, conventional, in the habit of **14** consuetudinary

**ace**
**01** A **03** jot, one, Tib **04** cool, neat, unit **05** basto, brill, great, whizz **06** expert, genius, grouse, master, superb, wicked, winner **07** dab hand, hotshot, maestro, perfect **08** champion, spadille, terrific, top-notch, very good, virtuoso **09** brilliant, excellent **10** first-class **11** outstanding

**acerbic**
**05** harsh, sharp, spiky **06** biting **07** caustic, mordant **08** abrasive, stinging **09** rancorous, sarcastic, trenchant, vitriolic **10** astringent **11** acrimonious

**ache**
**01** H **03** die, yen **04** hurt, itch, kill, long, pain, pang, pine, work **05** agony, aitch, crave, pound, smart, sting, throb, yearn **06** be sore, desire, hanker, hunger, play up, stound, stownd, suffer, thirst, twinge **07** agonize, anguish, craving, longing **08** pounding, smarting, soreness, stinging, yearning **09** be in agony, be painful, hankering, suffering, throbbing

**achieve**
**02** do **03** get, win **04** earn, gain **05** reach **06** attain, effect, finish, fulfil, manage, obtain, wrap up **07** acquire, execute, perform, procure, produce, realize, succeed **08** carry out, complete **09** polish off **10** accomplish, bring about, consummate, effectuate

**achievement**
**03** act **04** deed, feat **06** action, effort, stroke **07** exploit, success, triumph **08** activity, fruition **09** execution **10** attainment, chevisance, completion, fulfilment **11** acquirement, performance, procurement, realization **12** consummation, effectuation **14** accomplishment, stroke of genius

**achiever**
**04** doer **08** go-getter, live wire, whizz kid **09** high-flyer, performer, succeeder **12** success story

**Achilles' heel**
**05** fault **07** failing **08** weakness, weak spot **09** weak point **12** imperfection **15** vulnerable point

**acid**
**04** keen, sour, tart **05** catty, harsh, sharp, sugar **06** acidic, biting, bitter, morose, unkind **07** acerbic, acetous, caustic, cutting, hurtful, mordant, pungent **08** critical, incisive, stinging, vinegary **09** acidulous, corrosive, sarcastic, trenchant, vitriolic **10** astringent, ill-natured **11** unsweetened

*Acids include:*

**03** DNA, LSD, RNA
**04** acyl, EDTA, uric
**05** amino, boric, fatty, folic
**06** acetic, citric, formic, lactic, nitric, oxalic, phenol, tannic
**07** acrylic, benzoic, boracic, chloric, nitrous, nucleic, prussic, pyruvic, silicic, stearic
**08** abscisic, ascorbic, carbolic, carbonic, ethanoic, lysergic, palmitic, periodic, retinoic, tartaric
**09** methanoic, nicotinic, propionic, salicylic, sulphonic, sulphuric
**10** aqua fortis, barbituric, carboxylic, phosphoric, sulphurous
**11** hydrocyanic, ribonucleic
**12** hydrochloric, hydrofluoric
**13** thiosulphuric, tricarboxylic

*See also* **amino acid**

• **acid test**
**02** pH
• **work with acid**
**04** etch

**acknowledge**
**03** con, own **04** avow, hail, mark **05** admit, allow, grant, greet, thank **06** accede, accept, affirm, agnize, answer, avouch, honour, notice, salute, wave to **07** address, agree to, concede, confess, confirm, declare, own up to, react to, reply to **08** signal to **09** acquiesce, celebrate, recognize, respond to **10** be grateful **11** say thank you, write back to **13** give thanks for

**acknowledged**
**06** avowed **08** accepted, admitted, approved, attested, declared **09** confirmed, professed **10** accredited, recognized

**acknowledgement**
**03** nod **04** wave **05** reply, smile **06** answer, avowal, credit, homage, notice, praise, thanks **07** tribute, welcome **08** bouquets, cognovit, comeback, granting, greeting, reaction, response **09** admission, allowance, deference, gratitude **10** acceptance, confession, profession, salutation **11** declaration, recognition **12** appreciation, gratefulness, recognizance

**acme**
**04** apex, peak **05** crown, prick **06** apogee, climax, comble, height, summit, zenith **07** optimum **08** pinnacle **09** high point **11** culmination, sublimation **12** highest point

**acolyte**
**06** helper **08** adherent, altar boy, follower, hanger-on, sidekick, thurifer **09** assistant, attendant **11** acolouthite

**acorn**
**04** mast **05** glans **07** oak mast, valonea, valonia **08** racahout, vallonia **09** raccahout

**acoustic**
**05** aural, sound **06** audile **07** hearing **08** auditory

**acquaint**
**04** tell **05** brief **06** advise, inform, notify, reveal **07** apprise, divulge, let know, possess **08** accustom, announce, disclose **09** enlighten **11** familiarize, make aware of **14** make conversant **15** put in the picture

**acquaintance**
**04** mate **06** friend, pick-up **07** contact, homeboy **08** confrère, habitude, hanger-on, intimacy **09** associate, awareness, colleague, companion, knowledge **10** cognizance, connection, experience, fellowship **11** association, conversance, familiarity **12** relationship **13** companionship, social contact, understanding

**acquainted**
**05** aware **06** au fait, versed **07** abreast **08** apprised, familiar, friendly, intimate **09** au courant, cognizant, in the know, up to speed **10** conversant, well-versed **11** on good terms **13** knowledgeable **15** on friendly terms
• **be acquainted with**
**03** ken **04** know

**acquiesce**
**05** agree, allow, defer **06** accede, accept, assent, concur, give in, permit, submit **07** approve, consent **12** give the nod to

**acquiescence**
**03** nod **05** say-so **06** assent **07** consent, go-ahead **08** approval, thumbs-up, yielding **09** agreement, deference **10** acceptance, compliance, green-light, submission **11** concurrence, countenance

**acquiescent**
**07** servile **08** acceding, agreeing, amenable, obedient, yielding **09** accepting, agreeable, approving, compliant **10** concurring, consenting, submissive **11** complaisant, deferential

**acquire**
◇ *containment indicator*
**03** bag, buy, cop, ern, get, net, win **04** earn, gain, grab **05** amass **06** attain, collar, come by, gather, obtain, pick up, secure, snap up, take on **07** achieve, collect, procure, realize, receive, snaffle, usucapt **08** purchase **10** accumulate **11** appropriate, splash out on

**acquisition**
**03** buy **04** gain **05** prize **07** acquest, gaining **08** property, purchase, securing, takeover **09** accession, obtaining, usucapion **10** attainment, investment, possession, usucaption **11** achievement, procurement **13** appropriation

**acquisitive**
**04** avid **06** greedy **08** covetous, grasping, hoarding **09** predatory, rapacious, voracious **10** avaricious **12** accumulative

**acquisitiveness**
**05** greed **07** avarice, avidity **08** cupidity, rapacity, voracity **12** covetousness, graspingness **13** predatoriness

**acquit**
**02** do **03** act **04** bear, free **05** clear, prove, repay **06** assoil, behave, bestow, excuse, let off, settle **07** absolve, comport, conduct, deliver, dismiss, perform, release, relieve, satisfy, set free **08** liberate, reprieve, uncharge **09** discharge, exculpate, exonerate, vindicate **11** make a bad job **12** make a good job **13** let off the hook

**acquittal**
**06** relief **07** freeing, release **08** clearing, excusing, reprieve **09** clearance, discharge, dismissal **10** absolution, liberation **11** deliverance, exculpation, exoneration, vindication **12** compurgation

**acre**
**01** a **02** ac

**acrid**
**04** acid, sour, tart **05** harsh, nasty, sharp **06** biting, bitter **07** acerbic, burning, caustic, cutting, mordant, pungent **08** incisive, sardonic, stinging, venomous, virulent **09** malicious, sarcastic, trenchant, vitriolic **10** astringent **11** acrimonious

**acrimonious**
**05** sharp **06** bitchy, biting, bitter, severe **07** abusive, acerbic, caustic, crabbed, cutting, waspish **08** petulant, spiteful, venomous, virulent **09** irascible, rancorous, splenetic, trenchant, vitriolic **10** astringent, censorious **11** atrabilious, ill-tempered

**acrimony**
**04** gall **05** spite, venom **06** spleen **07** ill will, rancour, sarcasm, vitriol **08** acerbity, acridity, asperity, mordancy **09** harshness, ill temper, petulance, virulence **10** bitterness, causticity, ill feeling, resentment, trenchancy **11** astringency **12** irascibility

**acrobat**
**05** speel **07** gymnast, speeler, tumbler **08** balancer, posturer, stuntman

**09** aerialist, posturist **10** rope-dancer, rope-walker, stuntwoman, wing-walker **11** equilibrist, funambulist **12** somersaulter, trick cyclist **13** contortionist, trapeze artist **15** tightrope-walker

**acrobatics**
◇ *anagram indicator*
**06** stunts **09** balancing **10** gymnastics **11** equilibrity, funambulism, rope-walking, wire-walking **13** somersaulting

**across**
**01** a **02** ac **03** dia-, tra- **04** over, tran- **05** trans- **06** thwart **07** athwart **08** à travers

**act**
**02** be, do **03** bit, gig, kid, law **04** bill, deal, deed, fake, feat, item, mime, move, part, play, sham, show, skit, step, turn, work **05** canon, doing, edict, enact, feign, front, mimic, put on, react, serve **06** action, affect, assume, be busy, behave, decree, number, ruling, sketch, stroke **07** episode, exploit, go about, imitate, measure, operate, perform, portray, pretend, respond, routine, section, statute **08** be active, division, feigning, function, pretence, put-up job, simulate **09** dissemble, execution, manoeuvre, operation, ordinance, represent, take steps **10** do the job of, enterprise, resolution, subsection, take action, take effect **11** achievement, affectation, counterfeit, dissimulate, impersonate, make-believe, performance, undertaking **12** characterize, dissemblance, go on the stage, have an effect, take measures **13** be efficacious, dissimulation, exert yourself **14** accomplishment, acquit yourself **15** comport yourself, conduct yourself

*See also* **law**

**• act badly**
**03** ham

**• act on**
**04** heed, obey, take **05** alter **06** affect, change, follow, fulfil, modify, work on **08** carry out **09** conform to, influence, transform **10** comply with

**• act the part of**
**04** come

**• act up**
**04** fail **06** pack up, play up **07** carry on, conk out, go kaput, go wrong, not work **09** break down, mess about, misbehave **10** give bother, muck around **11** behave badly, malfunction, stop working **12** cause trouble

**acting**
◇ *anagram indicator*
**01** a **03** act **04** actg **05** drama **06** action, deputy, fill-in, pro tem, relief, supply **07** interim, reserve, showbiz, stand-by, stand-in, stopgap, theatre **08** artistry, covering **09** dramatics, imitating, in place of, luvviedom, melodrama, portrayal, short-term, surrogate, temporary **10** footlights, performing, play-acting, stagecraft, substitute **11** histrionics, performance, provisional, theatricals, Thespianism **12** show business **13** impersonation, standing in for **14** performing arts

**actinium**
**02** Ac

**actinon**
**02** an

**action**
◇ *anagram indicator*
**03** act, pas **04** case, deed, feat, fray, move, step, suit, work **05** clash, doing, fight, force, power **06** affray, battle, combat, effect, effort, energy, events, motion, result, spirit, vigour **07** exploit, lawsuit, measure, pizzazz, process, warfare **08** activity, conflict, exercise, exertion, fighting, goings-on, movement, practice, skirmish, vitality **09** encounter, endeavour, influence, mechanism, operation **10** activities, engagement, enterprise, excitement, get-up-and-go, happenings, litigation, liveliness, proceeding **11** achievement, functioning, hostilities, performance, proceedings, prosecution, stimulation, undertaking **12** exhilaration, forcefulness **14** accomplishment, course of action

**• check action**
**04** stay

**• course of action**
**04** path

**• critical time of action**
**04** D-day

**activate**
◇ *anagram indicator*
**04** fire, move, stir, trip **05** impel, put on, rouse, start **06** arouse, bestir, excite, prompt, propel, set off, turn on **07** actuate, animate, trigger **08** energize, get going, initiate, mobilize, motivate, set going, switch on **09** derepress, galvanize, kick-start, stimulate **10** trigger off **11** set in motion **12** start working **13** push the button **14** press the button, throw the switch

**active**
◇ *anagram indicator*
**01** a **03** act **04** at it, busy, go-go, spry **05** agile, alert, astir, manic, quick, vital, yauld, zippy **06** birkie, lively, mobile, nimble, quiver, wimble **07** devoted, engaged, forward, in force, on the go, running, springe, vibrant, working **08** activist, animated, diligent, forceful, frenetic, involved, militant, occupied, practive, spirited, vigorous **09** committed, effectual, energetic, operative, sprightly, stirabout **11** functioning, hard-working, hyperactive, industrious, in operation, light-footed, operational **12** contributing, enterprising, enthusiastic **13** indefatigable

**• be active**
**02** do **03** hum

**activist**
**07** inciter, stirrer **08** agitator, fomenter, henchman, militant **09** firebrand **10** incendiary, subversive **12** troublemaker **13** revolutionary

*Activists include:*

**04** **Bono**, **King** (Martin Luther)
**05** **Nader** (Ralph), **Parks** (Rosa)
**06** **Gandhi** (Mahatma), **Geldof** (Bob)
**07** **Angelou** (Maya), **Chomsky** (Noam), **Guevara** (Che), **Jackson** (Jesse), **Mandela** (Nelson), **Mandela** (Winnie)
**08** **Malcolm X**, **Silkwood** (Karen)
**09** **Pankhurst** (Christabel), **Pankhurst** (Emmeline), **Pankhurst** (Sylvia)

*See also* **aboriginal**

**activity**
◇ *anagram indicator*
**02** do, go **03** act, job **04** deed, life, play, stir, task, work **05** hobby **06** action, bustle, labour, motion, scheme **07** pastime, project, pursuit, venture **08** business, exercise, exertion, industry, interest, movement **09** avocation, commotion, diversion, endeavour **10** activeness, enterprise, hurly-burly, liveliness, occupation **11** distraction, undertaking **13** something to do **14** toing and froing **15** a hive of activity, a hive of industry, hustle and bustle

**• bustling activity**
**04** rush **06** bustle **07** beehive

**• focus of activity**
**03** hub

**• furious activity**
**04** rage

**• increase in activity**
**04** boom

**actor, actress**
**03** ham **04** feed, mime, mute, supe **05** buffa, buffo, comic, extra, luvvy, super, thesp **06** artist, luvvie, mummer, player, stager, stooge, walk-on **07** artiste, comique, histrio, ingénue, Roscius, starlet, support, trouper **08** comedian, epilogue, film star, histrion, juvenile, thespian **09** bit player, film actor, hamfatter, movie star, performer, play actor, principal, tragedian **10** leading man, mime artist, movie actor, understudy, utility man **11** leading lady, matinée idol, pantomimist, protagonist, straight man, tragedienne, tritagonist **12** impersonator, spear carrier **13** deuteragonist, supernumerary **14** character actor, dramatic artist, stage performer **15** strolling player

*Actors include:*

**03** **Cox** (Brian), **Fox** (James), **Fox** (Michael J), **Fry** (Stephen), **Law** (Jude), **Lee** (Bruce), **Lee** (Christopher), **Lee** (Spike), **Lom** (Herbert), **Sim** (Alastair)
**04** **Cage** (Nicolas), **Chan** (Jackie), **Chow** (Yun-Fat), **Dean** (James), **Depp** (Johnny), **Ford** (Harrison), **Gere** (Richard), **Holm** (Sir Ian), **Hope** (Bob), **Hurt** (John), **Kaye** (Danny),

**Kean** (Edmund), **Lowe** (Rob), **Peck** (Gregory), **Penn** (Sean), **Pitt** (Brad), **Reed** (Oliver), **Sher** (Sir Antony), **Tati** (Jacques), **Thaw** (John), **Tree** (Sir Herbert Beerbohm), **Wood** (Elijah)

**05** **Allen** (Woody), **Bacon** (Kevin), **Bates** (Alan), **Brody** (Adrien), **Caine** (Sir Michael), **Clift** (Montgomery), **Craig** (Daniel), **Crowe** (Russell), **Dafoe** (Willem), **Damon** (Matt), **Dance** (Charles), **Firth** (Colin), **Flynn** (Errol), **Fonda** (Henry), **Gable** (Clark), **Grant** (Cary), **Grant** (Hugh), **Grant** (Richard E), **Hanks** (Tom), **Hardy** (Oliver), **Irons** (Jeremy), **Kelly** (Gene), **Kempe** (Will), **Kline** (Kevin), **Leung** (Tony), **Lewis** (Jerry), **Lloyd** (Harold), **Lorre** (Peter), **Mason** (James), **Mills** (Sir John), **Moore** (Roger), **Neill** (Sam), **Nimoy** (Leonard), **Niven** (David), **Nolte** (Nick), **Price** (Vincent), **Quinn** (Anthony), **Reeve** (Christopher), **Robey** (Sir George), **Scott** (George C), **Sheen** (Charlie), **Sheen** (Martin), **Smith** (Will), **Spall** (Timothy), **Stamp** (Terence), **Sydow** (Max von), **Tracy** (Spencer), **Wayne** (John)

**06** **Alleyn** (Edward), **Beatty** (Warren), **Bogart** (Humphrey), **Brando** (Marlon), **Brooks** (Mel), **Burton** (Richard), **Cagney** (James), **Carrey** (Jim), **Chaney** (Lon), **Coburn** (James), **Cooper** (Gary), **Cruise** (Tom), **Curtis** (Tony), **De Niro** (Robert), **DeVito** (Danny), **Dillon** (Matt), **Finney** (Albert), **Gambon** (Sir Michael), **Gibson** (Mel), **Glover** (Danny), **Harris** (Richard), **Heston** (Charlton), **Hopper** (Dennis), **Howard** (Trevor), **Hudson** (Rock), **Irving** (Sir Henry), **Jacobi** (Sir Derek), **Jolson** (Al), **Jouvet** (Louis), **Keaton** (Buster), **Keitel** (Harvey), **Kemble** (John Philip), **Laurel** (Stan), **Laurie** (Hugh), **Lemmon** (Jack), **Lugosi** (Bela), **Martin** (Steve), **Murphy** (Eddie), **Murray** (Bill), **Neeson** (Liam), **Newman** (Paul), **Oldman** (Gary), **O'Toole** (Peter), **Pacino** (Al), **Phelps** (Samuel), **Quayle** (Sir Anthony), **Reagan** (Ronald), **Reeves** (Keanu), **Rooney** (Mickey), **Rourke** (Mickey), **Sharif** (Omar), **Sinden** (Sir Donald), **Slater** (Christian), **Spacey** (Kevin), **Swayze** (Patrick), **Walken** (Christopher), **Welles** (Orson), **Wilder** (Gene), **Willis** (Bruce), **Wolfit** (Sir Donald)

**07** **Astaire** (Fred), **Auteuil** (Daniel), **Aykroyd** (Dan), **Benigni** (Roberto), **Berkoff** (Steven), **Bogarde** (Sir Dirk), **Branagh** (Kenneth), **Bridges** (Jeff), **Bridges** (Lloyd), **Bronson** (Charles), **Brosnan** (Pierce), **Brynner** (Yul), **Burbage** (Richard), **Carlyle** (Robert), **Chaplin** (Charlie), **Clooney** (George), **Connery** (Sir Sean), **Costner** (Kevin), **Crystal** (Billy), **Cushing** (Peter), **Douglas** (Kirk), **Douglas** (Michael), **Everett** (Rupert), **Fiennes** (Joseph), **Fiennes** (Ralph), **Forrest** (Edwin), **Freeman** (Morgan), **Garrick** (David), **Gielgud** (Sir John), **Hoffman** (Dustin), **Hopkins** (Sir Anthony), **Hordern** (Sir Michael), **Jackson** (Samuel L), **Karloff** (Boris), **Marceau** (Marcel), **Matthau** (Walter), **McQueen** (Steve), **Mitchum** (Robert), **Montand** (Yves), **Nielsen** (Leslie), **Olivier** (Laurence, Lord), **Poitier** (Sidney), **Redford** (Robert), **Rickman** (Alan), **Robbins** (Tim), **Robeson** (Paul), **Roscius**, **Russell** (Kurt), **Savalas** (Telly), **Selleck** (Tom), **Sellers** (Peter), **Shatner** (William), **Steiger** (Rod), **Stewart** (James), **Ustinov** (Sir Peter)

**08** **Atkinson** (Rowan), **Barrault** (Jean-Louis), **Day-Lewis** (Daniel), **DiCaprio** (Leonardo), **Dreyfuss** (Richard), **Eastwood** (Clint), **Goldblum** (Jeff), **Guinness** (Sir Alec), **Harrison** (Sir Rex), **Kingsley** (Ben), **Laughton** (Charles), **Macready** (William Charles), **McGregor** (Ewan), **McKellen** (Sir Ian), **Redgrave** (Sir Michael), **Reynolds** (Burt), **Robinson** (Edward G), **Scofield** (Paul), **Stallone** (Sylvester), **Travolta** (John), **Van Cleef** (Lee), **Van Damme** (Jean-Claude), **von Sydow** (Max), **Williams** (Robin), **Woodward** (Edward)

**09** **Barrymore** (Lionel), **Broadbent** (Jim), **Broderick** (Matthew), **Chevalier** (Maurice), **Courtenay** (Sir Tom), **Depardieu** (Gérard), **Fairbanks** (Douglas), **Fernandel**, **Hawthorne** (Sir Nigel), **Lancaster** (Burt), **Malkovich** (John), **Nicholson** (Jack), **Pleasence** (Donald), **Strasberg** (Lee), **Valentino** (Rudolph)

**10** **Richardson** (Sir Ralph), **Sutherland** (Donald), **Sutherland** (Kiefer), **Washington** (Denzel)

**11** **Mastroianni** (Marcello), **Weissmuller** (Johnny)

**12** **Attenborough** (Richard, Lord), **Garcia Bernal** (Gael), **Stanislavsky** (Konstantin)

**14** **Schwarzenegger** (Arnold)

*See also* **comedian**

*Actresses include:*

**03** **Bow** (Clara), **Cox** (Courteney), **Day** (Doris), **Loy** (Myrna)

**04** **Ball** (Lucille), **Dern** (Laura), **Diaz** (Cameron), **Dors** (Diana), **Duse** (Eleonora), **Gish** (Lillian), **Gwyn** (Nell), **Hawn** (Goldie), **Hird** (Dame Thora), **Rigg** (Dame Diana), **Ryan** (Meg), **West** (Mae), **Wood** (Natalie), **York** (Susannah)

**05** **Allen** (Gracie), **Berry** (Halle), **Bloom** (Claire), **Close** (Glenn), **Davis** (Bette), **Davis** (Geena), **Dench** (Dame Judi), **Derek** (Bo), **Evans** (Dame Edith), **Fonda** (Jane), **Gabor** (Zsa Zsa), **Garbo** (Greta), **Jolie** (Angelina), **Kelly** (Grace), **Lange** (Jessica), **Leigh** (Janet), **Leigh** (Vivien), **Lopez** (Jennifer), **Loren** (Sophia), **Mills** (Hayley), **Moore** (Demi), **Ryder** (Winona), **Smith** (Dame Maggie), **Stone** (Sharon), **Swank** (Hilary), **Terry** (Dame Ellen), **Welch** (Raquel)

**06** **Adjani** (Isabelle), **Bacall** (Lauren), **Bardot** (Brigitte), **Bisset** (Jacqueline), **Cheung** (Maggie), **Curtis** (Jamie Lee), **Farrow** (Mia), **Fisher** (Carrie), **Foster** (Jodie), **Grable** (Betty), **Hannah** (Daryl), **Harlow** (Jean), **Hedren** (Tippi), **Hunter** (Holly), **Huston** (Anjelica), **Keaton** (Diane), **Kemble** (Fanny), **Kidman** (Nicole), **Kinski** (Nastassja), **Lamarr** (Hedy), **Lumley** (Joanna), **Midler** (Bette), **Mirren** (Helen), **Monroe** (Marilyn), **Moreau** (Jeanne), **Robson** (Dame Flora), **Rogers** (Ginger), **Spacek** (Sissy), **Streep** (Meryl), **Suzman** (Janet), **Tautou** (Audrey), **Taylor** (Dame Elizabeth), **Temple** (Shirley), **Turner** (Kathleen), **Turner** (Lana), **Ullman** (Tracey), **Weaver** (Sigourney), **Winger** (Debra)

**07** **Andress** (Ursula), **Andrews** (Dame Julie), **Aniston** (Jennifer), **Bergman** (Ingrid), **Binoche** (Juliette), **Colbert** (Claudette), **Deneuve** (Catherine), **Gardner** (Ava), **Garland** (Judy), **Hepburn** (Audrey), **Hepburn** (Katharine), **Jackson** (Glenda), **Johnson** (Dame Celia), **Langtry** (Lillie), **Lombard** (Carole), **Paltrow** (Gwyneth), **Roberts** (Julia), **Russell** (Jane), **Seymour** (Jane), **Siddons** (Sarah), **Swanson** (Gloria), **Walters** (Julie), **Winslet** (Kate)

**08** **Ashcroft** (Dame Peggy), **Bancroft** (Anne), **Bankhead** (Tallulah), **Basinger** (Kim), **Campbell** (Mrs Patrick), **Charisse** (Cyd), **Christie** (Julie), **Crawford** (Joan), **Dietrich** (Marlene), **Fontaine** (Joan), **Goldberg** (Whoopi), **Griffith** (Melanie), **Hayworth** (Rita), **MacLaine** (Shirley), **Minnelli** (Liza), **Pfeiffer** (Michelle), **Pickford** (Mary), **Rampling** (Charlotte), **Redgrave** (Vanessa), **Sarandon** (Susan), **Shepherd** (Cybill), **Signoret** (Simone), **Stanwyck** (Barbara), **Thompson** (Emma)

**09** **Barrymore** (Drew), **Bernhardt** (Sarah), **Blanchett** (Cate), **Johansson** (Scarlett), **MacDowell** (Andie), **Mansfield** (Jayne), **Plowright** (Joan Ann), **Streisand** (Barbra), **Thorndike** (Dame Sybil), **Zellweger** (Renée), **Zeta Jones** (Catherine)

**10** **Rossellini** (Isabella), **Rutherford** (Dame Margaret)

**11** **Bracegirdle** (Anne), **de Havilland** (Olivia), **Mistinguett**, **Scott-Thomas** (Kristin)

**12** **Bonham Carter** (Helena), **Lollobrigida** (Gina)

*See also* **comedian**

**• actor's portrayal**
**04** part, role
**• bad actor**
**03** ham

**actors**
**04** cast **07** company

**actress** *see* **actor, actress**

**actual**
**04** real, true, very **07** certain, de facto, factual, genuine **08** absolute, bona fide, concrete, definite, existent, material, physical, positive, real life, tangible, truthful, verified
**09** authentic, confirmed, realistic
**10** legitimate **11** substantial
**12** indisputable **14** unquestionable

**actuality**
**03** ens **04** fact **05** truth **07** realism, reality **08** solidity **09** entelechy, existence, substance **10** factuality
**11** historicity, materiality
**12** corporeality **14** substantiality

**actually**
**04** even **05** truly **06** indeed, in fact, really **07** de facto, insooth, in truth, soothly **09** in reality **10** absolutely
**11** as it happens **12** surprisingly
**14** believe it or not **15** as a matter of fact

**actuate**
**04** move, stir **05** rouse, start
**06** arouse, kindle, prompt, set off, turn on **07** animate, trigger **08** activate, motivate, set going, switch on
**09** instigate, stimulate **10** trigger off
**11** set in motion **12** start working

**acumen**
**03** wit **05** sense **06** wisdom **07** insight
**08** gumption, keenness, sagacity, sapience **09** ingenuity, intuition, judgement, quickness, sharpness, smartness **10** astuteness, cleverness, perception, shrewdness
**11** discernment, penetration, percipience, perspicuity
**12** intelligence, perspicacity
**13** judiciousness **14** discrimination

**acupressure**
**04** do-in **07** shiatsu, shiatzu **09** Jin Shin Do®

**acute**
**04** dire, keen **05** canny, grave, sharp, smart, vital **06** astute, clever, severe, shrewd, urgent **07** crucial, cutting, drastic, extreme, intense, sapient, serious, violent **08** critical, decisive, incisive, peracute, piercing, poignant
**09** dangerous, judicious, observant, sensitive **10** discerning, insightful, perceptive, percipient, unbearable
**11** distressing, penetrating, sharp-witted **13** perspicacious

**acutely**
**04** very **06** keenly **07** gravely, sharply **08** markedly, severely, strongly **09** extremely, intensely, seriously

**adage**
**03** saw **05** axiom, gnome, maxim
**06** byword, saying **07** precept, proverb **08** aphorism, paroemia
**10** apophthegm, whakatauki

**adamant**
**03** set **04** firm, hard **05** fixed, rigid, stiff, tough **07** diamond **08** obdurate, resolute, stubborn **09** immovable, insistent, lodestone, unbending
**10** determined, inflexible, unshakable, unwavering, unyielding **11** unrelenting, unshakeable **12** intransigent
**14** uncompromising

**Adamson**
**04** Abel, Cain, Seth

**adapt**
◇ *anagram indicator*
**03** apt, fit **04** suit **05** alter, apply, frame, match, shape, tally **06** adjust, change, comply, modify, reduce, tailor
**07** arrange, conform, convert, exploit, fashion, get used, prepare, qualify, remodel **08** attemper, settle in
**09** contemper, customize, harmonize
**10** specialize **11** accommodate **13** get accustomed

**adaptable**
◇ *anagram indicator*
**07** open-end, plastic, pliable
**08** amenable, flexible, variable
**09** alterable, compliant, easy-going, malleable, open-ended, versatile
**10** adjustable, changeable, modifiable
**11** conformable, convertible

**adaptation**
◇ *anagram indicator*
**05** shift **06** change **07** fitting, shaping
**08** matching, revision **09** refitting, reshaping, reworking, variation
**10** adjustment, alteration, conformity, conversion, fashioning **11** getting used, habituation, preparation, remodelling
**12** conformation, modification, refashioning **13** accommodation, customization, harmonization
**14** transformation **15** acclimatization, familiarization

**add**
◇ *juxtaposition indicator*
**03** eik, eke, put, sum, tot **04** go on, join, tote **05** affix, annex, boost, count, put in, put on, raise, top up, total, tot up
**06** adjoin, append, attach, deepen, extend, hike up, prefix, suffix, tack on
**07** augment, build on, carry on, combine, count up, enhance, improve, include, postfix, summate, throw in
**08** complete, continue, heighten, increase **09** aggravate, go on to say, increment, intensify, introduce
**10** supplement **15** work out the total
**• add up**
**03** fit **04** cast, make, mean **05** count, run to, spell, sum up, tally, total, tot up
**06** amount, come to, reckon
**07** compute, count up, include, signify, stack up **08** figure up, indicate, ring true
**09** calculate, make sense **10** constitute
**11** add together, be plausible **12** be consistent, be reasonable, hang together **13** stand to reason

**added**
**03** new **04** more **05** extra, fresh, spare
**07** adjunct, another, further
**10** additional **13** supplementary

**addendum**
**02** PS **03** add **05** annex **07** adjunct, allonge, codicil **08** addition, appendix
**09** appendage **10** attachment, postscript, supplement
**11** endorsement **12** augmentation

**addict**
**03** fan **04** buff, head, hype, user
**05** fiend, freak, hound, junky
**06** junkie, stoner **07** devotee, druggie, fanatic, hop-head, tripper
**08** adherent, coke-head, drug user, follower, snowbird **09** clay eater, crackhead, dope-fiend, drug fiend, drug taker, mainliner, smackhead
**10** enthusiast **14** cruciverbalist

**addicted**
**04** daft, fond, nuts, wild **05** crazy, given, potty **06** hooked **07** devoted
**08** absorbed, bibulous, frequent, inclined, obsessed **09** confirmed, dedicated, dependent, fanatical, strung out **10** dissipated **13** drug-dependent

**addiction**
**04** need **05** habit, mania, thing
**06** monkey **07** craving **08** caffeism, opiumism, vinosity **09** cocainism, ergomania, obsession **10** caffeinism, compulsion, dependence, dependency, femininism **11** a colt's tooth, etheromania

**addictive**
**09** obsessive **10** compulsive **12** habit-forming, irresistible **14** uncontrollable

**addition**
**02** PS **03** eik, eke, PPS **04** also, gain, plus **05** extra, rider **06** adding, annexe
**07** adjunct, codicil **08** addendum, additive, appendix, counting, increase
**09** accession, accessory, accretion, appendage, extension, inclusion, increment, reckoning, summing-up, totalling, totting-up **10** annexation, attachment, increasing, postscript, supplement **11** computation, enlargement **12** afterthought, appurtenance, augmentation
**• in addition**
**03** too **04** also **05** forby **06** as well, to boot, withal **07** besides, further, thereto **08** as well as, moreover
**09** thereunto **11** furthermore
**12** additionally, not to mention, over and above **14** for good measure, into the bargain

**additional**
**03** new, odd **04** more, plus **05** added, extra, fresh, other, spare **07** another, further **09** increased **10** excrescent
**12** adscititious, adventitious, supervenient, supplemental
**13** supplementary

**additionally**
**03** too **04** also **05** forby **06** as well, to boot, withal **07** besides, further **08** moreover **10** in addition **11** furthermore **12** over and above **14** for good measure, into the bargain

**additive**
**04** MTBE **05** extra **07** E-number **08** addition **09** oxygenate, summative **10** emulsifier, stabilizer, supplement **12** preservative **13** canthaxanthin **14** canthaxanthine

**addle**
**03** bad **04** daze, faze **05** empty **06** barren, muddle, putrid **07** confuse, fluster, muddled, perplex **08** befuddle, bewilder

**addled**
**04** lost **05** fazed **07** mixed-up, muddled **08** confused **09** befuddled, flustered, perplexed **10** bewildered

**address**
**03** add **04** call, flat, hail, home, lord, mail, post, send, talk **05** abode, greet, house, label, orate, place, remit, spiel, uncle **06** accost, convey, direct, invoke, mister, prayer, sermon, speech, talk to **07** accoast, bespeak, lecture, lodging, oration, speak to, welcome, write to **08** diatribe, dwelling, greeting, harangue, location, mistress, petition, preach to **09** apartment, designate, discourse, epirrhema, inaugural, intend for, monologue, philippic, residence, rhetorize, sermonize, situation, soliloquy **10** allocution, apostrophe, directions, invocation, salutation **11** communicate, give a talk to, inscription, make a speech, superscribe, superscript, valedictory, whereabouts **12** disquisition, dissertation **13** give a speech to, poste restante **14** deliver a speech

• **address yourself to**
**06** tackle **07** focus on **08** attend to, deal with, engage in **09** undertake **10** take care of **12** buckle down to **13** concentrate on **15** apply yourself to

**adduce**
**04** cite, lead, name **05** quote **06** assign, object **07** mention, present, proffer, refer to, trot out, upbraid **08** allude to, evidence, point out **10** put forward

**adept**
**03** ace, don **04** able, deft, good **05** handy, sharp, swell **06** adroit, clever, deacon, expert, genius, master, nimble, versed, wicked, wizard **07** capable, dab hand, maestro, mahatma, skilled, veteran **08** hot stuff, masterly, polished **09** competent, practised **10** proficient **11** experienced, nobody's fool **12** accomplished

**adequacy**
**07** ability, fitness, measure **08** fairness **10** capability, competence, mediocrity **11** passability, sufficiency, suitability **12** indifference, tolerability **13** acceptability, requisiteness, tolerableness **14** reasonableness, serviceability

**adequate**
**02** OK **03** fit **04** able, enow, good **05** equal, ho-hum, valid **06** enough, patchy, will do, worthy **07** average, capable, working **08** all right, passable, suitable **09** competent, requisite, tolerable **10** acceptable, reasonable, sufficient **11** appropriate, indifferent, serviceable **12** commensurate, could be worse, run of the mill, satisfactory **13** could be better, no great shakes, unexceptional **14** fair to middling **15** undistinguished

**adequately**
**08** passably, suitably **09** tolerably **10** acceptably, reasonably **12** sufficiently **13** appropriately **14** satisfactorily

**adhere**
**03** fix **04** bond, glue, grip, heed, hold, join, keep, link, obey **05** cling, paste, stick **06** attach, cement, cleave, cohere, defend, fasten, follow, fulfil, solder **07** abide by, accrete, combine, espouse, observe, respect, stand by, support **08** cleave to, coalesce, hold fast **10** comply with, stick up for **11** go along with **13** stick together

**adherence**
**05** cling **07** defence, respect, support **08** advocacy, fidelity **10** compliance, fulfilment, observance

**adherent**
**03** bur, fan, nut **04** buff, burr, Jain, Sikh, Sofi, Sufi **05** Bahai, child, freak, Hindu, Jaina **06** Hindoo, Maoist, Sabean, votary **07** admirer, devotee, engager, Genevan, gnostic, Patarin, Sabaean, sceptic, sectary, skeptic **08** advocate, believer, catholic, disciple, follower, groupist, hanger-on, henchman, Jacobite, loyalist, partisan, partizan, Patarine, rightist, royalist, sectator, servitor, sticking, upholder, Vichyite, Wesleyan **09** Caesarean, Caesarian, Communard, Gothicist, ideologue, Oliverian, Samaritan, satellite, socialist, Spinozist, supporter, Wagnerist, Wagnerite **10** aficionado, Bourbonist, enthusiast, Protestant **12** episcopalian, hereditarian **13** sun worshipper **14** restorationist **15** hereditarianist, parliamentarian

**adhesion**
**04** bond, grip **08** cohesion, purchase, sticking, synechia **09** adherence **10** attachment **12** adhesiveness **15** holding together

**adhesive**
**03** gum **04** bond, glue, tape **05** glair, gluey, gummy, paste, tacky **06** Blu-tak®, cement, clammy, Cow Gum®, gummed, sticky **07** Band-aid®, Blu-tack®, holding, hot melt, stick-on **08** adherent, adhering, clinging, cohesive, fixative, goldsize, mountant, mucilage, sticking **09** attaching, emplastic, glutinous, Sellotape®, Superglue® **10** sticky tape **11** Elastoplast®, hot-melt glue **12** mucilaginous, passe-partout, rubber cement, self-adhesive

**ad hoc**
**05** ad-lib **09** extempore, makeshift **10** improvised, off the cuff, unprepared, unscripted **11** spontaneous, unrehearsed **13** spontaneously

**adieu**
**03** bye **04** ciao, ta-ta **05** adios **06** bye-bye, cheers, kia ora, see you, so long **07** cheerio, goodbye, haere ra **08** au revoir, farewell, take care **10** all the best **11** arrivederci, be seeing you, leave-taking, see you later, valediction, valedictory **12** have a nice day, mind how you go, see you around **14** auf Wiedersehen

**ad infinitum**
**03** aye **07** for ever **08** evermore **09** endlessly, eternally **10** at all times, constantly **11** continually, incessantly, permanently, perpetually **12** till doomsday

**adjacent**
◇ *juxtaposition indicator*
**04** near, next, nigh **05** close **06** beside **07** closest, nearest, vicinal **08** abutting, next-door, touching **09** adjoining, alongside, bordering, proximate **10** contiguous, coterminal, juxtaposed **11** conterminal, coterminant, coterminate, coterminous **12** conterminant, conterminate, conterminous, neighbouring

**adjective**
**01** a **03** adj

**adjoin**
◇ *juxtaposition indicator*
**03** add **04** abut, join, link, meet **05** annex, touch, unite, verge **06** append, attach, be next, border, couple **07** combine, connect **09** juxtapose, neighbour **12** interconnect

**adjoining**
◇ *juxtaposition indicator*
**04** near, next **07** joining, linking, uniting, verging, vicinal **08** abutting, adjacent, next door, touching **09** bordering, combining, impinging, proximate **10** conjoining, connecting, contiguous, juxtaposed **12** neighbouring **15** interconnecting

**adjourn**
**04** stay **05** defer, delay, pause **06** put off, recess, repair, retire **07** retreat, suspend **08** break off, continue, postpone, prorogue, withdraw **09** interrupt **11** discontinue **14** betake yourself **15** stop temporarily

**adjournment**
**04** stay **05** break, delay, let-up, pause **06** recess **08** deferral, interval **09** deferment **10** moratorium, putting-off, suspension **11** continuance, dissolution, prorogation **12** intermission, interruption, postponement **15** discontinuation

**adjudge**
**04** aret, cide, deem, side **05** aread, arede, arett, award, judge **06** addeem, addoom, assign, decide, decree, reckon, regard **07** arreede **08** consider **09** determine

**adjudicate**
**04** pass **05** award, judge **06** decide, settle, umpire **07** adjudge, referee **09** arbitrate, determine, pronounce

**adjudication**
**06** decree, ruling **07** verdict **08** decision **09** judgement **10** conclusion, settlement **11** arbitration **13** determination, pronouncement

**adjudicator**
**03** ref, ump **05** judge **06** umpire **07** arbiter, referee **08** mediator **10** arbitrator

**adjunct**
**05** added **06** joined **07** apanage **08** addition, appanage **09** accessory, appendage, appendant **10** complement, supplement **11** concomitant **13** accompaniment

**adjust**
◇ *anagram indicator*
**03** fit, fix, set **04** gang, sort, suit, tram, true, tune **05** adapt, align, alter, amend, coapt, frame, shape, tweak **06** change, modify, reduce, repair, revise, settle, square, temper **07** arrange, balance, compose, concert, conform, convert, dispose, measure, rectify, remodel, reshape **08** fine-tune, modulate, register, regulate **09** get used to, harmonize, reconcile, refashion **11** accommodate **14** grow accustomed **15** make adjustments

**adjustable**
**07** movable **08** flexible **09** adaptable, alterable, versatile **10** modifiable **11** convertible

**adjustment**
◇ *anagram indicator*
**03** adj **04** COLA **06** change, fixing, tuning **07** fitting, setting, shaping **08** ordering, revision, tweaking **09** amendment, arranging **10** adaptation, alteration, coaptation, conforming, conversion, fine-tuning, regulation, settlement, settling in **11** arrangement, habituation, orientation, rearranging, remodelling **12** modification, settling down **13** accommodation, getting used to, harmonization, rearrangement, rectification **14** naturalization, reconciliation **15** acclimatization

**adjutant**
**03** adj **04** adjt **06** argala **07** marabou **08** marabout

**ad-lib**
**06** freely, invent, made-up, make up, wing it **09** extempore, impromptu, improvise **10** improvised, off the cuff, unprepared **11** extemporize, impulsively, play it by ear, spontaneous, unrehearsed **12** extemporized **13** spontaneously **14** extemporaneous, unpremeditated **15** speak off the cuff

**administer**
◇ *anagram indicator*
**03** run **04** drug, give, head, lead, rule **05** anele, apply, fetch, guide **06** direct, govern, impose, manage, supply **07** adhibit, conduct, control, deliver, dole out, execute, exhibit, give out, mete out, oversee, provide **08** disburse, dispense, organize, regulate **09** discharge, officiate, supervise **10** distribute, measure out **11** preside over, superintend

**administration**
**05** admin **06** regime, ruling, senate **07** cabinet, command, control, council, red tape, running **08** congress, ministry **09** direction, discharge, execution, executive, governing, paperwork, provision, supplying **10** government, imposition, leadership, management, overseeing, parliament **11** application, supervision **12** directorship, dispensation, organization, powers that be, term of office **13** administering, governing body **15** superintendence

**administrative**
**09** executive **10** management, managerial, regulatory **11** directorial, legislative, supervisory **12** governmental **13** authoritative, gubernatorial **14** organizational

*Administrative areas include:*

**04** area, city, town, ward, zila, zone
**05** shire, state, theme
**06** county, oblast, parish, region, sector, zillah
**07** borough, commune, enclave, pargana, village
**08** district, division, precinct, province, township
**09** pergunnah, territory
**11** conurbation
**12** constituency, municipality

*See also* **borough**; **council**; **county**; **department**; **district**; **province**; **state**

**administrator**
**04** boss, head **05** chief, elder, ruler **06** bigwig, leader, top dog **07** manager, trustee **08** big noise, chairman, director, governor, guardian, overseer **09** big cheese, commander, custodian, executive, organizer, patrician, president **10** controller, supervisor **11** dispensator **14** chief executive, judicial factor, superintendent **15** director-general, judicial trustee

**admirable**
**04** cool, fine, rare **05** brill **06** choice, wicked, worthy **07** slammin' **08** laudable, masterly, slamming, superior, terrific, valuable **09** deserving, estimable, excellent, exquisite, respected, wonderful **10** creditable **11** commendable, exceptional, magnificent, meritorious **12** praiseworthy, second to none **14** out of this world

**admirably**
**09** eminently, supremely **11** commendably, deservingly, excellently, wonderfully **13** exceptionally, magnificently

**admiral**
**02** AF, RA, VA **03** Adm **07** capitan, navarch, vanessa

*Admirals include:*

**04** **Byng** (George, Viscount Torrington), **Hood** (Samuel, Viscount), **Howe** (Richard, Earl), **Togo** (Heihachiro, Count)
**05** **Blake** (Robert), **Croft**, **Doria** (Andrea), **Hawke** (Edward, Lord), **Rooke** (Sir George)
**06** **Beatty** (David, Earl), **Benbow** (John), **Dönitz** (Karl), **Fisher** (John, Lord), **Grasse** (François, Comte de), **Halsey** (William F, Jnr), **Nelson** (Horatio, Lord), **Nimitz** (Chester), **Raeder** (Erich), **Vernon** (Edward)
**07** **Old Grog**, **Tirpitz** (Alfred von), **Wrangel** (Ferdinand, Baron von)
**08** **Cochrane** (Thomas), **Jellicoe** (John, Earl)
**09** **Artemisia**
**10** **Villeneuve** (Pierre Charles)
**11** **Collingwood** (Cuthbert, Lord), **Mountbatten** (Louis, Earl)

**admiration**
**03** yen **04** mana **05** kudos **06** esteem, fureur, praise, regard, wonder **07** acclaim, delight, idolism, respect, worship **08** approval, pleasure, surprise **09** adoration, adulation, affection, amazement, reverence **10** high esteem, high regard, veneration **11** approbation, hero-worship **12** appreciation, astonishment, commendation

• **expression of admiration**
**01** O **02** oh **03** man, wow **05** golly, wowee **06** by Jove **07** caramba, gee whiz, respect

**admire**
**04** laud, like **05** adore, prize, value **06** esteem, praise, revere, wonder **07** applaud, approve, iconize, idolize, respect, worship **08** look up to, venerate **09** approve of **10** appreciate **11** hero-worship **12** esteem highly, like very much **13** think highly of **14** put on a pedestal **15** think the world of

**admirer**
**03** fan **04** beau, buff **05** fiend, freak, lover, wooer **06** suitor **07** amateur,

beloved, devotee, gallant
**08** adherent, disciple, follower, idolater, idolator, idolizer
**09** boyfriend, supporter
**10** aficionado, enthusiast, girlfriend, sweetheart, worshipper

**admissible**
**02** OK **05** legit, licit **06** lawful
**07** allowed **08** passable **09** allowable, permitted, tolerable, tolerated
**10** acceptable, legitimate **11** justifiable, permissible

**admission**
**06** access, avowal, entrée, exposé
**07** ingress, peccavi **08** entrance, granting, mea culpa **09** allowance
**10** acceptance, admittance, concession, confession, confidence, disclosure, divulgence, ordination, permission, profession, revelation
**11** affirmation, declaration, entrance fee, entry charge, recognition
**12** admission fee, asseveration, grande entrée, right of entry **13** right of access
**14** acknowledgment
**15** acknowledgement, enfranchisement

**admit**
◇ *containment indicator*
**03** gie, own **04** give, take **05** adopt, agree, allow, enter, grant, let in, own up, yield **06** accept, affirm, fess up, ordain, reveal, take in **07** adhibit, concede, confess, declare, divulge, embrace, profess, receive, swear in, welcome
**08** blurt out, disclose, initiate, intromit
**09** come clean, introduce, recognize
**10** allow entry, give access
**11** acknowledge, matriculate **12** allow to enter, eat your words **13** give admission

**admittance**
**05** entry **06** access, entrée **07** ingress
**08** audience, entrance **09** admission, admitting, letting in, reception
**10** acceptance, initiation
**12** introduction, right of entry **13** right of access

**admitted**
**05** given **07** confest, granted
**08** accepted, affirmed, declared
**09** confessed, confirmed, professed
**10** recognized **12** acknowledged

**admittedly**
**07** granted **08** avowedly **09** allowedly, certainly **11** confessedly

**admitting**
**03** tho' **06** though

**admixture**
**03** mix **05** alloy, blend **06** fusion
**07** amalgam, mixture **08** compound, tincture **10** commixture
**11** combination **12** amalgamation, intermixture

**admonish**
**04** warn **05** chide, scold **06** berate, exhort, rebuke, school **07** censure, correct, counsel, reprove, tell off, upbraid **09** reprimand **10** discipline
**13** tear a strip off

**admonition**
**05** pi-jaw **06** advice, earful, rebuke
**07** censure, counsel, reproof, warning, wigging **08** berating, moniment, monument, scolding **09** reprimand
**10** correction, telling-off, ticking-off
**11** exhortation **12** dressing-down, reprehension

**ad nauseam**
**08** boringly **09** endlessly
**10** constantly **11** continually, perpetually **12** continuously, interminably, monotonously

**ado**
**04** flap, fuss, stir, to-do **05** hoo-ha, tizzy **06** bother, bustle, hassle
**07** stashie, stishie, stushie, trouble
**08** stooshie **09** commotion
**10** difficulty, hurly-burly **11** piece of work **12** song and dance

**adolescence**
**05** teens, youth **07** boyhood, puberty
**08** girlhood, minority **10** boyishness, immaturity, juvenility, pubescence
**11** development, girlishness
**12** juvenescence, teenage years, youthfulness **14** young adulthood

**adolescent**
**03** ned, Ted **04** teen **05** minor, young, youth **06** boyish, neanic **07** girlish, growing, puerile, teenage **08** childish, immature, juvenile, subadult, Teddy boy, teenager, youthful **09** infantile, pubescent, Teddy girl **10** bobbysoxer, developing, young adult
**11** juvenescent, young person

**adopt**
◇ *containment indicator*
**04** back, take, vote **05** elect **06** accept, assume, borrow, choose, father, follow, foster, mother, ratify, select, take in, take on, take up **07** appoint, approve, embrace, endorse, espouse, support
**08** arrogate, decide on, maintain, nominate, settle on **10** naturalize
**11** appropriate **13** take as your own

**adoption**
**04** vote **06** choice **07** backing, support
**08** approval, election, espousal, taking-in, taking-on, taking-up **09** embracing, fostering, selection **10** acceptance, nomination **11** appointment, approbation, embracement, endorsement **12** ratification
**13** appropriation **15** taking as your own

**adorable**
**04** dear **05** sweet **07** darling, lovable, winning, winsome **08** charming, fetching, pleasing, precious
**09** appealing, wonderful **10** attractive, bewitching, delightful, enchanting
**11** captivating

**adoration**
**04** love **06** esteem, homage, praise, regard **07** worship **08** devotion, doting on, idolatry **09** laudation, reverence **10** admiration, cherishing, exaltation, high regard, veneration
**11** idolization **12** thanksgiving
**13** glorification, magnification

**adore**
**04** love **05** enjoy **06** admire, dote on, esteem, honour, relish, revere, savour
**07** cherish, worship **08** be fond of, hold dear, venerate **10** idolatrize **11** be devoted to, be partial to **12** enjoy greatly, esteem highly, like very much
**15** think the world of

**adorn**
**04** deck, dink, do up, gild, trim
**05** array, begem, besee, crown, dight, dress, grace, paint **06** aguise, attire, attrap, bedeck, doll up, enrich, honour, invest, ornate, set out, tart up
**07** adonize, apparel, bedight, bedizen, bejewel, bestick, commend, emblaze, enhance, festoon, furbish, garnish, impearl, miniate **08** beautify, decorate, emblazon, ornament **09** bespangle, embellish **10** illustrate

**adornment**
**05** frill **06** fallal **07** decking, falbala, figgery, flounce, garnish, gilding
**08** frippery, furbelow, ornament
**09** accessory, fallalery, fandangle, garnishry, garniture, jewellery, trappings, trimmings **10** decorating, decoration, enrichment, ornateness, tawdry lace **11** bedizenment
**13** embellishment, ornamentation
**14** beautification

**adrift**
◇ *anagram indicator*
**04** lost **05** at sea **07** aimless
**08** drifting, goalless, insecure, rootless
**09** off course, unsettled **10** anchorless, unanchored **11** disoriented
**13** directionless, disorientated

**adroit**
**04** able, deft, neat, pert **05** adept, slick, trick **06** clever, expert, habile
**07** skilful **08** dextrous, tactical
**09** dexterous, ingenious, masterful
**10** proficient **11** resourceful

**adroitly**
**04** ably **06** deftly **08** cleverly, expertly
**09** skilfully **11** dexterously, masterfully
**12** proficiently **13** resourcefully

**adroitness**
**05** skill **07** ability, address, finesse, mastery **08** deftness, facility
**09** adeptness, dexterity, expertise
**10** cleverness, competence
**11** proficiency, skilfulness
**15** resourcefulness

**adulation**
**06** praise **07** fawning, incense
**08** flattery **10** admiration, sycophancy
**11** assentation, bootlicking, hero worship, idolization **12** blandishment
**13** pats on the back **15** personality cult

**adulatory**
**07** fawning, fulsome, servile
**08** praising, unctuous **10** flattering,

obsequious **11** blandishing, bootlicking, sycophantic **13** complimentary

**adult**
**01** A, X **03** man **04** blue, ripe **05** of age, woman **06** fruity, mature, sleazy, X-rated **07** grown-up, obscene, raunchy, ripened **08** hard-core, indecent **09** developed, full-grown **10** fully-grown **11** grown person, near the bone **12** fully-fledged, pornographic **14** near the knuckle

**adulterate**
**04** card, lime, load **05** taint, water **06** debase, defile, dilute, weaken **07** corrupt, degrade, devalue, falsify, pollute, vitiate **09** attenuate, water down **10** bastardize, make impure **11** contaminate, deteriorate **12** sophisticate

**adulteration**
**08** dilution **09** pollution, vitiation, weakening **10** corruption, debasement, defilement **13** contamination, deterioration

**adulterer**
**03** cad **04** rake, roué, stud, wolf **05** flirt **06** lecher **07** Don Juan, playboy **08** Casanova, deceiver **09** avouterer, ladies' man, libertine, womanizer **10** lady-killer, profligate **11** philanderer

**adulterous**
**05** false **08** cheating, disloyal **09** deceitful, faithless, two-timing **10** inconstant, unfaithful

**adultery**
**06** affair **07** avoutry, liaison **08** cheating **09** two-timing **10** flirtation, infidelity, misconduct, unchastity **11** fornication **12** entanglement **13** a bit on the side, playing around **14** unfaithfulness **15** extramarital sex, playing the field

**advance**
**01** a **03** pay, sub **04** ante, cite, give, grow, help, lend, loan, pass, push, rise, seek, step **05** early, march, offer, prior, raise **06** adduce, allege, assist, avaunt, better, come on, credit, foster, growth, incede, move on, submit, supply, thrive **07** benefit, deposit, develop, forward, furnish, further, go ahead, headway, imprest, improve, leading, present, proceed, proffer, promote, prosper, provide, suggest, support, upgrade **08** flourish, get ahead, increase, move in on, progress, retainer, vanguard **09** go forward **10** betterment, facilitate, forge ahead, gain ground, prepayment, put forward **11** advancement, come forward, development, down payment, furtherance, improvement, make earlier, make headway, move forward, preliminary, progression, step forward **12** amelioration, breakthrough, bring forward, going forward, make progress, pay in advance, surge forward **13** expeditionary, moving forward, pay beforehand **14** onward movement **15** forward movement, marching forward

**• in advance**
**02** on **05** ahead, early **06** sooner **07** earlier, forward, in front, up front **09** aforehand, in the lead **10** beforehand, previously **11** ahead of time **14** in the forefront

**advanced**
**01** a **03** far **04** high, lent, shot **05** ahead, early **06** higher, hi-tech, onward **07** complex, forward, leading **08** foremost, high-tech, up-to-date **09** high-level **10** avant-garde, precocious **11** progressive, ultra-modern **13** sophisticated, state-of-the art **14** forward-looking **15** ahead of the times

**advancement**
**04** gain, rise **06** ascent, growth **07** advance, headway **08** progress **09** evolution, promotion, upgrading **10** betterment, furthering, preferment, proceeding, upward step **11** development, furtherance, improvement **12** kick upstairs

**advances**
**05** moves, offer **08** approach **09** addresses, overtures **10** approaches, attentions, suggestion **11** proposition

**advantage**
**02** ad **03** aid, pro, use, van **04** boon, boot, edge, gain, good, head, help, lead, odds, plus, pull, sake, sted, sway **05** asset, avail, cause, favor, fruit, prise, prize, stead, value **06** beauty, favour, ground, pay-off, profit, reward, virtue **07** account, benefit, box-seat, service, utility, vantage, welfare **08** blessing, eminence, interest, leverage, whip hand **09** dominance, emolument, good point, head start, obvention, plus point, privilege, upper hand **10** assistance, percentage, perquisite, precedence, proceeding, usefulness, whip handle **11** convenience, helpfulness, pre-eminence, superiority, weather gage **12** weather gauge **14** on the windy side

**advantageous**
**04** plus **06** useful **07** gainful, helpful **08** valuable **09** favorable, of service, opportune, rewarding **10** beneficial, convenient, favourable, profitable, propitious, worthwhile **11** furthersome, serviceable **12** of assistance, remunerative

**advent**
**03** adv **04** dawn **05** birth, onset **06** coming **07** arrival, looming **08** approach, entrance **09** accession, beginning, emergence, inception **10** appearance, occurrence **12** introduction

**adventitious**
**07** foreign **09** unplanned **10** accidental, additional, fortuitous, unexpected, unforeseen, unintended **12** uncalculated

**adventure**
**04** gest, kick, risk **05** kicks, peril, quest **06** aunter, chance, danger, hazard, thrill **07** exploit, romance, venture **08** escapade, incident **09** happening **10** enterprise, excitement, experience, occurrence **11** speculation, undertaking

**adventurer**
**04** hero **06** pirate **07** heroine, Ulysses, voyager **08** Argonaut, Odysseus, venturer, wanderer **09** daredevil, traveller **10** filibuster, speculator **11** bandeirante, enterpriser, opportunist **12** carpetbagger, swashbuckler

**adventurous**
**04** bold, rash **05** gutsy, risky **06** daring, spunky **07** dareful **08** exciting, intrepid, perilous, reckless, romantic **09** audacious, dangerous, daredevil, hazardous, impetuous **10** headstrong, precarious **11** venturesome **12** enterprising **13** swashbuckling

**adversary**
**03** foe **05** enemy, rival, Satan **07** opposer **08** attacker, copemate, opponent **09** assailant, copes-mate **10** antagonist, competitor, contestant

**adverse**
**05** cross **06** thwart **07** awkward, counter, harmful, hostile, hurtful, opposed, unlucky **08** contrary, negative, opposing, opposite, perverse, untoward **09** injurious **10** unfriendly **11** conflicting, detrimental, inexpedient, inopportune, uncongenial, unfortunate **12** antagonistic, inauspicious, unfavourable, unpropitious **15** disadvantageous

**adversely**
**09** harmfully, unluckily **10** negatively **12** unfavourably **13** detrimentally, unfortunately **14** inauspiciously, unpropitiously

**adversity**
**03** woe **04** hell **05** cross, trial **06** misery, sorrow **07** bad luck, ill luck, reverse, the pits, trouble **08** calamity, disaster, distress, hardship, traverse **09** hard times, suffering **10** affliction, ill fortune, living hell, misfortune, perversity **11** catastrophe, tribulation **12** wretchedness

**advertise**
**04** bark, bill, hype, plug, post, puff, push, sell, tout **05** boost, quack, trail **06** inform, market, notify, poster, praise, talk up **07** declare, display, promote, publish **08** announce, proclaim **09** broadcast, make known, publicize **10** make public, promulgate **11** merchandize

**advertisement**
**02** ad, PR **04** bill, hype, plug, puff **05** blurb, promo **06** advert, jingle, notice, poster, teaser, tele-ad, want ad **07** display, handout, leaflet, placard, trailer **08** banner ad, bulletin, circular, handbill **09** marketing, promotion, publicity, throwaway **10** commercial, propaganda **12** announcement

**advice**
**03** tip **04** help, rede, reed, view, word **05** reede **06** notice, wisdom **07** caution, conseil, counsel, opinion, warning **08** guidance **09** direction **10** admonition, injunction, memorandum, suggestion **11** counselling, dos and don'ts, information, instruction **12** notification **13** communication, encouragement **14** recommendation
- **source of advice**
**03** CAB **10** counsellor

**advisability**
**06** wisdom **07** aptness **08** prudence **09** soundness **10** expediency **11** suitability **12** desirability **13** judiciousness, preferability **15** appropriateness

**advisable**
**03** apt, fit **04** best, well, wise **05** sound **06** proper, wisest **07** correct, fitting, politic, prudent **08** sensible, suitable **09** desirable, expedient, judicious, suggested **10** beneficial, preferable, profitable **11** appropriate, recommended

**advise**
**04** read, rede, tell, urge, vise, warn **05** guide, reede, teach, tutor **06** enjoin, inform, notify, preach, report **07** apprise, caution, commend, counsel, suggest **08** acquaint, fill in on, forewarn, instruct **09** make known, recommend **10** give notice **11** give counsel **12** give guidance **14** give the low-down **15** give suggestions, make suggestions

**advisedly**
**06** wisely **09** carefully, prudently **10** cautiously **11** judiciously **13** intentionally

**adviser**
**03** IFA **04** aide, guru **05** angel, coach, guide, tutor **06** Egeria, helper, lawyer, mentor, minder **07** counsel, monitor, starets, staretz, teacher **08** assessor **09** agony aunt, authority, confidant, therapist, town clerk **10** confidante, consultant, counsellor, instructor, law-officer, pensionary **12** amicus curiae, right-hand man **13** company doctor **14** right-hand woman **15** Attorney-General

**advisory**
**03** adv **07** helping **08** advising **10** consulting **11** counselling **12** consultative, consultatory, recommending

**advocacy**
**06** avowry **07** backing, defence, pushing, support **08** adoption, espousal, proposal **09** patronage, promotion, upholding **11** advancement, campaigning, championing, propagation **12** promulgation **13** encouragement, justification **14** recommendation

**advocate**
**02** KC, QC **03** adv **04** back, peat, plug, urge **05** adopt, be pro, lobby **06** advise, back up, defend, favour, lawyer, preach, syndic, uphold **07** counsel, endorse, espouse, justify, pleader, promote, propose, push for, speaker, support **08** argue for, attorney, be behind, champion, defender, exponent, plead for, preacher, press for, promoter, upholder **09** barrister, believe in, encourage, paraclete, patronize, prescribe, proponent, recommend, solicitor, spokesman, supporter **10** campaigner, evangelist, vindicator **11** campaign for, countenance, protagonist, spokeswoman, subscribe to **12** King's Counsel, spokesperson **13** Queen's Counsel **14** sympathize with

**aegis**
**04** wing **06** favour **07** backing, support **08** advocacy, auspices **09** patronage **10** protection **11** sponsorship **12** championship, guardianship

**aeon**
**03** age, eon, era **04** span, time, year **05** epoch, years **08** duration, eternity **10** generation

**aerate**
**06** excite, gasify **07** lighten, perturb, refresh **09** oxygenate, ventilate **10** put air into **13** charge with air, charge with gas

**aerial**
**04** aery, dish, yagi **05** aerie **06** dipole, duplex, midair **07** aeolian, antenna, booster, scanner **08** air-to-air, in the air, radiator, receiver, squarial **13** satellite dish **14** above the ground

**aeroplane**
**03** bus **04** kite **05** crate
*See also* **aircraft**

**aesthetic**
**04** arty, fine **07** elegant, stylish **08** adorning, artistic, tasteful **10** decorative, ornamental **11** beautifying **12** embellishing **15** greenery-yallery

**afar**
**06** far off **07** far away **08** a long way **09** distantly **13** a long distance

**affability**
**06** warmth **08** courtesy, facility, matiness, mildness, openness **09** benignity, geniality, palliness **10** amiability, chumminess, cordiality, good humour, good nature, kindliness **11** amicability, benevolence, sociability **12** congeniality, friendliness, graciousness, obligingness, pleasantness **15** approachability, conversableness

**affable**
**04** maty, mild, open, warm **05** matey, pally, suave **06** chummy, facile, genial, kindly **07** amiable, cordial **08** amicable, friendly, gracious, obliging, pleasant, sociable **09** agreeable, congenial, courteous, expansive **10** benevolent, soft-spoken **11** good-natured **12** approachable, good-humoured

**affair**
**02** go **03** biz **04** gear, love, ploy, shew, show **05** amour, cause, event, fling, issue, thing, topic **06** effeir, effere, matter, pidgin, pigeon **07** affaire, carry-on, concern, episode, funeral, liaison, pidgeon, project, romance, shebang, subject **08** activity, amour fou, business, hypothec, incident, interest, intrigue, question **09** happening, operation **10** love affair, occurrence, proceeding **11** transaction, undertaking **12** circumstance, relationship **13** affaire d'amour, grande passion **14** affaire de coeur, responsibility

**affect**
**03** hit **04** do to, fake, faze, move, sham, stir, sway, take **05** act on, adopt, alter, amove, assay, feign, pinch, put on, taint, throw, touch, up-end, upset **06** assume, attack, change, impact, modify, regard, salute, strike **07** apply to, concern, disturb, imitate, impress, involve, perturb, pretend, profess, trouble **08** bear upon, come home, interest, overcome, relate to, simulate **09** influence, transform **10** do things to, take hold of **11** counterfeit, impinge upon, prevail over **14** have an effect on

**affectation**
**03** act **04** airs, pose, sham, show **06** façade **07** charade, foppery, ladyism **08** pretence, pretense **09** affection, imitation, mannerism **10** appearance, minauderie, simulation **11** insincerity, theatricism **12** false display **13** airs and graces, artificiality **15** pretentiousness

**affected**
◇ *anagram indicator*
**04** camp, fake, posy, sham, twee **05** ditsy, ditzy, posey, put-on, stiff **06** chichi, la-di-da, phoney **07** assumed, feigned, foppish, mincing, minikin, pompous, stuck up, studied **08** literose, mannered, precious **09** contrived, insincere, simpering, simulated, unnatural **10** artificial, euphuistic, histrionic, hoity-toity **11** counterfeit, highfalutin, pretentious **12** highfaluting, histrionical, niminy-piminy

**affecting**
**03** sad **06** moving **07** piteous, pitiful **08** pathetic, pitiable, poignant,

powerful, stirring, touching
**09** troubling **10** impressive **12** heart-rending **13** heartbreaking

**affection**
**03** luv **04** care, love **05** amity
**06** caring, desire, favour, liking, storge, warmth **07** feeling, passion, worship
**08** calf-love, devotion, fondness, goodwill, kindness, localism, penchant
**10** attachment, endearment, partiality, proclivity, propensity, tenderness, topophilia **11** inclination
**12** friendliness, predilection
**14** predisposition

**affectionate**
**04** fond, kind, warm **05** eager
**06** caring, doting, loving, tender
**07** adoring, amiable, cordial, devoted, fervent, fulsome **08** attached, friendly, Platonic, sisterly **09** brotherly
**10** passionate **11** warm-hearted

**affectionately**
**06** dearly, fondly, kindly, warmly
**07** amiably **08** lovingly, tenderly
**09** adoringly, cordially, devotedly

**affiliate**
**04** ally, join **05** annex, merge, unite
**06** team up **07** combine, conjoin, connect, filiate **09** associate, syndicate
**10** amalgamate, fraternize
**11** confederate, incorporate **12** band together

**affiliated**
**06** allied **07** related **08** in league
**09** connected **10** associated, integrated **11** amalgamated
**12** incorporated **13** in partnership

**affiliation**
**03** tie **04** bond, link **05** union
**06** league, merger **07** joining
**08** alliance **09** coalition, filiation
**10** connection, federation, membership **11** association, combination **12** amalgamation, relationship **13** confederation, incorporation

**affinity**
**03** kin **04** bond **06** kinred, liking
**07** analogy, empathy, kindred, kinship, rapport **08** affiance, fondness, homology, likeness, sympathy
**09** chemistry, good terms
**10** attraction, partiality, propensity, similarity, similitude **11** resemblance
**12** relationship **13** comparability, compatibility **14** correspondence, predisposition

**affirm**
**03** say **04** aver, avow **05** state, swear
**06** adhere, assert, attest, avouch, ratify, uphold **07** certify, confirm, declare, endorse, support, testify, witness
**08** maintain **09** predicate, pronounce
**10** asseverate **11** corroborate

**affirmation**
**02** ay **03** aye, yes **04** oath **06** avowal
**07** protest, witness **08** averment
**09** assertion, statement, testimony
**10** affirmance, avouchment, deposition **11** attestation, declaration, endorsement **12** asseveration, confirmation, ratification
**13** certification, corroboration, pronouncement

**affirmative**
**02** ay, OK **03** aye, yea, yes
**08** agreeing, dogmatic, emphatic, positive **09** agreement, approving, assenting, asserting, assertory
**10** acceptance, concurring, confirming, consenting
**11** concurrence, predicatory
**12** acquiescence, confirmation, ratification **13** corroborative

**affix**
**03** add, put, tag **04** bind, glue, join, tack **05** annex, paste, pin on, set to, stick **06** adhere, adjoin, append, attach, fasten, prefix, suffix
**07** connect, subjoin **09** privative
**13** frequentative

**afflict**
**03** ail, try **04** harm, hurt, pain, prey
**05** assay, beset, curse, gripe, smite, visit, wound **06** bother, burden, grieve, harass, plague, strain, stress, strike
**07** anguish, inflict, oppress, scourge, torment, torture, trouble **08** distress, lacerate **09** persecute **12** bear hard upon

**afflicted**
◇ *anagram indicator*
**03** ill, sad **04** hurt, sick, sore **05** beset, woful **06** cursed, humble, pained, struck, woeful **07** injured, laid low, plagued, wounded, wracked
**08** affected, bothered, burdened, harassed, strained, stricken, tortured, troubled **09** aggrieved, anguished, depressed, disturbed, miserable, oppressed, sorrowful, suffering, tormented **10** distressed, overthrown
**11** traumatized **13** grief-stricken

**affliction**
**03** woe **04** care, pain, sore, teen, tene, tine, tyne **05** anger, cross, curse, grief, night, teene, trial **06** misery, ordeal, plague, sorrow, unweal **07** disease, furnace, illness, languor, scourge, torment, trouble **08** calamity, disaster, distress, hardship, sickness
**09** adversity, suffering **10** depression, heart-grief, misfortune, visitation
**11** tribulation **12** wretchedness

**affluence**
**06** inflow, plenty, riches, wealth
**07** fortune, tidy sum **08** opulence, property **09** abundance, megabucks, profusion, substance **10** easy street, prosperity **11** wealthiness

**affluent**
**04** rich **05** flush **06** loaded
**07** moneyed, opulent, wealthy, well-off **08** well-to-do **09** abounding, inflowing **10** in the money, prosperous, well-heeled **11** comfortable, rolling in it **12** on easy street

**afford**
**04** bear, give **05** allow, grant, offer, spare, yield **06** answer, impart, manage, pay for, supply **07** furnish, present, produce, provide, sustain
**08** generate **09** stretch to **11** be able to pay **13** have enough for **15** have the money for

**affordable**
**05** cheap **06** budget **07** low-cost
**08** moderate **09** dirt cheap, low-priced **10** economical, manageable, reasonable **11** inexpensive, sustainable

**affray**
**03** row **04** fear, feud, fray, riot
**05** brawl, brush, fight, mêlée, scrap, set-to **06** fracas, tussle **07** contest, disturb, punch-up, quarrel, scuffle, startle, wrangle **08** frighten, skirmish, squabble **10** fisticuffs, free-for-all
**11** disturbance

**affront**
**03** vex **04** face, slur, snub **05** abuse, anger, annoy, facer, pique, wrong
**06** injury, insult, offend, slight
**07** incense, offence, outrage, provoke
**08** confront, dishonor, irritate, rudeness, vexation **09** aspersion, dishonour, displease, indignity
**10** disrespect **11** discourtesy, provocation **13** slap in the face **14** kick in the teeth

**affronted**
**05** angry, vexed **06** piqued
**07** annoyed, injured **08** incensed, insulted, offended, outraged, slighted
**09** irritated **10** displeased

**Afghanistan**
**03** AFG

**aficionado**
**03** fan, nut **04** buff **05** fiend, freak
**06** expert **07** admirer, devotee
**09** authority **10** enthusiast, specialist
**11** connoisseur

**aflame**
**02** in **03** lit **05** aglow, lit up **06** ablaze, alight, bright, on fire **07** burning, ignited, lighted, radiant, shining
**11** illuminated

**afloat**
**05** aswim, at sea, awash, sound
**06** viable **07** buoyant, solvent, unfixed
**08** drifting, floating, swimming, watching **09** out of debt **10** in the black, unsinkable

**afoot**
**02** up **05** about, agate, astir
**06** abroad, around **07** brewing, current, going on **08** in the air **09** in the wind **10** going about **11** circulating
**13** in the pipeline

**aforementioned**
**04** this **07** the same **09** aforesaid
**10** aforenamed

**afraid**
**03** rad **04** nesh **05** adrad, adred, afear, sorry, timid **06** afeard, aghast, craven,

feared, scared **07** affeard, alarmed, anxious, daunted, fearful, nervous **08** affrayed, cowardly, effraide, timorous **09** concerned, petrified, regretful, reluctant, terrified, tremulous **10** apologetic, frightened, suspicious **11** distrustful, in a blue funk, intimidated **12** apprehensive, faint-hearted, in a cold sweat **13** having kittens, panic-stricken, scared to death

**• be afraid**
**05** quake

**afresh**
◇ *anagram indicator*
**04** anew **05** again, newly **08** once more **09** once again, over again

**Africa**

*African countries include:*

**04** Chad, Mali, Togo
**05** Benin, Congo, Egypt, Gabon, Ghana, Kenya, Libya, Niger, Sudan
**06** Angola, Guinea, Malawi, Rwanda, Uganda, Zambia
**07** Algeria, Burundi, Comoros, Eritrea, Lesotho, Liberia, Morocco, Namibia, Nigeria, Senegal, Somalia, Tunisia
**08** Botswana, Cameroon, Djibouti, Ethiopia, Tanzania, Zimbabwe
**09** Cape Verde, Mauritius, Swaziland, The Gambia
**10** Madagascar, Mauritania, Mozambique, Seychelles
**11** Burkina Faso, Côte d'Ivoire, Sierra Leone, South Africa
**12** Guinea-Bissau
**13** Western Sahara
**16** Equatorial Guinea
**18** São Tomé and Príncipe
**22** Central African Republic
**28** Democratic Republic of the Congo

*African landmarks include:*

**04** Giza, Nile
**05** Congo, Luxor
**06** Karnak, Sphinx
**07** Zambezi
**08** Aswan Dam, Kalahari, Lake Chad, Okavango, Pyramids
**09** Lake Nyasa, Masai Mara, River Nile, Serengeti, Suez Canal
**10** Lake Malawi, Lake Nasser, River Congo, River Niger
**11** Drakensberg, Great Sphinx, Kilimanjaro, Luxor Temple
**12** Aswan High Dam, Great Pyramid, Lake Victoria, Sahara Desert, Zambezi River
**13** Mt Kilimanjaro, Okavango Delta, Table Mountain, Victoria Falls
**14** Atlas Mountains, Cape of Good Hope, Kalahari Desert, Lake Tanganyika
**15** Great Rift Valley

**African**

*Africans include:*

**03** Ibo, Kru, Twi
**04** Boer, Efik, Igbo, Kroo, Moor, Susu, Tshi, Zulu
**05** Masai, Swazi, Temne, Tonga
**06** Griqua, Herero, Kenyan, Kikuyu, Libyan, Malian, Somali, Tuareg, Yoruba
**07** Angolan, Basotho, Chadian, Gambian, Guinean, Ivorian, Mosotho, Rwandan, Sahrawi, Swahili, Ugandan, Zambian
**08** Algerian, Batswana, Beninese, Egyptian, Eritrean, Gabonese, Ghanaian, Liberian, Malagasy, Malawian, Moroccan, Motswana, Namibian, Nigerian, Nigerien, Sahraoui, Sudanese, Togolese, Tunisian
**09** Burkinabé, Burundian, Congolese, Ethiopian, Sahrawian, Santoméan, São Toméan, Tanzanian
**10** Djiboutian, Mozambican, Sahraouian, Senegalese, Zimbabwean
**11** Cameroonian, Cape Verdean, Mauritanian
**12** South African
**13** Equatoguinean, Sierra Leonean
**14** Central African, Guinea-Bissauan

**after**
◇ *juxtaposition indicator*
**02** on **03** epi-, for **04** past **05** about, since **06** behind **07** chasing, owing to, wanting **09** because of, following, posterior, regarding **10** concerning, in honour of **11** as a result of, in pursuit of, on account of, trying to get **12** subsequent to, with regard to **15** in consequence of

**• after all**
**08** in the end **09** most of all, primarily **10** first of all **12** nevertheless **15** most importantly

**• after that**
**04** then **05** later

**• after which**
**04** when

**• immediately after**
**04** next

**• not after**
**02** by

**• until after**
**04** over

**after-effect**
**06** result, upshot **07** spin-off **09** aftermath **11** consequence **12** repercussion

**aftermath**
**03** end **04** rawn, wake **05** rowan **06** rawing, rowing, upshot **07** effects, fallout, outcome, results **08** backwash **10** lattermath **11** aftergrowth **12** after-effects, consequences **13** repercussions

**afternoon**
**01** a **02** pm **04** arvo **06** undern **07** evening **12** postmeridian

**• pleasant Sunday afternoon**
**03** PSA

**afterpiece**
**03** jig **05** exode

**afterthought**
**02** PS **03** PPS **05** rider **07** codicil **10** postscript

**afterwards**
**03** eft **04** next, syne, then **05** later **07** later on **09** after that, thereupon **12** subsequently

**again**
**02** do, re **03** eft **04** anew, back, more, over, then **05** ditto **06** afresh, encore, iterum **07** further **08** once more, yet again **09** once again, over again **11** another time, one more time

**• again and again**
**05** often **10** constantly, frequently, repeatedly **11** continually **12** time and again

**against**
◇ *juxtaposition indicator*
**01** v **02** on, to, vs **03** con **04** anti **06** facing, versus **07** harmful **08** abutting, fronting, in case of, opposing, touching **09** close up to, hostile to, opposed to, resisting **10** adjacent to, opposite to **11** confronting, detrimental, in the face of, prejudicial **12** in contrast to, in defiance of, unfavourable **13** in contact with **14** antagonistic to, in opposition to **15** disadvantageous

**agate**
**04** onyx **05** afoot, astir, murra **06** astray, murrha, pebble **10** Mocha stone **11** chalcedonyx, dendrachate **12** Scotch pebble

**agave**
**05** sisal **06** maguey **08** henequen, henequin, heniquin **12** American aloe, century plant

**age**
**03** day, eon, era, yug **04** aeon, date, days, span, time, yuga **05** epoch, ripen, years **06** dotage, grow up, mature, mellow, old age, period, season, wither **07** century, decline, grow old **08** duration, maturity, senility **09** become old, come of age, seniority **10** degenerate, generation, senescence **11** decrepitude, deteriorate, elderliness **14** advancing years, declining years

*See also* **old age**

**aged**
**02** ae, of **03** aet, old **04** grey **05** aging, hoary **06** ageing, mature, past it, senior **07** ancient, doddery, elderly **08** advanced, wintered **09** geriatric, getting on, senescent **11** over the hill, patriarchal **13** superannuated **15** advanced in years, no spring chicken

**agency**
**04** firm, work **05** force, means, power **06** action, bureau, effect, medium, office **07** company, vehicle **08** activity, business, workings **09** influence, mechanism, operation **10** department **11** involvement **12** intervention, organization **15** instrumentality

*See also* **news**; **spy**

**agenda**
**04** list, menu, plan **05** diary
**06** scheme **08** calendar, schedule, to-do list **09** programme, timetable
**12** scheme of work

**agent**
**03** agt, Fed, rep, spy, way **04** Bond, doer, G-man, mole, narc, nark, root, spie, wait **05** cause, envoy, force, means, mover, narco, plant, proxy, route, spial, spook **06** agency, beagle, broker, deputy, engine, factor, medium, setter, shadow, source, worker **07** channel, liaison, sleeper, trustee, vehicle **08** assignee, delegate, emissary, Mata Hari, minister, mouchard, operator **09** go-between, middleman, operative, performer
**10** instrument, negotiator, substitute
**11** double agent, functionary
**12** intermediary **14** representative
*See also* **publicity**

**age-old**
**03** old **04** aged **07** ancient, antique, very old **08** primeval, time-worn
**09** long-lived, primaeval

**agglomeration**
**04** mass **05** stash, store **07** build-up
**08** increase **09** aggregate, gathering, stockpile **10** collection **11** aggregation
**12** accumulation, augmentation

**aggrandize**
**05** exalt, widen **06** enrich **07** advance, amplify, dignify, elevate, enhance, enlarge, ennoble, glorify, inflate, magnify, promote, upgrade
**09** glamorize **10** exaggerate, make richer

**aggrandizement**
**09** elevation, promotion **10** exaltation
**11** advancement, enhancement, enlargement **12** exaggeration
**13** magnification

**aggravate**
**03** irk, try, vex **05** annoy, get at, tease
**06** harass, needle, pester, wind up, worsen **07** incense, inflame, magnify, provoke **08** compound, heighten, increase, irritate **09** intensify, make worse **10** exacerbate, exaggerate, exasperate

**aggravation**
**05** aggro **06** hassle **07** teasing
**08** vexation **09** annoyance
**10** irritation **11** irksomeness, provocation **12** exasperation **15** thorn in the flesh

**aggregate**
**03** ore, ped, sum **04** full, mass **05** gross, total, whole **06** amount, domain, entire
**08** assemble, combined, complete, dendrite, detritus, entirety, manifold, point set, potstone, sum total, totality
**09** complexus, inclusive, summation
**10** collection, generality, grand total
**11** accumulated, combination, total amount, whole amount
**12** accumulation **13** comprehensive, hypersthenite

**aggression**
**04** rage, raid **06** attack, injury, strike
**07** air rage, assault, offence
**08** invasion, road rage **09** hostility, incursion, intrusion, militancy, offensive, onslaught, pugnacity
**10** antagonism **11** bellicosity, provocation **12** belligerence, encroachment, forcefulness, infringement **13** combativeness
**14** aggressiveness

**aggressive**
**04** bold **05** lairy, pushy **06** bad-ass, brutal, chippy, feisty, full-on, savage
**07** bullish, go-ahead, hostile, kick-ass, zealous **08** forceful, invasive, ruthless, vigorous **09** assertive, bellicose, combative, cut-throat, ferocious, incursive, intrusive, in-yer-face, offensive, truculent **10** in-your-face, pugnacious **11** bareknuckle, belligerent, competitive, contentious, destructive, provocative, quarrelsome
**12** bareknuckled **13** argumentative

**aggressor**
**07** invader **08** attacker, intruder, offender, provoker **09** assailant, assaulter **10** instigator

**aggrieved**
◇ *anagram indicator*
**04** hurt, sore **05** angry, upset **06** bitter, miffed, pained, peeved **07** annoyed, ill-used, injured, unhappy, wronged
**08** insulted, offended, saddened
**09** pissed off, resentful **10** distressed, maltreated **11** disgruntled

**aghast**
**06** amazed **07** shocked, stunned
**08** appalled, dismayed, startled
**09** astounded, horrified, stupefied
**10** astonished, confounded **12** horror-struck **13** thunderstruck

**agile**
◇ *anagram indicator*
**04** deft, spry **05** acute, alert, brisk, fleet, lithe, nifty, quick, sharp, swank, swift, withy **06** active, astute, clever, limber, lissom, lively, mobile, nimble, supple **07** lissome **08** athletic, flexible **09** dexterous, sprightly
**11** quick-witted

**agility**
**08** deftness, mobility **09** alertness, briskness, quickness, sharpness, swiftness **10** activeness, astuteness, liveliness, nimbleness, suppleness
**11** flexibility **15** quick-wittedness

**agitate**
◇ *anagram indicator*
**03** vex **04** beat, faze, fuss, heat, poss, rile, rock, stir, toss **05** alarm, argue, blend, churn, fight, rouse, shake, upset, whisk, worry **06** arouse, battle, betoss, dither, excite, flurry, incite, rattle, ruffle, rumble, stir up, wind up, work up
**07** commove, confuse, disturb, ferment, fluster, inflame, perturb, torment, trouble, unnerve
**08** campaign, convulse, disquiet, distract, kefuffle, unsettle **09** carfuffle, curfuffle, kerfuffle, stimulate
**10** discompose, disconcert, perturbate

**agitated**
◇ *anagram indicator*
**04** wild **05** het up, upset **06** heated, hectic, mobled, stormy **07** agitato, anxious, excited, nervous, ruffled, worried **08** hopped-up, in a tizzy, troubled, unnerved **09** disturbed, ebullient, flustered, in a lather, steamed up, troublous, unsettled, wrought up
**10** distraught, tumultuous
**11** highwrought **12** all of a dither, all of a doodah, disconcerted **14** hot and bothered

**agitation**
**04** fret **05** alarm, tweak, worry
**06** battle, flurry, frenzy, jabble, lather, motion, moving, pucker, ruffle, taking
**07** anxiety, beating, concern, crusade, emotion, fanteeg, ferment, fluster, flutter, shaking, tempest, tension, tossing, trouble, turning **08** blending, disquiet, distress, fantigue, fighting, kefuffle, movement, stirring, striving, struggle, whisking **09** carfuffle, commotion, curfuffle, kerfuffle
**10** ebullition, excitement
**11** campaigning, distraction, disturbance, jactitation, trepidation
**12** perturbation, restlessness

**agitator**
**07** inciter, stirrer **08** activist, fomenter
**09** Bolshevik, firebrand **10** instigator, subversive **12** rabble-rouser, troublemaker **13** revolutionary

**agnostic**
**07** doubter, sceptic **08** doubting
**09** sceptical **10** questioner, unbeliever
**11** questioning, unbelieving
**12** disbelieving **14** doubting Thomas

**ago**
**04** back, gone, past, syne **05** since
**06** before **07** earlier **09** in the past
**10** previously **12** from that time

**agog**
**04** avid, keen **05** eager **07** anxious, curious, excited, pop-eyed
**09** impatient **10** enthralled, in suspense **12** enthusiastic **13** on tenterhooks

**agonize**
**04** fret **05** worry **06** labour, strain, strive **07** contend, trouble, wrestle
**08** struggle

**agonizing**
**07** painful, racking **08** piercing, worrying **09** harrowing, torturous
**10** tormenting **11** distressing
**12** excruciating, heart-rending

**agony**
**03** woe **04** hurt, pain **05** spasm
**06** misery, throes **07** anguish, torment, torture **08** distress **09** suffering
**10** affliction **11** tribulation
**12** wretchedness

**agrarian**
**07** bucolic, farming, georgic, predial **08** geoponic, praedial **09** agronomic **10** cultivated **12** agricultural

**agree**
**02** OK **03** fit, yes **04** gree, jibe, jump, okay, sort, suit **05** admit, align, aline, allow, apply, atone, chime, close, fadge, get on, grant, match, tally, yield **06** accede, accept, accord, adhere, assent, assort, attone, clinch, comply, concur, cotton, decide, go with, permit, settle, square **07** be at one, comport, concede, concord, conform, congree, congrue, consent, consort, paction **08** coincide, compound, hit it off, say yes to, strike in **09** determine, harmonize, subscribe, symbolize **10** compromise, condescend, correspond, fall in with, homologate, underwrite **11** acquiesce in, be of one mind, go along with, meet halfway, rubber-stamp, see eye to eye **12** be consistent, share the view **14** give the go-ahead, strike a bargain **15** give the thumbs-up, make concessions

**agreeable**
**04** fine, kind, nice **05** jolly, sapid **07** likable, willing **08** amenable, amicable, charming, euphonic, friendly, likeable, pleasant **09** compliant, congenial, desirable, enjoyable, toothsome **10** acceptable, attractive, delightful, euphonical, euphonious **11** complaisant, conformable, good-natured, sympathetic **12** approachable **13** companionable, consentaneous

**agreeably**
**09** enjoyably **10** acceptably, pleasantly, pleasingly **11** accordingly **12** attractively, delightfully

**agreement**
**03** agt, FTA **04** amen, band, deal, deed, GATT, pact, repo, whiz **05** chime, covin, NAFTA, tally, union, whizz **06** accord, assent, comart, covyne, pre-nup, treaty, unison **07** analogy, bargain, closing, compact, concert, concord, consent, consort, contrat, entente, fitting, harmony, syntony **08** affinity, contract, covenant, matching, Mercosur, sortance, sponsion, sympathy **09** Ausgleich, collusion, community, concordat, consensus, indenture, unanimity **10** compliance, conformity, congruence, congruency, consonance, convention, settlement, similarity, uniformity **11** arrangement, concordance, concurrence, consistence, consistency, respondence, supersedere, transaction **12** complaisance **13** compatibility, embellishment, understanding **14** correspondence, correspondency

*See also* **treaty**

**• expression of agreement**
**01** I **02** ay, OK **03** aye, oke, olé **04** amen, done, good, okay, sure **05** right, uh-huh, wilco **06** quotha, rather, righto **07** d'accord, right-ho

**agricultural**
**05** rural **06** farmed **07** bucolic, farming, georgic **08** agrarian, geoponic, pastoral, praedial **09** agronomic **10** cultivated, geoponical **11** countryside

*See also* **farm**

**agriculture**
**03** agr **04** plow **06** plough **07** farming, tillage, tilling **08** agronomy **09** geoponics, husbandry **10** agronomics **11** agroscience, cultivation **12** agribusiness

*Agriculturists include:*

**04** **Coke** (Thomas William), **Tull** (Jethro)
**05** **Lawes** (Sir John Bennet), **Young** (Arthur)
**06** **Carver** (George Washington)
**07** **Borlaug** (Norman), **Burbank** (Luther)
**08** **Bakewell** (Robert)
**09** **McCormick** (Cyrus)
**12** **Boussingault** (Jean-Baptiste)

**aground**
**05** stuck **06** ashore, neaped **07** beached, wrecked **08** grounded, marooned, stranded **09** foundered **10** high and dry, on the rocks

**ague**
◇ *anagram indicator*
**05** exies, fever **07** malaria **10** the shivers

**ah**
**02** ay, la **10** alas the day **12** alas the while

**ahead**
◇ *juxtaposition indicator*
**02** up **05** forth **06** before, onward **07** forward, in front, leading, onwards, winning **08** advanced, forwards, headlong, superior **09** at the head, earlier on, in advance, in the lead, to the fore **13** at an advantage, in the vanguard **14** in the forefront

**aid**
**04** ease, gift, hand, help, prop **05** boost, grant, serve **06** a leg up, assist, backup, favour, hasten, oblige, relief, second **07** backing, benefit, charity, funding, promote, relieve, service, speed up, subsidy, succour, support, sustain **08** donation, expedite **09** encourage, patronage, subsidize **10** assistance, facilitate, rally round, subvention **11** accommodate, helping hand, sponsorship **12** contribution **13** a shot in the arm, co-operate with, encouragement

**aide**
**02** PA **06** minder, Sherpa **07** adviser, attaché **08** adjutant, advocate, disciple, follower **09** assistant, confidant, supporter **10** aide-de-camp, confidante **12** right-hand man **14** right-hand woman

**ail**
**04** fail, pain **05** upset, worry **06** bother, sicken, weaken **07** afflict, trouble **08** distress, irritate **13** indisposition

**ailing**
**03** ill **04** poor, sick, weak **05** frail, unfit **06** feeble, infirm, poorly, sickly, unwell **07** failing, invalid, unsound **08** diseased **09** deficient, insolvent, off-colour, suffering **10** foundering, inadequate, indisposed, out of sorts **11** debilitated, languishing **12** in poor health **15** under the weather

**ailment**
**03** ill, pip **04** waff, worm **05** cough **06** malady **07** disease, illness, passion **08** disorder, sickness, weakness **09** complaint, infection, infirmity **10** affliction, disability **11** dog's disease **13** indisposition

**aim**
**03** end, eye, try **04** bend, goal, gole, hope, mark, mean, plan, sake, seek, vizy, want, wish **05** dream, ettle, level, point, sight, telos, train, visie **06** aspire, course, design, desire, direct, intend, intent, line up, motive, object, scheme, strive, target, vizzie **07** attempt, mission, propose, purpose, resolve, shoot at, take aim **08** ambition, zero in on **09** direction, endeavour, intention, objective **10** aspiration **11** work towards **15** set your sights on

**aimless**
**05** stray **06** chance, futile, random **07** erratic, wayward **08** drifting, goalless, rambling, unguided **09** haphazard, pointless, shiftless, unsettled, wandering **10** irresolute, undirected **11** purposeless, unmotivated **13** directionless, unpredictable

**air**
**03** sky **04** aero-, aria, aura, ayre, lift, lilt, look, mien, puff, song, tell, tune, waft, wind **05** blast, dirge, ditty, ether, ozone, state, utter, voice, whiff **06** aerate, allure, aspect, breath, breeze, demean, effect, expose, manner, oxygen, reveal, screen, zephyr **07** arietta, bearing, canzona, canzone, declare, demaine, demayne, demeane, divulge, draught, express, feeling, freshen, heavens, publish **08** ambience, carriage, cavatina, disclose, fresh air, serenade **09** broadcast, character, circulate, demeanour, make known, publicize, ventilate **10** appearance, atmosphere, expression, give vent to, impression, make public **11** chansonette, communicate, disseminate, have your say **13** speak your mind

**• air defence**
**02** AD

**• Air Transport Association**
**03** ATA

**airbed**
**04** Lilo®

**airborne**
**02** a/b **06** flying **07** winging
**08** hovering, in flight, in the air

**aircraft**

*Aircraft include:*

**01** B, F
**03** jet, MiG
**04** Hawk, kite, Moth, STOL, VTOL
**05** blimp, Comet, jumbo, Piper, plane, Stuka
**06** Airbus®, Boeing, bomber, Cessna, copter, Fokker, glider, Mirage, Nimrod
**07** airship, air taxi, balloon, biplane, Chinook, chopper, fighter, Halifax, Harrier, jump-jet, prop-jet, Tornado, Tristar, Typhoon
**08** airliner, Blenheim, Concorde, Hercules, jumbo jet, Mosquito, seaplane, Spitfire, spy plane, superjet, triplane, turbojet, warplane, Zeppelin
**09** aeroplane, amphibian, aquaplane, Boeing 747, delta-wing, dirigible, freighter, Gipsy Moth, Hurricane, Lancaster, monoplane, swing-wing, Tiger Moth, turboprop, two-seater
**10** dive-bomber, hang-glider, helicopter, microlight, Sunderland, Wellington, whirlybird
**11** battleplane, de Havilland, Flying Tiger, intercepter, rocket plane, Thunderbolt
**12** air ambulance, single-seater, Sopwith Camel, troop-carrier
**13** hot-air balloon, Messerschmitt, Stealth Bomber

*Aircraft include:*

**04** R101
**06** Bell X-1
**07** Voyager
**08** Enola Gay
**09** Winnie Mae
**10** Hindenburg
**11** Air Force One, Lucky Lady II, Spruce Goose, Wright Flyer
**12** Graf Zeppelin, Memphis Belle
**15** Spirit of St Louis

*Aircraft parts include:*

**03** fin, rib
**04** cowl, flap, hood, skid, wing
**05** cabin, radar, radio, stick
**06** canopy, engine, rudder
**07** aileron, ammeter, cockpit, cowling, fairing, tail fin, winglet
**08** elevator, fuselage, intercom, joystick, tail boom, turbojet, wing flap
**09** altimeter, nose wheel, propeller, tailplane, tail wheel
**10** flight deck
**11** chronometer, landing flap, landing gear, vertical fin
**12** control stick, equilibrator, radio compass, rudder pedals
**13** accelerometer, control column, undercarriage
**14** radar altimeter
**15** landing-carriage, magnetic compass

**aircraftsman, aircraftswoman**
**02** AC **03** ACW, erk, LAC **04** LACW

**air force**
**03** RAF **04** RAAF, RCAF, USAF, WAAF, WRAF **05** RNZAF, WRAAF
**06** RAuxAF **09** Luftwaffe **11** Flying Corps
*See also* **rank**

**airily**
**07** lightly, readily **08** breezily, casually, jauntily **10** flippantly **12** nonchalantly
**14** light-heartedly

**airing**
**07** venting, voicing **08** aeration, exposure, uttering **09** broadcast, statement **10** disclosure, divulgence, expression, freshening, refreshing, revelation **11** circulation, declaration, making known, publication, ventilation **13** communication, dissemination

**airless**
**05** close, heavy, muggy, musty, stale
**06** stuffy, sultry **08** stifling
**10** breathless, oppressive
**11** suffocating **12** unventilated
**15** badly ventilated

**airline**

*Airlines include:*

**02** BA, UA
**03** BEA, BMI, JAL, KLM, PIA, SAS, TWA
**04** BOAC, El Al
**05** Pan Am
**06** Qantas
**07** EasyJet, Ryanair
**08** Aeroflot, Alitalia
**09** Aer Lingus, Air Canada, Air France, Lufthansa
**13** Air New Zealand, Cathay Pacific
**14** British Airways, British Midland, United Airlines, Virgin Atlantic

**airman**
**02** AC, AR **03** ace, erk, LAC

**airport**
**08** STOLport **09** aerodrome, vertiport

*Airports include:*

**03** JFK, Zia
**04** Orly
**05** Luton, McCoy, O'Hare
**06** Cannon, Changi, Dulles, Midway, V C Bird
**07** Ataturk, Bradley, D F Malan, Entebbe, Gatwick, Hopkins, Lincoln, Lubbock, Roberts
**08** Ciampino, El Dorado, G Marconi, Heathrow, Jan Smuts, La Aurora, McCarran, Mohamed V, Sangster, Schiphol, Stansted
**09** Ben Gurion, Charleroi, Fiumicino, James M Cox, J F Kennedy, Jose Marti, Lindbergh, Marco Polo, Queen Alia
**10** George Bush, Golden Rock, Hellenikon, John Lennon, King Khaled, Louis Botha, Sky Harbour, Will Rogers
**11** Capodichino, Jorge Chavez, Las Americas, Ninoy Aquino, Owen Roberts, Pointe Noire, Tito Menniti
**12** Benito Juarez, Berline-Tegel, Eduardo Gomes, Hancock Field, Indira Gandhi, Jomo Kenyatta, Norman Manley, Queen Beatrix, Simon Bolivar
**13** Château Bougon, Chiang Kai Shek, Grantley Adams, King Abdul Aziz, Mariscal Sucre, Robert Mueller
**14** Galileo Galilei, Juan Santa Maria, Kingsford Smith, Lester B Pearson, Murtala Mohamed
**15** Augusto C Sandino, Charles de Gaulle, General Mitchell, Hamilton Kindley, Leonardo da Vinci, Theodore Francis

**airs**
**05** swank **06** frills, posing **07** hauteur
**09** arrogance, pomposity
**10** snootiness **11** affectation, haughtiness, pretensions
**12** affectedness **13** artificiality
**15** pretentiousness

**airtight**
**06** closed, sealed **08** flawless
**09** windtight **10** conclusive
**11** impermeable, indubitable, irrefutable **12** impenetrable, indisputable, tight-fitting **13** beyond dispute, incontestable **14** beyond question, unquestionable

**airy**
**04** open **05** blowy, fresh, gusty, happy, roomy, windy **06** aerial, breezy, casual, jaunty, lively **07** offhand **08** cheerful, draughty, ethereal, etherial, flippant, spacious **09** spiritual, sprightly
**10** immaterial, intangible, nonchalant, spirit-like **11** incorporeal **12** high-spirited, light-hearted **13** unsubstantial
**14** well-ventilated

**aisle**
**04** lane, path **07** gangway, passage, walkway **08** alleyway, corridor
**10** passageway **12** deambulatory

**ajar**
**04** agee, ajee, open **08** half open, unbolted, unclosed, unlocked
**09** unlatched **10** unfastened
**12** slightly open

**akin**
**03** sib **04** like, near, sibb **05** close, sybbe **07** related, similar **08** congener
**10** comparable, equivalent
**13** corresponding

**Alabama**
**02** AL **03** Ala

**alacrity**
**06** ardour **07** fervour **08** keenness
**09** briskness, eagerness, readiness
**10** enthusiasm, impatience, promptness **11** willingness

**alarm**
◇ *anagram indicator*
**03** din **04** bell, fear, horn **05** alert, daunt, larum, panic, scare, shock, siren **06** arouse, beat up, dismay, fright, horror, rattle, terror, tirrit, tocsin **07** agitate, anxiety, perturb, startle, terrify, unnerve, warning, whistle **08** affright, distress, frighten, Teasmade® **09** alarm-bell **10** make afraid, uneasiness **11** nervousness, trepidation **12** apprehension, danger signal, perturbation, put the wind up **13** consternation, smoke detector **14** distress signal

**alarming**
**05** scary **07** ominous **08** daunting, dreadful, shocking, worrying **09** dismaying, startling, unnerving **10** disturbing, perturbing, terrifying **11** distressing, frightening, threatening

**alarmist**
**09** doomsayer, jitterbug, pessimist **11** doomwatcher, scaremonger **12** doom-merchant **13** prophet of doom

**alas**
**02** ay **03** out **04** haro, waly **06** harrow **07** welaway **08** waesucks, welladay, wellaway **09** alack-a-day, wellanear

**Alaska**
**02** AK

**Albania**
**02** AL **03** ALB

**albatross**
**10** gooneybird, Quaker-bird

**Alberta**
**02** AB

**album**
**04** disc

**albumin**
**05** ricin **06** myogen **08** leucosin

**alchemist**
**05** adept **06** chemic **08** spagyric **09** spagyrist

**alcohol**
**03** jar **04** bowl, diol, grog, lush, slug **05** booze, drink, juice, mahua, mahwa, sauce, skink, tinct **06** fuddle, gutrot, liquor, sterol, strunt, tiddly, tipple **07** butanol, ethanol, liqueur, mannite, shebeen, spirits, xylitol **08** catechol, farnesol, geraniol, glycerin, glycerol, linalool, mannitol, methanol, propanol, stimulus **09** aqua vitae, firewater, glycerine, hard stuff, the bottle **10** intoxicant **11** jungle juice, sphingosine, strong drink, the creature, tickle-brain **12** Dutch courage, spirit of wine

*See also* **drink**

• **low in alcohol**
**04** lite

**alcoholic**
**03** sot **04** alky, hard, lush, soak, wino **05** alkie, bloat, dipso, drunk, souse, toper **06** ardent, boozer, brewed, sponge, strong **07** Bacchus, drinker, tippler, tosspot **08** drunkard, habitual **09** distilled, fermented, inebriate **10** spirituous, wine-bibber **11** dipsomaniac, hard drinker, inebriating **12** heavy drinker, intoxicating

*See also* **drink**

• **very alcoholic**
**04** hard

**alcove**
**03** bay **04** nook **05** booth, niche **06** carrel, corner, recess, shrine **07** carrell, cubicle, dinette, opening **09** cubbyhole, ingleneuk, inglenook **11** compartment

**alderman**
**02** CA **03** Ald **09** ealdorman

**Alderney**
**03** GBA

**ale**
**03** nog **04** beer, mild, nogg, purl **05** nappy, swats **06** alegar, tipper **07** morocco, October **08** heavy wet, twopenny **10** barley-bree, barley-broo **11** barley-broth

**alehouse** *see* **pub**

**alert**
**04** gleg, warn, wary **05** agile, alarm, awake, brisk, quick, ready, shake, sharp **06** active, inform, lively, nimble, notice, notify, signal, sprack, tip off, tip-off **07** apprise, careful, caution, heedful, warning **08** all there, forewarn, prepared, spirited, vigilant, watchful **09** attentive, observant, on the ball, on the spot, sharp-eyed, up to snuff, wide-awake **10** on your toes, perceptive, presential, wake-up call **11** circumspect, sharp-witted **12** notification, on the lookout, on the qui vive

**alertness**
**08** wariness **09** vigilance **10** observance **12** watchfulness **14** attentivenenss, perceptiveness **15** sharp-wittedness

**alga, algae**

*Algae and lichens include:*

**05** chara, manna, usnea
**06** archil, corkir, crotal, desmid, diatom, korkir, nostoc, volvox
**07** crottle, cup moss, euglena, oak lump, parella, seaweed, Valonia
**08** anabaena, conferva, frustule, lecanora, lungwort, pond scum, red algae, sea ivory, stonerag, stoneraw, tree moss, Ulothrix, wall moss, wartwort
**09** chlorella, cup lichen, Isokontae, rock tripe, spirogyra, stonewort
**10** brown algae, Conjugatae, cyanophyte, fallen star, green algae, heterocont, heterokont, rock violet, water bloom
**11** blanketweed, Iceland moss, manna-lichen, Protococcus
**12** Cyanophyceae, Phaeophyceae, reindeer moss, Rhodophyceae, stromatolite, water flowers
**13** chlamydomonas, Protococcales, Schizophyceae, witches' butter
**14** blue-green algae, cyanobacterium, dinoflagellate

*See also* **seaweed**

**Algeria**
**02** DZ **03** Alg, DZA

**alias**
**03** aka, née **06** anonym **07** allonym, moniker, pen name **08** formerly, monicker, nickname **09** false name, otherwise, pseudonym, sobriquet, stage name **10** also called, nom de plume, soubriquet **11** also known as, assumed name, nom de guerre **14** under the name of

**alibi**
**05** story **06** excuse, reason **07** cover-up, defence, pretext **11** explanation, vindication **13** justification

**alien**
**02** ET **03** LGM, odd **05** metic **06** exotic, remote **07** foreign, incomer, Martian, opposed, strange, unusual **08** contrary, forinsec, inimical, newcomer, outsider, peculiar, stranger **09** estranged, foreigner, immigrant, non-native, offensive, repugnant **10** extraneous, forinsecal, outlandish, unfamiliar **11** conflicting, incongruous **12** antagonistic, incompatible **14** little green man

**alienate**
**05** sever **06** cut off, devest **07** divorce, turn off **08** amortize, estrange, separate, turn away **09** disaffect **10** antagonize, set against **11** make hostile

**alienation**
**07** divorce, rupture **08** disunion **09** diversion, isolation, severance **10** detachment, remoteness, separation **11** turning away **12** disaffection, estrangement, indifference **14** antagonization

**alight**
**02** in **03** lit, pop **04** fall, land, rest **05** alive, avail, avale, fiery, light, lit up, perch, pitch **06** ablaze, aflame, availe, bright, debark, get off, lively, on fire, settle, strike **07** blazing, burning, descend, detrain, flaming, get down, ignited, lighted, radiant, shining **08** come down, dismount, gleaming **09** brilliant, disembark, touch down **10** come to rest, disentrain **11** illuminated

**align**
**04** ally, even, join, side, tram **05** agree, order, range, unite **06** adjust, even up, line up **07** arrange, combine **08** regulate **09** affiliate, associate, co-operate, orientate **10** co-ordinate, join forces, regularize, straighten, sympathize **12** make parallel

**alignment**
**04** line **05** order **06** lining, siding **07** ranging **08** alliance, lining up, sympathy **09** agreement **10** alineation **11** affiliation, allineation, arrangement, association, co-operation **13** straightening

**alike**
**04** akin, even **05** equal, samey **06** at once **07** cognate, equally, similar, the same, uniform **08** in common, matching, parallel **09** analogous, duplicate, identical, similarly **10** comparable, equivalent, resembling **11** analogously, much the same **12** in the same way **13** corresponding **15** correspondingly

**alimony**
**06** upkeep **07** aliment, support **08** palimony **09** allowance **11** maintenance **12** child support

**alive**
**04** live, vive **05** alert, awake, brisk, quick, vital **06** active, chirpy, extant, full of, lively, living **07** alert to, animate, awake to, aware of, in force, running, vibrant, working, zestful **08** animated, existent, spirited, vigorous **09** breathing, energetic, heedful of, on the hoof, surviving, to the fore, vivacious **10** carrying on, full of life, having life, in the flesh **11** abounding in, above-ground, cognizant of, conscious of, functioning, going strong, in existence, in operation, sensitive to, teeming with **12** crawling with, swarming with, thronged with **15** overflowing with

**alkaloid**
**06** emetin, harmin, theine **07** atropin, betaine, brucine, caffein, cocaine, codeine, coniine, emetine, harmine, morphia, narceen **08** atropine, caffeine, curarine, cytisine, daturine, harmalin, hyoscine, ibogaine, lobeline, mescalin, morphine, narceine, nicotine, piperine, thebaine, veratrin **09** aconitine, bebeerine, berberine, chaconine, ephedrine, gelsemine, harmaline, mescaline, muscarine, narcotine, quinidine, rhoeadine, sparteine, veratrine, yohimbine **10** apomorphia, cinchonine, colchicine, corydaline, ergotamine, papaverine, pilocarpin, strychnine **11** apomorphine, gelseminine, hyoscyamine, pilocarpine, scopolamine, theobromine, vincristine **15** castanospermine

**all**
**01** a' **03** sum **04** each, even, full, just **05** every, fully, quite, total, tutti, utter, whole **06** apiece, entire, the lot, utmost, wholly **07** perfect, totally, utterly **08** complete, entirely, entirety, everyone, greatest, outright **09** aggregate, everybody, wholesale **10** altogether, completely, every bit of, every one of, everything, infinitely, the whole of **11** every single, total amount, whole amount **12** each and every, universality **13** in its entirety

**• at all**
**03** any, ava, eer **04** ever **10** oughtlings **14** in the slightest

**allay**
**04** calm, cool, ease, stay **05** blunt, check, quell, quiet, slake **06** alegge, allege, lessen, pacify, reduce, smooth, soften, solace, soothe, stanch, subdew, subdue **07** allegge, appease, assuage, compose, mollify, relieve, smoothe, staunch **08** decrease, diminish, moderate **09** alleviate **12** tranquillize

**allegation**
**04** plea **05** claim, story **06** avowal, charge **07** surmise **08** averment, citation **09** assertion, statement, testimony **10** accusation, deposition, profession **11** affirmation, declaration **12** asseveration

**allege**
**04** aver, hold, urge **05** allay, claim, plead, state, trump **06** affirm, assert, attest, insist, obtend **07** contend, declare, profess **08** maintain **09** alleviate, represent **10** asseverate, put forward

**alleged**
**06** stated **07** claimed, dubious, reputed, suspect **08** declared, doubtful, inferred, putative, so-called, supposed **09** described, professed, purported **10** designated, ostensible

**allegedly**
**09** dubiously **10** apparently, doubtfully, ostensibly, putatively, reportedly, supposedly **11** purportedly **13** by all accounts

**allegiance**
**03** foy **04** duty **06** fealty **07** loyalty, support **08** devotion, fidelity, liegedom **09** adherence, constancy, obedience **10** friendship, obligation, solidarity **12** faithfulness

**allegorical**
**06** mystic **07** typical **08** symbolic **09** parabolic **10** emblematic, figurative **11** symbolizing **12** metaphorical **13** significative **14** representative

**allegory**
**04** myth, tale **05** fable, story **06** emblem, legend, symbol **07** analogy, parable **08** apologue, metaphor **09** symbolism **10** comparison

**allergic**
**06** averse **07** hostile, opposed **08** affected **09** sensitive **11** disinclined, dyspathetic, susceptible **12** antagonistic **14** hypersensitive

**allergy**
**08** aversion, dyspathy **09** antipathy, hostility **10** antagonism, opposition **11** sensitivity **14** disinclination, susceptibility

**alleviate**
**04** alay, dull, ease, kill **05** abate, aleye, allay, check **06** alegge, allege, deaden, lessen, reduce, soften, soothe, subdue, temper **07** allegge, assuage, cushion, mollify, relieve **08** diminish, mitigate, moderate, palliate **14** take the edge off

**alleviation**
**06** easing, relief **07** dulling **08** soothing **09** abatement, deadening, lessening, reduction **10** allegeance, diminution, mitigation, moderation, palliation **11** aleggeaunce, assuagement, consolation **13** mollification

**alley**
**03** taw **04** gate, lane, mall, road, walk, wynd **05** close **06** ginnel, marble, street, vennel **07** dead end, passage, pathway **08** alleyway, cul-de-sac, pall-mall, rope-walk **10** back street, passageway

**alliance**
**04** axis, bloc, bond, NATO, pact **05** Anzus, guild, union **06** cartel, league, treaty **07** compact, kinship **08** marriage **09** agreement, coalition, concordat, syndicate **10** connection, consortium, federation, Warsaw Pact **11** affiliation, association, combination, confederacy, partnership **12** conglomerate, consociation, popular front **13** confederation

**allied**
**03** wed **05** bound, joint **06** agnate, joined, linked, united **07** cognate, connate, coupled, kindred, married, related, unified **08** combined, in league **09** connected, federated, in cahoots **10** affiliated, associated **11** amalgamated, confederate, hand in glove **12** confederated

**allocate**
**04** mete, task **05** allot, allow, issue **06** assign, budget, divide, ration **07** deal out, dole out, earmark, mete out **08** dispense, set aside, share out **09** admeasure, apportion, designate, parcel out **10** distribute

**allocation**
**03** cut, lot **05** grant, quota, share, stint, whack **06** budget, ration **07** measure, portion **09** allotment, allowance, giving-out **10** sharing-out **12** distribution **13** apportionment **14** slice of the cake

**allot**
**03** lot **04** aret, mete, rate, sort **05** allow, arett, grant, stint, teene **06** affect, assign, budget, divide, ration **07** dole out, earmark, mete out, portion **08** allocate, dispense, set aside, share out **09** admeasure, apportion, designate **10** distribute

**allotment**
**03** cut, lot **04** land, plot **05** grant, quota, share, stint, whack **06** ration **07** measure, portion **08** division **09** allowance, partition **10** allocation,

percentage, plot of land **12** distribution **13** apportionment **14** slice of the cake

**all-out**
**04** full **05** total **06** utmost
**07** maximum **08** complete, forceful, powerful, resolute, thorough, vigorous
**09** energetic, full-scale, intensive, undivided, unlimited, unstinted, wholesale **10** determined, exhaustive, forcefully, powerfully, resolutely, thoroughly, vigorously **11** intensively, unremitting **12** determinedly, exhaustively, unrestrained
**13** comprehensive, energetically, no-holds-barred, thoroughgoing, unremittingly

**allow**
**02** OK **03** let, own **04** give, okay
**05** admit, agree, allot, grant, spare
**06** afford, assign, beteem, enable, endure, permit, suffer **07** agree to, approve, beteeme, concede, confess, consent, earmark, provide, warrant
**08** allocate, sanction, say yes to, set aside, tolerate **09** apportion, authorize, consent to, give leave, put up with **11** acknowledge **15** give your consent
• **allow for**
**07** foresee, include, plan for
**08** consider **09** budget for **10** arrange for, bear in mind, keep in mind, provide for **15** take into account

**allowable**
**02** OK **04** okay **05** legal, legit, licit
**06** lawful **07** rulable **08** all right, approved **09** excusable
**10** acceptable, admissible, legitimate
**11** appropriate, justifiable, permissible
**12** sanctionable

**allowance**
**03** DLA, fya, ICA, JSA, law, lot, RDA
**04** diet, feed, mags, size, tare, tret
**05** batta, cloff, grant, maggs, quota, ratio, share, stint **06** amount, budget, corody, income, livery, milage, ration, rebate, sequel **07** aliment, alimony, annuity, benefit, bursary, charter, corrody, dietary, leakage, mileage, payment, pension, portion, provand, provend, stipend, subsidy, windage
**08** discount, expenses, latitude, pittance, proviant **09** baby bonus, deduction, reduction, risk money, salt-money, strike pay, weighting
**10** allocation, assistance, concession, exhibition, husbandage, percentage, privy purse, remittance, table money, toleration **11** appointment, deferred pay, maintenance, pocket money
**12** child benefit, contribution, severance pay **15** capitation grant
• **make allowances**
**06** excuse, pardon **07** condone, forgive **08** bear with, consider, overlook **10** bear in mind, keep in mind
**15** take into account

**allowed**
**02** OK **03** let **04** luit, okay **05** legal, legit, licit **06** lawful **08** accepted, all right, approved **09** of warrant, permitted, tolerated **10** authorized

**alloy**
◇ *anagram indicator*
**04** bras **05** blend, brass, Invar®, metal, potin, terne **06** Alnico®, Babbit, billon, bronze, eureka, fusion, latten, Magnox®, occamy, ormolu, oroide, pewter, solder, tambac, tombac, tombak **07** amalgam, Babbitt, chromel, mixture, Nitinol, shakudo, similor, tinfoil, tutenag **08** cast iron, compound, electron, gunmetal, Manganin®, Nichrome®, orichalc, pot metal, zircaloy, Zircoloy®
**09** admixture, bell-metal, composite, Duralumin®, Dutch gold, Dutch leaf, eutectoid, magnalium, oricalche, pinchbeck, platinoid, shibuichi, type metal **10** constantan, Dutch metal, iridosmine, iridosmium, mischmetal, Monel metal®, mosaic gold, nicrosilal
**11** coalescence, combination, cupronickel, white copper **12** fusible metal, German silver, prince's metal
**13** Babbitt's metal, speculum metal
**14** Britannia metal, high-speed steel, phosphor bronze **15** aluminium bronze, Corinthian brass
*See also* **metal**

**all-powerful**
**05** great **07** supreme **08** absolute, almighty **10** omnipotent, pre-eminent
**12** totalitarian

**all-purpose**
**08** all-round, flexible **09** adaptable, versatile **12** multi-purpose **14** general-purpose

**all right**
**02** OK **03** A-OK, yes **04** fair, fine, okay, safe, well **05** hunky, right, sound, sweet, whole **06** agreed, indeed, secure, unhurt **07** average, healthy, no doubt **08** adequate, passable, passably, suitable, suitably, unharmed, very well **09** allowable, all serene, certainly, hunky-dory, uninjured
**10** absolutely, acceptable, acceptably, adequately, definitely, good enough, reasonable, reasonably, unimpaired, well enough **11** right as rain
**12** satisfactory **13** appropriately
**14** satisfactorily **15** unobjectionable, unobjectionably, without question

**allspice**
**07** pimento **11** calycanthus **13** Jamaica pepper

**allude**
**04** hint **05** imply, infer, refer **06** remark
**07** mention, speak of, suggest, touch on **08** intimate **09** adumbrate, insinuate, touch upon

**allure**
**02** it, SA **03** air, win **04** coax, draw, gait, lure, mien, pull **05** charm, decoy, tempt, train, troll **06** appeal, cajole, disarm, entice, lead on, seduce, work on **07** attract, beguile, enchant, glamour, win over **08** entrance, interest, persuade, sirenize
**09** captivate, fascinate, magnetism, seduction **10** attraction, come-hither, enticement, temptation **11** captivation, enchantment, fascination **13** give the come-on

**alluring**
**04** sexy **05** siren **06** taking
**07** agaçant, winning **08** agaçante, arousing, engaging, enticing, fetching, inviting, sensuous, tempting, to die for
**09** beguiling, desirable, glamorous, seductive **10** attractive, bewitching, come-hither, enchanting, intriguing
**11** captivating, fascinating, interesting

**allusion**
**04** hint **06** glance, remark
**07** comment, mention **08** citation
**09** quotation, reference **10** intimation, side glance, suggestion **11** implication, insinuation, observation

**ally**
**03** taw **04** join, link, side **05** marry, unify, unite **06** friend, helper, league, marble, team up **07** combine, connect, consort, partner **08** co-worker, sidekick **09** accessory, affiliate, associate, colleague, supporter
**10** accomplice, amalgamate, foederatus, fraternize, join forces
**11** collaborate, confederate **12** band together, collaborator

**almanac**
**06** annual, Wisden **08** calendar, register, yearbook **09** ephemeris, Whitaker's

**almighty**
**04** huge **05** awful, great **06** severe
**07** immense, intense, supreme
**08** absolute, enormous, terrible
**09** desperate, very great **10** invincible, omnipotent **11** all-powerful, exceedingly, plenipotent **12** irresistible, overpowering, overwhelming

**almond**
**06** comfit **07** amygdal, praline

**almost**
◇ *tail deletion indicator*
**03** nie, sub- **04** near, nigh **05** about, quasi- **06** all but, nearly, next to, nighly, nigh on, uneath **07** close on, close to, nearing **08** as good as, nigh-hand, not quite, well-nigh **09** just about, virtually
**10** more or less, not far from, pretty much, pretty well **11** approaching, practically **12** pretty nearly
**13** approximately

**alms**
**05** gifts **06** awmous **07** charity
**08** devotion, handouts, largesse
**09** donations, endowment
**13** contributions

**aloft**
**02** up **04** high **05** above **06** high up
**07** aheight **08** in the air, in the sky, overhead **12** off the ground

**alone**
**03** sad **04** just, only, sola, sole, solo
**05** apart, solus **06** lonely, simply,

single, singly, solely, unique **07** forlorn, herself, himself, insular, private, unaided, unhappy **08** by itself, deserted, desolate, detached, forsaken, high-lone, isolated, lonesome, rejected, separate, solitary, uniquely **09** destitute, miserable, on your own, on your tod **10** by yourself, cloistered, unassisted, unattended, unescorted **11** exclusively, sequestered, without help **12** single-handed **13** companionless, independently, off your own bat, unaccompanied

**along**
**02** on, up **04** down, near **05** ahead **06** beside, next to **07** close to, further, onwards, with you **09** alongside, as company **10** adjacent to, as a partner **11** at the side of
• **all along**
**06** always **07** for ever **10** all the time, constantly **11** continually
• **along with**
**09** including **12** in addition to, not to mention, over and above, together with **14** to say nothing of

**alongside**
◇ *juxtaposition indicator*
**02** by **04** near **05** aside **06** beside **08** adjacent

**aloof**
**03** off **04** cold, cool **05** chill **06** abeigh, chilly, formal, offish, remote, skeigh **07** distant, haughty, insular, stuck-up **08** detached, reserved **09** exclusive **10** antisocial, forbidding, unfriendly, unsociable **11** indifferent, standoffish **12** inaccessible, supercilious, uninterested, unresponsive **13** unforthcoming, unsympathetic **14** unapproachable

**aloud**
◇ *homophone indicator*
**06** loudly **07** audibly, clearly, noisily, out loud, plainly **10** à haute voix, distinctly, sonorously **12** for all to hear, intelligibly, resoundingly, vociferously

**alpha**
**01** A

**alphabet**
**05** abcee, absey **06** script **13** criss-cross-row **14** Christ-cross-row

*Alphabets and writing systems include:*

**03** ABC, IPA, ITA
**04** Cree, kana, ogam
**05** Greek, kanji, Kufic, Latin, ogham, Roman, runic
**06** Arabic, Brahmi, finger, Glagol, Hebrew, nagari, naskhi, Pinyin, romaji
**07** Braille, futhark, futhorc, futhork, Glossic, linear A, linear B
**08** Cyrillic, Georgian, Gurmukhi, hiragana, katakana, phonetic
**09** Byzantine, cuneiform, ideograph, logograph, syllabary
**10** Chalcidian, devanagari, estrangelo, pictograph
**11** estranghelo, hieroglyphs
**14** Augmented Roman
**15** Initial Teaching

*Letters of the Arabic alphabet:*

**02** ba, fa, ha, ra, ta, ya, za
**03** ayn, dad, dai, jim, kaf, kha, lam, mim, nun, qaf, sad, sin, tha, waw, zay
**04** alif, dhai, shin
**05** ghayn

*Letters of the English alphabet:*

**01** A, B, C, D, E, F, G, H, I, J, K, L, M, N, O, P, Q, R, S, T, U, V, W, X, Y, Z
**02** ar, ay, ee, ef, el, em, en, es, ex, oh, wy
**03** bee, cee, cue, dee, eff, eks, ell, enn, ess, eye, gee, jay, kay, kew, pee, see, tee, vee, you, zed, zee
**05** aitch
**06** haitch
**07** double-u
**09** double-you

*Letters of the Greek alphabet:*

**02** mu, nu, pi, xi
**03** chi, eta, phi, psi, rho, san, tau, vau
**04** beta, iota, zeta
**05** alpha, delta, gamma, kappa, koppa, omega, sampi, sigma, theta
**06** lambda
**07** digamma, epsilon, omicron, upsilon, ypsilon
**08** episemon

*Letters of the Hebrew alphabet:*

**02** fe, he, pe
**03** bet, heh, het, kaf, mem, nun, peh, qof, sin, tav, taw, tet, vav, waw, yod
**04** alef, ayin, beth, chaf, heth, kaph, khaf, koph, qoph, resh, sade, shin, teth, yodh
**05** aleph, cheth, dalet, gimel, lamed, sadhe, tsadi, tzade, zayin
**06** daleth, lamedh, saddhe, samech, samekh

*Letters of the NATO phonetic alphabet:*

**04** echo, golf, kilo, lima, mike, papa, xray, zulu
**05** alpha, bravo, delta, hotel, india, oscar, romeo, tango
**06** juliet, quebec, sierra, victor, yankee
**07** charlie, foxtrot, uniform, whiskey
**08** november

**already**
**05** by now **06** by then, so soon **07** even now, just now, so early, thus far **08** even then, hitherto **09** before now **10** beforehand, by that time, by this time, heretofore, previously **12** so soon as this

**alright** *see* **all right**

**also**
◇ *juxtaposition indicator*
**03** and, eke, too **04** item, plus **06** as well **07** besides, further **08** as well as, likewise, moreover **09** along with, including **10** in addition **11** furthermore **12** additionally

**alter**
◇ *anagram indicator*
**04** turn, vary **05** adapt, amend, emend, shift, tweak **06** adjust, bushel, change, deform, modify, recast, reform, revise, rework **07** antique, convert, disform, distort, improve, qualify, remodel, reshape **08** airbrush, innovate **09** diversify, transform, transmute, transpose **10** manipulate, metaphrase **12** metamorphose **13** make different
• **alter ego**
**04** Hyde (Mr)

**alteration**
◇ *anagram indicator*
**05** shift, tweak **06** change **07** massage **08** revision, variance **09** amendment, reshaping, reworking, variation **10** adaptation, adjustment, conversion, difference, emendation **11** reformation, remodelling, vicissitude **12** modification **13** metamorphosis, transmutation, transposition **14** transformation **15** diversification, transfiguration

**altercation**
**03** row, wap **04** beef, miff, whid, yike **05** broil, clash, scrap, set-to **06** barney, bicker, breach, breeze, bust-up, dust-up, fracas, fratch, ruffle, square **07** brattle, discord, dispute, punch-up, quarrel, wrangle **08** argument, squabble **09** high words, logomachy **10** dependence, difference, difficulty, dissension **12** disagreement **13** slanging match

**alternate**
◇ *hidden alternately indicator*
**03** alt **04** vary **05** alter, other **06** change, rotate, second **07** in turns **08** rotating **09** fluctuate, oscillate, take turns **10** every other, reciprocal, substitute **11** alternating, consecutive, every second, interchange, intersperse, reciprocate **13** chop and change, interchanging, take it in turns

**alternative**
◇ *anagram indicator*
**02** or **05** other, wacky **06** back-up, choice, fringe, option, second **07** another, oddball, unusual **08** alterant, fall-back, recourse, uncommon **09** different, duplicate, selection, surrogate **10** preference, substitute, unorthodox **12** second string **14** nontraditional, unconventional

**alternatively**
◇ *anagram indicator*
**02** or **06** or else **07** instead **09** otherwise **13** as a substitute **14** on the other hand **15** as another option

**although**
**03** and **04** albe, as if, when **05** while **06** albeit, even if, much as, though, whilst **07** howbeit **08** as much as

**09** howsoever **10** even though **11** granted that **13** even supposing **15** notwithstanding

**altitude**
**03** alt **05** depth **06** height **07** stature **08** tallness **09** elevation, loftiness

**alto**
**01** a **03** alt

**altogether**
◇ *juxtaposition indicator*
**04** alto **05** all-to, fully, in all, joint, quite, slick, whole **06** algate, in toto, wholly **07** algates, all told, in total, overall, totally, utterly **08** all in all, all to one, entirely **09** perfectly **10** absolutely, completely, holus-bolus, thoroughly **12** first and last

**altruism**
**06** unself **10** generosity **11** benevolence, disinterest, magnanimity **12** selflessness **13** self-sacrifice, unselfishness **15** considerateness

**altruistic**
**06** humane **08** generous, selfless **09** unselfish **10** benevolent, charitable **11** considerate, magnanimous **12** humanitarian **13** disinterested, philanthropic **14** public-spirited **15** self-sacrificing

**aluminium**
**02** Al

**alumnus**
**02** OB **06** old boy **07** old girl

**always**
**02** ay **03** aye, e'er **04** ever **05** still **06** algate, semper, sempre **07** algates, forever **08** evermore **09** endlessly, eternally, every time, regularly **10** all the time, constantly, habitually, invariably, repeatedly **11** continually, in perpetuum, perpetually, unceasingly, unfailingly **12** consistently **13** again and again **14** on each occasion **15** on every occasion

**amalgam**
**05** alloy, blend, union **06** fusion, merger **07** mixture **08** compound **09** admixture, aggregate, synthesis **10** commixture **11** coalescence, combination

**amalgamate**
**04** ally, fuse **05** alloy, blend, merge, unify, unite **06** mingle **07** combine **08** coalesce, compound, intermix **09** commingle, integrate **10** homogenize, synthesize **11** incorporate

**amalgamation**
**05** blend, union, unity **06** fusion, merger **07** joining, merging **08** alliance, blending, compound **09** admixture, synthesis **11** coalescence, combination, commingling, integration, unification **13** incorporation **14** homogenization

**amass**
**04** gain, heap, pile **05** hoard, store **06** accrue, garner, gather, heap up, pile up **07** acquire, collect, store up **08** assemble **09** aggregate **10** accumulate, foregather **11** agglomerate, agglutinate

**amateur**
**01** A **02** Am **03** DIY, ham **04** buff **06** layman **07** admirer, dabbler, fancier, varment, varmint **08** armchair **09** lay person **10** aficionado, Corinthian, dilettante, enthusiast **11** afficionado **12** do-it-yourself **15** non-professional

**amateurish**
**03** lay **05** crude, hammy, inept **06** clumsy, unpaid **08** bungling, inexpert **09** unskilful, untrained **10** blundering **11** incompetent, unqualified **14** unprofessional **15** non-professional

**amatory**
**04** fond **05** randy **06** erotic, loving, sexual, tender **07** amorous, lesbian **10** passionate **11** impassioned **12** affectionate

**amaze**
**03** wow **04** daze, kill, stun **05** floor, panic, shock **06** awhape, dazzle, dismay **07** astound, flatten, stagger, startle, stupefy **08** astonish, bewilder, bowl over, confound, gobsmack, surprise **09** dumbfound **10** disconcert, strike dumb **11** flabbergast, knock for six **12** blow your mind

**amazed**
**05** dazed **06** agazed **07** floored, stunned **08** startled **09** astounded, surprised **10** astonished, bewildered, gobsmacked, speechless **11** dumbfounded, open-mouthed **13** flabbergasted, thunderstruck

**amazement**
**04** maze **05** shock **06** dismay, marvel, wonder **08** surprise **09** confusion **10** admiration, perplexity, wonderment **11** incredulity **12** astonishment, bewilderment, stupefaction **13** consternation

**amazing**
◇ *anagram indicator*
**06** awsome, far-out, unreal **07** awesome **08** dazzling, exciting, fabulous, stunning **09** thrilling, wonderful **10** astounding, formidable, impressive, incredible, marvellous, monumental, staggering, surprising **11** astonishing, bewildering, jaw-dropping, magnificent, spectacular **12** awe-inspiring, overwhelming **13** disconcerting

**amazon**
**06** virago **09** shield-may **10** shield-maid **12** shield-maiden

**ambassador**
**05** agent, elchi, envoy **06** backer, consul, deputy, elchee, eltchi, ledger, legate, leiger, lieger, nuncio **07** leaguer, leidger **08** advocate, delegate, diplomat, emissary, minister **09** pronuncio, supporter **10** campaigner **14** representative **15** plenipotentiary

**ambience**
**03** air **04** aura, feel, mood, tone **05** tenor, vibes **06** milieu, spirit **07** climate, feeling, flavour **09** character **10** atmosphere, impression, vibrations **11** environment **12** surroundings

**ambiguity**
**05** doubt **06** enigma, puzzle **07** dubiety, paradox **08** polysemy **09** confusion, obscurity, vagueness **10** double-talk, woolliness **11** ambivalence, double-speak, dubiousness, imprecision, uncertainty, unclearness **12** doubtfulness, equivocality, equivocation **13** double meaning **14** double entendre

**ambiguous**
**05** vague **06** double, louche, woolly **07** cryptic, dubious, obscure, unclear **08** confused, doubtful, oracular, puzzling, two-edged **09** confusing, enigmatic, equivocal, imprecise, oraculous, uncertain **10** back-handed, homonymous, indefinite, multivocal **11** double-edged, paradoxical **12** inconclusive **13** double-meaning, indeterminate

**ambit**
**04** area **05** range, realm, scope, sweep **06** bounds, extent, sphere **07** breadth, compass **08** confines

**ambition**
**03** aim **04** goal, hope, push, wish, zeal **05** dream, drive, graal, grail, ideal **06** design, desire, grayle, hunger, intent, object, target, thrust **07** craving, longing, purpose **08** striving, yearning **09** eagerness, hankering, holy grail, objective **10** aspiration, commitment, enterprise, get-up-and-go, initiative **11** what it takes **13** determination **15** fire in your belly

**ambitious**
**04** bold, hard, keen **05** eager, pushy **06** driven, intent **07** arduous, driving, emulate, go-ahead, hopeful, zealous **08** aspirant, aspiring, desirous, exacting, full of go, striving **09** assertive, demanding, difficult, elaborate, energetic, go-getting, grandiose, strenuous **10** determined, formidable, impressive, purposeful **11** challenging, industrious, power-hungry, pretentious **12** enterprising, enthusiastic

**ambivalence**
**05** clash, doubt **08** conflict, wavering **09** confusion **10** hesitation, opposition, unsureness **11** fluctuation, uncertainty, vacillation **12** equivocation **13** contradiction, inconsistency **14** irresoluteness

**ambivalent**
**05** mixed **06** unsure **07** opposed, warring **08** clashing, confused, doubtful, hesitant, wavering
**09** debatable, equivocal, uncertain, undecided, unsettled **10** irresolute, unresolved **11** conflicting, fluctuating, vacillating **12** inconclusive, inconsistent **13** contradictory

**amble**
**04** pace, walk **05** drift **06** dawdle, ramble, stroll, toddle, wander
**07** meander, saunter **09** promenade
**10** mosey along, single-foot
**11** perambulate

**ambulance**
**07** pannier **09** meat wagon **10** blood-wagon

**ambush**
**04** jump, trap, wait **05** await, lurch, snare **06** attack, entrap, turn on, waylay
**07** ensnare, forelay, lay wait
**08** embusqué, lie perdu, pounce on, surprise **09** ambuscade, bushwhack, emboscata, lie in wait, lie perdue, waylaying **11** lay a trap for **14** surprise attack

**ameliorate**
**04** ease, mend **05** amend **06** better, remedy **07** benefit, elevate, enhance, improve, promote, rectify, relieve
**08** mitigate **09** alleviate **10** make better

**amelioration**
**04** help **07** benefit **09** amendment, bettering **10** mitigation, refinement
**11** alleviation, enhancement, improvement **13** rectification

**amenable**
**04** open **06** docile **07** pliable, subject, willing **08** biddable, flexible
**09** agreeable, compliant, tractable
**10** responsive, submissive
**11** acquiescent, complaisant, persuadable, responsible, susceptible
**13** accommodating

**amend**
◇ *anagram indicator*
**03** fix **04** cure, heal, mend **05** alter, emend **06** adjust, better, change, modify, reform, remedy, repair, revise
**07** correct, enhance, improve, qualify, recover, rectify, redress **08** emendate
**10** ameliorate

**amendment**
◇ *anagram indicator*
**03** ERA **05** Fifth **06** change, reform, remedy **07** adjunct **08** addendum, addition, revision **10** adjustment, alteration, attachment, correction, emendation **11** corrigendum, enhancement, improvement, reformation **12** modification
**13** clarification, qualification, rectification

**amends**
**07** redress **08** requital **09** atonement, expiation, indemnity **10** recompense, reparation **11** restitution, restoration
**12** compensation, satisfaction
**15** indemnification
• **make amends**
**05** atone

**amenity**
**07** service, utility **08** civility, facility, resource **09** advantage
**11** arrangement, convenience, opportunity

**America**
**01** A **02** Am, US **03** USA **04** Amer
*See also* **United States of America**

*Countries of the Americas include:*

**04** Cuba, Peru
**05** Chile, Haiti
**06** Belize, Brazil, Canada, Guyana, Mexico, Panama
**07** Bolivia, Ecuador, Grenada, Jamaica, St Lucia, Uruguay
**08** Colombia, Dominica, Honduras, Paraguay, Suriname
**09** Argentina, Costa Rica, Guatemala, Nicaragua, Venezuela
**10** El Salvador, The Bahamas
**15** St Kitts and Nevis
**17** Antigua and Barbuda, Dominican Republic, Trinidad and Tobago
**21** United States of America
**25** St Vincent and the Grenadines

*South American landmarks include:*

**04** moai
**05** Andes, Colca, llano, Plata, Plate, selva
**06** Amazon, Iguaçu, Itaipu, Osorno, pampas, Paraná
**07** Atacama, Ipanema, Orinoco
**08** Cape Horn, Cotopaxi, Titicaca
**09** Aconcagua, Cartagena, Galápagos, Gran Chaco, Itaipu Dam, Patagonia
**10** Angel Falls, Copacabana, Mato Grosso, River Plate, Salto ángel
**11** Colca Canyon, Iguaçu Falls, Machu Picchu, Mt Aconcagua, Pico Bolívar
**12** Easter Island, Lake Titicaca, Perito Moreno, Río de la Plata
**13** Atacama Desert, Kaieteur Falls
**14** Cristo Redentor, Tierra del Fuego
**15** Guiana Highlands

• **Central America**
**02** CA
• **South America**
**02** SA

**American**
◇ *dialect word indicator*
**01** A **02** Am, US **04** Amer, Yank
**06** Yankee, yanqui **08** Jonathan
**09** stateside
*See also* **president**; **United States of America**

*Native American peoples include:*

**02** Ge
**03** Fox, Han, Mam, Ofo, Ute, Zia
**04** Adai, Coos, Cree, Crow, Erie, Hopi, Hupa, Inca, Innu, Iowa, Maya, Pomo, Suma, Tewa, Yana, Yuit, Yuma, Zuñi
**05** Aztec, Carib, Creek, Haida, Huron, Inuit, Kaska, Mayan, Olmec, Omaha, Opata, Osage, Sioux, Tache, Wappo, Wiyot, Yupik
**06** Apache, Arawak, Beaver, Bororo, Cayuga, Chiaha, Dakota, Haihai, Haisla, Iquito, Jumano, Kitsai, Konkow, Lakota, Micmac, Mixtec, Mohawk, Mojave, Nakipa, Navaho, Navajo, Nootka, Ojibwa, Oneida, Ottawa, Paipai, Paiute, Pawnee, Pueblo, Quapaw, Santee, Seneca, Toltec, Yakama, Yamana
**07** Arapaho, Atakapa, Bannock, Chibcha, Chinook, Choctaw, Hohokam, Huastec, Ingalik, Koskimo, Koyukon, Kwatami, Mahican, Miskito, Mohegan, Mohican, Nahuatl, Natchez, Secotan, Shawnee, Tlingit, Walapai, Wanapum, Zapotec
**08** Algonkin, Cherokee, Cheyenne, Comanche, Delaware, Iroquois, Kwakiutl, Menomini, Onondaga, Seminole, Shoshone, Shoshoni, Squamish, Tarascan, Yanomamo
**09** Algonquin, Blackfoot, Chickasaw, Menominee, Tuscarora, Winnebago
**10** Athabascan, Athabaskan, Potawatomi, Wallawalla

• **North American**
**04** Yank **06** Yankee **08** Canadian

**American football**

*American football teams:*

**11** New York Jets, St Louis Rams
**12** Buffalo Bills, Chicago Bears, Detroit Lions
**13** Dallas Cowboys, Denver Broncos, Houston Texans, Miami Dolphins, New York Giants
**14** Atlanta Falcons, Oakland Raiders
**15** Baltimore Ravens, Cleveland Browns, Green Bay Packers, Seattle Seahawks, Tennessee Titans
**16** Arizona Cardinals, Carolina Panthers, Kansas City Chiefs, Minnesota Vikings, New Orleans Saints, San Diego Chargers
**17** Cincinnati Bengals, Indianapolis Colts, San Francisco 49ers
**18** New England Patriots, Philadelphia Eagles, Pittsburgh Steelers, Tampa Bay Buccaneers, Washington Redskins
**19** Jacksonville Jaguars

*American football-related terms include:*

**03** AFC, NFC, NFL
**04** down, flag, pass, play, punt, sack, snap
**05** blitz, block, drive, field, guard, sneak
**06** center, fumble, huddle, pocket, punter, safety, tackle
**07** defense, end zone, lateral, lineman, offense, quarter, rushing, shotgun, time out
**08** fullback, gridiron, halfback, linesman, overtime, receiver, scramble, tailback, tight end

**09** field goal, reception, secondary, Super Bowl, touchdown
**10** completion, cornerback, extra point, linebacker, nose tackle
**11** quarterback, running back
**12** defensive end, interception, interference, special teams, wide receiver
**13** defensive back
**15** run interference

*American footballers include:*

**04** **Camp** (Walter Chauncy), **Monk** (Art), **Rice** (Jerry)
**05** **Allen** (Marcus), **Baugh** (Sammy), **Brown** (Jim), **Brown** (Paul), **Craig** (Roger), **Elway** (John), **Favre** (Brett), **Fouts** (Dan), **Halas** (George), **Perry** (Joe), **Perry** (William), **Shula** (Don), **Smith** (Emmitt), **White** (Reggie)
**06** **Blanda** (Frederick), **Butkus** (Dick), **Graham** (Otto), **Grange** (Red), **Greene** (Joe), **Hutson** (Don), **Landry** (Tom), **Madden** (John), **Marino** (Dan), **Namath** (Joe Willie), **Payton** (Walter), **Rockne** (Knute), **Sayers** (Gale), **Taylor** (Lawrence), **Thorpe** (Jim), **Unitas** (Johnny Constantine)
**07** **Lambeau** (Curly), **Montana** (Joe), **Sanders** (Barry), **Sanders** (Deion), **Simpson** (OJ)
**08** **Campbell** (Earl), **Lombardi** (Vince), **Staubach** (Roger)
**09** **Tarkenton** (Frank)

**American Samoa**
**03** ASM

**americium**
**02** Am

**amiability**
**06** warmth **08** kindness **10** cordiality, likability **11** likeability **12** cheerfulness, friendliness, pleasantness **15** warm-heartedness

**amiable**
**04** kind, maty, warm **05** matey, pally, sweet **06** chummy, genial, gentle **07** affable, cordial, likable, lovable **08** charming, cheerful, engaging, friendly, likeable, loveable, obliging, pleasant, sociable **09** agreeable, clubbable, congenial, gemütlich **11** good-natured, warm-hearted **12** approachable, good-tempered **13** companionable **15** easy to get on with

**amicable**
**05** civil **07** cordial **08** friendly, peaceful **09** civilized **10** harmonious **11** good-natured

**amicably**
**07** civilly **09** cordially, peaceably **12** harmoniously **13** good-naturedly

**amid, amidst**
◇ *hidden indicator*
◇ *insertion indicator*
**05** among, midst **06** amidst **07** amongst **12** in the midst of, in the thick of, surrounded by **13** in the middle of

**Amin**
**03** Idi

**amino acid**

*Amino acids include:*

**04** dopa
**06** glycin, leucin, lysine, serine, valine
**07** alanine, glycine, leucine, proline
**08** arginine, cysteine, tyrosine
**09** glutamine, histidine, ornithine, threonine
**10** asparagine, citrulline, domoic acid, isoleucine, methionine, tryptophan
**11** tryptophane
**12** aspartic acid, glutamic acid, phenylalanin
**13** phenylalanine
**14** glutaminic acid

**amiss**
◇ *anagram indicator*
**02** up **03** ill **04** awry, evil **05** false, wonky, wrong **06** astray, faulty **07** misdeed, wrongly **08** faultily, improper, untoward **09** defective, imperfect, incorrect **10** improperly, inaccurate, out of order, unsuitable **11** out of kilter **13** inappropriate

**amity**
**05** peace **06** accord, comity **07** concord, harmony **08** goodwill, kindness, sympathy **10** cordiality, fellowship, fraternity, friendship **12** friendliness, peacefulness **13** brotherliness, understanding

**ammo** *see* **ammunition**

**ammonia**
• **derivative of ammonia**
**05** amide, amine

**ammunition**
**04** ammo, mine, shot **05** bombs, round, slugs **06** rounds, shells **07** bullets, rockets **08** grenades, missiles **09** gunpowder **10** cartridges, explosives **11** projectiles

**amnesty**
**05** mercy **06** pardon **07** freedom, liberty, release **08** immunity, lenience, oblivion, reprieve **09** discharge, remission **10** absolution, indulgence **11** forgiveness **12** dispensation

**amok**
◇ *anagram indicator*
**05** crazy, madly **06** wildly **07** berserk **08** frenzied, insanely **09** in a frenzy, violently **12** like a lunatic, on the rampage, out of control **14** uncontrollably

**among**
◇ *hidden indicator*
◇ *insertion indicator*
**02** in, of **04** amid, with **05** midst **06** amidst **07** amongst, between **12** in the midst of, in the thick of, surrounded by, together with **13** in the middle of **14** in the company of

**amorous**
**04** fond, warm **05** kissy, nutty, randy **06** erotic, in love, lovely, loving, sexual, tender, wanton **07** amatory, gallant, lustful **08** lovesick **10** cupidinous, passionate **11** flirtatious, impassioned **12** affectionate

**amorphous**
**05** vague **08** formless, inchoate, nebulous, unformed, unshapen **09** irregular, shapeless, undefined **10** indistinct **11** featureless **12** unstructured **13** indeterminate

**amount**
**03** lot, sum **04** bulk, come, mass **05** quota, total, whole **06** degree, extent, figure, number, supply, volume **07** expanse, measure, quantum **08** entirety, quantity, sum total **09** aggregate, magnitude
• **amount to**
**04** come, make, mean **05** equal, run to, spell, total, tot up **06** come to, number **07** add up to, run into, tot up to **09** aggregate, inventory **10** boil down to, come down to **12** correspond to **14** be equivalent to, be tantamount to
• **large amount**
**03** lot **04** peck, slew, slue, tons
• **small amount**
**03** tad **04** haet, ha'it, hate, iota, whit

**amphetamine**
**04** whiz **05** benny, crank, speed, whizz **06** bomber **07** crystal **10** Benzedrine®, Methedrine®

**amphibian**
**04** duck **06** weasel **07** amtrack
*See also* **animal**

*Amphibians include:*

**03** ask, eft, olm
**04** frog, hyla, newt, pipa, Rana, toad
**05** Anura
**06** Anoura, peeper
**07** axolotl, paddock, proteus, puddock, tadpole
**08** bullfrog, cane-toad, mudpuppy, platanna, tree frog, tree toad
**09** Ambystoma, caecilian, green toad, marsh frog, Nototrema, warty newt
**10** Amblystoma, common frog, common toad, edible frog, flying frog, hellbender, horned toad, natterjack, salamander, smooth newt
**11** midwife toad, painted frog, Surinam toad
**12** springkeeper, spring peeper
**14** common treefrog, fire salamander, natterjack toad
**15** arrow-poison frog, common spadefoot

**amphitheatre**
**04** bowl, ring **05** arena **06** circus

**ample**
**03** big **04** full, good, rich, wide **05** broad, great, large, roomy, wally **06** enough, plenty **07** copious, liberal, profuse **08** abundant, adequate, generous, handsome, spacious **09** expansive, extensive, plenteous, plentiful **10** commodious, sufficient,

voluminous **11** substantial **12** considerable, unrestricted **14** more than enough

**amplification**
**07** raising **08** addition, boosting, increase **09** expansion, loudening **10** supplement **11** development, elaboration, enlargement **12** augmentation, making louder **13** strengthening **15** intensification

**amplify**
**05** add to, boost, raise, widen **06** deepen, expand, extend, louden **07** augment, broaden, bulk out, develop, enhance, enlarge, fill out **08** enlargen, flesh out, heighten, increase, lengthen **09** enlarge on, intensify **10** make louder, strengthen, supplement **11** elaborate on, expatiate on **13** go into details

**amplitude**
**04** bulk, mass, size **05** throw, width **06** extent, volume **07** expanse **08** capacity, fullness, vastness **09** greatness, largeness, magnitude, plenitude, profusion **11** copiousness **12** spaciousness **13** capaciousness

**ampoule**
**04** vial

**amputate**
**03** lop **04** dock **05** sever **06** cut off, lop off, remove **07** chop off, curtail, hack off **08** dissever, separate, truncate

**amulet**
**04** juju, tiki **05** charm **06** fetish, grigri, mascot, scarab **07** abraxas, periapt, sea bean **08** churinga, greegree, grisgris, pentacle, talisman **09** toadstone **10** lucky charm, phylactery

**amuse**
**04** play, slay **05** charm, cheer, crack, jolly, relax, sport, swing **06** absorb, crease, divert, engage, occupy, please, popjoy, regale, tickle, trifle **07** cheer up, delight, disport, engross, enthral, gladden **08** distract, interest, recreate **09** entertain, make laugh

**amusement**
**03** fun, toy **04** game, play **05** flume, hobby, mirth, R and R, sport, swing **06** solace **07** cockshy, delight, Dodgems®, pastime **08** cottabus, flip-flop, hilarity, interest, laughter, pleasure **09** big dipper, diversion, enjoyment, merriment, parish top **10** recreation **11** distraction **12** fruit machine **13** entertainment, scenic railway **15** shooting gallery

**amusing**
**03** fun **04** zany **05** a hoot, drôle, droll, funny, jolly, light, witty **07** a scream, comical, jocular, killing, waggish **08** charming, humorous, pleasant **09** diverting, enjoyable, facetious, funny ha-ha, hilarious, laughable, ludicrous, quizzical **10** delightful, recreative **11** interesting **12** entertaining

**amusingly**
**07** wittily **09** comically, enjoyably **10** humorously, pleasantly **11** hilariously **12** delightfully **13** interestingly **14** entertainingly

**anaconda**
**04** boma **08** sucurujú, water boa

**anaemic**
**03** wan **04** lame, pale, poor, tame, weak **05** ashen, bland, frail, livid, pasty, stale **06** chalky, feeble, infirm, pallid, sallow, sickly **07** insipid **09** bloodless, enervated, hackneyed, whey-faced **10** colourless, exsanguine, uninspired, unoriginal **11** ineffective, ineffectual **12** exsanguinous **13** unimaginative

**anaesthetic**
**05** local **06** number, opiate, premed **07** anodyne, general **08** epidural, narcotic, sedative **09** analgesic, soporific **10** nerve block, painkiller, palliative **12** stupefacient, stupefactive **13** premedication

*Anaesthetics include:*

**03** gas, PCP
**05** ether, trike
**06** eucain, Evipan®, spinal
**07** Avertin®, cocaine, eucaine, urethan
**08** ketamine, metopryl, procaine, stovaine, urethane
**09** Fluothane®, halothane, lidocaine, Pentothal®
**10** benzocaine, chloroform, lignocaine, nerve block, orthocaine, thiopental
**11** Dutch liquid, laughing gas, thiopentone
**12** cyclopropane, hexobarbital, nitrous oxide
**13** hexobarbitone, phencyclidine
**14** methyl chloride
**15** tribromoethanol

**anaesthetize**
**04** dope, drug, dull, numb **06** deaden, freeze **07** stupefy **09** cocainize **10** put to sleep **11** desensitize

**analgesic**
**10** painkiller

*Analgesics include:*

**06** Calpol®
**07** aspirin, codeine, Disprin®, Disprol®, menthol, metopon, morphia, Nurofen®, Panadol®, quinine, salicin
**08** Cuprofen®, fentanyl, ketamine, morphine, salicine, stovaine
**09** Calprofen®, co-codamol, ibuprofen, pethidine
**10** diclofenac
**11** aminobutene, Distalgesic®, indometacin, paracetamol, pentazocine
**12** indomethacin, salicylamide
**13** carbamazepine, phencyclidine
**14** phenylbutazone

**analogous**
**04** like **07** kindred, similar **08** agreeing, matching, parallel, relative **10** comparable, equivalent, resembling **11** correlative **13** corresponding

**analogy**
**06** simile **08** likeness, metaphor, parallel, relation **09** agreement, semblance **10** comparison, similarity, similitude **11** correlation, equivalence, resemblance **14** correspondence

**analyse**
◇ *anagram indicator*
**04** scan, sift, test **05** assay, judge, parse, study **06** divide, reduce, review **07** dissect, examine, inquire, process, resolve **08** calendar, consider, construe, critique, estimate, evaluate, separate **09** anatomize, break down, criticize, interpret, metricize, take apart **10** scrutinize **11** investigate, phonemicize

**analysis**
◇ *anagram indicator*
**04** test **05** assay, check, study **06** review **07** anatomy, check-up, inquiry, opinion, sifting **08** division, scrutiny **09** blood test, breakdown, judgement, reasoning, reduction **10** dissection, estimation, evaluation, exposition, inspection, resolution, separation **11** examination, explanation, explication, navel-gazing **13** anatomization, introspection, investigation **14** interpretation

**analyst**
**06** prober, tester **07** assayer, chemist **08** analyser, inquirer **09** dissector **10** researcher **12** experimenter **15** experimentalist

**analytical**
**07** in-depth, logical **08** analytic, clinical, critical, detailed, rational, studious **09** inquiring, searching **10** diagnostic, dissecting, expository, methodical, systematic **11** explanatory, inquisitive, questioning **13** investigative **14** interpretative

**anarchic**
◇ *anagram indicator*
**07** chaotic, lawless, riotous **08** confused, mutinous, nihilist **10** disordered, rebellious, ungoverned **11** anarchistic, libertarian **12** disorganized **13** revolutionary

**anarchism**
**05** chaos **07** mob-rule **08** disorder, rent-a-mob, sedition **09** mobocracy, rebellion **10** insurgency, ochlocracy, revolution **11** lawlessness **12** insurrection, racketeering

**anarchist**
**05** rebel **08** nihilist **09** Bolshevik, insurgent, terrorist **11** libertarian **13** revolutionary

**anarchy**
**04** riot **05** chaos **06** mutiny, unrule **07** misrule **08** disorder, nihilism

**09** anarchism, confusion, rebellion **10** revolution **11** lawlessness, pandemonium **12** insurrection

**anathema**
**04** bane **05** curse, taboo **07** bugbear **08** aversion **09** bête noire **10** abhorrence **11** abomination **12** proscription

**anatomy**
**05** build, frame **06** make-up **07** zootomy **08** analysis, topology **09** framework, phytotomy, sarcology, structure **10** dissection **11** composition, vivisection **12** anthropotomy, constitution, construction

*Anatomical terms include:*

**04** bone, hock, limb, oral, vein, womb
**05** aorta, aural, bowel, digit, elbow, gland, groin, helix, ileum, nasal, pedal, renal, spine, uvula, volar, vulva
**06** artery, axilla, biceps, buccal, carpal, carpus, dental, dermal, dorsal, gullet, lumbar, muscle, neural, ocular, septum, tendon, thymus, uterus
**07** abdomen, alveoli, auricle, cardiac, cochlea, gastric, glottis, gristle, hepatic, jugular, mammary, membral, optical, patella, sternum, thyroid, triceps
**08** cerebral, duodenal, foreskin, gingival, ligament, mandible, pectoral, thoracic, vena cava, vertebra, voice-box, windpipe
**09** capillary, cartilage, diaphragm, epidermis, funny bone, genitalia, hamstring, lachrymal, lymph node, pulmonary, sphincter, umbilicus, ventricle
**10** cerebellum, epiglottis, oesophagus
**11** intercostal, solar plexus
**14** Fallopian tubes

*See also* **bone**; **brain**; **ear**; **eye**; **gland**; **heart**; **hormone**; **mouth**; **muscle**; **teeth**; **vein**

*Anatomists include:*

**04** Baer (Karl), Bell (Sir Charles), Dart (Raymond), Knox (Robert)
**05** Clark (Sir Wifred le Gros), Graaf (Regnier de), Monro (Alexander)
**06** Adrian (Edgar, Lord), Cowper (William), Cuvier (Georges, Lord), Haller (Albrecht von), Stubbs (George), Tobias (Phillip)
**07** Colombo (Matteo Realdo), Galvani (Luigi)
**08** Alcmaeon, Malpighi (Marcello), Vesalius (Andreas)
**09** Bartholin (Caspar), Eustachio (Bartolomeo), Fallopius (Gabriel), Zuckerman (Solly, Lord)
**10** Herophilus
**13** Waldeyer-Hartz (Wilhelm)

**ancestor**
**04** sire **05** elder **06** father, mother, tipuna, tupuna **07** forbear **08** forebear **09** ascendant, ascendent, grandsire, precursor **10** antecedent, antecessor, forefather, forerunner, progenitor **11** predecessor **12** primogenitor **13** primogenitrix

**ancestral**
**06** avital, lineal **07** genetic **08** familial, parental **09** inherited **10** hereditary **12** genealogical

**• ancestral image**
**04** tiki

**ancestry**
**04** line, race **05** blood, roots, stock **06** family, linage, lynage, origin, stirps **07** descent, lignage, lineage **08** breeding, heredity, heritage, pedigree **09** ancestors, ancientry, forebears, genealogy, offspring, parentage, whakapapa **10** derivation, extraction, family tree **11** forefathers, progenitors

**anchor**
**03** fix **04** hook, host, moor **05** affix, berth, tie up **06** attach, fasten **07** bulwark, compère, mooring, mudhook, recluse, support **08** backbone, linchpin, mainstay, make fast **09** anchorman, announcer, presenter **10** foundation, newsreader **11** anchorwoman **15** tower of strength

*Anchors include:*

**03** car, CQR, ice, sea
**04** navy, rond
**05** bower, drift, kedge, sheet, waist
**06** drogue, plough, stream
**07** grapnel, killick, killock, stocked, weather
**08** mushroom
**09** admiralty, stockless, yachtsman
**12** double fluked

**• lie at anchor**
**04** ride

**anchorage**
**04** cell, road, rode **06** riding

**anchorite**
**04** monk **05** loner **06** anchor, hermit **07** ascetic, eremite, recluse, stylite **08** solitary **09** anchoress **10** solitarian

**ancient**
**03** old **04** aged **05** early, first, hoary, passé **06** age-old, antick, bygone, démodé **07** antique, archaic **08** earliest, obsolete, original, outmoded, primeval, pristine, time-worn, world-old **09** antiquary, atavistic, auld-warld, out-of-date, primaeval, primitive **10** antiquated, fossilized, immemorial, primordial **11** prehistoric **12** antediluvian, old-fashioned **13** superannuated **15** as old as the hills

*See also* **city**; **Egyptian**; **festival**

**ancillary**
**05** extra **07** helping **08** adjuvant **09** accessory, auxiliary, secondary **10** additional, subserving, subsidiary, supporting **11** adminicular, ministering, subordinate **12** contributory **13** supplementary

**and**
◇ *juxtaposition indicator*
**01** 'n' **02** an' **03** too **04** also, plus, then, with **06** as well **07** ampassy, besides **08** as well as, by the way, moreover, together **09** along with, ampersand, amperzand, including, what's more **10** ampussy-and, in addition **11** furthermore **12** in addition to, together with

**andiron**
**03** dog **06** chenet **07** firedog

**Andorra**
**03** AND

**androgynous**
**08** bisexual **09** polygamic **10** monoecious **11** monoclinous, protogynous **12** heterogamous **13** gynodioecious, hermaphrodite, male and female **14** androdioecious

**anecdotal**
**08** everyday, informal **09** narrative **10** unofficial **11** reminiscing **12** storytelling, unscientific

**anecdote**
**04** tale, yarn **05** story **06** sketch **08** exemplum **09** narrative, urban myth **11** urban legend **12** reminiscence

**anecdotes**
**03** ana

**anew**
◇ *anagram indicator*
**05** again **06** afresh, de novo, iterum **07** freshly **08** once more **09** de integro, once again **12** all over again

**angel**
**03** gem **05** ideal, saint **07** darling, paragon, watcher **08** guardian, treasure **09** nonpareil **13** heavenly being **14** messenger of God **15** divine messenger

*Angels include:*

**05** Ariel, Eblis, Iblis, Satan, Uriel
**06** Abdiel, Arioch, Azrael, Belial, Mammon, Moloch, Zephon
**07** Gabriel, Israfel, Lucifer, Michael, Raphael, Zadkiel
**08** Ithuriel
**09** Beelzebub

*Orders of angel include:*

**05** angel, power
**06** cherub, seraph, throne, virtue
**08** dominion
**09** archangel
**10** domination
**12** principality

**angelic**
**04** holy, pure **05** pious **06** divine, lovely **07** saintly **08** adorable, beatific, cherubic, empyrean, ethereal, heavenly, innocent, seraphic, virtuous **09** beautiful, celestial, unworldly **10** cherubical, cherubimic

**anger**
**03** bug, ire, irk, vex, wax **04** face, fuff, fury, gall, gram, huff, miff, mood, move,

nark, pelt, rage, rile, roil, teen, tene **05** annoy, blood, flake, get at, pique, teene, wrath **06** bother, choler, dander, emboil, enrage, madden, monkey, needle, nettle, offend, ruffle, temper, wind up **07** affront, air rage, bluster, chagrin, dudgeon, incense, inflame, kippage, offence, offense, outrage, provoke, rancour **08** bad blood, drive mad, irritate, paroxysm, road rage, vexation **09** aggravate, annoyance, infuriate, make angry **10** antagonism, antagonize, bitterness, conniption, drive crazy, exasperate, fit of anger, irritation, resentment **11** displeasure, indignation **12** boiling-point, drive bananas, exasperation, irritability **13** make sparks fly **14** drive up the wall

- **show anger**

**06** bridle

**angle**

**03** aim **04** bend, edge, face, fish, fork, hook, knee, nook, side, spin, take, tilt, turn **05** crook, elbow, facet, point, slant **06** aspect, corner, crotch, direct **07** flexure, outlook **08** approach, gradient, position **09** direction, viewpoint **10** projection, standpoint **11** inclination, perspective, point of view **12** intersection

- **angle for**

**03** aim **04** seek **05** go for **07** fish for **08** shoot for, try to get **11** make a bid for **12** seek to obtain

- **angle in botany**

**04** axil

- **angle in mining**

**04** hade

- **angle of 45°**

**05** mitre

- **reflex angle**

**02** in

**angler**

**03** rod **06** fisher, Walton **07** rodster, wide-gab **08** frogfish, monkfish, piscator **09** devilfish, fisherman, goose-fish, piscatrix, Waltonian

**Anglican**

**02** CE

**angling** *see* **fishing**

**Anglo-French**

**02** AF

**Angola**

**02** AN **03** AGO

**angrily**

◇ *anagram indicator*

**05** hotly **06** warmly **07** crossly, irately **08** bitterly **09** furiously, stroppily **10** wrathfully **11** indignantly, rancorously, resentfully **12** passionately

**angry**

◇ *anagram indicator*

**03** hot, mad **04** evil, high, warm, wild, yond **05** black, cross, het up, irate, livid, moody, radge, ratty, spewy, wrath **06** bitter, choked, heated, raging, sullen, sultry **07** annoyed, berserk, blazing, crooked, enraged, furious, ropable, stroppy, uptight **08** burned up, choleric, foribund, hairless, in a paddy, incensed, moody-mad, outraged, ropeable, seething, steaming, up in arms, wrathful **09** in a lather, in a temper, indignant, infuriate, irritated, pissed off, rancorous, raving mad, resentful, seeing red, splenetic, ticked off **10** aggravated, displeased, hopping mad, infuriated, passionate, stomachful, up in the air **11** disgruntled, exasperated, fit to be tied **12** on the rampage, on the warpath **14** beside yourself

- **make angry**

**07** incense

**angst**

**05** dread, worry **06** stress **07** anguish, anxiety, tension **08** distress **09** worriment **10** foreboding, uneasiness **11** disquietude **12** apprehension

**angstrom**

**01** A

**Anguilla**

**03** AIA

**anguish**

**03** woe **04** dole, pain, pang, rack **05** agony, dolor, grief **06** dolour, misery, sorrow **07** anxiety, torment, torture **08** distress **09** heartache, suffering **10** affliction, desolation, heartbreak **11** tribulation **12** wretchedness

**anguished**

**08** dolorous, harrowed, stressed, stricken, tortured, wretched **09** afflicted, miserable, suffering, tormented **10** distressed

**angular**

**04** bony, lank, lean, thin **05** gaunt, gawky, lanky, spare **06** skinny **07** scrawny **08** rawboned **12** sharp-pointed

**animal**

**03** pig **04** wild, zoic **05** beast, brute, swine **06** bodily, carnal, mammal, savage **07** bestial, brutish, critter, fleshly, inhuman, monster, sensual **08** animalic, creature, physical **09** barbarian **11** furry friend, instinctive **13** theriomorphic

*Animals include:*

**02** ai, ox, zo
**03** ape, asp, ass, bay, boa, bok, cat, cow, dog, dso, eft, elk, ewe, ewt, fox, gnu, hob, kob, olm, pig, ram, rat, roe, roo, sai, wat, yak
**04** anoa, anta, arna, atoc, axis, balu, bear, boma, bull, cavy, colt, cony, deer, dieb, douc, emys, euro, eyra, foal, frog, gila, goat, hare, hart, hyen, ibex, lion, mara, mare, mico, mink, mohr, mole, moyl, mule, naga, newt, oont, oryx, paca, paco, peba, pipa, pudu, puma, quey, rana, rusa, saki, scut, seal, seps, skug, stag, tahr, tegu, tehr, thar, titi, toad, unau, ursa, urus, urva, wolf
**05** adder, bison, camel, civet, coney, eland, horse, hyena, koala, lemur, llama, loris, moose, mouse, otter, panda, ratel, sheep, skunk, tiger, whale, zebra
**06** baboon, badger, beaver, cougar, ermine, ferret, gerbil, gibbon, impala, jaguar, monkey, ocelot, rabbit, racoon, walrus, weasel, wombat
**07** buffalo, caribou, cheetah, dolphin, gazelle, giraffe, gorilla, hamster, leopard, panther, polecat, sealion, wallaby
**08** aardvark, antelope, elephant, hedgehog, kangaroo, kinkajou, mongoose, platypus, reindeer, sea otter, squirrel
**09** armadillo, orang-utan, polar bear, wolverine
**10** camelopard, chimpanzee, giant panda, rhinoceros
**11** grizzly bear
**12** hippopotamus

*See also* **amphibian**; **ape**; **beetle**; **bird**; **butterfly**; **cat**; **cattle**; **chicken**; **collective**; **crustacean**; **deer**; **dinosaur**; **disease**; **dog**; **duck**; **farm**; **fish**; **game**; **horse**; **insect**; **invertebrate**; **lair**; **lizard**; **mammal**; **marsupial**; **mollusc**; **monkey**; **moth**; **pig**; **poultry**; **reptile**; **rodent**; **shark**; **sheep**; **snake**; **sound**; **spider**; **whale**; **worm**

*Animal lairs, nests and homes include:*

**03** den, nid, pen, sty
**04** bike, bink, byre, cage, coop, drey, fold, form, hive, hole, holt, nest, sett
**05** earth, eyrie, lodge, shell
**06** burrow, warren, wurley
**08** dovecote, fortress, vespiary
**09** formicary
**11** formicarium, termitarium

*Adjectives relating to animals include:*

**05** apian, avian, avine, ovine
**06** bovine, canine, equine, feline, hippic, larine, lupine, murine, simian, ursine
**07** acarine, anguine, asinine, caprine, cervine, corvine, hircine, leonine, milvine, otarine, pardine, phocine, piscine, porcine, saurian, sebrine, taurine, tigrine, turdine, vespine, vulpine
**08** anserine, aquiline, bubaline, cameline, chthyoid, elaphine, ichthyic, lemurine, leporine, limacine, ophidian, pavonine, sciurine, soricine, suilline, viperine, vituline
**09** caballine, chelonian, colubrine, columbine, crotaline, falconine, hirundine, musteline, ornithoid, viverrine, volucrine, vulturine
**10** psittacine, serpentine
**11** accipitrine, elephantine, fringilline, lacertilian

**12** gallinaceous, oryctolagine
**13** rhopalocerous
**14** papilionaceous

*Animal-related terms include:*

**03** ear, egg, eye, fin, fur, leg, paw, pet
**04** beak, bill, bite, claw, coat, crop, dock, gill, gula, hoof, horn, hump, jowl, loin, mane, mate, prey, rump, tail, teat, tusk, wild, wing, wool
**05** chine, crest, fangs, feral, moult, pouch, scale, shell, snout, spine, sting, trunk, udder, venom
**06** antler, barrel, dewlap, jubate, mantle, muzzle, thorax, ungula
**07** abdomen, antenna, feather, flehmen, flipper, gizzard, habitat, migrate, mimicry, pallium, segment, withers
**08** coupling, domestic, forefoot, forewing, halteres, hindfoot, hindwing, predator, torquate, ungulate, whiskers
**09** marsupium, oviparous, prehallux, proboscis, pygostyle, syndactyl, taligrade
**10** camouflage, gressorial, ovipositor, viviparous, webbed feet
**11** compound eye, lateral line, search image, swim bladder, waggle dance
**12** forked tongue
**13** electric organ, metamorphosis
**14** startle colours
**15** prehensile thumb

*Female animals include:*

**03** cow, doe, ewe, hen, pen, ree, sow
**04** gill, hind, jill, jomo, mare
**05** bitch, dsomo, jenny, nanny, queen, reeve, vixen, zhomo
**06** peahen
**07** greyhen, lioness, tigress
**08** water cow
**09** dolphinet, guinea hen, turkey hen
**10** leopardess, weasel coot

*Male animals include:*

**03** cob, dog, hob, nun, ram, tom, tup
**04** boar, buck, bull, cock, hart, jack, stag, zobo, zobu
**05** billy, drake, drone, dsobo
**06** gander, musket, old man, ramcat
**08** seecatch, stallion
**09** blackcock
**10** turkey cock
**12** throstle-cock

*Young animals include:*

**03** cub, elt, fry, kid, kit, nit
**04** brit, calf, colt, eyas, fawn, foal, gilt, grig, joey, lamb, maid, parr, peal, sild, slip, yelt
**05** chick, elver, owlet, piper, puppy, scrod, shote, smolt, squab, steer, whelp
**06** alevin, cygnet, eaglet, gimmer, grilse, heifer, hidder, kitten, lionet, piglet, pullet, samlet, weaner
**07** codling, eelfare, gosling, leveret, pigling, sardine, skegger, sounder, tadpole, wolfkin
**08** brancher, duckling, goatling, nestling, pea-chick
**09** fledgling

*Animals representing years in the Chinese calendar:*

**02** ox
**03** dog, pig, rat
**04** boar, cock, goat, hare
**05** horse, sheep, snake, tiger
**06** dragon, monkey, rabbit
**07** buffalo, rooster, serpent

**• animal display**
**03** zoo **09** menagerie
**• animal's body**
**04** soma
**• stock of animals**
**04** team, teme
**• tame animal**
**03** pet
**• unsuitable animal**
**04** cull

**animate**
**04** fire, goad, live, move, spur, stir, urge, wake **05** alive, impel, quick, rouse, spark, vital **06** arouse, buck up, ensoul, excite, incite, inform, insoul, kindle, living, revive, vivify **07** enliven, inspire, quicken **08** activate, embolden, energize, inspirit, vitalize
**09** breathing, conscious, encourage, galvanize, instigate, stimulate
**10** invigorate, reactivate **11** bring to life

**animated**
◇ *anagram indicator*
**03** hot **05** alive, brisk, eager, peppy, quick, vital, zappy **06** active, ardent, chirpy, lively **07** buoyant, chipper, excited, fervent, glowing, radiant, vibrant **08** instinct, spirited, vehement, vigorous **09** ebullient, energetic, sparkling, sprightly, vivacious
**10** passionate **11** full of beans, impassioned **12** enthusiastic **15** bright and breezy

**animatedly**
◇ *anagram indicator*
**05** mosso **07** briskly, eagerly
**08** actively, ardently **09** excitedly, fervently, radiantly, vibrantly
**10** vehemently, vigorously
**11** vivaciously **12** passionately
**13** energetically

**animation**
**02** go **03** pep **04** fire, heat, life, zeal, zest, zing **05** verve **06** action, energy, spirit, vigour **07** elation, fervour, passion, sparkle **08** activity, radiance, vibrancy, vitality, vivacity **10** claymation, ebullience, enthusiasm, excitement, liveliness **11** high spirits **12** exhilaration
**13** sprightliness, vivaciousness

**animosity**
**04** feud, hate **05** odium, pique, spite
**06** animus, enmity, hatred, malice **07** ill will, rancour **08** acrimony, friction, loathing **09** antipathy, hostility, malignity **10** abhorrence, antagonism, bitterness, ill feeling, race hatred, resentment **11** malevolence

**ankle**
**04** coot, cuit, cute, hock **05** hough, talus **06** tarsus

**annals**
**04** acta **05** fasti **07** history, memoirs, records, reports **08** accounts, archives, journals **09** registers
**10** chronicles

**annex**
**03** add **04** join **05** affix, seize, unite, usurp **06** adjoin, append, attach, fasten, occupy, take in **07** acquire, connect, conquer, purloin
**08** arrogate, take over **09** extension, mediatize **11** appropriate, incorporate

**annexation**
**07** seizure **08** conquest, takeover, usurping **10** arrogation, occupation
**11** acquisition **13** appropriation

**annexe**
**04** wing **08** addition **09** expansion, extension **10** attachment, supplement

**annihilate**
**04** raze, rout **05** erase **06** defeat, murder, rub out, thrash **07** abolish, conquer, destroy, take out, trounce, wipe out **09** eliminate, eradicate, extirpate, liquidate **10** extinguish, obliterate **11** assassinate, exterminate

**annihilation**
**03** end **06** defeat, murder **07** erasure
**09** abolition **10** extinction
**11** destruction, elimination, eradication, extirpation, liquidation
**12** obliteration **13** assassination, extermination

**anniversary**
**04** obit **07** jubilee **08** birthday, yahrzeit **09** centenary, millenary
**10** birthnight, centennial, millennium, wedding day **11** bicentenary, bimillenary, octingenary, semi-jubilee
**12** bicentennial, quinquennial, sexcentenary, tercentenary
**13** novocentenary, octocentenary, quincentenary, tercentennial
**14** octingentenary
**15** quatercentenary, sesquicentenary

*Anniversaries include:*

**04** D-Day
**05** VE Day, VJ Day
**07** Flag Day
**08** Anzac Day
**09** Canada Day, Empire Day
**10** Burns Night, Victory Day
**11** Bastille Day, Columbus Day, Dominion Day, Oak-apple Day, Republic Day, Waitangi Day
**12** Armistice Day, Australia Day, Discovery Day, Fourth of July, Thanksgiving
**13** King's Birthday, Liberation Day, Revolution Day
**14** Guy Fawkes Night, Queen's Birthday, Remembrance Day, Unification Day
**15** Constitution Day, Emancipation Day, Independence Day

*Wedding anniversaries include:*

**03** fur, tin
**04** gold, iron, jade, lace, ruby, silk, wood, wool
**05** china, coral, fruit, glass, ivory, linen, paper, pearl, steel, sugar
**06** bronze, clocks, copper, cotton, silver, willow
**07** crystal, diamond, emerald, flowers, leather, pottery, watches
**08** desk sets, platinum, sapphire, textiles
**09** aluminium
**10** appliances, silverware
**13** gold jewellery

**annotate**
**04** note **05** gloss **07** comment, explain **09** elucidate, explicate, interpret **10** add notes to **11** marginalize

**annotation**
**04** note **05** gloss **07** comment **08** exegesis, footnote, scholion, scholium **10** commentary **11** elucidation, explanation, explication **12** commentation

**announce**
◇ *homophone indicator*
**04** bill, post **05** sound, state **06** advise, blazon, notify, report, reveal **07** betoken, declare, divulge, gazette, give out, publish **08** denounce, disclose, intimate, proclaim, propound **09** advertise, broadcast, make known, preconize, publicize **10** make public, promulgate **12** blazon abroad **14** make a statement **15** issue a statement

**announcement**
**04** card **06** notice, report **07** message, release **08** bulletin, dispatch, handbill, obituary **09** broadcast, giving-out, ipse dixit, publicity, reporting, statement **10** communiqué, disclosure, divulgence, intimation, revelation **11** declaration, information, making known, publication, publicizing **12** making public, notification, proclamation, promulgation **13** advertisement **14** pronunciamento

**announcer**
**02** MC **04** host **06** anchor, herald **07** compère **09** anchorman, messenger, presenter, town crier **10** newscaster, newsreader, speakerine **11** anchorwoman, annunciator, broadcaster, commentator

**annoy**
**03** bug, din, hip, hyp, irk, nag, noy, try, vex **04** fash, gall, hump, miff, nark, ride, rile, roil **05** anger, cross, sturt, tease **06** bother, harass, hassle, hatter, hector, madden, molest, nettle, pester, plague, ruffle, tee off, wind up **07** chagrin, disturb, hack off, provoke, tick off, trouble **08** brass off, contrary, irritate **09** aggravate, cheese off, displease, drive nuts, importune **10** drive crazy, exasperate **11** get your goat **12** drive bananas **13** get on your wick, get up your nose, get your back up, make sparks fly **14** drive up the wall, get your blood up, give you the hump, piss someone off, take the michael **15** get on your nerves, get your dander up

**annoyance**
**04** bind, bore, drag, fash, hump, pain, pest **05** anger, sturt, tease **06** bother, injury, molest, pester, ruffle **07** bugbear, chagrin, noyance, trouble **08** headache, irritant, mischief, nuisance, vexation **09** bête noire **10** harassment, irritation **11** aggravation, displeasure, disturbance, provocation **12** exasperation, excruciation **13** pain in the butt, pain in the neck **14** thorn in the side

• **expression of annoyance**
**03** dam, dee, god, hey, sod, tut **04** damn, drat, heck, hell, hoot, phew, rats **05** blast, blimy, damme, devil, Jesus, my God!, shoot, waugh **06** blimey, bother, Christ, dammit, shucks, zounds **07** caramba, doggone **08** honestly, hoot-toot **09** cor blimey, do you mind?, good grief, gorblimey **10** hell's bells, hell's teeth, hoots-toots **11** botheration, for God's sake, for pete's sake, that's torn it **12** Donnerwetter **13** Gordon Bennett **14** for Christ's sake, for heaven's sake **15** for goodness sake

**annoyed**
**04** sore **05** angry, cross, fed up, upset, vexed **06** bugged, hipped, miffed, narked, peeved, piqued, shirty **07** chocker, hassled, in a huff, pig sick, stroppy **08** harassed, in a paddy, provoked **09** indignant, irritated, pissed off, ticked off **10** brassed off, cheesed off, displeased, driven nuts, got the hump **11** driven crazy, exasperated

**annoying**
**05** pesky **06** trying **07** galling, irksome, teasing **08** infernal, niggling, tiresome **09** harassing, intrusive, maddening, offensive, provoking, unwelcome, vexatious **10** bothersome, disturbing, irritating, plaguesome **11** aggravating, importunate, infuriating, pestiferous, troublesome **12** exasperating

**annual**
**06** yearly **07** almanac **08** calendar, register, yearbook

• **annual return**
**02** AR

**annul**
**04** undo, void **05** quash **06** cancel, defeat, negate, recall, reduce, repeal, revoke, vacate **07** abolish, cashier, nullify, rescind, retract, reverse, suspend, vacuate **08** abrogate, disannul, dissolve, overrule, set aside **10** invalidate **11** countermand

**annulment**
**06** defeat, recall, repeal **07** reverse, voiding **08** negation, quashing **09** abolition, cassation **10** abrogation, rescission, revocation, suspension **11** countermand, dissolution, rescindment **12** cancellation, invalidation **13** nullification

**anodyne**
**04** dull **05** bland **07** neutral **08** harmless, innocent **09** analgesic, deadening, innocuous **11** inoffensive

**anoint**
**03** oil, rub **04** balm, daub, nard, oint **05** anele, bless, salve, smear **06** grease, hallow, ordain, pomade **08** dedicate, sanctify, set apart **09** embrocate, lubricate **10** apply oil to, consecrate

**anomalous**
◇ *anagram indicator*
**03** odd **04** rare **05** freak **07** deviant, unusual **08** abnormal, atypical, freakish, peculiar, singular **09** eccentric, irregular **11** exceptional, incongruous **12** inconsistent

**anomaly**
◇ *anagram indicator*
**05** freak **06** misfit, oddity, rarity **09** departure, deviation, exception **10** aberration, divergence **11** abnormality, incongruity, peculiarity **12** eccentricity, irregularity **13** inconsistency

**anon**
**04** soon **06** coming **07** by and by, shortly **09** quite soon **10** before long **11** immediately **14** in a little while **15** in the near future

**anonymous**
**01** a **02** an **04** anon, gray, grey **07** unknown, unnamed **08** faceless, nameless, unsigned **09** incognito **10** authorless, impersonal, innominate, unattested **11** nondescript, unspecified **12** unattributed, unidentified, unremarkable **13** unexceptional **14** unacknowledged

**anorak**
**04** nerd, nurd, spod, wonk **06** cagoul, kagool, kagoul **07** cagoule, kagoule **11** windcheater **12** trainspotter

**another**
◇ *anagram indicator*
**04** more **05** added, extra, other, spare **06** second **07** further, variant **09** different, some other **10** additional, not the same **11** alternative

**answer**
**01** a **03** ans, fit, get, key **04** fill, meet, pass, rein, suit **05** agree, match, react, reply, serve **06** fulfil, pick up, refute, result, retort, return **07** conform, resolve, respond, riposte, satisfy **08** comeback, quick fix, reaction, rebuttal, rescript, response, solution **09** correlate, get back to, match up to,

rejoinder, retaliate, write back **10** come back to, resolution **11** acknowledge, explanation, replication, retaliation, unravelling **12** correspond to **15** acknowledgement

**• answer back**
**04** sass **05** argue, rebut **06** retort **07** dispute, riposte **08** backchat, disagree, talk back **09** retaliate **10** be cheeky to, contradict

**• answer for**
**06** pay for **08** speak for, vouch for **09** engage for, suffer for **11** be liable for **13** be punished for

**• answer to**
**08** report to **09** work under **15** be accountable to, be responsible to

**answerable**
**06** liable **07** to blame **08** suitable **10** chargeable, equivalent **11** accountable, blameworthy, responsible

**ant**
**05** emmet, nurse **06** ergate, nasute, neuter **07** ergates, pismire, termite

*Ants include:*

**03** red
**04** army, fire, leaf, wood
**05** black, crazy
**06** Amazon, driver, weaver
**07** bulldog, forager, pharaoh, soldier
**08** honeydew
**09** black lawn, carpenter, harvester
**10** leaf-cutter
**12** red harvester

**antagonism**
**06** enmity **07** discord, ill will, rivalry **08** conflict, friction **09** animosity, antipathy, hostility **10** antibiosis, contention, dissension, ill feeling, opposition, oppugnancy

**antagonist**
**03** foe **04** peer **05** enemy, rival **08** opponent **09** adversary, contender **10** competitor, contestant

**antagonistic**
**06** averse **07** adverse, hostile, opposed **08** opponent **10** at variance, unfriendly **11** adversarial, belligerent, conflicting, contentious, ill-disposed **12** incompatible

**antagonize**
**03** bug **04** miff, rile **05** anger, annoy, get at, repel **06** insult, needle, nettle, offend, wind up **07** incense, provoke **08** alienate, drive mad, embitter, estrange, irritate **09** aggravate, disaffect **10** drive crazy **12** drive bananas **13** make sparks fly **14** drive up the wall

**Antarctica**
**03** ATA

**Antarctic animal**
**07** Penguin

**antbear**
**08** aardvark, tamanoir **12** Myrmecophaga

**anteater**
**05** Manis **07** echidna, tamandu **08** aardvark, pangolin, tamandua

**antecedent**
**04** race **05** blood, roots, stock **06** stirps, tipuna, tupuna **09** ancestors, forebears, genealogy, precedent, preceding, precursor **10** extraction, forerunner, prevenient **11** forefathers, preparatory, progenitors

**antedate**
**07** precede, predate, prevene **08** antecede, go before **10** come before

**antediluvian**
**03** old **05** early, passé **06** bygone, old hat **07** archaic **08** outmoded **10** antiquated **11** out of the Ark **15** as old as the hills

**antelope**

*Antelopes include:*

**03** bok, doe, gnu, kid, kob
**04** kudu, oryx, puku, suni, thar, topi
**05** addax, bubal, chiru, eland, goral, nagor, nyala, oribi, sable, saiga, sasin, serow
**06** bosbok, dik-dik, duiker, duyker, dzeren, impala, inyala, koodoo, lechwe, nilgai, nilgau, pygarg, reebok
**07** blaubok, blesbok, bloubok, bubalis, chamois, chikara, gazelle, gemsbok, gerenuk, grysbok, madoqua, nylghau, sassaby
**08** Antilope, bontebok, boschbok, bushbuck, palebuck, reedbuck, steenbok, tsessebe
**09** blackbuck, sitatunga, situtunga, springbok, steinbock, tragelaph, waterbuck
**10** Alcelaphus, hartebeest, ox-antelope, wildebeest
**11** zebra duiker
**12** goat-antelope, klipspringer
**13** sable antelope

**antenna**
**04** horn **06** aerial, feeler

**anteroom**
**04** hall **05** foyer, lobby, porch **09** vestibule **11** antechamber, waiting-room **12** entrance hall, voiding-lobby

**anthem**
**04** hymn, song **05** chant, motet, paean, psalm **06** motett, waiata **07** chorale, introit **08** antiphon, canticle, isodicon **10** responsory **12** Marseillaise, song of praise

**anthology**
**06** digest **07** omnibus **08** treasury **09** selection, spicilege **10** collection, compendium, miscellany **11** compilation, florilegium **12** chrestomathy

**Anthony**
**04** Tony

**anthrax**
**04** sang

**anthropology**
**09** ethnology

*Anthropologists include:*

**04** **Boas** (Franz), **Buck** (Sir Peter), **Mead** (Margaret)
**05** **Hiroa** (Te Rangi), **Tylor** (Sir Edward)
**06** **Frazer** (Sir J G), **Leakey** (Louis), **Marett** (R R)
**07** **Métraux** (Albert)
**09** **Heyerdahl** (Thor)
**10** **Malinowski** (Bronislaw)
**11** **Lévi-Strauss** (Claude)
**14** **Radcliffe-Brown** (Alfred)

**antibiotic**

*Antibiotics include:*

**05** Cipro®
**08** neomycin, nystatin
**09** avoparcin, kanamycin, Neosporin®, polymyxin, quinolone
**10** ampicillin, Aureomycin®, bacitracin, gramicidin, lincomycin, meticillin, penicillin, polymyxin B, rifampicin, Terramycin®, vancomycin
**11** amoxicillin, amoxycillin, clindamycin, cloxacillin, cycloserine, doxorubicin, doxycycline, fusidic acid, methicillin
**12** erythromycin, griseofulvin, streptomycin, tetracycline, trimethoprim
**13** cephalosporin, ciprofloxacin, co-trimoxazole, metronidazole, spectinomycin, virginiamycin
**15** chloramphenicol, oxytetracycline

**antibody**
**03** MAB **06** reagin **10** agglutinin, amboceptor, immune body, precipitin **13** isoagglutinin

**antic**
**04** dido **05** caper, clown **07** buffoon **09** fantastic, grotesque **10** mountebank

**Antichrist**
**08** man of sin, the Beast **10** lawless one

**anticipate**
**05** await, guess **06** bank on, expect **07** count on, foresee, hope for, look for, obviate, precede, predict, pre-empt, prepare, prevene, prevent **08** antedate, beat to it, figure on, forecast, preclude, reckon on **09** apprehend, count upon, forestall, intercept **10** prepare for **11** preoccupate, second-guess, think likely **13** look forward to

**anticipation**
**04** hope, type **08** forecast **09** foretaste, intuition, prejudice, prolepsis **10** excitement, expectancy, prediction, prevention **11** bated breath, expectation, preparation **12** apprehension, presentiment

**anticlimax**
**06** bathos, fiasco **07** let-down

**08** comedown, non-event **09** damp squib **14** disappointment

**antics**
**06** capers, doings, pranks, stunts, tricks **07** foolery, frolics **08** clowning, mischief **09** horseplay, silliness **10** buffoonery, shenanigan, skylarking, tomfoolery **11** playfulness, shenanigans **12** monkey-tricks

**antidote**
**04** cure **05** serum **06** bezoar, remedy, senega **07** theriac, treacle **08** naloxone, Orvietan, theriaca **09** antitoxin, antivenin **10** corrective, mithridate **11** contrayerva, dimercaprol, neutralizer **12** alexipharmic, counter-agent **13** counter-poison, Venice treacle **14** alexipharmakon, countermeasure

**Antigua and Barbuda**
**03** ATG

**antimony**
**02** Sb

**antipathy**
**04** hate **05** odium **06** animus, enmity, hatred **07** allergy, disgust, dislike, ill will **08** aversion, bad blood, distaste, dyspathy, loathing **09** animosity, hostility, repulsion **10** abhorrence, antagonism, opposition, repugnance **15** incompatibility

**antiquated**
**05** dated, passé **06** bygone, démodé, fogram, fossil, old hat **07** ancient, archaic, outworn **08** obsolete, outdated, outmoded **09** out-of-date, primitive **10** fossilized **11** on the way out, prehistoric **12** antediluvian, old-fashioned **13** anachronistic, prehistorical

**antique**
◇ *archaic word indicator*
**03** old **05** curio, relic **06** bygone, quaint, rarity **07** ancient, archaic, veteran, vintage **08** Egyptian, heirloom, obsolete, outdated **09** antiquity, curiosity **10** antiquated **11** antiquarian, museum piece, period piece **12** old-fashioned **13** object of virtu **14** collector's item

*Antiques-related terms include:*

**04** Goss, Ming, ring, T'ang
**05** glaze, ivory
**06** barock, dealer, empire, Gothic, lustre, patina, period, rococo
**07** art deco, auction, barocco, baroque, ceramic, federal, impasto, opaline, pilgrim, pottery, Tiffany
**08** filigree, Georgian, Jacobean, majolica, Sheraton, trecento
**09** bone china, collector, Delftware, Edwardian, porcelain, Queen Anne, soft paste, stoneware, valuation, Victorian
**10** art nouveau, millefiori
**11** chinoiserie, Chippendale, cinquecento, haute époque, Hepplewhite, period piece, restoration
**12** antiques fair, arts and craft, blanc de Chine, blue and white, reproduction, transitional
**13** willow pattern
**15** churrigueresque

**antiquity**
**03** age, eld **06** old age **07** oldness **08** agedness **09** ancientry, olden days **10** days of yore **11** ancientness, distant past **12** ancient times **14** time immemorial

**antiseptic**
**04** pure **05** clean **07** aseptic, sterile **08** cleanser, germ-free, hygienic, purifier, sanitary **09** germicide, medicated, mouthwash, sanitized **10** sterilized, unpolluted **11** bactericide **12** disinfectant **14** uncontaminated

*Antiseptics include:*

**03** TCP®
**05** eupad, eusol
**06** cresol, Dettol®, flavin, formol, phenol, Savlon®, thymol
**07** benzoin, flavine
**08** creasote, creosote, formalin, iodoform
**09** cassareep, cassaripe, cetrimide, Germolene®, Listerine®, merbromin, zinc oxide
**10** acriflavin
**11** acriflavine
**12** carbolic acid, methyl violet
**13** chlorhexidine, crystal violet, flowers of zinc, gentian violet, silver nitrate
**14** Dakin's solution, rubbing alcohol, sodium benzoate, sodium chlorate
**15** hexachlorophane, hexachlorophene

**antisocial**
**07** asocial, hostile, lawless **08** anarchic, reserved, retiring **09** alienated, withdrawn **10** disorderly, disruptive, rebellious, unfriendly, unsociable **11** belligerent **12** antagonistic, misanthropic, unacceptable **13** unforthcoming **14** unapproachable **15** uncommunicative

**antisubmarine**
**02** AS

**antithesis**
**07** reverse **08** contrast, converse, opposite, reversal **10** opposition **13** contradiction **15** opposite extreme

**antithetical**
**07** opposed **08** clashing, contrary, opposing **11** conflicting **12** incompatible, in opposition **13** contradictory **14** irreconcilable

**antler**
**04** horn **08** staghorn **09** hartshorn

**antler**
**04** horn **08** staghorn **09** hartshorn

**Antony**
**04** Tony

**anxiety**
**03** tiz **04** care, cark, fear, rack, stew **05** angst, dread, sweat, tizzy, worry **06** fantad, fantod, hang-up, nerves, strain, stress **07** anguish, concern, fantads, fanteeg, fantods, jitters, tension, thought, willies **08** disquiet, distress, fantigue, suspense **09** dysthymia, misgiving, worriment **10** foreboding, impatience, solicitude, uneasiness **11** butterflies, disquietude, fretfulness, nervousness **12** apprehension, collywobbles, hypochondria, restlessness **13** consternation, heebie-jeebies **14** solicitousness

*See also* **phobia**

**• free from anxiety**
**04** ease

**anxious**
◇ *anagram indicator*
**04** keen, taut, toey **05** eager, het up, tense, upset **06** afraid, uneasy **07** careful, fearful, fretful, in a stew, jittery, longing, nervous, uptight, worried **08** desirous, dismayed, in a tizzy, insecure, restless, tortured, troubled, yearning **09** concerned, desperate, disturbed, expectant, ill at ease, impatient, on the rack, tormented **10** distressed, in suspense, solicitous **11** overwrought **12** apprehensive, enthusiastic **13** grandmotherly, on tenterhooks **14** hot and bothered, valetudinarian **15** a bundle of nerves

**anxiously**
**07** tensely **08** uneasily **09** fearfully, fretfully, nervously **10** restlessly **11** impatiently, tormentedly **12** solicitously **14** apprehensively

**any**
**03** ary, one **04** a few, some **05** arrow, at all **06** a bit of **09** whichever **10** a single one, in the least **11** the least bit, to any extent **12** to some extent

**anybody**
**03** one

**anyhow**
◇ *anagram indicator*
**06** anyway **07** anyways **08** at random, untidily **09** at any rate, in any case **10** carelessly, in any event, not in order, regardless **11** at all events, haphazardly **12** nevertheless, no matter what **13** indifferently

**anyone**
**03** you

**anything**
**03** owt **05** ought

**anyway**
◇ *anagram indicator*
**06** anyhow **07** anyroad **09** in any case **10** in any event, regardless **11** at all events **12** nevertheless, no matter what

**apace**
**04** fast **07** hastily, quickly, rapidly, swiftly **08** speedily **10** at top speed **11** at full speed, double-quick **12** without delay

**apart**
◇ *anagram indicator*
**04** afar, away **05** alone, aloof, aside **06** beside, cut off, in bits, singly, to bits **07** asunder, distant **08** by itself, distinct, divorced, excluded, in pieces, isolated, separate, to pieces **09** into parts, on your own, piecemeal, privately, separated, to one side **10** by yourself, separately **11** not together **12** individually **13** independently

• **apart from**
**04** save **06** beyond, but for, except **07** besides, outside **08** excepted **09** aside from, except for, excluding **11** not counting

**apartment**
**03** apt, pad **04** flat, gaff, room, unit **05** bower, condo, split **06** duplex, walk-up **07** chamber, mansion **08** home unit, paradise, tenement **11** condominium **12** privy chamber **13** accommodation **15** duplex apartment
*See also* **room**

**apathetic**
**04** cold, cool, numb **05** blasé, ho-hum **07** passive, unmoved **08** listless, lukewarm **09** impassive, lethargic, unfeeling **10** insouciant, uninvolved **11** emotionless, half-hearted, indifferent, unambitious, unconcerned, unemotional **12** uninterested, unresponsive

**apathy**
**06** acedia, torpor **07** accidie, inertia, languor **08** coldness, coolness, lethargy **09** passivity, unconcern **11** impassivity **12** indifference, listlessness, sluggishness **13** insensibility, lack of concern **14** lack of interest

**ape**
**04** copy, echo, mock **05** magot, mimic **06** affect, mirror, parody, parrot, send up, simian **07** imitate, take off **09** proconsul **10** anthropoid, caricature, jackanapes, troglodyte **11** counterfeit
*See also* **animal**; **monkey**; **primate**

*Apes include:*

**05** chimp, drill, jocko, orang, pigmy, pongo, pygmy, satyr
**06** baboon, bonobo, chacma, dog-ape, gelada, gibbon, monkey, wou-wou, wow-wow
**07** gorilla, hoolock, macaque, siamang
**08** hylobate, mandrill
**09** hamadryad, orang-utan
**10** chimpanzee, silverback
**11** orang-outang
**12** Cynocephalus, ourang-outang, paranthropus
**13** Kenyapithecus
**15** pygmy chimpanzee

**aperture**
**03** eye, gap **04** hole, rent, slit, slot, vent **05** chink, cleft, crack, light, mouth, space **06** breach, choana, oscule, rictus, throat, window **07** fissure, foramen, opening, orifice, osculum, passage, punctum, swallow **08** fenestra, overture, punctule **09** sight-hole **10** interstice **11** perforation **14** counter-opening

**apex**
**03** tip, top **04** acme, peak **05** crest, crown, point **06** apogee, climax, height, summit, vertex, zenith **08** pinnacle **09** fastigium, high point **10** apotheosis, pyramidion **11** culmination **12** consummation **13** crowning point

**aphid, aphis**
**06** ant cow **08** blackfly, greenfly **09** bark-louse **10** dolphin-fly, plant louse, smother-fly

**aphorism**
**03** saw **05** adage, axiom, gnome, maxim **06** dictum, saying **07** epigram, precept, proverb **08** sentence **09** witticism **10** apophthegm, whakatauki

**aphrodisiac**
**06** erotic **07** amative, amatory, philter, philtre **08** venerous **09** cantharis, erogenous, stimulant, venereous **10** love potion, Spanish fly **11** erotogenous, stimulative

**Aphrodite**
**05** Venus

**apiece**
**03** all **04** each **06** singly **07** per head **09** per capita, per person **10** separately **12** individually, respectively

**aplomb**
**05** poise **08** calmness, coolness **09** assurance, composure, sangfroid **10** confidence, equanimity **11** savoir-faire **13** self-assurance **14** self-confidence, self-possession, unflappability

**apocryphal**
**06** made-up **07** dubious **08** doubtful, fabulous, mythical, spurious **09** concocted, equivocal, imaginary, legendary **10** fabricated, fictitious, unverified **11** unsupported **12** questionable **15** unauthenticated, unsubstantiated

*Apocryphal books of the Bible include:*

**03** Bar, Esd, Jud, Sir, Sus, Tob
**04** Macc, Wisd
**05** Bel&Dr, Tobit (Book of)
**06** Baruch (Book of), Ecclus, Esdras (Books of), Judith (Book of)
**07** Pr of Man, Susanna (History of)
**08** Manasseh (Prayer of)
**09** Maccabees
**14** Ecclesiasticus (Book of)
**15** Bel and the Dragon, Wisdom of Solomon (Book of)

*See also* **Bible**

**apologetic**
**05** sorry **06** rueful **08** contrite, penitent **09** regretful, repentant **10** excusatory, remorseful

**apologetically**
**08** ruefully **10** contritely, penitently **11** regretfully, repentantly **12** remorsefully

**apologia**
**07** defence **08** argument **11** explanation, explication, vindication

**apologist**
**06** backer **08** advocate, defender, endorser, upholder **09** supporter **10** vindicator

**apologize**
**05** plead **06** grovel, regret **07** confess, explain, justify **08** say sorry **09** ask pardon **11** acknowledge **12** be apologetic, eat humble pie, eat your words **14** ask forgiveness, say you are sorry

**apology**
**04** oops, plea **05** sorry **06** excuse **07** defence, mockery, regrets **08** excuse me, pardon me, travesty **10** caricature, confession, corruption, distortion, palliation **11** explanation, saying sorry, vindication **12** poor specimen **13** justification **14** poor substitute **15** acknowledgement

**apoplectic**
**03** mad **04** high **05** cross, irate, livid, moody, radge, ratty, spewy, wrath, wroth **06** bitter, choked, raging, sullen, sultry **07** annoyed, crooked, enraged, furious, ropable, stroppy, uptight **08** burned up, choleric, foribund, hairless, in a paddy, incensed, outraged, seething, up in arms, wrathful **09** in a lather, in a temper, indignant, irritated, pissed off, rancorous, raving mad, resentful, seeing red, splenetic, ticked off, very angry **10** hopping mad, infuriated, passionate, up in the air **11** disgruntled, exasperated, fit to be tied **12** on the rampage, on the warpath **14** beside yourself

**apostasy**
**06** heresy **07** perfidy, rattery, ratting **09** defection, desertion, falseness, recreance, recreancy, treachery **10** disloyalty, renegation **12** renunciation **13** faithlessness **14** unfaithfulness

**apostate**
**03** rat **07** heretic, traitor **08** defector, deserter, recreant, renegade, runagate, turncoat **10** recidivist **13** tergiversator

**apostle**
**07** pioneer, teacher **08** advocate, champion, crusader, disciple, preacher, reformer **09** apologist, messenger, proponent, supporter **10** evangelist, missionary **12** proselytizer

**Apostles of Jesus Christ:**

**04** John
**05** James, Judas, Peter, Simon
**06** Andrew, Philip, Thomas
**07** Matthew
**08** Matthias, Thaddeus
**11** Bartholomew
**13** Judas Iscariot
**14** Simon the Zealot
**15** James of Alphaeus
**17** Simon the Canaanite

**apotheosis**
**03** tip **04** acme, apex, peak **05** crest, crown, point **06** apogee, climax, height, summit, vertex, zenith
**08** pinnacle **09** fastigium, high point
**11** culmination, deification
**12** consummation **13** crowning point, glorification

**appal**
**05** alarm, daunt, scare, shock
**06** dismay **07** disgust, horrify, outrage, terrify, unnerve **08** frighten
**10** disconcert, intimidate

**appalling**
◇ *anagram indicator*
**04** dire, grim, naff, poor, ropy **05** awful, lousy, pants, ropey **06** horrid
**07** ghastly, hideous, the pits, very bad
**08** alarming, daunting, dreadful, hopeless, horrible, horrific, inferior, pathetic, shocking, terrible
**09** atrocious, frightful, harrowing, loathsome, unnerving **10** disgusting, horrifying, inadequate, outrageous, terrifying **11** frightening, nightmarish
**12** intimidating, unacceptable
**14** unsatisfactory

**appallingly**
◇ *anagram indicator*
**07** awfully **08** horribly, terribly
**09** hideously **10** dreadfully, hopelessly, shockingly **11** frightfully **12** horrifically, pathetically, unacceptably

**apparatus**
**03** rig **04** bank, gear, tool **05** means, set-up, tools **06** device, gadget, outfit, system, tackle **07** machine, network
**08** utensils **09** appliance, equipment, framework, implement, machinery, materials, mechanism, structure
**10** implements, instrument
**11** contraption
*See also* **laboratory**

**apparel**
**03** kit **04** garb, gear, tire, togs
**05** besee, dress, get-up, weeds
**06** attire, outfit, robing, vestry
**07** clobber, clothes, costume, raiment, vesture **08** clothing, garments, wardrobe **09** garniture **11** habiliments

**apparent**
◇ *hidden indicator*
**02** ap **03** app **04** open **05** clear, overt, plain **06** marked, patent **07** evident, obvious, outward, seeming, visible
**08** declared, distinct, manifest
**10** detectable, noticeable, ostensible
**11** conspicuous, perceptible, superficial **12** unmistakable **13** be standing out

**apparently**
**02** ap **03** app **07** clearly, plainly
**08** patently **09** evidently, obviously, outwardly, reputedly, seemingly
**10** manifestly, ostensibly **12** on the surface **13** on the face of it, superficially

**apparition**
**05** fetch, ghost, shape, spook, taish
**06** double, spirit, taisch, vision, wraith
**07** chimera, eidolon, gytrash, phantom, specter, spectre **08** illusion, manifest, phantasm, presence, visitant
**09** hobgoblin, semblance
**10** appearance **12** doppelgänger
**13** manifestation **15** materialization

**appeal**
**02** it, SA **03** ask, beg, cry, SOS, sue
**04** call, draw, lure, peal, pele, plea, pray, suit **05** apply, charm, claim, oomph, plead, tempt **06** allure, ask for, avouch, beauty, call on, engage, entice, invite, invoke, orison, please, prayer, review
**07** address, attract, beseech, entreat, implore, provoke, reclaim, request, retrial, solicit **08** approach, call upon, charisma, entreaty, interest, petition
**09** fascinate, magnetism **10** adjuration, attraction, invocation, recusation, supplicate **11** application, conjuration, enchantment, fascination, imploration, winsomeness **12** re-evaluation, solicitation, supplication **13** re-examination **14** attractiveness
**15** reconsideration
• **solemn appeal**
**04** oath

**appealing**
**07** winning, winsome **08** alluring, charming, engaging, enticing, inviting, magnetic, pleasing, tempting
**10** attractive, enchanting
**11** charismatic, fascinating, interesting

**appear**
◇ *homophone indicator*
**03** act, eye **04** go on, look, loom, peer, play, rise, seem, shew, show, star
**05** arise, bob up, break, enter, issue, kithe, kythe, occur, pop up **06** arrive, attend, cast up, co-star, crop up, emerge, figure, show up, spring, turn up **07** come out, compear, develop, perform, surface, topline, turn out
**08** platform, take part **09** be on stage, be present, come along **10** be a guest in **11** be published, come to light, materialize, show signs of **12** come across as, come into view, show your face **13** become visible, come into sight **14** take the guise of **15** become available
• **begin to appear**
**03** ope **04** open

**appearance**
**03** air, hew, hue **04** broo, brow, face, form, garb, look, mien, rise, show, view
**05** debut, front, ghost, guise, image, looks **06** advent, aspect, coming, effeir, effere, façade, figure, manner, ostent, visage **07** arrival, bearing, outward **08** exterior, illusion, presence, pretence **09** appearing, demeanour, emergence, semblance
**10** apparition, attendance, complexion, expression, impression
**11** outward form **12** introduction
**14** coming into view
• **final appearance**
**08** swansong
• **personal appearance**
**02** PA

**appease**
**04** stay **05** allay, atone, quiet, still
**06** aslake, attone, defray, pacify, soothe
**07** mollify, placate, qualify, satisfy
**08** mitigate **09** reconcile
**10** conciliate, propitiate **13** make peace with

**appeasement**
**09** placation **11** peacemaking
**12** conciliation, pacification, satisfaction **14** reconciliation

**appellation**
**04** name **05** title **07** epithet
**08** monicker, nickname **09** most noble, sobriquet **10** soubriquet
**11** description, designation
**12** compellation, denomination

**append**
◇ *juxtaposition indicator*
**03** add, put, tag **04** join **05** affix, annex
**06** adjoin, attach, fasten, tack on
**07** conjoin, subjoin **08** pickback
**09** pickaback, pickapack, piggyback

**appendage**
**03** lug **04** aril **05** affix, aglet, whisk
**06** aiglet, arista, barbel, cercus, stipel, uropod **07** adjunct, arillus, auricle, foretop, maxilla, stipule **08** addendum, addition, appendix, gnathite, nose-leaf, pedipalp, pendicle **09** allantois, chelicera, swimmeret, tailpiece
**10** paraglossa, parapodium, supplement **11** aiguillette
**12** appurtenance

**appendix**
**03** app **05** annex, rider **07** adjunct, codicil, pendant, pendent
**08** addendum, addition, epilogue, schedule **09** appendage
**10** postscript, supplement

**appertain**
**05** apply, refer **06** bear on, effeir, effere, regard, relate **07** concern, pertain
**10** be relevant **14** have a bearing on

**appetite**
**03** maw, yen **04** lust, urge, zeal, zest
**05** taste, tooth, twist **06** desire, hunger, liking, orexis, relish, thirst
**07** craving, longing, malacia, passion, stomach **08** inner man, yearning
**09** eagerness **10** inner woman, propensity **11** inclination
**13** concupiscence
• **sharpness of appetite**
**04** edge

**appetizer**
**04** meze, tapa, whet **05** bhaji, mezze, tapas **06** bhagee, bhajee, canapé, dim sum, relish **07** starter **08** antepast, apéritif, cocktail **09** antipasto
**11** amuse-bouche, amuse-gueule, first course, hors d'oeuvre **13** prawn cocktail

**appetizing**
**05** tasty, yummy **06** morish
**07** moreish, piquant, savoury, scrummy **08** inviting, tempting
**09** appealing, delicious, palatable, succulent, toothsome **11** lip-smacking, scrumptious **13** mouthwatering

**applaud**
**03** hum **04** clap, laud, root, ruff
**05** cheer, extol **06** cry aim, praise
**07** acclaim, approve, commend
**08** eulogize **10** compliment
**12** congratulate **14** cheer to the echo, give a big hand to **15** give an ovation to

**applause**
**04** hand, ruff **05** éclat, salvo, vivat
**06** bravos, cheers, praise **07** acclaim, ovation, plaudit **08** a big hand, accolade, approval, cheering, clapping, encomium, plaudits
**11** acclamation, Kentish fire
**12** commendation **14** congratulation
**15** standing ovation

**apple**
**04** pome

*Apples include:*

**03** Cox
**04** Cox's, crab, snow
**05** Coxes, eater
**06** biffin, codlin, cooker, eating, idared, pippin, russet
**07** Baldwin, Bramley, codling, cooking, costard, crispin, ribston, Sturmer, wine-sap
**08** Braeburn, Jonathan, McIntosh, pearmain, Pink Lady, queening, ribstone, sweeting
**09** delicious, jenneting, king-apple, nonpareil, Royal gala
**11** Granny Smith, McIntosh red, russet apple
**12** Red Delicious
**13** Ribston pippin, Sturmer Pippin
**15** Golden Delicious

• **apple core**
**04** runt
• **big apple**
**02** NY **03** NYC

**appliance**
**03** use **04** iron, tool **05** gizmo, truss, value, waldo **06** device, gadget, praxis
**07** machine **08** function
**09** apparatus, implement, mechanism, relevance **10** fire engine, instrument
**11** application, carrying-out, contraption, contrivance
*See also* **domestic**; **utensil**

**applicable**
**03** apt, fit **04** live **05** valid **06** proper, suited, useful **07** fitting **08** apposite, relevant, suitable **09** pertinent
**10** legitimate **11** appropriate
• **not applicable**
**02** n/a

**applicant**
**06** suitor **08** aspirant, claimant, inquirer **09** candidate, postulant
**10** competitor, contestant, petitioner
**11** interviewee

**application**
**03** use **04** suit **05** claim, study, value
**06** appeal, demand, effort, praxis
**07** aptness, bearing, inquiry, program, purpose, request, rubbing
**08** function, hard work, industry, keenness, petition, smearing, software **09** anointing, assiduity, diligence, putting on, relevance, spreading, treatment **10** commitment, dedication, pertinence
**11** germaneness **12** perseverance, sedulousness, significance
**13** attentiveness **15** industriousness
• **make application**
**03** sue

**applied**
◇ *anagram indicator*
**04** real **06** actual, useful **07** hands-on **08** relevant **09** practical
**10** functional
• **applied to**
**02** on

**apply**
**03** fit, lay, ply, put, rub, set, sue, use
**04** give, suit, turn **05** brush, claim, exert, lay on, order, paint, put on, refer, smear, study, wield **06** affect, anoint, appeal, appose, ask for, assign, bestow, betake, commit, devote, direct, draw on, employ, engage, relate, resort
**07** address, adhibit, execute, harness, inquire, involve, pertain, present, request, solicit, utilize **08** dedicate, exercise, petition, practise, put in for, resort to, spread on, work hard
**09** appertain, cover with, implement, persevere, treat with **10** administer, be diligent, be relevant, buckle down, settle down **11** bring to bear, concentrate, knuckle down, requisition, write off for **12** make an effort, write away for **13** be industrious, be significant, bring into play **14** commit yourself, devote yourself, fill in a form for **15** put into practice
• **apply carelessly**
**04** slap

**appoint**
**03** fix, set **04** cast, hire, make, name, pick, post **05** allot, co-opt, elect, limit, place, put in, voice **06** assign, charge, choose, decide, decree, depute, detail, direct, employ, engage, ordain, select, settle, take on **07** arrange, command, destine, install, present, recruit, specify, station **08** delegate, nominate
**09** designate, determine, establish
**10** commission, constitute **13** be shortlisted

**appointed**
◇ *anagram indicator*
**03** due, set **05** fixed **06** chosen
**07** decided, decreed, settled
**08** allotted, arranged, assigned, destined, ordained **09** scheduled
**10** designated, determined
**11** established, pre-arranged, preordained

**appointment**
**03** job **04** date, post, room **05** place, tryst **06** choice, naming, office
**07** meeting **08** choosing, election, position **09** interview, selection, situation **10** delegation, engagement, nomination, rendezvous
**11** arrangement, assignation
**12** consultation **13** commissioning
• **keep an appointment**
**04** meet

**apportion**
**04** deal, mete **05** allot, carve, grant, share, stint, weigh **06** assign, divide, morsel, number, ration **07** deal out, dole out, hand out, mete out
**08** allocate, dispense, share out
**09** admeasure, ration out **10** distribute, measure out

**apportionment**
**05** grant, share **06** ration **07** dealing, handout, sharing **08** division
**09** allotment, rationing **10** allocation, assignment **12** dispensation, distribution

**apposite**
**03** apt **06** suited **07** apropos, germane, in point **08** relevant, suitable
**09** befitting, pertinent **10** applicable, to the point **11** appropriate **12** to the purpose

**appraisal**
◇ *anagram indicator*
**05** assay, prise, prize **06** rating, review, survey **07** opinion **08** estimate, once-over **09** judgement, reckoning, valuation **10** assessment, estimation, evaluation, inspection **11** examination
**12** appreciation

**appraise**
**04** rate **05** assay, judge, sum up, value
**06** assess, review, size up, survey
**07** examine, inspect, valuate
**08** estimate, evaluate, once-over

**appreciable**
**04** vast **08** definite, sensible
**10** noticeable, ponderable
**11** discernible, perceptible, significant, substantial **12** considerable, recognizable

**appreciably**
**08** markedly **10** definitely, noticeably
**11** perceptibly **12** considerably
**13** significantly, substantially

**appreciate**
**03** see **04** gain, go up, grow, know, like, rise **05** enjoy, grasp, mount, prize, sense, thank, value **06** admire, esteem, regard, relish, savour **07** apprise,

apprize, cherish, enhance, improve, inflate, realize, respect, welcome **08** increase, perceive, treasure **09** be aware of, recognize **10** comprehend, strengthen, understand **11** acknowledge **12** be indebted to, take kindly to **13** be conscious of, be grateful for, be sensitive to, give thanks for, think highly of **14** be appreciative, sympathize with

**appreciation**
**04** gain, rise **05** grasp, sense **06** esteem, growth, liking, notice, praise, regard, relish, review, thanks **07** feeling, respect, valuing **08** analysis, critique, increase, sympathy **09** awareness, enjoyment, gratitude, inflation, judgement, knowledge, valuation **10** admiration, assessment, cognizance, commentary, escalation, estimation, evaluation, obligation, perception, respecting **11** enhancement, high opinion, improvement, realization, recognition, sensitivity **12** gratefulness, indebtedness, thankfulness **13** comprehension, understanding **14** responsiveness **15** acknowledgement

• **expression of appreciation**
**02** ta **05** merci, mercy, super **06** cheers!, phwoah, phwoar, thanks **08** thank you **10** danke schon

**appreciative**
**07** mindful, obliged, pleased **08** admiring, beholden, grateful, indebted, thankful **09** conscious, sensitive **10** perceptive, respectful, responsive, supportive **11** encouraging **12** enthusiastic **13** knowledgeable

**apprehend**
**03** nab, see **04** bust, grab, nick, take, twig **05** catch, grasp, run in, seize **06** arrest, collar, detain, pick up, pull in **07** believe, capture, realize **08** conceive, consider, perceive **09** deprehend, recognize **10** comprehend, understand

**apprehension**
**04** fear **05** alarm, doubt, dread, grasp, qualm, worry **06** arrest, belief, noesis, taking, unease, uptake **07** anxiety, capture, concern, jitters, seizure, willies **08** disquiet, mistrust **09** detention, misgiving, suspicion **10** cognizance, conception, foreboding, perception, the willies, uneasiness **11** butterflies, discernment, nervousness, realization, recognition, trepidation **12** collywobbles, intellection, perturbation **13** comprehension, heebie-jeebies, understanding

**apprehensive**
**04** toey **06** afraid, uneasy **07** alarmed, anxious, fearful, nervous, worried **08** bothered, doubtful, insecure **09** concerned **10** suspicious **11** distrustful, mistrustful **13** on tenterhooks

**apprehensively**
**08** uneasily **09** anxiously, fearfully, nervously **10** doubtfully **12** suspiciously **13** distrustfully, mistrustfully

**apprentice**
**01** L **03** app, cub **04** snob, tiro, tyro **05** cadet, maiko, pupil **06** commis, indent, intern, novice, rookie **07** flat cap, learner, recruit, starter, student, trainee **08** beginner, improver, newcomer, prentice, servitor, turnover **11** probationer **13** printer's devil

**apprenticeship**
**09** Lehrjahre, novitiate **11** studentship, traineeship, trial period **14** training period

**apprise**
**04** tell, warn **05** brief **06** advise, inform, notify, tip off **08** acquaint, intimate **09** ascertain, enlighten **11** communicate

**approach**
◇ *juxtaposition indicator*
**03** nie, way **04** cost, draw, meet, near, nigh, plea, road **05** abord, anear, angle, begin, close, coast, coste, drive, greet, knock, means, reach, run-in, slant, style, treat **06** access, accost, advent, appeal, arrive, avenue, broach, coming, gain on, go near, invite, manner, method, stance, system, tackle, talk to **07** accoast, address, advance, apply to, arrival, catch up, contact, doorway, get onto, mention, opinion, passage, request, speak to, succeed, tactics **08** advances, appeal to, attitude, bear down, border on, commence, deal with, draw near, driveway, embark on, entrance, go nearer, landfall, oncoming, overture, position, proposal, set about, sound out, strategy **09** introduce, overtures, procedure, technique, threshold, undertake, viewpoint **10** buttonhole, come closer, come nearer, come near to, coming near, invitation, launch into, standpoint, suggestion **11** application, appropinque, approximate, come close to, coming close, compare with, get closer to, move towards, perspective, point of view, proposition, suggestions **12** make advances **13** appropinquate, make overtures, modus operandi **14** advance towards, course of action, get in touch with, proceed towards

**approachable**
**04** open, warm **07** affable **08** friendly, informal, pleasant, sociable **09** agreeable, congenial, get-at-able, reachable, welcoming **10** accessible, attainable **15** easy to get on with

**approbation**
**06** esteem, favour, praise **07** respect **08** applause, approval **09** allowance, laudation **10** acceptance, well-liking **11** countenance, endorsement, good opinion, recognition **12** commendation **13** encouragement

**appropriate**
**03** apt, fit, nab **04** jump, lift, meet, nick, sink, take **05** annex, filch, pinch, right, seize, steal, swipe, usurp **06** assume, choice, pilfer, pocket, proper, seemly, spot-on, suited, thieve, timely **07** apropos, correct, fitting, germane, impound, in order, pre-empt, purloin, trouser **08** accepted, arrogate, becoming, embezzle, glom on to, knock off, liberate, peculate, property, relevant, suitable **09** befitting, congruous, expedient, opportune, pertinent, well-timed **10** applicable, commandeer, confiscate, felicitous, seasonable, to the point, well-chosen **11** appurtenant, expropriate, in character, make off with, requisition **12** appertaining **14** misappropriate

**appropriately**
**07** apropos **08** properly, suitably **09** correctly, fittingly **10** relevantly **12** felicitously

**approval**
**02** OK **03** nod **04** okay, wink **05** favor, leave, voice **06** assent, esteem, favour, honour, liking, praise, regard **07** acclaim, approof, consent, go-ahead, licence, mandate, plaudit, respect, support **08** agrément, applause, blessing, sanction, thumbs-up **09** agreement **10** acceptance, admiration, green light, imprimatur, permission, validation **11** acclamation, approbation, concurrence, endorsement, good opinion, rubber stamp **12** appreciation, commendation, confirmation, ratification **13** authorization, certification **14** recommendation

• **expression of approval**
**02** ay, OK **03** aye, oke, olé, rah, yay **04** good, hear, okay, viva, vive **05** bravo, hurra, huzza, there, vivat **06** beauty, hooray, hurrah, hurray **07** attaboy, too much, top-hole, way to go! **08** attagirl, long live, zindabad **09** full marks, good on you **10** good for you, hubba hubba

**approve**
**02** OK **03** buy, dig **04** amen, back, like, pass **05** adopt, allow, bless, carry **06** accept, admire, concur, esteem, favour, permit, praise, ratify, regard, second, uphold **07** acclaim, agree to, applaud, commend, confirm, endorse, mandate, support **08** accede to, assent to, hold with, sanction, validate **09** authorize, consent to, recommend **10** appreciate, homologate **11** countenance, rubber-stamp, think well of **12** give the nod to **13** be pleased with, think highly of

**approved**
**03** app **06** proper **07** correct **08** accepted, favoured, official, orthodox **09** permitted, preferred **10** authorized, recognized, sanctioned **11** comme il faut, permissible, recommended **13** authoritative

**approving**
**08** admiring, praising **09** laudatory **10** favourable, respectful, supportive **12** appreciative, commendatory

**approvingly**
**10** admiringly, favourably **12** with pleasure **14** appreciatively

**approximate**
**03** app **04** like, near, wild **05** close, loose, rough, round **06** coarse **07** guessed, inexact, similar, verge on **08** approach, ballpark, border on, relative, resemble **09** estimated, imprecise **10** come near to **11** be similar to, come close to **14** be tantamount to

**approximately**
**01** c **02** ca **03** odd, say **04** or so, some **05** about, circa **06** around, nearly **07** close to, loosely, roughly **09** just about, not far off, rounded up **10** give or take, more or less, round about **11** approaching, rounded down **13** in the region of, or thereabouts, something like **14** in round figures, in round numbers **15** in the vicinity of

**approximation**
**05** guess **08** approach, estimate, likeness **09** rough idea, semblance **10** conjecture, estimation, similarity **11** guesstimate, resemblance **14** ballpark figure, correspondence

**appurtenance**
**09** equipment, trappings **10** belongings **11** accessories, impedimenta **13** paraphernalia

**April**
**03** Apr

**a priori**
**07** deduced **08** inferred **11** conjectural, theoretical **12** hypothetical **13** suppositional

**apron**
**03** bay, bib, rim **04** brat, edge, tier **05** dicky, skirt **06** border, dickey, dickie, fringe, napron, pinnie, tabard **07** placket, tablier **08** pinafore, standing **09** barm-cloth, forecourt, periphery **10** loading bay **12** hard-standing

**apropos**
**02** re **03** apt **05** right **06** proper, seemly, timely **07** correct, fitting **08** accepted, becoming, relevant, suitable **09** befitting, opportune, pertinent, regarding **10** applicable, felicitous, respecting, seasonable, to the point, well-chosen **11** in respect of **12** in relation to, with regard to **13** with respect to **14** on the subject of **15** with reference to

**apse**
**04** bema **06** concha, exedra **07** exhedra **09** apsidiole, prothesis

**apt**
**03** fit **04** gleg **05** given, happy, prone, ready **06** liable, likely, proper, seemly, spot-on, timely, toward **07** correct, fitting, germane, subject, tending **08** accurate, apposite, disposed, inclined, relevant, suitable **10** acceptable, applicable, seasonable **11** appropriate

**aptitude**
**04** bent, gift, turn **05** flair, skill **06** talent **07** ability, faculty, fitness, leaning **08** capacity, facility, tendency **09** endowment, quickness **10** capability, cleverness **11** disposition, inclination, proficiency **12** intelligence **14** natural ability

**aptly**
**05** fitly **08** suitably **09** fittingly **10** appositely, relevantly, to the point **13** appropriately

**aquatic**
**03** sea **05** fluid, river, water **06** liquid, marine, watery **07** fluvial **08** maritime, nautical

**aquiline**
**06** hooked **10** hooknosed

**Arab**
**02** Ar

*Arab League countries:*

**03** UAE
**04** Iraq, Oman
**05** Egypt, Libya, Qatar, Sudan, Syria, Yemen
**06** Jordan, Kuwait
**07** Algeria, Bahrain, Comoros, Lebanon, Morocco, Somalia, Tunisia
**08** Djibouti
**09** Palestine
**10** Mauritania
**11** Saudi Arabia
**18** United Arab Emirates

**Arabic**
**02** Ar **04** Arab
*See also* **alphabet**

**arable**
**03** lay, lea, lee, ley **06** fecund **07** fertile **08** farmable, fruitful, tillable **10** cultivable, ploughable, productive
*See also* **crop**

**arachnid** *see* **spider**

**arbiter**
**05** judge **06** expert, master, pundit, umpire **07** oddsman, referee **08** governor **09** authority, birlieman, byrlaw-man **10** controller **11** adjudicator

**arbitrarily**
**08** by chance, randomly **11** illogically **12** irrationally, subjectively, unreasonably **14** inconsistently

**arbitrary**
**06** chance, random **08** absolute, despotic, dogmatic, personal **09** illogical, imperious, whimsical **10** autocratic, capricious, dominative, high-handed, irrational, subjective, tyrannical, unreasoned **11** dictatorial, domineering, instinctive, magisterial, overbearing **12** conventional, inconsistent, unreasonable **13** discretionary

**arbitrate**
**05** judge **06** decide, settle, umpire **07** mediate, referee **09** determine **10** adjudicate **13** pass judgement **14** sit in judgement

**arbitration**
**08** decision **09** arbitrage, judgement, mediation **10** compromise, settlement **11** arbitrament, negotiation **12** adjudication, intervention **13** determination

**arbitrator**
**03** ref, ump **05** judge **06** umpire **07** arbiter, referee **08** mediator **09** go-between, moderator **10** negotiator **11** adjudicator **12** intermediary

**arbour**
**03** bay **05** bower **06** alcove, grotto, herbar, recess **07** pergola, retreat, shelter **09** sanctuary

**arc**
**03** bow **04** arch, bend, spin, turn **05** curve, round **06** swerve **09** curvature **10** curved line, semicircle

**arcade**
**04** mall, stoa **05** plaza **06** loggia, piazza **07** gallery, portico **08** cloister, galleria, precinct **09** colonnade, peristyle, triforium **10** covered way **12** shopping mall

**arcane**
**06** hidden, occult, secret **07** cryptic, obscure **08** abstruse, esoteric, mystical, profound **09** concealed, enigmatic, recondite **10** mysterious

**arch**
◇ *anagram indicator*
**03** arc, bow, hog, sly **04** bend, dome, hoop, span **05** chief, curve, embow, ogive, roach, vault **06** bridge, camber, diadem, girdle, invert, portal, shrewd, zygoma **07** archway, concave, cunning, playful, roguish, squinch, waggish **08** cross-rib, espiègle, platband **09** curvature, principal **10** manteltree, mysterious, semicircle **11** counterfort, mischievous **13** arc de triomphe

*Arches include:*

**04** keel, ogee, skew
**05** round, Tudor
**06** convex, corbel, Gothic, lancet, Norman, tented
**07** pointed, stilted, trefoil
**09** Ctesiphon, horseshoe, parabolic, segmental, triumphal
**10** four-centre, proscenium, shouldered
**11** equilateral
**12** basket handle

**archaeology**

*Archaeological terms include:*

**03** cup, dig, jar, jug, tor, urn
**04** adze, bowl, celt, cist, core, kist, site, tell
**05** blade, burin, cairn, ditch, flake, flask, flint, henge, hoard, mound, mummy, shard, sherd, stele, whorl
**06** barrow, beaker, bogman, dolmen, dromos, eolith, menhir, midden, mosaic, patina, strata, trench
**07** amphora, anomaly, cave art, crannog, handaxe, Iron Age, neolith, obelisk, papyrus, rock art, sondage, stratum, tumulus
**08** artefact, artifact, cromlech, excavate, hill fort, knapping, ley lines, megalith, post hole, Stone Age
**09** arrowhead, Bronze Age, cartouche, crop-marks, earthwork, enclosure, hypocaust, longhouse, Neolithic
**10** Anglo-Saxon, assemblage, excavation, geophysics, grave goods, inhumation, roundhouse, tear bottle
**11** burial mound, rock shelter, stone circle
**12** amphitheatre, archaeometry, carbon dating, field walking, Interglacial, Palaeolithic, stratigraphy
**13** kitchen-midden, standing stone, treasure trove, wattle and daub
**14** hunter-gatherer

*Archaeologists include:*

**04** **Uhle** (Max)
**05** **Clark** (Grahame), **Evans** (Sir Arthur)
**06** **Anning** (Mary), **Breuil** (Henri), **Carter** (Howard), **Childe** (Gordon), **Clarke** (David L), **Daniel** (Glyn), **Hawkes** (Jacquetta), **Kidder** (A V), **Layard** (Sir Austen), **Leakey** (Louis), **Leakey** (Mary), **Petrie** (Sir Flinders), **Putnam** (Frederic Ward)
**07** **Binford** (Lewis), **Renfrew** (Colin, Lord), **Thomsen** (Christian), **Wheeler** (Sir Mortimer), **Woolley** (Sir Leonard), **Worsaae** (Jens Jacob)
**08** **Breasted** (J H), **Cunliffe** (Barry), **Fiorelli** (Giuseppe), **Koldewey** (Robert), **Mallowan** (Sir Max), **Mariette** (Auguste), **Marshall** (Sir John)
**09** **Andersson** (Johan Gunnar)
**10** **Pitt-Rivers** (Augustus), **Schliemann** (Heinrich)
**11** **Champollion** (Jean François)

**archaic**
**03** old **05** passé **06** bygone, old hat, quaint **07** ancient, antique
**08** medieval, obsolete, outdated, outmoded **09** mediaeval, out-of-date, primitive **10** antiquated
**11** obsolescent, out of the ark
**12** antediluvian, old-fashioned

**archangel**
**08** hierarch **10** dead-nettle **14** garden angelica

*See also* **angel**

**archbishop**
**03** abp **07** primate **12** metropolitan

*See also* **cardinal**

*Archbishops include:*

**04** **Gray** (Gordon), **Hope** (David), **Hume** (Basil), **Kemp** (John), **Lang** (Cosmo), **Laud** (William), **Tutu** (Desmond)
**05** **Beran** (Josef), **Carey** (George), **Glemp** (Jozef)
**06** **Anselm**, **Beaton** (David), **Becket** (Thomas à), **Benson** (Edward White), **Blanch** (Stuart), **Coggan** (Donald), **Edmund** (St), **Fisher** (Geoffrey), **Heenan** (John Carmel), **Hilary** (of Poitiers, St), **Mannix** (Daniel), **Morton** (John), **Parker** (Matthew), **Potter** (John), **Ramsay** (Michael), **Runcie** (Robert), **Temple** (Frederick), **Temple** (William), **Trench** (Richard Chenevix), **Ussher** (James), **Walter** (Hubert), **Warham** (William), **Wolsey** (Thomas)
**07** **Arundel** (Thomas), **Cranmer** (Thomas), **Dunstan** (St), **Habgood** (John), **Langton** (Stephen), **Mendoza** (Pedro Gonzalez de), **Sentamu** (John), **Sheldon** (Gilbert), **Wiseman** (Nicholas)
**08** **Adalbert**, **Cuthbert**, **Davidson** (Randall), **Ethelred**, **Makarios**, **Whitgift** (John), **Williams** (Rowan)
**09** **Augustine** (St), **Wyszynski** (Stefan)
**10** **Damaskinos**, **Huddleston** (Trevor)

**archdiocese** *see* **diocese**

**archer**
**04** Eros, Tell **05** Cupid **06** bow-boy, bowman **09** sagittary **11** Sagittarius, toxophilite

**archetypal**
**05** ideal, model, stock **07** classic, typical **08** original, standard
**09** exemplary **12** paradigmatic
**14** characteristic, quintessential, representative

**archetype**
**04** form, idea, type **05** ideal, model
**06** entity **07** classic, epitome, pattern
**08** exemplar, original, paradigm, standard **09** precursor, prototype
**10** stereotype **12** quintessence, typification

**archipelago**

*Archipelagoes include:*

**04** Cuba, Fiji, Sulu
**05** Åland, Gulag, Japan, Malay, Malta, Tonga
**06** Arctic, Azores, Chagos, Kosrae, Tuvalu
**07** Bahamas, Mayotte, Tuamotu
**08** Bismarck, Cyclades, Kiribati, Maldives, Moluccas, Svalbard
**09** Alexander, Antarctic, Cape Verde, Catherine, Galápagos, Indonesia, Louisiade, Marquesas, North Land
**10** Ahvenanmaa, Les Iles d'Or, Seychelles, Vesterålen, West Indies
**11** Iles d'Hyères, Line Islands, Philippines, Spitsbergen, Vesteraalen
**12** Kuril Islands, Novaya Zemlya, Pearl Islands, Spice Islands, Sunda Islands
**13** Aegean Islands, Caicos Islands, Canary Islands, Ellice Islands, Ionian Islands, Tubuai Islands
**14** Austral Islands, Bijagos Islands, Channel Islands, Franz Josef Land, Gilbert Islands, Leeward Islands, Lofoten Islands, Nicholas II Land, Oki Archipelago, Papua New Guinea, Phoenix Islands, Solomon Islands, Tierra del Fuego, Visayan Islands
**15** Balearic Islands, Friendly Islands, Marshall Islands, Pitcairn Islands, Severnaya Zemlya, Wallis and Futuna, Windward Islands

**architect**
**05** maker **06** author, shaper
**07** creator, founder, planner
**08** designer, engineer, inventor
**10** instigator, mastermind, originator, prime mover **11** constructor, draughtsman **13** master builder

*Architects include:*

**04** **Adam** (Robert), **Drew** (Dame Jane), **Loos** (Adolf), **Nash** (John), **Shaw** (Norman), **Wren** (Sir Christopher)
**05** **Aalto** (Alvar), **Barry** (Sir Charles), **Costa** (Lucio), **Dudok** (Willem), **Gaudí** (Antonio), **Jones** (Inigo), **Meier** (Richard), **Nervi** (Pier Luigi), **Piano** (Renzo), **Pugin** (Augustus), **Scott** (Sir George Gilbert), **Scott** (Sir Giles Gilbert), **Soane** (Sir John), **Speer** (Albert), **Velde** (Henri van de)
**06** **Casson** (Sir Hugh), **Cubitt** (Thomas), **Foster** (Sir Norman), **Giotto**, **Howard** (Sir Ebenezer), **Lescot** (Pierre), **Morris** (William), **Paxton** (Sir Joseph), **Pisano** (Giovanni), **Rogers** (Sir Richard), **Semper** (Gottfried), **Serlio** (Sebastiano), **Spence** (Sir Basil), **Wright** (Frank Lloyd)
**07** **Alberti** (Leon Battista), **Asplund** (Erik Gunnar), **Behrens** (Peter), **Bernini** (Gian Lorenzo), **Gropius** (Walter), **Ictinus**, **Imhotep**, **Lutyens** (Sir Edwin), **Olmsted** (Frederick Law), **Vignola** (Giacomo da)
**08** **Bramante** (Donato), **Jacobsen** (Arne), **Miralles** (Enric), **Niemeyer** (Oscar), **Palladio** (Andrea), **Piranesi** (Giambattista), **Saarinen** (Eero), **Sottsass** (Ettore), **Stirling** (James), **Sullivan** (Louis), **Vanbrugh** (Sir John)
**09** **Borromini** (Francesco), **Haussmann** (Georges, Baron), **Hawksmoor** (Nicholas), **Libeskind** (Daniel), **Mackmurdo** (Arthur), **Vitruvius**
**10** **Mackintosh** (Charles Rennie)
**11** **Le Corbusier**
**12** **Brunelleschi** (Filippo), **Viollet-Le-Duc** (Eugène)
**14** **Mies van der Rohe** (Ludwig)
**15** **Leonardo da Vinci**

**architecture**
**04** form **05** frame, set-up, style **06** design, make-up, system **08** building, planning **09** designing, framework, structure **11** arrangement, composition **12** conformation, constitution, construction, organization **13** configuration **14** architectonics

*Architecture styles include:*

**04** Adam
**05** Greek, Saxon
**06** Gothic, modern, Norman, rococo
**07** barocco, baroque, Italian, Lombard, mission, mudéjar
**08** baronial, high tech
**09** beaux arts, brutalism, Byzantine, Cape Dutch, decorated, Palladian, Queen Anne
**10** art nouveau, Corinthian, Romanesque
**11** Elizabethan, Renaissance
**13** Gothic revival, international, neoclassicism, Perpendicular, post-modernism
**15** churrigueresque

*Architectural features include:*

**03** orb, web
**04** anta, apse, arch, base, bell, boss, cove, crop, cusp, cyma, dado, drum, list, neck, ribs, vase, void
**05** antae, attic, congé, crown, flute, gable, gavel, glyph, groin, gutta, hance, helix, mould, nerve, ogive, print, pylon, quirk, scape, socle, spire, stria, talon, tenia, tondo, torus, tower, truss, vault
**06** abacus, atrium, canton, caulis, chevet, cinque, cippus, column, concha, congee, coping, corona, coving, crenel, dentil, facade, fascia, fillet, finial, flèche, fornix, frieze, haunch, impost, lierne, metope, patera, patten, pillar, podium, portal, reglet, regula, rosace, scotia, severy, striae, taenia, turret, wreath
**07** aileron, annulet, balloon, bandrol, capital, cavetti, cavetto, conchae, corbeil, cornice, crocket, diglyph, doucine, echinus, fantail, festoon, fronton, fusarol, grecque, larmier, mullion, necking, nervure, pannier, parapet, Persian, pilotis, portico, rosette, solidum, squinch, surbase, tambour, telamon, tondino
**08** abutment, accolade, apophyge, astragal, baguette, bandelet, banderol, bannerol, bellcote, buttress, canephor, cartouch, chapiter, chaptrel, ciborium, cincture, crenelle, diastyle, dipteral, dipteros, entresol, epistyle, frontoon, fusarole, gorgerin, imperial, intrados, mascaron, moulding, pediment, pilaster, prostyle, pulpitum, rockwork, sept-foil, skewback, spandrel, spandril, terminus, triglyph, tympanum, voussoir
**09** apsidiole, archivolt, balection, banderole, bolection, cartouche, crossette, cul-de-four, decastyle, embrasure, embrazure, foliation, guilloche, hypostyle, mezzanine, modillion, octastyle, octostyle, peristyle, strap work, stylobate, tierceron, triforium, water leaf
**10** acroterion, architrave, ball-flower, bratticing, cauliculus, chambranle, clearstory, clerestory, demicupola, ditriglyph, egg-and-dart, eye-catcher, feathering, jerkinhead, pendentive, quatrefoil, subarcuate, water table, weathering
**11** brattishing, entablature, paternoster
**12** egg-and-anchor, egg-and-tongue, frontispiece
**13** chain moulding, interpilaster, quatrefeuille, vermiculation
**14** Catherine-wheel, flying buttress

*See also* **arch**

*Architectural and building terms include:*

**04** dado, dome, jamb, roof
**05** Doric, eaves, groin, Ionic, ridge, Tudor
**06** alcove, annexe, coving, duplex, façade, fascia, fillet, finial, frieze, Gothic, lintel, Norman, pagoda, plinth, reveal, rococo, scroll, soffit, stucco, Tuscan
**07** baroque, cornice, festoon, fletton, fluting, mullion, pantile, parapet, rafters, Regency, rotunda
**08** baluster, capstone, dogtooth, dry-stone, gargoyle, Georgian, pinnacle, sacristy, terrazzo, wainscot
**09** bas relief, classical, Edwardian, elevation, gatehouse, Queen Anne, roughcast
**10** architrave, barge-board, Corinthian, drawbridge, flamboyant, groundplan, Romanesque, weathering
**11** coping stone, corner-stone, Elizabethan, Flemish bond
**12** Early English, frontispiece, half-timbered

**archives**
**04** roll **05** deeds **06** annals, papers **07** ledgers, records **09** documents, memorials, registers **10** chronicles **11** memorabilia

**arctic**
**05** polar **06** boreal, frosty, frozen **07** glacial, subzero **08** Far North, freezing, Siberian **11** far northern, hyperborean **12** bitterly cold, freezing cold

**• arctic animal**
**09** polar bear

**ardent**
**03** hot **04** avid, keen, warm **05** eager, fiery **06** fervid, fierce, strong **07** burning, devoted, fervent, intense, mettled, zealous **08** sanguine, spirited, vehement **09** dedicated, perfervid, spiritous **10** mettlesome, passionate **11** empassioned, evangelical, impassioned, warm-blooded **12** enthusiastic **14** enthusiastical

**• be ardent**
**04** glow

**ardently**
**05** hotly **06** avidly, warmly **07** eagerly **08** strongly **09** devotedly, fervently, intensely, zealously **10** vehemently **12** passionately

**ardour**
**04** fire, heat, lust, rage, zeal, zest **05** flame, wrath **06** duende, fervor, spirit, warmth **07** avidity, fervour, passion **08** covetise, devotion, keenness **09** animation, eagerness, intensity, vehemence **10** dedication, enthusiasm **12** empressement

**arduous**
**04** hard **05** chore, harsh, heavy, steep, stiff, tough **06** severe, taxing, tiring, uphill **07** be a slog, onerous **08** be murder, daunting, rigorous, wearying **09** difficult, fatiguing, gruelling, laborious, punishing, strenuous **10** burdensome, exhausting, formidable **12** backbreaking

**are**
**01** A **04** live **05** exist

**area**
**01** A **04** beat, part, size, zone **05** field, manor, patch, place, range, realm, scope, tract, width, world **06** branch, domain, extent, parish, region, sector, sphere **07** breadth, compass, enclave, expanse, portion, quarter, section, stretch, terrain **08** district, environs, locality, precinct, province **09** territory **10** department **11** environment, reserve area **13** catchment area, neighbourhood

*See also* **administrative**; **council**; **county**; **district**

**arena**
**04** area, bowl, ring **05** field, realm, scene, world **06** domain, ground, sphere **07** stadium, theatre **08** coliseum, province **10** department, hippodrome **11** battlefield **12** amphitheatre, battleground **14** area of conflict

**Ares**
**04** Mars

**Argentina**
**02** RA **03** ARG

**argon**
**02** Ar

**argot**
**04** cant **05** idiom, slang **06** jargon **08** parlance

**arguable**
**04** moot **09** debatable, uncertain, undecided **10** disputable **11** contentious, open to doubt **12** questionable **14** controvertible, open to question

**arguably**
**05** maybe **08** possibly, probably **10** most likely **15** in all likelihood

**argue**
**03** rag, row **04** feud, hold, moot, show, spar **05** claim, fight, imply, nyaff, plead, prove **06** assert, bicker, cangle, debate, denote, haggle, hassle, reason **07** accurse, contend, declare, discuss, display, dispute, exhibit, fall out, quarrel, quibble, suggest, wrangle, wrestle **08** convince, disagree, dissuade, have a row, indicate, logicize, maintain, manifest, persuade, question, squabble **09** altercate, chop logic, have it out, have words, join issue, take issue, talk out of **10** chew the fat, chew the rag, contradict, hold a brief **11** cross swords, demonstrate, expostulate, remonstrate **13** be evidence for, have it out with **15** be at loggerheads, have a bone to pick

**argument**
**03** pro, row **04** beef, blue, case, feud, plot, spat, tiff, yike **05** claim, clash, fight, lemma, logic, run-in, set-to, theme, topic, yikes **06** barney, bust-up, contra, debate, dust-up, hassle, reason, ruckus, rumpus, tangle, thesis **07** contest, defence, dispute, fallacy, outline, polemic, quarrel, summary, wrangle **08** conflict, ding-dong, evidence, exchange, squabble, synopsis, trilemma **09** argy-bargy, assertion, enthymeme, objection, quodlibet, rationale, reasoning, syllogism **10** contention, discussion **11** altercation, controverse, controversy, declaration **12** antistrophon, disagreement **13** argumentation, demonstration, expostulation, justification, running battle, shouting-match, slanging-match **14** heated exchange

**argumentation**
**04** case **05** claim, logic **06** debate **07** defence **08** argument, disproof, evidence **09** rationale, reasoning **10** contention **13** expostulation, justification

**argumentative**
**06** chippy **07** stroppy **08** captious, contrary, perverse **09** litigious, polemical, truculent **11** belligerent, contentious, dissentious, opinionated, quarrelsome **12** cantankerous, disputatious

**arid**
**03** dry **04** drab, dull, flat **05** baked, vapid, waste **06** barren, boring, desert, dreary, jejune, meagre, torrid **07** parched, sterile, tedious **08** lifeless **09** infertile, torrefied, waterless **10** colourless, dehydrated, desiccated, monotonous, spiritless, uninspired **12** moistureless, shrivelled up, unproductive **13** uninteresting

**aright**
**02** OK **05** aptly, fitly, truly **07** exactly, rightly **08** properly, suitably **09** correctly **10** accurately

**arise**
◇ *reversal down indicator*
**04** come, flow, go up, lift, rise, soar, stem **05** begin, climb, ensue, get up, issue, mount, occur, start, tower **06** appear, ascend, come up, crop up, derive, emerge, follow, happen, result, rise up, spring **07** emanate, proceed, stand up **08** commence **10** be caused by **11** be a result of, come to light **12** straighten up **13** come into being, get to your feet, present itself

**aristocracy**
**04** nobs, rank **05** élite, lords, peers, toffs **06** gentry, ladies **07** peerage **08** nobility, noblemen **09** gentility, optimates, top drawer **10** haute monde, noblewomen, patricians, patriciate, upper class, upper crust **11** aristocrats, high society, ruling class **15** privileged class

**aristocrat**
**03** nob **04** lady, lord, peer, toff **05** noble **06** Junker **07** grandee, high-hat, peeress **08** eupatrid, nobleman, optimate **09** patrician **10** grande dame, noblewoman **13** grand seigneur

*See also* **nobility**

**aristocratic**
**01** U **05** élite, noble **06** lordly, titled **07** courtly, elegant, refined **08** highborn, well-born **09** dignified, patrician **10** upper-class, upper-crust **11** blue-blooded **12** thoroughbred

**arithmetic**
**07** algebra **08** algorism, logistic **11** computation

**Arizona**
**02** AZ **04** Ariz

**Arkansas**
**02** AR **03** Ark

**Arkwright**
**04** Noah

**arm**
**03** bay, fin, rig **04** barb, cove, gird, heel, iron, limb, loch, prop, whip, wing **05** array, brace, crank, creek, equip, firth, force, index, inlet, issue, might, power, prime, rearm, steel, wiper **06** branch, outfit, sleeve, supply, weapon **07** channel, estuary, euripus, forearm, fortify, furnish, passage, prepare, protect, provide, quillon, sea loch, section **08** accoutre, brachium, division, embattle, offshoot, strength **09** appendage, authority, extension, reinforce, upper limb **10** department, detachment, projection, strengthen **12** embranchment **15** windscreen-wiper

**armada**
**04** navy **05** fleet **08** flotilla, squadron **10** naval force

**armadillo**
**04** peba **05** tatou **07** Dasypus, tatouay **10** pichiciego

**armaments**
**04** arms, guns **06** cannon **07** weapons **08** ordnance, weaponry **09** artillery, munitions **10** ammunition

**armed**
**06** fitted **07** packing **08** tooled up
• **armed man**
**03** gun

**armed services** *see* **army**; **air force**; **military**; **navy**; **rank**

**Armenia**
**02** AM **03** ARM

**armistice**
**04** pact **05** peace, truce **09** ceasefire **10** still-stand **11** peace treaty

**armour**
**04** gear, gere, mail, weed **05** plate, proof, stand **06** corium, shield **07** panoply **08** armature **12** iron-cladding

*Armour includes:*

**04** cush, jack, jamb, lame, mail, suit, tace
**05** armet, brace, cuish, culet, curat, jambe, salet, tasse, visor
**06** beaver, byrnie, casque, couter, crinet, cuisse, curiet, faulds, gorget, greave, grille, gusset, helmet, jamber, morion, poleyn, rondel, salade, sallet, taslet, tasset, tonlet, tuille, voider
**07** ailette, barding, basinet, besagew, brasset, buckler, cap-à-pie, corslet, cuirass, harness, hauberk, jambeau, jambeux, jambier, lamboys, morrion, palette, placcat, placket, poitrel, puldron, sabaton, surcoat, ventail
**08** aventail, bascinet, brassard, brassart, chaffron, chamfron, chausses, corselet, gauntlet, giambeux, jambeaux, jazerant, pauldron, pectoral, placcate, pouldron, shynbald, solleret, spaulder, vambrace, ventaile, ventayle
**09** aventaile, backpiece, backplate, chain mail, chamfrain, garniture, habergeon, jesserant, mandilion, mandylion, nosepiece, rerebrace, vantbrace, vantbrass
**10** body armour, cataphract, coat-armour, coat of mail
**11** breastplate, genouillère, mentonnière, plate armour, scale armour
**12** splint armour

**armoured**
**06** plated **08** iron-clad, loricate **09** bomb-proof, protected, toughened **10** reinforced **11** bullet-proof, steel-plated **12** armour-plated

**armoury**
**05** depot, stock **07** arsenal **08** magazine **09** arms depot, garderobe, stockpile **10** repository **13** ordnance depot **14** ammunition dump

**armpit**
**05** oxter **06** axilla

**arms**
**04** guns **05** crest **06** cannon, emblem, shield **07** weapons **08** blazonry, firearms, heraldry, insignia, missiles, ordnance, weaponry **09** armaments, artillery, munitions **10** ammunition, coat-of-arms, escutcheon
**11** projectiles **14** heraldic device

**army**
**03** mob **04** host, pack, sena **05** crowd, horde, swarm **06** throng, troops
**07** cohorts, legions, militia
**08** brachial, infantry, military, soldiers, soldiery **09** multitude **10** armed force, arrière-ban, land forces **11** thin red line

*Armies include:*

**02** AA, SA, TA
**03** AVR, GAR, IRA, USA, WLA
**04** BAOR, INLA
**05** Sally
**06** Church, Tartan
**08** New Model
**09** Eurocorps, Salvation
**10** Blue Ribbon, Women's Land
**11** Grande Armée, Territorial

*See also* **rank**; **regiment**
• **army corps** *see* **regiment**
• **army regulation**
**02** AR

**aroma**
**04** nose **05** fumet, odour, scent, smell
**06** savour **07** bouquet, fumette, perfume **09** fragrance, redolence

**aromatic**
**05** balmy, fresh, spicy **07** pungent, savoury, scented **08** fragrant, perfumed, redolent **11** odoriferous
**12** sweet-scented **13** sweet-smelling

**around**
◇ *anagram indicator*
◇ *containment indicator*
◇ *reversal indicator*
**01** c **02** ca **04** near **05** about, circa, close, round **06** at hand, nearby, nearly
**07** all over, close by, close to, roughly
**08** framed by, to and fro **09** enclosing
**10** encircling, everywhere, more or less, on all sides, throughout
**11** surrounding, within reach
**12** circumjacent, encompassing, everywhere in, here and there, on all sides of, to all parts of
**13** approximately, circumambient, on every side of **15** in all directions

**arousal**
◇ *anagram indicator*
**06** firing **08** stirring **09** agitation, evocation **10** excitement
**11** provocation, titillation **12** getting going, inflammation

**arouse**
◇ *anagram indicator*
**04** fire, goad, move, spur, whet
**05** alarm, cause, evoke, incur, pique, rouse, spark, tease, waken **06** awaken, beat up, bestir, excite, incite, induce, kindle, prompt, stir up, turn on, wake up, whip up **07** agitate, animate, inflame, knock up, provoke, quicken, sharpen, startle, trigger, upraise **08** get going, summon up **09** call forth, eroticize, galvanize, impassion, instigate, stimulate, suscitate, titillate
**11** disentrance

**arraign**
**06** accuse, charge, impugn, indict
**07** appoint, empeach, impeach
**09** prosecute **11** incriminate **13** call to account

**arraignment**
**04** case **05** trial **06** charge
**07** summons **10** accusation, indictment **11** impeachment, legal action **13** incrimination

**arrange**
◇ *anagram indicator*
**02** do **03** fix, set **04** cast, comb, file, gang, list, make, plan, sift, size, sort, stow, tidy, tile, trim **05** adapt, agree, align, aline, array, braid, class, dress, fix up, grade, group, ink in, order, place, preen, range, score, set up, swing
**06** adjust, blouse, codify, decide, design, devise, digest, fettle, format, gather, lay out, line up, make up, ordain, set out, settle **07** address, article, blow-dry, concert, dispose, echelon, enrange, marshal, prepare, process, project, rummage, seriate, sort out, windrow **08** alphabet, classify, conclude, contrive, embattle, engineer, enraunge, organize, pencil in, position, regulate, rustle up, settle on, stratify **09** catalogue, collocate, determine, harmonize, methodize, negotiate, serialize **10** categorize, co-ordinate, distribute, foreordain, instrument, put in order, transcribe
**11** choreograph, configurate, orchestrate, systematize
**12** chronologize

**arranged**
**03** arr

**arrangement**
◇ *anagram indicator*
**03** lay **04** form, pack, plan **05** array, order, plans, score, set-up, taxis, terms
**06** design, detail, fixing, format, layout, line-up, method, scheme, system
**07** details, display, setting, version
**08** contract, disposal, grouping, ordnance, planning, position, schedule **09** agreement, Ausgleich, bandobast, bundobust, digestion, formation, preparing, structure
**10** adaptation, compromise, groundwork, schematism, settlement
**11** disposition, positioning, preparation
**12** modus vivendi, organization, preparations **13** configuration, harmonization, orchestration
**14** classification, interpretation
**15** instrumentation

**arranger**
**03** arr

**arrant**
**04** rank, vile **05** gross, utter **06** brazen
**07** blatant, extreme **08** absolute, complete, flagrant, infamous, outright, rascally, thorough **09** barefaced, downright, egregious, notorious, out-and-out **11** unmitigated **12** incorrigible
**13** thoroughgoing

**array**
◇ *anagram indicator*
**03** set **04** deck, garb, robe, show, trim
**05** adorn, align, dress, group, herse, order, range **06** attire, attrap, clothe, draw up, effeir, effere, lay out, line up, line-up, matrix, muster, parade, plight, spread **07** apparel, arrange, bedight, bedizen, display, dispose, exhibit, marshal, panoply **08** accoutre, assemble, decorate, position
**09** formation **10** assemblage, assortment, collection, exhibition, exposition, habilitate **11** arrangement, disposition, marshalling

**arrears**
**04** debt **05** debts **07** balance, deficit
**10** amount owed, money owing
**11** liabilities **14** sum of money owed
• **in arrears**
**04** late **05** owing **06** behind, in debt
**07** overdue **10** behindhand **11** back-ganging, outstanding

**arrest**
◇ *containment indicator*
**02** do **03** cop, lag, nab, nip, sus
**04** book, bust, grab, grip, halt, hold, lift, nail, nick, slow, stem, stop, suss
**05** block, catch, check, delay, pinch, rivet, run in, seize, stall **06** absorb, attach, collar, detain, engage, fixate, hinder, impede, nobble, pick up, pull in, retard, stasis, take up **07** attract, caption, capture, engross, inhibit, seizure, snabble, snaffle **08** intrigue, obstruct, restrain, slow down **09** apprehend, detention, epistasis, fascinate, interrupt
**11** nip in the bud **12** apprehension
**15** take into custody
• **under arrest**
**06** copped **09** in custody **11** in captivity

**arresting**
**07** amazing, notable **08** engaging, riveting, striking, stunning
**10** impressive, noteworthy, noticeable, remarkable, surprising **11** conspicuous, eye-catching, outstanding
**13** extraordinary

**arrival**
**03** arr **04** dawn **05** birth, comer, entry, guest, start **06** advent, blow-in, coming, income, origin **07** entrant, fresher, incomer, visitor **08** approach, debutant, entrance, freshman, newcomer, visitant **09** debutante, emergence, invention **10** appearance, homecoming, occurrence
**11** development

**arrive**
◇ *juxtaposition indicator*
**03** arr, get, hit **04** come, dock, gain, land, make, show **05** enter, fetch, get

to, occur, reach **06** accede, appear, attain, become, blow in, come in, come to, drop in, happen, make it, obtain, pull in, roll in, roll up, show up, swan in, swan up, turn up **07** achieve, check in, clock in, get here, pitch up, succeed, surface **08** get there **09** be present, hammer out, thrash out, touch down **10** accomplish, be a success, be produced, come to hand **11** get to the top, materialize **12** become famous **14** come on the scene **15** become available, come on the market

**arrogance**
**04** side **05** nerve, pride, scorn **06** hubris, hybris, morgue, vanity **07** conceit, disdain, egotism, hauteur, opinion **08** assuming, boasting, contempt, high hand, surquedy **09** contumely, insolence, lordiness, pomposity, surquedry **11** haughtiness, presumption, superiority **12** snobbishness **13** condescension, imperiousness **14** high-handedness, self-importance

**arrogant**
**04** high **05** cobby, proud, stout **06** lordly, uppity, wanton **07** haughty, stuck-up, topping **08** assuming, boastful, insolent, jumped-up, scornful, snobbish, superior **09** bigheaded, conceited, dangerous, egotistic, hubristic, imperious **10** disdainful, high-handed, hoity-toity **11** overbearing, overweening, patronizing, toffee-nosed **12** contemptuous, presumptuous, supercilious **13** condescending, high and mighty, self-important **14** full of yourself, on the high ropes

**arrogantly**
**04** high **07** proudly **09** haughtily **10** boastfully, insolently, scornfully, snobbishly **11** conceitedly, imperiously **12** disdainfully, high-handedly **13** hubristically, overbearingly, overweeningly, patronizingly **14** contemptuously, presumptuously, superciliously **15** condescendingly, self-importantly

**arrogate**
**05** seize, usurp **06** assume **07** presume **08** take over **10** commandeer **11** appropriate **14** misappropriate

**arrogation**
**07** seizure **10** assumption, possession, taking over **13** appropriation, commandeering

**arrow**
**03** any, ary **04** bolt, dart **05** shaft **06** flight, marker, quar'le **07** dogbolt, pointer, quarrel, sagitta **08** bird-bolt **09** butt-shaft, indicator **11** swallowtail **13** grey-goose wing **14** cloth-yard shaft, grey-goose quill, grey-goose shaft

**arrowhead**
**04** fork

**arrowroot**
**03** pia **07** Maranta

**arsenal**
**05** depot, stock **06** armory **07** armoury, weapons **08** magazine, weaponry **09** arms depot, garderobe, stockpile **10** repository **13** ordnance depot **14** ammunition dump

**arsenic**
**02** As

**arson**
**09** pyromania, saddlebow
**11** firebombing, fire-raising
**12** incendiarism

**arsonist**
**05** torch **07** firebug **10** firebomber, fire-raiser, incendiary, pyromaniac

**art**
**04** feat, gift **05** craft, flair, guile, knack, skill, trade **06** Arthur, deceit, design, method, talent **07** artwork, cunning, daubery, finesse, knowhow, mastery, sleight, slyness **08** aptitude, artistry, facility, strategy, trickery, wiliness **09** dexterity, expertise, ingenuity, technique **10** adroitness, artfulness, astuteness, craftiness, profession, shrewdness, virtuosity **12** creative work **13** craftsmanship **15** draughtsmanship

*See also* **Japanese**; **painting**; **sculpture**

*Arts and crafts include:*

**04** film
**05** batik, video
**06** fresco, mosaic, saikei
**07** carving, collage, crochet, drawing, etching, ikebana, origami, pottery, weaving
**08** ceramics, graphics, knitting, painting, pencraft, spinning, tapestry, tsutsumu
**09** animation, cloisonné, engraving, jewellery, marquetry, metalwork, modelling, patchwork, sculpture, sketching, woodcraft
**10** basketwork, caricature, embroidery, enamelling, needlework, xylography
**11** calligraphy, lithography, needlecraft, oil painting, photography, portraiture, psaligraphy, stitchcraft, watercolour, woodcarving, wood cutting
**12** animatronics, architecture, chalcography, illustration, stained glass
**13** digital design, graphic design, wood engraving
**14** relief printing, screenprinting

*See also* **picture**

*Schools, movements and styles of art include:*

**05** Nabis, Op Art, video
**06** Cubism, Gothic, Pop Art, Purism, Rococo
**07** Art Brut, Art Deco, Baroque, Bauhaus, Brit art, Dadaism, digital, Fauvism, folk art, Realism
**08** abstract, Barbizon, Bohemian, Futurism, Japonism, Venetian
**09** Byzantine, formalism, Mannerism, Modernism, Symbolism, Vorticism
**10** arte povera, Art Nouveau, automatism, classicism, Florentine, literalism, Minimal Art, Naturalism, New Realism, Romanesque, Surrealism
**11** Hellenistic, Pointillism, Primitivism, renaissance, Romanticism, Suprematism
**12** Aestheticism, magic realism, Quattrocento, Superrealism
**13** Arts and Crafts, Conceptual Art, Expressionism, Impressionism, Neoclassicism, Neo-Plasticism, Post-Modernism, Preraphaelite
**14** action painting, Constructivism

*Art materials and art-related terms include:*

**03** ink
**04** term, wash
**05** cameo, easel, fitch, liner, sable, smock, turps, video
**06** badger, crayon, fusain, pastel, pencil, relief, sketch, tusche
**07** atelier, cartoon, digital, modello, organic, palette, scumble, torchon
**08** abstract, alfresco, charcoal, gumption, intaglio, Luminism, monotint, paintbox, pastille
**09** lay-figure, pen and ink, stretcher
**10** delineavit, from nature, paint brush, sketchbook
**11** perspective, trompe l'oeil, wash drawing
**12** installation, underdrawing
**13** social realism
**15** oil of turpentine

• **work of art**
**06** doodle **09** Old Master

**artefact**
◇ *anagram indicator*
**04** item, tool **05** thing **06** object
**07** neolith **09** something
**10** palaeolith

**Artemis**
**05** Diana

**artery**
**02** M1 **04** duct, road, tube **06** vessel **07** channel, conduit **11** blood vessel

*See also* **vein**

**artful**
◇ *anagram indicator*
**03** sly **04** foxy, rusé, wily **05** dodgy, sharp, smart **06** cautel, clever, crafty, shrewd, subtle, tricky **07** cunning, devious, skilful, vulpine **08** masterly, scheming **09** cautelous, deceitful, designing, dexterous, ingenious **11** resourceful

**artfully**
◇ *anagram indicator*
**05** slyly **08** cleverly, craftily, shrewdly
**09** cunningly, deviously, skilfully
**11** deceitfully, ingeniously

**arthropod**

*Arthropods include:*

**09** trilobite, water bear
**10** tardigrade
**14** bear-animalcule

*See also* **crustacean**; **insect**; **invertebrate**; **spider**

**Arthurian legend** *see* **knight**; **legend**

**article**
**01** a **02** an, el, il, la, le, un **03** art, ein, les, the, une **04** eine, item, part, term, unit **05** curio, essay, paper, piece, point, story, thing **06** clause, exposé, object, report, review **07** account, exhibit, feature, portion, section, whatsit, write-up **08** artefact, offprint **09** commodity, editorial, monograph, paragraph, something, thingummy **10** boondoggle, commentary, subsection
**11** composition, constituent
**12** thingummybob, thingummyjig
**14** what-d'you-call-it

**articulate**
◇ *homophone indicator*
◇ *anagram indicator*
**03** say **04** talk **05** clear, frame, lucid, speak, state, utter, vocal, voice
**06** fluent, tongue, verbal **07** breathe, enounce, express, jointed, realize
**08** coherent, distinct, eloquent, vocalize **09** enunciate, pronounce, verbalize **10** expressive, meaningful, well-spoken **12** intelligible
**13** communicative
**14** comprehensible, understandable

**articulated**
◇ *homophone indicator*
◇ *anagram indicator*
**05** joint **06** hinged, joined, linked
**07** coupled, jointed **08** attached, fastened **09** connected, segmented
**10** vertebrate **11** interlocked **14** fitted together

**articulately**
**07** clearly, lucidly **08** fluently
**10** coherently, distinctly, eloquently
**12** expressively, intelligibly
**14** comprehensibly

**articulation**
**05** joint **06** saying **07** diction, segment, talking, voicing **08** coupling, delivery, jointing, junction, speaking, tonguing **09** arthrosis, clavation, consonant, gomphosis, utterance
**10** connection, expression
**11** diarthrosis, enunciation
**12** schindylesis, synarthrosis, vocalization **13** pronunciation, verbalization

**artifice**
**03** art, con, gin **04** ruse, scam, wile
**05** craft, dodge, fraud, guile, reach, set-up, shift, trick **06** deceit, device, scheme, tactic **07** cunning, shuffle, slyness **08** strategy, subtlety, trickery
**09** chicanery, deception, stratagem
**10** artfulness, cleverness, craftiness, subterfuge **11** contrivance, deviousness **12** contrivement
**14** davenport-trick

**artificial**
**03** art **04** fake, faux, mock, sham
**05** bogus, false, paste, pseud
**06** ersatz, forced, made-up, phoney, pseudo **07** assumed, feigned, man-made, plastic, studied **08** affected, mannered, specious, spurious
**09** contrived, imitation, insincere, pretended, processed, simulated, synthetic, unnatural **10** non-natural
**11** counterfeit **12** manufactured

**artificiality**
**04** sham **07** falsity **08** pretence
**10** simulation **11** insincerity
**12** speciousness, spuriousness
**13** theatricalism, theatricality, unnaturalness

**artificially**
**07** falsely **10** speciously, spuriously
**11** insincerely, unnaturally
**13** synthetically

**artillery**
**02** RA **03** AAA, art, RHA **04** arty, guns
**05** train **07** cannons, gunnery, weapons **08** cannonry, missiles, ordnance **09** heavy guns, munitions
**12** heavy weapons

**artisan**
**06** expert **07** pioneer **08** mechanic
**09** artificer, craftsman, operative
**10** journeyman, technician
**11** craftswoman **12** craftsperson
**13** skilled worker **14** handicraftsman

**artist**
**02** RA **03** ace, ARA, pro **04** poet
**05** actor, maker, maven, mavin
**06** author, dancer, expert, writer
**07** creator, dab hand, founder, maestro
**08** Bohemian, composer, inventor, musician **09** authority, mannerist, performer **10** originator, specialist, trecentist **12** professional
**13** perspectivist

*Artists, craftsmen and craftswomen include:*

**06** etcher, master, potter, weaver
**07** painter, printer
**08** animator, designer, engraver, sculptor
**09** architect, carpenter, goldsmith
**10** blacksmith, cartoonist, oil painter
**11** coppersmith, draughtsman, illustrator, miniaturist, portraitist, silversmith, web designer
**12** caricaturist, lithographer, photographer
**13** draughtswoman, graphic artist, screenprinter
**14** graffiti artist, pavement artist, watercolourist
**15** graphic designer

*See also* **painter**; **photograph**; **sculpture**

• **great artist**
**09** Old Master

**artiste**
**05** actor, comic **06** dancer, player, singer **07** actress, trouper
**08** comedian, musician **09** performer
**10** comedienne **11** entertainer
**12** vaudevillian **13** variety artist

**artistic**
**04** fine **06** gifted **07** elegant, refined, skilled, stylish **08** creative, cultured, graceful, original, talented, tasteful
**09** aesthetic, beautiful, exquisite, sensitive **10** attractive, cultivated, decorative, expressive, harmonious, ornamental **11** imaginative

**artistry**
**05** craft, flair, skill, style, touch
**06** genius, talent **07** ability, finesse, mastery **08** deftness **09** expertise
**10** brilliance, creativity **11** proficiency, sensitivity, workmanship
**13** craftsmanship **14** accomplishment

**artless**
**04** open, pure, true **05** frank, naive, naked, plain **06** candid, direct, honest, simple, unwary **07** genuine, natural, sincere **08** homespun, innocent, trusting **09** childlike, guileless, ingenuous, unworldly
**10** unaffected **11** undesigning
**13** unpretentious **15** straightforward, unsophisticated

**artlessly**
**05** truly **06** openly, purely, simply
**07** frankly, naively, plainly **08** candidly, directly **09** naturally, sincerely
**10** innocently **11** ingenuously
**15** unpretentiously

**Aruba**
**03** ABW

**as**
**02** eg, so, ut **03** als, qua **04** kame, like, when **05** being, esker, since, while
**06** just as, such as, whilst **07** arsenic, because, owing to, through
**09** forasmuch, similar to **10** for example, inasmuch as, seeing that
**11** as a result of, for instance, in the role of, on account of **12** in the guise of
**13** at the same time, functioning as, with the part of **14** simultaneously
**15** at the same time as, considering that

• **as for**
**07** apropos **09** as regards
**10** concerning, respecting **12** in relation to, with regard to **13** with respect to **14** on the subject of, with relation to **15** with reference to

• **as it were**
**05** quasi **06** in a way, kind of, second, sort of **07** so to say **09** in some way, so to speak **10** in some sort **11** as it might be

**asafoetida**
**04** hing

**asbestos**
**07** amosite **08** amiantus, rock wood
**09** amianthus, earthflax **10** chrysotile
**11** crocidolite **12** mountain wood

**ascend**
◇ *reversal down indicator*
**03** sty **04** go up, rise, soar, upgo **05** arise, climb, fly up, get up, mount, scale, tower **06** climax, come up, move up **07** float up, lift off, take off **10** gain height **12** slope upwards

**ascendancy**
**04** edge, sway **05** power
**07** command, control, mastery
**08** dominion, hegemony, lordship, prestige **09** authority, dominance, dominancy, influence, mobocracy, supremacy, upper hand
**10** domination, prevalence **11** pre-eminence, superiority
**12** predominance

**ascendant**
◇ *reversal down indicator*
**07** growing **08** dominant, powerful, superior **09** prevalent **10** developing **11** predominant **12** on the up and up **13** rising in power

**ascending**
**02** up

**ascent**
**04** hill, pull, ramp, rise **05** climb, slope **06** rising, uphill **07** advance, incline, scaling **08** anabasis, climbing, gradient, mounting, progress **09** acclivity, ascending, ascension, elevation
**10** escalation **11** advancement

**ascertain**
**03** fix, see **04** twig **05** learn, prove
**06** detect, locate, settle, verify
**07** confirm, find out, pin down, suss out **08** discover, identify, make sure
**09** determine, establish, get to know
**10** come to know, make sure of
**11** make certain

**ascetic**
**03** nun **04** Jain, monk, yogi **05** fakir, harsh, Jaina, plain, sadhu, stern
**06** Essene, hermit, saddhu, severe, strict **07** austere, dervish, Jainist, puritan, recluse, spartan, stylite
**08** celibate, Nazarite, rigorous, sannyasi, solitary **09** abstainer, abstinent, anchorite, Montanist, pillarist **10** abstemious **11** pillar-saint, puritanical, self-denying **14** self-controlled **15** self-disciplined

**asceticism**
**07** ascesis **08** severity **09** austerity, harshness **10** abstinence, self-denial
**11** monasticism, self-control **14** self-discipline

**ascidian**
**08** tunicate **09** sea squirt
**15** appendicularian

**ascribe**
**05** apply **06** assign, charge, credit, impute **07** put down, set down
**08** accredit, arrogate **09** attribute
**12** give credit to

**ash**
**04** kali, kelp, kilp **05** aizle, easle, rowan **06** embers, tephra **07** cinders, clinker, residue, witchen **08** charcoal, Ygdrasil **09** xanthoxyl, Yggdrasil **10** Yggdrasill
**11** nuée ardente **13** toothache tree
**15** Pharaoh's serpent

**ashamed**
**05** loath, sorry **06** guilty, modest
**07** abashed, bashful, humbled
**08** blushing, contrite, hesitant, penitent, red-faced, sheepish **09** mortified, reluctant, unwilling **10** apologetic, distressed, humiliated, remorseful, shamefaced **11** crestfallen, discomfited, discomposed, embarrassed **12** on a guilt trip **13** self-conscious

**ashen**
**03** wan **04** grey, pale **05** livid, pasty, white **06** leaden, pallid **07** anaemic, ghastly **08** blanched, bleached
**09** pale-faced **10** colourless

**ashore**
**05** aland **11** onto the land **12** onto the beach, onto the shore **15** towards the shore

**Asia**

*Asian countries include:*

**04** Laos
**05** Burma, China, India, Japan, Nepal
**06** Bhutan, Taiwan
**07** Myanmar, Vietnam
**08** Cambodia, Malaysia, Maldives, Mongolia, Pakistan, Sri Lanka, Thailand
**09** East Timor, Indonesia, Singapore
**10** Bangladesh, Kazakhstan, Kyrgyzstan, North Korea, South Korea, Tajikistan, Uzbekistan
**11** Afghanistan, Philippines
**12** Turkmenistan
**16** Brunei Darussalam

*Asian landmarks include:*

**05** Indus
**06** Ganges, Mekong, Mt Fuji
**07** Everest, Yangtze
**08** Krakatoa, Lake Sebu, Red River, Taj Mahal
**09** Angkor Wat, Annapurna, Great Wall, Himalayas, Hiroshima, Ming Tombs, Mt Everest
**10** Gobi Desert, River Indus, Sagarmatha, Sea of Japan, Thar Desert
**11** Brahmaputra, Mekong River, Three Gorges, Yellow River
**12** Golden Temple, Potala Palace, Raffles Hotel
**13** Forbidden City, Kangchenjunga
**14** Jaganath Temple
**15** Tiananmen Square

**Asian**

*Asians include:*

**03** Han, Lao
**04** Ainu, Cham, Nair, Shan, Sulu, Thai
**05** Bajau, Karen, Kazak, Nayar, Tajik, Tamil, Uzbeg, Uzbek, Vedda
**06** Afghan, Baluch, Gurkha, Indian, Kazakh, Kyrgyz, Manchu, Mongol, Pathan, Tadjik, Telugu
**07** Baluchi, Burmese, Chinese, Goanese, Goorkha, Karenni, Kirghiz, Laotian, Manchoo, Maratha, Russian, Tadzhik, Tagálog, Turkish, Turkmen
**08** Bruneian, Canarese, Filipina, Filipino, Japanese, Kanarese, Mahratta, Nepalese
**09** Bhutanese, Cambodian, Malaysian, Mongolian, Pakistani, Sri Lankan, Taiwanese
**10** Indonesian, Myanmarese, Vietnamese
**11** Azerbaijani, Bangladeshi, Kazakhstani, North Korean, Singaporean, South Korean, Tajikistani

**aside**
**02** by **04** away **05** alone, apart
**07** whisper **08** secretly **09** alongside, departure, monologue, on one side, privately, soliloquy, to one side
**10** apostrophe, digression, separately
**11** in isolation, out of the way, parenthesis **12** obiter dictum, stage whisper **13** cursory remark
**15** notwithstanding

**asinine**
**04** daft **05** crazy, inane, potty, silly
**06** absurd, stupid **07** fatuous, foolish, idiotic, moronic **08** gormless
**09** imbecilic, ludicrous, senseless
**10** half-witted **11** nonsensical

**ask**
**03** beg, bid, eft, sue **04** evet, newt, poll, pose, pray, pump, quiz, seek
**05** crave, grill, order, plead, posit, press, query, speer, speir, yearn
**06** appeal, demand, desire, invite, summon **07** beseech, bespeak, canvass, clamour, enquire, entreat, fire off, implore, inquire, propose, request, require, solicit, suggest **08** approach, have over, petition, propound, question **09** entertain, have round, interview, postulate **10** put forward, supplicate **11** interrogate, requisition
**12** cross-examine, put on the spot
**13** cross-question **14** put a question to
**15** give a grilling to

**askance**
**04** awry **07** asconce **08** sideways
**09** dubiously, obliquely **10** doubtfully, indirectly, scornfully **11** sceptically
**12** disdainfully, suspiciously
**13** distrustfully, mistrustfully
**14** contemptuously, disapprovingly

**askew**
◇ *anagram indicator*
**04** awry, skew **05** aglee, agley, tipsy
**06** skivie, squint **07** crooked, oblique
**08** lopsided, sideways **09** crookedly, obliquely, off-centre, out of line, skew-whiff **10** lopsidedly **12** asymmetrical
**14** asymmetrically

**asleep**
**04** numb **05** inert **06** dozing
**07** dormant, napping, resting
**08** comatose, inactive, reposing,

sleeping, snoozing **09** conked out, flaked out, nodded off, popped off **10** crashed out, fast asleep, sparked out **11** sound asleep, unconscious **13** out like a light **14** dead to the world, in the land of Nod, out for the count

**asparagus**
**05** sprew, sprue **06** smilax

**aspect**
**03** air **04** brow, face, look, side, view **05** angle, facet, light, phase, point, trine, visor, vizor **06** facies, factor, manner, phasis **07** bearing, contour, feature, outlook, respect, sextile **08** position, quartile, quincunx, quintile **09** dimension, direction, landscape **10** apparition, appearance, biquintile, complexion, expression, standpoint **11** conjunction, countenance, physiognomy, point of view **13** configuration

**asperity**
**08** acerbity, acrimony, severity, sourness **09** crossness, harshness, roughness, sharpness **10** bitterness, causticity **11** astringency, crabbedness, peevishness **12** abrasiveness, churlishness, irascibility, irritability

**aspersion**
**04** slur **07** calumny, slander

**• cast aspersions on**
**04** slur **05** knock, slate, smear **06** defame, vilify **07** censure, run down, slander **08** reproach **09** criticize, denigrate, deprecate, disparage **10** calumniate, sling mud at, throw mud at

**asphalt**
**08** uintaite **09** gilsonite, Jew's-pitch, uintahite **12** mineral pitch

**asphyxiate**
**03** gas **05** choke **06** stifle **07** smother **08** strangle, throttle **09** suffocate **11** strangulate

**asphyxiation**
**07** choking **08** stifling **10** smothering **11** suffocation **13** strangulation

**aspirant**
**06** donzel, squire **09** candidate

**aspirate**
**05** rough

**aspiration**
**03** aim, yen **04** goal, hope, wish **05** dream, ideal **06** desire, intent, object **07** craving, longing, purpose **08** ambition, yearning **09** breathing, endeavour, hankering, objective **10** pretension

**aspire**
**03** aim, yen **04** hope, long, mint, seek, wish **05** crave, dream, ettle, yearn **06** desire, hanker, intend, pursue **07** pretend, purpose **11** have as a goal, have as an aim

**aspiring**
**04** keen **05** eager **07** budding, hopeful, longing, wishful, would-be **08** aspirant, striving **09** ambitious, intending **10** optimistic **12** endeavouring, enterprising

**ass**
**03** fon, git, mug, nit, oaf, sot, yap **04** berk, cake, clot, cony, coof, dill, dope, dork, fool, geek, goop, gowk, gull, joss, moke, mule, nana, nerd, nerk, nong, pony, prat, soft, twit, yo-yo **05** burro, cluck, cuddy, dicky, dweeb, galah, hinny, idiot, Jenny, kiang, klutz, kulan, kyang, neddy, ninny, patch, schmo, snipe, sumph, twerp, wally **06** bampot, cretin, dickey, dimwit, donkey, dottle, drongo, koulan, nidget, nitwit, numpty, onager, quagga, sawney, turkey, wigeon **07** airhead, asinico, buffoon, gubbins, halfwit, jackass, jughead, lemming, muggins, natural, plonker, saphead, want-wit **08** dipstick, flathead, fondling, imbecile, innocent, lunkhead, mooncalf, numskull, omadhaun, Tom-noddy **09** blockhead, capocchia, dumb-cluck, dziggetai, lack-brain, lame brain, mumchance, schlemiel **10** nincompoop **11** jenny donkey, knuckle-head **13** Jerusalem pony, proper Charlie

*See also* **fool**

**assail**
**03** din, rag, row **04** peal, pelt, slam **05** assay, beset, go for, slate, worry **06** attack, invade, malign, plague, rattle, revile, strafe, straff, strike **07** barrage, bedevil, belabor, bestorm, bombard, disturb, lay into, perplex, rubbish, run down, set upon, slag off, torment, trouble **08** badmouth, ballyrag, belabour, bludgeon, bullyrag, maltreat, overfall, set about, tear into **09** criticize, pitch into **10** fall foul of, set against

**assailant**
**05** enemy **06** abuser, mugger **07** invader, reviler **08** assailer, attacker, onsetter, opponent **09** adversary, aggressor, assaulter

**assassin**
**04** thug **05** bravo, ninja **06** gunman, hit-man, killer, slayer **07** sworder **08** murderer **09** cut-throat **10** hatchet man, liquidator **11** contract man, executioner

*See also* **murderer**

**assassinate**
◇ *anagram indicator*
**03** hit **04** do in, kill, slay **06** murder **07** bump off, execute **08** dispatch **09** eliminate, liquidate, slaughter

**assassination**
◇ *anagram indicator*
**06** murder **07** killing **09** execution, slaughter, taking-off **11** termination

**assault**
**02** do **03** GBH, hit, mug **04** raid, rape **05** abuse, assay, blitz, feint, go for, onset, smite, stoor, storm, stour **06** affray, attack, beat up, charge, do over, fall on, insult, invade, molest, stound, stownd, stowre, strike **07** attempt, battery, bombard, lay into, mugging, offence, offense, set upon **08** invasion, storming **09** fusillade, incursion, offensive, onslaught **10** hamesucken, violent act **11** molestation **13** interfere with **15** act of aggression, throw yourself on

**assay**
**04** test **05** check, cupel, ELISA **08** analysis **09** appraisal, judgement **10** assessment, evaluation, inspection **11** examination

**assemblage**
**04** mass **05** crowd, flock, group, rally, shoal, strew **06** galaxy, school, throng **07** montage **09** aggregate, gathering, multitude **10** collection, collective, parliament **12** accumulation

**assemble**
◇ *anagram indicator*
**04** band, join, make, mass, meet **05** amass, build, flock, group, rally, relie, set up, troop **06** accoil, cobble, gather, join up, muster, relide, roll up, summon **07** collate, collect, compose, connect, convene, convoke, marshal, round up, summons **08** mobilize **09** aggregate, construct, fabricate **10** accumulate, congregate, rendezvous **11** fit together, get together, manufacture, put together **12** come together **13** bring together, piece together

**assembly**
**03** hui, mob **04** body, Dáil, diet, feis, meet, moot, Sejm **05** agora, bench, court, crowd, divan, flock, gemot, group, jirga, rally, synod, thing **06** indaba, kgotla, Majlis, Mejlis, muster, plenum, throng **07** chamber, chapter, company, council, gorsedd, Knesset, Landtag, meeting, squeeze, turnout, zemstvo **08** audience, building, bun fight, conclave, congress, ecclesia, folkmoot, panegyry, presence, Sobranje, Sobranye, Storting **09** Aula Regis, concourse, frequence, gathering, multitude, Skupstina, Storthing, synagogue, synedrion, synedrium, volksraad **10** assemblage, bear garden, collection, conference, consistory, convention, Curia Regis, Donnybrook, masquerade, Oireachtas, Skupshtina **11** church court, convocation, Dáil Eireann, fabrication, manufacture, Pandemonium **12** body of people, common vestry, congregation, construction, Pandaemonium **15** piecing together, putting together

*See also* **parliament**

**• General Assembly**
**02** GA

**assent**
**03** buy **05** agree, allow, grant, yield **06** accede, accept, accord, comply, concur, permit, submit **07** approve, concede, consent, go-ahead

**08** approval, sanction, thumbs-up **09** accession, acquiesce, agreement, subscribe **10** acceptance, compliance, concession, green light, permission, submission **11** approbation, concurrence **12** acquiescence, capitulation **14** give the go-ahead **15** give the thumbs-up

**• expression of assent**

**01** I **02** ay, OK **03** aye, oke, olé **04** done, good, okay **07** d'accord **09** I am agreed **10** I am content

**assert**

**03** put, say **04** have, hold, pose **05** argue, claim, state, swear, vouch **06** affirm, attest, avouch, defend, stress, uphold **07** confirm, contend, declare, lay down, profess, protest **08** constate, insist on, maintain **09** establish, predicate, pronounce, testify to, vindicate **10** stand up for **12** crack the whip

**assertion**

**03** vow **04** word **05** claim, vouch **06** avowal, threap, threep **08** averment, pretence, pretense, sentence **09** statement **10** affirmance, allegation, contention, insistence, profession **11** affirmation, attestation, declaration, jactitation, predication, testificate, vindication **12** constatation, gratis dictum **13** pronouncement

**assertive**

**04** bold, firm **05** perky, pushy **07** decided, forward **08** assuming, dogmatic, dominant, emphatic, forceful, immodest, positive **09** confident, insistent **10** aggressive, determined **11** domineering, opinionated, overbearing, self-assured **12** presumptuous, strong-willed **13** self-confident **14** sure of yourself **15** feeling your oats

**assertively**

**06** boldly, firmly **10** dominantly, forcefully, positively **11** confidently, insistently **12** aggressively **14** presumptuously **15** self-confidently

**assess**

**03** fix, tax **04** levy, rate **05** cense, gauge, Jenny, judge, stent, sum up, teind, value, weigh **06** affeer, assize, demand, extend, impose, modify, review, size up **07** compute **08** appraise, check out, consider, estimate, evaluate **09** calculate, determine **11** jenny donkey

**assessment**

**04** levy, rate, toll **05** recce, stent **06** demand, review, tariff **07** opinion, testing **09** appraisal, judgement, valuation **10** estimation, evaluation, imposition **11** computation **12** appraisement **13** consideration

**assessor**

**05** judge **06** expert, gauger, umpire, valuer **07** adviser, arbiter, referee **08** examiner, measurer, recorder, reviewer, valuator **09** appraiser, estimator, inspector **10** arbitrator, consultant, counsellor **11** adjudicator **12** loss adjuster **15** average adjuster

**asset**

**03** aid **04** boon, help, plus **05** funds, goods, means, money **06** estate, virtue, wealth **07** benefit, capital, savings **08** blessing, holdings, property, reserves, resource, seed corn, strength, tangible **09** advantage, liability, plus point, resources, valuables **10** securities **11** hot property, possessions, receivables, strong point

**asseverate**

**04** aver, avow **05** claim, state **06** affirm, assert, attest **07** confirm, declare, profess **08** maintain

**assiduity**

**08** devotion, hard work, industry, sedulity **09** constancy, diligence **10** dedication **11** persistence **12** perseverance **14** meticulousness **15** industriousness

**assiduous**

**06** steady **07** careful, devoted **08** constant, diligent, sedulous, studious, thorough, untiring **09** attentive, dedicated **10** meticulous, persistent, unflagging **11** hard-working, industrious, persevering **13** conscientious, indefatigable

**assign**

**03** fix, put, set **04** aret, cast, give, name, rank, sort **05** allot, allow, apply, arett, grant, range **06** affect, choose, convey, detail, impute, ordain, select **07** adjudge, appoint, ascribe, consign, endorse, hive off, indorse, install, put down, specify, station **08** accredit, allocate, arrogate, delegate, dispense, hand over, make over, nominate, relegate, transfer, transmit **09** apportion, attribute, chalk up to, designate, determine, stipulate **10** commission, distribute **11** appropriate

**assignation**

**04** date **05** tryst **10** engagement, rendezvous **11** appointment, arrangement **13** secret meeting

**assignment**

**03** job **04** duty, post, task **05** grant **06** charge, errand **07** project **08** position, transfer **09** selection **10** allocation, commission, conveyance, delegation, nomination, obligation **11** appointment, consignment, designation, disposition **12** distribution **14** responsibility

**assimilate**

◇ *containment indicator*

**03** mix **05** adapt, blend, grasp, learn, unite **06** absorb, adjust, imbibe, mingle, pick up, take in **08** accustom **09** integrate **11** acclimatize, accommodate, incorporate, internalize

**assimilation**

**07** osmosis **08** blending, grasping, learning, mixing in, taking in **09** digestion **10** absorption, adaptation, adjustment, resorption **11** integration **13** accommodation, incorporation **15** acclimatization, internalization

**assist**

**03** aid **04** abet, back, help **05** serve **06** back up, enable, second **07** advance, benefit, further, pitch in, relieve, succour, support, sustain **08** expedite **09** co-operate, do your bit, encourage, give a hand, lend a hand, reinforce **10** facilitate, make easier, rally round **11** collaborate **12** give a leg up to

**assistance**

**03** aid **04** hand, help **05** boost **06** a leg up, relief **07** backing, benefit, service, subsidy, succour, support **08** easement **09** adjutancy **10** friendship **11** co-operation, furtherance **12** a helping hand **13** collaboration, reinforcement

**assistant**

**02** PA **03** cad, PDA **04** aide, ally, mate **05** clerk, usher **06** backer, curate, deputy, helper, intern, leg-man, nipper, second, yeoman **07** abettor, acolyte, acolyth, best boy, fireman, matross, nobbler, omnibus, partner **08** chainman, leg-woman, mud-clerk, right arm, salesman, servitor **09** accessory, ancillary, associate, auxiliary, coadjutor, colleague, land-reeve, midinette, prorector, secretary, suffragan, supporter, toad-eater, whipper-in **10** accomplice, aide-de-camp, amanuensis, copyholder, evangelist, proproctor, reading-boy, roughrider, sales clerk, saleswoman, subsidiary **11** confederate, merry-andrew, salesperson, subordinate **12** brigade major, collaborator, demonstrator, driving force, right-hand man **13** counter-jumper **14** boatswain's mate, checkout person, Common Serjeant, counter-skipper **15** second-in-command, vice-chamberlain

**associate**

◇ *juxtaposition indicator*

**01** A **03** Ass, mix, pal **04** ally, band, chum, gang, herd, join, link, mate, mell, pair, peer, yoke **05** crony, haunt, unite **06** attach, couple, fellow, friend, helper, hobnob, league, mingle, relate **07** combine, company, compeer, comrade, connect, consort, goombah, hang out, partner, sociate **08** complice, confrère, co-worker, follower, identify, sidekick, sororize, yoke-mate **09** accompany, affiliate, assistant, coadjutor, colleague, companion, correlate, hang about, neighbour, socialize, syndicate **10** accomplice, amalgamate, be involved, coadjutrix, consociate, fraternize, hang around, yokefellow

**11** coadjutress, confederate, keep company **12** band together, collaborator, go hand in hand, rub shoulders **15** think of together

**associated**
◇ *juxtaposition indicator*
**03** Ass **05** alike **06** allied, linked
**07** coupled, related, similar
**08** combined, in league
**09** connected, consorted **10** affiliated, correlated, syndicated
**11** amalgamated **12** confederated
**13** corresponding, in partnership

**association**
**03** Ass, tie **04** band, bond, club, gild, hunt, link **05** group, guild, tie-up, union **06** cartel, chapel, clique, league, Probus, thrift, Verein **07** combine, company, contact, job club, society **08** alliance, clanship, intimacy, relation, sodality **09** coalition, goose-club, syndicate **10** connection, consortium, craft guild, federation, fellowship, fraternity, friendship, Jockey Club, Land League, propaganda, Young Italy
**11** affiliation, confederacy, corporation, correlation, familiarity, involvement, partnership, triumvirate
**12** consociation, Gesellschaft, organization, relationship
**13** companionship, confederation, incorporation, interrelation
**14** Burschenschaft, identification, Primrose League **15** friendly society

**assorted**
◇ *anagram indicator*
**05** mixed **06** divers, motley, sundry, varied **07** diverse, several, various
**08** manifold, sortable **09** different, differing **10** variegated **11** farraginous
**12** multifarious **13** heterogeneous, miscellaneous

**assortment**
**03** lot, mix **05** array, bunch, group
**06** choice, jumble, medley **07** farrago, mixture, variety **08** grouping, mixed bag **09** diversity, menagerie, potpourri, selection **10** collection, miscellany, salmagundi
**11** arrangement, olla-podrida, smörgåsbord **13** bits and pieces

**assuage**
**04** beet, bete, calm, ease, lull **05** allay, lower, mease, slake, swage **06** lenify, lessen, pacify, quench, reduce, soften, soothe **07** appease, lighten, mollify, relieve, satisfy **08** mitigate, moderate, palliate **09** alleviate

**assume**
◇ *containment indicator*
**03** don **04** bear, take **05** adopt, fancy, feign, guess, infer, posit, put on, seize, think, usurp **06** accept, affect, deduce, expect, strike, take it, take on
**07** acquire, believe, embrace, imagine, pre-empt, presume, pretend, suppose, surmise **08** arrogate, shoulder, simulate, take over **09** enter upon, postulate, undertake **10** come to have, commandeer, presuppose, take as read, understand **11** appropriate, counterfeit **14** take for granted

**assumed**
**04** fake, sham **05** bogus, false
**06** made-up, phoney **07** feigned
**08** affected, borrowed, putative, supposed **09** pretended, simulated
**10** fictitious **11** counterfeit
**12** adscititious, hypothetical, pseudonymous **14** supposititious

**assumption**
**04** idea **05** axiom, donné, fancy, guess
**06** belief, donnée, notion, theory
**07** embrace, premise, seizure, surmise
**08** adoption, takeover **09** inference, postulate **10** acceptance, arrogation, conclusion, conjecture, hypothesis, pre-emption, usurpation
**11** embarkation, expectation, postulation, presumption, shouldering, supposition, undertaking
**13** appropriation, commandeering
**14** presupposition

**assurance**
**03** vow **04** gall, oath, word **05** nerve, poise **06** aplomb, pledge **07** courage, promise, surance, warrant **08** audacity, boldness, security, sureness
**09** assertion, certainty, guarantee
**10** confidence, conviction, positivism
**11** affirmation, assuredness, declaration, undertaking **12** self-reliance **13** self-assurance **14** self-confidence, unflappability

**assure**
**03** vow **04** affy, hete, seal, tell
**05** hecht, hight, swear **06** affirm, attest, avouch, ensure, pledge, secure, soothe **07** certify, comfort, confirm, hearten, promise, resolve, warrant **08** convince, persuade, reassure **09** ascertain, encourage, guarantee

**assured**
**04** bold, calm, sure **05** fixed **06** secure
**07** certain, ensured, settled
**08** definite, positive, promised
**09** assertive, audacious, confident, confirmed, thoughten **10** guaranteed
**11** cut and dried, irrefutable, self-assured **12** indisputable **13** self-confident, self-possessed **14** sure of yourself

• **be assured of**
**04** know

**assuredly**
**05** pardi, pardy, perdy **06** pardie, perdie, surely **07** my certy **08** my certie **09** by my certy, certainly, of a verity **10** by my certie, definitely, for certain **12** and no mistake, indisputably, without doubt
**14** unquestionably **15** without question

**astatine**
**02** At

**astern**
**03** aft **04** baft **05** abaft, apoop

**asteroid**
**09** planetoid **11** minor planet

*Asteroids include:*

**04** Eros, Hebe, Iris, Juno
**05** Ceres, Flora, Metis, Vesta
**06** Apollo, Cybele, Davida, Europa, Hygiea, Icarus, Pallas, Psyche, Trojan
**07** Eunomia
**10** Interamnia

**astir**
**05** afoot, agate **07** abroach, humming
**09** in the wind

**astonish**
**03** wow **04** daze, stun **05** amaze, floor, shock, stony **07** astound, flummox, stagger, startle, stupefy
**08** bewilder, bowl over, confound, dumfound, gobsmack, surprise
**09** dumbfound, electrify, take aback
**11** flabbergast, knock for six **12** blow your mind

**astonished**
**05** dazed **06** amazed **07** shocked, stunned **08** open-eyed, startled, wide-eyed **09** astounded, staggered, surprised **10** bewildered, bowled over, confounded, gobsmacked, taken aback **11** dumbfounded **12** lost for words **13** flabbergasted, knocked for six, thunderstruck

**astonishing**
◇ *anagram indicator*
**07** amazing **08** shocking, striking, stunning **09** startling **10** astounding, impressive, marvellous, prodigious, staggering, surprising **11** bewildering, mind-blowing **12** awe-inspiring, breathtaking, mind-boggling, unbelievable

**astonishment**
**05** shock **06** dismay, marvel, wonder
**08** surprise **09** amazement, confusion, disbelief **10** admiration, wonderment
**12** bewilderment, stupefaction
**13** consternation

**astound**
**04** stun **05** abash, amaze, floor, shock
**06** stound **07** flummox, startle, stupefy
**08** astonish, bewilder, bowl over, surprise **09** overwhelm **11** knock for six

**astounding**
**07** amazing **08** shocking, stunning
**09** startling **10** staggering, stupefying, stupendous, surprising **11** astonishing, bewildering **12** breathtaking, overwhelming

**astray**
◇ *anagram indicator*
**04** awry, lost, miss, will, wull **05** abord, agate, amiss, wrong **06** abroad, adrift, errant, erring **07** missing **09** off course
**10** miswandred, off the mark **11** off the rails

**astride**
◇ *containment indicator*
**08** straddle **10** en cavalier **12** colossus-wise

**astringent**
**04** acid, hard, kino **05** harsh, rough, stern **06** biting, gambir, severe **07** acerbic, austere, caustic, gambier, guaraná, mordant, puckery, rhatany, styptic **08** alum-root, critical, krameria, scathing **09** obstruent, tormentil, trenchant, zinc oxide **10** astrictive, witch-hazel **11** restringent

**astrologer**
**09** stargazer **10** genethliac **11** horoscopist, Nostradamus **12** figure-caster **14** archgenethliac

**astronaut**
**08** lunanaut, spaceman **09** cosmonaut, lunarnaut, taikonaut **10** spacewoman **14** space traveller

*Astronauts and space travellers include:*

**03** **Ham**
**04** **Bean** (Alan), **Ride** (Sally), **Tito** (Dennis)
**05** **Foale** (Michael), **Glenn** (John), **Irwin** (James), **Laika**, **Scott** (David), **Titov** (Gherman), **White** (Edward)
**06** **Aldrin** (Buzz), **Conrad** (Pete), **Leonov** (Aleksei), **Lovell** (Jim)
**07** **Chaffee** (Roger), **Collins** (Michael), **Gagarin** (Yuri), **Grissom** (Gus), **Schirra** (Wally), **Sharman** (Helen), **Shepard** (Alan)
**08** **Mitchell** (Edgar)
**09** **Armstrong** (Neil)
**10** **Tereshkova** (Valentina)

• **would-be astronaut**
**10** space cadet

**astronomer**
**04** astr **06** astron **09** stargazer

*Astronomers and astrophysicists include:*

**04** **Airy** (Sir George), **Biot** (Jean-Baptiste), **Gold** (Thomas), **Hale** (George), **Lyot** (Bernard), **Oort** (Jan), **Pond** (John), **Rees** (Sir Martin), **Ryle** (Sir Martin), **Saha** (Meghnad), **Webb** (James E)
**05** **Adams** (John Couch), **Adams** (Walter S), **Baade** (Walter), **Baily** (Francis), **Bliss** (Nathaniel), **Brahe** (Tycho), **Dyson** (Sir Frank), **Gauss** (Carl Friedrich), **Hoyle** (Sir Fred), **Jeans** (Sir James), **Jones** (Sir Harold Spencer), **Moore** (Sir Patrick), **Sagan** (Carl), **Smith** (Sir Francis), **Vogel** (Hermann Carl)
**06** **Bessel** (Friedrich), **Halley** (Edmond), **Hewish** (Antony), **Hubble** (Edwin), **Jansky** (Karl), **Kepler** (Johannes), **Kuiper** (Gerard), **Lovell** (Sir Bernard), **Olbers** (Heinrich), **Piazzi** (Giuseppe), **Roemer** (Olaus)
**07** **Babcock** (Harold D), **Barnard** (Edward Emerson), **Bradley** (James), **Cassini** (Giovanni), **Celsius** (Anders), **Galilei** (Galileo), **Galileo**, **Hawking** (Stephen), **Huggins** (Sir William), **Langley** (Samuel), **Laplace** (Pierre), **Lockyer** (Sir Norman), **Maunder** (E W), **Penrose** (Roger), **Penzias** (Arno), **Ptolemy**, **Russell** (Henry Norris), **Sandage** (Allan), **Schmidt** (Maarten), **Seyfert** (Carl), **Shapley** (Harlow), **Whipple** (Fred), **Woolley** (Sir Richard)
**08** **Burbidge** (Geoffrey), **Burbidge** (Margaret), **Chandler** (Seth Carlo), **Christie** (Sir William), **Friedman** (Herbert), **Herschel** (Caroline), **Herschel** (Sir John), **Herschel** (Sir William), **Lemaître** (Georges), **Tombaugh** (Clyde W)
**09** **Eddington** (Sir Arthur), **Fabricius** (David), **Flamsteed** (John), **Maskelyne** (Nevil), **Sosigenes**
**10** **Carrington** (Richard), **Copernicus** (Nicolas), **Hipparchos**, **Wolfendale** (Sir Arnold)
**11** **Bell Burnell** (Jocelyn), **Graham-Smith** (Sir Francis), **Hertzsprung** (Ejnar), **Tsiolkovsky** (Konstantin)
**12** **Schiaparelli** (Giovanni)
**13** **Chandrasekhar** (Subrahmanyan), **Schwarzschild** (Karl)
**14** **Galileo Galilei**

**astronomical**
**04** astr, huge, vast **06** astron, cosmic **07** immense, mammoth, massive, stellar **08** colossal, enormous, gigantic, heavenly, infinite, thumping, whopping **09** celestial, planetary **10** tremendous **11** substantial **12** considerable, cosmological, immeasurable, interstellar

• **astronomical model**
**06** orrery

**astronomy**
**04** astr **06** astron **08** star-read **09** uranology

**astrophysicist** *see* **astronomer**

**astute**
**03** sly **04** cute, keen, sage, wide, wily, wise **05** canny, sharp **06** clever, crafty, shrewd, subtle **07** cunning, knowing, prudent **09** sagacious **10** discerning, perceptive **11** intelligent, penetrating, sharp-witted **13** perspicacious

**astutely**
**06** keenly, wisely **08** craftily, shrewdly **12** perceptively **13** intelligently, sharp-wittedly

**asunder**
**02** up **05** apart, in two **06** atwain **07** in twain **08** in pieces, to pieces

**asylum**
**03** bin **05** girth, grith, haven **06** bedlam, refuge **07** retreat, shelter **08** madhouse, Magdalen, nuthouse **09** dark-house, funny farm, sanctuary **10** frithsoken **11** institution **12** penitentiary, port in a storm **13** place of safety **14** mental hospital

**asymmetrical**
**04** awry, skew **06** uneven **07** anaxial, crooked, oblique, unequal **08** lopsided **09** distorted, irregular, malformed **10** unbalanced **13** unsymmetrical

**asymmetry**
**09** imbalance **10** distortion, handedness, inequality, unevenness, unsymmetry **11** crookedness **12** irregularity, lopsidedness, malformation

**at**
**02** in, to **08** astatine

**ate**
◇ *containment indicator*

**atheism**
**07** impiety **08** nihilism, paganism, unbelief **09** disbelief, non-belief **10** heathenism, infidelity, irreligion, scepticism **11** godlessness, rationalism, ungodliness **12** freethinking

**atheist**
**05** pagan **07** heathen, heretic, infidel, sceptic **08** humanist, nihilist **10** unbeliever **11** disbeliever, freethinker, non-believer, nullifidian, rationalist

**Athene**
**07** Minerva

**athlete**
**04** jock **05** miler **06** player, runner **07** gymnast, hurdler **09** contender, sportsman **10** competitor, contestant **11** sportswoman **12** quarter-miler

*Athletes include:*

**03** **Coe** (Sebastian, Lord)
**04** **Budd** (Zola), **Cram** (Steve), **Koch** (Marita), **Mota** (Rosa)
**05** **Bubka** (Sergey), **Jones** (Marion), **Keino** (Kip), **Lewis** (Carl), **Lewis** (Denise), **Moses** (Ed), **Nurmi** (Paavo), **Ottey** (Merlene), **Ovett** (Steve), **Owens** (Jesse), **Waitz** (Grete), **Wells** (Allan)
**06** **Aouita** (Said), **Barber** (Eunice), **Beamon** (Bob), **Devers** (Gail), **Foster** (Brendan), **Greene** (Maurice), **Holmes** (Kelly), **Mutola** (Maria), **Oerter** (Al), **Peters** (Mary)
**07** **Backley** (Steve), **Edwards** (Jonathan), **Fosbury** (Dick), **Freeman** (Cathy), **Gunnell** (Sally), **Jackson** (Colin), **Johnson** (Ben), **Johnson** (Michael), **Liddell** (Eric), **Zatopek** (Emil), **Zelezny** (Jan)
**08** **Christie** (Linford), **Guerrouj** (Hicham el-), **Kipketer** (Wilson), **McColgan** (Liz), **Pieterse** (Zola), **Thompson** (Daley)
**09** **Bannister** (Sir Roger), **O'Sullivan** (Sonia), **Radcliffe** (Paula), **Sanderson** (Tessa), **Whitbread** (Fatima)
**12** **Blankers-Koen** (Fanny), **Gebrselassie** (Haile), **Grey-Thompson** (Dame Tanni)
**14** **Griffith Joyner** (Florence 'Flo-Jo')

**athletic**
**01** A **03** fit **04** wiry **05** games, leish **06** active, brawny, muscly, robust, sinewy, sports, sporty, strong, sturdy

**08** muscular, powerful, sporting, vigorous, well-knit **09** energetic, gymnastic, strapping

**athletics**
**05** games, races **06** sports **07** matches **08** aerobics **09** exercises
**10** gymnastics **11** field events, track events **13** callisthenics

*See also* **sport**

*Athletics events include:*

**04** ball, shot, walk
**05** relay
**06** discus, hammer, sprint
**07** hurdles, javelin, shot put
**08** biathlon, high jump, long jump, marathon, tug-of-war
**09** broad jump, caber toss, decathlon, pole vault, sheaf toss, triathlon
**10** heptathlon, pentathlon, tetrathlon, triple jump
**11** discus throw, fell running, fifty metres, hammer throw, race walking
**12** cross-country, half marathon, javelin throw, steeplechase
**14** hop, step and jump
**15** tossing the caber

**athwart**
**04** awry **06** across, aslant **07** asklent

**atmosphere**
**03** air, atm, fug, sky **04** aura, feel, mood, tone **05** ether, miasm, tenor, vibes **06** miasma, milieu, spirit, welkin **07** climate, feeling, flavour, heavens, quality, setting **08** ambience, empyrean **09** aerospace, character, firmament **10** background
**11** environment **12** surroundings
**13** vault of heaven

*Atmosphere layers include:*

**09** exosphere, ionopause, mesopause
**10** ionosphere, mesosphere, ozone layer, tropopause
**11** stratopause, troposphere
**12** stratosphere, thermosphere

**atom**
**03** bit, jot **04** hint, iota, mite, spot, whit **05** crumb, grain, scrap, shred, speck, trace **06** morsel **08** fragment, molecule, particle **09** scintilla

*See also* **particle**

**atomic**
**01** A
• **atomic mass unit**
**03** amu
• **atomic number**
**04** at no **06** at numb
• **atomic weight**
**01** A **03** AWU **04** at wt

**atone**
**03** aby **04** abye **06** offset, pay for, ransom, redeem, remedy, repent
**07** appease, expiate, redress, satisfy
**08** make good **09** indemnify, make right, make up for, reconcile
**10** compensate, make amends, propitiate, recompense **14** make reparation

**atonement**
**06** amends, ransom **07** payment, penance, redress **08** requital
**09** expiation, indemnity, repayment
**10** recompense, redemption, reparation **11** appeasement, eye for an eye, restitution, restoration
**12** compensation, propitiation, satisfaction **13** acceptilation, reimbursement

**atrocious**
◇ *anagram indicator*
**05** awful, cruel, enorm **06** brutal, savage, wicked **07** ghastly, heinous, hideous, vicious **08** dreadful, enormous, fiendish, grievous, horrible, ruthless, shocking, terrible
**09** appalling, frightful, merciless, monstrous, nefarious **10** abominable, diabolical, disgusting, flagitious, horrendous

**atrociously**
**07** cruelly **08** brutally, horribly, terribly, wickedly **09** heinously **10** abominably, dreadfully, fiendishly, ruthlessly, shockingly **11** appallingly, monstrously

**atrocity**
**04** evil **06** horror **07** cruelty, outrage
**08** enormity, savagery, vileness, villainy
**09** barbarity, brutality, violation
**10** wickedness **11** abomination, heinousness, hideousness, monstrosity, viciousness
**13** atrociousness **14** flagitiousness

**atrophy**
**04** fade **05** decay, waste **06** shrink, sweeny, tabefy, wither **07** decline, dwindle, shrivel, wasting **08** diminish, emaciate, marasmus **09** waste away, withering **10** amyotrophy, degenerate, diminution, emaciation, involution
**11** deteriorate, shrivelling, tabefaction, wasting away **12** degeneration
**13** deterioration

**attach**
**03** add, fix, lay, pin, put, sew, tag, tie
**04** ally, bind, join, link, nail, send, tack, weld **05** add on, affix, annex, cling, place, put on, snell, stick, unite
**06** adhere, append, assign, belong, couple, detail, fasten, impute, limber, second, secure, solder **07** adhibit, ascribe, Blu-Tack®, connect, harness, plaster **08** allocate, relate to
**09** affiliate, align with, associate, attribute, factorize, latch onto, piggyback **10** articulate, make secure
**11** combine with **13** affiliate with, associate with

**attached**
**04** fond **06** liking, loving, tender
**07** devoted, engaged, married
**08** friendly **09** affianced, appendant, spoken for **11** going steady
**12** affectionate **15** in a relationship

**attachment**
**03** tie **04** bond, frog, link, love
**05** extra **06** fetich, fetish, liking
**07** adapter, adaptor, adjunct, codicil, fetiche, fitment, fitting, fixture, loyalty
**08** addition, adhesion, affinity, calf-love, devotion, fixation, fondness
**09** accessory, affection, appendage, closeness, extension **10** attraction, commitment, friendship, partiality, supplement, tenderness
**12** accoutrement, appurtenance
**13** grande passion

**attack**
**03** fit, gas, get, lam, mob, mug, pan, pin, TIA **04** bash, bomb, bout, chin, fake, flak, fork, gang, go at, jump, Mace®, nuke, prey, push, raid, rear, roll, rush, Scud, slam, tilt **05** abuse, alert, begin, blame, blast, blitz, board, brash, decry, fling, fly at, foray, glass, go for, ictus, knock, prang, sally, scrag, siege, slate, snipe, spasm, start, storm, touch
**06** access, affect, ambush, assail, batter, beat up, berate, bodrag, bottle, charge, come at, do over, duff up, extent, fall on, hold-up, impugn, infect, insult, invade, jump on, malign, molest, napalm, oppugn, pounce, rebuke, revile, rocket, savage, send in, shower, sortie, strafe, strike, stroke, tackle, tongue, vilify, wade in, waylay
**07** address, aggress, air-raid, assault, attempt, battery, besiege, blister, bombard, bulldog, censure, clobber, destroy, fly upon, focus on, handbag, hiccups, inveigh, kicking, lampoon, lay into, reprove, round on, rubbish, run down, sandbag, seizure, set upon, slag off, slating, torpedo **08** attend to, camisade, camisado, commence, deal with, denounce, dive-bomb, embark on, firebomb, invasion, knocking, paroxysm, pounce on, roasting, set about, slamming, storming, strike at, tear into, tomahawk **09** broadside, cannonade, criticism, criticize, go wilding, have a go at, hiccoughs, incursion, invective, irruption, light into, obsession, offensive, onslaught, pull apart, stand upon, submarine, undertake, weigh into **10** bitch about, calumniate, chuck off at, convulsion, coup de main, crise de foi, get stuck in, hatchet job, have a pop at, impugnment, revilement, take a pop at, vituperate, weight into
**11** bombardment, infestation, pick holes in **12** crise de nerfs, get started on, get stuck into, go over the top, leave for dead, Pearl Harbour, pull to pieces, put in the boot, put the boot in, tear to pieces, tear to shreds, vilification
**13** feeding frenzy, find fault with **14** a warm reception, make a dead set at
**15** act of aggression, apply yourself to, go for the jugular, throw yourself on

**attacker**
**06** abuser, critic, mugger, raider
**07** invader, reviler, striker
**09** aggressor, assailant, assaulter, detractor **10** persecutor

**attain**
**03** get, hit, net, win **04** earn, find, gain
**05** fetch, grasp, reach, seize, touch

**06** effect, fulfil, obtain, secure
**07** achieve, acquire, possess, procure, realize, recover **08** arrive at, complete
**10** accomplish

**attainable**
**06** at hand, doable, viable **08** feasible, possible, probable **09** potential, reachable, realistic **10** accessible, achievable, imaginable, manageable, obtainable **11** conceivable, practicable, within reach

**attainment**
**03** art **04** feat, gift **05** skill **06** talent
**07** ability, mastery, success
**08** aptitude, facility **10** capability, competence, completion, fulfilment
**11** achievement, acquirement, procurement, proficiency, realization
**12** consummation **14** accomplishment

**attempt**
**02** go **03** aim, bid, shy, try **04** bash, burl, fand, fond, make, mint, push, seek, shot, stab, trie **05** assay, crack, essay, foray, offer, trial, whack
**06** aspire, effort, set out, strive, tackle
**07** have a go, pretend, venture
**08** attentat, endeavor, have a try, struggle **09** endeavour, give it a go, have a bash, have a shot, have a stab, tentative, undertake **10** coup d'essai, experiment, give it a try, have a crack
**11** have a stab at, try your hand, undertaking **12** give it a whirl **13** see if you can do, try your hand at **15** do your level best

**attend**
**04** go to, hear, heed, help, mark, mind, note, page, show, stay, tend, wait
**05** audit, await, guard, holla, nurse, serve, usher, visit, watch **06** appear, assist, be here, escort, follow, listen, notice, show up, squire, turn up **07** be there, care for, give ear, go along, observe **08** chaperon, frequent, take note, wait upon **09** accompany, chaperone, come along, look after
**10** minister to, take care of, take notice, take part in **11** be present at, concentrate **12** pay attention

**• attend to**
**03** fix **04** heed, mind, sort, tent **05** see to, valet **06** direct, handle, manage, notice **07** control, oversee, process
**08** consider, cope with, deal with, follow up, see about **09** look after, supervise **10** follow up on, take care of
**11** give an eye to

**attendance**
**04** duty, gate **05** crowd, house
**06** escort, roll-up **07** showing, turnout
**08** audience, courting, presence
**09** appearing, showing up
**10** appearance

**attendant**
**03** man **04** aide, jack, mute, page, sice, syce **05** angel, gilly, guard, guide, jäger, saice, sowar, usher, woman
**06** batman, bedral, escort, gillie, helper, jaeger, keeper, porter, varlet, verger, waiter **07** acolyte, acolyth, bederal, best man, bulldog, checker, custrel, equerry, esquire, famulus, footboy, footman, ghillie, janitor, linkboy, linkman, marshal, orderly, related, servant, snuffer, steward
**08** attached, batwoman, beach boy, chaperon, chasseur, follower, footpage, handmaid, janitrix, retainer, waitress **09** assistant, auxiliary, boxkeeper, chaperone, chaprassi, chaprassy, chuprassy, companion, custodian, groomsman, janitress, kennelman, lady's-maid, observant, pew-opener, resultant, satellite
**10** associated, conclavist, consequent, handmaiden, incidental, kennelmaid, led captain, lock-keeper, ministrant, pursuivant, subsequent, vivandière
**11** apple-squire, body servant, concomitant, gentlewoman, loblolly-boy **12** accompanying, bottle-holder, shield-bearer **13** church officer, gillie-wetfoot **14** gentleman usher, valet de chambre **15** gillie-white-foot

**attention**
**03** ear, eye **04** care, gaum, gorm, heed, help, mind, 'shun **06** notice, regard **07** concern, respect, service, therapy, thought **08** civility, courtesy, scrutiny **09** alertness, awareness, gallantry, limelight, treatment, vigilance **10** advertence, advertency, attendance, politeness
**11** compliments, high profile, mindfulness, observation, recognition
**13** concentration, consideration, contemplation, preoccupation

**• expressions relating to attracting or directing attention**
**02** hi, ho, la, lo, oi, 'st, yo **03** hem, hey, hoa, hoh, hoi, hoy, pst, say, see, why
**04** ahem, ecce, ecco, here, hist, look, oyes, oyez, psst, 'shun, soho, what, yo-ho **05** cooee, cooey, hallo, hello, holla, hollo, hullo, voilà **06** behold, halloa, halloo, yo-ho-ho, yoo-hoo **07** whoa-hoa **08** whoa-ho-ho **10** view-halloo

**• pay attention**
**04** gaum, gorm, heed **06** listen
**07** focus on, hearken, observe **10** get a load of, take notice **13** concentrate on
**14** watch carefully **15** focus your mind on, listen carefully

**attentive**
**04** kind **05** alert, awake, aware, civil, tenty, whist **06** polite, tentie **07** all ears, careful, devoted, dutiful, gallant, heedful, listful, mindful **08** gracious, noticing, obliging, vigilant, watchful, watching **09** advertent, adviceful, avizefull, courteous, listening, observant, on the ball, regardant
**10** chivalrous, particular, thoughtful
**11** advertising, considerate, punctilious **12** on the qui vive
**13** accommodating, concentrating, conscientious

**attentively**
**09** carefully, mindfully **10** watchfully
**11** observantly **15** conscientiously

**attenuated**
**04** bony, fine, slim, thin **06** narrow, skinny, slight **07** scraggy, scrawny, slender

**attest**
**04** aver, show **05** prove **06** adjure, affirm, assert, depose, evince, verify
**07** certify, confirm, declare, display, endorse, witness **08** evidence, manifest, proclaim, vouch for
**10** asseverate **11** corroborate, demonstrate **13** bear witness to

**attic**
**04** loft **06** garret **07** mansard **10** sky parlour

**attire**
**04** garb, gear, suit, tire, togs, wear
**05** dress, habit **06** finery, outfit, rig-out
**07** apparel, clobber, clothes, costume
**08** clothing, garments **10** habiliment, habilitate **11** habiliments
**13** accoutrements

**attired**
**05** ready **07** adorned, arrayed, clothed, dressed **09** decked out, rigged out, turned out **11** habilitated

**attitude**
**04** mood, pose, song, view **05** piety, sense, stand **06** aspect, manner, stance **07** bearing, feeling, mindset, opinion, outlook, posture
**08** approach, carriage, position
**09** mentality, sentiment, viewpoint, world-view **10** Anschauung, deportment **11** disposition, perspective, point of view **13** way of thinking **14** Weltanschauung

**attorney**
**02** AG, DA, QC **03** Att **04** Atty **05** brief
**06** lawyer **07** counsel, proctor
**08** advocate **09** barrister, solicitor
**12** legal adviser

**attract**
**04** draw, hook, lure, pull **05** charm, rivet, swing, tempt **06** allure, engage, entice, excite, induce, invite, pull in, seduce **07** bewitch, bring in, enchant, incline **08** appeal to, interest
**09** captivate, fascinate, magnetize

**attraction**
**02** it, SA **04** bait, bond, draw, hook, lure, pull **05** charm, sight **06** allure, appeal, favour **07** draught, feature, glamour **08** activity, affinity, building, cohesion, interest **09** box office, diversion, magnetism, seduction
**10** enticement, inducement, invitation, temptation **11** captivation, enchantment, fascination, Ferris wheel
**13** entertainment

**• centre of attraction**
**04** clou

**attractive**
**03** bad, fit, hot **04** cute, fair, foxy, sexy, taky **05** bonny, dishy, hunky, tasty, triff
**06** catchy, comely, glossy, lovely, nubile, pretty, snazzy **07** dashing, elegant, nymphic, shapely, triffic,

winning, winsome **08** all right, beddable, catching, charming, engaging, enticing, epigamic, fetching, gorgeous, handsome, hot stuff, inviting, knockout, luscious, magnetic, pleasant, pleasing, striking, stunning, tempting, terrific **09** agreeable, appealing, appetible, beautiful, desirable, fanciable, glamorous, insidious, seductive, toothsome **10** adamantine, personable, photogenic, voluptuous **11** captivating, charismatic, fascinating, good-looking, interesting, picturesque **12** irresistible **13** prepossessing **14** a bit of all right

**attribute**
**03** lay **04** mark, note, side, sign **05** apply, blame, facet, point, quirk, refer, trait **06** aspect, assign, charge, credit, impute, reckon, streak, symbol, virtue **07** adjunct, apanage, ascribe, feature, put down, quality, set down **08** accredit, appanage, arrogate, property **09** affection, indicator **11** peculiarity **12** idiosyncrasy **14** characteristic

**attrition**
**07** chafing, erosion, rubbing **08** abrasion, friction, grinding, scraping **09** detrition, weakening **10** harassment **11** attenuation, wearing away, wearing down

**attuned**
**03** set **05** tuned **07** adapted **08** adjusted **09** regulated **10** accustomed, harmonized **11** assimilated, co-ordinated **12** acclimatized, familiarized

**atypical**
**07** deviant, unusual **08** aberrant, abnormal, freakish, uncommon **09** anomalous, divergent, eccentric, untypical **11** exceptional **13** extraordinary **14** unconventional

**aubergine**
**07** brinjal **08** eggplant, mad-apple

**auburn**
**04** rust **05** henna, tawny **06** copper, russet, Titian **07** dark-red **08** chestnut **12** reddish-brown

**auction**
**04** cant, roup, sale **06** outcry, vendue **07** outroop **09** trade sale **11** warrant sale **12** subhastation

**auctioneer**
**09** outrooper **11** rouping-wife

**audacious**
**04** bold, pert, rash, rude **05** brave, fresh, lippy, nervy, risky, saucy **06** brazen, cheeky, daring, plucky **07** assured, forward, valiant **08** assuming, fearless, impudent, insolent, intrepid, reckless **09** dauntless, shameless, unabashed **10** courageous **11** adventurous, impertinent, venturesome **12** devil-may-care, enterprising, presumptuous **13** disrespectful

**audacity**
**04** grit, guts, neck, risk **05** cheek, nerve, pluck **06** bottle, daring, valour **07** bravery, courage **08** boldness, defiance, forehead, pertness, rashness, rudeness **09** assurance, hardihead, hardihood, impudence, insolence **10** brazenness, effrontery, enterprise **11** forwardness, intrepidity, presumption **12** fearlessness, impertinence, recklessness **13** dauntlessness, shamelessness **15** adventurousness

**audible**
◇ *homophone indicator*
**05** clear, heard **08** distinct, hearable **10** detectable **11** appreciable, discernible, perceptible **12** recognizable

**audience**
**04** fans **05** audit, crowd, house **06** public **07** hearing, meeting, patrons, ratings, theater, theatre, turnout, viewers **08** assembly, auditory, devotees, regulars **09** followers, following, gathering, interview, listeners, onlookers, reception **10** auditorium, conference, discussion, spectators **11** bums on seats **12** congregation, consultation

**audit**
**05** check **06** go over, review, survey, verify **07** analyse, balance, examine, inspect **08** analysis, scrutiny **09** balancing, go through, statement **10** inspection, scrutinize **11** examination, investigate, work through **12** verification **13** investigation

**audition**
**05** trial **07** hearing

**auditorium**
**04** hall **05** front, house **07** chamber, theatre **09** playhouse, sphendone **10** opera house **11** concert hall **12** assembly room **14** conference hall

**au fait**
**05** aware **06** versed **07** abreast, in touch **08** familiar, up to date **09** au courant **10** conversant **13** knowledgeable

**augment**
**03** ech, ich **04** eche, eech, grow **05** add to, boost, put on, raise, swell **06** expand, extend **07** amplify, build up, enhance, enlarge, inflate, magnify **08** heighten, increase, multiply **09** intensify, reinforce **10** strengthen **11** make greater

**augmentation**
**05** boost **06** growth **07** build-up **08** increase **09** expansion, extension **11** enlargement **13** amplification, magnification, strengthening **15** intensification

**augur**
**04** bode, spae **06** herald **07** betoken, portend, predict, presage, promise, signify **08** forebode, foretell, prophesy **09** auspicate, be a sign of, harbinger

**augury**
**04** omen, sign **05** sooth, token **06** herald **07** portent, promise, warning **08** prodrome, prophecy **09** harbinger **10** foreboding, forerunner, prediction **11** forewarning **12** ornithoscopy **13** haruspication **15** prognostication

**august**
**03** Aug **05** grand, lofty, noble **06** solemn **07** exalted, stately, sublime **08** glorious, imperial, imposing, majestic **09** dignified, respected, venerable **10** impressive **11** magnificent **12** awe-inspiring **13** distinguished

**Augustines**
**03** OSA

**auk**
**04** roch **05** rotch **06** rotche **07** Alcidae, dovekie, penguin, rotchie, sea dove **08** garefowl **09** razorbill

**Auntie**
**03** BBC **04** Beeb

**aura**
**03** air **04** feel, hint, mood **05** vibes **06** nimbus **07** feeling, quality **08** ambience, mystique **09** emanation **10** atmosphere, genius loci, suggestion, vibrations

**aural**
◇ *homophone indicator*

**aurora**
**03** Eos **11** polar lights **12** merry dancers **14** northern lights, southern lights

**auspices**
• **under the auspices of**
**11** in the care of **13** in the charge of **15** under the aegis of

**auspicious**
**04** rosy **05** happy, lucky, white **06** bright, timely **07** hopeful **08** cheerful **09** fortunate, opportune, promising **10** fair-boding, favourable, felicitous, optimistic, propitious, prosperous **11** encouraging

**austere**
**04** cold, grim, hard **05** basic, bleak, grave, harsh, plain, rigid, sober, stark, stern, stoic, stoor, stour, sture **06** chaste, formal, frugal, severe, simple, solemn, sombre, stowre, strict **07** ascetic, Dantean, distant, killjoy, serious, spartan **08** exacting, rigorous **09** stringent, unadorned, unbending, unfeeling **10** abstemious, astringent, economical, forbidding, functional, inflexible, restrained, Waldensian **11** puritanical, self-denying **12** unornamented **14** self-abnegating **15** self-disciplined

**austerity**
**06** rigour **07** economy **08** coldness, hardness, severity **09** formality, harshness, plainness, solemnity

**10** abstinence, asceticism, puritanism, self-denial, simplicity **13** inflexibility **14** abstemiousness, self-discipline

**Australia**
**01** A **02** Oz **03** AUS **04** Aust **05** Austr **09** down under

*See also* **electorate**; **governor**; **Prime Minister**; **state**; **team**

*Australian cities and notable towns include:*

**05** Perth
**06** Cairns, Darwin, Hobart, Sydney
**08** Adelaide, Brisbane, Canberra
**09** Fremantle, Melbourne
**12** Alice Springs

*Australian landmarks include:*

**05** Uluru
**08** Lake Eyre, Shark Bay
**09** Ayers Rock, Botany Bay, Pinnacles, Purnululu
**10** Bondi Beach, Yarra River
**11** Barrier Reef, Mt Kosciusko, Murray River
**12** Darling River, Fraser Island, Gibson Desert, Hunter Valley, Rialto Towers
**13** Barossa Valley, Blue Mountains, Bungle Bungles, Devil's Marbles, Dividing Range, Flinders Range, Harbour Bridge, Simpson Desert
**14** Australian Alps, Nullarbor Plain, Pinnacle Desert, Snowy Mountains, Twelve Apostles, Uluru–Kata Tjuta, Victoria Desert

**Australian**
**01** A **02** Oz **03** gin **05** koori, myall, ocker **06** Aussie, Strine

*See also* **Aboriginal**; **state**

**Australian football**

*Australian football-related terms include:*

**03** AFL
**04** goal, mark, ruck, wing
**05** rover
**06** ball up, behind, centre, tackle, time on, umpire
**07** dispose, kick out, quarter, ruckman
**08** follower, free kick, full back, half back, handball, handpass, left wing, screamer, stab pass
**09** playfield, right wing, ruck rover
**10** back pocket, banana kick, behind post, centre line, goal square, goal umpire, off the boot
**11** Aussie Rules, daisy cutter, full forward, half forward
**12** boundary line, centre bounce, centre square, Magarey Medal
**13** Brownlow Medal, checkside punt, fifty-metre arc, forward pocket, half-back flank, Sandover Medal
**14** aerial pingpong, boundary umpire, centre half back
**15** chewy on your boot

*Australian football players include:*

**04** **Dyer** (Jack)
**05** **Carey** (Wayne)
**06** **Ablett** (Gary), **Blight** (Malcolm), **Bunton** (Haydn), **Capper** (Warwick), **Cazaly** (Roy), **Farmer** (Graham 'Polly')
**07** **Barassi** (Ron), **Jackson** (Mark), **Lockett** (Tony), **Whitten** (Ted)
**08** **Bartlett** (Kevin), **Brereton** (Dermot), **Brownlow** (Charles), **Matthews** (Leigh), **Richards** (Lou)
**10** **Jesaulenko** (Alex)

*Australian Football League team nicknames include:*

**04** Cats
**05** Blues, Crows, Hawks, Lions, Power, Swans
**06** Demons, Eagles, Saints, Tigers
**07** Bombers, Dockers, Magpies
**08** Bulldogs
**09** Kangaroos

**Austria**
**01** A **03** AUT

**authentic**
**04** echt, real, true **05** legal, valid **06** actual, dinkum, honest, kosher, lawful **07** certain, correct, factual, genuine **08** accurate, attested, bona fide, credible, faithful, reliable, sterling **10** dependable, historical, legitimate, true-to-life, undisputed **11** trustworthy **12** the real McCoy, the real thing

**authentically**
**04** echt **06** really **08** actually, credibly, lawfully, reliably **09** genuinely **10** accurately, faithfully **12** historically, legitimately

**authenticate**
**04** test **05** prove **06** attest, ratify, signet, verify **07** certify, confirm, endorse, warrant **08** accredit, notarize, validate, vouch for **09** authorize, guarantee **11** corroborate **12** substantiate

**authentication**
**10** validation **11** attestation, endorsement **12** confirmation, ratification, verification **13** accreditation, authorization, corroboration **14** substantiation

**authenticity**
**05** truth **07** honesty **08** accuracy, fidelity, legality, validity, veracity **09** certainty **10** legitimacy **11** correctness, credibility, genuineness, reliability **12** faithfulness, truthfulness **13** dependability **15** trustworthiness

**author**
**03** pen **04** hand, poet **05** maker, mover **06** parent, penman, writer **07** creator, founder, planner **08** composer, designer, essayist, inventor, lyricist, novelist, penwoman, producer, reporter, volumist **09** architect, dramatist, garreteer, initiator, ink-jerker, scribbler **10** biographer, ink-slinger, journalist, librettist, originator, playwright, prime mover, songwriter, trecentist **11** contributor, hedge-writer **12** man of letters, paper-stainer, screenwriter **13** Deuteronomist, revelationist **14** woman of letters

*See also* **writer**

*Authors include:*

**03** **Eco** (Umberto), **Kee** (Robert), **Lee** (Harper), **Lee** (Laurie), **Poe** (Edgar Allan), **Pym** (Barbara), **RLS**, **Roy** (Arundhati)
**04** **Amis** (Kingsley), **Amis** (Martin), **Behn** (Aphra), **Böll** (Heinrich), **Boyd** (William), **Buck** (Pearl S), **Cary** (Joyce), **Dahl** (Roald), **Dane** (Clemence), **Fine** (Anne), **Ford** (Ford Madox), **Gide** (André), **Grey** (Zane), **Hogg** (James), **Hope** (Anthony), **Hugo** (Victor), **Jane** (Fred T), **King** (Stephen), **Levi** (Primo), **Loos** (Anita), **Mann** (Thomas), **Okri** (Ben), **Puzo** (Mario), **Rhys** (Jean), **Roth** (Philip), **Sade** (Marquis de), **Saki**, **Sand** (George), **Seth** (Vikram), **Shah** (Eddy), **Snow** (C P), **Wain** (John), **West** (Dame Rebecca), **Wood** (Mrs Henry), **Zola** (Emile)
**05** **Adams** (Douglas), **Adams** (Richard), **Agnon** (Shmuel Yosef), **Banks** (Iain), **Banks** (Lynne Reid), **Bates** (H E), **Behan** (Brendan), **Benét** (Stephen), **Bowen** (Elizabeth), **Bragg** (Melvyn), **Brink** (André), **Brown** (George Mackay), **Bunin** (Ivan), **Byatt** (A S), **Camus** (Albert), **Chase** (James Hadley), **Craik** (Dinah), **Crane** (Stephen), **Dante**, **Defoe** (Daniel), **Desai** (Anita), **Doyle** (Roddy), **Doyle** (Sir Arthur Conan), **Dumas** (Alexandre, fils), **Dumas** (Alexandre, père), **Eliot** (George), **Ellis** (Alice Thomas), **Elton** (Ben), **Faure** (Edgar), **Frayn** (Michael), **Genet** (Jean), **Gogol** (Nikolai), **Gorky** (Maxim), **Grass** (Günter), **Hardy** (Thomas), **Hasek** (Jaroslav), **Hesse** (Hermann), **Heyer** (Georgette), **Innes** (Hammond), **James** (Henry), **James** (P D), **Joyce** (James), **Kafka** (Franz), **Keane** (Molly), **Kesey** (Ken), **Laski** (Marghanita), **Lewis** (C S), **Lewis** (M G 'Monk'), **Lewis** (Sinclair), **Lewis** (Wyndham), **Lodge** (David), **Lowry** (Malcolm), **Marsh** (Dame Ngaio), **Milne** (A A), **Moore** (Brian), **Moore** (Thomas), **Munro** (H H), **O'Hara** (John), **Paton** (Alan), **Peake** (Mervyn), **Plath** (Sylvia), **Powys** (John), **Queen** (Ellery), **Reade** (Charles), **Sagan** (Françoise), **Scott** (Paul), **Scott** (Sir Walter), **Shute** (Nevil), **Simon** (Claude), **Smith** (Dodie), **Smith** (Stevie), **Smith** (Wilbur), **Spark** (Dame Muriel), **Staël** (Madame de), **Stowe** (Harriet Beecher), **Swift** (Graham), **Swift** (Jonathan), **Twain** (Mark), **Tyler** (Anne), **Verne** (Jules), **Vidal** (Gore), **Waugh** (Auberon), **Waugh** (Evelyn), **Wells** (H G), **White** (Patrick), **White**

(T H), **Wilde** (Oscar), **Wolfe** (Thomas Clayton), **Wolfe** (Tom), **Woolf** (Virginia), **Yates** (Dornford), **Yonge** (Charlotte)

**06** **Achebe** (Chinua), **Alcott** (Louisa May), **Aldiss** (Brian), **Ambler** (Eric), **Aragon** (Louis), **Archer** (Jeffrey), **Asimov** (Isaac), **Atwood** (Margaret), **Austen** (Jane), **Auster** (Paul), **Balzac** (Honoré de), **Barker** (Pat), **Barnes** (Julian), **Barrie** (Sir J M), **Bellow** (Saul), **Binchy** (Maeve), **Blixen** (Karen, Lady), **Blyton** (Enid), **Borges** (Jorge Luis), **Braine** (John), **Bratby** (John), **Brazil** (Angela), **Brontë** (Anne), **Brontë** (Charlotte), **Brontë** (Emily), **Bryson** (Bill), **Buchan** (John), **Bunyan** (John), **Burney** (Fanny), **Butler** (Samuel), **Capote** (Truman), **Carter** (Angela), **Cather** (Willa), **Chopin** (Kate), **Clancy** (Tom), **Clarke** (Arthur C), **Conrad** (Joseph), **Cooper** (James Fenimore), **Cooper** (Jilly), **Cronin** (A J), **Faulks** (Sebastian), **Fowles** (John), **France** (Anatole), **Fuller** (Margaret), **Gibbon** (Lewis Grassic), **Godden** (Rumer), **Godwin** (William), **Goethe** (Johann Wolfgang von), **Graham** (Winston), **Graves** (Robert), **Greene** (Graham), **Haddon** (Mark), **Hamsun** (Knut), **Heller** (Joseph), **Hilton** (James), **Holtby** (Winifred), **Hornby** (Nick), **Hughes** (Thomas), **Huxley** (Aldous), **Ibáñez** (Vicente Blasco), **Jensen** (Johannes V), **Jerome** (Jerome K), **Keller** (Gottfried), **Kelman** (James), **Laclos** (Pierre Choderlos de), **Larkin** (Philip), **Le Fanu** (Sheridan), **Lively** (Penelope), **London** (Jack), **Mailer** (Norman), **Malouf** (David), **McEwan** (Ian), **Miller** (Henry), **Morgan** (Charles), **Nesbit** (E), **O'Brien** (Edna), **O'Brien** (Flann), **Orwell** (George), **Porter** (Katherine Anne), **Powell** (Anthony), **Proulx** (E Annie), **Proust** (Marcel), **Rankin** (Ian), **Sapper**, **Sartre** (Jean-Paul), **Sayers** (Dorothy L), **Sewell** (Anna), **Sharpe** (Tom), **Singer** (Isaac Bashevis), **Steele** (Danielle), **Sterne** (Laurence), **Stoker** (Bram), **Storey** (David), **Tagore** (Rabindranath), **Thomas** (Dylan), **Traven** (B), **Undset** (Sigrid), **Updike** (John), **Walker** (Alice), **Warner** (Marina), **Warren** (Robert Penn), **Weldon** (Fay), **Wesley** (Mary), **Wilder** (Thornton), **Wilson** (Sir Angus), **Wright** (Richard)

**07** **Ackroyd** (Peter), **Aksakov** (Sergei), **Angelou** (Maya), **Arrabal** (Fernando), **Baldwin** (James), **Ballard** (J G), **Beckett** (Samuel), **Bennett** (Arnold), **Bentine** (Michael), **Burgess** (Anthony), **Burnett** (Frances Hodgson), **Calvino** (Italo), **Canetti** (Elias), **Carroll** (Lewis), **Chatwin** (Bruce), **Chekhov** (Anton), **Clavell** (James), **Cleland** (John), **Cocteau** (Jean), **Coetzee** (J M), **Colette**, **Collins** (Wilkie), **Cookson** (Catherine), **Deledda** (Grazia), **Dickens** (Charles), **Diderot** (Denis), **Dineson** (Isaac), **Douglas** (Norman), **Drabble** (Margaret), **Durrell** (Gerald), **Durrell** (Lawrence), **Fleming** (Ian), **Forster** (E M), **Forster** (Margaret), **Forsyth** (Frederick), **Francis** (Dick), **Gaskell** (Mrs Elizabeth), **Gautier** (Théophile), **Gibbons** (Stella), **Gissing** (George), **Golding** (William), **Grahame** (Kenneth), **Grisham** (John), **Haggard** (Sir H Rider), **Hammett** (Dashiell), **Hartley** (L P), **Kerouac** (Jack), **Kipling** (Rudyard), **Kundera** (Milan), **Lardner** (Ring), **Laxness** (Halldór), **Le Carré** (John), **Lehmann** (Rosamond), **Lessing** (Doris), **Maclean** (Alistair), **Mahfouz** (Naguib), **Malamud** (Bernard), **Malraux** (André), **Manning** (Olivia), **Manzoni** (Alessandro), **Marryat** (Captain Frederick), **Maugham** (W Somerset), **Mauriac** (François), **Mérimée** (Prosper), **Mishima** (Yukio), **Mitford** (Nancy), **Moravia** (Alberto), **Murdoch** (Dame Iris), **Nabokov** (Vladimir), **Naipaul** (V S), **Peacock** (Thomas Love), **Prévost** (l'Abbé), **Pullman** (Philip), **Pushkin** (Alexander), **Pynchon** (Thomas), **Ransome** (Arthur), **Raphael** (Frederic), **Renault** (Mary), **Rendell** (Ruth), **Richler** (Mordecai), **Robbins** (Harold), **Rolland** (Romain), **Rowling** (J K), **Rushdie** (Salman), **Sassoon** (Siegfried), **Shelley** (Mary), **Shields** (Carol), **Simenon** (Georges), **Sitwell** (Sir Osbert), **Soyinka** (Wole), **Spender** (Sir Stephen), **Surtees** (Robert Smith), **Theroux** (Paul), **Tolkien** (J R R), **Tolstoy** (Leo, Count), **Tremain** (Rose), **Wallace** (Lewis), **Walpole** (Sir Hugh), **Wharton** (Edith), **Wyndham** (John)

**08** **Andersen** (Hans Christian), **Apuleius** (Lucius), **Asturias** (Miguel), **Barbusse** (Henri), **Beckford** (William Thomas), **Beerbohm** (Sir Max), **Björnson** (Björnstjerne), **Bradbury** (Malcolm), **Bradbury** (Ray), **Bradford** (Barbara Taylor), **Brittain** (Vera), **Brookner** (Anita), **Bulgakov** (Mikhail), **Caldwell** (Erskine), **Cartland** (Barbara), **Chandler** (Raymond), **Christie** (Dame Agatha), **Constant** (Benjamin), **Cornwell** (Patricia), **Crompton** (Richmal), **Day-Lewis** (Cecil), **Deighton** (Len), **De La Mare** (Walter), **Disraeli** (Benjamin), **Donleavy** (J P), **Faulkner** (William), **Fielding** (Henry), **Flaubert** (Gustave), **Forester** (C S), **Francome** (John), **Goncourt** (Edmond de), **Gordimer** (Nadine), **Hochhuth** (Rolf), **Huysmans** (J K), **Ishiguro** (Kazuo), **Jhabvala** (Ruth Prawer), **Kawabata** (Yasunari), **Keneally** (Thomas), **Kingsley** (Charles), **Koestler** (Arthur), **Lagerlöf** (Selma), **Lawrence** (D H), **Lockhart** (John Gibson), **Macaulay** (Dame Rose), **McCarthy** (Mary), **Melville** (Herman), **Meredith** (George), **Michener** (James A), **Milligan** (Spike), **Mitchell** (Margaret), **Morrison** (Toni), **Mortimer** (John), **Murasaki** (Shikibu), **Oliphant** (Margaret), **Ondaatje** (Michael), **Remarque** (Erich Maria), **Rousseau** (Jean Jacques), **Salinger** (J D), **Sillitoe** (Alan), **Sinclair** (Upton), **Smollett** (Tobias), **Spillane** (Mickey), **Stendhal**, **Tanizaki** (Junichiro), **Trollope** (Anthony), **Trollope** (Joanna), **Turgenev** (Ivan), **Voltaire**, **Vonnegut** (Kurt, Junior)

**09** **Allingham** (Margery), **Bernières** (Louis de), **Bleasdale** (Alan), **Burroughs** (Edgar Rice), **Burroughs** (William S), **Cervantes** (Miguel de), **Charteris** (Leslie), **Chatterji** (Bankim), **D'Annunzio** (Gabriele), **Delafield** (E M), **De La Roche** (Mazo), **De Quincey** (Thomas), **Dos Passos** (John), **Du Maurier** (Dame Daphne), **Du Maurier** (George), **Edgeworth** (Maria), **Gerhardie** (William), **Goldsmith** (Oliver), **Greenwood** (Walter), **Grossmith** (George), **Grossmith** (Weedon), **Guareschi** (Giovanni), **Hauptmann** (Gerhart), **Hawthorne** (Nathaniel), **Hemingway** (Ernest), **Highsmith** (Patricia), **Hölderlin** (Friedrich), **Hopkinson** (Sir Tom), **Isherwood** (Christopher), **Lampedusa** (Giuseppe Tomasi de), **Lermontov** (Mikhail), **Linklater** (Eric), **Llewellyn** (Richard), **Mackenzie** (Sir Compton), **Mankowitz** (Wolf), **Mansfield** (Katherine), **Marinetti** (Filippo Tommaso), **Masefield** (John), **McCullers** (Carson), **Mitchison** (Naomi), **Monsarrat** (Nicholas), **Pasternak** (Boris), **Pratchett** (Terry), **Priestley** (J B), **Radcliffe** (Ann), **Santayana** (George), **Sholokhov** (Mikhail), **Steinbeck** (John), **Stevenson** (Robert Louis), **Thackeray** (William Makepeace), **Wodehouse** (Sir P G)

**10** **Bainbridge** (Beryl), **Ballantyne** (R M), **Chesterton** (G K), **De Beauvoir** (Simone), **Dostoevsky** (Fyodor), **Fairbairns** (Zoë), **Fitzgerald** (F Scott), **Galsworthy** (John), **Lagerkvist** (Pär), **Maupassant** (Guy de), **Pirandello** (Luigi), **Richardson** (Dorothy M), **Richardson** (Samuel), **Strindberg** (August), **Van der Post** (Sir Laurens), **Waterhouse** (Keith)

**11** **Kazantzakis** (Nikos), **Sienkiewicz** (Henryk), **Vargas Llosa** (Mario)

**12** **Quiller-Couch** (Sir Arthur), **Robbe-Grillet** (Alain), **Saint-Exupéry** (Antoine de), **Solzhenitsyn** (Aleksandr)

**13** Alain-Fournier (Henri), García Márquez (Gabriel), Sackville-West (Vita)
**14** Compton-Burnett (Dame Ivy)
**15** Somerset Maugham (William)

*See also* **playwright**; **poet**

**authoritarian**
**05** harsh, rigid, tough **06** despot, severe, strict, tyrant **08** absolute, autocrat, despotic, dictator, dogmatic **09** imperious, Orwellian **10** absolutist, autocratic, inflexible, oppressive, tyrannical, unyielding **11** dictatorial, doctrinaire, domineering, magisterial **12** totalitarian **14** disciplinarian

**authoritarianism**
**06** Nazism **07** Fascism **09** autocracy, despotism **10** absolutism, oppression, repression **12** dictatorship **15** totalitarianism

**authoritative**
**04** bold, true **05** crisp, sound, valid **07** factual, learned **08** accepted, accurate, approved, decisive, faithful, imposing, official, reliable, truthful **09** assertive, audacious, authentic, confident, masterful, scholarly **10** authorized, commanding, convincing, definitive, dependable, imperative, legitimate, sanctioned **11** cathedratic, magisterial, self-assured, trustworthy **13** self-confident, self-possessed **14** sure of yourself

**authoritatively**
**06** boldly **08** reliably **09** factually **10** accurately, decisively, dependably, ex cathedra, faithfully **11** assertively, audaciously, confidently **12** convincingly, definitively **13** authentically **15** self-confidently

**authority**
**03** bar **04** buff, mana, name, rule, sage, sway, them, they **05** adept, bible, clout, force, leave, power, right, say-so, state **06** expert, master, muscle, permit, pundit **07** command, consent, control, council, faculty, go-ahead, licence, prelacy, royalty, scepter, sceptre, scholar, Vatican, warrant **08** dominion, lordship, sanction, thumbs-up **09** influence, provostry, supremacy, vicariate **10** domination, fatherhood, government, green light, inquirendo, management, permission, specialist **11** bureaucracy, connoisseur, credentials, imperialism, landlordism, officialdom, prerogative, sovereignty **12** carte blanche, jurisdiction, professional, protectorate **13** authorization, establishment **14** administration, patria potestas **15** the powers that be

• **emblem of authority**
**03** rod **04** vare, wand **05** sword **07** scepter, sceptre

• **post of authority**
**04** seat

**authorization**
**02** OK **04** okay, pass **05** leave, stamp **06** permit **07** consent, go-ahead, licence, mandate, warrant **08** approval, passport, retainer, sanction, thumbs-up, warranty **09** authority **10** commission, empowering, green light, permission, validation, warrantise **11** credentials, entitlement, procuratory **12** confirmation, ratification **13** accreditation

**authorize**
**02** OK **03** let **04** okay **05** allow **06** enable, permit, ratify **07** approve, confirm, empower, entitle, licence, license, mandate, warrant **08** accredit, legalize, sanction, validate **09** consent to, make legal, privilege **10** commission **15** give authority to

**authorized**
**05** legal, legit **06** lawful **08** approved, licensed, official **09** permitted, warranted **10** accredited, recognized **12** commissioned, under licence

**autobahn**
**02** AB

**autobiography**
**02** CV **05** diary **06** memoir **07** journal, memoirs **09** life story **15** story of your life

**autocracy**
**07** fascism, tyranny **08** autarchy **09** despotism **10** absolutism **12** dictatorship **15** totalitarianism

**autocrat**
**04** cham **06** Caesar, despot, Hitler, tyrant **08** dictator **10** absolutist, panjandrum **12** little Hitler, totalitarian **13** authoritarian

**autocratic**
**08** absolute, despotic **09** autarchic, imperious **10** tyrannical **11** all-powerful, dictatorial, domineering, overbearing **12** totalitarian **13** authoritarian

**autograph**
**04** mark, name, sign **07** endorse, initial **08** initials, monicker **09** signature **11** countersign, endorsement, inscription, put your mark **13** write your name

**automatic**
**06** reflex **07** certain, natural, robotic, routine **08** knee-jerk, unmanned, unwilled **09** automated, necessary, Pavlovian **10** inevitable, mechanical, mechanized, programmed, push-button, self-acting, unthinking **11** inescapable, instinctive, involuntary, spontaneous, unavoidable, unconscious **12** computerized **14** self-activating, self-propelling, self-regulating, uncontrollable

*See also* **gun**

**automatically**
**09** certainly, naturally, routinely **10** inevitably **11** inescapably, necessarily, robotically, unavoidably **12** mechanically, unthinkingly **13** instinctively, involuntarily, spontaneously, unconsciously **14** uncontrollably

**automobile**
**03** car **05** motor **07** vehicle **08** motor car **12** motor vehicle

*See also* **car**

**autonomous**
**04** free **09** sovereign **11** independent **13** self-directing, self-governing **15** self-determining

**autonomy**
**07** autarky, freedom **08** free will, home rule, self-rule **11** sovereignty **12** independence **14** rangatiratanga, self-government **15** self-sufficiency

**autopsy**
**08** necropsy **10** dissection, post-mortem

**autumn**
**04** fall **07** back-end, harvest **08** leaf-fall

**auxiliary**
**03** aid **05** extra, spare **06** aiding, backer, back-up, helper, second **07** helping, partner, reserve **09** accessory, adminicle, ancillary, assistant, assisting, emergency, secondary, supporter **10** additional, peripheral, subsidiary, substitute, supporting, supportive **11** subordinate **12** right-hand man **13** supplementary **14** right-hand woman **15** second-in-command

**avail**
**03** dow, use **04** doff, vail **05** lower, serve, stead **06** accept, alight, draw on **07** bestead, prevail, succeed, utilize **08** exercise, resort to **09** make use of **15** take advantage of

• **to no avail**
**06** in vain, vainly **11** fruitlessly **13** ineffectually **14** unsuccessfully, without success

**available**
**02** on **04** free, open **05** handy, on tap, ready, to let **06** at hand, on hand, single, to hand, usable, vacant **07** not busy, untaken **09** at liberty **10** accessible, convenient, disposable, obtainable, procurable, unoccupied, up for grabs **11** contactable, forthcoming, off the shelf, within reach **12** up your sleeve **13** at your command **14** at your disposal

**avalanche**
**04** wave **05** flood **06** deluge **07** barrage, cascade, lauwine, torrent **08** landslip, snowslip **09** landslide **10** inundation

**avant-garde**
**06** far-out, modern, way-out **07** go-ahead **08** advanced, original **09** inventive **10** futuristic, innovative, innovatory, pioneering **11** progressive **12** contemporary, enterprising,

experimental **14** forward-looking, ground-breaking, unconventional

**avarice**
**05** greed **06** misery **07** avidity **08** meanness **09** pleonexia, the gimmes **10** greediness **11** gourmandise, materialism, miserliness, selfishness **12** covetousness **15** acquisitiveness

**avaricious**
**04** avid, gare, mean **06** greedy, grippy, sordid **07** griping, gripple, miserly **08** covetous, grasping **09** mercenary, rapacious **10** pleonectic **11** acquisitive **12** curmudgeonly

**avatar** *see* **incarnation**

**avenge**
**05** repay, right, venge, wreak **06** punish **07** pay back, requite **09** get back at, retaliate, vindicate **11** get even with **14** get your own back, take revenge for

**avenger**
**04** goel

**avenue**
**02** Av **03** ave, way **04** line, road, walk **05** allée, corso, drive, grove, vista **06** dromos, method, midway, scheme, street **07** Madison, passage **08** approach, broadway **09** boulevard **10** cradlewalk **12** thoroughfare **13** modus operandi **14** course of action

**aver**
**04** avow **05** state **06** affirm, attest, cattle **07** confirm, declare **08** maintain **09** make known **11** possessions

**average**
**02** av **03** ave, par, run **04** fair, mean, mode, norm, rule, so-so **05** usual **06** centre, common, medial, median, medium, middle, Nikkei, normal **07** regular, routine, typical **08** Dow-Jones, everyday, mediocre, middling, mid-point, moderate, ordinary, passable, standard **09** tolerable **10** not much cop **11** indifferent, not up to much **12** intermediate, run-of-the-mill, satisfactory **13** no great shakes, unexceptional **14** common-or-garden, fair to middling, nothing special **15** undistinguished

• **on average**
**06** mainly, mostly **07** as a rule, chiefly, usually **08** normally **09** generally, in the main, routinely, typically **10** by and large, on the whole, ordinarily

**averse**
**05** loath **07** hostile, opposed **09** reluctant, unwilling **10** indisposed **11** disinclined, ill-disposed **12** antagonistic, antipathetic, unfavourable

**aversion**
**04** hate **06** hatred, horror, phobia **07** disgust, dislike **08** distaste, loathing **09** antipathy, hostility, repulsion, revulsion **10** abhorrence, antagonism, opposition, reluctance, repugnance **11** abomination, detestation **13** unwillingness **14** disinclination
*See also* **phobia**

**avert**
**03** wry **04** stop **05** avoid, evade, parry **07** deflect, fend off, forfend, head off, obviate, prevent, ward off **08** preclude, stave off, turn away **09** forestall, frustrate, turn aside

**aviary**
**06** volary

**aviation**
**06** flight, flying **11** aeronautics

*Aviation-related terms include:*

**04** dive, drag, flap, taxi
**05** fly-by, pilot, plane, prang
**06** airway, hangar, runway, thrust
**07** airline, air miss, airport, airship, captain, console, fly-past, landing, lift-off, spoiler, take-off
**08** aircraft, airfield, airplane, airspace, airstrip, altitude, black box, nose dive, subsonic, windsock, wingspan
**09** aeroplane, aerospace, crash dive, fixed-wing, fly-by-wire, jetstream, overshoot, parachute, sonic boom, test pilot, touchdown
**10** chocks away, flight crew, Mach number, solo flight, supersonic, test flight, undershoot
**11** ground speed, loop-the-loop, night-flying, vapour trail
**12** control tower, crash-landing, landing strip, maiden flight, sound barrier
**13** ground control, jet propulsion
**14** automatic pilot, flight recorder, holding pattern

**aviator**
**05** flyer, pilot **06** airman **08** airwoman **12** aircraftsman **14** aircraftswoman

*Aviators include:*

**04** **Byrd** (Richard Evelyn), **Rust** (Mathias), **Udet** (Ernst)
**05** **Bader** (Sir Douglas), **Balbo** (Italo, Count), **Brown** (Sir Arthur Whitten), **Johns** (Captain W E), **Smith** (Sir Ross)
**06** **Alcock** (Sir John), **Cessna** (Clyde), **Gibson** (Guy), **Harris** (Sir Arthur 'Bomber'), **Hughes** (Howard), **Nobile** (Umberto), **Wright** (Orville), **Wright** (Wilbur), **Yeager** (Chuck)
**07** **Bennett** (Floyd), **Blériot** (Louis), **Branson** (Richard), **Cochran** (Jacqueline), **Dornier** (Claudius), **Douglas** (Donald Wills), **Earhart** (Amelia), **Fossett** (Steve), **Giffard** (Henri), **Goering** (Hermann), **Hinkler** (Bert), **Johnson** (Amy), **Korolev** (Sergei), **Piccard** (Auguste), **Sopwith** (Sir Thomas)
**08** **Brabazon** (John, Lord), **Cheshire** (Leonard, Lord), **Zeppelin** (Count Ferdinand von)
**09** **Blanchard** (Jean Pierre), **Lindbergh** (Charles), **McDonnell** (James Smith)
**10** **Lindstrand** (Per), **Richthofen** (Manfred, Baron von)
**11** **Montgolfier** (Jacques), **Montgolfier** (Joseph)
**12** **Saint-Exupéry** (Antoine de)
**13** **Messerschmitt** (Willy)

**avid**
**03** mad **04** keen **05** crazy, eager, great **06** ardent, greedy, hungry **07** athirst, devoted, earnest, fervent, intense, thirsty, zealous **08** covetous, grasping, ravenous **09** dedicated, fanatical **10** insatiable, passionate **12** enthusiastic

**avidly**
**05** madly **06** keenly **07** eagerly **08** ardently, greedily, hungrily **09** devotedly, earnestly, fervently, intensely, thirstily, zealously **10** covetously, insatiably, ravenously **11** fanatically **12** passionately

**avocado**
**08** aguacate **09** guacamole **13** alligator pear

**avocet**
**07** awlbird, scooper

**avoid**
**03** fly **04** balk, duck, miss, shun **05** avert, dodge, elude, evade, evite, hedge, shirk **06** bypass, escape, eschew **07** decline, evitate, forbear, prevent **08** get out of, get round, sidestep **09** give a miss **10** circumvent **11** abstain from, make a detour, refrain from, run away from, shy away from **12** hold back from, keep away from, stay away from, steer clear of

**avoidable**
**08** eludible, evitable **09** avertible, escapable, stoppable **11** preventable

**avow**
**03** vow **04** aver **05** admit, state, swear **06** assert, attest, avouch **07** confess, declare, profess **08** maintain **11** acknowledge

**avowed**
**04** open **05** overt, sworn **07** confest **08** admitted, declared **09** barefaced, confessed, professed **10** professing **12** acknowledged **13** self-confessed **14** self-proclaimed

**await**
**04** bide, stay **05** tarry **06** expect, remain **07** hope for, look for, wait for **10** anticipate **12** be in store for, lie in wait for **13** look forward to

**awake**
**04** stir, wake **05** abray, alert, alive, aware, rouse, waken **06** abrade, abraid, arouse, awaken, wake up **07** aroused, mindful, wakeful **08** stirring, vigilant, watchful **09** attentive, conscious, observant, sensitive, wide awake **12** appreciative

**awaken**
**04** stir, wake **05** awake, rouse, waken **06** abraid, excite, wake up **07** inspire

**08** engender, generate **09** stimulate **11** disentrance **14** cause to realize

**awakening**
**05** birth **06** waking **07** arousal, awaking, revival, rousing **08** wakening **09** animating **10** activation, enlivening **11** reanimating, revivifying, stimulation **12** vivification

**award**
**03** cup **04** aret, gift, give, gong **05** allot, allow, arett, endow, grant, medal, order, prize **06** accord, addeem, addoom, adward, assign, bestow, confer, modify, reward, trophy **07** adjudge, bursary, honours, payment, present, rosette **08** accolade, allocate, bestowal, citation, decision, decorate, dispense **09** allotment, allowance, apportion, conferral, determine, endowment, judgement **10** adjudicate, decoration, distribute, palatinate, settlement, subvention **11** certificate, scholarship **12** adjudication, commendation, dispensation, presentation

*Awards and prizes include:*

**02** CH, MM, OM
**03** CBE, OBE
**04** Brit, Emmy, Tony
**05** Bafta, César, Nobel, Oscar
**06** Booker, Grammy, Orange, Turner
**07** Academy, Olivier
**08** Palme d'Or, Pulitzer, Stirling
**09** Grand Jury, Grand Prix, Man Booker, Templeton
**10** Golden Bear, Golden Palm
**11** Fields Medal, Golden Globe
**12** Prix Goncourt
**13** Whitbread Book

*See also* **honour**; **military**

**aware**
**03** hip **05** alert, awake, sharp **06** shrewd, sussed **07** alive to, clued up, heedful, knowing, mindful **08** apprised, familiar, informed, sensible, sentient, vigilant **09** attentive, au courant, cognizant, conscient, conscious, in the know, observant, on the ball, sensitive **10** acquainted, conversant **11** enlightened, recognizant **12** appreciative **13** knowledgeable
• **aware of**
**04** on to
• **be aware of**
**03** ken **04** feel, know

**awareness**
**03** sus **04** suss **05** grasp **06** vision **07** insight, samadhi **09** knowledge **10** cognizance, perception **11** familiarity, panesthesia, recognition, sensitivity **12** acquaintance, appreciation, panaesthesia **13** consciousness, sensitiveness, understanding

**awash**
**04** full **05** alive **06** packed, soaked **07** flooded, replete, teeming **08** crawling, drenched, swarming **09** inundated, saturated, submerged

**away**
◇ *anagram indicator*
**02** by **03** far, fro, off, out **04** from **05** apart, aside, hence **06** abroad, absent **08** from here **09** elsewhere, from there, not at home, not at work, on holiday **10** on vacation **11** at a distance

**awe**
**04** fear **05** dread **06** honour, terror, wonder **07** respect **09** amazement, reverence **10** admiration, veneration, wonderment **12** apprehension, astonishment, stupefaction

**awed**
**06** amazed, solemn **07** fearful, stunned **09** awe-struck **10** astonished **11** reverential **12** lost for words

**awe-inspiring**
**06** moving, solemn **07** amazing, awesome, exalted, sublime **08** daunting, dazzling, fearsome, imposing, majestic, numinous, striking, stunning **09** wonderful **10** formidable, impressive, stupefying, stupendous **11** astonishing, magnificent, spectacular **12** breathtaking, intimidating, mind-boggling, overwhelming

**awesome**
**07** amazing **08** daunting, stunning **10** formidable, impressive **11** astonishing, jaw-dropping, spectacular **12** breathtaking, intimidating, mind-boggling, overwhelming **13** extraordinary

**awestruck**
**04** awed **06** amazed **09** awe-struck, impressed **10** astonished **12** lost for words

**awful**
◇ *anagram indicator*
**03** ill **04** crap, dire, naff, sick **05** lousy, nasty, pants, rough, seedy, spewy **06** crummy, horrid, in pain, poorly, unwell **07** abysmal, fearful, ghastly, heinous, the pits **08** alarming, dreadful, gruesome, horrible, horrific, inferior, pathetic, shocking, terrible, very poor **09** appalling, atrocious, frightful, third-rate, washed out **10** disgusting, horrifying, inadequate, second-rate, unpleasant **11** distressing **14** a load of rubbish, unsatisfactory **15** under the weather

**awfully**
◇ *anagram indicator*
**04** very **06** deeply, really **07** greatly **08** terribly **09** extremely, immensely **10** absolutely, dreadfully, remarkably **12** particularly, tremendously, unbelievably

**awhile**
**10** for a moment **11** for some time **13** for a short time

**awkward**
◇ *anagram indicator*
**03** shy **04** rude **05** blate, gawky, inept, nasty **06** clumsy, clunky, fiddly, gauche, rustic, thumby, touchy, tricky, ungain **07** bashful, boorish, cubbish, loutish, prickly, spastic, stroppy, uncouth **08** annoying, bungling, clownish, delicate, handless, inexpert, lubberly, stubborn, ungainly, untoward, unwieldy **09** all thumbs, difficult, graceless, ham-fisted, ill at ease, inelegant, irritable, maladroit, obstinate, unskilful **10** cumbersome, left-handed, perplexing, ungraceful, unpleasant **11** disobliging, embarrassed, heavy-handed, obstructive, problematic, troublesome **12** bloody-minded, embarrassing, inconvenient **13** chuckle-headed, oversensitive, uncomfortable, unco-operative, unco-ordinated **15** unaccommodating

**awkwardly**
◇ *anagram indicator*
**05** shyly **07** ineptly **08** clumsily, uneasily, ungainly **09** bashfully **10** inexpertly **11** gracelessly, ham-fistedly, inelegantly, maladroitly, unskilfully **12** ungracefully **13** heavy-handedly, uncomfortably

**awkwardness**
**09** confusion, gawkiness, inaptness **10** clumsiness, inaptitude, inelegance, maladdress, uneasiness **11** bashfulness **12** discomfiture, ungainliness **13** embarrassment, gracelessness, left-handiness **15** heavy-handedness

**awl**
**04** brog, prod, stob **05** elsin **06** elshin

**awn**
**05** beard

**awning**
**04** tilt **05** blind, cover, shade **06** canopy **07** shelter **08** covering, shamiana, sunblind, sunshade, velarium **09** shamianah

**awry**
◇ *anagram indicator*
**03** cam, kam **04** skew **05** aglee, agley, amiss, askew, kamme, tipsy, wonky, wrong **06** skivie, uneven **07** askance, athwart, crooked, haywire, oblique, tortive, twisted **08** cockeyed **09** off-centre, skew-whiff **10** misaligned, out of joint **12** asymmetrical, by transverse

**axe**
**03** cut, hew **04** bill, celt, chop, fell, fire, sack **05** split **06** cancel, cleave, guitar, labrys, piolet, remove, sparth **07** chopper, cleaver, cut down, dismiss, gisarme, halberd, hatchet, sparthe, twibill **08** get rid of, palstaff, palstave, partisan, throw out, tomahawk, withdraw **09** battle-axe, discharge, eliminate, saxophone, terminate **11** coup de poing, discontinue, thunderbolt **12** Jeddart staff
• **get the axe**
**10** get the boot, get the chop, get the sack **11** be cancelled

**axiom**
**02** ax **05** adage, maxim, truth **06** byword, dictum, truism **07** precept **08** aphorism, petition **09** postulate, principle **11** fundamental

**axiomatic**
**05** given **06** gnomic **07** assumed, certain, granted **08** accepted, manifest **10** aphoristic, proverbial, understood **11** fundamental, indubitable, presupposed, self-evident **12** unquestioned **14** apophthegmatic, unquestionable

**axis**
**01** X, Y, Z **03** cob **04** axle **05** henge, hinge, pivot **06** chital, rachis **07** rhachis **08** backbone, modiolus, vertical **10** centre-line, horizontal **13** macrodiagonal **14** brachydiagonal

**• end of axis**
**04** pole

**axle**
**03** pin, rod **04** axis **05** pivot, shaft, truck **07** mandrel, mandril, spindle **11** paddle-shaft

**Azerbaijan**
**02** AZ **03** AZE

**azure**
**04** Saxe **07** sky-blue **08** cerulean, pale blue **09** light blue **11** nattier blue **13** Cambridge blue

# B

**B**
**04** beta **05** bravo

**babble**
**03** gab, jaw **05** babel, prate **06** burble, cackle, gabble, gibber, gurgle, hubbub, jabber, jawing, mumble, murmur, mutter, waffle, witter **07** blabber, brabble, chatter, clamour, prattle, twaddle, twattle **08** rabbit on **09** gibberish, wittering **10** tongue-work **12** bibble-babble

**babe**
**03** sis, tot **04** baby **05** child **06** infant **07** newborn, tiny tot **08** suckling **10** babe in arms **11** newborn baby

**babel**
**03** din **05** chaos **06** babble, bedlam, hubbub, tumult, uproar **07** clamour, turmoil **08** disorder **09** commotion, confusion **10** hullabaloo **11** pandemonium

**baboon**
**05** drill **06** chacma, dog-ape, gelada **08** mandrill **09** hamadryad **12** Cynocephalus

**baby**
**03** bub, sis, tot, wee **04** babe, dear, love, mini, mite, tiny **05** bairn, bubby, child, dwarf, honey, small, sprog, teeny **06** infant, little, midget, minute **07** darling, dearest, neonate, newborn, papoose, sweetie, tiny tot, toddler **08** killcrop, pint-size, suckling **09** miniature, pint-sized **10** diminutive, small-scale, sweetheart **11** newborn baby

**babyish**
**04** baby, soft **05** naive, silly, sissy, young **07** foolish, puerile **08** childish, immature, juvenile **09** infantile

**Babylonian** *see* **god, goddess**

**bacchanalian**
**• bacchanalian expression**
**04** euoi, evoe, upsy **05** evhoe, evohe, upsee, upsey

**Bacchus**
**08** Dionysus

**bachelor**
**01** B **02** BA **04** Bach **05** batch

**bacillus**
**02** TB **03** bcg **07** anthrax **08** coliform **11** micrococcus

**back**
◇ *reversal indicator*
◇ *tail selection indicator*
**03** aft, ago, aid, bet, bid, end, off **04** abet, ante, away, help, hind, past, rear, risk, tail **05** boost, other, spine, stake, stern, wager **06** assist, before, behind, bygone, chance, dorsum, far end, favour, former, gamble, rachis, recede, recoil, retire, second, tergum **07** bolster, confirm, earlier, elapsed, endorse, finance, promote, rear end, regress, retreat, reverse, sponsor, support, sustain, tail end, venture **08** advocate, back away, backbone, backside, be behind, champion, hindmost, hind part, obsolete, outdated, previous, sanction, side with, withdraw **09** backtrack, backwards, encourage, get behind, other side, out of date, posterior, speculate, subsidize, to the rear **10** previously, underwrite **11** countenance, countersign, go backwards, reverse side **12** hindquarters **13** move backwards

**• back and forth**
◇ *palindrome indicator*

**• back away**
**06** recede, recoil **07** retreat **08** draw back, fall back, move back, step back, withdraw **10** give ground

**• back down**
**05** yield **06** give in, submit **07** abandon, concede, retreat **08** withdraw **09** back-pedal, backtrack, climb down, surrender

**• back out**
◇ *reversal indicator*
**06** cancel, cry off, give up, recant, resign, resile **07** abandon, call off, pull out, retreat **08** crawfish, go back on, withdraw **10** chicken out **11** get cold feet

**• back up**
**03** aid **04** abet **06** assist, second, soothe, verify **07** bear out, bolster, confirm, endorse, reserve, stand by, stand to, support **08** champion, validate **09** reinforce **11** corroborate **12** substantiate

**• behind your back**
**05** slyly **08** covertly, secretly, sneakily **09** furtively **11** deceitfully **15** surreptitiously

**• turn your back on**
**04** quit **05** leave **06** ignore, reject **07** abandon, exclude **08** throw out **09** repudiate **15** wash your hands of

**backbiting**
**05** abuse, catty, libel, slurs, spite **06** bitchy, gossip, malice **07** abusive, calumny, cattish, insults, slander **08** spiteful **09** aspersion, cattiness, criticism, libellous, malicious, vilifying **10** bitchiness, defamation, detraction, revilement, rubbishing, slanderous **11** denigration, disparaging, mud-slinging, slagging off **12** back-wounding, spitefulness, vilification, vituperation **13** disparagement

**backbone**
**04** core, grit, guts **05** basis, chine, nerve, pluck, power, spine **06** bottle, mettle **07** courage, nucleus, resolve, stamina, support **08** firmness, mainstay, strength, tenacity **09** character, toughness, vertebrae, willpower **10** foundation, resolution **11** cornerstone **12** spinal column, vertebration **13** determination, steadfastness **15** vertebral column

**backbreaking**
**04** hard **05** heavy **07** arduous, killing, onerous **08** crushing, grueling **09** gruelling, laborious, punishing, strenuous **10** exhausting

**backchat**
**03** lip **04** face **05** cheek, mouth, nerve, snash **08** back talk, repartee, rudeness **09** brass neck, cross-talk, impudence, insolence, sauciness **12** impertinence

**backer**
**05** angel **06** friend, funder, patron, second **07** sponsor **08** advocate, champion, investor, promoter, seconder, stickler **09** supporter **10** benefactor, subscriber, subsidizer, well-wisher **11** underwriter **12** bottle-holder

**backfire**
◇ *reversal indicator*
**04** fail, flop **06** blow up, recoil **07** explode, misfire, rebound **08** detonate, miscarry, ricochet **09** boomerang, discharge **10** strike back **12** defeat itself **14** score an own goal **15** be self-defeating, come home to roost

**backgammon**
**08** tick-tack, tric-trac, verquere **10** trick-track

**background**
**04** fond **05** field, scene **06** canvas, family, milieu, record, status **07** context, culture, factors, history, origins, setting **08** backdrop, breeding, surround **09** backcloth, cyclorama, education, framework, grounding, tradition **10** experience, influences, upbringing **11** credentials, environment, preparation **12** surroundings **13** circumstances **14** qualifications, social standing

**backhanded**
**06** ironic **07** awkward, dubious, oblique, reverse **08** indirect, sardonic, two-edged **09** ambiguous, equivocal, insincere, sarcastic **11** double-edged

**backing**
◇ *reversal indicator*
**03** aid **04** help, vamp **05** funds, grant
**06** backup, facing, favour, lining
**07** finance, funding, helpers, padding, subsidy, support **08** advocacy, approval, sanction **09** obbligato, patronage, promotion, seconding
**10** assistance, stiffening
**11** championing, co-operation, endorsement, interlining, sponsorship
**12** commendation, moral support
**13** accompaniment, encouragement, reinforcement

**backlash**
**06** recoil **08** backfire, kickback, reaction, reprisal, response
**09** boomerang **11** retaliation
**12** repercussion **13** counteraction

**backlog**
**04** heap, pile **05** hoard, stock
**06** excess, supply **07** reserve
**08** mountain, reserves **09** resources
**12** accumulation

**back-pedal**
**05** yield **06** give in, renege, submit
**07** abandon, concede, retract, retreat
**08** do a U-turn, go back on, take back, withdraw **09** about-face, about-turn, backtrack, climb down, surrender
**12** tergiversate **14** change your mind

**backslide**
◇ *reversal indicator*
**03** sin **04** slip **05** lapse, stray
**06** defect, desert, go back, renege, revert **07** default, regress, relapse
**08** go astray, turn away **10** apostatize
**12** tergiversate, turn your back **13** fall from grace

**backslider**
**07** reneger **08** apostate, defector, deserter, recreant, renegade, turncoat
**09** defaulter **10** recidivist
**13** tergiversator

**backsliding**
◇ *reversal indicator*
**05** lapse **07** relapse **08** apostasy
**09** defection, desertion **10** defaulting, regression **14** tergiversation

**backtrack**
◇ *reversal indicator*
**06** renege **08** do a U-turn, go back on, withdraw **09** back-pedal, climb down **12** tergiversate **14** change your mind

**backup**
**03** aid **04** help **07** support
**10** assistance **11** endorsement
**12** confirmation **13** encouragement, reinforcement

**backward**
◇ *reversal indicator*
**03** shy **04** hind, slow **05** timid
**06** arrear, averse, behind **07** arriéré, bashful, reverse **08** hesitant, immature, rearward, retarded, reticent, retiring, wavering **09** reluctant, shrinking, subnormal, to the back, unwilling
**10** hesitating, regressive, retrograde
**11** undeveloped **13** retrogressive
**14** underdeveloped
**15** unsophisticated

**backwards**
◇ *reversal indicator*
**05** aback, retro- **09** rearwards, to the back **12** regressively
**15** retrogressively

**backwash**
**04** flow, path, wake, wash **05** swell, waves **06** result **07** results **08** reaction
**09** aftermath **11** after effect, consequence **12** after effects, consequences, repercussion
**13** repercussions **14** reverberations

**backwater**
**05** bogan, scrub **06** slough **08** Woop Woop **11** remote place **13** isolated place

**backwoods**
**04** bush **05** brush **07** outback
**08** backveld **09** backwater, the sticks
**10** back-blocks, the boonies **11** remote place **12** back of beyond, the boondocks **13** isolated place
**15** middle of nowhere

**bacon**
**04** bard, spek **05** Roger, speck
**06** collar, gammon, lardon, rasher
**07** Francis, lardoon **08** forehock, pancetta

**bacteria** *see* **bacterium**

**bacteriology**

*Bacteriologists include:*

**04** **Cohn** (Ferdinand), **Gram** (Hans), **Koch** (Robert), **Roux** (Émile)
**05** **Avery** (Oswald), **Smith** (Theobald), **Twort** (Frederick)
**06** **Enders** (John)
**07** **Behring** (Emil von), **Buchner** (Hans), **Ehrlich** (Paul), **Fleming** (Sir Alexander), **Löffler** (Friedrich)
**08** **Calmette** (Albert), **Kitasato** (Shibasaburo)
**10** **Wassermann** (August von)

*See also* **biology**

**bacterium**
**03** bug, rod **04** cell, germ **06** mother, packet, strain **07** microbe **08** parasite, serotype, superbug **13** micro-organism

*Bacteria include:*

**04** MRSA
**06** coccus, vibrio
**07** Proteus
**08** bacillus, listeria, Shigella, yersinia, zoogloea
**09** Azobacter, peritrich, ray fungus, Rhizobium, spirillum, treponema, treponeme
**10** gonococcus, Klebsiella, Leptospira, salmonella, saprophyte
**11** acidophilus, Actinomyces, Azotobacter, Bacillaceae, clostridium, Escherichia, Pasteurella, Penicillium, pseudomonad, pseudomonas, spirochaete
**12** enterococcus, helicobacter, pneumococcus, vinegar plant
**13** campylobacter, Eubacteriales, fission fungus, lactobacillus, Mycobacterium, streptococcus
**14** actinobacillus, Corynebacteria, staphylococcus, trichobacteria, Vibrio cholerae, Yersinia pestis
**15** Escherichia coli, intestinal flora, sulphur bacteria

**bad**
◇ *anagram indicator*
**03** hot, ill, mal-, off **04** blue, eale, edgy, evil, foul, high, hurt, lewd, mean, naff, nice, poor, poxy, ropy, rude, sick, sour, vile, wack, weak **05** acute, angry, awful, black, cross, crude, dirty, gammy, grave, gross, harsh, humpy, juicy, lousy, narky, nasty, onkus, pants, ratty, sorry, testy **06** aching, coarse, crabby, crummy, faulty, feisty, filthy, gallus, gloomy, grumpy, guilty, in pain, mouldy, poorly, putrid, rancid, rotten, severe, shirty, shoddy, sinful, smutty, snappy, spoilt, stingy, tetchy, unruly, unwell, vulgar, wicked **07** abusive, adverse, ashamed, bilious, bolshie, botched, corrupt, crabbed, decayed, gnarled, grouchy, harmful, hurtful, immoral, in a huff, in a sulk, injured, intense, naughty, obscene, painful, peppery, prickly, profane, raunchy, ruinous, serious, stroppy, tainted, the pits, unhappy, useless, wayward, wounded **08** choleric, contrite, criminal, critical, damaging, diseased, dreadful, hopeless, impaired, impolite, indecent, inferior, mediocre, pathetic, petulant, shameful, terrible
**09** appalling, atrocious, crotchety, dangerous, defective, deficient, difficult, dishonest, dyspeptic, fractious, impatient, imperfect, injurious, insulting, irascible, irritable, offensive, querulous, reprobate, splenetic, third-rate, unhealthy
**10** apologetic, capernoity, degenerate, deplorable, despondent, ill-behaved, inadequate, mismanaged, outrageous, putrescent, refractory, remorseful, second-rate, shamefaced, unpleasant, unsuitable **11** a load of crap, bad-tempered, blasphemous, carnaptious, deleterious, destructive, detrimental, disobedient, distressing, incompetent, ineffective, ineffectual, mischievous, substandard, thin-skinned, undesirable, unfortunate, unwholesome **12** badly-behaved, cantankerous, contaminated, disagreeable, discourteous, inauspicious, inconvenient, putrefactive, unacceptable, unfavourable **13** inappropriate, quick-tempered, reprehensible **14** a load of garbage, a load of rubbish,

uncontrollable, unsatisfactory
**15** under the weather
• **not bad**
**02** OK **04** fair, so-so **07** average
**08** adequate, all right, passable
**09** quite good, tolerable
**10** acceptable, reasonable
**12** satisfactory

**badge**
**03** mon **04** blue, logo, mark, sign, star **05** brand, crest, eagle, patch, stamp, token, wings **06** button, device, emblem, ensign, rondel, shield, symbol **07** cockade, insigne, kikumon, rosette **08** episemon, insignia, numerals, vernicle **09** indicator, trademark **10** cognizance, escutcheon, indication **14** identification

**badger**
**03** nag **04** bait, goad, ride **05** brock, bully, harry, hound, ratel **06** chivvy, go on at, harass, hassle, keep at, pester, plague, teledu **07** torment **08** ballyrag, bullyrag, keep on at **09** importune
• **badger-like animal**
**05** ratel
• **badgers**
**04** cete

**badinage**
**05** borak, chaff **06** banter, humour **07** mockery, ribbing, teasing, waggery **08** dicacity, drollery, raillery, repartee, wordplay **10** jocularity, persiflage **11** give and take

**badly**
◇ *anagram indicator*
**03** ill, mis- **06** deeply, evilly, poorly **07** acutely, awfully, cruelly, gravely, greatly, ineptly, wrongly **08** bitterly, faultily, severely, sinfully, terribly, unfairly, very much, wickedly **09** adversely, crucially, extremely, immorally, intensely, painfully, seriously, unhappily, uselessly **10** carelessly, criminally, critically, enormously, improperly, shamefully **11** appallingly, dangerously, defectively, desperately, dishonestly, exceedingly, imperfectly, incorrectly, negligently, offensively **12** inadequately, pathetically, tremendously, unacceptably, unfavourably **13** incompetently, ineffectually, unfortunately **14** unsuccessfully
• **badly off**
**04** poor **05** needy **06** in need

**bad-mannered**
**04** rude **05** crude **06** coarse **07** boorish, cubbish, ill-bred, loutish, uncivil, uncouth **08** churlish, impolite, insolent **10** ill-behaved, unmannerly **11** ill-mannered, insensitive **12** badly-behaved, discourteous

**badminton**

*Badminton-related terms include:*

**03** net, set
**04** bird, kill
**05** clear, court, drive, flick, rally, serve, smash
**06** racket
**07** doubles, racquet, singles
**08** drop shot, wood shot
**11** shuttlecock
**12** service court
**13** underarm clear

**badness**
**03** sin **04** evil **07** cruelty **08** foulness, vileness **09** depravity, nastiness **10** corruption, dishonesty, immorality, wickedness **12** shamefulness **14** unpleasantness

**bad-tempered**
**04** edgy, mean **05** black, cross, humpy, narky, ratty, sulky, testy, vixen **06** crabby, feisty, gnarly, grumpy, shirty, snappy, stingy, tetchy **07** bilious, crabbed, crabbit, gnarled, grouchy, in a huff, in a mood, in a sulk, peppery, prickly, stroppy, vicious, vixenly **08** choleric, petulant, scratchy, vixenish **09** crotchety, dyspeptic, fractious, impatient, irascible, irritable, querulous, splenetic **10** capernoity, ill-natured, in a bad mood **11** carnaptious, curnaptious, dyspeptical, ill-humoured, thin-skinned **12** cantankerous **13** quick-tempered

**baffle**
◇ *anagram indicator*
**03** bar, fox, get **04** daze, faze, foil, mate **05** block, check, elude, evade, stump, throw, upset **06** bemuse, defeat, fickle, hinder, puzzle, thwart **07** bumbaze, confuse, flummox, mystify, nonplus, perplex **08** bewilder, confound **09** bamboozle, dumbfound, frustrate **10** disconcert **13** bring to naught

**baffling**
◇ *anagram indicator*
**07** amazing, cryptic **08** bemusing, puzzling **09** confusing, enigmatic **10** astounding, mysterious, perplexing, stupefying, surprising **11** bewildering **12** unfathomable **13** disconcerting, extraordinary

**bag**
◇ *containment indicator*
**03** cod, get, net, pot, sac **04** gain, grab, kill, land, pock, poke, port, take, trap **05** catch, pouch, shoot **06** come by, corner, obtain, pocket, secure **07** acquire, capture, reserve **09** container **10** commandeer, receptacle **11** appropriate

*Bags include:*

**03** bum, jag, kit, pod
**04** caba, case, grip, hand, mail, pack, sack, tote, wash
**05** bulse, cabas, dilli, dilly, ditty, money, purse, scrip
**06** carpet, clutch, duffel, flight, sachel, saddle, tucker, valise, vanity, wallet
**07** carrier, evening, holdall, satchel, shopper, utricle
**08** backpack, carry-all, gripsack, knapsack, mailsack, meal-poke, pochette, reticule, rucksack, shopping, shoulder, suitcase, wineskin, woolpack
**09** briefcase, fanny pack, Gladstone, haversack, moneybelt, overnight
**10** sabretache
**11** attaché-case, portmanteau

**baggage**
**04** bags, gear, swag **05** cases **06** things **07** clobber, dunnage, effects, luggage **08** carriage, materiel **09** equipment, suitcases, viaticals **10** belongings **11** impedimenta **13** accoutrements, paraphernalia
*See also* **prostitute**

**baggy**
**05** kneed, loose, roomy, slack **06** bulged, droopy, floppy, pouchy, sloppy **07** bulging, sagging **08** oversize **09** billowing, shapeless **10** ballooning, extra large, ill-fitting **12** loose-fitting

**bagpipe**
**05** gaita, pipes **07** musette, piffero **08** dulcimer, zampogna **09** cornemuse **10** small-pipes, sourdeline **12** uillean pipes **13** uilleann pipes
• **bagpipe composition**
**04** port **07** pibroch

**Bahamas**
**02** BS **03** BHS

**Bahrain**
**03** BHR, BRN

**bail**
**04** bond, hoop **05** ladle **06** pledge, surety **07** caution, custody, replevy **08** security, warranty **09** guarantee **10** collateral **12** jurisdiction
• **bail out**
**03** aid **04** help, quit, save **05** eject, ladle, scoop **06** assist, escape, get out, rescue **07** back out, finance, relieve, retreat **08** get clear, withdraw

**bailiff**
**04** foud **05** agent, reeve **06** beagle **07** nut-hook **08** huissier **09** bum-baylie, hundreder, hundredor **10** philistine **11** land-steward **12** shoulder knot **15** shoulder-clapper

**bait**
**03** dap, irk, lug **04** goad, lure, rage **05** annoy, bribe, decoy, harry, hound, leger, slate, snare, squid, taunt, tease, tie-up, yabby **06** badger, berley, burley, caplin, gentle, harass, hassle, ledger, lidger, needle, plague, yabbie **07** capelin, catworm, lugworm, provoke, ragworm, torment **08** irritate **09** anchoveta, angleworm, brandling, incentive, killifish, persecute, propeller, white worm **10** allurement, attraction, enticement, incitement, inducement, temptation **11** hellgramite, refreshment **12** hellgrammite, night crawler **15** give a hard time to

**bake**
◇ *anagram indicator*
**03** dry **04** burn, cake, cook, fire, heat, shir **05** brown, parch, roast, shirr **06** harden, scorch, wither **07** shrivel

08 pot-roast 09 oven-roast, spit-roast 12 porcellanize

**balance**
03 bal, set 04 meet, rest, trim, tron 05 agree, level, Libra, match, pease, peaze, peise, peize, peyse, poise, pound, tally, weigh 06 adjust, aplomb, equate, equity, even up, excess, juggle, launce, make up, offset, parity, review, square, stasis, steady 07 compare, even out, librate, residue, surplus, weigh up 08 appraise, calmness, consider, equality, equalize, estimate, evaluate, evenness, symmetry 09 assurance, composure, equipoise, remainder, sangfroid, stability, stabilize 10 correspond, counteract, difference, equanimity, neutralize, set against, steadiness, uniformity 11 equilibrate, equilibrium, equivalence, self-control 12 counterweigh 13 compensate for, equiponderate 14 cool-headedness, correspondence, counterbalance, self-possession, unflappability 15 level-headedness

• **balance sheet**
02 bs

• **in the balance**
04 iffy 06 unsure 07 unknown 08 in the air 09 knife-edge, uncertain, undecided, unsettled 10 indefinite, touch and go 12 undetermined 13 unpredictable

• **on balance**
07 overall 08 all in all 09 generally 12 in conclusion

**balanced**
04 calm, even, fair 05 equal, level, sound 06 poised 07 assured, healthy, weighed 08 complete, sensible, straight, unbiased 09 equitable, impartial, objective 10 cool-headed, even-handed 11 level-headed, well-rounded 12 unprejudiced 13 dispassionate, self-possessed

**balcony**
04 gods 06 loggia 07 gallery, portico, sundeck, terrace, veranda 09 mezzanine 10 moucharaby 11 upper circle 14 quarter-gallery

**bald**
04 bare 05 bleak, blunt, naked, plain, stark 06 barren, direct, paltry, peeled, severe, simple, smooth 07 exposed, obvious, pollard, trivial 08 glabrate, glabrous, hairless, outright, straight, tonsured, treeless 09 depilated, downright, outspoken, unadorned, uncovered 10 bald-headed, forthright 11 bald as a coot, unambiguous, undisguised, unsheltered 15 straightforward

**balderdash**
03 rot 04 blah, bosh, bull, bunk, crap, guff, jazz 05 bilge, borak, hooey, trash, tripe 06 blague, bunkum, drivel, faddle, havers, hot air, piffle 07 baloney, eyewash, hogwash, rhubarb, rubbish, twaddle 08 blethers, bulldust, claptrap, cobblers, doggerel, malarkey, nonsense, tommyrot 09 bull's wool, gibberish, moonshine, poppycock 10 codswallop, galimatias 12 clamjamphrie

**balding**
04 bald 08 receding 09 thin on top 14 losing your hair

**baldmoney**
03 meu 07 spignel

**baldness**
07 fox-evil 08 alopecia, bareness, hair loss, psilosis 09 calvities, madarosis, starkness 12 glabrousness, hairlessness 14 alopecia areata, bald-headedness

**bale**
02 bl 04 lave, pack 05 ladle, seron, truss 06 bundle, parcel, seroon 07 confine, package 08 woolpack

• **bale out**
04 quit 06 escape, get out 07 back out, retreat 08 get clear, withdraw

**baleful**
04 evil 05 swart 06 deadly, malign, sullen, swarth 07 harmful, hurtful, malefic, noxious, ominous, painful, ruinous 08 menacing, mournful, sinister, venomous 09 injurious, malignant, sorrowful 10 lugubrious, malevolent, pernicious 11 destructive, threatening

**balefully**
09 harmfully, hurtfully 10 menacingly 11 dangerously 13 destructively, detrimentally, threateningly

**balk, baulk**
03 bar, hen, jib 04 chop, foil 05 avoid, check, demur, dodge, evade, reest, reist, shirk, stall 06 baffle, boggle, defeat, eschew, flinch, hinder, ignore, impede, pull up, recoil, refuse, resist, shrink, thwart 07 decline, prevent 08 hesitate, obstruct 09 discomfit, forestall, frustrate 10 counteract, disconcert 11 frustration 14 disappointment

**ball**
01 O 02 ba 03 cop, nur, orb 04 clew, clue, drop, knur, nurr, pill, shot, slug, tice 05 dance, fungo, globe, Jaffa, knurr, party 06 beamer, bullet, googly, pellet, soirée, sphere, strike, yorker 07 bouncer, globule, long hop, shooter, swinger 08 assembly, carnival, Chinaman, delivery, full toss, gazunder, leg break, off break 09 inswinger 10 masquerade, outswinger, projectile 11 daisy-cutter, dinner-dance 14 conglomeration

• **high ball**
03 lob

• **play ball**
07 go along, respond 09 co-operate, play along 11 collaborate, reciprocate, show willing

• **position of ball**
03 lie

**ballad**
03 jig 04 poem, song 05 carol, ditty, mento 06 shanty 07 ballant, calypso, romance 08 folk-song, singsong 09 cantilena 10 forebitter 12 Lillibullero

**ballet**
07 dancing 11 leg-business 13 ballet-dancing

*See also* **choreography**; **dance**; **dancer**

*Ballets include:*

05 Manon, Rodeo, Rooms
06 Apollo, Boléro, Carmen, Façade, Ondine, Onegin, Parade
07 Giselle, La Valse, Orpheus, Requiem
08 Coppélia, Les Noces, Nocturne, Swan Lake
09 Anastasia, Les Biches, Mayerling
10 Cinderella, Don Quixote, La Sylphide, Petroushka, Prince Igor, Pulcinella
11 Billy the Kid, Las Hermanas, The Firebird
12 Les Sylphides, Schéhérazade
13 Pineapple Poll, The Nutcracker
14 Daphnis et Chloé, Romeo and Juliet, The Prodigal Son
15 The Rite of Spring

*Ballet-related terms include:*

03 bar, pas
04 jeté, plié, posé, tutu
05 barre, battu
06 à terre, attack, ballon, chassé, écarté, en face, en l'air, pointe, school, splits
07 à pointe, bourrée, bras bas, ciseaux, company, danseur, en avant, fouetté, leotard, maillot, pointes, premier
08 attitude, batterie, cabriole, capriole, coryphée, couronne, danseuse, en pointe, ensemble, fish dive, glissade, première, stulchak
09 arabesque, ballerina, battement, cou de pied, elevation, entrechat, pas de chat, pas de deux, pas de seul, pirouette, point shoe, promenade, régisseur
10 ballet shoe, répétiteur
11 Laban system, ports de bras
12 ballet-dancer, ballet-master, choreography, labanotation
13 corps de ballet, five positions, sur les pointes
14 divertissement, maître de ballet, petit battement, premier danseur, prima ballerina
15 grande battement, principal dancer

**balloon**
03 bag 04 soar 05 belly, bulge, swell 06 billow, blow up, dilate, expand, rocket 07 distend, enlarge, fumetto, inflate, puff out 08 aerostat, escalate, snowball 09 dirigible, skyrocket 11 grow rapidly, montgolfier 12 ballon d'essai 15 increase rapidly

**ballot**
04 poll, vote 06 voting 07 polling 08 election 10 plebiscite, referendum

• **ballot-box**
03 urn

**ballyhoo**
**04** fuss, hype, to-do **05** noise **06** hubbub, racket, tumult **07** build-up, clamour **09** agitation, commotion, hue and cry, kerfuffle, promotion, publicity **10** excitement, hullabaloo, propaganda **11** advertising, disturbance

**balm**
**04** nard, tolu **05** cream, salve **06** balsam, lotion, relief **07** anodyne, bromide, comfort, unguent **08** curative, lenitive, ointment, sedative **09** calmative, emollient, opobalsam **10** palliative **11** consolation, embrocation, restorative

**balmy**
**04** mild, soft, warm **06** gentle **07** clement, summery **08** pleasant, soothing **09** temperate

**balsam**
**04** heal, Tolu **06** embalm **07** wood oil **09** impatiens, spikenard **13** noli-me-tangere

**Balt**
**04** Esth, Lett

**bamboozle**
◇ *anagram indicator*
**03** con **04** daze, dupe, fool, gull, rook **05** cheat, trick, upset **06** bemuse, diddle, puzzle **07** bumbaze, confuse, deceive, mystify, nonplus, perplex, swindle **08** bewilder, confound, hoodwink **09** dumbfound **10** disconcert **14** pull a fast one on

**ban**
**03** bar **04** band, tabu, tapu, veto **05** black, curse, taboo **06** banish, censor, forbid, outlaw **07** abolish, boycott, embargo, exclude **08** disallow, outlawry, prohibit, restrict, stoppage, suppress **09** ostracize, proscribe, sanctions **10** banishment, censorship, disqualify, injunction, moratorium **11** prohibition, restriction, suppression **12** anathematize, condemnation, denunciation, interdiction, proclamation, proscription

**banal**
**04** dull, flat **05** bland, corny, empty, inane, stale, stock, tired, trite, vapid **06** boring, old hat **07** cliché'd, humdrum, mundane, trivial **08** clichéed, cornball, everyday, ordinary, overused **09** hackneyed **10** threadbare, unoriginal **11** commonplace, nondescript, stereotyped, wearing thin **13** unimaginative

**banality**
**06** cliché, truism **07** bromide, fatuity **08** cornball, dullness, vapidity **09** emptiness, inaneness, platitude, staleness, tiredness, triteness **10** prosaicism, triviality **11** commonplace, old chestnut **12** ordinariness **13** unoriginality

**banana**
**08** plantain

**bananas**
◇ *anagram indicator*
**03** mad **04** hand, Musa **05** bunch, crazy

**• go bananas**
**04** flip **05** freak **08** freak out

**band**
**02** CB **03** bar, rib, rim, tie **04** ally, belt, body, bond, club, cord, core, crew, fess, frog, gang, ging, herd, hoop, join, line, link, ring, sash, tape, team, teme, tire, tyre, welt, with, zona, zone **05** chain, crowd, fesse, flock, group, horde, merge, music, party, strap, strip, thong, troop, unite, withe **06** clique, fetter, gather, girdle, ribbon, streak, stripe, swathe, team up, throng **07** bandage, binding, company, manacle, shackle, society **08** ensemble, federate, ligature, pop group **09** affiliate, gathering, orchestra **10** amalgamate, close ranks, connection, contingent, join forces, music group **11** association, collaborate, consolidate **12** club together, musical group, pull together **13** stand together, stick together

*See also* **singer**

**• raised band**
**03** rib

**• twisted band**
**04** torc, with **05** withe **06** torque

**bandage**
**01** T **04** bind, lint, wrap **05** cover, dress, gauze, spica **06** binder, bind up, swathe **07** Band-aid®, bandeau, plaster, scapula, swaddle **08** capeline, compress, dressing, ligature, Tubigrip® **09** capelline, suspensor **10** tourniquet **11** Elastoplast®

**bandicoot**
**05** bilby **06** pig-rat **10** Malabar-rat

**bandit**
**05** crook, thief **06** cowboy, gunman, mugger, outlaw, pirate, raider, robber **07** brigand **08** criminal, gangster, hijacker, marauder **09** buccaneer, desperado, plunderer, racketeer **10** highwayman

**bandsman**
**04** wait

**bandy**
◇ *anagram indicator*
**04** bent, pass, swap, toss **05** bowed, fight, fling, throw, trade **06** barter, curved, spread, strive **07** chaffer, crooked **08** exchange **09** bow-legged, misshapen **11** interchange, reciprocate

**bane**
**03** woe **04** evil, harm, pest, ruin **05** curse, death, trial **06** blight, burden, misery, ordeal, plague, poison **07** scourge, torment, trouble **08** calamity, disaster, distress, downfall, mischief, nuisance, vexation **09** adversity, annoyance, bête noire **10** affliction, irritation, misfortune, pestilence **11** destruction **14** thorn in the side **15** thorn in the flesh

**baneful**
**07** harmful, noxious, painful, ruinous **08** annoying **09** poisonous **10** disastrous, pernicious **11** destructive, distressing, troublesome **12** pestilential

**bang**
**03** hit, pop, rap **04** bash, benj, blow, boom, bump, clap, dead, drum, echo, hard, peal, shot, slam, slap, sock, thud, wham **05** burst, clang, clash, crack, crash, knock, noise, pound, punch, right, smack, spang, stamp, thump, whack **06** blow up, hammer, report, strike, stroke, thwack, wallop **07** clatter, exactly, explode, noisily, resound, thunder **08** abruptly, bump into, cannabis, detonate, directly, headlong, slap-bang, straight, suddenly **09** collision, crash into, explosion, precisely **10** absolutely, detonation

**banger**
**04** bomb, heap **05** crate **06** jalopy **07** clunker, jaloppy, sausage **09** tin lizzie

**Bangladesh**
**02** BD **03** BGD

**bangle**
**04** band, kara **06** anklet **07** circlet **08** bracelet, wristlet

**banish**
**03** ban, bar **04** band, oust **05** debar, eject, evict, exile, expel **06** deport, dispel, forsay, outlaw, remove **07** abandon, cast out, discard, dismiss, exclude, foresay, shut out **08** dislodge, get rid of, relegate, send away, throw out **09** drive away, eliminate, eradicate, extradite, ostracize, rusticate, transport **10** disimagine, expatriate, repatriate **13** excommunicate

**banishment**
**03** ban **05** exile **08** eviction, outlawry **09** exclusion, exilement, expulsion, ostracism **11** deportation, extradition **12** expatriation **14** transportation **15** excommunication

**banisters**
**04** rail **07** railing **08** handrail **10** balustrade

**bank**
**02** as, bk **03** bar, dam, row, tip **04** bink, brae, edge, fund, heap, keep, line, link, mass, pile, pool, rank, reef, rise, rive, save, side, sunk, tier, tilt **05** amass, array, bench, bluff, cache, drift, group, hoard, hurst, knoll, lay by, levee, mound, panel, pitch, ridge, shore, slant, slope, stack, stock, store, train **06** heap up, margin, pile up, rivage, save up, series, supply **07** deposit, hillock, incline, parados, pottery, rampart, reserve, savings, stack up **08** put aside, sequence, treasury **09** earthwork,

reservoir, stash away, stockpile **10** accumulate, depository, embankment, repository, succession **11** put together, savings bank **12** accumulation, clearing bank, finance house, merchant bank **14** finance company, high-street bank **15** building society

**• banking system**
**04** giro

**• bank on**
**05** bet on, trust **06** rely on **07** count on **08** depend on **09** bargain on, believe in **14** pin your hopes on

**• bank rate**
**02** br

**• banks**
◇ *ends selection indicator*

**• bank up**
**04** hele, hill

**banker**
**05** gnome **06** shroff **07** Lombard **09** exchanger
*See also* **river**

**banknote**
**03** fin **04** bill, note **05** fiver, scrip **06** flimsy, greeny, single, tenner, twenty **07** greenie, iron man, sawbuck **09** greenback **10** paper money **12** treasury note

**bankrupt**
**04** bung, bust, duck, ruin **05** break, broke, spent **06** beggar, bereft, broken, debtor, dyvour, failed, folded, hard up, pauper, ruined **07** cripple, lacking, wanting, without **08** beggared, depleted, deprived, in the red, lame duck **09** deficient, destitute, exhausted, gone under, insolvent, penurious, sequester **10** impoverish, on the rocks, stony broke, trade-falne **11** impecunious, trade-fallen **12** impoverished, on your uppers **13** gone to the wall, in liquidation

**bankruptcy**
**04** lack, ruin **05** smash **06** penury, stumer **07** beggary, dyvoury, failure **08** disaster **09** ruination **10** exhaustion, insolvency **11** Carey Street, liquidation **12** indebtedness **13** financial ruin, sequestration

**• to bankruptcy**
**04** scat **05** skatt

**banner**
**04** flag, sign **06** burgee, ensign, fanion, pennon **07** bandrol, colours, labarum, pennant, placard **08** banderol, bannerol, gonfalon, gumphion, standard, streamer, vexillum **09** banderole, bannerall, oriflamme

**banquet**
**04** dine, meal **05** feast, party, treat **06** dinner, junket, spread **11** dinner party **13** entertainment

**banter**
**03** kid, pun, rag, rib **04** jest, joke, josh, mock, quiz, rail **05** borak, borax, chaff, rally, roast, tease **06** deride, joking **07** jesting, kidding, mockery, ribbing **08** badinage, chaffing, derision, dicacity, raillery, repartee, ridicule, word play **09** make fun of **10** persiflage, pleasantry

**Bantu**
**04** Hutu, Xosa, Zulu **05** Nguni, Sotho, Swazi, Tonga, Tutsi, Xhosa **06** Herero, Nyanja, Tswana **07** Basotho, Lingala, Sesotho, Swahili **08** Congoese **09** Congolese

**baptism**
**05** debut **06** launch, naming **07** mersion **08** affusion **09** aspersion, beginning, immersion, launching **10** dedication, initiation, sprinkling **11** christening, parabaptism **12** inauguration, introduction, paedobaptism, purification

**baptize**
**03** dip **04** call, name, term **05** admit, enrol, style, title **06** purify **07** cleanse, immerse, recruit **08** christen, initiate, sprinkle **09** introduce

**bar**
**01** T, Z **03** ban, fen, fid, gad, inn, pub, rib, rod, zed, zee **04** bolt, cake, dive, howf, hunk, lock, lump, pole, rail, risp, rung, save, shet, shut, slab, slot, snug, spar, stop, swee, toll **05** block, check, chunk, court, debar, estop, grill, ingot, latch, lever, shaft, stake, stick, table, wedge **06** batten, bistro, boozer, but for, except, fasten, forbid, hinder, lounge, nugget, paling, saloon, secure, tavern **07** barrier, counsel, counter, exclude, lawyers, padlock, prevent, railing, suspend, taproom **08** blockade, drawback, hostelry, obstacle, obstruct, omitting, preclude, prohibit, restrain, snuggery, tribunal **09** advocates, apart from, aside from, barricade, brasserie, deterrent, except for, excepting, excluding, hindrance, lounge bar, stanchion **10** barristers, beer-parlor, crosspiece, disqualify, impediment **11** obstruction, public house **12** beverage room, watering-hole

**barb**
**03** dig, mow **04** gibe, harl, herl, tang, trim **05** arrow, beard, fluke, point, prong, ramus, scorn, shave, sneer, spike, sting, thorn **06** insult, needle, rebuff **07** affront, bristle, killick, killock, prickle

**Barbados**
**03** BDS, BRB

**barbarian**
**03** Hun, oaf **04** boor, Goth, lout, wild **05** brute, crude, rough **06** coarse, savage, vandal, vulgar **07** brutish, loutish, ruffian, uncouth **08** hooligan **09** Hottentot, ignoramus **10** illiterate, philistine, tramontane, uncultured, wild person **11** Neanderthal, uncivilized **12** uncultivated **15** unsophisticated

**barbaric**
◇ *anagram indicator*
**04** rude, wild **05** crude, cruel **06** brutal, coarse, fierce, savage, vulgar **07** bestial, brutish, foreign, inhuman, uncouth, vicious **08** ruthless **09** barbarous, ferocious, murderous, primitive **11** uncivilized

**barbarism**
**07** cruelty **08** enormity, ferocity, rudeness, savagery, wildness **09** brutality, crudeness, vulgarity **10** bestiality, coarseness, corruption, fierceness, heathenism **11** brutishness, inhumanness, uncouthness, viciousness **12** ruthlessness **13** murderousness **15** uncivilizedness

**barbarity**
**07** cruelty, outrage **08** atrocity, enormity, ferocity, savagery, wildness **09** brutality **10** inhumanity, savageness **11** brutishness, viciousness **12** ruthlessness **13** barbarousness

**barbarous**
◇ *anagram indicator*
**04** rude, wild **05** crude, cruel, harsh, rough **06** brutal, fierce, Gothic, savage, vulgar **07** bestial, brutish, corrupt, inhuman, vicious **08** barbaric, ignorant, ruthless **09** barbarian, ferocious, heartless, murderous, primitive, unrefined **10** uncultured, unlettered **11** uncivilized, unscholarly **15** unsophisticated

**barbecue**
**03** BBQ **04** bake, cook **05** braai, broil, brown, grill, roast **06** barbie **07** cookout, griddle, hibachi, stir-fry **09** spit-roast **10** braaivleis

**barbed**
**04** acid **05** armed, catty, jaggy, nasty, snide, spiky, spiny **06** bitchy, hooked, jagged, spiked, tanged, thorny, unkind **07** bearded, caustic, cutting, hostile, hurtful, pointed, prickly, pronged, toothed **08** barbated, critical, spiteful, wounding **09** sarcastic

**barber**
**04** Todd **05** shave, strap **06** Figaro, shaver, tonsor **07** scraper **11** hairdresser, Sweeney Todd

**bard** *see* **poet**

**bare**
**04** bald, cold, hard, lewd, mere, nude, peel, pure, very **05** basic, bleak, clear, empty, naked, plain, sheer, stark, strip, utter **06** barren, expose, reveal, simple, unmask, unveil, vacant **07** denuded, display, exposed, lay bare, uncover, undress **08** absolute, complete, desolate, in the nip, in the raw, stripped, treeless, unclothe, unwooded, woodless **09** essential, in the buff, in the nude, in the scud, unadorned, unclothed, uncovered, undressed, very least **10** defoliated, no more than, stark-naked, unforested **11** unfurnished, unsheltered **13** with nothing on **15** straightforward

**barefaced**
**04** bald, bold, open **05** brash, naked **06** arrant, avowed, brazen, patent **07** blatant, glaring, obvious **08** flagrant, impudent, insolent, manifest, palpable **09** audacious, bald-faced, beardless, shameless, unabashed **11** transparent, unconcealed, undisguised

**barefooted**
**06** unshod **08** barefoot, shoeless **09** discalced

**barely**
**04** just, only **05** scant **06** almost, hardly, openly, scrimp **07** halfway, nakedly, none too, plainly **08** narrowly, no sooner, only just, scarcely **10** by a whisker, explicitly **12** be a near thing, by a short head **13** be a close thing

**bargain**
**02** go **03** buy **04** deal, pact, sell, snip, whiz **05** broke, cheap, steal, trade, truck, whizz **06** barter, broker, clinch, haggle, indent, market, pledge, settle, treaty **07** chaffer, cheapen, good buy, promise, traffic **08** beat down, cheap buy, contract, covenant, discount, giveaway, purchase, transact, wanworth **09** agreement, bon marché, concordat, negotiate, reduction **11** arrangement, negotiation, transaction **12** special offer **13** understanding, value for money

• **bargain for**
**06** expect **07** foresee, imagine, include, look for, plan for **08** consider, contract, figure on, reckon on **10** anticipate **11** contemplate **13** be prepared for **15** take into account

• **into the bargain**
**04** also **06** as well **07** besides **10** in addition **11** furthermore **12** additionally

**bargaining**
**05** trade **06** barter, buying, dicker, outcry **07** chaffer, dealing, selling **08** dealings, haggling **09** bartering **11** negotiation, trafficking, transaction **12** horsetrading **14** wheeler-dealing

**barge**
◇ *anagram indicator*
**03** hit **04** bump, keel, pram, push, rush, scow **05** barca, butty, casco, elbow, praam, press, shove, smash **06** galley, hopper, jostle, plough, push in, wherry **07** birlinn, budgero, collide, gabbard, gabbart, lighter, piragua, pirogue, pontoon **08** budgerow, flatboat, keelboat, periagua **09** Bucentaur, canal-boat, houseboat **10** narrowboat **11** galley-foist, push your way **12** force your way

• **barge in**
**05** cut in **06** butt in **07** break in, burst in, intrude **09** gatecrash, interfere, interrupt

**baritone**
**03** bar

**barium**
**02** Ba

**bark**
**03** bay, cry, tan, wow, yap **04** bass, bast, bawl, cork, hide, howl, husk, kina, peel, rind, skin, snap, tapa, waff, woof, yaff, yawp, yell, yelp **05** china, cough, crust, growl, quest, quill, quina, shell, shout, snarl, suber, tappa **06** bellow, bowwow, casing, cortex **07** cascara, encrust, pereira, thunder **08** calisaya, cinchona, cinnamon, covering, simaruba, tan balls **09** bull's wool, quebracho, sassafras, simarouba, xanthoxyl **10** cascarilla, integument, quercitron **11** slippery elm **13** cascara amarga **14** cascara sagrada

**barking**
◇ *anagram indicator*
**03** bay, mad, odd **04** daft, nuts **05** barmy, batty, crazy, dippy, dotty, loony, loopy, nutty, potty **06** cuckoo, insane **07** bananas, bonkers **08** crackers **09** latration **10** off your nut, unbalanced **11** off your head **12** mad as a hatter, round the bend **13** off your rocker, round the twist **14** off your trolley

**barley**
**04** bear, bere, bigg, malt **07** Hordeum

**barmy**
**03** mad, odd **04** daft, nuts **05** batty, crazy, dippy, dotty, loony, loopy, nutty, silly **06** cuckoo, frothy, insane, stupid **07** foolish, idiotic **08** crackers **10** fermenting, off your nut, out to lunch, unbalanced **11** off your head **12** round the bend **13** off your rocker, round the twist **14** off your trolley

**barn**
**06** grange **07** skipper

**barometer**
**07** aneroid **09** barograph **10** statoscope **12** weather glass **13** sympiesometer

**baron**
**01** B **02** Bn **04** lord, peer **05** mogul **06** bigwig, fat cat, tycoon **07** big shot, magnate **08** nobleman **09** big cheese, executive **10** aristocrat, Münchausen **12** entrepreneur **13** industrialist

**baroness**
**04** lady, peer **07** baronne **10** aristocrat, noblewoman

**baronet**
**02** Bt **04** Bart

**baroque**
◇ *anagram indicator*
**04** bold **05** showy **06** florid, ornate, rococo **07** flowery **08** fanciful, vigorous **09** decorated, elaborate, exuberant, fantastic, grotesque, whimsical **10** convoluted, flamboyant **11** embellished, extravagant, overwrought **13** overdecorated, overelaborate **15** churrigueresque

**barrack**
**03** boo **04** hiss, jeer **05** taunt **06** casern, heckle **07** caserne **09** interrupt, shout down

**barracking**
**04** boos **07** hissing, jeering **08** heckling **12** interruption **13** interruptions

**barracks**
**03** bks **04** camp, fort **06** billet, casern **07** lodging **08** garrison, quarters **10** encampment, glasshouse, guardhouse **11** gendarmerie **13** accommodation

**barrage**
**03** dam **04** dyke, hail, mass, rain, wall **05** burst, flood, onset, salvo, storm **06** attack, deluge, shower, stream, volley **07** assault, barrier, battery, gunfire, torrent **08** shelling **09** abundance, barricade, broadside, cannonade, fusillade, onslaught, profusion **10** embankment **11** bombardment, obstruction

**barrel**
**01** b **02** bl **03** bbl, but, keg, tub, tun **04** butt, cade, cask, drum, pipe, wood **05** pièce **06** clavie, firkin, runlet, tierce, tumble **07** oil drum, rundlet **08** hogshead **09** water-butt **10** Morris-tube

**barren**
**03** dry **04** arid, dull, eild, flat, yeld, yell **05** addle, bleak, blunt, empty, gaunt, vapid, waste **06** desert, effete, meagre **07** hirstie, sterile, useless **08** desolate, infecund, teemless **09** childless, fruitless, infertile, pointless, unbearing, valueless **10** profitless, unfruitful, unprolific **11** purposeless, uninspiring, unrewarding **12** inhospitable, uncultivable, unproductive **13** uninformative, uninstructive, uninteresting

**barrenness**
**06** dearth **07** aridity, dryness **08** dullness **09** emptiness, sterility **11** infecundity, infertility, uselessness **13** pointlessness **14** unfruitfulness

**barricade**
**03** bar **04** shut **05** block, close, fence **06** defend **07** barrier, bulwark, close up, defence, fortify, protect, rampart, shut off **08** blockade, obstacle, obstruct, palisade, stockade **10** protection, strengthen **11** obstruction

**Barrie**
**02** JM

**barrier**
**03** bar, dam **04** bail, boom, doll, gate, ha-ha, wall **05** block, check, ditch, fence, hedge, rails, spina **06** haw-haw, hurdle **07** barrage, curtain, railing, rampart **08** blockade, boundary, bulkhead, division, drawback, frontier, handicap, obstacle, railings, stockade, tick gate, traverse, turnpike

**09** barricade, enclosure, hindrance, inclosure, partition, restraint, ring-fence, roadblock **10** breakwater, difficulty, dingo fence, impediment, limitation, tariff wall **11** iron curtain, mental block, obstruction, restriction **12** glass ceiling **13** bamboo curtain, fortification, kangaroo fence **14** stumbling-block **15** cordon sanitaire, dingo-proof fence

**barring**
**02** if **03** bar **06** except, unless **09** except for

**barrister**
**02** KC, QC **03** Bar **04** silk **05** brief **06** lawyer **07** counsel, Rumpole **08** advocate, attorney, recorder, serjeant **09** counselor, solicitor **10** counsellor **12** King's Counsel **13** Queen's Counsel, serjeant-at-law

*See also* **lawyer**

**barrow**
**03** how **04** cart, howe, tump **05** hurly, truck **07** tumulus **08** push-cart **11** horned cairn

**bartender**
**06** barman **07** barkeep, barmaid **08** publican **09** barkeeper **10** mixologist

**barter**
**04** chop, cope, coup, deal, sell, swap, swop **05** trade, truck **06** dicker, haggle, niffer **07** bargain, dealing, trading, traffic **08** exchange, haggling, swapping, truckage **09** negotiate **10** bargaining **11** negotiation, permutation, trafficking

**basalt**
**04** trap, whin **05** wacke **07** diabase **08** basanite, traprock **09** toadstone, whinstone

**base**
**01** e **02** HQ **03** bed, dog, key, low, ten **04** camp, core, evil, foot, home, mean, poor, post, prop, rest, root, seat, site, stay, vile **05** basis, build, depot, found, heart, hinge, layer, lowly, stand **06** abject, bottom, centre, depend, derive, fundus, ground, locate, origin, plinth, sordid, source, vulgar, wicked **07** bedrock, coating, corrupt, essence, immoral, install, pitiful, situate, station, support **08** backbone, covering, depraved, infamous, keystone, pedestal, position, shameful, wretched **09** component, construct, essential, establish, low-minded, miserable, principal, reprobate, thickness, valueless, worthless **10** despicable, foundation, groundwork, scandalous, settlement, substratum, underneath **11** disgraceful, fundamental, ignominious **12** contemptible, disreputable, have as a basis, headquarters, substructure, unprincipled **13** starting-point **14** understructure **15** foundation stone

• **base of**
◇ *tail selection down indicator*

**baseball**

*Baseball players include:*

**03** **Ott** (Mel)
**04** **Cobb** (Ty), **Mack** (Connie), **Mays** (Willie), **Ruth** (Babe), **Ryan** (Nolan)
**05** **Aaron** (Hank), **Bench** (Johnny), **Berra** (Yogi), **Paige** (Satchel), **Spahn** (Warren), **Young** (Cy)
**06** **Gehrig** (Lou), **Gibson** (Bob), **Gibson** (Josh), **Koufax** (Sandy), **Mantle** (Mickey), **Musial** (Stan), **Ripken** (Cal)
**07** **Clemens** (Roger), **Jackson** (Reggie), **McGwire** (Mark), **Stengel** (Casey)
**08** **Clemente** (Roberto), **DiMaggio** (Joe), **Robinson** (Brooks), **Robinson** (Jackie), **Williams** (Ted)
**09** **Alexander** (Grover Cleveland), **Mathewson** (Christy)

*Major league baseball teams:*

**11** Chicago Cubs, New York Mets
**12** Boston Red Sox, Texas Rangers
**13** Atlanta Braves, Detroit Tigers, Houston Astros
**14** Cincinnati Reds, Florida Marlins, Minnesota Twins, New York Yankees, San Diego Padres
**15** Chicago White Sox, Colorado Rockies, Seattle Mariners, Toronto Blue Jays
**16** Baltimore Orioles, Cleveland Indians, Kansas City Royals, Milwaukee Brewers, Oakland Athletics, St Louis Cardinals
**17** Los Angeles Dodgers, Pittsburgh Pirates, Tampa Bay Devil Rays
**18** San Francisco Giants
**19** Arizona Diamondbacks, Washington Nationals
**20** Philadelphia Phillies
**25** Los Angeles Angels of Anaheim

*Baseball terms include:*

**03** ace, ERA, hit, out, RBI, run, tag
**04** balk, ball, base, bunt, cage, mitt, safe, walk
**05** alley, bench, error, mound, pitch, plate
**06** assist, batter, bottom, closer, double, dugout, fly out, inning, on deck, single, sinker, slider, strike, triple, wind-up
**07** all-star, base hit, battery, bull pen, catcher, chopper, diamond, fly ball, home run, infield, pennant, pitcher, rundown, shutout
**08** ballpark, baseline, fair ball, fastball, foul ball, foul pole, nightcap, no-hitter, outfield, set-up man
**09** cut-off man, earned run, first base, gold glove, grand slam, ground out, hit-and-run, home plate, infielder, in the hole, left field, line drive, sacrifice, screwball, strike out, third base, wild pitch
**10** baserunner, batter's box, double play, ground ball, outfielder, passed ball, right field, second base, strike zone
**11** base on balls, basket catch, centre field, knuckleball, left fielder, perfect game, pinch hitter, pinch runner, run batted in, unearned run
**12** breaking ball, double-header, extra innings, load the bases, right fielder, warning track
**13** centre fielder, foul territory, relief pitcher, safety squeeze
**14** American League, backdoor slider, batting average, fielder's choice, National League, suicide squeeze
**15** starting pitcher

• **baseball statistic**
**03** ERA, RBI

**baseless**
◇ *tail deletion down indicator*
**04** idle **06** untrue **09** unfounded **10** fabricated, gratuitous, groundless, ill-founded, unattested **11** uncalled-for, unconfirmed, unjustified, unsupported **15** unauthenticated, unsubstantiated

**basement**
**05** crypt, dunny, vault **06** cellar

**bash**
**02** go **03** box, hit, ram, try **04** bang, beat, belt, biff, blow, bump, clip, dent, rave, shot, slug, sock, stab **05** blast, break, crack, crash, knock, party, punch, smack, smash, thump, whack, whirl **06** batter, rave-up, strike, thrash, wallop **07** attempt, clobber **11** celebration

**bashful**
**03** coy, shy **05** blate, timid **06** modest **07** abashed, laithfu', nervous **08** backward, blushing, hesitant, reserved, reticent, retiring, sheepish, timorous **09** diffident, inhibited, shamefast, shrinking **10** shamefaced, sheep-faced **11** embarrassed **12** self-effacing **13** self-conscious, unforthcoming

**bashfully**
**05** shyly **07** timidly **08** modestly **09** nervously **10** hesitantly, reticently, sheepishly **11** diffidently **14** self-effacingly **15** self-consciously

**bashfulness**
**05** shame **07** blushes, coyness, modesty, reserve, shyness **08** timidity **09** hesitancy, reticence **10** diffidence, inhibition **11** nervousness **12** sheepishness **13** embarrassment, mauvaise honte **14** self-effacement, shamefacedness

**basic**
**03** gut, key **04** bare, root **05** crude, first, plain, stark, vital **06** simple, staple **07** austere, bedrock, central, minimal, minimum, primary, radical, spartan **08** inherent, no-frills, standard, starting **09** essential, important, intrinsic, necessary, primitive, unadorned **10** elementary, underlying **11** bog standard, fundamental, lowest level, preparatory, rudimentary **12** down-and-dirty **13** indispensable **14** unsophisticate **15** unsophisticated

**basically**
**06** mainly **07** at heart **08** at bottom **09** in essence, in the main, primarily, radically **10** inherently **11** essentially, in principle, principally
**13** fundamentally, intrinsically, substantially

**basics**
**03** ABC **04** core **05** abcee, absey, facts **07** bedrock **08** alphabet, elements **09** realities, rudiments **10** brass tacks, essentials, principles, rock bottom
**11** necessaries, nitty-gritty
**12** fundamentals, introduction, nuts and bolts **14** practicalities **15** first principles

**basin**
**03** bed, dip, pan, pot **04** bowl, dish, dock, park, sink, tank **05** bidet, docks, gully, laver, playa **06** cavity, crater, hollow, lavabo, valley **07** channel, piscina **08** birdbath, washbowl
**09** impluvium, reservoir
**10** aquamanale, aquamanile, depression

**basis**
**03** key, way **04** base, core, fond, root **05** heart, radix, terms **06** bottom, ground, method, reason, status, system, thrust **07** bedrock, essence, footing, grounds, keynote, premise, reasons, support **08** approach, pedestal, platform **09** condition, essential, principle, procedure, rationale **10** conditions, essentials, foundation, grass-roots, groundwork, hypostasis, substratum
**11** arrangement, cornerstone, fundamental **12** fundamentals, quintessence **13** alpha and omega, starting-point **14** main ingredient
**15** first principles

**bask**
**03** lie, sun **04** laze, loll **05** bathe, enjoy, lap up, relax, revel **06** lounge, relish, savour, sprawl, wallow **08** apricate, sunbathe **09** delight in, luxuriate
**14** take pleasure in

**basket**
**03** bin, box, cob, fan, rip, van, wpb
**04** case, cauf, chip, coop, corf, crib, goal, hask, kipe, leap, skep, trug
**05** cabas, creel, frail, maund, scull, skull, willy **06** gabion, hamper, holder, junket, mocock, mocuck, murlan, murlin, petara, pottle, punnet, willey, wisket **07** corbeil, cresset, flasket, murlain, pannier, scuttle, seedlip, shopper, trolley **08** bassinet, calathus
**09** container, corbeille, fish-creel, peat-creel **10** receptacle **12** wagger-pagger

**basketball**

*Basketball teams:*

**08** Utah Jazz
**09** Miami Heat
**11** Phoenix Suns
**12** Atlanta Hawks, Chicago Bulls, Orlando Magic
**13** Boston Celtics, Denver Nuggets, Indiana Pacers, New Jersey Nets, New York Knicks
**14** Detroit Pistons, Houston Rockets, Milwaukee Bucks, Toronto Raptors
**15** Dallas Mavericks, Sacramento Kings, San Antonio Spurs
**16** Charlotte Bobcats, Los Angeles Lakers, Memphis Grizzlies
**17** New Orleans Hornets, Philadelphia 76ers, Washington Wizards
**18** Cleveland Cavaliers, Los Angeles Clippers, Seattle SuperSonics
**19** Golden State Warriors
**20** Portland Trail Blazers
**21** Minnesota Timberwolves

*Basketball players and associated figures include:*

**04** Bird (Larry)
**05** Belov (Sergei), Cousy (Bob), Lemon (Meadowlark), Mikan (George), O'Neal (Shaquille)
**06** Bryant (Kobe), Erving (Julius), Jordan (Michael), Malone (Karl), Miller (Cheryl), Pippen (Scottie), Rodman (Dennis)
**07** Barkley (Charles), Bradley (Bill), Iverson (Allen), Jackson (Phil), Johnson (Earvin 'Magic'), Russell (Bill)
**08** Auerbach (Arnold 'Red'), Olajuwon (Hakeem), Petrovic (Drazen), Stockton (John)
**09** Robertson (Oscar)
**11** Abdul-Jabbar (Kareem), Chamberlain (Wilt)

*Basketball-related terms include:*

**03** key, NBA
**04** dunk, hoop, trap
**05** block, drive, guard, lay-up, pivot, steal, tap-in
**06** assist, basket, box out, centre, post up, rim out, screen, tip-off
**07** dribble, forward, foul out, kick out, low post, rebound, sky hook, time-out
**08** alley oop, bank shot, charging, fadeaway, foul lane, foul line, hang time, high post, hook shot, inbounds, jump ball, jump hook, jump shot, slam dunk, turnover
**09** backboard, chest pass, fast break, field goal, free throw, perimeter, shot clock, violation
**10** bounce pass, double pump, foul circle, point guard, transition, travelling
**11** goal-tending, pick and roll, zone defence
**12** baseball pass, power forward, small forward
**13** shooting guard

**bass**
**01** B **03** low **04** base, bast, deep, full, rich **05** fibre, grave **06** burden, phloem **07** bourdon, burthen, matting, sea dace, sea wolf **08** continuo, diapason, low-toned, resonant, sea perch, sonorous **09** deep-toned, full-toned, loup de mer, succentor **10** low-pitched **11** deep-pitched

**bast**
**04** bass **05** fibre, liber **06** phloem, raffia **07** leptome, matting

**bastard**
◇ *anagram indicator*
**03** git **05** slink **06** basket, by-blow, mamzer **07** buzzard **08** sideslip, spurious **09** come-o'-will, love child
**10** lucky-piece, misfortune **12** come-by-chance, illegitimate, natural child
**13** filius nullius

**bastardize**
**06** debase, defile, demean
**07** cheapen, corrupt, degrade, devalue, distort, pervert, vitiate
**10** adulterate, degenerate, depreciate
**11** contaminate

**bastion**
**04** prop, rock **06** pillar **07** bulwark, citadel, defence, lunette, moineau, redoubt, support **08** defender, fortress, mainstay **10** protection, stronghold

**bat**
**04** blow, club, lath, rate **05** fungo, lingo, speed, spree, stick **06** paddle, racket, willow **07** batsman, battery, flutter
**09** battalion, rearmouse, reremouse, trap stick **10** battledoor, battledore, Scotch hand **12** flitter-mouse

*Bats include:*

**03** fox, red
**05** fruit, guano, hoary
**06** kalong, yellow
**07** leisler, mastiff, noctule, spectre, vampire
**08** big brown, big-eared, Leisler's, noctilio, serotine
**09** barbastel, flying fox, horseshoe, leaf-nosed, roussette
**10** free-tailed, frog-eating, mouse-eared
**11** barbastelle, little brown, pipistrelle
**12** false vampire
**14** Kitti's hog-nosed
**15** Mexican freetail

**batch**
**03** lot, set **04** mass, pack **05** bunch, crowd, group **06** amount, parcel
**07** cluster **08** quantity **09** aggregate
**10** assemblage, assortment, collection, contingent **11** consignment
**12** accumulation **14** conglomeration

**bath**
**03** dip, spa, tub **04** soak, stew, wash
**05** banya, bathe, clean, sauna, scrub, stove, therm **06** douche, hammam, hot tub, hummum, mikvah, mikveh, shower, therms **07** bathtub, hummaum, Jacuzzi®, spa pool, thermae **08** aerotone, balneary
**09** bain-marie, freshen up, have a bath, steam bath, steam room, take a bath, whirlpool **10** Aquae Sulis **11** slipper bath, Turkish bath

**bathe**
**03** bay, dip, tub, wet **04** bath, baye, dook, lave, soak, stew, surf, swim, wash

05 beath, clean, cover, embay, flood, rinse, steep **06** paddle **07** cleanse, embathe, imbathe, immerse, Jacuzzi®, moisten, suffuse **08** permeate, saturate, take a dip **09** encompass, skinny-dip

**bathos**
**07** let-down **08** comedown
**10** anticlimax **14** disappointment

**baton**
**03** rod **05** staff, stick **06** cudgel, warder **07** scepter, sceptre
**09** truncheon

**bats**
◇ *anagram indicator*
**03** mad **04** nuts **05** crazy
**07** Mormops **15** Megacheiroptera, Microchiroptera

**batsman**
**• first batsman**
**06** opener
**• weaker batsmen**
**04** tail

**battalion**
**02** bn **03** bat, mob **04** army, herd, host, mass, unit **05** crowd, force, horde
**06** battle, legion, throng, troops
**07** brigade, company, platoon, section
**08** division, garrison, regiment, squadron **09** multitude **10** contingent, detachment

**batten**
**03** bar, fix **04** bolt **05** board, strip
**06** fasten, secure **07** board up, tighten
**08** nail down **09** barricade, clamp down

**batter**
◇ *anagram indicator*
**03** hit, lam, ram **04** bash, beat, club, dash, hurt, lash, maul, pelt **05** abuse, erode, pound, smash, whack **06** beat up, bruise, buffet, damage, hatter, injure, mangle, pummel, strike, thrash, wallop **07** assault, bombard, destroy, lay into, rough up, wear out
**08** demolish, ill-treat, maltreat, wear down **09** cannonade, disfigure
**10** knock about **11** overweather
**• batter down**
**04** ruin **05** smash, wreck **07** destroy
**08** demolish **09** break down

**battered**
◇ *anagram indicator*
**03** hit **06** abused, beaten, shabby
**07** bruised, crushed, damaged, injured, run-down **09** crumbling
**10** ill-treated, maltreated, ramshackle, tumbledown **11** dilapidated
**13** weather-beaten

**battery**
**03** bat, row, set **04** bank, cell, guns, pram **05** array, cycle, force, group, nicad, praam **06** attack, cannon, series
**07** assault, beating, mugging
**08** cannonry, ordnance, sequence, striking, violence **09** artillery, thrashing
**10** button cell, succession
**12** emplacements

**batting**
◇ *anagram indicator*
**02** in

**battle**
**02** by **03** bye, row, war **04** feud, fray, race, wage **05** argue, brawl, clash, drive, field, fight, scrap, set-to, stoor, stour **06** action, affair, attack, buffet, combat, debate, engage, stoush, stowre, strife, strive **07** agitate, clamour, contend, contest, crusade, dispute, fertile, hosting, quarrel, warfare **08** campaign, conflict, darraign, disagree, naumachy, sea-fight, skirmish, struggle **09** battalion, encounter, naumachia
**10** Armageddon, engagement, free-for-all, nourishing, tournament
**11** altercation, competition, controversy, final battle, hostilities, turkey-shoot **12** disagreement
**13** armed conflict, confrontation

*See also* **siege**; **war**

*Battles include:*

**04** Jena, Loos, Neva, Nile, Zama
**05** Alamo, Anzio, Boyne, Bulge, Crécy, Issus, Liège, Maipó, Maipú, Marne, Mylae, Pavia, Rhine, Sedan, Sluys, Somme, Spurs, Valmy, Varna, Ypres
**06** Actium, Amiens, Arnhem, Cannae, Crimea, Harlaw, Kosovo, Lützen, Midway, Mohács, Mycale, Naseby, Pinkie, Quebec, Shiloh, Tobruk, Towton, Verdun, Wagram
**07** Antwerp, Britain, Bull Run, Cambrai, Cassino, Colenso, Corunna, Cowpens, Dresden, Dunkirk, Flodden, Iwo Jima, Jutland, Leipzig, Lepanto, Leuctra, Marengo, Okinawa, Plassey, Salamis, Salerno, Thapsus
**08** Atlantic, Ayacucho, Blenheim, Carabobo, Culloden, Fontenoy, Formigny, Granicus, Hastings, Mafeking, Marathon, Monmouth, Omdurman, Philippi, Poitiers, Pyramids, Saratoga, Spion Kop, St Albans, Waterloo, Yorktown
**09** Agincourt, Balaclava, Bay of Pigs, Chaeronea, El Alamein, Pharsalus, Ramillies, Sedgemoor, Seven Days, Solferino, Trafalgar, Vicksburg
**10** Aboukir Bay, Adrianople, Austerlitz, Brandywine, Bunker Hill, Charleston, Cold Harbor, Copenhagen, Gettysburg, Malplaquet, Oudenaarde, River Plate, Stalingrad, Tannenberg, Tel-El-Kebir, Wilderness
**11** Bannockburn, Guadalcanal, Hohenlinden, Marston Moor, Navarino Bay, Pearl Harbor, Prestonpans, Wounded Knee
**12** Mons Graupius, Monte Cassino, Tet offensive
**13** Bosworth Field, Cape St Vincent, Killiecrankie, Little Bighorn, Magersfontein, Passchendaele
**14** Fredericksburg

**battle-axe**
**03** axe, hag **04** bill, fury, wife **05** shrew, witch **06** dragon, poleax, sparth, Tartar, virago **07** gisarme, poleaxe, sparthe
**08** harridan, martinet **09** termagant
**12** Jeddart staff **14** disciplinarian

**battle-cry**
**05** motto **06** banzai, slogan, war cry
**07** war song **09** catchword, watchword **11** catchphrase, rallying cry
**12** rallying call

**battlefield**
**05** arena, field, front, place **07** war zone **09** front line **10** Armageddon, combat zone **12** battleground **13** field of battle

**battlement**
**07** barmkin **08** bartisan, bartizan

**batty**
◇ *anagram indicator*
**03** mad, odd **04** bats, daft, nuts
**05** barmy, buggy, crazy, dippy, dotty, loony, loopy, nutty, silly **06** insane, stupid **07** bonkers, foolish, idiotic
**08** crackers, demented, peculiar
**09** eccentric **10** off your nut, out to lunch **11** off your head **12** round the bend **13** off your rocker, round the twist

**bauble**
**03** toy **06** gewgaw, tinsel, trifle
**07** bibelot, flamfew, trinket
**08** gimcrack, kickshaw, ornament
**09** bagatelle, plaything **10** knick-knack

**baulk** *see* **balk, baulk**

**bawd**
**04** pimp **05** madam **08** procurer
**09** panderess, procuress **13** brothel-keeper

**bawdy**
**04** blue, lewd, rude **05** adult, dirty, gross **06** coarse, erotic, ribald, risqué, smutty, vulgar, X-rated **07** lustful, obscene, raunchy **08** improper, indecent, prurient **09** lecherous, salacious **10** indecorous, indelicate, lascivious, libidinous, licentious, sculduddry, suggestive **11** sculduddery, skulduddery **12** pornographic **14** near the knuckle

**bawl**
**03** cry, sob **04** call, gape, howl, roar, wail, weep, yell, yowl **05** shout
**06** bellow, cry out, gollar, goller, holler, scream, snivel, squall **07** blubber, call out, screech **10** vociferate
**• bawl out**
**05** scold **06** rebuke, yell at **07** rouse on, tell off **09** dress down, reprimand

**bay**
**03** arm, cry, vae, voe **04** bark, bawl, bell, cove, gulf, howl, loch, nook, roar, yelp, yowl **05** bathe, bight, booth, creek, firth, fleet, inlet, niche, reach, sound, stall **06** alcove, bellow, carrel, holler, lagoon, laurel, recess
**07** clamour, classis, cubicle, estuary,

opening **09** cubbyhole, embayment **11** compartment, indentation

*Bays include:*

**04** Acre, Clew, Daya, Kiel, Luce, Lyme, Pigs, Tees
**05** Algoa, Blind, Cloud, Enard, Evans, False, Fundy, Hawke, Shark, Table
**06** Baffin, Bantry, Bengal, Biscay, Botany, Broken, Colwyn, Dingle, Dublin, Galway, Hervey, Hudson, Lubeck, Mounts, Naples, Plenty, Tasman, Torbay, Walvis
**07** Bustard, Chaleur, Donegal, Dundalk, Fortune, Halifax, Hudson's, Montego, Moreton, Pegasus, Prudhoe, Thunder, Trinity, Volcano
**08** Campeche, Cardigan, Delaware, Georgian, Hang-Chow, Portland, Quiberon, San Pablo, Tremadog, Weymouth
**09** Admiralty, Discovery, Encounter, Frobisher, Galveston, Geographe, Hermitage, Mackenzie, Morecambe, Notre Dame, Placentia
**10** Barnstaple, Bridgwater, Carmarthen, Chesapeake, Conception, Heligoland, Providence, Robin Hood's
**11** Port Jackson, Port Phillip, Saint Bride's, Saint Magnus
**12** Saint George's, San Francisco

**• bay with spots**
**04** roan

**bayonet**
**04** pike, stab **05** blade, knife, spear, spike, stick, sword **06** dagger, impale, pierce **07** poniard **08** white arm

**bazaar**
**04** fair, fête, mart, sale, souk **06** market **07** alcázar **08** exchange **10** alcaicería, jumble sale **11** bring-and-buy, marketplace **13** nearly-new sale

**BBC**
**04** Beeb **06** Auntie

**be**
**03** lie **04** form, last, live, make, stay **05** abide, arise, dwell, exist, occur, stand **06** befall, endure, happen, make up, obtain, remain, reside **07** add up to, be alive, breathe, develop, inhabit, persist, prevail, survive **08** amount to, continue **09** be located, be present, beryllium, come about, represent, take place, transpire **10** account for, be situated, come to pass, constitute

**beach**
**04** hard, land, lido, sand **05** coast, plage, sands, shore **06** ground, strand **07** machair, seaside, shingle **08** go ashore, littoral, seaboard, seashore **09** coastline, run ashore **10** be grounded, be stranded, run aground, water's edge

*Beaches include:*

**04** Gold, Juno, Long, Palm, Utah
**05** Bells, Bondi, Cable, Manly, Miami, Omaha, Sword
**06** Chesil, Malibu, Sunset, Tahiti, Venice
**07** Daytona, Glenelg, Ipanema, Pattaya, Waikiki
**08** Hotwater, St Tropez, Virginia
**09** Blackpool
**10** Copacabana, Ninety Mile
**11** Coney Island
**13** Skeleton Coast
**15** Surfers Paradise

**beachcomber**
**06** loafer **07** forager **08** loiterer, wayfarer **09** scavenger

**beacon**
**04** beam, fire, sign **05** fanal, flare, light, racon **06** pharos, rocket, signal **07** bonfire **08** bale-fire, needfire **09** watch fire **10** lighthouse, watchtower **12** danger signal, warning light

**bead**
**03** dot **04** ball, bede, blob, drip, drop, gaud, glob, nurl, tear **05** bugle, jewel, knurl, ojime, pearl **06** bubble, pellet, prayer **07** cabling, droplet, globule **08** moulding, spheroid **10** adderstone **11** paternoster, spacer plate **13** cable-moulding

**beadle**
**06** bedral, Bumble **07** bederal **09** apparitor **10** bluebottle **13** church officer

**beak**
**02** JP **03** neb, nib, ram **04** bill, nose **05** becke, snout **07** rostrum **09** mandibles, proboscis, rostellum **10** magistrate **12** schoolmaster **14** schoolmistress

**beaker**
**03** cup, jar, mug **05** glass **07** tankard, tumbler

**beam**
**03** aim, bar, ray, RSJ, tie **04** balk, boom, emit, glow, grin, lath, send, spar, yard **05** baulk, board, chink, flare, flash, glare, gleam, glint, joist, laugh, plank, relay, shaft, shine, smile, smirk, stock, strut, trave **06** binder, bumkin, direct, gibbet, girder, hurter, lintel, needle, pencil, purlin, rafter, solive, streak, stream, summer, timber **07** bumpkin, carling, effulge, glimmer, glitter, radiate, sleeper, sparkle, support, transom, trimmer **08** herisson, kingpost, stanchel, stancher, streamer, stringer, transmit **09** broadcast, crosshead, outrigger, principal, queen post, scantling, stanchion, weigh-bauk **10** bressummer, cantilever **12** breastsummer

**• off beam**
**05** wrong **08** mistaken **09** incorrect, misguided, off target **10** inaccurate **11** wrong-headed **13** wide of the mark

**bean**

*Beans and pulses include:*

**03** dal, Goa, pea, soy, urd, wax
**04** dahl, dhal, fava, gram, guar, jack, Lens, lima, loco, mung, navy, okra, snap, soja, soya
**05** aduki, berry, black, broad, carob, dholl, green, horse, moong, pinto, sugar, tonga, tonka
**06** adsuki, adzuki, butter, cherry, chilli, coffee, cowpea, French, frijol, kidney, lablab, legume, lentil, locust, runner, string, winged
**07** alfalfa, Calabar, fasolia, frijole, haricot, jumping, Molucca, scarlet, snow pea, tonquin
**08** black-eye, borlotti, chickpea, garbanzo, pichurim, snuffbox, split pea, sugar pea, yard-long
**09** black-eyed, black gram, flageolet, green gram, jequirity, mangetout, pigeon pea, puy lentil, red kidney, red lentil
**10** cannellini, golden gram, prayer bead
**11** black-eye pea, garbanzo pea, green lentil
**12** asparagus pea, black-eyed pea, marrowfat pea, sassafras nut, St John's bread
**13** scarlet runner

**bear**
◇ *containment indicator*
**02** go **03** act, hae, owe, pay, sit **04** bend, dree, hack, have, hold, hump, keep, like, move, show, take, teem, tote, turn, veer **05** abear, abide, admit, allow, beget, breed, bring, brook, carry, curve, drive, fetch, stand, thole, yield **06** accept, acquit, behave, convey, endure, foster, give up, hold up, keep up, permit, suffer, swerve, uphold **07** abrooke, cherish, comport, conduct, deliver, develop, deviate, display, diverge, endorse, exhibit, harbour, produce, stomach, support, sustain **08** engender, fructify, generate, live with, maintain, shoulder, tolerate **09** entertain, propagate, put up with, transport **10** bring forth **11** give birth to **13** grin and bear it

*Bears include:*

**03** sea, sun
**04** balu, cave, Pooh, Yogi
**05** baloo, black, brown, Bruin, Great, honey, koala, Nandi, polar, sloth, teddy, water, white
**06** Little, native, Rupert, woolly
**07** grizzly, Malayan
**08** cinnamon
**09** Ursa Major, Ursa Minor
**10** giant panda, Paddington
**13** Teddy Robinson, Winnie the Pooh

**• bear down on**
**08** approach, browbeat, move in on
**09** advance on, close in on

**• bear in mind**
**04** mind, note **06** keep in **08** consider, remember **10** keep in mind **11** be mindful of **15** make a mental note, take into account

**• bear out**
**05** prove **06** back up, ratify, uphold, verify **07** confirm, endorse, justify, support, warrant **08** validate **09** vindicate **11** corroborate, demonstrate **12** substantiate

**• bear up**
**04** buoy, cope **06** endure, suffer **07** carry on, survive **09** persevere, soldier on, withstand **13** grin and bear it

**• bear with**
**06** endure, suffer **07** forbear **08** tolerate **09** put up with **13** be patient with

**bearable**
**07** livable **08** liveable, passable, portable **09** endurable, tolerable **10** acceptable, admissible, manageable, sufferable **11** supportable, sustainable

**beard**
**03** awn **04** dare, defy, face, kesh, peak, tuft, ziff **05** brave **06** beaver, goatee, oppose, pappus **07** bristle, Charley, Charlie, stubble, vandyke **08** confront, imperial, whiskers **09** challenge, moustache, sideburns **10** face-fungus, facial hair, sideboards **11** mutton chops **12** Newgate frill **13** Newgate fringe **14** stand up against

**bearded**
**05** awned, bushy, hairy **06** barbed, shaggy, tufted **07** bristly, hirsute, prickly, stubbly **08** barbated, unshaven **09** pogoniate, whiskered **11** bewhiskered

**bearer**
**05** agent, owner, payee **06** holder, porter, runner **07** carrier, courier, jampani **08** chairman, conveyor, jampanee **09** consignee, messenger, possessor **11** beneficiary, transporter

**bearing**
◇ *containment indicator*
**01** E, N, S, W **03** aim, air, way **04** east, gait, gest, mien, port, west **05** geste, north, poise, south, track **06** aspect, course, manner **07** concern, posture, stature **08** attitude, carriage, location, portance, position, relation **09** behaviour, demeanour, direction, influence, reference, relevance, situation **10** connection, deportment, pertinence **11** comportment, orientation, whereabouts **12** significance

**• strewn with bearings**
**04** semé **05** semée

**beast**
**03** pig **04** bête, ogre **05** brute, devil, fiend, swine **06** animal, savage, tarand **07** monster, salvage **08** behemoth, creature, opinicus **09** barbarian
*See also* **animal**

**• mark of the Beast**
**02** mb

**beastly**
**04** foul, mean, vile **05** awful, cruel, nasty **06** brutal, horrid, rotten **07** swinish **08** horrible, terrible **09** brutishly, repulsive **10** abominably, unpleasant **11** frightfully **12** disagreeable

**beat**
**02** do **03** box, gub, hit, lam, mix, pug, ram, tan, tap, way, wop **04** bang, bash, belt, best, biff, blow, cane, club, cuff, dash, ding, drub, dust, firk, flap, flay, flog, form, lash, lick, mall, maul, path, pelt, race, rout, ruin, slap, slat, stir, thud, tick, time, tund, walk, welt, wham, whip, whop, work, yerk, yirk **05** all in, birch, blend, clout, crush, excel, forge, knock, knout, metre, mould, outdo, paste, pound, pulse, punch, quake, quell, repel, rhyme, round, route, shake, shape, smack, smash, stamp, strap, swing, swipe, tempo, throb, thump, tired, whack, whisk, worst **06** accent, batter, bruise, buffet, bushed, course, cudgel, done in, exceed, fill in, granny, hammer, outrun, outwit, pooped, pummel, quiver, reject, rhythm, rounds, stress, strike, stroke, subdue, thrash, thresh, thwack, wallop, zonked **07** banging, cadence, circuit, clobber, combine, conquer, contuse, eclipse, fashion, flutter, journey, knubble, lambast, lay into, measure, outplay, pulsate, surpass, tremble, trounce, vibrate, wearied, whacked, worn out **08** dead-beat, dog-tired, fatigued, jiggered, knocking, malleate, outmatch, outscore, outsmart, outstrip, overcome, pounding, rib-roast, striking, throw out, tired out, vanquish, vapulate **09** devastate, discomfit, exhausted, knackered, marmelize, overpower, overthrow, overwhelm, palpitate, pooped out, pulsation, pulverize, slaughter, subjugate, territory, transcend, vibration, zonked out **10** annihilate, clapped-out, knock about **11** palpitation, tuckered out **13** have the edge on, put to the worse, run rings round **14** get the better of **15** make mincemeat of

**• beat against the wind**
**03** ply

**• beat off**
**05** repel **07** hold off, repulse, ward off **08** beat back, fight off, overcome, push back **09** drive back, force back, keep at bay

**• beats per minute**
**03** BPM **05** pulse **09** pulse rate

**• beat up**
◇ *anagram indicator*
**02** do **03** mug **05** scrag **06** arouse, attack, bang up, batter, donder, do over, duff up, switch **07** assault, clobber, disturb, rough up, scare up **08** duff over, work over **10** knock about **11** knock around

**beaten**
◇ *anagram indicator*
**04** flat, ybet **05** foamy, mixed, trite **06** forged, formed, frothy, shaped, worked **07** blended, moulded, stamped, stirred, trodden, whipped, whisked, wrought **08** foliated, hammered, trampled, well-used, well-worn **09** exhausted, fashioned, stonkered **11** well-trodden

**beatific**
**06** divine, joyful **07** angelic, blessed, exalted, sublime **08** blissful, ecstatic, glorious, heavenly, seraphic **09** rapturous

**beatification**
**10** exaltation **12** canonization **13** glorification **14** sanctification

**beatify**
**05** bless, exalt **07** glorify **08** canonize, macarize, sanctify

**beating**
**04** loss, rout, ruin, warm **05** laldy, pandy, pulse, socks **06** caning, defeat, hiding, lacing, laldie **07** battery, belting, duffing, hitting, lashing, pasting, pugging, tanning, the cane, warming **08** bruising, clubbing, conquest, downfall, drubbing, flogging, knocking, once-over, punching, slapping, smacking, the birch, the strap, thumping, whacking, whipping, whupping **09** bastinade, bastinado, battering, doing-over, duffing-up, going-over, hammering, overthrow, pulsation, pulsatory, slaughter, thrashing, trouncing, walloping **10** clobbering, loundering, outwitting, paddy-whack **11** duffing-over, outsmarting, vanquishing **12** annihilation, chastisement, overpowering, overwhelming

**beatitude**
**07** delight, ecstasy, elation, rapture **08** macarism **09** happiness **11** blessedness **13** contentedness

**beau**
**03** fop, guy **04** buck **05** dandy, lover, spark **06** Adonis, escort, fiancé, suitor **07** admirer, coxcomb **08** muscadin, popinjay **09** boyfriend **10** sweetheart

**beautician**
**07** friseur **09** visagiste **11** cosmetician, hairdresser **12** aesthetician

**beautiful**
**04** fair, fine **05** bonny, sheen **06** bright, comely, lovely, pretty, seemly **07** auroral, radiant, smicker **08** alluring, aurorean, becoming, charming, gorgeous, graceful, handsome, pleasing, smashing, specious, striking, stunning **09** appealing, exquisite, fair-faced, fairytale, ravishing **10** attractive, delightful, voluptuous **11** good-looking, hyacinthine, magnificent **14** out of this world, poetry in motion **15** pulchritudinous

**beautifully**
**06** fairly, lovely **09** radiantly
**10** charmingly, gracefully, pleasantly, pleasingly, strikingly, stunningly
**12** attractively, delightfully

**beautify**
**04** deck, gild **05** adorn, array, grace
**06** bedeck, doll up, tart up
**07** enhance, garnish, improve, smarten
**08** decorate, flourish, ornament, spruce up, titivate **09** embellish, glamorize, smarten up

**beauty**
**04** boon, dish, fair, form **05** asset, belle, bonus, charm, doozy, glory, grace, looks, merit, peach, pride, siren, Venus **06** allure, appeal, corker, doozer, glamor, virtue **07** benefit, charmer, cracker, delight, feature, glamour, harmony, smasher, stunner
**08** blessing, dividend, Greek god, knockout, radiance, strength, symmetry **09** advantage, beau ideal, good looks, good point, good thing, plus point **10** attraction, excellence, good-looker, loveliness, prettiness, seemliness **11** femme fatale, pulchritude **12** gorgeousness, gracefulness, handsomeness
**13** exquisiteness **14** attractiveness, beauté du diable

**beaver**
**04** flix **05** beard **06** castor **08** sewellel
• **beaver away**
**04** slog **06** work at **07** persist **08** plug away, work hard **09** persevere, slave away

**becalmed**
**04** idle **05** still, stuck **07** at a halt
**08** marooned, stranded **10** motionless
**13** at a standstill

**because**
**02** as **03** 'cos, for **05** due to, since
**06** for why **07** owing to, through
**08** seeing as, thanks to **09** forasmuch
**10** by reason of, by virtue of **11** as a result of, on account of
• **because of**
**02** in **07** owing to **08** what with **10** by virtue of, in virtue of **11** on account of

**beckon**
**03** nod **04** call, coax, draw, lure, pull, waft, wave **05** tempt **06** allure, entice, induce, invite, motion, signal, summon
**07** attract, gesture **08** persuade
**11** gesticulate

**become**
◇ *anagram indicator*
**02** go **03** get, run, set, wax, won
**04** come, fall, grow, suit, take, turn
**05** befit, grace, worth **06** beseem, besort, set off **07** enhance, flatter
**08** come to be, grow into, ornament, pass into **09** embellish, harmonize
**10** change into, look good on, mature into **11** develop into, turn out to be
**13** be changed into
• **become of**
**06** befall **08** happen to **11** be the fate of

**becoming**
**03** fit **06** comely, decent, pretty, seemly **07** elegant, fitting
**08** charming, decorous, fetching, graceful, gracious, handsome, suitable, tasteful **09** befitting, besitting, congruous **10** attractive, compatible, consistent, flattering **11** appropriate

**becomingly**
**09** elegantly **10** charmingly, fetchingly, gracefully, tastefully **12** attractively

**bed**
**03** fix, hay, kip, mat, pad, pit, row, set
**04** area, base, bury, doss, plot, sack
**05** basis, embed, floor, found, inlay, layer, patch, plant, space, strip
**06** border, bottom, garden, ground, insert, matrix, settle **07** channel, implant, stratum **09** establish
**10** foundation, groundwork, substratum **11** watercourse

*Beds include:*

**01** Z
**03** box, cot, day
**04** bunk, camp, cott, crib, sofa, twin
**05** berth, couch, divan, futon, water
**06** cradle, double, litter, pallet, Put-u-up®, single
**07** folding, hammock, trestle, truckle, trundle
**08** bassinet, foldaway, king-size, mattress, platform, put-you-up
**09** couchette, king-sized, lit bateau, palliasse, queen-size, shakedown
**10** adjustable, four-poster, mid sleeper, queen-sized
**11** high sleeper
**12** chaise longue

• **bed down**
**03** kip **05** sleep **06** turn in **07** go to bed, kip down **08** doss down **09** hit the hay **10** call it a day, get some kip, hit the sack, settle down
• **dry bed**
**04** wadi, wady
• **get out of bed**
**04** rise **07** surface, turn out **08** show a leg, tumble up **10** hit the deck **12** rise and shine
• **out of bed**
**02** up **05** astir, risen

**bedaub**
**04** clag, moil **05** smear **06** parget
**07** besmear, plaster **08** slaister
**09** beslubber

**bedbug**
**01** B **05** B flat **06** chinch

**bedclothes**
**06** covers **07** bedding **08** bed-linen

*Bedclothes include:*

**05** doona, duvet, quilt, sheet
**06** downie, pillow
**07** bedroll, blanket, bolster, valance
**08** coverlet
**09** bed canopy, bedspread, comforter, eiderdown, throwover
**10** duvet cover, pillowcase, pillow sham, pillowslip, quilt cover
**11** counterpane, fitted sheet, sleeping bag
**13** mattress cover, valanced sheet, Witney blanket
**14** patchwork quilt
**15** cellular blanket, electric blanket

**bedeck**
**04** deck, trim **05** adorn, array
**07** festoon, garnish, trick up
**08** beautify, decorate, ornament, trick out **09** embellish

**bedevil**
◇ *anagram indicator*
**03** irk, vex **04** fret **05** annoy, beset, tease, worry **06** harass, pester, plague
**07** afflict, besiege, torment, torture, trouble **08** confound, distress, irritate
**09** frustrate

**bedfellow**
**04** ally **06** fellow, friend **07** partner
**09** associate, colleague, companion

**bedlam**
◇ *anagram indicator*
**05** babel, chaos, noise **06** furore, hubbub, madman, tumult, uproar
**07** anarchy, clamour, turmoil
**08** madhouse **09** commotion, confusion **10** hullabaloo
**11** pandemonium

**bedraggled**
**03** wet **05** dirty, messy, muddy
**06** soaked, sodden, soiled, untidy
**07** muddied, scruffy, soaking, unkempt
**08** drenched, dripping, slovenly
**10** disordered, soaking wet
**11** dishevelled

**bedridden**
**06** bedrid, laid up **07** worn-out
**10** housebound **13** confined to bed, incapacitated **14** flat on your back

**bedrock**
**04** base, core **05** basis, heart
**06** basics, bottom, reason **07** essence, footing, premise, reasons, support
**09** rationale **10** essentials, foundation, rock bottom **12** fundamentals
**13** starting-point **15** first principles

**bedroom**
**02** br **06** dormer **07** cubicle
**08** roomette **09** bed-closet
**10** bedchamber

**bee**
**01** B **04** king **05** drone, nurse, queen
**06** hummer, neuter, worker **07** royalty
**10** drumbledor, dumbledore, leaf-cutter

**beech**
**05** Fagus **06** myrtle **15** Tasmanian myrtle

**beef**
**03** gag, sey **04** moan, rump, shin
**05** bully, chuck, filet, flank, gripe, keema, mouse, round, skink, steak, T-bone **06** grouse, object, runner
**07** charqui, dispute, grumble, sirloin, surloin, topside **08** bresaola, complain, disagree, pastrami, salt-junk

**09** aitchbone, criticize, rump steak, salt horse, tournedos **10** mousepiece, silverside **11** filet mignon, sauerbraten **12** mouse-buttock **13** Chateaubriand, Scotch collops **15** scotched collops

**• beef up**
**07** build up, toughen **08** flesh out
**09** establish, reinforce, toughen up
**10** invigorate, strengthen
**11** consolidate **12** substantiate **15** give new energy to

**beefeater**
**04** exon **06** ox-bird, yeoman
**07** Buphaga **08** oxpecker

**beefy**
**03** fat **05** bulky, burly, heavy, hefty, tubby **06** brawny, fleshy, robust, stocky, stolid, sturdy **07** hulking **08** muscular, stalwart **09** corpulent

**beehive**
**03** gum **04** skep

**beer**
**04** brew, grog, half, pint **06** liquor
**07** brewski **11** amber liquid

*Beers include:*

**03** ale, dry, ice, IPA, keg
**04** bock, mild, Pils, rice
**05** black, fruit, guest, heavy, honey, kvass, lager, plain, sixty, stout, wheat, white
**06** bitter, eighty, export, old ale, porter, shandy, Stella®
**07** bottled, draught, pale ale, Pilsner, real ale, seventy
**08** amber ale, brown ale, Guinness®, home brew, light ale, Pilsener, trappist
**09** microbrew, milk stout, snakebite, wheat beer
**10** barley wine, low-alcohol, malt liquor, sweet stout, Weisse Bier
**11** black-and-tan
**12** Christmas ale, India Pale Ale
**13** sixty shilling
**14** eighty shilling
**15** cask-conditioned, seventy shilling

*See also* **glass**

**beetle**
**03** nip, run, zip **04** dash, maul, rush, tear **05** hurry, scoot **06** batler, batlet, bustle, mallet, scurry **07** scamper

*See also* **animal**; **insect**

*Beetles include:*

**03** dor, may, oil
**04** bark, dorr, dung, leaf, musk, pine, rove, stag
**05** black, click, clock, shard, tiger, water
**06** carpet, chafer, dor-fly, ground, may bug, sacred, scarab, sexton, weevil
**07** burying, cadelle, carabid, carrion, goliath, hop-flea, hornbug, rose bug
**08** bum-clock, cardinal, Colorado, glow-worm, Hercules, Japanese, ladybird, longhorn, wireworm, woodworm
**09** furniture, goldsmith, longicorn, tumblebug, whirligig
**10** bombardier, cockchafer, deathwatch, rhinoceros, rose chafer, scarabaean, scarabaeid, tumbledung, turnip flea
**11** coprophagan, typographer

**• beetle-crusher**
**03** cop **09** policeman **11** infantryman

**beetling**
**07** jutting, pendent **09** poking out, prominent **10** projecting, protruding
**11** leaning over, overhanging, sticking out

**befall**
**04** fall **05** ensue, occur **06** arrive, astart, betide, chance, follow, happen, result, strike **07** fortune **08** bechance, come over, come upon, fall upon, happen to **09** befortune, overwhelm, supervene, take place **11** materialize

**befit**
**03** set, sit **04** seem, sort, suit **05** match
**06** become, befall, behove, beseem, besort **10** complement **13** harmonize with

**befitting**
**03** apt, fit **04** like, meet **05** right
**06** decent, proper, seemly **07** correct, fitting **08** becoming, sortable, suitable
**11** appropriate **12** well-becoming
**13** well-beseeming

**before**
◇ *juxtaposition indicator*
**01** a **02** an, or, to **03** bef, ere, pre, pro-
**04** ante, once, onst, prae- **05** ahead
**07** ahead of, already, earlier, in front, prior to **08** formerly **09** in advance, in front of **10** on the eve of, previously, previous to, sooner than **11** earlier than
**12** in the sight of, not later than **15** in the presence of

**• as before**
**02** do **05** ditto

**beforehand**
**03** pre- **04** fore-, prae- **05** afore, early
**06** before, former, sooner **07** already, earlier **08** paravant **09** aforehand, in advance, paravaunt **10** previously
**11** ahead of time **13** preliminarily

**befriend**
**03** aid **04** back, help **06** assist, defend, favour, uphold **07** benefit, comfort, protect, stand by, succour, support, sustain, welcome **09** encourage, get to know, look after **10** fall in with, stick up for **11** keep an eye on **13** make a friend of **15** make friends with

**befuddle**
◇ *anagram indicator*
**04** daze, faze **06** baffle, muddle, puzzle **07** confuse, nonplus, perplex, stupefy **08** bewilder **09** disorient

**beg**
**03** ask, bum **04** pray, prog, thig
**05** cadge, crave, maund, mooch, mouch, plead **06** appeal, ask for, desire, fleech, sponge, turn to
**07** beseech, beseeke, entreat, implore, intreat, maunder, request, require, schnorr, skelder, solicit **08** governor, mooch off, petition, scrounge, stand pad **09** importune, panhandle
**10** supplicate **11** ask for money
**13** touch for money

**beget**
**03** get **04** kind, sire **05** breed, cause, spawn **06** create, effect, father, gender, lead to **07** produce, propage
**08** engender, generate, occasion, result in **09** procreate, propagate
**10** bring about, give rise to

**beggar**
**03** bum **04** defy **05** randy, tramp
**06** baffle, blowse, blowze, cadger, canter, craver, exceed, mumper, pauper, randie, toerag **07** bludger, jarkman, maunder, moocher, ruffler, sponger, surpass, vagrant **08** Abram-man, beadsman, bedesman, besognio, besonian, bezonian, blighter, glassman, palliard, vagabond, whipjack
**09** challenge, lazzarone, mendicant, schnorrer, scrounger, sundowner, transcend **10** Abraham-man, beadswoman, down-and-out, freeloader, panhandler, supplicant, upright-man **11** gaberlunzie **12** down-and-outer, hallan-shaker

**beggarly**
**03** low **04** mean, poor **05** needy
**06** abject, meagre, modest, paltry, slight, stingy **07** miserly, pitiful
**08** pathetic, wretched **09** niggardly, worthless **10** despicable, inadequate
**12** contemptible **13** insubstantial

**begin**
**02** go **03** gin, ope **04** open, take
**05** arise, enter, found, get at, set in, set up, shoot, spark, start **06** appear, broach, come on, crop up, embark, emerge, incept, set off, set out, spring
**07** actuate, do first, enter on, kick off, take off **08** activate, commence, embark on, fire away, get going, inchoate, initiate, set about, shoot off, strike up **09** enter upon, instigate, institute, introduce, originate
**10** launch into **11** get cracking, give birth to, open the ball, set in motion
**13** take the plunge

**beginner**
◇ *head selection indicator*
**01** L **03** cub, deb **04** tiro, tyro **05** pupil, rooky **06** author, newbie, novice, rookie **07** fresher, learner, new chum, recruit, starter, student, trainee
**08** freshman, initiate, neophyte, newcomer **09** fledgling, greenhorn, Johnny-raw **10** apprentice, raw recruit, tenderfoot **11** abecedarian, probationer **13** alphabetarian

**beginning**
◇ *head selection indicator*
**03** ord **04** dawn, germ, rise, root, seed
**05** birth, debut, get-go, intro, onset, start **06** day one, launch, origin, outset, source **07** genesis, kick-off, new leaf, opening, preface, prelude
**09** emergence, first base, first part,

inception, square one, the word go **10** conception, fresh start, inchoation, incipience, initiation **11** institution, opening part, pastures new **12** commencement, fountainhead, inauguration, introduction **13** establishment, new beginnings, starting-point

• **from beginning to end**

**04** over **07** through **08** from A to Z

**begone**

**04** away **05** hence **06** avaunt **10** aroint thee **11** allez-vous-en

**begrudge**

**04** envy, mind **05** covet, stint **06** grudge, resent **08** object to **11** be jealous of **13** be resentful of

**beguile**

**04** dupe, fool, gull, wile **05** amuse, blend, charm, cheat, cozen, guile, guyle, trick **06** delude, divert, occupy, seduce **07** attract, bewitch, deceive, delight, enchant, engross, mislead **08** distract, hoodwink **09** captivate, entertain

**beguiling**

**08** alluring, charming, enticing **09** appealing, diverting, seductive **10** attractive, bewitching, delightful, enchanting, intriguing **11** captivating, interesting **12** entertaining

**behalf**

**04** name, part, sake **07** account, benefit **08** interest

• **on behalf of**

**02** pp **03** for **06** per pro **09** acting for **11** in support of, in the name of **12** for account of, for the good of, for the sake of, representing **13** to the profit of **15** for the benefit of

**behave**

**02** be, do **03** act, use **04** bear, go on, quit, walk, work **05** abear, carry, quite, quyte, react **06** acquit, be good, demean, deport, quight **07** comport, conduct, operate, perform, respond **08** function **10** act your age **11** act politely, act properly **12** not mess about, not muck about **13** be well-behaved **14** acquit yourself **15** comport yourself, conduct yourself, mind your manners, mind your p's and q's

**behaviour**

**04** form, ways **06** action, doings, habits, manner **07** conduct, manners **08** dealings, reaction, response **09** attitudes, demeanour, operation **10** deportment **11** comportment, functioning, performance, way of acting

**behead**

◇ *head deletion indicator*

**04** head, kill **07** execute **09** decollate **10** decapitate, guillotine, put to death

**behest**

• **at the behest of**

**11** at the hest of **12** at the order of **13** on the wishes of **14** at the bidding of, at the command of, at the request of

**behind**

◇ *juxtaposition indicator*

◇ *tail selection indicator*

**03** aft, ass, bum, for **04** back, baft, butt, late, next, post, rear, rump, slow **05** abaft, after, ahind, ahint, retro-, stern **06** arrear, astern, back of, bottom, heinie, in debt **07** backing, causing, close on, delayed, overdue **08** backside, buttocks, derrière, in back of **09** at the back, at the rear, endorsing, following, in arrears, in the rear, later than, posterior **10** behindhand, explaining, initiating, supporting **11** at the back of, at the rear of, instigating, on the side of, running late **12** giving rise to, subsequently **13** accounting for, at the bottom of **14** responsible for **15** slower than usual

**behindhand**

**03** lag **04** down, late, slow **05** tardy **06** behind, remiss **07** delayed **08** backward, dilatory **09** in arrears, out of date **14** behind schedule

**behold**

**02** la, lo **03** see **04** ecce, ecco, espy, look, mark, note, scan, view **05** voici, voilà, watch **06** descry, gaze at, look at, regard, survey **07** discern, observe, witness **08** consider, perceive **11** contemplate

**beholden**

**05** bound, owing **07** obliged **08** addebted, grateful, indebted, thankful **09** obligated **12** appreciative **15** under obligation

**behove**

**05** befit **06** import, profit **07** benefit, stand on **08** be proper, be seemly **11** be essential, be necessary **13** be suitable for **14** be advantageous

**beige**

**03** tan **04** buff, ecru, fawn **05** camel, khaki, sandy, suede, taupe **06** coffee, greige, oyster **07** neutral, oatmeal **08** mushroom

**being**

**03** ens, man **04** esse, life, soul, will **05** beast, heart, human, thing, woman **06** animal, entity, living, mortal, nature, person, psyche, spirit **07** essence, reality **08** creature, emotions **09** actuality, animation, existence, haecceity, inner self, substance **10** human being, individual, inner being **11** personality **13** heart of hearts

**belabour**

◇ *anagram indicator*

**03** hit **04** beat, belt, flay, flog, whip **05** sauce **06** attack, pummel, strike, thrash **07** dwell on **09** lay on load, reiterate **11** flog to death, harp on about **14** go on and on about

**Belarus**

**02** BY, SU **03** BLR

**belated**

**04** late **05** lated, tardy **07** delayed, overdue **09** benighted, out of date **10** behindhand, unpunctual **14** behind schedule

**belatedly**

**07** tardily **12** unpunctually **14** behind schedule

**belch**

**03** yex **04** boak, bock, boke, burp, emit, gush, rift, spew, vent, yesk **05** eject, eruct, issue **06** hiccup **07** give off, give out **08** disgorge, eructate **09** discharge **10** eructation **11** bring up wind

**beleaguered**

**05** beset, vexed **07** plagued, worried **08** badgered, besieged, bothered, harassed, pestered, troubled **09** blockaded, tormented **10** persecuted, surrounded, under siege

**Belgium**

**01** B **03** BEL **04** Belg

**belie**

**04** deny **06** negate, refute **07** conceal, confute, cover up, deceive, falsify, gainsay, mislead **08** disguise, disprove **10** contradict **12** misrepresent, run counter to

**belief**

**03** ism **04** idea, view **05** creed, dogma, ethic, faith, ideal, tenet, trust **06** credit, notion, theory, threap, threep **07** feeling, opinion **08** credence, doctrine, ideology, reliance, sureness, teaching **09** assurance, certainty, intuition, judgement, knowledge, principle, tradition, viewpoint **10** confidence, conviction, impression, persuasion **11** expectation, point of view, presumption

*Beliefs include:*

**06** holism, malism, racism
**07** animism, atheism, elitism
**08** demonism, feminism, hedonism, humanism, nihilism, Satanism
**09** pantheism, physicism, tritheism
**10** liberalism, Manicheism, monotheism, polytheism
**11** agnosticism, parallelism, supremacism, tetratheism
**12** Manicheanism
**13** ethnocentrism, individualism, structuralism
**14** fundamentalism, traditionalism, tripersonalism
**15** supernaturalism

*See also* **religion**

**believable**

**06** likely **07** credent **08** credible, possible, probable, reliable **09** plausible **10** acceptable, imaginable **11** conceivable, trustworthy **13** authoritative

**believe**

**03** buy, wis **04** deem, feel, hold, trow, wear, ween, wish, wist **05** faith, guess, judge, opine, think, trust **06** accept, assume, credit, figure, gather, reckon **07** fall for, imagine, suppose, swallow **08** consider, maintain, perceive **09** postulate, speculate **10** Adam and Eve, conjecture, understand **11** be certain of, take on board **13** be convinced by, be persuaded by

• **believe in**

**04** rate **05** trust **06** favour, follow, hold by, rely on **07** swear by **08** depend on **09** approve of, encourage, recommend **11** value highly **12** be in favour of **13** be convinced of, be persuaded by **15** set great store by

• **hard to believe**

**04** tall

**believer**

**06** zealot **07** convert, devotee **08** adherent, disciple, follower, upholder **09** proselyte, supporter

*Believers include:*

**03** Jew
**04** Babi, Jain, Sikh, Sofi, Sufi
**05** Babee, Hindu, Jaina
**06** holist, Muslim
**07** Alawite, animist, Bahaist, Genevan, Lollard, Scotist
**08** Arminian, Buddhist, Calixtin, Catholic, demonist, Erastian, Glassite, humanist, Lutheran, Nazarean, Nazarene, Pelagian, Salesian, Satanist, Wesleyan
**09** animalist, Calixtine, Christian, Confucian, Eutychian, Gregorian, Methodist, Nestorian, Origenist, pantheist, Sabellian, Simeonite, Wyclifite
**10** Bergsonian, Berkeleian, Cameronian, Capernaite, Holy Roller, Marcionite, polytheist, Wycliffite
**11** Sandemanian, Valentinian
**12** Apollinarian, Southcottian
**13** Hutchinsonian, Roman Catholic, Swedenborgian
**14** fundamentalist, the Oxford group
**15** supernaturalist

**belittle**

**04** slag, slam **05** abase, decry, knock, scorn, slate **06** demean, deride, do down, dump on, lessen **07** dismiss, rubbish, run down, slag off **08** diminish, minimize, play down, ridicule **09** deprecate, disparage, downgrade, sell short, underrate **10** trivialize, understate, undervalue **11** detract from, pick holes in **12** pull to pieces, tear to shreds **13** underestimate **15** do a hatchet job on

**Belize**

**02** BH, BZ **03** BLZ

**bell**

**03** tom **04** gong, horn, peal, ring **05** bleep, chime, knell, larum, siren **06** alarum, curfew, hooter, signal, tocsin, vesper **07** angelus, bleeper, tinkler, warning **08** pavilion **13** tintinnabulum

• **sound of bell, sound of bells**

**04** clam, dong, peal, ring, ting, tink, toll **05** chime, knell **06** firing, tinkle **08** ding-dong **09** ding-a-ling

**bellbird**

**08** araponga, arapunga **09** campanero

**belle**

**05** peach, siren, Venus **06** beauty, corker **07** charmer, cracker, smasher, stunner **08** knockout **10** good-looker **11** femme fatale

**bellicose**

**07** violent, warlike, warring **08** bullying, militant **09** combative **10** aggressive, pugnacious **11** belligerent, contentious, quarrelsome **12** antagonistic **13** argumentative

**belligerence**

**03** war **08** bullying, violence **09** militancy, pugnacity **10** aggression, antagonism **11** provocation **12** warmongering **13** combativeness, sabre-rattling **14** unfriendliness **15** contentiousness, quarrelsomeness

**belligerent**

**06** chippy **07** hostile, scrappy, violent, warlike, warring **08** bullying, militant **09** combative, truculent **10** aggressive, pugnacious **11** contentious, provocative, quarrelsome **12** antagonistic, disputatious, warmongering **13** argumentative, sabre-rattling

**bellow**

**03** cry **04** bawl, howl, roar, rout, yell **05** shout, troat **06** buller, holler, scream, shriek **07** clamour, thunder **14** raise your voice

**belly**

**03** gut, pot, tum, wem **04** bulk, bunt, guts, kite, kyte, puku, wame, wemb **05** gastr-, tummy, weamb **06** gastro-, paunch, venter **07** abdomen, gastero-, insides, stomach **08** pot-belly **09** beer belly **10** intestines **11** bread basket, corporation

**belong**

**02** go **03** fit **04** be in, long **05** fit in **06** go with **07** be found, be yours, pertain **08** attach to, be part of, be sorted, relate to **09** appertain, be owned by, tie up with **10** be included, be situated, link up with **11** be a member of **12** be classified **13** be categorized, have as its home **14** be affiliated to, be an adherent of, have as its place **15** be connected with, be the property of

**belonging**

**04** link **05** links **07** kinship, loyalty, rapport **08** affinity **09** closeness **10** acceptance, attachment, fellowship **11** affiliation, association **12** relationship **13** compatibility, fellow-feeling

• **belonging to**

◇ *hidden indicator*

**belongings**

**03** kit **04** gear **05** goods, stuff, traps **06** tackle, things **07** clobber, effects **08** chattels, property **11** possessions **13** accoutrements, appurtenances, paraphernalia

**beloved**

**02** jo **03** joe, joy, pet **04** baby, bird, dear, duck, leve, lief, love, wife **05** angel, fella, honey, lieve, loved, lover, sweet **06** adored, fiancé, liking, prized, spouse, tender **07** admired, darling, dearest, fiancée, husband, partner, revered, sweetie **08** endeared, lady-love, loved one, precious, true-love **09** belamoure, betrothed, boyfriend, cherished, favourite, heart-dear, inamorata, inamorato, much loved, treasured **10** bellamoure, girlfriend, sweetheart, worshipped **12** alder-liefest **13** special friend

**below**

◇ *juxtaposition down indicator*

**03** inf, sub- **04** down **05** infra, later, lower, under **07** beneath **09** further on, hereunder, lower down, lower than, subject to **10** inferior to, lesser than, underneath **13** at a later place, subordinate to **15** lower in rank than

**belt**

◇ *anagram indicator*

**03** box, fly, hit, tan, zip **04** area, band, bang, bash, biff, blow, cane, cord, dash, flay, flog, lash, loop, pelt, rush, sash, slap, tear, whip, zona, zone **05** apron, birch, chain, clout, girth, knock, layer, mitre, punch, slosh, smack, speed, strap, strip, swipe, thump, tract, wanty, whack **06** bruise, career, cestus, charge, corset, extent, girdle, region, sector, strike, swathe, thwack, wallop, waspie **07** baldric, bashing, clobber, harness, stretch, zonulet **08** baldrick, ceinture, cincture, cingulum, district **09** bandoleer, bandolier, hip-girdle, Sam Browne, waistband **10** cummerbund

*See also* **karate**

• **below the belt**

**05** dirty **06** unfair, unjust **09** dishonest, underhand, unethical **10** out of order **11** uncalled-for, unjustified **12** unscrupulous

• **belt up**

**02** sh, st **03** shh **04** hist **05** shush, whish, whist **06** shut up, whisht, wrap up **07** be quiet, wheesht **08** button up, cut it out, pipe down **10** keep shtoom, stay shtoom **12** put a sock in it, shut your face **13** button your lip, shut your mouth

**belvedere**

**06** gazebo **07** mirador

**bemoan**

**03** rue **04** moan, pity, wail **05** mourn **06** bewail, lament, regret **07** deplore, sigh for, weep for **09** grieve for **10** sorrow over

**bemuse**
◇ *anagram indicator*
**04** daze, faze **05** floor, throw
**06** baffle, muddle, puzzle **07** confuse, perplex, stupefy **08** befuddle, bewilder **09** bamboozle

**bemused**
◇ *anagram indicator*
**05** dazed, fazed, mused **07** baffled, floored, muddled, puzzled
**08** confused **09** astounded, befuddled, perplexed, pixilated, stupefied **10** astonished, bamboozled, bewildered, pixillated
**11** overwhelmed **12** disconcerted

**bemusement**
**04** daze **09** confusion **10** bafflement, perplexity, puzzlement
**12** bewilderment, stupefaction
**14** disorientation

**Ben**
**03** Hur

**bench**
**03** pew **04** banc, bank, bink, form, seat **05** board, court, judge, ledge, stall, table, thoft **06** banker, exedra, settle, thwart **07** counter, exhedra, tribune **08** rout-seat, tribunal
**09** courtroom, judiciary, shopboard, workbench, worktable **10** judicature, knife-board, magistrate **13** judgement-seat

**benchmark**
**04** norm **05** basis, gauge, level, model, scale **07** example, pattern **08** standard
**09** criterion, guideline, reference, yardstick **10** guidelines, touchstone
**14** reference-point

**bend**
◇ *anagram indicator*
**01** S, U, Z **02** es **03** arc, bow, ess, out, ply, sag **04** arch, curb, flex, genu, hook, hump, kink, knot, lean, loop, ramp, sway, trap, turn, veer, warp, wind
**05** angle, bight, courb, crimp, crook, curve, elbow, embow, hinge, hunch, kneel, mould, ox-bow, plash, round, shape, squat, stoop, trend, twist, wring
**06** affect, bought, buckle, compel, corner, crouch, cut-off, deflex, direct, dog-leg, recede, reflex, spring, swerve, wimple, zigzag **07** compass, contort, crankle, decline, deflect, deviate, dip-trap, diverge, flexion, flexure, incline, incurve, inflect, meander, recline, recurve, reflect, turning, whimple, wriggle **08** persuade, swan neck
**09** curvature, genuflect, incurvate, inflexure, influence, prostrate, retroflex
**10** circumflex, deflection, divergence, make curved, manipulate
**11** circumflect, hairpin bend, inclination, incurvation
• **bend over**
**04** lean **08** double up
• **bend over backwards**
**08** go all out **10** do your best **11** try very hard **13** exert yourself **14** put yourself out **15** trouble yourself

**bendy**
◇ *anagram indicator*
**08** flexible

**beneath**
◇ *juxtaposition down indicator*
**03** sub **05** below, lower, neath, under
**06** aneath **09** lower down, lower than
**10** unbecoming, underneath, unworthy of **11** unbefitting

**Benedictines**
**03** OSB

**benediction**
**05** grace **06** favour, prayer **07** benison
**08** blessing **10** invocation
**11** blessedness **12** consecration, thanksgiving

**benefactor**
**05** angel, donor, giver **06** backer, friend, helper, patron **07** sponsor
**08** promoter, provider **09** supporter
**10** subscriber, subsidizer, well-wisher
**11** contributor **14** fairy godmother, philanthropist

**beneficent**
**04** kind **06** benign **07** benefic, helpful, liberal **08** generous **09** bountiful, unselfish **10** altruistic, benevolent, charitable, munificent
**12** Grandisonian **13** compassionate

**beneficial**
**04** good **06** useful **07** helpful
**08** edifying, salutary, valuable
**09** benignant, improving, promising, rewarding, wholesome **10** favourable, profitable, propitious, worthwhile
**11** serviceable **12** advantageous
• **beneficial to**
**03** for

**beneficiary**
**04** heir **05** payee **07** heiress, legatee
**08** receiver **09** inheritor, recipient, successor **10** the assured

**benefit**
**03** ACC, aid, DPB, pay, use **04** boon, broo, dole, gain, good, help, perk, sake
**05** asset, avail, bonus, buroo, compo, merit, serve **06** assist, behalf, behoof, better, credit, favour, income, milage, pay-off, profit, reward **07** advance, bespeak, enhance, further, improve, mileage, payment, pension, promote, service, sick pay, spin-off, support, vantage, welfare **08** blessing, dividend, do good to, interest, kindness
**09** advantage, allowance, good point
**10** assistance, perquisite
**11** benefaction **13** be of service to, fringe benefit, income support
**14** social security **15** be of advantage to

**benevolence**
**04** care, pity **05** grace, mercy
**08** altruism, goodness, goodwill, kindness **09** tolerance **10** compassion, generosity, humaneness, liberality
**11** magnanimity, munificence
**12** friendliness, philanthropy
**14** charitableness **15** considerateness, humanitarianism, kind-heartedness

**benevolent**
**04** good, guid, kind **06** benign, caring, humane, kindly **07** liberal **08** friendly, generous, gracious, merciful, tolerant
**10** altruistic, charitable, munificent
**11** considerate, kind-hearted, magnanimous, soft-hearted
**12** humanitarian, well-disposed
**13** compassionate, philanthropic
**15** philanthropical

**benevolently**
**06** kindly **08** benignly, humanely
**09** liberally **10** charitably, generously, graciously, mercifully, tolerantly
**13** considerately, kind-heartedly, magnanimously, soft-heartedly
**14** altruistically **15** compassionately

**benighted**
**07** belated, nighted **08** backward, ignorant **09** unknowing **10** illiterate, uncultured, uneducated, unlettered, unschooled **11** unfortunate
**13** inexperienced, unenlightened

**benign**
**04** good, kind, mild, warm **05** sweet, trine **06** genial, gentle, kindly
**07** affable, amiable, benefic, cordial, curable, healthy, liberal **08** benedict, friendly, generous, gracious, harmless, innocent, obliging **09** agreeable, avuncular, opportune, temperate, treatable, wholesome **10** auspicious, beneficial, benevolent, charitable, favourable, propitious, refreshing, salubrious **11** restorative, sympathetic, warm-hearted
**12** advantageous, non-malignant, providential

**benignly**
**06** kindly **07** affably, amiably
**08** genially **10** charitably, generously, graciously, obligingly **12** benevolently
**15** sympathetically

**Benin**
**02** DY, RB **03** BEN

**bent**
◇ *anagram indicator*
**04** curb, gift, turn **05** bowed, corbe, courb, dodgy, flair, forte, knack, wrong
**06** angled, arched, curved, fiorin, folded, redtop, reflex, talent, warped
**07** ability, corrupt, crooked, curvate, doubled, embowed, faculty, falcate, hunched, illegal, leaning, stooped, strepto-, twafald, twisted **08** aptitude, capacity, criminal, cup of tea, curvated, facility, falcated, fondness, inclined, inflexed, penchant, reflexed, retorted, tendency **09** contorted, dishonest, infracted, refracted, retroflex, swindling **10** fraudulent, geniculate, preference, proclivity, propensity
**11** disposition, geniculated, inclination
**12** predilection **13** untrustworthy
**14** predisposition
• **bent on**
**05** set on **07** fixed on **08** intent on
**10** disposed to, inclined to, resolved to
**11** insistent on **12** determined to

**bequeath**
**04** give, will **05** endow, grant, leave **06** assign, bestow, commit, demise, devise, impart, pass on **07** consign, entrust **08** hand down, make over, transfer, transmit

**bequest**
**04** gift **05** trust **06** estate, legacy **07** devisal **08** bestowal, donation, heritage, pittance **09** endowment **10** bequeathal, settlement **11** inheritance **13** mortification

**berate**
**05** blast, chide, scold, slate **06** rail at, rebuke, revile **07** censure, chew out, reprove, start on, tell off, upbraid **08** chastise, give hell, reproach **09** castigate, criticize, dress down, fulminate, reprimand, start in on **10** vituperate **13** give a rocket to, tear a strip off

**bereaved**
**03** orb **04** lost **06** robbed **07** widowed **08** deprived, divested, grieving, orphaned **12** dispossessed

**bereavement**
**04** loss **05** death, grief **06** orbity, sorrow **07** passing, sadness **08** deprival **11** deprivation, passing-away **13** dispossession

**bereft**
• **bereft of**
**05** minus **07** lacking, wanting **08** devoid of, robbed of **10** cut off from, deprived of, parted from, stripped of **11** destitute of

**berkelium**
**02** Bk

**Berlin**
**06** Irving

**Bermuda**
**03** BMU

**berry**
**05** bacca **06** acinus

*Berries include:*

**05** lichi
**06** lichee, litchi, lychee
**07** bramble, leechee
**08** bilberry, dewberry, goosegog, mulberry, tayberry
**09** blaeberry, blueberry, cranberry, raspberry, whimberry
**10** blackberry, cloudberry, elderberry, gooseberry, loganberry, redcurrant, strawberry
**11** boysenberry, huckleberry
**12** blackcurrant, serviceberry, whitecurrant, whortleberry

**berserk**
◇ *anagram indicator*
**03** mad **04** nuts, wild **05** angry, barmy, batty, berko, crazy, manic, rabid **06** crazed, insane, raging, raving **07** frantic, furious, violent **08** baresark, demented, deranged, frenzied, maniacal **10** hysterical **11** off your head **13** off the deep end, out of your mind **14** beside yourself, uncontrollable

**berth**
**03** bed **04** bunk, dock, land, moor, port, quay **05** tie up, wharf **06** anchor, billet **07** hammock, harbour, mooring, sleeper **09** anchorage, couchette **10** cast anchor, drop anchor
• **give a wide berth to**
**04** shun **05** avoid, dodge, evade **06** eschew **09** give a miss **12** steer clear of

**beryl**
**07** emerald **08** emeraude, heliodor **09** morganite **10** aquamarine

**beryllium**
**02** Be

**beseech**
**03** ask, beg, sue **04** pray **05** crave, plead **06** adjure, call on, desire, exhort **07** entreat, implore, intreat, solicit **08** appeal to, petition **09** deprecate, importune, obsecrate **10** supplicate

**beset**
◇ *containment indicator*
**03** lay, rag **04** bego **05** belay, hem in, press, worry **06** assail, attack, bestad, bested, harass, hassle, obsess, pester, plague, preace, prease **07** bedevil, besiege, bestead, preasse, torment **08** bestadde, entangle, scabrous, surround

**besetting**
**08** constant, dominant, habitual **09** harassing, obsessive, prevalent, recurring **10** compulsive, inveterate, persistent **11** troublesome **12** irresistible **14** uncontrollable

**beside**
◇ *juxtaposition indicator*
**02** by, on, to **04** near **06** next to **07** close to, upsides **08** abutting, adjacent **09** abreast of, alongside, bordering **10** next door to **11** by the side of, overlooking **12** neighbouring
• **beside yourself**
**03** mad **05** crazy **06** crazed, insane **07** berserk, frantic **08** demented, deranged, frenetic, frenzied, overcome, unhinged **09** delirious **10** distraught, unbalanced **13** out of your mind

**besides**
**02** by **03** too, yet **04** also, else **05** forby **06** as well, either, forbye, foreby, withal **07** au reste, further **08** as well as, moreover **09** apart from, aside from, excluding, other than, otherwise, what's more **10** in addition **11** furthermore **12** additionally, in addition to, over and above

**besiege**
◇ *containment indicator*
**03** nag **05** belay, beset, besit, hem in, hound, worry **06** assail, badger, bother, harass, invest, obsess, pester, plague, shut in **07** assiege, confine, oppress, torment, trouble **08** blockade, encircle, surround **09** beleaguer, encompass, importune, overwhelm **10** lay siege to

**besmirch**
**04** slur, soil **05** dirty, smear, stain, sully **06** damage, defame, defile **07** besmear, blacken, slander, tarnish **08** besmutch **09** dishonour

**besom**
**03** cow, kow **05** broom

**besotted**
**03** mad **04** wild **05** crazy, potty **06** doting, sotted, stupid **07** bedazed, drunken, smitten **08** obsessed **09** bedazzled, bewitched, stupefied **10** bowled over, hypnotized, infatuated, spellbound **11** intoxicated

**bespatter**
**04** dash, drop, soil **05** bemud, dirty, smear, spray, stain **06** bedash, befoam, defame, shower, splash **07** asperse, scatter, spatter, splodge **08** splatter, sprinkle

**bespeak**
**04** show **05** imply **06** attest, denote, engage, evince, reveal **07** betoken, display, exhibit, signify, suggest **08** evidence, indicate, proclaim, speak for **11** demonstrate

**bespoke**
◇ *anagram indicator*
**09** dedicated **10** tailor-made

**best**
**02** A1 **03** ace, cap, top **04** beat, lick, most, pick, plum, rout, star, tops **05** cream, élite, first, ideal, jewel, prime, worst **06** choice, defeat, finest, flower, hammer, outwit, subdue, thrash, utmost **07** clobber, conquer, greatly, hardest, highest, largest, leading, optimal, optimum, outplay, perfect, premium, supreme, the tops, trounce **08** foremost, greatest, outsmart, overcome, peerless, ultimate, vanquish **09** damnedest, excellent, extremely, favourite, first-rate, highlight, matchless, nonpareil, number one, overpower, overwhelm, slaughter, supremely, top-drawer, worthiest **10** annihilate, first-class, pre-eminent, unbeatable, unequalled, unrivalled **11** excellently, matchlessly, outstanding, superlative, unsurpassed **12** incomparable, incomparably, second to none **13** exceptionally, have the edge on, one in a million, outstandingly, superlatively, unsurpassedly **14** crème de la crème, get the better of, greatest effort, record-breaking

**bestial**
**04** rude, vile **05** cruel, feral, gross **06** animal, brutal, carnal, savage, sordid **07** beastly, brutish, inhuman, sensual **08** barbaric, degraded, depraved **09** barbarous, unrefined

**bestiality**
**07** cruelty **08** savagery **09** barbarism

**10** inhumanity, sordidness **15** animal behaviour

**bestir**
**05** exert **06** arouse, awaken, incite **07** actuate, animate **08** activate, energize, motivate **09** galvanize, stimulate

**bestow**
**02** do **04** give **05** allot, award, endow, grant, spend, wreak **06** accord, commit, confer, donate, estate, impart, lavish **07** dispose, entrust, present **08** bequeath, transmit **09** apportion **11** communicate

**bestride**
**05** cross **06** defend **07** command, protect **08** dominate, straddle **10** bestraddle, overshadow, sit astride **12** stand astride

**bestseller**
**03** hit **07** success, triumph **08** smash hit **11** blockbuster, brand leader

**bestselling**
**03** top **06** famous **07** leading, popular **08** unbeaten

**bet**
**02** go **03** bid, lay, pot, put **04** ante, back, hold, punt, risk, view **05** place, pound, stake, wager **06** be sure, chance, choice, expect, gamble, hazard, notion, option, pledge, theory **07** feeling, flutter, lottery, opinion, venture **09** be certain, intuition, judgement, speculate, viewpoint **10** conviction, impression, prediction **11** alternative, be convinced, point of view, speculation **12** have a flutter, play for money **14** course of action, not be surprised

*See also* **gambling**

*Bets and betting systems include:*

**03** TAB
**04** tote
**06** double, parlay, roll-up, tierce, treble, triple, Yankee
**07** à cheval, each way
**08** ante-post, forecast, perfecta, quinella, trifecta
**09** on the nose, quadrella
**10** martingale, pari-mutuel, superfecta, sweepstake
**11** accumulator, daily double
**13** double or quits

• **accept bet**
**03** see

**betel**
**03** pan **04** paan, pawn, siri **05** sirih

**bête noire**
**04** bane **05** curse **07** bugbear, pet hate **08** anathema, aversion **11** abomination, pet aversion **14** thorn in the side **15** thorn in the flesh

**betide**
**05** ensue, occur **06** befall, betime, chance, happen **07** develop **08** overtake **09** supervene, take place

**betoken**
**04** bode, mark, mean, sign **05** augur, token **06** betide, denote, signal **07** bespeak, declare, portend, presage, promise, signify, suggest **08** evidence, forebode, indicate, manifest **09** represent, symbolize **13** prognosticate

**betray**
**03** dob **04** dupe, sell, shop, show, tell **05** abuse, cross, dob in, grass, peach, rat on **06** bewray, delude, desert, expose, reveal, rumble, tell on, unmask **07** abandon, confess, deceive, divulge, forsake, let down, let slip, mislead, sell out, split on, stool on **08** disclose, give away, go back on, inform on, manifest, renege on, squeal on **09** play false, walk out on **11** double-cross, turn traitor **12** be disloyal to, bring to light **13** stab in the back **14** be unfaithful to, break faith with

**betrayal**
**05** abuse **06** duping **07** perfidy, sell-out, treason **08** giveaway, trickery **09** deception, duplicity, falseness, treachery **10** disloyalty **11** double-cross **13** breaking faith, double-dealing, stab in the back **14** double-crossing, traitorousness, unfaithfulness

**betrayer**
**05** grass, Judas **07** stoolie, traitor **08** apostate, deceiver, informer, renegade, traditor, treacher **09** treachour **10** supergrass **11** backstabber, conspirator, stool pigeon **13** double-crosser, whistle-blower

**betrothal**
**03** vow **04** vows **05** troth **07** promise **08** affiance, contract, espousal, handfast **09** assurance **10** engagement **11** fiançailles, handfasting, hand-promise, subarration, trothplight **12** subarrhation

**betrothed**
**05** troth **07** assured, engaged, pledged **08** espoused, promised **09** affianced, combinate **10** contracted **11** trothplight **13** trothplighted

**better**
**03** cap, top **04** beat, best, mend, well **05** cured, finer, outdo, raise **06** bigger, enrich, exceed, fitter, healed, larger, longer, punter, reform **07** correct, enhance, forward, further, gambler, greater, improve, promote, rectify, surpass **08** improved, outstrip, overtake, restored, stronger, superior, worthier **09** a cut above, healthier, improve on, improving, on the mend, recovered **10** ameliorate, make better, preferable, recovering, speculator, surpassing **11** more fitting, progressing **12** more valuable **14** fully recovered, more acceptable **15** go one better than, of higher quality

**betterment**
**10** enrichment **11** advancement, edification, enhancement, furtherance, improvement, melioration **12** amelioration

**betting** *see* **bet**

**between**
◇ *insertion indicator*
**03** bet, mid **04** amid **05** among, inter- **06** amidst **07** amongst, halfway **11** in the middle **13** in the middle of

**bevel**
**04** bias, cant, tilt **05** angle, basil, bezel, mitre, slant, slope, splay **07** chamfer, oblique **08** diagonal

**beverage**
**04** brew **05** drink **06** liquid, liquor **07** draught, potable **08** ambrosia, potation **11** refreshment

*See also* **drink**

**bevy**
**04** band, gang, pack **05** bunch, crowd, flock, group, troop **06** gaggle, throng, troupe **07** company **08** assembly **09** gathering **10** collection

**bewail**
**03** rue **04** keen, moan **05** mourn **06** bemoan, lament, regret, repent **07** cry over, deplore **08** sigh over **10** grieve over, sorrow over **14** beat your breast

**beware**
**04** cave, mind, shun, ware **05** avoid, watch **06** be wary, caveat **07** look out, mind out **08** take heed, watch out **09** be careful **10** be cautious **12** guard against, steer clear of **13** be on your guard

**bewilder**
◇ *containment indicator*
**04** daze, faze, lose, maze **05** amaze, floor, mix up, stump **06** baffle, bemuse, fickle, muddle, puzzle, wander, wilder **07** buffalo, bumbaze, confuse, flummox, mystify, nonplus, perplex, stupefy **08** confound **09** bamboozle, disorient, obfuscate **10** disconcert, take to town **12** tie up in knots

**bewildered**
◇ *anagram indicator*
**04** lost, will, wull **05** at sea, dizzy, fazed, muzzy **06** fogged, tavert **07** baffled, bemazed, bemused, floored, mixed up, muddled, pixy-led, puzzled, stunned, taivert **08** all at sea, confused, jiggered, pathless, wandered **09** flummoxed, mystified, perplexed, pixilated, surprised, trackless, uncertain **10** bamboozled, distracted, nonplussed, pixillated, speechless, taken aback **11** disoriented

**bewildering**
**05** dizzy **07** amazing, cryptic **08** baffling, puzzling **09** confusing, enigmatic **10** astounding, mysterious, mystifying, perplexing, surprising **12** unfathomable

**bewilderment**
**03** awe, fog **04** daze, maze **05** amaze **06** muddle, puzzle **07** mizmaze **08** surprise **09** amazement, confusion, égarement, puzzledom **10** amazedness, perplexity, puzzlement **11** uncertainty **12** stupefaction **13** disconcertion, mystification **14** disorientation

**bewitch**
**03** hex, obi **04** obia, take, wish **05** charm, obeah, witch **06** allure, hoodoo, obsess, seduce, strike, voodoo, voudou **07** beguile, delight, enchant, enthral, glamour, possess **08** elf-shoot, entrance, forspeak, intrigue, overlook, sirenize, transfix **09** captivate, enrapture, ensorcell, fascinate, forespeak, hypnotize, mesmerize, spellbind, tantalize

**beyond**
**04** over, past **05** above, after, ayont, trans- **08** away from **09** apart from, later than, upwards of **10** remote from **11** further than, greater than **12** out of range of, out of reach of **14** on the far side of

**Bhutan**
**03** BTN

**bias**
**04** bent, load, sway, warp **05** angle, cross, poise, slant, twist **06** colour, earwig, weight **07** bigotry, distort, leaning, oblique **08** diagonal, jaundice, penchant, tendency **09** influence, parti pris, prejudice, preoccupy, slantwise **10** distortion, partiality, partialize, predispose, prepossess, proclivity, propensity, unfairness **11** favouritism, inclination, intolerance, load the dice, prejudicate **12** one-sidedness, predilection, stereotyping **13** prepossession

**biased**
◇ *anagram indicator*
**04** skew **06** angled, loaded, skewed, swayed, unfair, warped **07** bigoted, partial, slanted, twisted **08** one-sided, partisan, partizan, weighted **09** blinkered, distorted, jaundiced **10** influenced, interested, prejudiced, subjective, tendential **11** predisposed, prejudicate, tendencious, tendentious **12** prepossessed **14** discriminatory

**bib**
**04** pout **05** Bible, blain **06** brassy, feeder

**Bible**
**02** NT, OT **03** ABC, Bib, law **05** canon **06** fardel, manual, omasum, primer **07** Gospels, letters, lexicon **08** epistles, good book, handbook, holy writ, prophets, textbook, writings **09** Apocrypha, authority, companion, directory, guidebook, Holy Bible, manyplies **10** dictionary, Pentateuch, psalterium, revelation, Scriptures **12** encyclopedia, New Testament, Old Testament **13** reference book **14** holy Scriptures

*See also* **plague**; **scripture**

*Versions of the Bible include:*

**02** AV, EV, RV
**03** NEB, RSV
**05** Douai, Douay, Itala, Reims
**06** Geneva, Gideon, Italic, Wyclif
**07** Matthew, Peshito, Tyndale, Vulgate
**08** Breeches, Peshitta, Peshitto, Wycliffe
**09** Coverdale, King James
**10** New English, Septuagint
**14** English Version, Revised Version

*Books of the Bible include:*

**02** **Am, Ch, Dt, Ec, Ex, Ez, Is, Jg, Jl, Jn, Kg, Lk, Mk, Mt, Ob, Pr, Ps, Ru, Th**
**03** **Bar, Chr, Col, Cor, Dan, Eph, Esd, Est, Gal, Gen, Hab, Hag, Heb, Hos, Isa, Jas, Jer, Job** (Book of), **Jon, Jos, Jud, Lam, Lev, Mal, Mic, Nah, Neh, Num, Pet, Rev, Rom, Sam, Sir, Sus, Tim, Tit, Tob**
**04** **Acts, Amos** (Book of), **Deut, Eccl, Epis, Esth, Exod, Ezek, Ezra** (Book of), **Hebr, Joel** (Book of), **John** (Gospel according to), **John** (Letters of), **Josh, Jude** (Letter of), **Luke** (Gospel according to), **Macc, Mark** (Gospel according to), **Numb, Obad, Phil, Prov, Ruth** (Book of), **S of S, Wisd, Zech, Zeph**
**05** **Bel&Dr, Hosea** (Book of), **James** (Letter of), **Jonah** (Book of), **Kings** (Books of), **Levit, Micah** (Book of), **Nahum** (Book of), **Peter** (Letters of), **Thess, Titus** (Letter of Paul to), **Tobit** (Book of)
**06** **Baruch** (Book of), **Coloss, Daniel** (Book of), **Eccles, Ecclus, Esdras** (Books of), **Esther** (Book of), **Exodus** (Book of), **Haggai** (Book of), **Isaiah** (Book of), **Joshua** (Book of), **Judges** (Book of), **Judith** (Book of), **Philem, Psalms** (Book of), **Romans** (Letter of Paul to the), **Samuel** (Books of), **Sirach** (Book of)
**07** **Ezekiel** (Book of), **Genesis** (Book of), **Gospels, Hebrews** (Letter of Paul to the), **Malachi** (Book of), **Matthew** (Gospel according to), **Numbers** (Book of), **Obadiah** (Book of), **Pr of Man, Susanna** (History of), **Timothy** (Letters of Paul to)
**08** **Habakkuk** (Book of), **Jeremiah** (Book of), **Jeremiah** (Letter of), **Nehemiah** (Book of), **Philemon** (Letter of Paul to), **Proverbs** (Book of)
**09** **Apocrypha, Ephesians** (Letter of Paul to the), **Galatians** (Letter of Paul to the), **Hexateuch, Leviticus** (Book of), **Maccabees, Zechariah** (Book of), **Zephaniah** (Book of)
**10** **Apocalypse, Chronicles** (Books of), **Colossians** (Letter of Paul to the), **Heptateuch, Pentateuch, Revelation**
**11** **Corinthians** (Letters of Paul to the), **Deuteronomy** (Book of), **Philippians** (Letter of Paul to the)
**12** **Ecclesiastes** (Book of), **Lamentations, New Testament, Old Testament**
**13** **Song of Solomon, Thessalonians** (Letters of Paul to the)
**14** **Ecclesiasticus** (Book of), **Pauline Letters**
**15** **Bel and the Dragon, Pastoral Letters, Prayer of Azariah, Wisdom of Solomon**
**16** **Prayer of Manasseh, Revelation of John**
**17** **Acts of the Apostles**
**22** **Song of the Three Young Men**

*Biblical characters include:*

**03** Dan, Eve, Gad, Ham, Job, Lot
**04** Abel, Adam, Ahab, Amos, Anna, Baal, Cain, Esau, Ezra, Joel, John, Leah, Levi, Luke, Mark, Mary, Noah, Paul, Ruth, Saul, Seth, Shem
**05** Aaron, Abner, Asher, Caleb, David, Enoch, Hagar, Herod (the Great), Hosea, Isaac, Jacob, James, Jesus, Jonah, Judah, Judas, Magog, Micah, Moses, Nahum, Naomi, Peter, Rhoda, Sarah, Sheba (Queen of), Simon, Titus, Tobit, Uriah
**06** Andrew, Baruch, Christ, Daniel, Elijah, Elisha, Esther, Gideon, Isaiah, Joseph, Joshua, Josiah, Judith, Martha, Miriam, Nathan, Nimrod, Philip, Pilate, Rachel, Reuben, Salome, Samson, Samuel, Simeon, Thomas, Uzziah
**07** Abigail, Abraham, Absalom, Azariah, Delilah, Ephraim, Ezekiel, Gabriel, Goliath, Ishmael, Japheth, Jezebel, Lazarus, Malachi, Matthew, Michael, Obadiah, Rebecca, Rebekah, Solomon, Stephen, Susanna, Tabitha, Timothy, Zebedee, Zebulun
**08** Barabbas, Barnabus, Benjamin, Caiaphas, Habbakuk, Hezekiah, Issachar, Jeremiah, Jeroboam, Jonathan, Manasseh, Matthias, Mordecai, Naphtali, Nehemiah, Thaddeus, Zedekiah
**09** Bathsheba, Beelzebub, Nathanael, Nathaniel, Nicodemus, Priscilla, Zechariah, Zephaniah
**10** Adam and Eve, Bartimaeus, Belshazzar, Methuselah, Simon Magus, Simon Peter
**11** Bartholomew, Gog and Magog, Jehoshaphat, Jesus Christ
**12** Herod Agrippa, Herod Antipas, Queen of Sheba
**13** Judas Iscariot, Mary Magdalene, Pontius Pilate, Simon of Cyrene
**14** John the Baptist, Nebuchadnezzar, Simon the Zealot

*Biblical placenames include:*

**03** Nod
**04** Eden, Gaza, Rome, Zion
**05** Babel, Egypt, Judah, Sinai, Sodom
**06** Ararat, Canaan, Cyrene, Israel, Jordan, Judaea, Mt Zion, Red Sea
**07** Babylon, Calvary, Galilee, Jericho, Mt Sinai, Nineveh

**08** Bethesda, Dalmatia, Damascus, Golgotha, Gomorrah, Mt Ararat, Nazareth
**09** Bethlehem, Jerusalem, Palestine
**10** Alexandria, Gethsemane
**11** River Jordan
**12** Garden of Eden, Sea of Galilee

*See also* **apocryphal**

**bibliography**
**06** record **08** book list **09** catalogue **10** bibliology **11** bibliotheca, list of books

**bicker**
**03** row **04** spar, spat **05** argue, clash, fight, scrap **06** patter, quiver **07** dispute, fall out, glitter, quarrel, wrangle **08** disagree, squabble **09** altercate

**bickering**
**06** at odds **07** arguing **08** clashing **09** scrapping **10** squabbling **11** disagreeing, quarrelling **13** at loggerheads **15** like cats and dogs

**bicycle**
**04** bike **05** cycle, wheel **10** pedal cycle

*Bicycles include:*

**03** BMX
**04** push, quad, solo
**05** hobby, racer
**06** safety, tandem
**07** chopper, Raleigh®, touring
**08** draisene, draisine, exercise, kangaroo, mountain, ordinary, push-bike, tricycle, unicycle
**09** recumbent
**10** all-terrain, boneshaker, dandy-horse, fairy-cycle, fixed-wheel, stationary, two-wheeler, velocipede
**12** mountain bike
**13** penny farthing
**14** all-terrain bike

*Bicycle parts include:*

**03** hub
**04** bell, fork, gear, lamp, pump, tire, tyre
**05** brake, chain, crank, frame, pedal, spoke, wheel
**06** dynamo, fender, hanger, pulley, saddle, spokes
**07** bar ends, carrier, headset, hub gear, pannier, rim tape, toe clip, tool bag, top tube
**08** aero bars, cassette, chainset, crankset, crossbar, down tube, head tube, mudguard, rim brake, rod brake, seat post, seat tube, sprocket, wheel nut, wheel rim
**09** brake shoe, chain link, chain ring, disc brake, drum brake, gear cable, gear lever, gearwheel, inner tube, kickstand, prop stand, reflector, seat stays, tyre valve, wheel lock
**10** brake block, brake cable, brake lever, chain guard, chain guide, chain stays, chain wheel, crank lever, derailleur, drive train, handlebars, seat pillar, stabilizer, Woods® valve
**11** gear shifter, lamp bracket, Presta® valve, roller chain, speedometer
**12** brake caliper, coaster brake, diamond frame, spoke nipples, steering head, steering tube, stirrup guide, wheel bearing, wheel spindle
**13** bottom bracket, clipless pedal, freewheel unit, handlebar stem, Schrader® valve, shock absorber, sprocket wheel
**14** drop handlebars, side-pull brakes

**bid**
**02** go **03** ask, say, sum, try, vie
**04** bode, call, pray, tell, wave, wish
**05** greet, offer, order, price, put up
**06** amount, charge, demand, desire, direct, effort, enjoin, invite, submit, summon, tender **07** advance, attempt, call for, command, proffer, propose, request, require, solicit, venture
**08** instruct, proposal **09** endeavour
**10** put forward, submission
• **no bid**
**04** pass

**biddable**
**04** meek **08** amenable, obedient
**09** compliant, easy-going, malleable, tractable **10** submitting **11** subservient

**bidding**
**04** call **05** order **06** behest, charge, demand, desire **07** command, request, summons **09** direction **10** injunction, invitation **11** instruction, requirement
• **bidding system**
**04** Acol **06** canapé **09** blackwood

**big**
**02** OS **03** fat **04** huge, loud, main, mega, tall, vast **05** adult, beefy, build, bulky, burly, elder, giant, great, hefty, jumbo, large, major, obese, older, stout
**06** brawny, bumper, famous, mature, pile up, valued **07** eminent, grown-up, hulking, immense, leading, mammoth, massive, pompous, radical, salient, serious, sizable, weighty **08** boastful, colossal, critical, enormous, generous, gigantic, gracious, muscular, powerful, sizeable, spacious, whopping
**09** cavernous, corpulent, extensive, ginormous, humungous, important, momentous, principal, prominent, unselfish, well-built, well-known
**10** benevolent, extra large, munificent, noteworthy, voluminous
**11** fundamental, influential, kind-hearted, magnanimous, outstanding, pretentious, significant, substantial
**12** considerable **13** distinguished

**bigheaded**
**04** vain **05** cocky **07** haughty, stuck-up **08** arrogant **09** conceited **11** swell-headed **12** vainglorious **13** self-important, self-satisfied, swollen-headed **14** full of yourself

**bigot**
**03** MCP **06** racist, sexist, zealot **07** fanatic **08** partisan **09** dogmatist, homophobe, sectarian **10** chauvinist **11** religionist

**bigoted**
**06** biased, closed, narrow, swayed, warped **07** partial, twisted
**08** dogmatic, one-sided **09** blinkered, fanatical, hidebound, illiberal, jaundiced, obstinate **10** influenced, intolerant, prejudiced **11** opinionated **12** narrow-minded

**bigotry**
**04** bias **06** racism, sexism **08** jingoism **09** dogmatism, injustice, prejudice, racialism **10** chauvinism, fanaticism, partiality, unfairness **11** intolerance, religionism **12** sectarianism
**14** discrimination

**bigwig**
**03** nob, VIP **04** tuan **05** mogul, swell **06** big gun, honcho, worthy **07** big shot, notable **08** big noise, somebody **09** big cheese, celebrity, dignitary, personage **10** panjandrum
**11** heavyweight

**bijou**
**03** wee **04** tiny **05** jewel, small
**06** little, minute, petite, pocket
**07** compact, trinket **10** diminutive

**bile**
**04** gall **05** anger **06** choler, spleen
**07** rancour **09** bad temper, ill-humour, testiness **10** bitterness, melancholy
**11** peevishness, short temper
**12** irascibility, irritability

**bilge**
**03** rot **04** crap **05** balls, trash, tripe
**06** drivel, faddle, hot air, piffle
**07** rubbish, twaddle **08** blethers, claptrap, cobblers, nonsense, tommyrot **09** gibberish, poppycock
**10** codswallop **12** clamjamphrie

**bilious**
**04** edgy, sick **05** cross, lurid, testy
**06** crabby, garish, grumpy, queasy, sickly **07** grouchy, peevish
**08** choleric **09** crotchety, irritable, nauseated **10** disgusting, nauseating, out of sorts **11** bad-tempered, ill-humoured, ill-tempered **13** short-tempered

**bilk**
**02** do **03** con **05** cheat, elude, sting, trick **06** diddle, fleece **07** deceive, defraud, do out of, swindle
**09** bamboozle **14** pull a fast one on

**bill**
**02** a/c, ad, ax **03** acc, act, axe, fin, IOU, neb, nib, tab **04** acct, beak, chit, note, post **05** check, debit, flyer, score, tally
**06** advert, charge, notice, poster
**07** account, charges, handout, invoice, leaflet, measure, placard, promote, rostrum, statute, William **08** announce, banknote, bulletin, circular, handbill, mandible, playbill, proposal
**09** advertise, list costs, programme, reckoning, statement **10** broadsheet,

give notice **11** legislation
**12** announcement **13** advertisement, send an account, send an invoice
**14** send a statement

**• bill of sale**

**02** bs

**billet**

**03** job **04** post **05** berth, lodge, put up, rooms **06** casern, coupon, office
**07** caserne, housing, lodging, quarter, station **08** barracks, position, quarters
**09** situation **10** employment, occupation **11** accommodate
**13** accommodation **14** living quarters

**billow**

**04** mass, rise, roil, roll, rush, wave
**05** bulge, cloud, flood, heave, surge, swell **06** expand **07** balloon, breaker, fill out, puff out **08** undulate

**billowy**

**06** waving **07** heaving, rolling, surging, tossing **08** rippling, swelling, swirling
**09** billowing **10** undulating

**Billy**

**06** Bunter

**bin**

**03** box **04** bing, bunk **05** chest
**06** basket, bucket, holder **07** wheelie
**09** container **10** garbage can, receptacle **11** waste basket

**bind**

**03** oop, oup, tie, wap **04** bond, bore, gage, gird, hold, hole, join, lash, pain, rope, spot, tape, whip, wrap, yoke
**05** chain, clamp, cover, dress, force, impel, leash, stick, strap, thirl, tie up, truss, unify, unite **06** attach, compel, embale, fasten, fetter, hamper, objure, oblige, secure, swathe, tether
**07** astrict, bandage, combine, confine, dilemma, embrace, impasse, require, shackle **08** astringe, enfetter, nuisance, quandary, restrain, restrict **09** colligate, constrain, tight spot **10** close ranks, difficulty, irritation **11** necessitate, predicament **12** knit together, pull together **13** embarrassment, inconvenience, pain in the neck, stand together

**binding**

**04** tape, yapp **05** cover, tight, valid
**06** border, edging, strict **07** bandage
**08** covering, ligation, rigorous, trimming, wrapping **09** mandatory, necessary, permanent, requisite, stringent **10** compulsory, conclusive, obligatory **11** irrevocable, unalterable, unbreakable
**12** indissoluble

**bindweed**

**08** bearbine, bellbind, withwind, woodbind, woodbine **09** withywind
**11** convolvulus

**binge**

**02** do **03** jag **04** bout, orgy, sesh, toot, tout **05** beano, blind, fling, spree
**06** bender, guzzle **07** blow-out, session

**biochemistry**

*Biochemists include:*

**04** **Abel** (John Jacob), **Cori** (Carl), **Duve** (Christian de)
**05** **Boyer** (Herbert), **Brown** (Rachel Fuller), **Chain** (Sir Ernst B), **Doisy** (Edward A), **Krebs** (Sir Edwin G), **Krebs** (Sir Hans), **Monod** (Jacques), **Moore** (Stanford)
**06** **Asimov** (Isaac), **Beadle** (George), **Domagk** (Gerhard), **Martin** (Archer), **Mullis** (Kary B), **Oparin** (Alexandr), **Perutz** (Max), **Porter** (Rodney R), **Sanger** (Frederick)
**07** **Edelman** (Gerald M), **Fischer** (Edmond H), **Hopkins** (Sir Frederick), **Khorana** (Har Gobind), **Stanley** (Wendell M), **Waksman** (Selman), **Warburg** (Otto)
**08** **Anfinsen** (Christian B), **Chargaff** (Erwin), **Kornberg** (Arthur), **Meyerhof** (Otto), **Northrop** (John H), **Weinberg** (Robert)
**09** **Bergström** (Sune), **Butenandt** (Adolf), **Michaelis** (Leonor)
**11** **Hoppe-Seyler** (Felix)
**12** **Szent-Györgyi** (Albert von)

*See also* **biology**

**biography**

**02** CV **03** bio **04** biog, life **05** diary
**06** biopic, letter, memoir, record, résumé **07** account, diaries, history, journal, letters, memoirs, profile
**08** journals **09** life story
**11** hagiography **12** recollection
**13** autobiography, prosopography, recollections **15** curriculum vitae

*Biographers include:*

**05** **Spark** (Dame Muriel), **Weems** (Mason Locke)
**06** **Aubrey** (John), **Morley** (John, Viscount), **Motion** (Andrew), **Napier** (Mark), **Wilson** (Andrew Norman)
**07** **Ackroyd** (Peter), **Bedford** (Sybille), **Bolitho** (Hector), **Boswell** (James), **Debrett** (John), **Ellmann** (Richard), **Holroyd** (Michael), **Lubbock** (Percy), **Pearson** (Hesketh), **Sitwell** (Sacheverell)
**08** **Lockhart** (John Gibson), **Plutarch**, **Strachey** (Lytton)
**09** **Aldington** (Richard), **Kingsmill** (Hugh), **Suetonius**

**biology**

*Biological terms include:*

**02** GM
**03** DNA, RNA
**04** cell, gene
**05** class, genus, virus
**06** coccus, enzyme, family, fossil, tissue
**07** meiosis, microbe, mitosis, nucleus, osmosis, protein, species
**08** bacillus, bacteria, cultivar, genetics, membrane, molecule, mutation, organism, parasite, ribosome, stem cell
**09** amino acid, cell cycle, corpuscle, cytoplasm, diffusion, ecosystem, ectoplasm, evolution, food chain, Mendelism, pollution, reticulum, symbiosis
**10** alpha helix, chromosome, extinction, Lamarckism, metabolism, parasitism, protoplasm
**11** Haeckel's law, homeostasis, respiration
**12** conservation, mitochondria, reproduction
**13** flora and fauna, micro-organism, mitochondrion
**14** Golgi apparatus, photosynthesis
**15** nuclear membrane, ribonucleic acid

*Biologists and naturalists include:*

**03** **His** (Wilhelm)
**04** **Axel** (Richard), **Baer** (Karl Ernst von), **Berg** (Paul), **Hess** (Walter), **Hunt** (Tim), **Katz** (Sir Bernard), **Koch** (Ludwig), **Lyon** (Mary)
**05** **Arber** (Werner), **Bacon** (Francis, Viscount), **Bates** (Henry Walter), **Beebe** (William), **Bruce** (Sir David), **Crick** (Francis), **Golgi** (Camillo), **Lewis** (Edward B), **Luria** (Salvador), **Lwoff** (André), **Nurse** (Sir Paul M), **Sabin** (Albert), **Scott** (Sir Peter), **Sharp** (Phillip), **Smith** (Hamilton), **White** (Gilbert)
**06** **Altman** (Sidney), **Anning** (Mary), **Bishop** (Michael), **Blobel** (Günter), **Boveri** (Theodor), **Buffon** (George-Louis, Comte de), **Cairns** (Hugh), **Cannon** (Walter), **Carson** (Rachel), **Claude** (Albert), **Darwin** (Charles), **Friend** (Charlotte), **Huxley** (Sir Julian), **Huxley** (T H), **Isaacs** (Alick), **Kandel** (Eric), **Lartet** (Edouard), **Morgan** (Thomas Hunt), **Palade** (George), **Sloane** (Sir Hans), **Varmus** (Harold), **Watson** (James), **Wilson** (Edward)
**07** **Adamson** (Joy), **Agassiz** (Louis), **Andrews** (Roy), **Beneden** (Edouard), **Brenner** (Sydney), **Dawkins** (Richard), **Driesch** (Hans), **Durrell** (Gerald), **Epstein** (Sir Anthony), **Flavell** (Richard), **Gilbert** (Walter), **Haeckel** (Ernst), **Haldane** (J B S), **Hershey** (A D), **Jackson** (Barbara, Lady), **Kendrew** (Sir John), **Lamarck** (Jean), **Lubbock** (Sir John), **Nathans** (Daniel), **Pasteur** (Louis), **Roberts** (Richard), **Steptoe** (Patrick), **Wallace** (Alfred)
**08** **Cousteau** (Jacques), **Delbrück** (Max), **Flemming** (Walther), **Franklin** (Rosalind), **Hartwell** (Lee), **Humboldt** (Alexander, Baron von), **Jeffreys** (Sir Alec), **Linnaeus** (Carl), **Li Shizen**, **Margulis** (Lynn), **Meselson** (Matthew), **Milstein** (Cesar), **Purkinje** (Jan), **Sielmann** (Heinz), **Starling** (Ernest), **Tonegawa** (Susumu), **Weismann** (August)
**09** **Lederberg** (Joshua), **Schaudinn** (Fritz), **Wieschaus** (Eric)

**10** Ingen-Housz (Jan)
**11** Deisenhofer (Johan), Leeuwenhoek (Antoni van), Metchnikoff (Elie), Ramón y Cajal (Santiago), Spallanzani (Lazaro)
**12** Attenborough (Sir David), Maynard Smith (John)
**13** Du Bois-Reymond (Emil Heinrich)
**14** Levi-Montalcini (Rita)
**15** Nusslein-Volhard (Christiane)

*See also* **bacteriology**; **biochemistry**; **palaeontologist**; **physiology**

## birch

**03** rod **04** birk, flog, twig **05** swish
**06** Betula

## bird

**03** jug **04** avis, babe, gaol, girl, jail, nick, quod, shop, stir, time **05** choky, clink **06** chokey, lumber, prison
**07** college, slammer **10** girlfriend

*See also* **animal**; **chicken**; **duck**; **game**; **hen**; **poultry**

### *Birds include:*

**02** ka
**03** ani, auk, bat, cob, daw, doo, emu, hae, hen, jay, kea, kia, mag, maw, mew, moa, owl, pie, roc, tit, tui
**04** barb, chat, cirl, cobb, cock, coot, crow, dodo, dove, duck, emeu, erne, eyas, fowl, gled, guan, gull, hawk, hern, huia, ibis, jynx, kagu, kaka, kite, kiwi, knot, kora, kuku, lark, loom, loon, lory, mina, myna, nene, nyas, pavo, pern, pica, piet, pyat, pyet, pyot, rail, rhea, rook, ruff, runt, ruru, rype, shag, skua, smee, sora, swan, taha, teal, tern, tody, weka, wren, xema, yite
**05** agami, ariel, booby, capon, chick, crane, diver, eagle, egret, eider, finch, fleet, flier, galah, glede, goose, grebe, heron, hobby, macaw, mynah, ousel, piper, pipit, pitta, potoo, quail, raven, robin, scops, snipe, solan, squab, stilt, stork, swift, tewit, twite, vireo, wader
**06** avocet, bantam, barbet, budgie, bulbul, canary, chough, condor, cuckoo, curlew, cushat, darter, dipper, drongo, dunlin, falcon, fulmar, gannet, godwit, grouse, hoopoe, houdan, jabiru, jacana, kakapo, linnet, magpie, martin, merlin, mesite, motmot, oriole, osprey, parrot, peahen, peewit, petrel, pigeon, plover, puffin, pullet, raptor, redcap, roller, sea-mew, shrike, siskin, takahe, thrush, tom-tit, toucan, trogon, turaco, turkey, yaffle, zoozoo
**07** antbird, apteryx, babbler, barn owl, bittern, bluecap, blue jay, bluetit, bullbat, bunting, bustard, buzzard, chicken, coal-tit, cotinga, courser, cowbird, creeper, dottrel, dunnock, fantail, finfoot, goshawk, grackle, halcyon, harrier, hoatzin, jacamar, jackdaw, kestrel, lapwing, leghorn, limpkin, mallard, manakin, moorhen, mudlark, oilbird, ostrich, peacock, pelican, penguin, phoenix, pintail, poultry, quetzal, redpoll, redwing, rooster, ruddock, seagull, seriema, skimmer, skylark, spadger, sparrow, sunbird, swallow, tanager, tiercel, tinamou, titlark, touraco, vulture, wagtail, warbler, waxbill, wrybill, wryneck
**08** aasvogel, accentor, adjutant, aigrette, bee-eater, bellbird, blackcap, bobolink, cockatoo, currasow, dabchick, dotterel, fish-hawk, flamingo, great tit, grosbeak, hernshaw, hornbill, landrail, laverock, leafbird, lorikeet, lovebird, lyrebird, megapode, myna bird, nightjar, nuthatch, ovenbird, ox-pecker, palmchat, parakeet, pheasant, puffbird, rainbird, redshank, redstart, ringtail, screamer, sea eagle, shoebill, starling, tapaculo, water-hen, whimbrel, white-eye, woodcock
**09** aepyornis, albatross, bald eagle, bergander, blackbird, blackhead, bowerbird, broadbill, bullfinch, cassowary, chaffinch, chickadee, cockatiel, cormorant, corncrake, eider duck, fairy tern, fieldfare, frogmouth, gerfalcon, gnateater, goldfinch, goosander, guillemot, jack-snipe, kittiwake, little owl, merganser, mollymawk, mousebird, mynah bird, nighthawk, ossifrage, partridge, peregrine, phalarope, ptarmigan, razorbill, sandpiper, scrub-bird, sheldrake, thornbill, trumpeter, turnstone, wind-hover
**10** budgerigar, chiff-chaff, fledgeling, flycatcher, goatsucker, gobemouche, greenfinch, greenshank, guinea fowl, hammerhead, harpy eagle, honeyeater, honeyguide, kingfisher, kookaburra, nutcracker, sanderling, sandgrouse, shearwater, sheathbill, song thrush, sunbittern, tropicbird, turtledove, wattlebird, woodpecker, wood pigeon
**11** butcherbird, frigatebird, golden eagle, hummingbird, mockingbird, nightingale, plantcutter, reed-warbler, snow bunting, song sparrow, sparrowhawk, stone-curlew, storm petrel, thunderbird, tree-creeper, woodcreeper, wood-swallow
**12** adjutant bird, cuckoo-roller, diving petrel, flowerpecker, golden plover, honeycreeper, missel-thrush, mistle-thrush, sedge warbler, yellowhammer
**13** archaeopteryx, barnacle goose, oystercatcher, secretary bird, willow warbler
**14** bird of paradise, plains wanderer
**15** blue-footed booby, passenger pigeon, peregrine falcon

### *Birds of prey include:*

**03** owl
**04** erne, hawk, kite, pern
**05** eagle, hobby
**06** falcon, lanner, merlin, osprey, raptor
**07** barn owl, buzzard, goshawk, harrier, hawk owl, kestrel, red kite
**08** bateleur, berghaan, duck-hawk, eagle owl, fish-hawk, Scops owl, sea eagle, spar-hawk, tawny owl
**09** bald eagle, black kite, eagle-hawk, fish eagle, gyrfalcon, little owl, marsh hawk, peregrine, stone hawk
**10** harpy eagle, hen harrier, tawny eagle
**11** booted eagle, chicken hawk, Cooper's hawk, golden eagle, sparrowhawk, stone falcon
**12** great grey owl, honey buzzard, long-eared owl, marsh harrier
**13** American eagle, Iceland falcon, imperial eagle, lesser kestrel, pallid harrier, secretary bird, short-eared owl
**14** short-toed eagle
**15** Montagu's harrier, peregrine falcon, red-footed falcon

### *Flightless birds include:*

**03** emu
**04** dodo, emeu, kiwi, rhea, weka
**06** kakapo, ratite, takahe
**07** ostrich, penguin
**08** great auk, notornis
**09** cassowary, owl-parrot, solitaire

### *Mythical birds include:*

**03** fum, roc, rok, ruc
**04** fung, huma, rukh
**07** phoenix
**08** whistler
**09** impundulu
**11** thunderbird
**12** bird of wonder

### *Seabirds include:*

**03** auk, cob, maw, mew
**04** cobb, guga, gull, shag, skua, tern, Xema
**05** solan
**06** fulmar, gannet, petrel, puffin
**07** pickmaw, seagull
**08** comorant
**09** black tern, great skua, guillemot, kittiwake, little auk, mallemuck, razorbill, swart-back
**10** Arctic skua, Arctic tern, common gull, common tern, little gull, little tern, saddleback, solan goose
**11** herring gull, Iceland gull, roseate tern, Sabine's gull, storm petrel
**12** glaucous gull, Leach's petrel, pomarine skua, sandwich tern
**14** black guillemot, long-tailed skua, Manx shearwater
**15** black-backed gull, black-headed gull

### *Wading birds include:*

**03** ree
**04** hern, ibis, knot, ruff
**05** crake, crane, heron, reeve, snipe, stilt, stint, stork

**06** avocet, curlew, dunlin, godwit, plover
**07** bittern, bustard, lapwing
**08** dotterel, flamingo, redshank, whimbrel, woodcock
**09** dowitcher, grey heron, phalarope, sandpiper, turnstone
**10** greenshank, sanderling
**11** little stint, stone curlew
**12** golden plover, great bustard, ringed plover
**13** little bustard, oystercatcher

**• birds**
**04** Aves **05** ornis

**birth**
**04** dawn, line, race, rise, root, seed
**05** blood, house, start, stock
**06** advent, family, labour, origin, source, strain **07** arrival, descent, genesis, lineage, origins **08** ancestry, breeding, delivery, nativity, pedigree
**09** beginning, emergence, genealogy, parentage **10** appearance, background, childbirth, derivation, extraction **11** confinement, parturition
**12** commencement, fountainhead
**13** starting-point

*Birth flowers:*

**04** rose
**05** aster, daisy, holly, poppy
**06** cosmos, violet
**07** jonquil
**08** hawthorn, larkspur, primrose, snowdrop, sweet pea
**09** calendula, carnation, gladiolus, narcissus, water lily
**10** poinsettia
**11** honeysuckle
**12** morning glory
**13** chrysanthemum
**15** lily of the valley

*Birth stones:*

**04** opal, ruby
**05** pearl, topaz
**06** garnet, zircon
**07** diamond, emerald, peridot
**08** amethyst, sapphire, sardonyx
**09** moonstone, turquoise
**10** aquamarine, bloodstone, tourmaline
**11** alexandrite

**• give birth to**
**03** cub, ean, kid, lay, pig, pup **04** bear, drop, fawn, foal, have, lamb, yean
**05** calve, found, throw **06** create, farrow, kitten, litter, mother **08** initiate
**09** establish **10** bring forth, give rise to, inaugurate **12** cause to exist

**birthday**
**03** dob **10** day of birth **11** anniversary

**birthmark**
**04** mole **05** naeve, nevus, patch
**06** naevus **07** blemish **10** beauty spot, mother spot **13** discoloration, port-wine stain **14** strawberry mark

**birthplace**
**02** bp **03** b pl **04** home, root **05** fount, roots **06** cradle, source **08** home town
**10** fatherland, incunables, incunabula, native town, provenance **12** place of birth **13** mother country, native country, place of origin

**birthright**
**03** due **06** legacy **08** birthdom
**09** privilege **11** inheritance, prerogative

**biscuit**
**04** bake, cake **05** biccy **06** bickie

*Biscuits include:*

**03** dog, nut, sea, tea
**04** kiss, Nice, puff, rice, rusk, ship, snap, tack, thin, Twix®, wine
**05** Marie, ship's, wafer, water
**06** cookie, hob-nob, Kit-Kat®, parkin, perkin
**07** Bourbon, cracker, fig roll, Gold Bar®, iced gem, Lincoln, oatcake, Penguin®, pretzel, ratafia, rich tea, saltine
**08** biscotto, captain's, cracknel, flapjack, hardtack, macaroon, Zwieback
**09** Abernethy, Breakaway®, chocolate, digestive, four-by-two, garibaldi, ginger nut, jaffa cake, party ring, petit four, pink wafer, shortcake
**10** Bath Oliver, Blue Riband®, brandy snap, butter-bake, crispbread, dunderfunk, florentine, gingersnap, malted milk, shortbread, Wagon Wheel®
**11** brown George, fly cemetery, soda cracker, squashed fly
**12** cream cracker, custard cream, jammie dodger, langue de chat
**14** gingerbread man

**• soften biscuit**
**04** dunk

**bisect**
◇ *insertion indicator*
**04** fork **05** cross, halve, split **06** divide
**08** cut in two, separate **09** bifurcate, cut in half, intersect **13** divide into two

**bisexual**
**02** bi **04** AC/DC **07** epicene
**11** androgynous, monoclinous
**12** ambidextrous, switch hitter
**13** hermaphrodite
**15** gynandromorphic

**bishop**
**01** B **02** Bp, DD, RR **04** abba, lord
**06** exarch, magpie, primus **07** pontiff, prelate, primate **08** diocesan
**09** coadjutor, patriarch, suffragan
**10** archbishop, episcopant, metropolis
**11** intercessor **12** metropolitan
**13** spiritual peer **14** vicar-apostolic

*Bishops include:*

**05** **Aidan** (St), **Peter** (St)
**06** **Blaise**, **Ninian** (St), **Osmund** (St)
**07** **Ambrose** (St), **Carroll** (John), **Hadrian**, **Patrick** (St)
**08** **Geoffrey** (of Monmouth), **Holloway** (Richard), **Nicholas** (St), **Sheppard** (David)
**11** **Elphinstone** (William), **Odo of Bayeux**

*See also* **archbishop**

**bishopric**
**03** see **07** diocese, Holy See
**10** episcopacy, episcopate
*See also* **diocese**

**bismuth**
**02** Bi

**bison**
**04** gaur **06** wisent **07** aurochs, bonasus, buffalo **08** bonassus

**bit**
◇ *hidden indicator*
**03** ate, dot, jot, ort, tad **04** atom, chip, curb, dash, doit, drap, drop, haet, hint, iota, lump, mite, part, what, whit
**05** chunk, crumb, drill, flake, fleck, grain, piece, scrap, shred, slice, speck, touch, trace **06** cannon, morsel, nibble, pelham, sliver, tittle
**07** kenning, portion, segment, snaffle, soupçon, vestige **08** fragment, mouthful, particle **09** scintilla **10** small piece **12** small portion

**• a bit**
**04** tick **05** jiffy **06** a while, fairly, minute, moment, rather **07** a little, a moment, not much, not very
**08** slightly **10** a short time, few minutes, few moments **12** a little while

**• bit by bit**
**06** slowly **08** in stages **09** gradually, piecemeal **10** step by step **14** little by little

**• bit of**
◇ *head selection indicator*

**• last bit of**
◇ *tail selection indicator*

**bitch**
**03** cat, cow, pig **04** moan, slut
**05** brach, gripe, harpy, shrew, swine, trial, vixen, whine **06** ordeal, virago, whinge **07** doggess, grumble, torment
**08** badmouth, complain **09** criticize, female dog, nightmare **13** find fault with **15** be spiteful about

**bitchiness**
**05** spite, venom **06** malice **07** cruelty
**08** meanness **09** cattiness, nastiness
**13** maliciousness

**bitchy**
**04** mean **05** catty, cruel, nasty, snide
**07** cutting, vicious **08** shrewish, spiteful, venomous, vixenish
**09** malicious, rancorous
**10** backbiting, vindictive

**bite**
◇ *containment indicator*
**03** bit, eat, nip **04** chew, crop, gnaw, grip, hold, kick, peck, pick, rend, snap, take, tang, tear, work **05** champ, chomp, crush, force, gnash, munch, piece, pinch, power, prick, punch, seize, smart, snack, spice, sting, taste, wound **06** begnaw, crunch, effect, impact, lesion, morsel, nibble, pierce, tingle **07** morsure, remorse

**08** mouthful, piquancy, puncture, pungency, smarting, strength **09** influence, light meal, masticate, sharpness, spiciness **10** impression, take effect **11** refreshment

**biting**
◇ *containment indicator*
**03** raw **04** acid, cold, keen, tart **05** acrid, harsh, nippy, sharp **06** bitter, severe, shrewd, toothy **07** caustic, cutting, cynical, hurtful, mordant, nipping, pointed, pungent, vicious **08** freezing, incisive, piercing, scathing, stinging **09** sarcastic, trenchant, vitriolic **10** astringent, mordacious **11** penetrating

**bitter**
**03** ale, raw, sad, wry **04** acid, keen, sore, sour, tart **05** acerb, acidy, acrid, angry, aygre, cruel, eager, harsh, nippy, parky, sharp, tangy, wersh **06** arctic, biting, fierce, morose, porter, savage, severe, sullen, tragic **07** acerbic, caustic, cynical, hostile, intense, painful, pungent, unhappy
**08** freezing, piercing, sardonic, scathing, spiteful, stinging, venomous, vinegary, virulent **09** aggrieved, harrowing, indignant, jaundiced, merciless, rancorous, resentful, vitriolic **10** astringent, begrudging, embittered, malevolent, vindictive, wry-mouthed **11** acrimonious, disgruntled, distressing, penetrating, unsweetened **12** freezing cold, gut-wrenching, heart-rending, vituperative
**13** disappointing, heartbreaking

**bitterly**
**05** wryly **06** sourly **07** angrily, cruelly **08** bitingly, morosely, savagely, severely, sullenly **09** cynically, hostilely, intensely, painfully **10** grievously, grudgingly, piercingly, scathingly, spitefully, venomously **11** acerbically, caustically, indignantly, rancorously, resentfully, with vitriol **12** begrudgingly, embitteredly, malevolently, sardonically, vindictively **13** acrimoniously, penetratingly **14** vituperatively

**bittern**
**05** Ardea **06** bittor, bittur **07** bittour **08** mire-drum **10** butter-bump **11** mossbluiter **12** bull-of-the-bog

**bitterness**
**04** bite, edge, fell, gall, pain **05** anger, marah, spite, venom **06** enmity, grudge, rancor, spleen **07** acidity, cruelty, iciness, rancour, rawness, sadness, tragedy, vinegar **08** acrimony, coldness, cynicism, distress, ferocity, jaundice, pungency, severity, sourness, tartness, wormwood **09** harshness, hostility, intensity, sharpness, tanginess, virulence **10** acerbicity, antagonism, chilliness, frostiness, moroseness, resentment, sullenness **11** indignation, malevolence, painfulness, penetration, unhappiness **12** embitterment, heart-rending **13** heartbreaking
**14** disappointment, vindictiveness

**bitty**
**06** broken, fitful **07** scrappy **09** piecemeal **10** disjointed, fragmented, incoherent
**12** disconnected

**bitumen**
**03** tar **05** slime **09** albertite, elaterite **11** pissasphalt

**bivalve**
**06** cockle, oyster, tellen, tellin **07** geoduck, scallop, scollop **08** ark-shell **10** otter shell

**bizarre**
◇ *anagram indicator*
**03** odd **05** funny, gonzo, outré, queer, wacky, weird **06** way-out **07** comical, curious, deviant, oddball, offbeat, strange, surreal, unusual **08** abnormal, freakish, peculiar, uncommon
**09** eccentric, fantastic, grotesque, left-field, ludicrous **10** off the wall, outlandish, ridiculous **11** extravagant, Pythonesque **13** extraordinary
**14** unconventional

**bizarrely**
◇ *anagram indicator*
**05** oddly **07** weirdly **09** comically, curiously, strangely, unusually
**10** abnormally, freakishly, peculiarly **11** ludicrously **12** outlandishly, ridiculously **13** extravagantly

**blab**
**04** blat, leak, tell **05** prate **06** gossip, reveal, squeal, tattle **07** blister, divulge, let slip, tattler **08** blurt out, disclose, tattling **11** blow the gaff **15** give the game away

**blabber**
**04** chat **06** babble, gabble, gossip, jabber, witter **07** blather, blether, chatter, prattle, swollen, twattle, twitter

**black**
**01** B **03** bad, dim, sad **04** dark, evil, inky, sick, slae, sloe, vile **05** angry, awful, bleak, cruel, dingy, dirty, dusky, grimy, gross, gungy, muddy, raven, sooty, unlit, wrong **06** bitter, dismal, filthy, gloomy, grotty, grubby, odious, soiled, sombre, sullen, tragic, vulgar, wicked **07** cynical, demonic, heinous, immoral, satanic, stained, Stygian, subfusc, swarthy, unclean, unhappy
**08** coloured, devilish, funereal, hopeless, menacing, moonless, mournful, overcast, starless
**09** Cimmerian, depressed, malicious, miserable, nefarious, resentful, tasteless, tenebrous **10** depressing, diabolical, fuliginous, in bad taste, lugubrious, malevolent, melancholy, melanistic, nigrescent, pitch-black
**11** black as coal, crepuscular, dark-skinned, distressing, threatening
**13** unilluminated

*Blacks include:*

**03** jet
**04** blae, ebon, jeat
**05** dwale, ebony, sable
**08** jet-black
**09** coal-black

- **black and white**

**02** b/w **04** gray, grey **05** plain
**07** brocked, brockit, on paper, piebald, printed, pyebald, written **08** clear-cut, definite, distinct, on record
**11** categorical, unambiguous, unequivocal, well-defined, written down **12** monochromist **13** pepper-and-salt

- **black eye** *see* **eye**
- **black out**

**03** gag **05** faint **06** censor, darken
**07** conceal, cover up, eclipse, pass out
**08** collapse, flake out, keel over, suppress, withhold

- **in the black**

**03** ban, bar, hit **05** punch, taboo
**06** bruise, injure **07** blacken, boycott, embargo, solvent **08** in credit
**09** blacklist, out of debt **11** without debt

- **very black**

**02** BB **04** inky

**blackball**
**03** ban, bar, pip **04** oust, pill, snub, veto
**05** debar, expel **06** reject **07** drum out, exclude, shut out **08** throw out
**09** blacklist, ostracize, repudiate
**11** vote against

**blacken**
**03** ink, tar **04** cork, soil **05** black, cloud, decry, dirty, libel, smear, smoke, stain, sully, taint **06** besmut, darken, defame, defile, impugn, malign, revile, smudge, vilify **07** detract, nigrify, run down, slander, tarnish **08** besmirch
**09** denigrate, discredit, dishonour, make dirty **10** calumniate

**blackguard**
**05** crook, devil, knave, rogue, sweep, swine **06** rascal, rotter, wretch
**07** bleeder, bounder, scumbag, stinker, villain **08** blighter **09** miscreant, reprobate, scoundrel **10** vituperate

**blackleg**
**03** leg **04** fink, scab, snob
**09** knobstick

**blacklist**
**03** ban, bar **04** snub, veto **05** debar, expel, taboo **06** outlaw, reject
**07** boycott, exclude, shut out
**08** disallow, preclude **09** ostracize, proscribe, repudiate

**blackmail**
**04** milk **05** black, bleed, chout, exact, force **06** coerce, compel, demand, extort, lean on, ransom, strike
**07** bribery, squeeze **08** chantage, exaction, threaten **09** extortion, greenmail, hush money, shakedown
**10** pressurize **12** hold to ransom, intimidation **14** put the screws on

**blackmailer**
**07** vampire **08** hijacker **10** highbinder, highjacker **11** bloodsucker, extortioner
**12** extortionist

**blackout**
**04** coma **05** faint, swoon **07** cover-up, embargo, secrecy, silence, syncope
**08** brownout, oblivion, power cut
**10** censorship, flaking-out, passing out
**11** concealment, suppression, withholding **12** power failure
**15** unconsciousness

**blacksmith**
**06** vulcan **09** hammerman, ironsmith
**11** burn-the-wind

**bladder**
**04** swim **05** sound **06** vesica
**07** blister, utricle, vesicle **09** cholecyst

**blade**
**03** fan, oar **04** edge, peel, vane, wash
**05** float, knife, lance, razor, skate, spear, sword **06** dagger, lamina, paddle, scythe, Toledo **07** bayonet, scalpel, spatula **10** cream-slice, paperknife **11** cutting edge
*See also* **dagger**; **sword**

**blame**
**03** rap, tax **04** onus, wite, wyte
**05** chide, decry, fault, guilt, odium, stick, thank, wight **06** accuse, berate, charge, dirdam, dirdum, injury, rebuke
**07** appoint, censure, condemn, pin it on, reproof, reprove, upbraid
**08** admonish, berating, reproach, tear into **09** criticism, criticize, dispraise, inculpate, liability, name names, reprehend, reprimand, scapegoat
**10** accusation, confounded, disapprove, discommend, find guilty, hold liable **11** culpability
**12** condemnation, name and shame
**13** find fault with, incrimination, recrimination **14** accountability, responsibility **15** hold accountable, hold responsible

**blameless**
**05** clear **07** perfect, sinless, upright
**08** innocent, virtuous, witeless
**09** faultless, guiltless, lily-white, stainless **10** inculpable, unblamable, unreproved **11** unblemished
**12** irreprovable, without fault **13** above reproach, unimpeachable
**14** irreproachable **15** irreprehensible

**blameworthy**
**06** guilty **07** at fault **08** culpable, shameful, unworthy **10** flagitious
**11** inexcusable, responsible
**12** disreputable, indefensible, reproachable **13** discreditable, reprehensible

**blanch**
**04** boil **05** scald **06** blench, whiten
**07** go white, lighten **08** etiolate, grow pale, turn pale **09** turn white
**10** become pale, grow pallid
**11** become white **12** become pallid

**blancmange**
**04** mold **05** mould **08** flummery

**bland**
**04** dull, flat, mild, weak **05** suave
**06** boring, smooth, spammy
**07** anodyne, humdrum, insipid, mundane, tedious, vanilla **08** ordinary
**09** tasteless **10** antiseptic, monotonous, unexciting **11** flavourless, inoffensive, nondescript, uninspiring
**13** characterless, uninteresting

**blandishments**
**05** sooth, spiel **07** blarney, coaxing, fawning, flannel, treacle **08** cajolery, flattery, lipsalve, soft soap
**09** agréments, sweet talk, wheedling
**10** sycophancy **11** compliments, enticements, inducements
**12** ingratiation, inveiglement
**14** persuasiveness

**blank**
**03** gap **04** bare, void **05** break, clean, clear, empty, plain, space, white
**06** glazed, vacant, vacuum
**07** deadpan, vacancy, vacuity, vacuous
**08** lifeless, unfilled, unmarked
**09** apathetic, emptiness, impassive, unwritten **10** empty space, poker-faced **11** emotionless, indifferent, inscrutable, nothingness
**12** uninterested **14** expressionless, without feeling **15** uncomprehending

**blanket**
**04** coat, film, hide, mask **05** bluey, cloak, cloud, cover, layer, manta, quilt, sheet, total **06** afghan, carpet, deaden, global, mantle, muffle, poncho, sarape, serape, stroud **07** coating, conceal, eclipse, obscure, overall, overlay, whittle, wrapper **08** bedcover, coverage, covering, coverlet, envelope, mackinaw, suppress, surround, sweeping, wrapping
**09** bedspread, eiderdown, inclusive, wholesale **11** wide-ranging **12** all-embracing, all-inclusive, underblanket
**13** comprehensive **14** across-the-board, indiscriminate

**blankly**
**08** vacantly **09** vacuously **10** lifelessly
**11** impassively **13** apathetically, emotionlessly, indifferently
**14** uninterestedly, without feeling

**blare**
**04** boom, honk, hoot, peal, ring, roar, toot **05** blast, clang **07** boom out, clamour, resound, thunder, trumpet
**08** blast out **11** sound loudly

**blarney**
**05** spiel, taffy **06** cajole, sawder
**07** coaxing, flannel **08** cajolery, flattery, soft soap **09** sweet talk, wheedling **10** soft sawder, soft sowder
**13** blandishments **14** persuasiveness

**blasé**
**04** cool **05** bored, jaded, weary
**07** offhand, unmoved **08** lukewarm
**09** apathetic, impassive, unexcited
**10** nonchalant, phlegmatic, uninspired
**11** indifferent, unconcerned, unimpressed **12** uninterested

**blaspheme**
**04** cuss, damn **05** abuse, curse, swear
**06** revile **07** profane **08** execrate
**09** desecrate, imprecate **10** utter oaths
**12** anathematize

**blasphemous**
**07** godless, impious, profane, ungodly
**10** irreverent, sulphurous
**11** imprecatory, irreligious
**12** sacrilegious

**blasphemously**
**09** profanely **12** irreverently
**14** sacrilegiously **15** disrespectfully

**blasphemy**
**05** curse, oaths **07** cursing, impiety, outrage **08** swearing **09** expletive, profanity, sacrilege, violation
**10** execration, unholiness
**11** desecration, impiousness, imprecation, irreverence, profaneness, ungodliness

**blast**
◇ *anagram indicator*
**03** dee, wap **04** bang, blow, bomb, boom, clap, dang, drat, gale, gust, honk, hoot, parp, peal, puff, roar, ruin, rush, shot, slam, toot, tout, waff, wail, zonk **05** blare, burst, clang, crack, crash, pryse, scath, slate, sound, storm, trump, whiff, whift **06** assail, attack, bellow, berate, blow up, blow-up, flatus, flurry, jigger, rebuke, scaith, scathe, scream, shriek, skaith, squall, strike, volley, wuther **07** blaring, blatter, bluster, booming, boom out, clamour, destroy, draught, explode, gun down, reprove, roaring, shatter, tantara, tell off, tempest, thunder, upbraid, whither **08** blare out, demolish, outburst, siderate
**09** criticize, discharge, explosion, reprimand, shoot down, tantarara
**10** detonation, sideration **12** blow to pieces **13** thunder-stroke
• **blast off**
**07** lift off, take off **10** be launched

**blasted**
◇ *anagram indicator*
**05** ruddy **06** cursed, damned, darned
**07** flaming **08** annoying, blighted, blooming, dratting, flipping, infernal
**10** confounded, unpleasant **12** planet-struck **14** planet-stricken

**blatant**
**04** bald, open **05** naked, overt, sheer
**06** arrant, brazen, coarse, full-on, patent **07** glaring, obvious **08** flagrant, hard-core, manifest, outright **09** bald-faced, barefaced, clamorous, obtrusive, out-and-out, prominent, shameless, unashamed
**10** pronounced **11** conspicuous, undisguised, unmitigated
**12** ostentatious

**blatantly**
**06** openly **08** brazenly, patently
**09** glaringly, obviously, out-and-out
**10** flagrantly, manifestly **11** shamelessly, unashamedly **13** conspicuously

**blaze**
**03** low **04** beam, boil, burn, fire, glow, lowe, lunt, rage **05** blast, burst, erupt,

flame, flare, flash, glare, gleam, light, shine, shoot **06** blow up, flames, ignite, let fly, let off, see red, seethe, set off **07** bonfire, explode, flare up, flare-up, glitter, inferno **08** be alight, be on fire, outburst, radiance **09** be radiant, catch fire, discharge, explosion, fire-storm **10** brilliance **11** be brilliant **13** conflagration **15** burst into flames

**blazing**
◇ *anagram indicator*
**05** angry **06** on fire **07** burning

**blazon**
**05** vaunt **06** flaunt, herald **07** trumpet **08** announce, flourish, proclaim **09** broadcast, celebrate, make known, publicize

**bleach**
**04** fade, pale **06** blanch, whiten **07** lighten **08** decolour, etiolate, make pale, peroxide, turn pale **09** make white, turn white **10** decolorize

**bleak**
**03** raw **04** arid, bare, blae, blay, bley, cold, dark, drab, dull, grim, open **05** ablet, empty, harsh, windy **06** barren, chilly, dismal, dreary, gloomy, leaden, sombre **07** exposed, joyless, spartan **08** desolate, hopeless, soulless, wretched **09** cheerless, desperate, miserable, windswept **10** depressing **11** comfortless, unpromising, unsheltered **12** discouraging, unfavourable **13** disheartening, weather-beaten

**bleakly**
**06** grimly **08** dismally, drearily, gloomily, sombrely **09** joylessly, miserably **10** wretchedly **11** cheerlessly **12** unfavourably **13** unpromisingly

**bleary**
**03** dim **05** tired **06** blurry, cloudy, drowsy, rheumy, watery **07** blurred **09** unfocused **10** bleary-eyed

**bleat**
**03** baa, cry, maa **04** beef, blat, bray, call, moan **05** gripe, whine **06** grouse, kvetch, whinge **07** grumble, whicker **08** complain **09** complaint

**bleed**
**03** run, sap **04** flow, gush, melt, milk, ooze, seep, weep **05** blood, drain, exude, flood, glide, merge, spurt **06** extort, reduce **07** deplete, exhaust, extract, squeeze, suck dry, trickle **08** let blood **09** lose blood, shed blood **10** bleed white **11** extravasate, haemorrhage **12** exsanguinate, phlebotomize

**blemish**
**03** mar **04** blot, blur, flaw, mark, mote, tash, vice, want **05** botch, fault, speck, spoil, stain, sully, taint, touch **06** blotch, damage, deface, defame, defect, impair, smudge **07** tarnish **08** disgrace **09** deformity, disfigure, dishonour **10** compromise **12** imperfection **13** discoloration, disfigurement

*Blemishes include:*

**03** zit
**04** acne, boil, bump, corn, mole, scab, scar, spot, wart
**06** bunion, callus, naevus, pimple
**07** blister, freckle, pustule, verruca
**08** pockmark
**09** birthmark, blackhead, carbuncle, chilblain, whitehead
**14** strawberry mark

**blench**
**03** shy **05** cower, quail, quake, start, wince **06** falter, flinch, quiver, recoil, shrink **07** shudder **08** draw back, hesitate, pull back

**blend**
◇ *anagram indicator*
**03** fit, mix **04** beat, fuse, meld, melt, stir, suit **05** admix, alloy, match, merge, union, unite, whisk **06** commix, fusion, go with, mingle, set off **07** amalgam, combine, merging, mixture, uniting **08** coalesce, compound, intermix **09** admixture, commingle, composite, contemper, harmonize, synthesis **10** amalgamate, commixture, complement, concoction, go together, go well with, homogenize, intertwine, interweave, synthesize **11** combination, portmanteau, run together **12** amalgamation

**bless**
**04** laud **05** exalt, extol, thank, wound **06** anoint, favour, hallow, honour, ordain, praise, thrash **07** glorify, magnify, worship **08** brandish, dedicate, sanctify **10** consecrate, lay hands on **13** be grateful for, be thankful for, give thanks for

• **bless you**
**10** benedicite, Gesundheit

**blessed**
◇ *anagram indicator*
**04** glad, holy **05** happy, lucky **06** adored, divine, graced, joyful, joyous, sacred **07** endowed, revered **08** benedict, favoured, hallowed, heavenly, provided **09** benedight, contented, fortunate **10** prosperous, sanctified **11** consecrated

**blessing**
**02** OK **04** boon, gain, gift, help **05** grace, leave **06** bounty, favour, profit **07** backing, benefit, benison, consent, darshan, go-ahead, godsend, kiddush, service, support **08** approval, felicity, sanction, thumbs-up, windfall **09** advantage, agreement, authority, good thing **10** benedicite, dedication, green light, invocation, permission **11** approbation, benediction, concurrence, good fortune **12** commendation, consecration, thanksgiving

**blight**
◇ *anagram indicator*
**03** mar, rot, woe **04** bane, dash, evil, kill, ruin, take **05** blast, check, crush, curse, decay, spoil, wreck **06** cancer, canker, damage, fungus, injure, mildew, strike, wither **07** destroy, disease, scourge, scowder, setback, shatter, shrivel, trouble **08** calamity, scouther, scowther **09** blastment, fire-blast, frustrate, pollution, undermine **10** affliction, annihilate, corruption, disappoint, misfortune, sideration **11** infestation **13** contamination

**blimey**
**03** coo, lor

**blind**
**03** mad **04** hood, mask, rash, seal, seel, slow, trap, wild **05** blend, chick, cloak, cover, front, hasty, shade, trick **06** bisson, closed, dazzle, façade, hidden, screen **07** confuse, cover-up, curtain, deceive, eyeless, mislead, shutter, unaware, winking **08** careless, heedless, ignorant, mindless, obscured, reckless, unseeing, Venetian **09** concealed, impetuous, impulsive, make blind, oblivious, sightless, unmindful, unsighted **10** beetle-eyed, camouflage, intimidate, irrational, masquerade, neglectful, obstructed, out of sight, uncritical, unthinking, visionless **11** distraction, inattentive, indifferent, injudicious, insensitive, roller blind, smokescreen, thoughtless, unconscious, unobservant, unreasoning, window shade **12** festoon blind, imperceptive **13** Austrian blind, inconsiderate, Venetian blind **14** deprive of sight, indiscriminate **15** block your vision, deprive of vision, put the eyes out of
*See also* **sight**

**blindly**
**05** madly **06** rashly, wildly **10** carelessly, mindlessly, recklessly, unseeingly **11** impetuously, impulsively, senselessly, sightlessly **12** incautiously, irrationally, uncritically, unthinkingly, without sight **13** thoughtlessly, without vision

**blink**
**04** peep, pink, wink **05** flash, gleam, shine, twink **06** glance, wapper **07** flicker, flutter, glimmer, glimpse, glitter, nictate, sparkle, twinkle **09** nictitate **11** scintillate

**blip**
**03** pip **04** buzz **05** bleep **06** glitch, hiccup, squeal **07** screech

**bliss**
**03** joy **06** heaven, utopia **07** ecstasy, elation, nirvana, rapture **08** euphoria, gladness, paradise **09** happiness **11** blessedness **12** blissfulness **13** seventh heaven

**blissful**
**05** happy **06** elated, joyful, joyous **07** idyllic **08** ecstatic, euphoric, seraphic **09** delighted, enchanted, rapturous **10** enraptured, seraphical

**blister**
**03** wen **04** blab, bleb, boil, cyst, sore **05** blain, bulla, ulcer **06** canker,

papula, pimple **07** abscess, measles, papilla, pustule, vesicle **08** cold sore, furuncle, overgall, swelling, vesicate, vesicula **09** carbuncle, phlyctena, pompholyx **10** phlyctaena

**blistering**
**03** hot **05** cruel **06** fierce, savage **07** caustic, extreme, intense, vicious **08** scathing, vesicant, virulent **09** ferocious, sarcastic, scorching, withering **10** epispastic

**blithe**
**05** happy, merry **06** casual, cheery **08** carefree, careless, cheerful, heedless, uncaring **10** unthinking, untroubled **11** thoughtless, unconcerned **12** light-hearted

**blithely**
**08** casually **10** carelessly **12** unthinkingly **13** thoughtlessly

**blitz**
**04** raid **06** attack, effort, strike **07** attempt **08** campaign, exertion **09** endeavour, offensive, onslaught **10** blitzkrieg **11** bombardment **12** all-out effort

**blizzard**
**05** buran, storm **06** squall **07** tempest **08** white-out **09** snowstorm

**bloated**
**04** full **05** puffy **06** sodden **07** blown up, dilated, stuffed, swollen **08** enlarged, expanded, inflated, puffed up **09** distended, puffed out

**blob**
**01** O **03** dab, gob **04** ball, bead, drop, duck, glob, lump, mass, pill, spot, tear **05** pearl **06** bubble, pellet, splash **07** droplet, globule

**bloc**
**04** axis, ring **05** block, cabal, group, union **06** cartel, clique, league **07** entente, faction **08** alliance **09** coalition, syndicate **10** federation **11** association

**block**
◇ *insertion indicator*
**03** bar, dam, dit, jam, let, ped **04** cake, clog, cube, halt, hunk, lump, mass, plug, seal, slab, stop **05** batch, brick, check, choke, chunk, close, dam up, delay, deter, group, piece, wedge **06** arrest, bung up, clog up, hamper, hinder, impede, scotch, series, square, stop up, thwart **07** barrier, cluster, complex, occlude, section **08** blockage, building, drawback, obstacle, obstruct, quantity, stoppage **09** deterrent, frustrate, hindrance, stonewall, structure **10** be in the way, impediment, resistance **11** development, obstruction **14** stumbling-block

• **block off**
**04** seal, stop **05** close **06** stop up **07** close up, shut off

• **block out**
**04** hide, mask, veil **06** screen **07** blot out, conceal, eclipse, obscure, repress, shut out **08** blank out, suppress **10** obliterate

• **block up**
**03** ram **04** cloy

**blockade**
**03** ram **04** cloy, stop **05** block, check, siege **06** hinder **07** barrier, besiege, choke up, closure, prevent **08** encircle, keep from, obstacle, obstruct, oppilate, stoppage, surround **09** barricade **10** investment **11** obstruction, restriction **12** encirclement, prevent using **15** prevent entering, prevent reaching

**blockage**
**03** jam **04** clot **05** block **06** log jam **08** blocking, snifters, stoppage **09** hindrance, occlusion **10** bottleneck, congestion, impediment **11** obstruction

**blockhead**
**03** git **04** dope, dork, fool, geek, jerk, mome, mutt, nerd, prat, twit **05** chump, dunce, goosy, idiot, ninny, twerp, wally **06** dimwit, goosey, nitwit, noodle, oxhead, tumphy **07** dizzard, jackass, log-head, plonker **08** bonehead, clotpoll, dipstick, imbecile, jolthead, lunkhead, numskull **09** besom-head, doddipoll, doddypoll, dottipoll, numbskull, pigsconce, thickhead, thickskin **10** bufflehead, jolterhead, loggerhead, muddle-head, nincompoop, thick-skull, woodenhead **11** chuckle-head, leather-head

**bloke**
**03** boy, guy, man, oik **04** chap, male **05** fella **06** fellow **09** character **10** individual

*See also* **boy**

**blond, blonde**
**04** fair **05** light **06** cendré, flaxen, golden **08** bleached **10** fair-haired **11** tow-coloured **12** golden-haired **13** light-coloured

**blood**
**03** nut **04** Blut, gore, knut, ruby, sang **05** birth **06** claret, family **07** descent, kindred, kinship, lineage **08** ancestry **09** lifeblood, relations **10** extraction, vital fluid **11** descendants **12** relationship

• **draw blood**
**03** cup **05** bleed

• **mass of blood**
**04** clot

**bloodcurdling**
**05** scary **06** horrid **07** fearful **08** chilling, dreadful, horrible, horrific **09** appalling **10** horrendous, horrifying, terrifying **11** frightening, hair-raising **13** spine-chilling

**bloodgroup**
**01** A, B, O **02** AB

**bloodhound**
**04** lime, lyam, lyme **06** sleuth **07** coondog **09** coonhound, detective, lime-hound, lyam-hound, lyme-hound **11** sleuth-hound

**bloodless**
**03** wan **04** cold, dead, pale **05** ashen, pasty, white **06** chalky, feeble, pallid, sallow, sickly, torpid **07** anaemic, drained, insipid, languid **08** lifeless, listless, peaceful **09** unfeeling, unwarlike **10** colourless, non-violent, spiritless, strife-free **11** passionless, unemotional

**bloodshed**
**04** gore **06** murder, pogrom **07** carnage, killing, slaying **08** butchery, massacre **09** bloodbath, slaughter **10** decimation **12** bloodletting

**bloodsucker**
**04** flea, gnat, tick **05** lamia, leech **06** gadfly **07** deer fly, sponger, tabanid, vampire **08** birch fly, black fly, mosquito, parasite, simulium **09** stable fly **10** horseleech, vampire bat **11** blackmailer, buffalo gnat, extortioner **12** extortionist, sucking louse

**bloodthirsty**
**05** cruel **06** brutal, savage **07** inhuman, vicious, warlike **08** barbaric, ruthless **09** barbarous, ferocious, homicidal, murderous **10** sanguinary

**bloody**
**03** red **04** gory, rare **05** bally, cruel, ruddy **06** bluggy, brutal, fierce, purple, savage **08** bleeding, blinking, blooming, sanguine **09** ferocious, homicidal, murderous **10** sanguinary **11** ensanguined, sanguineous **12** bloodstained, bloodthirsty, sanguinolent **13** ensanguinated

**bloody-minded**
**05** cruel **06** touchy **07** awkward, stroppy **08** stubborn **09** difficult, irritable, obstinate, unhelpful **11** obstructive **13** unco-operative

**bloom**
**03** bud **04** blow, glow, grow, open **05** blush, chill, flush, prime **06** beauty, flower, health, heyday, lustre, mature, pruina, sprout, thrive, vigour **07** blossom, develop, prosper, red tide **08** flourish, radiance, rosiness, strength **09** freshness **10** perfection **11** florescence **13** efflorescence

• **in bloom**
**03** out

**bloomer** *see* **flower**; **mistake**

**blooming**
**04** rosy **05** bonny, primy, ruddy **07** healthy **09** flowering **10** blossoming, florescent

**blossom**
**03** bud, may, pip **04** blow, grow **05** bloom **06** flower, mature, pruina, thrive **07** bloosme, burgeon, develop,

prosper, succeed **08** flourish, progress **10** effloresce **11** florescence **13** efflorescence

### blot

**03** dot, dry, mar **04** blur, flaw, mark, soak, spot **05** dry up, fault, smear, spawn, speck, spoil, stain, sully, taint **06** absorb, blotch, defect, smudge, soak up **07** blacken, blemish, splodge, tarnish **08** disgrace **09** black mark, disfigure **10** tarnishing **12** imperfection, obliteration

**• blot out**

**04** bury, hide **05** blank, erase **06** cancel, darken, delete, efface, screen, shadow **07** conceal, eclipse, expunge, obscure **08** black out **10** obliterate

### blotch

**04** blot, dash, mark, monk, spot **05** patch, stain **06** smudge, splash **07** blemish, pustule, splodge, splotch **08** heatspot

### blotched

**06** marked, pimply, spotty **07** blotchy, freckly, scarred, spotted, stained **09** blemished, centonate, scratched

### blotchy

◇ *anagram indicator*

**06** patchy, smeary, spotty, uneven **07** spotted **08** inflamed, reddened **09** blemished

### blouse

**05** middy, shirt, smock, tunic, waist **09** garibaldi **10** shirtwaist

### blow

**03** bat, bob, bop, box, cut, dad, fan, hit, rap, tip, wap **04** bang, bash, belt, biff, buff, butt, chop, clap, clip, conk, cuff, daud, dint, flow, flub, fuse, gale, gust, hook, jolt, lick, melt, oner, paik, pant, pash, pelt, pipe, play, plug, puff, ruin, rush, scat, slap, snot, sock, stot, swat, tear, toot, waff, waft, welt, whop, wind, wipe, yank **05** appel, blare, blast, botch, break, burst, carry, clout, drift, drive, fling, float, fluff, knock, one-er, peise, punch, shock, skiff, smack, sound, souse, spang, split, spoil, sweep, swipe, thump, upset, waste, whack, whang, whirl, whisk, wreck **06** buffet, bungle, cock up, devvel, exhale, flurry, inhale, stream, stroke, thwack, wallop, whammy, wunner, wuther **07** blow out, breathe, flutter, lounder, puff out, reverse, rupture, screw up, setback, shocker, trumpet, whample, whirret **08** calamity, comedown, disaster, misspend, puncture, squander, surprise **09** bombshell, dissipate, miss out on **10** affliction, breathe out, concussion, exsufflate, insufflate, misfortune **11** catastrophe, fritter away, make a mess of, miss the boat, spend freely **12** short-circuit **13** rude awakening **14** disappointment, spend like water **15** bolt from the blue

**• blow out**

**04** tear **05** burst, snift, split **06** put out **07** rupture, smother **08** puncture, snuff out **10** extinguish

**• blow over**

**03** end **04** pass **05** abate, cease **06** finish, vanish **07** die down, subside **08** peter out **09** disappear, dissipate, fizzle out **10** settle down **11** be forgotten

**• blow up**

◇ *anagram indicator*

**04** bomb, fill, flip, gale, go up, gust, puff, wind **05** blast, bloat, blore, burst, go ape, go mad, go off, scold, storm, swell **06** dilate, expand, flurry, puff up, pump up, squall **07** balloon, distend, draught, enlarge, explode, fill out, inflate, magnify, tempest **08** detonate **09** overstate **10** exaggerate, hit the roof **11** become angry, blow your top, flip your lid, go ballistic **12** get into a rage **14** lose your temper **15** fly off the handle

**• gentle blow**

**03** tip **04** peck

**• heavy blow**

**02** KO **04** bang, bash, bump, oner, slog, slug, swat **05** douse, dowse, one-er, slosh, souse, swash, thump **06** lander, wallop, wunner **07** lounder **08** knockout **11** neck-herring

### blow-out

**04** bash, flat, rave **05** binge, feast, party **06** rave-up **07** knees-up **08** flat tyre, puncture **09** beanfeast, burst tyre **11** celebration

### blowpipe

**03** hod **06** sumpit **07** blowgun **08** sumpitan **09** sarbacane

### blowy

**05** fresh, gusty, windy **06** breezy, stormy **07** squally **08** blustery

### blowzy

**05** messy **06** sloppy, untidy **07** tousled, unkempt **08** slipshod, slovenly **09** ungroomed **10** bedraggled **11** dishevelled

### blubber

**03** cry, sob **04** blub, spek, weep **05** speck **06** bubble, snivel **07** sniffle, snotter, whimper **09** jellyfish

### bludgeon

**03** hit, sap **04** beat, club, cosh **05** baton, bully, force **06** badger, batter, coerce, compel, cudgel, harass, hector, strike **07** clobber, dragoon **08** browbeat, bulldoze **09** terrorize, truncheon **10** intimidate, pressurize

### blue

◇ *anagram indicator*

**03** low, sad **04** down, glum, lewd, rude, Tory **05** adult, bawdy, dirty, fed up, saucy **06** coarse, dismal, erotic, fruity, gloomy, morose, risqué, smutty, steamy, vulgar, X-rated **07** obscene, raunchy, unhappy **08** dejected, downcast, improper, indecent **09** depressed, miserable, off-colour, offensive **10** despondent, dispirited, melancholy **11** downhearted, near the bone **12** Conservative, pornographic **14** down in the dumps, near the knuckle

*Blues include:*

**03** sky
**04** anil, aqua, bice, blae, cyan, navy, Saxe, teal
**05** azure, perse, smalt
**06** cerule, cobalt, haüyne, indigo
**07** caerule, gentian, ice-blue, jacinth, sea-blue, sky-blue, watchet
**08** baby blue, cerulean, dark blue, mazarine, navy blue, Nile blue, sapphire, Saxe blue
**09** caerulean, royal blue, steel-blue, turquoise
**10** aquamarine, Berlin blue, cornflower, kingfisher, Oxford blue, periwinkle, petrol blue, powder blue
**11** duck-egg blue, lapis lazuli, nattier blue, peacock-blue, ultramarine
**12** air-force blue, dumortierite, electric blue, midnight blue, Prussian blue, Wedgwood blue
**13** Cambridge blue, robin's-egg blue
**15** lapis lazuli blue

### bluebottle

**06** beadle **07** blawort, blewart, blowfly, brommer **09** policeman

### blueprint

**04** plan **05** draft, guide, model, pilot **06** design, scheme, sketch **07** outline, pattern, project **08** strategy **09** archetype, cyanotype, programme, prototype **14** representation

### blues

**05** dumps, gloom **06** cafard **07** sadness **08** doldrums, glumness, miseries **09** dejection, moodiness **10** depression, gloominess, melancholy **11** despondency, unhappiness

### bluff

**03** lie **04** bank, brow, crag, fake, fool, open, peak, sham, show **05** blind, blunt, cliff, feign, feint, frank, fraud, ridge, scarp, surly, trick **06** candid, deceit, delude, direct, escarp, genial, hearty, height, humbug **07** affable, bravado, deceive, leg-pull, mislead, pretend **08** foreland, headland, hoodwink, pretence **09** bamboozle, deception, downright, four-flush, idle boast, outspoken, precipice **10** blustering, escarpment, promontory, subterfuge **11** braggadocio, good-natured, plain-spoken **15** straightforward

### blunder

◇ *anagram indicator*

**03** err **04** bish, boob, flub, gaff, goof, slip **05** bevue, boner, botch, break, error, fault, fluff, gaffe **06** bêtise, booboo, bumble, bungle, cock up, cock-up, goof up, howler, mess up, muck up, muddle, ricket, slip up, slip-up **07** bloomer, clanger, faux pas, floater, go wrong, mistake, screw up, stumble **08** flounder, get wrong, misjudge, pratfall, solecism **09** mismanage, oversight **10** inaccuracy **12** drop a clanger, indiscretion, make a mistake, miscalculate, misjudgement

**blunt**
**04** bald, bate, curt, dull, numb, rude, worn **05** abate, allay, frank, stark **06** abrupt, candid, dampen, deaden, direct, honest, obtund, obtuse, rebate, retund, soften, unedge, weaken **07** brusque, disedge, rounded, stubbed, uncivil **08** edgeless, explicit, hebetate, impolite, not sharp, tactless **09** alleviate, downright, outspoken, pointless **10** forthright, point-blank **11** insensitive, plain-spoken, unsharpened **12** anaesthetize **13** unceremonious **14** take the edge off **15** straightforward

**bluntly**
**06** rudely **07** frankly, roundly **08** candidly, directly **09** brusquely **10** explicitly, impolitely, point-blank, tactlessly **12** forthrightly **13** insensitively **15** unceremoniously

**blur**
◇ *anagram indicator*
**03** dim, fog **04** dull, fuzz, haze, mask, mist, muzz, slur, spot, veil **05** befog, blear, cloud, mudge, smear, stain **06** blotch, darken, mackle, muddle, smudge, soften **07** becloud, blemish, conceal, confuse, dimness, obscure **09** confusion, disfigure, fuzziness, make vague, obscurity **10** cloudiness **14** indistinctness, make indistinct

**blurb**
**04** copy, hype, puff **05** spiel **12** commendation **13** advertisement

**blurred**
◇ *anagram indicator*
**03** dim **04** hazy, soft **05** blear, faint, foggy, fuzzy, misty, muzzy, vague, woozy **06** bleary, cloudy **07** clouded, obscure, unclear **08** confused **10** ill-defined, indistinct, out of focus

**blurt**
**• blurt out**
**03** cry **04** blab, blat, gush, leak, tell **05** plump, spout, utter **06** cry out, let out, reveal **07** call out, divulge, exclaim, let slip **08** disclose **09** ejaculate **11** come out with **13** spill the beans **15** give the game away

**blush**
**03** red **04** glow **05** flush, go red, rouge **06** colour, mantle, redden **07** crimson, scarlet, turn red **08** colour up, rosiness **09** reddening, ruddiness

**blushing**
**03** red **04** rosy **06** modest **07** ashamed, flushed, glowing, red face **08** confused **09** rubescent **10** erubescent **11** embarrassed **12** apple-cheeked

**bluster**
**04** brag, crow, huff, rage, rant, roar **05** bluff, boast, bully, storm, strut, vaunt **06** hector, ruffle **07** bravado, crowing, roister, royster, show off, swagger, talk big **08** boasting, harangue **11** braggadocio, domineering, fanfaronade, rodomontade

**blustery**
**04** wild **05** gusty, windy **06** stormy **07** squally, violent **10** boisterous, swaggering **11** tempestuous

**boar**
**03** hog **05** brawn **06** barrow, tusker **07** sounder **08** sanglier

**board**
**02** bd **04** beam, deal, food, grub, jury, nosh, slab, slat, tray **05** catch, embus, enter, get in, get on, meals, mount, Ouija®, panel, plank, sheet **06** embark, timber **07** council, emplane, entrain, get into, rations **08** advisers, trustees, victuals **09** committee, directors, governors **10** commission, head office, management, provisions, step aboard, sustenance **11** directorate **12** working party **13** advisory group
**• board up**
**04** seal, shut **05** close, cover **06** shut up **07** close up, cover up
**• on board**
**02** SS
**• put on board**
**04** lade **06** embark
**• remove from board**
**04** bear

**boarder**
**02** PG **09** pensioner

**board game** *see* **game**

**boast**
**03** gab, gem, joy **04** blow, brag, crow, have, yelp **05** claim, crack, crake, enjoy, glory, prate, pride, skite, strut, swank, vapor, vaunt **06** avaunt, bounce, hot air, vapour **07** big-note, bluster, crowing, exhibit, possess, show off, swagger, talk big, trumpet **08** mouth off, sound off, talk tall, treasure **09** gasconade, gasconism, jactation, loudmouth, overstate, vainglory **10** blustering, exaggerate, self-praise **11** fanfaronade, rodomontade **12** cry roast-meat **13** overstatement **15** blow your own horn, pride yourself on

**boastful**
**03** big **04** vain **05** cocky, proud, windy **06** hot-air, swanky **07** crowing **08** arrogant, braggart, bragging, glorious, immodest, puffed up **09** bigheaded, blustrous, cock-a-hoop, conceited, thrasonic **10** blusterous, swaggering **11** egotistical, spread-eagle, swell-headed, thrasonical **12** self-glorious, vainglorious **13** swollen-headed **14** self-flattering
**• boastful talk**
**03** gas **05** mouth

**boastfully**
**03** big **07** cockily, proudly **09** crowingly **10** arrogantly **11** conceitedly **13** egotistically **14** vaingloriously

**boat**
**03** tub
*See also* **sail**; **ship**

**boatman**
**05** rower **06** bargee, sailor **07** oarsman **08** ferryman, hoveller, voyageur, waterman, water rat **09** gondolier, oarswoman, yachtsman **11** yachtswoman

**bob**
**01** s **03** bow, dop, hod, hop, nod, tap **04** dock, jerk, jolt, jump, leap, skip **05** float **06** bobble, bounce, curtsy, popple, quiver, Robert, spring, twitch, wobble **08** shilling **09** oscillate
**• bob up**
**04** rise **05** arise, pop up **06** appear, arrive, crop up, emerge, show up **07** surface **08** spring up **11** materialize

**bobbin**
**04** bone, pirn, reel **05** quill, spool

**bobby** *see* **police officer**

**bobsleigh run**
**04** lauf

**bode**
**03** bid **04** sign, warn **05** augur, dwelt, offer **06** herald, waited **07** betoken, endured, portend, predict, presage, purport, signify **08** forebode, foreshow, foretell, forewarn, indicate, intimate, prophesy, remained, threaten **09** adumbrate, foretoken **10** foreshadow **13** prognosticate

**bodge**
**04** flub, goof, mess, ruin **05** botch, fluff, spoil **06** bungle, foul up, goof up, mess up, muck up **07** blunder, louse up, screw up **11** make a hash of

**bodice**
**04** body **05** choli, gilet, jumps, waist **06** Basque, corset, halter **07** bustier, corsage **08** camisole, jirkinet, overslip **10** chemisette

**bodily**
**04** real **05** as one, fully **06** actual, carnal, in toto, wholly **07** en masse, fleshly, totally **08** as a whole, concrete, entirely, material, physical, tangible **09** corporeal **10** altogether, completely **11** substantial **12** collectively
*See also* **humour**

**body**
◇ *anagram indicator*
**03** bod, lot, mob, nub **04** area, band, bloc, bouk, buik, buke, bulk, clay, core, form, lich, mass, soma **05** build, crowd, frame, group, heart, range, shell, stiff, torso, trunk **06** amount, cartel, casing, corpse, extent, figure, kernel, throng, volume, weight **07** anatomy, cadaver, carcase, chassis, company, council,

density, essence, expanse, phalanx, society, stretch **08** congress, dead body, firmness, fullness, main part, physique, quantity, richness, skeleton, solidity **09** authority, framework, multitude, structure, substance, syndicate **10** collection **11** association, central part, consistency, corporation, largest part **12** organization **13** confederation

• **body odour**

**02** BO

**bodyguard**

**02** SS **05** guard **06** minder **08** defender, guardian **09** lifeguard, protector **10** triggerman **11** Swiss Guards **13** Schutzstaffel **15** praetorian guard

**boffin**

**05** brain **06** expert, genius, wizard **07** egghead, planner, thinker **08** designer, engineer, inventor **09** intellect, scientist **10** mastermind **11** backroom-boy **12** intellectual

**bog**

**02** WC **03** can, fen, lav, loo **04** dike, dyke, john, kazi, mire, moss, quag, sink, spew, spue, sump **05** dunny, gents, karsy, karzy, khazi, lavvy, marsh, privy, swamp, yarfa **06** carsey, karsey, ladies', lavabo, morass, muskeg, office, petary, slough, stodge, throne, toilet, yarpha **07** cludgie, latrine **08** bathroom, dunnakin, quagmire, washroom, wetlands **09** cloakroom, marshland, swampland **10** facilities, quicksands **11** convenience, water closet **12** smallest room

• **bog down**

**04** halt, mire, sink, trap **05** delay, stall, stick **06** deluge, hinder, hold up, impede, retard, slow up **07** set back **08** encumber, slow down **09** overwhelm

• **bog myrtle**

**04** gale **06** Myrica **09** sweet-gale

• **hole in bog**

**03** hag **04** hagg

**boggle**

**03** jib **05** alarm, amaze, demur **06** bungle, marvel, wonder **07** astound, confuse, scruple, stagger, startle **08** bowl over, hesitate, surprise **09** objection, overwhelm **11** flabbergast

**boggy**

**04** miry, oozy, soft **05** fenny, moory, mossy, muddy, soggy, spewy **06** marshy, quaggy, sodden, spongy, swampy **07** moorish, morassy, paludal, queachy, queechy **11** waterlogged

**bogus**

◇ *anagram indicator*

**03** bad **04** fake, sham **05** dummy, false, pseud, spoof **06** forged, phoney, pseudo **08** spurious **09** imitation **10** artificial, fraudulent **11** counterfeit, make-believe **13** disappointing

**bohemian**

**04** arty, boho **06** exotic, hippie, way-out **07** beatnik, bizarre, drop-out, oddball, offbeat **08** artistic, original **09** eccentric **10** avant-garde, off-the-wall, unorthodox **11** alternative **12** trustafarian **13** nonconformist **14** unconventional

**bohrium**

**02** Bh

**boil**

◇ *anagram indicator*

**03** jug **04** brew, cook, fizz, foam, fume, heat, leep, rage, rave, sore, stew **05** blain, botch, erupt, froth, steam, storm, ulcer **06** bubble, bunion, decoct, growth, gurgle, pimple, see red, seethe, simmer, tumour, wallop **07** abscess, anthrax, blister, explode, gumboil, parboil, pustule **08** furuncle, ganglion, swelling **09** blow a fuse, carbuncle, fulminate, gathering **10** effervesce, hit the roof **11** blow your top **12** fly into a rage, inflammation **13** come to the boil **14** bring to the boil **15** fly off the handle, go off the deep end

• **boil down**

**06** amount, digest, distil, reduce **07** abridge **08** abstract, condense **09** summarize **11** concentrate

**boiled**

◇ *anagram indicator*

**03** sod **06** sodden

**boiler**

**06** kettle

**boiling**

◇ *anagram indicator*

**03** hot **05** angry, surge **06** baking, fuming, torrid **07** coction, enraged, flaming, furious **08** broiling, bubbling, gurgling, incensed, roasting, scalding, steaming **09** indignant, scorching, turbulent **10** blistering, ebullition, infuriated, sweltering **12** effervescent

**boisterous**

◇ *anagram indicator*

**04** loud, wild **05** noisy, randy, rough, rowdy **06** active, bouncy, lively, randie, stormy, unruly **07** laddish, riotous, romping **08** animated, roisting, roysting, spirited **09** clamorous, energetic, exuberant, goustrous, turbulent **10** disorderly, knockabout, rollicking, strepitoso, tumultuous **11** dithyrambic, hyperactive, rumbustious **12** obstreperous, rambunctious, unrestrained

**boisterously**

**06** loudly, wildly **07** noisily, roughly, rowdily **08** actively **09** riotously **10** animatedly, spiritedly **11** clamorously, exuberantly, turbulently **12** tumultuously **13** energetically, hyperactively **14** obstreperously, unrestrainedly

**bold**

**02** bf **04** free, loud, pert **05** brash, brave, heavy, saucy, showy, steep, thick, vivid **06** abrupt, brassy, brazen, bright, cheeky, daring, flashy, heroic, manful, plucky, strong **07** assured, defiant, forward, gallant, haughty, naughty, valiant **08** definite, distinct, fearless, impudent, insolent, intrepid, malapert, outgoing, spirited, striking, valorous **09** audacious, bald-faced, barefaced, chivalric, colourful, confident, dauntless, foolhardy, prominent, shameless, unabashed, undaunted **10** chivalrous, courageous, diastaltic, flamboyant, in-your-face, noticeable, pronounced **11** adventurous, bold as a lion, bold as brass, conspicuous, eye-catching, venturesome **12** enterprising, high-spirited, presumptuous

• **be bold**

**04** dare

**boldly**

**06** crouse **07** bravely, vividly **08** brightly, daringly, pluckily, risoluto, strongly **09** valiantly **10** definitely, distinctly, fearlessly, heroically, intrepidly, strikingly **11** audaciously, confidently, prominently **12** courageously **13** adventurously

**Bolivia**

**03** BOL

**bolshie**

**04** rude **06** touchy **07** awkward, prickly, problem, stroppy **08** stubborn **09** difficult, irritable, obstinate, unhelpful **10** unpleasant **12** bloody-minded **13** oversensitive, unco-operative

**bolster**

**03** aid, pad **04** help, prop, stay **05** boost, brace **06** assist, buoy up, firm up, pillow **07** augment, cushion, shore up, stiffen, support **08** buttress, maintain **09** Dutch wife, reinforce **10** invigorate, revitalize, strengthen, supplement

**bolt**

**01** U **03** bar, fly, peg, pin, rat, ray, rod, run **04** cram, dart, dash, flee, gulp, lock, rush, slot, sneb, snib, stud, wolf **05** arrow, blaze, burst, catch, elope, flare, flash, gorge, latch, rivet, scoff, screw, shaft, shoot, spark, stuff **06** devour, escape, fasten, gobble, guzzle, hurtle, pintle, run off, secure, sperre, sprint, streak **07** abscond, run away, scarper **08** fastener, wolf down

**Boltzmann constant**

**01** k

**bomb**

◇ *anagram indicator*

**03** egg **05** prang, speed **06** attack, blow up, device, mortar **07** bombard, destroy **09** bombshell, explosive **10** projectile

*Bombs include:*

**01** A, H
**02** V-1, V-2
**03** car

**04** aero, atom, buzz, dumb, fire, mine, MOAB, nail, pipe, time
**05** dirty, E-bomb, Mills, shell, smart, smoke, stink
**06** binary, candle, cobalt, drogue, flying, fusion, letter, parcel, petrol, radium, rocket
**07** bomblet, cluster, fission, grenade, missile, neutron, nuclear, plastic, tallboy, torpedo
**08** bouncing, firebomb, hydrogen, landmine
**09** doodlebug, Grand Slam, pineapple
**10** incendiary
**11** blockbuster, daisy-cutter, depth charge, penetration, sensor fuzed, stun grenade, thermobaric
**12** bunker buster, rifle grenade
**13** fragmentation, thermonuclear
**15** Molotov cocktail

**bombard**
**04** bomb, pelt, raid **05** blast, blitz, flood, hound, pound, shell, stone, swamp **06** assail, attack, batter, bother, deluge, harass, mortar, pellet, pester, strafe, straff **07** besiege, torpedo **08** inundate **09** blackjack

**bombardment**
**04** fire, flak, hail **05** blitz, salvo, stonk **06** attack **07** air raid, assault, barrage, bombing, stonker **08** hounding, pounding, shelling **09** besieging, bothering, cannonade, fusillade, harassing, onslaught, pestering, shellfire

**bombast**
**03** pad **04** rant **05** stuff **06** hot air **07** bluster, fustian, heroics, inflate, padding **08** euphuism, inflated, stuffing **09** dithyramb, pomposity, verbosity, wordiness **10** sophomoric, turgidness **11** ampullosity **13** magniloquence **14** grandiloquence **15** pretentiousness

**bombastic**
**04** tall **05** puffy, tumid, windy, wordy **06** turgid **07** bloated, fustian, pompous, verbose **08** affected, inflated **09** grandiose, high-flown **10** euphuistic, portentous, sophomoric **11** pretentious, spread-eagle **12** magniloquent, ostentatious, sophomorical **13** grandiloquent

**bomber**
**01** B

*Bombers include:*

**03** B-10, B-17, B-19, B-52, MB-1
**04** dive
**05** Stuka
**06** Gotha G, Harris, Sukhoi
**07** Avenger, Heinkel, Junkers, stealth, suicide, Tupolev, Warthog
**08** Mitchell
**09** Lancaster, Liberator
**13** Superfortress
**14** Flying Fortress

**bona fide**
**04** real, true **05** legal, valid **06** actual, dinkum, honest, kosher, lawful **07** genuine **09** authentic **10** legitimate **12** the real McCoy

**bonanza**
**04** boon **07** godsend **08** blessing, windfall **12** stroke of luck, sudden wealth

**bond**
**02** bd **03** gum, tie, vow **04** band, bind, cord, deal, fuse, glue, join, knot, link, pact, seal, ties, weld, word, yoke **05** chain, nexus, noose, paste, starr, stick, union, unite **06** attach, cement, copula, fasten, fetter, league, pledge, treaty **07** binding, connect, liaison, linkage, manacle, promise, rapport, shackle, statute, valence **08** affinity, contract, covenant, ligament, mateship, relation, vinculum, yearling **09** agreement, chemistry **10** attachment, connection, friendship, obligation **11** affiliation, transaction **12** relationship

**bondage**
**04** yoke **06** thrall **07** serfdom, slavery **08** nativity, thraldom **09** captivity, restraint, servitude, thralldom, vassalage **10** subjection, villeinage **11** confinement, enslavement, subjugation **12** imprisonment, subservience **13** incarceration

**bone**
**03** nab, tot **05** seize **06** bobbin

*Bones include:*

**01** T
**02** os
**03** hip, jaw, luz, rib
**04** back, coxa, knee, shin, ulna
**05** ankle, anvil, cheek, costa, femur, funny, hyoid, ilium, incus, jugal, pubis, skull, spine, talus, thigh, thumb, tibia, vomer, wrist
**06** breast, carpal, coccyx, collar, fibula, hammer, pecten, pelvis, radius, sacrum, saddle, stapes, tarsus
**07** cranium, ethmoid, humerus, ischium, kneecap, knuckle, malleus, ossicle, patella, phalanx, scapula, sternum, stirrup
**08** clavicle, lower jaw, mandible, parietal, scaphoid, shoulder, upper jaw, vertebra
**09** calcaneum, calcaneus, occipital, trapezium, zygomatic
**10** metacarpal, metatarsal
**12** pelvic girdle
**13** shoulder-blade

**bones**
**02** Dr, GP, MO **03** doc **04** dice, ossa **06** doctor **08** skeleton

**bonfire**
**04** pyre **08** bale-fire **09** feu de joie

**bonhomie**
**08** sympathy **09** geniality **10** affability, amiability, good nature, tenderness **12** conviviality, friendliness **15** kind-heartedness, warm-heartedness

**bon mot**
**04** quip **07** riposte **08** one-liner, repartee **09** wisecrack, witticism **10** pleasantry

**bonnet**
**03** cap **04** hood, poke **06** kiss-me, toorie, tourie **08** balmoral, bongrace **11** kiss-me-quick

• **bonnet monkey**
**04** zati

**bonny**
**04** fair, fine **05** bonie, merry, plump **06** cheery, comely, joyful, lovely, pretty **07** smiling **08** blooming, bouncing, cheerful, handsome **09** beautiful **10** attractive, sweetheart

**bonus**
**03** tip **04** gain, gift, perk, plus **05** bribe, extra, prize **06** reward **07** benefit, handout, premium **08** dividend, gratuity **09** advantage, lagniappe **10** commission, honorarium, perquisite **14** fringe benefits

**bony**
**04** lean, thin **05** drawn, gaunt, gawky, lanky **06** skinny **07** angular, osseous, scraggy, scrawny **08** gangling, rawboned, sclerous, skeletal **09** emaciated

**book**
**01** b **02** bk **03** bag, lib, log, vol **04** text, tome, work **05** Bible, blame, enter, folio, order, tract **06** accuse, arrest, charge, engage, script, volume **07** arrange, booklet, charter, procure, reserve **08** accuse of, libretto, organize, schedule **09** programme **10** prearrange **11** publication

*Books include:*

**03** pad
**04** A to Z, bath, chap, cook, copy, days, hand, hymn, note, text, work, year
**05** album, atlas, audio, board, cloth, comic, diary, e-book, guide, novel, pop-up, scrap, story
**06** annual, gradus, hymnal, jotter, ledger, manual, missal, phrase, prayer, primer, sketch
**07** almanac, fiction, Filofax®, journal, lexicon, omnibus, picture, psalter
**08** exercise, grimoire, hardback, libretto, self-help, softback, thriller
**09** anthology, biography, catalogue, children's, detective, directory, gazetteer, paperback, reference, thesaurus
**10** bestseller, compendium, dictionary, large print, lectionary, manuscript
**11** coffee-table, concordance, instruction, travel guide
**12** encyclopedia
**13** penny dreadful, travel journal
**15** pocket companion

*See also* **apocryphal**; **Bible**

• **book in**
**05** enrol **07** check in **08** register

• **book of rules**
**03** pie, pye **07** ordinal **11** penitential

**bookbinding**
**10** bibliopegy

*Bookbinding terms include:*

**03** aeg
**04** case, head, limp, tail, yapp
**05** bolts, hinge, spine
**06** boards, gather, jacket, lining, Linson®, sewing
**07** binding, buckram, drawn-on, flyleaf, headcap, morocco
**08** backbone, blocking, casing-in, doublure, drilling, endpaper, fore edge, hardback, headband, open-flat, shoulder, smashing, stamping, tailband
**09** backboard, book block, casebound, debossing, dust cover, embossing, full bound, half bound, loose-leaf, millboard, paperback, signature, soft-cover
**10** back lining, binder's die, front board, laminating, pasteboard, raised band, side-stitch, square back, stab-stitch, strawboard, varnishing, whole bound
**11** comb binding, ring binding, velo binding, wire binding, wiro binding
**12** all edges gilt, binder's board, binder's brass, cloth binding, flexi binding, notch binding, quarter bound, saddle-stitch, thread sewing
**13** back cornering, blind blocking, spiral binding, unsewn binding, wire stitching
**14** library binding, perfect binding
**15** adhesive binding, cloth-lined board, hot foil stamping

**booking**
**11** appointment, arrangement, reservation

**bookish**
**07** donnish, erudite, inkhorn, learned **08** academic, cultured, highbrow, lettered, literary, pedantic, studious, well-read **09** scholarly **10** scholastic **12** bluestocking, intellectual

**booklet**
**06** folder, notice **07** handout, leaflet
**08** brochure, circular, pamphlet
**09** programme

**books**
**02** bb, NT, OT **03** bks **07** ledgers, records **08** accounts **12** balance sheet

**boom**
**03** jib **04** bang, clap, gain, grow, jump, leap, roar, roll, spar **05** blare, blast, boost, burst, crash, spurt, surge, swell **06** bellow, do well, expand, growth, rumble, thrive, upturn **07** advance, burgeon, develop, explode, prosper, resound, succeed, success, thunder, upsurge, upswing **08** escalate, flourish, increase, mushroom, progress, snowball **09** bombilate, bombinate, expansion, explosion, intensify, loud noise, resonance, skyrocket **10** escalation, strengthen **11** development, improvement, reverberate **13** reverberation

**boomerang**
◇ *reversal indicator*
**05** kiley, kylie **06** recoil **07** rebound, reverse **08** backfire, ricochet
**10** bounce back, spring back, throw stick

**boon**
**04** bene, gift, help, plus **05** bonus, grant **06** favour, jovial **07** benefit, godsend, present, request **08** blessing, gratuity, intimate, kindness, petition, windfall **09** advantage, convivial

**• boon companion**
**06** cupman, Trojan **07** franion
**09** confidant **10** best friend, confidante, dear friend **11** bosom friend, close friend **13** special friend

**boor**
**03** hog, lob, oaf, oik, yob **04** clod, Jack, kern, lout, pleb, slob **05** chuff, clown, kerne, ocker, yahoo, yobbo, yokel
**06** chough, keelie, rustic **07** Grobian, peasant **08** plebeian **09** barbarian, lager lout, vulgarian **10** clodhopper, philistine **14** country bumpkin

**boorish**
**04** rude **05** borel, crass, crude, gross, gruff, ocker, rough, swain **06** borrel, coarse, jungli, lumpen, oafish, rustic, vulgar **07** borrell, ill-bred, loutish, uncouth **08** ignorant, impolite, swainish **09** unrefined **10** uneducated
**11** clodhopping, ill-mannered, uncivilized

**boost**
**03** aid, rap **04** boom, help, hype, lift, plug, rise, spur, wrap **05** put up, raise, steal **06** assist, expand, fillip, foster, play up, praise, talk up, uplift
**07** advance, amplify, augment, bolster, develop, ego-trip, enhance, enlarge, further, improve, inspire, promote, support **08** addition, heighten, increase, maximize, shoplift, stimulus
**09** advertise, encourage, expansion, increment, promotion, publicity, publicize, stimulate **10** assistance, potentiate, supplement
**11** development, enhancement, enlargement, furtherance, improvement, inspiration
**12** augmentation, shot in the arm
**13** advertisement, amplification, encouragement

**boot**
**04** kick **05** shove, trunk **06** profit
**09** advantage

*Boots include:*

**03** gum, top, ugg
**04** crow, half, jack, lace, moon, snow
**05** ankle, kamik, rugby, thigh, wader, welly
**06** bootee, buskin, chukka, combat, finsko, galosh, golosh, hiking, jemima, mucluc, mukluk, riding
**07** blucher, bottine, Chelsea, cracowe, finnsko, galoche, Hessian, walking
**08** balmoral, bootikin, climbing, finnesko, football, high shoe, larrigan, muckluck, overshoe
**09** scarpetto
**10** Doc Martens®, wellington
**13** beetle-crusher

**• boot out**
**04** fire, sack, shed **05** eject, expel
**06** lay off **07** dismiss, kick out, suspend
**10** give notice **12** give the heave
**13** make redundant

**• to boot**
**03** too **06** as well **07** besides **10** in addition **14** into the bargain

**booth**
**03** box, hut **05** crame, kiosk, stall, stand **06** bothan, carrel **07** cubicle
**11** compartment, luckenbooth

**bootleg**
**05** wrong **06** banned, barred, pirate
**07** illegal, illicit, pirated, smuggle
**08** criminal, outlawed, smuggled, unlawful **09** forbidden **10** prohibited, proscribed **11** black-market, interdicted **12** unauthorized **15** under-the-counter

**bootless**
**04** vain **06** barren, futile **07** sterile, useless **09** fruitless, pointless
**10** profitless, unavailing **11** ineffective
**12** unprofitable, unsuccessful

**booty**
**04** haul, loot, prey, swag **05** bribe, gains, prize, spoil **06** bottom, creach, creagh, shikar, spoils **07** pillage, plunder, profits, takings **08** pickings, purchase, winnings

**booze**
**03** jar **04** grog, slug, tank **05** drink, juice, skink, tinct **06** fuddle, liquor, strunt, tiddly, tipple **07** alcohol, indulge, liqueur, spirits **08** stimulus
**09** firewater, get pissed, hard stuff, the bottle, the cratur **10** have a drink, intoxicant **11** jungle juice, strong drink, the creature **12** Dutch courage, hit the bottle **14** drink like a fish

*See also* **beer**; **cocktail**; **drink**; **liqueur**; **liquor**; **spirits**; **wine**

**boozer**
**03** bar, inn, pub, sot **04** howf, lush, soak, wino **05** alkie, bloat, dipso, drunk, local, souse, toper **06** lounge, saloon, sponge, tavern **07** Bacchus, drinker, tippler, tosspot **08** drunkard, habitual, hostelry **09** alcoholic, inebriate, lounge bar **10** wine-bibber
**11** dipsomaniac, hard drinker, public house **12** heavy drinker, watering-hole

**boozy**
◇ *anagram indicator*

*See* **drunken**

**bop**
**03** hop, jig **04** blow, jive, jump, leap, rock, spin, sway **05** dance, stomp, twirl, twist, whirl **06** boogie, gyrate, hoof it, strike **09** pirouette, shake a leg
**11** move to music

**borage**
**07** alkanet, anchusa, bugloss, comfrey, manjack, myosote **08** gromwell, lungwort, myosotis, sebesten
**09** stickseed, Symphytum **10** dog's-tongue, heliotrope, Pulmonaria
**11** cool-tankard, oyster plant
**12** hound's-tongue, lithospermum
**13** viper's bugloss

**border**
**03** bed, hem, mat, rim **04** abut, bank, bord, brim, cost, curb, dado, edge, join, kerb, limb, line, list, mark, mete, orle, rand, roon, rund, side, trim, welt
**05** apron, board, boord, borde, bound, brink, coast, coste, flank, frill, limit, march, skirt, swage, touch, verge
**06** accost, adjoin, boorde, bounds, cotise, frieze, fringe, margin, purfle, screed, trench, weeper **07** accoast, bordure, confine, connect, cottise, enclose, engrail, impinge, marches, margent, selvage, valance, valence, wayside **08** be next to, boundary, confines, dentelle, emborder, frontier, furbelow, headland, roadside, selvedge, surround, trimming
**09** cartouche, guilloche, lie next to, perimeter, periphery, state line
**10** borderline, limitrophe, marchlands
**11** demarcation **12** be adjacent to, circumscribe **13** circumference

*Borders and boundaries include:*

**07** Rubicon
**09** Green Line
**10** Berlin Wall, no-man's-land
**11** Iron Curtain, Maginot Line
**13** Bamboo Curtain
**14** Mason–Dixon line
**15** cordon sanitaire

• **border on**
**07** verge on **08** approach, be almost, be nearly, resemble **13** approximate to
**14** be tantamount to

• **borders of**
◇ *ends selection indicator*
**08** purlieus

**borderline**
**04** iffy, line **05** limit **06** divide
**08** boundary, division, doubtful, marginal **09** uncertain **10** ambivalent, indecisive, indefinite **11** problematic
**12** dividing-line **13** indeterminate
**15** demarcation line, differentiation
*See also* **border**

**bore**
**03** awl, dig, irk, sap, sat, tap, vex
**04** bare, bind, drag, eger, jade, mine, pain, sink, tire **05** annoy, drill, eager, eagre, ennui, grind, weary, worry
**06** bother, burrow, dig out, hollow, jostle, pall on, pierce, tunnel
**07** exhaust, fatigue, sondage, trouble, turn off, turn-off, wear out
**08** headache, irritate, nuisance, puncture **09** hollow out, make tired, penetrate, perforate, terebrant, terebrate, undermine **11** be tedious to, send to sleep **13** pain in the neck
**15** bore the pants off

• **enlarge bore**
**04** ream, rime

**bored**
**05** fed up, tired **06** ennuyé, in a rut
**07** ennuied, wearied **09** exhausted, turned off, unexcited **10** bored stiff, brassed off, browned off, cheesed off
**12** bored to tears, sick and tired, uninterested

**boredom**
**05** ennui **06** acedia, apathy, tedium
**07** humdrum, malaise, taedium, vapours **08** dullness, flatness, monotony, sameness **09** weariness
**11** frustration, tediousness
**12** listlessness **14** world-weariness

**boring**
**03** dry **04** dull, flat, slow, tedy **05** dully, ho-hum, samey, stale, trite **06** draggy, dreary, flatly, jejune, stupid, tiring
**07** humdrum, insipid, mundane, prosaic, routine, tedious, tritely
**08** drearily, tiresome, unvaried
**09** insipidly, tediously **10** long-winded, monotonous, tiresomely, uneventful, unexciting, uninspired
**11** commonplace, prosaically, repetitious, stultifying, uninspiring
**12** long-windedly, monotonously, uneventfully, unexcitingly
**13** repetitiously, stultifyingly, unimaginative, uninteresting **14** soul-destroying **15** unimaginatively, uninterestingly

• **boring piece**
**05** drill

**born**
**01** b, n **02** né **03** nat, née **05** natus

**boron**
**01** B

**borough**
**03** bor **04** area, port, town **05** borgo, burgh **06** parish **08** district
**09** community **12** constituency
*See also* **London**; **New York**

**borrow**
**03** use **04** draw, hire, rent, take
**05** adopt, cadge, lease, lever, usurp
**06** derive, obtain, pledge, scunge, sponge, surety, take up **07** acquire, charter **08** scrounge, take over
**10** have on loan, take on loan
**11** appropriate **12** have the use of, take out a loan **14** use temporarily

**borrowing**
**03** IOU, use **04** debt, hire, loan
**06** calque, rental **07** charter, leasing
**08** adoption, loan-word, takeover
**10** derivation **11** acquisition
**12** temporary use **15** loan-translation

**Bosnia and Herzegovina**
**03** BIH

**bosom**
**03** pap, tit **04** boob, boon, bust, core, dear **05** booby, chest, close, diddy, heart, midst **06** breast, centre, desire, loving **07** breasts, devoted, shelter
**08** faithful, intimate **09** sanctuary
**10** protection **12** confidential

**boss**
◇ *anagram indicator*
**03** cow, don, gov, guv **04** calf, head, knob, knot, stud, umbo **05** bully, chief, empty, jewel, owner, stock **06** bigwig, gaffer, hollow, honcho, leader, manage, master, oubaas, pellet, top dog, top man **07** cacique, captain, cazique, control, foreman, manager, mistake, supremo **08** browbeat, bulldoze, bull's-eye, chairman, director, dominate, domineer, employer, governor, omphalos, overseer, superior, top woman **09** big cheese, excellent, executive, top banana, tyrannize **10** chairwoman, order about, push around, supervisor
**11** chairperson, order around **12** give orders to **13** administrator, lay down the law **14** superintendent

**bossiness**
**07** tyranny **09** autocracy, despotism
**13** assertiveness, imperiousness
**14** high-handedness

**bossy**
**03** cow **04** calf **06** lordly **08** despotic, exacting **09** assertive, demanding, imperious, insistent **10** autocratic, dominating, high-handed, oppressive, tyrannical **11** dictatorial, domineering, overbearing **13** authoritarian

**botany**
**03** bot **09** phytology **11** phytography

*Botanists include:*

**03** **Mee** (Margaret Ursula), **Ray** (John)
**04** **Bary** (Heinrich Anton de), **Bose** (Sir Jagadis Chandra), **Cohn** (Ferdinand Julius), **Gray** (Asa)
**05** **Banks** (Sir Joseph), **Brown** (Robert), **Hales** (Stephen), **Sachs** (Julius von), **Vries** (Hugo de)
**06** **Biffen** (Sir Rowland Harry), **Carver** (George Washington), **Haller** (Albrecht von), **Hooker** (Sir Joseph Dalton), **Hudson** (William), **Mendel** (Gregor Johann), **Nägeli** (Karl Wilhelm von), **Torrey** (John)
**07** **Bartram** (John), **Bellamy** (David), **Bentham** (George), **De Vries** (Hugo Marie), **Pfeffer** (Wilhelm), **Tansley** (Sir Arthur George), **Vavilov** (Nikolai)
**08** **Blackman** (Frederick Frost), **Candolle** (Augustin Pyrame de), **Linnaeus** (Carolus)
**09** **Boerhaave** (Hermann), **Schleiden** (Matthias Jakob)
**10** **Camerarius** (Rudolph Jacob), **Hofmeister** (Wilhelm Friedrich Benedikt), **Pringsheim** (Nathaniel)

**botch**
◇ *anagram indicator*
**03** mar, mux **04** boil, flop, flub, goof, hash, mess, muff, ruin, sore **05** bodge, farce, fluff, patch, spoil **06** bungle, clatch, cock up, cock-up, foul up, goof up, mess up, muck up, muddle, pimple

**07** blemish, blunder, butcher, clamper, failure, louse up, screw up
**08** shambles **09** mismanage **11** make a hash of, make a mess of, miscarriage
**13** make a bad job of

## both
**04** each **06** as well, the two **07** the pair

## bother
◇ *anagram indicator*
**03** ado, bug, irk, nag, vex **04** drat, fash, fuss, pest **05** aggro, alarm, annoy, deave, deeve, grief, grind, pains, tease, upset, worry **06** bovver, bustle, dismay, effort, flurry, harass, hassle, molest, pester, plague, put out, rumpus, shtook, shtuck, strain, unrest
**07** concern, disturb, fluster, perplex, problem, schtook, schtuck, trouble
**08** disorder, distress, exertion, fighting, irritate, nuisance, vexation
**09** annoyance, incommode
**10** aggravate, difficulty, irritation
**11** disturbance **12** make an effort
**13** inconvenience, make the effort, pain in the neck **14** think necessary
**15** concern yourself

## bothersome
**05** pesky **06** boring, vexing **07** brickle, irksome, tedious **08** annoying, fashious, tiresome **09** laborious, vexatious, wearisome **10** irritating
**11** aggravating, distressing, infuriating, troublesome **12** exasperating, inconvenient

## Botswana
**02** BW, RB **03** BWA

## bottle
◇ *anagram indicator*
◇ *hidden indicator*
**03** bot **04** grit, guts **05** nerve, spunk
**06** daring, valour **07** bravery, courage
**08** boldness **09** container
**11** intrepidity **12** Dutch courage

*Bottles include:*

**03** bed, gas, ink, pig
**04** beer, case, codd, jack, junk, mick, milk, tear, vial, wash, wine
**05** bidon, cruet, cruse, dumpy, flask, gourd, Klein, phial, scent, snuff, water
**06** carafe, carboy, cutter, feeder, fiasco, flacon, flagon, hottie, inkpot, lagena, magnum, poison, pooter, siphon, stubby, syphon, Woulfe
**07** amphora, ampulla, costrel, feeding, flacket, pilgrim, pitcher, squeezy, sucking, torpedo, vinegar, washing
**08** calabash, decanter, demijohn, hip flask, hot-water, magnetic, medicine, screwtop, smelling, weighing
**09** Aristotle
**10** apothecary, lachrymary, winchester
**11** vinaigrette, water bouget
**12** Bologna phial, lachrymatory, Thermos® flask

*See also* **wine**

### • bottle up
**04** curb, hide **06** cork up, shut in
**07** conceal, confine, contain, enclose, inhibit, repress **08** disguise, hold back, keep back, restrain, restrict, suppress
**11** keep in check

## bottleneck
**05** block **06** hold-up **07** snarl-up
**08** blockage, clogging, gridlock, obstacle **09** narrowing **10** congestion, traffic jam **11** obstruction, restriction
**12** constriction

## bottom
◇ *tail selection down indicator*
**03** ass, bed, bum, end **04** base, butt, coit, foot, prat, rear, rump, seat, sill, sole, tail, tush **05** basis, batty, booty, botty, floor, lower, nadir, quoit, tushy
**06** behind, depths, far end, fundus, ground, heinie, lowest, plinth, seabed, tushie **07** bedrock, staddle, support
**08** backside, buttocks, pedestal, sea floor **09** posterior, undermost, underside **10** foundation, underneath
**11** farthest end, furthest end, lowest level **12** substructure, underpinning

*See also* **buttocks**

## bottomless
◇ *tail deletion down indicator*
**04** deep **07** abysmal, abyssal
**08** infinite, profound **09** boundless, depthless, limitless, subjacent, unfounded, unlimited, unplumbed
**10** fathomless, unbottomed, unfathomed
**11** measureless **12** immeasurable, unfathomable **13** inexhaustible

## bough
**04** limb **06** branch **07** gallows, roughie

## bought
**04** coft

## boulder
**04** rock **05** stone **06** gibber
**07** bowlder **10** niggerhead

## boulevard
**04** Blvd, Boul, mall, road **05** drive
**06** avenue, parade, street **08** corniche, prospect **09** promenade
**12** thoroughfare

## bounce
**02** go **03** bob, dap, lie, zip **04** bang, beat, give, jump, leap, stot, thud
**05** boast, boing, boink, bound, pitch, stoit, styte, throw **06** energy, morgay, recoil, spring, vigour **07** dogfish, rebound **08** boasting, dynamism, ricochet, vitality, vivacity
**09** animation, dismissal **10** ebullience, elasticity, exaggerate, exuberance, get-up-and-go, liveliness, resilience, spring back **11** springiness **12** spiritedness

### • bounce back
**07** improve, recover **09** get better
**13** make a comeback **15** get back to normal

## bouncer
**03** dud **04** liar **05** bully **06** bumper
**10** chucker-out

## bouncing
◇ *anagram indicator*
**05** bonny **06** hearty, lively, robust, strong
**07** healthy **08** blooming, thriving, vigorous **09** energetic, walloping

## bouncy
◇ *anagram indicator*
**04** spry **05** alive **06** active, lively, spongy **07** dynamic, elastic, rubbery, springy **08** flexible, spirited, stretchy, vigorous **09** energetic, resilient, sprightly, vivacious **11** full of beans

## bound
◇ *containment indicator*
**02** bd **03** bob, hop, lep, off **04** curb, edge, held, jump, leap, line, mere, skip, sten, stot, sure, tied, tyde **05** brink, caper, check, dance, fated, fixed, flank, frisk, going, limit, off to, roped, scoup, scowp, skelp, skirt, sling, spang, stend, sworn, vault, verge **06** border, bounce, cavort, coming, doomed, forced, fringe, frolic, gambol, headed, hurdle, lashed, liable, limits, lollop, margin, prance, spring, tied up **07** affined, certain, chained, clamped, confine, contain, control, enclose, galumph, gambado, heading, obliged, outline, pledged, secured, trussed **08** articled, attached, bandaged, beholden, confines, definite, destined, fastened, fettered, gallumph, handfast, moderate, regulate, required, restrain, restrict, shackled, strapped, surround, tethered **09** committed, compelled, duty-bound, extremity, perimeter, restraint **10** borderline, covenanted, limitation, proceeding, restricted, travelling **11** constrained, demarcation, on your way to, restriction, termination
**12** circumscribe **13** circumference

### • bound up with
**07** involve **09** related to **10** linked with, tied up with **11** dependent on
**13** connected with **14** associated with, hand in hand with

## boundary
**02** IV, VI **03** six **04** edge, four, goal, gole, limb, line, list, mark, mere, mete, pale, term **05** bourn, brink, limes, limit, march, meith, score, verge **06** border, bounds, bourne, fringe, limits, margin
**07** barrier, confine, marches, Rubicon, surface **08** confines, frontier
**09** extremity, parameter, perimeter, periphery **10** borderline
**11** demarcation, termination **15** point of no return

*See also* **border**

## bounded
**05** edged **07** cramped, defined, limited **08** bordered, confined, enclosed, hemmed in, walled in
**09** delimited, encircled **10** controlled, demarcated, restrained, restricted, surrounded **11** encompassed
**13** circumscribed

## bounder
**03** cad, cur, pig, rat, roo **04** euro
**05** cheat, knave, rogue, swine

**06** hopper, jumper, rotter **07** dastard, wallaby **08** blighter, dirty dog **09** miscreant **10** blackguard

### boundless

**04** vast **06** untold **07** endless, immense **08** infinite, unending **09** countless, limitless, shoreless, unbounded, unlimited **10** numberless, unconfined, unflagging **11** everlasting, illimitable, innumerable, measureless, never-ending **12** immeasurable, incalculable, interminable **13** indefatigable, inexhaustible

### bounds

◇ *ends selection indicator*

**05** edges, scope **06** limits **07** borders, fringes, marches, margins **08** confines **09** perimeter, periphery **10** boundaries, parameters **11** extremities **12** demarcations, restrictions **13** circumference

**• out of bounds**

**02** OB **04** tapu **05** taboo **06** banned, barred **09** forbidden, off limits **10** disallowed, not allowed, prohibited

### bountiful

**05** ample **06** lavish **07** copious, liberal, profuse **08** abundant, generous, princely, prolific **09** boundless, bounteous, exuberant, luxuriant, plenteous, plentiful **10** munificent, open-handed, ungrudging, unstinting **11** magnanimous, overflowing

### bounty

**03** tip **04** gift **05** bonus, grant **06** reward **07** charity, premium, present **08** donation, gratuity, kindness, largesse **09** allowance **10** almsgiving, generosity, liberality, recompense **11** beneficence, magnanimity, munificence **12** philanthropy

### bouquet

**04** nose, posy **05** aroma, bunch, odour, scent, smell, spray **06** eulogy, favour, honour, praise, wreath **07** corsage, garland, nosegay, perfume, tribute **08** accolade, approval **09** fragrance, redolence **10** buttonhole, compliment **11** boutonnière **12** commendation, felicitation, pat on the back **15** congratulations, odoriferousness

### bourgeois

**04** dull **05** banal, trite **06** square **07** humdrum **08** ordinary **09** hidebound, Pooterish **10** capitalist, conformist, pedestrian, uncreative, uncultured, uninspired, unoriginal **11** Biedermeier, commonplace, middle-class, traditional **12** conservative, conventional **13** materialistic, unadventurous, unimaginative **15** money-orientated

### bout

**02** go **03** fit, jag, run **04** bend, bust, dose, fall, game, heat, lush, sesh, term, time, turn **05** binge, boose, booze, bouse, brash, burst, drunk, fight, match, round, set-to, spasm, spell, spree, stint, touch, veney, venue **06** attack, battle, beer-up, bottle, course, fuddle, period, screed, venewe **07** booze-up, carouse, contest, session, splurge, stretch, wassail, wrestle **08** struggle **09** encounter **10** engagement, makunouchi **11** competition

### bovine

**04** dull, dumb, slow **05** dense, thick **06** stupid **07** cowlike, doltish **09** dim-witted **10** cattlelike, slow-witted

**• bovine animals**

**04** cows, neat **06** cattle

### bow

**03** arc, bob, nod, tie, yew **04** arch, arco, beak, beck, bend, duck, eugh, head, jook, jouk, knot, loop, lout, lowt, move, prow, ring, stem **05** crook, crush, curve, defer, dicky, drail, front, slope, stick, stoop, yield **06** accede, accept, circle, comply, crouch, curtsy, dickey, dickie, give in, humble, kowtow, salaam, subdue, submit **07** bending, concede, conquer, consent, incline, namaste, rostrum, succumb **08** forepart, namaskar, vanquish **09** acquiesce, genuflect, give way to, humiliate, lavaliere, obeisance, overpower, subjugate, surrender **10** capitulate, lavallière, salutation **11** fiddlestick, genuflexion, inclination, prostration **12** dorsiflexion **13** make obeisance **15** acknowledgement

**• bow out**

**04** quit **05** leave **06** defect, desert, give up, resign, retire **07** abandon, back out, pull out **08** step down, withdraw **09** stand down **10** chicken out

**• part of bow**

**03** nut **04** frog, heel, luff

**• with bow**

**04** arco

### bowdlerize

**03** cut **04** edit **05** purge **06** censor, excise, modify, purify **07** clean up, expunge **09** expurgate **10** blue-pencil

### bowels

**04** core, guts **05** belly, colon, heart **06** cavity, centre, depths, inside, middle **07** innards, insides, viscera **08** entrails, interior **09** entralles **10** intestines

### bower

**03** bay **05** arbor **06** alcove, arbour, grotto, recess **07** retreat, shelter **09** sanctuary

### bowl

**03** cap, cog, pan **04** caup, dish, hurl, race, roll, rush, sink, spin, wood **05** basin, cogie, fling, hurry, joram, jorum, mazer, motor, pitch, speed, tazza, throw, whirl **06** beaker, bicker, career, coggie, crater, goblet, krater, piggin, propel, rotate, vessel **07** brimmer, cage-cup, chalice, écuelle, revolve **08** jeroboam, monteith **09** container, porringer, posset cup, pottinger **10** receptacle **11** fingerglass **12** move steadily

**• bowled**

**01** b

**• bowl over**

**03** wow **04** fell, stun **05** amaze, floor, shock **06** topple **07** astound, stagger, startle **08** astonish, push into, surprise **09** dumbfound, knock down, overwhelm, unbalance **11** flabbergast **12** affect deeply **14** impress greatly

### bowler

**03** hat **04** skip **05** Derby **06** pot hat, seamer **07** Christy, hard hat, spinner **08** Christie

### box

◇ *containment indicator*

**02** tv **03** ark, dan, hit, pew, pix, pyx, urn **04** butt, case, cuff, etui, fist, fund, inro, loge, mill, pack, slap, slug, sock, spar, tele, wrap **05** bijou, chest, clout, fight, lodge, punch, pyxis, telly, thump, whack **06** batter, buffet, carton, casket, coffin, encase, packet, parcel, strike, wallop **07** coffret, package, present **09** baignoire, container **10** receptacle, television

**• box in**

**04** cage, trap **05** hem in **06** bail up, coop up, corner, shut in **07** block in, confine, contain, enclose, fence in **08** imprison, restrain, restrict, surround **09** cordon off **12** circumscribe

### boxer

**03** ham, pug **07** cruiser, fighter **08** pugilist, southpaw **12** prizefighter **15** sparring partner

*Boxers, managers and promoters include:*

**03** Ali (Muhammad)
**04** Benn (Nigel), Clay (Cassius), Khan (Amir), King (Don)
**05** Bruno (Frank), Duran (Roberto), Hamed ('Prince' Naseem), Lewis (Lennox), Louis (Joe), Moore (Archie), Tyson (Mike)
**06** Cooper (Henry), Dundee (Angelo), Eubank (Chris), Holmes (Larry), Liston (Sonny), Spinks (Leon)
**07** Dempsey (Jack), Foreman (George), Frazier (Joe), Leonard (Sugar Ray)
**08** Marciano (Rocky), McGuigan (Barry), Robinson (Sugar Ray)
**09** Armstrong (Henry), Holyfield (Evander), Honeyghan (Lloyd)
**11** Fitzsimmons (Bob), Queensberry (Sir John Sholto Douglas, Marquis of)

### boxing

**04** ring **06** savate **08** fighting, pugilism, sparring **10** fisticuffs, infighting, the science **11** the noble art **13** prizefighting **15** the noble science

*See also* **sport**

*Professional boxing weight divisions include:*

**09** flyweight
**11** heavyweight, lightweight, strawweight

12 bantamweight, middleweight, welterweight
13 cruiserweight, featherweight, mini flyweight, minimum weight
14 light flyweight, super flyweight
15 junior flyweight

**• boxing match**
**04** bout, mill, spar **10** glove-fight, prizefight

## boy

**03** bub, cub, kid, lad, son, tad **04** boyo, loon, lown, male, tama **05** bubby, bucko, child, gilpy, groom, knave, lowne, sprog, youth **06** chield, chokra, chummy, fellow, garçon, junior, loonie, nickum, nipper, shaver **07** galopin, gorsoon, gossoon **08** man-child, spalpeen, teenager, young man
**09** dandiprat, dandyprat, Jack-a-Lent, schoolboy, stripling, youngster
**10** adolescent, knave-bairn
**11** guttersnipe, kinchin-cove
**14** whippersnapper

*Boys' names include:*

02 Al, Cy, Ed, Ik, Jo
03 Abe, Alf, Ali, Asa, Bat, Baz, Ben, Bob, Dai, Dan, Deb, Dee, Del, Den, Dev, Dob, Don, Gay, Gaz, Gil, Gus, Guy, Hew, Huw, Ian, Ike, Iky, Ira, Ivo, Jay, Jem, Jim, Joe, Jon, Jos, Ken, Kim, Kit, Lal, Lee, Len, Leo, Lew, Mat, Max, Nat, Ned, Nye, Pat, Pip, Rab, Rae, Ray, Reg, Rex, Rob, Rod, Ron, Roy, Sam, Sim, Sol, Tam, Ted, Tim, Tom, Val, Vic, Viv, Wat, Wyn, Zia
04 Adam, Adil, Alan, Alec, Aled, Alex, Algy, Alun, Amin, Andy, Anil, Arch, Arun, Bart, Bert, Bill, Bram, Bryn, Carl, Ceri, Chad, Chae, Chay, Clem, Colm, Dave, Davy, Dean, Dewi, Dick, Dirk, Doug, Drew, Eddy, Egon, Eoin, Eric, Eryl, Euan, Evan, Ewan, Ewen, Ezra, Finn, Fred, Gabi, Gary, Gaye, Gene, Glen, Glyn, Gwyn, Hani, Hank, Hari, Hope, Huey, Hugh, Hugo, Iain, Ifor, Ivan, Ivon, Ivor, Jack, Jake, Jeff, Jock, Joel, Joey, John, Josh, Joss, Jude, Jule, Karl, Kirk, Kurt, Liam, Luke, Mark, Matt, Mick, Mike, Neal, Neil, Nick, Noam, Noel, Omar, Owen, Ozzy, Paul, Pete, Phil, Rana, Ravi, Raza, René, Rhys, Rick, Rolf, Rory, Ross, Ryan, Saul, Sean, Seth, Siôn, Theo, Thos, Toby, Tony, Trev, Umar, Walt, Will, Yves, Zach, Zack
05 Aaron, Abd-al, Abdul, Abram, Adeel, Adnan, Ahmad, Ahmed, Aidan, Aiden, Alfie, Allan, Allen, Alwin, Alwyn, Amrit, Andie, Angel, Angus, Anwar, Archy, Arran, Barry, Basil, Bazza, Benny, Billy, Bobby, Boris, Brent, Brett, Brian, Bruce, Bruno, Bryan, Bunny, Cahal, Calum, Cecil, Chaim, Chris, Chuck, Claud, Clint, Clive, Clyde, Colin, Colum, Conor, Corin, Cosmo, Craig, Cyril, Cyrus, Damon, Danny, David, Davie, Denis, Denny, Denys, Derek, Dicky, Dilip, Dipak, Donal, Duane, Dwane, Dylan, Eddie, Edgar, Edwin, Elroy, Elton, Elvis, Elwyn, Emlyn, Emrys, Enoch, Ernie, Errol, Farid, Faruq, Felix, Fionn, Floyd, Frank, Gabby, Gamal, Garry, Gavin, Geoff, Gerry, Giles, Glenn, Gopal, Hamza, Harry, Harun, Hasan, Haydn, Henry, Homer, Howel, Humph, Husni, Hywel, Idris, Ieuan, Inigo, Isaac, Jacob, Jamal, James, Jamie, Jamil, Jared, Jason, Jerry, Jesse, Jimmy, Jools, Kamal, Kasim, Keith, Kelly, Kenny, Kerry, Kevan, Kevin, Kiran, Kumar, Lance, Larry, Leigh, Lenny, Leroy, Lewie, Lewis, Linus, Lloyd, Logan, Lorne, Louie, Louis, Lucas, Madoc, Manny, Micky, Miles, Moray, Moses, Moshe, Mungo, Murdo, Myles, Neale, Neddy, Niall, Nicky, Nicol, Nigel, Ollie, Orson, Oscar, Ozzie, Paddy, Patsy, Percy, Perry, Peter, Piers, Qasim, Rajiv, Ralph, Randy, Ricky, Roald, Robin, Roddy, Roger, Rowan, Rufus, Sacha, Salim, Sammy, Sandy, Sasha, Scott, Shane, Shaun, Shawn, Silas, Simon, Solly, Steve, Sunil, Taffy, Tariq, Teddy, Terry, Tommy, Tudor, Ulric, Ultan, Vijay, Vinay, Waldo, Walid, Wally, Wasim, Wayne, Willy, Wynne
06 Adrian, Albert, Alexei, Alexej, Alexis, Alfred, Andrew, Antony, Archie, Arnold, Arthur, Ashley, Ashraf, Aubrey, Austin, Barney, Benjie, Bernie, Bertie, Bharat, Billie, Blaise, Bobbie, Callum, Calvin, Caspar, Cathal, Cedric, Ciaran, Clancy, Claude, Clovis, Colley, Connor, Conrad, Dafydd, Damian, Damien, Daniel, Darren, Declan, Deepak, Delroy, Dennis, Denzil, Dermot, Deryck, Devdan, Dicken, Dickie, Dickon, Dilwyn, Dobbin, Donald, Donnie, Dougal, Dudley, Dugald, Duggie, Duncan, Dustin, Eamonn, Eamunn, Edmund, Edward, Ernest, Esmond, Eugene, Faisal, Fareed, Faysal, Fergus, Finbar, Fingal, Finlay, Finley, Fintan, Freddy, Gareth, Garret, George, Georgy, Gerald, Gerard, Gerrie, Gideon, Gobind, Gordon, Govind, Graeme, Graham, Gussie, Hamish, Harold, Haroun, Harvey, Hassan, Hayden, Haydon, Hector, Herbie, Hervey, Hilary, Horace, Howard, Howell, Hubert, Hughie, Husain, Isaiah, Iseult, Ismail, Israel, Jarvis, Jasper, Jeremy, Jerome, Jervis, Jethro, Jimmie, Jolyon, Jordan, Joseph, Joshua, Julian, Julius, Justin, Kelvin, Kennie, Kieran, Kieron, Laurie, Lawrie, Lennie, Leslie, Lester, Lionel, Lorcan, Lucius, Luther, Lynsey, Magnus, Mahmud, Marcel, Marcus, Marlon, Martin, Martyn, Marvin, Melvin, Melvyn, Mervyn, Milton, Morgan, Morris, Murray, Nathan, Neddie, Nichol, Ninian, Norman, Oliver, Osbert, Oswald, Pascal, Pearce, Philip, Pierce, Rajesh, Randal, Ranulf, Reggie, Reuben, Richie, Robbie, Robert, Rodney, Roland, Ronald, Rudolf, Rupert, Saleem, Samuel, Sanjay, Seamas, Seamus, Seumas, Shamus, Sharif, Sidney, Sorley, Steven, Stevie, St John, Stuart, Sydney, Teddie, Thomas, Timmie, Tobias, Trevor, Tyrone, Vernon, Victor, Vikram, Virgil, Vivian, Vyvian, Vyvyan, Walter, Willie, Xavier
07 Abraham, Alister, Ambrose, Aneurin, Anthony, Auberon, Barnaby, Bernard, Bertram, Brendan, Chandra, Charles, Charley, Charlie, Christy, Clement, Crispin, Derrick, Desmond, Dominic, Douglas, Eustace, Feargal, Finbarr, Francie, Francis, Frankie, Freddie, Gabriel, Geordie, Georgie, Geraint, Gervase, Gilbert, Godfrey, Grahame, Gwillym, Herbert, Humphry, Hussain, Hussein, Ibrahim, Isadore, Isidore, Isodore, Jeffrey, Johnnie, Kenneth, Killian, Krishna, Lachlan, Leonard, Leopold, Lindsay, Lindsey, Ludovic, Malcolm, Matthew, Maurice, Michael, Murdoch, Mustafa, Neville, Nicolas, Orlando, Patrick, Peredur, Phillip, Quentin, Quintin, Quinton, Randall, Randolf, Ranulph, Raymond, Reynold, Richard, Rowland, Rudolph, Russell, Shankar, Shelley, Solomon, Stanley, Stephen, Stewart, Terence, Timothy, Torquil, Tristan, Vaughan, Vincent, Wilfred, Wilfrid, William, Winston, Zachary
08 Alasdair, Alastair, Algernon, Alistair, Augustus, Barnabas, Benedick, Benedict, Benjamin, Beverley, Christie, Clarence, Clifford, Crispian, Cuthbert, Dominick, Emmanuel, Frederic, Geoffrey, Humphrey, Jonathan, Jonathon, Kimberly, Kingsley, Lancelot, Laurence, Lawrence, Llewelyn, Matthias, Meredith, Mordecai, Muhammad, Nicholas, Perceval, Percival, Randolph, Reginald, Roderick, Ruaidhri, Ruairidh, Ruaraidh, Rupinder, Terrance, Theodore, Tristram
09 Alexander, Archibald, Augustine, Christian, Ferdinand, Frederick, Kimberley, Launcelot, Nathaniel, Peregrine, Sebastian, Siegfried, Somhairle, Sylvester, Valentine
10 Maximilian
11 Bartholomew, Christopher

## boycott

**03** ban, bar **04** snub **05** avoid, black, spurn **06** eschew, ignore, outlaw, refuse, reject **07** embargo, exclude, refusal **08** disallow, prohibit, spurning
**09** blacklist, exclusion, ostracism, ostracize, proscribe, rejection
**11** prohibition **12** cold-shoulder, proscription **14** send to Coventry

## boyfriend

**03** ami, guy, man **04** beau, date
**05** bloke, fella, lover **06** fellow, fiancé, steady, suitor, toyboy **07** admirer, best

boy, partner, squeeze **08** young man **09** cohabitee **10** sweetheart **11** live-in lover **15** common-law spouse

**boyish**
**05** gamin, green, young **06** gamine, tomboy **07** puerile **08** childish, immature, innocent, juvenile, youthful **09** childlike **10** adolescent, unfeminine, unmaidenly

**brace**
**02** II, PR **03** duo, tie, two **04** beam, bend, bind, pair, prop, stay, vice **05** clamp, nerve, shore, steel, strap, strut, truss **06** couple, fasten, gear up, hold up, prop up, secure, steady, wimble **07** bandage, bolster, compose, fortify, prepare, psych up, shore up, shoring, support, tighten, twosome **08** accolade, bridging, buttress, fastener, get ready **09** reinforce, stanchion, undergird **10** strengthen **13** reinforcement

**bracelet**
**04** band **05** armil **06** bangle **07** armilla, circlet **08** handcuff, wristlet

**bracing**
**05** brisk, crisp, fresh, tonic **07** rousing **08** reviving, vigorous **09** energetic **10** energizing, enlivening, fortifying, refreshing **11** stimulating **12** exhilarating, invigorating **13** strengthening

**bracken**
**04** tara **05** brake

**bracket**
◇ *containment indicator*
**03** lot **04** prop, rest, stay **05** batch, brace, class, frame, group **06** becket, cohort, corbel, gusset, holder, mutule, trivet **07** cripple, potence, support **08** category, grouping **09** goose-neck, modillion **10** cantilever, misericord **11** misericorde, parenthesis **14** classification

**brackish**
**04** brak, salt **05** briny, salty **06** bitter, saline **07** saltish **11** salsuginous

**bract**
**05** glume, palea **06** spathe **08** phyllary **10** hypsophyll

**brad**
**04** nail

**brag**
**03** gab **04** bull, crow **05** boast, proud, vapor, vaunt **06** vapour **07** big-note, bluster, proudly, show off, swagger, talk big **08** mouth off **10** shoot a line **11** hyperbolize, rodomontade **12** cry roast-meat, lay it on thick **15** blow your own horn

**braggart**
**06** gascon **07** bluffer, boaster, show-off, swasher, windbag **08** bangster, big mouth, boastful, fanfaron, puckfist **09** blusterer, loud-mouth, swaggerer **11** braggadocio **12** rodomontader, swashbuckler

**bragging**
**06** hot air **07** bluster, bravado **08** boasting, vauntery **09** thrasonic **10** showing-off **11** jactitation, thrasonical **12** boastfulness, exaggeration **13** tongue-doubtie

**braid**
**04** cord, lace, tail, wind, yarn **05** plait, pleat, queue, ravel, tress, twine, twist, weave **06** caddis, ric-rac, sennit, sinnet, thread **07** caddice, embraid, entwine **08** reproach, rick-rack, soutache **09** interlace, passement **10** intertwine, interweave **13** scrambled eggs

**brain**
◇ *anagram indicator*
**03** wit **04** head, mind, nous **05** savvy, sense **06** acumen, boffin, brains, expert, genius, pundit, reason **07** egghead, prodigy, scholar **08** brainbox, highbrow, pia mater, sagacity **09** intellect, sensorium **10** encephalon, grey matter, mastermind, shrewdness **11** cleverclogs, common sense, upper storey **12** intellectual, intelligence **13** understanding

*Brain parts include:*

**04** falx, lobe, lobi, pons
**06** cortex
**07** cinerea
**08** amygdala, cerebrum, meninges, midbrain, thalamus
**09** brainstem, forebrain, hindbrain, ventricle
**10** Broca's area, cerebellum, grey matter, pineal body, spinal cord
**11** frontal lobe, hippocampus, white matter
**12** hypothalamus, limbic system, parietal lobe, Purkinje cell, temporal lobe, visual cortex
**13** choroid plexus, mesencephalon, occipital lobe, olfactory bulb, optic thalamus, Wernicke's area
**14** cerebral cortex, corpus callosum, left hemisphere, pituitary gland
**15** right hemisphere, substantia nigra

**brainless**
**04** daft **05** crazy, inept, silly **06** stupid **07** foolish, idiotic **08** mindless **09** hen-witted, senseless **10** half-witted **11** incompetent, thoughtless **12** simple-minded

**brains**
**02** IQ **03** wit **04** loaf, nous **05** harns, savey, savvy **06** common, savvey, sconce, wisdom **08** gumption **10** grey matter

**brainteaser**
**05** poser **06** puzzle, riddle **07** problem **09** conundrum **10** mind-bender **12** brain-twister

**brainwashing**
**08** grilling **09** menticide **10** persuasion **11** mind-bending, re-education **12** conditioning, pressurizing **14** indoctrination

**brainy**
**04** wise **05** smart **06** bright, clever, gifted **07** sapient **09** brilliant **11** intelligent **12** intellectual

**brake**
**04** curb, drag, fern, halt, rein, slow, stop **05** check **06** harrow, pull up, retard **07** bracken, control, slacken, thicket **08** moderate, slow down **09** restraint **10** constraint, decelerate, retardment **11** reduce speed, restriction

- **braking system**

**03** ABS

**bramble**
**05** Rubus **06** lawyer **08** dewberry **10** blackberry, cloudberry **12** Penang-lawyer

**bran**
**06** chesil, chisel, shorts **07** pollard **08** roughage

**branch**
**02** br **03** arm, cow, leg, lye **04** axis, fork, limb, lobe, loop, part, reis, rice, stem, whip, wing **05** bough, corps, prong, ramus, scrog, shoot, sprig, withy **06** agency, bureau, office **07** braunch, cladode, section **08** division, offshoot **09** affiliate, succursal, tributary **10** department, discipline, subsection, subsidiary **11** local office, phylloclade, subdivision **12** ramification **14** regional office

- **branch off**

**04** fork **06** divide, offset, spring **07** deviate, diverge, furcate **08** separate **09** bifurcate

- **branch out**

**04** vary **05** add to **06** expand, extend, ramify **07** develop, enlarge **08** increase, multiply **09** diversify, spread out, subdivide **10** broaden out **11** proliferate

**brand**
**03** tag **04** burn, chop, kind, line, logo, make, mark, sear, sere, sign, sort, type, wipe **05** class, grill, label, stain, stamp, taint **06** burn in, emblem, marque, symbol **07** censure, quality, species, variety **08** besmirch, denounce, disgrace, hallmark, typecast **09** brand-name, discredit, trademark, tradename **10** stigmatize **14** identification **15** identifying mark

**brandish**
**03** wag **04** wave **05** bless, flash, raise, shake, swing, wield **06** flaunt, hurtle, parade, waving **07** display, exhibit, vibrate, wampish **08** flourish

**brandy**
**03** dop **04** fine, marc **05** bingo, mobby, Nantz, peach, smoke **06** Cognac, grappa, mobbie **07** quetsch **08** Armagnac, Calvados, eau de vie, mahogany, slivovic **09** apple-jack, aqua vitae, Cape smoke, mirabelle, slivovica, slivovitz, slivowitz **10** ball of fire **11** aguardiente, cold-without, water of life **12** cherry bounce **13** fine Champagne

**brash**
**04** bold, rash, rude **05** cocky, crude, hasty, pushy **06** brazen, flashy
**07** assured, brittle, forward
**08** impudent, insolent, reckless
**09** assertive, audacious, bumptious, foolhardy, heartburn, impetuous, impulsive **10** incautious, indiscreet
**11** impertinent, precipitate **13** self-confident

**brashly**
**06** boldly, rashly, rudely **07** cockily, hastily, pushily **08** brazenly
**09** assuredly, forwardly **10** impudently, insolently, recklessly **11** assertively, audaciously, foolhardily, impetuously, impulsively **12** incautiously, indiscreetly **13** impertinently, precipitately **15** self-confidently

**brashness**
**08** audacity, boldness, rashness, rudeness **09** hastiness, impudence, incaution, insolence, pushiness
**10** brazenness **12** impertinence, recklessness **13** assertiveness, foolhardiness **14** self-confidence

**brass**
**04** gall, loot, sass **05** cheek, money, nerve **06** latten **08** audacity, chutzpah, orichalc, rudeness, temerity
**09** brass neck, impudence, insolence, necessary, oricalche **10** brass nerve, brazenness, effrontery **11** presumption
**12** impertinence
**• top brass**
**04** VIPs

**brassy**
**04** bold, hard, loud **05** brash, cocky, harsh, noisy, pushy, sassy, saucy
**06** brazen **07** blaring, forward, grating, jarring, raucous **08** insolent, jangling, piercing, strident **09** dissonant, shameless **11** loud-mouthed

**brat**
**03** get, imp, kid **04** gait, geit, gyte
**05** brach, puppy **06** nipper, rascal
**07** brachet **08** bantling, bratchet
**09** youngster **10** jackanapes
**11** guttersnipe **14** whippersnapper

**bravado**
**04** show, talk **05** boast, brave
**06** parade **07** bluster, bombast, bravery, swagger **08** boasting, bragging, pretence, vaunting
**09** swaggerer **10** showing-off
**11** braggadocio, fanfaronade, rodomontade

**brave**
**04** bear, bold, dare, defy, face
**05** bravo, bully, gutsy, hardy, manly, noble, showy **06** daring, endure, feisty, gritty, heroic, plucky, spunky, suffer
**07** doughty, gallant, stoical, valiant
**08** confront, face up to, fearless, handsome, intrepid, resolute, stalwart, unafraid, valorous, yeomanly
**09** audacious, challenge, dauntless, excellent, put up with, stand up to, undaunted, withstand **10** courageous
**11** indomitable, lion-hearted, unflinching **12** face the music, not turn a hair, stout-hearted **14** game as Ned Kelly, keep your chin up

**bravely**
**06** boldly **07** hardily **08** daringly, pluckily, yeomanly **09** doughtily, gallantly, stoically, valiantly
**10** fearlessly, heroically, intrepidly, resolutely, stalwartly, valorously
**11** audaciously, dauntlessly, indomitably, undauntedly
**12** courageously **13** unflinchingly
**14** stout-heartedly

**bravery**
**04** grit, guts **05** pluck, spunk, valor
**06** daring, finery, mettle, spirit, valour
**07** bravado, courage, heroism, prowess **08** audacity, boldness, chivalry, tenacity, valiance
**09** fortitude, gallantry, hardiness
**10** resolution **11** intrepidity
**12** fearlessness, stalwartness
**13** dauntlessness **14** courageousness, indomitability

**bravo**
**01** B **03** olé **04** euge **08** well done
**09** excellent, spadassin

**bravura**
**04** dash, élan **06** spirit **07** sparkle
**10** brilliance **12** magnificence

**brawl**
**03** row **04** dust, fray, rout **05** argue, broil, clash, fight, flite, flyte, mêlée, scold, scrap **06** affray, bundle, bust-up, dust-up, fracas, fratch, ruckus, rumpus, stoush, tussle **07** bagarre, brabble, brangle, dispute, punch-up, quarrel, scuffle, tuilyie, tuilzie, wrangle, wrestle
**08** argument, disorder, skirmish, squabble **09** altercate
**10** Donnybrook, fisticuffs, free-for-all, rough-house **11** altercation

**brawn**
**04** beef, boar, bulk **05** might, power
**06** muscle, sinews **07** muscles
**08** beefcake, strength **09** beefiness, bulkiness **10** headcheese, robustness
**11** muscularity

**brawny**
**05** beefy, bulky, burly, hardy, hefty, hunky, husky, meaty, solid **06** fleshy, robust, sinewy, strong, sturdy
**07** hulking, massive **08** athletic, muscular, powerful, stalwart, vigorous
**09** strapping, well-built

**bray**
**04** bell, hoot, roar **05** blare, neigh
**06** bellow, heehaw, whinny
**07** screech, trumpet

**brazen**
**04** bold, pert **05** brash, pushy, saucy
**06** brassy **07** blatant, defiant, forward
**08** flagrant, immodest, impudent, insolent **09** audacious, bald-faced, barefaced, shameless, unabashed, unashamed **10** hard-boiled, in-your-face

**• brazen it out**
**04** defy **09** be defiant **11** be unashamed **12** be impenitent

**brazenly**
**06** boldly **09** blatantly, defiantly
**10** flagrantly, immodestly, impudently, insolently **11** audaciously, shamelessly, unashamedly

**brazier**
**06** hearth, mangal **07** brasero
**08** scaldino **10** fire-basket

**Brazil**
**02** BR **03** BRA **04** Braz

**breach**
**03** gap **04** gulf, hole, rift, slap
**05** break, chasm, cleft, crack, lapse, space, split, unlaw **06** open up, saltus, schism **07** crevice, fissure, offence, offense, opening, parting, quarrel, rupture, violate **08** aperture, breakers, breaking, division, fraction, infringe, solution, trespass, variance **09** break open, severance, violation
**10** alienation, contravene, difference, disruption, dissension, infraction, separation **12** break through, burst through, disaffection, disagreement, disobedience, dissociation, estrangement, infringement
**13** contravention, transgression

**bread**
**03** fat, tin **04** cash, diet, dosh, fare, food, pane **05** dough, dumps, funds, lolly, money, sugar **06** crusts
**07** shekels **08** sandwich, victuals
**09** nutriment **10** livelihood, provisions, sustenance **11** necessities, nourishment, spondulicks, subsistence
**12** the necessary

*Bread and rolls include:*

**03** bap, cob, nan, rye, tea
**04** azym, cake, corn, diet, farl, flat, loaf, milk, naan, pita, pone, roti, soda
**05** arepa, azyme, bagel, black, brown, cheat, fancy, horse, matza, matzo, pitta, plait, poori, ravel, white
**06** burger, damper, French, garlic, graham, hoagie, hot dog, Indian, injera, lavash, matzah, matzoh, panini, panino, simnel, stotty, wastel
**07** bannock, bloomer, brioche, brownie, buttery, challah, chapati, currant, ficelle, granary, jannock, manchet, paratha, pretzel, stollen, stottie, wheaten
**08** baguette, barm cake, chapatti, ciabatta, corn pone, focaccia, grissini, leavened, milk loaf, ravelled, ryebread, schnecke, standard, tortilla
**09** bara brith, barmbrack, batch loaf, burger bun, cornbread, croissant, flatbread, hamburger, petit pain, schnecken, shewbread, showbread, sourdough, wholemeal
**10** breadstick, bridge roll, finger roll, French loaf, stotty cake, unleavened, vienna loaf, wholewheat

**11** cottage loaf, French stick, morning roll, potato bread, potato scone
**12** pumpernickel
**13** farmhouse loaf
**14** pain au chocolat

**• bread and butter**
**11** maintenance
**• bread in milk**
**03** sop

**breadbasket**
**03** tum **05** tummy **07** stomach

**breadth**
**01** b **04** beam, size, span **05** range, reach, scale, scope, sweep, width **06** extent, spread **07** compass, expanse, measure **08** latitude, vastness, wideness **09** amplitude, beaminess, broadness, dimension, magnitude, thickness **10** distension **13** extensiveness

**break**
◇ *anagram indicator*
◇ *insertion indicator*
**03** gap, vac **04** beat, bust, dash, dawn, fail, gash, halt, hole, kick, lash, luck, lull, open, part, quit, rend, rest, rift, rise, ruin, snap, stop, tame, tear, tell, vary **05** begin, cleft, crack, crash, crush, excel, flout, let-up, outdo, pause, pound, sever, smash, solve, split **06** appear, be born, better, breach, chance, change, cut off, cut out, decode, divide, emerge, exceed, falter, give up, go phut, impair, impart, inform, lessen, open up, pack up, pierce, reduce, reveal, schism, shiver, soften, strike, subdue, weaken, worsen **07** abandon, conk out, crevice, cushion, decrypt, destroy, disobey, disturb, divulge, fissure, fortune, go kaput, holiday, improve, lighten, opening, respite, rupture, shatter, smoke-ho, stammer, stumble, stutter, surpass, suspend, time off, time-out, unravel, violate, work out **08** announce, breather, decipher, demolish, diminish, disclose, enfeeble, fracture, infringe, interval, outstrip, overcome, puncture, separate, shake off, splinter, vacation **09** advantage, dishonour, figure out, interlude, interrupt, perforate, undermine **10** contravene, demoralize, relinquish, separation **11** discontinue, malfunction, opportunity, stop working **12** bring to an end, disintegrate, estrangement, go on the blink, intermission, interruption, stroke of luck **13** interfere with

**• break away**
**03** fly **04** flee, quit **05** leave, split, start **06** depart, detach, escape, secede **07** run away **08** separate, split off **11** part company **13** make a run for it

**• break down**
**02** go **04** cark, conk, fail, kark, stop **05** crash, crock, crush, plash, smash **06** detail, go down, go phut, pack up **07** analyse, burn out, conk out, crack up, crock up, destroy, dissect, founder, give way, itemize, seize up **08** collapse, demolish, separate **09** attenuate, decompose, knock down **10** be overcome, categorize, go to pieces **11** fall through, lose control, stop working **13** come to nothing

**• break in**
**03** rob **04** raid, tame, wear **05** cut in, prime, start, train **06** burgle, butt in, irrupt **07** impinge, intrude **08** accustom, encroach **09** condition, cultivate, get used to, interject, interpose, interrupt, intervene **14** enter illegally

**• break off**
**03** end **04** halt, part, stop **05** cease, pause, sever **06** detach, divide, finish **07** snap off, suspend **08** dissever, separate **09** interrupt, terminate **10** disconnect **11** discontinue **12** bring to an end

**• break out**
**03** rip **04** bolt, flee **05** arise, begin, erupt, occur, shout, start **06** blow up, emerge, escape, happen **07** abscond, exclaim, flare up **08** burst out, commence **09** come out in, interject **13** begin suddenly

**• break through**
**04** pass **06** emerge **07** succeed **08** fracture, overcome, progress **09** penetrate **10** gain ground **11** leap forward, make headway

**• break up**
◇ *anagram indicator*
◇ *containment indicator*
**04** part, stop **05** sever, split, stave **06** divide, finish, reduce, reform **07** adjourn, destroy, disband, divorce, resolve, split up, suspend **08** demolish, diffract, disperse, dissolve, separate, splinter, to-bruise **09** dismantle, dismember, take apart, terminate **11** come to an end, discontinue, part company **12** bring to an end, disintegrate

**• break with**
**04** drop, jilt **05** ditch **06** reject **08** part with, renounce **09** repudiate **10** finish with **12** separate from

**breakable**
**05** frail **06** flimsy **07** brittle, fragile, friable **08** delicate **09** frangible **10** jerry-built **12** easily broken **13** insubstantial

**breakaway**
**05** rebel **06** escape, revolt **08** apostate, renegade, seceding **09** defection, heretical, secession **10** dissenting, schismatic, separatist, withdrawal **12** secessionist

**breakdown**
**07** failure **08** analysis, collapse, stoppage **10** cracking-up, dissection **11** itemization, malfunction **12** interruption **13** going to pieces **14** categorization, classification, disintegration

**• breakdown service**
**02** AA **03** RAC

**breaker**
**04** wave **06** billow, buster, roller **10** roughrider **11** white horses

**breakfast**
**07** dejeune, disjune **08** déjeuner **10** chota hazri **13** petit déjeuner
*See also* **cereal**

**break-in**
**04** raid **07** larceny, robbery **08** burglary, invasion, trespass **09** intrusion **13** house-breaking

**breakneck**
**05** rapid, swift **06** speedy **07** express **08** headlong, very fast **09** very quick **11** precipitate **13** like lightning

**breakthrough**
**04** find, gain, leap, step **07** advance, finding, headway **08** progress **09** discovery, invention, milestone **10** innovation **11** development, improvement, leap forward, quantum leap, step forward

**break-up**
**03** end **04** rift **05** split **06** finish **07** debacle, divorce, parting, upbreak **09** crumbling, dispersal **10** separation **11** dissolution, splitting-up, termination **14** disintegration

**breakwater**
**04** dock, mole, pier, quay, spur **05** jetty, wharf **06** groyne **07** bulwark, sea wall

**bream**
**03** tai **05** porgy **06** braise, braize, porgie, sargos, sargus **08** tarwhine

**breast**
**03** dug, pap, tit **04** boob, bust, stem, teat **05** booby, bosom, chest, diddy, front, heart, mamma, titty **06** nipple, thorax **07** brisket, bristol, knocker **08** breaskit

**breastplate**
**06** byrnie, thorax **07** cuirass, placket **08** pectoral, plastron, rational

**breath**
**03** air **04** gasp, gulp, gust, hint, pant, puff, sigh, waft, wind **05** aroma, odour, prana, smell, whiff **06** breeze, flatus, murmur, pneuma, spirit **07** whisper **09** breathing, suspicion, undertone **10** exhalation, inhalation, suggestion **11** inspiration, respiration

**breathe**
**04** gasp, pant, puff, sigh, tell **05** imbue, snore, utter, voice **06** exhale, expire, impart, infuse, inhale, inject, instil, murmur **07** express, inspire, respire, suspire, whisper **09** embreathe, inbreathe, transfuse **10** articulate, insufflate

**breather**
**04** gill, halt, lung, nare, rest, walk **05** break, pause **06** recess **07** respite **10** relaxation **14** breathing space, constitutional

**breathless**
**04** agog, dead **05** eager **06** pooped,

puffed, winded **07** airless, anxious, choking, excited, gasping, panting, puffing **08** feverish, wheezing
**09** exhausted, expectant, impatient, pooped out, puffed out **10** in suspense
**11** open-mouthed, out of breath, short-winded, tuckered out

**breathtaking**
**06** moving **07** amazing **08** drop-dead, exciting, stirring, stunning
**09** thrilling **10** astounding, impressive, stupendous **11** astonishing, magnificent, spectacular **12** awe-inspiring, overwhelming

**breathtakingly**
**09** amazingly **10** excitingly, stirringly, stunningly **11** thrillingly
**12** impressively, stupendously
**13** astonishingly, spectacularly
**14** awe-inspiringly, overwhelmingly

**breeches**
**04** hose **05** slops **06** breeks, tights, trouse, trunks **07** plushes, trusses
**08** chausses, jodhpurs, leathers, trossers, trousers **09** buckskins, knee-cords, strossers, trunk hose
**12** galligaskins, pedal pushers, small-clothes **14** knickerbockers

**breed**
**04** bear, kind, line, make, race, rear, sort, type **05** cause, class, hatch, raise, stamp, stock **06** arouse, create, family, foster, hybrid, strain **07** bring up, calibre, develop, lineage, nourish, nurture, produce, progeny, species, variety **08** engender, generate, multiply, occasion, pedigree
**09** cultivate, originate, procreate, propagate, pullulate, reproduce
**10** bring about, bring forth, give rise to
**11** give birth to

**breeding**
**05** stock **06** polish **07** culture, lineage, manners, nurture, raising, rearing
**08** ancestry, civility, gentrice, training, urbanity **09** education, gentility
**10** politeness, refinement, upbringing
**11** cultivation, development, good manners, procreation, savoir-vivre
**12** reproduction
• **breeding establishment**
**04** stud

**breeding-ground**
**04** nest **06** cradle, hotbed, school
**07** nursery **08** hothouse **14** training ground

**breeze**
◇ *anagram indicator*
**03** air **04** flit, gust, puff, sail, trip, waft, wind **05** glide, hurry, sally, slant, snift, sweep **06** breath, doctor, flurry, wander, zephyr **07** cat's paw, draught, saunter, snifter **08** sniffler **12** periodic wind

**breezy**
**04** airy **05** blowy, brisk, fresh, gusty, light, windy **06** blithe, bright, casual, jaunty, lively **07** blowing, buoyant, relaxed, squally **08** animated, blustery, carefree, cheerful, debonair, informal **09** confident, easy-going, vivacious **12** exhilarating, light-hearted

**Brenda**
**02** ER

**brevity**
**07** economy, fewness **08** curtness, laconism **09** briefness, concision, crispness, pithiness, shortness, terseness **10** abruptness, transience
**11** compactness, conciseness
**12** ephemerality, impermanence, incisiveness, succinctness
**14** transitoriness

**brew**
◇ *anagram indicator*
**04** boil, cook, loom, make, mash, plan, plot, soak, stew **05** blend, drink, hatch, steep **06** devise, excite, foment, gather, infuse, liquor, potion, scheme, seethe **07** build up, concoct, develop, ferment, mixture, prepare, project
**08** beverage, compound, contrive, infusion **10** be on its way, concoction
**11** combination, preparation
**12** distillation, fermentation **13** be in the offing **15** be in preparation

**bribe**
**03** buy, fix, sop **04** bung, dash, gift, palm, vail, wage **05** bonus, booty, drink, sling, spoil, touch, vails, vales
**06** boodle, buy off, carrot, grease, hamper, nobble, pay off, pay-off, payola, reward, square, suborn **07** buy over, corrupt, douceur, palm-oil, pension **08** kickback, the drink
**09** hush money, incentive, keep sweet, lubricate, refresher, slush fund, sweetener **10** allurement, back-hander, enticement, inducement, palm-grease, take care of
**12** straightener **13** gratification
**15** protection money

**bribery**
**05** graft **09** embracery **10** corruption, inducement, protection
**11** subornation **12** malversation, palm-greasing

**bric-à-brac**
**06** curios **07** baubles, gewgaws
**08** antiques, bibelots, trinkets, trumpery **09** gimcracks, ornaments
**10** Japanesery, rattletrap, Victoriana
**11** knick-knacks, odds and ends **13** bits and pieces

**brick**
**03** bar, bur, pal **04** burr, chum, lump, mass, mate, rock, slab **05** adobe, block, buddy, gault, piece, stone, wedge **06** header, rubber, rustic
**07** clinker, fletton, klinker, nogging, soldier **09** briquette, firebrick, stretcher **10** real friend **11** breeze block
**12** Dutch clinker
• **brick waste**
**04** grog
• **piece of brick**
**03** bat

**bridal**
**07** marital, nuptial, wedding
**08** conjugal, marriage **09** connubial
**11** matrimonial

**bride**
**04** wife **06** spouse **07** GI bride
**08** newly-wed, war bride, wife-to-be
**09** bride-to-be **11** honeymooner
**15** marriage partner

**bridegroom**
**05** groom **06** spouse **07** husband
**08** newly-wed **11** honeymooner, husband-to-be **15** marriage partner

**bridge**
**02** br **03** tie **04** bind, bond, fill, join, link, pons, rest, span **05** cross, unite
**06** couple, go over **07** connect, spanner **08** traverse **10** connection
**11** reach across

*Bridge types include:*

**03** air, fly
**04** arch, beam, deck, draw, foot, leaf, over, raft, road, rope, skew, toll, wire
**05** chain, pivot, swing
**06** Bailey, flying, girder
**07** bascule, flyover, lattice, lifting, pontoon, railway, through, viaduct
**08** aqueduct, causeway, floating, humpback, overpass
**09** box girder
**10** cantilever, suspension, traversing
**11** cable-stayed

*Bridges include:*

**03** Tay
**04** Skye, Tyne
**05** Forth, Sighs, Tower
**06** Bailey, Humber, Kintai, London, Rialto, Severn
**07** Bifrost, Clifton, Rainbow, Tsing Ma, Yichang
**08** Bosporus, Brooklyn, Jiangyin, Mackinac, Waterloo
**09** Evergreen, Forth Road, Kurushima, River Kwai
**10** Bosporus II, Golden Gate, Höga Kusten, Ironbridge, Millennium, Pont du Gard, Storebaelt
**11** Brocade Sash
**12** Akashi-Kaikyo, Pont d'Avignon, Ponte Vecchio
**13** Great Belt East, Kita Bisan-seto, Millau Viaduct, Sydney Harbour
**14** Ponte 25 de Abril, Quebec Railroad
**15** Minami Bisan-Seto

• **bridge player**
**01** e, n, s, w **04** east, west **05** north, south
• **bridge support**
**04** pier
• **bridge system**
**04** Acol **06** canapé **09** blackwood

**bridle**
**05** check **06** branks, govern, halter, master, subdue **07** bristle, contain, control, repress **08** hold back, moderate, restrain **09** hackamore, restraint **12** be offended by
**15** become indignant

*Bridle parts include:*

**03** bit
**04** curb
**05** cheek
**06** musrol, pelham
**07** bridoon, eye-flap, snaffle
**08** browband, noseband
**09** headstall
**10** cheekpiece

*See also* **horse**

**brief**
◇ *tail deletion indicator*
**02** KC, QC **04** case, curt, data, tell **05** blunt, breve, crisp, gen up, guide, hasty, pithy, prime, quick, remit, sharp, short, surly, swift, terse **06** abrupt, advice, advise, digest, direct, fill in, flying, inform, lawyer, orders, précis **07** brusque, compact, concise, cursory, defence, dossier, explain, laconic, limited, mandate, outline, passing, prepare, summary **08** abridged, abstract, argument, breviate, briefing, capsular, evidence, fleeting, instruct, succinct **09** barrister, condensed, directive, ephemeral, fugacious, laconical, momentary, temporary, thumbnail, tout court, transient **10** aphoristic, compressed, directions, evanescent, short-lived, transitory **11** abridgement, information **12** instructions **13** bring up to date, short and sweet **14** responsibility

**briefing**
**03** gen **06** advice, orders **07** low-down, meeting, priming, run-down **08** guidance **09** filling-in **10** conference, directions, intimation **11** information, preparation **12** instructions

**briefly**
◇ *tail deletion indicator*
**05** in few, short **07** in a word, in brief, in short, quickly, shortly, tersely **09** concisely, cursorily, precisely, summarily **10** succinctly, to the point **11** in a few words, in a nutshell

**brigade**
**03** Bde **04** band, body, crew, team, unit **05** corps, force, group, party, squad, troop **07** company **10** contingent
• **Boys' Brigade**
**02** BB

**brigand**
**06** bandit, haiduk, outlaw, robber **07** cateran, heyduck, ruffian **08** gangster, marauder **09** desperado, plunderer **10** bushranger, freebooter, highwayman **11** trailbaston

**bright**
**03** gay, lit, net **04** fine, glad, keen, nett, rosy **05** acute, clear, happy, jolly, light, merry, quick, sharp, smart, sunny, vivid **06** astute, brainy, clever, genial, joyful, lively **07** beaming, blazing, glaring, glowing, hopeful, intense, radiant, shining **08** blinding, cheerful, dazzling, flashing, gleaming, glorious, luminous, lustrous, pleasant, splendid **09** beautiful, brilliant, cloudless, effulgent, promising, refulgent, sparkling, twinkling, unclouded, vivacious **10** auspicious, favourable, glistening, glittering, optimistic, perceptive, propitious, shimmering **11** encouraging, illuminated, illustrious, intelligent, quick-witted, resplendent **12** incandescent **15** bright as a button

**brighten**
**03** rub **04** glow, jazz **05** gleam, pep up, rub up, shine **06** buck up, buoy up, jazz up, perk up, polish **07** burnish, cheer up, clear up, enhance, enliven, gladden, hearten, lighten, light up, liven up **09** encourage, irradiate, refurbish, smarten up **10** illuminate, make bright

**brightly**
**06** ablaze, gladly **07** happily **08** joyfully **09** glaringly, glowingly, intensely, radiantly **10** blindingly, cheerfully, dazzlingly, splendidly **11** brilliantly, vivaciously

**brilliance**
**04** tone **05** glare, glory, gloss, sheen **06** dazzle, genius, lustre, talent **07** bravura, glamour, prowess, sparkle **08** aptitude, fulgency, radiance, splendor **09** greatness, intensity, splendour, vividness **10** brightness, cleverness, effulgence, excellence, refulgence, virtuosity **11** coruscation, distinction **12** magnificence, resplendence

**brilliant**
**03** ace, def **04** cool, hard, mega, neat, pear, star **05** brill, gemmy, great, quick, showy, vivid **06** astute, brainy, bright, clever, expert, famous, gifted, glossy, superb, wicked **07** blazing, crucial, erudite, fulgent, glaring, intense, lambent, radical, shining, skilful **08** dazzling, glorious, masterly, smashing, splendid, talented, terrific, top-notch **09** effulgent, excellent, fantastic, refulgent, sparkling, splendent, sunbright, wonderful **10** brightsome, celebrated, glittering, remarkable **11** exceptional, illustrious, intelligent, magnificent, outstanding, resourceful, resplendent **12** accomplished, enterprising, second to none **13** scintillating **14** out of this world

**brilliantly**
**07** vividly **08** brightly, cleverly, superbly **09** intensely, skilfully **10** dazzlingly, gloriously, splendidly **11** masterfully, wonderfully **13** magnificently, resplendently

**brim**
**03** lip, rim, top **04** edge, poke **05** brink, limit, verge **06** border, margin **09** perimeter **10** be full with **12** be filled with, overflow with **13** circumference

**brimful**
**04** full **05** abrim **06** filled, jammed **07** bulging, crammed, stuffed **09** packed out **11** chock-a-block, overflowing

**brindled**
**04** pied **05** tabby **06** dotted **07** dappled, flecked, mottled, piebald **08** speckled, stippled, streaked **10** variegated

**bring**
**03** fet, get, lay **04** bear, lead, take **05** carry, cause, fetch, force, guide, usher **06** convey, create, escort, prompt, submit **07** conduct, deliver, present, produce, provoke **08** engender, initiate, result in **09** accompany, transport **10** make happen, put forward
• **bring about**
**04** make **05** cause, frame, wreak **06** create, effect, fulfil, manage **07** achieve, compass, inspire, operate, perform, procure, produce, provoke, realize **08** contrive, generate, occasion, purchase **09** encompass, instigate **10** accomplish
• **bring back**
◇ *reversal indicator*
**05** evoke, recal **06** call up, recall, reduce, relate, remind **07** recover, reverse, suggest **13** take you back to **14** make you think of
• **bring down**
**04** drop, oust, pull, stop **05** abate, lower, shoot **06** defeat, depose, derive, embace, embase, humble, imbase, reduce, sadden, topple, unseat **07** destroy **08** decrease, dismount, vanquish **09** knock down, overthrow, shoot down **11** cause to drop, cause to fall
• **bring forward**
**05** raise **06** adduce, allege, object **07** advance, prepone, present, produce, propose, suggest, trot out **10** put forward **11** make earlier
• **bring in**
◇ *containment indicator*
**03** net **04** earn, make, wind **05** fetch, gross, set up, yield **06** accrue, import, induce, launch, return **07** pioneer, produce, realize, usher in **08** initiate **09** introduce, originate, pronounce **10** inaugurate
• **bring off**
**03** win **06** fulfil, rescue **07** achieve, execute, perform, pull off **09** discharge, put across, succeed in **10** accomplish, consummate
• **bring on**
**05** cause, infer **06** foster, induce, lead to, prompt **07** advance, improve, inspire, nurture, provoke **08** expedite, generate, occasion **10** accelerate, give rise to, make happen **11** precipitate
• **bring out**
**05** issue, print **06** launch, stress **07** draw out, enhance, produce, publish **09** emphasize, highlight, introduce **10** accentuate
• **bring round**
◇ *containment indicator*
**04** coax **05** rouse **06** awaken, cajole, revive, wake up **07** bring to, convert,

win over **08** convince, persuade **11** resuscitate

**• bring up**

◇ *reversal down indicator*

**03** cat **04** barf, form, puke, rear **05** breed, nurse, raise, teach, train, vomit **06** broach, foster, nousle, nuzzle, submit **07** care for, educate, mention, nourish, noursle, nousell, nurture, propose, throw up, touch on **09** introduce **11** regurgitate

**brink**

**03** lip, rim **04** bank, brim, edge **05** limit, marge, verge **06** border, fringe, margin **08** boundary **09** extremity, threshold

**brio**

**03** pep, zip **04** dash **05** force, gusto, oomph, verve **06** energy, spirit, vigour **08** dynamism, vivacity **09** animation **10** liveliness

**brisk**

**04** busy, cant, cold, fast, good, perk, pert, yare **05** agile, alert, cobby, crisp, fresh, kedge, kedgy, kidge, quick, rapid, sharp, smart **06** active, crouse, lively, nimble, snappy **07** allegro, bracing **08** brushing, bustling, friskful, galliard, spirited, vigorous **09** energetic, sprightly **10** no-nonsense, refreshing **11** stimulating **12** businesslike, exhilarating, invigorating

**briskly**

**04** well **06** busily, nimbly **07** allegro, con moto, quickly, rapidly, sharply **08** abruptly **09** brusquely **10** decisively, vigorously **13** energetically

**bristle**

**03** awn **04** barb, hair, rise, seta **05** birse, quill, spine, thorn **06** arista, bridle, chaeta, seethe, setule, stilet, striga, stylet **07** hum with, prickle, stubble, whisker **08** abound in, bridle at, teem with, vibrissa **09** swarm with **10** seethe with, stand on end, vibraculum **11** be thick with, horripilate **12** be incensed at **14** draw yourself up

**bristly**

**05** hairy, rough, spiky, spiny **06** hispid, thorny **07** bearded, hirsute, prickly, stubbly **08** echinate, unshaven **09** echinated, whiskered **10** barbellate

**British**

**01** B **02** Br, GB, UK **03** pom **04** Brit **05** pommy

*See also* **monarch**

**• British Columbia**

**02** BC

**brittle**

◇ *anagram indicator*

**04** curt, edgy, hard **05** birsy, brash, crisp, frail, frowy, frush, harsh, nervy, sharp, short, spall, spalt, tense **06** frowie **07** bruckle, crackly, crumbly, fragile, friable, froughy, grating, nervous, redsear, shivery **08** delicate, hot-short, redshare, redshire, redshort, shattery, unstable **09** breakable, cold-short, crumbling, frangible, irritable, sensitive **12** easily broken

**broach**

◇ *anagram indicator*

**03** tap **04** open, spit **05** begin, raise **06** hint at, open up, pierce, strike **07** bring up, mention, propose, refer to, suggest **08** allude to **09** introduce

**broad**

**04** free, open, vast, wide **05** ample, clear, large, plain, roomy, vague **06** coarse, direct, marked, strong, vulgar **07** evident, general, obvious **08** catholic, eclectic, spacious, sweeping, unsubtle **09** capacious, extensive, inclusive, outspoken, universal, unlimited **10** noticeable, widespread **11** compendious, far-reaching, not detailed, unconcealed, undisguised, wide-ranging **12** all-embracing, encyclopedic, latitudinous **13** comprehensive

**broadcast**

◇ *anagram indicator*

◇ *homophone indicator*

**03** air, sow **04** beam, show **05** aired, cable, relay **06** repeat, report, spread **07** network, publish, radiate, scatter, trailer, webcast **08** announce, newscast, teletext, televise, transmit **09** advertise, cablecast, circulate, make known, programme, publicize, simulcast, soap opera **10** promulgate, sportscast, telebridge **11** disseminate **12** transmission **15** access broadcast

**• outside broadcast**

**02** OB **06** remote

**broaden**

**05** widen **06** expand, extend, open up, spread **07** augment, develop, enlarge, stretch **08** increase **09** branch out, diversify

**broadly**

**05** fully **06** mainly, mostly, widely **07** as a rule, largely, usually **08** commonly, normally **09** generally **10** by and large, more or less, on the whole, thoroughly **11** extensively, in most cases, in principle **14** for the most part **15** comprehensively

**broad-minded**

**07** liberal **08** tolerant, unbiased **09** impartial, indulgent, receptive **10** forbearing, open-minded, permissive **11** enlightened, progressive **12** free-thinking, unprejudiced **13** dispassionate

**broadside**

**04** tire **05** blast, salvo, stick **06** attack, volley **07** assault, censure **08** brickbat, diatribe, harangue **09** battering, cannonade, criticism, invective, philippic **11** bombardment, fulmination **12** counterblast, denunciation

**brochure**

**05** flyer **06** folder **07** booklet, handout, leaflet **08** circular, handbill, pamphlet **09** throwaway **10** broadsheet, prospectus

**broil**

**03** fry **04** cook **05** grill, roast, toast **08** barbecue, stramash

**broiling**

**03** hot **06** baking **07** boiling **08** roasting **09** scorching **10** blistering, sweltering

**broke**

◇ *anagram indicator*

**04** bust, poor **05** skint, stony **06** hard up, ruined **07** bargain **08** bankrupt, indigent, strapped **09** destitute, insolvent, negotiate, penniless, penurious **10** cleaned out, stony-broke **11** impecunious **12** impoverished, on your uppers **14** on your beam ends **15** poverty-stricken, strapped for cash

**broken**

◇ *anagram indicator*

**04** bust, down, duff, rent, weak **05** burst, ended, kaput, tamed, wonky **06** beaten, failed, faulty, feeble, fitful, pakaru **07** crushed, damaged, erratic, halting, severed, smashed, subdued **08** defeated, divorced, ruptured **09** defective, destroyed, disturbed, exhausted, faltering, fractured, gone wrong, imperfect, knackered, oppressed, separated, shattered, spasmodic **10** demolished, disjointed, dispirited, hesitating, not working, on the blink, on the fritz, out of order, stammering, vanquished **11** demoralized, fragmentary, inoperative, interrupted, out of action **12** disconnected, intermittent **13** discontinuous **14** malfunctioning

**• not to be broken**

**04** iron

**broken-down**

**03** ill **04** bust, duff **05** kaput **06** broken, faulty, ruined **07** damaged, decayed, rickety, worn-out **08** decrepit **09** collapsed, defective **10** on the blink, on the fritz, out of order, ramshackle **11** dilapidated, in disrepair, inoperative

**broken-hearted**

**03** sad **04** down **07** forlorn, unhappy **08** dejected, desolate, dolorous, mournful, wretched **09** miserable, sorrowful **10** despairing, despondent, devastated, prostrated **11** crestfallen, heartbroken **12** disappointed, disconsolate, inconsolable **13** grief-stricken **14** down in the dumps

**broker**

**03** job **04** deal **05** agent, agree, bania **06** banian, banyan, clinch, dealer, factor, jobber, settle **07** arrange, bargain, execute, handler, mediate **08** complete, conclude, organize **09** arbitrate, go-between, land agent, middleman, negotiate **10** negotiator **11** arbitrageur, stockbroker, stockjobber **12** intermediary

**bromide**
**06** cliché, downer, opiate, truism **07** anodyne **08** banality, narcotic, sedative **09** calmative, platitude **10** stereotype **11** barbiturate, commonplace **12** sleeping pill **13** tranquillizer

**bromine**
**02** Br

**bronze**
**02** br **03** tan **04** rust **05** brass **06** auburn, copper, Titian **07** aeneous, vermeil **08** chestnut **09** impudence **10** horseflesh **12** reddish-brown **14** copper-coloured

**bronzed**
**05** brown **06** bronze, tanned **07** browned **08** hardened, sunburnt **09** sunburned, suntanned

**brooch**
**03** pin **04** clip, ouch, prop **05** badge, broch, clasp **06** fibula, tiepin **08** lapel pin **09** breastpin

**brood**
**03** eye, nid, nye, sit **04** aery, clan, eyry, fret, kind, mope, muse, nest, nide, race, sulk, team **05** aerie, ayrie, breed, cleck, clock, cover, covey, eyrie, hatch, issue, spawn, sperm, tribe, young **06** chicks, clutch, family, go over, kindle, litter, ponder **07** agonize, dwell on, eelfare, progeny **08** children, clecking, incubate, meditate, mull over, rehearse, ruminate **09** bairn-team, bairn-time, fret about, household, offspring, parentage **10** extraction, worry about

**brook**
**04** bear, beck, burn, gill, kill, purl, rill **05** allow, creek, fleet, ghyll, inlet, stand **06** accept, branch, endure, permit, runnel, stream **07** abrooke, channel, rivulet, stomach, support **08** tolerate **09** put up with, withstand **11** countenance, watercourse

**broom**
**04** wisp **05** besom, scrub, spart **06** retama **07** cytisus, hag-weed **09** knee-holly, Turk's head **10** Jew's-myrtle **15** shepherd's myrtle

**broth**
◇ *anagram indicator*
**04** kail, kale, soup **05** ramen **06** brewis, cullis **08** bouillon, hotchpot **09** pot liquor **10** beef-brewis, hodgepodge, hotchpotch, muslin-kale

**brothel**
**03** kip **04** crib, stew **05** stews **06** bagnio, bordel **07** Corinth **08** bordello, cathouse, hothouse, red light **10** bawdy-house, flash-house, whorehouse **12** knocking-shop, leaping-house **13** sporting house, vaulting-house **14** house of ill fame, massage parlour **15** disorderly house

**brother**
**02** br **03** bro, fra, pal, sib **04** bhai, brer, chum, mate, monk, sibb **05** billy, buddy, frère, friar **06** billie, fellow, friend, german **07** comrade, partner, sibling **08** relation, relative **09** associate, colleague, companion **11** full brother, half-brother, twin-brother **12** blood-brother **13** brother-german
• **big brother**
**05** prior **08** dictator

**brotherhood**
**03** PRB **05** guild, union **06** clique, league **07** society **08** alliance, confrère **09** community, confrérie, Félibrige **10** fellowship, fraternity, friendship **11** association, cameraderie, comradeship, confederacy **12** fraternalism, friendliness **13** confederation, confraternity

**brotherly**
**04** kind **05** loyal **06** caring, loving **08** amicable, friendly **09** fraternal **10** benevolent **11** sympathetic **12** affectionate **13** philanthropic

**brow**
**03** tip, top **04** peak **05** brink, cliff, ridge, verge **06** summit **07** pit-head, temples **08** forehead

**browbeat**
**05** bully, force, hound **06** coerce, hector **07** dragoon, oppress **08** bulldoze, domineer, overbear, threaten **09** tyrannize **10** intimidate

**brown**
**02** br **03** fry **04** cook, fusc, seal **05** grill, singe, toast **06** tanned **07** bronzed, browned, embrown, fuscous **08** sunburnt **09** infuscate

*Browns include:*

**03** bay, dun, tan
**04** buff, drab, ecru, fawn, pine, rust, sand, teak
**05** beige, camel, cocoa, dusky, hazel, honey, khaki, mocha, ochre, rusty, sepia, taupe, tawny, tenné, umber
**06** auburn, bister, bistre, bronze, burnet, coffee, copper, ginger, russet, sorrel, walnut
**07** biscuit, caramel, chamois, filemot, oatmeal, oxblood
**08** brunette, chestnut, cinnamon, mahogany, mushroom, nut-brown, philamot, raw umber
**09** chocolate, earth-tone
**10** burnt umber, café au lait, terracotta
**11** burnt sienna, orange-tawny
**12** vandyke brown

**browned off**
**05** bored, fed up, weary **07** annoyed **09** hacked off, irritated, pissed off **10** bored stiff, brassed off, cheesed off, dispirited **11** discouraged, disgruntled, downhearted, exasperated **12** discontented, disheartened

**brownie**
**03** hob, nis **05** nisse

**browse**
**03** eat **04** feed, look, scan, skim, surf **05** graze **06** nibble, peruse, survey **07** dip into, pasture **09** quick read **11** leaf through **12** flick through, flick-through

**bruise**
◇ *anagram indicator*
**04** beat, hurt, mark, stun **05** break, clour, crush, frush, pound, spoil, upset, wound **06** damage, grieve, injure, injury, insult, intuse, lesion, offend, shiner **07** blacken, blemish, contuse, rainbow, surbate **08** black eye, to-bruise **09** contusion, discolour **10** ecchymosis **13** discoloration

**bruiser**
**04** thug **05** bully, rough, tough **07** hoodlum, ruffian **08** bully boy **09** bovver boy, roughneck **12** prize-fighter

**Brunei**
**03** BRN, BRU

**brunt**
**05** force, shock **06** burden, impact, strain, thrust, weight **07** impetus **08** pressure **09** main force **10** full weight

**brush**
**03** hog, rub **04** bush, dust, kiss, swab, wipe **05** besom, broom, clash, clean, clear, fight, fitch, flick, frith, graze, scrap, scrub, scuff, set-to, shine, sweep, touch, whisk **06** badger, bushes, caress, duster, dust-up, fracas, pallet, polish, putois, scrape, shrubs, stroke, tussle **07** burnish, contact, fox-tail, stipple, sweeper, thicket, tickler **08** argument, conflict, skirmish **09** brushwood, currycomb, encounter, pope's head, underwood **10** hair-pencil **11** ground cover, overgrainer, undergrowth **12** disagreement **13** confrontation
• **brush aside**
**05** flout **06** ignore **07** dismiss **08** belittle, override, pooh-pooh **09** disregard
• **brush off**
**04** snub **05** spurn **06** disown, ignore, rebuff, reject, slight **07** dismiss, repulse **09** disregard, repudiate **12** cold-shoulder
• **brush up**
**04** cram, swot, tidy **05** clean, study **06** go over, read up, revise, tidy up **07** improve, refresh, relearn **08** bone up on, polish up **09** freshen up **15** clean yourself up, refresh yourself

**brush-off**
**04** snub **06** rebuff, slight **07** kiss-off, refusal, repulse **09** dismissal, rejection **11** repudiation **12** cold shoulder **14** discouragement

**brushwood**
**03** hag **04** hagg, reis, rice **05** bavin, firth, frith, scrub **06** jungle **07** fascine **08** mattress, ovenwood **09** chaparral **10** underscrub

**brusque**
**04** curt **05** blunt, brief, gruff, sharp, short, surly, terse **06** abrupt **07** uncivil **08** impolite, tactless **09** downright **12** discourteous, undiplomatic

**brutal**
**05** cruel, frank, harsh, plain, tough **06** animal, coarse, savage, severe **07** beastly, bestial, boarish, brutish, callous, doggish, inhuman, ruffian, vicious, violent **08** inhumane, pitiless, ruthless **09** barbarous, ferocious, heartless, merciless, unfeeling, unsparing **10** Rottweiler **11** insensitive, iron-hearted, remorseless **12** bloodthirsty, down-and-dirty **15** straightforward

**brutality**
**07** cruelty **08** atrocity, ferocity, savagery, violence **09** barbarism, barbarity, callosity, roughness **10** coarseness, inhumanity **11** brutishness, callousness, viciousness **12** ruthlessness

**brutalize**
**03** hit **04** beat, flog **05** inure, pound **06** attack, batter, deaden, harden, thrash **07** assault, degrade **09** animalize **10** dehumanize **11** desensitize

**brutally**
**07** cruelly, frankly, harshly **08** savagely, severely **09** brutishly, callously, viciously **10** inhumanely, pitilessly, ruthlessly **11** barbarously, ferociously, heartlessly, mercilessly, unfeelingly **13** insensitively

**brute**
**04** bête, lout, ogre **05** beast, bully, crude, devil, fiend, gross, swine, yahoo **06** animal, bodily, carnal, coarse, sadist, savage, stupid **07** Caliban, fleshly, monster, ruffian, sensual **08** creature, depraved, mindless, physical **09** senseless **10** irrational, Rottweiler, unthinking **11** instinctive

**brutish**
**05** crass, crude, cruel, feral, gross **06** animal, brutal, coarse, ferine, savage, stupid, vulgar **07** bestial, loutish, uncouth **08** barbaric **09** barbarian, barbarous **11** uncivilized

**bubble**
**04** ball, bead, bell, bleb, boil, drop, fizz, foam, head, lock, seed, suds **05** fraud, froth, gloop, spume **06** bounce, burble, dimple, gurgle, lather, mantle, seethe, trifle, vanity, wallop **07** air-bell, air-lock, blister, blubber, droplet, fantasy, globule, sparkle, vesicle **08** be elated, be filled, blowhole, delusion, fleeting, illusion, rowndell **09** ball of air, be excited, deceptive, transient **10** depression, effervesce **13** effervescence, insubstantial

**bubbly**
◇ *anagram indicator*
**04** fizz **05** fizzy, happy, merry, sudsy **06** bouncy, elated, frothy, lively **07** excited, foaming **08** animated, champers **09** champagne, ebullient, exuberant, sparkling, vivacious **10** carbonated **12** effervescent

**buccaneer**
**06** pirate **07** corsair, sea wolf **08** sea rover **09** privateer, sea robber **10** filibuster, freebooter

**buck**
◇ *anagram indicator*
**03** bok **04** soar, sore **05** cheer, dandy, soare, sorel **06** buoy up, dollar, ignore, marker, oppose, resist, sorell, sorrel **07** counter, hearten, pricket **08** reassure **09** encourage **10** contradict **13** break the rules
**• buck up**
**05** cheer, gee up, hurry, rally **06** hasten, perk up **07** cheer up, enliven, hearten, hurry up, improve **08** inspirit, step on it **09** encourage, stimulate, take heart **10** get a move on **14** rattle your dags **15** get your skates on

**bucket**
**03** can, dip, tub **04** bail, bale, pail **05** ladle, stoop, stope, stoup **06** dipper, kibble, situla, stoope, vessel **07** pitcher, scuttle **09** clamshell
**• bucket down**
**04** pour **08** pelt down, pour down **11** rain heavily **15** rain cats and dogs
**• bucket chain**
**05** noria **12** Jacob's ladder

**buckle**
◇ *anagram indicator*
**04** bend, clip, fold, hasp, hook, kink, warp **05** bulge, catch, clasp, close, hitch, twist **06** cave in, fasten, secure **07** connect, crumple, distort, wrinkle **08** collapse, fastener **10** contortion, distortion
**• buckle down**
**08** go all out **11** get down to it, knuckle down **15** start to work hard

**buckler**
**05** pelta **06** target **08** rondache **09** protector **10** protection

**bucolic**
**05** rural **06** rustic **07** country **08** agrarian, pastoral **11** countrified **12** agricultural

**bud**
**03** eye, gem **04** bulb, germ, grow, knop, knot **05** caper, clove, gemma, knosp, shoot, sprig **06** bulbel, bulbil, button, embryo, friend, sprout, turion **07** brother, burgeon, cabbage, develop, plumule **09** débutante, pullulate **11** heart of palm, palm-cabbage **12** hibernaculum

**Buddhist**
**03** Zen **04** lama **05** bonze **08** talapoin **09** Dalai Lama
**• Buddhist dome**
**04** tope **05** stupa **06** dagaba, dagoba

**budding**
**07** growing, nascent **09** embryonic, fledgling, flowering, gemmation, germinant, incipient, potential, promising **10** burgeoning, developing **11** up-and-coming

**buddy**
**03** pal **04** chum, mate **05** crony **06** cobber, friend **07** brother, comrade **09** companion **10** buddy-buddy, good friend

**budge**
**03** jee **04** bend, give, move, push, roll, stir, sway **05** bodge, bouge, shift, slide, stiff, yield **06** change, give in, remove **07** give way, pompous **08** convince, dislodge, persuade **09** influence **13** not compromise **14** change your mind

**budget**
**04** plan **05** allot, allow, funds, means, quota **06** afford, bouget, bowget, ration **08** allocate, estimate, finances, schedule, set aside **09** allotment, allowance, apportion, economics, resources **10** allocation **13** financial plan

**buff**
**03** fan, rub, tan **04** blow, fawn **05** beige, brush, fiend, freak, khaki, maven, rub up, sandy, shine, straw **06** addict, expert, nankin, polish, smooth, stroke **07** admirer, burnish, devotee, fanatic, nankeen, natural **09** yellowish **10** aficionado, enthusiast **11** connoisseur **14** yellowish-brown
**• in the buff**
**04** bare, nude **05** naked **08** in the raw, starkers, stripped **09** unclothed, uncovered, undressed **10** stark-naked **12** not a stitch on **13** with nothing on **15** in the altogether

**buffalo**
**04** anoa, arna **05** bison, bugle **07** Bubalus, carabao, overawe, tamarao, tamarau, timarau, zamouse **08** bewilder, water cow

**buffer**
**03** pad **06** absorb, bumper, deaden, fender, lessen, pillow, reduce, screen, shield, soften **07** bulwark, cushion, protect **08** diminish, mitigate, polisher, suppress **12** intermediary **13** shock absorber

**buffet**
**03** box, hit, jar, tax **04** bang, beat, blow, buff, bump, café, cuff, harm, jolt, push, slap **05** clout, knock, pound, shove, smack, thump, weigh **06** batter, battle, blight, burden, pummel, strike **07** afflict, counter, disturb, oppress, trouble **08** cold meal, distress, snackbar **09** cafeteria, cold table, weigh down **11** self-service, smorgasbord **12** help yourself

**buffeted**
◇ *anagram indicator*

**buffoon**
**03** wag **04** fool, mime, mome, Vice, zany **05** antic, clown, comic, droll, joker **06** antick, jester, Scogan

07 anticke, antique, farceur, Scoggin, tomfool 08 comedian, farceuse, Iniquity 09 harlequin 10 mountebank, Scaramouch 11 Jack-pudding, merry-andrew, Punchinello, Scaramouche

**buffoonery**
05 farce 07 jesting, zanyism
08 clowning, drollery, nonsense
09 pantomime, silliness 10 tomfoolery
11 waggishness 12 harlequinade, pantaloonery 13 Pantagruelism

**bug**
03 fad, irk, tap, vex, wog 04 flaw, flea, germ, mite, snag 05 annoy, craze, error, fault, mania, thing, virus
06 bother, cootie, defect, harass, insect, needle, pester, wind up
07 blemish, disease, disturb, failing, gremlin, illness, microbe, monitor, wiretap 08 irritate, listen in, phone-tap
09 aggravate, bacterium, eavesdrop, infection, obsession 10 listen in on, listen in to 11 eavesdrop on 12 creepy-crawly, imperfection 13 micro-organism 15 listening device

**bugbear**
03 bug 04 bane, bogy 05 bogey, bogle, dread, fiend, poker 06 horror 07 pet hate, rawhead 08 anathema 09 bête noire, nightmare 10 Mumbo-jumbo

**bugle**
10 flügelhorn 11 hunting-horn

**bugle-call**
04 post, taps 07 hallali, retreat 08 last post, reveille 09 first post, lights out
15 boots and saddles

**build**
03 big, set 04 body, form, make, rear, size 05 begin, edify, erect, frame, mason, put up, raise, shape, start
06 extend, figure, timber 07 augment, develop, enlarge, fashion, upbuild
08 assemble, escalate, increase, initiate, physique, throw out
09 construct, fabricate, institute, intensify, overbuild, structure, substruct
10 constitute, inaugurate 11 put together 13 knock together

• **build up**
03 add 04 grow, hype, plug, rear
05 amass, boost, mount, set up
06 expand, extend, gather
07 aggrade, amplify, augment, collect, develop, enhance, enlarge, fortify, improve, mount up, promote
08 assemble, escalate, heighten, increase, snowball 09 advertise, construct, elaborate, establish, intensify, publicize, reinforce, structure
10 accumulate, strengthen 11 put together 13 piece together

**builder**
05 jerry, mason 06 waller 08 labourer
09 craftsman 11 craftswoman
12 craftsperson, manual worker
13 skilled worker

**building**
◇ *anagram indicator*
04 pile 07 edifice 08 dwelling, erection 09 structure 11 development, fabrication 12 architecture, construction

*See also* **architecture**

*Building types include:*

03 inn, pub
04 barn, café, fort, mews, mill, pier, shed, shop, silo
05 abbey, arena, cabin, hotel, house, store, villa
06 castle, chapel, church, cinema, garage, gazebo, mandir, mosque, museum, pagoda, palace, prison, school, stable, temple
07 chateau, college, cottage, factory, library, low-rise, mansion, theatre
08 barracks, beach hut, bungalow, dovecote, fortress, gurdwara, high-rise, hospital, monument, outhouse, pavilion, showroom, skilling, skillion, windmill
09 apartment, boathouse, cathedral, farmhouse, gymnasium, mausoleum, monastery, multiplex, synagogue, warehouse
10 lighthouse, maisonette, restaurant, skyscraper, sports hall, tower block, university
11 condominium, observatory, office block, public house, summerhouse
12 block of flats, power station
14 apartment house, sliver building

*See also* **accommodation**; **house**; **tent**

*Buildings include:*

05 Duomo
07 BT Tower, CN Tower, Kremlin, La Scala, St Paul's, UN Plaza
08 Casa Milà, Cenotaph, Chrysler, Flatiron, Pantheon, St Peter's, Taj Mahal
09 Acropolis, Coit Tower, Colosseum, Notre Dame, Old Bailey, Parthenon, Reichstag, St Pancras, Taipei 101, The Louvre, US Capitol
10 Guggenheim, Sears Tower, Tate Modern, The Gherkin, Trump Tower, Versailles, White House
11 Canary Wharf, Eden Project, Eiffel Tower, Empire State, Musée d'Orsay, Space Needle, The Alhambra, The Panthéon, The Pentagon, Tower Bridge, Tower of Pisa
12 Globe Theatre, Great Pyramid, Mont St Michel, Telecom Tower, The Parthenon, Winter Palace
13 Crystal Palace, Dome of the Rock, Musée du Louvre, Royal Crescent, Somerset House, Tower of London
14 Balmoral Castle, Barbican Centre, Blenheim Palace, Centre Pompidou, Hoover Building, Millennium Dome, Petronas Towers, Pompidou Centre, Sagrada Familia, UN Headquarters, Wells Cathedral
15 Ashmolean Museum, Banqueting House, Brandenburg Gate, Capitol Building, Edinburgh Castle, Lincoln Memorial, Post Office Tower, Royal Opera House, Statue of Liberty, Westminster Hall

*See also* **religious**; **tower**

*Building materials include:*

03 MDF
04 clay, sand, tile, wood
05 brick, glass, grout, slate, steel, stone
06 ashlar, cement, girder, gravel, gypsum, lintel, lumber, marble, mastic, mortar, pavior, siding, tarmac, thatch, timber
07 asphalt, bitumen, decking, drywall, fixings, granite, lagging, plaster, plastic, plywood, sarking, shingle
08 asbestos, cast iron, cladding, concrete, hard core, roof tile, wall tile
09 aggregate, aluminium, chipboard, clapboard, flagstone, floor tile, hardboard, sandstone, steel beam
10 glass fibre, insulation, matchboard
11 breeze block, paving stone, roofing felt
12 plasterboard
13 building block, wattle and daub
14 foam insulation, stainless steel

• **building area**
04 site

**build-up**
04 gain, heap, hype, load, mass, plug, puff 05 drift, stack, store 06 growth
08 increase 09 accretion, expansion, marketing, promotion, publicity, stockpile 10 escalation 11 advertising, development, enlargement
12 accumulation

**built**
◇ *anagram indicator*

**built-in**
05 fixed 06 fitted 07 in-built
08 implicit, included, inherent, integral
09 essential, intrinsic, necessary
11 fundamental, inseparable
12 incorporated

**bulb**
03 set 05 globe 11 Rupert's drop

*Plants grown from bulbs and corms include:*

04 cive, eddo, iris, ixia, lily, taro
05 camas, chive, onion, tulip
06 allium, camash, camass, chives, crinum, crocus, garlic, nerine, scilla, squill
07 anenome, jonquil, muscari, peacock, quamash
08 amarylis, bluebell, camassia, curtonis, cyclamen, daffodil, endymion, galtonia, gladioli, harebell, hyacinth, scallion, snowdrop, sparaxis
09 amaryllis, colchicum, crocosmia, galanthus, gladiolus, narcissus, snowflake, tiger lily
10 agapanthus, chionodoxa, fritillary, giant rouge, montbretia, ranunculus, snake's head, solfaterre, wand flower

**11** acidanthera, African lily, erythronium, fritillaria, hippeastrum, lapeirousia, naked ladies, spring onion, sternbergia, tiger flower
**12** autumn crocus, ornithogalum, Solomon's seal, wild hyacinth
**13** crown imperial, grape hyacinth, lily-of-the-Nile, striped squill, winter aconite
**14** belladonna lily, chincherinchee, glory of the snow, Ithuriel's spear
**15** dog's tooth violet, lily-of-the-valley

---

**bulbous**
**06** convex, puffed **07** bloated, bulging, rounded, swollen
**08** swelling, tuberous **09** distended, puffed out, pulvinate **10** pulvinated

**Bulgaria**
**02** BG **03** BGR **04** Bulg

**bulge**
**03** bag, bug, sag **04** bias, bulb, bump, hump, lump, rise **05** belly, pouch, strut, surge, swell **06** billow, dilate, expand, strout **07** blister, distend, enlarge, project, puff out, upsurge **08** increase, protrude, shoulder, swelling
**10** distension, projection
**12** protuberance **15** intensification

**bulk**
**04** body, bouk, feck, hold, hull, mass, most, size **05** cargo, great, gross
**06** extent, volume, weight **07** bigness
**08** majority, quantity, roughage
**09** amplitude, immensity, largeness, magnitude, nearly all, substance
**10** dimensions, lion's share
**13** preponderance
**• bulk out, bulk up**
**04** fill **06** expand, extend, fill up, pad out **07** fill out **08** increase **10** make bigger

**bulky**
**03** big **04** huge **05** ample, gross, heavy, hefty, large, lofty, lusty
**07** awkward, hulking, immense, lumping, mammoth, massive, volumed, weighty **08** colossal, enormous, unwieldy **10** cumbersome, voluminous **11** substantial
**12** unmanageable

**bull**
**02** ox **03** rot **04** brag, male, mick, neat
**05** micky **06** mickey, strong, Taurus
**07** massive **08** nonsense
**09** policeman **10** Unigenitus
**11** Hibernicism **12** Hibernianism

**bulldoze**
**04** push, raze **05** bully, clear, force, level **06** coerce **07** flatten
**08** browbeat, demolish **09** knock down **10** intimidate **11** push through, steamroller

**bullet**
**04** ball, shot, slug **06** dumdum, pellet
**07** missile **08** Biscayan **09** cartouche, cartridge, lead towel, Minié ball
**10** projectile, propellant

**bulletin**
**06** report, update **07** leaflet, message, release **08** dispatch **09** newsflash, newspaper, news sheet, statement
**10** communiqué, newsletter
**12** announcement, notification
**13** communication

**bullfight**
**07** corrida **10** tauromachy **14** corrida de toros

**bullfighter**
**07** matador, picador **08** matadore, toreador **10** rejoneador
**12** banderillero

**bullish**
**06** upbeat **07** buoyant, hopeful
**08** cheerful, positive, sanguine
**09** confident, obstinate **10** aggressive, optimistic

**bully**
◇ *anagram indicator*
**03** cow **04** good, haze, huff, prey, thug
**05** brave, bucko, great, heavy, tough, tyran **06** coerce, cuttle, hector, pick on, tyrant **07** bluster, bouncer, hoodlum, killcow, oppress, ruffian, torment **08** browbeat, bulldoze, bully-boy, bullyrag, domineer, overbear
**09** excellent, persecute, souteneur, terrorize, tormentor, tyrannize, victimize **10** blustering, browbeater, Drawcansir, intimidate, persecutor, push around **11** intimidator
**12** swashbuckler

**bulrush**
**04** tule **08** cat's-tail

**bulwark**
**04** wall **05** guard **06** buffer
**07** bastion, defence, outwork, rampart, redoubt, sea-wall, support
**08** buttress, mainstay, security
**09** partition, safeguard **10** breakwater, embankment, protection
**13** fortification

**bum**
◇ *anagram indicator*
**03** ass, bad, beg, dud, low **04** butt, coit, duff, hobo, hurl, loaf, naff, poor, rear, rump, seat, tail, toss **05** awful, booty, cadge, false, quoit, spree, tramp, wrong **06** behind, borrow, bottom, crummy, dosser, sponge **07** adverse, gangrel, rubbish, sponger, useless, vagrant **08** backside, beach boy, buttocks, scrounge, terrible, vagabond
**09** imperfect, worthless
**10** despicable, inadequate, unpleasant
**12** disagreeable, unacceptable
**14** unsatisfactory

**bumble**
◇ *anagram indicator*
**05** drone, idler, lurch **06** beadle, bungle, falter, teeter, totter **07** blunder, bungler, stagger, stumble

**bumbling**
◇ *anagram indicator*
**05** inept **06** clumsy **07** awkward, muddled **08** botching, bungling
**09** lumbering, maladroit, stumbling
**10** blundering **11** incompetent, inefficient

**bump**
**03** hit, jar **04** bang, blow, hump, jerk, jole, joll, jolt, jowl, knur, lump, slam, thud, whap, whop **05** barge, bulge, crash, dunch, dunsh, joule, knock, prang, shake, shock, shove, smash, thump **06** bounce, impact, injury, jostle, jounce, nodule, rattle, strike
**07** collide, papilla **08** dislodge, swelling **09** collision, speed bump
**10** protrusion, tumescence **11** collide with **12** irregularity, protuberance
**• bump into**
**04** meet **07** run into **09** encounter, light upon **10** chance upon, come across, happen upon **12** meet by chance
**• bump off**
**03** top **04** do in, kill **06** murder, remove, rub out **08** blow away
**09** eliminate, liquidate **11** assassinate

**bumper**
**03** big **04** rich **05** great, jumbo, kelty, large, rouse **06** keltie **07** bouncer, massive **08** abundant, enormous, whopping **09** excellent, ginormous, plentiful **11** exceptional
**12** supernaculum

**bumpkin**
**03** oaf, put, yap **04** boor, hick, lout, lowt, putt, rube **05** clown, yokel
**06** rustic **07** hawbuck, hayseed, peasant **08** clodpate, clodpole, clodpoll **09** hillbilly **10** clodhopper, provincial **11** bushwhacker **12** country yokel **14** country bumpkin

**bumptious**
**04** coxy **05** brash, cocky, pushy
**06** cocksy, uppish **07** forward, pompous **08** arrogant, boastful, impudent **09** assertive, conceited, egotistic, officious **10** swaggering
**11** overbearing **12** presumptuous
**13** over-confident, self-important
**14** full of yourself

**bumpy**
**05** jerky, lumpy, rough **06** bouncy, choppy, knobby, uneven **07** jolting, knobbly **08** pot-holed **09** irregular

**bun**
**03** wad **04** chou **05** brick **06** cookie
**07** Bath bun, huffkin, teacake **08** black bun, cream bun, crescent, cross bun, rock cake **09** burger bun **10** Chelsea bun, currant bun, Eccles cake **11** hot cross bun **12** mosbolletjie

**bunch**
**03** bob, lot, mob, wad **04** band, club, crew, gang, heap, herd, hump, lump, mass, pack, pile, posy, team, tuft, wisp
**05** batch, clump, crowd, flock, group, party, sheaf, spray, stack, swarm, troop
**06** bundle, gather, huddle, number, string **07** bouquet, cluster, collect, corsage, nosegay **08** assemble, boughpot, fascicle, quantity, swelling

**09** fascicule, gathering, multitude **10** assortment, châtelaine, collection, congregate, fasciculus, racemation **11** concentrate **12** tussie mussie **13** agglomeration

**bundle**

◇ *anagram indicator*

**03** bag, box, jag, kit, set, tie, wad, wap **04** bale, bind, drum, heap, mass, pack, pile, roll, rush, swag, wisp, wrap, yelm **05** batch, bavin, bluey, brawl, bunch, group, hurry, sheaf, shook, shove, skein, stack, truss, whisk **06** bottle, carton, faggot, fasces, fasten, gather, huddle, hustle, knitch, packet, parcel, tumble **07** cluster, dorlach, fascine, package **08** fascicle, quantity, shiralee, woolpack **09** fascicule, shirralee, trousseau **10** assortment, collection, fasciculus **11** consignment, push roughly **12** accumulation

**bung**

**03** pay, tip **04** cork, dead, dook, plug, seal **05** bribe, purse, shive **06** spigot **07** stopper, useless **08** bankrupt, cutpurse **10** pickpocket

**bungle**

◇ *anagram indicator*

**03** mar **04** boob, duff, flub, goof, mash, mess, muff, mull, ruin **05** blunk, bodge, botch, fluff, fudge, spoil **06** bobble, boggle, bumble, bummle, cock up, foozle, foul up, goof up, mangle, mess up, muck up, muddle **07** bauchle, blunder, louse up, screw up **09** misguggle, mishandle, mismanage **10** mishguggle **11** make a mess of

**bungler**

**04** muff **05** blunk **06** bumble, bummle, duffer, tinker **07** blunker, botcher, bumbler **08** shlemiel **09** blunderer, schlemiel, schlemihl **11** incompetent **13** butterfingers

**bungling**

**05** inept, messy **06** clumsy **07** awkward **08** botching **09** ham-fisted, ham-handed, maladroit, unskilful **10** amateurish, blundering, cack-handed **11** incompetent

**bunk**

**04** flee **05** berth, sleep **06** humbug **08** claptrap

**bunker**

**03** bin **04** fuel, trap **06** hazard **07** shelter **08** sand trap

**bunkum**

**02** BS **03** rot **04** blah, bosh, bull, bunk **05** balls, bilge, hooey, trash, tripe **06** humbug, piffle **07** baloney, garbage, hogwash, rubbish, twaddle **08** blah-blah, bulldust, claptrap, cobblers, malarkey, nonsense, tommyrot **09** poppycock **10** balderdash, codswallop **12** blah-blah-blah **13** horsefeathers

**bunting**

**04** cirl **05** flags, junco **07** ortolan **08** longspur **09** snowflake, snowfleck, snowflick **10** dickcissel **11** decorations, reed-sparrow, yellow-ammer **12** yellowhammer **13** writing-master

**buoy**

**03** dan **04** rise **05** float **06** beacon, marker, signal **07** dolphin, mooring

**• buoy up**

**04** lift **05** boost, cheer, raise **06** bear up **07** cheer up, hearten, support, sustain **09** encourage

**buoyancy**

**03** joy, pep **06** bounce, growth, vigour **07** flotage **08** floatage, gladness, optimism, strength **09** geniality, happiness, jolliness, lightness, toughness **10** brightness, confidence, enthusiasm, resilience **11** development, good spirits **12** cheerfulness, floatability

**buoyant**

**05** happy, hardy, light, peppy, tough **06** afloat, blithe, bouncy, bright, joyful, lively, strong **07** bullish, growing **08** animated, carefree, cheerful, debonair, floating, thriving, youthful **09** adaptable, floatable, resilient, vivacious **10** developing, optimistic, weightless **12** light-hearted

**burble**

**03** lap **04** purl **06** babble, gurgle, murmur, tangle **07** confuse

**burden**

**03** bob, tax **04** bear, care, cark, duty, lade, load, onus, task, tote, yoke **05** beare, cargo, cross, crush, drone, trial, worry **06** bother, charge, fading, impose, lumber, monkey, saddle, sorrow, strain, stress, weight **07** anxiety, burthen, holding, oppress, present, refrain, trouble **08** carriage, encumber, handicap, incumber, land with, overbulk, overload, pressure **09** agistment, cumbrance, grievance, lie hard on, millstone, overpress, overwhelm, undersong, weigh down **10** affliction, dead-weight, imposition, lie heavy on, obligation, overburden, overextend, overstress **11** encumbrance **14** responsibility

**burdensome**

**05** heavy **06** taxing, trying **07** irksome, onerous, weighty **08** crushing, exacting, grievous **09** chargeful, difficult, importune, wearisome **10** chargeable, oppressive **11** importunate, troublesome

**burdock**

**04** gobo **05** clote **07** clotbur, hardoke **08** clotebur **09** cocklebur

**bureau**

**04** desk **06** agency, branch, office **07** counter, service **08** division **10** department **11** writing-desk

**bureaucracy**

**07** red tape **08** city hall, ministry **09** beadledom, paperwork, the system **10** government **11** officialdom **12** civil service **13** officiousness **14** administration, the authorities

**bureaucrat**

**04** suit **07** officer **08** Eurocrat, mandarin, minister, official **09** chinovnik **11** apparatchik, functionary **12** civil servant, office-holder **13** administrator **15** committee member

**bureaucratic**

**05** rigid **08** official **10** inflexible, procedural **11** complicated, ministerial **12** governmental **14** administrative

**burgeon**

**04** grow **05** swell **06** expand, extend **07** develop, enlarge **08** escalate, increase, snowball **11** proliferate

**burglar**

**04** yegg **05** thief **06** robber **07** yeggman **08** pilferer **09** cracksman **10** cat-burglar, trespasser **12** housebreaker

**burglary**

**05** heist, theft **07** break-in, larceny, robbery **08** stealing, trespass **09** pilferage **13** housebreaking

**burgle**

**03** rob **05** screw **09** break into, burst into, steal from **10** burglarize

**burial**

**07** burying, funeral **08** exequies **09** committal, interment, obsequies, sepulchre **10** entombment, inhumation

**burial place**

**05** crypt, grave, vault **06** kurgan **07** charnel, tumulus **08** catacomb, cemetery, God's acre, Golgotha, Pantheon **09** graveyard, mausoleum, sepulcher, sepulchre **10** churchyard, necropolis **12** potter's field

*See also* **cemetery**

**Burkina Faso**

**02** BF **03** BFA

**burlesque**

**04** mock **05** comic, spoof **06** parody, satire, send-up **07** mockery, mocking, take-off **08** derisive, farcical, ridicule, travesty **09** parodying, satirical **10** caricature, heroi-comic **11** caricatural, hudibrastic **12** heroi-comical, mickey-taking **13** Pantagruelism

**burly**

**03** big **05** beefy, heavy, hefty **06** brawny, knotty, stocky, strong, sturdy **07** buirdly, hulking **08** athletic, muscular, powerful, thickset **09** strapping, well-built

**burn**

**03** fry, gut **04** bite, bren, char, fume, glow, hurt, itch, long, plot, sear, sere **05** blaze, brand, brook, cense, chark, flame, flare, flash, grill, inure, light, parch, ploat, scald, singe, smart, smoke, sting, swale, swayl, sweal, sweel, toast, yearn **06** brenne, desire, emboil, ignite, kindle, scorch, seethe, simmer, stream, tingle **07** be eager, combust, consume, corrode, cremate, destroy, flare up, flicker, glimmer, inflame, scowder, shrivel **08** be ablaze, be on fire, burn down, scouther, scowther, smoulder **09** catch fire, cauterize, incremate, set alight, set fire to **10** be in flames, deflagrate, incinerate **11** catch ablaze, conflagrate, go up in smoke, put a match to **12** be consumed by, go up in flames **13** put to the torch **15** burst into flames

## burning

**02** in **03** hot, lit **04** live, sear **05** acrid, acute, afire, eager, fiery, quick, seare, urent, vital **06** ablaze, aflame, alight, ardent, biting, cauter, fervid, urgent, ustion **07** blazing, caustic, cautery, crucial, earnest, fervent, flaming, frantic, glowing, intense, pungent, searing **08** flagrant, flashing, frenzied, gleaming, piercing, pressing, scalding, smarting, stinging, swealing, tingling, vehement **09** consuming, essential, important, inburning, prickling, scorching **10** passionate **11** conflagrant, illuminated, impassioned, significant, smouldering **12** incendiarism **13** conflagration

## burnish

**04** buff **05** glaze, shine **06** lustre, polish **08** brighten, polish up

## burp

**04** wind **05** belch **08** eructate **10** eructation **11** bring up wind

## burrow

**03** den, dig, set **04** bury, hole, howk, lair, mine, root, sett **05** delve, earth, wroot **06** gopher, nuzzle, search, tunnel, warren **07** retreat, rummage, shelter **08** excavate, fox-earth **09** undermine **10** rabbit hole

## bursar

**06** purser **07** cashier **09** treasurer

## bursary

**05** award, grant **09** endowment **10** exhibition, fellowship **11** scholarship

## burst

◇ *anagram indicator*

**03** fit, fly, pop, run **04** bang, blow, clap, dart, gush, gust, loup, part, race, rush, tear **05** barge, blaze, blitz, brash, break, crack, erupt, flash, go off, go pop, hurry, plump, salvo, spate, split, spout, spurt, start, surge **06** blow up, bounce, go bang, shiver, spring, volley **07** blow-out, dehisce, disrupt, explode, rupture, shatter, torrent **08** distrain, fragment, outbreak, outburst, puncture **09** break in on, break open, discharge, fusillade, pull apart, split open **10** outpouring **11** push your way **12** disintegrate

### • burst out

**03** cry **04** buff **05** begin, flash, start, utter **06** cry out, irrupt **07** call out, exclaim, explode **08** blurt out, commence **10** break forth

## Burundi

**02** RU **03** BDI

## bury

◇ *containment indicator*

**04** eard, hide, sink, tomb, yerd, yird **05** cover, earth, embed, grave, inter, plant, yeard **06** absorb, burrow, engage, engulf, entomb, inhume, occupy, shroud **07** conceal, enclose, engross, immerse, implant, inearth, inherce **08** enshroud, inhearse, submerge **09** lay to rest, sepulchre **15** put six feet under

## bus

**03** ISA, PCI, USB **05** coach, trunk **06** jitney, pirate **09** two-decker, vaporetto **10** mammy-wagon, service car **11** park-and-ride **12** double-decker, single-decker

## bush

**03** tod **05** brush, crude, hedge, plant, scrog, scrub, shrub, todde, wilds **06** busket, tavern **07** bramble, outback, thicket **09** backwoods, makeshift, primitive, scrubland **11** uncivilized **13** rough and ready

### • not beat about the bush

**11** speak openly **12** speak plainly **14** come to the point, commit yourself

## bushbaby

**06** galago **07** nagapie **08** night-ape

## bushel

**02** bu **03** fou

## bushranger

**06** outlaw **07** brigand **10** highwayman **12** backwoodsman

*Bushrangers include:*

**04** **Cash** (Martin), **Hall** (Ben), **Howe** (Michael)
**05** **Brady** (Matthew), **Kelly** (Ned)
**06** **Caesar** (John 'Black Caesar'), **Morgan** (Dan 'Mad Dog'), **Palmer** (George)
**07** **Donohoe** (Jack), **Gilbert** (Johnny)
**08** **Flash Dan** (Daniel Charters), **Gardiner** (Frank), **Governor** (Jimmy), **Governor** (Joe), **Melville** (Frank McCallum, 'Captain'), **Moonlite** (Andrew Scott, 'Captain')
**09** **Armstrong** (George), **Starlight** (Frank Pearson, 'Captain')
**11** **Thunderbolt** (Frederick Ward, 'Captain')
**12** **Jackey Jackey** (William Westwood)

## bushy

**04** wiry **05** bosky, fuzzy, rough, stiff, thick, woody **06** dumose, dumous, fluffy, shaggy, unruly **07** bristly **09** bristling, luxuriant, spreading **12** dasyphyllous

## busily

**04** hard **07** briskly **08** actively, speedily **09** earnestly **10** diligently **11** assiduously, strenuously **12** purposefully **13** energetically, industriously

## business

**02** co **03** biz, bus, job **04** baby, deal, duty, firm, gear, line, task, work **05** issue, point, topic, trade **06** affair, buying, career, matter, métier, outfit, pigeon **07** calling, company, concern, problem, selling, subject, trading, venture **08** commerce, dealings, flagship, industry, question, vocation **09** franchise, operation, syndicate **10** bargaining, consortium, employment, enterprise, occupation, profession **11** corporation, partnership **12** conglomerate, organization, transactions **13** establishment, manufacturing, merchandizing, multinational, parent company **14** holding company, responsibility

*Businesses include:*

**02** BA, BP
**03** BAA, BAE, BAT, BHS, BMW, BSB, EMI, HMV, IBM, ICI, MFI, NCP, NEC, RAC, RBS
**04** Asda, BASF, Esso, Fiat, HBOS, HSBC, Rank, Sony
**05** Abbey, Alcan, Bayer, Boots, Canon, Corus, Enron, Exxon, Heinz, Honda, Intel, Mazda, Nokia, Ricoh, Sharp, Shell, Tesco, Volvo
**06** Adecco, Arriva, Boeing, Diageo, Dixons, Du Pont, Hanson, L'Oreal, Nestlé, Nissan, Pfizer, Suzuki, Texaco, Toyota, Virgin, Wimpey
**07** Alcatel, Arcadia, Aventis, Chevron, EasyJet, Fujitsu, Harrods, Hitachi, Hyundai, Lafarge, Marconi, Matalan, Minerva, Pearson, Pepsico, Peugeot, Renault, Reuters, Samsung, Siemens, Toshiba, Wal-Mart, W H Smith
**08** AXA Group, Barclays, Burberry, Centrica, Chrysler, Coca-Cola, Goodyear, JP Morgan, Michelin, Olivetti, Rentokil, Rio Tinto, Unilever, Vodafone, Waitrose
**09** Akzo Nobel, John Laing, Ladbrokes, Lloyds TSB, McDonald's, Microsoft, Morrisons, Schroders, Whitbread
**10** Exxon Mobil, Greene King, J Sainsbury, Kingfisher, Mitsubishi, Nationwide, Pilkington, Prudential, Rolls-Royce, Sainsbury's, Somerfield, Stagecoach, Telefonica, Volkswagen, Walt Disney, Woolworths
**11** AstraZeneca, Caterpillar, Isuzu Motors, Nippon Steel, Standard Oil, William Hill
**12** Allied Domecq, Eastman Kodak, Hilton Hotels, Merrill Lynch, Northern Rock, Philip Morris, Philips Group, Reed Elsevier, Sears Roebuck, Total Fina Elf, Union Carbide, Union Pacific, Western Union
**13** Abbey National, Anglo American, Balfour Beatty, General Motors, Harvey Nichols, Lever Brothers, Sanyo Electric, Taylor Woodrow, Travis Perkins
**14** Alfred McAlpine, British Airways, Credit Agricole, Hewlett-Packard, Virgin Atlantic

**15** American Express, DaimlerChrysler, Deutsche Telekom, Electrolux Group, General Electric, GlaxoSmithKline, Legal and General, Marks and Spencer, National Express, News Corporation

- **business centre**

**04** city

- **do business**

**04** deal, sell

- **go out of business**

**04** fold

**businesslike**

**05** slick **06** formal **07** correct, orderly, precise **08** thorough **09** efficient, organized, practical, pragmatic
**10** impersonal, methodical, systematic
**11** painstaking, well-ordered
**12** matter-of-fact, professional

**businessman, businesswoman**

**06** trader, tycoon, wallah **07** Babbitt, magnate **08** city gent, employer, merchant **09** boxwallah, executive, financier **10** capitalist **12** entrepreneur, manufacturer **13** industrialist

*Businesspeople include:*

**04** **Benz** (Karl Friedrich), **Bond** (Alan), **Boot** (Sir Jesse), **Cook** (Thomas), **Ford** (Henry), **Jobs** (Steven), **Mond** (Ludwig), **Shah** (Eddy), **Tate** (Sir Henry), **Wang** (An)
**05** **Arden** (Elizabeth), **Astor** (John, Lord), **Bosch** (Carl), **Fayed** (Mohamed al-), **Forte** (Charles, Lord), **Gates** (Bill), **Getty** (Jean Paul), **Grade** (Michael), **Heinz** (Henry John), **Honda** (Soichiro), **Krupp** (Friedrich), **Laker** (Sir Freddie), **Leahy** (Sir Terry), **Lyons** (Sir Joseph), **Marks** (Simon, Lord), **Nobel** (Alfred), **Rolls** (Charles), **Royce** (Sir Henry), **Sugar** (Sir Alan), **Trump** (Donald), **Zeiss** (Carl)
**06** **Ansett** (Sir Reg), **Boeing** (William Edward), **Browne** (John, Lord), **Butlin** (Billy), **Conran** (Sir Terence), **Cunard** (Sir Samuel), **Dunlop** (John Boyd), **du Pont** (Pierre Samuel), **Fugger** (Johannes), **Gamble** (Josias), **Hammer** (Armand), **Hilton** (Conrad Nicholson), **Hoover** (William Henry), **Hughes** (Howard), **Mellon** (Andrew William), **Morgan** (J Pierpont), **Packer** (Kerry), **Turner** (Ted)
**07** **Agnelli** (Giovanni), **Barclay** (Robert), **Branson** (Sir Richard), **Bugatti** (Ettore), **Cadbury** (George), **Cadbury** (John), **Citroën** (André Gustave), **Iacocca** (Lee), **Kennedy** (Joseph P), **Maxwell** (Robert), **Murdoch** (Rupert), **Onassis** (Aristotle), **Roddick** (Anita), **Sotheby** (John), **Tiffany** (Charles Lewis)
**08** **Birdseye** (Clarence), **Carnegie** (Andrew), **Christie** (James), **Gillette** (King Camp), **Guinness** (Sir Benjamin Lee), **Michelin** (André), **Nuffield** (William Richard Morris, Viscount), **Olivetti** (Adriano), **Pulitzer** (Joseph), **Rathenau** (Walther), **Rowntree** (Joseph), **Sinclair** (Sir Clive)
**09** **Arkwright** (Sir Richard), **Carothers** (Wallace), **Firestone** (Harvey Samuel), **Sainsbury** (Alan John, Lord), **Selfridge** (Harry Gordon), **Woolworth** (Frank Winfield)
**10** **Berlusconi** (Silvio), **Guggenheim** (Meyer), **Leverhulme** (William Hesketh Lever, Viscount), **Pilkington** (Sir Alastair), **Rothschild** (Meyer Amschel), **Vanderbilt** (Cornelius)
**11** **Beaverbrook** (Max, Lord), **Harvey-Jones** (Sir John), **Rockefeller** (John D)

**busker**

**14** street-musician

**bust**

◇ *anagram indicator*
**04** duff, head, herm, phut, raid, term **05** boobs, bosom, break, chest, crack, herma, kaput, punch, smash, spree, torso, wonky **06** arrest, breast, broken, damage, demote, faulty, ruined, statue
**07** breasts, destroy, shatter
**08** terminus **09** defective, penniless, sculpture **10** on the blink, on the fritz, out of order **11** out of action

- **go bust**

**04** fail, flop, fold **05** crash **06** go bung **07** founder **08** collapse **09** close down **11** go to the wall **14** become bankrupt **15** become insolvent

**bustle**

◇ *anagram indicator*
**03** ado **04** belt, buzz, dash, fuss, rush, stir, tear, to-do, trot, whew **05** haste, hurry **06** bestir, bumble, bummle, flurry, hasten, pother, ruffle, rustle, scurry, tumult **07** fluster, scamper, the rush **08** activity, rush hour, scramble, to and fro, tournure **09** agitation, commotion, stirabout **10** excitement, hurly-burly **11** hurry-scurry, hurry-skurry **12** rush to and fro **13** dress-improver **15** a hive of activity, hustle and bustle

**bustling**

◇ *anagram indicator*
**04** busy, full **05** astir **06** active, hectic, lively **07** abustle, buzzing, crowded, humming, rushing, teeming
**08** eventful, restless, stirring, swarming, thronged **09** energetic, on the trot

**busy**

◇ *anagram indicator*
**04** at it, full **05** manic **06** absorb, active, bustle, eident, embusy, employ, engage, hectic, lively, occupy, red-hot, throng, tied up, tiring **07** concern, crowded, engaged, engross, frantic, go about, immerse, involve, on the go, teeming, vibrant, working **08** bustling, diligent, employed, eventful, hard at it, interest, involved, meddling, occupied, on the job, restless, sedulous, swarming, tireless **09** assiduous, detective, energetic, engrossed, on the trot, stirabout, strenuous **10** busy as a bee **11** industrious, snowed under, unavailable **12** having a lot on, in conference **13** under pressure **14** fully stretched, having a lot to do, in the thick of it

- **be busy**

**03** hum

**busybody**

**03** pry **05** snoop **06** gossip
**07** meddler, snooper **08** intruder, quidnunc **09** pragmatic **10** interferer
**11** Nosey Parker **12** eavesdropper, troublemaker **13** mischief-maker, scandalmonger **14** pantopragmatic

**but**

**03** bar, nay, sed **04** just, only, save
**06** anyway, at most, even so, except, merely, purely, simply **07** barring, besides, however **08** omitting
**09** apart from, aside from, excepting, excluding, objection, other than **10** all the same, for all that, leaving out, no more than **11** just the same, nonetheless **12** nevertheless
**15** notwithstanding

- **all but**

**04** near **06** almost

**butch**

**04** male **05** macho, tough **06** virile
**07** manlike, mannish **09** masculine

**butcher**

◇ *anagram indicator*
**04** kill, slay **05** botch, spoil **06** killer, slayer **07** destroy, flesher **08** massacre, murderer, mutilate **09** destroyer, liquidate, slaughter **10** meat trader
**11** assassinate, exterminate, meat counter, slaughterer, supermarket
**12** mass murderer, meat retailer

**butchery**

**06** murder **07** carnage, killing
**08** abattoir, butcher's, massacre, shambles **09** bloodshed, meat trade, slaughter **10** mass murder **11** meat-selling **12** blood-letting **13** meat retailing **14** slaughterhouse **15** mass destruction

**butler**

**03** RAB **08** khansama **09** khansamah, sommelier **12** bread-chipper

**butt**

**03** box, bum, but, end, hit, jab, keg, nip, nut, ram, tip, tun **04** base, bump, bunt, cask, dout, dupe, foot, haft, horn, mark, pipe, poke, prod, push, stub
**05** dunch, dunsh, knock, punch, roach, shaft, shove, snipe, stock, stump
**06** barrel, bottom, buffet, bumper, dog-end, fag end, firkin, handle, object, stooge, target, thrust, tierce, victim **07** butt end, remnant, rundlet, subject, tail end **08** buttocks, hogshead **09** posterior, scapegoat
**10** table-sport **12** jesting-stock
**13** laughing-stock

**• butt in**
**05** cut in **06** horn in, meddle **07** break in, intrude **09** interfere, interject, interpose, interrupt **12** put your oar in **15** stick your nose in

**butter**
**03** ghi, ram **04** drop, ghee, goat **06** beurre **08** flattery

**• butter producer**
**04** mowa, shea **05** mahua, mahwa, mowra

**• butter up**
**04** coax **06** cajole, kowtow, praise **07** blarney, flatter, wheedle **08** kowtow to, pander to, soft-soap, suck up to **14** be obsequious to

**buttercup**
**06** gilcup **07** giltcup, kingcup **08** crowfoot **10** goldilocks, ranunculus

**butterfingers**
**04** muff

**butterfly**
**05** light **07** flighty **10** dilettante
*See also* **animal**; **insect**; **moth**

*Butterflies include:*

**03** map
**04** blue, wall
**05** argus, comma, elfin, heath, satyr, white
**06** apollo, copper, hermit, morpho, pierid, psyche
**07** admiral, cabbage, monarch, Papilio, peacock, ringlet, satyrid, skipper, thistle, Ulysses, vanessa
**08** birdwing, cardinal, grayling, hesperid, milk-weed
**09** brimstone, cleopatra, Hesperian, holly-blue, nymphalid, orange-tip, wall brown, wood white
**10** brown argus, common blue, fritillary, gatekeeper, hairstreak, red admiral
**11** large copper, meadow-brown, painted lady, Scotch argus, swallowtail
**12** cabbage-white, dingy skipper, Essex skipper, marbled-white, white admiral
**13** chalkhill blue, clouded yellow, mourning cloak, purple emperor, tortoiseshell
**15** black hairstreak, brown hairstreak, green hairstreak, grizzled skipper, heath fritillary, Lulworth skipper, marsh fritillary, mountain ringlet

**buttocks**
**03** ass, bum, can, fud **04** buns, butt, coit, doup, duff, prat, rear, rump, seat, tail, tush **05** booty, fanny, nates, pratt, quoit, tushy **06** behind, bottom, breech, cheeks, heinie, tushie **07** crouper, croupon, gluteus, hurdies, keister, sit-upon **08** backside, derrière, haunches **09** fundament, hinder-end, posterior **10** hinderlans, hinderlins **11** hinderlands, hinderlings **12** hindquarters
*See also* **bottom**

**button**
**04** disc, frog, knob, link, stud **05** catch, clasp, lever **06** barrel, olivet, switch, toggle **08** bell push, fastener **09** fastening

**buttonhole**
**03** nab **04** grab **05** catch **06** accost, collar, corner, detain, waylay **09** importune, take aside **11** boutonnière

**buttress**
**04** pier, prop, stay **05** brace, shore, strut **06** back up, hold up, prop up **07** shore up, support, sustain, tambour **08** abutment, mainstay, underpin **09** bolster up, reinforce, stanchion **10** strengthen **11** counterfort **13** reinforcement

**buxom**
**05** ample, busty, jolly, plump, sonsy **06** bosomy, chesty, comely, lively, sonsie, zaftig **07** bucksom, elastic **08** yielding **09** Junoesque, pneumatic **10** Rubenesque, voluptuous **11** full-figured, well-endowed, well-rounded, well-stacked **12** full-breasted **13** large-breasted

**buy**
**03** fix, get, job **04** chop, coff, deal, take **05** bribe, hedge, scalp, trade **06** buy off, market, nobble, obtain, pay for, pick up, redeem, snap up, suborn **07** acquire, bargain, emption, engross, overbuy, procure, shop for **08** invest in, panic-buy, purchase, underbuy **09** speculate, stock up on, subsidize **10** go shopping, shop around **11** acquisition, merchandize, splash out on **13** do the shopping

**buyer**
**06** broker, client, dealer, emptor, patron, vendee **07** shopper **08** consumer, customer **09** purchaser

**buzz**
**03** fad, hum **04** call, high, kick, purr, race, ring, zing **05** craze, drone, kicks, pulse, throb, throw, whirr **06** bustle, gossip, latest, murmur, rumour, thrill **07** buzzing, hearsay, resound, scandal **08** resonate, susurrus, tinnitus **09** bombilate, bombinate, phone call, susurrate **10** enthusiasm, excitement **11** bombilation, bombination, reverberate, stimulation, susurration **15** word on the street

**buzzard**
**04** pern **05** buteo **07** bee-kite, puttock **08** zopilote **09** gallinazo

**buzzer**
**03** bee **08** telltale **09** whisperer

**by**
◇ *juxtaposition indicator*
**01** X **02** at, in, of, on **03** gin, per, via **04** away, near, over, past, with **05** along, aside, close, forby, handy, times, using **06** at hand, before, beside, beyond, next to **07** close by, close to, through **09** alongside, by means of **11** according to, no later than **12** in relation to **15** under the aegis of

**bygone**
**04** lost, past **05** olden **06** former **07** ancient, antique, one-time **08** departed, forepast, previous **09** erstwhile, forgotten **10** antiquated, dinosauric

**bypass**
**04** CABG, omit **05** avoid, dodge, evade, shunt, skirt **06** detour, ignore **07** neglect **08** ring road, sidestep, slip road **09** diversion, sidetrack **10** circumvent **12** steer clear of **13** find a way round

**by-product**
**06** result **07** fallout, spin-off **10** derivative, entailment, side effect **11** after-effect, concomitant, consequence **12** repercussion **13** epiphenomenon, knock-on effect

**bystander**
**07** watcher, witness **08** looker-on, observer, onlooker, passer-by, talesman **09** spectator **10** eyewitness, rubberneck

**byword**
**03** saw **05** adage, ideal, maxim, model, motto **06** ayword, dictum, saying, slogan **07** epitome, example, nayword, paragon, precept, proverb **08** aphorism, exemplar, overcome, standard **09** catchword, watchword **10** apophthegm, embodiment **14** perfect example

**Byzantine**
◇ *anagram indicator*
**06** knotty **07** complex **08** tortuous **09** intricate **11** complicated **12** labyrinthine

# C

**C**
**03** cee, san, see **07** Charlie

**cab**
**04** taxi **05** cabin, noddy **06** drosky, fiacre, hansom **07** droshky, growler, minicab, taxicab, vettura **08** quarters **10** two-wheeler **11** compartment, four-wheeler **15** hackney carriage

**cabal**
**03** set **04** plot **05** junta, junto, party **06** clique, league **07** coterie, faction **08** conclave, intrigue, plotters **09** camarilla, coalition

**cabaret**
**04** acts, club, show **05** turns **06** comedy **07** dancing, singing, variety **09** night club **10** restaurant **11** performance **13** entertainment

**cabbage**
**04** chou, cole, gobi, kail, kale, wort **05** savoy, steal **06** greens **07** bok choy, castock, custock, pak choi, purloin **08** colewort, drumhead, kohlrabi **09** banknotes **10** choucroute, greenstuff, paper money, sauerkraut **11** cauliflower, sea colewort **13** Chinese leaves **14** Brussels sprout

**cabbage-head**
**04** loaf

**cabin**
**03** hut **04** room, shed **05** berth, bothy, coach, cuddy, lodge, shack **06** cabana, chalet, refuge, saloon, shanty **07** cottage, gondola, shelter **08** log-house, quarters **09** signal box, stateroom **10** roundhouse **11** compartment

**cabinet**
**04** case **05** bahut, chest, filer, store **06** closet, locker, senate, shrine **07** almirah, console, dresser **08** cupboard, vargueño **09** executive, ministers **10** chiffonier, encoignure, government, leadership, secretaire **11** chiffonnier **12** Privy Council **14** administration, official family

**cable**
**03** fax, guy **04** co-ax, cord, flex, lead, line, rope, stay, wire **05** chain, e-mail, radio **06** feeder, halser, hawser **07** coaxial **08** telegram, transmit **09** facsimile, send a wire, telegraph **11** Telemessage® **13** send a telegram **15** send by telegraph

**cache**
**04** fund, hide **05** hoard, stash, stock, store **06** garner, supply **07** reserve **09** stockpile **10** collection, repository, storehouse **12** accumulation **13** treasure-store **14** hidden treasure

**cachet**
**06** esteem, favour, status **08** approval, eminence, prestige **10** estimation, reputation, street cred **11** distinction

**cack-handed**
**05** gawky, inept **06** clumsy **07** awkward **08** bungling **09** all thumbs, ham-fisted, unskilful **10** blundering, left-handed, ungraceful **11** heavy-handed **13** unco-ordinated

**cackle**
**04** crow **05** clack **06** gabble, gaggle, giggle, keckle, titter **07** chortle, chuckle, snigger **09** loud laugh **11** laugh loudly **15** unpleasant laugh

**cacophonous**
**04** loud **05** harsh **07** grating, jarring, raucous **08** strident **09** dissonant **10** discordant **11** horrisonant **12** inharmonious

**cacophony**
**03** din **06** racket **07** discord, jarring **09** charivari, harshness, stridency **10** disharmony, dissonance **11** raucousness **12** caterwauling

**cactus**

*Cacti include:*

**04** crab, toad, tuna
**05** dildo, nopal
**06** barrel, cereus, cholla, Easter, mescal, old man, orchid, peanut, peyote
**07** jointed, old lady, opuntia, rainbow, saguaro
**08** dumpling, gold lace, hedgehog, rat's tail, snowball, starfish, Turk's cap
**09** bunny ears, Christmas, goat's horn, gold charm, Indian fig, mistletoe, sea-urchin
**10** cotton-pole, sand dollar, silver ball, strawberry, zygocactus
**11** grizzly bear, mammillaria, prickly pear, scarlet ball, silver torch
**12** golden barrel
**13** Bristol beauty, schlumbergera
**14** drunkard's dream
**15** queen of the night, snowball cushion

**cad**
**03** oik, rat **04** heel **05** devil, knave, rogue, swine **06** rascal, rotter, wretch **07** bleeder, bounder, scumbag, stinker, villain **08** blighter, deceiver **09** miscreant, reprobate, scoundrel **10** blackguard

**cadaver**
**04** body **05** stiff **06** corpse **07** carcase, remains **08** dead body

**cadaverous**
**03** wan **04** pale, thin **05** ashen, gaunt **07** ghostly, haggard **08** skeletal **09** death-like, emaciated **10** corpse-like

**caddy**
**05** chest

**cadence**
**04** beat, fall, lilt, rate **05** close, metre, pulse, swing, tempo, throb, trope **06** accent, euouae, evovae, rhythm, stress **07** falling, measure, pattern, sinking **09** half-close **10** inflection, intonation, modulation

**cadge**
**03** beg, bot, bum **05** mooch, mouch, ponce **06** sponge **08** scrounge

**cadmium**
**02** Cd

**cadre**
**03** set **04** band, crew, gang, team **05** corps, squad **10** small group

**caesium**
**02** Cs

**café**
**04** caff **06** bistro, buffet, pull-in **07** noshery, tea room, tea shop, wine bar **08** snackbar **09** brasserie, cafeteria, coffee bar, cybercafé, estaminet, truck stop **10** coffee shop, restaurant **11** greasy spoon

**cafeteria**
**04** café, caff **06** buffet **07** canteen **10** restaurant **15** self-service café

**cage**
**03** mew, pen **04** coop, corf, dray, drey **05** cavie, grate, hutch, pound **06** aviary, corral, keavie, lock-up **07** tumbler **09** enclosure

**caged**
**05** mewed **06** shut up **07** encaged **08** confined, cooped up, fenced in, locked up **09** impounded **10** imprisoned, restrained **12** incarcerated

**cagey**
**04** wary, wily **05** chary **06** shrewd **07** careful, guarded **08** cautious, discreet **09** secretive **11** circumspect **12** non-committal

**cahoots**
• **in cahoots**
**08** in league **09** colluding
**10** conspiring, in alliance **11** hand in glove, in collusion **13** collaborating

**cairn**
**03** man **04** barp **05** raise

**cajole**
**04** coax, dupe, lure, wile, work
**05** moody, tempt **06** beflum, chat up, diddle, entice, humbug, seduce, soothe, whilly **07** beguile, blarney, cuittle, flatter, mislead, wheedle
**08** blandish, butter up, get round, inveigle, persuade, soft-soap
**09** sweet-talk, whillywha
**10** whillywhaw **12** work yourself

**cajolery**
**05** wiles **06** duping **07** blarney, coaxing **08** flattery, soft soap **09** sweet talk, wheedling, whillywha
**10** cajolement, enticement, inducement, inveigling, misleading, persuasion, whillywhaw
**11** beguilement, inducements
**12** blandishment, inveiglement
**13** blandishments

**cake**
**03** bar, dry, pan **04** coat, cube, farl, loaf, lump, mass, pone, slab **05** block, chunk, cover, fancy, farle **06** harden, pastry, tablet **07** congeal, encrust, plaster, thicken **08** solidify
**09** coagulate **11** consolidate

*Cakes, pastries and puddings include:*

**03** bun, pie
**04** baba, flan, fool, puri, roti, tart
**05** bombe, crêpe, jelly, poori, scone, sweet, torte
**06** éclair, gateau, junket, mousse, muffin, parkin, sponge, trifle, waffle, yum-yum
**07** baklava, Banbury, bannock, Bath bun, brioche, brownie, crumble, crumpet, cupcake, fig roll, fritter, iced bun, jam roll, jam tart, oatcake, pancake, Pavlova, plum pie, ratafia, rum baba, saffron, savarin, soufflé, stollen, strudel, tartlet, teacake, wedding, Yule log
**08** apple pie, black bun, doughnut, flummery, macaroon, malt loaf, meringue, mince pie, pecan pie, plum-cake, rock cake, sandwich, seedcake, syllabub, tiramisu, turnover, whim-wham
**09** angel cake, cherry-pie, clafoutis, cranachan, cream cake, cream horn, cream puff, drop scone, fairy cake, fruitcake, fruit tart, fudge cake, Genoa cake, lamington, lardy cake, lemon tart, madeleine, panettone, pound cake, queen cake, Sally Lunn, shortcake, Swiss roll
**10** banana cake, Battenburg, carrot cake, cheesecake, Chelsea bun, coffee cake, Dundee cake, Eccles cake, ginger cake, girdle cake, key lime pie, marble cake, panna cotta, pumpkin pie, simnel cake, sponge cake, tarte tatin
**11** baked Alaska, banana bread, banoffee pie, crème brulée, currant cake, custard tart, gingerbread, hot cross bun, jam roly-poly, lady's finger, Linzertorte, Madeira cake, plum pudding, profiterole, rice pudding, Sachertorte, sago pudding, spotted dick, treacle tart, wedding cake
**12** apfel strudel, Bakewell tart, birthday cake, chocolate log, custard slice, Danish pastry, figgy pudding, hasty pudding, pease pudding, sandwich cake
**13** apple dumpling, apple turnover, chocolate cake, Christmas cake, Scotch pancake, sponge pudding, summer pudding
**14** apple charlotte, charlotte russe, Pontefract cake, steamed pudding, toasted teacake, upside-down cake, Victoria sponge
**15** chocolate éclair, queen of puddings

*See also* **bun**

**calamitous**
◇ *anagram indicator*
**04** dire **05** fatal **06** deadly, tragic, woeful **07** ghastly, ruinous
**08** dreadful, grievous, wretched
**10** disastrous **11** cataclysmic, devastating **12** catastrophic

**calamity**
**02** wo **03** wae, woe **04** blow, Jane, ruin, ruth, woes **05** trial **06** mishap
**07** reverse, scourge, tragedy, trouble
**08** disaster, distress, downfall
**09** adversity, mischance **10** affliction, misfortune **11** catastrophe, tribulation
**12** misadventure **15** sword of Damocles

**calcium**
**02** Ca

**calculate**
**03** aim **04** cast, make, plan, rate, work
**05** add up, count, gauge, judge, tally, think, value, weigh **06** assess, cipher, cypher, derive, design, figure, intend, reckon **07** compute, measure, purpose, suppose, work out
**08** consider, estimate, reckon up
**09** determine, enumerate

**calculated**
**06** wilful **07** planned **08** computed, intended, measured, purposed, reckoned, tactical **10** considered, deliberate, purposeful, well-judged
**11** intentional **12** premeditated

**calculating**
**03** sly **04** wily **05** sharp **06** crafty, shrewd **07** cunning, devious
**08** scheming **09** designing
**10** contriving **11** circumspect
**12** manipulative **13** Machiavellian
• **calculating aid**
**03** log **04** abac **06** abacus **07** soroban
**08** computer, isopleth, nomogram
**09** nomograph, slide rule **10** calculator
**12** arithmometer **14** alignment chart
**15** digital computer

**calculation**
**03** sum **06** answer, result **08** estimate, figuring, forecast, logistic, planning
**09** evolution, judgement, reckoning
**10** alligation, arithmetic, assessment, estimation, figurework, working-out
**11** computation, mensuration
**12** deliberation

**calculus**
**04** lith- **06** tartar **07** urolith
**08** fluxions **09** sialolith
**11** quaternions

**calendar**

*Calendars include:*

**05** Bahà'í, Hindu, lunar, Roman, solar
**06** Coptic, Hebrew, Jewish, Julian
**07** Chinese, Islamic, Persian
**09** arbitrary, Gregorian, lunisolar
**10** republican
**13** revolutionary

*See also* **animal**; **month**

**calf**
**04** boss, dogy, veal **05** bossy, dogie, poddy, slink **06** vealer **08** maverick

**calibre**
**03** cal **04** bore, gage, size **05** gauge, gifts, merit, worth **06** league, talent
**07** ability, faculty, measure, quality, stature **08** capacity, diameter, strength
**09** character **10** competence, endowments, excellence
**11** distinction

**California**
**02** CA **05** Calif

**californium**
**02** Cf

**call**
**02** ca', go **03** bid, caa', cap, cry, dub, mot, run **04** bawl, bell, buzz, caul, cite, hail, name, need, nemn, pink, plea, ring, roar, term, toll, yell **05** brand, cause, claim, cleep, clepe, cooee, cooey, hight, label, order, phone, pop in, right, shout, style, title, visit
**06** appeal, ask for, bellow, call in, come by, cry out, demand, drop in, excuse, invite, market, reason, reckon, rename, ring up, scream, shriek, signal, stop by, summon, tinkle **07** baptize, command, contact, convene, enstyle, entitle, exclaim, grounds, hallali, phone up, request, send for, summons, warning
**08** assemble, christen, occasion
**09** call round, designate, pay a visit, telephone **10** denominate, describe as, invitation **11** ask to come in, exclamation **12** announcement
**13** justification **14** ask to come round
• **call for**
**04** levy, need, take **05** claim, fetch, go for **06** demand, entail, pick up
**07** collect, involve, justify, push for, require, solicit, suggest, warrant
**08** occasion, press for **11** necessitate
**13** make necessary

**• call off**
**04** drop **05** scrub **06** cancel, revoke, shelve **07** abandon, rescind **08** break off, withdraw **11** discontinue
**• call on**
**03** ask, bid, gam, put, see **04** urge **05** plead, visit **06** appeal, demand, invoke, summon, wait on **07** entreat, request **08** appeal to, go and see, look in on, press for, wait upon **10** supplicate
**• call up**
**04** buzz, pick, ring **05** phone, raise **06** choose, enlist, invite, ring up, select, sign up, summon, take on **07** contact, display, phone up, recruit **08** settle on **09** conscript, telephone
**• on call**
**05** ready **06** on duty **09** on standby **10** standing by

**called**
**03** hot **04** hote **05** nempt

**call girl**
**04** tart **05** whore **06** harlot, hooker **07** hustler **10** loose woman, prostitute **12** street-walker **14** lady of the night

**calling**
**03** job **04** line, work **05** field, trade **06** career, métier **07** mission, pursuit **08** business, province, vocation **10** employment, line of work, occupation, profession **14** line of business

**callous**
**04** cold **05** cruel, harsh, horny, stony, tough **06** seared **08** hardened, indurate, obdurate, uncaring **09** heartless, insensate, unfeeling **10** hard-bitten, hard-boiled, insensible, iron-headed **11** cold-blooded, cold-hearted, hard as nails, hard-hearted, indifferent, insensitive **12** case-hardened, stony-hearted, thick-skinned **13** unsympathetic

**callously**
**06** coldly **07** harshly **11** heartlessly, unfeelingly **13** cold-bloodedly, hard-heartedly, insensitively

**callow**
**03** raw **05** green, naive **06** jejune, rookie **07** puerile, untried **08** immature, innocent, juvenile **09** fledgling, guileless, unbearded, unfledged **11** uninitiated **13** inexperienced **15** unsophisticated

**calm**
**03** cam **04** alay, came, caum, cool, ease, even, hush, loun, lown, lull, mild **05** aleye, allay, lound, lownd, peace, quiet, relax, sleek, still **06** becalm, pacify, placid, poised, repose, sedate, serene, settle, smooth, soothe, steady, stilly **07** appease, assuage, compose, halcyon, mollify, placate, quieten, relaxed, reposed, restful, unmoved **08** ataraxia, calmness, composed, cool down, dead-wind, laid-back, peaceful, pipeclay, quietude, serenity, tranquil, waveless, windless **09** collected, composure, impassive, lighten up, limestone, nerveless, placidity, sangfroid, stillness, supercool, unclouded, unexcited, unruffled **10** cool-headed, equanimity, phlegmatic, settle down, simmer down, untroubled **11** contentment, impassivity, restfulness, undisturbed, unemotional, unexcitable, unflappable, unflustered, unpassioned, unperturbed **12** even-tempered, keep your head, on an even keel, peacefulness, tranquillity, tranquillize, unpassionate **13** dispassionate, impassiveness, imperturbable, self-possessed, unimpassioned **14** presence of mind, self-controlled, unapprehensive, unflappability **15** cool as a cucumber

**calmly**
**08** steadily **11** impassively **12** on an even keel **13** unemotionally **14** phlegmatically **15** dispassionately

**calorie**
**03** cal

**calumny**
**05** abuse, libel, lying, smear **06** attack, insult, mud pie **07** obloquy, slander **09** aspersion **10** backbiting, defamation, derogation, detraction, revilement **11** denigration, slagging-off **12** vilification, vituperation **13** disparagement

**camaraderie**
**08** affinity, intimacy **09** closeness **10** fellowship, friendship **11** brotherhood, comradeship, sociability **12** togetherness **13** brotherliness, companionship, esprit de corps **14** fraternization, good fellowship

**Cambodia**
**01** K **03** KHM

**Cambridge University** *see* **college**

**camel**
**04** oont **08** Bactrian **09** dromedare, dromedary **15** ship of the desert

**camera**

*Cameras include:*

**02** TV
**03** APS, SLR, TLR
**04** CCTV, cine, disc, film, Fuji®, view
**05** Canon®, Kodak®, Leica®, Nikon®, plate, press, sound, still, video
**06** Konica®, Pentax®, reflex, Rollei®, stereo, Super 8®, Webcam
**07** bellows, compact, digital, Minolta®, obscura, Olympus®, pinhole, Yashica®
**08** dry-plate, Polaroid®, Praktica®, security, wet-plate
**09** automatic, binocular, camcorder, half-plate, miniature, panoramic, Rolliflex®, single use, Steadicam®
**10** box Brownie®, disposable, Instamatic®, sliding box
**11** large-format
**12** quarter-plate, subminiature, surveillance
**13** daguerreotype, folding reflex, point-and-press
**14** twin-lens reflex
**15** cinematographic

**• move camera**
**03** pan **05** track

**Cameroon**
**03** CAM, CMR

**camouflage**
◇ *anagram indicator*
**04** hide, mask, veil **05** blind, cloak, cover, front, guise **06** façade, screen **07** conceal, cover up, cover-up, deceive, obscure **08** disguise **09** deception **10** maskirovka, masquerade **11** concealment, counterfeit

**camp**
**03** set **04** duar, laer, side, tent **05** campy, crowd, douar, dowar, group, gypsy, party, tents **06** caucus, clique, encamp, laager, outlie **07** bivouac, faction, leaguer, rough it, section **08** affected, campsite, mannered **09** pitch camp, posturing, set up camp **10** artificial, effeminate, encampment, over the top, pitch tents, theatrical **11** camping-site, exaggerated **12** ostentatious **13** camping-ground, sleep outdoors
**• confined to camp**
**02** CC

**campaign**
**03** war **04** push, work **05** blitz, drive, fight, jehad, jihad, lobby **06** attack, battle, strive **07** canvass, crusade, journey, promote **08** advocate, movement, strategy, struggle **09** offensive, operation, promotion **10** expedition **14** course of action

**campaigner**
**06** zealot **07** fighter **08** activist, advocate, champion, crusader, promoter, reformer **10** enthusiast

**camp-follower**
**03** boy **05** toady **06** bummer, lackey, lascar **08** hanger-on, henchman **11** leaguer-lady, leaguer-lass

**can**
**03** dow, jar, jug, lav, loo, mug, tin **04** dows, jail, pail, stir **06** prison, toilet **08** canister, jerrycan, lavatory, preserve **09** container **10** chimney pot, receptacle **11** depth charge
*See also* **prison**; **toilet**
**• can it** *see* **quiet**; **shut up** *under* **shut**

**Canada**
**03** CAN, CDN
*See also* **Prime Minister**; **province**

*Canadian cities and notable towns include:*

**06** Ottawa, Quebec, Regina
**07** Calgary, Halifax, Toronto
**08** Edmonton, Montreal, Victoria, Winnipeg
**09** Saskatoon, Vancouver

*Canadian landmarks include:*

**06** Mt Thor
**07** CN Tower, Mt Logan, Niagara, Rockies, Sky Dome
**08** Lake Erie
**09** Hudson Bay, Lake Huron, Mt Seymour
**10** Great Lakes, St Lawrence
**11** Lake Ontario
**12** Lake Superior, Niagara Falls
**13** Algonquin Park, Parc Olympique
**14** Horseshoe Falls, Rocky Mountains

**Canadian**
**03** Can, Cdn **06** Canuck

**canal**
**03** Can, gut **04** duct, foss, moat, tube **05** ditch, fosse, zanja **06** groove, trench **07** channel, enteron, passage, shipway **08** waterway **10** navigation **11** watercourse **14** digestive tract

*Canals include:*

**04** Erie, Kiel, Suez
**05** Grand
**06** Panama, Rideau
**07** Corinth, Midland, Welland
**10** Caledonian, Mittelland
**11** Welland Ship
**14** Manchester Ship

**cancel**
**03** axe, nix **04** drop, kill, stop, undo, wipe **05** abort, adeem, annul, erase, quash, scrap, scrub **06** delete, offset, repeal, revoke, shelve, strike **07** abandon, abolish, call off, nullify, red-line, rescind, retract, vitiate, wash out **08** abrogate, break off, cross out, dissolve, override, postpone, suppress, withdraw, write off **09** eliminate, strike out **10** declare off, invalidate, obliterate, scrub round **11** countermand, discontinue **14** counterbalance
• **cancel out**
**06** offset, redeem **07** balance, nullify **09** make up for **10** compensate, counteract, neutralize **14** counterbalance

**cancellation**
**06** repeal **08** deletion, dropping, quashing, shelving, stopping **09** abolition, annulment, scrubbing **10** abandoning, calling-off, nullifying, revocation **11** abandonment, elimination **12** invalidation **14** neutralization

**cancer**
**03** rot **04** Big C, Crab, evil **06** blight, canker, growth, plague, tumour **07** disease, scourge, the Big C, the Crab **08** cancroid, sickness **09** carcinoma **10** corruption, malignancy, pestilence **15** malignant growth

**candelabrum**
**07** menorah **09** lampadary **11** candlestick

**candid**
**04** fair, open **05** blunt, clear, frank, plain, round, white **06** honest, simple **07** liberal, shining, sincere, unposed **08** informal, truthful, unbiased **09** guileless, impartial, ingenuous, outspoken **10** forthright **11** plain-spoken, unequivocal, unrehearsed **12** heart-to-heart **15** straightforward

**candidate**
**03** PPC **06** runner, seeker **07** entrant, nominee **08** aspirant, examinee **09** applicant, contender, postulant, pretender **10** competitor, contestant **11** possibility
• **candidate list**
**04** leet **06** ticket

**candidly**
**06** openly, simply **07** bluntly, clearly, frankly, plainly, roundly, up-front **08** honestly **09** liberally, sincerely **10** truthfully **11** guilelessly, ingenuously, outspokenly **12** forthrightly **13** unequivocally

**candle**
**03** dip **04** slut **05** cerge, sperm, taper, torch **06** bougie, ulicon, ulikon **07** oolakan, oulakan, shammes, ulichon **08** amandine, eulachan, eulachon, luminary, oulachon, shammash, wax light **09** tallow dip **10** night-light **12** tallow candle

**candour**
**06** purity **07** honesty, naivety **08** kindness, openness **09** bluntness, franchise, frankness, plainness, sincerity, whiteness **10** directness, liberality, simplicity **11** artlessness, brusqueness **12** impartiality, plain-dealing, truthfulness **13** guilelessness, ingenuousness, outspokenness **14** forthrightness **15** unequivocalness

**candy**
**05** glacé, kandy **06** candie, sweets **07** cocaine, encrust, toffees **10** chocolates **11** crystallize **13** confectionery

**cane**
**03** rod **05** crook, ratan, staff, stick, swish, swits **06** ferule, jambee, rattan, switch **07** tickler, whangee **09** riding rod **10** alpenstock, supplejack **12** swagger-stick, walking-stick

**canine**
**01** c **04** tush **06** cuspid **08** dogtooth, eye tooth
*See also* **dog**

**canker**
**03** rot **04** bane, boil, evil, sore **05** decay, ulcer **06** blight, cancer, infect, lesion, plague **07** corrupt, destroy, disease, pollute, scourge **08** sickness **09** corrosion, infection **10** cankerworm, corruption, pestilence, ulceration

**cannabis**
**03** kef, kif, pot, tea **04** benj, blow, dope, gage, hash, hemp, kaif, leaf, puff, punk, toke, weed **05** bhang, blunt, ganja, gauge, grass, joint, roach, skunk, splay **06** bomber, greens, reefer, spliff **07** hashish **08** locoweed, Mary Jane **09** marihuana, marijuana, substance **10** sinsemilla, wacky baccy **12** electric puha

**cannibal**
**08** man-eater **09** Thyestean, Thyestian **11** people-eater **15** anthropophagite

**cannibalism**
**08** exophagy **09** endophagy, man-eating **12** people-eating **13** anthropophagy

**cannibalistic**
**09** man-eating, Thyestean
**10** exophagous **11** endophagous
**12** people-eating
**15** anthropophagous

**cannily**
**06** subtly **07** acutely, sharply **08** astutely, cleverly, shrewdly **09** knowingly, skilfully

**cannon**
**03** gun **05** carom, saker **06** barker, big gun, curtal, falcon, monkey, mortar, Quaker **07** battery, bombard, chamber, nursery **08** basilisk, culverin, field gun, great gun, howitzer, murderer, oerlikon, ordnance, spitfire **09** artillery, carambole, carronade, Quaker gun, zumbooruk **10** fieldpiece, serpentine **11** stern-chaser **12** demi-culverin **14** murdering-piece

**cannonade**
**05** salvo **06** volley **07** barrage **08** pounding, shelling **09** broadside **11** bombardment

**canny**
**03** sly **04** good, nice, wice, wise **05** acute, lucky, pawky, sharp **06** artful, astute, clever, gentle, shrewd, subtle **07** careful, knowing, prudent, skilful **08** cautious, innocent **09** fortunate, judicious, sagacious **11** circumspect, worldly-wise **13** perspicacious

**canoe**
**04** waka **05** kaiak, kayak **06** dugout **07** piragua **08** montaria, woodskin **09** monoxylon

**canon**
**03** can, law **04** line, rota, rule **05** round, vicar **06** priest, square, squier, squire **07** brocard, dictate, precept, statute **08** Mathurin, minister, reverend, standard, vice-dean **09** clergyman, criterion, Mathurine, principle, yardstick **10** prebendary, regulation **12** residentiary

**canonical**
**07** regular **08** accepted, approved, orthodox **10** authorized, recognized, sanctioned **13** authoritative
• **canonical hours**

*Canonical hours include:*

**04** none, sext
**05** lauds, nones, prime, terce
**06** matins, tierce

07 complin, orthros, vespers
08 compline, evensong

**canonize**
05 bless, saint 07 beatify, besaint
08 sanctify

**canopy**
03 sky 04 dais, tilt 05 cover, herse, shade, state 06 awning, estate, hearse, huppah, tester 07 chuppah, majesty, marquee, shelter, veranda
08 ciborium, covering, marquise, pavilion, shamiana, sunshade, umbrella, verandah 09 baldachin, baldaquin, clamshell, parachute, shamianah 10 cooker hood, tabernacle 11 baldacchino 12 cloth of state

**cant**
04 kant, tilt 05 argot, brisk, lingo, merry, slang, slope 06 jargon, lively, snivel 07 snuffle 09 hypocrisy
10 vernacular 11 insincerity, rogues' Latin 12 thieves' Latin
15 pretentiousness

**cantankerous**
05 cross, testy 06 crabby, crusty, grumpy, ornery 07 crabbed, grouchy, peevish, piggish 08 contrary, perverse, stubborn 09 crotchety, difficult, irascible, irritable 11 bad-tempered, carnaptious, curnaptious, ill-humoured, quarrelsome 13 quick-tempered

**canteen**
04 café 05 flask, Naafi 06 buffet
08 snackbar 09 cafeteria, refectory
10 commissary, restaurant

**canter**
03 jog, ren, rin, run 04 lope, trot
05 amble, titup 06 gallop, tittup
07 jogtrot, tripple 11 false gallop

**canton**
03 can 04 Vaud 05 space 06 corner
08 division, ordinary

**canvas**
04 tent 05 Binca®, sails, tents
06 burlap, muslin 08 oilcloth

**canvass**
04 poll, scan, sift 05 study 06 debate, survey 07 agitate, analyse, discuss, examine, explore, find out, inspect
08 campaign, evaluate 09 seek votes
10 scrutinize 11 ask for votes, electioneer, inquire into, investigate
12 solicit votes 13 drum up support

**canyon**
05 abyss, cañon, chasm, gorge, gully
06 cañada, ravine, valley

**cap**
03 hat, lid, mob, taj, tam, top 04 beat, bung, call, caul, coat, coif, curb, kepi, plug 05 beret, chaco, cover, crown, excel, kippa, limit, mutch, outdo, quoif, shako, tammy, toque, tuque
06 amorce, barret, berret, better, biggin, bonnet, bunnet, calpac, chapka, czapka, exceed, granny, kalpak, pileus, shacko 07 biretta, bycoket, calotte, calpack, control, eclipse, ferrule, grannie, montero, stopper, surpass 08 capeline, chaperon, gorblimy, outshine, outstrip, restrain, restrict, schapska, trencher, yarmulka, yarmulke, zuchetta, zuchetto 09 capelline, chaperone, cock's-comb, crown cork, glengarry, gorblimey, transcend, trenchard, zucchetto 10 cockernony, Kilmarnock
11 bonnet-rouge, mortarboard, Tam o' Shanter 12 cheesecutter
13 international 15 go one better than

*See also* **hat**

**capability**
05 means, power, skill 06 talent
07 ability, faculty 08 aptitude, capacity, facility 09 potential
10 competence, efficiency
11 proficiency, skilfulness
13 qualification 14 accomplishment

**capable**
04 able 05 adept, apt to, smart
06 clever, fitted, gifted, suited
07 needing, notable, skilful
08 allowing, liable to, masterly, talented 09 competent, efficient, qualified, tending to 10 disposed to, inclined to, proficient 11 experienced, intelligent 12 accomplished, businesslike 13 comprehensive

**capably**
04 ably 07 adeptly 08 cleverly
09 skilfully 11 competently, efficiently
12 proficiently 13 intelligently

**capacious**
03 big 04 huge, vast, wide 05 ample, broad, large, roomy, womby 07 liberal, sizable 08 generous, spacious
09 expansive, extensive
10 commodious, voluminous
11 comfortable, elephantine, substantial 13 comprehensive

**capacity**
03 cap, job 04 bind, gift, post, role, room, size 05 power, range, scope, skill, space 06 extent, genius, office, talent, volume 07 ability, compass, content, faculty 08 aptitude, function, position 09 largeness, magnitude, potential, readiness, resources
10 capability, cleverness, competence, competency, dimensions, efficiency
11 appointment, proficiency, proportions, sufficience
12 intelligence

• **in the capacity of**
03 qua

**cape**
01 C 03 ras 04 coat, head, naze, neck, ness, robe, scaw, skaw, wrap 05 amice, cloak, fanon, fichu, point, shawl, talma
06 almuce, domino, mantle, muleta, poncho, sontag, tippet, tongue
07 burnous, manteel, mozetta, pelisse
08 burnouse, headland, pelerine
09 peninsula 10 promontory

*See also* **cloak**; **peninsula**

*Capes include:*

03 Cod
04 Fear, Horn, York
05 Wrath
06 Cretin, Orange
07 Kennedy, Leeuwin, Lookout
08 Farewell, Foulwind, Good Hope, Suckling
09 Canaveral, Carbonara, St Vincent, Trafalgar, Van Diemen
10 Finisterre, Kidnappers, Providence
11 Three Points, Tribulation
12 Hopes Advance
13 Prince of Wales

**caper**
03 hop 04 dido, jape, jest, jump, lark, leap, romp, skip 05 antic, bound, crime, dance, flisk, frisk, prank, scoup, scowp, stunt 06 affair, antics, bounce, cavort, frolic, gambol, prance, spring
07 gambado 08 business, capriole, escapade, mischief 09 high jinks
10 pigeon-wing

**Cape Verde**
03 CPV

**capital**
◇ *head selection indicator*
02 A1, uc 03 cap 04 cash, head, main, seat 05 chief, first, fonds, funds, major, means, money, prime, stock 06 assets, uncial, wealth 07 central, finance, leading, primary, savings, serious
08 cardinal, foremost, main city, property, reserves 09 excellent, important, majuscule, principal, resources 10 investment 11 block letter, investments, wherewithal
12 block capital, liquid assets
13 capital letter 15 upper-case letter

*See also* **city**; **currency**

• **small capitals**
02 sc

**capitalism**
12 laissez-faire 14 free enterprise

**capitalist**
05 mogul 06 banker, fat cat, tycoon
07 magnate, moneyer 08 investor, moneyman 09 bourgeois, financier, moneybags, plutocrat 12 money-spinner 13 person of means

**capitalize**
• **capitalize on**
07 exploit 08 cash in on 10 profit from
13 make the most of 15 take advantage of

**capitulate**
05 yield 06 give in, give up, relent, submit 07 succumb 08 back down
09 surrender 15 throw in the towel

**capitulation**
08 giving-in, giving-up, yielding
09 relenting, surrender 10 submission, succumbing 11 backing-down

**caprice**
03 fad 04 whim 05 fancy, freak, humor, quirk 06 humour, megrim,

notion, spleen, vagary, vapour, whimsy **07** fantasy, impulse **08** humoresk, migraine, phantasy **09** capriccio **10** fickleness, fitfulness, humoresque **11** inconstancy **14** changeableness

**capricious**
◇ *anagram indicator*
**03** odd **05** freak, queer **06** fickle, fitful, kittle, quirky, wanton **07** erratic, wayward **08** fanciful, freakish, humorous, perverse, petulant, variable **09** arbitrary, fantastic, impulsive, mercurial, uncertain, whimsical **10** capernoity, changeable, humoursome, inconstant **11** capernoitie, cappernoity, fantastical **13** unpredictable

**capsize**
◇ *reversal indicator*
**04** purl **05** upset **06** invert **07** tip over, whemmle, whomble, whommle, whummle **08** keel over, overturn, roll over, turn over **10** turn turtle **11** overturning

**capsule**
**03** pod, urn **04** boll, pill **05** craft, jelly, probe, shell **06** bomber, caplet, cocoon, module, ovisac, sheath, tablet **07** habitat, lozenge, sandbox **08** pyxidium, spansule **09** container, poppy-head, radio pill **10** nidamentum, receptacle **11** sporogonium

**captain**
**03** cid **04** boss, head, lead, skip **05** chief, owner, pilot **06** direct, guider, leader, manage, master, old man, patron **07** command, control, officer, patroon, skipper **08** capitayn **09** commander, commodore, supervise **10** ritt-master, shipmaster **12** be in charge of **13** master-mariner, protospataire, whaling-master **14** protospathaire **15** protospatharius

*Captains include:*

**04** Ahab, Cook (James), Hook, Kidd (William), Nemo
**05** Bligh (William), Flint (Jim Turner), Johns (W E), Queeg, Smith (John), Swing
**07** Corelli (Antonio), Marryat (Frederick)
**08** Bobadill, Hastings (Arthur), MacHeath
**09** Singleton
**10** Hornblower (Horatio)

**caption**
**04** note **05** title **06** arrest, legend, titles **07** cutline, heading, wording **08** headline **09** underline **11** inscription

**captious**
**07** carping, peevish **08** critical, niggling **09** quibbling **10** nit-picking, scrupulous **13** hair-splitting, hypercritical

**captivate**
**03** get, win **04** lure, take **05** charm **06** allure, dazzle, seduce **07** attract, beguile, bewitch, delight, enamour, enchant, enthral **09** enrapture, fascinate, hypnotize, infatuate, mesmerize **11** take by storm

**captivating**
**06** taking **07** winsome **08** alluring, catching, charming, dazzling **09** beautiful, beguiling, seductive **10** attractive, bewitching, delightful, enchanting **11** enthralling, fascinating

**captive**
**03** POW **05** caged, slave **06** secure, shut up **07** caitive, convict, hostage, subject, triumph **08** confined, detained, detainee, enslaved, ensnared, interned, internee, jailbird, locked up, prisoner **09** enchained, in bondage **10** imprisoned, locked away, restrained, restricted **12** incarcerated **13** held in custody

**captivity**
**05** bonds, exile **06** duress **07** bondage, custody, slavery **09** detention, endurance, restraint, servitude **10** constraint, internment **11** confinement, enslavement **12** imprisonment **13** incarceration

**captor**
**05** guard **06** jailor, keeper, warder **09** custodian **12** incarcerator

**capture**
◇ *containment indicator*
**03** cop, nab, net, win **04** land, nick, rush, take, trap, with **05** carry, catch, mop up, seize, snare, withe **06** arrest, collar, cut out, entrap, occupy, pick up, record, secure, taking **07** embrace, ensnare, express, nabbing, nicking, run down, seizure, snabble, snaffle **08** catching, hit a blot, hunt down, imprison, surprise, trapping **09** apprehend, collaring, recapture, represent, reproduce **11** encapsulate **12** imprisonment, take prisoner **13** taking captive **14** taking prisoner

**• be captured**
**04** fall

**capuchin**
**03** sai **05** Cebus, sajou **07** sapajou

**car**
**04** auto, cart, heap **05** motor **07** chariot, clunker, vehicle, vettura **08** motor car **09** speedster **10** automobile, rust bucket **12** motor vehicle **13** shooting brake

*Car manufacturers include:*

**02** MG, RR, VW
**03** BMW, Kia
**04** Audi, Fiat, Ford, Jeep, Lada, Mini, Saab, Seat, Yugo
**05** Buick, Dodge, Honda, Isuzu, Lexus, Lotus, Mazda, Riley, Rover, Skoda, Smart, Volvo
**06** Austin, Daewoo, Datsun, Jaguar, Lancia, Morgan, Morris, Nissan, Proton, Subaru, Talbot, Toyota
**07** Bentley, Bugatti, Citroen, Daimler, Ferrari, Hillman, Hyundai, Peugeot, Pontiac, Porsche, Reliant, Renault, Trabant, Triumph
**08** Cadillac, Chrysler, Daihatsu, De Lorean, Maserati, Mercedes, Standard, Vauxhall, Wolseley
**09** Alfa Romeo, Chevrolet, Land Rover
**10** Mitsubishi, Oldsmobile, Rolls Royce, Vanden Plas, Volkswagen
**11** Aston Martin, Lamborghini
**12** Mercedes-Benz

*Car types include:*

**02** RR
**03** cab, MPV, SUV
**04** jeep, limo, Mini®, taxi
**05** brake, break, buggy, coupé, sedan
**06** banger, Beetle®, estate, hearse, jalopy, kit-car, saloon, tourer
**07** jaloppy, minivan
**08** fastback, hot hatch, panda car, roadster, runabout, Smart car®, stock car
**09** all-roader, bubble-car, cabriolet, hatchback, Land Rover®, limousine, off-roader, patrol car, sports car
**10** Model T Ford®, Range Rover®, Sinclair C5, subcompact, veteran car, vintage car
**11** convertible
**12** station wagon
**13** people carrier, shooting brake
**14** four-wheel drive

*Famous cars include:*

**04** FAB1
**08** Blue Bird
**09** Batmobile, Christine, Genevieve
**11** Flintmobile

*Car and motor vehicle parts include:*

**03** ABS
**04** axle, boot, door, gear, hood, horn, jack, sill, tyre, vent, wing
**05** bezel, clock, grill, shaft, trunk, wheel
**06** airbag, bonnet, bumper, clutch, dimmer, engine, fender, heater, hub-cap, towbar
**07** battery, chassis, fog lamp, gas tank, gearbox, kingpin, spoiler, sunroof
**08** air brake, air inlet, bodywork, brake pad, door-lock, fog light, headrest, ignition, jump lead, lift gate, oil gauge, roof rack, seat belt, silencer, solenoid, sun visor, track rod
**09** brake drum, brake shoe, crankcase, dashboard, disc brake, drum brake, filler cap, fuel gauge, gear-lever, gearshift, gear-stick, handbrake, headlight, indicator, monocoque, overrider, prop shaft, rear light, reflector, sidelight, spare tyre, stoplight, wheel arch
**10** brake light, drive shaft, petrol tank, power brake, rev counter, side mirror, stick shift, suspension, windscreen, windshield, wing mirror

**11** accelerator, anti-roll bar, exhaust pipe, ignition key, number plate, parcel shelf, speedometer
**12** licence plate, parking-light, quarterlight, transmission
**13** centre console, courtesy light, cruise control, flasher switch, pneumatic tyre, rack and pinion, radial-ply tyre, reclining seat, shock absorber, side-impact bar, steering-wheel
**14** air-conditioner, central locking, electric window, emergency light, four-wheel drive, hydraulic brake, rear-view mirror, reversing light, steering-column
**15** windscreen-wiper

*Car and motoring-related terms include:*

**02** AA
**03** dip, GPS, LRP, map, MOT, RAC, tow
**04** exit, park, skid, SORN, stop
**05** amber, brake, crash, cut up, flash, layby, on tow, prang, shunt
**06** diesel, fill up, filter, garage, hold-up, L-plate, octane, petrol, pile-up, pull in
**07** blowout, bollard, bus lane, car park, car wash, cat's-eye, give way, logbook, MOT test, neutral, pull out, reverse, road map, snarl-up, tax disc, traffic
**08** accident, change up, coasting, declutch, fast lane, flat tyre, gridlock, indicate, junction, main beam, overtake, puncture, red light, road rage, services, slip road, slow lane, speeding, tailback, taxi rank, turn left, unleaded
**09** blind spot, breakdown, collision, cycle lane, fifth gear, first gear, green card, hit-and-run, radar trap, road atlas, road studs, roadworks, sixth gear, third gear, T junction, turn right, wheelspin, white line
**10** accelerate, amber light, arm signals, bottleneck, change down, change gear, change lane, contraflow, crossroads, fourth gear, green light, inside lane, middle lane, pedestrian, petrol pump, roundabout, second gear, speed limit, stay in lane, straight on, tailgating, traffic jam, yellow line
**11** box junction, crawler lane, drink-driver, driving test, hand signals, highway code, outside lane, speed camera, traffic cone, traffic cops, traffic news, zigzag lines
**12** drink-driving, hard shoulder, left-hand lane, motorway toll, one-way system, parking meter, passing place, road junction, speeding fine, tyre pressure
**13** Belisha beacon, drink and drive, driving lesson, driving school, flashing amber, handbrake turn, jump the lights, left-hand drive, level crossing, no-claims bonus, parking ticket, pay and display, penalty points, petrol station, power steering, right-hand lane, super unleaded, traffic lights, traffic police, zebra crossing
**14** cadence braking, double declutch, driving licence, four-wheel drive, mini-roundabout, MOT certificate, motorway pile-up, overtaking lane, poor visibility, puffin crossing, right-hand drive, service station, speeding ticket, unleaded petrol
**15** pelican crossing, put your foot down, road fund licence, test certificate, traction control, warning triangle

*See also* **motor vehicle**

**carafe**
**03** jug **05** flask **06** bottle, flagon **07** pitcher **08** decanter

**caravan**
**02** RV **03** van **04** line **05** group, train **06** cafila, convoy, kafila **07** caffila, trailer **09** camper van, Dormobile®, motor home, Winnebago® **10** mobile home

**carbon**
**01** C **04** copy **07** diamond **08** graphite **09** buckyball

**• carbon copy**
**02** cc **03** bcc **06** flimsy **08** manifold

**carbuncle**
**04** boil, bump, lump, sore **06** bunion, pimple **07** anthrax, blister **12** inflammation

**carcase, carcass**
**04** body, hulk **05** shell **06** corpse, cutter **07** cadaver, remains **08** dead body, skeleton **09** framework, structure

*See also* **meat**

**card**
**03** ace, map, mix **04** Amex, club, comb, jack, king, tose, toze **05** deuce, heart, joker, knave, queen, spade, toaze **06** domino, master, meishi **07** diamond **10** adulterate **13** carte-de-visite

*See also* **eccentric**; **game**

**• cards suits**
**01** c, d, h, s **05** clubs **06** hearts, spades **08** diamonds

**• on the cards**
**06** likely **08** possible, probable **11** looking as if, looking like **13** the chances are

**• playing cards**
**04** deck, hand **11** devil's books

**cardinal**
**02** HE **03** key **04** main **05** basic, chief, first, pivot, prime **06** number, red hat **07** capital, central, highest, leading, primary **08** foremost, greatest, grosbeak **09** essential, important, paramount, principal **10** pre-eminent **11** fundamental **14** apostolic vicar

*See also* **archbishop**; **number**

*Cardinals include:*

**03** **Sin** (Jaime)
**04** **Gray** (Gordon), **Hume** (Basil), **Pole** (Reginald), **Retz** (Jean Françoise de)
**05** **Chigi** (Fabio)
**06** **Beaton** (David), **Borgia** (Rodrigo), **Fisher** (John), **Heenan** (John Carmel), **Medici** (Giovanni de'), **Newman** (John Henry), **Rovere** (Francesco della), **Stuart** (Henry, Duke of York), **Wolsey** (Thomas)
**07** **Bethune** (David), **Langham** (Simon), **Langton** (Stephen), **Mazarin** (Jules), **Mendoza** (Pedro Gonzalez de), **Pandulf**, **Vaughan** (Herbert), **Wiseman** (Nicholas), **Ximenes** (Francisco)
**08** **Alberoni** (Giulio), **Aubusson** (Pierre d'), **Beaufort** (Henry), **Stepinac**
**09** **Richelieu** (Armand Jean Duplessis, Duc de), **Wyszynski** (Stefan)
**10** **Bellarmine** (Robert), **Breakspear** (Nicolas), **Mindszenty** (József)
**13** **Murphy-O'Connor** (Cormac)

**• cardinal's office**
**03** hat

**care**
**04** cark, fear, heed, mind, reck, reke, ward **05** kaugh, pains, worry **06** bother, burden, charge, hang-up, kiaugh, regard, strain, stress, tender **07** anxiety, caution, concern, control, custody, keeping, minding, tending, thought, trouble **08** accuracy, disquiet, distress, interest, pressure, prudence, tutelage, vexation **09** attention, give a damn, oversight, vigilance **10** affliction, attendance, protection **11** be concerned, carefulness, forethought, heedfulness, safekeeping, supervision, tribulation **12** be interested, guardianship, looking-after, watchfulness, watching-over **13** consideration **14** circumspection, meticulousness, responsibility

**• care for**
**04** like, love, mind, tend, want **05** enjoy, nurse **06** attend, desire **07** cherish, protect **08** be fond of, be keen on, maintain **09** be close to, delight in, look after, watch over **10** minister to, provide for, take care of **12** be in love with

**• care of**
**01** c/- **02** c/o

**career**
◇ *anagram indicator*
**03** job, ren, rin, run **04** bolt, dash, life, past, race, rush, tear **05** shoot, speed, trade, whang **06** gallop, hurtle, métier **07** calling, cariere, pursuit **08** life-work, vocation **10** employment, livelihood, occupation, profession

**carefree**
**05** happy **06** blithe, breezy, cheery **07** halcyon **08** cheerful, debonair, laid-back **09** easy-going, fancy-free, unworried **10** debonnaire, insouciant, nonchalant, rollicking, untroubled **11** thoughtless, unconcerned **12** happy-go-lucky, light-hearted **13** irresponsible

**careful**
**04** mean, wary, wise **05** alert, aware, chary, close, heedy, tight **06** eyeful, frugal, stingy **07** anxious, guarded, heedful, mindful, miserly, precise, prudent, sparing, tactful, thrifty **08** accurate, cautious, detailed, diligent, discreet, rigorous, sensible, thorough, vigilant, watchful **09** assiduous, attentive, judicious, niggardly, penny-wise **10** deliberate, economical, fast-handed, fastidious, hard-fisted, methodical, meticulous, particular, scrupulous, solicitous, systematic, thoughtful **11** circumspect, close-fisted, close-handed, painstaking, punctilious, tight-fisted **12** parsimonious, softly-softly **13** conscientious, penny-pinching

**carefully**
**05** hooly **06** warily **07** charily, closely **09** guardedly, heedfully, mindfully, precisely, prudently, tactfully **10** accurately, cautiously, diligently, discreetly, handsomely, rigorously, solicitous, thoroughly, vigilantly, watchfully **11** assiduously, attentively, judiciously, punctilious **12** deliberately, fastidiously, methodically, meticulously, scrupulously, thoughtfully **13** circumspectly, painstakingly **14** systematically **15** conscientiously

**careless**
◇ *anagram indicator*
**03** lax **04** nice **05** hasty, messy, slack **06** breezy, casual, remiss, secure, shoddy, simple, sloppy, untidy **07** artless, cursory, négligé, offhand, untenty **08** carefree, cheerful, heedless, laid-back, reckless, slapdash, slipshod, tactless, uncaring **09** easy-going, forgetful, negligent, unguarded, unmindful, unworried **10** disorderly, inaccurate, incautious, indiscreet, insouciant, neglectful, nonchalant, regardless, unthinking, untroubled **11** inattentive, perfunctory, superficial, thoughtless, unconcerned **12** absent-minded, disorganized, happy as a clam, happy-go-lucky, light-hearted **13** inconsiderate, irresponsible **15** happy as a sandboy

**carelessly**
◇ *anagram indicator*
**06** anyhow **07** hastily **08** casually, remissly, shoddily, slam-bang, slapdash, sloppily **09** cursorily **10** heedlessly, recklessly, tactlessly, uncaringly **11** forgetfully, negligently, offhandedly, unguardedly, unmindfully **12** incautiously, indiscreetly, neglectingly, unthinkingly **13** inattentively, irresponsibly, perfunctorily, superficially, thoughtlessly, unconcernedly **14** absent-mindedly **15** inconsiderately

**caress**
**03** coy, hug, pat, pet, rub **04** bill, kiss **05** grope, touch **06** cuddle, feel up, fondle, nuzzle, stroke **07** embrace, petting, touch up **08** canoodle, lallygag, lollygag **10** endearment **13** butterfly kiss, slap and tickle

**caretaker**
**06** acting, fill-in, keeper, porter, pro tem, sexton, verger, warden **07** curator, dvornik, janitor, ostiary, shammes, stand-in, steward **08** janitrix, shammash, watchman **09** concierge, custodian, janitress, short-term, temporary **10** doorkeeper, substitute **11** provisional **14** superintendent

**careworn**
**04** worn **05** gaunt, tired, weary **07** anxious, haggard, worn-out, worried **08** fatigued **09** exhausted

**cargo**
**04** bulk, haul, last, load **05** goods **06** lading **07** baggage, fraught, freight, payload, tonnage **08** contents, deck-load, frautage, shipment **10** fraughtage **11** consignment, merchandise

**Caribbean**
**02** WI **10** West Indies

**caricature**
**04** mock **05** mimic **06** parody, satire, send up, send-up **07** cartoon, distort, lampoon, mimicry, take off, take-off **08** ridicule, satirize, travesty **09** burlesque, imitation **10** distortion, exaggerate **14** representation

**caring**
**04** fond, kind, warm **06** loving, tender **07** devoted, helpful **08** friendly **10** altruistic, benevolent, thoughtful **11** good-natured, kind-hearted, sympathetic **12** affectionate **13** compassionate, philanthropic, tender-hearted

**carnage**
**06** murder **07** killing **08** butchery, genocide, massacre **09** bloodbath, bloodshed, holocaust, slaughter **10** mass murder **15** ethnic cleansing

**carnal**
**04** lewd **05** belly, human **06** animal, bodily, erotic, impure, sexual **07** fleshly, lustful, natural, outward, sensual **08** physical **09** corporeal, lecherous, murderous **10** lascivious, libidinous, licentious **11** flesh-eating, unspiritual

**carnival**
**04** fair, fête, gala **05** carny **06** carney, fiesta **07** holiday, jubilee, revelry **08** Fasching, festival, jamboree **09** amusement, Mardi Gras, merriment **11** celebration, merrymaking

**carnivorous**
**10** meat-eating, zoophagous **11** creophagous, flesh-eating

**carol**
**04** hymn, noel, sing, song **06** carrel, chorus, strain **07** carrell, wassail **13** Christmas song

**carousal**
**04** upsy **05** feast, rouse, upsee, upsey

**carouse**
**04** birl **05** birle, booze, drink, party, quaff, revel, spree **06** imbibe **07** roister, wassail **09** celebrate, make merry **11** drink freely, wassail bout

**carousing**
**08** drinking, partying **11** celebrating, compotation, merrymaking **13** mallemaroking

**carp**
**02** id **03** ide, koi, nag **04** yerk **05** gibel, knock, pinch **06** go on at, twitch **07** censure, crucian, crusian, nit-pick, quibble **08** complain, cyprinid, goldfish, reproach **09** criticize, find fault, round fish **10** find faults, silverfish **11** have a shot at **14** ultracrepidate

**carpenter**
**05** chips **06** chippy, joiner, Joseph, Quince, wright **10** cartwright, shipwright, woodworker **12** cabinet-maker

**carpet**
**03** bed, mat, rug **04** cake, coat, wrap **05** cover, dress, layer **06** clothe, encase, spread **07** blanket, matting, overlay **08** covering **10** tablecloth **13** floor-covering

*Carpets and rugs include:*

**03** rag, red, rya
**04** kali
**05** Dutch, kelim, kilim, magic, pilch, stair, throw
**06** hearth, hooked, khilim, Kirman, numdah, runner, prayer, Turkey, Wilton
**07** bergama, flokati, Persian, Turkish
**08** Aubusson, bergamot, Brussels, moquette
**09** Axminster, prayer rug, sheepskin
**10** travelling
**11** Bessarabian, buffalo robe
**13** Kidderminster

**carping**
**07** nagging, Zoilism **08** captious **09** cavilling, quibbling **10** nit-picking **11** complaining, criticizing **12** fault-finding

**carriage**
**03** air, car, cge, job, set **04** gait, mien, port **05** guise, poise, tenue **06** burden, clatch, manner, stance **07** baggage, bearing, conduct, freight, portage, postage, posture, turnout, vehicle, voiture **08** attitude, carrying, delivery, equipage, portance, presence, truckage **09** behaviour, demeanour, porterage, transport **10** conveyance, deportment **14** transportation

*Carriages include:*

**03** cab, fly, gig
**04** arba, baby, chay, drag, dray, ekka, mail, pony, pram, rath, shay, trap

**05** araba, aroba, bandy, buggy, coach, coupé, dilly, ratha, stage, sulky, T-cart, wagon
**06** berlin, calash, chaise, drosky, go-cart, hansom, herdic, landau, pochay, purdah, spider, spring, surrey
**07** britska, britzka, cariole, caroche, chariot, dogcart, droshky, hackney, phaeton, pillbox, ricksha, tilbury, vettura, vis-à-vis
**08** barouche, britzska, brougham, carriole, carryall, clarence, diligent, jump-seat, po'chaise, rickshaw, rockaway, sociable, stanhope, victoria
**09** britschka, cabriolet, landaulet, wagonette
**10** four-in hand, post chaise, stagecoach
**11** family coach, hurly-hacket, village cart
**13** désobligeante, mourning coach, spider phaeton, thoroughbrace

## carried away
**04** rapt **06** enlevé, way-out
- **get carried away**
**06** lose it **13** become excited

*See also* **carry**

## carrier
**06** bearer, porter, runner, telfer, vector
**07** airline, telpher, tranter, vehicle
**08** conveyor, horseman, kurveyor
**09** messenger **10** plastic bag
**11** transmitter, transporter
**12** roundsperson **13** dispatch rider
**14** delivery-person, transport rider

## carrion
**03** ket
- **carrion feeder**
**04** hyen **05** hyena **06** hyaena
**07** vulture **08** aardwolf **09** scavenger

## carry
◇ *containment indicator*
**03** act, lug **04** bear, cart, gain, haul, have, hold, hump, lead, mean, move, pass, pipe, sell, show, take, tote, wain **05** adopt, bring, cover, drive, fetch, mount, print, reach, relay, shift, stand, stock **06** accept, acquit, behave, convey, effect, entail, hold up, lead to, pass on, ratify, retail, suffer, travel, uphold, wheech **07** approve, be heard, comport, conduct, contain, deliver, display, involve, present, publish, release, support, sustain, vote for **08** hand over, maintain, result in, sanction, shoulder, transfer, transmit, underpin **09** authorize, be audible, broadcast, transport **11** communicate, disseminate, have for sale, keep in stock **12** vote in favour **14** be infected with
- **carry away**
**03** rap **04** lift **06** asport, ravish
**08** bear away **09** transport
- **carry off**
**03** lag, net, rob, win **04** gain, hent, land, rape **05** crack **06** abduct, kidnap, pick up, secure **07** achieve **08** complete **09** succeed in, transport
**12** come away with
- **carry on**
**03** ren, rin, run **04** go on, hold, keep, last, wage **06** bash on, endure, keep on, keep up, manage, play up, pursue, resume **07** conduct, operate, persist, proceed, restart **08** continue, engage in, maintain, progress, return to
**09** misbehave, persevere
**10** administer, be involved, mess around, play around **12** have an affair
**15** behave foolishly
- **carry out**
**02** do **04** fill **05** mount **06** effect, fulfil
**07** achieve, conduct, deliver, execute, perform, realize **08** bring off
**09** discharge, implement, undertake
**10** accomplish **12** give effect to **13** put into effect **15** deliver the goods, put into practice

## carry-on
**04** flap, fuss, stir, to-do **05** hoo-ha
**06** bother, hassle **07** trouble
**09** commotion, kerfuffle

## cart
**03** car, jag, lug **04** bear, dray, gill, haul, hump, jill, lead, move, pram, tote
**05** bandy, carry, float, furby, gambo, shift, truck, wagon **06** barrow, convey, furphy, gurney **07** cariole, hackery, shandry, trailer, tumbrel, tumbril
**08** carriole, democrat, handcart, transfer **09** transport **11** wheelbarrow

## cartilage
**07** cricoid, gristle **08** chondrus, meniscus

## carton
**03** box, tub **04** case, pack **06** packet, parcel **07** package **09** container

## cartoon
**04** toon **05** anime, manga **06** bubble, parody, send-up, sketch **07** balloon, drawing, fumetto, lampoon, picture, take-off **09** animation, burlesque
**10** caricature, comic strip **12** animated film, strip cartoon

*Cartoon characters include:*

**03** PHB, Ren, Tom
**04** Bart, Fred, Huey, Kyle, Lisa, Stan
**05** Alice, Bluto, Dewey, Dumbo, Goofy, Homer, Jerry, Kenny, Louey, Marge, Mr Men, Robin, Rocky, Snowy, Wally
**06** Batman, Beavis, Boo Boo, Calvin, Daphne, Droopy, Hobbes, Maggie, Obelix, Popeye, Shaggy, Snoopy, Stimpy, Thelma, Tintin, Top Cat
**07** Asterix, Cartman, Custard, Dilbert, Gnasher, Muttley, Penfold, Roobarb
**08** Andy Capp, Butthead, Clouseau, Garfield, Krazy Kat, Olive Oyl, Super Man, Superted, Tank Girl, The Joker, Yogi Bear
**09** Betty Boop, Bugs Bunny, Chip 'n' Dale, Daffy Duck, Daisy Duck, Dastardly, Dick Tracy, Elmer Fudd, Marmaduke, Oor Wullie, Pepe le Pew, Scooby Doo, Spider Man, Sylvester, The Broons, Tweety Pie
**10** Bullwinkle, Donald Duck, Judge Dredd, Road Runner, Scrappy Doo, The Riddler
**11** Bart Simpson, Betty Rubble, Danger Mouse, Felix the Cat, Flash Gordon, Fred Bassett, Korky the Cat, Lisa Simpson, Mickey Mouse, Minnie Mouse, The Simpsons, Wile E Coyote
**12** Barney Rubble, Charlie Brown, Desperate Dan, Homer Simpson, Little Misses, Marge Simpson, Ren and Stimpy
**13** Dick Dastardly, Maggie Simpson, Modesty Blaise, Rupert the Bear, Scrooge McDuck
**14** Bash Street Kids, Foghorn Leghorn, Fred Flintstone, Incredible Hulk, The Pink Panther
**15** Calvin and Hobbes, Dennis the Menace, Penelope Pitstop, Steamboat Willie, Wilma Flintstone

*Cartoonists include:*

**02** HB
**03** Low (Sir David)
**04** Capp (Al), Kane (Bob), Rémi (Georges)
**05** Adams (Scott), Avery (Tex), Block (Herbert L), Davis (Jim), Doyle (John), Giles, Hanna (William), Hergé, Jones (Chuck), Lantz (Walter), McCay (Winsor), Segar (Elzie), Silas
**06** Addams (Charles), Disney (Walt), Fisher (Bud), Iwerks (Ub), Larson (Gary), Scarfe (Gerald), Schulz (Charles M), Searle (Ronald), Siegel (Jerry), Smythe (Reg)
**07** Barbera (Joseph), Shuster (Joseph), Tenniel (Sir John), Trudeau (Garry), Watkins (Dudley D), Webster (Tom)
**08** Goldberg (Rube), Groening (Matt), Herblock, Herriman (George), Robinson (Heath)
**09** Baxendale (Leo), Fleischer (Max), Watterson (Bill)
**12** Bairnsfather (Bruce), Hanna-Barbera

## cartridge
**04** case, tube **05** blank, round, shell
**06** charge **07** capsule, torpedo
**08** canister, cassette, cylinder, magazine, streamer **09** container
**11** central fire

## caruncle
**04** aril **08** arillode **10** strophiole

## carve
◇ *anagram indicator*
**03** cut, hew **04** chip, chop, etch, form, hack **05** cut up, kerve, mould, notch, sculp, shape, slice, write **06** chisel, entail, incise, indent, sculpt, unlace
**07** engrave, entayle, fashion, insculp, whittle **09** apportion, dismember, sculpture, truncheon **10** distribute
**11** insculpture
- **carve up**
◇ *anagram indicator*
**05** share, split **06** divide **07** split up
**08** separate, share out **09** parcel out, partition **10** distribute

**carving**
**03** cut **04** bust **05** model, round, tondo **06** statue **08** incision, knotwork, tympanum **09** scrimshaw, sculpture, statuette **10** lithoglyph, petroglyph, rosemaling **11** dendroglyph, scrimshandy **12** mezzo-relievo, mezzo-rilievo, scrimshander

**cascade**
**03** lin **04** fall, gush, linn, pour, rush **05** chute, falls, flood, pitch, spill, surge **06** deluge, plunge, shower, tumble **07** descend, torrent, trickle **08** cataract, fountain, overflow **09** avalanche, waterfall **10** outpouring, water chute, waterworks

**case**
◇ *ends selection indicator*
**03** bag, box **04** étui, sted, suit **05** cause, chest, cover, crate, crime, event, point, shell, state, stead, stede, trial, trunk **06** action, affair, carton, casing, casket, client, dative, essive, holder, jacket, sheath, valise, victim **07** attaché, cabinet, capsule, context, defence, dispute, elative, examine, example, grounds, holdall, inquiry, invalid, keister, lawsuit, patient, process, wrapper **08** abessive, ablative, adessive, allative, argument, canister, evidence, genitive, illative, incident, inessive, instance, kalamdan, locative, occasion, position, showcase, specimen, suitcase, vasculum, vocative **09** briefcase, cartridge, chrysalid, chrysalis, condition, container, flight bag, papeterie, portfolio, reasoning, situation, travel bag **10** accusative, comitative, nominative, occurrence, receptacle, subjective, vanity-case **11** attaché case, contingency, hand luggage, portmanteau, proceedings, reconnoitre, translative, writing desk **12** illustration, overnight bag **13** circumstances, investigation, particularity

**cases**
**02** ca

**cash**
**03** tin **04** cent, dime, dosh, loot **05** blunt, brass, bread, coins, dough, funds, gravy, lolly, money, notes, Oscar, ready, rhino, smash **06** change, encash, greens, moolah, stumpy **07** bullion, capital, finance, readies, realize, scratch, shekels **08** currency, exchange, greenies **09** banknotes, hard money, liquidate, megabucks, resources **10** ready money **11** legal tender, spondulicks, wherewithal **12** hard currency, turn into cash
• **cash return**
**07** jackpot

**cashier**
**04** fire, sack **05** annul, break, clerk, expel **06** banker, bursar, purser, teller **07** checker, discard, dismiss, drum out, unfrock **08** get rid of, throw out **09** bank clerk, discharge, treasurer **10** accountant

**casing**
◇ *containment indicator*
◇ *ends selection indicator*
**03** cup, tub **04** cast, core **05** cover, shell **06** jacket, sheath **07** cowling, housing **08** binnacle, covering, envelope, pair case, trunking, wrapping **09** air-jacket, crankcase, oil string, sheathing **10** protection **11** bell-housing, junction box, steam jacket, water jacket **13** cylinder block

**cask**
**03** but, keg, pin, tub, tun, vat **04** butt, cade, pipe, wood **05** flask **06** barrel, casket, casque, firkin, octave, tierce **07** barrico, breaker, leaguer **08** hogshead, puncheon **09** kilderkin **11** scuttlebutt

**casket**
**03** box **04** case, kist **05** chest, pyxis, shell **06** coffer, coffin, larnax **08** cassette, jewel-box **11** sarcophagus **12** pine overcoat, wooden kimono **14** wooden overcoat

**cassava**
**04** yuca **05** yucca **06** manioc **07** mandioc, manihoc, tapioca **08** mandioca **09** mandiocca

**casserole**
**04** stew **06** diable **07** cocotte, stew-pan, terrine, tzimmes **08** pot-au-feu **09** Dutch oven **10** slow cooker

**cast**
◇ *anagram indicator*
**03** die, lob, mew, put, see, shy **04** drop, emit, form, hurl, look, putt, seek, shed, slip, toss, turn, veer, view, vote, warp **05** add up, drive, fling, found, fusil, heave, impel, model, mould, moult, pitch, place, shape, shoot, sling, stamp, throw **06** actors, assign, chance, create, direct, fusile, glance, launch, look at, manner, record, reject, spread, thrown, troupe **07** appoint, casting, company, condemn, diffuse, discard, dismiss, fashion, give off, give out, glimpse, moulded, players, predict, project, quality, radiate, redound, reflect, scatter **08** covering, register, rejected **09** calculate, formulate **10** catch sight, characters, performers **12** entertainers **13** put in jeopardy **14** mark with a cross
• **cast aside**
**06** reject **07** discard, say no to **08** get rid of, turn down **12** dispense with
• **cast down**
**05** abase, crush **06** abattu, deject, sadden **07** depress **08** dejected, desolate **10** discourage, dishearten
• **cast out**
**09** ostracize

**caste**
**04** race, rank **05** class, grade, group, order **06** degree, estate, status **07** lineage, station, stratum **08** position **10** background **11** social class **14** social standing

**castigate**
**03** rap **04** slam **05** chide, emend, scold **06** berate, punish, rebuke **07** censure, chasten, correct, reprove, upbraid **08** admonish, chastise **09** criticize, dress down, reprimand **10** discipline **13** tear a strip off **15** give someone hell

**castle**
**01** R **04** fort, keep, rook **05** tower, villa **06** kasbah, palace **07** château, citadel, mansion, schloss **08** fastness, fortress **10** stronghold **11** stately home **12** country house

*Castles include:*

**03** Doe, Eye, Lea, Mey
**04** Clun, Drum, Leap, Peel, Trim, Ward, York
**05** Black, Burgh, Corfe, Croft, Doune, Flint, Knock, Leeds, Skibo, White
**06** Cawdor, Durham, Fraser, Glamis, Howard, Ludlow, Maiden, Sandal, Swords
**07** Alnwick, Arundel, Braemar, Caister, Culzean, Dunster, Harlech, Lismore, Old Wick, Peveril, Scotney, Warwick, Windsor
**08** Balmoral, Bamburgh, Bastille, Broughty, Corgarff, Dunottar, Dunvegan, Egremont, Elsinore, Goodrich, Jedburgh, Kilkenny, Monmouth, Pembroke, Stirling, Stokesay, Tintagel, Urquhart
**09** Beaumaris, Blackrock, Chipchase, Dunsinane, Edinburgh, Hermitage, Inverness, Lancaster, Lochleven, St Andrews, Tantallon
**10** Bridgnorth, Caernarvon, Caerphilly, Carmarthen, Jewel Tower, Kenilworth, Montgomery, Okehampton, Pontefract, Rockingham
**11** Castell Coch, Chillingham, Craigmillar, Eilean Donan, Fotheringay, Lindisfarne, Narrow Water, Ravenscraig, Scarborough, Tattershall, Thirlestane
**12** Conisborough
**13** Carrickfergus
**15** St Michael's Mount

*Castle parts include:*

**04** berm, keep, moat, ward
**05** ditch, fosse, motte, mound, scarp, tower
**06** bailey, chapel, corbel, crenel, donjon, merlon, turret
**07** bastion, dungeon, parados, parapet, postern, rampart
**08** approach, barbican, bartizan, brattice, buttress, crosslet, loophole, stockade, wall walk
**09** arrow-slit, courtyard, embrasure, gatehouse, inner wall
**10** drawbridge, murder hole, portcullis, watchtower
**11** battlements, curtain wall, outer bailey
**12** crenellation, lookout tower
**13** enclosure wall

• **castles**
**02** O-O **03** O-O-O

**castrate**
**03** cut, fix **04** geld, glib, swig **05** alter, unman, unsex **06** doctor, neuter **07** evirate, knacker **10** emasculate

**casual**
**03** odd **04** orra **05** blasé, stray **06** chance, random **07** cursory, leisure, offhand, passing, relaxed, scratch **08** careless, informal, laid-back, lukewarm, part-time **09** apathetic, easy-going, irregular, negligent, short-term, temporary, throwaway **10** accidental, fortuitous, incidental, insouciant, nonchalant, occasional, unexpected, unforeseen **11** comfortable, free-and-easy, indifferent, promiscuous, provisional, spontaneous, superficial, unconcerned **12** happy-go-lucky, intermittent **13** lackadaisical, serendipitous, unceremonious, unintentional **14** unpremeditated

**casually**
**06** overly **08** sportily **10** informally, off the cuff **11** comfortably **12** occasionally **13** spontaneously **15** parenthetically

**casualty**
**04** loss **05** death **06** caduac, injury, victim **07** injured, missing, wounded **08** accident, fatality, sufferer **10** dead person, misfortune **13** injured person

**casuistry**
**07** sophism **09** chicanery, sophistry **12** equivocation, speciousness

**cat**
**03** man, mog, tom **04** chap, puss **05** moggy, pussy, queen, rumpy **06** feline, kitten, mouser, neuter, tomcat **08** baudrons, pussy cat **09** catamaran, grimalkin

*See also* **animal**; **vomit**

*Domestic cats include:*

**03** rex
**04** Manx
**05** Korat, tabby
**06** Angora, Bengal, Birman, Bombay, Cymric, Havana, LaPerm, Ocicat, Somali
**07** Burmese, Persian, rag-doll, Siamese, Tiffany
**08** Balinese, Burmilla, Devon rex, Snowshoe, Tiffanie
**09** Himalayan, Maine Coon, Singapura, Tonkinese
**10** Abyssinian, Carthusian, chinchilla, Cornish rex, Selkirk Rex, Turkish Van
**11** Egyptian Mau, Foreign Blue, Russian Blue, silver tabby
**12** Foreign White, Scottish Fold
**13** domestic tabby, Tortoiseshell, Turkish Angora
**15** British longhair, Exotic shorthair, Japanese Bobtail, Norwegian Forest

*Wild and big cats include:*

**03** bob
**04** eyra, lion, lynx, pard, puma
**05** feral, tiger
**06** cougar, jaguar, kodkod, margay, ocelot, pampas
**07** cheetah, leopard
**08** mountain
**09** Geoffroy's
**10** jaguarundi
**11** snow leopard
**12** mountain lion, Scottish wild
**13** little spotted
**14** clouded leopard

*Famous cats include:*

**03** Tom
**04** Bast, Jess
**05** Dinah, Felix, Korky
**06** Arthur, Bastet, Ginger, Kaspar, Top Cat, Ubasti
**07** Bagpuss, Custard, Simpkin
**08** Beerbohm, Garfield, Humphrey, Krazy Kat, Macavity
**09** Mehitabel, Mrs Norris, Sylvester, Thomasina, Tom Kitten
**10** El Brooshna, Heathcliff
**11** Cat in the Hat, Cheshire Cat, Crookshanks, Korky the Cat, Pink Panther, Puss in Boots
**14** Bustopher Jones, Mr Mistoffelees, Old Deuteronomy, The Cat in the Hat

**cataclysm**
**04** blow **07** debacle **08** calamity, collapse, disaster, upheaval **10** convulsion **11** catastrophe, devastation

**cataclysmic**
**05** awful, fatal **06** tragic **08** dreadful, terrible **10** calamitous, disastrous **11** catastrophe, devastating

**catacomb**
**04** tomb **05** crypt, vault **07** ossuary **09** mausoleum **11** burial-vault

**catalogue**
**03** cat **04** file, list, roll **05** guide, index, table **06** litany, ragman, record, roster **07** catelog, magalog, notitia, ragment **08** brochure, bulletin, calendar, classify, manifest, register, schedule, tabulate **09** checklist, directory, gazetteer, inventory, make a list **10** categorize, prospectus **11** alphabetize, iconography, specialogue **12** compile a list **14** classification, Durchmusterung

**catapult**
**01** Y **04** fire, hurl, toss **05** fling, pitch, shoot, sling, throw **06** hurtle, launch, propel **07** balista, bricole **08** ballista, scorpion, shanghai **09** slingshot

**cataract**
**03** lin **04** linn **05** falls, force, pearl **06** deluge, rapids **07** cascade, torrent **08** downpour, overfall, pearl-eye **09** floodgate, pin and web, waterfall **10** portcullis, waterspout

**catastrophe**
**04** blow, doom, rear, ruin **06** fiasco **07** debacle, failure, reverse, tragedy, trouble **08** calamity, disaster, upheaval **09** adversity, cataclysm, mischance **10** affliction, misfortune **11** devastation

**catastrophic**
**05** awful, fatal **06** tragic **08** dreadful, terrible **10** calamitous, disastrous **11** cataclysmic, devastating

**catcall**
**03** boo **04** gibe, hiss, jeer, jibe **07** whistle **09** raspberry **10** barracking, Bronx cheer

**catch**
◇ *containment indicator*
**03** bag, cop, get, kep, nab, net **04** bolt, clip, draw, fang, find, fish, grab, grip, hank, hasp, haul, hear, hold, hook, lock, make, nail, nick, pawl, rope, sear, snag, sneb, snib, tack, take, trap, twig **05** board, clasp, get it, get on, grasp, hitch, latch, phang, seize, snare, sneck, watch **06** arrest, clutch, collar, corner, detect, detent, engage, entrap, expose, fathom, follow, pick up, snatch, take in, unmask **07** attract, capture, develop, discern, ensnare, find out, make out, problem, round up, seizure, startle **08** contract, discover, drawback, fastener, holdfast, hunt down, obstacle, overtake, perceive, surprise **09** apprehend, deprehend, lay hold of, recapture, recognize, succumb to **10** comprehend, difficulty, go down with, understand **11** be in time for **12** disadvantage, get the hang of **13** become ill with, catch in the act **14** catch red-handed

*See also* **haul**; **song**

• **catch on**
**05** grasp **06** fathom, follow, take in **10** comprehend, understand **13** become popular

• **catch up**
**06** gain on **08** overtake **09** draw level

**catching**
◇ *containment indicator*
**06** taking **10** attractive, contagious, infectious **11** captivating **12** communicable **13** transmissible, transmittable

**catchphrase**
**05** motto **06** byword, jingle, saying, slogan, wheeze **07** formula **08** password **09** catchword, parrot-cry, watchword **10** shibboleth

**catchy**
**07** melodic, popular, tuneful **08** haunting **09** appealing, deceptive, memorable **10** attractive **11** captivating **13** unforgettable

**catechize**
**04** test **05** drill, grill **07** examine **08** instruct, question **11** interrogate **12** cross-examine

**categorical**
**05** clear, total, utter **06** direct **07** express **08** absolute, definite, emphatic, explicit, positive **09** downright **10** conclusive,

unreserved **11** unequivocal, unqualified **13** unconditional

**categorically**
**07** clearly, utterly **08** directly
**09** expressly **10** absolutely, definitely, explicitly, positively **12** emphatically, unreservedly **13** unequivocally
**15** unconditionally

**categorization**
**07** listing, ranking, sorting
**08** grouping, ordering **11** arrangement
**14** classification

**categorize**
**03** peg **04** list, rank, sort **05** class, grade, group, order **06** docket
**07** arrange, docquet **08** classify, tabulate **09** phenotype
**10** pigeonhole, stereotype

**category**
**04** head, kind, list, rank, sort, type
**05** class, genre, grade, group, order, stirp, stuff, taxon, title **06** rubric, stirps
**07** bracket, chapter, heading, listing, section, variety **08** division, grouping
**10** department, superclass, superorder **11** superphylum
**14** classification

**cater**
**05** serve **06** pander, supply **07** furnish, indulge, provide, satisfy, victual
**09** provision

**caterwaul**
**03** cry **04** bawl, howl, wail, yowl
**05** miaow, wrawl **06** scream, shriek, squall **07** screech

**catharsis**
**07** purging, release **09** cleansing, epuration, purifying **10** abreaction, abstersion, lustration **12** purification

**cathartic**
**07** lustral, purging, release, scourer
**09** cleansing, purgative, purifying
**10** abreactive, abstersive, eccoprotic

**cathedral**
**04** dome **05** duomo **07** minster
**12** procathedral
*See also* **church**

*Cathedrals in the UK include:*

**03** Ely
**05** Derby, Isles, Leeds, Ripon, Truro, Wells
**06** Bangor, Brecon, Dundee, Durham, Exeter, Oxford
**07** Arundel, Bristol, Cardiff, Chester, Clifton, Dornoch, Glasgow, Lincoln, Newport, Norwich, Salford, St Asaph, St John's, St Mary's, St Paul's, Swansea, Wrexham
**08** Aberdeen, Bradford, Carlisle, Coventry, Hereford, Llandaff, Plymouth, St Albans, St Davids
**09** Blackburn, Brentwood, Edinburgh, Guildford, Inverness, Lancaster, Leicester, Lichfield, Liverpool, Newcastle, Rochester, Salisbury, Sheffield, Southwark, St Andrews, Wakefield, Worcester
**10** Birmingham, Canterbury, Chelmsford, Chichester, Gloucester, Manchester, Nottingham, Portsmouth, Shrewsbury, Winchester
**11** Northampton, York Minster
**12** Christ Church, Peterborough
**13** Middlesbrough, St Edmundsbury

*Cathedrals worldwide include:*

**04** Lund
**05** Milan
**06** Aachen, Rheims
**07** Cologne, Córdoba, Orvieto, St Mark's
**08** Chartres, Florence, St Basil's, St Peter's
**09** Notre-Dame
**10** Strasbourg
**11** Hagia Sophia

**• cathedral city**
**03** see

**catholic**
**01** C **02** RC **04** Tory, wide **05** broad, Latin, Roman **06** global, varied
**07** diverse, general, liberal **08** eclectic, Jebusite, Romanish, Romanist, tolerant
**09** inclusive, universal **10** broad-based, left-footer, open-minded, Tridentine, widespread **11** broad-minded, wide-ranging **12** all-embracing, all-inclusive
**13** comprehensive **15** all-encompassing

**catholicism**
**04** Rome **06** popery **08** Romanism

**catmint**
**03** nep, nip **06** catnep, catnip, nepeta

**cats and dogs**
**04** rain

**cattle**
**02** ky **03** fee, kye **04** aver, cows, kine, kyne, neat, nout, nowt, oxen **05** bulls, stock **06** beasts, beeves **09** livestock
*See also* **animal**

*Cattle include:*

**02** zo
**03** dso, dzo, gir, gur, gyr, zho
**04** dzho, jomo, tuli, zebu, zobo, zobu
**05** Angus, black, Devon, dsobo, dsomo, Kerry, Luing, sanga, wagyu, white, zhomo
**06** ankole, dexter, Durham, Jersey, Salers, Sussex, watusi
**07** beefalo, brahman, brahmin, brangus, cattabu, cattalo, Latvian, red poll
**08** Alderney, Ayrshire, Chianina, Friesian, Galloway, gelbvieh, Guernsey, Hereford, Highland, Holstein, illawara, Limousin, longhorn, Shetland
**09** Afrikaner, braunvieh, Charolais, Corriente, Romagnola, shorthorn, Simmental, Teeswater, Ukrainian, white park
**10** Africander, beefmaster, Brown Swiss, Canadienne, Charollais, Lincoln Red, Murray grey, Piemontese, Simmenthal, South Devon, Tarentaise, Welsh Black
**11** Belgian Blue, Chillingham, Piedmontese
**12** British White, Simmenthaler
**13** Aberdeen Angus, droughtmaster, Texas longhorn
**14** Belted Galloway, Santa Gertrudis

**catty**
**03** kin **04** kati, mean **05** katti
**06** bitchy **07** vicious **08** spiteful, venomous **09** malicious, rancorous
**10** backbiting, ill-natured, malevolent

**caucus**
**03** set **06** clique, parley **07** meeting, session **08** assembly, conclave
**09** gathering **10** convention **11** get-together

**caught**
◇ *containment indicator*
**01** c **02** ct **03** had **04** held **06** keight, netted **11** in by the week

**cauliflower**
**04** gobi
**• head of cauliflower**
**04** curd

**causative**
**04** root **07** causing, factive
**09** factitive

**cause**
**03** aim, end, gar **04** call, make, root, sake **05** agent, basis, beget, begin, breed, causa, force, garre, ideal, maker, mover **06** agency, author, belief, compel, create, effect, factor, incite, induce, lead to, motive, object, origin, parent, prompt, reason, render, source, spring **07** because, creator, grounds, impulse, produce, provoke, purpose, trigger **08** generate, motivate, movement, occasion, producer, result in, stimulus **09** beginning, incentive, originate, principle, stimulate, wherefore **10** accusation, bring about, conviction, enterprise, give rise to, inducement, mainspring, make happen, motivation, originator, prime mover, trigger off **11** explanation, precipitate, undertaking **12** be the cause of **13** be at the root of, justification

**caustic**
**04** acid, keen, tart **05** snide **06** biting, bitter, severe **07** burning, cutting, erodent, mordant, pungent
**08** scathing, stinging, virulent
**09** acidulent, acidulous, corroding, corrosive, sarcastic, trenchant, vitriolic
**10** astringent, escharotic
**11** acrimonious, destructive

**caustically**
**08** bitterly, severely **10** scathingly, virulently **11** trenchantly
**13** acrimoniously, sarcastically, vitriolically

**cauterize**
**04** burn, fire, sear **05** singe **06** scorch
**09** carbonize, disinfect, sterilize

**caution**
**04** bail, care, heed, urge, warn **05** alert, deter, guard **06** advice, advise, cautel, caveat, surety, tip off, tip-off **07** counsel, warning **08** admonish, prudence, security, wariness **09** alertness, reprimand, vigilance **10** admonition, discretion, injunction **11** carefulness, forethought, heedfulness, mindfulness **12** deliberation, watchfulness **14** circumspection
• **lacking caution**
**04** rash

**cautious**
**04** safe, ware, wary **05** alert, cagey, chary **06** Fabian, shrewd **07** careful, guarded, heedful, prudent, tactful **08** discreet, gingerly, vigilant, watchful **09** cautelous, defensive, judicious, tentative **10** deliberate **11** circumspect **12** conservative, softly-softly **13** unadventurous

**cautiously**
**08** gingerly **09** carefully, prudently, tactfully **10** discreetly **11** defensively, judiciously, tentatively **12** deliberately **13** circumspectly **14** conservatively

**cavalcade**
**05** array, train, troop **06** parade **07** cortège, retinue, sowarry **08** sowarree **09** march-past, motorcade **10** procession

**cavalier**
**04** curt **05** lofty, spahi **06** casual, escort, knight, lordly **07** gallant, haughty, offhand, partner, warlike **08** arrogant, chasseur, horseman, insolent, Ironside, royalist, scornful **09** chevalier, gentleman, Malignant **10** cavalryman, disdainful, equestrian, incautious, swaggering **11** Bashi-Bazouk, free-and-easy, patronizing **12** devil-may-care, horse soldier, supercilious **13** condescending

**cavalry**
**05** horse **07** hussars, lancers, reiters **08** dragoons, horsemen, sabreurs, troopers **09** chasseurs, Ironsides, risaldars **10** cavalrymen, light-horse, the heavies **11** equestrians, ritt-masters **13** horse soldiers, mounted troops

**cave**
**03** den **04** grot, hole **05** antar, antre, delve **06** beware, cavern, cavity, dugout, grotto, hollow, tunnel **07** pothole **09** Domdaniel

*Caves include:*

**04** Zitu
**06** Berger, Vqerdi
**08** Badalona
**09** G E S Malaga, Snezhnaya
**10** Schneeloch
**11** Batmanhöhle, Jean Bernard
**14** Lamprechstofen, Pierre-St-Martin, Sistema Huautla

• **cave in**
**04** fall, slip **05** yield **06** fall in **07** give way, subside **08** collapse

**caveat**
**05** alarm **06** notice **07** caution, proviso, warning **10** admonition

**cavern**
**03** den **04** cave, cove **05** vault **06** cavity, dugout, Erebus, grotto, hollow, tunnel **07** pothole **08** catacomb, vaultage

**cavernous**
**04** dark, deep, huge, vast **05** large **06** gaping, gloomy, hollow, sunken **07** concave, echoing, immense, yawning **08** resonant, spacious **09** depressed **10** bottomless **12** unfathomable

**cavil**
**03** nag **04** carp **06** haggle **07** censure, nit-pick, quarrel, quibble **08** complain, reproach **09** criticize **10** find faults

**cavity**
**03** gap, pit, sac, vug **04** bore, cell, dent, hole, mine, tear, vein, well, womb **05** celom, crypt, druse, geode, lumen, purse, sinus, vitta **06** antrum, atrium, camera, coelom, concha, cotyle, crater, hollow, lacuna, pelvis, pocket **07** chamber, cochlea, coelome, eardrum, glenoid, orifice, vacuole, vesicle **08** aperture, brood-sac **09** ventricle, vestibule **10** acetabulum, blastocoel, brood-pouch, cavitation, excavation, hollowness, thunder-egg **11** conceptacle, haematocele, mediastinum, rhynchocoel **13** neuroblastoma, splanchnocele

**cavort**
◇ *anagram indicator*
**04** romp, skip **05** caper, dance, frisk, sport **06** frolic, gambol, prance

**cavy** *see* **guinea pig**

**Cayman Islands**
**03** CYM

**cease**
**03** die, end, lin **04** blin, fail, halt, poop, quit, stay, stop, unbe **05** abate, cesse, leave, let up, stint **06** desist, devall, finish, lay off, pack in **07** poop out, refrain, suspend **08** break off, conclude, give over, leave off, peter out, surcease **09** call a halt, cessation, fizzle out, terminate **11** come to a halt, come to an end, discontinue **12** bring to a halt, bring to an end

**ceaseless**
**07** endless, eternal, non-stop **08** constant, unending, untiring **09** continual, incessant, perpetual, unceasing **10** continuous, persistent **11** everlasting, never-ending, unremitting **12** interminable **13** uninterrupted

**ceaselessly**
**07** for ever **09** endlessly, eternally **10** constantly, unendingly **11** day in day out, incessantly, unceasingly **12** continuously, interminably **13** everlastingly, unremittingly **14** for ever and ever **15** uninterruptedly

**cedar**
**06** arolla, deodar **11** cryptomeria

**cede**
**05** allow, grant, yield **06** convey, give up, resign **07** abandon, concede, deliver **08** abdicate, hand over, renounce, transfer, turn over **09** surrender **10** relinquish

**ceiling**
**04** loft, most, roof **05** beams, limit, vault **06** awning, canopy, cupola, soffit **07** lacunar, maximum, plafond, rafters, seeling **08** overhead **09** laquearia **10** upper limit **11** cut-off point

**celebrate**
**03** wet **04** hold, hymn, keep, laud, mark, rave, sing, tune **05** binge, bless, carol, chant, extol, go out, revel, sound, toast **06** besing, chaunt, honour, record, renown, repeat, shrove, sonnet **07** drink to, emblaze, have fun, maffick, observe, perform, poetize, rejoice, triumph, trumpet **08** emblazon, live it up, memorize, remember **09** have a ball, solemnize, whoop it up **10** have a party, procession **11** commemorate, throw a party **12** concelebrate **13** enjoy yourself, go on the razzle **14** go out on the town, push the boat out, put the flags out **15** paint the town red

**celebrated**
**03** cel **05** famed, great, noted **06** famous **07** admired, eminent, exalted, notable, popular, revered **08** fabulous, glorious, renowned **09** acclaimed, legendary, prominent, well-known **11** illustrious, outstanding **13** distinguished

**celebration**
**02** do **03** ale, jol **04** fete, gala, orgy, rave **05** beano, binge, feast, jolly, spree **06** hooley, junket, rave-up **07** jubilee, revelry, shindig **08** festival, jamboree, occasion, Olympiad **09** festivity, gaudeamus **10** observance **11** merrymaking **13** jollification
*See also* **festival**

*Celebrations include:*

**04** fête, gala
**05** feast, party
**06** May Day
**07** banquet, baptism, jubilee, name-day, reunion, tribute, wedding
**08** birthday, festival, hen night, marriage
**09** centenary, Labour Day, reception, saint's day, stag night
**10** bar mitzvah, bat mitzvah, dedication, graduation, homecoming, retirement
**11** anniversary, christening, coming-of-age, harvest-home
**12** thanksgiving
**13** commemoration
**15** harvest festival, Independence Day

**celebratory**
**06** festal

**celebrity**
**03** VIP **04** fame, lion, name, note, star **05** celeb **06** bigwig, esteem, legend, renown, worthy **07** big name, big shot, notable, stardom **08** eminence, luminary **09** dignitary, greatness, notoriety, personage, superstar **10** notability, prominence, reputation **11** distinction, personality **12** famous person, living legend **13** household name **15** illustriousness

**celerity**
**05** haste, speed **08** dispatch, fastness, rapidity, velocity **09** fleetness, quickness, swiftness **10** expedition, promptness

**celestial**
**06** astral, divine, starry, uranic **07** angelic, Chinese, elysian, eternal, godlike, sublime **08** empyrean, ethereal, heavenly, immortal, seraphic, supernal **09** spiritual, unearthly **10** paradisaic, superlunar **11** superlunary, translunary **12** supernatural **14** transcendental

**celestially**
**08** divinely **09** eternally, sublimely **10** immortally **11** angelically, spiritually **14** supernaturally

**celibacy**
**06** purity **08** chastity **09** virginity **10** abnegation, abstinence, continence, maidenhood, self-denial, singleness **12** bachelorhood, spinsterhood **13** self-restraint

**celibate**
**04** pure **05** unwed **06** chaste, single, virgin **08** bachelor, spinster **09** abstinent, unmarried

**cell**
**03** set **04** coop, cyte, jail, room, unit **05** ascus, crowd, crypt, group, party, peter, spore **06** caucus, clique, lock-up, matrix, prison, zygote **07** battery, chamber, cubicle, dungeon, faction, nucleus, section **08** organism **09** anchorage, black hole, cytoplasm, enclosure, hermitage, reclusory **10** protoplasm, protoplast **11** compartment, electric eye

*Cells include:*

**01** B, T
**03** egg, PEC, red, rod, sex, wet
**04** cone, fuel, germ, HeLa, mast, ovum, stem
**05** blood, guard, nerve, plant, solar, sperm, water, white
**06** animal, cancer, collar, diaxon, gamete, goblet, Hadley, killer, memory, mother, neuron, oocyte, plasma, target, tumour
**07** cadmium, Daniell, gravity, helper T, initial, neurone, primary, Schwann, Sertoli, somatic, voltaic
**08** akaryote, basophil, daughter, galvanic, gonidium, gonocyte, monocyte, myoblast, neoblast, parietal, platelet, Purkinje, red blood, retinula, sclereid, selenium, tracheid, zooblast
**09** acidophil, antipodal, astrocyte, coenocyte, corpuscle, fibrocyte, haemocyte, hybridoma, idioblast, Leclanché, leucocyte, leukocyte, macrocyte, microcyte, myofibril, phagocyte, photocell, prokaryon, sclereide, secondary, spermatid, syncytium, thymocyte, tracheide
**10** choanocyte, cnidoblast, enterocyte, eosinophil, fibroblast, gametocyte, hepatocyte, histiocyte, histoblast, leucoblast, leukoblast, lymphocyte, macrophage, melanocyte, myeloblast, neuroblast, neutrophil, osteoblast, osteoclast, spherocyte, suppressor, thread-cell, white blood
**11** B lymphocyte, erythrocyte, granulocyte, lymphoblast, megaloblast, odontoblast, poikilocyte, thrombocyte, T lymphocyte
**12** chondroblast, erythroblast, haematoblast, red corpuscle, reticulocyte, spermatocyte, spermatozoid, spermatozoon
**13** chromatophore, natural killer, photoelectric, spermatoblast
**14** blood corpuscle, spermatogonium, white corpuscle

• **mass of cells**
**05** nodus **06** morula

**cellar**
**04** vaut **05** crypt, dunny, vault, vaute **08** basement, coal hole, vaultage **09** storeroom, wine vault **10** wine cellar, wine vaults

**Celtic** *see* **mythology**

**cement**
**03** fix, gum **04** bind, bond, glue, join, lime, lute, weld **05** affix, compo, grout, paste, putty, stick, trass, union, unite **06** attach, cohere, fasten, gunite, maltha, mastic, matrix, mortar, screed, slurry, solder, stucco **07** bonding, combine, mastich, plaster **08** adhesive, concrete, fixative, grouting, pointing, rice glue, solution **11** ciment fondu

**cemetery**
**05** tombs **06** graves **08** boneyard, God's acre, urnfield **09** graveyard **10** burial site, campo santo, churchyard, necropolis **11** burial place **12** burial ground, charnel house

*Cemeteries and burial places include:*

**07** Nunhead
**08** Brompton, Highgate, Panthéon
**09** Abney Park, Arlington
**10** El Escorial, La Almudena, Montmartre, Mount Holly, San Michele, Weissensee
**11** Kensal Green, Mount Olivet, West Norwood
**12** Golders Green, Les Invalides, Montparnasse, Père Lachaise, Tower Hamlets
**13** Mount of Olives
**15** Island of the Dead

**censor**
**03** ban, cut **04** Cato, edit **06** delete, editor **08** examiner, make cuts **09** expurgate, inspector **10** blue-pencil, bowdlerize, expurgater **11** bowdlerizer

**censorious**
**06** severe **07** carping **08** captious, critical, negative **09** cavilling **10** fuddy-duddy **11** disparaging **12** condemnatory, disapproving, fault-finding, overcritical **13** hypercritical

**censoriously**
**08** severely **10** captiously, critically **13** disparagingly **14** disapprovingly, overcritically **15** hypercritically

**censure**
**03** rap **04** damn, Hell, slam **05** blame, chide, fault, judge, scold, strop, taunt **06** jump on, rebuke, taxing **07** appeach, condemn, obloquy, reproof, reprove, scandal, tell off, trounce, upbraid **08** admonish, denounce, reproach, scolding, sentence **09** castigate, criticism, criticize, dispraise, reprehend, reprimand, reprobate, syndicate **10** admonition, imputation, perstringe, reflection, telling-off, upbraiding **11** castigation, disapproval, remonstrate, reprobation **12** admonishment, condemnation, denunciation, disapprove of, pull to pieces, remonstrance, reprehension, vituperation **15** come down heavy on

**cent**
**01** c **02** ct **03** red **05** penny

**centimes**
**01** c

**centipede**
**08** scutiger **11** scolopendra **12** scolopendrid, thousand-legs

**central**
◇ *hidden indicator*
◇ *middle selection indicator*
**03** cen, key, mid **04** cent, core, main **05** basic, chief, focal, inner, major, prime, vital **06** centre, medial, median, middle **07** crucial, pivotal, primary **08** dominant, foremost, interior **09** essential, principal **11** fundamental, significant **13** most important

• **central heating**
**02** ch

**Central African Republic**
**03** CAF, RCA

**Central America** *see* **America**; **god, goddess**

**centralization**
**08** focusing **11** convergence, unification **12** amalgamation, streamlining **13** concentration, consolidation, incorporation **15** rationalization

**centralize**
**05** focus, unify **07** compact
**08** condense, converge
**10** amalgamate, streamline
**11** concentrate, consolidate, incorporate, rationalize **13** bring together **14** gather together

**centre**
◇ *middle selection indicator*
**03** hub, mid **04** core, crux **05** arena, focus, heart, hinge, pivot **06** kernel, middle, resort **07** nucleus, revolve
**08** bull's-eye, converge, linchpin, midpoint, omphalos **09** gravitate
**10** focal point, metropolis, stronghold
**11** concentrate
• **in centre**
◇ *hidden indicator*

**centre-forward**
**02** cf

**centre-half**
**02** ch

**centrepiece**
**04** best, peak **05** cream **06** climax
**07** epergne **08** duchesse, high spot
**09** highlight, high point **13** duchesse cover

**century**
**01** c **03** age, cen, ton **04** cent
**09** centenary
• **half century**
**01** l

**cephalopod**
**05** Sepia, squid **06** cuttle, loligo
**07** octopus **08** ammonite, nautilus
**09** goniatite, nautiloid **10** cuttlefish
**13** paper nautilus **14** pearly nautilus

**ceramics**
**04** raku, ware **06** bisque **07** faience, pottery **09** ironstone, porcelain
**11** earthenware

**cereal**
**05** grain

*Cereals include:*

**03** oat, rye, tef, zea
**04** bear, bere, corn, oats, rice, sago, teff, yuca
**05** bajra, emmer, maize, spelt, wheat
**06** barley, bulgur, manioc, millet
**07** bulghur, cassava, mandioc, manihoc, oatmeal, sorghum, tapioca
**08** amaranth, amelcorn, couscous, mandioca, semolina
**09** buckwheat, mandiocca, sweetcorn, triticale
**10** guinea corn, Indian corn, Kaffir corn
**11** pearl millet
**12** common millet
**13** bulrush millet, foxtail millet, grain amaranth, Italian millet

*Breakfast cereals include:*

**04** bran
**05** Alpen®
**06** muesli
**07** All Bran®, granola
**08** Cheerios®, Coco Pops®, Frosties®, porridge, Ricicles®, Special K®, Weetabix®
**09** Ready Brek®, Shreddies®
**10** Bran Flakes®, cornflakes, Quaker Oats®, Sugar Puffs®
**11** Fruit'n'Fibre®, Puffed Wheat®, Sultana Bran®
**12** Country Crisp®, Rice Krispies®
**13** Fruit and Fibre®, Golden Grahams®, Honey Nut Loops®, Shredded Wheat®

---

**ceremonial**
**04** rite **05** state **06** custom, formal, ritual, solemn **07** mummery, stately
**08** ceremony, official, protocol
**09** dignified, formality, solemnity
**11** ritualistic

**ceremonially**
**08** formally, ritually, solemnly
**10** officially

**ceremonious**
**05** civil, exact, grand, stiff **06** formal, polite, ritual, solemn **07** courtly, precise, starchy, stately **08** imposing, majestic, official **09** courteous, dignified **10** scrupulous **11** deferential, punctilious

**ceremoniously**
**07** civilly, exactly, grandly, stiffly
**08** formally, politely, solemnly
**09** precisely, starchily **10** officially
**11** courteously **12** scrupulously
**13** deferentially, punctiliously
**15** ritualistically

**ceremony**
**04** form, gaud, pomp, rite, show
**05** order **06** custom, parade, ritual
**07** decorum, liturgy, service
**08** exercise, festival, function, niceties, occasion, protocol **09** etiquette, formality, induction, ordinance, pageantry, propriety, punctilio, sacrament, solemnity, tradition, unveiling **10** ceremonial, coronation, dedication, graduation, initiation, observance **11** anniversary, celebration, investiture
**12** circumstance, commencement, inauguration **13** commemoration, spit and polish

*Ceremonies include:*

**05** amrit, doseh, tangi
**06** maundy, nipter
**07** baptism, capping, chanoyu, chuppah, matsuri, wedding
**08** marriage, nuptials
**09** committal, matrimony
**10** bar mitzvah, bat mitzvah, corroboree, graduation, initiation
**11** christening, fire-walking
**12** confirmation

---

• **funeral ceremonies**
**04** obit

**Ceres**
**07** Demeter

**cerium**
**02** Ce

**certain**
**04** safe, some, sure, true **05** bound, clear, fated, fixed, plain, small
**06** doomed, siccar, sicker **07** assured, dead set, decided, evident, express, limited, obvious, partial, perfect, precise, regular, settled, special
**08** absolute, definite, destined, in the bag, positive, reliable, resolved, specific **09** confident, convinced, indubious, persuaded, undoubted, unfailing **10** conclusive, convincing, dependable, determined, home and dry, individual, inevitable, inexorable, particular, undeniable **11** cut and dried, established, indubitable, ineluctable, inescapable, irrefutable, open-and-shut, unavoidable
**12** indisputable, no ifs and buts
**13** bound to happen, meant to happen
**14** unquestionable
• **a certain**
**03** one **04** some
• **make certain**
**06** ensure

**certainly**
**02** OK **03** oke, yes **04** iwis, okay, sure, ywis **06** and how!, certes, siccar, sicker, surely, you bet **07** clearly, for sure, no doubt, plainly **08** forsooth, of course, to be sure **09** assuredly, doubtless, naturally, obviously, sure thing **10** absolutely, by all means, definitely, in very deed, positively, undeniably **11** beyond doubt, doubtlessly, if you please, indubitably, past dispute, undoubtedly **12** as sure as a gun, bang to rights, questionless, without doubt **13** beyond dispute, without a doubt **14** beyond question, unquestionably, without dispute **15** in all conscience

**certainty**
**03** nap **04** cert, fact, lock, snip
**05** cinch, faith, moral, trust, truth
**06** banker, surety **07** natural, reality, safe bet **08** dead cert, security, sureness, validity **09** assurance, constancy, sure thing **10** confidence, conviction, positivism **11** assuredness
**12** positiveness **13** inevitability
**14** matter of course

**certificate**
**04** pass **05** award, lines, proof, scrip, title **06** cocket, docket, patent, ticket
**07** diploma, licence, voucher, warrant
**08** aegrotat, document, navicert, register, testamur **09** clearance, debenture, guarantee, land-scrip
**10** securities **11** credentials, endorsement, smart-ticket, testimonial
**12** bill of health, Tyburn-ticket
**13** authorization, certificatory, marriage-lines, qualification

**certify**
**04** aver **05** vouch **06** assure, attest, inform, ratify, verify **07** confirm, declare, endorse, license, testify, warrant, witness **08** accredit, validate
**09** authorize, guarantee, pronounce, recognize **11** corroborate

12 authenticate, substantiate 13 bear witness to

**certitude**
08 sureness 09 assurance, certainty 10 confidence, conviction, plerophory 11 assuredness, plerophoria 12 positiveness 13 full assurance

**cessation**
02 ho 03 end, hoa, hoh 04 blin, halt, rest, stay, stop 05 break, cease, let-up, pause, stint 06 ending, hiatus, recess 07 ceasing, failure, halting, respite 08 abeyance, breakoff, interval, stoppage, stopping, surcease, suspense 09 remission 10 conclusion, desistance, standstill, suspension 11 termination 12 intermission, interruption 13 discontinuing 14 discontinuance 15 discontinuation

**Chad**
03 TCD, TCH

**chafe**
03 rub, vex 04 bind, fret, rasp, wear 05 anger, annoy, grate, peeve 06 abrade, chaufe, chauff, enrage, scrape 07 be angry, incense, inflame, provoke, scratch 08 irritate, wear away, wear down 09 excoriate 10 exasperate

**chaff**
03 kid, rag, rib, rot 04 chip, jest, joke, josh, mock, pods 05 cases, husks, tease 06 banter, have-on, joking, shells 07 jesting, kidding, ribbing, rubbish, teasing 08 badinage, repartee 09 make fun of

**chagrin**
03 irk, vex 05 annoy, peeve, shame 07 mortify 08 disquiet, irritate, shagreen, vexation, wormwood 09 annoyance, displease, embarrass, humiliate 10 disappoint, dissatisfy, exasperate, irritation 11 displeasure, fretfulness, humiliation, indignation 12 discomfiture, discomposure, exasperation 13 embarrassment, mortification 14 disappointment 15 dissatisfaction

**chain**
02 ch 03 row, set, tie 04 bind, bond, boom, curb, firm, line, link, rode, seal, team 05 group, guard, hitch, range, slang, train, union 06 albert, catena, fasten, fetter, secure, series, string, tether, traces 07 company, confine, creeper, enslave, manacle, measure, shackle, trammel 08 coupling, handcuff, restrain, sequence 09 fanfarona, restraint 10 succession, watchguard 11 progression 13 concatenation

**chair**
02 MC 04 lead, seat 05 emcee 06 direct 07 convene, speaker 08 chairman, convenor, director, moderate 09 organizer, president, supervise 10 chairwoman 11 chairperson, preside over, toastmaster 13 act as chairman, professorship 15 act as chairwoman

*Chairs include:*

03 arm, lug, pew
04 Bath, camp, cane, deck, easy, form, high, push, wing
05 bench, elbow, king's, night, potty, sedan, stool, wheel
06 basket, carver, curule, dining, estate, jampan, Morris, pouffe, rocker, sag bag, sledge, swivel, throne, wicker
07 beanbag, Berbice, bergère, commode, guérite, kitchen, lounger, nursing, rocking, Windsor
08 captain's, electric, fauteuil, prie-dieu, recliner, wainscot
09 director's
10 boatswain's, fiddle-back, frithstool, ladder-back
11 Cromwellian, gestatorial
12 ducking-stool

*See also* **seat**

**chairman, chairwoman**
02 MC 03 Chm 04 chmn, prof 05 emcee 06 preses 07 praeses 08 convenor, director 09 organizer, president, professor, spokesman 10 prolocutor 11 chairperson, spokeswoman 12 spokesperson

**chalcedony**
04 sard 05 agate 06 plasma 07 sardius 09 hornstone, moss agate 10 bloodstone 11 chrysoprase

**chalk**
• **chalk up**
03 log 04 gain 05 score, tally 06 attain, charge, credit, record 07 achieve, ascribe, put down 08 register 09 attribute 10 accumulate

**chalky**
03 wan 04 pale 05 ashen, dusty, white 06 ground, pallid 07 crushed, powdery 10 calcareous, colourless, cretaceous, granulated

**challenge**
03 hen, tax, try, vie 04 call, dare, defy, gage, risk, test 05 assay, brave, claim, demur, query, stand, stump, trial 06 accost, accuse, appeal, cartel, charge, hazard, henner, hurdle, invite, strain, summon, tackle, why-not 07 bidding, darrain, darrayn, deraign, dispute, problem, protest, provoke, stretch, summons 08 champion, confront, darraign, darraine, defiance, object to, obstacle, question 09 darraigne, objection, stimulate, ultimatum 10 accusation, opposition 11 opportunity, provocation, questioning 12 disagreement, disagree with 13 confrontation, interrogation 14 call in question 15 take exception to

**challenging**
06 gnarly, taxing 07 testing 08 exacting, exciting 09 demanding 10 stretching

**chamber**
02 po 03 pot 04 hall, room, silo 05 divan, fogou, house, jerry, potty, vault 06 camera, cavern, cavity, chanty, durbar, hollow, jordan, serdab, urinal 07 bedroom, boudoir, confine, council 08 assembly, casemate, gazunder, hypogeum, moot-hall, thalamus 09 apartment, combustor, hypogaeum, mattamore, stokehold, ventricle 10 auditorium, close-stool, parliament, souterrain, subterrain, subterrane, thunderbox 11 compartment, legislature 12 assembly room, meeting-place

*See also* **room**

**champagne**
03 fiz, pop 04 fizz 06 bubbly, simkin 07 Sillery, simpkin 08 champers, the Widow 10 gooseberry

*See also* **wine**

**champion**
02 Ch 03 ace, Cid, gun 04 back, hero, kemp 05 angel, champ, ozeki 06 backer, defend, expert, kemper, knight, patron, uphold, victor, winner 07 apostle, espouse, messiah, promote, protect, saviour, support, tribune 08 advocate, asserter, assertor, defender, douzeper, guardian, maintain, Palmerin, stand for, upholder, yokozuna 09 campeador, challenge, conqueror, deliverer, doucepere, excellent, promachos, proponent, protector, supporter 10 kemperyman, stand up for, vindicator 11 excellently, protagonist, title-holder 13 hold a brief for

*See also* **seven**

**chance**
03 hap, run, try 04 cast, fate, luck, odds, risk, show, time 05 arise, break, essay, fluke, occur, stake, wager 06 crop up, fair go, flukey, follow, gamble, happen, hazard, random, result, strike, upcast 07 destiny, develop, fortune, opening, venture 08 accident, Buckley's, fortuity, occasion, prospect 09 arbitrary, come about, haphazard, speculate, take place 10 likelihood, play a hunch, providence 11 bet your life, coincidence, contingency, opportunity, possibility, probability, serendipity, speculation, take a chance 12 bet your boots, happenstance, push your luck, your best shot 14 Buckley's chance, chance your luck
• **by chance**
07 happily 08 bechance, randomly 09 by mistake 10 by accident 11 haphazardly, unwittingly 12 accidentally, fortuitously, incidentally, peradventure, unexpectedly 13 inadvertently 14 adventitiously 15 serendipitously, unintentionally
• **chance on, chance upon**
04 meet 06 casual, flukey, random 07 run into 08 bump into, discover 09 arbitrary, haphazard, run across, stumble on 10 accidental, come across, fortuitous, incidental,

unexpected, unforeseen, unintended **11** inadvertent, unlooked-for **12** find by chance **13** serendipitous, unanticipated, unintentional

- **decision by chance**

**03** lot **04** draw **07** lottery

**Chancellor of the Exchequer**
**02** CE

**chancy**
**04** safe **05** dicey, dodgy, lucky, risky **06** tricky **07** fraught **09** dangerous, hazardous, uncertain **11** speculative **13** problematical, unpredictable

**chandelier**
**06** corona, lustre **09** girandola, girandole **11** corona lucis, electrolier

**change**
◇ *anagram indicator*
**02** go **03** mew **04** cash, chop, move, pass, peal, swap, turn, vary **05** adapt, alter, amend, coins, renew, shift, trade, trend, U-turn, waver **06** adjust, barter, become, evolve, modify, mutate, reform, revise, rotate, silver, switch **07** commute, connect, convert, coppers, develop, novelty, remodel, renewal, replace, shake-up, variate, variety **08** do a U-turn, exchange, movement, mutation, reversal, revision, rotation, transfer, upheaval **09** about-face, about-turn, alternate, amendment, customize, diversion, evolution, fluctuate, transform, transpose, turnabout, vacillate, variation, volte-face **10** adaptation, adjustment, alteration, conversion, difference, ebb and flow, innovation, reorganize, revolution, substitute, transition **11** alternation, development, fluctuation, interchange, remodelling, replacement, restructure, state of flux, transfigure, transmutate, vacillation, vicissitude **12** metamorphose, modification, substitution **13** chop and change, customization, make different, metamorphosis, restructuring, transmutation, transposition **14** reconstruction, reorganization, transformation **15** become different, make a connection, transfiguration

**changeable**
◇ *anagram indicator*
**05** fluid, windy **06** fickle, labile, mobile, wankle, whimsy **07** erratic, flighty, movable, mutable, Protean, various, varying, voluble, whimsey **08** moveable, shifting, skittish, unstable, unsteady, variable, volatile, wavering **09** changeful, irregular, mercurial, uncertain, unsettled, versatile **10** capricious, inconstant, unreliable **11** chameleonic, fluctuating, vacillating **12** inconsistent **13** chameleon-like, kaleidoscopic, unpredictable **15** vicissitudinous

**changeless**
**05** final, fixed **06** static **07** eternal **08** constant, timeless **09** immutable, permanent **10** invariable, unchanging **11** unalterable **12** unchangeable

**changeling**
**03** auf, oaf **08** elf-child, killcrop

**channel**
**02** ea **03** bed, eau, gut, sny, sow, use, way **04** duct, feed, gate, kill, lake, lane, lead, main, neck, path, race, send, snye, sure, tube **05** agent, canal, chime, ditch, drain, falaj, flume, focus, force, glyph, guide, gully, latch, letch, level, major, means, radio, rigol, route, sewer, sloot, sluit, sound, stank, trunk **06** agency, airway, artery, avenue, convey, course, cut-off, direct, furrow, gravel, groove, grough, gullet, gulley, gutter, hollow, limber, medium, narrow, rigoll, sheuch, siphon, sluice, strait, trench, trough **07** chamfer, conduct, conduit, culvert, fairway, limbers, narrows, offtake, passage, raceway, shingle, station, wireway **08** approach, aqueduct, headrace, millrace, overflow, tailrace, transmit, wash-away, waterway **11** canaliculus, concentrate, katabothron, katavothron, spill-stream, watercourse

*Channels include:*

**03** Kii
**04** Foxe
**05** Bashi, Bungo, Kaiwi, Kauai, Lamma, Minas, Minch, North
**06** Akashi, Kalohi, Manche, Queens
**07** Babuyan, Bristol, English, Jamaica, Massawa, Pailolo, Sandwip, St Lucia, Yucatán
**08** Dominica, La Manche, Nicholas, Santaren, Sicilian, St Andrew, The Minch
**09** Balintang, Capricorn, East Lamma, Geographe, Kaulakahi, Northwest, Old Bahama, Skagerrak, St George's, West Lamma
**10** Alalakeiki, Alenuihaha, McClintock, Mozambique, North Minch
**11** Little Minch
**12** Kealaikahiki, Santa Barbara

*See also* **television**

- **Channel Islands**

**02** CI

*The Channel Islands:*

**04** Herm, Sark
**06** Jersey, Jethou
**07** Brechou
**08** Alderney, Guernsey
**10** the Caskets
**11** the Chauseys
**12** the Minquiers

**chant**
**03** cry **04** haka, sing, song, yo-ho **05** ditty, psalm, shout **06** cantus, chorus, incant, intone, mantra, melody, recite, slogan, warcry, yo-ho-ho **07** refrain **09** decantate, plainsong, yo-heave-ho **10** cantillate, intonation, recitation **11** Hare Krishna, incantation

**chaos**
◇ *anagram indicator*
**04** mess, muss, riot **05** abyss, havoc, musse, snafu **06** bedlam, mayhem, tumult, uproar **07** anarchy **08** disarray, disorder, madhouse, shambles, tohu bohu, upheaval **09** confusion **10** disruption, dog's dinner **11** lawlessness, pandemonium **13** pig's breakfast **14** Rafferty's rules **15** disorganization

**chaotic**
◇ *anagram indicator*
**05** snafu **06** unruly **07** lawless, riotous **08** anarchic, confused, deranged **09** disrupted, orderless, shambolic **10** disordered, disorderly, topsy-turvy, tumultuary, tumultuous **12** disorganized, uncontrolled **14** all over the shop **15** all over the place

**chap**
**03** boy, cat, cod, guy, jaw, man, mun, oik, sod **04** boyo, chop, cove, hack, sort, type **05** bloke, bucko, cheek, crack, knock, spray **06** codger, fellow, Johnny, shaver, strike **07** bastard, Johnnie, spreaze, spreeze **08** spreathe, spreethe **09** character **10** individual, male person

**chapel**
**05** crypt **06** Beulah **07** chantry, galilee, martyry, oratory **08** chauntry, feretory, parabema, sacellum **09** bead-house, prothesis **13** Nonconformist **15** chapelle ardente

**chaperon, chaperone**
**04** mind **05** guard **06** attend, duenna, escort **07** protect **08** sheepdog, shepherd **09** accompany, companion, look after, matronize, safeguard, watch over **10** take care of

**chapped**
**03** raw **04** sore **06** chafed **07** cracked, sprayed

**chapter**
**01** c **02** ch **03** cap **04** chap, part, sura, time **05** caput, phase, stage, surah, topic **06** branch, clause, period **07** capital, episode, portion, section **08** division **10** department

**char**
**02** do **03** tea **04** burn, coal, sear **05** brown, singe, togue, woman **06** Mrs Mop, scorch **07** blacken, Mrs Mopp, torgoch **08** redbelly, saibling **09** carbonize, cauterize **10** accomplish, brook trout **11** Dolly Varden

**character**
**04** aura, card, case, hair, logo, mark, part, role, rune, sign, sort, tone, type **05** charm, ethos, image, stamp, style, trait, write **06** appeal, cipher, device, emblem, figure, honour, letter, make-up, nature, oddity, person, psyche, status, symbol, temper **07** calibre, courage, engrave, essence, feature, honesty, imprint, oddball, persona, quality **08** backbone, describe, identity, interest, original, position, property, strength **09** delineate, eccentric, ideograph, integrity, reference, represent **10** attributes,

hieroglyph, human being, individual, moral fibre, reputation **11** disposition, peculiarity, personality, specialness, temperament, uprightness
**12** constitution **13** determination, individuality **14** attractiveness
**15** characteristics, eccentric person
*See also* **alphabet**; **Bible**; **cartoon**; **fairy tale**; **legend**; **letter**; **literary**; **mythology**; **opera**; **pantomine**; **Shakespeare**

**• character part**
**04** role

**• characters in**
◇ *hidden indicator*

**• proper character**
**03** him

**characteristic**
**04** mark, note **05** point, right, trait
**06** factor **07** feature, quality, special, symptom, typical **08** hallmark, peculiar, property, specific, symbolic
**09** attribute, mannerism, trademark
**10** individual **11** distinctive, peculiarity, symptomatic **12** idiosyncrasy
**13** idiosyncratic **14** discriminative, distinguishing, representative

**characteristically**
**09** typically **10** peculiarly
**12** individually **13** distinctively

**characterization**
**09** depiction, portrayal **11** description
**12** presentation **14** representation

**characterize**
**04** mark **05** brand, stamp **06** depict, typify **07** portray, present, qualify, specify **08** describe, identify, indicate
**09** designate, represent **10** stereotype
**11** distinguish

**• be characterized by**
**04** have

**characterless**
**05** inane **12** invertebrate

**charade**
**04** fake, sham **05** farce **06** parody, riddle **07** mockery **08** pretence, travesty **09** pantomime

**charge**
**01** Q **03** ask, chg, due, fee, ion, rap, tax
**04** bill, care, cost, debt, dues, duty, fill, levy, load, mine, rate, rent, rush, shot, tear, tilt, toll, ward **05** blame, debit, exact, imbue, onset, order, price, prime, storm, terms, trust **06** accuse, affect, amount, ask for, assail, attack, burden, demand, dittay, impose, impute, indict, infuse, onrush, outlay, rental, sortie, tariff, thrill **07** arraign, assault, command, custody, expense, impeach, keeping, mandate, payment, pervade, suffuse **08** godchild, saturate, storming **09** challenge, fix a price, inculpate, incursion, offensive, onslaught, overwhelm, put down to, set a price **10** accusation, accusement, allegation, imputation, indictment, objuration, obligation, protection
**11** arraignment, expenditure, impeachment, incriminate, rush forward, safekeeping **12** guardianship
**13** incrimination **14** responsibility
**15** ask someone to pay, demand in payment
*See also* **heraldry**

**• clear of charges**
**03** net **04** nett

**• in charge of**
**02** i/c **07** leading **08** managing
**09** directing, heading up
**10** overseeing **11** controlling, supervising **12** looking after, taking care of **14** responsible for

**charged**
**04** live **08** instinct

**chariot**
**03** car **04** biga, rath, wain **05** ratha, wagon **06** charet, vimana, waggon
**08** quadriga

**charioteer**
**03** Hur **04** Jehu **06** Ben-Hur
**07** wagoner **08** waggoner

**charisma**
**04** draw, lure, pull **05** charm **06** allure, appeal **09** magnetism **10** attraction
**12** drawing-power

**charismatic**
**08** charming, magnetic **09** appealing, glamorous **10** attractive **11** captivating, fascinating **12** irresistible

**charitable**
**04** kind **06** benign, kindly **07** lenient, liberal **08** generous, gracious, tolerant
**09** bounteous, forgiving, indulgent
**10** beneficent, benevolent, open-handed **11** broad-minded, considerate, magnanimous, sympathetic **12** eleemosynary, humanitarian **13** compassionate, philanthropic, understanding

**• charitable person**
**04** Lion

**charitably**
**06** kindly **09** liberally **10** generously, graciously, tolerantly **11** bounteously
**12** open-mindedly **13** considerately
**15** compassionately, sympathetically

**charity**
**03** aid **04** alms, fund, gift, love **05** trust
**06** relief **07** caritas, concern, funding, handout, mission **08** altruism, clemency, donation, goodness, goodwill, hospital, humanity, kindness, leniency, sympathy **09** affection, tolerance **10** almsgiving, assistance, benignness, compassion, foundation, generosity, indulgence **11** beneficence, benevolence, institution, munificence
**12** contribution, graciousness, philanthropy **13** bountifulness, confraternity, consideration, unselfishness **14** thoughtfulness
**15** considerateness, kind-heartedness

*Charities include:*

**03** DEC, NCH
**04** PDSA, RNIB, RNLI, RSPB, WRVS
**05** CAFOD, NSPCC, Oxfam, RSPCA, Scope
**09** ActionAid, Barnardo's
**10** Greenpeace
**11** Comic Relief, Help the Aged
**12** Christian Aid
**13** National Trust, Wellcome Trust, Woodland Trust
**15** Leonard Cheshire, Save the Children, St John Ambulance

*Charity fundraising events include:*

**06** fun run, raffle
**08** telethon
**09** radiothon, swimathon
**10** jumble sale
**12** slave auction
**13** coffee morning, sponsored swim, sponsored walk
**14** charity auction
**15** bring-and-buy sale

**charlatan**
**04** fake, sham **05** cheat, fraud, quack
**06** con man, phoney **08** impostor, swindler **09** pretender, trickster
**10** confidence, mountebank **11** bogus caller, illywhacker **13** bogus official

**charlie**
**01** C
*See also* **fool**

**charm**
**02** it **03** obi, win **04** draw, idol, ju-ju, mojo, obia, take, tiki **05** aroma, magic, obeah, spell, weird **06** allure, amulet, appeal, cajole, enamor, fetish, glamor, grigri, mascot, please, seduce
**07** abraxas, attract, becharm, beguile, bewitch, delight, enamour, enchant, encharm, glamour, hei tiki, periapt, sorcery, trinket, windbag **08** comether, greegree, grisgris, intrigue, medicine, nephrite, ornament, prestige, talisman
**09** captivate, cramp-bone, enrapture, fascinate, magnetism, mesmerize
**10** allurement, attraction, night-spell, phylactery **11** abracadabra, captivation, enchantment, fascination, hand of glory, what it takes
**12** desirability, porte-bonheur
**14** attractiveness, delightfulness

**charming**
**04** cute, nice **05** elfin, sweet **06** lovely, pretty, quaint, smooth **07** winning, winsome **08** adorable, alluring, engaging, fetching, pleasant, pleasing, tasteful, tempting **09** appealing, disarming, glamorous, seductive
**10** attractive, bewitching, delectable, delightful, enchanting, entrancing
**11** captivating, fascinating
**12** chocolate-box, irresistible

**charmingly**
**07** sweetly **09** winsomely
**10** alluringly, delectably, pleasantly, pleasingly **11** glamorously
**12** attractively, delightfully, enchantingly, irresistibly

**chart**
**02** ch **03** map **04** abac, draw, list, mark, note, plan, plot **05** draft, graph,

place, table **06** follow, league, map out, record, sketch **07** diagram, monitor, observe, outline, sea card **08** bar chart, document, isopleth, nomogram, pie chart, register **09** blueprint, delineate, flow chart, flow sheet, hit parade, modulator, nomograph, sociogram, top twenty **10** hyetograph, organogram **11** put on record **13** keep a record of

**charter**
**04** bond, deed, hire, rent **05** carta, grant, lease, right **06** charta, employ, engage, patent, permit **07** licence, license, warrant **08** contract, covenant, document, sanction **09** allowance, authority, authorize, franchise, indenture, novodamus, privilege **10** commission, concession **11** prerogative **13** accreditation, authorization

**chary**
**03** shy **04** cagy, slow, wary **05** cagey, leery **06** tender, uneasy **07** careful, guarded, heedful, prudent **08** cautious, precious **09** reluctant, unwilling **10** fastidious, suspicious **11** circumspect

**chase**
◇ *juxtaposition indicator*
**03** sic **04** fall, hunt, rush, seek, sick, tail **05** chevy, chivy, drive, expel, hound, hurry, track, trail **06** chivvy, course, follow, groove, pursue, quarry, scorse, shadow **07** engrave, hot-trod, hunting, pursuit **08** coursing, run after, send away **09** give chase, prosecute **12** running after **13** hare and hounds

**chasm**
**03** gap **04** gape, gulf, rift, void, yawn **05** abyss, cleft, crack, gorge, split **06** breach, canyon, cavity, crater, hollow, ravine **07** divorce, fissure, opening, quarrel **08** crevasse **10** alienation, separation **12** disagreement, estrangement

**chassis**
**05** frame **08** bodywork, fuselage, skeleton **09** framework, structure **12** substructure **13** undercarriage

**chaste**
**03** ren, rin, run **04** bare, pure, sick **05** moral, plain, worry **06** decent, demure, graced, honest, modest, scorse, simple, single, vestal **07** austere, classic **08** celibate, innocent, virginal, virtuous **09** abstinent, continent, unadorned, undefiled, unmarried, unsullied **10** immaculate, restrained **13** unembellished

**chasten**
**04** curb, tame **06** humble, punish, purify, refine, soften, subdue, temper **07** correct, repress, reprove **08** chastise, moderate, restrain **09** castigate, humiliate **10** discipline

**chastise**
**03** fix **04** beat, cane, flog, lash, whip **05** scold, smack, spank, strap **06** berate, disple, punish, purify, refine, reform, swinge, wallop **07** censure, correct, reprove, scourge, upbraid **08** admonish, moderate, restrain **09** castigate, dress down, reprimand **10** discipline, take to task

**chastisement**
**07** beating, censure, what for **08** flogging, scolding, smacking, spanking, whipping **09** walloping **10** admonition, correction, discipline, punishment **11** castigation **12** dressing-down

**chastity**
**05** honor **06** honour, purity, virtue **07** honesty, modesty **08** celibacy **09** innocence, virginity **10** abstinence, continence, continency, maidenhood, moderation, singleness **13** temperateness **14** immaculateness, unmarried state

**chat**
**03** gas, jaw, rap **04** coze, talk **05** crack, louse, visit, wongi **06** babble, confab, cosher, gossip, jabber, natter, rabbit, waffle, yabber **07** blather, blether, chatter, chinwag, prattle, schmooz, shmoose, shmooze **08** causerie, chitchat, converse, cosy chat, rabbit on, schmooze **09** small talk, tête-à-tête **10** chew the fat, chew the rag **11** confabulate **12** conversation, heart-to-heart, tittle-tattle **13** confabulation **14** clash-ma-clavers, shoot the breeze

**• chat up**
**03** eye **04** ogle **06** leer at **08** come on to **09** flirt with **11** make a pass at **14** make advances to **15** try to get off with

**chatter**
**03** gab, gas, jaw, mag, yap **04** chat, talk **05** clack, clash, froth, skite **06** babble, cackle, confab, gabble, gammon, gossip, jabber, jargon, natter, patter, rabbit, rattle, tattle, waffle, witter, yatter **07** blether, chinwag, chitter, chunder, chunner, chunter, clatter, earbash, gabnash, nashgab, palaver, prattle, twattle **08** chitchat, chounter, rabbit on, rattle on **09** tête-à-tête **10** talky-talky, tongue-work **12** conversation, gibble-gabble, talkee-talkee, tittle-tattle, yada yada yada **14** clitter-clatter **15** yadda yadda yadda

**chatterbox**
**06** gabber, gasbag, gasser, gossip, talker **07** babbler, gabnash, tattler, windbag **08** big mouth, jabberer, natterer **09** chatterer, gossipper, loudmouth **12** blabbermouth **13** tittle-tattler **14** telephone kiosk

**chatterer**
**03** pie **06** chewet, gabber, tatler **07** gabnash, nashgab, tattler

**chatty**
**04** glib **05** dirty, gabby, lousy, newsy **06** casual, mouthy **07** gossipy, gushing, verbose **08** effusive, familiar, friendly, informal **09** garrulous, talkative **10** colloquial, long-winded, loquacious **13** communicative **14** conversational

**chauvinism**
**04** bias **06** sexism **08** jingoism **09** prejudice **10** flag-waving **11** nationalism **12** partisanship **14** male chauvinism

**chauvinist**
**03** MCP **05** jingo **06** biased, sexist **08** jingoist **10** flag-waving, prejudiced **11** nationalist **14** male chauvinist

**chauvinistic**
**06** biased, sexist **10** jingoistic, prejudiced **13** nationalistic

**cheap**
**03** low **04** mean, poor, sale **05** a snip, tacky, tatty **06** a steal, budget, cheapo, chintz, common, jitney, paltry, shoddy, sordid, tawdry, two-bit, vulgar **07** bargain, chintzy, economy, low-cost, reduced, slashed **08** a good buy, cut-price, dog-cheap, giveaway, inferior, low-price, no-frills, sixpenny, twopenny **09** bon marché, cheapjack, cheap-rate, dirt-cheap, good-cheap, knock-down, rinky-dink, tasteless, ten a penny, throwaway, worthless **10** à bon marché, affordable, despicable, discounted, economical, improvised, marked-down, ramshackle, reasonable, rock-bottom, second-rate **11** a dime a dozen, gingerbread, inexpensive, reduced-rate **12** contemptible **13** cheap and nasty, going for a song, on a shoestring, value-for-money **14** on special offer **15** bargain-basement

**cheapen**
**05** lower **06** demean **07** degrade, devalue **08** belittle, derogate **09** denigrate, discredit, disparage, downgrade **10** depreciate

**cheaply**
**09** at low cost, bon marché **10** à bon marché, affordably, reasonably **12** at a cheap rate, economically, with no frills **13** inexpensively **14** at a reduced rate, on special offer

**cheat**
**02** do **03** bam, bob, cog, con, fix, fob, fox, gum, gyp, jew, rig **04** bilk, chiz, clip, colt, deny, dupe, fake, fool, gull, have, jink, mump, slur, snap, swiz, take, trim **05** biter, bluff, check, chess, chizz, cozen, crook, cully, dingo, fraud, fudge, hocus, queer, rogue, screw, shark, stiff, sting, touch, trick, welsh **06** baffle, begunk, cajole, chisel, chouse, con man, diddle, dodger, do down, fiddle, fleece, intake, rip off, smouch, take in, thwart **07** beguile, cheater, cozener, deceive, defraud, deprive, escheat, forfeit, gudgeon, mislead, prevent, sharper, skelder, swindle, swizzle, twister, two-time **08** deceiver, hoodwink, impostor, picaroon, swindler **09** bamboozle, charlatan,

chiseller, cony-catch, deception, duckshove, frustrate, trickster, victimize **10** do a flanker **11** cony-catcher, do one over on, double-cross, extortioner, gull-catcher, hornswoggle, short-change **12** do the dirty on, take for a ride **13** double-crosser

**check**

**02** ch **03** bar, nip, tab **04** balk, bill, curb, damp, foil, halt, rein, scan, slow, sneb, snub, stem, stop, test, tick **05** audit, baulk, crush, delay, limit, pinch, probe, punch, sneap, study, stunt, tally, token **06** arrest, blight, bridle, coupon, hinder, impede, look at, police, rebuff, rebuke, rein in, retard, screen, tartan, thwart, ticket, verify **07** account, analyse, charges, check-up, compare, confirm, contain, control, examine, inhibit, inquiry, inspect, invoice, monitor, repress, repulse, setback, shorten, staunch **08** analysis, holdback, make sure, obstruct, once-over, research, restrain, scrutiny, slow down, suppress, validate **09** going-over, go through, reckoning, reprimand, restraint, statement, take stock **10** cross-check, inspection, monitoring, scrutinize **11** corroborate, counterfoil, examination, inquire into, investigate **12** confirmation, substantiate, verification **13** investigation, look at closely **15** give the once-over

**• check in**

**05** enrol **06** book in **08** register

**• check out**

**04** case, test **05** leave, recce, study **06** depart **07** examine, inspect **08** look into, settle up **10** pay the bill **11** investigate

**• check up**

**04** test **05** probe **06** assess, verify **07** analyse, confirm, examine, inspect **08** evaluate, make sure **09** ascertain **11** inquire into, investigate

**• hold in check, keep in check**

**04** curb, stop **06** arrest, bridle, hinder, impede, rein in **07** control, prevent, repress **08** hold back, keep back, obstruct, restrain, suppress

**check-up**

**04** test **05** audit, probe **07** inquiry **08** analysis, research, scrutiny **09** appraisal **10** evaluation, inspection, monitoring **11** examination **12** confirmation, verification **13** investigation

**cheek**

**03** jaw, lip **04** chap, chop, gall, gena, jole, joll, jowl, neck, sass, wang **05** chaft, mouth, nerve, sauce **06** chafts, dimple **08** attitude, audacity, chutzpah, temerity **09** brass neck, impudence, insolence **10** brazenness, disrespect, effrontery **12** impertinence

**cheekily**

**06** pertly **10** impudently, insolently **13** impertinently **15** disrespectfully

**cheeky**

**04** pert, rude **05** fresh, lippy, sassy, saucy **06** brazen, mouthy **07** forward **08** impudent, insolent **09** audacious **11** impertinent **12** overfamiliar **13** disrespectful

**cheep**

**04** peep, pipe, sing **05** chirp, trill, tweet **06** warble **07** chirrup, twitter, whistle

**cheer**

**03** hip, joy, olé, rah **04** buck, buoy, clap, face, fare, food, glad, hail, hoop, warm, yell **05** bravo, elate, shout, whoop **06** buck up, buoy up, cherry, hurrah, perk up, salute, solace, spirit, uplift **07** acclaim, applaud, comfort, console, enliven, fanfare, gladden, hearten, ovation, revelry, root for, support, welcome **08** applause, brighten, clapping, gladness, inspirit, plaudits, semblant **09** celebrate, encourage, enhearten, happiness, merriment **10** barrack for, exhilarate, joyfulness **11** acclamation, high spirits, hopefulness, merrymaking **12** cheerfulness **13** entertainment

**• cheer up**

**05** liven, rally **06** buck up, perk up **07** chirrup, comfort, console, hearten, liven up **08** brighten **09** encourage, take heart **10** brighten up

**• be cheered**

**04** rise

**cheerful**

**03** gay **04** glad, joco, warm **05** bonny, cadgy, canty, happy, jolly, light, merry, riant, sunny **06** blithe, bonnie, breezy, bright, bubbly, cheery, chirpy, genial, hearty, jaunty, jocund, jovial, joyful, joyous, kidgie, lively, smiley, upbeat **07** buoyant, chipper, holiday, smiling, winsome **08** animated, carefree, chirrupy, eupeptic, laughing, pleasant, pleasing, spirited, stirring **09** agreeable, contented, exuberant, inspiring, lightsome, sparkling **10** attractive, comforting, delightful, heartening, optimistic **11** encouraging **12** enthusiastic, good-humoured, high-spirited, light-hearted **13** in good spirits

**cheerily**

**06** gladly **07** happily **08** brightly, jovially **10** cheerfully **14** light-heartedly

**cheerio**

**03** bye **04** ta-ta **05** adieu **06** bye-bye, cheers, hooray, hooroo, see you, so long **07** goodbye, haere ra **08** au revoir, farewell **11** see you later

*See also* **farewell**

**cheerless**

**03** sad **04** cold, dank, dark, dead, drab, dull, grim **05** bleak, dingy **06** barren, dismal, dreary, gloomy, lonely, sombre, sullen, wintry **07** austere, forlorn, joyless, sunless, unhappy, wintery **08** dejected, desolate, dolorous, mournful, winterly **09** miserable, sorrowful **10** depressing, despondent, melancholy, uninviting **11** comfortless **12** disconsolate

**cheers**

**02** ta **03** bye **04** rivo, skol, ta-ta, tope **05** adieu, skoal **06** bye-bye, health, prosit, see you, so long **07** cheerio, goodbye, haere ra, slàinte, wassail **08** au revoir, bless you, chin-chin, farewell, thank you, waes hail **09** bottoms up, drink hail **10** all the best, here's to you, many thanks, thanks a lot **11** much obliged, see you later **12** down the hatch, mud in your eye **13** happy landings **14** your good health **15** to absent friends

**cheery**

**03** gay **04** glad **05** happy, jolly, merry **06** breezy, bright, chirpy, genial, hearty, jaunty, jovial, joyful, lively **07** buoyant, smiling **08** animated, carefree, cheerful, laughing, spirited **09** contented, exuberant, sparkling **10** optimistic **12** back-slapping, enthusiastic, light-hearted **13** in good spirits

**cheese**

*Cheeses include:*

**03** ewe, Oka
**04** Brie, curd, Edam, feta, goat, hard, skyr, soft
**05** Caboc, Carré, Derby, Gouda, quark
**06** Cantal, chèvre, Dunlop, junket, Orkney, paneer, Romano, Tilsit
**07** Boursin, Cheddar, crottin, crowdie, Fontina, Gruyère, kebbock, kebbuck, Limburg, Münster, ricotta, sapsago, Stilton®
**08** bel paese, Cheshire, Churnton, Emmental, halloumi, Huntsman, manchego, Parmesan, pecorino, raclette, Taleggio, vacherin
**09** Amsterdam, Blue Vinny, Cambozola®, Camembert, chevreton, Emmenthal, ewe-cheese, Ilchester, Jarlsberg®, Killarney, Leicester, Limburger, Lymeswold®, mouse-trap, Port Salut, processed, provolone, reblochon, Roquefort, sage Derby
**10** blue cheese, Caerphilly, curd cheese, Danish blue, dolcelatte, Emmentaler, Gloucester, Gorgonzola, hard cheese, Lancashire, mascarpone, mozzarella, Neufchâtel, Red Windsor, soft cheese, stracchino, vegetarian
**11** Coulommiers, cream cheese, Petit Suisse, Pont l'Évêque, Saint-Paulin, Wensleydale
**12** Blue Cheshire, fromage frais, Monterey Jack, Philadelphia®, Red Leicester
**13** Bleu d'Auvergne, cottage cheese

**• big cheese**

**03** nob, VIP **04** tuan **05** mogul, swell **06** big gun, bigwig, honcho, worthy **07** big shot, notable **08** big noise, somebody **09** celebrity, dignitary, personage **10** panjandrum **11** heavyweight

### cheesed off

**05** bored, fed up **07** annoyed **09** depressed, disgusted, hacked off, pissed off **10** brassed off, browned off **11** disgruntled **12** disappointed, discontented, dissatisfied, sick and tired

### chef

*Chefs, restaurateurs and cookery writers include:*

**03** **Hom** (Ken)
**04** **Gray** (Rose), **Roux** (Albert), **Roux** (Michel), **Spry** (Constance)
**05** **Allen** (Betty), **Blanc** (Raymond René), **David** (Elizabeth), **Delia**, **Floyd** (Keith), **Leith** (Prue), **Roden** (Claudia), **Smith** (Delia), **Soyer** (Alexis), **Stein** (Rick), **White** (Marco Pierre)
**06** **Appert** (Nicolas François), **Beeton** (Mrs Isabella Mary), **Carême** (Marie Antoine), **Farmer** (Fannie), **Lawson** (Nigella), **Oliver** (Jamie), **Ramsay** (Gordon), **Rhodes** (Gary), **Rogers** (Ruth), **Slater** (Nigel), **Wilson** (David)
**07** **Cradock** (Fanny), **Erikson** (Gunn), **Grigson** (Jane), **Grigson** (Sophie), **Jaffrey** (Madhur), **Ladenis** (Nico)
**08** **Dimbleby** (Josceline), **Grossman** (Loyd), **Harriott** (Ainsley), **Mosimann** (Anton), **Paterson** (Jennifer)
**09** **Carluccio** (Antonio), **Escoffier** (Auguste), **McCartney** (Linda)
**12** **Two Fat Ladies**
**13** **Dickson Wright** (Clarissa)
**14** **Brillat-Savarin** (Anthelme)
**15** **Worrall Thompson** (Antony)

### chemical

*Chemical compounds include:*

**03** PVC
**04** alum, DEET, urea
**05** epoxy
**06** phenol
**07** ammonia, borazon, chloral, ethanol, styrene, toluene
**08** kerosene, methanol, paraffin
**10** chloramine, chloroform
**12** benzaldehyde, borosilicate
**13** carbon dioxide, chlorhexidine, chlorobromide
**14** carbon monoxide, chloral hydrate
**15** organophosphate, sodium hydroxide

*See also* **element**

### chemist

*Chemists include:*

**03** **Lee** (Yuan T)
**04** **Abel** (Sir Frederick), **Davy** (Sir Humphry), **Hess** (Germain Henri), **Kuhn** (Richard), **Mond** (Ludwig), **Urey** (Harold Clayton)
**05** **Abegg** (Richard), **Black** (Joseph), **Boyle** (Robert), **Curie** (Marie), **Darby** (Abraham), **Dewar** (Sir James), **Haber** (Fritz), **Hooke** (Robert), **Kroto** (Sir Harold), **Libby** (Willard Frank), **Meyer** (Lothar), **Nobel** (Alfred), **Soddy** (Frederick)
**06** **Baeyer** (Adolf von), **Barton** (Sir Derek), **Bunsen** (Robert Wilhelm), **Dalton** (John), **Eyring** (Henry), **Hevesy** (George Charles von), **Liebig** (Justus von), **Miller** (Stanley Lloyd), **Nernst** (Walther), **Porter** (George, Lord), **Ramsay** (Sir William)
**07** **Abelson** (Philip H), **Bergius** (Friedrich), **Buchner** (Eduard), **Faraday** (Michael), **Fischer** (Emil Hermann), **Fischer** (Hans), **Hodgkin** (Dorothy), **Pasteur** (Louis), **Pauling** (Linus Carl), **Scheele** (Carl Wilhelm), **Seaborg** (Glenn Theodore)
**08** **Avogadro** (Amedeo), **Chevreul** (Michel Eugène), **Hadfield** (Sir Robert Abbott), **Klaproth** (Martin Heinrich), **Langmuir** (Irving), **Lonsdale** (Dame Kathleen), **Lovelock** (James), **Mulliken** (Robert Sanderson), **Regnault** (Henri Victor), **Robinson** (Sir Robert), **Sidgwick** (Nevil Vincent), **Svedberg** (Theodor), **Tiselius** (Arne Wilhelm Kaurin)
**09** **Arrhenius** (Svante August), **Baekeland** (Leo Hendrik), **Berzelius** (Jöns Jacob), **Cavendish** (Henry), **Gay-Lussac** (Joseph Louis), **Lavoisier** (Antoine Laurent), **Priestley** (Joseph), **Prigogine** (Ilya, Vicomte)
**10** **Cannizzaro** (Stanislao), **Mendeleyev** (Dmitri)
**12** **Boussingault** (Jean Baptiste Joseph)

**• chemists**
**03** ICI, RSC **04** BASF **06** IChemE

### chemistry

*Chemistry terms include:*

**02** IR, pH
**03** cis, gas, ion
**04** acid, atom, base, bond, mass, mole, rate, salt, weak
**05** assay, block, cycle, ester, group, IUPAC, lipid, order, phase, polar, redox, shell, solid, trans, yield
**06** alkali, alkane, alkene, buffer, chiral, dalton, dilute, dipole, fusion, halide, isomer, ketone, ligand, liquid, matter, period, phenyl, pi bond, proton, strong, symbol
**07** chelate, chemist, colloid, crystal, element, entropy, fission, formula, halogen, isotope, lattice, mixture, neutral, neutron, nucleus, orbital, organic, polymer, product, racemic, reagent, soluble, solvent, valency
**08** analysis, aromatic, catalyst, compound, cracking, dialysis, electron, emulsion, end point, enthalpy, fixation, half life, inert gas, miscible, molecule, noble gas, reactant, reaction, solution
**09** aliphatic, allotrope, anhydrous, catalysis, corrosion, diffusion, electrode, empirical, hydroxide, indicator, inorganic, insoluble, ionic bond, oxidation, reduction, saturated, side chain, sigma bond, substance, synthesis, titration
**10** amphoteric, atomic mass, combustion, curly arrow, double bond, exothermic, free energy, hydrolysis, immiscible, litmus test, reversible, single bond, suspension, triple bond, zwitterion
**11** crystallize, diffraction, electrolyte, endothermic, equilibrium, evaporation, free radical, ground state, hydrocarbon, litmus paper, precipitate, respiration, sublimation
**12** atomic number, atomic radius, atomic weight, biochemistry, chemical bond, chlorination, concentrated, condensation, covalent bond, dissociation, distillation, electrolysis, fermentation, hydrogen bond, melting point, metallic bond, spectroscopy
**13** chain reaction, decomposition, fractionation, periodic table, radioactivity, stoichiometry
**14** Avogadro number, Brownian motion, buffer solution, chromatography, saponification
**15** atomic structure, aufbau principle, chemical element, collision theory, transition metal, transition state

### cheque

**03** dud **04** giro **06** stumer **07** bouncer **11** counterfoil

### chequer

**04** dice **09** interrupt, variegate **10** chessboard **13** counterchange

### chequered

**05** diced, mixed **06** checky, chequy, varied **07** checked, diverse, striped **08** eventful **10** variegated **13** multicoloured, particoloured **15** with ups and downs

### cherish

**03** hug **04** love **05** adore, brood, nurse, prize, value **06** foster, nestle, tender **07** brood on, care for, harbour, nourish, nurture, shelter, support, sustain **08** enshrine, hold dear, treasure **09** encourage, entertain, look after **10** make much of, take care of **11** have at heart, refocillate **14** take good care of

### cherished

**03** pet **08** precious

### cherry

**04** gean **05** cheer, morel, ruddy **06** cornel, mazard **07** may-duke, mazzard, morello **08** hagberry **09** Malpighia **10** blackheart

### cherub

**05** angel **06** seraph

**cherubic**
**04** cute **05** sweet **06** lovely
**07** angelic, lovable **08** adorable, heavenly, innocent, loveable, seraphic
**09** appealing

**chess**

*Chess players include:*

**03** **Tal** (Mikhail), **Xie** (Jun)
**04** **Euwe** (Max)
**05** **Anand** (Viswanathan), **Short** (Nigel)
**06** **Karpov** (Anatoli), **Lasker** (Emanuel), **Morphy** (Paul), **Polgar** (Judit), **Polgar** (Zsuzsa), **Thomas** (Sir George), **Timman** (Jan), **Xie Jun**
**07** **Fischer** (Bobby), **Kramnik** (Vladimir), **Smyslov** (Vasili), **Spassky** (Boris)
**08** **Alekhine** (Alexander), **Deep Blue**, **Kasparov** (Garry), **Korchnoi** (Viktor), **Philidor** (François André), **Steinitz** (Wilhelm)
**09** **Botvinnik** (Mikhail), **Khalifman** (Alexander), **Petrosian** (Tigran)
**10** **Capablanca** (José)
**13** **Chiburdanidze** (Maya)

*Chess pieces include:*

**04** king, pawn, rook
**05** queen
**06** bishop, castle, knight

*Chess-related terms include:*

**01** R
**03** man, pin, row
**04** bind, FIDE, fork, move, play
**05** black, board, check, flank, march, piece, white
**06** attack, centre, double, gambit, master, patzer, square
**07** chequer, defence, endgame, en prise, j'adoube, opening, promote, retract, squeeze
**08** back rank, castling, diagonal, exchange, kingside, opponent, queening, zugzwang
**09** bad bishop, checkmate, Elo rating, en passant, fool's mate, miniature, promotion, queenside, stalemate
**10** fianchetto, good bishop, major piece, middle game, minor piece, passed pawn
**11** counterplay, grandmaster, zwischenzug
**12** backward pawn, problem child
**13** counter attack, fifty move rule
**14** perpetual check
**15** knight's progress

**chest**
**03** ark, box, cub **04** case, kist
**05** bahut, caddy, crate, hutch, trunk
**06** breast, bunker, bureau, casket, coffer, girnel, larnax, scrine, shrine, thorax **07** cap-case, cassone, commode, dresser, meal-ark, sternum, tallboy **08** corn-kist, treasury, wakahuia **09** slop-chest, strongbox
**10** chiffonier

**chestnut**
**02** ch **05** favel **06** cliché, conker, favell, sorrel **07** badious, buckeye, caltrop, horn-nut, saligot **08** bean tree, Castanea **09** chincapin, chinkapin
**10** chinquapin **14** Castanospermum

**chevron**
**01** V **06** stripe **08** dancette

**chew**
◇ *anagram indicator*
**03** eat **04** bite, chaw, gnaw, quid
**05** champ, chomp, grind, munch
**06** crunch **07** reflect **08** meditate, ruminate **09** manducate, masticate
• **chew over**
**06** muse on, ponder **07** weigh up
**08** consider, mull over **10** meditate on, ruminate on **14** deliberate upon

**chic**
**05** smart, style **06** chichi, dapper, modish, snazzy, trendy, with it **07** à la mode, elegant, stylish **08** elegance
**11** fashionable **13** sophisticated

**chicanery**
**05** dodge, fraud, guile, wiles
**08** artifice, cheating, intrigue, trickery
**09** deception, duplicity, quibbling, sophistry **10** dishonesty, subterfuge
**11** deviousness, hoodwinking
**13** deceitfulness, double-dealing, jiggery-pokery, sharp practice
**15** underhandedness

**chick**
**04** bird

**chicken**
**03** hen **04** poot, pout **05** biddy, chook, chuck, poule, poult, rumpy, squab **06** scared **07** broiler, chookie, chuckie, poussin **08** coq au vin, cowardly, springer, yakitori
**09** howtowdie **10** frightened

*See also* **animal**; **cowardly**; **hen**

*Chickens include:*

**06** Ancona, bantam, Cochin, houdan, sultan
**07** Dorking, Hamburg, leghorn, Minorca
**08** Hamburgh, Langshan
**09** Orpington, Welsummer, wyandotte
**10** Andalusian, Australorp, chittagong, jungle fowl
**11** Cochin-China, Spanish fowl
**12** Plymouth Rock
**14** Rhode Island Red

**chickpea**
**04** gram **05** chana, chich **08** garbanzo

**chide**
**03** row **04** rate, twit **05** blame, dress, scold, shend **06** berate, rebuke
**07** censure, lecture, quarrel, reprove, tell off, upbraid **08** admonish, chastise, reproach **09** criticize, objurgate, reprehend, reprimand

**chief**
**02** Ch **03** cid, key, oba **04** arch, boss, cock, head, jarl, kaid, khan, lead, lord, main, raja, ratu **05** ariki, chair, first, grand, great, major, prime, rajah, ratoo, ruler, sheik, vital **06** big gun, gaffer, honcho, leader, master, primal, sachem, sheikh, sudder, top dog
**07** cacique, captain, cazique, central, headman, highest, leading, manager, mugwump, premier, primary, supreme, supremo **08** big noise, cardinal, chairman, director, dominant, foremost, governor, intimate, overlord, sagamore, superior, suzerain **09** big cheese, chieftain, commander, directing, essential, head-woman, important, number one, paramount, pendragon, president, principal, rangatira, top banana, uppermost
**10** chairwoman, coryphaeus, head bummer, pre-eminent, prevailing, ringleader **11** chairperson, controlling, outstanding, predominant, supervising
**13** most important, prime minister
**14** chief executive, superintendent

*See also* **emperor**; **empress**; **governor**; **king**; **president**; **queen**; **ruler**

**chiefly**
**06** mainly, mostly **07** usually
**09** capitally, generally, in the main, primarily **10** especially, on the whole
**11** essentially, principally
**13** predominantly **14** for the most part

**child**
**02** ch, it **03** boy, elf, get, imp, kid, son, tot **04** babe, baby, brat, chit, dalt, gait, geit, girl, gyte, mite, puss, tama, tike, tiny, trot, tyke, waif, wean **05** bairn, chick, dault, elfin, issue, mardy, minor, scamp, slink, smout, smowt, sprog, totty, wench, youth **06** cherub, enfant, infant, kidlet, moppet, nipper, pledge, rug rat, toddle, tottie, urchin, wanton
**07** bambino, dilling, gangrel, hellion, kinchin, littlin, name-son, neonate, papoose, preteen, prodigy, progeny, subteen, tiny tot, toddler, young 'un
**08** adherent, bantling, Benjamin, daughter, disciple, godchild, innocent, juvenile, little 'un, littling, munchkin, suckling, tamariki, teenager, weanling, young one **09** kiddywink, littleane, little boy, little one, monthling, offspring, stepchild, underfive, youngster **10** adolescent, ankle-biter, changeling, descendant, eyas-musket, fosterling, grandchild, inhabitant, jackanapes, kiddiewink, knave-bairn, little girl, orphanmite, ragamuffin, wunderkind, young adult **11** ankle-nipper, butter-print, encumbrance, guttersnipe, olive branch, preschooler, schoolchild, weeny-bopper, young person **12** kiddiewinkie
• **only child**
**02** oc

**childbirth**
**05** pains **06** labour **07** lying-in, travail
**08** delivery **09** maternity, pregnancy, puerperal **11** confinement, parturition
**12** accouchement, child-bearing

**childhood**
**05** youth **07** boyhood, infancy
**08** babyhood, girlhood, minority
**09** early days **10** early years,

immaturity, schooldays
**11** adolescence

**childish**
**05** silly **06** boyish **07** babyish, foolish, girlish, puerile **08** immature, juvenile, trifling **09** frivolous, infantile
**10** namby-pamby **13** irresponsible

**childishly**
**09** foolishly **10** immaturely
**13** irresponsibly

**childless** *see* **without issue** *under* **issue**

**childlike**
**05** naive **06** docile, simple **07** artless, natural **08** innocent, trustful, trusting
**09** credulous, guileless, ingenuous
**10** unaffected

**children**
**05** issue

**Chile**
**03** CHL, RCH

**chill**
**03** flu, ice, icy, nip, raw **04** bite, cold, cool, fear **05** algid, aloof, bleak, dread, fever, nippy, oorie, ourie, owrie, parky, relax, scare, sharp, virus **06** biting, chilly, dampen, dismay, freeze, frigid, frosty, shiver, wintry **07** anxiety, depress, iciness, petrify, rawness, terrify **08** coldness, cool down, coolness, freezing, frighten, make cold
**09** crispness, influenza **10** become cold, depressing, discourage, dishearten, make colder, unfriendly
**11** refrigerate **12** apprehension, become colder
• **chilled**
**05** on ice **07** relaxed
• **chill out**
**05** relax **06** unwind **08** calm down
**09** have a rest **10** take it easy

**chilly**
**03** icy, raw **04** cold, cool **05** aloof, bleak, brisk, crisp, fresh, gelid, nippy, parky, sharp, stony **06** biting, frigid, wintry **07** distant, hostile **08** freezing
**10** unfriendly **11** unwelcoming
**12** unresponsive **13** unsympathetic
**14** unenthusiastic

**chime**
**04** boom, ding, dong, peal, ring, tink, toll **05** agree, clang, rhyme, sound
**06** accord, jingle, strike, tinkle
**07** harmony, resound **11** reverberate
**13** reverberation **14** tintinnabulate
• **chime in**
**05** agree, blend, cut in, fit in **06** butt in, chip in **09** be similar, harmonize, interject, interpose, interrupt
**10** correspond **12** be consistent

**chimera**
**05** dream, fancy **07** fantasy, ratfish, spectre **08** delusion, illusion **09** idle fancy **12** will-o'-the-wisp
**13** hallucination

**chimney**
**03** lum **04** flue, vent **05** cleft, shaft, stack, stalk **06** funnel, tunnel
**07** chimley, chumley, crevice
**08** femerall **10** flare stack, smokestack
**12** chimney stalk
• **chimney pot**
**03** can **06** top-hat

**china**
**02** Ch, RC **03** CHN, TWN **04** Chin, kina, mate **05** quina **06** dishes, plates
**07** ceramic, pottery, quinine
**08** crockery **09** porcelain, tableware
**10** terracotta **11** earthenware
**13** dinner service **14** cups and saucers, the flowery land **15** Celestial Empire, People's Republic
*See also* **friend**; **porcelain**

**Chinese**
**02** Ch **03** Han **04** Chin, Sino-
**05** Seric, Sinic **07** Cataian, Catayan, Sinaean **08** Cathaian, Cathayan
*See also* **animal**; **dynasty**
• **Chinese society**
**04** tong

**chink**
**03** cut, gap **04** gasp, rift, rima, rime, slit, slot **05** cleft, crack, money, space, split **06** cavity, cranny, rictus
**07** crevice, fissure, opening
**08** aperture

**chip**
**03** bit, fry **04** dent, disc, EROM, flaw, gash, nick, pare **05** break, chaff, crack, crisp, EPROM, flake, nacho, notch, piece, scrap, shard, shred, slice, snick, spale, spall, tease, token, wafer
**06** chisel, damage, gallet, paring, sliver
**07** blitter, counter, crumble, Pentium®, pinning, scratch, shaving, whittle
**08** break off, fragment, splinter
**09** French fry **10** transputer **11** fried potato **14** microprocessor
*See also* **computer**
• **chip in**
**03** pay **05** cut in **06** butt in, donate
**07** chime in **09** interject, interpose, interrupt, subscribe **10** contribute
**12** club together **13** make a donation
**14** have a whip-round **15** have a collection

**chirp**
**03** pip **04** peep, pipe, sing **05** cheep, chirk, chirm, chirr, trill, tweet **06** chirre, warble **07** chirrup, chitter, twitter, whistle **10** tweet-tweet

**chirpy**
**03** gay **04** glad **05** happy, jolly, merry, perky **06** blithe, bright, cheery, jaunty, lively **08** cheerful

**chisel**
**03** gad **04** bran, burr **05** burin, cheat, drove, gouge **06** firmer, gravel
**07** boaster, bolster, scauper, scorper, shingle **12** pitching tool
*See also* **carve**; **cheat**; **sculpt**

**chit-chat**
**04** chat, talk **06** confab, gossip, natter
**07** chatter, chinwag, prattle **08** cosy chat **09** small talk, tête-à-tête **10** idle gossip **12** conversation, heart-to-heart, tittle-tattle

**chivalrous**
**04** bold **05** brave, noble **06** heroic, polite **07** gallant, valiant **08** gracious, knightly **09** courteous **10** courageous, honourable **11** gentlemanly **12** well-mannered

**chivalry**
**06** honour **07** bravery, bushido, courage **08** boldness, courtesy, noblemen **09** gallantry, integrity
**10** politeness **11** courtliness, good manners **12** graciousness, truthfulness
**15** gentlemanliness

**chivvy**
**03** bug, nag **04** goad, hunt, prod, urge
**05** annoy, chase, hound, hurry
**06** badger, harass, hassle, pester, plague **07** hurry up, pursuit, torment
**08** pressure **09** importune

**chlorine**
**02** Cl

**chock-a-block**
**04** full **06** jammed, packed **07** brimful, chocker, crammed, crowded
**08** overfull **09** congested, jam-packed
**14** full to bursting

**choice**
**03** try **04** best, fine, list, plum, rare, trye, wale, will **05** prime, prize, range, taste **06** answer, dainty, finest, opting, option, select **07** Auslese, picking, special, variety **08** choosing, decision, druthers, election, precious, solution, superior, valuable **09** excellent, exclusive, exquisite, first-rate, selection
**10** first-class, hand-picked, preference
**11** alternative, appropriate
**14** discrimination

**choke**
**03** bar, dam, gag **04** clog, glut, plug, silt, stap, stop **05** block, close, cough, dam up, retch, worry **06** accloy, silt up, stifle **07** congest, occlude, smother
**08** obstruct, strangle, suppress, throttle
**09** constrict, overpower, overwhelm, suffocate **10** asphyxiate
• **choke back**
**04** curb **05** check **07** contain, control, inhibit, repress **08** restrain, strangle, suppress **09** fight back

**chokey, choky** *see* **prison**

**choleric**
**05** angry, fiery, testy **06** crabby, touchy
**07** crabbed, peppery **08** petulant
**09** crotchety, irascible, irritable
**10** passionate **11** bad-tempered, hot-tempered, ill-tempered **13** quick-tempered

**choose**
**03** opt **04** list, pick, take, wale, want, will, wish **05** adopt, chuse, elect, fix on, go for **06** decide, desire, favour, opt for, prefer, see fit, select, take up
**07** appoint, espouse, extract, pick out, vote for **08** decide on, plump for, settle on **09** designate, determine,

single out **10** predestine **14** make up your mind

**choosy**
**05** faddy, fussy, picky **07** finicky **08** exacting **09** selective **10** fastidious, particular, pernickety **11** persnickety **14** discriminating

**chop**
**02** ax **03** axe, cut, eat, hew, jaw, lop, saw **04** chap, clap, dice, fell, food, hack, hash, seal, snap **05** brand, carve, crack, cut up, mince, sever, share, slash, slice, split **06** barter, change, cleave, divide, thrust **07** dissect, fissure **08** exchange, truncate **09** côtelette

**• chop up**
◇ *anagram indicator*
**03** cut **04** cube, dice **05** cut up, grate, grind, mince, shred, slice **06** divide **07** slice up **13** cut into pieces

**choppy**
◇ *anagram indicator*
**04** wavy **05** rough **06** broken, stormy, uneven **07** ruffled, squally **08** blustery **09** turbulent **11** tempestuous

**chore**
**03** job **04** duty, task **05** truck **06** burden, errand **07** routine **11** piece of work

**choreography**

*Choreographers include:*

**04** **Bolm** (Adolph), **Dean** (Laura), **Feld** (Eliot), **Kidd** (Michael)
**05** **Bruce** (Christopher), **Cohan** (Robert), **Dolin** (Anton), **Jooss** (Kurt), **Laban** (Rudolf von), **Lifar** (Serge), **North** (Robert), **Sleep** (Wayne), **Tharp** (Twyla)
**06** **Ashton** (Sir Frederick), **Béjart** (Maurice), **Blasis** (Carlo), **Bourne** (Matthew), **Clarke** (Michael), **Cranko** (John), **Davies** (Siobhan), **Duncan** (Isadora), **Fokine** (Michel), **Graham** (Martha), **Morris** (Mark), **Petipa** (Marius), **Valois** (Dame Ninette de), **Wigman** (Mary)
**07** **Darrell** (Peter), **de Mille** (Agnes George), **Joffrey** (Robert), **Massine** (Léonide)
**08** **Berkeley** (Busby), **de Valois** (Dame Ninette), **Helpmann** (Sir Robert), **Humphrey** (Doris), **Nijinska** (Bronislava), **Nijinsky** (Vaslav)
**09** **Beauchamp** (Pierre), **Macmillan** (Sir Kenneth)
**10** **Balanchine** (George), **Cunningham** (Merce)
**11** **Baryshnikov** (Mikhail)

**choristers**
**05** choir

**chortle**
**04** crow **05** laugh, snort **06** cackle, guffaw **07** chuckle, snigger

**chorus**
**04** call **05** choir, shout **06** burden, strain **07** refrain, singers **08** ensemble, response **09** vocalists **10** choristers **11** choral group

**Christ**
**01** X **02** Ch, JC, XP, Xt **03** Chr, I am **04** Lord **06** the Son **07** Holy One, Messiah, Saviour **08** Immanuel, Redeemer, Son of God, Son of Man **09** deliverer, Lamb of God, Word of God **11** King of kings, Lord of lords, the Redeemer **12** Good Shepherd **13** Prince of Peace

**christen**
**03** dub **04** call, name, term **05** style, title **07** baptize, immerse **08** sprinkle **09** designate **10** begin using, inaugurate **11** give a name to

**Christian**
**02** Xn **03** Chr **04** Copt, Xian **05** Xtian

**Christmas**
**02** Xm **04** Noel, Xmas, Yule **05** Nowel **06** Crimbo, Nowell **08** Chrissie, Nativity, Yuletide

*Gifts for the Twelve Days of Christmas:*

**09** gold rings
**10** French hens
**11** turtle doves
**12** calling birds, geese a-laying, pipers piping
**13** ladies dancing, lords a-leaping, maids a-milking
**14** swans a-swimming
**16** drummers drumming
**20** partridge in a pear tree

*Gifts from the Three Wise Men:*

**04** gold
**05** myrrh
**12** frankincense

*See also* **wise man** *under* **wise**

**Christmas Island**
**03** CXR

**Christ's-thorn**
**04** nabk

**chromium**
**02** Cr

**chromosome**
**• part of chromosome**
**02** id **07** cistron

**chronic**
**04** naff, ropy **05** awful, pants **07** abysmal, the pits **08** constant, dreadful, habitual, hardened, long-term, terrible **09** appalling, atrocious, confirmed, continual, frightful, incessant, ingrained, recurring **10** deep-rooted, deep-seated, deplorable, inveterate, persistent **11** long-lasting **12** incorrigible, long-standing **14** a load of rubbish

**chronically**
**08** long-term **10** constantly, habitually **11** continually, incessantly, recurrently **12** deep-rootedly, incorrigibly, inveterately, persistently

**chronicle**
**04** epic, list, saga, tell **05** chron, diary, enter, story **06** annals, record, relate, report **07** account, history, journal, narrate, recount, set down **08** archives, calendar, register **09** narrative, write down **11** put on record

**• entry in chronicle**
**05** annal

**chronicler**
**06** scribe **07** diarist **08** annalist, narrator, recorder, reporter **09** archivist, historian **11** chronologer **13** chronographer **15** historiographer

**chronological**
**06** serial **07** in order, ordered **10** historical, in sequence, sequential **11** consecutive, progressive

**chubby**
**03** fat **04** full **05** fubby, fubsy, plump, podgy, round, stout, tubby **06** flabby, fleshy, portly, rotund **07** paunchy **08** roly-poly

**chuck**
**03** put, shy **04** cast, dump, food, hurl, jilt, lump, quit, toss **05** chunk, fling, heave, pitch, sling, throw **06** give up, pack in, pebble, reject **07** abandon, chicken, discard, dismiss, forsake **08** get rid of, jettison **12** give the elbow **15** give the brush-off

**chuckle**
**04** crow **05** laugh, snort **06** cackle, clumsy, giggle, titter **07** chortle, snigger **12** laugh quietly

**chum**
**03** pal **04** mate, tosh **05** buddy, butty, crony **06** cobber, friend **07** comrade **09** accompany, associate, companion

*See also* **friend**

**chummy**
**04** maty **05** close, matey, pally, thick **08** criminal, friendly, intimate, sociable **12** affectionate

**chunk**
**03** nub **04** hunk, junk, lump, mass, slab **05** block, chuck, piece, wedge, wodge **06** dollop **07** portion

**chunky**
**05** broad, bulky, dumpy, heavy, large, solid, thick **06** blocky, stocky **07** awkward, weighty **08** thickset, unwieldy **09** well-built **10** cumbersome **11** substantial

**church**
**02** CE, Ch **04** cult, fold, kirk, sect **05** abbey, flock **06** bethel, chapel, shrine, temple **07** chantry, minster **08** assembly, basilica, Bethesda, ecclesia, grouping **09** cathedral, community, tradition **10** fellowship, house of God, Lord's house, tabernacle **11** people of God **12** body of Christ, congregation, denomination, meeting-house, procathedral **13** bride of Christ, house of prayer **14** house of worship, place of worship, preaching-house

*See also* **cathedral**

*Church and cathedral parts include:*

**03** pew
**04** apse, arch, font, nave, rood, tomb
**05** aisle, altar, choir, crypt, porch, slype, spire, stall, stoup, tower, vault
**06** adytum, arcade, atrium, belfry, chapel, chevet, corona, parvis, portal, pulpit, sedile, shrine, squint, vestry
**07** almonry, chancel, frontal, gallery, lectern, lucarne, narthex, piscina, reredos, steeple, tambour
**08** cloister, credence, crossing, keystone, parclose, pinnacle, predella, sacellum, sacristy, transept
**09** antechoir, bell tower, sacrarium, sanctuary, sepulchre, stasidion, triforium
**10** ambulatory, baptistery, bell screen, clerestory, diaconicon, fenestella, frithstool, misericord, presbytery, retrochoir, rood screen
**12** chapterhouse, confessional, deambulatory
**14** ringing chamber, schola cantorum

**churchman** *see* **clergyman, clergywoman**

**churchyard**
**05** house **07** charnel **08** boneyard, cemetery, God's acre, kirkyard **09** graveyard, kirkyaird **10** burial site, necropolis **11** burial place **12** burial ground

**churlish**
**04** rude **05** harsh, rough, surly **06** morose, oafish, sullen **07** boorish, brusque, carlish, crabbed, doggish, ill-bred, loutish, uncivil **08** impolite **10** ungracious, unmannerly, unsociable **11** bad-tempered, ill-mannered, ill-tempered **12** discourteous **13** unneighbourly **14** ill-conditioned

**churn**
◇ *anagram indicator*
**04** beat, boil, foam, kirn, puke, stir, toss, turn **05** froth, heave, retch, swirl, vomit **06** be sick, seethe, writhe **07** agitate, disturb, throw up **08** convulse

• **churn out**
**07** knock up, pump out, turn out **13** throw together

**chute**
**03** lin **04** linn, ramp **05** flume, rapid, shaft, shoot, shute, slide, slope, spout, trunk **06** funnel, gutter, runway, trough **07** channel, incline **09** parachute, waterfall **10** water shoot

**chutzpah**
**03** lip **04** gall **05** cheek, mouth, nerve, sauce **08** audacity **09** brass neck, impudence, insolence **10** brazenness, disrespect, effrontery **12** impertinence

**cicada**
**06** tettix **10** harvest-fly **11** balm-cricket

*Cicadas include:*

**05** Myer's
**06** red-eye
**09** Union Jack
**10** blue prince
**11** black prince, floury baker, greengrocer, green Monday, masked devil
**12** floury miller, yellow Monday
**13** double drummer

**cigarette**
**03** cig, fag, tab **04** weed **05** cigar **06** dog end, fag end **10** coffin-nail, paper-cigar **11** cancer-stick

*Cigarettes and cigars include:*

**04** bidi, burn
**05** beedi, blunt, ciggy, claro, joint, paper, roach, segar, smoke, snout, stogy, whiff
**06** beedie, bomber, ciggie, concha, gasper, Havana, low-tar, manila, reefer, roll-up, spliff, stogey, stogie
**07** cheroot, high-tar, manilla, menthol, regalia
**08** king-size, long-nine, perfecto
**09** cigarillo, filter tip, panatella
**10** tailor-made
**11** corona lucis, roll-your-own

**cinch**
**04** snip **06** doddle, scoosh, stroll **08** cakewalk, duck soup, pushover, walkover **09** certainty **10** child's play **11** piece of cake

**cinders**
**04** coal, coke, slag **05** ashes **06** dander, embers **07** clinker **08** charcoal

**cinema**
**05** films, scope **06** flicks, movies **07** drive-in, fleapit, theatre **08** bioscope, bughouse, pictures **09** big screen, multiplex **10** movie house **11** film theatre, nickelodeon **12** movie theatre, picture-house, silver screen **13** picture-palace **14** motion pictures, moving pictures

*Cinema and theatre names include:*

**03** ABC, MGM, Rex, Rio, UCI, UGC
**04** Gala, IMAX, Ritz, Roxy
**05** Byron, Cameo, Forum, Grand, Kings, Lyric, Metro, Odeon, Orion, Plaza, Regal, Royal, Savoy, Scala, Tower
**06** Albany, Apollo, Cannon, Casino, Curzon, Empire, Gaiety, Lyceum, Marina, New Vic, Old Vic, Palace, Queens, Regent, Rialto, Robins, Tivoli, Virgin
**07** Adelphi, Almeida, Arcadia, Astoria, Capitol, Carlton, Central, Century, Circuit, Classic, Coronet, Embassy, Essoldo, Gaumont, Granada, La Scala, Locarno, Mayfair, Orpheum, Paragon, Phoenix, Picardy
**08** Alhambra, Broadway, Charlton, Cineplex, Citizens, Coliseum, Colonial, Dominion, Electric, Everyman, Festival, Imperial, Landmark, Majestic, Memorial, Pavilion, Windmill
**09** Alexandra, Cineworld, Filmhouse, Hollywood, Palladium, Paramount, Playhouse
**10** Ambassador, Hippodrome, Lighthouse
**11** Her Majesty's, His Majesty's, New Victoria, Ster Century
**12** Metropolitan, Picturedrome, Picturehouse, Thefilmworks
**13** Lyceum Theatre, Picture Palace, Warner Village
**14** Electric Palace
**15** Screen on the Hill

**cipher**
**01** O **03** nil **04** code, null, zero **05** zilch **06** Enigma, naught, nobody, nought, yes-man **07** nothing **09** calculate, character, nonentity **10** cryptogram **11** cryptograph **12** coded message, secret system **13** secret writing

**circa**
**01** c **02** ca **03** cir, odd **04** circ, some **05** about **06** around, nearly **07** close to, loosely, roughly **09** just about, not far off **10** more or less, round about **11** approaching **13** approximately, in the region of, or thereabouts, something like **15** in the vicinity of

**circle**
◇ *containment indicator*
**01** O **03** set **04** club, gang, gird, wind **05** crowd, group, hem in, pivot, whirl **06** clique, gyrate, rotate, swivel **07** circlet, company, coterie, cycloid, enclose, envelop, hedge in, revolve, rondure, rounder, society **08** assembly, encircle, surround **09** circulate, encompass, move round **10** fellowship, fraternity **12** circumscribe **14** circumnavigate

*Circles include:*

**03** lap, orb
**04** ball, band, belt, coil, corn, crop, curl, disc, eddy, gyre, halo, hoop, hour, loop, oval, ring, turn, tyre
**05** crown, cycle, dress, globe, grand, great, magic, mural, orbit, pitch, plate, polar, round, stone, upper, wheel
**06** Arctic, circus, cordon, discus, girdle, rundle, saucer, sphere, spiral, tropic, vortex, wreath
**07** annulet, annulus, circuit, compass, coronet, ellipse, equator, roundel, traffic, transit, turning, vicious
**08** epicycle, gyration, meridian, rotation, roundure, striking, virtuous
**09** Antarctic, perimeter, whirlpool, whirlwind
**10** almacantar, almucantar, Circassian, revolution
**13** circumference

• **stone circle**
**08** cromlech **09** cyclolith **10** Stonehenge **11** peristalith

**circuit**
**02** IC **03** lap **04** area, beat, eyre, tour **05** ambit, limit, orbit, range, round, route, track **06** bounds, course, diadem, region **07** compass, rondure, rounder **08** boundary, district, progress, roundure **09** perimeter, race track **10** revolution **12** running-track **13** circumference, perambulation

**• closed circuit**
**02** CC

**• logic circuit**
**02** OR **03** AND, NOR, NOT, XOR **04** NAND

**circuitous**
**07** devious, oblique, winding **08** indirect, rambling, tortuous **09** meandrian, meandrous **10** meandering, roundabout **11** anfractuous **12** labyrinthine, periphrastic

**circular**
**05** flyer, orbed, round **06** folder, letter, notice **07** annular, leaflet **08** handbill, pamphlet **09** spherical **10** disc-shaped, hoop-shaped, ring-shaped, round robin **12** announcement **13** advertisement

**circulate**
◇ *anagram indicator*
**04** flow, pass, walk **05** float, issue, rumor, swirl, troll, utter, whirl **06** gyrate, report, rotate, rumour, spread **07** diffuse, give out, go about, go round, publish, revolve **08** go abroad, go around, put about, transmit **09** broadcast, get around, pass round, propagate, publicize, send round **10** distribute, promulgate **11** disseminate, go the rounds, spread about **12** spread around **13** make the rounds

**circulation**
**04** flow **05** cycle **06** motion, spread **07** issuing **08** circling, currency, cyclosis, movement, rotation **09** blood-flow, publicity **10** readership **11** propagation, publication **12** distribution, transmission **13** dissemination

**• in circulation**
◇ *anagram indicator*
**05** in use **06** afloat, around, issued **07** current, printed **09** available, published **11** distributed, spread about **12** spread around

**circumference**
**03** arc, rim **04** edge **05** girth, round, verge **06** border, bounds, circle, fringe, limits, margin **07** circuit, compass, outline **08** boundary, confines **09** extremity, perimeter, periphery

**circumlocution**
**06** ambage **08** pleonasm **09** euphemism, prolixity, tautology, verbosity, wordiness **10** periphrase, redundancy **11** convolution, diffuseness, periphrasis **12** indirectness **14** discursiveness, roundaboutness

**circumlocutory**
**05** wordy **06** prolix **07** diffuse, verbose **08** elliptic, indirect **09** ambagious, redundant **10** convoluted, discursive, elliptical, long-winded, pleonastic, roundabout **11** euphemistic **12** periphrastic, tautological

**circumscribe**
**04** trim **05** bound, hem in, limit, pen in **06** define **07** abridge, confine, curtail, delimit, enclose **08** encircle, restrain, restrict, surround **09** delineate, demarcate, encompass

**circumspect**
**04** wary, wise **05** canny **07** careful, guarded, politic, prudent **08** cautious, discreet, vigilant, watchful **09** attentive, judicious, observant, sagacious **10** deliberate **11** calculating **14** discriminating

**circumspection**
**04** care **07** caution **08** prudence, wariness **09** canniness, chariness, examining, vigilance **10** discretion **11** carefulness, guardedness **12** deliberation, watchfulness

**circumstance**
**03** lot **04** case, fact, fate, item, nark, this **05** event, means, state, thing **06** detail, factor, plight, status **07** element, fortune, respect, situate **08** accident, ceremony, position **09** condition, happening, lifestyle, resources, situation **10** background, occurrence, particular **11** arrangement, environment **12** lie of the land **14** how the land lies, state of affairs

**circumstantial**
**04** tiny **06** minute **07** deduced, hearsay **08** indirect, inferred, presumed **10** contingent, evidential, incidental **11** conjectural, inferential, presumptive, provisional

**circumvent**
**04** dish **05** avoid, dodge, evade **06** bypass, outwit, thwart **07** get past **08** get out of, get round, go beyond, outflank, sidestep **09** encompass **12** steer clear of

**circumvention**
**07** dodging, evasion **09** avoidance, bypassing, thwarting **12** sidestepping **13** steering clear

**circus**
**06** cirque **10** hippodrome

*Circus-related terms include:*

**03** top
**04** geek, ring, tent
**05** clown
**06** big top, pie car
**07** acrobat, balloon, juggler, sawdust, trapeze, tumbler
**08** carnival, conjurer, conjuror, drum roll, high wire, magician, sideshow, unicycle
**09** aerialist, fire-eater, lion tamer, menagerie, safety net, strongman, tightrope
**10** acrobatics, acrobatism, candy floss, custard pie, ringmaster, roustabout, somersault, trick-rider, unicyclist
**11** funambulist, greasepaint
**12** escape artist, roll up! roll up!, stiltwalking, trick cyclist
**13** bareback rider, contortionist, trapeze artist

**cissy**
**03** wet **04** baby, soft, tonk, weak, wimp, wuss **05** pansy, softy **06** coward, feeble **07** crybaby, milksop, unmanly, wimpish **08** cowardly, weakling **09** mummy's boy **10** effeminate, namby-pamby

**cistern**
**03** vat **04** sink, tank **05** basin **08** feed-head, flush-box **09** reservoir

**citadel**
**04** fort, keep **05** tower **06** castle **07** bastion, kremlin **08** fortress **09** acropolis **10** stronghold **13** fortification

**citation**
**03** cit **05** award, quote **06** honour, source **07** cutting, excerpt, mention, passage **08** allusion, epigraph **09** quotation, reference **10** allegation **12** commendation, illustration

**cite**
**04** call, name **05** bring, quote, state, vouch **06** adduce, allege, summon **07** advance, bring up, convent, mention, refer to, specify **08** allude to, evidence **09** enumerate, exemplify **13** give an example

**citizen**
**03** cit **05** local, voter **07** burgher, denizen, freeman, oppidan, subject **08** civilian, national, resident, taxpayer, townsman, urbanite **10** inhabitant, townswoman **11** city-dweller, householder

**city**
**02** EC **04** seat, town **08** big smoke, downtown, precinct **09** inner city, metroplex, Weltstadt **10** city centre, cosmopolis, metropolis, micropolis, pentapolis **11** conurbation, megalopolis, urban sprawl **12** municipality **13** urban district **14** concrete jungle

*Ancient cities include:*

**02** Ur
**04** Acre, Axum, Ebla, Nuzi, Rome, Susa, Troy, Tula, Tyre, Uruk
**05** Aksum, Argos, Bosra, Bursa, Copán, Cuzco, Eridu, Hatra, Huari, Mitla, Moche, Petra, Saida, Sidon, Tikal, Uxmal
**06** Athens, Byblos, Cyrene, Jabneh, Jamnia, Napata, Nippur, Sardis, Shiloh, Sparta, Thebes, Ugarit
**07** Antioch, Babylon, Bukhara, Corinth, El Tajin, Ephesus, Megiddo, Miletus, Mycenae, Nineveh, Paestum,

Plataea, Pompeii, Samaria, Sybaris, Vergina
**08** Carthage, Damascus, Hattusas, Hattusha, Kerkuane, Palenque, Pergamon, Pergamum, Sigiriya, Tashkent, Thysdrus
**09** Byzantium, Cartagena, Epidaurus, Sukhothai
**10** Alexandria, Angkor Thom, Carchemish, Heliopolis, Hierapolis, Monte Albán, Persepolis
**11** Chichén Itzá, Herculaneum, Machu Picchu, Polonnaruwa, Teotihuacán
**12** Anuradhapura
**13** Halicarnassus
**14** Constantinople

*Capital cities include:*

**04** Apia, Baku, Bern, Dili, Doha, Kiev, Lima, Lomé, Malé, Oslo, Riga, Rome, San'a, Suva
**05** Abuja, Accra, Amman, Berne, Cairo, Dacca, Dakar, Dhaka, Hanoi, Kabul, Koror, La Paz, Minsk, Paris, Praia, Quito, Rabat, Sana'a, Seoul, Sofia, Sucre, Tokyo, Tunis, Vaduz
**06** Akmola, Ankara, Asmara, Astana, Athens, Bamako, Bangui, Banjul, Beirut, Berlin, Bissau, Bogotá, Dodoma, Dublin, Harare, Havana, Kigali, Lisbon, London, Luanda, Lusaka, Madrid, Majuro, Malabo, Manama, Manila, Maputo, Maseru, Monaco, Moroni, Moscow, Muscat, Nassau, Niamey, Ottawa, Peking, Prague, Riyadh, Roseau, Skopje, T'aipei, Tarawa, Tehran, Tirana, Vienna, Warsaw, Yangon, Zagreb
**07** Abidjan, Algiers, Alma-Ata, Baghdad, Bangkok, Beijing, Belfast, Bishkek, Caracas, Cardiff, Cayenne, Colombo, Conakry, Cotonou, El Aaiún, Godthab, Honiara, Jakarta, Kampala, Lobamba, Managua, Mbabane, Nairobi, Nicosia, Palikir, Papeete, Rangoon, San José, San Juan, São Tomé, St John's, Tallinn, Tbilisi, Teheran, Thimphu, Tripoli, Valetta, Vilnius, Yaoundé, Yerevan
**08** Abu Dhabi, Ashgabat, Asunción, Belgrade, Belmopan, Brasília, Brussels, Budapest, Canberra, Cape Town, Castries, Chisinau, Damascus, Djibouti, Dushanbe, Freetown, Gaborone, Helsinki, Khartoum, Kingston, Kinshasa, Kishinev, Lilongwe, Monrovia, N'Djamena, New Delhi, Port-Vila, Pretoria, Santiago, Sarajevo, Tashkent, The Hague, Tórshavn, Valletta, Victoria, Windhoek
**09** Amsterdam, Ashkhabad, Bucharest, Bujumbura, Edinburgh, Fongafale, Islamabad, Jerusalem, Kathmandu, Kingstown, Ljubljana, Mogadishu, Nuku'alofa, Phnom Penh, Port Louis, Porto Novo, Pyongyang, Reykjavík, San Marino, Singapore, St George's, Stockholm, Ulan Bator, Vientiane
**10** Addis Ababa, Basseterre, Bratislava, Bridgetown, Copenhagen, Georgetown, Kuwait City, Libreville, Luxembourg, Mexico City, Montevideo, Nouakchott, Panama City, Paramaribo, Wellington, Willemstad
**11** Brazzaville, Buenos Aires, Kuala Lumpur, Monaco-Ville, Ouagadougou, Port Moresby, Port of Spain, San Salvador, Tegucigalpa, Vatican City
**12** Antananarivo, Bloemfontein, Fort-de-France, Port-au-Prince, Santo Domingo, Tel Aviv-Jaffa, Washington DC, Yamoussoukro
**13** Guatemala City, Yaren District
**14** Andorra la Vella
**17** Bandar Seri Begawan
**23** Sri Jayawardenepura Kotte

*Cities and towns include:*

**02** Bo, LA, NY
**03** Åbo, Ayr, Ely, Fès, Fez, Gao, Hué, Lae, Nis, NYC, Pau, Qom, Ufa, Ulm, Vac, Zug
**04** Acre, Aden, Agra, Ajme, Amoy, Bari, Bath, Bonn, Brno, Bury, Caen, Cali, Cebu, Como, Cork, Dazu, Deal, Edam, Elat, Eton, Faro, Gand, Gent, Gifu, Graz, Györ, Homs, Hove, Hull, Iasi, Icel, Ipoh, Jima, Jixi, Kano, Kiel, Kobe, Köln, Kota, La-sa, León, Linz, Lódz, Lugo, Luik, Lund, Lvov, Metz, Mold, Mons, Naas, Naha, Nara, Nice, Nuuk, Oban, Oita, Omsk, Oran, Oulu, Pécs, Pegu, Perm, Pisa, Pula, Pune, Rand, Reno, Rhyl, Ruse, Ryde, Safi, Sale, Salt, Sfax, Sian, Sion, Soul, St-Lô, Suez, Sumy, Tema, Thun, Tula, Tyre, Umeå, Vasa, Vigo, Waco, Wick, Wien, Wuhu, Wuxi, Xi'an, York, Zibo, Zörs
**05** Adana, Ahvaz, Åland, Al Ayn, Aosta, Aqaba, Argos, Århus, Arica, Arles, Arras, Aspen, Aswan, Ávila, Baden, Banff, Baoji, Basle, Basra, Beira, Belém, Benxi, Blida, Blyth, Boise, Bondi, Borga, Bouar, Breda, Brest, Braga, Bursa, Busan, Cádiz, Canea, Cavan, Ceuta, Chiba, Chita, Colón, Conwy, Cowes, Crewe, Cuzco, Davao, Davos, Delft, Delhi, Derby, Dijon, Dover, Duala, Dubai, Dukou, Eilat, Elche, Epsom, Essen, Eupen, Évora, Fiume, Frome, Fuxin, Genoa, Ghent, Gijón, Gomel, Gorky, Gouda, Gweru, Hagen, Haifa, Halle, Hefei, Hohot, Honan, Ichun, Ieper, Iwaki, Izmir, Jaffa, Jedda, Jilin, Jinan, Jinja, Kaédi, Kandy, Karaj, Kazan, Kelso, Kirov, Kitwe, Kochi, Konya, Köseg, Kursk, Kyoto, Lagos, Leeds, Lewes, Lhasa, Liège, Lille, Limbe, Luton, Luxor, Lyons, Mâcon, Mainz, Malmö, Masan, Mecca, Medan, Miami, Milan, Mitla, Mopti, Mosul, Namen, Namur, Nancy, Nasik, Natal, Ndola, Nîmes, Ohrid, Omagh, Omaha, Omiya, Oryol, Osaka, Otley, Oujda, Padua, Parma, Patan, Patna, Pavia, Penza, Perth, Plzen, Ponce, Poole, Poona, Pusan, Reims, Resit, Ripon, Ronda, Rouen, Rovno, Rugby, Sakai, Salem, Salta, Sebha, Ségou, Sidon, Siena, Skien, Sochi, Sopot, Split, Suita, Surat, Suwon, Taegu, Talca, Tampa, Tanga, Tanta, Tempe, Thane, Thiès, Tomar, Tomsk, Torun, Tours, Trier, Troon, Truro, Tulsa, Tunja, Turin, Turku, Tzu-po, Udine, Ulsan, Urawa, Utica, Vaasa, Varna, Vejle, Vlorë, Wells, Wigan, Worms, Wuhan, Ypres, Zadar, Zaria, Zarqa
**06** Aachen, Aarhus, Agadez, Agadir, Albany, Aleppo, Amiens, Annaba, Annecy, Anshan, Anvers, Anyang, Arezzo, Armagh, Arnhem, Arusha, Ashdod, Atbara, At Taif, Austin, Avarua, Baguio, Bangor, Baotou, Bastia, Bengpu, Bergen, Bhopal, Bilbao, Biloxi, Bitola, Bochum, Bolton, Bombay, Bootle, Boston, Brasov, Bremen, Bruges, Brugge, Burgos, Buxton, Cairns, Calais, Callao, Calmar, Camden, Campos, Cancún, Cannes, Canton, Carlow, Casper, Chania, Chi-nan, Chonju, Cochin, Cracow, Crosby, Cuenca, Dalian, Dallas, Da Nang, Danzig, Daqing, Darhan, Darwin, Datong, Dayton, Denver, Dieppe, Douala, Dudley, Duluth, Dundee, Durban, Durham, Durrës, El Gîza, El Paso, Eugene, Evreux, Exeter, Fatima, Fresno, Frunze, Fu-chou, Fushun, Fuzhou, Galway, Gdansk, Gdynia, Geneva, Gitega, Grodno, Grozny, Guelph, Guilin, Guimar, Gujrat, Guntur, Ha'apai, Hamina, Handan, Han-kou, Harbin, Harlem, Harlow, Harrow, Hebron, Hegang, Himeji, Hobart, Howrah, Ibadan, Inchon, Indore, Jaffna, Jaipur, Jarash, Jarrow, Jeddah, Jiddah, Jilong, Juneau, Kalmar, Kaluga, Kankan, Kanpur, Kaolan, Kassel, Kaunas, Kendal, Khulna, Kirkby, Kirkuk, Kosice, Kraków, Kumasi, Kurgan, Lahore, Lanark, Leiden, Le Mans, Leshan, Leuven, Leyden, Lübeck, Lublin, Ludlow, Lugano, Maceio, Madras, Makale, Málaga, Malang, Manaus, Mantua, Matrah, Medina, Meerut, Mekele, Meknès, Meshed, Mobile, Mukden, Multan, Muncie, Munich, Murcia, Mysore, Nablus, Nagano, Nagoya, Nagpur, Nantes, Napier, Naples, Narvik, Newark, Ningbo, Nouméa, Odense, Odessa, Oldham, Olinda, Oporto, Örebro, Osasco, Osijek, Ostend, Oviedo, Oxford, Padang, Paphos, Phuket, Piatra, Pierre, Pilsen, Porvoo, Potosí, Poznan, Presov, Puebla, Quebec, Queluz, Quetta, Raipur, Rajkat, Ranchi, Recife, Redcar, Reggio, Regina, Rennes, Rheims, Rijeka, Ryazan, Saigon, Salala, Samara, Santos, Schwyz, Sefadu, Sendai, Shiraz, Silves, Sining, Sintra, Skikda, Sliema, Slough, Smyrna, Sokodé, Sousse, Soweto, Sparta, St Ives, St John, St Malo, St Paul, Stroud, Stuart, Suchow, Sukkur, Suzhou,

Sydney, Szeged, Tabriz, Tacoma, Tadmur, Taejon, Tahoua, Tainan, Tamale, Tambov, Tarbes, Tarsus, Ta-t'ung, Teruel, Thurso, Tipasa, Tobruk, Toledo, Toluca, Topeka, Torbay, Toulon, Toyama, Toyota, Tralee, Trento, Treves, Tromsø, Troyes, Tsinan, Tubruq, Tucson, Tyumen, Urumqi, Vannes, Vargas, Venice, Verona, Viborg, Weimar, Whitby, Widnes, Woking, Xiamen, Xining, Xuzhou, Yangku, Yantai, Yeovil, Yichun, Yunnan, Zabrze, Zigong, Zinder, Zurich, Zwolle

**07** Aberfan, Airdrie, Aligarh, Alnwick, Antibes, Antioch, Antwerp, Aracaju, Atlanta, Augusta, Auxerre, Avignon, Baalbek, Badajoz, Bairiki, Banares, Banbury, Bandung, Baoding, Barnaul, Barossa, Bayamón, Bedford, Beeston, Benares, Bendigo, Berbera, Bergama, Bergamo, Bexhill, Bizerta, Blarney, Bologna, Bolzano, Boulder, Bourges, Braemar, Brescia, Bristol, Bryansk, Buffalo, Burnley, Cáceres, Calgary, Calicut, Cardiff, Catania, Chalcis, Changan, Cheadle, Cheddar, Chelsea, Chengde, Chengdu, Cheng-tu, Chester, Chicago, Chifeng, Chi-lung, Chongju, Chungho, Clonmel, Coblenz, Coimbra, Cologne, Concord, Córdoba, Corinth, Corinto, Corunna, Crawley, Dandong, Detroit, Devizes, Donetsk, Douglas, Dresden, Dundalk, Dunedin, Dunkirk, Durango, Entebbe, Erdenet, Esbjerg, Evesham, Exmouth, Falkirk, Fareham, Ferrara, Foochow, Fukuoka, Funchal, Ganzhou, Geelong, Glasgow, Goiânia, Gosport, Granada, Grimsby, Guiyang, Gwalior, Gwangju, Haerbin, Halifax, Hamburg, Hamhung, Hanover, Harwich, Henzada, Heredia, Houston, Huaibai, Huainan, Ipswich, Iquique, Iquitos, Irkutsk, Isfahan, Ivanovo, Izhevsk, Jackson, Jericho, Jiamusi, Jinzhou, Jodhpur, Kaesong, Kaifeng, Kalinin, Kananga, Karachi, Kassala, Kayseri, Keelung, Kenitra, Keswick, Kharkov, Kherson, Koblenz, Kolding, Kuching, Kunming, Kutaisi, Lansing, Lanzhou, La Plata, Larnaca, Latakia, Leghorn, Le Havre, Leipzig, Lerwick, Liberia, Limoges, Lincoln, Lipetsk, Liuzhou, Livorno, Logroño, Louvain, Lucerne, Lucknow, Lugansk, Lumbini, Luoyang, Machida, Madison, Madurai, Malvern, Manzini, Maracay, Marburg, Margate, Mashhad, Massawa, Matlock, Matsudo, Melilla, Memphis, Mendoza, Mildura, Mindelo, Miskolc, Mitsiwa, Mogilev, Mombasa, Morpeth, Münster, Nanjing, Nanking, Nanning, Nantong, Newbury, Newport, Newquay, New Ross, New York, Niigata, Niterói, Norfolk, Norwich, Novi Sad, Oakland, Okayama, Okinawa, Olympia, Orlando, Orleans, Ostrava, Pahsien, Paisley, Palermo, Panshan, Pattaya, Peebles, Penrith, Perugia, Phoenix, Piraeus, Pistoia, Pitesti, Plovdiv, Poltava, Popayán, Portree, Potsdam, Preston, Prizren, Qingdao, Qiqihar, Quimper, Raleigh, Randers, Ravenna, Reading, Redwood, Reigate, Roanoke, Rosario, Rostock, Rotorua, Runcorn, Sagunto, Salamis, Salerno, Salford, Sandown, Santa Fe, São Luis, Sapporo, Saransk, Saratov, Sassari, Seattle, Segovia, Setúbal, Seville, Shannon, Shantou, Shihezi, Shikoku, Shkodër, Sialkot, Sinuiju, Songnam, Spokane, Spoleto, Staines, Stanley, St Denis, St Louis, Sudbury, Swansea, Swindon, Taiyuan, Tampere, Tampico, Tangier, Taunton, Tel Aviv, Telford, Tétouan, Tianjin, Tijuana, Tilburg, Tilbury, Toronto, Torquay, Tournai, Trenton, Trieste, Tucumán, Ulan-Ude, Uppsala, Utrecht, Ventnor, Vicenza, Vitebsk, Vitosha, Walsall, Warwick, Watford, Weifang, Wenzhou, Wexford, Wichita, Windsor, Wrexham, Wroclaw, Wuhsien, Yakeshi, Yichang, Yingkou, Yonkers, Zermatt, Zhuzhou, Zwickau

**08** Aberdeen, Acapulco, Adelaide, Akureyri, Alajuela, Albacete, Alicante, Amarillo, Amritsar, Arbroath, Arequipa, Auckland, Augsburg, Aviemore, Ayia Napa, Ballarat, Banghazi, Bareilly, Barnsley, Bathurst, Bayreuth, Beauvais, Belgorod, Benghazi, Benguela, Benidorm, Besançon, Bhadgaon, Biarritz, Bismarck, Blantyre, Bobruysk, Bordeaux, Boulogne, Bradford, Braganza, Brighton, Brindisi, Brisbane, Bulawayo, Burgundy, Cagliari, Calcutta, Campinas, Carlisle, Changsha, Chartres, Chemnitz, Chepstow, Cheyenne, Chiclayo, Chimbote, Chimkent, Ching-tao, Chongjin, Clevedon, Columbia, Columbus, Contagem, Coventry, Culiacán, Curitiba, Dartford, Dearborn, Debrecen, Djakarta, Dortmund, Drogheda, Duisburg, Dumfries, Dunhuang, Dunleary, Durgapur, Dzhambul, Ebbw Vale, Edmonton, El Kharga, Elsinore, Europort, Falmouth, Florence, Flushing, Freeport, Fribourg, Fujisawa, Fukuyama, Gaoxiong, Gisborne, Gorlovka, Grantham, Grasmere, Greenock, Grenoble, Guernica, Hachioji, Haiphong, Hakodate, Hamilton, Hangchow, Hangzhou, Hannover, Hartford, Hastings, Hengyang, Hereford, Hertford, Hirakata, Holyhead, Holywell, Hong Kong, Honolulu, Huangshi, Hunjiang, Ichikawa, Iowa City, Istanbul, Jabalpur, Jaboatoa, Kairouan, Kanazawa, Kandahar, Karlsbad, Katowice, Kawasaki, Keflavik, Kemerovo, Kilkenny, Kirkwall, Kismaayo, Klosters, Kolhapur, Konstanz, Koriyama, Kuei-yang, Kumamoto, Laâyoune, La Laguna, Las Vegas, Lausanne, Legoland, Leskovac, Liaoyang, Liaoyuan, Limassol, Limerick, Londrina, Longford, Lüderitz, Ludhiana, Lyallpur, Makassar, Mandalay, Mannheim, Marbella, Mariupal, Mariupol, Mayaguez, Mazatlán, Medellín, Mercedes, Mexicali, Montreal, Montreux, Montrose, Mufulira, Mulhouse, Murmansk, Myingyan, Nagasaki, Namangan, Nanchang, Nazareth, New Haven, Newhaven, Nijmegen, Novgorod, Nuneaton, Nürnberg, Oak Ridge, Omdurman, Oostende, Orenburg, Oswestry, Pago Pago, Pamplona, Panchiao, Pasadena, Pavlodar, Penzance, Peshawar, Piacenza, Ploiesti, Plymouth, Poitiers, Portland, Portrush, Port Said, Pristina, Ramsgate, Rancagua, Randstad, Redditch, Richmond, Road Town, Rochdale, Rockford, Roskilde, Rosslare, Sabadell, Salonica, Salonika, Saltillo, Salvador, Salzburg, San Diego, Santa Ana, Santarém, São Paulo, Satu Mare, Savannah, Schwerin, Semarang, Shanghai, Shanklin, Shaoguan, Shenyang, Shizuoka, Sholapur, Silk Road, Simbirsk, Skegness, Smolensk, Solihull, Solingen, Sorocaba, Southend, Srinagar, Stafford, St Albans, Stamford, St David's, St Gallen, St Helens, St Helier, Stirling, St Moritz, Stockton, Strabane, St-Tropez, Subotica, Suicheng, Surabaya, Swan Hill, Syracuse, Szczecin, Taganrog, Taichung, Tamworth, Tangshan, Teresina, Thetford, Thonburi, Tiberias, Tientsin, Timbuktu, Titograd, Tolyatti, Tongeren, Toulouse, Toyohasi, Toyonaka, Trujillo, Tsingtao, Tübingen, Uleaborg, Ullapool, Vadodara, Valencia, Valletta, Varanasi, Veracruz, Vila Real, Vinnitsa, Vittoria, Vladimir, Voronezh, Wakayama, Wallasey, Wallsend, Warangal, Weymouth, Winnipeg, Worthing, Würzburg, Xiangfan, Xiangtan, Xinxiang, Yangchow, Yangquan, Yangzhou, Yinchuan, Yin-hsien, Yokohama, Yokosuko, Yorktown, Zakopane, Zanzibar, Zhitomir

**09** Adis Abeba, Ahmadabad, Alba Iulia, Albufeira, Aldershot, Algeciras, Allahabad, Amagasaki, Ambleside, Anchorage, Annapolis, Archangel, Asahikawa, Astrakhan, Audenarde, Aylesbury, Bakhtaran, Baltimore, Bangalore, Barcelona, Beersheba, Berbérati, Bethlehem, Bhavnagar, Bialystok, Blackburn,

Blackpool, Bossangoa, Botany Bay, Brunswick, Bydgoszcz, Cambridge, Cartagena, Castlebar, Changchun, Changzhou, Charleroi, Charlotte, Chengchow, Cherbourg, Chernobyl, Chiang Mai, Chihuahua, Choluteca, Chongqing, Chungking, Cleveland, Colwyn Bay, Constance, Constanta, Des Moines, Doncaster, Dordrecht, Dubrovnik, Dudelange, Dumbarton, Dungannon, Dunstable, Eastleigh, Eindhoven, Eskisehir, Esztergom, Fairbanks, Famagusta, Faridabad, Fishguard, Fleetwood, Fortaleza, Fort Worth, Frankfort, Frankfurt, Fremantle, Funabashi, Galveston, Gateshead, Gaziantep, Gippsland, Gold Coast, Gorakhpur, Gravesend, Greenwich, Groningen, Guangzhou, Guarulhos, Guayaquil, Guildford, Hallstatt, Hamamatsu, Harrogate, Haslemere, Helsingør, Heraklion, Hilversum, Hiroshima, Humpty Doo, Hyderabad, Immingham, Innsbruck, Inverness, Ismailiya, Jalandhar, Jamestown, Johnstone, Jönköping, Kagoshima, Kamchatka, Kaohsiung, Karaganda, Karlsruhe, Kawaguchi, Killarney, Kimberley, King's Lynn, Kirkcaldy, Kisangani, Kishinyov, Kitzbühel, Kórinthos, Kozhikode, Krasnodar, Krivoy Rog, Kurashiki, Kuybyshev, Kwang-chow, Lancaster, Las Cruces, Leicester, Lexington, Lichfield, Liverpool, Llangefni, Long Beach, Lowestoft, Lymington, Magdeburg, Mahajanga, Maidstone, Makeyevka, Mamoudzan, Manizales, Mansfield, Maracaibo, Maralinga, Marrakesh, Matsuyama, Melbourne, Middleton, Milwaukee, Monterrey, Moradabad, Morecambe, Mullingar, Nashville, Neuchâtel, Newcastle, Newmarket, Nikolayev, Nuremberg, Ogbomosho, Osnabrück, Palembang, Pamporovo, Perpignan, Peterhead, Pingxiang, Pontianak, Port Natal, Port Sudan, Pressburg, Prestwick, Princeton, Qinghai Hu, Querétaro, Riverside, Rochester, Rotherham, Rotterdam, Rovaniemi, Salisbury, Samarkand, San Miguel, Santa Cruz, Santander, Saragossa, Saskatoon, Shanchung, Sheerness, Sheffield, Sioux City, South Bend, Southport, Southwark, St Andrews, Stavanger, Stavropol, St-Étienne, Stevenage, St-Nazaire, Stockport, Stornoway, St-Quentin, Stranraer, Stuttgart, Sukhothai, Sundsvall, Surakarta, Takamatsu, Takatsuki, Tarragona, Tenkodogo, T'ien-ching, Timisoara, Toamasina, Togliatti, Toowoomba, Trondheim, Tullamore, Ulyanovsk, Vancouver, Velingrad, Vicksburg, Volgograd, Wakefield, Walvis Bay, Waterford, Wiesbaden, Wimbledon, Wolfsburg, Worcester, Wuppertal, Xiangyang, Yaroslavl, Zamboanga, Zaozhuang, Zhengzhou, Zhenjiang, Zrenjanin

**10** Alexandria, Baton Rouge, Belize City, Birkenhead, Birmingham, Bridgeport, Bridgwater, Broken Hill, Caernarvon, Caerphilly, Canterbury, Carmarthen, Carnoustie, Carson City, Casablanca, Chandigarh, Charleston, Cheboksary, Chelmsford, Cheltenham, Cheng-hsien, Chichester, Chittagong, Cienfuegos, Cincinnati, Cluj-Napoca, Coatbridge, Cochabamba, Coimbatore, Colchester, Concepción, Darjeeling, Darlington, Diyarbakir, Dorchester, Düsseldorf, Dzerzhinsk, Eastbourne, El Mansoura, Faisalabad, Felixstowe, Folkestone, Fray Bentos, Galashiels, George Town, Gillingham, Glenrothes, Gloucester, Goose Green, Gothenburg, Gujranwala, Haddington, Harrisburg, Hartlepool, Heidelberg, Hermosillo, Hildesheim, Huntingdon, Huntsville, Jamshedpur, Jingdezhen, Joao Pessoa, Juiz de Fora, Kakopetria, Kalgoorlie, Kansas City, Kenilworth, Khabarovsk, Kilmarnock, Kita-Kyushu, Kompong Som, Lake Placid, Las Piedras, Launceston, Leeuwarden, Letchworth, Linlithgow, Little Rock, Liupanshui, Livingston, Llangollen, Los Angeles, Louisville, Lubumbashi, Luluabourg, Maastricht, Maidenhead, Manchester, Marseilles, Medjugorje, Miami Beach, Monte Carlo, Montego Bay, Montgomery, Montpelier, Mostaganem, Motherwell, Mudanjiang, New Orleans, Nottingham, Nouadhibou, Nova Iguacu, Oranjestad, Oudenaarde, Palmerston, Petersburg, Pittsburgh, Pontefract, Portishead, Portsmouth, Providence, Quezon City, Quinnipiac, Rawalpindi, Regensburg, Sacramento, Sagamihara, San Antonio, San Ignacio, Santa Marta, Santo André, São Gonçalo, Scunthorpe, Sebastopol, Shepparton, Shreveport, Shrewsbury, Simferapol, Sioux Falls, Södertälje, Strasbourg, Sunderland, Sverdlovsk, Talcahuano, Tammerfors, Tananarive, Thunder Bay, Townsville, Trivandrum, Trowbridge, Tsaochuang, Utsunomiya, Valladolid, Valparaíso, Vijayawada, Viña del Mar, Vlissingen, Wadi Medani, Wagga Wagga, Warrington, Washington, Whitehorse, Wilmington, Winchester, Windermere, Winterthur, Wittenberg, Wollongong, Workington, Yogyakarta, Yoshkar Ola, Zaporozhye

**11** Aberystwyth, Albuquerque, Antofagasta, Bahía Blanca, Banjarmasin, Basingstoke, Bhilai Nagar, Bognor Regis, Bournemouth, Brandenburg, Bremerhaven, Bridlington, Broadstairs, Brownsville, Bucaramanga, Campo Grande, Carcassonne, Charlestown, Chattanooga, Chelyabinsk, Cherepovets, Cirencester, Cleethorpes, Cockermouth, Coney Island, Conisbrough, Constantine, Cumbernauld, Dar es Salaam, Differdange, Downpatrick, Dunfermline, Enniskillen, Farnborough, Fort William, Francistown, Fraserburgh, Fredericton, Glastonbury, Grangemouth, Guadalajara, Guisborough, Hälsingborg, Helsingborg, Helsingfors, High Wycombe, Johor Baharu, Juan-les-Pins, Kaliningrad, Kampong Saom, Karlovy Vary, Kompong Saom, Komsomolosk, Krasnoyarsk, Lianyungang, Londonderry, Lossiemouth, Makhachkala, Mar del Plata, Medicine Hat, Medway Towns, Minneapolis, Montpellier, Narayanganj, Newport News, New York City, Nishinomiya, Northampton, Novosibirsk, Palm Springs, Pointe-Noire, Polonnaruwa, Port Augusta, Porto Alegre, Prestonpans, Punta Arenas, Qinhuangdao, Resistencia, Rockhampton, Rostov-on-Don, Saarbrücken, Scarborough, Southampton, Spanish Town, Springfield, Stourbridge, Szombathely, Tallahassee, Trincomalee, Tselinograd, Vladivostok, Westminster, White Plains, Wu-lu-k'o-mu-shi, Yellowknife, Zhangjiakou

**12** Alice Springs, Anuradhapura, Atlantic City, Barquisimeto, Barranquilla, Beverly Hills, Bloemfontein, Buenaventura, Caloocan City, Chesterfield, Christchurch, Ciudad Juárez, East Kilbride, Great Malvern, Higashiosaka, Hubli-Dharwar, Huddersfield, Indianapolis, Jacksonville, Johannesburg, Keetmanshoop, Kota Kinabalu, Kristianstad, Léopoldville, Lisdoonvarna, Loughborough, Luang Prabang, Ludwigshafen, Macclesfield, Magnitogorsk, Mazar-e-Sharif, Milton Keynes, New Amsterdam, Nizhniy Tagil, Novokuznetsk, Oklahoma City, Petaling Jaya, Peterborough, Philadelphia, Pingdingshan, Pointe-à-Pitre, Ponta Delgada, Port Harcourt, Puerto Cortes, Rio de Janeiro, Salt Lake City, San Cristobal, San Francisco, San Pedro Sula, San Sebastian, Santa Barbara, Schaffhausen, Shijiazhuang,

Shuangyashan, Sidi bel Abbès, Skelmersdale, South Shields, Speightstown, Stanleyville, St Catherines, Stoke-on-Trent, St Petersburg, Tel Aviv-Jaffa, Tennant Creek, Thessaloníki, Trichinopoly, Ujung Pandang, Villahermosa, West Bromwich, Williamsburg, Winston-Salem

**13** Aix-en-Provence, Belo Horizonte, Bobo-Dioulasso, Charlottetown, Ciudad Guayana, Duque de Caxias, Ellesmere Port, Epsom and Ewell, Great Yarmouth, Ho Chi Minh City, Jefferson City, Kidderminster, Kirkcudbright, Kirkintilloch, Leamington Spa, Lytham St Anne's, Middlesbrough, Ordzhonikidze, Port Elizabeth, Portlaoighise, Quezaltenango, Ribeirao Preto, San Bernardino, San Luis Potosí, Semipalatinsk, Sihanoukville, Veliko Turnovo, Virginia Beach, Visakhapatnam, Wolverhampton, Yekaterinburg, Zlatni Pyasaci

**14** Andorra-la-Vella, Dnepropetrovsk, Elisabethville, Feira de Santana, Hemel Hempstead, Henley-on-Thames, Louangphrabang, Santiago de Cuba, Shihchiachuang, Stockton-on-Tees, Székesfehérvár, Tunbridge Wells, Ust-Kamenogorsk, Voroshilovgrad

**15** Alcalá de Henares, Angra do Heroísmo, Barrow-in-Furness, Burton-upon-Trent, Charlotte Amalie, Charlottesville, Chester-le-Street, Clermont-Ferrand, Colorado Springs, Frankfurt am Main, Netzahaulcoyotl, Nizhniy Novgorod, Palma de Mallorca, Palmerston North, São João de Meriti, Sekondi-Takoradi, Shoubra el-Kheima, Sutton Coldfield, Weston-super-Mare

*See also* **Australia**; **Canada**; **Ireland**; **New Zealand**; **Russia**; **United Kingdom**; **United States of America**

**• city area**
**02** EC

**civet**
**05** genet, rasse, zibet **07** genette, linsang, nandine, Viverra
**08** mongoose, suricate, toddy cat
**09** binturong, delundung, ichneumon, weasel cat **10** paradoxure

**civic**
**04** city, town **05** local, urban **06** public
**07** borough **08** communal
**09** community, municipal
**12** metropolitan

**civil**
**03** civ, lay **04** fair, home **05** civic, local, state **06** polite, public, urbane
**07** affable, courtly, refined, secular
**08** civilian, communal, domestic, interior, internal, mannerly, national, obliging, polished, temporal, well-bred **09** civilized, community, compliant, courteous, municipal
**10** cultivated, respectful
**11** complaisant **12** well-mannered
**13** accommodating, parliamentary

**civilian**
**03** civ **05** civvy, mufti **07** citizen, gownman **08** gownsman **12** non-combatant

**civility**
**04** tact **06** comity, notice **07** amenity, manners, respect **08** breeding, courtesy, urbanity **09** attention
**10** affability, politeness, refinement
**11** good manners **12** graciousness, pleasantness **13** courteousness

**civilization**
**06** Kultur, people **07** culture, customs, society **08** progress, urbanity
**09** community, education
**10** refinement **11** advancement, cultivation, development **12** human society **13** enlightenment
**14** sophistication

**civilize**
**04** tame **05** edify **06** polish, refine
**07** educate, improve, perfect
**08** humanize, instruct **09** cultivate, enlighten, socialize **12** sophisticate

**civilized**
**06** polite, urbane **07** refined
**08** advanced, cultured, educated, sensible, sociable **09** courteous, developed **10** cultivated, reasonable
**11** enlightened **12** well-mannered
**13** sophisticated

**civilly**
**07** courtly **08** mannerly, politely, urbanely **10** obligingly **11** courteously
**12** respectfully

**clad**
**06** vested **07** attired, clothed, covered, dressed, wearing

**claim**
**03** ask, bag, own, sue **04** aver, avow, call, hold, kill, need, plea, pose, take
**05** cause, clame, exact, right, shout, state **06** affirm, allege, assert, assume, avowal, demand, insist **07** collect, contend, darrain, darrayn, declare, deraign, deserve, pretend, profess, purport, request, require **08** averment, darraign, darraine, maintain, petition, put in for **09** assertion, challenge, darraigne, postulate, privilege
**10** allegation, contention, insistence, lay claim to, pretension, profession
**11** affirmation, application, declaration, entitlement, requirement, requisition **12** asseveration, be entitled to, have a right to

**claimant**
**06** titler **08** litigant **09** applicant, candidate, pretender, suppliant
**10** challenger, petitioner, pretendant, pretendent, supplicant

**clairvoyance**
**03** ESP **09** telepathy **11** second sight
**13** psychic powers **14** cryptaesthesia, fortune-telling, hyperaesthesia

**clairvoyant**
**04** seer **05** augur **06** oracle **07** diviner, prophet, psychic **08** telepath
**09** prophetic, visionary **10** prophetess, soothsayer, telepathic **12** extrasensory
**13** fortune-teller

**clam**
**03** Mya **05** cohog **06** quahog
**07** quahaug, scallop **08** tridacna
**11** black quahog

**clamber**
**04** claw, shin **05** climb, mount, scale
**06** ascend, shinny **08** scrabble, scramble, sprackle **09** spraickle

**clammy**
**04** damp, dank **05** close, heavy, moist, muggy, slimy **06** sticky, sweaty, viscid
**08** sweating

**clamorous**
**04** loud **05** lusty, noisy, vocal
**07** blaring, blatant, riotous **08** blattant, vehement **09** deafening, insistent
**10** boisterous, strepitant, tumultuous, uproarious, vociferant, vociferous
**11** open-mouthed **12** obstreperous

**clamour**
**03** cry, din, hue **04** bark, rout, urge, utis
**05** blare, claim, noise, raird, reird, rumor **06** demand, hubbub, insist, outcry, racket, rumour, uproar
**07** brabble, call for, outrage
**08** brouhaha, press for, shouting, stramash **09** agitation, commotion, hue and cry **10** complaints
**11** vociferance **12** katzenjammer, vociferation **13** ask for noisily

**clamp**
**03** fix **04** grip, heap, hold, vice
**05** brace, clasp, press, stack, tread
**06** clench, clinch, fasten, secure
**07** bracket, squeeze **08** fastener
**09** hand-screw, pinchcock, potato pit
**10** Denver boot, immobilize
**11** immobilizer

**• clamp down on**
**04** stop **05** limit **07** confine, control, prevent **08** restrain, restrict, suppress
**10** put a stop to **11** crack down on
**14** come down hard on

**clampdown**
**04** stop **05** limit **07** control
**09** crackdown, restraint **10** prevention
**11** restriction, suppression

**clan**
**03** set **04** band, gens, hapu, line, name, race, sect, sept **05** group, horde, house, tribe **06** circle, clique, family, kinred **07** coterie, faction, kindred, society **10** fraternity **11** brotherhood
**13** confraternity

*See also* **Scottish**

**clandestine**
**03** sly **06** closet, covert, hidden, secret, sneaky **07** furtive, private
**08** backdoor, backroom, stealthy
**09** concealed, underhand **10** behind-door, fraudulent, undercover
**11** underground **13** surreptitious

14 cloak-and-dagger 15 under-the-counter

**clandestinely**
05 slyly 07 on the QT 08 covertly, secretly, sneakily 09 furtively, privately 10 on the quiet, stealthily 12 fraudulently 15 surreptitiously, under the counter

**clang**
04 bong, peal, ring, toll 05 chime, clank, clash, clink, clunk, klang 06 jangle, timbre 07 clatter, resound 11 reverberate 13 reverberation

**clanger**
04 boob, flub, goof, slip 05 boner, error, fault, gaffe 06 booboo, cock-up, howler, slip-up, stumer 07 bloomer, blunder, faux pas, mistake 08 solecism 09 oversight 10 inaccuracy 12 indiscretion, misjudgement

**clank**
04 ring, toll 05 clang, clash, clink, clunk 06 jangle 07 clatter, resound 10 resounding 11 reverberate 13 reverberation

**clannish**
06 narrow, select 07 cliquey, insular 08 cliquish 09 exclusive, parochial, sectarian 10 unfriendly

**clap**
03 hit, pat, ray 04 bang, bolt, chop, slap 05 blaze, burst, cheer, crack, flare, flash, shaft, smack, spark, whack 06 streak, strike, wallop 07 acclaim, applaud, ovation 08 applause, handclap, plaudite 11 thunderbolt 15 round of applause, standing ovation

**claptrap**
03 rot 04 blah, bosh, bull, bunk, guff 05 balls, bilge, hokum, trash, tripe 06 bunkum, drivel, faddle, hot air, piffle 07 baloney, blarney, eyewash, hogwash, rhubarb, rubbish, twaddle 08 blethers, buncombe, cobblers, nonsense, tommyrot 09 gibberish, poppycock 10 codswallop

**clarification**
05 gloss 10 definition, exposition 11 elucidation, explanation 12 illumination 14 interpretation, simplification

**clarify**
05 clear, gloss, purge 06 define, filter, purify, refine 07 clear up, explain, resolve 08 simplify, spell out 09 elucidate, make clear, make plain 10 illuminate 11 shed light on 12 throw light on

**clarity**
08 lucidity 09 chiarezza, clearness, plainness, precision, sharpness 10 definition, simplicity, visibility 11 obviousness 12 explicitness, transparency 15 intelligibility, unambiguousness

**clash**
03 jar, war 04 bang, feud, slam, snap 05 brush, clang, clank, crash, fight, noise, swash 06 gossip, hurtle, jangle, rattle, scream, strike 07 chatter, clatter, collide, contend, co-occur, grapple, jarring, quarrel, warring, wrangle 08 argument, coincide, conflict, disagree, fall foul, fighting, mismatch, not match, showdown, striking 09 collision, not go with 10 fall foul of 11 altercation, discordance, misalliance 12 be discordant, disagreement, irregularity 13 confrontation, not go together 14 be incompatible, look unpleasant 15 incompatibility

**clasp**
◇ *containment indicator*
03 hug, pin 04 clip, grip, hasp, hold, hook, tach 05 bosom, catch, grasp, press, slide, spang, tache, unite 06 attach, brooch, buckle, clutch, cuddle, enfold, fasten, preace, prease, tassel 07 agraffe, cling to, connect, embosom, embrace, enclasp, grapple, preasse, squeeze 08 fastener 09 fastening, hair slide, interlock, safety pin 10 infibulate

**class**
03 set 04 chic, form, kind, race, rank, rate, sort, type, year 05 brand, caste, genre, genus, grade, group, level, order, style, taste 06 course, league, lesson, period, phylum, reckon, sphere, status, stream 07 arrange, lecture, quality, section, seminar, species, teach-in 08 category, classify, division, elegance, grouping, standing, tutorial, workshop 09 designate 10 background, categorize, department, pigeonhole, study group 11 distinction, social order, stylishness 12 denomination, pecking order, social status 14 classification, social division, social standing, sophistication

*See also* **classification**

**classic**
04 best, Oaks, true 05 Derby, great, ideal, model, prime, usual 06 finest, simple 07 abiding, ageless, elegant, lasting, regular, St Leger, The Oaks, typical, undying 08 Augustan, enduring, exemplar, immortal, masterly, standard, timeless 09 brilliant, excellent, exemplary, first-rate, prototype 10 archetypal, consummate, definitive, first-class, masterwork 11 established, masterpiece, outstanding, traditional, undecorated, understated 12 paradigmatic, time-honoured 13 authoritative 14 characteristic, quintessential, representative 15 established work, unsophisticated

**classical**
04 pure 05 Attic, Latin, plain 06 humane, simple 07 concert, elegant, Grecian, refined, serious 08 Hellenic 09 excellent, symphonic 10 harmonious, restrained 11 symmetrical, traditional 12 ancient Greek, ancient Roman

*See also* **musician**; **singer**

**classically**
06 purely, simply 07 as a rule, plainly, usually 08 normally 09 elegantly, typically 10 ordinarily, originally 11 customarily 12 harmoniously, historically 13 symmetrically, traditionally

**classification**
05 group 06 method 07 grading, sorting 08 classing, grouping, taxonomy 10 tabulation 11 arrangement, cataloguing 12 codification, distribution 14 categorization 15 systematization

*Classifications of living organisms include:*

05 class, genus, order
06 domain, empire, family, phylum
07 kingdom, species
08 division

*Kingdoms, domains and empires include:*

05 fungi
06 monera, plants
07 animals, archaea
08 bacteria, protista
10 eubacteria, eukaryotes
11 prokaryotes
14 archaebacteria

*Classes include:*

04 Aves
07 Insecta
08 Amphibia, Bivalvia, Mammalia
09 Arachnida, Bryopsida, Pinopsida
10 Gastropoda, Liliopsida
11 Cephalopoda
12 Malacostraca
13 Magnoliopsida

**classify**
03 peg 04 file, rank, sort, type 05 class, grade, group, order, range 06 assort, codify, divide 07 arrange, dispose, include, sort out 08 regiment, serotype, stratify, tabulate 09 catalogue 10 categorize, distribute, pigeonhole 11 systematize

**classy**
04 fine, posh 05 grand, ritzy 06 select, smooth, swanky 07 elegant, stylish 08 gorgeous, superior, up-market 09 exclusive, expensive, exquisite, high-class 13 sophisticated

**clatter**
03 jar 04 bang 05 clang, clank, clunk, crash 06 gossip, hotter, jangle, rattle, strike 07 blatter, chatter

**clause**
04 item, part 05 point, rider, salvo 06 phrase 07 adjunct, article, chapter, heading, passage, proviso, section 08 clausula, loophole, particle, tenendum 09 condition, novodamus, paragraph, provision, reddendum 10 subsection 13 specification

**claw**
**03** rip **04** clat, crab, fang, maul, nail, sere, tear **05** chela, claut, cloye, graze, griff, seize, talon **06** clutch, griffe, mangle, nipper, pincer, pounce, scrape, unguis **07** falcula, flatter, gripper, scratch **08** lacerate, scrabble **11** clapperclaw

**clay**
**03** cam, pug, wax **04** bole, calm, caum, glei, gley, loam, lute, marl, pisé, slip, soil, tile, till **05** argil, blaes, brick, cloam, earth, fango **06** blaise, blaize, clunch, ground, kaolin **07** kaoline, pottery **08** ceramics, cimolite, illuvium, laterite **09** bentonite **10** lithomarge, meerschaum, plastilina
• **clay-chalk mixture**
**04** malm

**clean**
**03** net, new, rub **04** char, even, fair, good, just, neat, nett, pure, tidy, wash, wipe **05** blank, crisp, empty, final, fresh, fully, moral, quite, rinse, scour, sweep, total, utter, whole **06** chaste, decent, emunge, hollow, honest, modest, proper, scrape, simple, smooth, soogee, soogie, unused, washed **07** aseptic, elegant, ethical, launder, perfect, regular, sterile, totally, upright **08** clean-cut, cleansed, clear-cut, complete, decisive, directly, entirely, flawless, graceful, hygienic, innocent, pristine, purified, sanitary, smoothly, spotless, straight, unerring, unmarked, unsoiled, virtuous **09** faultless, guiltless, laundered, reputable, righteous, speckless, unspotted, unstained, unsullied, wholesome **10** above board, antiseptic, completely, conclusive, even-handed, honourable, immaculate, sterilized, unpolluted, upstanding **11** appropriate, respectable, unblemished, uncorrupted, well-defined **12** spick and span, squeaky-clean **13** unadulterated **14** clean as a new pin, decontaminated, uncontaminated

*Cleaning products include:*

**04** soap
**06** bleach, polish
**07** shampoo, solvent
**09** detergent, shower gel
**10** bubble bath, soap powder
**12** disinfectant
**13** washing powder
**14** scouring powder
**15** washing-up liquid

• **clean out**
**03** fay, fey
• **come clean**
**05** admit, own up **06** fess up, reveal **07** confess, tell all **11** acknowledge **13** spill the beans

**clean-cut**
**04** neat, tidy, trim **05** fresh, natty, smart, terse **06** spruce **07** orderly **11** uncluttered

**cleaner**
**03** vac **04** char **05** daily, wiper **06** Hoover®, Mrs Mop, vacuum **07** Mrs Mopp, orderly **08** charlady **09** charwoman

**cleanliness**
**06** purity **09** cleanness, freshness **10** perfection **12** spotlessness

**cleanse**
**04** pure, wash **05** bathe, clean, clear, flush, porge, purge, rinse, scour **06** garble, purify **07** absolve, deterge, launder, mundify **08** absterge, lustrate, scavenge **09** disinfect, sterilize **12** make free from

**cleanser**
**04** soap **07** cleaner, scourer, solvent **08** purifier **09** detergent **10** soap powder **12** disinfectant **14** scouring powder

**clear**
**02** go **03** net, rid **04** earn, fair, fine, free, full, gain, jump, keen, land, make, move, neat, nett, open, pass, pure, quit, sure, tidy, void, wipe **05** allow, bring, clean, empty, erase, let go, light, lucid, overt, plain, quick, quite, sharp, sheer, shift, sunny, vault **06** acquit, bright, decode, excuse, filter, glassy, go over, limpid, liquid, loosen, pardon, patent, permit, pocket, refine, remble, remove, serene, settle, unclog, unload, unstop, vacate, vanish, wholly **07** absolve, approve, audible, bring in, certain, cleanse, evident, express, fogless, hyaline, justify, logical, obvious, plainly, precise, release, through, unblock **08** apparent, coherent, definite, distinct, evacuate, evanesce, explicit, get rid of, innocent, jump over, leap over, liberate, luculent, luminous, manifest, melt away, pellucid, positive, pregnant, sanction, sensible, take away, take home, undimmed, undulled **09** authorize, blameless, cloudless, convinced, decongest, disappear, discharge, evaporate, exculpate, exonerate, extricate, guiltless, unblocked, unclouded, unimpeded, vindicate **10** articulate, colourless, diaphonous, disengaged, in the clear, perceptive, pronounced, reasonable, see-through, unhindered, unscramble, untroubled **11** acquittance, beyond doubt, conspicuous, crystalline, disentangle, make a profit, penetrating, perceptible, translucent, transparent, unambiguous, unequivocal, well-defined **12** clear as a bell, crystal-clear, intelligible, recognizable, twenty-twenty, unmistakable, unobstructed **13** find not guilty **14** beyond question, comprehensible, give permission, give the go-ahead, having no qualms, understandable, unquestionable
• **all clear**
**09** copacetic, copasetic, kopasetic
• **clear away**
**03** mop
• **clear off**
**04** quit **06** get out, go away **07** buzz off, gertcha, push off **08** cheese it, run along, shove off
• **clear out**
**03** get **04** sort, tidy **05** empty, hop it, leave, scour **06** beat it, depart, get out, go away, tidy up, vacate **07** get lost, push off, sort out **08** clear off, shove off, throw out, withdraw
• **clear up**
**03** red **04** fair, redd, sort, tidy **05** crack, order, salve, solve **06** answer, remove **07** clarify, explain, improve, iron out, resolve, sort out, unravel **08** brighten **09** elucidate, liquidate, rearrange **10** become fine, brighten up, put in order, straighten **11** become sunny, stop raining **12** straighten up **13** straighten out
• **not clear**
**02** nl **09** non liquet

**clearance**
**02** OK **03** gap **04** room **05** leave, say-so, space, sweep **06** margin, moving **07** consent, freeing, go-ahead, removal **08** clearing, emptying, headroom, riddance, sanction, shifting, vacating **09** allowance, cleansing, unloading **10** demolition, evacuation, green light, permission, taking-away **11** endorsement **13** authorization

**clear-cut**
**05** clean, clear, plain, sharp **07** precise **08** definite, distinct, explicit, sharp-cut, specific **09** trenchant **11** cut and dried, unambiguous, unequivocal, well-defined **13** black and white **15** straightforward

**clear-headed**
**04** wise **05** sober **08** rational, sensible **09** practical, realistic **11** intelligent

**clearing**
**03** gap **04** dell **05** glade, slash, space **06** assart **07** opening **08** scouring, slashing

**clearly**
**04** well **05** plain **06** bright, openly **07** lucidly, plainly **08** markedly, patently **09** evidently, obviously **10** coherently, distinctly, explicitly, manifestly, undeniably **11** undoubtedly **12** indisputably, intelligibly, unmistakably, without doubt **13** conspicuously, incontestably **14** comprehensibly

**cleave**
◇ *insertion indicator*
**03** cut, hew **04** chop, hold, open, part, rend, rift **05** cling, crack, halve, sever, share, slice, split, stick, unite **06** adhere, attach, cohere, divide, pierce, remain, sunder **07** fissure **08** dissever, disunite, separate **09** crack open, split open

**cleft**
◇ *containment indicator*
**03** gap, jag **04** rent, rift, riva **05** break, chasm, chink, cloff, crack, slack, split

06 breach, cranny, parted, sexfid 07 chimney, crevice, divided, fissure, octofid, opening, pharynx 08 cleaving, crevasse, fissured, fracture, scissure 09 bisulcate, quadrifid, septemfid 13 quadripartite

**clemency**
04 pity 05 mercy 06 lenity 08 humanity, kindness, leniency, mildness, sympathy 10 compassion, generosity, indulgence, moderation, tenderness 11 forbearance, forgiveness, magnanimity 12 mercifulness 15 soft-heartedness

**clench**
04 grip, grit, hold, seal, shut 05 clasp, close, grasp, press 06 clinch, clutch, double, fasten 07 squeeze 08 double up 12 close tightly 13 press together

**clergy**
06 church 07 clerics 08 learning, ministry, the cloth 09 churchmen, clergymen, education, the church 10 holy orders, priesthood 11 churchwomen, clergywomen, spiritualty 12 spirituality

**clergyman, clergywoman**
02 DD, RR 03 Rev 04 dean, imam, papa 05 canon, clerk, padre, rabbi, vicar 06 bishop, cleric, curate, deacon, divine, father, josser, Levite, mother, mullah, parson, pastor, priest, rector 07 diocese, dominie, muezzin, prelate, secular 08 cardinal, chaplain, man of God, minister, Nonjuror, preacher, reverend, sky pilot, spintext, squarson, vartabed 09 churchman, deaconess, presbyter, rural dean 10 arch-priest, prebendary, woman of God 11 churchwoman 12 ecclesiastic 13 man of the cloth 14 superintendent 15 woman of the cloth

**clerical**
06 filing, office, typing 08 official, pastoral, priestly, reverend 09 canonical, episcopal 10 pen-pushing, sacerdotal 11 keyboarding, ministerial, secretarial, white-collar 14 administrative, ecclesiastical

*See also* **vestment**

**clerk**
04 babu 05 baboo 06 circar, notary, priest, scribe, sircar, sirkar, teller, typist, writer 07 actuary, copyist, scholar 08 cursitor, official, Petty Bag, quillman, servitor 09 assistant, clergyman, pen-driver, pen-pusher, secretary 10 book-keeper 11 paper-pusher, protocolist, protonotary, quill-driver 12 prothonotary, receptionist, record-keeper, stenographer 13 account-keeper, administrator, shop-assistant

**clever**
03 apt 04 able, cute, deft, gleg, keen 05 natty, quick, sharp, smart, witty 06 adroit, artful, brainy, bright, expert, gifted, pretty, shrewd, souple 07 capable, cunning, knowing, notable, sapient, skilful 08 rational, sensible, talented 09 brilliant, conceited, dexterous, ingenious, inventive, sagacious, spiritual 10 discerning, perceptive 11 intelligent, quick-witted, resourceful, sharp-witted 12 apprehensive 13 knowledgeable

**cleverly**
04 ably 07 capably 08 artfully, astutely, craftily, expertly, shrewdly 09 skilfully 11 ingeniously 12 discerningly 13 intelligently, knowledgeably, quick-wittedly

**cliché**
06 truism 07 bromide 08 banality, chestnut 09 platitude 10 stereotype 11 commonplace, old chestnut 15 hackneyed phrase

**cliché'd, clichéed**
04 dull, worn 05 banal, corny, stale, stock, tired, trite 06 common 07 routine, worn-out 08 overused, time-worn 09 hackneyed 10 overworked, pedestrian, threadbare 11 commonplace, stereotyped, wearing thin 12 run-of-the-mill 13 platitudinous, unimaginative

**click**
04 beat, snap, snip, tick, twig 05 clack, clink, forge, get on, snick 08 cotton on, get along, hit it off 09 get on well, implosive, make sense 10 understand 11 become clear, suction stop 13 fall into place, suctional stop

**client**
04 user 05 buyer 06 patron, punter, vassal 07 patient, regular, shopper 08 consumer, customer, hanger-on 09 applicant, dependant, purchaser

**clientèle**
05 trade, users 06 buyers, market 07 clients, patrons 08 business, regulars, shoppers 09 consumers, customers, following, patronage 10 purchasers

**cliff**
03 tor 04 clef, crag, face, scar 05 bluff, cleve, scarp, scaur 06 cleeve 08 overhang, rock-face 09 precipice 10 escarpment, promontory

**climactic**
05 final 07 crucial 08 critical, decisive, exciting 09 paramount

**climate**
04 mood 05 trend 06 milieu, region, spirit, temper 07 feeling, setting, weather 08 ambience, tendency 10 atmosphere 11 disposition, environment, temperament, temperature

**climax**
03 top 04 acme, apex, head, peak 06 apogee, finale, height, summit, zenith 08 pinnacle 09 crescendo, highlight, high point 11 catastrophe, culmination

**climb**
◇ *reversal down indicator*
03 sty, top 04 go up, move, ramp, rise, scan, shin, soar, stie, stir, stye 05 jumar, mount, scale, sclim, shift, sklim, speel, swarm 06 ascend, ascent, prusik, shin up 07 clamber, going up, shoot up 08 increase, scramble, surmount 11 herringbone, mountaineer, upward slope 14 uphill struggle

• **climb down**
05 yield 07 concede, descend, retract, retreat 08 back down 09 surrender 12 eat your words

• **climbing party**
04 rope

**climb-down**
07 retreat 08 yielding 09 surrender 10 concession, retraction, withdrawal

**climber**
03 ivy 04 Jack, Jill, vine 07 speeler 10 nasturtium 11 balloon-vine, honeysuckle, Jack and Jill, mountaineer 12 kangaroo vine, morning glory 13 scarlet runner 14 Scotch attorney

**clinch**
03 pun 04 land, seal 05 clink, close, rivet 06 clench, decide, secure, settle, verify 07 confirm, embrace, grapple 08 conclude 09 determine

**cling**
03 hug 04 grip, hold 05 clasp, grasp, stick 06 adhere, attach, cleave, clutch, defend, fasten, hold on, shrink 07 embrace, shrivel, stand by, support 08 hold on to, stay true 09 adherence 10 be faithful

**clinic**
07 doctor's 08 hospital 09 infirmary 10 sanatorium 12 health centre 13 medical centre

**clinical**
04 cold 05 basic, plain, stark 06 simple 07 austere, medical, patient 08 analytic, detached, hospital 09 impassive, objective, unadorned, unfeeling 10 analytical, antiseptic, impersonal, scientific, uninvolved 11 emotionless, unemotional 12 businesslike 13 disinterested, dispassionate

**clinically**
09 medically 14 scientifically

**clink** *see* **prison**

**clip**
◇ *tail deletion indicator*
03 box, cut, dod, fix, hit, pin 04 crop, cuff, dock, hold, mute, pare, poll, slap, snip, trim 05 cheat, clout, D-ring, graze, jumar, prune, punch, shear, smack, thump, tough, whack 06 attach, crutch, cut off, cut out, fasten, reduce, staple, strike, tingle, wallop 07 Bulldog®, curtail, cutting, embrace, excerpt, extract, passage, pollard, run into, section, shorten, snippet 08 citation, cut short, encircle, fastener, truncate 09 crash into,

quotation **10** abbreviate, clothes-peg, clothes-pin, jumar clamp, overcharge **11** collide with, music holder
*See also* **cut**

**clipping**
**04** clip **05** scrow, shear, shred
**06** paring **07** cutting, excerpt, extract, passage, section, snippet, topiary
**08** citation, snipping, trimming
**09** quotation

**clique**
**03** set **04** band, clan, club, gang, pack, ring **05** bunch, crowd, group **06** circle, set-out **07** coterie, faction, in-crowd, society **08** grouplet **10** fraternity

**cloak**
**04** cape, coat, hide, mask, pall, rail, robe, veil, wrap **05** blind, cloke, cover, front **06** mantle, screen, shield, shroud
**07** conceal, obscure, pretext
**08** covering, disguise **10** camouflage

*Cloaks include:*

**04** capa
**05** amice, grego, jelab, manta, pilch, sagum, shawl, talma
**06** abolla, capote, dolman, domino, poncho, visite
**07** chlamys, galabea, galabia, jellaba, korowai, manteel, mantlet, paenula, pelisse, pluvial, rocklay, rokelay, sarafan
**08** capuchin, cardinal, djellaba, galabeah, galabiah, gallabea, gallabia, himation, mantelet, mantilla, palliate
**09** djellabah, gabardine, gaberdine, gallabeah, gallabiah, gallabieh, gallabiya
**10** gallabiyah, gallabiyeh, paludament, roquelaure
**11** buffalo robe
**12** mousquetaire, paludamentum

**clobber**
◇ *anagram indicator*
**03** hit, kit, zap **04** bash, beat, belt, capa, garb, gear, lick, rout, ruin, slap, sock, togs **05** clout, crush, knock, punch, stuff, thump, whack **06** attack, defeat, hammer, strike, tackle, things, thrash, wallop **07** baggage, conquer, trounce **08** clothing, garments
**09** equipment, overpaint, overwhelm
**10** belongings **11** bits and bobs, possessions **13** bits and pieces, paraphernalia

**clock**
**03** hit, sit **04** face **05** brood, cluck
**06** beetle, notice **07** observe
**08** ornament **10** mileometer, timekeeper **11** speedometer

*Clocks and watches include:*

**03** fob, Tim
**04** ring, stop
**05** alarm, wrist
**06** atomic, cuckoo, mantel, quartz
**07** bracket, digital, pendant, sundial
**08** analogue, carriage, longcase, speaking
**09** repeating
**10** travelling
**11** chronograph, chronometer, grandfather, grandmother

**• clock up**
**03** log **05** reach **06** attain, record
**07** achieve, archive, chalk up, notch up
**08** register

**• round the clock**
**10** constantly **11** ceaselessly, day and night **12** continuously **15** twenty-four seven, without stopping

**clod**
**04** hunk, lump, mass, mool, pelt, slab
**05** block, chunk, clump, glebe, throw, wedge **06** ground

**clog**
**03** dam, jam, log, mud **04** ball, gaum, gorm **05** block, choke, dam up, sabot
**06** accloy, ball up, bung up, burden, chopin, galosh, golosh, hamper, hinder, hobble, impede, patten, pester, stop up **07** chopine, clutter, congest, galoche, occlude **08** encumber, obstruct

**cloister**
**05** aisle **06** arcade **07** portico, walkway **08** corridor, pavement
**10** ambulatory

**cloistered**
**08** confined, enclosed, hermitic, isolated, secluded, shielded
**09** cloistral, insulated, protected, reclusive, sheltered, withdrawn
**10** restricted **11** sequestered

**close**
**03** bar, Clo, end, row **04** best, bolt, clog, cork, dear, fail, fill, flop, fold, fuse, good, hard, join, keen, lane, like, lock, mean, mews, mure, near, plug, road, seal, shet, shut, slam, stop, true
**05** block, bosom, cease, court, dense, exact, fixed, fuggy, heavy, humid, muggy, pause, place, quiet, solid, tight, union, unite **06** at hand, clinch, decide, direct, ending, fasten, finale, finish, gain on, go bust, hidden, lessen, lock up, loving, marked, narrow, nearby, nearly, not far, packed, secret, secure, settle, shut up, square, sticky, stingy, stop up, strait, street, strict, strong, stuffy, sultry, verify, wind up
**07** adjourn, airless, block up, cadence, careful, close by, compact, confirm, cramped, crowded, densely, devoted, grapple, intense, literal, miserly, occlude, padlock, precise, private, similar, terrace, tightly **08** accurate, adjacent, approach, attached, block off, collapse, complete, conclude, conflict, cul-de-sac, detailed, distinct, faithful, familiar, imminent, intimate, junction, obstruct, reserved, reticent, rigorous, round off, secluded, secretly, shut down, stifling, straight, streight, taciturn, thorough **09** adjoining, cessation, close down, close-knit, condensed, courtyard, determine, enclosure, encounter, establish, immediate, impending, niggardly, searching, secretive, terminate, winding-up **10** come closer, comparable, completion, conclusion, dénouement, go bankrupt, hard-fought, methodical, oppressive, quadrangle, sweltering
**11** adjournment, approaching, catch up with, culmination, discontinue, draw to an end, get closer to, go to the wall, inseparable, neck and neck, painstaking, suffocating, termination, well-matched **12** a stone's throw, bring to an end, concentrated, confidential, neighbouring, on the brink of, on the verge of, parsimonious, unventilated
**13** corresponding, evenly matched, in the vicinity, penny-pinching, unforthcoming **14** cease operating, on your doorstep **15** cease operations, uncommunicative

**• close in**
**04** shut **08** approach, draw near, encircle, surround **10** come nearer

**• close to**
**02** on **04** near, nigh **06** fast by, nearby

**• keep close to**
**03** hug

**closed**
**02** to **04** dark, shut **05** drawn
**06** lucken

**• not closed**
**04** agee, ajar, ajee, open

**closet**
**04** zeta **05** press, privy **06** covert, hidden, recess, secret **07** cabinet, confine, furtive, isolate, private, seclude **08** cloister, cupboard, shut away, wardrobe **10** undercover, unrevealed **11** storage room, underground **13** surreptitious

**closure**
**03** gag **05** block **07** cloture, failure, folding **08** blocking, shutdown, shutting **09** stricture, winding-up
**10** bankruptcy, guillotine, stopping-up
**11** closing-down, obstruction
**12** laryngospasm

**clot**
**03** gel, git, mug, nit, set **04** clag, dope, dork, fool, glob, lump, mass, nerd, prat, twit **05** clump, cruor, grume, idiot, twerp, wally **06** curdle, gobbet, lapper, lopper **07** congeal, embolus, plonker, splatch, thicken **08** clotting, coalesce, imbecile, solidify, thrombus
**09** blockhead, coagulate
**10** bufflehead, nincompoop, thrombosis **11** coagulation, obstruction **12** crassamentum

**cloth**
**03** lap, rag **05** sails, stuff, towel
**06** duster, fabric, lappie **07** flannel, textile **08** material **09** churchmen, clergymen, dishcloth, facecloth, the church, the clergy **10** floorcloth, holy orders, upholstery **11** churchwomen, clergywomen, the ministry
*See also* **fabric**

**• measure of cloth**
**03** ell, end

**• piece of cloth**
**03** lap, rag **04** fent, gair, pane, sash **05** clout, godet, lapje **06** lappie **07** remnant

**clothe**
**03** rig **04** coat, cour, deck, gird, robe, vest, wrap **05** cover, drape, dress, endew, endue, equip, habit, indew, indue, put on **06** attire, carpet, emboss, enrobe, fit out, invest, outfit **07** apparel, bedizen, blanket, envelop, garment, overlay, vesture **08** accoutre **09** caparison

**clothes, clothing**
**03** kit **04** drag, duds, garb, gear, togs, wear, weed **05** braws, claes, dress, get-up **06** attire, outfit **07** apparel, clobber, costume, raiment, threads, toggery, uniform, vesture **08** cast-offs, clothing, dressing, garments, glad rags, wardrobe **09** trousseau, vestiture, vestments **11** habiliments, hand-me-downs

*See also* **boot**; **cloak**; **coat**; **dress**; **footwear**; **hat**; **headdress**; **jacket**; **scarf**; **vestment**

*Clothes include:*

**02** gi
**03** aba, boa, bra, fur, gie, obi, PJs, tie, top
**04** 501s®, abba, belt, body, buff, capa, cape, coat, furs, gown, kilt, maud, midi, mink, mitt, muff, rami, ruff, sack, sari, sash, slip, slop, sock, spat, suit, sulu, toga, toge, veil, vest, wrap
**05** abaya, burka, cloak, cords, dhoti, dress, frock, glove, ihram, jeans, kanzu, Levis®, lungi, pants, parka, ruana, scarf, shawl, shift, shirt, shrug, skirt, smock, stole, teddy, thong, tunic
**06** basque, bikini, blouse, bodice, boorka, bow-tie, boxers, braces, briefs, caftan, corset, cravat, denims, dirndl, fleece, garter, girdle, jersey, jubbah, jumper, kaross, kimono, mitten, poncho, sacque, samfoo, sarong, shorts, slacks, tabard, tights, T-shirt
**07** catsuit, crop top, doublet, g-string, hosiery, jimjams, leotard, muffler, necktie, nightie, overall, panties, pyjamas, singlet, spattee, sweater, tank top, twin-set, uniform, vest top, wet suit, yashmak, Y-fronts
**08** bathrobe, bedsocks, breeches, camisole, cardigan, culottes, earmuffs, flannels, guernsey, hipsters, hot pants, jodhpurs, jumpsuit, leggings, lingerie, negligee, pashmina, pinafore, polo-neck, pullover, raincoat, swimsuit, tee-shirt, trousers
**09** balaclava, bed-jacket, brassière, coveralls, dress suit, dungarees, hair shirt, housecoat, jockstrap, mini skirt, outerwear, pantihose, petticoat, plus-fours, polo shirt, salopette, separates, shahtoosh, shell suit, Sloppy Joe, stockings, tracksuit, underwear, waistcoat
**10** boiler suit, Capri pants, cummerbund, dinner-gown, drainpipes, dress-shirt, flying suit, leg-warmers, lounge suit, nightdress, nightshirt, romper suit, rugby shirt, string vest, suspenders, sweat-shirt, turtle-neck, underpants
**11** bell-bottoms, boiled shirt, boxer-shorts, leisure suit, morning suit, pencil-skirt, thermal vest, trouser suit
**12** body stocking, camiknickers, divided-skirt, dressing-gown, evening-dress, palazzo pants, pedal-pushers, shirtwaister
**13** Bermuda shorts, cycling shorts, liberty bodice, pinafore skirt, shalwar-kameez, suspender belt
**14** bathing-costume, combat trousers, double-breasted, French knickers, jogging bottoms, single-breasted, swimming trunks, three-piece suit
**15** swimming costume

**• plain clothes**
**05** mufti

**• shabby clothes**
**03** tat

**cloud**
**03** dim, fog **04** blur, dull, mist, puff, rack, veil, weft **05** chill, cover, shade **06** billow, darken, defame, mantle, muddle, shadow, shroud **07** confuse, eclipse, obscure **08** dullness, woolpack **09** obfuscate **10** overshadow

*Clouds include:*

**06** cirrus, nimbus
**07** cumulus, stratus
**10** mare's-tails
**11** altocumulus, altostratus
**12** cirrocumulus, cirrostratus, cumulonimbus, nimbostratus
**13** fractocumulus, fractostratus, stratocumulus

**cloudless**
**03** dry **04** fair, fine **05** clear, sunny **06** bright **08** pleasant **09** unclouded

**cloudy**
**01** c **03** dim **04** dark, dull, grey, hazy **05** foggy, heavy, milky, misty, muddy, murky, vague **06** blurry, gloomy, leaden, opaque, sombre **07** blurred, muddled, obscure, sunless **08** confused, lowering, nebulous, nubilous, overcast **10** indistinct

**clout**
**03** box, hit **04** blow, cuff, pull, slap, slug, sock **05** patch, power, punch, smack, thump, whack **06** muscle, strike, wallop, weight **07** garment **08** prestige, standing **09** authority, influence

**cloven**
**05** cleft, split **07** divided **08** bisected

**clown**
**04** dork, fool, geek, jerk, jest, joke, nerd, twit, zany **05** antic, chuff, comic, idiot, joker, ninny, twerp, wally **06** antick, august, chough, dimwit, jester, joskin, nitwit, Pompey, rustic **07** anticke, antique, auguste, buffoon, bumpkin, Costard **08** comedian, dipstick, gracioso, imbecile, numskull **09** blockhead, grotesque, harlequin, muck about, patchocke, Whiteface **10** act the fool, fool around, goof around, mess around, nincompoop, patchcocke, Touchstone **11** carpet clown, merry-andrew, play the fool **12** act foolishly **13** pickle-herring

*Clowns include:*

**04** Bozo, Coco, Hobo, Joey
**05** Tramp
**07** Pierrot
**08** Grimaldi, Owl-glass, Trinculo
**09** Owle-glass
**10** Howleglass, Owlspiegle
**14** Joseph Grimaldi

**cloying**
**04** icky **06** sickly **07** choking, fulsome **08** luscious **09** excessive, oversweet, sickening **10** disgusting, nauseating

**club**
**03** hit, set **04** bash, beat **05** bunch, clout, group, guild, order, union **06** batter, beat up, circle, clique, fascio, league, priest, pummel, strike **07** chapter, clobber, combine, company, society, sorosis **08** hetairia **09** auxiliary **10** federation, fraternity, sisterhood **11** association, brotherhood, combination, free-and-easy **12** organization **13** life-preserver

*See also* **football**; **golf club**

*Clubs include:*

**03** bar, bat
**04** cosh, mace, patu, polt
**05** bandy, billy, caman, nulla, staff, stick, waddy
**06** cudgel, hurley
**07** bourdon
**08** bludgeon, trunnion
**09** blackjack, truncheon
**10** knobkerrie, nulla-nulla
**12** shinty-stick

*Club types include:*

**03** fan, job
**04** boat, book, glee, golf
**05** disco, field, goose, night, slate, strip, yacht, youth
**06** bridge, health, social, tennis
**07** cabaret, country, singles
**09** warehouse
**10** investment
**11** discotheque
**12** Darby and Joan

*Club names include:*

**03** MCC, RAC, Ski
**04** Arts, Turf
**05** Buck's, Naval
**06** Alpine, Cotton, Drones, Jockey, Kennel, Kitcat, Pratt's, Queen's, Reform, Rotary, Savage, Savile, United, White's

**07** Almack's, Authors', Boodle's, Brooks's, Canning, Carlton, Country, Farmers, Garrick, Groucho, Kiwanis, Leander, Railway, Variety
**08** Hell-fire, National, Oriental, Portland
**09** Athenaeum, Beefsteak, East India, Green Room, Lansdowne, Wig and Pen
**10** Caledonian, City Livery, Crockford's, Flyfishers', Hurlingham, Oddfellows, Roehampton, Travellers
**11** Army and Navy, Arts Theatre, Chelsea Arts
**12** Anglo-Belgian, City of London, London Rowing, New Cavendish, Thames Rowing
**13** Royal Air Force
**14** American Women's, City University
**15** National Liberal, Royal Automobile, Victory Services

**• club together**
**06** chip in **09** give money **10** contribute, join forces **12** share the cost **14** have a whip-round
**• in the club** *see* **pregnant**

**clubhouse**
**02** ch **14** nineteenth hole

**clubs**
**01** C
**• jack of clubs**
**03** pam

**clue**
**03** tip **04** hint, idea, lead, sign **05** fix up, light, trace **06** clavis, notion, thread, tip-off **07** inkling, pointer **08** evidence, signpost **09** master-key, suspicion **10** indication, intimation, suggestion

**clueless**
**04** dumb **05** dense, thick **06** stupid **08** helpless, ignorant **09** unlearned **10** uninformed, unschooled **11** not all there, uninitiated **13** inexperienced

**clump**
**03** lot, mot **04** beat, blow, clot, knot, mass, mott, plod, thud, tuft, tump **05** amass, bluff, bunch, clomp, group, motte, plump, stamp, stomp, thump, tramp **06** bundle, lumber, spinny, trudge **07** cluster, spinney, stumble, thicket, tussock **10** accumulate, collection **11** agglutinate **12** accumulation **13** agglomeration, agglutination

**clumsy**
◇ *anagram indicator*
**03** ham **04** rude **05** bulky, crude, Dutch, gawky, heavy, hulky, inept, looby, rough, squab **06** clunky, gauche, oafish, thumby, wooden **07** awkward, chuckle, hulking, ill-made, spastic, uncouth, unhandy **08** bungling, clumping, tactless, ungainly, unheppen, unwieldy **09** all thumbs, ham-fisted, ham-handed, lumbering, maladroit, shapeless, two-fisted, unskilful **10** blundering, cack-handed, cumbersome, Dutch-built, kack-handed, ungraceful, unhandsome **11** heavy-handed, insensitive **12** hippopotamic, unmanageable **13** accident-prone, chuckle-headed, hippopotamian, unco-ordinated **14** banana-fingered

**cluster**
**03** bob **04** band, knot, mass, tuft **05** batch, bunch, clump, crowd, flock, group, plump, strap, truss **06** gather, huddle, raceme **07** collect, panicle **08** assemble, assembly **09** gathering **10** assemblage, assortment, collection, congregate, racemation **11** constellate **12** come together **13** agglomeration, group together, inflorescence

**clustered**
**06** massed **07** bunched, grouped **08** gathered **09** assembled, glomerate **11** agglomerate

**clutch**
◇ *containment indicator*
**03** set **04** claw, grab, grip, hold, jaws, sway **05** brood, catch, clasp, claws, grasp, gripe, group, hands, hatch, mercy, power, seize **06** clench, graple, number, snatch **07** claucht, claught, cling to, control, custody, embrace, grapple, gripper, keeping, setting, sitting **08** dominion, hang on to, hatching **09** get hold of **10** incubation, possession, take hold of

**clutter**
**04** fill, mess, stir **05** chaos, cover, noise, strew **06** jumble, litter, mess up, midden, muddle **07** scatter **08** disarray, disorder, encumber **09** confusion, make a mess **10** make untidy, untidiness **12** fill untidily

**coach**
**03** bus, cab, car, gig **04** coch, cram, drag, post, trap **05** drill, prime, teach, train, tutor, wagon **06** fiacre, hansom, landau, mentor, school **07** droshky, grinder, hackney, minibus, prepare, railbus, rattler, tally-ho, teacher, trainer **08** barouche, brougham, carriage, educator, instruct, motor-bus **09** battlebus, buffet car, cabriolet, charabanc, Greyhound **10** four-in-hand, griddle car, instructor, motor-coach, répétiteur **12** express coach
*See also* **carriage**

**coagulate**
**03** gel, ren, rin, run, set **04** cake, clot, melt **06** curdle **07** clotted, clotter, congeal, curdled, thicken **08** solidify

**coagulation**
**08** clotting **10** congealing, thickening **11** solidifying

**coal**
**03** jet, jud, nut **04** char, jeat, smut **05** dross, ember, small **06** cinder, splint **07** lignite **10** anthracite **13** black diamonds
**• coal dust**
**04** coom, culm, duff
**• coal scuttle**
**03** hod **09** purdonium
**• coal yard**
**03** ree **04** reed

**coalesce**
**03** mix **04** fuse, join **05** blend, merge, unite **06** cohere, commix **07** combine **09** affiliate, commingle, integrate **10** amalgamate **11** consolidate, incorporate **12** join together

**coalescence**
**06** fusion, merger **07** mixture **08** blending **09** immixture **11** affiliation, combination, integration **12** amalgamation, concrescence **13** consolidation, incorporation

**coalition**
**04** bloc **05** union **06** fusion, league, merger **07** compact, joining **08** alliance **10** federation **11** affiliation, association, combination, confederacy, conjunction, integration, partnership **12** amalgamation **13** confederation

**coarse**
**03** ham **04** base, blue, rank, rude **05** bawdy, broad, brute, crass, crude, gross, hairy, harsh, lumpy, rough, rudas, scaly **06** blowsy, blowzy, brutal, common, earthy, incult, ribald, ribaud, rugged, shaggy, smutty, uneven, vulgar **07** abusive, boorish, bristly, loutish, obscene, prickly, raunchy, rybauld, uncivil **08** gorblimy, immodest, impolite, improper, indecent, inferior, porterly, unbolted **09** gorblimey, off-colour, offensive, unrefined **10** indelicate, unfinished, unpolished, unpurified **11** foul-mouthed, ill-mannered, unprocessed

**coarsely**
**06** rudely **07** bawdily, crudely, roughly **08** ruggedly, unevenly, vulgarly **09** boorishly, loutishly, obscenely **10** immodestly, impolitely, improperly, indecently **11** irregularly, offensively

**coarsen**
**04** dull **05** blunt **06** deaden, harden **07** roughen, thicken **08** indurate **11** desensitize

**coarseness**
**04** smut **06** raunch **07** crudity, hoggery **08** ribaldry **09** bawdiness, hairiness, immodesty, indecency, obscenity, roughness, vulgarism, vulgarity **10** crassitude, earthiness, indelicacy, ruggedness, smuttiness, unevenness **11** grossièreté, prickliness **12** irregularity **13** offensiveness

**coast**
**04** cost, sail, side, taxi **05** beach, coste, drift, glide, limit, shore, slide, terms **06** border, cruise, region, strand **07** footing, seaside **08** littoral, seaboard, seashore **09** coastline, direction, foreshore, freewheel
**• coast road**
**04** prom

**coaster**
**04** grab **05** doily, doyly, smack
**07** beermat

**coat**
**04** cake, daub, film, hair, hide, mack, pave, pelt, skin, wool **05** apply, cover, glaze, layer, paint, put on, quote, sheet, skirt, smear **06** clothe, enamel, finish, mantle, spread, veneer **07** coating, encrust, overlay, plaster, put over, varnish **08** cladding, covering, laminate, pellicle **10** integument, lamination

*Coats include:*

**03** box, car, fur, mac
**04** baju, buff, cape, jack, jump, maxi, midi, over, pink, rain, sack, tail, warm
**05** acton, cimar, cloak, cymar, drape, dress, frock, gilet, great, grego, jupon, lammy, loden, parka, sayon, wamus
**06** achkan, Afghan, anorak, Basque, blazer, bolero, cagoul, covert, dolman, duffel, fleece, jacket, jerkin, kagool, kagoul, kirtle, lammie, poncho, reefer, riding, sacque, sports, tabard, taberd, trench, tuxedo, Zouave
**07** Barbour®, blanket, blouson, cagoule, cutaway, kagoule, Mae West, matinée, morning, overall, snorkel, surtout, swagger, vareuse, zamarra, zamarro
**08** Burberry®, camisole, gambeson, haqueton, mackinaw, sherwani
**09** bed jacket, gabardine, gaberdine, hacqueton, macintosh, Mao-jacket, newmarket, pea-jacket, petticoat, redingote, shortgown
**10** body-warmer, bumfreezer, bush jacket, carmagnole, claw-hammer, Eton jacket, flak jacket, half-kirtle, life jacket, mackintosh, mess jacket, roundabout, windjammer
**11** biker jacket, puffa jacket, shell jacket, swallowtail, Windbreaker®, windcheater
**12** bomber jacket, combat jacket, dinner jacket, donkey jacket, lumberjacket, monkey jacket, Prince Albert, pyjama jacket, safari jacket, sports jacket, straitjacket
**13** hacking jacket, matinee jacket, Norfolk jacket, reefing-jacket
**14** shooting jacket

**coating**
**03** fur **04** coat, film, skin, wash
**05** crust, glaze, layer, sheet **06** crusta, enamel, finish, patina, resist, slough, veneer **07** blanket, dusting, overlay, varnish, washing **08** covering, membrane **10** colourwash, lamination, pebbledash

**coax**
**03** pet **04** draw, wile **05** carny, tempt
**06** allure, cajole, carney, entice, fleech, humour, induce, soothe **07** beguile, cuittle, flatter, wheedle, win over
**08** blandish, collogue, get round, inveigle, persuade, soft-soap, talk into, win round **09** sweet-talk, whillywha
**10** whillywhaw **11** prevail upon

**cobalt**
**02** Co

**cobber** *see* **friend**

**cobble**
**04** pave
**• cobble together**
**07** knock up **09** improvise **11** make quickly, make roughly, put together
**13** throw together **14** prepare quickly, prepare roughly, produce quickly, produce roughly

**cobbler**
**04** snab, snob **05** sutor **06** cosier, cozier, soutar, souter, sowter

**cobblers** *see* **rubbish**

**cobra**
**03** asp **04** naga, Naia, Naja **05** aspic
**09** hamadryad

**cocaine**
**01** C **04** blow, coke, snow **05** candy, crack **07** charlie, crystal **08** freebase
**09** nose candy, ready-wash **10** white stuff

**cock**
**03** dog, tap, tip **04** bend, lift, tilt
**05** capon, henny, point, raise, slant, strut **07** chicken, gobbler, incline, rooster, swagger **08** cockerel, nonsense, shake-bag **10** bubbly-jock, roadrunner **11** chanticleer, game-chicken
**• cock up**
◇ *anagram indicator*
**04** hash, muff, ruin **05** bodge, farce, fluff **06** bungle, foul up, mess up, muck up **07** blunder, screw up **08** shambles
**11** make a hash of, make a mess of

**cockeyed**
**04** awry, daft **05** askew, barmy, crazy, tipsy **06** absurd **07** crooked
**08** lopsided **09** half-baked, ludicrous, senseless, skew-whiff **11** nonsensical
**12** asymmetrical, preposterous

**cockily**
**08** cheekily **10** impudently, insolently
**13** impertinently **15** disrespectfully

**Cockney**
◇ *dialect indicator*
**04** 'Arry **06** 'Arriet **09** Londonese
**10** pearly king **11** pearly queen

**cocksure**
**04** vain **05** brash, cocky **08** arrogant
**09** conceited **10** swaggering
**11** egotistical, self-assured, swell-headed **13** overconfident, self-confident, self-important, swollen-headed

**cocktail**
◇ *anagram indicator*

*Cocktails include:*

**04** Sour
**05** Bronx
**06** eggnog, Gimlet, Mai tai, mojito, Rickey, Rob Roy
**07** Bellini, Collins, Martini®, negroni, pink gin, Sazerac®, Sidecar, Slammer, Stinger
**08** Acapulco, Brown Cow, Bullshot, Daiquiri, Pink Lady, salty dog, snowball
**09** buck's fizz, Kir Royale, long vodka, Manhattan, Margarita, Rusty Nail, Sea Breeze, whisky mac, White Lady
**10** Bloody Mary, blue lagoon, Caipirinha, Horse's Neck, margharita, Moscow Mule, piña colada, Tom Collins, whisky sour
**11** black velvet, gin-and-tonic, gloom raiser, Screwdriver
**12** Black Russian, Cosmopolitan, Old Fashioned, White Russian
**13** Planter's Punch
**14** American Beauty, Singapore Sling, tequila slammer, Tequila Sunrise
**15** Brandy Alexander

*See also* **liqueur**; **spirits**

**cocky**
**04** pert, vain **05** brash, perky
**06** bouncy **08** arrogant, cocksure, jumped-up **09** bumptious, conceited, hubristic **10** swaggering **11** egotistical, self-assured **13** overconfident, self-confident, self-important, swollen-headed

**cocoon**
**03** pod **04** wrap **05** cover **06** defend, dupion, swathe **07** cushion, envelop, isolate, protect **08** cloister, insulate, preserve **11** overprotect

**coddle**
**03** pet **04** baby **05** spoil **06** cosher, cosset, humour, pamper **07** indulge, protect **11** mollycoddle, overprotect

**code**
◇ *anagram indicator*
**03** law **04** laws **05** codex, fuero, Morse, rules, signs **06** cipher, codify, custom, cypher, ethics, morals, system, volume **07** bar code, conduct, letters, manners, numbers, symbols, zip code
**08** morality, postcode, practice
**09** etiquette, iddy-umpty, local code, Morse code **10** convention, cryptogram, postal code, principles
**11** cryptograph, machine code, regulations **12** dialling code, national code **13** secret message, secret writing
**14** secret language

**codify**
**05** group, order **06** digest **07** marshal, sort out **08** classify, organize
**09** catalogue **11** systematize

**coerce**
**05** bully, drive, force **06** compel, lean on **07** dragoon **08** bludgeon, browbeat, bulldoze, pressure, railroad, threaten, use force **09** constrain, pressgang, strongarm **10** intimidate, pressurize **14** put the screws on

**coercion**
**04** heat **05** force **06** duress
**07** duresse, threats **08** big stick,

bullying, pressure **09** restraint **10** compulsion, constraint **11** arm-twisting, browbeating **12** direct action, intimidation

**coffee**
**03** joe

*Coffee roasts and blends include:*

**04** Java
**05** decaf
**06** filter, ground, Kenyan
**07** Arabica, instant
**09** Colombian, dark roast
**10** Costa Rican, light roast, percolated
**11** French roast
**12** Blue Mountain
**13** decaffeinated

*Coffees include:*

**05** black, Irish, latte, milky, Mocha, white
**06** filter, Gaelic
**07** Turkish
**08** café noir, espresso
**09** Americano, cafetière, demitasse
**10** café au lait, café filtre, cappuccino
**11** skinny latte

**• coffee house**
**04** cafe, caff

**coffer**
**03** ark, box **04** case, cash, safe **05** chest, funds, hoard, means, money, store, trunk **06** assets, casket, wealth **07** backing, capital, coffret, finance, lacunar **08** moneybox, treasury **09** resources, strongbox **10** repository

**coffin**
**03** box **04** kist **05** flask, shell **06** casket, larnax **11** sarcophagus **12** pine overcoat, wooden kimono **14** wooden overcoat

**cogency**
**05** force, power **06** weight **07** potency, urgency **08** strength **09** influence **12** forcefulness, plausibility **13** effectiveness

**cogent**
**06** potent, strong, urgent **07** weighty **08** forceful, forcible, powerful, pregnant **09** effective **10** compelling, conclusive, convincing, persuasive **11** influential **12** irresistible, unanswerable

**cogently**
**08** forcibly, potently, strongly, urgently **10** forcefully, powerfully **11** effectively **12** compellingly, conclusively, convincingly, persuasively

**cogitate**
**04** mull, muse **06** ponder **07** reflect **08** consider, meditate, mull over, ruminate **09** cerebrate **10** deliberate **11** contemplate, think deeply

**cognate**
**03** cog **04** akin **05** alike **06** agnate, allied, kinred **07** kindred, related, similar **09** analogous, conjugate, connected **10** affiliated, associated, congeneric **11** consanguine **13** corresponding

**cognition**
**06** reason **07** insight **08** learning, thinking **09** awareness, knowledge, reasoning **10** perception **11** discernment, rationality **12** apprehension, intelligence **13** comprehension, consciousness, enlightenment, understanding

**cognizance**
**• take cognizance of**
**06** accept, regard **09** recognize **11** acknowledge **12** take notice of **13** become aware of

**cognizant**
**05** aware **06** versed **07** witting **08** acknowne, apprised, familiar, informed **09** conscious **10** acquainted, conversant **13** knowledgeable

**cohabit**
**03** bed **06** occupy **07** company, shack up **08** live with **09** live in sin, live tally **12** live together **13** sleep together

**cohere**
**04** bind, fuse, hold **05** add up, agree, cling, stick, unite **06** adhere, square **07** combine **08** coalesce **09** harmonize, make sense **10** correspond **11** consolidate **12** be consistent, hang together, hold together

**coherence**
**05** sense, union, unity **07** harmony **09** agreement, congruity, connexion **10** connection, consonance, logicality **11** concordance, consistency **14** correspondence

**coherent**
**05** clear, lucid **07** logical, orderly **08** joined-up, rational, reasoned, sensible **09** connected, organized **10** articulate, consistent, meaningful, systematic **11** well-planned **12** intelligible **14** comprehensible, well-structured

**cohesion**
**05** sense, union, unity, whole **07** harmony **09** agreement **10** connection, solidarity **11** consistency **12** togetherness **14** correspondence

**cohesive**
**05** close **06** joined, united **08** coherent, together **09** connected, tenacious **10** continuous **12** interrelated

**cohort**
**03** lot, set **04** band, body, mate, unit **05** batch, buddy, class, group, squad, troop **06** column, legion **07** bracket, brigade, company, partner **08** category, division, follower, myrmidon, regiment, sidekick, squadron **09** assistant, associate, companion, supporter **10** accomplice, contingent **11** combination **14** categorization, classification

**coil**
**04** clew, clue, curl, fake, fank, fuss, hank, loop, ring, roll, turn, wind **05** bight, choke, helix, noise, round, skein, snake, spire, twine, twirl, twist, whorl, wring **06** bought, hubbub, spiral, toroid, tumult, wreath, writhe **07** entwine, primary, rouleau, wreathe **08** solenoid, volution **09** convolute, corkscrew **11** convolution

**coin**
**04** bean, cash, cast, dump, mint **05** forge, money, piece, quoin, stamp **06** change, create, devise, invent, make up, silver, specie, strike **07** dream up, produce, think up **08** brockage, conceive, hard cash **09** fabricate, formulate, hard money, neologize, originate **10** lucky-piece **11** cornerstone, loose change, small change

*See also* **currency**

*Coins include:*

**02** as, at, xu
**03** bit, bob, cob, dam, écu, esc, fen, hao, joe, mag, mil, mna, moy, ore, pul, pya, rap, sen, sol, sou, ure, zuz
**04** anna, buck, cent, chon, dime, doit, duro, fals, fils, jane, jiao, joey, kuru, lion, lwei, maik, make, merk, mina, mite, mule, obol, para, paul, peni, quid, real, rial, ryal, sent, tael, zack
**05** angel, baisa, bodle, brock, brown, butut, conto, copec, crown, ducat, eagle, gerah, gopik, groat, khoum, kopek, laari, lepta, livre, louis, mopus, noble, obang, paolo, pence, penny, piece, pound, royal, scudo, scute, stamp, taler, thebe, unite
**06** aureus, bezant, boddle, copeck, copper, denier, dirham, dollar, double, escudo, florin, guinea, hansel, kopeck, nickel, obolus, pagoda, pesewa, satang, sequin, stater, talent, tanner, thaler
**07** austral, carolus, centavo, centime, centimo, chetrum, crusado, drachma, guilder, ha'penny, jacobus, moidore, Pfennig, piastre, pistole, pollard, quarter, sextant, solidus, spanker
**08** denarius, doubloon, ducatoon, farthing, Groschen, half anna, half mark, imperial, louis d'or, millième, napoleon, new penny, picayune, qindarka, sesterce, shilling, sixpence, solidare, stotinka, ten pence, two pence, two pound
**09** centesimo, dandiprat, five pence, gold crown, gold penny, half-crown, half groat, halfpenny, pound coin, sovereign, yellow-boy
**10** broadpiece, fifty pence, half florin, half guinea, krugerrand, sestertius
**11** bonnet-piece, double eagle, sixpenny bit, spade guinea, twenty pence, twopenny bit

12 antoninianus, silver dollar, two pound coin
13 brass farthing, half sovereign, quarter dollar, sixpenny piece, ten pence piece, tenpenny piece, threepenny bit, two pence piece, twopenny piece
14 five pence piece
15 fifty pence piece, threepenny piece

• **counterfeit coin**
**03** rag **04** shan, slip **05** shand
**06** doctor, duffer, stumer
• **material for coin**
**04** flan
• **supposed coin**
**03** moy

**coincide**
**05** agree, clash, match, tally **06** accord, concur, square **07** coexist **09** be the same, harmonize **10** correspond
**11** synchronize **14** happen together

**coincidence**
**04** luck, step **05** clash, fluke
**06** chance **08** accident, clashing, conflict, fortuity, synastry
**11** coexistence, concurrence, conjunction, consilience, correlation, eventuality, serendipity, synchronism
**12** simultaneity **13** synchronicity
**14** correspondence
**15** synchronization

**coincident**
**04** like **05** alike, close **07** related, similar, the same **09** in harmony
**10** coexisting, coinciding, comparable, concurrent, consistent, equivalent
**11** coterminous, in agreement
**12** conterminous, simultaneous
**13** corresponding
**15** contemporaneous

**coincidental**
**05** lucky **06** casual, chance, flukey
**09** unplanned **10** accidental, fortuitous **13** serendipitous, unintentional

**coincidentally**
**07** luckily **08** by chance
**12** accidentally **15** unintentionally

**coke** *see* **cocaine**

**cold**
**01** c **03** ice, icy, raw **04** brrr, cool, dead, jeel, keen, numb, rimy, rume, snow
**05** agued, aloof, bleak, cauld, chill, fremd, fresh, frore, frost, gelid, nippy, parky, polar, rheum, stony **06** arctic, biting, bitter, brumal, chilly, frigid, frosty, frozen, numbed, remote, winter, wintry **07** brumous, callous, catarrh, chilled, cutting, distant, glacial, hostile, ice-cold, iciness, rawness, shivery, unmoved **08** clinical, coldness, coolness, freezing, lukewarm, reserved, Siberian, uncaring, unheated
**09** chillness, frigidity, heartless, repulsive, unfeeling **10** chilliness, Decemberly, impersonal, phlegmatic, spiritless, unfriendly **11** Decemberish, indifferent, insensitive, passionless, standoffish, unemotional, unexcitable
**12** antagonistic, unresponsive
**13** unsympathetic **15** undemonstrative
• **cold and wet**
**04** sour

**cold-blooded**
**05** cruel **06** brutal, savage **07** callous, inhuman **08** barbaric, pitiless, ruthless
**09** barbarous, heartless, merciless, unfeeling **10** iron-headed
**14** poikilothermal, poikilothermic

**cold-hearted**
**04** cold **06** flinty, unkind **07** callous, inhuman **08** detached, uncaring
**09** heartless, unfeeling **10** iron-headed **11** indifferent, insensitive
**12** stony-hearted **13** unsympathetic
**15** uncompassionate

**coldly**
**09** callously **11** heartlessly, unfeelingly
**13** insensitively, unemotionally

**colic**
**03** bot **04** bott **05** batts **10** mulligrubs

**collaborate**
**04** join **05** unite **06** assist, betray, team up **07** collude **08** conspire **09** co-operate **10** fraternize, join forces
**11** participate, turn traitor, work jointly
**12** work together **13** associate with, combine forces **14** work as partners

**collaboration**
**05** union **08** alliance, teamwork
**09** collusion **10** conspiring
**11** association, co-operation, joint effort, partnership **12** fraternizing
**13** participation **14** combined effort

**collaborator**
**07** partner, traitor **08** betrayer, colluder, co-worker, quisling, renegade, teammate, turncoat
**09** assistant, associate, colleague
**10** accomplice **11** conspirator, fraternizer **12** fellow worker

**collapse**
◇ *anagram indicator*
**03** rot **04** blow, bust, fail, fall, flop, fold, ruin, sink **05** break, close, faint, slump, swoon **06** attack, cave in, cave-in, fall in, finish, fold up, go bung, tumble
**07** burst-up, crack up, crumble, crumple, debacle, deflate, failure, founder, give way, pancake, pass out, sinking, subside **08** black out, blackout, downfall, fainting, fall down, flake out, keel over **09** break down, breakdown, come apart, fall about, fall apart, falling-in, giving way
**10** concertina, foundering, go to pieces, passing-out, subsidence
**11** come to an end, coming apart, falling-down, fall through, go to the wall, keeling-over, lose control
**12** disintegrate, fall to pieces **13** come to nothing, loss of control
**14** disintegration, falling-through, have a breakdown **15** falling to pieces

**collar**
**03** bag, nab **04** band, bust, grab, nick, ring, stop **05** catch, seize **06** arrest, haul in **07** capture **08** neckband
**09** apprehend

*Collars include:*

**03** dog
**04** Eton, flea, roll, ruff, wing
**05** horse, ox-bow, shawl, steel, storm, whisk
**06** bertha, choker, collet, gorget, jampot, rabato, rebato
**07** brecham, partlet, rebater, stick-up, tie-neck, vandyke
**08** carcanet, clerical, granddad, mandarin, Peter Pan, polo neck, rabatine, turn-down
**09** holderbat, piccadell, piccadill
**10** chevesaile, piccadillo, piccadilly
**11** falling band
**12** mousquetaire

**collate**
**04** edit, sort **05** order **06** gather
**07** arrange, collect, compare, compile, compose **08** organize **10** put in order
**11** put together

**collateral**
**05** funds, rival **06** pledge, surety
**07** deposit **08** security **09** assurance, guarantee **10** additional, subsidiary
**12** contemporary **13** corresponding

**collation**
**07** editing **08** ordering **09** gathering
**11** arrangement, compilation, composition **12** organization
**15** putting together

**colleague**
**04** aide, ally **06** helper, winger
**07** comrade, partner **08** confrère, conspire, co-worker, teammate, workmate **09** assistant, associate, auxiliary, bedfellow, companion
**11** confederate **12** collaborator, fellow worker

**collect**
◇ *containment indicator*
**03** get **04** form, heap, mass, meet, save
**05** amass, fetch, hoard, rally **06** gather, make up, muster, pick up, pile up, semble, take up, uplift **07** acquire, call for, come for, compose, convene, prepare, recover, solicit **08** assemble, converge, go and get **09** aggregate, go and take, stockpile **10** accumulate, congregate, go and bring, raise money
**11** ask for money **12** come together, have as a hobby **14** be interested in, gather together **15** ask people to give

**collected**
◇ *anagram indicator*
◇ *insertion indicator*
**04** calm, cool **06** placid, poised, serene **07** unfazed **08** composed, unshaken **09** unruffled **10** controlled
**11** unflappable, unperturbed
**13** imperturbable, self-possessed
**14** self-controlled

**collection**
◇ *anagram indicator*
**03** set **04** gift, heap, mass, pack, pile, sort **05** gifts, group, hoard, plate, store

**06** basket, job-lot, rickle, series
**07** boiling, cluster, variety
**08** assembly, caboodle, donation, jingbang, offering **09** anthology, composure, congeries, donations, gathering, offertory, selection, stockpile, whip-round **10** assemblage, assortment **11** compilation, ingathering, olla-podrida
**12** accumulation, conglomerate, contribution, subscription
**13** contributions **14** collected works, conglomeration, omnium-gatherum

**collective**
**05** joint **06** common, moshav, shared, united **07** commune, kibbutz, kolkhoz **08** combined **09** aggregate, community, composite, concerted, corporate, gathering, unanimous
**10** assemblage, cumulative, democratic **11** congregated, co-operative **13** collaborative

*Collective nouns for animals include:*

**03** **bed** (clams, oysters), **cry** (hounds), **gam** (whales), **mob** (kangaroos), **nid** (pheasants), **nye** (pheasants), **pod** (seals, whales)
**04** **army** (caterpillars, frogs), **bale** (turtles), **band** (gorillas), **bask** (crocodiles), **bevy** (larks, pheasants, quail, swans), **cete** (badgers), **dole** (doves, turtles), **erst** (bees), **herd** (buffalo, cattle, deer, elephants, goats, horses, kangaroos, oxen, seals, whales), **hive** (bees), **pace** (asses), **pack** (dogs, grouse, hounds, wolves), **romp** (otters), **rout** (wolves), **safe** (ducks), **span** (mules), **team** (ducks), **trip** (goats, sheep), **zeal** (zebras)
**05** **bloat** (hippopotami), **brace** (ducks), **brood** (chickens, hens), **charm** (finches, goldfinches), **covey** (partridges, quail), **crash** (rhinoceros), **drift** (hogs, swine), **drove** (cattle, horses, oxen, sheep), **flock** (birds, ducks, geese, sheep), **grist** (bees), **shoal** (fish), **siege** (cranes, herons), **skein** (geese), **swarm** (ants, bees, flies, locusts), **tower** (giraffes), **tribe** (goats), **troop** (baboons, kangaroos, monkeys), **watch** (nightingales), **wedge** (swans)
**06** **ambush** (tigers), **cackle** (hyenas), **colony** (ants, bees, penguins, rats), **gaggle** (geese), **kindle** (kittens), **labour** (moles), **litter** (kittens, pigs), **murder** (crows), **muster** (peacocks, penguins), **parade** (elephants), **parcel** (penguins), **rafter** (turkeys), **school** (dolphins, fish, porpoises, whales), **string** (horses, ponies), **tiding** (magpies)
**07** **bouquet** (pheasants), **clowder** (cats), **company** (parrots), **prickle** (porcupines), **turmoil** (porpoises)
**08** **building** (rooks), **paddling** (ducks)
**09** **intrusion** (cockroaches), **mustering** (storks), **obstinacy** (buffalo)
**10** **exaltation** (larks), **parliament** (owls, rooks), **shrewdness** (apes), **unkindness** (ravens)
**11** **convocation** (eagles), **murmuration** (starlings), **ostentation** (peacocks), **pandemonium** (parrots)
**12** **congregation** (plovers)

**collector**

*Collectors and enthusiasts include:*

**05** gamer
**07** gourmet
**08** neophile, zoophile
**09** antiquary, cinephile, ex-librist, logophile, oenophile, philomath, xenophile
**10** arctophile, audiophile, cartophile, discophile, ephemerist, gastronome, hippophile, monarchist
**11** ailurophile, balletomane, bibliophile, canophilist, etymologist, notaphilist, numismatist, oenophilist, philatelist, scripophile, technophile, toxophilite
**12** ailourophile, cartophilist, coleopterist, Dantophilist, deltiologist, entomologist, incunabulist, ophiophilist, phillumenist, stegophilist
**13** arachnologist, campanologist, chirographist, lepidopterist, ornithologist, tegestologist, timbrophilist
**14** cruciverbalist
**15** conservationist, stigmatophilist

**college**
**01** c **04** coll, Eton, hall, poly, tech
**06** lyceum, prison, school
**07** academy, madrasa **08** madrasah, madrassa, seminary **09** institute, madrassah, medresseh **10** university
**11** polytechnic

*See also* **educational**; **university**

*Colleges and halls of Cambridge University:*

**05** Clare, Jesus, King's
**06** Darwin, Girton, Queens', Selwyn
**07** Christ's, Downing, New Hall, Newnham, St John's, Trinity, Wolfson
**08** Emmanuel, Homerton, Pembroke, Robinson
**09** Churchill, Clare Hall, Magdalene, St Edmund's
**10** Hughes Hall, Peterhouse
**11** Fitzwilliam, Trinity Hall
**12** Sidney Sussex, St Catharine's
**13** Corpus Christi, Lucy Cavendish
**16** Gonville and Caius

*Colleges and halls of Oxford University:*

**03** New
**05** Green, Jesus, Keble, Oriel
**06** Exeter, Merton, Queen's, Wadham
**07** Balliol, Kellogg, Linacre, Lincoln, St Anne's, St Cross, St Hugh's, St John's, Trinity, Wolfson
**08** All Souls, Hertford, Magdalen, Nuffield, Pembroke, St Hilda's, St Peter's
**09** Brasenose, Mansfield, St Antony's, Templeton, The Queen's, Worcester
**10** Somerville, University
**11** Campion Hall, Regent's Park
**12** Christ Church, St Benet's Hall, St Catherine's, St Edmund Hall, Wycliffe Hall
**13** Corpus Christi
**14** Greyfriars Hall
**15** Blackfriars Hall, St Stephen's House
**16** Harris Manchester, Lady Margaret Hall

• **at college**
**02** up
• **college head**
**04** dean
• **college square**
**04** quad

**collide**
**03** hit, war **04** bump, feud, foul
**05** clash, crash, fight, prang, smash
**06** cannon, go into **07** contend, grapple, quarrel, run into, wrangle
**08** bump into, conflict, disagree
**09** crash into, smash into **10** meet head on, plough into **12** be in conflict

**collision**
**04** bump, feud **05** brush, clash, crash, fight, prang, shunt, smash, wreck
**06** impact, pile-up **07** quarrel, warring, wrangle **08** accident, clashing, conflict, disaster, fighting, showdown **09** rencontre
**10** opposition, rencounter
**12** disagreement, fender bender
**13** confrontation

**colloid**
**03** gel, sol **08** emulsoid **10** suspensoid
**11** carrageenan, carrageenin
**12** carragheenin

**colloquial**
**06** casual, chatty **07** demotic, popular
**08** everyday, familiar, informal
**09** idiomatic **10** vernacular
**14** conversational

**colloquially**
**09** popularly **10** familiarly, informally

**collude**
**04** plot **06** scheme **07** connive
**08** conspire, intrigue **09** machinate
**11** be in cahoots, collaborate

**collusion**
**04** plot **06** deceit, league, scheme
**07** cahoots **08** artifice, intrigue, scheming **10** complicity, connivance, conspiracy **11** machination
**13** collaboration

**Colombia**
**02** CO **03** COL

**colonist**
**04** boor **05** colon **07** pioneer, planter, settler **08** colonial, emigrant, Siceliot, Sikeliot **09** colonizer, immigrant, inhabiter **12** Australasian

*See also* **governor**

**colonize**
**05** found, plant **06** occupy, people, settle **07** pioneer **08** populate

**colonnade**
**04** stoa **05** porch **06** arcade, xystus
**07** eustyle, portico **08** diastyle
**09** areostyle, cloisters, peristyle
**10** araeostyle **11** covered walk
**12** columniation

**colony**
**04** hive **05** apery, group, swarm
**07** outpost **08** dominion, province
**09** coenobium, community, formicary, hydrosoma, hydrosome, polyzoary, satellite, territory **10** dependency, plantation, possession, settlement
**11** association, formicarium, polyzoarium **12** protectorate
**14** satellite state

**Colorado**
**02** CO **04** Colo

**colossal**
**04** huge, vast **05** great, jumbo
**07** immense, mammoth, massive
**08** enormous, gigantic, whopping
**09** herculean, monstrous
**10** gargantuan, monumental
**14** Brobdingnagian

**colossus**
**04** ogre **05** giant, titan **07** Cyclops, Goliath, monster **08** Hercules

**colour**
**03** dye, hew, hue, ink, kit **04** bias, flag, glow, kick, leer, life, race, sway, tint, tone, wash **05** badge, blush, flush, get-up, go red, oomph, paint, shade, slant, stain, strip, taint, tinge **06** affect, banner, crayon, emblem, ensign, reason, redden, tackle, timbre
**07** distort, falsify, pervert, pigment, pizzazz, pretext, redness, turn red, variety **08** clothing, colorant, disguise, insignia, pinkness, richness, rosiness, standard, tincture **09** animation, highlight, influence, overstate, prejudice, ruddiness, vividness
**10** appearance, brilliance, coloration, complexion, exaggerate, liveliness, skin colour **11** ethnic group, nationality, racial group **12** misrepresent, pigmentation, plausibility

*Colours include:*

**03** dun, jet, red, sky, tan
**04** anil, blae, blue, buff, cyan, dove, drab, ecru, fawn, gold, gray, grey, guly, hoar, jade, navy, opal, pink, plum, puce, roan, rose, rosy, ruby, rust, sage, sand, wine
**05** amber, beige, black, brown, coral, cream, ebony, green, khaki, lemon, lilac, mauve, milky, ochre, peach, sepia, taupe, topaz, umber, white
**06** auburn, bottle, bronze, canary, cerise, cherry, cobalt, copper, indigo, maroon, orange, purple, salmon, silver, violet, yellow
**07** apricot, avocado, crimson, emerald, gentian, magenta, saffron, scarlet
**08** burgundy, charcoal, chestnut, cinnamon, eau de nil, lavender, magnolia, mahogany, sapphire
**09** aubergine, chocolate, nile green, tangerine, turquoise, vermilion
**10** aquamarine, chartreuse, cobalt blue, grass-green
**11** burnt sienna, lemon yellow

*See also* **black**; **blue**; **dye**; **green**; **grey**; **orange**; **pigment**; **pink**; **purple**; **rainbow**; **red**; **white**; **yellow**

**• lose colour**
**04** fade, pale

**coloured**
**01** C **09** chromatic

**colourful**
**03** gay **04** deep, rich **05** gaudy, vivid
**06** bright, garish, lively **07** graphic, intense, vibrant **08** animated, exciting
**09** brilliant **10** flamboyant, polychrome, variegated **11** interesting, picturesque, stimulating **12** many-coloured **13** kaleidoscopic, multicoloured, parti-coloured

**colourfully**
**08** brightly **09** intensely, vibrantly
**11** brilliantly

**colourless**
**03** wan **04** drab, dull, fade, grey, pale, tame **05** ashen, bleak, faded, plain, white **06** boring, dreary, sickly
**07** anaemic, insipid, neutral
**08** bleached **09** washed out
**10** lacklustre, monochrome, uncoloured **11** transparent, unmemorable **13** characterless, uninteresting **14** complexionless **15** in black and white

**colt**
**01** c **04** beat, cade, stag **05** staig
**06** hogget

**Columbia** *see* **British**; **District of Columbia** *under* **district**

**column**
**03** col, row **04** anta, file, item, line, list, pier, pole, post, rank **05** Atlas, piece, queue, shaft, story **06** parade, pillar, string **07** article, columel, feature, obelisk, support, telamon, upright
**08** caryatid, pilaster **10** procession

**• shaft of column**
**04** fust, tige **05** scape, trunk
**06** scapus

**columnist**
**06** critic, editor, writer **08** reporter, reviewer **10** journalist **11** contributor
**13** correspondent

**coma**
**03** PVS **05** sopor **06** stupor, torpor, trance **08** hypnosis, lethargy, oblivion
**09** catalepsy **10** drowsiness, somnolence **13** insensibility
**15** unconsciousness

**comatose**
**03** out **05** dazed **06** drowsy, sleepy, torpid **07** in a coma, out cold, stunned
**08** sluggish, soporose **09** lethargic, somnolent, stupefied **10** cataleptic, insensible **11** unconscious

**comb**
**03** red **04** card, hunt, kaim, kame, kemb, rake, redd, sift, tidy, tose, toze
**05** combe, coomb, crest, dress, groom, scour, sweep, tease, toaze, trawl **06** coombe, hackle, kangha, neaten, screen, search **07** arrange, explore, ransack, rummage
**08** scribble, untangle **09** go through
**11** disentangle **14** turn upside down

**combat**
**03** war **04** agon, bout, defy, duel
**05** clash, fight, lists **06** action, battle, debate, oppose, resist, strive
**07** contend, contest, wage war, warfare **08** conflict, do battle, fighting, skirmish, struggle **09** encounter, monomachy, rencontre, withstand
**10** engagement, rencounter, take up arms **11** hostilities

**• unarmed combat**
**04** judo **06** karate **07** ju-jitsu **08** jiu-jitsu

**combatant**
**05** enemy **07** fighter, soldier, warrior
**08** opponent **09** adversary, contender, gladiator **10** antagonist, batteilant, serviceman **11** belligerent, protagonist
**12** servicewoman

**combative**
**06** bantam **07** hawkish, warlike, warring **08** militant **09** agonistic, bellicose, truculent **10** aggressive, pugnacious **11** adversarial, belligerent, contentious, quarrelsome
**12** antagonistic **13** argumentative

**combination**
**03** mix **04** club **05** blend, cross, group, union **06** fusion, merger **07** amalgam, combine, mixture, synergy
**08** alliance, clubbing, compound, junction, solution **09** coalition, composite, syndicate, synthesis
**10** collection, conflation, connection, consortium, federation **11** association, coalescence, composition, confederacy, conjunction, co-operation, integration, unification
**12** amalgamation, co-ordination
**13** confederation

**combine**
**03** mix **04** ally, bind, bond, club, fuse, join, link, meld, pool, stir, weld
**05** admix, alloy, blend, marry, merge, piece, trust, unify, unite **06** mingle, team up **07** conjoin, connect
**08** compound, conflate, cumulate, restrict **09** associate, coadunate, co-operate, integrate, syndicate
**10** amalgamate, homogenize, join forces, synthesize **11** incorporate, put together **12** club together **13** bring together

**• combined**
**08** together

**• combined with**
**03** cum

**combustible**
◇ *anagram indicator*
**05** tense **06** ardent, stormy **07** charged **08** volatile **09** excitable, explosive, flammable, ignitable, sensitive **10** incendiary, phlogistic **11** inflammable

**combustion**
**06** firing **07** burning **08** igniting, ignition
• **internal combustion**
**02** IC

**come**
**02** be **04** gain, hail, near, stem, turn **05** arise, enter, issue, occur, reach, yield **06** allons, appear, arrive, attain, attend, become, climax, dawn on, evolve, follow, happen, secure, show up, strike, turn up **07** achieve, advance, barge in, burst in, develop, get here, occur to, surface, think of **08** approach, draw near, get there, pass into, remember **09** be on offer, come about, go as far as, originate, take place, transpire **10** be caused by, be produced, come to pass, evolve into, move nearer, result from **11** be a native of, be available, develop into, materialize, move forward, move towards **13** be on the market, present itself, reach an orgasm, travel towards **14** have as your home **15** come to the mind of, have as its origin, have as its source
• **come about**
**04** fall, sort **05** arise, occur **06** arrive, befall, happen, result **09** take place, transpire **10** come to pass
• **come across**
**04** find, meet, seem **06** appear, notice **07** run into **08** bump into, come over, discover, meet in wi' **09** encounter **10** chance upon, happen upon, meet in with **11** communicate **12** find by chance, meet by chance **13** stumble across
• **come along**
**04** mend **05** rally **06** arrive **07** advance, develop, hurry up, improve, recover **08** progress **09** get better, shake a leg **10** get a move on, recuperate **11** get cracking, make headway **12** make progress **15** get your skates on
• **come apart**
**04** tear **05** break, split **07** break up, crumble **08** collapse, separate **10** fall to bits **12** disintegrate, fall to pieces
• **come back**
◇ *reversal indicator*
**06** go back, remind, return **07** get back **08** come home, reappear **10** be recalled **11** be suggested **12** be remembered **13** be recollected
• **come between**
**04** part **06** divide **07** split up **08** alienate, disunite, estrange, separate **09** interpose
• **come by**
**03** get **05** visit **06** obtain, secure **07** acquire, procure **09** get hold of
• **come down**
**04** drop, fall **05** avail, avale, light **06** availe, reduce, worsen **07** decline, descend **08** decrease, dismount **10** degenerate **11** deteriorate
• **come down on**
**05** blame, chide, knock, slate **06** berate, rebuke **07** reprove, upbraid **08** admonish, tear into **09** criticize, reprehend, reprimand **13** find fault with
• **come down to**
**04** mean **07** add up to **08** amount to **10** boil down to **12** correspond to **14** be equivalent to, be tantamount to
• **come down with**
**03** get **05** catch **06** pick up **07** develop **08** contract **09** succumb to **10** go down with **11** fall ill with **13** become ill with
• **come forward**
**05** offer **06** accede, step up **09** volunteer **11** step forward **13** offer yourself
• **come in**
**05** enter **06** appear, arrive, entrez, finish, show up **07** receive
• **come in for**
**03** get **04** bear **06** endure, suffer **07** receive, sustain, undergo **10** experience **13** be subjected to
• **come into**
**04** heir **06** be left **07** acquire, inherit, receive **08** be heir to, contract
• **come off**
**04** mend, work **05** end up, occur, rally, strip **06** appear, go well, happen, pay off, thrive **07** advance, develop, improve, proceed, recover, succeed, work out **08** progress **09** get better, take place **10** recuperate, take effect **11** be effective **12** be successful, make progress
• **come on**
**03** via **04** mend **05** begin, rally **06** allons, appear, thrive **07** advance, develop, improve, proceed, recover, succeed **08** progress **09** get better **10** recuperate **12** make progress
• **come out**
**03** end **05** admit, end up, erupt, issue **06** appear, emerge, finish, result, strike **07** leak out **08** conclude **09** terminate **10** be produced, be released, be revealed **11** become known, be published, come to light **12** be made public **13** declare openly **15** become available
• **come out with**
**03** say **05** state, utter **06** affirm **07** declare, divulge, exclaim **08** blurt out, disclose
• **come round**
**04** veer, wake **05** agree, allow, awake, grant, occur, recur, visit, yield **06** accede, come to, happen, relent **07** concede, recover **08** reappear **09** be won over, take place **11** be persuaded **13** be converted to **14** change your mind
• **come through**
**04** pass, ride **06** endure **07** achieve, prevail, ride out, succeed, survive, triumph **09** withstand **10** accomplish **11** pull through
• **come to**
**04** make, stop, wake **05** awake, equal, run to, total **06** obtain **07** add up to, recover **08** amount to **09** aggregate, come round
• **come together**
**03** gel **04** jell, meet **05** close, rally **07** collect, convene
• **come up**
◇ *reversal down indicator*
**04** rise **05** arise, occur **06** appear, crop up, happen, turn up **13** present itself
• **come up to**
**04** meet **05** equal, reach **08** approach, live up to **09** match up to **11** compare with, measure up to **12** make the grade
• **come up with**
**05** offer **06** devise, submit **07** advance, dream up, present, produce, propose, suggest, think of **08** conceive **10** put forward

**comeback**
**05** rally **06** retort, return **07** revival **08** recovery **09** rejoinder **10** resurgence **12** reappearance **13** recrimination
• **make a comeback**
◇ *reversal indicator*

**comedian**
**03** wag, wit **05** clown, comic, joker **06** gagman **07** gagster **08** funny man, humorist **10** comedienne, funny woman **11** entertainer

*Comedians include:*

**03** **Dee** (Jack), **Fry** (Stephen), **Lom** (Herbert), **Sim** (Alastair), **Wax** (Ruby)
**04** **Cook** (Peter), **Dodd** (Ken), **Hill** (Benny), **Hill** (Harry), **Hope** (Bob), **Idle** (Eric), **Kaye** (Danny), **Marx** (Chico), **Marx** (Groucho), **Marx** (Harpo), **Marx** (Zeppo), **Sims** (Joan), **Tati** (Jacques), **Wise** (Ernie), **Wood** (Victoria)
**05** **Abbot** (Russ), **Allen** (Dave), **Allen** (Woody), **Brand** (Jo), **Bruce** (Lenny), **Burns** (George), **Cosby** (Bill), **Davro** (Bobby), **Elton** (Ben), **Emery** (Dick), **Hardy** (Oliver), **Henry** (Lenny), **Inman** (John), **James** (Sid), **Jones** (Griff Rhys), **Jones** (Terry), **Kempe** (Will), **Lewis** (Jerry), **Lloyd** (Harold), **Lucas** (Matt), **Moore** (Dudley), **Oddie** (Bill), **Palin** (Michael), **Pryor** (Richard), **Robey** (Sir George), **Sayle** (Alexei), **Smith** (Mel), **Starr** (Freddie), **Sykes** (Eric)
**06** **Abbott** (Bud), **Bailey** (Bill), **Barker** (Ronnie), **Brooks** (Mel), **Cleese** (John), **Coogan** (Steve), **Cooper** (Tommy), **Dawson** (Les), **Fields** (W C), **French** (Dawn), **Garden** (Graeme), **Howerd** (Frankie), **Jordan** (Dorothy), **Keaton** (Buster), **Lauder** (Sir Harry), **Laurel** (Stan), **Laurie** (Hugh), **Martin** (Steve),

Mayall (Rik), Merton (Paul), Murphy (Eddie), Murray (Bill), Reeves (Vic), Ullman (Tracey), Wilder (Gene), Wisdom (Norman)
07 Aykroyd (Dan), Baddiel (David), Bentine (Michael), Bremner (Rory), Carrott (Jasper), Chaplin (Charlie), Chapman (Graham), Corbett (Ronnie), Deayton (Angus), Enfield (Harry), Everett (Kenny), Feldman (Marty), Gervais (Ricky), Hancock (Tony), Handley (Tommy), Jacques (Hattie), Manning (Bernard), Matthau (Walter), Newhart (Bob), Roscius, Secombe (Harry), Sellers (Peter), Tarbuck (Jimmy), Ustinov (Sir Peter)
08 Atkinson (Rowan), Coltrane (Robbie), Connolly (Billy), Coquelin (Benoît Constant), Costello (Lou), Grimaldi (Joseph), Milligan (Spike), Mitchell (Warren), Mortimer (Bob), Roseanne, Saunders (Jennifer), Seinfeld (Jerry), Sessions (John), The Goons, Walliams (David), Williams (Kenneth), Williams (Robin)
09 Edmondson (Adrian), Fernandel, Grossmith (George), Morecambe (Eric), Rhys Jones (Griff), Whitfield (June)
10 The Goodies, Whitehouse (Paul)
11 Monty Python, Terry-Thomas
12 Brooke-Taylor (Tim)
14 Laurel and Hardy, Little and Large
15 The Marx Brothers

*See also* **actor, actress**

**comedown**
**04** blow **06** bathos **07** decline, descent, let-down, reverse **08** demotion, reversal **09** deflation **10** anticlimax **11** degradation, humiliation **14** disappointment

**comedy**
**03** com, fun **06** humour, joking **07** jesting **08** clowning, drollery, hilarity **09** funniness, pantomime **13** entertainment, facetiousness

*Comedy types include:*

03 gag, low, pun, wit
04 high, joke, sick
05 black, farce, Greek
06 modern, satire, sitcom, visual
07 musical, stand-up
08 romantic
09 burlesque, satirical, screwball, situation, slapstick
10 comic opera, sketch show, television, theatrical, vaudeville
11 alternative, Pythonesque, restoration, tragicomedy
12 Chaplinesque, neoclassical
13 Shakespearian
15 comedy of humours, comedy of manners, improvisational, situation comedy

**comely**
**04** fair, fine, tidy **05** ample, bonny, buxom, sonsy **06** bonnie, gainly, goodly, likely, lovely, pretty, proper, sonsie **07** sightly, winsome **08** blooming, graceful, handsome, pleasing **09** beautiful, excellent **10** attractive **11** good-looking **15** pulchritudinous

**come-on**
**04** lure **10** allurement, attraction, enticement, inducement, persuasion, temptation **13** encouragement

**comet**

*Comets include:*

04 West, Wolf
05 Cruls, Encke, Kirch, Mrkos, Tycho
06 Donati, Halley, Lexell, Newton
07 Bennett, Humason, Tebbutt
08 Daylight, Hale-Bopp, Kohoutek
09 Hyakutake, Ikeya-Seki, Morehouse, Seki-Lines
10 De Chéseaux, Flauergues, Great Comet
11 Arend-Roland, Swift-Tuttle
12 Pons-Winnecke
13 Shoemaker-Levy
14 Tago-Sato-Kosaka

**comeuppance**
**04** dues **05** merit **06** rebuke **07** deserts **08** requital **10** chastening, punishment, recompense **11** just deserts, retribution **14** what you deserve

**comfort**
**03** aid **04** cosy, cozy, ease, help, stay **05** cheer **06** luxury, plenty, relief, repose, solace, soothe **07** assuage, console, encheer, enliven, gladden, hearten, refresh, relieve, succour, support **08** cosiness, opulence, reassure, snugness **09** alleviate, empathize, encourage, enjoyment, recomfort, wellbeing **10** condolence, easy street, invigorate, relaxation, strengthen, sympathize **11** alleviation, consolation, contentment, reassurance **12** compensation, satisfaction **13** bring solace to, encouragement, Gemütlichkeit **15** freedom from pain, speak to the heart

**comfortable**
**04** bein, bien, cosy, cozy, easy, lazy, safe, slow, snug, tosh, warm, well **05** comfy, cushy, happy, loose, roomy **06** at ease, couthy, gentle, homely, kindly, secure **07** couthie, opulent, relaxed, restful, well-off **08** affluent, armchair, carefree, homelike, laid-back, pleasant, relaxing, well-to-do **09** agreeable, confident, contented, enjoyable, gemütlich, leisurely, luxurious, rosewater, unhurried **10** commodious, convenient, delightful, prosperous **11** well-fitting **12** loose-fitting **13** unembarrassed

**• make yourself comfortable**
**04** cose

**comforting**
**07** helpful **08** cheering, soothing **09** analeptic, consoling **10** heartening, reassuring **11** consolatory, encouraging, inspiriting **12** heartwarming

**comic**
**03** wag, wit **04** card, rich, zany **05** buffo, clown, droll, funny, joker, light, witty **06** absurd, gagman, joking **07** amusing, buffoon, comical, gagster, jocular **08** comedian, farcical, funny man, humorist, humorous **09** diverting, facetious, hilarious, laughable, ludicrous, priceless **10** funny woman, ridiculous **11** entertainer **12** entertaining, knee-slapping **13** side-splitting

*Comics include:*

03 Viz
05 Beano, Bunty, Dandy
08 The Beano, The Dandy, The Eagle

**comical**
**05** droll, funny, witty **06** absurd **07** amusing **08** farcical, humorous **09** diverting, hilarious, laughable, ludicrous, quizzical **10** ridiculous **12** entertaining

**comically**
**07** funnily, wittily **08** absurdly **09** amusingly **10** farcically, humorously **11** hilariously, ludicrously **12** ridiculously

**coming**
**03** due **04** anon, dawn, near, next **05** birth **06** advent, future, rising **07** arrival, nearing **08** approach, aspiring, imminent, upcoming **09** accession, advancing, impending, promising **11** approaching, forthcoming, up-and-coming

**• coming out**
**09** emergence

**command**
**03** bid, get **04** fiat, gain, head, hest, lead, rule, sway, warn, will **05** edict, heast, order, power, reign **06** adjure, behest, behote, charge, compel, decree, demand, direct, enjoin, govern, heaste, impose, manage, obtain, secure **07** be given, behight, bidding, control, dictate, mandate, mastery, precept, receive, require **08** dominate, dominion, instruct, pleasure **09** authority, direction, directive, supervise **10** ascendancy, domination, government, injunction, leadership, management **11** commandment, instruction, preside over, requirement, superintend, supervision **12** be in charge of, give orders to **13** be in control of **15** superintendence

*Commands include:*

03 hie, hup, hye
04 easy, halt, high, mush
05 be off, enter, gee up
06 come by, entrez, gee hup, huddup
07 give way
09 stand easy
10 quick march
12 be off with you
15 stand and deliver

**commandeer**
**04** take **05** press, seize, usurp **06** hijack **07** impound **08** arrogate **09** sequester **10** confiscate **11** appropriate, expropriate, requisition, sequestrate

**commander**
**03** Cdr, Com **04** boss, Cmdr, comm, head **05** bloke, chief, Comdr **06** leader, master

*Commanders include:*

**03** aga, mir
**04** agha, meer
**06** sardar, sirdar
**07** admiral, captain, general, officer, prefect, warlord
**08** director, governor, hipparch, phylarch, risaldar, taxiarch, tetrarch
**09** chieftain, chiliarch, imperator, polemarch, privateer, seraskier, trierarch
**11** encomendero, turcopolier
**13** generalissimo
**14** superintendent

*See also* **admiral**; **field marshal**; **general**

**commanding**
**05** lofty **06** strong **08** dominant, forceful, imperial, imposing, powerful, superior **09** assertive, confident, directing, strategic **10** autocratic, dominating, impressive, peremptory **11** controlling **12** advantageous **13** authoritative

**commemorate**
**04** keep, mark **06** honour, salute **07** observe **08** remember **09** celebrate, recognize, solemnize **11** immortalize, memorialize **12** pay tribute to

**commemoration**
**04** mind, obit **06** honour, memory, salute **07** tribute **08** ceremony **09** honouring **10** dedication, observance **11** celebration, recognition, recordation, remembrance

**commemorative**
**07** marking **08** memorial, saluting **09** honouring **10** dedicatory, in honour of, in memoriam, in memory of **11** celebratory, remembering **12** as a tribute to **15** in recognition of, in remembrance of

**commence**
**04** open **05** begin, start **06** launch **07** go ahead **08** embark on, initiate **09** originate **10** inaugurate, make a start **14** make a beginning

**commencement**
**05** onset, start **06** launch, origin, outset **07** kick-off, opening **09** beginning **10** initiation

**commend**
**03** rap **04** give, laud, wrap **05** adorn, extol, trust, yield **06** commit, praise, set off **07** acclaim, applaud, approve, confide, consign, deliver, entrust, propose, suggest **08** advocate, eulogize, hand over **09** recommend **10** compliment **13** speak highly of

**commendable**
**04** good **05** noble **06** pretty, worthy **08** laudable **09** admirable, deserving, estimable, excellent, exemplary, well-found **10** creditable **11** meritorious **12** praiseworthy

**commendation**
**06** credit, praise **07** acclaim **08** accolade, applause, approval, encomion, encomium, good word **09** panegyric **10** approvance **11** acclamation, approbation, good opinion, high opinion, recognition **13** brownie points, encouragement **14** congratulation, recommendation, seal of approval, special mention **15** stamp of approval

**commensurate**
**03** due **05** equal **07** fitting **08** adequate **10** acceptable, comparable, equivalent, sufficient **11** according to **13** appropriate to, corresponding, proportionate **14** compatible with, consistent with, in proportion to **15** corresponding to

**comment**
**03** say **04** note, view **05** gloss, gloze, opine **06** remark **07** descant, explain, mention, observe, opinion, speak to **08** annotate, footnote, point out, scholion, scholium, sidenote **09** criticism, elucidate, interject, interpose, interpret, statement **10** annotation, commentary, exposition **11** elucidation, explanation, observation **12** illustration, marginal note, obiter dictum **13** give an opinion

**commentary**
**04** comm **05** notes **06** Gemara, postil, remark, report, review **07** account **08** analysis, Brahmana, critique, exegesis, treatise **09** narration, voice-over **10** annotation, exposition, play-by-play **11** description, elucidation, explanation **14** interpretation

**commentator**
**05** hakam **06** critic **07** exegete, glosser **08** narrator, reporter **09** annotator, commenter, expositor, glossator, scholiast **10** newscaster **11** broadcaster, interpreter **12** sportscaster **13** correspondent

*See also* **cricket**

**commerce**
**03** com **05** trade **07** dealing, traffic **08** business, dealings, exchange, industry **09** marketing, relations **11** intercourse, trafficking **13** merchandizing

**commercial**
**02** ad **04** bill, hype, plug **05** blurb, trade, venal **06** advert, jingle, notice, poster, shoppy **07** display, handout, leaflet, placard, popular, trading **08** business, circular, handbill, merchant, monetary, saleable, sellable **09** financial, lucrative, marketing, mercenary, promotion, publicity **10** industrial, mercantile, profitable, propaganda **11** moneymaking **12** announcement, profit-making **13** advertisement, materialistic, money-spinning **15** entrepreneurial

**commiserate**
**07** comfort, console, feel for **10** sympathize, understand **12** feel sorry for **13** offer sympathy **15** express sympathy, send condolences

**commiseration**
**04** pity **06** solace **07** comfort **08** sympathy **10** compassion, condolence **11** condolences, consolation **13** consideration, understanding

**commission**
**03** cut, fee, job **04** duty, send, task, work **05** board, order, share, trust **06** ask for, assign, charge, depute, employ, engage, errand, select **07** appoint, arrange, council, empower, mandate, mission, rake-off, request, royalty, warrant **08** contract, delegate, function, nominate, poundage **09** allowance, authority, authorize, brokerage, committee **10** assignment, delegation, deputation, employment, percentage **11** appointment, piece of work **12** advisory body, compensation **13** advisory group **14** representative, responsibility **15** put in an order for

**commit**
**02** do **03** put, sin **04** aret, bind, give, hete, send **05** admit, arett, enact, enure, hecht, hight, inure, trust **06** assign, decide, effect, engage, pledge **07** commend, confide, confine, consign, deliver, deposit, entrust, execute, get up to, intrust, perform, promise, put away **08** bequeath, carry out, covenant, dedicate, delegate, hand over, obligate **09** indulge in, recommend **10** perpetrate **15** cross the Rubicon

**commitment**
**03** tie, vow **04** duty, word **06** effort, pledge **07** loyalty, promise **08** covenant, devotion, hard work **09** adherence, assurance, guarantee, liability **10** allegiance, dedication, engagement, obligation **11** involvement, undertaking **12** imprisonment **14** responsibility

**committal**
**06** pledge **07** sending **09** admission **11** confinement, consignment **12** imprisonment

**committed**
**05** loyal **06** active, engagé, paid up, red-hot **07** devoted, engaged, fervent, sold out, zealous **08** diligent, involved, studious **09** dedicated, sold out on **11** evangelical, hardworking, industrious **12** card-carrying, enthusiastic

**committee**
**03** com **05** board, table **08** delegacy **09** Politburo **10** Propaganda **11** Politbureau

**commodious**
**05** ample, large, roomy **08** spacious, suitable **09** capacious, expansive, extensive **10** convenient **11** comfortable, serviceable

**commodity**
**04** item **05** goods, stock, thing, wares **06** output, profit **07** article, produce, product **08** material **09** advantage, privilege **10** expediency **11** convenience, merchandise

**common**
**03** com, low **05** crude, daily, joint, plain, sense, share, stray, usual **06** coarse, mutual, normal, public, shared, simple, vulgar **07** average, general, ill-bred, loutish, popular, regular, routine, uncouth **08** accepted, communal, everyday, familiar, frequent, habitual, inferior, ordinary, plebeian, standard, tritical, workaday **09** community, customary, prevalent, ten a penny, two a penny, universal, unrefined **10** collective, customable, dime a dozen, prevailing, widespread **11** bog standard, commonplace **12** common as muck, conventional, run-of-the-mill **13** unexceptional **15** undistinguished

**commoner**
**02** MP **04** pleb **07** plebean **08** plebeian

**common land**
**03** tie, tye **04** mark

**commonly**
**05** often, vulgo **07** as a rule, usually **08** normally **09** generally, regularly, routinely, typically **10** frequently **14** for the most part

**commonplace**
**05** banal, stale, stock, trite, usual **06** boring, common, modern, ornery, vulgar **07** humdrum, mundane, obvious, ordinar, prosaic, routine, worn out **08** bromidic, copybook, everyday, exoteric, frequent, ordinary, overused **09** hackneyed, prosaical, quotidian **10** pedestrian, threadbare, widespread **11** a dime a dozen **13** unexceptional, uninteresting

**common sense**
**04** nous **05** savey, savvy, sense **06** brains, reason, sanity, savvey, wisdom **07** realism **08** gumption, prudence **09** good sense, judgement, mother wit, soundness **10** astuteness, experience, pragmatism, shrewdness **11** discernment, rumgumption **12** practicality, sensibleness **13** judiciousness, rumelgumption, rumlegumption **14** hard-headedness, rumblegumption, rummelgumption, rummlegumption **15** level-headedness

**commonsense**
**04** sane, wise **05** sound **06** astute, shrewd **07** prudent **08** sensible **09** judicious, practical, pragmatic, realistic **10** discerning, hard-headed, reasonable **11** down-to-earth, experienced, level-headed **12** matter-of-fact **14** commonsensical

**commonwealth**
**03** Com **04** weal **12** Protectorate

*Commonwealth member countries:*

**04** Fiji
**05** Ghana, India, Kenya, Malta, Nauru, Samoa, Tonga
**06** Belize, Brunei, Canada, Cyprus, Guyana, Malawi, Tuvalu, Uganda, Zambia
**07** Grenada, Jamaica, Lesotho, Namibia, Nigeria, St Lucia, Vanuatu
**08** Barbados, Botswana, Cameroon, Dominica, Kiribati, Malaysia, Maldives, Pakistan, Sri Lanka, Tanzania, Zimbabwe
**09** Australia, Mauritius, Singapore, Swaziland, The Gambia
**10** Bangladesh, Mozambique, New Zealand, Seychelles, The Bahamas
**11** Sierra Leone, South Africa
**13** United Kingdom
**14** Papua New Guinea, Solomon Islands
**15** St Kitts and Nevis
**16** Brunei Darussalam
**17** Antigua and Barbuda, Trinidad and Tobago
**21** St Christopher and Nevis
**24** United Republic of Tanzania
**25** St Vincent and the Grenadines

*Commonwealth of Independent States members:*

**06** Russia
**07** Armenia, Belarus, Georgia, Moldova, Ukraine
**10** Azerbaijan, Kazakhstan, Kyrgyzstan, Tajikistan, Uzbekistan
**12** Turkmenistan

**commotion**
**03** ado, row **04** fuss, Hell, riot, stir, to-do, toss **05** hurly, hurry, noise, steer, stire, storm, styre, whirl **06** bustle, bust-up, flurry, fracas, fraise, furore, hotter, hubbub, pother, pudder, racket, romage, rumpus, steery, tiswas, tizwas, tumult, uproar **07** burst-up, clamour, ferment, rummage, tempest, turmoil **08** ballyhoo, brouhaha, disorder, disquiet, kefuffle, tirrivee, tirrivie, upheaval **09** agitation, carfuffle, confusion, curfuffle, hurricane, kerfuffle, stirabout **10** excitement, hullabaloo, hurly-burly **11** disturbance

**communal**
**05** joint **06** common, public, shared **07** general **09** community **10** collective

**communally**
**07** jointly **08** commonly **09** community, generally **12** collectively

**commune**
**03** com, mir **06** colony **07** kibbutz **08** converse **09** community, discourse **10** collective, fellowship, get close to, get in touch, settlement **11** communicate, co-operative, feel close to, feel in touch, make contact **12** municipality

**communicable**
**08** catching **09** infective **10** contagious, conveyable, infectious, spreadable **12** transferable **13** transmissible, transmittable

**communicate**
**04** talk **05** phone, reach, relay, speak, write **06** bestow, convey, empart, impart, inform, liaise, notify, pass on, report, reveal, spread, unfold **07** commune, contact, declare, deliver, diffuse, divulge, express, get over, mediate, publish, put over **08** acquaint, announce, converse, disclose, intimate, proclaim, transmit **09** be in touch, broadcast, get across, make known, put across, telephone **10** correspond, get in touch **11** demonstrate, disseminate

**communication**
**05** touch **07** contact, message **09** telephony **10** connection, disclosure, intimation **11** information, intercourse **12** intelligence, transmission **13** dissemination **14** correspondence

*Communication forms include:*

**02** IT, TV
**03** fax, MMS, Net, PDA, SMS
**04** memo, Moon, news, note, post, wire, word
**05** cable, e-mail, media, pager, pay TV, press, radar, radio, telex, video
**06** gossip, letter, notice, poster, report, speech, tannoy, the net
**07** bleeper, Braille, cable TV, journal, leaflet, message, Prestel®, webcast, website
**08** access TV, aerogram, brochure, bulletin, circular, computer, dialogue, dispatch, Intelsat, intercom, Internet, junk mail, magazine, mailshot, pamphlet, postcard, telegram, teletext, wireless
**09** broadband, catalogue, digital TV, facsimile, grapevine, mass media, megaphone, Morse code, newsflash, newspaper, publicity, satellite, semaphore, statement, telephone, voice mail
**10** communiqué, dictaphone, loud-hailer, pay-per-view, television, typewriter
**11** advertising, chain letter, satellite TV, Telemessage®, teleprinter, text message, the Internet
**12** announcement, broadcasting, conversation, press release, sign language, walkie-talkie, World Wide Web
**13** video-on-demand, word processor
**14** correspondence, subscription TV

**communicative**
**04** free, open **05** frank **06** candid, chatty **07** voluble **08** friendly, outgoing, sociable **09** expansive, extrovert, talkative **10** unreserved **11** forthcoming, informative, intelligent

**communion**
**02** HC **04** Mass **05** agape, unity **06** accord **07** concord, empathy, harmony, rapport **08** affinity, occasion, sympathy **09** closeness, communing, community, Eucharist, Sacrament **10** fellowship **11** intercourse, Lord's Supper **12** togetherness **13** participation **15** sharing feelings, sharing thoughts

**communiqué**
**06** report **07** message **08** bulletin, dispatch **09** newsflash, statement **12** announcement, press release **13** communication

**communism**
**06** Maoism **07** Marxism, Titoism **08** Leninism **09** socialism, sovietism, Stalinism **10** Bolshevism, Trotskyism **11** revisionism **12** collectivism **15** totalitarianism

**communist**
**03** com, red **04** Trot **05** commo, commy, tanky **06** commie, Maoist, soviet **07** comrade, leftist, Marxist **08** Leninist, Viet Cong **09** communard, socialist, Stalinist **10** Bolshevist, Spartacist, Spartakist, Trotskyist, Trotskyite **11** revisionist **12** collectivist

**community**
**04** body, town, umma **05** biome, group, order, state, tribe, ummah **06** ashram, colony, locale, nation, people, public, region, sangha **07** commune, dogtown, kibbutz, phalanx, section, society **08** district, Greekdom, locality, populace **09** Agapemone, agreement, coenobium, residents, sociation **10** commonness, fellowship, fraternity, population, settlement, sisterhood **11** association, brotherhood **13** neighbourhood

**commute**
**05** remit **06** adjust, lessen, modify, reduce, soften **07** curtail, journey, lighten, shorten, shuttle **08** decrease, exchange, mitigate **10** substitute **12** travel to work

**commuter**
**09** passenger, traveller **11** strap-hanger, suburbanite

**Comoros**
**03** COM

**compact**
**03** ram **04** bond, cram, deal, firm, neat, pact, snug, tamp **05** brief, close, dense, pithy, short, small, solid, terse, tight, union **06** accord, league, little, pocket, settle, treaty **07** bargain, concise, entente, flatten, squeeze **08** alliance, compress, condense, contract, covenant, flapjack, pack down, smallish, succinct, well-knit **09** agreement, concordat, condensed, indenture, press down, telescope **10** compressed, settlement **11** arrangement, close-packed, consolidate, transaction **12** close-grained, close-pressed, impenetrable **13** press together, understanding **15** pressed together

**companion**
**03** lad, pal **04** aide, ally, feer, fere, mate **05** buddy, crony, feare, fiere **06** cohort, co-mate, cupman, escort, fellow, friend, marrow, pheere, potman, shadow, Trojan **07** compeer, comrade, consort, convive, franion, partner **08** barnacle, beau-pere, book-mate, chaperon, compadre, copemate, Ephesian, follower, intimate, playmate, sidekick, workmate **09** assistant, associate, attendant, bon vivant, chaperone, colleague, confidant, copes-mate, pew-fellow **10** accomplice, bon vivante, compotator, confidante, goodfellow **11** compotation, confederate, inseparable, skaines mate

*See also* **boon**

**companionable**
**06** genial **07** affable, amiable, cordial **08** familiar, fellowly, friendly, informal, outgoing, sociable **09** agreeable, congenial, convivial, extrovert **10** gregarious **11** neighbourly, sympathetic **12** approachable

**companionship**
**07** company, rapport, society, support **08** intimacy, sympathy **09** closeness **10** fellowship, friendship **11** association, camaraderie, comradeship **12** consociation, conviviality, togetherness **13** esprit de corps

**company**
**02** AG, BV, Co, SA **03** Cia, Cie, Coy, PLC, set **04** band, body, cast, core, crew, firm, gang, ging, GmbH, heap, push, sort, team **05** crowd, group, house, party, troop, trust **06** cartel, circle, guests, throng, troupe **07** callers, concern, contact, society, support **08** assembly, business, ensemble, jingbang, presence, visitors **09** closeness, community, gathering, syndicate **10** attendance, consortium, fellowship, friendship, subsidiary **11** association, comradeship, corporation, partnership **12** conglomerate, conviviality, togetherness **13** companionship, establishment, multinational **14** holding company, limited company

*See also* **business; dance company** *under* **dance**

**comparable**
**04** akin, like, near **05** alike, close, equal **07** cognate, related, similar **08** parallel **09** analogous **10** equivalent, tantamount **12** commensurate, proportional **13** corresponding, proportionate

**comparably**
**07** equally **09** similarly **11** analogously **14** proportionally **15** correspondingly, proportionately

**comparative**
**02** -er **03** -est **08** relative **12** by comparison, in comparison

**comparatively**
**10** relatively **12** by comparison, in comparison

**compare**
**02** cf, cp **03** get, vie **04** even, like, link **05** equal, liken, match, touch, weigh **06** confer, equate **07** balance, compeer, compete, measure, paragon, provide, stack up **08** confront, contrast, parallel, resemble **09** analogize, correlate, juxtapose **10** be as good as, comparison, set against **13** hold a candle to, set side by side **14** bear comparison, be comparable to **15** regard as the same

• **beyond compare**
**06** superb **07** supreme **08** peerless **09** brilliant, matchless, nonpareil, unmatched **10** unequalled, unrivalled **11** superlative, unsurpassed **12** incomparable, without equal **15** without parallel

**comparison**
**07** analogy, parable **08** contrast, likeness, parallel **10** similarity, similitude **11** correlation, differences, distinction, parallelism, resemblance **12** relationship **13** comparability, juxtaposition **15** differentiation

**compartment**
**03** bay, box, pew, pod **04** area, cage, cell, pane, part, room, till **05** berth, booth, niche, panel, stall **06** alcove, carrel, locker, locule **07** chamber, cubicle, loculus, section, sleeper **08** carriage, casemate, category, division, traverse **09** cubbyhole, partition **10** pigeonhole **11** subdivision

**compartmentalize**
**03** tag **04** file, slot, sort **05** group **08** classify **09** catalogue **10** categorize, pigeonhole **11** alphabetize **12** sectionalize

**compass**
**04** area, bend, dial, plot, zone **05** ambit, curve, field, gamut, grasp, limit, range, reach, realm, round, scale, scope, space, sweep, swing **06** bounds, circle, extent, limits, obtain, realms, sphere, spread **07** achieve, circuit, enclose, pelorus, stretch, trammel **08** boundary, contrive, diapason, register, surround **09** enclosure **10** accomplish, comprehend **13** circumference

*Compass points:*

**01** E, N, S, W
**02** NE, NW, SE, SW

**03** ENE, ESE, NNE, NNW, SSE, SSW, WNW, WSW
**04** east, E by N, E by S, N by E, N by W, S by E, S by W, W by N, W by S, west
**05** NE by E, NE by N, north, NW by N, NW by W, SE by E, SE by S, south, SW by S, SW by W
**09** north-east, north-west, south-east, south-west
**11** east by north, east by south, north by east, north by west, south by east, south by west, west by north, west by south
**13** east-north-east, east-south-east, west-north-west, west-south-west
**14** north-north-east, north-north-west, south-south-east, south-south-west
**15** north-east by east, north-west by west, south-east by east, south-west by west
**16** north-east by north, north-west by north, south-east by south, south-west by south

**compassion**
**04** care, pity **05** heart, mercy
**06** bowels, sorrow, ubuntu
**07** concern, remorse **08** humanity, kindness, leniency, sympathy
**10** condolence, gentleness, tenderness **11** benevolence
**13** commiseration, consideration, fellow-feeling, understanding

**compassionate**
**06** benign, caring, gentle, humane, kindly, tender **07** clement, feeling, lenient, piteous, pitiful, pitying
**08** bleeding, merciful **09** forgiving
**10** benevolent, charitable, forbearing, passionate, remorseful, supportive
**11** kind-hearted, sympathetic, warm-hearted **12** humanitarian **13** tender-hearted, understanding

**compatibility**
**05** match **07** harmony, rapport
**08** sympathy **11** consistence, consistency, suitability **12** adaptability
**14** like-mindedness

**compatible**
**06** suited **07** similar **08** matching, suitable **09** accordant, adaptable, congruent, congruous, consonant, in harmony **10** consistent, harmonious, like-minded, well-suited
**11** conformable, sympathetic, well-matched **12** reconcilable **13** having rapport

**compatriot**
**10** countryman **12** countrywoman
**13** fellow citizen **14** fellow national

**compel**
**03** gar **04** make, urge **05** bully, coact, drive, force, garre, impel **06** coerce, hustle, lean on, oblige **07** dragoon, efforce, enforce **08** browbeat, bulldoze, compulse, insist on, pressure
**09** constrain, press-gang, strongarm
**10** intimidate, pressurize
**11** necessitate **14** put the screws on

**compelling**
**06** cogent, urgent **07** weighty
**08** coercive, forceful, gripping, mesmeric, powerful, pressing, riveting
**09** absorbing **10** compulsive, compulsory, conclusive, convincing, imperative, overriding, persuasive
**11** enthralling, fascinating, irrefutable
**12** irresistible, spellbinding
**13** unputdownable

**compendious**
**05** brief, crisp, short, terse
**07** compact, concise, summary
**08** complete, succinct **09** condensed
**10** to the point **12** all-embracing
**13** comprehensive

**compendium**
**06** digest, manual, symbol
**07** summary **08** abstract, breviate, handbook, synopsis **09** anthology, companion, vade-mecum
**10** abridgment, collection, shortening
**11** abridgement, compilation

**compensate**
**05** atone, repay **06** cancel, make up, offset, recoup, redeem, refund, reward
**07** balance, nullify, redress, requite, restore, satisfy **08** make good, make up to **09** indemnify, make up for, reimburse **10** balance out, counteract, make amends, neutralize, recompense, remunerate
**11** countervail **12** counterpoise
**14** counterbalance, make reparation

**compensation**
**04** boot, bote **05** compo **06** amends, refund, return, reward **07** comfort, damages, payment, redress
**08** reprisal, requital, solatium
**09** atonement, demurrage, indemnity, repayment **10** blood money, correction, recompense, reparation
**11** consolation, restitution, restoration
**12** remuneration, satisfaction
**13** reimbursement **15** conscience money, indemnification

**compère**
**02** MC **04** host **05** emcee, front
**06** anchor **07** present **09** anchorman, announcer, presenter **10** link person
**11** anchorwoman

**compete**
**03** ren, rin, run, vie **04** play, race
**05** enter, fight, match, rival **06** battle, jostle, oppose, strive **07** compare, contend, contest, go in for **08** struggle, take part **09** challenge **11** participate, pit yourself

**competence**
**05** power, skill **07** ability, fitness, purview **08** aptitude, capacity, facility
**09** authority, expertise, technique
**10** capability, efficiency, experience
**11** proficiency, sufficience, sufficiency, suitability **12** jurisdiction **13** legal capacity

**competent**
**03** fit **04** able, good **05** adept, equal, tight **06** expert, habile, strong, useful
**07** capable, skilful, skilled, trained
**08** adequate, masterly, passable, suitable **09** efficient, qualified
**10** acceptable, consummate, legitimate, proficient, reasonable, sufficient **11** appropriate, experienced, respectable **12** accomplished, satisfactory **13** well-qualified

**competition**
**03** bee, cup **04** bout, game, goal, gole, meet, open, quiz, race **05** event, field, match, vying **06** rivals, strife, trials
**07** contest, cook off, rivalry
**08** concours, conflict, knockout, struggle **09** challenge, emulation, encounter, opponents, spelldown
**10** contention, opposition, tournament **11** challengers, competitors, spelling bee
**12** championship, cross-country
**13** combativeness **15** competitiveness

*Sporting competitions include:*

**02** TT
**05** Ashes, Derby, FA Cup
**06** Le Mans
**07** Grey Cup, Masters, Uber Cup, UEFA Cup
**08** Rose Bowl, Ryder Cup, Speedway, World Cup
**09** Motocross, Super Bowl, Thomas Cup, World Bowl
**10** Asian Games, Formula One, Solheim Cup, Stanley Cup
**11** Admiral's Cup, America's Cup, Kinnaird Cup, World Series
**12** Iditarod Race, Olympic Games, Tour de France
**13** Grand National, Kentucky Derby, Leonard Trophy
**15** Paralympic Games
**17** Commonwealth Games

**competitive**
**03** low **04** fair, just, keen **05** pushy
**06** modest **07** average, cut-rate
**08** moderate **09** ambitious, combative, cut-throat, dog-eat-dog
**10** aggressive, reasonable
**11** contentious, inexpensive
**12** antagonistic **15** bargain-basement

**competitively**
**03** low **06** fairly **08** modestly
**10** moderately, reasonably
**13** inexpensively

**competitiveness**
**07** rat race, rivalry **08** ambition, keenness **09** challenge, pugnacity, pushiness **10** aggression, antagonism
**13** ambitiousness, assertiveness, combativeness **14** aggressiveness
**15** contentiousness

**competitor**
**05** rival **06** player **07** agonist, entrant, roadman **08** corrival, emulator, Olympian, opponent, trialist
**09** adversary, candidate, contender, triallist **10** antagonist, challenger, contestant, opposition
**11** competition, pancratiast, participant, pentathlete

**compilation**
◇ *anagram indicator*
**04** opus, work **05** album, segue **06** corpus **07** omnibus **08** treasury **09** amassment, anthology, collation, potpourri, selection, thesaurus **10** assemblage, collection, compendium, miscellany **11** arrangement, collectanea, composition, florilegium **12** accumulation, chrestomathy, organization

**compile**
◇ *anagram indicator*
**04** cull, edit **05** amass **06** garner, gather **07** arrange, collate, collect, compose, marshal **08** assemble, organize **09** construct **10** accumulate **11** put together

• **compiler**
**01** I **02** me

• **compiler's**
**04** mine

**complacency**
**05** pride **07** triumph **08** gloating, pleasure, serenity, smugness **11** contentment, self-content **12** complaisance, satisfaction **13** gratification, self-assurance

**complacent**
**04** smug, vain **05** proud **06** serene **07** pleased **08** gloating, serenity **09** contented, gratified, satisfied **10** triumphant **11** complaisant, self-assured, unconcerned **13** self-contented, self-righteous, self-satisfied

**complain**
**03** nag **04** ache, beef, bind, carp, fuss, girn, hurt, mean, mein, mene, moan, mump **05** bitch, bleat, gripe, groan, growl, grump, meane, plain, whine **06** bemoan, bewail, endure, grouse, grutch, kvetch, lament, object, repine, snivel, squawk, squeal, whinge **07** carry on, grumble, protest, wheenge **08** be in pain, feel pain **09** bellyache, criticize, find fault, make a fuss **10** make a noise, suffer from **11** expostulate, kick up a fuss, raise a stink, remonstrate **12** moan and groan **14** file a complaint **15** have a bone to pick, lodge a complaint

**complainer**
**04** nark **06** kvetch, moaner, whiner **07** bleater, fusspot, grouser, niggler, whinger **08** grumbler, kvetcher **09** nit-picker **10** bellyacher, fussbudget **11** fault-finder

**complaint**
**04** beef, moan **05** bleat, gripe, groan, plain, upset **06** charge, grouch, grouse, grutch, malady, plaint, squawk, whinge **07** ailment, beefing, carping, censure, disease, grumble, illness, malaise, protest, quarrel, quibble, trouble, wheenge **08** bleating, disorder, plaining, sickness **09** annoyance, bellyache, condition, criticism, grievance, infection, objection, querimony, whingeing **10** accusation, affliction **11** bellyaching **12** fault-finding, inflammation **13** indisposition **14** representation **15** dissatisfaction

*See also* **disease**; **inflammation**

• **expression of complaint**
**02** ah

**complaisant**
**06** docile **07** amiable, willing **08** amenable, biddable, obedient, obliging **09** agreeable, compliant, tractable **10** complacent, solicitous **11** conformable, deferential **12** conciliatory **13** accommodating

**complement**
**03** set, sum **05** crown, match, quota, total **06** alexin, amount, number, set off **08** addition, capacity, complete, contrast, entirety, fullness, round off, strength, totality **09** accessory, accompany, aggregate, allowance, companion **10** completion, go well with **11** counterpart **12** consummation **13** accompaniment **14** go well together **15** combine well with

**complementary**
**04** twin **06** fellow **08** matching **09** companion, finishing **10** compatible, completing, harmonious, perfecting, reciprocal, supporting **11** correlative **12** interrelated **13** corresponding **14** interdependent

*See also* **medicine**

**complete**
**02** do **03** all, cap, end **04** done, full, over, real **05** clean, close, crown, ended, pakka, pucka, pukka, total, utter, whole **06** answer, clinch, damned, entire, fill in, finish, fulfil, intact, make up, settle, wind up **07** achieve, execute, fill out, fulfill, perfect, perform, plenary, realize, settled **08** absolute, achieved, conclude, detailed, finalize, finished, integral, outright, round off, thorough, unbroken, unedited **09** completed, concluded, discharge, downright, finalized, integrate, out-and-out, polish off, terminate, undivided **10** accomplish, consummate, exhaustive, terminated, unabridged **11** unmitigated, unqualified, unshortened **12** accomplished, unexpurgated **13** comprehensive, thoroughgoing, unabbreviated, unconditional

**completely**
**02** up **03** all, out **05** fully, quite, right, whole **06** hollow, in full, wholly **07** good and, sheerly, solidly, totally, utterly **08** entirely, outright **09** all ends up, all the way, every inch, perfectly, to the hilt, to the wide **10** absolutely, abundantly, altogether, thoroughly **11** back to front, neck and crop, up to the hilt **12** from top to toe, heart and soul, stoop and roop, stoup and roup, well and truly **13** bag and baggage, head over heels, root and branch **14** in every respect **15** down to the ground, from first to last

**completion**
**03** end, sum **05** close, crown **06** finish **08** fruition **09** discharge, execution **10** attainment, conclusion, fulfilling, fulfilment, perfection, settlement **11** achievement, culmination, realization, termination **12** consummation, finalization **14** accomplishment

**complex**
◇ *anagram indicator*
**05** mixed, thing **06** hang-up, phobia, scheme, system, varied **07** devious, diverse, network **08** compound, disorder, fixation, involved, multiple, neurosis, ramified, tortuous **09** Byzantine, composite, difficult, elaborate, institute, intricate, obsession, plexiform, structure **10** circuitous, complicate, convoluted **11** aggregation, complicated, development **12** organization **13** establishment, preoccupation, sophisticated

**complexion**
**03** rud **04** blee, cast, kind, leer, look, skin, sort, tone, type **05** guise, light, stamp **06** aspect, colour, nature **07** texture **08** attitude **09** character, colouring **10** appearance **11** perspective **12** pigmentation

**complexity**
**07** variety **09** intricacy **10** complicacy, complicity **11** convolution, deviousness, diverseness, elaboration, involvement **12** complication, entanglement, multiplicity, ramification, repercussion, tortuousness **13** compositeness **14** circuitousness **15** complicatedness

**compliance**
**01** C **06** assent **07** keeping **08** yielding **09** agreement, appliance, deference, obedience, passivity **10** accordance, conformity, submission **11** application, concurrence **12** acquiescence, complaisance **14** conformability, submissiveness

**compliant**
**05** civil **06** docile **07** passive, pliable **08** amenable, biddable, flexible, obedient, yielding **09** agreeable, appliable, indulgent, tractable **10** obsequious, sequacious, submissive **11** acquiescent, complaisant, conformable, deferential, subservient **13** accommodating

**complicate**
◇ *anagram indicator*
**05** mix up **06** jumble, muddle, puzzle, tangle **07** complex, confuse, involve, inweave, perplex **08** compound, entangle **09** elaborate **12** make involved **13** make difficult

**complicated**
◇ *anagram indicator*
**06** fiddly, implex, tricky **07** complex, cryptic **08** confused, involved,

puzzling, tortuous **09** Byzantine, difficult, elaborate, intricate **10** convoluted, perplexing **11** problematic **12** labyrinthine

**complication**
◇ *anagram indicator*
**03** web **04** node, snag **05** nodus **06** tangle **07** mixture, problem **08** drawback, obstacle **09** confusion, intricacy **10** complexity, difficulty **11** complexness, convolution, elaboration **12** ramification, repercussion **13** complexedness

**complicity**
**08** abetment, approval **09** agreement, collusion, knowledge **10** complexity, connivance **11** concurrence, involvement **13** collaboration **14** being in cahoots

**compliment**
**04** laud **05** extol **06** admire, eulogy, favour, homage, honour, praise, salute **07** applaud, bouquet, commend, devoirs, douceur, flatter, regards, tribute **08** accolade, approval, encomium, eulogize, flattery, respects **09** baisemain, greetings, laudation, sugarplum, trade-last **10** admiration, best wishes, felicitate, good wishes, salutation **11** speak well of **12** commendation, congratulate, felicitation, pat on the back, remembrances **13** speak highly of **15** congratulations

• **looking for compliments**
**07** angling, fishing

**complimentary**
**04** free **06** gratis **07** glowing **08** admiring, courtesy, honorary **09** approving **10** eulogistic, favourable, flattering, for nothing, on the house **11** meliorative, panegyrical **12** appreciative, commendatory **14** congratulatory

**comply**
**04** meet, obey **05** agree, all in, defer, yield **06** accede, accord, assent, follow, fulfil, oblige, submit **07** abide by, conform, consent, observe, perform, respect, satisfy **09** acquiesce, discharge **10** condescend **11** accommodate

**component**
◇ *anagram indicator*
**03** bit **04** item, part, unit **05** basic, piece **06** factor, module, widget **07** element, partial, section **08** inherent, integral **09** essential, intrinsic, spare part **10** ingredient **11** constituent **12** constitutive, integral part **15** constituent part

*See also* **electrical**

**comport**
**03** act, use **04** bear **05** abear, carry **06** acquit, behave, demean, deport **07** conduct, perform

**compose**
◇ *anagram indicator*
**03** pen, set **04** calm, dite, form, lull, make **05** build, frame, quell, quiet, still, write **06** create, devise, draw up, indite, invent, make up, pacify, settle, soothe, steady **07** arrange, assuage, collect, compile, concoct, control, fashion, produce, stickle, think of, think up **08** assemble, calm down, comprise **09** construct, reconcile **10** constitute **11** choreograph, orchestrate, put together **12** tranquillize

**composed**
◇ *anagram indicator*
**04** calm, cool **05** quite **06** at ease, placid, sedate, serene **07** relaxed **08** together, tranquil **09** collected, confident, unruffled, unworried **10** calmed down, controlled **11** level-headed, unflappable **13** imperturbable, quietened down, self-possessed **14** self-controlled **15** cool as a cucumber

**composer**
**04** bard, poet **05** lyric, maker **06** author, master, writer **07** creator, maestro **08** arranger, melodist, musician, producer, psalmist, triadist **09** epitapher, songsmith, tunesmith **10** epitaphist, operettist, originator, songwriter, symphonist **12** balladmonger, variationist, vaudevillist **13** contrapuntist, dodecaphonist, orchestralist

*Composers include:*

**03** **Bax** (Sir Arnold), **Sor** (Fernando)
**04** **Adam** (Adolphe), **Arne** (Thomas), **Bach** (Carl Philipp Emanuel), **Bach** (Johann Christian), **Bach** (Johann Sebastian), **Berg** (Alban), **Bull** (John), **Byrd** (William), **Cage** (John), **Ives** (Charles), **Orff** (Carl), **Pärt** (Arvo), **Weir** (Judith)
**05** **Adams** (John), **Auric** (Georges), **Berio** (Luciano), **Bizet** (Georges), **Bliss** (Sir Arthur), **Boito** (Arrigo), **Boyce** (William), **Bruch** (Max), **D'Indy** (Vincent), **Dufay** (Guillaume), **Dukas** (Paul), **Durey** (Louis), **Elgar** (Sir Edward), **Falla** (Manuel de), **Fauré** (Gabriel), **Glass** (Philip), **Gluck** (Christoph), **Grieg** (Edvard), **Haydn** (Joseph), **Holst** (Gustav), **Lehár** (Franz), **Liszt** (Franz), **Lully** (Jean Baptiste), **Ogdon** (John), **Parry** (Sir Hubert), **Ravel** (Maurice), **Satie** (Erik), **Verdi** (Giuseppe), **Weber** (Carl Maria von)
**06** **Barber** (Samuel), **Bartók** (Béla), **Bishop** (Sir Henry Rowley), **Boulez** (Pierre), **Brahms** (Johannes), **Busoni** (Ferruccio), **Casals** (Pablo), **Chopin** (Frédéric), **Clarke** (Jeremiah), **Coates** (Eric), **Delius** (Frederick), **Dvorák** (Antonín), **Franck** (César), **German** (Sir Edward), **Glinka** (Mikhail), **Gounod** (Charles), **Gurney** (Ivor), **Handel** (George Frideric), **Kodály** (Zoltán), **Ligeti** (György), **Mahler** (Gustav), **Morley** (Thomas), **Mozart** (Wolfgang Amadeus), **Previn** (André), **Rameau** (Jean Philippe), **Rubbra** (Edmund), **Tallis** (Thomas), **Varèse** (Edgard), **Wagner** (Richard), **Walton** (Sir William), **Webern** (Anton von), **Wilbye** (John)
**07** **Albéniz** (Isaac), **Allegri** (Gregorio), **Bellini** (Vincenzo), **Bennett** (Sir Richard Rodney), **Berlioz** (Hector), **Borodin** (Alexander), **Britten** (Benjamin), **Campion** (Thomas), **Copland** (Aaron), **Corelli** (Arcangelo), **Debussy** (Claude), **Delibes** (Léo), **Dowland** (John), **Duruflé** (Maurice), **Fricker** (Peter), **Gibbons** (Orlando), **Górecki** (Henryk), **Janácek** (Leos), **Menotti** (Gian-Carlo), **Milhaud** (Darius), **Nicolai** (Otto), **Nielsen** (Carl), **Poulenc** (Francis), **Puccini** (Giacomo), **Purcell** (Henry), **Rossini** (Gioacchino), **Salieri** (Antonio), **Shankar** (Ravi), **Smetana** (Bedrich), **Strauss** (Johann), **Strauss** (Richard), **Tavener** (John), **Tippett** (Sir Michael), **Vivaldi** (Antonio), **Xenakis** (Iannis)
**08** **Berkeley** (Sir Lennox), **Bruckner** (Anton), **Couperin** (François), **Goossens** (Sir Eugene), **Grainger** (Percy), **Hoffmann** (Ernst Theodor Wilhelm), **Holliger** (Heinz), **Honegger** (Arthur), **Maconchy** (Dame Elizabeth), **Mascagni** (Pietro), **Massenet** (Jules), **Messiaen** (Olivier), **Respighi** (Ottorino), **Schubert** (Franz), **Schumann** (Robert), **Scriabin** (Aleksandr), **Sibelius** (Jean), **Sondheim** (Steven), **Stanford** (Sir Charles Villiers), **Sullivan** (Sir Arthur), **Telemann** (Georg Philipp), **Victoria** (Tomás Luis de), **Williams** (John)
**09** **Beethoven** (Ludwig van), **Boulanger** (Nadia), **Buxtehude** (Diderik), **Donizetti** (Gaetano), **Hindemith** (Paul), **Meyerbeer** (Giacomo), **Offenbach** (Jacques), **Pachelbel** (Johann), **Prokofiev** (Sergei), **Scarlatti** (Alessandro), **Scarlatti** (Domenico), **Tortelier** (Paul)
**10** **Birtwistle** (Sir Harrison), **Boccherini** (Luigi), **Kabalevsky** (Dmitri), **Monteverdi** (Claudio), **Mussorgsky** (Modeste), **Praetorius** (Michael), **Rubinstein** (Anton), **Saint-Saëns** (Camille), **Schoenberg** (Arnold), **Stravinsky** (Igor), **Villa-Lobos** (Hector)
**11** **Humperdinck** (Engelbert), **Leoncavallo** (Ruggiero), **Mendelssohn** (Felix), **Rachmaninov** (Sergei), **Stockhausen** (Karlheinz), **Tchaikovsky** (Piotr), **Theodorakis** (Mikis)
**12** **Shostakovich** (Dmitri)
**13** **Khatchaturian** (Aram), **Maxwell Davies** (Sir Peter)
**14** **Rimsky-Korsakov** (Nikolai)
**15** **Vaughan Williams** (Ralph)

*See also* **libretto**

**composite**
**05** alloy, blend, fused, mixed **06** fusion **07** amalgam, blended, complex, mixture **08** combined, compound, pastiche **09** patchwork, synthesis **10** conflation **11** agglutinate, combination, synthesized **12** amalgamation, conglomerate **13** agglutination, heterogeneous

**composition**
◇ *anagram indicator*
**02** op **04** book, dite, fine, form, opus, poem, port, task, text, work **05** compo, essay, motet, novel, opera, paper, piece, story, study, thing, verse **06** design, erotic, layout, make-up, making, motett, review, satire, sonata, thesis **07** article, balance, drawing, harmony, mixture, morceau, picture, writing **08** creation, devising, exercise, oratorio, painting, pencraft, rhapsody, symmetry, symphony, treatise **09** album-leaf, arranging, capriccio, character, exaration, formation, impromptu, invention, structure, work of art **10** adaptation, assignment, compromise, concoction, confection, consonance, mock-heroic, production, proportion, whipstitch **11** arrangement, combination, compilation, formulation **12** conformation, constitution, dissertation, organization **13** accompaniment, choral prelude, configuration **15** putting together
*See also* **musical**

**compost**
**04** peat **05** humus, mulch **06** manure **07** grow-bag, mixture **08** dressing, leaf-soil **09** leaf-mould **10** fertilizer, growing-bag

**composure**
**04** calm, ease **05** poise **06** aplomb, temper **07** dignity **08** calmness, coolness, serenity **09** assurance, character, placidity, sangfroid **10** collection, confidence, dispassion, equanimity **11** composition, impassivity, self-control, temperament **12** tranquillity **13** self-assurance **14** self-possession **15** level-headedness

**compound**
◇ *anagram indicator*
**03** Cpd, mix, pen **04** fold, fuse, yard **05** add to, alloy, blend, court, fused, mixed, pound, put up, unite **06** corral, fusion, hybrid, make up, medley, mingle, worsen **07** amalgam, augment, blended, combine, complex, magnify, mixture, paddock **08** coalesce, combined, dispense, heighten, increase, multiple, stockade **09** admixture, aggravate, composite, enclosure, intensify, intricate, synthesis **10** amalgamate, complicate, exacerbate, synthesize **11** combination, complicated, composition, intermingle, put together, synthesized **12** amalgamation, conglomerate
*See also* **chemical**

**comprehend**
◇ *containment indicator*
**03** see **04** know, twig **05** catch, cover, get it, grasp, sense **06** fathom, take in, tumble **07** catch on, compass, contain, discern, embrace, include, involve, make out, realize **08** comprise, conceive, perceive, tumble to **09** apprehend, encompass, penetrate **10** appreciate, assimilate, generalize, understand **11** make sense of **15** put your finger on

**comprehensible**
**05** clear, lucid, plain **06** simple **08** coherent, explicit **09** graspable **10** accessible **11** conceivable, discernible **12** intelligible **14** understandable **15** straightforward

**comprehension**
**03** ken **05** grasp, sense **07** insight **09** judgement, knowledge **10** conception, perception **11** discernment, realization **12** appreciation, apprehension, intelligence **13** understanding

**comprehensive**
**04** full, wide **05** all-in, broad **06** global **07** blanket, capable, general, overall **08** complete, elliptic, sweeping, thorough **09** extensive, inclusive, universal **10** elliptical, exhaustive, widespread **11** compendious **12** all-embracing, all-inclusive, encyclopedic **14** across-the-board, encyclopedical

**comprehensively**
**05** fully **06** widely **07** broadly **10** completely, thoroughly, widespread **11** extensively **12** exhaustively

**compress**
**03** jam, ram, zip **04** cram, lace, pack, pump, tamp **05** crowd, crush, pinch, press, screw, stuff, wedge **06** impact, reduce, squash, strain **07** abridge, astrict, compact, embrace, flatten, shorten, squeeze **08** astringe, condense, contract, shoehorn **09** coarctate, constrict, summarize, synopsize, telescope **10** abbreviate, pressurize **11** concentrate, consolidate, strangulate

**compression**
**07** packing, pumping **08** pinching, pressing, stuffing, thlipsis **09** squashing **10** condensing, flattening **12** constriction **13** concentration, consolidation

**comprise**
◇ *containment indicator*
**04** form **05** cover **06** embody, make up, take in **07** compose, contain, embrace, include, involve **09** consist of, encompass **10** comprehend, constitute **11** incorporate **12** be composed of

**compromise**
◇ *anagram indicator*
**04** deal, risk **05** adapt, agree, shame **06** adjust, damage, expose, settle, weaken **07** balance, bargain, concede, imperil, involve **08** endanger, trade-off **09** agreement, arbitrate, discredit, dishonour, embarrass, implicate, mediation, middle way, negotiate, prejudice, settle for, undermine **10** adjustment, concession, jeopardize, settlement **11** arbitration, composition, co-operation, give and take, meet halfway, negotiation, temperament **12** bring shame to, modus vivendi **13** accommodation, understanding **15** make concessions

**compulsion**
**04** need, urge **05** drive, force **06** demand, desire, duress **07** duresse, impulse, longing **08** coaction, coercion, distress, pressure **09** necessity, obsession **10** constraint, insistence, obligation, temptation **11** enforcement **13** preoccupation

**compulsive**
**06** hooked, urgent **07** chronic, driving **08** addicted, gripping, habitual, hardened, hopeless, mesmeric, riveting **09** absorbing, besetting, dependent, incurable, obsessive **10** compelling, inveterate **11** enthralling, fascinating, unavoidable **12** incorrigible, irredeemable, irresistible, overpowering, overwhelming, pathological, spellbinding **14** uncontrollable

**compulsively**
**09** incurably **10** habitually, inevitably **11** chronically, obsessively, unavoidably **12** incorrigibly, irresistibly **13** involuntarily **14** pathologically

**compulsory**
**03** set **06** forced **07** binding **08** coactive, required **09** de rigueur, essential, mandatory, necessary, requisite **10** compelling, imperative, obligatory, stipulated **11** contractual

**compunction**
**05** guilt, qualm, shame **06** qualms, regret, sorrow, unease **07** remorse **09** misgiving, penitence **10** contrition, hesitation, misgivings, reluctance, repentance, uneasiness

**computation**
**03** sum **06** answer, result **08** estimate, figuring, forecast **09** reckoning **10** arithmetic, estimation, working-out **11** calculation, forecasting

**compute**
**03** sum **04** rate **05** add up, count, tally, total **06** assess, figure, reckon **07** count up, measure, work out **08** estimate, evaluate **09** calculate, enumerate

**computer**
**02** NC, PC **03** MPC **10** calculator **15** electronic brain

*Computers include:*

**03** HAL, IBM, Mac, SAL
**04** iMac, VIKI
**05** Eddie, ENIAC, Holly, iBook
**06** UNIVAC

**08** Colossus, Deep Blue, Spectrum
**09** The Matrix
**11** DeepThought
**12** Commodore Pet

*Computer scientists include:*

**04** **Bell** (Gordon), **Bush** (Vannevar), **Cray** (Seymour), **Hurd** (Cuthbert Corwin), **Jobs** (Steven), **Zuse** (Konrad)
**05** **Aiken** (Howard Hathaway), **Burks** (Arthur Walter), **Gates** (William Henry 'Bill'), **Olsen** (Kenneth Harry), **Sugar** (Alan)
**06** **Amdahl** (Gene Myron), **Backus** (John), **Comrie** (Leslie John), **Eckert** (John Presper), **Hopper** (Grace Murray), **Huskey** (Harry Douglas), **Michie** (Donald), **Milner** (Robin Gorell), **Porter** (Arthur), **Turing** (Alan), **Wilkes** (Maurice Vincent)
**07** **Babbage** (Charles), **Kilburn** (Tom), **Mauchly** (John William), **Shannon** (Claude Elwood), **Stibitz** (George Robert), **Wheeler** (David John)
**08** **Lovelace** (Ada, Countess), **Shockley** (William Bradford), **Sinclair** (Sir Clive), **Williams** (Sir Frederic Calland)
**09** **Atanasoff** (John Vincent), **Forrester** (Jay Wright), **Goldstine** (Herman Heine), **Hollerith** (Herman), **Wilkinson** (James Hardy)
**10** **Berners-Lee** (Tim), **Fairclough** (John Whitaker), **Michaelson** (Sidney), **Von Neumann** (John)

*Computing and Internet terms include:*

**02** CD, IT, PC, VR
**03** bit, bot, bug, bus, CD-R, CPU, DOS, DTP, DVD, FAQ, FTP, GUI, hit, IDE, ISP, Mac®, net, P2P, PDF, RAM, ROM, RTF, URL, VDU, WAN, Web, WWW
**04** BIOS, boot, byte, card, CD-RW, cell, chip, data, disk, dump, file, game, HTML, icon, iMac®, ISDN, menu, port, ring, SGML, Unix®, worm
**05** ASCII, BASIC, cache, CD-ROM, e-mail, iBook®, JANET®, Linux, login, log on, Mac OS, macro, modem, mouse, MS-DOS®, pixel, shell, virus
**06** access, backup, binary, bitmap, buffer, cursor, DVD-ROM, editor, format, Google®, laptop, log off, memory, plug-in, reboot, screen, script, server, the Net, the Web, toggle, window
**07** browser, crawler, default, desktop, hacking, monitor, network, palmtop, Pentium®, pointer, printer, program, scanner, toolbar, Unicode, upgrade, Web page, Web site, Windows®, WYSIWYG, zip disk
**08** Apple Mac®, autosave, bookmark, chat room, database, emoticon, firewall, freeware, gigabyte, graphics, handheld, hard disk, hardware, home page, Internet, joystick, keyboard, kilobyte, megabyte, mouse mat, notebook, password, platform, protocol, software, template, terabyte, terminal, user name
**09** character, debugging, directory, disk drive, e-commerce, hard drive, hyperlink, hypertext, interface, mainframe, newsgroup, shareware, sound card, utilities, video card
**10** domain name, floppy disk, multimedia, netiquette, peer-to-peer, peripheral, rewritable, serial port
**11** abandonware, application, compact disc, compression, cut and paste, floppy drive, motherboard, optical disk, screen saver, silicon chip, spreadsheet, Trojan horse, workstation
**12** circuit board, graphics card, installation, laser printer, parallel port, search engine, spellchecker, subdirectory, World Wide Web
**13** file extension, ink-jet printer, microcomputer, user interface
**14** electronic mail, internal memory, microprocessor, read only memory, rich text format, virtual reality, word processing
**15** operating system, wide area network

*See also* **key**; **language**

**• connected computers**
**03** net, web **07** network

## comrade

**03** pal **04** aide, ally, mate **05** billy, buddy, butty, crony **06** billie, escort, fellow, frater, friend **07** Achates, consort, partner **08** chaperon, follower, intimate, sidekick, tovarich, tovarish **09** assistant, associate, attendant, bully-rook, chaperone, colleague, communist, companion, confidant, tovarisch **10** accomplice, confidante **11** bon camarade, confederate **12** pot companion

## comradeship

**08** affinity **09** closeness **10** fellowship, friendship, sisterhood **11** brotherhood, camaraderie, sociability **12** sisterliness, togetherness **13** brotherliness, companionship, esprit de corps

## con

**02** do **04** dupe, hoax, know, rook, scam, scan, show **05** bluff, cheat, fraud, knock, learn, teach, trick
**06** fiddle, fleece, racket, rip off
**07** against, deceive, defraud, mislead, swindle, tweedle **08** cheating, hoodwink, inveigle, prisoner
**09** bamboozle, deception
**11** acknowledge, double-cross
**15** confidence trick

## concatenation

**05** chain, nexus, trail, train **06** course, series, string, thread **07** linking
**08** progress, sequence **10** connection, procession, succession **11** progression
**12** interlinking, interlocking

## concave

**04** arch **05** vault **06** cupped, hollow, sunken **07** invexed, scooped
**08** curved in, hollowed, incurved, indented **09** depressed, excavated, incurvate **14** bending inwards

## conceal

◇ *containment indicator*
◇ *hidden indicator*
**04** bury, feal, heal, heel, hele, hide, mask, sink, veil **05** cloak, cloke, cover, stash **06** closet, hush up, keep in, pocket, screen, shroud, vizard
**07** cover up, obscure, secrete, smother
**08** disguise, keep dark, submerge, suppress, tuck away **09** dissemble, keep quiet, overgreen, whitewash
**10** camouflage, keep hidden, keep secret, subterfuge **11** dissimulate, put the lid on **14** keep out of sight, keep under wraps

## concealed

◇ *containment indicator*
◇ *hidden indicator*
**05** perdu **06** covert, hidden, latent, masked, perdue, unseen **07** covered
**08** screened **09** disguised, submerged
**10** tucked away **11** clandestine
**13** inconspicuous

## concealment

◇ *containment indicator*
◇ *hidden indicator*
**04** mask, veil **05** cloak, cover, wraps
**06** hiding, screen, shroud **07** cover-up, hideout, mystery, privacy, secrecy, shelter **08** disguise, hideaway
**09** secretion, whitewash
**10** camouflage, protection **11** keeping dark, smokescreen, suppression
**13** keeping secret

## concede

**03** owe, own **04** cede **05** admit, allow, grant, own up, yield **06** accede, accept, give up **07** confess, forfeit
**08** hand over **09** recognize, sacrifice, surrender **10** condescend, relinquish
**11** acknowledge

## conceit

**03** ego **04** fume, wind **05** image, pride, think **06** device, simile, vanity
**07** bighead, egotism, imagine, swagger, thought **08** conceive, concetto, metaphor, puppyism, self-love **09** arrogance, cockiness, immodesty, vainglory **10** comparison, narcissism **11** complacency, haughtiness **12** boastfulness
**13** bigheadedness, conceitedness, understanding **14** figure of speech, self-admiration, self-assumption, self-importance

## conceited

**04** smug, vain **05** cocky, flory, proud, windy, witty **06** clever, snotty
**07** haughty, stuck-up **08** arrogant, boastful, immodest, puffed up
**09** bigheaded, cat-witted, egotistic, upsetting **10** complacent, toffee-nose
**11** egotistical, fantastical, overweening, swell-headed, toffee-nosed

12 narcissistic, supercilious, vainglorious **13** above yourself, self-important, self-satisfied, swelled-headed, swollen-headed **14** full of yourself

**conceivable**
**06** likely **07** tenable **08** credible, possible, probable **09** cogitable, plausible, thinkable **10** believable, imaginable

**conceivably**
**08** possibly, probably **09** plausibly **10** imaginably

**conceive**
**03** see **04** form, take **05** brain, fancy, grasp, guess, start, think **06** create, design, devise, enwomb, invent **07** believe, conceit, develop, express, fantasy, gestate, imagine, picture, produce, realize, suppose, think of, think up **08** contrive, envisage, perceive **09** apprehend, be fertile, formulate, originate, reproduce, visualize **10** appreciate, come up with, comprehend, understand **11** get pregnant, give birth to **14** become pregnant **15** get into your head

**concentrate**
**04** mind **05** amass, bunch, crowd, focus, juice, rivet, think **06** apozem, attend, centre, direct, distil, elixir, gather, reduce **07** cluster, collect, essence, extract, thicken **08** boil down, compress, condense, consider, converge **09** decoction, decocture, evaporate, intensify **10** accumulate, centralize, congregate **11** consolidate, dephlegmate, put your mind **12** distillation, keep your mind, pay attention, quintessence **13** apply yourself **15** devote attention

**concentrated**
**04** conc, deep, hard, rich **05** dense **06** all-out, strong **07** intense, reduced **08** vigorous **09** concerted, condensed, distilled, intensive, strenuous, thickened, undiluted, undivided **10** compressed, evaporated

**concentration**
**04** conc, heed, mass, mind **05** crowd **07** cluster **08** devotion, focusing, grouping **09** attention, denseness, intensity, reduction, thickness **10** absorption, collection **11** application, boiling-down, compression, convergence, deep thought, engrossment, evaporation **12** accumulation, close thought, congregation, distillation **13** agglomeration, consolidation **14** centralization, conglomeration

**concept**
**04** idea, idée, plan, view **05** image **06** notion, theory, vision **07** picture, thought **09** dimension, intention, universal **10** conception, hypothesis, impression **11** abstraction **13** visualization

**conception**
**04** clue, idea, plan, view **05** birth, image **06** design, notion, origin, outset, theory, vision **07** concept, genesis, inkling, picture, thought **09** beginning, formation, inception, intention, invention, knowledge, launching, pregnancy **10** conceiving, hypothesis, impression, initiation, perception **11** abstraction, fecundation, origination **12** appreciation, impregnation, inauguration, insemination, reproduction **13** comprehension, fertilization, understanding, visualization

**conceptual**
**05** ideal **08** abstract, notional, thematic **11** speculative, theoretical **12** hypothetical **14** classificatory

**concern**
**03** job **04** baby, busy, care, cern, duty, firm, heed, part, reck, reke, task **05** alarm, cover, field, issue, point, stake, topic, touch, upset, worry **06** affair, affect, bear on, bother, charge, debate, devote, indaba, matter, meddle, pidgin, pigeon, reckon, regard, sorrow, strain, tender, unease **07** anguish, anxiety, apply to, be about, company, disturb, involve, lookout, perturb, pidgeon, problem, refer to, subject, thought, trouble **08** argument, business, deal with, disquiet, distress, interest, pressure, question, relate to **09** attention, pertain to, syndicate **10** enterprise, solicitude **11** appertain to, association, concernment, corporation, disturbance, involvement, make anxious, make worried, partnership **12** apprehension, have to do with, organization, perturbation **13** attentiveness, consideration, establishment **14** prey on your mind, responsibility **15** be connected with

*See also* **company**; **business**

**concerned**
◇ *anagram indicator*
**04** kind **05** upset **06** caring, uneasy **07** anxious, helpful, related, unhappy, versant, worried **08** affected, bothered, gracious, involved, troubled **09** attentive, connected, disturbed, perturbed, sensitive, unselfish **10** altruistic, charitable, distressed, implicated, interested, solicitous, thoughtful **11** considerate **12** apprehensive

• **be concerned**
**04** care, mell

• **concerned with**
**02** in, re **05** about

**concerning**
**02** of, on, re **04** in re, over **05** about, after, anent **07** apropos **08** to do with, touching **09** as regards, regarding **10** relating to, relevant to, respecting **11** referring to **12** with regard to **13** in the matter of, with respect to **14** on the subject of **15** with reference to

**concert**
**03** gig **04** prom, show **05** quill, union **06** accord, smoker, soirée, unison **07** concord, harmony, recital **09** agreement, rendering, rendition, unanimity **10** appearance, consonance, engagement, hootenanny, jam session, production **11** concordance, co-operation, partnership, performance **12** presentation **13** collaboration, entertainment

**concerted**
**05** joint **06** shared, united **07** planned **08** combined **09** organized **10** collective **11** co-operative, co-ordinated, interactive, prearranged **12** concentrated **13** collaborative

**concession**
**03** cut, sop **05** grant, right **06** ceding, favour **07** forfeit **08** decrease, discount, giving-up, handover, yielding **09** admission, allowance, exception, franchise, privilege, reduction, sacrifice, surrender **10** acceptance, adjustment, compromise **11** recognition, synchoresis **12** special right **14** relinquishment **15** acknowledgement

• **expression of concession**
**02** ou, ow

**conciliate**
**06** disarm, pacify, soften, soothe **07** appease, mollify, placate, satisfy **09** reconcile **10** propitiate **11** disembitter

**conciliation**
**09** placation **11** appeasement, peacemaking **12** pacification, propitiation **13** mollification **14** reconciliation

**conciliator**
**04** dove **06** broker **08** mediator **09** go-between, middleman **10** negotiator, peacemaker, reconciler **11** intercessor **12** intermediary

**conciliatory**
**06** irenic **07** pacific **09** appeasing, assuaging, disarming, peaceable, placatory **10** mollifying **11** peacemaking **12** pacificatory, propitiative, propitiatory, smooth-spoken **13** smooth-talking, smooth-tongued **14** reconciliatory

**concise**
**04** curt **05** brief, crisp, pithy, short, terse, tight **07** compact, laconic, summary **08** abridged, elliptic, mutilate, succinct, synoptic **09** condensed, thumbnail **10** aphoristic, compressed, elliptical, to the point **11** abbreviated, compendious **12** epigrammatic **14** epigrammatical

**concisely**
**06** curtly **07** briefly, crisply, in a word, in brief, in short, pithily, tersely

10 succinctly, to the point 11 in a nutshell, laconically

**conclave**
05 cabal 06 parley, powwow
07 cabinet, council, meeting, session
08 assembly 09 gathering
10 conference 13 confabulation, secret meeting

**conclude**
03 end 04 amen, make 05 agree, allow, cease, close, debar, infer, judge, uptie 06 assume, clinch, decide, deduce, effect, finish, gather, reason, reckon, settle, top off, wind up, wrap up
07 arrange, enclose, pull off, resolve, suppose, surmise, work out 08 bring off, complete, restrain 09 culminate, determine, establish, negotiate, polish off, terminate 10 accomplish, conjecture, consummate 11 come to an end, discontinue, draw to an end
12 bring to an end

**conclusion**
03 con, end 04 coda, fine 05 close, finis, issue, omega, point 06 answer, ending, finale, finish, result, riddle, upshot 07 come-off, finding, opinion, outcome, problem, verdict 08 decision, epilogue, explicit, illation, pirlicue, settling, solution 09 agreement, brokering, cessation, clinching, deduction, effecting, inference, judgement, punchline 10 assumption, completion, consectary, conviction, experiment, peroration, pulling-off, resolution, settlement, working-out
11 arrangement, consequence, culmination, negotiation, termination
12 consummation 13 determination, establishment 14 accomplishment, discontinuance

**• in conclusion**
04 ergo 06 in fine 07 finally, to sum up
09 in closing 10 to conclude

**conclusive**
03 net 04 nett 05 clear, final
08 decisive, definite, ultimate
10 convincing, definitive, unarguable, undeniable 11 irrefutable
12 indisputable, unanswerable, unappealable

**conclusively**
07 clearly, finally 10 decisively, definitely, ultimately, unarguably, undeniably 11 irrefutably
12 convincingly, definitively, indisputably

**concoct**
◇ *anagram indicator*
03 fix, mix 04 brew, cook, make, plan, plot 05 blend, frame, hatch 06 cook up, decoct, devise, invent, make up, mature 07 develop, dream up, prepare, think up 08 contrive, rustle up
09 fabricate, formulate
11 manufacture, put together

**concoction**
◇ *anagram indicator*
04 brew, myth 05 blend, fable, story
06 potion 07 fiction, mixture, untruth
08 compound, creation 09 hell-broth, love-juice 10 fairy story
11 combination, fabrication, preparation, witches' brew

**concomitant**
07 symptom 09 attendant, by-product, conjoined, secondary, syndromic 10 co-existent, concurrent, incidental, side effect 11 associative, synchronous 12 accompanying, coincidental, conterminous, contributing, simultaneous
13 accompaniment, complementary, epiphenomenon
15 contemporaneous

**concord**
04 pact 05 agree, amity, peace, union
06 accord, treaty, unison 07 compact, concent, entente, harmony, rapport
09 agreement, concentus, consensus, harmonize, unanimity 10 consonance, friendship 11 amicability

**concourse**
04 hall 05 crowd, crush, foyer, lobby, plaza, press, swarm 06 lounge, piazza, repair, resort, throng 07 meeting
08 assembly, entrance 09 gathering, multitude 10 collection, confluence

**concrete**
04 firm, real 05 béton, solid 06 actual
07 factual, genuine, Siporex®, visible
08 definite, explicit, material, physical, positive, specific, tangible
09 touchable 11 perceptible, substantial

**concubine**
05 leman, lover, madam 07 lorette, sultana 08 mistress, paramour
09 courtesan, guinea-hen, kept woman 11 apple-squire

**concupiscence**
04 lust 06 desire, libido 07 concupy, lechery 08 appetite, lewdness
09 horniness, lubricity, randiness
11 lustfulness 12 sexual desire
14 lasciviousness, libidinousness

**concupiscent**
04 lewd 05 horny, randy 07 lustful
09 lecherous 10 lascivious, libidinous, lubricious

**concur**
05 agree 06 accede, accord, assent, comply 07 approve, consent
08 coincide 09 acquiesce, co-operate, harmonize 11 be in harmony

**concurrence**
06 assent 07 consent 08 approval, syndrome 09 agreement, synchrony
10 acceptance, conspiracy
11 association, coexistence, coincidence, consilience, convergence
12 acquiescence, common ground, simultaneity 13 juxtaposition
15 contemporaneity

**concurrent**
10 coexistent, coexisting, coincident, coinciding 11 concomitant, synchronous 12 accompanying, simultaneous 15 contemporaneous

**concussion**
10 head injury 11 brain injury, water hammer 15 unconsciousness

**condemn**
◇ *anagram indicator*
03 ban, bar 04 cast, damn, doom, hiss, kest, slam 05 blame, decry, force, judge, knock, slate 06 berate, coerce, compel, ordain, punish, revile
07 accurse, censure, consign, convict, deplore, destine, destroy, reprove, run down, upbraid 08 demolish, denounce, reproach, sentence
09 castigate, criticize, deprecate, disparage, reprehend 10 disapprove, find guilty 12 declare unfit 13 declare unsafe, give a sentence, pass a sentence

**condemnation**
◇ *anagram indicator*
03 ban 04 doom 05 blame
07 censure, reproof 08 judgment, reproach, sentence 09 criticism, damnation, judgement 10 conviction, thumbs-down 11 castigation, deprecation, disapproval, reprobation
12 denunciation 13 disparagement

**condemnatory**
08 accusing, critical 09 damnatory, reprobate 10 accusatory, censorious
11 deprecatory, judgemental, reprobative, reprobatory
12 denunciatory, disapproving, discouraging, proscriptive, unfavourable 13 incriminating

**condensation**
05 steam 06 digest, précis
07 summary 08 moisture, synopsis
09 reduction 11 abridgement, boiling-down, compression, contraction, curtailment, evaporation
12 distillation, liquefaction
13 concentration, consolidation, deliquescence, precipitation

**condense**
03 cut 06 distil, précis, reduce
07 abridge, compact, curtail, cut down, shorten, thicken 08 boil down, compress, contract, solidify
09 capsulize, coagulate, epitomize, evaporate, intensify, summarize
10 abbreviate, condensate, deliquesce, inspissate 11 concentrate, encapsulate, precipitate

**condensed**
03 cut 04 rich 05 dense 06 potted, strong 07 capsule, clotted, compact, concise, cut down, reduced, summary
08 capsular 09 curtailed, shortened, thickened, undiluted 10 abstracted, coagulated, compressed, contracted, evaporated, summarized
12 concentrated

**condescend**
04 bend 05 agree, deign, grant, stoop
06 comply, see fit 07 concede, consent, decline, descend, specify

09 patronize, vouchsafe 10 talk down to 12 be snobbish to 13 lower yourself 14 demean yourself, humble yourself

**condescending**
05 lofty 06 lordly, snooty 07 haughty, stuck-up 08 gracious, snobbish, superior 09 imperious 10 disdainful 11 patronizing, toffee-nosed 12 supercilious

**condescendingly**
10 snobbishly 11 imperiously 12 disdainfully 13 patronizingly 14 superciliously

**condescension**
04 airs 05 stoop 07 disdain 09 loftiness 10 lordliness 11 haughtiness, superiority 12 snobbishness

**condiment**
04 salt 05 spice 06 ginger, pepper, relish, season 07 caraway, chutney, mustard, pickles, vinegar 08 carraway, chow-chow 09 seasoning 11 horseradish, tracklement 13 French mustard 14 English mustard

**condition**
◇ *anagram indicator*
02 do, if 03 -dom, ply 04 case, form, nick, pass, rule, sted, tone, trim, tune 05 adapt, equip, groom, limit, mould, order, prime, set-up, shape, state, stead, stedd, stede, steed, teach, terms, train, treat 06 adjust, defect, demand, factor, fettle, health, kilter, malady, milieu, plight, revive, season, stedde, temper 07 ailment, climate, context, disease, educate, factors, fitness, illness, improve, nourish, prepare, problem, proviso, restore, setting 08 accustom, disorder, position, quandary, restrict, weakness 09 brainwash, complaint, essential, infirmity, influence, necessity, provision, situation, transform, way of life 10 atmosphere, background, limitation, obligation 11 environment, familiarize, make healthy, predicament, requirement, restriction, stipulation 12 indoctrinate, precondition, prerequisite, surroundings, working order 13 circumstances, qualification, state of health

*See also* **disease**; **psychological**; **skin**

**• in good condition**
02 OK 03 fit 04 okay, taut, tidy, well 05 sound 07 in flesh, in shape, thrifty 13 well-preserved

**• in perfect condition**
02 go 06 groovy 12 sound as a bell

**• in such condition**
02 so

**• in what condition**
03 how

**conditional**
04 tied 05 based 07 limited, subject 08 relative 09 dependent, provisory, qualified 10 contingent, restricted 11 provisional

**conditionally**
09 limitedly 10 relatively 11 qualifiedly 13 provisionally

**conditioning**
07 shaping 08 moulding 09 influence 10 adaptation, adjustment 11 preparation 12 transforming

**condolence**
04 pity 07 comfort, support 08 sympathy 10 compassion 11 consolation 13 commiseration

**condom**
04 safe 06 johnny, rubber, sheath 07 Femidom®, johnnie, scumbag 10 protective 12 female condom, French letter, prophylactic 13 contraceptive

**condone**
05 allow, brook 06 accept, excuse, ignore, pardon 07 forgive, let pass 08 overlook, tolerate 09 disregard 15 turn a blind eye to

**conducive**
06 useful 07 helpful, leading, tending 09 promoting 10 beneficial, favourable, productive 11 encouraging, ministerial 12 advantageous, contributing, contributory, instrumental

**conduct**
02 do 03 act, ren, rin, run 04 bear, hold, keep, lead, show, take, ways 05 bring, carry, chair, guide, pilot, steer, usher 06 acquit, behave, convey, direct, escort, handle, manage 07 actions, bearing, comport, control, manners, operate, perform, running, solicit 08 attitude, behavior, carry out, guidance, organize, practice, regulate, transmit 09 accompany, behaviour, demeanour, direction, operation 10 administer, deportment, leadership, management 11 comportment, orchestrate, supervision 12 be in charge of, organization 14 administration

**conductance**
01 G

**conductor**
06 leader 07 clippie, maestro, manager 11 non-electric

*Conductors include:*

04 **Böhm** (Karl), **Wood** (Sir Henry)
05 **Boult** (Sir Adrian), **Bülow** (Hans von), **Davis** (Sir Andrew), **Davis** (Sir Colin), **Elgar** (Sir Edward), **Hallé** (Sir Charles), **Kempe** (Rudolf), **Solti** (Sir Georg), **Sousa** (John Philip)
06 **Abbado** (Claudio), **Boulez** (Pierre), **Casals** (Pablo), **Gibson** (Sir Alexander), **Maazel** (Lorin), **Mahler** (Gustav), **Previn** (André), **Rattle** (Sir Simon), **Walter** (Bruno)
07 **Beecham** (Sir Thomas), **Gergiev** (Valery), **Haitink** (Bernard), **Harding** (Daniel), **Jansons** (Mariss), **Karajan** (Herbert von), **Lambert** (Constant), **Nicolai** (Otto), **Richter** (Hans), **Sargent** (Sir Malcolm), **Smetana** (Bedrich), **Strauss** (Johann), **Strauss** (Richard)
08 **Goossens** (Sir Eugene)
09 **Ashkenazy** (Vladimir), **Barenboim** (Daniel), **Bernstein** (Leonard), **Boulanger** (Nadia), **Klemperer** (Otto), **Mackerras** (Sir Charles), **Stokowski** (Leopold), **Tortelier** (Paul), **Toscanini** (Arturo)
10 **Barbirolli** (Sir John), **Villa-Lobos** (Heitor)
11 **Furtwängler** (Wilhelm)
12 **Rostropovich** (Mstislav)

**conduit**
04 duct, main, pipe, tube 05 canal, chute, ditch, drain, flume, trunk 06 gutter, trough, tunnel 07 channel, culvert, passage, wireway 08 fountain, penstock, waterway 10 passageway 11 watercourse

**cone**
03 puy 05 spire 06 cornet, funnel 09 monticule, strobilus

**confection**
◇ *anagram indicator*
*See* **dessert**

**confectionery**
05 candy 06 sweets 07 bonbons, goodies, junkets, toffees 08 licorice, sweeties 09 liquorice 10 chocolates, confiserie, sweetmeats, sweet-stuff
*See also* **sweet**

**confederacy**
04 band, Bund 05 junta, junto, union 06 league 07 compact 08 alliance 09 coalition 10 conspiracy, federation 11 Five Nations, partnership 13 confederation

**confederate**
04 ally, band 05 cover 06 allied, friend, united 07 abettor, fedarie, federal, partner 08 combined, federary, federate, foedarie 09 accessory, assistant, associate, colleague, federarie, supporter 10 accomplice, associated 11 conspirator 12 collaborator

**confederation**
04 zupa 05 union 06 league 07 compact 08 alliance 09 coalition, hermandad 10 federation 11 association, confederacy, partnership 12 amalgamation

**confer**
02 cf, do 03 pay 04 give, lend, talk 05 award, grant, parle, pawaw 06 accord, bestow, debate, impart, parley, powwow 07 compare, consult, discuss, give out, present 08 converse 10 deliberate 13 exchange views

**conference**
03 hui 04 diet, pear 05 forum 06 debate, huddle, indaba, parley, powwow, summit 07 meeting, palaver, seminar 08 colloquy, congress, dialogue 09 symposium 10 colloquium, convention,

discussion, imparlance, pourparler **11** convocation, emparlaunce, get-together **12** consultation, council of war

**confess**
**03** own **04** avow, sing **05** admit, cough, grant, own up **06** affirm, agnize, assert, expose, fess up, reveal, shrive, squeak **07** concede, confide, declare, divulge, profess, tell all, unbosom **08** disclose, unburden **09** come clean, make known, recognize **11** accept blame, acknowledge **13** come out with it, spill the beans, spill your guts **15** get off your chest

**confession**
**06** avowal, shrift **08** exposure, owning-up **09** admission, assertion **10** disclosure, divulgence, profession, revelation, submission, unbosoming **11** affirmation, declaration, making known, short shrift, unburdening **14** acknowledgment **15** acknowledgement, amende honorable

**confidant, confidante**
**03** pal **04** chum, mate **05** buddy, crony **06** friend **08** alter ego, intimate **09** companion **10** best friend, bosom buddy, repository **11** bosom friend, close friend

**confide**
**04** affy, tell **05** admit **06** impart, reveal **07** breathe, confess, divulge, entrust, unbosom, whisper **08** disclose, intimate, unburden **11** tell a secret **15** get off your chest

**confidence**
**03** con **04** hope **05** faith, poise, trust **06** aplomb, belief, secret **07** courage **08** boldness, calmness, credence, forehead, intimacy, reliance **09** assurance, certainty, composure **10** conviction, dependence, self-belief **11** assuredness **12** positiveness, self-reliance **13** private matter, self-assurance **14** self-confidence, self-possession

• **in confidence**
**08** in secret, secretly **09** entre nous, in privacy, in private, privately **10** personally **11** just quietly **12** under the rose **14** confidentially **15** between you and me

**confident**
**04** bold, calm, cool, sure **05** happy, hardy **06** crouse, secure, upbeat **07** assured, certain **08** composed, definite, fearless, positive, sanguine **09** convinced, dauntless, unabashed **10** courageous, optimistic, sure-footed **11** comfortable, self-assured, self-reliant **12** unhesitating **13** self-confident, self-possessed **14** sure of yourself **15** unselfconscious

**confidential**
**04** pack **05** bosom, privy **06** inward, secret **07** a latere, private **08** hush-hush, intimate, man-to-man, personal **09** sensitive, tête-à-tête, top secret **10** classified, restricted **12** off-the-record, woman-to-woman

**confidentially**
**07** privily, sub rosa **08** in camera, in secret **09** entre nous, in privacy, in private, privately **10** on the quiet, personally **12** in confidence **15** between you and me

**confidently**
**06** boldly, calmly, coolly, surely **09** assuredly **10** composedly, fearlessly, positively **11** comfortably **12** courageously **14** optimistically, unhesitatingly

**configuration**
**04** cast, face, form **05** shape **06** figure **07** contour, outline **11** arrangement, composition, disposition **12** conformation

**confine**
**03** fix, mew, pen **04** bail, bale, bind, cage, coop, crib, edge, gate, hold, keep, mure, shut **05** bound, cramp, emmew, enmew, immew, limit, pound, scope, stick, thirl **06** border, coop up, immure, inhoop, intern, keep in, lock up, narrow, prison, shut in, shut up **07** chamber, control, delimit, enclose, impound, inclose, inhibit, repress, shackle, trammel **08** bottle up, boundary, frontier, imprison, lock away, regulate, restrain, restrict, shut away **09** constrain, immanacle, parameter, perimeter, prescribe **10** limitation **11** hold captive, incarcerate, restriction **12** circumscribe, hold prisoner **13** circumference, hold in custody

**confined**
**04** pent, poky **05** caged, close, pokey, small **06** narrow, penned, poking **07** captive, cramped, limited, squeezy **08** enclosed **09** chambered **10** controlled, housebound, imprisoned, restricted **11** constrained, constricted **13** circumscribed

**confinement**
**05** birth **06** burden, labour **07** custody, lying-in **08** delivery, solitary **09** captivity, detention, restraint **10** childbirth, constraint, internment, prisonment **11** house arrest, parturition **12** imprisonment **13** incarceration

**confirm**
**03** fix, tie **04** aver, back **05** check, prove **06** affirm, assert, assure, bishop, clinch, harden, obsign, pledge, ratify, settle, soothe, uphold, verify **07** approve, certify, endorse, fortify, gazette, promise, qualify, support, warrant **08** evidence, reassure, sanction, validate **09** authorize, establish, guarantee, obsignate, reinforce **10** asseverate, homologate, strengthen **11** corroborate, demonstrate **12** authenticate, substantiate **14** give credence to

**confirmation**
**05** proof **06** assent, chrism **07** backing, support **08** approval, evidence, sanction **09** agreement, testimony **10** acceptance, affirmance, validation **11** affirmation, approbation, endorsement **12** ratification, verification **13** accreditation, corroboration **14** authentication, substantiation

**confirmed**
**03** set **04** firm **05** fixed, sworn, vowed **06** inured, rooted **07** affear'd, chronic, settled **08** addicted, affeered, habitual, hardened, seasoned **09** incurable **10** double-dyed, entrenched, inveterate **11** corroborate, established **12** incorrigible, long-standing **13** dyed-in-the-wool **15** long-established

**confiscate**
**05** seize **06** remove **07** escheat, forfeit, impound **08** arrogate, take away **09** forfeited, sequester **10** commandeer **11** appropriate, expropriate

**confiscation**
**07** escheat, removal, seizure **08** takeover **09** distraint **10** forfeiture, impounding **12** distrainment **13** appropriation, commandeering, expropriation, sequestration

**conflagration**
**04** fire **05** blaze **06** flames **07** burning, inferno **09** holocaust **12** deflagration

**conflate**
**04** fuse **05** blend, merge **07** combine **08** compound **09** integrate **10** amalgamate, synthesize **11** incorporate, put together **13** bring together

**conflict**
**03** jar, row, war **04** agon, camp, feud, muss **05** agony, brawl, clash, close, fight, mêlée, musse, scrap, set-to **06** battle, bust-up, combat, differ, dust-up, fracas, oppose, scrape, strife, strive, tangle, thwart, unrest **07** collide, contend, contest, discord, dispute, ill-will, quarrel, warfare **08** antinomy, be at odds, clashing, disagree, friction, skirmish, struggle, variance **09** antipathy, collision, encounter, front line, go against, hostility **10** antagonism, contention, contradict, dissension, dissonance, engagement, opposition **12** be at variance, disagreement **13** be incongruous, confrontation **14** be in opposition **15** be at loggerheads, incompatibility
*See also* **battle**; **war**

**conflicting**
**06** at odds, off-key **08** clashing, contrary, opposing **09**

**conflicting**
**06** at odds, off-key **08** clashing, contrary, opposing **09** competing, dissonant **10** at variance

11 incongruous 12 antithetical, incompatible, inconsistent
13 contradictory

**confluence**
05 union 06 infall 07 conflux, meeting
08 junction 09 concourse
10 watersmeet 11 concurrence, convergence 12 meeting-point

**conform**
03 fit 04 obey, suit 05 adapt, agree, match, tally 06 accord, adjust, comply, follow, square 07 abide by, observe
08 parallel, quadrate 09 be uniform, harmonize 10 comply with, correspond, fall in with, toe the line
11 accommodate 12 fall into line 13 go with the flow 14 be conventional, do the same thing, follow the crowd 15 go with the stream

**conformist**
03 Con 06 yes-man 11 rubber-stamp
13 stick-in-the-mud 14 traditionalist
15 conventionalist

**conformity**
07 harmony 08 affinity, likeness
09 agreement, congruity, obedience, orthodoxy 10 accordance, accordancy, adjustment, compliance, consonance, observance, similarity, uniformity 11 resemblance
13 accommodation
14 correspondence, traditionalism
15 conventionality

**confound**
◇ *anagram indicator*
03 mix 04 beat, dash, faze, mate, ruin, stun 05 abash, amaze, floor, knock, stump, throw, upset 06 awhape, baffle, defeat, puzzle, rabbit, thwart
07 astound, confuse, destroy, flummox, mystify, nonplus, perplex, stagger, startle, stupefy, unshape
08 astonish, bewilder, demolish, surprise 09 bamboozle, discomfit, dumbfound, frustrate, overthrow, overwhelm 10 spiflicate
11 flabbergast, spifflicate

**confront**
04 defy, face, meet, show 05 brave, cross 06 accost, appose, attack, oppose, resist, tackle 07 address, affront, assault, compare, eyeball, present 08 cope with, deal with, face down, face up to 09 challenge, encounter, stand up to, withstand
10 meet head on, reckon with
11 contend with 12 face the music
15 come to grips with, come to terms with

**confrontation**
05 brush, clash, fight, set-to 06 battle
07 contest, face-off, quarrel
08 conflict, showdown 09 collision, encounter 10 engagement
12 disagreement

**confuse**
◇ *anagram indicator*
03 fog 04 faze, lose, maze 05 addle, bemud, dizzy, floor, mix up, mudge, stump, throw, upset 06 baffle, bemuse, burble, didder, dither, fickle, flurry, fuddle, jumble, mess up, mingle, mither, mizzle, moider, muddle, puzzle, tangle 07 bumbaze, flummox, fluster, involve, mistake, moither, mortify, mystify, perplex 08 bemuddle, bewilder, compound, confound, disorder, distract, dumfound, entangle, surprise 09 bamboozle, disorient, dumbfound, elaborate, embarrass, embrangle, imbrangle, obfuscate
10 complicate, disarrange, discompose, disconcert, tie in knots
12 disorientate, make involved, mingle-mangle 13 make difficult

*See also* **baffle**; **tangle**

**confused**
◇ *anagram indicator*
04 hazy, lost, mazy, mixt, mixy
05 dazed, dizzy, messy, mixed, muddy
06 addled, untidy 07 baffled, bemused, chaotic, floored, in a flap, jumbled, maffled, mixed-up, muddled, puzzled 08 all at sea, flustery
09 delirious, disturbed, flummoxed, flustered, mystified, perplexed
10 bamboozled, bewildered, confounded, désorienté, disordered, disorderly, distracted, hurly-burly, indistinct, nonplussed, out of order, topsy-turvy, unbalanced, up a gumtree
11 complicated, disarranged, in a flat spin, muddy-headed 12 disconcerted, disorganized, inextricable
13 disorientated, helter-skelter, muddle-brained 15 all over the place

**confusing**
◇ *anagram indicator*
05 dizzy 07 cryptic, unclear
08 baffling, involved, muddling, puzzling, tortuous 09 ambiguous, difficult 10 misleading, perplexing
11 bewildering, complicated
12 inconclusive, inconsistent
13 contradictory

**confusion**
◇ *anagram indicator*
02 pi 03 fog, pie, pye 04 mess, muss, toss 05 chaos, lurry, mix-up, musse, shame 06 baffle, bumble, bummle, cock-up, dudder, fuddle, guddle, huddle, jumble, mess-up, muddle
07 clutter, flutter, turmoil, whemmle, whomble, whommle, whummle
08 disarray, disorder, mish-mash, shambles, upheaval 09 commotion, égarement, overthrow, perdition
10 bafflement, hurly-burly, perplexity, puzzlement, topsy-turvy, untidiness
12 bewilderment, entanglement, hubble-bubble, hugger-mugger
13 disconcertion, embarrassment, indistinction, mystification
14 disarrangement 15 disorganization

**confute**
05 rebut, refel 06 debunk, negate, refute 07 put down 08 disprove, redargue 09 discredit 10 contradict, controvert, prove false

**congeal**
03 gel, set 04 cake, clot, fuse, geal, jeel
05 jelly 06 curdle, freeze, harden
07 pectize, stiffen, thicken
08 coalesce, solidify 09 coagulate
11 concentrate

**congenial**
04 cosy 06 genial, homely, kinred
07 kindred 08 friendly, pleasant, pleasing, relaxing, suitable
09 agreeable, simpatico
10 compatible, delightful, favourable, like-minded, well-suited
11 complaisant, sympathetic, sympathique 13 companionable

**congenital**
05 utter 06 inborn, inbred, innate, inured 07 chronic, connate, natural
08 complete, habitual, hardened, inherent, seasoned, thorough
09 incurable, inherited 10 compulsive, connatural, entrenched, hereditary, inveterate 12 incorrigible
14 constitutional

**congested**
04 full 06 choked, jammed, packed
07 blocked, clogged, crammed, crowded, stuffed, teeming
08 engorged 11 overcharged, overcrowded, overflowing

**congestion**
03 jam 07 choking, snarl-up
08 blockage, blocking, clogging, crowding, gridlock 10 bottleneck, pinchpoint, traffic jam
12 overcrowding

**conglomerate**
04 firm 05 group, trust 06 cartel, merger 07 combine, company, concern 08 business, fullness
10 consortium, traffic jam
11 association, corporation, engorgement, partnership
13 establishment, multinational

**conglomeration**
04 mass 06 medley 09 composite
10 assemblage, assortment, collection, hotchpotch 11 aggregation
12 accumulation 13 agglomeration

**Congo**
03 COD, COG, RCB, ZRE

**congratulate**
05 greet 06 praise 08 wish well
09 gratulate 10 compliment, felicitate
12 pat on the back 13 say well done to
15 wish happiness to
• **congratulate yourself**
05 plume, preen, pride 09 delight in

**congratulations**
04 euge 07 bouquet 08 bouquets, congrats, mazeltov, well done 09 good on you, greetings 10 best wishes, good for you, good wishes 11 compliments
12 pat on the back 13 felicitations

**congregate**
04 form, mass, meet 05 clump, crowd, flock, rally 06 gather, muster, throng
07 cluster, collect, convene

**08** assemble, converge
**10** accumulate, rendezvous **12** come together

**congregation**
**04** fold, host, mass **05** crowd, flock, group, laity **06** parish, people, throng **07** meeting **08** assembly **09** multitude **10** fellowship **12** parishioners

**congress**
**03** hui **04** diet **05** forum, synod
**07** council, meeting **08** assembly, conclave **09** gathering **10** conference, convention, parliament
**11** convocation, legislature

**congruence**
**05** match **07** harmony **08** identity
**09** agreement **10** concinnity, conformity, consonance, similarity
**11** coincidence, concurrence, consistency, parallelism, resemblance
**13** compatibility **14** correspondence

**congruent**
**07** similar **08** parallel, suitable
**09** consonant **10** compatible, concurrent, consistent, harmonious
**13** corresponding

**conical**
**06** spired **07** pointed, tapered
**08** tapering **09** pyramidal, turbinate
**10** cone-shaped, fastigiate **12** funnel-shaped, infundibular **13** infundibulate, pyramid-shaped

**conifer** *see* **pine; tree**

**conjectural**
**07** assumed, posited **08** academic, supposed, surmised **09** tentative
**10** divinatory, postulated, stochastic
**11** speculative, theoretical
**12** divinatorial, hypothetical
**13** suppositional

**conjecture**
**03** aim **05** augur, fancy, guess, infer
**06** assume, notion, reckon, theory
**07** imagine, presume, suppose, surmise, suspect **08** estimate, theorize
**09** guesswork, inference, speculate, suspicion **10** assumption, conclusion, divination, estimation, hypothesis, presuppose, projection
**11** guesstimate, hypothesize, presumption, speculation, supposition
**13** extrapolation **14** presupposition

**conjoin**
**04** join, link **05** match, unify, unite
**06** concur **07** combine, connect
**08** alligate **10** amalgamate, synthesize
**12** join together

**conjugal**
**06** bridal, wedded **07** marital, married, nuptial, spousal **08** hymeneal
**09** connubial **11** epithalamic, matrimonial
• **conjugal union**
**03** bed

**conjunction**
**05** synod, union **06** syzygy **07** unition
**10** alligation, connection, copulative, injunction **11** association, coexistence, coincidence, colligation, combination, concurrence, unification
**12** amalgamation, co-occurrence
**13** juxtaposition
• **in conjunction with**
**04** with **09** alongside, along with
**12** combined with, together with **13** in company with

**conjure**
**05** charm, evoke, raise, rouse **06** call up, compel, invoke, juggle, summon
**07** bewitch, do magic **08** do tricks
**09** fascinate **10** make appear
**11** materialize **12** perform magic
**13** perform tricks
• **conjure up**
**05** evoke **06** awaken, create, excite, invoke, recall **07** produce **08** summon up **09** recollect **10** call to mind
**11** bring to mind

**conjurer**
**06** wizard **08** magician, sorcerer
**10** mystery-man **11** illusionist, thaumaturge **12** prestigiator
**13** miracle-worker **15** prestidigitator
• **conjurer's skill**
**11** legerdemain **13** sleight of hand
• **conjurer's words**
**09** hey presto **10** hocus-pocus
**11** abracadabra

**conk**
**04** head, nose
• **conk out**
**03** die **04** fail **06** go bust, go phut, pack up **07** go kaput **08** collapse
**09** break down, go haywire **12** go on the blink

**con man**
**04** liar **05** bunco, cheat, crook
**06** rorter, usurer **07** blagger, grifter, hustler **08** deceiver, swindler, tweedler **09** con artist **11** bunco artist, illy whacker, overcharger **12** bunko-steerer, extortionist, rip-off artist

**connect**
**03** put, tie **04** ally, bolt, bond, fuse, join, link **05** affix, clamp, unite
**06** attach, bridge, couple, equate, fasten, relate, secure **07** bracket, combine **08** identify, relate to
**09** associate, correlate **10** articulate
**11** compaginate, concatenate **12** hang together

**connected**
**04** akin, tied **06** allied, joined, linked, united **07** coupled, related, secured
**08** coherent, combined, fastened
**09** associate, conjugate **10** affiliated, associated

**Connecticut**
**02** CT **04** Conn

**connection**
**03** tie **04** bond, link, pons **05** clasp, joint, tie-in, tie-up **06** friend, hook-up, link-up **07** analogy, contact, context, liaison, linkage, rapport, sponsor
**08** alliance, coupling, intimacy, junction, parallel, relation, relative
**09** coherence, fastening, reference, relevance **10** attachment
**11** association, colligation, conjunction, correlation, intercourse
**12** acquaintance, relationship
**13** communication, consanguinity, interrelation **14** correspondence
• **in connection with**
**02** re **04** as to **05** about **07** apropos
**09** as regards, regarding
**10** concerning, in regard to **12** in relation to, with regard to **13** with respect to **14** on the subject of **15** with reference to

**conning-tower**
**04** sail

**connivance**
**07** consent **08** abetment, abetting
**09** collusion, condoning
**10** complicity, conspiracy, lenocinium

**connive**
**04** plot, wink **05** allow, brook, cabal, coact, let go **06** ignore, scheme, wink at **07** collude, complot, condone, let pass **08** conspire, intrigue, overlook, pass over, tolerate **09** disregard, gloss over **11** collaborate **15** turn a blind eye to

**conniving**
**05** nasty **07** corrupt, immoral
**08** plotting, scheming **09** colluding
**10** conspiring **12** manipulative, unscrupulous

**connoisseur**
**04** buff **05** judge **06** expert, pundit
**07** arbiter, devotee, epicure, gourmet
**08** aesthete, oenophil, virtuoso
**09** authority **10** aficionado, gastronome, specialist
**11** cognoscente, gastronomer, oenophilist **12** iconophilist

**connotation**
**04** hint **06** intent, nuance **08** allusion, overtone **09** colouring, undertone
**10** intimation, suggestion
**11** association, implication, insinuation
**12** undercurrent **13** comprehension

**connote**
**05** imply **06** hint at, import
**07** betoken, purport, signify, suggest
**08** allude to, indicate, intimate
**09** associate, connotate, insinuate

**conquer**
**03** win **04** beat, best, rout, take
**05** annex, crush, debel, quell, seize, worst **06** defeat, humble, master, obtain, occupy, subdew, subdue
**07** acquire, control, overrun, possess, succeed, trounce **08** overcome, suppress, surmount, vanquish
**09** overpower, overthrow, rise above, subjugate **11** appropriate, prevail over, triumph over **14** get the better of

**conqueror**
**04** hero, lord, Moor **05** champ, Mogul
**06** master, victor, winner **08** champion
**10** subjugator, vanquisher
**12** conquistador

**conquest**
**03** win **04** coup, rout **05** catch, lover **06** defeat **07** beating, captive, capture, mastery, seizing, success, triumph, victory **08** crushing, invasion **09** overthrow, trouncing **10** annexation, occupation, possession, subjection **11** acquisition, overrunning, subjugation **12** overpowering, vanquishment **13** appropriation

**conscience**
**05** inwit **06** ethics, morals, qualms **08** scruples **09** diligence, moral code, standards **10** moral sense, principles, syneidesis, synteresis **11** voice within **12** sense of right **14** scrupulousness **15** still small voice

**conscience-stricken**
**05** sorry **06** guilty **07** ashamed **08** contrite, penitent, troubled **09** disturbed, regretful, repentant **10** remorseful **11** guilt-ridden **12** compunctious, on a guilt trip

**conscientious**
**06** honest **07** careful, dutiful, upright **08** diligent, faithful, thorough **09** assiduous, attentive, dedicated **10** methodical, meticulous, particular, scrupulous **11** hard-working, industrious, painstaking, punctilious, responsible

**conscious**
**05** alert, alive, awake, aware **06** wilful **07** heedful, knowing, mindful, studied, witting **08** rational, sensible, sentient **09** cognizant, conscient, on purpose, reasoning, voluntary **10** calculated, deliberate, percipient, responsive, volitional **11** intentional, recognizant **12** premeditated **13** self-conscious
• **be conscious of**
**04** feel **06** savour

**consciously**
**08** wilfully **09** knowingly, on purpose **11** voluntarily **12** deliberately **13** intentionally

**consciousness**
**04** mind **06** psyche **07** thought **09** alertness, awareness, intuition, knowledge, sentience **10** being awake, cognizance, perception **11** cenesthesia, cenesthesis, realization, recognition, sensibility, wakefulness **12** apprehension **13** coenaesthesia, coenaesthesis

**conscript**
**05** draft **06** call up, enlist, induct, muster, take on **07** draftee, recruit, round up **08** enlistee, enrolled, inductee **10** registered

**conscription**
**05** draft **08** drafting

**consecrate**
**03** vow **05** bless, exalt **06** anoint, devote, hallow, ordain, revere **07** devoted **08** dedicate, make holy, sanctify, venerate **10** sanctified

**consecutive**
**06** in a row, in turn, serial **07** running, sequent, seriate **08** parallel, straight, unbroken **09** following, on the trot **10** back to back, continuous, sequential, succeeding, successive **13** uninterrupted

**consecutively**
**06** in a row, in turn **09** on the trot **10** back to back **11** hand-running **12** continuously, sequentially, successively **15** uninterruptedly

**consensus**
**05** unity **07** concord, consent, harmony **09** agreement, unanimity **10** consension **11** concurrence **12** consentience, majority view

**consent**
**05** admit, agree, allow, grant, yield **06** accede, accept, afford, assent, comply, concur, permit, submit **07** affoord, approve, concede, go-ahead **08** approval, sanction **09** acquiesce, agreement, authorize, clearance **10** acceptance, compliance, concession, condescend, green light, homologate, permission **11** concurrence, go along with **12** acquiescence **13** authorization **14** give the go-ahead **15** give the thumbs-up

**consequence**
**03** end **04** note **05** issue, value **06** effect, import, moment, result, upshot, weight **07** concern, outcome **08** eminence, sequence **09** aftermath, inference, substance **10** importance, importancy, prominence, side effect **11** distinction, eventuality, implication **12** repercussion, significance **13** reverberation

**consequent**
**07** ensuing, sequent **09** appendant, corollary, following, resultant, resulting **10** consectary, sequential, subsequent, successive

**consequential**
**03** key **05** vital **07** crucial, ensuing, serious, weighty **08** material, relevant, valuable **09** following, important, momentous, prominent, resultant, resulting **10** noteworthy, sequential, subsequent, successive **11** far-reaching, significant, substantial

**consequently**
**04** ergo, then, thus **05** hence **06** so that **09** as a result, therefore **11** accordingly, necessarily **12** subsequently **13** inferentially **15** consequentially

**conservation**
**03** con **04** care **06** saving, upkeep **07** custody, ecology, economy, keeping **09** husbandry **10** protection **11** maintenance, safe-keeping **12** preservation, safeguarding

**conservationist**
**05** green **06** econut **07** greenie **08** ecofreak **09** ecologist **10** tree-hugger **15** preservationist
• **conservationists**
**02** NT **03** WWF

**conservatism**
**09** orthodoxy **14** traditionalism **15** conventionalism

**conservative**
**01** C **03** Con **04** blue, cons, Tory **05** right, sober **06** hunker **07** careful, diehard, guarded, old-line **08** cautious, moderate, old-liner, orthodox, Unionist, verkramp **09** bourgeois, hidebound, right-wing **10** inflexible **11** reactionary, right-winger, traditional **12** buttoned-down, conventional **13** set in your ways, stick-in-the-mud, unprogressive **14** traditionalist **15** backward-looking, middle-of-the-road

**conservatory**
**06** school **07** academy, college **08** hothouse **09** institute **10** glasshouse, greenhouse, storehouse **11** music school **12** drama college, preservative **13** conservatoire

**conserve**
**03** jam **04** keep, save **05** guard, gumbo, hoard, jelly **06** retain **07** husband, protect, store up **08** keep back, maintain, preserve **09** comfiture, marmalade, safeguard **10** take care of **13** keep in reserve

**consider**
**03** see **04** deem, feel, hold, muse, note, rate, view, vise **05** count, judge, study, think, weigh **06** debate, devise, esteem, ponder, regard, reward **07** believe, bethink, examine, reflect, respect, toy with, weigh up **08** chew over, cogitate, envisage, meditate, mull over, prepense, regard as, remember, ruminate, see about **09** apprehend, kick about **10** animadvert, bear in mind, deliberate, keep in mind, kick around **11** contemplate **13** give thought to **15** take into account

**considerable**
**03** big, gay, gey **04** some, tidy, vast **05** ample, great, large, smart **06** lavish, marked, pretty **07** healthy, notable, serious, sizable **08** abundant, generous, sizeable **09** important, plentiful, tolerable **10** noteworthy, noticeable, reasonable **11** appreciable, influential, perceptible, respectable, significant, substantial, substantive **13** distinguished

**considerably**
**03** gay, gey **04** much **07** greatly **08** markedly **10** abundantly, noticeably, remarkably **11** appreciably **13** significantly, substantially

**considerate**
**04** kind **06** caring **07** helpful, tactful **08** discreet, generous, gracious, obliging, selfless **09** attentive, concerned, courteous, sensitive, unselfish **10** altruistic, charitable,

deliberate, respective, solicitous, thoughtful **11** sympathetic **13** compassionate

**consideration**
**04** care, fact, heed, tact **05** count, issue, point **06** factor, motive, notice, reason, regard, review **07** account, concern, payment, respect, thought **08** altruism, analysis, kindness, scrutiny, sympathy **09** attention, reckoning **10** cogitation, compassion, discretion, generosity, importance, inspection, meditation, recompense, reflection, rumination **11** examination, helpfulness, sensitivity **12** circumstance, deliberation, graciousness, selflessness **13** contemplation, unselfishness **14** thoughtfulness

• **lacking consideration**
**04** nude

• **take into consideration**
**05** study **07** plan for **08** allow for, consider **10** bear in mind, keep in mind **13** give thought to **15** take into account

**considering**
**08** all in all, in view of **10** respecting **12** in the light of **13** bearing in mind

**consign**
**04** seal, send, ship, sign **06** assign, banish, commit, convey, devote **07** commend, deliver, entrust **08** give over, hand over, relegate, transfer, transmit **09** recommend

**consignment**
**04** load **05** batch, cargo, goods **08** delivery, shipment

**consist**
**03** lie **05** exist **06** embody, inhere, reside **07** contain, embrace, include, involve, subsist **08** amount to, be formed, be made up, comprise **10** be composed **11** be contained, incorporate

**consistency**
**07** density, harmony, keeping **08** cohesion, evenness, firmness, identity, sameness **09** agreement, coherence, coherency, congruity, constancy, stability, substance, thickness, viscosity **10** accordance, conformity, consonance, continuity, regularity, smoothness, steadiness, uniformity **11** persistence, reliability **12** lack of change **13** compatibility, dependability, steadfastness **14** correspondence

**consistent**
**04** same **06** stable, steady **07** logical, regular, uniform **08** agreeing, coherent, constant, matching, straight **09** accordant, congruous, consonant, unfailing **10** coinciding, compatible, conforming, dependable, harmonious, persistent, unchanging **11** predictable, undeviating **13** consentaneous, corresponding **15** hanging together

**consistently**
**09** regularly, uniformly **10** constantly, dependably **11** predictably, unfailingly **12** persistently

**consolation**
**03** aid **04** ease, help **05** cheer **06** relief, solace **07** comfort, succour, support **08** soothing, sympathy **11** alleviation, assuagement, reassurance **12** recomforture **13** commiseration, encouragement

**console**
**04** calm, help, Xbox® **05** ancon, board, cheer, dials, knobs, panel **06** levers, solace, soothe **07** buttons, comfort, hearten, relieve, succour, support **08** controls, Gamecube®, keyboard, Nintendo®, reassure, switches **09** consolate, dashboard, encourage, recomfort **11** instruments, PlayStation® **12** control panel **14** sympathize with **15** commiserate with

**consolidate**
**03** pun **04** fuse, join **05** merge, unify, unite **06** cement, secure, united **07** combine, compact, fortify **09** reinforce, stabilize **10** amalgamate, make secure, make stable, make strong, strengthen **12** make stronger **14** make more secure, make more stable

**consolidation**
**06** fusion, merger **07** joining, uniting **08** alliance, securing **09** cementing **10** federation **11** affiliation, association, combination, unification **12** amalgamation **13** confederation, fortification, reinforcement, stabilization, strengthening

**consonance**
**07** concord, harmony **09** agreement, congruity **10** accordance, conformity **11** consistency, suitability **13** compatibility **14** correspondence

**consonant**
**05** lenis, velar **06** fortis, sonant, uvular **08** agreeing, alveolar, bilabial, ejective, emphatic, suitable **09** accordant, according, congruous, implosive, in harmony **10** compatible, conforming, consistent, harmonious **11** in agreement **12** articulation, in accordance **13** correspondent

**consort**
**03** mix **04** lady, maik, make, mate, wife **05** agree, troop **06** accord, escort, mingle, spouse **07** husband, partner **09** accompany, agreement, associate, companion, spend time **10** fraternize **11** keep company

**consortium**
**04** bloc, bond, pact **05** guild, union **06** cartel, league, treaty **07** compact, company **08** alliance, marriage **09** agreement, coalition, syndicate **10** federation, fellowship **11** affiliation, association, combination, corporation, partnership **12** conglomerate, organization **13** confederation

**conspicuous**
**05** clear, showy **06** flashy, garish, marked, patent **07** blatant, eminent, evident, glaring, obvious, shining, visible **08** apparent, flagrant, kenspeck, manifest, remarked, striking **09** prominent **10** easily seen, kenspeckle, noticeable, observable, remarkable **11** discernible, perceptible **12** ostentatious, recognizable **13** easily noticed

**conspicuously**
**07** clearly, showily, visibly **08** flashily, garishly, markedly, patently **09** blatantly, evidently, glaringly, obviously **10** flagrantly, manifestly, noticeably, observably, remarkably, strikingly **11** discernibly, perceptibly, prominently **12** recognizably **14** ostentatiously

**conspiracy**
**03** fix **04** plot **05** cabal, covin, set-up **06** covyne, league, scheme **07** complot, consult, frame-up, treason **08** intrigue **09** collusion, stratagem **10** connivance **11** concurrence, confederacy, machination **13** collaboration

**conspirator**
**05** Casca, Cinna **06** Brutus **07** Cassius, plotter, schemer, traitor **08** Catiline, colluder **09** conspirer, intriguer **10** highbinder, practisant **12** collaborator

• **group of conspirators**
**04** band **05** cabal

**conspire**
**04** ally, join, link, plan, plot **05** unite **06** devise, scheme **07** collude, combine, complot, conjure, connect, connive **08** intrigue **09** associate, colleague, co-operate, machinate, manoeuvre **10** hatch a plot, join forces **11** act together, collaborate **12** work together

**constable**
**02** PC, SC **03** cop, WPC **04** Dull **05** jawan, wolly **06** cotwal, harman, kotwal **09** catchpole, catchpoll **10** harman-beck **11** headborough **12** thirdborough

*See also* **police officer**

**constancy**
**05** truth **07** loyalty **08** devotion, fidelity, firmness, tenacity **09** certainty, fixedness, stability **10** permanence, regularity, resolution, steadiness, uniformity **11** consistency, persistence **12** faithfulness, perseverance **13** dependability, steadfastness **15** trustworthiness, unchangeability

**constant**
**01** c, G, h, k **04** even, firm, trew, true **05** daily, fixed, loyal **06** stable, stanch, steady **07** chronic, devoted, endless, eternal, non-stop, regular, staunch, uniform **08** faithful, resolute, unbroken **09** ceaseless, continual, immutable, incessant, permanent, perpetual,

steadfast, unfailing, unvarying
**10** changeless, consistent, continuous, dependable, invariable, persistent, relentless, unchanging, unflagging, unwavering **11** everlasting, never-ending, persevering, trustworthy, unalterable, unremitting
**12** interminable, unchangeable
**13** uninterrupted **14** without respite

**constantly**
**03** aye **05** daily, still **06** always **07** for ever, non-stop, on and on **09** ad nauseam, endlessly **10** all the time, invariably **11** ceaselessly, continually, day in day out, incessantly, perennially, permanently, perpetually
**12** continuously, interminably, relentlessly **13** everlastingly
**15** twenty-four seven

**constellation**

*Constellations include:*

**03** Ara, Cup, dog, Fly, Fox, Leo, Net, Ram
**04** Apus, Argo, Bull, Crab, Crow, Crux, Dove, Grus, Hare, Harp, Keel, Lion, Lynx, Lyra, Pavo, Swan, Vela, Wolf
**05** Altar, Aries, Arrow, Cetus, Clock, Crane, Draco, Eagle, Easel, Hydra, Indus, Lepus, Level, Libra, Lupus, Mensa, Musca, Norma, Orion, Pyxis, Sails, Table, Twins, Virgo, Whale
**06** Antlia, Aquila, Archer, Auriga, Boötes, Caelum, Cancer, Carina, Chisel, Corvus, Crater, Cygnus, Dorado, Dragon, Fishes, Fornax, Gemini, Hydrus, Indian, Lizard, Octans, Octant, Pictor, Pisces, Puppis, Scales, Scutum, Shield, Taurus, Toucan, Tucana, Virgin, Volans
**07** Air Pump, Centaur, Cepheus, Columba, Dolphin, Furnace, Giraffe, Lacerta, Peacock, Pegasus, Perseus, Phoenix, Sagitta, Sea Goat, Serpens, Serpent, Sextans, Sextant, Unicorn
**08** Aquarius, Circinus, Equuleus, Eridanus, Great Dog, Hercules, Herdsman, Leo Minor, Scorpion, Scorpius, Sculptor, Triangle
**09** Andromeda, Centaurus, Chameleon, Compasses, Delphinus, Great Bear, Little Dog, Monoceros, Ophiuchus, Reticulum, Swordfish, Telescope, Ursa Major, Ursa Minor, Vulpecula
**10** Canis Major, Canis Minor, Cassiopeia, Chamaeleon, Charioteer, Flying Fish, Horologium, Little Bear, Little Lion, Microscope, Sea Serpent, Ship's Stern, Triangulum, Water Snake
**11** Capricornus, Hunting Dogs, Little Horse, Sagittarius, Telescopium, Water Bearer, Winged Horse
**12** Microscopium, Southern Fish
**13** Berenice's Hair, Canes Venatici, Coma Berenices, Northern Crown, River Eridanus, Serpent Bearer, Southern Cross, Southern Crown
**14** Bird of Paradise, Camelopardalis, Corona Borealis
**15** Corona Australis, Mariner's Compass, Piscis Austrinus

**consternation**
**03** awe **04** fear **05** alarm, dread, panic, shock **06** dismay, fright, horror, terror
**07** anxiety **08** distress **11** disquietude, trepidation **12** bewilderment, perturbation

**constipated**
**05** bound

**constituency**
**04** area, seat, ward, zone **05** burgh, shire **06** parish, region, Riding
**07** borough **08** district, division, Euroseat, marginal, precinct
**09** community **10** electorate

**constituent**
◇ *anagram indicator*
**03** bit **04** part, unit **05** basic, voter
**06** factor **07** content, elector, element, section **08** electing, inherent, integral
**09** component, essential, intrinsic, principle **10** ingredient **12** constitution
**13** component part

**constitute**
**02** be **04** form, make, mean **05** found, set up **06** create, make up, strike
**07** add up to, appoint, charter, compose, empower **08** amount to, comprise, initiate **09** authorize, establish, institute, represent
**10** commission, inaugurate **12** be regarded as **14** be equivalent to, be tantamount to

**constitution**
**03** set **04** code, laws **05** fuero, habit, rules, state **06** health, make-up, nature, policy, polity, temper, upmake
**07** charter **08** habitude, physique, statutes **09** character, condition, formation, structure **10** social code
**11** codified law, composition, disposition, temperament, temperature **12** bill of rights, idiosyncrasy, organization
**13** configuration **15** basic principles

**constitutional**
**04** turn, walk **05** amble, by law, legal
**06** airing, lawful, stroll, vested
**07** politic, saunter **08** codified, ratified
**09** promenade, statutory
**10** authorized, legitimate **11** legislative
**12** governmental

**constrain**
**03** put **04** bind, curb, rein, urge
**05** check, drive, force, impel, limit
**06** coerce, compel, hinder, oblige, strain **07** confine **08** hold back, obligate, pressure, restrain, restrict
**09** constrict **10** perstringe, pressurize
**11** necessitate

**constrained**
**04** hard **05** stiff **06** forced, uneasy
**07** awkward, guarded **08** reserved, reticent **09** compelled, inhibited, unnatural **11** embarrassed

**constraint**
**04** curb, rein **05** check, force
**06** damper, demand, duress
**07** duresse, shackle **08** coercion, pressure **09** hindrance, necessity, restraint, reticence, stiffness
**10** compulsion, forcedness, impediment, inhibition, insistence, limitation, obligation **11** awkwardness, confinement, guardedness, restriction, self-control **13** embarrassment, unnaturalness

**constrict**
**04** bind, curb **05** check, choke, close, cramp, limit, pinch **06** hamper, hinder, impede, narrow, shrink **07** confine, inhibit, squeeze, tighten **08** compress, contract, hold back, obstruct, restrict, strangle **09** constrain **10** make narrow
**11** strangulate

**constriction**
**04** curb **05** check, choke, cramp
**07** isthmus **08** blockage, pressure, stenosis, thlipsis **09** hindrance, narrowing, reduction, squeezing, stegnosis, stricture, tightness
**10** constraint, impediment, limitation, tightening **11** compression, contraction, restriction
**13** constringency, incarceration

**construct**
◇ *anagram indicator*
**04** form, make **05** build, craft, erect, found, model, patch, put up, raise, set up, shape, weave **06** create, design, devise, fabric **07** compile, compose, elevate, fashion, knock up, throw up
**08** assemble, engineer **09** carpenter, establish, fabricate, formulate, structure **11** manufacture, put together
**13** knock together, throw together

**construction**
**04** form **05** model, order, shape
**06** fabric, figure, make-up, making
**07** edifice, meaning, reading
**08** assembly, building, erection
**09** deduction, elevation, formation, framework, inference, structure
**11** arrangement, composition, disposition, fabrication, manufacture
**12** organization **13** configuration, establishment **14** interpretation

**constructive**
**06** useful **07** helpful **08** inferred, positive, valuable **09** practical
**10** beneficial, productive
**12** advantageous **13** architectonic

**constructively**
**08** usefully **09** helpfully **10** positively
**11** practically **12** beneficially, productively **14** advantageously

**construe**
◇ *anagram indicator*
**04** read **05** infer, see as **06** deduce, render **07** analyse, explain, expound
**08** regard as **09** interpret **10** take to mean, understand

**consul**
**03** Con **05** agent, elchi, envoy

**06** ledger, legate, nuncio **07** leaguer **08** delegate, diplomat, emissary, minister **10** ambassador **14** representative **15** plenipotentiary

**consult**
**03** see **04** talk, vide **06** confer, debate, look up, turn to **07** discuss, refer to **08** question **09** ask advice **10** deliberate, seek advice **11** interrogate **14** ask information **15** seek information

**consultant**
**06** expert **07** adviser **09** associate, authority **10** specialist

**consultation**
**04** talk **05** forum **07** counsel, hearing, meeting, session **08** dialogue **09** interview **10** conference, discussion **11** appointment, examination **12** deliberation

**consultative**
**07** helping **08** advising, advisory **10** consulting **11** counselling **12** consultatory, recommending

**consume**
◇ *containment indicator*
**03** eat, gut, use **04** burn, grip, kill, pine, take, wear **05** drain, drink, eat up, scoff, shift, snarf, spend, touch, use up, waste **06** absorb, bezzle, burn up, damage, devour, expend, gobble, guzzle, ingest, murder, obsess, punish, ravage, tuck in **07** deplete, destroy, discuss, drink up, engross, exhaust, swallow, torment, utilize **08** demolish, dominate, lay waste, mainline, squander, wear down **09** devastate, dispose of, dissipate, go through, overwhelm, polish off, preoccupy **10** annihilate, get through, monopolize **11** fritter away **12** get stuck into

**consumer**
**04** user **05** buyer, mouth **06** client, patron **07** end-user, shopper **08** customer **09** purchaser

**consuming**
◇ *containment indicator*
**07** wasting, wearing **08** gripping **09** absorbing, devouring, obsessive **10** compelling, destroying, dominating, engrossing, immoderate, tormenting **12** monopolizing, overwhelming, preoccupying

**consummate**
**03** cap, end **05** crown, exact, total, utter **06** finish, fulfil, gifted, made up, superb **07** achieve, execute, perfect, perform, realize, skilled, supreme **08** absolute, complete, conclude, finished, polished, superior, ultimate **09** competent, exemplary, matchless, practised, terminate **10** accomplish, effectuate, proficient **11** replenished, unqualified **12** accomplished, transcendent **13** distinguished

**consummation**
**03** end **04** pass **06** finish **07** capping **08** crowning **09** execution **10** completion, conclusion, fulfilment, perfection **11** achievement, culmination, performance, realization, termination **12** effectuation **13** actualization **14** accomplishment

**consumption**
**02** TB **05** waste **06** eating **07** decline, using-up **08** draining, drinking, guzzling, scoffing, spending **09** depletion, devouring, expending, ingestion, tucking-in **10** absorption, exhaustion, swallowing **11** expenditure, squandering, utilization **12** going-through, tuberculosis **14** getting-through

**contact**
**03** fax **04** call, ring **05** e-mail, phone, reach, touch, union **06** friend, impact, notify **07** apply to, get onto, meeting, speak to, sponsor, taction, write to **08** approach, junction, relation, relative, tangency, touching **09** get hold of, proximity, telephone **10** connection, contiguity **11** association, contingence **12** acquaintance, get through to **13** communication, juxtaposition **14** get in touch with **15** communicate with

**• in contact with**
**02** to **04** into

**contagion**
**06** poison **08** tainting **09** infection, pollution **10** corruption, defilement **13** contamination

**contagious**
**07** noxious **08** catching, epidemic, pandemic **09** spreading **10** compelling, infectious **12** communicable, irresistible **13** transmissible, transmittable

**contain**
◇ *containment indicator*
◇ *hidden indicator*
**04** curb, hold, seat, stop, take **05** carry, check, limit **06** embody, enseam, enwomb, hold in, rein in, retain, stifle, take in **07** control, embrace, enclose, include, involve, repress **08** comprise, keep back, restrain, suppress **09** keep under **10** have inside **11** accommodate, incorporate, keep in check

**container**
◇ *hidden indicator*
**06** holder, vessel **10** receptacle, repository

*Containers include:*

**03** bag, bin, box, can, cup, jar, jug, keg, mug, pan, pot, tin, tub, urn, vat
**04** bowl, case, cask, dish, drum, Esky®, pack, pail, sack, silo, tank, tube, vase, vial, well
**05** basin, chest, churn, crate, crock, glass, purse, trunk
**06** barrel, basket, beaker, bottle, bucket, carton, casket, hamper, kettle, locker, packet, punnet, teapot, trough, tureen
**07** cistern, dustbin, pannier, pitcher, tumbler
**08** canister, cauldron, cylinder, suitcase, tea caddy, tea chest, waste bin
**09** water-butt

**containment**
**04** curb **05** check **07** control **08** stifling **09** restraint **10** limitation, repression **11** suppression

**contaminate**
◇ *anagram indicator*
**04** foul, harm, soil **05** decay, spike, spoil, stain, sully, taint **06** debase, defile, infect **07** corrupt, deprave, pollute, tarnish, vitiate **10** adulterate, make impure

**contamination**
◇ *anagram indicator*
**04** harm **05** decay, filth, stain, taint **07** soiling, tarnish **08** foulness, impurity, spoiling, sullying **09** infection, pollution, vitiation **10** corruption, debasement, defilement, rottenness **11** desecration **12** adulteration

**contemplate**
**04** muse, plan, view **05** spell, study, weigh **06** behold, design, expect, intend, look at, ponder, regard, survey **07** dwell on, examine, foresee, inspect, observe, propose, weigh up **08** cogitate, consider, envisage, meditate, mull over, ruminate **09** reflect on **10** deliberate, have in mind, have in view, scrutinize, think about **11** have an eye to **13** give thought to

**contemplation**
**04** muse, view **05** dwell, study **06** gazing, musing, regard, survey **07** purpose, thought, viewing **08** mind's eye, scrutiny, weighing **09** beholding, pondering, regarding **10** cogitation, inspection, meditation, reflection, rumination, weighing up **11** cerebration, examination, mulling-over, observation **12** deliberation, recollection **13** consideration

**contemplative**
**04** rapt **06** intent, musing **07** pensive **08** cerebral **10** meditative, reflective, ruminative, thoughtful **13** deep in thought, introspective

**contemporaneous**
**06** coeval **10** coetaneous, coexistent, concurrent **11** synchronous **12** simultaneous

**contemporary**
**02** AD **03** now **04** peer **05** equal **06** coeval, fellow, latest, modern, recent, today's, trendy, with it **07** current, partner, present, topical **08** confrère, co-worker, parallel, up-to-date **09** associate, colleague **10** avant-garde, coetaneous, coexistent, collateral, concurrent, futuristic, new-fangled, present-day

**11** counterpart, fashionable, present-time, synchronous, ultra-modern
**12** simultaneous **13** up-to-the-minute
**14** contemporanean
**15** contemporaneous

**contempt**
**05** scorn **06** hatred **07** disdain, dislike, mockery, neglect **08** derision, despisal, disgrace, loathing, ridicule
**09** contumely, dishonour, disregard
**10** disrespect **11** detestation
**13** condescension
**• expression of contempt**
**02** ho **03** ach, aha, bah, boo, foh, gup, hoa, hoh, mew, och, pho, poh, rot, sis, yah **04** booh, nuts, phew, phoh, pish, poof, pooh, push, quep, rats, tush, yech
**05** pshaw, snoot, sucks! **06** phooey
**10** sucks to you!
**• sign of contempt**
**04** fico, figo **05** sneer **11** Harvey Smith
**• term of contempt**
**03** cit, dog, nit **05** sprat **06** monkey
**07** jive-ass **08** whipster

**contemptible**
**03** low **04** base, mean, vile **05** petty
**06** abject, cruddy, ornery, paltry, scurvy, shabby **07** hateful, pelting, pitiful **08** pitiable, shameful, unworthy, wretched **09** loathsome, miserable, worthless **10** degenerate, despicable, detestable, lamentable **11** ignominious
**• contemptible person**
**04** crud, scut, snot, toad **05** crumb, diddy, droob, snipe, squit, twerp
**06** fellow, louser **07** dogbolt, hangdog
**08** dirty dog, scullion, whiffler

**contemptuous**
**05** tossy **06** snorty **07** cynical, haughty, jeering, mocking
**08** arrogant, derisive, derisory, insolent, scornful, sneering
**09** insulting, withering **10** despiteful, disdainful, dispiteous
**12** contumelious, supercilious
**13** condescending, disrespectful, high and mighty

**contend**
**03** vie, war **04** aver, cope, deal, face, hold, wage **05** argue, brave, claim, clash, fight, rival, state **06** affirm, allege, assert, battle, combat, debate, oppose, reckon, strive, tackle, tussle
**07** address, agonize, compete, contest, declare, dispute, grapple, profess, wrestle **08** conflict, face up to, maintain, militate, struggle
**09** challenge **10** asseverate, meet head on **11** come to grips, come to terms

**content**
◇ *hidden indicator*
**04** ease, gist, glad, load, size, text
**05** happy, ideas, items, parts, peace, theme, topic **06** amount, at ease, be glad, burden, humour, matter, pacify, please, soothe, volume **07** appease, be happy, chapter, comfort, delight, essence, gratify, indulge, meaning, measure, placate, pleased, satisfy, section, subject, willing **08** capacity, cheerful, contents, division, elements, gladness, material, pleasure, serenity
**09** be pleased, contented, fulfilled, happiness, satisfied, substance, unworried **10** components, equanimity, fulfilment, proportion, untroubled **11** comfortable, contentment, ingredients
**12** cheerfulness, constituents, peacefulness, satisfaction, significance, things inside
**13** gratification, subject matter
**14** component parts **15** what is contained
**• remove contents**
**03** gut **05** empty **10** disembowel

**contented**
**04** glad **05** happy **07** content, perfect, pleased, relaxed **08** cheerful
**09** fulfilled, satisfied, unworried
**10** untroubled **11** comfortable

**contention**
**04** bate, case, plea, toil, view **05** claim, stand, sturt, words **06** belief, debate, enmity, jangle, notion, strife, theory, thesis **07** discord, dispute, feeling, feuding, opinion, rivalry **08** argument, position, struggle **09** assertion, hostility, intuition, judgement, logomachy, viewpoint, wrangling
**10** conviction, difference, differency, dissension, impression, persuasion
**11** controversy, point of view
**12** disagreement

**contentious**
**07** hostile **08** captious, disputed, doubtful, perverse **09** bellicose, bickering, debatable, polemical, querulous **10** debateable, disputable, pugnacious **11** dissentious, quarrelsome, tendentious
**12** antagonistic, questionable
**13** argumentative, controversial

**contentment**
**04** ease **05** peace **07** comfort, content **08** gladness, pleasure, serenity **09** happiness **10** equanimity, fulfilment **11** complacency
**12** cheerfulness, peacefulness, satisfaction **13** contentedness, gratification

**contest**
**03** vie, war **04** bout, deny, game, jump, race **05** doubt, event, fight, match, pairs, set-to, vying **06** battle, combat, debate, defend, oppose, pingle, refute, strife, strive, tussle
**07** brabble, compete, contend, dispute, matchup **08** argument, concours, conflict, litigate, object to, question, skirmish, struggle
**09** challenge, emulation, encounter, try to beat **10** tournament
**11** competition, controversy **12** argue against, championship, contestation
**• in contest against**
**04** with
**• part of contest**
**03** leg

**contestant**
**05** rival **06** player, prizer **07** entrant
**08** aspirant, opponent **09** adversary, candidate, contender, disputant
**10** competitor **11** participant

**context**
**07** factors, setting **08** position
**09** connexion, framework, situation
**10** background, conditions, connection **12** surroundings
**13** circumstances **14** state of affairs

**contiguous**
**04** near, next **05** close **06** beside
**07** vicinal **08** abutting, adjacent, touching **09** adjoining, bordering
**10** coadjacent, conjoining, juxtaposed, tangential
**12** conterminous, neighbouring
**15** juxtapositional

**continent**
**08** mainland, virtuous **09** temperate
**10** terra firma

*Continents:*

**04** Asia
**06** Africa, Europe
**07** Oceania
**10** Antarctica
**11** Australasia
**12** North America, South America

**contingency**
**05** event **06** chance **07** contact
**08** accident, fortuity, incident, juncture
**09** emergency, happening
**10** incidental, randomness **11** chance event, eventuality, possibility, uncertainty **13** arbitrariness

**contingent**
**03** set **04** band, body **05** based, batch, group, party, quota, share
**07** company, mission, section, subject
**08** division, relative **09** dependant, dependent **10** accidental, complement, delegation, deputation, detachment **11** conditional
**15** representatives

**continual**
**05** still **07** abiding, eternal, regular
**08** constant, frequent, repeated
**09** incessant, perpetual, recurrent, unceasing **10** persistent, repetitive
**11** everlasting **12** interminable

**continually**
**03** e'er **04** ever **06** always **07** forever, non-stop, on and on **09** endlessly, eternally, regularly **10** all the time, constantly, frequently, habitually, repeatedly **11** ceaselessly, incessantly, perpetually, recurrently
**12** interminably, persistently
**13** everlastingly

**continuance**
**04** stay, term **06** period **07** abiding, durance **08** duration, dwelling, standing **09** endurance
**10** permanence **11** adjournment, maintenance, persistence, protraction
**12** continuation

**continuation**
**06** return, sequel **07** renewal **08** addition, progress **09** extension **10** carrying-on, resumption, supplement **11** development, furtherance, lengthening, maintenance, persistence, protraction **12** prolongation **13** starting again **14** recommencement
• **in continuance**
**02** on

**continue**
**02** on **04** dure, go on, hold, keep, last, rest, stay **05** abide, renew **06** endure, extend, hold on, keep on, keep up, move on, pursue, remain, resume **07** adjourn, carry on, hold out, not stop, persist, press on, proceed, project, prolong, stick at, subsist, survive, sustain **08** lengthen, maintain, progress **09** keep going, persevere, persist in, soldier on **10** begin again, keep moving, keep on with, press ahead, recommence, start again **11** keep walking, persevere in, take up again **12** proceed again **14** keep travelling

**continuity**
**04** flow **07** linkage **08** cohesion, sequence, synaphea **09** synapheia **10** connection, succession **11** progression **14** continuousness

**continuous**
◇ *hidden indicator*
◇ *juxtaposition indicator*
**05** solid **07** endless, flowing, lasting, non-stop, running **08** constant, extended, seamless, unbroken, unending **09** ceaseless, continued, prolonged, unceasing **10** persistent, relentless **11** consecutive, never-ending, not stopping, unremitting, with no let-up **12** interminable **13** uninterrupted, without a break

**continuously**
◇ *hidden indicator*
◇ *juxtaposition indicator*
**04** away **08** together **09** endlessly **10** all the time, at a stretch, constantly **11** ceaselessly **12** interminably, persistently, relentlessly **13** consecutively, unremittingly **15** twenty-four seven, uninterruptedly

**contort**
◇ *anagram indicator*
**03** wry **04** knot, warp **05** gnarl, twist **06** deform, squirm, wrench, writhe **07** distort, screw up, wreathe, wriggle **08** misshape **09** convolute, disfigure **14** bend out of shape

**contortionist**
**07** acrobat, gymnast, tumbler **08** balancer, stuntman **09** aerialist **10** rope-dancer, rope-walker, stuntwoman **11** equilibrist, funambulist **12** posture-maker, somersaulter **13** posture-master, trapeze artist

**contour**
**04** form **05** curve, lines, shape **06** aspect, figure, relief **07** isobase, isobath, outline, profile, surface **08** contorno, tournure **09** character **10** silhouette

**contraband**
**08** hot goods, smuggled **09** smuggling **10** prohibited **11** banned goods, bootlegging **13** unlawful goods **14** illegal traffic **15** prohibited goods, proscribed goods

**contraceptive**

*Contraceptives include:*

**03** cap, IUD
**04** coil, IUCD, loop, pill, safe
**06** condom, johnny, rubber, sheath, Vimule®
**07** Femidom®, johnnie, the pill
**08** Dutch cap, minipill
**09** birth pill, diaphragm, prolactin
**10** Lippes loop, protective
**11** Depo-Provera®
**12** female condom, French letter, prophylactic

**contract**
◇ *tail deletion indicator*
**03** get **04** bond, deal, knit, make, pact **05** agree, catch, purse, tense **06** draw in, engage, lessen, narrow, pick up, pledge, reduce, settle, shrink, take in, treaty **07** abridge, appalto, arrange, bargain, betroth, compact, curtail, develop, promise, shorten, shrivel, tighten, wrinkle **08** compress, condense, covenant, decrease, diminish, handfast **09** agreement, betrothal, champerty, concordat, constrict, indenture, negotiate, stipulate, succumb to, undertake **10** abbreviate, agree terms, commitment, constringe, convention, engagement, go down with, settlement **11** arrangement, make shorter, make smaller, stipulation, transaction **12** come down with **13** become ill with, become shorter, become smaller, understanding **14** be taken ill with
• **contract out**
**06** get out **07** drop out, farm out **08** delegate, withdraw **09** outsource **11** subcontract **12** give to others, pass to others

**contraction**
**06** shrink **07** systole, tensing **09** drawing-in, lessening, narrowing, reduction, shrinkage **10** abridgment, shortening, tightening **11** abridgement, astringency, compression, curtailment, shrivelling **12** abbreviation, constriction **13** shortened form

**contradict**
**03** nay **04** deny **05** argue, belie, rebut **06** impugn, naysay, negate, oppose, refute, threap, threep **07** confute, counter, dispute, gainsay, outface, sublate **08** contrary, traverse **09** argue with, challenge, clash with, disaffirm, go against **12** be at odds with, conflict with, contrast with, disagree with **14** fly in the face of

**contradiction**
**04** odds **05** clash **06** denial **07** démenti, dispute, paradox **08** antilogy, antinomy, conflict, negation, rebuttal, traverse, variance **09** challenge **10** antithesis, opposition, refutation **11** confutation, incongruity **12** disagreement **13** disaffirmance, inconsistency **14** disaffirmation **15** counter-argument

**contradictory**
**07** opposed **08** clashing, contrary, opposing, opposite **09** dissonant, repugnant **10** discordant, discrepant **11** conflicting, dissentient, incongruous, paradoxical **12** antagonistic, antithetical, incompatible, inconsistent **14** irreconcilable

**contralto**
**01** c **04** alto

**contraption**
**03** rig **05** gizmo, waldo **06** device, doodad, doodah, doofer, gadget, widget **07** machine **08** thingamy **09** apparatus, invention, mechanism **11** contrivance, thingamybob, thingamyjig **12** what's-its-name

**contrary**
◇ *reversal indicator*
**05** annoy **06** oppose **07** adverse, awkward, counter, hostile, opposed, reverse, stroppy, wayward **08** clashing, converse, opposing, opposite, perverse, stubborn **09** difficult, obstinate **10** antipathic, antithesis, discrepant, headstrong, overthwart, refractory **11** conflicting, disobliging, intractable **12** antagonistic, cantankerous, cross-grained, incompatible, inconsistent **13** unco-operative **14** irreconcilable
• **contrary to**
**10** at odds with **14** at variance with, in conflict with, in opposition to
• **on the contrary**
◇ *reversal indicator*
**08** not at all **09** far from it, per contra **10** conversely, e contrario **11** al contrario, au contraire **14** just the reverse **15** just the opposite, quite the reverse, tout au contraire

**contrast**
**04** foil **05** clash **06** differ, oppose, relief, set-off **07** compare **08** be at odds, chiasmus, conflict, disagree, opposite **09** disparity, go against **10** antithesis, comparison, contradict, difference, divergence, opposition **11** counter-view, distinction, distinguish **12** be at variance, be in conflict, discriminate **13** counterchange, differentiate, dissimilarity, dissimilitude **14** contraposition **15** differentiation
• **in contrast to**
**09** as against, opposed to **10** rather than **14** in opposition to

**contravene**
**04** defy **05** break, flout **06** breach, oppose **07** disobey, violate **08** infringe **10** transgress

**contravention**
**06** breach **08** breaking **09** violation **11** dereliction **12** infringement **13** transgression

**contretemps**
**04** tiff **05** brush, clash, hitch **06** mishap **08** accident, argument, squabble **10** difficulty, misfortune **11** predicament **12** disagreement, misadventure

**contribute**
**04** edit, give, help, make **05** add to, cause, endow, grant, write **06** bestow, chip in, create, donate, kick in, lead to, submit, supply **07** chuck in, compile, compose, conduce, furnish, prepare, present, produce, promote, provide **08** generate, occasion, result in **09** originate, subscribe **10** bring about, give rise to, make happen **11** be a factor in, play a part in **13** give a donation

**contribution**
**03** tax **04** gift, item, koha, levy, mite, shot **05** grant, input, paper, piece, story **06** column, report, review **07** article, feature, handout, present **08** addition, bestowal, donation, gratuity, offering **09** endowment **10** feuilleton, proportion, submission **11** Peter's pence **12** subscription **14** superannuation

**contributor**
**05** donor, giver **06** author, backer, critic, patron, writer **07** sponsor **08** compiler, reporter, reviewer **09** columnist, freelance, supporter **10** benefactor, journalist, subscriber **13** correspondent

**contrite**
**05** sorry **06** humble **07** ashamed **08** penitent, red-faced **09** chastened, regretful, repentant **10** remorseful **11** guilt-ridden, penitential

**contrition**
**05** shame **06** regret, sorrow **07** remorse **09** penitence **10** repentance **11** compunction, humiliation **12** self-reproach

**contrivance**
**03** art, gin **04** gear, plan, plot, ploy, ruse, tool **05** dodge, gizmo, shift, trick **06** design, device, doodad, doodah, doofer, engine, gadget, scheme, tactic, widget **07** machine, project **08** artifice, intrigue, thingamy **09** apparatus, appliance, equipment, expedient, implement, invention, mechanism, stratagem **10** compassing **11** contraption, imagination, machination, thingamybob, thingamyjig **12** excogitation, what's-its-name

**contrive**
◇ *anagram indicator*
**04** brew, cook, form, plan, plot, work **05** frame, set up, spend, weave **06** create, cut out, design, devise, effect, engine, invent, manage, scheme, tamper, wangle **07** arrange, compass, concoct, imagine, succeed **08** conceive, engineer, find a way **09** construct, fabricate, manoeuvre **10** bring about, understand **11** orchestrate, stage-manage

**contrived**
◇ *anagram indicator*
**05** false, hokey, set-up **06** forced **08** laboured, mannered, overdone, strained **09** elaborate, unnatural **10** artificial, factitious

**control**
**03** ren, rin, run **04** curb, dial, head, keep, knob, lead, rein, ride, rule, sway, work **05** brake, check, lever, limit, power, reign **06** adjust, button, charge, direct, govern, make go, manage, reduce, subdue, switch, verify **07** command, contain, mastery, monitor, operate, oversee, repress **08** dominate, guidance, hold back, modulate, regulate, restrain, restrict **09** authority, be the boss, constrain, constrict, direction, dominance, hindrance, influence, oversight, reduction, restraint, supervise, supremacy **10** constraint, discipline, government, impediment, instrument, limitation, management, perstringe, regulation, repression, run the show **11** call the tune, keep in check, preside over, restriction, self-control, superintend, supervision **12** be in charge of, call the shots, jurisdiction, rule the roost **13** be in the saddle, self-restraint **14** pull the strings, put the brakes on, self-discipline **15** superintendence, wear the trousers
• **lose control**
**04** slip, spaz **05** spazz **07** flip out
• **numerical control**
**02** NC

**controversial**
**04** moot **07** at issue, eristic, polemic **08** disputed, doubtful **09** debatable, polemical **10** disputable **11** contentious, tendentious **12** questionable **13** argumentative

**controversy**
**06** debate, strife **07** discord, dispute, polemic, quarrel, wrangle **08** argument, friction, squabble **10** contention, debatement, discussion, dissension, war of words **11** altercation **12** cause célèbre, disagreement

**contusion**
**04** bump, lump, mark **05** knock **06** bruise, injury **07** blemish **08** swelling **10** ecchymosis **13** discoloration

**conundrum**
**05** guess, poser **06** enigma, puzzle, riddle, teaser **07** anagram, problem **08** quandary, word game **10** difficulty **11** brainteaser **12** brain-twister

**conurbation**
**04** city, town **06** ghetto **08** big smoke, downtown, precinct, suburbia **09** inner city, metroplex, urban area **10** city centre, cosmopolis, metropolis, micropolis, pentapolis **11** megalopolis, urban sprawl **12** municipality **13** urban district **14** concrete jungle

**convalesce**
**05** rally **06** pick up, revive **07** get well, improve, recover **09** get better **10** recuperate **11** get stronger, pull through

**convalescence**
**08** recovery **09** anastasis **11** improvement, restoration **12** recuperation **13** getting better **14** rehabilitation

**convene**
**04** call, meet **05** bring, rally **06** gather, muster, summon **07** collect, convoke **08** assemble **10** congregate **12** call together, come together **13** bring together

**convenience**
**03** bog, lav, loo, use **04** help **06** behoof, device, gadget, toilet **07** amenity, benefit, fitness, service, utility **08** facility, lavatory, resource **09** advantage, appliance, commodity, ease of use, handiness, usability **10** expediency, usefulness **11** propinquity, suitability, water closet **12** availability **13** accessibility, accommodation, opportuneness **14** propitiousness, serviceability **15** appropriateness
*See also* **toilet**

**convenient**
**03** fit **04** easy, gain, hend **05** handy **06** at hand, fitted, nearby, suited, timely, useful **07** adapted, favored, fitting, helpful **08** favoured, handsome, suitable **09** available, expedient, opportune, well-timed **10** accessible, beneficial, commodious, near at hand **11** appropriate, close at hand, within reach **12** labour-saving **13** advantageable **14** at your disposal

**conveniently**
**04** well **05** patly **06** at hand, nearby **08** suitably, usefully **09** helpfully **10** accessibly, near at hand **11** close at hand, within reach **13** appropriately

**convent**
**04** cite **05** abbey, house **06** fratry, friary, priory, summon **07** convene, fratery, nunnery **08** cloister **09** monastery
*See also* **monastery**

**convention**
**03** use **04** bond, code, deal, pact **05** ethos, mores, synod, usage **06** accord, custom, treaty **07** bargain, compact, council, fashion, meeting **08** assembly, ceremony, conclave, congress, contract, covenant, practice,

protocol **09** agreement, Blackwood, concordat, delegates, etiquette, formality, gathering, propriety, punctilio, tradition **10** commitment, conference, engagement, settlement **11** arrangement, convocation, transaction **12** matter of form **13** understanding **15** representatives

**conventional**
**04** lame **05** nomic, trite, usual **06** common, formal, normal, proper, ritual **07** correct, pompier, regular, routine, uptight **08** accepted, copybook, expected, ordinary, orthodox, received, standard, straight **09** bourgeois, customary, hidebound, prevalent **10** conformist, mainstream, pedestrian, prevailing, unoriginal **11** commonplace, respectable, stereotyped, traditional **12** conservative, run-of-the-mill **14** common-or-garden

**conventionally**
**07** usually **08** commonly, formally, normally **09** regularly, routinely **10** ordinarily **13** traditionally

**converge**
**04** form, join, mass, meet **05** focus, merge, unite **06** gather **07** close in, combine **08** approach, coincide **09** intersect **11** concentrate, move towards **12** come together

**convergence**
**05** union **07** meeting, merging **08** approach, blending, junction **10** confluence **11** coincidence, combination **12** intersection **13** concentration

**conversant**
**• conversant with**
**08** versed in **09** skilled in **10** apprised of, au fait with **11** practised in **12** familiar with, proficient in **13** experienced in, informed about **14** acquainted with

**conversation**
◇ *homophone indicator*
**03** rap **04** chat, talk **05** board, convo, crack, craic, wongi **06** confab, gossip, natter, yabber **07** chinwag, purpose **08** chitchat, colloquy, cosy chat, dialogue, exchange, parlance, question, speaking **09** discourse, small talk, table talk, tête-à-tête **10** discussion, pillow talk **12** heart-to-heart **13** communication, interlocution

**conversational**
◇ *homophone indicator*
**06** casual, chatty **07** relaxed **08** informal **09** talkative **10** colloquial **13** communicative

**converse**
◇ *homophone indicator*
**04** chat, talk **05** speak, wongi **06** confer, dialog, gossip, natter, reason, relate **07** chatter, commune, counter, discuss, obverse, propose, purpose, reverse **08** chitchat, collogue, colloquy, contrary, dialogue, opposing, opposite, question, reversed **09** discourse **10** antithesis, chew the fat, chew the rag, colloquize, transposed **11** communicate **12** antithetical **13** other way round

**conversely**
**09** e converso, obversely **10** contrarily **12** contrariwise **13** on the contrary **14** antithetically, on the other hand

**conversion**
◇ *anagram indicator*
**06** change, switch **07** rebirth, turning **08** exchange, metanoia, mutation **09** preaching, reshaping **10** adaptation, adjustment, alteration, conviction, persuasion **11** proselytism, reformation, remodelling, translation **12** modification, regeneration, substitution **13** customization, metamorphosis, transmutation **14** evangelization, reconstruction, reorganization, transformation **15** proselytization, transfiguration

**convert**
◇ *anagram indicator*
**03** put **04** goal, make, turn **05** adapt, alter **06** adjust, change, modify, mutate, reform, revise, switch **07** rebuild, remodel, reshape, restyle, win over **08** adherent, believer, convince, disciple, exchange, go over to, move over, neophyte, persuade, transfer, turn into **09** bring over, customize, new person, proselyte, refashion, transform, transmute **10** evangelize, reorganize, substitute, switch from **11** jump the dyke, loup the dyke, proselytize, reconstruct, restructure, transfigure **12** metamorphose **13** change beliefs, changed person **14** change religion

**convertible**
◇ *anagram indicator*
**06** ragtop **07** soft top **09** adaptable, landaulet **10** adjustable, changeable, modifiable, permutable **11** landaulette **12** exchangeable **15** interchangeable

**convex**
**04** nowy **05** bombé **07** bulging, gibbous, rounded **08** swelling **09** curved out **10** bow-fronted **11** protuberant **15** bending outwards

**convey**
**03** put, tip **04** bear, have, lead, move, pipe, send, take, tell, wain **05** bring, carry, drive, fetch, guide, shift, steal **06** hand on, impart, import, pass on, relate, reveal **07** channel, conduct, deliver, express, forward, mediate, present **08** announce, disclose, transfer, transmit **09** make known, transport **11** communicate

**conveyance**
**03** bus, cab, car, sac, van **04** cart, taxi **05** coach, grant, lorry, truck, wagon **06** ceding **07** bicycle, express, transit, vehicle **08** carriage, delivery, granting, mortgage, movement, transfer **09** transport **10** bequeathal, motorcycle **11** consignment **12** transference, transmission **13** transportance **14** transportation
*See also* **aircraft**; **bicycle**; **car**; **carriage**; **ship**

**convict**
**03** con, lag **05** crime, crook, felon, judge **06** canary, forçat, inmate **07** approve, attaint, condemn, culprit, old hand, reprove, villain **08** criminal, imprison, jailbird, offender, prisoner, sentence, yardbird **09** wrongdoer **10** canary-bird, emancipist, find guilty, lawbreaker

**conviction**
**04** view **05** creed, faith, prior, tenet **06** belief **07** fervour, opinion **08** firmness, sentence **09** assurance, certainty, certitude, judgement, principle **10** confidence, persuasion, plerophory **11** earnestness, plerophoria **12** condemnation, imprisonment, satisfaction

**convince**
**04** sell, sway **06** assure, induce, prompt **07** prove to, resolve, satisfy, win over **08** persuade, perswade, talk into, talk over **09** bring home, influence **10** bring round **11** prevail upon

**convincing**
**06** cogent, likely **07** certain, telling **08** credible, forceful, luculent, positive, powerful, pregnant, probable **09** plausible **10** compelling, conclusive, conclusory, impressive, persuasive **12** satisfactory

**convincingly**
**08** cogently, credibly **09** all ends up, plausibly, tellingly **10** forcefully, powerfully **12** compellingly, conclusively, impressively, persuasively

**convivial**
**04** boon **05** jolly, merry **06** genial, hearty, jovial, lively, social **07** affable, cordial, festive **08** cheerful, friendly, sociable **09** fun-loving **11** Anacreontic

**conviviality**
**03** fun **05** cheer, mirth **06** gaiety **07** jollity **08** bonhomie **09** festivity, geniality, joviality **10** cordiality, liveliness **11** good feeling, merrymaking, sociability **12** friendliness **14** goodfellowship

**convocation**
**04** diet **05** forum, synod **07** council, meeting **08** assembly, conclave, congress **10** assemblage, conference, convention **12** congregation, forgathering

**convoluted**
◇ *anagram indicator*
**04** mazy **07** complex, unclear, winding, writhen, wrythen **08** involved, tortuous, twisting **09** convolute, intricate, Vitruvian **10** meandering **11** complicated

**convolution**
**04** coil, fold, loop, turn **05** gyrus, helix, twist, whorl **06** spiral **07** coiling, winding **08** curlicue **09** intricacy, sinuosity **10** complexity
**11** involvement, sinuousness
**12** complication, entanglement, tortuousness

**convoy**
**04** line **05** fleet, group, guard, train
**06** escort **07** company **10** attendance, protection

**convulse**
◇ *anagram indicator*
**04** jerk **05** seize **07** disturb, shudder
**08** unsettle **10** suffer a fit **14** shake violently, suffer a seizure

**convulsion**
**03** fit, tic **05** cramp, ictus, spasm
**06** attack, furore, tremor, tumult, unrest **07** seizure, turmoil **08** disorder, eruption, laughter, outburst, paroxysm, upheaval **09** agitation, commotion
**10** turbulence **11** contraction, disturbance **13** electric shock

**convulsive**
**05** jerky **06** fitful **07** violent
**08** sporadic **09** spasmodic
**11** spasmodical **12** uncontrolled
• **convulsive disorder**
**03** DTs **15** delirium tremens

**cook**
◇ *anagram indicator*
**02** do **03** pan **04** burn, chef, fake, heat, make, peep, ruin, warm **05** fryer, put on, spoil **06** doctor, greasy, overdo
**07** babbler, concoct, falsify, prepare, scare up, underdo **08** overcook, rustle up **09** cuisinier, improvise, undercook
**11** put together **13** throw together
*See also* **chef**

*Cooking methods include:*

**03** fry
**04** bake, boil, sear, stew
**05** broil, brown, curry, grill, poach, roast, sauté, steam, toast
**06** braise, coddle, flambé, pan-fry, simmer
**07** deep-fry, parboil, stir-fry
**08** barbecue, pot-roast, scramble
**09** casserole, char-grill, fricassee, microwave, oven-roast, spit-roast
**10** flame-grill

• **cook up**
◇ *anagram indicator*
**04** brew, edit, plan, plot **06** devise, invent, make up, scheme **07** concoct, falsify, prepare **08** contrive **09** fabricate

**cooked**
◇ *anagram indicator*
• **lightly cooked**
**04** rare, rear

**cookery**

*Cookery styles include:*

**04** Thai
**05** Greek, halal, Irish, mezze, rural, tapas, vegan, Welsh
**06** French, fusion, German, Indian, kosher, Tex-Mex
**07** African, British, Chinese, Eastern, English, Italian, Mexican, seafood, Spanish, Turkish
**08** American, fast food, Japanese, Scottish
**09** Cantonese, Caribbean, Malaysian, Provençal
**10** cordon bleu, Far Eastern, gluten-free, Indonesian, Pacific Rim, vegetarian
**11** home cooking, lean cuisine
**12** haute cuisine
**13** Mediterranean, Middle Eastern
**14** cuisine minceur
**15** nouvelle cuisine

*Cookery-related terms include:*

**03** Aga, dip, gut, hob, ice
**04** chef, chop, cook, cure, dice, mash, oven, rise, whip
**05** baste, brown, carve, chill, chump, curry, daube, devil, dress, glaze, grate, knead, mince, mould, press, purée, score, shave, smoke, steep, stuff, whisk
**06** batter, blanch, de-bone, entrée, fillet, fondue, infuse, kosher, leaven, recipe, reduce, season, spread
**07** garnish, nibbles, proving, starter, tandoor, topping
**08** cookbook, devilled, marinade, marinate, preserve
**09** antipasto, percolate, reduction, tenderize
**10** caramelize
**11** hors d'oeuvre

**Cook Islands**
**03** COK

**cool**
**03** ace, fan, ice **04** calm, chic, cold, iced, keel, mega, neat **05** abate, allay, aloof, brill, chill, crisp, fresh, great, nervy, nippy, parky, poise, quiet, smart, tepid **06** breeze, breezy, caller, chilly, dampen, freeze, frigid, frosty, lessen, placid, poised, quench, reduce, sedate, temper, trendy, wicked **07** assuage, bracing, chilled, control, distant, draught, elegant, get cold, ice-cold, relaxed, stylish, subside, unmoved
**08** calmness, coldness, composed, coolness, diminish, draughty, impudent, laid-back, lukewarm, make cold, moderate, reserved, smashing, terrific, turn cold **09** admirable, apathetic, collected, composure, crispness, excellent, fantastic, freshness, get colder, impassive, nippiness, sangfroid, unexcited, unruffled, wonderful **10** acceptable, become cold, chilliness, make colder, marvellous, refreshing, streetwise, turn colder, unfriendly, untroubled
**11** fashionable, half-hearted, indifferent, level-headed, refrigerate, self-control, standoffish, undisturbed, unemotional, unexcitable, unflappable, unflustered, unperturbed, unwelcoming **12** air-condition, become colder, second to none, uninterested, unresponsive
**13** collectedness, defervescence, defervescency, disinterested, dispassionate, imperturbable, self-possessed, sophisticated **14** out of this world, self-discipline, self-possession, unapprehensive, unenthusiastic
**15** cool as a cucumber, uncommunicative, undemonstrative

**cooler** *see* **jail, gaol**

**cooling**
**08** chilling, freezing **10** refreshing
**11** refrigerant, ventilation
**13** defervescence, defervescency, refrigeration, refrigerative, refrigeratory **15** air-conditioning

**coolly**
**06** calmly, coldly **07** quietly **08** frostily, placidly, sedately **09** distantly
**10** composedly, impudently, reservedly **11** collectedly, impassively, unexcitably, unexcitedly
**13** apathetically, half-heartedly, imperturbably, indifferently, level-headedly, standoffishly, unemotionally
**14** uninterestedly, unresponsively
**15** dispassionately

**coop**
**03** box, mew, pen, ren, rin, rip, run
**04** cage **05** cavie, hutch, pound
**06** keavie **09** enclosure
• **coop up**
**03** pen **04** cage, shut **06** bail up, immure, keep in, lock up, shut in, shut up **07** close in, confine, enclose, impound **08** imprison, lock away
**11** incarcerate

**Cooper**
**04** Gary

**co-operate**
**03** aid **04** ally, help, play, pool
**05** share, unite **06** assist, team up
**07** combine, pitch in **08** conspire, play ball **09** play along **10** contribute, join forces **11** collaborate, participate, string along **12** band together, pull together, work together **14** pull your weight, work side by side

**co-operation**
**03** aid **04** help **05** unity **08** teamwork
**10** assistance, team spirit **11** give-and-take, helpfulness, helping hand, joint action **12** contribution, co-ordination
**13** collaboration, esprit de corps, participation **15** concerted action, concerted effort, working together

**co-operative**
**05** joint **06** shared, united **07** helpful, helping, willing **08** coactive, combined, obliging **09** assisting, compliant, concerted **10** collective, responsive, supportive **11** co-ordinated **13** accommodating, collaborative **15** working together

**co-ordinate**
**01** x, y, z **02** go **04** mesh **05** adapt, blend, match, order **06** go well, join up

07 absciss, arrange, blend in
08 abscissa, abscisse, ordinate, organize, regulate, tabulate 09 co-operate, correlate, harmonize, integrate, mix 'n' match
10 complement, go together
11 collaborate, synchronize, systematize 12 be compatible, work together 14 make compatible

**co-ordination**
07 harmony 08 blending, matching, ordering 10 ordonnance
11 arrangement, co-operation, integration 12 organization
13 collaboration, compatibility
15 complementation

**cop**
02 PC 03 get, pig, top 04 bull, head, nark 05 bizzy, bobby, catch 06 arrest, copper, obtain, rozzer 07 acquire, capture, officer 08 flatfoot
09 constable, policeman 10 bluebottle
11 policewoman 13 police officer
*See also* **police officer**
**• cop out**
04 balk, duck, shun 05 avert, avoid, dodge, elude, evade, hedge, shirk
06 bypass, escape 07 prevent 08 get out of, get round, sidestep 09 give a miss 11 abstain from, make a detour, run away from, shy away from 12 hold back from, keep away from, stay away from, steer clear of

**cope**
04 meet 05 get by, match 06 barter, make do, manage 07 carry on, chlamys, contend, pluvial, subsist, succeed, survive 08 exchange
09 encounter 10 get through
**• cope with**
04 hack 05 touch, treat 06 endure, handle, manage, take up 07 weather
08 deal with 09 encounter 11 contend with, grapple with, wrestle with
12 struggle with

**coping**
04 skew

**copious**
04 full, huge, rich 05 ample, great, large 06 bags of, lavish 07 fulsome, liberal, profuse, teeming 08 abundant, generous, numerous 09 abounding, bounteous, bountiful, extensive, luxuriant, plenteous, plentiful, redundant 11 overflowing
13 inexhaustible

**cop-out**
05 alibi, dodge, fraud 06 excuse, get-out 07 evasion, pretext 08 pretence, shirking 14 passing the buck

**copper**
01 p 02 Cu
*See also* **coin**; **police officer**

**cops** *see* **police**

**copse**
04 bush, carr, wood 05 brush, grove
06 spinny, spring 07 coppice, spinney, thicket

**copulate**
03 tup 04 mate 07 have sex 08 make love 10 fool around, get off with, make it with 11 go all the way, go to bed with

**copulation**
03 sex 06 coitus, mating 07 coition
08 congress, coupling, embraces, intimacy 09 relations 10 commixtion, love-making 15 carnal knowledge

**copy**
02 cc 03 ape, bcc, CRC, fax 04 crib, echo, fake, scan 05 clone, forge, image, issue, mimic, model, print, stuff, trace, Xerox® 06 borrow, carbon, ectype, follow, mirror, parrot, pirate, repeat, sample 07 emulate, estreat, example, forgery, imitate, pattern, replica, tracing, vidimus 08 apograph, knock-off, likeness, manifold, simulate, specimen 09 archetype, borrowing, duplicate, facsimile, imitation, photocopy, Photostat®, polygraph, replicate, reproduce, semblance
10 carbon copy, mimeograph, plagiarism, plagiarize, transcribe, transcript, triplicate 11 counterfeit, counterpart, engrossment, impersonate, replication
12 reproduction 13 transcription
14 representation 15 exemplification

**coquettish**
06 flirty 07 amorous, flighty, teasing, vampish 08 dallying, inviting
09 seductive 10 come-hither
11 flirtatious, provocative

**cord**
03 guy, tie 04 bond, flex, lace, line, link, rope 05 cable, match, twine, twist
06 bobbin, myelon, ribbon, strand, string, tendon, thread 07 funicle, service 08 bell pull, chenille
09 funiculus 10 connection, draw-string 11 navel-string 12 spinal marrow

**cordial**
04 warm 05 shrub 06 genial, hearty
07 affable, cardiac, earnest, persico, ratafia, rosolio, sincere 08 amicable, anisette, cheerful, friendly, persicot, pleasant, rosoglio, sociable
09 agreeable, heartfelt, hippocras, rosa-solis, welcoming 10 pousse-café
11 Benedictine, stimulating, warm-hearted 12 affectionate, invigorating, wholehearted 13 aqua caelestis, aurum potabile

**cordiality**
05 heart 06 warmth 07 earnest, welcome 09 affection, geniality, sincerity 10 affability, heartiness
11 sociability 12 cheerfulness, friendliness 13 agreeableness

**cordially**
06 warmly 07 affably 08 amicably, genially, sociably 10 cheerfully, pleasantly 13 warm-heartedly
14 wholeheartedly

**cordon**
04 line, ring 05 chain, fence, plant
06 column, ribbon 07 barrier

**• cordon off**
07 enclose, isolate, seal off 08 close off, encircle, fence off, separate, surround

**core**
03 key, nub 04 crux, gang, gist, lead, main, nife, runt 05 basic, heart, shift, vital 06 centre, innate, kernel, middle
07 campana, central, company, corncob, crucial, essence, nucleus, typical 08 inherent, interior
09 essential, intrinsic, principal, substance 10 barysphere, definitive, underlying 11 constituent, fundamental, nitty-gritty 12 axis cylinder, quintessence
14 characteristic

**cork**
03 lid 04 bung, plug, seal, stop
05 cover, shive, suber 07 phellem, stopper

**corm** *see* **bulb**

**cormorant**
04 shag 05 scart, skart 06 duiker, duyker, scarth, skarth 07 sea crow

**corn**
03 mow, rye, Zea 04 oats 05 grain, maize, wheat 06 barley, cereal, farina, kernel, pinole 10 arable crop, cereal crop, intoxicate

**corner**
03 cor, fix, hog, jam 04 bend, fork, hole, nook, trap, tree 05 angle, catch, crook, curve, joint, niche 06 bail up, cantle, cavity, cranny, cut off, dièdre, pickle, plight, recess, scrape
07 confine, control, crevice, hideout, retreat, straits, turning 08 block off, dominate, hardship, hideaway, hunt down, junction 09 ingleneuk, inglenook, situation, tight spot
10 monopolize, run to earth
11 predicament 12 intersection
13 nowhere to turn 15 force into a place
**• around the corner**
04 near 05 close, local 06 at hand, coming, nearby 07 close by, looming
08 imminent, in the air 09 impending
10 accessible, convenient
11 approaching, within range, within reach 12 a stone's throw, neighbouring
13 about to happen
**• cut corners**
05 skimp

**cornerstone**
03 key 04 base, coin, core 05 basis, heart, quoin 06 thrust 07 bedrock, essence, keyhole, skew-put, support
08 keystone, mainstay 09 essential, principle, skew-table 10 essentials, groundwork, skew-corbel
11 fundamental 12 fundamentals
13 alpha and omega, starting-point
14 basic principle, main ingredient
15 first principles

**Cornwall**
02 SW

**corny**
**04** dull **05** banal, horny, stale, trite **06** feeble, spammy **07** buckeye, cliché'd, maudlin, mawkish **08** clichéed, overused **09** hackneyed **11** commonplace, Mickey Mouse, sentimental, stereotyped **12** old-fashioned **13** platitudinous

**corollary**
**05** rider **06** porism, result, upshot **08** function, illation **09** deduction, induction, inference **10** conclusion, consectary, consequent **11** consequence **13** supplementary

**coronation**
**08** crowning **12** enthronement

**coronet**
**05** crown, tiara **06** cornet, diadem, wreath **07** circlet, crownet, garland

**corporal**
**03** Cpl, NCO, Nym **04** corp, naik, pall **06** actual, bodily, carnal **07** fleshly, somatic **08** concrete, material, physical, tangible **09** brigadier, corporeal **10** anatomical **11** substantial **13** lance sergeant

**corporate**
**05** joint **06** allied, common, merged, pooled, shared, united **08** combined, communal **09** concerted **10** collective, collegiate **11** amalgamated **13** collaborative

**corporation**
**04** firm, gild **05** belly, guild, house, trust **06** cartel, paunch **07** commune, company, concern, council, guildry **08** business, industry, pot-belly, township **09** authority, beer belly, syndicate **10** consortium **11** association, authorities, City Company, partnership **12** conglomerate, organization **13** burgh of barony, establishment, governing body, multinational **14** holding company
*See also* **paunch**; **stomach**

**corporeal**
**05** human, hylic **06** actual, bodily, carnal, mortal **07** fleshly **08** concrete, corporal, material, physical, tangible **11** substantial

**corps**
**01** C **02** CD **03** RAC **04** band, body, crew, team, unit **05** squad **07** brigade, company **08** division, regiment, squadron **10** contingent, detachment

**corpse**
**04** body, like, mort **05** corse, mummy, relic, stiff, zombi **06** deader, relics, zombie **07** cadaver, carcase, carcass, remains **08** dead body, skeleton **09** flatliner

**corpulent**
**03** fat **05** beefy, bulky, burly, large, obese, plump, poddy, podgy, stout, tubby **06** fleshy, portly, rotund **07** adipose, fattish **08** roly-poly **10** overweight, pot-bellied, well-padded **11** Falstaffian

**corpus**
**04** body **05** whole **08** entirety **10** collection **11** aggregation, compilation

**corral**
**03** sty **04** coop, fold **05** kraal, pound, stall **09** enclosure

**correct**
◇ *anagram indicator*
**02** OK **03** fix **04** cure, edit, jake, just, mend, okay, real, sort, true **05** amend, debug, emend, exact, right, scold, tweak **06** actual, adjust, bang on, proper, punish, rebuke, reform, remedy, revise, seemly, spot-on, strict **07** fitting, improve, precise, rectify, redress, regular, reprove, right-on, sort out **08** accepted, accurate, admonish, disabuse, faithful, flawless, put right, regulate, set right, standard, suitable, truthful, unerring **09** faultless, reprimand **10** acceptable, ameliorate, blue-pencil, discipline **11** appropriate, comme il faut, put straight, put to rights, set to rights, word-perfect **12** conventional, rehabilitate **14** counterbalance

**correction**
◇ *anagram indicator*
**05** tweak **06** rebuke, reform **07** reproof **08** equation, grafting, scolding **09** amendment, reduction, remedying, reprimand **10** adjustment, admonition, alteration, diorthosis, discipline, emendation, punishment **11** improvement, reformation **12** amelioration, chastisement, compensation, modification **13** rectification **14** rehabilitation

**corrective**
**05** penal **08** curative, punitive, remedial **09** corrigent, medicinal **10** amendatory, emendatory, palliative **11** reformatory, restorative, therapeutic **12** disciplinary **14** rehabilitative

**correctly**
◇ *anagram indicator*
**02** OK **04** okay **05** right **07** exactly, rightly **08** actually, properly, suitably **09** about east, fittingly, precisely **10** acceptably, accurately, flawlessly, unerringly **11** faultlessly **13** appropriately **14** conventionally

**correlate**
**04** link **05** agree, tally, tie in **06** equate, relate **07** compare, connect **08** analogue, interact, parallel **09** associate **10** co-ordinate, correspond **15** show a connection

**correlation**
**03** fit **04** link **10** connection **11** association, equivalence, interaction, interchange, reciprocity **12** relationship **14** correspondence **15** interdependence

**correspond**
**03** fit, pen **05** agree, match, rhyme, tally, write **06** accord, answer, concur, square **07** balance, conform, match up **08** assonate, coincide, dovetail, register **09** be similar, correlate, harmonize, represent **10** complement, sympathize **11** be analogous, communicate, fit together, keep in touch **12** be consistent, be equivalent **13** be in agreement **15** exchange letters

**correspondence**
**03** fit **04** mail, post **05** e-mail, match **07** analogy, harmony, letters, writing **08** relation **09** agreement, assonance, congruity **10** comparison, conformity, consonance, similarity **11** coincidence, concurrence, correlation, equivalence, resemblance, suitability **13** communication, comparability
*See also* **letter**

**correspondent**
**06** keypal, pen pal, writer **08** agreeing, reporter, suitable **09** answering, columnist, pen friend **10** journalist, responsive **11** contributor, responsible **12** letter-writer

**corresponding**
**04** like **07** similar, suiting **08** agreeing, matching, parallel, relative **09** accordant, analogous, answering, congruent, facsimile, identical **10** collateral, comparable, equivalent, reciprocal **12** commensurate, interrelated **13** complementary

**corridor**
**04** hall **05** aisle, lobby **07** gallery, gangway, hallway, passage **08** alleyway **09** penthouse **10** passageway

**corroborate**
**05** prove **06** attest, back up, ratify, uphold, verify **07** bear out, certify, confirm, endorse, support, sustain **08** document, evidence, underpin, validate **09** confirmed **12** authenticate, substantiate

**corroboration**
**10** validation **11** attestation, endorsement **12** confirmation, ratification, verification **14** authentication, substantiation

**corroborative**
**09** endorsing, verifying **10** confirming, evidential, supporting, supportive, validating **11** evidentiary **12** confirmative, confirmatory, verificatory **14** substantiating

**corrode**
**03** eat, rot **04** burn, etch, fret, rust **05** eat in, erode, waste **06** abrade, impair **07** consume, crumble, destroy, eat away, eat into, oxidize, tarnish **08** wear away **11** deteriorate **12** disintegrate

**corrosion**
**03** rot **04** rust **07** burning, erosion, rotting, rusting, wasting **08** abrasion **09** prerosion **10** tarnishing **13** deterioration **14** disintegration

**corrosive**
**04** acid **07** caustic, cutting, erosive, wasting, wearing **08** abrasive
**09** consuming, corroding
**11** destructive

**corrugated**
**06** fluted, folded, ridged **07** creased, grooved, rumpled, striate **08** crinkled, furrowed, wrinkled **10** channelled

**corrupt**
◇ *anagram indicator*
**03** buy, mar, rot **04** bent, evil, lure, warp **05** bribe, decay, shady, spoil, taint, venal **06** blight, bribed, buy off, canker, debase, defile, doctor, impure, infect, poison, putrid, rotten, seduce, sleazy, suborn, wicked **07** abusive, crooked, debauch, defiled, deprave, falsify, immoral, obscene, pervert, pollute, putrefy, subvert, tainted, vitiate
**08** bribable, depraved, empoison
**09** barbarize, barbarous, debauched, dishonest, dissolute, inquinate, unethical **10** adulterate, bastardize, degenerate, demoralize, fraudulent, lead astray, tamper with
**11** contaminate **12** contaminated, unprincipled, unscrupulous
**13** untrustworthy **15** be a bad influence

**corruption**
**03** rot **04** evil, vice **05** abuse, bobol, fraud, graft **06** sleaze **07** bribery, leprosy **08** impurity, iniquity, villainy
**09** depravity, extortion, pollution, shadiness **10** adaptation, alteration, debauchery, dishonesty, distortion, immorality, perversion, rottenness, subversion, wickedness **11** criminality, crookedness, degradation, subornation **12** degeneration, modification **13** contamination, sharp practice

**corset**
**04** belt, busk **05** stays **06** bodice, girdle, roll-on, shaper, waspie
**08** corselet **11** panty girdle

**cortège**
**05** suite, train **06** column, parade
**07** retinue **09** cavalcade, entourage
**10** procession

**cosh** *see* **weapon**

**cosily**
**06** safely, snugly, warmly **08** securely
**10** intimately **11** comfortably

**cosmetic**
**04** fard **05** minor **06** beauty, make-up, slight **07** shallow, surface, trivial
**08** external, skin-deep **10** maquillage, peripheral **11** beautifying, superficial

*Cosmetics include:*

**05** rouge, toner
**07** blusher, bronzer, mascara, perfume
**08** cleanser, eyeliner, face mask, face pack, lip gloss, lip liner, lipstick, panstick
**09** concealer, eye shadow, face cream
**10** face powder, foundation, kohl pencil, nail polish
**11** greasepaint, moisturizer, nail varnish
**13** eyebrow pencil, pressed powder

**cosmic**
**04** huge, mega, vast **05** large
**07** immense, in space, massive, mundane, orderly, seismic **08** colossal, enormous, infinite **09** from space, grandiose, limitless, universal, worldwide **11** measureless, significant
**12** immeasurable

**cosmonaut**
**08** lunanaut, spaceman **09** astronaut, lunarnaut, taikonaut **10** spacewoman
**14** space traveller

**cosmopolitan**
**06** urbane **07** worldly **08** cultured
**09** universal **11** broad-minded, multiracial, worldly-wise
**12** unprejudiced **13** international, multicultural, sophisticated, well-travelled

**cosmos**
**06** galaxy, nature, system, worlds
**08** creation, universe

**cosset**
**03** pet **04** baby **05** spoil **06** coddle, cuddle, fondle, pamper **07** cherish, indulge **11** mollycoddle, overindulge

**cost**
**03** fee, pay, tab **04** exes, harm, hurt, levy, loss, rate, take, toll **05** coast, fetch, go for, price, quote, value, worth
**06** amount, ask for, budget, buy for, charge, come to, damage, figure, injure, injury, outlay, tariff **07** be worth, cost out, deprive, destroy, expense, payment, penalty, sell for, set back, stand in, work out **08** amount to, estimate, expenses, retail at, spending
**09** calculate, cause harm, detriment, knock back, outgoings, overheads, quotation, sacrifice, suffering, valuation **10** be priced at, be valued at
**11** asking price, cause injury, deprivation, expenditure
**12** disbursement, selling price
**13** disbursements **14** cause the loss of

**Costa Rica**
**02** CR **03** CRI

**costly**
**04** dear, posh, rich, salt **05** steep
**06** lavish, pricey **07** harmful, premium, ruinous, sky-high **08** damaging, high-cost, precious, splendid, valuable
**09** big-ticket, chargeful, excessive, expensive, priceless, sumptuous
**10** disastrous, exorbitant, high-priced, loss-making, overpriced
**11** deleterious, destructive, detrimental
**12** catastrophic, costing a bomb, extortionate **15** costing the earth, daylight robbery

**costume**
**02** gi **03** gie, tog **04** garb, suit **05** dress, get-up, habit, robes **06** attire, bather, bikini, cossie, judogi, livery, outfit, rig-out, toilet **07** apparel, clobber, clothes, fashion, threads, uniform
**08** clothing, ensemble, garments
**09** gala-dress, vestments **10** diving suit, fancy dress **11** diving dress
**12** style of dress
*See also* **clothes, clothing**

**cosy**
**04** cosh, safe, snug, warm **05** comfy
**06** homely, intime, secure **08** intimate
**09** congenial, gemütlich, sheltered
**11** comfortable

**Côte d'Ivoire**
**02** CI **03** CIV

**coterie**
**03** set **04** camp, club, gang **05** cabal, group **06** caucus, circle, clique
**07** cenacle, faction **09** camarilla, community **11** association

**cottage**
**03** cot, hut **04** crib, gite **05** bothy, cabin, dacha, lodge, shack, villa
**06** bothie, chalet, shanty
**08** bungalow **09** home-croft

**cotton**
**04** lint **05** ceiba

*Cotton fabrics include:*

**04** aida, duck, jean
**05** chino, denim, dhoti, drill, jaspé, jeans, kanga, piqué, surat, toile
**06** Bengal, calico, canvas, chintz, coutil, dhooti, diaper, dimity, humhum, jersey, khanga, madras, moreen, muslin, nankin, Oxford, pongee, sateen, T-cloth
**07** batiste, buckram, challis, duvetyn, fustian, galatea, gingham, jaconet, kitenge, Mexican, nankeen, percale, printer, silesia
**08** chambray, corduroy, coutille, cretonne, drilling, frocking, lambskin, marcella, nainsook, organdie, osnaburg, shantung, thickset
**09** cottonade, huckaback, longcloth, percaline, sailcloth, satin jean, swans-down, velveteen
**10** Balbriggan, candlewick, monk's cloth, seersucker, winceyette
**11** cheesecloth, flannelette, mutton cloth, nettle-cloth, Oxford cloth, sponge cloth
**13** casement cloth

• **foreign particle in cotton**
**04** moit, mote

**couch**
**03** bed, set **04** bear, sofa, word
**05** divan, frame, quick, utter **06** cradle, day bed, litter, pallet, phrase, quitch, scutch, settee, twitch **07** express, lounger, ottoman, quicken, sofa bed, support, vis-à-vis **08** dog-grass, dog-wheat **10** quack grass, quick grass, triclinium **11** quitch grass, scutch grass, twitch grass **12** chaise-longue, chesterfield

**cough**
**03** hem, ugh **04** ahem, bark, hack, hawk, kink, rasp **05** croak, hoast

**06** tisick, tussis **07** hawking **08** kink-host **09** chincough, kink-cough, pertussis **15** clear your throat

**• cough up**

**03** pay **04** give **05** pay up **06** ante up, pay out **07** fork out, stump up **08** hand over, shell out

**could**

**• could be, could become**

◇ *anagram indicator*

**council**

**04** body, diet, duma, jury **05** board, boule, cabal, crowd, divan, douma, flock, forum, group, jirga, junta, panel, rally, shura, synod, witan **06** senate, soviet, throng **07** cabinet, chamber, company, conseil, consult, meeting **08** advisers, assembly, congress, ministry, trustees **09** committee, directors, executive, gathering, governors, Landsting, Loya Jirga, multitude, panchayat, Sanhedrim, Sanhedrin, syndicate **10** commission, conference, convention, focus group, government, Landsthing, management, parliament, presidency **11** city fathers, convocation, corporation, directorate, witenagemot **12** advisory body, ayuntamiento, body of people, congregation, working party **13** advisory group, governing body **14** administration, local authority

*Council areas of Scotland:*

**04** Fife
**05** Angus, Moray
**07** Falkirk
**08** Highland, Stirling
**10** Dundee City, Eilean Siar, Inverclyde, Midlothian
**11** East Lothian, Glasgow City, West Lothian
**12** Aberdeen City, East Ayrshire, Renfrewshire
**13** Aberdeenshire, Argyll and Bute, North Ayrshire, Orkney Islands, South Ayrshire
**15** City of Edinburgh, Perth and Kinross, Scottish Borders, Shetland Islands
**16** Clackmannanshire, East Renfrewshire, North Lanarkshire, South Lanarkshire
**18** East Dunbartonshire, West Dunbartonshire
**19** Dumfries and Galloway

*Council areas of Wales:*

**05** Conwy, Powys
**07** Cardiff, Gwynedd, Newport, Swansea, Torfaen, Wrexham
**08** Bridgend
**10** Caerphilly, Ceredigion, Flintshire
**12** Blaenau Gwent, Denbighshire
**13** Merthyr Tydfil, Monmouthshire, Pembrokeshire
**14** Isle of Anglesey
**15** Carmarthenshire, Neath Port Talbot, Vale of Glamorgan
**16** Rhondda Cynon Taff

**councillor**

**02** CC, Cr, PC **04** Cllr **05** vezir, vizir **06** induna, visier, vizier, wizier **07** burgess, provost **08** decurion

**counsel**

**02** KC, QC **04** read, rede, silk, urge, warn **05** aread, arede, guide, teach **06** advice, advise, direct, exhort, lawyer **07** arreede, caution, opinion, suggest **08** admonish, advising, advocate, attorney, guidance, instruct, moralism **09** barrister, direction, recommend, solicitor, viewpoint **10** admonition, advisement, conference, conferring, suggestion **11** exhortation, forethought, information **12** amicus curiae, consultation, deliberation, give guidance **13** consideration **14** recommendation **15** give your opinion

**counsellor**

**04** guru **05** coach, guide, tutor **06** mentor, Nestor **07** teacher **08** director **09** authority, barrister, confidant, directrix, therapist **10** Achitophel, Ahithophel, confidante, consultant, directress, instructor

**count**

**03** add, Ory, sum **04** deem, feel, Graf, hold, list, poll, tell **05** add up, check, compt, Fosco, grave, judge, score, sum up, tally, think, total, tot up, whole **06** census, county, esteem, matter, number, reckon, regard **07** account, compute, Dracula, include, qualify, signify **08** allow for, consider, look upon **09** calculate, enumerate, landgrave, numbering, palsgrave, reckoning, totting-up **10** cut some ice, full amount, Rhinegrave **11** be important, calculation, carry weight, computation, enumeration **13** mean something, take account of **15** make a difference, take into account

*See also* **nobility**

**• count in**

**05** put in **06** rope in **07** include, involve, let in on **08** allow for **09** introduce

**• count on**

**05** trust **06** bank on, expect, lean on, rely on **07** bargain, believe, swear by **08** depend on, reckon on **10** bargain for

**• count out**

**04** omit, tell **06** ignore **07** exclude **08** leave out, pass over **09** disregard, eliminate **10** include out

**countenance**

**04** back, face, look, mien **05** agree, allow, brook **06** endure, favour, permit, uphold, visage **07** approve, condone, endorse **08** features, sanction, semblant, stand for, tolerate **09** patronage, put up with **10** appearance, expression **11** approbation, physiognomy **12** acquiescence

**counter**

**03** bar **04** buck, chip, coin, desk, disc, dump, fish, meet **05** merel, meril, parry, piece, stand, table, token **06** answer, buffet, combat, marker, merell, offset, oppose, resist, retort, return **07** adverse, against, dispute, opposed, respond, surface, worktop **08** contrary, opposing, opposite **09** hit back at, retaliate, shopboard **10** contradict, conversely **11** conflicting, contrasting, work surface **12** in opposition **13** contradictory

**counteract**

**04** foil, undo **05** annul, check **06** defeat, hinder, negate, offset, oppose, remedy, resist, thwart **07** prevent **09** frustrate **10** act against, invalidate, neutralize **11** countervail **14** counterbalance

**counterbalance**

**04** undo **05** poise **06** cancel, offset, set-off **07** balance, correct, requite **08** equalize **09** make up for **10** compensate, neutralize **11** countervail **12** counterpoise **13** compensate for

**counterfeit**

**03** dud **04** base, copy, fake, sham **05** bogus, dummy, faked, false, feign, forge, fraud, phony, pseud, queer, snide **06** copied, forged, phoney, pirate, pseudo **07** falsify, feigned, forgery, imitate, pretend, simular **08** borrowed, disguise, phantasm, postiche, simulate, spurious **09** brummagem, fabricate, imitation, pretended, reproduce, simulated **10** artificial, camouflage, fraudulent **11** impersonate **12** reproduction

*See also* **counterfeit coin** *under* **coin**

**countermand**

**05** annul, quash **06** cancel, repeal, revoke **07** rescind, reverse, unorder **08** abrogate, override, overturn **10** revocation

**counterpart**

**04** copy, mate, peer, twin **05** equal, match, moral, tally **06** double, fellow **07** obverse **08** parallel **09** duplicate **10** complement, equivalent, supplement **14** opposite number

**counterpoint**

**04** foil **06** relief, set off, set-off **07** descant, enhance **08** contrast, faburden, heighten, opposite **09** intensify **10** complement **11** counterpane **13** differentiate **15** differentiation, throw into relief

**countless**

**06** legion, myriad, untold **07** endless, umpteen **08** infinite **09** boundless, limitless **10** numberless, unnumbered, without end **11** innumerable, measureless **12** immeasurable, incalculable **13** inexhaustible

**countrified**

**04** hick **05** rural **06** rustic **07** bucolic,

idyllic, outback **08** agrarian, pastoral **10** provincial **12** agricultural

**country**

**04** area, bush, land, pays, soil
**05** power, realm, rural, state, wilds
**06** landed, nation, people, public, region, rustic, sticks, voters **07** bucolic, idyllic, kingdom, outback, terrain
**08** agrarian, citizens, district, electors, farmland, locality, moorland, pastoral, populace, republic **09** backwater, backwoods, community, green belt, provinces, residents, rural area, territory **10** population, provincial
**11** countryside, inhabitants
**12** agricultural, back of beyond, principality **13** neighbourhood
**15** middle of nowhere

*Countries:*

**02** UK
**03** PRC, UAE, USA
**04** Chad, Cuba, Fiji, Iran, Iraq, Laos, Mali, Oman, Peru, Togo
**05** Benin, Burma, Chile, China, Congo, Egypt, Gabon, Ghana, Haiti, India, Italy, Japan, Kenya, Libya, Malta, Nauru, Nepal, Niger, Palau, Qatar, Samoa, Spain, Sudan, Syria, Tonga, Yemen
**06** Angola, Belize, Bhutan, Brazil, Canada, Cyprus, España, France, Greece, Guinea, Guyana, Israel, Italia, Jordan, Kuwait, Latvia, Malawi, Mexico, Monaco, Norway, Panama, Poland, Russia, Rwanda, Sweden, Taiwan, Turkey, Tuvalu, Uganda, Zambia
**07** Albania, Algeria, Andorra, Armenia, Austria, Bahrain, Belarus, Belgium, Bolivia, Burundi, Comoros, Croatia, Denmark, Ecuador, Eritrea, Estonia, Finland, Georgia, Germany, Grenada, Holland, Hungary, Iceland, Ireland, Jamaica, Lebanon, Lesotho, Liberia, Moldova, Morocco, Myanmar, Namibia, Nigeria, Romania, Senegal, Somalia, St Lucia, Tunisia, Ukraine, Uruguay, Vanuatu, Vatican, Vietnam
**08** Barbados, Botswana, Bulgaria, Cambodia, Cameroon, Colombia, Djibouti, Dominica, Ethiopia, Honduras, Kiribati, Malaysia, Maldives, Mongolia, Pakistan, Paraguay, Portugal, Slovakia, Slovenia, Sri Lanka, Suriname, Tanzania, Thailand, Zimbabwe
**09** Argentina, Australia, Cape Verde, Costa Rica, East Timor, Guatemala, Indonesia, Lithuania, Macedonia, Mauritius, Nicaragua, San Marino, Singapore, Swaziland, The Gambia, Venezuela
**10** Azerbaijan, Bangladesh, El Salvador, Kazakhstan, Kyrgyzstan, Luxembourg, Madagascar, Mauritania, Mozambique, New Zealand, North Korea, Seychelles, South Korea, Tajikistan, The Bahamas, Uzbekistan
**11** Afghanistan, Burkina Faso, Côte d'Ivoire, Deutschland, Philippines, Saudi Arabia, Sierra Leone, South Africa, Switzerland
**12** Guinea-Bissau, Turkmenistan
**13** Czech Republic, Liechtenstein, United Kingdom, Western Sahara
**14** Papua New Guinea, Solomon Islands, The Netherlands
**15** Marshall Islands, St Kitts and Nevis
**16** Brunei Darussalam, Equatorial Guinea
**17** Antigua and Barbuda, Dominican Republic, Trinidad and Tobago
**18** São Tomé and Príncipe, United Arab Emirates
**19** Serbia and Montenegro
**20** Bosnia and Herzegovina
**21** United States of America
**22** Central African Republic
**25** St Vincent and the Grenadines
**27** Federated States of Micronesia
**28** Democratic Republic of the Congo

*Country codes include:*

**03** ABW, AFG, AGO, AIA, ALB, AND, ANT, ARE, ARG, ARM, ASM, ATA, ATF, ATG, AUS, AUT, AZE, BDI, BEL, BEN, BFA, BGD, BGR, BHR, BHS, BIH, BLR, BLZ, BMU, BOL, BRA, BRB, BRN, BTN, BVT, BWA, CAF, CAN, CCK, CHE, CHL, CHN, CIV, CMR, COD, COG, COK, COL, COM, CPV, CRI, CUB, CXR, CYM, CYP, CZE, DEU, DJI, DMA, DNK, DOM, DZA, ECU, EGY, ERI, ESH, ESP, EST, ETH, FIN, FJI, FLK, FRA, FRO, FSM, GAB, GBR, GEO, GHA, GIB, GIN, GLP, GMB, GNB, GNQ, GRC, GRD, GRL, GTM, GUF, GUM, GUY, HGK, HMD, HND, HRV, HTI, HUN, IDN, IMN, IND, IOT, IRL, IRN, IRQ, ISL, ISR, ITA, JAM, JOR, JPN, KAZ, KEN, KGZ, KHM, KIR, KNA, KOR, KWT, LAO, LBN, LBR, LBY, LCA, LIE, LKA, LSO, LTU, LUX, LVA, MAC, MAR, MCO, MDA, MDG, MDV, MEX, MHL, MKD, MLI, MLT, MMR, MNG, MNP, MOZ, MRT, MSR, MTQ, MUS, MWI, MYS, MYT, NAM, NCL, NER, NFK, NGA, NIC, NIU, NLD, NOR, NPL, NRU, NZL, OMN, PAK, PAN, PCN, PER, PHL, PLW, PNG, POL, PRI, PRK, PRT, PRY, PYF, QAT, REU, ROU, RUS, RWA, SAU, SDN, SEN, SGP, SHN, SJM, SLB, SLE, SLV, SMR, SOM, SPM, STP, SUR, SVK, SVN, SWE, SWZ, SYC, SYR, TCA, TCD, TGO, THA, TJK, TKL, TKM, TLS, TON, TTO, TUN, TUR, TUV, TWN, TZA, UGA, UKR, URY, USA, UZB, VAT, VCT, VEN, VGB, VIR, VNM, VUT, WLF, WSM, YEM, YUG, ZAF, ZMB, ZWE

*Former country names include:*

**04** Siam, USSR
**05** Burma, Zaire
**06** Bengal, Ceylon, Persia, Urundi
**07** Dahomey, Formosa
**08** Rhodesia
**09** Abyssinia, Indochina, Kampuchea, Nyasaland
**10** Basutoland, Ivory Coast, Senegambia, Tanganyika, Upper Volta, Yugoslavia
**11** Dutch Guiana, French Sudan, New Hebrides, Ubangi Shari
**12** Bechuanaland, French Guinea, Ruanda-Urundi
**13** British Guiana, Ellice Islands, Khmer Republic, Spanish Guinea, Spanish Sahara, Trucial States
**14** Czechoslovakia, French Togoland, Gilbert Islands
**15** British Honduras, British Togoland, Dutch East Indies, South West Africa

*See also* **Africa**; **America**; **Arab**; **Asia**; **commonwealth**; **Europe**; **Middle East**

**• open country**

**03** lay, lea, lee, ley **04** moor, veld, wold
**05** field, heath, plain, range, veldt, weald

**countryman, countrywoman**

**03** hob **04** boor, hick, hind **05** Hodge, yokel **06** farmer, rustic, yeoman
**07** bumpkin, hayseed, landman, peasant **09** hillbilly **10** clodhopper, compatriot, provincial **11** bushwhacker
**12** backwoodsman **13** fellow citizen
**14** fellow national

**countryside**

**06** nature **07** country, scenery
**08** farmland, moorland, outdoors
**09** green belt, landscape, rural area

**countrywoman** *see* **countryman, countrywoman**

**county**

**02** Co **04** area **05** count, shire, state
**06** parish, region **08** district, province
**09** comitatus, territory **10** department

*Counties and administrative areas of England:*

**04** Kent, York
**05** Derby, Devon, Essex, Luton, Poole
**06** Dorset, Durham, Halton, London, Medway, Slough, Surrey, Torbay
**07** Cumbria, Norfolk, Reading, Rutland, Suffolk, Swindon
**08** Cheshire, Plymouth, Somerset, Thurrock
**09** Blackpool, Hampshire, Leicester, Wiltshire, Wokingham
**10** Darlington, Derbyshire, East Sussex, Hartlepool, Lancashire, Merseyside, Nottingham, Portsmouth, Shropshire, Warrington, West Sussex
**11** Bournemouth, Isle of Wight, Oxfordshire, Southampton, Tyne and Wear
**12** Bedfordshire, Lincolnshire, Milton Keynes, Peterborough, Stoke-on-Trent, Warwickshire, West Midlands
**13** City of Bristol, Herefordshire, Hertfordshire, Middlesbrough, North Somerset, Southend-on-Sea, Staffordshire, West Berkshire, West Yorkshire
**14** Cambridgeshire, Leicestershire, Northumberland, North Yorkshire,

South Yorkshire, Stockton-on-Tees, Worcestershire
**15** Bracknell Forest, Brighton and Hove, Buckinghamshire, Gloucestershire, Nottinghamshire
**16** Northamptonshire, Telford and Wrekin
**17** Greater Manchester, North Lincolnshire
**18** Redcar and Cleveland
**19** Blackburn with Darwen
**20** South Gloucestershire, Windsor and Maidenhead
**21** East Riding of Yorkshire, North East Lincolnshire
**22** City of Kingston upon Hull
**24** Bath and North East Somerset, Cornwall and Isles of Scilly

*County abbreviations include:*

**02** Mx
**03** Dev, Dur, Ess, Mon, Som, Sur, War
**04** Beds, Camb, Ches, Corn, Cumb, Dors, Glos, Mont, Oxon, Suff
**05** Berks, Bucks, Cambs, Cards, Derby, E Suss, Hants, Herts, Lancs, Leics, Lincs, Middx, Notts, Wilts, Worcs, Yorks
**06** Caerns, Shrops, Staffs
**08** Northumb
**09** Northants

*Counties of Ireland:*

**04** Cork, Leix, Mayo
**05** Cavan, Clare, Kerry, Laois, Louth, Meath, Sligo
**06** Carlow, Dublin, Galway, Offaly
**07** Donegal, Kildare, Leitrim, Wexford, Wicklow
**08** Kilkenny, Laoighis, Limerick, Longford, Monaghan
**09** Roscommon, Tipperary, Waterford, Westmeath

*See also* **district**

• **home counties**
**02** SE
• **county town** *see* **town**

**coup**
**04** blow, deed, feat **05** stunt, upset **06** action, barter, putsch, revolt, stroke **07** exploit, success, triumph **08** exchange, overturn, takeover, uprising **09** coup d'état, manoeuvre, overthrow, rebellion **10** revolution **11** tour de force **12** insurrection, masterstroke **14** accomplishment

**coup de grâce**
**04** kill **06** kibosh **07** quietus **08** clincher **09** death blow **11** kiss of death **13** finishing blow

**coup d'état**
**04** coup **06** putsch, revolt **08** takeover, uprising **09** overthrow, rebellion **10** revolution **12** insurrection

**couple**
◇ *repetition indicator*
**03** duo, two, wed **04** ally, bind, join, link, mate, meng, ming, pair, tway, yoke **05** brace, clasp, hitch, marry, match, menge, twain, unite **06** attach, buckle, fasten, lovers, marrow **07** combine, conjoin, connect, diarchy, shackle, twosome **08** double up, partners **09** accompany, associate, integrate, newlyweds **12** Darby and Joan **14** husband and wife

**coupon**
**04** form, slip, stub **05** check, token **06** billet, docket, ticket **07** voucher **11** certificate, counterfoil

**courage**
**04** grit, guts **05** balls, heart, metal, moxie, nerve, pluck, spunk, valor **06** bottle, daring, mettle, spirit, valour **07** bravery, cojones, heroism, stomach **08** audacity, backbone, boldness, coraggio, gumption **09** fortitude, gallantry **10** resolution **11** intrepidity **12** fearlessness **13** dauntlessness, determination

**courageous**
**04** bold, game **05** brave, gutsy, hardy, wight **06** ballsy, daring, feisty, heroic, manful, plucky, spunky **07** gallant, valiant **08** fearless, generous, intrepid, resolute, valorous **09** audacious, dauntless **10** determined, stomachous **11** adventurous, full-hearted, high-hearted, indomitable, lion-hearted **12** stout-hearted
• **courageous person**
**04** hero, lion

**courageously**
**06** boldly **07** bravely **09** gallantly, valiantly **10** fearlessly, heroically, intrepidly, resolutely **11** audaciously, dauntlessly, indomitably **13** adventurously

**courier**
**03** rep **05** envoy, guide **06** bearer, escort, herald, legate, nuncio, runner **07** carrier, postman **08** emissary **09** estafette, messenger, tour guide **10** pursuivant **11** travel guide **13** dispatch rider **14** representative

**course**
**03** ren, rin, run, way **04** beat, dash, dish, flow, gush, hunt, lane, line, mess, mode, move, part, path, plan, pour, race, rise, road, rota, span, tack, term, time **05** ambit, chase, lapse, march, orbit, order, route, spell, stage, surge, sweet, track, trail **06** entrée, follow, ground, manner, method, period, policy, pursue, remove, series, stream, system, voyage **07** advance, channel, circuit, classes, current, dessert, lessons, passage, passing, process, pudding, regimen, starter, studies **08** approach, duration, lectures, movement, progress, run after, schedule, sequence, syllabus **09** appetizer, direction, entremets, procedure, programme, racetrack, unfolding **10** curriculum, flight path, golf course, main course, racecourse, succession, trajectory **11** development, furtherance, hors d'oeuvre, progression
*See also* **compass**; **golf**; **race**; **racecourse**
• **alter course**
**04** gybe, jibe, tack, wear
• **deviate from course**
**03** bag, yaw
• **direct course**
**03** aim **04** head
• **fixed course**
**03** rut **04** race
• **in due course**
**02** so **06** in time **07** finally **09** in due time **10** eventually **13** all in good time, sooner or later
• **of course**
**02** ay **03** aye **04** sure **05** natch **06** surely **07** no doubt **08** to be sure **09** certainly, naturally **10** by all means, definitely **11** bien entendu, doubtlessly, indubitably, undoubtedly **12** indisputably **13** needless to say, without a doubt **14** not unnaturally
• **part of course**
**03** leg

**court**
**02** ct **03** bar, Hof, see, sew, sue, woo, wow **04** date, quad, ring, risk, seek, yard **05** alley, arena, bench, chase, green, patio, plaza, suite, track, train **06** castle, go with, ground, incite, invite, palace, piazza, prompt, pursue, square **07** attract, cortège, flatter, provoke, retinue, solicit **08** cloister, game area, go steady, pander to, try to win **09** courtyard, cultivate, curtilage, enclosure, entourage, esplanade, forecourt, go out with, household, judiciary, peristyle **10** attendants, cozy up with, judicatory, judicature, praetorium, quadrangle **11** conservancy, go round with, playing area **12** go around with **13** spheristerion **14** royal residence **15** curry favour with

*Courts include:*

**03** law
**04** eyre, Fehm, high, Lyon, moot, open, Vehm
**05** burgh, civil, crown, prize, trial, World, youth
**06** appeal, Arches, church, claims, county, family, Honour, police, record
**07** appeals, assizes, borough, circuit, Diplock, divorce, federal, justice, Probate, Session, sheriff, Supreme
**08** chancery, coroner's, criminal, district, juvenile, kangaroo, Requests, superior, tribunal
**09** children's, Exchequer, Faculties, municipal, Old Bailey, Piepowder, Sanhedrim, Sanhedrin, the Arches
**10** Commercial, commissary, consistory, Divisional, Piepowders, Protection
**11** Arbitration, Common Bench, Common Pleas, High Justice, magistrates', police-court, Prerogative, small claims
**12** Aulic Council, court-martial, House of Lords, Privy Council
**13** first instance

**14** Criminal Appeal, High Commission, High Justiciary
**15** Central Criminal, European Justice, Lord Chancellor's

• **bring to court**
**04** file
• **court case**
**04** suit **05** trial **06** action **07** lawsuit
• **court house**
**02** ch
• **in court**
**02** up **08** at the bar
• **right to hold court**
**03** sac, soc
• **take to court**
**03** law, sue

**courteous**
**04** hend, kind **05** civil **06** polite, urbane **07** affable, courtly, gallant, refined, tactful **08** debonair, gracious, ladylike, mannerly, obliging, polished, well-bred **09** attentive **10** chivalrous, debonnaire, diplomatic, respectful, well-spoken **11** considerate, deferential, gentlemanly **12** well-mannered

**courteously**
**06** kindly **07** civilly **08** politely, urbanely **09** gallantly, refinedly, tactfully **10** graciously, obligingly **11** attentively **12** chivalrously, respectfully **13** considerately, deferentially **14** diplomatically

**courtesy**
**04** tact **06** comity, curtsy, devoir, favour, gentry **07** manners, respect **08** breeding, chivalry, civility, kindness, urbanity **09** attention, deference, etiquette, gallantry, gentility **10** generosity, gentilesse, politeness, refinement **11** good manners **12** good breeding, graciousness **13** consideration

**courtier**
**04** lady, lord, page **05** noble, toady **07** steward, subject **08** follower, liegeman, nobleman **09** attendant, cup-bearer, flatterer, sycophant **11** train-bearer **13** lady-in-waiting

**courtly**
**05** aulic, civil **06** formal, lordly, polite **07** elegant, gallant, refined, stately **08** decorous, gracious, high-bred, obliging, polished **09** dignified **10** chivalrous, flattering **11** ceremonious **12** aristocratic

**courtship**
**04** suit **05** spoon **06** affair, dating, wooing **07** chasing, pursuit, romance **08** courting, going-out, love-suit **10** attentions, lovemaking **11** going steady

**courtyard**
**04** area, quad, ward, yard **05** court, garth, marae, patio, plaza **06** atrium, square **07** cortile **08** cloister **09** enclosure, esplanade, forecourt **10** quadrangle

**cove**
**03** bay, man **04** chap **05** bight, creek, fiord, firth, inlet **06** cavern **07** estuary

**covenant**
**03** vow **04** bond, deed, pact **05** agree, trust **06** engage, pledge, treaty **07** compact, promise **08** contract, warranty **09** agreement, concordat, indenture, stipulate, testament, undertake **10** commitment, convention, engagement **11** arrangement, stipulation, undertaking **12** dispensation

**cover**
◇ *containment indicator*
◇ *hidden indicator*
**02** do, go **03** cap, cup, hap, hat, lay, lep, lid, set, top **04** bury, cake, case, coat, cour, cowl, daub, deck, film, heal, heel, hele, hide, hood, leap, mask, pall, skin, tell, tilt, veil, vele, wrap **05** apron, brood, cloak, cloke, coure, cross, dress, duvet, front, guard, layer, paten, quoit, throw, treat **06** attire, be over, canopy, carpet, clothe, defend, embody, encase, extend, façade, incase, insure, jacket, mantle, pay for, refuge, report, review, screen, shield, shroud, sleeve, spread, survey, take in, toilet, travel **07** analyse, bedding, binding, blanket, coating, conceal, contain, cover-up, defence, embrace, envelop, examine, garment, include, involve, journey, measure, narrate, obscure, overlay, package, plaster, present, pretext, protect, put over, relieve, replace, shelter, stretch, swaddle, wrapper, wreathe **08** accoutre, bedcover, bespread, blankets, clothing, comprise, consider, continue, covering, deal with, deputize, describe, disguise, enshroud, envelope, go across, overveil, pretence, security, traverse **09** assurance, bedspread, encompass, fill in for, indemnify, indemnity, insurance, make up for, place over, safeguard, sanctuary, talk about, whitewash **10** balance out, bedclothes, camouflage, complicity, conspiracy, extend over, overspread, protection, provide for, recompense, stand in for, travel over, underwrite, write about **11** be enough for, concealment, confederate, hiding-place, incorporate, investigate, pinch-hit for, smokescreen **12** compensation, take over from **13** compensate for, give details of **14** counterbalance **15** give an account of, indemnification
• **cover up**
◇ *hidden indicator*
**03** hap **04** hide **05** blank, fudge **06** hush up **07** conceal, repress **08** enshroud, hoodwink, keep dark, suppress **09** dissemble, gloss over, whitewash **10** keep secret
• **original cover**
**02** OC

**coverage**
**04** item **05** story **06** report **07** account, blanket, reports **08** analysis **09** reportage, reporting **11** description **13** investigation

**covering**
**03** cap, lag, rug, top **04** aril, cape, case, coat, cope, film, hood, husk, mask, pall, roof, skin **05** armor, cloak, cloke, cover, crust, layer, shell **06** armour, awning, carpet, casing, sheath, tegmen, veneer **07** blanket, coating, housing, overlay, roofing, shelter **08** clothing, pavilion, sheeting, wrapping **09** tarpaulin **10** encasement, incasement, integument, overlaying, protection **11** descriptive, explanatory **12** accompanying, introductory

**covert**
**06** hidden, secret, sneaky, veiled **07** furtive, private, shelter **08** sidelong, stealthy, ulterior **09** concealed, disguised, underhand **10** dissembled **11** clandestine, unsuspected **13** subreptitious, surreptitious, under the table

**covertly**
**08** secretly **09** furtively, privately **15** surreptitiously

**cover-up**
**05** front **06** façade, screen **08** pretence **09** deception, whitewash **10** complicity, conspiracy **11** concealment, smokescreen

**covet**
**04** envy, want **05** crave, fancy **06** desire **07** long for **08** begrudge, yearn for **09** hanker for, hunger for, lust after, thirst for

**covetous**
**06** greedy **07** craving, envious, jealous, longing, wanting **08** desirous, grasping, yearning **09** hankering, hungering, rapacious, thirsting **10** avaricious, insatiable **11** acquisitive, close-fisted, close-handed

**covey**
**03** nid, set **04** band, bevy **05** brood, flock, group, hatch, party, skein **06** flight **07** cluster, company

**cow**
**02** ox **03** mog **04** boss, mart, neat, quey, runt **05** besom, bossy, bully, daunt, doddy, moggy, mooly, muley, scare, stirk **06** crummy, dismay, hawkey, hawkie, heifer, humlie, Jersey, milker, moggie, mulley, rattle, rother, subdue **07** kouprey, overawe, unnerve **08** Alderney, browbeat, domineer, Friesian, frighten, springer **09** terrorize **10** discourage, dishearten, intimidate

**coward**
**03** cat **04** Noel, sook, wimp, wuss **05** dingo, sissy **06** craven **07** chicken, cowherd, crybaby, dastard, hilding, nithing, viliaco, viliago **08** cowheard, deserter, poltroon, recreant, renegade, villagio, villiaco, villiago, weakling **10** faint-heart, poultroone,

Scaramouch, scaredy-cat **11** Scaramouche, yellow-belly

**cowardice**
**08** timidity **11** fearfulness **12** cowardliness, timorousness **13** pusillanimity, spinelessness **14** spiritlessness

**cowardly**
**04** nesh, soft, weak **05** faint, mangy, timid **06** coward, cowish, craven, mangey, maungy, scared, yellow **07** chicken, dastard, fearful, gutless, hilding, jittery, meacock, nithing, unmanly, wimpish **08** timorous, unheroic **09** dastardly, spineless, weak-kneed **10** spiritless **11** lily-livered, milk-livered **12** faint-hearted, weak-spirited, white-livered **13** pusillanimous, yellow-bellied **14** chicken-hearted, chicken-livered

**cowboy**
**05** cheat, rogue, waddy **06** drover, gaucho, herder, rascal, waddie **07** bungler, cowhand, cowpoke, herdboy, rancher, vaquero **08** buckaroo, buckayro, buckeroo, herdsman, ranchero, stockman, swindler, wrangler **09** cattleman, fraudster, scoundrel **10** cowpuncher **11** incompetent **12** bronco-buster, cattleherder

**cower**
**04** ruck **05** quail, quake, shake, skulk, wince **06** cringe, crouch, flinch, grovel, recoil, shiver, shrink **07** croodle, tremble **08** draw back

**cowhouse**
**04** byre **07** shippen, shippon

**co-worker**
**04** aide, ally **06** helper **07** comrade, partner **08** confrère, teammate, workmate **09** assistant, associate, auxiliary, colleague, companion **11** confederate **12** collaborator, fellow worker

**cows**
**02** ky **03** kye **04** kine, neat

**coxcomb**
**03** fop **04** head, prig **07** princox **08** popinjay, princock

**coy**
**03** shy **04** arch, nice, prim **05** squab, timid **06** caress, demure, modest, skeigh **07** bashful, disdain, evasive, prudish **08** backward, reserved, retiring, skittish **09** diffident, kittenish, reticence, shrinking, squeamish, withdrawn **10** coquettish **11** flirtatious **12** self-effacing

**coyly**
**06** primly **07** timidly **08** demurely, modestly **09** bashfully, evasively, prudishly **11** diffidently **12** coquettishly **13** flirtatiously **14** self-effacingly

**crab**
**04** claw, cock **05** decry, scrog, wreck **06** Cancer, hermit, partan, scrawl **07** fiddler, limulus, pagurid, souring, wilding **08** horseman, obstruct, ochidore, pagurian **09** criticize, frustrate, scrog-bush, scrog-buss, soft-shell **12** saucepan-fish

**crabbed, crabby**
**04** sour, tart **05** acrid, cross, harsh, surly, testy, tough **06** cranky, morose, snappy **07** awkward, cankery, fretful, grouchy, iracund, prickly **08** cankered, captious, churlish, perverse, petulant, snappish **09** crotchety, difficult, fractious, irascible, irritable, splenetic **10** ill-natured **11** acrimonious, bad-tempered, ill-tempered **12** cantankerous, iracundulous, misanthropic

**crack**
◇ *anagram indicator*
**02** go **03** ace, dig, gag, gap, hit, pop, try **04** bang, bash, beat, blow, boom, bump, chap, chat, chip, chop, clap, dope, dunt, fent, flaw, gibe, jest, joke, leak, line, quip, rent, rift, rima, rock, shot, slap, snap, stab, star **05** boast, break, burst, check, chink, cleft, clout, craic, crash, craze, joint, shake, slash, smack, solve, split, whack, whirl **06** breach, cave in, cavity, choice, cleave, cranny, decode, effort, expert, go bang, gossip, report, spring, strike, wallop **07** attempt, crackle, crevice, decrypt, dope out, explode, fissure, resolve, rupture, shatter, skilful, skilled, unravel, work out **08** collapse, crevasse, decipher, detonate, fracture, fragment, one-liner, repartee, splinter, superior, top-notch **09** break down, brilliant, excellent, explosion, figure out, first-rate, ready-wash, wisecrack, witticism **10** detonation, first-class, go to pieces, hand-picked **11** lose control, outstanding **15** find the answer to

• **crack down on**
**03** end **04** stop **05** check, crush, limit **07** confine, control, repress **08** restrict, suppress **10** act against, get tough on, put a stop to **11** clamp down on

• **crack up**
◇ *anagram indicator*
**05** go mad, laugh **06** praise **07** go crazy **08** collapse **09** break down, fall about, fall apart **10** go to pieces **11** go ballistic, lose control **14** split your sides

**crackdown**
**03** end **04** stop **05** check **08** crushing **09** clampdown **10** repression **11** suppression

**cracked**
◇ *anagram indicator*
**03** mad **04** bats, daft, nuts, torn **05** barmy, batty, crazy, harsh, loony, nutty, split **06** broken, crazed, faulty, flawed, insane **07** chapped, chipped, damaged, foolish, idiotic, starred **08** crackpot, deranged, dingbats, fissured **09** defective, imperfect **12** crackbrained, round the bend **13** off your rocker, out of your tree

**crackers**
◇ *anagram indicator*
**03** mad **04** daft, nuts **05** batty, crazy, loony, matza, matzo, nutty **06** matzah, matzoh **07** cracked, foolish, idiotic **08** crackpot **10** unbalanced **12** crackbrained, round the bend

**crackle**
**04** snap **05** crack, money **06** rustle, sizzle **08** crepitus **09** banknotes, crepitate **10** paper money **11** crepitation, decrepitate **13** decrepitation

**crackpot**
◇ *anagram indicator*
**04** fool **05** freak, idiot, loony **06** nutter, weirdo **07** nutcase, oddball **10** basket case

**cradle**
**03** bed, cot **04** base, crib, hold, lull, prop, rest, rock, tend **05** fount, frame, mount, nurse, stand **06** holder, nestle, origin, rocker, source, spring **07** berceau, infancy, nurture, shelter, support **08** bassinet, carry-cot, cunabula, mounting **09** beginning, framework, travel-cot **10** birthplace, gold-washer, incunabula, wellspring **11** Moses basket **12** fountain-head **13** starting-point

**craft**
◇ *anagram indicator*
**03** art, job **04** boat, line, ship, work **05** flair, guile, knack, skill, trade, wiles **06** deceit, talent, vessel **07** ability, calling, cunning, finesse, foxship, mastery, pursuit, sleight, slyness **08** activity, aircraft, aptitude, artistry, business, deftness, subtlety, trickery, vocation **09** dexterity, expertise, handiwork, ingenuity, sharpness, spaceship, technique **10** adroitness, artfulness, astuteness, cleverness, craftiness, employment, expertness, handicraft, occupation, shrewdness, spacecraft **11** cunningness, deviousness, skilfulness, workmanship **12** fiendishness, landing craft **13** deceitfulness, inventiveness **15** imaginativeness, resourcefulness

*See also* **art**; **ship**

**craftily**
◇ *anagram indicator*
**05** slyly **08** artfully, astutely, shrewdly **09** cunningly, deviously **10** guilefully **11** deceitfully **12** fraudulently

**craftsman, craftswoman**
**05** maker, smith **06** artist, expert, master, wright **07** artisan, artsman, workman **08** mechanic **09** artificer, tradesman **10** technician **11** tradeswoman **12** craftsperson, tradesperson **13** skilled worker

*See also* **artist**

**craftsmanship**
**05** skill **07** mastery **08** artistry **09** dexterity, expertise, technique **11** skilfulness, workmanship

**craftswoman** *see* **craftsman, craftswoman**

**crafty**
◇ *anagram indicator*
**03** sly **04** foxy, slim, wily **05** canny, loopy, sharp **06** artful, astute, knacky, shrewd, subtle **07** crooked, cunning, devious, tricksy, versute **08** guileful, knackish, scheming **09** conniving, deceitful, designing, subdolous **10** fraudulent **11** calculating, duplicitous **12** disingenuous **13** Machiavellian

**crag**
**03** tor **04** neck, noup, peak, rock **05** bluff, cliff, craig, heuch, heugh, ridge, scarp, stoss **06** throat **08** pinnacle **10** escarpment

**craggy**
**05** rocky, rough, stony **06** cliffy, jagged, marked, rugged, uneven **07** cliffed, cragged **09** rough-hewn **11** precipitous **13** weather-beaten

**cram**
**03** bag, jam, lie, ram **04** crap, fill, glut, pack, pang, stap, stop, swot, tuck **05** crowd, crush, farce, force, frank, gorge, grind, mug up, press, prime, stuff **06** fill up, revise, stodge **07** compact, squeeze **08** bone up on, compress, overfeed, overfill **09** overcrowd, study hard

**cramp**
**03** tie **04** ache, pain, pang, rein **05** check, crick, limit, spasm **06** arrest, bridle, hamper, hinder, impede, narrow, stitch, stymie, thwart, twinge **07** confine, cramped, inhibit, shackle **08** handicap, obstruct, restrain, restrict **09** constrain, constrict, frustrate, hamstring, restraint, stiffness **10** convulsion **11** contraction **14** pins and needles **15** overuse syndrome, scrivener's palsy

**cramped**
**04** full, poky **05** small, tight **06** narrow, packed **07** bounded, crabbed, crowded, squeezy **08** closed in, confined, hemmed in, niggling, overfull, squashed, squeezed **09** congested, jam-packed **10** compressed, restricted **11** constricted, overcrowded **12** incommodious **13** uncomfortable

**crane**
**05** davit, hoist, Jenny, sarus, winch **06** brolga, hooper, jigger, tackle **07** cranium, derrick, whooper **08** adjutant **10** demoiselle **12** adjutant bird, cherry picker **14** block and tackle **15** native companion

**crank**
**04** kook, whim **05** freak, idiot, loony, wince, winch **06** madman, nutter, weirdo **07** oddball **08** crackpot **09** character, eccentric **11** amphetamine
• **crank up**
**05** add to **06** hike up, step up **07** build up, further **08** increase **09** intensify **10** strengthen

**cranky**
◇ *anagram indicator*
**03** fey, odd **04** tart **05** cross, dotty, harsh, queer, shaky, surly, testy, wacky **06** crabby, Fifish, screwy, snappy **07** awkward, bizarre, crabbed, grouchy, prickly, strange **08** freakish, peculiar, unsteady **09** crotchety, difficult, eccentric, irritable **11** bad-tempered, ill-tempered **12** cantankerous **13** idiosyncratic **14** unconventional

**cranny**
**03** gap **04** hole, nook, rent, slit **05** chink, cleft, crack **07** crevice, fissure, opening **08** cleavage **10** interstice

**crash**
◇ *anagram indicator*
**03** din, hit, ram **04** bang, bash, boom, bump, clap, dash, fail, fall, fold, rack, ruin, thud, wham **05** break, clang, clank, clash, ditch, frush, knock, pitch, pound, prang, rapid, shunt, smash, thump, wreck **06** batter, bingle, cut out, fold up, fragor, go bust, go into, go phut, pack up, pile-up, plunge, racket, shiver, topple, urgent **07** clatter, collide, failure, founder, go kaput, go under, run into, shatter, smash-up, thunder **08** accident, collapse, downfall, fracture, fragment, meltdown, splinter **09** break down, collision, drive into, emergency, explosion, immediate, intensive, smash into **10** bankruptcy, depression, plough into, telescoped **11** accelerated, black Monday, come a gutser, go to the wall, malfunction, stop working, thunderclap **12** concentrated, disintegrate, go on the blink **13** round-the-clock

**crass**
**04** naff, rude **05** crude, dense, gross, ocker **06** clumsy, coarse, oafish, obtuse, stupid **07** boorish, witless **08** tactless, unsubtle **09** tasteless, unrefined **10** blundering, indelicate **11** insensitive **15** unsophisticated

**crassly**
**06** rudely **07** crudely **08** clumsily, coarsely, stupidly **10** tactlessly **11** tastelessly **12** indelicately **13** insensitively

**crate**
**03** box, car **04** case, kist **05** chest, plane, seron **06** seroon **08** tea chest **09** container **10** packing-box **11** packing-case

**crater**
**03** dip, pit **04** bowl, hole, maar **05** abyss, basin, chasm **06** cavity, hollow **07** caldera **09** shell-hole **10** depression

**cravat**
**05** scarf, stock **06** o'erlay **07** overlay, owrelay, soubise **09** neckcloth, steenkirk, steinkirk

**crave**
**03** beg **04** need, want, wish **05** claim, covet, fancy **06** desire, hunger **07** dream of, long for, longing, pant for, pine for, require, sigh for **08** yearn for **09** hunger for, lust after, thirst for **10** be dying for **11** hanker after

**craven**
**04** soft, weak **05** timid **06** afraid, coward, scared, yellow **07** chicken, fearful, gutless **08** cowardly, poltroon, recreant, timorous, unheroic **09** spineless, weak-kneed **10** spiritless **11** lily-livered **12** faint-hearted, mean-spirited, weak-spirited, white-livered **13** pusillanimous **14** chicken-hearted, chicken-livered

**craving**
**04** lust, need, pica, urge, wish **06** desire, greedy, hunger, pining, thirst **07** longing, malacia, panting, sighing **08** appetent, appetite, yearning **09** hankering **10** dipsomania, hydromania, methomania **11** toxicomania **13** morphinomania

**crawl**
**04** drag, edge, fawn, inch, knee, swim, teem **05** creep, snail, swarm, toady **06** cringe, grovel, kowtow, seethe, squirm, suck up, writhe **07** bristle, flatter, slither, wriggle **08** be full of **09** be all over, freestyle **10** move slowly **11** curry favour **12** bow and scrape, go on all fours **13** advance slowly **14** be obsequious to
• **crawler**
**06** insect

**crayfish**
**05** yabby **06** gilgie, jilgie, marron, yabbie

**craze**
**03** bug, fad **04** buzz, flaw, mode, rage, ramp, whim **05** crack, mania, thing, trend, vogue **06** frenzy, furore, impair, weaken **07** fashion, novelty, passion **08** insanity **09** melomania, obsession, the latest, typomania **10** anglomania, anthomania, enthusiasm **11** acronymania, infatuation, tulipomania **12** orchidomania, potichomania, theatromania **13** preoccupation

**crazed**
◇ *anagram indicator*
**03** mad **04** nuts, wild **05** berko, crazy, loony **06** insane **07** berserk, lunatic **08** demented, deranged, unhinged **09** up the pole **10** moonstruck, unbalanced **12** moon-stricken, round the bend **13** off your rocker, out of your mind, round the twist

**crazily**
◇ *anagram indicator*
**05** madly **06** wildly **08** insanely **09** manically **11** frantically **12** frenetically

**crazy**
◇ *anagram indicator*
**03** mad, odd, wet **04** avid, bats, daft,

fond, gaga, gyte, keen, loco, nuts, wild, zany **05** barmy, batty, buggy, daffy, dippy, dotty, flaky, gonzo, loony, loopy, manic, nutty, potty, silly, wacko, wacky, wiggy **06** absurd, ardent, crazed, cuckoo, dottle, fruity, insane, maniac, mental, raving, screwy, stupid, unwise **07** bananas, barking, berserk, bonkers, cracked, devoted, dottled, foolish, frantic, haywire, idiotic, lunatic, meshuga, rickety, smitten, strange, zealous **08** crackers, crackpot, demented, deranged, dingbats, doolally, frenetic, peculiar, unhinged **09** disturbed, enamoured, fanatical, foolhardy, half-baked, imprudent, infuriate, ludicrous, lymphatic, pixilated, senseless, up the wall **10** bestraught, distracted, distraught, frantic-mad, infatuated, off the wall, off your nut, outrageous, out to lunch, passionate, pixillated, ridiculous, unbalanced **11** hare-brained, impractical, nonsensical, not all there, off the rails, off your head, unrealistic **12** crackbrained, enthusiastic, mad as a hatter, off your chump, preposterous, round the bend **13** impracticable, irresponsible, off your rocker, out of your head, out of your mind, out of your tree, round the twist **14** off your trolley, wrong in the head

**• go crazy**

◇ *anagram indicator*

**04** flip **05** go ape, go mad **06** blow up, wig out **09** go bananas **11** flip your lid, go ballistic **15** lose your marbles

**creak**

**04** rasp **05** grate, grind, groan **06** scrape, screak, squeak, squeal **07** scratch, screech

**creaky**

**05** rusty **07** grating, rasping, squeaky, unoiled **08** grinding, groaning, scraping **09** squeaking, squealing **10** scratching, screeching

**cream**

**03** oil **04** best, pale, pick, ream, skim **05** creme, élite, ivory, milky, paste, pasty, prime, salve, sweet **06** finest, flower, lotion, thrash **07** unguent **08** cleanser, cosmetic, emulsion, liniment, off-white, ointment **09** emollient **10** choice part, select part **11** application, preparation **13** whitish-yellow **14** crème de la crème, pick of the bunch, yellowish-white

**creamy**

**04** oily, pale, rich **05** ivory, milky, pasty, reamy, thick **06** smooth **07** buttery, velvety **08** off-white **13** cream-coloured, whitish-yellow **14** yellowish-white

**crease**

**04** fold, kris, line, ruck, tuck **05** crimp, pleat, ridge **06** creese, furrow, groove, kreese, pucker, ruckle, rumple, runkle **07** crinkle, crumple, wreathe, wrinkle **09** corrugate **10** line of life **11** corrugation

**• crease up**

**05** amuse **09** make laugh

**create**

**04** coin, form, make **05** build, cause, erect, found, frame, hatch, mould, set up, shape **06** design, devise, invent, invest, lead to, ordain **07** appoint, compose, concoct, develop, install, produce **08** engender, generate, initiate, occasion, result in **09** construct, establish, fabricate, formulate, institute, originate **10** bring about, give rise to, inaugurate **13** cause to happen **14** bring into being

**creation**

◇ *anagram indicator*

**04** life, work **05** birth, world **06** cosmos, design, making, nature, origin **07** concept, genesis, product **08** universe **09** formation, handiwork, handywork, invention, work of art **10** biopoiesis, brainchild, conception, concoction, everything, foundation, generation, initiation, innovation, production **11** achievement, chef d'oeuvre, composition, development, fabrication, institution, masterpiece, origination, procreation **12** constitution, construction **13** establishment

**creative**

**06** clever, gifted **07** fertile **08** artistic, inspired, naturing, original, talented **09** forgetive, ingenious, intuitive, inventive, visionary **10** innovative, productive **11** full of ideas, imaginative, resourceful

**creativity**

**04** gift **06** talent, vision **08** artistry **09** fertility, ingenuity **10** cleverness **11** imagination, inspiration, originality **13** inventiveness **14** productiveness **15** imaginativeness, resourcefulness

**creator**

**03** God **05** maker **06** author, Brahma, father, mother, Ormazd, Ormuzd **07** builder, founder **08** composer, demiurge, designer, inventor, producer **09** architect, Artificer, demiurgus, initiator **10** Ahura Mazda, first cause, originator, prime mover

**creature**

**03** man **04** bird, body, fish, soul, zoon **05** beast, being, human, thing, wight, woman **06** animal, cratur, insect, mortal, person, wretch **07** crathur, critter, crittur **08** organism **10** human being, individual **11** living thing

*See also* **animal**; **mythical**; **poison**

**credence**

**05** faith, trust **06** belief, credit **07** support **08** reliance **09** sideboard **10** acceptance, confidence, dependence **11** credibility

**credentials**

**04** deed **05** title **06** papers, permit **07** diploma, licence, warrant **08** passport **09** documents, reference **11** certificate, testimonial **12** identity card **13** accreditation, authorization **14** recommendation **15** proof of identity

**credibility**

**04** cred **09** integrity **10** likelihood **11** probability, reliability **12** plausibility **14** reasonableness **15** trustworthiness

**credible**

**06** honest, likely **07** credent, sincere, tenable **08** possible, probable, reliable **09** plausible, thinkable **10** believable, convincing, dependable, imaginable, persuasive, reasonable **11** conceivable, trustworthy

**credibly**

**08** honestly, possibly, reliably **09** plausibly, sincerely, thinkably **10** believably, dependably, imaginably, reasonably **11** conceivably **12** convincingly, persuasively **13** trustworthily

**credit**

**02** cr, HP **03** buy **04** fame, tick **05** asset, boast, faith, glory, kudos, mense, pride, strap, tally, trust **06** accept, assign, belief, charge, esteem, honour, impute, praise, rely on, thanks **07** acclaim, ascribe, believe, put down, swallow, tribute **08** accredit, approval, credence, plaudits, prestige **09** attribute, have faith, laudation **10** confidence, estimation, reputation **11** distinction, pride and joy, recognition, subscribe to **12** commendation **15** acknowledgement

**• in credit**

**07** solvent **10** beforehand, in the black

**• on credit**

**06** on tick **07** on lay-by, on trust **08** on the tab **09** on account **10** on the slate **12** on the knocker **13** by instalments **14** on hire purchase **15** on the never-never

**creditable**

**04** good **06** worthy **08** laudable **09** admirable, deserving, estimable, excellent, exemplary, reputable **10** honourable **11** commendable, meritorious, respectable, trustworthy **12** praiseworthy

**creditably**

**04** well **09** admirably **10** honourably **11** commendably, excellently, respectably

**creditor**

**02** cr **06** debtee, lender **07** Shylock **08** apprizer **09** loan shark **11** moneylender

**credulity**

**07** naivety **09** silliness, stupidity **10** dupability, simplicity **11** gullibility **13** credulousness **14** uncriticalness

**credulous**

**04** fond **05** naive **06** simple **07** credent, dupable **08** gullable,

gullible, trusting, wide-eyed
**10** uncritical **12** overtrusting, unsuspecting

**creed**
**05** canon, credo, dogma, faith
**06** belief, Ophism, symbol, tenets
**08** articles, doctrine, ideology, standard, teaching **09** catechism, the belief **10** persuasion, principles

**creek**
**03** bay, geo, gio, goe, pow, voe
**04** cove, wick **05** bight, brook, crick, fiord, firth, fjord, fleet, inlet **06** slough, stream **07** estuary

**creep**
**04** edge, fawn, fear, geek, grew, grue, inch, worm **05** alarm, crawl, slink, snake, sneak, steal, toady **06** cringe, fawner, grovel, horror, squirm, terror, tiptoe, unease, writhe, yes-man
**07** shudder, slither, wriggle **08** disquiet
**09** revulsion, sycophant **10** bootlicker
**13** move unnoticed

**creeper**
**04** vine **05** liana, plant **06** runner
**07** climber, rambler, trailer **08** trailing, woodbind, woodbine **09** Boston ivy
**10** ampelopsis, monkey rope, tropaeolum **13** climbing plant, trailing plant
*See also* **snake**

**creepy**
**05** eerie, scary, weird **06** crawly, spooky **07** macabre, ominous
**08** gruesome, horrible, horrific, menacing, sinister **10** disturbing, horrifying, mysterious, terrifying, unpleasant **11** frightening, hair-raising, nightmarish, threatening
**13** bloodcurdling, spine-chilling

**crescent**
**04** Cres **06** waxing **07** growing
**09** croissant **10** increasing

**crescent-shaped**
**05** moony **06** lunate **07** falcate, lunated, lunular **08** falcated **09** bow-shaped, falciform **12** sickle-shaped

**crest**
**03** mon, top **04** apex, comb, edge, head, knap, mane, peak, tuft **05** badge, chine, crown, plume, ridge **06** cimier, copple, crista, device, emblem, summit, symbol, tassel **07** cornice, feather, panache, regalia, topknot
**08** aigrette, caruncle, insignia, pinnacle, surmount **09** cockscomb
**10** coat of arms

**crestfallen**
**03** sad **08** dejected, downcast
**09** depressed **10** cheesed off, despondent, dispirited
**11** discouraged, downhearted
**12** disappointed, disconsolate, disheartened **13** in the doldrums
**14** down in the dumps

**cretin**
**03** ass, mug, nit **04** clot, dolt, dope, dork, fool, geek, jerk, prat, twit
**05** chump, dumbo, dunce, idiot, moron, ninny, schmo, twerp, wally
**06** dimwit, nitwit, sucker **07** fathead, halfwit, jughead, pillock, plonker, schmuck **08** imbecile **09** birdbrain, blockhead, ignoramus, simpleton
**10** bufflehead, nincompoop

**crevasse**
**03** gap **05** abyss, chasm, cleft, crack, split **07** fissure **11** bergschrund

**crevice**
**03** gap **04** hole, rift, slit **05** break, chink, cleft, crack, split **06** cranny
**07** fissure, opening **10** interstice

**crew**
**03** lot, man, mob, set **04** band, crue, gang, pack, ship, team, unit **05** bunch, corps, crowd, eight, force, group, party, squad, troop **06** torpid **07** company
**09** lower deck **10** complement

**crew member** *see* **sailor**; **ship**

**crib**
**03** bed, cot, key **04** copy, lift, pony, putz, trot **05** cheat, horse, pinch, stall, steal **06** cratch, pirate **07** brothel, purloin **08** bassinet, carry-cot, cribbage **09** reproduce, travel-cot
**10** plagiarize **11** Moses basket

**crick**
**04** kink, pain, rick **05** cramp, creek, spasm **06** twinge **09** stiffness
**10** convulsion

**cricket**
**04** grig **05** stool **09** churr-worm

*Cricket teams include:*

**04** Kent
**05** Essex
**06** Durham, Surrey, Sussex
**08** Somerset, Victoria
**09** Glamorgan, Hampshire, Middlesex, Yorkshire
**10** Derbyshire, Lancashire, Queensland
**12** Warwickshire
**13** New South Wales
**14** Leicestershire, South Australia, Worcestershire
**15** Gloucestershire, Nottinghamshire

*Cricket terms include:*

**01** b, c, M, w
**02** by, CC, in, lb, nb, no, on, ro
**03** bat, box, bye, CCC, cut, ECB, ICC, lbw, leg, MCC, net, ODI, off, pad, peg, run, six, ton
**04** bail, ball, blob, bowl, deep, draw, duck, edge, four, go in, grub, hook, Oval, over, pair, poke, pull, slip, tail, test, tice, walk, wide
**05** Ashes, break, c and b, catch, cover, dolly, drive, extra, glide, gully, knock, Lords, mid-on, pitch, plumb, point, silly, skyer, snick, stump
**06** appeal, beamer, bowled, bowler, caught, crease, doosra, eleven, glance, googly, ground, howzat, leg bye, long on, maiden, middle, mid-off, no-ball, not out, opener, play on, run out, single, square, stumps, the leg, umpire, whites, wicket, yorker
**07** batsman, batting, bouncer, century, declare, dismiss, fielder, grubber, infield, innings, last man, leg side, leg slip, leg spin, long hop, long leg, long off, off spin, on the up, spinner, striker, stumped, wrong'un
**08** bodyline, boundary, chinaman, delivery, fielding, flannels, follow on, full toss, how's that, leg guard, long slip, long stop, misfield, off break, off drive, off guard, one-dayer, outfield, pavilion, short leg, sledging, the Ashes, third man
**09** batswoman, deep field, fieldsman, hit wicket, inswinger, leg before, leg theory, long field, mid-wicket, overpitch, short slip, square leg, test match, tip and run
**10** all-rounder, cover drive, draw stumps, fast bowler, golden duck, leg spinner, maiden over, pace bowler, right guard, scoreboard, seam bowler, silly mid-on, skittle out, spin bowler, twelfth man
**11** clean bowled, daisy-cutter, diamond duck, fast bowling, fieldswoman, grass-cutter, ground staff, half-century, limited-over, net practice, one-day match, pace bowling, seam bowling, sight screen, silly mid-off, spin bowling
**12** carry your bat, wicketkeeper
**13** break your duck, county cricket, keep your end up, maiden century, night-watchman, popping crease
**14** off the back foot
**15** bowl a maiden over, caught and bowled, leather on willow, leg before wicket, square leg umpire

*See also* **delivery**

*Cricketers, commentators and umpires include:*

**03** **Fry** (Charles Burgess)
**04** **Ames** (Leslie), **Bedi** (Bishen), **Bird** (Dicky), **Hall** (Wesley), **Hick** (Graeme), **Khan** (Imran), **Lara** (Brian), **Lock** (Tony), **Lord** (Thomas)
**05** **Abbas** (Zaheer), **Akram** (Wasim), **Allen** (Sir Gubby), **Amiss** (Dennis), **Crowe** (Martin), **Evans** (Godfrey), **Gibbs** (Lance), **Gooch** (Graham), **Gough** (Darren), **Gower** (David), **Grace** (W G), **Greig** (Tony), **Healy** (Ian), **Hobbs** (Sir Jack), **Knott** (Alan), **Laker** (Jim), **Lawry** (William), **Lloyd** (Clive), **Marsh** (Rodney), **Pilch** (Fuller), **Walsh** (Courtney), **Warne** (Shane), **Waugh** (Mark), **Waugh** (Steve)
**06** **Arlott** (John), **Bailey** (Trevor), **Benaud** (Richie), **Border** (Allan), **Botham** (Ian), **Cronje** (Hansie), **Dexter** (Ted), **Donald** (Allan), **Dravid** (Rahul), **Edrich** (Bill), **Edrich** (John), **Garner** (Joel), **Hadlee** (Sir Richard), **Haynes** (Desmond), **Hutton** (Len), **Jessop** (Gilbert), **Lillee** (Dennis), **Miller** (Keith), **Rhodes** (Wilfred),

Sobers (Sir Garfield), Thorpe (Graham), Titmus (Fred), Turner (Glenn), Warner (Sir Pelham 'Plum')
07 **Ambrose** (Curtley), **Boycott** (Geoffrey), **Bradman** (Sir Donald), **Compton** (Denis), **Cowdrey** (Colin, Lord), **Denness** (Michael), **De Silva** (Aravinda), **Gatting** (Mike), **Holding** (Michael), **Hussain** (Nasser), **Jardine** (Douglas), **Larwood** (Harold), **Miandad** (Javed), **Pollock** (Graeme), **Simpson** (Robert), **Stewart** (Alec), **Thomson** (Jeff), **Trueman** (Fred)
08 **Atherton** (Michael), **Chappell** (Greg), **Chappell** (Ian), **Chappell** (Trevor), **Flintoff** (Andrew), **Gavaskar** (Sunil), **Kapil Dev** (Nikhanj), **Richards** (Barry), **Richards** (Vivian), **Sheppard** (David)
09 **D'Oliveira** (Basil), **Greenidge** (Gordon), **Ranatunga** (Arjuna)
10 **Azharuddin** (Mohammad), **Barrington** (Ken), **Lillywhite** (William)
11 **Heyhoe Flint** (Rachel), **Illingworth** (Raymond), **Trescothick** (Marcus)

## crier

**06** beadle, herald **07** bellman
**09** announcer, messenger, outrooper, town crier **10** proclaimer **15** bearer of tidings

## crime

**03** rap, sin **04** evil, fact, vice
**06** crimen, felony **07** misdeed, offence, offense, outrage, villany
**08** atrocity, enormity, iniquity, thievery, villainy **09** violation **10** illegal act, misconduct, wickedness, wrongdoing
**11** delinquency, lawbreaking, lawlessness, malefaction, malfeasance, unlawful act **12** misdemeanour
**13** transgression

*Crimes include:*

03 ABH, GBH
04 rape
05 arson, fraud, theft
06 hijack, murder, piracy
07 assault, battery, bribery, forgery, larceny, mugging, perjury, robbery, treason
08 burglary, filicide, homicide, poaching, sabotage, stalking
09 blackmail, extortion, hate crime, joy-riding, matricide, parricide, patricide, pilfering, terrorism, uxoricide, vandalism
10 corruption, cybercrime, fratricide, kidnapping
11 drug dealing, hooliganism, infanticide, shoplifting, sororicide, trespassing
12 drink-driving, embezzlement, manslaughter
13 assassination, drug smuggling, housebreaking
14 counterfeiting, insider dealing, insider trading
15 computer hacking

## criminal

◇ *anagram indicator*
**03** con **04** bent, crim, evil **05** felon, tough, wrong **06** chummy, guilty, outlaw, wicked **07** convict, corrupt, crooked, culprit, illegal, illicit, lawless, obscene, villain **08** crimeful, culpable, infamous, offender, prisoner, shameful, unlawful **09** dishonest, felonious, miscreant, nefarious, wrongdoer
**10** delinquent, deplorable, disgusting, indictable, iniquitous, lawbreaker, malefactor, outrageous, scandalous, villainous **11** disgraceful, lawbreaking
**12** preposterous **13** reprehensible

*Criminal types include:*

03 dip, lag
04 hood, thug, yegg
05 crook, thief
06 bandit, forger, gunman, killer, mugger, pirate, rapist, robber, vandal
07 abactor, brigand, burglar, filcher, hoodlum, mobster, poacher, prigger, rustler, stalker, tea leaf, yeggman
08 arsonist, assassin, batterer, bigamist, car-thief, gangster, hijacker, jailbird, joyrider, murderer, pederast, perjurer, receiver, saboteur, smuggler, swindler
09 buccaneer, cracksman, embezzler, kidnapper, larcenist, racketeer, ram-raider, strangler, terrorist
10 bootlegger, cat burglar, dope pusher, drug dealer, fire-raiser, highwayman, paedophile, pickpocket, shoplifter, trespasser
11 armed robber, blackmailer, bogus caller, drink-driver, kerb-crawler, safecracker, war criminal
12 drug smuggler, extortionist, housebreaker, sexual abuser
13 counterfeiter

*Criminals include:*

03 **Ray** (James Earl)
04 **Aram** (Eugene), **Hare** (William), **Hood** (Robin), **Kray** (Reginald), **Kray** (Ronnie), **Rais** (Gilles de), **Todd** (Sweeney), **West** (Frederick), **West** (Rosemary)
05 **Biggs** (Ronald), **Blood** (Thomas), **Booth** (John Wilkes), **Brady** (Ian), **Burke** (William), **Ellis** (Ruth), **James** (Jesse), **Kelly** (Ned), **Lucan** (Richard John Bingham, Lord)
06 **Barrow** (Clyde), **Bonney** (William H), **Borden** (Lizzie), **Capone** (Al), **Corday** (Charlotte), **Meehan** (Patrick), **Nilsen** (Dennis), **Oswald** (Lee Harvey), **Parker** (Bonnie), **Rob Roy**, **Sirhan** (Sirhan), **Turpin** (Dick)
07 **Bathori** (Elizabeth), **Chapman** (Mark), **Crippen** (Hawley), **Hindley** (Myra), **Huntley** (Ian), **Ireland** (William), **Luciano** (Charles 'Lucky'), **Shipman** (Harold), **Winters** (Larry)
08 **Barabbas**, **Christie** (John), **Hanratty** (James), **Sheppard** (Jack), **Son of Sam**
09 **Berkowitz** (David), **Dillinger** (John), **Sutcliffe** (Peter)
11 **Billy the Kid**
13 **Jack the Ripper**
14 **Moors Murderers**
15 **Yorkshire Ripper**

*See also* **highwayman**; **pirate**

## crimp

**04** bend, curl, fold, pote, tuck, wave
**05** flute, pleat, quill, ridge **06** crease, furrow, gather, goffer, groove, hinder, pucker, rumple, thwart **07** crinkle, crumple, gauffer, wrinkle **09** corrugate

## cringe

**03** bow, shy **04** bend, duck, fawn
**05** cower, crawl, creep, quail, sneak, start, stoop, toady, wince **06** blench, crouch, flinch, grovel, kowtow, quiver, recoil, shrink, suck up **07** flatter, tremble **08** draw back **09** be all over
**11** curry favour **12** bow and scrape
**14** tug the forelock

## crinkle

**04** curl, fold, line, ruck, tuck, wave
**05** crimp, money, pleat, ridge, twist
**06** crease, furrow, groove, pucker, ruffle, rumple **07** crumple, wrinkle
**09** corrugate **10** paper money
**11** corrugation

## crinkly

**05** curly, kinky, money **06** fluted, folded, frizzy, ridged, tucked
**07** creased, crimped, grooved, pleated, rumpled, wrinkly **08** crinkled, crumpled, furrowed, gathered, puckered, wrinkled **10** corrugated, paper money

## cripple

**04** lame, maim, ruin **05** spoil
**06** damage, hamper, impair, impede, injure, weaken **07** destroy, disable, lameter, lamiger, lamiter, vitiate
**08** handicap, lammiger, mutilate, paralyse, sabotage **09** hamstring, undermine **10** debilitate, immobilize
**12** incapacitate

## crippled

**04** halt, lame, maim **08** deformed, disabled **09** paralysed
**11** handicapped **13** incapacitated

## crisis

**03** fit, fix, jam **04** acme, hole, mess, stew, turn **05** brunt, crise **06** crunch, pickle, scrape **07** dilemma, problem, trouble **08** calamity, disaster, exigency, hot water, quandary, solution
**09** emergency, extremity
**10** crossroads, difficulty **11** catastrophe, predicament **12** turning-point

## crisp

**04** chip, cool, firm, hard, neat **05** brief, brisk, clear, crump, fresh, pithy, short, terse **06** chilly, crispy, crumpy, snappy
**07** bracing, brittle, chippie, concise, crackly, crumbly, crunchy, friable
**08** decisive, incisive, succinct
**09** breakable **10** refreshing
**12** invigorating **13** authoritative

**criterion**
**03** law **04** norm, rule, test **05** basis, canon, gauge, model, scale **06** square **07** measure **08** exemplar, standard **09** benchmark, principle, yardstick **10** shibboleth, touchstone

**critic**
**05** judge **06** carper, censor, expert, pundit **07** analyst, knocker, monitor, Zoilist **08** attacker, censurer, observer, overseer, reviewer **09** Aristarch, authority, backbiter, find-fault, nit-picker **11** commentator, fault-finder

*See also* **literary**

**critical**
**04** crit, nice **05** fatal, grave, major, vital **06** severe, urgent **07** carping, crucial, exigent, fateful, gingery, pivotal, probing, serious **08** captious, deciding, decisive, historic, niggling, perilous, pressing, scathing, venomous **09** cavilling, dangerous, essential, important, momentous, quibbling, vitriolic **10** analytical, censorious, compelling, derogatory, diagnostic, discerning, evaluative, expository, nit-picking, perceptive, precarious **11** climacteric, disparaging, explanatory, judgemental, penetrating, significant **12** all-important, condemnatory, disapproving, fault-finding, hypercorrect, life-and-death, sharp-tongued, vituperative **13** hypercritical **14** disapprobative, interpretative **15** uncomplimentary

• **critical position**
**04** pass

**critically**
**07** acutely, gravely, vitally **08** urgently **09** crucially, seriously **10** captiously, decisively, perilously **11** dangerously **12** analytically **13** disparagingly, significantly **14** diagnostically, disapprovingly **15** hypercritically

**criticism**
**04** flak **05** blame, snipe, stick, strop **06** attack, niggle, review **07** censure, comment, reproof, ripping, slating, write-up, Zoilism **08** analysis, bad press, brickbat, critique, knocking, niggling, slamming **09** appraisal, judgement, stricture **10** assessment, commentary, evaluation, exposition, nit-picking, textualism **11** disapproval, explanation, explication **12** appreciation, condemnation, fault-finding **13** animadversion, disparagement **14** interpretation

**criticize**
**03** bag, nag, pan, rip **04** carp, crab, flay, slag, slam, zing **05** blame, cut up, decry, judge, knock, roast, score, slash, slate, snipe, trash **06** assess, attack, hammer, impugn, niggle, peck at, review, tilt at **07** analyse, canvass, censure, condemn, dissect, explain, nit-pick, rip into, rubbish, run down, scarify, slag off, snipe at **08** appraise, badmouth, denounce, evaluate, wade into **09** castigate, denigrate, disparage, excoriate, have a go at, interpret, pull apart, slaughter, take apart, tear apart **10** animadvert, come down on, go to town on, have a pop at, speak ill of, take a pop at, vituperate **11** have a shot at, pick holes in **12** disapprove of, pick to pieces, pull to pieces, put the boot in, tear to shreds **13** find fault with, tear a strip off **14** cast aspersions, ultracrepidate **15** do a hatchet job on, pass judgement on

**critique**
**05** essay **06** review **07** write-up **08** analysis **09** appraisal, criticism, judgement **10** assessment, commentary, evaluation, exposition **11** explanation, explication **12** appreciation **14** interpretation

**croak**
**03** caw, die **04** crow, gasp, kill, rasp **05** crake, croup, grunt **06** squawk, wheeze **07** grumble **12** speak harshly

**Croatia**
**02** HR **03** HRV

**crock**
**03** jar, pig, pot, urn **04** dirt, smut **06** vessel **07** disable **08** potsherd **09** break down

**crocked**
◇ *anagram indicator*
*See* **drunk**

**crockery**
**05** china **06** dishes **07** pottery **08** brockage **09** porcelain, stoneware, tableware **11** earthenware **12** breakfast-set

**crocodile**
**04** croc **06** caiman, cayman, garial, gavial, mugger **07** gharial **09** leviathan, teleosaur **11** river-dragon, Teleosaurus

**croft**
**04** farm, plot **07** pightle **08** farmland **12** smallholding

**Cronus**
**06** Saturn

**crony**
**03** pal **04** ally, chum, mate **05** buddy **06** friend **07** comrade **08** familiar, follower, intimate, sidekick **09** associate, colleague, companion, confidant **10** accomplice, confidante

**crook**
◇ *anagram indicator*
**03** bow, ill **04** bend, flex, hook, kink, sick, tilt, warp **05** angle, angry, cheat, cromb, crome, cross, curve, fraud, nasty, rogue, shark, slant, thief, twist, wrong **06** con man, deform, gibbet, kebbie, robber, unfair, unwell **07** crosier, crozier, distort, dubious, villain **08** criminal, crummack, crummock, inferior, offender, operator, swindler **09** card sharp, dishonest, sheep-hook **10** distortion, lawbreaker, unpleasant **13** pastoral staff

**crooked**
◇ *anagram indicator*
**04** awry, bent **05** askew, bowed, shady, wrong **06** angled, camsho, curved, hooked, shifty, thrawn, tilted, uneven, warped, zigzag **07** buckled, corrupt, illegal, illicit, sinuous, twisted, winding **08** camshoch, criminal, deformed, lopsided, slanting, thraward, thrawart, tortuous, unlawful **09** camsheugh, contorted, deceitful, dishonest, distorted, irregular, misshapen, nefarious, off-centre, skew-whiff, underhand, unethical **10** asymmetric, fraudulent **11** anfractuous, treacherous **12** unprincipled, unscrupulous

**crookedly**
**04** agee, ajee, awry **05** askew **08** unevenly **09** off-centre **10** lopsidedly **14** asymmetrically

**croon**
**03** hum **04** lilt, sing **06** warble **08** vocalize

• **crooner**
**04** Bing

*See also* **singer**

**crop**
**03** cut, lop, lot, mow, rod, set **04** clip, crap, craw, pare, poll, reap, snip, stow, trim **05** batch, gorge, group, prune, shear, stand, yield **06** finial, fruits, gather, growth, reduce **07** curtail, harvest, produce, reaping, shorten, vintage **08** gleaning, wool clip **09** gathering, ingluvies **10** collection

*Arable crops include:*

**03** pea, rye, yam
**04** bean, corn, flax, hemp, kale, milo, oats, rape, rice
**05** colza, maize, swede, wheat
**06** barley, kharif, millet, potato, turnip
**07** alfalfa, cassava, linseed, lucerne, oilseed, popcorn, sorghum, soy bean
**08** mung bean, soya bean, teosinte
**09** milo maize, sugar beet, sugar cane, sunflower, sweetcorn, triticale
**11** oilseed rape, sweet potato
**12** mangel wurzel

• **crop up**
**05** arise, occur **06** appear, arrive, come up, emerge, happen, turn up **09** take place **10** come to pass **13** present itself

**cross**
◇ *anagram indicator*
**01** X **03** cut, ill, irk, mix, woe, wry **04** arch, crux, defy, edgy, foil, ford, join, lace, load, meet, pain, sign, sore, span, vext, wade **05** angry, annoy, blend, block, check, grief, harsh, irate, short, surly, thraw, trial, vexed, worry **06** bridge, burden, crabby, franzy, grumpy, hamper, hinder, hybrid, impede, misery, oppose, peeved, put out, resist, shirty, snappy, sullen, thwart **07** adverse, amalgam, annoyed, awkward, fretful, grouchy, mixture,

mongrel, oblique, peevish, prickly, trouble **08** bestride, confront, converge, diagonal, disaster, go across, obstruct, opposite, pass over, snappish, traverse, walk over
**09** adversity, balancing, crosswise, crotchety, decussate, difficult, dishonest, fractious, frustrate, hybridize, impatient, intersect, irascible, irritable, splenetic, suffering
**10** affliction, criss-cross, crossbreed, displeased, interbreed, intertwine, interweave, misfortune, mixed breed, mongrelize, overthwart, reciprocal, transverse **11** bad-tempered, catastrophe, combination, ill-tempered, tribulation
**12** cantankerous, disagreeable, interchanged, intersecting, neutralizing, travel across **14** cross-fertilize, cross-pollinate

*See also* **hybrid**

*Crosses include:*

**01** T
**03** Red, tau
**04** ankh, high, Iron, ring, rood, rose, rosy
**05** fiery, Greek, Latin, papal, Rouen
**06** ansate, botoné, Celtic, fleury, fylfot, Geneva, George, market, moline, potent, Y-cross
**07** Avelian, Calvary, capital, Cornish, Maltese, Russian, saltire, Weeping
**08** Buddhist, capuchin, cardinal, crosslet, crucifix, holy-rood, Lorraine, military, pectoral, quadrate, rood-tree, Southern, St Peter's, swastika, Victoria
**09** encolpion, encolpium, Jerusalem, preaching, St Andrew's, St George's
**10** St Anthony's
**11** patriarchal
**13** Constantinian, crux decussata
**14** archiepiscopal

• **cross out**
**06** cancel, cut out, delete, remove, rub out **07** edit out **09** strike out **10** blue-pencil, obliterate
• **make cross**
**04** vote
• **make sign of cross over**
**04** sain

**cross-examination**
**04** quiz **08** grilling, quizzing
**11** examination, questioning
**13** interrogation **14** the third degree

**cross-examine**
**04** pump, quiz **05** grill, targe
**07** examine **08** question
**11** interrogate **13** cross-question

**crossing**
◇ *containment indicator*
**04** ford, trip **06** voyage **07** journey, passage, traject **08** junction, traverse
**09** crosswalk, overgoing
**10** crossroads, trajection
**12** intersection **13** zebra crossing
**14** Toucan crossing **15** grade separation, pelican crossing

**crossover value**
**03** COV

**crosswise**
**04** awry, over **06** across, aslant, thwart **07** athwart **08** sideways **09** crossways, obliquely **10** crisscross, diagonally, overthwart, transverse **11** catercorner
**12** transversely **13** catercornered

**crossword**

*Crosswords and crossword setters include:*

**03** Phi
**04** Apex, Azed, Duck, Mass, Monk, Paul, Shed
**05** Afrit, Owzat, Rufus, Wynne (Arthur)
**06** Aelred, Crispa, Custos, Gemini, Merlin, Portia
**07** Columba, Cyclops, Fidelio, Quixote, Spurius, Ximenes
**08** Everyman, Giovanni, Mephisto, Pasquale
**09** Araucaria, Beelzebub, Bunthorne, Cinephile, Virgilius
**10** Enigmatist, Torquemada

**crotch**
**04** fork **05** groin **06** crutch **08** genitals
**11** bifurcation

**crotchet**
**03** toy **04** whim **11** quarter note

**crotchety**
**05** cross, surly, testy **06** crabby, crusty, grumpy **07** awkward, crabbed, grouchy, iracund, maggoty, peevish, prickly **08** contrary, petulant
**09** difficult, fractious, irascible, irritable, whimsical **11** bad-tempered, ill-tempered **12** cantankerous, disagreeable, iracundulous, obstreperous **13** short-tempered

**crouch**
**03** bow **04** bend, dare, duck, fawn, ruck **05** cower, hunch, kneel, squat, stoop **06** cringe

**crow**
**03** daw, jay **04** brag, rook **05** boast, crake, exult, gloat, raven, vaunt
**06** chough, corbie, corvid, hoodie
**07** bluster, jackdaw, rejoice, show off, talk big, triumph **08** flourish **09** flute-bird **10** nutcracker, saddleback **12** cry roast-meat **13** Cornish chough
**14** cock-a-doodle-doo **15** blow your own horn

**crowd**
**03** jam, lot, mob, set **04** army, band, cram, gate, herd, host, mass, mong, pack, pile, push, raft, rout **05** bunch, crush, crwth, drove, elbow, flock, group, horde, house, meiny, press, shove, stuff, surge, swarm, three
**06** bundle, circle, clique, gather, huddle, hustle, jostle, masses, meiney, meinie, menyie, muster, people, public, rabble, roll-up, squash, stream, throng, thrust **07** cluster, company, congest, scrooge, scrouge, squeeze, the many, turnout, viewers
**08** assembly, audience, caboodle, compress, converge, frequent, overflow, populace, riff-raff, scrowdge, varletry, watchers **09** frequence, gathering, listeners, multitude, revel-rout **10** attendance, collection, congregate, fraternity, spectators
**12** grex venalium

**crowded**
**04** busy, full, pang **05** close, thick
**06** filled, jammed, mobbed, packed, throng **07** chocker, crammed, cramped, crushed, teeming
**08** frequent, overfull, swarming, thronged **09** congested, jam-packed
**11** chock-a-block, overcrowded, overflowing **13** overpopulated **14** full to bursting

**crown**
**02** cr **03** cap, taj, tip, top **04** acme, apex, bays, king, noll, pate, peak, tiar
**05** adorn, award, crest, glory, kudos, prize, queen, ruler, tiara, title
**06** anoint, cantle, climax, corona, diadem, empire, fulfil, height, honour, induct, invest, krantz, reward, sconce, summit, trophy, vertex, wreath
**07** aureola, aureole, circlet, coronal, coronet, dignify, emperor, empress, festoon, foretop, garland, install, laurels, monarch, perfect, pschent, royalty, thick'un **08** complete, enthrone, finalize, kingship, laureate, monarchy, pinnacle, round off
**09** sovereign **10** consummate
**11** culmination, distinction, sovereignty **13** ultimus haeres

**crowning**
**03** top **05** final **07** highest, perfect, supreme **08** greatest, ultimate
**09** climactic, paramount, sovereign, unmatched **10** consummate, coronation **11** culminating, investiture, unsurpassed **12** enthronement, inauguration, incoronation, installation

**crucial**
**03** key **05** major, vital **06** trying, urgent **07** central, pivotal, testing
**08** critical, deciding, decisive, historic, pressing **09** essential, important, momentous, searching **10** compelling
**12** all-important

**crucially**
**07** vitally **09** centrally **10** critically, decisively **11** essentially, importantly, momentously

**crucify**
**04** mock, rack, slam **05** knock, slate
**06** punish **07** execute, rubbish, run down, torment, torture **08** ridicule
**09** criticize, denigrate, excoriate, persecute **10** put to death **12** pull to pieces, tear to pieces, tear to shreds
**14** kill on the cross

**crude**
◇ *anagram indicator*
**03** hot, raw **04** blue, lewd, rude
**05** basic, bawdy, brash, brute, dirty, gross, juicy, rough **06** coarse, earthy, risqué, simple, smutty, vulgar

07 natural, obscene, raunchy, uncouth 08 immature, indecent 09 half-baked, makeshift, offensive, primitive, unrefined, untreated 10 inartistic, undigested, unfinished, unpolished, unprepared 11 barrelhouse, rudimentary, unconcocted, undeveloped, unprocessed 12 down-and-dirty 13 rough and ready

**crudely**
◇ *anagram indicator*
06 rudely, simply 07 roughly
08 coarsely 09 basically, obscenely
10 indecently 11 offensively, primitively

**cruel**
◇ *anagram indicator*
03 raw 04 evil, fell, grim, mean
05 felon, nasty 06 bitter, bloody, brutal, fierce, flinty, immane, savage, severe, unkind, wanton, wicked
07 callous, cutting, hellish, inhuman, painful, vicious 08 barbaric, diabolic, felonous, fiendish, indurate, inhumane, Neronian, pitiless, ruthless, sadistic, spiteful, vengeful 09 atrocious, barbarous, butcherly, ferocious, heartless, malicious, merciless, murderous, truculent, unfeeling
10 blistering, heathenish, implacable, inexorable, iron-headed, malevolent
11 cold-blooded, hard-hearted, remorseless, unrelenting
12 bloodthirsty, bloody-minded, excruciating, stony-hearted
13 marble-hearted 14 marble-breasted

**cruelly**
08 brutally, fiercely, immanely, savagely, unkindly 09 callously, inhumanly, painfully, viciously 10 implacably, inhumanely, pitilessly, ruthlessly, spitefully 11 ferociously, heartlessly, maliciously, mercilessly, truculently
13 cold-bloodedly, hard-heartedly, remorselessly

**cruelty**
05 abuse, spite, venom 06 malice, sadism 07 tyranny 08 bullying, ferocity, immanity, meanness, savagery, severity, violence 09 barbarity, brutality, harshness 10 bestiality, inhumanity, unkindness 11 callousness, viciousness 12 ruthlessness
13 heartlessness, mercilessness, murderousness 15 hard-heartedness

**cruise**
04 busk, sail, taxi, trip 05 coast, drift, glide, slide 06 travel, voyage
07 holiday, journey 09 freewheel

**crumb**
03 bit, jot 04 atom, iota, mite, nirl
05 flake, grain, piece, scrap, shred, speck 06 morsel, sliver, titbit
07 granule, snippet, soupçon
08 fragment, particle

**crumble**
◇ *anagram indicator*
03 rot 04 fail, mull, murl 05 crush, decay, grind, pound 06 powder
07 break up, moulder 08 collapse, come away, fragment 09 break down, decompose, fall apart, pulverize
10 degenerate 11 deteriorate
12 disintegrate, fall to pieces

**crumbly**
◇ *anagram indicator*
04 nesh 05 frush, short 07 brittle, friable, powdery 11 pulverulent

**crummy**
04 poor, weak 05 cheap 06 grotty, rotten, shoddy, trashy 07 useless
08 inferior, pathetic, rubbishy 09 half-baked, miserable, third-rate, worthless
10 second-rate, unpleasant
11 substandard 12 contemptible

**crumpet**
04 head 05 woman, women
06 muffin 07 pikelet

**crumple**
04 fall, fold 05 crush 06 crease, pucker, raffle, rumple 07 crinkle, wrinkle 08 collapse, scrumple

**crunch**
04 bite, chew, crux, test 05 champ, chomp, crush, grind, munch, pinch, sit-up, smash 06 crisis 07 graunch, scranch, scrunch 09 emergency, masticate 13 critical point, moment of truth

**crusade**
03 war 04 push, work 05 cause, drive, fight, jihad 06 attack, battle, strive
07 holy war, promote 08 advocate, campaign, movement, strategy, struggle 09 offensive 10 expedition
11 undertaking

**crusader**
06 zealot 07 battler, fighter 08 activist, advocate, champion, promoter, reformer 10 campaigner, enthusiast, missionary

**crush**
◇ *anagram indicator*
03 jam 04 cram, love, mash, mill, mush, pack, pash, pulp, ruin 05 abash, break, chack, champ, check, crowd, grind, horde, pinch, pound, press, quash, quell, shame, smash, stamp, tread, upset 06 bruise, crease, crunch, defeat, liking, mangle, rumple, squash, squish, step on, subdue, throng
07 break up, conquer, contuse, crinkle, crumble, crumple, mortify, oppress, passion, put down, screw up, scrunch, shatter, squeeze, squelch, thrutch, wrinkle 08 compress, demolish, overcome, scrumple, squabash, suppress, vanquish 09 break down, comminute, devastate, humiliate, obsession, overpower, overwhelm, pulverize, telescope, triturate
10 annihilate 11 infatuation, steam-roller

**• crush down**
03 bow

**crust**
03 fur, reh 04 coat, film, husk, rind, scab, skin 05 argol, layer, shell, skull
06 caking, casing, gratin, pastry
07 caliche, capping, clinker, coating, outside, salband, surface, topping
08 beeswing, covering, exterior
09 wine-stone 10 concretion, livelihood 11 lithosphere
12 encrustation, impertinence, incrustation 13 efflorescence

*Parts of the earth's crust include:*

03 sal
04 sial, sima
06 craton, mantle

**crustacean**

*Crustaceans include:*

04 crab
05 krill, prawn, yabby
06 gilgie, hermit, jilgie, marron, partan, scampi, scrawl, shrimp, squill, yabbie
07 camaron, copepod, daphnia, dog-crab, fiddler, limulus, lobster, pagurid, pea-crab, pill bug
08 barnacle, crawfish, crayfish, crevette, king crab, land crab, ochidore, pagurian
09 centipede, devil-crab, fish louse, king prawn, langouste, millipede, phyllopod, schizopod, sea slater, shore crab, soft-shell, water flea, woodlouse
10 acorn-shell, edible crab, hermit crab, mitten-crab, robber crab, sandhopper, seed shrimp, spider crab, stomatopod, tiger prawn, velvet-crab, velvet worm, whale louse
11 brine shrimp, calling-crab, coconut crab, common prawn, Dublin prawn, fairy shrimp, fiddler crab, langoustine, rock lobster, soldier crab, spectre crab, tiger shrimp
12 common shrimp, mantis shrimp, mussel shrimp, saucepan-fish, sentinel crab, spiny lobster, squat lobster
13 acorn-barnacle, common lobster, goose barnacle, horseshoe crab, noble crayfish, Norway lobster, opossum shrimp, spectre shrimp, tadpole shrimp, velvet-fiddler
14 Dublin Bay prawn, skeleton shrimp, woolly-hand crab

*See also* **animal**

**crusty**
04 firm, hard 05 baked, cross, gruff, surly, testy 06 crabby, crispy, grumpy, snappy, touchy 07 awkward, brittle, brusque, crabbed, crumbly, crunchy, friable, grouchy, peevish, prickly
08 contrary, petulant, well-done
09 breakable, difficult, fractious, irascible, irritable, splenetic, well-baked 11 bad-tempered
12 cantankerous, disagreeable, obstreperous 13 short-tempered

**crux**
03 nub 04 core 05 cross, heart
06 centre, kernel, puzzle 07 essence, nucleus 13 the bottom line
*See also* **cross**

**cry**
**03** caw, mew, sab, sob **04** bawl, blub, call, gowl, hoop, hoot, howl, keen, mewl, pipe, plea, rivo, roar, wail, weep, word, yawp, yell, yelp, yowl **05** bleat, chevy, chivy, clock, greet, havoc, mouth, neigh, pewit, shout, skirl, tears, whine, whoop **06** bellow, bubble, chivvy, lament, peewee, peewit, prayer, report, rumour, scream, shriek, slogan, snivel, squawk, squeal, yoicks **07** bawling, blubber, call out, clamour, exclaim, screech, tantivy, vagitus, whimper **08** peesweep, proclaim **09** alalagmos, be in tears, peaseweep, shed tears, watchword **11** ejaculation, exclamation, lamentation **14** burst into tears, cry your eyes out
*See also* **shout**; **war cry** *under* **war**

• **cry off**
**06** cancel **07** back out **08** withdraw **13** decide against **14** change your mind, excuse yourself

• **cry out for**
**04** need, want **06** demand **07** call for, require **11** necessitate

• **cry up**
**04** sell **06** praise

**crypt**
**04** tomb **05** vault **08** catacomb **09** mausoleum **10** undercroft **13** burial chamber

**cryptic**
**04** dark **06** hidden, occult, secret, unseen, veiled **07** bizarre, obscure, strange **08** abstruse, esoteric, puzzling **09** ambiguous, enigmatic, equivocal **10** mysterious, perplexing

**cryptically**
**08** secretly **09** bizarrely, obscurely, strangely **11** ambiguously **12** mysteriously **13** enigmatically

**crystal**
**04** spar **05** macle, table **06** needle, raphis **07** cocaine, raphide, rhaphis, spicule **08** cut glass, rhaphide **09** microlite **10** watchglass **11** amphetamine, seeing stone

**crystallize**
**04** form **05** candy, shoot **06** appear, emerge, harden **07** clarify **08** solidify **09** make clear **11** become clear, materialize **12** make definite **13** become clearer **14** become definite

**cub**
**03** pup **04** baby, tiro **05** chest, puppy, whelp, young, youth **06** newbie, novice, rookie **07** fresher, learner, recruit, starter, student, trainee **08** beginner, freshman, initiate, neophyte **09** fledgling, greenhorn, offspring, youngster **10** apprentice, raw recruit, tenderfoot **11** probationer

**Cuba**
**01** C **02** CU **03** CUB

**cubbyhole**
**03** den **04** hole, slot **05** booth, niche **06** recess **07** cubicle **08** hideaway, tiny room **10** pigeonhole **11** compartment

**cube**
**03** die **04** dice **05** block, solid **06** cuboid **10** hexahedron, triplicate

**cuckoo**
◇ *anagram indicator*
**03** ani, mad **04** daft, gouk, gowk, koel, loco, nuts **05** batty, crazy, loony, nutty, silly **07** cracked, foolish, idiotic **08** crackpot, rainbird **12** crackbrained, round the bend **13** chaparral cock **14** brain-fever bird
*See also* **fool**; **foolish**

**cucumber**
**05** choko, wolly **07** gherkin **10** dill pickle **11** bitter-apple

**cuddle**
**03** hug, pet **04** hold, neck, snog **05** clasp, nurse **06** caress, enfold, fondle, nestle, smooch **07** embrace, smuggle, snuggle **08** canoodle

**cuddly**
**04** cosy, soft, warm **05** plump **07** lovable **08** huggable, loveable **10** cuddlesome

**cudgel**
**03** bat, hit **04** bash, beat, club, cosh, mace, patu, rung **05** clout, plant, pound, shrub, stick, towel **06** alpeen, ballow, batter, souple, strike, thwack, waster **07** clobber **08** bludgeon **09** bastinado, crabstick, fustigate, truncheon **10** shillelagh **12** an oaken towel

**cue**
**01** Q **03** nod, rod **04** hint, mace, sign **06** prompt, signal **08** feed-line, half-butt, reminder, stimulus **09** catchword, incentive **10** indication, intimation, suggestion

**cuff**
**03** box, hit **04** beat, belt, biff, clip, gowf, slap **05** clout, knock, scuff, smack, thump, whack **06** buffet, scruff, strike **07** armband, clobber, manacle **08** bracelet, gauntlet, handcuff, snitcher, wristlet **09** muffettee

• **off the cuff**
**05** ad lib **09** extempore, impromptu **10** improvised, off the wall, unprepared, unscripted **11** unrehearsed **13** spontaneously

**cuisine**
**07** cookery, cooking **10** cordon bleu **12** haute cuisine **15** nouvelle cuisine

**cul-de-sac**
**04** loke **05** close **07** dead end **10** blind alley **13** no through road

**cull**
**04** dupe, kill, pick, sift, thin **05** amass, glean, pluck **06** choose, gather, select **07** collect, destroy, pick out, thin out **09** slaughter

**culminate**
**03** end **04** peak **05** close, crest, end up **06** climax, finish, wind up **08** conclude **09** terminate **10** consummate **11** come to a head **13** come to a climax

**culmination**
**03** sum, top **04** acme, apex, head, peak, roof, turn **05** crown, point **06** apogee, climax, finale, height, heyday, summit, zenith **08** meridian, pinnacle **09** high point **10** completion, conclusion, perfection, perihelion **12** consummation

**culpability**
**05** blame, fault, guilt **09** liability **13** answerability **14** accountability, responsibility **15** blameworthiness

**culpable**
**05** wrong **06** faulty, guilty, liable, sinful **07** at fault, peccant, to blame **08** blamable, criminal **09** blameable, offending **10** answerable, censurable, in the wrong **11** blameworthy, responsible **13** reprehensible

**culprit**
**05** felon **07** convict, villain **08** criminal, offender **09** miscreant, wrongdoer **10** delinquent, lawbreaker **11** guilty party

**cult**
**03** fad **04** sect **05** craze, faith, mania, party, trend, vogue, Wicca **06** belief, cultus, school, Shinto **07** faction, fashion, in-thing, macumba **08** fixation, movement, navalism, religion **09** obsession **11** affiliation **12** denomination, macrobiotics

**cultivate**
◇ *anagram indicator*
**03** aid, dig, sow, woo **04** back, farm, grow, help, tend, till, work **05** court, fancy, groom, plant, raise, train **06** assist, enrich, foster, garden, labour, manure, plough, polish, pursue, refine, work on **07** advance, bring on, cherish, culture, develop, enhance, forward, further, harvest, husband, improve, nurture, prepare, produce, promote, support **08** civilize **09** encourage, enlighten, fertilize

**cultivated**
**04** tame **06** polite, sative, urbane **07** genteel, refined **08** advanced, cultured, educated, highbrow, polished, well-read **09** civilized, scholarly **10** discerning **11** enlightened **12** well-informed **13** sophisticated **14** discriminating

**cultivation**
**05** tilth **06** sowing **07** backing, culture, farming, growing, nurture, support, tilling, working **08** planting **09** advancing, fostering, manurance, nurturing **10** assistance, cherishing, forwarding, furthering, harvesting, refinement **11** agriculture, development, improvement, preparation **12** civilization **13** encouragement

**cultural**
**04** folk **06** ethnic, tribal **07** liberal **08** artistic, communal, edifying, national, societal **09** aesthetic, educative, elevating, enriching,

improving **10** broadening, civilizing, humanizing **11** educational, traditional **12** enlightening **13** developmental **15** anthropological

**culture**
**04** arts, crop **05** mores, music **06** growth, habits **07** customs, history, society, the arts **08** heritage, learning, painting **09** behaviour, cultivate, education, lifestyle, nurturing, tendering, way of life **10** humanities, literature, philosophy, production, refinement, traditions **11** cultivation **12** civilization

**cultured**
**04** arty **06** polite, urbane **07** erudite, genteel, learned, refined **08** advanced, artistic, educated, highbrow, polished, tasteful, well-bred, well-read **09** arty-farty, civilized, scholarly **10** cultivated **11** enlightened **12** intellectual, well-educated, well-informed **13** sophisticated

**culvert**
**04** duct **05** drain, sewer **06** gutter **07** channel, conduit, ponceau **11** watercourse

**cumbersome**
**04** slow **05** bulky, heavy **07** awkward, complex, onerous, weighty **08** cumbrous, involved, unwieldy, wasteful **09** difficult **10** burdensome **11** complicated, inefficient **12** incommodious, inconvenient, unmanageable **14** badly organized

**Cumbrian**
◇ *dialect indicator*

**cumulative**
**07** growing **08** mounting **09** enlarging **10** collective, increasing **11** multiplying, progressive, snowballing

**cunning**
**03** art, fly, sly **04** arch, deep, deft, foxy, rusé, slee, wily **05** canny, carny, craft, guile, guyle, leery, sharp, skill, wiles **06** artful, astute, carney, cautel, clever, crafty, dainty, deceit, knacky, policy, quaint, shifty, shrewd, slight, sneaky, subtle, tricky **07** crabbit, devious, finesse, knowing, practic, skilful, sleekit, sleight, slyness, varment, varmint, vulpine **08** artifice, deftness, fiendish, guileful, knackish, slippery, subtlety, trickery **09** deceitful, dexterous, ingenious, ingenuity, insidious, inventive, knowledge, sharpness **10** adroitness, artfulness, astuteness, cleverness, craftiness, shrewdness **11** cunningness, deviousness, imaginative, resourceful **12** fiendishness, manipulative **13** cunning as a fox, deceitfulness, inventiveness **15** imaginativeness, resourcefulness

**cup**
**03** mug, nut, pot, tig, tot **04** bowl, tass, wine **05** award, bidon, calix, cruse, medal, plate, prize, punch **06** beaker, bumper, cotyle, goblet, hollow, noggin, quaich, quaigh, reward, rhyton, tassie, trophy **07** chalice, cyathus, scyphus, tankard, tumbler **08** pannikin **09** cantharus, gripe's egg **11** doch-an-doris **12** deuch-an-doris, doch-an-dorach **13** deoch-an-doruis

*See also* **drinking**

**cupbearer**
**04** Hebe **08** Ganymede

**cupboard**
**05** ambry, awmry, chest, press, store **06** almery, aumbry, awmrie, closet, locker, pantry **07** almirah, armoire, cabinet, dresser, tallboy **08** cellaret, hot press, meat safe, wardrobe **09** sideboard **12** clothes-press, Welsh dresser **14** Coolgardie safe

**Cupid**
**04** Eros

**cupidity**
**05** greed **06** hunger **07** avarice, avidity, itching, longing **08** rapacity, voracity, yearning **09** eagerness, hankering **10** greediness **12** covetousness, graspingness **13** rapaciousness **14** avariciousness **15** acquisitiveness

**curable**
**08** operable **09** medicable, reparable, treatable **10** reformable, remediable **11** rectifiable

**curative**
**05** tonic **07** healing **08** medcinal, remedial, salutary **09** healthful, medicinal, vulnerary **10** corrective, febrifugal **11** alleviative, restorative, therapeutic **12** health-giving

**curator**
**06** keeper, warden, warder **07** steward **08** guardian **09** attendant, caretaker, custodian **11** conservator

**curb**
**03** bit **04** bend, bent, rein **05** brake, check, corbe, courb **06** bridle, damper, hamper, hinder, impede, muzzle, rebuff, reduce, retard, subdue **07** contain, control, inhibit, refrain, repress **08** hold back, keep back, moderate, restrain, restrict, suppress **09** constrain, deterrent, hindrance, kerbstone, restraint, retardant **10** constraint, impediment, limitation, repression, unofficial **11** holding-back, keep in check, restriction, suppression

**curdle**
**03** run **04** clot, earn, grew, grue, sour, turn, whig **05** yearn **06** lapper, lopper, posset **07** congeal, cruddle, ferment, thicken **08** solidify, turn sour **09** coagulate

**curd, curds**
**04** skyr **06** junket
• **bean curd**
**04** tofu

**cure**
◇ *anagram indicator*
**03** dry, dun, fix **04** ease, heal, help, mend, salt **05** amend, break, reast, reest, reist, smoke, treat **06** elixir, hobday, kipper, pickle, remedy, repair **07** correct, cure-all, dry-salt, healing, panacea, recover, rectify, relieve, restore, therapy **08** antidote, barbecue, make well, medicine, preserve, recovery, smoke-dry, solution, specific, unpoison **09** alleviate, treatment **10** corrective, make better **11** alleviation, restorative **12** fever therapy

**cure-all**
**06** elixir **07** nostrum, panacea **10** catholicon **12** panpharmacon **13** diacatholicon **15** universal remedy

**curfew**
**04** gate

**curie**
**02** Ci

**curio**
**06** bygone **07** antique, bibelot, trinket **09** curiosity, objet d'art **10** knick-knack **12** objet de vertu **13** object of virtu **14** article of virtu

**curiosity**
**05** curio, freak **06** bygone, gabion, marvel, oddity, prying, rarity, search, wonder **07** antique, exotica, inquiry, novelty, trinket **08** interest, nosiness, querying, snooping **09** objet d'art, spectacle **10** knick-knack, phenomenon **11** peculiarity, questioning **12** interference **15** inquisitiveness

**curious**
◇ *anagram indicator*
**03** odd **04** agog, nosy, rare **05** funny, nosey, novel, queer, weird **06** exotic, prying, quaint, unique **07** bizarre, strange, unusual **08** freakish, meddling, peculiar, puzzling, querying, singular, snooping **09** inquiring, intrigued, searching **10** fascinated, interested, keen to know, meddlesome, mysterious, remarkable, unorthodox **11** inquisitive, interfering, questioning **13** extraordinary **14** unconventional, wanting to learn
• **be curious**
**03** pry

**curiously**
◇ *anagram indicator*
**05** oddly **08** quaintly **09** bizarrely, strangely, unusually **10** peculiarly, remarkably **11** inquiringly **12** meddlesomely, mysteriously **13** inquisitively, interferingly, questioningly

**curium**
**02** Cm

**curl**
**04** bend, coil, eddy, friz, kink, loop, purl, ring, roll, tong, turn, wave, wind **05** crimp, curve, dildo, frizz, helix, pinch, snake, swirl, twine, twirl, twist, whorl **06** becurl, ripple, scroll, spiral,

wreath, writhe **07** crimple, crinkle, earlock, frizzle, frounce, meander, ringlet, wreathe **08** curlicue, kiss-curl, lovelock **09** corkscrew, favourite **12** heartbreaker **13** permanent wave

**curly**
**04** wavy **05** fuzzy, kinky **06** curled, frizzy, permed **07** coiling, crimped, curling, looping, turning, winding **08** twirling, twisting **09** corkscrew, spiralled, wreathing **10** spiralling

**currant**
**05** Ribes **06** rizard, rizzar, rizzer **07** rizzart

**currency**
**03** tin **04** cash **05** bills, brass, coins, money, notes, vogue **07** coinage **08** exposure **09** publicity **10** acceptance, popularity, prevalence **11** circulation, legal tender **13** dissemination

*Currencies include:*

**02** nu
**03** ecu, kip, lat, lei, lek, leu, lev, som, sum, won, yen
**04** baht, birr, cedi, dong, dram, euro, kina, kuna, kyat, lari, lats, lira, loti, mark, peso, pula, punt, rand, real, rial, riel, taka, tala, vatu, yuan
**05** colón, denar, dinar, dobra, franc, frank, krona, krone, kroon, kunar, leone, litas, manat, marka, naira, nakfa, pence, pound, riyal, rupee, sucre, tenge, tolar, zaïre, zloty
**06** ariary, balboa, dalasi, dirham, dollar, escudo, forint, gourde, gulden, hryvna, koruna, kwacha, kwanza, maloti, markka, new sol, pa'anga, pataca, peseta, rouble, rupiah, shekel, somoni, tugrik, tugrug
**07** afghani, bolivar, cordoba, drachma, guarani, guilder, hyrvnia, lempira, metical, new peso, ouguiya, quetzal, ringgit, rufiyaa
**08** new dinar, ngultrum, nuevo sol, renminbi, shilling, sterling, US dollar
**09** boliviano, lilangeni, new dollar, schilling
**10** emalangeni, Swiss franc
**11** Deutschmark, French franc, karbovanets, Turkish lira
**12** Belgian franc, Deutsche mark, renminbi yuan
**14** Canadian dollar

*See also* **coin**

*Former currencies include:*

**01** m
**02** DM
**03** pie
**04** inti, lira, mark, pice, punt, reis
**05** belga, franc, krone, sucre, zaïre
**06** décime, ekuele, escudo, gilder, lepton, markka, peseta
**07** austral, cruzado, drachma, guilder, milreis
**08** cruzeiro, groschen
**09** schilling
**11** Deutschmark

**current**
**01** I **02** AC, DC, in **03** amp, cur, ebb, jet, now **04** curt, eddy, flow, live, mood, race, rife, rill, soom, swim, tide **05** drift, going, juice, swirl, tenor, trend, valid **06** abroad, common, course, extant, modern, outset, stream, trendy **07** backset, bombora, draught, exhaust, feeling, flowing, general, indraft, instant, in vogue, ongoing, outflow, popular, present, running, thermal, topical **08** accepted, backwash, existing, movement, progress, reigning, tendency, tide race, up-to-date **09** direction, indraught, in fashion, prevalent **10** mainstream, present-day, prevailing, widespread **11** back-draught, fashionable, going around, present-time **12** contemporary, undercurrent **13** in circulation, up-to-the-minute

**currently**
**03** now **05** today **07** just now **08** right now **09** at present, presently, these days **10** at this time **11** at the moment **15** for the time being

**curriculum**
**06** course, module **07** program **08** subjects, syllabus **09** programme, timetable **10** discipline **13** course of study **14** core curriculum **15** course of studies

**curry**
**04** beat **06** madras, quarry **07** cuittle, scratch **08** vindaloo

**curse**
**02** wo **03** ban, eff, hex, moz, pox, woe **04** bane, blow, cuss, damn, evil, harm, jinx, mozz, oath, ruin **05** beset, blast, blind, shrew, spell, swear, weary, winze **06** berate, blight, maugre, ordeal, plague **07** accurse, afflict, beshrew, condemn, malison, scourge, torment, trouble **08** anathema, calamity, cussword, denounce, disaster, execrate, maledict **09** blaspheme, blasphemy, curse-word, expletive, fulminate, imprecate, obscenity, profanity, swear-word, vengeance **10** affliction, execration, Indian sign, misfortune, put a jinx on **11** bad language, eff and blind, imprecation, malediction, tribulation **12** anathematize, damn and blast **13** excommunicate **14** four-letter word, use bad language

**cursed**
**04** vile **05** curst **06** bloody, cussed, damned, darned, dashed, odious **07** blasted, flaming, hateful, unlucky **08** annoying, blinking, blooming, dratting, fiendish, flipping, infamous, infernal **09** execrable, loathsome **10** abominable, confounded, detestable, pernicious, unpleasant

**cursory**
**05** brief, hasty, quick, rapid **06** casual, slight **07** hurried, offhand, passing, summary **08** careless, fleeting, slapdash **09** desultory **10** dismissive **11** perfunctory, superficial

**curt**
**04** rude, tart **05** blunt, brief, gruff, pithy, sharp, short, squab, terse **06** abrupt **07** brittle, brusque, concise, laconic, offhand, summary, uncivil **08** snappish, succinct **10** ungracious **11** short-spoken **13** short and sweet, unceremonious

**curtail**
◇ *tail deletion indicator*
**03** cut **04** clip, dock, pare, slim, trim **05** abate, limit, prune **06** hamper, lessen, reduce, shrink **07** abridge, cut back, cut down, shorten **08** cut short, decrease, pare back, pare down, restrict, truncate **09** cut back on **10** abbreviate, guillotine **12** circumscribe

**curtailment**
◇ *tail deletion indicator*
**03** cut **06** paring **07** cutback, docking, pruning **08** decrease, slimming, trimming **09** lessening, reduction, shrinkage **10** abridgment, guillotine, limitation, shortening, truncation **11** abridgement, contraction, restriction **12** abbreviation, retrenchment

**curtain**
**04** pall, swag, vail, veil **05** blind, cover, drape, scene **06** purdah, screen **07** drapery, hanging, shutter, vitrage **08** backdrop, portière, tapestry, traverse **10** net curtain **13** window hanging
• **theatre curtain**
**03** tab **04** drop, iron **05** cloth

**curtly**
**05** short **06** rudely **07** bluntly, briefly, gruffly, pithily, sharply, shortly, tersely **08** abruptly **09** brusquely, concisely, uncivilly **10** succinctly **11** laconically **12** ungraciously **15** unceremoniously

**curtsy**
**03** bob, bow, dop **06** kowtow, salaam **08** courtesy **09** genuflect

**curvaceous**
**05** buxom, curvy **06** bosomy, comely **07** shapely **09** curvesome **10** voluptuous **11** well-rounded, well-stacked

**curve**
**03** arc, bow **04** arch, bend, coil, hook, kink, loop, ogee, turn, wind **05** bulge, crook, graph, helix, rhumb, round, swell, twist **06** bought, camber, circle, record, spiral, spiric, swerve **07** caustic, cissoid, compass, flexure, incurve, quadric, quartic, winding **08** apophyge, catenary, conchoid, crescent, envelope, liquidus, parabola, sinusoid, trochoid **09** curvature, loxodrome **10** epicycloid, isoseismal, meandering, trajectory **11** catacaustic, harmonogram **12** hypotrochoid **15** brachistochrone, Lissajous figure

**curved**
**04** bent **05** bowed, wrong **06** arched, convex, cupped, humped, warped **07** arcuate, bending, bulging, concave, crooked, rounded, scooped, sinuous, twisted **08** sweeping, swelling, tortuous **09** curviform, incurvate **10** incurvated, serpentine

**cushion**
**03** cod, mat, pad **04** bank, tyre **05** squab **06** absorb, buffer, dampen, deaden, lessen, muffle, pillow, prop up, reduce, soften, stifle **07** beanbag, bolster, bum roll, hassock, kneeler, padding, pillion, protect, sandbag, support **08** buttress, diminish, headrest, mitigate, pulvinus, suppress **09** pulvillus, upholster **10** lace-pillow, protection **11** booster seat **13** shock absorber **14** vegetable sheep

**cushy**
**04** easy, plum, soft **05** jammy **11** comfortable, undemanding

**cusp**
**04** horn **05** point **07** spinode

**custard**
**04** flam **05** flamm, flawn **06** flaune **07** sabayon **08** zabaione **10** zabaglione

**custodian**
**05** guard **06** custos, keeper, warden, warder **07** curator **08** claviger, guardian, overseer, watchdog, watchman **09** caretaker, castellan, protector **11** conservator **12** conservatrix **14** superintendent

**custody**
◇ *containment indicator*
**04** bail, care, hand, hold, ward **05** hands **06** arrest, charge, prison **07** keeping **08** guarding, guidance, handfast, security, wardship, watching **09** captivity, detention, retention **10** possession, protection **11** confinement, safekeeping, supervision, trusteeship **12** guardianship, imprisonment, preservation **13** custodianship, incarceration **14** responsibility

**custom**
**03** use, way, won **04** form, rite, thew **05** ethos, habit, mores, style, trade, usage **06** manner, policy, ritual **07** fashion, routine **08** business, ceremony, practice **09** etiquette, formality, patronage, procedure, rusticism, sacred cow, tradition **10** consuetude, convention, observance **11** institution **13** way of behaving

**customarily**
**07** as a rule, usually **08** commonly, normally **09** generally, popularly, regularly, routinely **10** habitually, ordinarily **11** fashionably **13** traditionally **14** conventionally

**customary**
**03** set **04** used **05** nomic, usual **06** common, normal, vulgar, wonted **07** general, popular, regular, routine **08** accepted, everyday, familiar, habitual, ordinary **10** obligatory, prevailing **11** established, fashionable, traditional **12** conventional, prescriptive **14** consuetudinary

**customer**
**05** buyer, trick **06** client, patron, punter **07** regular, shopper **08** consumer, prospect **09** purchaser, shillaber

**customize**
**03** fit **04** suit **05** adapt, alter, tweak **06** adjust, modify, tailor **07** convert **08** fine-tune **09** transform **11** personalize

**customs**
**04** dues **05** mores, taxes **06** duties, excise, impost, levies **07** tariffs **08** protocol

**cut**
◇ *anagram indicator*
◇ *deletion indicator*
◇ *insertion indicator*
◇ *tail deletion indicator*
**02** ax **03** axe, bit, end, hew, lop, mow, rip, saw **04** blow, burn, chop, clip, crop, curb, dash, dice, dock, edit, form, gash, hack, halt, kerf, make, nick, omit, pare, part, race, rase, raze, reap, sawn, shun, skip, slit, sned, snee, snip, snub, stab, stop, tape, trim **05** avoid, blank, block, break, carve, cross, fault, grate, joint, knife, lance, lower, mince, notch, piece, prune, quota, scalp, score, scorn, sever, shape, share, shave, shear, shred, slash, slice, slish, sneck, snick, split, spurn, style, whack, wound **06** chisel, chop up, cleave, delete, design, dilute, divide, excise, ignore, incise, insult, lessen, pierce, précis, ration, rebuff, record, reduce, saving, slight, stroke, trench **07** abridge, curtail, cutback, cut dead, diluted, dissect, economy, engrave, failure, fashion, incised, portion, profile, rake-off, scratch, section, shorten, suspend **08** break off, castrate, cleaving, condense, decrease, diminish, dividing, excision, incision, lacerate, lowering, obstruct, renounce, stoppage **09** breakdown, expurgate, intercept, interrupt, intersect, lessening, reduction, summarize, videotape **10** abbreviate, adulterate, allocation, cutting-out, diminution, disconnect, laceration, proportion, tape-record **11** adulterated, discontinue, make shorter **12** breaking-down, bring to an end, cold-shoulder, retrenchment **14** malfunctioning, send to Coventry, slice of the cake **15** pretend not to see

*See also* **hairstyle**; **meat**

**• cut across**
**08** go beyond, surmount **09** intersect, rise above, transcend **11** leave behind

**• cut and dried**
**05** clear, fixed **06** sewn up **07** certain, decided, settled **08** definite **09** automatic, organized **11** prearranged **13** predetermined

**• cut back**
**03** lop **04** crop, curb, trim **05** check, lower, prune, slash **06** lessen, reduce **07** coppice, curtail **08** decrease, downsize, retrench **09** economize, scale down

**• cut down**
**02** ax **03** axe, hew, lop, mow, saw **04** curb, fell, kill, maim, raze, reap **05** level, lower, prune, slash **06** lessen, reduce **07** curtail **08** chop down, decrease, diminish

**• cut in**
**05** nip in **06** butt in **07** barge in, break in, intrude **09** interject, interpose, interrupt, intervene

**• cut off**
**03** end **04** clip, halt, nick, stop **05** block, sever, shred **06** detach, excide, remove, unhook **07** abscind, chop off, exscind, handsel, isolate, seclude, shelter, suspend, take off, tear off **08** amputate, break off, insulate, obstruct, prescind, retrench, separate, smite off **09** intercept, interrupt, keep apart **10** disconnect, interclude, stormbound **11** discontinue **12** bring to an end

**• cut out**
**04** clip, drop, edit, fail, omit, quit, stop **05** block, cease, debar, shape, sneck, snick **06** delete, desist, excise, exsect, go phut, lay off, pack in, pack up, remove **07** conk out, eclipse, exclude, extract, go kaput, go wrong, refrain, ride out, take out, tear out **08** carve out, contrive, knock off, leave off, leave out, separate, supplant **09** break down **11** discontinue, malfunction, stop working **12** go on the blink

**• cut out for**
**04** good, made **05** right **06** suited **08** suitable **09** qualified **11** appropriate

**• cut short**
◇ *tail deletion indicator*
**04** crop, dock, snub **05** roach **07** abridge, bobtail, chapped, concise, curtail **08** prescind, truncate **10** detruncate

**• cut slantwise**
**04** bias

**• cut square across**
**03** bob **04** bang

**• cut up**
**04** chop, dice, hurt **05** break, carve, het up, mince, slash, slice, upset **06** chop up, divide, put out **07** annoyed, dissect, slice up, unhappy **08** bothered, saddened, tomahawk, troubled, worked up **09** dismember **10** distressed

**cutback**
◇ *reversal indicator*
**03** cut **06** saving **07** economy **08** decrease, lowering, slashing **09** lessening, reduction **11** curtailment **12** retrenchment

**cute**
**04** twee **05** ankle, sweet **06** astute, clever, lovely, pretty **07** lovable

**08** adorable, charming, loveable
**09** appealing, endearing **10** attractive, delightful

**cutlery**
**06** silver **07** canteen **08** flatware

*Cutlery items include:*

**04** fork
**05** knife, ladle, spoon
**08** fish fork, teaspoon
**09** fish knife, fish slice, salt spoon, soupspoon
**10** bread knife, caddy spoon, cake server, chopsticks, pickle fork, steak knife, sugar tongs, tablespoon
**11** butter knife, carving fork, cheese knife, corn holders
**12** apostle spoon, carving knife, dessertspoon, salad servers
**14** vegetable knife

**cutlet**
**04** chop **09** côtelette, schnitzel
**15** Wiener schnitzel

**cut-price**
**04** sale **05** cheap **07** bargain, cut-rate, reduced **08** discount **09** low-priced
**10** marked-down

**cutpurse**
**03** nip **04** bung **06** nipper
**10** pickpocket

**cutter**
**04** pone **05** axman **06** axeman
**08** lapidary

*Cutters include:*

**03** axe, fox, saw, sax
**04** adze, bill, celt
**05** bilbo, blade, brand, knife, mower, plane, razor, saber, sabre, sword
**06** chisel, colter, culter, dagger, ice axe, jigsaw, labrys, lopper, meat-ax, piolet, poleax, rapier, scythe, shears, sickle, sparth
**07** chopper, cleaver, coulter, cutlass, fretsaw, gisarme, hacksaw, halberd, hatchet, meat-axe, poleaxe, poll-axe, sparthe, twibill
**08** battle-ax, billhook, chainsaw, claymore, clippers, palstaff, palstave, partisan, scimitar, scissors, shredder, stone axe, Strimmer®, tomahawk
**09** battle-axe, double-axe, Excalibur, holing-axe, lawnmower, secateurs
**10** broadsword, coal-cutter, cork-cutter, guillotine, putty-knife, spokeshave
**11** chaff-cutter, coup de poing, glass-cutter, grass-cutter, Lochaber axe, paper-cutter, straw-cutter
**12** cookie-cutter, hedgetrimmer, Jeddart staff, marble-cutter
**13** mowing machine, pinking shears

*See also* **dagger**; **knife**; **saw**; **weapon**

**cut-throat**
**04** keen, thug **05** cruel, razor
**06** brutal, cutter, fierce **07** ruffian, sworder **08** assassin, pitiless, ruthless
**09** dog-eat-dog, merciless, murderous
**10** relentless **15** keenly contested

**cutting**
◇ *insertion indicator*
**03** raw **04** acid, clip, keen, sect, sien, slip, syen **05** chill, piece, plant, scion, scrap, sharp, snide **06** bitchy, biting, bitter, secant **07** caustic, coupure, excerpt, extract, gingery, hurtful, mordant, pointed **08** clipping, incision, incisive, piercing, quickset, scathing, scission, scissure, stinging, wounding **09** malicious, sarcastic, trenchand, trenchant **11** penetrating

**cuttle-bone**
**03** pen **06** pounce, sepium

**cycle**
**03** age, eon, era, orb **04** aeon, bike, rota **05** epoch, order, phase, round, trike **06** circle, period, rhythm, series
**07** pattern **08** go-around, rotation, sequence **09** biorhythm, body clock
**10** revolution, succession **11** oscillation

**cyclical**
**06** cyclic **07** regular **08** repeated
**09** recurrent, recurring **10** repetitive

**cyclist**

*Cyclists include:*

**03** Hoy (Chris)
**04** Gaul (Charly)
**05** Binda (Alfredo), Bobet (Louison), Coppi (Fausto), Kelly (Sean), Moser (Francesco), Zabel (Erik)
**06** Burton (Beryl), Fignon (Laurent), Harris (Reg), LeMond (Greg), Merckx (Eddy)
**07** Bartali (Gino), Hinault (Bernard), Museeuw (Johan), Pantani (Marco), Queally (Jason), Simpson (Tom), Ullrich (Jan), Van Looy (Rik)
**08** Anquetil (Jacques), Boardman (Chris), Indurain (Miguel), Maertens (Freddy), Opperman (Sir Hubert), Poulidor (Raymond), Virenque (Richard)
**09** Armstrong (Lance), Zoetemelk (Joop)
**10** Bahamontes (Federico), van Moorsel (Leontien Ziljaard-)
**11** De Vlaeminck (Roger)
**13** Longo-Ciprelli (Jeannie)

**cyclone**
**05** storm **07** monsoon, tempest, tornado, typhoon **09** hurricane, whirlwind, windstorm **10** cockeye bob, depression, willy-willy
**11** cockeyed bob **13** tropical storm

**cylinder**
**04** drum, reel, roll **05** spool **06** barrel, bobbin, column, roller **07** spindle

**cymbal**
**03** zel **07** symbole

**cynic**
**05** surly **07** doubter, killjoy, knocker, sceptic, scoffer **08** Diogenes, snarling
**09** pessimist **10** spoilsport
**11** misanthrope

**cynical**
**05** surly **06** bitter, ironic **07** mocking
**08** critical, derisive, Diogenic, doubtful, doubting, negative, sardonic, scoffing, scornful, snarling, sneering
**09** hardnosed, sarcastic, sceptical
**10** embittered, hard-boiled, streetwise, suspicious **11** distrustful, pessimistic, worldly-wise
**12** contemptuous, disenchanted
**13** disillusioned, unsentimental
**14** Mephistophelic
**15** Mephistophelean, Mephistophelian

**cynically**
**08** bitterly **09** mockingly **10** critically, derisively, negatively, scornfully
**11** sceptically **12** suspiciously
**13** distrustfully **14** contemptuously
**15** pessimistically

**cynicism**
**05** doubt, irony, scorn **07** mocking, sarcasm **08** contempt, distrust, scoffing, sneering **09** disbelief, pessimism, surliness, suspicion
**10** scepticism **11** misanthropy
**13** heartlessness **14** disenchantment
**15** disillusionment

**Cyprus**
**02** CY **03** CYP

**cyst**
**03** sac, wen **04** bleb **06** growth, ranula
**07** abscess, bladder, blister, capelet, dermoid, hydatid, utricle, vesicle
**08** atheroma, capellet, steatoma
**09** chalazion

**Czech Republic**
**02** CZ **03** CZE

# D

**D**
**03** dee **05** delta

**dab**
**03** bit, mop, pat, tad, tap **04** blot, dash, daub, drop, peck, spot, swab, wipe **05** fleck, press, smear, speck, tinge, touch, trace **06** dollop, smudge, splash, stroke **07** smidgen, trickle **08** sprinkle **09** lemon sole **10** sandsucker

**• dab hand**
**03** ace, dip, toy, wet **04** play **05** adept, dally **06** dampen, expert, paddle, potter, splash, tinker, trifle, wizard **07** amateur, dallier, moisten, trifler **08** splatter, sprinkle, tinkerer **09** lay person **10** dilettante, past master

**dabble**
**03** dip, toy, wet **04** play **05** dally, flirt, plash **06** clatch, dampen, fiddle, guddle, muddle, paddle, potter, putter, splash, tinker, trifle **07** immerse, moisten, plotter, plouter, plowter, smatter **08** splatter, sprinkle

**dabbler**
**07** amateur, dallier, trifler **08** tinkerer **09** lay person, literator **10** dilettante

**dad** *see* **father**

**daemon**
**04** deva **05** demon, devil, force, geist **06** animus, genius, spirit **09** cacodemon **10** evil spirit, genius loci, good spirit

**daft**
◇ *anagram indicator*
**03** dim, mad, odd **04** avid, dull, dumb, fond, keen, nuts, slow, wild **05** barmy, batty, crazy, daffy, dense, dopey, dotty, inane, loony, loopy, nutty, potty, silly, sweet, thick, wacky **06** absurd, ardent, crazed, insane, mental, simple, stupid, unwise **07** berserk, bonkers, devoted, fatuous, foolish, glaiket, glaikit, idiotic, lunatic, smitten, touched, zealous **08** crackpot, demented, deranged, dingbats, farcical, gormless, obsessed, peculiar, unhinged **09** dim-witted, disturbed, enamoured, fanatical, foolhardy, half-baked, imprudent, laughable, ludicrous, senseless **10** infatuated, irrational, outrageous, passionate, ridiculous, slow-witted, unbalanced **11** hare-brained, nonsensical, unrealistic **12** addle-brained, crackbrained, enthusiastic, preposterous, round the bend, simple-minded **13** impracticable, irresponsible, off your rocker, out of your mind, round the twist, thick as a plank

**dagger**
**05** blade, knife **06** obelus

*Daggers include:*

**04** dirk, kris
**05** kukri, skean, skene
**06** anlace, bodkin, crease, creese, hanjar, kirpan, kreese
**07** anelace, dudgeon, handjar, jambiya, khanjar, poniard, yatagan
**08** baselard, jambiyah, puncheon, skean-dhu, skene-dhu, stiletto, yataghan
**10** bowie knife, misericord, skene-occle
**11** misericorde

*See also* **knife**; **sword**

**Dáil member**
**02** TD

**daily**
**04** char **05** adays **06** common **07** cleaner, diurnal, journal, per diem, regular, routine **08** constant, day by day, day-to-day, everyday, habitual, ordinary **09** circadian, customary, quotidian, regularly **10** constantly **11** commonplace, day after day

*See also* **newspaper**

**dainty**
**04** cate, fine, neat, nice, trim **05** dinky, faddy, fancy, fussy, genty, juicy, small, tasty **06** bonbon, choice, choosy, friand, little, luxury, mignon, morsel, petite, pretty, sunket, titbit **07** cunning, elegant, finicky, friande, genteel, minikin, refined, savoury **08** charming, delicacy, delicate, graceful, luscious, mignonne, tasteful **09** delicious, enjoyable, exquisite, lickerish, liquorish, succulent, sweetmeat **10** appetizing, delectable, delightful, fastidious, particular, scrupulous **11** bonne-bouche **12** hard to please **14** discriminating

**dairy**

*Dairy produce includes:*

**04** ghee, milk, whey
**05** cream, curds, quark
**06** beurre, butter, cheese, yogurt
**07** UHT milk, yoghurt
**08** ice cream, yoghourt
**09** butter oil, goat's milk, milk shake, sour cream, whole milk
**10** buttermilk, milk powder
**11** double cream, semi-skimmed, single cream, skimmed milk, soured cream
**12** clotted cream, crème fraîche, fromage frais, long-life milk, powdered milk
**13** condensed milk, full cream milk, low-fat yoghurt, whipping cream
**14** evaporated milk, sterilized milk, unsalted butter
**15** clarified butter, homogenized milk, semi-skimmed milk

**dairymaid**
**03** dey **08** dey-woman

**dais**
**05** stage, stand **06** estate, podium **07** haut pas, rostrum, staging **08** footpace, platform

**daisy**
**05** gowan, ox-eye **07** felicia, guayule **08** feverfew, ox-tongue **10** cupid's dart, horse-gowan, marguerite, moonflower **14** hen-and-chickens

**dale**
**03** cwm, den, ria **04** dean, dell, dene, gill, glen, vale **05** coomb, griff, grike, gulch, heuch, slade **06** dingle, strath, valley

**dalliance**
**04** play **05** delay, sport **06** toying **07** playing **08** dawdling, flirting, sporting, tarrying, trifling **09** loitering, pottering

**dally**
**03** toy **04** play **05** delay, flirt, tarry **06** coquet, dawdle, frivol, linger, loiter, pingle, trifle **07** carry on **08** coquette **10** tick and toy **12** take your time **13** procrastinate

**dam**
**03** pen **04** bund, stem, sudd, wall, wear, weir **05** block, cauld, check, stank **06** anicut, mother **07** annicut, barrage, barrier, confine, staunch **08** blockage, obstruct, restrict **09** barricade, decametre, hindrance, restraint **10** draughtman, embankment, millstream **11** obstruction

*Dams include:*

**04** Guri, Hume, Kiev, Mica
**05** Aswan, Ertan, Nurek, Rogun
**06** Beaver, Bratsk, Hoover, Inguri, Itaipu, Kariba, Vaiont
**07** Benmore, Boulder, Tarbela
**08** Akosombo, Chapetón, Gezhouba
**09** Aswan High, Mauvoisin, Owen Falls
**10** Glen Canyon

**11** Afsluitdijk, Grand Coulee, La Esmeralda, Three Gorges
**13** Alberto Lleras, Alvaro Obregon, Grande Dixence, Manuel M Torres
**14** Afsluitdijk Sea
**15** Sayano-Shushensk

**damage**
◇ *anagram indicator*
**03** mar, rip **04** cost, dent, fine, harm, hurt, loss, ruin **05** abuse, havoc, price, spoil, wreck, wrong **06** charge, deface, impair, injure, injury, weaken **07** blemish, destroy, empeach, expense, impeach, vitiate **08** decimate, mischief, mutilate, sabotage **09** desecrate, detriment, disprofit, indemnity, suffering, vandalism, vandalize **10** defacement, defilement, impairment, mutilation, recompense, reparation, tamper with **11** depredation, desecration, destruction, devastation, restitution **12** compensation, disadvantage, incapacitate, satisfaction **13** play havoc with, reimbursement, vandalization **14** wreak havoc with **15** indemnification

**damaged**
◇ *anagram indicator*
**04** mard **07** cracked, unsound **08** impaired

**damaging**
**03** bad **07** harmful, hurtful, ruinous **09** injurious **10** pernicious **11** deleterious, destructive, detrimental, prejudicial **12** unfavourable **15** disadvantageous

**dame**
**03** DBE, DCB **04** Edna, lady **05** broad, woman **06** female, matron, mother **07** dowager, peeress **08** baroness **10** aristocrat, noblewoman

**damn**
**01** d **03** dee, jot, pan **04** dang, darn, dash, doom, hang, hoot, iota, sink, slag, slam, toss **05** blank, blast, curse, decry, knock, slate, swear **06** attack, berate, jigger, revile **07** accurse, censure, condemn, inveigh, monkey's, run down, slag off **08** denounce, execrate, maledict, two hoots **09** blaspheme, castigate, criticize, denigrate, excoriate, fulminate, imprecate **10** come down on, denunciate **11** pick holes in, tinker's cuss **12** anathematize, pull to pieces, tear to shreds **13** brass farthing **14** use bad language

**damnable**
**06** cursed, damned, wicked **07** hateful, hellish **08** horrible, infernal **09** atrocious, execrable, offensive **10** abominable, despicable, detestable, diabolical, iniquitous, pernicious, unpleasant **12** disagreeable **13** objectionable

**damnation**
**04** doom, hell **08** anathema, hell-fire **09** perdition **12** condemnation, denunciation, proscription **15** excommunication

**damned**
**04** lost, very, vile **05** pocky **06** blamed, bloody, cursed, darned, dashed, deuced, doomed, effing, odious **07** blasted, flaming, hateful **08** accursed, annoying, blinking, blooming, complete, dratting, fiendish, flipping, infernal, jiggered, thorough **09** condemned, execrable, execrated, loathsome, reprobate **10** abominable, confounded, despicable, detestable, pernicious, unpleasant **11** exceedingly **13** anathematized, blankety-blank **14** blankety-blanky

**damning**
**09** damnatory **10** condemning **11** implicating, implicative, inculpatory **12** accusatorial, condemnatory **13** incriminating

**damp**
**03** dew, fog, wet **04** dank, dewy, dull, mist, rain **05** check, foggy, gloom, humid, misty, mochy, moist, muggy, rainy, soggy **06** clammy, fousty, mochie, moisty, rheumy, vapour **07** drizzle, drizzly, wetness, wettish **08** dampness, dankness, humidity, moisture, vaporous **09** moistened **10** clamminess, discourage **14** discouragement, unenthusiastic

**• damp down**
**04** calm, dull **05** check **06** deaden, lessen, quench, reduce **08** decrease, diminish, moderate, restrain

**dampen**
**03** wet **04** damp, dash, dull **05** check, deter, spray **06** deaden, dismay, lessen, muffle, reduce, stifle **07** depress, inhibit, moisten, smother **08** damp down, decrease, diminish, moderate, restrain **10** discourage, dishearten **12** put a damper on

**damper**
**04** mute **07** sordino **10** wet blanket **13** register-plate

**• put a damper on**
**04** dash, dull **05** check, deter **06** deaden, dismay, lessen, muffle, reduce, stifle, subdue **07** depress, inhibit, smother **08** damp down, decrease, diminish, moderate, restrain **10** discourage, dishearten

**dampness**
**03** dew, fog, wet **04** damp, mist, rain **06** vapour **07** drizzle, wetness **08** dankness, humidity, moisture **09** mugginess **10** clamminess

**damsel**
**04** girl, lass **06** lassie, maiden **09** young lady **10** young woman

**dance**
◇ *anagram indicator*
**04** juke, jump, leap, play, rock, skip, spin, sway **05** caper, flash, frisk, swing, twirl, waver, whirl **06** bounce, cavort, frolic, gambol, gyrate, hoof it, prance, ripple, spring **07** flicker, shimmer, sparkle, twinkle **09** pirouette, shake a leg **11** move lightly, move to music **13** tread a measure

*See also* **ballet**

*Dances include:*

**03** bop, hay, hey, jig, war
**04** dump, fado, giga, haka, hula, jive, jota, juba, kolo, nach, polo, reel, shag
**05** conga, gigue, mambo, natch, polka, rumba, salsa, samba, skank, stomp, sword, tango, twist, waltz
**06** Balboa, bolero, can-can, cha-cha, hustle, minuet, morris, valeta, veleta
**07** beguine, csárdás, foxtrot, gavotte, hoe-down, Lancers, mazurka, morrice, musette, one-step, tordion
**08** boogaloo, cakewalk, excuse-me, fandango, flamenco, galliard, hay-de-guy, hey-de-guy, hornpipe, hula-hula, kantikoy, lindy hop, Playford, the twist
**09** bossanova, cha-cha-cha, clogdance, écossaise, jitterbug, paso doble, passepied, Paul Jones, quadrille, quickstep, rock 'n' roll, roundelay
**10** Charleston, corroboree, hokey-cokey, slow rhythm, turkey-trot
**11** black bottom, Lambeth Walk, morris-dance, schottische, varsovienne
**12** boogie-woogie, mashed potato
**13** Highland fling, Viennese waltz
**15** military two-step

*Dance types include:*

**03** tap
**04** clog, folk, jazz, line
**05** belly, break, disco, Irish, limbo, salsa, swing
**06** ballet, hip-hop, modern, morris, square
**07** bogling, country, morrice, old-time
**08** ballroom, flamenco, Highland, robotics, skanking
**10** bellydance, breakdance
**12** contemporary
**13** Latin-American

*Dance functions include:*

**02** ba'
**03** hop
**04** ball, prom, rave
**05** disco
**06** social
**07** ceilidh, knees-up, shindig
**08** hunt ball, tea dance
**09** barn dance
**10** thé dansant
**11** charity ball, dinner dance
**14** fancy dress ball

*Dance steps include:*

**03** dig, dip, fan, pas, set
**04** buck, chop, chug, clip, comb, dame, drag, draw, drop, ocho, riff, spin, turn, vine, whip
**05** abajo, brush, catch, corté, cramp, flare, galop, glide, grind, hitch, pivot, scuff, seven, spike, stamp,

stomp, strut, Suzi-Q, three, twist, whisk
**06** aerial, breaks, bronco, chassé, circle, jockey, paddle, riffle, shimmy, uprock
**07** box step, fan kick, feather, jig step, locking, lollies, popping, pop turn, rocking, scuffle, shuffle, six-step, swivels, toprock, twinkle
**08** back step, crab walk, flat step, four-step, hair comb, headspin, heel pull, heel turn, hook turn, neck wrap, pas-de-bas, push spin, rock step, shedding, spot turn, swingout, throwout, time step, windmill
**09** allemagne, applejack, crazy legs, cross over, cross turn, dile que no, grapevine, lindy turn, pas de deux, poussette, promenade, quick stop, sugarfoot, sugarpush
**10** ball-change, chainé turn, change step, charleston, chassé turn, come-around, Cuban walks, cucarachas, inside turn, jackhammer, rubber legs, spiral turn, texas tommy, triple step
**11** alemana turn, impetus turn, natural turn, outside turn, pas de basque, quarter turn, reverse turn, setting step
**12** last shedding, shake and turn, under-arm turn
**13** double-shuffle, fall off the log, first shedding
**14** change of places, kick-ball-change, transition step, travelling step

## • dance company

**03** set

*Dance companies include:*

**10** Ballet West
**11** Kirov Ballet, Royal Ballet
**12** Sadler's Wells, Kirov Ballet, Royal Ballet
**13** Ballet Rambert, Ballets Russes, Bolshoi Ballet, Joffrey Ballet
**14** National Ballet

## dancer

**04** alma, alme **05** almah, almeh **06** bopper, exotic, hoofer **07** baladin, danseur, kachina, morisco, skipper, slammer, waltzer **08** coryphee, danseuse, figurant, joncanoe, junkanoo, matachin, première, showgirl **09** ballerina, figurante, John Canoe, John Kanoo, tap-dancer **10** pyrrhicist **11** belly-dancer, comprimario **12** ballet dancer **13** terpsichorean **14** Jack-in-the-green

*Dancers include:*

**03** **Lee** (Gypsy Rose)
**04** **Bull** (Deborah), **Edur** (Thomas), **Oaks** (Agnes)
**05** **Ailey** (Alvin, Jnr), **Baker** (Josephine), **Cohan** (Robert), **Dolin** (Anton), **Kelly** (Gene), **Laban** (Rudolf von), **Lifar** (Serge), **Perón** (Isabelita), **Sleep** (Wayne), **Tharp** (Twyla)
**06** **Ashton** (Sir Frederick), **Béjart** (Maurice), **Blasis** (Carlo), **Childs** (Lucinda), **Clarke** (Michael), **Cooper** (Adam), **Davies** (Siobhan), **Dowell** (Anthony), **Duncan** (Isadora), **Fokine** (Michel), **Graham** (Martha), **Paxton** (Steve), **Petipa** (Marius), **Rogers** (Ginger), **Sibley** (Antoinette), **Wigman** (Mary)
**07** **Astaire** (Fred), **Bussell** (Darcey), **Durante** (Viviana), **Edwards** (Leslie), **Fonteyn** (Dame Margot), **Guillem** (Sylvie), **Markova** (Dame Alicia), **Massine** (Léonide), **Nureyev** (Rudolf), **Pavlova** (Anna), **Rambert** (Dame Marie), **Seymour** (Lynn), **Ulanova** (Galina)
**08** **Danilova** (Alexandra), **De Valois** (Dame Ninette), **Hayworth** (Rita), **Helpmann** (Sir Robert), **Humphrey** (Doris), **Nijinska** (Bronislava), **Nijinsky** (Vaslav)
**09** **Diaghilev** (Sergei), **Macmillan** (Sir Kenneth)
**10** **Balanchine** (George), **Cunningham** (Merce), **Mukhamedov** (Irek)
**11** **Baryshnikov** (Mikhail), **Mistinguett**

*See also* **ballet**

## dandelion

**09** kok-saghyz, taraxacum

## dandle

**03** pet **04** toss **05** dance **06** bounce, cradle, cuddle, doodle, fondle, jiggle

## dandy

**03** fop **04** beau, buck, dude, fine, lair, posh, toff **05** blade, blood, great, smart, swell **06** Adonis, masher **07** capital, coxcomb, jessamy, musk-cat, peacock, princox **08** macaroni, muscadin, popinjay, splendid **09** excellent, exquisite, fantastic, first-rate **10** beau garçon, dapperling, fantastico **12** man about town **13** puss-gentleman

*Dandies include:*

**04** **Nash** (Richard 'Beau')
**05** **Crisp** (Quentin), **Wilde** (Oscar)
**06** **Coward** (Noel)
**08** **Beerbohm** (Max), **Brummell** (George 'Beau')
**12** **Yankee Doodle**

## danger

**04** risk **05** nasty, peril, power
**06** hazard, menace, risque, threat
**07** pitfall **08** jeopardy **09** liability
**10** insecurity **11** imperilment
**12** endangerment, perilousness
**13** vulnerability **14** precariousness
**15** snake in the grass

## • danger signal

**03** red **08** red light

## • hidden danger

**04** trap **07** pitfall

## dangerous

**03** hot **05** dicey, dodgy, grave, hairy, nasty, risky, tight **06** chancy, daring, severe, unsafe **07** exposed, no'canny, ominous, serious **08** alarming, arrogant, critical, high-risk, insecure, menacing, perilous, reckless, unchancy **09** breakneck, hazardous, minacious, mischancy **10** jeopardous, periculous, precarious, vulnerable **11** defenceless, stand-offish, susceptible, threatening, treacherous

## dangerously

**07** acutely, gravely **08** severely
**09** seriously **10** alarmingly, critically, menacingly, perilously **12** precariously
**13** threateningly

## dangle

**03** sag **04** fall, flap, hang, loll, lure, sway, wave **05** droop, offer, swing, tempt, trail **06** entice, flaunt, seduce
**07** hold out **08** flourish **09** tantalize

## dank

**03** wet **04** damp, dewy **05** madid, moist, musty, slimy, soggy **06** chilly, clammy, sticky

## Daphne

**08** lacebark, mezereon, mezereum
**09** eaglewood, widow wail **12** spurge laurel

## dapper

**04** chic, neat, spry, tidy, trim **05** brisk, natty, smart **06** active, dainty, nimble, spruce **07** stylish **08** debonair, sprauncy **11** well-dressed, well-groomed **13** well-turned-out

## dappled

**04** pied **06** dotted **07** blotchy, flecked, mottled, piebald, spotted **08** blotched, freckled, speckled, stippled, streaked
**09** chequered **10** bespeckled, variegated

## dare

**04** dace, dart, daze, defy, doze, face, goad, lurk, risk **05** brave, flout, stake, stare, stump, taunt **06** crouch, gamble, hazard, invite, resist, shrink
**07** daunton, presume, provoke, venture **08** boldness, confront, endanger, frighten, gauntlet
**09** adventure, challenge, go so far as, stand up to, ultimatum **11** provocation
**12** be bold enough, go out on a limb
**13** be brave enough **14** have the courage

## daredevil

**04** bold, rash **05** brave, hasty
**06** daring, madcap, plucky
**07** hothead, valiant **08** fearless, intrepid, reckless, stuntman
**09** audacious, dauntless, desperado, hotheaded, impetuous, impulsive
**10** adventurer **11** adventurous
**12** swashbuckler

## daring

**04** bold, gall, grit, guts, rash, wild
**05** brave, hardy, moxie, nerve, pluck, spunk **06** bottle, plucky, spirit, valour
**07** bravery, courage, gallows, prowess, valiant **08** audacity, boldness, defiance, fearless, intrepid, rashness, reckless, shocking, ventrous, wildness
**09** audacious, dauntless, foolhardy, impulsive, undaunted, venturous
**10** courageous, jeopardous
**11** adventurous, intrepidity, venturesome **12** fearlessness,

high-spirited, recklessness
**13** foolhardiness **15** adventurousness

**daringly**
**06** boldly **07** bravely **10** fearlessly
**11** audaciously **12** courageously
**13** adventurously

**dark**
**02** dk **03** bad, dim, fog, sad, wan
**04** base, drab, dusk, evil, foul, grim, mirk, mist, murk, vile **05** awful, black, bleak, blind, brown, dingy, dirty, dusky, foggy, gloom, misty, moody, murky, night, olive, sable, shade, shady, tawny, unlit, wrong **06** arcane, auburn, cloudy, dismal, gloomy, hidden, morose, opaque, secret, sombre, tanned, tragic, veiled, wicked
**07** bronzed, crooked, cryptic, dimness, evening, immoral, joyless, mystery, obscure, ominous, pit-mirk, privacy, secrecy, shadows, shadowy, sunless, swarthy **08** abstruse, badly lit, brunette, chestnut, darkness, dejected, dimly lit, esoteric, hopeless, horrible, menacing, mournful, overcast, puzzling, sinister, twilight, worrying
**09** blackness, cheerless, concealed, enigmatic, half-light, ignorance, intricate, murkiness, nightfall, night-time, obscurity, poorly lit, recondite, shadiness, suntanned, tenebrity, tenebrose, tenebrous **10** caliginous, cloudiness, dark-haired, despicable, disastrous, forbidding, gloominess, iniquitous, mysterious, tenebrious, unpleasant **11** concealment, crepuscular, dark-skinned, distressing, frightening, inscrutable, sunlessness, tenebrosity **12** crepusculous
**13** unenlightened, unilluminated
**14** unintelligible

**darken**
**03** dim, fog **04** fade **05** blind, cloud, colly, frown, sable, shade, sully
**06** deject, sadden, shadow
**07** benight, blacken, depress, eclipse, embrown, imbrown, obscure **08** cast down **09** cloud over, grow angry, look angry, obfuscate, overshade, weigh down **10** grow darker, make gloomy, obnubilate, overshadow, sclerotize
**11** become angry **12** become darker
**13** disilluminate

**darkly**
**05** dimly **06** glumly **07** at night, blackly, by night **08** dismally, gloomily, sullenly **09** obscurely **11** cryptically, inscrutably **12** in the shadows, mysteriously **13** enigmatically

**darkness** *see* **dark**

**darling**
**03** hon, luv, pet **04** dear, duck, hero, idol, love, peat **05** angel, honey, loved, sugar, sweet **06** adored, dautie, dawtie, minion, poppet, prized
**07** acushla, asthore, beloved, dearest, dilling, minikin, sweetie **08** dearling, precious, sweeting, treasure
**09** celebrity, cherished, favourite, treasured **10** delightful, mavourneen, sweetheart **11** blue-eyed boy, teacher's pet, white-haired **13** fair-haired boy **14** apple of your eye

**darmstadtium**
**02** Ds

**darn**
**03** sew **04** drat, mend **05** patch, sew up **06** cobble, repair, stitch

**dart**
**03** fly, run **04** barb, bolt, cast, cook, dace, dare, dash, flit, hurl, leap, plan, race, rush, send, skit, tear, toss
**05** arrow, bound, flash, fling, lance, lanch, scoot, shaft, shoot, sling, start, throw **06** endart, flight, glance, launch, pounce, propel, scheme, scurry, spring, sprint, strike, wheech
**07** feather, harpoon, project
**08** spiculum **09** fléchette, love-arrow, love-shaft **10** banderilla

**dash**
◇ *anagram indicator*
**03** bit, cut, dad, dah, fly, hie, jaw, nip, pop, run, tad, zip **04** bang, beat, bolt, brio, dart, daud, ding, dive, drop, élan, hint, hurl, lash, life, pash, race, ramp, rash, ruin, rule, rush, slam, spot, tear, toss **05** blank, blash, bound, break, bribe, crash, crush, fling, force, grain, gusto, hurry, pinch, plash, pound, scart, shine, smash, souse, spang, speck, speed, spoil, spurt, swash, swill, throw, tinge, touch, trace, verve, wreck
**06** blight, dampen, energy, hurtle, jabble, little, relish, sadden, sluice, spirit, splash, sprint, streak, strike, stroke, thwart, vigour, wheech
**07** depress, destroy, fervour, flavour, let down, passion, pizzazz, scuttle, shatter, smidgen, soupçon, sparkle, viretot **08** confound, gratuity, scramble, vitality, vivacity
**09** animation, devastate, frustrate
**10** disappoint, discourage, dishearten, enthusiasm, liveliness, suggestion

• **dash off**
**06** scrawl **07** jot down **08** scribble

**dashing**
◇ *anagram indicator*
**04** bold **05** doggy, showy, smart
**06** dapper, daring, lively, plucky, rakish
**07** elegant, gallant, go-ahead, raffish, stylish, varment, varmint **08** animated, debonair, slap-bang, slashing, smashing, spirited, vigorous
**09** energetic, exuberant **10** attractive, flamboyant **11** fashionable

**dastard**
**06** coward **07** hilding

**dastardly**
**03** low **04** base, evil, mean, vile
**06** craven, wicked **07** nithing
**08** cowardly, fiendish **09** underhand
**10** despicable, diabolical, iniquitous
**11** lily-livered **12** contemptible, faint-hearted

**data**
**04** info **05** facts, input **07** details, figures **08** features, material, research
**09** documents **10** statistics
**11** information, particulars

• **collection of data**
**04** file

**date**
**01** d **03** age, day, era **04** ides, time, week, year **05** court, epoch, go out, month, stage, tryst **06** belong, decade, epocha, escort, friend, go back, go with, period, steady **07** century, meeting, partner, take out **08** come from, young man **09** boyfriend, exist from, go out with, man friend, obsolesce, originate, young lady **10** be together, engagement, girlfriend, go out of use, lady friend, millennium, rendezvous, show its age
**11** appointment, assignation, woman friend **12** go steady with **14** become obsolete, be involved with

• **to date**
**03** yet **05** as yet, so far **07** up to now
**08** until now **14** up to the present

• **without date**
**02** sa, sd

**dated**
**05** passé **06** old hat, square **07** archaic
**08** obsolete, outdated, outmoded
**09** out-of-date, unstylish
**10** antiquated, superseded
**11** obsolescent **12** old-fashioned
**13** unfashionable

**daub**
**03** dab **04** blot, coat, gaum, gorm, spot, teer **05** cover, paint, slake, smalm, smarm, smear, stain, sully
**06** bedaub, blotch, clatch, smirch, smudge, splash **07** plaster, slubber, spatter, splodge, splotch **08** splatter
**09** beplaster, bespatter **10** blottesque

**daughter**
**01** d **03** dau **04** girl, lass **05** child, fille
**06** lassie **08** disciple **09** offspring
**10** descendant, inhabitant

*Daughters include:*

**04** Anne (Princess), Hero, Kate, Page (Anne)
**05** Freud (Anna), Lloyd (Emily), Mills (Hayley), O'Neal (Tatum), Regan
**06** Bhutto (Benazir), Bianca, Fatima, Fisher (Carrie), Forbes (Emma), Gandhi (Indira), Imogen, Juliet, Marina
**07** Electra, Forsyte (Fleur), Goneril, Jessica, Lavinia, Miranda, Ophelia, Perdita, Presley (Lisa Marie)
**08** Cordelia, Lovelace (Ada), Minnelli (Liza), Williams (Shirley)
**09** Cassandra, du Maurier (Daphne), Katharina, McCartney (Stella), Pankhurst (Christabel)
**10** Beckinsale (Kate), Richardson (Joely), Richardson (Natasha), Rossellini (Isabella)
**13** Princess Royal

**daunt**
**03** cow **04** adaw, faze, pall **05** abash, alarm, amate, deter, quail, scare, shake
**06** dismay, put off, rattle, ruffle, subdue

**07** overawe, unnerve **08** dispirit, frighten **09** take aback **10** demoralize, disconcert, discourage, dishearten, intimidate **11** disillusion

**daunted**
**04** mate **05** quayd

**daunting**
**05** scary **08** alarming **09** unnerving **11** dispiriting, frightening **12** demoralizing, discouraging, intimidating **13** disconcerting, disheartening

**dauntingly**
**07** scarily **10** alarmingly **11** unnervingly **13** dispiritingly, frighteningly **14** demoralizingly, discouragingly, intimidatingly **15** disconcertingly, dishearteningly

**dauntless**
**04** bold **05** brave, stout **06** daring, plucky **07** doughty, valiant **08** fearless, intrepid, resolute **09** undaunted **10** courageous, determined **11** indomitable

**dawdle**
**03** lag **05** dally, delay, drawl, tarry, trail **06** diddle, linger, loiter, potter, putter **07** saunter **08** go slowly **09** faff about, hang about **10** dilly-dally **11** take too long **12** drag your feet, take your time

**dawn**
**04** open, rise **05** begin, birth, break, gleam, onset, start, sun-up **06** advent, appear, arrive, Aurora, be born, emerge, origin, spring **07** arrival, day-peep, develop, genesis, glimmer, lighten, morning, sunrise **08** brighten, cock-crow, commence, daybreak, daylight **09** beginning, dayspring, emergence, grow light, inception, originate **10** break of day, first light **11** become light, crack of dawn **12** commencement **13** come into being

• **dawn on**
**03** hit **05** click **06** sink in, strike **07** occur to, realize **12** register with

**day**
**01** d **03** age, era **04** date, dies, Ides, jour, peak, time **05** bloom, epoch, flush, Nones, prime **06** heyday, period **07** calends, daytime, kalends **08** daylight **09** golden age **10** generation **13** daylight hours

*Days of the week:*

**03** Fri, Mon, Sat, Sun, Thu, Tue, Wed
**04** Thur, Tues, Weds
**05** Thurs
**06** Friday, Monday, Sunday
**07** Tuesday
**08** Saturday, Thursday
**09** Wednesday

*French day names:*

**05** jeudi, lundi, mardi
**06** samedi
**08** dimanche, mercredi, vendredi

*German day names:*

**06** Montag
**07** Freitag, Samstag, Sonntag
**08** Dienstag, Mittwoch
**10** Donnerstag

*Italian day names:*

**06** lunedì, sabato
**07** giovedì, martedì, venerdì
**08** domenica
**09** mercoledì

*Latin day names:*

**09** Jovis dies, Lunae dies, Solis dies
**10** Martis dies
**11** Saturni dies, Veneris dies
**12** Mercurii dies

*Spanish day names:*

**05** lunes
**06** jueves, martes, sàbado
**07** domingo, viernes
**09** miércoles

*Named days include:*

**02** VE, VJ
**09** Fig Sunday, Low Sunday, Red Friday, Red Letter
**10** Good Friday, Holy Friday, Palm Sunday, Whit Sunday
**11** Bible Sunday, Black Friday, Black Monday, Egg Saturday, Fat Thursday
**12** Advent Sunday, Ash Wednesday, Black Tuesday, Bloody Monday, Bloody Sunday, Easter Monday, Easter Sunday, Golden Friday, Stir-up Sunday
**13** Passion Sunday, Shrove Tuesday, Trinity Sunday
**14** Easter Saturday, Maundy Thursday, Pancake Tuesday, Rogation Sunday
**15** Mothering Sunday

*See also* **Christmas**

• **day after day**
**09** endlessly, regularly **10** repeatedly **11** continually, perpetually **12** monotonously, persistently, relentlessly, time and again **13** again and again

• **day by day**
**08** steadily **09** gradually **13** progressively **15** slowly but surely

• **day in, day out**
**08** every day **09** endlessly, regularly **10** repeatedly **11** continually **12** monotonously, persistently, time and again **13** again and again

• **day's end**
**03** e'en, ene, eve **04** even **07** evening

• **have had its day**
**08** be past it **11** be out of date

• **number of days**
**04** week, year **05** month **07** weekend **09** fortnight

• **these days**
**02** AD

• **three times a day**
**03** tid

• **time of day**
**04** seal, seel, seil, sele

**daybreak**
**04** dawn, morn **05** sun-up **06** Aurora **07** morning, sunrise **08** cock-crow, daylight **10** break of day, first light **11** crack of dawn **12** skreigh of day

**daydream**
**04** muse, wish **05** dream, fancy **06** musing, trance, vision **07** fantasy, figment, imagine, reverie **09** fantasize, imagining, pipe dream, switch off **11** inattention **13** be lost in space, woolgathering **14** stare into space **15** be in a brown study, castles in the air, not pay attention

**daydreamer**
**06** rêveur **07** dreamer, rêveuse **08** idealist, romantic **09** fantasist, visionary **10** Don Quixote, fantasizer **11** Walter Mitty

**daylight**
**03** day **04** dawn **05** light, sun-up **07** daytime, high day, morning, sunrise **08** broad day, cock-crow, daybreak, sunlight **10** break of day, first light **11** crack of dawn **12** natural light

**daze**
**04** dare, numb, spin, stun **05** amaze, blind, gally, knock, shock, whirl **06** baffle, dazzle, stupor, trance **07** astound, confuse, perplex, stagger, startle, stupefy **08** astonish, bewilder, blow away, bowl over, knock out, numbness, paralyse, surprise **09** confusion, dumbfound, take aback **11** distraction, flabbergast, knock for six **12** bewilderment

**dazed**
◇ *anagram indicator*
**03** out **05** muzzy, silly, totty, woozy **06** amazed, groggy, numbed, punchy **07** baffled, dazzled, shocked, stunned **08** confused, startled **09** astounded, blown away, paralysed, perplexed, staggered, stupefied, surprised **10** astonished, bewildered, bowled over, punch-drunk, speechless, taken aback **11** dumbfounded, unconscious **13** flabbergasted

**dazzle**
**03** awe, wow **04** blur, daze **05** amaze, blaze, blend, blind, flare, flash, glare, gleam **06** bedaze, strike **07** bewitch, confuse, glitter, impress, overawe, sparkle, stupefy **08** astonish, bedazzle, bowl over, knock out **09** dumbfound, fascinate, hypnotize, overpower, overwhelm, splendour **10** brightness, brilliance, razzmatazz **11** scintillate **12** magnificence **13** scintillation

**dazzling**
**05** glaik, grand **06** bright, superb **07** glaring, radiant, shining **08** blinding, glorious, splendid, stunning **09** brilliant, ravishing, sparkling **10** foudroyant, glittering, impressive **11** psychedelic, sensational, spectacular **12** awe-inspiring, breathtaking **13** scintillating

**dazzlingly**
**08** brightly, superbly **09** glaringly, radiantly **10** blindingly, gloriously **11** brilliantly **12** impressively **13** sensationally, spectacularly **14** breathtakingly

**deactivate**
**04** stop **07** disable **08** paralyse **10** immobilize **14** put out of action

**dead**
**01** d **03** dec **04** bang, bung, bust, cold, dull, flat, gone, late, numb, very **05** dated, exact, inert, kaput, napoo, passé, quiet, quite, smack, stiff, tired, total, utter, waned **06** asleep, barren, benumb, boring, broken, deaden, entire, frigid, no more, old hat, really, sleepy, torpid **07** awfully, defunct, disused, exactly, expired, extinct, humdrum, perfect, tedious, utterly, worn out **08** absolute, ad patres, benumbed, complete, dead beat, deceased, departed, directly, inactive, lifeless, lukewarm, obsolete, outright, passed on, perished, straight, terribly, thorough, tired out, unerring **09** apathetic, bloodless, conked out, deathlike, downright, exanimate, exhausted, extremely, inanimate, inelastic, insensate, knackered, out of date, paralysed, thanatoid, unfeeling **10** absolutely, breathless, broken-down, brown bread, completely, insentient, not working, on the blink, on the fritz, out of order, passed away, spiritless, unexciting **11** dead as a dodo, emotionless, gone to sleep, immediately, indifferent, ineffective, insensitive, off the hooks, ready to drop, unemotional, unqualified **12** discontinued, six feet under, unresponsive **13** exceptionally, uninteresting, unsympathetic **14** no longer spoken **15** dead as a doornail

**deaden**
**04** dull, hush, mute, numb **05** abate, allay, blunt, check, slake **06** benumb, dampen, harden, lessen, muffle, obtund, reduce, soothe, stifle, subdue, weaken **07** assuage, mortify, quieten, smother **08** diminish, mitigate, moderate, paralyse, suppress **09** alleviate **11** desensitize **12** anaesthetize **14** take the edge off **15** make insensitive

**deadline**
**04** term, time **06** time up **08** timeline **09** time limit **10** target date

**deadlock**
**04** halt **05** stale **06** log jam **07** dead end, impasse **08** stand-off, stoppage **09** checkmate, stalemate **10** standstill

**deadly**
**04** dull, fell, grim, sure, true **05** fatal, feral, great, hated, quite, toxic **06** bitter, boring, fierce, funest, lethal, marked, mortal, savage **07** deathly, extreme, humdrum, intense, killing, noxious, perfect, precise, serious, tedious, totally, utterly **08** accurate, deathful, entirely, flawless, mortific, unerring, venomous **09** dangerous, deathlike, effective, extremely, malignant, murderous, perfectly, pestilent, thanatoid, unfailing **10** absolutely, completely, dreadfully, implacable, monotonous, pernicious, thoroughly, unexciting **11** destructive, internecine, internecive **12** death-dealing **13** uninteresting **14** irreconcilable **15** life-threatening

**deadpan**
**05** blank, empty **09** impassive **10** poker-faced **11** emotionless, inscrutable **12** inexpressive, unexpressive **13** dispassionate, straight-faced **14** expressionless

**deaf**
**04** surd **05** dunny **07** unmoved **08** heedless **09** oblivious, stone-deaf, unmindful, untouched **10** cloth-eared, impervious, unaffected **11** deaf as a post, inattentive, indifferent, unconcerned **13** hard of hearing **15** hearing-impaired

**deafening**
**07** booming, ringing, roaring **08** piercing, very loud **09** very noisy **10** resounding, thundering, thunderous **11** ear-piercing **12** ear-splitting, overwhelming **13** reverberating

**deal**
**02** go **03** act, buy, lot **04** flog, hand, load, mart, mete, pact, push, vend **05** allot, reach, round, serve, share, stock, trade, treat **06** amount, assign, bestow, degree, direct, divide, export, extent, handle, market, strike **07** bargain, deliver, dish out, dole out, give out, inflict, mete out, operate, portion, traffic **08** contract, covenant, dispense, quantity **09** agreement, apportion, negotiate, treatment **10** administer, buy and sell, distribute, do business **11** arrangement, transaction **12** distribution **13** understanding

**• deal out**
**04** dole, help **06** divide **08** dispense **10** distribute

**• deal with**
**04** cope, sort **05** cover, see to, touch, treat **06** handle, manage, tackle **07** be about, concern, process, sort out **08** attend to, consider, cope with **09** look after **10** take care of **12** have to do with **14** get to grips with

**• good deal**
**07** bargain

**• great deal**
**03** lot **04** heap, mort, much, some **05** heaps, power, sight, world

**dealer**
**03** dlr **04** tout **05** agent, coper **06** broker, couper, hawker, monger, pedlar, pusher, seller, totter, trader, vendor **07** chapman, fripper **08** marketer, merchant, retailer, salesman, supplier **09** brinjarry, fripperer **10** saleswoman, trafficker, wholesaler **11** distributor, salesperson **12** merchandizer

**dealing, dealings**
**05** trade, truck **07** trading, traffic **08** business, commerce **09** marketing, operation, relations **10** chevisance, operations **11** association, connections, intercourse, merchandise, trafficking, transaction **12** negotiations, transactions **13** communication

**dean**
**03** den **04** dell, dene, head **05** doyen, slade, Swift **08** director **09** principal, rural dean **11** chapter head, vicar-forane **12** Very Reverend **13** head of faculty **14** cardinal-bishop

**• rural dean**
**02** RD **10** arch-priest **11** vicar-forane

**dear**
**03** joy, pet **04** cher, chou, high, lamb, leve, lief, love, posh, salt **05** angel, chère, close, honey, lieve, loved, steep, sugar, sweet **06** adored, costly, pricey, scarce, valued **07** beloved, darling, earnest, machree, sky-high, sweetie **08** esteemed, familiar, favoured, grievous, high-cost, intimate, loved one, not cheap, precious, treasure **09** big-ticket, chargeful, cherished, endearing, excessive, expensive, favourite, respected, treasured **10** exorbitant, high-priced, mavourneen, overpriced, sweetheart **11** well-beloved **12** au poids de l'or, costing a bomb, extortionate **15** costing the earth, daylight robbery

**dearer**
**04** loor

**dearly**
**06** deeply, fondly **07** greatly **08** lovingly, tenderly, very much **09** adoringly, devotedly, earnestly, extremely **10** a great deal, intimately, profoundly, with favour **11** with respect **12** at a great cost, at a high price **13** with affection, with great loss **14** affectionately

**dearth**
**04** lack, need, want **06** famine **07** absence, paucity, poverty **08** dearness, scarcity, shortage, sparsity **10** barrenness, deficiency, inadequacy, meagreness, scantiness **12** exiguousness **13** insufficiency

**death**
**03** end **04** loss, ruin **06** finish **07** decease, undoing **08** curtains, downfall, the grave **09** cessation, departure, mortality, perishing **10** defunction, expiration, extinction **11** destruction, dissolution, eradication, extirpation, termination **12** annihilation, obliteration **13** extermination

*Death-related terms include:*

**03** DOA, RIP, urn
**04** bier, cist, mort, obit, pall, pyre, sati, soul, toll, tomb, wake, will
**05** ashes, bardo, cairn, dirge, elegy, éloge, elogy, grave, mourn, shiva, tangi, vigil, widow
**06** Azrael, bedral, burial, chadar, coffin, corpse, demise, entomb, eulogy, exequy, fossor, grieve, hearse, lament, lethal, martyr, monody, mortal, orphan, rosary, shibah, shivah, shroud, suttee, wreath
**07** autopsy, bederal, bereave, coroner, cortège, cremate, crucify, elogium, epitaph, funeral, inquest, karoshi, keening, mastaba, mourner, passing, quietus, requiem, widower
**08** casualty, cemetery, cenotaph, deathbed, death row, deceased, disinter, dispatch, eulogium, fatality, grieving, hara-kiri, interred, last post, long home, mortbell, mortuary, mourning, necropsy, necrosis, obituary, yahrzeit
**09** committal, cremation, dead march, death mask, graveside, graveyard, headstone, interment, last rites, mass grave, mausoleum, mortician, obsequies, passing on, sacrifice, sepulchre, testament, tombstone, year's mind
**10** death knell, euthanasia, grim reaper, necropolis, obituarist, pall-bearer, posthumous, predecease, strae death, undertaker
**11** bereavement, crematorium, eternal rest, funeral home, grave-digger, last honours, passing away, passing bell, requiem mass, rest in peace, rigor mortis, sarcophagus, suicide pact
**12** burial ground, debt of nature, disinterment, last farewell, mercy killing, resting place, the other side
**13** burial society, natural causes
**14** extreme unction, funeral parlour
**15** funeral director, resurrectionist

**• after death**
**02** PM **10** posthumous, post-mortem
**• approach of death**
**03** fit
**• by reason of death**
**02** cm
**• put to death**
**03** gas **04** do in, hang, kill **05** lynch, press, shoot, waste **06** behead, martyr, rub out **07** bump off, crucify, execute, take out **08** blow away, despatch, dispatch, knock off **09** transport **10** decapitate, guillotine **11** electrocute, exterminate
**• repose of death**
**04** rest

**deathless**
**07** eternal, undying **08** immortal, timeless **09** memorable **10** ever-living **11** everlasting, never-ending **12** imperishable **13** incorruptible, unforgettable

**deathly**
**03** wan **04** grim, pale **05** ashen, fatal, white **06** deadly, mortal, pallid, utmost **07** extreme, ghastly, ghostly, haggard, harmful, intense **08** terrible **09** deathlike, ghost-like, thanatoid **10** cadaverous, colourless

**debacle**
**04** hash, rout, ruin **05** farce, havoc **06** cock-up, defeat, fiasco, foul-up **07** failure, screw-up, turmoil, washout **08** collapse, disaster, downfall, reversal, stampede **09** cataclysm, overthrow, ruination **11** catastrophe, devastation **14** disintegration

**debar**
**03** ban, bar **04** deny, stop **05** eject, expel **06** cut out, forbid, hamper, hinder **07** exclude, keep out, prevent, shut out, suspend **08** conclude, obstruct, preclude, prohibit, restrain **09** blackball, proscribe, segregate **10** disqualify

**debarred**
**03** out

**debase**
**05** abase, allay, alloy, lower, shame, taint **06** bemean, defile, demean, dilute, embace, embase, humble, imbase, reduce **07** cheapen, corrupt, degrade, devalue, pollute, vitiate **08** disgrace **09** discredit, dishonour, humiliate **10** adulterate, bastardize, sensualize **11** contaminate

**debased**
**03** low **04** base, vile **05** hedge **06** abased, fallen, impure, shamed, sinful, sordid, vulgar **07** corrupt, defiled, humbled, immoral, tainted **08** degraded, devalued, polluted, reversed **09** cheapened, debauched, disgraced, perverted **10** degenerate, humiliated, prostitute **11** adulterated, discredited, dishonoured **12** contaminated

**debasement**
**05** shame **08** disgrace **09** abasement, dishonour, pollution **10** cheapening, corruption, defilement, perversion **11** degradation, depravation, devaluation, humiliation **12** adulteration, degeneration **13** contamination

**debatable**
**04** moot **06** unsure **07** dubious, unclear **08** arguable, doubtful **09** uncertain, undecided, unsettled **10** disputable **11** contentious, contestable **12** questionable **13** controversial, problematical **14** open to question

**debate**
**05** argue, fight, flyte, forum, weigh **06** combat, ponder, powwow, reason **07** contend, contest, discept, discuss, dispute, flyting, polemic, reflect, teach-in, wrangle, wrestle **08** argument, cogitate, consider, mull over, polemics, talk over **09** altercate, forensics, kick about, talk about, talkathon, think over, thrash out **10** contention, deliberate, discussion, kick around, knock about, meditate on, reflection **11** altercation, controversy, disputation, knock around, talk through **12** cut and thrust, deliberation **13** consideration **15** exchange of views

**debauch**
**03** wet **04** ruin **05** whore **06** debosh, ravish, seduce **07** corrupt, deprave, pervert, pollute, subvert, violate, vitiate **10** lead astray **11** over-indulge

**debauched**
**04** lewd **06** wanton **07** corrupt, debased, immoral, riotous **08** decadent, degraded, depraved, rakehell **09** abandoned, carousing, corrupted, dissolute, excessive, perverted **10** degenerate, dissipated, licentious, profligate **11** intemperate, promiscuous **13** overindulgent

**debauchery**
**04** lust, orgy, riot **05** revel **06** excess **07** licence, license **08** carousal, lewdness **09** decadence, depravity **10** corruption, degeneracy, immorality, rakishness, wantonness **11** degradation, dissipation, libertinage, libertinism **12** intemperance **13** dissoluteness **14** licentiousness, overindulgence
**• place of debauchery**
**03** sty

**debenture**
**04** bond

**debilitate**
**03** sap **04** tire **05** drain **06** impair, weaken **07** cripple, exhaust, fatigue, wear out **08** enervate, enfeeble **09** undermine **10** devitalize **12** incapacitate

**debilitating**
**06** tiring **09** crippling, fatiguing, impairing, weakening **10** enervating, enervative, enfeebling, exhausting, wearing out **11** undermining **14** incapacitating

**debility**
**05** atony **07** fatigue, frailty, languor, malaise **08** asthenia, weakness **09** atonicity, faintness, infirmity, tiredness, weariness **10** enervation, exhaustion, feebleness, incapacity, myasthenia **11** decrepitude **12** enfeeblement, lack of energy, neurasthenia **14** lack of vitality

**debit**
**• direct debit**
**02** DD

**debonair**
**05** suave **06** breezy, jaunty, smooth, urbane **07** affable, buoyant, dashing, elegant, refined, stylish **08** carefree, charming, cheerful, cultured, well-bred **09** courteous, dignified **12** light-hearted **13** sophisticated

**debrief**
**05** grill **07** examine **08** question **09** interview **11** interrogate **12** cross-examine **13** cross-question

**debris**
◇ *anagram indicator*
**04** bits, muck **05** drift, dross, ruins, scrap, trash, waste, wreck **06** bahada, bajada, litter, pieces, refuse, rubble, tephra **07** eluvium, remains, rubbish **08** detritus, wreckage **09** fragments, sweepings **12** pyroclastics
• **pile of debris**
**03** tel **04** tell

**debt**
**03** dew, due, IOU, sin **04** bill, duty, hock **05** claim, debit, score **06** charge **07** account, arrears **08** money due **09** amount due, liability, overdraft **10** aes alienum, commitment, money owing, obligation **11** amount owing **12** indebtedness
• **in debt**
**06** in hock **08** in the red **09** gone under, in arrears, insolvent **10** owing money **11** in overdraft **13** gone to the wall, in Queer Street
• **indication of debt**
**03** red
• **in someone's debt**
**07** obliged **08** beholden, indebted, thankful **11** honour-bound **12** appreciative

**debtor**
**02** Dr **07** debitor **08** bankrupt, borrower, deadbeat **09** defaulter, insolvent, mortgagor **10** abbey-laird, fly-by-night

**debunk**
**04** mock **05** quash **06** expose, show up **07** deflate, explode, lampoon **08** disprove, puncture, ridicule **13** cut down to size

**debut, début**
**05** start **06** launch **08** entrance, première **09** beginning, coming-out, first time, launching **10** first night, initiation **12** inauguration, introduction, presentation **14** first recording **15** first appearance

**debutante, débutante**
**03** bud, deb **05** debby

**decadence**
**04** fall **05** decay **07** decline **09** depravity **10** corruption, debasement, debauchery, degeneracy, immorality, perversion **11** dissipation, dissolution **12** degeneration **13** deterioration, retrogression **14** degenerateness, licentiousness, self-indulgence

**decadent**
**06** effete **07** corrupt, debased, immoral **08** decaying, degraded, depraved **09** debauched, declining, dissolute, symbolist **10** Babylonian, degenerate, dissipated, licentious **12** degenerating, unprincipled **13** deteriorating, self-indulgent

**decamp**
**03** fly, guy **04** bolt, flee, flit **05** lam it, scrap, slide, slope, split **06** desert, escape, hook it, levant, mizzle, run off **07** abscond, do a bunk, make off, run away, scamper, scarper, take off, vamoose **08** light out, slope off, up sticks **09** do a runner, skedaddle **10** hightail it, make tracks **12** absquatulate **14** take in on the lam

**decant**
**03** tap **05** drain **07** draw off, pour out **08** transfer **09** siphon off

**decapitate**
◇ *head deletion indicator*
**06** behead, unhead **07** execute **10** guillotine

**decay**
**03** rot **04** blet, doat, dote, fail, ruin, rust, sink **05** faint, go bad, go off, mould, spoil, waste **06** blight, canker, caries, dry rot, empare, fading, fester, fungus, impair, mildew, perish, weaken, wet rot, wither **07** atrophy, corrode, crumble, decline, dwindle, empaire, empayre, failing, failure, forfair, go to pot, putrefy, rotting, shrivel, wasting **08** collapse, downfall, foxiness, going bad, wear away **09** crumbling, decadence, decadency, decompose, perishing, putridity, waste away, weakening, withering **10** debasement, declension, decompound, degenerate, go downhill **11** deteriorate, go to the dogs, labefaction, putrescence **12** degeneration, disintegrate, putrefaction **13** consenescence, consenescency, decomposition, deterioration, labefactation **14** disintegration

**decayed**
**03** bad, off **04** rank, sour **05** druxy, stale **06** addled, failed, mouldy, putrid, rotten, sleepy, wasted **07** carious, carrion, doddard, rotting, ruinous, spoiled **08** corroded, doddered, mildewed, perished, withered **09** putrefied **10** decomposed, dirt-rotten, putrescent **12** impoverished

**decease**
**03** die, end **04** rest **05** death, dying **06** demise **07** passing **09** departure, passing on **10** expiration **11** dissolution, passing away

**deceased**
**03** dec **04** dead, gone, late, lost **06** asleep, former, no more **07** defunct, expired, extinct **08** departed, finished **12** six feet under **15** dead as a doornail

**deceit**
**03** con **04** fake, game, ruse, sham, wile **05** abuse, dodge, feint, fraud, guile, guyle **06** barrat **07** cunning, forgery, glozing, slenter, slinter, slyness, swindle **08** artifice, cheating, coquetry, cozenage, pretence, trickery, wiliness **09** chicanery, deception, duplicity, falseness, gold brick, hypocrisy, invention, malengine, phenakism, stratagem, treachery **10** craftiness, imposition, subterfuge **11** fraudulence **13** double-dealing **14** monkey business **15** underhandedness

**deceitful**
**03** sly **04** foxy, jive, rusé **05** false, lying, Punic, sharp **06** braide, crafty, double, forked, sneaky, tricky **07** crooked, cunning, devious, elusory, knavish **08** coloured, guileful, illusory, two-faced **09** deceiving, deceptive, designing, dishonest, insincere, underhand **10** deceptious, fraudulent, Janus-faced, mendacious, perfidious, untruthful **11** counterfeit, dissembling, duplicitous, prestigious, treacherous **12** false-hearted, hypocritical **13** double-dealing, double-tongued, untrustworthy

**deceitfully**
**05** slyly **06** double **07** falsely **08** craftily, sneakily **09** cunningly **11** deceivingly, deceptively, dishonestly, insincerely **12** fraudulently, mendaciously, perfidiously, untruthfully **13** duplicitously, treacherously, underhandedly **14** hypocritically

**deceive**
**02** do **03** cog, con, gag, kid, lie **04** bite, do in, dupe, flam, fool, gull, hoax, mock **05** abuse, blind, bluff, cheat, false, put on, trick, trump **06** befool, betray, delude, entrap, have on, humbug, lead on, misuse, outwit, seduce, slip up **07** beguile, cheat on, chicane, defraud, ensnare, mislead, swindle, two-time **08** hoodwink, misguide, outsmart **09** bamboozle, dissemble, mislippen **10** camouflage, disappoint, impose upon **11** double-cross, hornswoggle, set a trap for, string along **12** put one over on, take for a ride **13** put a cheat upon **14** pull a fast one on

**deceiver**
**04** fake **05** cheat, crook, fraud **06** abuser, con man, falser, guiler, guyler, hoaxer **07** deluder, diddler, seducer **08** betrayer, impostor, swindler, treacher **09** charlatan, hypocrite, inveigler, treachour, tregetour, trickster **10** dissembler, mountebank **11** treachetour **12** double-dealer

**decelerate**
**04** slow **05** brake **06** retard **08** slow down **11** reduce speed **12** go more slowly **14** put the brakes on

**December**
**03** Dec

**decency**
**07** decorum, fitness, modesty **08** civility, courtesy, fairness **09** etiquette, good taste, integrity, propriety **10** politeness, seemliness **11** correctness, helpfulness, uprightness **14** respectability

**decent**
**02** OK **03** fit **04** fair, kind, nice, pure **05** civil **06** chaste, honest, modest, polite, proper, seemly, worthy **07** correct, ethical, fitting, gradely, helpful, upright **08** adequate, becoming, decorous, generous, gracious, graithly, moderate, obliging, passable, pleasant, suitable, tasteful, virtuous, wise-like **09** befitting, competent, courteous, dignified, tolerable **10** acceptable, dependable, reasonable, salubrious, sufficient, thoughtful **11** appropriate, presentable, respectable, trustworthy **12** satisfactory **13** accommodating

**decently**
**06** fairly, nicely **08** honestly, politely, properly, suitably **09** correctly, ethically, helpfully, tolerably **10** acceptably, adequately, becomingly, decorously, generously, graciously, obligingly, reasonably **11** courteously, presentably, respectably **12** sufficiently, thoughtfully **13** appropriately **14** satisfactorily

**decentralize**
**07** devolve **08** delegate, localize **11** regionalize **13** deconcentrate **14** spread outwards **15** spread downwards

**deception**
**03** cog, con, fib, kid, lie **04** hoax, hype, ruse, scam, sell, sham, wile **05** bluff, cheat, fraud, glaik, guile, kiddy, moody, set-up, snare, sting, trick **06** deceit, have-on, humbug, take-in **07** abusion, cunning, eyewash, fallacy, fubbery, gullery, leg-pull, swindle **08** artifice, cheating, flim-flam, illusion, nonsense, pretence, put-up job, trickery **09** chicanery, chicaning, duplicity, hypocrisy, imposture, stratagem, treachery **10** craftiness, hocus-pocus, maskirovka, pious fraud, subterfuge **11** dissembling, fraudulence, insincerity, supercherie **13** deceptiveness, double-dealing, funny business, jiggery-pokery **14** false pretences **15** smoke and mirrors, underhandedness

**deceptive**
**03** sly **04** fake, foxy, mock, sham **05** bogus, false, sharp **06** bubble, catchy, crafty, hollow **07** amusive, crooked, cunning, elusive **08** cheating, delusive, delusory, fraudful, illusive, illusory, imposing, specious, spurious **09** ambiguous, dishonest, faithless, underhand **10** fallacious, fraudulent, misleading, unreliable **11** dissembling, duplicitous

**deceptively**
**07** falsely **10** illusively, speciously, spuriously **11** ambiguously, dishonestly **12** fraudulently, misleadingly

**decibel**
**02** dB

**decide**
**03** end, fix, opt **04** pick, rule, seal **05** aread, arede, go for, judge, opt in **06** choose, clinch, define, make up, opt for, select, settle, wrap up **07** adjudge, arreede, darrain, darrayn, deraign, discuss, resolve, work out **08** conclude, darraign, darraine, plump for **09** arbitrate, darraigne, determine, establish **10** adjudicate, dijudicate **11** give a ruling **12** turn the scale **13** make a decision **14** commit yourself, give a judgement, make up your mind, reach a decision **15** come to a decision

**decided**
**04** ared, firm **05** clear **06** marked **07** certain, express, obvious **08** absolute, clear-cut, decisive, definite, distinct, emphatic, positive, resolute **10** deliberate, determined, forthright, pronounced, purposeful, undeniable, undisputed, unswerving, unwavering, well-marked **11** categorical, unambiguous, unequivocal **12** indisputable, unhesitating, unmistakable **14** unquestionable

**decidedly**
**04** very **05** quite **07** clearly **08** markedly **09** certainly, downright, obviously **10** absolutely, decisively, definitely, distinctly, noticeably, positively **12** unmistakably **13** unequivocally **14** unquestionably

**decider**
**08** clincher **10** determiner **11** coup de grâce

**deciding**
**03** key **05** chief, final, prime **06** crunch **07** crucial, supreme **08** critical, decisive **09** principal **10** conclusive **11** determining, influential, significant

**decimate**
**05** tithe, tythe **07** destroy, flatten **09** devastate, eliminate, eradicate **10** annihilate, obliterate

**decipher**
**04** dope **05** break, crack, solve **06** decode, detect, reveal **07** dope out, make out, suss out, unravel, work out **08** construe **09** figure out, interpret, translate **10** descramble, understand, unscramble **11** make sense of **13** transliterate

**decision**
**05** arrêt, award, parti **06** decree, firman, result, ruling **07** finding, opinion, outcome, purpose, resolve, verdict **08** firmness, last word, sentence **09** judgement **10** conclusion, resolution, settlement **11** arbitration **12** adjudication, decisiveness, forcefulness **13** determination, pronouncement **14** recommendation

**decisive**
**03** key **04** firm **05** crisp, fatal, final, prime **06** strong **07** crucial, decided, fateful **08** absolute, critical, deciding, definite, forceful, positive, resolute **09** effectual, momentous, principal **10** conclusive, definitive, determined, forthright, purposeful, unswerving, unwavering **11** determinate, determining, influential, significant **12** single-minded, strong-minded

**decisively**
**06** firmly **08** strongly **09** crucially, fatefully **10** absolutely, critically, forcefully, positively, resolutely **11** momentously **12** conclusively, definitively, determinedly, forthrightly, purposefully, unswervingly, unwaveringly **13** influentially, significantly **14** single-mindedly

**deck**
**02** dk **03** rig, tog **04** pack, prim, trap, trim **05** adorn, array, cover, grace **06** bedeck, betrim, clothe, enrich, ground, tart up **07** festoon, garland, garnish, trick up **08** beautify, covering, decorate, ornament, platform, prettify, trick out **09** embellish

• **deck out**
**03** rig, tog **04** do up, garb, robe **05** adorn, array, dress, get up, prick **06** clothe, doll up, tart up **07** dress up **08** decorate

**declaim**
**04** rant **05** mouth, orate, spiel, spout **06** recite **07** bespout, elocute, lecture **08** disclaim, harangue, perorate, proclaim, sound off **09** hold forth, pronounce, sermonize **11** expostulate, speak boldly

**declamation**
**04** rant **06** sermon, speech, tirade **07** address, lecture, oration **08** harangue **10** recitation **12** speechifying

**declamatory**
**04** bold **05** stagy **07** fustian, orotund, pompous, stilted **08** dramatic, inflated, parlando **09** bombastic, grandiose, high-flown, overblown **10** discursive, oratorical, rhetorical, theatrical **12** magniloquent **13** grandiloquent

**declaration**
**03** dec **04** call, dick, word **05** edict **06** avowal, decree **08** averment **09** affidavit, assertion, assurance, broadcast, manifesto, outgiving, statement, testimony **10** confession, deposition, disclosure, profession, revelation **11** affirmation, attestation, certificate, enunciation **12** announcement, asseveration, confirmation, denunciation, notification, proclamation, promulgation, protestation **13** communication, pronouncement **15** acknowledgement

**declare**
**02** go **03** say, vie **04** aver, avow, read, show **05** aread, arede, claim, speak, state, swear **06** affirm, assert, attest, decree, notify, reveal **07** arreede,

certify, confess, confirm, discuss, express, profess, protest, publish, signify, testify, witness **08** announce, disclose, maintain, manifest, proclaim, set forth, validate **09** broadcast, make known, pronounce **10** asseverate, promulgate **11** communicate

**declared**
**04** ared **06** avowed, stated **07** confest **09** confessed, professed

**decline**
**03** dip, ebb, rot, sag, set **04** balk, deny, drop, fade, fail, fall, flag, hill, nill, sink, slip, wane, welk **05** abate, avoid, baulk, decay, droop, forgo, lapse, quail, slant, slide, slope, slump, stoop, traik **06** devall, forego, go down, lessen, plunge, recede, reduce, refuse, reject, sunset, waning, weaken, wither, worsen **07** descend, descent, deviate, drop-off, dwindle, evening, failing, failure, fall off, get less, go to pot, incline, plummet, regress, say no to, subside, tail off **08** come down, decrease, diminish, downturn, fall away, lowering, nosedive, peter out, turn down **09** abatement, catabasis, decadence, decadency, declivity, deviation, downswing, dwindling, lessening, recession, reduction, repudiate, weakening, worsening **10** become less, condescend, de-escalate, degenerate, diminution, divergence, falling-off, go downhill, go to pieces, sunsetting **11** declination, dégringoler, deteriorate **12** de-escalation, degeneration **13** deterioration, retrogression

**decode**
**04** dope **05** clear, crack **07** decrypt, dope out, make out, unravel, work out **08** construe, decipher, uncipher **09** figure out, interpret, translate **10** understand, unscramble **13** transliterate

**decomposable**
**10** degradable **12** destructible **13** biodegradable **14** decompoundable

**decompose**
◇ *anagram indicator*
**03** rot **05** decay, go bad, go off, spoil **06** fester **07** break up, crumble, degrade, putrefy **08** dissolve, fragment, pyrolyse, separate **09** break down **10** decompound **12** depolymerize, disintegrate

**decomposition**
**03** rot **05** decay **07** rotting **08** going bad, going off **09** perishing, putridity, pyrolysis **10** corruption, hydrolysis, photolysis, radiolysis **11** degradation, dissolution, putrescence **12** electrolysis, fermentation, putrefaction **14** disintegration

**decontaminate**
**05** clean, purge **06** purify **07** cleanse **08** fumigate, sanitize **09** disinfect, sterilize

**décor**
**07** scenery **10** decoration **11** furnishings **12** colour scheme **13** ornamentation

**decorate**
**03** ice **04** cite, deck, do up, hang, pink, trim **05** adorn, array, chase, crown, grace, paint, paper **06** bedaub, colour, daiker, enrich, fangle, honour, parget, reward, tart up **07** bedizen, bemedal, deck out, embrave, festoon, furbish, garland, garnish, smarten, trick up **08** beautify, damaskin, ornament, prettify, renovate, spruce up, trick out **09** damascene, damaskeen, damasquin, embellish, guilloche, refurbish, scrimshaw, wallpaper **10** damasceene **12** give a medal to **13** give an award to **14** give an honour to

**decoration**
**04** paua, star **05** award, badge, cross, crown, décor, frill, honor, medal, mural, order, title **06** bauble, doodad, doodah, emblem, honour, laurel, parget, ribbon, scroll, wreath **07** bunting, colours, garland, garnish, trinket **08** diamanté, flourish, frou-frou, insignia, ornament, parament, trimming **09** adornment **10** enrichment, Japanesery, knick-knack **11** elaboration, enhancement, furnishings **12** colour scheme **13** embellishment, ornamentation **14** beautification

*See also* **honour**; **military**

**decorative**
**05** fancy **06** flashy, ornate, pretty, rococo **08** adorning **09** elaborate, enhancing **10** ornamental **11** beautifying, prettifying **12** embellishing **13** non-functional

**decorous**
**03** fit **05** staid **06** comely, decent, modest, polite, proper, sedate, seemly **07** correct, courtly, refined **08** becoming, mannerly, menseful, suitable **09** befitting, dignified **11** appropriate, comme il faut, well-behaved **13** parliamentary

**decorum**
**05** grace **07** decency, dignity, honesty, modesty **08** breeding, courtesy, good form, protocol **09** behaviour, etiquette, propriety, restraint **10** conformity, deportment, politeness, seemliness **11** good manners **14** respectability

**decoy**
**04** bait, draw, lead, lure, tice, tole, toll, trap **05** dummy, piper, roper, shill, snare, stale, stall, tempt **06** allure, bonnet, button, entice, entrap, seduce, trepan **07** attract, deceive, ensnare, pitfall, roper-in **08** inveigle, pretence **09** diversion **10** allurement, attraction, enticement, inducement, red herring, temptation **11** ensnarement, stool pigeon, tame cheater

**decrease**
**03** ebb **04** drop, ease, fall, loss, slim, trim, wane **05** abate, decay, let up, lower, slide, taper, wanze **06** decrew, go down, lessen, plunge, reduce, shrink **07** curtail, cut back, cutback, cut down, decline, dwindle, fall off, plummet, slacken, subside **08** come down, contract, diminish, downturn, lowering, make less, peter out, rollback, slim down, step-down, taper off **09** abatement, decrement, dwindling, lessening, reduction, scale down, shrinkage **10** become less, de-escalate, degression, diminution, falling-off, subsidence **11** contraction **12** de-escalation

**decree**
**03** act, law, saw **04** fiat, rule, will **05** edict, enact, grace, irade, novel, order, ukase, write **06** decern, decide, direct, enjoin, firman, modify, ordain, ruling **07** command, dictate, lay down, mandate, novelle, precept, statute **08** proclaim, psephism, rescript **09** determine, directive, enactment, indiction, interdict, judgement, manifesto, ordinance, prescribe, pronounce, testament **10** regulation **11** hatti-sherif **12** interlocutor, proclamation, promulgation **13** interlocution **14** senatus consult

**decrepit**
**03** old **04** aged, weak **05** frail, warby **06** feeble, infirm, past it **07** elderly, rickety, run-down, worn-out **08** battered, spavined **09** crumbling, doddering, enfeebled, getting on, senescent, tottering **10** broken-down, clapped-out, in bad shape, ramshackle, tumbledown **11** dilapidated, over the hill **12** falling apart **13** falling to bits **14** in bad condition **15** falling to pieces

**decrepitude**
**04** ruin **05** decay **06** dotage, old age **08** debility, senility, weakness **09** infirmity **10** disability, feebleness, incapacity, senescence **11** ricketiness **12** degeneration, dilapidation **13** deterioration **14** incapacitation

**decriminalize**
**05** allow **06** permit, ratify **07** approve, license, warrant **08** legalize, sanction, validate **09** authorize **10** legitimize

**decry**
**03** pan **04** carp, crab, slam **05** blame, knock, slate, snipe **06** attack **07** censure, condemn, devalue, nit-pick, run down, traduce **08** belittle, denounce, derogate **09** criticize, denigrate, disparage, excoriate, underrate **10** animadvert, come down on, depreciate, preach down, undervalue **12** disapprove of, pull to pieces, tear to shreds **13** find fault with, tear a strip off **14** declaim against, inveigh against **15** do a hatchet job on

**dedicate**
**04** bind, give, name, open **05** bless, offer **06** assign, commit, devote,

hallow, pledge **07** address, devoted, present **08** inscribe, make holy, sanctify, set apart **09** sacrifice, surrender **10** consecrate, give over to, inaugurate

**dedicated**

**06** oblate **07** bespoke, devoted, sold out, staunch, zealous **08** diligent **09** committed, sold out on **10** customized, purposeful **11** custom-built, given over to, hard working, industrious **12** card-carrying, enthusiastic, single-minded, wholehearted **13** dyed-in-the-wool, single-hearted

**dedication**

**04** wake, zeal **07** address, loyalty **08** blessing, devotion **09** adherence, hallowing **10** allegiance, attachment, commitment, enthusiasm **11** benediction, inscription **12** consecration, faithfulness, presentation **13** self-sacrifice **14** sanctification

**deduce**

**04** dope, draw, suss **05** glean, infer **06** derive, gather, reason **07** dope out, surmise, work out **08** conclude **09** figure out, syllogize **10** understand

**deduct**

**04** dock **06** deduce, reduce, remove, weaken **07** take off **08** knock off, reduce by, separate, subtract, take away, take from, withdraw **09** strike off **10** decrease by

**deduction**

**04** dock **06** result **07** finding, removal, reprise **08** decrease, discount **09** abatement, allowance, corollary, inference, reasoning, reduction, surmising, taking off **10** assumption, conclusion, consectary, diminution, hypothesis, taking away, withdrawal **11** consequence, presumption, subtraction **12** off-reckoning

• **clear of deductions**

**03** net **04** nett

**deed**

**03** act **04** fact, feat, work **05** issue, starr, title, truth **06** action, escrow, factum, record **07** charter, exploit, reality **08** activity, contract, document, mortgage, valiance, valiancy **09** actuality, agreement, endeavour, indenture, quitclaim, specialty **10** attainment, backletter, bill of sale **11** achievement, disposition, enfeoffment, infeudation, performance, transaction, undertaking **14** accomplishment

**deem**

**03** see **04** hold **05** judge, think **06** esteem, reckon, regard **07** account, adjudge, believe, imagine, opinion, suppose **08** conceive, consider, estimate

**deep**

**03** far, low, sea **04** bass, dark, full, lost, main, rapt, rich, warm, wise **05** briny, grave, ocean, quiet, sound, thick, vivid **06** arcane, ardent, astute, clever, gaping, intent, severe, strong **07** abysmal, abyssal, booming, cunning, earnest, extreme, faraway, fervent, glowing, intense, learned, obscure, serious, yawning **08** absorbed, abstruse, a long way, esoteric, high seas, immersed, powerful, profound, reserved, resonant, sonorous, the drink, vigorous **09** brilliant, cavernous, difficult, engrossed, excessive, full-toned, heart-felt, intensely, recondite, sagacious, unplumbed, very great **10** bottomless, discerning, fathomless, low-pitched, mysterious, passionate, perceptive, profoundly, resounding, unfathomed **11** deep as a well, impassioned, preoccupied, uncrossable **12** immeasurable, intellectual, wholehearted **13** knowledgeable, perspicacious **14** a great distance

**deepen**

**04** grow **06** bump up, dig out, extend, hike up, hollow, step up, worsen **07** build up, magnify **08** excavate, get worse, heighten, increase, mushroom, scoop out **09** intensify, reinforce, scrape out **10** strengthen **11** deteriorate

**deeply**

**04** upsy **05** sadly, upsee, upsey **06** keenly **07** acutely, gravely, greatly, sharply **08** ardently, movingly, severely, strongly, very much **09** earnestly, extremely, feelingly, fervently, intensely, seriously **10** completely, mournfully, profoundly, thoroughly, to the quick, vigorously **12** passionately **13** distressingly

**deep-seated**

**04** deep **05** fixed **07** chronic, settled **08** intimate, Plutonic, profound **09** confirmed, ingrained **10** deep-rooted, entrenched **11** fundamental

**deer**

**03** doe **04** buck, fawn, hart, hind, spay, stag **05** Bambi, spade, spayd **06** cervid, rascal, spayad **07** pricket, spitter **08** staggard

*Deer include:*

**03** elk, hog, red, roe
**04** axis, mule, musk, pudu, rusa, sika
**05** moose, water
**06** chital, fallow, forest, sambar, sambur, tufted, wapiti
**07** barking, brocket, caribou, jumping, muntjac, muntjak
**08** cariacou, carjacou, Irish elk, reindeer, Virginia
**09** barasinga
**10** barasingha, chevrotain, Père David's
**11** black-tailed, white-tailed
**12** Chinese water, Indian sambar
**13** Indian muntjac

**deface**

◇ *head deletion indicator*

**03** mar **04** ruin **05** spoil, sully **06** damage, defame, deform, impair, injure **07** blemish, destroy, tarnish **08** mutilate **09** disfigure, vandalize **10** disfeature, obliterate

**de facto**

**04** real **06** actual, in fact, really **08** actually, existing, in effect **10** in practice

**defamation**

**04** slur **05** libel, smear **07** calumny, obloquy, scandal, slander **08** innuendo, slamming **09** aspersion **10** backbiting, derogation, opprobrium **11** badmouthing, denigration, malediction, mud-slinging, slagging-off, traducement **12** vilification **13** disparagement, smear campaign

**defamatory**

**09** aspersory, injurious, insulting, libellous, vilifying **10** calumnious, derogatory, pejorative, scandalous, scurrilous, slanderous **11** denigrating, disparaging, maledictory, mud-slinging **12** contumelious

**defame**

**04** slag, slam **05** cloud, libel, smear **06** deface, infame, infamy, malign, vilify **07** asperse, blacken, blemish, detract, run down, scandal, slag off, slander, traduce **08** badmouth, besmirch, disgrace, infamize **09** bespatter, denigrate, discredit, dishonour, disparage **10** calumniate, sling mud at, stigmatize, throw mud at, vituperate **11** speak evil of **14** cast aspersions

**default**

**04** fail, lack, loss, want **05** dodge, evade, fault, lapse **06** defect **07** absence, defraud, failing, failure, neglect, offence, swindle **08** omission **09** backslide **10** deficiency, negligence, non-payment **11** dereliction

**defaulter**

**04** duck **08** absentee, lame duck, non-payer, offender **11** non-appearer

**defeat**

**03** gub, lam, war **04** balk, beat, best, drub, foil, kill, lick, loss, rout, ruin, tank, tonk, undo, whip **05** annul, block, crush, excel, paste, quell, repel, smash, stump, throw, thump, worst **06** baffle, granny, hammer, outwit, puzzle, reject, subdue, thrash, thwart **07** beating, clobber, conquer, debacle, eclipse, failure, inch out, outplay, pasting, perplex, reverse, setback, surpass, tanking, trounce **08** confound, conquest, crushing, downfall, drubbing, obstruct, outmatch, outscore, outsmart, overcome, squabash, throw out, vanquish, Waterloo, whipping, whupping **09** breakdown, checkmate, defeature, devastate, discomfit, disfigure, frustrate, marmelize, overmatch, overpower, overthrow, overwhelm, pulverize, rejection, repulsion, shoot down, slaughter, subjugate, thrashing, thwarting, trouncing **10** annihilate, defeasance, disappoint, disconcert, overcoming **11** frustration, subjugation **12** annihilation, pip at the post, vanquishment **13** have the edge on, put to the worse, run rings round **14** disappointment, get the better of **15** make mincemeat of

**defeatist**

**06** gloomy **07** quitter, yielder **08** helpless, hopeless, negative, resigned **09** doomsayer, pessimist **10** despairing, despondent, fatalistic **11** doomwatcher, pessimistic **13** prophet of doom

**defecate**

**03** poo **04** crap, mute, plop, poop **05** egest **07** excrete, scumber, skummer **08** evacuate **11** do number two, pass a motion **12** cover the feet, ease yourself **13** void excrement **14** do your business, move your bowels **15** empty your bowels, relieve yourself

**defect**

**03** bug **04** flaw, lack, snag, spot, want **05** craze, error, fault, rebel, taint **06** desert, hiatus, renege, revolt, wreath **07** abandon, abscond, absence, blemish, default, demerit, failing, frailty, mistake **08** hamartia, omission, psellism, weakness, weak spot **09** deformity, shortfall **10** apostatize, break faith, deficience, deficiency, inadequacy **11** change sides, jump the dyke, loup the dyke, shortcoming, turn traitor **12** imperfection, tergiversate

**defection**

**06** mutiny, revolt **07** perfidy, treason **08** apostasy, betrayal **09** breakaway, desertion, rebellion **10** absconding, disloyalty, renegation **11** abandonment, backsliding, defalcation, dereliction **14** tergiversation

**defective**

◇ *anagram indicator*

**04** bust, duff **05** kaput, trick, wrong **06** broken, faulty, flawed **08** abnormal **09** deficient, imperfect **10** on the blink, on the fritz, out of order **11** in disrepair **12** insufficient **14** malfunctioning

**defector**

**03** rat **05** Judas, rebel **07** traitor **08** apostate, betrayer, deserter, mutineer, quisling, recreant, renegade, turncoat **10** backslider **13** tergiversator

**defence**

**04** army, case, keep, navy, plea, wall **05** alibi, cover, guard **06** excuse, screen, shield, troops **07** apology, bastion, bulwark, outpost, rampart, shelter, weapons **08** advocacy, air force, apologia, argument, buttress, fortress, garrison, immunity, military, munition, pleading, security, soldiers, weaponry **09** armaments, barricade, deterrent, safeguard, testimony **10** apologetic, deterrence, munifience, protection, resistance, stronghold **11** armed forces, exoneration, explanation, explication, extenuation, vindication **12** propugnation **13** fortification, justification

• **air defence**

**02** AD

*See also* **fortification**

**defenceless**

**04** weak **05** naked, silly **07** exposed, unarmed **08** helpless, impotent **09** guardless, powerless, unguarded **10** undefended, vulnerable **11** susceptible, unprotected **12** open to attack

**defend**

**04** back, fend, hold **05** cover, deter, guard, plead **06** assert, forbid, oppose, resist, screen, secure, shield, uphold **07** bolster, bulwark, contest, endorse, enguard, explain, fortify, justify, protect, shelter, stand by, support, warrant **08** argue for, bestride, buttress, champion, garrison, maintain, preserve, prohibit **09** barricade, exonerate, safeguard, vindicate, watch over, withstand **10** go to bat for, speak up for, stand up for, stick up for **12** keep from harm, make a case for **15** fight your corner, stand your corner

**defendant**

**03** def, dft **07** accused **08** litigant, offender, prisoner **09** appellant **10** respondent

**defender**

**04** back **05** guard **06** backer, keeper, patron **07** bastion, counsel, sponsor, warrant **08** advocate, asserter, assertor, champion, endorser, guardian, upholder **09** apologist, bodyguard, defendant, preserver, promachos, protector, supporter **10** vindicator

**defensible**

**04** safe **05** valid **06** secure **07** tenable **08** arguable **09** plausible **10** pardonable, vindicable **11** impregnable, justifiable, permissible **12** maintainable, unassailable

**defensive**

**04** wary **08** cautious, opposing, watchful **09** defending **10** apologetic, protecting, protective **12** safeguarding **13** Maginot-minded, oversensitive, self-defensive **14** self-justifying

• **defensive ring**

**04** laer **06** corral, laager

**defer**

**03** bow **05** delay, waive, yield **06** accede, comply, give in, put off, shelve, submit **07** adjourn, give way, put back, rejourn, respect, suspend **08** hold over, postpone, prorogue, protract, put on ice, roll over **09** acquiesce, surrender **10** capitulate **13** procrastinate

**deference**

**04** duty **06** esteem, honour, regard **07** respect **08** civility, courtesy, yielding **09** obedience, reverence, servility **10** compliance, politeness, submission **12** acquiescence **13** attentiveness, consideration **14** respectfulness, submissiveness, thoughtfulness

**deferential**

**05** civil **06** humble, polite **07** dutiful **08** obeisant, reverent **09** attentive, courteous, regardful **10** morigerous, obsequious, respectful **11** complaisant, reverential **12** ingratiating

**deferment**

**04** stay **05** delay **07** waiving **08** deferral, shelving **10** moratorium, putting-off, suspension **11** adjournment, holding-over, prorogation **12** postponement **15** procrastination

**defiance**

**08** contempt **09** challenge, contumacy, disregard, insolence **10** opposition, resistance, truculence **12** disobedience **13** confrontation, recalcitrance **14** rebelliousness **15** insubordination

• **expression of defiance**

**03** yah **04** nuts **05** ya-boo **06** yah-boo **10** ya-boo sucks **11** yah-boo sucks

**defiant**

**04** bold **08** insolent, militant, roisting, roysting, scornful **09** obstinate, resistant, truculent **10** aggressive, rebellious, refractory **11** challenging, disobedient, provocative **12** antagonistic, contemptuous, contumacious, intransigent, recalcitrant **13** insubordinate, unco-operative

**defiantly**

**05** acock **06** boldly **10** insolently, militantly, scornfully **11** obstinately, truculently **12** aggressively, rebelliously **13** disobediently, provocatively **14** contemptuously, contumaciously, intransigently, recalcitrantly **15** insubordinately, unco-operatively

**deficiency**

**04** flaw, lack, want **05** fault, minus **06** dearth, defect, shorts **07** absence, deficit, failing, frailty, poverty, wantage **08** scarcity, shortage, weakness **10** inadequacy, scantiness **11** shortcoming **12** imperfection **13** insufficiency

*Deficiencies include:*

**07** acapnia, amentia, hypoxia
**09** cytopenia, hypinosis, hypoxemia, oligaemia, spanaemia

**10** hypoxaemia
**11** hypospadias, sideropenia
**14** leucocytopenia, oligocythaemia

### deficient
◇ *anagram indicator*
**03** low **04** poor, weak **05** minus, scant, short **06** meagre, scanty, scarce, skimpy **07** lacking, wanting
**08** bankrupt, exiguous, inferior
**09** imperfect **10** defectible, inadequate, incomplete **12** insufficient
**14** unsatisfactory

### deficit
**04** lack, loss **07** arrears, default
**08** shortage **09** shortfall **10** deficiency

### defile
◇ *anagram indicator*
**03** col, ray **04** file, gate, moil, pass, soil
**05** dirty, gorge, gully, halse, hause, hawse, spoil, stain, sully, taint
**06** debase, defame, defoul, enseam, infect, ravine, valley **07** blacken, corrupt, degrade, passage, pollute, profane, tarnish, violate, vitiate
**08** disgrace, maculate **09** denigrate, desecrate, dishonour, inquinate
**10** make impure **11** contaminate, make unclean

### defilement
**04** moil **08** foulness, impurity, staining, sullying, tainting, tainture **09** pollution, profanity, violation **10** debasement, defamation, tarnishing **11** degradation, denigration, desecration
**13** conspurcation, contamination

### definable
**05** exact, fixed **07** precise
**08** definite, specific **10** explicable
**11** describable, perceptible
**12** determinable, identifiable
**13** ascertainable

### define
**03** fix **05** bound, limit **06** decide, detail **07** clarify, delimit, explain, expound, mark out, pin down, specify
**08** describe, pinpoint, spell out
**09** delineate, demarcate, designate, determine, elucidate, establish, interpret **12** characterize, circumscribe

### definite
**04** firm, hard, sure **05** clear, exact, fixed **06** marked **07** assured, certain, decided, obvious, precise, settled
**08** clear-cut, distinct, explicit, positive, specific **10** determined, guaranteed, noticeable, particular
**12** unmistakable

### definitely
**06** easily, indeed, surely **07** clearly, for sure, plainly **09** certainly, doubtless, expressly, no denying, obviously, out-and-out **10** absolutely, distinctly, in terminis, positively, undeniably
**11** indubitably, undoubtedly
**12** unmistakably, without doubt
**13** categorically, determinately, unmistakeably **14** unquestionably
**15** without question

### definition
**03** def **05** focus, sense **07** clarity, diorism, meaning **08** contrast
**09** clearness, precision, sharpness
**10** denotation, exposition, visibility
**11** description, elucidation, explanation **12** distinctness, significance **13** clarification, determination **14** interpretation

### definitive
**05** exact, final **07** classic, correct, perfect **08** absolute, complete, decisive, positive, reliable, standard, ultimate **09** classical **10** conclusive, exhaustive **11** categorical, terminative
**13** authoritative

### definitively
**07** finally **10** absolutely, completely, decisively **12** conclusively
**13** categorically **15** authoritatively

### deflate
**04** dash, slow, void **05** empty, lower
**06** debunk, humble, lessen, reduce, shrink, squash, subdue **07** chasten, depress, devalue, exhaust, flatten, let down, mortify, put down, squeeze
**08** collapse, contract, decrease, diminish, dispirit, puncture, slow down
**09** humiliate **10** depreciate, disappoint, disconcert

### deflect
**04** bend, draw, turn, veer, wind
**05** avert, drift, snick, twist **06** glance, swerve **07** deviate, diverge, head off, refract **08** ricochet, withdraw
**09** glance off, sidetrack, turn aside
**12** change course

### deflection
**04** bend, veer **05** drift, snick, throw
**06** swerve **07** turning **08** ricochet, twisting **09** deviation, diversion
**10** aberration, divergence, refraction
**11** glancing-off **12** sidetracking, turning aside **14** changing course

### deflower
**03** mar **04** harm, rape, ruin **05** force, spoil **06** defile, molest, ravish, seduce
**07** assault, despoil, violate
**09** deflorate, desecrate

### deform
◇ *anagram indicator*
**03** mar **04** maim, ruin, warp **05** spoil, twist **06** buckle, damage, deface
**07** contort, distort, hideous, malform, pervert **08** misshape, mutilate
**09** disfigure, unshapely

### deformation
**04** bend, warp **05** curve, twist
**06** buckle **08** twisting **10** cataclasis, contortion, defacement, distortion, mutilation **11** compression
**12** diastrophism, malformation
**13** disfiguration, misshapenness

### deformed
◇ *anagram indicator*
**04** bent **06** camsho, inform, maimed, marred, ruined, warped **07** buckled, crooked, defaced, dismayd, gnarled, mangled, misborn, mishapt, twisted
**08** camshoch, crippled
**09** camsheugh, contorted, corrupted, distorted, malformed, miscreate, misshaped, misshapen, mutilated, perverted **10** disfigured, miscreated, out of shape

### deformity
**06** defect **08** claw-foot, misshape, ugliness, vileness **09** grossness
**10** corruption, defacement, distortion, misfeature, perversion **11** abnormality, contracture, crookedness, monstrosity
**12** imperfection, irregularity, malformation **13** disfigurement, misproportion, misshapenness

### defraud
**02** do **03** con, rob **04** dupe, fool, nick, rook, rush, swiz **05** cheat, cozen, lurch, screw, sting, trick, wrong **06** delude, diddle, fiddle, fleece, outwit, rip off
**07** beguile, deceive, mislead, swindle, swizzle **08** embezzle, hoodwink

### defray
**03** pay **04** meet **05** cover, repay
**06** refund, settle, square **07** appease, satisfy **09** discharge, reimburse
**10** recompense

### defrost
**04** melt, thaw **08** defreeze

### deft
**04** able, feat, neat **05** adept, agile, handy, natty, nifty **06** adroit, clever, expert, nimble **07** skilful **09** dexterous
**10** proficient

### deftly
**04** ably **05** slick **06** neatly, nimbly
**07** adeptly **08** cleverly, expertly
**09** skilfully **12** proficiently

### defunct
**04** dead, gone **05** passé **06** bygone, unused **07** disused, expired, extinct, invalid **08** deceased, departed, finished, obsolete, outmoded
**11** inoperative

### defuse
◇ *anagram indicator*
**04** calm, cool **06** disarm **07** disable, quieten, relieve **08** calm down, cool down, disorder **09** alleviate
**10** deactivate, immobilize **11** clear the air

### defy
**04** dare, face, foil, mock **05** avoid, beard, brave, elude, flout, repel, scorn, spurn **06** baffle, defeat, ignore, resist, slight, thwart **07** despise, discard, dislike, disobey, outdare, provoke
**08** confront **09** challenge, disregard, frustrate, stand up to, withstand
**10** disrespect **12** rebel against **14** fly in the face of

### degeneracy
**08** vileness **09** decadence
**10** corruption, debasement, debauchery, effeteness, fallenness, immorality, perversion, sinfulness, wickedness **11** degradation,

depravation **12** degeneration **13** deterioration, dissoluteness

**degenerate**
**03** low, rot **04** base, fail, mean, rake, roué, sink, slip, vile **05** decay, knave, lapse, rogue, scamp **06** effete, fallen, rascal, recoil, sinful, sinner, wicked, worsen, wretch **07** corrupt, dastard, debased, decline, fall off, go to pot, ignoble, immoral, regress, villain **08** criminal, decadent, decrease, degender, degraded, depraved, derogate, evildoer, vagabond **09** abandoned, debauched, dissolute, miscreant, perverted, reprobate, scallywag, scoundrel, wrongdoer **10** bastardize, go downhill, ne'er-do-well, profligate **11** degenerated, deteriorate, off the rails **12** deteriorated, troublemaker **13** mischief-maker **14** go down the tubes

**degeneration**
**03** rot **04** drop, slip **05** decay, lapse, slide **06** dry rot **07** atrophy, decline, failure, sinking **08** decrease **09** caseation, steatosis, worsening **10** debasement, falling-off, involution, regression, retrogress **11** degradation **13** deterioration

**degradation**
**05** shame **07** decline **08** comedown, demotion, disgrace, ignominy, vileness **09** abasement, decadence, demission, dishonour **10** corruption, culvertage, debasement, debauchery, degeneracy, fallenness, immorality, perversion, sinfulness, wickedness **11** depravation, downgrading, humiliation **12** degeneration, immiseration **13** decomposition, deterioration, dissoluteness, mortification **14** immiserization

**degrade**
**04** sink **05** abase, erode, lower, shame, sully **06** debase, defile, demean, demote, depose, embace, embase, humble, imbase, impair, reduce, unseat, weaken **07** cashier, cheapen, corrupt, declass, deprive, devalue, drum out, embrute, imbrute, mortify, pervert, put down **08** belittle, diminish, disgrace, dishonor, relegate **09** brutalize, decompose, discredit, dishonour, downgrade, humiliate **10** adulterate, disennoble, prostitute **11** deteriorate, lower in rank **12** reduce in rank

**degrading**
**04** base **07** ignoble **08** debasing, lowering, shameful, unworthy **09** demeaning **10** belittling, cheapening, mortifying **11** disgraceful, humiliating, undignified **12** contemptible, discrediting **13** dishonourable

**degree**
**01** d **02** BA, MA **03** deg, pin **04** mark, rank, rate, rung, step, unit **05** class, first, grade, level, limit, order, point, range, stage, third **06** amount, extent, second, status **07** Desmond, measure **08** position, standard, standing, strength **09** intensity **11** double first **13** baccalaureate

*See also* **qualification**

**• in a high degree**
**02** so **03** far **04** much, very **05** great

**• in a lower degree**
**04** less

**• in whatever degree**
**02** as

**dehydrate**
**03** dry **05** drain, dry up, parch **06** dry out **09** desiccate, evaporate, exsiccate, lose water **10** effloresce

**dehydration**
**06** drying **08** parching **11** desiccation, evaporation **13** dehumidifying

**• treatment for dehydration**
**03** ORT

**deification**
**07** worship **08** revering **09** elevation, extolling, reverence **10** apotheosis, exaltation, veneration **11** ennoblement, idolization **12** divinization, idealization **13** glorification **14** divinification **15** immortalization

**deify**
**03** god **05** exalt, extol **06** revere **07** elevate, ennoble, glorify, idolize, worship **08** idealize, venerate **10** aggrandize **11** immortalize

**deign**
**05** daine, stoop **07** consent **10** condescend **13** lower yourself **14** demean yourself

**deity**
**03** god **04** idol **05** numen, power **06** avatar, heaven, spirit **07** demigod, eternal, goddess, godhead, godhood **08** divinity, immortal, numinous **10** genius loci **11** divine being **12** supreme being

*See also* **God**; **god, goddess**

**dejected**
**03** low, sad **04** blue, down, flat, glum **05** amort **06** abattu, dismal, gloomy, morose **07** alamort, crushed, doleful, subdued **08** cast down, downcast, wretched **09** depressed, jaw-fallen, miserable, sorrowful **10** chopfallen, despondent, dispirited, melancholy, spiritless **11** crestfallen, demoralized, discouraged, downhearted, melancholic **12** disconsolate, disheartened **14** down in the dumps

**dejectedly**
**05** sadly **06** glumly **08** dismally, gloomily, morosely **09** miserably **10** wretchedly **12** despondently **14** disconsolately

**dejection**
**04** crab **05** blues, dumps, gloom **06** misery, sorrow **07** despair, sadness **09** faintness **10** depression, gloominess, low spirits, melancholy, moroseness **11** despondence, despondency, dolefulness, melancholia, unhappiness **12** wretchedness **14** disconsolation, discouragement, dispiritedness **15** downheartedness

**de jure**
**05** legal **07** legally **08** rightful **10** rightfully

**Delaware**
**02** DE **03** Del

**delay**
**03** lag, let **04** halt, keep, lull, mora, slow, stay, stop, wait **05** check, dally, defer, frist, sit on, stall, stave, tarry **06** dawdle, detain, dilute, dither, hamper, hang on, hinder, hold up, hold-up, impede, linger, loiter, put off, retard, shelve, temper, weaken **07** adjourn, forsloe, forslow, put back, respite, set back, setback, suspend, waiving **08** dawdling, foreslow, hang fire, hesitate, hold back, hold over, interval, obstruct, postpone, put on ice, reprieve, restrain, shelving, stalling, stoppage, tarrying **09** dalliance, deferment, demurrage, detaining, detention, faff about, hesitance, hesitancy, hindrance, lag behind, lingering, loitering, stonewall, tarriance **10** cunctation, dilly-dally, filibuster, hesitation, impediment, moratorium, putting-off, suspension **11** adjournment, holding-over, obstruction, retardation **12** interruption, postponement **13** dilly-dallying, procrastinate **15** procrastination

**delayed**
**04** late **08** retarded

**delectable**
**05** tasty, yummy **06** dainty, lovely **07** savoury **08** adorable, charming, engaging, exciting, luscious, pleasant, pleasing **09** agreeable, beautiful, delicious, palatable, succulent **10** appetizing, attractive, delightful, enchanting **11** flavoursome, scrumptious **13** mouthwatering

**delectation**
**06** relish **07** comfort, delight **08** pleasure **09** amusement, diversion, enjoyment, happiness **11** contentment, refreshment **12** satisfaction **13** entertainment, gratification

**delegate**
**03** del **04** give, name **05** agent, envoy, leave, proxy, vicar **06** assign, charge, commit, depute, deputy, legate, ordain, pass on, second, syndic **07** appoint, consign, deputed, devolve, empower, entrust **08** emissary, hand over, nominate, pass over **09** authorize, designate, messenger, secondary, spokesman **10** ambassador, amphictyon, commission, substitute **11** spokeswoman **12** commissioner, spokesperson **14** representative

**delegation**
**07** embassy, mission **08** legation
**09** committal, passing on
**10** assignment, commission, contingent, deputation, devolution, entrusting **11** consignment, empowerment, passing over
**12** substitution, transference
**15** representatives

**delete**
**01** d **03** cut **04** dele, edit **05** erase
**06** cancel, cut out, efface, excise, remove, rub out, strike **07** blot out, destroy, edit out, expunge, scratch, take out **08** cross out, white out
**09** strike out **10** blue-pencil, obliterate

**deleterious**
**03** bad **07** harmful, hurtful, noxious, ruinous **08** damaging **09** injurious, poisonous, predatory **10** pernicious
**11** destructive, detrimental, prejudicial

**deliberate**
**03** set **04** muse, slow **05** think, voulu, weigh **06** advise, debate, ponder, steady, wilful, willed **07** advised, careful, consult, discuss, heedful, knowing, planned, prudent, reflect, studied, weigh up, willful, witting
**08** cautious, cogitate, consider, designed, evaluate, measured, meditate, mull over, propense, resolute, ruminate, studious, volitive
**09** conscious, leisurely, ponderous, think over, unhurried **10** calculated, considered, excogitate, methodical, preplanned, think about, thoughtful, unwavering **11** circumspect, considerate, intentional, prearranged
**12** preconceived, premeditated, professional, unhesitating

**deliberately**
**06** slowly **08** by design, steadily, wilfully **09** carefully, knowingly, on purpose, pointedly, prudently, wittingly
**10** cautiously, studiously
**11** consciously, in cold blood, ponderously, unhurriedly
**12** methodically, thoughtfully
**13** calculatingly, circumspectly, coldbloodedly, intentionally

**deliberation**
**04** care **05** study **06** debate, musing
**07** caution, counsel, mulling, thought
**08** brooding, calmness, coolness, prudence, slowness **09** pondering
**10** advisement, cogitation, conferring, discussion, evaluation, excogitate, meditation, reflection, rumination, steadiness, weighing-up
**11** calculation, carefulness, forethought **12** consultation
**13** consideration, unhurriedness
**14** circumspection, thoughtfulness

**delicacy**
**04** care, cate, tact **05** goody, taste, treat **06** dainty, delice, junket, luxury, nicety, relish, sunket, tidbit, titbit
**07** finesse, savoury, trinket
**08** elegance, fineness, kickshaw, niceness, subtlety, weakness
**09** diplomacy, fragility, kickshaws, lightness, precision, sweetmeat
**10** daintiness, discretion, morbidezza, refinement, speciality, tenderness
**11** bonne-bouche, sensitivity
**12** niminy-piminy **13** consideration, exquisiteness, luxuriousness
**14** discrimination

**delicate**
**04** fine, mild, nesh, nice, pale, soft, weak **05** bland, dorty, exact, faint, fairy, frail, light, muted **06** ailing, dainty, flimsy, friand, gentle, incony, infirm, luxury, pastel, polite, sickly, slight, subtle, tender, touchy, tricky, unwell
**07** awkward, band-box, brittle, careful, elegant, fragile, friande, inconie, precise, subdued, tactful **08** accurate, critical, delicacy, discreet, graceful, hothouse, kid-glove, ladylike **09** airy-fairy, breakable, difficult, exquisite, fairylike, fingertip, luxurious, precision, sensitive **10** diaphanous, diplomatic, fastidious **11** considerate, debilitated, problematic **12** easily broken, in poor health, niminy-piminy, softly-softly
**13** controversial, easily damaged, insubstantial

**delicately**
**06** finely, gently, mildly, palely, softly, subtly **07** blandly, faintly **08** daintily
**09** carefully, elegantly, tactfully
**10** critically, gracefully **11** exquisitely, sensitively **14** diplomatically

**delicious**
**04** good **05** juicy, tasty, yummy
**06** choice, delish, morish **07** moreish, savoury, scrummy **08** charming, pleasant, pleasing, tempting
**09** agreeable, ambrosial, enjoyable, exquisite, palatable, succulent, toothsome **10** appetizing, delectable, delightful, enchanting, goloptious, goluptious, gratifying, nectareous
**11** captivating, fascinating, lip-smacking, pleasurable, scrumptious
**12** entertaining **13** mouth-watering

**delight**
**03** joy **04** fain, glee, like, love, rape
**05** amuse, bliss, charm, cheer, enjoy, feast, mirth **06** delice, excite, please, ravish, relish, savour, thrill, tickle
**07** boast of, ecstasy, elation, enchant, gladden, glory in, gratify, rapture, revel in **08** bowl over, entrance, euphoria, felicity, gladness, pleasure, wallow in
**09** amusement, captivate, enjoyment, enrapture, entertain, happiness, transport **10** appreciate, exultation, jubilation, tickle pink **11** contentment, delectation, take pride in
**13** entertainment, gratification **14** take pleasure in **15** give enjoyment to

**delighted**
**04** glad **05** happy **06** elated, joyful, joyous, made up, stoked **07** charmed, excited, gleeful, pleased **08** ecstatic, euphoric, jubilant, thrilled
**09** enchanted, entranced, gratified, overjoyed **10** captivated, enraptured
**11** over the moon, tickled pink
**12** happy as Larry **14** pleased as Punch
**15** happy as a sandboy

**delightful**
**03** ace **04** nice **05** great, magic, super, sweet **06** divine, groovy, lovely, wizard
**07** amusing, darling, the tops
**08** charming, engaging, exciting, glorious, luscious, pleasant, pleasing
**09** agreeable, appealing, beautiful, diverting, enjoyable, ravishing, thrilling
**10** attractive, delectable, enchanting, entrancing, felicitous, gratifying
**11** captivating, fascinating, pleasurable, scrumptious
**12** entertaining **14** out of this world
• **something delightful**
**03** gas

**delimit**
**03** fix, set **04** mark **05** bound
**06** define **09** demarcate, determine, establish

**delineate**
**03** fix **04** draw, line, mark **05** bound, chart, stell, trace **06** define, depict, design, render, sketch **07** outline, portray **08** describe, set forth
**09** determine, establish, represent

**delineation**
**06** sketch **07** tracing **09** depiction, portrayal, rendering **11** description, presentment **14** representation

**delinquency**
**05** crime, fault **07** misdeed, offence
**10** misconduct, wrongdoing
**11** criminality, lawbreaking
**12** misbehaviour, misdemeanour
**13** transgression

**delinquent**
**03** ned, ted **06** bodgie, guilty, remiss, vandal, widgie **07** culprit, lawless, ruffian **08** criminal, culpable, hooligan, offender **09** miscreant, negligent, offending, wrongdoer **10** lawbreaker, malefactor **11** Halbstarker, lawbreaking **13** young offender

**delirious**
◇ *anagram indicator*
**03** mad **04** gone, wild **05** crazy, light
**06** elated, insane, raving **07** frantic
**08** babbling, demented, deranged, ecstatic, euphoric, frenetic, frenzied, jubilant, rambling, unhinged
**09** overjoyed, phrenetic, rapturous, spaced out, wandering **10** hysterical, incoherent, irrational **11** carried away, light-headed, over the moon **13** out of your mind **14** beside yourself

**deliriously**
◇ *anagram indicator*
**10** jubilantly **11** rapturously
**12** ecstatically, hysterically

**delirium**
**03** joy **05** fever **06** frenzy, lunacy, raving **07** ecstasy, elation, jimjams, madness, passion, rapture
**08** dementia, euphoria, hysteria, insanity, wildness **09** craziness,

phrenesis **10** excitement, jubilation **11** derangement, incoherence **13** hallucination, irrationality

• **delirium tremens**
**03** DTs **05** jumps **07** jimjams **09** Joe Blakes **10** the horrors **11** the dingbats

**deliver**
**02** do **03** aim, rid **04** bowl, cede, deal, free, give, hand, make, save, send, take **05** bring, carry, grant, serve, speak, utter, voice, yield **06** commit, convey, direct, fulfil, launch, nimble, ransom, redeem, render, rescue, strike, supply **07** declare, entrust, express, give out, inflict, manumit, present, provide, release, set free **08** announce, carry out, dispatch, hand over, liberate, live up to, proclaim, transfer, turn over **09** enunciate, implement, pronounce, surrender **10** administer, distribute, emancipate, relinquish **11** give voice to **15** help give birth to

**deliverance**
**06** escape, ransom, rescue **07** freedom, release **08** riddance **09** salvation **10** liberation, redemption **11** extrication **12** emancipation

**deliveries**
**04** over

**delivery**
**04** ball, dlvy, load **05** batch, birth **06** labour, speech, supply **07** travail **08** carriage, dispatch, shipment, transfer **09** elocution, transport, utterance **10** childbirth, conveyance, intonation **11** confinement, consignment, enunciation, parturition **12** accouchement, articulation, distribution, transmission **13** pronunciation **14** transportation

*Cricket deliveries include:*

**06** doosra, googly, teesra, yorker
**07** bouncer, swinger
**08** Chinaman, fastball, leg break, off break
**09** inswinger, leg-cutter, off-cutter
**10** outswinger
**11** daisy-cutter

• **deliveries**
**04** over

**dell**
**04** dale, dean, hole, vale **05** slade, trull **06** dargle, dimble, dingle, hollow, valley **10** prostitute

**delta**
**01** D

**delude**
**03** kid **04** dupe, fool, hoax **05** blend, cheat, elude, kiddy, trick **06** cajole, have on, lead on, take in **07** beguile, deceive, mislead, two-time **08** hoodwink, misguide **09** bamboozle, misinform **11** double-cross **12** take for a ride **14** pull a fast one on, put the change on

**deluge**
**04** rush, soak, wave **05** drown, flood, spate, swamp **06** drench, engulf **07** barrage, torrent **08** downpour, inundate, submerge **09** avalanche, overwhelm, snow under **10** inundation **11** overflowing

**delusion**
**05** error, fancy **07** fallacy **08** illusion, tricking **09** deception, misbelief **11** false belief **13** hallucination, misconception **14** misinformation **15** false impression, misapprehension

**de luxe, deluxe**
**04** fine, rich **05** grand, plush, swish **06** choice, costly, lavish, luxury, select **07** elegant, opulent, quality, special **08** palatial, splendid, superior **09** exclusive, expensive, luxurious, sumptuous

**delve**
**04** cave, hole, poke, root **05** probe **06** burrow, go into, hollow, hunt in, search **07** dig into, examine, explore, ransack, rummage **08** look into, research, scrabble **10** depression **11** hunt through, investigate

**demagogue**
**06** orator **07** speaker **08** agitator **09** firebrand, haranguer **10** tub-thumper **12** rabble-rouser **13** public speaker

**demand**
**03** ask, run **04** call, need, plea, sale, take, tell, urge, want **05** claim, draft, exact, order **06** ask for, desire, market **07** call for, clamour, command, dictate, inquire, inquiry, involve, request, require, solicit **08** exaction, exigency, insist on, petition, press for, pressure, question **09** cry out for, necessity, stipulate, ultimatum **10** hold out for, insistence **11** interrogate, necessitate, requirement **13** interrogation

• **in demand**
**02** in **03** big **06** trendy **07** desired, popular **08** asked for **09** requested **11** fashionable, of the moment, sought after

**demanding**
**04** hard **05** tough **06** taxing, trying, urgent **07** exigent, nagging, testing, wearing **08** exacting, pressing **09** difficult, harassing, insistent **10** a tall order, exhausting **11** challenging **12** back-breaking

**demarcate**
**03** fix **04** mark **05** bound, limit **06** define, divide **07** delimit, mark off, mark out **08** separate **09** determine, establish

**demarcation**
**04** line **05** bound, limit **06** fixing, margin **08** boundary, division **09** enclosure **10** definition, marking off, marking out, separation **11** distinction **12** delimitation **13** determination, establishment **15** differentiation

**demean**
**03** air **04** bear **05** abase, lower, stoop, treat **06** behave, debase, demote, humble **07** bearing, conduct, degrade, descend **08** belittle, ill-treat **09** deprecate, humiliate, treatment **10** condescend

**demeaning**
**04** base **07** ignoble **08** debasing, shameful, unworthy **09** degrading **10** belittling, cheapening, mortifying **11** disgraceful, humiliating, undignified **12** contemptible, discrediting **13** dishonourable

**demeanour**
**03** air **04** mien, port **06** manner **07** bearing, conduct **08** carriage, semblant **09** behaviour **10** deportment **11** comportment, countenance

**demented**
◇ *anagram indicator*
**03** ape, mad **04** bats, gyte, loco, nuts, wild **05** barmy, batty, buggy, crazy, daffy, dippy, dotty, flaky, gonzo, loony, loopy, nutty, potty, wacko, wacky, wiggy **06** crazed, cuckoo, fruity, insane, maniac, mental, raving, screwy **07** bananas, barking, berserk, bonkers, cracked, frantic, lunatic, meshuga **08** crackers, deranged, dingbats, doolally, frenetic, unhinged **09** disturbed, infuriate, lymphatic, up the wall **10** bestraught, distracted, distraught, frantic-mad, off the wall, off your nut, out to lunch, unbalanced **11** not all there, off the rails, off your head **12** mad as a hatter, off your chump, round the bend **13** off your rocker, out of your head, out of your mind, out of your tree, round the twist **14** off your trolley, wrong in the head

**Demeter**
**05** Ceres

**demigod**
**04** aitu, hero **05** pagod **06** garuda, pagoda

**demise**
**03** end **04** fall, ruin **05** death, dying **07** decease, failure, passing **08** collapse, downfall **09** cessation, departure **10** expiration **11** termination **14** disintegration

**demobilize**
**05** demob **07** break up, disband, dismiss **08** disperse

**democracy**
**08** autonomy, republic **12** commonwealth **14** self-government

**democratic**
**01** D **04** left **07** elected, popular **08** populist **10** autonomous, republican **11** egalitarian **12** Jeffersonian **13** self-governing **14** representative

**Democratic Republic of the Congo**
**03** COD, ZRE

**demolish**
◇ *anagram indicator*
**04** beat, lick, rase, raze, rout, ruin, undo **05** abate, crush, excel, level, quash, quell, repel, wreck **06** hammer, subdue, thrash **07** break up, conquer, destroy, flatten, ruinate, surpass, unbuild **08** bulldoze, knock out, lay waste, massacre, overcome, overturn, pull down, take down, tear down, vanquish **09** break down, devastate, dismantle, knock down, overpower, overthrow, overwhelm, pulverize, slaughter, subjugate, throw down **10** annihilate **14** get the better of

**demolition**
**04** rout, ruin **06** razing **07** beating, licking **08** massacre **09** hammering, levelling, overthrow, slaughter, thrashing **10** breaking-up, clobbering, flattening, surpassing **11** destruction, dismantling, pulling-down, tearing-down **12** annihilation, knocking-down, overpowering, overwhelming

**demon**
**03** ace, imp **04** atua, buff, ogre, Rahu **05** afrit, beast, brute, devil, fiend, freak, ghoul, rogue, satyr **06** addict, afreet, daemon, duende, nicker, savage, wizard **07** dab hand, fanatic, incubus, monster, rakshas, villain, warlock **08** familiar, succubus **09** blue devil, cacodemon **10** evil spirit **11** fallen angel

**demonic**
**03** mad **05** manic **06** crazed **07** frantic, furious, hellish, satanic **08** devilish, fiendish, frenetic, frenzied, infernal, maniacal **09** possessed **10** diabolical

**demonstrable**
**05** clear **07** certain, evident, obvious **08** arguable, positive, provable **09** evincible **10** attestable, verifiable **11** self-evident

**demonstrate**
**04** show **05** march, prove, rally, sit in, teach **06** betray, evince, parade, picket, verify **07** approve, bespeak, betoken, display, exhibit, explain, expound, express, protest **08** describe, indicate, manifest, register, validate **09** determine, establish, make clear, testify to **10** illustrate **11** communicate, remonstrate **12** substantiate **13** bear witness to

**demonstration**
**04** demo, show, test **05** march, proof, rally, sit-in, trial **06** morcha, muster, parade, picket **07** display, protest **08** evidence **09** événement, mass rally, testimony **10** evincement, exhibition, exposition, expression, indication, validation **11** affirmation, description, elucidation, explanation, hunger march **12** confirmation, illustration, presentation, verification **13** communication, manifestation **14** substantiation

**demonstrative**
**04** open, warm **06** loving **07** gushing **08** effusive **09** emotional, expansive, extrovert **10** expressive, scientific, unreserved **12** affectionate

**demonstratively**
**06** openly, warmly **08** lovingly **11** emotionally **12** expressively **14** affectionately

**demonstrator**
**06** shower

**demoralize**
**05** crush, daunt, lower **06** debase, defile, deject, weaken **07** corrupt, deprave, depress, pervert **08** cast down, dispirit **09** undermine **10** disconcert, discourage, dishearten **11** contaminate **14** make despondent

**demoralizing**
**08** daunting **09** weakening **10** depressing **11** dispiriting **12** discouraging **13** disconcerting, disheartening

**demote**
**04** bust **05** break **06** humble **07** cashier, degrade **08** relegate **09** downgrade **12** reduce in rank

**demotic**
**06** vulgar **07** popular **08** enchoric **09** enchorial **10** colloquial, vernacular

**demotion**
**09** degrading **10** relegation **11** downgrading

**demur**
**04** balk, stop **05** cavil, doubt, pause, qualm **06** boggle, object, refuse **07** dispute, dissent, protest, scruple **08** demurral, disagree, hesitate, question **09** misgiving, objection **10** hesitation **11** be unwilling, compunction, reservation **12** disagreement, make question **13** express doubts, take exception

**demure**
**03** coy, mim, shy **04** prim **05** grave, mimsy, quiet, sober, staid, timid **06** chaste, mimsey, modest, prissy **07** primsie, prudish, serious **08** reserved, reticent, retiring **10** unassuming **11** strait-laced

**demurely**
**05** coyly, shyly **06** primly **07** quietly, staidly, timidly **08** modestly **09** seriously **10** reticently **12** unassumingly

**den**
**04** dive, Hell, hole, home, lair, lare, nest **05** haunt, joint, patch, pitch, study **06** bothan, hollow, hotbed, studio **07** hideout, retreat, shelter, spieler **08** hideaway **09** Domdaniel, rock house, sanctuary **12** meeting-place

**denial**
**02** no **03** nay **04** veto **05** denay **06** rebuff **07** démenti, dissent, gainsay, refusal **08** negation, rebuttal, traverse **09** disavowal, dismissal, disowning, forsaking, rejection **10** abjuration, denegation, disclaimer, opposition, refutation **11** prohibition, repudiation **12** disagreement, renunciation **13** contradiction **14** disaffirmation

**denigrate**
**03** bag **05** abuse, decry **06** assail, defame, impugn, malign, revile, vilify **07** blacken, run down, slander **08** belittle, besmirch, fling mud, sling mud, talk down, throw mud, vilipend **09** blackened, criticize, deprecate, disparage **10** calumniate **11** pick holes in

**denigration**
**05** abuse **07** calumny, slander **10** belittling **11** degradation, deprecation **12** vilification **13** disparagement

**denizen**
**07** citizen, dweller, habitué, inhabit **08** habitant, occupant, resident, townsman **10** inhabitant, townswoman

**Denmark**
**02** DK **03** DNK

**denomination**
**04** cult, kind, sect, sort, unit **05** class, creed, faith, grade, order, value, worth **06** belief, Church, parish, school **08** religion **09** communion, face value, tradition **10** persuasion **11** designation **12** constituency **13** religious body **14** religious group

**denote**
**04** mark, mean, note, show **05** imply **06** typify **07** betoken, express, refer to, signify, suggest **08** indicate, stand for **09** be a sign of, designate, represent, symbolize

**dénouement**
**05** close, event **06** climax, finale, finish, pay-off, upshot **07** last act, outcome **08** solution **10** conclusion, resolution **11** culmination, unravelling **13** clarification

**denounce**
**04** post, slag **05** decry, knock, slate **06** accuse, attack, betray, impugn, indict, revile, vilify **07** arraign, censure, condemn, declaim, deplore, rubbish, run down, slag off, thunder, trumpet **08** announce, badmouth, execrate, proclaim **09** castigate, criticize, fulminate, inculpate, pronounce, proscribe **10** denunciate, stigmatize **11** pick holes in **12** pull to pieces, put the boot in, tear to pieces **13** inform against

**dense**
**03** dim **04** dull, dumb, rank, slow **05** close, dopey, heavy, solid, stiff, thick **06** obtuse, opaque, packed, stupid **07** compact, crammed, crowded, intense **08** gormless **09** close-knit, condensed, dim-witted **10** compressed, slow-witted **11** close-packed **12** concentrated,

impenetrable **13** tightly packed **14** jammed together

### densely
**05** close **06** firmly **07** closely, heavily, solidly, thickly, tightly **09** compactly

### density
**01** d **04** body, bulk, mass **08** solidity **09** closeness, denseness, solidness, thickness, tightness **10** spissitude **11** compactness, consistency **15** impenetrability

**• of little density**
**04** thin

### dent
**03** cut, dip, pit **04** bash, dint, drop, fall **05** gouge **06** crater, damage, dimple, hollow, indent, lessen, push in, reduce, weaken **07** depress **08** diminish **09** concavity, deduction, lessening, reduction **10** depression **11** indentation

### dentist
**03** BDS, DDS, LDS, MDS **06** doctor **08** odontist **09** gum-digger **13** dental surgeon

### denude
**04** bare **05** clear, strip **06** divest, expose **07** uncover **08** deforest **09** defoliate

### denunciation
**03** ban **06** attack, threat **07** censure, decrial, obloquy, thunder **09** criticism, invective **10** accusation **11** castigation, commination, fulmination **12** condemnation, counterblast, denouncement **13** incrimination

### deny
**03** nay **04** nick, reny, veto **05** denay, rebut, renay, reney, renig, unget **06** abjure, disown, forbid, naysay, negate, oppose, rebuff, recant, refuse, refute, reject, renege **07** decline, disavow, dismiss, gainsay, nullify, renague, renegue, sublate **08** abnegate, disallow, disclaim, disprove, forswear, prohibit, renounce, traverse, turn down, withhold **09** disaffirm, repudiate **10** contradict **12** disagree with **14** turn your back on

### deodorant
**05** scent **06** roll-on **08** fumigant **09** fumigator **10** deodorizer **12** air-freshener, disinfectant **14** anti-perspirant

### deodorize
**06** aerate, purify **07** freshen, refresh, sweeten **08** fumigate **09** disinfect, ventilate

### depart
**02** go **03** dep, die, off **04** blow, exit, fork, part, quit, scat, vade, vary, veer, walk, wend **05** go off, lam it, leave, quite, quyte, scoot, scram, skive, split **06** avaunt, decamp, differ, divide, egress, escape, go away, quight, remove, retire, set off, set out, swerve, vamose, vanish **07** bunk off, deviate, digress, diverge, do a bunk, drop off, make off, migrate, pull out, push off, retreat, scarper, swan off, take off, tear off, vamoose, walk off **08** check out, clear off, drop away, get going, make wing, separate, shove off, start out, take wing, turn away, up sticks, withdraw **09** branch off, disappear, do a runner, evaporate, push along, skedaddle, turn aside **10** hightail it, hit the road, make tracks **11** hit the trail, take the road **12** shoot through **13** sling your hook, take your leave **14** absent yourself, make a bolt for it, rattle your dags, take it on the lam **15** make a break for it, take to your heels

### departed
**04** dead, gone, late, lost, went **07** expired **08** deceased **10** passed away

### department
**01** D **03** Dep, dpt **04** area, Dept, line, nome, part, unit, wing **05** field, realm **06** agency, branch, bureau, domain, office, region, sector, sphere **07** concern, section, station **08** district, division, function, interest, province **10** cost centre, speciality **11** subdivision **12** organization **14** responsibility

*Départements of France:*

**03** Ain, Lot, Var
**04** Aube, Aude, Cher, Eure, Gard, Gers, Jura, Nord, Oise, Orne, Tarn
**05** Aisne, Doubs, Drôme, Indre, Isère, Loire, Marne, Meuse, Paris, Rhône, Somme, Yonne
**06** Allier, Ariège, Cantal, Creuse, Landes, Loiret, Lozère, Manche, Nièvre, Sarthe, Savoie, Vendée, Vienne, Vosges
**07** Ardèche, Aveyron, Bas-Rhin, Corrèze, Côte-d'Or, Essonne, Gironde, Hérault, Mayenne, Moselle
**08** Ardennes, Calvados, Charente, Dordogne, Haut-Rhin, Morbihan, Val-d'Oise, Vaucluse, Yvelines
**09** Finistère, Puy-de-Dôme
**10** Corse-du-Sud, Deux-Sèvres, Haute-Corse, Haute-Loire, Haute-Marne, Haute-Saône, Loir-et-Cher, Val-de-Marne
**11** Côtes-d'Armor, Eure-et-Loire, Hautes-Alpes, Haute-Savoie, Haute-Vienne, Pas-de-Calais
**12** Haute-Garonne, Hauts-de-Seine, Indre-et-Loire, Lot-et-Garonne, Maine-et-Loire, Saône-et-Loire, Seine-et-Marne, Ville de Paris
**13** Ille-et-Vilaine, Seine-Maritime, Tarn-et-Garonne
**14** Alpes-Maritimes, Bouches-du-Rhône, Hautes-Pyrénées
**15** Loire-Atlantique, Seine-Saint-Denis
**16** Charente-Maritime, Meurthe-et-Moselle
**18** Pyrénées-Orientales
**19** Pyrénées-Atlantiques, Territoire de Belfort
**20** Alpes-de-Haute-Provence

### departs
**01** d **03** dep

### departure
**03** dep **04** exit **05** going, lucky, shift **06** change, egress, escape, exodus **07** forking, leaving, removal, retreat, veering **08** farewell, going off **09** branching, decession, deviation, egression, going away, variation **10** difference, digression, divergence, innovation, retirement, setting-off, setting-out, withdrawal **11** leave-taking **12** branching out

### depend
**03** lie **04** need, rely, turn **06** bank on, expect, hang on, lean on, lippen, rely on, rest on, ride on, turn on **07** cling to, count on, hinge on, trust in **08** reckon on **09** be based on, build upon **11** be decided by, be subject to, calculate on **13** be dependent on, revolve around **14** be contingent on, be determined by

### dependable
**04** sure **06** honest, stable, steady, trusty **07** certain **08** faithful, reliable **09** rock-solid, steadfast, unfailing **11** responsible, trustworthy **13** conscientious **14** tried and tested

### dependant
**04** ward **05** child, minor **06** charge, client, feeder, minion, vassal **07** protégé, relying **08** creature, hanger-on, henchman, parasite, relative, retainer **09** pensioner **10** contingent **11** subordinate

### dependence
**04** need **05** abuse, faith, trust **08** reliance **09** addiction, vassalage **10** attachment, confidence, dependency **11** expectation **12** helplessness, subservience **13** subordination

### dependency
**05** abuse, habit **06** colony **07** support **08** dominion, pendicle, province, reliance, weakness **09** addiction, satellite, territory **10** attachment, immaturity **12** helplessness, protectorate, subservience **13** subordination **14** submissiveness

### dependent
**04** weak **05** based **07** decided, leaning, reliant, relying, subject **08** dictated, helpless, immature, relative **09** adjective, supported, sustained **10** contingent, controlled, determined, influenced, vulnerable **11** conditional, subordinate

### depict
**04** draw, show **05** paint, trace **06** detail, devise, record, render, sketch **07** depaint, impaint, outline, picture, portray, present, recount **08** describe, resemble **09** delineate, represent, reproduce **10** illustrate **12** characterize

### depiction
**05** image **06** sketch **07** drawing, outline, picture **08** likeness

**09** detailing, portrayal, rendering **10** caricature **11** delineation, description **12** illustration **14** representation

**deplete**
**05** drain, empty, erode, spend, use up **06** expend, lessen, reduce, weaken **07** consume, eat into, exhaust, run down **08** bankrupt, decrease, diminish, evacuate **09** attenuate **10** impoverish **11** whittle away

**depletion**
**07** using-up **08** decrease, lowering **09** dwindling, lessening, reduction, shrinkage, weakening **10** deficiency, diminution, evacuation, exhaustion **11** attenuation, consumption, expenditure **14** impoverishment

**deplorable**
◇ *anagram indicator*
**03** sad **04** dire **05** woful **06** rueful, woeful **07** chronic, ghastly **08** criminal, grievous, pitiable, shameful, wretched **09** appalling, miserable **10** abominable, despicable, disastrous, lamentable, melancholy, outrageous, scandalous **11** blameworthy, disgraceful, distressing, regrettable, unfortunate **12** disreputable **13** dishonourable, heartbreaking, reprehensible

**deplorably**
**08** shocking **09** miserably **10** abominably, despicably, lamentably, shamefully **11** appallingly **12** outrageously, scandalously **13** disgracefully, unfortunately

**deplore**
**03** cry, rue **04** pine, slam, weep **05** blame, mourn, slate **06** bemoan, berate, bewail, lament, regret, revile **07** censure, condemn, reprove, upbraid **08** denounce, reproach **09** castigate, criticize, deprecate, disparage, grieve for, reprehend, shed tears **12** disapprove of

**deploy**
◇ *anagram indicator*
**03** use **04** open **06** extend, unfold **07** arrange, dispose, scatter, station, utilize **08** position **09** make use of, spread out **10** distribute

**depopulate**
**05** empty **08** unpeople **09** dispeople

**deport**
**03** act **04** bear, hold, oust **05** carry, exile, expel **06** acquit, banish, behave, manage **07** comport, conduct, perform **09** extradite, ostracize, transport **10** repatriate

**deportation**
**05** exile **07** ousting **09** expulsion, ostracism **10** banishment **11** extradition **12** repatriation **14** transportation

**deportment**
**03** air **04** gait, mien, port, pose **06** aspect, manner, stance **07** address, bearing, conduct, manners, posture **08** behavior, carriage **09** behaviour, demeanour, etiquette **10** appearance **11** comportment

**depose**
**04** fire, oust, sack **05** swear **06** attest, demote, remove, topple, unseat **07** degrade, dismiss, unfrock **08** dethrone, displace, down with **09** discharge, downgrade, overthrow **12** disestablish

**deposit**
◇ *hidden indicator*
**03** bed, dep, dew, fan, lay, put, set, sit **04** bank, bung, drop, dump, file, gage, land, lees, park, save, silt, soot, stow, ware, warp **05** amass, dregs, hoard, lay-by, lodge, pay in, place, plant, put by, stake, store **06** depone, locate, margin, pledge, settle, tophus **07** consign, earnest, entrust, fall-out, lay down, put away, put down, reposit, saburra, set down, sublime **08** alluvium, oviposit, retainer, security, sediment, stratify **10** deposition, hypostasis, instalment **11** down payment, part payment, precipitate **12** accumulation

**deposition**
**07** ousting, removal **08** evidence, sediment, toppling **09** affidavit, dismissal, overthrow, statement, testimony, unseating **11** attestation, declaration, illuviation, information **12** dethronement, displacement **13** sedimentation

**depository**
**05** cache, depot, store **07** arsenal **09** warehouse **10** repository, storehouse **15** bonded warehouse

**depot**
**04** camp **05** cache, store **06** garage **07** arsenal, station **08** terminal, terminus **09** barracoon, warehouse **10** depository, repository, storehouse **14** receiving-house

**deprave**
**04** warp **06** debase, defile, infect, seduce **07** corrupt, debauch, degrade, pervert, pollute, subvert, viciate, vitiate **10** demoralize, lead astray **11** contaminate

**depraved**
**04** base, evil, vile **06** sinful, warped, wicked **07** bestial, corrupt, debased, immoral, obscene, vicious **08** criminal **09** debauched, dissolute, felonious, graceless, perverted, reprobate, shameless **10** degenerate, iniquitous, licentious

**depravity**
**04** evil, vice **08** baseness, iniquity, vileness **09** reprobacy, turpitude **10** corruption, debasement, debauchery, degeneracy, immorality, perversion, sinfulness, wickedness **13** dissoluteness

**deprecate**
**04** slam **05** blame, knock, slate **06** berate, reject, revile **07** censure, condemn, deplore, reprove, rubbish, run down, upbraid **08** denounce, object to, reproach **09** castigate, criticize, disparage, protest at, reprehend **12** disapprove of

**deprecatory**
**09** regretful **10** apologetic, censorious, dismissive, protesting **11** reproachful **12** condemnatory, disapproving

**depreciate**
**04** drop, fall **05** lower, slump **06** defame, lessen, malign, reduce, revile, slight **07** decline, deflate, devalue, disable, run down **08** belittle **09** denigrate, disparage, downgrade, underrate **10** undervalue **11** fall in value, make light of **13** go down in value, underestimate **15** decrease in value

**depreciation**
**04** fall **05** slump **08** mark-down, ridicule **09** deflation **10** cheapening, depression, derogation, detraction **11** denigration, devaluation **12** belittlement **13** disparagement **15** underestimation

**depredation**
**04** prey **05** theft **06** damage **07** looting, pillage, plunder, raiding, robbery **08** hardship, harrying, ravaging **09** marauding **10** denudation, desolation, despoiling, plundering, ransacking **11** destruction, devastation, laying waste

**depress**
**03** cut, sap **04** down, push, tire **05** daunt, drain, level, lower, press, slash, upset, weary **06** burden, deject, hammer, humble, impair, lessen, reduce, sadden, weaken **07** cheapen, devalue, exhaust, get down, make sad, oppress **08** cast down, enervate, hold down, push down **09** bring down, press down, undermine, weigh down **10** debilitate, depreciate, discourage, dishearten, overburden

**depressant**
**06** downer **07** calmant **08** relaxant, sedative **09** calmative **13** tranquillizer

**depressed**
**03** low, sad **04** blue, down, glum, poor **05** cowed, doomy, fed up, moody, needy **06** dented, gloomy, hollow, moping, morose, sunken **07** accablé, concave, dumpish, humbled, lowered, run-down, unhappy **08** cast down, dejected, deprived, downbeat, downcast, indented, pushed in, recessed **09** destitute, exanimate, flattened, heartsick, jaw-fallen, miserable **10** a peg too low, despondent, dispirited, distressed, emarginate, melancholy **11** crestfallen, discouraged, downhearted, low-spirited, pessimistic **12** disheartened, low in spirits, out of spirits, under hatches **13** broken-hearted,

disadvantaged **14** down in the dumps **15** poverty-stricken

**depressing**
**03** sad **04** grey, grim **05** black, bleak, doomy, grave **06** dismal, dreary, gloomy, leaden, sombre **07** unhappy **08** daunting, downbeat, hopeless **09** cheerless, dejecting, saddening, upsetting **10** melancholy **11** dispiriting, distressing **12** discouraging **13** disheartening, heartbreaking

**depressingly**
**05** sadly **07** bleakly **08** drearily, gloomily **09** unhappily **10** dauntingly **11** cheerlessly **13** dispiritingly, distressingly **14** discouragingly **15** dishearteningly, heartbreakingly

**depression**
**03** col, dip, pit, PND **04** bowl, dent, dint, dish, glen, hole, sink, slot, swag **05** basin, blues, crash, delve, dumps, fossa, gloom, slump **06** cafard, cavity, dimple, downer, hollow, recess, trough, valley **07** cyclone, decline, despair, foveola, foveole, megrims, sadness, sinkage, sinking **08** black dog, doldrums, glumness, lowering, slowdown **09** baby blues, concavity, dejection, demission, hard times, pessimism, recession, umbilicus **10** desolation, excavation, gloominess, impression, inactivity, low spirits, melancholy, scrobicule, stagnation, standstill, the horrors **11** despondency, indentation, melancholia, unhappiness **12** hopelessness **14** discouragement **15** downheartedness

**deprivation**
**04** lack, loss, need, want **06** denial, penury **07** poverty, removal **08** hardship **09** privation **10** withdrawal **11** bereavement, destitution, withholding **12** disadvantage **13** dispossession **14** impoverishment

**deprive**
**03** rob **04** deny, geld, twin **05** spoil, strip, twine **06** amerce, denude, divest, refuse **07** bereave **08** take away, withhold **09** destitute **10** confiscate, dispossess **11** expropriate

**deprived**
**04** gelt, poor **05** needy **06** bereft, in need **07** lacking **09** destitute **12** impoverished **13** disadvantaged **15** underprivileged

**• be deprived of**
**04** lose

**depth**
**01** d **03** bed **04** deep, drop, glow, gulf **05** abyss, floor, midst, range, scope **06** acumen, amount, bottom, extent, middle, vigour, warmth, wisdom **07** fervour, gravity, insight, measure, passion **08** darkness, deepness, richness, severity, strength **09** awareness, intensity, intuition, vividness **10** astuteness, brilliance, cleverness, perception, profundity, shrewdness **11** discernment, earnestness, penetration, seriousness **12** profoundness, remotest area, thoroughness **13** extensiveness **14** third dimension

**• depth charge**
**03** can

**• in depth**
**08** in detail, thorough **09** extensive **10** thoroughly **11** extensively **12** exhaustively **13** comprehensive **15** comprehensively

**deputation**
**07** embassy, mission **08** legation **09** committee **10** commission, delegation **15** representatives

**depute**
**06** charge, second **07** appoint, consign, empower, entrust, mandate **08** accredit, delegate, hand over, nominate **09** authorize, designate **10** commission

**deputize**
**05** cover **06** act for, double, sub for **07** relieve, replace **08** take over **09** fill in for, represent **10** stand in for, substitute, understudy **11** pinch-hit for **14** take the place of

**deputy**
**02** TD **03** Dep **04** Dept, mate, vice- **05** agent, envoy, locum, nawab, prior, proxy, vicar **06** commis, -depute, legate, second, vidame **07** stand-in **08** delegate, official, prioress, sidekick, sidesman, Tanaiste, vicaress, viscount **09** alternate, assistant, secondary, surrogate **10** ambassador, commissary, lieutenant, subchanter, substitute, vice-consul, vice-regent **11** locum tenens, subordinate **12** commissioner, spokesperson, under-sheriff, vice-chairman, vice-governor **13** pro-chancellor, sheriff depute, vice-president **14** representative **15** second-in-command, vice-chairperson, vice-chamberlain

**derail**
**05** ditch, upset **06** impede **07** disrupt, disturb, prevent **08** displace, hold back, obstruct **14** throw off course

**deranged**
◇ *anagram indicator*
**03** ape, fey, mad **04** bats, loco, nuts, wild **05** barmy, batty, buggy, crazy, daffy, dippy, dotty, flaky, gonzo, loony, loopy, manic, nutty, potty, wacko, wacky, wiggy **06** crazed, cuckoo, fruity, insane, maniac, mental, raving, screwy, skivie **07** bananas, barking, berserk, bonkers, cracked, frantic, lunatic, meshuga **08** confused, crackers, demented, dingbats, doolally, frenetic, frenzied, maniacal, unhinged, unstable **09** brainsick, delirious, disturbed, lymphatic, psychotic, unsettled, up the wall **10** bestraught, disordered, distracted, distraught, frantic-mad, irrational, off the wall, off your nut, out to lunch, unbalanced **11** not all there, off the rails, off your head **12** mad as a hatter, off your chump, round the bend **13** off your rocker, of unsound mind, out of your head, out of your mind, out of your tree, round the twist **14** off your trolley, wrong in the head **15** non compos mentis, out of your senses

**derangement**
**05** mania **06** frenzy, lunacy **07** madness **08** delirium, dementia, disarray, disorder, insanity, neurosis **09** agitation, confusion **10** aberration **11** dislocation, distraction, disturbance **13** hallucination

**Derek**
**02** Bo **03** Del

**derelict**
**04** hobo **05** jakey, tramp **06** beggar, dosser, no-good, ruined, wretch **07** drifter, no-hoper, outcast, run-down, swagman, vagrant **08** deserted, desolate, forsaken, vagabond **09** abandoned, discarded, neglected **10** down-and-out, ne'er-do-well, ramshackle, tumbledown **11** dilapidated, in disrepair **12** down-and-outer **14** good-for-nothing **15** falling to pieces

**dereliction**
**04** ruin **05** ruins **07** evasion, failure, neglect **08** apostasy, betrayal **09** desertion, disrepair, forsaking **10** abdication, desolation, negligence, remissness, renegation **11** abandonment **12** dilapidation, renunciation **13** faithlessness **14** relinquishment

**deride**
**03** rag **04** gibe, jeer, mock, slag **05** knock, laugh, scorn, taunt, tease **06** bemock, chiack, chyack, insult, jeer at **07** disdain, laugh at, scoff at, slag off, sneer at **08** belittle, pooh-pooh, ridicule, satirize **09** disparage, make fun of

**de rigueur**
**04** done **05** right **06** decent, proper **07** correct, fitting **08** decorous, expected, required **09** necessary **10** compulsory **11** fashionable **12** conventional, the done thing

**derision**
**05** scorn **06** insult, satire **07** disdain, hissing, mockery, ragging, teasing **08** contempt, ridicule, scoffing, sneering, taunting **10** disrespect **13** disparagement

**• expression of derision**
**02** ho **03** gup, hoa, hoh, mew, yah **05** sucks!, te-hee, ya-boo **06** tee-hee, yah-boo **07** so there **10** get knotted!, sucks to you!, ya-boo sucks **11** yah-boo sucks

**derisive**
**06** ribald **07** jeering, mocking **08** irrisory, scoffing, scornful, taunting **09** insulting **10** disdainful, irreverent **12** contemptuous **13** disrespectful

**derisively**
**10** scornfully **12** disdainfully, irreverently **14** contemptuously **15** disrespectfully

**derisory**
**04** tiny **05** small **06** absurd, paltry **07** risible **08** pathetic, scoffing **09** insulting, laughable, ludicrous **10** inadequate, outrageous, ridiculous **12** contemptible, insufficient, preposterous

**derivation**
**03** der **04** root **05** basis, deriv **06** origin, source **07** descent **08** ancestry, pedigree **09** beginning, deduction, etymology, genealogy, inference **10** extraction, foundation **13** parasynthesis

**derivative**
**03** der **05** deriv, trite **06** branch, copied **07** cribbed, derived, product, spin-off **08** acquired, borrowed, obtained, offshoot, rehashed **09** by-product, formative, hackneyed, imitative, outgrowth, secondary **10** derivation, descendant, second-hand, unoriginal **11** development, plagiarized

**derive**
**03** get **04** draw, flow, gain, reap, stem, take **05** arise, fetch, infer, issue **06** borrow, deduce, evolve, follow, obtain, spring **07** acquire, descend, develop, emanate, extract, proceed, procure, receive **09** originate **14** have its roots in **15** have as the source, have its origin in

• **derived from**
**02** of

**derogatory**
**05** snide **06** snidey **08** critical **09** injurious, insulting, offensive, slighting, vilifying **10** belittling, defamatory, detracting, detractive, detractory, pejorative **11** denigratory, disparaging **12** depreciative, disapproving, unfavourable **15** uncomplimentary

**descend**
**03** dip **04** dive, drop, fall, sink, stem **05** deign, issue, pitch, slope, stoop, storm, swoop **06** alight, arrive, derive, go down, invade, plunge, spring, tumble **07** decline, emanate, go to pot, incline, pancake, plummet, proceed, subside **08** come down, dismount, move down, take over **09** originate, parachute **10** condescend, degenerate, go downhill **11** dégringoler, deteriorate, go to the dogs **13** lower yourself **14** arrive suddenly

**descendant**
**03** son **04** cion, sien, slip, syen **05** child, niece, scion **06** nephew, sprout **08** daughter

• **descendant of**
**01** O'

**descendants**
**04** line, race, seed **05** heirs, issue **06** family, scions **07** descent, lineage, progeny **08** children, mokopuna **09** offspring, posterior, posterity **10** generation, posteriors, successors

**descended**
**04** alit

**descent**
**03** dip **04** dive, down, drop, fall, line, raid **05** blood, pitch, slant, slope, stock, stoop **06** origin, plunge **07** decline, incline, lineage, sinking **08** ancestry, comedown, gradient, heredity, invasion, pedigree **09** decadence, declivity, genealogy, going-down, parentage, subsiding **10** debasement, declension, degeneracy, extraction, family tree **11** degradation **12** degeneration, dégringolade **13** deterioration

**describe**
◇ *containment indicator*
**04** call, draw, hail, talk, tell **05** brand, label, style, sweep, think, trace, write **06** define, depict, detail, relate, report, scrive, sketch, strike **07** explain, express, mark out, narrate, outline, portray, present, recount, scrieve, specify **08** consider, descrive **09** character, delineate, designate, elucidate, represent **10** illustrate **12** characterize **13** give details of

**description**
**04** kind, make, sort, type **05** brand, breed, class, order, style **06** report, sketch **07** account, outline, picture, profile, variety **08** category, portrait **09** chronicle, depiction, narration, portrayal, statement **10** commentary, definement, exposition **11** delineation, designation, elucidation, explanation, portraiture **12** presentation **13** particularism, specification **14** representation

**descriptive**
**05** vivid **07** graphic **08** detailed, striking **09** colourful, pictorial **10** blottesque, expressive **11** elucidatory, explanatory **12** illustrative

**descry**
**03** get, see **04** espy, mark, spot **06** detect, notice, reveal **07** discern, glimpse, make out, observe **08** discover, perceive **09** discovery, recognize **11** distinguish **12** catch sight of

**desecrate**
◇ *anagram indicator*
**05** abuse **06** damage, debase, defile, insult **07** pervert, pollute, profane, violate **09** blaspheme, dishallow, dishonour, vandalize **10** unsanctify **11** contaminate

**desecration**
**06** damage, insult **07** impiety **09** blasphemy, pollution, sacrilege, violation **10** debasement, defilement **11** profanation **12** dishonouring

**desegregate**
**04** join **05** blend, merge **08** intermix **09** harmonize, integrate **10** assimilate **11** incorporate

**desert**
**03** dry, due, fly, rat **04** arid, bare, deny, fail, flee, jilt, quit, void, wild **05** empty, leave, merit, rat on, right, waste, wilds, worth **06** barren, betray, bug out, decamp, defect, forhow, give up, go AWOL, lonely, maroon, recant, return, reward, strand, virtue **07** abandon, abscond, cast off, demerit, deserts, dried up, forsake, parched, payment, run away, sterile **08** desolate, dust bowl, renounce, run out on, solitary, solitude **09** infertile, throw over, walk out on, wasteland **10** apostasize, barrenness, chicken out, recompense, relinquish, wilderness **11** change sides, comeuppance, retribution, uninhabited **12** moistureless, remuneration, tergiversate, uncultivated, unproductive **14** turn your back on, what you deserve **15** leave high and dry, leave in the lurch

*Deserts include:*

**04** Gobi, Thar
**05** Kavir, Namib, Ordos, Sturt
**06** Gibson, Mojave, Nubian, Sahara, Syrian, Ust'-Urt
**07** Alashan, Arabian, Atacama, Kara Kum, Simpson, Sonoran
**08** Kalahari, Kyzyl Kum
**09** Dzungaria
**10** Bet-Pak-Dala, Chihuahuan, Great Basin, Great Sandy, Patagonian, Takla Makan
**13** Great Victoria
**14** Bolson de Mapimi

**deserted**
**01** d **04** left, lorn, void **05** empty **06** bereft, lonely, vacant **08** betrayed, derelict, desolate, forsaken, isolated, solitary, stranded **09** abandoned, neglected **10** unoccupied **11** god-forsaken, uninhabited **14** underpopulated

**deserter**
**03** rat **06** bug-out, truant **07** escapee, runaway, traitor **08** apostate, betrayer, defector, fugitive, renegade, turncoat **09** absconder **10** backslider, delinquent

**desertion**
**06** bug-out, denial, flight, give up **07** jilting, leaving, truancy **08** apostasy, betrayal, giving-up, quitting **09** decamping, defection, forsaking, going AWOL **10** absconding, casting-off, renegation **11** abandonment, dereliction, running-away **12** renunciation **14** relinquishment, tergiversation

**deserve**
**03** win **04** earn, rate **05** incur, merit **07** justify, warrant **10** be worthy of **12** be entitled to, have a right to, have it coming

**deserved**
**03** apt, due **04** fair, just, meet **05** right **06** earned, proper **07** condign, fitting, merited **08** apposite, rightful, suitable **09** justified, warranted **10** legitimate, well-earned **11** appropriate, justifiable

**deservedly**
**04** duly **06** fairly, justly **07** rightly **08** by rights, properly, suitably **09** fittingly **10** rightfully **11** justifiably **13** appropriately

**deserving**
**05** worth **06** worthy **07** upright **08** laudable, virtuous **09** admirable, estimable, exemplary, righteous **11** commendable, meritorious **12** praiseworthy

**desiccated**
**03** dry **04** arid, dead **05** dried **07** drained, dried up, parched, sterile **08** lifeless, powdered **10** dehydrated, exsiccated

**desiccation**
**07** aridity, dryness **08** parching, xeransis **09** sterility **11** dehydration, exsiccation

**desideratum**
**04** must, need, want **09** essential, necessity, requisite **10** sine qua non **11** requirement **12** prerequisite

**design**
◇ *anagram indicator*
**03** aim, end, lay, map **04** draw, etch, form, gear, goal, hope, logo, make, mean, plan, plot, seal, tatu, tool, wish **05** draft, dream, guide, hatch, model, motif, point, shape, style, think **06** cipher, create, desire, device, devise, draw up, emblem, figure, format, intend, intent, invent, make-up, object, scheme, sketch, slight, tailor, target, tattoo **07** destine, develop, diagram, drawing, fashion, meaning, outline, pattern, project, propose, purpose, sleight, think up, thought **08** conceive, contrive, indicate, monogram **09** blueprint, construct, delineate, fabricate, intention, objective, originate, prototype, structure **10** assignment, compassing, enterprise **11** arrangement, composition, delineation, destination, undertaking **12** construction, contrivement, organization

• **by design**
**08** wilfully **09** knowingly, on purpose, pointedly, wittingly **11** consciously **12** deliberately **13** calculatingly, intentionally

**designate**
**03** dub **04** call, name, show, term **05** class, elect, style, title **06** assign, choose, define, denote, select **07** appoint, earmark, entitle, express, specify **08** christen, classify, describe, indicate, nominate, set aside **09** stipulate

**designation**
**03** tag **04** name, term, type **05** label, style, title **07** epithet, marking **08** category, denoting, election, nickname **09** selection, sobriquet **10** definition, indication, nomination **11** appellation, appellative, appointment, description, stipulation **12** denomination **13** specification **14** classification

**designer**
**05** maker **06** author, deccie **07** creator, deviser, planner, plotter, stylist **08** inventor, producer **09** architect, contriver, couturier, fashioner **10** originator **11** draughtsman

*See also* **fashion**

**designing**
**03** sly **04** wily **05** sharp **06** artful, crafty, shrewd, tricky **07** couture, cunning, devious **08** guileful, plotting, scheming **09** deceitful, underhand **10** conspiring, intriguing **11** calculating

**desirability**
**05** merit, worth **06** allure, appeal, profit **07** benefit **08** sexiness **09** advantage **10** attraction, excellence, popularity, preference, usefulness **12** advisability **13** seductiveness **14** attractiveness

**desirable**
**03** fit, hot **04** good, sexy **06** plummy **07** popular, wishful **08** alluring, beddable, eligible, fetching, in demand, pleasant, pleasing, sensible, tempting **09** advisable, agreeable, appetible, expedient, seductive **10** attractive, beneficial, preferable, profitable, worthwhile **11** appropriate, sought-after, tantalizing **12** advantageous

**desire**
**03** ask, yen **04** Cama, earn, envy, erne, fain, itch, Kama, lech, like, list, lust, need, salt, urge, vote, want, will, wish **05** bosom, covet, crave, fancy, greed, mania, yearn **06** ardour, besoin, demand, libido, take to **07** avidity, burn for, craving, erotism, gasp for, long for, longing, passion, wish for **08** appetite, covetise, feel like, sex drive, yearn for, yearning **09** cacoëthes, hankering, hunger for, lust after, sexuality **10** aphrodisia, aspiration, be dying for, desiderate, preference, proclivity, sensuality **11** hanker after **12** be crazy about, ephebophilia, have a crush on, predilection, take a shine to **13** concupiscence, have designs on **14** have the hots for, have your eyes on, lasciviousness, predisposition, set your heart on **15** give the world for

**desired**
**05** exact, right **06** proper, wanted **07** correct, fitting **08** accurate, expected, in demand, required **09** necessary **10** particular **11** appropriate **13** in great demand

**desirous**
**04** avid, keen **05** eager, ready **06** fervid, hoping, hungry **07** anxious, burning, craving, fervent, hopeful, itching, longing, wanting, willing, wishful, wishing **08** aspiring, yearning **09** ambitious, desirable **10** cupidinous **12** enthusiastic

**desist**
**03** end **04** halt, stay, stop **05** cease, leave, pause, remit, stash **06** give up **07** abstain, forbear, refrain, suspend **08** break off, have done, leave off, peter out **09** supersede **11** discontinue

**desk**
**04** ambo **05** desse, table **06** bureau, carrel, pulpit **07** carrell, lectern, lecturn, lettern, rolltop **08** prie-dieu, vargueño **09** davenport, écritoire, faldstool, secretary **10** secretaire **11** litany-stool, reading-desk **12** writing-table **13** bonheur-du-jour

**desolate**
**03** sad **04** arid, bare, wild **05** bleak, floor, gaunt, upset, waste **06** barren, bereft, desert, dismal, dreary, gloomy, gousty, lonely **07** forlorn, get down, nonplus, shatter, unhappy **08** confound, dejected, deserted, downcast, forsaken, isolated, solitary, unpeeled, wasteful, wretched **09** abandoned, depressed, devastate, discomfit, miserable, overwhelm, take aback, wasteland **10** depressing, despondent, disconcert, distressed, drearisome, melancholy, unoccupied **11** comfortless, god-forsaken, heartbroken, uninhabited **12** disheartened, god-forgotten, unfrequented **13** broken-hearted

**desolation**
**04** ruin **05** gloom, grief, waste **06** misery, sorrow **07** anguish, despair, ravages, sadness **08** distress, solitude, wildness **09** bleakness, dejection, emptiness, isolation **10** barrenness, depression, loneliness, melancholy, remoteness, wilderness **11** despondency, destruction, devastation, forlornness, laying waste, unhappiness **12** wretchedness

**despair**
**05** gloom **06** give in, give up, misery **07** anguish, wanhope **08** collapse, distress, lose hope **09** dejection, dysthymia, lose heart, pessimism, surrender **10** depression, melancholy **11** desperation, despondency **12** be despondent, hopelessness, wretchedness **13** be discouraged, hit rock bottom **15** throw in the towel

**despairing**
**08** dejected, desolate, dismayed, downcast, hopeless, suicidal, wretched **09** anguished, depressed, desperate, miserable, sorrowful **10** despondent, distraught **11** au désespoir, desperation, discouraged, heartbroken, pessimistic **12** disconsolate, disheartened, inconsolable **13** grief-stricken

**despatch** *see* **dispatch, despatch**

**desperado**
**04** thug **06** badman, bandit, gunman, mugger, outlaw **07** brigand, hoodlum, ruffian **08** criminal, gangster **09** cut-throat, terrorist **10** lawbreaker

**desperate**
◇ *anagram indicator*
**04** bold, dire, rash, wild **05** acute, dying, grave, great, hasty, risky
**06** daring, severe, urgent **07** acharné, crucial, do-or-die, extreme, frantic, furious, lawless, serious, violent
**08** critical, dejected, desolate, dismayed, downcast, frenzied, hairless, hopeless, pressing, reckless, suicidal, wretched **09** abandoned, anguished, audacious, dangerous, depressed, foolhardy, hazardous, impetuous, miserable, sorrowful
**10** compelling, despondent, determined, distraught, incautious, on the ropes **11** discouraged, heartbroken, in great need, pessimistic, precipitate **12** at rock-bottom, crying out for, disconsolate, disheartened, inconsolable **13** grief-stricken **15** needing very much, wanting very much

**desperately**
◇ *anagram indicator*
**05** badly **07** acutely, gravely, greatly
**08** severely, urgently **09** extremely, fearfully, seriously **10** critically, dreadfully, hopelessly **11** à corps perdu, dangerously, frightfully

**desperation**
**04** fury, pain **05** agony, gloom, worry
**06** misery, sorrow **07** anguish, anxiety, despair, trouble **08** distress
**10** depression, despairing
**11** despondency **12** hopelessness, recklessness, wretchedness

**despicable**
**03** bum, low **04** base, mean, vile
**05** dirty, spewy **07** caitiff, lowdown, pitiful **08** dwarfish, shameful, wretched **09** dastardly, degrading, loathsome, reprobate, worthless
**10** abominable, detestable, disgusting
**11** disgraceful **12** contemptible, disreputable **13** reprehensible
**15** beneath contempt

**despise**
**04** hate, mock, shun **05** abhor, scorn, sneer, spurn **06** deride, detest, forhow, loathe, revile, slight **07** condemn, conspue, contemn, deplore, disdain, dislike **08** vilipend **10** look down on, undervalue **11** set at naught, set at nought **14** hold in contempt

**despite**
**07** against, defying **09** in spite of **11** in the face of **12** regardless of, undeterred by **15** notwithstanding

**despoil**
**03** rob **04** loot, rape **05** pluck, rifle, spoil, strip, wreck **06** bezzle, denude, divest, maraud, ravage **07** bereave, deprive, destroy, pillage, plunder, ransack **08** spoliate **09** depredate, devastate, vandalize **10** disgarnish, dispossess, untreasure

**despondency**
**04** hump **05** blues, gloom, grief
**06** misery, sorrow **07** despair, sadness
**08** distress, glumness **09** dejection, heartache, pessimism **10** depression, melancholy **11** desperation, melancholia **12** hopelessness, wretchedness **14** discouragement, dispiritedness **15** downheartedness, inconsolability

**despondent**
**03** low, sad **04** blue, down, glum
**06** gloomy **07** doleful **08** dejected, downcast, mournful, wretched
**09** depressed, heartsick, miserable, sorrowful **10** despairing, distressed, melancholy **11** discouraged, heartbroken **12** disheartened, inconsolable **14** down in the dumps

**despot**
**04** boss, czar, tsar, tzar **06** sultan, tyrant **08** autocrat, dictator
**09** oppressor **10** absolutist
**13** absolute ruler

*Despots include:*

**03** Idi
**04** Amin (Idi)
**05** Timur
**06** Caesar (Julius), Führer, Hitler (Adolf), Stalin (Joseph)
**07** Papa Doc
**08** Duvalier (François)
**09** Ceausescu (Nicolae), Mao Zedong, Tamerlane
**10** Mao Tse-tung
**11** Robespierre (Maximilien de), Tamburlaine
**15** Ivan the Terrible

**despotic**
**08** absolute, arrogant **09** arbitrary, imperious, tyrannous **10** autocratic, high-handed, oppressive, tyrannical
**11** dictatorial, domineering, overbearing **13** authoritarian

**despotism**
**07** tyranny **09** autocracy
**10** absolutism, oppression, repression
**11** stratocracy **12** dictatorship
**15** totalitarianism

**dessert**
**03** pud **05** sweet **06** afters **07** pudding
**09** sweet dish **11** aftersupper, sweet course

*Desserts and puddings include:*

**03** ice, pie
**04** flan, fool, sago, tart
**05** bombe, jelly, kulfi
**06** mousse, mud pie, sorbet, sundae, trifle, yogurt
**07** baklava, cobbler, compote, crumble, parfait, pavlova, soufflé, tapioca, tartufo, yoghurt
**08** Eton mess, ice cream, pandowdy, plum-duff, syllabub, tiramisu, vacherin, yoghourt
**09** clafoutis, cranachan
**10** blancmange, Brown Betty, cheesecake, egg custard, frangipane, fruit salad, panna cotta, peach Melba, zabaglione
**11** baked Alaska, banana split, banoffee pie, crème brûlée, Eve's pudding, milk pudding, plum pudding, rice pudding, spotted dick
**12** crème caramel, crêpe suzette, fruit crumble, profiteroles
**13** fruit cocktail, millefeuilles, summer pudding
**14** charlotte russe
**15** clootie dumpling, queen of puddings, roly-poly pudding

*See also* **cake**

**destabilize**
◇ *anagram indicator*
**05** upset **08** unsettle

**destination**
**03** aim, end **04** fate, goal, gole, list, stop **06** design, object, target
**07** purpose, station **08** ambition, terminus **09** intention, objective
**10** aspiration **11** journey's end **12** end of the line, landing place **15** final port of call, jumping-off place

**destined**
**04** born **05** bound, fatal, fated, meant
**06** booked, doomed, headed, marked, routed **07** certain, en route, heading
**08** assigned, designed, directed, intended, ordained, set apart
**09** appointed, scheduled **10** inevitable
**11** inescapable, preordained, unavoidable **12** foreordained
**13** predetermined

**destiny**
**03** lot **04** doom, fate, luck **05** karma, Moera, Moira **06** future, kismet
**07** fortune, portion **09** necessity
**10** predestiny **14** predestination

**destitute**
**04** poor **05** broke, needy, skint
**06** bereft, hard up, rooked **07** lacking, wanting **08** badly off, bankrupt, depleted, deprived, devoid of, dirt-poor, forsaken, helpless, indigent
**09** deficient, penniless, penurious
**10** cleaned out, distressed, down-and-out, friendless, innocent of, stony-broke **11** impecunious, necessitous, on the street **12** impoverished **14** on the breadline, on your beam-ends
**15** poverty-stricken, strapped for cash

**destitution**
**06** penury **07** beggary, poverty, straits
**08** distress **09** indigence, pauperdom
**10** bankruptcy, starvation
**13** pennilessness **14** impoverishment
**15** impecuniousness

**destroy**
◇ *anagram indicator*
**03** eat, end, gut, zap **04** kill, raze, ruin, slay, undo **05** break, crush, erase, fordo, harry, level, smash, spoil, waste, wreck **06** banjax, canker, defeat, delete, finish, perish, quench, ravage,

subdue, thwart, wither **07** attrite, deep-six, flatten, handbag, kill off, nullify, put down, ransack, ruinate, scuttle, shatter, stonker, torpedo, unshape, vitiate **08** decimate, demolish, dispatch, knock out, lay waste, overturn, pull down, sabotage, stamp out, tear down **09** devastate, dismantle, eliminate, eradicate, extirpate, knock down, marmelize, overthrow, pulverize, slaughter, undermine **10** annihilate, do away with, extinguish, obliterate, put to sleep, spiflicate **11** spifflicate

**destroyer**
**06** locust, vandal **07** flivver, ravager, stew-can, wrecker **08** Apollyon
**09** desolater, despoiler, ransacker
**10** demolisher, destructor
**11** annihilator, kiss of death

**destruction**
◇ *anagram indicator*
**03** end **04** bane, loss, rack, ruin
**05** death, havoc, stroy, waste, wrack, wreck **06** defeat, murder, razing
**07** killing, undoing, wastage
**08** crushing, downfall, massacre, smashing, wreckage **09** levelling, overthrow, ruination, shipwreck, slaughter, vandalism **10** demolition, desolation, extinction, killing-off, ravagement, shattering **11** depredation, devastation, dismantling, elimination, eradication, extirpation, liquidation, pulling-down, tearing-down
**12** annihilation, depopulation, knocking-down, obliteration
**13** extermination, nullification

**destructive**
**05** fatal **06** deadly, lethal **07** adverse, baneful, harmful, hostile, hurtful, killing, noxious, ruinous, vicious
**08** contrary, damaging, deathful, negative **09** injurious, malignant, withering **10** derogatory, disastrous, disruptive, nullifying, pernicious, subversive, unfriendly **11** deleterious, denigrating, detrimental, devastating, disparaging, mischievous, undermining **12** antagonistic, catastrophic, discouraging, pestilential, slaughterous, unfavourable

**destructively**
**08** lethally **09** harmfully, hurtfully
**12** disastrously **13** detrimentally

**desultorily**
**07** loosely **08** casually, fitfully
**09** aimlessly **11** erratically **13** half-heartedly

**desultory**
◇ *anagram indicator*
**05** hasty, loose **06** casual, fitful, random **07** aimless, chaotic, erratic
**08** rambling **09** haphazard, irregular, spasmodic **10** capricious, discursive, disorderly, undirected **11** half-hearted
**12** disconnected, inconsistent, unmethodical, unsystematic **13** uncoordinated

**detach**
**04** free, undo **05** calve, draft, sever, split, unfix **06** cut off, divide, loosen, remove, unglue **07** disjoin, divorce, isolate, take off, tear off, unhitch, unloose, unrivet **08** break off, disunite, estrange, separate, take away, uncouple, unfasten, unloosen, withdraw **09** disengage, segregate
**10** disconnect, dissociate
**11** disentangle

**detachable**
**07** movable **08** moveable
**09** removable, separable
**10** eradicable, removeable
**12** transferable

**detached**
**04** cold, free **05** aloof, loose
**06** remote **07** divided, neutral, severed **08** clinical, discreet, discrete, outlying, separate **09** impartial, objective, uncoupled, withdrawn
**10** disengaged, impersonal, unattached, undivested, unfastened
**11** dissociated, independent, indifferent, unconcerned, unconnected, unemotional
**12** disconnected **13** disinterested, dispassionate

**detachment**
**04** unit **05** corps, force, party, squad
**06** detail, patrol **07** brigade, removal, reserve, undoing **08** coolness, disunion, fairness, squadron
**09** aloofness, isolation, loosening, severance, task force, unconcern
**10** dispassion, lack of bias, neutrality, remoteness, separation, uncoupling, withdrawal **11** impassivity, objectivity, unfastening **12** impartiality, indifference, provost guard
**13** disconnection, disengagement, disentangling, lack of emotion

**detail**
◇ *tail deletion indicator*
**04** fact, item, list, unit **05** corps, force, point, squad **06** aspect, assign, charge, choose, depict, factor, nicety, patrol, relate, set out **07** appoint, brigade, element, feature, itemize, portray, present, recount, respect, specify **08** allocate, delegate, describe, minutiae, point out, rehearse, specific, spell out, tabulate
**09** attribute, catalogue, component, delineate, enumerate, intricacy, precision, task force **10** commission, complexity, ingredient, ins and outs, particular, refinement, triviality
**11** elaboration, nitty-gritty
**12** circumstance, complication, nuts and bolts, technicality, thoroughness
**13** particularity, specification
**14** characteristic, meticulousness

**• in detail**
**05** fully **07** in depth **08** at length
**09** carefully, piecemeal **10** item by item, thoroughly **12** exhaustively, in particular, particularly, point by point
**15** comprehensively

**detailed**
◇ *tail deletion indicator*
**04** full **05** close, exact **06** minute, narrow **07** complex, in-depth, precise, special **08** complete, itemized, specific, thorough **09** elaborate, intricate **10** blow-by-blow, convoluted, exhaustive, meticulous, particular **11** complicated, descriptive
**13** comprehensive

**detain**
**04** hold, keep, slow, stay, stop
**05** check, delay **06** arrest, hinder, hold up, impede, intern, lock up, retard
**07** confine, inhibit **08** hold back, imprison, keep back, make late, restrain, withhold **09** detention
**11** incarcerate, put in prison **13** hold in custody, keep in custody **15** take into custody

**detainee**
**03** POW

**detect**
**03** spy **04** find, nose, note, spot, take
**05** catch, sense, sight, trace **06** accuse, expose, notice, reveal, turn up, unmask
**07** discern, find out, make out, nose out, observe, uncover, unearth
**08** decipher, disclose, discover, identify, perceive **09** ascertain, deprehend, recognize, track down
**11** distinguish **12** bring to light
**13** become aware of

**detectable**
◇ *containment indicator*
**05** clear **07** visible **08** apparent, distinct **10** noticeable **11** discernible, perceivable, perceptible
**12** discoverable, identifiable, recognizable **14** before your eyes

**detection**
**04** note **06** exposé **08** exposure, noticing, sighting **09** discovery, unmasking **10** disclosure, perception, revelation, uncovering, unearthing
**11** discernment, observation, recognition, smelling-out, sniffing-out
**12** ascertaining, tracking-down
**14** distinguishing, identification

**detective**
**02** DC, DI, DS, PI **03** Det, eye, 'tec
**04** busy, dick, jack, tail **05** plant
**06** shadow, shamus, sleuth
**07** gumshoe **08** prodnose, sherlock
**09** operative **10** bloodhound, private eye, thief-taker **11** sleuth-hound
**12** investigator, thief-catcher **13** police officer

*Detectives include:*

**03** **Zen** (Aurelio)
**04** **Bony** (Napoleon Bonaparte), **Chan** (Charlie), **Cuff** (Richard), **Dean** (Sam), **Gray** (Cordelia), **Vane** (Harriet)
**05** **Brown** (Father), **Drake** (Paul), **Duffy** (Nicholas), **Dupin** (C Auguste), **Ghote** (Inspector Ganesh), **Grant** (Alan), **Lewis** (Sergeant), **Mason** (Perry), **Morse** (Inspector

Endeavour), **Queen** (Ellery), **Rebus** (John), **Spade** (Sam), **Vance** (Philo), **Wolfe** (Nero)
**06** **Alleyn** (Roderick), **Archer** (Lew), **Essrog** (Lionel), **Hanaud** (Inspector), **Holmes** (Sherlock), **Marple** (Miss Jane), **Pascoe** (Peter), **Poirot** (Hercule), **Silver** (Miss Maude), **Vidocq** (Eugène Françoise), **Watson** (Dr John), **Wimsey** (Lord Peter)
**07** **Appleby** (John), **Cadfael** (Brother), **Campion** (Albert), **Charles** (Nick), **Columbo** (Lieutenant), **Dalziel** (Andy), **Fansler** (Kate), **Laidlaw** (Jack), **Maigret** (Inspector), **Marlowe** (Philip), **Milhone** (Kinsey), **Moseley** (Hoke), **Wexford** (Reginald)
**08** **Bergerac** (Jim), **Lestrade** (Inspector), **Ramotswe** (Precious)
**09** **Bonaparte** (Napoleon), **Dalgliesh** (Adam), **Hawksmoor** (Nicholas), **Pinkerton** (Allan), **Scarpetta** (Kay)
**10** **Van Der Valk** (Piet), **Warshawski** (V I)
**13** **Continental Op**

**• detectives**
**03** CID, FBI

**detention**
**05** delay **07** custody, jankers
**09** captivity, hindrance, restraint, slowing-up **10** constraint, detainment, internment, punishment, quarantine
**11** confinement, holding-back
**12** imprisonment **13** incarceration

**deter**
**04** stop, warn **05** check, daunt
**06** hinder, put off **07** caution, inhibit, prevent, turn off **08** dissuade, frighten, prohibit, restrain, scare off **09** talk out of **10** discourage, disincline, intimidate

**detergent**
**04** soap **07** cleaner **08** cleanser
**09** cetrimide, detersive **10** abstergent, surfactant **13** washing powder
**15** washing-up liquid

**deteriorate**
**03** ebb **04** drop, fade, fail, slip, wane
**05** decay, go bad, go off, lapse, slide, spoil **06** go down, starve, weaken, worsen **07** break up, decline, degrade, fall off, go to pot, relapse, tail off **08** get worse, go to seed, tail away
**09** decompose, fall apart, grow worse, run to seed **10** degenerate, depreciate, go downhill, retrograde, retrogress
**11** become worse **12** disintegrate, fall to pieces **13** go down the tube

**deterioration**
◇ *anagram indicator*
**03** ebb **04** drop **05** decay, lapse, slide
**06** waning **07** atrophy, decline, failure, relapse **08** downturn, senility, slipping
**09** corrosion, worsening
**10** debasement, falling-off, pejoration
**11** degradation, dégringoler
**12** degeneration, exacerbation
**13** retrogression **14** disintegration

**determinate**
**05** fixed **07** certain, decided, defined, express, limited, precise, settled
**08** absolute, clear-cut, decisive, definite, distinct, explicit, positive, specific **09** specified **10** conclusive, definitive, quantified **11** established

**determination**
◇ *ends selection indicator*
**03** end **04** grit, guts, push, will
**05** assay, drive, value **06** decree, ruling, thrust **07** opinion, purpose, resolve, stamina, verdict **08** backbone, decision, firmness, sentence, tenacity
**09** fortitude, judgement, willpower
**10** conclusion, conviction, dedication, insistence, resolution, settlement
**11** arbitrament, arbitrement, persistence **12** perseverance, resoluteness **13** steadfastness

**determine**
**03** fix, set **04** rule **05** check, elect, fix on, guide, hight, impel, learn, limit, point, shape **06** affect, assign, choose, clinch, decide, define, detect, direct, finish, govern, ordain, prompt, settle, verify **07** agree on, control, dictate, find out, purpose, resolve
**08** conclude, discover, identify, regulate **09** ascertain, condition, establish, influence **12** turn the scale
**14** make up your mind

**determined**
**03** out, set **04** bent, dour, firm **05** fixed
**06** dogged, gritty, intent, single, strong
**07** certain, dead set, decided **08** hell-bent, resolute, resolved, stubborn
**09** convinced, dedicated, insistent, steadfast, tenacious **10** iron-willed, persistent, purposeful, unwavering
**11** ascertained, persevering, tough-minded, unflinching, well-defined
**12** single-minded, strong-minded, strong-willed **14** uncompromising

**determinedly**
**06** firmly **08** strongly **09** decidedly
**10** resolutely, stubbornly **11** insistently, steadfastly, tenaciously **12** persistently, purposefully **13** unflinchingly
**14** single-mindedly, strong-mindedly

**deterrence**
**09** avoidance, hindrance, obviation
**10** dissuasion, heading-off, prevention, warding-off **11** elimination

**deterrent**
**03** bar **04** curb **05** block, check
**07** barrier **08** obstacle **09** hindrance, repellent, restraint **10** difficulty, impediment **11** obstruction
**12** disincentive **14** discouragement

**detest**
**04** hate **05** abhor **06** loathe
**07** deplore, despise, dislike
**08** execrate **09** abominate, can't stand
**10** recoil from

**detestable**
**04** vile **06** horrid, odious, sordid
**07** hateful, heinous **08** accursed, horrible, shocking **09** abhorrent, execrable, loathsome, obnoxious, offensive, repellent, repugnant, repulsive, revolting, villanous
**10** abominable, despicable, disgusting, villainous **11** abhominable, distasteful **12** contemptible, insufferable, pestilential
**13** reprehensible

**detestation**
**04** hate **05** odium **06** hatred
**07** dislike **08** anathema, aversion, loathing **09** animosity, antipathy, hostility, revulsion **10** abhorrence, execration, repugnance
**11** abomination

**dethrone**
**04** oust **06** depose, topple, unseat
**07** uncrown **08** unthrone

**detonate**
**04** pink **05** blast, go off, knock, shoot
**06** blow up, ignite, kindle, let off, set off
**07** explode **08** spark off **09** discharge, fulminate

**detonation**
**04** bang, boom **05** blast, burst
**06** blow-up, report **08** igniting, ignition **09** blowing-up, discharge, explosion **11** fulmination

**detour**
◇ *anagram indicator*
**05** byway **06** bypass, bypath, byroad
**09** deviation, diversion **10** digression
**11** scenic route **13** indirect route
**15** circuitous route, roundabout route

**detract**
**03** mar **04** take **05** abate, lower, spoil
**06** defame, lessen, reduce **08** belittle, derogate, diminish, distract, take away
**09** devaluate, disparage **10** depreciate
**12** subtract from, take away from

**detractor**
**05** enemy **06** critic **07** defamer, reviler
**08** traducer, vilifier **09** backbiter, belittler, muck-raker, slanderer
**10** denigrator, disparager
**11** substractor **13** scandalmonger

**detriment**
**03** ill **04** evil, harm, hurt, loss
**05** wrong **06** damage, injury
**07** empeach, impeach **08** mischief
**09** prejudice **10** diminution, disservice, impairment
**12** disadvantage

**detrimental**
**07** adverse, harmful, hurtful
**08** damaging, inimical, scathing
**09** injurious **10** pernicious
**11** deleterious, destructive, mischievous, prejudicial
**15** disadvantageous

**detritus**
**04** junk, scum **05** waste **06** debris, litter, rubble **07** garbage, remains, rubbish **08** wreckage **09** fragments

**devalue**
**04** slag, slam **05** knock, lower, slate
**06** demean, reduce **07** deflate,

dismiss, run down, slag off
**08** decrease, minimize, play down
**09** devaluate, disparage, underrate
**10** devalorize, undervalue **11** make light of **12** pull to pieces, tear to pieces

**devastate**
◇ *anagram indicator*
**04** raze, ruin, sack **05** floor, level, shock, spoil, waste, wreck **06** ravage **07** despoil, destroy, flatten, nonplus, perturb, pillage, plunder, ransack, shatter **08** confound, demolish, desolate, lay waste, overcome, populate **09** discomfit, overwhelm, take aback **10** discompose, disconcert, traumatize

**devastated**
◇ *anagram indicator*
**05** upset, waste **06** gutted **07** crushed, shocked, stunned **08** appalled, desolate, overcome **09** horrified, in anguish **10** distressed, taken aback
**11** heartbroken, overwhelmed, traumatized **13** knocked for six

**devastating**
**05** great **06** lovely **07** harmful, ruinous, wasting **08** crushing, damaging, dazzling, fabulous, gorgeous, incisive, ravaging, shocking, smashing, striking, stunning **09** brilliant, effective, wonderful **10** disastrous, impressive, marvellous, remarkable, shattering, staggering **11** destructive, magnificent, spectacular
**12** catastrophic, overwhelming, traumatizing **13** extraordinary

**devastation**
**04** ruin, sack **05** havoc, ruins, waste, wrack **06** damage, ravage **07** pillage, plunder, ravages **08** wreckage
**09** wasteness **10** demolition, desolation, spoliation **11** destruction
**12** annihilation, fire and sword

**develop**
◇ *anagram indicator*
**03** get **04** grow **05** arise, begin, catch, educe, ensue, found, hatch, ripen, shape, start **06** create, evolve, expand, follow, foster, happen, invent, mature, pick up, result, set off, spread, unfold
**07** acquire, advance, amplify, enhance, enlarge, improve, nurture, open out, produce, prosper, shape up, work out
**08** argument, commence, contract, dilate on, disclose, expand on, fetch out, flourish, generate, initiate, progress, set about **09** branch out, come about, elaborate, establish, institute, originate, succumb to **10** go down with **11** fall ill with, materialize, set in motion **13** become ill with

**development**
◇ *anagram indicator*
**04** area, land **05** block, event, issue
**06** centre, change, estate, growth, result, spread **07** advance, complex, outcome **08** genetics, incident, increase, maturing, maturity, progress, upgrowth **09** evolution, expansion, extension, happening, promotion, situation, unfolding **10** blossoming, occurrence, phenomenon, prosperity, refinement, upbuilding **11** elaboration, enlargement, flourishing, furtherance, improvement, progression
**12** circumstance, turn of events
**• stage of development**
**04** pupa

**deviance**
**07** anomaly **08** variance **09** disparity
**10** aberration, divergence, perversion
**11** abnormality **12** eccentricity, irregularity

**deviant**
◇ *anagram indicator*
**04** bent, geek, goof, kook **05** crank, freak, kinky **06** misfit, oddity, quirky, weirdo **07** bizarre, dropout, oddball, odd sort, pervert, twisted, variant, wayward **08** aberrant, abnormal, freakish, perverse **09** anomalous, disparate, divergent, eccentric, irregular, perverted **13** nonconformist
**15** with a screw loose

**deviate**
◇ *anagram indicator*
**03** bag, err, yaw **04** part, seam, turn, vary, veer **05** drift, sheer, sport, stray
**06** change, depart, differ, swerve, wander **07** decline, deflect, digress, diverge, incline, oblique, turn off
**08** aberrate, go astray, turn away
**09** turn aside **11** prevaricate **13** go off the rails

**deviation**
◇ *anagram indicator*
**03** yaw **05** break, drift, error, freak, quirk, sheer, shift **06** change, detour, swerve **07** anomaly, decline, turning
**08** variance **09** deflexion, deflexure, departure, disparity, excursion, inflexion, variation **10** aberration, alteration, deflection, difference, digression, divergence, inflection
**11** abnormality, declination, discrepancy, fluctuation, inclination
**12** eccentricity, inordination, irregularity, turning-aside
**13** inconsistency, prevarication

**device**
**04** bomb, logo, plan, plot, ploy, ruse, seal, sign, tool, wile **05** badge, crest, dodge, gizmo, motif, motto, stunt, token, trick, waldo **06** design, emblem, gadget, gambit, masque, scheme, shield, symbol, tactic **07** conceit, machine, slinter, utensil **08** artifice, colophon, insignia, strategy
**09** apparatus, appliance, implement, manoeuvre, mechanism, stratagem
**10** coat of arms, instrument
**11** contraption, contrivance, machination

*Devices include:*

**04** iPod®, Xbox®
**05** clock, phone, razor, torch, watch
**06** juicer, scales, shaver
**07** Game Boy®, lighter, stapler, Walkman
**08** CD player, egg timer, Gamecube®, nail file, scissors, tweezers
**09** can opener, cell phone, corkscrew, hairdryer, hole punch, magnifier, pedometer, staple gun, stopwatch, telephone, tin opener
**10** calculator, coin sorter, fax machine, ice scraper, wine cooler
**11** answerphone, baby monitor, electric fan, manicure set, mobile phone, PlayStation®, thermometer
**12** bottle opener, curling tongs, games console, kitchen timer, nail clippers
**13** remote control, smoke detector, staple remover
**14** personal stereo, Swiss army knife

*See also* **electrical**; **optical**; **rhetorical**

**devil**
**03** div, imp, Pug **04** bogy, fend, Nick, ogre **05** beast, bogey, brute, demon, deuce, fiend, fient, rogue, Satan, sorra, worry **06** Belial, Cloots, daemon, daimon, drudge, Hornie, Mahoun, Old One, pester, ragman, rascal, savage, sorrow, terror, wretch **07** bogyman, Clootie, dickens, Evil One, goodman, incubus, Lucifer, Mahound, monster, Old Nick, Scratch, succuba, the deil
**08** Apollyon, bogeyman, firework, goodyear, man of sin, Mephisto, mischief, Old Harry, Old Poker, succubus, the enemy, wirricow, worricow, worrycow **09** Adversary, arch-fiend, Beelzebub, cacodemon, Davy Jones, goodyears, Nickie-ben, yoke-devil **10** cacodaemon, evil spirit, Old Scratch, Ragamuffin, the evil one, the Tempter **11** arch-traitor, the old enemy **12** the wicked one
**14** Mephistopheles, Mephistophilis, Mephostophilus

**devilish**
◇ *anagram indicator*
**04** evil, very, vile **05** cruel, jolly
**06** highly, knotty, really, thorny, tricky, wicked **07** awfully, awkward, demonic, greatly, hellish, satanic
**08** accursed, damnable, delicate, diabolic, dreadful, fiendish, infernal, severely, shocking, terribly, ticklish
**09** atrocious, difficult, execrable, extremely, intensely, malignant, nefarious, sensitive, unusually
**10** diabolical, disastrous, dreadfully, outrageous, remarkably, thoroughly, uncommonly **11** complicated, exceedingly, excessively, frightfully, problematic **12** excruciating, immoderately, unreasonably
**13** exceptionally **15** extraordinarily

**devil-may-care**
**04** rash **06** casual **08** careless, cavalier, flippant, heedless, reckless
**09** audacious, easy-going, frivolous, unworried **10** insouciant, nonchalant, swaggering **11** unconcerned
**12** happy-go-lucky **13** swashbuckling

**devilry**
**03** sin **04** evil **07** impiety **08** atrocity, enormity, foulness, iniquity, vileness

**09** amorality, depravity, diabolism, reprobacy **10** corruption, immorality, sinfulness, wickedness **11** abomination, corruptness, heinousness
**12** fiendishness, shamefulness
**13** dissoluteness **15** unrighteousness

**devious**
◇ *anagram indicator*
**03** sly **04** wily **06** artful, crafty, erring, subtle, tricky **07** crooked, cunning, erratic, evasive, winding **08** indirect, rambling, scheming, slippery, tortuous **09** deceitful, designing, deviating, dishonest, insidious, insincere, underhand, wandering **10** circuitous, misleading, roundabout **11** calculating, treacherous **12** disingenuous, unscrupulous **13** double-dealing, surreptitious

**devise**
**02** do **04** cast, form, plan, plot, talk, will **05** forge, frame, guess, hatch, hit on, shape, study **06** cook up, create, decoct, depict, design, invent, scheme
**07** arrange, compose, concoct, dream up, hit upon, imagine, project, purpose, suppose, think up, work out
**08** bequeath, conceive, consider, conspire, contrive, describe, meditate
**09** construct, fabricate, formulate, originate **10** come up with **11** put together

**devoid**
**04** bare, free, vain, void **05** empty
**06** barren, bereft, vacant **07** lacking, wanting, without **08** deprived
**09** deficient, destitute

**devolution**
**09** dispersal **12** distribution

**devolve**
**06** convey, depute, fall to, pass on
**07** consign, deliver, entrust, succeed
**08** delegate, hand down, pass down, rest with, transfer **10** commission

**Devon**
**02** SW

**devote**
**04** doom, give **05** allot, apply, offer, put in **06** assign, commit, pledge
**07** appoint, consign, reserve
**08** allocate, dedicate, enshrine, set apart, set aside **09** sacrifice, surrender
**10** consecrate **11** appropriate **12** give yourself

**devoted**
**04** fond, true **05** loyal **06** ardent, caring, devout, doomed, loving, sacred **07** staunch, zealous
**08** constant, dedicate, faithful, tireless
**09** attentive, committed, concerned, dedicated, steadfast **10** unswerving

**devotedly**
**06** fondly **07** loyally **08** ardently, caringly, devoutly, lovingly
**09** staunchly **10** faithfully, tirelessly
**11** attentively, committedly, dedicatedly, steadfastly
**12** unswervingly

**devotee**
**03** bum, fan **04** buff **05** fiend, freak, hound, lover **06** addict, votary, voteen, zealot **07** admirer, fanatic
**08** adherent, disciple, follower, merchant **09** supporter **10** aficionado, enthusiast

**devotion**
**04** alms, love, zeal **05** faith, piety
**06** ardour, prayer, regard **07** fervour, loyalty, passion, support, worship
**08** fidelity, fondness, holiness, sanctity, trueness, warmness **09** adherence, adoration, affection, closeness, constancy, godliness, reverence
**10** admiration, allegiance, attachment, commitment, dedication, devoutness, observance, solidarity **11** earnestness, schwärmerei, staunchness
**12** consecration, faithfulness, heart-service, spirituality **13** religiousness, steadfastness

**• object of devotion**
**03** god **09** Jugannath **10** Juggernaut

**devotional**
**04** holy **05** pious **06** devout, sacred, solemn **07** dutiful **09** pietistic, religious, spiritual **11** reverential

**devour**
◇ *insertion indicator*
**03** eat **04** bolt, cram, gulp **05** eat up, enjoy, gorge, raven, scarf, scoff, skoff, snarf, stuff, worry **06** absorb, engulf, gobble, guzzle, ravage, relish, take in
**07** consume, destroy, drink in, engorge, envelop, feast on, put away, revel in, swallow **08** dispatch, lay waste, tuck into, wolf down
**09** depredate, devastate, finish off, knock back, polish off **10** appreciate, gormandize **13** be engrossed in, gourmandize

**devout**
**04** deep, holy **05** godly, pious
**06** ardent, solemn **07** devoted, earnest, fervent, genuine, intense, saintly, serious, sincere, staunch, zealous **08** constant, faithful, orthodox, profound, reverent, vehement **09** committed, dedicated, heartfelt, prayerful, religious, steadfast
**10** passionate, practising, unswerving
**11** church-going **12** wholehearted

**devoutly**
**06** deeply **07** piously **08** ardently
**09** earnestly, fervently, sincerely, staunchly, zealously **10** faithfully, reverently **11** prayerfully, religiously, steadfastly **12** passionately
**14** wholeheartedly

**dewy**
**05** roral, roric, rorid **06** roscid
**07** bedewed **08** blooming, innocent, youthful **10** starry-eyed

**dexterity**
**03** art **05** craft, knack, skill **06** slight
**07** ability, address, agility, finesse, mastery, sleight **08** aptitude, artistry, deftness, facility **09** adeptness, expertise, handiness, ingenuity, readiness **10** adroitness, expertness, nimbleness **11** legerdemain, proficiency, skilfulness
**14** effortlessness **15** right-handedness

**dexterous**
**04** able, deft **05** adept, agile, handy, nifty, nippy, ready **06** adroit, artful, clever, expert, facile, habile, nimble, subtle, wieldy **07** featous, skilful
**08** feateous, featuous **10** neat-handed, proficient **11** right-handed
**12** accomplished **14** nimble-fingered

**diabolical**
◇ *anagram indicator*
**04** evil, vile **05** nasty **06** sinful, wicked
**07** demonic, hellish, satanic
**08** absolute, complete, damnable, devilish, dreadful, fiendish, infernal, shocking **09** appalling, atrocious, execrable, monstrous **10** disastrous, outrageous **12** excruciating

**diacritic**
**05** acute, breve, grave, haček, tilde
**06** accent, macron, umlaut **07** cedilla
**08** dieresis, modifier

**diadem**
**05** crown, mitre, round, tiara **07** circlet, circuit, coronet **08** headband

**diagnose**
**06** detect **07** analyse, explain, isolate
**08** identify, pinpoint **09** determine, interpret, recognize **11** distinguish, investigate

**diagnosis**
**06** answer **07** opinion, verdict
**08** analysis, scrutiny **09** detection, judgement **10** conclusion
**11** diagnostics, examination, explanation, recognition
**13** investigation **14** identification, interpretation

**diagnostic**
**10** analytical, indicative
**11** symptomatic **12** interpretive, recognizable **13** demonstrative
**14** distinguishing, interpretative
**15** differentiating

**diagonal**
**05** cater, cross **06** angled **07** crooked, oblique, sloping **08** crossing, slanting
**09** crosswise **10** cornerways
**11** catercorner, catty-corner
**13** catercornered, catty-cornered, kitty-cornered

**diagonally**
**05** cater **06** aslant **08** bendwise **09** at an angle, crossways, crosswise, obliquely, on the bias, slantwise
**10** cornerways, cornerwise, on the cross, on the slant **11** catercorner, catty-corner **13** catercornered, catty-cornered, kitty-cornered

**diagram**
**03** key **04** abac, plan, plat, tree
**05** chart, draft, graph, table
**06** figure, layout, schema, scheme, sketch **07** cutaway, drawing, outline,

picture **08** bar chart, isopleth, nomogram, pie chart, run chart **09** floor plan, flow chart, indicator, nomograph, schematic **10** family tree, stereogram **11** delineation **12** exploded view, illustration **14** alignment chart, representation

**diagrammatic**
**07** graphic, tabular **09** schematic **12** illustrative **14** diagrammatical

**dial**
**03** map, pan **04** bass, call, disc, face, mush, ring **05** clock, phone, tuner, watch **06** call up, circle, treble **07** control **09** give a bell, give a buzz, hourplate, telephone

**• compass dial**
**04** card

**dialect**
**03** Twi **04** Norn **05** argot, idiom, lingo **06** accent, jargon, patois, speech **07** diction, variety **08** language, localism **10** vernacular **11** regionalism **13** provincialism

**• dialect society**
**03** EDS

**dialectic**
**05** logic **06** debate **07** logical **08** analysis, logistic, polemics, rational **09** deduction, deductive, induction, inductive, polemical, rationale, reasoning **10** analytical, contention, dialectics, discussion **11** dialectical, disputation **12** disputatious **13** argumentation, argumentative, ratiocination, rationalistic

**dialogue**
**04** chat, talk **05** lazzo, lines **06** debate, gossip, script **08** colloquy, converse, exchange **09** discourse, tête-à-tête **10** conference, discussion **11** interchange, pastourelle **12** conversation, stichomythia **13** communication, interlocution

**diameter**
**01** d **03** dia **04** diam

**diametrically**
**07** utterly **08** directly **10** absolutely, completely **14** antithetically

**diamond**
**04** bort, pick, rock **05** boart, spark **06** carbon, lasque **07** adamant, paragon, rhombus **08** sparkler **09** brilliant, solitaire **10** Rhinestone

*Diamonds include:*

**04** Hope
**05** Orlov, Sancy
**06** Orloff, Regent
**07** Tiffany
**08** Blue Hope, Cullinan, Idol's Eye, Koh-I-Noor
**09** Centenary, Excelsior, Hortensia
**10** Florentine, Great Mogul
**12** Star of Africa, Taylor-Burton

**• diamonds**
**01** D **03** ice

**Diana**
**02** Di **07** Artemis

**diaphanous**
**04** fine, thin **05** clear, filmy, gauzy, light, sheer, veily **08** chiffony, cobwebby, delicate, gossamer, pellucid **09** gossamery **10** see-through **11** translucent, transparent

**diarrhoea**
**05** scour **06** scours **07** the runs **08** lientery, the trots, wood-evil **09** dysentery, looseness **10** Delhi belly, gippy tummy, gyppy tummy **12** Aztec two-step, holiday tummy, Spanish tummy, weaning brash

**diary**
**03** log **06** memoir **07** day-book, diurnal, Filofax®, journal, logbook **08** year-book **09** chronicle **13** journal intime **14** engagement book **15** appointment book

*Diarists include:*

**03** **Lee** (Lorelei)
**04** **Byrd** (William), **Gide** (André), **Mole** (Adrian), **Ooka** (Shohei)
**05** **Birde** (William), **Frank** (Anne), **Grant** (Elizabeth), **Jones** (Bridget), **Pasek** (Jan Chryzostom), **Pepys** (Samuel), **Reyes** (Alfonso), **Scott** (Robert Falcon), **Torga** (Miguel)
**06** **Burney** (Fanny), **Evelyn** (John), **Pooter** (Charles)
**07** **Andrews** (Pamela), **Carlyle** (Jane Welsh), **Chesnut** (Mary), **Creevey** (Thomas), **Kilvert** (Francis), **Régnier** (Paule)
**08** **Greville** (Charles Cavendish Fulke), **Melville** (James), **Robinson** (Henry Crabb)
**09** **Schreiber**, **Slaveykov** (Petko)
**10** **Ooka Shohei**
**11** **Lichtenberg** (Georg Christoph), **Thermopolis** (Mia)
**12** **Bashkirtseva** (Marya)

**diatribe**
**05** abuse **06** attack, insult, rebuke, tirade **07** reproof, slating **08** harangue, knocking, reviling, slamming **09** criticism, invective, onslaught, philippic, reprimand **10** upbraiding **11** running-down **12** denunciation, vituperation

**dice**
**04** bale **05** bones **09** astragals **11** devil's bones

**• spot on dice**
**03** pip **04** peep **05** peepe

**dicey**
**04** iffy **05** dodgy, hairy, risky **06** chancy, tricky **07** dubious **09** dangerous, difficult, uncertain **11** problematic **13** unpredictable

**dichotomy**
**08** conflict, division, variance **09** deviation, disparity, variation **10** difference, divergence, opposition **11** discrepancy **13** dissimilarity **15** differentiation

**dicky**
◇ *anagram indicator*
**03** ass **04** weak **05** frail, shaky **06** ailing, infirm **07** unsound **08** unsteady

**dictate**
**03** law, say **04** dite, read, rule, word **05** edict, order, speak, utter **06** behest, charge, decree, demand, direct, impose, indite, insist, ruling **07** bidding, command, lay down, mandate, precept, read out, set down, statute **08** announce, instruct, transmit **09** direction, ordinance, prescribe, principle, pronounce, read aloud, ultimatum **10** injunction, promulgate **11** requirement **12** give orders to, promulgation

**dictator**
**04** dict, duce **06** despot, tyrant **07** supremo **08** autocrat **09** oppressor **10** autarchist, Big Brother **12** little Hitler **13** absolute ruler

*See also* **despot**

**dictatorial**
**05** bossy **08** absolute, despotic, dogmatic **09** arbitrary, autarchic, imperious, unlimited **10** autocratic, omnipotent, oppressive, peremptory, repressive, tyrannical **11** all powerful, domineering, magisterial, overbearing **12** totalitarian, unrestricted **13** authoritarian, authoritative

**dictatorship**
**07** fascism, tyranny **09** autocracy, despotism, Hitlerism **11** police state **12** absolute rule **13** reign of terror **15** totalitarianism

**diction**
**05** lexis, style **06** saying, speech **07** fluency **08** delivery, language, locution, phrasing, speaking **09** elocution **10** expression, inflection, intonation **11** enunciation **12** articulation **13** pronunciation

**dictionary**
**03** DNB, OED, TCD **04** dict **06** gradus **07** alveary, lexicon **08** Chambers, glossary, wordbook **09** gazetteer, thesaurus **10** vocabulary **11** concordance, onomasticon, synonymicon **12** encyclopedia, etymologicon, etymologicum

**dictum**
**04** fiat **05** axiom, edict, maxim, order **06** decree, ruling, saying **07** command, dictate, precept, proverb **08** aphorism **09** direction, ipse dixit, utterance **12** proclamation **13** pronouncement

**did**
**01** 'd

**didactic**
**05** moral **08** pedantic **09** educative, pedagogic **10** didascalic, moralizing, preceptive, protreptic **11** educational, informative, instructive **12** prescriptive

**die**
**02** go **03** dee, ebb, end, pip **04** ache, cark, exit, fade, fail, kark, long, pass, pine, sink, stop, wane, wilt **05** be mad, choke, croak, decay, drown, go off, lapse, merge, punch, quell, swelt, yearn **06** be nuts, be wild, cut out, depart, desire, expire, famish, finish, go bung, go west, pass on, peg out, perish, pip out, pop off, starve, sterve, vanish, wither **07** be crazy, conk out, decease, decline, dwindle, kick off, kiss off, long for, pass out, pine for, snuff it, subside, succumb **08** be raring, decrease, dissolve, flatline, intaglio, melt away, pass away, pass over, peter out, spark out **09** break down, disappear, go belly up, have had it, lose power **10** hop the twig **11** be desperate, bite the dust, come to an end **12** lose your life, pop your clogs, slip the cable **13** close your eyes, kick the bucket, meet your maker, push up daisies **14** depart this life, give up the ghost, turn up your toes **15** breathe your last, cash in your chips, join the majority

• **die away**
**04** fade, fall **07** evanish, fall off **09** disappear **10** become weak **11** become faint

• **die down**
**04** drop, stop **05** abate, slake **06** quench **07** decline, quieten, subside **08** blow over, decrease

• **die out**
**06** vanish **08** peter out **09** disappear **10** extinguish **11** become rarer

• **soon to die**
**03** fay, fey, fie **05** fated

**died**
**01** d **02** ob **05** obiit

**diehard**
**05** blimp **06** zealot **07** fanatic **08** hardline, old fogey, rightist **09** fanatical, hardliner **11** reactionary **12** conservative, intransigent **13** dyed-in-the-wool, stick-in-the-mud **14** traditionalist

**diet**
**04** bant, fare, fast, food, slim, VLCD **06** reduce, regime, viands **07** abstain, cut down, Landtag, rations, regimen **08** fishmeal, victuals **09** nutrition **10** abstinence, conference, foodstuffs, lose weight, provisions, sustenance **11** comestibles, subsistence, weight-watch

**differ**
**04** vary **05** argue, clash **06** debate, oppose **07** contend, deviate, dispute, dissent, diverge, fall out, quarrel **08** be unlike, conflict, contrast, disagree **09** altercate, take issue **10** contradict, depart from, disconsent **11** deviate from **12** be at odds with, be at variance, be dissimilar **14** not see eye to eye

**difference**
**03** row **04** rest, spat, tiff **05** clash, set-to **07** balance, dispute, quarrel, residue, variety **08** argument, conflict, contrast, variance **09** deviation, dichotomy, disparity, diversity, exception, remainder, variation **10** antithesis, contention, divergence, inequality, unlikeness **11** altercation, controversy, discrepancy, disputation, distinction, incongruity, singularity **12** disagreement, distinctness **13** dissimilarity, dissimilitude **14** discrimination **15** differentiation

**different**
◇ *anagram indicator*
**03** new, odd **04** allo-, many, rare **05** novel, other **06** at odds, sundry, unique, unlike, varied **07** a far cry, another, awkward, bizarre, diverse, opposed, several, special, strange, unusual, variant, various, varying **08** assorted, clashing, discrete, distinct, ill-timed, mixed bag, numerous, original, peculiar, separate, untimely **09** anomalous, deviating, disparate, divergent, otherwise **10** at variance, dissimilar, individual, poles apart, remarkable, unsuitable **11** contrasting, distinctive, inopportune, worlds apart **12** heterologous, inconsistent, inconvenient, poles asunder, streets apart, unfavourable, unmanageable **13** extraordinary, miscellaneous **14** unconventional

**differential**
**03** gap **08** contrast, separate, variance **09** different, disparate, disparity, divergent **10** difference, divergence **11** contrasting, discrepancy, distinctive **14** discriminating

**differentiate**
**06** modify **07** mark off **08** contrast, separate **09** diversify, tell apart **10** specialize **11** distinguish **12** discriminate **13** individualize, particularize

**differentiation**
**08** contrast **10** separation **11** demarcation, distinction **12** modification **14** discrimination, distinguishing

**differently**
◇ *anagram indicator*
**06** at odds **07** a far cry **09** diversely **10** at variance, poles apart **11** worlds apart **12** dissimilarly, incompatibly **13** contrastingly **14** inconsistently

**difficult**
**03** ill **04** dark, hard, high **05** rough, steep, stiff, tough **06** arcane, Augean, badass, gnarly, knotty, thorny, tiring, tricky, trying, uneath, uphill **07** arduous, awkward, complex, Gordian, obscure, onerous, testing **08** abstract, abstruse, badassed, baffling, esoteric, exacting, involved, perverse, puzzling, stubborn, ticklish, tiresome **09** demanding, difficile, gruelling, intricate, laborious, obstinate, recondite, strenuous, wearisome **10** burdensome, exhausting, formidable, perplexing, refractory **11** complicated, intractable, troublesome **12** back-breaking, hard to please, recalcitrant, unmanageable **13** problematical, unco-operative

**difficulty**
**03** ado, fix, ill, jam, net, rub **04** hole, knot, mess, node, snag, spot, stew **05** bitch, block, devil, nodus, trial **06** aporia, bother, hang-up, hassle, hiccup, hobble, hurdle, labour, pickle, plight, strain **07** barrier, dilemma, nonplus, perplex, pitfall, problem, quarrel, scruple, straits, trouble **08** distress, exigency, hardship, hot water, obstacle, quandary, struggle **09** deep water, hindrance, how-d'you-do, Lob's pound, nineholes, objection, tall order, tight spot **10** cleft stick, disability, impediment, opposition, perplexity, pretty pass, struggling **11** arduousness, awkwardness, dire straits, obstruction, painfulness, predicament, tribulation **12** complication **13** embarrassment, laboriousness, strenuousness **14** stumbling-block

• **get through difficulty**
**04** pass

• **in difficulties**
**06** in a fix, in a jam **07** in a hole, in a mess, in a stew, stumped, up a tree **08** bunkered **09** in a scrape, in the soup, in trouble **10** hard-pushed, in hot water, up the creek **11** hard-pressed, in deep water, up against it **12** in a tight spot **13** in dire straits **14** having problems, out of your depth

• **with difficulty**
**03** ill **04** hard **06** hardly, scarce, uneath **10** at a stretch

**diffidence**
**07** modesty, reserve, shyness **08** humility, meekness, timidity **09** hesitancy, self-doubt **10** inhibition, insecurity, reluctance **11** bashfulness **12** backwardness, self-distrust **14** self-effacement **15** unassertiveness

**diffident**
**03** shy **04** meek **05** timid **06** modest, unsure **07** abashed, bashful, nervous **08** hesitant, insecure, reserved, sheepish **09** inhibited, reluctant, shrinking, tentative, unassured, withdrawn **10** shamefaced **11** distrusting, unassertive **12** self-effacing **13** self-conscious

**diffuse**
**03** ren, rin, run **05** large, vague, wordy **06** prolix, spread, winnow **07** profuse, publish, scatter, send out, verbose **08** diffused, dispense, disperse, permeate, rambling, waffling **09** circulate, dispersed, dissipate, imprecise, propagate, scattered **10** discursive, distribute, long-winded, loquacious, promulgate **11** disseminate **12** disconnected, periphrastic **14** circumlocutory, unconcentrated

**diffusion**
**07** osmosis **08** bleeding **09** dispersal, extension, spreading **10** permeation, scattering **11** circulation, dissipation, propagation **12** distribution, promulgation **13** dissemination

**dig**
**03** get, jab **04** cast, fork, gibe, gird, grub, howk, jeer, mine, poke, prod, spit, spud, till, twig, work **05** click, crack, delve, ditch, gouge, graft, grasp, grave, lodge, probe, punch, scoop, sneer, spade, taunt **06** burrow, follow, go into, grub up, harrow, hollow, insult, pierce, plough, quarry, search, take in, thrust, trench, tunnel **07** approve, break up, channel, fossick, grub out, realize, scratch, unearth **08** disinter, entrench, excavate, research, turn over **09** cultivate, figure out, make a hole, penetrate, undermine, wisecrack **10** appreciate, compliment, excavation, understand **11** insinuation, investigate **12** get the hang of

**• dig up**
**04** find **06** exhume, expose **07** root out, uncover, unearth **08** discover, disinter, excavate, retrieve **09** extricate, track down **12** bring to light

**• digging implement**
**02** ko **04** spud **05** spade

**digest**
◇ *anagram indicator*
**04** code **05** endew, endue, grasp, indew, indue, study **06** absorb, codify, ponder, précis, reduce, résumé, take in **07** abridge, process, shorten, stomach, summary **08** abstract, canon law, compress, condense, consider, dissolve, macerate, meditate, mull over, synopsis **09** break down, reduction, summarize **10** assimilate, compendium, comprehend, understand **11** abridgement, compression, contemplate, incorporate **12** abbreviation

**digestion**
**08** eupepsia **09** ingestion **10** absorption, maceration **12** assimilation, breaking-down **14** transformation

**digit**
**03** toe **05** index, thumb **06** dactyl, figure, finger, hallux, number **07** integer, numeral **10** forefinger, ring finger **12** little finger, middle finger

**dignified**
**04** high **05** grand, grave, lofty, manly, noble **06** august, formal, lordly, sedate, solemn **07** courtly, exalted, stately **08** decorous, handsome, imposing, majestic, reserved **10** honourable, impressive **11** ceremonious **13** distinguished

**dignify**
**05** adorn, crown, exalt, grace, raise **06** honour **07** advance, elevate, enhance, ennoble, glorify, promote **10** aggrandize **11** apotheosize, distinguish

**dignitary**
**03** VIP **04** dean, name **05** canon **06** big gun, bigwig, high-up, worthy **07** big name, big shot, grandee, notable, provost **08** alderman, luminary, somebody, top brass **09** personage **10** archdeacon

**dignity**
**05** poise, pride, state **06** honour, status **07** decorum, majesty, worship **08** cathedra, eminence, grandeur, nobility, standing **09** elevation, greatness, loftiness, nobleness, propriety, solemnity **10** excellence, importance, preferment, self-esteem **11** courtliness, self-respect, stateliness **13** honourability **14** respectability, self-importance, self-possession

**digress**
**05** drift, stray **06** depart, ramble, wander **07** deviate, diverge, excurse **08** divagate **09** turn aside **13** be sidetracked **15** go off at a tangent, go off the subject

**digression**
**05** aside **06** ecbole, flight, vagary **08** excursus, footnote, straying **09** departure, deviation, diversion, evagation, excursion, wandering **10** apostrophe, divagation, divergence **11** parenthesis **12** extravagance, obiter dictum

**digs**
**03** pad **05** place, rooms **06** billet **08** lodgings, quarters **13** accommodation, boarding-house

**dilapidated**
◇ *anagram indicator*
**05** shaky **06** beat-up, ruined, shabby **07** decayed, in ruins, rickety, run-down, worn-out **08** decaying, decrepit **09** crumbling, neglected **10** broken-down, ramshackle, tumbledown, uncared-for **12** falling apart

**dilapidation**
**04** ruin **05** decay, waste **08** collapse **09** disrepair **10** demolition **11** destruction **13** deterioration **14** disintegration

**dilate**
**04** tent **05** bloat, swell, widen **06** expand, extend, spread **07** broaden, distend, enlarge, inflate, stretch **08** increase **09** spread out

**dilatory**
**04** lazy, slow **05** slack, tardy **08** dawdling, delaying, sluggish, stalling, tarrying **09** lingering, loitering, snail-like **10** postponing, prolixious **11** time-wasting **13** lackadaisical **15** procrastinating

**dilemma**
**03** fix **04** mess, spot **06** plight, puzzle, why-not **07** problem **08** conflict, quandary **10** cleft stick, difficulty, double bind, perplexity **11** predicament, tight corner **13** embarrassment, vicious circle **14** no-win situation

**dilettante**
**07** amateur, dabbler, trifler **08** aesthete, potterer, sciolist **15** non-professional

**diligence**
**04** care **08** industry **09** assiduity, attention, constancy **10** conscience, dedication, intentness **11** application, earnestness, painstaking, pertinacity **12** perseverance, sedulousness, thoroughness **13** assiduousness, attentiveness, laboriousness

**diligent**
**04** busy **06** eident **07** careful, earnest **08** constant, sedulous, studious, thorough, tireless **09** assiduous, attentive, dedicated **10** meticulous, persistent **11** hard-working, industrious, painstaking, persevering **13** conscientious

**dilly-dally**
**05** dally, delay, hover, tarry, waver **06** dawdle, dither, falter, linger, loiter, potter, trifle **08** hesitate **09** faff about, vacillate, waste time **12** shilly-shally, take your time **13** procrastinate

**dilute**
**03** cut, dil **04** kill, thin **05** allay, delay, lower, small, water **06** lessen, reduce, temper, weaken **07** diffuse, thin out **08** decrease, diminish, mitigate, moderate, tone down, waterish **09** attenuate, water down **10** adulterate, attenuated, make weaker **11** make thinner

**diluted**
**03** cut **04** weak **06** watery **07** thinned **10** thinned out, wishy-washy **11** watered down

**dim**
**04** blur, dark, dull, dumb, dusk, fade, grey, hazy, pale, paly, slow, weak **05** appal, bedim, blear, cloud, dense, dingy, dopey, dusky, faint, foggy, fuzzy, misty, shade, thick, unlit, vague **06** bleary, cloudy, darken, feeble, gloomy, leaden, obtuse, simple, sombre, stupid **07** adverse, becloud, blurred, doltish, obscure, shadowy, tarnish, unclear **08** clouding, confused, gormless, overcast **09** dim-witted, imperfect, make faint, tenebrous **10** caliginous, ill-defined, indistinct, lacklustre, obfuscated, slow-witted **11** become faint, crepuscular, make blurred, unpromising **12** crepusculous, discouraging, inauspicious, simple-minded, unfavourable **13** become blurred

**dimension**
**01** D **03** dim **04** area, bulk, mass, side, size **05** depth, facet, range, scale, scope, width **06** aspect, extent, factor, height, length, volume **07** breadth, element, feature, measure **08** capacity

09 greatness, largeness, magnitude 10 importance 11 measurement, proportions

**diminish**
03 cut, ebb 04 bate, damp, drop, fade, pare, sink, wane 05 abate, lower, mince 06 defame, die out, impair, lessen, minify, minish, rebate, recede, reduce, shrink, vilify, weaken 07 assuage, attrite, decline, deflate, degrade, detract, devalue, die away, drop off, dwindle, slacken, subside, whittle 08 belittle, contract, decrease, derogate, grow less, minimize, pare down, peter out, retrench, taper off, wear down 09 denigrate, deprecate, disparage 10 become less, deactivate, grow weaker 11 whittle away, whittle down 12 become weaker 14 take the edge off

**diminuendo**
03 dim 04 fade 11 decrescendo

**diminution**
03 cut, ebb 04 loss 05 decay, taper 07 atrophy, cutback, decline 08 decrease, drawdown 09 abatement, deduction, detriment, lessening, reduction, shrinkage, weakening 10 shortening, subsidence 11 contraction, curtailment, defalcation 12 retrenchment

**diminutive**
03 dim, wee 04 mini, tiny 05 dinky, elfin, pigmy, pygmy, small, teeny 06 little, midget, minute, petite, pocket, tottie 07 compact, minikin 08 dwarfish, pint-size 09 miniature, pint-sized 10 contracted, homuncular, hypocorism, small-scale, teeny-weeny, undersized 11 hypocorisma, Lilliputian, microscopic, pocket-sized 13 infinitesimal

**dimly**
05 dully 06 darkly, feebly, hazily, weakly 07 dingily, faintly, mistily 08 gloomily, sombrely 09 obscurely, unclearly 12 indistinctly

**dimness**
04 dusk, mist 06 caligo 08 darkness, dullness, greyness, twilight 09 dinginess, half-light 10 cloudiness, crepuscule 12 caliginosity

**dimple**
04 dint 05 fovea 06 hollow 09 concavity, umbilicus 10 depression 11 indentation

**dimwit**
03 git 04 berk, clot, dope, dork, fool, geek, prat, twit 05 dumbo, dunce, dweeb, idiot 06 nitwit 07 dullard, halfwit, plonker 08 bonehead, numskull 09 blockhead, ignoramus 10 dunderhead 11 knuckle-head

*See also* **fool**

**din**
03 row 04 deen, reel, utis 05 alarm, chirm, clash, crash, noise, noyes, raird, reird, shout 06 babble, hubbub, outcry, racket, randan, stound, stownd, tumult, uproar 07 clamour, clatter, yelling 08 brouhaha, clangour, shouting 09 charivari, commotion, loud noise 10 hullabaloo 11 pandemonium

**dine**
03 eat, sup 04 feed, mess 05 feast, lunch 06 dinner 07 banquet 10 have dinner

**dingy**
03 dim, dun 04 dark, drab, dull, fusc, worn 05 dirty, dusky, faded, grimy, murky, oorie, ourie, owrie, seedy 06 dismal, dreary, gloomy, isabel, shabby, soiled, sombre 07 fuscous, obscure, run-down, squalid 08 isabella 09 cheerless 10 colourless, isabelline 11 discoloured 12 disreputable

**dinky**
04 fine, mini, neat, trim 05 natty, small 06 dainty, little, petite 07 trivial 09 miniature 13 insignificant

**dinner**
03 tea 04 dine, hall, kail, kale, meal 05 feast 06 repast, spread, supper 07 banquet, blow-out 08 main meal 09 beanfeast, refection, wasegoose, wayzgoose 11 evening meal

• **dinner time**
07 evening

**dinosaur**

*Dinosaurs include:*

04 T Rex
06 Raptor
08 Coelurus, Sauropod, Theropod
09 Hadrosaur, Iguanodon, Oviraptor
10 Allosaurus, Anatotitan, Barosaurus, Diplodocus, Megalosaur, Ophiacodon, Torosaurus, Utahraptor
11 Apatosaurus, Ceteosaurus, Coelophysis, Coelurosaur, Deinonychus, Dromaeosaur, Polacanthus, Prosauropod, Saurischian, Stegosaurus, Triceratops, Tyrannosaur
12 Ankylosaurus, Brontosaurus, Camptosaurus, Ceratosaurus, Megalosaurus, Ornithischia, Ornithomimus, Plateosaurus, Titanosaurus, Velociraptor
13 Atlantosaurus, Brachiosaurus, Compsognathus, Corythosaurus, Dwarf Allosaur, Edmontosaurus, Herrerasaurus, Ornitholestes, Styracosaurus, Tyrannosaurus
14 Leaellynasaura
15 Cryolophosaurus, Parasaurolophus

**dint**
04 blow, dent 05 force 06 hollow, indent, stroke 09 concavity 10 depression, impression 11 indentation

• **by dint of**
09 by means of 10 by virtue of 13 by the agency of

**diocese**
03 see 04 Ebor, Exon, Oxon 06 Cantab, Dunelm 07 Cantuar, eparchy 09 bishopric, eparchate

*Dioceses and archdioceses of the UK:*

03 Ely
04 York
05 Derby, Derry, Leeds, Truro
06 Armagh, Bangor, Connor, Durham, Exeter, Hallam, London, Oxford
07 Brechin, Bristol, Cardiff, Chester, Clifton, Clogher, Dromore, Dunkeld, Glasgow, Kilmore, Lincoln, Menevia, Norwich, Paisley, Salford, St Asaph, Wrexham
08 Aberdeen, Bradford, Carlisle, Coventry, Galloway, Hereford, Llandaff, Monmouth, Plymouth, St Albans, St Davids
09 Blackburn, Brentwood, Edinburgh, Guildford, Lancaster, Leicester, Lichfield, Liverpool, Newcastle, Rochester, Salisbury, Sheffield, Southwark, Southwell, Wakefield, Worcester
10 Birmingham, Canterbury, Chelmsford, Chichester, East Anglia, Gloucester, Manchester, Motherwell, Nottingham, Portsmouth, Shrewsbury, Winchester
11 Northampton, Sodor and Man (Anglican), Westminster
12 Bath and Wells, Peterborough
13 Down and Connor, Middlesbrough, Ripon and Leeds
14 Derry and Raphoe, Down and Dromore
16 Swansea and Brecon
17 Aberdeen and Orkney, Argyll and the Isles
18 Arundel and Brighton, Glasgow and Galloway, Hexham and Newcastle
21 Moray, Ross and Caithness, St Andrews and Edinburgh
23 St Edmundsbury and Ipswich
27 St Andrews, Dunkeld and Dunblane

**Dionysus**
07 Bacchus 10 Liber Pater

**dip**
03 dap, dib, dim, dop, nod, sag 04 bath, dent, dive, drop, duck, dunk, fall, hole, pawn, plot, sink, soak, swim 05 basin, bathe, cream, delve, douse, lower, merge, ploat, sauce, slope, slump, souse 06 dibble, go down, hollow, plunge, relish 07 baptize, decline, descend, descent, ducking, immerge, immerse, incline, moisten, sloping, soaking, subside, suffuse 08 decrease, dressing, infusion, lowering, mortgage, submerge 09 concavity, drenching, immersion, lessening, reduction 10 depression, pickpocket 11 indentation

• **dip into**
03 use 04 skim 05 spend 06 browse, draw on, look at 10 run through 11 leaf through, look through 12 flick through, thumb through

**diplomacy**
**04** tact **05** craft, skill **07** finesse **08** delicacy, politics, prudence, subtlety **10** cleverness, discretion, statecraft **11** manoeuvring, negotiation, savoir-faire, sensitivity, tactfulness **12** negotiations **13** judiciousness, statesmanship

**diplomat**
**02** CD, HE **05** envoy **06** consul, legate **07** attaché **08** emissary, mediator **09** go-between, moderator, statesman **10** ambassador, arbitrator, negotiator, peacemaker, politician **11** conciliator **12** ambassadress **15** plenipotentiary

**diplomatic**
**06** clever, subtle **07** politic, prudent, skilful, tactful **08** consular, discreet **09** judicious, sensitive **13** ambassadorial

• **diplomatic corps**
**02** CD

• **period of diplomatic service**
**04** tour

**diplomatically**
**09** prudently, skilfully, tactfully **10** discreetly **11** judiciously, politically, sensitively **13** by negotiation, with diplomacy **14** conciliatorily

**dipsomaniac**
**03** sot **04** lush, soak, wino **05** alkie, bloat, dipso, drunk, souse, toper **06** boozer, sponge **07** Bacchus, drinker, tippler, tosspot **08** drunkard, habitual **09** alcoholic, inebriate **10** wine-bibber **11** hard drinker **12** heavy drinker

**dire**
◇ *anagram indicator*
**04** fell **05** awful, grave, vital **06** urgent **07** crucial, drastic, extreme, ominous **08** alarming, dreadful, horrible, pressing, shocking, terrible **09** appalling, atrocious, desperate, frightful **10** calamitous, disastrous, portentous **11** distressing **12** catastrophic

**direct**
◇ *anagram indicator*
**03** aim, con, run, set **04** airt, conn, hold, lead, mean, near, show, tell, turn **05** apply, bluff, blunt, focus, frank, guide, level, order, point, ready, right, shape, steer, teach, usher **06** adjure, candid, charge, escort, govern, handle, honest, intend, manage, market, target **07** address, command, conduct, control, incline, non-stop, oversee, primary, sincere, through, up-front **08** directly, explicit, instruct, organize, personal, regulate, straight, unbroken **09** first-hand, immediate, outspoken, supervise **10** administer, face-to-face, forthright, give orders, mastermind, point-blank, show the way, unswerving **11** be the boss of, plainspoken, point the way, preside over, superintend, unambiguous, undeviating, unequivocal **12** be in charge of, call the shots **13** be in control of, uninterrupted **15** straightforward, uninterruptedly

• **directed towards**
**02** on

• **direct from**
**02** ex

**direction**
**03** set, way **04** airt, goal, lead, line, path, plan, road **05** brief, drift, route, rules, tenor, track, trend **06** course, orders **07** bearing, command, control, running **08** briefing, guidance, handling, tendency **10** current aim, government, guidelines, indication, leadership, management, overseeing, regulation **11** inclination, information, orientation, regulations, supervision **12** instructions **14** administration **15** recommendations, superintendency

*See also* **compass**

• **directions**
**06** recipe

• **general direction**
**03** ren, rin, run

• **in the direction of**
**02** on, to **03** for **07** towards

• **in the wrong direction**
**03** wry

• **sharp change in direction**
**03** zig

• **take a different direction**
**07** diverge

• **take a direction**
**02** go **04** chop **06** strike

**directive**
**04** fiat **05** edict, order **06** charge, decree, notice, ruling **07** bidding, command, concern, dictate, mandate **09** direction, ordinance, speech act **10** imperative, injunction, regulation **11** instruction

**directly**
**03** due **04** bang, dead, full, just, slap, soon **05** plumb, right, smack **06** at once, pronto, square **07** bluntly, clearly, exactly, frankly, plainly, quickly **08** candidly, honestly, outright, promptly, slap-bang, speedily, squarely, straight **09** forthwith, instantly, precisely, presently, right away, sincerely **10** explicitly, point-blank, straightly **11** immediately, straight out, straightway **12** straightaway, straightways, unswervingly, without delay **13** unambiguously, unequivocally **15** instantaneously

**directness**
**07** honesty **09** bluntness, frankness, immediacy **10** candidness **13** immediateness, outspokenness **14** forthrightness **15** plainspokenness

**director**
**01** D **03** Dir **04** boss, head **05** chair, chief **06** auteur, leader, top dog **07** manager **08** chairman, governor, overseer, Pole Star, producer **09** conductor, corrector, executive, film-maker, intendant, organizer, president, principal, régisseur, top banana **10** chairwoman, controller, counsellor, supervisor **11** agonothetes, chairperson, choirmaster, symposiarch **12** chapel master, chorus master, contributory, manufacturer **13** administrator, kapellmeister **14** chief executive, superintendent **15** Astronomer Royal

*Film and theatre directors and producers include:*

**03** **Cox** (Brian), **Lee** (Spike), **May** (Elaine), **Ozu** (Yasujiro), **Ray** (Satyajit), **Woo** (John)
**04** **Alda** (Alan), **Axel** (Gabriel), **Bond** (Edward), **Coen** (Ethan), **Coen** (Joel), **Eyre** (Sir Richard), **Ford** (John), **Gray** (Simon), **Hall** (Sir Peter), **Hare** (David), **Hart** (Moss), **Hill** (George Roy), **Lang** (Fritz), **Lean** (Sir David), **Nunn** (Trevor), **Reed** (Sir Carol), **Roeg** (Nicolas), **Tati** (Jacques), **Todd** (Mike), **Weir** (Peter), **Wise** (Robert)
**05** **Allen** (Woody), **Barba** (Eugenio), **Boyle** (Danny), **Brook** (Peter), **Capra** (Frank), **Carné** (Marcel), **Clair** (René), **Craig** (Gordon), **Cukor** (George Dewey), **Dante** (Joe), **Demme** (Jonathan), **Fosse** (Bob), **Gance** (Abel), **Hands** (Terry), **Hawks** (Howard), **Ivory** (James), **Kazan** (Elia), **Kelly** (Gene), **Korda** (Sir Alexander), **Leigh** (Mike), **Leone** (Sergio), **Losey** (Joseph), **Lucas** (George), **Lumet** (Sidney), **Lynch** (David), **Malle** (Louis), **Mamet** (David), **Marsh** (Dame Ngaio), **Mayer** (Louis B), **Miles** (Bernard, Lord), **Noble** (Adrian), **Pabst** (Georg Wilhelm), **Perry** (Antoinette), **Roach** (Hal), **Scott** (Ridley), **Stein** (Peter), **Stone** (Oliver), **Vadim** (Roger), **Varda** (Agnès), **Verdy** (Violette), **Vidor** (King), **Wajda** (Andrzej), **Wells** (John), **Wolfe** (George C), **Wyler** (William)
**06** **Abbott** (George), **Altman** (Robert), **Ang Lee**, **Artaud** (Antonin), **Arzner** (Dorothy), **August** (Bille), **Badham** (John), **Barton** (John), **Beatty** (Warren), **Besson** (Luc), **Brecht** (Bertolt), **Brooks** (Mel), **Bryden** (Bill), **Buñuel** (Luis), **Burton** (Tim), **Callow** (Simon), **Cooney** (Ray), **Copeau** (Jacques), **Corman** (Roger), **Curtiz** (Michael), **Cusack** (Cyril), **Daldry** (Stephen), **Davies** (Howard), **Davies** (Terence), **De Sica** (Vittorio), **Devine** (George), **Dexter** (John), **Disney** (Walt), **Donner** (Richard), **Dunlop** (Frank), **Dybwad** (Johanne), **Ephron** (Nora), **Forbes** (Bryan), **Forman** (Milos), **Frears** (Stephen), **Fugard** (Athol), **Gibson** (Mel), **Godard** (Jean-Luc), **Godber** (John), **Haydee** (Marcia), **Herzog** (Werner), **Hopper** (Dennis), **Hughes** (Howard), **Huston** (John), **Jarman** (Derek), **Jordan** (Neil), **Jouvet** (Louis), **Kantor** (Tadeusz), **Kasdan** (Lawrence), **Landis** (John), **Lupino**

(Ida), **Mendes** (Sam), **Miller** (George), **Miller** (Jonathan), **Moreau** (Jeanne), **Murnau** (F W), **Ophuls** (Max), **Parker** (Alan), **Powell** (Michael), **Prince** (Hal), **Prowse** (Philip), **Quayle** (Sir Anthony), **Reiner** (Carl), **Renoir** (Jean), **Siegal** (Don), **Tairov** (Aleksandr), **Usigli** (Rodolfo), **Warhol** (Andy), **Warner** (Deborah), **Warner** (Jack), **Welles** (Orson), **Wilder** (Billy), **Wilson** (Robert), **Zanuck** (Darryl)

**07** **Akerman** (Chantal), **Aldrich** (Robert), **Asquith** (Anthony), **Belasco** (David), **Benigni** (Roberto), **Bennett** (Alan), **Bennett** (Michael), **Bergman** (Ingmar), **Berkoff** (Steven), **Bigelow** (Kathryn), **Boorman** (John), **Branagh** (Kenneth), **Bresson** (Robert), **Cameron** (James), **Campion** (Jane), **Chabrol** (Claude), **Chaikin** (Joseph), **Chaplin** (Charlie), **Clavell** (James), **Clooney** (George), **Clurman** (Harold), **Cocteau** (Jean), **Coppola** (Francis Ford), **Costner** (Kevin), **De Mille** (Cecil Blount), **De Palma** (Brian), **Douglas** (Bill), **Douglas** (Michael), **Fellini** (Federico), **Fleming** (Tom), **Fleming** (Victor), **Forsyth** (Bill), **Gaumont** (Léon), **Gilliam** (Terry), **Goldwyn** (Samuel), **Guthrie** (Sir Tyrone), **Hartley** (Hal), **Heiberg** (Gunnar), **Holland** (Agnieszka), **Jackson** (Peter), **Joffrey** (Robert), **Kaufman** (George S), **Kaufman** (Philip), **Kubrick** (Stanley), **McBride** (Jim), **McGrath** (John), **Nichols** (Mike), **Olivier** (Sir Laurence), **Poitier** (Sidney), **Pollack** (Sydney), **Redford** (Robert), **Resnais** (Alain), **Robbins** (Tim), **Russell** (Ken), **Sellars** (Peter), **Sennett** (Mack), **Stiller** (Mauritz), **Sturges** (Preston), **Webster** (Margaret), **Wenders** (Wim)

**08** **Anderson** (Lindsay), **Barrault** (Jean-Louis), **Berkeley** (Busby), **Björnson** (Björnstjerne), **Bogdanov** (Michael), **Brustein** (Robert), **Carrière** (Jean-Claude), **Clements** (Sir John), **Crawford** (Cheryl), **Eastwood** (Clint), **Friedkin** (William), **Griffith** (David Wark), **Houseman** (John), **Jarmusch** (Jim), **Kurosawa** (Akira), **Levinson** (Barry), **Lubitsch** (Ernst), **Luhrmann** (Baz), **Lyubimov** (Yuri), **Marshall** (Penny), **Merchant** (Ismail), **Minnelli** (Vincente), **Mitchell** (Arthur), **Miyazaki** (Hayao), **Ninagawa** (Yukio), **Pasolini** (Pier Paulo), **Piscator** (Erwin), **Polanski** (Roman), **Pudovkin** (Vsevolod), **Schepisi** (Fred), **Scorsese** (Martin), **Selznick** (David Oliver), **Sjöström** (Victor), **Stroheim** (Erich von), **Truffaut** (François), **Visconti** (Luchino), **von Trier** (Lars), **Zemeckis** (Robert)

**09** **Alexander** (Bill), **Almodóvar** (Pedro), **Antonioni** (Michelangelo), **Armstrong** (Gillian), **Carpenter** (John), **Chen Kaige**, **Fernández** (Emilio), **Greenaway** (Peter), **Grotowski** (Jerzy), **Hitchcock** (Sir Alfred), **Malkovich** (John), **Meyerhold** (Vsevolod), **Minghella** (Anthony), **Mizoguchi** (Kenji), **Mountford** (Charles P), **Peckinpah** (Sam), **Plowright** (Joan), **Preminger** (Otto), **Spielberg** (Steven), **Stevenson** (Robert), **Strasberg** (Lee), **Streisand** (Barbra), **Tarantino** (Quentin), **Tavernier** (Bertrand), **Von Trotta** (Margarethe), **Wanamaker** (Sam), **Zinnemann** (Fred)

**10** **Bertolucci** (Bernardo), **Cronenberg** (David), **Eisenstein** (Sergei), **Fassbinder** (Rainer Werner), **Kaurismäki** (Aki), **Kiarostami** (Abbas), **Kieslowski** (Krzystof), **Littlewood** (Joan), **Makhmalbaf** (Mohsen), **Mankiewicz** (Joseph L), **Mnouchkine** (Ariane), **Rossellini** (Roberto), **Saint-Denis** (Michel), **Sucksdorff** (Arne E), **Vakhtangov** (Evgeny), **Wertmuller** (Lina), **Zeffirelli** (Franco), **Zetterling** (Mai), **Zhang Yimou**

**11** **Bogdanovich** (Peter), **Dingelstedt** (Franz von), **Mackendrick** (Alexander), **Pressburger** (Emeric), **Riefenstahl** (Leni), **Roddenberry** (Gene), **Schlesinger** (John)

**12** **Attenborough** (Sir Richard), **Espert Romero** (Nuria), **Stanislavsky**, **Von Sternberg** (Josef)

**13** **Aguilera Malta** (Demetrio), **Gutiérrez Alea** (Tomás), **Stafford-Clark** (Max)

---

**• directors**
**05** board

**• managing director**
**02** MD **06** Man Dir

**directory**
**04** list **05** guide, index **06** folder **07** listing, red book, who's who **09** catalogue, inventory **10** court guide **11** Yellow Pages®

**dirge**
**05** elegy **06** dirige, lament, monody **07** requiem **08** coronach, threnody **09** dead-march **11** funeral song

**dirk**
**07** whinger **08** skean-dhu, skene-dhu, whiniard, whinyard **10** skene-occle

**dirt**
**03** mud **04** clay, crap, crud, dust, grot, gunk, loam, mess, mire, muck, pick, smut, soil, soot, yuck **05** bilge, clart, crock, earth, filth, grime, gunge, scuzz, slime, stain **06** clarts, grunge, ordure, scunge, sleaze, sludge, smudge **07** gutters, rubbish, tarnish **08** impurity, lewdness **09** excrement, indecency, obscenity, pollution **10** sordidness **11** pornography **13** salaciousness

**dirty**
**03** bad, mud, ray **04** blue, dark, dull, foul, lewd, mean, mess, miry, poxy, soil, soss **05** bawdy, black, clart, dusty, grimy, manky, messy, mucky, muddy, nasty, slimy, smear, sooty, spoil, stain, sully, yucky **06** assoil, chatty, clarty, cloudy, coarse, cruddy, defile, filthy, greasy, grotty, grubby, grungy, mess up, mingin', muck up, ribald, risqué, scungy, shabby, skanky, sleazy, smirch, smudge, smutty, soiled, sordid, splash, stormy, unfair, vulgar, X-rated **07** begrime, blacken, clouded, corrupt, defiled, draggle, grufted, immoral, minging, obscene, piggish, pollute, raunchy, scruffy, squalid, stained, sullied, tarnish, unclean **08** bedaggle, besmirch, discolor, enormous, improper, indecent, polluted, unwashed **09** bedraggle, deceitful, discolour, dishonest, salacious, tarnished **10** adulterate, despicable, flea-bitten, insanitary, suggestive, unhygienic, unpleasant **11** contaminate, treacherous, undesirable **12** contaminated, contemptible, pornographic, unscrupulous

**disability**
**04** maim **06** defect, malady **07** ailment, illness **08** disorder, handicap, weakness **09** complaint, inability, infirmity, unfitness **10** affliction, difficulty, impairment, incapacity **11** disablement **12** incapability

**disable**
**04** lame, maim, stop **05** crock, wreck **06** damage, defuse, impair, weaken **07** cripple, invalid **08** enfeeble, handicap, knock out, paralyse **09** disparage, hamstring, make unfit, prostrate **10** deactivate, debilitate, depreciate, disqualify, immobilize, invalidate, undervalue **12** incapacitate **14** put out of action

**disabled**
**04** lame, weak **05** unfit **06** infirm, maimed **07** invalid, wrecked **08** crippled, impaired, weakened **09** bed-ridden, enfeebled, paralysed **10** indisposed **11** debilitated, handicapped, immobilized, out of action **12** hors de combat **13** incapacitated

**disabuse**
**09** enlighten, undeceive **10** disappoint, disenchant **11** disillusion

**disadvantage**
**03** out **04** flaw, harm, hurt, lack, loss, snag **05** catch, minus **06** damage, defect, hang-up, injury **07** own goal, penalty, trouble **08** downside, drawback, handicap, hardship, nuisance, weakness **09** detriment, hindrance, liability, prejudice, privation, weak point **10** disamenity, disbenefit, disservice, disutility, impediment, limitation **11** disinterest **12** Achilles heel **13** inconvenience

**disadvantaged**
**04** poor **06** in need, in want **08** deprived **10** in distress, struggling

**11** handicapped **12** impoverished
**15** poverty-stricken, underprivileged

**disadvantageous**
**07** adverse, hapless, harmful, hurtful, unlucky **08** damaging, ill-timed
**09** injurious **11** deleterious, detrimental, inexpedient, inopportune, prejudicial, unfortunate
**12** inconvenient, unfavourable

**disaffected**
**07** hostile **08** disloyal, mutinous
**09** alienated, estranged, malignant, seditious **10** rebellious, unfriendly
**11** disgruntled, ill-disposed
**12** antagonistic, discontented, dissatisfied

**disaffection**
**07** discord, dislike, ill-will **08** aversion, coolness **09** animosity, hostility
**10** alienation, antagonism, disharmony, disloyalty, resentment
**12** disagreement, estrangement
**14** discontentment, disgruntlement, unfriendliness **15** dissatisfaction

**disagree**
**04** vary **05** argue, clash, fight, upset
**06** bicker, differ, object, oppose, sicken **07** contend, contest, discord, dispute, dissent, diverge, fall out, quarrel, wrangle **08** conflict, nauseate, squabble **09** be against, disaccord, take issue **10** contradict, make unwell, think wrong **11** beg to differ **12** argue against, be at odds with, cause illness, disapprove of **13** agree to differ, take issue with

**disagreeable**
**03** bad **04** evil, rude, sour **05** cross, nasty, surly **07** awkward, beastly, brusque, grouchy, peevish **08** churlish, contrary, dreadful, horrible, impolite
**09** difficult, irritable, obnoxious, offensive, repellent, repugnant, repulsive, unhelpful, unsavoury
**10** abominable, disgusting, ill-natured, unfriendly, ungrateful, unpleasant
**11** bad-tempered, disobliging, displeasing, distasteful, ill-humoured, unpalatable **13** objectionable

**disagreeably**
**07** nastily **08** horribly **10** dreadfully
**11** obnoxiously, offensively, repulsively
**12** disgustingly, unpleasantly
**13** objectionably

**disagreement**
**03** row **04** flak, tiff **05** clash, fight
**06** bust-up, strife **07** discord, dispute, dissent, quarrel, wrangle **08** argument, clashing, conflict, disunion, friction, squabble, variance **09** deviation, disparity, dissensus, diversity
**10** conformity, contention, difference, disharmony, dissension, dissidence, dissonance, divergence, falling-out, unlikeness **11** altercation, contretemps, discrepancy, disputation, incongruity
**13** dissimilarity, dissimilitude, inconsistency **14** unpleasantness, unsuitableness **15** incompatibility

**• expression of disagreement**
**02** ah, h'm **03** boo, gup, hmm, hum, nah, naw, rot **04** booh, quep, uh-uh
**05** arrah **06** hardly **08** nonsense
**09** do you mind?

**disallow**
**03** ban **04** veto **05** debar **06** abjure, cancel, disown, forbid, rebuff, refuse, reject **07** disavow, dismiss, embargo, exclude, say no to **08** disclaim, overrule, prohibit **09** disaffirm, dispraise, interdict, proscribe, repudiate, surcharge

**disappear**
◇ *deletion indicator*
**02** go **03** ebb, end, fly **04** exit, fade, flee, hide, melt, pass, walk, wane
**05** cease, ghost, slope **06** depart, die out, escape, expire, go cold, perish, recede, retire, vanish **07** die away, drop off, drop out, get lost, pass off, scarper, vamoose **08** dissolve, drop away, evanesce, melt away, peter out, withdraw **09** dissipate, evaporate, go missing **10** make tracks, take flight
**12** go out of sight **13** become extinct, dematerialize, pass from sight **14** go like hot cakes **15** take French leave

**disappearance**
◇ *deletion indicator*
**03** end **04** exit, loss **05** going
**06** expiry, fading, flight **07** passing
**08** dying-out, fade-away
**09** departure, desertion, immersion, vanishing **10** extinction, karyolysis, resolution, withdrawal
**11** evanescence, evaporation, melting away

**disappoint**
**03** vex **04** fail, foil, mock **06** baffle, betray, defeat, delude, dismay, hamper, hinder, sadden, slip up, thwart
**07** deceive, depress, let down
**08** dispirit, mistryst **09** devastate, frustrate, mislippen **10** disconcert, discourage, disenchant, disgruntle, dishearten, dissatisfy **11** disillusion, make a fool of

**disappointed**
**04** sick **05** upset, vexed **06** balked, choked, gutted, miffed **07** let-down
**08** betrayed, cast down, deflated, saddened, thwarted **09** depressed
**10** despondent, devastated, dischuffed, distressed, frustrated, unequipped **11** discouraged, disgruntled, downhearted, ill-equipped **12** disconsolate, disenchanted, disheartened, dissatisfied **13** disillusioned, sick as a parrot

**disappointing**
**03** sad **05** bogus, sorry **07** unhappy
**08** inferior, pathetic, unworthy
**10** depressing, inadequate
**12** disagreeable, discouraging, insufficient **13** anticlimactic, disconcerting, underwhelming
**14** unsatisfactory

**disappointment**
**04** balk, blow, sell, swiz **05** baulk, frost, lemon **06** bummer, fiasco, fizzer, regret, suck-in, take-in **07** chagrin, failure, let-down, sadness, setback, swizzle, washout, wipeout
**08** calamity, comedown, disaster, distress, non-event **09** damp squib
**10** anticlimax, bitter pill, discontent, misfortune **11** cold comfort, despondency, displeasure, frustration
**14** discouragement, disenchantment, dispiritedness **15** disillusionment, dissatisfaction

**• expression of disappointment**
**02** aw **04** nuts, pity **05** shoot
**06** shucks

**disapprobation**
**05** blame **07** censure, dislike, mislike, reproof **08** reproach **09** criticism, disfavour, exception, objection
**11** disapproval, displeasure
**12** condemnation, denunciation
**13** disparagement, remonstration
**14** discountenance **15** dissatisfaction

**disapproval**
**04** veto **05** blame **06** rebuke
**07** censure, disgust, dislike, reproof
**08** reproach **09** criticism, exception, misliking, objection, rejection
**11** displeasure **12** condemnation, denunciation, disallowance
**13** disparagement, remonstration, the thumbs-down **14** disapprobation
**15** dissatisfaction

**• expression of disapproval**
**01** O **02** oh **03** boo, fie, tut **04** booh, toot, tuts, umph, what **05** humph, toots **06** tut-tut **07** fie upon **10** hoity-toity

**• indication of disapproval**
**03** boo **04** booh, hiss **05** frown
**07** catcall, walk out **09** dirty look, raspberry **10** Bronx cheer, thumbs down **12** slow handclap **13** shake your head

**disapprove**
**04** veto **05** blame, spurn **06** reject
**07** censure, condemn, deplore, dislike, frown on, mislike **08** denounce, disallow, disfavor, disprove, harrumph, object to **09** be against, deprecate, disesteem, disfavour, disparage, disproove, reprobate **10** animadvert, look down on **11** not hold with **12** think badly of **13** think little of
**14** discountenance, hold in contempt, take a dim view of **15** take exception to

**disapproving**
**04** prim **07** killjoy **08** critical, frowning
**09** reproving **10** censorious, derogatory, pejorative **11** deprecatory, disparaging, improbative, improbatory, reproachful **12** condemnatory
**14** disapprobative, disapprobatory

**disarm**
**05** charm, unarm **07** appease, disable, disband, mollify, placate, unsteel, win over **08** persuade, unweapon
**10** conciliate, deactivate, demobilize,

immobilize **11** lay down arms **12** demilitarize **13** make powerless **14** lay down weapons, put out of action

**disarmament**
**11** arms control **12** deactivation **13** arms reduction **14** arms limitation, demobilization

**disarming**
**07** winning **08** charming, likeable **10** mollifying, persuasive **12** conciliatory, irresistible

**disarmingly**
**10** charmingly, pleasantly **12** irresistibly, persuasively

**disarrange**
◇ *anagram indicator*
**04** mess, muss **05** musse **06** jumble, tousle, touzle, untidy **07** confuse, derange, disturb, shuffle **08** dishevel, disorder, displace, unsettle **09** dislocate **10** discompose **11** disorganize **13** put out of place

**disarray**
◇ *anagram indicator*
**04** mess, tash **05** chaos, rifle, upset **06** jumble, muddle, tangle **07** clutter, undress **08** disorder, shambles **09** confusion **10** unruliness, untidiness **11** derangement **12** dishevelment, indiscipline **13** unsettledness **15** disorganization

**disassemble**
**08** separate **09** dismantle, pull apart, take apart **12** pull to pieces, take to pieces

**disassociate**
**05** break **06** cut off, remove **08** separate, withdraw **10** disconnect, dissociate

**disaster**
**04** blow, flop, ruin **06** fiasco, mishap, mucker, stroke **07** debacle, failure, reverse, screw-up, setback, tragedy, trouble, washout, wipeout **08** accident, act of God, calamity, reversal **09** adversity, cataclysm, holocaust, mischance, ruination, shipwreck, sticky end **10** misfortune, providence **11** catastrophe, horror story **12** misadventure

**disastrous**
◇ *anagram indicator*
**04** dire **05** fatal **06** gloomy, tragic **07** adverse, harmful, ruinous, unlucky **08** dreadful, ill-fated, ravaging, shocking, terrible, tragical **09** appalling, injurious, miserable **10** calamitous, ill-starred **11** cataclysmic, destructive, devastating, unfortunate **12** catastrophic

**disavow**
**04** deny **06** abjure, disown, reject **08** disvouch, renounce **09** disaffirm, disavouch, repudiate **10** contradict **15** wash your hands of

**disavowal**
**06** denial **07** dissent **09** rejection **10** abjuration, disclaimer **11** repudiation **12** disclamation, renunciation **13** contradiction **14** disaffirmation

**disband**
◇ *anagram indicator*
**05** demob **06** disarm, reduce, reform **07** break up, dismiss, scatter **08** disperse, dissolve, separate **10** demobilize **11** part company **14** go separate ways

**disbelief**
**05** doubt **07** atheism, dubiety, scruple **08** acosmism, distrust, mistrust, unbelief **09** discredit, rejection, suspicion **10** infidelity, scepticism **11** incredulity, questioning
• **expression of disbelief**
**03** huh, tut **04** as if!, hoot **05** hoots **06** heaven, indeed, phooey, Walker **07** get away, says you **08** honestly, hoot-toot **09** away you go! **11** away with you, Betty Martin **12** Hookey Walker **13** what do you know?

**disbelieve**
**05** doubt **06** reject **07** suspect **08** discount, distrust, mistrust, question **09** discredit, miscredit, repudiate **13** be unconvinced

**disbeliever**
**07** atheist, doubter, sceptic, scoffer **08** agnostic **10** questioner, unbeliever **11** non-believer, nullifidian **14** doubting Thomas

**disbelieving**
**07** cynical, infidel **08** doubtful, doubting **09** sceptical, uncertain **10** suspicious **11** distrustful, incredulous, unbelieving, unconvinced

**disburse**
**05** spend **06** expend, lay out, pay out **07** cough up, dish out, fork out **08** shell out

**disbursement**
**06** outlay **07** payment **08** disposal, spending **09** disbursal, outgiving **11** expenditure

**disc**
**01** O **02** CD, EP, LP **03** DVD **04** disk, face, gong, ring **05** album, CD-ROM, elpee, paten, plate, round, vinyl, wheel **06** button, circle, discus, record, saucer **07** counter, rosette, roundel **08** diskette, hard disk, roundlet **10** floppy disk **11** compact disk, microfloppy

**discard**
**03** bin **04** cast, defy, drop, dump, jilt, junk, kill, shed **05** ditch, scrap, trash **06** reject, remove **07** abandon, cashier, cast off, dismiss, forsake, lay away, toss out **08** chuck out, get rid of, jettison, lay aside, throw out **09** cast aside, chuck away, discharge, dismissal, dispose of, repudiate, supersede, throw away, throw over **10** pension off, relinquish **11** abandonment **12** dispense with

**discards**
**04** crib

**discern**
**03** get, see, wit **04** spot, tell **05** judge **06** descry, detect, notice, scerne **07** make out, observe, pick out **08** discover, perceive, tell from **09** ascertain, determine, recognize **11** distinguish **12** discriminate **13** differentiate

**discernible**
**05** clear, plain **06** patent **07** obvious, visible **08** apparent, distinct, manifest **10** detectable, noticeable, observable **11** appreciable, conspicuous, perceptible **12** discoverable, recognizable **15** distinguishable

**discerning**
**04** wise **05** acute, quick, sharp, sound **06** astute, clever, seeing, shrewd, subtle **07** prudent, sapient, trained **08** critical, piercing, tasteful **09** clear-eyed, eagle-eyed, ingenious, judicious, sagacious, selective, sensitive **10** perceptive, percipient **11** intelligent, penetrating **12** clear-sighted, eagle-sighted **13** perspicacious, understanding **14** discriminating

**discernment**
**05** flair, sense, taste **06** acumen, wisdom **07** insight **08** keenness, sagacity, sapience **09** acuteness, awareness, good taste, ingenuity, judgement, sharpness **10** cleverness, perception, shrewdness **11** penetration, percipience **12** intelligence, perspicacity **13** ascertainment, understanding **14** discrimination, perceptiveness

**discharge**
**02** do **03** arc, axe, pay, pus, ren, rin, run **04** emit, fire, flow, free, gush, leak, meet, ooze, oust, pass, pour, sack, vent, void **05** clear, congé, doing, drain, egest, eject, empty, expel, exude, issue, let go, loose, rheum, salvo, shoot, spout **06** acquit, congee, firing, forbid, fulfil, honour, let fly, let off, let out, pardon, remove, sanies, set off, settle, unload **07** absolve, boot out, discard, dismiss, excrete, explode, exuding, fire off, fluxion, give off, ousting, outflow, payment, perform, release, relieve, removal, sacking, satisfy, send out, set free, the boot, the sack, turf out **08** carry out, detonate, disgorge, dispense, displode, ejection, emission, evacuate, get rid of, liberate, settling, the elbow, turn away **09** acquittal, bowler-hat, broadside, clearance, colluvies, disburden, dismissal, excretion, exculpate, execution, exonerate, expulsion, honouring, quitclaim, repayment, secretion, unfraught, unloading **10** absolution, cashiering, disburthen,

disembogue, fulfilment, liberation, the heave-ho **11** achievement, carrying-out, exculpation, exoneration, performance, suppuration **12** give the elbow **13** give the boot to **14** accomplishment

**disciple**
**03** son **05** chela, child, pupil **06** votary **07** apostle, convert, devotee, learner, scholar, student **08** adherent, believer, follower, upholder **09** proselyte, supporter
*See also* **apostle**

**disciplinarian**
**06** despot, ramrod, tyrant **08** autocrat, martinet, stickler **10** taskmaster **13** authoritarian **14** hard taskmaster

**discipline**
**04** bull, curb, judo **05** check, drill, inure, limit, order, teach, train, tutor **06** branch, disple, govern, ground, moguls, punish, rebuke, school **07** break in, chasten, control, correct, educate, regimen, reprove, routine, subject **08** chastise, dressage, exercise, feng shui, instruct, mathesis, penalize, practice, regulate, restrain, restrict, training **09** castigate, direction, inculcate, reprimand, restraint, schooling **10** correction, punishment, regulation, speciality, strictness **11** area of study, castigation, keep in check, orderliness, self-control **12** chastisement, field of study **13** course of study, mortification, self-restraint **14** self-discipline **15** make an example of

**disclaim**
**04** deny **06** abjure, disown, refuse, reject **07** abandon, declaim, decline, disavow **08** renounce **09** repudiate **15** wash your hands of

**disclaimer**
**06** denial **09** disavowal, rejection **10** abjuration, abnegation, disownment, retraction **11** repudiation **12** renunciation **13** contradiction **14** disaffirmation

**disclose**
**04** blab, leak, open, show, tell **05** hatch, let on, unrip **06** betray, evolve, expose, impart, open up, relate, reveal, squeal, unfold, unheal, unhele, unlock, unveil **07** confess, develop, divulge, exhibit, lay bare, let drop, let slip, open out, propale, publish, unclose, uncover **08** blurt out, develope, discover **09** broadcast, make known, tell a tale **10** disclosure, make public **11** blow the gaff, communicate **12** bring to light **13** spill the beans **14** blow the whistle **15** give the game away, take the wraps off

**disclosure**
**04** leak **06** exposé **08** exposure, overture **09** admission, broadcast, discovery **10** apocalypse, confession, divulgence, laying bare, revelation, uncovering **11** declaration, publication **12** announcement **15** acknowledgement, bringing to light

**discoloration**
**04** blot, mark, spot **05** patch, stain **06** blotch, foxing, streak **07** blemish, blue-rot, pink-eye, splotch, tarnish **08** cyanosis, dyschroa, foxiness **09** dyschroia, melanosis **10** ecchymosis **12** acrocyanosis, weather stain **13** xanthochromia

**discolour**
**03** fox, mar **04** fade, mark, rust, soil **05** dirty, stain, tinge **06** bruise, streak **07** tarnish, weather **09** disfigure

**discomfit**
◇ *anagram indicator*
**04** balk, faze, rout **05** abash, shend, throw **06** baffle, defeat, outwit, rattle, ruffle, thwart **07** confuse, fluster, perplex, perturb **08** confound, unsettle **09** embarrass, frustrate **10** demoralize, discompose, disconcert

**discomfiture**
**05** lurch **06** unease **07** chagrin **09** abashment, confusion **10** uneasiness **11** frustration, humiliation **12** discomposure **13** embarrassment **14** demoralization, disappointment

**discomfort**
**04** ache, hell, hurt, pain, pang **05** worry **06** bother, hassle, jet lag, misery, twinge, unease **07** malaise, trouble **08** disquiet, distress, drawback, hardship, nuisance, soreness, vexation **09** annoyance, purgatory **10** cardialgia, difficulty, irritation, tenderness, uneasiness **12** apprehension, disadvantage, restlessness, unpleasantry **13** embarrassment, inconvenience

**discompose**
◇ *anagram indicator*
**06** ruffle **07** agitate, disturb **08** disorder **10** disarrange

**discomposure**
**05** upset **06** unease **07** anxiety, fluster **09** agitation, annoyance **10** inquietude, irritation, uneasiness **11** disquietude, disturbance **12** perturbation, restlessness

**disconcert**
◇ *anagram indicator*
**04** faze **05** abash, alarm, blank, quell, shake, tease, throw, upset **06** baffle, defeat, dismay, put off, put out, rattle, ruffle **07** break up, confuse, disturb, fluster, nonplus, perplex, perturb, startle, stumble, unnerve **08** bewilder, disunion, surprise, throw off, throw out, unsettle **09** discomfit, embarrass, frustrate, knock back, take aback **14** discomboberate, discombobulate **15** throw off balance

**disconcerting**
◇ *anagram indicator*
**07** awkward **08** alarming, baffling, daunting **09** confusing, dismaying, unnerving, upsetting **10** bothersome, disturbing, off-putting, perplexing, perturbing, unsettling **11** bewildering, distracting **12** embarrassing

**disconnect**
**04** part, undo **05** loose, sever, split **06** cut off, detach, divide, ungear, unhook, unplug **07** disjoin, unhitch **08** disjoint, separate, uncouple **09** disengage **10** de-energize

**disconnected**
**05** loose **06** abrupt **07** garbled, jumbled, mixed-up, scrappy **08** confused, rambling, staccato **09** illogical, separated, wandering **10** disjointed, incoherent, irrational **12** inconsequent **13** unco-ordinated **14** unintelligible

**disconnection**
**07** undoing **08** division **09** severance **10** detachment, separation, uncoupling, unplugging **13** disengagement

**disconsolate**
**03** low, sad **04** down **06** gloomy **07** crushed, forlorn, unhappy **08** dejected, desolate, downcast, hopeless, wretched **09** depressed, miserable **10** despondent, dispirited, melancholy **11** heartbroken, low-spirited **12** heavy-hearted, inconsolable **13** grief-stricken **14** down in the dumps

**disconsolately**
**05** sadly **09** miserably, unhappily **10** dejectedly, desolately, wretchedly **12** despondently, inconsolably **14** heavy-heartedly

**discontent**
**06** misery, regret, unrest **08** disquiet, vexation **09** fed-upness **10** impatience, uneasiness **11** displeasure, fretfulness, unhappiness **12** disaffection, dissatisfied, heartburning, restlessness, wretchedness **15** dissatisfaction

**discontented**
**05** fed up **07** unhappy **08** restless, wretched **09** impatient, miserable, pissed off **10** browned off, cheesed off, displeased, malcontent **11** complaining, disaffected, disgruntled, exasperated **12** dissatisfied

**discontinue**
**03** end **04** drop, halt, quit, stop **05** cease, scrap **06** cancel, finish **07** abandon, abolish, refrain, suspend **08** break off, knock off, withdraw **09** interrupt, terminate **10** do away with **11** come to an end, come to a stop

**discontinued**
**03** dis, off **07** at an end

**discontinuity**
**05** break, comma **06** breach **07** rupture **08** disunion **09** nickpoint **10** disruption, knickpoint

**11** incoherence **12** interruption
**13** disconnection **14** disjointedness

**discontinuous**
**06** broken, fitful **08** discrete, periodic, sporadic **09** irregular, separated, spasmodic **10** punctuated
**11** interrupted **12** disconnected, intermittent

**discord**
◇ *anagram indicator*
**03** row **05** split **06** jangle, strife
**07** dispute, dissent, jarring
**08** argument, clashing, conflict, disagree, disunity, division, friction, jangling **09** cacophony, disaccord, harshness, wrangling **10** contention, difference, disharmony, dissension, dissonance, opposition, suspension
**11** discordance **12** disagreement
**13** inharmonicity **15** discord of sounds, incompatibility

**discordant**
◇ *anagram indicator*
**04** flat **05** harsh, sharp **06** at odds, atonal, hoarse, off-key **07** grating, hostile, jarring **08** absonant, clashing, jangling, opposing, strident
**09** differing, dissonant **10** at variance, dissenting **11** cacophonous, conflicting, disagreeing, disharmonic, incongruous, unagreeable
**12** incompatible, inconsistent, inharmonious **13** contradictory

**discount**
**03** cut **04** agio **05** slash **06** deduct, ignore, rebate, reduce **07** dismiss, take off **08** cut price, knock off, mark down, mark-down, overlook, pass over, pooh-pooh **09** allowance, deduction, disregard, gloss over, reduction
**10** concession, disbelieve, rebatement

**discourage**
**04** damp **05** chill, daunt, deter
**06** dampen, deject, dismay, hinder, put off **07** depress, prevent, unnerve
**08** cast down, choke off, dispirit, dissuade, hold back, restrain **09** talk out of **10** demoralize, disappoint, dishearten **12** put a damper on
**13** advise against **14** discountenance
**15** pour cold water on

**discouraged**
**04** glum **06** dashed **07** daunted, let down **08** deflated, dejected, dismayed, downcast **09** depressed
**10** dispirited **11** crestfallen, demoralized, pessimistic
**12** disheartened **14** down in the dumps

**discouragement**
**04** curb, damp **05** gloom **06** damper, dismay, rebuff **07** barrier, despair, setback **08** obstacle **09** dejection, deterrent, hindrance, pessimism, restraint **10** depression, impediment, opposition **11** despondency
**12** disincentive, hopelessness
**14** disappointment
**15** downheartedness

**discouraging**
**08** daunting **09** dampening
**10** depressing, dissuasive, dissuasory, off-putting **11** dehortatory, dispiriting
**12** demoralizing, inauspicious, unfavourable, unpropitious
**13** disappointing, disheartening

**discourse**
**04** chat, tale, talk **05** essay, speak, spell
**06** confer, debate, homily, preach, reason, sermon, speech, tongue
**07** address, discuss, lecture, oration
**08** chit-chat, colloquy, converse, dialogue, exercise, treatise
**09** discursus, hold forth, rigmarole
**10** discussion, exposition, meditation, preachment **11** exhortation, highfalutin **12** conversation, disquisition, dissertation, exercitation, highfaluting **13** communication, confabulation

**discourteous**
**04** curt, rude **05** gruff, short **06** abrupt
**07** boorish, brusque, ill-bred, offhand, uncivil, uncouth **08** ignorant, impolite, impudent, insolent **09** offensive, truculent **10** ungracious, unmannerly, unpleasant **11** bad-mannered, ill-mannered, impertinent
**13** disrespectful, unceremonious

**discourteously**
**06** curtly, rudely **07** gruffly
**08** abruptly **09** brusquely, uncivilly
**10** impolitely, impudently, insolently
**11** offensively, offhandedly
**12** ungraciously, unpleasantly
**13** impertinently **15** disrespectfully, unceremoniously

**discourtesy**
**04** snub **06** insult, rebuff, slight
**07** affront **08** curtness, rudeness
**09** indecorum, insolence **10** bad manners, disrespect, incivility
**11** brusqueness, ill-breeding
**12** impertinence, impoliteness
**14** indecorousness, ungraciousness, unmannerliness

**discover**
◇ *anagram indicator*
◇ *hidden indicator*
**03** see, spy, sus **04** espy, find, spot, suss, twig **05** dig up, hit on, learn, trace
**06** create, descry, detect, devise, fathom, invent, locate, notice, reveal, rumble, sus out, turn up, unmask
**07** analyse, compose, discern, discure, exhibit, find out, get onto, hit upon, light on, make out, pioneer, realize, suss out, uncover, unearth, work out
**08** disclose, discoure, perceive, smoke out, sound out **09** ascertain, determine, establish, fathom out, ferret out, get wind of, get wise to, originate, recognize, stumble on **10** come across, come to know, excogitate
**11** come to light **12** find out about
**13** stumble across

**discoverer**
**05** scout **06** author, finder **07** creator, deviser, founder, pioneer **08** explorer, informer, inventor **09** initiator
**10** originator

**discovery**
**04** find **06** descry, eureka **07** finding, heureka **08** devising, findings, learning, location, research
**09** detection, invention **10** disclosure, innovation, pioneering, revelation
**11** discernment, exploration, origination, realization, recognition
**12** breakthrough, introduction
**13** determination
• **expression of discovery**
**05** bingo, hallo, hello, hullo **06** eureka
**07** heureka

**discredit**
**04** deny, slag, slur **05** blame, doubt, shame, slate, smear **06** damage, debunk, defame, infamy, refute, reject, stigma, vilify **07** censure, degrade, discard, explode, rubbish, run down, scandal, slag off, slander, tarnish
**08** badmouth, belittle, disgrace, disprove, distrust, ignominy, mistrust, question, reproach **09** aspersion, challenge, dishonour, disparage, disrepute, ill-repute, reflect on
**10** disbelieve, invalidate, opprobrium
**11** humiliation **14** put in a bad light, reflect badly on

**discreditable**
**06** shabby **08** improper, infamous, shameful, unworthy **09** degrading
**10** scandalous **11** blameworthy, disgraceful **12** disreputable
**13** dishonourable, reprehensible

**discreet**
**04** wary, wise **05** witty **06** modest
**07** careful, guarded, politic, prudent, tactful **08** cautious, delicate, detached, reserved, sensible, separate
**09** judicious **10** diplomatic
**11** circumspect, considerate
**13** unpretentious

**discreetly**
**06** wisely **08** sensibly **09** carefully, prudently, tactfully **10** cautiously, delicately **11** judiciously
**13** circumspectly, considerately
**14** diplomatically

**discrepancy**
**08** conflict, variance **09** deviation, disparity, variation **10** difference, divergence, inequality **11** discordance, incongruity **12** disagreement
**13** contradiction, dissimilarity, inconsistency

**discrete**
**08** abstract, detached, disjunct, distinct, separate **09** disjoined
**10** individual, unattached
**12** disconnected **13** discontinuous

**discretion**
**04** care, tact, will, wish **06** choice, desire, wisdom **07** caution, freedom, reserve **08** prudence, volition, wariness **09** diplomacy, good sense, judgement **10** preference
**11** carefulness, discernment,

guardedness, inclination **12** predilection **13** consideration, judiciousness **14** circumspection

**discretionary**
**04** open **08** elective, optional **09** voluntary **12** unrestricted

**discriminate**
**06** secern **07** discern **08** be biased, separate **09** segregate, tell apart, victimize **11** distinguish **12** be intolerant, be prejudiced **13** differentiate, show prejudice, treat unfairly

**discriminating**
**04** keen **05** acute **06** astute, nasute, shrewd **08** critical, delicate, tasteful **09** invidious, selective, sensitive **10** cultivated, discerning, fastidious, particular, perceptive, respective **12** differential, preferential

**discrimination**
**04** bias **05** skill, taste **06** acumen, ageism, racism, sexism, sizism **07** ableism, bigotry, fattism, insight, Jim Crow, lookism, sizeism **08** classism, inequity, judgment, keenness, subtlety **09** acuteness, colour bar, judgement, prejudice **10** astuteness, difference, differency, homophobia, perception, refinement, shrewdness, unfairness **11** discernment, distinction, favouritism, intolerance, penetration, segregation, sensitivity **12** heterosexism, perspicacity **14** male chauvinism

**discriminatory**
**06** biased, loaded, unfair, unjust **07** partial **08** one-sided, partisan, weighted **09** favouring **10** prejudiced **11** inequitable, prejudicial **12** preferential **14** discriminative

**discursive**
**05** wordy **06** prolix **07** diffuse, verbose **08** rambling **09** wandering **10** circuitous, digressing, long-winded, meandering **11** wide-ranging

**discuss**
**03** vex **04** sift, toss **05** argue, study, treat **06** confer, debate, decide, dispel, go into, handle, parley, reason, review, settle, take up **07** agitate, analyse, belabor, beprose, canvass, consult, declare, examine, speak to, weigh up **08** belabour, consider, converse, critique, deal with, question, talk over **09** discourse, kick about, pro and con, talk about, thrash out **10** deliberate, interplead, kick around, knock about, politicize **11** confabulate, expostulate, knock around **12** go into detail **15** exchange views on

**discussion**
**03** rap **04** chat, conf, moot, talk **05** forum, study, talks **06** debate, korero, parley, powwow, review, talk-in **07** gabfest, palaver, seminar **08** analysis, argument, dialogue, exchange, question, scrutiny, speaking, talkfest **09** discourse, symposium, talkathon **10** colloquium, conference, rap session **11** examination **12** consultation, conversation, deliberation, negotiations **13** consideration

**disdain**
**03** coy **04** snub **05** scorn, sdayn, sdein, spurn **06** deride, ignore, rebuff, reject, sdaine, sdeign, slight **07** contemn, despise, disavow, dislike, sdeigne, sneer at **08** belittle, contempt, derision, pooh-pooh, sneering, turn down **09** arrogance, contumely, disregard **10** look down on, sour grapes, undervalue **11** deprecation, haughtiness **12** cold shoulder, snobbishness, think scorn of **13** disparagement

**• expression of disdain**
**04** pooh, tush **06** powwaw

**• show disdain**
**04** geck

**disdainful**
**05** aloof, proud, saucy **07** haughty, pompous **08** arrogant, derisive, insolent, scornful, sneering, superior **09** slighting **11** disparaging **12** contemptuous, supercilious

**disease**
**03** bug, pox **05** virus **06** malady **07** ailment, illness **08** disorder, epidemic, sickness **09** complaint, condition, contagion, ill-health, infection, infirmity **10** affliction, disability, uneasiness **13** indisposition, unhealthiness

*Diseases and medical conditions include:*

**02** CF, ME, MS, TB
**03** CFS, CJD, DVT, flu, FMS, IBS, PID, PKU, PVS, tic, TSS
**04** AIDS, clap, cold, coma, gout, kuru, Lyme, mono, rash, SARS
**05** colic, croup, favus, lupus, mumps, polio, Weil's
**06** angina, apnoea, asthma, autism, cancer, chorea, Crohn's, dropsy, eczema, emesis, goitre, Grave's, hernia, herpes, oedema, otitis, Paget's, quinsy, rabies, scurvy, stroke, thrush, tumour, typhus
**07** abscess, allergy, anaemia, anthrax, anxiety, atrophy, Batten's, bird flu, Bright's, bulimia, cholera, coeliac, kissing, leprosy, lockjaw, malaria, Marburg, measles, myalgia, mycosis, rickets, rubella, sarcoma, scabies, tetanus, typhoid, vertigo
**08** Addison's, alopecia, aneurism, anorexia, avian flu, beriberi, botulism, bursitis, cachexia, coxalgia, Cushing's, cynanche, cystitis, dementia, diabetes, embolism, epilepsy, fibroids, gangrene, glaucoma, Hodgkin's, impetigo, jaundice, kala-azar, listeria, lymphoma, melanoma, Ménière's, migraine, necrosis, orchitis, pyelitis, Raynaud's, rhinitis, ringworm, sciatica, shingles, smallpox, stenosis, syphilis, tapeworm, Tay-Sachs, tinnitus, trachoma, venereal, viraemia
**09** arthritis, arthrosis, bilharzia, chlamydia, chlorosis, cirrhosis, cri du chat, distemper, dysentery, eclampsia, emphysema, enteritis, hepatitis, influenza, ketonuria, leukaemia, neoplasia, nephritis, nephrosis, neuralgia, paralysis, parotitis, pertussis, pneumonia, psoriasis, pyorrhoea, silicosis, sinusitis, sunstroke, Sydenham's, toothache, urticaria, varicella
**10** acromegaly, Alzheimer's, amoebiasis, asbestosis, Bell's Palsy, Black Death, bronchitis, chickenpox, common cold, depression, diphtheria, gingivitis, gonorrhoea, laryngitis, Lassa fever, meningitis, Parkinson's, rhinorrhea, thrombosis
**11** anaphylaxis, brucellosis, cholestasis, consumption, dehydration, dengue fever, farmer's lung, green monkey, haemophilia, haemorrhage, heart attack, Huntington's, hydrophobia, hyperplasia, hypertrophy, hypotension, listeriosis, mastoiditis, motor neuron, myocarditis, peritonitis, pharyngitis, pneumonitis, proteinuria, psittacosis, sarcoidosis, septicaemia, spina bifida, tonsillitis, trench fever, yellow fever
**12** appendicitis, athlete's foot, cor pulmonale, encephalitis, endocarditis, foot-and-mouth, heart failure, Legionnaires', liver failure, osteoporosis, pericarditis, scarlet fever, tuberculosis
**13** bronchiolitis, bubonic plague, cerebral palsy, coronary heart, Down's syndrome, elephantiasis, endometriosis, German measles, kidney failure, leishmaniasis, mononucleosis, osteomyelitis, poliomyelitis, Rett's syndrome, Reye's syndrome, schizophrenia, toxoplasmosis, varicose veins, West Nile virus, whooping cough
**14** angina pectoris, break-bone fever, conjunctivitis, cystic fibrosis, glandular fever, osteoarthritis, pneumoconiosis, rheumatic fever, river blindness, sleepy sickness, thyrotoxicosis
**15** anorexia nervosa, atherosclerosis, bipolar disorder, gastro-enteritis, Gulf War syndrome, manic depression, phenylketonuria, schistosomiasis

*See also* **skin**

*Animal diseases include:*

**03** BSE, FMD, gid, orf
**04** gape, gout, loco, roup, wind
**05** bloat, braxy, farcy, frush, hoove, pearl, surra, vives
**06** canker, Johne's, mad cow, Marek's,

nagana, rabies, spavie, spavin, sturdy
**07** anthrax, blue ear, dourine, hard pad, measles, mooneye, moorill, murrain, roaring, rubbers, scrapie, yellows
**08** bovine TB, fowl-pest, glanders, pullorum, scaly-leg, seedy-toe, sheep-pox, staggers, swayback, swine-pox, wildfire, wire-heel
**09** Aujeszky's, blackhead, distemper, Newcastle, scratches, sheep scab, spauld-ill, St Hubert's, strangles
**10** blue tongue, louping-ill, ornithosis, rinderpest, sallenders, swamp fever, swine fever, Texas fever, water-brain
**11** blood-spavin, brucellosis, mad staggers, myxomatosis, parrot fever, psittacosis
**12** black-quarter, bush sickness, cattle-plague, foot-and-mouth, furunculosis, gall-sickness
**13** grass sickness, grass staggers, leptospirosis
**14** sleepy staggers
**15** Rift Valley fever, stomach staggers

*Plant diseases include:*

**04** bunt, curl, rust, smut
**05** ergot
**06** blight, blotch, canker, mildew, mosaic, red rot
**07** ferrugo, oak wilt, ring rot, rosette, soft rot, yellows
**08** blackleg, black rot, clubroot, crown rot, Dutch elm, leaf curl, loose-cut, wheat eel
**09** crown gall, potato rot, tulip root
**10** fire-blight, leaf mosaic, silver leaf, sooty mould, vine-mildew
**11** anthracnose, wheat mildew
**12** finger-and-toe, peach-yellows, potato blight
**13** powdery mildew
**14** psyllid yellows

*Disease symptoms include:*

**04** pain, rash
**05** cramp, fever, hives, sniff
**06** aching, lesion, tremor
**07** anxiety, fatigue, fitting, itching
**08** bruising, coughing, deafness, fainting, headache, insomnia, numbness, sickness, sneezing, swelling, tingling, vomiting, weakness
**09** blindness, diarrhoea, dizziness, heartburn, impotence, lassitude, nosebleed, paralysis, stiffness, twitching
**10** congestion, depression, flatulence, irritation, sore throat, tenderness
**11** convulsions, indigestion, loss of voice, trapped wind
**12** constipation, incontinence, inflammation, irritability, loss of libido, muscle cramps
**13** loss of hearing, stomach cramps, swollen glands
**14** loss of appetite, pins and needles
**15** high temperature, loss of sensation

**• abatement of disease**
**05** lysis
**• infectious diseases**
**02** ID

**diseased**
◇ *anagram indicator*
**03** ill **04** poxy, sick **06** ailing, infirm, unwell **07** unsound **08** blighted, infected, soul-sick **09** unhealthy **12** contaminated, distemperate

**disembark**
**04** land **05** leave **06** alight, arrive, debark, get off **07** deplane, detrain, disbark, step off **08** dismount

**disembarkation**
**07** arrival, landing **09** alighting

**disembodied**
**07** ghostly, phantom **08** bodiless, spectral **09** spiritual **10** discarnate, immaterial, intangible **11** incorporeal **12** discorporate

**disembowel**
◇ *middle deletion indicator*
**03** gut **04** draw **06** paunch **07** embowel **08** disbowel, gralloch **09** viscerate **10** eviscerate, exenterate

**disenchanted**
**05** blasé, fed up **06** soured **07** cynical, let down **09** jaundiced **11** discouraged, indifferent **12** disappointed, dissatisfied **13** disillusioned

**disenchantment**
**08** cynicism **09** fed-upness, revulsion **11** disillusion **14** disappointment **15** disillusionment, dissatisfaction

**disengage**
**04** free, slip, undo **05** untie **06** detach, loosen, remove, unhook **07** release, unhitch **08** disunite, liberate, separate, throw off, uncouple, unfasten, withdraw **09** extricate **10** disconnect **11** disentangle

**disengaged**
**04** free **05** clear, freed, loose **08** detached, released, separate **09** liberated, separated, unhitched **10** unattached, unoccupied **11** unconnected **12** disentangled

**disengagement**
**07** release, removal, retreat **09** loosening, releasing **10** detachment, retirement, separating, taking away, withdrawal **13** disconnection **15** disentanglement

**disentangle**
**03** red **04** free, redd, undo **05** loose, ravel **06** detach, unfold, unknot, unwind **07** clarify, release, resolve, unravel, unsnarl, untwist **08** distance, ravel out, separate, simplify, unfasten, untangle **09** debarrass, disengage, extricate **10** disconnect, disinvolve, straighten **11** distinguish **13** straighten out

**disfavour**
**06** oppose **07** disgust, dislike **08** distaste, ignominy **09** discredit, disesteem, disregard, disrepute, hostility **10** disapprove, low opinion, opprobrium **11** disapproval, displeasure **12** unpopularity **14** disapprobation **15** dissatisfaction

**disfigure**
◇ *anagram indicator*
**03** mar **04** blad, blur, flaw, maim, ruin, scar, tash **05** blaud, spoil **06** agrise, agrize, agryze, beweep, damage, deface, defeat, deform, injure, mangle **07** blemish, distort **08** discolor, make ugly, mutilate **09** defeature, discolour

**disfigurement**
**04** scar, spot, wart **05** stain **06** blotch, defect, injury **07** blemish **08** disgrace **09** defeature, deformity **10** defacement, distortion, impairment, mutilation **12** uglification

**disgorge**
**04** hawk, spew **05** belch, eject, empty, expel, spout, vomit **06** effuse **07** pour out, throw up **09** discharge **11** regurgitate

**disgrace**
**04** blot, slur **05** abase, atimy, blame, shame, shend, smear, stain, sully, taint **06** baffle, debase, defame, ignomy, infamy, stigma **07** attaint, degrade, obloquy, reproof, scandal, villany **08** belittle, contempt, dishonor, ignominy, reproach, ugliness, villainy **09** attainder, black mark, denigrate, discredit, disfavour, dishonour, disparage, disrepute, humiliate, indignify, indignity **10** debasement, defamation, disrespect, disworship, loss of face, opprobrium, put to shame, scandalize, stigmatize **11** degradation, humiliation **12** bring shame on **13** disfigurement **14** disapprobation **15** cause to lose face

**disgraced**
**06** shamed **07** branded **08** degraded **10** humiliated **11** discredited, dishonoured, stigmatized, under a cloud **13** in the doghouse

**disgraceful**
**05** awful **06** indign **08** culpable, dreadful, infamous, shameful, shocking, terrible, unworthy **09** appalling, degrading **10** despicable, inglorious, outrageous, scandalled, scandalous **11** blameworthy, ignominious, opprobrious, reproachful **12** contemptible, dishonorable, disreputable **13** discreditable, dishonourable, reprehensible

**disgracefully**
**07** awfully **08** terribly **10** despicably, dreadfully, shamefully, shockingly **11** appallingly **12** contemptibly, disreputably, outrageously, scandalously **13** dishonourably, ignominiously, reprehensibly

**disgruntled**
◇ *anagram indicator*
**05** fed up, sulky, testy, vexed

**06** grumpy, peeved, put out, sullen **07** annoyed, chuffed, peevish **08** petulant **09** hacked off, irritated, resentful **10** brassed off, browned off, cheesed off, displeased, malcontent **11** exasperated **12** discontented, dissatisfied

**disguise**
◇ *anagram indicator*
**04** face, fake, hide, mask, ring, veil **05** cloak, cloke, color, cover, feign, front, fudge, visor, vizor **06** colour, façade, immask, mantle, screen, shroud, veneer, vizard **07** conceal, costume, cover up, deceive, dress up, falsify, pretend, repress **08** palliate, pretence, suppress, travesty **09** coverture, deception, dissemble, gloss over, whitewash **10** camouflage, masquerade **11** concealment, dissimulate, impersonate **12** be under cover, cook the books, false picture, misrepresent **15** put on a brave face

**disguised**
◇ *anagram indicator*
**04** fake **05** false **06** covert, hidden, made up, masked, veiled **07** cloaked, feigned **09** incognito **10** under cover **11** camouflaged **14** unrecognizable

**disgust**
**03** irk, pip **04** cloy **05** repel, shock **06** hatred, nausea, offend, put off, revolt, sicken, turn up **07** outrage, scunner, turn off **08** aversion, distaste, gross out, loathing, nauseate, scomfish **09** disfavour, displease, disrelish, repulsion, revulsion **10** abhorrence, repugnance **11** detestation, disapproval, displeasure **15** turn your stomach

**• expression of disgust**
**02** aw, fy **03** bah, fie, foh, huh, pah, paw, pho, sis, ugh, wow, yah, yuk **04** damn, phoh, pooh, tush, whow, yech, yuck **05** faugh, shoot, wowee **06** powwaw **07** brother **11** for God's sake **14** for heaven's sake

**disgusted**
**04** sick **06** put off **08** appalled, offended, outraged, repelled, repulsed, revolted, sickened, up in arms **10** cheesed off

**disgusting**
**03** bad **04** foul, vile **05** grody, gross, nasty, slimy, yucky, yukky **06** odious, putrid, ugsome **07** mawkish, noisome, obscene **08** nauseous, shocking **09** appalling, offensive, repellent, repugnant, repulsive, revolting, sickening **10** abominable, detestable, nauseating, off-putting, outrageous, unpleasant **11** disgraceful, distasteful, rebarbative, unpalatable **12** unappetizing **13** objectionable

**dish**
◇ *anagram indicator*
**04** bowl, fare, food, ruin, tray **05** plate **06** course, recipe, tureen **07** platter **08** delicacy **10** speciality
*See also* **food**

**• dish out**
◇ *anagram indicator*
**07** dole out, give out, hand out, inflict, mete out **08** allocate, dispense, share out **09** hand round, pass round **10** distribute

**• dish up**
**05** ladle, offer, scoop, serve, spoon **07** present **08** dispense

**disharmony**
**05** clash **06** strife **07** discord, dissent **08** conflict, friction **09** disaccord **10** dissonance **11** discordance, incongruity **12** disagreement **15** incompatibility

**dishearten**
**04** dash **05** chill, crush, daunt, deter **06** dampen, deject, dismay **07** depress, unheart **08** cast down, dispirit **09** disparage, weigh down **10** demoralize, disappoint, discourage **12** put a damper on **13** make depressed

**disheartened**
◇ *middle deletion indicator*
**04** down **07** crushed, daunted **08** dejected, dismayed, downcast **09** depressed **10** dispirited **11** crestfallen, demoralized, discouraged, downhearted **12** disappointed

**dishevelled**
◇ *anagram indicator*
**04** wild **05** daggy, messy **06** blowsy, blowzy, untidy **07** in a mess, ruffled, rumpled, scruffy, tousled, unkempt **08** slovenly, uncombed **09** windswept **10** bedraggled, disordered **11** disarranged

**dishonest**
**03** sly **04** bent, iffy **05** cross, dirty, dodgy, false, fishy, lying, shady, snide **06** crafty, shifty, untrue **07** corrupt, crooked, cunning, devious, knavish **08** cheating, unchaste **09** deceitful, deceptive, insincere, irregular, swindling **10** fraudulent, mendacious, perfidious, untruthful **11** duplicitous, treacherous **12** disreputable, unprincipled, unscrupulous **13** dishonourable, double-dealing, untrustworthy

**dishonestly**
**05** false **07** falsely **09** corruptly, deviously **10** on the cross **11** deceitfully, deceptively **12** disreputably, fraudulently, perfidiously **13** dishonourably, treacherously **14** unscrupulously

**dishonesty**
**05** fraud **06** deceit **07** falsity, knavery, perfidy **08** cheating, trickery **09** chicanery, duplicity, falsehood, improbity, shadiness, treachery **10** corruption, dirty trick **11** criminality, crookedness, fraudulence, insincerity **12** irregularity **13** double-dealing, sharp practice **14** untruthfulness

**dishonour**
**04** slur **05** abuse, shame, stain, sully, wrong **06** debase, defame, defile, demean, ignomy, infamy, insult, offend, refuse, reject, seduce, slight, stigma **07** affront, debauch, degrade, offence, outrage, scandal **08** disgrace, ignominy, reproach, turn down **09** abasement, aspersion, discredit, disfavour, disparage, disrepute, humiliate, indignity **10** debasement, disworship, opprobrium **11** degradation, discourtesy, humiliation

**dishonourable**
**05** shady **07** corrupt, disleal, ignoble, low-down **08** infamous, shameful, unhonest, unworthy **09** shameless, unethical **10** despicable, perfidious, scandalous **11** disgraceful, ignominious, treacherous **12** contemptible, disreputable, unprincipled, unscrupulous **13** discreditable, untrustworthy

**dishy**
**04** sexy **05** hunky **08** charming, gorgeous, handsome **10** attractive **11** good-looking

**disillusion**
**08** disabuse **09** undeceive **10** disappoint, disenchant **14** disappointment, disenchantment **15** disillusionment

**disillusioned**
**07** let-down **09** disabused **10** undeceived **12** disappointed, disenchanted

**disincentive**
**06** damper **07** barrier, turn-off **08** obstacle **09** determent, deterrent, hindrance, repellent **10** constraint, dissuasion, impediment **11** restriction **14** discouragement

**disinclination**
**07** dislike **08** aversion **09** antipathy, loathness, objection **10** alienation, averseness, hesitation, opposition, reluctance, repugnance, resistance **13** indisposition, unwillingness

**disinclined**
**05** loath **06** averse **07** opposed **08** hesitant **09** reluctant, resistant, unwilling **10** indisposed, undisposed **14** unenthusiastic

**disinfect**
**05** clean, purge **06** bleach, purify **07** cleanse **08** fumigate, sanitize **09** sterilize **13** decontaminate

**disinfectant**
**05** lysol **06** cineol, cresol, phenol **07** cineole **08** fumigant, sheep-dip, terebene **09** germicide, sanitizer **10** antiseptic, sterilizer **11** bactericide **12** methyl violet **13** decontaminant **14** glutaraldehyde

**disingenuous**
**03** sly **04** wily **06** artful, crafty, shifty **07** cunning, devious, feigned

**08** guileful, two-faced, uncandid **09** deceitful, designing, dishonest, insidious, insincere **11** duplicitous

**disingenuously**
**05** slyly **08** artfully **09** cunningly, deviously **11** deceitfully, dishonestly, insidiously, insincerely

**disinherit**
**06** cut off, reject **07** abandon **08** renounce **09** repudiate **10** dispossess, exheredate, impoverish **14** turn your back on

**disintegrate**
◇ *anagram indicator*
**03** rot **05** decay, smash **06** reduce **07** break up, crumble, moulder, shatter **08** separate, splinter **09** decompose, fall apart **10** break apart **12** fall to pieces, self-destruct

**disintegration**
◇ *anagram indicator*
**03** rot **05** decay **07** breakup **08** biolysis, decaying **09** breakdown, crumbling **10** karyolysis, separation, shattering **11** dissolution **12** falling-apart **13** decomposition, radioactivity, spondylolysis

**disinter**
**05** dig up **06** exhume, expose, reveal, unbury **07** uncover, unearth **08** excavate, exhumate **09** disentomb, disinhume, resurrect **12** bring to light

**disinterest**
**08** fairness **09** unconcern **10** detachment, neutrality **12** disadvantage, impartiality, unbiasedness

**disinterested**
**04** cool, fair, just **07** neutral **08** detached, generous, unbiased **09** equitable, impartial, objective, unselfish **10** even-handed, open-minded, uninvolved **12** unprejudiced **13** dispassionate

**disjointed**
◇ *anagram indicator*
**05** bitty, loose, split **06** abrupt, broken, fitful **07** aimless, divided **08** confused, rambling **09** displaced, disunited, separated, spasmodic, wandering **10** dislocated, disordered, incoherent **11** unconnected **12** disconnected **13** directionless **14** disarticulated

**dislike**
**04** defy, down, hate, lump, mind, shun **05** abhor, derry, scorn, thing **06** animus, detest, enmity, hatred, loathe, needle **07** allergy, despise, disgust, mislike **08** aversion, disfavor, distaste, dyspathy, execrate, loathing, object to **09** abominate, animosity, antipathy, disesteem, disfavour, disrelish, hostility, objection **10** antagonism, disapprove, repugnance, resentment **11** detestation, disapproval, displeasure, take against **12** have a derry on **14** disapprobation, disinclination, take a scunner to

**dislocate**
◇ *anagram indicator*
**04** do in, pull, slip **05** shift, twist **06** luxate, put out, sprain, strain **07** confuse, disrupt, disturb **08** disjoint, disorder, displace, disunite, misplace **09** disengage **10** disconnect **11** disorganize **13** put out of joint, put out of place

**dislocation**
◇ *anagram indicator*
**04** slip **05** fault **08** disarray, disorder, luxation **10** disruption **11** disturbance **12** displacement **15** disorganization

**dislodge**
**04** bump, move, oust, tuft **05** eject, shift **06** remove, uproot **08** displace, force out, untenant **09** extricate

**disloyal**
**05** false **06** untrue **07** disleal **08** apostate, two-faced **09** deceitful, faithless **10** perfidious, traitorous, un-American, unfaithful **11** treacherous, unpatriotic **13** double-dealing

**disloyalty**
**06** deceit **07** falsity, perfidy, treason **08** adultery, apostasy, betrayal, sedition **09** falseness, treachery **10** infidelity **11** inconstancy, waka-jumping **12** disaffection **13** breach of trust, double-dealing **14** perfidiousness, unfaithfulness

**dismal**
**03** bad, sad **04** blue, dark, drab, dull, glum, gray, grey, grim, naff, poor, ropy **05** awful, black, bleak, dingy, dowie, lousy, morne, trist, wormy **06** crummy, dreary, dreich, gloomy, somber, sombre, sullen, triste **07** forlorn, useless **08** desolate, dolesome, dreadful, funereal, ghastful, hopeless, terrible **09** cheerless, frightful, ghastfull, long-faced, miserable, sorrowful **10** depressing, despondent, grimlooked, lugubrious, melancholy, sepulchral **11** low-spirited **12** discouraging, unsuccessful

**dismally**
**05** badly, sadly **06** darkly, drably **08** drearily, gloomily, terribly **09** miserably **10** dreadfully **11** frightfully **12** despondently **14** unsuccessfully

**dismantle**
◇ *anagram indicator*
**05** derig, strip **06** strike **08** demolish, pull down, separate, take down **09** pull apart, strip down, take apart **11** disassemble **12** take to pieces

**dismay**
**04** fear **05** alarm, amate, appal, daunt, dread, scare, shake, shock, upset, worry **06** bother, fright, horror, put off, terror **07** concern, depress, disturb, horrify, perturb, unnerve **08** cast down, dispirit, distress, frighten, unsettle **09** agitation, take aback **10** disappoint, disconcert, discourage, dishearten **11** consternate, disillusion, heart-strike, trepidation **12** apprehension **13** consternation **14** disappointment, discouragement

• **expression of dismay**
**02** ha **03** hah **04** argh, heck, hell, oops, whew **05** aargh **06** crumbs, dear me, heaven, oh dear!, wheugh **07** cravens, crivens, deary me, heavens **08** crivvens, dearie me **09** good grief **11** that's done it, that's torn it

**dismember**
**04** limb **05** sever **06** divide **07** break up, disject, dislimb, dissect, quarter **08** amputate, disjoint, mutilate, separate **09** dislocate, piecemeal, pull apart

**dismemberment**
**07** breakup **08** division **10** amputation, dissection, mutilation, separation

**dismiss**
◇ *deletion indicator*
**04** boot, daff, drop, fire, free, sack **05** chuck, eject, expel, lay by, let go, spurn **06** banish, bounce, chassé, lay off, reject, remove, shelve **07** boot out, cashier, discord, fall out, kick out, kiss off, put away, release, send off, suspend, turn off **08** brush off, discount, dispatch, dissolve, relegate, send away, set aside **09** bowler-hat, discharge, disregard, repudiate **10** brush aside, give notice, give the air, pension off **11** send packing **13** give the bucket, make redundant **15** pour cold water on

**dismissal**
◇ *deletion indicator*
**01** b, c **02** ax, hw, ro, st **03** axe, lbw **04** bird, boot, push, road, sack **05** chuck, congé, elbow **06** avaunt, bounce, bowled, caught, congee, firing, mitten, notice, papers, run-out **07** discard, heave-ho, kiss-off, removal, sacking, stumped **08** brush-off, bum's rush, despatch, dispatch, mittimus **09** discharge, expulsion, hit wicket, laying-off **10** cashiering, redundancy **11** cashierment **12** golden bowler **13** walking-orders, walking papers, walking-ticket **14** marching-orders **15** leg before wicket

• **expression of dismissal**
**03** och, out, via **04** poof, pooh, tush **06** avaunt, begone, powwaw **07** voetsak

**dismissed**
**03** out

**dismissive**
**07** off-hand **08** scornful, sneering **10** disdainful, dismissory **12** contemptuous **13** disrespectful, inconsiderate

**dismissively**
**10** scornfully, sneeringly **11** off-handedly **12** disdainfully **14** contemptuously

**dismount**
**04** lite **05** light **06** alight, get off **07** descend, get down, unmount **09** disembark

**disobedience**
**06** mutiny, revolt **08** defiance **09** contumacy, rebellion **10** infraction, unruliness, wilfulness **11** contumacity, waywardness **12** contrariness, indiscipline **13** recalcitrance **15** insubordination

**disobedient**
**06** unruly, wilful **07** defiant, froward, naughty, wayward **08** contrary, recusant **10** disorderly, rebellious, refractory **11** intractable, mischievous **12** contumacious, obstreperous, recalcitrant **13** insubordinate

**disobey**
**04** defy **05** flout, rebel **06** ignore, resist **07** violate **08** infringe, overstep **09** disregard **10** contravene, transgress **13** step out of line

**disobliging**
**04** rude **06** unkind **07** awkward, uncivil **09** unhelpful, unwilling **11** inofficious **12** bloody-minded, disagreeable, discourteous **13** unco-operative **15** unaccommodating

**disorder**
◇ *anagram indicator*
**03** ADD, OCD, SAD **04** ADHD, mess, muss, PMDD, PTSD, riot, rout **05** brawl, chaos, deray, fight, mêlée, musse **06** defuse, fracas, jumble, malady, muddle, ruffle, rumple, rumpus, tumble, tumult, unrest, uproar **07** ailment, anarchy, clamour, clutter, confuse, derange, disease, flutter, garboil, illness, misrule, overset, quarrel **08** brouhaha, confound, disarray, pell-mell, shambles, sickness **09** commotion, complaint, condition, confusion, mistemper **10** affliction, disability, disarrange, discompose, disruption, untidiness **11** derangement, disturbance **12** confusedness **14** disorderliness **15** disorganization

**disordered**
◇ *anagram indicator*
**03** mad **04** wild **05** messy, mussy, oncus, onkus, upset **06** turbid, untidy **07** jumbled, muddled, unkempt **08** confused, deranged, madbrain, troubled **09** betumbled, cluttered, disturbed **10** madbrained, out of joint, unbalanced, upside-down **11** distempered, maladjusted **12** disorganized, disreputable

**disorderly**
◇ *anagram indicator*
**04** wild **05** messy, rough, rowdy **06** ragtag, unruly, untidy **07** chaotic, jumbled, lawless **08** confused **09** cluttered, irregular, turbulent **10** boisterous, confusedly, in disarray, ragmatical, rebellious, refractory, tumultuous **11** disobedient **12** disorganized, hugger-mugger, obstreperous, unmanageable **13** undisciplined **14** uncontrollable

**disorganization**
◇ *anagram indicator*
**05** chaos **06** muddle **08** disarray, disorder, shambles **09** confusion **10** disruption, untidiness **11** dislocation

**disorganize**
◇ *anagram indicator*
**05** mix up, upset **06** jumble, mess up, muddle **07** break up, confuse, destroy, disrupt, disturb **08** disorder, unsettle, unstring **09** dislocate **10** disarrange, discompose **11** unmechanize **12** play hell with **13** play havoc with

**disorganized**
◇ *anagram indicator*
**07** chaotic, jumbled, muddled **08** careless, confused, unsorted **09** haphazard, shambolic **10** disordered, topsy-turvy, untogether **11** unorganized **12** unmethodical, unstructured, unsystematic **13** undisciplined **14** unsystematized

**disorientate**
◇ *anagram indicator*
**04** faze **05** upset **06** muddle, puzzle **07** confuse, mislead, perplex **09** disorient

**disorientated**
◇ *anagram indicator*
**04** lost **05** at sea, upset **06** adrift, astray **07** mixed up, muddled, puzzled **08** all at sea, confused **09** perplexed, unsettled **10** bewildered, unbalanced **11** disoriented

**disorientation**
◇ *anagram indicator*
**06** muddle **08** lostness **09** confusion **10** perplexity, puzzlement **12** bewilderment

**disown**
**04** deny **05** unget **06** reject **07** abandon, cast off, disavow, forsake **08** abnegate, disallow, disclaim, renounce **09** reprobate, repudiate **14** disacknowledge, turn your back on

**disparage**
**04** mock, slag, slam, slur **05** decry, knock, scorn, slate **06** defame, deride, lessen, malign, vilify **07** cry down, degrade, disable, disdain, dismiss, empeach, impeach, rubbish, run down, slag off, slander, traduce **08** belittle, derogate, disvalue, minimize, ridicule, vilipend **09** criticize, denigrate, deprecate, discredit, dishonour, sell short, underrate **10** calumniate, depreciate, dishearten, undervalue **11** detract from **13** underestimate

**disparagement**
**04** slur **05** scorn **07** decrial, disdain, slander **08** contempt, decrying, derision, ridicule **09** aspersion, contumely, criticism, discredit **10** debasement, derogation, detraction **11** degradation, deprecation **12** belittlement, condemnation, denunciation, depreciation, vilification **15** underestimation

**disparaging**
**05** snide **07** mocking **08** critical, derisive, knocking, scornful **09** insulting **10** derogatory, dismissive, pejorative **11** deprecating, deprecatory

**disparate**
**06** unlike **07** diverse, unequal **08** contrary, distinct **09** different **10** discrepant, dissimilar **11** contrasting

**disparity**
**03** gap **04** bias, gulf **08** contrast, inequity **09** imbalance **10** difference, inequality, unevenness, unfairness, unlikeness **11** discrepancy, distinction, incongruity **13** disproportion, dissimilarity, dissimilitude, inconsistency

**dispassionate**
**04** calm, cool, fair **07** neutral **08** composed, detached, unbiased **09** equitable, impartial, objective, unexcited **10** impersonal **11** unemotional **12** unprejudiced **13** disinterested, self-possessed **14** self-controlled

**dispassionately**
**06** coolly, fairly **09** equitably **11** impartially, objectively, unexcitedly **12** impersonally **13** unemotionally **15** disinterestedly

**dispatch, despatch**
**04** do in, item, kill, mail, news, post, send, ship **05** haste, piece, remit, speed **06** convey, finish, letter, murder, report, settle **07** account, article, bump off, consign, dépêche, dismiss, execute, express, forward, mailing, message, perform, posting, sending, send off, special **08** alacrity, bulletin, celerity, conclude, deal with, expedite, knock off, rapidity, transmit **09** discharge, dismissal, dispose of, slaughter, swiftness **10** accelerate, communiqué, expedience, expedition, forwarding, promptness, put to death **11** assassinate, consignment, promptitude, transmittal **13** communication

**dispel**
◇ *anagram indicator*
**03** rid **04** rout **05** allay, expel **06** assoil, banish **07** discuss, dismiss, scatter **08** disperse, get rid of, melt away **09** chase away, dissipate, drive away, eliminate **11** disseminate

**dispensable**
**07** useless **08** needless **10** disposable, expendable, gratuitous, pardonable **11** inessential, replaceable, superfluous, unnecessary **12** non-essential

**dispensation**
**04** plan **05** issue, order **06** relief, scheme, system **07** economy, licence, release **08** bestowal, covenant, immunity, reprieve **09** allotment, authority, direction, discharge, endowment, exception, exemption, provision, remission **10** allocation, handing out, permission, sharing out **11** application, arrangement **12** distribution, organization **13** apportionment **14** administration

**dispense**
**05** allot, apply, issue, share **06** assign, bestow, confer **07** deal out, deliver, dole out, enforce, execute, expense, give out, hand out, mete out, operate **08** allocate, carry out, compound, share out, supplies **09** apportion, discharge, divide out, implement, pass round **10** administer, distribute, effectuate **11** expenditure **12** dispensation

**• dispense with**
**02** ax **03** axe **04** omit, want **05** forgo, waive **06** cancel, forego, give up, ignore, revoke **07** abolish, discard, not need, rescind **08** get rid of, renounce **09** dispose of, disregard, do without **10** do away with, relinquish

**dispersal**
**07** breakup **09** dismissal **10** breaking-up, disbanding, scattering, separation **11** segregation **12** distribution

**disperse**
◇ *anagram indicator*
**04** melt, shed **05** break, scail, scale, skail **06** dispel, spread, vanish **07** break up, diffuse, disband, dismiss, resolve, scatter, split up, thin out **08** dissolve, melt away, separate, squander **09** dissipate **10** distribute **11** disseminate

**dispersion**
◇ *anagram indicator*
**07** scatter **08** diaspora **09** broadcast, diffusion, dispersal, spreading **10** scattering **11** circulation, dissipation **12** distribution **13** dissemination

**dispirit**
**04** damp, dash **05** deter **06** dampen, deject, sadden **07** depress **10** demoralize, discourage, dishearten **12** put a damper on

**dispirited**
**03** low, sad **04** down, glum **05** fed up **06** feeble, gloomy, morose **08** cast down, dejected, downcast, sackless **09** depressed **10** brassed off, browned off, cheesed off, despondent, spiritless **11** crestfallen, demoralized, discouraged, pale-hearted **12** disheartened **14** down in the dumps

**displace**
**04** move, oust **05** eject, evict, expel, heave, shift **06** depose, luxate, remove **07** boot out, dismiss, disturb, replace, succeed, turf out **08** dislodge, force out, misplace, relocate, supplant **09** discharge, dislocate, supersede **10** disarrange

**displacement**
**03** jee **04** warp **05** heave, hitch, shift, throw **06** ectopy, moving, ptosis **07** ectopia, upthrow **08** shifting **09** proptosis **10** aberration, compliance, dislodging **11** dislocation, disturbance, heterotaxis, heterotopia, subluxation, superseding, supplanting **12** misplacement, retroversion **14** Chandler wobble, disarrangement **15** Chandler's wobble

**display**
**03** air, HUD, LCD **04** expo, pomp, shaw, show, wear **05** array, boast, state **06** betray, blazon, evince, expose, flaunt, layout, muster, parade, reveal, set out, splash, unfold, unfurl, unveil **07** airshow, bravura, breathe, étalage, exhibit, pageant, parafle, present, promote, show off, splurge **08** disclose, evidence, flourish, manifest, paraffle, put forth, set forth, showcase **09** advertise, pageantry, publicize, put on show, spectacle, spread out, unfolding **10** disclosure, displaying, evincement, exhibition, exposition, revelation, tournament **11** demonstrate **12** presentation **13** demonstration, manifestation

**displease**
**03** bug, irk, vex **05** anger, annoy, upset **06** offend, put out **07** dislike, disturb, incense, mislike, perturb, provoke **08** irritate **09** aggravate, infuriate, misplease **10** discompose, disgruntle, dissatisfy, exasperate **11** displeasure

**displeased**
**05** angry, cross, upset, vexed **06** peeved, piqued, put out **07** annoyed, furious **08** offended **09** irritated **10** aggravated, dischuffed, infuriated **11** disgruntled, exasperated, out of humour

**displeasure**
**03** ire **05** anger, pique, wrath **07** chagrin, disgust, offence, offense **08** distaste **09** annoyance, disfavour **10** irritation, resentment **11** disapproval, indignation **12** exasperation, perturbation **14** disapprobation, discontentment, disgruntlement **15** dissatisfaction

**disport**
◇ *anagram indicator*
**04** play, romp **05** amuse, cheer, frisk, revel, sport **06** cavort, divert, frolic, gambol **07** delight, get down **09** entertain

**disposable**
**09** throwaway **10** expendable **11** replaceable **13** biodegradable, non-returnable

**disposal**
**05** order **07** command, control, liberty, removal, service **08** bestowal, grouping, ordering, riddance **09** clearance, direction, scrapping **10** deployment, discarding, management **11** arrangement, jettisoning, positioning **12** getting rid of, throwing-away

**• at someone's disposal**
**05** on tap, ready **06** at hand, to hand **09** available **10** obtainable

**dispose**
◇ *anagram indicator*
**03** put, set **04** do in, dump, kill, plot, shed, sort **05** align, group, order, place, posit, scrap, see to, sew up, tempt **06** battle, decide, finish, handle, line up, murder, settle, tackle, wrap up **07** arrange, bump off, destroy, discard, dismiss, dispone, incline, situate, sort out **08** attend to, chuck out, clear out, deal with, dispatch, get rid of, jettison, organize, position, throw out **09** clear away, determine, get shot of, look after, polish off, throw away **10** distribute, do away with, put to death, take care of **15** make short work of

**• try to dispose of**
**04** hawk

**disposed**
◇ *anagram indicator*
**03** apt **04** bent **05** dight, eager, prone, ready **06** liable, likely, minded **07** subject, willing **08** inclined, pregnant, prepared **11** affectioned, predisposed

**disposition**
◇ *anagram indicator*
**03** lay, lie **04** bent, make, mood, trim **05** cheer, habit, humor, order **06** humour, kidney, layout, line-up, make-up, nature, spirit, system, talent, temper **07** leaning, pattern, placing, stomach **08** disposal, grouping, ordnance, position, sequence, tendency, transfer **09** affection, alignment, character, proneness **10** allocation, conveyance, deployment, giving-over, proclivity, propension, propensity **11** arrangement, inclination, personality, positioning, temperament **12** constitution, distribution, ministration, predilection, propenseness **14** predisposition

**dispossess**
**03** rob **04** oust **05** eject, evict, expel, strip **06** divest **07** deprive **08** dislodge, take away **11** expropriate

**disproportion**
**09** asymmetry, disparity, imbalance **10** inadequacy, inequality, unevenness **11** discrepancy **12** lopsidedness **13** insufficiency

**disproportionate**
**06** uneven **07** unequal **09** excessive **10** inordinate, unbalanced **12** unreasonable **14** incommensurate **15** incommensurable, out of proportion

**disproportionately**
**08** unevenly **11** excessively **12** inordinately, unreasonably

**disprove**
**04** deny **05** rebut, refel **06** debunk, expose, negate, refute **07** confute, reprove **08** blow away **09** discredit **10** contradict, controvert, invalidate, prove false **12** give the lie to

**disputable**
**04** moot **07** dubious **08** arguable, doubtful **09** debatable, litigious, uncertain **12** questionable **13** controversial

**disputation**
**03** act **06** debate **07** dispute, schools **08** argument, diatribe, exercise, polemics **09** quodlibet **10** apposition, discussion, dissension **11** controversy **12** deliberation, kilfud-yoking **13** argumentation

**disputatious**
**08** captious **09** litigious, polemical **10** pugnacious **11** contentious, quarrelsome **12** cantankerous **13** argumentative

**dispute**
**03** row **04** deny, feud, moot, odds, plea, spar, spat, tilt **05** argue, clash, doubt **06** bicker, cangle, debate, differ, strife, threap **07** contend, contest, discept, discuss, gainsay, quarrel, wrangle, wrestle **08** argument, conflict, litigate, question, squabble, traverse, variance **09** altercate, challenge, have words, tug-of-love **10** contention, contradict, controvert, litigation **11** altercation, controverse, controversy, cross swords **12** disagreement, disceptation

**disqualification**
**03** ban, bar **04** veto **10** disability, incapacity, preclusion **11** elimination, prohibition **13** ineligibility **14** disentitlement

**disqualified**
**06** banned **08** debarred **09** incapable, precluded, struck off **10** eliminated, ineligible **11** disentitled

**disqualify**
**03** ban, bar **05** debar, unfit **06** impair **07** disable, rule out, suspend **08** handicap, preclude, prohibit **09** eliminate, strike off **10** debilitate, disentitle, immobilize, invalidate **12** incapacitate **13** dishabilitate

**disquiet**
**03** vex **04** faze, fear, fret **05** alarm, annoy, dread, shake, upset, worry **06** bother, harass, hassle, pester, plague, ruffle, unease, uneasy, unrest **07** agitate, anguish, anxiety, concern, disturb, perturb, trouble, turmoil, unnerve **08** distress, restless, unsettle **09** agitation, incommode **10** discompose, foreboding, inquietude, make uneasy, uneasiness **11** disquietude, disturbance, fretfulness, make anxious, nervousness **12** perturbation, restlessness

**disquieting**
**04** ugly **06** trying **07** anxious **08** worrying **09** unnerving, upsetting **10** disturbing, nail-biting, perturbing, unsettling **11** distressing, troublesome

**disquisition**
**05** essay, paper **06** sermon, thesis **07** descant **08** treatise **09** discourse, monograph **10** exposition **11** explanation **12** dissertation

**disregard**
◇ *deletion indicator*
**04** bend, omit, pass, shun, snub **05** flout, waive **06** ignore, insult, offend, slight **07** affront, despise, disdain, disobey, neglect, oversee, smile at **08** brush-off, contempt, discount, laugh off, overlook, pass over, set aside **09** denigrate, disesteem, disoblige, disparage, gloss over, oversight, sacrilege **10** brush aside, disrespect, negligence **11** denigration, desperation, inattention, make light of, set at naught, walk all over **12** carelessness, cold shoulder, cold-shoulder, dispense with, indifference **13** give the go-by to, non-regardance, put out of court **14** rule out of court, take no notice of **15** close your eyes to, turn a blind eye to

**disrepair**
**04** ruin **05** decay **08** collapse **10** shabbiness **11** rack and ruin **12** dilapidation **13** deterioration

**disreputable**
**03** low **04** base, mean **05** dodgy, seamy, seedy, shady **06** louche, shabby, shifty, untidy **07** corrupt, dubious, scruffy, unkempt **08** infamous, shameful, shocking, slovenly, unworthy **09** notorious, unsavoury **10** outrageous, scandalous, suspicious **11** disgraceful, dishevelled, ignominious, opprobrious **12** contemptible, unprincipled **13** discreditable, dishonourable, unrespectable

**disrepute**
**05** shame **06** infamy **07** ill fame, obloquy **08** disgrace, ignominy **09** discredit, disesteem, disfavour, dishonour **13** disreputation

**disrespect**
**05** cheek, scorn **08** contempt, rudeness **09** dishonour, disregard, impudence, insolence, misesteem **10** incivility **11** discourtesy, irreverence **12** impertinence, impoliteness

**disrespectful**
**04** rude **05** sassy **06** cheeky **07** uncivil **08** flippant, impolite, impudent, insolent **09** insulting **10** dismissive, irreverent, unmannerly **11** impertinent **12** contemptuous, discourteous **13** inconsiderate

**disrespectfully**
**06** rudely **08** cheekily **09** uncivilly **10** impolitely, impudently, insolently **11** insultingly **12** irreverently **13** impertinently **14** contemptuously, discourteously

**disrobe**
**04** bare, shed **05** strip **06** denude, divest, remove **07** take off, uncover, undress **08** unclothe **10** disapparel

**disrupt**
◇ *anagram indicator*
**05** burst, split, upset **06** butt in, hamper, impede **07** blemish, break up, confuse, disturb, intrude, screw up **08** sabotage, unsettle **09** dislocate, interrupt **10** disarrange **11** disorganize **13** interfere with

**disruption**
◇ *anagram indicator*
**05** upset **06** bust-up **07** burst-up, turmoil **08** disarray, disorder, stoppage, upheaval **09** cataclasm, confusion **11** disordering, disturbance **12** interference, interruption **14** disorderliness **15** disorganization

**disruptive**
**05** noisy, rogue **06** unruly **09** turbulent, upsetting **10** boisterous, disorderly, disturbing, unsettling **11** distracting, troublesome **12** obstreperous **13** troublemaking, undisciplined

**dissatisfaction**
**05** anger **06** regret **07** chagrin, dislike **08** vexation **09** annoyance **10** discomfort, discontent, irritation, resentment, uneasiness **11** disapproval, displeasure, frustration, unhappiness **12** disaffection, exasperation, restlessness **14** disappointment, disapprobation

• **expression of dissatisfaction**
**02** oh **03** boo, huh, tut **04** booh, umph, whow **05** humph

**dissatisfied**
**05** angry, fed up **07** annoyed, unhappy **09** irritated, pissed off **10** brassed off, browned off, cheesed off, discontent, displeased, frustrated, malcontent **11** disaffected, disgruntled, exasperated, unfulfilled, unsatisfied **12** disappointed, discontented, disenchanted, malcontented **13** disillusioned

**dissatisfy**
**03** vex **05** anger, annoy **06** put out **07** let down **08** irritate **09** displease, frustrate **10** disappoint, discontent, disgruntle, exasperate

**dissect**
**05** cut up, probe, study **07** analyse, examine, explore, inspect **08** pore over, vivisect **09** anatomize, break down, dismember **10** scrutinize **11** investigate

**dissection**
**05** probe, study **07** anatomy, autopsy, zootomy **08** analysis, necropsy, scrutiny **09** breakdown, cutting up, necrotomy **10** inspection

**11** cephalotomy, examination, exploration, vivisection **13** dismemberment, encephalotomy, investigation

**dissemble**
**04** fain, fake, hide, mask, sham **05** cloak, faine, fayne, feign **06** affect **07** conceal, cover up, falsify, pretend **08** disguise, simulate **10** camouflage, play possum **11** counterfeit, dissimulate

**dissembler**
**04** fake, liar **05** fraud **06** con man **07** feigner **08** deceiver, impostor **09** charlatan, hypocrite, pretender, trickster **12** dissimulator **15** whited sepulchre

**disseminate**
**03** sow **05** scale **06** spread **07** diffuse, publish, scatter **08** disperse, proclaim **09** broadcast, circulate, propagate, publicize, scattered **10** distribute, promulgate

**dissemination**
**06** spread **09** broadcast, diffusion, spreading **10** dispersion, publishing **11** circulation, propagation, publication **12** broadcasting, distribution, promulgation

**dissension**
**04** flak **06** square, strife **07** discord, dispute, dissent, faction, quarrel **08** argument, conflict, dispeace, disunion, disunity, friction, variance **10** contention **12** disagreement

**dissent**
**05** demur **06** differ, object, refuse **07** discord, dispute, protest, quibble **08** disagree, friction **09** objection **10** difference, disconsent, disharmony, dissension, opposition, resistance **11** controversy **12** disagreement

**dissenter**
**05** rebel **07** heretic, sectary **08** objector, recusant **09** disputant, dissident, protester, Raskolnik **10** protestant, schismatic, separatist **11** dissentient, Old Believer **12** demonstrator **13** nonconformist, revolutionary

**dissentient**
**08** opposing, recusant **09** differing, dissident, heretical **10** dissenting, protesting, rebellious **11** conflicting, disagreeing **13** nonconformist, revolutionary

**dissertation**
**05** essay, paper **06** thesis **08** critique, excursus, treatise **09** discourse, monograph **10** exposition **11** prolegomena **12** disquisition, propaedeutic

**disservice**
**04** harm, hurt **05** wrong **06** injury **07** bad turn **08** con trick, mischief **09** disfavour, injustice **10** dirty trick, unkindness **13** sharp practice **14** kick in the teeth

**dissidence**
**04** feud **06** schism **07** dispute, dissent, rupture **08** variance **09** recusancy **11** discordance **12** disagreement

**dissident**
**05** rebel **07** heretic **08** agitator, frondeur, objector, opposing, recusant, refusnik **09** differing, dissenter, heretical, heterodox, protester, refusenik **10** discordant, dissenting, protesting, rebellious, schismatic **11** conflicting, disagreeing **13** nonconformist, revolutionary

**dissimilar**
**06** unlike **07** diverse, unalike, various, varying **08** bifacial, distinct **09** deviating, different, disparate, divergent, unrelated **10** mismatched **11** contrasting, hemimorphic **12** incompatible **13** heterogeneous

**dissimilarity**
**07** variety **08** contrast **09** disparity, diversity **10** difference, differency, divergence, inequality, unlikeness **11** discrepancy, distinction **13** dissimilitude, heterogeneity, unrelatedness **15** incomparability, incompatibility

**dissimulate**
**03** lie **04** fake, hide, mask **05** cloak, feign **06** affect **07** conceal, cover up, pretend **08** disguise **09** dissemble **10** camouflage

**dissipate**
◇ *anagram indicator*
**04** blow **05** drain, spend, use up, waste **06** burn up, dispel, expend, lavish, vanish, wanton **07** break up, consume, deplete, diffuse, exhaust, resolve, scatter, splurge **08** disperse, dissolve, melt away, squander **09** disappear, drive away, evaporate **10** get through, run through **11** fritter away

**dissipated**
◇ *anagram indicator*
**03** gay **04** wild **06** rakish, wasted **07** corrupt **08** depraved **09** abandoned, debauched, dissolute **10** degenerate, licentious, profligate **11** intemperate **13** self-indulgent

**• be dissipated**
**04** melt **08** peter out

**dissipation**
**06** excess, racket **07** licence **08** pleasure **09** depletion, depravity, diffusion, dispersal **10** corruption, debauchery, immorality **11** abandonment, consumption, evaporation, expenditure, prodigality, squandering **12** extravagance, intemperance **13** disappearance **14** licentiousness, self-indulgence

**dissociate**
**04** quit **05** sever **06** cut off, detach, secede **07** break up, disband, disrupt, divorce, isolate **08** break off, distance, disunite, separate, set apart, withdraw **09** disengage, segregate, separated **10** disconnect **12** disassociate

**dissociation**
**05** break, split **07** divorce **08** disunion, division, severing **09** isolation, severance **10** cutting-off, detachment, distancing, separation **11** dissevering, segregation **12** setting apart **13** disconnection, disengagement **14** disassociation

**dissolute**
◇ *anagram indicator*
**04** fast, lewd, wild **05** loose **06** rakish, wanton **07** corrupt, immoral, outward **08** depraved **09** abandoned, debauched **10** Corinthian, degenerate, dissipated, licentious, profligate **11** Falstaffian, intemperate **12** unrestrained **13** self-indulgent

**dissolution**
**06** ending, Repeal **07** break-up, divorce, melting **08** collapse, dialysis, disposal, division **09** annulment, cessation, loosening, overthrow **10** conclusion, karyolysis, separation, suspension **11** destruction, evaporation, termination, thermolysis **13** decomposition, disappearance **14** disintegration **15** discontinuation

**dissolve**
**03** end **04** melt **05** annul, begin, break, burst, solve, start **06** digest, finish, revoke, vanish, wind up **07** break up, crumble, disband, dismiss, divorce, dwindle, liquefy, nullify, rescind, solvate, unmarry **08** collapse, discandy, disperse, evanesce, melt away, separate **09** disappear, discandie, dissipate, evaporate, terminate **10** deliquesce, invalidate **11** discontinue, lose control **12** bring to an end, disintegrate **14** be overcome with, go into solution

**dissonance**
**03** jar **04** wolf **05** clash **06** jangle **07** discord, grating, jarring **08** variance **09** cacophony, disparity, harshness, stridency **10** difference, disharmony, dissension **11** discordance, discrepancy, incongruity **12** disagreement **13** inconsistency **15** incompatibility

**dissonant**
◇ *anagram indicator*
**05** harsh **07** grating, jarring, raucous **08** clashing, jangling, strident, tuneless **09** anomalous, differing, irregular, unmusical **10** discordant **11** cacophonous, conflicting, disagreeing, incongruous, unmelodious **12** incompatible, inconsistent, inharmonious **13** contradictory **14** irreconcilable

**dissuade**
**04** stop **05** deter **06** dehort, nobble, put off **07** prevent **09** talk out of **10** discounsel, discourage, disincline **13** persuade not to

**dissuasion**
**07** caution **09** deterring **10** deterrence **11** dehortation **12** remonstrance

**13** expostulation, remonstration
**14** discouragement

**distance**
**03** gap, way **04** span, step **05** break, depth, lunar, piece, range, reach, space, width **06** cut off, detach, extent, height, length, remove, secede
**07** breadth, faraway, farness, reserve, stretch **08** coldness, coolness, interval, separate, throw out, withdraw
**09** aloofness, formality, stiffness
**10** detachment, dissociate, opposition, remoteness, separation
**11** mountenance **12** disassociate, mountenaunce **13** codeclination
**14** unfriendliness **15** inaccessibility, standoffishness
*See also* **measurement**

**• at a distance**
**04** afar, wide **06** afield **12** at arm's length

**• short distance**
**03** wee **06** bittie **11** stone's-throw

**distant**
**03** far, icy **04** cold, cool, deep
**05** aloof, blank, stiff **06** abroad, dreamy, far-off, formal, remote, slight, vacant **07** faraway, glacial
**08** detached, far-flung, indirect, isolated, not close, outlying, reserved
**09** dispersed, withdrawn
**10** antisocial, distracted, indistinct, restrained, unfriendly **11** daydreaming, out-of-the-way, preoccupied, stand-offish, up the Boohai **12** absent-minded, back of beyond, unresponsive
**14** unapproachable
**15** uncommunicative

**distantly**
**05** dimly, miles **06** coldly, coolly
**07** faintly, far away, stiffly, vaguely
**08** a long way, formally, remotely, slightly, vacantly **10** not closely
**11** imprecisely **12** some distance
**13** great distance, unemotionally
**14** unresponsively

**distaste**
**06** dégoût, horror, offend **07** disgust, dislike, offence **08** aversion, loathing
**09** antipathy, disfavour, disrelish, revulsion **10** abhorrence, repugnance
**11** displeasure

**• expression of distaste**
**03** ugh, wow, yuk **04** whow, yech, yuck **05** wowee

**distasteful**
**04** gory, icky **08** god-awful
**09** abhorrent, loathsome, obnoxious, offensive, repellant, repellent, repugnant, repulsive, revolting, unsavoury **10** detestable, disgusting, uninviting, unpleasant **11** displeasing, undesirable, unpalatable
**12** disagreeable **13** objectionable

**distend**
**04** puff **05** bloat, bulge, swell, widen
**06** dilate, expand **07** balloon, enlarge, fill out, inflate, stretch **09** intumesce
**10** exaggerate

**distended**
**05** puffy **06** astrut, puffed **07** bloated, dilated, distent, swollen **08** enlarged, expanded, inflated, varicose
**09** puffed-out, stretched, tumescent
**10** ventricose, ventricous
**13** emphysematous

**distension**
**05** swell **06** spread **07** breadth
**08** bloating, dilation, swelling
**09** emphysema, expansion, extension
**10** flatulence, flatulency, tumescence, tympanites, wind dropsy
**11** enlargement, turgescence
**12** intumescence **14** hydronephrosis

**distil**
**04** drip, flow, leak **05** still **06** derive, purify, refine **07** draw out, express, extract, rectify, trickle **08** condense, press out, vaporize **09** evaporate, sublimate

**distillation**
◇ *anagram indicator*
**06** spirit **07** essence, extract
**10** extraction **11** evaporation
**12** condensation, purification

**distinct**
**05** clear, plain, sharp **06** marked
**07** defined, diverse, evident, obvious, several **08** apparent, clear-cut, definite, detached, discrete, manifest, separate **09** different, disparate, trenchant **10** dissimilar, individual, noticeable, variegated
**11** unambiguous, unconnected, well-defined **12** recognizable, unassociated, unmistakable
**13** distinguished **14** differentiated

**distinction**
**04** fame, mark, note **05** éclat, honor, merit, siege, worth **06** credit, honour, luster, lustre, renown, repute
**07** diorism, feature, quality
**08** contrast, division, eminence, prestige **09** celebrity, greatness
**10** difference, excellence, importance, prominence, reputation, separation
**11** consequence, discernment, peculiarity, superiority **12** distinctness, significance **13** dissimilarity, dissimilitude, individuality
**14** characteristic, discrimination
**15** differentiation, distinguishment
*See also* **honour**

**distinctive**
**06** unique **07** special, typical
**08** original, peculiar, singular
**09** different **10** individual, noteworthy, particular **13** extraordinary, idiosyncratic **14** characteristic, distinguishing

**distinctiveness**
**10** uniqueness **11** originality, peculiarity, singularity **12** idiosyncrasy
**13** individuality **14** noteworthiness

**distinctly**
**05** plain **07** clearly, plainly
**08** markedly **09** decidedly, evidently, obviously **10** definitely, manifestly, noticeably **12** unmistakably
**13** unambiguously, unmistakeably

**distinguish**
**03** see **04** dist, mark **05** excel, judge, stamp **06** descry, detect, divide, do well, notice, pick up, secern, typify
**07** dignify, discern, ennoble, glorify, make out, mark off, pick out **08** classify, identify, perceive, set apart, tell from
**09** ascertain, determine, recognize, signalize, single out, tell apart
**10** categorize **11** bring fame to
**12** characterize, discriminate **13** bring honour to, differentiate, particularize
**14** bring acclaim to

**distinguishable**
**05** clear, plain **07** evident, obvious
**08** dividant, manifest **10** noticeable, observable **11** appreciable, conspicuous, discernible, perceptible, plainly seen **12** recognizable

**distinguished**
**04** fine **05** famed, noble, noted
**06** famous, marked, of note
**07** eminent, notable, refined, shining
**08** distinct, especial, esteemed, eximious, honoured, identify, renowned, striking **09** acclaimed, egregious, prominent, well-known
**10** celebrated, nameworthy
**11** conspicuous, illustrious, outstanding
**12** aristocratic **13** extraordinary

**distinguishing**
**06** marked, unique **07** typical
**08** peculiar, singular **09** diacritic, different **10** diagnostic, episematic, individual **11** diacritical, distinctive
**14** characteristic, discriminative, discriminatory **15** differentiating, differentiation, individualistic

**distort**
◇ *anagram indicator*
**04** bend, bias, rack, skew, warp
**05** color, fudge, slant, thraw, twist, wrest, wring **06** buckle, colour, deform, detort, garble, hamper, jumble, mangle, wrench, writhe
**07** contort, falsify, pervert, screw up, torment, torture **08** misshape
**09** disfigure, pull about **10** tamper with **12** cook the books, misrepresent

**distorted**
◇ *anagram indicator*
**03** wry **04** awry, bent, skew **05** false, thraw **06** biased, skewed, thrawn, warped **07** twisted **08** deformed, tortured **09** falsified, misshapen, perverted **10** disfigured, out of shape
**14** misrepresented

**distortion**
**04** bend, bias, skew, warp **05** slant, twist **06** buckle **07** warping
**08** cinching, garbling, twisting
**09** colouring, deformity
**10** contortion, perversion
**11** crookedness **13** falsification

**distract**
◇ *anagram indicator*
**05** amuse **06** divert, harass, madden,

occupy, put off, puzzle **07** confuse, deflect, detract, disturb, embroil, engross, fluster, perplex **08** bewilder, confound, draw away, forhaile, throw out, turn away **09** entertain, sidetrack, turn aside **10** discompose, disconcert

**distracted**
◇ *anagram indicator*
**03** mad **04** wild **05** crazy, upset **06** éperdu, raving **07** anxious, éperdue, frantic, madding **08** agitated, confused, diverted, dreaming, frenetic, harassed, maddened, worked up **09** miles away, not with it, scattered, up the wall, wandering **10** abstracted, bestraught, bewildered, distraught, distressed, hysterical **11** inattentive, overwrought, preoccupied **12** absent-minded **13** grief-stricken **14** beside yourself

**distracting**
**07** diverse **08** annoying **09** confusing **10** disturbing, irritating, off-putting, perturbing, unsettling **11** bewildering **13** disconcerting

**distraction**
**04** game **05** hobby, sport **07** madness, pastime **09** agitation, amusement, avocation, confusion, diversion **10** perplexity, recreation, relaxation **11** derangement, disturbance, interrupted **12** interference **13** entertainment **14** divertissement
• **drive to distraction**
**05** anger, annoy, upset **06** madden **10** drive crazy, exasperate

**distraint**
**03** nam **04** naam **06** stress

**distraught**
◇ *anagram indicator*
**03** mad **04** wild **05** crazy, elvan, elven, het up, upset **06** elfish, elvish, raving **07** anxious, frantic, worried **08** agitated, in a state, worked up, wretched **09** perplexed **10** distracted, distressed, hysterical **11** overwrought **14** beside yourself

**distress**
**03** irk, vex, woe **04** hurt, need, pain, prey **05** agony, cut up, grief, peril, trial, upset, worry **06** danger, grieve, harass, harrow, misery, penury, sadden, sorrow, unease **07** afflict, agonize, anguish, anxiety, disturb, misease, oppress, perturb, poverty, put to it, sadness, torment, torture, trouble **08** aggrieve, calamity, distrain, exigence, exigency, hardship, straiten **09** adversity, extremity, heartache, indigence, privation, suffering **10** affliction, compulsion, desolation, difficulty, discomfort, exhaustion, misfortune **11** destitution, make anxious, tribulation **12** deforciation, difficulties, perturbation, wretchedness **13** make miserable

**distressed**
**03** ill **04** hurt, sore **05** upset **06** pained, put out **07** uptight, worried **08** bothered, dismayed, in a state, perished, troubled, worked up **09** aggrieved, disturbed, heart-sore, on the rack, perturbed, strung out, unsettled **11** discomposed **12** impoverished

**distressing**
**05** sorry **06** crying, tragic, trying, uneath **07** painful **08** alarming, tragical, worrying **09** harrowing, startling, upsetting **10** afflicting, disturbing, off-putting, perturbing, unsettling **11** frightening **13** disconcerting

**distribute**
◇ *anagram indicator*
**04** deal, dish, part **05** allot, carve, issue, ladle, share **06** assort, digest, divide, spread, supply **07** deal out, deliver, diffuse, dish out, dispose, dole out, give out, hand out, mete out, pass out, prorate, scatter **08** allocate, dispense, disperse, ladle out, serve out, transmit **09** apportion, circulate, discharge, pass round **10** measure out, reticulate **11** disseminate

**distribution**
◇ *anagram indicator*
**05** range **06** supply **07** dealing, sharing **08** delivery, division, grouping, handling, position **09** allotment, diffusion, dispersal, giving-out, placement, proration, spreading, transport **10** allocation, conveyance, handing-out, scattering **11** arrangement, circulation, disposition, repartition **12** organization **13** apportionment, dissemination **14** classification, transportation

**district**
**03** gau, way **04** area, belt, hunt, land, leet, pale, ride, side, soke, walk, ward, zila, zone **05** block, patch, place, shire **06** barrio, bounds, circar, county, domain, locale, parish, region, riding, sector, sircar, sirkar, suburb **07** circuit, quarter, section **08** faubourg, highland, locality, precinct, province, quartier, stannary, vicinity **09** community, territory **12** constituency, municipality, neighborhood **13** neighbourhood **15** circumscription

*Districts of Northern Ireland:*

**04** Ards, Down
**05** Derry, Larne, Moyle, Omagh
**06** Antrim, Armagh
**07** Belfast, Lisburn
**08** Limavady, Strabane
**09** Ballymena, Banbridge, Coleraine, Cookstown, Craigavon, Dungannon, Fermanagh, North Down
**10** Ballymoney
**11** Castlereagh, Magherafelt
**12** Newtownabbey
**13** Carrickfergus
**14** Newry and Mourne

*See also* **county**; **London**; **New York**; **Paris**

• **District of Columbia**
**02** DC
• **outer district**
**03** end
• **squalid district**
**04** slum

**distrust**
**05** doubt, qualm **07** suspect **08** be wary of, misfaith, mistrust, question, wariness **09** chariness, disbelief, discredit, misgiving, mislippen, suspicion **10** disbelieve, scepticism **11** questioning **12** doubtfulness **14** be suspicious of **15** have doubts about

**distrustful**
**04** wary **05** chary **06** uneasy **07** cynical, dubious **08** doubtful, doubting **09** sceptical **10** suspicious, untrustful, untrusting **11** distrusting, mistrustful **12** disbelieving

**disturb**
◇ *anagram indicator*
**03** jee, vex **04** fret, stir **05** annoy, rouse, shake, sturt, touch, upset, worry **06** affray, beat up, bother, dismay, hassle, infest, muddle, pester, put off, racket, ruffle, tumult, turn up **07** agitate, commove, concern, concuss, confuse, disrupt, fluster, inquiet, mismake, perturb, trouble **08** butt in on, disorder, disquiet, distract, distress, unsettle **09** discomfit, dislocate, interrupt **10** disarrange, discompose, disconcert, distrouble, perturbate **11** disorganize, make anxious

**disturbance**
◇ *anagram indicator*
**03** row **04** dust, fray, muss, riot, rout **05** brawl, broil, musse, sturt, upset **06** bother, cangle, fracas, hassle, hoop-la, kick-up, muddle, racket, ruckus, rumble, rumpus, tumult, turn-up, unrest, uproar, upturn **07** illness, ruction, stashie, stishie, stushie, trouble, turmoil **08** disorder, neurosis, outbreak, sickness, stooshie, stramash, upheaval, williwaw **09** agitation, annoyance, commotion, complaint, confusion, hindrance, intrusion **10** convulsion, disruption, hullabaloo, inquietude, perplexity, rough-house **11** derangement, distraction, embroilment, molestation **12** interference, interruption **13** collieshangie **14** distemperature
• **freedom from disturbance**
**04** ease

**disturbed**
◇ *anagram indicator*
**04** vext **05** upset, vexed **06** hung-up, uneasy **07** anxious, inquiet, unquiet, worried **08** bothered, confused, neurotic, paranoid, troubled, unstable **09** concerned, flustered, psychotic, screwed-up, turbulent **10** mistrysted, unbalanced **11** discomposed, maladjusted, mentally ill **12** apprehensive **13** dysfunctional

**disturbing**
◇ *anagram indicator*
**08** alarming, worrying **09** agitating, confusing, dismaying, startling, troubling, troublous, upsetting
**10** disturbant, perturbing, unsettling
**11** bewildering, disquieting, distressing, frightening, threatening
**12** discouraging, disturbative
**13** disconcerting

**disunited**
**05** split **07** divided **09** alienated, disrupted, estranged, separated
**10** dissevered

**disunity**
**05** split **06** breach, schism, strife
**07** discord, dissent, rupture
**08** conflict, division **10** alienation, dissension **11** discordance
**12** disagreement, estrangement

**disuse**
**05** decay **07** neglect **09** desuetude
**11** abandonment, inusitation
**14** discontinuance

**disused**
**04** idle **06** unused **07** decayed
**08** obsolete **09** abandoned, neglected
**12** discontinued

**ditch**
**04** delf, dike, drop, dump, dyke, foss, grip, ha-ha, lode, moat, rean, reen, sike, syke **05** canal, chuck, delph, drain, fosse, graft, gripe, gully, level, rhine, rhyne, scrap, stank **06** derail, furrow, gulley, gutter, haw-haw, sheuch, sheugh, the sea, trench, trough
**07** abandon, channel, discard, euripus
**08** get rid of, jettison, throw out
**09** dispose of, sunk fence, throw away
**11** watercourse

**dither**
◇ *anagram indicator*
**04** faff, flap, stew, tizz **05** delay, panic, quake, tizzy, waver **06** bother, dicker, falter, pother, shiver **07** agitate, confuse, fluster, flutter, perturb, tremble **08** hang back, hesitate **09** faff about, vacillate **10** dilly-dally, indecision **12** be in two minds, perturbation, shilly-shally, take your time

**ditto**
**02** do

**divan**
**04** sofa **05** couch, dewan **06** day bed, lounge, settee **07** council, lounger, ottoman, sofa bed **08** assembly
**12** chaise-longue, chesterfield

**dive**
**03** bar, dip, fly, ken, pub **04** bolt, club, dart, dash, drop, duck, dump, fall, hole, jump, leap, rush, tear **05** hurry, joint, lunge, pitch, sound, swoop **06** go down, header, plunge, refuge, saloon, spring, subway **07** descend, go under, plummet **08** nose-dive, submerge, tailspin **09** belly-flop, jackknife, nightclub **11** move quickly

**diver**
**04** loom, loon **05** grebe **08** aquanaut, urinator **09** guillemot **10** pickpocket
*See also* **swimmer**

**diverge**
**04** fork, part, vary **05** clash, drift, split, stray **06** branch, depart, differ, divide, spread, wander **07** deflect, deviate, digress, dissent, radiate **08** conflict, disagree, divagate, separate
**09** bifurcate, branch off, spread out, subdivide **10** contradict, divaricate
**12** be at variance

**divergence**
**03** gap **05** clash, slant **07** parting
**08** conflict **09** departure, deviation, dichotomy, disparity, variation
**10** deflection, difference, digression, separation **12** branching-out, disagreement, divarication

**divergent**
**07** diverse, variant, varying
**08** separate **09** deviating, different, differing, diverging **10** dissimilar, divaricate, tangential **11** conflicting, disagreeing

**divers**
**04** many, some **06** sundry, varied
**07** several, various, varying
**08** manifold, numerous **09** different
**12** multifarious **13** miscellaneous

**diverse**
◇ *anagram indicator*
**05** mixed **06** sundry, unlike, varied
**07** several, various, varying
**08** assorted, discrete, distinct, manifold, separate **09** different, differing, multiform **10** all means of, dissimilar **11** contrasting, distracting
**13** heterogeneous, miscellaneous

**diversification**
**09** extension, variation **10** alteration
**11** variegation **12** branching-out, modification, spreading-out

**diversify**
**03** mix **04** vary **05** alter, paint, spice
**06** assort, change, expand, extend, modify **08** sprinkle **09** branch out, spread out, variegate **11** intersperse
**13** differentiate **14** bring variety to

**diversion**
◇ *anagram indicator*
**03** fun **04** game, play **05** hobby, sport
**06** change, detour **07** pastime
**09** amusement, avocation, deviation, switching **10** alteration, recreation, relaxation, rerouteing **11** distraction, redirection **13** divertisement, entertainment **14** divertissement

**diversionary**
**09** divertive **10** deflecting
**11** distracting

**diversity**
**05** range **06** medley **07** mixture, variety **08** variance **09** pluralism
**10** assortment, difference, embroidery, miscellany **11** variegation
**12** biodiversity **13** dissimilarity, dissimilitude, heterogeneity
**15** diversification

**divert**
◇ *anagram indicator*
**04** sway **05** amuse, avert **06** absorb, baffle, occupy, put off, siphon, switch, syphon **07** deflect, delight, engross, hive off, pervert, reroute, turn off
**08** call away, distract, draw away, estrange, interest, intrigue, redirect, turn away **09** entertain, sidetrack

**diverting**
◇ *anagram indicator*
**03** fun **05** funny, witty **07** amusing
**08** humorous, pleasant **09** enjoyable
**11** pleasurable **12** entertaining

**divest**
**04** doff **05** strip **06** denude, remove
**07** deprive, despoil, disrobe, undress
**08** unclothe **09** disentail
**10** dispossess

**divide**
◇ *insertion indicator*
**03** cut, div, gap **04** deal, divi, fork, gulf, part, rank, rift, sort **05** allot, break, cut up, grade, group, order, sever, share, split **06** bisect, branch, breach, cantle, cleave, depart, detach **07** arrange, break up, carve up, deal out, discide, dispart, diverge, dole out, fissure, hand out, opening, sort out, split up
**08** alienate, allocate, classify, dispense, disunite, division, estrange, polarize, separate, share out **09** apportion, break down, segregate, watershed
**10** categorize, disconnect, distribute, divergence, drive apart, measure out, separation **11** come between, distinguish

• **divide up**
**05** allot, share **07** dole out **08** allocate, share out **09** apportion, dismember, parcel out **10** measure out

**dividend**
**03** cut, div, FID **04** divi, gain, perk, plus
**05** bonus, divvy, extra, share, whack
**07** benefit, portion, surplus
**09** advantage **10** percentage, perquisite

**divination**
**05** -mancy **06** augury **07** presage
**08** divining, prophecy **10** conjecture, prediction **11** foretelling, hariolation, second sight, soothsaying **14** fortune-telling **15** prognostication

*Divination and fortune-telling techniques include:*

**04** dice
**05** runes, tarot
**06** I Ching, sortes
**07** dowsing, scrying
**08** geomancy, myomancy, taghairm, zoomancy
**09** aeromancy, astrology, belomancy, ceromancy, gyromancy, oenomancy, palmistry, pyromancy, sortilege, tea leaves, theomancy
**10** axinomancy, capnomancy, cartomancy, chiromancy,

cleromancy, dukkeripen, hieromancy, hydromancy, lithomancy, numerology, spodomancy
**11** bibliomancy, botanomancy, crithomancy, gastromancy, hepatoscopy, oneiromancy, onychomancy, rhabdomancy, tephromancy
**12** clairvoyance, coscinomancy, lampadomancy, omphalomancy, ornithomancy, radiesthesia, scapulomancy
**13** Book of Changes, crystal gazing, dactyliomancy, fortune cookie, omoplatoscopy
**14** crystallomancy

---

**divine**
**04** holy, spae **05** godly, guess, infer **06** cleric, deduce, intuit, lovely, parson, pastor, priest, sacred **07** angelic, exalted, godlike, prelate, saintly, suppose, supreme, surmise, suspect **08** charming, foretell, glorious, heavenly, minister, mystical, perceive, reverend, seraphic, splendid **09** apprehend, beautiful, celestial, churchman, clergyman, excellent, prescient, religious, spiritual, wonderful **10** conjecture, delightful, sanctified, superhuman, theologian, understand **11** churchwoman, clergywoman, consecrated **12** ecclesiastic, supernatural, transcendent **13** prognosticate

*See also* **clergyman, clergywoman**; **religious**

**divinely**
**08** heavenly **10** charmingly, gloriously, mystically **11** angelically, celestially, excellently, spiritually, wonderfully **12** delightfully **14** supernaturally

**diviner**
**04** seer **05** augur, sibyl **06** dowser, oracle **07** prophet **08** haruspex **09** divinator, visionary **10** astrologer, soothsayer **11** clairvoyant, conjecturer, water-finder **12** crystal-gazer

**diving** *see* **swimming**

**divinity**
**02** RE, RI **03** god **05** deity **06** spirit **07** goddess, godhead, godship **08** holiness, numinous, religion, sanctity, theology **09** godliness **10** divineness

*See also* **God**; **god, goddess**

**division**
**03** arm, div **04** feud, part, rift, side **05** class, group, limit, share, split, tribe, tuath, world **06** border, branch, breach, divide, region, schism, sector **07** barrier, cutting, discord, parting, portion, rupture, scruple, section, segment, sharing **08** boundary, category, conflict, disunion, disunity, dividing, frontier, scission, scissure, townland **09** allotment, cutting up, detaching, partition, severance **10** alienation, allocation, department, digitation, dividing up, separation, sharing out, subsection **11** compartment, distinction **12** disagreement, distribution, dividing-line, estrangement **13** apportionment **15** demarcation line

**divisive**
**08** damaging **09** injurious **10** alienating, discordant, disruptive, estranging, schismatic **11** troublesome **12** inharmonious **13** troublemaking

**divorce**
**03** div **04** part **05** annul, sever, split, talak, talaq **06** breach, bust up, detach, divide **07** break up, break-up, isolate, put away, rupture, split up, split-up **08** dissolve, disunion, disunite, division, separate **09** annulment, partition, repudiate, severance **10** disconnect, dissociate, separation **11** dissolution, divorcement **13** diffarreation

**divorced**
**03** div

**divorcee**
**02** ex

**divulge**
**04** leak, talk, tell **05** let on, split **06** babble, betray, bewray, expose, impart, repeat, reveal **07** confess, declare, let slip, publish, uncover **08** disclose, evulgate, proclaim **09** broadcast, make known, unconfine **10** promulgate **11** blow the gaff, communicate **12** break the news **13** spill the beans

**dizziness**
**06** megrim **07** megrims, vertigo **09** faintness, giddiness, mirligoes, wooziness **10** scotodinia **15** light-headedness, vertiginousness

**dizzy**
◇ *anagram indicator*
**04** mazy **05** dazed, ditsy, faint, giddy, shaky, silly, woozy **06** wobbly **07** confuse, extreme, foolish, muddled, reeling **08** confused, Disraeli **09** airheaded, confusing, Gillespie **10** bewildered, off-balance **11** addle-headed, bewildering, light-headed, vertiginous **13** irresponsible, rattle-brained **14** feather-brained, scatterbrained, weak at the knees

**Djibouti**
**03** DJI

**do**
◇ *anagram indicator*
**02** ut **03** act, con, dae, end, fix, put, rob **04** bash, char, comb, cook, dope, do up, dupe, fare, fuss, go at, have, hoax, make, raid, read, take, tidy, tour, wash, work **05** brush, cause, cheat, clean, crack, event, feast, get on, learn, mimic, offer, party, place, put on, reach, serve, solve, study, style, treat, trick, visit **06** adjust, affair, beat up, behave, bestow, come on, confer, create, finish, fleece, fulfil, manage, master, rave-up, render, rip off, soirée, supply, tackle, tart up, thrash, thrive, tidy up, work as, work at, work on **07** achieve, arrange, assault, clean up, deceive, defraud, develop, dope out, execute, exhaust, explore, furnish, go round, knees-up, major in, perform, prepare, present, proceed, produce, provide, resolve, satisfy, sort out, suffice, swindle, work out **08** activity, be enough, carry out, complete, conclude, deal with, decorate, function, get along, get ready, hoodwink, occasion, organize, progress, sightsee, travel at **09** come along, discharge, figure out, gathering, implement, look after, overreach, prosecute, puzzle out, reception, undertake **10** accomplish, be adequate, effectuate, fit the bill, have as a job, take care of, try to solve **11** celebration, impersonate, travel round **12** be employed as, be in charge of, be sufficient, take for a ride **13** earn a living as, make a bad job of **14** acquit yourself, be satisfactory, make a good job of **15** comport yourself, conduct yourself, find the answer to, put into practice

**• do away with**
**04** do in, kill, slay **05** annul, scrap **06** murder, remove **07** abolish, bump off, destroy, discard, nullify **08** get rid of, knock off **09** dispose of, eliminate, finish off, liquidate, slaughter **10** put to death **11** assassinate, discontinue, exterminate

**• do down**
**04** slag, slam **05** blame, cheat **06** dump on, subdue **07** censure, condemn, put down, rubbish, slag off **08** badmouth, belittle **09** criticize, disparage **13** find fault with

**• do in**
**04** kill, ruin, slay **06** murder **07** bump off, deceive, exhaust **08** knock off **09** slaughter **10** put to death **11** assassinate, exterminate

**• do out of**
**06** fleece **08** con out of **09** deprive of **10** cheat out of, trick out of **11** diddle out of **12** swindle out of

**• dos and don'ts**
**04** code **05** rules **07** customs **09** etiquette, standards **11** regulations **12** instructions

**• do up**
**03** tie **04** lace, pack **05** tie up, zip up **06** button, fasten, repair **07** arrange, restore **08** decorate, renovate **09** modernize, refurbish **10** redecorate **11** recondition

**• do without**
**04** miss, want **05** forgo, spare **06** eschew, forego, give up **07** refrain **09** go without **10** relinquish **11** abstain from **12** deny yourself, dispense with **13** manage without

**• that will do**
**02** so **03** sae

**docile**
**07** dutiful, willing **08** amenable, flexible, obedient, obliging, yielding

09 childlike, compliant, tractable
10 controlled, manageable, submissive 11 co-operative
12 controllable

## docilely
08 amenably 09 dutifully, willingly
10 obediently, obligingly
11 compliantly 13 co-operatively

## docility
07 pliancy 08 meekness 09 ductility, obedience 10 compliance, pliability
11 amenability 12 biddableness, complaisance, tractability
13 manageability 14 submissiveness

## dock
◇ *tail deletion indicator*
02 dk 03 bob, cut, pen 04 clip, crop, land, moor, pier, quay, rump 05 basin, berth, jetty, put in, Rumex, tie up, wharf
06 anchor, deduct, detail, lessen, marina, reduce, remove, sorrel
07 bistort, curtail, harbour, shorten
08 boat yard, canaigre, decrease, diminish, patience, quayside, subtract, truncate, withhold 09 grapetree, polygonum 10 drop anchor, tidal basin, waterfront 12 monk's rhubarb, submarine pen 15 fitting-out basin

**• docked**
02 in

**• in the dock**
07 on trial

## docker
04 ship 06 lumper 08 labourer
09 stevedore 11 farmer's wife
12 longshoreman

## docket
03 tab, tag 04 bill, chit, file, mark
05 index, label, tally 06 chitty, coupon, record, ticket 07 receipt, voucher
08 document, register 09 catalogue, paperwork 10 categorize
11 certificate, counterfoil
13 documentation

## doctor
◇ *anagram indicator*
02 Dr 03 doc 04 cook, drug, fake, lace, load, pill, spay 05 alter, bones, medic, quack, spike 06 change, crocus, dilute, fiddle, mganga, neuter, repair, weaken 07 falsify, massage, pervert, sangoma 08 castrate, disguise, marabout, medicate, medicine, sawbones 09 body-curer, clinician, physician, sterilize 10 add drugs to, adulterate, manipulate, tamper with 11 add poison to, contaminate, witch-finder
12 misrepresent, sophisticate
13 interfere with

*Doctor types include:*

02 BM, GP, MB, MD, MO
03 vet
05 locum
06 intern
07 dentist, surgeon
08 houseman, resident
09 registrar
10 consultant
12 family doctor
14 hospital doctor, medical officer

*See also* **medical**

*Doctors include:*

03 Who
04 **Bell** (Sir Charles), **Koch** (Robert), **Lind** (James), **Mayo** (Charles), **Razi** (ar-), **Reed** (Walter), **Ross** (Sir Ronald)
05 **Broca** (Paul Pierre), **Bruce** (Sir David), **Galen**, **Lower** (Richard), **Osler** (Sir William), **Paget** (Sir James), **Remak** (Robert), **Steno** (Nicolaus)
06 **Bichat** (Marie), **Bright** (Richard), **Carrel** (Alexis), **Celsus** (Aulus), **Cooper** (Sir Astley), **Fernel** (Jean), **Finsen** (Niels), **Garrod** (Sir Archibald), **Harvey** (William), **Hunter** (John), **Jekyll**, **Jenner** (Edward), **Lister** (Joseph, Lord), **Manson** (Sir Patrick), **Mesmer** (Franz), **Watson** (John), **Willis** (Thomas)
07 **Addison** (Thomas), **Barnard** (Christiaan), **Beddoes** (Thomas), **Burkitt** (Denis), **Cushing** (Harvey), **Eijkman** (Christiaan), **Gilbert** (William), **Hodgkin** (Thomas), **Laënnec** (René), **Laveran** (Charles), **Linacre** (Thomas), **MacEwen** (Sir William), **McIndoe** (Sir Archibald), **Nicolle** (Charles), **Winston** (Robert, Lord)
08 **Anderson** (Elizabeth Garrett), **Barnardo** (Thomas), **Beaumont** (William), **Billroth** (Theodor), **Charnley** (Sir John), **Duchenne** (Guillaume), **Magendie** (François), **Morgagni** (Giovanni Battista), **Sydenham** (Thomas), **Tournier** (Paul)
09 **Bartholin** (Erasmus), **Boerhaave** (Hermann), **Dutrochet** (Henri), **Fabricius** (Johannes), **Hahnemann** (Samuel), **Mackenzie** (Sir James), **Parkinson** (James)
10 **Fracastoro** (Girolamo), **Paracelsus**, **Sanctorius**
11 **Hippocrates**, **Ramón y Cajal** (Santiago)
12 **Erasistratus**

*See also* **surgeon**

## doctrinaire
05 rigid 06 biased 08 armchair, dogmatic, pedantic 09 fanatical, insistent 10 inflexible 11 impractical, opinionated, theoretical

## doctrine
03 ism 04 lore 05 canon, credo, creed, dogma, tenet 06 belief
07 esotery, mystery, opinion, precept
08 teaching 09 principle 10 conviction

*See also* **philosophy**

## document
04 chop, cite, deed, form, list, roll, writ
05 chart, paper, proof, prove 06 back up, billet, detail, patent, record, report, verify 07 charter, support, warning, write up 08 evidence, register, validate
09 affidavit, chronicle, write down
10 chirograph, commission, instrument 11 certificate, corroborate, instruction, put on record
12 command paper, commit to film, give weight to, keep on record, substantiate 13 commit to paper

## documentary
07 charted, factual, written
08 detailed, recorded 09 reportage
10 chronicled, documented, featurette

## documentation
06 papers, record 08 evidence
09 authority, paperwork
12 verification 14 qualifications

## doddering
◇ *anagram indicator*
04 aged, weak 05 frail 06 feeble, infirm, senile 07 elderly 08 decrepit
09 tottering

## doddery
◇ *anagram indicator*
04 aged, weak 05 shaky 06 feeble, infirm 07 tottery 08 unsteady
09 doddering, faltering, tottering
10 staggering

## dodge
03 tip 04 bolt, dart, dash, dive, duck, fake, jink, jook, jouk, lurk, ploy, ruse, rush, shun, veer, wile 05 avoid, elude, evade, fudge, shift, shirk, trick
06 bypass, device, racket, scheme, swerve 07 evasion, fend off, quibble, shuffle, slinter, wrinkle 08 fakement, get out of, get round, gimcrack, jimcrack, jump away, side-step
09 deception, manoeuvre, stratagem
10 subterfuge 11 contrivance, machination 12 move suddenly, steer clear of 13 sharp practice

## dodger
06 evader, skiver 07 avoider, dreamer, goof-off, shirker, slacker 08 layabout, slyboots 09 lazybones, trickster
11 goldbricker, lead-swinger

## dodgy
◇ *anagram indicator*
04 iffy 05 crook, dicey, fishy, risky
06 artful, chancy, tricky, unsafe
07 dubious, fraught, suspect
08 doubtful, unstable 09 dangerous, dishonest, uncertain 10 unreliable
12 disreputable 13 problematical

## doer
04 hand 05 agent 06 dynamo, factor, worker 07 bustler 08 achiever, activist, executor, go-getter, live wire
09 organizer 10 powerhouse
12 accomplisher 14 mover and shaker

## doff
03 tip 04 lift, shed, vail 05 avail, avale, raise, strip, touch 06 availe, lay off, remove 07 discard, take off, undight
08 throw off

## dog
03 cur, pup, tag 04 cock, Fido, mutt, stag, tail, tike, tyke 05 bitch, harry,

haunt, hound, piper, pooch, puppy, rogue, Rover, stalk, track, trail, worry **06** barker, bitser, canine, follow, infest, plague, pursue, rascal, shadow, touser, towser, wretch, yapper **07** andiron, mongrel, traitor, trouble, villain, whiffet, yapster **08** informer **09** scoundrel **10** tripehound **11** Montmorency, trendle-tail, trindle-tail, trundle-tail

*See also* **animal**

*Dogs include:*

**03** gun, lab, Pom, pug
**04** chow, kuri, Peke, tosa
**05** akita, boxer, corgi, dhole, dingo, husky, hyena, laika, spitz
**06** badger, bandog, beagle, bitser, borzoi, briard, collie, gun dog, moppet, poodle, saluki, Scotty, setter, vizsla, Westie
**07** basenji, bouvier, bulldog, bush dog, coondog, griffon, lurcher, Maltese, mastiff, pitbull, pointer, Samoyed, Scottie, Shar-Pei, sheltie, shih tzu, sloughi, spaniel, terrier, volpino, whippet
**08** Airedale, alsatian, chow-chow, coach dog, Doberman, elkhound, foxhound, keeshond, komondor, Labrador, malamute, papillon, Pekinese, Sealyham, sheepdog, warrigal
**09** boar-hound, chihuahua, coonhound, dachshund, Dalmatian, Eskimo dog, Great Dane, greyhound, Kerry Blue, lhasa apso, Pekingese, red setter, retriever, schnauzer, St Bernard, wolfhound
**10** bloodhound, fox terrier, Iceland-dog, Maltese dog, otter hound, Pomeranian, raccoon dog, Rottweiler, sausage-dog, spotted dog, St Bernard's
**11** Afghan hound, basset-hound, bichon frise, bull-mastiff, bull terrier, carriage dog, Irish setter, Jack Russell, kangaroo dog, wishtonwish
**12** Border collie, cairn terrier, Irish terrier, Japanese tosa, Newfoundland
**13** affenpinscher, bearded collie, Boston terrier, cocker spaniel, Scotch terrier
**14** English terrier, German Shepherd, Irish wolfhound, pit bull terrier
**15** golden retriever, Scottish terrier, springer spaniel

*See also* **spaniel**; **terrier**

*Dog types include:*

**02** pi
**03** gun, hot, lap, pet, pie, pye, sea, top, toy, war
**04** corn, rach, wild
**05** guard, guide, house, pooch, rache, ratch, sheep, under, watch, water, zorro
**06** kennet, pariah, police, ranger, ratter, sleeve, yellow
**07** harrier, hearing, leading, mongrel, tracker, truffle
**08** huntaway, turnspit
**09** retriever
**10** sheep-biter, shin-barker
**11** sleuth-hound

*Famous dogs include:*

**03** Lad
**04** Lucy, Nana, Odie, Shep, Spot, Toby, Toto
**05** Balto, Butch, Flush, Goofy, Laika, Petra, Pluto, Pongo, Sadie, Snowy, Timmy
**06** Buster, Droopy, Gelert, Gromit, Hector, Lassie, Missis, Nipper, Sirius, Snoopy
**07** Charley, Gnasher, Perdita, Roobarb
**08** Bullseye, Cerberus, Dogmatix
**09** RinTinTin, Scooby Doo
**10** Deputy Dawg, Fred Basset
**12** Real Huntsman
**13** Master McGrath, Mick the Miller
**15** Greyfriars Bobby, The Littlest Hobo

• **dog's breakfast, dog's dinner**
**04** mess
• **reproof to dog**
**04** rate

## dogged

**04** firm **06** intent, steady, sullen **07** staunch **08** obdurate, resolute, stubborn, tireless **09** obstinate, steadfast, tenacious **10** determined, persistent, relentless, unflagging, unshakable, unyielding **11** indomitable, persevering, unfaltering, unshakeable **12** pertinacious, single-minded **13** indefatigable

## doggedly

**06** firmly **09** staunchly **10** resolutely, stubbornly, tirelessly, unshakably **11** obstinately, steadfastly, tenaciously, unshakeably **12** persistently, relentlessly **13** indefatigably **14** single-mindedly

## doggedness

**08** firmness, tenacity **09** endurance, obstinacy **10** resolution, steadiness **11** persistence, pertinacity **12** perseverance, stubbornness **13** determination, steadfastness, tenaciousness **14** indomitability, relentlessness

## doggerel

**03** jig **08** nonsense, rat-rhyme **11** cramboclink **12** crambo-jingle

## dogma

**04** code **05** credo, creed, maxim, tenet **06** belief **07** article, opinion, precept **08** doctrine, teaching **09** principle **10** conviction **12** code of belief **14** article of faith

## dogmatic

**08** arrogant, emphatic, pontific, positive **09** arbitrary, assertive, canonical, doctrinal, imperious, insistent **10** ex cathedra, intolerant, peremptory, pontifical **11** affirmative, categorical, dictatorial, doctrinaire, domineering, opinionated, overbearing, pragmatical **13** authoritarian, authoritative **14** unquestionable **15** unchallengeable

## dogmatically

**10** arrogantly **11** assertively, imperiously, insistently **12** emphatically, intolerantly **13** categorically, dictatorially, domineeringly **15** authoritatively

## dogmatism

**07** bigotry **11** presumption **12** positiveness **13** arbitrariness, assertiveness, imperiousness **14** peremptoriness **15** dictatorialness, opinionatedness

## dogsbody

**05** gofer, slave **06** drudge, lackey, menial, skivvy **07** doormat **08** factotum **11** galley-slave **12** bottle-washer, man-of-all-work **13** maid-of-all-work

## doings

**04** acts, work **05** deeds, feats **06** events **07** actions, affairs **08** concerns, dealings, exploits, goings-on **09** handiwork **10** activities, adventures, happenings **11** enterprises, proceedings **12** achievements, transactions

## doldrums

**05** blues, dumps, ennui, gloom **06** acedia, apathy, tedium, torpor **07** boredom, inertia, malaise, megrims **08** dullness **09** dejection, lassitude **10** depression, melancholy, stagnation **12** listlessness, sluggishness **15** downheartedness, low-spiritedness

## dole

**03** JSA **04** broo, pain, vail **05** grief, guile, share, vails, vales **06** credit, income **07** benefit, payment, support **08** pittance **09** allowance **12** state benefit **14** social security
• **dole out**
**04** deal **05** allot, issue, share **06** assign, divide, ration **07** deal out, dish out, give out, hand out, mete out **08** allocate, dispense, divide up, share out **09** apportion **10** administer, distribute

## doleful

**03** sad **04** blue **06** dismal, dreary, gloomy, rueful, sombre, woeful **07** forlorn, painful, pitiful **08** dolorous, mournful, pathetic, wretched **09** cheerless, miserable, sorrowful, woebegone **10** depressing, lugubrious, melancholy **11** distressing **12** disconsolate **14** down in the dumps

## dolefully

**05** sadly **08** dismally, gloomily **09** forlornly, miserably, unhappily **10** mournfully, wretchedly **12** pathetically **14** disconsolately

## doll

**03** toy **04** babe **05** dolly **06** figure **08** figurine **09** plaything

*Dolls include:*

**03** kid, rag, wax
**04** baby
**05** China, cloth, Dutch, metal, paper, Paris, Sindy®
**06** artist, Barbie®, bisque, blow-up, ethnic, fabric, Hamble, kewpie, modern, moppet, poppet, puppet, voodoo, wooden
**07** fashion, jointed, kachina, kokeshi, nesting, rag baby, Russian
**08** golliwog, gollywog
**09** miniature, porcelain, tachibina, Tiny Tears
**10** marionette, matryoshka, Raggedy Ann, topsy-turvy
**11** composition, papier-mâché, Polly Pocket
**12** reproduction
**15** Cabbage Patch Kid, frozen Charlotte

**• doll up**
**05** preen, primp **06** tart up **07** deck out, dress up, trick up **08** titivate, trick out

**dollar**
**03** cob, dol **04** buck, peso **05** scrip, wheel **06** loonie, single **07** iron man, Mexican, smacker **09** greenback
**• eighth of a dollar**
**04** real
**• five dollars**
**03** fin **04** spin **05** fiver

**dollop**
**03** gob **04** ball, blob, glob, lump **05** bunch, clump **06** gobbet, slairg

**dolly**
**05** peggy **06** maiden, Parton, Varden

**dolorous**
**03** sad **06** rueful, sombre, woeful **07** doleful, painful **08** grievous, mournful, wretched **09** anguished, harrowing, miserable, sorrowful, woebegone **10** lugubrious, melancholy **11** distressing **12** heart-rending

**dolour**
**04** pain **05** grief **06** misery, sorrow **07** anguish, sadness **08** distress, mourning **09** heartache, suffering **10** heartbreak **11** lamentation

**dolphin**
**06** sea-pig **07** grampus **08** porpoise **09** coryphene, Delphinus, mere swine **10** bottle-nose

**dolt**
**03** ass, git, oaf **04** clot, dope, dork, fool, geek, nerd, twit **05** chump, clunk, golem, idiot, ninny, twerp, wally **06** dimwit, nitwit **07** nutcase, plonker **08** dipstick, imbecile, mooncalf, numskull **09** blockhead, simpleton **10** clodhopper, nincompoop, sheep's-head **11** chuckle-head

**domain**
**04** area **05** arena, bourn, field, lands, realm, reame, reign, world **06** bourne, empire, estate, region, sphere **07** concern, kingdom, section **08** dominion, province, seignory, universe **09** ownership, seigneury, seigniory, territory **10** department, discipline, seigneurie, speciality **12** jurisdiction

*See also* **classification**

**dome**
**04** tope **05** igloo, mound, stupa, vault **06** bubble, cupola, dagaba, dagoba, tholus **07** rotunda **09** astrodome, macrodome **10** brachydome, hemisphere

**domestic**
**03** dom, pet **04** char, cook, esne, help, home, maid, tame **05** daily, house, local, tamed **06** au pair, broken, family, homely, native **07** cleaner, private, servant **08** broken in, char lady, familiar, fireside, home-bred, home help, internal, national, personal **09** charwoman, daily help, household **10** home-loving, indigenous, stay-at-home **11** domiciliary **12** domesticated, domestic help, housekeeping, house-trained

*Domestic appliances include:*

**03** Aga®, hob, Vax®
**04** iron, oven, spit
**05** grill, mixer, radio, stove
**06** cooker, fridge, Hoover®, juicer, kettle, washer
**07** blender, fan oven, freezer, griddle, ionizer, toaster
**08** barbecue, gas stove, hotplate, wireless
**09** deep fryer, Dutch oven, DVD player, steam iron
**10** coffee mill, deep-freeze, dishwasher, humidifier, liquidizer, percolator, rotisserie, slow cooker, steam press, television, waffle iron
**11** tumble-drier, washer-drier
**12** kitchen range, refrigerator, stereo system, trouser press
**13** carpet sweeper, electric grill, floor polisher, food processor, fridge-freezer, ice-cream maker, microwave oven, sandwich maker, vacuum cleaner, video recorder
**14** electric cooker, juice extractor, upright cleaner, washing machine
**15** carpet shampooer, cylinder cleaner

**domestically**
**06** at home **07** locally **08** near home **09** in private **10** internally, nationally

**domesticate**
**04** tame **05** break, train **07** break in **08** accustom **09** habituate **10** assimilate, house-train, naturalize **11** acclimatize, familiarize

**domesticated**
**03** pet **04** tame **05** tamed **06** broken, homely **08** broken in, domestic **10** home-loving, house-proud **11** housewifely, naturalized **12** house-trained

**domestication**
**06** taming **08** training **10** breaking-in **11** habituation **12** assimilation **13** house-training **14** naturalization

**domesticity**
**09** homecraft **10** homemaking, housecraft **12** housekeeping **13** domestication, home economics **15** domestic science

**domicile**
**04** home, live **05** abode, house **06** settle **07** lodging, mansion **08** dwelling, lodgings, quarters **09** establish, residence, residency **10** habitation, settlement **12** make your home, put down roots **15** take up residence

**dominance**
**04** rule, sway **05** power **07** command, control, mastery **08** hegemony **09** authority, supremacy **10** ascendancy, centrality, domination, government, leadership **11** paramountcy, pre-eminence, superiority

**dominant**
**03** key **04** main **05** chief, major, prime **06** ruling, strong **07** central, leading, primary, supreme **08** powerful **09** assertive, besetting, governing, important, paramount, presiding, prevalent, principal, prominent **10** commanding, overriding, pre-eminent, prevailing **11** all-powerful, controlling, influential, outstanding, predominant **13** authoritative, most important

**dominate**
**04** lead, rule **05** dwarf **06** direct, govern, master, rule OK **07** command, control, eclipse, preside, prevail **08** domineer, overbear, overgang, overlook, overrule **09** mesmerize, tower over, tyrannize **10** intimidate, monopolize, overmaster, overshadow, run the show **11** have on toast, predominate **12** hold the floor **15** have over a barrel, wear the trousers

**dominating**
**06** strong **08** dominant, powerful, superior **09** assertive, confident, directing **10** commanding, overruling **11** controlling **12** advantageous **13** authoritative

**domination**
**04** rule, sway **05** power **07** bossism, command, control, mastery, tyranny **09** authority, despotism, influence, prelatism, supremacy **10** ascendancy, government, leadership, militarism, oppression, repression, subjection **11** pre-eminence, superiority, suppression **12** dictatorship, predominance **13** subordination

**domineer**
**04** boss, ride **07** henpeck **08** jackboot

**domineering**
**05** bossy, pushy **07** haughty, kick-ass

**08** arrogant, coercive, despotic, forceful, managing **09** imperious, masterful, tyrannous **10** aggressive, autocratic, high-handed, iron-handed, oppressive, peremptory, tyrannical **11** dictatorial, overbearing **13** authoritarian

**Dominica**
**02** WD **03** DJI, DMA

**Dominican**
**03** Dom

**Dominican Republic**
**03** DOM

**Dominicans**
**02** OP

**dominion**
**03** Dom **04** rule, sway **05** power, realm **06** colony, domain, empire **07** command, control, country, kingdom, mastery **08** lordship, province **09** authority, direction, supremacy, territory **10** ascendancy, dependency, domination, government **11** sovereignty **12** jurisdiction, protectorate **14** rangatiratanga

**don**
◇ *insertion indicator*
**04** Juan **05** adept, put on, swell, tutor **06** assume, expert, fellow, reader **07** address, dress in, get into, scholar, teacher **08** academic, Giovanni, lecturer, slip into **09** professor

**donate**
**03** gie **04** give **06** bestow, chip in, confer, pledge **07** cough up, fork out, present **08** bequeath, give away, shell out **09** make a gift, subscribe **10** contribute **12** club together **13** make a donation

**donation**
**04** alms, gift, koha, wakf, waqf **05** grant **07** bequest, charity, largess, present **08** gratuity, largesse, memorial, offering **11** benefaction **12** contribution, presentation, subscription

**done**
◇ *anagram indicator*
**02** OK **04** over **05** baked, crisp, ended, fried, ready, right **06** agreed, boiled, cooked, proper, seemly, stewed, tender **07** browned, correct, decided, fitting, roasted, settled **08** accepted, arranged, complete, decorous, executed, finished, prepared, realized, suitable, well-done **09** completed, concluded, fulfilled **10** absolutely, acceptable, terminated **11** appropriate, consummated **12** accomplished, conventional

• **done for**
**04** lost **06** beaten, broken, dashed, doomed, foiled, ruined, undone **07** wrecked **08** defeated, finished, spitcher, washed-up **09** destroyed **10** vanquished **14** for the high jump

• **done in**
**04** dead **05** all in, weary **06** bushed, pooped, zonked **07** whacked, worn out **08** dead beat, dog-tired, fatigued, tired out **09** exhausted, fagged out, fit to drop, flaked out, knackered, pooped out, shattered, stonkered **11** bushwhacked, tuckered out **14** on your last legs, worn to a frazzle

• **have done with**
**04** stop **05** cease **06** desist, give up **08** over with **09** throw over **10** finish with, thrash with **12** finished with **13** be through with **15** over and done with, wash your hands of

**Don Juan**
**04** rake **05** lover, romeo **06** gigolo **08** Casanova **09** ladies' man, philander, womanizer **10** lady-killer **11** philanderer

**donkey**
**03** ass **04** moke, mule **05** burro, cuddy, genet, hinny, jenny, neddy **06** cuddie, gennet, jennet **07** jackass **11** cardophagus **13** Jerusalem pony

**donnish**
**07** bookish, erudite, learned, serious **08** academic, pedantic, studious **09** pedagogic, scholarly **10** scholastic **11** formalistic **12** intellectual

**donor**
**05** angel, giver **06** backer **07** donator **08** provider **09** supporter **10** benefactor **11** contributor **14** fairy godmother, philanthropist

**doom**
**03** lot **04** damn, date, dome, fate, ruin **05** death, judge, weird **06** decree, devote **07** condemn, consign, destine, destiny, fortune, portion, verdict **08** disaster, downfall, judgment, sentence **09** destinate, judgement, pronounce, ruination **10** death-knell, predestine **11** catastrophe, destruction, rack and ruin **12** condemnation **13** pronouncement

**doomed**
**03** fay, fey, fie **05** fated **06** cursed, damned, marked, ruined **07** accurst, devoted, unlucky **08** accursed, destined, hopeless, ill-fated, luckless **09** condemned, ill-omened **10** bedevilled, ill-starred **11** star-crossed

**door**
**03** way **04** exit, haik, hake, heck, road, yett **05** entry, hatch, route, way in **06** access, portal **07** doorway, gateway, opening, postern **08** entrance, open door **11** opportunity

• **guard door**
**04** tile

**doorkeeper**
**05** tiler, tyler, usher **06** porter **07** doorman, janitor, ostiary **08** huissier **09** caretaker, concierge **10** gatekeeper **14** commissionaire

**doorpost**
**04** dern, durn

**dope**
**01** E **03** gen, git, LSD, oaf, pot, tea **04** acid, berk, clot, coke, dolt, dork, drug, fool, geek, hash, info, lace, prat, twit, weed **05** crack, drugs, dunce, facts, grass, idiot, ninny, opium, speed, spike, twerp **06** dimwit, doctor, heroin, inject, nitwit, opiate, sedate **07** buffoon, details, Ecstasy, halfwit, low-down, plonker, stupefy **08** cannabis, knock out, medicate, narcotic **09** absorbent, blockhead, marijuana, narcotize, simpleton, specifics **10** nincompoop **11** amphetamine, barbiturate, information, particulars **12** anaesthetize, hallucinogen

*See also* **fool**

**dopey**
**04** daft, dozy **05** silly **06** drowsy, groggy, simple, sleepy, stupid, torpid **07** foolish, muddled, nodding **08** confused, narcotic **09** lethargic, somnolent, stupefied **12** addle-brained **14** not the full quid

**dormancy**
**04** rest **05** sleep **07** latency, slumber **09** inertness **10** estivation, inactivity **11** aestivation, hibernation

**dormant**
**05** inert, joist **06** asleep, fallow, latent, torpid **07** resting **08** comatose, inactive, latitant, sleeping, sluggish **09** crossbeam, lethargic, potential, quiescent **10** slumbering, unrealized **11** hibernating, undeveloped, undisclosed

**dormouse**
**04** loir

**dosage**
**04** dose **06** amount **07** measure, portion **08** quantity

**dose**
**03** fix, hit **04** pill, shot **05** bolus, treat **06** amount, dosage, drench, potion, powder **07** booster, draught, measure, portion **08** dispense, medicate, quantity **09** prescribe **10** administer **11** horse-drench **12** prescription

• **lethal dose**
**02** LD

**dosh** *see* **money**

**dossier**
**04** case, data, file **05** brief, notes **06** folder, papers, report **09** documents, portfolio **11** information

**dot**
**03** dab, dit, hit, jot, set **04** atom, iota, limp, mark, spot, stud, tick **05** fleck, point, prick, speck **06** bullet, circle, pepper, stigme, tittle **07** punctum, scatter, speckle, stipple **08** full stop, particle, pin-point, punctule, sprinkle **09** punctuate **11** bullet point **12** decimal point

• **on the dot**
**05** sharp **06** on time **07** exactly

**08** promptly **09** precisely
**10** punctually **13** exactly on time

**dotage**
**06** old age **07** anility **08** agedness, senility, weakness **09** infirmity
**10** feebleness, imbecility
**11** decrepitude, elderliness **12** autumn of life **13** evening of life **15** second childhood

**dote**
• **dote on**
**04** love **05** adore, spoil **06** admire, pamper **07** idolize, indulge, worship
**08** hold dear, treasure

**doting**
**04** fond, soft **06** loving, tender
**07** adoring, devoted **09** indulgent
**12** affectionate

**dotty**
◇ *anagram indicator*
**03** ape **04** bats, loco, nuts **05** barmy, batty, buggy, crazy, daffy, dippy, flaky, gonzo, loony, loopy, nutty, potty, wacko, wacky, weird, wiggy
**06** cuckoo, fruity, mental, raving, screwy **07** bananas, barking, bonkers, cracked, meshuga, touched
**08** crackers, demented, dingbats, doolally, peculiar, unsteady
**09** eccentric, lymphatic, up the wall
**10** bestraught, frantic-mad, off the wall, off your nut, out to lunch **11** not all there, off the rails, off your head
**12** feeble-minded, mad as a hatter, off your chump, round the bend **13** off your rocker, out of your head, out of your tree, round the twist **14** off your trolley, wrong in the head

**double**
◇ *repetition indicator*
**02** bi-, di- **03** dbl, twi-, twy- **04** copy, dual, fold, twin **05** clone, duple, image, match, trick, twice **06** binate, clench, do also, duplex, fill in, paired, repeat, ringer, two-ply **07** coupled, doubled, enlarge, magnify, replica, stand in, twofold **08** geminate, geminous, increase, turn down, two-edged
**09** ambiguous, bifarious, deceitful, duplicate, equivocal, facsimile, insincere, lookalike **10** ambivalent, substitute, understudy **11** counterpart, deceitfully, double-edged, paradoxical, reduplicate
**12** doppelgänger, hypocritical, impersonator **13** double-meaning, have a dual role, multiply by two, spitting image **14** be an understudy, have a second job **15** have a second role
• **at the double**
**06** at once **07** quickly **09** right away
**11** at full speed, immediately
**12** straight away, without delay
• **double back**
**04** loop **05** dodge, evade **06** circle, return **07** reverse **09** backtrack

**double-cross**
**03** con **05** cheat, trick **06** betray
**07** defraud, mislead, swindle, two-time **08** hoodwink **12** take for a ride **14** pull a fast one on

**double-dealing**
**07** perfidy **08** betrayal, cheating, tricking **09** duplicity, mendacity, swindling, treachery, two-timing
**10** defrauding, misleading
**11** crookedness, dissembling, hoodwinking **12** ambidextrous, two-facedness

**double entendre**
**03** pun **08** innuendo, wordplay
**09** ambiguity **11** play on words
**13** double meaning **14** suggestiveness

**doubling**
**04** fold, loop **05** plait, trick
**08** mantling **10** gemination
**11** duplicature **12** diplogenesis
**13** reduplication

**doubly**
**03** bis **05** again, extra, twice
**07** twofold **10** especially

**doubt**
**04** fear **05** demur, qualm, query, waver
**06** aporia, danger, mammer, wonder
**07** dilemma, dubiety, impeach, problem, scepsis, scruple, skepsis, suspect **08** distrust, dubitate, hesitate, misdoubt, mistrust, quandary, question, wavering **09** ambiguity, be dubious, confusion, hesitance, hesitancy, misgiving, suspicion, vacillate **10** difficulty, disbelieve, hesitation, indecision, perplexity, scepticism, skepticism, uneasiness
**11** be uncertain, be undecided, incredulity, reservation, uncertainty
**12** apprehension, be suspicious, mixed feeling **14** call in question **15** have qualms about
• **expression of doubt**
**02** ha, h'm, um **03** erm, hah, hmm, hum **05** humph
• **in doubt**
**04** moot **08** doubtful **09** ambiguous, debatable, uncertain, undecided **10** in question, unreliable, unresolved, up in the air **12** open to debate, questionable **14** open to question
• **no doubt**
**04** iwis, ywis **06** surely **08** of course, probably **09** certainly, doubtless, no denying **10** definitely, most likely, presumably, sure enough
**11** undoubtedly **12** bang to rights, without doubt **13** in anyone's book
**14** unquestionably

**doubter**
**05** cynic **06** Thomas **07** sceptic, scoffer **08** agnostic **10** questioner, unbeliever **11** disbeliever, non-believer, questionist **14** doubting Thomas

**doubtful**
**04** iffy **05** crook, fishy, shady, vague
**06** uneasy, unsure **07** dubious, in doubt, obscure, suspect, unclear
**08** hesitant, insecure, unlikely, wavering **09** ambiguous, debatable, sceptical, skeptical, tentative, uncertain, undecided
**10** improbable, in two minds, irresolute, suspicious, touch and go
**11** distrustful, vacillating
**12** apprehensive, inconclusive, questionable **14** open to question

**doubtfully**
◇ *anagram indicator*
**08** uneasily **10** hesitantly
**11** sceptically, uncertainly
**12** irresolutely **14** apprehensively

**doubtless**
**04** sure **05** truly **06** surely **07** clearly, no doubt **08** of course, probably
**09** assuredly, certainly, dreadless, precisely, seemingly **10** most likely, presumably, supposedly
**11** indubitably, undoubtedly **12** bang to rights, indisputably, without doubt
**13** in anyone's book
**14** unquestionably

**dough**
**04** cake, duff, masa **05** knish, money, pasta, paste **08** kreplach **09** hush puppy
*See also* **money**

**doughnut**
**05** torus **06** sinker **07** olycook, olykoek **09** friedcake

**doughty**
**04** able, bold, fell, tall **05** brave, gutsy
**06** daring, gritty, heroic, plucky, spunky, strong **07** gallant, valiant
**08** fearless, intrepid, unafraid, valorous
**09** confident, dauntless, unabashed, undaunted **10** courageous, unblinking
**11** indomitable, lion-hearted, unblenching, unflinching
**14** unapprehensive

**doughy**
**03** sad **04** soft **05** heavy, pasty
**06** pallid, sodden

**dour**
**04** grim, hard, sour **05** gruff, harsh, rigid, stern **06** dismal, dreary, gloomy, morose, severe, strict, sullen
**07** austere **08** churlish, rigorous
**09** obstinate, unsmiling
**10** determined, forbidding, inflexible, unfriendly, unyielding

**douse, dowse**
**03** dip, wet **04** duck, dunk, soak
**05** flood, snuff, souse, steep
**06** deluge, drench, plunge, put out, quench, splash, strike **07** blow out, immerge, immerse, smother
**08** saturate, submerge **10** extinguish
**13** pour water over

**dove**
**03** doo **06** culver, pigeon, rocker, turtle **07** rockier **10** rock pigeon

**dovetail**
**04** join, link **05** agree, match, tally
**06** accord **07** conform **08** coincide
**09** harmonize, interlock
**10** correspond **11** fit together

**dowdy**
**04** drab **05** dingy, mopsy, tacky, tatty **06** frowsy, frumpy, shabby **08** frumpish, slovenly **10** ill-dressed **12** old-fashioned **13** unfashionable

**down**
**01** d **02** dn **03** ill, low, nap, sad **04** à bas, blue, bust, fell, flue, fuzz, gulp, oose, ooze, pile, shag, swig, wool **05** along, bloom, drink, floor, floss, fluff, kaput, swill, throw, wonky **06** pappus, topple **07** consume, crashed, depress, descent, floccus, put away, swallow, toss off, unhappy **08** dejected, downcast, feathers, fine hair, gulp down, wretched **09** bring down, conked out, depressed, knock back, knock down, miserable, overthrow, prostrate, southward **10** behindhand, dispirited, melancholy, not working, on the blink, on the fritz, out of order, to the floor **11** downhearted, inoperative, out of action, to the bottom, to the ground **12** soft feathers **13** to a lower level **14** down in the dumps, malfunctioning

**• down with**
**03** hip **04** à bas **06** depose **07** abolish, put down, swallow **08** away with, get rid of **10** in tune with

**• set down**
**03** lay **04** drop, dump, land, snub, take **05** judge, state **06** depose, esteem, record, regard **07** ascribe, deposit, detrain **09** attribute, discharge **10** disentrain

**down-and-out**
**03** bum **04** hobo, wino **05** caird, jakey, loser, piker, rogue, tramp **06** dosser, ruined, toerag, truant, vagrom, walker **07** dingbat, floater, gangrel, tinkler, vagrant **08** clochard, cursitor, deadbeat, derelict, homeless, straggle, stroller, vagabond **09** destitute, landloper, penniless, sundowner **11** rinthereout, scatterling, Weary Willie **12** down-and-outer, hallan-shaker, impoverished, on your uppers **15** knight of the road

**down-at-heel**
**04** drab, poor **05** dingy, dowdy, seedy, tacky, tatty **06** frayed, frowsy, ragged, shabby **07** run-down **08** slovenly, tattered **09** neglected **10** ill-dressed, ramshackle, tumbledown, uncared for **11** dilapidated, in disrepair

**downbeat**
**03** low **04** calm **06** casual, gloomy **07** cynical, relaxed **08** downcast, informal, laid-back, negative **09** cheerless, depressed, easy-going, unhurried, unworried **10** despondent, insouciant, nonchalant **11** pessimistic **15** fearing the worst

**downcast**
**03** low, sad **04** blue, down, dull, glum **05** fed up **06** gloomy **07** daunted, hanging, unhappy **08** dejected, dismayed, wretched **09** depressed, miserable **10** despondent, dispirited, downlooked **11** crestfallen, discouraged, downhearted, low-spirited **12** disappointed, disconsolate, disheartened

**downfall**
**04** fall, ruin **05** decay **07** debacle, failure, undoing **08** collapse, disgrace **09** overthrow **10** debasement **11** degradation, destruction, humiliation

**downgrade**
**05** decry, lower **06** defame, demote, depose, do down, humble **07** deflate, degrade, run down **08** belittle, minimize, relegate **09** denigrate, disparage, sell short, underrate **11** lower in rank, make light of **12** reduce in rank

**downhearted**
**03** sad **04** glum **06** gloomy **07** daunted, unhappy **08** dejected, dismayed, downcast **09** depressed **10** browned off, despondent, dispirited **11** discouraged, low-spirited **12** disappointed, disconsolate, disheartened

**down-market**
**04** poor, sale **05** cheap, tacky, tatty **06** budget, cheapo, common, shoddy, tawdry **07** bargain, economy, low-cost, reduced **08** cut-price, giveaway, inferior, low-price, no-frills **09** cheapjack, cheap-rate, knock-down, throwaway, worthless **10** affordable, discounted, economical, marked-down, ramshackle, rock-bottom, second-rate **11** inexpensive **15** bargain-basement

**downpour**
**04** pelt, rain **05** flood, plash **06** deluge **07** torrent **09** rainstorm **10** cloudburst, inundation, waterspout

**downright**
**04** flat **05** clear, plain, plump, sheer, total, utter **06** arrant, simply **07** brusque, clearly, plainly, totally, utterly **08** absolute, complete, even-down, outright, positive, straight, thorough **09** out-and-out, up-and-down, wholesale **10** absolutely, completely, forthright, positively, thoroughly **11** categorical, plain-spoken, unequivocal, unqualified **13** categorically

**downside**
**04** flaw, snag **05** minus **06** defect **07** penalty, trouble **08** drawback, nuisance, weakness **09** liability, weak point **10** impediment, limitation **12** Achilles heel, disadvantage **13** inconvenience

**downsize**
**04** slim **06** reduce, shrink **08** contract, diminish, minimize, moderate **11** make smaller

**down-to-earth**
**04** sane **07** mundane **08** sensible **09** practical, realistic **10** hard-headed, no-nonsense **11** commonsense, plain-spoken **12** matter-of-fact **13** plain-speaking, unsentimental **14** commonsensical

**downtrodden**
**06** abused **07** bullied **08** burdened, helpless **09** exploited, oppressed, powerless **10** subjugated, trampled on, tyrannized, victimized **11** overwhelmed, subservient, weighed-down

**down under**
**02** Oz **09** Australia

**downward**
**07** sliding **08** downhill, slipping **09** declining, going down **10** descending, moving down

**downy**
**04** fine, soft **05** fuzzy, nappy **06** fleecy, fluffy, smooth, woolly **07** cottony, dowlney, knowing, pappose, pappous, velvety **08** feathery **09** plumulate **10** lanuginose, lanuginous

**dowry**
**03** dot **04** gift **05** share **06** legacy, talent, tocher **07** faculty, portion **09** endowment, provision **11** inheritance **12** wedding-dower **15** marriage portion

**dowse** *see* **douse, dowse**

**doxology**
**04** hymn, song **05** chant, psalm **06** anthem, gloria, praise **07** chorale **08** response **11** recessional **12** hymn of praise, song of praise **13** glorification

**doze**
**03** kip, nap **04** dare, zizz **05** dover, go off, sleep **06** catnap, drowse, nod off, siesta, snooze **07** drop off, shut-eye **08** drift off, take a nap **10** forty winks

**• doze off**
**06** catnap, nod off, snooze **08** drift off **10** fall asleep **14** have forty winks

**dozen**
**02** dz **03** doz, XII **04** twal **06** twelve **07** stupefy

**dozy**
**04** daft **05** dopey, silly, tired, weary **06** dreamy, drowsy, simple, sleepy, stupid, torpid **07** foolish, nodding, yawning **09** somnolent **10** half-asleep

**drab**
**04** dull, flat, grey **05** dingy, whore **06** boring, dismal, dreary, gloomy, isabel, shabby, sombre **07** tedious **08** isabella, lifeless **09** cheerless **10** colourless, isabelline, lacklustre **11** featureless **12** Quaker-colour **13** uninteresting

**drabness**
**05** gloom **08** dullness, greyness **09** dinginess **10** dreariness, shabbiness, sombreness **12** lifelessness **13** cheerlessness **14** colourlessness

**Draconian**
**04** grim, hard **05** cruel, harsh, stern **06** brutal, savage, severe, strict **07** inhuman **08** abrasive, pitiless, ruthless **09** merciless, unfeeling **10** iron-fisted, iron-handed **13** unsympathetic

**draft**
**03** dft **04** bill, draw, plan **05** essay, rough **06** cheque, design, detach, draw up, scroll, sketch **07** compose, drawing, ébauche, outline, paste-up **08** abstract, bank-bill, protocol **09** blueprint, delineate, formulate, treatment **10** money order **11** delineation, postal order, rough sketch **14** bill of exchange, letter of credit

**drag**
**03** lag, lug, tow, tug **04** bind, bore, draw, hale, harl, haul, pain, pest, pull, rash, shoe, sled, snig, trek, tump, yank **05** crawl, creep, shlep, snake, sweep, trail, train **06** bother, drogue, schlep, wear on **07** schlepp, skidpan, trouble **08** go slowly, headache, nuisance **09** annoyance, go on and on, influence **11** go on for ever **12** become boring **13** become tedious, pain in the neck

**• drag on**
**04** go on **05** run on **07** persist **08** continue **09** be lengthy **14** be long-drawn-out

**• drag out**
**06** extend, hang on **07** draw out, persist, prolong, spin out **08** lengthen, protract

**• drag up**
**05** raise **06** rake up, remind, revive **07** bring up, mention **09** introduce

**dragon**
**04** worm **05** Draco, drake **08** lindworm **09** firedrake **12** flying lizard

**dragonfly**
**05** naiad, nymph **07** Odonata **10** demoiselle

**dragoon**
**05** bully, drive, force, impel **06** coerce, compel, harass **08** browbeat, pressure **09** constrain, press-gang, strongarm **10** intimidate, pressurize

**drain**
**02** ea **03** dry, eau, pot, sap, sew, tap, tax **04** buzz, delf, duct, grip, leak, milk, nala, ooze, pipe, pour, sink, suck, tile, void **05** bleed, cundy, ditch, drink, empty, exude, fleet, gripe, gully, ladle, leach, leech, nalla, nulla, quaff, sewer, siver, sough, stank, syver, use up **06** condie, effuse, emulge, filter, gutter, nallah, nullah, outlet, remove, sheuch, sheugh, sluice, sponge, strain, trench **07** channel, conduit, consume, culvert, cunette, deplete, dewater, draw off, drink up, exhaust, extract, flow out, piscina, pump off, seep out, swallow, trickle, unwater **08** bleed dry, evacuate, withdraw **09** depletion, discharge, lickpenny **10** bleed white, exhaustion, underdrain **11** common-shore, consumption, watercourse **12** exsanguinate

**• drained**
**05** tired

**dram**
**02** dr **03** tot, wet **04** shot, suck, tiff, tift **06** chasse, drachm **07** caulker, morning, nobbler, snifter, tickler **08** chota peg, meridian **10** stirrup cup

*See also* **drink**

**drama**
**02** no **03** noh **04** auto, play, show **05** opera, piece, scene **06** acting, azione, comedy, crisis, kabuki, thrill **07** dilemma, tension, theater, theatre, tragedy, turmoil **08** operetta **09** dramatics, melodrama, sensation, spectacle **10** dramaturgy, excitement, stagecraft **11** histrionics

*See also* **play**

**• drama students**
**04** RADA

**dramatic**
**05** stage, tense, vivid **06** abrupt, marked, sudden **07** drastic, graphic **08** distinct, exciting, stirring, striking, Thespian **09** effective, thrilling **10** artificial, expressive, flamboyant, histrionic, impressive, noticeable, theatrical, unexpected **11** exaggerated, personative, sensational, significant, spectacular, substantial **12** considerable, melodramatic

**dramatically**
**07** vividly **08** abruptly, suddenly **10** noticeably, strikingly **12** considerably, expressively, impressively **13** significantly, spectacularly, substantially

**dramatist**
**06** writer **08** comedian **09** tragedian **10** dramaturge, playwright, play-writer **12** dramaturgist, screen writer, scriptwriter

*See also* **playwright**

**dramatization**
**07** staging **10** adaptation **11** arrangement **12** presentation

**dramatize**
**03** act, ham **05** adapt, ham up, put on, stage **06** overdo **07** play-act **09** overstate **10** arrange for, exaggerate **12** lay it on thick **14** present as a film, present as a play **15** make a big thing of

**drape**
◇ *containment indicator*
**04** drop, fold, hang, veil, vest, wrap **05** adorn, cloak, cover, droop **06** shroud **07** arrange, envelop, overlay, suspend **08** decorate

**drapery**
**05** arras, blind, cloth **06** blinds **07** curtain, hanging, valance, valence **08** backdrop, covering, curtains, hangings, mantling, tapestry **09** coverings **10** jardinière, lambrequin

**drastic**
◇ *anagram indicator*
**03** bad **04** dire **05** harsh **06** severe, strong **07** extreme, radical, serious, violent **08** dramatic, forceful, forcible, rigorous **09** desperate, Draconian, swingeing **10** unpleasant **11** far-reaching

**drastically**
**07** greatly **08** severely, strongly **09** extremely, radically, seriously **10** forcefully, rigorously

**draught**
**03** cup **04** flow, gulp, puff, pull, rush, swig **05** draft, drink, privy, quaff, swill **06** breath, drench, influx, potion, waucht, waught **07** current, drawing, pulling, swallow **08** cesspool, dragging, movement, potation, quantity, quencher, traction **10** attraction **12** williewaught

**draw**
**02** go **03** get, lug, tap, tie, tow, tug **04** bait, come, drag, haul, limn, lure, milk, move, pick, pull, pump, suck, take, walk **05** chart, drain, drive, frame, go for, infer, paint, sweep, trace, trail **06** allure, appeal, be even, choose, come to, deduce, depict, design, doodle, elicit, entice, gather, infuse, inhale, map out, obtain, pencil, prompt, raffle, reason, remove, resort, select, siphon, sketch, travel **07** advance, attract, be equal, bring in, extract, inspire, lottery, portray, proceed, procure, produce, pull out, receive, respire, take out, tombola **08** approach, bring out, conclude, dead heat, decide on, describe, interest, lengthen, persuade, plump for, progress, scribble, withdraw **09** breathe in, delineate, influence, magnetism, represent, stalemate, unsheathe **10** attraction, enticement, eviscerate, sweepstake **11** be all square

**• draw back**
**04** cock, funk **05** wince **06** boggle, flinch, recoil, retire, shrink **07** fall off, retract, retreat **08** withdraw **09** start back **10** disadvance

**• draw in**
◇ *containment indicator*
**04** pull, suck **05** hunch, rough **06** absorb, inhale **07** involve, retract **08** contract

**• draw near**
**04** come, nigh **08** approach

**• draw on**
**03** use **05** apply, train **06** allure, call on, employ, induce, lead on, quarry, rely on **07** exploit, utilize **08** approach, put to use **09** make use of **14** have recourse to

**• draw out**
**04** make, spin, tose, toze **05** educe, evoke, leave, start, toaze **06** depart, extend, set out **07** drag out, extract,

move out, prolong, pull out, spin out, stretch **08** continue, elongate, lengthen, protract **09** put at ease
**12** induce to talk **13** induce to speak
**15** encourage to talk

**• draw together**
**04** knit **06** gather **07** close up
**08** astringe, contract **10** constringe

**• draw up**
**04** halt, stop **05** draft, frame, run in
**06** pull up **07** compile, compose, make out, prepare **08** write out
**09** formulate **12** put in writing

**• goalless draw**
**02** 0-0

**drawback**
**03** out **04** flaw, snag **05** catch, fault, hitch **06** damper, defect, hurdle
**07** barrier, problem, take-off, trouble
**08** handicap, nuisance, obstacle, pullback, weak spot **09** hindrance, liability **10** deficiency, difficulty, disamenity, disbenefit, disutility, impediment, limitation
**12** disadvantage, imperfection
**14** discouragement, stumbling-block

**drawer**
**02** dr **04** till **07** shottle, shuttle

**• bottom drawer**
**08** glory box **09** hope chest

**drawing**
**05** study **06** pencil, pin-man, sketch
**07** cartoon, diagram, graphic, outline, picture **08** graffito, portrait, scribble
**09** attrahent, depiction, pen-and-ink, portrayal **11** composition, delineation, scenography **12** illustration
**14** representation

**drawl**
**03** haw **05** drant, drone, twang
**06** dawdle, draunt, haw-haw
**08** protract **09** say slowly **11** speak slowly

**drawn**
◇ *anagram indicator*
**04** taut, worn **05** gaunt, tense, tired
**06** closed, sapped **07** fraught, haggard, hassled, pinched **08** fatigued, harassed, strained, stressed
**09** etiolated, washed out
**10** unsheathed **11** eviscerated

**dread**
**03** awe, shy **04** dire, fear, funk, fury
**05** alarm, awful, quail, qualm, worry
**06** dismay, feared, flinch, fright, grisly, horror, terror **07** dreaded, ghastly, shudder, tremble **08** alarming, blue funk, cringe at, disquiet, dreadful, frighten, gastness, gruesome, horrible, terrible **09** cold sweat, frightful, gastnesse, ghastness, misgiving **10** be afraid of, be scared of, blind panic, shrink from, terrifying **11** fit of terror, frightening, trepidation
**12** apprehension, awe-inspiring, perturbation **13** be terrified by **14** be anxious about, be frightened by, be worried about

*See also* **phobia**

**dreadful**
◇ *anagram indicator*
**04** dern, dire, grim **05** awful, dearn, nasty **06** awsome, tragic **07** awesome, ghastly, heinous, hideous **08** alarming, grievous, horrible, horrific, shocking, terrible, terrific **09** appalling, frightful
**10** abortional, calamitous, horrendous, outrageous, terrifying, tremendous, unpleasant **11** frightening

**dreadfully**
◇ *anagram indicator*
**04** very **07** awfully **08** terribly
**09** extremely **10** shockingly
**11** appallingly, atrociously, exceedingly, frightfully **12** horrendously

**dream**
**03** aim, joy **04** dwam, goal, hope, long, mare, muse, plan, wish **05** crave, dwalm, dwaum, fancy, ideal, mirth, model, music, sound, yearn **06** beauty, design, desire, marvel, superb, sweven, trance, vision **07** aisling, delight, fantasy, imagine, perfect, phantom, reverie, supreme **08** ambition, daydream, delusion, envisage, illusion, somniate, yearning **09** excellent, fantasize, nightmare, pipe dream, switch off, wonderful **10** aspiration, minstrelsy, perfection **11** expectation, hallucinate, imagination, inattention, speculation **12** want very much **13** be lost in space, hallucination
**14** phantasmagoria, stare into space
**15** castles in the air, not pay attention

**• dream up**
**04** spin **05** hatch **06** create, devise, invent **07** concoct, imagine, think up
**08** conceive, contrive **09** conjure up, fabricate

**• not dream of**
**08** not think **10** not imagine **11** not conceive, not consider

**dreamer**
**07** Utopian **08** idealist, romancer, romantic **09** fantasist, stargazer, theorizer, visionary **10** daydreamer, fantasizer

**dreamily**
**06** gently, softly **08** absently
**10** peacefully, pleasantly
**12** romantically

**dreamlike**
**06** unreal **07** phantom, surreal
**08** ethereal, illusory **09** fantastic, visionary **10** chimerical, trance-like
**13** hallucinatory, insubstantial, unsubstantial **14** phantasmagoric

**dreamy**
**03** dim **04** hazy, soft **05** faint, misty, moony, spacy, vague **06** absent, gentle, lovely, musing, spacey, unreal
**07** calming, faraway, lulling, pensive, shadowy, unclear **08** ethereal, fanciful, relaxing, romantic, soothing
**09** fantastic, imaginary, visionary
**10** abstracted, idealistic, indistinct, thoughtful **11** daydreaming, fantasizing, impractical, preoccupied
**12** absent-minded **13** wool-gathering

**drearily**
**08** boringly, dismally **09** routinely, tediously **11** monstrously
**12** depressingly

**dreary**
**03** sad **04** dark, drab, dull **05** bleak, oorie, ourie, owrie **06** boring, dismal, dreich, gloomy, gousty, sombre
**07** humdrum, routine, tedious
**08** desolate, ghastful, lifeless, mournful, overcast, unvaried
**09** cheerless, ghastfull, wearisome
**10** colourless, depressing, monotonous, uneventful
**11** commonplace, featureless **12** run-of-the-mill **13** uninteresting

**dredge**

**• dredge up**
**05** dig up, raise **06** drag up, draw up, fish up, rake up **07** scoop up, uncover, unearth **08** discover

**dregs**
**04** lags, lees, scum **05** draff, dross, legge, trash, waste **06** bottom, dunder, faeces, fecula, graves, mother, rabble, tramps, ullage **07** bottoms, deposit, dossers, greaves, grounds, residue, taplash **08** detritus, outcasts, residuum, riff-raff, sediment, tailings, vagrants **09** excrement, scourings, sublimate **10** faex populi **11** down-and-outs, precipitate

**drench**
**03** wet **04** duck, soak **05** douse, drook, drouk, drown, flood, imbue, souse, steep, swamp **06** embrue, imbrue, sluice **07** embrewe, immerse
**08** inundate, permeate, saturate
**09** milk shake **13** soak to the skin

**dress**
◇ *anagram indicator*
**02** do **03** don, fig, fit, ray, rig, tog
**04** boun, busk, comb, deck, doll, draw, garb, gear, gown, rail, robe, tend, tidy, tiff, tift, tire, togs, trim, wear **05** adorn, array, bowne, chide, clean, cover, drape, erect, frock, get-up, groom, guise, habit, preen, primp, put on, style, treat **06** adjust, attire, betrim, bind up, clothe, finish, fit out, graith, manure, outfit, smooth, swathe, thrash
**07** apparel, arrange, bandage, bravery, clobber, clothes, costume, deck out, dispose, flatten, garment, garnish, get into, prepare, throw on, turn out
**08** accoutre, clothing, decorate, ensemble, garments, get ready, slip into **10** habiliment, straighten **13** put a plaster on **14** wearing-apparel

*See also* **clothes, clothing**

*Dresses include:*

**03** mob
**04** ball, coat, maxi, sack, sari, tent
**05** shift, shirt, smock, tasar
**06** caftan, dirndl, jumper, kaftan, kimono, muu-muu, sheath, tusser
**07** bathing, chemise, evening, gym slip, kitenge, matinee, matinée, tussore, wedding

**08** ball-gown, cocktail, gym tunic, negligée, pinafore, princess, sundress
**09** cheongsam, farandine, going-away, minidress, slammakin, trollopee
**10** dinner-gown, farrandine, slammerkin, wraparound
**11** d'écolletage, Dolly Varden, riding habit
**12** shirtwaister

**• dress down**
**05** chide, scold **06** berate, carpet, rebuke, thrash **07** reprove, rouse on, tell off, tick off, upbraid **09** castigate, reprimand **13** dress casually, give a rocket to, tear off a strip, tear strips off **15** dress informally

**• dress up**
◇ *anagram indicator*
**04** deck, gild, perk **05** adorn, dizen, tog up **06** buck up, doll up, dude up, jazz up, tart up **07** dandify, improve **08** beautify, decorate, disguise, ornament **09** embellish
**10** masquerade **12** dress smartly
**13** dress formally

## dresser

**• showy dresser**
**03** cat **04** beau

**• special dresser**
**03** Mod

## dressing

◇ *anagram indicator*
**03** jus, pad **04** lint **05** gauze, patch, sauce, spica **06** coulis, relish
**07** bandage, Band-aid®, clothes, plaster **08** compress, ligature, poultice
**09** condiment **10** tourniquet
**11** Elastoplast®, vinaigrette

*See also* **salad**

## dressmaker

**06** tailor **07** modiste **09** couturier, midinette, tailoress **10** couturière, seamstress **11** mantua-maker, needlewoman, sewing woman
**12** garment-maker

## dressy

**05** natty, ritzy, sharp, showy, smart, swish **06** classy, formal, ornate
**07** elegant, stylish **09** elaborate

## dribble

**03** run **04** drib, drip, drop, foam, leak, ooze, seep, spit **05** drool, exude, froth, gloop **06** drivel, saliva, slaver
**07** droplet, seepage, slobber, trickle
**10** sprinkling

## dried

**04** arid, sear, sere **06** wilted
**07** drained, parched, wizened
**08** withered **09** mummified
**10** dehydrated, desiccated, exsiccated, shrivelled

## drier

**04** oast **07** tumbler

## drift

◇ *anagram indicator*
**03** aim, sag **04** bank, core, crab, flow, ford, gist, heap, hull, mass, pile, rack, roam, rove, rush, vein, waft, wisp
**05** amass, coast, drive, drove, float, mound, point, scope, shift, stray, sweep, tenor, trend **06** course, design, gather, heap up, import, leeway, pierce, pile up, stream, thrust, tunnel, wander, wreath **07** current, driving, essence, meaning, purport **08** movement, tendency **09** direction, freewheel, intention, substance, variation
**10** accumulate, digression
**11** implication **12** accumulation, significance **14** be carried along **15** go with the stream

## drifter

**04** hobo **05** nomad, rover, tramp
**06** drover **07** swagger, swagman, vagrant **08** vagabond, wanderer
**09** itinerant, sundowner, traveller
**11** beachcomber **12** rolling stone

## drill

**02** PE, PT **03** awl, bit **04** bore **05** borer, coach, prick, punch, teach, train
**06** gimlet, ground, jumper, manual, pierce, reamer, school, seeder
**07** routine, tuition, wildcat
**08** coaching, exercise, instruct, practice, practise, puncture, rehearse, training **09** exercises, grounding, inculcate, penetrate, perforate, procedure **10** discipline, jackhammer, repetition
**11** counterbore, inculcation, instruction, make a hole in, preparation
**13** square-bashing **14** indoctrination, manual exercise

## drink

**03** bib, cup, jar, lap, nip, one, peg, sea, sip, sup, tot **04** brew, down, dram, grog, gulp, have, lush, neck, pint, pull, shot, suck, swig, tass, tiff, tift, tope, toss
**05** booze, drain, hooch, juice, plonk, quaff, revel, sauce, smoke, swill, tinct, toast **06** absorb, grog on, guzzle, hootch, imbibe, liquid, liquor, rotgut, salute, swally, tank up, tiddly, tipple
**07** alcohol, carouse, draught, drink to, indulge, shicker, spirits, swallow
**08** aperitif, beverage, get drunk, infusion **09** firewater, get pissed, hard stuff, knock back, overdrink, partake of, polish off, soft drink, stiffener, the bottle, throw back **10** amber fluid
**11** have too much, jungle juice, refreshment, strong drink, the creature, tickle-brain **12** Dutch courage, go on the shout, hit the bottle **13** knock back a few **14** be a hard drinker, drink like a fish, have one too many, thirst-quencher **15** be a heavy drinker, propose a toast to

*See also* **glass**

*Alcoholic drinks include:*

**02** it
**03** ale, dop, gin, kir, mum, nog, rum, rye, tay
**04** arak, beer, bull, fine, flip, grog, hock, mead, nipa, ouzo, pils, port, purl, sake, saki, sour, sura, vino, wine
**05** cider, G and T, lager, perry, Pimm's®, plonk, stout, vodka
**06** arrack, bishop, brandy, bubbly, Cognac, eggnog, grappa, porter, poteen, Scotch, shandy, sherry, whisky
**07** alcopop, aquavit, Bacardi®, bourbon, Campari, Gordon's®, liqueur, Marsala, Martell®, martini, oloroso, pink gin, red wine, retsina, sangria, sloe gin, spirits, tequila, vin rosé, whiskey
**08** advocaat, Armagnac, Calvados, cold duck, Guinness®, hot toddy, schnapps, Smirnoff®, vermouth, vin blanc, vin rouge
**09** badminton, Beefeater®, champagne, cocktails, Laphroaig®, snakebite, white wine, Wincarnis®
**10** ginger wine, Remy Martin®
**11** black-and-tan, boilermaker, Courvoisier®, gin-and-tonic, Glenfiddich®, Irish coffee, Jack Daniel's®
**12** Famous Grouse®, Glenmorangie®, malternative
**13** peach schnapps, Scotch and soda
**14** Bombay Sapphire®

*See also* **beer**; **cocktail**; **liqueur**; **spirits**; **wine**

*Non-alcoholic drinks include:*

**03** cha, pop, tea
**04** Coke®, cola, kola, milk, soda
**05** assai, Assam, cocoa, float, julep, latte, mixer, Pepsi®, tonic, water
**06** coffee, Indian, Irn-Bru®, Ribena®, squash, tisane
**07** beef tea, cordial, limeade, Perrier®, seltzer
**08** café noir, China tea, Coca-Cola®, Earl Grey, espresso, expresso, fruit tea, green tea, Horlicks®, lemonade, lemon tea, Lucozade®, Ovaltine®, root beer, smoothie
**09** Aqua Libra®, ayahuasco, Canada Dry®, cherryade, cream soda, ginger ale, herbal tea, milk shake, mint-julep, orangeade, soda water
**10** café au lait, café filtre, cappuccino, fizzy drink, fruit juice, ginger beer, rosehip tea, still water, tonic water, Vichy water
**11** barley water, bitter lemon, camomile tea
**12** hot chocolate, mineral water, sarsaparilla
**13** peppermint tea, Turkish coffee
**14** sparkling water
**15** lapsang souchong

*Drinks of the gods include:*

**06** amrita, nectar
**08** ambrosia

*Special drinks include:*

**03** ava
**04** kava, soma
**05** haoma
**09** ayahuasco

**• drink hard**
**04** bend, tank **06** bezzle

**• drink in**
**05** grasp **06** absorb, digest, imbibe, take in **07** inhaust, realize **10** appreciate

**drinkable**
**04** safe **05** clean **07** potable **10** fit to drink

**drinker**
**03** sot **04** lush, soak, wino **05** alkie, dipso, drunk, toper **06** barfly, boozer, sponge, sucker **07** imbiber, pint-pot, tippler, tosspot **08** drunkard **09** fuddle-cap, inebriate **10** winebibber **11** dipsomaniac, froth-blower, hard drinker **12** heavy drinker **14** serious drinker
**• reformed drinkers**
**02** AA

**drinking**
◇ *insertion indicator*
**• drinking cup**
**03** nut, tig, tot **04** bowl, tass **05** cylix, kylix **06** cotyle, goblet, quaich, quaigh, rhyton **07** chalice, scyphus **09** cantharus **10** parting-cup
**• drinking session**
**03** bat, bum **04** bend, bevy, bout, bust, lush, sesh **05** bevvy, binge, blind, booze, drunk, spree **06** beer-up, bender, bottle, fuddle, grog-on, grog-up, razzle, screed **07** blinder, booze-up, carouse, session, wassail
**• expressions relating to drinking**
**04** evoe, rivo, skol **05** evhoe, evohe, skoal **06** cheers, prosit **07** slàinte **08** chin-chin **10** good health **12** mud in your eye
**• given to drinking**
**03** wet

**drip**
**02** IV **03** wet **04** bead, bore, drop, leak, ooze, plop, tear, weed, weep, wimp **05** gloop, ninny, pansy, sissy, softy **06** filter, splash **07** dewdrop, dribble, drizzle, trickle **08** sprinkle, weakling **09** percolate **10** stillicide
**• dripping**
**03** fat

**drive**
**02** ca', Dr, go **03** caa', dig, put, ram, ren, rin, run, tax, vim, zip **04** bear, come, dash, firk, goad, herd, hunt, hurl, lash, lead, move, need, prod, push, rack, rate, ride, road, send, sink, spin, spur, take, trip, turn, urge, will **05** carry, chase, drift, fight, force, guide, impel, jaunt, knock, motor, pilot, power, press, screw, steer, surge, thump, verve **06** action, appeal, avenue, battle, burden, coerce, compel, convey, desire, direct, effort, energy, hammer, handle, incite, manage, oblige, outing, pizazz, plunge, prompt, propel, spirit, strike, thrust, travel, vigour **07** actuate, control, crusade, dragoon, enforce, go by car, impulse, journey, operate, overtax, provoke, resolve, roadway, round up **08** ambition, appetite, approach, campaign, driveway, instinct, motivate, movement, overdo it, overwork, persuade, pressure, struggle, tenacity **09** chauffeur, come by car, constrain, excursion, transport **10** enterprise, get-up-and-go, initiative, motivation, overburden, pressurize, propulsion **11** give a lift to, travel by car, work too hard **12** be at the wheel, kill yourself, transmission **13** determination **14** propeller shaft **15** be at the controls
**• drive at**
**04** hint, mean **05** aim at, get at, imply **06** intend **07** refer to, signify, suggest **08** allude to, indicate, intimate **09** insinuate **10** have in mind
**• drive away**
**04** hunt, shoo **05** chase **06** banish, dispel **07** repulse **08** exorcize
**• drive down**
**03** ram
**• drive fast**
**04** race **05** speed
**• drive inconsiderately**
**03** hog
**• drive out**
**04** fire **05** expel, wreak **07** turn out **11** exterminate
**• prepare to drive**
**03** tee

**drivel**
**03** rot **04** blah, bull, crap, drip, guff **05** balls, bilge, drool, hooey, slush, tripe **06** bunkum, slaver, waffle **07** baloney, dribble, eyewash, garbage, hogwash, maunder, rhubarb, rubbish, slabber, twaddle **08** claptrap, malarkey, nonsense **09** gibberish, poppycock **10** balderdash, mumbo-jumbo **12** gobbledygook

**driver**
**02** Dr **04** Jehu, whip **05** mizen, rider **06** cabbie, jarvey, jarvie, mizzen **07** locoman, taximan, trucker, truckie **08** bullocky, motorist, muleteer, roadsman, truckman **09** chauffeur **12** motorcyclist **15** knight of the road
*See also* **racing**
**• new driver**
**01** L

**drivers**
**02** AA **03** RAC

**driving**
**05** heavy **07** dynamic, violent **08** forceful, sweeping, vigorous **09** energetic **10** compelling, forthright

**drizzle**
**04** drip, drop, mist, pour, rain, smir, smur, spit, spot **05** smirr, spray **06** mizzle, shower **07** dribble, scowder, skiffle, trickle **08** fine rain, scouther, scowther, sprinkle **09** light rain **10** rain finely, Scotch mist **11** rain lightly

**droll**
**03** odd, rum **04** jest, zany **05** comic, funny, queer, witty **06** jester **07** amusing, bizarre, comical, jocular, risible, waggish **08** clownish, farcical, humorous, peculiar **09** diverting, eccentric, laughable, ludicrous, whimsical **10** ridiculous **12** entertaining

**drone**
**03** dor, hum **04** buzz, dorr, purr **05** chant, drant, drawl, idler, leech, thrum, whirr **06** bumble, bummle, dog-bee, doodle, draunt, intone, loafer **07** bourdon, dreamer, goof-off, slacker, sponger, vibrate **08** hanger-on, layabout, parasite, whirring **09** bombilate, bombinate, go on and on, lazybones, murmuring, scrounger, vibration **10** lazy person **11** goldbricker

**drool**
**04** dote, gush **05** gloat **06** drivel, slaver **07** dribble, enthuse, slobber **08** salivate **11** slobber over **15** water at the mouth

**droop**
**03** bow, lob, nod, sag **04** bend, drop, fade, flag, peak, sink, weep, wilt **05** faint, slink, slump, stoop **06** dangle, falter, nutate, slouch, wither **07** decline **08** fall down, hang down, languish, pendency **09** lose heart

**droopy**
**03** lax **04** lank, limp, weak **05** loose, saggy, slack **06** feeble, floppy **07** falling, sagging **08** drooping, dropping

**drop**
◇ *deletion indicator*
**02** gt **03** bit, can, dab, end, lay, nip, sip, tad, tot **04** bead, blob, cast, dash, dive, drib, drip, fall, fire, glob, gout, jilt, land, leak, omit, plop, quit, sack, shed, sink, spat, spot, stop, take, tear **05** abyss, bring, candy, carry, cease, chasm, chuck, cliff, ditch, droop, forgo, gutta, lapse, let go, lower, pinch, slope, slump, sweet, trace **06** bonbon, bubble, desert, disown, dragée, drappy, finish, forego, give up, goutte, humbug, lessen, little, plunge, put off, reject, splash, tumble, weaken **07** abandon, boot out, cutback, decline, deliver, descend, descent, dismiss, drappie, dribble, driblet, droplet, dwindle, exclude, fall off, forsake, globule, let fall, let go of, lozenge, miss out, modicum, pendant, plummet, smidgen, sweetie, trickle, turf out **08** decrease, diminish, downturn, dribblet, globulet, leave out, lowering, mouthful, pastille, renounce, run out on, spheroid, sprinkle **09** bespatter, declivity, discharge, precipice, reduction, repudiate, terminate, throw over, transport, walk out on **10** falling-off, finish with, relinquish, slacken off **11** devaluation, discontinue **12** depreciation, dispense with **13** deterioration, make redundant
**• drop back**
**03** lag **07** retreat **08** fall back **09** lag behind **10** fall behind
**• drop in**
**04** call **05** pop in, visit **06** call by, come

by, instil **07** instill **08** come over **09** call round, come round

**• drop off**
**04** doze, sink **05** go off **06** catnap, depart, hand in, lessen, nod off, plunge, snooze, unload **07** decline, deliver, deposit, doze off, dwindle, fall off, plummet, set down **08** decrease, diminish, drift off **09** disappear **10** fall asleep, slacken off **14** have forty winks

**• drop out**
**04** quit **05** leave **06** cry off, give up **07** abandon, back out, forsake **08** renounce, withdraw

**• drop out of**
**04** quit **05** leave **06** opt out, renege **07** abandon, pull out **08** opt out of, renege on, renounce **09** back out of **10** cry off from **12** withdraw from

**dropout**
**05** loner, rebel **06** hippie **07** beatnik, deviant **08** Bohemian, renegade **09** dissenter **10** malcontent **11** dissentient **13** nonconformist

**droppings**
**04** dung, scat, skat **06** egesta, faeces, manure, ordure, stools **07** excreta, spraint **09** excrement

**dross**
**04** junk, lees, rust, scum, slag **05** dregs, lucre, slack, trash, waste **06** debris, refuse, scoria **07** remains, rubbish **08** impurity **09** recrement

**drought**
**04** want **06** drouth, thirst **07** aridity, dryness **08** shortage **11** dehydration, desiccation, parchedness

**drove**
**03** mob **04** herd, host, pack **05** crowd, crush, drift, flock, horde, press, swarm **06** string, throng **07** company **09** gathering, multitude

**drown**
**02** go **03** die **04** sink **05** flood, swamp **06** deluge, drench, engulf, perish **07** founder, go under, howl out, immerse, silence, wipe out **08** drown out, inundate, outvoice, overcome, submerge **09** overpower, overwhelm **10** extinguish **12** lose your life

**drowsily**
**06** dopily, dozily **07** wearily **08** sleepily **10** sluggishly **13** lethargically

**drowsiness**
**06** torpor **08** dopiness, doziness, lethargy, narcosis **09** oscitancy, tiredness, weariness **10** grogginess, sleepiness, somnolence, somnolency **12** sluggishness

**drowsy**
**04** dozy, dull **05** dopey, dozed, heavy, tired, weary **06** bleary, dozing, dreamy, sleepy, torpid **07** nodding, slumbry, yawning **08** comatose, slumbery **09** lethargic, somnolent **10** half-asleep **11** heavy-headed

**drubbing**
**06** defeat **07** beating, licking **08** flogging, pounding, whipping **09** hammering, thrashing, trouncing, walloping **10** clobbering, cudgelling, pummelling

**drudge**
**04** drug, hack, moil, plod, toil, work **05** devil, droil, grind, grunt, scrub, slave, snake, sweat **06** beaver, labour, lackey, menial, skivvy, slavey, stooge, toiler, worker **07** servant **08** dogsbody, factotum, labourer, plug away, slog away, trauchle **09** packhorse **10** after-guard, Cinderella **11** galley-slave

**drudgery**
**03** fag **04** slog, toil **05** chore, grind, sweat, yakka **06** labour, yacker, yakker **07** faggery, slavery **08** hackwork, trauchle **09** skivvying, slaistery, spadework, treadmill **10** collar-work, donkey-work, menial work **13** sweated labour

**drug**
**04** cure, dose, numb **06** deaden, drudge, potion, remedy, sedate **07** stupefy **08** knock out, medicate, medicine, shanghai **09** stimulant **10** medication **12** anaesthetize, tranquillize **15** make unconscious

*See also* **medicine**

*Medicinal drugs include:*

**03** AZT
**04** Soma®
**05** Intal®, NSAID, salep, Taxol®, Zyban®
**06** opiate, Prozac®, statin, sulpha, Valium®, Viagra®, Zantac®
**07** antacid, aspirin, codeine, heparin, insulin, Nurofen®, quinine, Relenza®, Ritalin®, Seroxat®, steroid
**08** Antabuse®, diazepam, diuretic, hyoscine, methadon, morphine, narcotic, neomycin, orlistat, Rohypnol®, sedative, warfarin
**09** aciclovir, acyclovir, analgesic, co-codamol, cortisone, digitalis, ibuprofen, methadone, oestrogen, stimulant, tamoxifen, temazepam
**10** antibiotic, anxiolytic, chloroform, chloroquin, dimorphine, interferon, penicillin, ranitidine, salbutamol
**11** allopurinol, amoxycillin, amyl nitrate, anaesthetic, beta-blocker, chloroquine, cyclosporin, haloperidol, ipecacuanha, neuroleptic, paracetamol, propranolol, vasodilator
**12** ACE-inhibitor, chlorambucil, methotrexate, progesterone, sleeping pill, streptomycin, sulphonamide, tetracycline
**13** antibacterial, anticoagulant, antihistamine, streptokinase, tranquillizer
**14** anticonvulsant, antidepressant, azidothymidine, bronchodilator, corticosteroid, erythropoietin, hallucinogenic, hydrocortisone
**15** chloramphenicol, vasoconstrictor

*Recreational drugs include:*

**01** C, E, H
**03** hop, ice, kef, kif, LSD, PCP, pot, tab
**04** acid, bang, barb, blow, coca, coke, dope, dove, gage, hash, hemp, junk, kaif, pill, scag, skag, snow, weed
**05** bhang, crack, crank, dagga, horse, jelly, opium, shmek, smack, speed, sugar, upper
**06** basuco, charas, downer, heroin, mescal, peyote, pituri, popper
**07** charlie, churrus, cocaine, crystal, ecstasy, fantasy, guaraná, pep pill, roofies, schmeck
**08** cannabis, freebase, ketamine, laudanum, meconium, mescalin, methadon, moonrock, morphine, nepenthe, Rohypnol, snowball, Special K
**09** angel dust, dance drug, marijuana, mescaline, methadone, nose candy, peace pill, ready-wash, speedball, temazepam
**10** white stuff
**11** amphetamine, barbiturate, purple heart
**12** date-rape drug
**13** phencyclidine

*See also* **cannabis**; **cocaine**; **heroin**

**• drug dose**
**03** fix **05** bolus

**• drug experience**
**04** trip

**drug addict**
**04** head, hype, user **05** freak **06** junkie **07** druggie, hop-head, tripper **08** coke-head, snowbird **09** dope-fiend, mainliner

**drugged**
**04** high **05** doped **06** ripped, stoned, wasted, zonked **07** on a trip **08** comatose, hopped-up, turned on **09** spaced out, stupefied **10** knocked out

**drum**
**03** rap, tap **04** beat, dhol, reel, swag **05** bongo, conga, daiko, house, knock, naker, ridge, tabor, taiko, throb, thrum **06** atabal, barrel, bundle, cannon, kettle, rigger, tabour, tabret, tam-tam, tattoo, timbal, tom-tom, tum-tum, tymbal **07** bodhrán, drumlin, mridang, pulsate, tambour, timpano, tympano **08** mridanga, tympanum **09** mridamgam, mridangam **11** reverberate

**• drum into**
**06** hammer, harp on, instil **07** din into **09** drive home, inculcate, reiterate

**• drum out**
**05** expel **07** dismiss **08** throw out **09** discharge

**• drum up**
**03** get **06** gather, obtain, summon **07** attract, canvass, collect, round up, solicit **08** petition

**drumbeat**
**04** flam, roll, ruff, touk, tuck **05** hurry

**06** rafale, rappel, rattan, tattoo
**08** assembly **10** paradiddle

## drummer

**02** Dr **07** swagman **09** timpanist, tympanist

## drunk

◇ *anagram indicator*
**03** fap, fou, lit, sot, wat, wet **04** full, high, inky, lush, paid, soak, wino **05** alkie, dipso, foxed, happy, inked, lit up, merry, moppy, slued, tight, tipsy, toper, woozy **06** blotto, bombed, boozer, canned, corked, in wine, jagged, jarred, juiced, loaded, mashed, mellow, mortal, ratted, ripped, slewed, soused, sponge, stewed, stinko, stoned, tanked, tiddly, wasted **07** bevvied, bonkers, bottled, crocked, drinker, drunken, ebriose, fairish, half-cut, legless, maggoty, pickled, pie-eyed, shicker, sloshed, smashed, sozzled, squiffy, tiddled, tiddley, tippler, tosspot, trashed, wrecked **08** bibulous, drunkard, footless, hammered, in liquor, juiced up, liquored, moon-eyed, overseen, overshot, sow-drunk, stocious, stotious, tanked up, whiffled, whistled **09** alcoholic, blootered, crapulent, incapable, inebriate, inebrious, paralytic, plastered, saturated, shickered, stonkered, up the pole, well-oiled **10** blind drunk, capernoity, inebriated, obfuscated **11** capernoitie, cappernoity, dipsomaniac, hard drinker, high as a kite, intoxicated, on the tiddly, slaughtered **12** drunk as a lord, drunk as a newt, heavy drinker, roaring drunk **13** drunk as a piper, drunk as a skunk, having had a few, under the table **14** Brahms and Liszt **15** a sheet in the wind, one over the eight, the worse for wear, under the weather

### • getting drunk

**02** on **12** half-seas-over **13** mops and brooms

### • make drunk

**03** cup **05** sew up, souse **07** tipsify **09** inebriate **10** intoxicate

## drunkard

**03** sot **04** lush, soak, wino **05** alkie, bloat, dipso, drunk, souse, toper **06** boozer, sponge **07** bloater, drinker, fuddler, hophead, shicker, tippler, tosspot **08** bacchant, habitual **09** alcoholic, inebriate **10** wine-bibber **11** dipsomaniac, hard drinker **12** heavy drinker

## drunken

◇ *anagram indicator*
**03** wat **05** boozy, drunk, happy, lit up, merry, tight, tipsy **06** bombed, boozey, loaded, spongy, stoned, tiddly **07** Bacchic, drucken, riotous, sloshed **08** Bacchian, besotted **09** crapulent, debauched, inebriate, worthless **10** dissipated **11** baccanalian, intemperate, intoxicated

## drunkenness

**07** ebriety, ivresse **08** methysis **09** ebriosity, inebriety, temulence, tipsiness **10** alcoholism, crapulence, debauchery, dipsomania, insobriety **11** inebriation **12** bibulousness, hard drinking, intemperance, intoxication **13** St Martin's evil **15** serious drinking

## dry

**02** TT **03** air, sec, xer- **04** arid, brut, dull, fair, flat, kiln, sear, seco, sere, welt, wilt, wipe, xero- **05** baked, drain, droll, husky, parch, secco, witty, xeric **06** barren, boring, clever, dreary, formal, frigid, ironic, low-key, rizzar, rizzer, rizzor, scorch, subtle, torrid, wilted, wither **07** cutting, cynical, deadpan, drouthy, gasping, hirstie, laconic, make dry, parched, precise, shrivel, tedious, thirsty, trocken **08** droughty, rainless, scorched, teetotal, withered **09** abstinent, become dry, dehydrate, desiccate, dry as dust, sarcastic, temperate, unwatered, waterless, wearisome **10** abstemious, dehumidify, dehydrated, desiccated, dry as a bone, monotonous, on the wagon, shrivelled, unbuttered, unexciting **11** alcohol-free **12** moistureless **13** uninteresting **14** prohibitionist

### • dry up

**04** fade, fail, sear, stop, wane **05** arefy **06** die out, ensear, scorch, shut up **07** dwindle **09** desiccate, disappear, exsiccate **11** come to an end, stop talking **15** forget your lines

## dryness

**06** drouth, thirst **07** aridity, drought, siccity, xerasia, xerosis **08** aridness **09** xerostoma **10** barrenness, xerostomia **11** dehydration, thirstiness

## dual

**04** twin **06** binary, double, duplex, paired **07** coupled, matched, twofold **08** combined, two-piece **09** duplicate

## duality

**07** twoness **09** duplicity **10** doubleness, opposition, separation **11** combination, duplication **12** polarization

## dub

**03** tag **04** call, name, term, trim **05** label, style **06** bestow, confer, puddle **07** entitle **08** christen, nickname **09** designate

## dubiety

**05** doubt, qualm **08** mistrust **09** misgiving, suspicion **10** hesitation, indecision, scepticism **11** incertitude, uncertainty **12** doubtfulness

## dubious

◇ *anagram indicator*
**04** iffy **05** crook, fishy, shady **06** shifty, unsure **07** obscure, suspect **08** doubtful, elliptic, hesitant, wavering **09** ambiguous, debatable, sceptical, uncertain, undecided, unsettled **10** backhanded, elliptical, irresolute, left-handed, suspicious, unreliable **11** vacillating **12** questionable **13** untrustworthy

## dubiously

**09** debatably **10** hesitantly **11** ambiguously, uncertainly, undecidedly **12** questionably, suspiciously

## dubnium

**02** Db

## duchy

**07** dukedom

## duck

**01** O **03** bob, dip, wet **04** bend, dive, dook, drop, dunk, jook, jouk, shun, zero **05** avoid, dodge, douse, drake, elude, evade, lower, shirk, skive, souse, squat, stoop, yield **06** cringe, crouch, plunge **07** bow down, darling, immerse **08** bankrupt, sidestep, submerge **09** defaulter **10** sweetheart **12** steer clear of, wriggle out of

*See also* **animal**

*Ducks include:*

**04** blue, musk, smee, smew, surf, teal, wood
**05** eider, Pekin, ruddy, scaup
**06** burrow, hareld, herald, magpie, Peking, runner, scoter, smeath, smeeth, spirit, tufted, velvet, wigeon
**07** crested, gadwall, mallard, moulard, muscovy, old wife, pintail, pochard, steamer
**08** garganey, hookbill, mandarin, old squaw, shelduck
**09** Cuthbert's, goldeneye, goosander, harlequin, merganser, sheldrake, shielduck, shoveller
**10** bufflehead, canvasback, long-tailed, ring-necked
**11** ferruginous, St Cuthbert's, white-headed
**12** common scoter, Indian runner, velvet scoter
**13** ruddy shelduck

### • string of ducks

**04** sord, team

### • two ducks

**02** OO **04** pair

## duct

**03** vas **04** pipe, tube **05** canal **06** funnel, ureter, vessel **07** channel, conduit, fistula, passage, Venturi, wireway **08** deferent, diffuser **09** emunctory, excretory **11** Venturi tube

## ductile

**06** pliant **07** plastic, pliable **08** amenable, biddable, flexible, tractile, yielding **09** compliant, malleable, tractable **10** manageable **11** manipulable

## dud

**03** bum **04** bust, duff, flop **05** kaput **06** broken, failed, faulty, stumer **07** failure, let-down, washout **08** bum steer, nugatory **09** conked out, valueless, worthless **11** counterfeit, inoperative **14** disappointment

**dude**
**03** cat, fop, Roy **04** buck, lair **05** dandy

**dudgeon**
**04** hilt **05** pique **10** resentment

**due**
**03** fee, fit, lot **04** dead, just, levy, owed, toll **05** ample, owing, right **06** charge, direct, earned, enough, merits, proper, rights, unpaid **07** awaited, charges, correct, deserts, dewfull, exactly, fitting, merited, payable, tribute **08** adequate, deserved, directly, expected, plenty of, required, rightful, straight, suitable **09** appointed, in arrears, justified, precisely, privilege, repayable, requisite, scheduled **10** birthright, sufficient **11** anticipated, appropriate, comeuppance, just deserts, long-awaited, outstanding, prerogative **12** contribution, subscription **13** membership fee

**• due to**
**07** owing to **08** caused by **09** because of **11** as a result of

**duel**
**04** tilt **05** clash, fight **06** battle, combat, duello **07** contest, rivalry **08** struggle **09** encounter, monomachy **10** dependence, engagement, monomachia **11** competition **14** affair of honour **15** affaire d'honneur

**duff**
◇ *anagram indicator*
**03** bad **04** naff, poor, poxy, ropy, rump, weak **05** awful, dough, lousy, pants **06** broken, bungle, crummy, faulty **07** botched, the pits, useless **08** buttocks, hopeless, inferior, mediocre, pathetic, terrible **09** defective, deficient, imperfect, third-rate **10** inadequate, mismanaged, second-rate **11** incompetent, ineffective, poor-quality, substandard **12** unacceptable **14** a load of garbage, a load of rubbish, unsatisfactory

**duffer**
**03** git, oaf **04** clod, clot, dolt, dork, fool, geek, muff, prat **05** fogey, idiot **06** dimwit **07** bungler, halfwit, plonker, rustler **08** bonehead **09** blunderer, ignoramus **11** cattle-thief

**dugong**
**06** sea cow, sea-pig **08** halicore, sirenian

**duke**
**01** D **04** fist, lord

**dulcet**
**04** soft **05** sweet **06** gentle, mellow **08** pleasant, soothing **09** agreeable, melodious **10** harmonious **11** mellifluous **13** sweet-sounding

**dulcimer**
**06** santir, santur **07** cembalo, cymbalo, santoor, santour **08** cimbalom **09** pantaleon

**dull**
**03** dim, dry, mat, sad **04** blah, damp, dark, dead, dowf, dozy, drab, drug, dumb, fade, flat, gray, grey, idle, logy, matt, mild, mull, numb, slow, soft, tame, weak **05** allay, bland, blunt, cloud, corny, dense, dingy, dopey, dowdy, dowie, dusty, faint, gross, heavy, ho-hum, inert, lower, matte, murky, muted, plain, prose, prosy, quiet, rusty, slack, thick, vapid **06** barren, boring, bovine, cloudy, dampen, darken, deaden, deject, dismal, dreary, drowsy, feeble, gloomy, leaden, lessen, mopish, obtund, obtuse, opaque, opiate, rebate, reduce, sadden, sleepy, soften, sombre, sopite, stodgy, stupid, subdue, sullen, torpid, wooden **07** assuage, blacken, depress, disedge, doltish, humdrum, insipid, insulse, lumpish, muffled, mumpish, obscure, prosaic, relieve, stupefy, tedious, wash out **08** blockish, Boeotian, decrease, diminish, downcast, edgeless, hebetate, inactive, lifeless, mitigate, moderate, overcast, paralyse, sluggish, tiresome, tone down, toneless, workaday **09** alleviate, cheerless, dead-alive, dimwitted, inanimate, lethargic, ponderous, prosaical, wearisome **10** discourage, dishearten, indistinct, insensible, lackluster, lacklustre, monochrome, monotonous, pedestrian, perstringe, uneventful, unexciting **11** birdbrained, blunt-witted, desensitize, distressing, heavy-headed, stereotyped, stultifying, thick-witted, troublesome, unsharpened **12** dead-and-alive, thick-skulled, tranquillize **13** uncomfortable, unimaginative, unintelligent, uninteresting **15** slow on the uptake

**• become dull**
**04** rust **05** blunt **07** tarnish **08** hebetate

**dullard**
**03** git, oaf, owl **04** clod, clot, dolt, dope, dork, prat **05** chump, dumbo, dunce, idiot, moron **06** dimwit, nitwit **07** plonker **08** bonehead, imbecile, numskull **09** blockhead, ignoramus, simpleton **10** bufflehead, dunderhead

*See also* **fool**

**dullness**
**04** drab, yawn **05** cloud **06** fadeur, tedium, torpor **07** dryness, vacuity **08** flatness, monotony, slowness, vapidity **09** emptiness, plainness **10** dreariness, oppression **12** sluggishness

**duly**
**05** fitly **08** properly, suitably **09** correctly, fittingly **10** decorously, deservedly, rightfully, sure enough **11** accordingly, befittingly **13** appropriately

**dumb**
**03** mum **04** dozy, mute **05** dense, dopey, shtum, stumm, thick **06** shtoom, shtumm, silent, stupid **07** foolish, schtoom **08** gormless **09** brainless, dim-witted, soundless **10** speechless, tongue-tied **12** inarticulate, lost for words **13** unintelligent, without speech **15** at a loss for words

**• dumb down**
**07** deskill **08** simplify

**dumbfound**
**03** wow **04** daze, stun **05** amaze, floor, shock **07** astound, flummox, stagger, startle, stupefy **08** astonish, bewilder, bowl over, confound, gobsmack, surprise **09** take aback **11** flabbergast, knock for six **12** blow your mind **15** knock all of a heap

**dumbfounded**
**04** dumb **06** amazed, thrown **07** baffled, floored, stunned, stupent **08** confused, overcome, startled **09** astounded, paralysed, staggered **10** astonished, bewildered, bowled over, confounded, gobsmacked, nonplussed, speechless, taken aback **11** overwhelmed **12** lost for words **13** flabbergasted, knocked for six

**dumbly**
**06** mutely **08** silently **11** soundlessly **12** speechlessly **14** inarticulately

**dumbo** *see* **fool**

**dumbstruck**
**03** mum **04** dumb, mute **06** aghast, amazed, silent **07** shocked **09** astounded **10** speechless, tongue-tied **11** dumbfounded, obmutescent **12** inarticulate **13** thunderstruck

**dummy**
**03** git, oaf **04** clot, copy, dork, fake, fool, form, mock, prat, sham, teat **05** bogus, chump, false, idiot, model, trial **06** dimwit, figure, mock-up, nitwit, phoney, sample, silent **07** feigned, plonker, soother **08** imbecile, numskull, pacifier, practice **09** blockhead, comforter, duplicate, imitation, lay-figure, mannequin, simulated **10** artificial, bufflehead, substitute **11** counterfeit **12** reproduction **14** representation

*See also* **fool**

**dump**
**03** tip **04** bung, drop, hole, jilt, mess, park, pool, slum **05** chuck, ditch, hovel, joint, leave, place, plonk, scrap, shack, shoot, store **06** desert, marble, midden, pigpen, pigsty, shanty, tip out, unload **07** abandon, counter, deposit, discard, forsake, lay down, let fall, offload, pour out, put down, set down **08** empty out, get rid of, jettison, junkyard, throw out **09** chuck away, discharge, dispose of, fling down, scrapyard, throw away, throw down, walk out on **10** rubbish tip **11** rubbish heap **14** give the elbow to

**• down in the dumps**
**03** low, sad **04** blue **07** unhappy **08** dejected, downcast **09** depressed,

miserable **10** dispirited, melancholy **11** downhearted

**• dumps**

**08** doldrums

**dumpling**

**06** dim sum, perogi, pirogi, won ton **07** gnocchi, knaidel, kneidel, pierogi **08** doughboy, quenelle **09** doughball, matzo ball **10** corn dodger

**dumpster**

**04** skip

**dumpy**

**05** plump, podgy, pudgy, short, squab, squat, stout, tubby **06** chubby, chunky, stubby

**dun**

**04** dull, hill **05** dingy, dusky **06** harass, pester, plague **11** mud-coloured **12** greyish-brown **13** mouse-coloured

**dunce**

**01** d **03** git **04** dork, fool, nerd, prat, twit **05** idiot, ninny, twerp, wally **06** dimwit, nitwit **07** dullard, plonker **08** bonehead, dipstick, imbecile, numskull **09** blockhead **10** bufflehead, loggerhead, nincompoop

**dune** *see* **sand dune, sand dunes** *under* **sand**

**dung**

**04** chip, cock, dirt, muck, soil, tath **05** argol, dreck, guano, mulch, shard, sharn, siege **06** cowpat, doo-doo, faeces, fumets, manure, ordure **07** buttons, fewmets, scumber, skummer, spraint **08** spraints **09** droppings, excrement, spawn cake **10** spawn brick **11** animal waste **12** album Graecum, buffalo chips

**• devil's dung**

**04** hing

**• dog's dung**

**04** pure

**• plaster with dung**

**04** leep

**dung-beetle**

**03** dor **04** dorr **06** scarab **11** coprophagan

**dungeon**

**04** cage, cell, gaol, jail, keep **05** vault **06** lock-up, prison **09** oubliette

**dupe**

**03** con, gum, mug **04** cony, cull, flat, fool, geck, gull, hoax, pawn **05** cheat, coney, cully, shaft, trick **06** chouse, delude, diddle, outwit, plover, puppet, rip off, sitter, stooge, sucker, take in, victim **07** deceive, defraud, dottrel, fall guy, swindle **08** dotterel, hoodwink, pushover, soft mark **09** bamboozle, goldbrick, simpleton **10** instrument **11** make a fool of

**duplicate**

**03** dup, fax **04** copy, echo, fold, like, mate, twin **05** clone, ditto, match, model, Roneo®, spare, Xerox® **06** carbon, double, paired, repeat, ringer **07** do again, forgery, matched, replica, twofold **08** matching **09** facsimile, identical, imitation, lookalike, photocopy, Photostat®, replicate, reproduce **10** carbon copy, dead ringer, equivalent, transcript **11** alternative, counterpart **12** reproduction **13** corresponding, spitting image

**duplication**

**04** copy **05** clone **07** cloning, copying **08** doubling **09** photocopy **10** gemination, repetition **11** dittography, replication **12** photocopying, reproduction

**duplicity**

**05** fraud, guile **06** deceit **07** perfidy **08** artifice, betrayal **09** chicanery, deception, falsehood, hypocrisy, mendacity, treachery **10** dishonesty, doubleness **11** insincerity **13** deceitfulness, dissimulation, double-dealing

**durability**

**04** wear **07** durance, wearing **08** strength **09** constancy, endurance, longevity, stability **10** permanence **11** durableness, lastingness, persistence **15** imperishability

**durable**

**04** fast, firm **05** fixed, hardy, pakka, pucka, pukka, solid, sound, tough **06** robust, stable, strong, sturdy **07** abiding, lasting **08** constant, enduring, reliable, unfading **09** heavy-duty, permanent, resistant **10** dependable, persistent, persisting, reinforced, unchanging **11** hard-wearing, long-lasting, serviceable, substantial

**duration**

**04** span, term, time **05** spell **06** extent, length, period **07** stretch **08** fullness, standing, time span **09** endurance, time scale **10** protension **11** continuance, persistence, persistency, running time **12** continuation, length of time, perpetuation, prolongation

**duress**

**05** force **06** threat **08** coercion, exaction, pressure **09** restraint **10** compulsion, constraint **11** arm-twisting, enforcement **12** imprisonment

**during**

◇ *insertion indicator*

**02** in, of **03** dia-, for **04** over **07** pending **10** throughout **11** all the while, at the time of, in the time of **12** for the time of **13** in the course of, in the middle of

**dusk**

**03** dim, eve **04** dark **05** gloom, shade **06** sunset **07** darkish, evening, shadows, sundown **08** darkness, gloaming, owl-light, twilight **09** nightfall **10** crepuscule **11** candlelight

**dusky**

**03** dim, dun, sad **04** dark, hazy **05** black, brown, foggy, misty, murky, swart, tawny **06** cloudy, gloomy, phaeic, swarth, twilit **07** shadowy, subfusc, subfusk, swarthy, umbrose **09** tenebrous **10** fuliginous **11** crepuscular, dark-skinned **12** dark-coloured

**dust**

**03** ash, mop **04** bort, clay, coom, culm, dirt, duff, fuzz, grit, mote, seed, smut, soil, soot, wipe **05** ashes, boart, brawl, brush, clean, cover, earth, grime, lemel, money, smoke, spray, stour **06** bedust, ground, limail, polish, pother, powder, pudder, spread **07** burnish, fallout, scatter, smother, turmoil **08** bulldust, sprinkle, stardust **09** particles, pozzolana **10** cryoconite, haemoconia **11** disturbance **13** meteor streams **14** micro-meteorite

**• dust storm**

**05** devil **06** calima **07** Shaitan

**dust-up**

**05** brawl, brush, fight, scrap, set-to **06** barney, bust-up, fracas, tussle **07** punch-up, quarrel, scuffle **08** argument, conflict, skirmish **09** argy-bargy, commotion, encounter **11** disturbance **12** disagreement

**dusty**

**03** bad **04** dull **05** dirty, grimy, sandy, sooty **06** chalky, filthy, grubby, stoury **07** crumbly, friable, powdery **08** granular, lifeless **09** pulverous **11** dust-covered **12** contemptible, old-fashioned

**Dutch**

**01** D **02** Du

**• Cape Dutch**

**04** Taal

**dutiful**

**05** pious **06** filial **07** devoted **08** obedient **09** compliant, officious **10** obsequious, respectful, submissive, thoughtful **11** considerate, deferential, reverential **13** conscientious

**duty**

**03** job, tax **04** debt, dues, levy, onus, part, role, task, toll, work **05** chore **06** burden, charge, excise, office, tariff **07** calling, customs, loyalty, mission, respect, service **08** business, fidelity, function **09** deference, obedience **10** allegiance, assignment, attendance, commission, obligation **11** requirement **12** faithfulness **14** responsibility

**• active duty**

**02** AD

**• duty list**

**04** rota

**• off duty**

**03** off **04** free **07** off work, resting **08** inactive **09** at leisure, not at work, on holiday **10** not working

**• on duty**

**04** busy **06** active, at work, on call,

tied up **07** engaged, working **08** occupied

**dwarf**
**03** elf, toy **04** baby, Mime, mini, tiny, trow **05** check, gnome, pigmy, pygmy, small, stunt, troll **06** arrest, droich, durgan, goblin, little, midget, minute, petite, pocket, retard **07** atrophy, manikin, stunted **08** Alberich, dominate, homuncle, mannikin, Tom Thumb **09** homuncule, miniature, tower over **10** diminutive, homunculus, overshadow, undersized **11** Lilliputian

*Snow White's dwarfs:*

**03** Doc
**05** Dopey, Happy
**06** Grumpy, Sleepy, Sneezy
**07** Bashful

**dwell**
**03** won **04** bide, home, live, rest, stay **05** abide, lodge, stall **06** people, remain, reside, settle, tenant **07** hang out, inhabit, sojourn **08** populate **11** be domiciled
• **dwell on**
**06** harp on **07** brood on **08** mull over **09** elaborate, emphasize, expatiate, reflect on **10** linger over, meditate on, ruminate on, think about

**dweller**
**07** denizen **08** occupant, occupier, resident **10** inhabitant

**dwelling**
**03** cot, dug, hut, won **04** flat, home, roof, tent, tipi, weem, woon **05** abode, bothy, bower, donga, gundy, house, hovel, humpy, lodge, place, tepee **06** grange, gunyah, mia-mia, pondok, shanty, teepee, wurley **07** cottage, doghole, lodging **08** domicile, messuage, quarters, tenement **09** apartment, penthouse, residence, single-end **10** habitation, pied-à-terre **11** continuance **13** dwelling-house, establishment
*See also* **accommodation**; **house**

**dwindle**
**03** ebb **04** fade, fail, fall, wane **06** die out, lessen, reduce, shrink, vanish, weaken, wither **07** decline, shrivel, subside, tail off **08** decrease, diminish, fall away, grow less, peter out, taper off **09** disappear, waste away **10** become less
• **dwindle away**
**05** peter

**dye**
**03** hew, hue **04** tint, wash **05** agent, imbue, shade, stain, tinct, tinge **06** colour, embrue, imbrue **07** embrewe, pigment **09** colouring
*See also* **colour**; **pigment**

*Dyes include:*

**04** anil, Saxe, wald, weld, woad
**05** chica, eosin, henna, mauve
**06** anatto, archil, corkir, flavin, fustic, indigo, kamala, korkir, madder, mauvin, orcein, orchel, orchil
**07** alkanet, annatto, azurine, cudbear, flavine, magenta, mauvein, mauvine, para-red, ponceau, saffron
**08** amaranth, fuchsine, mauveine, orchella, orchilla, safranin, turnsole
**09** cochineal, nigrosine, primuline, safranine, Saxon blue, Turkey red, Tyrian red
**10** carthamine, Saxony blue, tartrazine
**12** Tyrian purple

• **dyeing technique**
**04** ikat
• **source of dye**
**04** chay

**dyed-in-the-wool**
**05** fixed **07** diehard, settled **08** complete, hard-core, hardened, thorough **09** confirmed **10** deep-rooted, entrenched, inflexible, inveterate, unshakable **11** established, unshakeable **12** card-carrying, long-standing, unchangeable **14** uncompromising

**dying**
**04** last **05** final, going, waned **06** ebbing, ending, fading, mortal **07** closing, failing, passing **08** expiring, moribund **09** declining, finishing, perishing, vanishing **10** concluding **11** near to death **12** at death's door, close to death **14** on your deathbed, on your last legs

**dynamic**
◇ *anagram indicator*
**05** vital **06** active, causal, lively, potent, strong **07** driving, go-ahead **08** forceful, powerful, spirited, vigorous **09** effective, energetic, go-getting **11** high-powered **12** full of energy, self-starting

**dynamically**
**07** vitally **08** actively, strongly **10** forcefully, powerfully, vigorously **11** effectively **13** energetically

**dynamism**
**02** go **03** pep, vim, zap, zip **04** push **05** drive **06** energy, spirit, vigour **07** pizzazz **10** enterprise, get-up-and-go, initiative, liveliness **12** forcefulness

**dynasty**
**04** line, rule **05** house **06** empire, regime **07** lineage **08** dominion **09** authority **10** government, succession **11** sovereignty **12** jurisdiction

*Dynasties include:*

**02** Yi
**03** Jin, Qin, Sui
**04** Asen, Avis, Chin, Lodi, Ming, Qing, Song, Sung, Tang, Vasa, Yuan, Zhou
**05** Ch'ing, Piast, Qajar, Shang
**06** Chakri, Sayyid, Valois, Wettin, Zangid
**07** 'Abbasid, Ayyubid, Chakkri, Fatimid, Romanov, Safavid, Tughlaq
**08** Capetian, Habsburg, Ilkhanid
**09** Jagiellon
**10** Qarakhanid
**11** Plantagenet
**12** Hohenstaufen, Hohenzollern
**14** Petrovic-Njegos

**dyspepsia**
**07** acidity, pyrosis **08** dyspepsy **09** heartburn **10** cardialgia, water-brash

**dyspeptic**
**04** edgy **05** humpy, ratty, testy **06** crabby, feisty, gloomy, shirty, touchy **07** crabbed, grouchy, in a huff, in a sulk, peevish, stroppy **08** snappish **09** crotchety, irritable **10** indigested **11** bad-tempered, cacogastric, indigestive **13** short-tempered

**dysprosium**
**02** Dy

# E

**E**
**04** echo **07** epsilon

**each**
**02** ea **03** ilk, per **05** every **06** apiece, singly **07** each one, per head **09** per capita, per person **10** separately **11** every single **12** individually, respectively **15** each and every one, every individual

• **for each**
**03** per

**eager**
**04** agog, avid, bore, fain, keen, rath, toey **05** antsy, dying, frack, hasty, prone, rathe, sharp **06** ardent, greedy, gung-ho, hungry, intent, raring, watery **07** anxious, earnest, fervent, longing, thirsty, up for it, willing, wishful, wishing, zealous **08** desirous, diligent, empressé, yearning **09** desperate, impatient, perfervid **12** affectionate, enthusiastic, wholehearted

**eagerly**
**04** sore **06** avidly, keenly **08** ardently, greedily, intently **09** earnestly, fervently, zealously **11** impatiently **14** wholeheartedly

**eagerness**
**03** yen **04** lust, zeal **05** ardor, greed **06** ardour, hunger, thirst **07** avidity, fervour, longing **08** fainness, fervency, keenness, yearning **09** fervidity **10** enthusiasm, greediness, impatience, intentness **11** earnestness, impetuosity

**eagle**
**04** erne **05** harpy **06** Aquila **07** alerion, lectern **08** allerion, bateleur, berghaan **11** king of birds

**ear**
◇ *homophone indicator*
**03** ere, lug **04** heed, till **05** skill, souse, taste **06** notice, plough, regard **07** ability, earhole, hearing, lughole **09** attention, shell-like **10** perception **11** sensitivity **12** appreciation **13** attentiveness **14** discrimination

*Ear parts include:*

**04** drum, lobe
**05** anvil, helix, incus, pinna, scala
**06** concha, cupola, hammer, stapes, tragus
**07** alveary, auricle, cochlea, eardrum, ear lobe, malleus, saccule, stirrup, utricle
**08** pavilion, sacculus, tympanum
**09** columella, endolymph, labyrinth, perilymph, vestibule
**10** oval window
**11** Corti's organ, round window
**12** organ of Corti
**13** auditory canal, auditory nerve
**14** columella auris, Eustachian tube
**15** vestibular nerve

• **of the ear**
**04** otic

• **play it by ear**
**05** ad-lib **06** busk it, wing it **09** improvise **11** extemporize **15** think on your feet

**earlier**
**02** ex **06** before **07** already, prior to **08** formerly, previous **10** previously

**early**
**02** am **04** auld, rare, rath, rear, soon **05** first **06** at dawn **07** advance, ancient, forward, initial, morning, opening, too soon **08** advanced, primeval, untimely **09** in advance, premature, primaeval, primitive **10** at daybreak, beforehand, in good time, precocious, primordial **11** ahead of time, prematurely, undeveloped **12** in the morning **13** autochthonous **15** ahead of schedule, with time to spare

**earmark**
**03** tag **05** label **07** mark out, reserve **08** allocate, keep back, lay aside, put aside, set aside **09** designate

**earn**
**03** ern, get, net, win **04** draw, gain, make, rate, reap **05** clear, gross, merit **06** attain, be owed, be paid, curdle, obtain, pocket, pull in, rake in, secure **07** achieve, acquire, bring in, collect, deserve, get paid, realize, receive, warrant **08** take home

**earnest**
**03** sad **04** dear, firm, keen **05** arles, eager, fixed, grave, token, truth **06** ardent, devout, intent, pledge, solemn, steady, urgent **07** deposit, devoted, fervent, forward, intense, promise, serious, sincere, wistful, zealous **08** diligent, resolute, security **09** assiduous, assurance, committed, dedicated, guarantee, heartfelt, sincerity **10** persistent, press-money, resolution, thoughtful **11** down payment, impassioned, seriousness **12** earnest-penny, enthusiastic **13** conscientious, determination

• **in earnest**
**07** genuine, serious, sincere, stand-up **08** ardently, intently, steadily **09** not joking, seriously, zealously **10** resolutely **12** passionately, purposefully **14** wholeheartedly **15** conscientiously

**earnestly**
**04** hard **06** dearly, firmly, keenly, warmly, wistly **07** eagerly **08** intently **09** fervently, seriously, sincerely, zealously **10** resolutely

**earnestness**
**04** zeal **06** ardour, warmth **07** fervour, gravity, passion **08** devotion, fervency, keenness **09** eagerness, sincerity, vehemence **10** enthusiasm, intentness, resolution **11** seriousness **13** determination **14** purposefulness

**earnings**
**03** fee, pay **04** gain **05** wages **06** income, net pay, return, reward, salary **07** profits, revenue, stipend **08** gross pay, proceeds, receipts **09** emolument **10** honorarium **11** take home pay **12** remuneration

**earring**
**04** drop, hoop, snap, stud **06** clip-on **07** pendant, pendent, sleeper

**earshot**
**04** hail **05** sound **07** hearing

• **beyond earshot**
**10** out of range

**earth**
**01** E **02** Ge **03** orb, sod **04** clay, dirt, dust, eard, Gaea, Gaia, land, loam, mold, soil, turf, yerd, yird **05** globe, humus, mould, world **06** ground, planet, sphere **07** topsoil

• **rammed earth**
**04** pisé

**earthenware**
**03** pig, pot **04** delf, pots, waly **05** cloam, delft, delph, wally **07** faience, pottery **08** ceramics, crockery, figuline, maiolica, majolica **09** creamware, ironstone, porcelain, stoneware **10** Samian ware, terracotta **14** terra sigillata

**earthly**
**04** vile **05** human **06** likely, mortal **07** fleshly, mundane, profane, secular, sensual, terrene, worldly **08** feasible, material, physical, possible, sublunar, telluric, temporal **09** slightest, sublunary, tellurian **10** imaginable **11** conceivable, terrestrial **13** materialistic

**earthquake**
**05** quake, seism, shake, shock **06** tremor **07** temblor **08** trembler,

upheaval **10** aftershock, convulsion **11** earth-tremor

**earthwork**
**04** berm, ring **06** cursus, sconce **07** parados **10** breastwork, embankment, roundabout **12** entrenchment, intrenchment, maiden castle

**earthy**
**04** blue, rude **05** bawdy, crude, gross, rough **06** cloddy, coarse, direct, ribald, simple, vulgar **07** natural, raunchy, terrene **08** claylike, dirtlike, soil-like **09** earthlike, unrefined **10** indecorous **11** down to earth, uninhibited **15** unsophisticated

**ease**
**04** calm, edge, inch, rest **05** abate, allay, guide, peace, quiet, relax, salve, slide, steer **06** lessen, reduce, relent, repose, smooth, soothe, wealth **07** assuage, comfort, leisure, lighten, quieten, relieve **08** deftness, diminish, facility, grow less, mitigate, moderate, opulence, otiosity, palliate **09** affluence, alleviate, dexterity, enjoyment, happiness, manoeuvre **10** adroitness, ameliorate, become less, bed of roses, cleverness, easy street, facilitate, otioseness, prosperity, relaxation **11** contentment, lap of luxury, life of Riley, naturalness, skilfulness **12** peacefulness **14** effortlessness

**• at ease**
**04** calm **06** secure **07** natural, relaxed **08** composed, sans gêne **11** comfortable

**• ease off**
**04** wane **05** abate **06** relent **07** die away, die down, slacken, subside **08** decrease, diminish, moderate, slack off **10** become less, slacken off

**easily**
◇ *anagram indicator*
**04** eath, ethe, well **05** by far, eathe **06** simply, surely **07** clearly, readily **08** fluently, probably **09** certainly **10** definitely, far and away, undeniably **11** comfortably, doubtlessly, undoubtedly **12** effortlessly, indisputably, without doubt

**• easily handled**
**04** yare

**east**
**01** E **04** Asia **06** Levant, Orient **07** sunrise **08** Old World **09** sunrising **11** morning-land

**• East End**
◇ *dialect indicator*

**• from the east, goes east**
◇ *reversal indicator*

**Easter**
**04** Pace **05** Pasch

**eastern**
**01** E **06** exotic, Levant, Orient **08** Oriental

**East German** *see* **German**

**East Timor**
**03** TLS

**easy**
◇ *anagram indicator*
**04** calm, eath, ethe, glib, soft **05** cushy, eathe **06** a cinch, casual, dégagé, facile, simple, smooth **07** a doddle, natural, relaxed, running **08** carefree, homelike, informal, laid-back, painless, unforced **09** a cakewalk, a pushover, easy as ABC, easy as pie, easy-going, easy-peasy, foolproof, leisurely, unstudied **10** child's play, effortless, manageable, unlaboured **11** comfortable, undemanding **12** a piece of cake **13** uncomplicated **14** a walk in the park **15** straightforward

**• easy thing**
**03** pie **08** pushover

**• take it easy**
**04** loll **05** relax

**easy-going**
**04** calm **06** placid, serene **07** equable, lenient, relaxed **08** amenable, carefree, indolent, laid-back, tolerant **10** insouciant, nonchalant **11** undemanding **12** even-tempered, happy-go-lucky **13** imperturbable

**eat**
◇ *containment indicator*
**02** go **03** hog, pig, rot, sup **04** bite, chew, chop, cram, dine, feed, fret, grub, guts, mess, nosh, peck, pick, take **05** binge, decay, erode, feast, graze, hog it, lunch, munch, scoff, snack, snarf, taste, twist, upset, worry **06** begnaw, devour, gobble, guttle, ingest, pig out, slairg, tuck in **07** consume, corrode, crumble, predate, put away, swallow **08** bite into, bolt down, chow down, demolish, dissolve, gulp down, irritate, tuck into, wear away, wolf down **09** breakfast, have a bite, knock back, manducate, partake of, polish off, undermine **10** gormandize, have a snack

*Eating places include:*

**04** hall, mess
**06** frater, fratry
**07** canteen
**08** takeaway
**09** refectory
**10** commissary, dining-hall
**11** frater-house

*See also* **restaurant**

**• eat away**
**04** etch, gnaw **05** erode **06** begnaw **07** corrode

**• eat quickly**
**04** bolt, cram, gulp

**eatable**
**04** good **06** edible **08** esculent **09** palatable, wholesome **10** comestible, digestible

**eavesdrop**
**03** bug, spy, tap **05** snoop **06** earwig **07** monitor **08** listen in, overhear **10** stillicide

**eavesdropper**
**03** spy **05** snoop **07** monitor, snooper **08** listener

**ebb**
**04** drop, fall, flag, sink, wane **05** abate, decay, go out **06** lessen, recede, reflow, reflux, shrink, waning, weaken **07** decline, dwindle, ebb tide, lagging, low tide, retreat, slacken, subside **08** decrease, diminish, fade away, fall back, flow back, going-out, low water, peter out, receding **09** abatement, dwindling, lessening, refluence, retrocede, subsiding, weakening **10** degenerate, slackening, subsidence **11** deteriorate, flowing-back **12** degeneration **13** deterioration

**ebony**
**03** jet **04** dark, inky **05** black, heben, jetty, sable, sooty **08** jet-black **09** cocuswood **10** calamander, coromandel

**ebullience**
**04** zest **07** elation **08** buoyancy, vivacity **10** breeziness, brightness, bubbliness, chirpiness, enthusiasm, excitement, exuberance **11** high spirits **12** effusiveness, exhilaration

**ebullient**
**06** breezy, bright, bubbly, chirpy, elated **07** buoyant, excited, gushing, zestful **08** agitated, effusive **09** exuberant, vivacious **11** exhilarated **12** effervescent, enthusiastic **13** irrepressible

**eccentric**
◇ *anagram indicator*
**03** cam, dag, fay, fey, fie, nut, odd, off **04** card, case, cure, ditz, geek, kook, loon, wack, zany **05** crank, ditsy, ditzy, dotty, flake, flaky, freak, geeky, kinky, kooky, loony, loopy, nutty, queer, spacy, wacko, wacky, weird **06** cranky, kookie, nutjob, nutter, oddity, quirky, screwy, spacey, way-out, weirdo, whacko **07** bizarre, cupcake, dingbat, erratic, nutcase, oddball, odd fish, off-beat, strange, weirdie **08** aberrant, abnormal, crackpot, freakish, peculiar, singular **09** character, ding-a-ling, screwball **10** loony tunes, off the wall, outlandish **13** idiosyncratic, nonconformist **14** fish out of water, unconventional

**eccentricity**
**01** e **05** quirk **06** oddity **07** anomaly **09** weirdness **10** aberration, quirkiness, screwiness **11** abnormality, bizarreness, peculiarity, singularity, strangeness, unorthodoxy **12** freakishness, idiosyncrasy **13** nonconformity **14** capriciousness

**ecclesiastic**
**04** abbé, dean **05** canon, padre, vicar **06** bishop, cleric, curate, deacon, father, lector, parson, pastor, priest, rector **08** chaplain, man of God, minister, preacher, reverend **09** churchman, clergyman, deaconess, presbyter **10** archbishop, woman of God **11** churchwoman, clergywoman

**13** man of the cloth **15** woman of the cloth

*See also* **clergyman, clergywoman**

**ecclesiastical**
**04** holy **06** church, divine **07** canonic **08** churchly, clerical, pastoral, priestly **09** canonical, religious, spiritual **10** sacerdotal **11** ministerial

**echelon**
**04** rank, rung, tier **05** grade, level, place **06** degree, status **08** position

**echinoderm**
**07** crinoid, cystoid, sea-lily, trepang **08** starfish **09** sea-urchin **10** bêche-de-mer **11** brittlestar, sea-cucumber

**echo**
**01** E **04** copy, hint, ring **05** angel, clone, ditto, image, mimic, reply, trace **06** answer, memory, mirror, parrot, repeat, report **07** imitate, rebound, reflect, remains, resound, respeak, ringing, vestige **08** allusion, imitator, parallel, rebellow, reminder, resemble **09** duplicate, evocation, flashback, imitation, reiterate, repercuss, reproduce **10** reflection, repetition, resounding **11** mirror image, reiteration, remembrance, replication, reverberate **12** reproduction **13** reverberation

**éclat**
**04** fame, show **05** glory, style **06** effect, lustre, renown **07** acclaim, display, success **08** applause, approval, plaudits **09** celebrity, splendour **10** brilliance **11** acclamation, distinction, flamboyance, ostentation, stylishness

**eclectic**
**04** wide **05** broad **06** varied **07** diverse, general, liberal **08** catholic **09** many-sided, selective **11** diversified, wide-ranging **12** all-embracing, multifarious **13** comprehensive, heterogeneous

**eclipse**
**03** dim, ebb **04** fall, loss, veil **05** block, cloud, cover, decay, dwarf, excel, outdo **06** darken, exceed, shroud **07** blot out, conceal, decline, dimming, failure, obscure, shading, surpass, veiling **08** covering, darkness, outshine **09** darkening, deliquium, transcend, weakening **10** concealing, overshadow **11** blotting-out, obscuration **13** overshadowing **14** run rings around **15** cast a shadow over, put into the shade

**economic**
**05** cheap, trade **06** fiscal, viable **08** business, monetary **09** budgetary, financial, pecuniary, rewarding **10** commercial, industrial, productive, profitable **11** moneymaking **12** profit-making, remunerative **13** cost-effective

**economical**
**05** cheap, tight **06** budget, frugal, modest, saving **07** careful, low-cost, prudent, sparing, thrifty **08** low-price, skimping **09** efficient, low-budget, low-priced, provident, scrimping **10** reasonable **11** inexpensive **12** parsimonious **13** cost-effective **15** bargain-basement

**economics**

*Economics theories and schools include:*

**07** Marxian
**09** Keynesian
**10** game theory
**11** physiocracy
**12** mercantilism, neo-classical, neo-Keynesian, neo-Ricardian, new classical
**13** Chicago school, post-Keynesian
**14** Austrian school
**15** classical school

*Economic problems include:*

**08** scarcity
**09** deflation, inflation, skills gap
**10** depression
**12** trade barrier, trade deficit, unemployment
**13** budget deficit

**economist**
**10** chrematist

*Economists include:*

**03** **Say** (Jean-Baptiste), **Sen** (Amartya)
**04** **Nash** (John), **Ward** (Dame Barbara), **Webb** (Sidney)
**05** **Arrow** (Kenneth J), **Meade** (James Edward), **North** (Douglass C), **Petty** (Sir William), **Smith** (Adam), **Solow** (Robert Merton), **Stone** (Sir Richard), **Tobin** (James)
**06** **Allais** (Maurice), **Cobden** (Richard), **Cripps** (Sir Stafford), **Debreu** (Gerard), **Erhard** (Ludwig), **Frisch** (Ragnar), **Horner** (Francis), **Keynes** (John Maynard), **Myrdal** (Gunnar), **Tawney** (Richard Henry)
**07** **Bagehot** (Walter), **Kuznets** (Simon), **Malthus** (Thomas Robert), **Ricardo** (David), **Robbins** (Lionel, Lord), **Scholes** (Myron), **Stigler** (George Joseph), **Toynbee** (Arnold), **Vickrey** (William)
**08** **Buchanan** (James McGill), **Friedman** (Milton), **Leontief** (Wassily), **Marshall** (Alfred), **Mirrlees** (James), **Robinson** (Joan Violet), **Schiller** (Karl), **Shatalin** (Stanislav), **Youngson** (Alexander John)
**09** **Beveridge** (William, Lord), **Galbraith** (John Kenneth), **Greenspan** (Alan), **Tinbergen** (Jan)
**10** **Modigliani** (Franco)
**11** **Kantorovich** (Leonid)

**economize**
**03** eke **04** save **06** budget **07** cut back, use less **08** cut costs, retrench **10** buy cheaply, cut corners **12** be economical **13** keep down costs, scrimp and save **14** cut expenditure, live on the cheap **15** tighten your belt

**economy**
**04** care **06** saving, thrift, wealth **08** prudence, skimping **09** frugality, husbandry, parsimony, plutology, plutonomy, restraint, scrimping **10** providence **11** carefulness **12** catallactics, retrenchment **13** chrematistics **14** financial state, system of wealth **15** financial system

**ecstasy**
**01** E **03** joy, tab **04** dove **05** bliss **06** frenzy **07** delight, elation, fervour, rapture **08** euphoria, pleasure **09** transport **10** exultation, jubilation **11** sublimation **12** disco biscuit
• **rouse to ecstasy**
**04** send

**ecstatic**
**04** rapt, sent **06** elated, joyful, Pythic **07** fervent **08** blissful, euphoric, frenzied, jubilant **09** delirious, overjoyed, rapturous, rhapsodic **10** blissed-out, enraptured, in raptures **11** high as a kite, on cloud nine, over the moon, tickled pink **13** jumping for joy **15** in seventh heaven

**Ecuador**
**02** EC **03** ECU

**ecumenical**
**07** general **08** catholic **09** universal **10** broad-based **12** all-embracing, nonsectarian

**eddy**
**04** curl, pirl, purl, reel, roll, spin, turn, weal, weel, well **05** rotor, swirl, swish, twirl, twist, whirl **06** vortex **07** backset **08** swirling **09** maelstrom, whirlpool, whirlwind

**edge**
◇ *ends selection indicator*
◇ *head selection indicator*
**03** hem, lip, rim **04** bite, brim, ease, head, inch, kerb, lead, line, side, worm, zest **05** brink, crawl, creep, elbow, force, limit, sidle, steal, sting, verge **06** border, fringe, margin **07** outline **08** acerbity, boundary, frontier, keenness, pungency, severity, whip-hand **09** acuteness, advantage, dominance, extremity, perimeter, periphery, sharpness, threshold, upper hand **10** ascendancy, causticity, outer limit, trenchancy **11** pick your way, superiority **12** incisiveness
• **on edge**
**04** edgy, toey **05** jumpy, nervy, tense **06** touchy **07** anxious, keyed-up, nervous, twitchy, uptight **09** ill at ease, irritable **12** apprehensive, highly-strung
• **rough edge**
**03** bur **04** burr
• **straight edge**
**04** lute, rule

**edgy**
**05** nervy, tense **06** on edge, touchy **07** anxious, brittle, keyed-up, nervous, uptight **09** ill at ease, irritable **12** highly-strung

**edible**
**04** good **07** eatable **08** fit to eat, harmless **09** palatable, safe to eat, wholesome **10** comestible, digestible
**• edible shoots**
**03** udo

**edict**
**03** act, law **04** bull, fiat, rule **05** order, ukase **06** decree, ruling **07** command, mandate, process, statute **08** decretal, rescript **09** forbiddal, manifesto, pragmatic **10** golden bull, injunction, regulation **11** forbiddance **12** proclamation **13** pronouncement **14** pronunciamento

**edification**
**07** tuition **08** coaching, guidance, teaching **09** education, elevation, uplifting **10** upbuilding **11** improvement, instruction **13** enlightenment

**edifice**
**08** building, erection **09** structure **12** construction

**edify**
**05** build, coach, guide, teach, tutor **06** inform, school, uplift **07** build up, educate, elevate, improve, nurture **08** instruct **09** enlighten, establish

**edit**
◇ *anagram indicator*
◇ *deletion indicator*
**04** head **05** adapt, amend, check, emend **06** censor, choose, direct, garble, gather, head up, modify, polish, redact, revise, reword, select **07** arrange, collect, compile, correct, reorder, rewrite, subedit **08** annotate, assemble, copy-edit, organize, rephrase **09** proofread, rearrange **10** blue-pencil, bowdlerize **11** put together **12** be in charge of

**edition**
**02** ed **04** Aufl, copy, edit **05** extra, issue, print **06** number, urtext, volume **07** hexapla, omnibus, reprint, version **08** printing, tetrapla, variorum **10** impression **11** publication **12** extra-special, reproduction
**• limited edition**
**04** Aufl

**editor**
**02** ed **04** hack **06** journo, writer **07** amender, checker, newsman, reviser **08** director, overseer, reporter, reviewer, rewriter **09** corrector, newswoman, publisher, subeditor **10** copy editor, desk editor, journalist, newscaster, undertaker **11** factchecker, proofreader **12** newspaperman **13** correspondent **14** newspaperwoman
*See also* **journalist**
**• assistant editor**
**03** sub

**editorial**
**06** column

**educable**
**09** teachable, trainable **12** instructible

**educate**
**05** coach, drill, edify, prime, teach, train, tutor **06** inform, school **07** bring up, develop, improve, nourish, nurture, prepare, train up, uptrain **08** hothouse, instruct **09** cultivate, enlighten, inculcate, institute **10** discipline, take in hand **12** indoctrinate

**educated**
**02** ed **04** wise **06** brainy, taught **07** erudite, learned, refined, trained, tutored **08** all there, cultured, informed, lettered, literate, schooled, well-bred, well-read **09** civilized, sagacious **10** cultivated, instructed **11** enlightened **12** clever-clever **13** knowledgeable

**education**
**02** ed **07** culture, letters, nurture, tuition **08** coaching, drilling, guidance, learning, teaching, training, tutoring **09** fostering, informing, knowledge, schooling **10** upbringing **11** cultivation, development, edification, improvement, inculcation, instruction, preparation, scholarship **13** enlightenment **14** indoctrination
**• basic education**
**03** RRR
**• education journal**
**03** TES
**• further education**
**02** FE
**• higher education**
**02** HE

**educational**
**08** academic, cultural, didactic, edifying, learning, teaching **09** educative, improving, pedagogic **10** scholastic **11** informative, instructive, pedagogical **12** enlightening **13** instructional **14** institutionary

*Educational establishments include:*

**03** CFE, CTC, uni
**04** poly, tech
**07** academy, college
**08** seminary
**10** high school, playschool, prep school, university
**11** city academy, faith school, polytechnic, upper school
**12** beacon school, infant school, junior school, kindergarten, middle school, public school, summer school, Sunday school
**13** comprehensive, convent school, grammar school, nursery school, primary school, private school
**14** boarding school, business school, combined school, flagship school
**15** community school, finishing school, grant-maintained, secondary modern, secondary school, voluntary school

**educative**
**08** didactic, edifying **09** improving **10** catechetic **11** catechismal, catechistic, educational, informative, instructive **12** enlightening **13** catechistical

**educator**
**05** coach, tutor **06** master, mentor **07** teacher, trainer **08** academic, lecturer, mistress **09** pedagogue, professor, schoolman **10** instructor **11** headteacher **12** schoolmaster **13** schoolteacher **14** educationalist, schoolmistress

**educe**
**05** infer **06** elicit **07** develop, draw out, extract

**Edward**
**02** Ed **03** Ted

**eel**

*Eels and similar fish include:*

**03** hag, sea
**04** grig, lant, sand, snig, tuna
**05** elver, lance, moray, murry, siren, snake, wheat
**06** conger, gulper, gunnel, launce, murena, murray, murrey
**07** hagfish, muraena
**08** Anguilla, electric, sandling
**09** sand lance, wheatworm
**10** spitchcock

**• bait for eel**
**03** bob

**eerie**
**05** scary, unked, unket, unkid, weird **06** creepy, spooky **07** ghostly, scaring, strange, uncanny **08** sinister, timorous **09** unearthly, unnatural **10** mysterious **11** frightening **13** bloodcurdling, spine-chilling

**eerily**
**07** weirdly **09** strangely, uncannily **11** unnaturally **12** mysteriously

**efface**
**04** dele **05** erase **06** cancel, delete, excise, remove, rub out **07** blot out, destroy, dislimn, expunct, expunge, wipe out **08** blank out, cross out, wear away **09** eliminate, eradicate, extirpate, strike out **10** obliterate

**effect**
**03** win **04** gear, make **05** carry, cause, drift, force, fruit, goods, issue, power, sense, stuff, tenor **06** action, create, fulfil, impact, import, result, things, thread, upshot **07** achieve, baggage, clobber, execute, luggage, meaning, outcome, perform, produce, purport **08** carry out, chattels, complete, contrive, efficacy, generate, initiate, movables, property, strength **09** aftermath, influence, moveables, repulsion, trappings **10** accomplish, belongings, bring about, conclusion, effectuate, give rise to, impression **11** consequence, possessions **12** significance **13** accoutrements, paraphernalia
**• in effect**
**06** in fact, really **07** en effet, in truth **08** actually **09** in reality, virtually **10** in

practice **11** effectively, essentially **12** in actual fact **13** substantially **14** produce results

• **produce an effect**

**03** act

• **special effects**

**02** FX **03** SFX

• **take effect**

**04** bite, take, talk, vest, work **05** begin **06** kick in **07** come off, succeed **08** function **09** become law **11** become valid, be effective **13** be implemented, come into force **14** produce results **15** become operative, come into service

**effective**

**04** home, neat **05** legal, valid **06** active, actual, cogent, potent, superb, useful **07** capable, current, helpful, in force, operant, telling, virtual **08** adequate, exciting, forceful, fruitful, in effect, powerful, striking **09** efficient, energetic, essential, operative, practical **10** attractive, compelling, convincing, impressive, persuasive, prevailing, productive, successful, sufficient, worthwhile **11** devastating, efficacious, energetical, functioning, implemental, in operation, serviceable

**effectively**

**04** home, well **06** in fact, really **07** in truth **08** actually, in effect **09** in reality, virtually **10** fruitfully, in practice **11** efficiently, essentially **12** in actual fact, productively, successfully

**effectiveness**

**03** use **05** clout, force, power **06** vigour, weight **07** ability, cogency, potence, potency, success **08** efficacy, strength, validity **09** influence **10** capability, efficacity, efficiency, usefulness **12** fruitfulness **14** productiveness **15** efficaciousness

**effectual**

**05** legal, sound, valid **06** lawful, proper, useful **07** binding, capable **08** decisive, forcible, powerful **09** authentic, effective, magistral, operative **10** perficient, productive, successful **11** influential, serviceable **13** authoritative

**effeminate**

**04** soft **05** cissy, minty, pansy, sissy **06** prissy, queeny **07** epicene, meacock, unmanly, wimpish, womanly **08** delicate, feminine, womanish **11** limp-wristed

**effervesce**

**04** boil, fizz, foam **05** froth **06** bubble **07** ferment, sparkle **08** be lively **10** be animated **11** be ebullient, be vivacious **13** be exhilarated

**effervescence**

**03** gas, vim, zip **04** fizz, foam, zing **05** froth **07** bubbles, ferment, foaming, sparkle **08** bubbling, buoyancy, frothing, vitality, vivacity **09** animation, fizziness, gassiness **10** ebullience, enthusiasm, excitement, exuberance, liveliness **11** excitedness, high spirits **12** exhilaration, fermentation

**effervescent**

◇ *anagram indicator*

**05** fizzy, gassy, vital **06** bubbly, frothy, lively **07** aerated, buoyant, excited, fizzing, foaming **08** animated, bubbling **09** ebullient, exuberant, sparkling, vivacious **10** carbonated, fermenting **11** exhilarated **12** enthusiastic **13** irrepressible

**effete**

**04** weak **05** spent **06** barren, feeble, used up, wasted **07** corrupt, debased, decayed, drained, shotten, spoiled, sterile, worn out **08** decadent, decrepit, infecund, tired out **09** enervated, enfeebled, exhausted, fruitless, played out **10** degenerate, unfruitful, unprolific **11** debilitated, ineffectual **12** unproductive

**efficacious**

**06** active, potent, strong, useful **07** capable **08** adequate, powerful **09** competent, effective, effectual, operative, potential, sovereign **10** productive, successful, sufficient

**efficacy**

**03** use **04** feck **05** force, power, value **06** effect, energy, virtue **07** ability, potency, success **08** strength **09** influence **10** capability, competence, usefulness **13** effectiveness **14** successfulness

**efficiency**

**05** order, skill **07** ability **09** expertise **10** capability, competence, competency **11** orderliness, proficiency, skilfulness **12** organization, productivity **13** effectiveness

**efficient**

**04** able **05** smart **06** expert, strong **07** capable, skilful, well-run **08** powerful **09** competent, effective, organized, practical **10** methodical, productive, proficient, systematic **11** streamlined, well-ordered, workmanlike **12** businesslike, rationalized **13** well-conducted, well-organized

**effigy**

**03** guy **04** icon, idol, sign **05** dummy, image **06** figure, statue **07** carving, picture **08** likeness, portrait **09** Jack-straw **14** representation

**efflorescence**

**03** reh

**effluent**

**05** waste **06** efflux, sewage **07** outflow **08** emission **09** discharge, effluence, effluvium, emanation, pollutant, pollution **10** exhalation **11** liquid waste

**effort**

**02** go **03** try **04** bash, beef, deed, feat, opus, push, shot, stab, toil, work **05** crack, essay, force, nisus, pains, power, sweat, whirl **06** energy, labour, result, strain, stress **07** attempt, exploit, muscles, product, travail, trouble **08** creation, exertion, hard work, striving, struggle **09** endeavour **10** attainment, production **11** achievement, application, elbow-grease, muscle power **14** accomplishment **15** sweat of your brow

• **calling for effort**

**02** yo

• **sudden effort**

**03** fit

• **utmost efforts**

**03** all

**effortless**

**04** easy **06** facile, simple, smooth **07** passive **08** painless **10** unexacting **11** undemanding **13** uncomplicated **15** straightforward

**effrontery**

**03** lip **04** face, gall, sass **05** brass, cheek, nerve **07** hutzpah **08** audacity, boldness, brazenry, chutzpah, temerity **09** arrogance, brashness, brass neck, impudence, insolence **10** brazenness, cheekiness, disrespect **11** presumption **12** impertinence **13** shamelessness

**effulgent**

**07** glowing, radiant, shining **08** glorious, splendid **09** brilliant, refulgent **11** resplendent **12** incandescent

**effusion**

**04** gush **06** efflux, stream **07** outflow **08** emission, outburst, shedding, voidance **09** discharge, effluence **10** outpouring

**effusive**

**03** OTT **05** gabby, gassy, gushy **06** lavish **07** fulsome, gushing, lyrical, profuse, voluble **08** all mouth **09** ebullient, expansive, exuberant, rhapsodic, talkative **10** big-mouthed, over the top, unreserved **11** extravagant, overflowing **12** enthusiastic, unrestrained **13** demonstrative

**eg**

**02** as, zB **03** say **06** such as **10** for example, par exemple **11** zum Beispiel **13** exempli gratia

**egalitarian**

**04** fair, just **07** sharing **09** equitable **10** democratic **12** equalitarian

**egg**

**01** O **03** nit **04** blow, bomb, mine, ovum **05** berry, ovule **06** oocyte **08** oosphere

• **egg on**

**03** set, tar **04** abet, coax, edge, goad, prod, push, spur, urge **05** drive, prick **06** excite, exhort, incite, prompt, urge on **08** talk into **09** encourage, stimulate

• **egg-supplier** *see* **bird**

**• lower half of egg**
**04** doup, dowp
**• spot on egg**
**03** eye

**egghead**
**03** don **05** brain **06** boffin, genius **07** know-all, scholar, thinker **08** academic, bookworm, brainbox, Einstein **09** intellect, know-it-all **12** intellectual

**eggs**
**02** OO **03** ova, roe **06** clutch, graine **11** pullet-sperm

**ego**
**01** I **03** sel **04** self, soul **07** egotism **08** identity **09** self-image, self-worth **10** self-esteem **14** self-confidence, self-importance **15** sense of identity

**egocentric**
**07** selfish **09** egotistic **11** egotistical, self-centred, self-seeking, self-serving **12** narcissistic, self-absorbed **14** self-interested

**egoism**
**07** egotism **08** egomania, self-love **10** narcissism, self-regard **11** amour-propre, selfishness, self-seeking **12** self-interest **13** egocentricity **14** self-absorption, self-importance **15** self-centredness

**egoist**
**07** egotist **09** egomaniac **10** narcissist, self-seeker

**egoistic**
**09** egotistic **10** egocentric, egoistical **11** egomaniacal, egotistical, self-centred, self-seeking **12** narcissistic, self-absorbed, self-involved, self-pleasing **13** self-important

**egotism**
**03** ego **05** pride, swank **06** egoism, vanity **08** egomania, self-love, selfness, snobbery **10** narcissism, self-regard **11** braggadocio, self-conceit, selfishness, superiority **12** boastfulness **13** bigheadedness, conceitedness, egocentricity **14** self-admiration, self-importance **15** self-centredness

**egotist**
**06** egoist **07** bighead, bluffer, boaster, show-off **08** big mouth, braggart **09** egomaniac, smart alec, swaggerer **10** clever dick **11** braggadocio, clever clogs, self-admirer

**egotistic**
**04** vain **05** proud **07** selfish **08** boasting, bragging, egoistic, superior **09** bigheaded, conceited **10** egocentric **11** self-centred, swell-headed **12** narcissistic, self-admiring **13** self-important, swollen-headed

**egregious**
**04** fine, rank **05** gross **06** arrant **07** glaring, heinous **08** flagrant, grievous, infamous, precious, shocking **09** appalling, monstrous, notorious, prominent **10** outrageous, scandalous **11** intolerable **12** insufferable **13** distinguished

**egress**
**04** exit, vent **05** issue **06** depart, escape, exodus, outlet, way out **07** leaving **09** departure, emergence **11** escape route

**Egypt**
**02** ET **03** EGY

**Egyptian**
**07** Thebaic

*Ancient Egyptian rulers include:*

**05** Khufu
**06** Ahmose, Cheops
**07** Ptolemy, Rameses
**08** Berenice, Thutmose
**09** Akhenaten, Amenhotep, Cleopatra, Nefertiti, Sesostris, Tuthmosis
**10** Hatshepsut
**11** Tut'ankhamun

*See also* **god, goddess; pharaoh**

**eight**
**04** VIII **05** octad, octet **06** octave, octett, ogdoad **07** octette **08** octonary

**eighteen**
**05** XVIII

**eighty**
**04** LXXX

**einsteinium**
**02** Es

**ejaculate**
**03** cry **04** call, come, emit, yell **05** blurt, eject, expel, shout, spurt, utter **06** cry out, scream **07** call out, exclaim, release **08** blurt out, shout out **09** discharge

**ejaculation**
**03** cry **04** call, yell **05** shout, spurt **06** climax, coming, scream **07** release **08** ejection, emission **09** discharge, expulsion, utterance **11** exclamation **12** interjection

**eject**
**04** emit, fire, oust, sack, spew, spit **05** belch, degas, evict, exile, expel, exude, spout, vomit **06** banish, bounce, deport, get out, propel, remove **07** bail out, boot out, dismiss, exclude, excrete, expulse, kick out, release, turf out, turn out **08** chuck out, disgorge, drive out, evacuate, get rid of, splutter, throw out **09** discharge, ejaculate, thrust out **11** expectorate

**ejection**
**05** exile **06** firing, ouster, outing **07** ousting, removal, sacking, the boot, the sack **08** eviction, vomiting **09** discharge, dismissal, exclusion, expulsion **10** banishment **11** deportation, ejaculation

**eke**
**• eke out**
**03** ech, ich **04** eche, eech **05** add to, get by **06** scrape **07** fill out, help out, husband, scratch, spin out, stretch, survive **08** increase, piece out **10** go easy with, supplement **11** economize on **12** feel the pinch **13** scrimp and save

**elaborate**
◇ *anagram indicator*
**05** exact, fancy, fussy, showy **06** devise, minute, ornate, polish, quaint, refine, rococo, work up **07** amplify, careful, complex, develop, enhance, explain, improve, precise, studied, work out **08** detailed, develope, expand on, flesh out, involved, laboured, thorough **09** decorated, enlarge on, expatiate, extensive, intricate, perfected, storiated **10** ornamental **11** complicated, extravagant, highwrought, historiated, overwrought, painstaking **12** ostentatious

**élan**
**04** brio, dash, zest **05** flair, oomph, style, verve **06** esprit, pizazz, spirit, vigour **07** panache, pizzazz **08** flourish, vivacity **09** animation **10** confidence, liveliness **11** impetuosity, stylishness

**elapse**
**02** go **03** ren, rin, run **04** go by, go on, pass **05** lapse **06** go past, slip by **07** passing **08** overpass, pass away, slip away

**elastic**
◇ *anagram indicator*
**04** easy **05** buxom, fluid **06** bouncy, pliant, supple **07** buoyant, plastic, pliable, rubbery, springy **08** flexible, stretchy, tolerant, yielding **09** adaptable, compliant, resilient **10** adjustable **11** elasticated, stretchable **13** accommodating

**elasticity**
**04** give, play **05** tonus **06** bounce, spring **07** stretch **08** buoyancy **09** tolerance **10** plasticity, pliability, resilience, suppleness **11** flexibility, springiness **12** adaptability, stretchiness **13** adjustability

**elated**
**04** high **05** happy **06** joyful, joyous **07** excited **08** blissful, ecstatic, euphoric, exultant, glorious, jubilant, thrilled **09** delighted, overjoyed, rapturous, rhapsodic **11** exhilarated, on cloud nine, over the moon

**elation**
**03** joy **04** glee, lift, ruff **05** bliss, ruffe **06** thrill **07** delight, ecstasy, rapture **08** euphoria **09** happiness **10** exaltation, exultation, joyfulness, joyousness, jubilation **11** high spirits **12** exhilaration, intoxication

**elbow**
**04** bump, push **05** ancon, barge, crowd, force, knock, nudge, shove **06** jostle, justle **08** shoulder

**elbow-grease**
**04** beef **06** effort, energy **07** muscles **08** exertion, hard work, strength **11** muscle power **15** sweat of your brow

**elbow-room**
**04** play, room **05** scope, space **06** leeway **07** freedom **08** latitude **10** Lebensraum **14** breathing space

**elder**
**03** OAP **04** aîné, sire **05** aînée, older, oldie **06** deacon, father, leader, senior **07** ancient, wise man **08** ancestor, boortree, bountree, bourtree, kaumatua **09** first-born, old person, pensioner, presbyter **11** older person

**elderly**
**03** old **04** aged, OAPs **05** aging, hoary **06** ageing, mature, oldies, past it, senile **07** fossils **08** badgerly, has-beens **09** old people, senescent, wrinklies **10** grey-haired, pensioners **11** golden agers, older adults, over the hill **13** retired people **14** long in the tooth, senior citizens **15** older generation

**eldest**
**05** first **06** oldest **09** first-born **13** first-begotten

**elect**
**03** opt **04** pick, -to-be, vote **05** adopt, co-opt, élite, voice **06** choose, chosen, future, opt for, picked, prefer, return, select, vote in **07** appoint, vote for **08** decide on, nominate, plump for, selected **09** cast a vote, chosen few, designate, determine, preferred **10** hand-picked **11** prospective **12** go to the polls

**elected**
**02** in

**election**
**04** poll, vote **06** ballot, choice, return, voting **07** picking, primary **08** choosing, decision, free will, hustings **09** rectorial, selection **10** preference, referendum **11** appointment **13** determination

**electioneering**
**08** fighting, hustings, lobbying **09** crusading, promotion **10** canvassing, struggling **11** campaigning, championing **13** mainstreeting

**elector**
**05** voter **08** selector **10** electorate **11** constituent

**electorate**

*Australian electorates:*

**04** Bass, Cook, Grey, Holt, Hume, Indi, Lowe, Lyne, Mayo, Page, Reid, Ryan, Swan
**05** Aston, Banks, Blair, Brand, Bruce, Casey, Corio, Cowan, Forde, Groom, Lalor, Lyons, Makin, Moore, Oxley, Perth, Sturt, Wills
**06** Barker, Barton, Batman, Bonner, Bowman, Calare, Cowper, Curtin, Dawson, Deakin, Dobell, Fadden, Farrer, Fisher, Fowler, Fraser, Gorton, Gwydir, Hotham, Hughes, Hunter, Isaacs, Lilley, Mallee, McEwan, Murray, Parkes, Pearce, Petrie, Rankin, Sydney, Wannon, Watson
**07** Bendigo, Berowra, Boothby, Braddon, Calwell, Canning, Chifley, Denison, Dickson, Dunkley, Fairfax, Forrest, Gilmore, Hasluck, Herbert, Higgins, Hinkler, Kennedy, Kooyong, La Trobe, Lindsay, Longman, Maranoa, Menzies, Moreton, O'Conner, Scullin, Solomon, Tangney, Throsby, Werriwa, Wide Bay
**08** Adelaide, Ballarat, Blaxland, Brisbane, Canberra, Charlton, Chisholm, Flinders, Franklin, Greenway, Griffith, Jagajaga, Kingston, Lingiari, McMillan, Mitchell, Paterson, Prospect, Richmond, Riverina, Stirling
**09** Bennelong, Bradfield, Fremantle, Gippsland, Goldstein, Grayndler, Hindmarsh, Macarthur, Mackellar, Macquarie, McPherson, Melbourne, Moncrieff, Newcastle, Robertson, Shortland, Wakefield, Warringah, Wentworth
**10** Cunningham, Eden-Monaro, Gellibrand, Kalgoorlie, Leichhardt, New England, Parramatta
**11** Capricornia, Corangamite, Maribyrnong, North Sydney
**12** Port Adelaide
**14** Kingsford Smith, Melbourne Ports

*New Zealand electorates:*

**04** Ilam, Mana
**05** Epsom, Otago, Otaki, Piako, Taupo
**06** Aoraki, Napier, Nelson, Rakaia, Rodney, Tainui, Tamaki, Wigram
**07** Mangere, New Lynn, Rotorua, Te Atatu
**08** Clevedon, Manurewa, Mt Albert, Rimutaka, Rongotai, Tauranga, Tukituki, Waiariki
**09** East Coast, Hutt South, Mt Roskill, Northcote, Northland, Pakuranga, Wairarapa, Waitakere, Whanganui, Whangarei
**10** Coromandel, North Shore, Rangitikei, Te Tai Tonga
**11** Bay of Plenty, Helensville, Manukau East, New Plymouth, Port Waikato, Waimakariri
**12** Dunedin North, Dunedin South, Hamilton East, Hamilton West, Invercargill, Maungakiekie, Te Tai Hauauru, Te Tai Tokerau
**13** East Coast Bays, Ikaora-Rawhiti, Ohariu-Belmont
**14** Banks Peninsula, Tamaki Makaurau
**15** Auckland Central, Clutha-Southland, Palmerston North, West Coast-Tasman
**16** Christchurch East
**17** Wellington Central
**19** Christchurch Central, Taranaki-King Country

**electric**
**04** live **05** tense **07** charged, dynamic, powered, rousing **08** cordless, exciting, stirring **09** startling, thrilling **11** stimulating **12** electrifying, rechargeable **13** mains-operated **15** battery-operated, electric-powered

• **electric fluid**
**04** vril

**electrical**

*Electrical components and devices include:*

**04** fuse
**05** cable
**06** socket
**07** adaptor, ammeter, battery, conduit, fusebox
**08** armature, neon lamp, test lamp
**09** light bulb
**10** lampholder, multimeter, transducer, two-pin plug
**11** ceiling rose, earthed plug, fuse carrier, transformer
**12** dimmer switch, three-pin plug
**13** extension lead
**14** bayonet fitting, circuit breaker, dry-cell battery, insulating tape, three-core cable, voltage doubler
**15** copper conductor, fluorescent tube

**electrify**
**04** fire, jolt, stir **05** amaze, rouse, shock **06** charge, excite, thrill **07** animate, astound, stagger **08** astonish **09** electrize, galvanize, stimulate **10** invigorate

**elegance**
**04** chic **05** grace, poise, style, taste **06** beauty, luxury, polish **07** dignity **08** grandeur **09** gentility, propriety, smartness **10** concinnity, politeness, refinement **11** discernment, distinction, stylishness **12** gracefulness, tastefulness **13** exquisiteness, sumptuousness **14** sophistication **15** fashionableness

**elegant**
**04** chic, fine, jimp, neat **05** bijou, ritzy, smart **06** dainty, humane, la-di-da, lovely, modish, smooth, snazzy, swanky, urbane **07** genteel, refined, stylish **08** artistic, charming, cultured, debonair, delicate, graceful, gracious, handsome, lah-di-dah, polished, tasteful **09** beautiful, excellent, exquisite **10** concinnous, cultivated, debonnaire **11** fashionable **13** sophisticated

**elegiac**
**03** sad **07** doleful, keening **08** funereal, mournful **09** epicedial, epicedian, lamenting, plaintive, threnetic, threnodic **10** threnodial **11** melancholic, threnetical, valedictory

**elegy**
**05** dirge **06** lament, plaint **07** requiem **08** threnode, threnody **10** burial hymn **11** funeral poem, funeral song

**element**
**03** set **04** hint, part **05** grain, group, haunt, niche, party, piece, touch, trace **06** basics, clique, factor, member, storms, strand **07** climate, faction, feature, habitat, soupçon, weather **08** filament, fragment **09** component, electrode, rudiments, suspicion, territory **10** essentials, individual, ingredient, principles **11** constituent, foundations, individuals, small amount, wind and rain **12** fundamentals **15** first principles

*Elements and their symbols include:*

**01** B (boron), C (carbon), F (fluorine), H (hydrogen), I (iodine), K (potassium), N (nitrogen), O (oxygen), P (phosphorus), S (sulphur), U (uranium), V (vanadium), W (tungsten), Y (yttrium)
**02** Ac (actinium), Ag (silver), Al (aluminium), Am (americium), Ar (argon), As (arsenic), At (astatine), Au (gold), Ba (barium), Be (beryllium), Bh (bohrium), Bi (bismuth), Bk (berkelium), Br (bromine), Ca (calcium), Cd (cadmium), Ce (cerium), Cf (californium), Cl (chlorine), Cm (curium), Co (cobalt), Cr (chromium), Cs (caesium), Cu (copper), Db (dubnium), Ds (darmstadtium), Dy (dysprosium), Er (erbium), Es (einsteinium), Eu (europium), Fe (iron), Fm (fermium), Fr (francium), Ga (gallium), Gd (gadolinium), Ge (germanium), Ha (hahnium), He (helium), Hf (hafnium), Hg (mercury), Ho (holmium), Hs (hassium), In (indium), Ir (iridium), Kr (krypton), La (lanthanum), Li (lithium), Lr (lawrencium), Lu (lutetium), Lw (lawrencium), Md (mendelevium), Mg (magnesium), Mn (manganese), Mo (molybdenum), Mt (meitnerium), Na (sodium), Nb (niobium), Nd (neodymium), Ne (neon), Ni (nickel), No (nobelium), Np (neptunium), Os (osmium), Pa (protactinium), Pb (lead), Pd (palladium), Pm (promethium), Po (polonium), Pr (praseodymium), Pt (platinum), Pu (plutonium), Ra (radium), Rb (rubidium), Re (rhenium), Rf (rutherfordium), Rg (roentgenium), Rh (rhodium), Rn (radon), Ru (ruthenium), Sb (antimony), Sc (scandium), Se (selenium), Sg (seaborgium), Si (silicon), Sm (samarium), Sn (tin), Sr (strontium), Ta (tantalum), Tb (terbium), Tc (technetium), Te (tellurium), Th (thorium), Ti (titanium), Tl (thallium), Tm (thulium), Xe (xenon), Yb (ytterbium), Zn (zinc), Zr (zirconium)
**03** tin (Sn)
**04** gold (Au), iron (Fe), lead (Pb), neon (Ne), zinc (Zn)
**05** argon (Ar), boron (B), radon (Rn), xenon (Xe)
**06** barium (Ba), carbon (C), cerium (Ce), cobalt (Co), copper (Cu), curium (Cm), erbium (Er), helium (He), indium (In), iodine (I), nickel (Ni), osmium (Os), oxygen (O), radium (Ra), silver (Ag), sodium (Na)
**07** arsenic (As), bismuth (Bi), bohrium (Bh), bromine (Br), cadmium (Cd), caesium (Cs), calcium (Ca), dubnium (Db), fermium (Fm), gallium (Ga), hafnium (Hf), hahnium (Ha), hassium (Hs), holmium (Ho), iridium (Ir), krypton (Kr), lithium (Li), mercury (Hg), niobium (Nb), rhenium (Re), rhodium (Rh), silicon (Si), sulphur (S), terbium (Tb), thorium (Th), thulium (Tm), uranium (U), yttrium (Y)
**08** actinium (Ac), antimony (Sb), astatine (At), chlorine (Cl), chromium (Cr), europium (Eu), fluorine (F), francium (Fr), hydrogen (H), lutetium (Lu), nitrogen (N), nobelium (No), platinum (Pt), polonium (Po), rubidium (Rb), samarium (Sm), scandium (Sc), selenium (Se), tantalum (Ta), thallium (Tl), titanium (Ti), tungsten (W), vanadium (V)
**09** aluminium (Al), americium (Am), berkelium (Bk), beryllium (Be), germanium (Ge), lanthanum (La), magnesium (Mg), manganese (Mn), neodymium (Nd), neptunium (Np), palladium (Pd), plutonium (Pu), potassium (K), ruthenium (Ru), strontium (Sr), tellurium (Te), ytterbium (Yb), zirconium (Zr)
**10** dysprosium (Dy), gadolinium (Gd), lawrencium (Lr, Lw), meitnerium (Mt), molybdenum (Mo), phosphorus (P), promethium (Pm), seaborgium (Sg), technetium (Tc)
**11** californium (Cf), einsteinium (Es), mendelevium (Md), roentgenium (Rg)
**12** darmstadtium (Ds), praseodymium (Pr), protactinium (Pa)
**13** rutherfordium (Rf)

**• old element**
**03** air **04** fire **05** earth, water

**elemental**
**05** basic **07** immense, natural, primary, radical **08** forceful, powerful **09** primitive, principal **11** fundamental, rudimentary **12** uncontrolled

**elementary**
**04** easy **05** basic, clear **06** simple **07** primary **09** principal **10** principial **11** fundamental, rudimentary **12** introductory, uncompounded **13** uncomplicated **15** straightforward

**elephant**
**05** Babar, jumbo, rogue **07** mammoth **08** oliphant **09** pachyderm **13** megaherbivore **14** megavertebrate
**• elephant carrier**
**03** roc, rok, ruc **04** rukh

**elephantine**
**04** huge, vast **05** bulky, great, heavy, large **06** clumsy **07** awkward, hulking, immense, massive, weighty **08** enormous **09** lumbering

**elevate**
◇ *reversal down indicator*
**04** lift **05** boost, cheer, exalt, hoist, raise, rouse **06** buoy up, hike up, refine, uplift **07** advance, ennoble, gladden, magnify, promote, upgrade **08** brighten, heighten **09** intensify, sublimate **10** aggrandize, exhilarate **11** give a lift to **12** kick upstairs **14** put on a pedestal **15** move up the ladder

**elevated**
◇ *anagram indicator*
◇ *reversal down indicator*
**04** high **05** grand, great, lofty, moral, noble **06** aerial, lifted, raised, rising **07** exalted, hoisted, stilted, sublime, uplying **08** advanced, lifted up, towering, uplifted **09** dignified, high-flown, high-toned, important **10** high-raised, high-reared **11** exhilarated

**elevation**
**04** back, face, hill, rise, side **05** agger, arsis, front, leg-up, mound, mount, ridge **06** aspect, façade, height, random, uplift **07** dignity, majesty, upright **08** altitude, eminence, foothill, grandeur, monticle, nobility, tallness, upheaval **09** go-getting, loftiness, monticule, promotion, sublimity, upgrading **10** exaltation, monticulus, preferment **11** advancement, sublimation **14** aggrandizement **15** step up the ladder

**elevator**
**04** jack, lift

**eleven**
**02** XI

**elf**
**03** imp **04** peri, puck **05** dwarf, fairy, gnome, pigmy, pixie, pygmy, troll **06** goblin, sprite, urchin **07** banshee, brownie **08** entangle **09** hobgoblin **10** leprechaun
**• elf's child**
**03** auf

**elfin**
**03** fay, fey, fie **05** small **06** dainty, elfish, impish, petite **07** elflike, playful, puckish **08** charming, delicate **09** sprightly **10** frolicsome **11** mischievous

**elicit**
**04** pump, tose, toze **05** cause, educe, evoke, exact, sweep, toaze, wrest **06** derive, extort, obtain **07** draw out, extract, mole out, worm out **08** bring out, outlearn **09** call forth

**eligibility**
**09** allowance, condition **11** entitlement, suitability

**12** desirability **13** acceptability, qualification

**eligible**
**03** fit **06** proper, worthy **07** fitting **08** entitled, suitable **09** desirable, qualified **10** acceptable **11** appropriate

**eliminate**
**03** ice, rid **04** beat, cure, do in, drop, kill, lick, omit, wipe **05** expel, whack **06** cancel, cut out, defeat, delete, hammer, murder, reject, remove, rub out, thrash **07** abolish, bump off, conquer, deep-six, exclude, take out, wipe out **08** get rid of, knock out, preclude, stamp out **09** cancel out, dispose of, disregard, eradicate, liquidate, overwhelm **10** annihilate, do away with, extinguish, put an end to, put a stop to **11** exterminate **12** dispense with

**elimination**
**07** quietus, removal **08** deletion, disposal, omission **09** abolition, exclusion, expulsion, rejection **11** eradication

**élite**
**04** best, pick **05** cream, elect, noble **06** choice, gentry, jet set **08** nobility, selected **09** exclusive **10** first-class, upper-class **11** aristocracy, high society **12** aristocratic, upper classes **13** establishment **14** crème de la crème, pick of the bunch

**elixir**
**04** pith **05** daffy, syrup, tinct **06** potion, remedy **07** arcanum, cure-all, essence, extract, mixture, nostrum, panacea **08** solution, tincture **09** principle **11** concentrate **12** quintessence

**elliptical**
**04** oval **05** ovoid, terse **07** concise, cryptic, dubious, laconic, oblique, obscure, oviform, ovoidal **08** abstruse, succinct **09** ambiguous, condensed, egg-shaped, recondite **12** concentrated, unfathomable **13** comprehensive

**elocution**
**06** speech **07** diction, oratory **08** delivery, phrasing, rhetoric **09** eloquence, utterance **11** enunciation **12** articulation **13** pronunciation **15** voice production

**elongate**
**06** extend **07** draw out, prolong, stretch **08** lengthen, protract **10** make longer, stretch out

**elongated**
**04** long, shot **08** extended **09** prolonged, stretched **10** lengthened, protracted

**elope**
**04** bolt, flee **05** leave **06** decamp, escape, run off **07** abscond, do a bunk, make off, run away, scarper, vamoose **08** slip away **09** disappear, do a runner, skedaddle, steal away **10** hightail it, hit the road **11** hit the trail **14** make a bolt for it **15** make a break for it

**eloquence**
**07** blarney, diction, fluency, oratory **08** facility, rhetoric **09** elocution, facundity, gassiness **10** expression **11** flow of words **12** forcefulness, gift of the gab **14** articulateness, expressiveness, persuasiveness

**eloquent**
**04** glib **05** vivid, vocal **06** fluent, moving **07** voluble **08** forceful, graceful, stirring **09** effective, Mercurial, plausible **10** articulate, Ciceronian, expressive, persuasive, well-spoken **11** Demosthenic **12** honey-tongued **13** silver-tongued, well-expressed

**El Salvador**
**02** ES **03** SLV

**elsewhere**
**06** abroad, absent **07** not here, removed **10** otherwhere **13** somewhere else **14** in another place, to another place

**• and elsewhere**
**04** et al **07** et alibi

**elucidate**
**06** fill in, unfold **07** clarify, clear up, explain, expound **08** simplify, spell out **09** exemplify, explicate, interpret, make clear **10** dilucidate, illuminate, illustrate **11** shed light on, state simply **12** throw light on **13** give an example

**elucidation**
**05** gloss **07** comment **08** footnote **10** annotation, commentary, exposition, marginalia **11** explanation, explication **12** illumination, illustration **13** clarification **14** interpretation

**elude**
◇ *deletion indicator*
**04** bilk, duck, flee, foil, jink, slip **05** avoid, dodge, evade, shirk, stump **06** baffle, delude, escape, puzzle, thwart **08** confound, shake off **09** frustrate **10** circumvent **11** get away from

**elusive**
**05** dodgy **06** shifty, slippy, subtle, tricky **07** evasive **08** baffling, puzzling, slippery **09** deceptive, transient **10** intangible, misleading, transitory **11** hard to catch, indefinable **12** unanalysable **15** difficult to find

**elusiveness**
**06** puzzle **08** subtlety **10** transience **11** evasiveness **13** intangibility **14** indefinability, transitoriness

**emaciated**
**04** bony, lean, thin **05** drawn, gaunt **06** meagre, skinny, wasted **07** haggard, pinched, scrawny **08** anorexic, skeletal **10** attenuated, cadaverous, wanthriven **11** thin as a rake **14** all skin and bone

**emaciation**
**07** atrophy **08** boniness, leanness, thinness **09** gauntness, symptosis **11** haggardness, scrawniness, tabefaction

**emanate**
**04** come, emit, flow, stem **05** arise, exude, issue **06** derive, emerge, exhale, spring, vanish **07** give off, give out, proceed, radiate, send out **09** discharge, originate

**emanation**
**04** aura, flow **06** efflux **08** effluent, effusion, emission **09** discharge, effluence, effluvium, effluxion, radiation **10** exhalation

**emancipate**
**04** free **05** loose, untie **06** unyoke **07** deliver, manumit, release, set free, unchain **08** liberate, set loose, unfetter **09** discharge, unshackle **11** enfranchise **14** forisfamiliate

**emancipation**
**07** freedom, freeing, liberty, release **09** discharge, unbinding **10** liberation, unchaining **11** deliverance, manumission, setting free, unfettering **15** enfranchisement

**emasculate**
**04** geld, spay **06** neuter, soften, weaken **07** cripple **08** castrate, enervate **10** debilitate, impoverish

**emasculation**
**09** abatement, lessening, reduction, weakening **10** moderation **12** debilitation, diminishment **14** impoverishment

**embalm**
**04** balm **05** store **06** balsam, lay out **07** cherish, mummify **08** conserve, enshrine, preserve, treasure **10** consecrate

**embankment**
**03** dam **04** bank, bund **05** levee, mound **06** staith **07** banking, rampart, remblai, seabank, staithe **08** causeway, stopbank **09** earthwork

**embargo**
**03** ban, bar **04** stop, tapu **05** block, check, seize **06** impede **07** barrier, seizure **08** blockage, obstruct, prohibit, restrain, restrict, stoppage **09** hindrance, interdict, proscribe, restraint **10** impediment **11** obstruction, prohibition, restriction **12** interdiction, proscription

**embark**
**04** ship **05** board **06** inship **08** go aboard, take ship **09** board ship

**• embark on**
**05** begin, enter, start **06** engage **07** enter on **08** commence, initiate, set about **09** undertake **10** launch into **11** venture into

**embarkation**
**06** vessel **08** boarding, entrance, mounting **09** embussing, emplaning, getting-on **11** entrainment

**embarrass**
◇ *anagram indicator*
**05** shame, upset **06** show up
**07** chagrin, confuse, fluster, mortify, perplex **08** distress, encumber, incumber **09** discomfit, humiliate
**10** discompose, disconcert **11** make ashamed, make awkward
**14** discountenance

**embarrassed**
◇ *anagram indicator*
**03** red **05** upset **06** guilty, shamed, uneasy **07** abashed, ashamed, awkward, shown up **08** confused, sheepish **09** ill at ease, mortified, perplexed, unnatural **10** distressed, humiliated **11** constrained, discomfited
**12** disconcerted **13** self-conscious, uncomfortable

**embarrassing**
**06** touchy, tricky **07** awkward, painful, shaming **08** shameful **09** sensitive, upsetting **10** indelicate, mortifying
**11** distressing, humiliating
**12** compromising, cringe-making, cringeworthy, discomfiting
**13** disconcerting, uncomfortable

**embarrassment**
**03** fix, jam **04** gene, mess **05** guilt, shame **06** excess, pickle, plight, scrape, unease **07** chagrin, dilemma, surplus **08** distress, embarras
**09** abundance, confusion, profusion
**10** constraint, difficulty, perplexity, uneasiness **11** awkwardness, bashfulness, humiliation, predicament
**12** difficulties, discomfiture, discomposure, sheepishness
**13** mortification, overabundance
**14** superabundance

**embassy**
**07** mission **08** legation, ministry
**09** consulate, embassade, embassage
**10** commission, delegation, deputation

**embed**
**03** bed, fix, lay, set **04** dock, nest, root, sink **05** drive, inlay, plant **06** hammer, insert **07** implant

**embellish**
**03** pan **04** deck, gild, trim, vary
**05** adorn, grace **06** bedeck, enrich
**07** dress up, enhance, festoon, garnish
**08** beautify, decorate, ornament
**09** bespangle, elaborate, embroider
**10** exaggerate

**embellishment**
**07** garnish, gilding **08** ornament, trimming, vignette **09** adornment, agreement **10** decoration, embroidery, enrichment **11** elaboration, enhancement **13** ornamentation
• **musical embellishment**
**04** turn **07** melisma, roulade
**09** fioritura, grace note

**embers**
**05** ashes, coals **06** gleeds **07** cinders, clinker, residue **08** charcoal **09** live coals

**embezzle**
**03** nab, rob **04** nick **05** filch, pinch, steal **06** impair, pilfer, rip off
**07** purloin, swindle **08** peculate, shoulder **09** defalcate **11** appropriate
**14** misappropriate

**embezzlement**
**05** fraud, theft **07** nabbing, nicking, swindle, swizzle **08** filching, stealing
**09** pilfering **11** defalcation
**13** appropriation

**embezzler**
**05** cheat, crook, fraud, thief **06** con man, robber **07** diddler **08** swindler
**09** peculator **10** defalcator

**embittered**
**04** sour **05** angry **06** bitter, piqued, soured **07** rankled **08** enfested
**09** rancorous, resentful **11** disaffected, discouraged, exasperated
**12** disenchanted, disheartened
**13** disillusioned

**emblazon**
**04** laud **05** adorn, extol, paint
**06** blazon, colour, depict, praise
**07** display, glorify, publish, trumpet
**08** decorate, ornament, proclaim
**09** celebrate, embellish, publicize
**10** illuminate

**emblem**
**04** flag, logo, mark, sign, type
**05** badge, crest, image, token, totem
**06** device, figure, symbol
**08** colophon, insignia **09** symbolize
**11** service mark **14** representation
*See also* **emblem of authority** *under* **authority**

*Floral and plant emblems include:*

**04** rose
**06** wattle
**07** thistle, waratah
**08** daffodil, shamrock
**09** maple leaf, maple tree
**10** fleur-de-lis, fleur-de-lys, silver fern
**11** common heath, kangaroo paw
**12** golden wattle
**13** royal bluebell
**14** Cooktown orchid
**15** Sturt's desert pea
**16** Sturt's desert rose, Tasmanian blue gum

**emblematic**
**07** typical **08** symbolic **10** figurative, symbolical **11** allegorical
**12** emblematical, representing
**14** representative

**embodiment**
**04** soul, type **05** model **06** vessel
**07** epitome, example **10** expression
**11** incarnation, realization
**12** quintessence **13** concentration, incorporation, manifestation
**14** representation, representative
**15** exemplification, personification

**embody**
◇ *containment indicator*
**05** shape **06** take in, typify **07** collect, combine, contain, express, include
**08** manifest, organize, stand for
**09** corporify, exemplify, incarnate, integrate, personify, represent, symbolize **10** assimilate, synonymize
**11** encarnalize, impersonate, incorporate **12** substantiate **13** bring together

**embolden**
**04** fire, stir **05** cheer, nerve, rouse
**07** animate, hearten, inflame, inspire
**08** make bold, reassure, vitalize
**09** encourage, make brave, stimulate
**10** invigorate, strengthen **13** give courage to

**embrace**
◇ *containment indicator*
◇ *hidden indicator*
**03** hug **04** bind, clip, coll, fold, hold, lock, neck, pash, snog, span, wrap
**05** admit, adopt, bosom, brace, clasp, cover, grasp, halse, hause, hawse, inarm **06** abrazo, accept, clinch, cuddle, enfold, enlace, fasten, inclip, infold, inlace, smooch, strain, take in, take up **07** colling, contain, espouse, include, involve, necking, receive, squeeze, welcome **08** accolade, canoodle, complect, compress, comprise **09** embrasure, encompass
**10** tangle with **11** incorporate, take on board **13** slap and tickle **14** receive eagerly

**embrocation**
**03** rub **05** cream, salve **06** lotion
**07** epithem **08** liniment, ointment

**embroider**
**03** sew **04** darn, purl, work **05** sprig
**06** colour, enrich, stitch **07** dress up, enhance, garnish, tambour
**08** decorate **09** elaborate, embellish, hemstitch **10** exaggerate **11** cross-stitch

**embroidery**
**04** work **05** braid **06** crewel, sewing
**07** apparel, cutwork, orphrey, sampler, tambour, tatting **08** braiding, fagoting, tapestry **09** faggoting, fancywork, stump work **10** canvas-work, needlework **11** needlecraft, needlepoint **13** embellishment, ornamentation

*Embroidery stitches include:*

**04** back, long, moss, stem, tent
**05** chain, cross, queen, satin
**07** blanket, bullion, chevron, feather, running
**08** couching, fishbone, straight, wheat-ear
**09** gros point, half-cross, honeycomb, lazy daisy
**10** French knot, longstitch
**11** herringbone
**12** long-and-short, Swiss darning

**embroil**
◇ *anagram indicator*
**05** mix up **06** enmesh **07** involve
**08** distract, draw into, entangle
**09** catch up in, implicate **11** incriminate

**embryo**
**04** germ, root, seed **06** basics, foetus **07** nucleus **08** gastrula, plantule **09** beginning, rudiments **11** unborn child

• **embryo transfer**
**02** ET

**embryonic**
**05** early **07** primary **08** emerging, germinal, immature, inchoate, unformed **09** beginning, fledgling, incipient **10** elementary **11** rudimentary, undeveloped

**emend**
◇ *anagram indicator*
**03** fix **04** edit **05** alter, amend **06** polish, redact, refine, repair, revise **07** correct, improve, rectify, rewrite **09** castigate

**emendation**
◇ *anagram indicator*
**07** editing **08** revision **09** amendment, redaction, rewriting **10** alteration, correction, refinement **11** corrigendum, improvement **13** rectification

**emerald**
**07** smaragd

**emerge**
◇ *anagram indicator*
◇ *hidden indicator*
**03** out **04** rise **05** arise, issue **06** appear, cast up, crop up, turn up **07** come out, debouch, develop, emanate, outcrop, proceed, surface, turn out **09** come forth, transpire **10** be revealed **11** become known, come to light, materialize **12** come into view **14** become apparent

**emergence**
**04** dawn, rise **05** issue **06** advent, coming **07** arrival, outcrop **08** disclose, eclosion **09** unfolding **10** appearance, disclosure **11** development, springing-up

**emergency**
**03** fix **04** mess **05** extra, pinch, spare **06** back-up, crisis, crunch, danger, pickle, plight, scrape, strait, urgent **07** dilemma, reserve **08** accident, calamity, disaster, exigence, exigency, fall-back, hot water, quandary **09** extremity, immediate **10** difficulty, substitute **11** alternative, catastrophe, predicament, top-priority **13** extraordinary

**emergent**
**06** coming, rising **07** budding **08** emerging **09** coming out, embryonic, fledgling **10** burgeoning, developing **11** independent

**emetic**
**04** puke **05** puker, vomit **06** emetin, ipecac **07** emetine **08** emetical, vomitary, vomitive, vomitory **11** ipecacuanha, sanguinaria

**emigrate**
**04** move **06** depart **07** migrate **08** relocate, resettle **10** move abroad **13** leave your home

**emigration**
**06** exodus **07** journey, removal **09** departure, migration **10** relocation **12** expatriation, moving abroad

**eminence**
**03** tor **04** berg, fame, hill, knob, note, rank **05** ridge **06** esteem, height, renown **07** dignity, stature **08** altitude, majority, prestige **09** advantage, celebrity, greatness, prelation **10** importance, notability, prominence, promontory, reputation, trochanter **11** distinction, pre-eminence, sovereignty, superiority **14** honourableness **15** illustriousness

**eminent**
**04** high **05** first, grand, great, noted **06** famous **07** notable **08** elevated, esteemed, renowned, superior **09** important, prominent, respected, well-known **10** celebrated, noteworthy, pre-eminent **11** conspicuous, high-ranking, illustrious, outstanding, prestigious, superlative **13** distinguished

**eminently**
**04** high, most, very, well **06** highly **07** greatly, notably **08** signally **09** extremely, obviously **10** remarkably, strikingly **11** exceedingly, prominently **12** surpassingly **13** conspicuously, exceptionally, outstandingly, par excellence

**emissary**
**03** spy **05** agent, envoy, scout **06** deputy, herald **07** courier **08** delegate, diplomat, outgoing **09** go-between, messenger **10** ambassador **12** intermediary **14** representative

**emission**
**04** vent **05** issue **06** escape **07** release **08** effusion, ejection **09** diffusion, discharge, emanation, exudation, giving-off, giving-out, radiation **10** exhalation, outpouring, production **11** ejaculation **12** transmission

**emit**
**03** ren, rin, run, say **04** boak, bock, boke, leak, ooze, pass, shed, spew, vent, void **05** eject, eruct, exude, issue, sound, speak, throw, utter, voice **06** exhale, expire, let out **07** diffuse, emanate, excrete, express, give off, give out, pour out, produce, radiate, release, send out **08** eructate, throw out, vocalize **09** discharge, give forth, send forth, verbalize

**emollient**
**03** oil **04** balm **05** cream, salve **06** lotion **07** calming, lenient, unguent **08** balsamic, lenitive, liniment, ointment, poultice, soap-ball, soothing **09** appeasing, assuaging, assuasive, demulcent, placatory, softening **10** mitigative, mollifying, palliative **11** moisturizer **12** conciliatory, moisturizing, propitiatory

**emolument**
**03** fee, pay **04** gain, hire **05** wages **06** charge, profit, return, reward, salary **07** benefit, payment, profits, stipend **08** earnings **09** advantage, allowance **10** honorarium, recompense **12** compensation, remuneration

**emotion**
**03** ire, joy **04** envy, fear, hate, pang, turn **05** anger, dread, grief, sense, shock, spasm, whirl **06** affect, ardour, motion, sorrow, spirit, thrill, warmth **07** anoesis, despair, ecstasy, feeling, fervour, passion, sadness, upsurge **08** movement, reaction, surprise **09** affection, happiness, reverence, sensation, sentiment, sublimity, transport, vehemence **10** excitement **11** sensibility

• **expression of emotion**
**01** O **02** ha, oh **03** hah, hoo, wow **05** arrah, hoo-oo, wowee

• **sign of emotion**
**04** tear

**emotional**
**04** warm **05** fiery, moved, soppy **06** ardent, fervid, heated, loving, moving, red-hot, roused, tender **07** emotive, feeling, fervent, glowing, gushing, radiant, soulful, tearful, zealous **08** effusive, exciting, hysteric, pathetic, poignant, stirring, swelling, touching, white-hot **09** excitable, schmaltzy, sensitive, thrilling **10** hot-blooded, hysterical, passionate, responsive **11** full-hearted, impassioned, overcharged, sentimental, susceptible, tear-jerking, tempestuous **12** enthusiastic, gut-wrenching, heartwarming, soul-stirring **13** demonstrative, psychological, temperamental

**emotionally**
**06** warmly **07** tensely **08** ardently, lovingly, tenderly **09** awkwardly, fervently, nervously, zealously **10** delicately, poignantly, touchingly **11** sensitively **12** passionately **13** sentimentally, under pressure **14** heartwarmingly **15** controversially, demonstratively, psychologically, temperamentally

**emotionless**
**04** cold, cool **05** blank **06** frigid, remote **07** deadpan, distant, glacial, unmoved **08** clinical, cold-fish, detached, toneless **09** impassive, unfeeling **10** antiseptic, impassible, insensible, phlegmatic, unaffected, unblinking **11** cold-blooded, indifferent, unemotional **13** imperturbable **15** undemonstrative

**emotive**
**06** touchy **07** awkward **08** delicate **09** emotional, sensitive **12** inflammatory **13** controversial

**empathize**
**05** share **07** comfort, feel for, support **10** understand **12** have a rapport, identify with

**emperor**
**03** Emp, Imp **04** czar, Inca, king, tsar **05** kesar, tenno **06** kaiser, keasar, mikado, purple, shogun **08** imperial, padishah **09** imperator, sovereign **12** kaisar-i-Hindi

*Emperors include:*

**03** Leo
**04** John, Nero, Otho, Otto, Paul, Pu Yi
**05** Akbar (the Great), Babur, Basil, Boris, Galba, Henry, Louis, Murad, Nerva, Pedro, Peter, Selim, Titus
**06** Caesar (Julius), Conrad, Joseph, Jovian, Julian, Justin, Mehmet, Philip (the Arab), Rudolf, Trajan
**07** Agustín (de Itúrbide), Akihito, Alamgir, Alexius, Baldwin, Charles, Charles (the Bald), Charles (the Fat), Francis, Gordian, Hadrian, Leopold, Lothair, Marcian, Michael, Severus, William
**08** Augustus, Aurelius, Caligula, Claudius, Commodus, Constans, Domitian, Galerius, Hirohito, Honorius, Jahangir, Licinius, Matthias, Maximian, Napoleon, Nicholas, Süleyman, Tiberius, Valerian
**09** Alexander, Antoninus, Atahualpa, Aurangzeb, Caracalla, Carausius, Ferdinand, Frederick, Gallienus, Heraclius, Justinian, Maxentius, Montezuma, Mutsuhito, Shah Jahan, Sigismund, Vespasian, Vitellius, Yoshihito
**10** Andronicus, Augustulus, Diocletian, Elagabalus, Kublai Khan, Maximilian, Meiji Tenno, Theodosius
**11** Charlemagne, Constantine, Constantius, Jean Jacques, Valentinian
**12** Chandragupta, Heliogabalus, John Comnenus, Samudragupta
**13** Antoninus Pius, Francis Joseph, Haile Selassie
**14** Marcus Aurelius
**15** Alexius Comnenus

*See also* **Roman**

**emphasis**
**04** birr, mark **05** focus, force, power **06** accent, moment, stress, weight **07** urgency **08** priority, strength **09** attention, intensity **10** importance, insistence, prominence **11** pre-eminence **12** accentuation, positiveness, significance, underscoring

**• expression of emphasis**
**04** Jeez **05** Jeeze **07** you know

**emphasize**
**06** accent, play up, stress, weight **07** dwell on, enforce, feature, point up **08** heighten, insist on **09** highlight, intensify, press home, punctuate, spotlight, underline **10** accentuate, foreground, strengthen **11** put stress on **14** bring to the fore **15** call attention to, draw attention to

**emphatic**
**04** firm **05** vivid **06** direct, marked, strong **07** certain, decided, earnest, marcato, telling **08** absolute, decisive, definite, distinct, forceful, forcible, positive, powerful, striking, vehement, vigorous **09** energetic, important, insistent, momentous **10** conclusive, expressive, impressive, pronounced, punctuated **11** categorical, distinctive, significant, unequivocal **12** unmistakable **13** unmistakeable

**emphatically**
**06** firmly **08** in spades, strongly **09** certainly **10** absolutely, definitely, forcefully, vehemently, vigorously **11** insistently **13** categorically, distinctively, unequivocally

**empire**
**03** Emp **04** firm, rule, sway **05** power, realm **06** domain, empery **07** command, company, control, kingdom **08** business, dominion, province **09** authority, supremacy, territory **10** consortium, government **11** corporation, sovereignty **12** commonwealth, conglomerate, jurisdiction, organization **13** multinational

*Empires and kingdoms include:*

**04** Cush, Kush, Moab
**05** Akkad, Alban, Media, Mogul, Roman
**06** Naples
**07** Argolis, Assyria, Bohemia, British, Chinese, Galicia, Ottoman, Persian
**08** Dalriada, Lombardy, Sardinia
**09** Abyssinia, Byzantine, Holy Roman
**10** New Kingdom, Old Kingdom
**11** Northumbria
**13** Middle Kingdom
**15** Austro-Hungarian

*See also* **classification**

**• part of empire**
**04** land

**empirical**
**08** observed **09** practical, pragmatic **11** a posteriori **12** experiential, experimental

**empirically**
**11** practically **13** pragmatically **14** experientially, experimentally

**employ**
**03** ply, use **04** fill, hire **05** apply, exert, spend **06** bestow, draw on, engage, enlist, expend, occupy, retain, sign up, take on, take up **07** appoint, exploit, recruit, service, utilize **08** exercise, put to use **09** make use of **10** apprentice, commission **11** bring to bear **13** bring into play **15** put on the payroll, take advantage of

**employed**
**04** busy, used **05** hired **06** active, in work **07** earning, engaged, working **08** occupied, with a job **11** preoccupied **12** in employment

**employee**
**03** cog, man **04** hand, help **05** gofer, woman **06** casual, worker **08** labourer, munchkin **09** assistant, job-holder, operative, rainmaker **10** wage-earner, waterclerk, working man **12** working woman **13** member of staff, working person

**employer**
**03** guv **04** boss, firm, head, user **05** malik, melik, owner **06** gaffer, master, old man **07** company, manager, padrone, skipper **08** business, director, governor, mistress **09** executive **10** management, proprietor, taskmaster, workmaster **12** entrepreneur, organization, taskmistress, workmistress **13** establishment

**employment**
**03** job, use **04** hire, line, ploy, post, work **05** craft, place, trade **06** employ, hiring, métier **07** calling, pursuit, service **08** business, position, taking-on, vocation **09** signing-up, situation **10** engagement, enlistment, livelihood, occupation, profession **11** application, recruitment **12** exercitation **14** apprenticeship

**emporium**
**04** fair, mart, shop **05** store **06** bazaar, market **08** boutique **11** market-place **13** establishment **15** department store

**empower**
**05** equip **06** enable, permit **07** certify, entitle, license, qualify, set free, warrant **08** accredit, delegate, sanction **09** authorize **10** commission **11** give means to, give power to

**empress**
**03** Emp, Imp **05** queen, ruler **07** czarina, tsarina **08** czaritsa, imperial, kaiserin, tsaritsa **09** imperator, sovereign

*Empresses include:*

**02** Lü, Wu
**03** Zoë
**04** Anna, Cixi
**05** Irene, Livia
**06** Helena (St), Tz'u Hsi, Wu Chao, Wu Zhao
**07** Eugénie, Wu Zhaov
**08** Adelaide (St), Cunegund (St), Faustina, Nur Jahan, Theodora, Victoria
**09** Agrippina (the Younger), Alexandra, Catherine, Catherine (the Great), Elizabeth, Joséphine, Kunigunde (St), Messalina, Old Buddha, Theophano
**11** Marie Louise
**12** Anna Ivanovna, Maria Theresa
**13** Livia Drusilla

**emptiness**
**04** void **05** blank **06** hiatus, hollow, hunger, vacuum **07** inanity, vacancy,

vacuity **08** bareness, futility, voidness **09** unreality **10** barrenness, desolation, flatulence, hollowness, vacantness **11** aimlessness, uselessness **13** senselessness, worthlessness **15** ineffectiveness, meaninglessness, purposelessness

**empty**
◇ *middle deletion indicator*
**03** gut **04** bare, boss, free, idle, lade, pump, teem, toom, vain, void **05** addle, blank, clear, drain, go out, inane, issue, leave, strip, use up, waste **06** barren, devoid, frothy, futile, gousty, hollow, hot-air, hungry, unload, unpack, unreal, vacant, vacate **07** aimless, deadpan, deplete, exhaust, flow out, pour out, trivial, turn out, useless, vacuate, vacuous, viduous **08** clear out, deserted, desolate, evacuate, soulless, unfilled **09** available, discharge, fruitless, insincere, pointless, senseless, worthless **10** unoccupied **11** ineffective, ineffectual, meaningless, purposeless, unfurnished, uninhabited **13** insubstantial **14** expressionless, unsatisfactory **15** with nothing in it

**empty-headed**
**04** daft, vain **05** batty, dippy, ditsy, ditzy, dopey, dotty, inane, silly **06** scatty, stupid **07** foolish, vacuous **09** frivolous **13** rattle-brained, unintelligent **14** feather-brained, scatter-brained

**emulate**
**04** copy, echo **05** emule, match, mimic, rival **06** aemule, follow **07** imitate, vie with **09** ambitious, reproduce **11** compete with, contend with **15** model yourself on

**emulation**
**06** strife **07** contest, copying, echoing, mimicry, paragon, rivalry **08** matching **09** challenge, following, imitation, rivalship **10** contention **11** competition **12** contestation

**enable**
**03** fit, let **04** able, help **05** allow, endue, equip **06** permit **07** empower, entitle, further, license, prepare, qualify, warrant **08** accredit, sanction, validate **09** authorize **10** commission, facilitate, make easier **12** make possible **13** pave the way for **14** clear the way for

**enact**
**04** pass, play, rule **05** order **06** act out, decree, depict, ordain, ratify **07** approve, command, make law, perform, portray **08** appear as, sanction **09** authorize, establish, legislate, represent

**enactment**
**03** act, law **04** bill, play, rule **05** edict, order **06** acting, decree **07** command, measure, passing, playing, purview, staging, statute **08** approval, sanction **09** ordinance, portrayal **10** performing, regulation **11** commandment, institution, legislation, performance **12** ratification **13** authorization **14** representation

**enamoured**
**03** mad **04** fond, keen, wild **05** taken **07** charmed, smitten **08** besotted **09** bewitched, enchanted, entranced **10** captivated, enthralled, fascinated, infatuated, in love with

**en bloc**
**05** as one **07** en masse, in a body **08** as a group, as a whole, ensemble **09** all at once, wholesale **11** all together

**encampment**
**04** base, camp, duar, laer **05** douar, dowar, tents **06** laager **07** bivouac, hutment, manyata **08** barracks, campsite, manyatta, quarters **13** camping-ground

**encapsulate**
◇ *containment indicator*
**03** pot **05** sum up **06** digest, précis, take in, typify **07** abridge, capture, contain, include **08** compress, condense **09** epitomize, exemplify, represent, summarize

**encapsulation**
**06** digest, précis **07** summary **10** expression **14** representation **15** exemplification

**encase**
**04** line, wrap **05** bound, cover, frame **07** confine, enclose, envelop **08** surround

**enchant**
**05** charm, spell **06** allure, appeal, thrill **07** attract, becharm, beguile, bewitch, delight, enamour, enthral, glamour **08** entrance, sirenize **09** captivate, enrapture, fascinate, hypnotize, mesmerize, spellbind

**enchanter**
**05** magus, witch **06** wizard **07** warlock **08** conjurer, magician, sorcerer **09** archimage, mesmerist **10** reim-kennar **11** necromancer, spellbinder

**enchanting**
**06** lovely **07** magical, winsome **08** alluring, charming, pleasant **09** appealing, endearing, ravishing, wonderful **10** attractive, bewitching, delightful, entrancing **11** captivating, fascinating, mesmerizing **12** irresistible

**enchantment**
**05** bliss, charm, magic, spell **06** allure, appeal, glamor **07** delight, ecstasy, glamour, gramary, rapture, sorcery **08** gramarye, malefice, witching, wizardry **09** hypnotism, mesmerism **10** allurement, necromancy, witchcraft **11** conjuration, fascination, incantation **14** attractiveness

**enchantress**
**04** vamp **05** Circe, fairy, lamia, siren, witch **07** charmer **08** conjurer, magician **09** sorceress **10** seductress **11** femme fatale, necromancer, spellbinder

**encircle**
◇ *containment indicator*
**04** belt, clip, gird, hoop, pale, ring, wind **05** crowd, girth, hem in, inorb, orbit, twine, wheel **06** circle, embail, enfold, engird, enlace, enring, girdle, inlace, stemme **07** close in, compass, enclose, envelop, environ, enwheel **08** surround **09** encompass **12** circumscribe

**enclose**
◇ *containment indicator*
**02** in **03** box, pen, pin **04** cage, case, coop, hold, ring, seal, tine, womb, wrap **05** bound, bower, clasp, cover, fence, frame, hedge, hem in, pound, put in **06** circle, cocoon, corral, embale, emboss, encase, enfold, enlock, girdle, immure, incase, infold, inhoop, insert, pocket, prison, shut in, take in **07** close in, compass, confine, contain, embound, embowel, embrace, enchase, envelop, include, seclude **08** conclude, encircle, send with, surround **09** encompass, ring-fence **10** comprehend, interclude **12** circumscribe

**enclosed**
**03** enc **04** encl, pend, pent **07** bosomed, recluse **08** included

**enclosure**
**03** box, enc, haw, pen, pit, ree, ren, rin, run, sty **04** area, bawn, boma, cage, camp, encl, fank, fold, hope, lair, pale, peel, pele, reed, ring, town, yard **05** arena, close, court, garth, kraal, pound, sekos, stell **06** corral, runway **07** enclave, fencing, haining, paddock, parrock, pightle, pinfold **08** addition, cloister, compound, enceinte, seraglio, stockade, townland **09** inclusion, insertion **10** encincture

**encode**
**05** ravel **06** cipher, garble **07** encrypt, obscure **08** disguise, encipher, scramble **11** put into code **14** make mysterious

**encompass**
◇ *containment indicator*
**04** gird, hold, ring, span **05** admit, bathe, brace, cover, hem in **06** begird, circle, embody, enfold, infold, shut in, sphere, take in **07** close in, confine, contain, embrace, enclose, envelop, include, involve, procure **08** cincture, comprise, encircle, surround **10** circumvent, comprehend **11** incorporate **12** circumscribe

**encore**
**03** bis **06** ancora, repeat, replay **10** repetition

**encounter**
**04** cope, face, meet, tilt **05** brush, clash, close, fight, joust, match, run-in,

set-to **06** action, battle, combat, engage, oppose, ruffle, strive, tackle, tussle **07** contact, contend, contest, dispute, meeting, run into **08** bump into, conflict, confront, cope with, deal with, happen on, skirmish, struggle **09** clash with, collision, rencontre, run across **10** chance upon, come across, engagement, experience, rencounter, rendezvous **11** be faced with, be up against, compete with, grapple with **12** do battle with **13** come up against, confrontation, passage of arms, stumble across **15** cross swords with

**encourage**
**03** aid **04** abet, back, coax, fuel, help, lift, root, spur, stir, sway, urge **05** boost, cheer, egg on, gee up, jolly, pep up, rally, rouse **06** assist, buck up, buoy up, exhort, favour, foster, incite, induce, prompt, second, spirit, spur on, stroke **07** advance, animate, cheer on, cherish, comfort, console, forward, further, hearten, inspire, promote, support, sustain, upcheer, win over **08** accorage, advocate, convince, embolden, inspirit, motivate, persuade, reassure, talk into **09** accourage, enhearten, influence, stimulate **10** barrack for, strengthen **14** be supportive to

**encouragement**
**03** aid **04** help **05** boost, cheer **06** come-on, urging **07** backing, coaxing, comfort, pep talk, succour, support **08** cheering, stimulus **09** incentive, promotion **10** assistance, heartening, incitement, motivation, persuasion **11** consolation, endorsement, exhortation, furtherance, inspiration, reassurance, stimulation **12** shot in the arm

**• expression of encouragement**
**02** ha, on **03** hah, olé, via, yay **04** come, sa sa **05** heigh, hollo, there **06** giddap, now now **07** attaboy, come now **08** attagirl, come come **09** ups-a-daisy, upsy-daisy

**encouraging**
**04** rosy **06** bright **07** hopeful **08** cheerful, cheering **09** hortative, hortatory, incentive, inspiring, promising, uplifting **10** auspicious, comforting, heartening, protreptic, reassuring, supportive **11** cohortative, stimulating **12** satisfactory **14** proceleusmatic

**encroach**
**03** jet **05** pinch, usurp **06** invade, trench **07** impinge, intrude, overrun **08** entrench, infringe, intrench, overstep, trespass **10** infiltrate, muscle in on **11** make inroads

**encroachment**
**06** inroad **08** invasion, trespass **09** incursion, intrusion **11** purpresture, trespassing **12** entrenchment, infiltration, infringement, intrenchment, overstepping

**encrypt**
**05** ravel **06** cipher, encode, garble **07** obscure **08** disguise, encipher, scramble **11** put into code **14** make mysterious

**encumber**
**03** jam **04** cram, load, pack **05** block, check, cramp, stuff **06** accloy, burden, hamper, hinder, impede, retard, saddle, strain, stress **07** bog down, burthen, congest, oppress, overlay, prevent **08** handicap, obstruct, overload, restrain, slow down **09** constrain, embarrass, weigh down **13** inconvenience

**encumbrance**
**04** load **05** cross **06** burden, strain, stress, weight **08** handicap, obstacle **09** albatross, cumbrance, hindrance, liability, millstone, restraint **10** constraint, difficulty, impediment, obligation **11** obstruction **13** inconvenience **14** responsibility

**encyclopedia**
**04** ency **05** encyc

**encyclopedic**
**04** vast **05** broad **07** in-depth **08** complete, thorough **09** universal **10** exhaustive **11** compendious, wide-ranging **12** all-embracing, all-inclusive **13** comprehensive, thoroughgoing **15** all-encompassing

**end**
◇ *tail selection indicator*
**01** Z **03** aim, tip **04** abut, area, butt, doom, edge, fine, goal, part, ruin, side, stop, stub, tail, term **05** cease, close, death, dying, field, issue, limit, omega, point, scrap **06** aspect, be over, border, branch, demise, design, die out, ending, expire, finale, finish, intent, margin, motive, object, period, reason, region, result, run out, target, upshot, wind up **07** abolish, destroy, outcome, purpose, remnant, section, vestige **08** boundary, break off, complete, conclude, dissolve, downfall, epilogue, fade away, fragment, round off **09** cessation, checkmate, culminate, extremity, intention, leftovers, objective, remainder, terminate **10** annihilate, completion, conclusion, dénouement, department, extinction, extinguish **11** come to an end, consequence, culmination, destruction, discontinue, dissolution, exterminate, termination **12** bring to an end **13** extermination

**• at an end**
**02** up **03** oer **04** over

**• at the end of**
◇ *juxtaposition indicator*
◇ *tail selection indicator*

**• at the far end**
**03** out

**• east end**
**04** apse

**• ends**
◇ *ends selection indicator*

**• nearly at an end**
**04** late

**• the end**
**06** enough **07** too much **08** the limit, the worst **10** unbearable **11** intolerable, unendurable **12** insufferable, the final blow, the last straw **15** beyond endurance

**endanger**
**04** risk **06** expose, hazard, risque **07** imperil **08** threaten **09** prejudice, put at risk **10** compromise, jeopardize **11** periclitate, put in danger **13** put in jeopardy

**endearing**
**04** cute **05** sweet **07** lovable, winsome **08** adorable, charming, engaging, loveable **09** appealing **10** attractive, delightful, enchanting **11** captivating

**endearment**
**04** love **07** pet-name **08** fondness **09** affection, sweet talk **10** attachment, diminutive, hypocorism **12** sweet nothing **15** term of affection

**• term of endearment**
**03** bud, hon, luv, pet, pug **04** burd, cony, dear, dove, fool, love, peat **05** chick, chuck, coney, ducks, ducky, heart, hinny, honey, jarta, lovey, mopsy, mouse, popsy, puggy, sugar, yarta, yarto **06** flower, monkey, moppet, pigsny **07** alannah, chuckie, cupcake, pigsney, pigsnie, princox **08** honeybun, precious, princock, treasure **09** pillicock, sugarplum **10** honeybunch, honey-chile, sweetie-pie **11** chick-a-biddy **12** chick-a-diddle

**endeavour**
**02** go **03** aim, try **04** bash, seek, shot, stab **05** assay, crack, Morse **06** aspire, effort, labour, strive **07** attempt, venture, working **08** striving, struggle **09** take pains, undertake **10** do your best, enterprise **11** undertaking **13** try your hand at

**ended**
**02** up **04** over, past

**ending**
◇ *tail selection indicator*
**03** end **04** last **05** close, death, dying **06** climax, finale, finish **07** closing, closure **08** epilogue, terminal **09** cessation, desinence, extremity, finishing **10** completing, completion, concluding, conclusion, dénouement, resolution **11** culmination, termination **12** consummation

**endless**
◇ *ends deletion indicator*
◇ *tail deletion indicator*
**05** whole **06** boring, entire **07** eternal, undying **08** constant, fineless, infinite, termless, unbroken, unending **09** boundless, ceaseless, continual, incessant, limitless, perpetual, Sisyphean, unlimited **10** continuous, monotonous, objectless, without end

**11** everlasting, measureless **12** interminable **13** inexhaustible, uninterrupted

**endlessly**
◇ *tail deletion indicator*
**09** eternally **10** constantly, infinitely, unendingly, without end **11** ceaselessly, continually, day after day, day in day out, limitlessly, perpetually **12** continuously, interminably **15** uninterruptedly, without stopping

**endmost**
◇ *tail selection indicator*
**04** last **07** extreme **08** farthest, hindmost

**endorse**
**02** OK **04** back, okay, sign **05** adopt **06** affirm, endoss, favour, ratify, uphold **07** approve, confirm, initial, support, sustain, warrant **08** advocate, be behind, sanction, vouch for **09** authorize, get behind, recommend **11** countersign, subscribe to **15** sign on the back of

**endorsement**
**02** OK **04** okay, visa, visé **07** backing, support, warrant **08** advocacy, approval, sanction, thumbs-up **09** signature **10** green light **11** affirmation, approbation, initialling, testimonial **12** commendation, confirmation, ratification, subscription **13** authorization **14** recommendation, seal of approval

**endow**
**04** fund, gift, give, have, vest, will **05** award, boast, dower, endew, enjoy, found, grant, leave, state **06** bestow, confer, donate, pay for, supply **07** finance, furnish, possess, present, provide, support **08** bequeath, make over **12** be endued with **13** be blessed with

**endowment**
**04** fund, gift, wakf, waqf **05** award, dower, dowry, flair, grant, power **06** genius, income, legacy, talent **07** ability, bequest, faculty, finance, funding, present, quality, revenue **08** aptitude, bestowal, capacity, donation, dotation **09** attribute, character, provision **10** capability, fellowship, settlement **11** benefaction, studentship **13** qualification

**endurable**
**07** lasting **08** bearable, portable **09** tolerable **10** manageable, sufferable **11** supportable, sustainable **13** withstandable

**endurance**
**04** guts, stay **05** spunk **06** bottle **07** lasting, stamina **08** backbone, duration, patience, stoicism, strength, tenacity **09** captivity, fortitude, stability, tolerance **10** durability, resolution, sufferance, toleration **11** continuance, persistence, resignation **12** perseverance, staying power, stickability **13** long-suffering

**endure**
**03** aby **04** abye, bear, bide, dree, dure, face, have, hold, keep, last, live, lump, meet, stay, take, wear **05** abear, abide, allow, brave, brook, stand, stick, thole **06** harden, hold up, permit, remain, suffer **07** abrooke, hold out, perdure, persist, prevail, stick it, stomach, support, survive, sustain, swallow, undergo, weather **08** continue, cope with, outstand, stand for, submit to, tolerate **09** encounter, go through, put up with, withstand **10** experience, sweat it out, tough it out

**enduring**
**04** firm **05** stout **06** stable, steady **07** abiding, chronic, durable, dureful, eternal, lasting **08** immortal, livelong, patience, tolerant **09** permanent, perpetual, remaining, steadfast, surviving **10** continuing, persistent, persisting, prevailing, undergoing, unwavering **11** long-lasting, substantial, unfaltering **12** imperishable, long-standing

**enemy**
**03** foe **04** time **05** Devil, rival **06** foeman **07** anemone, hostile, opposer **08** opponent **09** adversary, other side **10** antagonist, competitor, philistine **13** the opposition **14** the competition

**energetic**
**04** wick **05** brisk, pithy, vital, zappy, zippy **06** active, lively, potent, punchy, strong **07** dynamic, go-ahead, rackety, slammin', zestful **08** animated, bouncing, forceful, forcible, powerful, slamming, spirited, tireless, vigorous **09** effective, go-getting, strenuous **10** boisterous **11** full of beans, high-powered, throughgaun **12** through-going **13** indefatigable

**energize**
**04** stir **05** liven, pep up **06** arouse, excite, fire up, vivify **07** animate, enliven, quicken **08** activate, motivate, vitalize **09** electrify, galvanize, stimulate **10** invigorate

**energy**
**01** E **02** go **03** pep, vim, zip **04** brio, fire, fuel, gism, head, jism, life, push, zeal, zest, zing **05** drive, force, might, power, verve **06** ardour, spirit, vigour **07** pizzazz, potency, sparkle, stamina **08** activity, dynamism, exertion, strength, vitality, vivacity **09** animation, intensity **10** efficiency, enthusiasm, get-up-and-go, liveliness, propellant **11** motive power **12** forcefulness **13** effectiveness, effervescence, kinetic energy **15** potential energy

• **lacking energy**
**04** nesh, poky **05** pokey **09** out of curl

• **lose energy**
**04** flag, wilt

• **primitive energy**
**02** id

• **renewable energy department**
**04** ETSU

**enervated**
**04** limp, weak **05** spent, tired **06** beaten, done in, effete, feeble, pooped, sapped **07** run-down, worn out **08** fatigued, unmanned, unnerved, weakened **09** enfeebled, exhausted, paralysed, pooped out, washed-out **10** undermined **11** debilitated, devitalized, tuckered out **13** incapacitated

**enervating**
**04** hard **05** tough **06** taxing, tiring **07** arduous **08** draining, exacting, relaxing, wearying **09** demanding, difficult, fatiguing, laborious, strenuous, wearisome **10** exhausting

**enfeeble**
**03** sap **04** geld **05** waste **06** reduce, weaken **07** deplete, exhaust, fatigue, unhinge, unnerve, wear out **08** diminish, enervate **09** undermine **10** debilitate, devitalize

**enfold**
◇ *containment indicator*
**03** hug, lap **04** fold, hold, wind, wrap **05** clasp, imply **06** clutch, enwrap, inclip, inwrap, plight, shroud, swathe, wimple, wrap up **07** embrace, enclose, envelop, whimple **08** encircle **09** encompass, implicate

**enforce**
**04** urge **05** apply, drive, exact, force **06** coerce, compel, fulfil, impose, lean on, oblige, strive **07** execute, impress, require **08** carry out, insist on, pressure **09** constrain, discharge, emphasize, implement, prosecute, reinforce **10** administer, pressurize **11** necessitate **14** put the screws on

**enforced**
**06** forced **07** binding, imposed, obliged **08** dictated, ordained, required **09** compelled, mandatory, necessary **10** compulsory, obligatory, prescribed **11** constrained, involuntary, unavoidable

**enforcement**
**08** coaction, coercion, pressure **09** discharge, execution **10** compulsion, constraint, fulfilment, imposition, insistence, obligation **11** application, prosecution, requirement **14** administration, implementation

**enfranchise**
**04** free **07** manumit, release **08** liberate **10** emancipate **13** give the vote to **14** give suffrage to

**enfranchisement**
**07** freedom, freeing, release **08** suffrage **10** liberating, liberation **11** manumission **12** emancipation, voting rights

**engage**
**02** do **03** win **04** book, busy, draw, fill, gain, grip, hire, hold, join, lock, mesh,

take **05** catch, charm, enrol, fight, share, tie up **06** absorb, allure, assail, attach, attack, combat, employ, enlist, enmesh, fasten, occupy, pledge, sign on, sign up, take on, take up
**07** appoint, attract, betroth, capture, engross, involve, recruit, reserve
**08** contract, embark on, entangle, interact, intrigue, practise, take part
**09** captivate, clash with, encounter, enter into, guarantee, interlock, partake of, preoccupy, undertake
**10** battle with, commission **11** fit together, participate, wage war with
**12** interconnect **15** put on the payroll

**• engage in**

◇ *insertion indicator*

**04** play, wage **05** enter **07** enter on
**08** voutsafe **09** enter upon, prosecute, undertake, vouchsafe

## engaged

**04** busy **05** in use, taken **06** active, in mesh, tied up **07** pledged
**08** absorbed, employed, espoused, immersed, involved, occupied, plighted, promised **09** affianced, betrothed, committed, engrossed, intrigued, spoken for **11** preoccupied, unavailable **12** in conference

## engagement

**03** gig, vow, war **04** bond, date, snap
**05** clash, fight, troth **06** action, attack, battle, combat, pledge, plight, strife
**07** assault, booking, contest, fixture, meeting, promise, sharing **08** conflict, contract, espousal, struggle
**09** agreement, assurance, betrothal, encounter, interview, offensive, partaking **10** commitment, employment, obligation, rendezvous, taking part **11** appointment, arrangement, assignation, betrothment, hand-promise, involvement, reservation, undertaking
**13** confrontation, participation

## engaging

**05** sweet **07** likable, lovable, winning, winsome **08** adorable, charming, fetching, likeable, loveable, pleasant, pleasing **09** agreeable, appealing
**10** attractive, delightful, enchanting
**11** captivating, fascinating

## engender

**04** bear **05** beget, breed, cause
**06** arouse, create, effect, excite, incite, induce, kindle, lead to **07** inspire, nurture, produce, provoke
**08** generate, occasion **09** encourage, instigate, procreate, propagate
**10** bring about, give rise to

## engine

**03** way **04** tool **05** agent, cause, means, motor, snare, trick **06** device, dynamo, factor, genius, medium, source **07** ability, channel, machine, vehicle **09** apparatus, appliance, generator, implement, ingenuity, machinery, mechanism **10** instrument, locomotive **11** contraption, contrivance

*Engines include:*

**03** air, gas, ion, jet, oil
**04** aero, beam, heat
**05** motor, steam, water
**06** diesel, donkey, petrol, Petter, radial, rocket, rotary, Wankel
**07** orbital, turbine, V-engine
**08** compound, Stirling, traction, turbojet
**09** aerospike, turboprop
**10** stationary
**11** atmospheric, sleeve-valve
**13** fuel-injection, reciprocating
**15** linear aerospike

*Engine parts include:*

**04** pump, sump
**05** choke
**06** con-rod, gasket, piston, tappet
**07** fan belt, oil pump, oil seal, push-rod
**08** camshaft, flywheel, radiator, rotor arm
**09** air filter, drive belt, oil filter, rocker arm, spark plug
**10** alternator, cooling fan, crankshaft, inlet valve, petrol pump, piston ring, thermostat, timing belt
**11** carburettor, rocker cover
**12** cylinder head, exhaust valve, fuel injector, ignition coil, starter motor, timing pulley, turbocharger
**13** camshaft cover, connecting rod, cylinder block, inlet manifold, power-steering
**15** exhaust manifold

## engineer

◇ *anagram indicator*

**02** BE, CE, ME **03** BAI, eng, rig **04** plan, plot **05** cause **06** create, devise, direct, driver, effect, manage, sapper, scheme **07** arrange, builder, control, deviser, greaser, handler, planner
**08** contrive, designer, inventor, mechanic, operator **09** architect, machinist, manoeuvre, originate
**10** bring about, controller, manipulate, mastermind, originator, technician
**11** orchestrate, stage-manage
**12** engine driver **13** civil engineer, sound engineer

*Engineers include:*

**03** **Fox** (Sir Charles)
**04** **Bell** (Alexander Graham), **Benz** (Karl), **Eads** (James Buchanan), **Ford** (Henry), **Otto** (Nikolaus August), **Page** (Sir Frederick Handley), **Watt** (James)
**05** **Baird** (John Logie), **Baker** (Sir Benjamin), **Braun** (Wernher von), **Dodge** (Grenville), **Gooch** (Sir Daniel), **Grove** (Sir George), **Locke** (Joseph), **Maxim** (Sir Hiram Stevens), **Reber** (Grote), **Rolls** (Charles Stewart), **Royce** (Sir Henry), **Ruska** (Ernst August Friedrich), **Smith** (William), **Tesla** (Nikola)
**06** **Brunel** (Isambard Kingdom), **Brunel** (Sir Marc Isambard), **Carnot** (Sadi), **Cayley** (Sir George), **Claude** (Georges), **Cugnot** (Nicolas Joseph), **Diesel** (Rudolf Christian Karl), **Donkin** (Bryan), **Eckert** (John Presper), **Edison** (Thomas Alva), **Eiffel** (Gustave), **Fokker** (Anthony Herman Gerard), **Fuller** (Buckminster), **Fulton** (Robert), **Jansky** (Karl Guthe), **Jessop** (William), **Lenoir** (Jean Joseph Étienne), **McAdam** (John Loudon), **Napier** (Robert), **Nipkow** (Paul), **Rennie** (John), **Savery** (Thomas), **Séguin** (Marc), **Sperry** (Elmer Ambrose), **Taylor** (Frederick Winslow), **Vauban** (Sebastien le Prestre de), **Wallis** (Sir Barnes Neville), **Wankel** (Felix), **Wright** (Orville), **Wright** (Wilbur)
**07** **Balfour** (George), **Boulton** (Matthew), **Carlson** (Chester Floyd), **Citroën** (André Gustave), **Daimler** (Gottlieb), **Dornier** (Claude), **Eastman** (George), **Fleming** (Sir John Ambrose), **Giffard** (Henri), **Goddard** (Robert Hutchings), **Gresley** (Sir Nigel), **Heinkel** (Ernst), **Houston** (Edwin J), **Junkers** (Hugo), **Keldysh** (Mstislav), **Lesseps** (Ferdinand Marie, Vicomte de), **Nasmyth** (James), **Parsons** (Sir Charles Algernon), **Porsche** (Ferdinand), **Rankine** (William John Macquorn), **Siemens** (Sir William), **Siemens** (Werner von), **Smeaton** (John), **Sopwith** (Sir Thomas Octave Murdoch), **Telford** (Thomas), **Thomson** (Elihu), **Tupolev** (Andrei), **Whittle** (Sir Frank)
**08** **Bertrand** (Henri Gratien, Comte), **Bessemer** (Sir Henry), **Brindley** (James), **De Forest** (Lee), **Ericsson** (John), **Ferranti** (Sebastian Ziani de), **Huntsman** (Benjamin), **Ilyushin** (Sergei), **Kennelly** (Arthur Edwin), **Korolyov** (Sergei), **Leonardo** (da Vinci), **Maudslay** (Henry), **Mitchell** (Reginald Joseph), **Poncelet** (Jean Victor), **Reynolds** (Osborne), **Roebling** (John Augustus), **Sikorsky** (Igor), **Sinclair** (Sir Clive), **Zeppelin** (Ferdinand, Graf von)
**09** **Armstrong** (Edwin Howard), **Clapeyron** (Emile), **Cockerell** (Sir Christopher Sydney), **Fairbairn** (Sir William), **Fessenden** (Reginald Aubrey), **Issigonis** (Sir Alec), **Trésaguet** (Pierre Marie Jerome), **Whitworth** (Sir Joseph)
**10** **Bazalgette** (Sir Joseph William), **Freyssinet** (Marie Eugène Léon), **Hounsfield** (Sir Godfrey Newbold), **Lilienthal** (Otto), **Stephenson** (George), **Stephenson** (Robert), **Trevithick** (Richard)
**11** **De Havilland** (Sir Geoffrey), **Montgolfier** (Joseph Michel)
**12** **Westinghouse** (George)
**13** **Messerschmitt** (Willy)
**15** **Leonardo da Vinci**

## engineers

**02** RE, SE **04** REME **07** sappers

**England**
**03** Eng
*See also* **county**; **town**

**English**
**01** E **03** Eng **04** side
*See also* **alphabet**; **monarch**

**• early English**
**02** EE
**• English as a second language**
**03** ESL
**• English language teaching**
**03** ELT
**• in English**
**03** Ang **07** Anglice

**engorged**
**04** full **05** puffy **07** swollen
**08** enlarged, expanded, inflated, overfull

**engrave**
**03** cut, fix, set **04** etch, mark **05** brand, carve, chase, embed, inter, lodge, print, scalp, sculp, stamp, write
**06** chisel, incise **07** enchase, engrain, impress, imprint, insculp **08** inscribe
**09** character, mezzotint

**engraving**
**03** cut, eng **04** mark **05** block, plate, print, steel **06** niello **07** carving, cutting, etching, imprint, woodcut
**08** cerotype, dry-point, glyptics, intaglio **09** headpiece, mezzotint, sculpture, tailpiece **10** chiselling, heliograph, impression, lithoglyph, photoglyph, xylography **11** inscription, stylography, zincography
**12** glyptography, heliogravure, photo-etching, photogravure
**15** photoxylography

**engross**
**04** grip, hold **05** rivet **06** absorb, arrest, engage, enwrap, inwrap, occupy, take up, wrap in **07** enthral, immerse, involve **08** interest, intrigue
**09** captivate, fascinate, preoccupy
**10** monopolize

**engrossed**
**04** deep, lost, rapt **06** intent
**07** engaged, fixated, gripped, riveted, taken up, wrapped **08** absorbed, caught up, immersed, occupied
**09** intrigued **10** captivated, enthralled, fascinated, mesmerized
**11** preoccupied **13** up to the elbows

**engrossing**
**08** gripping, riveting **09** absorbing, consuming **10** compelling, intriguing
**11** captivating, enthralling, fascinating, interesting, suspenseful
**12** monopolizing **13** unputdownable

**engulf**
◇ *containment indicator*
**04** bury **05** drown, flood, gulph, swamp **06** absorb, deluge, devour, plunge, suck in **07** consume, engross, envelop, immerse, overrun, swallow **08** inundate, overtake, submerge **09** overwhelm, swallow up

**enhance**
**04** lift **05** add to, boost, exalt, raise, swell **06** enrich, stress **07** augment, elevate, improve, magnify, upgrade
**08** heighten, increase **09** embellish, emphasize, intensify, reinforce
**10** strengthen

**enhancement**
**05** boost **06** stress **08** emphasis, increase **09** elevation **10** enrichment
**11** heightening, improvement
**12** augmentation **13** magnification, reinforcement **15** intensification

**enigma**
**04** egma **05** poser **06** puzzle, riddle
**07** dilemma, mystery, paradox, problem **08** quandary **09** conundrum
**11** brain-teaser **12** brain-twister

**enigmatic**
◇ *anagram indicator*
**06** arcane **07** cryptic, obscure, strange
**08** baffling, esoteric, puzzling, riddling
**09** recondite **10** mysterious, mystifying, perplexing, sphinxlike
**11** inscrutable, paradoxical
**12** inexplicable, unfathomable

**enjoin**
**03** ban, bar **04** urge **05** order
**06** advise, charge, decree, demand, direct, forbid, impose, ordain
**07** command, require **08** disallow, encharge, instruct, prohibit
**09** encourage, interdict, prescribe, proscribe

**enjoy**
**03** joy **04** have, like, love **05** fancy, go for, taste, wield **06** relish, savour
**07** possess, revel in, undergo **08** be fond of **09** delight in, partake of, rejoice in **10** appreciate **11** benefit from, go a bundle on **12** have the use of
**13** be blessed with, be endowed with, get a buzz out of, get a kick out of **14** be favoured with, take pleasure in
**• enjoy yourself**
**03** jol **04** ball, rage **05** party, sport
**07** have fun, large it **08** live it up
**09** have a ball, make merry **10** have a blast **11** have it large **12** get your kicks
**13** have a good time **14** get your jollies
**15** let your hair down, paint the town red

**enjoyable**
**03** ace, bad, fab, fun **04** cool, fine, good, mega, neat, nice, wild **05** brill, rorty, super, triff **06** lekker, lovely, wicked, wizard **07** amusing, gustful, kicking, radical, triffic **08** fabulous, glorious, pleasant, pleasing, smashing, terrific **09** agreeable, beautiful, brilliant, delicious, fantastic
**10** delectable, delightful, gratifying, satisfying **11** pleasurable
**12** entertaining

**enjoyment**
**03** fun, joy, use **04** glee, zest **05** gusto
**06** favour, relish **07** benefit, comfort, delight **08** blessing, fruition, gladness, pleasant, pleasure **09** advantage, amusement, diversion, happiness, pleasance, privilege **10** indulgence, possession, recreation, suffisance
**11** delectation **12** satisfaction
**13** entertainment, gratification

**enlarge**
**03** pan **04** ream, zoom **05** add to, piece, swell, widen **06** blow up, dilate, expand, extend, let out **07** amplify, augment, broaden, develop, distend, inflate, magnify, stretch **08** dilate on, elongate, expand on, heighten, increase, jumboize, lengthen, multiply
**09** expatiate, intumesce **10** make bigger, make larger, supplement
**11** elaborate on, expatiate on
**12** become bigger, become larger
**13** go into details

**enlargement**
**05** swell, tumor **06** blow-up, bouton, goiter, goitre, growth, oedema, spavin, tumour **07** release **08** aneurism, aneurysm, dilation, increase, root-knot
**09** exostosis, expansion, extension
**10** ampliation, distension, stretching, varicocele **11** countersink, development **12** augmentation, cardiomegaly, hepatomegaly, intumescence, splenomegaly
**13** amplification, magnification
**14** multiplication

**enlighten**
**05** edify, teach, tutor **06** advise, inform, notify **07** apprise, counsel, educate **08** civilize, instruct
**09** cultivate, make aware **10** illuminate, illustrate **12** open your eyes

**enlightened**
**03** lit **04** wise **05** aware **07** erudite, learned, liberal, refined **08** cultured, educated, informed, literate
**09** civilized **10** conversant, cultivated, illuminate, Illuminati, open-minded, reasonable **11** broad-minded
**12** intellectual **13** knowledgeable, sophisticated

**enlightenment**
**05** light **06** satori, wisdom **07** insight
**08** learning, literacy, sapience, teaching **09** awareness, education, erudition, eye-opener, knowledge
**10** Aufklärung, refinement
**11** cultivation, edification, information, instruction **12** civilization, illumination
**13** comprehension, understanding
**14** open-mindedness, sophistication
**15** broad-mindedness

**enlist**
**03** get, win **04** hire, join, list **05** enrol, enter, prest **06** employ, engage, enroll, gather, induct, join up, muster, obtain, rope in, secure, sign up, take on
**07** procure, recruit **08** register
**09** conscribe, conscript, volunteer
**14** join the colours

**enliven**
◇ *anagram indicator*
**04** fire, jazz **05** cheer, juice, liven, pep up, rouse, spark **06** buoy up, excite,

ginger, jazz up, kindle, perk up, soup up, vivify, wake up **07** animate, cheer up, gladden, hearten, inspire, juice up, liven up, quicken **08** brighten, ginger up **09** stimulate **10** brighten up, exhilarate, invigorate, revitalize **11** give a lift to

**en masse**
**05** as one **06** en bloc, in sort **07** in a body **08** as a group, as a whole, as one man, ensemble, together **09** all at once, wholesale **10** in the quill **11** all together

**enmeshed**
**07** mixed up **08** caught up, involved **09** concerned, entangled **10** associated

**enmity**
**04** feud, hate **05** venom **06** hatred, malice, needle, rancor, strife **07** discord, ill-will, rancour **08** acrimony, aversion, bad blood, ill blood **09** animosity, antipathy, hostility **10** antagonism, bitterness, ill feeling **11** malevolence **14** unfriendliness

**ennoble**
**05** exalt, raise **06** gentle, honour, uplift **07** dignify, elevate, enhance, glorify, magnify **10** aggrandize, nobilitate **11** distinguish

**ennui**
**04** bore **05** weary **06** acedia, tedium **07** accidie, boredom, languor, malaise **09** lassitude, tiredness **11** the doldrums **12** listlessness **15** dissatisfaction

**enormity**
**04** evil **05** crime **06** horror **07** outrage **08** atrocity, evilness, iniquity, vastness, vileness **09** depravity, violation **10** wickedness **11** abnormality, abomination, immenseness, monstrosity, viciousness **13** atrociousness **14** outrageousness

**enormous**
**04** huge, mega, vast **05** dirty, giant, gross, jumbo **07** immense, mammoth, massive, monster, Titanic, whaling **08** colossal, gigantic, great big, plonking, whacking, whopping **09** abounding, atrocious, ginormous, humongous, humungous, monstrous, walloping **10** astronomic, gargantuan, hellacious, large-scale, monstruous, outrageous, prodigious, stupendous, tremendous **11** God-almighty **12** considerable, hulking great

**enormously**
**04** dead, very, well **05** jolly **06** hugely **08** devilish, terribly **09** extremely, immensely, massively **10** especially **11** exceedingly, God-almighty **12** tremendously **13** exceptionally, to a huge extent, to a vast extent **15** extraordinarily

**enormousness**
**07** expanse **08** hugeness, vastness **09** greatness, immensity, largeness, magnitude **11** immenseness, massiveness **13** extensiveness

**enough**
**04** anow, enow, nuff **05** ample, amply, basta, belay **06** fairly, plenty **08** abundant, adequacy, adequate, passably **09** abundance, amplitude, tolerably **10** adequately, moderately, reasonably, satisfying, sufficient **11** ample supply, sufficience, sufficiency **12** sufficiently **14** satisfactorily

**en passant**
**02** ep **08** by the way **09** cursorily, in passing **12** incidentally **15** parenthetically

**enquire, enquirer, enquiring, enquiringly, enquiry** *see* **inquire, enquire**; **inquirer, enquirer**; **inquiring, enquiring**; **inquiringly, enquiringly**; **inquiry, enquiry**

**enrage**
**03** bug, irk, vex **04** rile **05** anger, annoy **06** incite, madden, needle, wind up **07** agitate, hack off, incense, inflame, provoke **08** irritate **09** enranckle, infuriate, make angry **10** exasperate, push too far

**enraged**
**03** mad **04** wild **05** angry, irate, livid **06** fuming, raging **07** angered, annoyed, furious, horn-mad **08** incensed, inflamed, seething, storming **09** infuriate, irritated, pissed off **10** aggravated, infuriated **11** exasperated

**enrapture**
**05** charm **06** ravish, thrill **07** beguile, bewitch, delight, enchant, enthral **08** enravish, entrance **09** captivate, fascinate, spellbind, translate, transport **10** emparadise, imparadise **13** please greatly

**enrich**
**04** gild, lard **05** add to, adorn, endow, grace **06** fatten, manure, refine **07** augment, develop, enhance, fortify, garnish, improve **08** beautify, decorate, ornament, treasure **09** cultivate, embellish, fertilize **10** aggrandize, ameliorate, supplement

**enrol**
**03** tax **04** list, note **05** admit, enter **06** attest, engage, enlist, enwrap, join up, muster, record, sign on, sign up **07** go in for, put down, recruit **08** inscribe, muster in, register **10** enregister **15** put your name down

**enrolment**
**04** list **09** admission, enlisting, joining up, signing on, signing up **10** acceptance, enlistment **11** recruitment **12** conscription, registration

**en route**
**05** march **08** on the way **09** in transit, on the move, on the road **12** on the journey

**ensconce**
**03** put **05** lodge, niche, place **06** locate, nestle, screen, settle, shield **07** install, protect, shelter **08** entrench **09** establish

**ensemble**
**03** set, sum **04** band, cast, suit, unit **05** get-up, group, total, whole **06** chorus, circle, entity, outfit, rig-out, troupe **07** company, costume **08** entirety **09** aggregate, orchestra **10** collection, whole shoot **11** co-ordinates **12** accumulation **13** corps de ballet, whole caboodle **14** whole bang shoot

**enshrine**
**05** exalt, guard **06** embalm, hallow, revere, shield **07** cherish, enchase, idolize, lay down, protect, set down **08** dedicate, preserve, sanctify, treasure **10** consecrate **11** apotheosize, immortalize

**enshroud**
**04** hide, pall, veil, wrap **05** cloak, cloud, cover **06** enfold, enwrap, shroud **07** conceal, enclose, envelop, obscure

**ensign**
**03** Ens **04** flag, jack, mark, sign, waft **05** badge, color, crest **06** banner, colors, colour, pennon, shield **07** ancient, colours, pennant **08** gonfalon, pavilion, standard **10** coat of arms

**enslave**
**04** bind, trap, yoke **05** thirl **06** thrall **07** enchain, subject **08** bethrall, dominate **09** subjugate **14** disenfranchise

**enslavement**
**07** bondage, dulosis, serfdom, slavery **08** thraldom **09** captivity, servitude, vassalage **10** oppression, repression, subjection **11** enthralment, subjugation

**ensnare**
◇ *containment indicator*
**03** net **04** hook, lime, trap **05** benet, catch, snare, snarl **06** enmesh, entoil, entrap, trepan **07** capture, embroil **08** entangle **09** mousetrap **10** illaqueate

**ensue**
**04** flow, stem **05** arise, issue, occur **06** befall, derive, follow, happen, result **07** develop, proceed, succeed, turn out **08** come next **09** transpire

**ensure**
**05** guard **06** effect, secure **07** betroth, certify, protect, warrant **08** make safe, make sure **09** guarantee, safeguard **11** make certain

**entail**
**03** cut **04** need **05** carve, cause, infer **06** demand, lead to, tailye **07** call for, fashion, involve, produce, require, taillie, tailzie **08** occasion, result in **10** bring about, give rise to **11** necessitate

**entangle**
◇ *anagram indicator*
**03** elf **04** ball, knot, wrap **05** catch, mix up, ravel, snare, twist **06** emmesh, engage, enlace, enmesh, enroot, entoil, entrap, fankle, immesh, inlace, inmesh, jumble, muddle, puzzle, taigle, tangle **07** confuse, embroil, ensnare, ensnarl, involve, perplex, trammel **08** quagmire **09** implicate, interlace **10** complicate, intertwine

**entanglement**
◇ *anagram indicator*
**03** tie **04** knot, mesh, mess, trap **05** mix-up, snare, tie-up **06** affair, jumble, muddle, tangle **07** entrail, liaison, snarl-up **09** confusion **10** difficulty, entrapment, perplexity **11** ensnarement, involvement, predicament **12** complication, relationship **13** embarrassment

**entente**
**04** deal, pact **06** treaty **07** compact **09** agreement **10** friendship **11** arrangement **13** understanding **15** entente cordiale

**enter**
◇ *insertion indicator*
**03** log, ren, rin, run **04** come, go in, join, list, note **05** begin, board, enrol, get in, input, lodge, pop in, start **06** arrive, come in, enlist, go in to, insert, occupy, pierce, record, sign up, submit, take up **07** break in, burst in, get in to, go in for, put down, set down, sneak in **08** come in to, commence, embark on, engage in, inscribe, register, set about, take down, take part **09** introduce, penetrate, undertake, write down **10** embark upon, infiltrate, launch into **11** participate, put on record **12** gain access to **13** get involved in, worm your way in **15** become a member of

**enterprise**
**03** SME **04** firm, plan, push, show, task **05** drive, oomph **06** design, effort, energy, scheme, spirit, voyage **07** company, concern, courage, emprise, project, venture **08** ambition, boldness, business, campaign, gumption, industry, vitality **09** adventure, endeavour, operation, programme, undertake **10** assignment, designment, enthusiasm, expedience, get-up-and-go, initiative **11** imagination, undertaking **13** establishment, strong feeling **15** adventurousness, resourcefulness

**enterprising**
**04** bold, goey, keen **05** eager, pushy **06** active, daring **07** go-ahead, pushful, pushing, zealous **08** aspiring, spirited, vigorous **09** ambitious, energetic, ingenious **11** adventurous, imaginative, resourceful, self-reliant, undertaking, venturesome **12** enthusiastic **13** self-motivated **14** self-motivating **15** entrepreneurial

**entertain**
◇ *containment indicator*
**04** fête, have, host, meet, wine **05** amuse, charm, cheer, put up, treat **06** divert, engage, foster, harbor, junket, occupy, please, regale **07** accourt, ask over, cherish, delight, engross, harbour, imagine, nurture, receive **08** ask round, conceive, consider, distract, interest, maintain **09** captivate, flirt with, have round **10** experience, have guests, invite over, play host to, think about **11** accommodate, contemplate, countenance, invite round

**entertainer**
**04** host **06** diseur **07** diseuse, hostess **09** top banana **10** Amphitryon

*See also* **actor, actress**; **comedian**; **musician**; **singer**

*Entertainers include:*

**02** DJ
**04** bard, fool, Joey
**05** actor, clown, comic, mimic
**06** artist, august, busker, cowboy, dancer, jester, mummer, player, singer
**07** acrobat, actress, artiste, auguste, juggler, Pierrot
**08** comedian, conjuror, go-go girl, gracioso, jongleur, magician, minstrel, musician, showgirl, stripper
**09** bunny girl, chanteuse, ecdysiast, fire-eater, harlequin, hypnotist, ice-skater, lap dancer, lion tamer, performer, pierrette, presenter, puppeteer, strong man
**10** comedienne, disc jockey, go-go dancer, knockabout, mime artist, mind-reader, pole dancer, ring master, rope-walker, unicyclist, wire-dancer
**12** chat-show host, escapologist, exotic dancer, game-show host, impersonator, snake charmer, stand-up comic, street singer, trick cyclist, vaudevillean, vaudevillian
**13** contortionist, impressionist, thimblerigger, trapeze artist, ventriloquist
**14** pavement artist, sword-swallower
**15** jerry-come-tumble, song-and-dance act, tightrope walker

**entertaining**
◇ *containment indicator*
**03** fun **05** funny, jolly, witty **07** amusing, amusive, comical **08** humorous, pleasant, pleasing **09** diverting, enjoyable **10** delightful **11** interesting, pleasurable **12** recreational

**entertainment**
**03** fun **04** boff, olio, show **05** cheer, drama, hobby, sport, table **07** leisure, pastime, variety **08** activity, pleasure, semblant **09** amusement, diversion, enjoyment, honky-tonk, spectacle **10** confection, recreation **11** distraction, merrymaking, performance **12** extravaganza, presentation **14** divertissement

*Entertainments include:*

**03** BBQ, DVD, gig
**04** fête, film, play, show
**05** dance, disco, opera, radio, revue, rodeo, video
**06** circus
**07** airshow, cabaret, concert, karaoke, musical, pageant, recital, showbiz
**08** barbecue, carnival, festival, gymkhana, waxworks
**09** burlesque, fireworks, floor show, magic show, music hall, nightclub, pantomime, video game
**10** puppet show, television, vaudeville
**11** discothèque, variety show
**12** computer game, Punch-and-Judy, show business
**13** firework party
**14** laser-light show
**15** greyhound racing

*See also* **television**; **theatrical**

*Entertainment places include:*

**03** pub, zoo
**04** club, dogs, fair, hall
**05** arena, disco
**06** big top, casino, cinema, circus, museum, nitery
**07** cabaret, funfair, gallery, hot spot, ice rink, marquee, niterie, stadium, theatre
**08** ballroom, carnival, dog track, flesh pot
**09** bandstand, bingo hall, dance hall, music hall, nightclub, strip club
**10** auditorium, fairground, opera house, restaurant, social club
**11** boîte de nuit, concert hall, discothèque, public house, skating rink
**12** amphitheatre, bowling alley, cattle market
**13** leisure centre
**15** amusement arcade

• **entertainment industry**
**12** show business

• **undemanding entertainment**
**03** pap

**enthral**
◇ *containment indicator*
**04** grip **05** charm, rivet **06** absorb, thrill **07** beguile, bewitch, delight, enchant, engross **08** entrance, intrigue **09** captivate, enrapture, fascinate, hypnotize, mesmerize, spellbind

**enthralling**
◇ *containment indicator*
**08** charming, gripping, mesmeric, riveting **09** beguiling, thrilling **10** compelling, compulsive, enchanting, entrancing, intriguing **11** captivating, fascinating, hypnotizing, mesmerizing **12** spellbinding

**enthuse**
**04** fire, gush, rave **05** drool **06** excite, fire up, praise **07** inspire **08** motivate

**10** bubble over, effervesce, wax lyrical **14** go into raptures

**enthusiasm**
**04** brio, buzz, fire, hype, rage, zeal, zest **05** ardor, craze, estro, furor, hobby, mania, oomph, thing, verve **06** ardour, frenzy, furore, relish, spirit, warmth **07** ecstasy, fervour, passion, pastime **08** appetite, delirium, devotion, interest, keenness **09** eagerness, vehemence **10** commitment, ebullience, ebulliency, excitement, fanaticism **11** acclamation, earnestness, schwärmerei **12** entraînement **13** preoccupation
**• expression of enthusiasm**
**03** boy, gee **04** Jeez **05** Jeeze, oh boy!, whack **06** whacko **10** hubba hubba
**• lose enthusiasm**
**04** cool **08** languish

**enthusiast**
**03** bug, fan, nut **04** buff, zeal **05** fiend, freak, lover **06** maniac, zealot **07** admirer, amateur, devotee, fanatic **08** follower **09** supporter **10** aficionado **11** eager beaver
*See also* **collector**

**enthusiastic**
**03** mad **04** avid, daft, into, keen, nuts, rave, warm, wild **05** crazy, eager, potty **06** ardent, gung-ho, hearty, mad for **07** devoted, earnest, excited, fervent, intense, up for it, zealous **08** empressé, gaga over, mad about, spirited, vehement, vigorous **09** committed, ebullient, exuberant, fanatical, gaga about **10** passionate **11** rhapsodical **12** rootin'-tootin', wholehearted **13** keen as mustard, self-motivated

**entice**
**04** coax, draw, lure, tice, tole **05** tempt **06** allure, cajole, induce, lead on, seduce **07** attempt, attract, beguile, wheedle **08** inveigle, persuade **09** sweet-talk, tantalize

**enticement**
**04** bait, lure, tice **05** decoy **06** allure, carrot, come-on **07** coaxing **08** cajolery **09** seduction, sweet-talk **10** allurement, attraction, inducement, invitation, persuasion, temptation **11** beguilement **12** inveiglement **13** blandishments

**enticing**
**08** alluring, charming, inviting, tempting **09** appealing, seductive **10** attractive **11** captivating **12** irresistible

**entire**
**04** full, meer **05** round, sound, total, utter, whole **06** intact, within **07** genuine, plenary, untired **08** absolute, complete, integral, livelong, outright, stallion, thorough **09** sincerely, unmingled **10** unimpaired **11** unmitigated, unqualified **12** completeness

**entirely**
**03** all **04** inly, only, tout **05** clean, fully, quite **06** in toto, merely, purely, quight, solely, wholly **07** all over, totally, utterly **08** every bit, properly **09** every inch, every whit, perfectly, tout à fait **10** absolutely, altogether, completely, in every way, thoroughly **11** exclusively **12** unreservedly **14** in every respect

**entirety**
**03** all, sum **05** total, whole **08** fullness, totality **09** wholeness **12** completeness

**entitle**
**03** dub **04** call, name, term **05** allow, label, style, title **06** enable, know as, permit **07** empower, ennoble, license, qualify, warrant **08** accredit, christen, sanction **09** authorize, designate **12** give the title, make eligible
**• to be entitled to**
**04** bear **07** deserve

**entitlement**
**03** due **05** claim, right, title **07** warrant **09** authority, privilege **11** opportunity, prerogative

**entity**
**03** ens, Tao **04** body **05** being, thing **06** object, tensor **08** creature, organism **09** existence, substance **10** individual

**entomb**
**04** bury, tomb **05** inter, inurn, plant **06** inhume, shroud, wall up **07** inearth **09** lay to rest, sepulcher, sepulchre, sepulture **15** put six feet under

**entombment**
**06** burial **09** interment, sepulture **10** inhumation **12** laying to rest

**entourage**
**04** gang **05** court, posse, staff, suite, train **06** escort **07** company, cortège, coterie, retinue **09** followers, following, hangers-on, retainers **10** associates, attendants, companions

**entrails**
**04** guts **05** offal, tripe **06** bowels, haslet, inside, quarry, umbles **07** giblets, harslet, humbles, innards, insides, inwards, numbles, pudding, viscera **08** chawdron, gralloch, puddings **10** intestines **11** vital organs **14** internal organs

**entrance**
**03** eye **04** adit, door, gate, hall, ingo, pend, pipe **05** charm, debut, drive, entry, foyer, gorge, inlet, lobby, mouth, porch, start, way in **06** access, atrium, avenue, dromos, entrée, income, infare, ingate, portal, ravish **07** arrival, Avernus, beguile, bewitch, delight, doorway, enchant, enthral, gateway, hallway, ingoing, ingress, jawhole, opening **08** anteroom, approach, driveway **09** admission, captivate, closehead, enrapture, fascinate, hypnotize, introitus, mesmerize, spellbind, threshold, transport, vestibule **10** admittance, appearance, initiation, passageway **12** introduction, porte-cochère, right of entry
**• narrow entrance**
**04** jaws **06** throat

**entranced**
**04** rapt **10** spellbound

**entrancing**
**06** lovely **07** winsome **08** alluring, charming, pleasant **09** appealing, endearing, ravishing, wonderful **10** attractive, bewitching, delightful, enchanting **11** captivating, fascinating, mesmerizing **12** irresistible

**entrant**
**05** entry, pupil, rival **06** novice, player **07** convert, fresher, learner, starter, student, trainee **08** beginner, freshman, initiate, newcomer, opponent **09** applicant, candidate, contender **10** apprentice, competitor, contestant, new arrival **11** participant, probationer

**entrap**
**03** net **04** lure, trap **05** catch, decoy, snare, tempt, trick **06** allure, ambush, delude, enmesh, entice, seduce **07** beguile, capture, deceive, embroil, ensnare **08** entangle, inveigle **09** crossbite, implicate, underfong

**entreat**
**03** ask, beg, sew, sue **04** pray, prig **05** crave **06** induce, invoke, objure **07** beseech, beseeke, implore, request, solicit **08** appeal to, petition **09** flagitate, importune, plead with **10** supplicate

**entreaty**
**03** cry **04** plea, suit **06** appeal, prayer **07** beseech, request **08** petition, pleading **09** exoration **10** cri de coeur, invocation **11** conjuration **12** solicitation, supplication

**entrée**
**05** entry **06** access **07** ingress, prelude, starter **08** main dish **09** admission, appetizer **10** admittance, main course **11** first course **12** introduction, right of entry

**entrench**
**03** fix, set **04** root, seat **05** dig in, embed, lodge, plant, wound **06** anchor, sconce, settle **07** ingrain, install **08** ensconce, stop a gap **09** establish **14** take up position

**entrenched**
**03** set **04** firm **05** fixed **06** inbred, rooted **07** diehard **09** implanted, indelible, ingrained **10** deep-rooted, deep-seated, inflexible, unshakable **11** established, unshakeable **12** ineradicable, intransigent **13** dyed-in-the-wool, stick-in-the-mud **15** well-established

**entrepreneur**
**05** agent **06** broker, dealer, tycoon **07** magnate, manager **08** promoter **09** financier, middleman **10** contractor, impresario, moneymaker, speculator, undertaker

**11** businessman, enterpriser
**13** businesswoman, industrialist

**entrepreneurial**
**05** trade **08** business, economic, monetary **09** budgetary, financial
**10** commercial, industrial, managerial
**11** contractual **12** professional

**entrust**
**04** aret **05** arett, endow, trust
**06** assign, charge, commit, depute, invest, resign **07** commend, confide, consign, deliver, deposit **08** delegate, encharge, hand over, turn over
**09** authorize **11** put in charge

**entry**
**04** door, gate, hall, item, note **05** annal, foyer, lobby, porch, rival, way in
**06** access, entrée, minute, player, record **07** account, arrival, doorway, entrant, gateway, ingress, listing, opening, passage **08** anteroom, approach, entrance, opponent, register, registry **09** admission, applicant, candidate, contender, statement, threshold, vestibule
**10** admittance, appearance, competitor, contestant, memorandum
**11** description, participant
**12** introduction, right of entry

**entwine**
◇ *anagram indicator*
**04** coil, knit, knot, mesh, warp, wind
**05** braid, plait, ravel, twine, twist, weave **06** enlace, inlace **07** embroil, entrail, intwine, wreathe **08** entangle
**09** implicate, interlace, interlink
**10** intertwine, intervolve, interweave

**enumerate**
**04** cite, list, name, tell **05** count, quote, score **06** detail, number, recite, reckon, relate **07** compute, itemize, mention, recount, specify
**08** rehearse, spell out **09** calculate, catalogue **13** particularize

**enunciate**
**03** say **05** sound, speak, state, utter, voice **06** affirm **07** declare, enounce, express, propose **08** announce, proclaim, propound, vocalize
**09** pronounce **10** articulate, promulgate, put forward

**enunciation**
**05** sound **06** speech **07** diction
**08** sounding **09** statement, utterance
**10** expression **11** affirmation, declaration, proposition
**12** announcement, articulation, proclamation, promulgation, vocalization **13** pronunciation

**envelop**
◇ *containment indicator*
**04** hide, pack, veil, wrap **05** cloak, cover **06** encase, enfold, engulf, enwrap, muffle, shroud, swathe, wrap up **07** blanket, conceal, enclose, obscure, smother **08** encircle, enshroud, surround **09** encompass, enwreathe, inwreathe

**envelope**
**03** sae **04** case, skin, wrap **05** cover, frank, shell **06** casing, entire, gasbag, holder, jacket, sachet, sheath, sleeve
**07** coating, utricle, wrapper
**08** covering, Jiffy bag®, wrapping
**09** involucre

**enviable**
**04** fine **05** lucky **07** blessed
**08** favoured **09** desirable, excellent, fortunate, invidious **10** attractive, privileged **11** sought-after
**12** advantageous

**envious**
**05** green **07** jealous **08** covetous, grudging, spiteful **09** green-eyed, jaundiced, resentful **10** begrudging
**12** dissatisfied **13** green with envy

**enviously**
**08** with envy **09** jealously
**10** covetously, desirously, grudgingly
**11** resentfully **12** begrudgingly

**environment**
**04** Gaia, mood **05** earth, scene, world
**06** domain, locale, medium, milieu, nature **07** climate, context, element, habitat, setting **08** ambiance, ambience, creation **09** situation, territory **10** atmosphere, background, conditions, influences **11** mother earth
**12** mother nature, natural world, surroundings **13** circumstances **15** the lie of the land

*Environmental problems include:*

**06** litter
**07** drought
**08** acid rain, landfill, oil slick, oil spill
**09** pollution
**10** extinction, fossil fuel, toxic waste
**11** soil erosion
**12** air pollution, nuclear waste
**13** climate change, deforestation, global dimming, global warming, water shortage
**14** light pollution, ozone depletion, water pollution
**15** desertification, greenhouse gases

**environmentalist**
**05** green **06** econut **07** greenie
**08** ecofreak **09** ecologist **10** tree-hugger **15** conservationist, preservationist
• **environmentalists**
**03** FOE **10** Green Party

**environs**
**07** suburbs **08** district, locality, purlieus, vicinage, vicinity
**09** outskirts, precincts
**12** surroundings **13** neighbourhood
**15** circumjacencies, surrounding area

**envisage**
**03** see **05** image **07** foresee, imagine, picture, predict, think of **08** envision
**09** see coming, visualize **10** anticipate, conceive of **11** contemplate, preconceive

**envision**
**03** see **07** imagine, picture, think of
**08** envisage **09** see coming, visualize
**11** contemplate

**envoy**
**05** agent **06** consul, deputy, legate
**07** attaché, courier, plenipo
**08** delegate, diplomat, emissary, mediator, minister **09** go-between, messenger **10** ambassador
**12** intermediary **14** representative
**15** plenipotentiary

**envy**
**05** covet, crave, spite **06** desire, grudge, malice, resent **07** ill-will
**08** begrudge, jealousy **09** hostility
**10** resentment **12** covetousness
**13** resentfulness **15** dissatisfaction

**enzyme**

*Enzymes include:*

**05** DNase, lyase, renin, RNase
**06** cytase, kinase, ligase, lipase, papain, pepsin, rennin, zymase
**07** amylase, emulsin, erepsin, inulase, lactase, maltase, oxidase, pepsine, plasmin, trypsin, uricase
**08** bromelin, catalase, ceramide, elastase, esterase, lysozyme, nuclease, permease, protease, thrombin
**09** amylopsin, bromelain, cellulase, coagulase, hydrolase, invertase, isomerase, peptidase, reductase, urokinase
**10** insulinase, luciferase, peroxidase, polymerase, sulphatase, telomerase, tyrosinase
**11** collagenase, glutaminase, histaminase, hydrogenase, lecithinase, nitrogenase, phosphatase, transferase
**12** alpha amylase, asparaginase, chymotrypsin, endonuclease, fibrinolysin, ribonuclease, transaminase
**13** decarboxylase, dehydrogenase, DNA polymerase, neuraminidase, penicillinase, phosphorylase, RNA polymerase, streptokinase, thrombokinase, transcriptase
**14** cholinesterase, thromboplastin

**Eos**
**06** Aurora

**ephemeral**
**05** brief, short **07** fungous, passing
**08** fleeting, flitting **09** fugacious, momentary, temporary, transient
**10** evanescent, short-lived, transitory
**11** impermanent

**epic**
**04** epos, huge, long, myth, saga, vast
**05** grand, great, Iliad, large, lofty
**06** epopee, heroic, legend
**07** Dunciad, exalted, history, Homeric, Odyssey, romance, sublime
**08** colossal, elevated, epopoeia, imposing, Kalevala, long poem, majestic, Ramayana, rhapsody
**09** ambitious, colubriad, long story, narrative **10** heroic poem, impressive, large-scale **13** grandiloquent

**epicure**
**06** friand **07** friande, glutton, gourmet **08** gourmand, hedonist, Sybarite **09** bon vivant, bon viveur, epicurean **10** gastronome, sensualist, voluptuary **11** connoisseur, gastronomer

**epicurean**
**04** lush **07** gourmet, sensual **08** luscious **09** libertine, luxurious, Sybaritic **10** gluttonous, hedonistic, sensualist, voluptuous **11** gastronomic **12** gormandizing, unrestrained **13** self-indulgent

**epidemic**
**04** pest, rash, rife, rise, wave **05** spate **06** growth, plague, spread **07** endemic, rampant, scourge, upsurge **08** increase, outbreak, pandemia, pandemic, sweeping **09** extensive, pervasive, prevalent **10** prevailing, widespread **11** wide-ranging

**epigram**
**03** pun **04** quip **05** gnome, maxim **06** bon mot, saying **07** proverb **08** aphorism **09** witticism **10** apophthegm **11** old chestnut, play on words

**epigrammatic**
**05** brief, pithy, sharp, short, terse, witty **06** ironic **07** concise, laconic, piquant, pointed, pungent **08** incisive, succinct **10** aphoristic

**epilepsy**
**08** eclampsy, grand mal, petit mal **09** eclampsia **15** falling sickness
**• sensation before epilepsy**
**04** aura

**epilogue**
**02** PS **04** coda **08** appendix, swan song **09** afterword **10** conclusion, postscript

**episcopate**
**03** see

**episode**
**03** fit **04** bout, part **05** event, scene, spasm, spell **06** affair, attack, matter, period **07** chapter, passage, section **08** business, incident, occasion **09** adventure, happening **10** experience, instalment, occurrence **12** circumstance

**episodic**
**08** periodic, sporadic **09** anecdotal, irregular, spasmodic **10** digressive, disjointed, occasional, picaresque **12** disconnected, intermittent

**epistle**
**02** Ep **04** Epis, line, note **06** letter **07** message, missive, preface **08** bulletin **10** encyclical **13** communication **14** correspondence

**epitaph**
**03** RIP **05** elegy **08** obituary **11** inscription, rest in peace **13** commemoration **14** funeral oration

**epithet**
**03** tag **04** name, term **05** title **06** by-name, to-name **08** cognomen, nickname **09** apathaton, sobriquet **10** expression **11** appellation, description, designation **12** denomination

**epitome**
**04** type **05** model **06** digest, précis, résumé **07** essence, example, outline, summary **08** abstract, exemplar, synopsis **09** archetype, prototype **10** abridgment, embodiment **11** abridgement **12** quintessence **14** representation **15** personification

**epitomize**
**03** cut, pot **05** sum up **06** embody, précis, reduce, typify **07** abridge, curtail, shorten **08** abstract, compress, condense, contract **09** exemplify, incarnate, personify, represent, summarize, symbolize **10** abbreviate, illustrate **11** encapsulate, incorporate

**epoch**
**03** age, era **04** date, span, time **06** period
*See also* **geology**

**equable**
**04** calm, even **05** equal **06** placid, serene, smooth, stable, steady **07** regular, unfazed, uniform **08** composed, constant, laid-back, moderate, tranquil **09** easy-going, temperate, unvarying **10** consistent, even-minded, unchanging **11** level-headed, unexcitable, unflappable **12** even-tempered **13** imperturbable

**equably**
**06** calmly **08** placidly, serenely **10** tranquilly **11** unexcitably **13** level-headedly

**equal**
**02** eq **03** fit, par **04** able, egal, even, fair, fear, feer, fere, just, like, maik, make, mate, peer, twin, view **05** alike, feare, fiere, level, match, reach, rival, total **06** fellow, pheere, strong, suited **07** add up to, balance, capable, coequal, compeer, contend, emulate, matched, neutral, peregal, regular, the same, uniform **08** adequate, amount to, balanced, come up to, constant, corrival, equalize, parallel, suitable, unbiased **09** competent, identical, impartial, match up to, semblable, tally with, unvarying **10** be as good as, comparable, equate with, equivalent, even-steven, fifty-fifty, keep up with, square with, sufficient, unchanging **11** be a match for, be level with, be the same as, compare with, counterpart, even-stevens, measure up to, neck and neck, non-partisan, symmetrical **12** be on a par with, coincide with, commensurate, correspond to, well balanced **13** corresponding, evenly matched **14** be equivalent to

**equality**
**03** par, tie **05** match **06** owelty, parage, parity **07** balance, egality, justice **08** evenness, fairness, identity, likeness, rivality, sameness, symmetry **10** neutrality, proportion, similarity, uniformity **11** equal rights, equivalence, parallelism **12** impartiality, partisanship **13** comparability **14** correspondence, egalitarianism

**equalization**
**08** matching **09** balancing, levelling **10** evening-out **12** compensation **15** standardization

**equalize**
**05** equal, level, match **06** equate, even up, smooth, square **07** balance, even out **08** keep pace, make even **09** draw level **10** compensate, regularize **11** standardize

**equally**
**02** as **05** alike **06** evenly, fairly, just as, justly **07** ex aequo **08** likewise **09** similarly, uniformly **11** as important **12** in like manner, in the same way, on equal terms **14** by the same token, proportionally **15** correspondingly, proportionately

**equanimity**
**04** calm, ease **05** poise **06** aplomb **07** dignity **08** calmness, coolness, serenity **09** assurance, composure, placidity, sangfroid **10** confidence **11** impassivity, self-control **12** tranquillity **13** self-assurance **14** self-possession, unflappability **15** level-headedness

**equate**
**06** offset **07** balance, be equal, compare, liken to **08** equalize, link with, pair with, parallel **09** agree with, compare to, match with, tally with **10** square with **11** compare with, connect with **12** correspond to, identify with **13** juxtapose with **14** correspond with **15** bracket together, regard as the same

**equation**
**02** eq **05** cubic, match **07** pairing **08** equality, identity, likeness, matching, parallel **09** agreement, balancing, quadratic **10** comparison, similarity **11** calculation, equivalence **13** juxtaposition **14** correspondence, identification

**equator**
**07** the line **11** aclinic line
**• near the equator**
**03** low

**Equatorial Guinea**
**03** GNQ

**equestrian**
**05** rider **06** cowboy, equine, herder, hussar, jockey, knight, riding **07** courier, cowgirl, mounted, rancher, trooper **08** cavalier, horseman **10** cavalryman, horse-rider, horsewoman **11** horse-riding

*Equestrians and showjumpers include:*

**03** Hoy (Andrew), Hoy (Bettina)
**04** Anne (Princess), Leng (Virginia), Tait (Blyth), Todd (Mark)
**05** Green (Lucinda), Meade (Richard), Smith (Harvey)
**06** Astley (Philip), Broome (David), D'Inzeo (Raimondo), Klimke (Reiner), Smythe (Pat)
**07** Winkler (Hans-Günther)
**08** Phillips (Mark), Whitaker (John), Whitaker (Michael)

*See also* **horseman, horsewoman**

**equilibrium**
**05** poise **06** aplomb, stasis
**07** balance, dignity **08** calmness, coolness, evenness, serenity, symmetry **09** assurance, composure, equipoise, sangfroid, stability
**10** confidence, equanimity, steadiness
**11** self-control **12** counterpoise, tranquillity **13** self-assurance **14** self-possession, unflappability **15** level-headedness

**equip**
**03** arm, fit, rig **04** tool **05** array, dight, dress, endow, fit up, issue, rig up, stock
**06** aguise, aguize, clothe, fit out, kit out, outfit, supply **07** apparel, appoint, bedight, deck out, furnish, prepare, provide **08** accouter, accoutre, equipage **10** accomplish

**equipment**
**03** kit, rig **04** gear **05** stock, stuff, tools
**06** doings, graith, outfit, rig-out, tackle, things **07** baggage, battery, clobber, fixings, luggage **08** articles, hardware, material, materiel, supplies
**09** apparatus, furniture, inventory
**10** appliances **11** accessories, apparelment, furnishings
**12** appointments **13** accoutrements, paraphernalia

*See also* **farm**; **gardening**; **laboratory**; **medical**; **office**; **photographic**; **plumbing**; **sport**

**equipoise**
**05** poise **07** balance, ballast
**08** evenness, symmetry **09** libration, stability **10** steadiness **11** equibalance, equilibrium **12** counterpoise
**13** counter-weight **14** counterbalance, equiponderance

**equitable**
**03** due **04** fair, just **05** equal, right
**06** honest, proper, square **07** ethical
**08** rightful, unbiased **09** impartial, objective **10** even-handed, legitimate, reasonable **12** unprejudiced
**13** disinterested, dispassionate, fair-and-square

**equitably**
**06** fairly, justly **07** ex aequo
**08** honestly **09** ethically
**10** reasonably, rightfully **11** impartially
**12** even-handedly **15** disinterestedly, dispassionately

**equity**
**05** right **06** square **07** honesty, justice
**08** fairness, fair play, justness
**09** integrity, rectitude **11** objectivity, uprightness **12** impartiality
**13** equitableness, righteousness
**14** even-handedness, fair-mindedness, reasonableness

**equivalence**
**06** amount, parity **08** equality, identity, likeness, parallel, sameness
**09** agreement **10** conformity, similarity **11** correlation
**13** comparability, identicalness
**14** correspondence

**equivalent**
**02** eq **04** even, like, peer, same, twin
**05** alike, equal, match, value
**06** double, fellow **07** similar
**08** parallel **09** homologue, identical
**10** comparable, homologous, tantamount **11** alternative, correlative, counterpart, equipollent
**12** commensurate **13** correspondent, corresponding, substitutable
**14** opposite number
**15** interchangeable

**equivocal**
**05** fishy, vague **07** dubious, evasive, oblique, obscure **08** oracular
**09** ambiguous, confusing, oraculous, uncertain **10** ambivalent, homonymous, indefinite, misleading, suspicious **12** questionable

**equivocate**
**05** dodge, evade, fence, hedge, mudge
**06** boggle, palter, waffle, weasel
**07** mislead **09** pussyfoot, vacillate
**11** prevaricate **12** shilly-shally, tergiversate **13** chop and change, hedge your bets **14** change your mind, change your tune

**equivocation**
**06** waffle **07** evasion, flannel, hedging
**08** shifting **09** quibbling, shuffling
**10** double talk **11** weasel words
**12** pussyfooting **13** prevarication
**14** tergiversation **15** dodging the issue

**era**
**03** age, day **04** aeon, date, days, time
**05** cycle, epoch, stage, times
**06** period, season **07** century
**10** generation

*See also* **geology**

• **bygone era**
**02** BC

• **common era**
**02** CE

• **current era**
**02** AD

**eradicate**
**04** root, wipe **05** erase **06** efface, remove, uproot **07** abolish, destroy, expunge, root out, weed out, wipe out
**08** get rid of, stamp out, suppress
**09** eliminate, extirpate **10** annihilate, do away with, extinguish, obliterate
**11** crack down on, exterminate

**eradication**
**07** removal **08** riddance **09** abolition
**10** effacement, expunction, extinction
**11** destruction, elimination, extirpation, suppression
**12** annihilation, deracination, obliteration **13** extermination

**erasable**
**08** washable **09** removable
**10** effaceable, eradicable

**erase**
**03** rub, zap **04** race, rase, raze
**06** cancel, delete, efface, excise, remove, rub off, rub out, scrape
**07** blot out, destroy, expunge, rub away, scratch, wipe out **08** get rid of
**09** eradicate **10** obliterate, scratch out

**erasure**
**06** rasure, razure **07** removal
**08** deletion **09** cleansing, erasement, wiping-out **10** effacement, expunction, rubbing-out **11** blotting-out, elimination, eradication
**12** cancellation, obliteration

**erbium**
**02** Er

**erect**
**04** firm, form, hard, lift, rear **05** build, dress, found, mount, on end, pitch, prick, put up, raise, right, rigid, set up, stiff **06** create, raised **07** elevate, prick up, stand-up, upright **08** assemble, initiate, organize, standing, straight, vertical **09** construct, displayed, establish, institute, tumescent
**10** upstanding **11** orthostatic, put together **13** perpendicular, straight-pight

**erection**
**04** pile **07** edifice, raising **08** assembly, building, creation, priapism, rigidity
**09** elevation, stiffness, structure
**10** tumescence **11** fabrication, manufacture **12** construction
**13** establishment

**ergo**
**02** so **04** then, thus **05** argal, hence
**09** therefore **11** accordingly
**12** consequently **13** for this reason, in consequence

**Erica**
**04** ling **07** heather

**Eritrea**
**03** ERI

**erode**
**05** spoil **06** abrade **07** consume, corrode, degrade, deplete, destroy, eat away, eat into **08** fragment, wear away, wear down **09** excoriate, grind down, undermine **11** deteriorate
**12** disintegrate

**Eros**
**05** Cupid

**erosion**
**04** wash, wear **07** wash-out
**08** abrasion, scouring, wash-away

**09** attrition, corrosion **10** denudation **11** degradation, destruction, excoriation, undermining, wearing away **13** deterioration **14** disintegration

**erotic**

**03** hot **04** blue, go-go, sexy **05** adult, dirty, horny **06** carnal, steamy **07** amatory, amorous, lustful, raunchy, sensual **08** erogenic, venereal **09** erogenous, seductive **10** lascivious, suggestive, voluptuous **11** Anacreontic, aphrodisiac, stimulating, titillating **12** pornographic

**erotically**

**08** steamily **09** raunchily, sensually **10** explicitly **11** seductively **12** suggestively **15** anacreontically

**err**

◇ *anagram indicator*

**03** sin **04** boob, flub, goof **05** fluff **06** cock up, duff it, goof up, mess up, offend, slip up, wander **07** be wrong, blunder, deviate, do wrong, louse up, mistake, screw up, stumble **08** go astray, misjudge **09** make a slip, misbehave **10** transgress **11** be incorrect, make a booboo, misconstrue **12** come a cropper, drop a clanger, make a mistake, miscalculate **13** fall from grace, misunderstand **15** put your foot in it

**errand**

**03** job **04** duty, task **05** chore **06** charge **07** message, mission **10** assignment, commission **11** undertaking

**• person who runs errands**

**03** cad **05** caddy, cadee, cadie **06** caddie **07** express, galopin **10** message-boy **11** message-girl **13** printer's devil

**errant**

◇ *anagram indicator*

**05** loose, stray, wrong **06** erring, roving, sinful **07** deviant, lawless, nomadic, peccant, roaming, sinning, wayward **08** aberrant, criminal, quixotic, rambling, straying, thorough **09** itinerant, offending, wandering **10** journeying **11** disobedient, peripatetic

**erratic**

◇ *anagram indicator*

**06** fitful **07** vagrant, varying **08** aberrant, abnormal, shifting, sporadic, unstable, unsteady, variable, volatile **09** desultory, eccentric, irregular, planetary, unsettled, wandering **10** capricious, changeable, inconstant, meandering, unbalanced, unreliable **11** fluctuating **12** inconsistent, intermittent **13** unpredictable

**erratically**

◇ *anagram indicator*

**08** fitfully, variably **10** changeably, unreliably **11** irregularly **12** inconstantly, sporadically **13** unpredictably **14** inconsistently, intermittently

**erring**

◇ *anagram indicator*

**05** loose, stray, wrong **06** errant, guilty, sinful **07** deviant, devious, lawless, peccant, sinning, wayward **08** criminal, culpable, straying **09** misguided, offending, wandering **11** disobedient

**erroneous**

◇ *anagram indicator*

**05** false, wrong **06** erring, faulty, flawed, untrue **07** inexact, invalid **08** mistaken, specious, spurious, straying **09** illogical, incorrect, misguided, misplaced, unfounded, wandering **10** fallacious, inaccurate

**error**

◇ *anagram indicator*

**04** boob, flaw, flub, goof, slip, typo **05** fault, fluff, gaffe, lapse, mix-up, wrong **06** booboo, cock-up, foul-up, glitch, hickey, howler, slip-up **07** blooper, blunder, clanger, erratum, fallacy, faux pas, jeofail, literal, miscopy, mistake, own goal **08** delusion, mesprize, misprint, omission, solecism **09** oversight **10** aberration, inaccuracy, misjudgment **12** misjudgement **13** misconception **14** miscalculation **15** misapprehension, slip of the tongue, spelling mistake

**• errors excepted**

**02** EE

**• in error**

**03** out **07** falsely, wrongly **08** unfairly, unjustly **09** by mistake **10** mistakenly **11** erroneously, incorrectly, misguidedly **12** fallaciously, inaccurately **15** inappropriately

**• sign of error**

**01** X

**ersatz**

**04** fake, sham **05** bogus **06** phoney **07** man-made **09** imitation, simulated, synthetic **10** artificial, substitute **11** counterfeit

**erstwhile**

**02** ex **03** old **04** late, once, past **06** bygone, former **07** one-time **08** previous, sometime

**erudite**

**04** wise **06** brainy **07** learned **08** academic, cultured, educated, highbrow, lettered, literate, profound, well-read **09** scholarly **12** intellectual, well-educated **13** knowledgeable

**erudition**

**05** facts **06** wisdom **07** culture, letters **08** learning **09** education, knowledge **10** profundity **11** learnedness, scholarship **13** reconditeness, scholarliness

**erupt**

◇ *anagram indicator*

**04** emit, gush, spew, vent **05** belch, burst, eject, expel, spout **06** blow up **07** come out, explode, flare up **08** break out, emit lava **09** burst open, discharge, pour forth **13** discharge lava, pour forth lava

**eruption**

◇ *anagram indicator*

**04** rash, spot **06** blow-up, eczema, lichen, red gum, tetter **07** ecthyma, flare-up, morphew, prurigo, Purpura, venting **08** ejection, emission, empyesis, exanthem, malander, outbreak, outburst, rose drop **09** discharge, emphlysis, exanthema, explosion, mallander, mallender, pompholyx, salt rheum **12** inflammation

**erysipelas**

**04** rose **10** sideration **14** St Anthony's fire

**escalate**

**04** grow, rise, soar **05** climb, mount, raise **06** ascend, expand, extend, rocket, spiral, step up **07** amplify, develop, enlarge, magnify, shoot up **08** heighten, increase, mushroom **09** intensify **10** accelerate, hit the roof

**escalation**

**04** rise **06** growth **07** soaring **08** increase **09** expansion, extension **11** development, heightening, mushrooming **12** acceleration **13** magnification **15** intensification

**escalator**

**04** lift **08** elevator **10** travelator, travolator **13** moving walkway **15** moving staircase

**escapable**

**08** eludible, evadable **09** avertible, avoidable

**escapade**

**04** hoot, lark, ploy, romp **05** antic, caper, fling, prank, scape, spree, stunt, trick **06** escape, frolic, scheme, splore **07** exploit **08** escapado, fredaine **09** adventure, excursion **10** skylarking **11** monkey shine

**escape**

**03** esc, fly, lam, out **04** bolt, bunk, duck, flee, flit, flow, go-by, gush, hole, leak, ooze, pass, scat, seep, shun, skip, slip, vent **05** avoid, break, ditch, dodge, drain, elope, elude, evade, issue, lam it, leg it, prank, sally, scape, scoot, scram, spurt **06** blower, decamp, efflux, flight, forget, get off, outlet **07** abscond, bail out, do a bunk, dodging, ducking, evasion, fantasy, get away, getaway, leakage, not know, outflow, outpour, overrun, pastime, pour out, run away, scarper, seepage, trickle, wilding **08** break out, breakout, dreaming, emission, escapism, loophole, not place, run for it, shake off, sidestep, slip away **09** avoidance, breakaway, break free, cut and run, discharge, diversion, do a runner, emanation, jailbreak, pour forth **10** absconding, break loose, circumvent, decampment, have it away, hop the twig, Houdini act, recreation, relaxation **11** distraction, fantasizing, safety-valve **12** steer clear of **13** circumvention, extravasation, not be recalled, transgression **14** make a bolt for it, make your escape, run for your life, take it on the lam, take to the boats **15** make a break for it, make your getaway, not be remembered, take to your heels, wishful thinking

- **allow to escape**

**03** let **04** vent

- **means of escape**

**04** hole, loop **08** loophole

- **way of escape**

**03** out **04** mews, muse **05** meuse **06** get-out **08** bolthole

**escapee**
**06** truant **07** escaper, refugee, runaway **08** defector, deserter, fugitive **09** absconder **11** jailbreaker

**escapism**
**07** fantasy, pastime **08** dreaming **09** diversion **10** recreation, relaxation **11** distraction, fantasizing, pie in the sky, safety-valve **15** castles in the air, wishful thinking

**escapist**
**07** dreamer, ostrich **09** Billy Liar **10** daydreamer, Don Quixote, fantasizer, non-realist **11** Walter Mitty **14** wishful thinker

**eschew**
**04** shun **05** avoid, forgo, spurn **06** abjure, forego, give up **07** abandon, disdain **08** forswear, renounce **09** repudiate **11** abstain from, keep clear of, refrain from

**escort**
**03** see, set **04** aide, beau, date, hand, lead, take, tend, wait, walk **05** bring, guard, guide, suite, train, usher **06** convoy, defend, gigolo, squire **07** company, conduct, cortège, esquire, janizar, partner, protect, retinue, take out **08** attend on, chaperon, come with, defender, janizary, shepherd, take down **09** accompany, attendant, bodyguard, chaperone, companion, entourage, janissary, protector **10** attendance, attendants, javelin-man **13** come along with, guard of honour

**esoteric**
**05** inner **06** arcane, hidden, inside, mystic, occult, Orphic, secret **07** cryptic, obscure, private **08** abstruse, mystical, rarefied **09** recondite **10** acroamatic, mysterious **11** inscrutable **12** acroamatical, confidential

**esparto grass**
**04** alfa **05** halfa

**especial**
**06** marked, signal, unique **07** express, notable, special, unusual **08** peculiar, singular, specific, striking, uncommon **09** exclusive, principal **10** noteworthy, particular, pre-eminent, remarkable **11** distinctive, exceptional, outstanding **13** distinguished, extraordinary

**especially**
**03** esp **04** very **05** espec **06** mainly, mostly, namely **07** chiefly, largely, notably **08** above all, markedly, uniquely **09** expressly, in special, most of all, primarily, specially, supremely, unusually **10** remarkably, strikingly, uncommonly **11** exclusively, principally **12** in particular, particularly, pre-eminently **13** exceptionally, outstandingly **15** extraordinarily

**espionage**
**05** scout **06** spying **07** bugging, probing **08** snooping **10** tradecraft **11** fifth column, penetration, wiretapping **12** infiltration, intelligence, intercepting, surveillance **13** investigation, secret service **14** reconnaissance, undercover work

**espousal**
**06** choice **07** backing, defence, support, wedding **08** adoption, advocacy, taking-up **09** embracing, promotion **11** championing, maintenance **12** championship

**espouse**
**04** back **05** adopt **06** choose, defend, opt for, take up **07** embrace, support **08** advocate, champion, maintain **09** patronize **10** stand up for

**esprit de corps**
**10** team spirit **12** group loyalty, mutal respect, public spirit **13** mutual feeling

**espy**
**03** see, spy **04** spot **05** sight, watch **06** behold, descry, detect, notice **07** discern, glimpse, make out, observe **08** discover, perceive **11** distinguish **12** catch sight of

**essay**
**02** go **03** try **04** bash, push, shot, stab, test **05** assay, crack, go for, offer, paper, piece, study, theme, tract, trial **06** leader, review, sketch, strain, strive, tackle, take on, thesis **07** article, attempt, have a go, venture **08** causerie, critique, struggle, treatise **09** discourse, endeavour, have a bash, have a stab, prolusion, undertake **10** assignment, commentary, experiment, have a crack **11** composition **12** disquisition, dissertation

**essayist**

*Essayists include:*

**04** **Greg** (William Rathbone), **Hunt** (Leigh), **Lamb** (Charles), **Lynd** (Robert), **Rodó** (José Enrique)
**05** **Bacon** (Francis), **Gould** (Stephen Jay), **Lucas** (Edward Verrall), **Pater** (Walter Horatio), **Smith** (Sydney), **White** (E B)
**06** **Borges** (Jorge Luis), **Breton** (André), **Orwell** (George), **Ruskin** (John), **Steele** (Sir Richard)
**07** **Addison** (Joseph), **Calvino** (Italo), **Carlyle** (Thomas), **Chapone** (Hester), **Emerson** (Ralph Waldo), **Hayward** (Abraham), **Hazlitt** (William), **Lazarus** (Emma), **Meynell** (Alice Christiana Gertrude), **Montagu** (Lady Mary Wortley),**Thoreau** (Henry David)
**08** **Beerbohm** (Sir Max), **Macaulay** (Thomas Babington, Lord)
**09** **De Quincey** (Thomas), **Dickinson** (Goldsworthy Lowes), **Montaigne** (Michel Eyquem de)
**10** **Chesterton** (G K), **Crèvecoeur** (Michel Guillaume Jean de)
**12** **Quiller-Couch** (Sir Arthur)

**essence**
**03** nub **04** alma, core, crux, esse, life, otto, pith, soul **05** being, heart, juice, point, stuff **06** centre, entity, kernel, marrow, nature, spirit **07** alcohol, extract, meaning, quality, quiddit, ratafia, reality, spirits **08** bergamot, quiddity, whatness **09** actuality, character, principle, substance **10** attributes, distillate, heart-blood, hypostasis, ylang-ylang **11** concentrate, heart's-blood **12** distillation, quintessence, significance **13** concentration, individuation, ylang-ylang oil **15** characteristics, sum and substance

- **in essence**

**07** in grain **08** at bottom **09** basically **11** essentially **13** fundamentally, substantially

- **of the essence**

**05** vital **06** needed **07** crucial **08** required **09** essential, important, necessary, requisite **13** indispensable

**essential**
**03** key **04** gist, main, must, pure **05** basic, vital **06** formal, innate, needed **07** central, crucial, typical **08** inherent, key point, required, rudiment **09** important, intrinsic, key points, main point, necessary, necessity, principal, principle, requisite **10** definitive, main points, sine qua non, underlying **11** constituent, fundamental, requirement, substantial **12** all-important, constitutive, prerequisite **13** indispensable **14** characteristic

**essentially**
**05** per se **07** at heart **08** deep down **09** basically, in essence, primarily **10** inherently **13** fundamentally, intrinsically

**establish**
**03** fix **04** base, form, haft, make, open, seat, show **05** begin, build, edify, erect, found, lodge, pitch, plant, prove, raise, set up, start, state, stell **06** affirm, attest, create, ordain, ratify, secure, settle, verify **07** certify, confirm, install, start up **08** nail down, organize, validate **09** institute, introduce **10** constitute, inaugurate **11** corroborate, demonstrate **12** authenticate, substantiate **14** bring into being

**established**
**03** est, set **05** fixed **06** proved, proven, rooted, secure, stable, stated
**07** settled **08** accepted, radicate, ratified, standing **09** ensconced, radicated, respected, steadfast
**10** entrenched **11** experienced, traditional **12** conventional **14** tried and tested
• **to be established**
**04** root **06** obtain

**establishment**
**03** fix **04** firm, shop, them **05** store
**07** company, concern, forming
**08** business, creation, founding
**09** formation, inception, institute, setting up, the system **10** enterprise, foundation **11** corporation, down-sitting, institution, ruling class
**12** inauguration, installation, organization **13** the government
**14** the authorities **15** the powers that be

**estate**
**03** pen **04** alod, area, land, odal, park, rank, site, udal **05** allod, class, goods, lands, manor, place, state, taluk, tract, trust **06** assets, centre, domain, entail, having, realty, region, status
**07** demesne, effects, grounds, havings
**08** allodium, executry, hacienda, holdings, position, property, standing
**09** condition, patrimony, princedom, situation **10** belongings, latifundia, personalty, plantation, real estate
**11** development, landholding, possessions **14** conditional fee

**estate agent**
**07** realtor **09** land agent **13** property agent **15** real-estate agent

**esteem**
**03** way **04** deem, have, hold, love, pass, rate, view **05** compt, count, favor, izzat, judge, prise, prize, set by, store, think, value **06** admire, credit, favour, honour, make of, reckon, regard, revere **07** account, adjudge, believe, cherish, respect, set down
**08** consider, judgment, treasure, venerate **09** judgement, reckoning, reverence **10** admiration, estimation, veneration **11** approbation, good opinion **12** appreciation, regard highly
**13** consideration, put a premium on

**esteemed**
**06** prized, valued, worthy **07** admired, revered **08** favorite, honoured, precious **09** admirable, excellent, favourite, of warrant, reputable, respected, treasured, venerated
**10** honourable **11** prestigious, respectable **13** distinguished, of good warrant, well-respected, well-thought-of **14** highly regarded

**estimable**
**04** good **06** valued, worthy
**07** notable **08** esteemed, laudable, valuable **09** admirable, excellent, reputable, respected **10** creditable, honourable, noteworthy, worthwhile
**11** commendable, meritorious, respectable, warrantable
**12** praiseworthy **13** distinguished

**estimate**
**03** aim **04** cost, gage, rate, view
**05** carat, gauge, guess, judge, level, value, weigh **06** assess, belief, carrat, reckon, strike **07** compute, opinion
**08** appraise, evaluate, judgment, thinking **09** calculate, judgement, quotation, reckoning, valuation
**10** appreciate, assessment, conclusion, conjecture, estimation, evaluation, reputation, rough guess
**11** calculation, computation, guesstimate **13** approximation, consideration **14** ballpark figure
**15** approximate cost

**estimated**
**03** est

**estimation**
**04** rate, view **05** guess, honor, sight, stock **06** belief, credit, esteem, honour, regard **07** account, feeling, opinion, respect **08** estimate, judgment, thinking **09** judgement, reckoning, valuation **10** assessment, conception, conclusion, conjecture, evaluation, importance, reputation, rough guess **11** calculation, computation **12** appreciation
**13** consideration, way of thinking
**15** approximate cost

**Estonia**
**03** EST

**estrange**
**04** part **05** alien, sever **06** cut off, divide, remove **07** break up, divorce, split up **08** alienate, disunite, separate, withdraw, withhold **09** disaffect
**10** antagonize, drive apart, set against
**13** set at variance

**estranged**
**05** alien, apart, fraim, fremd **06** fremit
**07** aliened, divided **08** alienate, divorced, separate **09** alienated, separated **11** antagonized, disaffected

**estrangement**
**05** split **06** breach **07** break-up, parting **08** disunion, disunity, division
**09** antipathy, hostility, severance
**10** alienation, antagonism, separation, withdrawal **11** withholding
**12** disaffection, dissociation
**14** unfriendliness

**estuary**
**03** arm, bay, Est **04** cove **05** creek, firth, fiord, fjord, inlet, mouth **07** sea-loch

**et cetera**
**01** &c **03** etc **04** et al **07** and so on
**10** and all that, and so forth, and the like, and the rest, or whatever **11** and suchlike, and whatever **14** and what have you

**etch**
**03** cut, dig **04** bite, burn **05** carve, eat in, stamp **06** furrow, groove, incise
**07** corrode, eat away, engrave, impress, imprint, ingrain **08** inscribe

**etching**
**03** cut **05** print **06** sketch **07** carving, imprint **08** aquatint **09** aquatinta, engraving **10** aqua fortis, impression
**11** inscription

**eternal**
**07** abiding, aeonian, endless, lasting, non-stop, undying **08** constant, enduring, immortal, infinite, timeless, unending **09** ceaseless, deathless, eviternal, incessant, limitless, perennial, perpetual **10** continuous, persistent, relentless, unchanging
**11** everlasting, never-ending, remorseless, unremitting
**12** imperishable, interminable, unchangeable **14** indestructible

**eternally**
**04** ever **06** always **07** for ever
**09** endlessly, lastingly **10** constantly
**11** ceaselessly, continually, incessantly, permanently, perpetually
**12** interminably **13** everlastingly
**14** indestructibly

**eternity**
**03** age, eon **04** aeon, ages **05** yonks
**06** heaven **07** forever **08** Ewigkeit, infinity, long time, paradise **09** after-life, hereafter, next world **10** perpetuity
**11** ages and ages, endlessness, everlasting, immortality, world to come **12** donkey's years, immutability, timelessness **13** deathlessness
**15** everlasting life, everlastingness, imperishability, world without end

**ethereal**
**04** airy, fine **05** light **06** dainty, subtle
**07** refined, tenuous **08** delicate, empyreal, empyrean, gossamer, heavenly, rarefied **09** airy-fairy, celestial, elemental, exquisite, spiritual, unearthly, unworldly **10** diaphanous, immaterial, impalpable, intangible
**13** insubstantial

**ethical**
**04** fair, good, just **05** moral, noble, right **06** decent, honest, proper, seemly **07** correct, fitting, upright
**08** decorous, virtuous **09** righteous
**10** high-minded, honourable, principled **11** commendable, responsible **13** above reproach

**ethically**
**05** nobly **06** justly **07** morally, rightly
**08** honestly **09** reputably
**10** honourably, virtuously
**11** responsibly **12** high-mindedly, respectfully **13** ideologically
**14** moralistically

**ethics**
**04** code **05** rules **06** equity, morals, values **07** beliefs **08** morality
**09** moral code, propriety, standards
**10** conscience, deontology, principles
**11** moral values **13** descriptivism, moral theology **14** moral standards
**15** moral philosophy, moral principles

**Ethiopia**
**03** ETH

**ethnic**
**04** folk **06** exotic, native, racial, tribal **07** foreign **08** cultural, national, societal **10** aboriginal, indigenous **11** traditional **12** ethnological **13** autochthonous **15** anthropological

**ethnically**
**08** racially, socially, tribally **10** culturally, societally **13** traditionally **14** humanistically

**ethos**
**04** code **05** tenor **06** ethics, spirit **07** beliefs, flavour, manners **08** attitude, morality **09** character, rationale, standards **10** atmosphere, principles **11** disposition

**etiquette**
**04** code, form, kawa **05** rules **07** customs, decency, decorum, manners **08** ceremony, civility, courtesy, good form, protocol **09** propriety, standards **10** politeness **11** convenances, conventions, correctness, formalities, good manners **12** unwritten law **13** code of conduct **14** code of practice **15** code of behaviour

**etymology**
**03** ety **06** origin, source **08** word-lore **09** philology, semantics **10** derivation, lexicology **11** linguistics, word history, word origins

**eucalyptus**
**03** box, gum **05** karri, marri, sally, tuart **06** jarrah, mallee, red gum, sallee, tewart, tooart, wandoo **07** blue gum, gum tree **08** coolabah, coolibah, coolibar, ghost gum, ironbark, sugar gum **09** black butt, bloodwood, fever tree **10** tallow wood, woollybutt **11** mountain ash

**eulogize**
**04** hype, laud, plug **05** exalt, extol **06** honour, praise **07** acclaim, applaud, approve, commend, glorify, magnify **09** celebrate, rave about **10** compliment, panegyrize, wax lyrical **12** congratulate

**eulogy**
**04** laud **05** paean **06** praise **07** acclaim, plaudit, tribute **08** accolade, applause, encomion, encomium **09** laudation, laudative, laudatory, panegyric **10** compliment, exaltation **11** acclamation **12** commendation **13** glorification

**euphemism**
**07** evasion **09** softening **10** genteelism, politeness, polite term, substitute **12** substitution **14** understatement **15** mild alternative
*See also* **oath**

**euphemistic**
**04** mild **05** vague **06** polite **07** evasive, genteel, neutral **08** indirect **09** soft-toned **10** substitute **11** understated

**euphonious**
**04** soft **05** clear, sweet **06** dulcet, mellow **07** melodic, musical, silvery, tuneful **08** canorous, euphonic, pleasant **09** consonant, melodious **10** harmonious, sweet-toned **11** dulcifluous, mellifluous, symphonious **12** dulciloquent **13** sweet-sounding

**euphoria**
**03** joy **04** glee, high, rush **05** bliss **07** ecstasy, elation, rapture **08** buoyancy **09** happiness, transport, wellbeing **10** enthusiasm, exaltation, exultation, jubilation **11** high spirits **12** cheerfulness, exhilaration, intoxication

**euphoric**
**04** high **05** happy **06** elated, joyful, joyous **07** buoyant, exulted, gleeful **08** blissful, cheerful, ecstatic, exultant, jubilant **09** rapturous **10** enraptured **11** exhilarated, intoxicated **12** enthusiastic

**Europe**

*European countries include:*

**02** UK
**05** Italy, Malta, Spain
**06** Cyprus, France, Greece, Latvia, Monaco, Norway, Poland, Russia, Sweden, Turkey
**07** Albania, Andorra, Austria, Belarus, Belgium, Croatia, Denmark, Estonia, Finland, Germany, Hungary, Iceland, Ireland, Moldova, Romania, Ukraine, Vatican
**08** Bulgaria, Portugal, Slovakia, Slovenia
**09** Lithuania, Macedonia, San Marino
**10** Luxembourg
**11** Switzerland, Vatican City
**13** Czech Republic, Liechtenstein, United Kingdom
**14** The Netherlands
**19** Serbia and Montenegro
**20** Bosnia and Herzegovina

*European landmarks include:*

**02** Po
**04** Alps, Arno, Como, Etna, Lido, Main, Oder
**05** Delos, Eiger, Garda, Loire, Prado, Rhine, Rhône, Seine, Somme, Tiber, Urals, Volga
**06** Azores, Dachau, Danube, Delphi, Fátima, Geysir, Liffey, Rhodes, Tatras, Tivoli
**07** Algarve, Kremlin, Lapland, La Scala, Madeira, Moselle, Pompeii, Shannon, Siberia
**08** Alhambra, Ardennes, Auvergne, Canaries, Caucasus, Dordogne, Jungfrau, Lake Como, Legoland, Oude Kerk, Pantheon, Provence, Pyrenees, St Peter's, Strokkur, Tenerife, Vesuvius
**09** Acropolis, Balearics, Bantry Bay, Campanile, Colosseum, Connemara, Dolomites, Dublin Bay, Keukenhof, Lake Garda, Lanzarote, Menin Gate, Mont Blanc, Mount Etna, Notre Dame, Parc Güell, Parthenon, Red Square, Reichstag, Temple Bar, Zuider Zee
**10** Bran Castle, Grand Canal, IJsselmeer, Interlaken, Julian Alps, Lake Geneva, Lenin's tomb, Matterhorn, Nieuwe Kerk, Pont du Gard, Rubenshuis, Schönbrunn, Versailles, Wienerwald
**11** Afsluitdijk, Black Forest, Eiffel Tower, Königsplatz, Manneken Pis, Mount Elbrus, Rijksmuseum, Simplon Pass, Vatican City, Vienna Woods
**12** Abbey Theatre, Bavarian Alps, Blarney Stone, Frauenkirche, Lake Maggiore, Leaning Tower, Mont St Michel, Mount Olympus, Mozart's House, Ponte Vecchio, Rialto Bridge, Rubens's House, Summer Palace, Tower of Belém, Winter Palace
**13** Anne Frank Huis, Arc de Triomphe, Bridge of Sighs, Canary Islands, Ha'penny Bridge, Lake Constance, Little Mermaid, Massif Central, Millau Viaduct, Mount Vesuvius, Museo del Prado, Oresund Bridge, Sistine Chapel, St Mark's Square, Uffizi Gallery, Ural Mountains, Vatican Palace
**14** Bolshoi Theatre, Mount Parnassus, O'Connell Street, Palazzo Vecchio, Piazza San Marco, Potsdamer Platz, Sagrada Familia, Trinity College
**15** Anne Frank's house, Balearic Islands, Brandenburg Gate, Dingle Peninsula, Hermitage Museum, Rock of Gibraltar, Stedelijk Museum

**European**
◇ *foreign word indicator*
**01** E **03** Eur **04** Euro

*Europeans include:*

**04** Balt, Brit, Dane, Esth, Finn, Flem, Lapp, Pict, Pole, Scot, Serb, Slav, Turk
**05** Angle, Czech, Croat, Greek, Latin, Vlach, Swede, Swiss
**06** Almain, Basque, Briton, German, Nordic, Sabine, Salian, Teuton, Zyrian
**07** Belgian, Bosnian, Cypriot, Fleming, Iberian, Italian, Latvian, Lombard, Maltese, Manxman, Monacan, Russian, Samnite, Serbian, Walloon
**08** Albanian, Andorran, Austrian, Croatian, Dutchman, Estonian, Irishman, Moldovan, Romanian, Scotsman, Siberian, Silurian, Spaniard, Welshman
**09** Britisher, Bulgarian, Englander, Englisher, Frenchman, Hungarian, Icelander, Manxwoman, Norwegian, Sardinian, Slovakian, Slovenian, Ukrainian
**10** Anglo-Saxon, Belarusian, Dutchwoman, Englishman, Irishwoman, Lithuanian, Macedonian, Monégasque,

Portuguese, Welshwoman
11 Belarussian, Frenchwoman, Montenegrin, Sammarinese
12 Luxembourger, Scandinavian
13 Englishwoman, Herzegovinian
15 Liechtensteiner

**• European Union**
02 EU

*European Union member countries include:*

05 Italy, Malta, Spain
06 Cyprus, France, Greece, Latvia, Poland, Sweden
07 Austria, Belgium, Denmark, Estonia, Finland, Germany, Hungary, Ireland
08 Portugal, Slovakia, Slovenia
09 Lithuania
10 Luxembourg
13 Czech Republic, United Kingdom
14 The Netherlands

**europium**
02 Eu

**euthanasia**
07 quietus, release 12 happy release, mercy killing 15 assisted suicide, merciful release

**evacuate**
04 ease, quit, void 05 clear, eject, empty, expel, leave, purge, stool 06 decamp, depart, desert, getter, remove, vacate 07 abandon, excrete, forsake, nullify, relieve, retreat, vacuate 08 clear out, defecate, withdraw 09 discharge, eliminate, make empty, move out of, pull out of 10 go away from, relinquish, retire from, stercorate

**evacuation**
06 exodus, flight 07 Dunkirk, leaving, purging, removal, retreat 08 ejection, emptying, quitting, vacating 09 clearance, departure, desertion, discharge, expulsion, forsaking, gettering, urination, vacuation 10 defecation, retirement, withdrawal 11 abandonment, elimination 14 relinquishment

**evade**
04 balk, duck, shun 05 avoid, blink, burke, dodge, elude, fence, fudge, hedge, parry, sheer, shift, shirk, skive, waive 06 baffle, bludge, bypass, cop out, escape 07 fend off, quibble, shuffle, wriggle 08 get round, sidestep, skive off 09 back out of, duckshove, gold brick, weasel out 10 chicken out, circumvent, equivocate, scrimshank, skrimshank 11 prevaricate 12 steer clear of, wriggle out of

**evaluate**
04 rank, rate 05 gauge, judge, value, weigh 06 assess, reckon, size up 07 compute, measure 08 appraise, estimate 09 calculate, determine 15 get the measure of

**evaluation**
05 audit 06 rating 07 opinion 08 estimate, judgment 09 appraisal, judgement, reckoning, valuation 10 assessment, estimation 11 calculation, computation 13 determination

**evanescent**
05 brief 06 fading 07 passing 08 fleeting, unstable 09 ephemeral, momentary, temporary, transient, vanishing 10 perishable, short-lived, transitory 11 evaporating, impermanent 12 disappearing 13 insubstantial

**evangelical**
03 Sim 06 Marist 07 zealous 08 biblical, orthodox, Stundist 09 crusading, High-flier, High-flyer, Simeonite 10 converting, missionary, Morisonian, scriptural 11 campaigning 12 Bible-bashing, enthusiastic, evangelistic, propagandist 13 Bible-punching, Bible-thumping, proselytizing 14 Bible-believing, fundamentalist, propagandizing

**• Evangelical Union**
02 EU

**evangelist**
04 John, Luke, Mark 07 Matthew 08 crusader, preacher 09 gospeller, missioner 10 campaigner, missionary, revivalist 12 hot gospeller, proselytizer 13 televangelist

**evangelize**
06 preach 07 baptize, convert, crusade 08 campaign 09 gospelize 10 missionize 11 proselytize 12 missionarize, propagandize 13 spread the word

**evaporate**
03 dry, end 04 fade, melt 05 steme, vapor 06 depart, dispel, distil, exhale, vanish, vapour 08 boil away, disperse, dissolve, evanesce, melt away, vaporize 09 dehydrate, desiccate, disappear, dissipate 10 volatilize 13 dematerialize

**evaporation**
06 drying, fading 07 melting 09 vanishing 10 exhalation 11 dehydration, desiccation, dissolution 12 condensation, distillation, vaporization

**evasion**
04 go-by 05 dodge, fudge, quirk 06 cop-out, deceit, escape, excuse, put-off 07 dodging, ducking, elusion, fencing, fig leaf, fudging, hedging, quibble, shuffle, skiving 08 go-around, shirking, shunning, trickery 09 avoidance, deception, quibbling, shuffling 10 scrimshank, skrimshank, subterfuge 12 equivocation 13 circumvention, prevarication 14 tergiversation 15 steering clear of

**evasive**
03 coy 05 cagey, vague 06 shifty, slippy, tricky 07 cunning, devious, elusive, elusory, fudging, oblique 08 indirect, slippery, waffling 09 deceitful, deceptive, quibbling, secretive, shuffling 10 misleading 12 equivocating 13 prevaricating, unforthcoming

**evasiveness**
06 deceit 07 cunning, fudging, secrecy 08 caginess 09 quibbling, vagueness 12 equivocation, indirectness 13 deceptiveness, prevarication

**eve**
03 e'en 04 edge 05 brink, verge, vigil 09 day before, threshold 10 time before 12 period before

**even**
◇ *hidden alternately indicator*
03 all, e'en, too, yet 04 also, calm, cool, eevn, fair, flat, just, like, more, same, true 05 align, alike, at all, clean, drawn, eeven, equal, exact, flush, level, match, oddly, plain, plane, quits, still 06 as well, hardly, indeed, in fact, nearly, placid, serene, smooth, square, stable, steady 07 balance, compare, eevning, equable, exactly, flatten, neutral, regular, similar, uniform 08 actually, balanced, composed, constant, equalize, likewise, matching, parallel, scarcely, so much as, straight, tranquil 09 equitable, identical, impartial, make equal, stabilize, still more, unexcited, unruffled, unusually, unvarying 10 all the more, balance out, consistent, even-handed, fifty-fifty, horizontal, regularize, side by side, straighten, unchanging, unwavering 11 make uniform, more exactly, neck and neck, non-partisan, symmetrical, unexcitable, unflappable 12 even-tempered, surprisingly, unexpectedly 13 evenly matched, more precisely, unperturbable 14 strike a balance

**• even so**
03 but, yet 05 still 07 however 10 all the same 11 despite that, nonetheless 12 nevertheless 13 in spite of that

**• get even**
05 repay 06 avenge 07 pay back, requite 11 have revenge, reciprocate 12 settle a score 14 get your own back 15 revenge yourself, take your revenge

**• not even**
06 odd 06 uneven

**even-handed**
04 fair, just 06 square 07 neutral 08 balanced, unbiased 09 equitable, impartial 10 reasonable 12 unprejudiced 13 disinterested, dispassionate, fair and square

**evening**
03 e'en, ene, eve 04 dusk, eevn, even 05 eeven, night 06 sunset, vesper 07 eevning, sundown 08 eventide, twilight 09 forenight, nightfall 10 close of day

**evenly**
◇ *hidden alternately indicator*
04 flat 06 calmly, square, stably 07 equally 08 placidly, serenely, steadily 09 regularly, similarly, uniformly 10 constantly, tranquilly 12 consistently 13 evenly matched, symmetrically

**event**
**03** end **04** case, fact, fate, gala, game, item, meet, pass, race **05** issue, match, round **06** affair, effect, matter, result, upshot **07** contest, episode, fixture, fortune, meeting, ongoing, outcome **08** business, incident, occasion **09** adventure, aftermath, happening, milestone **10** conclusion, engagement, experience, occurrence, proceeding, tournament **11** competition, consequence, eventuality, possibility, termination **12** circumstance

• **in any event**
**06** anyhow, anyway **09** in any case **11** whether or no **12** no matter what, whether or not **15** whatever happens

**even-tempered**
**04** calm, cool **06** placid, serene, stable, steady **07** equable, unfazed **08** composed, laid-back, peaceful, tranquil **09** peaceable **11** level-headed, unflappable **13** imperturbable

**eventful**
**04** busy, full **06** active, lively **07** crucial, notable **08** critical, exciting, historic **09** checkered, chequered, important, memorable, momentous **10** noteworthy, remarkable **11** interesting, ripsnorting, significant **12** action-packed **13** unforgettable

**eventual**
**04** last **05** final, later **06** future **07** closing, ensuing, planned **08** ultimate **09** impending, projected, resulting **10** concluding, subsequent **11** prospective

**eventuality**
**04** case **05** event **06** chance, crisis, mishap **07** outcome **09** emergency, happening, incidence **10** likelihood, occurrence **11** contingency, possibility, probability **12** circumstance, happenstance

**eventually**
**06** at last, in time **07** finally **08** after all, at length, in the end **10** ultimately **11** in due course **12** in the long run, subsequently **13** sooner or later

**ever**
**02** ay **03** aye, e'er **05** at all **06** always **07** for ever **08** evermore **09** at any time, endlessly, eternally, in any case **10** at all times, constantly **11** continually, incessantly, permanently, perpetually **12** on any account, till doomsday **13** on any occasion

• **ever so**
**04** very **05** jolly **06** really **07** awfully **08** terribly, very much **09** extremely, immensely **11** exceedingly, frightfully **12** tremendously **13** exceptionally

**evergreen** *see* **pine**; **tree**

**everlasting**
**07** endless, eternal, non-stop, undying **08** cat's-foot, constant, immortal, infinite, timeless, unending **09** continual, deathless, incessant, permanent, perpetual, unceasing **10** continuous, immortelle, perdurable, persistent, relentless **11** Helichrysum, never-ending, remorseless, sempiternal, strawflower, unremitting, xeranthemum **12** imperishable, interminable **14** indestructible

**evermore**
**04** ever **06** always **07** for ever **09** eternally, ever after, hereafter **10** henceforth **11** in perpetuum, unceasingly **12** in perpetuity, till doomsday **14** for ever and a day, for ever and ever, to the end of time

**every**
**03** all, per **04** each, full, tout **05** total **06** entire **08** complete **11** all possible, every single **15** every individual

**everybody**
**03** all **05** a'body **07** each one **08** everyman, everyone **09** one and all **10** each person **11** all the world, every person, tout le monde **12** all and sundry, every man Jack **13** the whole world

**everyday**
**05** basic, daily, plain, stock, usual **06** common, folksy, modern, normal, simple **07** average, regular, routine **08** day-to-day, familiar, frequent, habitual, informal, ordinary, standard, workaday **09** customary, quotidian **10** accustomed, monotonous **11** commonplace **12** conventional, run-of-the-mill **13** unimaginative **14** common-or-garden

**everyone**
**03** all **07** each one **08** universe **09** allcomers, everybody, one and all **10** each person **11** every person **12** all and sundry, every man Jack **13** the whole world

**everything**
**03** all **04** lock **06** a'thing, the lot, the sum **08** the total, the works **09** all things, each thing **11** all the world, the entirety, the whole lot **12** the aggregate **14** stock and barrel **15** the whole shebang

**everywhere**
**04** left **06** a'where, passim, ubique **07** all over **09** all around, eachwhere **10** every place, far and near, far and wide, high and low, near and far, throughout, ubiquitous **11** at every turn, in all places, in each place, to all places, to each place **12** the world over **14** right and centre

**evict**
**04** oust **05** eject, expel **06** put out, remove **07** cast out, kick out, turf out, turn out **08** chuck out, dislodge, force out, throw out **10** dispossess **11** expropriate **12** force to leave

**eviction**
**07** removal, the boot, the push **08** ejection, the elbow **09** clearance, expulsion **11** the bum's rush **12** dislodgement **13** dispossession, expropriation **14** defenestration

**evidence**
**04** data, deed, hint, mark, show, sign, test **05** proof, prove, stamp, title, token, trace, vouch **06** affirm, assert, attest, avouch, betray, denote, evince, reveal **07** bespeak, confirm, display, exhibit, grounds, signify, support, symptom, witness **08** argument, document, indicate, instance, manifest, surrebut, warranty **09** adminicle, affidavit, establish, guarantee, testimony **10** indication, smoking gun, suggestion **11** affirmation, attestation, credentials, declaration, demonstrate **12** compurgation, confirmation, precognition, verification **13** corroboration, demonstration, documentation, manifestation **14** substantiation

• **in evidence**
**05** clear, plain **06** patent **07** obvious, visible **08** apparent, clear-cut **10** noticeable **11** conspicuous **12** unmistakable

**evident**
**05** clear, naked, overt, plain **06** patent **07** confest, obvious, visible **08** apparent, clear-cut, distinct, manifest, sensible, tangible **09** confessed, undoubted **10** noticeable **11** conspicuous, discernible, perceptible, transparent **12** indisputable, unmistakable **13** incontestable

**evidently**
**07** clearly, plainly, visibly **08** patently **09** doubtless, obviously, outwardly, seemingly, so it seems **10** apparently, manifestly, ostensibly **11** doubtlessly, so it appears, undoubtedly **12** indisputably **13** as it would seem, on the face of it **15** as it would appear

**evil**
**03** bad, ill, sin, woe **04** bale, base, blow, dire, eale, foul, harm, hurt, pain, ruin, vice, vile **05** amiss, black, cruel, curse, hydra, nasty, wrong **06** deadly, injury, misery, sinful, sorrow, wicked **07** adverse, badness, corrupt, demonic, disease, harmful, heinous, hurtful, illness, immoral, noisome, noxious, ruinous, unlucky, vicious **08** baseness, calamity, depraved, devilish, diabolic, disaster, distress, iniquity, mischief, sinister, stinking, vileness **09** adversity, depravity, injurious, malicious, malignant, malignity, nefarious, offensive, poisonous, suffering **10** affliction, calamitous, corruption, disastrous, immorality, iniquitous, malevolent, misconduct, misfortune, pernicious, sinfulness, wickedness, wrongdoing **11** catastrophe, deleterious, destructive, detrimental, heinousness,

mischievous, unfortunate, viciousness **12** catastrophic, devilishness, inauspicious, unfavourable, unpropitious **13** reprehensible

**evildoer**
**05** rogue **06** sinner **07** badmash, budmash, villain **08** criminal, offender **09** bad person, miscreant, reprobate, scoundrel, wrongdoer **10** delinquent, malefactor **12** transgressor

**evildoing**
**03** sin **07** badness, cruelty **08** iniquity, vileness **09** depravity, nastiness **10** corruption, immorality, sinfulness, wickedness **11** malefaction, malfeasance

**evince**
**04** show **06** attest, betray, reveal **07** bespeak, betoken, confess, declare, display, exhibit, express, signify, witness **08** evidence, indicate, manifest, overcome **09** establish, make clear, overpower **11** demonstrate

**eviscerate**
**03** gut **04** draw **06** paunch **08** gralloch **10** disembowel, exenterate

**evocation**
**04** echo **06** recall **07** arousal, calling **08** inducing, kindling, stirring **10** activation, excitation, invocation, suggestion **11** elicitation, stimulation, summoning-up

**evocative**
**05** vivid **07** graphic **08** redolent **09** memorable **10** expressive, indicative, suggestive **11** reminiscent

**evoke**
**04** call, draw, stir **05** cause, raise, waken **06** arouse, awaken, call up, elicit, excite, induce, invoke, kindle, recall, summon **07** provoke **08** summon up **09** call forth, conjure up, stimulate **10** bring about, call to mind **11** bring to mind

**evolution**
◇ *anagram indicator*
**06** growth **07** biogeny, descent **08** increase, progress, ripening **09** expansion, phytogeny, unfolding, unrolling **10** derivation, noogenesis, opening-out, working-out **11** development, progression, unravelling **12** cladogenesis, Neo-Darwinism, orthogenesis, phytogenesis, transformism

**evolve**
◇ *anagram indicator*
**04** grow **06** derive, emerge, expand, mature, result, unfold, unroll **07** advance, descend, develop, enlarge, open out, unravel, work out **08** develope, disclose, generate, increase, progress **09** elaborate

**ewe**
**03** keb, yow **04** yowe **05** crone, yowie **06** gimmer, lamber, theave

**ex**
**01** X **03** old **04** dead, late **06** former **07** outside, without

**exacerbate**
**03** vex **06** deepen, enrage, worsen **07** inflame, provoke, sharpen **08** embitter, heighten, increase, irritate **09** aggravate, infuriate, intensify, make worse **10** exaggerate, exasperate **12** fan the flames **15** make things worse

**exacerbation**
**09** worsening **10** irritation **11** aggravation **12** embitterment, exaggeration, exasperation **15** intensification

**exact**
**04** even, flat, just, milk, true **05** bleed, claim, close, force, right, wrest, wring **06** bang on, compel, dead on, demand, extort, impose, insist, minute, spot on, square, strict **07** call for, careful, command, correct, estreat, express, extract, factual, literal, orderly, perfect, precise, require, squeeze **08** accurate, definite, detailed, exacting, explicit, faithful, finished, flawless, insist on, punctual, rigorous, specific, thorough, unerring **09** faultless, identical, on the nail, religious, veracious **10** blow-by-blow, consummate, methodical, meticulous, on the money, particular, scrupulous **11** on the button, painstaking, point-device, point-devise, punctilious, word-perfect

**exacting**
**04** firm, hard **05** harsh, stern, tough **06** severe, strict, taxing, tiring **07** arduous, exigent, onerous **08** exigeant, rigorous **09** demanding, difficult, exigeante, laborious, stringent, unsparing **10** fastidious, unyielding **11** challenging, painstaking

**exactitude**
**04** care **05** print **06** detail, rigour **08** accuracy **09** exactness, precision **10** strictness **11** carefulness, correctness, orderliness **12** rigorousness, thoroughness **13** faultlessness, perfectionism **14** meticulousness, scrupulousness **15** painstakingness

**exactly**
**02** on **03** due, e'en, yes **04** dead, even, flat, jump, just, to a T, true **05** plumb, quite, right, smash, spang, truly **06** agreed, bang on, dead on, indeed, just so, spot on, to a tee **07** quite so, to a hair **08** of course, on the dot, strictly, verbatim, you got it **09** carefully, certainly, correctly, expressly, literally, on the nail, precisely **10** absolutely, accurately, definitely, explicitly, faithfully, rigorously, that's right, unerringly **11** faultlessly, on the button, religiously, to the letter, veraciously **12** methodically, particularly, scrupulously, specifically, without error **13** point for point, unequivocally

**• exactly what's looked for**
**02** it

**exactness**
**04** care **06** rigour **08** accuracy, justness **09** precision **10** exactitude, strictness **11** carefulness, correctness, orderliness **12** rigorousness, thoroughness **13** faultlessness **14** meticulousness, scrupulousness

**exaggerate**
**05** color **06** bounce, colour, overdo, stress **07** amplify, distend, enhance, enlarge, lay it on, magnify, stretch **08** overdo it, overdraw, overplay, oversell, pile it on **09** dramatize, embellish, embroider, emphasize, intensify, overstate **10** aggrandize, goliathize, shoot a line **11** overstretch **12** come it strong, lay it on thick, overdo things **13** make too much of, overdramatize, overemphasize, pile it on thick **15** stretch the truth

**exaggerated**
**04** camp, tall **05** steep **07** exalted **08** inflated, overdone **09** amplified, bombastic, excessive, overblown **10** burlesqued, cartoonish, euphuistic, hyperbolic, overstated, theatrical **11** caricatured, embellished, extravagant, overcharged, pretentious **12** overstrained **13** overestimated **14** larger than life

**exaggeration**
**06** excess, parody **07** stretch **08** emphasis **09** burlesque, hyperbole, stretcher **10** caricature **11** enlargement **12** extravagance, overemphasis **13** amplification, embellishment, magnification, overstatement **14** overestimation **15** pretentiousness

**exalt**
**04** laud **05** adore, bless, deify, elate, erect, extol, honor, raise, set up **06** excite, honour, praise, prefer, refine, revere, throne, uplift **07** acclaim, advance, applaud, delight, dignify, elevate, enliven, glorify, magnify, overjoy, promote, sublime, upgrade, upraise, worship **08** enthrone, eulogize, venerate **09** reverence, subtilize, transport **10** aggrandize, enthronize, exhilarate

**exaltation**
**03** joy **05** bliss, glory, larks **06** eulogy, honour, praise **07** acclaim, ecstasy, elation, raising, rapture, worship **08** erection **09** adoration, elevation, promotion, rejoicing, reverence **10** enthusiasm, excitement, jubilation, veneration **11** advancement, high spirits **12** exhilaration **13** glorification **14** aggrandizement

**exalted**
**04** haut, high **05** elate, grand, happy, hault, lofty, moral, noble, regal **06** elated, haught, joyful, lordly **07** eminent, stately, sublime **08** blissful, ecstatic, elevated, exultant, jubilant, magnific, supernal, virtuous **09** dignified, rapturous **10** idealistic, magnifical **11** exaggerated **13** high and

mighty, in high spirits **15** in seventh heaven

**exam, examination**
**02** ex **03** bac, CSE, GCE, MOT, mug **04** exam, GCSE, mods, oral, quiz, scan, test, viva **05** audit, check, final, paper, probe, study, trial **06** Abitur, A-level, biopsy, Greats, higher, O-level, prelim, review, search, survey **07** canvass, check-up, great go, inquiry, perusal **08** analysis, concours, critique, little go, necropsy, once-over, research, scrutiny, viva voce **09** appraisal, exercises, going-over, practical, questions **10** agrégation, assessment, inspection, post-mortem **11** exploration, inquisition, observation, preliminary, questioning **13** baccalaureate, interrogation, investigation

• **reject at examination**
**04** fail, plow, spin **06** plough

**examine**
**03** eye, pry, try, vet **04** case, jerk, palp, pump, quiz, scan, seek, sift, test, view, viva **05** assay, audit, check, grill, probe, quote, study **06** appose, assess, depose, go into, go over, jerque, look at, peruse, ponder, reason, review, revise, search, survey **07** analyse, canvass, check up, collate, discuss, dissect, explore, eyeball, inquire, inspect, observe, palpate, process, weigh up **08** appraise, check out, cognosce, consider, look into, look over, overhale, overhaul, pore over, question, research, traverse, viva voce, work over **09** catechize, check over, check up on, overhaile, speculate **10** go to town on, scrutinize **11** interrogate, investigate **12** cross-examine **13** cross-question **14** put the screws on

**examinee**
**07** entrant **09** applicant, candidate **10** competitor, contestant **11** interviewee

**examiner**
**05** judge, juror **06** censor, critic, marker, reader, tester **07** analyst, arbiter, assayer, auditor **08** assessor, external, reviewer **09** examinant, inspector, moderator, scrutator **10** questioner, scrutineer **11** adjudicator, interviewer, scrutinizer **12** interlocutor

**example**
**02** ex **04** case, lead, type **05** guide, ideal, model, peach, pearl, piece, thing **06** corker, lesson, mirror, muster, sample **07** caution, epitome, exemple, pattern, warning **08** ensample, exemplar, exemplum, exponent, instance, monument, paradigm, specimen, standard **09** archetype, criterion, exemplify, footsteps, precedent, prototype, role model **10** admonition, apotheosis, assay-piece, peacherino, punishment **11** case in point, typical case **12** illustration **14** representative **15** exemplification

• **for example**
**02** as, eg, zb **03** say **04** like **06** such as **10** par exemple **11** as an example, for instance, zum Beispiel **12** as an instance, to illustrate **13** exempli gratia

**exasperate**
**03** bug, irk, vex **04** bait, gall, goad, rile **05** anger, annoy, get to, rouse **06** enrage, madden, needle, rankle, wind up **07** incense, provoke **08** irritate **09** aggravate, infuriate, irritated **14** drive up the wall

**exasperated**
**05** angry, fed up, irked, riled, vexed **06** bugged, galled, goaded, peeved, piqued **07** angered, annoyed, needled, nettled **08** incensed, maddened, provoked **09** indignant, irritated **10** aggravated, infuriated

**exasperating**
**06** vexing **07** galling, irksome **08** annoying, infernal **09** maddening, provoking, vexatious **10** bothersome, confounded, irritating, pernicious **11** aggravating, infuriating, troublesome **12** disagreeable

**exasperation**
**04** fury, rage **05** anger **07** chagrin **09** annoyance **10** discontent, irritation **11** aggravation, indignation, stroppiness **12** exulceration **14** disgruntlement

**excavate**
**03** cut, dig **04** mine, sink **05** delve, dig up, drive, gouge, navvy, scoop, stope **06** burrow, dig out, exhume, hollow, quarry, reveal, tunnel **07** uncover, unearth **08** disinter **09** hollow out

**excavation**
**03** cut, dig, pit **04** delf, hole, mine **05** delph, ditch, drift, graft, heuch, heugh, shaft, stope **06** burrow, cavity, crater, dugout, hollow, mining, quarry, trench, trough **07** cutting, digging, sondage **08** catacomb, colliery, diggings, open-cast **09** burrowing, glory hole, hollowing **10** digging out, exhumation, tunnelling, unearthing **11** countermine, side cutting **12** hollowing out

**exceed**
**03** cap, top **04** beat, pass **05** excel, outdo **06** better, go over, outrun, overdo, overgo **07** eclipse, o'ergang, outrace, overtop, surpass **08** go beyond, outreach, outshine, outstrip, outweigh, overgang, overpass, overstep, overtake **09** outnumber, overshoot, transcend **10** be more than, transgress **12** be larger than, be superior to **13** be greater than

**exceedingly**
**04** main, very **05** amain, dooms **06** damned, highly, hugely, proper, vastly **07** greatly, not half, passing **08** almighty, devilish, heavenly, powerful, very much, wondrous **09** amazingly, extremely, immensely, monstrous, unusually, vengeance **10** consumedly, enormously, especially **11** excessively **12** inordinately, out of all nick, surpassingly **13** astonishingly, exceptionally, superlatively **14** with a vengeance **15** extraordinarily, unprecedentedly

**excel**
**03** war **04** beat, ring **05** outdo, shine **06** better, exceed, outtop, overdo **07** eclipse, outpeer, outrank, succeed, surpass **08** outclass, outrival, overpeer, stand out **09** be skilful **10** outperform **11** be excellent, go one better, predominate **12** be better than, be pre-eminent, be superior to **13** be outstanding **15** go one better than

**excellence**
**05** merit, skill, value, worth **06** purity, virtue, worthy **07** quality **08** eminence, fineness, goodness, nobility **09** greatness, supremacy **10** choiceness, perfection **11** distinction, high quality, pre-eminence, superiority **13** transcendence

**excellent**
**02** A1, ME **03** ace, def, exc, fab, rad **04** best, boss, cool, fine, good, high, mean, mega, neat, pure, rare, tops **05** beaut, boffo, brave, bravo, brill, bully, crack, dicty, dilly, great, hunky, jammy, lummy, noble, noted, prime, socko, triff, wally **06** beauty, beezer, bonzer, castor, cushty, dickty, divine, famous, goodly, groovy, grouse, peachy, purler, ripper, select, spot-on, superb, way-out, whizzo, whizzy, wicked, worthy **07** capital, classic, corking, cracker, crucial, elegant, eminent, kicking, notable, perfect, radical, ripping, shining, stellar, supreme, tipping, topping, triffic, trimmer, Utopian **08** champion, clinking, cracking, eximious, fabulous, flawless, heavenly, inspired, jim-dandy, knockout, smashing, spiffing, splendid, sterling, stonking, stunning, superior, terrific, top-notch, very good, whizbang **09** admirable, brilliant, copacetic, copasetic, exemplary, fantastic, faultless, first-rate, hunky-dory, kopasetic, matchless, righteous, top-drawer, whizz-bang, wonderful **10** first-class, marvellous, noteworthy, not half bad, pre-eminent, remarkable, surpassing, unequalled **11** commendable, exceptional, high-quality, magnificent, outstanding, sensational, superlative **12** praiseworthy, second to none, the bee's knees, unparalleled **13** above reproach, distinguished **14** out of this world **15** unexceptionable

**excellently**
**04** well **06** goodly **08** champion, divinely, superbly **09** admirably, capitally, eminently, first-rate, perfectly **10** remarkably, splendidly **11** brilliantly, commendably, wonderfully

12 marvellously, terrifically
13 exceptionally, fantastically, sensationally, superlatively

**except**
02 ex, sa' 03 bar, but, exc 04 less, omit, only, save, than 05 minus
06 bating, but for, nobbut, reject
07 barring, besides, exclude, outtake, rule out, short of, without 08 leave out, omitting, pass over 09 apart from, aside from, except for, excepting, excluding, other than, outside of
10 leaving out 11 not counting

**exception**
02 ex 03 exc 05 freak, quirk
06 oddity, rarity 07 anomaly, offence
09 departure, deviation, exclusion, objection 11 abnormality, peculiarity, special case 12 irregularity
13 inconsistency
**• take exception**
05 argue, demur, rebut 06 object, oppose, refuse, resist 07 protest
08 complain 09 challenge, repudiate, take issue, withstand 10 disapprove
11 beg to differ, expostulate, remonstrate
**• with the exception of**
03 bar, but 04 less, save 05 minus
07 barring, besides 08 omitting
09 apart from, except for, excepting, excluding, other than 10 leaving out
11 not counting

**exceptionable**
09 abhorrent, offensive, repugnant
10 deplorable, disgusting, unpleasant
12 disagreeable, unacceptable
13 objectionable

**exceptional**
03 odd 04 rare 06 way-out
07 notable, special, strange, unusual
08 aberrant, abnormal, atypical, peculiar, singular, superior, uncommon
09 anomalous, brilliant, excellent, irregular 10 marvellous, noteworthy, phenomenal, prodigious, remarkable, unequalled 11 outstanding
13 extraordinary, one in a million
14 one in a thousand

**exceptionally**
05 extra 06 rarely 07 notably
09 amazingly, extremely, unusually
10 abnormally, especially, remarkably, uncommonly 11 irregularly, wonderfully 13 outstandingly
15 extraordinarily

**excerpt**
04 clip, part 05 piece, quote, scrap
07 cutting, extract, passage, portion, section 08 citation, clipping, fragment, pericope 09 quotation, selection

**excess**
04 glut, rest 05 extra, spare 06 gutful, spilth 07 backlog, nimiety, o'ercome, residue, surfeit, surplus, too much
08 bellyful, left-over, overcome, overflow, overkill, owrecome, plethora, residual 09 leftovers, redundant, remainder, remaining
10 additional, debauchery, oversupply
11 dissipation, exorbitance, exorbitancy, prodigality, superfluity, superfluous, unrestraint
12 extravagance, immoderation, intemperance 13 dissoluteness, overabundance, supernumerary
14 immoderateness, more than enough, overindulgence, superabundance
**• in excess of**
04 over 05 above 08 more than

**excessive**
03 OTT 04 deep, over, rank 05 steep, stiff, undue 06 lavish 07 burning, extreme, fulsome, too much
08 needless, overdone, unneeded
09 exceeding, overblown
10 exorbitant, immoderate, inordinate, over the top 11 extravagant, superfluous, uncalled-for, unnecessary, unwarranted
12 overabundant, unreasonable
13 superabundant

**excessively**
06 overly, troppo, unduly 07 too much
08 overmuch, to a fault, woundily
09 extremely 10 needlessly 11 God-almighty 12 exorbitantly, immoderately, inordinately, out of all cess, unreasonably 13 beyond measure, exaggeratedly, extravagantly, intemperately, superfluously, unnecessarily

**exchange**
◇ *anagram indicator*
02 ex 04 chat, chop, cope, exch, swap, swop 05 bandy, bazar, swits, trade, trock, troke, truck 06 barter, bazaar, change, excamb, market, niffer, scorse, switch 07 bargain, commute, convert, dealing, replace, traffic 08 argument, commerce, dialogue, trade-off
09 transpose 10 discussion, stand in for, substitute 11 give and take, interchange, reciprocate, reciprocity, replacement 12 conversation, substitution

**excise**
03 cut, GST, tax, VAT 04 duty, levy, toll
05 erase 06 cut off, cut out, delete, impost, remove, tariff 07 customs, destroy, expunge, extract, rescind
09 eradicate, expurgate, extirpate, surcharge 11 exterminate

**excision**
◇ *deletion indicator*
03 cut 07 removal 08 deletion
10 expunction 11 destruction, eradication, expurgation, extirpation
13 extermination

**excitable**
04 edgy 05 fiery, hasty, nappy, nervy
06 feisty 07 nervous, rackety
08 choleric, volatile 09 emotional, hot-headed, irascible, mercurial, sensitive 10 passionate
11 combustible, hot-tempered, susceptible 12 highly-strung 13 quick-tempered, temperamental

**excite**
◇ *anagram indicator*
04 fire, move, stir, sway, urge, wake, warm, whet, yerk 05 evoke, flush, hop up, impel, rouse, steer, stire, styre, touch, upset, waken 06 accite, aerate, arouse, awaken, emmove, enmove, fire up, ignite, incite, induce, kindle, stir up, thrill, tickle, turn on, wind up, work up
07 agitate, animate, commove, disturb, enliven, ferment, impress, inflame, inspire, provoke, upraise 08 blow away, energize, engender, enkindle, generate, irritate, motivate
09 electrify, galvanize, instigate, sensitize, set on edge, stimulate, suscitate, titillate 10 bring about, intoxicate

**excited**
◇ *anagram indicator*
02 up 03 het, hot 04 high, warm, wild
05 antsy, astir, eager, hyper, moved, nervy, proud, radge, randy 06 elated, juiced, randie, roused 07 aroused, fevered, fired up, flushed, frantic, hyped up, sexed-up, stirred, uptight
08 agitated, animated, frenzied, hopped-up, restless, revved-up, thrilled, turned on, worked up
09 delirious, red-headed, wrought-up
10 corybantic, stimulated, up in the air
11 exhilarated, overwrought
12 enthusiastic 13 in high spirits, on tenterhooks 14 beside yourself, thrilled to bits

**excitement**
03 ado, rut, tew 04 fume, fuss, kick, ruff, spin, stir 05 fever, furor, kicks, pride, ruffe 06 action, didder, dither, flurry, furore, hoop-la, thrill, tumult, unrest 07 arousal, elation, emotion, ferment, passion 08 activity, brouhaha, delirium, erethism, flat spin, hilarity, pleasure 09 adventure, agitation, animation, commotion, eagerness, fleshment, rousement, sensation 10 enthusiasm, salutation
11 fun and games, stimulation
12 discomposure, exhilaration, Hobson-Jobson, intoxication, perturbation, restlessness
**• expression of excitement**
04 whee 05 yahoo 06 yippee 07 way to go! 08 hey-go-mad
**• seeking excitement**
04 fast
**• state of excitement**
10 fever pitch

**exciting**
03 hot 04 sexy 05 heady, magic
06 moving 07 rousing 08 dramatic, excitant, gripping, stirring, striking
09 inspiring, thrilling 10 nail-biting
11 aphrodisiac, enthralling, hair-raising, interesting, provocative, sensational, stimulating 12 action-packed, breathtaking, cliff-hanging, electrifying, exhilarating, intoxicating
13 swashbuckling
**• something exciting**
03 gas

**exclaim**
**03** cry **04** call, roar, yell **05** blurt, shout, utter **06** bellow, cry out, outcry, shriek **07** declare **08** blurt out, proclaim **09** ejaculate, interject **10** vociferate **11** come out with, exclamation

**exclamation**
**02** ho, wo **03** boo, cry, fen, hip, olé, pah, tut, ugh, woe, wow, yah, yay **04** call, go on, hech, I say!, oops, phew, pish, poof, pooh, push, roar, sa sa, shoo, skol, upsy, when, yell **05** bingo, fancy, house, hurra, my hat!, shout, skoal, upsee, upsey, yahoo **06** banzai, bellow, by Jove, hooray, hurrah, hurray, outcry, phooey, shriek, shucks, walker, whoops, zounds **07** bless me!, crivens, good egg, good-now, heigh-ho, hosanna, right on, whoopee **08** crivvens, hear hear!, here goes!, man alive, stroll on! **09** expletive, fancy that, good grief, unberufen, utterance **10** ecphonesis, epiphonema, Great Scott!, hoity-toity, how dare you!, upon my soul! **11** bless my soul!, bumpsadaisy, ejaculation, good heavens, marry come up **12** boomps-a-daisy, Hookey Walker, interjection, strike a light! **15** shiver my timbers
• **exclamation mark**
**05** pling **06** shriek **08** screamer

**exclude**
**03** ban, bar **04** drop, omit, skip, veto **05** debar, eject, evict, expel, hatch **06** delete, except, forbid, ice out, ignore, refuse, reject, remove **07** boot out, boycott, keep out, kick out, lock out, miss out, push out, rule out, shut off, shut out, turf out **08** count out, disallow, leave out, preclude, prohibit, throw out **09** blacklist, eliminate, freeze out, interdict, ostracize **10** include out **13** excommunicate **14** send to Coventry

**excluding**
◇ *deletion indicator*
**06** except **07** barring **08** omitting **09** debarring, except for, excepting, ruling out **10** leaving out **11** exclusive of, not counting **12** not including

**exclusion**
**03** ban, bar **04** veto **07** boycott, embargo, refusal, removal **08** ejection, eviction, omission **09** exception, expulsion, interdict, rejection, ruling out **10** preclusion **11** elimination, prohibition, repudiation **12** proscription

**exclusive**
**03** few **04** chic, coup, only, posh, sole **05** plush, ritzy, scoop, swish, total, whole **06** choice, classy, cliquy, closed, clubby, exposé, narrow, select, single, snazzy, unique **07** cliquey, elegant, limited, private **08** boutique, cliquish, complete, peculiar, rarefied, snobbish, unshared, up-market **09** high-class, sectarian, sensation, undivided **10** individual, restricted, revelation, upper-crust **11** fashionable, inside story, restrictive **12** incompatible **14** discriminative
• **exclusive of**
**06** except **07** barring **08** omitting **09** debarring, except for, excepting, excluding, ruling out **10** leaving out **11** not counting **12** not including

**excommunicate**
**03** ban, bar **05** curse, debar, eject, expel **06** banish, outlaw, remove **07** exclude **08** denounce, execrate, unchurch **09** blacklist, proscribe, repudiate **12** anathematize **13** disfellowship

**excommunication**
**07** banning, barring **08** ejection **09** exclusion, expulsion, outlawing **10** banishment **11** unchurching **12** denunciation **13** disfellowship

**excoriate**
**03** nag **04** carp, slam **05** blame, decry, knock, slate, snipe **06** attack **07** censure, condemn, nit-pick, run down **08** denounce **09** denigrate, disparage **10** animadvert, come down on, vituperate **12** disapprove of **13** find fault with

**excrement**
**03** poo **04** crap, crud, dung, flux, mess, poop **05** frass, guano, scats, stool **06** doo-doo, egesta, faeces, ordure **09** droppings, excretion **11** waste matter **12** rejectamenta, sir-reverence

**excrescence**
**03** bur, pin **04** blot, boil, bump, burr, knob, lump, moss, nail, nurl, wart, wolf **05** knurl **06** cancer, growth, tumour, wattle **07** eyesore, rat-tail, sarcoma, twitter **08** rat's-tail, swelling **09** appendage, carnosity, misgrowth, outgrowth **10** projection, prominence, proud flesh **11** monstrosity, twitter-bone **12** intumescence, protuberance **13** disfigurement

**excrete**
**03** poo **04** crap, pass, void **05** eject, expel, exude **07** secrete, urinate **08** defecate, evacuate **09** discharge

**excretion**
**03** poo **04** crap, dung **05** stool **06** faeces, ordure **07** excreta **09** discharge, droppings, excrement, urination **10** defecation, evacuation **12** perspiration

**excruciate**
◇ *anagram indicator*
**04** rack **07** torture **08** irritate

**excruciating**
**05** acute, sharp **06** bitter, savage, severe **07** burning, extreme, intense, painful, racking **08** piercing **09** agonizing, atrocious, harrowing, torturing **10** tormenting, unbearable **11** intolerable **12** cringe-making, cringeworthy, insufferable

**excruciatingly**
**07** acutely **08** severely **09** extremely, intensely, painfully **10** unbearably **11** atrociously, intolerably

**exculpate**
**04** free **05** clear **06** acquit, excuse, let off, pardon **07** absolve, deliver, forgive, justify, release **09** discharge, exonerate, vindicate

**excursion**
**02** ex **03** exc **04** raid, ride, tour, trip, walk **05** drive, jaunt, jolly, sally, visit **06** airing, detour, junket, outing, picnic, ramble, sashay, sortie, vagary **07** day trip, journey, outleap **08** breather, escapade, straying **09** departure, diversion, wandering **10** digression, expedition **11** mystery tour **12** pleasure trip

**excusable**
**05** minor **06** slight, venial **09** allowable **10** defensible, forgivable, pardonable **11** explainable, justifiable, permissible **14** understandable

**excuse**
**04** faik, free, hook, plea **05** alibi, front, salvo, scuse, shift, spare **06** acquit, cop-out, defend, essoin, exempt, get-out, ignore, let off, pardon, reason **07** absolve, apology, condone, cover-up, defence, essoyne, evasion, explain, forgive, grounds, indulge, justify, pretext, release, relieve **08** liberate, mitigate, occasion, overlook, palliate, pretence, tolerate **09** allowance, discharge, exculpate, exonerate, vindicate **10** indulgence, mitigation, substitute **11** exoneration, explanation, forgiveness, vindication **12** apologize for **13** justification **14** whittie-whattie

**execrable**
**04** foul, vile **05** awful **06** odious **07** hateful, heinous **08** accursed, damnable, dreadful, horrible, nauseous, shocking **09** abhorrent, appalling, atrocious, loathsome, obnoxious, offensive, repulsive, revolting **10** abominable, deplorable, despicable, detestable, disgusting

**execrate**
**04** damn, hate **05** abhor, blast, curse **06** detest, loathe, revile, vilify **07** condemn, deplore, despise **08** denounce **09** abominate, excoriate, fulminate, imprecate **10** denunciate **12** anathematize **14** inveigh against

**execute**
**02** do **03** cut, fry, run **04** hang, kill, take **05** dance, enact, serve, shoot, stage, throw **06** behead, effect, finish, fulfil, render **07** achieve, crucify, deliver, enforce, garotte, garrote, perform, produce, realize **08** bring off, carry out, complete, despatch, dispatch, engineer, expedite, garrotte, validate **09** discharge, implement, liquidate **10** accomplish, administer, consummate, decapitate, guillotine,

perpetrate, put to death **11** electrocute **13** put into effect **15** put into practice

**execution**
**03** run **04** mode **05** style **06** effect, manner **07** killing, staging **08** delivery, dispatch **09** discharge, effecting, enactment, operation, rendering, rendition, technique **10** completion, fulfilment **11** achievement, carrying-out, enforcement, performance, realization **12** consummation, death penalty, presentation **13** death sentence **14** accomplishment, administration, implementation, putting to death

*Execution methods include:*

**06** noyade
**07** burning, gassing, hanging, stoning
**08** lynching, shooting
**09** beheading
**10** garrotting
**11** crucifixion, firing squad, stringing up
**12** decapitation, guillotining
**13** electric chair, electrocution
**15** lethal injection

**executioner**
**06** axeman, hit man, killer, slayer **07** hangman **08** assassin, carnifex, headsman, murderer **09** deathsman, Jack Ketch, tormenter, tormentor **10** liquidator **11** firing squad **12** exterminator **15** Monsieur de Paris

**executive**
**02** ex **04** exec, suit **06** leader **07** big guns, guiding, leading, manager **08** big shots, chairman, director, governor, official, superior, top brass **09** directing, governing, hierarchy, lawmaking, organizer **10** chairwoman, controller, government, leadership, management, managerial, organizing, regulating **11** chairperson, controlling, directorial, ministerial, supervisory **13** administrator **14** administration, administrative, decision-making, organizational, superintendent

**exegesis**
**09** opening-up **10** exposition, expounding **11** explanation, explication **13** clarification **14** interpretation

**exemplar**
**04** copy, type **05** ideal, model **07** epitome, example, paragon, pattern, sampler **08** instance, paradigm, specimen, standard **09** archetype, criterion, prototype, yardstick **10** embodiment **12** illustration **15** exemplification

**exemplary**
**04** good **05** ideal, model **06** worthy **07** correct, perfect, warning **08** flawless, laudable **09** admirable, estimable, excellent, faultless **10** admonitory, cautionary, honourable **11** commendable, meritorious **12** praiseworthy

**exemplify**
**03** sum **04** cite, show, type **06** depict, embody, typify **07** display, example, exhibit **08** instance, manifest **09** epitomize, personify, represent **10** illustrate, synonymize **11** demonstrate **12** characterize **13** be an example of

**exempt**
**04** free **05** clear, exeem, exeme, spare, waive **06** excuse, immune, let off, spared **07** absolve, dismiss, exclude, excused, release, relieve **08** absolved, excluded, liberate, released **09** discharge, dismissed, exonerate, liberated, not liable **10** discharged, not subject **11** grandfather **15** grant immunity to, make an exception

**exemption**
**07** freedom, release **08** immunity, variance **09** discharge, exception, exclusion, indemnity, privilege **10** absolution, indulgence, indulgency, overslaugh **11** exoneration **12** dispensation

**exercise**
◇ *anagram indicator*
**02** PE, PT **03** gym, jog, try, use, vex **04** task, work **05** annoy, apply, drill, exert, sport, theme, train, upset, wield, worry **06** burden, effort, employ, labour, lesson, sports, warm up, warm-up **07** afflict, agitate, concern, disturb, exploit, perturb, problem, project, running, trouble, utilize, work out, workout **08** activity, ceremony, distress, exertion, movement, practice, practise, pump iron, training, warm down, warm-down **09** discharge, discourse, implement, make use of, operation, preoccupy, quodlibet **10** assignment, discipline, employment, fulfilment, gymnastics, isometrics **11** application, bring to bear, do exercises, piece of work, utilization **12** exercitation **13** bring into play, exert yourself **14** accomplishment, implementation

*Exercises include:*

**04** yoga
**05** Medau
**06** qigong, t'ai chi
**07** aquafit, chi kung, jogging, keep fit, Pilates, press-up
**08** aerobics
**09** boxercise, hatha yoga
**10** aquarobics, daily dozen, dancercise
**11** Callanetics, eurhythmics
**12** body-building, calisthenics, step aerobics
**13** callisthenics, cross-training, physical jerks
**15** circuit training

**exert**
**02** do **03** use **05** apply, spend, wield **06** employ, expend, extend, put out **07** utilize **08** exercise, put forth **11** bring to bear **13** bring into play
• **exert yourself**
**04** hump, pull, toil, work **05** sweat **06** labour, pingle, strain, strive **07** try hard **08** go all out, slog away, struggle **09** endeavour, take pains **10** do your best **11** give your all **12** do your utmost **13** apply yourself **15** make every effort

**exertion**
**03** use **04** toil, work **05** graft, pains, trial **06** action, effort, labour, pingle, strain, stress **07** attempt, travail, trouble **08** endeavor, exercise, industry, striving, struggle **09** diligence, endeavour, hard graft, operation **10** employment **11** application, utilization **12** perseverance **13** assiduousness

**exhalation**
**04** mist **06** meteor, vapour **08** emission, fumosity, mephitis **09** discharge, effluvium, emanation, expulsion **10** expiration **11** evaporation, respiration **12** breathing-out

**exhale**
**04** blow, emit, reek **05** expel, issue, smoke, steam **06** expire, vanish **07** blow out, breathe, emanate, give off, respire **08** perspire **09** discharge, evaporate, transpire **10** breathe out

**exhaust**
**02** do **03** beg, dry, sap, tax **04** do in, jade, kill, poop, suck, tire, wear **05** drain, empty, fordo, fumes, smoke, spend, steam, use up, waste, weary, whack **06** expend, fag out, finish, strain, vapour, weaken **07** consume, deplete, fatigue, knacker, overrun, overtax, play out, tire out, wash out, wear out, work out **08** bankrupt, emission, enervate, forspend, forswink, knock out, overlive, override, overteem, overtire, overwork, squander, weary out **09** discharge, dissipate, emanation, forespend, overshoot, overspend, overweary, overwrite, tucker out **10** almost kill, exhalation, impoverish, nearly kill, run through **11** take it out of

**exhausted**
**03** dry **04** done, mate, shot, void, weak, worn **05** all in, empty, jaded, spent, tired, weary **06** all out, beaten, bushed, done in, effete, pooped, used up, wabbit, wasted, zonked **07** at an end, drained, emptied, euchred, fainted, fordone, puggled, shagged, shotten, waygone, whacked, worn out **08** a cot case, burnt out, consumed, dead-beat, depleted, dog-tired, fatigued, finished, forfairn, half-dead, jiggered, tired out, wiped out **09** burned out, dead tired, enervated, enfeebled, fagged out, knackered, played-out, pooped out, prostrate, shattered, stonkered, washed-out, zonked out **10** clapped-out, euchred out, forfeuchen, forfoughen, shagged out **11** bush whacked, forfoughten, ready to drop, stressed-out, tuckered out

**exhausting**
**04** hard **06** severe, taxing, tiring
**07** arduous, killing, testing, wearing
**08** draining, grueling, wearying
**09** depletion, gruelling, laborious, punishing, strenuous **10** enervating, formidable **12** backbreaking, debilitating

**exhaustion**
**06** jet-lag **07** fatigue **08** distress, lethargy, weakness **09** tiredness, weariness **10** enervation, feebleness

**exhaustive**
**04** full **05** total **06** all-out **07** in-depth
**08** complete, detailed, sweeping, thorough **09** extensive, full-scale, intensive **10** definitive **11** far-reaching
**12** all-embracing, all-inclusive, encyclopedic **13** comprehensive

**exhaustively**
**05** fully **07** totally **10** completely, thoroughly **11** extensively, intensively
**12** definitively **14** all-inclusively
**15** comprehensively

**exhibit**
**03** air **04** hang, shew, show, wear
**05** array, exude, model, offer, sport
**06** expose, flaunt, parade, reveal, set out, unveil **07** display, express, present, propose, showing **08** disclose, discover, indicate, manifest, set forth, showcase **09** make clear, make plain, showpiece **10** exhibition
**11** demonstrate **12** illustration, presentation, put on display
**13** demonstration

**exhibition**
**04** demo, expo, fair, gift, show
**05** grant, rodeo, Salon, simul **06** airing
**07** academy, diorama, display, exhibit, ice show, preview, showing
**08** aquacade, pavilion, showcase, sideshow, waxworks **09** allowance, spectacle **10** cattle show, disclosure, exposition, expression, flower show, indication, panopticon, puppet show, revelation **11** performance
**12** presentation, simultaneous
**13** cinematograph, demonstration, manifestation, retrospective
**14** representation

**exhibitionism**
**09** dramatics, flaunting, staginess
**10** overacting, showing-off
**11** flamboyance, histrionics, self-display **12** boastfulness

**exhibitionist**
**05** poser **06** poseur **07** show-off
**09** extrovert **14** self-advertiser

**exhilarate**
**04** lift **05** cheer, elate **06** excite, perk up, thrill **07** animate, cheer up, delight, elevate, enliven, gladden **08** brighten, vitalize **09** inebriate, make happy, stimulate **10** intoxicate, invigorate, revitalize **11** make excited

**exhilarating**
**05** heady, sapid **06** breezy
**08** cheerful, cheering, exciting
**09** heartsome, thrilling **10** delightful, enlivening, gladdening **11** mind-blowing, stimulating **12** breathtaking, intoxicating, invigorating, revitalizing
**13** heart-stirring

**exhilaration**
**03** joy **04** dash, élan, glee, zeal
**05** gusto, mirth **06** ardour, gaiety, thrill
**07** delight, elation **08** euphoria, gladness, hilarity, vivacity
**09** animation, happiness
**10** enthusiasm, exaltation, excitement, joyfulness, joyousness, liveliness
**11** high spirits, stimulation
**12** cheerfulness, invigoration
**14** revitalization

**exhort**
**03** bid **04** goad, spur, urge, warn
**05** press **06** advise, call on, enjoin, incite, prompt **07** beseech, caution, counsel, entreat, implore, inflame, inspire **08** admonish, call upon, persuade **09** encourage, instigate

**exhortation**
**04** call **06** advice, appeal, sermon, urging **07** bidding, caution, counsel, goading, lecture, warning **08** entreaty
**09** enjoinder, parenesis
**10** admonition, allocution, beseeching, incitement, injunction, invitation, paraenesis, persuasion, protreptic **13** encouragement

**exhumation**
**10** excavation, unearthing
**12** disinterment **13** disentombment

**exhume**
**05** dig up **06** unbury **07** unearth
**08** disinter, excavate **09** disentomb, disinhume, resurrect

**exigency**
**04** need, turn **06** crisis, demand, plight, stress **07** urgency **08** distress, pressure, quandary **09** emergency, necessity **10** difficulty **11** predicament, requirement **12** criticalness
**14** imperativeness

**exigent**
**06** urgent **07** crucial **08** critical, exacting, pressing **09** demanding, extremity, insistent, necessary, stringent

**exiguous**
**04** bare, slim **05** scant **06** meagre, scanty, slight, sparse **07** slender
**10** inadequate, negligible
**12** insufficient

**exile**
**03** ban, bar **04** exul, oust **05** eject, expat, expel, Galut **06** banish, deport, émigré, Galuth, outlaw, pariah, uproot, wretch **07** Babylon, cast out, outcast, refugee **08** deportee, Diaspora, drive out, fugitive, separate **09** expulsion, extradite, ostracism, ostracize, uprooting **10** banishment, expatriate, repatriate, separating, separation
**11** deportation **12** expatriation
**13** excommunicate **14** transportation
**15** displaced person

**exist**
**02** be **04** last, live **05** abide, occur, stand **06** endure, happen, remain
**07** be alive, be found, breathe, consist, persist, prevail, subsist, survive
**08** continue, have life **09** be present, have being **10** have breath **11** be available **13** eke out a living, have existence

**existence**
**03** ens **04** esse, fact, life **05** being, thing **06** breath, entity, living
**07** inbeing, reality **08** creation, creature, survival, the world
**09** actuality, endurance, lifestyle, way of life **11** continuance, subsistence, way of living **12** continuation, mode of living **13** individuation
• **loss of independent existence**
03 LIE

**existent**
**04** real **05** alive **06** actual, around, extant, living **07** abiding, current, present **08** enduring, existing, standing **09** obtaining, remaining, surviving **10** prevailing **11** in existence

**exit**
**02** go **03** die **04** door, gate, vent
**05** death, going, go out, issue, leave
**06** depart, egress, exodus, flight, log off, log out, outlet, retire, way out
**07** doorway, leaving, off-ramp, outgate, retreat **08** farewell, withdraw
**09** departure **10** going forth, retirement, withdrawal **11** leave-taking
**13** take your leave

**exodus**
**02** Ex **04** exit, Exod **06** escape, flight, hegira **07** fleeing, leaving, retreat
**09** departure, long march, migration
**10** evacuation, retirement, withdrawal
**13** mass departure **14** mass evacuation

**exonerate**
**04** free **05** clear, spare **06** acquit, excuse, exempt, let off, pardon
**07** absolve, justify, release, relieve
**08** liberate **09** discharge, exculpate, vindicate **15** declare innocent

**exoneration**
**06** pardon, relief **07** amnesty, freeing, release **08** clearing, excusing, immunity **09** acquittal, discharge, dismissal, exemption, indemnity
**10** absolution, liberation
**11** exculpation, vindication
**13** justification

**exorbitant**
**05** steep, undue **07** a rip-off
**08** enormous **09** excessive, monstrous
**10** immoderate, inordinate
**11** extravagant, unwarranted
**12** extortionate, preposterous, unreasonable **15** daylight robbery

**exorbitantly**
**06** unduly **11** excessively
**12** immoderately, inordinately,

unreasonably **13** extravagantly **14** extortionately, through the nose

**exorcism**
**07** freeing **09** expulsion **10** adjuration, casting out **11** deliverance **12** exsufflation, insufflation, purification

**exorcize**
**03** lay **04** free **05** expel **06** adjure, purify **07** cast out **08** drive out **10** exsufflate, insufflate

**exotic**
◇ *anagram indicator*
**05** alien **06** ethnic, way-out **07** bizarre, curious, foreign, strange, unusual **08** external, imported, peculiar, striking, tropical **09** colourful, different, glamorous, non-native, recherché **10** impressive, introduced, outlandish, outrageous, remarkable, unfamiliar **11** extravagant, fascinating, sensational **13** extraordinary

**exotically**
**09** curiously, strangely, unusually **10** remarkably, strikingly, tropically **12** impressively, outlandishly **13** sensationally **15** extraordinarily

**expand**
**03** pad **04** grow **05** swell, widen **06** blow up, dilate, extend, fatten, intend, put out, spread, unfold, unfurl, work up **07** amplify, broaden, develop, distend, enlarge, fill out, inflate, magnify, open out, puff out, stretch, thicken **08** dispread, enlargen, escalate, increase, lengthen, multiply, mushroom **09** branch out, diversify, intensify, intumesce **10** decompress, make bigger, make larger **12** become bigger, become larger
• **expand on**
**08** dilate on, flesh out **09** embroider, enlarge on **11** elaborate on, expatiate on **13** go into details

**expanse**
**03** sea **04** area, main, mass, moor, muir, vast **05** field, ocean, plain, range, sheet, space, sweep, tract, vague, waste **06** extent, region, spread **07** breadth, stretch **08** vastness **09** champaign, immensity, outspread **11** immenseness **13** extensiveness

**expansion**
**04** boom **06** growth, spread **07** expanse **08** dilation, increase, swelling **09** diffusion, explosion, extension, inflation, unfolding, unfurling **10** broadening, dilatation, distension, thickening **11** development, enlargement, lengthening **12** augmentation **13** amplification, decompression, magnification **14** multiplication **15** diversification

**expansive**
**04** open, warm, wide **05** broad **06** genial **07** affable, growing **08** effusive, friendly, outgoing, sociable, sweeping, thorough **09** diffusive, enlarging, expanding, extensive, talkative **10** developing, increasing, loquacious, magnifying, widespread **11** expatiative, expatiatory, forthcoming, multiplying, uninhibited, wide-ranging **12** all-embracing, diversifying **13** communicative, comprehensive

**expatiate**
**06** dilate, expand **07** amplify, develop, dwell on, enlarge, expound **08** enlargen **09** elaborate, embellish, give forth **11** hold forth on

**expatriate**
**04** oust **05** exile, expat, expel **06** banish, deport, émigré, exiled, uproot **07** outcast, refugee **08** banished, deported, drive out, emigrant, expelled, uprooted **09** extradite, ostracize, proscribe **10** repatriate **15** displaced person

**expect**
**04** hope, look, wait, want, ween, wish **05** await, guess, think, trust **06** ask for, assume, bank on, demand, lippen, look to, reckon, rely on **07** believe, call for, count on, foresee, hope for, imagine, look for, predict, presume, project, require, suppose, surmise **08** envisage, figure on, forecast, insist on, think for, watch for **09** bargain on, look after **10** anticipate, bargain for, conjecture **11** contemplate **13** look forward to

**expectancy**
**04** hope **07** waiting **08** suspense **09** curiosity, eagerness **10** conjecture **11** expectation **12** anticipation

**expectant**
**05** eager, great, quick, ready **06** gravid **07** anxious, curious, excited, hopeful **08** awaiting, carrying, enceinte, preggers, pregnant, watchful **09** expecting, in the club, in trouble, with child **10** big-bellied, in suspense **11** open-mouthed **12** anticipating, apprehensive **13** on tenterhooks **14** in the family way, looking forward **15** with bated breath

**expectantly**
**07** eagerly **09** hopefully **10** in suspense **11** expectingly **14** apprehensively, in anticipation, optimistically

**expectation**
**04** hope, view, want, wish **05** trust **06** belief, demand **07** outlook, promise, suppose, surmise **08** forecast, optimism, prospect, reliance, suspense, tendance **09** assurance, eagerness **10** assumption, confidence, conjecture, insistence, looking-for, prediction, projection **11** calculation, possibility, presumption, probability, requirement, supposition **12** anticipation

**expecting**
**05** great, quick **06** gravid **08** carrying, enceinte, preggers, pregnant **09** expectant, in the club, in trouble, with child **10** big-bellied **14** in the family way

**expedience**
**05** haste **07** aptness, benefit, fitness, utility **08** despatch, dispatch, prudence **09** advantage, propriety **10** enterprise, expediency, pragmatism, properness, usefulness **11** convenience, helpfulness, suitability **12** advisability, desirability, practicality **13** effectiveness, judiciousness, profitability **14** profitableness, utilitarianism **15** appropriateness

**expedient**
**04** plan, ploy **05** dodge, means, salvo, shift, trick **06** device, method, scheme, tactic, useful **07** fitting, measure, politic, prudent, stopgap **08** artifice, resource, sensible, suitable, tactical **09** advisable, manoeuvre, opportune, practical, pragmatic, stratagem **10** beneficial, convenient, profitable **11** appropriate, contrivance, expeditious **12** advantageous

**expedite**
**05** hurry, press, quick **06** assist, hasten, prompt, step up **07** further, promote, quicken, speed up **08** despatch, dispatch **09** discharge **10** accelerate, facilitate **11** precipitate **12** hurry through, unencumbered

**expedition**
**03** dig **04** crew, hike, raid, sail, team, tour, trek, trip **05** group, haste, party, quest, shoot, speed **06** outing, ramble, safari, voyage **07** company, crusade, hosting, journey, mission, project, warpath **08** alacrity, campaign **09** adventure, excursion, field trip, swiftness **10** enterprise, pilgrimage, promptness **11** exploration, undertaking

**expeditious**
**04** fast **05** alert, brisk, hasty, quick, rapid, ready, swift **06** active, prompt, speedy **07** express, instant **08** diligent, meteoric **09** efficient, expedient, immediate

**expel**
**03** ban, bar, rid **04** hoof, oust, void **05** belch, eject, evict, exile **06** banish, deport, let out, outlaw, put out, reject **07** boot out, cast out, dismiss, drum out, expulse, extrude, fire out, kick out, read out, spew out, turn out **08** chuck out, drive out, evacuate, send down, sideline, throw out **09** discharge, eliminate, proscribe, turn forth **10** expatriate

**expend**
**03** buy, pay, sap, use **04** blow **05** drain, empty, spend, use up, waste **06** afford, employ, lay out, outlay, pay out **07** consume, deplete, dispend, exhaust, fork out, fritter, procure, utilize

**08** disburse, purchase, shell out, squander **09** dissipate, go through, overspend, splash out **10** get through

**expendable**
**09** throwaway **10** disposable
**11** dispensable, inessential, replaceable, unimportant, unnecessary **12** non-essential

**expenditure**
**03** use **04** mise **05** costs, outgo, waste **06** outlay, output **07** expense, payment, sapping **08** dispense, draining, expenses, outgoing, spending **09** goings-out, outgoings **10** employment **11** application, consumption, dissipation, squandering, utilization
**12** disbursement
• **reduction of expenditure**
**02** ax **03** axe **06** saving
**11** economizing

**expense, expenses**
**03** fee **04** cost, harm, loss, rate
**05** costs, price **06** charge, outlay
**07** payment **08** spending
**09** detriment, outgoings, overheads, paying-out, sacrifice **11** expenditure, incidentals **12** disadvantage, disbursement
• **share of expense**
**03** law

**expensive**
**04** dear, posh, salt **05** fancy, pricy, steep **06** costly, lavish, pricey **07** sky-high **08** high-cost, splendid **09** big-ticket, chargeful, excessive, executive
**10** exorbitant, high-priced, overpriced
**11** costing a lot, extravagant **12** costing a bomb, extortionate **15** costing the earth, daylight robbery

**experience**
**03** see, try **04** case, face, feel, find, have, know, meet, pass, spin **05** event, skill, taste **06** affair, endure, expert, ordeal, suffer **07** contact, episode, knowhow, receive, sustain, undergo
**08** exposure, incident, learning, perceive, practice, training
**09** adventure, encounter, go through, happening, knowledge **10** occurrence
**11** familiarity, involvement, live through, observation, pass through
**12** circumstance **13** participate in, participation, understanding
• **cause to experience**
**04** lead
• **irritating experience**
**03** rub **06** rubber
• **lacking experience**
**05** green, naive
• **painful experience**
**03** fit

**experienced**
**03** old **04** wise **05** adept, suave, tried
**06** around, au fait, expert, mature
**07** capable, skilful, skilled, trained, veteran, weighed **08** familiar, schooled, seasoned, traveled **09** au courant, competent, practised, qualified, travailed, travelled
**10** proficient, streetwise, well-versed
**11** worldly wise **12** accomplished, experimented, professional
**13** knowledgeable, sophisticated

**experiment**
**03** exp, try **04** test **05** assay, essay, proof, trial **06** dry run, sample, try out, try-out, verify **07** attempt, examine, explore, inquiry, observe, testing, venture **08** analysis, dummy run, piloting, research, trial run
**09** procedure **10** conclusion, experience, pilot study **11** examination, investigate, observation **13** carry out tests, demonstration, investigation, trial and error **15** experimentation

**experimental**
**03** exp **04** test **05** pilot, trial
**09** empirical, peirastic, tentative
**10** scientific **11** exploratory, preliminary, provisional, speculative
**13** investigative, observational, trial-and-error **15** at the trial stage

**experimentally**
**11** empirically, tentatively
**12** innovatively, provisonally **13** by rule of thumb, speculatively
**14** scientifically **15** by trial and error, investigatively

**experimentation**
**07** zoopery **08** research
**10** empiricism, pragmatism
**11** exploration, rule of thumb
**12** verification **13** inventiveness, investigation

**expert**
**03** ace, dab, don, gun, pro, sly **04** able, buff, nark, oner, up on **05** adept, crack, fundi, maven, mavin, one-er, whizz
**06** boffin, master, pundit, wunner
**07** dab hand, egghead, hotshot, maestro, old hand, skilful, skilled, wise guy **08** dextrous, masterly, top-notch, virtuoso, well up on **09** authority, brilliant, dexterous, excellent, old master, practised, qualified
**10** experience, past master, proficient, specialist **11** cognoscente, connoisseur, experienced
**12** accomplished, practitioner, professional **13** knowledgeable

**expertise**
**05** knack, skill **07** ability, command, finesse, knowhow, mastery
**08** deftness, facility **09** dexterity, knowledge **10** cleverness, expertness, tradecraft, virtuosity **11** proficiency, savoir-faire, skilfulness
**13** understanding **15** professionalism

**expertly**
**04** ably **07** capably **08** masterly
**09** skilfully **11** competently, efficiently, excellently **12** proficiently
**14** professionally

**expiate**
**05** atone, purge **06** attone, pay for
**07** redress, work out **08** atone for
**09** make up for **12** do penance for
**13** make amends for

**expiation**
**06** amends, ransom, shrift
**07** penance, redress **09** atonement
**10** recompense, redemption, reparation

**expire**
**03** die, end **04** emit, stop **05** cease, close, lapse **06** depart, finish, pass on, peg out, perish, pop off, run out
**07** decease, snuff it **08** conclude, pass away, pass over **09** have had it, terminate **11** bite the dust, come to an end, discontinue **12** lose your life, pop your clogs **13** kick the bucket, meet your maker **14** depart this life, give up the ghost **15** be no longer valid, breathe your last, cash in your chips

**expiry**
**03** end, exp, ish **05** close, lapse
**06** finish **09** cessation **10** conclusion, expiration **11** termination
**15** discontinuation

**explain**
**04** tell **05** gloze, solve, teach
**06** decode, defend, define, excuse, open up, set out, unfold **07** clarify, expound, justify, resolve, unravel
**08** decipher, describe, disclose, simplify, spell out, untangle
**09** delineate, elaborate, elucidate, enucleate, explicate, interpret, lie behind, make clear, translate, vindicate
**10** account for, illustrate
**11** demonstrate, explain away, rationalize, shed light on **12** throw light on **14** give a reason for

**explanation**
**04** note **05** alibi, gloss **06** answer, excuse, motive, reason, report
**07** account, comment, defence, meaning, warrant **08** apologia, decoding, exegesis, footnote, solution
**09** unfolding **10** annotation, commentary, definition, exposition, expounding **11** deciphering, delineation, description, elucidation, explication, vindication **12** illustration
**13** clarification, demonstration, justification **14** interpretation, reconciliation, simplification
**15** éclaircissement, rationalization

**explanatory**
**08** exegetic **10** exegetical, expositive, expository, justifying **11** declaratory, descriptive, elucidative, elucidatory, explicative **12** illustrative, interpretive
**13** demonstrative **14** interpretative

**expletive**
**04** cuss, oath **05** curse **08** anathema, cussword **09** blasphemy, obscenity, profanity, swear-word **10** execration
**11** bad language, imprecation **14** four-letter word

**explicable**
**08** solvable **09** definable, exponible
**10** resolvable **11** accountable, explainable, justifiable
**12** determinable, intelligible
**13** interpretable **14** understandable

**explicate**
**06** define, unfold **07** clarify, develop, explain, expound, unravel, work out **08** describe, set forth, spell out, untangle **09** elucidate, interpret, make clear **10** illustrate **11** demonstrate

**explication**
**10** exposition **11** description, elucidation, explanation **12** illustration **13** clarification **14** interpretation

**explicit**
**04** open **05** adult, bawdy, clear, dirty, exact, frank, plain **06** candid, direct, filthy, full-on, smutty, stated, X-rated **07** certain, express, obscene, pointed, precise **08** absolute, declared, definite, detailed, distinct, hard-core, positive, shocking, specific **09** offensive, outspoken **10** forthright, uncensored, unreserved **11** categorical, near the bone, plain-spoken, unambiguous, unequivocal, uninhibited **12** pornographic, unrestrained **14** near the knuckle **15** straightforward

**explicitly**
**06** barely **07** clearly, in terms, overtly, plainly **08** directly **09** expressly **10** definitely **12** specifically **13** in so many words, unambiguously, unequivocally

**explode**
◇ *anagram indicator*
**04** blow, boom, go up, leap **05** blast, burst, erupt, go off, rebut, surge **06** blow up, debunk, go bang, refute, rocket, see red, set off, spring **07** flare up **08** boil over, burst out, detonate, displode, disprove, escalate, mushroom **09** blow a fuse, discharge, discredit, do your nut, fulminate, repudiate **10** accelerate, hit the roof, invalidate **11** blow your top, go up the wall, grow rapidly, lose your rag **12** blow your cool, fly into a rage, give the lie to, lose your cool **13** hit the ceiling **14** lose your temper **15** fly off the handle, go off the deep end

**• cause to explode**
**04** fire **06** spring **08** detonate **09** fulminate

**exploit**
**03** act, tap, use **04** deed, feat, gest, milk, mine **05** abuse, apply, bleed, geste, stunt **06** action, draw on, employ, fleece, misuse, rip off **07** oppress, utilize **08** activity, cash in on, ill-treat, impose on, profit by **09** adventure, make use of, profiteer **10** attainment, manipulate **11** achievement, walk all over **12** capitalize on, put to good use, take for a ride **13** take liberties, turn to account **14** accomplishment, play off against, pull a fast one on **15** take advantage of

**exploitation**
**03** use **05** abuse **06** misuse, rip-off **07** milking **08** bleeding, fleecing **10** employment, oppression **11** application, cashing in on, making use of, utilization **12** manipulation **14** taking for a ride **15** taking advantage

**exploration**
**04** tour, trip **05** probe, study **06** safari, search, survey, travel, voyage **07** inquiry **08** analysis, research, scrutiny **10** expedition, inspection **11** examination, observation **13** investigation **14** reconnaissance

**exploratory**
**05** pilot, trial **07** probing, wildcat **08** analytic **09** searching, tentative **11** fact-finding **12** experimental **13** investigative

**explore**
**02** do **04** feel, palp, tour **05** probe, scout, study **06** review, search, survey, travel **07** analyse, examine, inspect **08** consider, look into, prospect, research, traverse **10** scrutinize **11** inquire into, investigate, reconnoitre, see the world

**explorer**
**05** scout **06** tourer **08** surveyor **09** navigator, traveller **10** discoverer, prospector **11** bandeirante **12** reconnoitrer

*Explorers and pioneers include:*

**03** **Cam**, **Caõ**, **Rae** (John)
**04** **Byrd** (Richard Evelyn), **Cano** (Juan Sebastian del), **Cook** (James), **Diaz** (Bartolomeu), **Eyre** (Edward John), **Gama** (Vasco da), **Park** (Mungo), **Polo** (Marco), **Ross** (Sir James Clark), **Soto** (Fernando de), **Soto** (Hernando de)
**05** **Barth** (Heinrich), **Beebe** (Charles William), **Boone** (Daniel), **Bruce** (James), **Cabot** (John), **Clark** (William), **Drake** (Francis), **Fuchs** (Sir Vivian Ernest), **Hanno**, **Lewis** (Meriwether), **Newby** (Eric), **Oates** (Lawrence), **Peary** (Robert Edwin), **Scott** (Robert Falcon), **Speke** (John Hanning)
**06** **Baffin** (William), **Balboa** (Vasco Núñez de), **Bering** (Vitus), **Burton** (Sir Richard), **Cabral** (Pedro Alvares), **Carson** (Kit), **Nansen** (Fridtjof), **Tasman** (Abel Janszoon), **Torres** (Luis de)
**07** **Andrews** (Roy Chapman), **Fiennes** (Sir Ranulph), **Fleming** (Peter), **Hillary** (Sir Edmund), **La Salle** (Robert Cavelier, Sieur de), **Pytheas**, **Raleigh** (Sir Walter), **Stanley** (Sir Henry Morton)
**08** **Amundsen** (Roald), **Columbus** (Christopher), **Cousteau** (Jacques), **Flinders** (Matthew), **Franklin** (Sir John), **Linnaeus** (Carolus), **Magellan** (Ferdinand), **Standish** (Myles), **Thesiger** (Sir Wilfred), **Vespucci** (Amerigo), **Williams** (Roger)
**09** **Emin Pasha**, **Frobisher** (Sir Martin), **Heyerdahl** (Thor), **Rasmussen** (Knud), **Vancouver** (George)
**10** **Erik the Red**, **Oglethorpe** (James Edward), **Shackleton** (Sir Ernest Henry), **Van der Post** (Sir Laurens)
**11** **Livingstone** (David)
**12** **Leif Eriksson**, **Younghusband** (Sir Francis)
**14** **Bellingshausen** (Fabian Gottlieb von), **Blashford-Snell** (Colonel John), **Hanbury-Tenison** (Robin Airling)

**explosion**
**03** fit, pop **04** bang, boom, chug, clap, leap, rage, roll **05** blast, burst, crack, pluff, surge **06** blow-up, report, rumble **07** Big Bang, flare-up, tantrum, thunder **08** airburst, eruption, outbreak, outburst, paroxysm **09** discharge **10** detonation, displosion **14** dramatic growth, sudden increase

**explosive**
◇ *anagram indicator*
**02** HE **04** bomb, mine, wild **05** angry, fiery, jelly, rapid, tense **06** abrupt, raging, stormy, sudden, touchy **07** charged, fraught, violent **08** critical, dramatic, meteoric, perilous, powerful, unstable, volatile, volcanic, worked-up **09** dangerous, fulminant, hazardous, initiator, plastique, rocketing, sensitive **10** burgeoning, propellant, unexpected **11** exponential, mushrooming, overwrought **12** nerve-racking, unrestrained

*Explosives include:*

**03** RDX, TNT
**04** ANFO
**06** amatol, dualin, Semtex®, tonite
**07** ammonal, cordite, dunnite, lyddite, plastic
**08** cheddite, dynamite, melinite, roburite, xyloidin
**09** cyclonite, gelignite, guncotton, gunpowder, xyloidine
**11** nitrocotton
**14** nitrocellulose, nitroglycerine, trinitrotoluol
**15** trinitrotoluene

**explosively**
**06** wildly **07** angrily, fierily, rapidly, tensely **08** suddenly, unstably **09** violently **10** critically, powerfully **11** dangerously, hazardously **12** dramatically, unexpectedly, volcanically **13** destructively, exponentially

**exponent**
**05** adept, index, power **06** backer, expert, master, player **08** adherent, advocate, champion, defender, promoter, upholder **09** performer, proponent, spokesman, supporter **10** specialist **11** spokeswoman **12** practitioner, spokesperson

**export**
**02** ex **03** exp **05** trade **08** deal with, Klondike, Klondyke, re-export, transfer **09** traffic in, transport **10** sell abroad

12 foreign trade, sell overseas
13 exported goods 15 exported product

**expose**
03 ope 04 open, risk, show 05 flash, strip 06 betray, detect, hazard, reveal, show up, unmask, unveil 07 display, divulge, exhibit, imperil, lay bare, lay open, present, uncover, unearth
08 denounce, disclose, endanger, manifest 09 lay open to, make known, put at risk, subject to 10 jeopardize
11 introduce to, present with
12 acquaint with, bring to light 13 put in jeopardy, take the lid off 14 blow the whistle, make vulnerable 15 familiarize with

**exposé**
07 account, article 08 exposure
10 disclosure, divulgence, revelation, uncovering

**exposed**
03 out 04 bare, open 05 naked, shown 06 object, on show, on view
07 subject 08 laid bare, revealed
09 exhibited, in the open, on display
10 vulnerable 11 susceptible, unprotected

**exposition**
04 expo, fair, show 05 moral, paper, study 06 aperçu, exposé, theory, thesis 07 account, display, exposal, Midrash, working 08 analysis, critique, exegesis 09 discourse, monograph, unfolding 10 commentary, enarration, exhibition 11 description, elucidation, explanation, explication
12 illumination, illustration, presentation 13 clarification, demonstration 14 interpretation

**expository**
08 exegetic 11 declaratory, descriptive, elucidative, explanatory, explicatory, hermeneutic
12 illustrative, interpretive
14 interpretative

**expostulate**
05 argue, claim, plead 06 reason
07 protest 08 disagree, dissuade
11 remonstrate

**exposure**
03 air 04 hype, plug, risk 05 flash
06 airing, danger, exposé, hazard
07 contact, display, exposal, showing
08 jeopardy 09 awareness, detection, discovery, exposture, knowledge, notoriety, promotion, publicity, unmasking, unveiling 10 disclosure, divulgence, exhibition, experience, revelation, uncovering 11 advertising, familiarity 12 acquaintance, denunciation, presentation
13 manifestation, vulnerability
14 susceptibility 15 public attention

**expound**
04 open, read, rede 06 open up, preach, set out, unbolt, unfold
07 analyse, clarify, dissect, explain, unravel 08 describe, prophesy, set forth, spell out, untangle 09 comment on, elucidate, explicate, interpret, sermonize 10 illuminate, illustrate
11 demonstrate

**express**
02 ex 03 air, exp, put, say 04 emit, fast, have, show, sole, tell, vent, word
05 brisk, clear, couch, exact, plain, quick, rapid, speak, state, swift, utter, voice 06 assert, convey, denote, depict, embody, intend, report, reveal, speedy, stated, strain 07 certain, declare, divulge, exhibit, get over, non-stop, precise, put over, signify, special, testify 08 announce, clear-cut, conceive, definite, disclose, distinct, explicit, indicate, intimate, manifest, point out, positive, register, specific, stand for 09 designate, enunciate, estafette, formulate, high-speed, pronounce, put across, represent, specially, symbolize, ventilate, verbalize 10 articulate, particular
11 categorical, communicate, demonstrate, expeditious, give voice to, unambiguous, unequivocal, well-defined 12 put into words

**expression**
◇ *homophone indicator*
03 air 04 look, mien, show, sign, term, tone, word 05 adage, axiom, depth, force, idiom, maxim, power, scowl, style, voice 06 aspect, phrase, saying, speech, symbol, vigour 07 diction, emotion, feeling, gesture, grimace, passion, proverb, voicing, wording
08 aphorism, artistry, delivery, language, locution, phrasing
09 assertion, intensity, set phrase, statement, utterance, verbalism, vividness 10 appearance, creativity, embodiment, exhibition, indication, intimation, intonation, modulation
11 countenance, declaration, enunciation, imagination
12 announcement, articulation, illustration, proclamation, turn of phrase, vocalization
13 communication, demonstration, manifestation, pronouncement, verbalization 14 representation
• **prevent free expression**
03 gag

**expressionless**
04 dull 05 blank, empty 06 glassy, glazed 07 deadpan, vacuous
08 toneless 09 impassive, unmeaning
10 poker-faced 11 emotionless, inscrutable, meaningless 13 straight-faced

**expressive**
05 vivid 06 lively, moving 07 showing, telling 08 animated, eloquent, emphatic, forceful, poignant, striking
09 evocative, revealing, speechful
10 articulate, indicative, meaningful, suggesting, suggestive, thoughtful
11 informative, significant, sympathetic
13 communicative, demonstrating, demonstrative

**expressively**
07 vividly 09 meaningly
10 eloquently, espressivo
11 evocatively 12 emphatically, meaningfully, suggestively
13 informatively 15 demonstratively

**expressiveness**
09 poignancy, vividness 10 articulacy
13 evocativeness 14 articulateness, meaningfulness

**expressly**
◇ *homophone indicator*
06 solely 07 clearly, exactly, plainly
09 decidedly, on purpose, pointedly, precisely, purposely, specially
10 absolutely, definitely, distinctly, especially, explicitly, manifestly
12 particularly, specifically
13 categorically, intentionally, unambiguously, unequivocally

**expropriate**
04 take 05 annex, seize, usurp
06 assume 07 impound, unhouse
08 arrogate, disseise, take away
09 sequester 10 commandeer, confiscate, dispossess 11 appropriate, requisition

**expropriation**
07 seizure 10 arrogation, impounding, taking-away 12 confiscation
13 appropriation, dispossession, sequestration

**expulsion**
05 exile, purge 07 removal, sacking, the boot, the sack, voiding
08 belching, ejection, eviction
09 discharge, dismissal, ejectment, exclusion, excretion, extrusion, ostracism, rejection 10 banishment, evacuation 11 throwing out

**expunge**
04 raze 05 annul, erase 06 cancel, delete, efface, remove, rub out
07 abolish, blot out, destroy, wipe out
08 cross out, get rid of 09 eradicate, extirpate 10 annihilate, extinguish, obliterate 11 exterminate

**expurgate**
03 cut 04 geld 05 emend, purge
06 censor, purify 07 clean up
08 sanitize 10 blue-pencil, bowdlerize

**exquisite**
04 fine, keen, pink, rare 05 acute, sharp 06 choice, dainty, lovely, picked, pretty, too-too 07 elegant, fragile, intense, perfect, refined 08 abstruse, charming, cultured, delicate, flawless, piercing, pleasing, poignant, precious
09 beautiful, delicious, excellent, sensitive 10 attractive, cultivated, delightful, discerning, far-fetched, fastidious, impeccable, meticulous
11 outstanding 14 discriminating

**exquisitely**
06 finely 08 daintily 09 elegantly
10 charmingly, delicately, pleasingly
11 beautifully 12 attractively, delightfully

**ex-serviceman**
**03** vet **07** veteran

**extant**
**05** alive **06** living **08** existent, existing **09** remaining, surviving **10** subsistent, subsisting **11** in existence **13** still existing

**extempore**
**05** ad-lib **07** offhand **08** suddenly **09** ad libitum, impromptu, unplanned **10** improvised, off the cuff, unprepared, unscripted **11** spontaneous, unrehearsed **13** spontaneously **14** extemporaneous

**extemporize**
**04** pong **05** ad-lib **06** make up, wing it **09** improvise **11** play it by ear **15** speak off the cuff, think on your feet

**extend**
**02** go **03** lap, run **04** draw, give, grow, last, pass, span **05** cover, grant, offer, range, reach, renew, seize, value, widen **06** assess, bestow, come to, confer, deploy, expand, go up to, impart, intend, put out, spread, step up, take in, unfold, unwind **07** amplify, augment, broaden, carry on, develop, drag out, draw out, embrace, enlarge, hold out, include, involve, present, produce, proffer, prolong, spin out, stretch **08** come up to, continue, elongate, go down to, increase, lengthen, protract, put forth, reach out **09** go as far as, intensify **10** come down to, comprehend

**extendable**
**07** elastic **08** stretchy **09** dilatable, extensive **10** expandable **11** enlargeable, magnifiable, stretchable

**extended**
**04** long, wide **06** spread **07** distent, lengthy **08** at length, enlarged, expanded **09** amplified, continued, developed, expansive, increased, prolonged **10** diastaltic, lengthened

**extension**
**03** ext **04** wing **05** add-on, delay **06** annexe **07** adjunct, stretch **08** addendum, addition, appendix, deferral, increase, more time, protense, quantity, widening **09** diffusion, expansion **10** broadening, elongation, production, stretching, supplement **11** development, enhancement, enlargement, lengthening, protraction **12** continuation, postponement, prolongation **13** proliferation **14** additional time

**extensive**
**04** huge, long, main, vast, wide **05** broad, large, roomy **07** general, in depth, lengthy **08** complete, extended, far-flung, sizeable, spacious, thorough **09** boundless, capacious, fair-sized, pervasive, prevalent, universal, unlimited, wholesale **10** commodious, large-scale, voluminous, widespread **11** far-reaching, substantial, wide-ranging **12** all-inclusive **13** comprehensive

**extensively**
**06** widely **07** greatly, largely **09** generally, wholesale **10** completely, thoroughly **11** boundlessly **13** substantially **15** comprehensively

**extent**
**04** area, bulk, play, size, span, term, time **05** level, limit, range, reach, scope, sweep, width **06** amount, attack, bounds, degree, length, sphere, spread, volume **07** breadth, compass, expanse, lengths, measure, seizure, stretch **08** coverage, duration, quantity **09** dimension, magnitude **10** dimensions

• **to full extent**
**04** hard, much

• **to some extent**
◇ *hidden indicator*

• **to that extent**
**02** as

• **to the extent of**
**02** by **03** for

**extenuate**
**06** excuse, lessen, modify, soften **07** qualify **08** diminish, minimize, mitigate, palliate

**extenuating**
**08** excusing **09** lessening, modifying, softening **10** justifying, minimizing, mitigating, moderating, palliating, palliative, qualifying **11** diminishing, exculpatory, extenuative, extenuatory

**exterior**
**03** ext **04** face, skin **05** glaze, outer, shell **06** façade, finish **07** coating, foreign, outside, outward, surface **08** covering, external **09** externals, extrinsic, objective, outermost **10** appearance, peripheral **11** superficial, surrounding **12** outer surface **15** external surface

**exterminate**
**04** do in, kill **06** kill up **07** abolish, bump off, destroy, kill off, wipe out **08** knock off, massacre **09** eliminate, eradicate, extirpate, liquidate, slaughter **10** annihilate, do away with

**extermination**
**07** killing **08** genocide, massacre **09** ethnocide **11** destruction, elimination, eradication, extirpation **12** annihilation

**external**
**03** ext, out **05** outer **07** foreign, outside, outward, surface, visible **08** apparent, cortical, exterior, visiting **09** extrinsic, outermost **10** accidental, extramural, extraneous, peripheral **11** independent, non-resident, superficial

**externally**
**03** ext **07** visibly **09** outwardly **10** apparently **12** extraneously, peripherally **13** superficially

**extinct**
**03** ext, old, out **04** dead, gone, lost **05** ended, passé **06** bygone, former **07** defunct, died out, expired, invalid **08** burnt out, inactive, obsolete, outmoded, quenched, squashed, vanished, wiped out **09** abolished **10** antiquated, terminated **11** non-existent **12** exterminated, extinguished

**extinction**
**05** death **07** quietus **08** dying-out, excision **09** abolition, vanishing **11** destruction, eradication, termination **12** annihilation, obliteration **13** disappearance, extermination

**extinguish**
**03** end **04** dout, kill **05** choke, douse, dowse, drown, erase, quash, quell, slake **06** die out, put out, quench, remove, rub out, sloken, stifle **07** abolish, blow out, destroy, expunge, slocken, smother, stub out **08** snuff out, suppress **09** eliminate, eradicate, extirpate **10** annihilate, dampen down **11** exterminate

**extirpate**
**04** root **05** erase **06** cut out, remove, uproot **07** abolish, destroy, expunge, root out, weed out, wipe out **08** stamp out **09** eliminate, eradicate **10** annihilate, deracinate, extinguish **11** exterminate

**extol**
**04** laud, puff **05** exalt, raise **06** lift up, praise **07** acclaim, advance, applaud, commend, glorify, magnify **08** eulogize **09** celebrate **10** rhapsodize, wax lyrical

**extort**
**04** milk, rack **05** bleed, bully, exact, force, screw, wrest, wring **06** coerce **07** extract, squeeze **08** get out of, outwrest **09** blackmail, shake down

**extortion**
**05** chout, force **06** demand **07** milking **08** chantage, coercion, exaction **09** blackmail **10** oppression **12** malversation, racketeering

**extortionate**
**04** hard **05** harsh **06** severe **08** exacting, grasping, grinding **09** excessive, rapacious **10** exorbitant, immoderate, inordinate, oppressive, outrageous **12** preposterous, unreasonable

**extortionist**
**05** screw, shark **06** yakuza **07** bleeder, exacter, exactor, menacer **09** exactress, exploiter, profiteer, racketeer **11** blackmailer, bloodsucker, extortioner

**extra**
**01** w **02** ex, lb, nb **03** bye, ext, new, odd, too **04** also, gash, more, over, wide **05** added, bonus, fresh, other, spare, super- **06** as well, excess, leg bye, no ball, unused, walk-on

**07** adjunct, and so on, another, besides, further, reserve, surplus **08** addendum, addition, additive, buckshee, left-over, let alone, unneeded **09** accessory, along with, ancillary, appendage, auxiliary, bit player, excessive, extension, extremely, minor role, redundant, unusually **10** additional, attachment, complement, especially, in addition, remarkably, subsidiary, supplement, uncommonly, walk-on part **11** superfluous, unnecessary **12** additionally, not to mention, particularly, spear-carrier, together with **13** exceptionally, extraordinary, not forgetting, supernumerary, supplementary **14** above and beyond, into the bargain **15** extraordinarily

**extract**
◇ *anagram indicator*
◇ *hidden indicator*
**03** ext, get, gut, try **04** cite, clip, copy, cull, draw, grog, milk, pick, pull, suck, worm **05** educe, exact, glean, juice, pluck, prise, quote, wrest, wring **06** choose, cut out, decoct, derive, distil, elicit, extort, gather, get out, gobbet, obtain, quarry, remove, render, select, uproot, wrench **07** cutting, derived, draw out, essence, estreat, excerpt, extrait, logwood, passage, pull out, recover, spirits, take out **08** abstract, boil down, citation, clipping, euonymin, pericope, withdraw **09** decoction, enucleate, quotation, reproduce, selection **10** deracinate, distillate **11** concentrate **12** distillation

**extraction**
**04** race **05** birth, blood, brood, stock **06** family, origin **07** descent, drawing, extreat, lineage, pulling, removal **08** ancestry, pedigree **09** obtaining, parentage, retrieval, taking-out, uprooting **10** derivation, drawing-out, separation, withdrawal

**extradite**
**05** exile, expel **06** banish, deport **08** hand over, send back, send home **10** repatriate

**extradition**
**05** exile **08** handover **09** expulsion **10** banishment **11** deportation, sending back **12** repatriation

**extraneous**
**05** alien, extra, inapt **07** foreign, strange **08** exterior, external, needless, unneeded **09** extrinsic, redundant, unrelated **10** additional, immaterial, inapposite, incidental, irrelevant, peripheral, tangential **11** inessential, superfluous, unconnected, unessential, unnecessary **12** inapplicable, non-essential **13** inappropriate, supplementary

**extraordinarily**
◇ *anagram indicator*
**05** oddly **07** notably **08** uniquely **09** amazingly, bizarrely, curiously, specially, strangely, unusually **10** remarkably, uncommonly **12** astoundingly, particularly, unexpectedly **13** exceptionally, significantly

**extraordinary**
◇ *anagram indicator*
**03** odd **04** rare **06** unique **07** amazing, bizarre, curious, notable, special, strange, unusual **08** peculiar, singular, uncommon **09** by-ordinar, emergency, fantastic, wonderful **10** astounding, marvellous, noteworthy, particular, portentous, remarkable, surprising, tremendous, unexpected **11** astonishing, exceptional, outstanding, significant **13** unprecedented **14** out of this world, unconventional

**extrapolate**
**04** plan **05** gauge **06** expect, reckon, sample **07** project **08** estimate **09** calculate **11** approximate

**extraterrestrial**
**02** ET **05** alien

**extravagance**
**05** extra, folly, treat, waste **06** excess, luxury, vanity **07** riotise, splurge **08** wildness **09** profusion **10** digression, enthusiasm, imprudence, lavishness, ornateness, profligacy **11** dissipation, ostentation, prodigality, squandering **12** exaggeration, immoderation, improvidence, overspending, recklessness, wastefulness **13** excessiveness **14** outrageousness, thriftlessness **15** pretentiousness

**extravagant**
◇ *anagram indicator*
**03** OTT **04** dear, wild **05** outré, steep **06** costly, flashy, lavish, ornate, pricey, rococo **07** baroque, bizarre, profuse, sky-high **08** fanciful, prodigal, reckless, romantic, wasteful **09** excessive, expensive, fanatical, fantastic, high-flown, imprudent, irregular, wasterful **10** exorbitant, extra modum, flamboyant, high-flying, immoderate, outrageous, overpriced, over the top, profligate, thriftless **11** exaggerated, improvident, pretentious, spendthrift, squandering **12** costing a bomb, extortionate, ostentatious, preposterous, unrestrained **15** churrigueresque, costing the earth, daylight robbery

**extravaganza**
**04** show **06** féerie **07** display, pageant **09** spectacle **11** spectacular

**extreme**
◇ *head selection indicator*
◇ *tail selection indicator*
◇ *ends selection indicator*
**03** end, top **04** acme, apex, dire, edge, last, line, mark, peak, pink, pole, wack **05** acute, depth, final, great, gross, harsh, limit, rigid, stern, ultra, utter **06** climax, excess, far-off, height, red-hot, severe, strict, utmost, zenith **07** distant, drastic, endmost, faraway, highest, intense, maximum, outside, radical, serious, supreme, zealous **08** farthest, greatest, hardline, outlying, pinnacle, remotest, terminal, ultimate **09** desperate, downright, Draconian, excessive, extremist, extremity, fanatical, out-and-out, outermost, stringent, uttermost **10** immoderate, inordinate, iron-fisted, iron-handed, most remote, pre-eminent, remarkable, unyielding **11** exceptional, termination, unrelenting **12** unreasonable **13** extraordinary **14** uncompromising

**• in the extreme**
**04** very **06** highly **07** awfully, greatly, utterly **08** terribly **09** intensely **10** dreadfully, remarkably, uncommonly **11** exceedingly, excessively, frightfully **12** immoderately, inordinately, terrifically **13** exceptionally **15** extraordinarily

**• opposite extreme**
**04** pole

**extremely**
◇ *ends selection indicator*
**03** too **04** high, mega, very **05** jolly **06** deuced, highly, mighty, mortal, pretty, really **07** acutely, awfully, greatly, majorly, only too, parlous, utterly **08** deucedly, severely, terribly **09** decidedly, intensely, seriously, unusually **10** dreadfully, remarkably, thoroughly, uncommonly **11** exceedingly, excessively, frightfully **12** immoderately, inordinately, terrifically, tremendously, unreasonably **13** exceptionally **15** extraordinarily

**extremism**
**04** zeal **08** zealotry **09** terrorism **10** fanaticism, radicalism **13** excessiveness

**extremist**
**05** ultra **06** zealot **07** diehard, fanatic, Jacobin, radical **08** militant **09** hardliner, terrorist **11** merveilleux **12** merveilleuse **14** fundamentalist

**extremity**
**03** arm, end, fix, jam, leg, tip, toe, top **04** acme, apex, edge, foot, hand, hole, limb, mess, peak, pole, spot, tail **05** bound, brink, depth, limit, point, verge **06** apogee, border, crisis, danger, ending, excess, finger, height, margin, pickle, plight, zenith **07** exigent, extreme, maximum, minimum, trouble **08** boundary, exigency, frontier, hardship, outrance, pinnacle, terminal, terminus, ultimate **09** adversity, emergency, indigence, periphery, tight spot, utterance **10** misfortune **11** dire straits, termination

**extricate**
**04** free **05** clear **06** detach, get out, remove, rescue **07** deliver, extract,

outwind, release, relieve, set free
**08** let loose, liberate, withdraw
**09** disengage **11** disentangle

**extrinsic**
**05** alien **06** exotic **07** foreign, outside
**08** exterior, external, imported
**10** extraneous, forinsecal

**extrovert**
**03** lad **05** mixer **06** joiner **07** mingler
**08** outgoing **10** socializer **14** outgoing person, sociable person

**extroverted**
**06** hearty **07** amiable **08** amicable, friendly, outgoing, sociable
**09** exuberant **13** demonstrative
**14** outward-looking

**extrude**
**05** expel, mould **08** force out, press out, protrude, put forth **09** thrust out
**10** squeeze out

**exuberance**
**04** life, zest **05** pride **06** energy, vigour **07** elation, pizzazz **08** buoyancy, lushness, outburst, rankness, richness, vitality, vivacity **09** abundance, animation, eagerness, plenitude, profusion **10** ebullience, enthusiasm, excitement, lavishness, liveliness, luxuriance, luxuriancy, redundancy
**11** copiousness, fulsomeness, high spirits, joie de vivre, prodigality
**12** cheerfulness, effusiveness, exaggeration, exhilaration
**13** effervescence, excessiveness
**14** superabundance

**exuberant**
**03** mad **04** lush, rank, rich **06** elated, lavish, lively, skippy **07** buoyant, excited, fulsome, profuse, zestful
**08** abundant, animated, cheerful, effusive, spirited, thriving, vigorous
**09** ebullient, energetic, luxuriant, luxurious, plenteous, plentiful, sparkling, vivacious **10** boisterous, full of life **11** exaggerated, exhilarated, overflowing **12** effervescent, enthusiastic, high-spirited, rambunctious, unrestrained
**13** irrepressible **15** on top of the world

**exude**
**03** gum **04** emit, leak, ooze, seep, show, weep, well **05** bleed, issue, still, sweat, swelt **07** display, emanate, excrete, exhibit, flow out, give off, give out, guttate, radiate, secrete, swelter, trickle **08** manifest, perspire
**09** discharge

**exult**
**03** joy **04** crow **05** gloat, glory, revel
**06** relish **07** delight, rejoice, triumph
**08** be joyful, jubilate **09** celebrate
**10** tripudiate **11** be delighted **13** be over the moon

**exultant**
**06** elated, joyful, joyous **07** gleeful
**08** exulting, jubilant, thrilled **09** cock-a-hoop, delighted, overjoyed, rejoicing, revelling **10** enraptured, triumphant **11** on cloud nine, over the moon **12** transporting **15** in seventh heaven

**exultation**
**03** joy **04** glee, pean **05** glory, paean
**06** eulogy **07** crowing, delight, elation, triumph **08** gloating, glorying
**09** jubilance, jubilancy, merriness, rejoicing, revelling, transport
**10** joyfulness, joyousness, jubilation
**11** celebration

**eye**
**02** ee **03** aim, orb, see **04** glim, glom, lamp, mind, ogle, peep, scan, view
**05** brood, light, optic, sight, study, taste, watch **06** appear, assess, belief, gaze at, keeker, look at, notice, ocular, peeper, peruse, regard, survey, vision, winker **07** blinker, examine, goggler, inspect, lookout, observe, ocellus, opinion, pigsney, stare at **08** eyesight, glance at, ommateum **09** attention, awareness, judgement, viewpoint, vigilance, water pump **10** estimation, perception, scrutinize **11** contemplate, discernment, observation, point of view, recognition, sensitivity
**12** appreciation, surveillance, watchfulness **13** look up and down, power of seeing, way of thinking
**14** discrimination, faculty of sight

*Eye parts include:*

**03** rod
**04** cone, irid, iris, lens, uvea
**05** fovea, pupil, white
**06** areola, cornea, eyelid, retina, sclera
**07** choroid, eyeball, eyelash, papilla, vitreum
**08** chorioid, tear duct
**09** blind spot, optic disc
**10** optic nerve
**11** ciliary body, conjunctiva, lower eyelid, upper eyelid
**12** chorioid coat, lacrimal duct, ocular muscle
**13** aqueous humour, lachrymal duct, sclerotic coat
**14** lachrymal gland, vitreous humour
**15** anterior chamber, crystalline lens, hyaloid membrane

---

**• black eye**
**05** mouse **06** keeker, shiner
**• keep an eye on**
**04** mind **07** monitor **08** attend to
**09** look after **10** keep tabs on, take care of **12** watch closely
**• reflection in eye**
**04** baby
**• see eye to eye**
**05** agree **06** concur, go with **07** be at one **11** be of one mind, go along with
**• set eyes on**
**03** see **04** meet **06** behold, notice
**07** observe **08** come upon
**09** encounter, lay eyes on **10** clap eyes on, come across
**• up to your eyes**
**04** busy **06** tied up **08** involved, occupied **09** engrossed, inundated
**11** overwhelmed, snowed under
**13** overstretched **14** fully stretched

**eyebrow**
**04** bree

**eye-catching**
**05** showy **08** gorgeous, imposing, striking, stunning **09** arresting, beautiful, prominent **10** attractive, impressive, noticeable **11** captivating, conspicuous, spectacular

**eye-opener**
**06** wonder **10** disclosure, revelation
**14** quite something, surprising fact
**15** surprising thing

**eyes**
**03** een **04** eine, eyne

**eyeshadow**
**04** kohl

**eyesight**
**04** view **05** sight **06** vision
**10** perception **11** observation
**13** power of seeing **14** faculty of sight

**eyesore**
**03** sty **04** blot, mess, scar, stye
**06** blight, horror **07** blemish
**08** atrocity, disgrace, ugliness
**09** carbuncle **10** defacement
**11** monstrosity **13** disfigurement

**eyewitness**
**06** viewer **07** watcher, witness
**08** looker-on, observer, onlooker, passer-by **09** bystander, spectator

# F

**F**
**02** ef **07** foxtrot

**fable**
**03** lie **04** epic, myth, saga, tale, yarn
**05** feign, story **06** invent, legend
**07** fiction, Märchen, parable, untruth
**08** allegory, apologue **09** falsehood, invention, moral tale, tall story
**11** fabrication **12** old wives' tale

*Fable writers include:*

**03** **Ade** (George), **Fay** (András), **Gay** (John)
**04** **Esop**, **Ruiz** (Juan)
**05** **Aesop**, **Boner** (Ulrich), **Torga** (Miguel)
**06** **Bidpai**, **Dryden** (John), **Halévy** (Lon), **Krylov** (Ivan), **Ramsay** (Allan), **Tessin** (Carl-Gustaf)
**07** **Arreola** (Juan José), **Babrius**, **Fénelon** (François de Salignac de la Mothe), **Gellert** (Christian Fürchtegott), **Iriarte** (Tomás de), **Kipling** (Rudyard), **Sologub** (Fyodor)
**08** **Andersen** (Hans Christian), **de France** (Marie), **Phaedrus**, **Saltykov** (Michail)
**09** **Furetière** (Antoine)
**10** **La Fontaine** (Jean de)
**15** **Iriarte y Oropesa** (Tomás de)

**fabled**
**05** famed **06** famous **07** feigned
**08** mythical, renowned **09** legendary
**10** celebrated, remarkable

**fabric**
**03** web **05** cloth, frame, stuff
**06** make-up **07** textile, texture
**08** material **09** construct, framework, structure **10** contexture
**11** foundations **12** constitution, construction, organization
**14** infrastructure

*Fabrics include:*

**03** aba, abb, kid, net, rep, rug, say, tat
**04** abba, aida, baft, buff, ciré, cord, drab, duck, ecru, felt, harn, ikat, jean, kelt, lace, lamé, lawn, leno, line, lyne, mull, nude, pall, piña, puke, repp, reps, roan, silk, wool
**05** abaya, baize, batik, beige, braid, camel, chino, crape, crash, crêpe, denim, dhoti, doily, doyly, drill, duroy, foulé, gauze, gazar, gunny, jaspé, kente, khaki, linen, lisle, llama, loden, Lurex®, Lycra®, moire, ninon, nylon, Orlon®, panne, piqué, plaid, plush, rayon, satin, scrim, serge, suede, surah, tabby, tamin, tammy, terry, Tibet, toile, tulle, tweed, twill, voile, wigan
**06** alpaca, angora, armure, barège, Bengal, bouclé, broché, burlap, burnet, burrel, byssus, calico, camlet, canvas, chintz, cloqué, coburg, cotton, coutil, cubica, Dacron®, damask, dévoré, dowlas, doyley, Dralon®, duffel, durant, durrie, faille, fleece, frieze, gloria, harden, jersey, kersey, kincob, linsey, madras, merino, mohair, moreen, muslin, Oxford, plissé, poplin, rateen, ratine, russet, samite, satara, sateen, saxony, sendal, shoddy, sindon, Tactel®, tamine, tartan, Thibet, tissue, tricot, tusser, velour, velvet, vicuña, wadmal, wincey, winsey
**07** alepine, baracan, batiste, brocade, buckram, bunting, cambric, camelot, caracul, challis, chamois, Cheviot, chiffon, cramesy, cypress, doeskin, dornick, drabbet, droguet, drugget, duvetyn, façonné, fake fur, flannel, foulard, fustian, gingham, Gore-Tex®, grogram, hessian, holland, hopsack, jaconet, karakul, khaddar, kidskin, leather, lockram, Mexican, mockado, morocco, nacarat, nankeen, oil silk, organza, orleans, paisley, percale, rabanna, raschel, raw silk, sagathy, scarlet, schappe, seating, silesia, Spandex®, stammel, suiting, tabaret, taffeta, ticking, veiling, Viyella®, webbing, woolsey, worsted
**08** barathea, barracan, bayadère, box-cloth, buckskin, cashmere, casimere, chambray, chenille, corduroy, coutille, cramoisy, cretonne, diamanté, drilling, frocking, gambroon, gossamer, homespun, jacquard, lambskin, marcella, mazarine, moleskin, oilcloth, organdie, osnaburg, pashmina, plaiding, pleather, quilting, sarsenet, shagreen, shalloon, shantung, sheeting, shirting, spun silk, suedette, swanskin, Terylene®, toilinet, waxcloth, whipcord
**09** astrakhan, baldachin, bombasine, calamanco, carmelite, cassimere, Chantilly, Crimplene®, crinoline, farandine, folk-weave, fur fabric, gaberdine, georgette, grenadine, grosgrain, haircloth, horsehair, huckaback, interlock, kalamkari, macintosh, matelassé, Moygashel®, open-weave, organzine, paramatta, petersham, pinstripe, polyester, raven-duck, sackcloth, sailcloth, satinette, sharkskin, sheepskin, stockinet, swans-down, tarpaulin, velveteen
**10** Balbriggan, broadcloth, brocatelle, candlewick, farrandine, florentine, grass cloth, habit-cloth, hop-sacking, kerseymere, mackintosh, microfibre, monk's cloth, mousseline, mummy-cloth, needlecord, paper-cloth, peau-de-soie, pilot cloth, polycotton, seersucker, sicilienne, Tattersall, toilinette, winceyette
**11** cheesecloth, flannelette, Harris tweed®, interfacing, Kendal green, marquisette, mutton cloth, nettle-cloth, sempiternum, stockinette
**12** bolting cloth, Brussels lace, butter-muslin, cavalry twill, crêpe de chine, leather-cloth, Lincoln green, Shetland wool
**13** boulting cloth, casement cloth, foundation-net, linsey-woolsey
**14** heather mixture, terry towelling

*See also* **cotton**

**fabricate**
◇ *anagram indicator*
**04** coin, fake, form, make **05** build, erect, forge, frame, hatch, shape, weave **06** cook up, create, devise, invent, make up **07** concoct, falsify, fashion, produce, trump up
**08** assemble **09** construct
**11** counterfeit, manufacture, put together

**fabrication**
**03** fib, lie, web **04** fake, myth **05** fable, story **06** mock-up **07** coinage, fiction, figment, forgery, untruth **08** assembly, building, erection **09** falsehood, invention **10** assemblage, concoction, fairy story, production **11** manufacture
**12** construction

**fabulous**
**03** def, fab, rad **04** cool, mean, mega, neat **05** false, great, magic, super, triff
**06** divine, fabled, grouse, made-up, mythic, superb, unreal, way-out, wicked **07** amazing, cracker, crucial, feigned, immense, radical **08** heavenly, invented, mythical, stonking, top-notch **09** excellent, fantastic, fictional, imaginary, legendary, wonderful
**10** apocryphal, astounding, fictitious, incredible, marvellous, mythologic, not half bad, phenomenal, remarkable,

tremendous **11** astonishing, sensational, spectacular
**12** breathtaking, mythological, unbelievable, unimaginable
**13** inconceivable **14** out of this world

**façade**
**04** face, mask, show, veil **05** cloak, cover, front, guise **06** veneer
**07** frontal **08** disguise, exterior, frontage, pretence **09** semblance
**10** appearance, storefront

**face**
◇ *head selection indicator*
**03** air, jib, mug, pan **04** clad, coat, dare, defy, dial, form, head, line, look, meet, mien, moue, name, phiz, pout, puss, side, trim **05** anger, brave, clock, cover, dress, flank, front, frown, looks, pitch, scowl **06** aspect, esteem, façade, favour, honour, kisser, nature, oppose, polish, resist, smooth, tackle, veneer, visage **07** affront, grimace, outside, overlay, profile, respect, surface
**08** boldness, confront, cope with, deal with, exterior, face up to, features, frontage, give on to, look onto, overlook, presence, prestige, standing
**09** demeanour, encounter, look out on, withstand **10** admiration, appearance, be opposite, effrontery, experience, expression, reputation
**11** countenance, look towards, physiognomy **13** come up against

*Face parts include:*

**03** ear, eye, gum, jaw, lip
**04** brow, chin, hair, iris, jowl, lips, neck, nose, skin
**05** beard, cheek, mouth, pupil, teeth
**06** eyelid, sclera, septum, temple, tongue
**07** earlobe, eyeball, eyebrow, eyelash, freckle, jawbone, nostril, wrinkle
**08** philtrum
**09** cheekbone, moustache
**10** complexion, double chin

*See also* **hair**

• **face to face**
**06** facing **07** vis-à-vis **08** eye to eye, in person, opposite **09** confronté, tête-à-tête **11** confronting **12** a quattr'occhi
**14** across-the-table **15** in confrontation

• **face up to**
**04** nose **06** accept **08** confront, cope with, deal with **09** recognize, stand up to **10** meet head-on **11** acknowledge
**15** come to terms with

• **flat face**
**04** pane

• **fly in the face of**
**04** defy **05** clash **06** insult, oppose
**08** be at odds, conflict, contrast, disagree **09** go against **10** contradict
**12** be at variance, be in conflict

• **on the face of it**
**07** clearly, plainly **08** patently
**09** obviously, outwardly, reputedly, seemingly **10** apparently, manifestly, ostensibly **12** on the surface
**13** superficially

• **pull a face**
**03** moe, mow **04** girn, gurn, lour, pout, sulk **05** fleer, frown, scowl **06** glower
**07** grimace **13** knit your brows

• **tilted face**
**04** cant

**facelift**
**05** refit **08** makeover **10** renovation
**11** restoration **12** redecoration, rhytidectomy **13** refurbishment
**14** plastic surgery, transformation
**15** cosmetic surgery

**facet**
**04** face, side **05** angle, plane, point, slant **06** aspect, factor **07** element, feature, surface **10** ommatidium
**14** characteristic

**facetious**
**04** glib **05** comic, droll, funny, witty
**06** jocose, joking **07** amusing, comical, jesting, jocular, playful, waggish **08** flippant, humorous
**09** frivolous **12** light-hearted
**13** tongue-in-cheek

**facile**
**04** easy, glib **05** hasty, light, quick, ready, slick **06** fluent, simple, smooth
**07** affable, shallow **08** yielding
**09** plausible **10** simplistic
**11** superficial **13** uncomplicated

**facilitate**
**04** ease, help **06** assist, grease, smooth **07** advance, forward, further, promote, speed up **08** expedite
**09** encourage, lubricate **10** accelerate, make easier **12** smooth the way

**facilitation**
**07** helping **09** promotion
**10** assistance, expediting, forwarding, furthering **12** acceleration
**13** encouragement

**facility**
**03** aid **04** ease, gift **05** knack, means, skill **06** mod con, talent **07** ability, amenity, feature, fluency, pliancy, service, utility **08** aptitude, resource
**09** advantage, appliance, dexterity, eloquence, equipment, provision, quickness, readiness **10** affability
**11** convenience, opportunity, proficiency, skilfulness **12** prerequisite
**14** articulateness, effortlessness

**facing**
**06** façade, lining, veneer **07** coating, overlay, surface **08** cladding, covering, dressing, trimming **09** revetment
**10** false front **13** reinforcement

**facsimile**
**03** fax **04** copy **05** image, print, repro, Xerox® **06** carbon **07** replica, telefax
**09** duplicate, imitation, photocopy, Photostat®, reproduce **10** carbon copy, mimeograph, transcript
**11** electrotype **12** reproduction
**13** telefacsimile

**fact**
**03** act, gen **04** deed, info, item, poop
**05** datum, event, point, score, thing, truth **06** detail, factor **07** element, feature, low-down, reality **08** incident, specific **09** actuality, certainty, component, happening **10** factuality, ins and outs, occurrence, particular
**11** information **12** circumstance, fait accompli

• **in fact**
**03** e'en, nay, yes **04** even **05** truly
**06** indeed, really **07** de facto, en effet, in truth **08** actually **09** in reality
**10** come to that, in practice **12** in actual fact **13** in point of fact **15** as a matter of fact

**faction**
**03** set **04** band, camp, ring, side
**05** cabal, group, junta, junto, lobby, party **06** caucus, clique, sector, strife
**07** coterie, discord, section, trouble
**08** argument, conflict, division, fraction, friction, grouplet, minority, quarrels, tendency **10** contention, contingent, disharmony, dissension, infighting **11** ginger group
**12** disagreement **13** pressure group, splinter group

**factious**
**05** rival, split **06** at odds **07** divided, warring **08** clashing, divisive, mutinous, partisan **09** dissident, sectarian, seditious, turbulent
**10** discordant, rebellious, refractory, tumultuous **11** conflicting, contentious, quarrelling, quarrelsome
**12** disputatious **13** at loggerheads, troublemaking **15** insurrectionary

**factitious**
**04** made, sham **05** bogus, false
**09** contrived, imitation, pretended, unnatural **10** artificial, fabricated
**11** counterfeit

**factor**
**04** fact, gene, item, part **05** cause, facet, point **06** aspect, detail
**07** divisor, element, feature
**09** component, influence
**10** ingredient **11** constituent, contingency, determinant, submultiple
**12** circumstance **13** consideration
**14** characteristic

• **unknown factor**
**01** x, y, z

**factory**
**04** mill, yard **05** plant, works
**07** foundry **08** workshop **09** shop floor **11** manufactory **12** assembly line, assembly shop

**factotum**
**05** do-all **06** circar, sircar, sirkar
**07** famulus **08** handyman **09** Man Friday, odd-jobman **10** Girl Friday
**12** bottle-washer **13** maid-of-all-work
**15** jack-of-all-trades

**facts**
**04** data, poop **05** truth **09** bare bones

**factual**
**04** real, true **05** close, exact **06** actual, strict **07** correct, genuine, literal, precise **08** accurate, detailed, faithful,

truthful, unbiased **09** authentic, objective, realistic **10** historical, true-to-life **12** unprejudiced

**factually**
**05** truly **06** really **08** actually **09** genuinely, in reality **10** truthfully **12** historically

**faculties**
**04** wits **06** powers, reason, senses **12** capabilities, intelligence

**faculty**
**03** ear, wit **04** bent, bump, gift, nose **05** flair, knack, power, sight, skill, taste **06** school, talent **07** ability, licence, section **08** aptitude, capacity, division, facility, function **10** capability, department **11** proficiency **12** organization

**fad**
**04** buzz, cult, mode, rage, whim **05** craze, fancy, mania, trend, vogue **06** maggot **07** fashion **10** enthusiasm **11** affectation **14** passing fashion

**faddy**
**05** exact, fussy, picky **06** choosy **07** finicky **10** fastidious, nit-picking, particular, pernickety **11** persnickety **12** hard-to-please

**fade**
**03** die, dim, ebb **04** dull, fail, fall, flag, melt, miff, pale, vade, wane, weak, wilt **05** appal, droop, faint **06** blanch, bleach, blench, die out, perish, recede, vanish, wallow, weaken, whiten, wither **07** decline, die away, dwindle, ebb away, shrivel, wash out **08** diminish, dissolve, etiolate, evanesce, grow pale, melt away, peter out, tone down, wear away **09** disappear, discolour, fizzle out, waste away **10** become pale, lose colour **11** become paler **12** become weaker

**faeces**
**04** crap, crud, dung, flux, mute, poop, pure **05** frass, guano, scats, stool **06** doo-doo, egesta, ordure, stools **07** excreta, motions **09** body waste, droppings, excrement, number two **11** waste matter **12** rejectamenta, sir-reverence

**fag**
**03** cig, tab **04** bind, bore, drag, pest, slog **05** chore, ciggy, grind, joint, smoke, weary, whiff **06** bother, ciggie, dog end, fag end, gasper, low-tar, roll-up **07** high-tar **08** drudgery, king-size, nuisance **09** cigarette, filter-tip **10** coffin-nail, irritation **11** cancer-stick, roll-your-own **13** inconvenience

**fagged**
**04** beat, done **05** all in, jaded, weary **06** beaten, bushed, done in, pooped, wasted, zonked **07** euchred, whacked, worn out **08** burnt out, dead-beat, dog-tired, fatigued, jiggered **09** exhausted, knackered, pooped out **10** euchred out **11** ready to drop, tuckered out **14** on your last legs

**fail**
**02** go **03** die, ebb, mis, sod **04** bomb, fade, feal, flag, flop, fold, lose, miss, omit, plow, sink, stop, turf, wane **05** abort, crash, decay, droop, flunk, fudge, leave, smash **06** blow it, cut out, desert, falter, forget, go bung, go bust, go phut, pack up, play up, plough, weaken **07** abandon, conk out, crap out, deceive, decline, dwindle, forsake, founder, go broke, go kaput, go under, go wrong, let down, misluck, neglect, not work **08** bottle it, collapse, diminish, fall down, fall flat, miscarry, not start **09** break down, come short, fall apart, fizzle out, go belly-up, not make it **10** come undone, disappoint, draw a blank, get nowhere, go bankrupt, not come off **11** bite the dust, come a gutser, come to grief, come unglued, come unstuck, dégringoler, deteriorate, fall through, go to the wall, malfunction **12** come a cropper, come to naught, go into the red, go on the blink, go on the fritz, underachieve **13** come to nothing **14** be unsuccessful, not do something, score an own goal **15** become insolvent, blow your chances

• **without fail**
**08** reliably **09** regularly **10** constantly, dependably, faithfully, punctually **11** predictably, religiously, unfailingly **13** like clockwork **15** conscientiously

**failing**
**03** sin **04** flat, flaw **05** error, fault, lapse **06** defect, foible **07** blemish, default, failure, lacking, wanting, without **08** drawback, on the ebb, weakness, weak spot **10** deficiency **11** in default of, shortcoming **12** imperfection **14** in the absence of

**failure**
**03** dud **04** flop, hash, mess, miss, no go, no-no, ruin **05** botch, crash, decay, flunk, loser **06** cock-up, defeat, demise, ebbing, fading, fiasco, misfit, reject, slip-up, victim, waning **07** also-ran, burst-up, debacle, decline, default, dropout, flivver, folding, has-been, let-down, neglect, no-hoper, screw-up, sinking, washout, wipeout **08** abortion, calamity, collapse, dead loss, disaster, downfall, flagging, meltdown, omission, shambles, shutdown, stalling, stopping, write-off **09** born loser, breakdown, disregard, oversight, packing-up, unsuccess, weakening **10** bankruptcy, conking-out, cutting-out, foundering, going under, ill success, insolvency, misfortune, negligence, non-starter, remissness **11** dereliction, frustration, malfunction, miscarriage **12** waste of space **13** deterioration, forgetfulness, lack of success **14** disappointment, going to the wall, malfunctioning **15** coming to nothing

**faint**
**03** dim, low, wan **04** drop, dull, fade, gone, hazy, mild, pale, soft, weak **05** decay, dizzy, droop, faded, giddy, light, muted, queer, quiet, sound, swarf, swelt, swerf, swoon, swoun, vague, woozy **06** feeble, hushed, slight, stanck, swarve, swerve, swound, vanish **07** blurred, ghostly, languid, muffled, obscure, pass out, subdued, syncope, unclear **08** black out, blackout, bleached, collapse, flake out, keel over, unsteady **09** exhausted **10** indistinct, oppressive **11** half-hearted, lightheaded **14** unenthusiastic **15** unconsciousness

**faint-hearted**
**04** soft, weak **05** timid, wussy **06** craven, scared, yellow **07** chicken, fearful, gutless, jittery, wimpish **08** cowardly, timorous **09** diffident, spineless, weak-kneed **10** hen-hearted, irresolute, spiritless **11** half-hearted, lily-livered **12** weak-spirited, white-livered **13** pusillanimous, yellow-bellied **14** chicken-hearted, chicken-livered

**faintly**
**04** a bit **06** feebly, softly, weakly **07** a little, vaguely **08** slightly, somewhat

**fair**
**02** OK **03** dry **04** even, expo, fete, fine, full, gaff, gala, good, just, mela, open, pale, pure, show, so-so, warm **05** blond, civil, clean, clear, cream, ivory, legit, light, quite, right, sunny, tryst, white, woman **06** bazaar, beauty, blonde, bright, decent, flaxen, golden, honest, kosher, lawful, likely, market, modest, not bad, proper, square, yellow **07** upright **08** adequate, all right, carnival, detached, directly, exchange, festival, handsome, mediocre, middling, moderate, passable, pleasing, specious, sporting, unbiased **09** beautiful, cloudless, craft fair, equitable, impartial, objective, out-and-out, plausible, tolerable, trade fair, unclouded, veritable **10** above board, acceptable, even-handed, exhibition, exposition, fair-haired, fair-headed, favourable, honourable, legitimate, on the level, prosperous, reasonable, straight up, sufficient **11** light-haired, respectable, trustworthy **12** satisfactory, unobstructed, unprejudiced **13** disinterested, dispassionate, done by the book **14** going by the book **15** played by the book

**fairground**
• **fairground attraction**
**04** ride

*Fairground attractions include:*

**06** hoop-la
**07** Dodgems®
**08** carousel, waltzers
**10** bumper cars, coconut shy, ghost train, swing boats
**11** Ferris wheel, wall of death
**12** bouncy castle, chair-o-planes, merry-go-round, tunnel of love
**13** helter-skelter, rollercoaster

**fairly**
**03** gay, gey **05** fully, quite **06** enough, gently, justly, neatly, pretty, quight, rather, really, square **07** legally, plainly **08** honestly, lawfully, middling, passably, properly, somewhat **09** equitably, neutrally, tolerably, veritably **10** absolutely, adequately, moderately, positively, reasonably, unbiasedly **11** beautifully, impartially, objectively

**fair-minded**
**04** fair, just **05** right **06** honest, proper, square **07** upright **08** detached, unbiased **09** equitable, impartial, objective **10** even-handed, honourable, on the level, straight up **11** trustworthy **12** unprejudiced **13** disinterested, dispassionate

**fairness**
**06** equity, square **07** decency, justice **09** rightness **10** legitimacy **11** uprightness **12** impartiality, rightfulness, unbiasedness **13** equitableness **14** even-handedness, honourableness, legitimateness

**fairy**
**03** elf, fay, fée, hob, imp, Mab **04** peri, pixy, Puck **05** faery, nymph, pisky, pixie, pouke **06** faerie, sprite **07** brownie, rusalka, sandman **08** delicate, fanciful **09** hobgoblin, Puck-hairy, whimsical **10** leprechaun **11** enchantress **15** Robin Goodfellow

**fairy tale**
**03** fib, lie **04** myth **07** fantasy, fiction, romance, untruth **08** folk-tale **09** invention, tall story **10** fairy story **11** fabrication

*Fairy tales include:*

**07** Aladdin, Ali Baba, The Bell
**08** Momo Taro, Peter Pan, Rapunzel, Snowdrop, The Angel, The Daisy, The Raven, Tom Thumb
**09** Ashputtel, Bluebeard, Briar Rose, Pinocchio, Snow White, The Shadow, The Storks
**10** Cinderella, Clever Hans, Goldilocks, Hans in Luck, The Fir Tree, The Rose-Elf, Thumbelina
**11** Clever Elsie, Hop o' my Thumb, Little Thumb, Mother Elder, Mother Goose, Puss in Boots, The Old House, The Red Shoes
**12** Holger Danske, Little Red-Cap, The Elderbush, The Goose Girl, The Pied Piper, The Snow Queen, The Tinderbox, The Wild Swans, Urashima Taro
**13** Chicken Licken, Red Riding Hood, The Frog Prince, The Golden Bird, The Neighbours, The Tin Soldier, The White Snake, The Wizard of Oz
**14** Babes in the Wood, Sleeping Beauty, The Flying Trunk, The Golden Goose, The Juniper Tree, The Nightingale, The Seven Ravens, The Water of Life
**15** Dick Whittington, Hansel and Gretel, Rumpelstiltskin, The Elfin Hillock, The Little Lovers, Three Little Pigs, The Ugly Duckling

*Fairy tale characters include:*

**03** Cat, Dog
**04** Duck, Jack, John, Liza, Nana, Nibs
**05** Beast, Curly, Wendy
**06** Beauty, Conrad, Donkey, Falada, Gretel, Hansel
**07** Michael, Rooster, Rose Red, The King, The Ogre, The Wolf, Tootles
**08** Baby Bear, Foxy Loxy, Geppetto, Peter Pan, Rapunzel, Slightly, The Elves, The Giant, The Queen, The Troll, The Twins, Tom Thumb
**09** Briar Rose, Daddy Bear, Good Fairy, Mummy Bear, Pinocchio, Snow White, The Miller, The Mirror, The Prince
**10** Cinderella, Ducky Lucky, Goldilocks, Henny Penny, Stepmother, The Emperor, Thumbelina, Tinker Bell
**11** Captain Hook, Grandmother, Pedlar Woman, Puss in Boots, The Huntsman, The Lost Boys, The Princess, Ugly Sisters, Wicked Fairy, Wicked Witch
**12** Goosey Loosey, The Goose Girl, The Shoemaker
**13** Band of Robbers, Chicken Licken, Red Riding Hood
**14** Fairy Godmother, The Golden Goose, The Seven Dwarfs
**15** Alice Fitzwarren, Billy Goats Gruff, Dick Whittington, Fairy Godmothers, Mr and Mrs Darling, Rumpelstiltskin, The Little Red Hen, The Rich Merchant, The Ugly Duckling, Three Little Pigs

**faith**
**03** fay, lay **04** faix, sect **05** creed, dogma, fides, troth, trust **06** belief, church, credit, fealty, honour, indeed **07** believe, honesty, loyalty **08** credence, devotion, doctrine, fidelity, reliance, religion, teaching **09** assurance, obedience, sincerity **10** allegiance, commitment, confidence, conviction, dedication, dependence, persuasion **12** denomination, faithfulness, truthfulness

• **in faith**
**04** fegs

**faithful**
**04** feal, leal, true **05** afald, close, exact, loyal **06** aefald, afawld, strict, trusty **07** aefauld, devoted, precise, staunch **08** accurate, brethren, constant, obedient, reliable, soothful, truthful **09** adherents, believers, believing, committed, dedicated, followers, soothfast, steadfast **10** dependable, supporters, unflagging, unswerving, unwavering **11** true-hearted, trustworthy **12** communicants, congregation

**faithfully**
**04** true **05** truly **06** firmly **07** closely, exactly, loyally **08** reliably, solemnly, strictly **09** devotedly, precisely, staunchly **10** accurately, constantly, dependably **11** steadfastly

**faithfulness**
**05** truth **06** fealty **07** loyalty **08** accuracy, devotion, fidelity **09** closeness, constancy, exactness **10** allegiance, commitment, dedication, strictness **11** reliability, staunchness **13** dependability, steadfastness **14** scrupulousness **15** trustworthiness

**faithless**
**05** false **06** fickle, untrue **08** agnostic, disloyal, doubting **09** atheistic, deceptive **10** adulterous, inconstant, perfidious, traitorous, unfaithful, unreliable, untruthful **11** nullifidian, treacherous, unbelieving **12** disbelieving, false-hearted **13** untrustworthy

**faithlessness**
**06** deceit **07** perfidy **08** adultery, apostasy, betrayal **09** treachery **10** disloyalty, fickleness, infidelity **11** inconstancy **14** unfaithfulness

**fake**
◇ *anagram indicator*
**03** rob **04** coil, cook, copy, faux, fold, hoax, mock, sham **05** bogus, dodge, false, feign, filch, flake, forge, fraud, fudge, phony, pseud, put on, quack **06** affect, assume, attack, bodgie, doctor, ersatz, forged, phoney, pirate, pseudo **07** assumed, forgery, hyped-up, imitate, pretend, replica, swindle **08** affected, impostor, simulate, spurious **09** charlatan, fabricate, imitation, simulated **10** artificial, fraudulent, mountebank, simulation **11** counterfeit **12** reproduction

**falcon**

*Falcons include:*

**05** hobby, saker
**06** gentle, lanner, merlin
**07** Iceland, kestrel
**08** duck-hawk
**09** gerfalcon, gyrfalcon, jerfalcon, peregrine, stone hawk
**11** tassell-gent
**12** falcon-gentil, falcon-gentle, tassel-gentle, tercel-gentle, tercel-jerkin

**Falkland Islands**
**03** FLK

**fall**
◇ *anagram indicator*
◇ *reversal indicator*
**02** fa **03** cut, die, ebb, get, lot, sin **04** dive, drip, drop, grow, hang, purl, rain, ruin, rush, sink, slip, soss, trap, trip, turn **05** abate, chute, crash, falls, lapse, occur, onset, pitch, slant, slide, slope, slump, souse, spill, yield **06** alight, autumn, become, be lost, chance, dangle, defeat, demise, give in, go down, gutzer, happen, lessen, perish, plunge, recede, revert, shower, submit, topple, tumble **07** be slain, be taken,

cadence, capture, cascade, decline, descend, descent, dwindle, failure, fall off, fall-off, fortune, impinge, incline, offence, plummet, stumble, subside, torrent **08** be killed, cataract, collapse, come down, come to be, conquest, decrease, diminish, down-come, downfall, fall down, giving-in, grow into, keel over, nose-dive, yielding **09** come about, declivity, dwindling, lessening, overthrow, reduction, surrender, take place, terminate, waterfall **10** be defeated, capitulate, plummeting, submission, topple over, wrongdoing **11** be conquered, come a gutser, destruction, keeling-over, lose control, original sin, precipitate, resignation **12** be vanquished, capitulation, come a cropper, disobedience, lose your life, pitch forward, precipitance, precipitancy **13** loss of control, transgression

**• fall apart**

**03** rot **04** fail **05** break, decay **06** divide **07** break up, crack up, crumble, shatter **08** collapse, come away, dissolve, disunite, go to bits **09** break down, decompose **10** fall to bits, go to pieces **11** lose control **12** come to pieces, disintegrate, fall to pieces **15** break into pieces

**• fall asleep**

**04** doze **06** get off, nod off, pop off **07** doze off, drop off **08** crash out, drift off, flake out, spark out **13** pass into sleep **15** go out like a light

**• fall away**

**04** drop, fail **05** lapse **06** go down, revolt **07** decline, drop off, dwindle, relapse **08** drop away, languish **09** slope away, slope down

**• fall back**

**06** depart, recoil, recule, revert **07** back off, give way, recoyle, recuile, relapse, retreat **08** draw back, pull back, withdraw **09** disengage **10** give ground, lose ground

**• fall back on**

**03** use **06** call on, employ, look to, turn to **08** resort to **09** make use of **12** call into play **14** have recourse to

**• fall behind**

**03** lag **05** trail **08** drop back, straggle **09** lag behind, not keep up

**• fall down**

**04** fail, flop **07** founder **08** collapse **09** break down **11** come unglued, come unstuck **12** come a cropper **13** come to nothing **14** be unsuccessful

**• fall for**

**03** buy **05** fancy **06** accept, desire, take to **07** swallow **10** be fooled by **11** be taken in by **12** be attached to, be crazy about, be deceived by, have a crush on **14** fall in love with

**• fall in**

**04** sink **05** array, crash **06** cave in, line up, revert **07** give way, subside **08** collapse, come down **11** stand in line **14** get in formation

**• fall in with**

**06** accept **07** support **08** assent to, hang with **09** agree with **10** comply with **11** go along with, hang out with **12** go around with **13** co-operate with, hang about with **14** hang around with **15** get involved with

**• fall off**

**04** drop, shed, slow **05** crash, slump **06** lessen, perish, worsen **07** decline, die away, drop off, slacken, slip off **08** decrease, draw back **11** deteriorate

**• fall on**

**04** meet **06** assail, attack, snatch **07** assault, lay into, set upon **08** pounce on **09** descend on

**• fall out**

**05** argue, clash, fight **06** bicker, differ, happen **07** dismiss, quarrel **08** disagree, squabble

**• fall slightly**

**04** ease

**• fall through**

**04** fail **05** abort **07** founder, go wrong **08** collapse, miscarry **11** come to grief **13** come to nothing

**• fall to**

**05** begin, set to, start **07** stand to **08** commence, set about **10** get stuck in **11** be the duty of, be the task of **13** apply yourself

**fallacious**

**05** false, wrong **06** untrue **07** inexact **08** delusive, delusory, illusory, mistaken, spurious **09** deceptive, erroneous, illogical, incorrect, sophistic **10** fictitious, inaccurate, misleading **11** casuistical, sophistical

**fallacy**

**04** flaw, myth **05** error **06** idolon, idolum **07** idolism, mistake, sophism **08** delusion, illusion **09** deception, falsehood, false idea, sophistry **12** equivocation, misjudgement **13** deceitfulness, inconsistency, misconception **14** miscalculation, mistaken belief **15** misapprehension

**fallen**

**04** dead, died, lost **05** loose, slain **06** killed, ruined, shamed **07** immoral, seduced **08** murdered, perished **09** disgraced **10** degenerate, overthrown **11** promiscuous, slaughtered

**fallibility**

**07** failing **08** weakness **09** mortality **10** inaccuracy **12** imperfection **13** unreliability

**fallible**

**04** weak **05** frail, human **06** errant, erring, flawed, mortal **08** ignorant **09** imperfect, uncertain **10** unreliable

**fallow**

**03** lay, lea, ley **04** idle **06** barren, unsown, unused **07** dormant, resting **08** inactive **09** unplanted **10** unploughed **11** undeveloped **12** uncultivated, unproductive

**false**

◇ *anagram indicator*

**03** bum **04** fake, faux, mock, sham **05** bogus, lying, pseud, wrong **06** faulty, forged, phoney, pseudo, untrue **07** assumed, bastard, feigned, inexact, invalid, pretend **08** disloyal, fabulous, illusive, illusory, invented, mistaken, postiche, pseudish, recreant, spurious, strumpet, two-faced **09** deceitful, dishonest, erroneous, faithless, imitation, incorrect, insincere, pretended, simulated, synthetic, trumped-up **10** artificial, fabricated, fallacious, fictitious, fraudulent, inaccurate, misleading, perfidious, traitorous, unfaithful, ungrounded, unreliable **11** counterfeit, double-faced, duplicitous, treacherous **12** hypocritical **13** double-dealing, untrustworthy

**falsehood**

**03** fib, lie **04** flam **05** fable, porky, story **06** deceit **07** fiction, leasing, perfidy, perjury, untruth, whopper **09** deception, duplicity, hypocrisy, invention, mendacity, tall story, treachery **10** dishonesty, fairy story **11** fabrication, insincerity **12** two-facedness **13** deceitfulness, double dealing **14** untruthfulness

**falsely**

**07** in error, untruly, wrongly **09** by mistake, deviously **10** mistakenly, wrongfully **11** deceitfully, dishonestly, erroneously, incorrectly, insincerely **12** artificially, fallaciously, fraudulently **13** counterfeitly, treacherously **14** hypocritically

**falsetto**

**04** alto **08** high note **09** high pitch, high voice **10** shrillness **12** head register

**falsification**

**06** change, deceit **07** forgery **08** adultery **09** tampering **10** alteration, distortion, perversion **12** adulteration **13** dissimulation

**falsify**

◇ *anagram indicator*

**03** lie, rig **04** cook, fake, rort **05** alter, belie, false, feign, forge, twist **06** diddle, doctor, fiddle, garble, wangle **07** distort, massage, pervert **08** misstate **10** adulterate, manipulate, tamper with **11** counterfeit **12** misrepresent, sophisticate

**falter**

**04** fail, flag **05** delay, quail, shake, waver **06** flinch, hiccup, totter **07** be shaky, stammer, stoiter, stumble, stutter, tremble **08** hesitate, hiccough **09** vacillate **10** be unsteady, dilly-dally **12** be in two minds, drag your feet, shilly-shally, take your time, unsteadiness **13** sit on the fence **14** fluff your lines

**faltering**

◇ *anagram indicator*

**04** weak **05** timid **06** broken **07** failing **08** flagging, hesitant, unsteady **09** stumbling, tentative, uncertain **10** irresolute, stammering

**fame**
**04** name, note **05** glory, kudos **06** esteem, honour, renown, report, repute, rumour **07** stardom **08** eminence **09** celebrity, greatness **10** importance, notability, prominence, reputation **11** distinction **15** illustriousness

**famed**
**05** noted **06** famous **08** esteemed, renowned **09** acclaimed, prominent, well-known **10** celebrated, recognized **11** widely known

**familiar**
**03** fam, old **04** bold, dear, easy, free, maty, near, open **05** aware, close, known, matey, pally, privy, usual **06** au fait, casual, chummy, common, homely, smarmy, versed, well up **07** abreast, clued up, forward, natural, relaxed, routine **08** everyday, fireside, frequent, friendly, genned up, habitual, homelike, informal, intimate, ordinary, repeated, sociable **09** au courant, customary, household, up to speed, well-known **10** accustomed, acquainted, conversant, recognized, unreserved **11** comfortable, commonplace, free-and-easy, impertinent **12** confidential, conventional, over-familiar, over-friendly, presumptuous, recognizable, run-of-the-mill, unmistakable **13** disrespectful, knowledgeable, unceremonious

**familiarity**
**04** ease **05** grasp, habit, skill **07** liberty, mastery **08** boldness, intimacy, nearness, openness **09** awareness, closeness, impudence, knowledge, liberties, palliness, pushiness **10** casualness, chumminess, consuetude, disrespect, experience, inwardness **11** conversance, conversancy, forwardness, informality, naturalness, presumption, sociability **12** acquaintance, friendliness, impertinence **13** comprehension, intrusiveness, understanding **15** over-familiarity

**familiarize**
**05** brief, coach, gen up, prime, teach, train **06** clue up, school **08** accustom, acquaint, instruct **09** habituate, make aware **11** acclimatize **12** get up to speed, indoctrinate, make familiar **13** keep up to speed **14** make acquainted

**family**
**03** fam, kin **04** clan, folk, gens, kids, kind, line, name, race, stem, type **05** birth, blood, brood, class, flesh, genus, group, house, issue, order, stock, tribe **06** kinred, people, scions, stirps, strain, whanau **07** descent, dynasty, kiddies, kindred, kinsmen, lineage, parents, progeny, species **08** ancestry, children, pedigree, subclass **09** ancestors, forebears, household, next of kin, offspring, parentage, relations, relatives **10** extraction, generation, little ones **11** descendants, you and yours **13** nuclear family **14** classification, extended family **15** one-parent family

**• member of family**
**08** relation, relative

*See also* **relative**

**• family tree**
**04** line **06** stemma **07** descent, lineage **08** ancestry, pedigree **09** genealogy, whakapapa **10** background, extraction

**famine**
**04** lack, want **05** death **06** dearth, hunger **08** scarcity **10** starvation **11** deprivation, destitution **12** exiguousness, malnutrition **14** shortage of food

**famished**
**06** hungry **07** starved **08** ravenous, starving **09** famishing, voracious **14** undernourished

**famous**
**04** name **05** famed, great, noted **06** legend, signal **07** eminent, notable, popular **08** esteemed, glorious, honoured, infamous, renowned **09** acclaimed, celebrity, excellent, legendary, notorious, prominent, respected, venerable, well-famed, well-known **10** celebrated, remarkable **11** illustrious, world-famous **13** distinguished

**famously**
**04** well **07** greatly, happily, notably **08** superbly **09** eminently, popularly **10** infamously, splendidly, swimmingly **11** brilliantly, notoriously, prominently, wonderfully **13** conspicuously

**fan**
◇ *anagram indicator*
**03** air, nut **04** blow, buff, cone, cool, vane, wing **05** fiend, freak, lover, punka, rouse **06** addict, aerate, arouse, backer, blower, Colmar, cooler, excite, groupy, ignite, incite, kindle, punkah, stir up, whip up, winnow, work up **07** admirer, agitate, air-cool, devotee, flutter, freshen, groupie, provoke, refresh **08** adherent, follower, increase **09** air cooler, extractor, flabellum, instigate, intensify, propeller, rhipidion, stimulate, supporter, ventilate **10** aficionado, enthusiast, ventilator **11** afficionado **12** air-condition, extractor fan **14** air-conditioner

**• fan out**
**04** open **06** spread, unfold, unfurl **07** move out, open out **09** spread out

**fanatic**
**03** nut **05** bigot, fiend, freak **06** addict, maniac, zealot **07** devotee, radical **08** activist, militant **09** extremist, visionary **10** enthusiast **14** fundamentalist

**fanatical**
**03** mad **04** wild **05** rabid **07** bigoted, burning, extreme, fervent, radical, zealous **08** activist, dogmatic, frenzied, militant **09** extremist, obsessive **10** immoderate, passionate **11** extravagant **12** narrow-minded, single-minded **14** fundamentalist

**fanaticism**
**04** zeal **06** frenzy **07** bigotry, fervour, madness **08** activism, wildness, zealotry **09** dogmatism, extremism, militancy, monomania **10** dedication, enthusiasm **11** infatuation, schwärmerei **13** obsessiveness **14** fundamentalism

**fancier**
**03** fan **05** fiend, freak **06** keeper **07** breeder, devotee **08** follower **10** enthusiast

**fanciful**
◇ *anagram indicator*
**04** wild **05** fairy **06** exotic, ornate, quaint, unreal **07** curious, flighty **08** chimeric, creative, fabulous, illusory, mythical, notional, romantic, vaporous **09** airy-fairy, decorated, elaborate, fairytale, fantastic, imaginary, legendary, visionary, whimsical **10** chimerical **11** extravagant, fantastical, imaginative, make-believe, unrealistic **12** metaphysical

**fancy**
◇ *anagram indicator*
**03** yen **04** flam, idea, itch, like, love, urge, want, ween, whim, wish **05** covet, dream, go for, guess, humor, showy, taste, think **06** desire, fangle, favour, humour, lavish, liking, notion, ornate, prefer, raving, reckon, rococo, take to, vision **07** adorned, baroque, believe, caprice, chimera, dream of, elegant, fantasy, imagine, impulse, long for, longing, not mind, opinion, picture, suppose, surmise, thought, wish for **08** chimaera, conceive, crotchet, delusion, fanciful, fantasia, feel like, fondness, illusion, penchant, phantasy, superior, yearn for, yearning **09** decorated, elaborate, expensive, fantastic, lust after **10** be mad about, conception, conjecture, creativity, far-fetched, have in mind, impression, not say no to, ornamented, preference **11** be wild about, embellished, extravagant, have eyes for, imagination, inclination **12** be crazy about, have a crush on, ostentatious, predilection, take a shine to **13** be attracted to, particoloured, take a liking to **14** be interested in, find attractive, have the hots for **15** think the world of

**fanfare**
**04** fuss, show **05** trump **06** parade, sennet, tucket **07** display **08** flourish **09** fanfarade, pageantry, publicity, tarantara **11** flamboyance, ostentation, taratantara, trumpet call

**fang**
**04** claw, grip, tang, tusk **05** catch, prong, talon, tooth **10** venom-tooth

**fantasize**
**05** dream **06** invent **07** imagine, romance **08** daydream **11** hallucinate **12** live in a dream

**fantastic**
◇ *anagram indicator*
**03** ace, odd **04** cool, mega, neat, wild **05** antic, brill, fancy, great, magic, outré, super, weird **06** absurd, antick, exotic, superb, unreal, wicked
**07** amazing, anticke, antique, bizarre, extreme, foppish, radical, strange
**08** enormous, fabulous, fanciful, illusory, romantic, smashing, terrific, top-notch **09** brilliant, eccentric, excellent, first-rate, grotesque, imaginary, storybook, visionary, whimsical, wonderful **10** capricious, impressive, incredible, marvellous, outlandish, phenomenal, remarkable, tremendous **11** extravagant, imaginative, sensational
**12** overwhelming, transcendent, unbelievable **14** out of this world

**fantastically**
**09** amazingly, extremely **10** incredibly **12** phenomenally, terrifically, tremendously, unbelievably

**fantasy**
**03** GBH, GHB **04** idol, love, myth
**05** dream, fancy **06** mirage, vision, whimsy **07** caprice, reverie, whimsey
**08** daydream, delusion, fantasia, illusion **09** fantasque, invention, moonshine, nightmare, pipe dream, unreality **10** apparition, creativity
**11** imagination, inspiration, originality, pie in the sky, speculation
**12** fancifulness **13** flight of fancy, hallucination, inventiveness, misconception **15** cloud-cuckoo-land, imaginativeness, resourcefulness

**far**
**03** way **04** away, much **05** miles, other **06** far-off, remote **07** distant, faraway, further, greatly, removed **08** a good way, a long way, far-flung, markedly, opposite, outlying, secluded, very much **09** decidedly, distantly, extremely **10** far-removed **11** back o' Bourke, godforsaken, nowhere near, out-of-the-way, up the Boohai
**12** considerably, immeasurably, inaccessible, incomparably, in the boonies, in the wop-wops, some distance **13** great distance, significantly, the black stump **14** in the boondocks

**• as far as**
**02** to, up **04** up to

**• far and wide**
**06** widely **07** broadly **08** all about **09** worldwide **10** everywhere, far and near **11** extensively, in all places
**13** from all places

**• far end, far side**
◇ *tail selection indicator*

**• far out**
**05** weird **06** exotic, way out
**07** bizarre, extreme, radical, strange, unusual **10** outlandish, unorthodox
**14** unconventional

**• go far**
**05** get on **06** arrive **07** succeed **08** go places **12** be successful, make your mark **14** achieve success **15** get on in the world

**• not far**
**02** nl

**• so far**
**02** as **03** als **06** to date **07** thus far, till now, up to now **08** hitherto **12** to some extent, within limits **13** up to this point

**faraway**
**03** far **04** lost **06** absent, dreamy, far-off, remote **07** distant **08** far-flung, outlying **10** abstracted **11** preoccupied
**12** absent-minded

**farce**
**03** jig **04** cram, joke, mime, sham
**05** exode, lazzo, stuff **06** comedy, parody, satire **07** mockery **08** burletta, nonsense, shambles, stuffing, travesty
**09** absurdity, burlesque, forcemeat, pantomime, slapstick **10** buffoonery
**11** opera bouffe **14** ridiculousness

**farcical**
**05** comic, silly **06** absurd, stupid
**08** derisory **09** diverting, laughable, ludicrous **10** ridiculous **11** nonsensical
**12** preposterous

**fare**
**02** be, do, go **03** fee **04** cost, diet, eats, food, go on, menu, nosh, tack, what
**05** board, cheer, get on, meals, price, speed, table **06** charge, course, happen, manage, ticket, travel, viands
**07** make out, passage, proceed, prosper, rations, succeed, turn out
**08** eatables, get along, progress, victuals **09** nutriment, passenger
**10** provisions, sustenance
**11** nourishment **12** passage-money

**farewell**
**02** BV **03** bye **04** ciao, ta-ta, vale
**05** adieu, adios, aloha, later, leave
**06** bye-bye, cheers, see you, so long, valete **07** cheerio, goodbye **08** au revoir, take care **10** all the best
**11** arrivederci, be seeing you, leave-taking, see you later, valediction, valedictory **12** have a nice day, mind how you go, see you around **14** auf Wiedersehen

**• expression of farewell**
**03** bye **04** ciao, ta-ta, vale **05** addio, adieu, adiós, aloha, later **06** hooray, hooroo, see you, shalom, sheers, so long **07** cheerio, goodbye **08** au revoir, chin-chin, sayonara, toodle-oo
**11** arrivederci, be seeing you, see you later **14** auf Wiedersehen, shalom aleichem

**far-fetched**
**05** crazy **06** forced **07** dubious
**08** fanciful, unlikely **09** exquisite, fantastic, recherché, unnatural
**10** improbable, incredible
**11** implausible, unrealistic
**12** preposterous, unbelievable, unconvincing

**farm**
**03** mas **04** ferm, land, sted, till
**05** acres, mains, plant, ranch
**06** bowery, grange, plough, shamba
**07** acreage, holding, mailing, operate, station **08** farmland, hacienda, property **09** cultivate, farmstead, homestead **11** co-operative, work the land

*Farms and farming types include:*

**03** dry, ley, pig
**04** deer, fish, hill, stud, wind
**05** croft, dairy, mixed, store, trash, trout
**06** arable, estate, salmon, turkey
**07** factory, organic, ostrich, poultry
**09** extensive, free-range, intensive
**10** collective, plantation
**11** cattle ranch, monoculture, subsistence
**12** sheep station, smallholding, stock station

*Farm animals include:*

**02** ox
**03** ass, cow, ewe, hen, pig, ram, sow
**04** bull, calf, cock, duck, foal, goat, lamb, mare, mule
**05** goose, horse, sheep
**06** cattle, donkey, piglet, rabbit, turkey
**07** chicken, rooster
**08** cockerel, stallion
**09** billy goat

*Farming equipment includes:*

**03** ard, ATV, axe, hoe, saw
**04** fork, plow, rake, wain
**05** baler, drill, flail, gambo, mower, share, spade
**06** harrow, plough, ricker, ripple, scythe, shovel, sickle, tanker, tedder
**07** combine, draw hoe, grubber, hayfork, hayrake, mattock, scuffle, sprayer, tractor, trailer
**08** buckrake, chainsaw, hay knife, haymaker, scuffler, spreader
**09** corn drill, drop-drill, harvester, irrigator, pitchfork, power lift, rotary hoe, Rotavator®, Rotovator®, scarifier, seed drill, whetstone
**10** cropduster, cultivator, disc harrow, disc plough, earth-board, flail mower, seed-harrow
**11** bale wrapper, broadcaster, chaff-cutter, chaff-engine, drill-harrow, hedgecutter, mole drainer, reaping hook, wheelbarrow, wheel plough
**12** muckspreader, slurry tanker
**13** fork-lift truck, potato planter, slurry sprayer
**14** field sprinkler, front end loader, milking machine

**• farm out**
**08** delegate **09** outsource **11** contract out, subcontract **12** give to others, pass to others

**• farm worker**
**03** dey **04** peon **06** sheepo **07** orra man **08** farmhand

**• healthy farm animal**
**04** doer

**farmer**
**04** Boer, ryot **05** cocky, colon, gebur **06** cockie, mailer, raiyat, yeoman **07** crofter, grazier, métayer, rancher **08** cockatoo **09** campesino, cow-cockie, sodbuster **10** agronomist, estanciero, husbandman **11** flock-master, share-milker, smallholder, stock-farmer, store farmer **12** sharecropper **13** agriculturist **15** agriculturalist

**farming**
**06** arable **07** tilling **08** agronomy, crofting **09** geoponics, husbandry **11** agriculture, agroscience, cultivation **12** agribusiness, share-milking

**Faroe Islands**
**02** FO **03** FRO

**far-off**
**03** far **06** remote **07** distant, faraway **08** far-flung, outlying

**farrago**
**04** hash **06** jumble, medley **07** mélange, mixture **08** mishmash **09** pot-pourri **10** dog's dinner, hodgepodge, hotchpotch, miscellany, salmagundi **11** gallimaufry **13** dog's breakfast

**far-reaching**
**04** wide **05** broad **06** global **08** profound, sweeping, thorough **09** extensive, important, momentous **10** widespread **11** significant, wide-ranging **13** comprehensive

**far-sighted**
**04** wise **05** acute, canny **06** shrewd **07** politic, prudent **08** cautious **09** far-seeing, judicious, prescient, provident **10** discerning **11** circumspect **14** forward-looking

**farther**
**07** further, remoter **11** more distant, more extreme

**farthest**
**08** furthest, remotest **11** most distant, most extreme

**farthing**
**01** f **03** rag **06** farden **07** farding

**fascia**
**04** band, sign **05** board, front, panel **06** fillet **07** console **08** platband **09** dashboard **15** instrument panel

**fascinate**
**04** draw, lure **05** charm, rivet, witch **06** absorb, allure, entice **07** attract, beguile, bewitch, delight, enchant, engross, enthral **08** intrigue, transfix **09** captivate, enrapture, hypnotize, mesmerize, spellbind

**fascinated**
**06** hooked **07** charmed, curious, enticed, smitten **08** absorbed, beguiled **09** bewitched, delighted, engrossed, entranced, intrigued **10** captivated, enthralled, hypnotized, infatuated, mesmerized, spellbound

**fascinating**
**04** sexy **07** killing **08** alluring, charming, engaging, enticing, exciting, fetching, gripping, riveting, tempting, witching **09** absorbing, seductive **10** bewitching, compelling, compulsive, delightful, enchanting, engrossing, intriguing **11** captivating, interesting, mesmerizing, stimulating **12** irresistible

**fascination**
**04** draw, lure, pull **05** charm, magic, spell **06** allure, appeal **07** delight, sorcery **08** interest, witchery **09** magnetism **10** attraction, compulsion **11** captivation, enchantment **13** preoccupation

**fascism**
**09** autocracy, Falangism, Hitlerism **10** absolutism, Sinarchism **12** dictatorship **15** totalitarianism

**fascist**
**04** duce, Nazi **08** autocrat **09** Falangist, Hitlerist, Hitlerite **10** absolutist, autocratic, Blackshirt, Brownshirt, sinarchist **12** totalitarian **13** authoritarian

**fashion**
◇ *anagram indicator*
**03** cut, fad, fit, ton, way **04** fain, feat, form, kind, line, look, make, mode, rage, sort, suit, turn, twig, type, wear, work **05** adapt, alter, build, craze, faine, fayne, feign, model, mould, shape, smith, style, trend, vogue **06** adjust, aguise, aguize, create, custom, design, entail, latest, manner, method, system, tailor **07** clothes, couture, entayle, in thing, pattern **08** approach, practice, rag trade, tendency **09** construct **10** appearance, convention **11** high fashion, manufacture **12** haute couture **13** designer label **15** clothes industry, fashion business

*Fashion designers include:*

**04** Choo (Jimmy), Dior (Christian), Erté, Lang (Helmut), Muir (Jean)
**05** Amies (Sir Hardy), Dolce (Domenico), Farhi (Nicole), Karan (Donna), Kenzo (Takada), Klein (Calvin), Ozbek (Rifat), Patou (Jean), Pucci (Emilio), Quant (Mary), Ricci (Nina), Smith (Sir Paul)
**06** Armani (Giorgio), Ashley (Laura), Cardin (Pierre), Chanel (Coco), Conran (Jasper), Davies (Betty), Lauren (Ralph), Miyake (Issey), Rhodes (Zandra), Ungaro (Emanuel)
**07** Balmain (Pierre), Fassett (Kaffe), Gabbana (Stefano), Hamnett (Katharine), Lacroix (Christian), Laroche (Guy), McQueen (Alexander), Missoni (Tai Otavio), Versace (Gianni)
**08** Galliano (John), Gaultier (Jean-Paul), Givenchy (Hubert James Marcel Taffin de), Hartnell (Sir Norman), Hilfiger (Tommy), Molyneux (Edward), Oldfield (Bruce), Richmond (John), Westwood (Dame Vivienne), Yamamoto (Yohji)
**09** Claiborne (Liz), Courrèges (André), Lagerfeld (Karl), McCartney (Stella), Valentino
**10** Balenciaga (Cristobal), Mainbocher, Vanderbilt (Gloria)
**12** Saint Laurent (Yves), Schiaparelli (Elsa)

---

**• after a fashion**
**08** in a sense **11** not very well **12** to some extent

**• current fashion**
**02** go

**• out of fashion**
**03** out **05** dated, passé **06** démodé, old hat, square **08** dismoded, obsolete, outmoded **09** out of date, unpopular **10** antiquated **12** old-fashioned **13** unfashionable

**fashionable**
**02** in **03** fly, hip, hot **04** chic, cool, tony **05** culty, flash, funky, natty, ritzy, smart, toney, vogue **06** chichi, glitzy, latest, modern, modish, snappy, snazzy, swanky, trendy, with it **07** à la mode, cultish, current, elegant, genteel, in vogue, mondain, popular, stylish, swagger **08** all the go, designer, fantoosh, mondaine, swinging, up-to-date **09** exclusive, happening, high-toned **10** all the rage, prevailing **11** in the groove **12** contemporary **13** up-to-the-minute

**fast**
**03** pdq **04** diet, firm, pacy, rash, shut, slim, wild **05** apace, brisk, faced, fiery, fixed, fleet, fully, hasty, nippy, pacey, quick, rapid, sound, swift, thick, tight **06** closed, deeply, firmly, flying, presto, secure, speedy, starve **07** abstain, express, fasting, fixedly, hastily, hurried, immoral, like mad, quickly, rapidly, refrain, riotous, swiftly, tightly **08** cracking, doggedly, exciting, fastened, go hungry, immobile, in a hurry, securely, speedily **09** breakneck, dissolute, fortified, high-speed, hurriedly, immovable, immovably, indelible, like a shot, like crazy, permanent, shameless, thrilling, turbulent **10** abstinence, blistering, boisterous, dissipated, like a flash, resolutely, starvation, stubbornly **11** accelerated, double-quick, lickety-spit, like the wind, ripsnorting **12** action-packed, deny yourself, dissipatedly, exhilarating, hunger strike, like the devil **13** extravagantly, like lightning, self-indulgent, unflinchingly **14** at a rate of knots, hell for leather **15** like the clappers

*Fast-days and fasting periods include:*

**04** Lent
**06** Ashura
**07** Ramadan
**08** Moharram, Muharram, Muharrem, Ramadhan, Tisha Bov

**09** Ember-days, Tisha Baav, Tisha be'Ab, Tisha Be'Av, Tishah b'Ab, Tishah B'Av, Yom Kippur
**10** Holy Friday
**12** Golden Friday

**fasten**
**03** aim, bar, fix, pin, tag, tie **04** bind, bolt, clip, do up, grip, join, lace, link, lock, moor, nail, seal, shut, spar, tack, zero **05** affix, chain, clamp, close, focus, hitch, latch, point, rivet, steek, unite, zip up **06** anchor, attach, buckle, button, direct, secure, take up, tether **07** connect **09** interlock **11** concentrate

**fastened**
**02** to **05** bound

**fastener, fastening**

*Fasteners include:*

**03** bar, fly, pin, tie, zip
**04** bond, clip, frog, hasp, hook, knot, lace, link, lock, loop, nail, stud, tach, tack
**05** catch, clasp, hinge, latch, morse, rivet, screw, tache
**06** buckle, button, clinch, cotter, eyelet, holder, staple, stitch, tassel, toggle, Velcro®, zipper
**07** padlock, tacking
**08** cufflink, shoelace, split pin
**09** paperclip, press stud, strapping
**10** collar stud, hook-and-eye
**11** bulldog clip, Chelsea clip, treasury tag
**12** espagnolette
**13** alligator clip, crocodile clip

**fast food** *see* **food; restaurant**

**fastidious**
**04** nice **05** chary, faddy, fussy, picky **06** choosy, dainty, quaint, queasy, queazy, spruce **07** choosey, finicky, precise **08** delicate, overnice, precious **09** difficult, exquisite, niff-naffy, squeamish, superfine **10** meticulous, niffy-naffy, particular, pernickety, scrupulous **11** persnickety, punctilious **12** hard-to-please **13** hypercritical **14** discriminating

**fat**
**02** OS **03** big, ghi, oil, pot, wax **04** bard, bulk, flab, fozy, ghee, lard, oily, rich, spek, suet, wide **05** beefy, broad, buxom, cream, dumpy, fatty, gross, heavy, keech, large, money, obese, plump, podgy, porky, pursy, round, solid, sonsy, speck, squab, stout, thick, tubby **06** butter, cheese, chubby, creesh, degras, flabby, fleshy, grease, greasy, lipoid, paunch, portly, rotund, tallow **07** adipose, blubber, fatness, fleshed, fulsome, in flesh, lanolin, obesity, paunchy, pinguid, sizable, tubbish **08** dripping, fruitful, generous, handsome, palmitin, pot belly, sizeable **09** animal fat, corpulent, fat as a pig, margarine, plumpness, sebaceous, solidness, spare tyre, stoutness **10** chubbiness, corpulence, deutoplasm, gor-bellied, kitchen-fee, oleaginous, overweight, pot-bellied, profitable **11** chylomicron, lipomatosis, substantial, well-endowed **12** considerable, saturated fat, steatopygous, vegetable fat **15** well-upholstered

**fatal**
**05** final, vital **06** deadly, lethal, mortal **07** fateful, killing **08** critical, decisive, destined, terminal **09** incurable, malignant **10** calamitous, disastrous **11** destructive, mortiferous, unavoidable **12** catastrophic

**fatalism**
**08** stoicism **09** endurance, passivity **10** acceptance **11** resignation

**fatalistic**
**07** passive, patient, stoical **08** resigned, yielding **09** defeatist **10** reconciled, submissive **11** acquiescent **13** long-suffering, philosophical

**fatality**
**04** dead, loss **05** death **08** casualty, disaster **09** lethality, mortality **10** deadliness **11** catastrophe

**fate**
**03** end, lot **04** doom, joss, luck, Norn, ruin **05** cavel, death, event, issue, karma, Moera, Moira, Norna, stars, weird **06** chance, defeat, future, kismet **07** destiny, fortune, outcome **08** disaster, God's will **09** horoscope **10** ill-fortune, predestiny, providence **11** catastrophe, destruction **14** predestination

*The Greek Fates:*

**06** Clotho
**07** Atropos
**08** Lachesis

*The Norse Fates:*

**03** Urd
**05** Skuld
**08** Verdande

**fated**
**03** fay, fey, fie **04** sure **06** doomed **07** certain **08** destined **09** enchanted **10** inevitable **11** ineluctable, inescapable, predestined, preordained, unavoidable **12** foreordained, predestinate

**fateful**
**05** fatal **07** crucial, pivotal **08** critical, decisive **09** important, momentous, prophetic **10** portentous **11** significant

**fatefully**
**09** crucially **10** critically, decisively **11** importantly, momentously **13** significantly

**father**
**02** da, Fr, pa **03** dad, gov, guv, pop **04** abba, abbé, bapu, curé, male, papa, père, pops, sire **05** adopt, beget, daddy, elder, maker, padre, pappy, pater **06** author, invent, leader, old man, parent, parson, pastor, patron, priest **07** creator, founder, genitor, produce **08** ancestor, beau-pere, begetter, engender, forebear, governor, inventor, minister **09** architect, clergyman, initiator, originate, patriarch, procreate **10** forefather, give life to, originator, prime mover, procreator, progenitor **11** birth father, predecessor **12** guiding light **13** paterfamilias

**Father Christmas**
**05** Santa **06** St Nick **10** Santa Claus **11** Kris Kringle **12** Kriss Kringle
*See also* **reindeer**

**fatherland**
**04** home **08** homeland **10** motherland, native land, old country **13** mother-country **15** land of your birth

**fatherly**
**04** kind **06** benign, kindly, tender **08** paternal **09** avuncular, indulgent **10** benevolent, forbearing, protective, supportive **11** patriarchal **12** affectionate

**fathom**
**01** f **02** fm **03** fth, get, see **04** fthm, twig **05** gauge, grasp, plumb, probe, sound **06** rumble **07** measure, plummet, suss out, work out **08** estimate, perceive **09** interpret, latch onto, penetrate, search out **10** comprehend, understand **12** get the hang of

**fathomless**
**04** deep **07** complex, endless **08** infinite **09** enigmatic, intricate **10** bottomless, mysterious **11** complicated **12** immeasurable, impenetrable

**fatigue**
**02** ME **03** CFS, sap, tax **04** do up, PVFS, tire, toil **05** drain, weary **06** overdo, weaken **07** exhaust, wear out **08** debility, enervate, lethargy, overwork, weakness **09** lassitude, tiredness, weariness, yuppie flu **10** debilitate, enervation, exhaustion **11** take it out of **12** listlessness **13** wearisomeness

**fatigued**
**04** beat **05** all in, jaded, tired, weary **06** beaten, bushed, done in, fagged, pooped, swink't, wasted, zonked **07** euchred, swinked, wappend, whacked **08** dead-beat, jiggered, tired out **09** exhausted, fagged out, knackered, overspent, overtired, pooped out **10** euchred out **11** tuckered out

**fatness**
**04** bulk, flab **06** grease **07** obesity **08** richness **09** bulkiness, fertility, grossness, heaviness, largeness, plumpness, podginess, rotundity, stoutness, tubbiness **10** corpulence, corpulency, overweight, pinguidity, pinguitude, portliness

**fatten**
**04** cram, feed, lard, soil **05** bloat, flesh, frank, stuff, swell, widen **06** batten, battle, enrich, expand, feed up, spread **07** broaden, build up, engross, fill out, nourish, nurture, thicken **08** overfeed, pinguefy, saginate **09** stall-feed

**fatty**
**03** fat **04** oily, waxy **05** oleic, suety **06** creamy, fleshy, greasy, lipoid, suetty **07** adipose, buttery, pinguid **08** unctuous **09** aliphatic, sebaceous **10** oleaginous

**fatuous**
**04** daft, gaga **05** dense, inane, moony, silly **06** absurd, stupid **07** asinine, foolish, idiotic, lunatic, moronic, puerile, vacuous, witless **08** imbecile, mindless **09** brainless, ludicrous **10** ridiculous, weak-minded

**fault**
◇ *anagram indicator*
**03** bug, nag, sin **04** beam, boob, carp, flaw, flub, gall, goof, slam, slip, trap, vice **05** blame, error, fluff, hitch, judge, knock, lapse, pinch, scold, slate, wrong **06** booboo, defect, foible, glitch, impugn, nibble, slip-up **07** blemish, blunder, censure, default, demerit, failing, impeach, misdeed, mistake, offence, quarrel **08** omission, weakness **09** criticize, inculpate, liability, oversight, reprehend, weak point **10** culpa levis, deficiency, negligence, peccadillo, wrongdoing **11** culpability, delinquency, pick holes in, shortcoming **12** imperfection, indiscretion, misdemeanour, pull to pieces **13** answerability, call to account, find fault with **14** accountability, responsibility **15** blameworthiness

**• at fault**
◇ *anagram indicator*
**03** out **05** wrong **06** guilty **07** at a loss, to blame **08** culpable **10** in the wrong **11** accountable, blameworthy, responsible

**• to a fault**
**06** unduly **07** too much **09** extremely **10** over the top, to extremes **11** excessively **12** immoderately, inordinately, in the extreme **13** unnecessarily

**fault-finding**
**04** crab **07** carping, nagging **08** captious, critical, niggling **09** cavilling, complaint, criticism, grumbling, querulous, quibbling **10** censorious, nit-picking **11** complaining **12** captiousness, pettifogging **13** hair-splitting, hypercritical **14** finger-pointing, hypercriticism

**faultless**
**04** pure **05** model **07** correct, perfect **08** accurate, flawless, spotless **09** blameless, exemplary, lily-white, unsullied **10** immaculate, impeccable **11** unblemished **13** unimpeachable **14** irreproachable, without blemish

**faulty**
◇ *anagram indicator*
**03** bad **04** bust, duff, weak **05** kaput, wonky, wrong **06** broken, flawed **07** damaged, invalid, vicious **08** culpable **09** casuistic, conked out, defective, erroneous, illogical, imperfect, incorrect, playing up **10** fallacious, inaccurate, not working, on the blink, out of order **11** inoperative, out of action **14** malfunctioning

**Faunas**
**03** Pan

**faux pas**
**04** boob, goof **05** error, gaffe **06** booboo, howler, slip-up **07** blunder, clanger, mistake **08** solecism **11** impropriety **12** indiscretion

**favour**
**03** aid **04** back, boon, gree, help, like, pick **05** go for, grace, spoil **06** assist, choose, esteem, opt for, pamper, prefer, select **07** aggrace, approve, backing, benefit, endorse, indulge, make for, promote, service, succour, support **08** advocate, approval, befriend, champion, courtesy, good deed, good turn, goodwill, kindness, plump for, resemble, sanction, sympathy **09** advantage, encourage, patronage, recommend **10** acceptance, act of grace, assistance, attraction, indulgence, obligation, partiality, preference **11** approbation, countenance, favouritism **12** commendation, friendliness, take kindly to **13** act of kindness

**• in favour of**
**03** for, pro **06** all for, behind **07** backing **10** supporting **11** on the side of

**• obtain favour**
**03** win

**favourable**
**04** fair, good, kind **05** white **06** benign, toward **08** amicable, Favonian, friendly, pleasing, positive, suitable, towardly **09** agreeable, approving, benignant, effective, opportune, promising **10** auspicious, beneficial, convenient, heartening, propitious, reassuring **11** appropriate, encouraging, meliorative, sympathetic **12** advantageous, enthusiastic, well-disposed **13** complimentary, understanding

**favourably**
**04** well **09** agreeably, helpfully **10** in good part, positively, profitably **11** approvingly, fortunately, opportunely **12** auspiciously, conveniently, propitiously **14** advantageously **15** sympathetically

**favoured**
**05** élite, fa'ard, faurd **06** chosen, graced **07** blessed, fancied **08** selected **09** favourite, predilect, preferred **10** advantaged, privileged **11** predilected, recommended

**favourite**
**03** nap, pet **04** fave, idol, peat, pick **05** great **06** choice, chosen, minion, winger **07** beloved, best boy, darling, dearest, nostrum, special **08** Benjamin, best girl, esteemed, favoured, gracioso, white boy **09** best-loved, boyfriend, certainty, form horse, golden boy, most-liked, number one, preferred, treasured **10** girlfriend, particular, preference **11** blue-eyed boy, first choice, teacher's pet **12** likely winner **13** fair-haired boy **14** apple of your eye, white-headed boy **15** odds-on favourite

**favouritism**
**04** bias **08** inequity, nepotism **09** injustice, prejudice **10** inequality, partiality, preference, unfairness **12** one-sidedness, partisanship

**fawn**
**04** buff, claw **05** beige, court, crawl, creep, khaki, kotow, sandy, smalm, smarm, toady **06** cosy up, cozy up, cringe, crouch, grovel, kowtow **07** adulate, cervine, flatter, spaniel **08** bootlick, butter up, cosy up to, pay court, soft-soap, suck up to **09** pale brown **10** cozy up with **11** curry favour **12** bow and scrape, sand-coloured **14** be obsequious to, yellowish-brown

**fawning**
**06** abject, supple **07** servile, spaniel **08** crawling, cringing, toadying, toadyish, unctuous **10** flattering, grovelling, obsequious, oleaginous **11** bootlicking, deferential, sycophantic **12** ingratiating, knee-crooking

**fay** *see* **fairy**

**faze**
**03** rub **04** beat, rush, stun **05** drive, shake, shock, worry **06** dismay, put off, put out, puzzle, rattle **07** disturb, fluster, perturb, startle, unnerve **08** disquiet, drive off, surprise, unsettle **09** dumbfound, take aback **10** disconcert **12** perturbation

**FBI member**
**03** Fed **04** G-man

**fear**
**03** awe **04** risk **05** alarm, doubt, dread, panic, scope, worry **06** adread, affray, chance, dismay, expect, fright, honour, horror, phobia, qualms, regret, revere, terror, unease, wonder **07** anxiety, concern, foresee, phobism, redoubt, respect, shaking, suspect, terrify **08** aversion, be afraid, disquiet, distress, freak out, prospect, venerate, wonder at **09** agitation, bête noire, fear of God, nightmare, quivering, reverence, shudder at, suspicion, tremble at, trembling **10** anticipate, be afraid of, be scared of, foreboding, heart-quake, likelihood, likeliness, misgivings, shrink from, solicitude,

tremble for, uneasiness, veneration **11** expectation, fearfulness, pantophobia, possibility, probability, trepidation **12** affrightment, apprehension, get the wind up, stand in awe of, take fright at **13** be in a blue funk, be uneasy about, consternation, have a horror of, lose your nerve **14** be anxious about, be in a cold sweat, lose your bottle, your heart melts **15** have qualms about, hold in reverence

**• for fear that**
**04** lest

**fearful**
**04** dire, grim **05** adred, afear, awful, ferly, nervy, tense, timid **06** afraid, aghast, hunted, scared, uneasy, yellow **07** alarmed, anxious, ghastly, hideous, in dread, nervous, panicky, shaking **08** affrayed, agitated, dreadful, effraide, fearsome, gruesome, hesitant, horrible, horrific, shocking, terrible, timorous **09** appalling, atrocious, frightful, harrowing, monstrous, petrified, quivering, spineless, trembling, tremulous **10** frightened **11** distressing, in a blue funk **12** apprehensive, faint-hearted, in a cold sweat **13** having kittens, scared to death

**fearfully**
**04** most, very, well **05** jolly **06** highly **07** awfully, timidly **08** terribly, uneasily **09** anxiously, extremely, intensely, nervously, unusually **10** dreadfully, hesitantly, incredibly **11** exceedingly, frightfully **12** terrifically, unbelievably **13** exceptionally **14** apprehensively

**fearless**
**04** bold, game **05** brave, gutsy, proud **06** ballsy, daring, feisty, gritty, heroic, plucky, spunky **07** aweless, doughty, gallant, impavid, valiant **08** intrepid, unafraid, valorous **09** confident, dauntless, unabashed, undaunted **10** courageous, unblinking **11** indomitable, lion-hearted, unblenching, unflinching **14** unapprehensive

**fearsome**
**04** unco **05** awful **07** awesome, dreaded **08** alarming, daunting, horrible, horrific, menacing, terrible **09** appalling, dismaying, frightful, unnerving **10** formidable, horrendous, horrifying, terrifying **11** frightening, hair-raising **12** awe-inspiring

**feasibility**
**09** viability **10** expedience **11** possibility, workability **12** practicality **13** achievability **14** practicability, reasonableness

**feasible**
**02** on **06** doable, likely, viable **08** possible, probable, workable **09** expedient, practical, realistic **10** achievable, attainable, realizable, reasonable **11** practicable **14** accomplishable

**feast**
**02** do **03** ale, pig **04** fest, fete, gala, luau, wake, Yule **05** agape, beano, binge, gaudy, gorge, hangi, Purim, revel, treat **06** bridal, dinner, double, Isodia, junket, kaikai, Lammas, pig out, regale, repast, revels, spread, Sukkot, wealth **07** banquet, blow-out, convive, holiday, holy day, lamb-ale, name day, potlach, Rood Day, Shavuot, Sukkoth **08** carnival, carousal, feast day, festival, Id al-Adha, Id al-Fitr, Passover, potlatch, Shabuoth, Shavuoth, Shevuoth **09** abundance, Eid al-Adha, Eid al-Fitr, entertain, epulation, Hallowmas, indulge in, junketing, love-feast, Martinmas, Martlemas, partake of, Pentecost, profusion, saint's day **10** cornucopia, jour de fête, Roodmas Day, slap-up meal **11** celebration, eat your fill, festivities, Holy-rood Day, wine and dine **13** All-hallowmass

**feat**
**03** act, art **04** deed **05** point, skill **06** action, henner, splits, stroke **07** exploit **08** hat trick, shanghai **09** keepy-uppy **10** attainment, Houdini act **11** achievement, performance, tour de force, undertaking **14** accomplishment

**feather**
**03** pen **04** down, tuft **05** crest, egret, penna, pinna, plume, quill, wedge **06** covert, fletch, hackle, manual, pinion, sickle **07** plumage, plumula, plumule, primary, rectrix, tectrix **08** aigrette, standard, tertiary, vibrissa **09** condition, filoplume, secondary, semiplume

**• coil of feathers**
**03** boa

**• part of feather**
**04** harl, herl

**feathery**
**04** soft **05** downy, light, plumy, wispy **06** fledgy, fleecy, flimsy, fluffy, plumed **07** plumate, plumose, plumous **08** delicate **09** feathered, penniform **10** pennaceous **11** featherlike

**feature**
**03** act, mug, pan **04** chin, dial, face, form, item, mark, nose, phiz, show, side, star **05** clock, facet, focus, looks, piece, point, shape, story, trait **06** appear, aspect, beauty, column, factor, figure, kisser, phizog, play up, report, visage **07** article, comment, perform, phantom, present, promote, quality **08** hallmark, property **09** attribute, character, emphasize, highlight, lineament, spotlight **10** accentuate, attraction, focal point, lineaments, speciality **11** centrepiece, countenance, participate, peculiarity, physiognomy **14** characteristic **15** call attention to, draw attention to

**featureless**
**04** dull **05** bland, blank, plain, vague **07** anaemic, insipid, vanilla **08** ordinary **11** commonplace, nondescript, uninspiring **12** cookie cutter, run of the mill, unattractive, unclassified, unremarkable **13** indeterminate, undistinctive, unexceptional, uninteresting **14** common or garden **15** undistinguished

**febrile**
**03** hot **05** fiery **07** burning, fevered, flushed, pyretic **08** feverish, inflamed **09** delirious

**February**
**03** Feb

**feckless**
**03** wet **04** weak **06** feeble, futile, no-good **07** aimless, useless, wimpish **08** helpless, hopeless **09** shiftless, worthless **11** incompetent, ineffectual **13** irresponsible

**fecund**
**07** fertile, teeming **08** fruitful, prolific **09** feracious, fructuous **10** productive **12** fructiferous

**fecundity**
**08** feracity **09** fertility **12** fruitfulness **14** productiveness

**federal**
**03** Fed **06** allied, united **07** unified **08** combined, in league **10** associated, integrated **11** amalgamated **12** confederated

**federate**
**04** ally **05** unify, unite **06** league **07** combine **09** associate, integrate, syndicate **10** amalgamate **11** confederate **12** confederated, join together

**federation**
**05** union **06** league **08** alliance, federacy **09** coalition, syndicate **11** association, combination, confederacy **12** amalgamation **13** confederation, copartnership

**fed up**
**03** ate **04** blue, down, glum, jack **05** bored, jaded, sated, tired, weary **06** dismal, gloomy **07** annoyed, chocker, pig sick **09** depressed, hacked off, pissed off **10** brassed off, browned off, cheesed off **11** disgruntled **12** discontented, dissatisfied, sick and tired **13** have had enough

**fee**
**03** due, pay, sub **04** bill, cost, fine, hire, rent, toll, wage **05** money, price, terms, tithe, tythe **06** cattle, charge, hirage, mouter, reward, salary, towage **07** account, faldage, footing, hireage, moorage, multure, payment, premium, service, tuition **08** chummage, pilotage, property, retainer **09** emolument, livestock, obvention, ownership, refresher, vassalage **10** bell-siller, honorarium, possession, recompense **11** inheritance **12** remuneration, subscription **15** appearance money

**feeble**
**03** wet **04** lame, poor, puny, tame, thin, weak **05** faint, frail, silly, sober, washy, wersh, wussy **06** ailing, debile, effete, flabby, flimsy, futile, infirm, sickly, slight, weakly **07** failing, rickety, wastrel, wearish, wimpish **08** daidling, decrepit, delicate, feckless, helpless, lustless, pathetic, sackless
**09** enervated, exhausted, graspless, powerless, weak-kneed **10** dispirited, fizzenless, foisonless, impuissant, inadequate, indecisive, namby-pamby, spiritless, wishy-washy **11** debilitated, fushionless, incompetent, ineffective, ineffectual, vacillating
**12** unconvincing, unsuccessful

**feeble-minded**
**04** dumb **05** dotty, silly **06** simple, stupid **07** idiotic, moronic
**08** imbecile, retarded **09** deficient, dim-witted, imbecilic **10** half-witted, indecisive, slow-witted, weak-minded
**11** not all there **13** soft in the head
**14** mouth breathing, not the full quid
**15** slow on the uptake

**feebly**
**06** lamely, sickly, weakly **07** faintly
**08** slightly **10** helplessly
**11** powerlessly **12** dispiritedly, indecisively, pathetically
**13** ineffectively

**feed**
◇ *insertion indicator*
**03** eat, put **04** crop, dine, food, fuel, give, paid, slip, soil, tire **05** graze, slide
**06** battle, browse, dine on, fodder, forage, foster, insert, repast, silage, stooge, suckle, supply, take in, tuck-in
**07** consume, deliver, fortify, gratify, nourish, nurture, pasture, provide, support, victual **08** cater for, ruminate
**09** encourage, foodstuff, introduce, partake of, provender **10** give food to, provide for, strengthen

**feedback**
**05** reply **06** answer **08** comeback, response **11** respondence

**feel**
**02** be **03** air, paw, rub **04** aura, bear, bent, deem, gift, hand, hold, know, look, maul, mood, palp, poke, seem
**05** enjoy, flair, grasp, grope, judge, knack, nurse, sense, skill, think, touch, vibes **06** appear, caress, clutch, detect, endure, finger, finish, fondle, fumble, handle, notice, reckon, stroke, suffer, talent **07** ability, believe, contact, discern, faculty, feeling, harbour, massage, observe, quality, realize, surface, texture, undergo
**08** ambience, aptitude, consider, instinct, perceive **09** be aware of, give way to, go through **10** atmosphere, experience, impression, manipulate, understand **11** consistency, live through **12** be overcome by **15** feel in your bones
• **feel for**
**04** pity **07** weep for **09** be moved by, grieve for **10** be sorry for, sympathize
**11** commiserate **13** empathize with
**14** sympathize with **15** commiserate with
• **feel like**
**04** want, wish **05** fancy **06** desire
**09** would like

**feeler**
**04** horn, palp **05** probe **06** palpus
**07** advance, antenna **08** approach, overture, tentacle **09** overtures
**10** sense organ **12** ballon d'essai, trial balloon

**feeling**
**03** air, ego **04** aura, bent, care, feel, gift, idea, love, mood, pity, view
**05** flair, hunch, knack, sense, skill, touch, vibes **06** ardour, belief, motion, notion, spirit, talent, theory, warmth
**07** ability, concern, emotion, fervour, inkling, opinion, passion, pitying, quality, thought **08** aptitude, emotions, esthesia, fondness, instinct, passions, sympathy **09** aesthesia, aesthesis, affection, intensity, intuition, sensation, sentience, sentiment, suspicion **10** affections, atmosphere, compassion, Empfindung, impression, perception, self-esteem, tenderness
**11** point of view, sensibility, sensitivity, sympathetic **12** appreciation
**13** compassionate, sensibilities, sensitivities, understanding, way of thinking **14** natural ability, sentimentality, susceptibility
• **show feeling**
**05** emote
• **with no feeling**
**04** numb

**feign**
**03** act **04** fain, fake, sham **05** fable, faine, false, fayne, forge, put on, shape
**06** affect, assume, gammon, invent, make up **07** falsify, fashion, imagine, imitate, pretend, put it on **08** misfeign, simulate **09** dissemble, fabricate
**11** counterfeit, dissimulate, make a show of, make believe

**feint**
**04** play, ruse, sham, wile **05** blind, bluff, dodge, dummy **06** gambit **08** artifice, pretence **09** deception, expedient, manoeuvre, stratagem **10** subterfuge
**11** distraction, make-believe, mock-assault **12** dissemblance

**feisty**
**04** bold **05** brave, gutsy, tough
**06** gritty, lively, plucky, spunky, touchy
**08** spirited **09** excitable, irritable
**10** courageous, determined

**feldspar, felspar**
**06** albite **08** adularia, andesine, sanidine, sunstone **09** anorthite, moonstone **10** hyalophane, oligoclase, orthoclase **11** anorthosite, labradorite, peristerite, plagioclase

**felicitous**
**03** apt **05** happy **06** timely
**07** apropos, fitting **08** apposite, inspired, suitable **09** fortunate, opportune, well-timed **10** delightful, propitious, prosperous, well-chosen, well-turned **11** appropriate
**12** advantageous

**felicity**
**03** joy **05** bliss **07** aptness, delight, ecstasy, rapture **08** blessing, euphoria
**09** eloquence, happiness, propriety
**11** delectation, suitability
**12** suitableness **13** applicability
**15** appropriateness

**feline**
**03** cat, tom **04** eyra, puss **05** catty, felid, manul, moggy, ounce, pussy, queen, quoll, rumpy, sleek, tabby
**06** kitten, malkin, mouser, ocelot, serval, slinky, smooth, Tibert, tomcat
**07** catlike, cattish, leonine, sensual, sinuous, wildcat **08** alleycat, baudrons, graceful, stealthy **09** grimalkin, sealpoint, seductive **10** jaguarundi
*See also* **cat**

**fell**
**02** ax, KO **03** axe, hew, lit, log **04** alit, dire, gall, hide, hill, keen, moor, pelt, raze, skin, very **05** cruel, felon, floor, great, level **06** deadly, fierce, lay low, mighty, poleax **07** cut down, doughty, flatten, poleaxe, pungent **08** chop down, demolish, felonous, membrane, ruthless **09** knock down, overthrow, prostrate **10** bitterness, strike down
**15** raze to the ground

**fellow**
**01** F, m **02** bo, co-, he **03** boy, bud, cat, cod, don, guy, Joe, lad, man, pal, sod, wag **04** bozo, chap, chum, cove, dean, dude, gent, like, male, mate, oppo, peer, twin **05** bloke, buddy, crony, devil, equal, match **06** buffer, callan, double, friend, person, rascal, sister
**07** callant, compeer, comrade, partner, related, similar **08** confrère, co-worker
**09** associate, boyfriend, character, colleague, companion, semblable
**10** associated, compatriot, individual
**11** counterpart **12** contemporary
*See also* **boy**
• **little fellow**
**03** elf, imp

**fellow feeling**
**04** care **07** empathy, feeling
**08** sympathy **10** compassion
**13** commiseration, understanding

**fellowship**
**04** club **05** guild, order, union
**06** league **07** society **08** intimacy, matiness, sodality, sorority
**09** communion, palliness **10** affability, amiability, chumminess, consortium, fraternity, friendship, sisterhood
**11** affiliation, association, brotherhood, camaraderie, comradeship, familiarity, sociability
**13** companionship, compatibility

**felon** *see* **criminal**

**felspar** *see* **feldspar, felspar**

**felt**
**03** bat **04** batt

**female**
**01** f **03** doe, -ess, gal, hen, her, pen, rib, she **04** bird, girl, hind, miss **05** woman
**06** maiden **07** girlish, womanly
**08** feminine, ladylike, womanish
**09** petticoat **10** carpellate, pistillate
*See also* **animal**; **girl**

**feminine**
**01** f **03** fem **04** weak **05** cissy, girly
**06** female, gentle, pretty, tender
**07** girlish, unmanly, wimpish, womanly
**08** delicate, graceful, ladylike, womanish **09** petticoat **10** effeminate

**femininity**
**08** delicacy **09** sissiness, womanhood
**10** effeminacy, gentleness, muliebrity, prettiness, tenderness **11** girlishness, womanliness **12** feminineness, gracefulness, womanishness

**feminism**
**09** women's lib **12** women's rights
**14** women's movement

*Feminists include:*

**04** Daly (Mary), Hite (Shere), Mott (Lucretia), Shaw (Anna Howard), Wolf (Naomi)
**05** Abzug (Bella), Astor (Nancy), Beale (Dorothea), Greer (Germaine), Stone (Lucy)
**06** Callil (Carmen), Cixous (Hélène), Faludi (Susan), Friday (Nancy), Fuller (Margaret), Gilman (Charlotte Perkins), Grimké (Sarah Moore), Orbach (Susie), Rankin (Jeannette), Stopes (Marie), Weldon (Fay)
**07** Anthony (Susan B), Davison (Emily), Dworkin (Andrea), Egerton (Sarah), Fawcett (Dame Millicent), Friedan (Betty), Goldman (Emma), Kennedy (Helena, Baroness), Lenclos (Ninon de), Steinem (Gloria), Tennant (Emma)
**08** Beauvoir (Simone de), Brittain (Vera), MacPhail (Agnes), Rathbone (Eleanor)
**09** Blackwell (Elizabeth), Pankhurst (Adela), Pankhurst (Christabel), Pankhurst (Emmeline), Pankhurst (Sylvia)
**11** Burgos Seguí (Carmen de)
**14** Wollstonecraft (Mary)

**femme fatale**
**04** vamp **05** Circe, siren **06** Sirens
**07** charmer, Delilah, Lorelei **08** Mata Hari **09** temptress **10** seductress
**11** enchantress

**fen**
**03** bog **04** moss, quag, wash
**05** marsh, swamp **06** morass, slough
**08** quagmire

**fence**
◇ *containment indicator*
**03** hay, pen **04** coop, oxer, pale, rail, wall, wear, weir, wire **05** bound, dodge, evade, guard, hedge, parry **06** defend, fraise, paling, pusher, rasper, rustic, secure, shield, shut in
**07** barrier, confine, defence, enclose, fortify, inclose, protect, quibble, railing, rampart **08** encircle, palisade, palisado, restrict, separate, sepiment, stockade, surround **09** barricade, enclosure, pussyfoot, stonewall, vacillate, windbreak **10** digladiate, equivocate, trafficker **11** prevaricate
**12** circumscribe, shilly-shally, tergiversate

• **sit on the fence**
**06** dither **08** be unsure **09** vacillate
**11** be uncertain, be undecided **12** be irresolute, shilly-shally **13** be uncommitted **14** blow hot and cold

**fencing**
**07** railing **08** guarding **09** defending, swordplay

*Fencing terms include:*

**03** bib, cut, hit
**04** bout, épée, foil, pass, pink, volt, ward
**05** allez, appel, carte, feint, forte, lunge, parry, piste, prime, punto, sabre, sixte, touch, volte
**06** attack, button, come in, doigté, faible, flèche, foible, octave, parade, puncto, quarte, quinte, remise, thrust, tierce, touché
**07** barrage, counter, en garde, on guard, passado, reprise, riposte, seconde, septime, stop hit
**08** back edge, balestra, coquille, plastron, tac-au-tac, traverse
**09** disengage, repechage
**10** flanconade, imbroccata, time-thrust
**11** corps à corps, punto dritto
**12** colichemarde, counter-parry, punto reverso
**14** counter-riposte

**fend**
**05** avert, parry, repel **06** defend, divert, resist **07** beat off, deflect, head off, keep off, provide, repulse, shut out, support, sustain, ward off **08** maintain, stave off **09** hold at bay, look after, turn aside **10** take care of

**feral**
**04** wild **06** animal, brutal, deadly, fierce, savage **07** bestial, brutish, untamed, vicious **08** funereal, unbroken **09** ferocious
**12** uncultivated **14** undomesticated

**ferment**
◇ *anagram indicator*
**04** boil, brew, foam, fret, fuss, heat, rise, stew, stir, work, zyme **05** cause, fever, froth, mould, rouse, yeast
**06** arouse, bubble, enzyme, excite, fester, foment, frenzy, furore, hubbub, incite, leaven, seethe, stir up, tumult, unrest, uproar, work up **07** agitate, inflame, provoke, ptyalin, turmoil
**08** bacteria, brouhaha, smoulder
**09** agitation, commotion, confusion
**10** disruption, effervesce, excitement, turbulence

**fermium**
**02** Fm

**fern**

*Ferns include:*

**03** oak
**04** hard, lady, male, tree
**05** beech, brake, chain, crown, holly, marsh, royal, sword, water
**06** Boston, ribbon, shield, silver, tongue
**07** bladder, bracken, buckler, Dickie's, elkhorn, Goldie's, leather, ostrich, parsley, rockcap, wall rue, woodsia
**08** aspidium, cinnamon, climbing, hairy lip, licorice, moonwort, pillwort, polypody, staghorn
**09** asparagus, asplenium, bird's nest, hare's foot, rusty-back, sensitive
**10** Asian chain, Korean rock, maidenhair, soft shield, spleenwort
**11** hart's tongue, rabbit's foot
**12** broad buckler, elephant's ear, resurrection
**13** crested ribbon, Japanese holly, scolopendrium, squirrel's foot
**14** brittle bladder
**15** Japanese painted

**ferocious**
**04** deep, grim, wild **05** cruel, feral
**06** bitter, brutal, fierce, savage, severe, strong **07** extreme, inhuman, intense, salvage, untamed, vicious, violent
**08** barbaric, pitiless, ruthless, sadistic, Tartarly, vigorous **09** barbarous, merciless, murderous **12** bloodthirsty, catamountain, cat o' mountain

**ferocity**
**06** sadism **07** cruelty **08** savagery, severity, violence, wildness
**09** barbarity, brutality, extremity, intensity **10** fierceness, inhumanity
**11** viciousness **12** ruthlessness

**ferret**
**03** hob **04** gill, hunt, jill **05** rifle, scour
**06** forage, search **07** rummage **09** go through

• **ferret out**
**04** find **05** dig up, trace **06** elicit
**07** extract, nose out, root out, suss out, unearth, worm out **08** discover, hunt down **09** search out, track down
**10** fossick out, run to earth

**ferry**
**03** ply, run **04** boat, move, pont, ro-ro, ship, take, taxi **05** carry, drive, shift
**06** convey, packet, ponton, vessel
**07** passage, pontoon, shuttle, traject, tranect **08** car ferry **09** ferry-boat, transport **10** packet boat **12** flying bridge **13** Interislander®, roll-on roll-off

**fertile**
**04** rich **06** battle, broody, fecund, potent, virile **08** abundant, creative, fruitful, inspired, pregnant, prolific
**09** ingenious, inventive, luxuriant, visionary **10** generative, productive
**11** imaginative, resourceful
**12** reproductive

**fertility**
**07** fatness, potency **08** richness, virility **09** abundance, fecundity **10** luxuriance **12** fruitfulness, prolificness **14** generativeness, productiveness

**fertilization**
**03** IVF **04** ICSI **07** selfing **10** conception **11** fecundation, pollination, procreation, propagation, siphonogamy **12** implantation, impregnation, insemination **13** palmification, superfetation

**fertilize**
**04** dung, feed, self **05** dress, mulch **06** enrich, manure **07** compost **08** fructify, top-dress **09** fecundate, pollinate, procreate **10** impregnate, inseminate **12** make fruitful, make pregnant

**fertilizer**
**04** dung, marl **05** guano, humus, mulch **06** manure **07** compost, humogen, kainite, nitrate, tankage **08** bone meal, dressing **09** cyanamide, plant food, soda nitre **10** fish-manure **11** top-dressing **13** sodium nitrate **14** superphosphate **15** ammonium nitrate

**fervent**
**03** hot **04** warm **05** eager, fiery **06** ardent, devout **07** earnest, excited, intense, sincere, zealous **08** spirited, vehement, vigorous **09** emotional, energetic, heartfelt **10** passionate **11** full-blooded, impassioned **12** enthusiastic, wholehearted

**fervently**
**07** eagerly **08** ardently **09** earnestly, excitedly, intensely, sincerely **10** vigorously **11** emotionally **12** passionately **13** energetically **14** wholeheartedly

**fervour**
**04** fire, heat, hwyl, zeal **05** verve **06** ardour, energy, spirit, vigour, warmth **07** emotion, passion **09** animation, eagerness, intensity, sincerity, vehemence **10** enthusiasm, excitement **11** earnestness

**fester**
**03** irk, rot **04** brew, gall **05** anger, annoy, chafe, decay, go bad **06** gather, infect, perish, rankle **07** moulder, putrefy **08** maturate, smoulder, ulcerate **09** decompose, discharge, suppurate

**festival**
**03** ale **04** fair, fete, gala, play, tide, wake **05** feast, festa, party, revel **06** double, fiesta, pardon **07** gala day, high day, holiday, jubilee **08** carnival, high tide, panegyry **10** merry-night, semi-double **11** anniversary, celebration, festivities, merrymaking **13** commemoration, entertainment

*See also* **celebration**; **service**

*Ancient festivals and celebrations include:*

**03** Bon, Mod
**04** feis, Lots, Yule
**05** Purim, Saman, Weeks, Wesak
**06** Advent, Diwali, Easter, Floria, Lammas, May Day, Oimelc, Opalia, Pesach, Plebii
**07** Beltane, Equiria, Feralia, Fugalia, holy-ale, Imbolic, Lady Day, Lemuria, Mop Fair, Navrati, Palilia, Parilia, Ramadan, Samhain, Sukkoth, Sullani, Theseia, Vinalia
**08** Agonalia, Cerealia, Fasching, Faunalia, Floralia, Hanukkah, Hogmanay, Homstrom, Hull Fair, Id ul-Adha, Id ul-Fitr, Lucia Day, Lugnasad, Mahayana, Matralia, Nit de foc, Passover, Samhuinn, Setsubun, Shabuoth, Stow Fair, Tanabata, Vestalia
**09** Baishakhi, Boxing Day, Christmas, church-ale, Floralies, Goose Fair, Hallowe'en, Hallowmas, Ides of Mar, Liberalia, Ludi Magni, Lugnasadh, Magalesia, Magha-puja, Mardi Gras, Martinmas, Nemoralia, Paganalia, Pentecost, Puanepsia, Robigalia, Thargelia, Ullambana, Up-Helly-Aa, Wakes Week, Yom Kippur
**10** Allhallows, Ambarvalia, Barnet Fair, Fordicidia, Fornicalia, Good Friday, Larentalia, La Tomatina, Lee Gap Fair, Ludi Romani, Lupercalia, Matronalia, Mother's Day, Neptunalia, Palm Sunday, Pancake Day, Parentalia, Portunalia, Quirinalia, Regifugium, Saturnalia, Swan Upping, Terminalia, Volcanalia
**11** Acension Day, All Fools' Day, All Souls' Day, Bacchanalia, Carmentalia, Epulum Jovis, Hina Matsuri, Lady Luck Day, Oktoberfest, Oskhophoria, Panathenaea, Quinquatrus, Semo Sanctus, St David's Day, Tabernacles
**12** All Saints' Day, Annunciation, Armilustrium, Ash Wednesday, Barranquilla, Day of the Dead, Doll Festival, Holy Wells Day, Kanda Matsuri, Ludi Merceruy, Mahashivrati, Meditrinalia, Moon Festival, Nutters Dance, Rosh Hashanah, St Andrew's Day, St George's Day, Thanksgiving, Tubilustrium, Twelfth Night, Well-dressing
**13** April Fool's Day, Haxey Hood Game, Ludi Consualia, Ludi Martiales, Midsummer's Eve, Raksha Bandhan, Shrove Tuesday, St Patrick's Day, The Furry Dance, Water Festival, Widecombe Fair
**14** Chinese New Year, Maundy Thursday, St Nicholas's Day, Vinalia Rustica, Walpurgis Night
**15** Festival of Light, Harvest Festival, Lares Praestites, Ludi Apollinares, Mahavira Jayanti, Mothering Sunday, Priddy Sheep Fair, St Valentine's Day

*Modern festivals and celebrations include:*

**05** VE Day, VJ Day, WOMAD
**08** Anzac Day, Earth Day, Labor Day
**09** Canada Day, Labour Day
**10** Burns Night, Eisteddfod
**11** Bastille Day, Cinco de Mayo, Glastonbury, Republic Day, Waitangi Day
**12** Armistice Day, Australia Day, Bonfire Night, Glyndebourne, Groundhog Day
**13** New Zealand Day
**14** Guy Fawkes' Night, Remembrance Day
**15** Edinburgh Fringe, Edinburgh Tattoo, Independence Day

*Religious festivals include:*

**02** Id
**03** Eid
**04** Holi, Lent, Lots, mela, Obon, Oram, puja, Yule
**05** Litha, Pesah, Purim
**06** Advent, Bakrid, Basant, Dhamma, Divali, Diwali, Easter, Lammas, Pesach, Sukkot
**07** Baisaki, Beltane, holy day, matsuri, New Year, Ramadan, Samhain, Shavuot, Sukkoth
**08** All Souls, Baisakhi, Dipavali, Dusserah, Epiphany, feast day, Hanukkah, Id-al-Adha, Id al-Fitr, Id-ul-Zuha, Muharram, Passover
**09** All Saints, Ascension, Candlemas, Christmas, Deepavali, Dolayatra, Durga-puja, Easter Day, Eid-al-Adha, Eid al-Fitr, Mardi Gras, Navaratri, Oshogatsu, Pentecost, Up-Helly-Aa, Yom Kippur
**10** All Hallows, Assumption, Good Friday, Lughnasadh, Lupercalia, Michaelmas, Palm Sunday, Ramanavami, Rathayatra, Saturnalia, Vulcanalia, Whit Sunday
**11** All Souls' Day, Bacchanalia, Lakshmi-puja, Milad-un-Nabi, Panathenaea, Rosh Hashana
**12** All Saints' Day, Annunciation, Ascension Day, Ash Wednesday, Christmas Day, Easter Sunday, Holy Saturday, Holy Thursday, Night of Power, Ohinamatsuri, Prakash Utsav, Rosh Hashanah, Simchat Torah, Star Festival, Tango no Sekku
**13** Buddha Purnima, Corpus Christi, Holy Innocents, Night of Ascent, Passion Sunday, spring equinox, Trinity Sunday, vernal equinox
**14** Chinese New Year, Day of Atonement, Easter Saturday, Maundy Thursday, summer solstice, winter solstice
**15** autumnal equinox, Lantern Festival, Tanabata Matsuri, Transfiguration

• **day before a festival**
**03** eve

• **octave of a festival**
**04** utas

**festive**
**04** gala **05** happy, jolly, merry

**06** cheery, festal, hearty, jovial, joyful, joyous **07** cordial, holiday **08** carnival, cheerful, feastful, jubilant **09** convivial **11** celebratory **12** light-hearted

**festivity**
**03** fun, rag **04** gala, gaud **05** party, revel, sport **06** fiesta, gaiety, let-off **07** jollity, joyance, revelry, triumph **08** carousal, feasting, festival, pleasure **09** amusement, enjoyment, joviality, junketing, merriment **10** banqueting, cheeriness, joyfulness, jubilation **11** celebration, fun and games, merrymaking **12** cheerfulness, conviviality **13** entertainment, glorification, jollification

**festoon**
**04** deck, hang, swag **05** adorn, array, drape **06** bedeck, swathe, wreath **07** bedizen, chaplet, garland, garnish, wreathe **08** decorate, encarpus, ornament

**fetch**
**03** fet, get **04** earn, fett, make, take **05** bring, carry, ghost, go for, reach, yield **06** arrive, attain, convey, derive, double, escort **07** bring in, collect, conduct, deliver, realize, sell for **08** go and get **09** stratagem, transport **10** apparition

**• fetch up**
**05** end up, vomit **06** arrive, show up, turn up, wind up **07** recover **08** finish up **11** materialize

**fetching**
**04** cute **05** sweet **06** pretty **07** winsome **08** adorable, alluring, charming **09** appealing **10** attractive, enchanting **11** captivating, fascinating

**fête, fete**
**04** fair, gala **05** treat **06** bazaar, honour, regale **07** holiday, lionize, welcome **08** carnival, festival **09** entertain **10** sale of work **11** garden party

**fetid, foetid**
**04** foul, rank **05** pongy **06** filthy, rancid, sickly, smelly, whiffy **07** humming, noisome, noxious, odorous, reeking **08** mephitic, stinking **09** offensive **10** disgusting, graveolent, malodorous, nauseating

**fetish**
**03** obi **04** idol, ju-ju, obia **05** charm, image, mania, obeah, thing, totem **06** amulet **08** fixation, idée fixe, talisman **09** obsession **10** cult object

**fetter**
**03** tie **04** bind, curb, gyve, iron **05** chain, tie up, truss **06** hamper, hinder, hobble, impede **07** confine, hopples, leg-iron, manacle, shackle **08** encumber, obstruct, restrain, restrict **09** constrain, entrammel, hamstring **10** hamshackle

**fetters**
**05** bands, bonds, curbs, irons **06** chains, checks, slangs **07** bondage **08** manacles, shackles **09** bracelets, captivity, handcuffs **10** hindrances, restraints **11** constraints, inhibitions **12** obstructions, restrictions

**fettle**
◇ *anagram indicator*

**• in fine fettle**
**03** fit **04** trim **05** sound **06** on form, strong **07** healthy, in shape **09** shipshape **10** in fine form, in good nick **11** in good shape **12** in good health **13** hale and hearty **15** in good condition

**feud**
**03** row, war **04** duel, food **05** argue, brawl, clash, fight **06** bicker, enmity, strife **07** contend, discord, dispute, ill will, quarrel, rivalry, wrangle **08** argument, bad blood, be at odds, conflict, squabble, vendetta **09** altercate, animosity, bickering, hostility **10** antagonism, bitterness **12** disagreement

**fever**
**04** heat **06** frenzy, unrest **07** ecstasy, ferment, passion, pyrexia, turmoil **08** delirium **09** agitation, calenture **10** excitement **11** temperature **12** feverishness, restlessness **15** high temperature

*Fevers include:*

**01** Q
**03** hay, tap
**04** ague, camp, gaol, gold, jail, Rock, ship, tick, worm
**05** brain, cabin, dandy, Lassa, Malta, marsh, stage, swamp, swine, Texas
**06** dengue, dumdum, hectic, jungle, parrot, plague, rabbit, spring, trench, typhus, valley, yellow
**07** biliary, enteric, gastric, malaria, measles, ratbite, sandfly, scarlet, splenic, spotted, typhoid, verruga
**08** childbed, kala-azar, undulant
**09** breakbone, calenture, East Coast, glandular, phrenitis, puerperal, relapsing, remittent, rheumatic
**10** blackwater, Rift Valley, scarlatina, yellow Jack
**12** African coast
**13** cerebrospinal, leptospirosis, Mediterranean
**14** kissing disease
**15** acute rheumatism

**fevered**
**03** hot, red **07** burning, excited, febrile, flushed, frantic, nervous **08** feverish, frenzied, restless, worked up **09** impatient **10** passionate

**feverish**
◇ *anagram indicator*
**03** hot, red **05** hasty **06** hectic, rushed **07** burning, excited, febrile, flushed, frantic, hurried, in a tizz, nervous **08** agitated, bothered, febrific, frenzied, in a tizzy, restless, troubled, worked up **09** delirious, flustered, impatient, in a dither **10** passionate **11** overwrought **12** in a kerfuffle **14** hot and bothered

**few**
**04** rare, some, thin **05** scant, wheen **06** meagre, scanty, scarce, sparse **07** a couple, handful, not many, several **08** one or two, sporadic, uncommon **09** a minority, exclusive, hardly any **10** inadequate, infrequent, negligible, scattering, sprinkling, two or three **11** scarcely any **12** insufficient **13** in short supply **14** a small number of, inconsiderable **15** thin on the ground

**fey**
**03** fay, fie, odd, shy **05** dotty, droll, elfin, funny, weird **06** doomed, quaint, quirky **07** curious, playful, unusual **08** childish, fanciful, peculiar **09** eccentric, impulsive, whimsical **10** capricious **11** mischievous **12** supernatural **13** unpredictable

**fiancé, fiancée**
**08** intended, wife-to-be **09** betrothed, bride-to-be **10** future wife **11** husband-to-be **13** future husband **14** bridegroom-to-be **15** prospective wife

**fiasco**
**04** bomb, flop, mess, rout, ruin **05** flask **06** bottle, fizzer, lash-up **07** cropper, debacle, failure, screw-up, washout **08** calamity, collapse, disaster **09** damp squib **11** catastrophe

**fiat**
**02** OK **05** edict, order **06** decree, dictum, diktat **07** command, dictate, mandate, precept, warrant **08** sanction **09** directive, ordinance **10** injunction, permission **12** proclamation **13** authorization

**fib**
**03** gag, lie **04** tale, yarn **05** evade, fable, porky, punch, story **06** invent, pummel **07** evasion, falsify, fantasy, fiction, untruth, whopper **08** sidestep, white lie **09** dissemble, fabricate, falsehood, fantasize, invention **10** concoction, taradiddle **11** prevaricate, tarradiddle **13** prevarication

**fibre**
**04** coir, hair, pile, pita, silk **05** cloth, nerve, sinew, stuff, viver **06** fibril, make-up, nature, strand, thread **07** calibre, courage, funicle, resolve, stamina, tendril, texture **08** backbone, filament, firmness, material, roughage, strength **09** character, substance, toughness, willpower **10** resolution **11** disposition, temperament **12** resoluteness **13** determination

**fibres**
**03** tow **04** pons

**fickle**
◇ *anagram indicator*
**06** kittle, labile, volage **07** flighty, mutable **08** disloyal, unstable, unsteady, variable, volatile **09** choiceful, faithless, mercurial, volageous **10** capricious, changeable, inconstant, irresolute, unfaithful, unreliable **11** treacherous,

vacillating **12** inconsistent, wind-changing **13** unpredictable

**• be fickle**

**04** turn

**fickleness**

**06** change, levity **09** treachery **10** disloyalty, fitfulness, mutability, volatility **11** flightiness, inconstancy, instability **12** unsteadiness **13** changeability, faithlessness, unreliability **14** capriciousness, changeableness, unfaithfulness

**fiction**

**03** fib, lie **04** myth, pulp, tale, yarn **05** fable, story **06** legend, novels **07** fantasy, parable, romance, stories, untruth **08** chick lit, noveldom, pretence **09** falsehood, invention, tall story **10** concoction **11** fabrication **12** splatterpunk, storytelling **15** creative writing

*See also* **literature**; **non-fiction**

**• science fiction**

**02** SF **05** sci-fi **09** cyberpunk

**fictional**

**06** made-up, unreal **08** fabulous, invented, literary, mythical **09** imaginary, legendary **11** make-believe, non-existent **12** mythological

*See also* **literary**; **novel**

*Fictional places include:*

**02** Ix, Oz
**04** Alph, Rhun
**05** Arnor, Holby, Moria, Rohan
**06** Canley, Dibley, Gondor, Laputa, Leonia, Lorien, Mordor, Narnia, Titipu, Utopia, Vulcan, Wessex, Xanadu
**07** Avonlea, Bedrock, Camelot, Erewhon, Eriador, Eurasia, Midwich, Mole End, Prydain, Sun Hill, Toyland, Walford
**08** Ambridge, Blefuscu, Borduria, Calormen, Earthsea, Flatland, Hobbiton, Islandia, Lilliput, Llaregyb, Meccania, Mirkwood, New Crete, Polyglot, Ragnarok, Stepford, Syldavia, Sylvania, Tartarus, The Shire, Toad Hall
**09** Barataria, Brigadoon, Discworld, Emmerdale, Freedonia, Hollyoaks, Llareggub, Ringworld, Rivendell, River Alph, Ruritania, Shangri-La, Summer Bay, Venusberg, Westworld
**10** Archenland, Barchester, Borchester, Moominland, Shieldinch, Vanity Fair, Wonderland
**11** Airstrip One, Ankh-Morpork, Barsetshire, Borsetshire, Brobdingnag, Diagon Alley, Emerald City, Gormenghast, Middle-Earth, Orbitsville, Skull Island, The Wild Wood
**12** Albert Square, Celesteville, Erinsborough, Glubbdubdrib, Jurassic Park, Ramsay Street, Sleepy Hollow, Tralfamadore, Weatherfield
**13** Celestial City, Christminster, Montego Street
**14** Brookside Close, Doubting-Castle, Hogwarts School, Never-Never Land, Nightmare Abbey, Treasure Island
**15** Baskerville Hall

**fictitious**

**04** fake, sham **05** bogus, false **06** made-up, mythic, untrue **07** assumed, feigned, fictive **08** invented, mythical, romantic, spurious, supposed **09** concocted, imaginary **10** apocryphal, artificial, fabricated, improvised **11** counterfeit, non-existent

*Fictitious places include:*

**07** Speewah
**08** Woop Woop
**10** Snake Gully
**11** Bandywallop
**12** Bullamakanka, Oodnagalahbi, Waikikamukau
**13** the black stump

**fiddle**

**02** do, gu **03** con, fix, gju, gue, kit, toy **04** fuss, play, rasp, rote, scam **05** cheat, fraud, graft, viola **06** diddle, fidget, juggle, meddle, racket, rip-off, scrape, tamper, tinker, trifle, violin **07** falsify, sultana, swindle **09** gold brick, interfere, manoeuvre, racketeer **10** fool around, mess around **12** cook the books **13** sharp practice

**fiddling**

**05** petty **06** fiddly, paltry **07** trivial **08** trifling **10** negligible **13** insignificant

**fidelity**

**05** faith, fides, troth, trust **07** honesty, loyalty **08** accuracy, devotion **09** adherence, closeness, constancy, exactness, precision **10** allegiance, strictness **11** devotedness, reliability **12** authenticity, faithfulness **13** dependability **15** trustworthiness

**fidget**

**03** toy **04** fike, fret, fuss, jerk, jump **05** hotch **06** bustle, fiddle, footer, hirsle, jiggle, niggle, squirm, tamper, tinker, trifle, twitch, writhe **07** shuffle, twiddle, wriggle **09** mess about **10** play around **11** toss and turn **12** restlessness

**fidgety**

**05** jumpy **06** on edge, uneasy **07** excited, jittery, nervous, restive, twitchy, uptight **08** agitated, restless **09** impatient

**field**

**03** lea, ley **04** area, lawn, line, mead, play, slip, stop **05** catch, champ, close, forte, glebe, green, parry, pitch, put up, range, sawah, scene, scope, sward **06** answer, bounds, domain, ground, handle, lea-rig, limits, meadow, padang, pick up, regime, return, select, sphere **07** deflect, paddock, pasture, present, runners, send out, stubble **08** ball park, confines, cope with, deal with, entrants, province, retrieve **09** grassland, opponents, possibles, territory **10** applicants, candidates, contenders, department, discipline, opposition, speciality **11** competition, competitors, contestants, environment **12** choose to play, participants, playing-field

*See also* **athletics**; **cricket**

**• stubble field**

**05** arish **06** arrish

**Field Marshal**

**02** FM **13** velt-mareschal

*Field Marshals include:*

**04** **Haig** (Douglas, Earl)
**05** **Lucan** (George Bingham, Earl of), **Monty**
**06** **French** (Sir John), **Raglan** (Fitzroy Somerset, Lord)
**07** **Allenby** (Edmund Hynman, Viscount), **Roberts** (Frederick, Earl)
**08** **Ironside** (William, Lord), **Wolseley** (Garnet Joseph, Viscount)
**09** **Robertson** (Sir William)
**10** **Alanbrooke** (Alan Francis Brooke, Viscount), **Auchinleck** (Sir Claude John Eyre), **Kesselring** (Albert), **Montgomery** (Bernard, Viscount)

**fiend**

**03** fan, nut **04** buff, ogre **05** beast, brute, demon, devil, fient, freak, ghoul **06** addict, savage **07** devotee, fanatic, monster **10** aficionado, enthusiast, evil spirit

**fiendish**

**05** cruel **06** brutal, clever, savage, wicked **07** complex, cunning, inhuman, obscure, vicious **08** barbaric, devilish, infernal, involved, ruthless **09** difficult, ferocious, ingenious, intricate, monstrous **10** aggressive, diabolical, horrendous, malevolent **11** challenging, complicated, imaginative, resourceful, unspeakable **12** bloodthirsty **14** Mephistophelic **15** Mephistophelean, Mephistophelian

**fierce**

**03** hot, wud **04** fell, grim, keen, wild, wood **05** angry, breem, breme, cruel, felon, grave, stern, stout **06** brutal, raging, savage, severe, strong, wrathy **07** furious, intense, rampant, vicious, violent **08** menacing, powerful, ruthless, terrible, walleyed **09** cut-throat, dangerous, ferocious, merciless, murderous, truculent **10** aggressive, passionate, relentless **11** frightening, tempestuous, threatening **12** bloodthirsty, uncontrolled

**fiercely**

**06** keenly, wildly **07** cruelly, sternly **08** bitterly, brutally, savagely, severely, strongly, terribly **09** furiously, intensely, viciously, violently **10** implacably, menacingly, powerfully, ruthlessly **11** dangerously, fanatically, ferociously, mercilessly, murderously

12 aggressively, passionately, relentlessly, tooth and nail
13 tempestuously, threateningly

**fiery**
**03** hot **05** afire, aglow, sharp, spicy **06** ablaze, aflame, ardent, fierce, heated, red-hot, spiced, spunky, sultry, torrid **07** blazing, burning, fervent, flaming, flushed, frampal, glowing, piquant, pungent, violent
**08** frampold, inflamed, seasoned
**09** excitable, hot-headed, impatient, impetuous, impulsive, irritable
**10** passionate, phlogistic, sulphurous
**11** empassioned, high-mettled, impassioned

**fiesta**
**04** gala **05** feast, party **07** holiday, jubilee **08** carnival, festival **09** festivity
**11** celebration, merrymaking

**fifteen**
**02** XV

**fifty**
**01** L
**• fifty per cent**
**02** so

**fight**
**03** box, hit, row, wap, war **04** blue, bout, camp, curb, defy, duel, feud, fray, grit, guts, mill, riot, rout, ruck, spar, stem, yike **05** aggro, argue, bandy, brawl, brush, clash, drive, fence, joust, mêlée, mix-in, pluck, punch, rammy, scrap, set-to, spunk, yikes **06** action, attack, barney, battle, bicker, bottle, bovver, bundle, combat, debate, dust-up, engage, fracas, meddle, medley, oppose, repugn, resist, ruckus, ruffle, rumble, scrape, shindy, spirit, stifle, stoush, strike, strive, take on, thwart, tussle **07** bashing, be at war, contend, contest, crusade, discord, dispute, fall out, grapple, lay into, make war, pasting, punch-up, quarrel, repress, resolve, ruction, scuffle, smother, tuilyie, tuilzie, wage war, warfare, wrangle, wrestle **08** argument, be at odds, bottle up, campaign, champion, conflict, ding-dong, do battle, dogfight, exchange, firmness, gunfight, have a row, hold back, keep back, militate, movement, object to, pell-mell, restrain, set about, skirmish, squabble, struggle, suppress, tenacity
**09** altercate, bloodshed, cockfight, duke it out, encounter, force back, monomachy, skiamachy, stand up to, weigh into, willpower, withstand
**10** aggression, bandy words, digladiate, dissension, Donnybrook, engagement, fisticuffs, free-for-all, graplement, will to live **11** altercation, come to blows, cross swords, disturbance, hostilities, snickersnee, work against **12** disagreement, resoluteness **13** confrontation, determination, measure swords, take issue with **14** hold out against
**15** campaign against, do battle against, struggle against

**• fight back**
**04** curb **05** check, reply **06** resist, retort **07** contain, control, repress
**08** bottle up, hold back, restrain, suppress **09** force back, retaliate
**11** put up a fight **13** counter-attack
**14** defend yourself, hold out against
**• fight off**
**04** rout **05** repel **06** rebuff, resist
**07** beat off, hold off, ward off **08** stave off **09** hold at bay, keep at bay **11** put to flight
**• incite to fight**
**03** tar **05** tarre

**fighter**
**01** F **03** EFA, MiG **05** rival **07** bruiser, chetnik, fechter, jump jet, soldier, trouper, warrior **08** attacker, hired gun, opponent **09** adversary, combatant, contender, disputant, man-at-arms, mercenary **10** antagonist, contestant
**11** bushwhacker **13** Messerschmitt
**15** sparring partner

*Fighters include:*

**05** boxer, pugil
**06** fencer, hitman, knight
**07** matador, picador, sworder
**08** pugilist, toreador, wrestler
**09** gladiator, kick boxer, spadassin, swordsman
**10** rejoneador
**11** bullfighter, digladiator
**12** banderillero, prizefighter

*See also* **aeroplane**

**figment**
**• figment of your imagination**
**05** fable, fancy **07** fiction **08** delusion, illusion **09** deception, falsehood, invention **10** concoction **11** fabrication
**13** improvisation

**figurative**
**03** fig **07** typical **08** symbolic, tropical
**09** parabolic, pictorial **10** emblematic
**11** allegorical, descriptive
**12** metaphorical, naturalistic
**14** representative

**figure**
**03** fig, sum **04** body, form, icon, idol, ikon, sign, sums **05** build, digit, frame, guess, image, judge, maths, price, shape, think, torso, total, value
**06** amount, appear, crop up, design, emblem, leader, number, person, reckon, sketch, symbol, worthy
**07** believe, diagram, drawing, feature, integer, notable, numeral, outline, passage, pattern, picture, suppose
**08** conclude, consider, estimate, foreshow, physique **09** authority, celebrity, character, dignitary, horoscope, personage, symbolize
**10** appearance, silhouette, statistics
**11** mathematics, personality **12** be included in, calculations, illustration
**13** be mentioned in **14** representation

*Figures include:*

**04** cone, cube, kite, oval
**05** prism
**06** circle, cuboid, oblong, sector, sphere, square
**07** decagon, diamond, ellipse, hexagon, nonagon, octagon, polygon, pyramid, rhombus
**08** crescent, cylinder, heptagon, pentagon, quadrant, tetragon, triangle
**09** chiliagon, dodecagon, rectangle, trapezium, undecagon
**10** hemisphere, hendecagon, octahedron, polyhedron, quadrangle, semicircle
**11** pentahedron, tetrahedron
**13** parallelogram, quadrilateral
**15** scalene triangle

*See also* **circle**; **triangle**

**• figure of speech**
**05** image, trope **06** flower, simile, zeugma **07** imagery, meiosis
**08** diallage, metaphor, oxymoron
**09** prolepsis **10** abscission, antithesis, hyperbaton, synecdoche
**11** parenthesis **12** antimetabole, turn of phrase
**• figure on**
**04** plan **06** expect **07** plan for
**08** depend on, reckon on **10** bargain for **13** be prepared for **15** take into account
**• figure out**
**03** see **04** dope, make, twig **05** count
**06** fathom, reason, reckon
**07** compute, dope out, make out, resolve, work out **08** decipher, estimate, tumble to **09** calculate, latch onto, puzzle out **10** understand **13** get the picture

**figurehead**
**04** bust, name **05** dummy, image, token **06** figure, puppet **07** carving
**08** front man **10** man of straw, mouthpiece **11** nominal head, titular head

**Fiji**
**03** FJI

**filament**
**04** cord, hair, pile, wire **05** cable, fiber, fibre, seton **06** cirrus, elater, sleave, strand, string, thread **07** fimbria, tendril, whisker **08** fibrilla, tentacle
**09** microwire, protonema
**10** paraphysis **11** gonimoblast

**filch**
**03** nab, rob **04** crib, drib, fake, lift, nick, palm, prig, take **05** lurch, pinch, steal, swipe **06** nobble, pilfer, rip off, smouch, snitch, thieve **07** purloin, snaffle **08** embezzle, knock off, peculate **09** knock down
**14** misappropriate

**file**
**03** ask, box, row, rub **04** case, data, hone, line, list, make, note, rake, rasp, risp, roll, sand, text, whet **05** apply, enter, grate, march, plane, put in, queue, scour, shape, shave, store, trail, train, troop **06** abrade, binder, column, folder, format, papers, parade, polish, record, scrape, smooth, stream, string,

submit, thread **07** box file, cortège, data set, details, dossier, pollute, process, program, Rolodex®, rub down **08** classify, document, organize, register **09** catalogue, crocodile, lever arch, portfolio **10** categorize, pickpocket, pigeonhole, procession, put in place, walk in line **11** information, particulars

**filial**

**04** fond **05** loyal **06** loving **07** devoted, dutiful **10** daughterly, respectful **12** affectionate

**filibuster**

**05** delay, stall **06** hinder, impede, pirate, put off **07** prevent **08** obstruct, perorate **09** buccaneer, hindrance, speechify, waste time **10** impediment, peroration **11** obstruction **12** postponement, speechifying **13** procrastinate **15** delaying tactics, procrastination

**filigree**

**04** lace **07** lattice, tracery **08** fretwork, lacework, wirework **09** interlace **10** scrollwork **11** latticework

**fill**

◇ *insertion indicator*

**04** brim, bung, clog, cork, cram, glut, hold, line, pack, plug, seal, soak, stop **05** ample, block, close, crowd, imbue, prime, stack, stock, stuff **06** bishop, charge, englut, enough, fulfil, occupy, plenty, riddle, stop up, supply, take up **07** congest, furnish, implete, perform, pervade, provide, satisfy, suffuse **08** complete, make full, permeate, saturate **09** abundance, replenish **10** all you want, impregnate, sufficient **11** sufficiency **13** all you can take **14** more than enough

**• fill in**

**05** brief, write **06** act for, advise, answer, inform **07** cover in, fill out, replace, stand in **08** acquaint, complete, deputize **09** represent **10** substitute, understudy **11** pinch-hit for **13** bring up to date

**• fill out**

**06** answer, fill in **08** complete **10** gain weight, grow fatter **11** put on weight **12** become fatter **13** become plumper **14** become chubbier

**fillet**

**04** list **05** label **06** anadem, fascia, reglet, regula **07** annulet, cloison **09** sphendone, tournedos

**filling**

◇ *insertion indicator*

**03** big **04** full, rich **05** ample, heavy, large, solid **06** filler, hearty, inside, square, stodgy **07** padding, wadding **08** contents, generous, stuffing **09** impletion, substance **10** nutritious, satisfying **11** substantial

**fillip**

**04** goad, prod, push, spur **05** boost, flick, shove **06** incite, snitch **07** impetus **08** stimulus **09** incentive, stimulant, stimulate **10** inducement, motivation **11** stimulation **13** encouragement

**film**

**03** cel, ISO, pic, web **04** cell, cine-, coat, epic, haze, kell, mist, reel, skin, veil, weft **05** cloud, cover, flick, glaze, layer, movie, sheet, shoot, short, spool, video **06** cinema, deepie, screen, silent, tissue **07** blanket, coating, dusting, feature, footage, picture **08** cassette, covering, membrane, pellicle, televise **09** blue movie, cartridge, mistiness, skinflick, videogram, videotape **10** featurette, horse opera, photograph, screenplay, video nasty **11** documentary, feature film **12** record on film **13** motion picture, video cassette

*See also* **director**

*Films include:*

**02** ET, If...
**03** Big, JFK, Kes, Ran
**04** Antz, Babe, Dr No, Gigi, Heat, Jaws, MASH, Reds
**05** Alfie, Alien, Bambi, Bugsy, Crash, Dumbo, Fargo, Ghost, Giant, Rocky, Shrek
**06** Aliens, Amélie, Batman, Ben-Hur, Blow-Up, Casino, Gandhi, Grease, Heimat, Lolita, Mad Max, Misery, Psycho, The Fly, Top Gun, Top Hat
**07** Amadeus, Big Fish, Cabaret, Das Boot, Die Hard, Dracula, Rain Man, Rebecca, Robocop, Titanic, Tootsie, Traffic, Vertigo
**08** Apollo 13, Body Heat, Born Free, Cape Fear, Chocolat, Duck Soup, Fantasia, High Noon, Insomnia, Key Largo, Kill Bill, King Kong, Scarface, Star Wars, The Birds, The Piano, The Sting, The Thing, The Tramp, Toy Story
**09** 12 Monkeys, A Bug's Life, Annie Hall, Betty Blue, Cat Ballou, Chinatown, City of God, Easy Rider, Excalibur, Funny Girl, Get Shorty, Gladiator, GoldenEye, Home Alone, Local Hero, Manhattan, Moonraker, Nosferatu, Octopussy, Pinocchio, Rio Grande, Spartacus, Spider-Man, Stand by Me, Vera Drake
**10** Blue Velvet, Braveheart, Casablanca, Chicken Run, Cry Freedom, Dirty Harry, East of Eden, Goldfinger, GoodFellas, Grand Hotel, High Sierra, Men in Black, Metropolis, My Fair Lady, My Left Foot, Now Voyager, Paris Texas, Raging Bull, Rear Window, Stagecoach, Taxi Driver, The Big Easy, The Hustler, The Postman, The Shining, The Wild One, Unforgiven, Wall Street
**11** A Few Good Men, All About Eve, American Pie, Beetlejuice, Blade Runner, Citizen Kane, Deliverance, Don't Look Now, Finding Nemo, Forrest Gump, Gosford Park, Heaven's Gate, La Dolce Vita, Mary Poppins, Mean Streets, Monsters, Inc, Mystic River, Notting Hill, Out of Africa, Pretty Woman, Public Enemy, Pulp Fiction, The 400 Blows, The Big Sleep, The Evil Dead, The Exorcist, The Fugitive, The Gold Rush, The Graduate, The Lion King, The Red Shoes, The Third Man, Thunderball, Wayne's World, Wild at Heart
**12** A View to a Kill, Brighton Rock, Casino Royale, Cool Hand Luke, Eyes Wide Shut, Frankenstein, Ghostbusters, Gregory's Girl, Groundhog Day, Jurassic Park, Lethal Weapon, Philadelphia, Prizzi's Honor, Roman Holiday, Rome, Open City, Salaam Bombay!, Seven Samurai, Sleepy Hollow, The Apartment, The Godfather, The Searchers, The Wicker Man, The Wild Bunch, Whisky Galore!, Withnail and I
**13** Apocalypse Now, Basic Instinct, Batman Forever, Batman Returns, Burnt by the Sun, Death in Venice, Die Another Day, Doctor Zhivago, Educating Rita, Eight and a Half, His Girl Friday, Licence to Kill, Live and Let Die, Mildred Pierce, Raining Stones, Reservoir Dogs, Scent of a Woman, Some Like It Hot, The Crying Game, The Dam Busters, The Deer Hunter, The Dirty Dozen, The Fisher King, The Jazz Singer, The Jungle Book, The Right Stuff, The Terminator, To Catch a Thief, Trainspotting, West Side Story, Wings of Desire, Zorba the Greek
**14** A Day at the Races, American Beauty, American Psycho, As Good as it Gets, Blazing Saddles, Bonnie and Clyde, Brief Encounter, Bringing Up Baby, Central Station, Chariots of Fire, Cinema Paradiso, Dial M for Murder, Empire of the Sun, Enter the Dragon, Erin Brockovich, Five Easy Pieces, Gangs of New York, Goodbye Mr Chips, Jean de Florette, LA Confidential, Midnight Cowboy, Minority Report, Muriel's Wedding, Schindler's List, Secrets and Lies, The Big Lebowski, The Commitments, The Elephant Man, The Great Escape, The Ladykillers, The Last Emperor, The Life of Brian, The Lost Weekend, The Mask of Zorro, The Music Lovers, The Seventh Seal, Un Chien Andalou
**15** Annie Get Your Gun, A Passage to India, Back to the Future, Crocodile Dundee, Dog Day Afternoon, Do the Right Thing, Fatal Attraction, For Your Eyes Only, Full Metal Jacket, Gone With the Wind, Good Will Hunting, Heart of Darkness, Independence Day, Life Is Beautiful, Manon des Sources, Meet Me in St Louis, On the Waterfront, Return of the Jedi, Road to Perdition, Singin' in the Rain, Sunset Boulevard, Tarzan the Ape Man, The African Queen,

The Bicycle Thief, Thelma and Louise, The Piano Teacher, The Seven Samurai, The Sound of Music, Thirty-nine Steps

*Film types include:*

**03** spy, war
**04** blue, cult, epic, noir
**05** adult, anime, buddy, crime, farce, heist, short, spoof, vogue, weepy
**06** action, auteur, biopic, B-movie, comedy, Disney, erotic, family, horror, murder, police, re-make, rom-com, silent, weepie
**07** Carry-on, cartoon, classic, diorama, fantasy, musical, neo-noir, new wave, passion, realist, robbery, slasher, tragedy, war hero, western
**08** animated, disaster, escapist, film noir, gangster, newsreel, romantic, space-age, thriller
**09** adventure, Bollywood, burlesque, chopsocky, detective, film à clef, flashback, Hitchcock, Hollywood, James Bond, love story, low-budget, melodrama, political, road movie, satirical, skin flick, Spielberg, whodunnit
**10** avant-garde, bonkbuster, gay-lesbian, neo-realist, period epic, snuff movie, surrealist, tear-jerker, travelogue
**11** black comedy, blockbuster, cliff-hanger, documentary, kitchen sink, period drama, tragicomedy, underground
**12** cinéma-vérité, Ealing comedy, ethnographic, fly-on-the-wall, mockumentary, pornographic, rockumentary, social comedy
**13** comic-book hero, expressionist, multiple-story, murder mystery, nouvelle vague, sexploitation, sexual fantasy, social problem
**14** blaxploitation, Charlie Chaplin, comedy thriller, police thriller, rites of passage, romantic comedy, science-fiction
**15** animated cartoon, cowboy and Indian, romantic tragedy, screwball comedy

**• film classification**
**01** A, U, X **02** AA, PG
**• film company**
**05** indie **06** studio
**• film over**
**03** fog **04** blur, dull **05** glaze **08** mist over **09** cloud over **13** become blurred
**• horror film** *see* **horror**
**• part of film**
**04** reel

### filmy
**04** fine, thin **05** gauzy, light, sheer **06** flimsy, floaty **07** clouded, fragile **08** chiffony, cobwebby, delicate, gossamer **09** gossamery **10** diaphanous, see-through, shimmering **11** translucent, transparent **13** insubstantial

### filter
**04** leak, mesh, ooze, seep, sift **05** drain, gauze, leach, sieve **06** purify, refine, riddle, screen, sifter, strain **07** clarify, dribble, netting, trickle **08** colander, filtrate, membrane, strainer **09** percolate

### filth
**03** mud **04** crap, crud, dirt, dung, gore, grot, gunk, mire, muck, porn, smut, soil, yuck **05** addle, bilge, dreck, dross, grime, gunge, slime, trash **06** faeces, grunge, manure, refuse, sewage, sleaze, sludge, wallow **07** garbage, rubbish, squalor, sullage **08** effluent, foulness, hard porn, impurity **09** blue films, colluvies, excrement, indecency, obscenity, pollution, vulgarity **10** coarseness, corruption, defilement, dirty books, sordidness **11** pornography, putrescence, raunchiness, uncleanness **12** putrefaction **13** contamination, sexploitation

### filthy
**03** bad, low, wet **04** base, blue, foul, lewd, mean, vile, wild **05** adult, angry, bawdy, black, cross, dirty, grimy, gross, manky, mucky, muddy, nasty, rainy, ratty, rough, slimy, sooty, yucky **06** Augean, coarse, crabby, cruddy, faecal, grubby, impure, putrid, rotten, shirty, smutty, soiled, sordid, stormy, vulgar, X-rated **07** corrupt, obscene, raunchy, squalid, stroppy, swinish, unclean **08** decaying, depraved, explicit, indecent, polluted, unwashed, wretched **09** irritable, offensive, worthless **10** despicable, putrefying, suggestive **11** bad-tempered, foul-mouthed **12** contaminated, contemptible, disagreeable, pornographic

### fin
**03** arm **04** hand, skeg, tail, vane **05** fiver, pinna, skegg **06** dorsal **07** Finland, ventral **08** pectoral

### final
◇ *tail selection indicator*
**03** end, net **04** last, nett **05** dying **06** latest **07** closing, settled, supreme **08** decisive, definite, eventual, farewell, terminal, ultimate **09** finishing **10** concluding, conclusive, conclusory, definitive, last-minute, peremptory **11** determinate, irrefutable, irrevocable, terminating, unalterable **12** indisputable
**• final word**
**04** amen

### finale
◇ *tail selection indicator*
**03** end **05** close **06** climax, ending **07** curtain **08** epilogue, final act **10** conclusion, dénouement **11** culmination **13** crowning glory

### finality
**08** firmness, ultimacy **09** certitude **10** conviction, resolution **11** decidedness **12** decisiveness, definiteness **13** inevitability **14** conclusiveness, inevitableness, irrevocability, unavoidability **15** irreversibility

### finalize
**03** end **05** agree, close, sew up **06** clinch, decide, finish, settle, wrap up **07** resolve, work out **08** complete, conclude, round off

### finally
◇ *tail selection indicator*
**04** last **06** at last, in fine, lastly **07** for ever, for good **08** at length, in the end **10** decisively, definitely, eventually, to conclude, ultimately **11** irrevocably, permanently **12** conclusively, in conclusion, irreversibly **13** for good and all, once and for all

### finance
**04** back, cash, fund **05** float, funds, means, money, set up, trade **06** assets, budget, income, pay for, wealth **07** affairs, banking, capital, funding, revenue, savings, sponsor, subsidy, support **08** accounts, bankroll, business, commerce **09** economics, guarantee, liquidity, resources, subsidize **10** accounting, capitalize, habilitate, investment, underwrite **11** bank account, sponsorship, stock market, wherewithal **15** money management

### financial
**05** money **06** fiscal **08** economic, monetary **09** budgetary, pecuniary **10** commercial **15** entrepreneurial
**• financial expert**
**09** economist **10** monetarist

### financier
**05** bania, gnome **06** banian, banker, banyan, trader **07** swindle **08** investor **10** moneymaker, speculator **11** stockbroker, white knight **12** financialist, Wall-Streeter **13** industrialist

### finch
**05** spink, twite **06** canary, linnet, siskin, towhee, whidah, whydah **07** bunting, chewink, manikin, redbird, waxbill **08** grosbeak, mannikin, snowbird, wheatear **09** brambling, crossbill, grassquit **10** fallow-chat, indigo bird, marsh-robin, weaver bird, whidah bird, whydah bird **11** green linnet, tree sparrow **12** cardinal-bird **13** indigo bunting

### find
**02** be **03** get, try, win **04** boon, coup, deem, earn, gain, meet, rate, rule, spot **05** asset, catch, exist, gauge, judge, learn, occur, reach, think, trace **06** attain, come by, decree, detect, dig out, expose, locate, notice, obtain, regain, reveal, review, secure, turn up, umpire **07** achieve, acquire, adjudge, bargain, believe, declare, examine, get back, godsend, good buy, mediate, observe, procure, realize, recover, referee, uncover, unearth **08** come upon, consider, discover, perceive, retrieve, sentence **09** arbitrate, be

present, discovery, encounter, recognize, stumble on, track down **10** adjudicate, chance upon, come across, experience, happen upon, lay hands on, run to earth, trouvaille **11** acquisition **12** bring to light, pass sentence **13** give a sentence, stumble across **14** sit in judgement **15** deliver a verdict

• **find in**

◇ *anagram indicator*

◇ *hidden indicator*

◇ *insertion indicator*

• **find out**

**03** see, sus **04** note, suss, take, twig **05** catch, get at, learn **06** detect, expose, gather, reveal, rumble, show up, unmask **07** extract, lay bare, observe, realize, suss out, uncover **08** disclose, discover, identify, perceive, pinpoint, tumble to **09** ascertain, establish, expiscate, get wind of **10** cotton on to, understand **11** make certain **12** bring to light **13** make certain of

**finding**

**04** find **05** award, order **06** decree **07** verdict **08** decision, judgment **09** discovery, judgement **10** conclusion, innovation **12** breakthrough **13** pronouncement **14** recommendation

**fine**

**01** F **02** A1, OK **03** A-OK, dry, end, fit, log, oke, yes **04** braw, eric, fair, good, jake, keen, mooi, nice, pawn, phat, pure, safe, slim, thin, well **05** beaut, bonny, clear, dandy, exact, gauzy, great, light, mulct, nifty, right, sharp, sheer, showy, smart, sound, sting, sunny, unlaw **06** agreed, amerce, assess, bonnie, bright, choice, dainty, flimsy, goodly, ground, incony, lovely, minute, narrow, on form, pledge, punish, purify, refine, sconce, select, slight, strong, subtle **07** clement, crushed, damages, elegant, forfeit, fragile, gradely, healthy, immense, inconie, in shape, penalty, powdery, precise, radical, refined, slender, stylish **08** accurate, all right, critical, delicate, gossamer, graithly, handsome, jim-dandy, narrowly, penalize, precious, properly, splendid, striking, superior, very good, very well, vigorous **09** admirable, agreeable, beautiful, brilliant, cloudless, correctly, egregious, excellent, expensive, exquisite, first-rate, sensitive, shipshape, temperate **10** acceptable, acceptably, amercement, attractive, diaphonous, discerning, first-class, forfeiture, punishment, remarkable, tickety-boo **11** amerciament, exceptional, fashionable, fine-grained, flourishing, in good shape, lightweight, magnificent, outstanding, pretentious, tickettyboo, up to scratch **12** in good health, satisfactory, successfully **13** distinguished, hair-splitting, hale and hearty **14** satisfactorily **15** in good condition

**fine-looking**

**04** waly **05** wally

**finely**

**05** wally **06** nicely, subtly, thinly **07** exactly, lightly, sharply **08** minutely **09** admirably, precisely **10** critically, delicately, splendidly **11** brilliantly, excellently **12** attractively **13** magnificently

**finery**

**07** bravery, gaudery, regalia, wallies **08** frippery, glad rags **09** jewellery, ornaments, showiness, splendour, trappings **10** rattletrap, Sunday best **11** bedizenment, best clothes, decorations

**finesse**

◇ *anagram indicator*

**04** tact **05** bluff, evade, flair, skill, trick **06** polish **07** knowhow **08** deftness, delicacy, elegance, neatness, strategy, subtlety **09** adeptness, diplomacy, expertise, manoeuvre, quickness **10** adroitness, cleverness, discretion, manipulate, refinement **11** savoir-faire, tactfulness **12** gracefulness **14** sophistication

**finger**

**03** paw **04** feel, name **05** pinky, share, talon, touch **06** agency, caress, fondle, handle, medius, paddle, pilfer, pinkie, stroke **07** annular, toy with **08** interest, virginal **09** prepollex **10** fiddle with, manipulate, meddle with **13** play about with

• **put your finger on**

**05** place **06** locate, recall **07** find out, hit upon, isolate, pin down **08** discover, identify, indicate, pinpoint, remember

**fingerhole**

**04** lill, lilt, stop **07** ventage, ventige

**finial**

**03** tee **04** crop **06** pommel **09** pineapple, poppy-head

**finicky**

◇ *anagram indicator*

**05** faddy, fussy, picky **06** choosy, fiddly, tricky **08** critical, delicate **09** difficult, finickety, intricate, selective **10** fastidious, meticulous, nit-picking, particular, pernickety, scrupulous **11** persnickety **13** hypercritical **14** discriminating

**finish**

◇ *tail selection indicator*

**02** do **03** eat, end, use **04** coat, coda, down, rout, ruin, stop **05** apply, cease, close, crush, drain, drink, empty, glaze, gloss, grain, scoff, sew up, shine, use up **06** attain, be over, defeat, devour, ending, expend, finale, fulfil, guzzle, lustre, pack in, polish, settle, topple, veneer, wind up, wind-up, wrap up **07** absolve, achieve, coating, conquer, consume, deplete, destroy, exhaust, lacquer, outwork, perfect, surface, texture, varnish, wipe out **08** carry out, complete, conclude, curtains, deal with, get rid of, overcome, round off, run out of **09** be through, bring down, cessation, culminate, discharge, get shot of, overpower, overthrow, overwhelm, polish off, put paid to, terminate, winding-up **10** accomplish, annihilate, appearance, be done with, call it a day, completion, conclusion, consummate, do away with, fulfilment, get through, lamination, perfection, smoothness **11** achievement, come to an end, culmination, destruction, discontinue, exterminate, termination **12** bring to an end **14** accomplishment, get the better of

• **finish off**

**03** end, ice, top **04** do in, slay **05** drain, mop-up, quash, quell, still, use up **06** defeat, murder **07** bump off, destroy, execute, put down, wipe out **08** despatch, dispatch, knock off **09** dispose of, eliminate, eradicate, liquidate, polish off, slaughter **10** annihilate, do away with, extinguish, put an end to, put to death, put to sleep **11** assassinate, exterminate

**finished**

**02** up **04** arch, dead, done, lost, neat, over, past, ripe **05** empty, exact, spent **06** doomed, expert, made up, ruined, sewn up, undone, urbane, zonked **07** all done, at an end, defunct, done for, drained, perfect, refined, rounded, through, useless **08** complete, defeated, flawless, masterly, polished, unwanted, virtuoso **09** completed, concluded, dealt with, exhausted, faultless, played out, unpopular, wrapped up **10** consummate, impeccable, proficient **11** all over with, consummated **12** accomplished, professional **13** sophisticated **15** over and done with

• **before it is finished**

**03** yet

**finite**

**05** fixed **07** bounded, limited **08** numbered **09** countable, definable **10** calculable, demarcated, measurable, restricted, terminable

**Finland**

**03** FIN

**fire**

**03** axe, can, fan **04** bake, flak, heat, hurl, kiln, life, sack, stir, whet, zeal **05** blame, blaze, eject, let go, light, rouse, salvo, shoot, start, stick, torch, verve **06** ardour, arouse, attack, energy, excite, firing, flames, heater, ignite, incite, kindle, launch, let off, set off, spirit, stir up, vigour **07** animate, barrage, bombing, bonfire, boot out, burning, censure, dismiss, enliven, explode, feeling, fervour, gunfire, inferno, inflame, inspire, kick out, passion, reproof, slating, sniping, sparkle, trigger **08** brickbat, detonate, dynamism, get rid of, knocking, motivate, radiance, radiator, shelling, slamming, spark off, vivacity **09** animation, cannonade, cauterize,

convector, criticism, discharge, eagerness, electrify, fusillade, galvanize, holocaust, intensity, lightning, set ablaze, set alight, set fire to, set on fire, stimulate **10** combustion, creativity, enthusiasm, excitement, liveliness, trigger off **11** bombardment, disapproval, put a match to
**12** condemnation, fault-finding
**13** conflagration, disparagement, inventiveness

**• fire up**
**06** arouse

**• on fire**
**03** lit **05** eager, fiery **06** ablaze, aflame, alight, ardent **07** blazing, burning, excited, flaming, ignited
**08** creative, in flames, inspired
**09** energetic, inventive, sparkling
**10** passionate **12** enthusiastic

**firearm**
**03** gun **04** heat **05** rifle **06** musket, pistol, weapon **07** handgun, shotgun
**08** revolver **09** automatic **10** self-cocker **12** breech-loader, muzzle-loader, shooting iron, single-action
**13** semi-automatic
*See also* **gun**; **weapon**

**firebrand**
**05** rebel **07** fanatic, radical
**08** agitator, militant **09** extremist, insurgent **10** incendiary **12** rabble-rouser, troublemaker **13** revolutionary
**15** insurrectionist

**fireplace**

*Fireplaces include:*

**04** kiln, oven
**05** forge, grate, ingle, range, stove
**06** boiler, hearth
**07** bonfire, brazier, firebox, furnace, gas fire
**08** campfire, open fire
**09** wood stove
**10** backboiler
**11** incinerator
**12** electric fire
**13** paraffin stove

**firepower**
**04** ammo

**fireproof**
**10** flameproof **12** non-flammable
**13** fire-resistant, incombustible
**14** flame-resistant, non-inflammable

**fireside** *see* **fireplace**

**firewater** *see* **drink**

**fireworks**
**03** fit **04** rage, rows **05** storm
**06** frenzy, sparks, temper, uproar
**07** trouble **08** outburst **09** hysterics
**10** explosions **12** pyrotechnics **13** feux d'artifice, illuminations

*Fireworks include:*

**04** cake, mine, pioy
**05** devil, flare, gerbe, peeoy, pioye, shell, squib, wheel
**06** banger, fisgig, fizgig, maroon, petard, rocket
**07** cracker, serpent, volcano
**08** flip-flop, fountain, pinwheel, slap-bang, sparkler, whizbang
**09** firedrake, girandola, girandole, sky-rocket, throw-down, waterfall, whizz-bang
**10** golden rain, Indian fire, tourbillon
**11** firecracker, firewriting, jumping-jack, roman candle, tourbillion
**14** Catherine wheel, Chinese cracker, indoor firework
**15** Pharaoh's serpent, Waterloo cracker

**firm**
**02** Co, OK **03** Cie, oke, set **04** boon, fast, good, hard, oaky, sure, true
**05** close, crisp, dense, fixed, house, rigid, solid, stiff, tight **06** dogged, secure, siccar, sicker, stable, stanch, steady, steeve, stieve, strict, strong, sturdy, trusty **07** adamant, compact, company, concern, decided, riveted, secured, settled, staunch, unmoved
**08** anchored, business, constant, definite, embedded, fastened, forceful, hardened, obdurate, resolute, resolved, stubborn, unshaken, vigorous **09** committed, immovable, inelastic, obstinate, rock-solid, sclerotic, steadfast, syndicate, tenacious **10** compressed, dependable, determined, enterprise, inflexible, motionless, solidified, stationary, unchanging, unshakable, unswerving, unwavering, unyielding
**11** association, corporation, established, institution, long-lasting, partnership, substantial, substantive, unalterable, unfaltering, unflinching, unshakeable **12** close-grained, concentrated, conglomerate, long-standing, organization, unchangeable
**13** establishment

**firmament**
**03** sky **05** ether, skies, space
**06** heaven, welkin **07** expanse, heavens, the blue **08** empyrean
**10** atmosphere

**firmly**
**04** fast **06** fastly, stably, steeve, stieve, surely **07** tightly **08** doggedly, robustly, securely, steadily, strictly, strongly, sturdily **09** immovably, staunchly
**10** decisively, definitely, enduringly, inflexibly, resolutely, unshakably
**11** steadfastly, unalterably
**12** determinedly, unchangeably, unwaveringly **13** unflinchingly

**firmness**
**06** fixity, fixure **07** density, resolve, tension **08** fixation, hardness, obduracy, rigidity, solidity, strength, sureness, tautness **09** constancy, stability, stiffness, tightness, willpower
**10** conviction, doggedness, resistance, resolution, steadiness, strictness
**11** compactness, reliability, staunchness **12** immovability, inelasticity **13** dependability, determination, inflexibility, steadfastness **14** changelessness, indomitability, strength of will

**• body firmness**
**04** tone

**first**
◇ *head selection indicator*
◇ *juxtaposition indicator*
**01** A **03** 1st, key, one, top **04** arch-, best, head, main **05** basic, chief, prima, prime, primo, prior, proto-, start
**06** eldest, oldest, origin, outset, primal, rather, ruling, senior, sooner **07** at first, earlier, firstly, highest, initial, leading, opening, origins, premier, primary, supreme **08** cardinal, champion, earliest, foremost, greatest, original, paravant, première, primeval
**09** beginning, inaugural, inception, initially, paramount, paravaunt, primaeval, primitive, principal, prototype, sovereign, square one, the word go, unveiling, uppermost
**10** beforehand, elementary, first of all, originally, pre-eminent, primordial
**11** at the outset, fundamental, predominant, preliminary, rudimentary, to begin with, to start with **12** commencement, in preference, introduction, introductory
**14** at the beginning **15** in the first place

**• at first**
◇ *head selection indicator*
**04** erst **07** at first **09** initially **10** first of all **11** at the outset, to begin with, to start with **15** in the first place

**• come first**
◇ *juxtaposition indicator*
**04** lead **05** outdo **07** precede

**• first lady**
**03** Eve

**first-born**
**04** aîné **05** aînée, eigne, elder, older
**06** eldest, oldest, senior **10** primogenit
**12** primogenital **13** primogenitary, primogenitive

**first-class**
**01** A **02** A1 **03** ace, top **04** cool, fine, mean, mega **05** crack, prime, super
**06** slap-up, superb, way-out, wicked
**07** crucial, leading, premier, radical, supreme, top-hole **08** fabulous, peerless, splendid, superior, top-notch
**09** admirable, excellent, first-rate, matchless, top-flight **11** exceptional, outstanding, superlative **12** second-to-none **14** out of this world

**firsthand**
**06** direct **07** hands-on, primary
**08** directly, on the job, personal
**09** immediate, in service **10** personally
**11** immediately

**firstly**
**04** once **07** at first **09** initially **10** first of all **11** at the outset, to begin with, to start with **15** in the first place

**first name**
**08** forename **09** given name
**13** baptismal name, Christian name

**first-rate**

**01** A **02** A1 **03** ace, top **04** cool, fine, jake, mean, mega **05** crack, prime, super **06** superb, way-out, wicked **07** crucial, leading, premier, radical, supreme **08** fabulous, peerless, splendid, superior, top-notch **09** admirable, excellent, matchless, top-flight **10** first-class **11** excellently, exceptional, outstanding, superlative **12** second-to-none **14** out of this world

**firth**

*Firths include:*

**03** Tay
**04** Lorn, Wide
**05** Clyde, Forth, Lorne, Moray
**06** Beauly, Solway, Thames
**07** Dornoch, Westray
**08** Cromarty, Pentland, Stronsay, Szczecin
**09** Inverness
**14** North Ronaldsay

**fiscal**

**03** tax **05** money **06** bursal **07** capital **08** economic, monetary, treasury **09** budgetary, financial, pecuniary, treasurer

• **procurator fiscal**

**02** PF

**fiscally**

**09** moneywise **11** financially, pecuniarily **12** economically

**fish**

**03** ask, bob, dap, dib, dip, fry, jig, net **04** harl, hunt, look, sean, seek, spin, trot **05** angle, catch, delve, grope, otter, seine, spoon, trawl, troll, whiff **06** guddle, ledger, search **07** counter, ransack, skitter, snigger, sniggle **08** hand line, try to get **09** go fishing **11** try to obtain

*See also* **animal**

*Fish, crustaceans and shellfish include:*

**02** ai, id
**03** aua, ayu, bar, bib, cod, dab, eel, gar, ged, hag, ide, lax, par, ray, sar, sei, tai
**04** barb, bass, blay, bley, brit, carp, chad, char, chub, chum, clam, coho, crab, cray, cusk, dace, dare, dart, dory, fugu, gade, goby, hake, hoki, huso, huss, kelt, keta, kina, lant, ling, luce, lump, moki, opah, orfe, parr, paua, pawa, peal, peel, pike, pipi, pope, pout, pupu, rudd, scad, scar, scat, scup, seer, shad, sild, slip, snig, sole, spot, tang, tope, tuna, tusk
**05** ablet, allis, basse, bleak, bream, brill, bully, cohoe, coley, danio, flake, guppy, koura, lance, loach, molly, perch, platy, porgy, prawn, roach, shark, skate, smelt, sprat, squid, tench, tetra, torsk, trout, tunny, whelk, yabby, zebra
**06** allice, angler, barbel, blenny, braise, braize, cockle, doctor, dorado, gadoid, groper, hapuku, jilgie, kipper, kokopu, launce, marlin, marron, minnow, mullet, mussel, oyster, piraña, plaice, porgie, puffer, red cod, red-eye, salmon, saurel, shrimp, tailor, turbot, wrasse
**07** abalone, anchovy, bloater, blue cod, catfish, cavalla, cavally, cichlid, cobbler, codfish, cowfish, dhufish, dogfish, garfish, gourami, grouper, gurnard, haddock, halibut, herring, kahawai, lamprey, lobster, morwong, mudfish, octopus, piranha, sardine, scallop, sea bass, snapper, toheroa, warehou, whiting
**08** blowfish, bluefish, bluenose, brisling, calamari, characid, crawfish, crayfish, dragonet, flathead, flounder, goldfish, grayling, ichthyic, John Dory, kingfish, luderick, mackerel, monkfish, Moray eel, pilchard, pipefish, rockfish, sailfish, scuppaug, sea bream, seahorse, skipjack, stingray, sturgeon, tarakihi, toadfish, trevally, tuna fish
**09** allis shad, angel-fish, barracuda, conger eel, Dover sole, greenling, grenadier, king prawn, lemonfish, lemon sole, Murray cod, neon tetra, red mullet, sea urchin, stonefish, swordfish, trumpeter, tunnyfish, whitebait, wobbegong, zebrafish
**10** angler fish, Balmain bug, barracouta, barramundi, bluebottle, Bombay duck, brown trout, butterfish, cuttlefish, damsel fish, flying fish, grey mullet, gummy shark, jellied eel, mossbunker, parrot-fish, puffer fish, red snapper, rock salmon, tommy rough
**11** electric eel, rock lobster, stickleback
**12** jellyblubber, orange roughy, rainbow trout, scorpion fish, skipjack tuna
**13** butterfly fish, horse mackerel, leatherjacket, Moreton Bay bug, sergeant-major
**14** Arbroath smokie

*See also* **crustacean**; **mollusc**; **shark**; **seafood**

• **fish out**

**04** find **07** extract, haul out, produce, pull out, take out **08** dredge up, retrieve **10** come up with

• **fish tank**

**04** stew **08** aquarium

• **queer fish**

**04** cure

**fisherman**

**03** rod **05** liner **06** angler, banker, codder, fisher, rodman, Walton **07** crabber, drag-man, drifter, rodsman, rodster **08** peter-man, piscator, shareman **09** cockleman, rodfisher, sharesman, Waltonian, trawlerman **11** piscatorian

**fishing**

**07** angling **08** trawling **09** piscatory **11** piscatorial **12** catching fish

*Fishing- and angling-related terms include:*

**03** fly, net, rod, tag, tie
**04** bait, barb, bite, cast, drag, gimp, hook, lead, line, lure, reel, sean, weel, weir, whip
**05** angle, baker, catch, clean, creel, seine, snell, troll
**06** angler, bob-fly, coarse, dry-fly, fly-rod, leader, sagene, sinker, tackle, waders, wet-fly
**07** angling, bycatch, drifter, dropper, flyline, fly reel, harpoon, keepnet, piscary, setline, spinner
**08** backcast, drift net, roll cast, trotline
**09** brandling, drabbling, false cast, hairy Mary, halieutic, indicator, leger line, night-line, piscatory
**10** bait bucket, casting arc, casting-net, fly casting, fly fishing, halieutics, landing net, ledger bait, ledger line, net-fishing, sea-fishing, weigh sling
**11** forward cast, game fishing, line-fishing, paternoster
**12** drift fishing, night crawler, night-fishery, shooting line
**13** bottom-fishing, coarse fishing
**15** catch-and-release

*See also* **fly**

**fishy**

◇ *anagram indicator*

**03** odd **05** funny, queer, shady **06** unsafe **07** dubious, piscine, suspect **08** doubtful, fish-like **09** equivocal, irregular, piscatory **10** improbable, suspicious **11** implausible, piscatorial **12** questionable

**fission**

**06** schism **07** parting, rending, rupture **08** breaking, cleavage, cleaving, division, scission **09** severance, splitting

**fissure**

**03** gap **04** chop, gape, gash, hole, rent, rift, rime, slit, vein **05** break, chasm, chink, cleft, crack, fault, grike, gryke, porta, shake, split, zygon **06** breach, cleave, cranny, divide, groove, sulcus **07** crevice, foramen, opening, rupture **08** cleavage, crevasse, fracture, scissure, sink hole **10** interstice **11** swallow hole

**fist**

**03** paw, pud **04** dook, duke, hand, mitt, neif, nief, palm **05** index, neafe, neive, nieve, puddy **06** neaffe **08** knuckles **11** handwriting **12** bunch of fives, clenched hand

**fit**

◇ *anagram indicator*

**02** A1, go **03** apt, arm, cry, due, fix, gee, jag, pet, rig, sit **04** able, ague, bout, hard, huff, join, lune, mate, meet, song, sort, suit, well **05** adapt, agree, alter, burst, canto, coach, equal, equip, exies, flaky, gapes, groom, hardy, ictus, match, place, prime, put in, queme, ready, right, shape, sharp, sound, spasm, spell, surge, tally, train **06** access, adjust, attach, attack, belong, change, concur, crisis, didder, dither, dueful, follow, habile, insert, in trim, modify, passus, proper, robust, seemly, square, strong, sturdy, tailor, worthy **07** arrange, be right, capable, chipper, conform, connect, correct, debauch, dewfull, fashion, fitting, get into, gradely, healthy, in shape, install, prepare, provide, qualify, seizure, tantrum, trained **08** decorous, dovetail, eligible, equipped, eruption, graithly, outbreak, outburst, paroxysm, position, prepared, regulate, suitable, vigorous **09** agreement, befitting, competent, condition, explosion, harmonize, interlock, make ready, pertinent, qualified **10** able-bodied, be a good fit, be suitable, conformity, conniption, convenient, convulsion, correspond, good enough, in good form, put in place, the shivers **11** accommodate, appropriate, be consonant, concurrence, correlation, equivalence, flourishing, in good shape, put together **12** be consistent, in good health, make suitable, relationship **13** be appropriate, fit like a glove, hale and hearty, put in position **14** correspondence **15** in good condition

**• fit for use**

**04** ripe

**• fit in**

◇ *insertion indicator*

**04** slot **05** agree, match **06** accord, belong, concur, square **07** conform, squeeze **10** correspond

**• fit out, fit up**

**03** arm, rig **04** trim **05** equip, frame **06** kit out, outfit, rig out, supply **07** furnish, prepare, provide **08** accoutre

**• fit together**

**04** nest

**• in fits and starts**

**08** brokenly, fitfully, off and on, unevenly **11** erratically, irregularly **12** occasionally, sporadically **13** spasmodically **14** intermittently

**fitful**

**06** broken, catchy, patchy, uneven **07** erratic **08** sporadic **09** disturbed, haphazard, irregular, spasmodic **10** occasional **12** disconnected, intermittent

**fitfully**

**08** unevenly **11** erratically, haphazardly, irregularly **12** occasionally, sporadically **13** spasmodically **14** intermittently **15** by fits and starts, in fits and starts

**fitness**

**04** trim **05** shape **06** health, vigour **07** aptness **08** adequacy, aptitude, haleness, property, strength **09** condition, edibility, readiness **10** capability, competence, competency, edibleness, good health, pertinence, robustness **11** eligibility, healthiness, opportunity, suitability **12** preparedness **13** applicability **14** qualifications **15** appropriateness

**• condition of fitness**

**04** form

**fitted**

**03** fit **05** armed, fixed, right **06** cut out, shaped, suited **07** built-in **08** equipped, integral, prepared, provided, suitable, tailored **09** appointed, furnished, permanent, qualified, rigged out **10** integrated

**fitting**

**03** apt, fit **04** meet, part, unit **05** piece, right **06** extras, liable, proper, seemly, square **07** condign, correct, fitment, fixture **08** decorous, deserved, fitments, fixtures, suitable, wise-like **09** accessory, component, desirable, equipment, furniture **10** attachment, connection, convenable **11** accessories, appropriate, furnishings **12** appointments **13** accoutrements, installations

**fittings**

**04** trim **09** trimmings **11** furnishings

**five**

**01** V **06** pentad **07** quinary, quintet **08** quintett **09** quintette **10** quintuplet

**• one of five**

**04** quin

**five hundred**

**01** D

**fix**

◇ *anagram indicator*

**02** do **03** aim, hit, jam, pin, rig, set, tie **04** bang, bind, comb, cook, dose, draw, fake, glue, hang, hold, hole, join, link, make, mend, mess, nail, name, root, scam, seat, shoo, shot, slug, sort, spay, spot, tidy, turn **05** affix, clamp, dress, embed, emend, focus, groom, level, lodge, order, plant, point, rivet, score, screw, see to, set up, set-up, stell, stick **06** adjust, anchor, answer, assign, attach, cement, corner, couple, decide, define, direct, fasten, fiddle, freeze, harden, locate, muddle, neaten, pickle, plight, remedy, repair, scrape, secure, settle, strike, way out **07** agree on, appoint, arrange, attract, connect, correct, destine, dilemma, falsify, implant, install, knock up, patch up, prepare, rectify, resolve, restore, rigging, situate, specify, station, stiffen, the soup **08** arrive at, castrate, chastise, finalize, get ready, position, put right, quandary, solidify, solution, valorize **09** destinate, determine, establish, injection, manoeuvre, stabilize, tight spot **10** difficulty, manipulate, put in order, resolution, straighten, tamper with **11** concentrate, predicament, put together **12** manipulation **13** throw together

**• fix up**

**04** clew, clue, plan **05** equip, lay on, plant **06** settle, supply **07** agree on, arrange, furnish, produce, provide, sort out **08** organize **10** bring about

**fixated**

**03** set **06** phobic **07** gripped **08** hung up on, neurotic, obsessed **09** dominated **10** compulsive, infatuated **11** preoccupied **12** pathological

**fixation**

**05** mania, thing **06** fetich, fetish, hang-up, phobia **07** complex, fetiche, setting **08** firmness, idée fixe, neurosis **09** obsession **10** compulsion, steadiness **11** infatuation **13** preoccupation

**fixed**

◇ *anagram indicator*

**03** set **04** fake, fast, firm **05** false, rigid, tight **06** phoney, rooted, secure, steady **07** decided, lasting, planned, pretend, settled, well-set **08** arranged, constant, definite, immobile, standing **09** appointed, insincere, permanent, pretended **10** determined, entrenched, inflexible, persistent, set in stone, stationary **11** cast in stone, determinate, established

**fixedly**

**04** hard **07** closely **08** intently, steadily **09** staringly **10** watchfully **11** attentively, searchingly

**fixity**

**09** constancy, fixedness, stability **10** permanence, steadiness **11** persistence **12** immutability

**fixture**

**04** game, race, unit **05** event, match, round **06** fixing **07** contest, fitting, meeting **09** equipment, furniture **11** competition, furnishings **13** installations

**fizz**

**03** gas, vim, zip **04** foam, hiss, zing **05** froth **06** bubble, fizzle **07** bubbles, ferment, foaming, sparkle **08** bubbling, buoyancy, frothing, vitality, vivacity **09** animation, champagne, fizziness, gassiness **10** effervesce, enthusiasm, excitement, exuberance, liveliness **11** excitedness, high spirits **12** exhilaration, fermentation **13** effervescence

**fizzle**

**• fizzle out**

**04** fail, flop, fold, stop **07** die away, die down, subside **08** collapse, peter out, taper off **09** disappear, dissipate, evaporate **11** come to grief, fall through **13** come to nothing

**fizzy**

**05** gassy **06** bubbly, frothy **07** aerated, foaming **08** bubbling **09** sparkling **10** carbonated **12** effervescent

**flab**

**03** fat, pot **04** bulk **06** paunch **07** blubber, fatness, obesity **08** pot belly **09** plumpness, solidness, spare tyre, stoutness **10** chubbiness, corpulence, overweight

**flabbergasted**
◇ *anagram indicator*
**05** dazed **06** amazed **07** stunned **08** overcome **09** astounded, blown away, staggered **10** astonished, bowled over, confounded, gobsmacked, nonplussed, speechless **11** dumbfounded, overwhelmed **13** knocked for six

**flabby**
**03** fat, lax **04** limp, soft **05** loose, plump, slack **06** feeble, flaggy, fleshy, floppy, sloppy **07** flaccid, hanging, sagging **08** drooping, wasteful, yielding **09** lymphatic, nerveless **10** overweight **11** inefficient **12** disorganized, uneconomical

**flaccid**
**03** lax **04** lank, limp, soft, weak **05** loose, slack **06** clammy, droopy, flabby, floppy **07** relaxed, sagging **08** drooping, toneless **09** nerveless

**flag**
**03** die, ebb, rag, sag, tag **04** fade, fail, fall, flop, hail, iris, jade, mark, note, sink, slow, tire, waft, wane, wave, wilt **05** abate, color, droop, faint, label, slump, weary **06** Acorus, colors, colour, falter, lessen, marker, motion, salute, weaken **07** calamus, decline, dwindle, fall off, slacken, subside **08** diminish, hang down, indicate, languish, peter out, taper off, wave down **09** grow tired, reed-grass **12** signal to stop

*Flags include:*

**05** Union
**07** Saltier, Saltire
**08** Crescent, Old Glory, Red Cross
**09** Blue Peter, dannebrog, Red Dragon, Red Duster, Red Ensign, Rising Sun, Tricolour, Union Jack
**10** Blue Ensign, Jolly Roger, Yellow Jack
**11** Olympic Flag, Red Crescent, White Ensign
**12** Stars and Bars
**15** Cross of St George, Hammer and Sickle, Stars and Stripes

*Flag types include:*

**03** red
**04** blue, fane, jack, sick
**05** black, house, peter, pilot, union, whiff, whift, white
**06** banner, burgee, cornet, ensign, fanion, pennon, prayer, signal, yellow
**07** ancient, bunting, colours, pennant
**08** banderol, gonfalon, pavilion, penoncel, standard, streamer, tricolor, vexillum
**09** blackjack, chequered, oriflamme, pennoncel, pilot jack, tricolour
**10** penoncelle, quarantine
**11** pennoncelle, swallow tail
**13** defaced ensign

• **flags**
**07** bunting

**flagellation**
**07** beating, flaying, lashing, whaling **08** flogging, whipping **09** scourging, thrashing **10** vapulation **11** castigation, verberation, vice anglais **12** chastisement

**flagging**
**06** ebbing, fading, tiring, waning **07** abating, failing, languid, sagging, sinking, slowing, wilting **08** drooping, pavement **09** declining, dwindling, faltering, lessening, subsiding, weakening **10** decreasing **11** diminishing

**flagon**
**03** jug **04** ewer **05** flask, half-g, peter **06** bottle, carafe, vessel **07** pitcher **08** decanter **09** container

**flagrant**
**04** bold, open, rank **05** gross, naked, overt **06** arrant, brazen, raging **07** blatant, burning, glaring, heinous **08** blattant, dreadful, enormous, infamous **09** atrocious, audacious, barefaced, egregious, notorious, shameless, unashamed **10** outrageous, scandalous **11** conspicuous, disgraceful, undisguised **12** ostentatious

**flagstaff**
**03** pin

**flail**
◇ *anagram indicator*
**04** beat, whip **06** batter, strike, thrash, thresh **08** threshel, thresher **11** swing wildly

**flair**
**04** bent, feel, gift, nose **05** knack, skill, style, taste **06** acumen, genius, talent **07** ability, faculty, mastery, panache **08** aptitude, elegance, facility **11** discernment, stylishness **14** natural ability

**flak**
**02** AA **05** abuse, blame, stick **07** censure, panning **08** bad press, knocking **09** brickbats, criticism, hostility, invective **10** aspersions, complaints, opposition **11** disapproval **12** condemnation, fault-finding **13** disparagement **14** animadversions, disapprobation

**flake**
◇ *anagram indicator*
**03** bit **04** chip, flaw, peel, smut **05** flash, scale, scurf, shark, spark, wafer **06** furfur, paring, shiver, sliver, squama **07** blister, flaught, peeling, shaving, spangle **08** fragment, particle, splinter **09** eccentric, exfoliate, flocculus **10** desquamate **11** exfoliation **12** desquamation

• **flake out**
**04** drop **05** faint **07** pass out **08** collapse, keel over **10** fall asleep **15** relax completely

**flaky**
◇ *anagram indicator*
**03** dry **05** crazy, inept, scaly **06** scurfy, stupid **07** laminar, layered **08** scabrous, squamate, squamose, squamous **09** eccentric **10** flocculent **11** exfoliative, incompetent **12** desquamative, desquamatory, furfuraceous

**flamboyance**
**04** dash, élan **05** style **06** colour **07** glamour, panache, pizzazz **09** showiness **10** brilliance **11** ostentation **12** extravagance **13** theatricality

**flamboyant**
**04** rich **05** gaudy, showy **06** bright, flashy, florid, ornate, rococo **07** baroque, dashing **08** dazzling, exciting, striking **09** brilliant, colourful, elaborate, glamorous **10** theatrical **11** extravagant **12** ostentatious

**flame**
**03** low **04** beam, burn, fire, glow, heat, lowe, lunt, rage, zeal **05** blaze, flake, flare, flash, flush, glare, gleam, go red, light, lover, shine **06** ardour, redden, warmth **07** fervour, partner, passion, radiate, sparkle, turn red **08** fervency, flammule, keenness, radiance **09** become red, boyfriend, catch fire, eagerness, intensity **10** brightness, enthusiasm, excitement, girlfriend, sweetheart **13** conflagration **15** burst into flames

• **in flames**
**06** ablaze, aflame, alight, on fire **07** blazing, burning, flaming, ignited

• **old flame**
**02** ex

**flameproof**
**09** fireproof **12** non-flammable **13** fire-resistant, incombustible **14** flame-resistant, non-inflammable

**flaming**
**03** mad **04** vile **05** angry, fiery, gaudy, vivid **06** aflame, alight, bloody, bright, cursed, damned, darned, dashed, odious, on fire, raging, red-hot **07** blasted, blazing, burning, enraged, furious, glowing, hateful, intense, violent **08** annoying, blinking, blooming, dratting, fiendish, flipping, incensed, infamous, infernal, in flames, wretched **09** brilliant, execrable, loathsome **10** abominable, confounded, detestable, infuriated, pernicious, unpleasant **11** smouldering **13** scintillating

**flammable**
**08** burnable **09** ignitable **11** combustible, inflammable

**flank**
◇ *containment indicator*
**03** hip **04** edge, line, lisk, loin, side, wall, wing **05** bound, skirt, thigh **06** border, fringe, haunch, screen **07** confine, quarter

**flannel**
**03** rot **05** spiel **06** waffle **07** blarney, flatter, rubbish, washrag **08** flattery, nonsense, soft soap **09** facecloth, sweet talk, washcloth **10** smooth talk **13** blandishments

**flap**
◇ *anagram indicator*
**03** fly, lap, lug, tab, tag, wag, wap
**04** beat, fall, flag, flip, fold, fuss, loma, slat, stew, sway, tail, waff, wave
**05** apron, flaff, lapel, panic, shake, skirt, state, swing, swish, tizzy, tuner, visor
**06** dither, elevon, lappet, thrash, thresh, tiswas, tizwas, tongue, waggle, wallop, winnow **07** agitate, aileron, flacker, fluster, flutter, overlap, tent-fly, vibrate **08** aventail, barn-door, covering, epiploon, overhang
**09** agitation, aventaile, commotion
**10** clack valve, epiglottis, fluttering
**12** great omentum **13** move up and down

**flare**
**04** beam, burn, glow, Very **05** blaze, burst, erupt, flame, flash, glare, gleam, light, splay, torch, widen **06** beacon, dazzle, flanch, rocket, signal, spread
**07** broaden, explode, flaunch, flicker, glimmer, glitter, sparkle **08** flare out, widening **09** spread out, Very light
**10** broadening, Verey light **13** warning signal **14** distress signal
• **flare out**
**04** bell
• **flare up**
**05** blaze, erupt, go ape, go mad
**06** blow up **07** explode **08** boil over, break out, burst out, freak out **09** blow a fuse, do your nut, go berserk **10** go to market, hit the roof **11** blow your top, do your block, flip your lid, go ballistic, go up the wall, lose control, lose your rag **12** fly into a rage, lose your cool, throw a wobbly **14** foam at the mouth, lose your temper **15** fly off the handle, go off the deep end

**flare-up**
**04** rash **07** venting **08** ejection, emission, eruption, outbreak, outburst
**09** discharge, explosion
**12** inflammation

**flash**
◇ *anagram indicator*
**02** mo **03** fly, ray **04** beam, bolt, dart, dash, fork, pond, pool, race, rush, show, tear, zoom **05** blaze, blink, bound, burst, dance, flake, flare, gaudy, glaik, glare, gleam, glint, quick, shaft, shine, shoot, showy, smart, spark, speed **06** career, flaunt, glaiks, glance, kitsch, moment, streak, strobe, sudden, vulgar **07** bluette, display, flaught, flicker, glimmer, glisten, glitter, instant, lighten, light up, shimmer, show off, sparkle, twinkle **08** brandish, concetto, fire-flag, flourish, green ray, outbreak, outburst **09** coruscate, expensive, fulgurate, fulminate, glamorous, lightning **10** exhibition
**11** coruscation, fashionable, fire-flaught, fulguration, pretentious, scintillate **12** ostentatious
**13** scintillation **14** expose yourself
• **in a flash**
**03** pdq **06** pronto **08** in a jiffy, in a trice, in no time **09** in a moment, instantly **11** in an instant **12** in a twinkling **13** in no time at all **14** in a split second

**flashy**
**04** bold, loud **05** brash, cheap, flash, gaudy, jazzy, lairy, showy, tacky, vapid
**06** garish, glitzy, kitsch, snazzy, tawdry, vulgar **07** buckeye, raffish, tigrish
**08** tigerish **09** glamorous, tasteless
**10** bling-bling, flamboyant
**11** pretentious **12** meretricious, ostentatious
• **flashy person**
**04** lair, raff

**flask**
**04** cask, mick **05** dewar, micky
**06** bottle, carafe, coffin, fiasco, flagon, mickey, retort, vessel **07** ampulla, balloon, canteen, costrel, flacket, matrass, Thermos® **08** decanter, lekythos **09** aryballos, container, livery pot **10** powder horn **12** pocket-pistol

**flat**
**03** low, OYO, pad, set **04** bust, dead, down, duff, dull, even, firm, flew, flue, fool, slow, tame, true, unit, weak
**05** banal, bland, burst, empty, exact, final, fixed, haugh, kaput, level, plain, plane, prone, quiet, rigid, rooms, sheer, slack, stale, still, stock, suite, total, utter, vapid **06** bedsit, boring, callow, direct, evenly, planar, sleepy, smooth, supine, used up, watery **07** exactly, flatlet, insipid, not deep, not tall, plainly, planned, regular, shallow, tedious, totally, uniform, utterly **08** absolute, arranged, blown-out, complete, defeated, definite, deflated, dejected, directly, downcast, entirely, explicit, finished, home unit, inactive, levelled, lifeless, not thick, outright, positive, ruptured, sluggish, stagnant, standard, straight, tenement, toneless, unbroken
**09** apartment, bedsitter, collapsed, depressed, downright, miserable, out-and-out, penthouse, pointless, precisely, prostrate, punctured, reclining, recumbent, unvarying
**10** absolutely, completely, despondent, homaloidal, horizontal, lacklustre, maisonette, monotonous, point-blank, spiritless, unexciting
**11** categorical, discouraged, maisonnette, unequivocal, unqualified
**12** outstretched, spread-eagled
**13** categorically, no longer fizzy, unconditional, uninteresting **14** flat as a pancake
• **flat out**
**04** hard **06** all out **10** at top speed **11** at full speed
• **flat place**
**04** plat

**flatly**
**10** absolutely, completely, point-blank, positively **12** peremptorily
**13** categorically **14** unhesitatingly
**15** unconditionally

**flatness**
**06** tedium **07** boredom, languor
**08** dullness, evenness, monotony, vapidity **09** emptiness, levelness, platitude, staleness **10** insipidity, smoothness, uniformity
**13** horizontality, tastelessness

**flatten**
**02** KO **04** fell, iron, raze, roll
**05** amaze, crush, dress, floor, level, plane, press **06** defeat, smooth, squash, subdue **07** even out, planish
**08** compress, demolish, knock out, make even, make flat, tear down
**09** knock down, overwhelm, prostrate

**flatter**
**04** claw, coax, fawn, soap, suit, word
**05** befit, court, creep, gloze, grace, toady **06** become, butter, cozy up, cringe, fleech, humour, kowtow, phrase, praise, sawder, smooth, soothe, stroke **07** adulate, enhance, flannel, gratify, lay it on, palaver, show off, soother, wheedle **08** beslaver, blandish, butter up, collogue, eulogize, inveigle, make up to, play up to, smooth it, soft-soap, suck up to **09** beslobber, embellish, sweet-talk **10** bear in hand, compliment, cozy up with, look good on, overpraise, pay court to, soft sawder, soft sowder **12** sycophantize
**14** tickle the ear of **15** curry favour with, make fair weather, show to advantage

**flatterer**
**05** carny, creep, toady **06** carney, earwig, fawner, lackey, minion, yes-man **07** crawler, creeper, proneur
**08** adulator, incenser, incensor, smoother **09** encomiast, eulogizer, groveller, sycophant **10** bootlicker, foot-licker **11** lickspittle **12** court-dresser **13** back-scratcher

**flattering**
**04** kind **06** honied, sugary
**07** candied, fawning, fulsome, honeyed, servile, sugared
**08** becoming, effusive, unctuous
**09** adulatory, enhancing, gnathonic, laudatory **10** favourable, gratifying, obsequious **11** gnathonical, soft-soaping, sycophantic **12** honey-tongued, ingratiating, smooth-spoken, sweet-talking **13** complimentary, smooth-talking, smooth-tongued

**flattery**
**04** fawn, soap **05** carny, sugar, taffy
**06** butter, carney, eulogy, praise, sawder **07** blarney, fawning, flannel, glozing, mamaguy **08** cajolery, soft soap, toadyism **09** adulation, fair words, fleeching, laudation, servility, sweet talk **10** cajolement, flapdoodle, fleechment, soft sawder, soft sowder, sycophancy **11** compliments, fulsomeness **12** blandishment, ingratiation **13** blandishments **14** back scratching, court holy water

**flatulence**
**03** gas **04** wind **06** flatus **07** farting
**09** gassiness, ventosity, windiness
**10** eructation **11** borborygmus

**flatulent**
**05** gassy, windy **07** ventose

**flaunt**
**03** air **05** boast, flash, skyre, sport, strut, vaunt, wield **06** dangle, parade, strout **07** display, disport, exhibit, show off **08** brandish, flourish

**flavour**
**03** hop **04** feel, gust, hint, lace, race, soul, tack, tang, tone, zest, zing **05** aroma, flava, imbue, lemon, odour, sapor, savor, smack, spice, style, taste, tinge, touch, twang **06** aspect, infuse, nature, palate, pepper, relish, savour, season, spirit **07** essence, feeling, liqueur, quality, spice up **08** ginger up, piquancy, property **09** character **10** atmosphere, impression, indication, suggestion

**flavouring**
**04** hops, miso, sage, tang, zest, zing **05** caper, shoyu, spice **06** borage, Bovril®, cassis, cloves, relish, savory **07** bay leaf, bitters, caramel, essence, extract, flavour, ratafia, saffron, vanilla **08** additive, costmary, piquancy, rosemary, tarragon **09** coriander, fenugreek, pistachio, seasoning, spearmint **10** peach-water **11** citronellal, malt-extract, wintergreen **12** bouquet garni, butterscotch
*See also* **herb**

**flaw**
**04** chip, gall, mark, rent, rift, slip, spot, tear **05** brack, break, cleft, crack, craze, error, fault, flake, lapse, speck, split, thief **06** defect, foible, uproar **07** blemish, crevice, failing, fallacy, fissure, mistake **08** fracture, fragment, hamartia, splinter, weakness, weak spot **09** windshake **11** shortcoming **12** Achilles' heel, imperfection

**flawed**
◇ *anagram indicator*
**06** broken, faulty, marked, marred, spoilt **07** chipped, cracked, damaged, unsound **09** blemished, defective, erroneous, imperfect **10** fallacious

**flawless**
**05** sound, whole **06** intact **07** perfect **08** spotless, unbroken **09** faultless, stainless, undamaged **10** immaculate, impeccable, unimpaired **11** unblemished **12** indefectible **14** without blemish

**flax**
**03** tow **04** harl, herl, line, lint **05** hards, hurds **06** byssus **07** allseed **08** Phormium **12** mill-mountain

**flay**
**03** pan **04** flog, skin, slam **05** knock, slate **06** attack, flench, flense, flinch, revile, uncase **07** condemn, lambast, run down, scourge, upbraid **08** denounce, execrate, frighten **09** castigate, criticize, excoriate, pull apart, skin alive, tear apart **12** pull to pieces **13** find fault with, tear a strip off

**flea**
**05** Pulex **06** chigoe, chigre, jigger **07** chigger, Daphnia, daphnid **09** turnip fly **11** Aphaniptera **12** Siphonaptera

**fleck**
**03** dot **04** dust, mark, spot **05** point, speck, stain **06** dapple, mottle, streak **07** freckle, spatter, speckle, stipple **08** sprinkle

**fledgling**
**03** new **04** tiro **05** squab **06** coming, novice, rising, rookie **07** budding, learner, nascent, recruit, trainee **08** beginner, emergent, emerging, neophyte, newcomer **09** coming out, embryonic, greenhorn, novitiate **10** apprentice, burgeoning, developing, tenderfoot **11** independent

**flee**
**03** fly, lam, ren, rin, run **04** bolt, bunk, loup, quit, rush, scat **05** lam it, leave, scoot, scram, skive, split **06** decamp, depart, escape, get out, vanish **07** abscond, bunk off, do a bunk, get away, make off, push off, retreat, run away, scarper, take off, vamoose **08** clear off, shove off, up sticks, withdraw **09** cut and run, disappear, do a runner, push along, skedaddle **10** hightail it, hit the road, make tracks, take flight **11** hit the trail **13** sling your hook **14** make a bolt for it **15** make a break for it, take to your heels

**fleece**
**02** do **03** con, jib, rob, teg **04** bilk, coat, down, gull, plot, rook, skin, tegg, wool **05** bleed, cheat, mulct, ploat, pluck, shave, shear, steal, sting **06** diddle, fiddle, rip off, toison **07** defraud, plunder, squeeze, swindle **08** fetch off **09** shearling, toison d'or **10** overcharge **11** string along **12** pull a fast one, put one over on, take for a ride **13** have someone on

**fleecy**
**04** soft **05** downy, hairy, nappy **06** fluffy, pilose, shaggy, woolly **07** velvety **08** floccose **10** flocculate, lanuginose **11** eriophorous

**fleet**
**02** RN **04** fast, flit, flow, navy **05** agile, flitt, float, flota, quick, rapid, swift **06** armada, flying, marine, nimble, speedy, winged **07** caravan **08** flotilla, meteoric, navarchy, squadron **09** mercurial, task force, transient **10** naval force **11** expeditious, light-footed

**fleeting**
**04** flit **05** brief, flitt, quick, short **06** bubble, flying, hollow, rushed, sudden **07** passing **08** fugitive, volatile **09** ephemeral, fugacious, momentary, temporary, transient **10** evanescent, short-lived, transitory

**fleetingly**
**07** briefly, quickly **08** casually **10** for a moment, for a second **11** momentarily **12** for an instant

**flesh**
**03** fat **04** boar, body, meat, pith, pulp, skin **05** brawn, braxy, stuff **06** matter, muscle, tissue, weight **08** solidity **09** carnality, sexuality, substance **10** sensuality **11** human nature, physicality **12** carnal nature, corporeality, significance, sinful nature **14** physical nature

• **flesh and blood**
**03** kin **04** rels **05** folks **06** family **07** kindred, rellies **08** relative **09** relations

• **flesh out**
**08** expand on **09** elaborate **10** add details **11** elaborate on, give details **12** make complete

• **flesh round jaw**
**04** gill

• **in the flesh**
**05** alive **06** bodily **08** in person **09** incarnate **10** in real life **12** in actual life

**fleshly**
**05** human **06** animal, bodily, carnal, earthy, erotic, sexual **07** bestial, brutish, earthly, lustful, sensual, worldly **08** corporal, material, physical **09** corporeal

**fleshy**
**03** fat **05** ample, beefy, hefty, meaty, obese, plump, podgy, pulpy, stout, tubby **06** brawny, chubby, chunky, flabby, portly, rotund **07** carnose, paunchy **08** carneous **09** corpulent, succulent **10** overweight, well-padded

**flex**
**03** bow, ply **04** bend, cord, lead, wire **05** angle, cable, crook, curve **07** stretch, tighten **08** contract, double up

**flexibility**
**04** give **06** spring **07** flexion, pliancy **09** tensility **10** elasticity, pliability, resilience, suppleness **11** amenability, bendability, springiness **12** adaptability, agreeability, complaisance **13** adjustability

**flexible**
◇ *anagram indicator*
**04** open **05** agile, bendy, lithe, withy **06** docile, floppy, limber, lissom, mobile, pliant, supple **07** elastic, flexile, lissome, plastic, pliable, springy, willowy **08** amenable, bendable, stretchy, variable, yielding **09** adaptable, compliant, complying, malleable, mouldable, open-ended, tractable **10** adjustable, changeable, manageable **13** accommodating, double-jointed

**flick**
**03** dab, hit, rap, tap **04** flip, jerk, lash, lick, snap, whip **05** click, flirt, swish, touch **06** fillip, strike

• **flick through**
**04** scan, skim, skip **08** glance at

10 glance over, run through **11** flip through, leaf through **12** thumb through **13** browse through

**flicker**
**03** bat **04** atom, drop, iota, jump, lick, play, wink **05** blink, flare, flash, gleam, glint, spark, trace, waver **06** gutter, quiver, yucker **07** flaught, flutter, glimmer, glitter, shimmer, sparkle, twinkle, vibrate **08** lambency **09** flaughter **10** indication

**flier**
**02** FO, PO **07** handout, leaflet **08** brochure, bulletin, circular, pamphlet **09** statement **10** literature **12** press release

*See also* **bird**

• **expert flier**
**03** ace

• **non-flier** *see* **flightless birds** *under* **bird**

**fliers**
**03** RAF

**flight**
**03** fly, guy, lam, set **04** exit, pair, rout, rush, trap, trip, wing **05** steps **06** escape, exodus, flying, roding, stairs, voyage **07** fleeing, getaway, journey, retreat, roading, runaway, shuttle, soaring **08** aviation, stairway **09** air travel, breakaway, departure, skedaddle, staircase **10** absconding, exaltation, running off, volitation, withdrawal **11** aeronautics, running away **12** air transport **13** globetrotting

• **take flight**
**03** fly, run **04** bolt, flee, quit, rush, scat **05** lam it, leave, leg it, scoot, scram, skive, split **06** decamp, depart, escape, vanish **07** abscond, bunk off, do a bunk, get away, make off, push off, retreat, run away, scarper, take off, vamoose **08** clear off, shove off, up sticks, withdraw **09** cut and run, disappear, do a runner, push along, skedaddle **10** hightail it, hit the road, make tracks **11** hit the trail **13** sling your hook **14** make a bolt for it, take it on the lam **15** make a break for it, take to your heels

**flighty**
◇ *anagram indicator*
**04** wild **05** giddy, silly, swift **06** fickle, volage **07** erratic, flyaway **08** fanciful, hellicat, skipping, skittish, unstable, unsteady, volatile **09** butterfly, frivolous, impetuous, impulsive, mercurial, volageous **10** bird-witted, capricious, changeable, inconstant, unbalanced **11** birdbrained, flirtatious, hare-brained, lightheaded, loup-the-dyke, thoughtless, unballasted **12** bubble-headed, rattle-headed, whisky-frisky **13** irresponsible, rattle-brained, weather-headed **14** scatterbrained

• **flighty type**
**04** bird

**flimsy**
**04** fine, poor, thin, weak **05** filmy, light, shaky, sheer, wispy **06** feeble, meagre, slight, slimsy **07** band-box, fragile, rickety, shallow, trivial **08** banknote, delicate, ethereal, gossamer, trifling, vaporous **09** airy-fairy, cardboard, gossamery, makeshift, paper-thin **10** inadequate, jerry-built, ramshackle **11** implausible, lightweight, superficial **12** unconvincing **13** insubstantial

**flinch**
**04** balk, duck, flay, flee, funk **05** avoid, cower, dodge, quail, quake, shake, shirk, start, wince **06** blench, cringe, crouch, falter, recoil, shiver, shrink **07** retreat, shudder, shy away, tremble **08** draw back, pull back, withdraw **10** shrink back

**fling**
**02** go **03** lob, shy, try **04** cast, dart, dash, hurl, jerk, jibe, rush, send, shot, toss, turn **05** amour, binge, chuck, crack, heave, lance, lanch, pitch, sling, spang, spree, taunt, throw, trial, whirl **06** affair, gamble, launce, launch, let fly, propel **07** affaire, attempt, carry-on, flounce, liaison, romance, venture **08** catapult, good time, intrigue, spanghew, throw out **10** indulgence, love affair, send flying **12** relationship **13** affaire d'amour, grande passion

**flinty**
**03** icy **04** cold, hard **05** blank, cruel, stern, stony **06** chilly, frigid, frosty, severe, steely **07** adamant, callous, deadpan, hostile **08** obdurate, pitiless **09** heartless, merciless, unfeeling **10** inexorable, poker-faced **11** emotionless, indifferent, unforgiving **12** unresponsive **14** expressionless

**flip**
◇ *reversal indicator*
**04** cast, flap, jerk, pert, snap, spin, toss, turn **05** click, flick, pitch, throw, twirl, twist **09** pitch-pole, pitch-poll

• **flip through**
**04** scan, skim, skip **08** glance at **10** glance over **11** leaf through **12** flick through, thumb through **13** browse through

**flippancy**
**05** cheek **06** levity **08** glibness, pertness **09** frivolity, sauciness **10** cheekiness, disrespect, persiflage **11** irreverence, shallowness **12** impertinence **13** facetiousness **14** superficiality **15** thoughtlessness

**flippant**
**04** flip, glib, pert, rude **05** saucy **06** cheeky, nimble **07** offhand, playful, shallow **08** impudent **09** facetious, frivolous **10** insouciant, irreverent **11** impertinent, superficial, thoughtless **12** light-hearted **13** disrespectful, irresponsible

**flippantly**
**06** glibly, rudely **11** facetiously, frivolously **12** irreverently **13** impertinently, irresponsibly, superficially, thoughtlessly **14** light-heartedly **15** disrespectfully

**flipping**
**06** cursed, damned, darned, dashed **07** blasted **08** annoying, blinking, blooming, dratting, fiendish, infernal, wretched **10** confounded, unpleasant

**flirt**
**03** rap, toy **04** jerk, mash, ogle, vamp **05** dally, eye up, flick, hussy, tease **06** chat up, chippy, coquet, gillet, lead on, masher, wanton **07** carry on, pickeer, trifler **08** coquette, make up to **09** gillflirt, philander **10** make eyes at **11** make a pass at, philanderer **12** heart-breaker

• **flirt with**
**03** try **04** mash **05** hit on **06** coquet **07** carry on, hit upon, toy with **08** consider, coquette, dabble in, play with **09** entertain **10** trifle with

**flirtation**
**05** amour, sport **06** affair, come-on, lumber, toying **07** teasing **08** coquetry, dallying, intrigue, trifling **09** dalliance **10** chatting up **12** philandering

**flirtatious**
**05** loose **06** come-on, flirty, wanton **07** amorous, flighty, teasing **08** flirtish, sportive **10** come-hither, coquettish **11** promiscuous, provocative

**flit**
◇ *anagram indicator*
**03** bob, fly **04** dart, dash, pass, rush, skim, skip, slip, wing **05** dance, flash, fleet, light, speed, whisk **07** flitter, flutter **08** fleeting

**float**
**03** bob **04** cart, cork, hang, hull, pram, sail, swim, waft **05** balsa, camel, drift, fleet, glide, hover, quill, set up, slide, table **06** bobber, launch, smooth, submit, wander **07** oropesa, pontoon, present, promote, propose, suggest, suspend **08** get going, initiate, levitate, lifebuoy **09** be buoyant, establish, recommend **10** come up with, put forward, stay afloat **13** pneumatophore **15** get off the ground

**floating**
◇ *anagram indicator*
**04** free **06** afloat, natant **07** bobbing, buoyant, movable, sailing, wafting **08** drifting, hovering, swimming, variable **09** migratory, unsettled, wandering **10** indecisive, transitory, unattached, unsinkable **11** fluctuating, uncommitted

**flock**
**03** mob **04** band, bevy, fold, game, herd, host, mass, mill, pack, rout, sord, trip, tuft, walk, wing, wisp, wool **05** bunch, charm, chirm, covey, crowd, drove, flush, group, shoal, skein, swarm, troop, watch **06** flight, gaggle, gather, huddle, school, spring, throng

07 cluster, collect, company, dopping 08 assemble, assembly, converge, paddling 09 flocculus, gathering, multitude 10 collection, congregate, unkindness 11 murmuration 12 come together, congregation

**flog**

◇ *anagram indicator*

03 tan, tat, taw 04 beat, belt, cane, drub, flay, hawk, hide, lash, sell, whip 05 birch, knout, strap, swish, trade, whack, whang 06 breech, deal in, handle, larrup, peddle, punish, strike, thrash, wallop 07 scourge, sjambok 08 chastise, urticate, vapulate 09 horsewhip 10 flagellate 12 offer for sale, put up for sale

**flogging**

06 caning, hiding 07 beating, belting, flaying, lashing 08 birching, whacking, whipping 09 scourging, strapping, thrashing, walloping 10 vapulation 12 flagellation 13 horsewhipping, whipping-cheer

**flood**

04 bore, eger, fill, flow, glut, gush, pour, rage, rush, soak, tide 05 drown, eager, eagre, spate, speat, surge, swamp, swell 06 deluge, drench, engulf, excess, series, stream 07 debacle, freshet, immerse, smother, torrent 08 alluvion, brim over, diluvion, diluvium, downpour, inundate, overflow, plethora, saturate, submerge 09 abundance, cataclysm, overwhelm, profusion 10 flash flood, inundation, outpouring, spring tide, succession, transgress 11 superfluity 13 Ogygian deluge

**floor**

02 fl, KO 04 area, base, beat, dais, deck, fell, loft, tier 05 attic, basis, étage, level, stage, stump, throw 06 baffle, defeat, ground, planch, puzzle, storey 07 flummox, landing, nonplus, perplex 08 basement, bel étage, bewilder, confound, entresol, flooring, platform 09 discomfit, dumbfound, frustrate, knock down, overwhelm, prostrate 10 disconcert, downstairs, strike down 11 piano nobile

• **first floor**

11 ground level

• **floor material**

04 lino, pisé, rung

**floozy** *see* **tart**

**flop**

◇ *anagram indicator*

03 sag 04 bomb, drop, fail, fall, fold, hang, sink, swap, swop 05 crash, droop, flump, slump 06 dangle, fiasco, go bust, pack up, slip-up, topple, tumble 07 also-ran, debacle, failure, founder, go broke, has-been, misfire, no-hoper, washout 08 collapse, disaster, fall flat, lay an egg, shambles 10 non-starter 11 go to the wall 12 come a cropper, go into the red 14 be unsuccessful

• **flop down**

03 wop 04 whap, whop 05 plump

**floppy**

◇ *anagram indicator*

04 limp, soft 05 baggy, loose 06 droopy, flabby 07 flaccid, hanging, sagging 08 dangling, diskette, flexible 12 flexible disk

**flora**

06 botany, Cybele, plants 07 herbage 08 plantage 09 plant life 10 vegetation

**floral emblem** *see* **emblem**

**florid**

03 red 04 high 05 Asian, fussy, ruddy 06 ornate, purple, rococo 07 baroque, flowery, flushed, pompous, reddish, taffeta, verbose 08 beetroot, blushing, figurate, red-faced, rubicund, sanguine, taffetas 09 bombastic, elaborate, high-flown 10 coloratura, flamboyant, melismatic 11 embellished, extravagant 12 high-sounding 13 grandiloquent, overelaborate

**Florida**

02 FL 03 Fla

**flotsam**

04 junk 05 dreck 06 debris, jetsam 07 flotage, rubbish 08 detritus, floatage, oddments, wreckage 11 odds and ends

**flounce**

03 bob 04 jerk, toss 05 fling, frill, stamp, storm, throw, twist 06 bounce, fringe, ruffle, spring 07 falbala, valance 08 furbelow, trimming

**flounder**

◇ *anagram indicator*

05 fluke, grope, slosh 06 dither, falter, fumble, jumble, tolter, wallop, wallow 07 blunder, go under, stagger, stumble 08 struggle 10 be confused, flail about 11 thresh about 12 lose the place

**flour**

04 meal 06 red-dog 07 cribble, pollard 08 tailings 09 wheatmeal 11 strong wheat

**flourish**

◇ *anagram indicator*

03 wag, wax 04 boom, élan, grow, lick, mort, show, wave 05 bloom, get on, serif, shake, swash, sweep, swing, swirl, swish, twirl, twist, vaunt, wield 06 do well, flaunt, flower, parade, paraph, rubric, swinge, thrive, tucket 07 blossom, burgeon, cadenza, develop, display, exhibit, fanfare, gesture, panache, pizzazz, prosper, show off, succeed, wampish 08 be strong, brandish, curlicue, increase, ornament, progress 09 bear fruit 10 decoration

**flourished**

◇ *anagram indicator*

02 fl 04 flor

**flourishing**

◇ *anagram indicator*

04 pert 05 green, palmy 06 bloomy 07 booming 08 blooming, thriving 10 blossoming, burgeoning, prosperous, successful 11 going strong

**flout**

04 defy, gibe, jibe, lout, lowt, mock 05 break, scorn, scout, spurn 06 jeer at, reject 07 disdain, disobey, laugh at, scoff at, sneer at, violate 08 ridicule 09 disregard, go against 11 set at nought 15 show contempt for

**flow**

◇ *anagram indicator*

02 go 03 jet, ren, rin, run 04 drip, flux, gush, leak, make, melt, move, ooze, pour, rail, roll, rush, seep, slip, spew, stem, teem, tide, well, wend 05 arise, drift, flood, glide, issue, raile, rayle, slide, spate, spill, spout, spurt, surge, sweep, swirl, whirl 06 babble, bubble, course, deluge, derive, emerge, gurgle, morass, plenty, result, ripple, spring, squirt, stream 07 cascade, current, emanate, passage, proceed, trickle 08 effusion, movement, overflow, plethora, recourse 09 abundance, circulate, originate, quicksand 10 outpouring

**flower**

03 bud 04 acme, best, grow, open, peak, pick 05 bloom, cream, élite, prime 06 choice, finest, floret, height, heyday, mature, select, sprout, thrive, zenith 07 blossom, burgeon, come out, develop, prosper, succeed 08 best part, flourish, floweret, maturity, pinnacle 10 perfection 11 culmination, florescence 13 efflorescence, inflorescence 14 crème de la crème

*See also* **birth**; **river**

*Flower parts include:*

05 calyx, ovary, ovule, petal, sepal, spike, stalk, style, torus, umbel
06 anther, carpel, corymb, pistil, raceme, spadix, stamen, stigma
07 corolla, nectary, panicle, pedicel
08 filament, thalamus
09 capitulum, dichasium, gynoecium
10 receptacle
11 monochasium

*Garden flowers include:*

04 lis
04 aloe, daff, flag, glad, iris, lily, pink, rose, sego
05 aster, daisy, lotus, lupin, pansy, phlox, poppy, stock, tulip, viola
06 allium, azalea, crocus, dahlia, orchid, salvia, squill, violet, zinnia
07 alyssum, anemone, begonia, campion, day-lily, freesia, fuchsia, lobelia, nemesia, nigella, petunia, primula, verbena
08 arum lily, asphodel, bluebell, cyclamen, daffodil, dianthus, foxglove, gardenia, geranium, gladioli, hyacinth, marigold, pond lily, primrose, snowdrop, sweet pea
09 amaryllis, aubrietia, calendula, candytuft, carnation, digitalis, gladiolus, hollyhock, narcissus,

nicotiana, regal lily, sunflower, tiger lily, torch lily
**10** agapanthus, busy lizzie, cornflower, delphinium, Easter lily, fleur-de-lis, fleur-de-lys, fritillary, nasturtium, poinsettia, polyanthus, ragged-lady, snake's head, snapdragon, wallflower
**11** African lily, antirrhinum, forget-me-not, gillyflower, love-in-a-mist, Madonna-lily, naked ladies, red-hot poker, tiger flower
**12** devil-in-a-bush, flower of Jove, rose geranium, Solomon's seal, sweet william, wild hyacinth, Zantedeschia
**13** African violet, butcher's broom, chrysanthemum, grape hyacinth, lily of the Nile, winter aconite
**14** belladonna lily, glory of the snow, Ithuriel's spear
**15** dog's tooth violet, lily of the valley, star of Bethlehem

*See also* **lily**

*Wild flowers include:*

**03** kex, meu
**04** daff, geum, ling, nard, woad
**05** clary, daisy, gowan, laser, poppy
**06** clover, oxslip, teasel, violet, yarrow
**07** ale hoof, bistort, campion, comfrey, cowslip, dog rose, goldcup, heather, spignel
**08** bluebell, crowfoot, dog daisy, foxglove, harebell, lungwort, primrose, rock rose, self-heal, spicknel, toadflax, wild iris
**09** Aaron's rod, baldmoney, birthwort, broomrape, buttercup, celandine, columbine, edelweiss, goldenrod, horsetail, moneywort, stonecrop, water lily, wild pansy
**10** crane's bill, goatsbeard, heartsease, lady's smock, marguerite, masterwort, oxeye daisy, pennyroyal, wild endive, wild orchid
**11** ragged robin, wild chicory, wood anemone
**12** common mallow, cuckoo flower, great mullein, lady's slipper, solomon's seal, white campion, yellow rocket
**13** butter-and-eggs, field cow-wheat, shepherd's club, wild gladiolus
**14** black-eyed susan, bladder campion, common toadflax, multiflora rose
**15** New England aster

• **garland of flowers**
**03** lei **05** toran **06** torana
• **mass of flowers**
**04** head

**flowery**
**05** fancy **06** bloomy, floral, florid, ornate **07** baroque, chintzy, pompous, verbose **08** blossomy **09** bombastic, elaborate, high-flown **10** euphuistic, rhetorical **13** grandiloquent

**flowing**
**04** easy, flux **05** loose **06** floppy, fluent, liquid, moving, oozing, smooth **07** current, cursive, falling, flaccid, gushing, hanging, natural, pouring, rolling, running, rushing, seeping, surging, welling **08** bubbling, sweeping, unbroken **09** cascading, streaming **10** continuous, effortless **11** loose-bodied, overflowing **12** hanging loose **13** hanging freely, uninterrupted

**fluctuate**
◇ *anagram indicator*
**04** sway, trim, vary, yo-yo **05** alter, float, range, shift, swing, waver **06** change, differ, seesaw **07** balance **08** hesitate, undulate **09** alternate, come and go, oscillate, vacillate **10** ebb and flow **11** go up and down, rise and fall **13** chop and change

**fluctuation**
**05** range, shift, swing **06** change, seiche **08** floating, nutation, wavering **09** variation **10** fickleness **11** alternation, ambivalence, inconstancy, instability, oscillation, vacillation, variability **12** irresolution, unsteadiness **14** capriciousness

**flue**
**03** fur **04** duct, flat, pipe, vent **05** shaft, tewel **06** flared, tunnel, uptake **07** channel, chimney, passage, shallow, splayed **08** fluework **09** influenza

**fluency**
**04** ease, flow **07** command, control **08** facility, glibness **09** assurance, eloquence, facundity, flippancy, readiness, slickness **10** outpouring, smoothness, volubility **12** flippantness **13** copia verborum **14** articulateness

**fluent**
**04** easy, glib **05** fluid, ready, slick **06** facile, smooth **07** elegant, flowing, natural, voluble **08** eloquent, graceful **10** articulate, effortless **11** free-flowing, mellifluous **13** silver-tongued

**fluently**
**03** pat **05** patly **06** easily, glibly **08** smoothly **09** elegantly, naturally **10** eloquently, gracefully **12** articulately, effortlessly

**fluff**
◇ *anagram indicator*
**03** fug, nap **04** blow, boob, dowl, down, dust, flue, fuzz, lint, muff, oose, ooze, pile **05** botch, dowle, flosh, floss, spoil **06** bungle, cock up, foul up, fumble, mess up, muck up, muddle **07** do badly, screw up **09** dust bunny, mismanage **11** make a mess of **13** make a bad job of **15** put your foot in it

**fluffy**
**04** soft **05** downy, furry, fuzzy, hairy, silky **06** fleecy, pluffy, shaggy, woolly **07** velvety **08** feathery

**fluid**
◇ *anagram indicator*
**02** fl **03** gas **04** easy, open **05** chyle, grume, juice, runny **06** liquid, liquor, melted, mobile, molten, smooth, vapour, watery **07** aqueous, elegant, flowing, natural, protean, running **08** atrament, flexible, graceful, shifting, solution, unstable, unsteady, variable **09** adaptable, diffluent, liquefied, unsettled **10** adjustable, changeable, effortless, inconstant, karyolymph **11** fluctuating, free-flowing **12** unsolidified

**fluke**
**03** fan **04** barb, worm **05** break, freak, quirk **06** chance, stroke, upcast **07** killick, killock, scratch **08** accident, blessing, flounder, fortuity, windfall **09** trematode **10** lucky break **11** coincidence, serendipity **12** stroke of luck

**fluky**
**05** jammy, lucky **06** chance **08** freakish **09** fortunate, uncertain **10** accidental, fortuitous **12** coincidental, incalculable **13** serendipitous

**flummox**
**03** fox **04** faze **05** floor, stump **06** baffle, defeat, puzzle, stymie **07** confuse, mystify, nonplus, perplex **08** bewilder, confound **09** bamboozle

**flummoxed**
**05** at sea, fazed, foxed **07** at a loss, baffled, floored, puzzled, stumped, stymied **08** confused **09** mystified, perplexed **10** bamboozled, bewildered, confounded, nonplussed

**flunk**
**04** bomb, fail, flop, fold **06** blow it **07** failure, founder **08** fall flat **09** not make it **10** come undone, not come off **11** bite the dust, come to grief, come unglued, come unstuck **12** come a cropper **14** be unsuccessful **15** blow your chances

**flunkey**
**05** slave, toady, valet **06** drudge, Jeames, lackey, menial, minion, yes-man **07** cringer, footman, servant, steward **08** hanger-on **09** assistant, underling **10** bootlicker, manservant

**fluorine**
**01** F

**flurried**
◇ *anagram indicator*
**05** fazed, upset **07** in a flap, in a tizz, rattled **08** in a tizzy, unnerved **09** disturbed, flustered, perturbed, unsettled **12** all of a lather **13** having kittens

**flurry**
◇ *anagram indicator*
**04** bout, flap, fuss, gust, stir, to-do **05** blast, burst, hurry, spell, spurt, swirl, upset, whirl **06** bother, bustle, hassle, hubbub, hustle, rattle, ruffle, scurry, shower, squall, tumult **07** agitate, confuse, disturb, fluster, flutter, perturb, swither **08** bewilder, outbreak, unsettle **09** agitation, commotion

**10** disconcert, excitement
**11** disturbance **12** perturbation
**14** discountenance

**flush**
**03** rud **04** burn, even, flat, full, gild, glow, hose, rich, swab, true, wash
**05** bloom, blush, clear, eject, elate, empty, expel, flame, go red, level, plane, rinse, rouse, scour, start
**06** colour, hectic, heyday, lavish, puddle, redden, sluice, smooth, square, vigour **07** cleanse, crimson, disturb, moneyed, redness, replete, suffuse, turn red, uncover, wealthy, well-off **08** abundant, colour up, discover, drive out, evacuate, force out, generous, rosiness, well-to-do
**09** abounding, abundance, freshness, reddening, ruddiness **10** prosperous, run to earth, well-heeled
**11** overflowing

**flushed**
**03** hot, red **04** pink, rosy **05** aglow, rosed, ruddy **06** ablaze, aflame, blowsy, blowzy, elated, florid, hectic
**07** aroused, burning, crimson, excited, glowing, scarlet **08** animated, blushing, enthused, exultant, inspired, rubicund, sanguine, thrilled
**11** embarrassed, exhilarated, intoxicated

**fluster**
◇ *anagram indicator*
**04** faze, flap, heat, tizz **05** panic, state, tizzy, upset **06** bother, bustle, dither, flurry, pother, pudder, put off, rattle, ruffle **07** agitate, confuse, disturb, perturb, turmoil, unnerve
**08** confound, distract, hurrying, unsettle **09** agitation, commotion, confusion, embarrass, flustrate
**10** discompose, disconcert
**11** disturbance, flustration, make nervous **12** perturbation
**13** embarrassment

**flute**
**04** fife **05** quena, tibia **06** poogye, zufolo **07** chamfer, piccolo, poogyee, zuffolo **08** recorder **09** flageolet
**10** shakuhachi

**fluted**
**06** ribbed, ridged **07** grooved
**08** furrowed **10** channelled, corrugated

**flutter**
◇ *anagram indicator*
**03** bat, bet, fan, fly **04** beat, flap, play, punt, risk, toss, waff, wave **05** dance, flaff, hover, shake, wager, waver
**06** gamble, quiver, ripple, ruffle, shiver, tremor, twitch, winnow **07** agitate, flacker, flaffer, flicker, flitter, pulsate, shudder, tremble, twitter, vibrate
**08** flapping, flichter, volitate
**09** agitation, confusion, flaughter, fluctuate, palpitate, vibration
**11** palpitation, speculation

**flux**
**04** flow, fuse, melt **05** issue
**06** change, motion, unrest **08** fluidity, movement, mutation **10** alteration, transition **11** development, fluctuation, instability **12** modification
**13** changeability

**• electric flux displacement**
**01** D

**• magnetic flux density**
**01** B

**fly**
◇ *anagram indicator*
**03** jet, run, sly **04** bolt, dart, dash, flap, flee, flit, quit, race, rise, rush, scat, show, soar, tear, wave, wily, wing, zoom
**05** alert, canny, float, glide, guide, hover, hurry, leave, mount, pilot, scoot, scram, sharp, shoot, skive, smart, speed, split, steer **06** artful, ascend, astute, career, decamp, depart, escape, flight, get out, hasten, reveal, shrewd, slip by, sprint, stream, vanish, winnow **07** abscond, careful, control, cunning, display, do a bunk, exhibit, flutter, get away, go by air, make off, operate, present, prudent, push off, retreat, run away, scarper, stylish, take off, vamoose **08** clear off, shove off, volitate, withdraw **09** cut and run, disappear, do a runner, golden-eye, go quickly, manoeuvre, on the ball, push along, sagacious, skedaddle **10** hit the road, make tracks, take flight
**11** fashionable, hit the trail, nobody's fool, pass quickly, travel by air **14** make a bolt for it **15** make a break for it, take to your heels

*Flies include:*

**03** bee, bot, day, dor, gad, hop, ked, may, med
**04** beet, blow, boat, bulb, bush, cleg, corn, deer, dung, fire, frit, gnat, gout, kade, lamp, meat, pium, sand
**05** alder, birch, black, crane, drone, flesh, froth, fruit, horse, house, hover, march, midge, onion, sedge, snake, snipe, water, wheat
**06** blowie, caddis, carrot, cuckoo, forest, motuca, muscid, mutuca, pomace, robber, stable, tipula, tsetse, turnip, tzetse, tzetze, warble
**07** blister, brommer, cabbage, cluster, diptera, dolphin, harvest, Hessian, lantern, sciarid, smother, Spanish, vinegar
**08** glossina, ruby-tail, scorpion, sheep ked, simulium, tachinid
**09** cantharis, ichneumon, screw-worm
**10** bluebottle, Cecidomyia, drosophila, spittle bug
**11** biting midge, buffalo gnat, cabbage-root, greenbottle
**12** cheesehopper
**13** cheese skipper, spittle insect

*Fishing flies include:*

**03** bob
**04** harl, herl, tail
**05** sedge
**06** doctor, hackle, palmer, salmon
**07** watchet
**09** hairy Mary, Jock Scott
**10** cock-a-bondy

**• fly at**
**03** hit **05** go for **06** attack, charge, let fly, strike **07** assault, lay into **08** fall upon **09** have a go at, lash out at

**• fly open**
◇ *anagram indicator*
**05** burst **15** burst at the seams

**fly-by-night**
**05** shady **06** cowboy **07** dubious
**09** ephemeral **10** short-lived, unreliable **12** disreputable, questionable, undependable
**13** discreditable, irresponsible, untrustworthy

**flyer** *see* **flier**

**flying**
**04** fast **05** brief, hasty, rapid
**06** mobile, rushed, speedy, volant, winged **07** gliding, hurried, soaring, winging **08** airborne, flapping, fleeting, flighted, floating, hovering, volitant **09** on the wing, wind-borne
**10** fluttering, volitation **11** upon the wing, whistle-stop

**foam**
**03** fry **04** boil, fizz, head, scum, suds, surf **05** froth, spume, yeast
**06** befoam, bubble, lather, mousse, seethe **07** aerogel, bubbles **08** sea froth **10** effervesce **13** effervescence

**foamy**
**05** spumy, sudsy **06** bubbly, frothy, yeasty **07** foaming, lathery
**10** spumescent

**fob**
**• fob off**
**04** dump **05** foist **06** impose, put off, unload **07** deceive, inflict, palm off, pass off **08** get rid of

**focus**
**03** aim, fix, hub **04** axis, core, crux, join, meet, turn **05** heart, hinge, pivot
**06** accent, center, centre, direct, home in, kernel, stress, target, weight, zero in, zoom in **07** nucleus **08** converge, emphasis, linchpin, pinpoint, priority
**09** attention, spotlight **10** focal point, importance, metropolis, prominence
**11** concentrate, pre-eminence
**12** accentuation, significance, underscoring **13** concentration
**14** bring into focus

**• in focus**
**05** clear, crisp, sharp **08** distinct
**11** well-defined

**• out of focus**
**04** hazy **05** fuzzy, muzzy **06** blurry
**07** blurred **10** ill-defined, indistinct

**fodder**
**02** ti **03** hay **04** feed, food, milo
**05** grass, vetch **06** eatage, forage, fother, lucern, luzern, silage, stover
**07** alfalfa, lucerne, pabulum, provand, provend, rations, soilage, timothy
**08** browsing, goat's-rue, oat grass, proviant, rye grass, sainfoin, teosinte

**09** foodstuff, milk vetch, milo maize, provender, sago grass, saintfoin **10** cow parsnip, serradella, serradilla, Sudan grass **11** nourishment, white clover **12** meadow fescue, timothy grass **13** kangaroo grass

## foe

**05** enemy, rival **08** opponent, wrangler **09** adversary, combatant, ill-wisher **10** antagonist

**foetid** *see* **fetid, foetid**

## foetus

**06** embryo **10** unborn baby **11** unborn child

## fog

◇ *anagram indicator*

**03** dim **04** blur, daze, dull, haar, haze, mist, moss, smog **05** befog, brume, cloud, gloom, smoke **06** baffle, darken, muddle, stupor, trance **07** aerosol, confuse, obscure, pea-soup, perplex, sea fret, steam up **08** bewilder, haziness **09** confusion, mistiness, murkiness, obfuscate, obscurity, pease-soup, pea-souper, vagueness **10** bafflement, perplexity, puzzlement **12** bewilderment **14** disorientation

## foggy

**03** dim **04** damp, dark, grey, hazy **05** misty, muggy, murky, thick, vague **06** cloudy, gloomy, smoggy, stupid **07** brumous, clouded, muddled, obscure, shadowy, unclear **08** overcast **10** indistinct

## foible

**05** fault, habit, quirk **06** defect, faible, oddity **07** failing, oddness **08** penchant, weakness **09** weak point **11** peculiarity, shortcoming, strangeness **12** eccentricity, idiosyncrasy, imperfection

## foil

**03** pip **04** balk, stop **05** baulk, block, chaff, check, elude, foyle, stump **06** baffle, defeat, hamper, hinder, outwit, relief, set-off, thwart, window **07** balance, counter, fleuret, nullify, paillon, prevent, repulse, scupper, scuttle, setting **08** contrast, obstruct **09** frustrate **10** antithesis, background, beauty spot, circumvent, complement **11** frustration, silver paper

## foist

**03** fob **05** force **06** fob off, impose, saddle, thrust, unload, wish on **07** palm off, pass off **08** get rid of **09** introduce

## fold

**03** hug, lap, pen, ply **04** bend, cuff, dart, fail, fake, flop, hood, line, lirk, purl, ring, ruck, tuck, turn, wrap, yard **05** clasp, close, court, crash, crimp, flock, kraal, layer, paper, pleat, plica, pouch, pound, prank, quill, quire **06** church, crease, crista, diapir, dog-ear, double, enfold, furrow, gather, go bust, mantle, middle, pack up, pleach, plight, pranck, pucker, ruffle, rumple, wimple, wrap up **07** company, crinkle, crumple, dog's-ear, embrace, enclose, entwine, envelop, flexion, folding, go broke, go under, omentum, overlap, paddock, prancke, squeeze, whimple, wrinkle **08** assembly, collapse, compound, doubling, patagium, shut down, stockade, syncline, turn down, turn over **09** community, duplicate, enclosure, gathering, gill cover, inflexure, knife-edge, mesentery, monocline, plication, plicature, replicate, turn under **10** epicanthus, fellowship, go bankrupt, intertwine **11** convolution, corrugation, duplicature, go to the wall **12** congregation, parishioners **14** hospital corner **15** go out of business

## folder

**04** file **05** folio **06** binder, holder, jacket, pocket, wallet **08** envelope **09** directory, matchbook, portfolio **13** lever arch file

## foliage

**06** canopy, leaves **07** boscage, boskage, leafage, verdure **08** greenery **09** foliation, foliature, vernation **10** vegetation **12** frondescence

## folio

**01** f **02** fo **03** fol

## folios

**02** ff

## folk

**03** kin, men **04** clan, race **05** tribe **06** ethnic, family, humans, nation, native, people, public, tribal, tupuna **07** kindred, parents, persons, popular, society **08** kinsfolk, national **09** ancestral, relations, relatives **10** indigenous, population **11** ethnic group, traditional

*See also* **singer**

## folklore

**04** lore **05** myths, tales **06** fables **07** beliefs, customs, legends, stories **09** folktales, mythology, tradition **13** superstitions

## folksy

**04** fond, kind, maty, warm **05** basic, close, crude, matey, pally, plain, thick, tight **06** chummy, genial, kindly, rustic, simple **07** affable, amiable, cordial, helpful, natural **08** amicable, everyday, familiar, friendly, intimate, ordinary, outgoing, sociable **09** comradely, convivial, receptive **10** hospitable **11** good-natured, inseparable, neighbourly, sympathetic, traditional **12** affectionate, approachable, time-honoured **13** companionable **15** unsophisticated

## follow

◇ *juxtaposition indicator*

**03** ape, dog, ren, rin, run, sew, sue, use **04** copy, flow, heed, heel, hunt, mind, note, obey, stag, suss, tail, twig **05** arise, catch, chase, ensue, grasp, hound, issue, mimic, stalk, track, trail, watch **06** accept, attend, escort, fathom, go with, pursue, repeat, result, second, shadow, spring, take in **07** develop, emanate, emulate, go after, imitate, observe, proceed, replace, stick to, succeed, support, suss out, yield to **08** adhere to, be a fan of, carry out, come next, go behind, practise, run after, supplant, tag along **09** accompany, come after, conform to, give chase, latch onto, supersede **10** appreciate, come behind, comply with, comprehend, keep up with, understand, walk behind **11** be devoted to, go along with, tread behind **14** be a supporter of, be interested in, take the place of **15** take your cue from

- **follow slavishly**

**04** echo

- **follow through**

**06** finish, fulfil, pursue **08** complete, conclude, continue **09** implement **10** see through

- **follow up**

**06** pursue **07** succeed **08** check out, continue, look into, research **09** prosecute, reinforce **11** consolidate, investigate

## follower

**03** fan, man **04** buff **05** freak, pupil **06** backer, cohort, escort, helper, lackey, voteen **07** acolyte, acolyth, admirer, Anthony, apostle, convert, devotee, janizar, lacquey, sectary **08** adherent, believer, disciple, emulator, hanger-on, imitator, janizary, retainer, sidekick **09** attendant, companion, janissary, poodle-dog, satellite, supporter **10** aficionado, enthusiast, pursuivant, running dog **11** afficionado

## following

◇ *juxtaposition indicator*

**01** f **03** fol **04** fans, next **05** later, suite **06** circle, public **07** backers, backing, coterie, ensuing, patrons, retinue, sequent, support **08** admirers, audience, secundum **09** adherents, clientèle, entourage, favorable, followers, hereunder, patronage, resulting **10** consequent, favourable, subsequent, succeeding, succession, successive, supporters **13** body of support

- **following pages**

**02** ff

## folly

**03** sin **04** whim **05** folie, moria, tower **06** gazebo, idiocy, lunacy, vanity **07** foolery, foppery, idiotcy, inanity, madness **08** insanity, monument, nonsense, rashness **09** absurdity, belvedere, craziness, silliness, stupidity **10** imbecility, imprudence **11** fatuousness, foolishness **12** illogicality, indiscretion, recklessness **13** foolhardiness, ludicrousness, senselessness **14** ridiculousness

**foment**
**04** brew, goad, spur **05** raise, rouse **06** arouse, excite, foster, incite, kindle, prompt, stir up, whip up, work up **07** agitate, promote, provoke, quicken **08** activate, incubate **09** encourage, instigate, stimulate

**fond**
**03** hot, try **04** daft, dote, vain, warm **05** basis, naive **06** absurd, caring, doting, keen on, liking, loving, nuts on, spoony, tender **07** adoring, amatory, amorous, attempt, deluded, devoted, foolish, proceed **08** hooked on, mad about **09** credulous, daft about, indulgent, nuts about, partial to **10** addicted to, attached to, background, crazy about, dotty about, foundation **11** enamoured of, impractical **12** affectionate **14** over-optimistic

**fondle**
**03** hug, pat, pet **05** grope **06** caress, cocker, cosset, cuddle, dandle, stroke **07** smuggle, touch up

**fondly**
**06** warmly **08** lovingly, tenderly **09** amorously **14** affectionately
**• speak fondly**
**03** coo **04** bill

**fondness**
**04** love **05** fancy, taste **06** dotage, liking, tender, tendre **07** leaning **08** devotion, kindness, penchant, soft spot, weakness **09** affection, engoûment, tendresse **10** attachment, engouement, enthusiasm, partiality, preference, tenderness, well-liking **11** inclination **12** predilection **14** susceptibility

**font**
**08** bénitier, delubrum

**food**
**03** kai **04** chow, diet, dish, eats, fare, feed, feud, grub, meal, menu, nosh, tack, tuck **05** board, meals, scoff, scran, table **06** fodder, kaikai, staple, stores, tucker, viands **07** aliment, cooking, cuisine, pabulum, pasture, rations **08** delicacy, eatables, victuals **09** nutriment, nutrition, provender, repasture **10** foodstuffs, provisions, speciality, sustenance **11** comestibles, nourishment, subsistence **12** refreshments

*Foods include:*

**03** dal, dip, ham, pie, poi
**04** dhal, eddo, flan, fool, hash, luau, mash, olio, olla, pâté, rice, soss, soup, stew, taco, tart, tofu, wrap
**05** balti, bhaji, boxty, brose, broth, champ, chips, crêpe, curry, daube, dolma, grits, gumbo, jelly, kebab, kofta, laksa, latke, pasta, pasty, pesto, pilau, pizza, Quorn®, roast, salad, salmi, salsa, satay, sauce, sushi, tapas, tikka, toast
**06** bhajee, borsch, burger, canapé, caviar, cheese, cookie, faggot, fajita, fondue, fu yung, gratin, haggis, hotpot, hummus, kipper, mousse, paella, pakora, panini, pastry, pilaff, quiche, ragout, samosa, scampi, sorbet, tahina, tamale, trifle, waffle
**07** biryani, biscuit, borscht, burrito, chowder, chutney, cobbler, compote, cracker, crowdie, crumble, fajitas, falafel, felafel, fritter, friture, galette, gnocchi, goulash, gravlax, lasagne, oatcake, pancake, pavlova, polenta, pudding, rarebit, risotto, rissole, sashimi, sausage, seafood, soufflé, stir fry, stovies, tempura, terrine, timbale, tostada
**08** barbecue, biriyani, calamari, chop suey, chow mein, cocktail, coleslaw, consommé, coq au vin, couscous, dolmades, dumpling, fishcake, fricasee, gado-gado, gazpacho, ice cream, kedgeree, meringue, moussaka, nut roast, omelette, porridge, pot-roast, raclette, sandwich, souvlaki, syllabub, tandoori, teriyaki, tortilla, turnover, tzatziki, vindaloo, yakitori
**09** casserole, cassoulet, charlotte, colcannon, croquette, enchilada, fricassée, galantine, gravadlax, guacamole, Irish stew, jambalaya, macedoine, meatballs, nut cutlet, souvlakia, succotash, tabbouleh
**10** blancmange, cannelloni, cheesecake, corned beef, cottage pie, enchiladas, fish-finger, fruit salad, Greek salad, green salad, minestrone, mixed grill, peperonata, quesadilla, salmagundi, salmagundy, sauerkraut, spring roll, stroganoff
**11** baba ganoush, caesar salad, cockaleekie, French fries, fritto misto, gefilte fish, potato salad, ratatouille, rumblethump, smorgasbord, vichyssoise, winter salad
**12** eggs Benedict, fish and chips, mulligatawny, pease pudding, rumblethumps, Russian salad, shepherd's pie, taramasalata, Waldorf salad, welsh rarebit
**13** bouillabaisse, fisherman's pie, prawn cocktail, salade niçoise, toad-in-the-hole
**14** chilli con carne, macaroni cheese, pickled herring
**15** bubble-and-squeak, Wiener schnitzel

*See also* **bean**; **biscuit**; **bread**; **cake**; **cheese**; **fruit**; **herb**; **meat**; **mushroom**; **nut**; **pasta**; **pastry**; **sauce**; **sausage**; **sweet**; **vegetable**

*Fast food includes:*

**03** KFC®
**04** taco, wrap
**05** bagel, chips, donut, fries, kebab, pizza
**06** Big Mac®, burger, hot dog, nachos
**07** burrito, chalupa, falafel, noodles, shwarma, Whopper®
**08** doughnut, sandwich
**09** bacon roll, chip butty, hamburger, Happy Meal®, milkshake
**10** beanburger, beefburger, doner kebab, fish 'n' chips, fish supper, onion rings, shish kebab
**11** bacon burger, baked potato, French fries, sausage roll
**12** cheeseburger, chicken wings, club sandwich, fish and chips, tortilla wrap, veggie burger
**13** chicken burger, sausage supper
**14** chicken nuggets, quarter pounder

*See also* **restaurant**

**• provide food**
**05** cater

**fool**
**04** goof, hoax, jest, joke **05** bluff, cheat, feign, tease, trick **06** delude, diddle, have on, play up, take in, trifle **07** beguile, carry on, deceive, mislead, pretend, swindle **08** hoodwink **09** bamboozle, lark about, mess about, play about **10** mess around, play around, play tricks **11** horse around, monkey about, string along **12** monkey around, put one over on

*Fools include:*

**02** bf
**03** ass, auf, con, fon, git, kid, mug, nit, nut, oik, sap, sot, yap
**04** berk, bête, bozo, burk, butt, cake, calf, clot, cony, coof, coot, cuif, dill, dope, dork, dupe, geek, goat, goof, goon, goop, gouk, gowk, gull, gump, hash, jerk, kook, loon, lump, lunk, muck, mutt, nana, nerd, nerk, nong, ouph, poop, prat, punk, putz, sham, shmo, simp, soft, tony, twit, yo-yo
**05** chump, clown, cluck, comic, coney, divvy, droll, dumbo, dunce, dweeb, eejit, galah, idiot, moron, neddy, nelly, ninny, patch, patsy, prick, purée, schmo, snipe, softy, twerp, wally
**06** bampot, bauble, cretin, dimwit, donkey, doofus, dottle, drongo, dum-dum, jester, josser, madcap, monkey, motley, muppet, nitwit, nutter, sawney, schmoe, stooge, sucker, turkey, wallie, wigeon, Yorick
**07** airhead, barmpot, bourder, buffoon, Charley, Charlie, dingbat, fat-head, God's ape, gubbins, halfwit, haverel, jackass, jughead, lemming, muggins, pillock, plonker, saphead, tomfool, want-wit, wazzock, widgeon
**08** boofhead, dipstick, flathead, fondling, Fred Nerk, imbecile, Jack-fool, lunkhead, merryman, mooncalf, omadhaun, shlemiel, Tom-noddy, Trinculo
**09** April fool, birdbrain, blockhead, capocchia, chipochia, cloth head, court fool, dumb-cluck, ignoramus, joculator, lack-brain, lamebrain,

mumchance, philander, schlemiel, schlemihl, simpleton
**10** head-banger, nincompoop, silly-billy, Touchstone
**11** chowderhead, knuckle-head,
**13** laughing-stock, poisson d'avril, proper Charlie

**• play the fool**

**03** fon **04** daff **07** act dido **09** fool about, mess about, muck about **10** act the fool, fool around, mess around, muck around **11** clown around, horse around **12** monkey around

**foolery**

**05** farce, folly, larks **06** antics, capers, pranks **07** carry-on, daffing, fooling, waggery, zanyism **08** clowning, drollery, mischief, nonsense, trumpery **09** high jinks, horseplay, silliness **10** buffoonery, tomfoolery **11** shenanigans **12** childishness, monkey tricks **14** practical jokes

**foolhardiness**

**08** boldness, rashness **10** imprudence **12** recklessness **13** impulsiveness

**foolhardy**

**04** bold, rash **06** daring **08** kamikaze, reckless **09** daredevil, imprudent, impulsive **10** ill-advised, incautious **11** temerarious **13** irresponsible

**foolish**

◇ *anagram indicator*

**03** mad, twp **04** daft, dumb, fond, fool **05** barmy, batty, crazy, dilly, divvy, doilt, dotty, glaik, goofy, inane, inept, nutty, potty, seely, silly, wacky **06** absurd, doiled, dottle, insane, paltry, simple, stupid, unwise **07** dottled, étourdi, fatuous, glaiket, glaikit, goatish, gudgeon, idiotic, moronic, peevish, risible, sottish, tomfool, unwitty, vacuous **08** étourdie, gormless, ignorant, imbecile, overfond **09** half-baked, idiotical, ill-judged, ludicrous, pointless, senseless **10** half-witted, idle-headed, ill-advised, pea-brained, ridiculous **11** hare-brained, injudicious, nonsensical **12** crack-brained, short-sighted, simple-minded, unreasonable **13** cockle-brained, ill-considered, out of your mind, rattle-brained, unintelligent

**foolishly**

◇ *anagram indicator*

**05** fonly, madly **06** daftly **07** crazily, ineptly, wackily **08** absurdly, stupidly, unwisely **09** fatuously, shallowly **10** mistakenly **11** idiotically, imprudently, senselessly **12** ill-advisedly, incautiously, indiscreetly, ridiculously **13** injudiciously **14** short-sightedly

**foolishness**

**03** rot **04** bunk, crap **05** balls, bilge, folly **06** bunkum, lunacy, piffle **07** baloney, foolery, hogwash, inanity, madness, rubbish **08** claptrap, cobblers, daftness, nonsense, unreason, unwisdom, weakness **09** absurdity, craziness, incaution, meshugaas, mishegaas, niaiserie, poppycock, silliness, stupidity **10** imprudence, ineptitude **12** indiscretion **13** senselessness

**foolproof**

**04** safe, sure **07** certain **08** fail-safe, sure-fire **09** unfailing **10** dependable, guaranteed, idiot-proof, infallible **11** trustworthy

**foot**

**01** f **02** ft **03** end, leg, pad, paw, pes, toe **04** base, heel, hoof, kick, sole **05** dance, limit, paeon **06** border, bottom, dactyl, far end, iambus, tarsus **07** anapest, paeonic, pyrrhic, spondee, tootsie, trochee, trotter **08** anapaest, bacchius, choriamb, dochmius, molossus, tribrach **09** extremity **10** amphibrach, amphimacer, choriambus, foundation **12** antibacchius, tootsy-wootsy

**• discomfort of foot**

**04** corn

**• division of foot**

**04** inch

**• model of foot**

**04** last

**• part of foot**

**03** toe **04** arch, vola **06** instep

**football**

**02** RL, RU **04** camp **06** soccer

*See also* **American football**; **Australian football**

*English league football teams:*

**03** QPR
**04** Bury
**06** Barnet, Fulham, Yeovil
**07** Arsenal, Burnley, Chelsea, Everton, Reading, Walsall, Watford, Wrexham
**08** Barnsley, Hull City, Millwall, Port Vale, Rochdale
**09** Blackpool, Brentford, Liverpool, Luton Town, Stoke City
**10** Aston Villa, Darlington, Gillingham, Portsmouth, Sunderland
**11** Bournemouth, Bristol City, Cardiff City, Chester City, Derby County, Grimsby Town, Ipswich Town, Leeds United, Lincoln City, Norwich City, Notts County, Southampton, Swansea City, Swindon Town
**12** Boston United, Bradford City, Chesterfield, Coventry City, Leyton Orient
**13** Bristol Rovers, Crystal Palace, Leicester City, Mansfield Town, Middlesbrough, Torquay United, West Ham United, Wigan Athletic
**14** Birmingham City, Carlisle United, Cheltenham Town, Crewe Alexandra, Hereford United, Manchester City, Oldham Athletic, Plymouth Argyle, Shrewsbury Town, Southend United, Tranmere Rovers
**15** Blackburn Rovers, Bolton Wanderers, Doncaster Rovers, Newcastle United, Northampton Town, Preston North End, Rotherham United, Sheffield United, Stockport County
**16** Charlton Athletic, Colchester United, Hartlepool United, Huddersfield Town, Macclesfield Town, Manchester United, Milton Keynes Dons, Nottingham Forest, Scunthorpe United, Tottenham Hotspur, Wycombe Wanderers
**17** Accrington Stanley, Queen's Park Rangers
**18** Peterborough United, Sheffield Wednesday, West Bromwich Albion
**21** Brighton and Hove Albion
**22** Wolverhampton Wanderers

*Scottish league football teams:*

**04** Hibs
**05** Clyde
**06** Celtic, Dundee, Gretna, Hearts
**07** Falkirk, Rangers
**08** Aberdeen, Arbroath, East Fife, Montrose, St Mirren
**09** Ayr United, Dumbarton, Elgin City, Hibernian, Peterhead, Stranraer
**10** Kilmarnock, Livingston, Motherwell, Queen's Park, Ross County
**11** Brechin City, Cowdenbeath, Raith Rovers, St Johnstone
**12** Albion Rovers, Dundee United
**13** Airdrie United, Alloa Athletic, Stenhousemuir
**14** Berwick Rangers, Forfar Athletic, Greenock Morton, Partick Thistle, Stirling Albion
**15** Queen of the South
**17** East Stirlingshire, Heart of Midlothian
**18** Hamilton Academical
**19** Dunfermline Athletic
**26** Inverness Caledonian Thistle

*European football teams include:*

**04** Ajax
**05** Lazio, Malmö, Parma, Porto
**06** Alaves, AS Roma, Bastia, Monaco, Napoli, Torino
**07** AC Milan, Antwerp, Benfica, Cologne, Español, FC Porto, Hamburg, Schalke
**08** Bordeaux, Juventus, Mallorca, Mechelen, Salzburg, Valencia
**09** Barcelona, Feyenoord, FK Austria, Marseille, Sampdoria, St Etienne, Stuttgart, SV Hamburg, TSV Munich
**10** Anderlecht, Club Bruges, Club Brugge, Dynamo Kiev, Fiorentina, Inter Milan, Real Madrid
**11** FC Magdeburg, Ferencvaros, Galatasaray, MTK Budapest, Rapid Vienna, Ujpest Dozsa
**12** Bayern Munich, Dinamo Zagreb, Gornik Zabrze, Moscow Dynamo, PSV Eindhoven, Real Zaragoza, Stade de Reims, Werder Bremen
**13** Carl Zeiss Jena, Dynamo Tbilisi, IFK Gothenburg, Panathinaikos, Standard Liège
**14** Athletic Bilbao, Atletico Madrid, Paris St Germain, Sporting Lisbon, Twente Enschede

**15** Bayer Leverkusen, Red Star Belgrade, Steaua Bucharest

*Football club nicknames include:*

**02** O's, R's, U's
**03** Ton
**04** Bees, Boro, City, Dale, Dons, Gers, Jags, Owls, Pars, Pool, Posh, Rams, Reds, Sons, Well
**05** Arabs, Bhoys, Binos, Blues, Foxes, Gills, Gulls, Hoops, Irons, Lions, Loons, Shire, Spurs, Stags, Swans, Villa, Wasps
**06** Accies, Albion, Bairns, Blades, County, Eagles, Fifers, Hibees, Jambos, Killie, Latics, Pompey, Robins, Rovers, Royals, Saints, Tigers, United, Whites, Wolves
**07** Addicks, Baggies, Bantams, Buddies, Clarets, Glovers, Gunners, Hammers, Hatters, Hornets, Magpies, Pirates, Potters, Quakers, Red Imps, Shakers, Silkmen, Spiders, Terrors, Toffees, Villans
**08** Blue Toon, Bully Wee, Canaries, Cherries, Citizens, Cobblers, Diamonds, Filberts, Harriers, Jam Tarts, Mariners, Pilgrims, Saddlers, Seagulls, Sky Blues, Terriers, Trotters, Valiants, Villains, Warriors
**09** Black Cats, Bluebirds, Borderers, Chairboys, Cottagers, Cumbrians, Dark Blues, Honest Men, Red Devils, Seasiders, Shrimpers, Spireites, Throstles, Toffeemen, Wee Rovers
**10** Blue Brazil, Doonhamers, Light Blues, Lilywhites, Livvy Lions, Minstermen, Railwaymen, Tangerines, Teddy Bears
**11** Gable Endies, Red Lichties, Tractor Boys
**12** Caley Thistle, Merry Millers
**13** Blue and Whites
**14** Black and Whites

*Football-related terms include:*

**03** box, cap, lob, net
**04** back, dive, foul, goal, half, head, hole, loan, mark, pass, post, save, shot, trap, wall, wing
**05** bench, chest, pitch
**06** assist, corner, double, futsal, goalie, handle, header, keeper, libero, nutmeg, one-two, soccer, tackle, treble, volley, winger
**07** booking, caution, dribble, far post, forward, kick-off, offside, own goal, penalty, red card, referee, stopper, sweeper, throw-in, whistle
**08** back heel, crossbar, dead ball, defender, free kick, friendly, full back, goal kick, goal line, half time, hand ball, hat-trick, left back, linesman, midfield, near post, outfield, play-offs, set piece, transfer, wall pass, wingback
**09** extra time, five-a-side, formation, give-and-go, goalmouth, promotion, right back, touchline
**10** centre back, centre half, centre spot, corner flag, corner kick, goalkeeper, golden goal, half volley, injury time, man marking, midfielder, off-the-ball, penalty box, possession, relegation, sending off, silver goal, substitute, suspension
**11** bicycle kick, half-way line, keepie-uppie, obstruction, offside trap, penalty area, penalty kick, penalty spot, six-yard area, straight red, time wasting
**12** back-pass rule, Bosman ruling, centre circle, overhead kick, stoppage time
**13** centre forward, dangerous play, technical area
**14** fourth official, goal difference, relegation zone
**15** eighteen-yard box

## footballer

*Footballers and associated figures include:*

**03** **Fry** (Charles Burgess), **Law** (Denis)
**04** **Best** (George), **Dean** (Dixie), **Didi**, **Figo** (Luis), **Hall** (Sir John), **Owen** (Michael), **Pelé**, **Rush** (Ian), **Zico**, **Zoff** (Dino)
**05** **Adams** (Tony), **Banks** (Gordon), **Busby** (Sir Matt), **Carey** (Johnny), **Giggs** (Ryan), **Greig** (John), **Henry** (Thierry), **Hurst** (Sir Geoff), **James** (Alex), **Moore** (Bobby), **Revie** (Don), **Rimet** (Jules), **Rossi** (Paolo), **Stein** (Jock), **Young** (George)
**06** **Baggio** (Roberto), **Baresi** (Franco), **Barnes** (John), **Baxter** (Jim), **Bosman** (Jean-Marc), **Clough** (Brian), **Cruyff** (Johann), **Finney** (Sir Tom), **Ginola** (David), **Graham** (George), **Gullit** (Ruud), **Haynes** (Johnny), **Hoddle** (Glenn), **Keegan** (Kevin), **Lawton** (Tommy), **McColl** (Robert Smyth), **McStay** (Paul), **Mercer** (Joe), **Morton** (Alan Lauder), **Müller** (Gerd), **Puskas** (Ferenc), **Ramsey** (Sir Alf), **Robson** (Sir Bobby), **Robson** (Bryan), **Rooney** (Wayne), **Seaman** (David), **Stiles** (Nobby), **St John** (Ian), **Walker** (Tommy), **Wenger** (Arsene), **Wright** (Billy), **Wright** (Ian), **Yashin** (Lev), **Zidane** (Zinedine)
**07** **Ardiles** (Osvaldo), **Beckham** (David), **Bremner** (Billy), **Butcher** (Terry), **Cantona** (Eric), **Charles** (John), **DiCanio** (Paolo), **Eastham** (George), **Edwards** (Duncan), **Eusebio** (Silva), **Greaves** (Jimmy), **Lineker** (Gary), **Macleod** (Ally), **Mannion** (Wilfred), **McCoist** (Ally), **McNeill** (Billy), **Paisley** (Bob), **Platini** (Michel), **Rivaldo**, **Ronaldo**, **Shankly** (Bill), **Shearer** (Alan), **Shilton** (Peter), **Souness** (Graeme), **Toshack** (John), **Waddell** (Willie)
**08** **Bergkamp** (Dennis), **Charlton** (Sir Bobby), **Charlton** (Jack), **Dalglish** (Kenny), **Docherty** (Tommy), **Ferguson** (Sir Alex), **Fontaine** (Just), **Harkness** (Jack), **Jennings** (Pat), **Johnston** (Maurice), **Maradona** (Diego), **Matthaus** (Lothar), **Matthews** (Sir Stanley), **Mourinho** (José), **Nicholls** (Sir Douglas Ralph), **Rivelino** (Roberto)
**09** **Batistuta** (Gabriel), **Collymore** (Stan), **DiStefano** (Alfredo), **Garrincha**, **Gascoigne** (Paul 'Gazza'), **Greenwood** (Ron), **Johnstone** (Jimmy), **Klinsmann** (Jurgen), **Lofthouse** (Nat), **Van Basten** (Marco)
**10** **Schmeichel** (Peter)
**11** **Beckenbauer** (Franz)
**12** **Blanchflower** (Danny)

**• footballers**
**02** FA **03** SFA

## footing
**04** base, cost, grip, rank, trod **05** basis, coast, coste, dance, grade, state, terms, track, tread, troad, trode **06** ground, status, troade **07** balance, support, surface **08** foothold, position, roothold, standing **09** relations **10** conditions, foundation **12** relationship

## footling
**05** minor, petty **06** paltry **07** trivial **08** piffling, trifling **10** irrelevant **13** insignificant

## footloose
**04** free **09** available, fancy-free **10** unattached, uninvolved **11** uncommitted

## footnote
**04** note **05** gloss **07** comment, subtext **08** scholium **10** annotation, commentary, marginalia **12** marginal note

## footnotes
**04** note **05** gloss **07** scholia **10** annotation, commentary, marginalia **12** marginal note

## footprint
**03** pad, pug **04** mark, seal, step **05** prick, spoor, trace, track, trail, tread **07** ichnite, vestige **08** footmark, footstep **09** ichnolite **13** ornithichnite

## footprints
**04** slot

## footstep
**04** plod, step **05** track, tramp, tread **06** trudge **08** footfall, footmark

## footwear

*Footwear includes:*

**03** dap, tie
**04** boot, clog, geta, mule, pump, shoe, vibs
**05** jelly, sabot, tacky, thong, wader, welly
**06** bootee, brogue, casual, galosh, lace-up, loafer, Oxford, patten, sandal, slip-on
**07** gumboot, slipper, sneaker, tap shoe, trainer
**08** boat shoe, deck shoe, flip-flop, jazz shoe, Mary Jane, moccasin,

overshoe, pantofle, plimsoll, snow-shoe
**09** court shoe, Derry boot, rugby boot, slingback, wedge heel
**10** ballet shoe, combat boot, Doc Martens®, espadrille, hiking-boot, kitten-heel, riding boot, tennis shoe
**11** bowling shoe, Chelsea boot, Hush Puppies®, walking boot
**12** climbing boot, football boot, platform heel, stiletto heel
**13** beetle-crusher
**14** beetle-crushers, brothel creeper, wellington boot
**15** brothel-creepers

*See also* **boot**; **clothes, clothing**

**fop**
**04** beau, dude, toff **05** dandy, swell **07** coxcomb, peacock **08** muscadin, popinjay, skipjack **09** exquisite, fantastic **10** Jack-a-dandy **11** petit maître **12** barber-monger

**foppish**
**04** vain **05** apish, natty **06** dainty, dapper, dressy, fallal, la-di-da, spruce **07** fangled, finical **08** affected, dandyish, preening, swellish **09** coxcombic, dandified, fantastic **10** coxcomical **11** coxcombical, fantastical, overdressed

**for**
**03** pro

**forage**
**04** feed, food, guar, hunt, loot, prog, raid, seek **05** étape, foray, scour **06** fodder, invade, ladino, ravage, search **07** assault, pickeer, plunder, ransack, rummage, scratch **08** mung bean, scavenge **09** cast about, gama grass, pasturage, provender **10** foodstuffs, provisions

**foray**
**04** raid **05** sally, swoop **06** attack, creach, creagh, forray, inroad, ravage, sortie **07** assault, attempt, journey, spreagh, venture **08** invasion **09** incursion, offensive **14** reconnaissance

**forbear**
**04** hold, omit, stay, stop **05** avoid, cease, pause **06** desist, eschew **07** abstain, decline, refrain **08** ancestor, hesitate, hold back, keep from, withhold

**forbearance**
**05** mercy **06** pardon **08** clemency, leniency, mildness, patience **09** avoidance, endurance, restraint, tolerance **10** abstinence, indulgence, indulgency, moderation, refraining, self-denial, sufferance, temperance, toleration **11** longanimity, resignation, self-control **13** long-suffering

**forbearing**
**04** easy, mild **07** clement, lenient, patient **08** merciful, moderate, tolerant **09** forgiving, indulgent **10** restrained **13** long-suffering **14** self-controlled

**forbid**
**03** ban, bar **04** deny, tabu, veto, warn **05** block, debar, taboo **06** defend, enjoin, forsay, hinder, not let, outlaw, refuse **07** exclude, foresay, forwarn, inhibit, prevent, rule out **08** disallow, forewarn, forspeak, not allow, preclude, prohibit, restrain **09** blacklist, discharge, forespeak, interdict, proscribe **13** excommunicate **14** contraindicate

**forbidden**
**02** nl **04** tabu, tapu, tref **05** not on, taboo, trefa, treif **06** banned, vetoed **07** illicit, profane **08** debarred, defended, excluded, outlawed, unlawful, verboten **10** contraband, prohibited, proscribed, restrained **11** out of bounds

**forbidding**
**04** grim **05** harsh, stern **06** severe **07** awesome, hostile, ominous **08** daunting, menacing, sinister **09** repulsive **10** Acherontic, foreboding, formidable, off-putting, unfriendly, uninviting **11** frightening, hard-grained, prohibitory, threatening **15** unprepossessing

**force**
◇ *anagram indicator*
**01** F **02** od **03** put, vis, zap **04** army, body, care, cops, dint, gist, make, odyl, pull, push, sway, unit, urge **05** blast, bully, corps, crack, drive, exact, group, impel, might, odyle, power, press, prise, sense, squad, stuff, troop, wrest, wring **06** coerce, compel, duress, dynamo, effort, energy, extort, impose, lean on, muscle, oblige, patrol, propel, ravish, stress, strive, thrust, vigour, wrench **07** cogency, essence, extract, impetus, impulse, inflict, meaning, passion, platoon, stamina **08** armament, bulldoze, coercion, division, dynamism, emphasis, exertion, momentum, pressure, railroad, regiment, squadron, strength, validity, vehement, violence, vitality **09** battalion, break open, constrain, force open, influence, intensity, necessity, pressgang, substance, the screws, vehemence, waterfall **10** aggression, compulsion, constraint, detachment, pressurize **11** arm-twisting, enforcement **12** significance **13** determination, effectiveness, put pressure on **14** persuasiveness, put the screws on, the third degree

*See also* **army**; **police**

**• in force**
**05** valid **07** binding, current, working **08** in crowds, in droves, in flocks **09** effective, operative **10** in strength **11** functioning, in operation **14** in great numbers, in large numbers

**forced**
◇ *anagram indicator*
**02** sf **03** sfz **05** false, stiff **06** wooden **07** binding, feigned, stilted **08** affected, enforced, laboured, overdone, sforzato, strained **09** compelled, contrived, excessive, insincere, mandatory, sforzando, unnatural **10** artificial, compulsory, far-fetched, non-natural, obligatory **11** constrained, involuntary

**forceful**
**05** gutty, valid **06** cogent, mighty, potent, strong, urgent **07** dynamic, telling, weighty **08** emphatic, forcible, powerful, vehement, vigorous **09** assertive, effective, energetic **10** compelling, convincing, impressive, persuasive **11** high-powered **12** high-pressure

**forcefully**
**07** con brio **08** strongly **10** powerfully, vehemently, vigorously **11** assertively, effectively **12** convincingly, emphatically, persuasively **13** energetically

**forcible**
**04** vive **05** pithy **06** cogent, forced, mighty, potent, strong **07** by force, drastic, marrowy, telling, violent, weighty **08** coercive, forceful, powerful, vehement **09** effective, energetic **10** aggressive, compelling, compulsory, impressive, using force **11** energetical

**forcibly**
**03** out **04** hard **07** by force **09** vi et armis, violently **10** using force, vehemently, vigorously, willy-nilly **11** under duress **12** compulsorily, emphatically, obligatorily **15** against your will, under compulsion

**ford**
**04** rack, wade **05** drift **06** Model T **08** causeway, crossing **09** tin lizzie **11** Irish bridge **13** crossing place

**forebear**
**06** father, tupuna **08** ancestor **10** antecedent, forefather, forerunner, progenitor **11** predecessor **12** primogenitor

**foreboding**
**04** fear, omen, sign **05** dread, token, worry **06** hoodoo **07** anxiety, feeling, presage, warning **09** abodement, intuition, misgiving, suspicion **10** prediction, sixth sense **11** premonition **12** apprehension, presentiment **15** prognostication

**forecast**
**03** tip **04** omen, perm **05** augur, guess **06** augury, divine, expect, tip off **07** foresee, metcast, outlook, portend, predict, presage, project **08** estimate, foretell, forewarn, prophecy, prophesy **09** calculate, prognosis **10** anticipate, conjecture, prediction, projection **11** calculation, expectation, extrapolate, forewarning, guesstimate, permutation, second-guess, speculation **13** extrapolation, prognosticate, weather report **15** prognostication

*See also* **shipping**

**forefather**
**06** father **08** ancestor, forebear
**10** ancestress, antecedent, forerunner, progenitor **11** predecessor
**12** primogenitor

**forefront**
**03** van **04** fore, head, lead **05** front
**06** vaward **08** vanguard **09** front line, spearhead **10** avant-garde, firing line
**11** leading edge **15** leading position

**forego, forgo**
**05** leave, waive, yield **06** abjure, eschew, give up, pass up, resign
**07** abandon, forfeit, precede
**08** renounce **09** do without, go without, sacrifice, surrender
**10** relinquish **11** abstain from, refrain from

**foregoing**
**05** above, prior **06** former **07** earlier
**08** previous **09** aforesaid, precedent, preceding **10** antecedent
**14** aforementioned

**foregone**
**• foregone conclusion**
**04** fact **09** certainty, sure thing
**10** inevitable **13** inevitability

**foreground**
**04** fore **05** front **06** centre
**09** forefront, limelight **10** prominence
**15** leading position

**forehead**
**04** brow **05** front **06** metope, temple
**07** temples **08** audacity
**10** confidence

**foreign**
◇ *anagram indicator*
◇ *foreign word indicator*
**03** odd **05** alien, fraim, fremd
**06** ethnic, exotic, forane, forren, fremit
**07** distant, faraway, migrant, outside, strange, unknown **08** borrowed, étranger, exterior, external, imported, overseas, peculiar **09** barbarian, étrangère, extrinsic, immigrant
**10** extraneous, forinsecal, outlandish, tramontane, unfamiliar
**11** unconnected **12** adventitious
**13** international
*See also* **nationality**

**foreigner**
**05** alien **06** gaijin, taipan **07** incomer, visitor **08** étranger, newcomer, outsider, stranger **09** Ausländer, barbarian, étrangère, immigrant, outlander, uitlander **10** tramontane

**foreknowledge**
**09** foresight, prevision **10** prescience
**11** forewarning, premonition, second sight **12** clairvoyance, precognition
**15** prognostication

**foreleg**
**04** gamb

**foreman**
**04** bo's'n, boss **05** bosun **06** gaffer, ganger, honcho, induna, leader
**07** manager, overman, steward, topsman **08** gangsman, overseer
**09** boatswain, straw boss
**10** chancellor, charge hand, supervisor
**14** superintendent

**foremost**
◇ *head selection indicator*
**03** top, van **04** main **05** chief, first, front, prime **07** central, highest, leading, premier, primary, supreme, up front **08** advanced, cardinal, vanguard **09** paramount, principal, uppermost **10** pre-eminent **13** most important

**foreordained**
**05** fated **08** destined **09** appointed, predevote **10** foredoomed
**11** prearranged, predestined, preordained **12** predestinate
**13** predetermined

**forerunner**
**04** omen, sign **05** envoy, token
**06** herald **08** ancestor **09** harbinger, messenger, precurrer, precursor
**10** antecedent, forefather
**11** forewarning, predecessor **12** vaunt-courier
**• be a forerunner**
**04** lead, pace

**foresee**
**06** divine, expect, prevue **07** predict, preview, previse **08** envisage, forebode, forecast, foreknow, foretell, prophesy **10** anticipate
**13** prognosticate

**foreshadow**
**04** bode, mean, type **05** augur
**06** signal **07** portend, predict, presage, promise, signify, suggest **08** indicate, prophesy **09** adumbrate, forepoint, prefigure **13** prognosticate

**foreshore**
**04** hard

**foresight**
**04** care **06** vision **07** caution
**08** forecast, planning, prudence
**09** prevision, provision, readiness
**10** precaution, prescience, providence
**11** discernment, forethought, prospection **12** anticipation, perspicacity, preparedness
**13** judiciousness **14** circumspection, discrimination, far-sightedness
**15** forward planning

**forest**
**04** bosk, wood **05** Arden, trees, woods **06** rustic, sylvan, timber
**07** boscage **08** Sherwood, tree farm, woodland **09** backwoods

*Forests and woods include:*

**04** bush, gapó
**05** brush, igapò, monte, selva, taiga, urman
**06** boreal, jungle, mallee, maquis, pinery
**07** coastal, garigue, lowland, macchie, wetland
**08** caatinga, garrigue, littoral, mangrove
**09** broadleaf, chaparral, deciduous, evergreen, greenwood, temperate
**10** coniferous, equatorial, peat forest, plantation, rainforest
**11** cloud forest, heath forest, lignum-scrub, lignum-swamp, mallee scrub, moist forest
**12** vàrzea forest
**13** ancient forest, gallery forest, mangrove swamp, savanna forest
**14** moist evergreen

**forestall**
**03** bar **04** balk, beat, stop **05** avert, lurch, parry **06** hinder, impede, thwart
**07** head off, obviate, pre-empt, prevent, ward off **08** obstruct, preclude, stave off **09** frustrate, intercept **10** anticipate, get ahead of
**11** second-guess

**forested**
**05** bosky **06** wooded **12** reafforested

**forester**
**06** foster, walker **08** woodsman

**forestry**
**09** woodcraft **10** dendrology
**11** forestation, woodmanship
**12** silviculture, sylviculture
**13** afforestation, arboriculture

**foretaste**
**05** whiff **06** prevue, sample, taster
**07** earnest, example, pre-echo, preview, trailer, warning **08** antepast, specimen **09** appetizer, avant-goût, foretoken **10** anticipate, indication
**11** forewarning, prelibation, premonition **12** anticipation, pregustation

**foretell**
**04** bode, spae **05** augur, write
**06** divine **07** bespeak, foresay, foresee, predict, presage, signify
**08** forebode, forecast, foreread, forewarn, indicate, prophesy, soothsay
**10** foreshadow **13** prognosticate

**forethought**
**07** caution **08** planning, prudence
**09** foresight, provision **10** precaution
**11** discernment, preparation
**12** anticipation, perspicacity
**13** judiciousness **14** circumspection, far-sightedness **15** forward planning

**forever**
**02** ay **03** aye **04** ever **06** always **07** à jamais, for good **08** evermore
**09** endlessly, eternally **10** all the time, constantly, for all time **11** continually, incessantly, permanently, perpetually
**12** interminably, persistently, till doomsday **13** everlastingly **15** till kingdom come

**forewarn**
**04** warn **05** alert, weird **06** advise, forbid, tip off **07** apprise, caution, previse **08** admonish, dissuade **10** give notice, precaution **11** preadmonish

**forewarning**
**06** tip-off **10** forerunner
**11** premonition **12** early warning

**13** advance notice **14** advance warning

**foreword**
**07** preface, prelims **08** prologue **11** frontmatter **12** introduction, prolegomenon

**forfeit**
**04** fine, lose, loss **05** cheat, forgo **06** forego, give up, pass up, sconce **07** abandon, damages, penalty **08** hand over, renounce **09** sacrifice, surrender **10** amercement, confiscate, relinquish, rue-bargain **12** confiscation **13** sequestration **14** relinquishment

**forfeiture**
**04** loss **07** escheat **08** forgoing, giving up **09** attainder, déchéance, foregoing, sacrifice, surrender **12** confiscation **13** sequestration **14** relinquishment

**forge**
◇ *anagram indicator*
**04** cast, copy, fake, form, make, tilt, work **05** build, feign, found, frame, mould, shape, smith **06** create, devise, invent, smithy, stithy **07** beat out, falsify, fashion, imitate, stiddie **08** simulate **09** construct, hammer out **11** counterfeit, put together, rivet hearth **13** beat into shape

**• forge ahead**
**07** advance **08** progress **09** go forward **11** make headway, move forward, push forward **12** make progress, move steadily

**forged**
◇ *anagram indicator*
**04** fake, sham **05** bogus, faked, false, pseud, snide **06** copied, phoney, pirate, pseudo **07** feigned, simular **08** borrowed, spurious **09** imitation, pretended, simulated **10** artificial, fraudulent **11** counterfect, counterfeit

**forger**
**05** faker **06** coiner, framer **09** contriver, falsifier **10** fabricator **13** counterfeiter

**forgery**
**03** dud **04** copy, fake, sham **05** fraud **06** deceit, faking, phoney **07** replica **09** imitation **11** counterfeit, falsi crimen **12** reproduction **13** falsification **14** counterfeiting **15** counterfeisance, counterfesaunce

**forget**
**04** fail, omit, wipe **05** dry up **06** corpse, ignore **07** dismiss, let slip, neglect, unlearn **08** not place, overlook, put aside **09** disregard **11** disremember, leave behind, lose sight of, misremember **12** put behind you, slip your mind **13** think no more of **14** fail to remember

**• forget yourself**
**09** be naughty, misbehave **11** behave badly

**forgetful**
**03** lax **06** dreamy, remiss **08** careless, heedless **09** negligent, oblivious, unheeding **10** abstracted, distracted, neglectful **11** inattentive, not all there, preoccupied **12** absent-minded **14** scatterbrained

**forgetfulness**
**05** lapse **07** amnesia, laxness, neglect **08** oblivion **10** dreaminess **11** abstraction, inattention **12** carelessness, heedlessness, obliviscence **13** obliviousness, wool-gathering

**forgivable**
**05** minor, petty **06** slight, venial **08** innocent, trifling **09** excusable **10** condonable, pardonable

**forgive**
**05** clear, remit, spare **06** acquit, excuse, let off, pardon **07** absolve, condone, let it go **08** overlook **09** exculpate, exonerate, shake on it **10** shake hands **13** think no more of **14** bury the hatchet

**forgiveness**
**05** mercy **06** excuse, pardon **07** amnesty **08** clemency, leniency, oblivion **09** acquittal, remission **10** absolution, misericord **11** condonation, exoneration, misericorde

**forgiving**
**04** kind, mild **06** humane **07** clement, lenient, pitying **08** merciful, placable, tolerant **09** indulgent, remissive **10** forbearing **11** magnanimous, soft-hearted **13** compassionate

**forgo** *see* **forego, forgo**

**forgotten**
**04** gone, lost, past **06** buried, bygone **07** ignored, omitted **09** neglected, oblivious, out of mind **10** blotted out, in the shade, left behind, overlooked, past recall, unrecalled **11** disregarded, obliterated, unretrieved **12** unremembered **13** irrecoverable, irretrievable **15** in the wilderness

**fork**
**01** Y **04** part **05** grain, graip, prong, spear, split, twist **06** branch, crotch, divide **07** diverge, furcate, toaster **08** division, junction, separate **09** bifurcate, branching, branch off, furcation, tormenter, tormentor **10** divaricate, divergence, separation **11** bifurcation **12** divarication, intersection, toasting iron **14** go separate ways

**• fork out**
**03** pay **04** give **05** pay up **06** pony up **07** cough up, stump up **08** shell out

**forked**
**05** split, tined **06** furcal **07** divided, furcate, pronged, Y-shaped **08** biramous, branched, furcated, furcular **09** bifurcate, branching, deceitful, forficate, insincere, separated **10** trifurcate **11** divaricated

**forlorn**
◇ *anagram indicator*
**03** sad **04** lost **06** bereft, lonely **07** unhappy **08** deserted, desolate, forsaken, helpless, homeless, hopeless, pathetic, pitiable, wretched **09** abandoned, cheerless, desperate, destitute, forgotten, miserable, neglected **10** despairing, drearisome, friendless, uncared-for **12** disconsolate

**forlornly**
**05** sadly **06** in vain **09** miserably, to no avail, unhappily **10** hopelessly **11** desperately, pointlessly **12** despondently **14** unsuccessfully

**form**
◇ *anagram indicator*
**03** cut, set **04** cast, face, grow, kind, make, mode, rite, sort, trim, turn, type, year **05** bench, build, class, forge, found, frame, genre, genus, grade, guise, model, mould, order, paper, set up, shape, sheet, style, usage **06** appear, beauty, create, custom, design, devise, draw up, fettle, figure, format, health, line up, make up, manner, nature, ritual, show up, stream, system **07** acquire, arrange, compose, develop, fashion, fitness, manners, outline, pattern, produce, serve as, species, spirits, variety **08** assemble, ceremony, comprise, conceive, contrive, document, organize, planning, protocol **09** be a part of, behaviour, character, condition, construct, establish, etiquette, formation, formulate, framework, structure, take shape **10** appearance, constitute, convention, regularity, silhouette **11** application, arrangement, crystallize, description, disposition, manufacture, materialize, put together **12** construction, organization, the done thing **13** become visible, configuration, manifestation, questionnaire **15** application form, correct practice, polite behaviour

**formal**
**03** dry, set **04** prim, sane **05** aloof, exact, fixed, rigid, stiff **06** proper, pusser, remote, ritual, solemn, starch, strict **07** correct, ordered, orderly, outward, precise, regular, starchy, stately, stilted **08** academic, approved, arranged, black tie, literary, methodic, official, orthodox, reserved, standard **09** customary, essential, organized, unbending **10** ceremonial, controlled, inflexible, methodical, prescribed **11** ceremonious, established, perfunctory, punctilious, ritualistic, strait-laced, symmetrical, traditional **12** conventional

**formality**
**03** ice **04** form, rite, rule **06** custom, ritual, starch **07** decorum, red tape, wiggery **08** ceremony, pedantry, protocol **09** etiquette, procedure, propriety, punctilio, sociality, stiffness

**10** convention, politeness
**11** bureaucracy, correctness **12** matter of form **13** spit and polish
**15** ceremoniousness, conventionality

**formalization**
**08** ordering **09** arranging
**11** arrangement, structuring
**12** arrangements, confirmation, organization **15** standardization, systematization

**formalize**
**03** fix, set **05** order **06** affirm, ordain, ratify **07** arrange, confirm, stylize
**08** organize **09** ritualize, structure
**10** make formal, regularize
**11** standardize, systematize **12** make official

**formally**
**06** primly **07** exactly, rigidly
**08** properly, ritually, solemnly
**09** correctly, precisely **10** formaliter, inflexibly, officially **12** ceremonially, methodically **13** punctiliously
**14** conventionally

**format**
**03** GIF, PDF, PNG, RTF, ZIP **04** form, JPEG, look, plan, TIFF, type **05** order, shape, style **06** design, layout, make-up **07** pattern, tabloid **08** portrait
**09** landscape, letterbox, structure
**10** appearance, dimensions, widescreen **11** arrangement
**12** construction, presentation
**13** configuration

**formation**
**04** make **05** order **06** design, figure, format, layout, make-up, making, series **07** pattern, phalanx, shaping
**08** building, creation, founding, grouping, starting **09** emergence, structure **10** appearance, generation, production **11** arrangement, composition, development, disposition, institution, manufacture
**12** constitution, construction, inauguration, organization
**13** configuration, establishment

**formative**
**06** creant, pliant **07** growing, guiding, plastic, shaping **08** dominant, moulding **09** malleable, mouldable, sensitive, teachable **11** controlling, determining, influential, susceptible
**13** determinative, developmental
**14** impressionable

**former**
**02** ex- **03** old **04** auld, fore, late, once, onst, past **05** above, first, olden, prior
**06** bygone, of yore, whilom
**07** ancient, earlier, long ago, old-time, one-time, quondam **08** ci-devant, departed, long-gone, previous, pristine, sometime **09** erstwhile, foregoing, preceding **10** antecedent, historical **14** first-mentioned

**formerly**
**04** erst, once, onst **05** as was, earst, of old **06** before **07** earlier, whilere
**08** ci-devant, erewhile, hitherto, sometime, while-ere **09** at one time, erstwhile, in the past, yesterday
**10** heretofore, previously
**12** historically **15** at an earlier time

**formidable**
**04** huge **05** great, scary, stiff, stoor, stour, sture **06** gorgon, no mean, shrewd, spooky, stowre **07** awesome, fearful, mammoth, onerous
**08** alarming, colossal, daunting, dreadful, horrific, menacing, powerful, terrific **09** frightful, leviathan
**10** horrifying, impressive, prodigious, staggering, terrifying, tremendous
**11** challenging, frightening, mind-blowing, redoubtable, threatening
**12** intimidating, overwhelming

**formidably**
**07** awfully **09** fearfully **10** dreadfully, menacingly, shockingly **11** frightfully
**12** horrifically, tremendously
**14** overwhelmingly

**formless**
**05** vague **06** inform **07** chaotic
**08** confused, inchoate, indigest, nebulous, unformed, unshaped
**09** amorphous, shapeless
**10** incoherent, indefinite
**12** disorganized, invertebrate
**13** indeterminate

**formula**
**03** mix, way **04** code, form, rule
**05** spell **06** method, recipe, rubric
**07** precept, wording **08** equation, exorcism, fog index, proposal, protocol **09** blueprint, principle, procedure, technique **10** convention
**12** prescription **13** set expression
**15** fixed expression
- **Formula One** *see* **racing**

**formulate**
**04** cast, form, plan **05** found, frame, state **06** create, define, design, detail, devise, draw up, evolve, invent, map out **07** compose, develop, express, formate, itemize, lay down, prepare, propose, put down, set down, specify, think up, work out **08** conceive
**09** originate, symbolize **10** articulate

**formulation**
**07** formula, framing, product
**08** creating, devising **10** conception, definition, expression, production
**11** composition, development, preparation **13** specification

**fornication**
**06** affair **07** avoutry, liaison
**08** adultery, cheating, idolatry **09** two-timing **10** flirtation, infidelity, unchastity **12** entanglement **13** a bit on the side, playing around
**14** unfaithfulness **15** extramarital sex, playing the field

**forsake**
**04** jilt, quit **05** chuck, ditch, forgo, leave, waive **06** desert, disown, forego, give up, reject **07** abandon, cast off, discard, forlese **08** jettison, renounce, set aside **09** destitute, repudiate, surrender, throw over **10** relinquish
**12** have done with **14** turn your back on **15** leave in the lurch

**forsaken**
**04** lorn **06** dreary, jilted, lonely, remote
**07** cast off, forlorn, ignored, outcast, shunned **08** derelict, deserted, desolate, disowned, isolated, lasslorn, lovelorn, marooned, rejected, solitary
**09** abandoned, destitute, discarded, neglected **10** friendless
**11** godforsaken **14** left in the lurch

**forswear**
**03** lie **04** deny, drop, reny **05** forgo, renay, reney **06** abjure, cut out, disown, forego, give up, jack in, pack in, recant, reject, renege **07** abandon, disavow, forsake, retract **08** disclaim, renounce **09** do without, repudiate
**15** perjure yourself

**fort**
**02** Ft, pa **03** pah **04** camp, keep, rath
**05** tower **06** castle, donjon, turret
**07** citadel, parapet, redoubt, station
**08** fortress, garrison, martello, pentagon **09** castellum
**10** blockhouse, stronghold, watchtower **11** battlements
**13** fortification, martello tower

**forte**
**01** f **04** bent, gift, loud **05** skill
**06** métier, talent **08** aptitude, strength
**10** speciality **11** strong point

**forth**
**02** on **03** off, out **04** away **05** furth
**06** abroad, onward **07** forward, onwards, outside **08** forwards, into view **13** into existence

**forthcoming**
**04** open **05** frank, on tap, ready
**06** chatty, coming, direct, future
**07** voluble **08** expected, friendly, imminent, sociable, upcoming
**09** available, expansive, impending, projected, talkative **10** accessible, loquacious, obtainable, up for grabs **11** approaching, informative, in the offing, prospective
**13** communicative **14** at your disposal, conversational

**forthright**
**04** bold, open **05** blunt, frank, plain
**06** at once, candid, direct, honest
**07** up-front **09** outspoken, trenchand, trenchant **10** four-square **11** plain-spoken **15** straightforward

**forthwith**
**03** eft **04** asap, away **06** at once, pronto **07** quickly **08** directly, eftsoons **09** instantly, right away
**11** immediately **12** straightaway, there and then, without delay

**fortification**
**08** munition **09** munitions
**10** munifience, protection, stronghold **12** embattlement, entrenchment **13** reinforcement, strengthening

*Fortifications include:*

**02** pa
**03** pah
**04** bawn, fort, gate, keep, laer, moat, wall
**05** ditch, fence, hedge, limes, tower
**06** abatis, castle, glacis, laager, sconce, trench, Vauban
**07** barrier, bastion, bulwark, citadel, defence, flanker, moineau, outwork, parapet, pillbox, rampart, redoubt, sandbag
**08** buttress, cavalier, fortress, outworks, palisade, stockade
**09** barricade, earthwork, fieldwork, fortalice, gabionade, gatehouse, razor wire
**10** barbed wire, bridgehead, fieldworks, trou de loup
**11** battlements, buttressing, crémaillère
**13** cheval-de-frise, Martello tower
**14** motte-and-bailey
**15** circumvallation, contravallation

**fortify**
**04** fort, load, wall **05** boost, brace, cheer, cover, fence, guard, mound **06** buoy up, castle, defend, munify, munite, revive, secure **07** bulwark, hearten, protect, rampart, shore up, support, sustain **08** buttress, embattle, energize, entrench, garrison, intrench, reassure **09** encourage, reinforce **10** invigorate, strengthen

**fortitude**
**04** grit, guts **05** nerve, pluck, spine **06** mettle, valour **07** bravery, courage **08** backbone, firmness, patience, stoicism, strength, tenacity **09** endurance, hardihood, willpower **10** resolution **11** forbearance **12** perseverance **13** determination **14** strength of mind

**fortress**
**04** burg, fort, keep **05** guard, place, tower **06** casbah, castle, kasbah **07** alcázar, citadel, defence **08** bastille, fastness, garrison **09** fortalice **10** stronghold **11** battlements **13** fortification

**fortuitous**
**05** fluky, lucky **06** casual, chance, random **09** arbitrary, fortunate, haphazard, unplanned **10** accidental, incidental, unexpected, unforeseen **12** providential **13** unintentional

**fortuitously**
**07** luckily **08** at random, by chance, casually, randomly **11** arbitrarily, fortunately, haphazardly **12** accidentally, incidentally, unexpectedly **13** inadvertently **15** unintentionally

**Fortuna**
**05** Tyche

**fortunate**
**04** rich, well **05** canny, happy, lucky, seely **06** timely **07** blessed, well-off **08** favoured **09** fairytale, opportune, promising, well-timed **10** auspicious, convenient, favourable, felicitous, fortuitous, profitable, propitious, prosperous, successful **11** encouraging, flourishing **12** advantageous, providential

**fortunately**
**07** happily, luckily **10** thankfully **12** conveniently **13** encouragingly **14** providentially

**fortune**
**03** cup, hap, lot **04** bomb, doom, fall, fate, life, luck, mint, pile, seal, seel, seil, sele **05** means, speed **06** assets, befall, bundle, chance, estate, future, income, packet, riches, wealth **07** destiny, heiress, history, portion, success **08** accident, big bucks, opulence, position, property, treasure **09** affluence, condition, megabucks, situation, substance **10** experience, prosperity, providence **11** coincidence, possessions, serendipity **13** circumstances **14** state of affairs
• **loss of fortune**
**04** ruin **05** decay
• **sudden good fortune**
**08** windfall

**fortune-teller**
**04** seer **05** augur, sibyl **06** oracle **07** diviner, prophet, psychic **08** telepath **09** visionary **10** prophetess, soothsayer **11** clairvoyant

**fortune-telling** *see* **divination**

**forty**
**02** XL
• **forty winks**
**03** nap **04** rest **05** sleep

**forum**
**03** BBS **05** arena, stage **06** debate **07** meeting, rostrum **08** assembly **09** gathering, symposium **10** conference, discussion **12** meeting-place

**forward**
**02** on, to **03** aid, out **04** back, bold, fore, head, help, mail, post, send, ship **05** ahead, brash, cocky, early, first, forth, fresh, front, hurry, pushy, ready, speed **06** assist, avanti, brazen, cheeky, favour, foster, future, hasten, onward, pass on, send on, step up **07** advance, deliver, earnest, frontal, further, go-ahead, leading, onwards, promote, speed up, support **08** advanced, dispatch, expedite, familiar, foremost, forwards, impudent, into view, long-term, redirect **09** advancing, assertive, audacious, barefaced, confident, encourage, long-range, officious, premature, presuming, readdress, thrusting, transport **10** accelerate, aggressive, facilitate, medium-term, precocious **11** impertinent, into the open, medium-range, progressing, progressive, prospective **12** enterprising, overfamiliar, presumptuous, well-advanced **13** over-assertive, over-confident, progressively, well-developed **14** forward-looking

**forward-looking**
**04** goey **06** modern **07** dynamic, go-ahead, liberal **09** go-getting, reforming **10** avant-garde, far-sighted, innovative **11** enlightened, progressive **12** enterprising

**forwardness**
**04** neck **05** cheek **08** audacity, boldness, pertness **09** brashness, brass neck, impudence, pushiness **10** brazenness, cheekiness, confidence **11** presumption **12** forth-putting, impertinence **14** aggressiveness, over-confidence

**forwards**
**02** on **03** out **04** pack **05** ahead, forth **06** onward **07** forward, onwards **13** progressively

**fossil**
**05** relic **07** remains, remnant **09** reliquiae **10** antiquated

*Fossils include:*

**04** bone, cast
**05** amber, shell
**06** burrow
**07** bivalve, crinoid
**08** ammonite, baculite, dinosaur, echinoid, nautilus, skeleton
**09** belemnite, coccolith, coprolite, fish teeth, steinkern, trilobite
**10** cast fossil, gastrolith, graptolite, snakestone
**11** ichnofossil, microfossil, mould fossil, resin fossil, sharks' teeth, trace fossil
**12** Burgess shale, stromatolite

**fossilized**
**04** dead **05** passé, stony **07** archaic, extinct **08** hardened, obsolete, ossified, outmoded **09** out of date, petrified **10** antiquated **11** prehistoric **12** antediluvian, old-fashioned **13** anachronistic

**foster**
**03** aid **04** back, feed, help, hold, rear **05** boost, nurse, raise **06** assist, foment, mother, nousle, nuzzle, uphold **07** advance, bring up, care for, cherish, further, harbour, nourish, noursle, nousell, nurture, promote, support, sustain **08** forester, incubate **09** cultivate, encourage, entertain, look after, stimulate **10** make much of, take care of

**foster-child**
**04** dalt **05** dault

**foul**
◇ *anagram indicator*
**03** bad, jam, low, paw, wet **04** base, blue, clog, edgy, lewd, mean, rank, soil, ugly, vile, wild **05** angry, black, block, catch, choke, cross, dirty, fetid, gross, humpy, mucky, muddy, narky, nasty,

putid, rainy, ratty, reeky, rough, snarl, stain, sully, taint, testy, twist **06** coarse, crabby, defile, dreggy, feisty, filthy, foetid, foul up, grumpy, impure, odious, pawpaw, putrid, reekie, ribald, rotten, shirty, smelly, smutty, snappy, soiled, stingy, stormy, tangle, tetchy, unfair, untidy, virose, vulgar, wicked
**07** abusive, bilious, blacken, collide, crabbed, decayed, defiled, ensnare, gnarled, grouchy, heinous, obscene, peppery, pollute, prickly, profane, rotting, squalid, squally, stroppy, tainted, unclean, vicious **08** blustery, choleric, entangle, feculent, harlotry, horrible, indecent, infected, obstruct, polluted, shameful, stagnant, stinking
**09** abhorrent, crotchety, dyspeptic, entangled, execrable, fractious, impatient, inclement, irritable, loathsome, nefarious, off-colour, offensive, repellent, repulsive, revolting, sickening, splenetic, technical **10** abominable, capernoity, despicable, detestable, disfigured, disgusting, indelicate, iniquitous, nauseating, putrescent, unpleasant
**11** bad-tempered, blasphemous, carnaptious, contaminate, disgraceful
**12** contaminated, contemptible, disagreeable, foul-smelling, putrefactive, unfavourable **13** quick-tempered

**• foul play**
**05** crime **06** murder **08** violence
**09** deception, dirty work **13** double-dealing, funny business, sharp practice
**15** unfair behaviour

**foul-mouthed**
**06** coarse, ribald, ribaud **07** abusive, obscene, profane, rybauld
**09** offensive **10** foul-spoken
**11** blasphemous

**foul-smelling stuff**
**04** hing **10** asafoetida

**found**
**03** fix, met, set **04** base, cast, rest, root
**05** build, endow, erect, merit, plant, raise, set up, start **06** bottom, create, ground, locate, settle **07** develop
**08** initiate, organize, position
**09** construct, establish, institute, originate **10** constitute, inaugurate
**14** bring into being

**• found in**
◇ *anagram indicator*
◇ *containment indicator*
◇ *hidden indicator*

**foundation**
◇ *tail selection indicator*
**03** key **04** base, call, core, crib, fond, foot, fund, rock, root **05** basis, cause, heart, score **06** bottom, excuse, ground, motive, reason, rip-rap, thrust
**07** account, bedrock, charity, essence, footing, grounds, keynote, premise, reasons, roadbed, support
**08** argument, creation, cribwork, founding, grillage, occasion, pitching
**09** endowment, essential, grounding, institute, principle, rationale, setting-up, substance **10** essentials, grass-roots, groundwork, hypostasis, inducement, initiation, stereobate, substratum **11** fundamental, institution, vindication **12** constitution, fundamentals, inauguration, organization, quintessence, substructure, underpinning **13** alpha and omega, establishment, justification, starting-point **14** main ingredient, understructure **15** first principles

**founder**
◇ *anagram indicator*
**04** fail, fall, sink **05** abort, maker
**06** author, father, go down, mother, oecist, oikist **07** builder, capsize, creator, endower, go wrong, misfire, stumble, subside **08** belleter, collapse, designer, inventor, miscarry, submerge
**09** architect, break down, developer, initiator, organizer, patriarch
**10** benefactor, discoverer, institutor, originator, prime mover, progenitor
**11** come to grief, constructor, establisher, fall through **13** come to nothing, go to the bottom **14** be unsuccessful

**foundling**
**04** waif **05** stray **06** orphan, urchin
**07** outcast **12** enfant trouvé
**15** abandoned infant

**fount**
**04** font, rise, well **05** birth, cause
**06** origin, source, spring **08** wellhead
**09** beginning, inception
**10** mainspring **12** commencement, fountainhead

**fountain**
**03** jet **04** fons, font, pant, rise, well
**05** birth, cause, fount, gerbe, laver, spout, spray, spurt **06** origin, source, spring **07** bubbler, conduit, jet d'eau
**08** Aganippe, wellhead **09** beginning, Castalian, inception, reservoir
**10** Hippocrene, mainspring, waterworks, wellspring **11** Aonian fount, scuttlebutt, scuttle cask
**12** commencement, fountainhead

**four**
**02** IV **04** IIII, mess **06** tetrad
**07** quartet **08** quartett **09** quartette
**10** quaternary, quaternion, quaternity

**• one of four**
**04** quad

**four-square**
**05** frank **06** firmly, honest **07** frankly, solidly **08** honestly, squarely
**10** forthright, resolutely

**fourteen**
**03** XIV

**fowl**
**03** hen **04** bird, cock, coot, duck
**05** chook, goose, poult **06** bantam, boiler, Brahma, houdan, rumkin, sultan, turkey **07** chicken, Hamburg, leghorn, pintado, poultry **08** Hamburgh, pheasant, rose comb, wildfowl
**09** wyandotte **10** chittagong, spatchcock **11** brissel-cock **14** Rhode Island red

**fox**
**03** pug, tod **05** cheat, puggy, vixen, zerda, zorro **06** baffle, corsac, fennec, Lowrie **07** Charley, Charlie, deceive, Reynard **09** Lowrie-tod, Tod-lowrie
**10** Basil Brush

**foxglove**
**09** digitalis **13** dead-men's bells
**14** witches' thimble

**foxtrot**
**01** F

**foxy**
**03** fly, sly **04** wily **05** canny, sharp
**06** artful, astute, crafty, shrewd, tricky
**07** cunning, devious, knowing, vulpine
**08** guileful

**foyer**
**04** hall **05** lobby **07** hallway
**08** anteroom **09** reception, vestibule
**11** antechamber **12** entrance hall

**fracas**
**03** row **04** riot, rout, spat **05** aggro, brawl, fight, mêlée, scrap, set-to
**06** affray, barney, bust-up, ruckus, ruffle, rumpus, shindy, uproar
**07** quarrel, ruction, scuffle, trouble
**10** Donnybrook, free-for-all
**11** disturbance

**fraction**
**03** bit **04** half, part **05** ratio, third
**06** amount **07** decimal, ligroin, quarter
**08** repeater, tailings **10** proportion, sexagenary **11** sexagesimal, subdivision

**fractional**
**04** tiny **05** small **06** little, minute, slight, subtle **07** partial **10** negligible
**13** imperceptible, insignificant, insubstantial

**fractious**
**05** cross, testy **06** crabby, grumpy, touchy, unruly **07** awkward, fretful, grouchy, peevish **08** captious, choleric, petulant **09** crotchety, irritable, querulous **10** refractory
**11** bad-tempered, quarrelsome
**12** recalcitrant

**fracture**
◇ *anagram indicator*
**03** gap **04** chip, rent, rift, slit, snap
**05** break, cleft, crack, fault, split
**06** breach, schism **07** fissure, opening, rupture **08** aperture, breakage, breaking, splinter **09** splitting
**10** microcrack

**fragile**
**04** fine, weak **05** frail **06** dainty, feeble, flimsy, infirm, slight, tender
**07** brittle **08** delicate, unstable
**09** breakable, frangible **13** insubstantial

**fragility**
**07** frailty **08** delicacy, weakness
**09** infirmity **10** feebleness
**11** brittleness **12** frangibility
**13** breakableness

**fragment**
◇ *hidden indicator*
**02** fr **03** bit, end, ort **04** blad, chip, flaw, mite, part, rift, snip, spar **05** blaud, break, chink, crumb, frust, patch, piece, scrap, shard, shred, split **06** cinder, divide, morsel, sheave, shiver, sliver, snatch **07** break up, cantlet, crumble, flinder, flitter, fritter, morceau, portion, remains, remnant, shatter, snippet, split up **08** disunite, fraction, particle, potshard, potshare, potsherd, quantity, splinter, xenolith **09** come apart, remainder **10** sequestrum, smithereen **11** smithereens **12** come to pieces, disintegrate **13** smash to pieces

**fragmentary**
**05** bitty **06** broken, snippy, uneven **07** partial, scrappy, sketchy **08** separate, snippety **09** piecemeal, scattered **10** disjointed, incoherent, incomplete **11** fractionary **12** disconnected **13** discontinuous

**fragmentation**
**07** break-up **08** division **09** crumbling, splitting **10** separation, shattering **11** atomization, splitting-up **13** decomposition **14** disintegration

**fragmented**
**06** broken, in bits **07** divided **08** in pieces, separate **09** disunited **10** disjointed, incomplete **13** disintegrated

**fragrance**
**04** balm, otto **05** aroma, attar, odour, scent, smell **07** bouquet, perfume **09** redolence **10** sweet smell

**fragrant**
**04** nosy **05** balmy, nosey, spicy, sweet **07** balsamy, odorous, savoury, scented **08** aromatic, perfumed, redolent **09** ambrosial **10** suaveolent **11** odoriferous **12** sweet-scented **13** sweet-smelling

**frail**
**04** puny, rush, weak **05** shaky **06** feeble, flimsy, infirm, slight, slimsy, unwell **07** brittle, fragile, unsound **08** delicate **09** breakable, frangible **10** vulnerable **11** susceptible **12** easily broken **13** insubstantial

**frailty**
**04** flaw **05** fault **06** defect, foible **07** blemish, failing **08** delicacy, weakness **09** fragility, infirmity, weak point **10** deficiency **11** brittleness, fallibility, shortcoming **12** imperfection **13** vulnerability **14** susceptibility

**frame**
◇ *containment indicator*
◇ *ends selection indicator*
**03** set **04** body, case, draw, edge, form, husk, loom, make, plan, plot, sash, size, tent, trap **05** adapt, box in, build, draft, erect, fit up, forge, model, mould, mount, pin on, plant, set up, shape, shell **06** adjust, border, casing, cook up, create, devise, draw up, encase, fabric, figure, map out, redact, sketch **07** carcase, chassis, compose, concoct, enclose, fashion, monture, pretend, setting, support, taboret **08** assemble, bodywork, conceive, contrive, mounting, physique, skeleton, stitch up, surround, tabouret **09** construct, establish, fabricate, formulate, framework, structure **10** articulate, foundation **11** incriminate, manufacture, put together, scaffolding **12** construction, substructure **13** cook up a charge

**• frame of mind**
**04** mood, tune **05** state **06** humour, spirit, temper **07** outlook **08** attitude **09** condition **11** disposition, state of mind

**frame-up**
**03** fix **04** plot, trap **05** fit-up **08** put-up job **10** conspiracy **11** fabrication **15** trumped-up charge

**framework**
◇ *containment indicator*
**04** grid, plan, rack **05** frame, shell **06** casing, cradle, fabric, scheme **07** lattice, outline, tressel, trestle **08** scaffold, skeleton **09** bare bones, structure **10** foundation, groundwork, parameters **11** constraints, trestlework **12** substructure

**France**
**01** F **02** Fr **03** FRA **04** Gaul
*See also* **department**

**• in France**
◇ *foreign word indicator*

**• South of France**
**04** Midi **07** Riviera **09** Côte d'Azur

**franchise**
**05** right **07** candour, charter, consent, freedom, liberty, licence, warrant **08** immunity, suffrage **09** exemption, frankness, privilege **10** concession, permission **11** prerogative **13** authorization **15** enfranchisement

**francium**
**02** Fr

**frank**
**04** free, mark, open **05** bluff, blunt, plain, stamp **06** cancel, candid, direct, honest, pigsty **07** genuine, liberal, sincere, up-front **08** explicit, postmark, straight, truthful **09** downright, ingenuous, outspoken, Ripuarian **10** forthright, four-square **11** hard-hitting, open-hearted, plain-spoken, transparent, undisguised **12** unrestrained **13** simple-hearted **15** straightforward

**frankincense**
**04** thus **08** olibanum

**frankly**
**06** freely, openly **07** bluntly, in truth, plainly **08** candidly, directly, eye to eye, honestly, straight **09** to be blunt, to be frank **10** explicitly, to be honest, truthfully **11** straight out **14** without reserve

**frankness**
**06** candor **07** candour, freedom, honesty **08** openness **09** bluntness, franchise, sincerity **10** directness **12** truthfulness **13** ingenuousness, outspokenness, plain speaking **14** forthrightness

**frantic**
◇ *anagram indicator*
**03** mad **04** wild **06** hectic, raging, raving **07** berserk, fraught, furious **08** agitated, frenetic, frenzied **09** desperate **10** distracted, distraught, distressed **11** overwrought **12** out of control **13** at your wits' end, panic-stricken **14** beside yourself

**frantically**
◇ *anagram indicator*
**05** madly **06** wildly **09** furiously **11** desperately **12** hysterically, out of control **13** at your wits' end **14** beside yourself

**fraternity**
**03** set **04** clan, club **05** guild, order, union **06** circle, fratry, league **07** company, fratery, kinship, society **08** sodality **10** fellowship **11** association, brotherhood, camaraderie, comradeship **13** companionship

**fraternize**
**03** mix **04** move **05** unite **06** hobnob, mingle **07** consort **08** go around **09** affiliate, associate, forgather, hang about, pal up with, socialize **10** cordialize, foregather, gang up with, sympathize **11** keep company **12** rub shoulders

**fraud**
**03** con, fix **04** fake, hoax, scam, sham, swiz **05** cheat, guile, phony, quack, snare, trick **06** con man, deceit, diddle, hoaxer, humbug, hustle, phoney, racket, riddle, rip-off, take-in **07** bluffer, forgery, roguery, swindle, swizzle **08** cheating, fraus pia, impostor, pia fraus, swindler, trickery **09** charlatan, chicanery, deception, duplicity, embezzler, fraudster, gold brick, imposture, pretender, swindling, trickster **10** mountebank **11** counterfeit, fraudulence, stellionate, supercherie **12** double-dealer, embezzlement **13** double-dealing, sharp practice **15** salami technique

**fraudulent**
**04** sham **05** bogus, cronk, false, quack, shady **06** phoney **07** crooked, knavish **08** cheating, covinous, criminal **09** deceitful, deceptive, dishonest, shameless, swindling **11** counterfeit, duplicitous **12** exploitative, unscrupulous **13** double-dealing, surreptitious

**fraudulently**
**07** falsely **09** corruptly, illegally **11** deceitfully, dishonestly, shamelessly **14** unscrupulously

**fraught**
**04** full, load **05** cargo, laden, tense **06** filled **07** anxious, charged, freight, replete, uptight, worried **08** agitated, attended **09** abounding, bristling, freighted **10** distraught, distressed **11** accompanied, overwrought, stressed out, under stress

**fray**
**03** rag, row, tax, vex **04** riot, wear **05** aggro, brawl, clash, fight, scrap, set-to **06** affray, battle, bovver, combat, dust-up, fridge, rumpus, scrape, strain, stress **07** bashing, frazzle, overtax, pasting, punch-up, quarrel, scuffle, unravel, wear out **08** conflict, frighten, irritate, wear thin **09** challenge, make tense, put on edge **10** excitement, free-for-all, push too far **11** disturbance, make nervous **12** become ragged **14** wigs on the green

**frayed**
**04** thin, worn **06** ragged **08** tattered, worn thin **10** threadbare, unravelled

**freak**
◇ *anagram indicator*
**03** fan, nut, odd **04** buff, geek, turn, whim **05** fiend, fluky, queer, quirk, twist **06** addict, chance, mutant, oddity, vagary, weirdo **07** anomaly, bizarre, caprice, devotee, erratic, fanatic, monster, oddball, unusual **08** aberrant, abnormal, atypical, mutation, surprise **09** curiosity, deformity, eccentric **10** aberration, aficionado, capricious, enthusiast, fortuitous, unexpected **11** abnormality, exceptional, monstrosity **12** irregularity, lusus naturae, malformation **13** freak of nature, unpredictable

**• freak out**
◇ *anagram indicator*
**06** go wild, wig out **07** explode, go crazy **09** go bananas, go berserk **11** lose control **12** throw a wobbly **15** go off the deep end, go out of your mind

**freakish**
**03** odd **05** weird **06** fitful, freaky **07** erratic, strange, unusual **08** aberrant, abnormal, fanciful, peculiar **09** arbitrary, fantastic, grotesque, malformed, monstrous, whimsical **10** capricious, changeable, outlandish **13** unpredictable **14** unconventional

**freckle**
**04** spot **07** ephelis, lentigo **08** heatspot **09** fernticle **10** ferniticle, ferntickle, fernyticle **11** fairniticle, fairnyticle, fernitickle, fernytickle **12** fairnitickle, fairnytickle

**free**
◇ *anagram indicator*
**03** ope, out, rid **04** bold, easy, idle, open, quit, save **05** broad, clear, empty, fluid, let go, loose, rough, spare, unmew, untie, vague **06** acquit, casual, except, excuse, exempt, freely, giving, gratis, lavish, let out, ransom, redeem, rescue, smooth, solute, svelte, unbind, vacant **07** absolve, acquite, at large, clear of, deliver, for free, for love, general, inexact, lacking, liberal, natural, off duty, relaxed, release, relieve, set free, unbowed, unchain, unleash, untaken, without **08** acquight, at no cost, buckshee, devoid of, generous, immune to, indecent, laid-back, lavishly, liberate, safe from, set loose, unburden **09** at liberty, autarchic, available, copiously, debarrass, disburden, discharge, disengage, easy-going, extricate, imprecise, liberally, liberated, sovereign, turn loose, unblocked, unimpeded, unsecured, voluntary **10** abundantly, autonomous, charitable, democratic, disburthen, emancipate, exempt from, for nothing, generously, hospitable, munificent, on the house, on the loose, open-handed, self-ruling, unattached, unconfined, unemployed, unfastened, unhampered, unoccupied, unstinting **11** Anacreontic, disentangle, emancipated, free as a bird, independent, requiteless, spontaneous, uninhibited **12** free of charge, unaffected by, unobstructed, unrestrained, unrestricted **13** at no extra cost, complimentary, extravagantly, make available, self-governing, without charge **15** with compliments

**• free and easy**
**06** casual **07** relaxed **08** carefree, informal, laid-back, tolerant **09** easy-going **11** spontaneous **12** happy-go-lucky **13** unconstrained

**• free hand**
**05** power, scope **07** freedom, liberty, licence **08** free rein, latitude **09** authority **10** discretion, permission **12** carte blanche

**• setting free**
**03** lib **07** release **09** unbinding **10** liberation

**freebooter**
**07** cateran, pindari **08** pindaree **09** snaphance **10** snaphaunce, snaphaunch

**freedom**
**04** ease, play **05** power, range, right, scope **06** leeway, margin **07** liberty, licence, release **08** autarchy, autonomy, free hand, free rein, home rule, immunity, impunity, latitude **09** democracy, exemption, frankness, privilege **10** separation **11** deliverance, flexibility, open slather, opportunity, prerogative, sovereignty **12** emancipation, independence **13** outspokenness **14** self-government

**free-for-all**
**03** row **04** fray **05** brawl, broil, clash, fight, mêlée, rammy, scrap **06** affray, bust-up, dust-up, fracas, fratch, ruckus, rumpus, stoush **07** bagarre, brabble, brangle, dispute, punch-up, quarrel, scuffle, tuilyie **08** argument, disorder, skirmish, squabble **10** Donnybrook, fisticuffs **11** altercation, open slather

**freely**
◇ *anagram indicator*
**05** ad-lib, amply **06** easily, openly **07** bluntly, frankly, loosely, plainly, readily **08** candidly, lavishly, smoothly **09** liberally, naturally, willingly **10** abundantly, generously **11** voluntarily **12** unreservedly **13** extravagantly, spontaneously **14** frictionlessly, without jerking **15** in all directions

**freeman**
**05** ceorl, thete **07** burgess, burgher, citizen **09** liveryman

**freethinker**
**05** deist **07** doubter, infidel, sceptic **08** agnostic **09** libertine **10** esprit fort, unbeliever **11** independent, rationalist **13** nonconformist

**freethinking**
**07** liberal **08** agnostic **09** sceptical **10** open-minded **11** broad-minded, independent, rationalist **13** nonconformist **14** unconventional

**free will**
**07** autarky, freedom, liberty **08** autonomy, election, volition **11** spontaneity **12** independence **15** self-sufficiency

**• of your own free will**
**06** freely **08** by choice **09** purposely, willingly **11** consciously, voluntarily **12** deliberately **13** intentionally, spontaneously **15** of your own accord

**freeze**
**03** fix, ice, peg, set **04** cool, halt, hold, stay, stop, take **05** chill, frost, ice up **06** fixing, harden, quiver, shiver **07** congeal, embargo, get cold, ice over, stiffen, suspend **08** cold snap, enfreeze, freeze-up, glaciate, preserve, shutdown, solidify, stoppage **09** freeze-dry, stabilize **10** deep-freeze, immobilize, moratorium, stand still, standstill, suspension **11** catch a chill, refrigerate **12** anaesthetize, interruption, postponement **15** become paralysed

**• freeze out**
**03** cut **04** snub **05** eject, evict, expel **06** ice out, ignore, remove **07** boot out, boycott, exclude, kick out, lock out, turf out **08** brush off, throw out **09** ostracize **13** excommunicate **14** send to Coventry

**freezing**
**03** icy, raw **04** cold, numb **05** polar **06** arctic, baltic, biting, bitter, chilly, frosty, wintry **07** cutting, glacial, numbing **08** piercing, Siberian, stinging **09** perishing **10** frigorific **11** penetrating **12** bitterly cold, brass monkeys

**freight**
**04** hire, load **05** cargo, goods **06** lading, let out **07** fraught, haulage,

payload, portage **08** carriage, contents, shipment **10** conveyance, freightage **11** consignment, merchandise **14** transportation

**French**
◇ *foreign word indicator*
**02** Fr
*See also* **day**; **month**; **number**; **shop**
• **Old French**
**02** OF

**French Guiana**
**03** GUF

**Frenchman**
**01** M

*French first names include:*

**03** Luc
**04** Jean, Léon, Rémi, Rémy, René, Yves,
**05** Alain, André, Denis, Émile, Henri, Jules, Louis, Serge
**06** Claude, Didier, Gaston, Gérard, Honoré, Jérôme, Marcel, Michel, Pascal, Pierre, Xavier
**07** Antoine, Édouard, Étienne, Georges, Gustave, Jacques, Laurent, Olivier, Patrice, Thibaut, Thierry, Vincent
**08** Frédéric, Matthieu, Philippe, Stéphane, Thibault
**09** Guillaume

**French Revolutionary Calendar**
*see* **month**

**frenetic**
◇ *anagram indicator*
**03** mad **04** wild **05** manic **06** hectic, insane, madman **07** berserk, excited, frantic **08** demented, frenzied, maniacal **09** delirious, obsessive **10** distracted, distraught, hysterical, unbalanced **11** hyperactive, overwrought

**frenetically**
◇ *anagram indicator*
**05** madly **06** wildly **09** excitedly, intensely, manically **10** hectically **11** frantically **12** hysterically

**frenzied**
**03** mad **04** amok, wild **05** manic **06** crazed, hectic, raving **07** berserk, frantic, furious **08** demented, feverish, frenetic **09** desperate, obsessive, phrenetic, raving mad **10** distracted, distraught, hysterical **11** overwrought **12** out of control, uncontrolled **13** at your wits' end, panic-stricken **14** beside yourself

**frenzy**
◇ *anagram indicator*
**03** fit **04** bout, fury, must, rage **05** burst, fever, mania, musth, spasm **06** lunacy **07** madness, oestrum, oestrus, passion, seizure, turmoil **08** delirium, hysteria, insanity, outburst, paroxysm, tailspin, wildness **09** agitation, phrenesis, transport **10** convulsion **11** derangement, distraction, nympholepsy **13** furor poeticus
• **expression of frenzy**
**04** euoi, evoe **05** evhoe, evohe, yahoo

**frequency**
**01** f **06** resort **09** constancy, incidence, oftenness **10** commonness, prevalence, recurrence, repetition **11** commonality, periodicity **12** frequentness

**frequent**
**05** daily, haunt, lobby, often, thick, usual, visit **06** attend, common, hourly, normal, weekly **07** crowded, regular **08** addicted, constant, everyday, familiar, habitual, numerous, practise, repeated **09** continual, countless, customary, habituate, hang out at, incessant, patronize, prevalent, recurrent, recurring **10** accustomed, persistent, prevailing, visit often **11** commonplace, hang about at, predominant **13** associate with, go to regularly **14** go to frequently, happening often

**frequenter**
**06** client, patron **07** habitué, haunter, regular **08** customer, resorter **14** regular visitor

**frequently**
**02** fr **03** oft **04** much **05** daily, often, thick **06** hourly, weekly **08** commonly **09** many a time, many times, regularly **10** habitually, oftentimes, repeatedly **11** continually, customarily, half the time, over and over **12** persistently

**fresh**
◇ *anagram indicator*
**03** hot, new, raw **04** bold, cool, fair, firm, just, keen, more, pert, pink, pure, rosy, span, warm **05** alert, brisk, clean, clear, cocky, crisp, crude, extra, green, newly, novel, other, right, sassy, saucy, spick, sweet, vital, windy **06** afresh, brazen, bright, caller, cheeky, chilly, direct, latest, lively, maiden, modern, recent, rested **07** bracing, forward, freshly, further, glowing, healthy, natural, renewed, revived, span new, uncured, undried, unfaded, unusual, vibrant **08** blooming, bouncing, brand-new, dewy-eyed, exciting, familiar, impudent, insolent, original, pristine, restored, straight, up-to-date, vigorous, youthful **09** different, energetic, refreshed, virescent **10** additional, a new person, innovative, new-fangled, raring to go, refreshing, stimulated, unpolluted **11** impertinent, invigorated, unpreserved, unprocessed **12** enthusiastic, invigorating, overfamiliar, presumptuous, ready for more **13** disrespectful, fresh as a daisy, inexperienced, revolutionary, supplementary, yourself again **14** healthy-looking, unconventional
• **remain fresh**
**04** keep, last

**freshen**
◇ *anagram indicator*
**03** air **05** clean, clear, liven, rouse **06** purify, refill, revive, tart up **07** enliven, liven up, refresh, restore **09** deodorize, stimulate, ventilate, vernalize **10** revitalize **12** reinvigorate
• **freshen up**
**09** get washed, have a wash **12** get spruced up, wash yourself **14** tidy yourself up

**freshly**
◇ *anagram indicator*
**04** anew, just **05** newly **06** barely, lately, of late **08** recently **10** not long ago **13** a short time ago

**freshman**
**05** bajan, frosh **06** bejant, pennal **07** fresher **08** newcomer **09** first-year **13** underclassman

**freshness**
**04** glow **05** bloom, flush, shine **06** vigour, youths **07** May-morn, newness, novelty, sparkle, verdure **09** cleanness, clearness, fraîcheur, immediacy, vernality **10** brightness, May-morning **11** originality **13** wholesomeness
• **early freshness**
**03** dew

**fret**
**03** rub, vex **04** mope, pine, rile, stop **05** anger, annoy, brood, chafe, grate, worry **06** bother, nettle, ripple **07** agonize, anguish, be upset, concern, corrode, disturb, torment, trouble, whittle **08** irritate **09** be anxious, infuriate, make a fuss, variegate **10** exasperate **12** be distressed **15** concern yourself

**fretful**
**04** edgy **05** tense, upset **06** uneasy **07** anxious, fearful, peevish, unhappy, uptight, worried **08** restless, troubled **09** disturbed, impatient **10** distressed

**fretfully**
**06** edgily **07** tensely **08** uneasily **09** anxiously, fearfully, worriedly **10** restlessly

**friable**
**05** crisp, crump **07** brittle, crumbly, powdery **12** pulverizable

**friar**
**02** Fr **03** fra **04** monk **05** abbot, frate, frier, minim, prior **06** frater **07** brother, limiter **08** Capuchin, récollet **09** Carmelite, Cordelier, Dominican, mendicant, Observant, predicant, recollect, religieux, religious **10** Franciscan, religioner **12** Observantine **13** Redemptionist

**friction**
**06** strife **07** arguing, chafing, discord, dispute, erosion, gnawing, grating, jarring, rasping, rivalry, rubbing **08** abrading, abrasion, bad blood, clashing, conflict, disunity, scraping, traction **09** animosity, attrition, hostility **10** antagonism, bad feeling, disharmony, dissension, ill feeling, irritation, opposition, resentment, resistance **11** disputation, excoriation,

quarrelling, wearing away, xerotripsis **12** disagreement

**Friday**
**02** Fr **03** Fri

**fridge**
**03** rub **04** fray, frig **06** cooler, icebox **07** minibar **12** refrigerator **13** refrigeratory

**friend**
**03** ami, bud, pal **04** ally, amie, chum, ehoa, mate, tosh **05** amigo, buddy, crony, ingle, lover **06** backer, belamy, bon ami, cobber, co-mate, gossib, gossip, inward, mucker, patron **07** best boy, comrade, goombah, paisano, partner, privado, sponsor **08** alter ego, best girl, compadre, familiar, intimate, playmate, sidekick, soul mate **09** associate, belle amie, bonne amie, boyfriend, companion, confidant, confident, paranymph, pen friend, supporter **10** back-friend, benefactor, best friend, better half, buddy-buddy, confidante, girlfriend, good friend, subscriber, well-wisher **11** bosom friend, cater-cousin, close friend, condisciple **12** acquaintance, fidus Achates, schoolfriend **15** sparring partner

**• mans' best friend**
**03** dog

**friendless**
**05** alone **06** lonely **07** forlorn, shunned, unloved **08** deserted, forsaken, isolated, lonesome, solitary **09** abandoned, destitute, unbeloved, unpopular **10** by yourself, ostracized, unattached **11** lonely-heart **12** unbefriended **13** companionless **14** cold-shouldered

**friendliness**
**06** warmth **08** bonhomie, kindness, matiness **09** geniality, palliness **10** affability, amiability, chumminess, kindliness **11** sociability **12** congeniality, conviviality **13** Gemütlichkeit **15** approachability, neighbourliness

**friendly**
**04** fond, kind, maty, nice, tosh, warm **05** close, matey, pally, thick, tight **06** chummy, couthy, folksy, genial, kindly **07** affable, amiable, cordial, couthie, helpful **08** amicable, down-home, familiar, informal, intimate, outgoing, pleasant, sociable **09** agreeable, comradely, congenial, convivial, favorable, peaceable, receptive, welcoming **10** favourable, hospitable **11** forthcoming, good-natured, inseparable, neighbourly, sympathetic **12** affectionate, approachable, well-disposed **13** companionable

**friendship**
**04** love **05** amity, amour **06** warmth **07** company, concord, harmony, rapport **08** affinity, alliance, fondness, goodwill, intimacy, mateship **09** affection, closeness **10** amiability, attachment, fellowship, kindliness **11** camaraderie, comradeship, familiarity **12** friendliness **13** companionship, confraternity, understanding

**fright**
**04** fear, fleg, funk **05** alarm, dread, gliff, glift, panic, scare, shock, skrik **06** creeps, dismay, horror, terror, tirrit **07** jitters, shivers, willies **08** affright, blue funk, disquiet **09** bombshell, cold sweat **10** blind panic **11** fearfulness, trepidation **12** affrightment, apprehension, perturbation **13** consternation, heebie-jeebies, knocking knees **15** bolt from the blue

**• expression of fright**
**03** eek **04** yike **05** yikes

**frighten**
**03** awe **04** dare, flay, fleg, fley, fray, gast, shoo **05** afear, alarm, appal, daunt, dread, ghast, panic, scare, shock, spook, unman **06** affear, affray, boggle, dismay, gallow, rattle **07** affeare, horrify, petrify, scarify, startle, terrify, unnerve **08** affright **09** terrorize **10** affrighten, intimidate, scare silly, scare stiff **12** put the wind up

**frightened**
**04** frit **05** cowed, feart, windy **06** afraid, frozen, scared **07** alarmed, chicken, panicky, quivery, trembly **08** dismayed, startled, unnerved **09** petrified, terrified **10** terrorized **11** in a blue funk, scared stiff **13** having kittens, panic-stricken, scared to death **14** terror-stricken

**frightening**
**04** eery, grim **05** eerie, hairy, scary **06** creepy, scarey, spooky **08** alarming, daunting, fearsome, terrific **09** traumatic **10** forbidding, formidable, petrifying, terrifying **11** hair-raising **12** white-knuckle **13** bloodcurdling, spine-chilling

**frightful**
◇ *anagram indicator*
**04** dire, grim, huge, ugly **05** awful, great, nasty **06** grisly, horrid, odious **07** fearful, ghastly, hideous, macabre, very bad **08** alarming, dreadful, fearsome, gruesome, horrible, horrific, shocking, terrible **09** abhorrent, appalling, harrowing, loathsome, repulsive, revolting **10** frightsome, horrendous, unbearable, unpleasant **11** affrightful, schrecklich, unspeakable **12** disagreeable

**frightfully**
◇ *anagram indicator*
**04** much, very **07** awfully, beastly, greatly **08** terribly **09** decidedly, extremely **10** dreadfully, ghastfully, thoroughly **11** desperately, exceedingly

**frigid**
**03** dry, icy **04** cold, cool **05** aloof, chill, polar, stiff, stony **06** arctic, bitter, chilly, formal, frosty, frozen, remote, wintry **07** distant, glacial, passive, unmoved **08** clinical, freezing, lifeless, reserved, Siberian, unloving, very cold **09** unfeeling **10** impersonal, unanimated **11** indifferent, passionless, standoffish, unemotional, unexcitable **12** unresponsive **13** unsympathetic

**frigidity**
**05** chill **07** iciness **08** coldness **09** aloofness, passivity, stiffness **10** chilliness, frostiness **11** impassivity **12** lifelessness **15** cold-heartedness

**frill**
**04** fold, ruff, tuck **05** extra, jabot, ruche **06** finery, fringe, purfle, ruffle **07** armilla, flounce, orphrey, ruching, valance **08** addition, frippery, furbelow, trimming **09** accessory, fanciness, fandangle, gathering, trimmings **10** decoration, frilliness **11** chitterling, ostentation, superfluity **13** embellishment, ornamentation

**frilly**
◇ *anagram indicator*
**04** lacy **05** fancy **06** ornate **07** crimped, frilled, ruffled, trimmed **08** flounced, gathered

**fringe**
◇ *ends selection indicator*
**03** hem, rim **04** bang, edge, fall, loma, purl, trim **05** bangs, frill, limit, skirt, thrum, verge **06** border, edging, margin, pelmet, tassel **07** bullion, enclose, fimbria, macramé, macrami, off-beat, valance **08** frisette, surround, trimming **09** left-field, outskirts, perimeter, periphery, peristome **10** avant-garde, borderline, unofficial, unorthodox **11** alternative **12** experimental **14** unconventional

**fringed**
**05** edged **06** fringy, hemmed **07** trimmed **08** bordered, tasselly **09** fimbriate, tasselled **10** fimbriated

**frippery**
**05** froth **06** finery, frills, trivia **07** baubles, foppery, gewgaws, trifles, useless **08** glad rags, nonsense, trifling, trinkets **09** fanciness, fussiness, gaudiness, nick-nacks, ornaments, showiness **10** adornments, fandangles, flashiness, frilliness, tawdriness, triviality **11** decorations, knick-knacks, ostentation **15** pretentiousness

**frisk**
**03** hop **04** fisk, jump, leap, play, romp, skip, trip **05** caper, check, dance, sport **06** bounce, cavort, curvet, frolic, gambol, prance, search **07** inspect **09** shake down **10** body-search

**friskily**
**08** actively **09** playfully **10** spiritedly **11** exuberantly

**frisky**
◇ *anagram indicator*
**04** high **05** hyper **06** active, bouncy,

lively, wanton **07** buckish, coltish, dashing, playful, romping **08** skittish, spirited **09** exuberant **10** frolicsome, rollicking **11** full of beans **12** high-spirited **13** in high spirits **15** alive and kicking

**fritter**
**04** blow, idle **05** waste **06** misuse **07** beignet, friture **08** fragment, misspend, squander **09** dissipate, go through, overspend **10** get through **14** spend like water

**frivolity**
**03** fun **04** jest **05** folly, froth **06** gaiety, levity **07** inanity **08** nonsense **09** flippancy, pettiness, silliness **10** triviality **11** foolishness **13** facetiousness, senselessness **14** superficiality

**frivolous**
**04** idle, vain **05** inane, light, petty, silly **06** futile **07** étourdi, foolish, jocular, puerile, shallow, trivial **08** étourdie, flippant, juvenile, skittish, trifling **09** airheaded, facetious, pointless, senseless **11** empty-headed, giddy-headed, light-minded, superficial, unimportant **12** bubble-headed, light-hearted **13** irresponsible **14** featherbrained

• **frivolous person**
**09** butterfly

**frivolously**
**04** idly **06** vainly **09** foolishly, jocularly **11** pointlessly, senselessly, whimsically **13** irresponsibly **14** light-heartedly

**frizzle**
**03** fry **04** bend, coil, curl, hiss, kink, loop, purl, roll, spit, tong, turn, wave, wind **05** crimp, curve, frizz, twine, twirl, twist **06** becurl, scorch, scroll, sizzle, spiral **07** crackle, crimple, crinkle, sputter, wreathe

**frizzy**
**04** wiry **05** crisp, curly **06** curled **07** crimped, frizzed **10** corrugated

**frock**
**04** gown, robe **05** dress
*See also* **dress**

**frog**
**04** hyla, Rana **05** frush **06** peeper **07** paddock, puddock **08** platanna, tree toad **12** spring peeper **15** Cape nightingale

**frolic**
◇ *anagram indicator*
**03** fun, hop, rig **04** game, lark, leap, play, rant, romp, skip **05** caper, dance, frisk, merry, mirth, prank, revel, sport, spree **06** antics, bounce, buster, cavort, curvet, gaiety, gambol, prance, pranky, razzle, splore, wanton **07** disport, gambado, gammock, jollity, May-game, rollick, skylark, stashie, stishie, stushie **08** escapade, stooshie **09** amusement, galravage, gilravage, high jinks, make merry, merriment **10** galravitch, gillravage, gilravitch, lark around **11** fun and games, gillravitch, merrymaking **12** razzle-dazzle **13** barnsbreaking

**frolicsome**
◇ *anagram indicator*
**03** gay **05** ludic, merry **06** frisky, lively, skippy **07** coltish, kitteny, playful **08** skittish, sportive **09** kittenish, sprightly **10** rollicking

**from**
◇ *anagram indicator*
◇ *hidden indicator*
**01** à **02** ab-, ex, of, on **03** fro, off, out **04** frae **05** out of, since

**front**
◇ *head selection indicator*
**03** air, bow, top, van **04** face, fore, head, lead, look, mask, meet, prow, show **05** blind, cover, first **06** aspect, façade, facing, manner, oppose, vaward **07** cover-up, leading, obverse, outside, pretext **08** confront, disguise, exterior, foremost, forepart, frontage, look over, overlook, pretence, vanguard **09** forefront, front line, look out on **10** appearance, battle zone, expression, firing line, foreground **11** countenance

• **in front**
◇ *juxtaposition indicator*
**04** fore **05** ahead, first **06** before, en face **07** leading **08** anterior, paravant **09** in advance, paravaunt, preceding, to the fore

• **in front of**
◇ *juxtaposition indicator*
**06** before, facing **07** ahead of **11** in advance of **14** under the nose of **15** in the presence of

**frontier**
**04** edge **05** limit, verge **06** border, bounds **07** marches **08** boundary, confines **09** bordering, partition, perimeter **10** borderline

**front-runner**
**03** nap **07** top seed **08** finalist **09** certainty, favourite, form horse **12** likely winner **15** odds-on favourite

**frost**
**03** ice, mat **04** rime **06** freeze **08** coldness, freeze-up **09** hoar-frost, Jack Frost

**frostily**
**06** coldly, coolly **07** stiffly

**frosty**
**03** icy **04** cold, cool, rimy **05** aloof, chill, frore, frorn, nippy, parky, polar, stiff **06** arctic, chilly, frigid, froren, frorne, frozen, wintry **07** glacial, hostile **08** freezing, Siberian **10** unfriendly **11** standoffish, unwelcoming **12** bitterly cold, discouraging

**froth**
**03** pap **04** barm, fizz, foam, head, mill, ream, scum, suds **05** spume, yeast **06** bubble, lather, mantle, trivia **07** bubbles, chatter, ferment, sea foam, trifles **10** cuckoo-spit, effervesce **12** trivialities **13** cuckoo-spittle, effervescence, irrelevancies

**frothy**
**04** vain **05** barmy, empty, fizzy, foamy, light, nappy, reamy, spumy, sudsy **06** bubbly, slight, yeasty **07** foaming, spumous, trivial **08** bubbling, trifling **09** frivolous **10** spumescent **11** lightweight **13** insubstantial

**frown**
**03** mow **04** lour, moue, pout **05** glare, scowl **06** glower **07** frounce, grimace **09** dirty look **13** look daggers at, raised eyebrow

• **frown on**
**05** glare, scowl **06** glower **07** dislike, grimace **08** object to **10** discourage **12** disapprove of, think badly of **14** take a dim view of **15** not take kindly to

**frowsty**
**05** fuggy, fusty, musty **06** stuffy **07** airless **12** unventilated

**frowsy**
**05** dirty, fusty, messy **06** frumpy, sloppy, stuffy, untidy **07** scruffy, unkempt **08** frumpish, slovenly, sluttish, unwashed **09** offensive, ungroomed **10** slatternly **11** dishevelled

**frozen**
**03** icy, raw **04** hard, iced, numb **05** fixed, frore, frorn, glacé, polar, rigid, stiff **06** arctic, frigid, froren, frorne, frosty **07** chilled, frosted, glacial, ice-cold **08** freezing, icebound, Siberian **10** ice-covered, solidified **11** frozen-stiff **12** bitterly cold

**frugal**
**05** spare **06** meagre, paltry, saving, scanty, stingy **07** careful, miserly, prudent, sparing, spartan, thrifty **09** husbandly, niggardly, penny-wise, provident **10** economical, inadequate **12** parsimonious **13** penny-pinching

**frugality**
**06** saving, thrift **07** economy **08** prudence **09** husbandry, parsimony **11** carefulness **12** conservation

**frugally**
**05** spare **08** meagrely, scantily **09** carefully, prudently, thriftily **12** economically, inadequately **14** parsimoniously

**fruit**
**03** haw, hep, hip, nut, pod **04** crop **05** acorn, berry, yield **06** effect, profit, result, return, reward **07** benefit, harvest, outcome, produce, product, rosehip **08** fruitage **09** advantage **11** consequence

*Fruits include:*

**03** bel, Cox, fig
**04** bael, bhel, Cox's, date, gage, kaki, lime, pear, plum, sloe, Ugli®

**05** apple, carob, galia, grape, guava, Jaffa, lemon, mango, melon, olive, peach, prune
**06** banana, cherry, damson, loquat, litchi, lychee, medlar, orange, papaya, pawpaw, pippin, pomelo, quince, raisin, russet, tomato, wampee
**07** acerola, apricot, avocado, bramble, Bramley, chayote, kumquat, mineola, rhubarb, satsuma, Seville, soursop, tangelo, William
**08** bilberry, Braeburn, date plum, goosegog, honeydew, kalumpit, mandarin, minneola, mulberry, muscatel, physalis, Pink Lady, rambutan, sebesten, sunberry, tamarind
**09** beach plum, blueberry, cantaloup, carambola, cherimoya, crab apple, cranberry, greengage, Juneberry, kiwi fruit, nectarine, persimmon, pineapple, raspberry, rose apple, sapodilla, saskatoon, shadberry, star-apple, star fruit, tangerine, ugli®fruit
**10** blackberry, breadfruit, cantaloupe, clementine, Conference, damask plum, elderberry, gooseberry, granadilla, grapefruit, loganberry, mangosteen, redcurrant, salal berry, sour cherry, spiceberry, strawberry, watermelon
**11** blood orange, boysenberry, eating apple, Granny Smith, Jaffa orange, navel orange, pomegranate, sallal berry, sharon fruit, sweet cherry
**12** blackcurrant, buffalo-berry, cooking apple, costard apple, custard apple, passion fruit, Red Delicious, serviceberry, victoria plum, whitecurrant, winter cherry
**13** kangaroo-apple, morello cherry, sapodilla plum, Seville orange
**14** Cape gooseberry, pink grapefruit
**15** Golden Delicious

---

• **fruit juice**
**03** oil **05** mobby **06** mobbie
• **fruit refuse**
**04** marc
• **fruit stone**
**03** pip, pit **06** pyrene **07** putamen
• **fruit syrup**
**03** rob

**fruitful**
**03** fat **04** rich **06** fecund, useful **07** fertile, teeming **08** abundant, fructive, pregnant, prolific **09** effective, effectual, feracious, fructuous, plenteous, plentiful, rewarding, well-spent **10** beneficial, productive, profitable, successful, worthwhile **11** conceptious, efficacious, increaseful **12** advantageous, fruit-bearing

**fruitfully**
**08** usefully **10** profitably **11** effectively **12** beneficially, productively, successfully **14** advantageously

**fruitfulness**
**06** uberty **08** feracity **09** fecundity, fertility **10** usefulness **11** fecundation **13** profitability **14** productiveness

**fruition**
**07** success **08** maturity, ripeness **09** enjoyment **10** attainment, completion, fulfilment, maturation, perfection **11** achievement, realization **12** consummation **13** actualization

**fruitless**
**04** idle, vain **06** barren, futile **07** sterile, useless **08** abortive, hopeless **09** pointless, worthless **11** ineffectual, infructuous **12** unproductive, unsuccessful

**fruitlessly**
**06** in vain, vainly **09** uselessly **10** hopelessly **11** pointlessly **14** unproductively, unsuccessfully

**fruity**
**03** low **04** blue, deep, full, racy, rich, sexy **05** bawdy, crazy, juicy, saucy, spicy **06** mellow, risqué, smutty, vulgar **07** naughty **08** indecent, resonant **09** salacious **10** indelicate, suggestive **11** titillating

**frumpy**
**04** drab **05** dated, dingy, dowdy **06** dreary **08** frumpish **09** out of date **10** ill-dressed **12** badly dressed

**frustrate**
**03** bug **04** balk, beat, crab, dash, foil, miff, nark, rile, stop **05** anger, annoy, baulk, block, check, get at, spike, stimy **06** baffle, balked, blight, defeat, hamper, hinder, hogtie, impede, needle, nobble, scotch, stimie, stymie, thwart, wind up **07** counter, depress, inhibit, nullify, scupper, useless **08** drive mad, embitter, irritate, obstruct **09** aggravate, forestall, infuriate **10** disappoint, disconcert, discourage, dishearten, dissatisfy, drive crazy, exasperate, neutralize **11** ineffectual

**frustrated**
**05** angry **06** dished **07** annoyed **08** blighted, thwarted **09** repressed, resentful **10** embittered **11** discouraged **12** disappointed, discontented, disheartened, dissatisfied

**frustrating**
**08** annoying **09** maddening **10** irritating **11** infuriating **12** discouraging, exasperating **13** disappointing, disheartening

**frustration**
**04** balk, foil **05** anger, baulk **06** defeat, thwart **07** balking, curbing, failure, foiling **08** blocking, vexation **09** annoyance, thwarting **10** irritation, resentment **11** obstruction **12** exasperation **13** circumvention, contravention, non-fulfilment **14** disappointment, discouragement **15** dissatisfaction
• ***expression of frustration***
**11** for God's sake **12** for pete's sake **14** for Christ's sake, for heaven's sake **15** for goodness sake

**fry**
**04** burn, foam **05** sauté, spawn **06** scorch, sizzle **07** frizzle, skegger **09** whitebait

**frying-pan**
**03** wok **06** spider **07** skillet

**fuddled**
◇ *anagram indicator*
**03** fap **04** hazy **05** drunk, mused, muzzy, tipsy, woozy **06** addled, groggy, swipey, tavert **07** bemused, muddled, sozzled, taivert **08** confused **09** overtaken, stupefied **10** inebriated, tossicated, tosticated **11** intoxicated

**fuddy-duddy**
**04** prim **06** fossil, square, stuffy **07** carping **08** old fogey **10** back number, censorious, conformist **11** museum piece, old-fogeyish **12** buttoned-down, conservative, old-fashioned, stuffed shirt **13** stick-in-the-mud **14** traditionalist

**fudge**
◇ *anagram indicator*
**03** fix **04** cook, fail, fake **05** avoid, cheat, dodge, evade, hedge, stall, stuff **06** fiddle, humbug **07** distort, evasion, falsify, shuffle **08** nonsense **10** distortion, equivocate **12** misrepresent

**fuel**
**03** fan **04** feed, fire **05** boost **06** incite **07** goading, inflame, nourish, stoke up, sustain **08** material, stimulus **09** encourage, incentive, stimulate **10** ammunition, incitement, propellant **11** combustible, motive power, provocation **13** encouragement

*Fuels include:*

**03** gas, LNG, LPG, MOX, oil, RDF
**04** coal, coke, derv, logs, peat, slug, SURF, wood
**05** argol, eldin, fagot, vraic
**06** benzol, billet, borane, butane, diesel, elding, faggot, gas oil, hydyne, petrol, smudge, Sterno®
**07** astatki, benzine, benzole, biofuel, Coalite®, eilding, gasahol, gasohol, mesquit, methane, propane, uranium
**08** calor gas®, charcoal, firewood, gasoline, kerosene, kerosine, kindling, mesquite, paraffin, tan balls, triptane
**09** acetylene, biodiesel, Campingaz®, cane-trash, diesel oil, hydrazine, plutonium, red diesel
**10** anthracite, atomic fuel, fossil fuel, natural gas, Orimulsion®
**11** electricity, North Sea gas, nuclear fuel
**12** buffalo chips, nitromethane, nuclear power, vegetable oil
**13** smokeless fuel
**14** aviation spirit

---

*See also* **petrol**

**fug**
**04** reek **05** stink **09** fetidness, fustiness, staleness **10** foetidness, stuffiness **11** frowstiness

**fuggy**
**04** foul **05** close, fetid, fusty, stale **06** foetid, stuffy **07** airless, frowsty, noisome, noxious **11** suffocating **12** unventilated

**fugitive**
**04** AWOL **05** brief, exile, short **06** flying, maroon, runner **07** elusive, escapee, fleeing, passing, refugee, runaway **08** deserter, fleeting, hideaway, runagate **09** ephemeral, fugacious, momentary, temporary, transient **10** evanescent, short-lived, transitory

**fulfil**
**04** fill, keep, meet, obey **05** honor **06** answer, effect, finish, honour **07** achieve, act up to, execute, live out, observe, perfect, perform, qualify, realize, satisfy **08** carry out, complete, conclude, live up to, make good **09** conform to, discharge, implement, stand up to **10** accomplish, comply with, consummate **15** come up to scratch

**fulfilled**
**05** happy **07** content, pleased **09** gratified, satisfied

**fulfilling**
**08** pleasing **10** comforting, completion, completory, gratifying, satisfying **12** satisfactory **14** accomplishment

**fulfilment**
**04** pass **07** success **08** enacture, fruition **09** discharge, execution, impletion **10** completion, observance, perfection **11** achievement, performance, realization **12** consummation, satisfaction **14** accomplishment, implementation

**full**
◇ *anagram indicator*
**03** fat, fed, top **04** bang, busy, deep, loud, rich, vast, walk, warm, wauk, wide **05** ample, baggy, broad, buxom, clear, drunk, flush, laden, large, loose, obese, plump, quite, right, round, sated, smack, stout, total, truly, waulk, whole **06** active, chubby, entire, filled, fruity, gorged, hectic, intact, jammed, lively, loaded, packed, rotund, strong, tiring, utmost **07** bulging, chocker, copious, crammed, crowded, exactly, filling, frantic, highest, intense, maximum, perfect, profuse, replete, rounded, shapely, stuffed, swelled, vibrant, well fed **08** abundant, bursting, chockers, chockful, complete, detailed, directly, distinct, eventful, exciting, generous, greatest, resonant, satiated, sonorous, squarely, straight, thorough **09** abounding, chock-full, corpulent, extensive, packed out, plentiful, satisfied **10** exhaustive, full-bodied, overweight, sufficient, thoroughly, unabridged, voluminous **11** chock-a-block, overflowing, protuberant, well-rounded, well-stocked **12** all-inclusive, loose-fitting, unexpurgated **13** comprehensive, full to the brim

• **be full**
**04** teem

• **in full**
**05** fully, uncut **06** wholly **07** at large, in pleno, in total **08** at length, in detail **10** completely **13** in its entirety

• **to the full**
**05** fully **07** utterly **08** entirely **10** completely, thoroughly **11** to the utmost

**full-blooded**
**06** hearty **07** devoted **08** thorough, vigorous **09** committed, dedicated, out-and-out **11** sanguineous **12** enthusiastic, wholehearted

**full-blown**
**04** full **05** major, total **06** all-out **07** intense **08** complete, thorough **09** full-scale, out-and-out **11** full-fledged

**full-bodied**
**03** fat **04** deep, full, rich **06** fruity, strong **07** amoroso, intense

**full-frontal**
**05** total **06** direct, strong **08** absolute, complete, forceful, thorough **09** out-and-out **12** unexpurgated, unrestrained

**full-grown**
**04** ripe **05** adult, of age **06** mature, seeded **07** grown-up **09** developed, full-blown, full-scale **10** fully grown **12** fully fledged **14** fully developed

**fullness**
**04** body, fill, glut **05** depth, force, power, width **06** growth, plenty, wealth **07** breadth, fatness, pleroma, satiety **08** dilation, loudness, plethora, richness, solidity, strength, swelling, totality, vastness **09** abundance, ampleness, greatness, impletion, intensity, largeness, plenitude, plumpness, profusion, repletion, resonance, satedness, satiation, wholeness **10** complement, congestion, tumescence **11** enlargement, repleteness, shapeliness **12** completeness, inflammation, satisfaction, thoroughness **13** extensiveness **14** curvaceousness, voluptuousness

• **in the fullness of time**
**06** in time **07** finally **08** in the end **10** eventually, ultimately **11** in due course

**full-scale**
**05** major **06** all-out **07** in-depth **08** complete, sweeping, thorough **09** extensive, intensive **10** exhaustive **11** wide-ranging **13** comprehensive, thoroughgoing **15** all-encompassing

**fully**
**02** up **05** quite **06** fairly, wholly **07** totally, utterly **08** entirely **09** perfectly **10** altogether, completely, positively, thoroughly, to the nines **12** sufficiently, unreservedly **13** in all respects **14** satisfactorily, without reserve

**fully fledged**
**06** mature, senior **07** trained **08** graduate **09** full-blown, qualified **10** proficient **11** experienced **12** professional **14** fully developed

**fulminate**
**04** fume, rage, rail, slam **05** curse, decry, flash, slate **07** condemn, declaim, inveigh, protest, thunder **08** denounce, detonate **09** criticize **10** animadvert, vituperate

**fulmination**
**06** tirade **07** decrial, obloquy, slating **08** brickbat, diatribe **09** criticism, invective, philippic **10** detonation, thundering **11** thunderbolt **12** condemnation, denunciation

**fulsome**
**03** fat, OTT **05** gross, slimy **06** smarmy **07** buttery, cloying, fawning **08** effusive, luscious, nauseous, overdone, unctuous **09** adulatory, excessive, insincere, offensive, sickening **10** immoderate, inordinate, nauseating, obsequious, over the top, saccharine **11** extravagant, sycophantic, well-rounded **12** enthusiastic, ingratiating **13** well-developed

**fulsomely**
**10** effusively, over the top **11** excessively, insincerely, sickeningly **12** immoderately, inordinately, nauseatingly **13** extravagantly

**fumble**
◇ *anagram indicator*
**04** faff, feel **05** botch, grope, spoil **06** bobble, bungle, huddle, mumble **07** blunder **08** flounder, scrabble **09** faff about, feel about, mishandle, mismanage

**fume**
**04** boil, rage, rant, rave, reek, stum **05** go mad, nidor, smoke, steam, storm, vapor **06** blow up, seethe, vapour **07** be livid, explode **08** boil over, smoulder **09** be furious **10** hit the roof **11** blow your top, lose your rag, rant and rave **12** blow your cool, fly into a rage, lose your cool **15** fly off the handle, go off the deep end

**fumes**
**03** fog, gas **04** haze, reek, smog **05** gases, smell, smoke, stink **06** stench, vapour **07** exhaust, vapours **09** pollution **10** exhalation

**fumigate**
**05** smoke **06** purify, smudge **07** cleanse, incense, perfume **08** sanitize **09** deodorize, disinfect, sterilize

**fumigation**
**09** cleansing, purifying
**12** disinfecting, purification, sanitization **13** sterilization

**fuming**
**03** mad **05** angry, livid **06** raging
**07** boiling, enraged, furious, smoking, uptight **08** incensed, seething, up in arms **09** in a lather, raving mad, seeing red, steamed up, ticked off **10** hopping mad **11** disgruntled

**fun**
**03** gig, joy **04** game, hoax, jest, joke, lark, play, romp **05** bourd, crack, craic, mirth, music, sport, trick, witty
**06** joking, laughs, lekker, lively
**07** amusing, foolery, gammock, jesting, jollity **08** gladness, hilarity, laughter, pleasure **09** amusement, diversion, diverting, enjoyable, enjoyment, frivolity, horseplay, merriment **10** buffoonery, delightful, jocularity, recreation, relaxation, skylarking, tomfoolery **11** celebration, distraction, merrymaking, pleasurable
**12** cheerfulness, entertaining, recreational **13** entertainment
• **for fun**
**08** for kicks **09** for a laugh **12** for enjoyment **14** for the hell of it
• **in fun**
**06** in jest **07** as a joke, playful, to tease
**08** jokingly **09** for a laugh, playfully, teasingly **11** mischievous
**13** mischievously, tongue in cheek
• **make fun of**
**03** cod, guy, rib **04** goof, jeer, joke, mock **05** get at, jolly, sport, taunt, tease **06** banter, deride, jeer at, send up **07** laugh at, scoff at, sneer at
**08** ridicule **09** humiliate, poke fun at
**11** have a shot at, poke borak at **13** take the mickey **15** pull someone's leg

**function**
**02** do, go **03** act, cos, cot, job, log, run, sec, sin, tan, use **04** cosh, coth, duty, part, post, role, sech, sine, sinh, tanh, task, work **05** chore, cosec, party, serve **06** affair, behave, charge, cosech, cosine, dinner, office, result, upshot **07** concern, mission, operate, perform, purpose, tangent **08** activity, business, capacity, luncheon
**09** corollary, deduction, gathering, induction, inference, reception, situation **10** conclusion, employment, occupation **11** concomitant, consequence, social event **12** have the job of **13** play the part of
**14** responsibility

*See also* **dance**

**functional**
**05** plain **06** useful **07** running, utility, working **08** clinical **09** operative, practical **11** hard-wearing, operational, serviceable, utilitarian

**functionally**
**08** usefully **11** efficiently, practically
**13** operationally

**functionary**
**07** officer **08** employee, official
**09** dignitary **10** bureaucrat **12** office-bearer, office-holder

**fund**
**03** box, IMF **04** back, bank, cash, dosh, gelt, loot, mine, pool, well
**05** brass, bread, cache, dough, endow, float, fonds, grant, gravy, hoard, kitty, lolly, means, money, rhino, stack, stock, store **06** assets, greens, moolah, pay for, source, supply, wealth **07** backing, capital, finance, jackpot, promote, readies, reserve, savings, shekels, sponsor, support, tracker **08** treasury
**09** endowment, megabucks, reservoir, resources, slate club, subsidize
**10** capitalize, collection, foundation, investment, repository, storehouse, underwrite **11** spondulicks
**12** accumulation, the necessary
**14** community chest
• **reserve fund**
**04** rest
• **transfer funds**
**04** vire

**fundamental**
**03** key **04** main, root **05** basal, basic, chief, first, prime, vital **06** bottom, primal **07** bedrock, central, crucial, initial, organic, primary, radical
**08** cardinal, integral, original, profound, ultimate **09** elemental, essential, important, necessary, primitive, principal **10** elementary, underlying **11** rudimentary
**12** foundational **13** indispensable

**fundamentalist**
**05** fundy, rigid, Talib **06** fundie, strict
**08** orthodox, rigorous
**14** uncompromising

**fundamentally**
**05** à fond **06** deeply **07** acutely, at heart **08** at bottom, deep down
**09** basically, crucially, in essence, primarily, radically **10** cardinally, critically, inherently, profoundly
**11** essentially **13** intrinsically, substantially

**fundamentals**
**04** laws **05** facts, rules **06** basics
**09** rudiments **10** brass tacks, essentials
**11** necessaries, nitty-gritty **12** nuts and bolts **14** practicalities **15** first principles

**fundraising** *see* **charity**

**funeral**
**04** obit, wake **05** tangi **06** burial
**08** exequies **09** cremation, interment, obsequies **10** entombment, inhumation

**funereal**
**03** sad **04** dark **05** feral, grave
**06** dismal, dreary, gloomy, solemn, sombre, woeful **07** serious
**08** exequial, funebral, mournful
**09** deathlike, funebrial, lamenting
**10** depressing, lugubrious, sepulchral

**fungus**
**11** thallophyte

*Fungi include:*

**04** rust, scab, smut
**05** ergot, yeast
**06** blight
**07** candida
**08** botritis, brown rot, mushroom
**09** black spot, grey mould, toadstool
**10** saprophyte, slime mould, sooty mould
**11** downy mildew, penicillium, slime fungus
**12** brewer's yeast, potato blight
**13** powdery mildew

*See also* **mushroom**

**funk**
**04** fear, flap, fuss, stew **05** alarm, dodge, panic, spark, state, tizzy
**06** balk at, blench, cop out, dither, flinch, frenzy, fright, terror, tiswas, tizwas **07** fluster **08** blue funk
**09** agitation, cold sweat, commotion, duck out of, shirk from, touchwood
**10** flinch from, recoil from **12** chicken out of

**funnel**
**02** go **04** flue, horn, move, pass, pipe, pour, tube, vent **05** guide, shaft, stack
**06** choana, convey, direct, drogue, filter, siphon **07** channel, chimney, tun-dish **08** sink hole, transfer, windsail
**10** smokestack **11** swallow hole
**12** infundibulum

**funnily**
◇ *anagram indicator*
**09** amazingly **10** incredibly, remarkably **12** surprisingly
**13** astonishingly

**funny**
◇ *anagram indicator*
**03** odd, rum **04** rich **05** a hoot, comic, corny, droll, queer, shady, silly, wacky, weird, witty **06** absurd, way-out
**07** amusing, a scream, bizarre, comical, curious, dubious, killing, oddball, off-beat, riotous, risible, strange, unusual **08** farcical, humorous, peculiar, puzzling
**09** diverting, facetious, hilarious, laughable **10** hysterical, mysterious, perplexing, remarkable, ridiculous, suspicious, uproarious **12** entertaining, knee-slapping **13** side-splitting
• **something funny**
**04** hoot, yell

**fur**
**03** boa **04** coat, down, fell, flue, hair, hide, mane, muff, pane, pean, pelt, skin, wool **06** fleece, pelage
**07** necklet

*Furs include:*

**03** fox
**04** flix, gris, mink, vair
**05** budge, civet, fitch, genet, grise, otter, sable, skunk
**06** beaver, ermine, marten, nutria, ocelot, rabbit, racoon, zorino

**07** blue fox, caracal, caracul, crimmer, fitchet, fitchew, genette, karakul, krimmer, minever, miniver, muskrat, opossum, raccoon
**08** cony-wool, kolinsky, moleskin, musquash, ponyskin, sealskin, sea otter, zibeline
**09** broadtail, silver fox, wolverene, wolverine, zibelline
**10** chinchilla
**11** beech marten, Persian lamb, stone marten

**furbish**
**04** do up **05** refit, renew **06** polish, purify, reform, repair, revamp
**07** improve, remodel, restore
**08** overhaul, renovate **09** modernize, refurbish **10** redecorate
**11** recondition **12** rehabilitate
**15** give a facelift to

**furious**
◇ *anagram indicator*
**03** mad, wud **04** wild, wood, yond
**05** angry, irate, livid **06** fierce, fuming, raging, savage, stormy **07** acharné, boiling, enraged, flaming, frantic, in a huff, in a stew, intense, salvage, violent
**08** brainish, frenzied, in a paddy, incensed, inflamed, maenadic, seething, sizzling, up in arms, vehement, vigorous **09** desperate, in a lather, indignant **10** boisterous, hopping mad, infuriated, outrageous
**11** tempestuous **12** incandescent
**14** purple with rage

**furiously**
**05** madly **06** wildly **07** angrily, crossly, in anger, irately, like mad **08** fiercely, in a paddy, stormily, up in arms
**09** intensely, seeing red, violently
**10** like blazes, vehemently, vigorously
**11** indignantly **12** passionately
**13** infuriatingly, tempestuously **15** avec acharnement

**furnace** *see* **oven**

**furnish**
**03** fit, rig **04** gird, give, suit **05** besee, endue, equip, grant, offer, plant, stock, stuff, yield **06** afford, bestow, fit out, kit out, purvey, supply **07** appoint, bedight, garnish, present, provide
**08** decorate, minister

**furniture**
**06** things **07** effects **08** fitments, fittings, movables **09** equipment, moveables **10** appliances
**11** accessories, furnishings, possessions **12** appointments
**14** household goods

*Furniture items include:*

**03** bed, cot
**04** bunk, desk, sofa
**05** chair, chest, couch, divan, stool, suite, table, trunk, wagon
**06** buffet, bureau, carver, coffer, cradle, daybed, fender, lowboy, mirror, pouffe, settee, waggon
**07** armoire, beanbag, bunkbed, cabinet, camp-bed, commode, dresser, ottoman, sofa bed, tallboy, whatnot
**08** armchair, bar chair, bedstead, bookcase, cupboard, end table, hatstand, recliner, toy chest, tub chair, wall unit, wardrobe, water bed
**09** bed-settee, card table, coatstand, easy chair, fireplace, footstool, hallstand, high-chair, lamp table, sideboard, side table, step-stool, washstand, wine table
**10** blanket box, chiffonier, dumb-waiter, encoignure, escritoire, firescreen, four-poster, secretaire, truckle bed, vanity unit
**11** coffee table, dining chair, dining table, mantelpiece, room-divider, swivel chair
**12** bedside table, chaise-longue, chesterfield, china cabinet, computer desk, folding table, gateleg table, kitchen chair, kitchen table, magazine rack, nest of tables, rocking chair, Welsh dresser
**13** dressing table, four-poster bed, umbrella stand
**14** chest of drawers, display cabinet, extending table, refectory table
**15** bathroom cabinet, butcher's trolley, occasional chair, occasional table

*See also* **office**

*Furniture styles include:*

**04** Adam, buhl
**06** boulle, Empire, Gothic, rococo, Shaker
**07** Art Deco, Baroque, Regency, Windsor
**08** Colonial, Georgian, Sheraton
**09** Charles II, Edwardian, Queen Anne, Shibayama, Victorian, William IV
**10** Art Nouveau, Mackintosh, provincial
**11** Anglo-Indian, Biedermeier, Chippendale, Cromwellian, Hepplewhite, Louis-Quinze, Restoration
**12** Gainsborough, Transitional, Vernis Martin
**13** Anglo-Colonial, Arts and Crafts, Dutch Colonial, Louis Philippe, Louis-Quatorze
**14** William and Mary

**furore**
**04** flap, fury, fuss, rage, stir, to-do
**05** craze, stink, storm **06** frenzy, outcry, tumult, uproar **08** outburst
**09** commotion **10** excitement, hullabaloo **11** disturbance

**furrow**
**03** fur, rut **04** furr, knit, line, list, mill, plow, rill, seam **05** flute, gouge, stria, track **06** crease, feerin, groove, gutter, hollow, plough, sulcus, trench, trough
**07** chamfer, channel, crinkle, feering, wrinkle **08** engroove, ingroove
**09** corrugate, crow's foot, vallecula
**11** canaliculus, lister ridge **12** draw together

• **draw first furrow**
**04** feer

**furry**
**04** soft **05** downy, fuzzy, hairy
**06** fleecy, fluffy, woolly

**further**
**03** aid, als, new, too **04** agen, also, ease, help, more, push **05** again, extra, fresh, other, speed **06** assist, as well, foster, hasten **07** advance, besides, develop, farther, forward, promote, remoter, speed up **08** champion, expedite, moreover **09** encourage, what's more **10** accelerate, additional, facilitate, in addition
**11** furthermore, more distant, more extreme **12** additionally
**13** supplementary

**furtherance**
**04** help **07** backing, pursuit
**08** advocacy, boosting, speeding
**09** advancing, promoting, promotion **10** preferment
**11** advancement, carrying-out, championing **12** facilitation
**13** encouragement

**furthermore**
**03** too **04** also **06** as well **07** besides, further **08** moreover **09** what's more
**10** in addition **12** additionally **14** into the bargain

**furthermost**
**06** utmost **07** extreme, outmost
**08** farthest, furthest, remotest, ultimate **09** outermost, uttermost

**furthest**
**06** utmost **07** extreme, outmost
**08** farthest, remotest, ultimate
**09** outermost, uttermost
**11** furthermost

**furtive**
**03** sly **06** covert, hidden, secret, shifty, sneaky, veiled **07** cloaked **08** stealthy, thievish, weaselly **09** secretive, underhand **11** clandestine
**13** surreptitious

**furtively**
**05** slyly **08** covertly, secretly
**11** secretively **15** surreptitiously

**fury**
**03** ire **04** rage **05** anger, dread, force, furor, power, wrath **06** Erinys, frenzy
**07** madness, passion **08** ferocity, severity, violence, wildness
**09** Eumenides, intensity, vehemence
**10** fierceness, turbulence
**11** desperation

*The Furies:*

**06** Alecto, Megara
**07** Megaera
**09** Tisiphone

**furze**
**04** whin **05** gorse

**fuse**
**03** ren, rin, run **04** flux, join, meld, melt, weld **05** blend, fusee, fuzee, merge, smelt, unite **06** mingle, solder
**07** combine **08** ankylose, coalesce, conflate, intermix **09** anchylose,

commingle, integrate, interfuse **10** amalgamate, colliquate, synthesize **11** agglutinate, intermingle, put together

**fusillade**
**04** fire, hail **05** burst, salvo **06** volley **07** barrage **08** outburst **09** broadside, discharge

**fusion**
**05** blend, union **06** merger **07** melting, running, welding **08** blending, smelting **09** ankylosis, synthesis **10** anchylosis, conflation, federation **11** coalescence, integration **12** amalgamation, colliquation

**fuss**
**02** do **03** ado, row **04** coil, faff, flap, fret, rout, song, stir, to-do, work **05** hoo-ha, hurry, panic, tizzy, upset, worry **06** bother, bustle, chichi, create, fidget, fikery, flurry, furore, hassle, hoo-hah, pother, pudder, racket **07** agitate, carry-on, fluster, grumble, palaver, parafle, stashie, stishie, stushie, tamasha, trouble **08** ballyhoo, brouhaha, complain, paraffle, squabble, stooshie **09** agitation, be all over, commotion, confusion, kerfuffle, pantomime, take pains **10** be in a tizzy, excitement, make a thing **11** piece of work **13** a song and dance **14** storm in a teacup

**fussiness**
**08** busyness, niceness, niggling **09** finicking **10** choosiness, finicality **11** finicalness **13** particularity, perfectionism **14** meticulousness, pernicketiness

**fusspot**
**06** fantod, fidget **07** old maid, worrier **08** old woman, stickler **09** nit-picker **10** fussbudget **11** hyper-critic **13** perfectionist

**fussy**
◇ *anagram indicator*
**04** busy **05** faddy, fancy, picky, tatty **06** chichi, choosy, ornate, prissy, rococo, spoffy **07** baroque, finical, finicky **08** niggling, pedantic, spoffish **09** cluttered, demanding, difficult, elaborate, quibbling, selective **10** fastidious, nit-picking, old-maidish, particular, pernickety, scrupulous **11** old-womanish, persnickety **12** fiddle-faddle, hard to please, pettifogging **13** grandmotherly, overdecorated **14** discriminating

**fusty**
**04** damp, dank, rank **05** fuggy, musty, passé, stale **06** fousty, frowsy, frowzy, mouldy, stuffy **07** airless, archaic, frowsty **08** outdated **09** out-of-date **10** antiquated, malodorous, mouldering **11** ill-smelling, old-fogeyish **12** old-fashioned, unventilated

**futile**
**04** idle, no go, vain **05** empty, inept **06** barren, hollow, in vain, no good, otiose, wasted **07** forlorn, useless **08** abortive, feckless, nugatory, tattling, trifling **09** fruitless, pointless, to no avail, worthless **10** profitless, sleeveless, unavailing **11** ineffective, ineffectual, meaningless **12** unproductive, unprofitable, unsuccessful

**futility**
**05** waste **06** vanity **07** mockery **08** vainesse **09** emptiness **10** barrenness, hollowness **11** aimlessness, uselessness **12** nugatoriness **13** fruitlessness, pointlessness, worthlessness **15** ineffectiveness, meaninglessness

**future**
**03** fut **04** next, to be **05** fated, later **06** avenir, coming, to come, unborn **07** by-and-by, outlook, planned **08** destined, eventual, expected, imminent, tomorrow **09** designate, hereafter, impending, prospects **10** subsequent, time to come **11** approaching, coming times, forthcoming, in the offing, prospective **12** expectations

**• in future**
**04** once **05** hence **09** after this, from now on, hereafter **10** henceforth **11** hereinafter **12** henceforward **13** from this day on **14** from this time on

**fuzz**
**03** fug, nap **04** blur, down, hair, lint, pile **05** fibre, flock, floss, fluff **06** police

**fuzzy**
◇ *anagram indicator*
**04** hazy **05** downy, faint, foggy, furry, linty, muzzy, vague **06** fleecy, fluffy, frizzy, napped, woolly **07** blurred, fuddled, muffled, shadowy, unclear, velvety **08** confused **09** distorted, unfocused **10** ill-defined, indefinite, indistinct

# G

**G**
**03** gee **04** golf

**gab**
**03** jaw, yak **04** blab, brag, buzz, chat, jest, talk **05** boast, prate, vaunt **06** babble, drivel, gossip, jabber, tattle **07** blabber, blarney, blather, blether, chatter, mockery, prattle **08** chitchat **09** loquacity, prattling, small talk **10** blethering, yackety-yak **12** conversation, tittle-tattle **13** tongue-wagging

**gabble**
**04** blab **05** spout **06** babble, cackle, drivel, gaggle, gibber, jabber, patter, rabble, rattle, waffle **07** blabber, blether, chatter, prattle, sputter, twaddle **08** cackling, nonsense, splutter **09** gibberish **10** blethering **12** gibble-gabble, ribble-rabble

**Gabon**
**01** G **03** GAB

**gad**
**• gad about**
**04** fisk, roam, rove **05** jaunt, range, stray **06** ramble, travel, wander **07** traipse **08** dot about **09** flit about, gallivant, run around

**gadabout**
**05** rover **07** rambler **08** runabout, wanderer **10** stravaiger **11** gallivanter **14** pleasure-seeker

**gadget**
**03** toy **04** tool **05** gismo, gizmo, thing, waldo **06** device, doodad, doodah, hickey, jimjam, widget **07** gimmick, gubbins, novelty, whatnot, whatsit **08** thingamy **09** apparatus, appliance, doohickey, implement, invention, jigamaree, jiggumbob, mechanism, thingummy **10** instrument **11** contraption, contrivance, thingamybob **12** executive toy, thingummyjig **14** what-d'you-call-it

**gadolinium**
**02** Gd

**Gaelic**
**04** Erse

**gaffe**
◇ *anagram indicator*
**04** boob, flub, goof, slip **05** brick, error **06** boo-boo, howler, slip-up **07** bloomer, blunder, clanger, faux pas, mistake **08** solecism **09** gaucherie **12** indiscretion

**gaffer**
**03** gov, guv **04** boss **06** bigwig, ganger, honcho **07** foreman, manager, overman **08** overseer **09** big cheese **10** supervisor **14** superintendent

**gag**
**03** pun **04** clog, curb, hoax, jest, joke, plug, pong, quip **05** block, check, choke, crack, funny, heave, quiet, retch, still **06** muffle, muzzle, stifle, wheeze **07** deceive, silence, smother **08** one-liner, restrain, suppress, throttle **09** put a gag on, wisecrack, witticism **11** nearly vomit

**gaga**
**03** mad **04** nuts **05** barmy, batty, crazy, dotty, loony, loopy, potty **06** cuckoo, insane, raving **07** fatuous **08** demented, deranged, doolally, unhinged **09** disturbed **10** distracted, unbalanced **11** not all there, off the rails **12** mad as a hatter **13** off your rocker **14** wrong in the head

**Gaia**
**05** Terra

**gaiety**
**03** fun, joy **04** glee, show **05** mirth **06** colour, frolic, racket **07** daffing, delight, frolics, gayness, glitter, jollity, joyance, revelry, sparkle **08** buoyancy, gladness, hilarity, pleasure, vivacity **09** festivity, happiness, joviality, merriment, showiness **10** blitheness, brightness, brilliance, exuberance, good humour, liveliness **11** celebration, galliardise, high spirits, joie de vivre, merrymaking **12** cheerfulness **13** colourfulness

**gaily**
**07** happily, merrily **08** blithely, brightly, joyfully **10** cheerfully **11** brilliantly, colourfully **12** flamboyantly **14** light-heartedly

**gain**
**03** add, ern, get, nab, net, win **04** earn, make, near, nett, reap, rise **05** bunce, carry, clear, get to, gross, put on, reach, yield **06** attain, collar, come to, gather, growth, income, obtain, pick up, profit, rake in, return, reward, secure **07** achieve, acquire, advance, benefit, bring in, capture, collect, harvest, headway, improve, procure, produce, realize, revenue, takings **08** addition, arrive at, dividend, earnings, increase, interest, pickings, proceeds, progress, straight, winnings **09** accretion, advantage, emolument, increment **10** attainment, chevisance, convenient **11** achievement, acquisition, advancement, improvement **12** augmentation
**• gain on**
**07** catch up **08** approach, overtake **09** catch up on, close in on, close with, level with **11** catch up with, get closer to, get nearer to, outdistance **12** narrow the gap
**• gain time**
**05** delay, stall **09** temporize **10** dilly-dally **11** play for time **12** drag your feet **13** procrastinate
**• seek to gain**
**03** woo **09** cultivate

**gainful**
**04** paid **06** paying, useful **08** fruitful **09** fructuous, lucrative, rewarding **10** beneficial, productive, profitable, worthwhile **11** moneymaking **12** advantageous, remunerative

**gainfully**
**08** usefully **10** profitably **11** lucratively **12** beneficially, productively **14** advantageously

**gainsay**
**04** deny **06** oppose **07** dispute **09** challenge, disaffirm **10** contradict, contravene, controvert **12** disagree with

**gait**
**03** get **04** brat, gyte, pace, step, walk **05** child, going, tread **06** allure, manner, stride **07** bearing **08** carriage **10** deportment

**gaiter**
**04** spat **06** hogger **07** cutikin, spattee **08** cootikin, cuitikin **11** spatterdash

**gala**
**04** fair, fete **05** party **07** jubilee, pageant **08** carnival, festival, jamboree **09** festivity **10** procession **11** celebration

**galaxy**
**04** host, mass **05** array, stars **06** blazar, nebula **07** cluster **09** gathering, multitude **10** collection, star system **11** solar system **13** constellation, group assembly

*Galaxies include:*

**03** Leo
**04** Arp's, Lost, Mice
**05** Bode's, Helix, Malin
**06** Baade's, Carafe, Hydra A, Maffei, Spider, Virgo A, Zwicky

**07** Cannon's, Cygnus A, Pancake, Sextans, Spindle, The Eyes
**08** Antennae, Barnard's, Bear's Paw, Black Eye, Milky Way, Papillon, Perseus A, Pinwheel, Seashell, Sombrero
**09** Andromeda, Bear's Claw, Cartwheel, Centaurus, Hercules A, Sunflower, Whirlpool
**10** Draco Dwarf, Silver Coin, The Garland, Triangulum
**11** Carina Dwarf, Hardcastle's, Pisces Cloud, Pisces Dwarf, The Ringtail
**12** Atom For Peace, Integral Sign, Pegasus Dwarf, Siamese Twins, Virgo Cluster
**13** Aquarius Dwarf, Sculptor Dwarf, Serpens Sextet, Virgo Pinwheel
**14** Capricorn Dwarf, Copeland Septet, Reticulum Dwarf, Ursa Minor Dwarf
**15** Exclamation Mark, Horologium Dwarf, Magellanic Cloud, Miniature Spiral

---

**gale**
**03** fit **04** wind **05** blast, burst, storm **06** Myrica, squall, wester **07** cyclone, norther, sea turn, snorter, souther, tornado, typhoon **08** eruption, outbreak, outburst **09** bog myrtle, explosion, hurricane, sou'wester **10** ripsnorter **11** equinoctial, sweet willow

**gall**
**03** irk, nag, vex **04** bile, dyke, fell, flaw, neck, rile **05** annoy, brass, cheek, fault, get to, nerve, peeve, scoff, spite, venom **06** animus, bother, enmity, harass, malice, nettle, oak-nut, pester, plague, rankle, ruffle **07** ill-will, provoke, rancour **08** acrimony, bedeguar, chutzpah, irritate, oak apple, sourness, tacahout **09** aggravate, animosity, antipathy, assurance, brass neck, hostility, impudence, insolence, sage apple, sauciness, virulence **10** bitterness, brazenness, effrontery, exasperate **11** malevolence, presumption **12** impertinence, mycodomatium **13** get on your wick, get up your nose, get your back up, put your back up

**gallant**
**03** fop, gay **04** beau, bold **05** brave, dandy, lover, manly, noble **06** daring, heroic, plucky, polite **07** amorous, courtly, dashing, valiant **08** cavalier, cicisbeo, fearless, gracious, intrepid, splendid **09** attentive, audacious, chamberer, chevalier, chivalric, courteous, dauntless **10** chivalrous, courageous, honourable, thoughtful **11** considerate, gentlemanly, magnificent

**gallantly**
**05** nobly **07** bravely **08** politely **09** valiantly **10** fearlessly, graciously, heroically, honourably, intrepidly **11** audaciously, courteously, dauntlessly **12** chivalrously, courageously, thoughtfully **13** considerately

**gallantry**
**04** game **05** pluck **06** daring, honour, spirit, valour **07** bravery, courage, heroism **08** audacity, boldness, chivalry, courtesy, nobility, valiance **09** manliness **10** politeness **11** courtliness, intrepidity **12** fearlessness, graciousness **13** attentiveness, consideration, courteousness, dauntlessness **14** courageousness, thoughtfulness **15** gentlemanliness

**gallery**
**04** brow, gods, loft, mine, pawn, walk **05** alure, level **06** arcade, circle, dedans, museum **07** balcony, passage, terrace, veranda **08** bartisan, bartizan, brattice, brattish, brettice, casemate, rood loft, traverse, verandah **09** choir loft, triforium **10** art gallery, earth-house, hall of fame, pinakothek, scaffolage, spectators **11** display room, dress circle, pinacotheca, scaffoldage **14** exhibition area

*See also* **museum**

**galley** *see* **ship**

**galling**
**06** bitter, vexing **07** irksome **08** annoying, nettling, plaguing, rankling **09** harassing, provoking, vexatious **10** bothersome, irritating **11** aggravating, embittering, humiliating, infuriating **12** exasperating

**gallium**
**02** Ga

**gallivant**
**04** roam, rove **05** range, stray **06** ramble, travel, wander **07** traipse **08** dot about, gad about, stravaig **09** flit about, run around

**gallon**
**01** g **03** gal **04** cong, gall **07** congius

**gallop**
**03** fly, run **04** bolt, dart, dash, race, rush, tear, zoom **05** burst, hurry, shoot, speed **06** canter, career, hasten, scurry, sprint, wallop **07** cariere

**gallows**
**03** nub **04** tree, wild **05** bough, cheat, perky, saucy **06** daring, gallus, gibbet, plucky, woodie **07** stifler, the rope **08** damnably, dule-tree, impudent, scaffold, spirited, tiresome **09** sprightly **10** Tyburn-tree, villainous **11** mischievous **12** confoundedly, nubbing-cheat, unmanageable

**galore**
**06** lots of, plenty, tons of **07** aplenty, heaps of, to spare **08** stacks of **09** in numbers **10** everywhere, millions of **11** in abundance, in profusion

**galvanize**
**04** fire, jolt, move, prod, spur, stir, urge, zinc **05** rouse, shock **06** arouse, awaken, excite **07** animate, enliven, inspire, provoke, quicken, startle **08** energize, vitalize **09** electrify, stimulate **10** invigorate

**Gambia**
**03** GMB, WAG

**gambit**
**04** move, play, ploy, ruse, wile **05** trick **06** device, tactic **07** tactics **08** artifice **09** manoeuvre, stratagem **11** machination

**gamble**
**03** bet **04** back, dice, gaff, game, jeff, play, punt, risk, spec **05** stake, wager **06** chance, hazard, plunge, toss-up **07** flutter, lottery, pot luck, venture **08** chance it **09** speculate, take a risk **10** put money on **11** speculation, take a chance, try your luck **12** have a flutter, play for money **13** leap in the dark, play the horses

**gambler**
**06** better, punter **07** plunger, tinhorn, tipster **08** gamester **09** bookmaker, daredevil, desperado, risk-taker, throwster **14** turf accountant

**gambling**
**04** play **07** betting **10** risk-taking **11** speculation **15** playing for money

*Gambling-related terms include:*

**03** hit, lay, pot
**04** back, bust, dice, hold, odds, punt, shoe, tout
**05** bingo, cards, craps, jeton, lotto, motza, poker, pools, stake, stick, wager, welsh
**06** bookie, casino, chip in, fan-tan, fulham, gaming, jetton, lay off, motser, punter
**07** flutter, lottery, tipster
**08** levanter, long shot, outsider, roulette, teetotum
**09** blackjack, bookmaker, card shark, dog racing, favourite, place a bet, vingt-et-un
**10** put-and-take, put money on, sweepstake
**11** card-sharper, find the lady, go one better, horse racing, numbers game, rouge-et-noir, slot machine
**12** break the bank, card counting, debt of honour, pitch-and-toss, scoop the pool
**13** hedge your bets, shoot the works, spread betting
**14** shove-halfpenny, three-card trick, wheel of fortune
**15** cash in your chips, disorderly house, greyhound racing, make a clean sweep

---

*See also* **bet**

• **gambling place**
**04** hell **06** arcade, casino

**gambol**
◇ *anagram indicator*
**03** hop **04** jump, leap, romp, skip **05** bound, caper, dance, frisk **06** bounce, cavort, frolic, prance,

spring **07** disport **09** cut a caper, cut capers **15** kick up your heels

**game**

**03** bag, fun, jeu, pit, tie **04** ball, bold, bout, jest, joke, lame, meat, meet, play, prey, romp **05** brave, eager, event, flesh, match, prank, ready, round, sport, trick, up for **06** daring, frolic, gamble, plucky, quarry, spoils **07** contest, gallant, meeting, pastime, valiant, willing **08** activity, business, desirous, fearless, inclined, intrepid, prepared, resolute, spirited, wild fowl **09** amusement, diversion, gallantry, merriment, operation **10** courageous, interested, recreation, tournament **11** competition, distraction, lion-hearted, unflinching **12** enthusiastic **13** entertainment, practical joke

*Game animals and birds include:*

**03** elk, fox
**04** bear, boar, coot, deer, duck, guan, hare, lion, stag, teal, wolf
**05** bison, goose, hyena, moose, quail, scaup, snipe, tiger, zebra
**06** curlew, grouse, plover, rabbit, wigeon
**07** buffalo, caribou, giraffe, mallard, moorhen, muntjac, pintail, pochard, red deer, roe deer, widgeon
**08** antelope, elephant, kangaroo, pheasant, sika deer, squirrel, wild boar, woodcock
**09** blackcock, blackgame, crocodile, partridge, ptarmigan, waterfowl
**10** fallow deer, guinea fowl, tufted duck, wild turkey, wood grouse, woodpigeon
**11** Canada goose
**12** capercaillie, capercailzie, hippopotamus, mountain lion

*See also* **poultry**

*Games include:*

**03** loo, nap
**04** brag, crib, dice, faro, I-spy, ludo, pool, snap
**05** bowls, chess, clubs, craps, darts, halma, jacks, Jenga®, poker, rummy, whist
**06** bridge, Cluedo®, quinze
**07** bezique, bowling, canasta, hangman, mah-jong, marbles, old maid, picquet, pinball, pontoon, snooker
**08** baccarat, card game, charades, checkers, cribbage, dominoes, draughts, forfeits, gin rummy, Kim's game, Monopoly®, napoleon, patience, ping pong, reversis, roulette, sardines, Scrabble®
**09** bagatelle, billiards, blackjack, board game, draw poker, hopscotch, newmarket, Pelmanism, Simon says, solitaire, solo whist, stud poker, tic-tac-toe, twenty-one, vingt-et-un
**10** backgammon, Balderdash®, fivestones, jackstraws, Pictionary®, spillikins
**11** battleships, beetle drive, chemin de fer, hide-and-seek, table tennis, tiddlywinks
**12** consequences, partner whist, shove ha'penny
**13** blind man's buff, clock patience, happy families, musical chairs, pass the parcel, postman's knock, spin the bottle, table football, ten-pin bowling
**14** contract bridge, follow-my-leader, hunt-the-thimble, nine men's morris, Trivial Pursuit®
**15** Chinese checkers, Chinese whispers, duplicate bridge

*Board games include:*

**02** go
**04** ludo, Risk®, siga
**05** chess, darts, goose, halma, lurch, marls, nyout, senet, shogi, Sorry®
**06** Boggle®, Cluedo®, gobang, gomuku, merels, merils, morals, morris, tables, tabula, uckers
**07** Cranium®, mah-jong, mancala, marrels, merells, pachisi, petteia, reverse, reversi, Yahtzee
**08** checkers, chequers, cribbage, Dingbats®, draughts, miracles, Monopoly®, parchesi, Rummikub®, Scrabble®
**09** bagatelle, Buccaneer®, Operation®, Parcheesi®, solitaire, tic-tac-toe
**10** backgammon, Go for Broke®, latrunculi, Mastermind®, Pictionary®
**11** Battleships®, fox and geese, Frustration®
**12** pente grammai
**13** Concentration®, table skittles, The Game of Life®
**14** nine men's morris, Trivial Pursuit®
**15** Chinese checkers, Chinese chequers, duodecim scripta, fivepenny morris, ninepenny morris, three men's morris

*See also* **sport**

*Card games include:*

**03** don, nap, pig, war
**04** brag, bust, faro, fish, golf, king, loba, may I?, phat, pits, push, rook, scat, skat, snap, solo, spit, tunk, tute, ugly
**05** blitz, cheat, cinch, crash, flush, knack, nerts, pairs, pedro, pitch, poker, ronda, rummy, samba, shoot, speed, tarok, tarot, whist
**06** big two, boodle, bridge, casino, church, crates, cuckoo, dakota, deuces, écarté, euchre, fan tan, five up, go fish, hearts, henway, kaiser, knaves, oh hell!, palace, pepper, piquet, pounce, red dog, sevens, spades, spoons, squeal, stitch, switch, tarock, taroky, trumps, turtle, valets
**07** auction, authors, bezique, bone ace, canasta, clabber, last one, mah jong, old maid, pontoon, quartet, setback, spitzer, whipsaw
**08** ace-deuce, all fives, all fours, anaconda, baccarat, bid whist, blackout, carousel, cribbage, drunkard, elevator, gin rummy, high five, Michigan, napoleon, patience, pinochle, Pope Joan, sequence, shanghai, Welsh don
**09** abyssinia, bid euchre, blackjack, catch five, golden ten, king pedro, king rummy, let it ride, newmarket, Pelmanism, poker bull, president, quadrille, racehorse, solitaire, solo whist, stud poker, tic-tac-toe, tile rummy, vingt-et-un
**10** black maria, buck euchre, capitalism, chinese ten, cincinnati, crazy nines, dirty clubs, German solo, parliament, preference, ride the bus, sheepshead, strip poker, three in one, Wall Street
**11** cat and mouse, chase the ace, chemin de fer, chicken foot, crazy eights, English stud, find the lady, French tarot, French whist, German whist, high-low-jack, Indian poker, Mexican stud, nine-card don, Oklahoma gin, racing demon, Russian bank, six-card brag, speculation, Texas hold 'em
**12** Chinese poker, devil's bridge, draw dominoes, five-card brag, five-card draw, four-card brag, high-card pool, kings corners, Mexican sweat, Mexican train, nine-card brag, one and thirty, pick a partner, ruff and trump, Russian poker, shoot pontoon
**13** concentration, contract rummy, contract whist, happy families, knockout whist, lame-brain Pete, Michigan rummy, Romanian whist, sergeant major, seven-card brag, Shanghai rummy, three-card brag
**14** Caribbean poker, contract bridge, five hundred rum, fives and threes, follow the queen, good, better, best, jack the shifter, Liverpool rummy, Minnesota whist, rich man, poor man, ruff and honours, second hand high, spite and malice, spit in the ocean, three-card monte, trust–don't trust
**15** back alley bridge, cut-throat euchre, double solitaire, nomination whist, railroad canasta, stealing bundles

• **end to game**
**04** draw, mate **09** checkmate, stalemate

• **point out game**
**03** set

• **preliminary to game**
**04** toss

• **right to begin game**
**04** pose

**gamekeeper**

**06** keeper, warden **07** venerer

**gamely**

**06** boldly **07** bravely **09** valiantly
**10** fearlessly, intrepidly, resolutely
**12** courageously **13** unflinchingly

**gamut**
**04** area **05** field, gamme, range, scale, scope, sweep **06** series **07** compass, variety **08** sequence, spectrum

**gang**
**02** go **03** lot, mob, set **04** band, club, core, crew, crue, ging, herd, nest, pack, push, ring, team **05** coven, crowd, group, horde, party, posse, shift, squad **06** circle, clique, coffle, outfit, troupe **07** company, coterie, massive, ratpack **09** gathering **11** tribulation

• **gang up on, gang up against**
**12** unite against **13** team up against **15** conspire against

**gangling**
**04** bony, tall **05** gawky, lanky, rangy **06** gangly, gauche, skinny **07** angular, awkward, spindly **08** raw-boned, ungainly **12** loose-jointed

**gangrene**
**07** mortify **08** necrosis **09** phagedena **10** phagedaena, thanatosis

**gangster**
**02** Al **04** hood, thug **05** crook, heavy, rough, tough **06** bandit, Capone, robber, yakuza, Yardie **07** brigand, gangsta, goombah, greaser, hoodlum, mobster, ruffian, steamer, tumbler, wise guy **08** criminal, enforcer **09** desperado, goodfella, racketeer, terrorist

**gangway**
**04** brow **05** aisle **07** passage, walkway **08** corridor **10** passageway

**gannet**
**04** guga **05** booby, solan **10** solan goose

**gaol, gaoler** *see* **jail, gaol**; **jailer, gaoler**

**gap**
**04** gulf, hole, lack, leap, lull, rent, rift, rima, slap, void **05** blank, break, chasm, chink, cleft, crack, gorge, musit, notch, pause, shard, sherd, space **06** breach, bunker, cavity, cranny, divide, hiatus, lacuna, recess, spread, street, window **07** crevice, opening, orifice, passage, saw gate, saw kerf, vacancy, vacuity **08** aperture, distance, fontanel, fracture, interval, sliprail **09** disparity, interlude **10** difference, divergence, fontanelle, interstice, separation **12** intermission, interruption **13** discontinuity, node of Ranvier **14** expansion joint

**gape**
**04** bawl, gaup, gawk, gawp, gaze, open, part, yawn **05** crack, gerne, split, stare **06** goggle, rictus, wonder **07** dehisce **10** rubberneck

**gaper**
**03** Mya **06** comber

**gaping**
**04** open, vast, wide **05** broad, hiant **06** rictus **07** ringent, yawning **09** cavernous, fatiscent, interrupt **11** open-mouthed **12** fissirostral

**garage**
**04** barn **06** lock-up **07** car port **10** gas station **11** muffler shop **13** petrol station **14** service station

**garb**
**03** rig **04** form, gear, look, robe, togs, vest, wear **05** array, cover, dress, get-up, guise, robes, style **06** aspect, attire, clothe, livery, outfit, rig out, rig-out **07** apparel, clobber, clothes, costume, fashion, garment, raiment, regalia, uniform, vesture **08** clothing **09** semblance, vestiment, vestments **10** appearance, habiliment, habilitate

**garbage**
**03** rot **04** blah, bosh, bull, bunk, cock, crap, guff, junk, muck **05** balls, bilge, dross, filth, hooey, slops, swill, trash, tripe, waste **06** bunkum, debris, drivel, hot air, litter, piffle, refuse, scraps **07** baloney, eyewash, hogwash, remains, rhubarb, rubbish, twaddle **08** claptrap, cobblers, detritus, malarkey, nonsense, tommyrot **09** gibberish, leftovers, moonshine, poppycock, scourings, sweepings **10** codswallop **11** odds and ends **13** bits and pieces

**garble**
◇ *anagram indicator*
**04** edit, sift, warp **05** mix up, slant, twist **06** doctor, jumble, mangle, muddle **07** cleanse, confuse, corrupt, distort, falsify, pervert **08** mutilate, scramble **10** tamper with **12** misinterpret, misrepresent

**garbled**
◇ *anagram indicator*
**07** jumbled, mixed-up, muddled **08** confused **09** scrambled **14** undecipherable, unintelligible

**garden**
**03** erf **04** bagh, park, plot, yard **05** garth **06** herbar **08** backyard, paradise **09** curtilage

*Gardens include:*

**03** Kew
**04** Eden, Ness
**05** Stowe
**06** Het Loo, Monet's, Suzhou, Tivoli, Wisley
**07** Alnwick, Bodnant, Boxwood, Giverny, Heligan, Kane'ohe, Motsuji, Urakuen
**08** Alhambra, Biltmore, Blenheim, Claymont, Ermitage, Hopewood, Hyde Hall, Longwood, Mt Vernon, Nanzenji, Pleasure, Rikugien, Rosedown, Rosemoor, Sankeien
**09** Bagatelle, Claremont, Lingering, Lion Grove, Stourhead, Tuileries
**10** Capel Manor, Chatsworth, Harlow Carr, Kensington, Levens Hall, Schönbrunn, Versailles
**11** Chanticleer, Eden Project, Ji Chang Yuan
**12** Castle Howard, Hampton Court, Hidcote Manor, Jingshan Park, Katsura Rikyu, Royal Botanic, Sissinghurst, Studley Royal
**13** Dumbarton Oaks, Harewood House, Orange Botanic, Vaux le Vicomte
**14** Biddulph Grange, Drummond Castle, Hua Ching Palace, Stone Lion Grove
**15** Arnold Arboretum

*Garden types include:*

**03** tea
**04** beer, herb, knot, lawn, rock, roof, rose
**05** arbor, fruit, water
**06** alpine, arbour, border, flower, herbar, indoor, market, physic, rosary, rosery, sunken, walled, winter
**07** cottage, hanging, Italian, kitchen, olitory, orchard, rockery, rose bed
**08** chinampa, Japanese, kailyard, rosarium
**09** allotment, arboretum, botanical, cole-garth, flower bed, kailyaird, raised bed, shrubbery, terrarium, truck-farm, window box
**10** ornamental, rose arbour
**13** plantie-cruive, vegetable plot

**gardener**
**03** Eve **04** Adam, mali **06** mallee **07** trucker

*Gardeners include:*

**03** **Don** (Monty)
**04** **Kent** (William), **Page** (Russell)
**05** **Brown** (Lancelot 'Capability'), **Gavin** (Diarmuid), **Lloyd** (Christopher), **Monet** (Claude), **Wilde** (Kim)
**06** **Gilpin** (William Sawrey), **Ingram** (Collingwood 'Cherry'), **Jekyll** (Gertrude), **Paxton** (Sir Joseph), **Repton** (Humphry)
**07** **Clusius** (Carolus), **Dimmock** (Charlie), **Le Nôtre** (André), **Thrower** (Percy)
**08** **Hamilton** (Geoff), **Jellicoe** (Sir Geoffrey), **Robinson** (William)
**10** **Titchmarsh** (Alan), **Tradescant** (John, the Elder), **Tradescant** (John, the Younger)
**13** **Sackville-West** (Vita)

**garden flower** *see* **flower**

**gardening**

*Gardening tools include:*

**03** axe, hoe
**04** fork, pots, rake
**05** Flymo®, spade
**06** cloche, gloves, scythe, shears, trowel
**07** fan rake, hatchet, kneeler, loppers, netting, pruners, trellis, wellies
**08** chainsaw, clippers, hosepipe, shredder, strimmer
**09** cold frame, fruit cage, garden saw, lawn edger, lawnmower, lawn raker, secateurs, sprinkler, water butt
**10** compost bin, cultivator, fertilizer, garden cart, greenhouse, lawn

roller, soil tester, weedkiller
**11** incinerator, watering can, wheelbarrow
**12** hedge trimmer, potting table
**13** garden sprayer, lawn scarifier
**14** rotary spreader

*Gardening-related terms include:*

**03** bed
**04** bulb, clay, loam, plot, seed, soil, tree, weed
**05** bower, graft, hedge, mulch, plant, shrub
**06** annual, hoeing, hybrid, manure, raking
**07** climber, compost, cutting, digging, growing, organic, produce, pruning, staking, topiary, topsoil, weeding
**08** gardener, layering, planting, thinning, watering
**09** deciduous, germinate, leaf-mould, perennial, pesticide
**10** coniferous, fertilizer, hardy plant
**11** cultivation, green manure, ground cover, hydroponics, potting shed, propagation
**12** bedding plant, conservatory, horticulture, hybrid vigour
**13** double digging, growing season, transplanting
**15** window gardening

**Gardner**
**03** Ava

**gargantuan**
**03** big **04** huge, vast **05** giant, large **07** immense, mammoth, massive, titanic **08** colossal, enormous, gigantic, towering **09** ginormous, humongous, humungous, leviathan, monstrous **10** monumental, prodigious, tremendous **11** elephantine **14** Brobdingnagian

**garish**
**04** heal, loud, rory **05** cheap, flash, gaudy, jazzy, lurid, roary, rorie, showy **06** criant, flashy, glitzy, roarie, tawdry, vulgar **07** glaring, raffish **08** luminous, tinselly **09** flaunting, tasteless **10** glittering **12** meretricious

**garishly**
**06** loudly **07** gaudily, jazzily, luridly **08** glitzily **09** glaringly **11** tastelessly

**garland**
**03** lei **04** bays, deck **05** adorn, crown, glory, toran **06** crants, stemma, torana, wreath **07** chaplet, coronal, coronet, festoon, flowers, girlond, honours, laurels, wreathe **08** decorate, headband, ornament **09** engarland **10** decoration, naval crown

**garments**
**04** garb, gear, togs, wear **05** dress, get-up **06** attire, outfit **07** apparel, clothes, costume, uniform **08** clothing, menswear
*See also* **clothes, clothing**

**garner**
**04** cull, heap, save **05** amass, hoard, lay up, put by, store **06** gather, pile up **07** collect, deposit, granary, husband, reserve, stack up **08** assemble, stow away, treasure **09** stockpile **10** accumulate

**garnet**
**06** pyrope **08** melanite **09** almandine, andradite, carbuncle, demantoid, grossular, pyreneite, rhodolite, uvarovite **10** alabandine, topazolite **11** schorlomite, spessartine, spessartite **12** grossularite **13** cinnamon stone **14** Uralian emerald

**garnish**
**04** deck, lard, trim **05** adorn, grace **06** kit out, relish, set off, supply **07** deck out, enhance, festoon, furnish **08** beautify, decorate, ornament, trimming **09** adornment, embellish, gremolata **10** decoration **11** enhancement **13** embellishment, ornamentation

**garret**
**04** loft **05** attic, roost, solar **06** turret **07** mansard **09** roof space **10** watchtower

**garrison**
**03** man **04** base, camp, fort, post, unit **05** guard, mount, place, stuff **06** assign, casern, defend, occupy, troops, zareba **07** command, furnish, protect, station **08** barracks, fortress, position **10** armed force, detachment, encampment, engarrison, stronghold **13** fortification

**garrulous**
**04** glib **05** gabby, gassy, windy, wordy **06** chatty, mouthy, prolix **07** gushing, prating, verbose, voluble, wordish **08** babbling, effusive, gaggling **09** gossiping, prattling, talkative, yabbering **10** chattering, long-winded, loquacious

**garrulousness**
**09** loquacity, prolixity, verbosity **10** mouthiness, volubility **11** verboseness, wordishness **13** talkativeness **14** long-windedness, loquaciousness

**gas**

*Gases include:*

**02** CS
**03** air, LNG, LPG
**04** neon, tear, town
**05** ether, marsh, nerve, niton, ozone, radon, xenon
**06** butane, helium, ketene
**07** ammonia, krypton, methane, mustard, natural, propane
**08** cyanogen, ethylene, firedamp, laughing
**09** acetylene, black damp, chokedamp
**10** chloroform
**12** nitrous oxide
**13** carbon dioxide, dimethylamine
**14** carbon monoxide

*See also* **talk**

**gash**
**03** cut **04** hack, nick, rend, rent, slit, tear **05** extra, gouge, score, slash, spare, split, wound **06** incise, scotch, tattle **07** ghastly, hideous **08** incision, lacerate **09** talkative **10** laceration

**gasp**
**04** blow, gulp, kink, pant, puff **05** chink, choke, heave **06** breath, wheeze **07** breathe **11** exclamation **15** catch your breath

**gassy**
**06** bubbly, frothy **07** aerated, foaming, gaseous, verbose **08** bubbling **09** sparkling **10** carbonated **12** effervescent

**gastric**
**07** coeliac, enteric, stomach **09** abdominal, stomachic **10** intestinal

**gastropod** *see* **mollusc**

**gate**
**03** way **04** door, exit, goat, path, port, yate, yett **05** hatch, koker **06** access, portal, street, vimana, wicket **07** barrier, caisson, channel, doorway, gateway, opening, passage, pontoon, postern, shutter **08** aboideau, aboiteau, entrance, sliprail
*See also* **circuit**

**gatecrash**
**04** sorn

**gateway**
**04** arch, port **05** pylon, toran, torii **06** torana **08** propylon **09** sallyport **10** propylaeum

**gather**
◇ *containment indicator*
**02** in **03** add **04** camp, club, crop, cull, draw, fold, gain, grow, heap, hear, mass, meet, pick, pull, rake, reap, tuck **05** amass, build, crowd, flock, get in, glean, group, hoard, infer, learn, pleat, pluck, rally, shirr **06** assume, deduce, garner, muster, pick up, pile up, pucker, pull in, rake in, ruffle, select, summon, throng **07** accrete, advance, attract, believe, build up, cluster, collect, convene, develop, harvest, hoard up, improve, marshal, round up, surmise **08** assemble, conclude, converge, increase, progress **09** stash away, stockpile, suppurate **10** accumulate, congregate, understand **12** come together **13** bring together

**gathering**
◇ *containment indicator*
**03** bee, hui, lek, mob **04** band, feis, fest, mass, meet, rave, rout, ruck, shir **05** coven, crowd, flock, group, hangi, horde, party, rally, salon, shirr, spree **06** huddle, love-in, muster, rabble, social, throng **07** company, gabfest, husking, Kommers, meeting, reunion, round-up, turnout **08** assembly, conclave, function, jamboree, musicale, singsong, tea party **09** wapenshaw, wapinshaw **10** assemblage, collective, convention,

corroboree, logrolling, wapenschaw, wapinschaw, wappenshaw
**11** convocation, gallimaufry, get-together, wappenschaw
**12** congregation **14** belle assemblée

**gauche**
**03** shy **05** gawky, inept **06** clumsy
**07** awkward, ill-bred **08** farouche, ignorant, tactless, ungainly
**09** graceless, inelegant, maladroit
**10** uncultured, ungraceful, unpolished
**11** ill-mannered, insensitive
**15** unsophisticated

**gaudiness**
**08** loudness **09** harshness, showiness
**10** brightness, brilliance, flashiness, garishness, tawdriness **11** raffishness
**13** tastelessness

**gaudy**
**03** gay **04** loud **05** flash, harsh, merry, showy, stark, tacky **06** bright, flashy, garish, glitzy, kitsch, snazzy, tawdry, tinsel, vulgar **07** flaming, glaring, raffish **08** tinselly **09** brilliant, colourful, flaunting, shrieking, tasteless, too bright **12** meretricious, ostentatious **13** multicoloured

**gauge**
**04** area, bore, norm, rate, rule, size, span, test **05** basic, check, count, depth, guess, guide, judge, meter, model, scale, scope, sizer, value, weigh, width **06** assess, degree, extent, figure, height, reckon, sample
**07** apprise, calibre, compute, example, measure, pattern, scantle **08** capacity, estimate, evaluate, exemplar, standard
**09** ascertain, benchmark, calculate, criterion, determine, guideline, indicator, magnitude, marijuana, scantling, thickness, yardstick
**11** guesstimate

*Gauges include:*

**03** oil
**04** rain, ring, snap, tide, tyre, wind
**05** drill, paper, steam, taper, water
**06** feeler, radius, strain, vacuum
**07** Bourdon, cutting, loading, marking, mortise
**08** gauge rod, pressure, udometer
**09** Nilometer
**10** anemometer, gauge glass, gauge wheel, hyetograph, hyetometer, micrometer, ombrometer, planometer, touchstone
**11** pluviometer
**15** hyetometrograph

**gaunt**
**04** bare, bony, grim, lank, lean, thin, yawn **05** bleak, harsh, stark **06** barren, dismal, dreary, skinny, wasted
**07** angular, forlorn, haggard, rawbone, scraggy, scrawny, spindly **08** desolate, rawboned, skeletal **09** emaciated
**10** cadaverous, forbidding, hollow-eyed **12** skin and bones

**Gauss**
**01** G **02** gs

**gauze**
**04** film **07** tiffany **08** illusion
**11** cheesecloth

**gauzy**
**04** thin **05** filmy, light, sheer **06** flimsy
**08** delicate, gossamer **10** diaphanous, see-through **11** transparent
**13** insubstantial, unsubstantial

**gawk**
**04** gape, gawp, gaze, look, ogle
**05** stare **06** goggle

**gawky**
**05** inept, lanky **06** clumsy, gauche, oafish **07** awkward, loutish
**08** gangling, ungainly **09** graceless, lumbering, maladroit **13** uncoordinated

**gawp**
**04** gape, gawk, gaze, look, ogle
**05** stare **06** goggle

**gay**
**04** camp, pink, rich **05** gaudy, happy, jolly, merry, nitid, riant, showy, sunny, vivid **06** blithe, bright, flashy, garish, joyful, lively, wanton **07** festive, gallant, lesbian, playful, sapphic, spotted
**08** animated, bisexual, carefree, cheerful, debonair, speckled
**09** brilliant, colourful, exuberant, fun-loving, homophile, sparkling, sprightly, vivacious **10** dissipated, flamboyant, homosexual **12** light-hearted **13** in good spirits, in high spirits **15** pleasure-seeking

**gaze**
**03** eye **04** gape, gawk, look, moon, muse, pore, view **05** stare, watch
**06** goggle, regard, wonder
**08** aftereye, gazement, outstare, wait upon **09** fixed look, moon about
**10** moon around **11** contemplate
**12** look vacantly, stare fixedly **13** stare intently

**gazebo**
**03** hut **07** shelter **08** pavilion
**09** belvedere **11** summerhouse

**gazelle**
**03** goa **04** mohr **05** ariel, mhorr
**07** chikara **08** chinkara

**gazette**
**03** gaz **05** organ, paper **06** notice
**07** journal, tabloid **08** despatch, dispatch, magazine **09** newspaper, news-sheet **10** broadsheet, periodical

**gear**
**03** cog, fit, kit, low, top **04** garb, togs
**05** adapt, dress, drugs, first, get-up, shift, stuff, third, tools, works **06** affair, armour, attire, design, devise, doings, matter, outfit, second, tackle, tailor, things **07** apparel, baggage, clobber, clothes, effects, gearing, harness, luggage, prepare, ratchet, reverse, threads **08** business, clothing, cogwheel, garments, organize, supplies, utensils **09** apparatus, engrenage, equipment, gearwheel, machinery, mechanism **10** appliances, belongings, implements, link-motion, tooth-wheel, underdrive
**11** accessories, instruments, possessions, synchromesh
**12** contrivances, toothed wheel
**13** accoutrements, paraphernalia

*See also* **clothes, clothing**; **garments**

**geegee**
**02** GG

*See also* **horse**

**geezer**
**03** man **04** chap, cove **05** bloke
**06** fellow

**gel, jell**
**03** set **04** form **06** harden **07** congeal, stiffen, thicken **08** finalize, solidify
**09** coagulate, take shape **11** crystallize, materialize **12** come together

**gelatinous**
**05** gluey, gooey, gummy **06** sticky, viscid **07** jellied, rubbery, viscous
**09** congealed, glutinous, jelly-like
**12** mucilaginous

**geld**
**03** cut, lib, tax **04** sort, spay
**05** unman, unsex **06** neuter
**07** deprive **08** castrate, enfeeble
**09** expurgate **10** emasculate

**gem**
**03** bud **04** rose **05** cameo, jewel, prize, stone **06** scarab **08** gemstone, marquise, sparkler, treasure
**09** bespangle, brilliant, scaraboid
**11** masterpiece, pride and joy **12** the bee's knees **13** precious stone
**14** crème de la crème

*Gemstones include:*

**03** jet
**04** jade, onyx, opal, ruby
**05** agate, amber, beryl, coral, pearl, topaz
**06** garnet, jasper, zircon
**07** cat's eye, citrine, crystal, diamond, emerald, peridot
**08** amethyst, fire opal, sapphire, sunstone
**09** cairngorm, carbuncle, carnelian, cornelian, demantoid, malachite, marcasite, moonstone, morganite, soapstone, tiger's eye, turquoise, uvarovite
**10** aquamarine, bloodstone, chalcedony, chrysolite, rhinestone, rose quartz, serpentine, spinel ruby, tourmaline
**11** alexandrite, chrysoberyl, chrysoprase, lapis lazuli, spessartite
**13** cubic zirconia, mother-of-pearl, white sapphire

**gen**
**04** data, dope, info **05** facts **07** details, low-down **09** knowledge
**10** background **11** information

• **gen up on**
**05** study **08** bone up on, read up on, research, swot up on **09** brush up on
**12** find out about

**gene** *see* **genetics**

**genealogy**
**04** line **05** birth **06** family **07** dynasty **08** breeding **09** parentage, whakapapa **10** derivation, extraction **11** generations **13** family history

*Genealogy-related terms include:*

**03** DSP, IGI, née
**04** AGRA, clan, deed, heir, late, race, will
**05** issue, trace, widow
**06** census, degree, estate, legacy, relict
**07** archive, bastard, bequest, consort, descent, divorce, epitaph, kinship, lineage, peerage, probate, progeny, removed, surname, testate, trustee, widower, witness
**08** ancestor, ancestry, bachelor, bequeath, canon law, deceased, decedent, emigrant, forebear, maternal, paternal, pedigree, relation, spinster
**09** ascendant, given name, immigrant, indenture, intestate, necrology, offspring, sine prole, testament
**10** ahnentafal, descendant, family name, family tree, forefather, generation, maiden name, onomastics, progenitor, succession
**11** beneficiary, genealogist, record agent
**12** burial record, census record, cousin-german, Domesday Book, illegitimate, primogenitor, vital records
**13** Christian name, consanguinity, pedigree chart, primogeniture
**14** cemetery record, common ancestor, marriage record
**15** vital statistics

**general**
**05** broad, loose, mixed, rough, total, usual, vague **06** common, global, normal, public, varied **07** blanket, diverse, inexact, overall, popular, regular, typical **08** accepted, all-round, assorted, everyday, habitual, ordinary, standard, sweeping **09** customary, extensive, imprecise, panoramic, prevalent, universal **10** ill-defined, indefinite, prevailing, unspecific, variegated, widespread
**11** approximate, wide-ranging **12** all-inclusive, conventional
**13** comprehensive, heterogeneous, miscellaneous **14** across-the-board

*Generals include:*

**03** **Doe** (Samuel K), **Ike**, **Lee** (Robert E), **Ney** (Michel)
**04** **Alba** (Ferdinand Alvarez de Toledo, Duke of), **Alva** (Ferdinand Alvarez de Toledo, Duke of), **Asad** (Hafez al-), **Dyer** (Reginald), **Haig** (Alexander), **Prem** (Tinsulanonda)
**05** **Assad** (Hafez al-), **Booth** (William), **Clive** (Robert, Lord), **Gates** (Horatio), **Grant** (Ulysses S), **Scott** (Winfield), **Soult** (Nicolas Jean de Dieu), **Wolfe** (James)
**06** **Anders** (Wladyslaw), **Caesar** (Julius), **Custer** (George Armstrong), **Franco** (Francisco), **Moreau** (Jean Victor), **Napier** (Sir Charles), **Powell** (Colin), **Rommel** (Erwin), **Scipio** (the Younger), **Sharon** (Ariel), **Zhukov** (Georgi)
**07** **Agrippa** (Marcus Vipsanius), **Atatürk** (Mustapha Kemal), **Fairfax** (Thomas, Lord), **Masséna** (André), **Spínola** (António de)
**08** **Agricola** (Gnaeus Julius), **Badoglio** (Pietro), **Brisbane** (Sir Thomas Makdougall), **Camillus** (Marcus Furius), **Cardigan** (James Thomas Brudenell, Earl of), **de Gaulle** (Charles), **Hamilton** (Sir Ian Standish Monteith), **Hannibal**, **Montrose** (James Graham, Marquis of)
**09** **Antigonus**, **Aristides**, **Boulanger** (Georges), **MacArthur** (Douglas), **Omar Pasha**, **Santander** (Francisco de Paula), **Townshend** (George, Viscount and Marquess), **Townshend** (Sir Charles Vere Ferrers)
**10** **Abercromby** (Sir Ralph), **Eisenhower** (Dwight D 'Ike'), **Oglethorpe** (James Edward), **Timoshenko** (Semyon)
**11** **Baden-Powell** (Robert, Lord), **Jiang Jieshi**, **Schwarzkopf** (H Norman)
**12** **Clive of India**
**13** **Chiang Kai-shek**
**14** **Osman Nuri Pasha**

**General Electric**
**02** GE **03** GEC

**generality**
**03** run **04** bulk, many, most
**07** breadth, the many **08** majority
**09** broadness, looseness, nearly all, vagueness **10** commonness, larger part, popularity, prevalence
**11** catholicity, ecumenicity, greater part, inexactness **12** more than half, universality **13** extensiveness, impreciseness, miscellaneity
**14** generalization, indefiniteness
**15** approximateness

**generalization**
**09** looseness, vagueness
**11** inexactness **12** axioma medium, inexactitude **13** impreciseness
**14** indefiniteness **15** approximateness

**generalize**
**05** infer **06** assume, deduce
**08** conclude, theorize **11** standardize

**generally**
**06** mainly, mostly **07** as a rule, at large, broadly, chiefly, largely, overall, usually **08** commonly, normally **09** in general
**10** by and large, habitually, more or less, on the whole, ordinarily
**11** customarily, in most cases, universally **13** predominantly **14** for the most part

**generate**
◇ *anagram indicator*
**04** form, make **05** breed, cause, spawn **06** arouse, create, evolve, gender, whip up **07** produce **08** engender, initiate, occasion **09** originate, procreate, propagate **10** bring about, give rise to **11** give birth to **14** bring into being

**generation**
**03** age, era **04** days, kind, race, time
**05** class, epoch **06** family, period
**07** descent, genesis, progeny **08** age group, breeding, creation
**09** engendure, formation, offspring
**10** engendrure, production
**11** engendering, origination, procreation, propagation
**12** reproduction

**generic**
**04** wide **06** common **07** blanket, general **08** superior, sweeping
**09** inclusive, unbranded, universal
**10** collective **12** all-inclusive
**13** comprehensive, non-registered, untrademarked **14** non-proprietary, non-trademarked **15** all-encompassing

**generically**
**08** commonly **09** generally
**11** inclusively, universally **14** all-inclusively **15** comprehensively

**generosity**
**06** bounty **07** charity, largess
**08** goodness, kindness, largesse
**10** lavishness, liberality
**11** benevolence, magnanimity, munificence **12** philanthropy, selflessness **13** unselfishness **14** big-heartedness, open-handedness

**generous**
**03** big **04** free, full, good, kind, rich
**05** ample, large, lofty, noble, plump, roomy **06** giving, lavish **07** copious, liberal **08** abundant, handsome, menseful, selfless, sporting
**09** bounteous, bountiful, plentiful, unselfish, unsparing **10** altruistic, beneficent, benevolent, big-hearted, charitable, courageous, free-handed, high-minded, munificent, open-handed, unstinting **11** gentlemanly, magnanimous, open-hearted, overflowing, soft-hearted, warm-hearted **12** large-hearted, wholehearted **13** disinterested, philanthropic **14** public-spirited

**generously**
**05** amply, fully, nobly **06** freely, richly
**08** lavishly **09** copiously, liberally
**10** abundantly, charitably, handsomely, selflessly **11** bountifully, plentifully, unselfishly **12** open-handedly
**13** magnanimously

**genesis**
**03** Gen **04** dawn, root **05** birth, start
**06** origin, outset, source **08** creation, founding **09** beginning, formation, inception **10** foundation, generation, initiation, production **11** development, engendering, propagation
**12** commencement

**genetic**
**07** genomic **09** inherited **10** biological, hereditary **11** chromosomal

**genetics**
**06** origin **11** development

*Geneticists include:*

**05** Brown (Michael S), Jones (Steve), Leder (Philip), Ochoa (Severo), Sager (Ruth), Snell (George Davis)
**06** Beadle (George Wells), Biffen (Sir Rowland Harry), Bodmer (Sir Walter), Boveri (Theodor Heinrich), Cantor (Charles), Fisher (Sir Ronald Aylmer), Galton (Sir Francis), Gurdon (Sir John), Morgan (Thomas Hunt), Müller (Hermann Joseph), Zinder (Norton David)
**07** Bateson (William), Correns (Carl), De Vries (Hugo Marie), Gehring (Walter), Hopwood (Sir David), Lysenko (Trofim)
**08** Auerbach (Charlotte), Lewontin (Richard), Yanofsky (Charles)
**09** Baltimore (David), Goldstein (Joseph), Lederberg (Joshua)
**10** Darlington (Cyril Dean), Dobzhansky (Theodosius), Kettlewell (Henry Bernard David), McClintock (Barbara), Sturtevant (Alfred Henry), Waddington (C H), Weatherall (Sir David)
**12** Maynard Smith (John)

*Genetics-related terms include:*

**02** GM
**03** DNA, PCR, RNA
**04** base, gene
**05** allel, clone, codon, helix, sperm
**06** allele, gamete, genome, hybrid, intron, vector, zygote
**07** diploid, meiosis, mitosis
**08** autosome, dominant, heredity, mutation, promoter, sequence
**09** amino acid, homologue, inversion, karyotype, offspring, recessive, repressor, variation
**10** adaptation, chromosome, generation, geneticist, homozygous, nucleosome, nucleotide, polymerase, speciation
**11** double helix, epigenetics, genetic code, inheritance, nucleic acid, polypeptide, X-chromosome, Y-chromosome
**12** cell division, heterozygous, reproduction
**13** DNA sequencing, fertilization, recombination, transcription, translocation

**genial**
**04** kind, maty, mild, warm **05** happy, human, jolly, matey, pally, sunny
**06** chummy, hearty, jovial, kindly, mellow **07** affable, amiable, cordial
**08** amicable, cheerful, cheering, friendly, pleasant, sociable, sunshiny
**09** agreeable, convivial, easy-going, healthful **11** good-natured, sympathetic, warm-hearted **12** good-humoured

**geniality**
**06** warmth **07** jollity **08** bonhomie, gladness, kindness, sunshine
**09** happiness, joviality **10** affability, amiability, cheeriness, cordiality, good nature, kindliness **12** cheerfulness, conviviality, friendliness, pleasantness
**13** agreeableness, congenialness
**15** warm-heartedness

**genially**
**06** warmly **07** affably, amiably
**08** amicably, heartily **09** cordially
**10** cheerfully, pleasantly **13** warm-heartedly

**genie**
**04** jann **05** demon, fairy, jinni
**06** djinni, jinnee, spirit

**genitals**
**08** privates **09** genitalia **12** private parts, sexual organs

**genius**
**04** bent, gift, nous, sage **05** adept, brain, demon, flair, knack **06** boffin, brains, daemon, daimon, engine, expert, ingine, master, talent, wisdom, wizard **07** ability, egghead, faculty, maestro, prodigy **08** aptitude, capacity, fine mind, ingenium, virtuoso
**09** bel esprit, intellect **10** brightness, brilliance, cleverness, grey matter, mastermind, past master, propensity, time spirit **11** inclination
**12** intellectual, intelligence **15** little grey cells

**genocide**
**08** massacre **09** ethnocide, slaughter
**13** extermination **15** ethnic cleansing

**genre**
**04** epic, form, kind, sort, type
**05** brand, class, conte, genus, group, novel, sci-fi, style **06** comedy, satire, school, strain **07** fantasy, fashion, romance, variety **08** category, intimism, pastoral, prog rock
**09** character, chopsocky, cyberpunk, reality TV **10** rare groove, whodunitry
**11** fête galante, pastourelle, tragicomedy, whodunnitry
**12** splatterpunk **13** fête champêtre
**14** science fiction **15** progressive rock

**gent** *see* **gentleman**

**genteel**
**05** civil **06** dainty, formal, polite, urbane **07** courtly, elegant, refined, stylish **08** cultured, graceful, ladylike, mannerly, polished, well-bred
**09** courteous **10** cultivated **11** comme il faut, fashionable, gentlemanly, respectable **12** aristocratic, well-mannered

**gentile**
**03** goy **06** ethnic **13** uncircumcised

**gentility**
**04** rank **05** élite **06** gentry, nobles
**07** culture, decorum, manners
**08** breeding, civility, courtesy, elegance, nobility, poshness, urbanity
**09** blue blood, etiquette, formality, high birth, propriety **10** good family, politeness, refinement, upper class
**11** aristocracy, courtliness, gentle birth
**12** mannerliness **14** respectability

**gentle**
**04** calm, easy, gent, kind, meek, mild, slow, soft, tame **05** balmy, bland, canny, light, milky, quiet, sweet
**06** benign, humane, kindly, placid, serene, slight, smooth, tender
**07** amiable, clement, ennoble, gradual, lenient **08** delicate, lamb-like, maidenly, mansuete, merciful, moderate, peaceful, pleasant, soothing, tranquil, well-born
**10** charitable, low-pitched **11** soft-hearted, sympathetic
**13** compassionate, imperceptible, tender-hearted

**gentleman**
**02** Mr **03** rye, sir **04** gent **05** Señor
**06** gemman, knight, Signor, squire, stalko, yeoman **07** esquire, hidalgo, Signior, Signore, younker **08** cavalier
**09** caballero, Signorino **10** duniwassal, pukka sahib **11** duniewassal, gentilhomme **12** dunniewassal
**13** grand seigneur

**gentlemanly**
**04** gent **05** civil, janty, noble, suave
**06** jantee, jaunty, polite, urbane
**07** gallant, genteel, jauntee, refined
**08** generous, mannerly, obliging, polished, well-bred **09** civilized, courteous, reputable **10** chivalrous, cultivated, honourable **12** well-mannered **13** gentlemanlike

**gentleness**
**05** mercy **06** warmth **08** calmness, kindness, meekness, mildness, softness, sympathy **09** sweetness
**10** compassion, humaneness, tenderness

**gently**
**01** p **04** soft **05** small **06** calmly, fairly, mildly, slowly, stilly, warmly **07** lightly
**08** serenely, slightly, tenderly
**09** gradually **10** charitably, moderately, pleasantly, sordamente, tranquilly
**14** hooly and fairly
**15** compassionately, sympathetically

**gentry**
**05** élite **06** nobles **08** nobility, squirage **09** gentility, squireage, top drawer **10** upper class, upper crust
**11** aristocracy

**gents** *see* **toilet**

**genuflect**
**03** bow **05** kneel **11** bend the knee
**12** pay obeisance **13** make obeisance
**14** humble yourself **15** pay your respects

**genuine**
**04** echt, good, open, pure, real, true
**05** frank, legal, pakka, pucka, pukka, right, sound **06** actual, candid, dinkum, entire, honest, kosher, lawful, native, pusser **07** dinky-di, earnest,

factual, natural, sincere **08** bona fide, dinky-die, original, sterling, truthful, unartful **09** authentic, intrinsic, real McCoy, simon-pure, undoubted, veritable **10** fair dinkum, legitimate, ridgy-didge, sure-enough **11** honest-to-God, intrinsical **12** unadulterate **13** unadulterated, with integrity **14** unsophisticate **15** unsophisticated

**genuinely**
**04** echt **06** dinkum, really **07** dinky-di **08** actually, dinky-die, honestly **09** earnestly, sincerely

**genus**
**03** set **04** kind, race, sort, type **05** breed, class, genre, group, order, taxon **07** species **08** category, division **11** subdivision

**geography**

*Geographical regions include:*

**04** veld
**05** basin, coast, heath, plain, polar, veldt
**06** Arctic, desert, forest, jungle, orient, pampas, steppe, tundra
**07** outback, prairie, riviera, savanna, seaside, tropics
**08** lowlands, midlands, occident, savannah, woodland
**09** Antarctic, grassland, green belt, marshland, scrubland, wasteland
**10** Third World, wilderness
**11** countryside
**13** Mediterranean, rural district, urban district
**14** developed world
**15** developing world

*Geography terms include:*

**03** bay, col, cwm
**04** arid, crag, mesa, tail, veld, wadi, wady
**05** butte, delta, shott, taiga, veldt
**06** canyon, cirque, corrie, tundra, valley
**07** aggrade, caldera, equator, glacial, hachure, isthmus, tropics, volcano
**08** alluvium, altitude, landmass, landslip, latitude, meridian, prograde
**09** accretion, antipodes, base level, billabong, deviation, ethnology, landslide, longitude, metroplex, relief map
**10** co-ordinate, demography, glaciation, landlocked, topography
**11** archipelago, cartography, chorography, conurbation, demographic, hydrography, triangulate, vulcanology
**13** hanging valley, Ordnance Datum, shield volcano
**14** plate tectonics, roche moutonnée

*Geographers include:*

**03** **Dee** (John)
**04** **Cary** (John), **Mela** (Pomponius)
**05** **Barth** (Heinrich), **Cabot** (Sebastian), **Darby** (Clifford), **Guyot** (Arnold), **Hedin** (Sven), **Penck** (Albrecht), **Sauer** (Carl), **Stamp** (Sir Lawrence Dudley)
**06** **Batuta**, **Behaim** (Martin), **Bowman** (Isaiah), **Clüver** (Phillip), **Gmelin** (Johann Georg), **Harvey** (David), **Idrisi**, **Ritter** (Karl), **Strabo**
**07** **Haggett** (Peter), **Hakluyt** (Richard), **Markham** (Sir Clements), **Ogilvie** (Alan), **Ptolemy**
**08** **Büsching** (Anton Friedrich), **Filchner** (Wilhelm), **Humboldt** (Alexander, Baron von), **Mercator** (Gerhardus), **Ortelius** (Abraham Ortel), **Robinson** (Arthur)
**09** **Kropotkin** (Pyotr), **Mackinder** (Sir Halford John), **Muqaddasi**, **Pausanias**
**10** **Hartshorne** (Richard), **Huntington** (Ellsworth), **Richthofen** (Ferdinand Baron von), **Wooldridge** (Sydney)
**11** **Christaller** (Walter), **Hägerstrand** (Torsten), **Kingdon-Ward** (Frank)
**12** **Eratosthenes**, **Leo Africanus**
**15** **Eudoxus of Cnidus**, **Vidal de la Blache** (Paul)

**geology**

*Geological time periods include:*

**06** Eocene (Epoch)
**07** Miocene (Epoch), Permian (Period)
**08** Cambrian (Period), Cenozoic (Era), Devonian (Period), Holocene (Epoch), Jurassic (Period), Mesozoic (Era), Pliocene (Epoch), Silurian (Period), Tertiary (Period), Triassic (Period)
**09** Oligocene (Epoch)
**10** Cretaceous (Period), Ordovician (Period), Palaeocene (Epoch), Palaeozoic (Era), Quaternary (Period)
**11** Phanerozoic (Eon), Pleistocene (Epoch), Precambrian (Era), Proterozoic (Eon)
**13** Carboniferous (Period), Mississippian (Epoch), Pennsylvanian (Epoch)

*Geology-related terms include:*

**02** aa
**03** bar, cwm, mya, ore
**04** clay, dome, dune, fold, lava, limb, lode, Moho, Riss, till, trap, tuff, vein, wadi
**05** agate, atoll, basin, butte, chert, delta, epoch, esker, fault, fiord, fjord, focus, gorge, gully, guyot, horst, joint, Karst, lahar, levee, magma, plain, P-wave, ridge, S-wave, talus
**06** albite, arkose, arroyo, basalt, bolson, canyon, cirque, corrie, debris, gabbro, geyser, gneiss, graben, mantle, oolite, quartz, runoff, schist, scoria, stress, tephra, trench, uplift
**07** aquifer, barchan, bauxite, bed-load, blowout, breccia, caldera, drumlin, glacier, granite, hogback, igneous, isograd, lapilli, meander, mineral, moraine, orogeny, outwash, plateau, pothole, vesicle, volcano
**08** A-horizon, alluvium, backwash, basement, B-horizon, C-horizon, feldspar, fumarole, isostasy, leaching, lopolith, monolith, mountain, obsidian, oilfield, oil shale, pahoehoe, pediment, regolith, rhyolite, syncline, xenolith
**09** alabaster, batholith, carbonate, deflation, epicentre, flood tide, hot spring, intrusion, laccolith, landslide, limestone, Mohs scale, monadnock, monocline, oxidation, peneplain, rock cycle, rockslide, sandstone, slip fault, striation, tableland, viscosity, volcanism
**10** anthracite, astrobleme, block fault, cinder cone, deposition, depression, earthquake, flood plain, kettle hole, mineralogy, rift valley, subsidence, topography, travertine, water table, weathering
**11** alluvial fan, central vent, exfoliation, geosyncline, groundwater, maar volcano, metamorphic, normal fault, sublimation, swallow hole, thrust fault, volcanic ash
**12** artesian well, coastal plain, fringing reef, magma chamber, pyroclastics, stratigraphy, unconformity, volcanic bomb, volcanic cone, volcanic dome, volcanic pipe
**13** angle of repose, barrier island, drainage basin, geomorphology, hanging valley, recumbent fold, shield volcano, stratovolcano, U-shaped valley, V-shaped valley
**14** bituminous coal, eustatic change, lateral moraine, longshore drift, stratification, subduction zone, transform fault, wave-cut terrace
**15** million years ago, sedimentary rock, strike-slip fault, terminal moraine

**Georgia**
**02** GA, GE **03** GEO

**germ**
**03** bud, bug, wog **04** root, seed, zyme **05** cause, shoot, spark, start, virus **06** embryo, origin, source, sprout **07** microbe, nucleus **08** bacillus, fountain, rudiment **09** bacterium, beginning, inception, swarm-cell **10** seminality, swarm-spore **12** commencement **13** micro-organism

**German**
◇ *foreign word indicator*
**01** G **03** Ger, Hun **04** Jute, Ossi **05** boche, Gerry, Jerry, Wessi **06** Almain, bosche, Teuton

*German first names include:*

**03** Jan, Max, Uwe
**04** Dirk, Eric, Erik, Jens, Jörg, Ralf, Sven, Swen
**05** Bernd, Erich, Fritz, Jonas, Klaus, Lukas, Ralph
**06** Dieter, Jürgen, Markus, Niklas, Stefan, Tobias, Ulrich
**07** Andreas, Dominik, Mathias, Steffen, Stephan, Torsten

08 Kristian, Matthias, Thorsten, Wolfgang

*See also* **day**; **month**; **number**

- **East German**

**03** Ost

**germane**

**03** apt **04** akin **06** allied, proper **07** apropos, fitting, related **08** apposite, material, relevant, suitable **09** connected, pertinent **10** applicable **11** appropriate

**germanium**

**02** Ge

**Germany**

**01** D **03** DDR, DEU, FDR, FRG, GDR, Ger **05** Reich **06** Almany **07** Almaine **08** Alemaine

- **in Germany**

◇ *foreign word indicator*

**germinal**

**07** seminal **09** embryonic **10** developing, generative **11** preliminary, rudimentary, undeveloped

**germinate**

**03** bud **04** grow **05** shoot, swell **06** sprout **07** burgeon, develop **08** spring up, take root **09** originate

**gestation**

**08** drafting, planning, ripening **09** evolution, pregnancy **10** conception, incubation, maturation **11** development

**gesticulate**

**04** sign, wave **06** motion, signal **07** gesture **08** indicate **09** make a sign

**gesticulation**

**04** sign, wave **06** motion, signal **07** gesture **08** movement **09** chironomy **10** indication **12** body language

**gesture**

**03** act **04** geck, gest, mint, sign, wave **05** geste, point, snook **06** action, beckon, motion, signal **08** dumbshow, indicate, movement **09** beau geste, behaviour, chirology, reverence **10** indication **11** gesticulate **13** gesticulation

**get**

◇ *juxtaposition indicator*

**02** go **03** bug, buy, cop, fix, hit, nab, see, vex, wax, win **04** brat, bust, coax, come, cook, earn, gain, grab, grow, have, hear, kill, land, make, move, nick, rile, suss, sway, take, trap, turn, twig, urge **05** annoy, bring, catch, child, clear, fetch, get it, go for, grasp, learn, reach, seize, snare **06** answer, arrest, arrive, attain, baffle, become, bother, collar, come by, descry, fathom, follow, induce, manage, obtain, pick up, secure, take in, travel, wangle, wind up, work it **07** achieve, acquire, arrange, be given, bring in, capture, collect, develop, discern, make out, prepare, procure, provoke, realize, receive, succeed, suss out, win over, work out **08** come to be, contract, convince, find a way, get ready, hunt down, irritate, organize, persuade, purchase, rustle up, talk into **09** aggravate, apprehend, figure out, influence, infuriate, lay hold of, recognize, succumb to **10** comprehend, drive crazy, exasperate, go down with, understand **11** get the point, prevail upon, put together **12** come down with, get the hang of **13** be afflicted by

- **get about**

**02** go **06** travel **08** go widely **09** move about **10** move around **12** travel widely

- **get across**

**06** convey, impart **07** express, get over, put over **08** transmit **09** make clear, put across **11** bring home to, communicate

- **get ahead**

**05** get on **06** do well, make it, thrive **07** advance, prosper, succeed **08** flourish, get there, go places, make good, progress **11** go great guns **12** get somewhere, make your mark **14** go up in the world, make the big time

- **get along**

**04** cope, fare **05** agree, get by, get on **06** giddap, giddup, manage, relate **07** develop, giddy-up, make out, survive **08** hit it off, progress, rub along **09** harmonize

- **get around**

◇ *containment indicator*

**04** coax, move, sway **05** avoid, evade **06** bypass, cajole, induce, travel **07** win over **08** persuade **09** talk round **10** circumvent **11** prevail upon

- **get at**

**04** find, hint, mean, slam **05** begin, bribe, imply, knock, reach, slate, touch **06** areach, attack, attain, intend, nobble, obtain, pick on, suborn **07** corrupt, suggest **08** discover **09** criticize, influence, insinuate, make fun of **11** pick holes in **12** gain access to **13** find fault with

- **get away**

**04** flee, scat **05** be off, leave, never!, scoot, scram **06** begone, depart, escape, get out **07** do a bunk, run away, scarper **08** break out, run for it **09** break away, break free, do a runner **13** sling your hook **14** make a bolt for it, run for your life **15** make a break for it, take to your heels

- **get back**

**06** go back, go home, recoup, recure, redeem, regain, return **07** pay back, recover **08** come back, come home, retrieve **09** repossess, retaliate **11** get even with **13** take revenge on **15** take vengeance on

- **get by**

**04** cope, fare **05** exist **06** hang on, manage **07** subsist, survive **08** get along **12** make ends meet, see it through **13** scrape through **15** weather the storm

- **get down**

**06** alight, get off, sadden **07** depress, descend, make sad **08** dismount, dispirit **09** disembark **10** dishearten

- **get in**

◇ *insertion indicator*

**04** come, land **05** enter **06** arrive, embark **09** penetrate **10** infiltrate

- **get into**

◇ *insertion indicator*

**05** enjoy, enter, put on **06** arrive **09** penetrate **10** infiltrate

- **get off**

**04** shed **05** learn, leave **06** alight, detach, escape, get out, remove **07** descend, get down **08** climb off, dismount, get out of, memorize, separate **09** disembark **10** alight from

- **get on**

**03** age **04** cope, fare **05** agree, board, get in, mount, shift **06** ascend, embark, manage, relate, thrive **07** advance, climb on, get into, make out, press on, proceed, prosper, succeed **08** continue, get along, hit it off, progress **09** harmonize **12** hit it off with

- **get on well**

**03** gee

- **get out**

**04** away, flee, quit, scat **05** leave, scoot, scram **06** depart, escape, spread, vacate **07** come out, do a bunk, extract, leak out, produce, scarper, take out **08** be leaked, break out, clear off, clear out, evacuate, run for it, withdraw **09** circulate, do a runner **11** become known **12** become public, free yourself **14** make a bolt for it, run for your life **15** make a break for it, take to your heels

- **get out of**

**05** avoid, dodge, evade, shirk, skive **06** escape, outwin **07** goof off **09** gold-brick

- **get over**

**06** convey, defeat, impart, master **07** explain, get well, put over, survive **08** complete, deal with, get round, overcome, shake off, surmount **09** get across, get better, make clear **10** be restored **11** communicate, pull through, recover from **14** recuperate from

- **get ready**

**04** boun **05** bowne, fix up, ready **06** set out **07** arrange, prepare **08** rehearse

- **get round**

◇ *containment indicator*

**04** coax, move, sway **05** avoid, evade **06** bypass, cajole, induce, travel **07** win over **08** persuade **09** talk round **10** circumvent **11** prevail upon

- **get there**

**06** arrive, make it **07** advance, prosper, succeed **08** go places, make good

- **get through**

**04** pass

- **get together**

**04** join, meet **05** rally, unite **06** finish, gather **07** collect **08** assemble, organize **10** congregate **11** collaborate

**• get up**

**03** fig **04** rise, stir **05** arise, climb, mount, scale, stand **06** ascend, huddup **07** stand up **08** show a leg **11** get out of bed

**getaway**

**05** break, start **06** escape, flight **08** breakout **10** absconding, decampment

**get-together**

**02** do **04** bash **05** party, rally **06** social, soirée **07** meeting, reunion **08** assembly, function, sing-sing **09** gathering, reception

**get-up**

**03** kit, set **04** gear, togs **06** make-up, outfit, rig-out **07** clobber, clothes, threads, turnout **08** clothing, garments **09** equipment

**Ghana**

**02** GH **03** GHA

**ghastliness**

**08** grimness **09** awfulness, nastiness **11** hideousness **12** dreadfulness, gruesomeness **13** frightfulness

**ghastly**

**03** bad, ill **04** gash, grim, ropy, sick **05** awful, grave, lousy, lurid, nasty, ropey **06** grisly, horrid, poorly, rotten, unwell **07** greisly, griesly, hideous, macabre, serious **08** critical, dreadful, gruesome, horrible, shocking, terrible **09** appalling, dangerous, deathlike, frightful, loathsome, off colour, repellent **10** deplorable, horrendous, terrifying **11** frightening **12** unrepeatable **15** under the weather

**ghost**

**04** hint, soul, waff **05** duppy, fetch, haunt, jumby, larva, lemur, shade, spook, trace, umbra **06** duende, jumbie, shadow, spirit, wraith **07** gytrash, phantom, specter, spectre **08** manifest, presence, revenant, visitant **09** semblance **10** apparition, astral body, impression, suggestion **11** poltergeist

**ghostly**

**05** eerie, faint, spook, weird **06** creepy, spooky **07** phantom, shadowy **08** chthonic, illusory, spectral **09** chthonian, ghostlike, religious, spiritual, sprightly, unearthly **10** wraith-like **12** supernatural

**ghoulish**

**04** sick **06** grisly, morbid **07** macabre **08** gruesome **09** revolting, unhealthy **11** unwholesome

**giant**

**04** eten, huge, ogre, vast **05** ettin, jotun, jumbo, large, titan, troll **06** jötunn, ogress **07** immense, mammoth, massive, monster, titanic **08** behemoth, Briarean, colossal, colossus, cyclopic, enormous, gigantic, great big, king-size, titaness, whopping **09** cyclopean, cyclopian, ginormous, humongous, humungous, leviathan, rounceval **10** gargantuan, monumental, Patagonian, prodigious, tremendous **11** gigantesque **14** Brobdingnagian

*Giants include:*

**03** Gog
**04** Gaia, Gerd, Grid, Loki, Rhea, Ymir
**05** Aegir, Arges, Argus, Atlas, Grawp, Hymir, Jotun, Magog, Orion, Pan Gu, Skadi, Theia, Thrym
**06** Albion, Bestla, Cronus, Hagrid, Phoebe, Tethys, Themis, Thiazi, Titans
**07** Cyclops, Geirrod, Goliath, Iapetus, Oceanus, Suttung
**08** Angrboda, Cyclopes, Gigantes, Gogmagog, Hrungnir, Hyperion, Jarnsaxa, Morgante, Nephilim, Panoptes, Steropes
**09** Angerboda, Bergelmir, Enceladus, Gandareva, Gargantua, Mnemosyne, Olentzero
**10** Angerbotha, Epimetheus, Paul Bunyan, Prometheus
**11** Finn MacCool, Galligantus, Gog and Magog, Utgardaloki
**12** Giant Despair, Vafthruthnir
**15** Cerne Abbas Giant, Fionn MacCumhail

**gibber**

**04** blab, cant **05** stone **06** babble, cackle, gabble, jabber **07** blabber, blather, boulder, chatter, prattle

**gibberish**

**04** blah, bosh, guff **05** hooey **06** bunkum, drivel, jargon, linsey, yammer **07** baloney, eyewash, hogwash, prattle, ravings, rhubarb, rubbish, twaddle **08** cobblers, malarkey, nonsense, tommyrot **09** moonshine, poppycock **10** balderdash, codswallop, jabberwock, mumbo-jumbo **11** abracadabra, jabberwocky **12** gobbledygook **13** linsey-woolsey

**gibbet**

**05** crook, cross **07** gallows, potence

**gibbon**

**06** wou-wou, wow-wow **07** hoolock, siamang **08** hylobate

**gibe, jibe**

**03** bob, dig, shy **04** gird, goof, jeer, mock, poke, quip, wipe, yerk **05** crack, fleer, fling, flout, gleek, scoff, slant, sneer, taunt, tease **06** deride **07** brocard, mockery, sarcasm, teasing **08** derision, outfling, ridicule **09** make fun of, wisecrack, witticism

**Gibraltar**

**03** GBZ, GIB

**giddily**

◇ *anagram indicator*

**06** wildly **07** dizzily, woozily **09** excitedly **10** restlessly, unsteadily **11** frantically **12** euphorically **13** lightheadedly

**giddiness**

**06** frenzy, nausea, thrill **07** vertigo **08** staggers **09** animation, dizziness, faintness, wooziness **10** excitement, wobbliness **11** glaikitness **12** exhilaration **15** lightheadedness

**giddy**

◇ *anagram indicator*

**04** high, wild **05** dizzy, faint, light, queer, silly, woozy **06** elated, sturdy, volage **07** excited, flighty, glaiket, glaikit, reeling, stirred **08** frenzied, hellicat, skipping, thrilled, unsteady **09** volageous **10** capernoity, hoity-toity, stimulated **11** capernoitie, cappernoity, exhilarated, hair-brained, hare-brained, lightheaded, vertiginous

**gift**

**03** foy, tip **04** bent, boon, give, koha, turn **05** bonus, bribe, flair, grant, knack, offer, power, skill **06** befana, bestow, bounty, confer, donate, genius, hansel, legacy, talent **07** ability, aptness, beffana, bequest, cumshaw, étrenne, faculty, fairing, freebie, handsel, minding, present, pressie, prezzie, propine **08** aptitude, capacity, donation, donative, facility, gratuity, largesse, offering, thankyou **09** attribute, book token, endowment **10** capability, contribute, exhibition **11** beneficence, inheritance, proficiency **12** Christmas box, contribution

*See also* **Christmas**

**gifted**

**04** able **05** adept, sharp, smart **06** bright, clever, expert **07** capable, endowed, skilful, skilled **08** masterly, talented **09** brilliant **10** proficient **11** intelligent **12** accomplished

**gig**

**03** fun **04** moze **05** buggy, sport **06** dennet, whisky **07** whiskey **11** hurly-hacket

**gigantic**

**04** huge, mega, vast **05** giant, jumbo **07** immense, mammoth, massive, monster, titanic **08** colossal, enormous, great big, king-size, whopping **09** Atlantean, ginormous, Herculean, humongous, humungous, leviathan, rounceval **10** Babylonian, gargantuan, monumental, Patagonian **14** Brobdingnagian

**giggle**

**05** laugh **06** titter **07** chortle, chuckle, snicker, snigger

**gilbert**

**02** Gb

**• Gilbert and Sullivan**

**05** G and S

**gild**

**04** coat, deck, trim **05** adorn, array, grace, paint **06** bedeck, enrich, golden **07** dress up, enhance, festoon, garnish **08** beautify, brighten, ornament **09** elaborate, embellish, embroider

**gilded**
**04** gilt, gold **06** golden **07** aureate **08** inaurate **10** gold-plated **11** gold-layered

**gill**
**04** glen **05** brook **06** noggin, ravine **08** branchia **09** ctenidium

**gilt**
**03** elt

**gimcrack**
**05** cheap, dodge, tacky, trick **06** fisgig, fizgig, shoddy, tawdry, trashy **08** rubbishy, trumpery **10** jerry-built

**gimmick**
**04** hype, ploy, ruse **05** dodge, stunt, trick **06** device, gadget, scheme **07** novelty **09** publicity, stratagem **10** attraction **11** contrivance

**gimmickry**
**07** novelty **09** modernity **10** innovation

**gin**
**02** by, if **03** max **04** ruin, trap **05** snare **06** geneva, Old Tom, scheme, spring **07** schnaps, springe, twankay **08** artifice, blue ruin, Hollands, schiedam, schnapps **10** square-face **11** contrivance, mother's ruin

• **gin and tonic**
**02** gt **05** g and t

**ginger**
◇ *anagram indicator*
**03** pop **04** race, rase, raze **05** bluey, sandy **06** amomum, asarum, mettle **07** curcuma, enliven, reddish **08** cardamom, cardamon, cardamum, turmeric, zingiber **09** galingale **10** cassumunar **11** stimulation

**gingerbread**
**05** parly **06** parkin, parley, perkin **10** parliament, pepper-cake **14** parliament-cake

**gingerly**
**06** warily **07** charily **09** carefully, prudently **10** cautiously, delicately, hesitantly, watchfully **11** attentively, judiciously, tentatively, with caution

**Gipsy** *see* **Gypsy, Gipsy**

**gird**
**03** pen **04** belt, bind, girr, hoop, ring **05** brace, hem in, ready, steel, taunt **06** enfold, fasten, girdle **07** accinge, enclose, fortify, prepare **08** cincture, encircle, get ready, surround **09** encompass

**girder**
**04** beam, spar **05** H-beam, I-beam **06** rafter **07** box beam

**girdle**
**03** hem **04** band, belt, bind, gird, ring, sash, zona, zone **05** bound, mitre, waist **06** cestos, cestus, circle, corset **07** enclose, go round, griddle, zonulet **08** ceinture, cincture, cingulum, encircle, surround **09** encompass, surcingle, waistband **10** cummerbund, encincture **15** cingulum Veneris

**girl**
**03** bit, cub, gal, gel, gig, hen, her, kid, mor, tit **04** babe, baby, bint, bird, chit, dell, gill, jill, Judy, lass, maid, mawr, minx, miss, peat, puss, romp, tart **05** belle, chick, child, cutie, cutty, dolly, fille, filly, flirt, gerle, gilpy, hussy, madam, peach, popsy, quean, randy, tabby, wench **06** au pair, blowze, chokri, cummer, damsel, female, fizgig, gamine, geisha, giglet, kimmer, lassie, maiden, moppet, mousmé, nipper, number, pigeon, sheila, shiksa, tawpie, tomboy, tottie **07** blushet, chapess, chicken, colleen, flapper, mauther, mawther, mousmee, nymphet **08** chappess, daughter, grisette, jail-bait, princess, teenager **09** backfisch, dolly bird, maid-child, young lady, youngster **10** adolescent, bit of fluff, bit of skirt, bit of stuff, bobbysoxer, Cinderella, girlfriend, jeune fille, schoolgirl, sweetheart, young woman **11** beauty queen, kinchin-mort, maidservant, teeny-bopper **12** bachelorette, bobby-dazzler

*Girls' names include:*

**02** Di, Jo, Mo, Vi
**03** Ada, Ali, Amy, Ann, Ava, Bab, Bea, Bee, Bel, Bet, Cis, Con, Deb, Dee, Die, Dot, Edy, Emm, Ena, Eva, Eve, Fay, Flo, Gay, Ida, Ina, Isa, Ivy, Jan, Jay, Jen, Joe, Joy, Kay, Kim, Kit, Lea, Lee, Liv, Liz, Lou, Mae, Mag, Mat, May, Meg, Mia, Nan, Pam, Pat, Peg, Pen, Pia, Pru, Rae, Ray, Ria, Ros, Roz, Sal, Sue, Una, Val, Viv, Win, Zoë
**04** Abby, Addy, Afra, Aggy, Alex, Ally, Alma, Alme, Angy, Anna, Anne, Asma, Babs, Bell, Bess, Beth, Cara, Caro, Cass, Ceri, Cher, Cleo, Cora, Dana, Dawn, Dian, Dora, Edel, Edie, Edna, Ella, Elma, Elsa, Elva, Emma, Emmy, Enid, Erin, Evie, Faye, Floy, Fred, Gabi, Gaea, Gaia, Gail, Gale, Gaye, Gene, Gert, Gill, Gina, Gita, Gwen, Hope, Ibby, Ines, Inez, Inga, Inge, Iona, Iris, Irma, Isla, Jade, Jane, Jean, Jess, Jill, Joan, Jodi, Jody, Joey, Joni, Joss, Jozy, Jude, Judy, June, Kate, Kath, Katy, Kaye, Lara, Leah, Lena, Lian, Lily, Lina, Lisa, Lise, Livy, Liza, Lois, Lola, Lucy, Lynn, Maev, Mary, Maud, Meta, Mina, Moll, Mona, Myra, Nell, Nina, Nita, Noel, Nola, Nona, Nora, Olga, Page, Phyl, Poll, Prue, Rana, Rene, Rita, Rona, Rosa, Rose, Ruby, Ruth, Sara, Sian, Sìne, Siri, Suke, Suky, Susy, Suzy, Tess, Thea, Tina, Toni, Trix, Vera, Vita, Zara, Zena, Zola
**05** Addie, Adela, Adèle, Aggie, Agnes, Ailie, Ailsa, Aisha, Alexa, Alice, Allie, Amber, Amina, Anaïs, Angel, Angie, Anila, Anita, Annie, Annis, Annot, Aphra, April, Areta, Aruna, Avril, Aysha, Becky, Bella, Belle, Beryl, Bessy, Betsy, Betty, Biddy, Bride, Brona, Bunny, Bunty, Candy, Carla, Carly, Carol, Carys, Cathy, Celia, Cerys, Chère, Chloe, Chris, Ciara, Cindy, Cissy, Clara, Clare, Coral, Daisy, Debby, Debra, Delia, Della, Diana, Diane, Dilys, Dinah, Dolly, Donna, Doris, Edith, Effie, Eliza, Ellen, Ellie, Elsie, Emily, Emmie, Erica, Essie, Ethel, Ethna, Ethne, Faith, Fanny, Farah, Ffion, Fiona, Fleur, Flora, Freda, Freya, Gabby, Gauri, Gayle, Geeta, Gemma, Gerda, Ginny, Golda, Golde, Grace, Greta, Haley, Hatty, Hazel, Heidi, Helen, Helga, Hetty, Hilda, Holly, Honor, Ilana, Ilona, Irena, Irene, Isbel, Isold, Ivana, Jaime, Jamie, Janet, Janis, Jemma, Jenna, Jenny, Jessy, Jinny, Jodie, Joely, Josie, Joyce, Judie, Julia, Julie, Kanta, Karen, Karin, Karla, Kathy, Katie, Katya, Kelly, Kenna, Kerry, Kiera, Kitty, Kylie, Lalla, Lally, Laura, Leigh, Leila, Leona, Letty, Liana, Libby, Linda, Lindy, Lorna, Lorne, Louie, Lubna, Lucia, Lydia, Lynda, Lynne, Mabel, Madge, Maeve, Magda, Máire, Màiri, Mamie, Mandy, Margo, Maria, Marie, Matty, Maude, Maura, Mavis, Meena, Megan, Mercy, Meryl, Moira, Molly, Morag, Morna, Moyra, Myrna, Nabby, Nadia, Nance, Nancy, Nelly, Nerys, Nessa, Nesta, Netta, Netty, Ngaio, Niamh, Nicky, Noele, Norah, Norma, Nuala, Olive, Olwen, Olwin, Olwyn, Onora, Oprah, Paddy, Padma, Paige, Pansy, Patsy, Patty, Paula, Pearl, Peggy, Penny, Petra, Pippa, Polly, Priya, Raine, Rajni, Renée, Rhian, Rhoda, Rhona, Robin, Robyn, Rosie, Sacha, Sadie, Sally, Sarah, Sasha, Senga, Shona, Shula, Sibyl, Sindy, Sonia, Sonya, Sophy, Stacy, Sukie, Susan, Susie, Sybil, Tamar, Tammy, Tania, Tanya, Terry, Tessa, Thora, Tibby, Tilda, Tilly, Tracy, Trina, Trish, Trixy, Trudy, Unity, Viola, Wanda, Wendy, Wilma, Zahra, Zelda, Zowie
**06** Adella, Agatha, Aileen, Alexia, Alexis, Alicia, Alison, Althea, Amabel, Amanda, Amelia, Andrea, Angela, Anneka, Annika, Anthea, Aphrah, Aretha, Ashley, Astrid, Audrey, Auriel, Auriol, Aurora, Aurore, Averil, Ayesha, Babbie, Barbie, Beatty, Bertha, Bertie, Bessie, Bianca, Biddie, Blanch, Bonnie, Brenda, Bridie, Brigid, Brigit, Briony, Bryony, Bunnie, Caddie, Candia, Carina, Carlie, Carmel, Carmen, Carola, Carole, Carrie, Cassie, Cathie, Cecily, Celina, Cherie, Cherry, Cheryl, Cicely, Cissie, Claire, Connie, Daphne, Davina, Deanna, Deanne, Debbie, Delyth, Denise, Dervla, Dianne, Dionne, Dolina, Doreen, Dorrie, Dottie, Dulcie, Dympna, Eartha, Edwina, Eileen, Eilidh, Eirian, Eirlys, Eithna, Eithne, Elaine, Elinor, Eloisa, Eloise, Elspet, Eluned, Elvira, Esther, Eunice, Evadne, Evelyn, Evonne, Fatima, Fedora, Felice, Finola, Flavia, Freddy, Frieda, Gaynor, Gertie,

Gladys, Glenda, Glenys, Gloria, Glynis, Goldie, Gracie, Grania, Granya, Gudrun, Gwenda, Hannah, Hattie, Hayley, Helena, Hermia, Hester, Hilary, Honora, Honour, Imelda, Imogen, Indira, Ingrid, Isabel, Iseult, Ishbel, Isobel, Isolda, Isolde, Jamila, Jancis, Janice, Janina, Janine, Jeanie, Jemima, Jennie, Jessie, Joanie, Joanna, Joanne, Joelle, Joleen, Jolene, Judith, Juliet, Kamala, Karena, Karina, Kathie, Kirsty, Kittie, Kumari, Lalage, Lalita, Lallie, Laurel, Lauren, Laurie, Leanne, Leonie, Lesley, Lettie, Lianna, Lianne, Lilian, Lilias, Linnet, Lisbet, Lizzie, Lolita, Lottie, Louisa, Louise, Lynsey, Madhur, Maggie, Maisie, Marcia, Marian, Marina, Marion, Marsha, Martha, Mattie, Maxine, Melody, Meriel, Millie, Minnie, Miriam, Monica, Morven, Muriel, Myriam, Myrtle, Nabila, Nadine, Nellie, Nessie, Nettie, Nicola, Nicole, Noelle, Noreen, Odette, Olivia, Olwyne, Paloma, Pamela, Pattie, Petula, Phemie, Phoebe, Rachel, Rajani, Raquel, Regina, Renata, Rhonda, Robina, Rodney, Roisin, Roshan, Rosina, Rowena, Roxana, Roxane, Rubina, Sabina, Sabine, Salome, Sandra, Saskia, Selina, Seonag, Serena, Sharon, Shashi, Sheela, Sheena, Sheila, Sherry, Sheryl, Silvia, Simone, Sinéad, Sophia, Sophie, Stacey, Stella, Suhair, Sydney, Sylvia, Tamara, Tammie, Tamsin, Teenie, Teresa, Thelma, Tibbie, Tracey, Tricia, Trisha, Trixie, Ulrica, Ursula, Vanora, Verity, Vijaya, Vinaya, Violet, Vivian, Vivien, Vyvian, Vyvyan, Winnie, Winona, Wynona, Xanthe, Yasmin, Yvette, Yvonne, Zainab, Zaynab

**07** Abigail, Aisling, Allegra, Allison, Andrina, Annabel, Annette, Antonia, Anushka, Ariadne, Augusta, Barbara, Beatrix, Belinda, Bernice, Bethany, Bettina, Bharati, Blanche, Bridget, Bronach, Bronagh, Bronwen, Caitlín, Camilla, Candace, Candice, Candida, Carolyn, Cecilia, Chandra, Chantal, Charity, Charley, Chelsea, Christy, Clarice, Claudia, Colette, Colleen, Corinna, Corinne, Crystal, Cynthia, Daniela, Deborah, Deirdre, Désirée, Dolores, Dorothy, Eleanor, Elspeth, Emerald, Estella, Estelle, Eugenia, Eugénie, Felicia, Fenella, Floella, Florrie, Flossie, Frances, Francie, Frankie, Freddie, Georgia, Georgie, Gillian, Giselle, Gwennie, Gwenyth, Gwyneth, Harriet, Heather, Heloise, Isadora, Isidora, Jacinta, Jacinth, Janetta, Janette, Jasmine, Jeannie, Jessica, Jillian, Jocasta, Jocelin, Jocelyn, Johanna, Jonquil, Josette, Juliana, Justina, Justine, Kathryn, Katrina, Katrine, Kirstie, Kirstin, Lakshmi, Lavinia, Leonora, Letitia, Lettice, Lillian, Lillias, Lindsay, Lindsey, Linette, Lisbeth, Lisette, Lizbeth, Loretta, Lucilla, Lucille, Lucinda, Lynette, Madonna, Margery, Marilyn, Marjory, Marlene, Martina, Martine, Matilda, Maureen, Melanie, Melissa, Mildred, Miranda, Myfanwy, Nanette, Natalia, Natalie, Natasha, Nichola, Nigella, Ninette, Ophelia, Pandora, Parvati, Pascale, Paulina, Pauline, Phyllis, Queenie, Rachael, Rebecca, Roberta, Rosabel, Rosalie, Rosanna, Rosetta, Roxanne, Sabrina, Saffron, Sharifa, Shelagh, Shelley, Shirley, Sidonie, Silvana, Siobhán, Surayya, Susanna, Sybilla, Tabitha, Theresa, Tiffany, Valerie, Vanessa, Venetia, Yolanda, Zuleika

**08** Adelaide, Adrianne, Adrienne, Angelica, Angelina, Angharad, Arabella, Ashleigh, Beatrice, Berenice, Beverley, Caroline, Catriona, Charlene, Charmian, Chrissie, Clarinda, Clarissa, Claudine, Cordelia, Cornelia, Courtney, Cressida, Daniella, Danielle, Dorothea, Eleanore, Emmeline, Euphemia, Felicity, Florence, Francine, Georgina, Germaine, Gertrude, Griselda, Grizelda, Gurinder, Hermione, Isabella, Jacintha, Jacinthe, Jeanette, Jennifer, Joceline, Joscelin, Katerina, Kathleen, Kimberly, Kirsteen, Lauretta, Lorraine, Madeline, Magdalen, Margaret, Marigold, Marjorie, Mathilda, Meredith, Michaela, Michelle, Morwenna, Ottoline, Patience, Patricia, Paulette, Penelope, Philippa, Primrose, Prudence, Prunella, Rhiannon, Rosalind, Rosamond, Rosamund, Roseanna, Roseanne, Rosemary, Samantha, Scarlett, Susannah, Theodora, Tomasina, Veronica, Victoria, Virginia, Winifred

**09** Albertina, Alexandra, Anastasia, Annabella, Annabelle, Cassandra, Catharine, Catherina, Catherine, Charlotte, Charmaine, Christina, Christine, Claudette, Cleopatra, Constance, Elisabeth, Elizabeth, Frederica, Gabrielle, Genevieve, Georgette, Georgiana, Geraldine, Ghislaine, Guinevere, Gwendolen, Henrietta, Jaqueline, Jeannette, Josephine, Katharine, Katherine, Kimberley, Madeleine, Magdalene, Mélisande, Millicent, Nicolette, Parminder, Priscilla, Rosemarie, Sigourney, Silvestra, Stephanie, Sylvestra, Thomasina, Valentine

**10** Antoinette, Bernadette, Christabel, Clementina, Clementine, Jacqueline, Shakuntula, Wilhelmina

---

• **society girl**

**03** deb **09** débutante

## girlfriend

**03** mot **04** babe, baby, bint, bird, date, girl, lady, lass, moll **05** chick, lover, woman **06** steady **07** fiancée, partner, squeeze **08** best girl, mistress, old flame **09** cohabitee, young lady **10** sweetheart **11** live-in lover **15** common-law spouse

## girlish

**08** childish, immature, innocent, youthful **09** childlike **10** adolescent **11** unmasculine

## girth

**04** band, bulk, size **05** strap **06** asylum **07** compass, measure **08** encircle **09** perimeter, sanctuary, surcingle **13** circumference

## gist

**03** nub **04** core, crux, idea, pith **05** drift, point, sense **06** import, marrow, matter, thrust **07** essence, keynote, meaning, nucleus, purport **09** direction, substance **12** quintessence, significance **15** sum and substance

## give

◇ *juxtaposition indicator*

**02** do **03** aim, gie **04** bend, cede, fall, gift, have, lead, lend, make, move, play, show, sink, slip, tell, turn, will, yeve **05** admit, allow, award, break, cause, endow, focus, grant, lay on, leave, offer, put on, slack, throw, utter, yield **06** accord, afford, bestow, buckle, commit, confer, convey, create, devote, direct, donate, fetter, give up, impart, induce, permit, prompt, render, reveal, supply **07** arrange, concede, declare, deliver, display, dispose, entrust, exhibit, furnish, give way, incline, perform, present, produce, proffer, provide, publish, shackle, stretch **08** announce, bequeath, carry out, collapse, estimate, hand over, indicate, make over, manifest, occasion, organize, set forth, transfer, transmit, turn over, yielding **09** break down, fall apart, pronounce, surrender **10** administer, contribute, distribute, elasticity, give rise to **11** cause to have, communicate, concentrate, springiness **12** stretchiness, take charge of **14** cause to undergo, let someone have

• **give away**

**04** leak, shed, tell **06** betray, expose, let out, reveal **07** concede, divulge, let slip, uncover **08** disclose, inform on

• **give in**

**04** quit **05** yield **06** give up, jack in, submit **07** chuck up, concede, give way, succumb **08** pack it in **09** chuck it in, surrender **10** call it a day, capitulate, knock under **11** admit defeat **13** concede defeat **15** throw in the cards, throw in the towel, throw up the cards

• **give off**

**04** emit, fume, vent **05** exude **06** evolve, exhale **07** give out, pour out, produce, release, send out **08** liberate, throw out **09** discharge

• **give on to**

**06** lead to **08** open on to, overlook

• **give out**

**04** deal, emit, vent **05** allot, exude,

yield **06** exhale, impart, notify, pack up, report, run out **07** conk out, declare, dish out, dole out, give off, hand out, mete out, pour out, produce, publish, release, send out **08** announce, depleted, disperse, share out, throw out, transmit **09** advertise, be mixed up, break down, broadcast, circulate, discharge, make known **10** be depleted, distribute, pass around, relinquish **11** be exhausted, come to an end, communicate, disseminate, stop working **12** be all mixed up

**• give over**
**03** lin **07** chuck it **08** transfer

**• give up**
**03** cut **04** cede, quit, stop **05** cease, forgo, remit, waive **06** cut out, forego, give in, render, resign, turn in **07** abandon, chuck in, chuck up, concede, crap out, deliver, forbear, forgive, lay down, put down, respite, throw up **08** abdicate, forswear, leave off, renounce **09** sacrifice, surrender **10** capitulate, relinquish **11** admit defeat, discontinue **13** concede defeat **14** drop your bundle **15** throw in the towel

## give-and-take
**08** goodwill **10** compliance, compromise **11** co-operation, flexibility, negotiation, willingness **12** adaptability

## given
**05** prone **06** liable, likely, stated **08** assuming, definite, disposed, distinct, inclined, in view of, specific **09** specified **10** individual, particular **11** considering **12** in the light of **13** bearing in mind

## giver
**05** angel, donor **06** backer, friend, helper, patron **07** sponsor **08** promoter, provider **09** supporter **10** benefactor, subscriber, subsidizer, well-wisher **11** contributor **14** fairy godmother, philanthropist

## glacial
**03** icy, raw **04** cold **05** chill, gelid, polar, stiff **06** arctic, biting, bitter, chilly, frigid, frosty, frozen, wintry **07** brumous, distant, hostile **08** freezing, inimical, piercing, Siberian **10** unfriendly **12** antagonistic

## glaciation stage
**04** Günz, Riss, Würm **06** Mindel

## glad
**04** fain, keen **05** eager, happy, merry, ready **06** bright, cheery, elated, joyful **07** chuffed, gleeful, pleased, welcome, willing **08** cheerful, disposed, gladsome, inclined, prepared, thrilled **09** contented, delighted, gratified, overjoyed, satisfied **11** over the moon, tickled pink

## gladden
**05** cheer, elate **06** buck up, please **07** delight, enliven, gratify, hearten, rejoice **08** brighten **09** encourage **10** exhilarate

## glade
**03** gap **04** dell, land **05** laund, space **07** opening **08** clearing **09** cock-shoot

## gladiator
**07** Samnite, sworder **09** retiarius, Spartacus

## gladly
**04** fain **06** fainly, freely **07** happily, readily **09** willingly **10** cheerfully, gladsomely **12** with pleasure **13** with good grace

## gladness
**03** joy **04** glee **05** mirth **06** gaiety **07** delight, jollity **08** felicity, hilarity, pleasure **09** happiness **10** brightness, joyousness **11** high spirits **12** cheerfulness

## glamorous
**04** glam **05** ritzy, smart **06** exotic, flashy, glammy, glitzy, glossy, lovely **07** elegant **08** alluring, charming, dazzling, exciting, gorgeous **09** appealing, beautiful, colourful, thrilling **10** attractive, bewitching, enchanting, glittering **11** captivating, fascinating, well-dressed

## glamour
**02** it, SA **04** gilt, Ritz **05** charm, magic **06** allure, appeal, beauty, thrill **07** glitter **08** elegance, prestige, witchery **09** magnetism **10** attraction, excitement **11** captivation, enchantment, fascination **14** attractiveness

**• sentimental glamour**
**04** halo

## glance
**03** dip, ray **04** flip, leaf, leer, look, ogle, peek, peep, scan, skim, view **05** blink, dekko, eliad, flash, flick, glide, slant, squiz, thumb, tweer, twire **06** amoret, aspect, browse, eyliad, gander, gledge, illiad, shufti, shufty, skelly, squint, vision **07** deflect, eye-beam, eyeliad, eyeshot, eye-wink, glimpse, skellie **08** butcher's, oeillade, ricochet **09** brief look, quick look **10** redruthite **13** look briefly at, look quickly at **15** catch a glimpse of

**• at first glance**
**09** outwardly, seemingly **10** apparently, ostensibly, prima facie **12** at first sight, on the surface **13** on the face of it, superficially

**• glance off**
**07** rebound **08** ricochet **09** bounce off **10** spring back

## gland

*Glands include:*

**05** lymph, ovary
**06** cortex, pineal, thymus
**07** adrenal, eccrine, mammary, medulla, parotid, thyroid
**08** apocrine, exocrine, pancreas, prostate, testicle
**09** endocrine, holocrine, lachrymal, lymph node, merocrine, pituitary, sebaceous
**11** parathyroid

## glare
**04** beam, glow, look, lour **05** blaze, flame, flare, frown, lower, scowl, shine, stare **06** dazzle, glassy, glower **07** daggers, reflect **08** iceblink **09** black look, dirty look, limelight, look frown, spotlight **10** brightness, brilliance

## glaring
**04** open **05** glary, gross, lurid, overt **06** garish, patent **07** blatant, obvious **08** flagrant, manifest, walleyed **10** outrageous **11** conspicuous

## glaringly
**06** openly **07** overtly **08** patently **09** blatantly, obviously **10** flagrantly, manifestly **13** conspicuously

## glass
**04** lens, opal, pony **05** loupe, poney, specs **06** beaker, copita, cullet, goblet, mirror, psyche, rummer **07** brimmer, crystal, monocle, opaline, sleever, tumbler, vitrail, vitrics **08** pince-nez **09** barometer, glassware, lorgnette **10** avanturine, aventurine, dildo-glass, eyeglasses, spectacles **12** opera-glasses, supernaculum **13** contact lenses

*Glass sizes include:*

**03** pot, six, ten
**04** pint
**05** bobby, middy, seven
**06** handle
**07** butcher, sleever
**08** half pint, schooner

**• flaw in glass**
**04** tear

**• substitute for glass**
**04** mica

## glassy
**03** icy **04** cold, dull **05** blank, clear, dazed, empty, fixed, glare, shiny **06** glazed, glazen, glossy, smooth, vacant **07** deadpan, hyaline, vacuous **08** lifeless, polished, slippery, unmoving, vitreous **09** glasslike **10** mirrorlike **11** transparent **12** crystal clear **14** expressionless

## glaze
**04** ciré, coat **05** aspic, cover, glass, gloss, shine, smear **06** enamel, finish, luster, lustre, polish, sancai **07** burnish, celadon, coating, eggwash, lacquer, varnish **08** tiger eye **09** peach-blow, tiger's eye

## gleam
**03** ray **04** beam, glow, leam, leme **05** blink, flame, flare, flash, glint, gloss, light, shaft, sheen, shine **06** glance, lustre **07** flicker, glimmer, glimpse, glisten, glitter, radiate, shimmer, sparkle **08** sun-blink **10** brightness, shimmering **11** scintillate

**glean**
**04** cull, pick, reap **05** amass, learn, lease **06** garner, gather, pick up, select **07** collect, find out, harvest **10** accumulate

**glee**
**03** fun, joy **04** gley **05** mirth, verve **06** gaiety, squint **07** delight, elation, jollity, triumph **08** gladness, hilarity, pleasure **09** joviality, merriment **10** exuberance, exultation, jocularity, joyfulness, joyousness, liveliness **12** cheerfulness, exhilaration **13** gratification

**gleeful**
**05** happy, merry **06** elated, jovial, joyful, joyous **07** pleased **08** cheerful, exultant, jubilant, mirthful **09** cock-a-hoop, delighted, exuberant, gratified, overjoyed **10** triumphant **11** over the moon **14** beside yourself

**gleefully**
**07** happily, merrily **08** joyfully, joyously **10** cheerfully, jubilantly **11** exuberantly **12** triumphantly

**glen**
**03** cwm **04** gill **05** ghyll **10** depression

**glib**
**04** easy **05** gabby, gassy, quick, ready, slick, suave **06** facile, fluent, smooth **07** voluble **08** castrate **09** insincere, plausible, talkative **10** loquacious **13** silver-tongued, smooth-talking, smooth-tongued

**glibly**
**05** patly, slick **06** easily **07** quickly, slickly **08** fluently, smoothly **11** insincerely

**glide**
**03** fly, run **04** cost, flow, pass, roll, sail, skim, slip, slur, soar, swan, swim **05** coast, coste, drift, float, lapse, skate, sleek, slide **06** vanish **07** scrieve **08** volplane **10** portamento **12** move smoothly

**glimmer**
**03** ray **04** glow, hint, wink **05** blink, flash, gleam, glint, grain, shine, stime, styme, trace **07** flicker, glimpse, glisten, glitter, inkling, shimmer, sparkle, twinkle **10** suggestion

**glimmering**
**04** clue, hint, idea, sign **06** notion **07** inkling, pointer, whisper **08** allusion, faintest, foggiest, innuendo **09** suspicion **10** indication, intimation, suggestion **11** insinuation

**glimpse**
**03** spy **04** espy, glim, look, peek, peep, spot, view, waff **05** blink, flash, gliff, glift, glisk, sight, stime, styme, whiff **06** aperçu, glance, gledge, squint **08** sighting **09** brief look, foregleam, quick look **12** catch sight of

**glint**
**05** flash, gleam, shine **07** glimmer, glisten, glitter, reflect, shimmer, sparkle, twinkle **10** glistening, reflection **11** scintillate

**glisten**
**05** flash, gleam, glint, shine **07** flicker, glimmer, glitter, shimmer, sparkle, twinkle **09** coruscate

**glitch**
**04** snag **05** block, catch, check, delay **06** hiccup, hold-up, mishap **07** barrier, problem, setback, trouble **08** drawback, obstacle **09** hindrance **10** difficulty, impediment **11** obstruction

**glitter**
**04** gilt, glee **05** flare, flash, gleam, glint, glitz, sheen, shine **06** bicker, dazzle, lustre, tinsel **07** flicker, glamour, glimmer, glisten, glister, shimmer, spangle, sparkle, twinkle **08** radiance **09** coruscate, showiness, splendour **10** brightness, brilliance, flashiness, razzmatazz **11** coruscation, scintillate **12** razzle-dazzle **13** scintillation

**glitz**
**05** swank **07** glitter, pizzazz **09** gaudiness, showiness **10** flashiness, garishness, razzmatazz **11** flamboyance, ostentation **12** razzle-dazzle **13** tastelessness **14** attractiveness **15** pretentiousness

**glitzy**
**04** loud, posh **05** cheap, fancy, flash, gaudy, ritzy, showy, vivid **06** flashy, garish, ornate, swanky, tawdry **07** pompous **09** brilliant, tasteless **10** flamboyant, glittering **11** pretentious **12** ostentatious

**gloat**
**04** crow **05** boast, exult, glory, vaunt **06** relish **07** rejoice, revel in, rub it in, triumph **09** delight in

**global**
**05** total **07** general **08** thorough **09** spherical, universal, worldwide **10** exhaustive **11** wide-ranging **12** all-inclusive, encyclopedic **13** comprehensive, encyclopaedic, international **15** all-encompassing

**globally**
**09** generally, worldwide **10** everywhere **11** in every land, under the sun, universally **12** in every place **14** in every country **15** internationally

**globe**
**03** orb **04** ball, pome **05** earth, round, world **06** planet, sphere **08** roundure

**globular**
**05** round **07** globate **08** spheroid **09** orbicular, spherical **10** ball-shaped

**globule**
**04** ball, bead, blob, drop, pill **05** pearl **06** bubble, pellet **07** droplet, vesicle **08** globulet, particle, vesicula

**gloom**
**03** woe **04** damp, dark, dusk, mirk, mood, murk **05** cloud, drere, grief, scowl, shade **06** dreare, misery, shadow, sorrow **07** despair, dimness, sadness **08** darkness, dullness, glumness, the blues, twilight **09** blackness, dejection, murkiness, obscurity, pessimism **10** cloudiness, depression, desolation, low spirits, melancholy, sullenness **11** despondency, unhappiness **12** hopelessness **14** discouragement

**gloomily**
**05** sadly **06** glumly **08** dismally, drearily, morosely **09** miserably **11** cheerlessly **12** depressingly, despondently **13** downheartedly **15** pessimistically

**gloomy**
**03** dim, low, sad, wan **04** dark, down, dull, glum, grim, mirk, murk **05** dingy, drear, dusky, heavy, morne, murky, sable, unlit **06** cloudy, dismal, dreary, drumly, morose, somber, sombre **07** obscure, shadowy, Stygian **08** darksome, dejected, desolate, downbeat, downcast, frowning, overcast **09** cheerless, Cimmerian, depressed, dyspeptic, miserable, saturnine, sorrowful, tenebrose, tenebrous **10** Acherontic, depressing, despondent, disastrous, dispirited, downlooked, melancholy, sepulchral, tenebrious **11** crepuscular, downhearted, dyspeptical, pessimistic **12** disconsolate, in low spirits **14** down in the dumps

• **gloomy appearance**
**04** lour

**glorification**
**06** avatar, praise **07** lauding, worship **08** doxology, thanking **09** adoration, extolling, gratitude, honouring, reverence **10** apotheosis, veneration **11** celebration, idolization, lionization **13** magnification **15** romanticization, transfiguration

**glorify**
**04** hail, laud **05** adore, bless, exalt, extol, thank **06** honour, praise, revere **07** elevate, heroize, idolize, lionize, magnify, worship **08** emblazon, enshrine, eulogize, sanctify, venerate **09** celebrate **10** panegyrize **11** immortalize, romanticize, transfigure

**glorious**
**04** fine **05** famed, grand, great, noble, noted, super, tipsy **06** bright, elated, famous, superb **07** eminent, perfect, radiant, shining, supreme **08** boastful, dazzling, gorgeous, heavenly, honoured, majestic, renowned, splendid, terrific **09** beautiful, brilliant, excellent, wonderful **10** celebrated, delightful, marvellous, triumphant, victorious **11** illustrious, magnificent **13** distinguished

**glory**
**03** sun **04** crow, fame, halo, pomp **05** boast, crown, exult, gloat, kudos, revel, strut **06** beauty, diadem, gloire,

gloria, homage, honour, praise, relish, renown **07** acclaim, aureola, delight, dignity, garland, majesty, preface, rejoice, tribute, triumph, worship **08** accolade, blessing, doxology, eminence, gloriole, grandeur, prestige, radiance **09** adoration, celebrity, gratitude, greatness, splendour **10** brightness, brilliance, exaltation, veneration **11** distinction, recognition **12** magnificence, resplendence, thanksgiving **13** pride yourself **14** impressiveness **15** illustriousness

**gloss**
**04** mask, note, show, veil **05** front, gleam, sheen, shine **06** define, façade, luster, lustre, polish, postil, veneer **07** comment, explain, shimmer, sparkle, surface, varnish **08** annotate, construe, disguise, footnote, scholion **09** elucidate, interpret, semblance, translate **10** annotation, appearance, brightness, brilliance, camouflage, commentary, definition **11** elucidation, explanation, explication, translation **12** add glosses to **14** interpretation, window-dressing

• **gloss over**
**04** fard, gild, hide, mask, veil **05** avoid, evade **06** ignore, soothe **07** conceal, cover up **08** disguise **09** whitewash **10** camouflage, double-gild, smooth over **11** explain away **13** draw a veil over **15** deal with quickly

**glossary**
**05** index **06** clavis **07** lexicon **08** wordbook, word list **09** thesaurus **10** dictionary **11** concordance

**glossy**
**05** glacé, shiny, silky, sleek, slick **06** bright, glassy, glazed, polite, sheeny, silken, smooth **07** shining, wet-look **08** gleaming, lustrous, polished **09** brilliant, burnished, enamelled, sparkling **10** shimmering

**glove**
**03** kid **04** gage, left, mitt **05** right **06** beaver, cestus, mitten, muffle **07** caestus, chevron **08** cheveron, gauntlet **09** oven glove

**glow**
**04** burn, leam, leme, rose **05** bloom, blush, flush, gleam, glory, light, shine **06** ardour, colour, redden, warmth **07** burning, fervour, glimmer, passion, radiate, redness, sunglow **08** grow pink, look pink, outflush, pinkness, radiance, richness, rosiness, smoulder **09** afterglow, corposant, happiness, intensity, reddening, splendour, vividness **10** brightness, brilliance, enthusiasm, excitement, luminosity **11** gegenschein, St Elmo's fire **12** satisfaction **13** incandescence **15** phosphorescence

**glower**
**04** look **05** frown, glare, scowl, stare **09** black look, dirty look **11** look daggers

**glowing**
**03** red **04** rave, rich, warm **05** ruddy, vivid **06** bright, fervid **07** candent, flaming, flushed, lambent, radiant, vibrant **08** ecstatic, luminous, rutilant **09** laudatory, rhapsodic **10** candescent, eulogistic, favourable **11** noctilucent, noctilucous, panegyrical, smouldering **12** enthusiastic, incandescent **13** complimentary **14** phosphorescent

**glue**
**03** fix, gum **04** bond, grip, seal, size **05** affix, epoxy, paste, rivet, stick **06** absorb, cement, compel, engage, mortar **07** engross, gelatin **08** adhesive, Araldite®, fixative, gelatine, propolis **09** hypnotize, mesmerize **11** agglutinate **12** conglutinate, ichthyocolla **14** impact adhesive

**gluey**
**05** gummy **06** sticky, viscid **07** viscous **08** adhesive **09** glutinous

**glum**
**03** low, sad **04** down, sour **05** gruff, moody, sulky, surly **06** gloomy, grumpy, morose, solemn, sullen **07** crabbed, doleful, forlorn, unhappy **08** churlish, dejected **09** depressed, miserable **10** despondent **11** crestfallen, ill-humoured, pessimistic **14** down in the dumps

**glumly**
**05** sadly **06** sourly **08** gloomily, gruffily, grumpily, morosely, sullenly **09** forlornly, miserably, unhappily **10** dejectedly **12** despondently

**glut**
**04** clog, cram, fill, sate **05** choke, flood, gorge, stuff **06** deluge, excess **07** engorge, satiate, surfeit, surplus **08** inundate, overfeed, overflow, overload, saturate **10** oversupply, saturation **11** superfluity **13** overabundance **14** superabundance

**glutinous**
**04** limy, ropy **05** gluey, gummy, ropey **06** mucous, sticky, viscid **07** viscous **08** adhesive, cohesive **09** emplastic **12** mucilaginous

• **glutinous formation**
**04** rope

**glutton**
**03** pig **06** gorger, gutser, gutzer **07** gobbler, guzzler, lurcher **08** belly-god, carcajou, gourmand **09** cormorant, free-liver, wolverine **10** greedy guts **11** gormandizer

**gluttonous**
**05** gutsy **06** greedy **07** hoggish, piggish **08** edacious, esurient, gourmand, ravenous **09** rapacious, voracious **10** gluttonish, insatiable, omnivorous **12** gormandizing

**gluttony**
**05** greed **07** edacity, surfeit **08** gulosity, voracity **09** esurience **10** gormandize, greediness **11** gourmandism, piggishness **13** insatiability

**G-man**
**03** fed

**gnarled**
◇ *anagram indicator*
**05** bumpy, lumpy, rough **06** gnarly, knotty, knurly, rugged **07** gnarred, knarred, knotted, twisted **08** leathery, wrinkled **09** contorted, distorted **13** weather-beaten

**gnash**
**04** grit **05** grate, grind **06** scrape

**gnaw**
**03** eat, nag **04** bite, chew, fret, prey, wear **05** erode, harry, haunt, munch, worry **06** crunch, devour, harass, nibble, niggle, plague **07** consume, eat away, torment, trouble **09** masticate

**gnome**
**03** saw **05** adage, dwarf, maxim, motto **06** goblin, kobold, saying **07** proverb **08** aphorism **09** financier

**go**
**03** act, bet, bid, die, fit, gae, gee, get, pep, run, try, zip **04** bash, bout, cark, deal, emit, fail, fare, gang, go by, grow, hark, head, kark, lead, life, move, pass, push, quit, scat, shot, span, stab, suit, turn, walk, work, yead, yede, yeed, zing **05** begin, blend, crack, croak, drive, drown, end up, fit in, force, lapse, leave, match, occur, oomph, reach, ready, scoot, scram, sound, spell, stake, start, whirl **06** accord, affair, beat it, be axed, become, be kept, belong, cark it, depart, effort, elapse, energy, expire, extend, go away, kark it, manage, matter, pan out, pass by, pass on, peg out, perish, pop off, repair, result, roll on, set off, set out, slip by, spirit, spread, starve, travel, unfold, vanish, vigour **07** advance, attempt, bargain, be fired, be found, be given, be spent, carry on, decease, develop, give off, journey, make for, operate, perform, pizzazz, proceed, release, retreat, send out, snuff it, stretch, success, turn out, urinate, work out **08** activity, be sacked, be used up, clear off, come to be, continue, dynamism, function, get rid of, melt away, pass away, progress, slip away, tick away, vitality, withdraw **09** animation, be donated, be given to, be located, be pledged, be spent on, disappear, endeavour, eventuate, harmonize **10** be consumed, be finished, be situated, complement, co-ordinate, correspond, get-up-and-go, go together, make a sound, make tracks **11** be awarded to, be discarded, be dismissed, be exhausted, be presented, bite the dust **12** be allotted to, be assigned to, be thrown away, lose your life, pop your clogs, shoot through **13** be changed into, close your eyes, kick the bucket, push up daisies, take your leave **14** be given the push, be given the sack, be shown the door,

depart this life, give up the ghost **15** be made redundant, breathe your last, cash in your chips, go with each other

**• go about**

◇ *containment indicator*

**02** do **04** stir **05** begin **06** tackle **07** address, perform **08** approach, attend to, embark on, engage in, set about **09** undertake

**• go ahead**

**04** move **05** begin **07** advance, carry on, precede, proceed **08** continue, fire away, progress **12** make progress

**• go along with**

**04** obey **06** accept, follow **07** abide by, support **09** accompany, agree with **10** comply with, concur with, fall in with

**• go and get**

**03** fet **05** fetch

**• go around, go round**

◇ *anagram indicator*

◇ *containment indicator*

◇ *reversal indicator*

**04** reel, spin, turn **05** swirl, twirl, twist, wheel, whirl, whirr **06** bypass, circle, gyrate, rotate, swivel **07** go about, revolve **09** circulate, pirouette, turn round **13** be passed round, be talked about **14** be spread around

**• go at**

**05** argue, blame **06** attack, tackle **08** set about **09** criticize

**• go away**

**04** scat **05** choof, hence, imshi, imshy, leave, scoot, scram, swith **06** begone, depart, vanish **07** abscond, do a bunk, gertcha, nick off, rack off, retreat **08** choof off, run for it, withdraw **09** disappear, do a runner **10** get knotted **13** sling your hook **14** make a bolt for it, run for your life **15** make a break for it, take to your heels

**• go back**

◇ *reversal indicator*

**06** return, revert **07** regress, retreat **09** backslide

**• go back on**

◇ *reversal indicator*

**04** deny **05** break **08** renege on **09** default on

**• go by**

**04** flow, heed, obey, pass **05** lapse **06** elapse, follow **07** observe **10** comply with

**• go down**

**03** dip, set **04** drop, fail, fall, fold, lose, sink **07** decline, descend, founder, go under, sustain **08** be beaten, collapse, decrease, fall down **09** be met with, be reduced **10** be defeated, be honoured, be received, be recorded, degenerate **11** be reacted to, be submerged, deteriorate **12** be recognized, be remembered, come a cropper, suffer defeat **15** have as a response

**• go down with**

**05** catch **06** pick up **07** develop **08** contract **09** succumb to **12** come down with **13** be afflicted by

**• go for**

**04** like **05** enjoy **06** admire, aim for, assail, attack, choose, favour, prefer, rush at, select **07** assault, lunge at **08** set about

**• go forward**

**03** rip

**• go freely**

**03** run

**• go in for**

**05** adopt, enter **06** follow, go into, pursue, take up **07** embrace, espouse **08** engage in, practise **09** undertake **10** take part in **13** participate in

**• go into**

◇ *insertion indicator*

**05** probe, study **06** review **07** analyse, discuss, dissect, examine **08** check out, consider, look into, research **09** delve into **10** scrutinize **11** inquire into, investigate

**• go off**

◇ *anagram indicator*

**03** rot **04** quit, sour, turn **05** blast, burst, go bad, leave **06** blow up, depart, go bang, set out, vanish **07** abscond, be fired, explode, go stale **08** detonate **09** disappear **11** deteriorate **12** be discharged

**• go on**

**03** gab, gas, hup **04** last, stay **05** occur **06** endure, happen, natter, rabbit, remain, witter **07** carry on, chatter, persist, proceed **08** continue, ramble on **09** take place

**• go out**

**03** ebb **04** date, exit **05** court, leave **06** depart, go with **07** go round **08** go around, go steady, withdraw **11** be turned off **12** see each other **13** be switched off **14** be extinguished

**• go over**

**04** list, read, scan **05** check, study **06** peruse, repeat, review, revise **07** discuss, examine, inspect **08** look over, rehearse **10** think about

**• go quickly**

**03** cut, run, zap **04** hare, race, spin

**• go round**

**04** ring, turn **06** rotate

**• go slow**

**04** lose

**• go through**

**04** bear, face, hunt **05** check, spend, stand, use up **06** endure, search, suffer **07** consume, examine, exhaust, explore, undergo **08** be passed, be signed, rehearse, squander, tolerate **09** be adopted, be carried, withstand **10** be accepted, be approved, experience, get through **11** be confirmed, investigate, look through **12** be authorized **13** be subjected to

**• go together**

◇ *juxtaposition indicator*

**03** fit **04** suit **05** blend, match **06** accord **09** harmonize **10** complement, co-ordinate

**• go under**

◇ *juxtaposition down indicator*

**03** die **04** fail, flop, fold, sink **05** drown **06** go bust, go down **07** default, founder, succumb **08** collapse, submerge **09** close down **10** go bankrupt **11** go to the wall **15** go out of business

**• go with**

**03** fit **04** suit, take **05** blend, match, usher **06** escort **09** accompany, harmonize **10** complement, co-ordinate, correspond

**• go without**

**04** lack, want **05** forgo **06** forego **07** abstain **09** do without **12** deny yourself **13** manage without

**• tell to go**

**04** send

## goad

**03** gad, nag, vex **04** brod, jolt, prod, push, spur, urge **05** ankus, annoy, drive, hound, impel, prick, sound, sting, taunt **06** arouse, harass, incite, induce, needle, prompt **07** inspire, provoke **08** irritate, motivate **09** instigate, stimulate **10** cattle prod, pressurize

## go-ahead

**02** OK **05** pushy **06** assent **07** consent, dashing, dynamic, forward **08** approval, sanction, thumbs-up, vigorous, warranty **09** agreement, ambitious, clearance, energetic, go-getting **10** aggressive, green light, permission, pioneering **11** opportunist, progressive, resourceful, up-and-coming **12** confirmation, enterprising **13** authorization **14** forward-looking

## goal

**03** aim, end **04** cage, dool, dule, hail, home, mark, race **05** bourn, grail, ideal, limit **06** bourne, design, object, target **07** purpose **08** ambition, boundary, terminus **09** direction, equalizer, intention, objective **10** aspiration **11** competition, destination

**• prevent goal**

**04** save

## goat

**03** bok, kid **04** gate, ibex, tahr, tehr, thar **05** nanny **06** Angora, butter, caprid, lecher, Saanen **07** bucardo, markhor **09** Capricorn

## goat-antelope

**05** goral, serow **07** chamois

## goatsucker

**06** evejar **07** bullbat, dorhawk, fern-owl **08** churn-owl, nightjar, poorwill **09** nighthawk **10** moth-hunter, night-churr **11** screech-hawk **12** mosquito hawk, whippoorwill **15** chuck-will's-widow

## gobble

◇ *containment indicator*

**04** bolt, cram, gulp, wolf **05** gorge, scoff, snarf, stuff **06** devour, guzzle **07** consume, put away, slabber, slubber, swallow **10** eat quickly

## gobbledygook

**06** drivel, jargon **07** prattle, rubbish, twaddle **08** nonsense **09** buzz words, gibberish **10** balderdash, journalese

**11** computerese, officialese
**12** psychobabble

**go-between**
**05** agent **06** broker, dealer, factor, medium **07** contact, liaison **08** mediator **09** messenger, middleman **10** love-broker **11** ring-carrier **12** intermediary

**goblet**
**03** cup **05** glass, hanap **06** beaker **07** chalice, stem cup, tumbler

**goblin**
**03** elf, imp, nis, pug **04** bogy, puck **05** bogey, bogle, demon, fiend, gnome, nisse, nixie, pooka, pouke, troll **06** bodach, duende, Empusa, kelpie, kobold, redcap, spirit, sprite **07** bargest, brownie, gremlin, knocker, red-cowl **08** barghest **09** barghaist, gobbeline, hobgoblin **10** leprechaun, shellycoat **11** lubber fiend **12** esprit follet

**gobsmacked**
**04** dumb **06** amazed, thrown **07** baffled, floored, shocked, stunned **08** confused, overcome, startled **09** astounded, paralysed, staggered **10** astonished, bewildered, bowled over, confounded, nonplussed, speechless, taken aback **11** dumbfounded, overwhelmed **12** lost for words **13** flabbergasted, knocked for six

**God**
**01** D **02** od **03** dod, dog, gad, Gog, gum, Jah, odd **04** Dieu, gosh, King, Lord, Zeus **05** Allah, Deity, Judge, Maker, monad **06** Brahma, Elohim, Father, Yahweh **07** all-seer, Bhagwan, Creator, Eternal, Godhead, Holy One, Jehovah, Saviour **08** all-giver, Almighty, gracious, infinite **09** All-father **10** first cause, prime mover, Providence **11** Divine Being, Everlasting, king of kings **12** Supreme Being
• **God willing**
**02** DV **09** inshallah **10** Deo volente, volente Deo

**god, goddess**
**02** as **04** aitu, cock, deus, deva, Fate, faun, icon, idol, kami, Muse, Norn **05** deify, deity, Grace, Norna, power **06** spirit, sylvan **08** divinity **09** promachos **11** divine being, graven image

*Babylonian gods include:*

**02** Ea
**03** Anu, Bel, Sin
**04** Adad, Apsu, Baal, Enki, Nabu
**05** Ellil, Enlil, Hadad, Mummu
**06** Anshar, Dumuzi, Marduk, Nergal, Tammuz
**07** Ninurta, Shamash, Thammuz

*Babylonian goddesses include:*

**03** Aja
**04** Antu
**05** Antum, Belit, Nintu
**06** Ishtar, Kishar, Ningal, Ninlil, Nintur, Tiamat
**07** Anunitu, Damkina
**10** Ereshkigal

*Central and South American gods include:*

**04** Chac, Inti
**06** Tlaloc
**07** Huang-ti, Hunab Ku, Itzamma
**08** Catequil, Kukulkan
**09** the Bacabs, Viracocha, Xipe Totec
**10** Apu Punchau, Manco Capac, Pachacamac, Xochipilli
**12** Quetzalcoatl, Tezcatlipoca, Xiuhtecuhtli
**15** Huitzilopochtil

*Central and South American goddesses include:*

**05** Aknah
**06** Ixchel
**09** Coatlicue, Ixazaluoh, Mama Oella, Pachamama
**10** Mama Quilla
**11** Tlazolteotl
**12** Xochiquetzal
**15** Chalchiuhtlicue

*Egyptian gods include:*

**02** Ra, Re
**03** Bes, Geb, Nut
**04** Apis, Aten, Atum, Ptah, Seth
**05** Horus, Thoth
**06** Amun-Re, Anubis, Osiris
**07** Khonsou, Sarapis, Serapis

*Egyptian goddesses include:*

**03** Nut
**04** Isis, Maat
**05** Khnum
**06** Hathor, Sakmet, Sekmet
**07** Nepthys, Sakhmet, Sekhmet
**08** Nephthys

*Greek gods include:*

**03** Pan
**04** Ares, Atys, Eros, Zeus
**05** Atlas, Attis, Hades
**06** Adonis, Aeolus, Apollo, Boreas, Cronus, Helios, Hermes, Hypnos, Nereus
**07** Oceanus
**08** Dionysus, Ganymede, Morpheus, Poseidon, Thanatos
**09** Asclepius
**10** Hephaestus
**11** Aesculapius

*Greek goddesses include:*

**03** Eos, Nyx
**04** Gaea, Gaia, Hebe, Hera, Iris, Nike, Rhea
**05** Tyche
**06** Athene, Cybele, Hecate, Hestia, Hygeia, Selene, Themis, Thetis
**07** Alphito, Artemis, Demeter, Erinyes, Nemesis
**08** Arethusa, the Fates, the Horae, the Muses
**09** Aphrodite, the Furies, the Graces
**10** Persephone

*Hindu gods include:*

**04** Agni, Kama, Rama, Siva, Soma, Yama
**05** Indra, Kurma, Radha, Rudra, Shani, Shiva, Surya
**06** Brahma, Ganesa, Ganesh, Garuda, Iswara, Narada, Pushan, Ravana, Skanda, Varuna, Vishnu
**07** Ganesha, Hanuman, Krishna, Savitri
**08** Ganapati, Nataraja
**09** Kartikeya, Lakshmana, Narasimha, Prajapati
**10** Jagannatha

*Hindu goddesses include:*

**03** Uma
**04** Devi, Kali, Maya, Sita
**05** Aditi, Durga, Gauri, Radha, Sakti
**06** Shakti
**07** Lakshmi, Parvati
**09** Sarasvati

*Maori gods include:*

**02** Tu
**03** Uru
**04** Maui, Tane
**05** Rangi, Rongo
**06** Haumia
**07** Tawhiri
**08** Ranginui, Ruaumoko, Tangaroa
**10** Tane Mahuta
**11** Rongomatane, Tumatauenga
**12** Tawhiri Matea

*Maori goddesses include:*

**04** Papa
**10** Hinetitama
**11** Hinenuitepo, Papatuanuku

*Norse gods include:*

**03** Bor, Otr, Tyr, Ull
**04** Frey, Logi, Loki, Odin, Thor
**05** Aegir, Aesir, Alcis, Bragi, Donar, Freyr, Hoder, Mimir, Njord, Vanir, Vidar, Woden, Wotan
**06** Balder, Fafnir, Hermod, Hoenir, Kvasir, Weland
**07** Volundr, Wayland, Weiland
**08** Heimdall

*Norse goddesses include:*

**03** Hel, Ran, Sif
**04** Hela
**05** Frigg, Idunn, Nanna, Norns, Sigyn
**06** Freyja, Gefion
**07** Nerthus
**08** Fjorgynn
**09** Valkyries
**10** Nehallenia

*Roman gods include:*

**04** Mars
**05** Cupid, Fides, Janus, Lares, Orcus, Picus, Pluto
**06** Apollo, Consus, Faunus, Genius, Mithra, Saturn, Vulcan
**07** Bacchus, Jupiter, Mercury, Mithras, Neptune, Penates
**08** Portunus, Silvanus
**09** Vertumnus
**10** Liber Pater

*Roman goddesses include:*

**03** Ops
**04** Juno, Luna, Maia
**05** Ceres, Diana, Epona, Fauna, Flora, Pales, Venus, Vesta
**06** Pomona, Rumina
**07** Bellona, Egreria, Feronia, Fortuna, Minerva
**08** Libitina, Victoria
**10** Proserpina

*Gods and goddesses of other regions and cultures include:*

**03** Rod, Wak
**04** Amma, Kane, Tane
**05** Epona, Pan Gu, Perun
**06** Guan Di, Inanna, Kuan Ti, Mithra, Modimo, Moloch, Shango, Svarog, Tengri, Teshub, Vahagn
**07** Anahita, Astarte, Kumarbi, Taranis, Triglav, Zanhary
**08** Rosmerta, Skyamsen, Sucellus, Teutates
**09** Amaterasu, Sventovit
**10** Ahura Mazda
**11** Thunderbird
**15** Izanagi no Mikoto, Izanami no Mikoto

**god-forsaken**
**05** bleak **06** dismal, dreary, gloomy, lonely, remote **07** forlorn **08** deserted, desolate, isolated, wretched
**09** abandoned, miserable **10** depressing

**godless**
**03** bad **04** evil **05** pagan **06** sinful, unholy, wicked **07** atheous, heathen, immoral, impious, profane, ungodly
**08** agnostic **09** atheistic, faithless
**10** irreverent **11** irreligious, nullifidian, unrighteous **12** sacrilegious

**godlessness**
**07** atheism, impiety **08** paganism
**10** irreligion, wickedness
**11** agnosticism, irreverence, ungodliness **13** faithlessness
**14** unfaithfulness

**godlike**
**04** holy **06** divine, sacred **07** deiform, exalted, perfect, saintly, sublime
**08** heavenly, Olympian **09** celestial
**10** superhuman **11** theomorphic
**12** transcendent

**godliness**
**05** piety **06** belief, purity **08** holiness, morality, religion, sanctity
**10** devoutness **13** righteousness

**godly**
**04** good, holy, pure, wise **05** moral, pious **06** devout **07** saintly
**08** innocent, virtuous **09** believing, religious, righteous **10** God-fearing

**godsend**
**04** boon **07** bonanza, miracle
**08** blessing, windfall **11** benediction
**12** stroke of luck

**goggle**
**04** gawk, gawp, gaze, ogle **05** stare
**06** wonder **08** protrude

**going-over**
**03** row **05** check, study **06** attack, rebuke, review, survey **07** beating, check-up, chiding, pasting **08** analysis, scolding, scrutiny, whipping
**09** criticism, reprimand, thrashing, trouncing **10** inspection
**11** castigation, examination
**12** chastisement, dressing-down
**13** investigation

**goings-on**
**06** events, scenes **07** affairs
**08** business, mischief **09** behaviour
**10** activities, happenings
**11** occurrences **12** misbehaviour
**13** funny business

**gold**
**02** Au, or **03** bar, Sol **04** gool, gule, leaf
**05** goold, ingot **06** nugget, riches, yellow **07** bullion **12** king of metals
**13** precious metal
• **yield gold**
**03** pan

**golden**
**03** red **04** fair, gilt, gold, rosy **05** blond, happy, sunny **06** blonde, bright, flaxen, gilded, gilden, gylden, joyful, yellow
**07** aureate, goldish, luteous, shining
**08** aurelian, dazzling, gleaming, glorious, inaurate, lustrous, precious
**09** brilliant, excellent, promising, rewarding, Saturnian, treasured
**10** auspicious, delightful, favourable, millennial, propitious, prosperous, successful **11** flourishing, hyacinthine, resplendent **12** gold-coloured

**goldfinch**
**06** redcap **09** goldspink, gowdspink
**10** yellowbird

**golf**
**01** G **04** gowf

*Golf courses include:*

**04** Deal, Eden
**05** Troon
**06** Manito, Merion, Skokie
**07** Balgove, Buffalo, Hoylake, Jubilee, Medinah, Newport, Oak Hill, Oakmont, Oak Tree, Prince's, Sahalee
**08** Bethesda, Birkdale, Blue Hill, Glen View, Portland, Sandwich, Valhalla
**09** Aronimink, Baltimore, Baltusrol, Bellerive, Brookline, Englewood, Hazeltine, Inverness, Minikahda, Muirfield, New Course, Old Course, Onwentsia, Pinehurst, Prestwick, St Andrews, The Belfry, Turnberry
**10** Canterbury, Carnoustie, Garden City, Royal Troon, Shoal Creek, Tanglewood, Winged Foot
**11** Cherry Hills, Kemper Lakes, Miami Valley, Musselburgh, Olympic Club, Pebble Beach, Strathtyrum
**12** Crooked Stick, Laurel Valley, Oakland Hills
**13** Northwood Club, Olympia Fields, Royal Birkdale, Royal Portrush, Southern Hills
**14** Keller Golf Club, Myopia Hunt Club, NCR Country Club, Pelham Golf Club
**15** Augusta National, Chicago Golf Club, Shinnecock Hills

**golf club**

*Golf clubs include:*

**04** iron, wood
**05** baffy, blade, cleek, mashy, spoon, wedge
**06** brassy, bulger, driver, jigger, mashie, putter
**07** blaster, brassie, midiron, niblick
**08** long iron
**09** midmashie, sand wedge, short iron
**10** mashie iron
**11** belly putter, driving iron, fairway wood, spade mashie
**12** putting-cleek
**13** mashie-niblick, pitching wedge, two-ball putter
**15** pitching niblick

**golfer**
**06** gowfer, yipper

*Golfers include:*

**03** **Els** (Ernie)
**04** **Lyle** (Sandy), **Webb** (Karrie)
**05** **Braid** (James), **Brown** (Ken), **Duval** (David), **Faldo** (Nick), **Floyd** (Raymond), **Hagen** (Walter), **Hogan** (Ben), **Jones** (Bobby), **Locke** (Bobby), **Lopez** (Nancy), **Singh** (Vijay), **Snead** (Sam Jackson), **Woods** (Tiger)
**06** **Alliss** (Peter), **Cotton** (Sir Henry), **Davies** (Laura), **Garcia** (Sergio), **Langer** (Bernhard), **Nelson** (Byron), **Norman** (Greg), **O'Meara** (Mark), **Palmer** (Arnold), **Player** (Gary), **Taylor** (John), **Vardon** (Harry), **Watson** (Tom)
**07** **Charles** (Bob), **Couples** (Fred), **Jacklin** (Tony), **Sarazen** (Gene), **Stewart** (Payne), **Strange** (Curtis), **Thomson** (Peter), **Trevino** (Lee Buck), **Woosnam** (Ian), **Zoeller** (Fuzzy)
**08** **Crenshaw** (Ben), **Nicklaus** (Jack), **Olazábal** (Jose Maria), **Torrance** (Sam), **Westwood** (Lee), **Zaharias** (Babe)
**09** **Mickelson** (Phil), **Sorenstam** (Annika), **Whitworth** (Kathy)
**11** **Ballesteros** (Severiano), **Montgomerie** (Colin)

**gone**
◇ *anagram indicator*
**03** ago, ygo **04** away, dead, done, gane, lost, over, past, used, ygoe
**05** agone, spent **06** absent, astray
**07** defunct, elapsed, extinct, missing, worn-out **08** departed, finished, vanished **11** disappeared **15** over and done with

**goo**
**03** mud **04** crud, grot, gunk, mire, muck, ooze, scum, slop, yuck

**05** gloop, grime, gunge, slime, slush **06** grease, grunge, matter, sludge **10** stickiness **14** sentimentality

**good**
**01** g **02** OK **03** bad, bon, fab, fit, rum, top, use **04** able, best, dear, fair, fine, gain, kind, mega, neat, nice, safe, sake, true, well **05** adept, avail, beaut, bewdy, bonne, bosom, brill, bully, close, great, large, lucky, merit, moral, nasty, noble, pakka, pious, pucka, pukka, right, sound, super, valid, whole, worth **06** agreed, behalf, bonzer, bosker, castor, clever, corker, cushty, ethics, expert, gifted, honest, honour, indeed, just so, loving, morals, polite, profit, ripper, strong, superb, useful, virtue, wicked, worthy **07** awesome, benefit, capable, ethical, fitting, genuine, healthy, helpful, honesty, perfect, purpose, service, sizable, skilful, skilled, upright, welfare **08** adequate, all right, budgeree, cheerful, complete, cracking, fabulous, faithful, friendly, goodness, gracious, interest, intimate, morality, obedient, passable, pleasant, pleasing, reliable, sensible, sizeable, smashing, suitable, superior, talented, terrific, thorough, very well, vigorous, virtuous **09** admirable, advantage, agreeable, bodacious, brilliant, competent, compliant, desirable, dexterous, efficient, enjoyable, excellent, exemplary, fantastic, first-rate, fortunate, integrity, in the pink, rectitude, righteous, tolerable, wellbeing, wonderful **10** acceptable, altruistic, auspicious, beneficial, benevolent, charitable, convenient, convincing, dependable, favourable, first-class, good as gold, honourable, marvellous, persuasive, proficient, profitable, propitious, prosperity, reasonable, respectful, satisfying, sufficient, thoughtful, usefulness, worthwhile **11** appropriate, commendable, considerate, convenience, exceptional, kind-hearted, pleasurable, serviceable, substantial, sympathetic, trustworthy, uprightness, well-behaved **12** accomplished, advantageous, bewdy bottler, considerable, fit as a fiddle, professional, satisfactory, under control, well-disposed, well-mannered **13** hale and hearty, philanthropic, righteousness **14** salt of the earth

• **for good**
**04** ever **06** always **07** for ever **08** evermore, for keeps **09** eternally **10** for all time **11** irrevocably, permanently **15** till kingdom come

• **make good**
**02** do **04** abet **05** go far **06** arrive, effect, fulfil, make it, recoup, repair, supply **07** justify, perform, restore, succeed, support **08** carry out, get ahead, live up to, progress, put right, retrieve **09** establish **10** compensate **12** be successful **13** compensate for, make amends for, put into action **15** get on in the world

• **neither good nor bad**
**04** so-so **14** comme çi comme ça

• **no good**
**02** ng **03** bad, bum **04** duff **06** futile, no chop **07** useless **09** worthless

• **pretty good**
**04** fair, tidy **06** decent, not bad **08** middling **09** tolerable **14** fair to middling

• **unusually good**
**04** gear **10** incredible

• **very good**
**02** OK, so, vg **03** sae, top **04** keen, mega **05** bonza, grand **06** bangin', beezer, bonzer, boshta, bosker, grouse, peachy **07** banging, boshter, crucial, immense, ripping **08** all right, cracking, terrific **09** brilliant **10** marvellous, tremendous

**goodbye**
**03** bye **04** ciao, ta-ta **05** addio, adieu, adiós, later **06** bye-bye, cheers, hooray, hooroo, kia ora, haere ra, see you, so long, valete **07** bonsoir, cheerio, good-day, good-den, good-e'en, parting **08** au revoir, chin-chin, farewell, good-even, sayonara, swan song, take care, toodle-oo **09** bon voyage, good night, toodle-pip **10** all the best, a rivederci, good morrow **11** arrivederci, be seeing you, good evening, good morning, leave-taking, see you later, valediction, valedictory **12** have a nice day, mind how you go, see you around **13** good afternoon **14** auf Wiedersehen

*See also* **farewell**

**good-for-nothing**
**03** bum **04** idle, lazy **05** idler, lorel, losel, stiff **06** donnat, donnot, loafer, lozell, no-good, skiver, waster **07** bludger, lorrell, sculpin, slacker, useless, vaurien, wastrel **08** feckless, indolent, layabout, scalawag **09** lazybones, reprobate, scallawag, scallywag, worthless **10** black sheep, ne'er-do-weel, ne'er-do-well, profligate **11** scant-o'-grace **13** irresponsible

**good-humoured**
**05** happy **06** genial, jovial **07** affable, amiable **08** cheerful, friendly, pleasant **09** congenial **12** approachable, good-tempered

**good-looking**
**04** fair **05** dishy **06** comely, goodly, lovely, pretty **08** handsome, weel-far'd, weel-far't **09** beautiful, weel-faird, weel-faur'd, weel-faurt **10** attractive, personable **11** presentable **12** well-favoured

**goodly**
**04** fine, good, tidy **05** ample, large **06** comely, proper **07** sizable **08** sizeable **09** excellent **10** sufficient **11** good-looking, significant, substantial **12** considerable

**good-natured**
**04** kind, nice **05** sonsy **06** clever, gentle, kindly, sonsie **07** helpful, patient **08** friendly, generous, tolerant **10** benevolent **11** kind-hearted, neighbourly, sympathetic, warm-hearted **12** approachable, good-tempered

**goodness**
**02** my **03** boy, law, wow **05** mercy, value **06** virtue **07** benefit, honesty, probity **08** altruism, goodwill, kindness **09** integrity, rectitude **10** compassion, excellence, generosity **11** beneficence, benevolence, helpfulness, uprightness **12** friendliness, graciousness **13** righteousness, unselfishness, wholesomeness

**goods**
**04** bona, gear **05** lines, stock, stuff, wares **06** taonga, things **07** effects, freight **08** chattels, products, property **10** belongings **11** commodities, merchandise, possessions **13** accoutrements, appurtenances, paraphernalia

• **package of goods**
**04** bale, wrap

**good-tempered**
**04** kind **06** gentle, kindly **07** helpful, patient **08** friendly, generous, tolerant **10** benevolent **11** good-natured, kind-hearted, neighbourly, sympathetic, warm-hearted **12** approachable

**goodwill**
**04** gree, zeal **05** amity, favor **06** favour **08** kindness **10** compassion, friendship, generosity **11** benevolence, well-wishing **12** friendliness

**goody-goody**
**05** pious **08** priggish, unctuous **13** sanctimonious, self-righteous, ultra-virtuous

**gooey**
**04** soft **05** gluey, gucky, gungy, gunky, tacky, thick **06** gloopy, sickly, sloppy, slushy, sticky, syrupy, viscid **07** cloying, maudlin, mawkish, squidgy, viscous **09** glutinous **10** nauseating **11** sentimental **12** mucilaginous

**goose**
**04** nene, wavy **05** roger, wavey **06** gander, goslet **07** gosling, grey-lag **08** barnacle **09** whitehead **10** saddleback **13** brent barnacle

*See also* **fool**

• **goose's lungs**
**04** soul

**gooseberry**
**06** groser, groset **07** grosert **08** goosegob, goosegog, grossart **09** honey-blob **14** worcesterberry

**goosefoot**
**04** beet **05** blite, orach **06** fat hen, kochia, orache, quinoa, saxaul **07** pigweed, saksaul **08** saltbush, saltwort, seablite **10** greasewood, Mexican tea **13** good-King-Henry

**gore**
**02** Al **04** cloy, gair, horn, stab **05** blood, cruor, filth, grume, skirt, spear, stick, wound **06** engore, impale, pierce **07** carnage **08** butchery **09** bloodshed, penetrate, slaughter **10** bloodiness

**gorge**
**03** gap **04** bolt, cram, feed, fill, glut, gulp, pass, rift, sate, wolf **05** abyss, cañon, chasm, cleft, gully, stuff **06** canyon, defile, devour, gobble, guzzle, ravine, stodge **07** crevice, fissure, overeat, surfeit, swallow **08** barranca

*See also* **ravine**

**gorgeous**
**04** fine, good, rich, sexy **05** grand, showy, sweet **06** lovely, pretty, superb **07** opulent **08** dazzling, glorious, handsome, pleasing, splendid, stunning **09** beautiful, brilliant, enjoyable, glamorous, luxurious, ravishing, splendent, sumptuous, wonderful **10** attractive, delightful, impressive, marvellous **11** good-looking, magnificent, resplendent **15** pulchritudinous

**gorgeously**
**06** richly **08** superbly **10** gloriously, splendidly **11** brilliantly, luxuriously, sumptuously, wonderfully **12** delightfully, impressively, marvellously **13** magnificently

**gorilla**
**04** thug **05** pongo **08** King Kong **10** silverback

**gorse**
**04** ulex, whin **05** furze, gosse

**gory**
**05** goary **06** bloody, brutal, grisly, savage **07** violent **09** murderous **10** sanguinary **11** blood-soaked, distasteful **12** bloodstained

**gospel**
**04** fact, John, Luke, Mark **05** credo, creed, truth **06** verity **07** evangel, kerygma, Matthew **08** doctrine, good news, teaching **09** certainty **12** life of Christ, New Testament **14** Protevangelium **15** message of Christ

*See also* **Bible**

**gossamer**
**04** airy, fine, thin **05** gauzy, light, sheer, silky **06** flimsy **08** cobwebby, delicate **10** diaphanous, see-through, shimmering **11** translucent, transparent **13** insubstantial

**gossip**
**03** ana, gab, gas, gup, jaw **04** aunt, buzz, chat, dirt, goss, talk **05** clash, crack, rumor, yenta **06** babble, claver, cummer, gabble, jabber, kimmer, natter, rabbit, report, rumour, tatler, tattle, tittle, waffle **07** babbler, blather, blether, chatter, chinwag, clatter, hearsay, prattle, scandal, shmoose, shmooze, tattler, whisper **08** busybody, causerie, chitchat, clatters, idle talk, prattler, rabbit on, schmooze, tell-tale **09** reportage, tell tales, whisperer **10** chatterbox, chew the fat, chew the rag, clish-clash, newsmonger, talebearer **11** mud-slinging, Nosey Parker, scuttlebutt, sweetie-wife **12** gossip-monger, spread gossip, tittle-tattle **13** bush telegraph, clishmaclaver, scandal-bearer, scandalmonger, smear campaign, spread a rumour **14** clash-ma-clavers

**gouge**
**03** cut, dig **04** claw, gash, hack **05** scoop, score, slash, wench **06** chisel, groove, hollow, incise **07** extract, scratch, swindle

**gourd**
**05** guiro, loofa, luffa **06** bryony, cacoon, loofah **07** pumpkin **08** calabash **11** white bryony **12** Hercules' club

**Gourde**
**01** G **03** Gde

**gourmand**
**03** hog, pig **06** gorger **07** glutton, guzzler **08** omnivore **09** voracious **10** gluttonous **11** gormandizer

**gourmet**
**06** foodie **07** epicure **09** bon vivant, epicurean **10** gastronome **11** connoisseur

**gout**
**04** drop, spot **05** taste **06** relish **07** podagra **08** chiragra **09** arthritis **10** cephalagra **12** hamarthritis

**govern**
**03** run **04** curb, head, lead, rein, rule, sway, tame **05** check, guide, order, pilot, quell, reign, steer **06** bridle, direct, manage, master, rein in, subdue **07** command, conduct, contain, control, oversee, preside **08** dominate, hold back, keep back, regulate, restrain **09** be in power, constrain, determine, influence, supervise **10** administer, discipline, hold office **11** keep in check, superintend **12** be in charge of

**governess**
**05** guide **06** duenna, mentor **07** teacher, tutress **08** fräulein, tutoress **09** companion **11** gouvernante **12** instructress, mademoiselle

**governing**
**06** ruling **07** guiding, leading, supreme **08** dominant, reigning **09** kingcraft, uppermost **10** commanding, dominative, overriding, prevailing, regulatory **11** controlling, predominant **12** transcendent

**government**
**01** g **03** Gov, HMG, raj **04** Govt, rule, sway **05** power, state **06** charge, circar, papacy, policy, régime, sircar, sirkar **07** cabinet, command, conduct, control, council, regence, regency, regimen, serkali **08** congress, dominion, guidance, ministry, politics, steerage **09** archology, authority, direction, executive, restraint **10** domination, governance, leadership, management, parliament, regulation **11** authorities, sovereignty, supervision **12** powers that be, surveillance **13** Establishment **14** administration **15** superintendence

*Government systems include:*

**05** junta
**06** empire
**07** kingdom
**08** monarchy, republic
**09** autocracy, communism, democracy, despotism, theocracy
**10** absolutism, federation, hierocracy, plutocracy
**11** triumvirate
**12** commonwealth, dictatorship

• **member of government**
**02** in

**governor**
**02** Pa **03** Ban, beg, bey, Dad, dey, gov, guv **04** boss, head, khan, naik, vali, wali **05** chief, guide, hakim, mudir, pilot, ruler, tutor **06** eparch, exarch, grieve, leader, legate, master, Pilate, rector, satrap, tuchun, warden **07** alcaide, alcayde, catapan, harmost, manager, nomarch, podestà, rectrix, subadar, vaivode, viceroy, voivode **08** alderman, burgrave, director, ethnarch, gospodar, hospodar, kaimakam, overseer, pentarch, provedor, providor, resident, subahdar **09** beglerbeg, castellan, commander, corrector, directrix, dominator, executive, governess, intendant, president, proconsul, provedore, regulator **10** adelantado, controller, directress, gubernator, Lord Warden, proveditor, stadholder, supervisor **11** proveditore, stadtholder **12** commissioner **13** administrator **14** chief executive, superintendent

*Colonial governors of New South Wales:*

**04** **King** (Captain Philip Gidley)
**05** **Bligh** (Captain William), **Gipps** (Sir George)
**06** **Bourke** (Major-General Richard), **Hunter** (Captain John)
**07** **Darling** (Lieutenant-General Ralph), **Denison** (Sir William), **FitzRoy** (Sir Charles), **Phillip** (Captain Arthur)
**08** **Brisbane** (Sir Thomas)
**09** **Macquarie** (Colonel Lachlan)

*Governors-general of Australia:*

**04** **Kerr** (Sir John), **Slim** (Field-Marshal Sir William)
**05** **Casey** (Richard Gardiner, Baron), **Cowen** (Sir Zelman), **Deane** (Sir William)
**06** **Denman** (Thomas, Baron), **Dudley** (William Humble Ward, Earl of), **Gowrie** (Alexander Hore-Ruthven,

Baron), **Hayden** (William), **Isaacs** (Sir Isaac), **McKell** (Sir William)
**07 De L'Isle** (William, Viscount), **Forster** (Henry William, Baron), **Hasluck** (Sir Paul), **Stephen** (Sir Ninian)
**08 Hopetoun** (John Adrian Louis Hope, Earl of), **Tennyson** (Hallam, Baron)
**09 Dunrossil** (William, Viscount), **Northcote** (Henry, Baron)
**10 Gloucester** (Prince Henry, Duke of), **Stonehaven** (Sir John Lawrence Baird, Baron)
**12 Hollingworth** (Dr Peter)
**13 Munro-Ferguson** (Sir Ronald)

*Governors-general of New Zealand:*

**06 Cobham** (Charles George Lyttleton), **Galway** (Earl of), **Newall** (Cyril Louis Norton), **Norrie** (Lord), **Reeves** (Paul Alfred), **Tizard** (Catherine)
**07 Beattie** (David Stuart), **Porritt** (Arthur Espie)
**08 Blundell** (Edward Denis), **Freyberg** (Bernard Cyril), **Holyoake** (Keith Jacka), **Jellicoe** (John Henry Rushworth)
**09 Bledisloe** (Charles Bathurst), **Fergusson** (Bernard), **Fergusson** (Charles), **Liverpool** (Earl of)
**10 Hardie Boys** (Michael)

*Governors of New Zealand:*

**04 Grey** (George), **Weld** (Frederick Aloysius)
**05 Bowen** (Charles Ferguson)
**06 Browne** (Thomas Robert Gore), **Gordon** (Arthur Hamilton), **Hobson** (William), **Onslow** (Earl of), **Onslow** (William Hillier)
**07 FitzRoy** (Robert), **Glasgow** (Earl of), **Jervois** (William Francis Drummond), **Plunket** (Lord)
**08 Normanby** (Marquess of), **Ranfurly** (Earl of), **Robinson** (Hercules George Robert)
**09 Fergusson** (James), **Islington** (Lord), **Liverpool** (Earl of)

**gown**
**04** garb, robe, sack, silk **05** bania, dress, frock, habit, manto, shift, stole **06** banian, banyan, kirtle, mantua, sacque **07** costume, garment, manteau, negligé **08** mazarine, negligee, peignoir **09** sack dress, slammakin **10** slammerkin **12** bearing cloth, dressing-gown **13** Mother Hubbard

**grab**
◇ *containment indicator*
**03** bag, nab, rap **04** grip, nail, take **05** annex, catch, grasp, pluck, seize, swipe, usurp **06** arrest, clutch, collar, nobble, snap up, snatch **07** capture, impress **08** interest **09** lay hold of **10** commandeer, take hold of **11** appropriate, catch hold of
*See also* **steal**

**• up for grabs**
**06** at hand **07** to be had **09** available **10** obtainable **12** for the asking

**grace**
**04** ease, trim **05** adorn, charm, honor, mense, mercy, poise, Venus **06** beauty, become, enrich, favour, honour, pardon, polish, prayer, set off, virtue **07** aggrace, charity, decency, decorum, dignify, enhance, finesse, fluency, garnish, manners, quarter, unction **08** beautify, blessing, breeding, clemency, courtesy, decorate, elegance, goodness, goodwill, kindness, leniency, ornament, reprieve **09** bethankit, embellish, etiquette, good taste, propriety **10** benedicite, comeliness, compassion, generosity, indulgence, kindliness, loveliness, refinement, smoothness **11** benediction, beneficence, benevolence, cultivation, distinguish, forgiveness, shapeliness **12** gracefulness, mercifulness, tastefulness, thanksgiving **13** consideration **14** attractiveness, prayer of thanks

*The Three Graces:*

**06** Aglaia, Thalia
**10** Euphrosyne

**graceful**
**04** deft, easy, fine, kind **05** agile, fluid, genty, suave **06** comely, fluent, gainly, nimble, polite, smooth, supple, svelte **07** elegant, flowing, genteel, natural, refined, slender, tactful, willowy **08** charming, cheerful, cultured, generous, gracious, grazioso, pleasant, polished, sylphine, sylphish, tasteful **09** agreeable, appealing, beautiful, courteous, sylphlike **10** attractive, cultivated, diplomatic, respectful

**gracefully**
**06** deftly, nimbly **08** grazioso, politely, smoothly **09** agreeably, elegantly, naturally, tactfully **10** cheerfully, generously, graciously, pleasantly, tastefully **11** beautifully, courteously **12** attractively, respectfully **14** diplomatically

**graceless**
**04** rude **05** crude, gawky, rough **06** clumsy, coarse, forced, gauche, vulgar **07** awkward, uncouth **08** impolite, improper, ungainly **09** barbarous, inelegant, menseless, shameless **10** indecorous, ungraceful, unmannerly **11** ill-mannered **12** unattractive **15** unsophisticated

**gracelessly**
**06** rudely **07** roughly **08** clumsily **09** awkwardly **10** impolitely **11** inelegantly **12** ungracefully

**gracious**
**04** hend, kind, mild **05** sweet **06** benign, kindly, polite **07** affable, clement, elegant, lenient, refined **08** friendly, generous, handsome, menseful, merciful, obliging, pleasant, tasteful **09** benignant, courteous, forgiving, indulgent, luxurious, sumptuous **10** acceptable, beneficent, benevolent, charitable, favourable, hospitable **11** comfortable, considerate, kind-hearted, magnanimous **12** well-mannered **13** accommodating, compassionate, condescending

**graciously**
**06** goodly, kindly **07** civilly **08** politely **09** tactfully **10** handsomely, pleasantly **11** courteously **12** respectfully **14** diplomatically

**gradation**
**04** mark, rank, step **05** array, cline, level, stage **06** ablaut, change, degree, series **07** grading, shading, sorting **08** ordering, progress, sequence **10** succession **11** arrangement, progression

**grade**
**03** gon **04** mark, rank, rate, rung, size, sort, step, type **05** brand, class, group, label, level, notch, order, place, range, stage, value **06** assess, degree, rating, status **07** arrange, echelon, quality, station **08** category, classify, evaluate, position, standard, standing **09** condition **10** categorize, pigeonhole **14** classification

**• equivalent grade**
**02** EG

**• first grade**
**05** alpha

**• fourth grade**
**05** delta

**• make the grade**
**04** pass **07** succeed **10** win through **11** come through **13** cut the mustard **15** come up to scratch

**• second grade**
**04** beta

**• third grade**
**05** gamma

**gradient**
**04** bank, hill, rise **05** grade, lapse, slope **07** incline **09** acclivity, declivity

**gradual**
**04** easy, even, slow **05** grail **06** gentle, steady **07** regular **08** measured, moderate **09** leisurely, unhurried **10** continuous, step-by-step **11** progressive

**gradually**
**06** evenly, gently, slowly **08** bit by bit, gingerly, steadily **09** by degrees, piecemeal, regularly **10** cautiously, inch by inch, moderately, step by step **11** unhurriedly **12** continuously, successively **13** imperceptibly, progressively **14** little by little

**graduate**
**02** BA, MA **04** grad, pass, rank, sort **05** grade, group, order, ovate, range **06** alumna, doctor, expert, fellow, master, member, move up **07** advance, alumnus, arrange, go ahead, mark off, qualify **08** bachelor, classify, graduand, progress, whizz kid **09** calibrate **10** be promoted, categorize, consultant, forge ahead, licentiate, measure out,

proportion, specialist **11** make headway, move forward **12** professional **13** skilled person, valedictorian **15** complete studies, qualified person

*See also* **qualification**

**graft**
**03** bud, dig, imp **04** join, scam, slog, take, toil **05** affix, ditch, graff, plant, scion, shoot, sting **06** branch, effort, growth, inarch, insert, labour, rip-off, sleaze, splice, sprout, sucker **07** bribery, cuckold, engraft, implant **08** exertion, hard word **09** allograft, autograft, con tricks, extortion, homograft, inoculate, xenograft **10** corruption, dishonesty, excavation, transplant **11** dirty tricks, heterograft **12** implantation **13** dirty dealings, shady business **14** sharp practices **15** sweat of your brow

**grain**
**02** gr **03** bit, jot, nap, rye **04** atom, corn, curn, fork, hint, iota, mite, oats, ragi, rice, seed **05** berry, crumb, emmer, fibre, grits, maize, minim, piece, prong, scrap, speck, trace, weave, wheat **06** barley, branch, fabric, groats, kernel, maslin, morsel **07** cereals, graddan, granule, marking, mashlam, mashlim, mashlin, mashlum, modicum, pattern, soupçon, surface, texture **08** fragment, mashloch, molecule, particle **09** scintilla **10** suggestion

**• soften grain**
**04** cree

**gram**
**01** g **02** gm, gr **03** urd **05** anger, grief, pulse **07** trouble **08** chickpea

**grammar**
**05** Donat, Donet, style, usage **06** syntax **11** good English **14** correct English **15** linguistic rules

*See also* **speech**

**grammatical**
**07** correct **09** syntactic **10** acceptable, linguistic, structural, well-formed **11** appropriate, syntactical **14** well-structured

*See also* **tense**

**grand**
**01** G **03** fab **04** arch, cool, fine, head, main, mega **05** chief, final, great, large, lofty, noble, regal, showy, super **06** in full, lavish, lordly, pretty, senior, superb, wicked **07** exalted, highest, leading, opulent, pompous, stately, sublime, supreme **08** complete, exalting, glorious, imposing, majestic, palatial, precious, smashing, splendid, striking, terrific, thousand **09** ambitious, dignified, enjoyable, excellent, fantastic, first-rate, grandiose, inclusive, luxurious, mausolean, principal, sumptuous, wonderful **10** delightful, impressive, marvellous, monumental, pre-eminent **11** illustrious, magnificent, outstanding, pretentious **12** all-inclusive, ostentatious **13** comprehensive

**grandchild**
**02** oe, oy **03** oye

**grandeur**
**04** fame, pomp **05** state **06** renown **07** dignity, majesty **08** eminence, nobility, opulence, vastness **09** greatness, splendour **10** importance, lavishness, prominence **11** stateliness **12** magnificence **13** luxuriousness **14** impressiveness **15** illustriousness, pretentiousness

**grandfather**
**04** oupa, papa **06** gramps, granda **07** grandad, grandpa, granfer, gutcher **08** goodsire, granddad, gudesire **09** grandaddy, grandpapa, grandsire, luckie-dad **10** granddaddy **11** grandparent

**grandiloquent**
**06** rotund, turgid **07** flowery, fustian, orotund, pompous, swollen **08** inflated **09** bombastic, high-flown, ororotund **10** euphuistic, rhetorical **11** exaggerated, pretentious **12** high-sounding, magniloquent **13** grandiloquous

**grandiose**
**04** long **05** grand, lofty, showy **07** pompous, stately **08** imposing, majestic, splendid, striking **09** ambitious, bombastic, high-flown, mausolean **10** flamboyant, impressive, monumental, over-the-top **11** extravagant, magnificent, pretentious **12** high-sounding, magniloquent, ostentatious

**grandly**
**07** regally **09** pompously **10** gloriously, strikingly **11** excellently **12** impressively, majestically **13** magnificently, pretentiously

**grandmother**
**03** nan **04** gran, nana, ouma **05** nanna, nanny **06** beldam, granny **07** beldame, grandam, grandma, grannam, grannie **08** babushka, good-dame, gude-dame **09** grandmama **10** grandmamma **11** grandparent

**grandparental**
**04** aval **06** avital

**granite**
**07** greisen **08** resolute **09** pegmatite, protogine **10** china stone, unyielding **11** luxulianite, luxulyanite **12** luxullianite

**grant**
**03** aid, fee, feu, let **04** Cary, gift, give, lend, send **05** admit, allot, allow, award, feoff, yield **06** accept, accord, assign, bestow, beteem, confer, donate, impart, permit, supply **07** agree to, annuity, appoint, bequest, beteeme, bursary, charter, concede, consent, furnish, licence, license, pension, present, provide, subsidy **08** accede to, allocate, dispense, donation, granting, transmit **09** allowance, apportion, consent to, endowment, vouchsafe **10** concession, condescend, contribute, exhibition, honorarium, subvention **11** acknowledge, benefaction, expectative, scholarship **12** contribution

**• granted**
**06** agreed

**granular**
**04** corn **05** curny, lumpy, rough, sandy **06** curney, grainy, gritty **07** crumbly, friable **10** granulated

**granule**
**03** jot **04** atom, bead, iota, seed **05** crumb, grain, pearl, piece, scrap, speck **06** pellet **07** plastid **08** bioblast, fragment, molecule, particle **09** chondrule, microsome

**grape**
**03** uva

*See also* **wine**

**grapefruit**
**06** pomelo **07** pompelo **10** pompelmous, pumple-nose **11** pampelmoose, pampelmouse, pompelmoose, pompelmouse

**grapeskins**
**04** marc

**graph**
**04** grid, plot **05** chart, curve, ogive, table **07** diagram, profile **08** bar chart, bar graph, nomogram, pie chart, waveform **09** histogram, nomograph, waveshape **10** carpet plot **11** demand curve, supply curve **13** learning curve **14** scatter diagram

**graphic**
**05** clear, drawn, lucid, vivid **06** cogent, lively, visual **07** telling **08** detailed, explicit, specific, striking, symbolic **09** effective, pictorial, realistic **10** blow-by-blow, expressive **11** delineative, descriptive, well-defined **12** diagrammatic, illustrative

**graphically**
**07** clearly, vividly **10** explicitly, strikingly **12** expressively **13** descriptively, realistically

**graphite**
**04** kish, lead **08** plumbago **09** blacklead, pencil-ore **10** pencil-lead

**grapple**
**04** face, grab, grip, hold, lock **05** clash, clasp, close, fight, grasp, seize **06** battle, clinch, clutch, combat, craple, engage, snatch, tackle, tussle **07** address, contend, wrestle **08** confront, cope with, deal with, struggle **09** encounter, lay hold of **14** get to grips with

**grasp**
◇ *containment indicator*
**03** get, see **04** clat, grab, grip, have, hend, hent, hold, holt, rule **05** catch, clamp, clasp, claut, gripe, power, seize, sense **06** clench, clutch, follow, graple, griple, master, rumble, snatch, strain, take in **07** catch on, command, compass, control, embrace, grapple, gripple, mastery, prehend, realize, squeeze **08** clutches, conceive, dominion, handgrip, perceive
**09** apprehend, awareness, knowledge, latch onto, lay hold of
**10** comprehend, perception, possession, understand **11** familiarity
**12** apprehension, get a handle on, get the hang of **13** comprehension, understanding

**grasping**
◇ *containment indicator*
**04** mean **06** grabby, greedy, griple, stingy **07** griping, gripple, miserly, seizing, selfish **08** covetous
**09** mercenary, niggardly, rapacious
**10** avaricious **11** acquisitive, close-fisted, large-handed, tight-fisted
**12** parsimonious **13** money-grubbing

**grass**
**03** fog, hay, lea, pot, rat, rip **04** blab, lawn, mead, nark, shop, tell, turf, veld
**05** dob in, downs, field, green, rough, split, sward, veldt **06** betray, common, inform, snitch, squeal, steppe, tell on
**07** foggage, pasture, prairie, savanna, stool on **08** denounce, informer, stitch up **09** asparagus, grassland
**11** incriminate

*See also* **cannabis**

*Grasses include:*

**03** nit, nut, oat, poa, rye, sea, seg, tef
**04** alfa, bent, cane, cord, corn, crab, dari, diss, doob, dura, gama, holy, kans, knot, lyme, moor, nard, oats, ragi, reed, rice, rusa, sago, sand, star, tape, tath, teff
**05** alang, arrow, beard, brome, bunch, canna, chess, China, couch, doura, float, grama, halfa, lemon, maize, melic, paddy, panic, plume, quack, quick, ragee, raggy, roosa, spear, spike, starr, stipa, Sudan, wheat
**06** bamboo, barley, canary, cotton, darnel, dhurra, fescue, finger, fiorin, guinea, kikuyu, lalang, marram, marrum, meadow, melick, millet, pampas, panick, quitch, raggee, rattan, redtop, rescue, scutch, sesame, switch, twitch, vernal
**07** Bermuda, bristle, buffalo, cannach, esparto, feather, pannick, papyrus, quaking, sacaton, sorghum, timothy, wild oat
**08** cat's-tail, cockspur, dog's-tail, Flinders, kangaroo, moss-crop, ryegrass, spinifex, teosinte
**09** bluegrass, buckwheat, cocksfoot, danthonia, hare's-tail, marijuana, porcupine, sugar cane
**10** citronella
**12** creeping bent, Kentucky blue, squirrel-tail
**13** meadow foxtail
**15** English ryegrass, Italian ryegrass

• **grass after hay**
**03** fog **07** foggage
• **handful of grass**
**03** rip **04** ripp
• **stem of grass**
**04** cane, culm

**grasshopper**
**04** grig, weta **09** wart-biter

**grate**
**03** irk, jar, rub, vex **04** bray, cage, gall, grid, grit, rasp, risp **05** annoy, chirk, creak, gride, grind, gryde, mince, peeve, shred, stove **06** rankle, scrape, squeak **07** scratch, screech **08** irritate
**09** aggravate, pulverize, triturate
**10** exasperate **12** kitchen-range **15** get on your nerves

**grateful**
**07** obliged, pleased **08** beholden, indebted, thankful **09** obligated
**12** appreciative

**gratefully**
**10** thankfully **13** with gratitude
**14** appreciatively

**gratification**
**03** joy, tip **04** glee, gust **05** bribe, feast, kicks **06** relish, thrill **07** delight, elation
**08** easement, pleasure **09** enjoyment
**10** indulgence, indulgency, recompense **11** contentment
**12** satisfaction

**gratify**
**03** pay **05** charm, cheer, flesh, humor, spoil **06** arride, cosset, favour, fulfil, humour, pamper, please, thrill
**07** aggrate, delight, flatter, gladden, indulge, placate, satiate, satisfy
**08** pander to, recreate **09** make happy

**grating**
**04** grid, hack, haik, hake, heck, iron, rack **05** frame, grate, grill, harsh, siver, syver **06** grille **07** braying, galling, grizzly, irksome, jarring, lattice, rasping, raucous, squeaky, trellis
**08** annoying, cancelli, creaking, grinding, gritting, mort-safe, scrannel, scraping, scratchy, strident **09** fire-grate, graticule, offensive
**10** discordant, irritating, portcullis, scratching, screeching, unpleasant
**12** disagreeable, exasperating

**gratis**
**04** free **08** at no cost, buckshee **10** for nothing, on the house **12** free of charge **13** complimentary, without charge

**gratitude**
**06** thanks **10** obligation **11** recognition
**12** appreciation, gratefulness, indebtedness, thankfulness
**15** acknowledgement
• **expression of gratitude**
**02** ta **06** thanks **07** thankee
**08** bless you!, gramercy, thank you
**09** God-a-mercy **10** grand merci
**11** God bless you!

**gratuitous**
**04** free **06** gratis, unpaid, wanton
**08** buckshee, needless **09** unfounded, unmerited, voluntary **10** for nothing, groundless, unasked-for, undeserved, unprovoked, unrewarded
**11** superfluous, uncalled-for, unjustified, unnecessary, unsolicited, unwarranted **12** free of charge
**13** complimentary, without reason

**gratuitously**
**10** needlessly **12** undeservedly
**13** unjustifiably, unnecessarily

**gratuity**
**03** tip **04** boon, dash, gift, mags, perk
**05** bonus, maggs **06** bounty, reward
**07** bansela, cumshaw, present, primage **08** bonsella, donation, donative, lagnappe, largesse
**09** backshish, bakhshish, baksheesh, beer-money, lagniappe, pourboire
**10** backsheesh, drink-money, glove-money, gratillity, perquisite, recompense

**grave**
**03** dig, pit, sad **04** bass, bury, dust, grim, high, lair, loss, tomb **05** acute, cairn, count, crypt, death, graff, heavy, mouls, quiet, sober, staid, vault, vital
**06** barrow, demise, gloomy, moulds, sedate, severe, solemn, sombre, urgent
**07** austere, crucial, decease, earnest, exigent, passing, pensive, prefect, serious, subdued, tumulus, weighty
**08** Catonian, critical, curtains, fatality, long home, matronal, menacing, perilous, pressing, reserved
**09** dangerous, departure, dignified, hazardous, important, long-faced, mausoleum, momentous, plague-pit, saturnine, sepulchre **10** burial site, expiration, loss of life, restrained, thoughtful **11** bed of honour, burial mound, burial place, destruction, passing away, significant, threatening
**12** last farewell

**gravel**
**04** grit **05** grail **06** chesil, chisel, graile, grayle, hoggin, murram, stones
**07** channel, channer, hogging, pebbles, shingle
• **layer of gravel**
**04** hard

**gravelly**
**05** gruff, harsh, rough, thick **06** grainy, gritty, hoarse, pebbly **07** grating, shingly, throaty **08** glareous, granular, guttural, sabulose, sabulous

**gravely**
**07** acutely, quietly **08** gloomily, severely, solemnly, urgently **09** crucially, earnestly, pensively, seriously
**10** critically **11** dangerously, importantly
**12** thoughtfully **13** significantly

**gravestone**
**05** stone, table **08** memorial
**09** headstone, tombstone

**graveyard**
**08** cemetery, God's acre **10** burial site, churchyard, necropolis **11** burial place **12** burial ground, charnel house **13** burying ground

**gravitas**
**06** weight **07** gravity **09** solemnity **10** importance **11** earnestness, seriousness

**gravitate**
**04** drop, fall, lean, move, sink, tend **05** drift **06** settle **07** descend, head for, incline **09** be drawn to **11** precipitate **12** be attached to

**gravity**
**01** g **04** pull **05** peril, state **06** danger, hazard, weight **07** dignity, reserve, urgency **08** exigency, grimness, severity, sobriety **09** acuteness, graveness, heaviness, restraint, soberness, solemnity **10** attraction, gloominess, importance, sombreness **11** consequence, earnestness, gravitation, seriousness, weightiness **12** significance **13** momentousness **14** thoughtfulness

**gray**
**02** Gy
*See also* **grey**

**graze**
**03** rub **04** crop, feed, kiss, rake, rase, raze, skim, skin **05** brush, chafe, gride, gryde, scuff, shave, touch **06** abrade, browse, bruise, crease, fodder, scrape **07** pasture, scratch **08** abrasion, ruminate **09** depasture, glance off

**grease**
**03** fat, oil **04** dope, lard, seam **05** bribe, seame, smear **06** creesh, dubbin, enlard, enseam, tallow **07** dubbing **08** dripping **09** lubricate **10** facilitate **11** lubrication

**greasy**
**04** oily, waxy **05** fatty, lardy, oleic, slimy **06** smeary, smooth **07** adipose, buttery, obscene, shearer **08** slippery, unctuous **09** sebaceous **10** oleaginous **12** ingratiating
• **greasy substance**
**04** glit

**great**
**02** gt **03** ace, big, fit, gay, gey **04** able, bulk, cool, fell, fine, gran, huge, main, mass, mega, neat, tall, unco, up on, vast, well **05** adept, brill, chief, crack, eager, famed, grand, jumbo, large, major, noted, stoor, stour, sture, super, titan, vital, whole **06** august, awsome, bangin', cushty, expert, famous, grouse, lively, mickle, muckle, stowre, superb, wicked **07** awesome, banging, crucial, eminent, extreme, healthy, immense, leading, mammoth, massive, notable, primary, rousing, salient, serious, sizable, skilful, skilled, sublime, tearing, teeming, weighty **08** colossal, cracking, critical, dextrous, enormous, fabulous, gigantic, glorious, great big, habitual, imposing, masterly, powerful, pregnant, renowned, sizeable, smashing, spacious, splendid, terrific, top-notch, virtuoso, well up on, whopping **09** admirable, boundless, brilliant, dexterous, energetic, essential, excellent, excessive, extensive, fantastic, favourite, first-rate, ginormous, humongous, humungous, important, momentous, paramount, practised, principal, prominent, qualified, swingeing, wholesale, wonderful **10** celebrated, impressive, inordinate, marvellous, noteworthy, proficient, pronounced, remarkable, specialist, successful, tremendous **11** experienced, illustrious, magnificent, outstanding, significant, substantial **12** accomplished, considerable, enthusiastic, professional **13** distinguished, knowledgeable

**Great Britain**
**02** GB, UK **03** GBR

**greatly**
**04** much **06** highly, hugely, sorely, vastly **07** big-time, majorly, notably **08** markedly, mightily, very much **09** extremely, immensely **10** abundantly, enormously, noticeably, powerfully, remarkably **11** exceedingly **12** considerably, impressively, tremendously **13** significantly, substantially

**greatness**
**04** fame, note **05** glory, power **06** genius, renown, weight **07** heroism, success **08** eminence, grandeur, muchness **09** intensity, magnitude **10** excellence, excellency, importance, mightiness **11** distinction, seriousness **12** significance **13** momentousness **14** successfulness **15** illustriousness

**Greece**
**02** GR **03** GRC

**greed**
**06** desire, hunger **07** avarice, avidity, craving, edacity, longing **08** bingeing, cupidity, gluttony, rapacity, voracity **09** eagerness, esurience, pleonexia **10** impatience **11** gourmandise, gourmandism, hoggishness, itching palm, piggishness, selfishness **12** covetousness, ravenousness **13** insatiability **15** acquisitiveness

**greedily**
**06** avidly **07** eagerly **09** selfishly **10** esuriently, ravenously **11** impatiently, rapaciously **12** avariciously

**greedy**
**04** avid, gare **05** eager **06** grabby, griple, having, hungry **07** craving, gripple, hoggish, piggish, selfish **08** covetous, desirous, edacious, esurient, grabbing, grasping, ravenous, starving **09** impatient, on the make, rapacious, voracious **10** avaricious, cupidinous, gluttonous, insatiable, omnivorous, pleonectic **11** acquisitive, itchy-palmed, open-mouthed **12** gormandizing **13** money-grubbing

**Greek**
**02** Gk, Gr

*Greeks include:*

**04** Esop
**05** Aesop, Galen, Homer, Plato
**06** Euclid, Lucian, Pindar, Sappho, Thales
**07** Hypatia, Pytheas (of Marseilles)
**08** Damocles, Epicurus, Plotinus, Plutarch, Polybius, Socrates, Xenophon
**09** Aeschylus, Aristotle, Euripides, Herodotus, Sophocles
**10** Archimedes, Democritus, Empedocles, Heraclitus, Hipparchos, Hipparchus, Praxiteles, Protagoras, Pythagoras, Theocritus, Thucydides, Xenophanes
**11** Hippocrates
**12** Aristophanes, Theophrastus

*See also* **alphabet**; **god, goddess**; **muse**; **mythology**; **seven**

**green**
**03** eco, lea, new, raw **04** lawn, long, lush, pine, sage, turf **05** field, fresh, grass, leafy, naive, sward, virid, yearn, young **06** common, grassy, meadow, recent, simple, tender, unripe, virent **07** budding, envious, growing, healthy, jealous, pasture, undried, verdant **08** blooming, covetous, glaucous, grudging, gullible, ignorant, immature, inexpert, unversed, vigorous **09** grassland, resentful, untrained, verdurous, virescent **10** ecological, olivaceous, porraceous, smaragdine, unseasoned **11** eco-friendly, flourishing, unqualified, viridescent **13** environmental, inexperienced **15** conservationist, preservationist, unsophisticated

*Greens include:*

**04** jade, lime, teal, vert
**05** lovat, olive
**06** reseda, sludge
**07** avocado, celadon, corbeau, emerald
**08** eau de Nil, pea-green, sap-green, sea green
**09** moss green, Nile green, pistachio, sage green, turquoise
**10** apple-green, aquamarine, chartreuse, rifle green
**11** bottle green
**12** Lincoln green
**14** turquoise-green

**greenery**
**04** vert **07** foliage, verdure **08** verdancy, viridity **09** greenness **10** vegetation, virescence **12** viridescence

**greenhorn**
**03** put **04** putt, tiro **06** newbie, novice, rookie **07** learner, recruit **08** beginner,

initiate, neophyte, newcomer
**09** fledgling, Johnny-raw
**10** apprentice, tenderfoot

**greenhouse**
**06** vinery **08** hothouse, orangery, pavilion **09** coldhouse, coolhouse
**10** glasshouse **12** conservatory

**Greenland**
**03** GRL

**greet**
**03** bid, bow **04** hail, kiss, meet, weep, wish **05** halse, hongi, nod to
**06** accost, salute, wave to **07** address, receive, regreet, weeping, welcome
**08** congreet, remember **10** say hello to, shake hands, tip your hat
**11** acknowledge, doff your hat
**14** shake hands with **15** give someone five

**greeting**
**03** bow, nod **04** kiss, wave **05** hongi
**06** abrazo, accost, salute **07** accoast, address, air kiss, namaste **08** glad hand, high five, namaskar
**09** handshake, reception, time of day
**10** how-do-you-do, salutation **12** the time of day **15** acknowledgement
• **expression of greeting**
**02** hi, yo **03** ave, how **04** ciao, g'day, hail, heil!, hiya **05** aloha, chimo, hallo, hello, holla, howdy, hullo, jambo, salve, skoal **06** salaam, shalom, wotcha
**07** all-hail, bonjour, bonsoir, good-day, good-den, good-e'en, salaams, salvete, save you, welcome, well met, wotcher **08** chin-chin, good-even, haeremai **09** how are you?, son of a gun, what cheer? **10** benedicite, good-morrow, how do you do? **11** good-evening, good-morning **13** good afternoon **14** shalom aleichem

**greetings**
**04** love **05** salve **07** regards, regreet, salaams **08** regreets, respects **10** best wishes, good wishes **11** compliments, kind regards, salutations, warm regards
**12** remembrances **15** congratulations

**gregarious**
**04** warm **06** social **07** affable, cordial
**08** friendly, outgoing, sociable
**09** convivial, extrovert **10** hospitable
**13** companionable

**Grenada**
**02** WG **03** GRD

**grenade**
**09** Mills bomb, pineapple **15** Molotov cocktail

**grey**
**02** gr **03** dim, old, wan **04** dark, dull, gris, pale **05** ashen, bleak, foggy, grise, grisy, misty, murky **06** cloudy, dismal, dreary, gloomy, gryesy, leaden, mature, pallid **07** griesie, neutral, unclear
**08** bloncket, doubtful, griseous, grizzled, overcast **09** ambiguous, anonymous, canescent, cheerless, cinereous, debatable, uncertain
**10** colourless, depressing, dove-colour **13** uninteresting **14** open to question

*Greys include:*

**03** ash
**04** drab
**05** liard, liart, lyart, perse, stone, taupe
**06** isabel, pewter, silver
**07** grizzle
**08** charcoal, dove grey, feldgrau, graphite, gridelin, platinum
**09** field grey, pearl-grey, slate-grey, steel-grey
**10** dapple-grey, dove-colour

• **greyish-brown**
**03** dun **04** ecru **05** mousy **06** mousey
**07** chamois
• **greyish-white**
**04** hoar, hore

**greyhound**
**04** grew **07** lurcher, sapling, whippet
**08** long-tail **09** deerhound, grewhound

**grid**
**05** frame, grate, grill **06** grille
**07** grating, lattice, network, trellis
**08** gridiron **09** framework, graticule

**grief**
**02** wo **03** vex, woe **04** dole, dool, gram, pain, sore, teen, tene **05** agony, dolor, doole, grame, teene **06** bother, dolour, misery, regret, sorrow, tsuris
**07** anguish, despair, remorse, sadness, thought, trouble, tsouris, wayment
**08** distress, mourning **09** bemoaning, dejection, grievance, heartache, suffering, tristesse **10** affliction, depression, desiderium, desolation, heartbreak **11** bereavement, despondency, lamentation, tribulation, unhappiness **12** dolorousness
• **come to grief**
**04** bomb, flop, fold **05** crash, spill
**06** mucker **07** founder, go wrong, miswend **08** collapse, fall down, fall flat **09** break down **10** not come off
**11** bite the dust, come unglued, come unstuck, fall through **12** come a cropper **13** come to nothing **14** be unsuccessful
• **emblem of grief**
**03** yew
• **expression of grief**
**02** io, oh **03** wow **04** alas **05** ohone, waugh, wowee **06** dear me, ochone, oh dear! **07** deary me **08** dearie me
• **feel grief**
**04** earn **05** yearn

**grief-stricken**
**03** sad **06** broken **07** crushed, unhappy **08** dejected, desolate, grieving, mourning, overcome, troubled, wretched **09** afflicted, anguished, depressed, sorrowful, sorrowing, woebegone **10** despairing, despondent, devastated, distressed
**11** heartbroken, overwhelmed
**12** disconsolate, inconsolable
**13** broken-hearted

**grievance**
**04** beef, moan **05** grief, gripe, peeve, score, trial, wrong **06** charge, damage, grouse, injury **07** grumble, offence, protest, trouble **08** distress, gravamen, hardship **09** complaint, injustice, objection **10** affliction, bone to pick, resentment, unfairness **11** tribulation

**grieve**
**03** cry, rue, sob, vex **04** ache, hone, hurt, mope, pain, wail, weep **05** brood, crush, mourn, shock, upset, wound
**06** bemoan, dismay, lament, offend, sadden, sorrow, suffer **07** afflict, condole, horrify, sheriff, wayment
**08** distress, engrieve, governor, pine away

**grievous**
**04** dear, sore **05** deare, deere, grave, heavy **06** noyous, severe, strong, tragic **07** careful, glaring, harmful, hurtful, painful **08** damaging, dolorous, dreadful, flagrant, shameful, shocking, wounding **09** appalling, atrocious, dolorific, injurious, monstrous, plightful, sorrowful
**10** afflicting, burdensome, calamitous, deplorable, outrageous, unbearable
**11** devastating, distressing, intolerable
**12** doloriferous, overwhelming

**grievously**
**04** sore **06** dernly **07** dearnly
**08** severely **10** dolorously, dreadfully, shockingly, tragically, unbearably
**11** appallingly, intolerably
**12** outrageously

**grill**
**04** cook, grid, heat, pump **05** bar-b-q, broil, frame, roast, toast **06** grille, wicket **07** grating, lattice, scallop
**08** barbecue, barbeque, gridiron
**09** charbroil **10** flame-grill

**grim**
◇ *anagram indicator*
**03** ill **04** dire, dour **05** awful, grisy, gurly, harsh, stern, surly **06** dismal, dogged, fierce, gloomy, griesy, grisly, grysie, horrid, morose, severe, sullen
**07** ghastly **08** dreadful, fearsome, gruesome, horrible, menacing, obdurate, resolute, shocking, sinister, stubborn, terrible **09** appalling, ferocious, harrowing, repellent, tenacious **10** depressing, determined, forbidding, formidable, horrendous, inexorable, persistent, unpleasant, unshakable, unyielding **11** frightening, threatening, unappealing, unshakeable, unspeakable **12** unattractive

**grimace**
**03** moe, mop, mou, mow, mug
**04** face, girn, moue, mump, pout
**05** frown, mouth, scowl, smirk, sneer
**07** murgeon **09** make a face, pull a face **12** fit of the face

**grime**
**03** mud **04** coom, crud, dirt, dust, grot, muck, soot, yuck **05** filth, gunge
**06** grunge, smutch

**grimly**
**07** harshly, sternly **08** fiercely, gloomily, morosely, sullenly

**grimy**
**05** dirty, dusty, mucky, muddy, sooty **06** filthy, grubby, rechie, reechy, smudgy, smutty, soiled **07** reechie, stained **10** besmirched

**grin**
**04** beam, girn, gren, leer, trap **05** gerne, laugh, risus, smile, smirk, snare, sneer **06** giggle, titter **07** chuckle, snigger

**grind**
**03** pug, rub **04** bray, chew, file, grit, meal, mill, rasp, sand, task, toil, whet **05** chore, crush, gnash, grate, pound, round, slime, stamp, sweat **06** abrade, crunch, kibble, labour, polish, powder, scrape, smooth **07** chamfer, crumble, graunch, routine, sharpen, slavery **08** drudgery, exertion, levigate **09** comminute, granulate, masticate, pulverize, triturate

**• grind down**
**05** crush, harry, hound **06** harass, plague **07** afflict, oppress, torment, trouble **08** wear down **09** persecute, tyrannize

**grip**
◇ *containment indicator*
**03** bag, get, hug **04** bite, case, fang, grab, hold, vice, vise **05** catch, clasp, cling, ditch, drain, grasp, power, rivet, sally, seize **06** absorb, clench, clutch, compel, engage, graple, griple, kitbag, strain, thrill, trench, valise **07** command, control, embrace, engross, enthral, fingers, grapple, gripple, holdall, involve, mastery **08** clutches, entrance, foothold, handfast, suitcase, traction **09** fascinate, get hold of, hypnotize, influence, latch onto, mesmerize, spellbind **10** domination, grab hold of **11** catch hold of, shoulder bag **12** overnight bag **13** travelling bag

**• come to grips with, get to grips with**
◇ *containment indicator*
**05** grasp **06** handle, tackle, take on **08** confront, cope with, deal with, face up to **09** encounter, look after **10** take care of

**gripe**
**03** nag **04** beef, carp, moan **05** bitch, ditch, drain, groan, whine **06** grouch, grouse, trench, whinge **07** griffin, griping, grumble, protest, vulture **08** complain **09** bellyache, complaint, grievance, objection **15** have a bone to pick

**gripping**
◇ *containment indicator*
**06** griple **07** gripple **08** exciting, riveting **09** absorbing, thrilling **10** compelling, compulsive, enchanting, engrossing, entrancing **11** enthralling, fascinating, suspenseful **12** spellbinding **13** unputdownable

**• gripping instrument**
**04** grip, vice, vise **05** clamp **08** tweezers

**grisly**
**04** gory, grim **05** awful, grisy **06** griesy, grysie, horrid **07** ghastly, hideous, macabre **08** dreadful, gruesome, horrible, shocking, terrible **09** abhorrent, appalling, frightful, loathsome, repulsive, revolting **10** abominable, disgusting, horrifying

**gristly**
**04** hard **05** chewy, tough **06** sinewy **07** fibrous, rubbery, stringy **08** leathery **13** cartilaginous

**grit**
**04** dust, guts, rasp, sand **05** gnash, grate, great, grind, swarf **06** clench, gravel, mettle, scrape **07** bravery, courage, pebbles, resolve, shingle **08** backbone, hardness, strength, tenacity **09** endurance, toughness **10** doggedness, resolution **12** perseverance **13** determination, steadfastness

**gritty**
**05** brave, dusty, gutsy, gutty, hardy, rough, sandy, tough **06** dogged, feisty, grainy, pebbly, plucky, spunky **07** powdery, shingly **08** abrasive, granular, gravelly, resolute, sabuline, sabulose, sabulous, spirited **09** steadfast, tenacious **10** courageous, determined, mettlesome **14** uncompromising

**grizzle**
**03** cry **04** fret, moan **05** whine **06** snivel, whinge **07** grumble, sniffle, snuffle, whimper **08** complain

**grizzled**
**04** grey, hoar **05** hoary **07** greying **08** griseous **09** canescent **10** grey-haired, grey-headed **13** pepper-and-salt

**groan**
**03** cry **04** beef, moan, sigh, wail **05** whine **06** grouch, grouse, lament, object, outcry, whinge **07** griping, grumble, protest, whimper **08** complain **09** bellyache, complaint, grievance, objection

**grocer**
**06** dealer **07** épicier **08** pepperer, purveyor, supplier **10** victualler **11** greengrocer, storekeeper, supermarket

**groggy**
◇ *anagram indicator*
**04** weak **05** dazed, dizzy, dopey, faint, muzzy, shaky, woozy **06** wobbly **07** reeling, stunned **08** confused, unsteady **09** befuddled, stupefied **10** bewildered, punch-drunk, staggering

**groin**
**04** lisk **05** growl, grunt **06** crotch, crutch **07** grumble **08** genitals

**groom**
◇ *anagram indicator*
**02** do **03** fix **04** sice, syce, tidy **05** brush, clean, coach, curry, dress, drill, preen, prime, prink, saice, teach, train, tutor **06** adjust, neaten, school, smooth, spouse, tidy up **07** arrange, educate, husband, prepare, smarten, turn out **08** coistrel, coistril, instruct, newly-wed, spruce up, strapper **09** make ready, stableboy, stable lad, stableman **10** bridegroom, palfrenier, put in order, stable hand, stable lass **11** honeymooner, husband-to-be **15** marriage partner

**groove**
**03** cut, pod, rut **04** kerf, mark, oche, race, sipe, slot **05** canal, chase, croze, ditch, flute, gouge, quirk, ridge, rigol, score, slide, track **06** cullis, furrow, gutter, hollow, keyway, rabbet, raggle, rebate, riffle, scrobe, sulcus, throat, trench, trough **07** chamfer, channel, diglyph, fissure, fossula, key-seat **09** cannelure, vallecula **11** indentation

**grooved**
**06** fluted, rutted, scored, sulcal **07** exarate, sulcate **08** furrowed, rabbeted, sulcated **09** chamfered **10** channelled **12** canaliculate, scrobiculate **13** canaliculated

**grope**
**04** feel, fish, hunt, pick, poke, ripe **05** abuse, probe, touch **06** feel up, fondle, fumble, molest, search **07** grabble, touch up **08** flounder, scrabble **09** cast about **13** abuse sexually, interfere with

**gross**
◇ *anagram indicator*
**02** gr **03** big, fat **04** blue, dull, earn, foul, huge, lewd, make, rank, rude, slow, take **05** bawdy, bulky, crass, crude, dirty, heavy, large, nasty, obese, plain, sheer, solid, thick, total, utter, whole, yucky **06** coarse, earthy, entire, filthy, odious, pull in, rake in, ribald, risqué, smutty, strong, stupid, vulgar **07** blatant, boorish, bring in, extreme, glaring, hulking, immense, lumpish, massive, obscene, obvious, sensual, serious **08** colossal, complete, enormous, flagrant, grievous, improper, indecent, manifest, material, nauseous, outright, palpable, shameful, shocking **09** aggregate, before tax, corpulent, egregious, inclusive, offensive, repugnant, repulsive, revolting, sickening, tasteless, unrefined **10** accumulate, disgusting, earthbound, nauseating, off-putting, outrageous, overweight, salt-butter, uncultured, unpleasant **11** disgraceful, distasteful, insensitive, unpalatable **12** all-inclusive, pornographic, unappetizing, unrepeatable **13** coarse-grained, comprehensive **15** unsophisticated

**grossly**
**04** very **05** fatly **06** highly, really
**07** acutely, awfully, greatly, utterly
**08** severely, terribly **09** decidedly, extremely, intensely, unusually
**10** dreadfully, remarkably, thoroughly, uncommonly **11** exceedingly, excessively, frightfully
**12** immoderately, inordinately, terrifically, unreasonably
**13** exceptionally **15** extraordinarily

**grotesque**
◇ *anagram indicator*
**03** odd **04** ugly **05** antic, black, weird
**06** absurd, antick, Gothic, rococo
**07** anticke, antique, bizarre, hideous, macabre, strange, surreal, twisted
**08** deformed, fanciful, freakish, peculiar **09** distorted, fantastic, ludicrous, malformed, misshapen, monstrous, unnatural, unsightly, whimsical **10** outlandish, ridiculous
**11** extravagant

**grotesquely**
**09** bizarrely, hideously, strangely
**11** unnaturally **12** outlandishly, unpleasantly

**grotto**
**04** cave, grot **05** speos **06** cavern
**07** chamber **08** catacomb, Lupercal
**09** Mithraeum, nymphaeum
**10** subterrane

**grotty**
**03** ill **04** sick, ugly **05** dirty, grody, mangy, rough, seedy, tatty **06** ailing, crummy, groggy, poorly, shabby, sleazy, untidy, unwell **07** run-down, scruffy, squalid **08** decaying **09** off-colour
**10** out of sorts **11** dilapidated **15** under the weather

**grouch**
**04** moan **05** gripe, grump, sulks
**06** griper, grouse, kvetch, moaner, sulker, whiner, whinge **07** grouser, grumble, whinger **08** grumbler, kvetcher, murmurer, mutterer, sourpuss **09** complaint, grievance, objection **10** bellyacher, complainer, crosspatch, malcontent **11** fault-finder

**grouchy**
**05** cross, sulky, surly, testy **06** grumpy
**07** peevish **08** captious, churlish, petulant **09** crotchety, grumbling, irascible, irritable, querulous, truculent
**11** bad-tempered, complaining, ill-tempered **12** cantankerous, discontented, dissatisfied

**ground**
◇ *anagram indicator*
**03** fix, set, sod **04** base, call, clay, dirt, dust, eard, land, lees, loam, marl, park, plot, soil, yerd, yird **05** acres, arena, basis, cause, coach, dregs, drill, earth, field, found, lawns, pitch, score, teach, terra, train, tutor, yeard **06** bottom, campus, domain, estate, excuse, fields, inform, motive, reason, settle
**07** account, deposit, dry land, educate, gardens, holding, prepare, residue, stadium, surface, terrain
**08** argument, initiate, instruct, occasion, position, property, sediment
**09** advantage, background, establish, introduce, principle, scourings, territory **10** foundation, inducement, terra firma **11** precipitate, vindication
**12** acquaint with, surroundings
**13** justification **15** familiarize with
*See also* **stadium**

• **leave the ground**
**04** yump
• **patch of ground**
**03** lot, tee **04** area
• **run along ground**
**04** taxi

**groundbait**
**04** chum **06** berley, burley

**groundless**
**05** empty, false **08** baseless, illusory
**09** imaginary, unfounded
**10** unprovoked **11** uncalled-for, unjustified, unsupported, unwarranted
**13** without reason **15** unsubstantiated

**grounds**
**04** lees **05** dregs

**groundwork**
**04** base **05** basis **06** bottom
**07** footing **08** homework, research
**09** spadework **10** essentials, foundation, metaphysic
**11** cornerstone, preparation
**12** fundamentals **13** preliminaries, underpinnings

**group**
**03** lot, mob, set **04** band, body, club, crew, gang, knot, link, mass, pack, pool, rank, sort, team, unit **05** batch, bunch, class, clump, crowd, flock, genus, grade, guild, order, party, range, squad, troop, unite **06** circle, clique, cohort, family, gather, huddle, league, line up, school **07** arrange, bracket, cluster, collect, company, coterie, element, faction, marshal, society, species **08** assemble, assembly, category, classify, grouping, organize
**09** associate, formation, gathering
**10** categorize, collection, congregate, contingent, detachment
**11** association, combination
**12** congregation, organization
**14** classification, conglomeration
*See also* **singer**

• **group of women**
**02** WI **05** coven
• **unit group**
**04** cell

**grouse**
**04** beef, carp, good, moan, neat
**05** bitch, gripe, groan, peeve, whine
**06** grouch, whinge **07** grumble, protest **08** complain **09** bellyache, complaint, excellent, find fault, grievance, objection

*Grouse include:*

**03** red
**04** sage, sand
**05** black, hazel
**06** ruffed, willow
**07** gorcock, greyhen, pintail, prairie, red game
**08** hazel hen, heath-hen, moorcock, moorfowl, moor-poot, moor-pout, muir-poot, muir-pout, pheasant, sage cock
**09** blackcock, blackgame, heathbird, heathcock, heath-fowl, partridge, ptarmigan
**10** heath-poult, prairie hen
**11** prairie fowl, sharp-tailed
**12** capercaillie, capercailzie
**14** prairie chicken

*See also* **game**
• **grouse-shooters' lair**
**04** butt

**grove**
**03** Gro **04** tope, wood **05** copse, hurst
**06** arbour, avenue, covert, lyceum
**07** coppice, spinney, thicket
**08** woodland **10** plantation

**grovel**
**04** fawn **05** cower, crawl, creep, defer, kneel, kotow, stoop, toady **06** cheese, cringe, crouch, kowtow, lie low, suck up **07** bow down, flatter, lie down
**08** kiss up to **12** bow and scrape
**14** demean yourself **15** butter someone up, fall on your knees

**grow**
**02** go **03** bud, get, sow, wax **04** farm, rise, stem, turn **05** arise, breed, issue, plant, raise, shoot, swell, widen
**06** become, change, deepen, expand, extend, flower, mature, spread, spring, sprout, thrive **07** advance, broaden, burgeon, develop, enlarge, fill out, harvest, improve, produce, prosper, stretch, succeed, thicken
**08** bourgeon, come to be, elongate, escalate, flourish, increase, lengthen, multiply, mushroom, progress
**09** cultivate, germinate, get bigger, get taller, originate, propagate **11** make headway, proliferate **12** become bigger, become larger, become taller
**14** increase in size
• **grow up**
**03** age **06** mature

**growl**
**03** yap **04** bark, gnar, gurl, howl, roar, roin, snap, snar, yelp **05** groin, royne, snarl **06** rumble **07** grumble

**grown-up**
**03** big, man **05** adult, of age, woman
**06** mature **09** full-grown **10** fully grown **12** fully fledged **14** fully developed

**growth**
**04** crop, gall, lump, rise **05** plant
**06** antler, flower, spread, tumour
**07** advance, budding, flowers, headway, success **08** greenery, increase, progress, shooting, swelling
**09** deepening, evolution, expansion, extension, flowering, outgrowth, springing, sprouting **10** burgeoning,

maturation, prosperity
**11** development, enlargement, excrescence, germination, improvement **12** augmentation, intumescence, protuberance
**13** amplification, magnification, proliferation **14** aggrandizement, multiplication
• **halt growth**
**03** nip

**grub**
**03** dig, eat, wog **04** eats, food, hunt, nosh, pupa, root, rout, stub, tuck, worm **05** delve, grout, larva, meals, probe, scour, wroot **06** burrow, ferret, forage, gru-gru, maggot, muddle, rootle, search, tucker **07** explore, rummage, snuzzle, uncover, unearth **08** bookworm, excavate, flag-worm, groo-groo, muck-worm **09** chrysalis, nutrition, provision, witchetty **10** grugru worm, sustenance **11** caterpillar, refreshment **12** refreshments
**13** leatherjacket

**grubby**
**05** dirty, grimy, messy, mucky, seedy
**06** filthy, shabby, soiled, thumby
**07** scruffy, squalid **08** unwashed

**grudge**
**04** envy, hate, mind **05** covet, pique, score, spite, venom **06** animus, enmity, grutch, hatred, malice, malign, murmur, repine, resent **07** dislike, ill-will, rancour **08** aversion, begrudge, jealousy, object to **09** animosity, antipathy, grievance **10** antagonism, bitterness, resentment **11** be jealous of, malevolence **12** hard feelings **15** take exception to

**grudging**
**07** envious, jealous **08** hesitant
**09** reluctant, resentful, unwilling
**11** half-hearted **12** heartburning
**14** unenthusiastic

**gruel**
**05** kasha **06** congee, conjee, skilly
**07** brochan **08** loblolly **10** punishment
**11** skilligalee, skilligolee

**gruelling**
**04** hard **05** harsh, tough **06** severe, taxing, tiring, trying **07** arduous
**08** crushing, draining, grinding
**09** demanding, difficult, laborious, punishing, strenuous **10** exhausting
**12** backbreaking

**gruesome**
**04** grim, sick **05** awful **06** grisly, grooly, horrid **07** ghastly, hideous, macabre **08** dreadful, horrible, horrific, shocking, terrible
**09** abhorrent, appalling, frightful, loathsome, monstrous, repellent, repugnant, repulsive, revolting, sickening **10** abominable, disgusting

**gruesomely**
**06** grimly **08** horribly, terribly
**09** hideously **10** dreadfully
**11** frightfully, monstrously, repulsively

**gruff**
**04** curt, rude, sour **05** blunt, harsh, husky, rough, surly, testy, thick
**06** abrupt, grumpy, hoarse, sullen, tetchy **07** brusque, crabbed, rasping, throaty **08** churlish, croaking, guttural, impolite **09** crotchety
**10** unfriendly **11** bad-tempered
**12** discourteous

**gruffly**
**06** curtly, rudely **07** harshly, huskily, roughly **08** abruptly, hoarsely
**09** brusquely **10** gutturally, impolitely
**14** discourteously

**grumble**
**04** beef, carp, moan, mump, nark, roar
**05** bitch, bleat, croak, gripe, groin, growl, grump, whine **06** grouch, grouse, gurgle, mumble, murmur, mutter, object, rumble, whinge
**07** chunder, chunner, chunter, grizzle, maunder, protest **08** chounter, complain **09** bellyache, complaint, find fault, grievance, muttering, objection

**grumbler**
**04** moan **06** grouch, moaner, whiner
**07** croaker, fusspot, grouser, niggler, whinger **09** nit-picker **10** bellyacher, complainer, fussbudget **11** fault-finder

**grumpily**
**07** crossly, in a huff, in a sulk, sulkily
**08** sullenly **09** grouchily **10** churlishly

**grumpy**
**05** crabby, cross, moany, ratty, sulky, surly **06** snappy, sullen, tetchy
**07** crabbed, grouchy, in a huff, in a sulk
**08** churlish, grumpish, petulant
**09** crotchety, irritable **11** bad-tempered, ill-tempered
**12** cantankerous, discontented

**grunt**
**03** ugh **04** oink, rasp **05** cough, croak, grate, groin, power, snore, snort
**06** drudge, grumph **07** pig-fish, soldier
**08** labourer

**Guadeloupe**
**03** GLP

**Guam**
**03** GUM

**guarantee**
**04** back, bond, gage, oath **05** swear, token **06** assure, avouch, engage, ensure, insure, pledge, secure, surety
**07** certify, earnest, endorse, promise, protect, sponsor, support, warrant
**08** contract, covenant, guaranty, make sure, security, vouch for, warranty
**09** answer for, assurance, insurance, stipulate, undertake, vouchsafe
**10** collateral, underwrite, warrandice, warrantise **11** endorsement, make certain, testimonial **12** word of honour
**15** give an assurance

**guarantor**
**05** angel **06** backer, surety **07** referee, sponsor, voucher **08** bailsman, bondsman **09** guarantee, supporter, warrantor **10** covenantor
**11** underwriter

**guard**
◇ *containment indicator*
**03** pad **04** care, keep, mind, rail, save, wait, wall, ward, wear, weir **05** check, cover, fence, garda, hedge, scout, watch **06** beware, buffer, bumper, captor, charge, defend, escort, fender, keeper, minder, patrol, picket, police, screen, secure, sentry, shield, warden, warder **07** barrier, be alert, control, cushion, defence, enguard, look out, lookout, oversee, protect, shelter, watcher **08** bostangi, defender, fortress, guardian, preserve, savegard, scrutiny, security, sentinel, splasher, take care, watchman **09** bodyguard, conductor, custodian, direction, keep watch, protector, safeguard, supervise, vigilance **10** inspection, monitoring, protection, regulation **11** observation, stewardship, supervision
**12** guardianship, surveillance
**15** superintendence
• **officer of the Guard**
**04** exon
• **off your guard**
**06** unwary **07** napping, unaware, unready **08** careless, unawares
**09** red-handed, surprised
**10** unprepared **11** inattentive
**12** unsuspecting
• **on your guard**
**04** wary **05** alert, ready **07** careful
**08** cautious, excubant, prepared, vigilant, watchful **09** attentive, wide awake **10** on the alert **11** circumspect
**12** on the lookout

**guarded**
**04** wary **05** cagey, chary **07** careful, striped, trimmed **08** cautious, defended, discreet, reserved, reticent, watchful **09** reluctant, secretive
**10** restrained **11** circumspect **12** non-committal

**guardedly**
**06** warily **07** charily **09** carefully
**10** cautiously **11** reluctantly, secretively
**13** circumspectly **14** non-committally

**guardian**
**05** angel, guard, Janus, tutor **06** custos, escort, gryfon, keeper, patron, warden, warder **07** curator, Granthi, griffin, griffon, gryphon, steward, trustee, tutelar **08** Cerberus, champion, curatrix, defender, tutelary
**09** attendant, caretaker, custodian, preserver, protector **10** depositary, depository, protecting **11** conservator
**12** conservatrix
• **guardian of women**
**04** Juno

**guardianship**
**04** care, ward **05** aegis, guard, hands, trust **07** custody, defence, keeping, tuition **08** guidance, tutelage, wardenry, wardship **09** patronage
**10** attendance, protection, wardenship
**11** curatorship, safekeeping,

stewardship, trusteeship
**12** preservation, protectorate
**13** custodianship

**Guatemala**
**03** GCA, GTM

**Guernsey**
**03** GBG

**guerrilla**
**03** Che **06** haiduk, maquis, sniper
**07** chetnik, fedayee, heyduck
**08** komitaji, partisan, Viet Cong
**09** irregular, terrorist, Zapatista
**10** Tamil tiger **11** bushwhacker, franc-tireur, guerrillero **14** freedom fighter

**guess**
**03** aim, bet **04** feel, idea, shot
**05** aread, arede, augur, fancy, hunch, judge, level, think **06** assume, belief, devise, divine, notion, reckon, theory
**07** arreede, believe, feeling, imagine, opinion, predict, suppose, surmise, suspect, work out **08** consider, estimate **09** guesswork, intuition, judgement, postulate, reckoning, speculate, suspicion **10** assumption, conjecture, hypothesis, make a guess, prediction **11** guesstimate, hypothesize, speculation, supposition
**13** shot in the dark **14** a shot in the dark, a stab in the dark, ballpark figure, put something at

**guessing-game**
**04** mora **05** morra

**guesstimate**
**05** guess **09** judgement, quotation, reckoning, valuation **10** assessment, estimation, evaluation, rough guess
**11** computation **13** approximation
**14** ballpark figure **15** approximate cost

**guesswork**
**06** theory **07** surmise **09** intuition, reckoning **10** assumption, conjecture, estimation, hypothesis, prediction
**11** guesstimate, speculation, supposition

**guest**
**02** PG **05** umbra **06** caller, lodger, patron **07** boarder, invitee, regular, visitor **08** manuhiri, resident, symphile, visitant **09** synoecete, synoekete

**guesthouse**
**03** inn **05** hotel **06** hostel **07** Gasthof, hospice, pension, taverna
**08** Gasthaus, hostelry, minshuku
**11** xenodochium **12** rooming-house
**13** boarding-house **15** bed-and-breakfast

**guff**
**03** rot **04** blah, bosh, bull, bunk, cock, crap **05** balls, bilge, hooey, smell, stink, trash, tripe **06** bunkum, drivel, hot air, humbug, piffle **07** baloney, eyewash, hogwash, rhubarb, rubbish, twaddle
**08** claptrap, cobblers, malarkey, nonsense, tommyrot **09** gibberish, moonshine, poppycock
**10** codswallop

**guffaw**
**04** hoot, roar **05** laugh, whoop
**06** bellow, cackle, haw-haw, shriek
**09** loud laugh **11** laugh loudly

**guidance**
**03** tip **04** help, hint, lead, rule, tips
**05** hints **06** advice, charge
**07** conduct, control, counsel, leading, pointer **08** pointers, teaching
**09** direction **10** assistance, directions, guidelines, indication, leadership, management, suggestion
**11** counselling, indications, information, instruction, suggestions
**12** instructions **14** recommendation
**15** recommendations
• **Parental Guidance**
**02** PG

**guide**
**03** ABC, key **04** guru, lead, mark, norm, rule, show, sign, wise **05** abcee, absey, gauge, maxim, model, pilot, point, steer, teach, train, tutor, usher, weise, weize **06** advise, attend, beacon, direct, escort, govern, leader, manage, manual, marker, mentor, ranger, signal **07** adviser, command, conduct, control, counsel, courier, educate, example, inspire, labarum, measure, oversee, pattern, pointer, red book, shikari, teacher, waymark
**08** Bradshaw, chaperon, cicerone, cynosure, director, engineer, exemplar, Good Food, handbook, helmsman, instruct, landmark, navigate, Pole Star, regulate, road book, shikaree, signpost, standard **09** accompany, archetype, attendant, benchmark, catalogue, chaperone, companion, conductor, criterion, directory, guidebook, guideline, influence, manoeuvre, navigator, sightsman, steersman, supervise, tombstone, yardstick **10** counsellor, indication, instructor, show the way **11** preside over, superintend **12** be in charge of, valet de place **14** Tyrian cynosure
• **weaver's guide**
**04** card

**guidebook**
**03** ABC **04** A to Z® **05** guide
**06** manual **08** Baedeker, handbook
**09** companion **10** prospectus
**15** instruction book

**guideline**
**04** rule **05** terms **06** advice
**07** measure, road map **08** standard
**09** benchmark, criterion, direction, framework, parameter, principle, procedure, yardstick **10** constraint, indication, regulation, suggestion, touchstone **11** information, instruction
**14** recommendation

**guild**
**03** WAG **04** club, tong **05** artel, lodge, order, union **06** chapel, league
**07** basoche, company, mistery, mystery, society **08** alliance, sorority
**10** federation, fellowship, fraternity
**11** association, brotherhood, corporation **12** organization
**13** incorporation

**guile**
**04** dole, ruse **05** craft, fraud, trick
**06** deceit **07** cunning, knavery, slyness
**08** artifice, trickery, wiliness
**09** deception, duplicity, stratagem, treachery **10** artfulness, cleverness, craftiness, trickiness **11** deviousness
**12** gamesmanship **13** double-dealing

**guileless**
**04** open **05** frank, naive **06** candid, direct, honest, simple **07** artless, genuine, natural, sincere **08** innocent, sackless, straight, trusting, truthful
**09** ingenuous, unworldly
**10** unreserved **11** transparent
**13** simple-hearted **15** straightforward, unsophisticated

**guilt**
**03** sin **05** blame, shame, wrong
**06** regret **07** remorse **08** disgrace
**09** dishonour, guilt trip, penitence
**10** blood-guilt, conscience, contrition, misconduct, repentance, sinfulness, wrongdoing **11** compunction, criminality, culpability **12** self-reproach, unlawfulness
**14** responsibility, self-accusation
**15** blameworthiness

**guiltily**
**07** at fault, to blame, wrongly
**09** illegally, illicitly **10** contritely, shamefully, unlawfully, with sorrow
**11** regretfully, responsibly
**12** remorsefully, unforgivably
**13** penitentially, reprehensibly, without excuse **14** caught in the act **15** caught red-handed

**guiltless**
**04** free, pure **05** clean, clear **07** sinless
**08** innocent, spotless **09** blameless, faultless, stainless, undefiled, unspotted, unsullied, untainted **10** immaculate, impeccable, inculpable, unblamable
**11** untarnished **13** above reproach, unimpeachable **14** irreproachable

**guilty**
**03** bad **04** evil **05** sorry, wrong
**06** faulty, nocent, sinful, wicked
**07** ashamed, at fault, illegal, illicit, to blame **08** blamable, contrite, criminal, culpable, infamous, penitent, sheepish, unlawful **09** condemned, convicted, offending, regretful, repentant
**10** delinquent, flagitious, remorseful, shamefaced **11** blameworthy, guilt-ridden, responsible **12** bloodstained, compunctious

**guinea**
**02** Ls, RG **03** GIN **04** quid **06** canary, George **07** Geordie
• **guineas**
**02** gs

**Guinea-Bissau**
**03** GNB, RGB

**guinea pig**
**04** cavy, paca **05** aguti **06** agouti,

agouty **08** capybara **09** do-nothing, triallist

**Guinness**
**04** Alec

**guise**
**03** air **04** face, form, mask, show **05** dress, front, shape **06** aspect, custom, façade, manner **07** purport **08** disguise, features, likeness, pretence **09** behaviour, demeanour, semblance **10** appearance

**guitar**
**02** ax **03** axe, uke **04** bass
**05** Dobro®, sanko **06** sancho
**07** gittern, samisen, ukulele
**08** shamisen **09** humbucker

**• play guitar**
**05** strum

**gulf**
**03** bay, gap, maw **04** cove, hole, rift, void **05** abyss, basin, bight, chasm, cleft, gorge, inlet, split **06** breach, canyon, divide, hollow, ravine, vorago **07** crevice, fissure, opening **08** division **09** whirlpool **10** separation

*Gulfs include:*

**04** Aden, Huon, Lion, Moro, Oman, Riga, Siam, Suez
**05** Ancud, Aqaba, Càdiz, Davao, Dulce, Gabes, Gaeta, Genoa, Kutch, Lions, Maine, Panay, Papua, Penas, Ragay, Saros, Sidra, Sirte, Tunis
**06** Aegina, Alaska, Cambay, Chania, Darien, Gdansk, Guinea, Kavala, Mannar, Mexico, Naples, Nicoya, Orosei, Panama, Parita, Patras, St Malo, Tonkin, Triste, Venice
**07** Almeria, Arabian, Asinara, Boothia, Bothnia, Cazones, Corinth, Edremit, Exmouth, Finland, Fonseca, Hauraki, Kachchh, Lepanto, Obskaya, Persian, Salerno, San Blas, Saronic, Spencer, Taranto, The Gulf, Trieste, Udskaya
**08** Amundsen, Batabano, Cagliari, Campeche, Chiriqui, Honduras, Khambhat, Liaotung, Lingayen, Martaban, Mosquito, Oristano, Papagayo, San Jorge, Taganrog, Thailand, Valencia
**09** Buor-Khaya, Corcovado, Dvinskaya, Guayaquil, Queen Maud, San Matias, San Miguel, St Florent, St Vincent, Van Diemen, Venezuela
**10** California, Chaunskaya, Cheshskaya, Coronation, Kyparissia, Policastro, St Lawrence, Tazovskaya, Thermaikos
**11** Carpentaria, Guacanayabo, Manfredonia, Pechorskaya, Strymonikos, Tehuantepec
**12** los Mosquitos, Penzhinskaya
**13** Baydaratskaya, Santa Catalina
**15** Joseph Bonaparte

**gull**
**04** dupe, fool, hoax **05** cheat
**07** deceive

*See also* **bird**; **fool**

**gullet**
**03** maw **04** craw, crop, gula **06** throat **07** Red Lane, weasand **09** esophagus **10** oesophagus

**gullibility**
**07** naivety **09** credulity, innocence
**10** simplicity **11** foolishness
**12** trustfulness

**gullible**
**05** green, naive **07** foolish, verdant
**08** innocent, trustful, trusting
**09** credulous, ingenuous **11** suggestible
**12** overtrusting, unsuspecting
**13** inexperienced **14** easily deceived, impressionable **15** unsophisticated

**gully**
**03** geo, gio, goe **05** ditch, donga, gorge, gulch **06** canyon, grough, gutter, ravine, valley **07** channel, couloir **11** watercourse

*See also* **ravine**

**gulp**
◇ *containment indicator*
**04** bolt, slug, swig, wolf **05** gulch, quaff, stuff, swill, swipe **06** devour, gobble, gollop, guzzle **07** draught, swallow **08** mouthful, tuck into **09** knock back

**gum**
**03** fix, God, jaw **04** clog, dupe, glue, guar, seal **05** affix, cheat, myrrh, paste, resin, stick **06** acajou, angico, balata, cement, chewie, chicle, chuddy, humbug, mastic **07** benzoin, deceive, dextrin, gamboge, mastich **08** adhesive, bdellium, benjamin, dextrine, fixative, galbanum, mucilage, nonsense, olibanum, opopanax, scammony **09** courbaril, insolence, sagapenum, tacamahac, tacmahack **10** ammoniacum, asafoetida, caoutchouc, euphorbium, sarcocolla, tragacanth

**• gum tree**
**04** arar **05** karri **06** tupelo
**08** sandarac **10** eucalyptus

**• gum up**
**04** clog **05** choke **06** hinder, impede
**08** obstruct

**gummy**
**05** gluey, gooey, tacky **06** sticky, viscid
**07** viscous **08** adhesive **09** toothless

**gumption**
**03** wit **04** nous **05** savvy, sense
**06** acumen **07** ability, courage
**08** sagacity **09** acuteness
**10** astuteness, cleverness, enterprise, initiative, shrewdness **11** common sense, discernment **15** resourcefulness

**gumshoe** *see* **detective**

**gun**
**03** rod **05** piece, shoot **06** expert, heater, weapon **07** firearm, shooter **10** pre-eminent **12** shooting iron

*Guns include:*

**02** MG
**03** air, dag, gas, gat, ray, six, Uzi
**04** AK-47, Bren, burp, Colt®, hand, pump, punt, shot, sten, stun
**05** baton, field, fusil, Lewis, Maxim, rifle, siege, spear, tommy
**06** airgun, Archie, Bofors, cannon, mortar, musket, needle, pistol, pom-pom, Purdey®, Quaker, turret
**07** bazooka, carbine, chopper, gatling, Long Tom, machine, pounder, scatter
**08** air rifle, arquebus, elephant, falconet, firelock, howitzer, pederero, revolver, starting, Sterling
**09** Archibald, Big Bertha, flintlock, harquebus
**10** black Maria, demi-cannon, six-shooter, submachine, Winchester®
**11** blunderbuss, four-pounder, half-pounder, Kalashnikov
**12** fowling-piece, mitrailleuse, three-pounder

**• gun's catch**
**04** sear

**• row of guns**
**04** tier

**gunfire**
**04** flak **05** salvo **06** firing
**08** gunshots, pounding, shelling, shooting **09** cannonade
**11** bombardment

**gunman**
**04** thug **05** bravo **06** bandit, gunsel, hit man, killer, sniper **07** mobster
**08** assassin, gangster, murderer, shootist **09** desperado, terrorist
**10** gunslinger, hatchet man **11** armed robber

**gurgle**
**03** lap **04** crow **05** brawl, clunk, plash
**06** babble, bubble, buller, burble, guggle, murmur, ripple, ruckle, splash
**08** bubbling

**guru**
**04** sage **05** swami, tutor **06** expert, gooroo, leader, master, mentor, pundit
**07** Bhagwan, teacher, tohunga
**08** luminary, Svengali **09** authority, maharishi **10** instructor **12** guiding light

**gush**
**03** goo, jet, run **04** boak, bock, boke, emit, flow, fuss, go on, pour, rail, rave, rush, tide, well **05** burst, flood, issue, raile, rayle, slush, spate, spout, spurt, surge **06** babble, drivel, effuse, jabber, stream **07** blather, cascade, chatter, enthuse, outflow, regorge, torrent
**08** fountain, outburst **10** bubble over, effervesce, outpouring **11** regurgitate
**12** effusiveness **14** sentimentality

**gushing**
**05** gushy **06** sickly, too-too
**07** cloying, fulsome, mawkish
**08** effusive **09** emotional, excessive
**10** saccharine, scaturient
**11** sentimental

**gust**
**03** fit **04** blow, flaw, gale, puff, rush, scud, wind **05** blast, blore, burst,

erupt, storm, surge **06** breeze, flurry, relish, squall **07** bluster, flaught, flavour **08** burst out, eruption, outbreak, outburst, williwaw **13** gratification

**gustily**
**06** wildly **07** windily **08** breezily, stormily **13** tempestuously

**gusto**
**04** élan, zeal, zest **05** verve **06** energy, relish **07** delight, fervour, unction
**08** pleasure **09** enjoyment
**10** enthusiasm, exuberance
**12** appreciation, exhilaration

**gusty**
**05** blowy, windy **06** breezy, stormy
**07** savoury, squally **08** blustery
**10** blustering **11** tempestuous

**gut**
◇ *middle deletion indicator*
**03** rob **04** draw, gill, grit, lane, loot, sack **05** balls, basic, belly, clean, clear, dress, empty, nerve, pluck, rifle, spunk, strip **06** bottle, bowels, innate, mettle, paunch, ravage, strong **07** bravery, courage, destroy, enteron, innards, insides, natural, plunder, ransack, stomach, viscera **08** audacity, backbone, boldness, clean out, clear out, entrails, tenacity **09** devastate, emotional, fortitude, heartfelt, intuitive
**10** deep-seated, disembowel, eviscerate, exenterate, intestines, mesenteron, unthinking
**11** archenteron, instinctive, involuntary, spontaneous, vital organs **14** internal organs

**gutless**
◇ *middle deletion indicator*
**04** nesh, weak **05** timid **06** abject, craven, feeble **07** chicken
**08** cowardly **09** spineless
**10** irresolute **11** lily-livered **12** faint-hearted **14** chicken-hearted, chicken-livered

**gutsily**
**06** boldly **07** bravely **08** spunkily
**10** resolutely, staunchily
**11** indomitably **12** courageously, passionately

**gutsy**
**04** bold, game **05** brave, gutty, lusty
**06** ballsy, plucky, spunky **07** gallant, staunch **08** resolute, spirited
**10** courageous, determined, gluttonous, mettlesome, passionate
**11** indomitable

**gutter**
**04** duct, grip, pipe, roan, rone, tube
**05** ditch, drain, gripe, gully, rhone, rigol, sewer, swale, swayl, sweal, sweel
**06** cullis, gulley, kennel, rigoll, runnel, sluice, strand, trench, trough
**07** channel, conduit, culvert, passage
**08** downpipe, roanpipe, ronepipe
**09** guttering

**guttersnipe**
**04** waif **05** gamin **06** urchin
**07** mudlark **10** ragamuffin
**14** tatterdemalion

**guttural**
**03** low **04** deep **05** gruff, harsh, husky, rough, thick **06** hoarse **07** grating, rasping, throaty **08** croaking, gravelly

**guy**
**02** bo **03** boy, lad, man, sod **04** boyo, chap, cove, dude, joke, lark, stay, vang
**05** bloke, bucko, fella, youth
**06** decamp, Fawkes, fellow, flight, geezer, person **09** character, decamping **10** individual

**Guyana**
**03** GUY

**guzzle**
**04** bolt, cram, gulp, soak, swig, wolf
**05** quaff, scoff, stuff, swill **06** devour, gobble **07** put away, swallow **08** tuck into **09** knock back, polish off
**10** gormandize

**gymnastics**
**02** PE, PT **03** gym

*Gymnastics disciplines include:*

**04** ball, beam, hoop
**05** clubs, floor, rings, vault
**06** ribbon
**07** high bar
**08** tumbling
**10** horse vault, uneven bars
**11** balance beam, pommel horse
**12** parallel bars, trampolining
**13** horizontal bar
**14** asymmetric bars, floor exercises, side horse vault, sports aerobics

*Gymnastics-related terms include:*

**04** beam, pike, tuck
**05** cross, floor, giant, rings, salto, stick, twist, vault
**06** aerial, bridge, layout
**07** element, flyaway, Gaylord
**08** dismount, flic-flac, rotation, round-off, straddle, walkover, whip back
**09** all-around, apparatus, cartwheel, execution, handstand, Yurchenko
**10** double back, handspring, somersault, uneven bars
**11** balance beam, double twist, pommel horse, Swedish fall
**12** compulsories, parallel bars
**13** horizontal bar, inverted cross
**14** asymmetric bars

*Gymnasts include:*

**03** **Kim** (Nellie), **Ono** (Takashi)
**06** **Korbut** (Olga Valentinovna), **Miller** (Shannon), **Retton** (Mary Lou)
**07** **Scherbo** (Vitaly), **Tweddle** (Beth)
**08** **Comaneci** (Nadia), **Ditiatin** (Aleksandr), **Latynina** (Larissa Semyonovna), **Shakhlin** (Boris Anfiyanovich)
**09** **Andrianov** (Nikolai Yefimovich), **Cáslavská** (Vera)
**10** **Boginskaya** (Svetlana), **Turischeva** (Lyudmila Ivanovna)

**gym shoe**
**03** dap **08** plimsole, plimsoll, sandshoe

**Gypsy, Gipsy**
**03** chi, faw, rom, rye **04** chai, chal, Roma **05** caird, nomad, rover
**06** gipsen, gitana, gitano, hawker, roamer, Romani, Romany, tinker
**07** rambler, Rommany, tinkler, tsigane, tzigany, Zincala, Zincalo, Zingana, Zingano, Zingara, Zingaro
**08** Bohemian, diddicoy, Egyptian, huckster, wanderer, Zigeuner
**09** out-of-door, traveller
**14** unconventional

**gyrate**
**04** gyre, spin, turn **05** swirl, twirl, wheel, whirl **06** circle, rotate, spiral, swivel **07** revolve **09** pirouette

**gyration**
**04** spin, turn **05** swirl, twirl, twist, whirl, whorl **06** circle, spiral, swivel
**08** rotation, spinning, wheeling, whirling **09** pirouette **10** revolution
**11** convolution

# H

**H**
**05** aitch, hotel **07** hydrant

**habit**
**03** way, won **04** bent, cowl, gear, mode, robe, rule, togs, ways, wont **05** dress, ethos, get-up, knack, quirk, trick, usage **06** custom, manner, monkey, outfit, policy **07** costume, garment, leaning, routine, uniform **08** clothing, fixation, practice, tendency, vestment, weakness **09** addiction, assuetude, mannerism, obsession, procedure **10** dependence, proclivity, propensity **11** familiarity, inclination **12** second nature **14** accustomedness, matter of course

*See also* **clothes, clothing**

**• bad habit**
**04** vice **09** cacoethes

**habitable**
**07** livable **08** liveable **09** livable in **10** liveable in **11** fit to live in, inhabitable

**habitat**
**04** home **05** abode, niche **06** domain **07** element, station, terrain **08** dwelling, locality **09** territory **10** metropolis **11** environment **12** surroundings

**habitation**
**03** hut, pad **04** digs, flat, gaff, home **05** abode, house, joint **06** biding **07** cottage, housing, lodging, mansion, tenancy **08** domicile, dwelling, quarters, tenement **09** apartment, occupancy, residence, residency **10** occupation **11** inhabitance, inhabitancy **12** inhabitation **13** accommodation, dwelling-place **14** living quarters

**habitual**
**03** set **05** fixed, great, usual **06** common, normal, wonted **07** chronic, natural, regular, routine **08** addicted, constant, familiar, hardened, ordinary, standard **09** confirmed, customary, dependent, obsessive, recurrent **10** accustomed, inveterate, persistent, systematic **11** established, intemperate, traditional **12** pathological, systematical

**habitually**
**06** mainly, mostly **07** as a rule, chiefly, usually **08** commonly, normally **09** generally, in the main, on average, regularly, routinely, typically **10** by and large, on the whole, ordinarily **13** traditionally **14** for the most part

**habituate**
**03** use **04** tame **05** adapt, break, enure, inure, train **06** harden, school, season, settle **07** break in **08** accustom, make used, settle in **09** condition **10** discipline **11** acclimatize, familiarize

**habitué**
**06** patron **07** denizen, regular **10** frequenter **15** frequent visitor, regular customer

**hack**
**03** cut, hag, hew, saw **04** chop, fell, gash, hash, kick, pick, rack **05** clear, cough, hired, notch, slash, slave **06** drudge, mangle, writer **07** grating, hackney, mattock **08** lacerate, mediocre, mutilate, reporter, tomahawk **09** hackneyed, mercenary, scribbler **10** journalist **11** hedge-writer, penny-a-liner

*See also* **horse**

**• hack it**
**04** cope **05** get by, get on **06** manage **07** carry on, make out **08** get along **10** get through **13** muddle through

**hackle**
**• make someone's hackles rise**
**03** bug, irk, vex **04** gall, miff, nark, rile **05** anger, annoy, get at **06** bother, enrage, hassle, heckle, madden, needle, nettle, offend, ruffle, wind up **07** affront, hatchel, incense, outrage, provoke **08** flax-comb, irritate **09** aggravate, infuriate, make angry **10** antagonize, exasperate **13** make sparks fly **15** get on your nerves

**hackneyed**
**03** old **04** hack, worn **05** banal, corny, hoary, stale, stock, tired, trite **06** common **07** cliché'd, percoct, worn-out **08** clichéed, overused, time-worn **09** twice-told **10** overworked, pedestrian, prostitute, threadbare, uninspired, unoriginal, yawn-making **11** commonplace, stereotyped, wearing thin **12** cliché-ridden, run-of-the-mill **13** platitudinous, unimaginative

**had**
**01** 'd

**haddock**
**05** capon, scrod, smoky **06** finnan, rizzar, rizzer, rizzor, smokie **07** findram, speldin **08** spelding, speldrin **09** speldring **14** Arbroath smokie

**Hades**
**05** Pluto

**hafnium**
**02** Hf

**haft**
**04** grip, hilt, knob **05** shaft, stock **06** handle **07** dudgeon **08** handgrip

**hag**
**03** hew **04** fury, hack **05** crone, harpy, rudas, shrew, vixen, witch **06** beldam, gorgon, virago **07** beldame, hellcat **08** harridan **09** battle-axe, termagant

**haggard**
**03** wan **04** lean, pale, thin **05** drawn, gaunt, Rider **06** pallid, wasted **07** drained, ghastly, pinched, untamed **08** careworn, shrunken **10** cadaverous **11** intractable **13** hollow-cheeked

**haggle**
**04** prig **05** cavil **06** barter, bicker, dicker, higgle, mangle, niffer, palter **07** bargain, chaffer, dispute, quarrel, quibble, wrangle **08** beat down, huckster, squabble **09** negotiate

**hahnium**
**02** Ha

**hail**
**03** ave **04** ahoy, beat, come, goal, hale, heil, laud, pelt, rain, skol **05** cheer, exalt, greet, nod to, salve, score, skoal, sleet, sound, speak, storm **06** accost, assail, attack, batter, health, honour, praise, salute, shower, volley, wave to, what ho **07** acclaim, address, applaud, barrage, bombard, earshot, torrent, welcome **08** be born in, flag down, greeting, signal to, wave down, whoa-ho-ho **09** call out to, frozen ice, hail-storm, originate, whoa-ho-hoa **10** frozen rain, hailstones, say hello to **11** acknowledge, bombardment, communicate **13** precipitation **14** have your home in **15** have your roots in

**hail-fellow-well-met**
**05** jolly, merry **06** genial, hearty, jovial, lively **07** affable, cordial, festive **08** cheerful, friendly, sociable **09** convivial, fun-loving

**hair**
**03** fur, mop **04** coat, hide, pelt, pile, type, wool **05** fibre, locks, pilus, shock **06** fibril, fleece, lanugo, thatch, villus **07** bristle, tresses **08** strammel, strummel **09** character

*Hair-related terms include:*

**03** bob, cue, cut, dod, dye, gel, wax, wig
**04** bald, body, clip, coif, comb, crop, curl, down, fine, grip, hank, kesh, lank, lice, lock, mane, perm, pouf, tête, tint, tong, trim, tuft, wavy, wiry
**05** bangs, black, blond, bluey, braid, brown, brush, crimp, curly, frizz, henna, layer, moult, mousy, queue, quiff, rinse, roots, sandy, serum, shade, shaft, shine, short, slick, slide, snood, tease, thick, tress
**06** auburn, barber, barnet, blonde, bobble, brunet, coarse, colour, crinal, fillet, flaxen, fringe, frizzy, ginger, greasy, hairdo, kangha, mousey, mousse, peruke, pomade, pompom, pompon, pouffe, ribbon, roller, silver, tangle, titian
**07** balding, bandeau, blow-dry, cowlick, crinate, flyaway, frizzle, greying, haircut, hair gel, hair net, hair oil, hirsute, keratin, lacquer, parting, periwig, pin curl, rat-tail, redhead, ringlet, shampoo, streaks, stylist, tonsure, topknot, tow-head, tressed, wet-look, xerasia
**08** alopecia, ash-blond, back-comb, baldpate, barrette, bar slide, bouffant, brunette, canities, chestnut, clippers, coiffeur, coiffure, combover, cow's lick, crinated, dandruff, diffuser, elflocks, fixature, follicle, forelock, grizzled, hair band, hairless, hairline, headring, kisscurl, lovelock, peroxide, rat's-tail, receding, roulette, scrunchy, side comb, sidelock, split end, straight
**09** Alice band, ash-blonde, bandoline, blue rinse, Brylcreem®, capillary, chevelure, coiffeuse, colourant, curlpaper, finger-dry, fright wig, hairbrush, hairdryer, hairpiece, hair slide, hairspray, hairstyle, headdress, Kirbigrip®, lowlights, madarosis, mop-headed, papillote, redheaded, scalp lock, scrunchie, tow-headed, trichosis, water wave
**10** bad hair day, bald-headed, detangling, extensions, fair-haired, fair-headed, finger wave, hair-powder, highlights, leiotrichy, long-haired, perruquier, piliferous, pocket-comb, scrunch-dry, trichology, widow's peak
**11** conditioner, flame-haired, hairdresser, hairstylist, side-parting, tow-coloured, white-haired, white-headed
**12** bottle-blonde, brilliantine, Cain-coloured, close-cropped, curling tongs, cymotrichous, hair restorer, leiotrichous, straightener, trichologist
**13** centre-parting, corkscrew curl, Judas-coloured, lissotrichous, pepper-and-salt, permanent wave, platinum-blond
**14** shoulder-length
**15** strawberry blond, styling products

*Facial hair-related terms include:*

**05** beard, pluck, razor
**06** goatee, tweeze, waxing
**07** epilate, eyelash, goateed, shaving, stubble
**08** bumfluff, depilate, stubbled, sugaring, tweezers
**09** depilator, moustache, sideburns
**10** aftershave, depilation, depilatory, face-fungus, pogonotomy, shaving gel
**11** clean-shaven, shaving foam, shaving-soap
**12** electrolysis, shaving-brush, shaving-stick, side whiskers
**13** eyebrow pencil, eyelash curler
**15** designer stubble

**• let your hair down**
**05** relax **08** chill out, loosen up **09** hang loose **13** have a good time, let yourself go **15** let it all hang out

**• make someone's hair stand on end**
**03** jar **04** daze, jolt, numb, stun **05** amaze, appal, repel, shake, shock, upset **06** dismay, revolt **07** agitate, astound, disgust, horrify, outrage, perturb, stagger, startle, stupefy, terrify, unnerve **08** bewilder, confound, disquiet, distress, frighten, paralyse, unsettle **09** dumbfound, take aback **10** scandalize, traumatize

**• not turn a hair**
**04** calm **08** stay cool **10** remain calm **11** see it coming **12** keep your cool **14** not bat an eyelid, remain composed

**• piece of hair**
**03** cue **04** lock **05** tress

**• split hairs**
**05** cavil **07** nit-pick, quibble **08** pettifog **09** find fault **10** over-refine

**haircut, hairdo** *see* **hairstyle**

**hairdresser**
**06** barber **07** crimper, friseur, stylist **08** coiffeur **09** coiffeuse **11** hairstylist **12** trichologist

*Hairdressers include:*

**06** Clarke (Nicky), Sorbie (Trevor)
**07** Grateau (Marcel), Sassoon (Vidal)
**08** Collinge (Andrew), Mitchell (Paul)
**10** Teazy Weazy, Toni and Guy
**11** Worthington (Charles)

**hairless**
**04** bald **05** shorn **06** shaven, smooth **08** glabrate, glabrous, tonsured **09** beardless, desperate **10** bald-headed **11** clean-shaven

**hairpiece**
**03** jiz, rug, tie, wig **04** gizz, jasy, jazy **05** caxon, jasey, major, syrup **06** bagwig, bobwig, Brutus, merkin, peruke, tie-wig, toupee, toupet **07** buzz-wig, periwig, Ramilie, scratch, spencer **08** postiche, Ramilies, Ramillie **09** fright wig, Ramillies **10** full-bottom, scratch-wig **12** Gregorian wig **14** transformation

**hair-raising**
**05** eerie, scary **06** creepy **08** alarming, exciting, shocking **09** startling, thrilling **10** horrifying, petrifying, terrifying **11** frightening **13** bloodcurdling, spine-chilling

**hair's-breadth**
**03** jot **04** hair, inch **07** whisker **08** fraction

**hairstyle**
**03** cut, set **05** style **06** barnet, hairdo **07** haircut **08** coiffure

*Hairstyles include:*

**02** DA
**03** bob, bun, wig
**04** Afro, crop, perm, shed
**05** bangs, braid, plait, quiff, weave
**06** curled, dreads, fringe, mullet, pouffe, toupee
**07** beehive, bunches, chignon, cowlick, crewcut, crimped, mohican, pageboy, pigtail, shingle, tonsure, topknot
**08** bouffant, combover, corn rows, Eton crop, frizette, ponytail, ringlets, skinhead, undercut
**09** duck's arse, hair-piece, Hoxton fin, number one, pompadour, sideburns
**10** backcombed, dreadlocks, extensions, marcel wave, sideboards
**11** French pleat
**13** hair extension

**hairy**
◇ *anagram indicator*
**05** bushy, dicey, dodgy, furry, fuzzy, grave, nasty, risky **06** chancy, daring, fleecy, pilose, pilous, severe, shaggy, unsafe, woolly **07** bearded, crinite, crinose, exposed, hirsute, ominous, serious **08** alarming, critical, high-risk, insecure, menacing, perilous, reckless, unshaven **09** breakneck, dangerous, hazardous **10** precarious, vulnerable **11** crinigerous, frightening, susceptible, threatening, treacherous

**• hairy person**
**04** Esau

**Haiti**
**02** RH **03** HTI

**halcyon**
**04** calm, mild **05** balmy, happy, quiet, still **06** gentle, golden, placid, serene **07** pacific **08** carefree, peaceful, tranquil **10** kingfisher, prosperous **11** flourishing, undisturbed

**hale**
**03** fit **04** drag, hail, well **05** sound **06** hearty, raucle, robust, strong **07** healthy **08** athletic, blooming, vigorous, youthful **09** in the pink **10** able-bodied **11** flourishing **12** in fine fettle

**half**
◇ *deletion indicator*
◇ *insertion indicator*
**02** hf **04** demi-, hemi-, part, semi- **05** share **06** barely, halved, moiety,

partly, slight **07** à moitié, divided, limited, partial, portion, section, segment **08** bisected, fraction, moderate, slightly **09** bisection, equal part, partially **10** equal share, fractional, hemisphere, incomplete, moderately, semicircle **11** imperfectly **12** divided in two, fifty per cent, inadequately, incompletely **13** hemispherical **14** insufficiently

- **by half**

**03** too **04** very **11** excessively **12** considerably

- **by halves**

**05** à demi **07** à moitié **11** imperfectly **12** inadequately, incompletely **14** insufficiently

- **not half**

**04** very **06** indeed, really **08** not at all, very much **09** not nearly **11** exceedingly

- **other half**

**04** wife **06** spouse **07** husband, partner **08** alter ego

- **too ... by half**

**03** too **04** over **06** unduly **11** excessively **12** immoderately, inordinately, unreasonably **13** unjustifiably, unnecessarily

### half-baked
**05** crazy, crude, silly **06** stupid **07** foolish **08** crackpot, immature **09** ill-judged, senseless, underdone, unplanned **10** half-witted, incomplete **11** harebrained, impractical, undeveloped **12** ill-conceived, short-sighted

### half-caste
**05** griff, metif, Métis, sambo **06** Creole, griffe, mestee **07** mestiza, mestizo, Métisse, mongrel, mulatta, mulatto **08** miscegen, quadroon **09** miscegene, miscegine, quintroon **10** mulattress, quarteroon **12** quarter-blood

### half-cough
**03** hem

### half-hearted
◇ *middle deletion indicator*
**04** cool, weak **05** tepid **06** feeble **07** neutral, passive **08** listless, lukewarm **09** apathetic, Laodicean **10** lacklustre **11** indifferent, unconcerned **12** uninterested **14** unenthusiastic

### half-heartedly
◇ *middle deletion indicator*
**06** feebly **09** neutrally **10** listlessly **13** apathetically

### half-moon
**04** lune **08** demilune

### halfpenny
**03** mag, meg, rap **04** maik, mail, make, posh **05** maile **06** bawbee, magpie, obolus **07** patrick **10** portcullis

### halfway
**03** mid **04** mean **06** barely, median, middle, midway **07** central **08** slightly **09** centrally **11** equidistant, imperfectly, in the middle, to the middle **12** intermediate

- **meet someone halfway**

**09** make a deal, negotiate **10** compromise **11** give and take **15** make concessions

### halfwit
**03** ass, git, mug, nit **04** berk, butt, clot, dill, dope, dork, dupe, fool, geek, nerk, nong, prat, twit **05** chump, clown, comic, dumbo, dunce, eejit, galah, idiot, moron, ninny, prick, twerp, wally **06** cretin, dimwit, doofus, jester, nitwit, numpty, stooge, sucker **07** airhead, buffoon, fat-head, pillock, plonker **08** imbecile **09** birdbrain, blockhead, ignoramus, simpleton **10** nincompoop **13** laughing-stock

### half-witted
**04** dull, dumb **05** barmy, batty, crazy, dotty, nutty, potty, silly, wacky **06** simple, stupid **07** foolish, idiotic, moronic **08** crackpot **09** dim-witted **12** crack-brained, feeble-minded, simple-minded **14** not the full quid

### hall
**02** ha' **04** aula, gild **05** foyer, guild, lobby, odeon, salle **06** atrium, exedra **07** apadana, chamber, citadel, commons, exhedra, hallway, megaron, passage **08** basilica, corridor **09** concourse, Domdaniel, longhouse, vestibule **10** auditorium, passageway **11** concert hall **12** assembly hall, assembly room, entrance-hall **14** conference hall

*See also* **college**

### hallmark
**04** mark, sign **05** badge, stamp **06** device, emblem, symbol **09** brand-name, indicator, platemark, trademark **10** indication **12** official mark **13** official stamp **14** typical quality

### hallo
**02** hi **04** g'day **05** chimo, hello, hillo, hullo **06** holloa **07** welcome **09** greetings **11** good evening, good morning **13** good afternoon

### hallowed
**04** holy, tapu **06** age-old, sacred **07** blessed, revered **08** honoured **09** dedicated, venerable **10** inviolable, sacrosanct, sanctified **11** consecrated, established

### hallucinate
**04** trip **05** dream **07** imagine **08** daydream, freak out **09** fantasize, see things **10** see visions **13** imagine things

### hallucination
**04** trip **05** dream **06** mirage, vision **07** fantasy, figment **08** daydream, delirium, delusion, freak-out, illusion **09** autoscopy **10** apparition **14** phantasmagoria **15** hypnagogic image, hypnogogic image

### halo
**01** O **04** aura, ring **05** crown, glory **06** corona, gloria, nimbus **07** aureola, aureole **08** gloriole, halation, radiance **12** vesica piscis **13** circle of light

### halt
**03** alt, end **04** curb, lame, limp, quit, rest, stem, stop, wait **05** block, break, cease, check, close, crush, pause **06** arrest, desist, draw up, finish, impede, pull up **07** limping, respite **08** break off, crippled, deadlock, full stop, hold back, interval, obstruct, stoppage **09** cessation, stalemate, terminate, vacillate **10** call it a day, come to rest, desistance, put an end to, standstill **11** come to a rest, come to a stop, discontinue, termination **12** bring to a stop, draw to a close, interruption **13** bring to a close **14** breathing space, discontinuance **15** discontinuation

### halting
**06** broken **07** awkward **08** hesitant, laboured, unsteady **09** faltering, imperfect, stumbling, uncertain **10** stammering, stuttering

### halve
◇ *insertion indicator*
**05** sever, share, split **06** bisect, divide, lessen, reduce **07** cut down **09** cut in half **10** split in two **11** dichotomize **13** divide equally

### halved
**03** cut **05** split **06** shared **07** divided **08** bisected **09** dimidiate

### ham
◇ *anagram indicator*
**04** hock **05** hough **06** clumsy, coarse **07** amateur, overact, pigmeat **08** inexpert **10** prosciutto

### ham-fisted
**03** ham **05** gawky, inept **06** clumsy, thumby **07** awkward, unhandy **08** bungling **09** all thumbs, lumbering, maladroit, two-fisted, unskilful **10** blundering, cack-handed **11** heavy-handed **13** accident-prone, unco-ordinated

### hamlet
**05** aldea, thorp **06** thorpe

### hammer
◇ *anagram indicator*
**02** ax **03** axe, din, hit **04** bang, bash, beat, drum, form, lick, make, mall, maul, pane, pean, peen, pein, pene, pick, plug, rout, slam, slap, slog **05** blame, bully, decry, dolly, drive, force, forge, gavel, grind, knock, madge, mould, pound, rivet, shape, slate **06** attack, batter, beetle, defeat, drudge, instil, keep on, labour, mallet, martel, monkey, oliver, plexor, sledge, strike, thrash **07** censure, clobber, condemn, dog-head, fashion, malleus, Mjölnir, outplay, persist, plessor, run down, trounce **08** malleate, Mjöllnir, overcome, trouncer, work away **09** criticize, denigrate, drive home, overwhelm, percussor, persevere, reiterate, slaughter **10** annihilate, claw hammer, sheep's-foot, tack hammer,

tilt-hammer, trip hammer **11** about-sledge, steam hammer, stone hammer, walk all over, water hammer
**12** sledgehammer **13** run rings round, tear a strip off **14** knapping-hammer
**15** make mincemeat of

**• hammer out**
◇ *anagram indicator*
**06** finish, settle **07** produce, resolve, sort out, work out **08** complete
**09** negotiate, thrash out
**10** accomplish, bring about **12** carry through

**hammered**
◇ *anagram indicator*
**06** incuse **07** excudit

**hammerhead**
**04** pane, pean, peen, pein, pene
**05** umbre **07** Zygaena **08** umbrette
**09** umber-bird

**hammock support**
**04** clew, clue

**hamper**
◇ *anagram indicator*
◇ *containment indicator*
**03** box, pad, ped **04** curb, foil, stop, tuck **05** baulk, block, bribe, cabin, check, cramp, creel, pinch, seron
**06** basket, bridle, fetter, hinder, hobble, hold up, impede, retard, seroon, stymie, tangle, thwart **07** curtail, distort, inhibit, pannier, prevent, shackle **08** encumber, handicap, incumber, obstruct, restrain, restrict, slow down **09** container, frustrate, hamstring

**hamstring**
**03** hox **04** foil, hock, stop **05** baulk, block, check, cramp, hough
**06** hinder, hold up, impede, stymie, thwart **07** cripple, disable
**08** encumber, handicap, paralyse, restrain, restrict **09** frustrate
**12** incapacitate

**hand**
**03** aid, fin, paw, pud **04** care, doer, fist, give, help, hond, mitt, palm, part, pass, side **05** arrow, manus, offer, power, skill, style, touch, yield **06** author, charge, convey, marker, needle, pledge, script, stroke, submit, worker
**07** acclaim, command, conduct, control, custody, deliver, ovation, pointer, present, quarter, succour, support, workman, writing
**08** applause, cheering, clapping, clutches, employee, farm-hand, handclap, hand over, hireling, labourer, producer, transmit **09** authority, direction, handiwork, indicator, influence, operative, performer, signature, workwoman **10** assistance, management, penmanship, possession
**11** calligraphy, handwriting, helping hand, supervision **12** manual worker
**13** participation **14** responsibility
**15** instrumentality, round of applause

**• at hand**
**04** near, nigh **05** close, handy, ready
**06** to hand, toward **08** imminent
**09** available, to the fore **10** accessible
**11** forthcoming, in the offing **13** about to happen

**• by hand**
**07** à la main **08** manually **13** with your hands **14** using your hands

**• from hand to mouth**
**09** in poverty **10** insecurely
**11** dangerously, uncertainly **12** au jour le jour, from day to day, precariously
**14** on the breadline

**• hand down**
**04** give, will **05** grant, leave **06** pass on
**07** devolve **08** bequeath, pass down, transfer

**• hand in glove**
**09** in cahoots **11** very closely

**• hand in hand**
**12** holding hands **13** with hands held
**14** closely related **15** closely together, with hands joined

**• hand on**
**04** give **06** pass on, supply **08** transfer, transmit **09** surrender **14** let someone have

**• hand out**
**04** dole **07** deal out, dish out, give out, mete out, pass out **08** dispense, share out **10** distribute **11** disseminate

**• hand over**
**04** give, pass, turn **05** yield **06** donate, give up, render **07** consign, deliver, present, release **08** transfer, turn over
**09** surrender **10** relinquish

**• hollow of hand**
**04** vola

**• in hand**
**05** put by, ready, spare **07** à la main
**08** under way **09** available, in reserve
**10** attended to, considered **12** under control **14** being dealt with

**• on the other hand**
**03** but **04** then **05** again
**12** contrariwise

**• out of hand**
◇ *anagram indicator*
**06** at once **11** immediately **12** out of control

**• to hand**
**04** near **05** close, handy, ready **06** at hand, nearby **07** ad manum
**08** imminent **09** available
**10** accessible **13** about to happen

**• try your hand**
**03** try **04** seek **06** strive **07** attempt, have a go **09** have a shot, have a stab
**10** have a crack **13** see if you can do

**• win hands down**
**09** win easily **15** win effortlessly

**• winning hand**
**04** post

**handbag**
**04** caba, grip **05** cabas, purse
**07** holdall **08** handgrip, reticule
**09** clutch bag, flight bag, vanity bag
**10** pocketbook **11** shoulder bag

**handbill**
**05** flier **06** letter, notice **07** leaflet
**08** circular, flysheet, pamphlet
**09** throwaway **12** announcement
**13** advertisement

**handbook**
**03** ABC **05** guide **06** manual
**08** Baedeker **09** companion, guidebook, vade-mecum
**10** prospectus **11** enchiridion
**12** encheiridion **15** instruction book

**handcuff**
**03** tie **04** cuff **06** fasten, fetter, secure
**07** manacle, shackle **08** bracelet, snitcher, wristlet

**handcuffs**
**05** cuffs, snaps **07** darbies, fetters, mittens, nippers **08** manacles, shackles, snippers **09** bracelets, snitchers, wristlets

**handful**
**03** few, rip **04** hank, pain, pest, ripp
**05** bunch, pugil **06** bother, little
**07** fistful, looﬀul **08** nieveful, nuisance
**10** scattering, smattering, sprinkling
**11** small amount, small number
**13** pain in the neck **15** thorn in the flesh

**handgun**
**03** gat, gun, rod **04** iron **05** piece
**06** pistol **07** sidearm **08** culverin, revolver **09** derringer **10** six-shooter
**11** blunderbuss

*See also* **gun**

**handicap**
**03** hcp **04** curb **05** block, check, limit
**06** bridle, burden, defect, hamper, hinder, impair, impede, retard
**07** barrier, disable, half-one, penalty
**08** drawback, encumber, hold back, obstacle, obstruct, restrict
**09** hindrance **10** constraint, disability, impairment, impediment, limitation
**11** abnormality, encumbrance, obstruction, restriction, shortcoming
**12** disadvantage **14** stumbling-block

**• concede as handicap**
**03** owe

**• with adverse handicap**
**04** plus

**• with a handicap of**
**03** off

**handicapped**
**08** disabled **10** challenged
**13** disadvantaged, incapacitated

**handicraft**
**03** art **05** craft, skill **08** artifice, handwork **09** craftwork, handiwork, scrimshaw **11** scrimshandy, workmanship **12** scrimshander
**13** craftsmanship

**handily**
**06** at hand, nearly, to hand **07** adeptly, readily **08** adroitly, cleverly, usefully
**09** helpfully, skilfully **10** accessibly
**11** practically, within reach
**12** conveniently

**handiwork**
**03** art **04** hand, work **05** craft, doing, skill **06** action, design, result
**07** product **08** creation **09** craftwork, invention **10** handicraft, production
**11** achievement, artisanship,

workmanship **13** craftsmanship **14** responsibility

**handkerchief**
**03** rag **04** wipe **05** blind, fogle, hanky, romal, rumal **06** hankie, napkin, tissue **07** bandana, foulard, Kleenex®, nose-rag, orarium, snotrag **08** kerchief, monteith, mouchoir **09** muckender
**• keep in a handkerchief**
**04** mail

**handle**
**03** bow, lug, paw **04** bail, feel, grip, haft, hilt, hold, knob, name, work **05** brake, drive, grasp, shaft, staff, stale, steal, steel, steer, steil, stele, stock, sweep, touch, treat, wield **06** behave, deal in, finger, fondle, manage, market, pick up, steale, tackle **07** control, discuss, operate, trade in, traffic **08** cope with, deal with, handgrip **09** handstaff, supervise **10** plough-tree, take care of **11** plough-stilt **12** be in charge of, do business in

**handling**
**07** conduct, running **08** approach, managing **09** direction, operation, treatment **10** discussion, management **11** transaction **12** manipulation **14** administration

**handout**
**04** alms, dole **05** gifts, issue, share **07** charity, freebie, leaflet **08** brochure, bulletin, circular, largesse, pamphlet **09** statement **10** free sample, literature **12** press release

**handover**
**04** move **05** shift **06** change **07** removal **08** transfer **10** assignment, changeover, conveyance, relocation **12** displacement, transference, transmission **13** transposition

**hand-picked**
**05** elect, élite **06** choice, chosen, picked, select **08** screened, selected **09** recherché

**hands**
**02** hh

**handsome**
**04** fair, fine **05** ample, brave, dishy, hunky, large, noble **06** comely, lavish, seemly **07** elegant, featous, liberal, sizable, stately **08** abundant, becoming, feateous, featuous, generous, gorgeous, gracious, sizeable, suitable **09** bountiful, dignified, featurely, goodfaced, plentiful, unsparing **10** attractive, convenient, personable, unstinting **11** good-looking, magnanimous **12** considerable

**handsomely**
**05** amply **06** richly **08** lavishly **09** carefully, liberally **10** abundantly, generously, graciously **11** bountifully, plentifully, unsparingly **12** munificently, unstintingly **13** magnanimously

**handwriting**
**03** paw **04** fist, hand **05** Neski **06** Naskhi, Neskhi, niggle, scrawl, script **07** writing **08** half-text, join-hand, printing, scribble **09** autograph, character, court hand, scripture **10** penmanship **11** calligraphy, chirography, copperplate, running hand **13** secretary hand **15** Lombardic script

**handy**
**04** deft, near **05** adept, gemmy, jemmy, ready **06** adroit, at hand, clever, expert, nearly, nimble, to hand, useful **07** helpful, skilful, skilled **08** handsome **09** available, dexterous, practical **10** accessible, convenient, functional, proficient **11** practicable, within reach

**handyman**
**05** DIYer **08** factotum **09** odd-jobber, odd-jobman **10** bluejacket **15** Jack-of-all-trades

**hang**
**03** fix, nub, sag **04** bend, damn, drop, flit, flop, glue, kill, kilt, lean, loll, pend **05** affix, cling, drape, drift, droop, float, hover, lynch, paste, put up, run up, scrag, stick, strap, swing, trail, truss **06** append, attach, cement, dangle, fasten, impend, linger, remain, string **07** execute, flutter, justify, meaning, stretch, suspend, turn off **08** hang down, string up **09** declivity **10** put to death **11** be suspended **13** supercollate **15** send to the gibbet
**• get the hang of**
**04** twig **05** grasp, learn **06** fathom, master **10** comprehend, understand **13** get the knack of
**• hang about**
**04** lime, mike, stay **05** haunt **06** dawdle, linger, loiter, remain **07** hang out, persist **08** frequent **09** waste time **10** hang around **13** associate with **15** keep company with
**• hang back**
**05** demur, stall **06** recoil **07** shy away **08** hesitate, hold back **10** shrink back, stay behind **11** be reluctant
**• hang down loosely**
**03** lop
**• hang fire**
**04** stop, wait **05** delay, stall, stick **06** hold on **08** hang back, hesitate, hold back **09** vacillate **13** procrastinate
**• hang on**
**04** grip, wait **05** cling, grasp **06** append, clutch, endure, hold on, remain, rest on, turn on **07** carry on, hinge on, hold out, persist **08** continue, depend on, hold fast **09** persevere **14** be contingent on, be determined by **15** be conditional on
**• hang over**
**04** loom **06** impend, menace **08** approach, threaten **10** be imminent, overshadow

**hangdog**
**05** cowed **06** abject, guilty **07** furtive **08** cringing, defeated, downcast, sneaking, wretched **09** miserable **10** browbeaten, shamefaced

**hanger-on**
**05** toady **06** client, lackey, minion, sponge **07** flunkey, sponger **08** follower, henchman, parasite **09** courtling, dependant, dependent, sycophant **10** freeloader

**hanging**
**04** drop **05** drape, loose, tapis **06** dossal, dossel, floppy **07** curtain, drapery, draping, frontal, pendant, pendent, pending, pensile **08** dangling, downcast, drooping, flapping, flopping, parament, swinging **09** drop-scene, pendulous, suspended **10** suspending, unattached **11** antependium, unsupported

**hangman**
**07** lockman, topsman **08** rascally **09** Jack Ketch **11** nubbing-cove

**hang-out**
**03** den **04** dive, home **05** haunt, joint, local, patch **12** meeting-place, watering-hole **14** stamping-ground

**hangover**
**08** survival **10** crapulence **12** after-effects, katzenjammer, morning after

**hang-up**
**05** block, thing **06** phobia **07** problem **08** fixation, idée fixe, neurosis **09** obsession **10** difficulty, inhibition **11** mental block **13** preoccupation

**hank**
**04** coil, fank, loop, roll, tuft **05** catch, piece, skein, twist **06** length **07** handful **08** selvagee

**hanker**
**06** linger
**• hanker after, hanker for**
**04** want **05** covet, crave **06** desire **07** itch for, long for, pine for, wish for **08** yearn for **09** hunger for, thirst for **10** be dying for **14** set your heart on

**hankering**
**04** ache, itch, urge, wish **06** desire, hunger, pining, thirst **07** craving, longing **08** yearning

**hankie, hanky** *see* **handkerchief**

**hanky-panky**
**05** fling **06** affair, tricks **07** carry-on, devilry **08** adultery, cheating, mischief, nonsense, trickery **09** chicanery, deception **10** dishonesty, subterfuge **11** shenanigans **12** bit on the side, machinations **13** fooling around, funny business, jiggery-pokery, slap and tickle **14** how's-your-father, monkey business

**haphazard**
◇ *anagram indicator*
**04** wild **06** casual, chance, random, randon **07** aimless, wildcat **08** careless, slapdash, slipshod **09** arbitrary, hit-or-miss, irregular, orderless, unplanned **10** disorderly, hitty-missy, tumultuary, willy-nilly

**11** promiscuous **12** disorganized, unmethodical, unsystematic
**14** indiscriminate, rough-and-tumble

**haphazardly**
◇ *anagram indicator*
**06** wildly **08** by chance, randomly
**10** carelessly, willy-nilly **11** arbitrarily, irregularly **14** unmethodically

**hapless**
**06** cursed, jinxed **07** unhappy, unlucky
**08** ill-fated, luckless, wretched
**09** miserable **10** ill-starred **11** star-crossed, unfortunate

**happen**
**02** be **03** hap **04** come, fall, find, go on, pass, tide **05** arise, ensue, hit on, occur, worth **06** appear, arrive, befall, chance, crop up, follow, result, turn up
**07** develop, light on, perhaps, turn out
**08** become of, bump into, chance on, come true, discover **09** come about, eventuate, run across, stumble on, supervene, take place, transpire
**10** come across, come to pass **11** be the fate of, eventualize, materialize
**13** come into being, present itself

**happening**
**04** case **05** event, scene, thing, weird
**06** action, affair, chance **07** episode
**08** accident, business, incident, occasion **09** adventure, événement, occurrent **10** experience, occurrence, phenomenon **11** eventuality, fashionable, proceedings
**12** circumstance

**happily**
**06** gladly **07** luckily, merrily, perhaps
**08** by chance, heartily, joyfully, joyously **09** agreeably, feliciter, fittingly, gleefully, willingly
**10** cheerfully **11** contentedly, delightedly, fortunately, opportunely
**12** auspiciously, propitiously
**14** providentially

**happiness**
**03** joy **04** glee, life, seal, seel, seil, sele
**05** bliss **06** gaiety, heaven **07** delight, ecstasy, elation **08** delirium, euphoria, felicity, gladness, pleasure
**09** beatitude, enjoyment, eudaemony, hog heaven, merriment, merriness
**10** blitheness, cheeriness, eudaemonia, exuberance, joyfulness
**11** contentment, good spirits, high spirits **12** cheerfulness

**happy**
◇ *anagram indicator*
**03** apt, gay **04** glad **05** blest, jolly, lucky, merry, seely **06** blithe, elated, golden, jovial, joyful, joyous, proper
**07** blessed, chuffed, content, exalted, fitting, gleeful, halcyon, helpful, pleased, radiant, smiling **08** apposite, carefree, cheerful, ecstatic, euphoric, gruntled, thrilled **09** cock-a-hoop, confident, contented, delighted, delirious, exuberant, fortunate, gratified, high-blest, opportune, overjoyed, rapturous, satisfied, unworried **10** auspicious, beneficial, convenient, favourable, felicitous, propitious, starry-eyed, untroubled
**11** appropriate, in a good mood, on cloud nine, over the moon, tickled pink, unconcerned **12** advantageous, happy as a clam, happy as Larry, light-hearted, walking on air **13** floating on air, in good spirits, in high spirits
**15** happy as a sandboy, in seventh heaven, on top of the world
• **be happy**
**03** ave

**happy-go-lucky**
**06** blithe, casual **08** carefree, cheerful, heedless, reckless **09** easy-going, unworried **10** insouciant, nonchalant, untroubled **11** improvident, unconcerned **12** devil-may-care, light-hearted **13** irresponsible

**harangue**
**05** orate, spout **06** lay off, preach, sermon, speech, spruik, tirade
**07** address, declaim, lecture, oration
**08** diatribe, perorate **09** hold forth, speechify **10** peroration, talky-talky
**11** exhortation, paternoster **12** talkee-talkee

**harass**
◇ *anagram indicator*
**03** dun, nag, vex **04** bait, cark, fret, tire
**05** annoy, chevy, chivy, grind, harry, hound, pinch, press, trash, weary, worry **06** argufy, badger, bother, chivvy, harrow, hassle, infest, overdo, pester, pingle, plague, pursue, stress
**07** afflict, disturb, dragoon, exhaust, fatigue, provoke, torment, trouble, trounce, turmoil, wear out **08** distract, distress, irritate **09** importune, persecute **10** antagonize, exasperate
**11** have it in for **12** put the wind up

**harassed**
◇ *anagram indicator*
**05** vexed **06** hunted **07** harried, hassled, hounded, plagued, uptight, worried **08** careworn, pestered, strained, stressed, troubled
**09** pressured, tormented
**10** distracted, distraught, distressed
**11** pressurized, stressed-out, under stress **13** under pressure

**harassment**
**05** grief **06** bother, hassle, molest
**07** mobbing, torment, trouble
**08** distress, nuisance, vexation
**09** annoyance, badgering, pestering
**10** irritation, pressuring **11** aggravation, bedevilment, molestation, persecution

**harbinger**
**04** host, omen, sign **06** herald
**07** pioneer, portent, warning
**09** foretoken, messenger, precursor
**10** forerunner, indication **12** avant-courier

**harbour**
◇ *containment indicator*
**04** bear, dock, herd, hide, hold, keep, mole, port, quay **05** basin, haven, house, lodge, nurse, reset, wharf
**06** foster, marina, refuge, retain, shield, take in **07** believe, cherish, cling to, conceal, imagine, lodging, mooring, nurture, protect, receive, shelter
**08** maintain **09** anchorage, entertain

**hard**
**01** H **03** bad, raw, set **04** bony, busy, cold, firm, grim, keen, live, near, real, sore, true **05** badly, close, cruel, dense, flint, harsh, heavy, horny, irony, rigid, sharp, solid, stern, stiff, stony, tough
**06** actual, bitter, busily, crusty, deeply, flinty, keenly, knotty, marble, potent, severe, stingy, strict, strong, tiring, wooden **07** acutely, arduous, austere, callous, certain, closely, compact, complex, eagerly, harmful, harshly, heavily, hornish, intense, onerous, painful, sharply, violent, zealous
**08** baffling, definite, diligent, exacting, forceful, forcibly, freezing, intently, involved, narcotic, obdurate, pitiless, powerful, puzzling, reliable, rigorous, ruthless, scleroid, sedulous, severely, steadily, strongly, toilsome, uneasily, verified, vigorous **09** addictive, arduously, assiduous, carefully, compacted, condensed, difficult, earnestly, energetic, intensely, intricate, laborious, merciless, niggardly, resistant, strenuous, unfeeling, unpliable, unsparing, violently
**10** compressed, critically, diligently, exhausting, forcefully, hard as iron, hard as rock, implacable, inflexible, oppressive, perplexing, powerfully, tyrannical, undeniable, unpleasant, unyielding, vigorously **11** assiduously, attentively, bewildering, cold-hearted, complicated, constrained, distressing, hard as flint, hard as stone, hard-hearted, hard-working, industrious, insensitive, intractable, laboriously, strenuously, troublesome, unrelenting
**12** backbreaking, disagreeable, enthusiastic, habit-forming, impenetrable, indisputable
**13** conscientious, energetically, industriously, reverberating, uncomfortable, unsympathetic
**14** after a struggle, unquestionable, with difficulty **15** conscientiously
• **hard and fast**
**03** set **05** fixed, rigid **06** strict
**07** binding **08** definite **09** immutable, stringent **10** inflexible, invariable, unchanging **11** unalterable
**12** unchangeable **14** uncompromising
• **hard black**
**02** HB
• **hard up**
**04** bust, poor, puir **05** broke, short, skint **07** boracic, lacking **08** bankrupt, dirt-poor, in the red, strapped
**09** penniless **10** cleaned out, stony broke **11** impecunious, near the bone
**12** impoverished, on your uppers
**14** on your beam ends **15** strapped for cash
• **very hard**
**02** HH

**hard-bitten**
**05** tough **06** inured, shrewd **07** callous, cynical **08** ruthless **09** hard-nosed, practical, realistic, toughened **10** hard-boiled, hard-headed **11** down-to-earth **12** case-hardened, matter-of-fact **13** unsentimental

**hard-boiled**
**05** tough **06** brazen **07** callous, cynical **09** practical **10** hard-headed **11** down-to-earth **13** unsentimental

**hard-core**
**05** rigid **07** blatant, diehard, extreme, staunch **08** explicit **09** dedicated, obstinate, steadfast **12** intransigent **13** dyed-in-the-wool

**harden**
**03** set **04** bake, cake, geal, gird **05** brace, chill, enure, flesh, inure, nerve, steel, train **06** anneal, bronze, deaden, endure, freeze, season, temper **07** calcify, congeal, fortify, petrify, stiffen, toughen **08** accustom, buttress, concrete, indurate, sclerose, solidify **09** habituate, reinforce, vulcanize **10** case-harden, sclerotize, strengthen, work-harden

**hardened**
**03** set **06** inured **07** bronzed, callous, chilled, chronic, coctile, steeled **08** habitual, obdurate, scleroid, seasoned **09** reprobate, shameless, toughened, unfeeling **10** accustomed, habituated, inveterate **12** incorrigible, irredeemable

**hard-headed**
**05** sharp, tough **06** astute, shrewd **08** pitiless, rational, sensible **09** hard-nosed, practical, pragmatic, realistic **10** cool-headed, hard-bitten, hard-boiled **11** down-to-earth, level-headed, tough-minded **12** businesslike **13** clear-thinking, unsentimental

**hard-hearted**
**04** cold, hard **05** cruel, stony **06** unkind **07** callous, inhuman **08** pitiless, uncaring **09** heartless, merciless, unfeeling **10** flint-heart **11** cold-blooded, unconcerned **12** stony-hearted **13** unsympathetic **14** marble-breasted

**hard-hitting**
**04** bold **05** blunt, frank, tough **06** direct **08** critical, forceful, straight, vigorous **09** unsparing **10** forthright **12** condemnatory **13** no-holds-barred **14** uncompromising

**hardihood**
**04** grit, guts, risk **05** pluck **06** bottle, daring, valour **07** bravery, courage **08** audacity, boldness, rashness **10** enterprise, robustness **11** intrepidity **12** fearlessness, recklessness **13** dauntlessness **15** adventurousness

**hardiness**
**06** valour **07** courage **08** boldness **09** fortitude, toughness **10** resilience, resolution, robustness, ruggedness, sturdiness **11** intrepidity

**hardline**
**05** tough **06** strict **07** extreme **08** militant **10** immoderate, inflexible, unyielding **11** undeviating **12** intransigent **14** uncompromising

**hardly**
**04** jimp, just **06** barely, jimply, uneath **07** harshly, none too **08** not at all, not quite, only just, scarcely, severely **09** almost not, by no means **14** with difficulty

**hardness**
**06** rigour **07** granite **08** coldness, firmness, rigidity, severity **09** harshness, sternness, toughness **10** difficulty, inhumanity **12** pitilessness **13** insensitivity, laboriousness

**hard-nosed**
**05** tough **08** ruthless **09** practical, realistic **10** hard-bitten, hard-boiled, hard-headed, no-nonsense **13** unsentimental

**hard-pressed**
**06** pushed, strait **07** hard put, harried **08** harassed **09** in a corner, overtaxed **10** hard-pushed **11** under stress, up against it **12** in a tight spot, overburdened **13** under pressure

**hardship**
**04** need, pain, want **05** trial **06** misery, murder, rigour, strait, stress **07** burdens, penance, poverty, trouble **08** distress **09** adversity, austerity, grievance, privation, suffering **10** affliction, difficulty, misfortune **11** depredation, deprivation, destitution, tribulation **12** depredations

**hardware**
**03** kit **04** gear **05** stuff, tools **06** outfit, rig-out, tackle, things **08** articles, supplies **09** apparatus, equipment, furniture **10** appliances **11** accessories, apparelment, ironmongery **13** accoutrements, paraphernalia

**hard-wearing**
**05** stout, tough **06** rugged, strong, sturdy **07** durable, lasting **08** well-made **09** resilient **10** made to last **11** built to last

**hard-working**
**04** busy, keen **07** zealous **08** diligent, sedulous **09** assiduous, energetic **11** industrious **12** enthusiastic **13** conscientious

**hardy**
**03** fit **04** bold, Olly **05** brave, sound, stout, tough **06** daring, heroic, plucky, robust, strong, sturdy, trusty **07** durable, healthy, spartan, stoical **08** fearless, impudent, indurate, intrepid, resolute, stalwart, vigorous **09** confident, heavy-duty, indurated, iron-sided, undaunted **10** courageous **11** indomitable **12** stout-hearted

**hare**
**03** doe, wat **04** baud, bawd, buck, mara, pika, puss, scut **06** hasten, malkin, mawkin **07** leveret **08** baudrons **10** Dolichotis, jack rabbit, sage rabbit, springhaas **14** snowshoe rabbit
*See also* **rabbit**

**hare-brained**
**04** daft, rash, wild **05** giddy, inane, silly **06** scatty, stupid **07** foolish **08** careless, crackpot, headlong, heedless, reckless **09** half-baked **12** ill-conceived **14** scatterbrained

**harem**
**05** serai **06** zenana **08** seraglio
• **room in a harem**
**03** oda

**hark**
**04** hear, mark, note **06** listen, notice **07** give ear, hearken, pay heed, whisper **12** pay attention
• **hark back**
**06** go back, hoicks, recall, revert **07** regress, try back **08** remember, turn back **09** recollect

**harlequin**
**04** fool, zany **05** clown, comic, joker **06** jester **07** buffoon **10** variegated

**harlot**
**03** pro **04** base, lewd, loon, lown, slag, tart **05** hussy, lowne, tramp, whore **06** hooker **07** slapper, trollop, wagtail **08** callgirl, scrubber, strumpet **10** loose woman, prostitute **11** fallen woman, working girl **12** streetwalker

**harm**
◇ *anagram indicator*
**03** ill, mar **04** bane, evil, hurt, loss, pain, ruin **05** abuse, annoy, scath, spoil, touch, wound, wreak, wrong **06** damage, impair, injure, injury, misuse, molest, scathe **07** blemish, destroy **08** ill-treat, maltreat **09** adversity, detriment, prejudice, suffering, vengeance **10** disservice, impairment, misfortune **11** destruction, work against **12** do violence to **15** be detrimental to

**harmful**
**03** bad, ill **04** evil **05** toxic **06** wicked **07** hurtful, noxious **08** damaging, wounding **09** dangerous, hazardous, injurious, poisonous, unhealthy **10** pernicious **11** deleterious, destructive, detrimental, unwholesome

**harmless**
**04** mild, safe **05** silly **06** gentle **07** anodyne **08** -friendly, hurtless, innocent, non-toxic **09** blameless, innocuous, woundless **11** inoffensive

**harmonious**
**06** dulcet, in sync, mellow **07** amiable, cordial, in synch, musical, tuneful **08** amicable, balanced, friendly, matching, peaceful, pleasant, rhythmic **09** according, agreeable, congruous,

consonant, consonous, melodious, peaceable **10** Apollonian, compatible, concinnous, concordant, concordial, consistent, euphonious, like-minded **11** co-ordinated, harmonizing, mellifluous, sympathetic, symphonious **13** sweet-sounding

**harmoniously**
**08** amicably **09** agreeably, cordially **10** compatibly, peacefully **11** congruously **12** consistently **13** symmetrically **14** in a balanced way **15** sympathetically

**harmonization**
**08** matching **09** agreement, balancing **10** adaptation **11** arrangement **12** co-ordination **13** accommodation **14** correspondence, reconciliation

**harmonize**
**02** go **03** mix **04** mesh, rime, suit, tone **05** adapt, agree, atone, blend, fit in, match, rhyme, salve **06** accord, attone **07** arrange, balance, compose, concord **08** coincide **09** get on with, reconcile **10** co-ordinate, correspond, go together **11** accommodate, be congruent, be congruous

**harmony**
**04** tone, tune **05** amity, chime, music, peace, unity **06** accord, assent, melody, unison **07** balance, chiming, concent, concert, concord, euphony, keeping, oneness, rapport **08** blending, diapason, eurythmy, faburden, goodwill, symmetry, sympathy, symphony **09** agreement, concentus, eurhythmy, unanimity **10** concinnity, conformity, consonance, consonancy **11** amicability, concurrence, consistence, consistency, co-operation, tunefulness **12** co-ordination, friendliness, thorough bass **13** compatibility, melodiousness, understanding **14** correspondence, correspondency, like-mindedness **15** mellifluousness

• **in harmony**
**08** together **15** never a cross word

• **out of harmony**
**04** ajar

**harness**
**03** use **04** gear, tack, team **05** apply, hitch, put to, trace **06** employ, straps, tackle **07** channel, control, exploit, gearing, hitch up, utilize **08** mobilize, tackling **09** equipment, make use of **10** baby-jumper **11** baby-bouncer **13** accoutrements

• **in harness**
**04** busy **06** active, at work **07** working **08** employed, together **11** co-operating **13** collaborating, in co-operation

**harp**
**04** kora, lyre **05** nebel **06** trigon **07** sambuca **08** clarsach **09** harmonica **10** mouth organ

• **harp on**
**03** nag **05** grind, press, renew **06** labour, repeat **07** dwell on **09** go on about, reiterate **11** flog to death, keep on about **14** go on and on about

**harpoon**
**03** peg **04** barb, dart **05** arrow, spear **06** fisgig, fizgig, grains **07** fishgig, trident **10** toggle iron

**harpsichord**
**06** spinet **07** cembalo, spinnet **08** clavecin, spinette, virginal **09** virginals **12** clavicembalo **15** pair of virginals

**harridan**
**03** hag, nag **04** fury **05** harpy, scold, shrew, vixen, witch **06** dragon, gorgon, tartar, virago **07** hell-cat **09** battle-axe, termagant, Xanthippe

**harried**
**05** beset **07** anxious, hassled, plagued, ravaged, worried **08** agitated, bothered, harassed, troubled **09** pressured, tormented **10** distressed **11** hard-pressed, pressurized

**harrow**
**04** drag, haro **05** brake, herse, wring **09** pitch-pole, pitch-poll

• **point of harrow**
**04** tine

**harrowing**
**05** rough **08** alarming, daunting, lacerant **09** agonizing, traumatic, upsetting **10** disturbing, perturbing, terrifying, tormenting **11** distressing, frightening **12** excruciating, heart-rending, nerve-racking

**harry**
**03** nag, vex **05** annoy, hound, worry **06** badger, bother, chivvy, harass, hassle, molest, pester, plague, ravage **07** destroy, disturb, oppress, plunder, torment, trouble **09** persecute **10** pressurize

**harsh**
**03** raw **04** bold, grim, hard, iron, rude, wild **05** asper, bleak, cruel, gaudy, gruff, lurid, rough, sharp, showy, stark, stern, stoor, stour, sture **06** barren, bitter, bright, brutal, coarse, flashy, garish, hoarse, savage, severe, shrill, stowre, strict, unkind **07** acerbic, austere, cracked, glaring, grating, hostile, inhuman, jarring, rasping, raucous, spartan **08** abrasive, croaking, dazzling, desolate, gravelly, grinding, guttural, jangling, metallic, pitiless, rigorous, ruthless, scabrous, strident **09** barbarian, barbarous, dissonant, Draconian, inclement, merciless, unfeeling, untunable **10** discordant, unpleasant, untuneable **11** comfortless, ear-piercing **12** inhospitable **13** unsympathetic

**harshly**
**04** hard **06** grimly, hardly **07** cruelly, gruffly, roughly, sharply, sternly **08** brutally, hoarsely, severely, unkindly **10** pitilessly, ruthlessly, stridently **11** mercilessly **12** discordantly, unpleasantly

**harshness**
**06** rigour **07** tyranny **08** acerbity, acrimony, asperity, hardness, severity, sourness **09** austerity, brutality, ill-temper, roughness, starkness, sternness **10** bitterness, coarseness, strictness **12** abrasiveness

**harum-scarum**
**04** rash, wild **05** hasty **06** scatty **07** erratic **08** careless, reckless **09** haphazard, impetuous, imprudent **11** hare-brained, precipitate **12** disorganized **13** ill-considered, irresponsible **14** scatterbrained

**harvest**
**02** in **03** mow **04** crop, gain, kirn, pick, rabi, reap **05** amass, glean, horde, pluck, stock, store, yield **06** autumn, effect, fruits, garner, gather, hairst, hockey, obtain, result, return, secure, silage, supply **07** acquire, collect, hopping, produce, product, reaping, returns **08** gather in, ingather, Spätlese, vendange **10** accumulate, collection, harvesting **11** consequence, harvest-home, harvest-time, ingathering **12** accumulation **13** tattie-howking, tattie-lifting

**has**
◇ *juxtaposition indicator*
**01** 's **04** hath

• **has not, hasn't**
**03** an't

**hash**
◇ *anagram indicator*
**04** hack, mash, mess, stew **05** botch, mince, mix-up **06** bungle, hachis, hotpot, jumble, muddle, scouse **07** goulash, hashish **08** mishmash **09** confusion, lobscouse, pound sign **10** hotchpotch, lob's course **11** olla-podrida **13** mismanagement

**hashish**
**03** pot **04** dope, hash, hemp, weed **05** bhang, ganja, grass **08** cannabis **09** marijuana **12** electric puha

**hassium**
**02** Hs

**hassle**
**03** bug **04** fuss **05** aggro, annoy, fight, harry, hound, trial, upset **06** badger, bother, chivvy, harass, mither, moider, pester, strife **07** dispute, moither, problem, quarrel, trouble, wrangle **08** argument, nuisance, squabble, struggle **09** bickering **10** difficulty **11** altercation **12** disagreement **13** inconvenience

**hassled**
**05** vexed **07** harried, hounded, plagued, uptight, worried **08** careworn, harassed, pestered, strained, stressed, troubled **09** pressured, tormented **10** distraught, distressed **11** pressurized, stressed-out, under stress **13** under pressure

**hassock**
**04** pouf **06** pouffe **07** kneeler
**09** footstool

**haste**
**03** hie **04** post, rush **05** hurry, speed **06** bustle, hasten, hustle, scurry **07** urgency **08** alacrity, celerity, despatch, dispatch, fastness, rapidity, rashness, velocity **09** briskness, quickness, swiftness **10** expedience **11** impetuosity **12** carelessness, precipitance, precipitancy, recklessness **13** foolhardiness, impulsiveness, precipitation **15** expeditiousness

**• in haste**
**04** fast, rash **05** apace **06** subito **07** hotfoot, quickly, rapidly **08** in a hurry, promptly, speedily **12** straightaway

**hasten**
**03** aid, fly, hie, ren, rin, run **04** bolt, dash, help, race, rush, spur, tear, urge **05** boost, hurry, press, speed **06** assist, bustle, go fast, hustle, sprint, step up **07** advance, be quick, forward, hurry up, quicken, speed up **08** despatch, dispatch, expedite, step on it **09** go quickly, hotfoot it, make haste **10** accelerate, get a move on **11** precipitate, push forward **12** step on the gas **15** put your foot down

**hastily**
**04** fast **05** apace **06** rashly **07** quickly, rapidly **08** chop-chop, promptly, speedily **09** hurriedly **10** heedlessly, recklessly **11** double-quick, impetuously, impulsively **12** straightaway **13** precipitately

**hasty**
**04** fast, rash **05** brief, brisk, eager, quick, rapid, short, swift **06** prompt, rushed, speedy, sudden **07** cursory, hurried, running **08** careless, fleeting, headlong, heedless, reckless **09** desultory, festinate, hotheaded, impatient, impetuous, impulsive, irritable **10** transitory **11** expeditious, perfunctory, precipitant, precipitate, subitaneous, thoughtless

**hat**
**03** lid, nab **04** tile **06** titfer **09** headpiece **10** upper crust

*Hats include:*

**03** cap, fez, sun, taj, tam, tin, top, toy
**04** doek, hard, hood, kepi, poke, tall
**05** beret, Bronx, busby, derby, mitre, mutch, opera, shako, snood, straw, tammy, toque, tuque
**06** beanie, beaver, biggin, boater, bobble, bonnet, bowler, chapka, cloche, fedora, helmet, kalpak, mob-cap, panama, pileus, sailor, trilby, turban
**07** bicorne, biretta, bycoket, Cossack, flat-cap, Homburg, leghorn, montero, picture, pill-box, pork-pie, stetson, tricorn
**08** balmoral, bearskin, chaperon, fool's cap, nightcap, skullcap, sombrero, tricorne, yarmulka
**09** Balaclava, cock's-comb, dunce's cap, forage cap, glengarry, jockey cap, muffin-cap, peaked cap, school cap, sou'wester, stovepipe, sun bonnet, ten-gallon
**10** cockernony, college cap, hunting-cap, Kilmarnock, pith helmet, poke-bonnet
**11** baseball cap, crash helmet, deerstalker, mortar-board, tam-o'-shanter, trencher cap
**12** cheesecutter, hummle bonnet, Scotch bonnet

*See also* **straw hat** *under* **straw**

**• shade attached to hat**
**04** ugly

**hatch**
◇ *anagram indicator*
**04** plan, plot **05** breed, brood, cleck, covey, sit on **06** clutch, design, devise, invent, scheme **07** concoct, develop, dream up, exclude, guichet, project, think up **08** conceive, contrive, disclose, incubate **09** formulate, originate

**hatchet**
**03** axe **07** chopper, cleaver, machete, mattock, pickaxe **08** tomahawk **09** battle-axe, hedgebill **11** hedging-bill

**hate**
**02** ug **04** whit **05** abhor, spite **06** detest, enmity, grudge, hatred, loathe, regret **07** be loath, be sorry, despise, dislike, ill-will, rancour **08** aversion, execrate, loathing, not stand **09** abominate, animosity, apologize, hostility **10** abhorrence, antagonism, bitterness, recoil from, resentment **11** abomination, be reluctant, be unwilling **15** feel revulsion at

**• pet hate**
**04** bane, bogy **05** bogle, dread, fiend, poker **06** horror **07** bugbear, rawhead **08** anathema **09** bête noire, nightmare

**hateful**
**04** evil, foul, loth, vile **05** loath, nasty **06** cursed, damned, goddam, horrid, odious **07** goddamn, heinous **08** damnable, horrible **09** abhorrent, execrable, goddamned, loathsome, obnoxious, offensive, repellent, repugnant, repulsive, revolting **10** abominable, despicable, detestable, disgusting, unpleasant **11** abhominable **12** contemptible, disagreeable

**hating**
**04** miso-

**hatred**
**04** hate **05** odium, spite **06** animus, enmity, grudge, phobia **07** despite, disgust, dislike, ill-will, phobism, rancour **08** aversion, haterent, loathing **09** animosity, antipathy, hostility, malignity, revulsion **10** abhorrence, antagonism, bitterness, execration, repugnance, resentment **11** abomination, detestation

**haughtily**
**07** proudly **08** snootily **10** arrogantly, cavalierly, scornfully **11** imperiously **12** disdainfully **14** contemptuously, superciliously

**haughtiness**
**04** airs **05** pride **06** hubris, morgue **07** conceit, disdain, hauteur **08** contempt **09** aloofness, arrogance, insolence, loftiness, pomposity **10** hogen-mogen, snootiness **12** snobbishness

**haughty**
**04** bold, haut, high, vain **05** hault, lofty, proud, surly **06** haught, lordly, snooty, superb **07** paughty, stuck-up **08** arrogant, assuming, cavalier, fastuous, orgulous, scornful, snobbish, stomachy, superior, toplofty **09** conceited, imperious, orgillous **10** disdainful, hoity-toity, stomachful, stomachous **11** cavalierish, egotistical, overbearing, patronizing, stiff-necked, toploftical **12** contemptuous, supercilious **13** condescending, high and mighty, self-important, swollen-headed **14** proud-stomached **15** on your high horse

**haul**
**03** lug, rug, tow, tug **04** cart, drag, draw, find, gain, harl, hump, loot, mess, move, pull, push, ship, swag, wind **05** booty, bouse, bowse, brail, carry, catch, heave, scoop, slack, touse, touze, towse, towze, trail, trice, wince, winch, yield **06** convey, convoy, spoils **07** plunder, takings **09** transport

**haunches**
**04** hips, rump **05** hucks, nates **06** thighs **07** huckles, hunkers, rear end **08** buttocks

**haunt**
**03** den **04** houf, howf, walk **05** beset, curse, ghost, harry, houff, howff, local, recur, spook, visit, worry **06** burden, obsess, plague, prey on, resort, show up **07** disturb, hangout, inhabit, oppress, possess, spright, torment, trouble **08** frequent **09** honky-tonk, patronize **10** rendezvous **11** hang about in, materialize, spend time in **12** hang around in, meeting-place **13** appear often in, favourite spot **14** stamping-ground, visit regularly

**haunted**
**05** eerie **06** cursed, jinxed, spooky **07** ghostly, plagued, worried **08** infested, obsessed, troubled **09** hag-ridden, possessed, tormented **10** frequented **11** preoccupied

**haunting**
**08** poignant **09** evocative, memorable, nostalgic, recurrent **10** persistent **11** atmospheric **13** unforgettable

**hauteur**
**04** airs **05** pride **06** hubris **07** conceit, disdain **08** contempt **09** aloofness, arrogance, insolence, loftiness, pomposity **10** snootiness
**11** haughtiness **12** snobbishness

**have**
**02** ha', 've **03** ask, bid, con, eat, get, hae, han, own, put, use **04** bear, down, dupe, feel, find, fool, gain, gulp, hold, keep, know, make, meet, must, show, take, tell **05** abide, allow, beget, brook, cheat, drink, enjoy, force, order, ought, stand, trick **06** accept, assert, coerce, compel, devour, diddle, embody, endure, enjoin, esteem, guzzle, oblige, obtain, permit, secure, should, suffer, take in **07** acquire, arrange, be given, cause to, command, consume, contain, deceive, develop, display, embrace, exhibit, express, include, possess, procure, put away, receive, request, require, swallow, swindle, undergo
**08** be forced, comprise, contract, manifest, organize, persuade, submit to, talk into, tolerate, tuck into, wolf down **09** be obliged, consist of, encounter, go through, knock back, partake of, put up with, succumb to
**10** be required, bring forth, comprehend, experience, suffer from, take part in **11** be compelled, demonstrate, give birth to, incorporate, prevail upon **13** be delivered of, be subjected to, participate in
• **have had it**
**06** be lost **10** be defeated, have no hope **11** be exhausted, be in trouble, bite the dust
• **have on**
**03** kid, rag **04** hoax, wear **05** chaff, tease, trick **11** be clothed in, be dressed in, have planned, play a joke on
**12** have arranged, take for a ride
**13** wind someone up **15** pull someone's leg

**haven**
**03** bay **04** dock, port **05** basin, hithe, oasis **06** asylum, harbor, refuge
**07** harbour, retreat, shelter
**09** anchorage, sanctuary

**haversack**
**06** kitbag **08** backpack, knapsack, rucksack

**havoc**
◇ *anagram indicator*
**04** Hell, ruin **05** chaos, waste, wreck
**06** damage, mayhem **08** disorder, ravaging, shambles, wreckage
**09** confusion, ruination **10** desolation, disruption **11** destruction, devastation, rack and ruin **12** depopulation, despoliation

**Hawaii**
**02** HI

**hawk**
**03** cry **04** bark, eyas, kite, nyas, sell, soar, sore, tout, vend **05** offer, soare, trant **06** falcon, keelie, market, peddle, tarcel, tarsal, tarsel, tassel, tercel
**07** buzzard, goshawk, haggard, harrier, tassell, tiercel **08** brancher, huckster
**10** eyas-musket **11** sparrowhawk
**12** honey buzzard, offer for sale
• **accustom hawk to handling**
**03** man

**hawker**
**04** spiv **05** crier **06** auceps, cadger, coster, dealer, mugger, pedlar, seller, sutler, trader, vendor **07** camelot, chapman, slanger, tranter **08** huckster
**09** barrow-boy, cheap-jack, cheap John **10** colporteur **11** speech-crier
**12** costermonger
• **hawker's round**
**04** walk

**hawseholes**
**04** eyes

**hawthorn**
**05** quick, thorn **07** may tree
**08** cockspur **09** albespine, albespyne, mayflower, thornbush, thorntree
**10** quickthorn, whitethorn

**hay**
• **bundle of hay**
**03** wad, wap **04** wise, wisp **06** bottle
• **pile of hay**
**03** mow **04** cock, rick **05** stack
**07** haycock **08** haystack

**haywire**
◇ *anagram indicator*
**03** mad **04** wild **05** crazy, wrong
**07** chaotic, tangled **08** confused
**10** disordered, topsy-turvy
**12** disorganized, out of control

**hazard**
**04** jump, luck, risk, wage **05** offer, peril, stake, wager **06** bunker, chance, danger, gamble, menace, niffer, risque, submit, threat **07** pitfall, suggest, venture **08** accident, endanger, jeopardy **09** deathtrap, hazardize, put at risk, speculate **10** jeopardize, put forward **12** endangerment **13** put in jeopardy **14** expose to danger

**hazardous**
**04** nice **05** hairy, risky **06** chancy, queasy, queazy, tricky, unsafe
**07** chancey **08** insecure, menacing, perilous **09** dangerous, difficult, uncertain **10** jeopardous, precarious
**11** threatening **13** unpredictable

**hazardously**
**07** riskily **10** insecurely, perilously
**11** dangerously, uncertainly
**12** jeopardously, precariously
**13** unpredictably

**haze**
**03** fog, rag **04** blur, daze, film, mist, smog **05** bully, cloud, steam
**06** muddle, vapour **07** dimness
**09** confusion, fogginess, mistiness, obscurity, smokiness, vagueness
**10** cloudiness **11** uncertainty
**12** bewilderment **14** indistinctness

**hazelnut**
**03** cob **06** cobnut **07** filberd, filbert
**12** Barcelona nut

**hazy**
◇ *anagram indicator*
**03** dim **05** faint, foggy, fuzzy, milky, misty, muzzy, smoky, vague **06** cloudy, veiled, woolly **07** blurred, clouded, misting, obscure, unclear
**08** confused, nebulous, overcast
**09** uncertain **10** ill-defined, indefinite, indistinct

**head**
◇ *head selection indicator*
**03** cop, nab, nob, nut, pow, ras, ren, rin, run, tip, top, van, wit **04** apex, bean, bent, boss, cape, conk, face, fizz, foam, fore, gift, lead, loaf, main, mind, ness, pash, pate, peak, poll, rise, rule, suds, tête, wits **05** bonce, brain, caput, chair, chief, crest, crown, first, flair, fount, front, froth, guide, knack, onion, power, prime, ruler, sense, skill, skull, steer, title **06** bigwig, brains, charge, climax, crisis, crunch, direct, genius, govern, height, lather, leader, manage, mazard, napper, noddle, noggin, noodle, origin, source, spring, summit, talent, vertex, wisdom **07** ability, aptness, bubbles, captain, command, control, cranium, crumpet, dilemma, faculty, go first, heading, headway, highest, leading, manager, obverse, oversee, premier, supreme, thought, topknot, topmost **08** aptitude, calamity, capacity, chairman, controls, director, dominant, facility, foremost, governor, headland, pressure, strength, vanguard, wellhead **09** attribute, be first in, big cheese, capitulum, commander, emergency, endowment, forefront, intellect, mentality, president, principal, reasoning, supervise, top banana **10** administer, capability, chairwoman, controller, grey matter, headmaster, leadership, management, pre-eminent, supervisor, upper crust, upperworks, wellspring **11** catastrophe, chairperson, common sense, head teacher, proficiency, superintend, supervision, upper storey **12** be in charge of, directorship, headmistress, intelligence **13** administrator, be in control of, critical point, understanding
**14** be at the front of, superintendent
**15** little grey cells, mental abilities

*See also* **toilet**

• **fox's head**
**04** mask
• **go to your head**
**06** puff up **08** befuddle **09** inebriate, make dizzy, make drunk, make proud, make woozy **10** intoxicate **12** make arrogant **13** make conceited
• **head for**
**06** aim for **07** make for, point to, turn for **08** steer for **09** go towards
**11** move towards **13** direct towards, travel towards
• **head off**
◇ *head deletion indicator*
**04** stop **05** avert **06** cut off, divert
**07** deflect, fend off, prevent, ward off

**09** forestall, intercept, interpose, intervene, turn aside

• **head over heels**

◇ *reversal down indicator*

**06** wildly **07** utterly **08** headlong **09** intensely **10** completely, recklessly, thoroughly **14** uncontrollably, wholeheartedly

• **head up**

**04** lead **06** direct, manage **12** be in charge of, take charge of

• **keep your head**

**08** keep calm **12** keep your cool

• **lose your head**

◇ *head deletion indicator*

**04** flap **05** panic **08** freak out **12** lose your cool

• **muffle head**

**03** mob

• **top of head**

**04** nole, noll, noul, nowl **05** noule

**headache**

**04** bane, head, pest **05** worry **06** bother, hassle **07** problem, trouble **08** migraine, nuisance, splitter, vexation **09** neuralgia **10** hemicrania **11** cephalalgia **13** inconvenience, pain in the neck

**headdress**

*Headdresses include:*

**03** cap, taj
**04** coif, head, kell, tête, tire
**05** mitre, tower
**06** cornet, modius, pinner, turban
**07** commode, coronet, kufiyah
**08** coiffure, fontange, fool's cap, head-tire, joncanoe, junkanoo, kaffiyeh, keffiyeh, ship-tire, stephane
**09** John Canoe, John Kanoo, porrenger, porringer, war bonnet
**10** lappet-head
**11** tire-valiant
**13** feather-bonnet

*See also* **hat**; **helmet**; **scarf**

**headgear**

**03** hat, jiz, lid, wig **04** call, caul, gizz, hood, tiar **05** crown, tiara **07** coronet **08** silly-how

*See also* **hat**; **helmet**; **scarf**

**heading**

◇ *head selection indicator*

**04** head, name, text **05** class, point, title **06** header, rubric **07** bearing, caption, section, subject **08** category, division, headline **09** direction **10** capitulary, descriptor, letterhead **14** classification

*See also* **compass**

**headland**

**03** ras **04** cape, head, naze, ness, noup, scaw, skaw **05** morro, point **07** headrig **08** foreland **10** promontory

**headless**

◇ *head deletion indicator*

**07** trunked **10** acephalous, leaderless **11** decapitated

**headlong**

**04** rash **05** ahead, hasty, steep **06** rashly, wildly **07** hastily, ramstam, tantivy **08** careless, full tilt, pell-mell, proclive, reckless **09** breakneck, dangerous, head first, hurriedly, impetuous, impulsive **10** carelessly, heedlessly, recklessly **11** hair-brained, hare-brained, impetuously, impulsively, precipitate, prematurely **12** hand over head **13** precipitately, thoughtlessly **15** without thinking

**headman**

**05** chief, ruler **06** ataman, leader, sachem **07** captain **08** caboceer, mocuddum, mokaddam, muqaddam, starosta **09** chieftain

**head-on**

**06** direct **08** straight **10** straight-on **11** full-frontal

**headquarters**

**02** HQ **04** base, hall **05** depot, SHAPE **06** armory, Temple **07** station **08** base camp, Pentagon **10** head office, main office, officialty, praetorium **11** command post, nerve centre, officiality

**headstone**

**06** plaque **08** memorial **09** tombstone **10** gravestone **11** cornerstone

**headstrong**

**06** unruly, wilful **07** wayward, willful **08** contrary, obdurate, perverse, stubborn **09** obstinate, pigheaded **10** refractory, self-willed **11** intractable **12** intransigent, recalcitrant, ungovernable

**headway**

**03** way **06** ground **07** advance **08** distance, movement, progress **11** development, improvement

**headwear** *see* **headgear**

**heady**

**04** rash **05** nappy **06** potent, strong **07** huff-cap, rousing, violent **08** ecstatic, euphoric, exciting, inflamed **09** thrilling **11** stimulating **12** exhilarating, intoxicating, invigorating, overpowering

**heal**

**04** cure, hide, mend, sain **05** cover, salve, treat **06** balsam, garish, physic, recure, remedy, settle, soothe **07** assuage, comfort, conceal, guarish, improve, patch up, restore **08** make good, make well, palliate, put right, set right **09** cicatrize, incarnate, reconcile **10** make better **12** conglutinate

**healer**

**03** Asa

*See also* **doctor**

**health**

**04** form, heal, tone, trim **05** shape, state, toast **06** fettle, sanity, vigour **07** fitness, welfare **08** strength **09** condition, good shape, soundness, wellbeing **10** robustness **11** healthiness **12** constitution **13** good condition

• **good health**

**04** tope **06** cheers, kia-ora **07** cheerio, slàinte, wassail **08** chin-chin, waes hail **09** bene vobis, drink hail **10** Gesundheit **12** mud in your eye

**healthily**

**04** well **07** soundly **08** robustly, strongly **10** vigorously **11** in condition, in good shape **12** in fine fettle

**healthy**

**03** fit **04** fine, good, hale, well, wise **05** hardy, jolly, lusty, sound **06** robust, strong, sturdy **07** bracing, lustick, prudent **08** blooming, lustique, sensible, thriving, vigorous **09** healthful, in the pink, judicious, wholesome **10** able-bodied, beneficial, hartie-hale, healthsome, nourishing, nutritious, refreshing, salubrious, successful **11** flourishing, in condition, in good shape, right as rain, stimulating **12** considerable, fit as a fiddle, in fine fettle, invigorating, well-disposed **13** hale and hearty

**heap**

**03** lot, mow, pit, pot **04** a lot, bank, bing, bulk, cock, load, lots, mass, pile, pots, raff, raft, rick, ruck, ruin, tass, tons **05** amass, build, cairn, clamp, drift, hoard, loads, mound, stack, store **06** bestow, bundle, burden, confer, gather, lavish, lumber, midden, oodles, pile up, plenty, quarry, rickle, scores, shower, stacks, supply, toorie **07** collect, company, congest, cumulus, store up, uphoard **08** assemble, cumulate, dunghill, lashings, millions, molehill, mountain **09** abundance, congeries, embroglio, great deal, imbroglio, stockpile **10** accumulate, acervation, assemblage, coacervate, collection, quantities **12** accumulation **13** agglomeration, kitchen midden **14** clearance cairn

**hear**

◇ *homophone indicator*

**03** get, try **04** heed **05** catch, judge, learn **06** be told, gather, listen, pick up, take in **07** examine, find out, inquire, make out **08** consider, discover, overhear, perceive **09** ascertain, eavesdrop, latch onto **10** adjudicate, be informed, understand **11** investigate **12** pay attention **13** be in touch with, pass judgement

• **hearer**

**03** ear

**hearing**

◇ *homophone indicator*

**03** ear **04** case, news, oyer **05** audit, range, reach, sound, trial **06** review **07** earshot, inquest, inquiry **08** audience, audition, scolding **09** interview, judgement **10** perception **11** examination, inquisition **12** adjudication **13** chance to speak, investigation **15** hearing distance

**hearsay**
◇ *homophone indicator*
**04** buzz, talk **05** on-dit, rumor, say-so **06** gossip, report, rumour **10** common talk **11** word of mouth **12** tittle-tattle **15** common knowledge

**heart**
◇ *middle selection indicator*
**03** hub, nub **04** core, crux, guts, love, mind, pith, pity, soul **05** bosom, pluck, spunk **06** bottle, centre, kernel, marrow, middle, nature, spirit, vigour, warmth **07** bravery, concern, courage, emotion, essence, feeling, heroism, nucleus, passion, stomach **08** boldness, keenness, kindness, sympathy **09** affection, character, eagerness, fortitude, sentiment, substance **10** compassion, cordiality, enthusiasm, resolution, tenderness **11** disposition, intrepidity, temperament **12** fearlessness, quintessence **13** determination, essential part **14** responsiveness

*Heart parts include:*

**04** vein
**05** aorta, valve
**06** artery, atrium, AV node, muscle, SA node
**07** auricle
**08** vena cava
**09** sinus node, ventricle
**10** epicardium, left atrium, myocardium
**11** aortic valve, endocardium, mitral valve, pericardium, right atrium
**13** bicuspid valve, carotid artery, left ventricle
**14** ascending aorta, pulmonary valve, Purkinje fibres, right ventricle, sino-atrial node, tricuspid valve
**15** papillary muscle

• **at heart**
◇ *insertion indicator*
◇ *middle selection indicator*
**06** really **08** at bottom **09** basically, in essence **11** essentially **13** fundamentally

• **by heart**
**03** pat **06** by rote, off pat **08** verbatim **09** memoriter **10** from memory **11** word for word **13** parrot-fashion

• **change of heart**
**07** rethink **12** change of mind **14** second thoughts

• **from the bottom of your heart**
**06** deeply **08** devoutly **09** earnestly, fervently, sincerely **10** profoundly **12** passionately

• **heart and soul**
**06** gladly **07** eagerly **08** entirely, heartily **09** devotedly **10** absolutely, completely **12** unreservedly **14** wholeheartedly

• **hearts**
**01** H **10** black Maria

• **lose heart**
◇ *middle deletion indicator*
**08** collapse **13** be discouraged

• **set your heart on**
**05** crave, yearn **06** desire **07** long for, wish for

• **take heart**
**05** rally **06** buck up, perk up, revive **07** cheer up **10** brighten up **12** be encouraged

• **take to heart**
**09** be moved by, be upset by **12** be affected by **13** be disturbed by

**heartache**
**04** pain **05** agony, grief, worry **06** sorrow **07** anguish, anxiety, despair, remorse, torment, torture **08** distress **09** dejection, suffering **10** affliction, bitterness, heartbreak **11** despondency

**heartbreak**
**04** pain **05** agony, grief **06** misery, sorrow **07** anguish, despair, sadness **08** distress **09** dejection, suffering **10** crève-coeur, desolation

**heartbreaking**
**03** sad **05** cruel, harsh **06** bitter, crying, tragic **07** painful, pitiful **08** grievous, poignant **09** agonizing, harrowing **11** distressing **12** excruciating, heart-rending **13** disappointing

**heartbroken**
**03** sad **07** crushed, grieved **08** dejected, desolate, downcast **09** anguished, miserable, sorrowful, suffering **10** despondent, dispirited **11** crestfallen **12** disappointed, disheartened, in low spirits **13** broken-hearted

**heartburn**
**05** brash **07** pyrosis **09** cardialgy, dyspepsia **10** cardialgia **11** indigestion

**hearten**
**05** boost, cheer, pep up, rouse **06** buck up **07** animate, cheer up, comfort, console, inspire **08** energize, reassure **09** encourage, stimulate **10** invigorate, revitalize

**heartening**
**06** moving **08** cheering, pleasing, touching **09** affecting, rewarding, uplifting **10** gladdening, gratifying, satisfying **11** encouraging **12** heartwarming

**heartfelt**
**04** deep, warm **06** ardent, devout, honest **07** earnest, fervent, genuine, sincere **08** profound **09** unfeigned **12** wholehearted **13** compassionate

**heartily**
◇ *middle selection indicator*
**04** upsy, very **05** agood, upsee, upsey **06** deeply, gladly, warmly **07** cheerly, eagerly, hartely, lustily, totally **08** con amore, entirely **09** cordially, earnestly, extremely, feelingly, genuinely, sincerely, staunchly, zealously **10** absolutely, completely, profoundly, resolutely, thoroughly, upsey Dutch, vigorously **11** unfeignedly, upsey Friese **12** upsey English **13** warm-heartedly

**heartless**
◇ *middle deletion indicator*
**04** cold, hard **05** cruel, harsh **06** brutal, unkind **07** callous, inhuman, unmoved **08** pitiless, ruthless, sardonic, uncaring **09** merciless, unfeeling **11** cold-blooded, cold-hearted, hard-hearted **13** inconsiderate, unsympathetic

**heartlessly**
◇ *middle deletion indicator*
**06** coldly **07** cruelly, harshly **08** brutally **09** callously **10** pitilessly **11** mercilessly **13** cold-heartedly, hard-heartedly

**heart-rending**
**03** sad **06** moving, tragic **07** piteous, pitiful **08** pathetic, poignant **09** affecting, agonizing, harrowing **11** distressing **13** heartbreaking

**heartsick**
**03** sad **04** glum **08** dejected, downcast **09** depressed **10** despondent, melancholy **12** disappointed, heavy-hearted

**heart-throb**
**04** hunk, idol, star **05** pin-up **09** dreamboat

**heart-to-heart**
**08** cosy chat **09** tête-à-tête **10** honest talk **12** friendly talk

**heartwarming**
**06** moving **08** cheering, pleasing, touching **09** affecting, rewarding, uplifting **10** gladdening, gratifying, heartening, satisfying **11** encouraging

**hearty**
**04** maty, warm **05** ample, bluff, eager, hardy, large, lusty, matey, solid, sound **06** blokey, jovial, robust, stanch, strong **07** affable, cordial, filling, genuine, healthy, sincere, sizable, staunch **08** abundant, blokeish, bouncing, cheerful, effusive, friendly, generous, sizeable, stalwart, vigorous **09** ebullient, energetic, exuberant, heartfelt, unfeigned **10** boisterous, nourishing, nutritious, unreserved **11** substantial, warm-hearted **12** enthusiastic, unrestrained, wholehearted

**heat**
◇ *anagram indicator*
**03** hot **04** bake, boil, cook, fire, fury, glow, race, rost, stir, warm, zeal **05** anger, annoy, beath, fever, flush, roast, rouse, toast **06** ardour, arouse, calefy, enrage, excite, fervor, reheat, sizzle, warmth, warm up **07** agitate, animate, fervour, firearm, hotness, inflame, passion, swelter, trouble **08** fervency **09** closeness, eagerness, fieriness, heaviness, intensity, microwave, stimulate, vehemence

**10** enthusiasm, excitement, sultriness, torridness **11** calefaction, earnestness, impetuosity **12** feverishness **15** high temperature

• **dead heat**

**03** tie **04** draw

**heated**

**05** angry, fiery, fired **06** bitter, fierce, raging, roused, stormy **07** enraged, excited, furious, intense, stirred, violent **08** animated, frenzied, inflamed, vehement, worked-up **10** passionate, stimulated **11** impassioned, tempestuous

**heatedly**

**07** angrily **08** bitterly, fiercely **09** excitedly, furiously, intensely, violently **10** vehemently **12** passionately

**heater**

**03** gun **04** fire **06** boiler, pistol **08** Califont®, radiator **09** convector, fan heater, gas heater, immersion **11** solar heater **12** electric fire **13** storage heater **14** central heating, electric heater **15** immersion heater

**heath**

**03** Ted **04** bent, fell, ling, moor, muir **05** briar, brier, erica **06** kalmia, manoao, upland **07** arbutus, heather **08** moorland **09** andromeda, bearberry **10** gaultheria

**heathen**

**05** pagan **06** ethnic, paynim, savage **07** Gentile, godless, infidel, nations **08** barbaric, idolater **09** barbarian **10** idolatress, idolatrous, philistine, unbeliever **11** irreligious, nullifidian, unbelieving, uncivilized **13** unenlightened

**heather**

**04** ling **05** erica **07** calluna **08** foxberry **11** Labrador tea

**heave**

◇ *deletion indicator*

**03** cat, gag, tug **04** barf, boke, cast, drag, give, haul, honk, hump, hurl, lift, puke, pull, rise, send, sigh, spew, toss **05** chuck, fling, heeze, hitch, hoist, lever, pitch, raise, retch, sling, surge, swell, throw, utter, vomit **06** be sick, let fly, let out, popple, sick up, wallow **07** breathe, bring up, chuck up, chunder, cough up, express, fetch up, throw up, upchuck **08** disgorge, parbreak, swelling **10** egurgitate

**heaven**

**03** joy, sky **04** Zion **05** bliss, ether, glory, skies **06** Asgard, on high, Svarga, Swarga, Swerga, utopia, welkin **07** delight, ecstasy, Elysium, nirvana, Olympus, rapture, the blue, up there **08** empyrean, holy city, paradise, Valhalla **09** afterlife, firmament, happiness, hereafter, home of God, next world, Shangri-La **10** abode of God, life to come **12** Land o' the Leal, New Jerusalem, promised land, upper regions **13** elysian fields, fiddler's green, seventh heaven, vault of heaven

• **the heavens**

**03** sky **04** pole **06** region **08** empyrean **12** upper regions

**heavenly**

**04** holy, pure **06** cosmic, divine, lovely **07** angelic, blessed, godlike, perfect, sublime, Uranian **08** beatific, blissful, cherubic, empyreal, empyrean, ethereal, etherial, glorious, immortal, seraphic **09** ambrosial, beautiful, celestial, enjoyable, excellent, exquisite, rapturous, spiritual, unearthly, wonderful **10** delightful, enchanting, marvellous **12** other-worldly, supernatural **14** out of this world

**heaven-sent**

**05** happy **06** bright, timely **09** fortunate, opportune **10** auspicious, favourable

**heavily**

**04** hard, upsy **05** thick, upsee, upsey **06** slowly **07** closely, densely, roundly, solidly, soundly, thickly, too much, utterly **08** clumsily, to excess, woodenly **09** awkwardly, compactly, copiously, painfully, weightily **10** abundantly, completely, decisively, sluggishly, thoroughly, upsey Dutch **11** excessively, laboriously, ponderously, upsey Friese **12** immoderately, upsey English **14** with difficulty

**heaviness**

**04** bulk **05** depth, gloom **06** weight **07** density, languor, sadness **08** deadness, severity, solidity **09** dejection, greatness, heftiness, intensity, lassitude, thickness **10** depression, drowsiness, gloominess, melancholy, oppression, sleepiness, somnolence **11** despondency, onerousness, seriousness, weightiness **12** sluggishness **13** ponderousness **14** burdensomeness, oppressiveness

**heavy**

**03** big, dry, sad **04** dark, deep, dowf, dull, full, grey, hard, rich, sour, thug **05** bulky, close, dense, Dutch, grave, great, harsh, hefty, humid, laden, large, muggy, sharp, solid, tense, thick, tough **06** clammy, cloudy, clumpy, doughy, drowsy, gloomy, hearty, leaden, loaded, severe, sombre, steamy, sticky, stodgy, strong, sultry, taxing, trying, wooden **07** arduous, awkward, crushed, extreme, filling, hulking, intense, irksome, lumping, lumpish, massive, onerous, pesante, pompous, serious, starchy, tedious, violent, weighty **08** burdened, crushing, downcast, exacting, forceful, grievous, groaning, highbrow, overcast, pedantic, powerful, profound, strained **09** abounding, burdenous, demanding, depressed, difficult, emotional, excessive, important, laborious, miserable, ponderous, sorrowful, squabbish, strenuous, wearisome **10** burdensome, cumbersome, despondent, encumbered, immoderate, inordinate, oppressive, unbearable **11** discouraged, heavy as lead, intemperate, intolerable, substantial, troublesome, weighed down **12** considerable, indigestible, sodden-witted, weighing a ton **13** overindulgent, uninteresting

**heavy-duty**

**02** HD **05** solid, sound, tough **06** robust, strong, sturdy **07** abiding, durable, lasting **08** enduring **09** resistant **10** reinforced **11** hard-wearing, long-lasting, substantial

**heavy-handed**

**05** harsh, inept, stern **06** clumsy, severe **07** awkward **08** bungling, despotic, forceful, tactless, unsubtle **09** ham-fisted, maladroit **10** autocratic, blundering, cack-handed, oppressive **11** domineering, insensitive, overbearing, thoughtless

**heavy-hearted**

**03** sad **04** glum **06** gloomy, morose **07** crushed, forlorn **08** downcast, mournful **09** depressed, heartsick, miserable, sorrowful **10** despondent, melancholy **11** discouraged, downhearted **12** disappointed, disheartened

**Hebe**

**08** Juventas

**Hebrew**

**03** Heb, Jew

*See also* **alphabet**

**Hebrew alphabet** *see* **alphabet**

**Hecate**

**06** Trivia

**heckle**

**04** bait, gibe, jeer **05** taunt **06** needle, pester **07** barrack, catcall, disrupt **09** interrupt, shout down

**hectare**

**02** ha

**hectic**

◇ *anagram indicator*

**04** busy, fast, wild **06** heated, rushed **07** chaotic, excited, flushed, frantic, furious **08** agitated, bustling, feverish, frenetic, frenzied **09** turbulent **10** tumultuous **11** consumptive

**hector**

**03** nag **04** huff **05** annoy, bully, worry **06** badger, chivvy, harass, menace **07** bluster, provoke **08** browbeat, bulldoze, bullyrag, threaten **09** blusterer **10** intimidate

**hedge**

◇ *containment indicator*

**03** haw, hay, low **04** duck, dyke, edge **05** cover, dodge, evade, fence, guard, hem in, limit, mound, stall **06** insure, lay off, raddle, screen, shield, waffle,

zareba, zariba, zereba, zeriba
**07** barrier, confine, debased, enclose, fortify, ox-fence, protect, quibble, shuffle, wayside, zareeba
**08** boundary, encircle, hedgerow, obstruct, quickset, restrict, sepiment, sidestep, surround **09** safeguard, temporize, windbreak **10** equivocate, protection **11** prevaricate **13** sit on the fence

**• escape through hedge**
**04** mews, muse **05** meuse

**hedgehog**
**06** urchin **08** herisson **11** tiggywinkle

**hedonism**
**09** dolce vita, epicurism
**10** sensualism, sensuality, sybaritism
**12** Epicureanism **13** gratification, luxuriousness **14** self-indulgence, voluptuousness **15** pleasure-seeking

**hedonist**
**07** epicure **08** sybarite **09** bon vivant, bon viveur, epicurean **10** sensualist, voluptuary **14** pleasure-seeker

**hedonistic**
**09** epicurean, luxurious, sybaritic
**10** voluptuous **13** self-indulgent
**15** pleasure-seeking

**heed**
**03** ear **04** care, gaum, gorm, mark, mind, note, obey, reak, reck, tent
**06** follow, listen, notice, regard
**07** caution, hearken, observe, respect, thought **08** attend to, consider
**09** attention **10** bear in mind, observance, take note of
**11** heedfulness **12** take notice of, watchfulness **13** animadversion, consideration **14** pay attention to
**15** take into account

**heedful**
**04** wary **05** chary **07** careful, jealous, mindful, prudent **08** cautious, vigilant, watchful **09** advertent, attentive, observant, regardful **10** respective
**11** circumspect

**heedless**
**04** rash **06** blithe, remiss, unwary
**08** careless, reckless, tactless, uncaring
**09** foolhardy, forgetful, negligent, oblivious, unguarded, unmindful
**10** incautious, indiscreet, insouciant, regardless, unthinking **11** hair-brained, hare-brained, inattentive, inobservant, precipitate, thoughtless, unconcerned, unobservant **12** absent-minded
**13** inconsiderate, irresponsible

**heedlessly**
**06** rashly **09** blindfold **10** carelessly, recklessly **11** negligently
**12** neglectingly, unthinkingly
**13** inattentively, thoughtlessly

**heel**
**03** cad, cow, rat, tip **04** bank, hele, hide, knob, lean, list, puke, seel, spur, sway, tilt **05** angle, cover, slant, slope
**06** ratbag, toerag, wretch **07** conceal, incline, ratfink **08** lean over, stiletto

**hefty**
**03** big **04** hard, huge, very **05** ample, beefy, bulky, burly, heavy, large, solid, stout **06** brawny, robust, strong
**07** awkward, hulking, immense, massive, sizable, violent, weighty
**08** abundant, colossal, forceful, generous, muscular, powerful, sizeable, unwieldy, vigorous
**09** strapping **11** substantial
**12** considerable

**Hegira**
**• in the year of Hegira**
**02** AH

**heifer**
**04** quey

**height**
**01** H **02** ht **03** alp, sum, top, tor
**04** apex, hill, peak, torr **05** crest, crown, level, limit, pitch **06** apogee, climax, summit, vertex, zenith
**07** ceiling, hill top, maximum, stature
**08** altitude, eminence, highness, pinnacle, tallness, ultimate
**09** elevation, extremity, loftiness, uttermost **10** perfection
**11** culmination, mountain top, sublimation

**heighten**
**04** lift **05** add to, boost, elate, exalt, raise **07** amplify, augment, build up, elevate, enhance, improve, magnify, sharpen **08** increase **09** intensify
**10** strengthen

**heinous**
**04** evil **05** awful, grave **06** odious, wicked **07** hateful, hideous, vicious
**08** flagrant, infamous, shocking
**09** abhorrent, atrocious, execrable, loathsome, monstrous, nefarious, revolting, unnatural **10** abominable, despicable, detestable, facinorous, iniquitous, outrageous, villainous
**11** unspeakable **12** contemptible

**heir, heiress**
**03** her **05** scion **06** co-heir, tanist
**07** fortune, legatee **08** apparent, atheling, parcener **09** inheritor, successor **10** cesarevich, cesarewich, coparcener, fellow-heir, inheritrix, next in line, substitute **11** beneficiary, cesarevitch, cesarewitch, coinheritor, crown prince, inheritress, tsesarevich, tsesarewich **12** tsesarevitch, tsesarewitch **13** crown princess

**heist** *see* **robbery**

**held**
**• held by, held in**
◇ *insertion indicator*
◇ *hidden indicator*

**helicopter**
**05** hover **06** copter **07** chopper, medevac **08** sikorsky **09** egg beater
**10** rotorcraft, rotor plane, whirlybird
**12** air ambulance

**Helios**
**03** Sol

**helium**
**02** He

**helix**
**04** coil, curl, loop **05** screw, twist, whorl **06** spiral, volute **07** wreathe
**08** curlicue **09** corkscrew

**hell**
**03** Dis, pit **04** Ades, fire, heck, hele, ruin **05** abyss, agony, below, Hades, havoc, Sheol **06** Erebus, misery, ordeal, Tophet, uproar **07** Abaddon, Acheron, anguish, Gehenna, inferno, the heck, torment, torture **08** Tartarus, the deuce **09** commotion, down there, Malebolge, nightmare, perdition, suffering, the blazes
**10** other place, the dickens, underworld **11** netherworld, tribulation **12** lower regions, wretchedness **13** bottomless pit, nether regions **15** abode of the devil, infernal regions

**• give someone hell**
**03** vex **04** beat, flog **05** annoy, scold
**06** harass, pester, punish **07** tell off, torment, trouble **08** chastise
**09** criticize **13** tear off a strip

**• hell for leather**
**06** rashly, wildly **07** quickly, rapidly, swiftly **08** very fast **09** hurriedly, like crazy, post-haste **10** recklessly **11** very quickly **13** precipitately **15** like the clappers

**• raise hell**
**07** run riot **09** be furious **10** hit the roof
**11** be very angry, make trouble
**13** object noisily, protest loudly
**15** cause a commotion

**hell-bent**
**03** set **04** bent **05** fixed **06** dogged, intent **07** settled **08** obdurate, resolved **09** tenacious **10** determined, inflexible, unwavering **12** intransigent, unhesitating

**hellish**
◇ *anagram indicator*
**04** very **05** cruel, nasty **06** savage, wicked **07** awfully, demonic, satanic, Stygian **08** accursed, barbaric, damnable, devilish, dreadful, fiendish, infernal **09** atrocious, execrable, extremely, immensely, intensely, monstrous, nefarious **10** abominable, diabolical, dreadfully, unpleasant
**12** disagreeable, unpleasantly
**13** exceptionally

**hello**
**02** hi, yo **04** g'day **05** hallo, hillo, howdy, hullo **06** holloa **07** bonjour, welcome **08** chin-chin **09** greetings
**10** buon giorno **11** good evening, good morning **13** good afternoon

**helm**
**05** steer, stern, timon, wheel **06** direct, helmet, rudder, tiller

**• at the helm**
**07** leading **08** in charge **09** directing, in command, in control **11** in the saddle
**15** holding the reins

**helmet**
**03** pot, top **04** topi **05** armet, salet, topee **06** basnet, casque, heaume, morion, murren, murrin, sallet, tin hat **07** basinet, hard hat, morrion, murrion, pith hat, skid lid, sola hat **08** burganet, burgonet, knapscal, sola topi **09** Balaclava, headpiece, knapscull, knapskull, sola topee **11** pickelhaube

**helmsman**
**03** cox **08** coxswain, timoneer **09** cockswain, steersman **10** steersmate

**help**
**03** aid, use **04** back, balm, cure, ease, heal **05** avail, boost, guide, nurse, salve, serve, stead **06** advice, assist, backup, helper, Mrs Mop, oblige, relief, remedy, soothe, worker **07** assuage, backing, benefit, be of use, bestead, charity, cleaner, further, healing, improve, promote, relieve, service, stand by, succour, support, utility **08** adjuvant, employee, guidance, home help, mitigate **09** advantage, alleviate, charwoman, co-operate, do your bit, encourage, lend a hand, moderator **10** ameliorate, assistance, contribute, facilitate, mitigation, rally round **11** alleviation, collaborate, co-operation, helping hand, improvement, restorative **12** amelioration, contribute to, give a boost to, shot in the arm **13** collaboration, encouragement **14** be of assistance, do something for **15** tower of strength

**• call for help**
**03** SOS **06** mayday **09** au secours **14** distress signal

**• cannot help**
**14** be unable to stop

**helper**
**02** PA **03** aid **04** aide, ally, maid, mate **06** deputy, second, worker **07** partner, servant **08** adjutant, co-worker, employee, helpmate, treasure **09** assistant, associate, attendant, auxiliary, colleague, man Friday, paraclete, supporter **10** accomplice, girl Friday, subsidiary **11** subordinate **12** collaborator, right-hand man **14** right-hand woman **15** second-in-command

**helpful**
**04** kind **05** of use **06** caring, second, useful **08** friendly, obliging, valuable **09** of service, practical **10** beneficial, benevolent, charitable, profitable, supportive, worthwhile **11** considerate, co-operative, furthersome, neighbourly, sympathetic **12** advantageous, constructive, instrumental **13** accommodating

**helpfully**
**06** kindly **08** usefully **10** obligingly **12** conveniently, reassuringly **13** considerately **15** sympathetically

**helping**
**05** order, piece, share **06** aidant, amount, dollop, ration **07** bowlful, portion, serving **08** adjuvant, plateful, spoonful **09** assistant, auxiliary **12** contributive

**helpless**
**04** weak **06** feeble, infirm **07** exposed, forlorn **08** clueless, desolate, disabled, feckless, impotent **09** abandoned, dependent, destitute, incapable, paralysed, powerless **10** friendless, high and dry, vulnerable **11** debilitated, defenceless, incompetent, unprotected

**helplessly**
**06** feebly, weakly **10** desolately, impotently, vulnerably **11** powerlessly **13** defencelessly

**helpmate**
**04** wife **06** helper, spouse **07** consort, husband, partner, support **08** helpmeet **09** assistant, associate, companion, other half **10** better half

**helter-skelter**
◇ *anagram indicator*
**06** random, rashly, wildly **07** hastily, jumbled, muddled **08** confused, headlong, pell-mell **09** haphazard, hit-or-miss, hurriedly **10** carelessly, confusedly, disordered, recklessly, topsy-turvy **11** impulsively **12** disorganized, like hey-go-mad, tumultuously, unsystematic

**hem**
**04** bind, edge, fold, trim **05** frill, skirt **06** border, edging, fringe, margin **07** fimbria, flounce, valance **08** trimming **09** fimbriate

**• hem in**
**04** trap **05** box in, limit, pen in **06** pocket, shut in **07** close in, confine, enclose, hedge in **08** restrict, surround **09** constrain

**hemispherical**
**04** domy **07** rose-cut

**hemlock**
**05** Tsuga **07** cowbane **10** insane root **13** water dropwort

**hemp**
**03** tow **04** pita, sida, sunn **05** abaca, bhang, dagga, ganja, hards, hurds, murva **06** fimble, moorva **07** boneset, hashish **08** agrimony, cannabis, hasheesh, henequen, henequin, heniquin, love-drug, neckweed **09** marihuana, marijuana, true dagga **10** crotalaria **13** Pantagruelion

*See also* **cannabis**

**hen**
**04** balk **05** biddy, chook, layer, poule **06** Cochin, eirack, female, pullet **07** chookie, clocker, Partlet, poulard **08** Langshan **09** incubator **10** Australorp **11** Cochin-China, Spanish fowl

*See also* **chicken**

**hence**
**04** away!, ergo, thus **06** begone! **09** therefore **11** accordingly **12** consequently **13** for this reason **14** as a consequence

**henceforth**
**05** hence **09** from now on, hereafter **11** hereinafter, in the future **12** henceforward **14** from this time on

**henchman, henchwoman**
**04** aide, page **05** crony, heavy **06** hit man, lackey, minder, minion **07** servant **08** follower, sidekick **09** associate, attendant, bodyguard, supporter, underling **10** hatchet man, led captain **11** subordinate **12** right-hand man **14** right-hand woman

**henna**
**08** camphire

**henpecked**
**04** meek **05** timid **07** bullied **08** badgered, harassed, pestered **09** dominated, hag-ridden, tormented **10** browbeaten, criticized, subjugated, woman-tired **11** intimidated

**Henry**
**01** H, O **03** Hal

**Hephaestus**
**06** Vulcan

**her**
**04** elle

**Hera**
**04** Juno

**herald**
**04** Lyon, omen, show, sign **05** augur, crier, token, usher **06** augury, Hermes, signal **07** courier, fanfare, portend, portent, precede, presage, promise, trumpet, usher in **08** announce, blazoner, indicate, Lord Lyon, proclaim **09** advertise, announcer, broadcast, harbinger, make known, messenger, precursor, publicize **10** forerunner, foreshadow, indication, king-at-arms, king-of-arms, Lyon-at-arms, make public, pave the way, proclaimer, promulgate **14** Lyon King of arms

**heraldry**

*Heraldry terms include:*

**02** or
**04** arms, fess, lion, orle, pall, pile, semé, urdé, vert
**05** azure, badge, crest, eagle, eisen, fesse, field, gules, motto, sable, tawny, tenné, undee
**06** argent, bezant, blazon, canton, centre, charge, dexter, emblem, ensign, helmet, impale, mullet, murrey, sejant, shield, volant, wivern
**07** annulet, bordure, cendreé, chevron, dormant, griffin, gyronny, lozenge, martlet, passant, phoenix, quarter, rampant, regalia, roundel, saltire, statant, tierced, unicorn, urinant

**08** addorsed, antelope, caboched, couchant, insignia, mantling, sanguine, sinister, tincture
**09** carnation, displayed, hatchment
**10** camelopard, cinquefoil, coat of arms, cockatrice, emblazonry, escutcheon, fleur-de-lis, quatrefoil, supporters
**11** bleu celeste, compartment
**15** regaliamantling

**herb**
**04** forb, weed, wort **07** olitory

*Herbs and spices include:*

**03** bay, nep, nip
**04** balm, dill, mace, mint, sage
**05** anise, basil, cumin, curry, thyme
**06** borage, cassia, chilli, chives, cloves, fennel, garlic, ginger, hyssop, lovage, nutmeg, pepper, savory, sesame, sorrel
**07** catmint, chervil, comfrey, mustard, oregano, paprika, parsley, pimento, saffron, vanilla
**08** allspice, angelica, bergamot, camomile, cardamom, cardamum, cinnamon, lavender, marjoram, rosemary, tarragon, turmeric
**09** chamomile, coriander, fenugreek, hypericum, lemon balm
**10** gaillardia
**12** caraway seeds
**13** cayenne pepper

• **magic herb**
**04** moly **13** Pantagruelion

**herbal tea** *see* **tea**

**herbicide**
**06** diquat **08** paraquat, simazine **10** glyphosate **11** glufosinate, graminicide

**herculean**
**04** hard, huge **05** great, heavy, large, tough **06** strong **07** arduous, mammoth, massive, onerous **08** colossal, daunting, enormous, exacting, gigantic, powerful, toilsome **09** demanding, difficult, gruelling, laborious, strenuous **10** exhausting, formidable, tremendous

**herd**
**03** mob **04** band, goad, host, lead, mass, pack, race, rout, tail, urge **05** crowd, crush, drive, drove, flock, force, guide, horde, meiny, plebs, press, rally, swarm, troop **06** gather, huddle, meiney, meinie, menyie, muster, proles, rabble, throng **07** collect, round up, sounder, wrangle **08** assemble, riff-raff, shepherd **09** look after, multitude, the masses **10** congregate, take care of **11** get together

**herdsman**
**06** cowman, drover **07** cowherd, grazier, vaquero **08** shepherd, stockman, wrangler **10** stock rider

**here**
**02** in **03** ici, now **05** adsum **06** around **07** present **10** at this time **11** at this place, at this point, at this stage, in this place, to this place

• **here is**
**04** ecco

**hereabouts**
**04** here **08** near here **10** around here **11** in this place **12** in these parts

**hereafter**
**05** hence, later **06** beyond, heaven **08** paradise **09** afterlife, from now on, next world **10** eventually, henceforth, life to come **11** in the future **12** henceforward **13** elysian fields **14** life after death

**here and there**
**05** about, among **06** thinly **08** to and fro **11** irregularly **12** sporadically **15** in various places

**hereditary**
**04** left **06** family, inborn, inbred, innate, willed **07** genetic, natural **08** inherent **09** ancestral, inherited **10** bequeathed, congenital, handed down **11** transferred **13** transmissible

• **hereditary factor**
**02** id **04** gene

**heredity**
**03** DNA **04** gene **05** genes **08** genetics **11** chromosomes, inheritance **13** genetic make-up

**herein**
◇ *containment indicator*
**06** within **11** contained in **13** in this respect

**heresy**
**05** error **06** schism **07** atheism, dissent **08** apostasy, Docetism, unbelief **09** blasphemy, Montanism, recusance **10** dissension, dissidence, heterodoxy, scepticism, separatism **11** agnosticism, revisionism, unorthodoxy **12** free-thinking, sectarianism **13** nonconformity

**heretic**
**06** zendik **07** atheist, sceptic **08** agnostic, apostate, recusant, renegade **09** dissenter, dissident, miscreant, sectarian **10** schismatic, separatist, unbeliever **11** free-thinker, revisionist **13** nonconformist

**heretical**
**07** impious **08** agnostic, recusant, renegade **09** atheistic, dissident, heterodox, sceptical, sectarian **10** dissenting, irreverent, schismatic, separatist, unorthodox **11** blasphemous, revisionist, unbelieving **12** free-thinking, iconoclastic **13** rationalistic

**heritage**
**03** due, lot **04** past **05** share **06** estate, family, legacy **07** bequest, culture, descent, dynasty, history, lineage, portion **08** ancestry, cultural **09** endowment, tradition **10** background, birthright, extraction, traditions **11** inheritance
*See also* **world**

**hermaphrodite**
**08** bisexual **09** androgyne, polygamic **10** monoecious **11** androgynous, monoclinous, protogynous **12** heterogamous **13** gynodioecious, male and female **14** androdioecious

**Hermes**
**07** Mercury

**hermetic**
**04** shut **06** sealed **07** magical, obscure **08** abstruse, airtight **10** hermetical, watertight

**hermit**
**04** monk **05** loner, Peter **07** ancress, ascetic, eremite, pagurid, recluse, stylite **08** beadsman, marabout, pagurian, sannyasi, solitary **09** anchoress, anchorite, pillarist **10** robber crab, solitarian **11** Hieronymite, pillar-saint, soldier crab

**hermitage**
**05** haven **06** ashram, asylum, refuge **07** hideout, retreat, shelter **08** cloister, hideaway **09** sanctuary **11** hiding-place

**hero**
**03** cid, god **04** idol, lead, lion, star **05** ideal, pin-up, sheik **06** eponym, sheikh, victor **07** demigod, good guy, paragon **08** cavalier, champion, male lead **09** celebrity, conqueror, lead actor, superstar **10** heart-throb **11** brave person, demigoddess, protagonist **12** leading actor **15** leading male part, leading male role, person of courage

*Heroes include:*

**04** Ajax, Bond (James), Dare (Dan), Hood (Robin)
**05** Bruce (Robert), El Cid, Jason, Jones (Indiana), Kelly (Ned), Zorro
**06** Arthur, Barton (Dick), Batman, Brutus (Lucius Junius), Rogers (Buck), Sharpe (Richard), Tarzan
**07** Beowulf, Biggles, Glyn Dwr (Owain), Ivanhoe, Perseus, Theseus, Wallace (William)
**08** Achilles, Heracles, Hercules, Lancelot, Odysseus, Superman
**09** Churchill (Sir Winston), D'Artagnan, Glendower (Owain), MacGregor (Rob Roy), Schindler (Oskar), Spiderman
**10** Coriolanus, Cú Chulainn, Hornblower (Horatio), Little John, Lone Ranger, Richthofen (Manfred von 'the Red Baron')
**11** Bellerophon, Finn MacCool, Wilberforce (William)
**14** Finn MacCumhail, Robert the Bruce
**15** Three Musketeers

**heroic**
**04** bold, epic **05** brave, noble **06** daring **07** doughty, gallant, Homeric, valiant **08** fearless, intrepid, selfless, valorous **09** dauntless, undaunted **10** chivalrous, courageous,

determined **11** adventurous, lion-hearted **12** stout-hearted

**heroically**
**05** nobly **06** boldly **07** bravely **09** valiantly **10** fearlessly, selflessly **11** dauntlessly **12** courageously

**heroin**
**01** H **04** junk, scag, skag, snow **05** horse, shmek, smack, sugar **07** schmeck **10** white stuff **11** diamorphine

**heroine**
**04** diva, idol, lead, star **05** ideal, pin-up **06** Amazon, victor **07** goddess, paragon **08** champion **09** celebrity, conqueror, lead actor, superstar **10** brave woman, female lead, prima donna **11** leading lady, protagonist **14** leading actress, prima ballerina, woman of courage

*Heroines include:*

**04** Lane (Lois)
**05** Croft (Lara), Szabo (Violette)
**06** Cavell (Edith), Judith, Ripley (Ellen)
**07** Ariadne, Darling (Grace), Deirdre
**08** Antigone, Atalanta, Boadicea, Boudicca, Penelope
**09** Cassandra, Joan of Arc, Macdonald (Flora), Snow White
**10** Cinderella
**11** Helen of Troy, Nightingale (Florence), Wonderwoman

**heroism**
**06** daring, valour **07** bravery, courage, prowess **08** boldness, chivalry **09** fortitude, gallantry **11** doughtiness, intrepidity **12** fearlessness, selflessness **13** dauntlessness, determination **14** courageousness **15** lion-heartedness

**heron**
**04** hern **05** Ardea, egret **07** bittern, squacco **08** boatbill, hernshaw, heronsew **09** heronshaw

**hero-worship**
**07** worship **09** adoration, adulation **10** admiration, exaltation, veneration **11** deification, idolization **12** idealization **13** glorification

**herring**
**04** brit, sild **05** capon **06** kipper, matjes, mattie **07** anchovy, bloater, clupeid, maatjes, rollmop, soldier **08** buckling, clupeoid, menhaden, sea stick **09** gaspereau **10** mossbunker **12** Norfolk capon

• **measure of herring**
**04** cran, maze, warp **05** maise, maize, mease

**hesitancy**
**05** delay, demur, doubt, qualm **08** scruples, wavering **09** misgiving **10** indecision, reluctance, stammering **11** reservation, uncertainty **12** doubtfulness, irresolution **13** unwillingness **14** disinclination

**hesitant**
**03** shy **04** wary **05** timid **06** unsure **07** dubious, halting **08** delaying, doubtful, stalling, wavering **09** demurring, reluctant, sceptical, tentative, uncertain, unwilling **10** hesitating, indecisive, irresolute, stammering, stuttering **11** disinclined, half-hearted, vacillating

**hesitate**
**04** halt, wait **05** delay, demur, doubt, pause, stall, waver **06** boggle, dicker, dither, falter, mammer, tarrow, teeter **07** balance, scruple, stammer, stumble, stutter, swither, um and ah **08** dubitate, hang back, hang fire, hold back **09** hum and haw, vacillate **10** dilly-dally, shrink from, think twice **11** be reluctant, be uncertain, be unwilling **12** shilly-shally **13** be disinclined

**hesitation**
**05** delay, demur, doubt, dwell, pause, qualm **06** demure, qualms **07** scruple, waiting **08** misdoubt, scruples, stalling, wavering **09** faltering, hesitance, stumbling **10** cunctation, indecision, misgivings, reluctance, scepticism, stammering, stuttering, unsureness **11** hanging-back, holding-back, uncertainty, vacillation **12** doubtfulness, irresolution **13** dilly-dallying, unwillingness **14** disinclination, second thoughts **15** shilly-shallying

• **expression of hesitation**
**02** er, ha, um, ur **03** erm, hah **04** well

**Hestia**
**05** Vesta

**heterodox**
**07** unsound **09** dissident, heretical **10** dissenting, schismatic, unorthodox **11** revisionist **12** free-thinking, iconoclastic

**heterogeneous**
**05** mixed **06** motley, unlike, varied **07** diverse, opposed, piebald, pyebald **08** assorted, catholic, contrary **09** different, disparate, divergent, multiform, unrelated **10** contrasted, discrepant, dissimilar **11** diversified, incongruous, polymorphic **13** miscellaneous

**heterogeneously**
**09** diversely **10** contrarily **11** differently, disparately, divergently **12** dissimilarly **13** incongruously

**heterosexual**
**03** het **06** hetero **07** breeder **08** straight

**het up**
**05** angry, tense, upset **07** anxious, in a rage, uptight, worried, wound up **08** agitated, offended, stressed, worked up **09** indignant, pissed off, resentful **11** stressed-out **14** beside yourself

**hew**
**03** axe, cut, dye, hag, hue, lop, saw **04** chip, chop, fell, form, hack, make, tint, trim **05** carve, model, prune, sever, shape, split **06** chisel, colour, hammer, sculpt **07** fashion, whittle **09** sculpture **10** appearance

**heyday**
**04** peak **05** bloom, flush, prime **06** summer **08** boom time, pinnacle **09** flowering, golden age **11** culmination

**hiatus**
**03** gap **04** lull, rest, rift, void **05** blank, break, chasm, lapse, pause, space **06** breach, defect, lacuna **07** opening **08** aperture, interval **10** suspension **12** interruption **13** discontinuity **14** discontinuance

**hibernate**
**06** winter

**hibernating**
**06** torpid **07** dormant **08** latitant

**hibiscus**
**04** okra **07** roselle, rozelle **10** cotton tree, rose mallow **12** rose of Sharon

**hiccup**
**03** hic, yex **04** snag, yesk **05** block, catch, check, delay, hitch **06** glitch, hold-up, mishap **07** barrier, problem, setback, trouble **08** drawback, obstacle **09** hindrance **10** difficulty, impediment **11** obstruction

**hick** *see* **bumpkin**

**hickory**
**05** pecan **08** shagbark **09** scaly-bark, shellbark

**hidden**
◇ *hidden indicator*
**04** dark, dern **05** close, dearn **06** arcane, covert, latent, masked, occult, secret, unseen, veiled **07** covered, cryptic, obscure, unknown **08** abstruse, mystical, shrouded, ulterior **09** concealed, disguised, invisible, recondite **10** indistinct, mysterious, out of sight, under wraps **11** camouflaged, clandestine **12** subterranean, under hatches

**hide**
◇ *containment indicator*
◇ *hidden indicator*
**03** fur **04** buff, bury, coat, fell, flog, heal, heel, hele, hell, lurk, mask, pell, pelt, robe, skin, stow, veil, whip, wrap **05** cache, cloak, cloud, cover, earth, slink, store **06** darken, encave, fleece, hole up, incave, lie low, screen, shadow, shroud, spetch **07** abscond, conceal, eclipse, envelop, flaught, leather, obscure, secrete, shelter, tappice **08** bottle up, disguise, keep dark, lie doggo, lock away, obstruct, suppress, withhold **09** dissemble, stash away, take cover **10** camouflage, go to ground, keep secret **12** go into hiding **13** draw a veil over, put out of sight **14** keep out of sight, keep under wraps, lay a false scent **15** conceal yourself, cover your tracks, keep a low profile

**hideaway**
**03** den **04** hole, lair, nest **05** haven **06** refuge **07** hideout, retreat, shelter **08** cloister, fugitive **09** hermitage, sanctuary **11** hiding-place

**hidebound**
**03** set **05** fixed, rigid **06** narrow **07** bigoted **08** stubborn **09** obstinate **10** entrenched, intolerant **11** Biedermeier, intractable, reactionary, strait-laced **12** conventional, narrow-minded **14** uncompromising

**hideous**
◇ *anagram indicator*
**04** gash, grim, huge, ugly **05** awful **06** deform, horrid, ugsome **07** ghastly, loathly, macabre **08** dreadful, gruesome, horrible, shocking, terrible **09** appalling, frightful, grotesque, monstrous, repellent, repulsive, revolting, unsightly **10** abominable, disgusting, horrendous, horrifying, monstruous, outrageous, terrifying

**hideously**
**08** horribly, horridly, terribly **10** abominably, dreadfully, gruesomely, shockingly **11** frightfully, grotesquely, repulsively **12** disgustingly, horrendously, outrageously, terrifyingly

**hideout**
**03** den **04** hole, lair, nest **05** haven **06** refuge **07** retreat, shelter **08** cloister, hideaway **09** hermitage, sanctuary **11** hiding-place

**hiding**
◇ *containment indicator*
**04** dern, mask, veil **05** cover, dearn **06** caning, shroud **07** beating, belting, licking, tanning, veiling **08** disguise, drubbing, flogging, spanking, whacking, whipping **09** battering, screening, thrashing, walloping **10** camouflage **11** concealment

**hiding-place**
**03** den, mew **04** hide, hole, lair, nest **05** cache, cover, haven, stash **06** refuge **07** hideout, hidling, hidlins, retreat, shelter **08** cloister, hideaway, hidlings, hidy-hole **09** glory hole, hidey-hole, sanctuary

**hierarchy**
**05** scale **06** ladder, series, strata, system **07** grading, ranking **08** echelons **09** structure **12** pecking order

**hieroglyphics**
**04** code **05** runes, signs **06** cipher **07** scratch, symbols **08** scrabble, scribble, squiggle **10** bad writing, cacography, pictograms **13** secret symbols **14** picture writing

**higgledy-piggledy**
◇ *anagram indicator*
**06** anyhow, untidy **07** jumbled, muddled **08** confused, pell-mell, untidily **09** any old how, haphazard **10** confusedly, disorderly, topsy-turvy **11** haphazardly **12** disorganized, through-other **14** indiscriminate

**high**
◇ *anagram indicator*
**03** bad, off, top **04** dear, fine, gamy, good, haut, loud, peak, tall, trip **05** acute, aloft, angry, chief, doped, drunk, great, gusty, lofty, moral, nervy, noble, sharp, steep, tinny, wired **06** bombed, choice, classy, costly, de luxe, elated, height, loaded, piping, putrid, rancid, record, select, senior, severe, shrill, smelly, stoned, stormy, strong, summit, tiptop, treble, turn-on, wasted, worthy, zenith, zonked **07** blasted, blitzed, complex, decayed, eminent, ethical, exalted, extreme, haughty, intense, leading, notable, on a trip, out of it, perfect, quality, rotting, shrilly, soaring, soprano, squally, upright, violent **08** abstruse, admiring, advanced, arrogant, blue-chip, blustery, elevated, falsetto, forceful, freak-out, high-tech, inflated, piercing, positive, powerful, smelling, superior, top-class, towering, turned on, vigorous, virtuous **09** admirable, agreeable, approving, difficult, dignified, elaborate, eminently, excellent, excessive, exemplary, expensive, extremely, first-rate, gilt-edged, high-level, important, luxurious, principal, prominent, spaced out **10** arrogantly, exorbitant, favourable, first-class, freaked out, honourable, inebriated, noteworthy, powerfully, surpassing, unequalled **11** anticyclone, commendable, high-pitched, high-ranking, inebriation, influential, intoxicated, luxuriously, outstanding, penetrating, progressive, superlative, tempestuous, ultra-modern **12** altitudinous, appreciative, extortionate, intoxication, unparalleled, unreasonable, well-disposed **13** complimentary, distinguished, hallucinating, hallucination, high-frequency

• **high and dry**
**06** bereft, dumped **07** ditched **08** helpless, marooned, stranded **09** abandoned, destitute

• **high and low**
**07** all over **09** all around **10** every place, everywhere, far and near, throughout **11** in all places, in each place **12** in every place

• **high and mighty**
**05** proud **06** swanky **07** exalted, haughty, stuck-up **08** arrogant, cavalier, snobbish, superior, toplofty **09** conceited, egotistic, imperious **10** disdainful, hogen-mogen **11** overbearing, overweening, patronizing, toploftical **13** condescending, self-important

• **hit high**
**03** lob, sky

• **on high**
**02** up **05** ahigh, aloft **07** aheight **08** supernal **10** in excelsis

**high-born**
**05** noble **08** well-born **09** patrician **11** blue-blooded **12** aristocratic, thoroughbred

**highbrow**
**04** deep **05** heavy **06** boffin, brains, brainy, genius **07** bookish, egghead, scholar, serious **08** academic, brainbox, cultured, long-hair, profound **09** classical, know-it-all, scholarly **10** cultivated, long-haired, mastermind **11** clever clogs **12** intellectual **13** sophisticated **14** third-programme

**high-class**
**01** U **04** posh **05** dicty, élite, pakka, pucka, pukka, super **06** choice, classy, de luxe, dickty, select **07** elegant, quality **08** superior, top-class **09** excellent, exclusive, first-rate, luxurious, top-flight **10** upper-class **11** high-quality

**highest**
**03** top **04** best **05** chief **07** supreme, topmost **08** crowning **09** uppermost

**highfalutin, highfaluting**
**05** lofty **06** la-di-da, swanky **07** pompous **08** affected **09** bombastic, grandiose, high-flown **11** pretentious **12** high-sounding, magniloquent, supercilious

**high-flown**
**05** lofty **06** florid, la-di-da, ornate, turgid **07** pompous, stilted **08** affected, elevated **09** bombastic, elaborate, grandiose **10** artificial, flamboyant **11** exaggerated, extravagant, highfalutin, pretentious **12** high-sounding, ostentatious, supercilious **13** grandiloquent, grand-sounding

**high-handed**
**05** bossy **07** haughty **08** arrogant, despotic **09** arbitrary, imperious **10** autocratic, oppressive, peremptory, tyrannical **11** dictatorial, domineering, overbearing

**high-handedness**
**09** arrogance, bossiness **13** arbitrariness, imperiousness, inflexibility **14** peremptoriness

**high jinks**
**06** antics, capers, pranks **07** foolery, fooling, jollity **08** clowning **09** horseplay **10** buffoonery, skylarking, tomfoolery **11** fun and games **13** fooling around **14** monkey business, practical jokes, rough-and-tumble

**highland**
**04** hill, rise **05** mound, mount, ridge **06** height, upland **07** plateau **08** mountain **09** elevation

**Highlander**
**04** Gael **06** Gadhel, Goidel **07** nainsel' **08** nainsell, plaidman, teuchter **09** Irish Scot

**highlight**
**04** best, peak **05** cream, focus **06** accent, climax, play up, set off, show up, stress **07** feature, focus on, point up **08** high spot **09** emphasize, high point, spotlight, underline **10** accentuate, illuminate **11** main feature **13** put emphasis on **15** call attention to

**highly**
**04** most, very, well **06** hugely, really, thrice, vastly, warmly **07** greatly **08** very much **09** certainly, decidedly, extremely, immensely **10** favourably, thoroughly **11** approvingly **12** considerably, tremendously **13** exceptionally **14** appreciatively **15** extraordinarily

**highly-strung**
**04** edgy **05** jumpy, nervy, tense **06** on edge **07** nervous, uptight, wound up **08** neurotic, restless, stressed **09** excitable, sensitive **11** easily upset, overwrought **13** temperamental

**high-minded**
**04** fair, good, pure **05** lofty, moral, noble **06** worthy **07** ethical, upright **08** elevated, virtuous **09** righteous **10** honourable, idealistic, principled **14** high-principled

**high-pitched**
**05** acute, sharp, steep, tinny **06** piping, shrill, treble **07** orthian, soprano **08** falsetto, piercing **11** penetrating

**high-powered**
**05** pushy, valid **06** mighty, potent, strong, urgent **07** dynamic, go-ahead, telling, weighty **08** emphatic, forceful, forcible, powerful, vehement, vigorous **09** assertive, effective, energetic **10** compelling, convincing, impressive, persuasive

**high-priced**
**04** dear, high **05** steep, stiff **06** costly, pricey **09** excessive, expensive **10** exorbitant **12** extortionate, unreasonable

**high-sounding**
**06** florid **07** orotund, pompous, stilted **08** affected, imposing, strained **09** bombastic, grandiose, high-flown, overblown, ponderous **10** altisonant, artificial, flamboyant **11** extravagant, pretentious **12** magniloquent, ostentatious **13** grandiloquent

**high-speed**
**05** brisk, fleet, hasty, quick, rapid, swift **06** flying, speedy **07** express, hurried **11** accelerated

**high-spirited**
**04** bold **05** proud **06** active, bouncy, daring, lively **07** dashing, dynamic, mettled, playful, rampant, vibrant **08** animated, cheerful, spirited, vigorous **09** ebullient, energetic, exuberant, sparkling, vivacious **10** boisterous, frolicsome, hot-blooded, mettlesome **11** full of beans, high-mettled **12** effervescent, great-hearted, thoroughbred

**high spirits**
**06** bounce, capers, energy, heyday, spirit **07** elation, sparkle **08** boldness, buoyancy, hilarity, vivacity **09** animation, good cheer **10** ebullience, exuberance, liveliness **11** high feather, joie de vivre **12** exhilaration **14** boisterousness

**highway**
**04** road, rode **05** grove, route **06** avenue, bypass **07** flyover, freeway, roadway, tollway **08** Autobahn, broadway, clearway, main road, motorway, ring road, toll road, turnpike **09** autoroute, boulevard, trunk road **10** autostrada, camino real, expressway, high street, interstate **11** carriageway **12** arterial road, primary route, thoroughfare **15** dual carriageway

**highwayman**
**03** pad **05** scamp **06** bandit, hold-up, robber **07** footpad **08** hijacker **09** bandolero, rank-rider, road agent **10** bushranger, highjacker, land-pirate **15** knight of the road

*Highwaymen include:*

**04** King (Tom)
**05** Duval (Claude)
**06** Turpin (Dick)
**07** Brennan (Willie), Nevison (John), Nevison (William)
**08** MacHeath
**09** Abershawe (Jerry), Swift Nick
**12** Mack the Knife

**hijack**
**05** seize **07** carjack, skyjack **08** take over **10** commandeer **11** expropriate

**hike**
**03** tug **04** jack, jerk, lift, plod, pull, ramp, trek, walk, yank **05** hitch, hoist, march, put up, raise, tramp **06** jack up, pull up, push up, ramble, trudge, wander **08** bushwalk, increase

**hilarious**
**05** funny, jolly, merry, noisy **06** jovial **07** amusing, a scream, comical, killing, riotous, risible **08** farcical, humorous **09** laughable **10** boisterous, hysterical, rollicking, uproarious **12** entertaining **13** side-splitting

**hilariously**
**09** comically, laughably **10** farcically, humorously **12** boisterously, hysterically, uproariously

**hilarity**
**03** fun **05** mirth **06** comedy, gaiety, levity **07** jollity **08** laughter **09** amusement, frivolity, merriment **10** exuberance **11** high spirits **12** conviviality, exhilaration **14** boisterousness

**hill**
**03** dod, dun, how, kip, kop, law, low, man, pap, tel, tor **04** berg, cone, down, drop, dune, fell, holt, howe, knot, loma, mesa, pike, ramp, rise, tell, toot, torr **05** butte, coast, jebel, knoll, kopje, morro, mound, mount, slope **06** ascent, barrow, cuesta, djebel, height, koppie, pimple, rising **07** descent, hillock, hilltop, hummock, incline, mamelon **08** eminence, foothill, gradient, mountain **09** acclivity, declivity, elevation, monadnock, monticule, sugarloaf **10** prominence, saddleback **12** rising ground

*Rome's seven hills:*

**07** Caelian, Viminal
**08** Aventine, Palatine, Quirinal
**09** Esquiline
**10** Capitoline

**• over the hill**
**03** old **04** gone **06** past it **09** getting on **13** past your prime

**hillbilly**
**03** oaf **04** boor, hick, lout **06** rustic **07** bumpkin, hawbuck, hayseed, hoedown, peasant **08** clodpoll **10** clodhopper, provincial **11** bushwhacker **12** country yokel **14** country bumpkin

**hill fort**
**04** rath

**hillock**
**04** dune, knap, knob, toft, tump **05** knoll, knowe, mound **06** barrow **07** hommock, hummock **08** monticle **10** monticulus

**hill-slope**
**04** brae

**hilltop**
**03** dod, nab **05** crest

**hilt**
**04** grip, haft, heft **05** helve, shaft **06** basket, handle **08** coquille, handgrip

**• to the hilt**
**05** fully **06** wholly **07** utterly **08** entirely, to the end **09** all the way, to the full **10** completely, thoroughly **14** in every respect **15** from first to last

**him**
**02** un

**hind**
**04** back, rear, rump, tail **05** after, stern **06** caudal, hinder **09** posterior

**hinder**
**03** bar, let **04** balk, curb, foil, halt, hind, last, rear, stay, stop **05** block, check, crimp, debar, delay, deter, dwarf, embar, estop, imbar, stunt **06** arrest, cumber, hamper, hold up, impede, oppose, resist, retard, stymie, taigle, thwart **07** empeach, forelay, impeach, inhibit, keep off, porlock, prevent, set back, trammel **08** encumber, handicap, hold back, obstruct, preclude, slow down **09** forestall, frustrate, hamstring, interrupt, throw back, withstand **10** overslaugh **13** interfere with

**hindmost**
**03** lag **04** last, tail **05** final **07** aftmost, endmost **08** furthest, rearmost, remotest, terminal, trailing, ultimate **09** aftermost **10** concluding **12** furthest back **14** farthest behind

**hindrance**
**03** bar, let **04** curb, drag, foil, snag, stop **05** block, check, delay, hitch **06** hold-up, thwart **07** barrier, empeach, impeach, shackle **08** drawback, handicap, obstacle, pullback, stoppage **09** cumbrance, deterrent, impedance, restraint, thwarting **10** difficulty, impediment, limitation, prevention **11** encumbrance, obstruction, obstructive, restriction **12** disadvantage, interference, interruption **13** inconvenience **14** stumbling-block

**hindsight**
**06** review, survey **10** reflection, retrospect **11** remembrance **12** afterthought, recollection, thinking back **13** re-examination

**Hindu** *see* **god, goddess; month**

**Hindustani**
**04** Hind, Urdu **05** Hindi

**hinge**
◇ *reversal indicator*
**04** hang, rest, turn **05** gemel, pivot **06** centre, depend, garnet **07** revolve **09** ginglymus **11** cross-garnet **12** be contingent

**hint**
**03** cue, tip **04** clue, dash, help, mint, note, sign, tang, wind, wink, word **05** hunch, imply, light, point, savor, speck, taste, tinge, touch, trace, whiff **06** advice, allude, moment, nuance, office, prevue, prompt, savour, signal, squint, tip off, tip-off **07** glimmer, inkling, let fall, mention, pointer, preview, soupçon, suggest, thought, whisper, wrinkle **08** allusion, indicate, innuendo, intimate, reminder **09** insinuate, scintilla, suspicion **10** indication, intimation, sprinkling, suggestion **11** implication, insinuation, opportunity, subindicate

**hinterland**
**08** backveld, interior **10** back-blocks, hinderland **11** back-country

**hip**
**02** in **03** hep **04** cool, huck, loin, rump **05** croup, funky, thigh **06** dog-hep, dog-hip, groovy, haunch, huckle, modish, pelvis, trendy, with it **07** stylish, voguish **08** buttocks **09** happening, posterior **10** all the rage **11** fashionable **12** hindquarters, hypochondria **13** up to the minute

• **hip bone**
**04** coxa **10** huckle-bone **14** innominate bone

**hippie, hippy**
**05** loner, rebel **07** beatnik, deviant, dropout **08** bohemian **10** long-haired **11** flower child

**hire**
**03** fee, job, let, pay **04** book, cost, lend, rent, wage **05** lease, price **06** charge, employ, engage, enlist, rental, retain, salary, sign on, sign up, take on **07** appoint, charter, freight, reserve **10** commission

**hire-purchase**
**02** HP **09** easy terms **10** never-never **14** instalment plan

**hirsute**
**05** hairy, rough **06** crinal, hispid, shaggy **07** bearded, bristly, crinate, crinite, crinose **08** unshaven **11** bewhiskered, crinigerous

**hiss**
**03** boo **04** buzz, hish, hizz, hoot, jeer, mock **05** goose, scorn, taunt, whiss, whizz **06** deride, fizzle, shrill, siffle, sizzle **07** catcall, hissing, mockery, scoff at, the bird, whistle **08** contempt, derision, ridicule, scoffing, sibilant, sibilate, taunting **09** raspberry, shout down, sibilance **10** assibilate, effervesce, sibilation **15** blow raspberries

**historian**
**07** diarist **08** annalist, narrator, recorder **09** archivist **10** chronicler **11** chronologer **15** historiographer

*Historians include:*

**04** **Bede** (St, 'The Venerable'), **Bois** (William Edward Burghardt du), **Livy**, **Read** (Sir Herbert Edward), **Webb** (Sidney)
**05** **Barth** (Heinrich), **Blunt** (Anthony Frederick), **Clark** (Kenneth, Lord), **Ensor** (Sir Robert), **Gates** (Henry Louis, Jnr), **Henry** (of Huntingdon), **Lodge** (Henry Cabot), **Nepos** (Cornelius), **Paris** (Matthew), **Ranke** (Leopold von), **Renan** (Ernest), **Stone** (Norman)
**06** **Arrian**, **Berlin** (Sir Isaiah), **Bolton** (Geoffrey), **Briggs** (Lord Asa), **Eliade** (Mircea), **Froude** (James Anthony), **Gibbon** (Edward), **Guizot** (François), **Irving** (David), **Namier** (Sir Lewis), **O'Brien** (Conor Cruise), **Schama** (Simon), **Strabo**, **Strong** (Sir Roy), **Tabari** (Abu Jafar Mohammed Ben Jarir al-), **Tawney** (Richard Henry), **Taylor** (Alan John Percivale), **Terkel** (Studs), **Thiers** (Adolphe), **Vasari** (Giorgio)
**07** **Barbour** (John), **Bullock** (Alan, Lord), **Carlyle** (Thomas), **Comines** (Philippe de), **Mommsen** (Theodor), **Pevsner** (Sir Nikolaus Bernhard), **Sallust**, **Severin** (Timothy), **Starkey** (David), **Tacitus**, **Toynbee** (Arnold), **Vasarib** (Giorgio), **William** (of Malmesbury), **William** (of Tyre)
**08** **Foucault** (Michel), **Geoffrey** (of Monmouth), **Gombrich** (Sir Ernst Hans Josef), **Josephus** (Flavius), **Las Casas** (Emmanuel), **Macaulay** (Thomas Babington, Lord), **Michelet** (Jules), **Palgrave** (Sir Francis), **Panofsky** (Erwin), **Plutarch**, **Polybius**, **Wedgwood** (Dame Cicely), **Xenophon**
**09** **Dionysius** (of Halicarnassus), **Froissart** (Jean), **Herodotus**, **Holinshed** (Raphael), **Pausanias**, **Plekhanov** (Giorgiy), **Procopius**, **Rowbotham** (Sheila), **Suetonius**, **Trevelyan** (George Macaulay)
**10** **Baldinucci** (Filippo), **Burckhardt** (Jacob Christopher), **Dio Cassius**, **Thucydides**
**11** **Schlesinger** (Arthur Meier), **Tocqueville** (Alexis de), **Trevor-Roper** (Hugh Redwald)
**12** **Guicciardini** (Francesco)
**15** **Diodorus Siculus**

**historic**
**05** famed **06** famous **07** notable **08** renowned **09** important, memorable, momentous, red-letter **10** celebrated, remarkable **11** epoch-making, outstanding, significant **13** consequential, extraordinary

**historical**
**03** old **04** past, real **05** prior **06** actual, bygone, former, of yore **07** ancient, factual **08** attested, recorded, verified **09** authentic, confirmed **10** chronicled, documented, verifiable

*Historical periods include:*

**05** Bruce, Tudor
**06** Norman, Stuart
**07** Angevin, Cold War, Post-War, Regency, Stewart, Yorkist
**08** Civil War, Dark Ages, Medieval
**09** Edwardian, Mediaeval, Modern Age, Victorian
**10** Anglo-Saxon, Hanoverian, Middle Ages
**11** Interbellum, Interregnum, Lancastrian, Plantagenet, Reformation, Renaissance, Restoration, Roman Empire, Romanticism
**13** British Empire, Enlightenment, Ottoman Empire
**15** Byzantine Empire

**historically**
**04** once **07** long ago **08** formerly **09** in the past, yesterday **10** originally **11** some time ago **13** in former times, in years gone by

**history**
**04** life, saga, tale **05** story, study **06** annals, family, record, report **07** account, memoirs, records, reports, the past **08** archives **09** antiquity, biography, chronicle, days of old, education, narrative, olden days, yesterday **10** background, bygone days, chronology, days of yore, experience, the old days, yesteryear **11** credentials, former times **13** autobiography, circumstances **14** qualifications, the good old days

**histrionic**
**03** ham **05** bogus, stagy **06** forced **08** affected, dramatic, operatic

**09** insincere, unnatural **10** artificial, theatrical **11** exaggerated, sensational **12** hypocritical, melodramatic

**histrionics**
**05** scene **08** tantrums **09** dramatics, melodrama, staginess, theatrics **10** overacting **11** affectation, insincerity, performance **13** artificiality, theatricality, unnaturalness **14** sensationalism

**hit**
◇ *anagram indicator*
**03** bat, bop, box, cue, dod, dot, fit, get, hay, pat, tap, tip, wow, zap **04** bang, bash, beat, belt, biff, blow, boff, bonk, bump, clip, club, cuff, daud, dawd, harm, hurt, move, polt, shot, skit, slap, slew, slog, sock, suit, swap, swat, tonk **05** catch, clonk, clout, crash, knock, pound, prang, punch, smack, smash, smite, thump, touch, upset, whack **06** affect, batter, buffet, come to, damage, dawn on, impact, strike, stroke, thrash, wallop, winner **07** beating, clobber, disturb, occur to, perturb, run into, success, triumph, trouble **08** knockout **09** collision, crash into, devastate, overwhelm, smash into, thrashing **10** clobbering, come to mind, meet head-on, plough into **11** be thought of, blockbuster, collide with, knock for six **12** be remembered **13** enter your mind **14** have an effect on

*See also* **kill**

• **hit back**
**06** return **07** respond **09** retaliate **10** strike back **11** reciprocate **13** counter-attack

• **hit it off**
**05** agree, click, fadge **06** warm to **09** get on with **10** grow to like **12** get along with **13** become friends, get on well with **14** be friendly with

• **hit on**
**05** guess **06** invent **07** light on, realize, think of, uncover **08** arrive at, chance on, discover **09** stumble on

• **hit out**
**04** rail **05** flail **06** assail, attack, strike, vilify **07** condemn, inveigh, lash out **08** denounce **09** criticize, strike out

**hitch**
**03** rub, tie, tug **04** bind, hike, hook, jerk, join, limp, pull, snag, yank, yoke **05** block, catch, check, delay, heave, hoist, hotch, stick, unite **06** attach, couple, fasten, glitch, hiccup, hike up, hobble, hold-up, mishap, tether **07** barrier, cat's-paw, connect, harness, problem, setback, trouble **08** drawback, obstacle **09** hindrance **10** difficulty, impediment **11** contretemps, obstruction

**hitherto**
**03** yet **05** so far **07** thus far, till now, up to now **08** formerly, until now **10** beforehand, heretofore, previously

**hitman**
**03** gun **06** ice man **08** assassin

**hit-or-miss**
**06** casual, hobnob, random, uneven **07** aimless, cursory, offhand **08** careless **09** apathetic, haphazard, unplanned **10** undirected **11** perfunctory **12** disorganized **13** lackadaisical, trial-and-error **14** indiscriminate

**hive**
**03** gum **04** skep **07** alveary, bee-skep

**hoard**
**04** fund, heap, keep, mass, pile, pose, save **05** amass, buy up, cache, hoord, hutch, lay in, lay up, plant, put by, spare, stash, store, uplay **06** coffer, gather, heap up, mucker, pile up, supply **07** collect, put away, reserve, stack up, stock up, uphoard **08** hoarding, salt away, set aside, squirrel, treasure **09** reservoir, stash away, stockpile **10** accumulate, collection **11** aggregation **12** accumulation, squirrel away **13** treasure-trove **14** conglomeration

**hoarder**
**05** miser, saver **06** magpie **07** niggard **08** gatherer, squirrel **09** collector

**hoarse**
**05** gruff, harsh, husky, raspy, roopy, rough **06** croaky, roopit **07** grating, rasping, raucous, throaty **08** croaking, gravelly, growling, guttural **10** discordant

**hoarsely**
**07** gruffly, harshly, huskily, roughly **08** croakily **09** raucously **10** gutturally

**hoarseness**
**04** roop, roup

**hoary**
**03** old **04** aged, grey **05** banal, trite, white **06** old-hat **07** ancient, antique, archaic, cliché'd, silvery **08** clichéed, familiar, grizzled **09** canescent, senescent, venerable **10** antiquated, grey-haired **11** predictable, white-haired **12** overfamiliar

**hoax**
**02** do **03** bam, cod, con, fun, gag, hum, kid **04** dupe, fake, fool, gull, jest, joke, josh, quiz, ruse, scam, sham, skit **05** bluff, cheat, fraud, kiddy, prank, put-on, spoof, stuff, trick **06** canard, delude, gammon, have on, humbug, pigeon, string, take in **07** deceive, fast one, frame-up, leg-pull, mystify, swindle, two-time **08** hoodwink, put-up job **09** April-fish, April fool, bamboozle, deception, gold brick **10** huntiegowk **11** double-cross, hunt-the-gowk, supercherie **12** take for a ride **13** practical joke **14** pull a fast one on

**hoaxer**
**05** joker **06** humbug **07** sharper, spoofer **09** mystifier, prankster, trickster **10** bamboozler, hoodwinker **14** practical joker

**hobble**
**04** clog, limp, reel **05** hilch, hitch **06** dodder, falter, fetter, hamper, scrape, totter **07** pastern, perplex, shackle, shuffle, spancel, stagger, stumble, trammel **10** walk lamely **13** walk awkwardly, walk with a limp

**hobbling**
**04** game, lame **06** lamish

**hobby**
**03** fad **04** game **05** sport **07** pastime, pursuit **08** interest, play-mare, sideline **09** amusement, avocation, diversion **10** recreation, relaxation **13** entertainment **14** divertissement, leisure pursuit **15** leisure activity

*Hobbies and pastimes include:*

**05** batik, chess
**06** acting, baking, bonsai, hiking, poetry, raffia
**07** camping, CB radio, collage, cookery, crochet, dancing, drawing, macramé, mosaics, origami, pottery, quizzes, reading, singing, tatting, topiary, weaving, writing
**08** basketry, cat shows, dog shows, draughts, feng shui, knitting, knotting, lacework, lapidary, marbling, painting, quilling, quilting, spinning, tapestry
**09** astrology, astronomy, decoupage, gardening, genealogy, marquetry, millinary, model cars, philately, rug-making, sketching, strawwork, toy-making, train sets
**10** beekeeping, board games, crosswords, doll-making, embroidery, kite-flying, lace-making, pub quizzes, pyrography, renovating, upholstery, wine-making
**11** archaeology, beadworking, bell-ringing, book-binding, calligraphy, card playing, cat breeding, cross-stitch, dog breeding, dressmaking, home brewing, model-making, model trains, needlepoint, numismatics, ornithology, paper crafts, papier-mâché, photography, wine-tasting, woodcarving, woodworking
**12** amateur radio, basketmaking, candle-making, games playing, phillumenism
**13** bungee jumping, egg decorating, toy collecting
**14** book collecting, coin collecting, cruciverbalism, doll collecting, flower pressing, herpetoculture, metal detecting
**15** aquarium keeping, ballroom dancing, flower arranging, jewellery making, model aeroplanes, stamp collecting

**hobgoblin**
**03** elf, imp **05** bogey, dwarf, gnome **06** buggan, buggin, goblin, spirit, sprite **07** bugaboo, bugbear, buggane,

spectre **08** wirricow, worricow, worrycow **10** apparition, bull-beggar, evil spirit

### hobnob
**03** mix **06** mingle **07** consort **08** go around **09** associate, hang about, hit-or-miss, pal around, socialize **10** fraternize **11** keep company

### hock
**03** ham, hox **04** pawn **07** gambrel, Rhenish **09** Rhine wine **11** Rhenish wine

*See also* **pawn**

### hockey

*Hockey-related terms include:*

**01** D
**03** hit
**04** ball, feet, goal, push
**05** flick, scoop
**06** aerial, tackle
**07** dribble, free hit, red card, striker, sweeper
**08** back line, bully-off, left back, left half, left wing
**09** corner hit, drag flick, field goal, green card, right back, right half, right wing
**10** centre half, centre pass, goal circle, goalkeeper, inside left, long corner, yellow card
**11** field player, hockey stick, inside right, obstruction, short corner
**12** penalty flick, reverse stick
**13** centre forward, penalty corner, penalty stroke
**14** shooting circle, striking circle

### hocus-pocus
**04** cant, hoax **05** cheat, spell **06** deceit, humbug, jargon, juggle **07** juggler, swindle **08** artifice, delusion, hoky-poky, nonsense, trickery **09** chicanery, conjuring, deception, gibberish, imposture, rigmarole **10** hokey-pokey, magic words, mumbo-jumbo **11** abracadabra, legerdemain, trompe-l'oeil **12** gobbledygook **13** sleight of hand

### hodgepodge
**03** mix **04** mess **06** jumble, medley **07** melange, mixture **08** mishmash **09** confusion **10** collection, hotchpotch, miscellany

### hoe
**04** clat **05** claut **06** pecker **07** scuffle **10** promontory

### hog
**03** pig **04** boar **05** swine **06** corner, porker **07** control, grunter **08** babirusa, dominate, shilling, take over, wild boar **09** babirussa **10** babiroussa, monopolize **14** keep to yourself

### hogshead
**04** muid

• **two hogsheads**
**04** pipe

### hogwash
**03** rot **04** blah, bosh, bunk, crap, guff, tosh **05** balls, bilge, hooey, swill, trash, tripe **06** bunkum, drivel, hot air, piffle **07** baloney, eyewash, rubbish, twaddle **08** claptrap, cobblers, malarkey, nonsense, tommyrot **09** gibberish, moonshine, poppycock **10** balderdash

### hoi polloi
**07** the herd **08** riff-raff, the plebs, varletry **09** the masses, the proles, the rabble **11** the peasants, the populace **14** the proletariat, the third estate **15** the common people

### hoist
**04** jack, lift, rear, sway, wind **05** crane, erect, heave, hoise, raise, steal, wince, winch **06** jack up, pulley, tackle, teagle, uplift, wind up **07** capstan, elevate, winch up **08** elevator, windlass

### hoity-toity
**05** giddy, huffy, lofty, noisy, proud **06** snooty, uppity **07** haughty, pompous, stuck-up **08** arrogant, scornful, snobbish **09** conceited **10** disdainful **11** overweening, toffee-nosed **12** supercilious **13** high and mighty

### hold
◇ *containment indicator*
**02** ho **03** aim, bet, hoa, hoh, hug, own, ren, rin, run **04** bear, bind, bulk, call, curb, deem, fill, go on, grip, have, holt, hook, keep, last, soft, stay, stop, sway, take, view **05** apply, belay, brace, carry, catch, check, clasp, cling, clout, grasp, gripe, judge, power, rivet, seize, stick, think, treat **06** absorb, adhere, arrest, assume, clutch, detain, direct, endure, enfold, engage, esteem, fulfil, hold up, keep up, lock up, nelson, occupy, prop up, reckon, regard, remain, retain, summon, suplex, take up **07** adjudge, armlock, bear hug, believe, carry on, claucht, claught, cling to, conduct, confine, contain, control, convene, custody, embrace, enclose, engross, enthral, holding, impound, mastery, observe, persist, possess, presume, reserve, soft you, support, suppose, sustain, toehold **08** assemble, buttress, consider, continue, dominion, headlock, hold down, imprison, leverage, maintain, organize, purchase, restrain, scissors, tenacity **09** authority, be in force, captivate, celebrate, dominance, fascinate, influence **10** Boston crab, compromise, full nelson, half nelson, hammerlock, monopolize, remain true, stronghold **11** accommodate, backbreaker, have room for, incarcerate, preside over, remain valid, scissor hold **12** have space for, stranglehold **13** be in operation, hold in custody, remain in force **14** have in your hand **15** have a capacity of, have in your hands

*See also* **wrestling**

• **get hold of**
◇ *containment indicator*
**03** get **05** reach **06** obtain **07** acquire, contact, speak to **12** get through to **14** get in touch with, get your hands on **15** communicate with

• **hold back**
**03** bar **04** curb, hang, pull, stop **05** check, delay, pause **06** desist, impede, refuse, retain, retard, shrink, stifle **07** contain, control, forbear, inhibit, prevent, refrain, repress **08** hesitate, keep back, obstruct, restrain, strangle, suppress, withhold

• **hold down**
**03** pin **04** have, keep **06** occupy **07** oppress **08** dominate, keep down, restrain, suppress **09** tyrannize **10** continue in

• **hold fast**
**03** pin **04** clip, nail **05** avast, stick **07** enchain, pin down

• **hold forth**
**04** show, talk **05** orate, speak, spout **06** preach **07** declaim, lecture **08** harangue **09** discourse **12** talk at length **13** speak at length

• **hold off**
**04** wait **05** avoid, defer, delay, repel **06** put off, rebuff, resist **07** fend off, hang off, keep off, ward off **08** fight off, postpone, stave off **09** keep at bay

• **hold on**
**04** grip, stop, wait **05** clasp, cling, grasp, seize **06** clutch, endure, hang on, remain **07** carry on, cling to, survive **08** continue **09** keep going, persevere

• **hold out**
**04** give, last, stay **05** offer, reach **06** endure, extend, hang on, resist **07** carry on, last out, persist, present, proffer, protend, subsist **08** continue **09** persevere, stand fast, stand firm, withstand

• **hold over**
**05** defer, delay **06** put off, shelve **07** adjourn, put back, suspend **08** postpone

• **hold up**
◇ *reversal down indicator*
**03** mug, rob **04** bear, lift, rear, show, slow, stay **05** apply, brace, carry, delay, raise **06** burgle, detain, endure, hinder, impede, nobble, prop up, remain, retard, upbear, uphold **07** bolster, display, exhibit, present, put back, set back, shore up, stick up, support, sustain **08** hold high, knock off, obstruct **09** be in force, break into, knock over, steal from **10** burglarize, remain true **11** remain valid **13** be in operation, remain in force

• **hold with**
**06** accept **07** support **09** agree with, approve of **11** countenance, go along with, subscribe to

• **hold your own**
**06** resist **07** survive **09** stand fast, stand firm, withstand **15** stand your ground

**• put on hold**
**05** defer, delay **06** put off **07** hold off **08** postpone

**holder**
**04** case, rest **05** cover, haver, owner, stand **06** bearer, casing, keeper, sheath **07** housing **08** occupant **09** container, custodian, incumbent, possessor, purchaser **10** proprietor, receptacle

**holdings**
**04** land **05** bonds **06** assets, estate, shares, stocks, tenure **08** property **09** resources **10** real estate, securities **11** investments, possessions

**hold-up**
**03** jam **04** raid, snag, wait **05** delay, heist, hitch, theft **07** break-in, mugging, problem, robbery, setback, stick-up, trouble **08** burglary, stoppage **10** bottleneck, difficulty, stick-up job, traffic jam **11** obstruction

**hole**
**03** cup, den, eye, fix, gap, jam, pit, set, tip **04** bind, bore, cave, dent, drop, dump, flaw, gash, geat, lair, mess, mine, nest, pore, rent, rift, slit, slot, slum, snag, spot, stab, stew, tear, vent **05** break, chasm, crack, delve, error, fault, hovel, notch, scoop, shack, shaft, space, spike, split, thirl, whole **06** breach, burrow, cavern, cavity, corner, covert, crater, defect, dimple, eyelet, hollow, outlet, pickle, pierce, pigpen, pigsty, plight, pocket, recess, scrape **07** chamber, fissure, mistake, opening, orifice, pothole **08** aperture, hot water, loophole, puncture, quandary, weakness **09** deep water, perforate **10** depression, difficulty, excavation, pretty pass, subterfuge **11** discrepancy, perforation, predicament **13** inconsistency

*See also* **fingerhole**

**• hole in one**
**03** ace

**• hole up**
**04** hide **06** lie low **09** take cover **10** go to ground **12** go into hiding **15** conceal yourself

**• pick holes in**
**04** slag **05** slate **07** nit-pick, run down, slag off **09** criticize **12** pull to pieces **13** find fault with

**hole-and-corner**
**06** covert, secret, sneaky **07** furtive **08** back-door, hush-hush, stealthy **09** secretive, underhand **10** backstairs **11** clandestine **13** surreptitious **15** under-the-counter

**holiday**
**03** vac **04** fete, play, rest, trip, wake **05** break, festa, leave, wakes **06** day off, fiesta, recess **07** half-day, high day, holy day, play-day, time off **08** feast day, festival, fly-drive, furlough, half-term, leisure, vacation **09** honeymoon, minibreak, saint's day **11** anniversary, bank holiday, celebration, package tour **12** legal holiday, long vacation **13** public holiday **14** leave of absence

*National holidays include:*

**05** UN Day
**07** Flag Day
**08** Anzac Day, Unity Day
**09** Labour Day, Women's Day
**10** Culture Day, Freedom Day, Martyrs' Day, Mothers' Day, Victory Day
**11** Bastille Day, National Day, Republic Day
**12** Armistice Day, Australia Day, Children's Day, Discovery Day, Thanksgiving
**13** King's Birthday, Liberation Day, Revolution Day
**14** Armed Forces Day, Queen's Birthday, Remembrance Day, Unification Day
**15** Constitution Day, Emancipation Day, Independence Day

**holier-than-thou**
**04** smug **05** pious **08** priggish, unctuous **09** pietistic, religiose **10** complacent, goody-goody **13** sanctimonious, self-approving, self-righteous, self-satisfied

**holiness**
**05** piety **06** purity **07** halidom **08** divinity, goodness, sanctity **09** godliness **10** dedication, devoutness, perfection, sacredness, sanctimony **11** blessedness, saintliness, sinlessness **12** consecration, spirituality, virtuousness **13** religiousness, righteousness

**holler**
**03** cry **04** bawl, call, howl, roar, yell, yelp, yowl **05** cheer, shout, whoop **06** bellow, shriek **07** clamour

**hollow**
**03** cup, dig, dip, how, lap, low, pan, pit **04** boss, bowl, cave, comb, dale, deaf, deep, dell, dent, dish, dull, flat, glen, hole, howe, khud, nook, sham, vain, vale, void, vola, well **05** basin, chasm, clean, combe, coomb, delve, empty, false, gorge, gouge, niche, scoop, womby **06** burrow, cavern, cavity, cirque, coombe, cranny, crater, dimple, dingle, furrow, futile, groove, indent, ravine, recess, sunken, trough, tunnel, unreal, vacant, valley **07** caved-in, channel, concave, deep-set, dishing, echoing, muffled, Pyrrhic, unsound, useless, vacuity **08** coreless, excavate, fleeting, fossette, indented, inflated, rumbling, unfilled **09** cavernous, concavity, deceitful, deceptive, depressed, emptiness, fruitless, incurvate, insincere, of no avail, pointless, pretended, valueless, worthless **10** artificial, completely, depression, excavation, profitless, semicirque, unavailing **11** indentation, meaningless, reverberant **12** hypocritical

**• beat someone hollow**
**04** lick, rout **05** crash **06** hammer, thrash **07** clobber, trounce **09** devastate, overwhelm, slaughter **10** annihilate **13** defeat soundly

**holly**
**04** holm, ilex, mate **06** yaupon **13** Aquifoliaceae

**holmium**
**02** Ho

**holocaust**
**05** Shoah **06** flames, pogrom **07** carnage, inferno **08** disaster, genocide, hecatomb, massacre **09** cataclysm, sacrifice, slaughter **10** extinction, immolation, mass murder **11** catastrophe, destruction, devastation **12** annihilation **13** conflagration, extermination **15** ethnic cleansing

**holy**
**02** pi **04** good, pure **05** godly, moral, pious, saint **06** devout, divine, sacred **07** blessed, perfect, revered, saintly, sinless **08** faithful, hallowed, virtuous **09** dedicated, pietistic, religious, righteous, spiritual, venerated **10** God-fearing, sacrosanct, sanctified **11** consecrated **13** sanctimonious

**• holy book** *see* **Bible**

**holy of holies**
**05** altar **06** shrine **07** sanctum **12** inner sanctum **13** most holy place

**homage**
**03** awe **06** esteem, honour, manred, praise, regard **07** incense, manrent, respect, service, tribute, worship **08** devotion **09** adoration, adulation, deference, reverence **10** admiration, veneration **11** knee-tribute, recognition **15** acknowledgement

**home**
**02** in **03** den, pad **04** base, digs, flat, goal, nest, semi **05** abode, fount, house, local, place, roots, villa **06** asylum, centre, cradle, family, hostel, inland, libken, native, refuge, source **07** address, blighty, cottage, element, habitat, retreat **08** bungalow, domestic, domicile, dwelling, fireside, homeland, home town, interior, internal, national **09** apartment, effective, household, residence, safe place, searching **10** birthplace, fatherland, habitation, motherland, native town **11** effectively, institution, nursing home **13** children's home, dwelling-place, mother country, native country, place of origin **14** old people's home, retirement home **15** country of origin, residential home, somewhere to live

*See also* **animal**

**• at home**
**02** in **06** at ease, well up, within **07** relaxed, skilled **08** familiar **09** competent, confident **10** conversant **11** comfortable, experienced **13** knowledgeable

**• at home of**
**04** chez

**• bring home**
**05** prove **06** instil **07** impress **08** convince **09** emphasize, inculcate
**• home improvements**
**03** DIY
**• home in on**
**03** aim **05** focus **06** direct **08** pinpoint, zero in on, zoom in on **11** concentrate
**• not at home**
**03** out **04** away
**• nothing to write home about**
**02** OK **04** drab, dull **06** boring **08** inferior, mediocre, ordinary **11** not exciting, predictable **13** no great shakes **14** not interesting

**homecoming**
**06** return **07** arrival **10** coming-back, return home **13** arrival at home

**homeland**
**04** home **10** fatherland, motherland, native land **13** mother country, native country **15** country of origin

**homeless**
**06** exiled, tramps **07** dossers, dossing, evicted, nomadic, outcast, vagrant **08** forsaken, rootless, vagrants **09** abandoned, derelicts, destitute, displaced, itinerant, squatters, unsettled, vagabonds, wandering **10** down-and-out, travellers, travelling **11** down-and-outs, on the street **12** dispossessed, on the streets **13** on the pavement, sleeping rough **14** of no fixed abode
**• homeless person**
**04** hobo, waif **05** skell

**homelessness**
**07** dossing **08** vagrancy **11** abandonment, destitution **12** displacement, no fixed abode, rootlessness **13** sleeping rough

**homely**
**04** cosy, homy, snug, ugly **05** homey, mumsy, plain **06** folksy, modest, russet, simple **07** natural, relaxed **08** cheerful, domestic, everyday, familiar, friendly, homelike, homespun, informal, intimate, ordinary, unlovely **09** welcoming **10** hospitable, unassuming **11** comfortable **12** unattractive **13** unpretentious **15** not much to look at, unprepossessing, unsophisticated

**homer**
**03** cor **09** Maeonides

**homespun**
**04** rude **05** crude, plain, rough **06** coarse, folksy, homely, russet, rustic, simple **07** artless, raploch **08** home-made **09** inelegant, unadorned, unrefined **10** amateurish, unpolished **13** uncomplicated **15** unsophisticated

**homestead**
**04** toft

**homework**
**04** prep **09** spadework **10** groundwork **11** preparation

**homey**
**04** cosy, snug **07** relaxed **08** cheerful, familiar, friendly, homelike, informal, intimate **09** welcoming **10** hospitable **11** comfortable

**homicidal**
**06** bloody, deadly, lethal, mortal **07** violent **08** maniacal **09** murderous **10** sanguinary **12** bloodthirsty, death-dealing

**homicide**
**06** murder **07** killing, slaying **09** bloodshed, slaughter **12** chance-medley, manslaughter **13** assassination

**homily**
**04** talk **05** prone, spiel **06** postil, sermon, speech **07** address, lecture, oration **08** harangue **09** discourse, preaching

**homogeneity**
**07** oneness **08** likeness, sameness **09** agreement **10** consonancy, similarity, similitude, uniformity **11** consistency, resemblance **13** analogousness, comparability, identicalness **14** correspondence

**homogeneous**
**04** akin **05** alike **07** cognate, kindred, similar, the same, uniform **08** of a piece, unvaried **09** analogous, identical, unvarying **10** all the same, comparable, compatible, consistent, harmonious, indiscrete **11** all of a piece, correlative **13** corresponding, of the same kind

**homogeneously**
**07** the same **09** similarly, uniformly **10** all the same **11** all of a piece, identically **12** consistently **13** of the same kind **15** correspondingly

**homogenize**
**04** fuse **05** blend, merge, unite **07** combine **08** coalesce **10** amalgamate **11** make similar, make uniform

**homologous**
**04** like **07** related, similar **08** matching, parallel **09** analogous **10** comparable, equivalent **13** correspondent, corresponding

**homosexual**
**03** gay **04** pink **07** lesbian, same-sex **08** bisexual
*See also* **gay**

**Honduras**
**02** HN **03** HND

**hone**
**04** edge, file, whet **05** grind, point **06** polish **07** develop, sharpen

**honest**
**04** fair, jake, just, open, real, true **05** afald, blunt, clean, frank, legal, moral, plain, round, white **06** aefald, afawld, candid, chaste, dinkum, direct, lawful, seemly, simple, single, square, trusty **07** aefauld, dinky-di, ethical, genuine, sincere, up-front, upright **08** bona fide, dinky-die, even-down, outright, reliable, soothful, straight, truthful, virtuous, yeomanly **09** equitable, impartial, ingenuous, objective, outspoken, reputable, righteous, soothfast **10** above-board, dependable, fair dinkum, forthright, four-square, high-minded, honourable, law-abiding, legitimate, on the level, principled, scrupulous, upstanding **11** respectable, right-minded, trustworthy **12** on the up and up, plain-hearted **13** fair and square, incorruptible, plain-speaking, unpretentious **14** straight as a die **15** straightforward

**honestly**
**04** true **05** truly **06** dinkum, direct, fairly, justly, really, simply, square **07** dinky-di, frankly, legally, morally, plainly, up-front, upright **08** dinky-die, directly, lawfully, straight **09** equitably, ethically, no messing, sincerely, uprightly **10** above board, honourably, on the level, straight up, to be honest, truthfully **11** impartially, in good faith, objectively, on the square **12** legitimately **13** fair and square

**honesty**
**05** faith **06** equity, ethics, honour, lunary, morals, square, virtue **07** balance, candour, decorum, probity, realtie **08** chastity, fairness, fidelity, justness, legality, moonwort, morality, openness, veracity **09** bluntness, frankness, integrity, rectitude, sincerity **10** legitimacy, principles **11** genuineness, objectivity, uprightness **12** explicitness, impartiality, truthfulness **13** outspokenness, plain-speaking, righteousness **14** even-handedness, forthrightness, scrupulousness **15** trustworthiness

**honey**
**03** hon, mel, sis **04** babe **05** sweet **06** nectar **07** sweeten
**• honey buzzard**
**04** pern **07** bee-kite
**• honey guide**
**03** tui
**• honey possum**
**04** tait **08** Tarsipes

**honeyed**
**04** cute, dear, kind **05** sweet **06** lovely, pretty, tender **07** winning **08** charming, engaging, pleasant, pleasing, precious, unctuous **09** agreeable, appealing, beautiful, seductive **10** attractive, delightful, flattering **11** mellifluous **12** affectionate

**honeysuckle**
**06** abelia **08** Lonicera, rewarewa, suckling, woodbind, woodbine **09** anthemion, caprifoil, caprifole, eglantine, snowberry, wolfberry **14** Caprifoliaceae

**Hong Kong**
**02** HK **03** HGK

**honorarium**
**03** fee, pay **06** reward, salary
**07** payment **09** emolument
**10** recompense **12** remuneration

**honorary**
**03** Hon **06** formal, unpaid **07** nominal, titular **09** ex officio, honorific **10** in name only, unofficial

**honour**
**01** A, J, K, Q **03** pay **04** fame, keep, take **05** adorn, award, clear, crown, exalt, glory, izzat, pride, prize, title, value **06** accept, admire, credit, esteem, ethics, favour, fulfil, homage, laurel, morals, praise, purity, regard, renown, repute, revere, reward, trophy, virtue, worthy **07** acclaim, applaud, commend, decency, dignity, execute, glorify, honesty, modesty, observe, perform, probity, respect, tribute, worship **08** accolade, applause, be true to, carry out, celibacy, chastity, decorate, good name, goodness, morality, remember, venerate **09** adoration, celebrate, discharge, innocence, integrity, privilege, recognize, rectitude, reverence, virginity **10** abstinence, admiration, compliment, continence, continency, decoration, estimation, maidenhood, principles, reputation, singleness, veneration **11** acclamation, acknowledge, commemorate, distinction, pay homage to, recognition, self-respect, uprightness **12** commendation, pay tribute to, truthfulness **13** righteousness, temperateness **14** immaculateness, unmarried state **15** acknowledgement, trustworthiness

*Honours include:*

**02** GC, KG, OM, VC
**03** CBE, DBE, DSC, DSO, GBE, KBE, MBE, OBE
**09** Iron Cross
**10** Bronze Star, Grand Cross, knighthood, Silver Star
**11** George Cross, Purple Heart
**12** Order of Merit
**13** Croix de Guerre, Legion of Merit, Medal for Merit, Victoria Cross, Victoria Medal
**14** Légion d'Honneur

• **in honour of**
**02** to **05** after **11** celebrating

**honourable**
**03** Hon **04** fair, good, just, true **05** great, moral, noble, noted, right, white **06** decent, family, famous, honest, trusty, worthy **07** eminent, ethical, notable, sincere, upright **08** reliable, renowned, straight, truthful, virtuous, worthful **09** admirable, ingenuous, reputable, respected, righteous **10** dependable, high-minded, principled, upstanding **11** illustrious, prestigious, respectable, trustworthy **13** distinguished **14** high-principled

**honourably**
**04** well **05** nobly, truly **07** morally **08** decently, honestly, worthily **09** ethically, reputably, sincerely **10** virtuously **11** respectably

**hood**
**02** Al **04** cowl **05** amice, blind, Robin, scarf, snood, visor, vizor **06** almuce, biggin, bonnet, calash, domino, mantle **07** bashlik, capouch, capuche, hoodlum, surtout **08** calyptra, capeline, capuccio, chaperon, trot-cozy **09** calyptera, capelline, chaperone, condition, Nithsdale, trot-cosey

**hoodlum**
**03** yob **04** hood, lout, thug **05** brute, felon, rowdy, tough **06** gunman, mugger, vandal **07** mobster, ruffian **08** criminal, gangster, hooligan, offender **09** bovver boy **10** lawbreaker **11** armed robber

**hoodoo**
**04** jinx **05** magic, spell **06** voodoo **07** bewitch, sorcery **08** wizardry **09** occultism, the occult **10** black magic, divination, necromancy, witchcraft **11** conjuration, enchantment, incantation, the black art

**hoodwink**
**03** con **04** dupe, fool, gull, hide, hoax, rook, seel **05** blear, cheat, trick **06** baffle, delude, have on, outwit, take in **07** deceive, defraud, mislead, swindle **09** bamboozle, blindfold **12** take for a ride **14** get the better of, pull a fast one on

**hoof**
**04** foot, kick **05** cloot, expel **06** ungula **07** trotter **10** cloven hoof

**hoofed**
**08** ungulate **10** horn-footed **11** unguligrade **12** cloven-footed, cloven-hoofed

**hook**
**03** arc, bag, bow, box, dog, fix, hit, peg, rap **04** barb, bend, blow, clip, cuff, curl, gaff, grab, hasp, loop, snig, trap **05** angle, catch, chape, clasp, cleek, clout, crome, crook, curve, elbow, hinge, hitch, knock, punch, snare, thump, uncus **06** attach, becket, enmesh, entrap, excuse, fasten, griple, scythe, secure, sickle, strike, stroke, tenter, wallop **07** attract, cantdog, capture, ensnare, gripple, hamulus, pretext, sniggle **08** crotchet, crummock, entangle, fastener **09** goose-neck, tenaculum **10** tenterhook **13** grappling-iron
• **by hook or by crook**
**07** somehow **10** by any means **11** by some means, come what may **15** one way or another
• **hook, line and sinker**
**05** fully, quite **06** in full, wholly **07** solidly, totally, utterly **08** entirely **09** every inch, perfectly **10** absolutely, altogether, completely, thoroughly **12** heart and soul **13** root and branch **14** in every respect **15** from first to last
• **off the hook**
**07** cleared **08** scot free **09** acquitted, ready-made **10** exonerated, in the clear, vindicated

**hookah**
**06** kalian **07** chillum, nargile, nargily **08** narghile, narghily, nargileh, nargilly **09** narghilly, water pipe **12** hubble-bubble

**hooked**
**04** bent **05** adunc, beaky **06** barbed, beaked, curled, curved, hamate, hamose, hamous, uncate **07** devoted, falcate, hamular **08** addicted, aduncate, aduncous, aquiline, hamulate, obsessed, unciform, uncinate **09** aduncated, dependent, enamoured **10** enthralled **12** sickle-shaped

**hooligan**
**03** ned, yob **04** hoon, lout, thug **05** droog, rough, rowdy, tough **06** apache, mugger, skolly, tsotsi, vandal **07** hoodlum, mobster, ruffian, skollie **08** larrikin, tough guy **09** bovver boy, roughneck **10** delinquent

**hoop**
**04** bail, band, gird, girr, loop, ring, tire **05** round, wheel **06** basket, circle, girdle **07** circlet, sleeper, stirrup, trochus, trundle **08** encircle, hula-hoop **10** laggen-gird

**hoot**
**03** boo, cry, jot, wit **04** beep, call, care, hiss, hoop, howl, jeer, mock, riot, toot, yell **05** blare, comic, joker, laugh, shout, sneer, taunt, whoop **06** scream, shriek **07** screech, ululate, whistle **08** howl down, ridicule **09** character **12** tu-whit tu-whoo **13** amusing person
• **not give a hoot**
**12** not care a toss, not give a damn **13** not be bothered **15** not give a monkey's

**hooter**
**03** owl **04** horn, nose **05** siren
• **little hooter**
**05** owlet

**hop**
**03** fly, nip, pop **04** jump, leap, limp, skip, step, trip **05** bound, dance, disco, frisk, jaunt, opium, party, vault **06** bounce, flight, hobble, prance, social, spring **07** journey, knees-up, shindig **09** excursion **10** fly quickly **11** quick flight
• **caught on the hop**
**07** unready **11** ill-equipped **14** caught in the act, caught unawares
• **stem of hop**
**04** bind, bine

**hope**
**03** aim **04** fear, long, pray, rely, wish **05** await, combe, crave, dream, faith,

inlet, trust, yearn **06** aspire, assume, belief, desire, expect **07** believe, craving, foresee, longing, promise **08** ambition, optimism, prospect, reckon on, yearning **09** assurance, be hopeful, enclosure, esperance, pipe dream **10** anticipate, aspiration, assumption, confidence, conviction, expectance, expectancy **11** be ambitious, contemplate, expectation, hopefulness **12** anticipation **13** look forward to **14** have confidence, pin your hopes on **15** hope against hope

**hopeful**
**04** rosy **06** bright **07** assured, bullish, buoyant **08** aspirant, aspiring, cheerful, pleasant, positive, sanguine **09** confident, expectant, promising **10** auspicious, favourable, gladdening, heartening, optimistic, propitious, reassuring **11** encouraging

**hopefully**
**05** I hope **07** eagerly **08** probably, with hope, with luck **09** bullishly **10** expectedly, sanguinely **11** conceivably, confidently, expectantly **12** all being well **13** if all goes well **14** optimistically

**hopefulness**
**04** wish **05** faith, trust **06** belief, desire **07** craving, longing **08** ambition, optimism, prospect, yearning **09** assurance **10** aspiration, assumption, confidence, conviction **11** expectation **12** anticipation

**hopeless**
◇ *anagram indicator*
**03** bad **04** lost, poor, vain, weak **05** all up, awful, bleak, grave, lousy **06** futile, gloomy, no-hope **07** foolish, forlorn, useless **08** dejected, downcast, helpless, negative, pathetic, wretched **09** all up with, defeatist, desperate, incurable, pointless, worthless **10** despairing, despondent, impossible **11** demoralized, downhearted, incompetent, irreparable, pessimistic **12** beyond remedy, beyond repair, irremediable, irreversible, unachievable, unattainable **13** impracticable **14** past praying for

**hopelessly**
◇ *anagram indicator*
**05** badly **06** weakly **07** awfully **08** gloomily **09** unhappily, uselessly **10** dejectedly, negatively **11** desperately **12** despairingly, despondently, pathetically **13** incompetently, inefficiently **15** pessimistically

**hopelessness**
**05** blues, dumps, gloom **06** misery **07** despair, wanhope **09** dejection, pessimism **10** gloominess **11** despondency, forlorn hope **12** wretchedness **14** discouragement

**hophead** *see* **addict**

**horde**
**03** mob **04** army, band, crew, gang, herd, host, mass, pack **05** crowd, drove, flock, swarm, troop **06** throng **09** multitude

**horizon**
**05** range, scope, verge, vista **07** compass, outlook, skyline **08** prospect **10** experience, perception **11** perspective **13** range of vision

• **on the horizon**
**04** near **05** close **06** at hand, coming **07** brewing, looming **08** imminent, in the air, menacing, on the way **09** impending **11** approaching, forthcoming, in the offing, threatening **13** about to happen, almost upon you **15** fast approaching

**horizontal**
**04** flat **05** level, plane **06** smooth, supine **08** levelled, straight **09** on its side

**hormone**

*Hormones include:*

**05** kinin
**07** gastrin, insulin, relaxin
**08** abscisin, androgen, autacoid, estrogen, florigen, glucagon, oxytocin, secretin, thyroxin
**09** adrenalin, cortisone, melatonin, oestrogen, pituitrin, prolactin, thyroxine
**10** adrenaline, calcitonin
**11** thyrotropin, vasopressin
**12** androsterone, melanotropin, noradrenalin, progesterone, somatostatin, somatotropin, testosterone, thyrotrophin
**14** erythropoietin, glucocorticoid

**horn**
**04** butt, cusp, gore, push **05** bugle, corno, cornu **06** klaxon **07** keratin **08** cornicle, oliphant **09** telephone **10** corniculum **15** corno di bassetto

• **horn band**
**04** frog

• **horn sound**
**03** mot **04** beep, honk, hoot, parp **05** blast

• **part of horn**
**03** bay, bez **04** tray, trey, trez **07** bay-tine, bez-tine **08** brow-tine, trey-tine **09** bay-antler, bez-antler **10** brow-antler, trey-antler

**hornless**
**05** mooly, muley, poley **06** dodded, humble, hummel, mulley, polled

**horny**
**04** hard, sexy **05** corny, randy **06** ardent **07** aroused, callous, lustful, ruttish **08** ceratoid, corneous **09** lecherous **10** keratinous, lascivious, libidinous **12** concupiscent

**horrendous**
**08** dreadful, horrible, horrific, shocking, terrible **09** appalling, frightful **10** horrifying, terrifying **11** frightening

**horrible**
◇ *anagram indicator*
**04** foul, grim, ugly **05** awful, black, grisy, nasty, scary **06** griesy, grisly, grysie, horrid, unkind **07** ghastly, hideous **08** dreadful, gruesome, horrific, shocking, terrible **09** appalling, frightful, harrowing, loathsome, monstrous, obnoxious, offensive, repulsive, revolting **10** abominable, detestable, disgusting, horrendous, horrifying, monstruous, terrifying, unpleasant **11** frightening, hair-raising **12** disagreeable **13** bloodcurdling

**horribly**
◇ *anagram indicator*
**03** ill **06** grimly **07** awfully **08** terribly **09** hideously **10** dreadfully, gruesomely **11** appallingly, frightfully, repulsively **12** disagreeably, horrifically, unpleasantly

**horrid**
◇ *anagram indicator*
**04** grim, mean **05** awful, cruel, nasty, rough **06** shaggy, unkind **07** beastly, ghastly, hateful, hideous **08** dreadful, gruesome, horrific, shocking, terrible **09** appalling, bristling, frightful, harrowing, obnoxious, repellent, repulsive, revolting **10** abominable, detestable, horrifying, terrifying **11** frightening, hair-raising **13** bloodcurdling

**horrific**
◇ *anagram indicator*
**05** awful, scary **07** ghastly **08** dreadful, gruesome, shocking, terrible **09** appalling, frightful, harrowing **10** horrifying, terrifying **11** frightening **13** bloodcurdling

**horrifically**
**07** awfully **08** terribly **10** dreadfully, shockingly **11** appallingly, frightfully, repulsively **12** disagreeably

**horrify**
**05** abhor, alarm, appal, panic, repel, scare, shock, spook **06** agrise, agrize, agryze, dismay, offend, revolt, sicken **07** disgust, outrage, startle, terrify **08** frighten, nauseate **09** terrorize **10** intimidate, scandalize **12** put the wind up, scare to death

**horror**
**04** fear, hate **05** alarm, dread, panic, shock **06** dismay, fright, terror **07** disgust, outrage **08** distaste, loathing **09** awfulness, revulsion **10** abhorrence, raggedness, repugnance, shagginess, shuddering **11** abomination, detestation, ghastliness, hideousness, trepidation **12** apprehension **13** consternation, frightfulness **14** unpleasantness

• **horror film**
**07** chiller **10** hair raiser

**horror-struck**
**06** aghast **07** shocked, stunned **08** appalled **09** horrified, petrified,

terrified **10** frightened **11** scared stiff **14** horror-stricken

**hors d'oeuvre**
**04** meze **05** mezze **06** hummus, matjes **07** ceviche, maatjes, zakuska **08** crudités **09** antipasto, carpaccio **11** smörgåsbord

**horse**
**01** H **02** GG **03** pad **04** crib, hack, hoss, moke, pony, prad, yaud **05** filly, mount, neddy **06** dobbin, gee-gee, heroin, keffel, sorrel **07** broncho, cavalry, centaur, charger, trotter **08** yarraman

*See also* **animal**; **heroin**; **pony**

*Horses and ponies include:*

**03** Don
**04** Arab, Barb, Fell
**05** Dales, Iomud, Lokai, Pinto, Shire, Toric, Waler, Welsh
**06** Auxois, Breton, Brumby, Exmoor, Morgan, Nonius, Tersky
**07** Comtois, Criollo, Finnish, Furioso, Hackney, Hispano, Jutland, Masuren, Muraköz, Murgese, Mustang, Salerno
**08** Budyonny, Danubian, Dartmoor, Friesian, Highland, Holstein, Kabardin, Karabair, Karabakh, Lusitano, Palomino, Paso Fino, Poitevin, Shetland, Welsh Cob
**09** Akhal-Teké, Alter-Réal, Anglo-Arab, Appaloosa, Ardennias, Brabançon, Calabrese, Connemara, Falabella, Groningen, Kladruber, Knabstrup, Kustanair, Maremmana, New Forest, New Kirgiz, Oldenburg, Percheron, Sardinian, Tchenaran, Trakehner, Welsh Pony
**10** Andalusian, Boulonnais, Clydesdale, Einsiedler, Freiberger, Gelderland, Hanoverian, Lipizzaner, Mangalarga, Shagya Arab
**11** Anglo-Norman, Døle Trotter, Irish Hunter, Mecklenburg, Przewalski's, Trait du Nord, Württemberg
**12** Cleveland Bay, Dutch Draught, East Friesian, French Saddle, Irish Draught, Metis Trotter, North Swedish, Orlov Trotter, Suffolk Punch, Thoroughbred
**13** East Bulgarian, Frederiksborg, French Trotter, German Trotter, Welsh Mountain
**14** American Saddle, Latvian Harness, Plateau Persian
**15** American Quarter, American Trotter, Swedish Halfbred

*Points of a horse include:*

**03** ear, eye, hip
**04** back, chin, dock, face, head, heel, hock, hoof, knee, lips, mane, neck, nose, poll, ribs, rump, shin, tail
**05** atlas, belly, canon, cheek, chest, crest, croup, elbow, ergot, flank, girth, loins, mouth, thigh
**06** breast, cannon, gaskin, haunch, muzzle, sheath, stifle, temple, throat
**07** abdomen, brisket, buttock, coronet, crupper, fetlock, forearm, hind leg, pastern, quarter, shannon, tendons, withers
**08** chestnut, forefoot, forehead, forelock, lower jaw, lower lip, nostrils, shoulder, under lip, upper lip, windpipe
**09** hamstring, hock joint, nasal peak
**10** chin groove, point of hip, wall of foot
**11** back tendons, point of hock, stifle joint
**12** fetlock joint, hindquarters, hollow of heel, point of elbow
**13** dock of the tail, flexor tendons, jugular groove, root of the tail
**14** Achilles tendon, crest of the neck
**15** point of shoulder

*Horses' tack includes:*

**03** bit
**05** arson, cinch, girth, hames, reins
**06** bridle, cantle, collar, halter, numnah, pommel, saddle, traces
**07** alforja, crupper, housing, stirrup
**08** backband, blinders, blinkers, noseband, shabrack
**09** bellyband, breeching, hackamore, headstall, saddlebag, saddlebow, saddlepad, surcingle
**10** martingale, saddletree, shabracque, throatlash
**11** bearing rein, saddlecloth, saddle-girth, throatlatch
**13** saddle blanket

*See also* **bridle**

*Horse-related terms include:*

**03** bay, cob, dun, hie, hup, nag, shy
**04** bolt, buck, colt, foal, gait, grey, mare, roan, stud, trot, walk
**05** break, forge, gee up, groom, hands, lunge, mount, nappy, pinto, steed
**06** bronco, brumby, canter, equine, gallop, hippic, livery, manège, riding, stable
**07** astride, blanket, gelding, giddy-up, hacking, nosebag, paddock, passade, piebald
**08** chestnut, dismount, horse box, skewbald, stallion
**09** horseshoe, roughshod
**10** blood horse, draft horse, en cavalier, equestrian, heavy horse, side-saddle
**11** riding habit
**12** broken-winded, pony-trekking, thoroughbred
**13** champ at the bit, mounting block, put out to grass
**14** strawberry roan

*Racehorses include:*

**05** Arkle, Cigar, Pinza
**06** Nearco, Red Rum, Sir Ken
**07** Alleged, Dawn Run, Eclipse, Phar Lap, Sceptre, Shergar, Sir Ivor
**08** Aldaniti, Best Mate, Corbiere, Esha Ness, Hyperion, Istabraq, Mill Reef, Nijinsky
**09** John Henry, L'Escargot, Oh So Sharp
**10** Night Nurse, Persian War, Seabiscuit, See You Then, Sun Chariot
**11** Cottage Rake, Never Say Die, Pretty Polly
**12** Dancing Brave, Desert Orchid, Golden Miller, Hatton's Grace

*See also* **racecourse**; **racing**

• **call to horse**
**03** hie, hup **04** high, proo, pruh

• **inferior horse**
**03** nag, rip **04** moke

• **pair of horses**
**04** span

• **shying horse**
**03** jib **06** jibber

• **thin horse**
**04** rake

• **working horse**
**03** cut

• **worn-out horse**
**03** tit **04** jade, plug **07** knacker

**horsefly**
**04** cleg

**horseman, horsewoman**
**05** rider **06** hussar, jockey, knight **07** dragoon, hobbler, pricker **08** stradiot, wrangler **09** caballero **10** cavalryman, equestrian **12** horse soldier

*Horseriders, jockeys and trainers include:*

**04** **Anne** (Princess), **Hern** (Major Dick), **Leng** (Virginia), **Pipe** (Martin), **Tait** (Blyth), **Todd** (Mark)
**05** **Cecil** (Henry), **Green** (Lucinda), **Krone** (Julie), **Lukas** (D Wayne), **McCoy** (Tony), **Meade** (Richard), **Smith** (Harvey), **Smith** (Robyn)
**06** **Arcaro** (Eddie), **Archer** (Fred), **Carson** (Willie), **Eddery** (Pat), **Fallon** (Keiren), **O'Brien** (Vincent), **O'Neill** (Jonjo), **Pitman** (Jenny)
**07** **Dettori** (Frankie), **Francis** (Dick), **Gifford** (Josh), **Piggott** (Lester), **Winkler** (Hans Günter)
**08** **Champion** (Bob), **Donoghue** (Steve), **Dunwoody** (Richard), **Phillips** (Captain Mark), **Richards** (Sir Gordon)
**09** **Scudamore** (Peter), **Shoemaker** (Willie)

*See also* **equestrian**

**horseplay**
**03** rag **06** antics, capers, pranks **07** foolery, fooling **08** clowning **09** high jinks **10** buffoonery, skylarking, tomfoolery **11** fun and games **13** fooling around **14** monkey business, practical jokes, rough-and-tumble

**horsepower**
**02** CV, hp, PS

**horseradish tree**
**03** ben

**horsewoman** *see* **horseman, horsewoman**

**hortatory**
**03** pep **08** didactic, edifying, inciting **09** homiletic, hortative, practical **10** heartening, preceptive **11** encouraging, exhortative, exhortatory, inspiriting, instructive, stimulating

**horticulture**
**09** gardening **11** agriculture, cultivation **12** floriculture **13** arboriculture

**hosanna**
**06** praise, save us **07** worship **08** alleluia **09** laudation

**hose**
**03** sox **04** duct, pipe, tube **05** socks **06** piping, trunks, tubing **07** airline, channel, conduit **08** chausses **09** stockings **12** galligaskins

**hosiery**
**04** hose **05** socks **06** tights **07** hold-ups, stay-ups **08** leggings **09** stockings **12** leg-coverings

**hospitable**
**04** kind, warm **05** cadgy **06** genial, kidgie **07** cordial, helpful, liberal **08** amicable, friendly, generous, gracious, sociable **09** bountiful, congenial, convivial, receptive, welcoming **10** open-handed **11** kind-hearted, neighbourly

**hospital**
**01** H **03** CHE, san **04** GOSH, Guy's, home, lock, MASH **05** Bart's **06** clinic, spital **07** hospice, spittle **08** clinique, nuthouse, snake-pit **09** ambulance, funny farm, hôtel-Dieu, infirmary, institute, leprosery **10** booby hatch, leproserie, polyclinic, sanatorium **11** nursing home **12** health centre **13** lunatic asylum, medical centre

**• hospital department**
**03** ENT **04** gyny **05** A and E **08** casualty

**hospitality**
**05** cheer **06** warmth **07** welcome **08** kindness **09** open house **10** generosity, liberality, philoxenia **11** helpfulness, sociability **12** congeniality, conviviality, friendliness, housekeeping **13** accommodation, entertainment **14** open-handedness, tea and sympathy **15** neighbourliness

**host**
◇ *containment indicator*
**02** MC **03** mob **04** army, band, give, herd, mass, pack **05** array, crowd, crush, emcee, horde, swarm, troop **06** anchor, myriad, throng **07** compère, linkman, present **08** landlady, landlord, publican **09** anchorman, announcer, harbinger, innkeeper, introduce, multitude, presenter **10** party-giver, proprietor **11** anchorwoman, entertainer **12** proprietress

**hostage**
**04** pawn **06** pledge, surety **07** captive **08** detainee, prisoner, security

**hostel**
**01** Y **03** inn **04** hall, YMCA, YWCA **05** entry, hotel, motel **07** hospice, pension **08** hospital **09** dormitory, dosshouse, flophouse, residence **10** guesthouse **11** youth hostel **13** boarding-house **15** bed-and-breakfast

**hostelry**
**03** bar, inn, pub **05** hotel, motel **06** tavern **07** canteen, pension **09** public bar **10** guesthouse **11** public house **13** boarding-house

**hostile**
**03** icy **05** enemy **06** averse, infest, wintry **07** adverse, glacial, opposed, warlike, wintery **08** contrary, inimical, opposite **09** bellicose, oppugnant **10** aggressive, inveterate, malevolent, unfriendly **11** adversarial, belligerent, disinclined, ill-disposed **12** antagonistic, antipathetic, disapproving, inauspicious, inhospitable, unfavourable **13** unsympathetic **14** at daggers drawn

**• become hostile**
**04** rise

**hostilities**
**03** war **04** arms **06** action, battle, strife **07** warfare **08** conflict, fighting **09** bloodshed

**hostility**
**03** war **04** envy, hate **05** anger **06** animus, enmity, hatred, malice **07** cruelty, dislike, ill-will **08** aversion, disfavor **09** animosity, antipathy, disfavour, militancy, prejudice **10** abhorrence, aggression, antagonism, bitterness, opposition, resentment **11** bellicosity, malevolence **12** belligerence, estrangement, hard feelings **14** unfriendliness, unpleasantness

**hot**
**01** h **02** in **03** het, hip, new, red **04** chic, cool, keen, warm **05** angry, balmy, eager, fiery, fresh, funky, livid, quick, ritzy, sharp, spicy **06** ardent, baking, fervid, fierce, fuming, glitzy, heated, latest, modern, piping, raging, recent, red hot, snazzy, spiced, stolen, strong, sultry, swanky, torrid, trendy, uncool, with it **07** boiling, burning, candent, current, devoted, earnest, enraged, flushed, furious, illicit, intense, in vogue, lustful, peppery, piquant, popular, pungent, searing, stylish, summery, violent, zealous **08** animated, diligent, exciting, feverish, incensed, inflamed, parching, pilfered, powerful, roasting, scalding, seething, sizzling, steaming, swinging, toasting, tropical, up-to-date, vehement **09** cut-throat, dangerous, delirious, dog-eat-dog, ill-gotten, indignant, scorching **10** all the rage, blistering, candescent, contraband, passionate, prevailing, sweltering **11** fashionable **12** contemporary, enthusiastic, incandescent **13** up-to-the-minute

*See also* **warm**

**• be hot**
**04** boil

**• blow hot and cold**
**04** sway **05** haver, waver **08** hesitate, hum and ha **09** fluctuate, hum and haw, oscillate, temporize, vacillate **10** dilly-dally **12** shilly-shally

**• feel hot**
**04** burn

**• hot air**
**03** gas **04** bosh, bunk, crap, foam **05** bilge, froth **06** bunkum, piffle, vapour **07** baloney, blather, blether, bluster, bombast, eyewash, vapours **08** blethers, claptrap, cobblers, nonsense, verbiage **09** bullswool, emptiness, empty talk, mere words **10** balderdash, codswallop

**hotbed**
**03** den **04** hive, nest **06** cradle, school **07** nursery, seedbed **08** seed plot **12** forcing-house **14** breeding-ground

**hot-blooded**
**04** bold, rash, wild **05** eager, fiery, lusty **06** ardent, heated **07** fervent, lustful, sensual **08** spirited **09** excitable, impetuous, impulsive, irritable, perfervid **10** passionate **11** precipitate **12** high-spirited, homothermous **13** temperamental

**hotchpotch**
◇ *anagram indicator*
**03** mix, pie **04** mess **06** jumble, medley **07** melange, mixture **08** mishmash **09** confusion, potpourri **10** collection, hodgepodge, miscellany

**hotel**
**01** H **03** inn, pub **04** Ritz **05** botel, hydro, motel **06** boatel, hostel, tavern **07** Gasthof, pension **08** Gasthaus, hostelry **09** flophouse **10** aparthotel, guesthouse, trust house **11** hydropathic, public house **13** boarding-house, sporting house **15** bed and breakfast

**• hotel employee**
**04** chef, page **05** boots **06** porter **07** bell boy, bell hop **11** chambermaid

**hotfoot**
**07** flat out, hastily, in haste, quickly, rapidly, swiftly **08** pell-mell, speedily **09** hurriedly, posthaste **10** at top speed **11** at the double **12** lickety-split, without delay **13** helter-skelter **14** at a rate of knots, hell for leather **15** like the clappers

**• hotfoot it**
**04** belt, dash, pelt, race, rush, tear, zoom **05** hurry, speed **06** career, gallop, hurtle, sprint **07** quicken **08** step on it **09** bowl along **10** accelerate **15** put your foot down

**hothead**
**06** madcap, madman, terror
**07** hotspur **08** cacafogo, tearaway
**09** cacafuego, daredevil, desperado

**hotheaded**
**04** rash, wild **05** fiery, hasty
**08** reckless, volatile, volcanic
**09** excitable, explosive, foolhardy, impetuous, impulsive, irascible
**10** headstrong **11** hot-tempered
**13** quick-tempered, short-tempered

**hothouse**
**05** stove **06** vinery **07** brothel
**08** orangery **10** glasshouse, greenhouse **12** conservatory, forcing-house

**hotly**
**04** near, nigh **06** keenly, nearly
**07** closely, tightly **08** ardently, fiercely, narrowly, strongly **09** fervently, intensely **10** forcefully, vehemently, vigorously **12** at close range, passionately **15** at close quarters

**hot-tempered**
**05** fiery, hasty, ratty, testy **07** crabbit, stroppy, violent **08** choleric, petulant, volcanic **09** explosive, irascible, irritable **10** splenative **13** quick-tempered, short-tempered

**hound**
**03** dog, nag **04** goad, hunt, lime, lyam, lyme, prod, urge **05** brach, bully, chase, drive, force, harry, stalk, track, trail
**06** badger, basset, beagle, chivvy, follow, harass, jowler, pester, pursue, talbot, tufter **07** coondog, disturb, provoke **08** hunt down **09** persecute

**• pack of hounds**
**03** cry **04** hunt **06** kennel

**hour**
**01** h **02** hr

*Hours include:*

**04** rush
**05** flexi, happy, lunch, small
**06** dinner, golden, office, waking
**07** trading, working
**08** business, eleventh, midnight, unsocial, visiting, witching

*See also* **canonical**

**• early hours**
**02** am

**• outside hours**
**04** kerb

**house**
◇ *containment indicator*
**02** ho **03** Hse, inn, ken, mas, pad
**04** body, casa, clan, door, firm, gaff, hame, hold, home, keep, line, race
**05** bingo, blood, board, cover, crowd, guard, lodge, place, put up, store, tribe
**06** billet, family, ménage, reside, strain, take in **07** chamber, company, contain, convent, dynasty, harbour, kindred, lineage, protect, quarter, sheathe, shelter, turnout, viewers **08** ancestry, assembly, audience, building, business, congress, domestic, domicile, dwelling
**09** gathering, household, listeners, onlookers, residence **10** auditorium, enterprise, habitation, parliament, spectators **11** accommodate, corporation, have room for, legislature
**12** family circle, have space for, organization **13** establishment

*Houses include:*

**03** hut
**04** flat, hall, semi, weem
**05** croft, igloo, lodge, manor, manse, shack, villa, whare
**06** bedsit, chalet, duplex, grange, mia-mia, pondok, prefab, shanty, studio, wurley
**07** cottage, mansion, rectory
**08** bungalow, detached, hacienda, log cabin, terraced, vicarage
**09** apartment, but and ben, farmhouse, homestead, parsonage, penthouse, single-end, town house, treehouse, villa home, villa unit
**10** granny flat, maisonette, pied-à-terre, ranch house, state house
**11** condominium
**12** council house, semi-detached
**14** chalet bungalow
**15** thatched cottage

*See also* **accommodation**; **building**; **zodiac**

**• House of Commons**
**02** HC

**• House of Lords**
**02** HL

**• on the house**
**04** free **06** gratis **08** at no cost **10** for nothing **11** without cost **12** free of charge **13** at no extra cost, without charge **14** without payment

**household**
**04** home **05** house, plain, set-up
**06** common, family, famous, ménage, people **08** domestic, everyday, familiar, ordinary **09** well-known
**11** established **12** family circle
**13** establishment

*Household items include:*

**03** bin, mop
**04** comb, hook, pram, vase
**05** broom, brush, diary, match, potty, range, towel
**06** basket, candle, duster, pet bed, sponge
**07** ashtray, coaster, dustpan, flannel, key rack, key ring, wash bag
**08** aquarium, bassinet, birdcage, calendar, coat hook, dish rack, fish tank, flatiron, hat stand, hip flask, ornament, place mat, shoe rack, soap dish, suitcase, tea towel, waste bin, wine rack
**09** cat basket, dishcloth, dog basket, door wedge, fireguard, hairbrush, hearth rug, highchair, memo board, phone book, pushchair, sponge bag, stair gate, stepstool, towel rail, washboard, washcloth
**10** baby bottle, baby walker, coathanger, laundry bag, letter rack, oven gloves, photo album, photo frame, stepladder, storage box, toothbrush
**11** address book, candlestick, changing mat, first aid kit, paperweight, toilet brush
**12** clothes airer, clothes-brush, clothes horse, ironing board, magazine rack, perambulator, picnic basket, thermos flask
**13** feather duster, laundry basket, satellite dish, soap dispenser, umbrella stand, washing-up bowl
**14** hot water bottle, phone directory
**15** draught excluder, photograph album, photograph frame

**householder**
**05** owner **06** tenant **07** goodman, gude-man **08** landlady, landlord, occupant, occupier, resident
**09** home-owner **10** freeholder, proprietor **11** leaseholder **13** owner-occupier

**housekeeping**
**08** domestic **10** homemaking
**11** hospitality, housewifery
**12** domestic work, running a home
**13** home economics **15** domestic matters, domestic science

**houseman**
**05** valet **06** butler, doctor, intern
**07** interne, servant **08** resident, retainer **10** manservant **12** house-surgeon, junior doctor **14** house-physician

**house-trained**
**04** tame **05** tamed **11** house-broken
**12** domesticated, well-mannered

**housing**
◇ *containment indicator*
**04** case **05** cover, guard, homes
**06** casing, holder, houses, jacket, sheath **07** shelter **08** covering, shabrack **09** container, dwellings
**10** habitation, protection, shabracque
**13** accommodation

**hovel**
**03** hut **04** dump, hole, shed, slum
**05** cabin, shack, whare **06** kennel, shanty **07** shelter

**hover**
**03** fly **04** flap, hang, hove, wave
**05** drift, float, hoove, pause, poise, waver **06** linger, loiter, seesaw
**07** flutter **08** hesitate **09** alternate, fluctuate, hang about, oscillate, vacillate **10** helicopter **11** be suspended

**however**
**03** but, yet **05** howbe, still **06** anyhow, even so, though **07** howbeit
**08** actually **09** as it comes, howsoever, in any case, leastways, leastwise **10** howsomever, leastaways, regardless
**11** howsomdever, just the same, nonetheless **12** nevertheless
**13** at the same time
**15** notwithstanding

**howl**
**03** bay, cry, wow **04** bawl, gowl, hoot, moan, roar, wail, yawl, yell, yelp, yowl **05** groan, laugh, shout **06** bellow, scream, shriek

**howler**
**04** boob, flub, goof **05** boner, error, fluff, gaffe **07** bloomer, blunder, clanger, mistake, Mycetes **08** solecism **11** malapropism

**HQ** *see* **headquarters**

**hub**
**03** hob **04** axis, boss, core, nave **05** focus, heart, pivot **06** centre, middle **08** linchpin **10** focal point **11** nerve centre

**hubbub**
**03** din, row **04** coil, riot **05** chaos, noise **06** racket, rumpus, tumult, uproar **07** clamour, whoobub **08** disorder, hubbuboo, rowdedow, rowdydow **09** commotion, confusion, level-coil **10** hullabaloo, hurly-burly **11** disturbance, pandemonium

**hubris**
**05** nerve, pride, scorn **06** vanity **07** conceit, disdain, egotism, hauteur **08** boasting, contempt **09** arrogance, contumely, insolence, lordiness, pomposity **11** haughtiness, overweening, presumption, superiority **12** snobbishness **13** condescension, imperiousness **14** high-handedness, self-importance

**huckster**
**04** hawk **06** barker, dealer, hawker, kidder, peddle, pedlar, tinker, trader, vendor **07** haggler, kiddier, packman, pitcher **11** salesperson

**huddle**
**04** cram, heap, herd, knot, mass, meet, pack, ruck **05** clump, crowd, flock, hunch, press **06** bundle, crouch, cuddle, curl up, fumble, gather, hustle, jumble, muddle, nestle, pester, powwow, throng **07** cluster, meeting, snuggle, squeeze **08** conclave, converge **09** confusion, gravitate **10** conference, congregate, discussion **12** consultation

**hue**
**03** dye, hew **04** tint, tone **05** color, light, shade, tinge **06** aspect, chroma, colour, nuance **07** clamour **08** shouting **10** appearance, complexion

**hue and cry**
**03** ado **04** fuss, to-do **05** chase, hoo-ha, tizzy **06** furore, outcry, rumpus, uproar **07** carry-on, clamour, ruction **08** ballyhoo, brouhaha **09** commotion, kerfuffle **10** hullabaloo **13** a song and dance

**huff**
**03** pet **04** mood, rage, stew, tiff **05** anger, bully, paddy, pique, snuff, sulks **06** hector, strunt **07** bad mood, bluster, passion **09** blusterer

**huffily**
**07** angrily, crossly, in a huff **08** in a paddy, in a strop, morosely, snappily **09** in a temper, irritably, peevishly **11** resentfully

**huffy**
**05** angry, cross, moody, short, sulky, surly, testy **06** crusty, grumpy, miffed, moping, morose, shirty, snappy, snuffy, touchy **07** crabbed, peevish, stroppy, waspish **08** offended, petulant **09** crotchety, irritable, querulous, resentful **10** hoity-toity **11** disgruntled

**hug**
◇ *containment indicator*
**01** O **04** coll, grip, hold **05** clasp, press **06** clinch, clutch, cuddle, enfold **07** cherish, cling to, embrace, enclose, snuggle, squeeze **08** stay near **09** hold close **11** keep close to, stay close to **13** follow closely

**huge**
**02** OS **03** big **04** mega, vast **05** bulky, enorm, giant, great, heavy, jumbo, large **06** immane **07** hideous, hugeous, immense, mammoth, massive, socking, titanic **08** colossal, enormous, gigantic, unwieldy **09** cavernous, extensive, frightful, gigantean, ginormous, Herculean, humongous, humungous, monstrous, swingeing **10** Babylonian, gargantuan, monumental, prodigious, stupendous, tremendous **11** mountainous, stupendious

**hugely**
**04** very **06** highly, really, vastly **07** awfully, greatly, largely **08** terribly, very much **09** extremely, immensely, massively **10** enormously, thoroughly **11** frightfully **12** terrifically, tremendously **15** extraordinarily

**hugger-mugger**
**03** sly **06** closet, covert, hidden, secret, sneaky, untidy **07** chaotic, furtive, jumbled, mixed-up, muddled, private, secrecy **08** backroom, confused, stealthy **09** concealed, confusion, underhand **10** behind-door, disordered, disorderly, fraudulent, out of order, undercover **11** clandestine, disarranged, underground **12** disorganized **13** surreptitious **14** cloak-and-dagger **15** under-the-counter

**Hughes**
**03** Ted

**hulk**
**03** oaf **04** clod, hull, lout, lump **05** frame, shell, wreck **06** lubber **07** remains **08** derelict **09** shipwreck **10** clodhopper

**hulking**
**03** big **05** bulky, heavy, large **06** clumsy **07** awkward, massive, weighty **08** ungainly, unwieldy **09** lumbering **10** cumbersome

**hull**
**03** pod **04** body, bulk, husk, pare, peel, rind, skin, trim **05** frame, shell, shuck, strip **06** casing, legume **07** capsule, epicarp **08** covering, skeleton **09** framework, monocoque, structure

**hullabaloo**
**03** din, hue **04** fuss, to-do **05** hoo-ha, noise, tizzy **06** furore, hubbub, outcry, racket, rumpus, tumult, uproar **07** carry-on, palaver, ruction, turmoil **08** ballyhoo, brouhaha, razmataz **09** commotion, hue and cry, kerfuffle **10** razzmatazz **11** disturbance, pandemonium, razzamatazz **13** a song and dance

**hum**
**03** bum **04** buzz, hoax, lilt, purr, sing **05** chirm, croon, drone, pulse, sough, throb, thrum, whirr **06** be busy, mumble, murmur **07** applaud, buzzing, purring, vibrate **08** whirring **09** bombilate, bombinate, pulsation, throbbing, vibration **10** imposition

• **hum and haw**
**04** sway **05** waver **06** dither **08** hesitate **09** fluctuate, oscillate, vacillate **10** dilly-dally **12** be indecisive, shilly-shally **14** blow hot and cold

**human**
**03** man **04** body, kind, soul, weak **05** child, woman **06** genial, humane, mortal, person **07** fleshly **08** fallible, physical, rational, tolerant **09** anthropic **10** anthropoid, human being, individual, reasonable, vulnerable **11** anthropical, considerate, Homo sapiens, susceptible, sympathetic **13** compassionate, flesh and blood, understanding

• **human affairs**
**04** life

**humane**
**04** good, kind, mild **06** benign, gentle, kindly, loving, polite, tender **07** elegant, lenient **08** generous, merciful **09** classical, forgiving **10** benevolent, charitable, forbearing, humanizing, thoughtful **11** considerate, good-natured, kind-hearted, sympathetic **12** humanitarian **13** compassionate, understanding

**humanely**
**06** gently, kindly, mildly **08** lovingly, tenderly **10** generously, mercifully **12** thoughtfully **13** kind-heartedly **15** compassionately, sympathetically

**humanitarian**
**04** kind **06** humane **07** welfare **08** altruist, do-gooder, generous **09** unselfish **10** altruistic, benefactor, benevolent, charitable **11** considerate, sympathetic **13** compassionate, good Samaritan, philanthropic, understanding **14** philanthropist, public-spirited

**humanitarianism**
**07** charity **08** goodwill, humanism **10** generosity **11** beneficence, benevolence **12** philanthropy **14** charitableness, loving-kindness

**humanities**
**04** arts **08** classics **10** literature, philosophy **11** liberal arts

**humanity**
**03** man **04** pity **05** mercy **06** mandom, people, ubuntu **07** mankind, mortals **08** goodness, goodwill, kindness, sympathy **09** humankind, human race, mortality, tolerance, womankind **10** compassion, generosity, gentleness, humaneness, tenderness **11** benevolence, Homo sapiens **13** brotherly love, fellow-feeling, understanding **14** thoughtfulness **15** kind-heartedness

**humanize**
**04** tame **05** edify **06** better, polish, refine **07** educate, improve **08** civilize **09** cultivate, enlighten **11** domesticate

**humankind**
**03** man **06** people **07** mankind, mortals **08** humanity **09** human race, mortality, womankind **11** Homo sapiens

**humanness**
**08** goodness, goodwill, humanity, kindness, sympathy **09** tolerance **10** compassion, generosity, gentleness, tenderness **11** benevolence, human nature **13** understanding **14** thoughtfulness **15** kind-heartedness

**humble**
**03** low **04** base, mean, meek, poor, sink **05** abase, crush, lower, lowly, plain, pluck, shame, silly, small **06** abased, common, demean, demiss, hummel, modest, polite, simple, subdue **07** afflict, awnless, chasten, deflate, degrade, depress, mortify, servile **08** belittle, bring low, disgrace, hornless, inferior, ordinary, yeomanly **09** afflicted, bring down, demissive, discredit, disparage, humiliate, prideless, unrefined **10** low-ranking, obsequious, put to shame, respectful, submissive, unassuming **11** commonplace, deferential, subservient, sycophantic, unassertive, unimportant **12** self-effacing, supplicatory **13** cut down to size, insignificant, unpretentious **14** unostentatious **15** undistinguished

**humbleness**
**07** modesty **08** humility, meekness **09** deference, lowliness, servility **10** diffidence **13** self-abasement **14** self-effacement, submissiveness, unassumingness **15** unassertiveness

**humbly**
**03** low **06** meekly, simply **08** docilely, modestly **09** cap in hand, servilely **10** sheepishly **11** diffidently **12** obsequiously, respectfully, submissively, unassumingly **13** deferentially, subserviently **15** unpretentiously

**humbug**
**03** con, gum, rot **04** bunk, cant, fake, gaff, guff, hoax, sham **05** actor, balls, bluff, cheat, fraud, fudge, poser, rogue, trick **06** barney, berley, blague, bunkum, burley, cajole, con man, deceit, gammon, string **07** baloney, bluffer, deceive, eyewash, rubbish, swindle **08** buncombe, cheating, claptrap, cobblers, flummery, impostor, nonsense, pretence, swindler, trickery **09** charlatan, deception, gold brick, hypocrisy, kidstakes, poppycock, trickster **10** balderdash, hollowness

**humdrum**
**04** dull **05** banal, prosy **06** boring, dreary **07** droning, mundane, routine, tedious **08** everyday, monotony, ordinary, tiresome, unvaried **09** bourgeois **10** monotonous, uneventful **11** commonplace, repetitious **12** run-of-the-mill **13** uninteresting

**humid**
**03** wet **04** damp, dank **05** close, heavy, mochy, moist, muggy **06** clammy, mochie, steamy, sticky, sultry **10** oppressive

**humidity**
**03** dew **04** damp, mist **07** wetness **08** dampness, dankness, moisture **09** closeness, heaviness, humidness, moistness, mugginess, sogginess **10** clamminess, steaminess, stickiness, sultriness, vaporosity **12** vaporousness

**humiliate**
**05** abase, abash, break, crush, shame **06** demean, humble, wither **07** chasten, deflate, degrade, mortify, put down **08** bring low, confound, disgrace, take down **09** discomfit, discredit, embarrass **11** make a fool of **12** bring shame on, take down a peg

**humiliating**
**07** shaming **08** crushing, humbling, snubbing **09** deflating, degrading, humiliant, withering **10** chastening, disgracing, inglorious, mortifying **11** disgraceful, humiliative, humiliatory, ignominious **12** discomfiting, embarrassing

**humiliation**
**04** snub **05** shame **06** ignomy, rebuff **07** affront, put-down **08** crushing, disgrace, downfall, humbling, ignominy, take-down **09** abasement, deflation, discredit, dishonour, humble pie, indignity **10** chastening, loss of face **11** confounding, degradation **12** discomfiture **13** embarrassment, mortification

**humility**
**07** modesty **08** meekness **09** deference, lowlihead, lowliness, servility **10** diffidence, humbleness **13** self-abasement **14** self-effacement, submissiveness, unassumingness **15** unassertiveness

**humming** *see* **smelly**

**hummingbird**
**05** sylph, topaz **06** hermit, hummer **07** colibri, jacobin, rainbow **08** coquette **09** sabrewing, swordbill, trochilus **10** racket-tail, rubythroat, sicklebill **11** whitethroat **12** sapphire-wing

**hummock**
**04** hump **05** knoll, mound **06** barrow **07** hillock **09** elevation **10** prominence

**humorist**
**03** wag, wit **05** clown, comic, joker **06** gagman, jester **08** comedian, satirist **10** cartoonist **12** caricaturist

**humorous**
**04** zany **05** comic, droll, funny, pawky, witty **06** absurd **07** amusing, comical, giocoso, jocular, playful, risible, waggish **08** farcical **09** facetious, funny ha-ha, hilarious, irregular, laughable, ludicrous, satirical, whimsical **10** capricious, Gilbertian, humoristic, ridiculous **11** Falstaffian, Rabelaisian **12** entertaining, knee-slapping **13** side-splitting

**humour**
**03** fun, wit **04** coax, gags, mood, vein **05** jokes, jolly, spoil **06** comedy, cosset, favour, kidney, pamper, pecker, permit, please, temper **07** flatter, gratify, indulge, jesting, mollify, observe, satisfy, spirits **08** badinage, drollery, hilarity, pander to, repartee, tolerate **09** absurdity, amusement, wittiness **10** comply with, jocularity, wisecracks **11** accommodate, acquiesce in, disposition, frame of mind, go along with, state of mind, temperament **13** facetiousness **14** ridiculousness

*The four bodily humours include:*

**05** blood
**06** choler, phlegm
**09** black bile
**10** melancholy, yellow bile

*Humour includes:*

**03** dry
**04** blue, sick
**05** black
**07** gallows, surreal
**08** farcical
**09** satirical, slapstick
**10** lavatorial
**11** barrack-room, Pythonesque
**12** Chaplinesque

**humourless**
**02** po **03** dry **04** dour, dull, glum, grim **05** grave **06** boring, morose, solemn, sombre **07** earnest, po-faced, serious, tedious **09** long-faced, unsmiling **10** unlaughing

**hump**
**03** hog, lug, pip, vex **04** arch, bend, bump, haul, knob, lift, lump, mass, ramp **05** annoy, bulge, bunch, carry, crook, curve, heave, hoist, humph, hunch, hurry, mound, ridge **08** shoulder, swelling **09** outgrowth, speed bump **10** projection, prominence, protrusion **11** excrescence **12** intumescence, protuberance
• **get the hump**
**04** mope, sulk **09** be annoyed, get the pip **11** be irritated **13** be exasperated
• **give someone the hump**
**03** bug, irk, nag, vex **04** gall, rile **05** anger, annoy, tease **06** bother, harass, hassle, madden, pester, plague, ruffle, wind up **07** disturb, hack off, provoke, tick off, trouble **08** brass off, irritate **09** aggravate, cheese off **10** exasperate **13** make sparks fly **14** drive up the wall **15** get someone's goat
• **over the hump**
**12** over the worst **13** past the crisis

**hump-backed**
**06** humped **07** crooked, gibbose, gibbous, hunched, stooped **08** deformed, kyphotic **09** misshapen **11** bunch-backed, crookbacked, hunchbacked

**humped**
**04** bent **06** arched, curved **07** bunched, crooked, gibbose, gibbous, hunched

**humus**
**03** mor **04** mull **05** moder

**hunch**
**04** arch, bend, bump, hint, hump, idea, knob, lump, mass, ramp **05** bulge, curve, guess, mound, squat, stoop **06** crouch, curl up, draw in, huddle **07** feeling, inkling **08** swelling **09** intuition, outgrowth, suspicion **10** impression, projection, prominence, protrusion, sixth sense **11** premonition **12** presentiment, protuberance

**hundred**
**01** C **04** cent **05** centi- **06** centum **07** cantred, cantref **09** centenary

**hundredweight**
**03** cwt **07** quintal

**Hungary**
**01** H **03** HUN **04** Hung

**hunger**
**03** yen **04** ache, itch, long, need, pine, want, wish **05** crave, greed, raven, yearn **06** desire, famine, hanker, pining, starve, thirst **07** bulimia, craving, longing **08** appetite, voracity, yearning **09** emptiness, esurience, esuriency, hankering **10** famishment, greediness, hungriness, starvation **12** malnutrition, ravenousness **15** have a craving for, have a longing for

**hungrily**
**06** avidly **07** eagerly **08** greedily **09** longingly **10** covetously, insatiably, ravenously

**hungry**
**04** avid, lean, mean, poor, yaup **05** eager, empty, sharp **06** aching, greedy, hollow, pining, stingy **07** craving, itching, longing, needing, peckish, thirsty **08** covetous, desirous, esurient, famished, hungerly, ravenous, sharp-set, starving, underfed, yearning **09** ahungered, hankering, hungerful, voracious **10** insatiable **12** malnourished **14** could eat a horse, undernourished

**hunk**
**04** base, clod, dish, goal, lump, mass, safe, slab, stud **05** block, chunk, he-man, piece, wedge **06** dollop, gobbet, secure **08** beefcake, macho man **09** dreamboat, strong man **10** studmuffin

**hunt**
**03** cub, dog, rat, ren, rin, run **04** fish, hawk, meet, seal, seek, slug **05** chase, chevy, chivy, drive, hound, mouse, quest, scour, stalk, track, trail **06** battue, beagle, chivvy, course, ferret, follow, forage, halloo, prey on, pursue, rabbit, search, shadow, turtle **07** dismiss, look for, predate, pursuit, ransack, rummage, scare up **08** scouring, scrounge, stalking, tire down, tracking, venation **09** persecute, rummaging, still-hunt, try to find **11** investigate, run to ground **12** ride to hounds **13** investigation

**hunter**
**05** hound, jäger **06** chaser, hawker, jaeger, Nimrod, ratter, shikar, wolfer **07** Actaeon, beagler, montero, shikari, turtler, venator, venerer, woodman **08** chasseur, free-shot, huntsman, rabbiter, shikaree, woodsman **10** lion-hunter, seal-fisher **11** still-hunter **13** rabbit trapper

**hunting**
**05** chase **06** shikar, venery **07** birding, cubbing, ducking, lamping, ratting, wolfing, wolving **08** beagling, coursing, falconry, stalking, trapping, turtling, venation **11** field sports
• **expressions relating to hunting**
**04** alew, so-ho **05** chevy, chivy **06** chivvy, halloa, halloo, hoicks, yoicks **07** tally-ho, tantivy
• **hunting-coat**
**04** pink
• **hunting-cry**
**04** alew **05** chevy, chivy **06** chivvy, halloa, halloo
• **hunting ground**
**04** walk
• **hunting group**
**04** meet

**huntsman**
**04** Peel **05** jäger, yager **06** jaeger **07** montero, skirter, venator, woodman **08** chasseur, woodsman

**hurdle**
**03** bar **04** doll, jump, snag, wall **05** fence, flake, hedge **06** raddle, wattle **07** barrier, problem, railing **08** handicap, obstacle **09** barricade, hindrance **10** difficulty, impediment **11** obstruction **12** complication **14** stumbling-block

**hurl**
◇ *anagram indicator*
**03** bum, put **04** cast, dart, dash, fire, pelt, putt, send, toss **05** chuck, fling, heave, lanch, pitch, sling, swing, throw, wheel **06** hurtle, launch, let fly, propel **07** project **08** catapult **11** precipitate

**hurly-burly**
**05** chaos **06** bedlam, bustle, frenzy, furore, hassle, hubbub, hustle, racket, tumult, unrest, uproar **07** trouble, turmoil **08** brouhaha, disorder, upheaval **09** agitation, commotion, confusion **10** disruption, turbulence **11** distraction, pandemonium

**hurricane**
**04** gale, rout **05** storm **06** baguio, squall, tumult **07** cyclone, tempest, tornado, typhoon **09** commotion, whirlwind

**hurried**
**03** ran **04** fast **05** brief, hasty, quick, rapid, short, swift **06** hectic, rushed, speedy **07** cursory, offhand, passing, rush job, shallow **08** careless, fleeting, slapdash **09** breakneck, festinate, transient **10** transitory **11** perfunctory, precipitate, superficial

**hurriedly**
**07** flat out, hastily, hotfoot, in haste, quickly, rapidly, swiftly **08** pell-mell, speedily **09** posthaste **10** at top speed **11** at the double **12** lickety-split, without delay **13** helter-skelter **14** at a rate of knots, hell for leather **15** like the clappers

**hurry**
**03** fly, hie, ren, rin, run **04** belt, dash, hare, hump, push, race, rush, tear **05** chase, drive, haste, mosey, press, pronto, speed **06** buck up, bustle, flurry, giddap, hasten, hubbub, hustle, scurry **07** press on, quicken, speed up, urgency, vamoose **08** celerity, chop-chop, despatch, dispatch, expedite, fastness, go all out, jump to it!, rapidity, step on it **09** beetle off, commotion, confusion, cut and run, festinate, hastiness, look alive, look smart, make haste, quickness, swiftness **10** accelerate, expedition, hightail it, look slippy, look snappy **11** run like hell **12** get a wiggle on, make it snappy, step on the gas **13** precipitation

**hurt**
◇ *anagram indicator*
**03** ake, cut, hit, mar, noy, sad **04** ache, burn, gall, harm, maim, pain, sore **05** abuse, annoy, grief, smart, spoil, sting, throb, upset, wound, wring **06** aching, be sore, blight, bruise,

damage, grazed, grieve, impair, injure, injury, lesion, maimed, misery, offend, sadden, sorrow, tingle **07** afflict, annoyed, blemish, bruised, burning, disable, injured, painful, sadness, scarred, scratch, torture, wounded
**08** distress, ill-treat, lacerate, maltreat, mischief, nuisance, offended, saddened, smarting, soreness, tingling
**09** affronted, aggrieved, be painful, in anguish, lacerated, miserable, sorrowful, suffering, throbbing **10** affliction, debilitate, discomfort, distressed
**12** cause sadness **13** grief-stricken

**hurtful**
**03** bad, ill **04** mean **05** catty, cruel, nasty **06** naught, nocent, shrewd, unkind **07** baleful, cutting, harmful, nocuous, noysome, ruinous, vicious
**08** damaging, grievous, scathing, spiteful, wounding **09** injurious, malicious, obnoxious, offensive, pestilent, scatheful, upsetting
**10** derogatory, maleficent, maleficial, pernicious **11** deleterious, destructive, detrimental, distressing, malefactory

**hurtle**
**03** fly **04** belt, dash, dive, hurl, pelt, race, rush, spin, tear **05** clash, crash, shoot, speed **06** career, charge, plunge, rattle **08** brandish, step on it
**12** step on the gas **14** step on the juice
**15** put your foot down

**husband**
**01** h **03** man **04** lord, mate, save
**05** baron, groom, hoard, hubby, put by, store **06** budget, eke out, manage, master, old boy, old man, ration, save up, spouse **07** consort, goodman, manager, partner, reserve
**08** conserve, preserve, put aside
**09** cultivate, economize, other half
**10** better half, hoddy-doddy, married man **12** gander-mooner, use carefully, use sparingly **15** mari complaisant

• **husband and wife**
**04** pair **06** couple

• **without husband or wife**
**04** sole

**husbandry**
**06** saving, thrift **07** economy, farming, tillage **08** agronomy **09** frugality
**10** agronomics, management
**11** agriculture, cultivation, thriftiness
**12** agribusiness, conservation **14** farm management, land management

**hush**
**04** calm **05** peace, quiet, still
**06** repose, settle, silent, soothe, subdue **07** be quiet, bestill, compose, mollify, quieten, silence **08** calmness, serenity **09** quietness, stillness
**12** peacefulness, tranquillity

• **hush up**
**03** gag **04** smug **06** huddle, stifle
**07** conceal, cover up, smother
**08** keep dark, suppress **10** keep secret

**hush-hush**
**06** secret **09** top-secret **10** classified, restricted, under wraps **12** confidential

**husk**
**03** pod **04** bran, case, coir, hull, peel, pill, rind, skin **05** chaff, shale, sheal, sheel, shell, shiel, shill, shuck, strip
**06** legume **07** capsule, epicarp
**08** covering **09** corn shuck

**huskily**
**06** deeply **07** gruffly, harshly
**08** croakily, gravelly, hoarsely
**10** gutturally

**husky**
**03** dry, low **04** deep **05** beefy, burly, gruff, harsh, hefty, Inuit, rough, thick
**06** brawny, coarse, croaky, hoarse, strong **07** rasping, throaty
**08** croaking, gravelly, guttural, muscular **09** strapping, well-built

**hussy**
**04** minx, slag, slut, tart, vamp
**05** huzzy, tramp **06** hussif, limmer
**07** floozie **08** scrubber **09** housewife, temptress **10** loose woman

**hustle**
**03** fly, tew **04** dash, fuss, push, rush, sell, stir **05** crowd, elbow, force, fraud, hurry, nudge, shove **06** bounce, bundle, bustle, hasten, huddle, jostle, justle, rustle, thrust, tumult **07** swindle
**08** activity **09** agitation, commotion, manhandle **10** hurly-burly, pressurize

**hut**
**03** den **04** shed, skeo, skio, tilt
**05** banda, booth, bothy, cabin, hogan, humpy, shack, sheal, shiel, whare
**06** bothan, bothie, chalet, gunyah, lean-to, mia-mia, pondok, rancho, saeter, shanty, succah, sukkah, wiltja, wurley **07** caboose, shelter, wickiup
**08** log cabin, rondavel, shealing, shieling **09** pondokkie, rancheria

**hybrid**
◇ *anagram indicator*
**05** cross, mixed **06** mosaic
**07** amalgam, bigener, mixture, mongrel **08** combined, compound
**09** composite, crossbred, half-blood, half-breed **10** crossbreed
**11** combination, single-cross
**13** heterogeneous **14** conglomeration

*Hybrids include:*

**02** zo
**03** dso, dzo, zho
**04** dzho, mule, OEIC, Ugli®
**05** oxlip, topaz
**06** oxslip
**07** beefalo, Bourbon, cattabu, cattalo, Jersian, lurcher, plumcot, tangelo, tea rose
**08** citrange, noisette, sunberry, tayberry
**09** perpetual, tiger tail, triticale
**10** clementine, loganberry, polyanthus
**11** boysenberry, bull-mastiff, Jacqueminot, marionberry, miracle rice
**13** polecat-ferret

**hybridize**
**05** cross **10** bastardize, crossbreed, interbreed

**hydrant**
**01** H **02** FP **08** fireplug

**hydrocarbon**

*Hydrocarbons include:*

**03** wax
**05** halon
**06** aldrin, alkane, alkene, alkyne, butane, cetane, decane, ethane, hexane, indene, nonane, octane, olefin, picene, pyrene, retene
**07** benzene, heptane, methane, olefine, pentane, propane, styrene, terpene
**08** camphane, camphene, diphenyl, isoprene, pristane, stilbene
**09** butadiene
**10** benzpyrene, mesitylene
**11** hatchettite, naphthalane
**12** cyclopropane

**hydrogen**
**01** H

**hyena**
**09** tiger wolf **10** strandwolf

**hygiene**
**06** purity **09** sterility **10** sanitation
**11** cleanliness **12** disinfection, sanitariness **13** wholesomeness

**hygienic**
**04** pure **05** clean **07** aseptic, healthy, sterile **08** germ-free, sanitary
**09** wholesome **10** salubrious, sterilized **11** disinfected

**hymn**
**03** air **04** song **05** carol, chant, dirge, motet, paean, psalm **06** anthem, choral, chorus, mantra, Te Deum
**07** cantata, chorale, introit, mantram, Sanctus **08** canticle, cathisma, dies irae, doxology, hymeneal, sequence
**09** dithyramb, offertory, spiritual, sticheron, trisagion, troparion
**10** paraphrase, procession, Tantum ergo **11** recessional, Stabat Mater
**12** Marseillaise, processional, song of praise

**hype**
**04** fuss, plug, puff **06** racket, talk up
**07** build up, build-up, promote, puffery
**08** ballyhoo, plugging **09** advertise, deception, promotion, publicity, publicize **10** razzmatazz
**11** advertising **13** advertisement

**hyped up**
**04** fake, high, wild **05** eager, hyper, moved **06** elated **07** anxious, excited, fired up, frantic, stirred, uptight
**08** agitated, animated, frenzied, restless, thrilled, worked up
**09** wrought-up **10** artificial, stimulated
**11** exhilarated, overwrought
**12** enthusiastic **13** in high spirits, on tenterhooks **14** beside yourself, thrilled to bits

**hyperbole**
**06** excess **07** auxesis **08** overkill
**12** exaggeration, extravagance
**13** magnification, overstatement

**hypercritical**
**05** fussy, picky **06** choosy, strict
**07** carping, finicky **08** captious, niggling, pedantic **09** cavilling, quibbling **10** censorious, nit-picking, pernickety **11** persnickety **12** fault-finding **13** hair-splitting **14** over-particular

**Hypnos**
**06** Somnus

**hypnotic**
**07** numbing **08** magnetic, sedative
**09** soporific **10** compelling, magnetical **11** fascinating, mesmerizing, somniferous
**12** irresistible, spellbinding, stupefactive **13** sleep-inducing

**hypnotism**
**08** Braidism, hypnosis **09** mesmerism
**10** suggestion **12** neurypnology
**14** auto-suggestion, electrobiology, neurohypnology **15** animal magnetism

**hypnotize**
**06** dazzle **07** beguile, bewitch, enchant **08** entrance **09** captivate, fascinate, magnetize, mesmerize, spellbind **10** put to sleep

**hypochondria**
**03** hip, hyp **08** neurosis
**15** hypochondriasis

**hypochondriac**
**08** neurotic **10** melancholy, phrenesiac **11** atrabilious
**14** hypochondriast, valetudinarian
**15** hypochondriacal

**hypocrisy**
**04** cant **06** deceit **07** falsity
**08** pretence **09** deception, duplicity
**10** dishonesty, double-talk, lip service, pharisaism, phoneyness
**11** dissembling, insincerity **12** two-facedness, wearing a mask
**13** deceitfulness, dissimulation, double-dealing

**hypocrite**
**05** fraud, Janus, pseud **06** canter, mucker, phoney, pseudo **08** deceiver, impostor, Pharisee, Tartuffe
**09** charlatan, Pecksniff, pretender
**10** dissembler, Holy Willie, mountebank **15** whited sepulchre

**hypocritical**
**05** false, lying **06** double, hollow, phoney **08** specious, spurious, two-faced **09** deceitful, deceptive, dishonest, insincere, pharisaic, self-pious, Tartufian, Tartufish **10** false-faced, fraudulent, histrionic, Janus-faced, perfidious, Tartuffian, Tartuffish
**11** dissembling, double-faced, duplicitous, Janian-faced, pharisaical
**12** histrionical, Pecksniffian **13** double-dealing, sanctimonious, self-righteous

**hypothesis**
**03** hyp **05** axiom **06** notion, theory, thesis **07** premise, theorem
**09** postulate **10** assumption, conjecture **11** presumption, proposition, speculation, supposition

**hypothetical**
**03** hyp **07** assumed **08** imagined, notional, presumed, proposed, supposed **09** imaginary
**11** conjectural, speculative, theoretical
**13** suppositional

**hypothetically**
**07** ideally **08** in theory **10** supposedly
**13** conjecturally, speculatively, theoretically

**hysteria**
**05** mania, panic **06** frenzy, mother
**07** habdabs, madness **08** delirium, neurosis **09** agitation, hysterics **15** fits of the mother

**hysterical**
**03** mad **04** rich **06** crazed, raving
**07** berserk, frantic **08** demented, farcical, frenzied, in a panic, neurotic
**09** delirious, hilarious, ludicrous, priceless **10** ridiculous, uproarious
**11** overwrought **12** out of control
**13** side-splitting **14** beside yourself, extremely funny, uncontrollable

**hysterically**
**05** madly **08** absurdly, in a panic
**10** farcically **11** frantically, hilariously, ludicrously, screamingly
**12** neurotically, out of control, ridiculously, uproariously **13** out of your mind **14** beside yourself, uncontrollably

**hysterics**
**05** mania, panic **06** frenzy
**07** habdabs, madness **08** delirium, hysteria, neurosis **09** agitation **12** crise de nerfs

# I

**I**
**02** ch, me **03** aye, che, ego, ich, one, yes **05** India **06** indeed, iodine
**• I am**
**02** I'm **03** sum

**ice**
**04** cool, kill **05** chill, frost, glaze **06** freeze, harden **07** diamond, iciness, reserve **08** coldness, coolness, diamonds, distance, enfreeze **09** formality **10** freeze over, frostiness **11** frozen water, refrigerate

*Ice types include:*

**03** dry, pan, sea
**04** floe, grew, grue, hail, pack, rime, slob, snow
**05** black, brash, crust, drift, field, shelf, shell, sleet, virga
**06** anchor, frazil, ground, icicle, stream
**07** glacier, hummock, pancake, verglas
**10** silver thaw
**13** tickly-benders

**• ice cream**
**04** cone **05** bombe, kulfi **06** bucket, cornet, gelato, ripple, slider, sorbet, sundae **07** cassata, choc-bar, granita, sherbet, spumone, spumoni, tortoni **08** hoky-poky, macallum **10** hokey-pokey, Neapolitan **11** tutti-frutti
**• put on ice**
**05** defer, delay **06** put off, shelve **07** suspend **08** postpone **14** hold in abeyance **15** leave in abeyance

**iceberg**
**04** berg, calf **07** growler

**ice-cold**
**03** icy, raw **04** hard, iced, numb **05** algid, fixed, gelid, polar, rigid, stiff **06** arctic, baltic, frigid, frosty, frozen **07** chilled, frosted, glacial **08** freezing, icebound, Siberian **10** solidified **11** frozen-stiff **12** bitterly cold

**ice hockey**

*Ice hockey-related terms include:*

**04** cage, goal, puck
**05** bully, check, icing, stick, zones
**06** assist, boards, period, sin-bin
**07** face-off, forward, offside, penalty, red line, shut-out, Zamboni
**08** blue line, boarding, defender, five-hole, linesman, one-timer, overtime, slap shot, slashing, spearing
**09** blueliner, bodycheck, centreman, netminder, power play
**10** centre line, cross-check, defenceman, goaltender, penalty box
**11** penalty shot, short-handed, sudden-death
**12** icing the puck, penalty bench
**13** defending zone

**Iceland**
**02** IS **03** ISL

**ice skating**

*Ice skaters include:*

**04** **Dean** (Christopher), **Koss** (Johann Olav), **Kwan** (Michelle), **Witt** (Katarina), **Yang** (Yang 'A')
**05** **Baiul** (Oksana), **Blair** (Bonnie), **Curry** (John), **Heiss** (Carol), **Henie** (Sonja), **Kania** (Karin), **Syers** (Madge)
**06** **Button** (Dick), **Hamill** (Dorothy)
**07** **Boitano** (Brian), **Cousins** (Robin), **Fleming** (Peggy), **Grinkov** (Sergei), **Harding** (Tonya), **Rodnina** (Irina), **Salchow** (Ulrich), **Torvill** (Jayne), **Yagudin** (Alexei)
**08** **Browning** (Kurt), **Dijkstra** (Sjoukje), **Dmitriev** (Artur), **Eldredge** (Todd), **Gordeeva** (Ekaterina), **Hamilton** (Scott), **Kazakova** (Oksana), **Kerrigan** (Nancy), **Lipinski** (Tara), **Petrenko** (Viktor)
**09** **Yamaguchi** (Kristi)
**10** **Ballangrud** (Ivar)

*Ice skating-related terms include:*

**04** Axel, edge, flip, loop, Lutz
**05** blade, pairs, skate, waltz
**06** figure, Mohawk, rocker, walley
**07** bracket, Choctaw, Salchow, sit spin, toe jump, toe loop, toe pick
**08** ice dance, Ina Bauer, stag leap
**09** camel spin, crossover, free dance
**10** inside edge
**11** death spiral, flying camel, layback spin, outside edge, spread eagle, upright spin
**12** headless spin, speed skating
**13** Biellmann spin, figure skating, flying sit spin, free programme
**14** short programme
**15** compulsory dance, set pattern dance

**icily**
**06** coldly, coolly, rudely **07** stiffly **08** formally, morosely **12** forbiddingly

**icon**
**04** idol **05** image **06** figure, smiley, sprite, symbol **08** likeness, portrait **09** portrayal **14** representation

**iconoclast**
**05** rebel **06** critic **07** heretic, radical, sceptic **08** opponent **09** denouncer, dissenter, dissident **10** questioner, unbeliever **11** denunciator **12** image-breaker

**iconoclastic**
**07** impious, radical **08** critical **09** dissident, heretical, sceptical **10** innovative, irreverent, rebellious, subversive **11** dissentient, questioning **12** denunciatory

**icy**
**03** raw **04** cold, cool, rimy, rude **05** aloof, chill, gelid, polar, stiff, stony **06** arctic, biting, bitter, chilly, formal, frigid, frosty, frozen, glassy, morose, slippy **07** distant, glacial, hostile, ice-cold **08** chilling, freezing, icebound, reserved, Siberian, slippery **10** forbidding, frostbound, restrained, unfriendly **11** indifferent

**id**
**04** orfe

**Idaho**
**02** ID

**idea**
**03** aim, end **04** clou, clue, goal, idée, plan, view **05** fancy, guess, image, point **06** belief, design, notion, object, reason, scheme, target, theory, vision **07** conceit, concept, feeling, inkling, opinion, purpose, thought, wrinkle **08** proposal **09** brainwave, intention, judgement, objective, obsession, suspicion, viewpoint **10** conception, conjecture, hypothesis, impression, perception, suggestion **11** abstraction, connotation, inspiration, proposition **13** understanding **14** interpretation, recommendation

**ideal**
**04** acme, best, type **05** cause, dream, image, model **06** ethics, morals, unreal, Utopia **07** eidolon, epitome, example, highest, optimal, optimum, paragon, pattern, perfect, supreme, utopian **08** absolute, abstract, complete, exemplar, fanciful, notional, romantic, standard **09** archetype, benchmark, criterion, imaginary, nonpareil, principle, prototype, visionary, yardstick **10** archetypal, conceptual, consummate, idealistic, perfection **11** impractical, moral values, theoretical **12** hypothetical, unattainable **13** ethical values, philosophical **14** moral standards, quintessential
**• ideal state**
**06** Utopia **07** nirvana

**idealism**
**09** mentalism **10** utopianism **11** romanticism **13** perfectionism **14** impracticality

**idealist**
**07** dreamer **08** optimist, romantic **09** visionary **11** romanticist **13** perfectionist

**idealistic**
**07** utopian **08** quixotic, romantic **09** visionary **10** optimistic, starry-eyed **11** impractical, unrealistic **13** impracticable, perfectionist

**idealization**
**07** worship **10** apotheosis, exaltation **11** ennoblement, idolization **13** glamorization, glorification, romanticizing **15** romanticization

**idealize**
**05** exalt **07** glorify, idolize, worship **09** glamorize **10** utopianize **11** romanticize

**ideally**
**06** at best **08** in theory, mentally **09** perfectly **13** theoretically **14** hypothetically, in an ideal world **15** in a perfect world

**idée fixe**
**06** hang-up **07** complex **08** fixation **09** fixed idea, leitmotiv, monomania, obsession

**identical**
**04** like, same, self, twin **05** alike, equal, right **06** cloned **07** identic, numeric, precise, similar **08** matching, self-same **09** analogous, congruent, duplicate, syngeneic **10** coincident, consistent, equivalent **11** a dead ringer **12** doppelgänger **13** corresponding, one and the same, spitting image **15** interchangeable

**identically**
**05** alike **07** equally **09** similarly **11** analogously, congruently, just the same **12** consistently, equivalently, in the same way **15** correspondingly, interchangeably

**identifiable**
**05** known **10** detectable, noticeable **11** discernible, perceptible **12** recognizable, unmistakable **13** ascertainable **15** distinguishable

**identification**
**02** ID **03** tie **04** bond, link **05** badge, label **06** naming, papers **07** empathy, rapport **08** passbook, passport, relation, spotting, sympathy **09** biometric, detection, diagnosis, documents, labelling **10** connection **11** association, correlation, credentials, involvement, pointing-out, recognition **12** dactyloscopy, identity card, relationship **13** fellow feeling, interrelation **14** classification, driving licence, fingerprinting

**identify**
**03** tag **04** know, name, spot **05** label, place **06** couple, detect, finger, notice, relate **07** connect, discern, feel for, find out, involve, make out, pick out, pin down, specify **08** classify, diagnose, discover, perceive, pinpoint, point out, relate to **09** ascertain, associate, catalogue, establish, recognize, respond to, single out **11** distinguish **13** associate with, empathize with **14** put the finger on, sympathize with **15** think of together

**identity**
**02** ID **03** ego **04** face, name, self **05** image, roots, seity, unity **07** oneness, profile **08** equality, likeness, property, sameness, selfhood **09** character, closeness, existence **10** appearance, background, impression, personhood, public face, similarity, uniqueness **11** equivalence, personality, resemblance, singularity **12** selfsameness **13** individuality, particularity, public persona **14** correspondence **15** distinctiveness

**ideologist**
**07** teacher, thinker **08** theorist **09** ideologue, visionary **11** doctrinaire, philosopher

**ideology**
**05** credo, creed, dogma, faith, ideas **06** belief, tenets, theory, thesis **07** beliefs, opinion **08** doctrine, opinions, teaching **09** doctrines, world-view **10** philosophy, principles **11** convictions, metaphysics

*See also* **political**

**idiocy**
**05** folly **06** lunacy **07** inanity **08** daftness, insanity **09** absurdity, craziness, silliness, stupidity **10** imbecility **11** fatuousness **13** foolhardiness, senselessness

**idiom**
**04** talk **05** style, usage **06** jargon, phrase, speech, Syrism **07** Arabism, dialect, Grecism, Pahlavi, Pehlevi, Persism, Slavism, Syriasm **08** Aramaism, Graecism, Hebraism, idiotism, Irishism, language, Latinism, locution, parlance, polonism, prosaism, Saxonism, Semitism, Sinicism **09** anglicism, Celticism, Chaldaism, Gallicism, Germanism, Gothicism, Hellenism, Italicism, Scoticism, Syriacism, Syrianism **10** classicism, cockneyism, Englishism, expression, femininism, Italianism, Johnsonese, Scotticism, vernacular, Yiddishism **11** Americanism, Hibernicism, phraseology **12** classicalism, Hibernianism, turn of phrase **13** Australianism, colloquialism, vernacularism

**idiomatic**
**06** native **07** correct, natural **08** everyday **09** dialectal **10** colloquial, idiolectal, vernacular **11** dialectical, grammatical

**idiosyncrasy**
**03** way **05** freak, habit, quirk, trait **06** oddity **07** feature, quality **09** mannerism **10** speciality **11** peculiarity, singularity **12** eccentricity **13** individuality **14** characteristic

**idiosyncratic**
**03** odd **06** quirky **08** peculiar, personal, singular **09** eccentric **10** individual **11** distinctive **14** characteristic

**idiot**
**03** ass, mug, nit, nut, oaf **04** berk, clod, clot, dill, dope, dork, fool, geek, jerk, nana, nerd, nerk, nong, prat, putz, twit **05** chump, clown, divvy, dumbo, dunce, eejit, galah, klutz, moron, nelly, ninny, prick, schmo, twerp, wally **06** bammer, bampot, cretin, dimwit, doofus, drongo, dum-dum, muppet, nidget, nitwit, numpty, sucker **07** airhead, barmpot, dumb-ass, fat-head, halfwit, jughead, natural, pillock, plonker, schmuck, wazzock **08** boofhead, dipstick, flathead, imbecile, innocent, numskull, pea-brain **09** birdbrain, blockhead, cloth head, ignoramus, lame brain, malt-horse, simpleton, thickhead **10** bufflehead, nincompoop **11** chowderhead, knuckle-head

*See also* **fool**

**idiotic**
◇ *anagram indicator*
**03** mad, twp **04** daft, dozy, dumb **05** barmy, batty, crazy, dorky, dotty, goofy, inane, inept, nutty, potty, silly, wacky **06** absurd, insane, oafish, simple, stupid, unwise **07** asinine, dumb-ass, fatuous, foolish, moronic, risible **08** gormless, ignorant **09** dim-witted, half-baked, ludicrous, pointless, senseless **10** half-witted, ill-advised, ridiculous **11** hare-brained, injudicious, nonsensical, thick-headed **12** crack-brained, short-sighted, simple-minded, unreasonable **13** ill-considered, knuckle-headed, unintelligent

**idle**
**03** lig **04** dead, doss, laze, lazy, loaf, mike, move, vain **05** dally, empty, light, petty, relax, shirk, skive, slack, waste, while **06** bludge, casual, daidle, dawdle, fester, fiddle, futile, loiter, lollop, lounge, potter, putter, unused, wanton **07** dormant, dronish, foolish, fritter, goof off, jobless, loafish, shallow, sit back, trivial, useless, work-shy **08** baseless, bone-idle, inactive, indolent, kill time, lallygag, lollygag, slothful, sluggish, sod about, tick over, trifling **09** bum around, do nothing, fruitless, gold-brick, lethargic, on the dole, pointless, redundant, while away, worthless **10** mothballed, not working, take it easy, unedifying, unemployed, unoccupied, whip the cat **11** fiddle about, horse around,

ineffective, ineffectual, inoperative, unimportant **12** be ready to run, fiddle around, fiddle-faddle, unproductive, unsuccessful **13** be operational, be ready to work, insignificant, lackadaisical

**idleness**
**04** ease **05** sloth **06** lazing, torpor **07** idlesse, inertia, leisure, loafing, skiving, vacancy, vacuity **08** inaction, laziness, otiosity **09** indolence, pottering **10** inactivity, otioseness, vegetating **12** slothfulness, sluggishness, unemployment **13** shiftlessness **14** dolce far niente

**idler**
**04** slob, spiv **05** drone, sloth **06** bumble, bummle, dodger, donnat, donnot, dosser, loafer, skiver, truant, waster **07** bludger, dawdler, goof-off, laggard, Lollard, lounger, shirker, slacker, wastrel **08** do-naught, fine lady, layabout, sluggard **09** do-nothing, gold brick, lazybones **10** malingerer **11** couch potato **12** carpet-knight, clock-watcher **13** fine gentleman **14** good-for-nothing

**idol**
**03** god, pet **04** hero, icon, joss, sham, star, wood **05** deity, image, pagod, pin-up, swami **06** effigy, fetish, figure, mammet, maumet, mawmet, mommet, pagoda **07** beloved, darling, fantasy, goddess, heroine, phantom **08** Baphomet, impostor, likeness **09** favourite, semblance, superstar **11** blue-eyed boy, graven image

**idolater**
**06** adorer, votary **07** admirer, devotee, idolist **10** iconolater, idolatress, worshipper **14** idol-worshipper

**idolatrous**
**05** pagan **07** adoring **09** adulatory, heretical, idolizing, lionizing **10** glorifying, uncritical **11** reverential, worshipping **15** idol-worshipping

**idolatry**
**07** idolism **08** mammetry, maumetry, mawmetry, paganism, whoredom **09** adoration, adulation, fetishism, idolizing, reverence **10** admiration, exaltation, heathenism, iconolatry **11** deification, fornication, hero-worship, icon worship, worshipping **13** glorification

**idolize**
**04** love **05** adore, deify, exalt **06** admire, dote on, revere **07** adulate, glorify, lionize, worship **08** venerate **09** reverence **11** hero-worship **14** put on a pedestal

**idyllic**
**05** happy **06** rustic **07** perfect **08** blissful, charming, heavenly, pastoral, peaceful, romantic **09** idealized, unspoiled, wonderful **10** delightful **11** picturesque, Theocritean

**ie**
**02** so

**if**
**02** an **03** and, gin **06** though **07** suppose, whether **08** as long as, assuming, in case of, provided, so long as, whenever **09** condition, providing, supposing **11** supposition, uncertainty **12** assuming that, in the event of **13** supposing that **15** on condition that

**• even if**
**03** and, tho **04** albe **05** albee, all-be **06** albeit, though **07** suppose

**• if it**
**03** an't

**iffy**
**04** suss **05** dodgy, risky **07** dubious **08** doubtful, low-grade **09** defective, imperfect, tentative, uncertain, undecided, unsettled **10** second-rate **11** substandard **13** disappointing **14** not up to scratch, unsatisfactory

**ignite**
**04** burn, fire **05** light, torch **06** kindle **07** flare up, inflame **08** spark off, touch off **09** catch fire, set alight, set fire to, set on fire **11** conflagrate, put a match to **15** burst into flames

**ignoble**
**03** low **04** base, mean, vile **05** petty, small **06** vulgar **07** heinous **08** infamous, shameful, unworthy, wretched **09** worthless **10** despicable **11** disgraceful **12** contemptible **13** dishonourable

**ignobly**
**06** meanly, vilely **07** pettily **10** despicably, infamously, shamefully, wretchedly **12** contemptibly **13** disgracefully, dishonourably, without honour

**ignominious**
**04** base **05** sorry **06** abject **08** infamous, shameful **09** degrading **10** despicable, mortifying, scandalous **11** disgraceful, humiliating, undignified **12** contemptible, disreputable, embarrassing **13** discreditable, dishonourable

**ignominiously**
**10** despicably, shamefully **12** disreputably, scandalously **13** disgracefully, dishonourably

**ignominy**
**05** odium, shame **06** infamy, stigma **07** obloquy, scandal **08** contempt, disgrace, reproach **09** discredit, dishonour, disrepute, indignity **10** opprobrium **11** degradation, humiliation **13** mortification

**ignoramus**
**03** ass **04** dolt, fool **05** dunce **06** dimwit, duffer, ignaro **07** dullard, halfwit **08** bonehead, ignorant, imbecile, numskull **09** blockhead, simpleton **10** illiterate **11** know-nothing

**ignorance**
**05** night **07** naivety **08** oblivion **09** greenness, innocence, nescience, stupidity, thickness **10** illiteracy **11** unawareness **12** inexperience **13** obliviousness, unfamiliarity **14** unintelligence **15** unconsciousness

**ignorant**
**04** dumb, lewd, rude **05** blind, dense, naive, thick **06** ingram, ingrum, stupid, unread **07** ill-bred, redneck, unaware, unknown **08** backward, clueless, innocent, inscient, nescient, untaught **09** benighted, in the dark, lack-Latin, oblivious, unknowing, unlearned, untrained, unwitting **10** analphabet, illiterate, innumerate, uneducated, unfamiliar, uninformed, unschooled **11** analphabete, ill-educated, ill-informed, know-nothing, unconfirmed, unconscious, uninitiated **12** discourteous, having no idea, unacquainted **13** inexperienced, unenlightened

**ignore**
◇ *deletion indicator*
**03** cut **04** balk, omit, snub **05** baulk, blank, blink, spurn, waive **06** bypass, pass by, reject, slight **07** cut dead, high-hat, neglect, tune out **08** brush off, discount, overlook, pass over, set aside, shrug off **09** disregard **10** brush aside, scrub round, slight over **11** not listen to, run away from **12** cold-shoulder **13** be oblivious to, keep in the dark **14** shut your eyes to, take for granted, take no notice of, turn a deaf ear to, turn your back on **15** close your eyes to, look the other way, turn a blind eye to

**ilk**
**04** each, kind, make, same, sort, type, ylke **05** brand, breed, class, stamp, style **07** variety **09** character **11** description

**ill**
◇ *anagram indicator*
**03** bad **04** down, evil, harm, hurt, pain, sick, weak **05** amiss, badly, cronk, crook, dicky, frail, harsh, rough, seedy, trial **06** ailing, barely, crummy, feeble, groggy, grotty, hardly, infirm, injury, laid up, naught, poorly, queasy, severe, sorrow, trials, unkind, unweal, unwell, wicked **07** adverse, ailment, cruelty, grieved, harmful, hostile, hurtful, ominous, peevish, problem, ruinous, run down, trouble, unlucky **08** critical, damaging, disaster, diseased, scantily, scarcely, sinister, unkindly **09** adversely, afflicted, bedridden, by no means, difficult, in a bad way, incorrect, injurious, off-colour, resentful, suffering, unhealthy, unluckily **10** affliction, broken-down, distressed, indisposed, misfortune, out of sorts, unfriendly, unpleasant, wickedness, wrongfully **11** belligerent, deleterious, destruction, destructive, detrimental, incompetent, peelie-wally, threatening, tribulation,

unfortunate, unpromising
**12** antagonistic, inadequately, inauspicious, infelicitous, unfavourable, unfavourably, unpropitious **13** reprehensible, unfortunately **14** disapprovingly, inauspiciously, insufficiently, unpleasantness, unsuccessfully, valetudinarian **15** under the weather

**• ill at ease**
◇ *anagram indicator*
**04** edgy **05** tense **06** on edge, uneasy, unsure **07** anxious, awkward, fidgety, nervous, strange, worried **08** farouche, hesitant, restless **09** disturbed, unrelaxed, unsettled **10** disquieted **11** embarrassed **13** on tenterhooks, self-conscious, uncomfortable

**• speak ill of**
**03** nag, pan **04** carp, slag, slam
**05** blame, cut up, decry, knock, roast, score, slash, slate, trash **06** attack, hammer, impugn, niggle, peck at, tilt at **07** censure, condemn, nit-pick, rubbish, run down, scarify, slag off, snipe at **08** backbite, badmouth, denounce, wade into **09** castigate, criticize, denigrate, disparage, excoriate, have a go at, misreport, pull apart, take apart, tear apart
**10** animadvert, come down on, go to town on, vituperate **11** pick holes in **12** disapprove of, pull to pieces, put the boot in, tear to shreds **13** find fault with, tear a strip off **15** do a hatchet job on, pass judgement on

**ill-advised**
**04** rash **05** hasty **06** unwise **07** foolish **08** careless, overseen, reckless **09** ill-judged, imprudent, misguided
**11** injudicious, thoughtless **12** short-sighted **13** ill-considered, inappropriate

**ill-assorted**
◇ *anagram indicator*
**08** unsuited **09** misallied
**10** discordant, mismatched
**11** incongruous, uncongenial
**12** incompatible, inharmonious

**ill-bred**
◇ *anagram indicator*
**04** rude **05** crass, crude, ocker
**06** coarse, vulgar **07** boorish, loutish, uncivil, uncouth **08** ignorant, impolite, unseemly **10** indelicate, misbehaved, unmannerly, unnurtured **11** bad-mannered, ill-mannered, uncivilized
**12** discourteous

**ill-considered**
**04** rash **05** hasty **06** unwise **07** foolish **08** careless, heedless **09** ill-judged, imprudent, overhasty **10** ill-advised
**11** improvident, injudicious, precipitate
**12** misconceived

**ill-defined**
**03** dim **04** hazy **05** fuzzy, vague
**06** blurry, woolly **07** blurred, mongrel, shadowy, unclear **08** nebulous
**09** imprecise, shapeless **10** indefinite, indistinct

**ill-disposed**
**04** anti **06** averse **07** against, hostile, opposed **08** inimical **10** malevolent, unfriendly **11** disaffected, unwelcoming **12** antagonistic
**13** unco-operative, unsympathetic

**illegal**
**05** wrong **06** banned, barred
**07** bootleg, crooked, illicit
**08** criminal, outlawed, unlawful, wrongful, wrongous **09** felonious, forbidden **10** adulterine, fraudulent, prohibited, proscribed **11** black-market, interdicted **12** criminalized, illegitimate, unauthorized **15** under-the-counter

**illegality**
**05** crime, wrong **06** felony
**09** wrongness **11** criminality, illicitness, lawlessness, malfeasance
**12** illegitimacy, unlawfulness, wrongfulness

**illegally**
**07** wrongly **08** guiltily **09** illicitly
**10** criminally, unlawfully, wrongfully
**13** against the law, disobediently
**14** illegitimately

**illegible**
**05** faint **07** obscure **08** scrawled
**10** hard to read, indistinct, unreadable
**12** hieroglyphic **14** indecipherable, unintelligible

**illegitimacy**
**08** bastardy **10** bastardism **12** bend-sinister **13** baton-sinister
**14** fatherlessness

**illegitimate**
**04** base, love **07** bastard, illegal, illicit, invalid, lawless, natural, unsound
**08** base-born, improper, misbegot, nameless, spurious, unlawful
**09** illogical, incorrect **10** adulterine, fatherless, unfathered, unlicensed
**11** misbegotten, unwarranted
**12** inadmissible, unauthorized

**ill-equipped**
**07** exposed **10** unprovided, unsupplied **11** ill-supplied, underfunded, undermanned, unprotected **12** disappointed, understaffed **13** underfinanced, under strength, unprovided for **14** under-resourced

**ill-fated**
**06** doomed **07** hapless, unhappy, unlucky **08** blighted, luckless **09** ill-omened, star-crost **10** ill-starred
**11** star-crossed, unfortunate

**ill-favoured**
**04** ugly **05** plain **06** homely
**07** hideous **08** unlovely **09** repulsive, unsightly **12** unattractive
**15** unprepossessing

**ill-feeling**
**05** anger, odium, pique, spite, wrath
**06** animus, enmity, grudge, malice
**07** dudgeon, ill-will, offence, rancour
**08** bad blood, sourness **09** animosity, hostility **10** antagonism, bitterness, resentment, unkindness **11** frustration, indignation **12** hard feelings
**14** disgruntlement **15** dissatisfaction

**ill-founded**
**07** unsound **08** baseless
**10** groundless **11** unconfirmed, unjustified, unsupported
**15** unsubstantiated

**ill-gotten**
**03** hot **04** bent **05** dodgy, taken
**06** nicked, stolen, swiped **07** nobbled
**08** pilfered **09** purloined, ripped off
**10** knocked off

**ill-humour**
**03** dod **04** bile, dump **05** dumps, rheum **06** spleen **09** distemper

**ill-humoured**
**04** tart **05** cross, huffy, moody, ratty, sharp, sulky, testy **06** crabby, grumpy, morose, shirty, snappy, sullen
**07** crabbed, grouchy, peevish, stroppy, waspish **08** petulant, snappish
**09** crotchety, impatient, irascible, irritable **11** acrimonious, bad-tempered, distempered
**12** cantankerous, disagreeable
**13** quick-tempered

**illiberal**
**04** mean **05** petty, tight **06** stingy
**07** bigoted, miserly **08** verkramp
**09** hidebound, niggardly **10** intolerant, prejudiced, ungenerous **11** close-fisted, reactionary, small-minded, tight-fisted **12** narrow-minded, parsimonious, uncharitable
**13** unenlightened

**illicit**
**03** sly **05** black, wrong **06** banned, barred, shonky **07** bootleg, furtive, illegal **08** criminal, improper, stealthy, unlawful **09** forbidden, ill-gotten, secretive **10** contraband, prohibited, unlicensed **11** black-market, clandestine **12** illegitimate, unauthorized **13** surreptitious, under-the-table **15** under-the-counter

**illicitly**
**07** wrongly **08** guiltily **09** illegally
**10** criminally, unlawfully, wrongfully
**13** against the law, disobediently
**14** illegitimately

**Illinois**
**02** IL **03** Ill

**illiteracy**
**09** ignorance **15** inability to read, lack of education, lack of schooling

**illiterate**
**08** ignorant, untaught **09** benighted, unlearned, untutored **10** letterless, uncultured, uneducated, unlettered, unschooled **12** analphabetic

**ill-judged**
**04** daft, rash **05** hasty **06** unwise
**07** foolish **08** mistaken, reckless
**09** foolhardy, impolitic, imprudent, misguided, overhasty, unadvised

**10** ill-advised, incautious, indiscreet **11** injudicious, wrong-headed **12** short-sighted **13** ill-considered

**ill-mannered**
**04** rude **05** crude **06** coarse **07** boorish, cubbish, ill-bred, loutish, uncivil, uncouth **08** churlish, impolite, insolent **10** ill-behaved, unmannerly **11** bad-mannered, insensitive **12** badly behaved, discourteous

**ill-natured**
**03** wry **04** acid, mean, ugly **05** cross, nasty, sulky, surly **06** crabby, gnarly, shrewd, sullen, unkind **07** crabbed, vicious **08** churlish, perverse, petulant, shrewish, spiteful **09** malicious, malignant **10** malevolent, unfriendly, unpleasant, vindictive **11** bad-tempered **12** disagreeable

**illness**
**03** wog **04** bout, evil, tout, towt, weed, weid **05** touch **06** attack, malady **07** ailment, disease **08** disorder, sickness **09** complaint, condition, ill health, infirmity **10** affliction, disability, poor health **13** indisposition

*See also* **disease**

**illogical**
**05** crazy, wrong **06** absurd, faulty **07** invalid, unsound **08** fallible, specious, spurious **09** casuistic, incorrect, senseless, untenable **10** fallacious, irrational **11** meaningless, sophistical **12** inconsequent, inconsistent, unreasonable, unscientific, woolly minded

**illogicality**
**07** fallacy **08** unreason **09** absurdity **10** invalidity **11** unsoundness **12** speciousness **13** inconsistency, irrationality, senselessness **14** fallaciousness

**ill-starred**
**06** doomed **07** hapless, unhappy, unlucky **08** blighted, ill-fated **09** star-crost **11** star-crossed, unfortunate **12** inauspicious

**ill-tempered**
**04** curt **05** cross, curst, ratty, sharp, testy **06** crabby, cranky, girnie, grumpy, morose, shirty, tetchy, touchy **07** crabbed, grouchy, stroppy, vicious **08** choleric, spiteful **09** crotchety, impatient, irascible, irritable **10** ill-natured **11** acrimonious, bad-tempered, ill-humoured **12** cantankerous

**ill-timed**
**05** crass, inept **07** awkward **08** mistimed, tactless, untimely **09** unwelcome **10** wrong-timed **11** inopportune, unfortunate **12** inconvenient, unseasonable **13** inappropriate

**ill-treat**
◇ *anagram indicator*
**04** harm **05** abuse, wrong **06** damage, demean, injure, misuse **07** neglect, oppress **08** maltreat, misguide, mistreat **09** mishandle

**ill-treatment**
**04** harm **05** abuse **06** damage, ill-use, injury, misuse **07** neglect **11** manhandling, mishandling **12** maltreatment, mistreatment

**illuminate**
**04** limn **05** adorn, edify, light **07** clarify, clear up, explain, lighten, light up, miniate, shine on **08** brighten, decorate, illumine, instruct, ornament, twilight **09** back-light, elucidate, embellish, enlighten, limelight, overshine **10** floodlight, illustrate **12** throw light on

**illuminating**
**07** helpful **08** edifying **09** revealing **10** revelatory **11** explanatory, informative, instructive **12** enlightening

**illumination**
**03** ray **04** beam **05** flash, light **06** lights **07** insight **08** learning, lighting, radiance **09** adornment, awareness, education, miniature, theosophy **10** brightness, decoration, perception, revelation **11** candlelight, elucidation, instruction, irradiation **12** illustration **13** clarification, embellishment, enlightenment, ornamentation, understanding, zodiacal light

**illusion**
**04** maya **05** error, fancy **06** déjà vu, mirage **07** chimera, fallacy, fantasy, mocking, phantom, spectre **08** delusion, phantasm, prestige **09** deception, phantosme **10** apparition, fata Morgana **12** misjudgement, will-o'-the-wisp **13** hallucination, misconception **15** false impression, misapprehension

**illusory**
**04** sham **05** false **06** unreal, untrue **07** fancied, phantom, seeming **08** apparent, deluding, delusive, delusory, illusive, imagined, mistaken, specious **09** deceptive, erroneous, imaginary **10** chimerical, fallacious, misleading **11** illusionary **13** unsubstantial

**illustrate**
**04** draw, show **05** adorn **06** depict, sketch **07** clarify, exhibit, explain, miniate, picture **08** decorate, instance, ornament, renowned **09** elucidate, embellish, enlighten, exemplify, interpret **10** illuminate **11** demonstrate

**illustrated**
**08** miniated **09** decorated, pictorial **11** embellished, illuminated **12** with drawings, with pictures

**illustration**
**04** case, note **05** bleed, chart, gloss, plate, quote **06** blow-up, design, figure, remark, sample, sketch **07** analogy, artwork, comment, diagram, drawing, example, graphic, picture **08** exemplar, exponent, half-tone, instance, specimen, vignette **09** adornment, hors texte, quotation, sidelight **10** decoration, photograph **11** case in point, elucidation, explanation, observation **12** frontispiece **13** clarification, demonstration, embellishment, ornamentation **14** interpretation, representation **15** exemplification

**illustrative**
**06** sample **07** graphic, typical **08** specimen **09** pictorial **10** expository **11** delineative, descriptive, explanatory, explicatory **12** diagrammatic, exemplifying, illustratory **14** illustrational, interpretative, representative

**illustrious**
**04** dull **05** famed, great, noble, noted **06** bright, famous **07** eminent, exalted, notable **08** esteemed, glorious, honoured, luminous, renowned, splendid **09** acclaimed, brilliant, excellent, prominent, well-known **10** celebrated, honourable, pre-eminent, remarkable **11** magnificent, outstanding **13** distinguished

**ill-will**
**04** envy, gall **05** anger, odium, spite, wrath **06** animus, enmity, grudge, hatred, malice, maugre **07** dislike, envying, maulgre, rancour **08** aversion, bad blood **09** animosity, antipathy, hostility, maltalent **10** antagonism, ill-feeling, resentment **11** indignation, malevolence **12** disaffection, hard feelings **14** unfriendliness

**image**
**03** pic **04** bust, copy, doll, face, icon, idea, idol, tiki, twin **05** clone, fancy, match **06** double, effigy, figure, idolon, idolum, mirror, notion, reflex, ringer, shadow, simile, statue, typify, vision **07** concept, eidolon, fantasy, imagery, imagine, persona, picture, portray, profile, replica, thought **08** figurine, identity, likeness, metaphor, phantasy, portrait **09** depiction, duplicate, facsimile, lookalike, portrayal, statuette **10** appearance, conception, dead ringer, impression, perception, photograph, projection, public face, reflection **11** graven image, resemblance **12** doppelgänger, reproduction, turn of phrase **13** public persona, spitting image **14** figure of speech, representation

**imaginable**
**06** likely **08** credible, feasible, possible, probable **09** plausible, thinkable **10** believable, supposable **11** conceivable

**imaginary**
**06** dreamy, made-up, unreal **07** assumed, fancied, fictive, ghostly, phantom, pretend, shadowy **08** fabulous, fanciful, illusory,

imagined, invented, mythical, notional, spectral, supposed **09** fantastic, fictional, legendary, visionary **10** chimerical, fictitious **11** fantastical, make-believe, non-existent **12** hypothetical, mythological **13** hallucinatory, insubstantial

**imagination**
**03** wit **05** dream, fancy **06** schema, vision **07** chimera, fantasy, imagery, insight, project **08** illusion, mind's eye, phantasy **09** dreamland, ingenuity **10** creativity, enterprise, mental view **11** inspiration, originality **12** fancifulness **13** contemplation, flight of fancy, ingeniousness, inventiveness **15** imaginativeness, resourcefulness

**imaginative**
**05** vivid **06** clever, poetic **07** lyrical **08** creative, fanciful, inspired, original, poetical **09** fantastic, ingenious, inventive, visionary, whimsical **10** innovative **11** full of ideas, resourceful **12** enterprising

**imagine**
**03** see **04** deem, plan, ween **05** dream, fancy, feign, guess, image, judge, think **06** assume, create, devise, figure, gather, ideate, invent, reckon, scheme, take it, vision **07** believe, conceit, dream up, picture, presume, pretend, project, propose, suppose, surmise, think up **08** conceive, contrive, daydream, envisage **09** conjure up, fantasize, visualize **10** conjecture **11** make believe **14** form a picture of

**imbalance**
**04** bias **08** inequity, variance **09** disparity **10** inequality, partiality, unevenness, unfairness **13** disproportion

**imbecile**
◇ *anagram indicator*
**03** ass, mug, nit **04** berk, clot, daft, dope, dork, dumb, fool, geek, jerk, nana, nerd, nerk, nong, prat, putz, twit **05** anile, barmy, batty, chump, crazy, dorky, dotty, dumbo, dunce, eejit, goofy, idiot, inane, klutz, moron, ninny, nutty, potty, silly, twerp, wacky, wally **06** absurd, bammer, bampot, cretin, dimwit, doofus, dum-dum, nitwit, numpty, stupid, sucker **07** asinine, bungler, fatuous, foolish, halfwit, idiotic, jughead, moronic, pillock, plonker, wazzock, witless **08** flathead, innocent, numskull **09** birdbrain, blockhead, cloth head, lame brain, ludicrous, simpleton, thickhead **10** nincompoop **11** chowderhead, knuckle-head, thick-headed **12** crack-brained **13** knuckle-headed

**imbecility**
**06** idiocy **07** amentia, fatuity, idiotcy, inanity **08** daftness **09** asininity, craziness, cretinism, stupidity **11** foolishness **12** childishness, incompetence

**imbibe**
◇ *containment indicator*
**03** sip **04** gain, gulp, suck, swig **05** drink, lap up, quaff **06** absorb, gather, ingest, soak up, take in **07** acquire, consume, drink in, receive, swallow **09** knock back **10** assimilate

**imbroglio**
**04** mess **06** muddle, scrape, tangle **07** dilemma **08** quandary **09** confusion **10** difficulty **11** embroilment, involvement **12** complication, entanglement

**imbue**
**04** fill, tint **05** embay, steep, taint, tinct, tinge **06** charge, infuse, inject, instil, season **07** breathe, ingrain, inspire, moisten, pervade, possess, suffuse **08** permeate, saturate, tincture **09** inbreathe, inculcate, inoculate, transfuse **10** impregnate **12** indoctrinate

**imitate**
**03** act, ape, hit **04** copy, echo, fake, mock **05** feign, forge, mimic, spoof **06** follow, hit off, mirror, parody, parrot, repeat, send up **07** copycat, emulate, take off **08** simulate **09** duplicate, replicate, reproduce **10** caricature, do likewise, follow suit **11** counterfeit, impersonate **12** take as a model

**imitation**
**04** copy, echo, -ette, fake, faux, mock, sham **05** apery, aping, dummy, spoof **06** ersatz, parody, phoney, pseudo, send-up **07** forgery, man-made, mimesis, mimicry, mockery, mocking, replica, take-off **08** knock-off, likeness, parrotry, travesty **09** burlesque, duplicate, emulation, simulated, synthetic **10** artificial, caricature, impression, reflection, simulation **11** counterfeit, resemblance **12** reproduction **13** impersonation

**imitative**
**04** mock **05** apish, me-too, mimic **07** copying, mimetic, servile **09** emulating, mimetical, mimicking, simulated **10** derivative, parrot-like, second-hand, unoriginal **11** plagiarized **12** onomatopoeic

**imitator**
**03** ape **04** echo **05** mimic **06** copier, epigon, parrot **07** copycat, copyist, epigone **08** emulator, follower, parodist **10** plagiarist **12** impersonator **13** impressionist

**immaculate**
**04** pure **05** clean **07** perfect, sinless **08** flawless, innocent, pristine, spotless, unsoiled **09** blameless, faultless, guiltless, incorrupt, stainless, undefiled, unstained, unsullied, untainted **10** impeccable **11** unblemished **12** spick and span, squeaky clean

**immaculately**
**06** purely **09** perfectly, sinlessly **10** flawlessly, impeccably, innocently, spotlessly, without sin **11** blamelessly, faultlessly, guiltlessly, incorruptly **12** to perfection, without blame, without guilt

**immanent**
**06** innate **08** inherent **09** ingrained, intrinsic, pervading **10** permeating, ubiquitous **11** omnipresent **12** all-pervading

**immaterial**
**05** minor, petty **07** trivial **08** trifling **10** irrelevant **11** incorporeal, inessential, of no account, unessential, unimportant **13** insignificant **15** inconsequential

**immature**
◇ *tail deletion indicator*
**03** raw **05** crude, green, naive, vealy, young **06** callow, jejune, unripe **07** babyish, budding, puerile, unbaked, unready **08** childish, juvenile, under-age, unformed, untimely **09** beardless, embryonic, fledgling, half-baked, infantile, ingenuous, unfledged, unsizable **10** adolescent, incomplete, unmellowed, unprepared, unsizeable **11** undeveloped **13** inexperienced

**immaturity**
**05** youth **07** crudity, rawness **09** crudeness, greenness, puerility **10** callowness, juvenility, unripeness **11** adolescence, babyishness **12** childishness, immatureness, imperfection, inexperience **14** unpreparedness

**immeasurable**
**04** vast **07** endless, immense **08** infinite **09** boundless, limitless, unbounded, unlimited **10** bottomless, fathomless **11** illimitable, inestimable, never ending **12** immensurable, incalculable, interminable, unfathomable **13** inexhaustible

**immeasurably**
**06** vastly **09** endlessly, immensely **10** infinitely **11** boundlessly, illimitably, inestimably, limitlessly **12** incalculably, interminably **13** beyond measure, inexhaustibly

**immediacy**
**07** urgency **08** instancy **09** freshness, imminence, swiftness **10** directness, importance, promptness **11** spontaneity **12** criticalness, simultaneity **13** instantaneity

**immediate**
**04** main, near, next **05** basic, chief, close, swift, vital **06** direct, prompt, recent, speedy, sudden, urgent **07** closest, crucial, current, instant, nearest, present, primary, soonest **08** abutting, adjacent, critical, existing, next-door, pressing **09** adjoining, first-time, important, posthaste, principal, proximate **11** fundamental, top-priority **12** high-priority, without delay **13** instantaneous

**immediately**
**03** now, pdq **04** anon, ASAP, next, stat, then, tite **06** at once, belive, pronto, statim, subito **07** bang off, quickly **08** as soon as, directly, promptly, right now, speedily, straight, urgently **09** at a glance, forthwith, instantly, like a shot, on the spot, out of hand, presently, right away, thereupon, yesterday **10** this minute **11** incessantly, incontinent, in the wake of, on the morrow, straightway, therewithal, this instant, tout de suite **12** lickety-split, no sooner than, on the instant, on the knocker, straight away, straightways, there and then, without delay **13** incontinently, straightforth **14** unhesitatingly, without more ado **15** before you know it, instantaneously, without question

**immemorial**
**05** fixed, hoary **06** age-old, of yore **07** ancient, archaic **08** timeless **09** ancestral **11** traditional **12** long-standing, time-honoured

**immense**
**04** fine, huge, mega, vast **05** enorm, giant, great, jumbo **06** bumper, cosmic, myriad **07** mammoth, massive, titanic **08** colossal, cyclopic, enormous, fabulous, gigantic, whopping **09** cyclopean, cyclopian, extensive, ginormous, herculean, humungous, limitless **10** monumental, tremendous **11** Brobdingnag, elephantine **14** Brobdingnagian, extremely large

**immensely**
**04** very **05** jolly **06** highly, really, vastly **07** acutely, awfully, greatly, utterly **08** severely, terribly **09** decidedly, extremely, intensely, massively, unusually **10** dreadfully, enormously, remarkably, uncommonly **11** exceedingly, excessively, frightfully **12** immoderately, inordinately, terrifically, unreasonably **13** exceptionally **15** extraordinarily

**immensity**
**04** bulk **07** expanse **08** hugeness, infinity, vastness **09** expansion, greatness, magnitude **11** massiveness **12** enormousness, giganticness **13** extensiveness, limitlessness

**immerse**
◇ *hidden indicator*
**03** dip **04** bury, duck, dunk, sink, soak **05** bathe, douse, souse **06** absorb, blanch, drench, engage, engulf, occupy, plunge, wallow **07** baptize, demerge, demerse, embathe, engross, imbathe, immerge, involve **08** saturate, submerge, submerse, wrap up in **09** preoccupy

**immersed**
◇ *hidden indicator*
**04** busy, deep, rapt, sunk **06** buried **07** taken up **08** absorbed, consumed, involved, occupied **09** engrossed, wrapped up **11** preoccupied

**immersion**
**03** dip **05** bathe **07** baptism, dipping, dousing, ducking, dunking, sinking, soaking **08** plunging **09** drenching **10** absorption, engagement, engrossing, saturation, submersion **11** involvement **13** concentration, preoccupation

**immigrant**
**03** pom **04** Balt **05** alien, issei, pommy **06** merino **07** greener, incomer, migrant, new chum, settler, wetback **08** newcomer, outsider **09** foreigner, Pakistani **10** Aussiedler, new arrival, overstayer **13** new Australian

**immigrate**
**06** come in, move in, remove, settle **07** migrate **08** resettle

**imminence**
**06** menace, threat **08** approach, instancy, nearness **09** closeness, immediacy **11** propinquity

**imminent**
**04** near **05** close **06** at hand, coming **07** brewing, in store, jutting, looming **08** in the air, menacing, on the way, upcoming **09** impending **11** approaching, forthcoming, in the offing, overhanging, threatening **12** on the horizon **13** about to happen, almost upon you **14** round the corner **15** fast approaching

**immobile**
**05** fixed, rigid, stiff, still **06** at rest, frozen, rooted, static **07** riveted **08** moveless, unmoving **09** immovable **10** motionless, stationary, stock-still **11** immobilized

**immobility**
**06** fixity **08** catatony, firmness **09** catatonia, fixedness, inertness, stability, stillness **10** disability, steadiness **12** immovability **14** motionlessness

**immobilize**
**04** halt, stop **05** Taser® **06** freeze **07** cripple, disable **08** paralyse, transfix **10** deactivate, inactivate **14** put out of action

**immoderate**
**03** OTT **05** steep, undue **06** lavish, wanton **07** extreme, fulsome **08** enormous, uncurbed **09** egregious, excessive, hubristic, unbridled, unlimited **10** exorbitant, inordinate, outrageous, over the top, profligate **11** exaggerated, extravagant, intemperate, overweening, uncalled-for, unjustified, unwarranted **12** distemperate, uncontrolled, unreasonable, unrestrained, unrestricted **13** self-indulgent **14** unconscionable

**immoderately**
**06** unduly **08** to excess, wantonly **09** extremely **11** excessively **12** exorbitantly, inordinately, out of all cess, unreasonably **13** exaggeratedly, extravagantly, unjustifiably **14** unrestrainedly, without measure

**immoderation**
**06** excess **08** unreason **10** inordinacy, lavishness **11** dissipation, exorbitance, prodigality, unrestraint **12** extravagance, intemperance **13** excessiveness **14** immoderateness, overindulgence

**immodest**
**04** bold, lewd **05** cocky, fresh, saucy **06** brazen, cheeky, coarse, risqué **07** forward, immoral, obscene **08** boastful, improper, impudent, indecent **09** revealing, shameless **10** indecorous, indelicate

**immodesty**
**04** gall **05** brass **08** audacity, boldness, impurity, lewdness, temerity **09** bawdiness, impudence, indecorum, obscenity **10** coarseness, impudicity, indelicacy **11** forwardness **13** shamelessness **14** indecorousness

**immolate**
**04** burn, kill **05** offer **07** offer up **09** sacrifice

**immoral**
**03** bad **04** base, blue, evil, lewd, vile **05** juicy, loose, wrong **06** impure, naught, sinful, wanton, wicked **07** corrupt, godless, obscene, raunchy, vicious **08** depraved, indecent, unhonest **09** debauched, dishonest, dissolute, nefarious, reprobate, unethical **10** degenerate, iniquitous, licentious **11** promiscuous **12** pornographic, questionable, unprincipled, unscrupulous **13** against nature

• **immoral act**
**03** sin

**immorality**
**03** sin **04** evil, vice **05** wrong **07** badness **08** impurity, iniquity, lewdness, vileness **09** depravity, indecency, obscenity, turpitude **10** corruption, debauchery, dishonesty, profligacy, sinfulness, wickedness, wrongdoing **11** pornography **12** indiscretion **13** dissoluteness **14** licentiousness

**immortal**
**03** god **04** hero **05** deity, great **06** famous, genius **07** abiding, ageless, endless, eternal, goddess, lasting, undying **08** constant, divinity, enduring, fadeless, honoured, Olympian, timeless, unfading **09** amarantin, ambrosial, ceaseless, deathless, memorable, perennial, perpetual, well-known **10** celebrated, ever-living **11** divine being, everlasting, sempiternal **12** imperishable **13** distinguished, unforgettable **14** indestructible

**immortality**
**04** fame **05** glory **06** honour, renown **08** eternity **09** celebrity, greatness **10** amritattva, perpetuity

**11** distinction, endlessness, eternal life
**12** gloriousness, timelessness
**13** deathlessness, glorification
**15** everlasting life, imperishability

**immortalize**
**04** laud **07** glorify **08** enshrine, eternize
**09** celebrate **10** eternalize, perpetuate
**11** commemorate, memorialize

**immovable**
**03** set **04** fast, firm, real **05** fixed, stuck
**06** dogged, jammed, moored, rooted, secure, stable **07** adamant, riveted
**08** anchored, constant, immobile, resolute, stubborn **09** impassive, obstinate, steadfast **10** determined, inflexible, motionless, unshakable, unswerving, unwavering, unyielding
**11** unalterable, unshakeable
**12** intransigent **14** marble-constant, uncompromising

**immune**
**04** free, safe **05** clear, proof
**06** exempt, secure, spared **07** excused
**08** absolved, released, relieved
**09** protected, resistant **12** invulnerable
**13** unsusceptible

**immunity**
**05** right **06** safety **07** freedom, liberty, licence, release **08** impunity
**09** exception, exemption, franchise, indemnity, privilege **10** permission, protection, resistance **11** exoneration, inoculation, vaccination
**12** immunization, mithridatism

**immunization**
**03** jab **09** injection **10** protection
**11** inoculation, vaccination

**immunize**
**04** salt **06** inject, shield **07** protect
**09** inoculate, safeguard, vaccinate

**immure**
**04** cage, jail **06** enwall, shut up, wall in
**07** confine, enclose **08** cloister, imprison **11** incarcerate **13** put behind bars

**immutability**
**09** constancy, fixedness, stability
**10** durability, permanence
**13** immutableness, invariability
**14** changelessness **15** unalterableness

**immutable**
**05** fixed **06** stable **07** abiding, lasting
**08** constant, enduring **09** permanent, perpetual, steadfast **10** changeless, inflexible, invariable, sacrosanct
**11** unalterable **12** unchangeable

**imp**
**03** elf **04** brat, limb, minx, puck, ympe
**05** demon, devil, gamin, gnome, graft, Ralph, rogue, scamp, scion, shoot
**06** goblin, rascal, sprite, urchin
**09** hobgoblin, prankster, trickster
**12** troublemaker **13** mischief-maker
**15** flibbertigibbet

**impact**
**03** act, fix, hit **04** bang, belt, blow, bump, dush, jolt, work **05** brunt, clash, crash, crush, force, knock, poise, power, shock, smash, souse **06** affect, effect, glance, strike **07** apply to, collide, contact, impinge, meaning, results **09** collision, influence
**10** impression, percussion
**12** consequences, significance
**13** press together, repercussions
**14** have an effect on, reverberations

**impair**
◇ *anagram indicator*
**03** mar **04** harm, rust **05** alloy, blunt, craze, decay, spoil, wrong **06** damage, hinder, injure, lessen, reduce, weaken, worsen **07** cripple, disable, empeach, impeach, tarnish, vitiate, wear out
**08** decrease, diminish, embezzle, emperish, enervate, enfeeble, wear away, wear down **09** undermine
**10** debilitate **11** deteriorate

**impaired**
◇ *anagram indicator*
**04** poor, weak **05** rusty, stale **06** faulty, flawed, spoilt **07** damaged, unsound, vicious **08** disabled, vitiated, weakened **09** defective, imperfect
**10** challenged **11** handicapped

**impairment**
**04** flaw, harm, hurt, ruin, wear **05** allay, fault, spoil **06** damage, injury
**07** empeach, impeach **08** handicap, weakness **09** paralogia, reduction, vitiation **10** disability **11** disablement, dysfunction **13** deterioration
*See also* **sight**

**impale**
**04** spit, stab **05** ganch, lance, prick, spear, spike, stick **06** gaunch, pierce, skewer **08** puncture, transfix
**09** perforate **10** disembowel, run through

**impalpable**
**04** airy, fine, thin **06** subtle **07** elusive, shadowy, tenuous **08** delicate
**10** indistinct, intangible
**11** incorporeal, indefinable
**13** imperceptible, insubstantial, unsubstantial **15** inapprehensible

**impart**
**04** give, lend, shed, tell **05** break, grant, offer **06** accord, assign, bestow, confer, convey, pass on, relate, report, reveal **07** divulge **08** disclose, transmit
**09** make known **10** contribute
**11** communicate

**impartial**
**04** fair, just **05** equal **06** candid
**07** neutral **08** detached, judicial, unbiased **09** equitable, objective
**10** crossbench, even-handed, fair-minded, open-minded **11** non-partisan, uncommitted, unconcerned
**12** unprejudiced **13** disinterested, dispassionate

**impartiality**
**06** candor, equity **07** candour, justice
**08** equality, fairness **10** detachment, dispassion, neutrality **11** disinterest, objectivity **12** unbiasedness
**14** even-handedness, open-mindedness **15** non-partisanship

**impassable**
**06** closed **07** blocked, invious
**08** pathless **09** trackless **10** invincible, obstructed, unpassable **11** insuperable, unnavigable **12** impenetrable, unassailable, unvoyageable
**13** untraversable **14** insurmountable

**impasse**
**04** halt **06** log jam **07** dead end
**08** cul-de-sac, deadlock
**09** checkmate, stalemate **10** blind alley, standstill **15** Mexican standoff

**impassioned**
**05** eager, fiery **06** ardent, fervid, heated **07** blazing, earnest, excited, fervent, furious, glowing, intense, rousing, violent **08** animated, forceful, inflamed, inspired, spirited, stirring, vehement, vigorous **09** emotional, heartfelt **10** passionate **12** enthusiastic

**impassive**
**04** calm, cool **05** bland **06** stolid
**07** stoical, unmoved **08** composed, laid-back **09** apathetic, immovable, unfeeling, unruffled **10** impassible, phlegmatic **11** emotionless, indifferent, unconcerned, unemotional, unemotioned, unexcitable, unflappable **13** dispassionate, imperturbable **14** expressionless

**impassively**
**06** calmly, coolly **11** unfeelingly
**13** apathetically, emotionlessly, imperturbably, unemotionally
**14** phlegmatically **15** dispassionately

**impatience**
**05** haste **07** anxiety **08** curtness, edginess, keenness, rashness
**09** agitation, dysphoria, eagerness, shortness, tenseness **10** abruptness, indignance, uneasiness
**11** brusqueness, impetuosity, intolerance, nervousness
**12** excitability, irritability, restlessness
• **expression of impatience**
**03** ach, dam, och, poh, tut **04** chut, damn, phew, pish, push, toot, tush, tuts, when **05** damme, devil, pshaw, toots
**06** dammit, tut-tut **07** crimine, crimini
**10** tilly-fally, tilly-vally
**12** Donnerwetter, tilley-valley

**impatient**
**04** curt, edgy, keen **05** angry, eager, hasty, narky, ratty, short, tense, testy
**06** abrupt, snappy **07** anxious, brusque, fidgety, fretful, jittery, nervous
**08** restless **09** excitable, impetuous, irritable, querulous **10** intolerant
**11** hot-tempered **13** on tenterhooks, quick-tempered

**impeach**
**05** blame **06** accuse, attack, charge, damage, hinder, impair, impede, impugn, indict, revile **07** arraign, censure, prevent **08** denounce
**09** criticize, detriment, disparage, hindrance **10** impairment, prevention

**impeachment**
**06** appeal, charge **10** accusation, indictment **11** arraignment **13** disparagement

**impeccable**
**04** pure **05** exact **06** just so **07** correct, perfect, precise, upright **08** flawless, innocent **09** blameless, exemplary, faultless, stainless **10** immaculate **11** unblemished **12** squeaky clean **14** irreproachable

**impecunious**
**04** poor **05** broke, needy, skint **07** boracic **08** dirt-poor, indigent, strapped **09** destitute, insolvent, penniless, penurious **10** cleaned out, stony-broke **12** impoverished, on your uppers **15** poverty-stricken

**impedance**
**01** Z **09** hindrance
• **measure of impedance**
**03** ohm

**impede**
**03** bar, rub **04** clog, curb, slow, stop **05** block, check, delay **06** hamper, hinder, hogtie, hold up, retard, thwart **07** disrupt, empeach, impeach, trammel **08** encumber, handicap, hold back, incumber, obstruct, restrain, slow down, strangle

**impediment**
**03** bar, bur, log, rub **04** burr, clog, curb, halt, snag **05** block, check **06** burden, defect, rubber **07** barrier, setback, stammer, stutter **08** handicap, obstacle **09** hindrance, restraint **10** difficulty **11** encumbrance, obstruction, restriction **14** stumbling-block

**impedimenta**
**04** gear **05** stuff **06** things **07** baggage, effects, luggage **09** equipment **10** belongings **12** encumbrances **13** accoutrements, bits and pieces, paraphernalia

**impel**
**03** put **04** goad, move, prod, push, spur, urge **05** drive, force, press **06** compel, excite, incite, oblige, prompt, propel, strike **07** inspire **08** get going, motivate, pressure **09** constrain, instigate, stimulate **10** pressurize

**impending**
**04** near **05** close **06** at hand, coming, toward **07** brewing, looming **08** imminent, in the air, menacing, on the way, upcoming **11** approaching, forthcoming, in the offing, threatening **12** on the horizon **13** about to happen

**impenetrable**
**04** dark **05** dense, solid, thick **07** cryptic, obscure **08** abstruse, airtight, baffling, puzzling **09** enigmatic, overgrown, recondite **10** adamantine, impassable, impervious, mysterious, soundproof **11** inscrutable **12** unfathomable **13** indiscernible **14** unintelligible

**impenitence**
**08** defiance, obduracy **11** impenitency **12** stubbornness **15** hard-heartedness, incorrigibility

**impenitent**
**07** defiant **08** hardened, obdurate **09** unabashed, unashamed **10** uncontrite, unreformed **11** remorseless, unrepentant **12** incorrigible, unregenerate, unremorseful **13** without regret **14** without remorse

**imperative**
**05** vital **06** urgent **07** crucial **08** critical, pressing **09** essential, necessary **10** compulsory, obligatory, peremptory **13** authoritative, indispensable

**imperceptible**
**04** fine, tiny **05** faint, small, vague **06** minute, slight, subtle **07** gradual, muffled, obscure, unclear **09** inaudible, minuscule **10** impalpable, indefinite, indistinct, negligible, unapparent **11** microscopic **12** undetectable, unnoticeable **13** inappreciable, indiscernible, infinitesimal

**imperceptibly**
**06** slowly, subtly, unseen **08** bit by bit **09** gradually **10** insensibly **12** unnoticeably **13** inappreciably, indiscernibly, unobtrusively **14** little by little

**imperfect**
◇ *anagram indicator*
**04** lame **06** broken, faulty, flawed **07** chipped, damaged, sketchy **08** impaired **09** blemished, defective, deficient, embryonic, unperfect **10** inadequate, incomplete **12** insufficient

**imperfection**
**03** cut **04** blot, dent, flaw, kink, spot, tear **05** break, crack, fault, stain, taint **06** blotch, defect, foible, hickey, mackle **07** blemish, failing, scratch **08** weakness **09** deformity **10** deficiency, impairment, inadequacy **11** shortcoming **13** insufficiency **15** malconformation

**imperial**
**03** Imp **05** grand, great, lofty, noble, regal, royal **06** august, kingly **07** queenly, stately, supreme **08** absolute, glorious, majestic, splendid **09** sovereign **10** commanding **11** magnificent, monarchical

**imperialism**
**10** flag-waving **11** adventurism, colonialism, flag-wagging **12** expansionism **14** empire-building **15** acquisitiveness

**imperil**
**04** harm, risk **06** expose, hazard, injure **08** endanger, threaten **10** compromise, jeopardize **11** put in danger, take a chance **12** expose to risk **13** put in jeopardy

**imperious**
**06** lordly **07** haughty **08** arrogant, despotic **09** assertive, masterful **10** autocratic, commanding, high-handed, peremptory, tyrannical **11** dictatorial, domineering, overbearing, overweening

**imperishable**
**07** abiding, eternal, undying **08** enduring, immortal, unfading **09** deathless, perennial, permanent, perpetual **11** everlasting **13** immarcescible, incorruptible, unforgettable **14** indestructible

**impermanence**
**09** briefness **10** transience, transiency **11** elusiveness, inconstancy **12** ephemerality **13** temporariness **14** transitoriness

**impermanent**
**05** brief **06** flying, mortal **07** elusive, passing, unfixed **08** fleeting, fugitive, unstable **09** ephemeral, fugacious, momentary, temporary, transient, unsettled **10** evanescent, fly-by-night, inconstant, perishable, short-lived, transitory

**impermeable**
**05** proof **06** sealed **08** airtight, hermetic **09** damp-proof, non-porous, resistant **10** impassable, impervious, waterproof, watertight **11** greaseproof **12** impenetrable **14** water-repellent, water-resistant

**impersonal**
**04** cold, cool **05** aloof, stiff **06** formal, frigid, remote, stuffy **07** distant, neutral **08** clinical, detached, official, unbiased **09** objective, unfeeling **11** unemotional **12** businesslike, unprejudiced **13** dispassionate

**impersonally**
**06** fairly, justly **09** equitably, neutrally **11** objectively, without bias **12** open-mindedly **14** with an open mind **15** dispassionately

**impersonate**
**02** do **03** act, ape **04** mock **05** mimic **06** embody, parody, pose as, send up **07** imitate, portray, present, take off **09** incarnate, pass off as **10** caricature **12** masquerade as

**impersonation**
**05** apery, aping, fraud, spoof **06** parody, send-up **07** mimicry, take-off **09** burlesque, imitation **10** caricature, impression

**impertinence**
**03** lip **04** face, gall, sass **05** brass, cheek, crust, mouth, nerve, sauce, snash **08** attitude, audacity, backchat, boldness, chutzpah, rudeness **09** brass neck, flippancy, impudence, insolence, intrusion **10** brazenness, disrespect, effrontery **11** discourtesy, forwardness, presumption

12 flippantness, impoliteness
13 shamelessness

**impertinent**
04 bold, pert, rude 05 brash, fresh, sassy, saucy 06 brazen, cheeky 07 forward 08 impolite, impudent, insolent 09 audacious, intrusive, shameless 10 unmannerly 11 ill-mannered 12 discourteous, presumptuous 13 disrespectful

**imperturbability**
04 cool 08 calmness, coolness
09 composure, sangfroid
10 equanimity 11 complacency
12 tranquillity 14 self-possession

**imperturbable**
04 calm, cool 06 serene 07 unfazed, unmoved 08 composed, laid-back, tranquil 09 collected, impassive, supercool, unruffled 10 complacent, unruffable, untroubled 11 unexcitable, unflappable 12 even-tempered
13 self-possessed 15 cool as a cucumber

**impervious**
05 proof, tight 06 closed, immune, opaque, sealed 07 unmoved 08 gas-tight, hermetic 09 damp-proof, dustproof, non-porous, rainproof, resistant, star-proof, untouched
10 light-proof, smokeproof, smoketight, steamtight, unaffected, waterproof, watertight 11 adiathermic, impermeable, showerproof
12 impenetrable, invulnerable

**impetuosity**
04 birr, dash, élan, rush 05 haste
08 rashness 09 hastiness, vehemence
10 impatience 11 spontaneity
12 recklessness 13 foolhardiness, impetuousness, impulsiveness
15 precipitateness, thoughtlessness

**impetuous**
04 rash 05 brash, fiery, hasty 06 sturdy
07 violent 08 headlong, reckless, tearaway 09 foolhardy, hot-headed, impatient, impulsive, unplanned
10 bull-headed, unreasoned, unthinking 11 precipitate, spontaneous, thoughtless 12 ill-conceived, uncontrolled
14 unpremeditated 15 spur-of-the-moment

**impetuously**
06 rashly 10 recklessly, vehemently
11 impulsively 12 passionately, unthinkingly 13 precipitately, spontaneously

**impetus**
04 birr, goad, push, send, spur 05 boost, drive, force, power, sweep, swing
06 energy, travel, urging 07 impulse
08 momentum, stimulus 09 actuation, incentive, influence 10 motivation
11 inspiration 13 encouragement

**impiety**
06 hubris 08 iniquity 09 blasphemy, profanity, sacrilege 10 irreligion, sinfulness, unholiness, wickedness
11 godlessness, irreverence, profaneness, ungodliness
15 unrighteousness

**impinge**
03 hit 04 beat, fall 05 souse, touch
06 affect, invade, strike 07 intrude, touch on 08 encroach, infringe, trespass 09 influence

**impious**
06 sinful, unholy, wicked 07 godless, profane, ungodly 09 hubristic
10 iniquitous, irreverent
11 blasphemous, irreligious, unrighteous 12 sacrilegious

**impish**
05 elfin, gamin 07 naughty, puckish, roguish, tricksy, waggish 08 devilish, rascally, sportive 09 pranksome, tricksome 10 frolicsome
11 mischievous

**implacability**
12 pitilessness, ruthlessness, vengefulness 13 inexorability, inflexibility, intransigence, mercilessness, rancorousness
14 implacableness, intractability, relentlessness 15 remorselessness, unforgivingness

**implacable**
05 cruel 06 deadly, mortal
07 adamant 08 pitiless, ruthless, vengeful 09 heartless, impacable, merciless, rancorous 10 inexorable, inflexible, relentless, unyielding
11 intractable, remorseless, unforgiving, unrelenting
12 intransigent, unappeasable
14 irreconcilable, uncompromising

**implant**
03 fix, put, sow 04 root 05 embed, graft, inset, place, plant 06 enrace, enroot, insert, instil 07 embosom, engraft, imbosom 09 inculcate, introduce 10 inseminate, transplant

**implausible**
04 lame, thin, weak 06 flimsy
07 dubious, suspect 08 doubtful, unlikely 10 far-fetched, improbable, incredible 11 transparent
12 questionable, unbelievable, unconvincing 13 hard to believe, inconceivable

**implausibly**
10 doubtfully, improbably, incredibly
12 questionably, unbelievably
13 inconceivably

**implement**
02 do 04 celt, comb, loom, rake, tool
05 apply, brush, dolly, flail, raker, razor, steel, whisk 06 anchor, device, effect, eolith, fulfil, gadget, pusher, ricker, ripple, sickle, taster, tedder 07 enforce, execute, grubber, perform, realize, utensil 08 carry out, complete, fly whisk, scuffler, shoehorn, spreader, squeegee, squilgee, tint tool
09 apparatus, appliance, discharge, fire-stick, fish slice, microlith, poop scoop, requisite, scarifier
10 accomplish, bring about, cultivator, extirpator, fish-carver, fish-trowel, gold-washer, instrument, loggerhead, snowplough, sucket fork, wheel brace
11 contrivance, road scraper, sucket spoon, turfing iron 13 pooper-scooper, put into action, put into effect
14 rostrocarinate

**implementation**
06 action 09 discharge, effecting, execution, operation 10 completion, fulfilling, fulfilment, performing
11 application, carrying-out, enforcement, performance, realization
14 accomplishment

**implicate**
◇ *anagram indicator*
05 imply 06 enfold 07 concern, connect, embroil, include, involve
08 entangle 09 associate, be a part of, be party to, inculpate 10 be a party to, compromise 11 incriminate

**implicated**
◇ *anagram indicator*
07 party to 08 included, involved
09 concerned, connected, embroiled, entangled, suspected 10 associated, inculpated 11 compromised, responsible 12 incriminated

**implication**
06 effect 07 meaning 08 overtone
09 deduction, inference, undertone
10 conclusion, connection, suggestion
11 association, consequence, embroilment, inculpation, insinuation, involvement 12 entanglement, ramification, repercussion, significance 13 incrimination
15 subintelligitur

**implicit**
04 full 05 sheer, tacit, total, utter
06 entire, hidden, hinted, latent, unsaid
07 implied, perfect 08 absolute, complete, indirect, inferred, inherent, positive, unspoken, unstated
09 deducible, entangled, steadfast, suggested 10 insinuated, understood, unreserved 11 intertwined, unexpressed, unqualified
12 unhesitating, wholehearted
13 unconditional, unquestioning

**implicitly**
06 firmly 07 totally, utterly
10 absolutely, completely
11 steadfastly 12 unreservedly
14 unhesitatingly, wholeheartedly
15 unconditionally, unquestioningly

**implied**
05 tacit 06 hinted 07 assumed
08 implicit, indirect, inherent, unspoken, unstated 09 suggested
10 insinuated, undeclared, understood
11 unexpressed

**implore**
03 ask, beg 04 pray 05 crave, plead, press 06 appeal, invoke 07 beseech, beseeke, conjure, entreat, request,

solicit **09** importune, obsecrate **10** supplicate

**imply**
**04** hint, mean **05** infer, state **06** denote, enfold, entail, signal **07** connote, involve, point to, require, signify, suggest, suppose **08** indicate, intimate **09** implicate, insinuate, predicate **10** presuppose, understand **13** say indirectly

**impolite**
**04** rude **05** crude, rough **06** abrupt, cheeky, coarse, vulgar **07** boorish, ill-bred, loutish, uncivil **08** insolent **09** unrefined **10** indecorous, ungracious, unladylike, unmannerly **11** bad-mannered, ill-mannered, impertinent, uncivilized **12** discourteous **13** disrespectful, inconsiderate, ungentlemanly

**impolitely**
**06** rudely **07** crudely **09** uncivilly **10** insolently **12** indecorously, ungraciously **13** impertinently **14** discourteously **15** disrespectfully, inconsiderately

**impoliteness**
**08** rudeness **09** crassness, gaucherie, indecorum, insolence, roughness **10** abruptness, bad manners, coarseness, disrespect, incivility, indelicacy **11** boorishness, discourtesy **12** churlishness, impertinence **14** indecorousness, unmannerliness

**impolitic**
**04** daft, rash **06** unwise **07** foolish **09** ill-judged, imprudent, maladroit, misguided **10** ill-advised, indiscreet, unpolicied **11** inexpedient, injudicious **12** short-sighted, undiplomatic **13** ill-considered

**import**
**03** nub **04** gist **05** buy in, drift, sense, state **06** amount, behove, convey, moment, ship in, thrust, weight **07** bring in, content, essence, meaning, message, portend, purport, signify **08** reimport, tendency **09** importing, intention, introduce, substance **10** importance **11** consequence, implication, seriousness **12** foreign goods, foreign trade, significance **13** buy from abroad, imported goods **14** foreign product **15** imported product

**importance**
**04** mark, note, pith **05** power, state, value, worth **06** esteem, import, matter, status, weight **07** concern, urgency **08** eminence, gravitas, interest, prestige, standing **09** graveness, influence, magnitude, substance **10** prominence, usefulness **11** consequence, distinction **12** criticalness, significance **13** consideration, momentousness, signification **14** noteworthiness

• **anything of importance**
**04** much

• **anything of minor importance**
**02** by **03** bye

• **be of importance**
**04** mean **06** matter

**important**
**03** big, key, top **04** main **05** chief, grave, heavy, major, noted, vital **06** mighty, urgent, valued **07** big-time, capital, central, crucial, eminent, fateful, leading, notable, pivotal, pompous, primary, salient, seminal, serious, weighty **08** critical, esteemed, foremost, historic, material, powerful, priority, relevant, ultimate, valuable **09** essential, front-page, high-level, momentous, number one, of warrant, paramount, principal, prominent **10** meaningful, noteworthy, pre-eminent **11** epoch-making, far-reaching, fundamental, high-ranking, influential, outstanding, prestigious, significant, substantial **12** world-shaking **13** consequential, distinguished, of good warrant **15** world-shattering

**importunate**
**06** dogged, urgent **08** annoying, pressing **09** impatient, insistent, tenacious **10** burdensome, persistent **11** inopportune, troublesome **12** pertinacious

**importune**
**03** beg, dun, ply **04** prig, urge **05** annoy, beset, hound, press **06** appeal, badger, cajole, harass, import, pester, plague, urgent **07** besiege, request, signify, solicit **08** untimely **09** flagitate, plead with **10** burdensome, lay siege to, resistless, supplicate **11** inopportune

**importunity**
**06** urging **07** urgency **08** cajolery, hounding, pressing **09** harassing, pestering **10** entreaties, harassment, importance, insistence **11** persistence **12** solicitation

**impose**
**03** fix, lay, put, set **04** levy, palm **05** abuse, apply, clamp, exact, foist, force, lay on, place, put on **06** burden, butt in, charge, decree, enjoin, impone, saddle, thrust **07** break in, command, enforce, exploit, inflict, intrude, mislead, obtrude, place on, presume, put over, put upon **08** encroach, encumber, trespass **09** establish, institute, introduce **13** force yourself, take liberties **14** thrust yourself **15** take advantage of

**imposing**
**05** grand, lofty **06** august **07** stately **08** majestic, matronly, specious, splendid, striking **09** deceptive, dignified, grandiose, mausolean **10** commanding, impressive, statuesque **12** high-sounding

**imposition**
**03** hum, tax **04** bite, duty, levy, load, task, toll **05** impot **06** burden, charge, decree, fixing, hassle, pensum, tariff **07** levying, setting **08** exaction, pressure, trickery **09** intrusion **10** constraint, infliction, punishment **11** application, encumbrance, enforcement, institution, trespassing **12** encroachment, introduction **13** establishment

*See also* **tax**

**impossibility**
**04** no-no **09** absurdity, inability **10** non-starter **11** unviability **12** hopelessness, untenability **13** ludicrousness **14** ridiculousness **15** unacceptability

**impossible**
**03** out **06** absurd **08** hopeless **09** beyond you, insoluble, ludicrous **10** incredible, outlandish, ridiculous, unbearable, unworkable **11** intolerable, prohibitive, unthinkable **12** pigs might fly, preposterous, unacceptable, unachievable, unattainable, unbelievable, unimaginable, unobtainable, unrealizable, unreasonable **13** anybody's guess, impracticable, inconceivable **15** and pigs might fly

**impostor**
**04** fake, idol, sham **05** cheat, fraud, quack, rogue **06** bunyip, con man, faitor, phoney, ringer **07** deluder, faitour **08** deceiver, phantasm, swindler **09** charlatan, defrauder, pretender, trickster **10** hoodwinker, mountebank **12** impersonator

**imposture**
**03** con **04** hoax, sham **05** cheat, fraud, trick **07** swindle **08** artifice, con trick, pretence, quackery **09** deception **10** imposition **11** counterfeit **13** impersonation

**impotence**
**07** frailty **08** ligature, weakness **09** inability, infirmity, paralysis **10** disability, enervation, feebleness, inadequacy, incapacity, inefficacy **11** impuissance, uselessness **12** helplessness, incompetence **13** powerlessness **15** ineffectiveness

**impotent**
**04** weak **05** frail **06** feeble, futile, infirm, unable **07** useless, worn out **08** crippled, disabled, helpless **09** enervated, exhausted, incapable, paralysed, powerless, worthless **10** impuissant, inadequate **11** debilitated, incompetent, ineffective **12** unrestrained **13** incapacitated

**impound**
**04** cage **05** hem in, pen in, poind, seize **06** coop up, immure, keep in, lock up, remove, shut up **07** confine, pinfold **08** take away **10** commandeer, confiscate **11** appropriate, expropriate, incarcerate

**impoverish**
**04** ruin **05** break, drain, waste
**06** beggar, denude, reduce, weaken
**07** deplete, exhaust **08** bankrupt, diminish, distress, make poor
**09** pauperize **11** depauperate

**impoverished**
**04** bare, bust, dead, poor **05** broke, empty, needy, skint, waste **06** barren, ruined **07** boracic, decayed, drained, reduced **08** bankrupt, desolate, dirt-poor, indigent, weakened
**09** destitute, exhausted, penniless, penurious **10** cleaned out, distressed, down-and-out, stony-broke
**11** depauperate, impecunious
**12** on your uppers, without a bean
**14** on your beam ends **15** poverty-stricken

**impracticability**
**08** futility **11** unviability, uselessness
**12** hopelessness **13** impossibility, infeasibility, unworkability
**14** unsuitableness

**impracticable**
**04** wild **07** useless **08** unviable, wild-eyed **09** non-viable, visionary
**10** impossible, inoperable, unfeasible, unworkable **11** unrealistic
**12** unachievable, unattainable, unmanageable **13** unpracticable, unserviceable

**impractical**
**05** crazy **07** awkward **08** academic, romantic **09** visionary **10** idealistic, impossible, ivory-tower, starry-eyed, unworkable **11** doctrinaire, unrealistic
**12** inconvenient **13** impracticable, unserviceable

**impracticality**
**08** idealism **11** romanticism
**12** hopelessness **13** impossibility, infeasibility, unworkability
**14** unworkableness

**imprecation**
**04** oath, pize **05** abuse, curse
**08** anathema, goodyear
**09** blasphemy, goodyears, profanity
**10** execration **11** malediction
**12** denunciation, vilification, vituperation

**imprecise**
**04** hazy **05** loose, rough, vague
**06** sloppy, woolly **07** blurred, inexact
**09** ambiguous, equivocal, estimated
**10** ill-defined, inaccurate, indefinite, inexplicit **11** approximate

**imprecision**
**04** haze **08** estimate **09** ambiguity, vagueness **10** inaccuracy, sloppiness
**11** inexactness **12** inexactitude
**13** approximation

**impregnable**
**04** safe **05** solid **06** secure, strong
**09** fortified **10** adamantine, invincible, inviolable, unbeatable **11** irrefutable
**12** impenetrable, inexpugnable, invulnerable, unassailable
**13** unconquerable **14** indestructible, unquestionable

**impregnate**
**03** pad **04** fill, melt, milt, soak
**05** imbue, stain, steep **06** drench, infuse **07** pervade, suffuse
**08** permeate, saturate **09** fecundate, fertilize, penetrate **10** inseminate
**12** make pregnant

**impregnation**
**07** imbuing **10** saturation
**11** fecundation, fertilizing, fructifying
**12** insemination **13** fertilization
**14** fructification

**impresario**
**07** manager, showman **08** director, producer, promoter **09** exhibitor, organizer

**impress**
**03** gas, wow **04** drum, grab, mark, move, slay, stir, sway **05** knock, press, prest, print, rouse, stamp, touch
**06** affect, deboss, emboss, excite, incuse, indent, instil, stress, strike
**07** enforce, engrave, impresa, imprint, inspire, possess **08** astonish, bowl over, knock out **09** beglamour, bring home, emphasize, fix deeply, go over big, highlight, inculcate, influence, overwhelm, pressgang, underline, watermark **10** bear in upon, hammer home, prepossess **11** knock for six
**13** go over big with

**impressed**
**05** moved, taken, wowed **06** marked, struck **07** excited, grabbed, stamped, stirred, touched **08** affected, overawed **10** bowled over, influenced, knocked out **13** knocked for six

**impression**
**04** dent, feel, idea, mark, note, ring, seal, sway **05** fancy, hunch, power, print, sense, sound, spoof, stamp, vibes
**06** belief, effect, impact, memory, notion, parody, repute, send-up
**07** control, feeling, imprint, mimicry, opinion, outline, tableau, take-off, thought **08** illusion, pressure, printing
**09** awareness, burlesque, imitation, influence, sensation, suspicion
**10** caricature, conviction, gut feeling
**11** indentation **12** funny feeling, recollection **13** consciousness, impersonation

- **confused impression**

**04** blur

- **give false impression**

**03** lie

- **make an impression**

**03** let **08** register **10** come across

**impressionability**
**07** naivety **09** greenness **11** gullibility, receptivity, sensitivity
**13** ingenuousness, receptiveness, vulnerability **14** suggestibility, susceptibility

**impressionable**
**04** open, waxy **05** naive **07** pliable
**08** gullible **09** ingenuous, mouldable, receptive, sensitive **10** responsive, vulnerable **11** persuadable, susceptible

**impressive**
**04** epic **05** grand, noble **06** awsome, killer, moving, rotund, solemn, superb, whizzo, whizzy **07** awesome, rousing, stately **08** dazzling, dramatic, emphatic, exciting, imposing, lapidary, powerful, stirring, stonking, striking, touching **09** affecting, effective, inspiring **10** commanding, emphatical, monumental, portentous
**11** magnificent, spectacular **12** awe-inspiring, breathtaking **13** scintillating

**impressively**
**07** grandly **09** awesomely
**10** powerfully, strikingly **11** effectively
**12** emphatically **13** magnificently, spectacularly

**imprint**
**03** fix **04** etch, logo, mark, sign, tool
**05** badge, brand, power, press, print, stamp **06** burn in, effect, emblem, emboss **07** engrave, impress, meaning, results **08** colophon
**09** character, establish, influence
**10** impression **11** indentation, rubber-stamp **12** consequences, significance
**13** repercussions **14** reverberations

*See also* **publisher**

**imprison**
◇ *containment indicator*
**03** jug, lag, pen **04** cage, gaol, jail, quad, quod, shop **06** bang up, cage in, detain, immure, intern, lock up, lumber, shut in, shut up **07** confine, put away
**08** restrain, send down **11** incarcerate, put in prison **12** send to prison

**imprisoned**
◇ *insertion indicator*
**05** caged **06** inside, jailed **07** captive, immured, put away **08** banged up, confined, locked up, sent down
**09** doing bird, doing time **10** behind bars **12** incarcerated **13** doing porridge **15** under lock and key

**imprisonment**
**04** bird, life **05** bonds **06** duress
**07** custody, durance, duresse
**08** porridge **09** captivity, committal, detention **10** commitment, internment
**11** confinement **13** incarceration

**improbability**
**05** doubt **07** dubiety **11** dubiousness, uncertainty **12** doubtfulness, unlikelihood, unlikeliness **14** far-fetchedness, implausibility, ridiculousness

**improbable**
**06** farfet **07** dubious **08** doubtful, unlikely **09** uncertain **10** far-fetched, incredible, marvellous, ridiculous
**11** implausible **12** preposterous, questionable, unbelievable, unconvincing

**impromptu**
**05** ad-lib **07** offhand **09** ad libitum, extempore, makeshift **10** improvised,

off the cuff, unprepared, unscripted
**11** spontaneous, unrehearsed
**13** spontaneously **14** extemporaneous

**improper**
◇ *anagram indicator*
**04** rude **05** false, unfit, wrong
**06** risqué, vulgar **07** immoral
**08** immodest, indecent, shocking, unlawful, unseemly **09** erroneous, incorrect, irregular, unfitting
**10** inadequate, indecorous, indelicate, indiscreet, out of place, unbecoming, unsuitable **11** incongruous, inopportune **12** illegitimate
**13** inappropriate

**improperly**
◇ *anagram indicator*
**05** amiss, wrong **06** rudely **07** falsely, wrongly **09** immorally **10** immodestly, indecently, unlawfully, unsuitably
**11** erroneously, incorrectly, irregularly, unfittingly **12** indecorously, indiscreetly **13** incongruously
**15** inappropriately

**impropriety**
**04** slip **05** gaffe, lapse **07** blunder, faux pas, mistake **08** bad taste, solecism
**09** gaucherie, immodesty, indecency, indecorum, vulgarity **11** incongruity
**12** unseemliness **13** unsuitability
**14** indecorousness

**improve**
**04** beet, bete, do up, file, grow, help, mend, rise **05** amend, do for, emend, fix up, rally **06** better, buck up, enrich, look up, occupy, perk up, pick up, polish, reform, revamp, revise, uplift, work on **07** advance, correct, develop, enhance, perfect, recover, rectify, touch up, upgrade **08** increase, progress, put right, set right, work upon **09** get better, meliorate, modernize **10** ameliorate, convalesce, make better, recuperate, streamline
**11** make headway **12** gain strength, mend your ways, rehabilitate
**14** be on the up and up **15** give a facelift to

**improvement**
**04** gain, rise **05** rally **06** growth, pick-up, profit, reform **07** advance, headway, upswing **08** increase, progress, recovery, revision
**09** amendment, bettering, upgrading
**10** betterment, correction, rectifying, refinement **11** development, enhancement, furtherance, modernizing, reformation
**12** amelioration **13** rectification
**14** rehabilitation

**improvident**
**06** wastry **07** wastery **08** careless, heedless, prodigal, reckless, wasteful
**09** imprudent, negligent, shiftless, unthrifty **10** profligate, thriftless, unprepared **11** extravagant, inattentive, Micawberish, spendthrift, thoughtless **12** uneconomical
**13** underprepared

**improvisation**
**04** vamp **05** ad-lib **06** improv, lash-up
**08** ad hocery **09** ad-libbing, expedient, impromptu, invention, makeshift **11** spontaneity
**13** autoschediasm, extemporizing
**15** extemporization

**improvise**
**03** jam **04** vamp, wing **05** ad-lib, rig up, run up **06** busk it, devise, invent, make do, noodle, wing it **07** concoct, knock up **08** contrive **09** play by ear
**11** extemporize, play it by ear **13** throw together **14** cobble together, have a brainwave **15** speak off the cuff
• **improvise on**
**04** ride

**improvised**
◇ *anagram indicator*
**05** ad-lib, scrub **06** sudden **07** scratch
**08** drumhead, on the fly
**09** extempore, impromptu, makeshift
**10** off-the-cuff, unprepared, unscripted **11** spontaneous, unrehearsed **12** extemporized
**14** extemporaneous

**imprudence**
**05** folly, haste **08** rashness
**12** carelessness, heedlessness, recklessness **13** foolhardiness
**15** thoughtlessness

**imprudent**
**04** rash **05** hasty **06** unwise **07** foolish
**08** careless, heedless, reckless
**09** foolhardy, ill-judged, impolitic
**10** ill-advised, incautious, indiscreet, unthinking **11** improvident, injudicious, thoughtless **12** short-sighted **13** ill-considered, inconsiderate, irresponsible

**impudence**
**03** lip **04** face, gall, neck, sass
**05** cheek, front, mouth, nerve, snash
**06** bronze **07** hutzpah **08** attitude, boldness, chutzpah, pertness, rudeness **09** brass neck, insolence, sauciness **10** brazenness, effrontery
**11** presumption **12** impertinence, impertinency

**impudent**
**04** bold, calm, cool, pert, rude
**05** bardy, cocky, fresh, hardy, nervy, sassy, saucy **06** brazen, cheeky, gallus
**07** forward, gallows **08** immodest, impolite, insolent, malapert, petulant
**09** audacious, barefaced, boldfaced, out of line, shameless **10** brass-faced, unblushing **11** impertinent
**12** presumptuous **13** disrespectful

**impugn**
**06** assail, attack, berate, oppose, resist, revile, vilify **07** censure, dispute, traduce **08** question, vilipend
**09** challenge, criticize **10** vituperate
**14** call in question

**impulse**
**04** push, send, urge, whim, wish
**05** drive, force, nisus, pulse, spike, surge **06** desire, impact, motion, motive, notion, signal, thrust
**07** caprice, conatus, feeling, impetus, passion **08** instinct, momentum, movement, pressure, stimulus
**09** brainwave, impulsion, incentive, premotion **10** compulsion, incitement, inducement, motivation, propulsion
**11** inclination, stimulation, thought-wave
• **on impulse**
**06** rashly **07** hastily **08** suddenly
**10** recklessly **11** impatiently, impetuously, impulsively, intuitively
**13** automatically, instinctively, irresponsibly, spontaneously, thoughtlessly **15** without thinking

**impulsive**
**04** rash **05** hasty, quick **06** madcap, sudden **08** reckless **09** automatic, emotional, foolhardy, ill-judged, impatient, impetuous, intuitive
**10** headstrong, passionate, unthinking
**11** instinctive, precipitate, spontaneous, thoughtless **13** ill-considered

**impulsively**
**06** rashly **07** hastily **08** suddenly
**09** on impulse **10** recklessly
**11** impatiently, impetuously, intuitively
**13** automatically, instinctively, irresponsibly, spontaneously, thoughtlessly **15** without thinking

**impulsiveness**
**05** haste **07** emotion, passion
**08** instinct, rashness **09** hastiness, quickness **10** impatience, suddenness
**11** impetuosity, spontaneity
**12** recklessness **13** foolhardiness, impetuousness, intuitiveness, precipitation **15** precipitateness, thoughtlessness

**impunity**
**07** amnesty, excusal, freedom, liberty, licence **08** immunity, security
**09** exemption **10** permission
**12** dispensation
• **with impunity**
**06** freely, safely **08** in safety **11** without risk

**impure**
**04** foul, lewd, sexy **05** bawdy, crude, dirty, mixed **06** coarse, drossy, erotic, filthy, ribald, risqué, smutty, vulgar
**07** alloyed, blended, corrupt, debased, defiled, diluted, immoral, lustful, obscene, sullied, tainted, unclean, vicious **08** combined, depraved, immodest, improper, indecent, infected, polluted, unchaste
**09** lecherous, offensive, shameless, unrefined **10** licentious, suggestive
**11** adulterated, promiscuous
**12** contaminated, pornographic

**impurity**
**04** dirt, mark, smut, spot **05** blend, donor, dross, filth, grime, taint
**07** crudity, mixture **08** dilution, foulness, lewdness **09** dirtiness, eroticism, immodesty, indecency, infection, looseness, obscenity,

pollutant, pollution, vulgarity **10** coarseness, corruption, debasement, immorality, unchastity **11** contaminant, foreign body, impropriety, lustfulness, pornography, promiscuity **12** adulteration **13** contamination, offensiveness, shamelessness **14** licentiousness

**impute**
**03** lay, put **05** refer **06** assign, charge, credit, object **07** ascribe **08** accredit **09** attribute, put down to

**in**
◇ *hidden indicator*
◇ *insertion indicator*
**01** i' **02** at, by, of, on **03** hip, per **04** cool, each, into, with **05** abode, among, every, funky, smart **06** alight, during, inside, modish, trendy, within **07** current, enclose, in vogue, popular, stylish, through **10** all the rage, enclosed by, throughout **11** fashionable **12** surrounded by **15** during the time of
• **in for**
**12** due to receive **13** going to suffer
• **in itself**
**04** in se **05** per se **13** intrinsically
• **in on**
**07** aware of **09** clued up on **10** involved in **14** acquainted with
• **in with**
**07** liked by **12** friendly with **15** on good terms with

**inability**
**08** handicap, weakness **09** impotence **10** disability, inadequacy, incapacity, ineptitude **11** uselessness **12** incapability, incompetence **13** powerlessness **15** ineffectiveness

**inaccessibility**
**08** distance **09** isolation **10** remoteness, separation **15** unattainability

**inaccessible**
**06** remote **08** isolated **10** out of reach **11** beyond reach, god-forsaken, out of the way, unavailable, uncomatable, unget-at-able, unreachable **12** impenetrable, unattainable, uncomeatable, unfrequented **14** inapproachable, unapproachable

**inaccuracy**
**04** flub, goof, slip **05** error, fault, gaffe **06** boo-boo, defect, howler, slip-up **07** blunder, clanger, erratum, mistake **11** corrigendum, imprecision, inexactness **12** mistakenness **13** erroneousness, unreliability **14** fallaciousness, miscalculation

**inaccurate**
◇ *anagram indicator*
**03** out **05** false, loose, wrong **06** adrift, faulty, flawed, untrue **07** inexact, unsound **08** mistaken **09** defective, erroneous, imperfect, imprecise, incorrect **10** fallacious, unfaithful, unreliable
• **be inaccurate**
**03** err

**inaccurately**
**06** wildly **07** falsely, loosely, wrongly **08** clumsily **09** inexactly **10** carelessly, unreliably **11** defectively, erroneously, imperfectly, imprecisely, incorrectly **12** unfaithfully

**inaction**
**04** rest **06** torpor **07** inertia **08** idleness, lethargy, slowness **09** passivity **10** immobility, inactivity, stagnation **12** lifelessness, sluggishness **14** motionlessness

**inactivate**
**04** stop **07** cripple, disable, scupper **08** mothball, paralyse **09** stabilize **10** deactivate, immobilize

**inactive**
**04** dead, idle, lazy, slow **05** inert, still **06** shadow, sleepy, torpid, unused **07** dormant, passive **08** immobile, indolent, lifeless, slothful, sluggish, stagnant, unactive **09** dead-alive, lethargic, quiescent, sedentary **10** motionless, stationary, unemployed, vegetating **11** hibernating, inoperative **12** dead-and-alive

**inactivity**
**04** rest **05** sloth **06** stasis, torpor **07** inertia, languor, vacancy **08** abeyance, dormancy, dullness, idleness, inaction, laziness, lethargy **09** heaviness, indolence, inertness, lassitude, passivity **10** immobility, quiescence, quiescency, stagnation, vegetation **11** hibernation **12** dilatoriness, lifelessness, sluggishness, unemployment

**inadequacy**
**04** flaw, lack, want **05** fault **06** dearth, defect, foible **07** deficit, failing, paucity, poverty **08** scarcity, shortage, weakness **09** inability **10** deficiency, inefficacy, inequality, meagreness, scantiness **11** shortcoming **12** imperfection, incapability, incompetence **13** defectiveness, insufficiency **15** ineffectiveness

**inadequate**
**03** bad **04** poor **05** scant, short, unfit **06** faulty, meagre, scanty, scarce, skimpy, sparse, too few **07** sketchy, unequal, wanting **08** careless, derisory, inexpert, pathetic **09** defective, deficient, imperfect, incapable, niggardly, too little **11** incompetent, ineffective, ineffectual, substandard, unqualified **12** insufficient, unproficient **13** disappointing, inefficacious, not good enough **14** incommensurate, not up to scratch, unsatisfactory **15** thin on the ground

**inadequately**
**05** badly **06** poorly, thinly **08** meagrely, scantily, skimpily, sparsely **09** sketchily **10** carelessly **11** imperfectly **14** insufficiently

**inadmissible**
**08** improper **09** precluded **10** disallowed, immaterial, inapposite, irrelevant, prohibited **11** unallowable **12** unacceptable **13** inappropriate

**inadvertent**
**06** chance **08** careless **09** negligent, unadvised, unguarded, unplanned, unwitting **10** accidental, unintended **11** inattentive, involuntary, thoughtless, unconscious **12** uncalculated **13** unintentional **14** unpremeditated

**inadvertently**
**08** by chance, remissly **09** by mistake **10** by accident, carelessly, heedlessly, mistakenly **11** negligently, unwittingly **12** accidentally, unthinkingly **13** involuntarily, thoughtlessly, unconsciously **15** unintentionally

**inadvisable**
**05** silly **06** unwise **07** foolish **09** ill-judged, imprudent, misguided **10** ill-advised, indiscreet **11** inexpedient, injudicious **13** ill-considered

**inalienable**
**08** absolute, inherent **09** permanent **10** inviolable, sacrosanct **11** unremovable **12** unassailable **13** non-negotiable **14** untransferable **15** imprescriptible, non-transferable

**inane**
**04** vain, void **05** empty, silly, vapid **06** absurd, drippy, futile, stupid, vacant **07** fatuous, foolish, idiotic, puerile, vacuous **08** mindless, trifling **09** frivolous, ludicrous, senseless, worthless **10** ridiculous **11** nonsensical **13** characterless, unintelligent

**inanely**
**08** absurdly, futilely, stupidly **09** fatuously, foolishly, vacuously **11** idiotically, ludicrously **12** ridiculously **13** nonsensically

**inanimate**
**04** dead, dull, lazy **05** inert **06** torpid, wooden **07** abiotic, defunct, dormant, extinct **08** immobile, inactive, lifeless, stagnant **09** apathetic, insensate, lethargic **10** insentient, spiritless **11** unconscious

**inanity**
**05** folly **06** waffle **07** fatuity, vacancy, vacuity **08** daftness, vapidity **09** absurdity, asininity, emptiness, frivolity, puerility, silliness, stupidity **10** imbecility **11** foolishness **13** ludicrousness, senselessness **14** ridiculousness

**inapplicable**
**05** inapt **08** unsuited **09** unrelated **10** immaterial, inapposite, irrelevant, unsuitable **11** unconnected **12** inconsequent **13** inappropriate

**inapposite**
**10** immaterial, irrelevant, out of place, unsuitable **13** inappropriate

**inappreciable**
**04** fine, tiny **05** faint, small, vague **06** minute, slight, subtle **07** gradual, muffled, obscure, unclear
**09** inaudible, minuscule, priceless
**10** impalpable, indefinite, indistinct, negligible, unapparent **11** microscopic
**12** undetectable, unnoticeable
**13** imperceptible, indiscernible, infinitesimal

**inappropriate**
**05** inapt, undue **08** ill-timed, improper, tactless, unseemly, untimely
**09** facetious, ill-fitted, ill-suited, tasteless, unfitting **10** inapposite, indecorous, irrelevant, malapropos, out of place, unbecoming, unsuitable
**11** incongruous, inopportune
**12** infelicitous **13** unappropriate

**inappropriately**
**07** unfitly **08** off topic **10** malapropos, out of place, tactlessly, unsuitably **11** off the point, tastelessly **12** irrelevantly
**13** incongruously, inopportunely
**14** beside the point, infelicitously

**inapt**
**05** unfit **07** unhappy **08** ill-timed, unsuited **09** ill-fitted, ill-suited
**10** inapposite, irrelevant, malapropos, out of place, unsuitable
**11** inopportune, unfortunate, unqualified **12** infelicitous
**13** inappropriate

**inarticulacy**
**08** mumbling **09** hesitancy, stumbling
**10** stammering, stuttering
**11** incoherence **14** indistinctness, speechlessness, tongue-tiedness

**inarticulate**
**04** dumb, mute **07** blurred, halting, muffled, mumbled, quavery, shaking, unclear **08** hesitant **09** faltering, gibbering, soundless, stumbling, trembling, voiceless **10** disjointed, hesitating, incoherent, indistinct, speechless, stammering, stuttering, tongue-tied **14** unintelligible

**inattention**
**07** absence **09** disregard, misregard
**10** dreaminess, negligence
**11** daydreaming, distraction
**12** carelessness, heedlessness, unobservance **13** forgetfulness, preoccupation, unmindfulness
**15** inattentiveness, thoughtlessness

**inattentive**
**04** deaf **05** loose, slack **06** absent, asleep, dreamy, remiss **08** careless, distrait, heedless **09** forgetful, incurious, miles away, negligent, unmindful **10** distracted, neglectful, regardless **11** daydreaming, inadvertent, preoccupied, thoughtless
**12** absent-minded, disregarding, unrespective **13** somewhere else, wool-gathering

**inaudible**
**03** low **04** dull, soft **05** faint, muted **06** silent **07** muffled, mumbled, stifled **08** murmured, muttered **09** noiseless, whispered **10** indistinct
**13** imperceptible

**inaugural**
**05** first **06** maiden **07** initial, opening
**08** exordial, original **09** launching
**12** introductory

**inaugurate**
**04** open **05** begin, set up, start
**06** hansel, induct, invest, launch, ordain **07** handsel, install, instate, swear in, usher in **08** commence, dedicate, enthrone, get going, initiate
**09** auspicate, institute, introduce, originate **10** commission, consecrate
**11** set in motion **13** admit to office
**14** open officially

**inauguration**
**06** launch **07** opening **08** starting
**09** induction, launching, setting up
**10** initiation, installing, ordination, swearing-in **11** institution, investiture
**12** commencement, consecration, enthronement, installation

**inauspicious**
**03** bad **05** black **07** ominous, unlucky
**08** ill-fated, sinister, untimely **09** ill-boding, ill-omened **10** ill-starred, sinistrous **11** threatening, unfortunate, unpromising **12** discouraging, infelicitous, unfavourable, unpropitious

**inborn**
**06** inbred, innate, native **07** connate, natural **08** inherent, untaught
**09** ingrained, inherited, intuitive
**10** congenital, hereditary, ingenerate
**11** instinctive, in the family

**inbred**
**03** sib **06** innate, native **07** connate, natural **08** inherent **09** incrossed, ingrained **10** ingenerate
**14** constitutional

**inbuilt**
**05** basic **07** built-in **08** inherent, integral **09** elemental, essential
**11** constituent, fundamental

**incalculable**
**04** vast **06** untold **07** endless, immense, sumless **08** enormous, infinite **09** boundless, countless, limitless, unlimited **10** numberless
**11** inestimable, innumerable, measureless **12** immeasurable
**13** unpredictable, without number

**incandescence**
**04** fire, glow, leam **05** gleam, glory
**07** glimmer, sunglow **08** outflush, radiance, richness **09** afterglow, splendour, vividness **10** brightness, brilliance, luminosity
**15** phosphorescence

**incandescent**
**03** mad **05** aglow, angry, irate, livid
**06** bright, fuming, raging **07** boiling, enraged, furious, glowing, shining
**08** dazzling, frenzied, gleaming, incensed, inflamed, seething, sizzling, up in arms, white-hot **09** brilliant, in a lather, indignant **10** hopping mad, infuriated **14** purple with rage

**incantation**
**03** hex **04** rune **05** chant, charm, spell
**06** mantra **07** formula, karakia, mantram **10** invocation
**11** abracadabra, conjuration **12** magic formula

**incapable**
◇ *anagram indicator*
**04** weak **05** drunk, inept, unfit
**06** feeble, unable **07** useless
**08** helpless, impotent, unfitted, unsuited **09** powerless **10** inadequate
**11** incompetent, ineffective, ineffectual, unqualified
**12** disqualified, not hacking it **14** not up to scratch **15** out of your league

**incapacitate**
**05** lay up **07** cripple, disable, scupper
**08** paralyse **10** debilitate, disqualify, immobilize **14** put out of action

**incapacitated**
**05** drunk, tipsy, unfit **06** laid up, unwell
**08** crippled, disabled **09** hamstrung, paralysed, prostrate, scuppered
**10** indisposed **11** immobilized, out of action **12** disqualified

**incapacity**
**08** weakness **09** impotence, inability, unfitness **10** disability, feebleness, inadequacy, ineptitude, non-ability
**11** uselessness **12** incapability, incompetence, incompetency
**13** powerlessness **14** ineffectuality
**15** ineffectiveness

**incarcerate**
**04** cage, gaol, jail **06** bang up, commit, coop up, detain, encage, immure, intern, lock up, wall in **07** confine, impound, put away **08** imprison, restrain, restrict, send down **09** put in jail, put inside **11** put in prison

**incarceration**
**04** jail **07** bondage, custody
**09** captivity, detention, restraint
**10** internment **11** confinement, restriction **12** imprisonment

**incarnate**
**04** heal **05** human **07** fleshly
**08** embodied, typified **09** corporeal, made flesh, personify **10** in the flesh
**11** impersonate, incardinate, in human form, personified

**incarnation**
**06** avatar **09** human form
**10** embodiment **13** impersonation, manifestation **15** personification

*Incarnations include:*

**04** Rama
**07** Krishna
**09** Jugannath
**10** Juggernaut

**incautious**
**04** rash **05** hasty **06** unwary
**07** foolish **08** careless, cavalier,

reckless, wareless **09** foolhardy, ill-judged, imprudent, impulsive, unguarded **10** ill-advised, unthinking, unwatchful **11** inattentive, injudicious, precipitate, thoughtless, unobservant **13** ill-considered, inconsiderate, uncircumspect

**incendiary**
**04** bomb, mine **06** charge **07** carcase, carcass, firebug, grenade **08** agitator, arsonist, fireball, firebomb, inciting, stirring **09** demagogue, explosive, firebrand, flammable, insurgent, pétroleur, seditious **10** fire-raiser, petrol bomb, pétroleuse, pyromaniac, rick-burner, subversive **11** combustible, dissentious, fire-raising, provocative **12** inflammatory, rabble-rouser **13** rabble-rousing, revolutionary **14** proceleusmatic **15** Molatov cocktail

**incense**
**03** irk, vex **04** balm, rile, thus, urge **05** anger, aroma, myrrh, scent **06** enrage, excite, hassle, homage, incite, kindle, madden, nettle, stacte **07** agitate, benzoin, bouquet, inflame, perfume, provoke **08** irritate, pastille **09** adulation, aggravate, fragrance, infuriate, joss-stick **10** exasperate **12** frankincense **14** drive up the wall

**incensed**
**03** mad **04** waxy **05** angry, cross, irate, ratty, spewy **06** choked, fuming, ireful **07** crooked, enraged, furious, ropable, stroppy, uptight **08** burned up, furibund, hairless, in a paddy, in a strop, maddened, up in arms, wrathful **09** in a lather, indignant, pissed off, raving mad, seeing red, steamed up, ticked off **10** aggravated, hopping mad, infuriated **11** disgruntled, exasperated, fit to be tied **12** on the warpath

**incentive**
**04** bait, goad, lure, spur **06** carrot, motive, reason, reward **07** impetus **08** igniting, inciting, stimulus **09** stimulant, sweetener **10** enticement, incitation, incitement, inducement, motivation **11** encouraging **13** encouragement

**inception**
**04** dawn, rise **05** birth, start **06** origin, outset **07** kick-off, opening **09** beginning **10** initiation **12** commencement, inauguration, installation **13** establishment

**incessant**
**07** endless, eternal, non-stop **08** constant, unbroken, unending **09** ceaseless, continual, perpetual, recurrent, unceasing, weariless **10** continuous, persistent **11** everlasting, never-ending, unremitting **12** interminable **13** uninterrupted

**incessantly**
**07** for ever **09** endlessly, eternally **10** constantly, unendingly **11** at every turn, ceaselessly, immediately, unceasingly **12** continuously, interminably **13** everlastingly, unremittingly **14** for ever and ever **15** twenty-four seven, uninterruptedly

**incidence**
**04** rate **05** range **06** amount, degree, extent, to-fall **09** frequency **10** commonness, occurrence, prevalence

**incident**
**03** bar, row **04** baur, bawr, page **05** brush, clash, event, fight, scene, upset **06** affair, comedy, fracas, matter, mishap, period **07** affaire, episode, falling, passage, subject **08** conflict, instance, occasion, skirmish **09** adventure, commotion, happening **10** consequent, experience, occurrence, proceeding **11** disturbance **12** circumstance **13** confrontation **14** unpleasantness

**incidental**
**05** minor, petty, small **06** casual, chance, random **07** passing, related, trivial **08** by chance, striking **09** ancillary, attendant, impinging, occurrent, secondary **10** accidental, background, fortuitous, occasional, peripheral, subsidiary **11** concomitant, contingency, facultative, subordinate **12** accompanying, contributory, non-essential **13** supplementary

**incidentally**
**07** apropos, by the by **08** by chance, by the way, casually **09** as an aside, en passant, in passing **10** by accident **11** secondarily **12** accidentally, digressively, episodically, fortuitously, unexpectedly **13** as a digression **14** coincidentally **15** parenthetically

**incinerate**
**04** burn **07** cremate **09** carbonize **13** reduce to ashes

**incineration**
**07** burning **09** cremation **13** carbonization **14** turning to ashes

**incipient**
**07** nascent, newborn **08** inchoate, starting **09** beginning, embryonic, impending, inaugural, inceptive **10** commencing, developing **11** originating, rudimentary

**incise**
**03** cut **04** etch, gash, nick, slit **05** carve, notch, slash **06** chisel, scribe, sculpt **07** cut into, engrave **09** sculpture

**incision**
**03** cut **04** gash, nick, slit **05** notch, slash, wound **07** coupure, cutting, opening **08** colotomy, incisure, lobotomy, oncotomy **09** cystotomy, insection, iridotomy **10** craniotomy, discission, enterotomy, episiotomy, nephrotomy, phlebotomy, pleurotomy, sclerotomy, trenchancy **11** hysterotomy, myringotomy, thoracotomy, tracheotomy, venesection, venisection **12** pharyngotomy, tonsillotomy

**incisive**
**04** acid, keen **05** acute, sharp **06** astute, biting, shrewd **07** caustic, cutting, mordant, pungent **08** piercing, stinging, surgical **09** sarcastic, trenchant **10** perceptive **11** penetrating **13** perspicacious

**incisively**
**06** keenly, tartly **07** acutely, sharply **08** astutely **09** mordantly, pungently **10** piercingly **11** caustically, trenchantly **13** penetratingly, sarcastically

**incisiveness**
**04** bite, edge **07** acidity, sarcasm **08** astucity, keenness, pungency, tartness **09** acuteness, sharpness **10** astuteness, trenchancy **11** penetration **12** perspicacity

**incite**
**03** egg, hoi, hoy, put, set, sic, tar **04** abet, fuel, goad, poke, prod, sick, spur, urge, whet **05** drive, egg on, impel, prick, put on, rouse, tarre **06** arouse, excite, fillip, foment, induce, kindle, prompt, stir up, whip up, work up **07** actuate, agitate, animate, incense, inflame, premove, provoke, solicit **09** encourage, instigate, stimulate **13** stir the possum

**incitement**
**04** goad, prod, spur, whet **05** drive, sting **06** motive, urging **07** impetus, rousing **08** stimulus **09** agitation, animation, incentive, onsetting, prompting **10** inducement, motivation, suggestion **11** instigation, provocation, stimulation **13** encouragement

**inciting**
**08** stirring **09** hortative, hortatory, incentive, seditious **10** incendiary, subversive **11** provocative **12** inflammatory **13** rabble-rousing **14** proceleusmatic

**incivility**
**08** rudeness **09** indignity, roughness, vulgarity **10** bad manners, coarseness, disrespect, inurbanity **11** boorishness, discourtesy, ill-breeding **12** impoliteness **14** unmannerliness

**inclemency**
**07** rawness **08** foulness, severity **09** harshness, roughness **10** bitterness, storminess **15** tempestuousness

**inclement**
**03** raw, wet **04** cold, foul **05** harsh, nasty, rough **06** bitter, severe, stormy **07** squally **08** blustery **11** intemperate, tempestuous

**inclination**
**03** bow, maw, nod, set **04** bank, bend, bent, bias, cant, kant, lift, list, mind, rake, ramp, tilt **05** angle, pitch, slant, slope, study, taste, trend **06** ascent, liking, notion **07** incline, leaning

**08** affinity, fondness, gradient, penchant, tendency **09** acclivity, affection, declivity, deviation, steepness **10** attraction, partiality, preference, proclivity, propension, propensity **11** disposition **12** predilection, propenseness **14** predisposition

• **with inclination towards**

**02** on

**incline**

**03** bow, dip, kip, nod, tip **04** bank, bend, bias, hade, heel, hill, lean, list, peck, rake, ramp, rise, slip, stay, sway, tend, tilt, veer **05** curve, offer, slant, slope, stoop, swell, swing, tempt, verge **06** affect, ascent, direct, prefer, shelve, steeve **07** descent, deviate, dispose, diverge, propend, recline **08** gradient, persuade **09** acclivity, declivity, influence, prejudice

**inclined**

**03** apt **04** bent, wont **05** given, ready **06** liable, likely, minded **07** oblique, of a mind, sloping, tending, willing **08** disposed, proclive, propense **10** well-minded **11** predisposed

• **be inclined**

**04** care

• **inclined to**

**01** -y

**include**

◇ *containment indicator*
◇ *hidden indicator*

**03** add **04** hold, span **05** add in, admit, carry, cover, enter, put in **06** embody, insert, reckon, rope in, take in **07** connote, contain, count in, embrace, enclose, involve, let in on, subsume, throw in **08** allow for, classify, comprise, conclude **09** encompass, introduce **10** comprehend **11** incorporate **15** take into account

**including**

◇ *containment indicator*

**03** inc **04** incl, with **08** as well as, counting, included **11** inclusive of **12** together with

**inclusion**

**08** addition **09** insertion **10** embodiment **11** involvement, subsumption **12** encompassing **13** comprehension, incorporation

**inclusive**

**03** inc **04** full, incl **05** all-in **07** blanket, general, overall **08** catch-all, included, sweeping **09** enclosing **12** all-embracing, all-inclusive **13** comprehensive **14** across-the-board

**incognito**

**06** masked, veiled **07** unknown **08** nameless, unmarked **09** disguised **10** in disguise **11** camouflaged **12** unidentified **14** unidentifiable, unrecognizable **15** under a false name

**incognizant**

**07** unaware **08** ignorant **09** unknowing **10** uninformed **11** inattentive, unconscious, unobservant **12** unacquainted **13** unenlightened

**incoherence**

**05** mix-up **06** jumble, muddle, mumble, mutter **07** stammer, stutter **08** wildness **09** confusion **10** brokenness **11** garbledness **12** illogicality **13** inconsistency **14** disjointedness

**incoherent**

**05** loose **06** broken **07** garbled, jumbled, mixed-up, muddled, mumbled, unclear **08** confused, muttered, rambling, wandered **09** illogical, rigmarole, scrambled, unjointed, wandering **10** disjointed, disordered, stammering, stuttering **11** unconnected **12** disconnected, inarticulate, inconsistent **14** skimble-skamble, unintelligible

**incombustible**

**09** fireproof **10** flameproof, unburnable **12** non-flammable **13** fire-resistant **14** flame-resistant, flame-retardant, non-inflammable

**income**

**03** pay **05** gains, means, rente, wages **06** inflow, profit, salary **07** arrival, profits, returns, revenue, takings **08** benefice, earnings, entrance, interest, proceeds, receipts, rent roll **09** allowance, comings-in, penny-rent **10** emoluments **12** independency, remuneration

**incoming**

**03** new **04** next **06** coming **07** ensuing, revenue **08** accruing, arriving, entering, homeward **09** returning **10** succeeding **11** approaching

**incommensurate**

**07** extreme, unequal **09** excessive **10** inadequate, inordinate **11** extravagant, inequitable **12** insufficient **15** incommensurable

**incommunicable**

**09** ineffable **11** unspeakable, unutterable **12** unimpartable **13** indescribable, inexpressible

**incomparable**

**06** superb **07** supreme **08** peerless **09** brilliant, matchless, nonpareil, paramount, unmatched **10** inimitable, unequalled, unrivalled **11** superlative, unsurpassed **12** second to none, unparalleled, without equal **13** beyond compare **15** without parallel

**incomparably**

**05** by far **06** easily **08** superbly **09** eminently, supremely **10** far and away, infinitely **11** brilliantly **12** immeasurably **13** beyond compare, superlatively

**incompatibility**

**05** clash **08** conflict, mismatch, variance **09** antipathy, disparity **10** antagonism, difference **11** discrepancy, incongruity **12** disagreement **13** contradiction, disparateness, inconsistency **14** uncongeniality

**incompatible**

**05** alien, wrong **06** at odds **08** clashing, unsuited **09** disparate, dissonant, exclusive, repugnant **10** at variance, discordant, ill-matched, in conflict, insociable, mismatched **11** conflicting, disagreeing, ill-assorted, incongruous, uncongenial **12** antagonistic, inconsistent **13** contradictory **14** irreconcilable

**incompetence**

**08** bungling **09** inability, ineptness, stupidity, unfitness **10** inadequacy, ineptitude, inequality **11** uselessness **12** incapability, inefficiency **13** insufficiency, unsuitability **14** ineffectuality **15** ineffectiveness, ineffectualness

**incompetent**

**03** ill **04** naff, poxy, ropy **05** awful, flaky, lousy, pants, ropey, unfit **06** clumsy, crummy, stupid, unable **07** awkward, botched, the pits, useless **08** bungling, fumbling, handless, hopeless, inexpert, pathetic, schleppy, terrible **09** deficient, incapable, unskilful **10** amateurish, inadequate, unsuitable **11** a load of crap, ineffective, inefficient, unqualified **12** insufficient **14** a load of garbage, a load of rubbish

**incomplete**

◇ *tail deletion indicator*

**04** half, part **05** short **06** broken, patchy **07** lacking, partial, pendant, pendent, scrappy, sketchy, wanting **08** abridged **09** defective, deficient, embryonic, half-baked, imperfect, piecemeal, shortened **10** catalectic, unfinished **11** fragmentary, rudimentary, undeveloped **14** unaccomplished

**incomprehensible**

**04** deep **06** opaque **07** complex, obscure, unaware **08** abstruse, baffling, involved, profound, puzzling **09** enigmatic, limitless, recondite **10** mysterious, perplexing, unfamiliar, unreadable **11** complicated, double Dutch, inscrutable **12** impenetrable, mind-boggling, over your head, unfathomable **13** above your head, all Greek to you, inconceivable **14** unintelligible

**incomprehension**

**09** ignorance, obscurity **10** complexity, profundity **11** unawareness **12** incognizance **13** unfamiliarity **14** inscrutability, mysteriousness **15** impenetrability

**inconceivable**

**06** absurd **08** shocking **09** ludicrous, unheard-of **10** impossible, incredible, outrageous, ridiculous, staggering **11** implausible, unthinkable **12** mind-boggling, unbelievable, unimaginable

**inconclusive**
**04** open, weak **05** vague
**09** ambiguous, uncertain, undecided, unsettled **10** indecisive, indefinite, up in the air **11** left hanging
**12** unconvincing, unsatisfying
**13** indeterminate **14** open to question

**incongruity**
**05** clash **08** conflict **09** disparity, inaptness **10** disharmony
**11** discrepancy **13** contradiction, inconsistency, unsuitability
**14** dissociability **15** dissociableness, incompatibility

**incongruous**
**03** odd **06** absurd, at odds, patchy
**07** jarring, strange **08** clashing, contrary, out of key **09** dissonant
**10** out of place, unsuitable
**11** conflicting, disharmonic, dissociable **12** incompatible, inconsistent, out of keeping
**13** contradictory, inappropriate
**14** irreconcilable

**incongruously**
**08** off topic **10** out of place, unsuitably
**11** off the point **12** irrelevantly
**13** inopportunely **14** beside the point, infelicitously **15** inappropriately

**inconsequential**
**05** minor, petty **07** trivial **08** trifling
**09** small beer **10** immaterial, negligible
**11** unimportant **13** inappreciable, insignificant **14** of no importance

**inconsiderable**
**04** mean, weak **05** minor, petty, small
**06** slight **07** nominal, trivial **08** trifling
**10** negligible **11** unimportant
**13** insignificant

**inconsiderate**
**04** rash, rude **06** unkind **07** selfish
**08** careless, heedless, tactless, uncaring **09** egotistic, imprudent
**10** dismissive, intolerant, regardless, unthinking, unweighing **11** insensitive, light-minded, self-centred, thoughtless, unconcerned **12** light-hearted, uncharitable, undiscerning

**inconsiderateness**
**08** rudeness **09** unconcern
**10** unkindness **11** intolerance, selfishness **12** carelessness, tactlessness **13** insensitivity **15** self-centredness, thoughtlessness

**inconsistency**
**04** odds **07** paradox **08** conflict, variance **09** disparity **10** divergence, fickleness, repugnance **11** contrariety, discrepancy, gallimaufry, incongruity, inconstancy, instability
**12** disagreement, unsteadiness
**13** contradiction, unreliability
**14** changeableness **15** incompatibility

**inconsistent**
**05** alien **06** at odds, fickle, spotty
**07** erratic, jarring, varying **08** contrary, in and out, unstable, unsteady, variable
**09** differing, irregular, mercurial, repugnant **10** at variance, capricious, changeable, discordant, dissimilar, inconstant, out of place **11** conflicting, incongruent, incongruous, unagreeable **12** incompatible, in opposition, out of keeping
**13** contradictory, self-repugnant, unpredictable **14** disconformable, irreconcilable

**inconsolable**
**08** desolate, wretched **09** miserable
**10** despairing, devastated
**11** heartbroken **12** disconsolate
**13** broken-hearted, grief-stricken

**inconspicuous**
**05** plain, quiet **06** hidden, low-key, modest **07** obscure **08** discreet, ordinary, retiring **09** concealed
**10** indistinct, unassuming
**11** camouflaged, unobtrusive
**12** unremarkable **13** insignificant **15** in the background, undistinguished

**inconspicuously**
**07** faintly, quietly **08** modestly
**12** unassumingly **13** unobtrusively
**15** insignificantly, in the background

**inconstancy**
**05** range, shift, swing **06** change
**08** wavering **09** variation **10** fickleness
**11** alternation, ambivalence, fluctuation, instability, oscillation, vacillation, variability **12** irresolution, unsteadiness, variableness

**inconstant**
**06** fickle, giglet, giglot **07** erratic, moonish, mutable, Protean, vagrant, varying, wayward **08** strumpet, unstable, unsteady, variable, volatile, wavering **09** changeful, faithless, fluxional, mercurial, uncertain, unsettled **10** capricious, changeable, fluxionary, irresolute, unfaithful, unreliable **11** fluctuating, vacillating
**12** inconsistent, undependable

**incontestable**
**04** sure **05** clear **07** certain, evident, obvious **08** cast-iron **10** undeniable
**11** indubitable, irrefutable, self-evident
**12** indisputable **14** unquestionable

**incontinent**
**04** lewd **05** loose **06** wanton
**07** lustful **08** unchaste **09** debauched, dissolute, lecherous, unbridled, unchecked **10** dissipated, lascivious, licentious, ungoverned, unstanched
**11** immediately, promiscuous, unstaunched **12** uncontrolled, ungovernable, unrestrained
**14** uncontrollable

**incontrovertible**
**05** clear **07** certain **10** undeniable
**11** beyond doubt, indubitable, irrefutable, self-evident
**12** indisputable **13** incontestable
**14** beyond question, unquestionable

**incontrovertibly**
**07** clearly **09** certainly **10** undeniably
**11** beyond doubt, indubitably, irrefutably **12** indisputably **14** beyond question, unquestionably

**inconvenience**
**03** irk **04** bind, bore, burr, drag, fuss, pain **05** annoy, upset, worry
**06** bother, burden, hassle, put out
**07** disrupt, disturb, problem, trouble, turn-off **08** drawback, flea-bite, headache, nuisance, vexation
**09** annoyance, disoblige, hindrance, incommode **10** difficulty, discommode, disruption, disutility, impose upon **11** awkwardness, disturbance, incommodity
**12** disadvantage, discommodity

**inconvenient**
**06** ungain **07** awkward **08** annoying, ill-timed, untimely, untoward, unwieldy
**09** difficult **10** bothersome, cumbersome, unhandsome, unsuitable
**11** inexpedient, inopportune, troublesome **12** embarrassing, incommodious, unmanageable, unseasonable **13** inappropriate

**incorporate**
◇ *containment indicator*
**03** mix **04** fuse **05** blend, merge, unify, unite **06** absorb, embody, imbody, take in **07** build in, combine, contain, embrace, include, piece up, subsume
**08** coalesce, incorpse **09** integrate, multiplex **10** amalgamate, assimilate
**11** consolidate

**incorporated**
**03** inc

**incorporation**
**05** blend, union **06** fusion, merger
**07** company, society **08** unifying
**09** inclusion, subsuming
**10** absorption, assumption, embodiment, federation
**11** association, coalescence, combination, integration, unification
**12** amalgamation, assimilation

**incorporeal**
**04** aery **05** aerie **06** unreal **07** ghostly
**08** bodiless, ethereal, illusory, spectral, unfleshy **09** spiritual, unfleshly
**10** immaterial, intangible, phantasmal, phantasmic

**incorrect**
◇ *anagram indicator*
**03** bad, ill **05** false, wrong **06** faulty, untrue **07** inexact, off beam
**08** improper, mistaken, not right
**09** erroneous, imprecise **10** fallacious, inaccurate, unsuitable, way off beam
**12** illegitimate **13** inappropriate, ungrammatical

**incorrectly**
**05** false, wrong **07** falsely, in error, wrongly **08** unfairly, unjustly **09** by mistake **10** mistakenly **11** erroneously, misguidedly **12** fallaciously, inaccurately **15** inappropriately

**incorrectness**
**05** error **07** fallacy **09** falseness, wrongness **10** faultiness, inaccuracy

**11** imprecision, inexactness, unsoundness **12** inexactitude, mistakenness, speciousness **13** erroneousness, impreciseness, unsuitability

**incorrigible**
**08** hardened, hopeless **09** incurable **10** beyond hope, inveterate **12** irredeemable **13** dyed-in-the-wool, irreclaimable

**incorruptibility**
**06** honour, virtue **07** honesty, probity **08** justness, morality, nobility **09** integrity **11** uprightness **15** trustworthiness

**incorruptible**
**04** just **05** moral **06** honest **07** ethical, upright **08** straight, virtuous **10** honourable, unbribable **11** trustworthy **14** high-principled

**increase**
**02** up **03** add, ech, eik, eke, ich, wax **04** eche, eech, gain, go up, grow, hike, rise, soar, wave **05** add to, boost, breed, bulge, climb, mount, raise, surge, swell, widen **06** bump up, deepen, expand, extend, flow-on, gather, growth, hike up, mark-up, profit, pump up, rocket, spiral, spread, step up, step-up, uplift, upturn **07** advance, augment, broaden, build up, build-up, develop, enhance, enlarge, further, improve, inflate, magnify, produce, progeny, prolong, scale up, upsurge **08** addition, escalate, heighten, interest, maximize, multiply, mushroom, progress, redouble, snowball **09** expansion, extension, increment, intensify, propagate, rocketing, skyrocket **10** accumulate, escalation, strengthen **11** development, enlargement, heightening, mushrooming, proliferate, snowballing **12** augmentation, bring to a head **13** become greater, proliferation **14** bring to the boil **15** be on the increase, intensification

**increasingly**
**06** more so **10** all the more **11** more and more **12** cumulatively **13** exponentially, on the increase, progressively

**incredible**
**04** tall **05** great, steep **06** absurd, unreal **07** amazing **08** smashing, terrific **09** fantastic, wonderful **10** astounding, cockamamie, far-fetched, formidable, impossible, improbable, marvellous, past belief, remarkable, surprising, tremendous **11** astonishing, cock-and-bull, exceptional, implausible, jaw-dropping, magnificent, unthinkable **12** beyond belief, mind-boggling, preposterous, unbelievable, unimaginable **13** extraordinary, inconceivable **14** out of this world

**incredibly**
**04** very **06** highly **07** greatly **09** amazingly, extremely **10** impossibly, remarkably **11** unspeakably, wonderfully **12** marvellously, surprisingly, terrifically, tremendously, unbelievably, unimaginably **13** exceptionally, fantastically, inconceivably, inexpressibly **15** extraordinarily

**incredulity**
**05** doubt **08** cynicism, distrust, mistrust, unbelief **09** amazement, disbelief, suspicion **10** scepticism

**incredulous**
**07** cynical, dubious **08** doubtful, doubting **09** sceptical, uncertain **10** suspicious **11** distrustful, distrusting, unbelieving, unconvinced **12** disbelieving, unbelievable

**increment**
**04** gain **06** growth, step-up **07** accrual **08** addendum, addition, increase **09** accretion, accrument, expansion, extension **10** growth ring, supplement **11** advancement, enlargement **12** augmentation

**incriminate**
**05** blame, set up **06** accuse, charge, indict **07** arraign, impeach, involve **08** stitch up **09** implicate, inculpate **13** put the blame on

**inculcate**
**03** fix **05** teach **06** infuse, instil, preach **07** din into, engrain, implant, impress, imprint **08** drum into **09** drill into **10** hammer into **12** indoctrinate

**inculpate**
**05** blame **06** accuse, charge, indict **07** arraign, censure, impeach, involve **09** implicate **11** incriminate, recriminate **13** put the blame on

**incumbent**
**04** up to **05** right **06** bearer, holder, member, parson **07** binding, officer **08** official **09** mandatory, necessary, overlying **10** compulsory, obligatory, prescribed **11** functionary, overhanging **12** office-bearer, office-holder **15** perpetual curate

**incur**
**03** ren, rin, run **04** earn, gain, risk **05** run up **06** arouse, suffer **07** provoke, sustain **08** contract, meet with **10** experience

**incurable**
**05** fatal **08** hardened, hopeless, terminal **10** beyond hope, inoperable, inveterate, remediless, unhealable, unrecuring **11** immedicable, untreatable **12** incorrigible **13** dyed-in-the-wool, unmedicinable

**incurably**
**07** fatally **10** beyond hope, hopelessly, inoperably, terminally **12** incorrigibly, inveterately

**incursion**
**04** raid, road, rode **05** foray, sally **06** attack, inroad, razzia, sortie **07** assault, inroads **08** invasion **09** intrusion, irruption, onslaught **11** penetration **12** infiltration

**indebted**
**05** owing **07** obliged **08** beholden, grateful, thankful **09** obligated **12** appreciative

• **be indebted**
**03** owe

**indebtedness**
**09** gratitude **10** obligation **12** appreciation **15** debt of gratitude

**indecency**
**07** crudity **08** foulness, impurity, lewdness **09** grossness, immodesty, indecorum, obscenity, vulgarity **10** coarseness **11** pornography **13** offensiveness **14** licentiousness

**indecent**
◇ *anagram indicator*
**04** blue, foul, free, lewd, ripe **05** bawdy, crude, dirty, gross, nasty **06** coarse, filthy, fruity, impure, ribald, risqué, sleazy, smutty, sultry, vulgar **07** corrupt, immoral, obscene, raunchy **08** depraved, immodest, improper, scabrous, shocking, uncomely, unhonest, unseemly **09** off colour, offensive, perverted **10** degenerate, indecorous, indelicate, licentious, outrageous, suggestive, unbecoming, unsuitable **11** near the bone, Rabelaisian **12** pornographic, unrepeatable **13** inappropriate **14** close to the bone, near the knuckle

**indecipherable**
**04** tiny **07** crabbed, cramped, unclear **09** illegible **10** indistinct, unreadable **14** unintelligible

**indecision**
**05** doubt **07** swither **08** suspense, wavering **09** hesitancy **10** hesitation **11** ambivalence, fluctuation, uncertainty, vacillation **12** irresolution **13** tentativeness **14** indecisiveness **15** shilly-shallying

**indecisive**
**04** open **06** unsure **07** unclear **08** doubtful, hesitant, wavering **09** faltering, tentative, uncertain, undecided, unsettled **10** ambivalent, hesitating, indefinite, in two minds, irresolute, undecisive, up in the air, weak-willed, wishy-washy **11** fluctuating, vacillating **12** feeble-minded, inconclusive, pussyfooting, undetermined **13** indeterminate **15** shilly-shallying

**indecorous**
**04** rude **05** crude, rough **06** coarse, vulgar **07** boorish, ill-bred, naughty, uncivil, uncouth **08** churlish, immodest, impolite, improper, indecent, seemless, unseemly, untoward **09** graceless, tasteless, unfitting **10** high-kilted, in bad taste,

seemelesse, unladylike, unmannerly, unsuitable **11** ill-mannered, undignified **13** inappropriate, ungentlemanly

**indecorum**
**07** crudity **08** bad taste, rudeness **09** immodesty, indecency, roughness, vulgarity **10** coarseness, uncivility **11** impropriety **12** impoliteness, unseemliness **13** tastelessness

**indeed**
**01** I **02** ay, la **03** aye, e'en, nay, yah, yea, yes **04** deed, even, faix, just **05** faith, haith, marry, quite, sooth, truly **06** atweel, in fact, quotha, rather, really **07** for sure, insooth, in truth, quite so, soothly **08** actually, forsooth, to be sure **09** certainly, soothlich **10** absolutely, definitely, in good time, positively, undeniably **11** doubtlessly, undoubtedly **12** without doubt **13** for that matter, in anyone's book, in point of fact

**indefatigable**
**06** dogged **07** patient, undying **08** diligent, tireless, untiring **09** unfailing, unresting, unwearied **10** relentless, unflagging, untireable, unwearying **11** indomitable, persevering, unremitting, unweariable **13** inexhaustible

**indefatigably**
**08** doggedly **09** patiently **10** diligently, tirelessly **11** indomitably, unfailingly, unrestingly **12** relentlessly, unflaggingly **13** unremittingly

**indefensible**
**05** wrong **06** faulty, flawed **07** exposed, unarmed **08** disarmed, specious **09** unguarded, untenable **10** unshielded, vulnerable **11** defenceless, ill-equipped, inexcusable, unfortified, unprotected **12** undefendable, unforgivable, unpardonable **13** insupportable, unjustifiable

**indefinable**
**03** dim **04** hazy **05** vague **06** subtle **07** obscure, unclear **08** nameless **10** impalpable, indistinct, unrealized **13** indescribable, inexpressible

**indefinite**
**04** hazy **05** fuzzy, loose, vague **07** blurred, general, inexact, obscure, unclear, unfixed, unknown **08** confused, doubtful, twilight **09** ambiguous, equivocal, imprecise, uncertain, undecided, undefined, unlimited, unsettled **10** ambivalent, ill-defined, indistinct, unresolved **11** nondescript, unspecified **12** inconclusive, undetermined **13** indeterminate

**indefinitely**
**06** always **07** for ever **09** endlessly, eternally **11** ad infinitum, continually, permanently **12** without limit

**indelible**
**04** fast **07** lasting **08** enduring, unfading **09** ingrained, permanent **12** imperishable, ineffaceable, ineradicable **14** indestructible

**indelibly**
**10** enduringly **11** permanently **12** ineradicably **14** indestructibly

**indelicacy**
**07** crudity **08** bad taste, rudeness **09** grossness, immodesty, indecency, obscenity, vulgarity **10** coarseness, smuttiness **11** impropriety **13** offensiveness, tastelessness **14** suggestiveness

**indelicate**
**03** low **04** blue, rude, warm **05** crude, gross **06** coarse, risqué, sultry, vulgar **07** obscene **08** immodest, improper, indecent, tactless, unseemly, untoward **09** off-colour, offensive, tasteless **10** in bad taste, indecorous, suggestive, unbecoming **12** embarrassing

**indemnify**
**03** pay **04** free **05** repay **06** exempt, insure, recoup, repair, secure **07** endorse, protect, requite, satisfy **09** guarantee, reimburse **10** compensate, remunerate, underwrite

**indemnity**
**07** amnesty, redress **08** immunity, requital, security **09** assurance, exemption, guarantee, insurance, repayment, safeguard **10** protection, reparation **11** restitution **12** compensation, remuneration **13** reimbursement

**indent**
**03** cut **04** dent, dint, mark, nick, pink **05** notch, order **06** ask for, crenel, demand, recess **07** bargain, impress, request, scallop, serrate **08** apply for, crenelle **09** penetrate **10** apprentice **11** requisition

**indentation**
**03** cut, dip, pit **04** dent, nick **05** gouge, notch, sinus **06** crenel, dimple, furrow, groove, hollow, recess **08** crenelle **09** serration **10** depression **11** engrailment

**indenture**
**04** bond, deal, deed **08** contract, covenant **09** agreement **10** commitment, settlement **11** certificate

**independence**
**01** I **05** uhuru **06** swaraj **07** autarky, freedom, liberty **08** autonomy, home rule, self-rule **10** competency, separation **11** nationalism, sovereignty **12** independency, self-reliance **13** individualism **14** decolonization, self-government **15** self-sufficiency

**independent**
**01** I **03** Ind **04** fair, free, just **07** neutral, private, unaided **08** absolute, autarkic, discrete, distinct, separate, unbiased **09** autarchic, freelance, impartial, liberated, objective, sovereign, unrelated **10** autogenous, autonomous, crossbench, individual, non-aligned, self-ruling, unattacked **11** self-reliant, unconnected **12** free-standing, free-thinking, self-standing, unprejudiced, unrestrained **13** autocephalous, disinterested, dispassionate, individualist, self-contained, self-governing, unconstrained **14** self-sufficient, self-supporting, unconventional **15** going your own way, individualistic, self-determining, self-legislating

**independently**
**04** solo **05** alone **07** unaided **09** on your own, on your tod **10** by yourself, separately **12** autonomously, individually

**indescribable**
**07** amazing **08** nameless **09** ineffable **10** incredible **11** exceptional, indefinable, inenarrable, undefinable, unspeakable, unutterable **13** extraordinary, inexpressible

**indescribably**
**04** very **06** highly **07** greatly **09** amazingly, extremely **10** incredibly **11** unspeakably, unutterably **13** exceptionally, inexpressibly **15** extraordinarily

**indestructible**
**05** tough **06** strong **07** abiding, durable, endless, eternal, lasting **08** enduring, immortal **09** permanent **10** undecaying **11** everlasting, infrangible, unbreakable **12** imperishable **15** tough as old boots

**indeterminate**
**04** hazy **05** vague **07** inexact, unclear, unfixed, unknown **08** unstated, variable **09** ambiguous, equivocal, imprecise, open-ended, uncertain, undecided, undefined **10** ambivalent, ill-defined, indefinite **11** unspecified **12** inconclusive, undetermined **13** unpredictable

**index**
**03** BMI, key, RPI **04** clue, dial, hand, hint, list, mark, nose, rate, sign **05** guide, power, ratio, scale, style, table, token **06** alidad, gnomon, needle, number **07** average, formula, pointer, preface, symptom **08** card file, exponent, fraction, prologue **09** catalogue, directory, indicator **10** difference, forefinger, indication, percentage, proportion **11** concordance **12** introduction **13** card catalogue **14** correspondence

**India**
**01** I **03** IND
*See also* **state**

**Indian** *see* **American**; **Asian**

**Indiana**
**02** IN **03** Ind

**indicate**
**03** put, say, tip **04** mark, mean, note, read, shew, show, sign, tell **05** argue, arrow, imply, point, spell, state, utter, voice **06** affirm, assert, denote, evince, record, report, reveal, set out **07** declare, display, divulge, express, point to, present, signify, specify, suggest **08** announce, disclose, evidence, manifest, point out, register **09** designate, formulate, make known, represent **10** articulate **11** communicate **15** be symptomatic of

**indicated**
**06** marked, needed **08** required **09** advisable, called-for, desirable, necessary, suggested **11** recommended

**indication**
**03** nod **04** clue, hint, lead, mark, note, omen, shew, show, sign **05** token, trace **06** augury, oracle, record, signal **07** glimpse, pointer, portent, symptom, warning **08** endeixis, evidence, monument, register, signpost **10** denotement, expression, intimation, suggestion **11** explanation **13** demonstration, manifestation

**indicative**
**07** typical **08** indicant, symbolic, telltale **10** denotative, exhibitive, indicatory, suggestive **11** significant, symptomatic **13** demonstrative, significative **14** characteristic

**indicatively**
**07** as a sign **09** as a symbol, typically **10** as evidence **12** symbolically **13** significantly **14** as an expression **15** symptomatically

**indicator**
**04** dial, hand, mark, sign **05** bezel, gauge, guide, index, meter, token **06** gnomon, marker, needle, signal, symbol **07** display, flasher, pointer **08** signpost **09** barometer **10** litmus test, turn signal

**indict**
**04** dite **06** accuse, charge, summon **07** arraign, article, impeach, summons, trounce **09** inculpate, prosecute **10** put on trial **11** incriminate

**indictment**
**06** charge, dittay **07** summons **10** accusation, allegation **11** arraignment, impeachment, inculpation, prosecution **13** incrimination, recrimination

**indifference**
**06** apathy, phlegm, slight **08** coldness, coolness **09** disregard, unconcern **10** negligence, neutrality **11** impassivity, inattention, nonchalance **12** heedlessness **13** lack of concern, lack of feeling **14** lack of interest

**indifferent**
**02** OK **03** bad **04** cold, cool, easy, fair, so-so **05** aloof, blasé **06** medium **07** average, callous, distant, easy-osy, neutral, not good, unmoved **08** adequate, careless, detached, heedless, inferior, jack easy, mediocre, middling, moderate, ordinary, passable, uncaring **09** apathetic, impassive, incurious, unexcited, unfeeling **10** insouciant, nonchalant, uninvolved **11** cold-hearted, pococurante, unconcerned, unemotional **12** could be worse, run of the mill, uninterested, unresponsive **13** could be better, disinterested, dispassionate, uninteresting, unsympathetic **14** unenthusiastic **15** all the same to you, undistinguished

**indigence**
**04** need, want **06** penury **07** poverty **08** distress **09** necessity, privation **11** deprivation, destitution

**indigenous**
**05** local **06** native **08** original **09** home-grown **10** aboriginal, vernacular **13** autochthonous

**indigent**
**04** bust, poor **05** broke, needy, skint **06** in need, in want **08** dirt-poor **09** destitute, penniless, penurious **10** cleaned out, down and out, stony-broke **11** impecunious, necessitous, up against it **12** impoverished, on your uppers **13** in dire straits **14** on your beam ends **15** poverty-stricken

**indigestion**
**07** acidity, apepsia, pyrosis **08** dyspepsy **09** dyspepsia, heartburn **10** cardialgia, water-brash **13** grass staggers **15** stomach staggers

**indignant**
**03** mad **05** angry, cross, irate, livid, riled **06** bitter, fuming, heated, miffed, narked, peeved **07** annoyed, enraged, furious, in a huff **08** in a strop, incensed, outraged, up in arms, wrathful **09** aggrieved, resentful, steamed up **10** got the hump, infuriated **11** acrimonious, disgruntled, exasperated

**indignantly**
**07** angrily, crossly, in a huff, irately **08** bitterly, up in arms **09** furiously, steamed up **11** resentfully **13** acrimoniously, reproachfully

**indignation**
**03** ire **04** fury, rage **05** anger, pique, scorn, wrath **06** furore **07** dudgeon, outrage **08** contempt **09** annoyance **10** resentment **12** exasperation **15** saeva indignatio

**indignity**
**04** snub **05** abuse, shame **06** injury, insult, slight **07** affront, obloquy, offence, outrage, putdown **08** contempt, disgrace, reproach **09** contumely, dishonour **10** disrespect, incivility, opprobrium **11** humiliation **12** cold shoulder, mistreatment, unworthiness **13** slap in the face **14** kick in the teeth

**indigo**
**04** anil

**indirect**
**02** by **03** bye **06** remote, squint, ungain, zigzag **07** curving, devious, mediate, oblique, winding **08** allusive, rambling, tortuous **09** ancillary, divergent, secondary, wandering **10** back-handed, circuitous, discursive, incidental, meandering, roundabout, subsidiary, unintended **11** subordinate **12** periphrastic **14** circumlocutory

**indirectly**
**05** round **09** deviously, hintingly, obliquely **10** allusively, second-hand **12** at second hand, incidentally, roundaboutly

**indiscernible**
**04** tiny **06** hidden, minute **07** obscure, unclear **09** invisible, minuscule **10** impalpable, indistinct, unapparent **11** microscopic **12** undetectable, unnoticeable **13** imperceptible, undiscernible

**indiscreet**
**04** rash **05** hasty **06** unwary, unwise **07** foolish **08** careless, heedless, immodest, reckless, tactless **09** foolhardy, ill-judged, impolitic, imprudent, shameless **10** ill-advised, indelicate, unthinking **11** injudicious, insensitive **12** undiplomatic **13** ill-considered

**indiscreetly**
**06** rashly **08** unwisely **09** foolishly **10** carelessly, heedlessly, immodestly, recklessly, tactlessly **11** shamelessly **12** indelicately **13** insensitively

**indiscretion**
**04** boob, flub, slip **05** error, folly, gaffe, lapse **06** slip-up **07** blunder, faux pas, mistake **08** rashness **09** immodesty **10** imprudence, indelicacy **11** foolishness **12** carelessness, recklessness, tactlessness **13** shamelessness

**indiscriminate**
◇ *anagram indicator*
**05** mixed **06** motley, random, varied **07** aimless, chaotic, diverse, general **08** careless, confused, pell-mell, sweeping **09** haphazard, hit or miss, wholesale **10** hit and miss **11** promiscuous, scattershot, unselective **12** unmethodical, unrespective, unsystematic **13** miscellaneous

**indiscriminately**
**08** randomly **09** aimlessly, generally, in the mass, wholesale **10** carelessly **11** haphazardly **13** unselectively **14** unmethodically **15** indistinctively

**indispensable**
**03** key **05** basic, vital **06** needed **07** crucial, needful **08** required **09** essential, important, necessary, requisite **10** absolutely, imperative **11** fundamental

**indisposed**
**03** ill **04** sick **05** crook, loath **06** ailing, averse, groggy, laid up, poorly, unwell **09** reluctant, unwilling **10** not of a mind, not willing, out of sorts **11** disinclined **12** not of a mind to **13** confined to bed, incapacitated **15** under the weather

**indisposition**
**03** ail **06** malady **07** ailment, disease, dislike, illness **08** aversion, disorder, distaste, sickness **09** bad health, complaint, hesitancy, ill health **10** reluctance **13** unwillingness **14** disinclination, distemperature

**indisputable**
**04** sure **06** liquid **07** certain, dead set **08** absolute, definite, positive **10** inarguable, unarguable, undeniable, undisputed **11** indubitable, irrefutable **13** incontestable **14** beyond question, uncontrollable, unquestionable

**indissoluble**
**05** fixed, solid **07** abiding, binding, eternal, lasting **08** enduring **09** permanent **10** inviolable **11** inseparable, sempiternal, unbreakable **12** imperishable **13** incorruptible **14** indestructible

**indistinct**
**03** dim, low **04** hazy, pale **05** blear, faded, faint, fuzzy, misty, muted, vague **06** grainy, woolly **07** blurred, clouded, distant, muffled, obscure, shadowy, unclear **08** confused, muttered **09** ambiguous, undefined **10** ill-defined, indefinite, out of focus **14** indecipherable, unintelligible

• **indistinct appearance**
**04** blur, loom

**indistinctly**
**05** dimly **06** hazily **07** fuzzily, vaguely **09** obscurely, unclearly **10** out of focus **14** unintelligibly

**indistinguishable**
**04** same, twin **05** alike **06** cloned **09** identical **10** tantamount **13** indiscernible **15** interchangeable

**indium**
**02** In

**individual**
**03** one, own **04** body, idio-, lone, poll, sole, sort, soul, type, unit **05** being, party **06** fellow, mortal, person, proper, single, unique, versal **07** private, several, special, typical **08** creature, distinct, isolated, original, peculiar, personal, separate, singular, solitary, specific **09** character, exclusive **10** human being, particular, respective, subjective **11** distinctive, inseparable **12** personalized **13** idiosyncratic **14** characteristic

**individualism**
**06** egoism **09** anarchism **11** freethought, originality **12** eccentricity, freethinking, independence, self-interest, self-reliance **13** egocentricity, self-direction **14** libertarianism

**individualist**
**05** loner **06** egoist **08** bohemian, lone wolf, maverick, original **09** anarchist, eccentric **10** egocentric, free spirit **11** freethinker, independent, libertarian **13** nonconformist

**individualistic**
**06** unique **07** special, typical **08** bohemian, egoistic, original **09** eccentric **10** egocentric, individual, particular, unorthodox **11** anarchistic, independent, libertarian, self-reliant **13** idiosyncratic, nonconformist **14** unconventional

**individuality**
**07** oneness **08** identity, property **09** character, propriety **10** uniqueness **11** distinction, originality, peculiarity, personality, singularity **12** separateness **15** distinctiveness

**individually**
**06** singly **08** one by one **09** in several, severally **10** one at a time, personally, separately **12** in particular, particularly **13** independently

**indivisible**
**10** impartible **11** inseparable, intrenchant, undividable **12** indissoluble **14** indiscerptible

**indoctrinate**
**05** drill, teach, train **06** ground, instil, school **07** impress **08** instruct **09** brainwash, inculcate **12** propagandize

**indoctrination**
**08** drilling, teaching, training **09** grounding, schooling **10** catechesis, instilling **11** catechetics, inculcation, instruction **12** brainwashing

**Indo-European**
**02** IE

*See also* **European**

**indolence**
**05** sloth **06** apathy, torpor **07** inertia, languor **08** idleness, laziness, lethargy, shirking, slacking **09** heaviness, inertness, torpidity, torpitude **10** inactivity, torpidness **11** languidness **12** do-nothingism, listlessness, sluggishness

**indolent**
**04** idle, lazy, slow **05** inert, slack **06** otiose, supine, torpid **07** languid, lumpish **08** bone-idle, fainéant, inactive, listless, slothful, sluggard, sluggish **09** apathetic, do-nothing, easy-going, lethargic, shiftless **13** lackadaisical

**indomitable**
**04** bold, firm **05** brave **07** staunch, valiant **08** fearless, intrepid, resolute, stalwart **09** steadfast, undaunted **10** courageous, determined, invincible, unbeatable, unyielding **11** impregnable, lion-hearted, unflinching **12** intransigent, unassailable, undefeatable **13** unconquerable

**Indonesia**
**02** RI **03** IDN

**indubitable**
**04** sure **07** certain, evident, obvious **08** absolute **09** undoubted **10** unarguable, undeniable **11** beyond doubt, irrefutable, undoubtable **12** indisputable, irrebuttable, irrefragable, unanswerable **13** beyond dispute, incontestable **14** unquestionable

**indubitably**
**05** truly **06** surely **07** clearly, no doubt **08** of course, probably **09** assuredly, certainly, doubtless, precisely **10** most likely, presumably **11** undoubtedly **12** indisputably, without doubt **14** unquestionably

**induce**
**03** get **04** coax, draw, lead, move, urge **05** cause, force, impel, press, tempt **06** effect, incite, lead to, prompt, seduce **07** actuate, bring on, entreat, inspire, intreat, procure, produce, provoke **08** generate, motivate, occasion, persuade, talk into **09** encourage, influence, instigate, originate **10** bring about, give rise to **11** prevail upon, set in motion

**inducement**
**04** bait, goad, lure, spur **05** bribe, cause, drink **06** carrot, motive, reason, reward **07** impetus **08** stimulus **09** incentive, influence, sweetener **10** attraction, back-hander, enticement, incitement, persuasion **11** seditionary **13** encouragement

**induct**
**05** admit, place, stall **06** enlist, invest, ordain **07** install, swear in **08** enthrone, initiate **09** conscript, introduce **10** consecrate, inaugurate

**inductance**
**01** L

• **measure of inductance**
**01** H **05** henry

**induction**
**07** epagoge, prelude **09** deduction, inference **10** conclusion, initiation, ordination **11** institution, investiture **12** consecration, enthronement, inauguration, installation, introduction **14** generalization

**indulge**
**03** pet **05** allow, spoil, treat **06** cocker, cosset, cuiter, favour, humour, pamper, pettle, regale **07** cater to, gratify, revel in, satisfy, yield to **08** give in to, pander to, wallow in **09** give way to, make merry **11** go along with, luxuriate in, mollycoddle **14** give free rein to

**indulgence**
**03** law **04** luxe, riot **05** favor, swing, treat **06** excess, excuse, favour, luxury,

pardon **08** lenience, spoiling
**09** pampering, remission, tolerance
**10** fulfilment, generosity, sensualism, sensuality **11** dissipation, forbearance
**12** extravagance, immoderation, intemperance, satisfaction
**13** dissoluteness, gratification, mollycoddling

**indulgent**
**04** fond, kind **06** humane, tender
**07** lenient, liberal, patient
**08** generous, merciful, spoiling, tolerant **09** compliant, cosseting, easy-going, forgiving, humouring, pampering **10** forbearing, permissive
**11** sympathetic **13** compassionate, mollycoddling, understanding

**indulgently**
**06** fondly, kindly **08** humanely, tenderly **09** leniently, liberally, patiently, with mercy **10** generously, mercifully, tolerantly **12** with sympathy
**14** with compassion
**15** compassionately, sympathetically

**industrial**
**05** trade **08** business **09** technical
**10** commercial **13** manufacturing

**industrialist**
**05** baron **06** tycoon **07** magnate
**08** producer **09** financier **10** capitalist
**12** manufacturer

**industrious**
**04** busy, hard **05** deedy **06** active, dogged, steady **07** notable, on the go, skilful, workful, zealous **08** diligent, sedulous, studious, tireless, vigorous, worksome **09** assiduous, dedicated, energetic, laborious **10** busy as a bee, determined, persistent, productive
**11** hard-working, persevering
**13** conscientious, indefatigable

**industriously**
**04** hard **08** doggedly, steadily
**10** diligently, sedulously **11** assiduously
**13** perseveringly **15** conscientiously

**industry**
**04** line, toil, zeal **05** field, trade
**06** effort, energy, labour, vigour
**07** service **08** activity, business, commerce, hard work, sedulity
**09** assiduity, diligence **10** enterprise, intentness, production, steadiness
**11** application, persistence
**12** perseverance, sedulousness, stickability, tirelessness
**13** assiduousness, concentration, determination, laboriousness, manufacturing **14** productiveness
**15** industriousness

**inebriated**
◇ *anagram indicator*
**04** full, high, inky **05** drunk, happy, inked, lit up, merry, moppy, tight, tipsy, woozy **06** blotto, bombed, canned, corked, jarred, juiced, loaded, mortal, pished, ripped, rotten, soused, stewed, stinko, stoned, tiddly, wasted
**07** bevvied, bonkers, bottled, crocked, drunken, half-cut, legless, maggoty, pickled, pie-eyed, sloshed, smashed, sozzled, squiffy, tiddled, wrecked
**08** bibulous, footless, hammered, in liquor, juiced up, liquored, moon-eyed, ossified, sow-drunk, steaming, stocious, tanked up, whiffled, whistled
**09** bladdered, crapulent, paralytic, plastered, shickered, up the pole, well-oiled **10** blind drunk, obfuscated
**11** intoxicated, off your face **12** drunk as a lord, drunk as a newt, roaring drunk **13** drunk as a piper, drunk as a skunk, having had a few, under the table **14** Brahms and Liszt **15** one over the eight, the worse for wear, under the weather

**inedible**
**03** bad, off **05** stale **06** deadly, rancid, rotten **07** harmful, noxious
**09** poisonous, uneatable **10** inesculent
**11** not fit to eat, unpalatable
**12** indigestible, unconsumable

**ineducable**
**08** indocile **11** unteachable
**12** incorrigible

**ineffable**
**07** fearful **10** remarkable **11** beyond words, unspeakable, unutterable
**12** unimpartible **13** indescribable, inexpressible **14** incommunicable

**ineffably**
**09** fearfully **10** absolutely, remarkably
**11** beyond words, unspeakably, unutterably **13** indescribably, inexpressibly

**ineffective**
**03** dud **04** idle, lame, vain, weak
**05** inept **06** feeble, futile **07** useless
**08** abortive, impotent **09** burned out, fruitless, powerless, to no avail, toothless, worthless **10** inadequate, profitless, unavailing, unpregnant
**11** incompetent, ineffectual
**12** unproductive, unsuccessful

**ineffectiveness**
**08** futility, weakness **10** feebleness, inadequacy **11** uselessness
**13** fruitlessness, worthlessness

**ineffectual**
**03** wet **04** lame, vain, void, weak
**05** inept, resty, wimpy **06** feeble, futile, unable **07** useless **08** abortive, chinless, feckless, impotent
**09** fruitless, frustrate, powerless, worthless **10** inadequate, unavailing
**11** incompetent **12** unproductive
**13** inefficacious, lackadaisical

**ineffectually**
**06** feebly, in vain, lamely, weakly **09** to no avail, uselessly **11** fruitlessly, to no purpose **14** unproductively, unsuccessfully

**inefficacy**
**08** futility **10** inadequacy
**11** uselessness **14** ineffectuality
**15** ineffectiveness, ineffectualness

**inefficiency**
**05** waste **06** laxity, muddle
**09** slackness **10** ineptitude, negligence, sloppiness
**12** carelessness, incompetence, wastefulness **15** disorganization

**inefficient**
**03** lax **05** inept, slack **06** flabby, sloppy **08** careless, inexpert, slipshod, wasteful **09** negligent, shiftless
**10** uneconomic **11** incompetent, ineffective, time-wasting, unorganized
**12** disorganized, money-wasting
**13** unworkmanlike

**inelegant**
**04** ugly **05** crude, rough **06** clumsy, gauche, vulgar **07** awkward, ill-bred, uncouth **08** homespun, laboured, ungainly, unpolite **09** graceless, unrefined **10** uncultured, unfinished, ungraceful, unpolished
**12** uncultivated **15** unsophisticated

**ineligible**
**05** unfit **08** ruled out, unfitted, unworthy **10** unequipped, unsuitable
**11** incompetent, undesirable, unqualified **12** disqualified, unacceptable

**ineluctable**
**04** sure **05** fated **07** assured, certain
**08** destined **10** ineludible, inevitable, inexorable **11** inescapable, irrevocable, unalterable, unavoidable

**inept**
◇ *anagram indicator*
**04** void **05** flaky, lousy, silly **06** clumsy, stupid **07** awkward, foolish, useless
**08** bungling, inexpert, pathetic
**09** appalling, ham-fisted, incapable, maladroit, unskilful **10** cack-handed, inadequate, unsuitable **11** heavy-handed, incompetent **12** unsuccessful

**ineptitude**
**07** fatuity **08** bungling **09** crassness, gaucherie, ineptness, stupidity, unfitness **10** clumsiness, gaucheness, incapacity **11** awkwardness, glaikitness, unhandiness, uselessness
**12** incapability, incompetence, inexpertness **13** unskilfulness

**inequality**
**03** rub **04** bias, odds, wave **05** whelk
**08** contrast, imparity **09** disparity, diversity, imbalance, prejudice, roughness, variation **10** difference, inadequacy, unevenness
**11** discrepancy, unequalness
**12** incompetence, irregularity
**13** disproportion, dissimilarity, nonconformity **14** discrimination

**inequitable**
**06** biased, unfair, unjust **07** bigoted, partial, unequal **08** one-sided, partisan, wrongful **10** intolerant, prejudiced **12** preferential
**14** discriminatory

**inequity**
**04** bias **05** abuse **09** injustice, prejudice **10** inequality, partiality, unfairness, unjustness

**12** maltreatment, mistreatment, one-sidedness, wrongfulness **14** discrimination

**inert**
**04** cold, dead, dull, idle, lazy **05** slack, still **06** leaden, sleepy, static, supine, torpid **07** dormant, languid, passive, restive **08** comatose, immobile, inactive, indolent, lifeless, listless, sluggish, stagnant, thowless, unmoving **09** apathetic, inanimate, lethargic, nerveless **10** motionless, stationary, stock-still **12** unresponsive

**inertia**
**05** sloth **06** apathy, torpor **07** languor **08** idleness, inaction, laziness, lethargy **09** indolence, inertness, passivity, stillness **10** immobility, inactivity, Oblomovism, stagnation **12** listlessness, slothfulness **14** motionlessness

**inescapable**
**04** sure **05** fated **07** assured, certain **08** destined **10** ineludible, inevitable, inexorable **11** ineluctable, irrevocable, unalterable, unavoidable

**inescapably**
**06** surely **09** assuredly, certainly **10** definitely, inevitably, inexorably **11** irrevocably, necessarily, unavoidably **13** automatically

**inessential**
**05** extra, spare **06** luxury **07** surplus **08** needless, optional, trimming **09** accessory, appendage, extrinsic, redundant, secondary **10** accidental, expendable, extraneous, immaterial, irrelevant, unasked-for **11** dispensable, superfluity, superfluous, uncalled-for, unessential, unimportant, unnecessary **12** extravagance, non-essential

**inestimable**
**04** vast **06** untold **07** immense **08** infinite, precious **09** priceless, unlimited **10** invaluable, prodigious **11** measureless, uncountable **12** immeasurable, incalculable, incomputable, mind-boggling, unfathomable **13** worth a fortune

**inevitability**
**04** fact **05** truth **07** reality, safe bet **08** dead cert, validity **09** certainty, sure thing **14** matter of course

**inevitable**
**04** sure **05** fated, fixed **07** assured, certain, decreed, fateful, settled, unshun'd **08** definite, destined, ordained **09** automatic, necessary, unavoided, unshunned **10** inexorable, infallible **11** ineluctable, inescapable, irrevocable, predestined, unalterable, unavoidable **13** unpreventable

**inevitably**
**06** surely **09** assuredly, certainly, fatefully, presently **10** definitely, inexorably, infallibly, willy-nilly **11** inescapably, irrevocably, necessarily, unavoidably **13** automatically

**inexact**
**03** lax **05** fuzzy, loose **06** untrue, woolly **07** muddled, of a sort, of sorts **09** erroneous, imprecise, incorrect **10** fallacious, inaccurate, indefinite, indistinct **11** approximate **13** indeterminate

**inexactitude**
**05** error **07** blunder, mistake **09** looseness **10** inaccuracy, woolliness **11** imprecision, inexactness **13** approximation, impreciseness, incorrectness **14** indefiniteness, miscalculation

**inexcusable**
**08** shameful **10** outrageous **11** blameworthy, intolerable **12** indefensible, unacceptable, unforgivable, unpardonable **13** reprehensible, unjustifiable

**inexcusably**
**10** shamefully **12** indefensibly, outrageously, unacceptably **13** reprehensibly, unjustifiably

**inexhaustible**
**07** endless **08** abundant, infinite, tireless, untiring **09** boundless, limitless, unbounded, unfailing, unlimited, unwearied, weariless **10** unflagging, unwearying **11** illimitable, measureless, never-ending **12** unrestricted **13** indefatigable

**inexorable**
**04** sure **05** fated **07** certain **08** definite, destined, ordained **09** immovable, incessant, unceasing **10** implacable, inevitable, relentless, unyielding **11** ineluctable, inescapable, irrevocable, remorseless, unalterable, unavertable, unfaltering, unrelenting, unstoppable **12** intransigent, irresistible **13** unpreventable

**inexorably**
**06** surely **09** certainly **10** definitely, implacably, inevitably, pitilessly **11** ineluctably, inescapably, irrevocably, mercilessly **12** irresistibly, relentlessly, resistlessly **13** remorselessly

**inexpedient**
**05** wrong **06** unwise **07** foolish **09** ill-chosen, ill-judged, impolitic, imprudent, misguided, senseless **10** ill-advised, indiscreet, unsuitable **11** detrimental, impolitical, impractical, inadvisable, injudicious, unadvisable, undesirable **12** inconvenient, undiplomatic, unfavourable **13** inappropriate **15** disadvantageous

**inexpensive**
**05** a snip, cheap **06** a steal, budget, modest **07** bargain, cut-rate, low-cost, reduced **08** dog-cheap, low-price, uncostly **09** dirt-cheap, low-priced, ten a penny **10** discounted, economical, reasonable **13** going for a song, on a shoestring

**inexperience**
**07** newness, rawness **09** freshness, ignorance, innocence, naiveness **10** immaturity **11** strangeness **12** inexpertness **13** unfamiliarity

**inexperienced**
**03** new, raw **04** puny **05** fresh, green, naive, young **06** callow, rookie, unseen **07** amateur **08** farouche, ignorant, immature, inexpert, innocent, unsifted, wide-eyed **09** fledgling, unfledged, unskilled, untrained, untutored **10** apprentice, fledgeling, unfamiliar, uninformed, unseasoned **11** new to the job, unexperient, unpractised, unqualified **12** probationary, unaccustomed, unacquainted **14** out of your depth, unsophisticate **15** unsophisticated

• **inexperienced person**
**03** cub **04** baby **09** fledgling **10** fledgeling

**inexpert**
**03** ham **05** inept **06** clumsy **07** amateur, awkward, unhandy **08** bungling, untaught **09** ham-fisted, maladroit, unskilful, unskilled, untrained, untutored **10** amateurish, blundering, cack-handed **11** incompetent, unpractised, unqualified **13** unworkmanlike **14** unprofessional

**inexplicable**
**05** weird **07** strange **08** abstruse, baffling, puzzling **09** enigmatic, insoluble **10** incredible, miraculous, mysterious, mystifying, perplexing **11** bewildering, inscrutable **12** inextricable, unbelievable, unfathomable **13** inexplainable, unaccountable, unexplainable **14** unintelligible

**inexplicably**
**09** strangely **10** bafflingly, incredibly, puzzlingly **12** miraculously, mysteriously, mystifyingly **13** unaccountably, unexplainably

**inexpressible**
**08** nameless, termless **09** ineffable, unsayable **10** untellable **11** indefinable, unspeakable, unutterable **12** inexpressive **13** indescribable, undescribable **14** incommunicable

**inexpressibly**
**09** ineffably **11** beyond words, unspeakably, unutterably **13** indescribably

**inexpressive**
**04** cold, dead **05** blank, empty **06** vacant **07** deadpan **08** lifeless **09** impassive **10** poker-faced **11** emotionless, inscrutable **12** unexpressive **14** expressionless

**inextinguishable**
**07** eternal, lasting, undying **08** enduring, immortal **09** deathless **11** everlasting, unquellable **12** imperishable, unquenchable **13** irrepressible, unconquerable **14** indestructible, unsuppressible

**inextricable**
**08** confused **09** intricate **11** indivisible, inescapable, inseparable
**12** indissoluble, inexplicable, irreversible **13** irretrievable

**inextricably**
**11** indivisibly, inescapably, inseparably, intricately, irresolubly
**12** indissolubly, irreversibly
**13** irretrievably

**infallibility**
**06** safety **08** accuracy, sureness
**09** inerrancy, supremacy
**10** perfection **11** omniscience, reliability **12** inerrability, unerringness
**13** dependability, faultlessness, impeccability **14** irrefutability
**15** trustworthiness

**infallible**
**04** sure **05** sound **07** certain, perfect
**08** accurate, fail-safe, flawless, reliable, sure-fire, unerring **09** faultless, foolproof, inerrable, unfailing
**10** dependable, impeccable, inevitable **11** trustworthy

**infamous**
**03** bad **04** base, evil, vile **06** wicked
**07** hateful **08** ill-famed, shameful, shocking **09** dastardly, egregious, nefarious, notorious **10** abominable, detestable, iniquitous, outrageous, scandalous **11** disgraceful, ignominious, opprobrious
**12** disreputable **13** discreditable, dishonourable

**infamy**
**04** evil **05** shame **06** defame, ignomy
**08** baseness, disgrace, ignominy, vileness, villainy **09** depravity, discredit, dishonour, disrepute, notoriety, turpitude **10** opprobrium, wickedness

**infancy**
**04** dawn, rise **05** birth, roots, seeds, start, youth **06** cradle, nonage, origin, outset **07** genesis, origins, silence
**08** babyhood **09** beginning, childhood, emergence, inception
**11** early stages **12** commencement
**14** speechlessness

**infant**
**03** new, tot **04** babe, baby **05** bairn, child, early, sprog, young **07** dawning, growing, initial, nascent, newborn, toddler **08** emergent, immature, juvenile, nursling, youthful
**09** beginning, fledgling, little one, nurseling **10** babe in arms, burgeoning, developing
**11** rudimentary

**infantile**
**05** young **07** babyish, puerile
**08** childish, immature, juvenile, youthful **10** adolescent
**11** undeveloped

**infantry**
**02** LI **03** inf **06** pultan, pulton, pultun, tercio, tertia **07** phalanx, pultoon

**infantryman**
**04** kern, naik, peon **05** grunt, kerne, Turco **06** ensign, evzone, Zouave
**07** dragoon, footman, hoplite, pandoor, pandour **08** chasseur, doughboy **10** voetganger **11** foot soldier, landsknecht **13** beetle-crusher

**infatuated**
**03** mad **06** assott, entêté, in love, sold on **07** entêtée, far gone, smitten, sweet on, wild for **08** assotted, besotted, mad about, obsessed, ravished
**09** bewitched, daft about, enamoured, nuts about, wild about **10** bowled over, captivated, crazy about, enraptured, fascinated, lovestruck, mesmerized, potty about, spellbound
**11** carried away **12** having a crush, having a thing, love-stricken

**infatuation**
**04** love, mash, pash, rave **05** craze, crush, mania, shine, thing **07** passion
**08** fixation, fondness **09** engoûment, obsession **10** engouement
**11** fascination **12** besottedness

**infect**
**03** mar, pox **04** clap, move, smit
**05** spoil, taint, touch **06** affect, blight, canker, defile, excite, measle, pass on, poison **07** animate, corrupt, inspire, overrun, pervert, pollute, tainted
**08** spread to, ulcerate **09** influence, stimulate, syphilize **10** parasitize
**11** contaminate, tuberculize

**infection**
**03** bug, wog **04** cold, germ, smit
**05** taint, virus **06** blight, poison, sepsis
**07** disease, fouling, illness **08** bacteria, epidemic, spoiling, tainting
**09** complaint, condition, contagion, influence, pollution **10** corruption, defilement, pestilence
**13** contamination
*See also* **disease**

**infectious**
**05** toxic **06** deadly, septic, taking
**07** noxious, smittle **08** catching, defiling, epidemic, virulent
**09** infective, polluting, spreading
**10** compelling, contagious, corrupting
**12** communicable, irresistible
**13** contaminating, transmissible, transmittable

**infelicitous**
**03** sad **05** inapt **07** unhappy, unlucky
**08** untimely, wretched **09** miserable, sorrowful, unfitting **10** despairing, unsuitable **11** incongruous, inopportune, unfortunate
**13** inappropriate **15** disadvantageous

**infer**
**05** educe, imply **06** allude, assume, deduce, derive, gather, induce, reason, render **07** conster, presume, surmise
**08** conclude, construe **09** figure out
**10** conjecture, generalize, understand
**11** extrapolate

**inference**
**07** reading, surmise **08** illation
**09** corollary, deduction, reasoning
**10** assumption, conclusion, conjecture
**11** consequence, presumption
**12** construction **13** extrapolation
**14** contraposition, interpretation

**inferior**
**03** bad, dog, inf, low **04** less, naff, poor, ropy, weak **05** awful, cheap, crook, grody, lousy, lower, lowly, minor, ropey
**06** coarse, crummy, faulty, grotty, humble, impair, junior, lesser, menial, minion, ornery, second, shoddy, vassal
**07** low-rent, of a sort, of sorts, provant, rubbish, shilpit, tinhorn, useless
**08** hopeless, mediocre, paravail, pathetic, slipshod, underman
**09** ancillary, cheap-jack, defective, deficient, imperfect, secondary, underling, underrate **10** fourth-rate, inadequate, low-quality, second-best, second-rate, subsidiary
**11** incompetent, indifferent, second-class, subordinate, subservient, substandard, under-sawyer
**12** unacceptable **14** unsatisfactory

**inferiority**
**08** meanness, ropiness **09** lowliness
**10** bad quality, crumminess, faultiness, grottiness, humbleness, inadequacy, low quality, mediocrity, shoddiness
**11** poor quality **12** imperfection, incompetence, slovenliness, subservience **13** defectiveness, subordination **14** insignificance

**infernal**
**04** evil, vile **06** cursed, damned, darned, dashed, Hadean, wicked
**07** blasted, demonic, fecking, flaming, hellish, satanic, Stygian **08** accursed, all-fired, blinking, blooming, devilish, fiendish, flipping, wretched
**09** atrocious, execrable
**10** confounded, diabolical, malevolent, outrageous, sulphurous

**infertile**
**04** arid **06** barren, effete **07** dried-up, parched, sterile **08** infecund
**09** childless **10** unfruitful
**11** unfructuous **12** unproductive
**13** non-productive

**infertility**
**07** aridity **08** aridness **09** sterility
**10** barrenness, effeteness
**11** infecundity **14** unfruitfulness

**infest**
**03** dog **04** teem **05** beset, crawl, flood, swarm **06** harass, invade, pester, plague, ravage, throng **07** bristle, disturb, overrun, pervade
**08** permeate, take over **09** penetrate
**10** infiltrate, overspread, parasitize, trichinize **13** spread through

**infestation**
**04** pest **05** crabs **06** blight, plague
**07** scourge **09** pervasion, taeniasis
**10** affliction, ascariasis, giardiasis, pestilence, visitation **11** molestation, overrunning, parasitosis, phthiriasis, shigellosis **12** infiltration, strongylosis,

uncinariasis **13** cysticercosis, helminthiasis, verminousness
**14** trichinization

**infested**
**04** mity **05** alive, batty, beset, buggy, lousy, midgy, mousy, ratty **06** chatty, grubby, mousey, ridden **07** haunted, overrun, plagued, rattish, ravaged, teeming, verminy, weevily
**08** crawling, pervaded, swarming, thievish, vermined, weeviled, weevilly
**09** bristling, permeated, verminous, weevilled **10** overspread, stylopized
**11** helminthous, infiltrated
**12** pestilential

**infidel**
**05** pagan **06** giaour **07** atheist, heathen, heretic, sceptic
**09** miscreant, sceptical **10** unbeliever
**11** disbeliever, freethinker, nullifidian, unbelieving **13** irreligionist

**infidelity**
**05** amour **06** affair **07** liaison, perfidy, romance **08** adultery, betrayal, cheating, intrigue **09** duplicity, falseness, treachery **10** disloyalty
**12** relationship **13** faithlessness, fooling around, playing around
**14** unfaithfulness

**infiltrate**
**04** seep, slip, soak **05** enter **06** filter, invade **07** intrude, pervade
**08** permeate **09** creep into, insinuate, penetrate, percolate

**infiltration**
**07** entrism **08** entryism, invasion
**09** intrusion, pervasion **10** permeation
**11** insinuation, penetration, percolation

**infiltrator**
**03** spy **07** entrist **08** entryist, intruder
**09** subverter **10** insinuator, penetrator, subversive **11** seditionary **14** fifth columnist

**infinite**
**03** all **04** huge, vast **05** total **06** untold
**07** endless, immense **08** absolute, enormous **09** boundless, countless, extensive, limitless, unbounded, unlimited **10** bottomless, fathomless, numberless **11** illimitable, inestimable, innumerable, never-ending, uncountable **12** immeasurable, incalculable, interminable, unfathomable **13** inexhaustible, unconditioned, without number
**14** indeterminable

**infinitely**
**03** all **09** endlessly, immensely
**10** absolutely, enormously, without end **11** ad infinitum, boundlessly, inestimably, limitlessly
**12** interminably, without limit
**13** inexhaustibly

**infinitesimal**
**03** wee **04** tiny **05** teeny **06** minute
**08** trifling **09** minuscule **10** negligible
**11** microscopic **13** imperceptible, inappreciable, insignificant
**14** inconsiderable

**infinitesimally**
**06** tinily **08** minutely **10** negligibly
**13** imperceptibly, inappreciably
**15** insignificantly, microscopically

**infinity**
**07** allness **08** eternity, vastness
**09** immensity **10** perpetuity
**11** endlessness **12** enormousness
**13** boundlessness, countlessness, extensiveness, limitlessness

**infirm**
**03** ill, old **04** lame, weak **05** frail, shaky
**06** ailing, feeble, poorly, sickly, unwell, wobbly **07** doddery, failing
**08** decrepit, disabled, unstable, unsteady **09** faltering **11** debilitated

**infirmity**
**06** malady **07** ailment, disease, failing, frailty, illness **08** debility, disorder, frailtee, senility, sickness, weakness
**09** complaint, frailness, ill health
**10** feebleness, sickliness
**11** decrepitude, dodderiness, instability **13** vulnerability

**inflame**
**03** fan **04** fire, fuel, heat, rile, stir
**05** anger, rouse **06** arouse, enrage, excite, foment, ignite, incite, kindle, madden, stir up, whip up, work up, worsen **07** agitate, incense, provoke
**08** enkindle, increase **09** aggravate, impassion, infuriate, intensify, make worse, stimulate **10** exacerbate, exasperate

**inflamed**
**03** het, hot, raw, red **04** sore **05** angry, heady **06** heated, septic **07** fevered, flushed, glowing, swollen **08** festered, feverish, infected, poisoned, reddened
**11** carbuncular

**inflammable**
**06** ardent **07** piceous **08** burnable
**09** flammable, ignitable **10** tinder-like
**11** combustible, combustious

**inflammation**
**04** fire, heat, rash **07** burning, hotness, redness **08** eruption, soreness, swelling **09** festering, infection
**10** irritation, tenderness **11** painfulness

*Inflammations include:*

**03** RSI, sty
**04** acne, boil, bubo, sore, stye
**05** croup, felon, mange
**06** ancome, angina, bunion, canker, otitis, quinsy, sepsis, thrush, ulitis
**07** abscess, colitis, empyema, pink-eye, sycosis, tylosis, whitlow
**08** bursitis, carditis, cynanche, cystitis, erythema, mastitis, myelitis, neuritis, orchitis, prunella, rhinitis, windburn
**09** arthritis, carbuncle, enteritis, fasciitis, frostbite, gastritis, glossitis, hepatitis, keratitis, laminitis, nephritis, phlebitis, retinitis, septicity, sinusitis, vaginitis
**10** bronchitis, cellulitis, dermatitis, erysipelas, gingivitis, intertrigo, laryngitis, meningitis, sore throat, tendinitis, tonsilitis, tracheitis, vasculitis
**11** mad staggers, myocarditis, peritonitis, pharyngitis, pneumonitis, prickly heat, shin splints, spondylitis, tennis elbow, thyroiditis, tonsillitis
**12** appendicitis, encephalitis, endocarditis, pancreatitis, pericarditis, vestibulitis
**13** jogger's nipple, labyrinthitis
**14** conjunctivitis, diverticulitis, housemaid's knee, sleepy staggers
**15** gastroenteritis

**inflammatory**
**04** sore **05** fiery, rabid **06** septic, tender **07** painful, riotous, swollen
**08** allergic, anarchic, inciting, infected
**09** demagogic, explosive, festering, inflaming, insurgent, seditious
**10** incendiary, incitative, phlogistic
**11** instigative, intemperate, provocative **13** rabble-rousing

**inflate**
**05** blast, bloat, boost, elate, raise, swell
**06** aerate, blow up, dilate, expand, extend, hike up, puff up, pump up, push up, step up **07** amplify, augment, balloon, bombast, distend, enlarge, magnify, puff out **08** escalate, increase, overrate, sufflate **09** intensify, overstate
**10** aggrandize, daisy-chain, exaggerate **11** fill with air
**12** overestimate

**inflated**
**04** tall **05** tumid **06** puffed, raised, turgid **07** bloated, blown up, bombast, bullate, dilated, pompous, swollen, upblown **08** extended, puffed up, rhetoric, tumefied **09** ballooned, bombastic, distended, escalated, high-blown, increased, overblown, puffed out **10** euphuistic, rhetorical
**11** exaggerated, intensified, overweening **12** magniloquent, ostentatious **13** grandiloquent

**inflation**
**04** rise **08** afflatus, cost push, increase
**09** expansion, turgidity **10** escalation
**11** inspiration **14** hyperinflation
• **measure of inflation**
**03** RPI

**inflection**
**04** tone **05** pitch **06** ending, rhythm, stress **07** bending, cadence
**08** emphasis **09** deviation
**10** comparison, modulation
**11** conjugation **12** change of tone

**inflexibility**
**06** fixity **08** hardness, obduracy, rigidity **09** obstinacy, stiffness
**10** stringency **12** immovability, immutability, incompliance, inelasticity, stubbornness, unsuppleness **13** immutableness, intransigence **14** intractability

**inflexible**
**03** set **04** fast, firm, hard, iron, taut **05** fixed, rigid, solid, stern, stiff **06** ramrod, steely, strict **07** adamant, uniform **08** obdurate, pitiless, resolute, rigorous, standard, stubborn, unsupple **09** calcified, immovable, immutable, merciless, obstinate, stringent, tramlined, unbending, unelastic, unvarying **10** entrenched, implacable, intolerant, relentless, unbendable, unyielding **11** hard and fast, intractable **12** intransigent, standardized, unchangeable **13** dyed-in-the-wool **14** uncompromising **15** unaccommodating

**inflict**
**03** hit, lay **04** deal, levy **05** apply, exact, lay on, wreak **06** burden, impose, strike, thrust **07** deal out, deliver, enforce, mete out **10** administer, perpetrate

**infliction**
**05** worry **06** burden **07** penalty, trouble **08** delivery, exaction, wreaking **10** affliction, imposition, punishment **11** application, castigation, enforcement, retribution **12** chastisement, perpetration **14** administration

**influence**
**03** say **04** bias, drag, hand, hold, mark, move, pull, rule, stir, sway, toll **05** alter, clout, force, guide, impel, mould, power, reign, rouse, shape **06** affect, arouse, change, colour, direct, effect, impact, incite, induce, inflow, modify, prompt, weight **07** control, dispose, holding, impress, incline, mastery **08** ambiance, ambience, dominate, guidance, impact on, interest, motivate, persuade, pressure, prestige, standing **09** authority, condition, determine, direction, dominance, have clout, instigate, manoeuvre, operation, prejudice, pull wires, restraint, supremacy, transform **10** domination, importance, manipulate **11** carry weight, pull strings **12** wheel and deal **14** have an effect on **15** hold over a barrel

• **easily influenced**
**09** malleable

• **unlucky influence**
**04** jinx

**influential**
**06** moving, potent, strong **07** guiding, leading, telling, weighty **08** dominant, powerful **09** effective, important, inspiring, momentous **10** compelling, convincing, meaningful, persuasive **11** charismatic, controlling, far-reaching, heavyweight, prestigious, significant, substantial **12** instrumental **13** authoritative

**influx**
**04** flow, rush, salt **05** flood **06** inflow, inrush, stream **07** arrival, ingress **08** invasion **09** accession, avalanche, incursion, influence, intrusion **10** inundation, visitation **11** instreaming

**inform**
◇ *homophone indicator*
**03** rat **04** blab, blow, fink, leak, mark, nark, shop, sing, tell **05** avail, brand, brief, cue in, dob in, grass, peach, split, stamp **06** advise, betray, clue in, clue up, direct, fill in, impart, notify, relate, rumble, snitch, squeak, squeal, tell on, tip off, typify, wise up **07** animate, apprise, certify, educate, inspire, let know, partake, possess, put wise, resolve, sing out, stool on **08** acquaint, announce, deformed, denounce, formless, identify, instruct, permeate, unformed **09** advertise, advertize, enlighten, misshapen, recommend **10** give notice, illuminate, keep posted **11** blow the gaff, communicate, distinguish, incriminate **12** characterize **13** spill the beans **15** put in the picture, sing like a canary

**informal**
**03** inf **04** easy, free **06** candid, casual, simple **07** invalid, natural, relaxed **08** everyday, familiar, friendly, unsolemn **09** easy-going, officious **10** colloquial, unofficial, vernacular **12** off the record **13** go-as-you-please, unceremonious, unpretentious

**informality**
**04** ease **07** freedom **08** cosiness **10** casualness, homeliness, relaxation, simplicity **11** familiarity, naturalness **12** congeniality **15** approachability

**informally**
**06** easily, freely, simply **08** casually **09** privately **10** familiarly, on the quiet **12** colloquially, off the record, unofficially **13** sans cérémonie **14** confidentially **15** unceremoniously, without ceremony

**information**
**02** SP **03** gen, inf, wit **04** bumf, data, dope, file, info, news, poop, word **05** clues, facts, input, score **06** advice, notice, record, report **07** counsel, details, dossier, good oil, low-down, message, tidings, witting **08** briefing, bulletin, databank, database, evidence, izvestia **09** hard stuff, izvestiya, knowledge **10** communiqué, propaganda **11** instruction, particulars **12** intelligence **13** enlightenment

• **measure of information**
**03** bit, nit **05** field, nepit, qubit **08** location **11** binary digit

**informative**
**05** newsy **06** chatty, useful **07** gossipy, helpful **08** edifying **09** revealing **11** educational, forthcoming, instructive **12** constructive, enlightening, illuminating **13** communicative

**informed**
**02** up **03** hep, hip **05** aware **06** au fait, expert, posted, primed, sussed, versed **07** abreast, briefed, clued-up, erudite, knowing, learned **08** educated, familiar, up to date, well-read **09** au courant, in the know, in the loop, up to speed **10** acquainted, conversant, well-versed **11** enlightened, intelligent, well-briefed **12** well-informed **13** authoritative, knowledgeable **14** well-researched

**informer**
**03** dog, rat, spy **04** fink, mole, nark, nose, stag **05** grass, Judas, shelf, sneak, snout **06** dobber, canary, finger, fizgig, moiser, singer, snitch **07** fizzgig, grasser, peacher, pentito, stoolie, traitor **08** animator, approver, betrayer, inspirer, promoter, snitcher, squeaker, squealer, tell-tale **09** informant, sycophant, whisperer **10** discoverer, supergrass **11** stool pigeon **13** whistle-blower

**infraction**
**06** breach **08** breaking **09** violation **12** encroachment, infringement **13** contravention, transgression

**infrared**
**02** ir

**infrequent**
**04** rare **06** scanty, seldom, sparse **07** unusual **08** sporadic, uncommon **09** spasmodic **10** occasional **11** exceptional **12** intermittent, like gold dust

**infringe**
**04** defy **05** break, flout **06** ignore, invade **07** disobey, impinge, infract, intrude, violate **08** encroach, overstep, trespass **10** contravene, transgress

**infringement**
**06** breach, piracy **07** evasion **08** breaking, defiance, invasion, trespass **09** intrusion, violation **10** infraction **12** disobedience, encroachment **13** contravention, non-compliance, non-observance, transgression

**infuriate**
**03** bug, vex **04** miff, nark, rile **05** anger, annoy, get at, rouse **06** enrage, madden, needle, nettle, wind up **07** incense, inflame, provoke **08** drive mad, irritate **09** aggravate **10** antagonize, drive crazy, exasperate **12** drive bananas **13** make sparks fly **14** drive up the wall

**infuriated**
**03** mad **04** wild **05** angry, cross, irate, radge, ratty, spewy, vexed **06** choked, heated, miffed, narked, peeved, roused **07** crooked, enraged, flaming, furious, ropable, stroppy, uptight, violent **08** agitated, burned up, hairless, in a paddy, incensed, maddened, provoked, up in arms **09** in a lather, irritated, pissed off, raving mad, seeing red, ticked off **10** aggravated, apoplectic, hopping mad **11** disgruntled, exasperated, fit to be tied **12** on the warpath **14** beside yourself

**infuriating**
**05** pesky **07** galling **08** annoying **09** maddening, provoking, thwarting, vexatious **10** irritating, unbearable **11** aggravating, frustrating, intolerable **12** exasperating

**infuse**
◇ *insertion indicator*
**04** brew, draw, fill, mash, mask, pour, shed, soak **05** imbue, immit, steep **06** inject, instil **07** implant, inspire, pervade **08** impart to, saturate **09** inculcate, introduce **11** breathe into

**infusion**
**03** tea **04** brew, mate **06** saloop, tisane **07** malt tea, sage tea, soaking, uva-ursi **08** infusing, senna tea, steeping, tar water **09** sassafras **10** capillaire **11** inculcation, inspiration **12** implantation, instillation

**ingenious**
**03** sly **04** neat, wily **05** adept, natty, nifty, sharp, slick, smart, witty **06** adroit, astute, bright, clever, crafty, gifted, patent, pretty, quaint, shrewd **07** cunning, skilful **08** creative, masterly, original, talented **09** brilliant, inventive **10** artificial, innovative **11** imaginative, resourceful

**ingeniously**
**07** niftily **08** cleverly **09** cunningly, skilfully **10** originally **11** brilliantly **13** imaginatively

**ingenuity**
**03** wit **04** gift **05** flair, knack, skill **06** engine, genius, ingine **07** cunning, faculty, slyness **08** deftness **09** invention, nattiness, niftiness, sharpness, slickness **10** adroitness, astuteness, cleverness, shrewdness **11** originality, skilfulness **12** creativeness **13** ingeniousness, ingenuousness, inventiveness **14** innovativeness **15** resourcefulness

**ingenuous**
**04** open **05** frank, naive, plain **06** candid, direct, honest, simple **07** artless, genuine, sincere **08** freeborn, innocent, trustful, trusting **09** guileless **10** forthright, honourable **11** transparent **12** single-minded **13** undissembling **14** unsophisticate **15** unsophisticated

**ingenuously**
**06** openly, simply **07** naively, plainly **08** directly, honestly **09** artlessly, genuinely, sincerely **10** innocently, trustingly **11** guilelessly **12** without guile

**ingenuousness**
**07** candour, honesty, naiveté, naivety **08** openness **09** frankness, innocence, unreserve **10** directness **11** artlessness, genuineness **12** trustfulness **13** guilelessness **14** forthrightness

**inglorious**
**06** unsung **07** ignoble, obscure, unknown **08** infamous, shameful, unheroic **10** irrenowned, mortifying, unhonoured **11** blameworthy, disgraceful, humiliating, ignominious **12** disreputable, unsuccessful **13** discreditable, dishonourable

**ingrain**
**03** dye, fix **04** root **05** embed, imbue, infix **06** instil **07** build in, engrain, implant, impress, imprint **08** entrench **09** establish, ingrained

**ingrained**
**05** fixed **06** inborn, inbred, rooted **07** built-in, inbuilt **08** embedded, inherent **09** immovable, implanted, permanent **10** deep-rooted, deep-seated, entrenched **11** established **12** ineradicable **13** thorough-going

**ingratiate**
**04** fawn, sook **05** crawl, creep, toady **06** cozy up, grovel **07** flatter **08** play up to, soft-soap, suck up to **09** get in with **10** cozy up with **11** curry favour **12** bow and scrape **15** butter someone up

**ingratiating**
**05** suave, sweet **06** greasy, silken **07** fawning, servile **08** crawling, toadying, unctuous **10** flattering, obsequious **11** bootlicking, sycophantic, time-serving **13** smooth-tongued

**ingratitude**
**13** thanklessness **14** ungraciousness, ungratefulness, unthankfulness

**ingredient**
◇ *anagram indicator*
**04** base, item, part, unit **05** basis **06** bottom, factor **07** amalgam, element, feature **09** component **11** constituent

*See also* **salad**

- **little boy ingredients**

**05** frogs, snips **06** snails **14** puppy dogs' tails

- **little girl ingredients**

**05** sugar, spice **13** all things nice **14** everything nice

**ingress**
**05** entry **06** access **08** entrance **09** admission **10** admittance **12** means of entry, right of entry **15** means of approach

**inhabit**
**05** dwell, haunt **06** live in, occupy, people, settle, stay in **07** denizen, dwell in, possess **08** colonize, populate, reside in **14** make your home in

**inhabitable**
**09** habitable **11** fit to live in

**inhabitant**
**03** son **05** child, towny **06** inmate, lodger, native, tenant **07** citizen, denizen, dweller, settler **08** habitant, occupant, occupier, resident **09** indweller **10** residenter **12** residentiary

**inhabited**
**04** held **07** lived-in, peopled, settled **08** occupied, populate, populous, tenanted **09** colonized, developed, populated, possessed

**inhalation**
**05** whiff **06** breath **07** suction **08** inhaling **09** breathing, spiration **11** inspiration, respiration

**inhale**
**04** draw, take, toot, tout **05** whiff **06** draw in, suck in **07** inspire, respire **09** breathe in, inbreathe

**inharmonious**
**03** out **04** sour **05** harsh **06** atonal, patchy **07** grating, jarring, raucous **08** clashing, jangling, perverse, strident, tuneless **09** dissonant, unmusical, untuneful **10** discordant, out of place, unfriendly **11** cacophonous, conflicting, disagreeing, inconsonant, quarrelsome, unmelodious **12** antipathetic, incompatible, unharmonious **13** contradictory, unsympathetic **14** irreconcilable

**inherent**
**05** basic **06** inborn, inbred, innate, native, natura **07** built-in, inbuilt, natural, radical **08** immanent, resident **09** essential, ingrained, inherited, intrinsic **10** hereditary, inexistant, inexistent, in the blood, subsistent **11** fundamental, intrinsical

**inherently**
**08** inwardly **09** basically, centrally **10** integrally **11** essentially **13** constituently, fundamentally, intrinsically

**inherit**
**04** heir **06** assume, be left **07** receive, succeed **08** accede to, be heir to, come into, take over **09** succeed to **10** fall heir to **12** be bequeathed

**inheritance**
**03** fee **06** legacy **07** bequest, descent **08** heredity, heritage **09** accession, endowment, patrimony **10** birthright, proportion, succession **13** primogeniture **15** secundogeniture

**inheritor**
**04** heir **05** scion **06** co-heir, tanist **07** devisee, heiress, heritor, legatee **08** heritrix, legatary **09** heritress, recipient, successor **10** fellow-heir, inheritrix, next in line, substitute **11** beneficiary, inheritress **12** reversionary

**inhibit**
**04** balk, curb, stem, stop **05** baulk, check **06** bridle, hamper, hinder, hold in, impede, rein in, stanch, thwart **07** prevent, repress, staunch **08** hold back, obstruct, restrain, restrict, slow down, suppress **09** constrain, frustrate **10** discourage **12** put a damper on, straitjacket **13** interfere with

**inhibited**
**03** shy **06** wooden **07** guarded, subdued, uptight **08** reserved, reticent **09** repressed, withdrawn **10** frustrated, restrained **11** constrained, embarrassed, introverted **13** self-conscious **14** self-restrained

**inhibition**
**03** bar **04** curb **05** check **06** hang-up **07** coyness, reserve, shyness **09** hampering, hindrance, restraint, reticence, thwarting **10** impediment, repression **11** frustration, obstruction, restriction **12** interference **13** embarrassment

**inhospitable**
**04** bare, cold, cool, wild **05** aloof, bleak, empty **06** barren, lonely, unkind **07** hostile, uncivil **08** desolate, inimical **09** hostlesse **10** antisocial, forbidding, unfriendly, ungenerous, uninviting, unsociable, xenophobic **11** uncongenial, unreceptive, unwelcoming **12** unfavourable **13** uninhabitable, unneighbourly

**inhuman**
**03** odd **05** cruel, harsh **06** animal, brutal, savage **07** bestial, strange, vicious **08** barbaric, fiendish, non-human, ruthless, sadistic **09** barbarous, merciless **10** diabolical **11** cold-blooded

**inhumane**
**05** cruel, harsh **06** brutal, unkind **07** callous **08** pitiless, uncaring **09** heartless, unfeeling **11** cold-hearted, dehumanized, hard-hearted, insensitive **13** inconsiderate, unsympathetic

**inhumanity**
**06** sadism **07** cruelty **08** atrocity **09** barbarism, barbarity, brutality **10** savageness, unkindness **11** brutishness, callousness, viciousness **12** pitilessness, ruthlessness **13** heartlessness **15** cold-bloodedness, cold-heartedness, hard-heartedness

**inimical**
**07** adverse, harmful, hostile, hurtful, noxious, opposed **08** contrary **09** injurious, repugnant **10** intolerant, pernicious, unfriendly **11** destructive, disaffected, ill-disposed, unwelcoming **12** antagonistic, antipathetic, inhospitable, unfavourable

**inimitable**
**06** unique **07** sublime, supreme **08** peerless **09** matchless, nonpareil, unmatched **10** consummate, unequalled, unexampled, unrivalled **11** distinctive, exceptional, superlative, unsurpassed **12** incomparable, unparalleled **13** unsurpassable

**iniquitous**
**04** base, evil **05** awful **06** sinful, unjust, wicked **07** heinous, immoral, vicious **08** accursed, criminal, dreadful, infamous **09** atrocious, nefarious, reprobate **10** abominable, facinorous, flagitious, outrageous **11** unrighteous **13** reprehensible

**iniquity**
**03** sin **04** evil, vice **05** crime, wrong **06** infamy **07** misdeed, offence **08** baseness, enormity **09** evil-doing, injustice **10** sinfulness, wickedness, wrongdoing **11** abomination, heinousness, lawlessness, ungodliness, viciousness **13** transgression **15** unrighteousness

**initial**
◇ *head selection indicator*
**04** sign **05** basic, early, first, prime **07** bloomer, endorse, opening, primary **08** inchoate, original, starting **09** autograph, beginning, formative, inaugural, inceptive, incipient **10** commencing, elementary **11** countersign **12** foundational, introductory

**initially**
◇ *head selection indicator*
**05** first **07** at first, firstly **08** first off **10** at the start, first of all, originally **11** at the outset, to begin with, to start with **14** at the beginning

**initiate**
**04** open, tiro **05** admit, begin, blood, cause, crash, drill, enrol, enter, lanch, let in, set up, start, teach, train, tutor **06** accept, induce, induct, instil, invest, launch, novice, ordain, prompt, rookie, sign up **07** convert, entrant, install, kick off, learner, pioneer, receive, recruit, start up, trigger, welcome **08** activate, beginner, bejesuit, commence, instruct, neophyte, newcomer **09** auspicate, establish, greenhorn, inculcate, instigate, institute, introduce, new member, novitiate, originate, proselyte, stimulate **10** bring about, catechumen, inaugurate, tenderfoot **11** get under way, probationer, set in motion **13** sow the seeds of **15** get off the ground, get things moving

**initiation**
**05** debut, entry, start **07** baptism, opening **08** entrance **09** admission, beginning, enrolment, inception, induction, launching, reception, setting-up **10** admittance, enlistment, ordination **11** investiture, origination **12** inauguration, installation, introduction **13** rite of passage
**• initiation rite**
**04** bora

**initiative**
**02** go **04** lead, plan, push **05** drive **06** action, energy, scheme **07** lead-off **08** ambition, démarche, dynamism, gumption, proposal **09** first move, first step **10** creativity, enterprise, get-up-and-go, suggestion **11** opening move, originality **12** introductory **13** inventiveness **14** innovativeness, recommendation **15** resourcefulness

**inject**
**03** add, hit, jab **04** bang, hype **05** bring, immit, shoot, spike **06** hype up, infuse, insert, instil **07** bring in, crank up, hit it up, inspire, shoot up, skin-pop, syringe **08** immunize, mainline **09** inoculate, introduce, vaccinate

**injection**
**03** fix, jab, jag **04** bang, dose, shot **06** needle **07** skin-pop **08** addition, infusion **09** insertion **10** hypodermic, instilling **11** inoculation, vaccination **12** immunization, introduction **13** a shot in the arm

**injudicious**
**04** rash **05** hasty **06** stupid, unwise **07** foolish **08** ill-timed **09** ill-judged, impolitic, imprudent, misguided **10** ill-advised, incautious, indiscreet, unthinking **11** inadvisable, inexpedient, wrong-headed **13** inconsiderate

**injunction**
**05** order **06** dictum, ruling **07** command, dictate, mandate, precept **09** direction, directive **10** admonition **11** conjunction, exhortation, instruction

**injure**
◇ *anagram indicator*
**03** cut, get, mar **04** bomb, burn, dere, harm, hurt, kill, lame, maim, maul, ruin, skin **05** abuse, annoy, break, chill, choke, deare, misdo, rifle, scald, scath, shend, spoil, touch, upset, waste, wound, wring, wrong **06** accloy, blight, damage, deface, deform, impair, mangle, nobble, offend, poison, put out, scaith, scathe, skaith, strain, weaken **07** blemish, carve up, cripple, disable, outrage, shoot up **08** aggrieve, fracture, ill-treat, maltreat, mutilate, override **09** disfigure, disoblige, humiliate, overshoot, prejudice, undermine **10** vitriolize **11** hospitalize **13** stab in the back

**injured**
◇ *anagram indicator*
**03** bad **04** hurt, lame, sore **05** upset **06** abused, harmed, pained, put out, tender **07** bruised, damaged, defamed, grieved, misused, unhappy, unsound, wounded, wronged **08** crippled, disabled, insulted, maligned, offended, weakened **09** aggrieved **10** displeased, ill-treated, maltreated, vulnerable **11** disgruntled, wither-wrung **13** cut to the quick
**• easily injured**
**04** nice

**injurious**
**03** bad **06** malign, noyous, unjust **07** adverse, baneful, harmful, hurtful, noxious, ruinous **08** damaging, wrongful **09** insulting, libellous, unhealthy **10** calumnious, corrupting, defamatory, derogatory, iniquitous,

offenceful, pernicious, slanderous **11** deleterious, destructive, detrimental, mischievous, prejudicial, unconducive **15** disadvantageous

**injury**
**03** cut, ill, RSI **04** bale, dere, gash, harm, hurt, maim, ruin, sore, teen, tene, tort **05** abuse, deare, teene, wound, wrong **06** bruise, damage, insult, lesion, scathe, trauma **07** offence, offense, outrage **08** abrasion, fracture, mischief, violence **09** annoyance, contusion, grievance, injustice, prejudice **10** affliction, contrecoup, disservice, impairment, laceration, mutilation, traumatism **12** endamagement, ill-treatment **13** disfigurement
- **after injury**
◇ *anagram indicator*

**injustice**
**04** bias **05** abuse, wrong **06** injury **07** offence, unright **08** inequity, iniquity, unreason **09** disparity, prejudice **10** inequality, oppression, partiality, unfairness, unjustness **11** favouritism **12** ill-treatment, one-sidedness, partisanship **14** discrimination

**inkling**
**04** clue, hint, idea, sign **06** notion **07** glimmer, pointer, umbrage, whisper **08** allusion, faintest, foggiest, innuendo **09** suspicion **10** glimmering, indication, intimation, suggestion **11** insinuation

**inky**
◇ *anagram indicator*
**03** jet **05** black, drunk, sooty **08** dark-blue, jet-black **09** coal-black **10** pitch-black
- **inky blotch**
**04** monk

**inlaid**
**03** set **05** inset, lined, tiled **06** mosaic **07** studded **08** enchased **09** empaestic, enamelled **10** damascened **11** tessellated

**inland**
**05** inner **06** upland **07** central, midland, refined **08** domestic, interior, internal, landward **09** up-country **10** within land **13** sophisticated

**inlay**
**05** embed, inset **06** enamel, insert, lining, mosaic, tiling **07** emblema, setting **08** damaskin, studding **09** damascene, damaskeen, damasquin **10** damasceene **12** tessellation

**inlet**
**03** arm, bay **04** cove, hope **05** bight, creek, fiord, firth, fjord, haven, sound **06** infall, ingate **07** opening, passage **08** entrance

**inmate**
**03** zek **04** case **06** client, intern **07** convict, patient **08** detainee, prisoner **09** collegian **10** collegiate

**inmost**
**04** deep **05** basic **06** buried, hidden, secret **07** central, closest, dearest, deepest, private **08** esoteric, intimate, personal **09** essential, innermost **12** confidential

**inn**
**03** bar, pub **04** khan **05** abode, hotel, house, howff, local, lodge, put up **06** boozer, hostel, imaret, posada, public, ryokan, shanty, tavern **07** albergo, auberge, canteen, potshop **08** bona fide, groggery, hostelry **09** free house, gin palace, lush-house, posthouse, roadhouse **11** caravansary, change-house, public house **12** caravansarai, caravanserai, halfway house **13** watering-house

**innards**
◇ *middle selection indicator*
**04** guts **05** works **06** entera, organs, umbles, vitals **07** giblets, insides, viscera **08** entrails, interior **09** mechanism **10** intestines **13** inner workings **14** internal organs

**innate**
**06** inborn, inbred, native **07** connate, natural **08** inherent, original **09** inherited, intrinsic, intuitive **10** congenital, hereditary, indigenous, ingenerate **11** instinctive

**innately**
**08** inwardly **09** basically, centrally **10** inherently, integrally **11** essentially **13** constituently, fundamentally, intrinsically

**inner**
**04** deep **06** entire, hidden, inside, inward, mental, middle, secret **07** central, obscure, private **08** esoteric, interior, internal, intimate, personal, profound **09** concealed, emotional, innermost, spiritual **10** restricted **13** psychological

**innermost**
**04** deep **05** basic **06** buried, hidden, inmost, secret **07** central, closest, dearest, deepest, private **08** esoteric, intimate, personal **09** essential **12** confidential

**innkeeper**
**04** host **07** hostess, manager, padrone **08** boniface, hotelier, landlady, landlord, mine host, publican **09** barkeeper, innholder **10** aubergiste, proprietor **11** hotel-keeper **12** restaurateur

**innocence**
**06** purity, safety, virtue **07** honesty, naivety **08** chastity, openness **09** credulity, frankness, ignorance, integrity, naiveness, virginity **10** simplicity **11** artlessness, gullibility, naturalness, playfulness, sinlessness **12** harmlessness, inexperience, spotlessness, trustfulness **13** blamelessness, childlikeness, faultlessness, guilelessness, guiltlessness, impeccability, inculpability, ingenuousness, innocuousness, righteousness, stainlessness, unworldliness **14** immaculateness **15** inoffensiveness

**innocent**
**04** babe, lamb, naif, open, pure, safe **05** bland, canny, child, clear, frank, fresh, green, idiot, naive, seely, white **06** benign, chaste, gentle, honest, infant, novice, simple **07** angelic, anodyne, artless, ingénue, natural, playful, sinless, upright **08** Arcadian, beginner, dewy-eyed, dovelike, gullible, harmless, imbecile, lamblike, neophyte, sackless, spotless, trustful, trusting, virginal, virtuous **09** blameless, childlike, credulous, crimeless, faultless, greenhorn, guileless, guiltless, incorrupt, ingenuous, innocuous, righteous, stainless, unsullied, untainted, unworldly **10** babe in arms, immaculate, impeccable, inculpable, tenderfoot **11** inoffensive, offenceless, unblemished, uncorrupted **12** prelapsarian, simple-minded, unsuspecting, unsuspicious **13** inexperienced, unblameworthy, unimpeachable **14** above suspicion, irreproachable, uncontaminated **15** unsophisticated

**innocently**
**06** simply **07** naively **09** artlessly **10** harmlessly, trustfully, trustingly **11** blamelessly, credulously, ingenuously, innocuously **13** inoffensively, unoffendingly **14** unsuspiciously

**innocuous**
**04** mild, safe **05** bland **07** anodyne, playful **08** harmless, innocent **11** inoffensive, unobtrusive **15** unobjectionable

**innovation**
**06** change, novity, reform **07** newness, novelty **08** novation, novelism, progress **09** departure, neologism, new method, variation **10** alteration, new product **12** introduction **13** modernization

**innovative**
**03** new **04** bold **05** fresh **06** daring **07** go-ahead **08** creative, original **09** inventive, reforming **10** avant-garde, Promethean **11** adventurous, imaginative, progressive, resourceful **12** enterprising, trail-blazing **14** groundbreaking

**innovator**
**06** source **07** creator, deviser, pioneer **08** novelist, reformer **09** developer **10** modernizer, originator **11** progressive, trailblazer **12** fresh thinker

**innuendo**
**04** hint, slur **07** whisper **08** allusion, overtone **09** aspersion **10** intimation, suggestion **11** implication, insinuation

**innumerable**
**04** many, tons **05** heaps, loads, piles **06** dozens, masses, oodles, stacks, untold **07** umpteen **08** hundreds, infinite, millions, numerous **09** countless, thousands **10** numberless, unnumbered **11** uncountable **12** incalculable

**inoculate**
**05** graft, imbue **06** inject **07** protect **08** immunize **09** safeguard, syphilize, vaccinate, variolate **10** give a jab to **11** give a shot to

**inoculation**
**03** jab, jag **04** shot **09** injection **10** protection **11** vaccination, variolation **12** immunization

**inoffensive**
**04** mild, safe **05** bland, quiet **07** anodyne **08** harmless, innocent, pleasant, retiring **09** innocuous, peaceable **11** unassertive, unobtrusive **15** unexceptionable, unobjectionable

**inoperable**
**05** fatal **06** deadly **08** hopeless, terminal **09** incurable **10** unhealable **11** intractable, irremovable, unremovable, untreatable

**inoperative**
**04** bust, duff, idle **05** kaput, resty **06** broken, futile, kaputt, silent, unused **07** invalid, useless **08** nugatory **09** defective, worthless **10** broken-down, inadequate, not working, on the blink, on the fritz, out of order, unworkable **11** ineffective, ineffectual, inefficient, inofficious, out of action **12** not operative, out of service **13** inefficacious, unserviceable **14** non-functioning **15** out of commission

**inopportune**
**06** clumsy **08** ill-timed, mistimed, tactless, untimely **09** ill-chosen, importune **10** unsuitable, wrong-timed **11** importunate, out of season, unfortunate **12** inauspicious, inconvenient, infelicitous, intempestive, unpropitious, unseasonable **13** inappropriate

**inordinate**
◇ *anagram indicator*
**03** OTT **05** great, undue **07** extreme **08** vaulting **09** excessive **10** exorbitant, immoderate, outrageous, over the top **11** God-almighty, unwarranted **12** preposterous, unmeasurable, unreasonable, unrestrained, unrestricted **14** unconscionable

**inorganic**
**04** dead **07** mineral **08** lifeless **09** inanimate **10** artificial, non-natural

**input**
**04** code, data, load **05** enter, facts, key in, put in, store **06** feed in, insert **07** capture, details, figures, process **08** material **09** resources **10** statistics **11** information, particulars **12** contribution

**inquest**
**07** hearing, inquiry **10** inspection, post-mortem **11** examination **13** investigation

**inquietude**
**05** worry **06** unease **07** anxiety **08** disquiet **09** agitation, jumpiness **10** solicitude, uneasiness **11** disquietude, disturbance, nervousness **12** apprehension, discomposure, perturbation, restlessness

**inquire, enquire**
**03** ask, see **04** call, quiz, scan, seek **05** probe, query, snoop, speer, speir, study **06** quaere, search **07** examine, explore, inquere, inspect **08** look into, question, research **10** scrutinize **11** interrogate, investigate

**inquirer, enquirer**
**06** seeker **07** querist, student **08** explorer, searcher **10** inquisitor, questioner, researcher **12** interrogator, investigator

**inquiring, enquiring**
**04** nosy **05** eager, nosey **06** prying **07** curious, probing, zetetic **08** doubtful **09** sceptical, searching, wondering **10** analytical, interested **11** inquisitive, questioning **13** interrogatory, investigative, investigatory **14** outward-looking

**inquiringly, enquiringly**
**06** keenly **07** eagerly **09** curiously **11** wonderingly **12** analytically **13** inquisitively, questioningly

**inquiry, enquiry**
**04** poll **05** probe, query, quest, study **06** demand, quaere, search, survey **07** hearing, inquest, inquire **08** etiology, question, scrutiny, sounding **09** aetiology **10** inspection **11** examination, exploration, inquisition, star chamber **12** perquisition **13** interrogation, interrogatory, investigation **14** reconnaissance

**inquisition**
**07** inquest, inquiry **08** grilling, quizzing **09** witch hunt **10** Holy Office **11** examination, questioning **13** interrogation, investigation **14** the third degree

**inquisitive**
**04** nosy **05** nosey **06** prying, snoopy, spying **07** curious, peeping, peering, probing **08** snooping **09** inquiring, intrusive, searching **10** meddlesome **11** interfering, questioning **12** scrutinizing

**inquisitively**
**06** keenly **07** eagerly **09** curiously **11** inquiringly, searchingly **12** meddlesomely **13** interferingly, questioningly

**inquisitor**
**04** Deza **07** Ximenes **10** Torquemada

**inroad**
**04** raid **05** foray, sally **06** attack, charge, infall, sortie **07** advance, assault **08** invasion, progress, trespass **09** incursion, intrusion, irruption, offensive, onslaught, sea breach **11** impingement, trespassing **12** encroachment

**insane**
◇ *anagram indicator*
**03** ape, fey, mad **04** bats, daft, gyte, loco, nuts, wild, wood, yond **05** barmy, batty, buggy, crazy, daffy, dippy, dotty, flaky, gonzo, loony, loopy, manic, nutty, potty, queer, wacko, wacky, wiggy **06** absurd, crazed, cuckoo, dement, fruity, maniac, mental, raving, red-mad, screwy, stupid **07** bananas, barking, berserk, bonkers, cracked, foolish, frantic, horn-mad, idiotic, lunatic, meshuga **08** bughouse, crackers, crackpot, demented, deranged, dingbats, doolally, frenetic, frenzied, maniacal, unhinged, unstable **09** delirious, disturbed, half-baked, lymphatic, psychotic, senseless, up the wall **10** bestraught, distracted, distraught, frantic-mad, off the wall, off your nut, out to lunch, ridiculous, stone-crazy, unbalanced **11** hare-brained, impractical, nonsensical, not all there, off the rails, off your head **12** crackbrained, mad as a hatter, off your chump, round the bend **13** off your rocker, of unsound mind, out of your head, out of your mind, out of your tree, round the twist **14** off your trolley, wrong in the head **15** non compos mentis, out of your senses

**insanely**
◇ *anagram indicator*
**05** madly **08** absurdly **09** foolishly **11** ludicrously, senselessly **12** outrageously, ridiculously

**insanitary**
**04** foul **05** dirty **06** filthy, impure **07** dirtied, noisome, noxious, unclean **08** feculent, infected, infested, polluted **09** unhealthy **10** unhygienic, unsanitary **11** unhealthful, unsanitized **12** contaminated, insalubrious **13** disease-ridden

**insanity**
◇ *anagram indicator*
**05** craze, folie, folly, mania **06** frenzy, lunacy **07** madness **08** daftness, delirium, dementia, neurosis **09** absurdity, craziness, psychosis, stupidity **10** insaneness **11** derangement, foolishness, hebephrenia, psychopathy **13** mental illness, senselessness **14** ridiculousness

*See also* **lunacy**

**insatiable**
**04** avid **06** greedy, hungry **07** craving **08** ravenous, sateless **09** rapacious,

voracious **10** gluttonous, immoderate, inordinate **12** unappeasable, unquenchable **13** unsatisfiable

**inscribe**
**03** cut **04** etch, mark, sign **05** brand, carve, enrol, enter, print, stamp, write **06** endoss, enlist, incise, record, scrive **07** address, engrave, impress, imprint, scrieve **08** dedicate, register **09** autograph

**inscription**
**04** ogam **05** ogham, title, words **06** legend **07** caption, epitaph, etching, message, trigram, wording, writing **08** colophon, epigraph, kakemono **09** autograph, engraving, lettering, signature, tetragram **10** chronogram, dedication **11** insculpture **15** circumscription

**inscrutable**
**04** deep **06** arcane, hidden, invis'd **07** cryptic **08** baffling, puzzling **09** enigmatic **10** mysterious, unreadable **12** impenetrable, inexplicable, unfathomable, unsearchable **13** unexplainable **14** unintelligible

**insect**

*Insects include:*

**03** ant, bee, bug, fly, ked, nit
**04** cleg, flea, frit, gnat, kade, moth, tick, wasp
**05** aphid, aphis, cimex, emmet, louse, midge, ox-bot, roach, sedge
**06** bedbug, beetle, bembex, capsid, cicada, cootie, drongo, earwig, gadfly, gru-gru, hornet, jigger, locust, maggot, mantis, may bug, mayfly, muscid, red ant, sawfly, thrips, tipula, tsetse, tzetse, tzetze, weevil
**07** antlion, blowfly, buzzard, chigger, cornfly, cricket, deer fly, fire ant, gallfly, gold-bug, hive bee, June bug, katydid, lace bug, lady bug, lamp fly, pill bug, rose bug, soldier, termite, wood ant
**08** berry bug, birch fly, blackfly, bookworm, cornworm, crane fly, fruit fly, gall wasp, glowworm, greenfly, honey bee, horse fly, house fly, hoverfly, lacewing, ladybird, mealy bug, mosquito, onion fly, sand wasp, sedge fly, snake fly, stink bug, white ant, whitefly, woodworm
**09** amazon ant, ant weaver, bumblebee, butterfly, caddis fly, carpet bug, cochineal, cockroach, coffee bug, damselfly, doodlebug, dragonfly, golden-eye, humble-bee, leaf miner, mason wasp, mining bee, mud dauber, paper wasp, shield bug, squash bug, stable fly, tsetse fly, tzetse fly, tzetze fly, velvet ant, wax insect, woodlouse
**10** blister fly, bluebottle, boll weevil, bulldog ant, cabbage-fly, cockchafer, dolphin-fly, drosophila, froghopper, grapelouse, kissing bug, leaf-cutter, leaf insect, Pharaoh ant, pondskater, silverfish, vinegar-fly, web spinner
**11** backswimmer, biting louse, biting midge, bristletail, bush cricket, caterpillar, froth-hopper, grasshopper, greenbottle, harvest mite, harvest tick, honeypot ant, stick insect, umbrella-ant, vine-fretter, walking leaf, walking twig
**12** house cricket, lightning bug, walking stick, water boatman
**13** daddy longlegs, diamond-beetle, leatherjacket, praying insect, praying mantis, water measurer, water scorpion

*See also* **animal**; **beetle**; **butterfly**; **invertebrate**; **moth**

*Insect parts include:*

**03** eye, jaw, leg
**04** head, vein, wing
**06** cercus, feeler, scutum, thorax
**07** abdomen, antenna, cuticle, maxilla, ocellus, pedicel, segment
**08** antennae, forewing, hindwing, mandible, peduncle, spiracle, tympanum
**09** mouthpart, proboscis
**10** epicuticle, integument, ovipositor
**11** compound eye

• **study of insects**
**03** ent **10** entomology

**insecticide**

*Insecticides include:*

**02** Bt
**03** BHC, DDT
**05** timbó, zineb
**06** aldrin, derris
**07** cinerin, safrole
**08** camphene, carbaryl, chlordan, chromene, diazinon, dieldrin, flyspray, rotenone
**09** chlordane, Gammexane®, Malathion®, parathion, toxaphene
**10** carbofuran, dimethoate, Paris green, piperazine
**15** organophosphate

**insectivore**
**04** mole, tody **05** shrew **06** agouta, desman, tanrec, tenrec, Tupaia **08** hedgehog, serotine **09** solenodon, tree shrew **10** golden mole, otter shrew **11** diamond bird, gnatcatcher **13** elephant shrew

• **insectivorous plant**
**06** sundew **07** Dionaea, drosera **10** butterwort, sarracenia **11** gobe-mouches **12** pitcher plant, Venus flytrap **13** Venus's flytrap

**insecure**
◇ *anagram indicator*
**04** weak **05** frail, loose, shaky **06** afraid, flimsy, tickle, unsafe, unsure **07** anxious, exposed, fearful, nervous, worried **08** doubtful, hesitant, perilous, unstable, unsteady **09** dangerous, hazardous, unassured, uncertain, unguarded **10** precarious, vulnerable **11** defenceless, unprotected **12** apprehensive, open to attack

**insecurity**
**04** fear **05** peril, worry **06** danger, hazard **07** anxiety **08** unsafety, weakness **09** frailness, shakiness **10** flimsiness, uneasiness, unsafeness, unsureness **11** instability, nervousness, uncertainty **12** apprehension, unsteadiness **13** vulnerability **14** precariousness **15** defencelessness

**insensate**
**04** deaf, numb **05** blind **07** unaware **08** comatose, ignorant **09** inanimate, oblivious, senseless, unfeeling, unmindful **10** insensible, insentient **11** unconscious **12** unresponsive **13** anaesthetized

**insensible**
**03** out **04** cold, deaf, dull, hard, numb **05** aloof, blind, faint **06** marble, slight, stupid, wooden, zonked **07** callous, distant, unaware, unmoved **08** comatose, detached, ignorant **09** oblivious, senseless, unfeeling, unmindful, untouched **10** insentient, iron-witted, knocked out, unaffected, unapparent **11** emotionless, hard-hearted, insensitive, unconscious **12** undetectable, unresponsive **13** anaesthetized, imperceptible, indiscernible **14** dead to the world, out for the count

**insensitive**
**04** dead, hard, iron **05** crass, tough **06** immune, obtuse **07** callous, unmoved **08** hardened, tactless, uncaring **09** anomalous, heartless, impassive, oblivious, resistant, unfeeling, untouched **10** hypalgesic, impervious, unaffected **11** hard-hearted, indifferent, thoughtless, unconcerned **12** case-hardened, impenetrable, thick-skinned, unresponsive **13** unsusceptible, unsympathetic **14** pachydermatous

**insensitivity**
**08** hardness, hypalgia, immunity **09** bluntness, crassness, toughness, unconcern **10** crassitude, hypalgesia, obtuseness, resistance **11** callousness **12** indifference, tactlessness **14** hard-headedness, imperviousness **15** hard-heartedness, impenetrability

**inseparable**
**05** bosom, close **07** devoted **08** constant, intimate **10** individual **11** individuate, indivisible, undividable **12** indissoluble, inextricable

**inseparably**
**05** as one **06** firmly **07** closely **08** arm in arm, together **10** hand in hand, intimately **11** indivisibly **12** indissolubly, inextricably

**insert**
**03** cue, put, set **04** sink **05** embed, enter, immit, infix, inlay, inset, let in,

place, plant, press, put in, stick **06** notice, push in, slip in **07** enchase, enclose, engraft, implant, ingraft, slide in, stick in **08** addition, circular, intromit, thrust in **09** enclosure, insertion, interject, interpose, introduce **10** interleave, supplement **11** intercalate, interpolate **13** advertisement

**insertion**
**05** entry, inset, miter, mitre **06** insert **07** implant **08** addition **09** inclusion, intrusion **10** supplement **12** introduction, intromission **13** intercalation, interpolation

**inside**
◇ *hidden indicator*
◇ *insertion indicator*
**04** core, guts **05** belly, heart, inner **06** centre, indoor, inward, middle, secret, within **07** content, indoors, private **08** contents, hush-hush, implicit, inherent, interior, internal, intromit, inwardly, reserved, secretly **09** innermost, intrinsic, privately **10** classified, internally, restricted **12** confidential

**insider**
**06** member **07** one of us **08** co-worker **11** participant, staff member **15** one of the in-crowd

**insides**
**04** guts **05** belly, tummy **06** bowels, organs **07** abdomen, giblets, innards, stomach, viscera **08** entrails **10** intestines **14** internal organs

**insidious**
**03** sly **04** wily **06** artful, crafty, sneaky, subtle, tricky **07** cunning, devious, furtive **08** sneaking, stealthy **09** cautelous, deceitful, deceptive, dishonest, insincere **10** perfidious **11** duplicitous, treacherous **13** Machiavellian, surreptitious

**insidiously**
**05** slyly **06** subtly **09** cunningly

**insight**
**05** grasp, sight **06** acumen, aperçu, vision, wisdom **08** epiphany **09** awareness, furniture, intuition, judgement, knowledge, sharpness **10** perception, shrewdness **11** discernment, observation, penetration, realization, sensitivity **12** apprehension, intelligence, perspicacity **13** comprehension, enlightenment, understanding

**insightful**
**04** wise **05** acute, sharp **06** astute, seeing, shrewd **07** prudent **08** inscient **09** observant, sagacious **10** discerning, perceptive, percipient **11** intelligent, penetrating **13** knowledgeable, perspicacious, understanding

**insignia**
**03** tab **04** arms, logo, mark, sign, type **05** armor, badge, brand, clasp, crest, eagle, order, signs **06** armour, emblem, ensign, ribbon, symbol **07** regalia **08** hallmark **09** hallmarks, medallion, trademark **10** coat of arms, decoration **11** cap and bells

**insignificance**
**08** meanness, tininess **09** pettiness, smallness **10** paltriness, triviality **11** irrelevance, nothingness **12** nugatoriness, unimportance **13** immateriality, inconsequence, negligibility, worthlessness **15** meaninglessness

**insignificant**
**04** tiny **05** C-list, dinky, minor, petit, petty, scrub, small **06** insect, meagre, paltry, puisne, puisny, scanty, slight **07** minimal, nebbich, scrubby, trivial **08** marginal, nugatory, piddling, trifling **09** jerkwater, no-account, small beer, small-time **10** fractional, immaterial, irrelevant, negligible, peripheral **11** meaningless, Mickey Mouse, unimportant **12** cutting no ice, non-essential **13** hole-in-the-wall, insubstantial, no great shakes **14** inconsiderable **15** inconsequential

**insincere**
**04** jive **05** false, lying **06** double, forked, hollow, phoney, untrue **07** devious, feigned, lip-deep **08** disloyal, rhetoric, two-faced **09** deceitful, dishonest, faithless, mouth-made, pretended, underhand, unnatural **10** backhanded, mendacious, perfidious, rhetorical, unfaithful, untruthful **11** dissembling, duplicitous, pretentious, treacherous **12** disingenuous, hypocritical, meretricious **13** double-dealing

**insincerely**
**07** falsely **09** deviously **10** disloyally **11** deceitfully, dishonestly **12** perfidiously, unfaithfully, untruthfully **13** duplicitously, pretentiously, treacherously **14** hypocritically

**insincerity**
**04** cant **06** humbug **07** falsity, perfidy **08** bad faith, pretence **09** duplicity, falseness, hypocrisy, mendacity, phoniness **10** dishonesty, hollowness, lip service **11** deviousness, dissembling, evasiveness **13** artificiality, deceitfulness, dissimulation, faithlessness **14** untruthfulness **15** pretentiousness

**insinuate**
**04** hint, wind **05** get at, imply **06** allude **07** mention, suggest, whisper **08** indicate, innuendo, intimate, work into **10** serpentine
• **insinuate yourself**
**04** work, worm **05** crawl, sidle **07** wriggle **09** get in with **10** ingratiate **11** curry favour

**insinuation**
**04** hint, slur **05** slant **08** allusion, innuendo **09** aspersion, inference **10** insinuendo, intimation, suggestion **11** implication **12** introduction

**insipid**
**03** dry **04** blah, drab, dull, fade, flat, lash, tame, thin, weak **05** banal, bland, trite, vapid, wersh **06** boring, pallid, watery **07** anaemic, insulse, mawkish, missish, shilpit, tedious, wearish **08** lifeless, waterish **09** inanimate, sapidless, tasteless, unsavoury, wearisome **10** albuminous, colourless, monotonous, spiritless, wishy-washy **11** flavourless **12** milk-and-water, unappetizing **13** characterless, unimaginative, uninteresting

**insist**
**03** vow **04** aver, hold, urge **05** claim, press, swear **06** assert, demand, harp on, repeat, strain, stress, threap **07** contend, declare, dwell on, entreat, persist, require, stand on **08** maintain **09** emphasize, reiterate, stand firm, stipulate **10** hang out for **11** state firmly, stick out for **12** ask for firmly **15** put your foot down, stand your ground, stick to your guns

**insistence**
**05** claim **06** demand, stress, urging **08** emphasis, entreaty, firmness **09** assertion **10** contention, repetition, resolution **11** declaration, exhortation, maintenance, persistence, reiteration, requirement **13** assertiveness, determination

**insistent**
**06** dogged, urgent **07** adamant, exigent **08** constant, emphatic, forceful, pressing, repeated, resolute **09** assertive, demanding, incessant, tenacious **10** determined, inexorable, persistent, relentless, unyielding **11** importunate, persevering, unrelenting, unremitting

**insobriety**
**09** inebriety, tipsiness **10** crapulence **11** drunkenness, inebriation **12** hard drinking, intemperance, intoxication

**insolence**
**03** gum, lip **04** gall, sass **05** abuse, cheek, mouth, nerve, sauce, snash **06** hubris, hybris **07** insults **08** attitude, audacity, boldness, chutzpah, defiance, pertness, rudeness **09** arrogance, contumely, impudence, sauciness **10** cheekiness, disrespect, effrontery, incivility **11** forwardness, presumption **12** impertinence **13** offensiveness **15** insubordination

**insolent**
**04** bold, rude **05** bardy, brash, fresh, lairy, lippy, sassy, saucy **06** brazen, cheeky, mouthy, wanton **07** abusive, defiant, forward **08** arrogant, impudent **09** audacious, insulting **10** purse-proud **11** ill-mannered, impertinent **12** contemptuous, contumelious, presumptuous **13** disrespectful, insubordinate

**insoluble**
**07** complex, obscure **08** baffling, involved, puzzling **09** enigmatic, intricate **10** mysterious, mystifying, perplexing, unsolvable **11** inscrutable **12** impenetrable, inexplicable, unfathomable **13** unexplainable **14** indecipherable

**insolvency**
**04** ruin **07** default, failure **10** bankruptcy **11** destitution, liquidation, queer street **12** indebtedness **13** impecuniosity, pennilessness **14** impoverishment

**insolvent**
**04** bust **05** broke, skint **06** failed, in debt, ruined **07** boracic **08** bankrupt, in the red, strapped **09** destitute, gone under, penniless **10** liquidated, on the rocks **11** impecunious **12** impoverished **13** gone to the wall, in queer street **14** on your beam ends **15** strapped for cash

**insomnia**
**11** wakefulness **12** insomnolence, restlessness **13** sleeplessness
• **insomnia drug**
**06** Ativan® **07** Mogadon® **08** Rohypnol® **09** lorazepam, Temazepam **10** nitrazepam

**insouciance**
**04** ease **08** airiness **09** flippancy, unconcern **10** breeziness, jauntiness **11** nonchalance **12** carefreeness, heedlessness, indifference

**insouciant**
**04** airy **06** breezy, casual, jaunty **07** buoyant **08** carefree, flippant, heedless **09** apathetic, easy-going, unworried **10** nonchalant, untroubled **11** free and easy, indifferent, unconcerned **12** happy-go-lucky, light-hearted

**inspect**
**03** vet **04** case, scan, tour, view **05** audit, check, study, visit **06** assess, go over, review, search, survey **07** examine, oversee, see over **08** appraise, check out, look into, look over, pore over **09** supervise **10** scrutinize **11** investigate, perlustrate, reconnoitre, superintend

**inspection**
**04** scan, tour, view **05** audit, check, dekko, recce, study, visit **06** alnage, muster, review, search, survey **07** autopsy, check-up, inspect, rag-fair, vetting, vidimus **08** analysis, autopsia, look-over, once-over, overview, scrutiny **09** appraisal, Cook's tour, look-round **10** assessment **11** examination, perspective, supervision **12** tracheoscopy **13** investigation

**inspector**
**06** conner, critic, exarch, keeker, tester, viewer **07** alnager, auditor, checker, officer, scanner, visitor **08** assessor, examiner, overseer, provedor, providor, reviewer, searcher, surveyor **09** appraiser, provedore **10** controller, proveditor, scrutineer, supervisor **11** proveditore **12** investigator **14** superintendent

**inspiration**
**04** goad, hoop, hwyl, idea, muse, spur **05** estro, whoop **06** breath, duende, fillip, genius **07** insight **08** afflatus, Aganippe, arousing, inflatus, infusion, stimulus, stirring, taghairm **09** afflation, awakening, brainwave, inflation, influence, theosophy **10** brainstorm, bright idea, creativity, enthusiasm, incitement, motivation, revelation **11** imagination, originality, stimulation, theopneusty **12** illumination **13** encouragement, enlightenment, inventiveness **14** stroke of genius

**inspirational**
**09** emotional, inspiring, spiritual **10** devotional, heartening, motivating, suggestive **11** encouraging, influential, instinctive **13** psychological

**inspire**
**04** fire, goad, spur, stir **05** guide, imbue, rouse **06** arouse, enamor, excite, inform, infuse, inject, kindle, prompt, thrill **07** animate, breathe, embrave, enamour, enliven, enthral, enthuse, hearten, impress, inflame, produce, provoke, quicken, trigger **08** energize, instruct, motivate, spark off, touch off **09** encourage, galvanize, infatuate, influence, instigate, stimulate **10** bring about, exhilarate

**inspired**
**05** vatic **08** afflated, creative, daemonic, daimonic, dazzling, exciting, splendid, talented, visioned **09** brilliant, memorable, thrilling, wonderful **10** impressive, marvellous, remarkable, theopneust **11** enthralling, exceptional, imaginative, outstanding, superlative **12** theopneustic

**inspiring**
**06** moving **07** rousing **08** exciting, stirring **09** affecting, memorable, thrilling, uplifting **10** heartening, impressive **11** encouraging, enthralling, interesting, stimulating **12** enthusiastic, exhilarating, invigorating **13** inspirational

**inspirit**
**04** fire, move **05** cheer, nerve, rouse **06** incite **07** animate, enliven, gladden, hearten, inspire, quicken, refresh **08** embolden **09** encourage, galvanize, stimulate **10** exhilarate, invigorate **12** reinvigorate

**instability**
**07** frailty **08** wavering **09** lubricity, shakiness **10** fickleness, fitfulness, flimsiness, insecurity, transience, unsafeness, volatility **11** flightiness, fluctuation, inconstancy, oscillation, temperament, uncertainty, unsoundness, vacillation, variability **12** impermanence, irresolution, unsteadiness **13** unreliability **14** capriciousness, changeableness, precariousness

**install**
**03** fit, fix, lay, put **04** site **05** lodge, place, plant, put in, set up, state **06** induct, insert, invest, locate, nestle, ordain, settle **07** instate, plumb in, situate, station, swear in **08** ensconce, enthrone, entrench, position **09** establish, institute, introduce **10** consecrate, inaugurate

**installation**
**02** HQ **04** base, camp, post, site **05** plant **06** centre, siting, system **07** artwork, fitting, placing, station **08** location **09** apparatus, equipment, induction, insertion, machinery **10** ordination, settlement, swearing-in **11** instatement, investiture, positioning **12** consecration, headquarters, inauguration **13** establishment

**instalment**
**02** HP **04** call, heft, part **06** lesson **07** chapter, episode, payment, portion, section, segment, tranche **08** division, rhapsody **09** repayment **11** part payment **12** continuation, hire purchase **13** the never-never

**instance**
**04** case, cite, give, name, suit **05** cause, proof, quote **06** adduce, behest, demand, motive, sample, urging **07** example, mention, point to, process, refer to, request, specify **08** citation, entreaty, evidence, occasion, pressure **09** exemplify, prompting **10** incitement, initiative, insistence, occurrence, particular **11** case in point, exhortation, importunity, instigation **12** illustration, solicitation **15** exemplification
• **for instance**
**02** as, eg, zB **10** for example **13** exempli gratia

**instant**
**02** mo **03** sec **04** fast, jiff, tick, time, whip **05** flash, jiffy, quick, rapid, swift, trice **06** direct, minute, moment, prompt, second, urgent **07** current, present **08** juncture, occasion **09** immediate, on-the-spot, twinkling **10** ready mixed **11** convenience, pre-prepared, split second **12** unhesitating **13** instantaneous **14** easily prepared **15** quickly prepared

**instantaneous**
**05** rapid **06** direct, prompt, snappy, sudden **07** instant **09** immediate, momentary, on-the-spot **12** momentaneous, unhesitating

**instantaneously**
**03** pdq **04** anon, ASAP **06** at once, pronto **07** quickly, rapidly **08** directly, in a jiffy, promptly, speedily **09** forthwith, instantly, on the spot, right away **11** immediately **12** straight away, there and then, without delay **14** unhesitatingly

**instantly**
**03** now, pdq **04** ASAP **06** at once, pronto **08** directly, in a jiffy, on the dot **09** forthwith, like a shot, on the spot, right away, zealously **11** immediately **12** straight away, there and then, without delay **13** importunately **15** instantaneously

**instead**
**04** else **06** rather **10** by contrast, in contrast, preferably, substitute **11** replacement **13** alternatively **15** as an alternative

**• instead of**
**04** vice **07** against **08** in lieu of **09** in place of **10** in favour of, on behalf of, rather than **11** as opposed to **12** in contrast to **14** in preference to

**instigate**
**04** goad, move, prod, spur, urge **05** begin, cause, impel, press, rouse, set on, spark, start **06** excite, foment, incite, induce, kindle, prompt, stir up, whip up **07** inspire, provoke **08** generate, initiate, persuade **09** encourage, influence, stimulate **10** bring about

**instigation**
**06** behest, motion, urging **07** bidding **09** incentive, prompting, prompture **10** incitement, inducement, initiation, initiative, insistence **11** fomentation **13** encouragement

**instigator**
**04** goad, spur **06** leader **07** inciter **08** agitator, fomenter, incensor, provoker, putter-on **09** firebrand, initiator, motivator **10** incendiary, prime mover, ringleader **12** troublemaker **13** mischief-maker

**instil**
**05** drill, imbue, plant, teach **06** infuse, inject **07** breathe, din into, implant, impress, ingrain **09** inculcate, insinuate, introduce, transfuse

**instinct**
**04** bent, feel, gift, urge **05** drive, flair, hunch, knack, moved **06** imbued, nature, talent **07** ability, charged, faculty, feeling, impulse, incited **08** animated, aptitude, tendency **09** intuition, principle **10** gut feeling, instigated, sixth sense **11** gut reaction **14** inbred response, predisposition **15** natural response

**instinctive**
**03** gut **06** inborn, innate, native, reflex **07** natural **08** inherent, knee-jerk, primeval, untaught, visceral **09** automatic, immediate, impulsive, intuitive, primaeval, unlearned **10** mechanical, unthinking **11** involuntary, spontaneous **13** unintentional **14** seat-of-the-pants, unpremeditated

**instinctively**
**09** naturally **11** intuitively **12** mechanically, unthinkingly **13** automatically, involuntarily, spontaneously **15** without thinking

**institute**
**01** I **03** law **04** Inst, open, rule **05** begin, enact, found, order, raise, set up, start **06** create, custom, decree, induct, invest, launch, ordain, school **07** academy, appoint, college, develop, educate, install, precept **08** commence, initiate, organize, seminary **09** establish, introduce, originate, principle **10** foundation, inaugurate, regulation **11** institution, put in motion, set in motion **12** conservatory, organization

*Institutes include:*

**02** IA, IM, WI
**03** BFI, CGI, CIB, CMI, EMI, ICA, MIT
**04** NICE, RIBA, RNIB, RNID, RTPI
**05** C and G, UMIST, UWIST
**07** Caltech

**institution**
**03** law **04** club, home, rule **05** guild, usage **06** center, centre, custom, league, ritual, system **07** college, concern, society **08** creation, founding, hospital, practice, starting **09** enactment, formation, inception, institute, setting-up, tradition **10** convention, foundation, initiation **11** association, corporation **12** commencement, installation, introduction, organization **13** establishment

**institutional**
**03** set **04** cold, drab, dull **06** dreary, formal **07** orderly, routine, uniform **08** accepted, clinical, orthodox **09** cheerless, customary, organized **10** forbidding, impersonal, methodical, monotonous, regimented, systematic **11** established, ritualistic, uninspiring, unwelcoming **12** bureaucratic, conventional **13** establishment

**instruct**
**03** bid **04** shew, show, tell, warn **05** brief, coach, drill, guide, order, prime, study, teach, train, tutor **06** advise, charge, demand, direct, enjoin, gospel, ground, inform, lesson, notify, school, taught **07** call out, command, counsel, educate, inspire, lecture, mandate, prepare, require **09** catechize, enlighten, make known **10** discipline **12** indoctrinate

**instruction**
**03** key **05** brief, order, rules **06** advice, charge, legend, lesson, manual, orders, ruling **07** classes, command, lecture, lessons, mandate, priming, telling, tuition **08** briefing, coaching, drilling, guidance, handbook, lectures, pedagogy, teaching, training, tutelage, tutoring **09** direction, directive, education, grounding, knowledge, schooling **10** directions, discipline, guidelines, injunction **11** book of words, edification, information, inspiration, preparation, requirement **13** enlightenment **14** indoctrination, recommendation **15** recommendations

**instructive**
**06** useful **07** helpful **08** didactic, edifying, teaching **09** doctrinal, educative, improving, uplifting **10** didactical **11** educational, informative, informatory **12** enlightening, illuminating

**instructor**
**04** guru **05** coach, guide, swami, tutor **06** master, mentor, sensei **07** adviser, teacher, trainer **08** educator, exponent, lecturer, mistress **09** maharishi, pedagogue, preceptor **10** counsellor, instituter, institutor **11** preceptress **12** demonstrator

**instrument**
**03** act, way **04** mean, rule, tool **05** agent, cause, gauge, gismo, means, meter, organ **06** agency, device, factor gadget, medium **07** channel, measure utensil, vehicle **09** apparatus, appliance, guideline, implement, indicator, mechanism, yardstick **11** contraption, contrivance

See also **measurement**; **optical**; **scientific**; **torture**; **writing**

*Musical instruments include:*

**02** gu
**03** gju, gue, lur, oud, sax, saz, uke, zel
**04** alto, bass, bell, drum, erhu, fife, gong, harp, horn, kora, koto, lure, lute, lyre, Moog®, oboe, pipe, rote, sang, tuba, vibe, vina, viol, zeze
**05** Amati, banjo, bells, bongo, bugle, cello, chime, crwth, flute, gusla, gusle, gusli, hi-hat, kazoo, mbira, organ, piano, pipes, rebec, shalm, shawm, sitar, strad, tabla, tabor, vibes, viola, zanze, zirna, zurna
**06** carnyx, cither, citole, cornet, cymbal, Fender, fiddle, guitar, rattle spinet, tom-tom, tympan, vielle, violin, zither
**07** alphorn, bagpipe, bandore, bandura, baryton, bassoon, bazouki, bodhran, buccina, celeste, cembalo, cithara, cithern, cittern, clarion, clavier, cowbell, hautboy, lyricon, maracas, marimba, ocarina, pandora, Pianola®, piccolo, sackbut, sambuca, sarangi, saxhorn, serpent, sistrum, tambura, theorbo, timpani, trumpet, ukulele, vihuela, whistle, zithern
**08** angklung, bagpipes, barytone, bass drum, bass viol, bouzouki, calliope, carillon, charango, cimbalom, clappers, clarinet, clarsach, cornpipe, crumhorn, dulcimer, handbell, hornpipe, humstrum, jew's harp, keyboard, mandolin, manzello, melodeon, Pan-pipes, polyphon, psaltery, recorder, side-drum, spinette, Steinway, surbahar, tamboura, theramin, theremin, timbales, triangle, trombone,

virginal, vocalion, zambomba
09 accordion, alpenhorn, balalaika, banjolele, bugle-horn, castanets, chime bars, decachord, euphonium, flageolet, harmonica, harmonium, Mellotron®, polyphone, saxophone, snare-drum, tenor-drum, wood block, Wurlitzer®, xylophone
10 arpeggione, bass guitar, bird-scarer, bongo-drums, bullroarer, clavichord, concertina, cor anglais, didgeridoo, double bass, eolian harp, flugelhorn, French horn, grand piano, hurdy-gurdy, kettle-drum, mouth organ, oboe d'amore, pentachord, pianoforte, sousaphone, squeeze-box, tambourine, thumb piano, tin whistle, vibraphone
11 aeolian harp, barrel organ, harpsichord, phonofiddle, player-piano, sleigh bells, synthesizer, violoncello
12 glockenspiel, harmonichord, penny whistle, stock and horn, Stradivarius, tubular bells, viola da gamba
13 contra-bassoon, Ondes Martenot, panharmonicon, slide trombone, Swanee whistle
14 acoustic guitar, electric guitar, jingling Johnny
15 Moog synthesizer®, wind synthesizer

**instrumental**
**06** active, useful **07** helpful, organic **08** involved **09** auxiliary, conducive, important **10** subsidiary **11** implemental, influential, ministerial, significant, subservient **12** contributory

**insubordinate**
**04** rude **06** unruly **07** defiant, riotous **08** impudent, mutinous **09** insurgent, seditious, turbulent **10** disorderly, rebellious, refractory **11** disobedient, impertinent **12** contumacious, recalcitrant, ungovernable **13** undisciplined

**insubordination**
**06** mutiny, revolt **08** defiance, rudeness, sedition **09** impudence, rebellion **11** riotousness **12** disobedience, impertinence, indiscipline, insurrection, mutinousness **13** recalcitrance **15** ungovernability

**insubstantial**
**04** idle, poor, thin, weak **05** false, frail, wispy **06** bubble, feeble, flimsy, frothy, meagre, slight, unreal, yeasty **07** tenuous **08** fanciful, illusory, tenuious, vaporous **09** airy-fairy, cardboard, ephemeral, imaginary, moonshine **10** chimerical, immaterial, intangible **11** incorporeal

**insufferable**
**08** dreadful, shocking **09** loathsome, repugnant, revolting **10** detestable, impossible, outrageous, unbearable **11** intolerable, unendurable **13** insupportable, too much to bear

**insufferably**
**10** impossibly, shockingly, unbearably **11** intolerably, repugnantly **12** outrageously

**insufficiency**
**04** lack, need, want **06** dearth **07** paucity, poverty **08** scarcity, shortage **10** deficiency, inadequacy **11** short supply **14** inadequateness

**insufficient**
**05** scant, short **06** meagre, scanty, scarce, sparse **07** lacking, wanting **09** defective, deficient, not enough **10** inadequate **13** in short supply

**insular**
**05** aloof, petty **06** biased, closed, cut off, narrow, remote **07** bigoted, limited **08** detached, isolated, separate, solitary **09** blinkered, insulated, parochial, withdrawn **10** prejudiced, provincial, restricted, xenophobic **12** narrow-minded, short-sighted **13** inward-looking

**insularity**
**04** bias **07** bigotry **09** isolation, pettiness, prejudice **10** detachment, xenophobia **12** parochiality, solitariness **13** parochialness

**insulate**
**03** lag, pad **04** wrap **05** cover **06** cocoon, cut off, detach, encase, shield **07** cushion, envelop, exclude, isolate, protect, shelter **08** separate **09** segregate, sequester

**insulation**
**05** cover **06** shield **07** lagging, padding, shelter **08** asbestos, cladding, covering, sleeving, stuffing, wrapping **09** cocooning, corkboard, exclusion, fibrefill, foam glass, isolation **10** cushioning, detachment, fiberglass, fibreglass, protection, separation, Thermalite® **11** segregation **12** foam plastics **13** building paper, double-glazing, triple glazing **14** foamed plastics, Willesden paper **15** contour feathers, vulcanized fibre

**insulator**

*Insulators include:*

03 lag
04 mica
07 bushing, tea cosy
08 rock wool
09 pink batts®
10 dielectric
11 vermiculite
12 friction tape
14 insulating tape, Willesden paper

**insult**
**04** bait, barb, gibe, hurt, slur, snub **05** abuse, libel, taunt, wound **06** damage, impugn, injure, injury, malign, mud pie, offend, rebuff, revile, slight, verbal **07** affront, mortify, offence, outrage, put-down, slander, traduce, trample, triumph **08** derogate, repriefe, ridicule, rudeness **09** call names, contumely, disparage, indignity, insolence **10** aspersions, calumniate, defamation, fling mud at, insultment, revilement, sling mud at, throw mud at **11** triumph over **13** disparagement, slap in the face **14** fly in the face of, kick in the teeth

**insulting**
**04** rude **07** abusive, hurtful **08** insolent, reviling **09** degrading, injurious, libellous, offensive, slighting **10** affronting, derogatory, outrageous, scurrilous, slanderous **11** disparaging, opprobrious **12** contemptuous, contumelious

**insuperable**
**10** formidable, impassable, invincible **12** overwhelming, unassailable **13** unconquerable **14** insurmountable

**insupportable**
**07** hateful **08** dreadful **09** loathsome, untenable **10** detestable, unbearable **11** intolerable, unendurable **12** indefensible, insufferable, irresistible, unacceptable **13** unjustifiable

**insuppressible**
**06** lively, unruly **09** energetic, go-getting **11** unstoppable, unsubduable **12** incorrigible, obstreperous, ungovernable **13** irrepressible **14** uncontrollable

**insurance**
**02** NI **03** ins **05** cover **06** policy, surety **07** premium **08** security, warranty **09** assurance, guarantee, indemnity, provision, safeguard **10** protection **15** indemnification

**insure**
**05** cover **06** assure, ensure **07** protect, warrant **08** reinsure **09** guarantee, indemnify **10** overinsure, underwrite

**insurer**
**07** assurer **09** abandonee, guarantor, protector, warrantor **11** indemnifier, underwriter

**insurgence**
**04** coup, riot **06** mutiny, putsch, revolt, rising **08** sedition, uprising **09** coup d'état, rebellion **10** revolution **12** insurrection

**insurgent**
**05** pandy, rebel **06** rioter, rising **07** riotous **08** Camisard, mutineer, mutinous, partisan, resister, revolted, revolter **09** revolting, seditious **10** rebellious **11** disobedient, seditionist **13** insubordinate, revolutionary, revolutionist **15** insurrectionary, insurrectionist

**insurmountable**
**08** hopeless **10** impossible, invincible **11** insuperable **12** overwhelming, unassailable **13** unconquerable

**insurrection**
**04** coup, riot **06** mutiny, putsch, revolt, rising, uproar **08** sedition, uprising
**09** coup d'état, rebellion
**10** insurgence, insurgency, revolution

**intact**
**05** sound, whole **06** entire, unhurt
**07** perfect **08** complete, flawless, integral, unbroken, unharmed
**09** faultless, undamaged, uninjured, unscathed, untouched **10** in one piece, unimpaired **12** undiminished
**13** all in one piece

**intangible**
**04** airy **05** vague **06** subtle, unfelt, unreal **07** elusive, obscure, shadowy, unclear **08** abstract, fleeting
**09** invisible, touchless **10** impalpable, indefinite **11** incorporeal, indefinable, undefinable **12** immeasurable, imponderable **13** indescribable, insubstantial

**integer**
**04** unit **05** digit, whole **06** figure, number **07** numeral **11** whole number

**integral**
**04** full **05** basic, total, whole **06** entire, intact **07** built-in, inbuilt, unitary
**08** complete, inherent **09** component, elemental, essential, intrinsic, necessary, requisite, undivided
**10** integrated, unimpaired
**11** constituent, fundamental
**13** indispensable

**integrate**
**03** mix **04** fuse, join, knit, mesh
**05** blend, merge, unite, whole
**06** mingle **07** combine **08** coalesce, complete, intermix **09** harmonize
**10** amalgamate, assimilate, co-ordinate, homogenize, mainstream
**11** consolidate, desegregate, incorporate

**integrated**
**05** fused, mixed **06** hybrid, joined, merged, meshed, united **07** blended, mingled, mongrel, unified
**08** cohesive, combined, joined-up
**09** coalesced, connected, one-nation, tight-knit **10** harmonious, harmonized
**11** amalgamated, assimilated, tightly knit, unseparated **12** consolidated, desegregated, incorporated, interrelated **13** part and parcel

**integration**
**03** mix **05** blend, unity **06** fusion, merger **07** harmony **11** combination, unification **12** amalgamation, assimilation **13** consolidation, desegregation, incorporation
**14** homogenization

**integrity**
**05** honor, unity **06** honour, purity, virtue **07** decency, honesty, justice, probity **08** cohesion, entirety, fairness, goodness, morality, totality
**09** coherence, principle, rectitude, sincerity, wholeness **10** entireness
**11** unification, uprightness
**12** completeness, impartiality, truthfulness **13** righteousness

**intellect**
**04** mind, nous **05** brain, sense
**06** brains, genius, noesis, reason, wisdom **07** egghead, noology, thinker, thought **08** academic, brainbox, highbrow **09** judgement
**10** brainpower, brilliance, mastermind
**12** intellectual, intelligence
**13** comprehension, understanding

**intellectual**
**04** blue **05** titan **06** boffin, brainy, far-out, genius, mental, noetic **07** bookish, egghead, erudite, learned, logical, thinker **08** academic, brainbox, cerebral, cultural, good mind, highbrow, studious, well-read
**09** intellect, scholarly **10** mastermind, noematical, thoughtful **11** intelligent
**12** bluestocking, pointy-headed, well-educated **15** rocket scientist

**intellectually**
**08** mentally **10** cerebrally, culturally, studiously **12** academically, conceptually, noematically

**intelligence**
**01** G **02** IQ **03** gen, wit **04** data, dope, news, nous, wits **05** brain, facts
**06** acumen, advice, brains, notice, reason, report, rumour, spying, tip-off
**07** account, low-down, thought, warning **08** aptitude, findings
**09** alertness, espionage, intellect, knowledge, quickness, sharpness
**10** brainpower, brightness, brilliance, cleverness, grey matter, perception
**11** discernment, information, observation **12** notification, surveillance **13** comprehension, understanding **15** little grey cells

• **intelligence service**
**02** MI **03** CIA, KGB, SIS **05** Stasi
**06** Mossad

**intelligent**
**05** acute, alert, quick, sharp, smart
**06** brainy, bright, clever **07** knowing
**08** all there, educated, informed, rational, sensible, thinking
**09** brilliant, sagacious **10** discerning, perceptive **11** quick-witted
**12** apprehensive, knowledgable, pointy-headed, well-informed
**13** communicative, knowledgeable, perspicacious, understanding, using your loaf

**intelligently**
**07** quickly **08** all there, cleverly, sensibly **09** knowingly **10** rationally
**11** sagaciously **12** discerningly, perceptively **13** using your loaf
**15** perspicaciously

**intelligentsia**
**06** brains **08** eggheads, literati
**09** academics, highbrows **10** illuminati
**11** cognoscenti **13** intellectuals

**intelligibility**
**07** clarity **08** lucidity **09** clearness, lucidness, plainness, precision
**10** legibility, simplicity **11** exotericism
**12** distinctness, explicitness

**intelligible**
**04** open **05** clear, lucid, plain
**07** legible **08** distinct, exoteric, explicit
**10** exoterical, fathomable, penetrable
**12** decipherable **14** comprehensible, understandable

**intemperance**
**06** excess **07** licence **10** crapulence, debauchery, insobriety
**11** drunkenness, inebriation, unrestraint **12** extravagance, immoderation, intoxication
**14** overindulgence, self-indulgence

**intemperate**
**03** OTT **04** wild **06** severe, strong
**07** drunken, extreme, violent
**08** prodigal **09** dissolute, excessive, unbridled **10** immoderate, inebriated, inordinate, licentious, over the top, passionate, profligate **11** dissipation, distempered, extravagant, incontinent, intoxicated, tempestuous
**12** uncontrolled, ungovernable, unreasonable, unrestrained **13** self-indulgent **14** irrestrainable, uncontrollable

**intend**
**03** aim **04** mean, plan, plot, turn
**05** ettle, hight, think **06** choose, design, devise, direct, expand, expect, extend, scheme, strain **07** be going, destine, earmark, express, mark out, project, propose, purport, purpose, resolve **08** foremean, meditate, set apart **09** be looking, calculate, destinate, determine, have a mind, intensify **10** have in mind
**11** contemplate **12** be determined

**intended**
**06** fiancé, future **07** fiancée, planned
**08** destined, proposed, purposed, wife-to-be **09** betrothed, designate
**10** deliberate, designated, future wife
**11** husband-to-be, intentional, prospective **13** future husband

• **as intended**
**15** according to plan

**intense**
**04** deep, full, keen **05** acute, dense, eager, great, harsh, heavy, sharp, tense, vivid **06** ardent, fervid, fierce, opaque, potent, severe, strong **07** burning, earnest, excited, extreme, fervent, nervous, serious, violent, zealous
**08** blinding, electric, forceful, powerful, profound, strained, vehement, vigorous **09** consuming, emotional, energetic, exquisite, intensive **10** heightened, passionate, thoughtful **11** impassioned
**12** concentrated, enthusiastic

**intensely**
**04** deep, very **06** deeply **07** greatly
**08** ardently, fiercely, strongly
**09** extremely, fervently, like stink
**10** profoundly **12** passionately **14** with a vengeance

**intensification**
**05** boost **07** build-up **08** emphasis, increase **09** deepening, intension, worsening **10** building-up, escalation, stepping-up **11** aggravation, enhancement, heightening **12** acceleration, augmentation, exacerbation **13** concentration, magnification, reinforcement, strengthening **14** exacerbescence

**intensify**
**03** fan **04** fire, fuel, whet **05** add to, boost, hot up, raise, widen **06** bump up, deepen, fester, hike up, intend, step up, worsen **07** augment, broaden, build up, enhance, magnify, quicken, sharpen **08** compound, escalate, heighten, increase, maximize **09** aggravate, emphasize, reinforce **10** exacerbate, exaggerate, strengthen **11** concentrate **12** bring to a head

**intensity**
**04** fire, zeal **05** depth, force, power **06** accent, ardour, energy, strain, vigour **07** emotion, fervour, passion, potency, tension **08** fervency, fullness, keenness, severity, strength **09** acuteness, eagerness, extremity, greatness, intension, vehemence **10** enthusiasm, fanaticism, fierceness, profundity **11** earnestness, intenseness **13** concentration

**intensive**
**04** full **05** total **06** all-out **07** in-depth, intense **08** detailed, rigorous, strained, thorough **10** exhaustive **11** unremitting **12** concentrated **13** comprehensive, thoroughgoing

**intensively**
**05** fully **07** closely, totally **09** intensely **10** completely, rigorously, thoroughly **11** extensively **12** exhaustively **15** comprehensively

**intent**
**03** aim, end, set **04** bent, firm, goal, hard, idea, keen, plan, rapt, view **05** alert, close, eager, ettle, fixed, point **06** design, enrapt, object, steady, target **07** earnest, focused, meaning, purpose, wistful **08** absorbed, occupied, resolved, watchful **09** attentive, committed, engrossed, intention, objective, searching, wrapped up **10** determined **11** connotation, preoccupied **13** concentrating

• **to all intents and purposes**
**06** almost, nearly **07** morally **08** as good as, in effect **09** in essence, just about, virtually **10** more or less, pretty much, pretty well **11** effectively, practically

**intention**
**03** aim, end **04** goal, hent, idea, plan, view, wish **05** point **06** animus, design, intent, object, target **07** concept, meaning, purpose, thought **08** ambition **09** objective **10** aspiration, attendment, designment **11** attendement

**intentional**
**03** set **05** meant **06** wilful **07** planned, studied, willful, willing **08** designed, intended, prepense, purposed **09** conscious, on purpose, voluntary, weighed-up **10** calculated, considered, deliberate, purposeful, systematic **11** prearranged **12** preconceived, premeditated, systematical

**intentionally**
**08** by design, wilfully **09** advisedly, knowingly, meaningly, on purpose, purposely, willingly **10** designedly, prepensely **11** in cold blood **12** deliberately

**intently**
**04** hard **06** keenly **07** closely, fixedly **08** steadily **09** carefully, earnestly, staringly **10** diligently, watchfully **11** attentively, searchingly

**inter**
**04** bury **05** earth, inurn **06** entomb, inhume **07** inearth **08** inhumate **09** lay to rest, sepulchre

**interbreed**
**03** mix **05** cross **09** hybridize **10** crossbreed, mongrelize **11** miscegenate **14** cross-fertilize

**interbreeding**
**07** syngamy **08** crossing **13** cross-breeding, hybridization, miscegenation

**intercede**
**05** plead, speak **07** beseech, entreat, mediate **08** moderate, petition **09** arbitrate, interpose, intervene, negotiate

**intercept**
◇ *insertion indicator*
**04** stop, take **05** block, catch, check, cut in, delay, seize **06** ambush, arrest, cut off, impede, thwart, waylay **07** deflect, head off **08** obstruct **09** frustrate, interrupt **10** commandeer

**interception**
◇ *insertion indicator*
**06** ambush **07** seizure **08** blocking, checking, stopping **10** cutting-off, deflection, heading-off **11** obstruction

**intercession**
**04** plea **06** agency, prayer **08** advocacy, entreaty, pleading **09** mediation **10** beseeching **11** arbitration, good offices, negotiation **12** intervention, solicitation, supplication **13** interposition **14** interpellation

**intercessor**
**04** mean **05** agent **06** broker, prayer **08** advocate, mediator **09** go-between, middleman, moderator, paraclete **10** arbitrator, negotiator **12** intermediary

**interchange**
**04** swap **05** trade **06** barter, switch **07** permute, replace, reverse, trading **08** crossing, exchange, junction **09** alternate, crossfire, crossroad, interplay, permutate, transpose **10** alternance, crossroads, substitute **11** alternation, give-and-take, reciprocate **12** intersection **13** reciprocation

**interchangeability**
**04** swap **06** barter **08** exchange, synonymy **10** congruence, similarity **11** equivalence, interaction, parallelism, reciprocity **13** comparability, reciprocation **14** correspondence **15** exchangeability, transposability

**interchangeable**
**07** similar, the same **08** fungible, standard **09** identical **10** comparable, equivalent, permutable, reciprocal, synonymous **11** commutative **12** exchangeable, transposable **13** corresponding

**interconnect**
**04** join, link **06** join up **07** network **09** interlink, interlock **10** interweave **11** communicate, interrelate

**intercourse**
**05** trade, trock, troke, truck **07** contact, traffic **08** commerce, congress, converse, dealings **10** connection **11** association **12** conversation **13** communication **14** correspondence

**interdependent**
**06** mutual, two-way **10** correlated, reciprocal **11** interlinked **12** interlocking, interrelated **13** complementary **14** interconnected

**interdict**
**03** ban, bar **04** tabu, veto **05** debar, taboo **06** forbid, outlaw **07** embargo, prevent, rule out **08** disallow, preclude, prohibit **09** proscribe **10** injunction, preclusion **11** prohibition **12** disallowance, interdiction, proscription

**interest**
**03** fad, int **04** care, gain, good, grip, heed, move, note, part, side **05** amuse, bonus, charm, claim, hobby, rivet, share, stake, stock, touch, value **06** absorb, allure, appeal, divert, engage, equity, moment, notice, occupy, profit, regard, return, weight **07** attract, benefit, concern, credits, engross, gravity, involve, pastime, portion, premium, pursuit, revenue, urgency **08** activity, appeal to, business, dividend, intrigue, priority, proceeds, receipts **09** advantage, amusement, attention, captivate, curiosity, diversion, fascinate, magnitude, relevance **10** attraction, engagement, importance, investment, percentage, prominence, recreation **11** consequence, fascination, involvement, seriousness **12** partisanship, significance

13 attentiveness, consideration, participation 15 inquisitiveness

**• in the interests of**
10 on behalf of 12 for the sake of 15 for the benefit of

**• lack of interest**
06 apathy 07 boredom

**• object of interest**
04 lion

**interested**
04 into, keen 05 hot on 06 intent 07 curious, devoted, engaged, gripped, riveted 08 absorbed, affected, involved 09 attentive, attracted, concerned, engrossed, intrigued 10 captivated, enthralled, fascinated, implicated 12 enthusiastic, having the bug

**interesting**
05 tasty 07 amusing, amusive, curious, unusual 08 engaging, exciting, gripping, readable, riveting, viewable 09 absorbing, appealing 10 attractive, compelling, compulsive, engrossing, intriguing 11 captivating, fascinating, stimulating 12 entertaining 13 unputdownable

**interestingly**
09 curiously 10 poignantly 11 ingeniously 12 intriguingly

**interfere**
03 jam, mar, pry 04 balk, rape 05 abuse, block, check, choke, clash, cramp, grope, upset 06 attack, butt in, feel up, hamper, hinder, impede, meddle, molest, tamper, thwart 07 assault, barge in, inhibit, intrude, touch up, trammel 08 conflict, handicap, intromit, mess with, obstruct, trespass 09 interpose, interrupt, intervene, mess about 10 mess around, muscle in on 11 intermeddle 12 put your bib in, put your oar in 13 get in the way of, poke your bib in, touch sexually 14 poke your nose in, stick your bib in, stick your oar in 15 sexually assault, stick your nose in

**interference**
03 EMI 05 noise, shash 06 prying, static 07 clutter, trammel 08 blocking, checking, clashing, conflict, handicap, meddling, trammels 09 cross-talk, hampering, hindrance, intrusion, thwarting 10 antagonism, impediment, inhibiting, opposition 11 disturbance, obstruction 12 interruption, intervention, intromission 13 interposition 14 meddlesomeness 15 intermodulation

**interfering**
04 nosy 05 nosey 06 prying 08 meddling 09 intruding, intrusive 10 meddlesome

**interim**
06 acting, pro tem 07 stand-in, stopgap 08 interval, meantime 09 caretaker, makeshift, meanwhile, temporary 10 improvised 11 interregnum, provisional

**interior**
03 int 04 core, home 05 heart, inner, local 06 centre, depths, hidden, inland, innate, inside, inward, mental, middle, remote, secret 07 central, innards, nucleus, private 08 domestic, internal, intimate, personal 09 emotional, impulsive, innermost, intrinsic, intuitive, spiritual, up-country 10 inside part 11 instinctive, involuntary, spontaneous 13 psychological

**interject**
03 cry 04 call 05 shout, utter 06 insert, pipe up 07 exclaim, throw in 09 ejaculate, interpose, interrupt, introduce 11 interpolate

**interjection**
03 cry 04 call 05 shout 09 utterance 11 ejaculation, exclamation 12 interruption 13 interpolation, interposition

**interlace**
04 knit 05 braid, cross, plait, twine, weave 06 enlace, inlace 07 entrail, entwine, intwine 08 intermix 09 interlock 10 intertwine, interweave, reticulate 11 intersperse 12 interwreathe

**interlink**
04 knit, link, mesh 07 network 09 intergrow, interlock 10 intertwine, interweave 12 interconnect, link together, lock together 13 clasp together

**interlock**
04 link, mesh 05 pitch, tooth 06 engage 10 intertwine 12 interconnect, link together, lock together 13 clasp together, interdigitate

**interloper**
07 invader 08 intruder 10 encroacher, trespasser 11 gatecrasher 14 uninvited guest

**interlude**
03 jig 04 halt, rest, stop, wait 05 break, delay, let-up, pause, spell 06 hiatus, kyogen, recess, verset 07 respite 08 antimask, breather, entr'acte, interact, interval, stoppage 09 interrupt 10 antimasque 11 parenthesis 12 intermission 14 breathing space, divertissement

**intermediary**
05 agent 06 broker 08 linguist, mediator 09 comprador, go-between, in-between, middleman 10 arbitrator, compradore, contact man, negotiator

**intermediate**
03 mid 04 mean 05 mesne 06 medial, median, medium, middle, midway 07 halfway 09 in-between 11 intervening 12 intermediary, transitional

**interment**
06 burial 07 burying, funeral, obsequy 08 exequies 09 obsequies, sepulture 10 inhumation

**interminable**
04 dull, long 06 boring, prolix 07 endless, eternal, tedious 08 dragging, infinite 09 boundless, ceaseless, limitless, perpetual, unlimited, wearisome 10 long-winded, loquacious, monotonous, without end 11 everlasting, never-ending 12 long-drawn-out

**intermingle**
03 mix 04 fuse, lace 05 blend, merge, mix up 06 commix 07 combine 08 intermix 09 commingle, interlace 10 amalgamate, interweave 11 mix together

**intermission**
04 halt, lull, rest, stop 05 break, let-up, pause 06 recess 07 respite 08 apyrexia, breather, interval, stoppage, suspense, vacation 09 cessation, interlude, remission 10 suspension 12 interruption 14 breathing space

**intermittent**
06 broken, cyclic, fitful 07 erratic 08 off and on, on and off, periodic, sporadic 09 irregular, spasmodic 10 occasional 11 spasmodical 13 discontinuous

**intermittently**
08 off and on, on and off 09 sometimes 11 erratically, irregularly 12 occasionally, periodically, sporadically 13 spasmodically 14 from time to time 15 by fits and starts, discontinuously, in fits and starts

**intern**
04 hold, jail, tiro 05 cadet, pupil 06 detain, inmate, novice 07 confine, learner, recruit, starter, student, trainee 08 beginner, graduate, imprison, newcomer, prentice 10 apprentice 11 probationer 13 hold in custody

**internal**
03 int 04 home 05 civil, inner, local 06 inside, inward, mental 07 in-house, private 08 domestic, interior, intimate, personal 09 emotional, intrinsic, spiritual 10 subjective 13 psychological

**internally**
06 inside, within 07 at heart, locally 08 deep down, inwardly, secretly 09 privately 10 to yourself 12 domestically, subjectively 13 deep inside you

**international**
01 I 03 cap, int 06 global, public 07 general 09 test match, universal, worldwide 12 cosmopolitan

**internecine**
05 civil, fatal 06 bloody, deadly, family, fierce, mortal 07 ruinous, violent 08 internal 09 murderous 11 destructive 13 exterminating

**Internet** *see* **computer**

**interplay**
**08** exchange **11** alternation, give-and-take, interaction, interchange **13** reciprocation, transposition

**interpolate**
**03** add **05** put in **06** insert **09** interject, interpose, intersert, introduce **10** spatchcock **11** intercalate

**interpolation**
**03** gag **05** aside **06** insert **08** addition **09** insertion **12** interjection, introduction **13** intercalation

**interpose**
**03** add **05** cut in, put in **06** butt in, chip in, horn in, insert, step in, strike **07** barge in, intrude, mediate, stickle **08** interlay, intermit, muscle in, strike in, thrust in **09** arbitrate, intercede, interfere, interject, interpone, interrupt, intervene, introduce **10** put between **11** come between, interpolate **12** place between, put your oar in **14** poke your nose in

**interpret**
**04** read, scan, take **05** aread, arede, solve **06** decode, define, open up, render, unfold **07** arreede, clarify, conster, explain, expound **08** construe, decipher **09** elucidate, explicate, make clear, translate **10** paraphrase, understand **11** make sense of, rationalize, shed light on **12** interpretate, throw light on

**interpretation**
**04** read, rede, spin, take **05** sense **07** anagoge, anagogy, meaning, opinion, reading, version **08** analysis, construe, decoding, exegesis **09** rendering **10** exposition, expounding, paraphrase **11** deciphering, elucidation, explanation, explication, performance, translation **12** construction **13** clarification, understanding

**interpretative**
**08** exegetic **10** expository **11** explanatory, explicatory, hermeneutic **12** interpretive **13** clarificatory

**interpreter**
**06** lawyer, munshi **07** dobhash, exegete, Latiner **08** dragoman, exponent, lingster, linguist, linkster, moonshee, truchman **09** annotator, expositor, expounder **10** elucidator, linguister, textualist, translator **11** commentator, expositress **12** hermeneutist, oneirocritic **13** interpretress, oneiroscopist

**interrelate**
**04** link **09** interlink, interlock **10** interweave **11** communicate **12** interconnect

**interrogate**
**04** pump, quiz **05** grill **07** debrief, examine **08** question **12** cross-examine **13** cross-question, give a roasting **14** give a going-over

**interrogation**
**04** quiz **07** inquest, inquiry, pumping **08** grilling, question, quizzing **09** going-over **11** examination, inquisition, questioning, third degree **14** the third degree

**interrogative**
**07** curious, probing **08** erotetic **09** inquiring, quizzical **11** inquisitive, questioning **12** catechetical **13** inquisitional, inquisitorial, interrogatory

**interrupt**
◇ *insertion indicator*
**03** cut, end **04** halt, stop **05** block, break, cut in, delay **06** butt in, cancel, chip in, chop in, cut off, heckle, hold up, snap up, take up **07** barge in, barrack, break in, chequer, disrupt, disturb, intrude, suspend **08** cut short, obstruct, postpone **09** intercept, interject, interlude, interpose, intervene, punctuate, take short **10** disconnect **11** interpolate, take up short **12** put your oar in **13** interfere with, interjaculate

**interruption**
◇ *insertion indicator*
**03** cut **04** halt, stop **05** break, delay, hitch, let-up, pause **06** cesure, hiatus, recess, remark **07** wipeout **08** blocking, breather, interval, obstacle, power cut, question **09** abatement, barging-in, butting-in, cessation, cutting-in, hindrance, interlude, intrusion **10** disruption, impediment, suspension **11** breaking-off, disturbance, obstruction **12** interference, interjection, intermission, solarization **13** disconnection, interpolation **14** discontinuance, interpellation

**intersect**
**03** cut **04** meet **05** cross **06** bisect, divide **07** overlap **08** converge **09** cut across, decussate, intervein **10** criss-cross

**intersection**
**04** edge, meet **06** carfax, carfox, chiasm, vertex **07** chiasma, meeting **08** crossing, junction **10** crossroads, roundabout **11** box junction, interchange **13** traffic circle **15** railway crossing

**intersperse**
**03** dot **06** pepper, spread **07** scatter **08** dispense, intermix, sprinkle **09** diversify, interlard, interpose, punctuate **10** distribute

**interstice**
**03** gap **04** gulf, hole, pore, rent, rift, void **05** blank, chink, cleft, crack, space **06** areola, breach, cavity, cranny, divide, lacuna **07** crevice, opening, orifice **08** aperture, fracture

**intertwine**
**03** mix **04** coil, knit, lace **05** blend, braid, cross, plait, pleat, twine, twirl, twist, weave **06** pleach, writhe **07** connect, entwine **08** empleach, impleach **09** interlace, interlink, interwind **10** interweave **12** link together

**interval**
**03** gap **04** leap, lull, rest, time, wait **05** break, comma, delay, pause, space, spell **06** period, recess, season **07** interim, opening **08** breather, distance, meantime **09** in-between, interlude, meanwhile **10** interspace **11** intervallum, parenthesis **12** intermission **14** breathing space

**intervene**
**04** pass **05** arise, occur **06** befall, elapse, happen, step in **07** intrude, mediate **08** separate **09** arbitrate, intercede, interfere, interrupt, negotiate **10** come to pass

**• intervene boldly**
**02** up

**intervening**
**06** middle **07** between, mediate **09** in-between **11** interjacent, interposing **12** intercurrent, intermediate, intervenient

**intervention**
**06** agency **09** intrusion, mediation **10** stepping-in **11** arbitration, involvement, negotiation **12** intercession, interference, interruption **13** interposition

**interview**
**03** vet **04** talk, viva **05** grill **06** assess, talk to **07** examine, meeting **08** audience, dialogue, evaluate, one-to-one, question, sound out **09** appraisal, encounter, tête-à-tête **10** assessment, conference, discussion, evaluation **11** interrogate **12** consultation, cross-examine **13** cross-question **15** oral examination, press conference

**interviewer**
**08** assessor, examiner, reporter **09** appraiser, evaluator **10** inquisitor, questioner **11** interrogant **12** interlocutor, interrogator, investigator **13** correspondent

**interweave**
**03** mat, mix **04** coil, knit **05** blend, braid, cross, plash, twine, twist, weave **06** raddle, splice, tissue **07** connect, entwine, perplex **08** complect **09** interlace, interlink, interlock, interwind, interwork **10** criss-cross, intertwine, intertwist, reticulate **11** intermingle, intertangle **12** interconnect, interwreathe, link together

**intestinal**
**05** ileac **07** coeliac, enteric, gastric **08** duodenal, internal, visceral **09** abdominal, stomachic **10** splanchnic

**intestines**
**04** guts **05** colon, offal **06** bowels, casing, vitals **07** innards, insides, viscera **08** entrails **09** chidlings, chitlings **11** chitterling **12** chitterlings

**intimacy**
**06** warmth **07** privacy **09** affection, closeness, connexion, knowledge **10** confidence, connection, friendship, inwardness **11** camaraderie, familiarity **13** understanding

**intimate**
**03** pal **04** boon, chum, cosy, cozy, dear, deep, hint, mate, maty, near, pack, snug, tell, tosh, warm **05** bosom, buddy, chief, china, close, crony, imply, matey, pally, palsy, privy, state, thick, tight **06** allude, belamy, chummy, friend, impart, intime, inward, secret, signal, strict, throng **07** Achates, comrade, declare, gremial, in-depth, private, special, suggest **08** alter ego, announce, detailed, familiar, friendly, indicate, informal, internal, personal, profound, thorough **09** associate, cherished, confidant, gemütlich, innermost, insinuate, make known, welcoming **10** best friend, better half, confidante, deep-seated, exhaustive, give notice, palsy-walsy **11** bosom friend, cater-cousin, close friend, communicate, penetrating **12** affectionate, confidential, fidus Achates, heart-to-heart, let it be known **13** boon companion **14** well-acquainted

*See also* **friend**

**intimately**
**04** well **05** fully **06** deeply, nearly, warmly **07** closely **08** commonly, in detail, tenderly **09** inside out, privately **10** familiarly, personally, thoroughly **11** confidingly, hand in glove **12** exhaustively, hand and glove, particularly **14** affectionately, confidentially

**intimation**
**04** hint, note **05** sniff **06** notice, signal **07** inkling, warning **08** allusion, innuendo, reminder **09** reference, statement **10** indication, suggestion **11** declaration, implication, insinuation **12** announcement **13** communication

**intimidate**
**03** cow **05** alarm, appal, bully, daunt, get at, scare **06** coerce, compel, dismay, extort, lean on, menace, subdue **07** overawe, terrify, warn off **08** ballyrag, browbeat, bulldoze, bullyrag, domineer, frighten, pressure, psych out, threaten **09** blackmail, terrorize, tyrannize **10** pressurize **13** turn the heat on **14** put the screws on

**intimidation**
**04** fear **06** screws, terror **07** menaces, threats **08** big stick, bullying, coercion, pressure **10** compulsion, terrifying **11** arm-twisting, browbeating, domineering, frighteners, frightening, terrorizing, threatening **12** scare tactics **13** sabre-rattling, terrorization, tyrannization

**intolerable**
**05** awful **06** the end, too bad **08** dreadful, the limit **09** loathsome **10** detestable, impossible, unbearable **11** unendurable **12** insufferable, the last straw, unacceptable **13** beyond the pale, insupportable

**intolerably**
**10** impossibly, shockingly, unbearably **11** repugnantly **12** insufferably, outrageously

**intolerance**
**06** ageism, racism, sexism **07** bigotry **08** jingoism **09** dogmatism, extremism, prejudice, racialism **10** chauvinism, fanaticism, impatience, insularity, narrowness, xenophobia **12** anti-Semitism, illiberality **14** discrimination **15** small-mindedness

**intolerant**
**06** ageist, biased, narrow, racist, sexist **07** bigoted, insular, redneck **08** dogmatic, one-sided, partisan **09** extremist, fanatical, illiberal, impatient, parochial, racialist **10** jingoistic, prejudiced, provincial, xenophobic **11** anti-Semitic, opinionated, persecuting, small-minded **12** chauvinistic, incompatible, narrow-minded, uncharitable **14** discriminating

**intonation**
**02** Om **04** lilt, tone **05** pitch, twang **06** stress, timbre **07** cadence **08** emphasis **10** expression, inflection, modulation **12** accentuation

**intone**
**03** say **04** sing **05** chant, croon, speak, utter, voice **06** chaunt, incant, recite **07** declaim **08** intonate, monotone **09** enunciate, pronounce **10** cantillate

**intoxicate**
◇ *anagram indicator*
**04** corn **05** elate **06** excite, fuddle, poison, sozzle, thrill **07** animate, enthuse, inflame, inspire, stupefy **08** befuddle, disguise **09** inebriate, make drunk, stimulate **10** exhilarate

**intoxicated**
◇ *anagram indicator*
**04** full, high, inky, winy **05** drunk, happy, inked, lit up, merry, moppy, moved, tight, tipsy, winey, woozy **06** blotto, bombed, canned, corked, elated, groggy, in wine, jarred, juiced, loaded, mortal, ripped, soused, stewed, stinko, stoned, tiddly, wasted, zonked **07** bevvied, blasted, blitzed, bonkers, bottled, coked-up, crocked, drunken, ebriate, ebriose, excited, half-cut, in drink, legless, maggoty, pickled, pie-eyed, sloshed, smashed, sozzled, squiffy, stirred, tiddled, wrecked **08** besotted, bibulous, ebriated, footless, hammered, in liquor, juiced up, liquored, moon-eyed, sow-drunk, steaming, stocious, tanked up, thrilled, whiffled, whistled, worked up **09** crapulent, inebriate, paralytic, pixilated, plastered, shickered, up the pole, well-oiled, zonked out **10** blind drunk, inebriated, obfuscated, pixillated, stimulated, whiskified **11** carried away, exhilarated, whiskeyfied **12** drunk as a lord, drunk as a newt, enthusiastic, roaring drunk **13** drunk as a piper, having had a few, in high spirits, under the table **14** Brahms and Liszt **15** one over the eight, the worse for wear, under the weather

*See also* **drunk**

**intoxicating**
**05** heady **06** moving, strong **07** rousing **08** dramatic, exciting, stirring **09** alcoholic, inebriant, inspiring, methystic, stimulant, thrilling **11** enthralling, stimulating **12** exhilarating **15** going to your head

**intoxication**
**06** fuddle, thrill **07** elation, rapture **08** euphoria, methysis, pleasure **09** animation, inebriety, poisoning, temulence, temulency, tipsiness **10** alcoholism, crapulence, debauchery, dipsomania, enthusiasm, excitement, insobriety **11** drunkenness, inebriation, stimulation **12** bibulousness, exhilaration, hard drinking, intemperance **15** serious drinking

**intractability**
**08** obduracy **09** obstinacy **10** perversity **11** awkwardness, waywardness **12** contrariness, indiscipline, perverseness, stubbornness **13** pig-headedness, unamenability **15** incorrigibility, ungovernability

**intractable**
**04** hard, wild **05** tough **06** kittle, unruly, wilful **07** awkward, frampal, haggard, problem, unwayed, wayward **08** contrary, frampold, obdurate, perverse, stubborn **09** difficult, fractious, obstinate, pig-headed, unbending **10** headstrong, monolithic, refractory, self-willed, unamenable, unyielding **11** disobedient, untreatable **12** cantankerous, cross-grained, intransigent, ungovernable, unmanageable **13** unco-operative, undisciplined **14** uncontrollable

**intransigence**
**08** obduracy, tenacity **09** toughness **10** obstinancy **12** stubbornness **13** determination, implacability, inflexibility, pig-headedness **14** intractability, relentlessness

**intransigent**
**05** rigid, tough **06** uppity **08** hardline, obdurate, stubborn **09** immovable, obstinate, pig-headed, tenacious, unbending **10** determined,

implacable, inexorable, inflexible, relentless, unamenable, unyielding **11** intractable, unbudgeable, unrelenting **12** bloody-minded **13** unpersuadable **14** irreconcilable, uncompromising

**intrepid**
**04** bold **05** brave, gutsy **06** daring, gritty, heroic, plucky, spunky **07** doughty, gallant, valiant **08** fearless, spirited, stalwart, unafraid, valorous **09** audacious, dauntless, undaunted **10** courageous, undismayed **11** lion-hearted, unflinching **12** stout-hearted

**intrepidness**
**04** grit, guts **05** nerve, pluck **06** daring, spirit, valour **07** bravery, courage, heroism, prowess **08** audacity, boldness **09** fortitude, gallantry **11** doughtiness, intrepidity **12** fearlessness **13** dauntlessness, undauntedness **15** lion-heartedness

**intricacy**
**06** enigma **09** obscurity **10** complexity, involution, knottiness, perplexity **11** complexness, convolution, involvement **12** complication, convolutions, entanglement **13** complexedness, elaborateness, intricateness **14** sophistication

**intricate**
◇ *anagram indicator*
**05** dedal, fancy **06** daedal, knotty, ornate, rococo, twisty **07** complex, finicky, Gordian, tangled **08** baffling, intrince, involved, puzzling, ravelled, tortuous **09** Byzantine, contrived, difficult, elaborate, enigmatic, entangled **10** convoluted, perplexing **11** complicated **12** intrinsicate, tirlie-wirlie **13** sophisticated

**intrigue**
**03** web **04** draw, pack, plot, pull, ruse, wile **05** amour, cabal, charm, dodge, junta, rivet **06** absorb, affair, brigue, puzzle, scheme **07** affaire, attract, connive, consult, liaison, romance, traffic **08** artifice, collogue, conspire, interest, intimacy, trickery **09** captivate, collusion, conniving, fascinate, gallantry, machinate, manoeuvre, stratagem, tantalize, undermine **10** conspiracy, courtcraft, dirty trick, love affair, manipulate **11** beguilement, machination **12** machinations **13** double-dealing, sharp practice, work the oracle **15** practise against

**intriguer**
**06** Jesuit **07** plotter, schemer, wangler **08** conniver **09** intrigant, trinketer **10** intrigante, machinator, politician, wire-puller **11** conspirator **12** collaborator **13** Machiavellian, wheeler-dealer

**intriguing**
**07** politic **08** charming, exciting, puzzling, riveting **09** absorbing, appealing, beguiling, diverting, stairwork **10** attractive, compelling **11** captivating, fascinating, interesting, tantalizing, titillating

**intrinsic**
**05** basic **06** inborn, inbred, inward, native **07** built-in, central, genuine, in-built, natural, radical **08** inherent, integral, interior, internal **09** elemental, essential **10** congenital, indigenous, underlying **11** fundamental **14** constitutional

**intrinsically**
**08** in itself, inwardly **09** basically, centrally **10** inherently, integrally **11** essentially **12** by definition **13** constituently, fundamentally

**introduce**
◇ *containment indicator*
**03** add **04** open **05** begin, float, found, immit, offer, plant, put in, start **06** induct, inject, insert, launch, lead in, prolog, submit **07** advance, bring in, develop, precede, preface, present, propose, suggest, usher in **08** acquaint, announce, commence, initiate, intromit, lead into, organize, prologue **09** establish, instigate, institute, originate **10** inaugurate, put forward **11** familiarize, put in motion, set in motion

**• be introduced to**
**04** meet

**introduction**
◇ *head selection indicator*
**05** debut, intro, proem, start **06** basics, entrée, launch, lead-in **07** baptism, opening, preface, prelude **08** exordium, foreword, overture, preamble, prologue **09** beginning, knock-down, rudiments **10** essentials, initiation **11** acquainting, development, front matter, institution, origination, prolegomena **12** announcement, commencement, fundamentals, inauguration, intromission, organization, presentation, prolegomenon **13** establishment, preliminaries **15** familiarization, first principles

**introductory**
**05** basic, early, first **07** initial, opening **08** exordial, isagogic, starting **09** beginning, essential, inaugural, prefatory, prelusory **10** elementary, initiative, initiatory, precursory **11** fundamental, preliminary, preparatory, rudimentary

**introspection**
**08** brooding **11** navel-gazing, pensiveness **12** introversion, self-analysis **13** contemplation, soul-searching **14** heart-searching, thoughtfulness **15** self-centredness, self-examination, self-observation

**introspective**
**06** musing **07** pensive **08** brooding, reserved **09** withdrawn **10** meditative, subjective, thoughtful **11** introverted, self-centred **12** self-absorbed **13** contemplative, inward-looking, self-analysing, self-examining, self-observing

**introverted**
**03** shy **05** quiet **08** reserved **09** withdrawn **11** self-centred **12** self-absorbed **13** introspective, inward-looking, self-examining

**intrude**
**04** sorn **05** abate **06** butt in, chip in, invade, meddle, thrust **07** aggress, barge in, impinge, obtrude, violate **08** encroach, infringe, trespass **09** gatecrash, interfere, interject, interlope, interrupt

**intruder**
**05** thief **06** raider, robber **07** burglar, invader, prowler **08** Derby dog, pilferer **10** interloper, trespasser **11** gatecrasher, infiltrator **12** housebreaker **14** unwelcome guest

**intrusion**
**04** vein **08** invasion, lopolith, meddling, trespass **09** incursion, obtrusion, phacolith, violation **12** encroachment, gatecrashing, impertinence, impertinency, infringement, interference, interruption

**intrusive**
**04** nosy **05** nosey, pushy **06** prying **07** forward **08** annoying, intruded, invasive, snooping, unwanted **09** go-getting, obtrusive, officious, uninvited, unwelcome **10** disturbing, irritating, meddlesome **11** impertinent, importunate, interfering, trespassing, troublesome, uncalled-for **12** interrupting, presumptuous

**intuition**
**03** ESP **05** hunch **06** belief **07** feeling, insight **08** instinct **10** gut feeling, perception, sixth sense **11** discernment, premonition **12** anticipation, presentiment **13** light of nature

**intuitive**
**06** inborn, innate **08** untaught, visceral **09** automatic, unlearned **11** instinctive, intuitional, involuntary, spontaneous

**intuitively**
**08** innately **10** by instinct **13** automatically, instinctively, spontaneously

**inundate**
**04** bury, soak **05** drown, flood, swamp **06** deluge, engulf **07** immerse, overrun **08** overflow, saturate, submerge **09** overwhelm **10** overburden

**inundation**
**04** glut **05** flood, spate, swamp **06** deluge, excess **07** surplus, torrent **08** diluvion, diluvium, overflow **09** land-flood, tidal wave **10** water flood

**inure**
**03** use **05** flesh, train **06** commit, harden, season, temper **07** toughen **08** accustom, practise **09** habituate **10** strengthen **11** acclimatize, desensitize, familiarize

**invade**
◇ *insertion indicator*
**04** raid **05** enter, seize, storm **06** attack, infest, maraud, occupy **07** assault, burst in, conquer, intrude, obtrude, overrun, pervade, pillage, plunder, violate **08** encroach, infringe, take over, trespass **09** descend on, interrupt, march into, penetrate, swarm over **10** infiltrate **12** enter by force

**invader**
**04** Dane **06** raider **08** attacker, intruder, marauder, pillager **09** aggressor, assailant, infringer, plunderer **10** trespasser

**invalid**
◇ *anagram indicator*
**03** ill **04** null, sick, void, weak **05** false, frail, wrong **06** ailing, feeble, infirm, poorly, sickly, unwell **07** chronic, expired, illegal, patient, quashed, revoked, unsound **08** baseless, disabled, informal, mistaken, sufferer **09** abolished, bedridden, cancelled, erroneous, illogical, incorrect, nullified, rescinded, unfounded, untenable, worthless **10** fallacious, groundless, ill-founded, irrational, overturned **11** debilitated, inoperative, null and void, unjustified, unwarranted **12** convalescent, unacceptable, unscientific **14** valetudinarian **15** unsubstantiated

**invalidate**
**04** undo, veto, void **05** annul, avoid, quash **06** cancel, negate, revoke, weaken **07** nullify, rescind, vitiate **08** abrogate, overrule **09** discredit, overthrow, terminate, undermine

**invalidity**
**07** fallacy, falsity, sophism **08** voidness **11** unsoundness **12** illogicality, speciousness **13** inconsistency, incorrectness, irrationality **14** fallaciousness

**invaluable**
**06** costly, useful **07** crucial **08** critical, precious, valuable **09** priceless **11** inestimable **12** incalculable **13** indispensable

**invariable**
**03** set **05** fixed, rigid **06** stable, steady **07** regular, uniform **08** constant, habitual **09** immutable, invariant, permanent, unvarying **10** changeless, consistent, inflexible, unchanging, unwavering **11** unalterable **12** unchangeable

**invariably**
**06** always **09** regularly **10** constantly, habitually, inevitably, repeatedly **11** unfailingly, without fail **12** consistently

**invasion**
**04** raid **05** foray **06** attack, breach, sepsis **07** descent **08** Overlord, storming **09** incursion, intrusion, irruption, offensive, onslaught, violation **10** occupation **11** penetration **12** encroachment, infiltration, infringement, interference, interruption

**invective**
**05** abuse **06** rebuke, satire, tirade, verbal **07** censure, obloquy, sarcasm **08** berating, diatribe, reproach, scolding **09** contumely, philippic, reprimand **10** revilement **11** castigation, fulmination **12** denunciation, vilification, vituperation **13** recrimination, tongue-lashing

**inveigh**
**04** rail **05** blame, scold **06** berate, revile **07** censure, condemn, lambast, thunder, upbraid **08** denounce, reproach, sound off **09** castigate, criticize, fulminate **10** tongue-lash, vituperate **11** expostulate, recriminate

**inveigle**
**03** con **04** coax, lure, wile **05** decoy **06** allure, cajole, entice, entrap, lead on, seduce **07** beguile, ensnare, wheedle **08** persuade **09** bamboozle, manoeuvre, sweet-talk **10** manipulate

**invent**
**04** coin, fain, find, mint, plan **05** fable, faine, fayne, feign, frame **06** cook up, create, design, devise, father, make up **07** concoct, dream up, hit upon, imagine, pioneer, think up, trump up **08** conceive, contrive, discover, innovate **09** fabricate, formulate, improvise, originate **10** come up with **11** confabulate, manufacture **12** swing the lead

**invented**
**03** inv **06** made up **09** trumped-up **10** fictitious

**invention**
◇ *anagram indicator*
**03** fib, lie, wit **04** baby, fake, gift, idea, myth **05** skill **06** deceit, design, device, gadget, genius, system, talent **07** coinage, coining, concept, fantasy, fiction, figment, forgery, machine, untruth **08** artistry, creation **09** discovery, falsehood, ingenuity, tall story **10** brainchild, concoction, contriving, creativity, innovation **11** contrivance, development, fabrication, imagination, inspiration, originality, origination **12** construction, contrivement, excogitation **13** falsification, inventiveness **15** resourcefulness

**inventive**
**06** clever, devise, gifted **07** fertile, skilful **08** artistic, contrive, creative, inspired, original, pregnant, talented **09** ingenious **10** innovative **11** imaginative, resourceful

**inventiveness**
**04** gift **05** power, skill **06** talent **10** creativity, enterprise, innovation **11** imagination, inspiration, originality **13** ingeniousness **14** innovativeness **15** imaginativeness, resourcefulness

**inventor**
**05** maker **06** author, coiner, father, framer, mother **07** creator, deviser **08** designer, engineer, producer **09** architect, developer, innovator, scientist, sloganeer **10** discoverer, mint master, originator **11** emblematist **12** palindromist

*Inventors include:*

**03** Sax (Antoine Joseph)
**04** Abel (Sir Frederick), Bell (Alexander Graham), Benz (Karl), Biro (Laszlo), Colt (Samuel), Davy (Sir Humphry), Hood (Thomas), Jobs (Steve), Land (Edwin Herbert), Moon (William), Otis (Elisha Graves), Swan (Sir Joseph Wilson), Tull (Jethro), Watt (James), Yale (Linus)
**05** Baird (John Logie), Boehm (Theobald), Boyle (Robert), Cyril (St), Dyson (James), Hertz (Heinrich), Kilby (Jack S), Maxim (Sir Hiram Stevens), Monge (Gaspard), Morse (Samuel), Nobel (Alfred), Rubik (Ernö), Sousa (John Philip), Tesla (Nikola), Volta (Alessandro, Count), Zeiss (Carl)
**06** Ampère (André Marie), Brunel (Isambard Kingdom), Brunel (Sir Marc Isambard), Bunsen (Robert Wilhelm), Diesel (Rudolf), Dunlop (John Boyd), Eckert (J Presper), Edison (Thomas Alva), Frisch (Otto), Hansom (Joseph Aloysius), Hornby (Frank), Hubble (Edwin Powell), Lenoir (Jean Joseph Étienne), Lister (Samuel, Lord), McAdam (John Loudon), Napier (John), Newton (Sir Isaac), Pascal (Blaise), Pitman (Sir Isaac), Schick (Jacob), Singer (Isaac Merritt), Sperry (Elmer Ambrose), Talbot (William Henry Fox), Wallis (Sir Barnes), Wright (Orville), Wright (Wilbur)
**07** Babbage (Charles), Blériot (Louis), Carlson (Chester Floyd), Daimler (Gottlieb), Drebbel (Cornelis), Eastman (George), Faraday (Michael), Gaumont (Léon), Giffard (Henri), Goddard (Robert Hutchings), Huygens (Christiaan), Jacuzzi (Candido), Janssen (Zacharias), Lumière (Auguste), Lumière (Louis Jean), Marconi (Guglielmo), Mauchly (John W), Maxwell (James Clerk), Pasteur (Louis), Pullman (George Mortimer), Thomson (Elihu), Whitney (Eli), Whittle (Sir Frank)
**08** Bessemer (Sir Henry), Birdseye (Clarence), Daguerre (Louis Jacques Mandé), De Forest (Lee), Ericsson (John), Ferranti (Sebastian Ziani de), Franklin (Benjamin), Gillette (King Camp), Goodyear

(Charles), **Huntsman** (Benjamin), **Newcomen** (Thomas), **Sandwich** (John Montagu, Earl), **Sinclair** (Sir Clive), **Zamenhof** (Lazarus Ludwig), **Zeppelin** (Ferdinand von, Count)
**09** **Arkwright** (Sir Richard), **Armstrong** (Edwin Howard), **Butterick** (Ebenezer), **Cockerell** (Sir Christopher Sydney), **Ctesibius**, **Fessenden** (Reginald Aubrey), **Gutenberg** (Johannes), **Hollerith** (Herman), **Macmillan** (Kirkpatrick), **McCormick** (Cyrus Hall), **Pinchbeck** (Christopher), **Remington** (Philo), **Whitworth** (Sir Joseph)
**10** **Archimedes**, **Berners-Lee** (Tim), **Cristofori** (Bartolommeo), **Fahrenheit** (Gabriel), **Lilienthal** (Otto), **Pilkington** (Sir Alastair), **Senefelder** (Aloys), **Stephenson** (George), **Torricelli** (Evangelista), **Trevithick** (Richard)
**11** **Montgolfier** (Jacques), **Montgolfier** (Joseph)
**12** **Friese-Greene** (William)

**inventory**
**04** file, list, roll **05** stock, sum up, tally **06** record, roster, scroll, supply **07** account, listing, terrier **08** register, schedule **09** catalogue, checklist, equipment **11** description, stocktaking

**inverse**
**05** other **07** counter, obverse, reverse **08** contrary, converse, inverted, opposite, reversed **10** reciprocal, retrograde, transposed, upside down **12** antistrophic

**inversion**
◇ *reversal indicator*
**07** reverse **08** contrary, converse, opposite, reversal **09** entropion, entropium **10** anastrophe, antithesis, transposal **11** contrariety **13** transposition **14** antimetathesis, contraposition

**invert**
◇ *reversal indicator*
**05** upset **06** turn up, upturn **07** capsize, reverse **08** overturn, turn down **09** transpose **10** homosexual, turn around, turn turtle **11** transsexual **13** turn inside out **14** turn upside down **15** turn back to front

**invertebrate**

*Invertebrates include:*

**05** coral, fluke, hydra, leech
**06** chiton, insect, spider, sponge
**07** bivalve, crinoid, mollusc, sea lily, sea wasp
**08** arachnid, flatworm, nematode, sea pansy, starfish, tapeworm
**09** arthropod, centipede, earthworm, gastropod, jellyfish, millipede, planarian, roundworm, sea spider, sea urchin, spoonworm, trilobite, water bear
**10** cephalopod, crustacean, echinoderm, sand dollar, sea anemone, tardigrade
**11** annelid worm, brittle star, chaetognath, feather star, sea cucumber
**12** box jellyfish, coelenterate, Venus's girdle
**13** crown-of-thorns, horseshoe crab, sea gooseberry
**15** dead-men's fingers

*See also* **animal**; **butterfly**; **crustacean**; **insect**; **mollusc**; **moth**; **spider**; **worm**

**invest**
◇ *hidden indicator*
◇ *insertion indicator*
**03** put **04** belt, fund, give, gown, robe, sink, vest **05** admit, adorn, cover, crown, endow, endue, frock, grant, imbue, place, put in, spend, tie up **06** bestow, clothe, confer, create, devote, enrobe, induct, lay out, lock up, ordain, supply **07** besiege, dignify, empower, entrust, install, mandate, provide, swear in **08** dedicate, sanction, surround **09** authorize, beglamour, subsidize **10** contribute, inaugurate

**investigate**
**03** spy, sus **04** case, comb, feel, sift, suss **05** probe, study, trawl **06** go into, muzzle, nuzzle, pry out, search **07** analyse, check up, examine, explore, inspect, suss out **08** check out, consider, look into, research **09** delve into **10** scrutinize **11** inquire into **15** give the once-over

**investigation**
**05** probe, quest, study **06** review, search, survey **07** enquiry, hearing, inquest, inquiry, sifting, zetetic **08** analysis, research, scrutiny **10** inspection **11** examination, exploration, inquisition **13** consideration
• **bear investigation**
**04** wash

**investigative**
**07** zetetic **08** research **09** heuristic **10** analytical, inspecting **11** exploratory, fact-finding, researching **13** investigating

**investigator**
**02** PI **04** dick **06** ferret, prober, sleuth **07** analyst **08** analyser, examiner, explorer, inquirer, quaestor, reviewer, searcher **09** detective, inspector **10** private eye, questioner, researcher, scrutineer **11** scrutinizer

**investiture**
**09** admission, induction, investing **10** coronation, investment, ordination, swearing-in **11** instatement **12** enthronement, inauguration, installation

**investment**
**04** cash, gilt, risk, spec **05** asset, funds, money, stake, stock **06** outlay, wealth **07** capital, finance, reserve, savings, venture **08** blockade, property **09** principal, resources **11** expenditure, investiture, speculation, transaction **12** contribution **14** venture capital

**inveterate**
**05** sworn **06** inured **07** chronic, diehard **08** addicted, habitual, hard-core, hardened, stubborn **09** confirmed, incurable, obstinate **10** double-dyed, entrenched **11** established **12** incorrigible, irreformable, long-standing **13** dyed-in-the-wool

**invidious**
**06** odious **07** awkward, hateful **08** enviable **09** difficult, obnoxious, offensive, repugnant, slighting **10** unpleasant **11** undesirable **13** objectionable **14** discriminating, discriminatory

**invigilate**
**05** watch **06** direct **07** inspect, monitor, oversee **09** look after, supervise, watch over **11** keep an eye on, superintend **12** be in charge of **13** be in control of

**invigilation**
**04** care **06** charge **07** control, running **08** guidance **09** direction, oversight **10** inspection **11** supervision **12** surveillance **15** superintendence

**invigilator**
**07** monitor, proctor **08** director, examiner, overseer **09** inspector **10** supervisor **14** superintendent

**invigorate**
**04** buck **05** brace, pep up, renew, rouse **06** buck up, excite, perk up, soup up **07** animate, enliven, fortify, freshen, inspire, liven up, quicken, refresh **08** energize, motivate, vitalize **09** stimulate **10** exhilarate, rejuvenate, revitalize, strengthen

**invigorating**
**05** brisk, fresh, tonic, vital **07** bracing **08** generous **09** animating, healthful, uplifting, vivifying **10** energizing, fortifying, life-giving, quickening, refreshing, salubrious **11** inspiriting, restorative, stimulating **12** exhilarating, rejuvenating

**invincibility**
**05** force, power **08** strength **13** inviolability **14** impregnability, insuperability **15** impenetrability, invulnerability, unassailability

**invincible**
**08** almighty **10** unbeatable, unshakable, unyielding **11** all-powerful, impregnable, indomitable, insuperable, unshakeable **12** impenetrable, invulnerable, unassailable, undefeatable **13** unconquerable **14** indestructible, unsurmountable

**inviolability**
**08** holiness, sanctity **09** inviolacy **10** sacredness **14** inalienability, inviolableness, sacrosanctness **15** invulnerability

**inviolable**
**04** holy **06** sacred **08** hallowed
**10** intemerate, sacrosanct
**11** inalienable, unalterable, untouchable

**inviolate**
**04** pure **05** whole **06** entire, intact, sacred, unhurt, virgin **08** complete, unbroken, unharmed **09** stainless, undamaged, undefiled, uninjured, unspoiled, unstained, unsullied, untouched **10** intemerate, unpolluted, unprofaned **11** undisturbed

**invisible**
**05** blind **06** hidden, unseen
**08** viewless **09** concealed, disguised, imaginary, occulting, sightless, unnoticed, unseeable **10** evaporated, out of sight, unobserved
**11** microscopic, non-existent
**12** undetectable **13** imperceivable, imperceptible, inconspicuous, indiscernible, infinitesimal, microscopical **14** dematerialized

**invitation**
**04** bait, call, draw, lure **06** appeal, come-on, invite **07** bidding, request, summons, welcome **08** overture, petition **09** challenge **10** allurement, attraction, come-hither, enticement, incitement, inducement, temptation
**11** proposition, provocation
**12** solicitation **13** encouragement

**invite**
**03** ask, bid, woo **04** call, draw, lead, seek, will **05** press, tempt **06** allure, appeal, ask for, entice, summon
**07** attract, bring on, look for, provoke, request, solicit, welcome **08** have over, petition **09** encourage, entertain, have round **15** give the come-on to

**inviting**
**07** winning **08** alluring, engaging, enticing, pleasant, pleasing, tempting
**09** agreeable, appealing, beguiling, seductive, welcoming **10** attractive, bewitching, come-hither, delightful, enchanting, entrancing, intriguing
**11** captivating, fascinating, tantalizing
**12** irresistible

**invocation**
**04** call **05** curse **06** appeal, prayer
**07** request, summons **08** entreaty, petition **09** epiclesis **10** beseeching
**11** benediction, conjuration, imploration **12** solicitation, supplication
• **expression of invocation**
**02** io

**invoice**
**03** inv **04** bill **07** account, charges
**08** manifest, pro forma **09** reckoning

**invoke**
**03** beg **04** cite, wish **05** curse, swear
**06** call on, pray to, rabbit, turn to
**07** beseech, conjure, entreat, implore, refer to, request, solicit, swear by
**08** appeal to, call down, call upon, petition, resort to **09** deprecate, imprecate, make use of **10** supplicate
**14** have recourse to

**involuntary**
**05** blind **06** forced, reflex **07** coerced
**08** knee-jerk, unwilled **09** automatic, compelled, impulsive, mandatory, reluctant, unwilling **10** compulsory, mechanical, obligatory, unthinking
**11** conditioned, instinctive, spontaneous, unconscious
**12** uncontrolled **13** unintentional

**involve**
◇ *anagram indicator*
◇ *insertion indicator*
**03** mix **04** cost, grip, hold, mean, wind, wrap **05** cover, imply, infer, mix up, rivet **06** absorb, affect, assume, commit, denote, draw in, engage, entail, mess in, occupy, take in
**07** concern, connect, connote, count in, dip into, embrace, embroil, engross, immerse, include, require **08** entangle, interest, mess with, walk into
**09** associate, embarrass, encompass, implicate, inculpate, preoccupy
**10** complicate, comprehend, compromise, presuppose
**11** incorporate, incriminate, necessitate **15** cause to take part

**involved**
◇ *anagram indicator*
**04** deep, held, in on **06** implex, knotty
**07** complex, engaged, gripped, jumbled, mixed up, riveted, tangled
**08** absorbed, caught up, confused, immersed, intorted, involute, occupied, plighted, tortuous
**09** concerned, confusing, difficult, elaborate, engrossed, intricate
**10** associated, convoluted, implicated, inculpated, interested, taking part
**11** anfractuous, complicated, preoccupied **12** incriminated, inextricable **13** participating
• **involved with**
◇ *insertion indicator*
**02** in

**involvement**
**04** part **05** share **06** action
**07** concern **08** interest **09** immersion
**10** attachment, connection
**11** association, implication
**12** contribution, entanglement
**13** participation **14** responsibility

**invulnerability**
**05** proof **06** safety **08** security, strength **13** invincibility, inviolability
**14** impregnability **15** impenetrability, unassailability

**invulnerable**
**04** safe **05** proof **06** secure
**09** woundless **10** impervious, invincible **12** impenetrable, unassailable **14** indestructible

**inward**
**02** in **05** inner **06** entire, hidden, infelt, inmost, inside, secret, toward
**07** private **08** entering, homefelt, incoming, interior, internal, intimate, introrse, involute, personal, turned-in
**09** heartfelt, incurrent, innermost, intrinsic **11** intrinsical **12** confidential

**inwardly**
**04** inly **06** inside, within **07** at heart
**08** deep down, secretly **09** privately
**10** to yourself **13** deep inside you

**inwards**
**06** inside, inward, within **07** indoors
**08** inwardly

**iodine**
**01** I

**iota**
**03** bit, jot, tad **04** atom, hint, mite, whit
**05** grain, scrap, speck, trace **06** morsel
**08** fraction, particle

**Iowa**
**02** IA

**Iran**
**02** IR **03** IRN

**Iraq**
**03** IRQ

**irascibility**
**06** choler **08** edginess **09** bad temper, crossness, fieriness, ill-temper, petulance, shortness, testiness
**10** crabbiness, impatience, irritation, touchiness **12** irritability, snappishness

**irascible**
**05** cross, hasty, narky, ratty, testy
**06** crabby, touchy **07** crabbed, iracund, prickly, toustie **08** choleric, petulant **09** irritable, querulous **10** ill-natured **11** bad-tempered, hot-tempered, ill-tempered
**12** cantankerous, iracundulous
**13** quick-tempered, short-tempered

**irate**
**03** mad **04** waxy **05** angry, livid, vexed
**06** fuming, raging **07** annoyed, enraged, furious, ranting **08** incensed, up in arms, worked up **09** indignant, irritated, pissed off, steamed up
**10** hopping mad, infuriated
**11** exasperated

**irately**
**07** angrily, crossly, in a huff **08** bitterly
**09** furiously **11** indignantly, resentfully
**13** acrimoniously, reproachfully

**ire**
**04** fury, rage **05** anger, wrath
**06** choler **07** passion **09** annoyance
**11** displeasure, indignation
**12** exasperation

**Ireland**
**03** IRL **04** Éire, Erin **08** Hibernia
**09** Green Isle **11** blarney-land, Emerald Isle

*Irish cities and notable towns include:*

**04** Cork
**05** Sligo
**06** Dublin, Galway
**07** Dundalk
**08** Drogheda, Limerick
**09** Waterford

*See also* **county**; **province**

**iridescent**
**04** shot **06** flambé, pearly **07** rainbow **08** dazzling **09** chatoyant, prismatic, sparkling **10** glittering, opalescent, shimmering, variegated **11** rainbow-like **13** multicoloured, polychromatic **15** rainbow-coloured

**iridium**
**02** Ir

**iris**
**03** lis, seg **04** flag, irid, ixia **05** orris, sedge **07** gladdon **09** water flag **10** fleur-de-lis, fleur-de-lys **12** flower-delice, flower-deluce **13** flower-de-leuce **14** roast-beef plant

**Irish**
**02** Ir **04** Erse **08** Milesian **09** Hibernian

*See also* **Ireland**

*Irish first names include:*

**03** Ena, Kit, Pat, Una
**04** Aine, Cait, Colm, Edel, Elva, Eoin, Erin, Euan, Ewan, Ewen, Finn, Kath, Kyra, Liam, Maev, Maud, Mona, Neal, Neil, Nola, Nora, Nora, Owen, Rory, Ryan, Sean, Sine, Tara
**05** Aidan, Aiden, Barry, Brona, Cahal, Ciara, Colum, Conor, Duane, Dwane, Elvis, Ethna, Ethne, Fionn, Kelly, Kerry, Kevan, Kevin, Kiera, Maeve, Maire, Maude, Maura, Moira, Moyra, Neale, Niall, Niamh, Norah, Norah, Nuala, Oscar, Paddy, Ronan, Rowan, Shane, Shaun, Shawn, Ultan
**06** Aileen, Ailish, Arthur, Cathal, Ciaran, Connor, Declan, Dervla, Dympna, Eamonn, Eamunn, Eileen, Eithna, Eithne, Finbar, Fingal, Finola, Finola, Fintan, Garret, Grania, Granya, Kieran, Kieron, Kilian, Lorcan, Noreen, Noreen, Roisin, Seamas, Seamus, Shamus, Sheila, Sinead, Sorcha, Tyrone
**07** Aisling, Brendan, Bronach, Bronagh, Caitlin, Christy, Clodagh, Colleen, Deirdre, Desmond, Dymphna, Feargal, Finbarr, Grainne, Killian, Mairead, Maureen, Padraic, Padraig, Patrick, Shannon, Shelagh, Siobhan
**08** Kathleen, Ruaidhri
**09** Fionnuala, Fionnuala

**irk**
**03** bug, get, vex **04** gall, miff, rile **05** anger, annoy, get at, get to, weary **06** needle, nettle, put out, ruffle, wind up **07** disgust, incense, provoke **08** distress, drive mad, irritate **09** aggravate, infuriate **10** drive crazy, exasperate **12** drive bananas **13** make sparks fly **14** drive up the wall, piss someone off

**irksome**
**06** boring, trying, vexing **07** painful, tedious **08** annoying, infernal, tiresome **09** vexatious, wearisome **10** bothersome, burdensome, confounded, irritating, ungrateful **11** aggravating, infuriating, troublesome **12** disagreeable, exasperating

**iron**
**02** Fe **04** airn, firm, hard, Mars **05** harsh, press, rigid, stern, tough **06** fetter, pistol, robust, smooth, steely, strong **07** adamant, flatten, grating, stirrup **08** decrease, revolver, strength **10** determined, inflexible **11** insensitive **14** uncompromising

**• iron out**
**06** settle **07** clear up, resolve, sort out **08** deal with, get rid of, put right **09** eliminate, eradicate, harmonize, reconcile **13** straighten out

**ironic, ironical**
**03** wry **04** rich **05** bland **07** mocking **08** derisive, sardonic, scoffing, scornful, sneering **09** sarcastic, satirical **10** ridiculing, ridiculous **11** paradoxical **12** antiphrastic, contemptuous **14** antiphrastical

**irons**
**05** bonds **06** chains **07** fetters **08** manacles, shackles, trammels

**irony**
**04** hard **05** scorn **06** satire **07** asteism, mockery, paradox, sarcasm **08** ridicule **10** enantiosis **11** antiphrasis, incongruity **12** contrariness **14** sting in the tail

**irradiate**
**06** expose, illume **07** lighten, light up, radiate, shine on **08** brighten, illumine **09** enlighten **10** illuminate

**irrational**
**04** surd, wild **05** brute, crazy, silly **06** absurd, phobic, unwise **07** brutish, foolish, invalid, unsound **08** paranoid **09** arbitrary, beastlike, illogical, senseless **10** groundless, ridiculous **11** implausible, nonsensical, unreasoning **12** inconsistent, unreasonable **14** beside yourself

**irrationality**
**06** lunacy **07** madness **08** insanity, unreason **09** absurdity **11** unsoundness **12** illogicality **13** senselessness **14** groundlessness, ridiculousness

**irreconcilable**
**05** alien **06** at odds **07** opposed **08** clashing, contrary, frondeur, hardline, opposite **10** implacable, in conflict, inexorable, inflexible, unatonable **11** conflicting, incongruous **12** incompatible, inconsistent, intransigent **13** contradictory, intransigeant **14** uncompromising

**irrecoverable**
**04** lost **09** unsavable **11** irreparable **12** irredeemable, irremediable **13** irreclaimable, irretrievable, unrecoverable, unsalvageable

**irredeemable**
**08** past hope **09** incurable **10** beyond hope **11** irreparable, irrevocable **12** incorrigible **13** irretrievable

**irrefutable**
**04** sure **07** certain **08** decisive, definite, positive **10** unarguable, undeniable **11** beyond doubt, indubitable **12** indisputable, unanswerable **13** incontestable **14** beyond question, unquestionable

**irregular**
◇ *anagram indicator*
**03** odd **04** bent, iffy **05** bumpy, false, fishy, freak, lumpy, rough, shady, shaky **06** fitful, haiduk, jagged, patchy, pitted, ragged, random, rugged, shifty, sniper, uneven **07** corrupt, crooked, devious, erratic, lawless, scraggy, snatchy, strange, unusual, wayward **08** aberrant, abnormal, cheating, improper, indecent, lopsided, partisan, peculiar, scraggly, sporadic, unsteady, variable, wavering **09** anomalous, deceitful, dishonest, guerrilla, haphazard, incondite, maquisard, spasmodic, terrorist **10** asymmetric, asyntactic, disorderly, fraudulent, immoderate, mendacious, occasional, out of order, perfidious, scraggling, unofficial, unorthodox **11** anomalistic, bushwhacker, duplicitous, exceptional, extravagant, fluctuating, fragmentary, franc-tireur, guerrillero, heteroclite **12** disorganized, disreputable, immethodical, inconsistent, intermittent, unmethodical, unprincipled, unscrupulous, unsystematic **13** against the law, anomalistical, dishonourable, extraordinary, unsymmetrical **14** freedom fighter, unconventional **15** against the rules

**irregularity**
**05** fraud, freak, spasm **06** breach, deceit, oddity **07** anomaly, falsity, perfidy **08** cheating, trickery, wavering **09** arhythmia, asymmetry, bumpiness, chicanery, deviation, duplicity, falsehood, improbity, lumpiness, obliquity, roughness, shadiness, treachery **10** aberration, arrhythmia, corruption, dirty trick, dishonesty, fitfulness, jaggedness, misconduct, patchiness, raggedness, randomness, unevenness **11** abnormality, criminality, crookedness, fluctuation, fraudulence, impropriety, inconstancy, insincerity, lawlessness, malpractice, obliqueness, peculiarity, singularity, uncertainty, unorthodoxy, unusualness, variability **12** eccentricity, inordination, lopsidedness, perturbation, unsteadiness **13** double-dealing, haphazardness, inconsistency, intermittence, sharp practice, unpunctuality **14** disorderliness, occasionalness, untruthfulness **15** disorganization

**irregularly**
**06** anyhow **07** jerkily **08** fitfully, off and on, unevenly **11** erratically,

haphazardly, now and again **12** here and there, occasionally
**13** eccentrically, interruptedly, spasmodically **14** disconnectedly, intermittently, unmethodically **15** by fits and starts, in fits and starts

**irrelevance**
**07** tangent **09** inaptness **10** digression, red herring **11** irrelevancy
**12** unimportance **13** inconsequence, unrelatedness **14** extraneousness, inappositeness **15** inapplicability

**irrelevant**
**05** inapt, inept **09** not matter, ungermane, unrelated **10** extraneous, immaterial, inapposite, irrelative, out of place, peripheral, tangential **11** off the point, unconnected, unimportant
**12** inapplicable, inconsequent
**13** beside the mark, inappropriate
**14** beside the point **15** having no bearing, not coming into it

**irreligious**
**05** pagan **06** sinful, unholy, wicked
**07** godless, heathen, impious, profane, ungodly **08** agnostic, undevout
**09** atheistic, heretical, sceptical
**10** heathenish, irreverent
**11** blasphemous, nullifidian, unbelieving, unreligious, unrighteous
**12** free-thinking, iconoclastic, sacrilegious **13** rationalistic

**irremediable**
**05** fatal, final **06** deadly, mortal
**08** hopeless, terminal **09** incurable
**10** inoperable, remediless
**11** irreparable **12** incorrigible, irredeemable, irreversible
**13** irrecoverable, irretrievable, unmedicinable

**irremovable**
**03** set **04** fast **05** fixed, stuck
**06** rooted **07** durable **08** obdurate
**09** immovable, ingrained, obstinate, permanent **10** inoperable, persistent
**12** ineradicable **14** indestructible

**irreparable**
**09** incurable **12** irremediable, irreversible, unrepairable
**13** irreclaimable, irrecoverable, irretrievable

**irreplaceable**
**05** vital **06** unique **07** special
**08** peerless, precious **09** essential, matchless, priceless, unmatched
**13** indispensable

**irrepressible**
**06** bubbly, lively **07** buoyant
**08** animated **09** ebullient, energetic, resilient, vivacious **10** boisterous
**11** uninhibited, unstoppable
**12** effervescent, ungovernable
**13** uncontainable **14** insuppressible, uncontrollable, unrestrainable

**irreproachable**
**04** pure **07** perfect, sinless
**08** flawless, innocent, spotless
**09** blameless, faultless, guiltless, stainless **10** immaculate, impeccable, unblamable **11** unblemished
**13** unimpeachable **14** beyond reproach **15** irreprehensible

**irresistible**
**06** potent, urgent **07** killing
**08** alluring, almighty, charming, enticing, forceful, pressing, tempting
**09** ravishing, seductive **10** compelling, compulsive, enchanting, imperative, importable, inevitable, inexorable, opposeless, resistless **11** captivating, fascinating, inescapable, tantalizing, unavoidable **12** overpowering, overwhelming **13** insupportable, irrepressible, overmastering, unpreventable **14** uncontrollable

**irresolute**
**04** weak **06** fickle, unsure **07** dubious
**08** doubtful, hesitant, shifting, unstable, unsteady, variable, wavering
**09** dithering, tentative, uncertain, undecided, unsettled **10** ambivalent, hesitating, indecisive, in two minds, on the fence, unresolved, weak-willed, wishy-washy **11** fluctuating, half-hearted, vacillating **12** faint-hearted, invertebrate, pussyfooting, undetermined **15** shilly-shallying

**irrespective**
**• irrespective of**
**07** however, whoever **08** ignoring, no matter, whatever **09** never mind, whichever **12** disregarding, not affecting, regardless of
**15** notwithstanding

**irresponsible**
**04** rash, wild **06** unwise **07** erratic, flighty **08** carefree, careless, heedless, immature, reckless **09** negligent
**10** fly-by-night, unreliable
**11** injudicious, thoughtless **12** light-hearted **13** ill-considered, untrustworthy **14** scatterbrained

**irretrievable**
**04** lost **06** damned **08** hopeless
**11** irreparable, irrevocable
**12** irredeemable, irremediable, irreversible, unrecallable
**13** irrecoverable, unrecoverable, unsalvageable

**irretrievably**
**10** hopelessly **11** irreparably, irrevocably **12** irredeemably, irreversibly **13** irrecoverably

**irreverence**
**05** cheek, sauce **06** heresy, levity
**07** impiety, mockery **08** rudeness
**09** blasphemy, flippancy, impudence, insolence, profanity, sacrilege
**10** cheekiness, disrespect, irreligion
**11** discourtesy, godlessness, ungodliness **12** impertinence, impoliteness

**irreverent**
**04** rude **05** saucy **06** cheeky
**07** godless, impious, mocking, profane, ungodly **08** flippant, impolite, impudent, insolent
**09** heretical **10** unreverend
**11** blasphemous, impertinent, irreligious **12** discourteous, sacrilegious **13** disrespectful

**irreversible**
**05** final **07** lasting **08** hopeless
**09** incurable, permanent
**11** irreparable, irrevocable, unalterable
**12** irremediable **13** irretrievable, unrectifiable

**irrevocable**
**05** final, fixed **07** settled
**09** immutable **10** changeless, invariable **11** unalterable
**12** irreversible, unchangeable
**13** irretrievable, predetermined

**irrevocably**
**07** for good **10** hopelessly, inevitably
**11** inescapably, insuperably, irreparably, unavoidably **13** for good and all

**irrigate**
**03** wet **04** soak **05** drink, flood, spray, water **06** dampen, deluge **07** moisten
**08** inundate, sprinkle

**irritability**
**04** bile, edge **08** edginess, erethism
**09** bad temper, crossness, hastiness, ill-temper, petulance, rattiness, testiness
**10** crabbiness, grumpiness, impatience, tetchiness, touchiness
**11** fretfulness, peevishness, prickliness, stroppiness **12** irascibility
**13** fractiousness

**irritable**
**04** edgy, sore **05** cross, fiery, gusty, hasty, humpy, narky, ratty, riley, short, spiky, techy, testy **06** chippy, crabby, crusty, feisty, grumpy, livery, on edge, shirty, snappy, tetchy, touchy
**07** bilious, crabbit, fretful, gustful, peckish, peevish, peppery, prickly, stroppy **08** liverish, scratchy, snappish
**09** crotchety, fractious, impatient, irascible, splenetic **10** capernoity, hot-blooded, nettlesome **11** bad-tempered, capernoitie, cappernoity, ill-tempered, out of temper, thin-skinned **12** cantankerous **13** quick-tempered, short-tempered
**14** hypersensitive

**irritant**
**04** gall, goad, pain **05** CS gas, savin
**06** bother, menace, savine **07** trouble
**08** nuisance, urushiol, vexation
**09** annoyance **11** provocation
**15** thorn in the flesh

**irritate**
**03** bug, eat, get, irk, jar, rub, try, vex
**04** fret, gall, goad, grig, hurt, itch, miff, nark, rile **05** anger, annoy, chafe, get at, grate, peeve, rouse, tease **06** bother, emboil, enrage, excite, gravel, harass, jangle, needle, nettle, niggle, put out, rattle, ruffle, tickle, wind up
**07** enchafe, incense, inflame, provoke
**08** acerbate, drive mad **09** aggravate, displease, drive nuts, infuriate, stimulate **10** drive crazy, exasperate, excruciate **12** drive bananas **13** get

your back up, make sparks fly **14** drive up the wall, piss someone off, rub the wrong way **15** get on your nerves, give the needle to

**irritated**
◇ *anagram indicator*
**03** mad **04** edgy, sore **05** angry, cross, irked, raggy, ratty, riled, spewy, vexed **06** choked, miffed, narked, peeved, piqued, put out, roused **07** annoyed, crooked, in a huff, nettled, ropable, ruffled, stroppy, uptight **08** bothered, harassed, in a paddy, in a strop, up in arms **09** flappable, flustered, impatient, in a lather, irritable, pissed off, raving mad, seeing red, splenetic, ticked off **10** aggravated, displeased, exasperate, hopping mad
**11** discomposed, disgruntled, exacerbated, exasperated, fit to be tied **12** on the warpath

**irritating**
**04** sore **05** itchy, pesky **06** thorny, trying, vexing **07** chafing, galling, grating, irksome, nagging, rubbing
**08** abrasive, annoying, infernal, ticklish, tiresome, urticant
**09** maddening, provoking, upsetting, vexatious, worrisome **10** bothersome, confounded, disturbing
**11** aggravating, displeasing, infuriating, troublesome **12** excruciating

**irritation**
**03** rub **04** bind, drag, fret, fury, pain, pest **05** anger, pique **06** bother
**07** scunner, trouble **08** nuisance, pinprick, vexation **09** annoyance, crossness, testiness **10** impatience, snappiness **11** aggravation, displeasure, disturbance, indignation, provocation, running sore, stimulation
**12** exasperation, excruciation, heeby-jeebies, irritability **13** heebie-jeebies, pain in the neck **15** dissatisfaction, thorn in the flesh

*See also* **itch**

**• display of irritation**
**04** tiff, tift

**is**
**01** 's **03** est

**Islamic** *see* **month**

**island**
**01** I **02** Is **03** ait, cay, île, Isl, key
**04** eyot, holm, inch, isle **05** atoll, islet
**06** skerry **07** isolate **11** archipelago

*Islands and island groups include:*

**03** Cos, Ely, Fyn, Hoy, IOM, Ios, IOW, Man, Rab, Rum
**04** Bali, Coll, Cook, Corn, Cuba, Eigg, Elba, Fiji, Gozo, Guam, Holy, Iona, Java, Jura, Line, Long, Mahe, Maui, Muck, Mull, Nias, Niue, Oahu, Rota, Sado, Sark, Skye, Uist, Wake
**05** Arran, Barra, Bioko, Bonin, Capri, Chios, Cocos, Coney, Corfu, Crete, Delos, Éfaté, Ellis, Farne, Faroe, Handa, Hondo, Hydra, Ibiza, Islay, Kauai, Kuril, Lanai, Lundy, Luzon, Malta, Melos, Nauru, Naxos, North, Öland, Orust, Palau, Paros, Pearl, Pemba, Samoa, Samos, South, Sunda, Timor, Tiree, Tonga, Wight
**06** Aegean, Aegina, Andros, Azores, Baffin, Bikini, Borneo, Caicos, Canary, Chagos, Comino, Cyprus, Devil's, Easter, Euboea, Flores, Flotta, Hainan, Harris, Hawaii, Honshu, Icaria, Ionian, Jersey, Kodiak, Komodo, Kosrae, Kyushu, Lemnos, Lesbos, Midway, Orkney, Patmos, Penghu, Rhodes, Scilly, Sicily, Skiros, Staffa, Staten, Tahiti, Taiwan, Tinian, Tobago, Tubuai, Tuvalu, Virgin
**07** Anjouan, Anthony, Antigua, Bahamas, Bahrain, Bermuda, Bonaire, Cabrera, Celebes, Channel, Chatham, Comoros, Corsica, Curaçao, Frisian, Gilbert, Gotland, Grenada, Iceland, Ireland, Iwo Jima, Jamaica, La Digue, Leeward, Lofoten, Loyalty, Madeira, Majorca, Mayotte, Menorca, Mikonos, Mindoro, Minorca, Molokai, Nicobar, Norfolk, Oceania, Okinawa, Palawan, Phoenix, Praslin, Rathlin, Réunion, Siberut, Society, Solomon, Stewart, St Kilda, St Lucia, Sumatra, Surtsey, Tokelau, Vanuatu, Visayan, Westman, Wrangel, Zealand
**08** Aleutian, Anglesey, Anguilla, Balearic, Bornholm, Colonsay, Coral Sea, Cyclades, Dominica, Falkland, Guernsey, Hawaiian, Hebrides, Hokkaido, Hong Kong, Jan Mayen, Johnston, Kiribati, Lord Howe, Maldives, Marshall, Mindanao, Moluccas, Pitcairn, Sakhalin, Sandwich, São Tiago, Sardinia, Shetland, Skiathos, Sri Lanka, Sulawesi, Svalbard, Tenerife, Trinidad, Victoria, Viti Levu, Windward, Zanzibar
**09** Admiralty, Ascension, Australia, Benbecula, Cape Verde, Christmas, Ellesmere, Galápagos, Greenland, Halmahera, Indonesia, Irian Jaya, Isle of Man, Kárpathos, Lanzarote, Las Palmas, Macquarie, Manhattan, Marquesas, Mascarene, Mauritius, Melanesia, Nantucket, New Guinea, North Uist, Rodrigues, Santorini, Singapore, South Seas, South Uist, Stromboli, Vanua Levu, Zacynthus
**10** Ahvenanmaa, Basse-Terre, Cape Breton, Cephalonia, Cook Strait, Dodecanese, Formentera, Heligoland, Hispaniola, Ile d'Oléron, Kalimantan, Kiritimati, Madagascar, Martinique, Micronesia, Montserrat, New Britain, New Ireland, Puerto Rico, Samothrace, Seychelles, Vesterålen, West Indies
**11** Gran Canaria, Grand Bahama, Grand Cayman, Grande-Terre, Guadalcanal, Iles d'Hyères, Iles du Salut, Isla Cozumel, Isle of Wight, North Island, Philippines, Saint Helena, Scilly Isles, South Island, South Orkney
**12** Bougainville, Grande Comore, Great Britain, Isla de Pascua, Newfoundland, Novaya Zemlya, Prince Edward, Prince Rupert, South Georgia
**13** American Samoa, British Virgin, Inner Hebrides, Isla Contadora, Isles of Scilly, New Providence, Outer Hebrides, South Shetland
**14** Oki Archipelago, Papua New Guinea, The Philippines, Tierra del Fuego, Tristan da Cunha, Turks and Caicos
**15** French Polynesia, Lewis with Harris, Martha's Vineyard, Wallis and Futuna

*See also* **Channel Islands** *under* **channel**

**• reef island**
**04** motu

**Isle of Man**
**03** GBM, IMN **11** Ellan Vannin

**isn't**
**03** nis, nys **04** ain't

**isolate**
**06** cut off, detach, enisle, inisle, island, maroon, remove, strand **07** divorce, exclude, seclude, shut out **08** abstract, alienate, insulate, separate, set apart, shut away **09** keep apart, ostracize, segregate, sequester **10** disconnect, quarantine **11** marginalize **12** cold-shoulder **14** send to Coventry

**isolated**
**04** lone **05** alone, apart, freak, stray
**06** cut off, lonely, remote, single, unique **07** insular, special, unusual
**08** abnormal, atypical, deserted, detached, outlying, secluded, solitary, uncommon **09** anomalous, separated, unrelated, untypical **10** segregated
**11** exceptional, god-forsaken, in the sticks, out-of-the-way
**12** unfrequented

**isolation**
**05** exile **08** solitude **09** aloneness, seclusion **10** alienation, detachment, insulation, loneliness, quarantine, remoteness, retirement, separation, withdrawal **11** abstraction, segregation
**12** dissociation, separateness, solitariness **13** disconnection, sequestration **15** marginalization

**Israel**
**02** IL **03** ISR
*See also* **tribe**

**issue**
**03** ish, jet, son **04** come, copy, emit, fall, fine, flow, flux, gush, mark, ooze, rise, rush, seed, seep, stem, turn
**05** ensue, equip, exude, fit up, heirs, point, proof, spurt, topic, young
**06** affair, debate, derive, effect, embryo, emerge, escape, family, finale, fit out, follow, kit out, matter, number, outlet, pay-off, put out, result, rig out, scions, spread, spring, stream, supply,

upshot **07** concern, deal out, debouch, deliver, develop, dispute, edition, emanate, give out, handout, outcome, outflow, problem, proceed, produce, profits, progeny, provide, publish, release, send out, subject, version **08** announce, argument, children, daughter, delivery, effusion, emission, printing, proclaim, question **09** broadcast, discharge, effluence, offspring, originate, supplying, terminate **10** break forth, burst forth, conclusion, dénouement, distribute, impression, instalment, promulgate, successors **11** circulation, consequence, controversy, descendants, disseminate, publication **12** announcement, distribution, promulgation **13** dissemination

• **at issue**
**10** in question **12** being debated **14** being discussed **15** under discussion

• **final issue**
**04** fate

• **side issue**
**02** by **03** bye

• **take issue**
**05** argue, fight **06** object **07** contest, dispute, protest, quarrel **08** be at odds, disagree **09** challenge **12** be at odds with **13** take exception

• **violent issue**
**04** gush

• **without issue**
**02** sp **03** dsp, osp **09** sine prole

**it**
**01** a, 't **02** SA **05** oomph **08** vermouth **09** sex appeal

• **it is not**
**05** 'taint, 'tisn't **06** aikona

• **it's**
**03** 'tis

• **on it**
**03** an't

**Italian**
◇ *foreign word indicator*
**01** I **02** It **03** Sig **04** Ital, trat **05** Roman, tratt **08** Ausonian, Sicilian, Venetian **09** trattoria **10** Neapolitan

*See also* **day**; **month**; **number**

• **Italian family**
**06** Medici

**Italy**
**01** I **03** ITA **04** Ital

**itch**
**03** die, euk, ewk **04** ache, burn, long, pine, yeuk, youk, yuck, yuke **05** crave, crawl, psora, yearn **06** desire, hanker, hunger, thirst, tickle, tingle **07** burning, craving, longing, passion, prickle, scabies **08** irritate, keenness, pruritus, tingling, yearning **09** cacoethes, eagerness, hankering, itchiness, prickling **10** irritation

**itching**
**03** euk, ewk **04** avid, yeuk, youk, yuck, yuke **05** dying, eager **06** aching, greedy, raring **07** burning, longing **08** prurient, pruritus **09** hankering, impatient **11** inquisitive

**item**
**03** job **04** also **05** entry, issue, piece, point, story, thing **06** aspect, detail, factor, matter, notice, number, object, report **07** account, article, element, feature **08** bulletin, likewise **09** component, paragraph **10** accidental, ingredient, particular **12** circumstance **13** consideration

**itemize**
**04** list **05** count **06** detail, number, record **07** mention, specify **08** document, instance, overname, tabulate **09** catalogue, enumerate **13** particularize **15** make an inventory

**itinerant**
◇ *anagram indicator*
**03** faw **04** hobo, Roma **05** caird, Gypsy, nomad, rover **06** gitano, hawker, pedlar, roamer, Romani, Romany, roving, tinker **07** chapman, didakai, didakei, didicoi, didicoy, nomadic, rambler, roadman, roaming, running, swagman, tzigany, vagrant, Zincalo, Zingaro **08** Bohemian, diddicoy, drifting, huckster, minstrel, preacher, rambling, rootless, stroller, vagabond, wanderer, Zigeuner **09** itinerary, migratory, muffin man, piepowder, strolling, sundowner, traveller, unsettled, wandering, wayfaring **10** evangelist, journeying, revivalist, travelling **11** gandy dancer, peripatetic, Scotch cuddy **12** on the wallaby, Scotch draper **15** New-Age Traveller, strolling player

**itinerary**
**03** way **04** plan, tour **05** route **06** course **07** circuit, journey **08** schedule **09** itinerant, programme, timetable **10** travelling **12** arrangements

**itself**
• **of itself**
**03** sui

**ivory**
**07** dentine **08** eburnean **09** eburneous **10** whale's bone

**IVR code** *see* **vehicle**

**ivy**
**03** tod, udo **04** gill **06** aralia, fatsia, Hedera **07** ale-hoof **08** cat's-foot

**Ivy League** *see* **university**

**izzard**
**01** Z **03** zed

# J

**J**
**03** jay **06** Juliet

**jab**
**03** box, dig, tap **04** poke, prod, push, shot, stab **05** elbow, lunge, nudge, punch **06** thrust **09** injection

**jabber**
**03** gab, jaw, yap **05** prate **06** babble, gabble, mumble, rabbit, ramble, rattle, tattle, witter, yabber, yatter **07** blather, blether, chatter, prattle, sputter

**jack**
**01** J **02** AB **03** Dee, jak, nob, pam, pur, tar **04** Jock, John, mark **05** bower, fed up, kitty, knave, makar, money, noddy, tired, winch **06** hopper, runner, sailor **07** pantine, sticker **08** mistress, saw-horse, turnspit **09** detective, hand-screw

- **jack up**

**04** hike, lift **05** hoist, put up, raise **06** hike up, push up, refuse, resist **07** elevate, inflate **08** increase

**jackal**
**04** dieb **13** lion's provider

**jackass**
**04** fool **09** blockhead **10** kookaburra

**jackdaw**
**02** ka **03** daw, kae **04** jack **07** dawcock

**jacket**
**02** DJ **03** tux **04** baju, beat, case, skin, wrap **05** acton, bania, cover, duvet, gilet, grego, jupon, polka, sayon, shell, tunic **06** anorak, banian, banyan, Basque, blazer, bolero, casing, dolman, folder, jerkin, railly, sheath, tuxedo, Zouave **07** Barbour®, Mae West, spencer, vareuse, wrapper **08** camisole, covering, envelope, water box, wrapping **09** night-rail, shortgown, slip cover **10** body-warmer, bumfreezer, duffel coat, sports coat, windjammer **11** Barbour® coat, windcheater

**jackpot**
**03** pot **04** mess, pool **05** award, kitty, prize **06** reward, stakes **07** big time, bonanza **08** winnings **10** first prize

- **hit the jackpot**

**05** score **06** arrive, make it **07** clean up, get rich, succeed **08** rake it in **09** make a pile **11** make a bundle, make a packet **13** hit the big time

**jade**
**02** yu **03** nag **06** limmer **08** axe-stone, nephrite **11** spleenstone

**jaded**
**04** done **05** all in, bored, fed up, spent, tired, weary **06** bushed, done in, dulled, fagged, pooped **07** wearied, whacked, worn out **08** fatigued, jiggered, tired out **09** disjaskit, exhausted, knackered, played-out, pooped out, shattered **10** cheesed off **11** ready to drop, tuckered out **14** unenthusiastic

**jag**
**03** dag, fit **04** barb, cart, load, snag, spur **05** cleft, notch, point, prick, slash, spell, spree, tooth **06** bundle, dentil, Jaguar, pierce **08** denticle, division, quantity **09** injection, saddlebag **10** projection, protrusion **11** inoculation

**jagged**
◇ *anagram indicator*
**04** rag'd **05** drunk, ragde, rough **06** barbed, broken, craggy, hackly, nicked, ragged, ridged, snaggy, spiked, uneven **07** notched, pointed, snagged, toothed **08** indented, saw-edged, serrated **09** irregular **11** denticulate

**jaggedness**
**09** roughness, serration, serrature **10** brokenness, raggedness, unevenness **12** irregularity

**jaguar**
**03** Jag **05** ounce, tiger **07** leopard, tigress **10** leopardess **13** American tiger

**jail, gaol**
**03** bin, can, jug, pen **04** nick, poky, quad, quod, stir **05** choky, clink, kitty, pokey **06** cooler, detain, immure, inside, intern, lock up, lock-up, prison **07** confine, custody, hoosgow, impound, put away, slammer **08** big house, hoosegow, imprison, porridge, send down **09** bridewell, jailhouse **10** guardhouse **11** incarcerate **12** penitentiary, send to prison **15** detention centre

*See also* **prison**

**jailbird** *see* **prisoner**

**jailer, gaoler**
**04** Adam **05** guard, screw **06** captor, keeper, warden, warder **07** alcaide, alcayde, turnkey **09** dungeoner **12** under-turnkey **13** prison officer

**jake**
**02** OK **04** fine, okay **05** yokel **06** honest **07** correct **09** first-rate

**jam**
**03** fix, mob, ram **04** bind, clog, cram, herd, hole, lock, pack, push, spot, stew **05** block, close, crowd, crush, force, horde, jeely, jelly, press, seize, stall, stick, stuff, swarm, wedge **06** hold-up, insert, jeelie, konfyt, pickle, plight, scrape, spread, squash, throng, thrust **07** confine, congest, seize up, squeeze, straits, the soup, trouble **08** close off, conserve, gridlock, obstruct, preserve, quandary **09** confiture, interfere, marmalade, multitude, tight spot **10** bottleneck, congestion **11** obstruction, predicament **12** damson cheese

**Jamaica**
**02** JA **03** JAM

**jamb**
**04** dern, durn, pole, post, prop **05** frame, shaft **06** greave, pillar **07** support, upright **08** doorpost, side post **09** stanchion **10** ingle-cheek

**jamboree**
**04** fête **05** party, rally, spree **06** frolic, junket **07** carouse, jubilee, revelry, shindig **08** carnival, festival, field day **09** festivity, gathering, merriment **10** convention **11** celebration, get-together

**jammy**
**05** lucky **06** timely **07** charmed **08** favoured **09** excellent, expedient, fortunate, opportune **10** auspicious, fortuitous, propitious, prosperous, successful **12** providential

**jangle**
◇ *anagram indicator*
**03** din, jar **05** chime, clang, clank, clash, clink, upset **06** bother, jingle, racket, rattle **07** clatter, discord, disturb, jarring, quarrel, stridor, trouble, vibrate, wrangle **08** clangour, irritate **09** cacophony **10** contention, dissonance **11** make anxious **13** reverberation

**janitor**
**06** porter **07** doorman, ostiary **08** servitor **09** attendant, caretaker, concierge, custodian **10** doorkeeper, servitress

**January**
**03** Jan

**japan**
**01** J **03** JPN **07** lacquer

**Japanese**
**03** eta **07** Japonic **09** Nipponese

*See also* **Asian**

*Japanese art forms include:*

**02** no
**03** noh
**04** raku
**05** haiku, Hizen, Imari, kendo
**06** gagaku, kabuki, nogaku, saikei, ukiyo-e
**07** bunraku, chanoyu, ikebana, nihonga, origami
**08** kakemono, kakiemon, tsutsumu
**11** linked verse, tea ceremony

**• Japanese title**
**03** san **04** sama

**jar**
◇ *anagram indicator*
**03** irk, jug, mug, pot, urn **04** jerk, jolt, olla, pint, rasp, turn, vase
**05** annoy, caddy, clash, crock, cruet, flask, grate, grind, shake, stave, upset
**06** bicker, carafe, dolium, flagon, jampot, jangle, jostle, justle, kalpis, nettle, offend, pithos, rattle, tinaja, tureen, vessel **07** agitate, amphora, disturb, pitcher, quarrel, stamnos, terrine, trouble, vibrate **08** be at odds, canister, conflict, disagree, irritate
**09** albarello, bell-glass, container, greybeard **10** receptacle **11** water monkey **12** be at variance, be in conflict

**jargon**
**04** cant, jive **05** argot, Greek, idiom, lingo, slang, usage **06** patois, patter, pidgin **07** chatter, Kennick, twitter
**08** legalese, nonsense, parlance, pig Latin **09** baragouin, buzz words, Eurospeak, gibberish **10** Eurobabble, greenspeak, journalese, mumbo-jumbo, twittering, vernacular
**11** computerese, diplomatese, lingoa geral, officialese, sociologese, technospeak **12** gobbledegook, gobbledygook, lingua franca, psychobabble, technobabble, telegraphese **13** commercialese, computerspeak, pidgin English

**jarring**
**04** ajar **05** harsh, shock **06** off-key
**07** grating, jolting, rasping
**08** backlash, clashing, friction, jangling, strident **09** dissonant, troubling, upsetting **10** discordant, disturbing, irritating **11** cacophonous

**jasmine**
**07** jessamy **09** gelsemium, gessamine, jessamine **10** frangipani

**jaundiced**
**05** jaded **06** biased, bitter **07** bigoted, cynical, envious, hostile, jealous
**09** distorted, resentful, sceptical
**10** prejudiced, suspicious
**11** distrustful, icteritious, pessimistic
**12** disbelieving, misanthropic, preconceived **14** unenthusiastic

**jaunt**
**04** ride, spin, tour, trip **05** drive, sally
**06** outing, ramble, stroll **07** holiday
**09** excursion

**jauntily**
**06** airily **07** perkily, smartly
**08** brightly, cheekily **10** cheerfully
**13** energetically **15** self-confidently

**jaunty**
◇ *anagram indicator*
**04** airy, pert, trim **05** perky, showy, smart **06** bouncy, breezy, cheeky, dapper, flashy, lively, rakish, spruce
**07** buoyant, stylish **08** carefree, cheerful, debonair, sparkish
**09** energetic, sprightly **11** gentlemanly, Micawberish **12** high-spirited **13** self-confident

**javelin**
**04** dart, pile **05** jerid, pilum, spear
**06** jereed **07** harpoon **08** gavelock
**09** handstaff

**jaw**
**03** gum, rap **04** chap, chat, chaw, chop, dash, jole, joll, jowl, talk, trap
**05** chaft, chops, claws, grasp, mouth, power, scold, visit, wongi **06** babble, chafts, confab, gabble, gossip, jabber, muzzle, natter, rabbit **07** chatter, chinwag, control, lecture, maxilla
**08** clutches, mandible, rabbit on, schmooze **09** threshold **10** discussion, masticator **12** conversation
**13** talkativeness

**• front of jaw**
**04** chin

**jay**
**01** J **10** whisky jack, whisky john

**jazz**
◇ *anagram indicator*

*Jazz types include:*

**03** bop, hot, rag
**04** acid, Afro, cool, jive, soul, trad
**05** bebop, blues, funky, kwela, modal, spiel, swing
**06** fusion, groove, modern
**07** classic, hard bop, New Wave, post-bop, ragtime
**08** free-form, high life
**09** Afro-Cuban, bossa nova, Dixieland, gutbucket, West Coast
**10** avant-garde, improvised, mainstream, neo-classic, New Orleans
**11** barrelhouse, third stream, traditional
**12** boogie-woogie

*See also* **singer**

**• jazz fan**
**03** cat

**• jazz up**
**07** enliven, liven up **08** ginger up
**09** smarten up **10** brighten up

**jazzy**
**04** bold, wild **05** fancy, gaudy, smart
**06** bright, flashy, lively, snazzy
**07** stylish, zestful **08** spirited, swinging
**09** vivacious

**jealous**
**04** wary **05** green **07** anxious, careful, envious, gealous, mindful
**08** covetous, desirous, doubting, grudging, insecure, vigilant, watchful
**09** defensive, green-eyed, jaundiced, resentful **10** begrudging, possessive, protective, solicitous, suspicious
**11** distrustful

**jealously**
**08** with envy **09** enviously
**10** covetously, desirously **11** resentfully
**12** possessively **13** distrustfully

**jealousy**
**04** envy **05** doubt, spite **06** gelosy, grudge **07** envying, ill-will **08** distrust, gealousy, mistrust, wariness
**09** emulation, suspicion, vigilance, zelotypia **10** bitterness, insecurity, resentment, yellowness **11** carefulness, mindfulness **12** covetousness, grudgingness, watchfulness
**13** defensiveness **14** possessiveness, protectiveness

**jeans**
**05** Levis®

**jeer**
**03** boo, dig **04** gibe, gird, goof, hiss, hoot, jest, jibe, mock, razz, twit
**05** abuse, chaff, fleer, flout, frump, geare, knock, scoff, scorn, sneer, taunt, tease **06** banter, chiack, deride, heckle
**07** barrack, catcall, mockery, teasing
**08** derision, ridicule **09** make fun of, shout down **10** sling off at **11** have a shot at, poke borak at **12** laugh to scorn

**jejune**
**03** dry **04** arid, dull **05** banal, empty, naive, silly, trite, vapid **06** barren, boring, callow, meagre, simple
**07** insipid, prosaic, puerile **08** childish, immature, juvenile **09** senseless
**10** colourless, spiritless, unoriginal, wishy-washy **13** uninteresting
**15** unsophisticated

**jell** *see* **gel, jell**

**jelly**
**03** gel **04** agar, jeel **05** aspic, jeely, shape **06** jeelie, kanten, napalm, Sterno® **07** congeal **08** agar-agar, quiddany, Vaseline® **09** calf's-foot, gelignite **10** petrolatum **14** liquid paraffin

**jellyfish**
**05** jelly **06** medusa **07** acaleph, aurelia, blubber, sea wasp
**08** acalephe, sea jelly **09** sea nettle
**10** nettle-fish, scyphozoan, sea blubber

**jeopardize**
**04** risk **05** stake **06** chance, expose, gamble, hazard, menace **07** imperil, venture **08** endanger, threaten **09** put at risk **11** take a chance **13** put in jeopardy **14** expose to danger

**jeopardy**
**04** risk **05** peril **06** danger, hazard, menace, threat **07** venture
**08** exposure **09** liability **10** insecurity
**12** endangerment **13** vulnerability
**14** precariousness

**jerk**
◇ *anagram indicator*
**03** ass, bob, git, jar, jig, jog, mug, nit, sap, tug **04** berk, cant, clot, coot, dope, dork, fool, geek, goat, goof, goop, hoik, jolt, jump, kick, kook, nerd, nerk, peck, prat, pull, toss, twit, yank **05** braid, chump, dumbo, dweeb, flirt, hitch, hoick, idiot, lurch, neddy, ninny, pluck, prick, quirk, shrug, surge, throw, twerp, wally **06** bounce, dum-dum, fillip, jiggle, josser, nitwit, sawney, sucker, switch, thrust, turkey, twitch, wrench **07** Charlie, charqui, gubbins, pillock, plonker, saphead, tosspot, wazzock **08** dipstick **09** birdbrain, cloth head, schlemiel **10** headbanger, nincompoop, silly-billy **11** kangaroo hop **13** proper Charlie

**jerkily**
**07** bumpily, jumpily, roughly **08** fitfully, unevenly **13** spasmodically

**jerky**
◇ *anagram indicator*
**05** bumpy, jumpy, rough, shaky **06** bouncy, fitful, uneven **07** charqui, jolting, shaking, twitchy **08** lurching, saccadic **09** spasmodic **10** convulsive, incoherent **12** disconnected, uncontrolled **13** unco-ordinated

**jerry-built**
**04** Lego® **05** cheap **06** faulty, flimsy, shoddy **07** rickety **08** slipshod, unstable **09** cheapjack, defective, slop-built **10** ramshackle **12** quickly built **13** insubstantial, unsubstantial **14** thrown together **15** built on the cheap

**jersey**
**03** GBJ, top **04** polo **05** frock **06** gansey, jumper, woolly, zephyr **07** maillot, sweater **08** guernsey, polo neck, pullover **10** sweatshirt

**Jerusalem**
**04** Zion

**jest**
**03** cod, fun, gab, gag, jig, kid, toy **04** fool, game, hoax, jape, jeer, joke, mock, quip **05** bourd, crack, droll, gleek, prank, taunt, tease, trick **06** banter **07** fooling, kidding, leg-pull **08** drollery **09** Joe Miller, tell jokes, wisecrack, witticism **13** practical joke
• **in jest**
**05** in fun **07** as a joke, to tease **08** jokingly **09** playfully **13** mischievously

**jester**
**03** wag, wit **04** fool, scop, zany **05** clown, comic, droll, joker, patch **06** gagman, motley, mummer **07** bourder, buffoon, juggler **08** comedian, humorist, merryman, quipster **09** court-fool, harlequin, joculator, pantaloon, prankster **11** Jack-pudding, merry-andrew

**Jesuits**
**02** SJ **09** Ignatians

**jet**
**03** fly, jut **04** flow, gush, inky, jeat, rush, zoom **05** black, ebony, jumbo, raven, sable, shoot, sooty, spirt, spout, spray, spurt, strut **06** Airbus®, candle, career, douche, spring, squirt, stream **07** sprayer **08** encroach, fountain **09** delta wing, sprinkler **10** pitch-black, tankbuster
*See also* **aircraft**

**jettison**
**04** drop, dump **05** chuck, ditch, eject, expel, heave, scrap **06** jetsam, unload **07** abandon, discard, offload **08** get rid of **09** throw away

**jetty**
**04** dock, mole, pier, quay **05** jutty, wharf **06** groyne **07** harbour **10** breakwater **12** landing-place, landing-stage

**jewel**
**03** gem **04** find, rock **05** bijou, pearl, prize **06** rarity **07** navette, paragon **08** gemstone, ornament, sparkler, treasure **09** jewellery, showpiece **10** ferronière **11** ferronnière, masterpiece, pride and joy **13** precious stone **14** crème de la crème

**jewellery**
**03** tom **04** gems **05** gauds **06** bijoux, finery, jewels **07** gemmery, regalia **08** treasure, trinkets **09** ornaments **10** bijouterie, tomfoolery **13** paraphernalia

*Jewellery types include:*

**04** prop, ring, stud
**05** beads, bindi, cameo, chain, tiara
**06** amulet, anklet, bangle, brooch, choker, corals, diadem, hatpin, locket, pearls, tiepin, torque
**07** armilla, coronet, earring, necklet, pendant, rivière, sautoir, toe ring
**08** bracelet, cufflink, necklace, negligee, nose ring, wristlet
**09** medallion, navel ring
**10** signet ring
**11** mangalsutra
**12** eternity ring
**13** charm bracelet, solitaire ring
**15** belly-button ring

**Jewish calendar** *see* **month**

**Jezebel**
**04** jade, tart, vamp **05** hussy, whore, witch **06** harlot, wanton **07** Delilah **08** man-eater, scrubber **09** temptress **10** loose woman, seductress **11** femme fatale **12** scarlet woman

**jib**
**03** shy **04** balk, face, stop **05** baulk, genoa, stall, strip **06** boggle, fleece, recoil, refuse, shrink **07** back off, retreat **09** stop short **10** standstill

**jibe** *see* **gibe**

**jiffy**
**02** mo **03** bit, sec **04** tick **05** flash, trice, whiff **06** minute, moment, no time, second **07** instant **08** two ticks **09** twinkling **11** split second

**jig**
◇ *anagram indicator*
**03** bob, hop **04** jerk, jest, jump, leap, skip **05** caper, prank, shake **06** bounce, jingle, prance, twitch, wiggle, wobble

**jigger**
**04** damn, jerk, ruin **05** blast, break, shake, spoil, wreck **06** chigoe, chigre, jolley, kibosh **07** botch up, chigger, destroy, louse up, scupper, vitiate **08** sand flea **09** undermine **14** make a pig's ear of

**jiggery-pokery**
**05** fraud **06** deceit **08** mischief, trickery **09** chicanery, deception **10** dishonesty, hanky-panky, subterfuge **13** funny business **14** monkey business

**jiggle**
◇ *anagram indicator*
**03** jig, jog **04** jerk, jump **05** shake, shift **06** bounce, fidget, joggle, twitch, waggle, wiggle, wobble **07** agitate

**jilt**
**04** drop, dump **05** chuck, ditch, leave, spurn **06** begunk, betray, desert, pack in, reject **07** abandon, discard **08** brush off **09** cast aside, throw over, walk out on

**jingle**
**03** jig **04** ding, poem, ring, song, tune **05** carol, chant, chime, chink, clang, clink, ditty, rhyme, verse **06** chorus, jangle, melody, rattle, slogan, tinkle **07** clatter, refrain, ringing **08** clangour, doggerel, limerick **14** tintinnabulate

**jingoism**
**10** chauvinism, flag-waving, insularity, patriotism **11** imperialism, nationalism **13** sabre-rattling

**jinx**
**03** hex, moz **04** doom, mozz **05** charm, curse, spell **06** hoodoo, plague, voodoo **07** bad luck, bedevil, bewitch, evil eye, gremlin **10** affliction, black magic, Indian sign **11** malediction **12** cast a spell on

**jitters**
◇ *anagram indicator*
**06** nerves **07** anxiety, fidgets, habdabs, jimjams **08** edginess **09** agitation, tenseness, the creeps, the shakes, trembling **10** the shivers, the willies, uneasiness **11** nervousness **12** collywobbles **13** heebie-jeebies

**jittery**
◇ *anagram indicator*
**04** edgy **05** het up, jumpy, nervy, shaky **06** on edge, uneasy **07** anxious, fidgety, in a stew, keyed up, nervous, panicky, quaking, shivery, twitchy, uptight, wound up **08** agitated, in a sweat, in a tizzy **09** flustered, perturbed, quivering, screwed-up, trembling

**job**
**04** char, darg, duty, part, peck, post, prod, role, spot, task, work **05** berth, chore, place, punch, share, stint, trade **06** affair, career, charge, errand, métier, office, thrust **07** calling, concern, mission, project, pursuit, venture **08** activity, business, capacity, function, position, province, sinecure, vocation **09** situation, soft thing **10** assignment, commission, employment, enterprise, line of work, livelihood, occupation, proceeding, profession **11** appointment, consignment, piece of work, undertaking **12** contribution **14** line of business, responsibility
*See also* **burglary**; **occupation**

• **have a job doing something**
**14** find it a problem

• **just the job**
**12** just the thing **13** just the ticket

**jobless**
**04** idle **07** laid off **08** inactive, workless **09** on the dole, out of work, redundant **10** unemployed **11** without work

**jock**
**02** DJ **03** Mac **04** jack **06** deejay **08** Scotsman **10** disc jockey

**jockey**
◇ *anagram indicator*
**04** coax, ease, edge **05** rider **06** cajole, induce, manage **07** wheedle **08** engineer, horseman, inveigle, jockette **09** manoeuvre, negotiate **10** equestrian, horsewoman, jump-jockey, manipulate
*See also* **equestrian**; **horseman, horsewoman**

**jocose**
**05** droll, funny, lepid, merry, witty **06** jovial, joyous **07** comical, jesting, playful, teasing, waggish **08** humorous, mirthful, pleasant, sportive **09** facetious **11** mischievous

**jocular**
**05** comic, droll, funny, witty **06** jocose, joking, jovial **07** amusing, comical, jesting, playful, roguish, scurril, teasing, waggish **08** humorous, scurrile **09** facetious, hilarious, whimsical **12** entertaining

**jocularity**
**03** wit **05** sport **06** gaiety, humour **07** fooling, jesting, teasing **08** drollery, hilarity, jocosity, laughter **09** amusement, funniness, jolliness, joviality, merriment **10** comicality, desipience, jocoseness, pleasantry **11** playfulness, roguishness, waggishness **12** sportiveness, whimsicality **13** entertainment, facetiousness

**jog**
◇ *anagram indicator*
**03** hod, jar, run **04** bump, jerk, jolt, poke, prod, push, rock, shog, stir, trot, whig **05** dunch, dunsh, elbow, hotch, mosey, nudge, shake, shove **06** arouse, bounce, canter, jig-jog, joggle, jostle, prompt, remind **08** activate **09** stimulate

**john**
**02** WC **03** bog, can, lat, lav, loo **04** jack, rear **08** lavatory
*See also* **toilet**

**joie de vivre**
**03** joy **04** zest **05** gusto, mirth **06** bounce, esprit, gaiety, relish **08** buoyancy, pleasure **09** enjoyment, merriment **10** blitheness, ebullience, enthusiasm, exuberance, get-up-and-go, joyfulness **12** cheerfulness

**join**
◇ *juxtaposition indicator*
**03** add, mix, oop, oup, sew, tie, wed **04** abut, ally, bind, fuse, glue, knit, link, meet, weld, yoke **05** annex, enrol, enter, marry, merge, touch, unify, unite **06** adhere, adjoin, attach, border, cement, couple, enlist, fasten, sign up, solder, splice **07** combine, conjoin, connect, injoint, verge on **08** border on, coincide, converge, splinter **09** accompany, affiliate, associate, co-operate, interjoin, march with **10** amalgamate, team up with **11** collaborate, compaginate **15** become a member of

• **join in**
**04** help **06** chip in, muck in **07** chime in, get in on, partake, pitch in **08** take part **09** co-operate, lend a hand **10** contribute, take part in **11** participate

• **join up**
**04** link **05** enrol, enter **06** accede, enlist, sign up

**joint**
**01** J **03** bar, fit, pub **04** club, dive, join, knot, lith, seam, weld **05** carve, cut up, haunt, hinge, nexus, place, roach, sever, stick, union, unite **06** common, couple, divide, fasten, joined, mutual, reefer, shared, spliff, united **07** connect, dissect, joining, segment **08** combined, communal, conjunct, coupling, junction, juncture **09** cigarette, concerted, dismember, ginglymus, nightclub **10** articulate, collective, commissure, connection, cup-and-ball **11** amalgamated, co-operative, co-ordinated, enarthrosis **12** articulation, consolidated, intersection
*See also* **bone**

**jointly**
**08** together, unitedly **09** in cahoots, in harmony **11** in agreement **13** co-operatively, in co-operation, in partnership **15** in collaboration

**joke**
**03** bar, cod, fun, gag, guy, kid, one, pun, rot **04** baur, bawr, fool, hoax, hoot, jape, jest, josh, lark, mock, play, quip, yarn **05** chaff, clown, crack, farce, funny, kiddy, laugh, prank, spoof, sport, stunt, tease, trick **06** banter, frolic, gambol, parody, wheeze, whimsy **07** leg-pull, mockery **08** chestnut, nonsense, one-liner, repartee, shambles, travesty **09** absurdity, booby trap, fool about, tell jokes, throwaway, wisecrack, witticism **10** break a jest, crack a joke, fool around, funny story, rib-tickler, running gag, whip the cat **11** apple-pie bed, old chestnut **12** take for a ride **13** have someone on, practical joke **14** pull a fast one on, ridiculousness

**joker**
**03** wag, wit **04** card **05** clown, comic, droll, laugh, sport **06** gagman, hoaxer, jester, kidder **07** buffoon, farceur, funster **08** comedian, farceuse, humorist, quipster **09** character, prankster, trickster **11** wisecracker **14** practical joker

**jollity**
**05** mirth **08** gladness **09** happiness, high jinks, merriment **11** high spirits, merrymaking **12** cheerfulness

**jolly**
**02** RM **03** gay **04** coax, dead, glad, spur, trip, urge, very, well **05** buxom, egg on, gaucy, gawcy, gawsy, happy, merry, party, plump **06** bootee, cheery, ever so, gaucie, hearty, highly, jovial, joyful, lively, outing, prompt, titupy **07** awfully, festive, gleeful, greatly, healthy, playful, tittupy **08** cheerful, mirthful, persuade, splendid, terribly **09** certainly, convivial, encourage, enjoyable, extremely, exuberant, influence, intensely **10** delightful **11** celebration, pleasurable, royal marine **12** entertaining **13** exceptionally **15** extraordinarily

**jolt**
◇ *anagram indicator*
**03** hit, jar, jog **04** bang, blow, bump, jerk, push, stun **05** amaze, floor, knock, lurch, nudge, shake, shock, shove, start, upset **06** bounce, hotter, impact, jostle, jounce, jumble **07** astound, disturb, perturb, setback, shake up, startle **08** astonish, reversal, surprise **09** bombshell **10** discompose, disconcert **11** knock for six, thunderbolt **15** bolt from the blue

**Jordan**
**03** HKJ, JOR

**jostle**
◇ *anagram indicator*
**03** jog, vie **04** bang, bump, jolt, push, tilt **05** crowd, elbow, fight, joust, shake, shove **06** battle, hustle, jockey, joggle, throng **07** collide, compete, contend, squeeze **08** shoulder, struggle **11** hog-shouther

**jot**
**03** ace, bit, dot, fig **04** atom, hint, hoot, iota, mite, whit **05** aught, gleam, grain, scrap, speck, stime, styme, trace

**06** detail, morsel, tittle, trifle **07** glimmer, smidgen **08** fraction, particle **09** scintilla

• **jot down**

**04** list, note **05** enter **06** record **07** put down **08** note down, register, scribble, take down **09** write down

## jotting

**04** line, memo, note **05** lines, notes **07** comment, message **08** reminder, scribble **10** memorandum

## journal

**01** J **03** log **04** blog **05** diary, e-zine, paper **06** record, review, weekly **07** account, daybook, diurnal, fanzine, gazette, logbook, monthly **08** magazine, register **09** chronicle, ephemeris, newspaper, waste book **10** periodical, trade paper **11** publication

*See also* **newspaper**

## journalism

**05** press **09** reportage, reporting **11** copy-writing, e-journalism, gutter press **12** broadcasting, fourth estate, news coverage **13** sportswriting, web journalism **14** correspondence, feature-writing, telejournalism

*Journalism-related terms include:*

**03** cub, cut, NPA, run, tip
**04** blat, bump, copy, deck, desk, kill, leak, news, op-ed
**05** angle, blatt, blurb, break, extra, local, media, pitch, quote, radio, scoop, squib, story, tie in
**06** anchor, Balaam, byline, column, editor, impact, kicker, leader, leg-man, rookie, source
**07** advance, article, caption, compact, editing, feature, journal, kill fee, spoiler, subhead, tabloid, topical, writing
**08** causerie, follow-up, headline, magazine, masthead, national, newshawk, news item, reporter, revision, stringer
**09** broadcast, columnist, editorial, exclusive, freelance, freesheet, front-page, interview, newshound, newspaper, paragraph, pull quote, reportage, scare-head, scare-line, soundbite, statement, stop-press, strapline
**10** broadsheet, centrefold, credit line, daily paper, journalist, leaderette, multimedia, newsreader, periodical, publishing, retraction, standfirst, television
**11** Fleet Street, Sunday paper
**12** breaking news, centre spread, press council, press release, scare-heading
**13** correspondent, human interest, middle article
**14** banner headline, blind interview, current affairs, leading article
**15** photojournalism, press conference

## journalist

**02** Ed **03** man, sub **04** hack **06** editor, journo, scribe **07** diarist, wireman **08** hackette, pressman, reporter, reviewer, stringer **09** columnist, freelance, gazetteer, ink-jerker, newshound, paparazzo, sob sister, subeditor, thunderer **10** diurnalist, hatchet man, ink-slinger, news-writer, presswoman **11** broadcaster, commentator, contributor, e-journalist **12** gossip-writer, newspaperman, sportswriter **13** correspondent, feature-writer, web journalist **14** newspaperwoman, telejournalist

*Journalists and editors include:*

**03** **Day** (Sir Robin), **Mee** (Arthur)
**04** **Adie** (Kate), **Bell** (Martin), **Birt** (John, Lord), **Ford** (Anna), **Gall** (Sandy), **Hogg** (Sarah, Baroness), **Jane** (Frederick), **Marr** (Andrew), **Neil** (Andrew), **Rook** (Jean), **Self** (Will), **Snow** (Jon), **Snow** (Peter), **Wade** (Rebekah), **Wark** (Kirsty)
**05** **Brown** (Helen Gurley), **Buerk** (Michael), **Cooke** (Alistair), **Dacre** (Paul), **Ensor** (Sir Robert), **Evans** (Sir Harold), **Frost** (Sir David), **Green** (Charlotte), **Hardy** (Bert), **James** (Clive), **Junor** (Sir John), **Laski** (Marghanita), **Levin** (Bernard), **Lewis** (Martyn), **Reith** (John, Lord), **Scott** (C P), **Waugh** (Auberon), **Wolfe** (Tom), **Young** (Toby)
**06** **Bailey** (Trevor), **Barron** (Brian), **Bierce** (Ambrose), **Burnet** (Sir Alastair), **Deedes** (Bill, Lord), **Fisher** (Archie), **Forman** (Sir Denis), **Gallup** (George), **Gordon** (John), **Greene** (Sir Hugh), **Hislop** (Ian), **Hulton** (Sir Edward), **Hutton** (Will), **Isaacs** (Sir Jeremy), **Martin** (Kingsley), **Morgan** (Charles), **Morgan** (Piers), **Murrow** (Edward R), **O'Brien** (Conor Cruise), **Paxman** (Jeremy), **Pilger** (John), **Proops** (Marjorie), **Reuter** (Paul Julius von, Lord), **Rippon** (Angela), **Stuart** (Moira), **Wilkes** (John)
**07** **Alagiah** (George), **Barclay** (William), **Boycott** (Rosie), **Bradlee** (Ben), **Brunson** (Michael), **Buckley** (William F, Jnr), **Cameron** (James), **Camrose** (William Berry, Viscount), **Cobbett** (William), **Dunnett** (Sir Alastair), **Edwards** (Huw), **Fairfax** (John), **Fleming** (Peter), **Gardner** (Frank), **Hellyer** (Arthur George Lee), **Ingrams** (Richard), **Jackson** (Dame Barbara), **Johnson** (Boris), **Kennedy** (Helena, Baroness), **Kennedy** (Sir Ludovic), **Leeming** (Jan), **Malcolm** (Derek), **Mencken** (H L), **Perkins** (Brian), **Rowland** (Tiny), **Simpson** (John), **Sissons** (Peter), **Stanley** (Sir Henry Morton), **Thomson** (Robert)
**08** **Burchill** (Julie), **Cronkite** (Walter), **Dimbleby** (David), **Dimbleby** (Jonathan), **Dimbleby** (Richard), **Douglass** (Frederick), **Drawbell** (James Wedgwood), **Gellhorn** (Martha), **Hanrahan** (Brian), **Hobhouse** (Leonard), **Horrocks** (Sir Brian), **Humphrys** (John), **Lippmann** (Walter), **McCarthy** (John), **McDonald** (Sir Trevor), **Naughtie** (James), **Nevinson** (Henry Wood), **Rees-Mogg** (William, Lord), **Robinson** (Henry Crabb), **Thompson** (Hunter S), **Woodward** (Bob)
**09** **Bernstein** (Carl), **Bosanquet** (Reginald), **Hopkinson** (Sir Tom), **Macdonald** (Gus, Lord), **MacGregor** (Sue), **Mackenzie** (Kelvin), **Magnusson** (Magnus), **Plekhanov** (Georgi), **Streicher** (Julius), **Trethowan** (Sir Ian)
**10** **Greenslade** (Roy), **Guru-Murthy** (Krishnan), **Muggeridge** (Malcolm), **Rusbridger** (Alan), **Waterhouse** (Keith), **Worsthorne** (Sir Peregrine)
**12** **Street-Porter** (Janet)

*See also* **newspaper**

## journey

**02** go, OE **03** fly, ren, rin, run, way **04** eyre, hike, mush, raik, rake, ride, roam, rove, sail, step, tour, trek, trip, went **05** drive, foray, jaunt, range, route, shlep, tramp **06** bummel, cruise, flight, outing, ramble, roving, safari, schlep, travel, voyage, wander **07** milk run, odyssey, passage, proceed, sailing, schlepp, stretch, travels **08** campaign, crossing, progress **09** excursion, gallivant, walkabout **10** expedition, pilgrimage, wanderings **11** peregrinate **13** globetrotting, peregrination

• **good journey, safe journey**

**08** godspeed **09** bon voyage

• **journey regularly**

**03** ply **07** commute

## journeyer

**07** pilgrim, rambler, tourist, trekker, tripper, voyager **08** wanderer, wayfarer **09** traveller **12** peregrinator

## joust

**03** vie **04** just, spar, tilt **05** fight, giust, trial **06** jostle, justle **07** compete, contest, quarrel, tourney, wrangle **08** skirmish **09** encounter, pas d'armes **10** engagement, tournament

## jovial

**03** gay **04** boon, glad **05** happy, jolly, merry **06** cheery, genial, joyous, lively, wanton **07** affable, Bacchic, buoyant, cordial, gleeful **08** animated, Bacchian, cheerful, mirthful, sociable **09** convivial **11** Falstaffian **13** in good spirits

## joviality

**03** fun **04** glee **05** mirth **06** gaiety **07** jollity **08** buoyancy, gladness, hilarity **09** happiness, merriment **10** affability, cheeriness, ebullience **12** cheerfulness

## joy

**03** gem **04** dear, glee, list, nuts **05** bliss, cheer, dream, exult, prize, treat **06** thrill **07** delight, ecstasy, elation, rapture, rejoice, success, victory **08** felicity, gladness, pleasure, treasure **09** cloud nine, enjoyment, happiness, rejoicing, transport **10** exultation, joyfulness, jubilation **11** achievement **12** entrancement, satisfaction **13** gratification, seventh heaven **14** accomplishment, positive result

• **expression of joy**
**02** ah, ha, ho, io **03** aha, hah, hey, hoa, hoh, ooh, rah, say, wow, yay **04** I say!, whee **05** heigh, hurra, huzza, oh boy!, tra-la, wowee, yahoo, yummy, zowie **06** banzai, gotcha, heyday, hooray, hurrah, hurray, yippee, yum-yum **07** whoopee

**joyful**
**04** fain, glad **05** happy, merry **06** elated **07** festive, gleeful, pleased **08** cheerful, ecstatic, euphoric, feastful, gleesome, jubilant, pleasing, thrilled **09** delighted, gratified, overjoyed **10** exhilarant, triumphant **11** on cloud nine, over the moon, tickled pink **15** in seventh heaven, on top of the world

**joyfully**
**06** gladly **07** happily **09** gleefully **10** cheerfully, jubilantly **12** ecstatically, euphorically, triumphantly

**joyless**
**03** sad **04** dour, glum, grim **05** bleak, sober **06** dismal, dreary, gloomy, sombre **07** doleful, forlorn, serious, unhappy **08** dejected, downcast **09** cheerless, miserable **10** depressing, despondent, dispirited **12** discouraging

**joyous**
**04** glad **05** happy, merry **06** festal, jovial, joyful **07** festive, gleeful **08** cheerful, ecstatic, frabjous, gladsome, jubilant **09** rapturous **10** blithesome, rollicking

**joyously**
**06** gladly **07** happily, merrily **08** joyfully **10** cheerfully, jubilantly **11** rapturously **12** ecstatically

**jubilant**
**06** elated, joyful **07** excited **08** ecstatic, euphoric, exultant, thrilled **09** delighted, exuberant, overjoyed, rejoicing, rhapsodic **10** triumphant **11** on cloud nine, over the moon, tickled pink **15** in seventh heaven, on top of the world

**jubilation**
**03** joy **07** ecstasy, elation, jubilee, triumph **08** euphoria, jamboree **09** festivity, rejoicing **10** excitement, exultation **11** celebration **13** jollification

**jubilee**
**04** fete, gala **07** holiday **08** carnival, feast day, festival **09** festivity **11** anniversary, celebration **13** commemoration **14** semi-centennial

**Judas**
**07** traitor **08** betrayer, deceiver, quisling, renegade, turncoat **11** backstabber **13** tergiversator

**judder**
◇ *anagram indicator*
**05** quake, shake **06** quiver **07** shudder, tremble, vibrate

**judge**
**01** J **03** lud, ref, see, try, ump, wig **04** beak, damn, deem, doom, find, lord, rate, rule, scan **05** award, gauge, hakim, think, value, weigh **06** assess, critic, decern, decide, decree, expert, puisne, puisny, reckon, review, syndic, umpire **07** account, adjudge, arbiter, believe, censure, condemn, convict, coroner, discern, examine, her nibs, his nibs, justice, Law Lord, mediate, referee, set down, sheriff, weigh up **08** appraise, assessor, conclude, consider, doomsman, estimate, evaluate, mediator, recorder, reviewer, sentence **09** arbitrate, ascertain, authority, criticize, determine, evaluator, judiciary, justiciar, moderator, ombudsman, seneschal, syndicate **10** adjudicate, arbitrator, dijudicate, magistrate **11** adjudicator, connoisseur, distinguish **12** pass sentence **13** form an opinion, give a sentence **14** sit in judgement **15** deliver a verdict

*Judges include:*

**04** **Coke** (Sir Edward)
**05** **Allen** (Florence Ellinwood), **Burgh** (Hubert de), **Draco**, Minos, **Solon**
**06** Aeacus, **Burger** (Warren Earl), **Gideon**, **Holmes** (Oliver Wendell), **Irvine** (Alexander, Lord), **Mackay** (James, Lord), **Warren** (Earl)
**07** **Brennan** (William J), **Denning** (Alfred, Lord), **Erskine** (Thomas, Lord), **O'Connor** (Sandra Day), **Scarman** (Leslie, Lord)
**08** **Gardiner** (Gerald, Lord), **Ginsburg** (Ruth Bader), **Hailsham** (Quintin McGarel Hogg, Viscount), **Jeffreys** (George, Lord), **Marshall** (John), **Marshall** (Thurgood)
**09** **Rehnquist** (William), **Vyshinsky** (Andrei)
**10** **Elwyn-Jones** (Frederick, Lord)
**11** **Butler-Sloss** (Dame Elizabeth), **Montesquieu** (Charles-Louis de Secondat, Baron de)
**12** **Rhadamanthus**

**judgement**
**04** doom, fate, mind, view **05** award, order, sense, sight, taste **06** acumen, belief, decree, result, ruling, wisdom **07** decreet, finding, opinion, verdict **08** decision, estimate, prudence, sagacity, sapience, sentence, thinking **09** appraisal, criticism, damnation, diagnosis, good sense, mediation, reckoning, sentiment **10** assessment, conclusion, conviction, evaluation, judication, misfortune, perception, punishment, shrewdness **11** arbitration, common sense, discernment, penetration, retribution **12** adjudication, condemnation, intelligence, perspicacity **13** enlightenment, judiciousness, understanding **14** discrimination

**judgemental**
**07** carping **08** critical, scathing **10** censorious, derogatory **11** disparaging **12** condemnatory, disapproving, fault-finding **13** hypercritical

**judicial**
**05** legal **08** critical, forensic, official **09** decretory, impartial, judiciary, magistral **14** discriminating

**judicially**
**07** legally **10** officially **11** impartially **12** forensically

**judiciary**
**06** judges, the law **07** justice **08** the bench **10** magistracy **11** court system, legal system

**judicious**
**04** wise **05** smart, sound **06** astute, clever, shrewd **07** careful, prudent **08** cautious, discreet, informed, rational, sensible, wise-like **09** sagacious, well-timed **10** considered, discerning, reasonable, thoughtful, well-judged **11** circumspect, common-sense, intelligent, well-advised **14** discriminating

**judiciously**
**06** wisely **08** astutely, sensibly, shrewdly **09** carefully, prudently **10** cautiously **11** sagaciously **12** discerningly, thoughtfully **13** circumspectly

**judo** *see* **martial art**

**jug**
**03** jar, urn **04** ewer, olpe, Toby **05** crock **06** carafe, flagon, pourie, prison, vessel **07** bombard, creamer, growler, pitcher, Toby jug **08** decanter, imprison **09** blackjack, container **10** aquamanale, aquamanile, bellarmine, receptacle **11** Enghalskrug

*See also* **prison**

**juggle**
◇ *anagram indicator*
**03** rig **04** cook, fake **05** alter **06** adjust, change, doctor, fiddle, tamper **07** balance, conjure, falsify, massage **08** disguise, equalize **09** rearrange **10** hocus-pocus, manipulate, tamper with **12** misrepresent

**juice**
**03** jus, oil, sap **04** must **05** fluid, serum **06** cremor, liquid, liquor, nectar, succus, walnut **07** enliven, essence, extract **08** piquancy, vitality **09** secretion **10** pancreatin

**juicy**
**03** hot, wet **04** lush, racy **05** lurid, moist, sappy, spicy, vivid **06** risqué,

watery **07** flowing **08** exciting **09** colourful, succulent, thrilling **10** profitable, scandalous, suggestive **11** interesting, sensational

**jujube**
**04** jube **05** lotus **08** zizyphus **12** Christ's-thorn

**Juliet**
**01** J

**July**
**02** Jy **03** Jul

**jumble**
◇ *anagram indicator*
**02** pi **03** mix, pie, pye **04** jolt, junk, mess **05** chaos, mix up, mix-up **06** garble, huddle, jabble, jumbal, medley, mingle, muddle, raffle, tangle, tumble, wuzzle **07** clutter, confuse, jolting, mixture, rummage, shuffle **08** cast-offs, disarray, disorder, hotchpot, mishmash, mixy-maxy, oddments, pastiche, shambles **09** bric-à-brac, confusion, pasticcio, potpourri, praiseach **10** disarrange, hodgepodge, hotchpotch, miscellany, mixty-maxty **11** disorganize, printer's pie **12** mingle-mangle, mixter-maxter, mixtie-maxtie **14** conglomeration

**jumbled**
◇ *anagram indicator*
**06** untidy **07** chaotic, garbled, huddled, mixed-up, muddled, tangled, tumbled **08** confused, shuffled, unsorted **10** disarrayed, disordered **11** farraginous **12** disorganized, mingle-mangle **13** miscellaneous

**jumbo**
**02** OS **04** huge, mega, vast **05** giant **07** immense, mammoth, massive, outsize, Titanic **08** colossal, elephant, enormous, gigantic, whopping **09** ginormous, walloping **10** extra-large

**jump**
◇ *anagram indicator*
**03** gap, hop, jar, lep, mug **04** axel, gain, gate, go up, hike, jerk, jolt, leap, lutz, miss, omit, rail, rise, risk, romp, skip **05** avoid, boost, bound, break, caper, clear, fence, frisk, halma, hedge, lapse, lurch, mount, ollie, quail, shake, shock, shoot, space, spasm, sport, start, surge, throb, vault, wince **06** ascend, attack, beat up, bounce, breach, bypass, cavort, cut out, do over, flinch, frolic, gambol, go over, hazard, hiatus, hurdle, ignore, lacuna, leap up, pounce, prance, quiver, recoil, shiver, spiral, spring, switch, twitch, upturn **07** advance, assault, barrier, digress, exactly, flicker, salchow, set upon, shoot up, swoop on, toe loop, upsurge, venture **08** batterie, bunny hop, escalate, go across, increase, interval, leave out, mounting, obstacle, omission, overlook, pass over, pounce on, spring on **09** barricade, disregard, elevation, increment, stage-dive **10** appreciate, escalation, quersprung, trampoline **12** Becher's Brook, interruption
**• jump at**
**04** grab **05** seize **06** accept, leap at, snatch **07** agree to, fall for, seize on, swallow **08** pounce on **13** accept eagerly, accept quickly
**• jump on**
**05** blame, chide, fly at, scold **06** berate, rebuke, revile **07** censure, reprove, tick off, upbraid **08** reproach **09** castigate, criticize, reprimand
**• jump the gun**
**10** act hastily, act too soon, anticipate **13** start too early **14** act prematurely

**jumper**
**03** roo **04** euro, flea **05** lammy **06** jersey, lammie, woolly **07** sweater **08** kangaroo, pullover, wallaroo **10** churn-drill, sweatshirt

**jumpy**
**04** edgy **05** bumpy, het up, jerky, nappy, nervy, rough, shaky, tense **06** bouncy, fitful, on edge, uneasy **07** anxious, fidgety, in a stew, jittery, jolting, keyed up, nervous, panicky, restive, shaking, twitchy, uptight, wound up **08** agitated, in a sweat, in a tizzy, lurching **09** spasmodic, squirrely **10** convulsive, incoherent, squirrelly **12** apprehensive, disconnected, uncontrolled **13** unco-ordinated

**junction**
**01** T **04** bond, cove, join, link, node, seam, toll **05** close, crown, graft, joint, raphe, union **06** circus, collar, infall, suture **07** cornice, joining, linking, meeting, welding **08** abutment, coupling, crossing, juncture, knitting **09** interface, symphysis, T-junction **10** confluence, connection, crossroads, match-joint **11** box junction, combination, interchange **12** intersection, meeting-point

**juncture**
**04** crux, time **05** point, stage, union **06** crisis, minute, moment, period **07** article, joining **08** occasion **09** emergency, situation **11** predicament

**June**
**03** Jun

**jungle**
**03** web **04** bush, heap, mass, maze **05** chaos, shola, snarl **06** growth, medley, tangle **07** clutter **08** disarray, disorder, mishmash **09** confusion, labyrinth **10** hotchpotch, miscellany, rainforest **14** tropical forest

**junior**
**02** Jr **03** Jnr, Jun, lad **04** fils, Junr **05** chota, lower, minor, young **06** lesser, minion, puisne, puisny, rating **07** servant, younger **08** dogsbody, inferior, under-boy **09** assistant, associate, secondary, underling **10** subsidiary **11** subordinate

**junk**
◇ *anagram indicator*
◇ *deletion indicator*
**04** dump, spam **05** chuck, chunk, ditch, dregs, scrap, trash, waste **06** debris, litter, refuse **07** clutter, discard, garbage, rubbish, rummage **08** cast-offs, get rid of, jettison, leavings, narcotic, nonsense, oddments, throw out, wreckage **09** bric-à-brac, dispose of, leftovers, throw away, worthless

**junket**
**02** do **04** bash, trip **05** beano, feast, spree, visit **06** outing, picnic, regale **07** banquet, journey **09** entertain **11** celebration

**Juno**
**04** Hera

**junta**
**03** set **04** gang, ring **05** cabal, group, party **06** cartel, clique, league **07** coterie, council, faction, meeting **08** conclave **09** camarilla **11** confederacy

**Jupiter**
**04** Zeus

**jurisdiction**
**04** area, bail, rule, soke, sway, zone **05** field, orbit, power, range, reach, right, scope, soken, verge **06** bounds, region, sphere **07** command, control, mastery **08** capacity, district, dominion, province **09** authority, influence, territory **10** cognizance, competence, domination, judicature, leadership **11** prerogative, sovereignty **14** administration

**jury**
**04** pais **05** panel, quest **06** assize, jurors **07** jurymen **09** grand jury, jurywomen, party-jury, petit jury, petty jury

**just**
**03** all, apt, due **04** egal, even, fair, good, only, to a T **05** equal, exact, joust, legal, moral, quite, right, sound, valid **06** bang on, barely, earned, hardly, honest, indeed, lately, lawful, merely, normal, proper, purely, simply, spot-on **07** ethical, exactly, fitting, merited, neutral, sincere, upright **08** deserved, recently, rightful, scarcely, suitable, truthful, unbiased, virtuous **09** equitable, impartial, justified, objective, perfectly, precisely, righteous **10** absolutely, a moment ago, completely, even-handed, fair-minded, honourable, legitimate, nothing but, principled, reasonable, upstanding **11** appropriate, well-founded **12** unprejudiced, well-deserved, well-grounded **13** a short time ago, disinterested, incorruptible, true-disposing **14** irreproachable
**• just about**
**06** all but, almost, nearly **08** as good as, well-nigh **09** virtually **10** more or less **11** practically

• **just after**
**02** on

**justice**
**01** J **02** CJ, JP, LJ **03** law **05** judge, right **06** amends, equity, ethics, honour, morals **07** honesty, nemesis, penalty, redress, sheriff **08** fairness, fair play, justness, legality, validity **09** integrity, propriety, rectitude, rightness, soundness **10** lawfulness, legitimacy, magistrate, neutrality, punishment, recompense, reparation **11** objectivity, uprightness **12** compensation, impartiality, rightfulness, satisfaction **13** equitableness, righteousness **14** even-handedness, fair-mindedness, reasonableness **15** justifiableness

**justifiable**
**03** fit **05** legal, right, sound, valid **06** lawful, proper **07** tenable **08** sensible **09** excusable, justified, plausible, warranted **10** acceptable, defensible, explicable, forgivable, legitimate, pardonable, reasonable **11** explainable, supportable, sustainable, warrantable, well-founded **12** within reason **14** understandable

**justifiably**
**07** legally, rightly, validly **08** lawfully, properly **09** excusably, plausibly **10** acceptably, defensibly, reasonably **12** legitimately, within reason **14** understandably

**justification**
**04** plea **05** basis **06** excuse, reason **07** apology, defence, defense, grounds, warrant **08** warranty **10** absolution, mitigation **11** explanation, vindication **12** confirmation, verification **15** rationalization

**justify**
**04** aver, avow **05** clear, prove **06** acquit, defend, excuse, pardon, punish, uphold, verify **07** absolve, bear out, confirm, darrain, darrayn, deraign, deserve, explain, forgive, support, sustain, warrant **08** darraign, darraine, maintain, make good, validate **09** authorize, darraigne, establish, exculpate, exonerate, vindicate **10** stand up for **11** rationalize **12** substantiate **13** show to be right **14** give grounds for, give reasons for

**justly**
**04** duly **05** right **06** fairly **07** equally, rightly **08** honestly, lawfully, properly **09** equitably **10** rightfully, with reason **11** deservingly, impartially, justifiably, objectively **12** even-handedly, legitimately

**jut, jut out**
**03** jet **04** butt **05** jetty, jutty, stick **06** beetle, extend **07** extrude, project **08** overhang, protrude, stick out **10** projection

**jute**
**03** tow **05** gunny, kenaf, urena **06** burlap **07** Hessian, hopsack **09** Corchorus **10** hop-sacking, Jews' mallow

**juvenile**
**03** boy, juv, kid **04** girl **05** child, green, minor, young, youth **06** callow, infant, junior **07** babyish, puerile, teenage **08** childish, immature, teenager, youthful **09** infantile, youngster **10** adolescent **11** young person **13** inexperienced **15** unsophisticated

**Juventus**
**04** Hebe

**juxtapose**
**06** empale, impale **11** put together **13** place together, put side by side **15** place side by side

**juxtaposition**
**07** contact **08** nearness, vicinity **09** closeness, immediacy, proximity **10** apposition, contiguity, impalement

# K

**K**
**03** Kay **04** kara, kesh, kilo **06** kaccha, kangha, kirpan

**kaleidoscopic**
**05** fluid **06** motley **08** manifold **10** changeable, poikilitic, polychrome, variegated **11** fluctuating **12** ever-changing, many-coloured, multifarious **13** multicoloured, parti-coloured, polychromatic **15** many-splendoured

**kame**
**02** ås **05** eskar, esker

**kangaroo**
**03** roo **04** euro, joey **06** boomer, old man **07** steamer, wallaby **08** forester, wallaroo

**Kansas**
**02** KS **04** Kans

**kaput**
**04** bust, phut **06** broken, ruined, undone **07** defunct, extinct, smashed, wrecked **08** finished **09** conked out, destroyed

**karate**
**08** Shotokan

*Shotokan belts include:*

**03** red
**05** black, brown, green, white
**06** orange, purple, yellow
**20** brown with white stripe
**21** purple with white stripe
**24** brown with two white stripes

*See also* **martial art**

**• karate costume**
**02** gi **03** gie

**kay**
**01** K

**Kazakhstan**
**02** KZ **03** KAZ

**keel**
**04** back, base, cool, ship, skeg **05** barge, skegg **06** bottom, carina, ruddle **07** keelson **08** backbone **10** stabilizer **11** centreboard **12** cheesecutter

**• keel over**
◇ *reversal down indicator*
**04** drop, fall **05** faint, swoon, upset **07** capsize, founder, pass out, stagger **08** black out, collapse, overturn **10** topple over, turn turtle **14** turn upside down

**keen**
**03** cry, mad, sob **04** acid, avid, cold, deep, fell, fine, gleg, howl, moan, nuts, wail, weep, wild, wise, yowl **05** acute, breem, breme, crazy, eager, groan, mourn, potty, quick, razor, sharp, smart, snell **06** argute, astute, biting, caring, clever, fierce, fond of, grieve, intent, lament, liking, loving, narrow, severe, shrewd, shrill, strong **07** anxious, devoted, earnest, fervent, hawking, hawkish, intense, mordant, nipping, pointed, pungent, sharpen, ululate **08** diligent, incisive, piercing, ruthless, stinging **09** assiduous, cut-throat, devoted to, dog-eat-dog, enamoured, impatient, quick-eyed, razor-like, sagacious, sensitive, trenchant, wide awake, wonderful **10** attached to, discerning, double-eyed, perceptive, razor-sharp **11** heavily into, industrious, lamentation, penetrating, quick-witted, sharp-witted **12** enthusiastic **13** conscientious, keen as mustard, perspicacious **14** discriminating

**keenly**
**06** deeply, shrewd **07** acutely, eagerly, quickly, sharply **08** astutely, cleverly, fiercely, shrewdly, strongly **09** earnestly, fervently, intensely **10** diligently, incisively **11** assiduously, sensitively **12** perceptively **13** penetratingly

**keenness**
**03** eye **04** edge **06** wisdom **08** industry, sagacity, sapience, sedulity **09** diligence, eagerness, sharpness **10** astuteness, cleverness, enthusiasm, shrewdness, trenchancy **11** discernment, earnestness, penetration, sensitivity **12** incisiveness **15** industriousness

**keep**
◇ *containment indicator*
◇ *hidden indicator*
**03** own, run **04** curb, feed, food, fort, have, heap, hold, last, mark, mind, obey, pile, rear, save, stay, tend **05** amass, block, board, breed, carry, check, delay, deter, guard, hoard, limit, means, place, raise, stack, stock, store, tower, watch **06** arrest, castle, deal in, defend, detain, donjon, endure, foster, fulfil, hamper, hinder, hold up, honour, impede, keep at, keep on, keep up, living, manage, pile up, remain, retain, retard, shield, upkeep **07** abide by, care for, carry on, citadel, collect, conduct, confine, control, deposit, dungeon, furnish, inhibit, nurture, observe, perform, persist, possess, prevent, protect, refrain, reserve, respect, shelter, store up, support, sustain **08** adhere to, carry out, conserve, continue, fortress, hang on to, hold back, hold on to, keep back, maintain, obstruct, preserve, restrain, withhold **09** celebrate, constrain, look after, persevere, recognize, safeguard, solemnize, subsidize, watch over **10** accumulate, comply with, effectuate, livelihood, perpetuate, provide for, stronghold, sustenance, take care of **11** commemorate, keep waiting, maintenance, not part with, nourishment, subsistence, superintend **12** be in charge of, have charge of **13** have custody of, interfere with, keep faith with **15** keep in good order

**• for keeps**
**06** always **07** for ever, for good **10** for all time

**• keep at**
**03** nag **04** last, stay, toil **05** grind **06** badger, drudge, endure, finish, labour, remain, slog at **07** carry on, persist, stick at **08** complete, continue, fight off, maintain **09** persevere **10** plug away at **11** be steadfast **12** beaver away at

**• keep back**
◇ *reversal indicator*
**04** curb, hide, save, stop **05** check, delay, hoard, limit, store **06** censor, hinder, hold up, hush up, impede, retain, retard, stifle **07** conceal, control, inhibit, repress, reserve **08** hold back, keep down, lay aside, prohibit, restrain, restrict, set aside, suppress, withhold **09** constrain, stockpile **10** accumulate, keep secret

**• keep from**
**04** halt, help, stop **06** desist, resist **07** forbear, prevent, refrain **08** restrain

**• keep in**
**04** hide **05** quell **06** coop up, detain, shut in, stifle, stop up **07** conceal, confine, control, inhibit, repress **08** bottle up, keep back, restrain, suppress

**• keep off**
**05** avoid, expel, fence, parry **07** stay off **08** hands off, keep away **09** not go near **10** body-swerve **12** stay away from, steer clear of **14** avoid going near

**• keep on**
**04** go on, last, stay **06** endure, hold on, remain, retain **07** carry on, persist **08** continue, keep at it, maintain **09** persevere, soldier on, stick at it **13** stay the course **14** continue to hire

**• keep on at**
**03** nag **05** harry **06** badger, chivvy, go

on at, harass, pester, plague, pursue **09** importune

• **keep secret**

**04** hide **07** conceal **08** keep back, keep dark, suppress **09** dissemble **14** keep under wraps

• **keep to**

**04** obey **06** fulfil **07** observe, respect, stick to **08** adhere to **10** comply with

• **keep up**

**03** vie **05** equal, match, rival **06** retain **07** compete, contend, emulate, persist, support, sustain **08** continue, keep pace, maintain, preserve **09** entertain, persevere **10** keep tabs on **11** go along with **13** keep abreast of **15** keep in touch with

**keeper**

**03** nab **05** guard **06** custos, escort, gaoler, jailer, mahout, minder, parker, parkie, warden, warder **07** curator, granger, marshal, steward **08** defender, governor, guardian, overseer, surveyor, vesturer **09** archivist, attendant, bodyguard, caretaker, castellan, constable, custodian, guard ring, inspector **10** austringer, châtelaine, proprietor, supervisor **11** conservator, park-officer **13** administrator **14** superintendent

**keep fit**

**02** PE, PT

**keeping**

**04** care, cure, hand, ward **05** aegis, hands, store, trust **06** accord, charge **07** balance, custody, harmony, support **08** auspices, tutelage **09** agreement, congruity, patronage, retention **10** compliance, conformity, observance, proportion, protection **11** consistency, maintenance, reservation, safe-keeping, supervision **12** guardianship, preservation, surveillance **14** correspondence

**keepsake**

**05** relic, token **06** emblem, pledge **07** memento **08** reminder, souvenir **11** remembrance

**keg**

**02** kg **03** tun, vat **04** butt, cask, drum **06** barrel, firkin **08** hogshead

**kelvin**

**01** K

**ken**

**04** know **05** field, grasp, range, reach, scope **06** notice **07** compass **09** awareness, knowledge **10** cognizance, perception **11** realization **12** acquaintance, appreciation **13** comprehension, understanding

**Kent**

**02** SE

**Kentucky**

**02** KY

**Kenya**

**03** EAK, KEN

**kerfuffle**

**03** ado **04** flap, fuss, to-do **05** hoo-ha, tizzy **06** bother, bustle, flurry, furore **07** agitate, carry-on, fluster, palaver **08** ballyhoo, brouhaha, disorder **09** agitation, commotion

**kernel**

**03** nub, nut **04** core, corn, crux, germ, gist, seed **05** copra, gland, grain, heart, stone **06** almond, centre, marrow, nutmeg **07** essence, innards, nucleus **08** pichurim **09** pistachio, substance **11** nitty-gritty, quandong-nut **12** nuts and bolts, quintessence

**kestrel**

**06** keelie **07** staniel, stannel, stanyel **08** stallion **09** windhover

**key**

**01** A, B, C, D, E, F, G, H **03** cue **04** clue, code, crib, kaie, main, mood, note, sign, tone **05** basic, chief, gloss, guide, index, major, means, pitch, style, table, vital, wedge **06** answer, clavis, legend, secret, timbre, winder **07** central, crucial, leading, pointer, spanner **08** decisive, glossary, solution **09** character, essential, important, indicator, necessary, principal **11** explanation, explication, fundamental, translation **12** passe-partout **14** interpretation

*See also* **island**

*Keys on a computer keyboard include:*

**03** alt, del, end, esc, ins, tab
**04** ctrl, home, pg dn, pg up
**05** alt gr, enter
**06** delete, insert, page up
**07** num lock
**08** caps lock, page down

• **key stem**

**03** pin

**keynote**

**01** C **04** core, gist, mese, pith **05** final, heart, point, theme, tonic **06** accent, centre, marrow, stress **07** essence **08** emphasis **09** substance

**keystone**

**04** base, core, crux, root **05** basis, quoin **06** ground, motive, source, spring **07** sagitta **08** linchpin **09** principle **10** foundation, mainspring **11** cornerstone

**kick**

◇ *anagram indicator*

**03** fun, hit, pep, toe, zip **04** bite, blow, boot, buzz, chip, foot, hack, heel, high, hoof, jolt, knee, lark, lift, punt, quit, shin, spur, stop, tang, yerk, zing **05** break, fling, pause, power, punce, punch, react, shoot, spurn, wince **06** effect, falter, give up, jack in, let out, pack in, recoil, strike, thrill **07** abandon, dropout, fly-kick, grubber, lash out, misfire, penalty, potency, project, rebound, spurn at, tap-kick **08** back-heel, drop-kick, free kick, goal kick, grub kick, high kick, jump back, leave off, move back, pleasure, pungency, set piece, sixpence, spot kick, stimulus, strength, striking **09** boomerang, cross-kick, garryowen, place kick **10** desist from, excitement, pile-driver, point after, resilience, resistance, spring back **11** stimulation **12** recalcitrate, spurn against

• **kick against**

**04** defy **05** rebel, spurn **06** oppose, resist **07** protest **09** withstand **14** hold out against

• **kick around**

**03** use **05** abuse **07** discuss, exploit, toy with **08** ill-treat, maltreat, play with **09** mess about, push about, talk about, trample on **10** mess around, push around **15** take advantage of

• **kick off**

**03** die **04** open **05** begin, start **08** commence, initiate **09** introduce **10** inaugurate **11** get under way

• **kick out**

**04** oust, sack, spur **05** eject, evict, expel **06** reject, remove **07** boot out, dismiss, turf out **08** chuck out, get rid of, throw out **09** discharge **13** give the boot to, give the push to, give the sack to **14** give the elbow to

**kickback**

**05** bribe **06** pay-off, recoil **07** rebound **08** backlash, reaction **09** incentive, sweetener **10** back-hander, inducement

**kick-off**

**02** KO **05** start **06** outset, word go **07** opening **09** beginning, inception **12** commencement, introduction

**kid**

**03** boy, con, imp, lad, rib, tot **04** brat, dupe, fool, girl, gull, hoax, jest, joke, wean **05** bairn, child, kiddy, sprog, tease, trick, youth **06** delude, faggot, have on, humbug, infant, nipper, rug rat, wind up **07** deceive, littlin, littl 'un, pretend, tiny tot, toddler, young 'un **08** cheverel, cheveril, hoodwink, juvenile, littling, teenager, yeanling, young one **09** bamboozle, deception, kiddywink, littleane, little boy, little one, youngster **10** adolescent, ankle-biter, little girl **11** young person

**kidnap**

**05** seize, steal **06** abduct, hijack, snatch **07** capture **08** carry off **12** hold to ransom **13** hold as hostage, take as hostage

**kill**

**03** axe, bag, end, ice, pip, sap, top, use, zap **04** ache, do in, dull, ease, fill, hang, hurt, pass, prey, ruin, slay **05** death, drain, mop-up, napoo, pound, quash, quell, shoot, smart, smite, spend, spoil, still, sting, throb, total, use up, waste, weary, whack **06** behead, be sore, climax, deaden, defeat, dilute, fag out, finish, lay low, muffle, murder, occupy, reject, rub out, settle, soothe, stifle, strain, suffer, twinge, weaken

**07** abolish, bump off, butcher, cut down, destroy, discard, execute, exhaust, fatigue, kiss off, knacker, nullify, put down, relieve, scupper, smother, stonker, take out, tire out, wipe out **08** blow away, decimate, despatch, dispatch, knock off, massacre, moderate, ring-bark, shoot-out, suppress **09** alleviate, be painful, cause pain, death-blow, devastate, dispose of, do to death, eliminate, eradicate, finish off, liquidate, overexert, polish off, shoot dead, slaughter, while away **10** annihilate, conclusion, decapitate, dénouement, do away with, extinguish, guillotine, neutralize, put an end to, put to death, put to sleep **11** assassinate, coup de grâce, electrocute, exterminate, stab to death, take it out of

**killer**
**03** gun, orc **04** orca **06** gunman, hit-man, ice man, slayer **07** butcher, matador, shooter **08** assassin, hired gun, homicide, murderer **09** cut-throat, destroyer **10** hatchet man, liquidator, man-queller, stupendous **11** axe murderer, executioner, slaughterer **12** exterminator, mass murderer, serial killer, woman-queller
**• natural killer**
**02** NK

**killing**
**03** hit **04** coup, gain, hard **05** booty, death, funny **06** absurd, big hit, deadly, murder, profit, taxing, tiring
**07** amusing, arduous, a scream, bonanza, carnage, clean-up, comical, fortune, slaying, success, wearing
**08** butchery, draining, fatality, genocide, homicide, massacre, windfall **09** bloodshed, execution, fatiguing, gruelling, hilarious, ludicrous, mactation, matricide, patricide, predation, slaughter, uxoricide **10** enervating, exhausting, fratricide, hysterical, lucky break, sororicide, uproarious **11** destruction, destructive, elimination, fascinating, infanticide, liquidation, rib-tickling
**12** back-breaking, debilitating, irresistible, manslaughter, stroke of luck **13** assassination, extermination, side-splitting

**killjoy**
**05** cynic **06** damper, grouch, misery, moaner, whiner **07** sceptic
**08** buzzkill, dampener **09** pessimist
**10** complainer, spoilsport, wet blanket
**11** Weary Willie **12** trouble-mirth
**13** prophet of doom

**kiln**
**04** oast **05** stove **06** muffle

**kilo**
**01** K

**kilt**
**07** filabeg, filibeg **08** fillibeg, philabeg, philibeg **09** phillabeg, phillibeg **10** fustanella

**kilter**
**• out of kilter**
**04** awry **05** askew **08** confused, lopsided **09** skew-whiff
**10** misaligned, unbalanced **12** out of balance

**kin**
**04** clan **05** blood, catty, stock, tribe
**06** family, people **07** cousins, kindred, lineage, related **08** affinity
**09** relations, relatives **10** extraction
**12** relationship **13** consanguinity, flesh and blood

**kina**
**01** K

**kind**
**03** ilk, set **04** form, good, mild, nice, race, sort, type, warm **05** beget, brand, breed, class, genre, genus, stamp, style **06** benign, family, genial, gentle, giving, humane, kindly, loving, manner, nature, strain **07** amiable, cordial, helpful, lenient, patient, pitying, species, tactful, variety
**08** amicable, category, friendly, generous, gracious, merciful, obliging, selfless, tolerant **09** agreeable, bounteous, character, congenial, courteous, indulgent, unselfish
**10** altruistic, benevolent, big-hearted, charitable, forbearing, persuasion, thoughtful **11** considerate, description, good-hearted, good-natured, kind-hearted, magnanimous, neighbourly, soft-hearted, sympathetic, temperament, warm-hearted
**12** affectionate, humanitarian
**13** compassionate, philanthropic, tender-hearted, understanding
**• in kind**
**08** in return, in specie **09** similarly, tit for tat **10** in exchange **12** in like manner
**• kind of**
◇ *anagram indicator*
**04** a bit **05** kinda, quite **06** fairly, pretty, rather, sort of **07** a little
**08** slightly, somewhat **10** moderately, relatively **12** to some degree, to some extent

**kind-hearted**
**04** kind, warm **06** benign, humane, kindly **07** helpful **08** amicable, generous, gracious, obliging
**10** altruistic, big-hearted
**11** considerate, good-hearted, good-natured, sympathetic, warm-hearted
**12** humanitarian **13** compassionate, philanthropic, tender-hearted

**kindle**
**03** fan **04** blow, fire, lunt, stir, tind, tine, tynd **05** brood, light, rouse, spark, teend, tynde **06** accend, arouse, awaken, excite, ignite, incite, induce, litter, thrill **07** enlight, incense, inflame, inspire, provoke **09** set alight, set fire to, set on fire, stimulate

**kindliness**
**06** nature, warmth **07** charity
**08** kindness, sympathy **09** benignity
**10** amiability, compassion, generosity
**11** beneficence, benevolence
**12** friendliness **14** loving-kindness

**kindly**
**04** fond, good, kind, mild, nice, warm
**06** benign, couthy, genial, gentle, gently, giving, goodly, humane, native, please, polite, tender, warmly
**07** benefic, cordial, couthie, helpful, natural, patient **08** amicable, benignly, friendly, generous, humanely, lovingly, pleasant **09** agreeable, avuncular, helpfully, indulgent, patiently, tactfully
**10** benevolent, big-hearted, charitable, charitably, favourable, generously, mercifully, selflessly, thoughtful, tolerantly **11** considerate, courteously, good-natured, kind-hearted, magnanimous, neighbourly, sympathetic, unselfishly
**12** benevolently, thoughtfully
**13** compassionate, considerately, grandfatherly, kind-heartedly, magnanimously, understanding
**14** affectionately, altruistically
**15** compassionately, sympathetically

**kindness**
**03** aid **04** help, love **05** grace
**06** favour, warmth **07** aggrace, benefit, candour, charity, service **08** altruism, courtesy, good deed, goodness, good turn, goodwill, humanity, leniency, mildness, niceness, patience, sympathy
**09** affection, benignity, tolerance
**10** assistance, benignancy, compassion, generosity, gentleness, humaneness, indulgence, kindliness **11** beneficence, benevolence, helpfulness, hospitality, magnanimity **12** friendliness, philanthropy, pleasantness
**13** consideration, fellow feeling, Gemütlichkeit, understanding
**14** loving-kindness, thoughtfulness
**15** considerateness, humanitarianism, warm-heartedness

**kindred**
**03** kin, sib **04** akin, clan, folk, hapu, like
**05** flesh, house, stock **06** allied, common, family, people **07** cognate, lineage, related, similar **08** affinity, kinsfolk, matching **09** congenial, connected, relations, relatives
**10** affiliated, similarity **11** connections
**12** relationship **13** consanguinity, corresponding, flesh and blood

**king**
**01** K, R **02** HM **03** Rex, Roi **04** Inca, lord, shah, star **05** chief, ruler
**06** bigwig, kaiser, leader, master, prince, top dog **07** big shot, emperor, kingpin, majesty, monarch, supremo
**08** big noise **09** big cheese, chieftain, sovereign **11** head of state, the greatest
**12** leading light

*Kings include:*

**03** Ban, Ida, Ine, Lot, Zog
**04** Ahab, Cnut, Cole, Edwy, Erik, Fahd, Ivan, Ivan (the Terrible), John, John (the Blind), Karl, Knut, Lear, Offa, Olaf, Olav, Otto, Paul, Quin, Saud, Saul, Zeus

**05** Boris, Brian, Bruce (Robert), Capet (Hugo or Hugh), Carol, Creon, David, Edgar, Edred, Edwin (St), Henri, Henry, Henry (the Fowler), Herod (the Great), Hiero, Ixion, James, Louis, Midas, Murat (Joachim), Penda, Pepin (the Short), Priam, Svein, Sweyn
**06** Alaric, Albert, Alboin, Alfred, Alonso, Arthur, Attila, Baliol (Edward de), Canute, Cheops, Clovis, Darius, Donald, Duncan, Edmund, Edmund (Ironside), Edward, Edward (the Confessor), Edward (the Elder), Edward (the Martyr), Egbert, Faisal, Farouk, George, Gustav, Haakon, Harald, Harold, Harold (Harefoot), Hassan, Khalid, Magnus, Oberon, Oswald (St), Philip, Ramses, Robert, Robert (the Bruce), Rudolf, Sargon, Xerxes
**07** Alfonso, Aragorn, Balliol (John de), Cepheus, Charles, Croesus, Emanuel, Francis, Fredrik, Humbert, Hussein, Ibn Saud, Kenneth, Leopold, Macbeth, Malcolm, Michael, Odoacer, Perseus, Ptolemy, Pyrrhus, Rameses, Richard, Romulus, Solomon, Stephen, Tarquin, Umberto, Wilhelm, William, William (the Conqueror), William (the Silent)
**08** Baudouin, Birendra, Ethelred, Ethelred (the Unready), Frederik, Gaiseric, Gustavus, Jeroboam, Leonidas, Matthias, Ramesses, Sihanouk (Norodom), Thutmose
**09** Aethelred, Akhenaten, Alexander, Alexander (the Great), Amenhotep, Antigonus, Antiochus, Athelstan, Christian, Cuchulain, Cymbeline, Ethelbert, Ethelwulf, Ferdinand, Frederick, Hammurabi, Hardaknut, Nadir Shah, Sigismund, Stanislaw, Taufa'ahau, Theodoric, Tuthmosis, Vortigern, Wenceslas, Wladyslaw, Zahir Shah (Mohammed)
**10** Aethelbert, Aethelstan, Aethelwulf, Artaxerxes, Carl Gustaf, Esarhaddon, Fisher King, Juan Carlos, Moshoeshoe, Ozymandias, Tarquinius, Wenceslaus
**11** Charlemagne, Constantine, Franz Joseph, Hardacanute, Hardicanute, Mithridates, Old King Cole, Sennacherib, Shalmaneser, Tut'ankhamun
**12** Assurbanipal, Boris Godunov, Herod Agrippa
**13** Chulalongkorn, Louis-Philippe
**14** Nebuchadnezzar, Philip Augustus, Victor Emmanuel
**15** Artaxerxes Ochus, Norodom Sihanouk

- **Three Kings** *see* **wise man** *under* **wise**

*See also* **Roman**

**kingdom**
**04** land **05** realm, reign, state **06** domain, empire, nation, sphere **07** country, dynasty **08** division, dominion, grouping, monarchy, province **09** territory **11** sovereignty **12** commonwealth, principality
*See also* **classification**; **empire**

**kingfisher**
**07** halcyon **10** kookaburra

**kingly**
**05** grand, noble, regal, royal **06** august, lordly **07** stately, sublime, supreme **08** glorious, imperial, imposing, majestic, splendid **09** dignified, grandiose, imperious, sovereign **11** monarchical

**Kingsley**
**03** Ben **04** Amis

**kink**
◇ *anagram indicator*
**03** bug **04** bend, coil, curl, dent, flaw, gasp, knot, loop, null, whim **05** chink, cough, crick, crimp, curve, hitch, quirk, twirl, twist **06** defect, fetish, foible, glitch, tangle **07** blemish, caprice, crinkle, failing, wrinkle **08** weakness **09** deviation, weak point **10** deficiency, perversion **11** indentation, peculiarity, shortcoming **12** eccentricity, entanglement, idiosyncrasy, imperfection

**kinkajou**
**05** potto **09** honey bear

**kinky**
◇ *anagram indicator*
**03** odd **04** wavy **05** crazy, curly, funky, queer, weird **06** coiled, curled, frizzy, quirky, warped **07** bizarre, crimped, deviant, strange, tangled, twisted, unusual **08** abnormal, crumpled, depraved, freakish, peculiar, wrinkled **09** eccentric, perverted, unnatural, whimsical **10** capricious, degenerate, licentious, outlandish **13** idiosyncratic **14** unconventional

**kinsfolk**
**03** kin **04** clan, hapu **06** family **07** cousins, kindred **09** relations, relatives **11** connections

**kinship**
**03** kin, sib, tie **04** ties **05** blood **06** family **07** kindred, lineage **08** affinity, alliance, ancestry, likeness, relation **09** community **10** conformity, connection, similarity **11** association, equivalence **12** relationship **13** consanguinity **14** correspondence

**kinsman**
**03** sib **04** ally **06** cousin **07** brother

**kiosk**
**03** box **05** booth, cabin, stall, stand **07** counter **09** bandstand, bookstall, news-stand

**Kiribati**
**03** KIR

**Kirkpatrick**
**01** K

**kismet**
**03** lot **04** doom, fate **05** karma **07** destiny, fortune, portion **10** predestiny, providence

**kiss**
**01** X **03** fan, lip, pax **04** buss, lick, neck, pash, peck, snog **05** brush, cross, graze, mouth, smack, touch **06** caress, scrape, smooch, smouch **07** plonker, smacker **08** canoodle, deep kiss, osculate, suck face **09** baisemain, glance off **10** bill and coo, contrecoup, French kiss, osculation **11** touch gently **12** touch lightly **13** butterfly kiss

**kit**
**03** rig, set **04** gear, togs **05** get-up, strip, stuff, tools **06** kitten, outfit, rig-out, tackle, things **07** baggage, clobber, clothes, colours, effects, luggage **08** clothing, supplies, utensils **09** apparatus, equipment, trappings **10** implements, provisions **11** instruments **13** accoutrements, appurtenances, paraphernalia

- **kit out**

**03** arm **05** dress, equip, fix up **06** fit out, outfit, rig out, supply **07** deck out, furnish, garnish, prepare, provide

**kitchen**
**03** but **06** galley **07** caboose, cookery, cuisine **08** scullery **10** percussion
*See also* **utensil**

**kite**
**04** gled **05** belly, glede **06** dragon, elanet, Milvus, paunch **07** puttock, rokkaku **08** aircraft

**kittenish**
**04** cute **05** ludic **06** frisky **07** playful **08** skittish, sportive **09** fun-loving **10** coquettish, frolicsome **11** flirtatious

**kittiwake**
**06** haglet **07** hacklet

**kitty**
**04** fund

**knack**
**03** art, toy **04** bent, feel, gift, hang, turn **05** flair, forte, habit, quirk, skill, trick **06** genius, talent **07** ability, faculty **08** aptitude, capacity, facility, ornament **09** dexterity, expertise, handiness, quickness, technique **10** adroitness, capability, competence, propensity **11** proficiency, skilfulness

**knapsack**
**03** bag **04** pack **06** kitbag **07** holdall, musette **08** backpack, rucksack **09** duffel bag, haversack

**knave**
**01** J **03** boy, cad, nob, pam, pur **04** jack **05** cheat, drôle, rogue, scamp, swine **06** fripon, rascal, rotter, varlet **07** bounder, custrel, dastard, villain **08** blighter, coistrel, coistril, swindler **09** reprobate, scallywag, scoundrel

**knavery**
**05** fraud **06** deceit, ropery **07** devilry, roguery **08** mischief, patchery,

trickery, villainy **09** chicanery, deception, duplicity, imposture **10** corruption, dishonesty, hanky-panky **11** caddishness, friponnerie, knavishness **13** double-dealing **14** monkey business

**knavish**
**06** rascal, wicked **07** caddish, corrupt, roguish **08** devilish, fiendish, rascally **09** dastardly, deceitful, deceptive, dishonest, reprobate **10** fraudulent, villainous **11** mischievous, scoundrelly **12** contemptible, unprincipled, unscrupulous **13** dishonourable

**knead**
◇ *anagram indicator*
**03** ply, rub **04** form, mold, work
**05** malax, mould, pound, press, shape
**06** conche, puddle, pummel
**07** knuckle, massage, squeeze
**08** malaxate **09** masticate
**10** manipulate

**kneel**
**03** bow **04** bend **05** stoop **06** curtsy, kowtow, revere **07** bow down, defer to **09** genuflect **13** make obeisance **15** fall to your knees

**knees**
**03** lap

**knell**
**03** end **04** peal, ring, toll **05** chime, knoll, sound **07** ringing

**knickers**
**05** pants, thong **06** briefs, smalls
**07** drawers, g-string, panties
**08** bloomers, frillies, lingerie, scanties
**09** underwear **10** underpants **12** bikini briefs, camiknickers
**14** knickerbockers

**knick-knack**
**04** quip **05** knack **06** bauble, gewgaw, jimjam, pretty, trifle **07** bibelot, trangam, trinket **08** gimcrack, jimcrack, nick-nack, ornament **09** bagatelle, bric-à-brac, plaything **11** whigmaleery **12** pretty-pretty, whigmaleerie

**knife**
**03** cut, rip **04** stab **05** blade, slash, wound **06** cutter, pierce **08** lacerate

*Knives include:*

**02** da
**03** dah, hay, pen
**04** bolo, case, chiv, dirk, fish, jack, moon, shiv, simi
**05** bowie, bread, clasp, craft, cutto, flick, fruit, gully, kukri, panga, paper, putty, skean, skene, spade, steak, table
**06** barong, butter, carver, chakra, cradle, cuttle, cuttoe, dagger, gulley, oyster, parang, pocket, sheath, trench
**07** bayonet, carving, catling, drawing, dudgeon, hunting, leather, machete, palette, pruning, scalpel, Stanley®, whittle
**08** bistoury, chopping, scalping, skean-dhu, skene-dhu, tranchet
**09** butterfly, jockteleg, Swiss army, toothpick
**10** skene-occle
**11** snickersnee, switchblade
**13** Kitchen Devils®, pusser's dagger

*See also* **dagger**; **sword**

• **knife stand**
**03** nef **05** block

**knight**
**01** K, N **02** AK, Kt **03** dub, Sir
**07** gallant, soldier, warrior, younker
**08** champion, horseman **09** freelance, man-at-arms **10** cavalryman, equestrian **12** carpet-knight, knight-errant

*Knights include:*

**04** grey
**05** black, white
**06** Bayard, carpet, errant, kemper, ritter
**07** paladin
**08** bachelor, banneret, cavalier, douzeper, vavasour
**09** chevalier, doucepere, valvassor
**10** kempery-man
**14** knight-bachelor, preux chevalier

*Knights of the Round Table in Arthurian legend include:*

**03** Kay
**05** Lucan, Safer
**06** Degore, Gareth
**07** Alymere, Dagonet, Galahad, Gawaine, Lamorak, Lionell, Mordred, Pelleas, Tristan
**08** Bedivere, Tristram
**09** Bleoberis, Palomedes, Percivale
**10** King Arthur
**11** Bors de Ganis
**12** Brunor le Noir, Ector de Maris
**13** Lancelot Du Lac
**15** La Cote Male Taile

**knightly**
**04** bold **05** noble **06** heroic
**07** courtly, gallant, valiant **08** gracious, intrepid, valorous **09** dauntless, soldierly **10** chivalrous, courageous, honourable

**knit**
**03** set, tie **04** ally, bind, join, knot, link, loop, mend **05** unite, weave
**06** crease, fasten, furrow, gather, secure **07** connect, tighten, wrinkle **08** contract, crotchet
**09** interlace **10** intertwine **12** draw together

*Knitting-related terms include:*

**03** rib, row
**04** aran, purl, wool
**05** chart, pearl, plain
**06** cast on, marker, needle, stitch
**07** cast off, chevron, four-ply, tension, twin rib
**08** ball band, fair isle, intarsia
**09** box stitch, double rib, fingering, garter rib, single rib
**10** double knit, French heel, moss stitch, rice stitch, row counter, seed stitch, tricoteuse
**11** basketweave, cable needle, cable stitch, drop a stitch, plain stitch, thumb method
**12** basket-stitch, garter-stitch, stitch holder
**13** fisherman's rib, stocking frame
**14** circular needle, double knitting, knitting needle, stocking stitch
**15** knitting machine, knitting pattern

**knob**
**03** bur, nub **04** ball, boll, boss, bump, burr, heel, knop, knot, knub, lump, node, noop, snub, stop, stud, umbo
**05** berry, gnarl, knurl, mouse, offer, plook, plouk, rowel, swell, tuber, tuner
**06** button, croche, handle, pommel, snubbe, switch, toorie, tourie, tumour
**07** chesnut **08** chestnut, doorstop, eminence, pulvinar, register, swelling, tubercle **10** doorhandle, projection, protrusion, push-button
**12** protuberance

**knock**
◇ *anagram indicator*
**02** ca' **03** box, caa', con, dod, hit, pan, rap, tap **04** bang, bash, belt, blow, bump, chap, clip, cuff, dash, daud, dawd, daze, ding, jole, joll, jolt, jowl, pink, punt, slag, slam, slap, stun
**05** clock, clour, clout, crash, joule, pound, punch, shock, slate, smack, stamp, swipe, thump, whack
**06** attack, batter, defeat, nubble, rebuff, strike, wallop, whammy **07** bad luck, banging, censure, collide, condemn, failure, innings, knobble, knubble, rubbish, run down, setback, slag off **08** bump into, confound, pounding, reversal **09** criticism, criticize, deprecate, disparage, hammering, pull apart, rejection
**10** misfortune **11** collide with, pick holes in **12** pull to pieces, tear to pieces **13** bad experience, find fault with

*See also* **beat**

• **knock about**
**03** gad, hit **04** bash, hurt, roam, rove
**05** abuse, punch, range, wound
**06** bang up, batter, beat up, bruise, buffet, damage, injure, ramble, strike, travel, wander **07** consort, saunter, traipse **08** go around, maltreat, mistreat **09** associate, gallivant, hang about, manhandle **10** hang around

• **knock back**
◇ *reversal indicator*
**04** cost, down, gulp, swig **05** drink, scoff, shock **06** devour, guzzle, rebuff, reject **07** swallow **08** gulp down
**10** disconcert

• **knock down**
**03** hit **04** fell, prop, raze **05** clout, floor, level, lower, pound, smash, wreck **06** batter, reduce, wallop
**07** destroy, run down, run over, skittle

**08** bowl over, decrease, demolish, pull down, take down **09** bring down, knock over

**• knocked down**

**02** KD

**• knock off**

**03** rob **04** do in, kill, lift, nick, slay, stop, whip **05** cease, filch, pinch, steal, swipe, waste **06** deduct, finish, murder, pack in, pilfer, pirate, rip off, snitch **07** bump off, snaffle **08** clock off, clock out, get rid of, pack it in, stop work, take away **09** polish off, terminate **10** do away with, finish work **11** assassinate, discontinue

**• knock out**

**02** KO **04** beat, fell, kayo, rout, stun **05** amaze, crush, floor, level, shock **06** defeat, hammer, thrash **07** astound, destroy, disable, flatten, impress, startle **08** astonish, bowl over, demolish, overcome, surprise **09** eliminate, overwhelm, prostrate **10** strike down **11** knock for six **13** run rings round **14** get the better of **15** make unconscious

**• knock over**

◇ *anagram indicator*

**04** fell **05** floor, level **07** run down, run over

**• knock up**

**04** call, stir **05** awake, rouse, waken **06** awaken, wake up **07** wear out **09** improvise **10** impregnate, jerry-build **11** make quickly **12** build quickly, make pregnant, put in the club

## knockout

**02** KO **03** hit **04** coup, kayo **05** smash, socko **06** winner **07** king-hit, stunner, success, triumph **08** smash-hit **09** sensation **10** attraction

## knoll

**04** hill, rise **05** knell, knowe, mound **06** barrow, koppie **07** hillock, hummock **09** elevation

## knot

◇ *anagram indicator*

**02** kn, kt **03** bud, nur **04** band, bind, bond, boss, gnar, hill, knag, knar, knit, knob, knub, knur, lash, lump, node, nurr, ring, tags **05** bunch, clump, crowd, gnarl, group, joint, knurl, knurr, leash, mouse, ravel, snarl, twist, weave **06** circle, gaggle, nodule, secure, splice, tangle, tether **07** chignon, cluster, entwine **08** entangle, ligature, swelling **09** fastening, gathering **10** concretion, difficulty **14** marriage-favour

*Knots include:*

**03** bow, tie
**04** bend, flat, loop, love, reef, wale, wall
**05** blood, chain, hitch, plait, thief, thumb, turle
**06** Domhof, granny, lover's, prusik, square
**07** bowline, Gordian, running, seizing, weaver's, Windsor
**08** overhand, slipknot, spade-end, surgeon's, true-love
**09** half hitch, lark's head, sheet bend, swab hitch, Turk's head
**10** clove hitch, common bend, fisherman's, Flemish eye, sheepshank, true-lover's
**11** carrick bend, donkey hitch, double blood, Englishman's, Hunter's bend, timber hitch
**12** marling hitch, rolling hitch, simple sennit, weaver's hitch
**13** drummer's chain, figure of eight, slippery hitch
**14** Blackwall hitch, common whipping, double Cairnton, double-overhand, double-overhang, Englishman's tie, fisherman's bend, Matthew Walker's, running bowline

## knotty

◇ *anagram indicator*

**04** hard **05** bumpy, nirly, rough **06** knaggy, knobby, nirlie, nodose, nodous, rugged, thorny, tricky **07** complex, gnarled, gnarred, knarred, knobbly, knotted, nodular **08** baffling, puzzling **09** Byzantine, difficult, intricate **10** mystifying, perplexing **11** anfractuous, complicated, troublesome **13** problematical

## know

**03** con, ken, kon, see, wis, wit, wot **04** have, tell, weet, wish, wist **05** conne, savey, savvy, sense, weete **06** fathom, notice, savvey, weeten **07** approve, be aware, discern, make out, realize, undergo **08** identify, perceive **09** apprehend, be clued up, go through, have taped, recognize, tell apart **10** comprehend, experience, understand **11** distinguish, know by sight **12** be au fait with, discriminate **13** associate with, be cognizant of, be conscious of, be friends with, differentiate **14** be familiar with, be well-versed in

**• I don't know**

**04** pass

## know-all

**06** Jowett **07** wise guy **08** polymath, wiseacre **09** know-it-all, smart alec **10** clever dick **11** clever clogs, smartypants

## know-how

**04** bent **05** flair, knack, savey, savvy, skill **06** savvey, talent **07** ability, faculty **08** aptitude, cum-savvy, gumption **09** adeptness, dexterity, expertise, ingenuity, knowledge **10** adroitness, capability, competence, experience **11** proficiency, savoir-faire

## knowing

**03** fly, hep, hip **05** aware, canny, downy **06** astute, shrewd, sussed **07** cunning, gnostic, skilful **08** informed **09** conscious, up to snuff **10** deliberate, discerning, expressive, meaningful, perceptive **11** intelligent, significant, worldly-wise

## knowingly

**08** by design, scienter, wilfully **09** on purpose, purposely, studiedly, willingly, wittingly **10** designedly **11** consciously **12** calculatedly, deliberately **13** intentionally

## knowledge

**03** art, gen, sus **04** data, suss **05** facts, grasp, jnana, light, skill, truth **06** gnosis, wisdom **07** ability, cunning, insight, knowhow, letters, tuition, witting **08** intimacy, learning, pansophy **09** awareness, cognition, education, erudition, expertise, judgement, schooling **10** cognizance **11** conversance, discernment, familiarity, information, instruction, proficiency, recognition, savoir-faire, scholarship **12** acquaintance, apprehension, intelligence **13** comprehension, consciousness, encyclopedism, enlightenment, understanding

**• full knowledge**

**11** omniscience

**• range of knowledge**

**03** ken

## knowledgeable

**02** up **05** aware, savey, savvy **06** au fait, expert, savvey **07** clued-up, erudite, learned **08** educated, familiar, genned up, informed, lettered, well-read, well up in **09** conscious, in the know, scholarly, up to speed **10** acquainted, conversant, well-versed **11** enlightened, experienced, intelligent **12** well-informed

## known

**04** kent **05** couth, noted, plain **06** avowed, famous, patent **07** obvious **08** admitted, familiar, revealed **09** confessed, published, well-known **10** celebrated, proclaimed, recognized **11** commonplace **12** acknowledged

**• also known as**

**03** aka **05** alias

## knuckle

**• knuckle down**

**10** buckle down **12** begin to study **15** start to work hard

**• knuckle under**

**05** defer, yield **06** accede, give in, submit **07** give way, succumb **09** acquiesce, surrender **10** capitulate **11** buckle under

## Koran

**05** Qoran, Quran **07** Alcoran

**• chapter of the Koran**

**04** sura **05** surah

**Korea**
**02** KP, KR **03** KOR, PRK, ROK

**kosher**
**• not kosher**
**04** tref **05** trefa, treif

**kowtow**
**04** fawn **05** defer, kneel, toady **06** cringe, grovel, pander, suck up **07** flatter **08** pay court **11** curry favour **12** bow and scrape

**krypton**
**02** Kr

**kudos**
**04** fame, mana **05** glory **06** cachet, credit, esteem, honour, praise, regard, renown, repute **07** acclaim, laurels **08** applause, plaudits, prestige **09** laudation **10** reputation **11** distinction

**Kuwait**
**03** KWT

**Kyrgyzstan**
**02** KS **03** KGZ

# L

**L**
**02** el **04** Lima

**label**
**03** dub, tab, tag **04** call, logo, make, mark, name, seal, term **05** badge, brand, class, flash, stamp, tally, title **06** define, docket, marker, number, sticky, ticket **07** address, crowner, epithet, sticker **08** classify, describe, identify, nickname **09** bookplate, brand name, designate, dripstone, trademark **10** categorize, identifier, pigeonhole **11** description, designation **12** characterize **13** bumper sticker **14** attach a label to, categorization, classification, identification **15** proprietary name

**laboratory**

*Laboratory apparatus includes:*

**05** clamp, flask, slide, stand, still, U-tube
**06** beaker, Bunsen, funnel, Gilson®, mortar, pestle, retort, tripod, trough
**07** bell jar, burette, cuvette, dropper, pipette, spatula, stirrer
**08** crucible, cylinder, fume hood, glove box, test tube
**09** autoclave, condenser, Petri dish, power pack, steam bath, stop clock
**10** centrifuge, desiccator, ice machine, microscope, PCR machine, Petri plate, watchglass
**11** boiling tube, filter flask, filter paper, fume chamber, thermometer
**12** Bunsen burner, cloud chamber, conical flask, fume cupboard, heating block, test tube rack, Woulfe bottle
**13** bubble chamber, Büchner funnel, top-pan balance
**14** Kipp's apparatus
**15** Erlenmeyer flask, evaporating dish, laminar flow hood, Liebig condenser, volumetric flask

**laborious**
**04** hard **05** heavy, tough **06** tiring, uphill **07** arduous, careful, onerous, operose, painful, slavish, tedious **08** diligent, tiresome, toilsome, wearying **09** assiduous, difficult, fatiguing, Sisyphean, strenuous, wearisome **10** laboursome, working-day **11** hard-working, industrious, painstaking **12** backbreaking **13** indefatigable

**laboriously**
**09** arduously, operosely, slavishly **10** drudgingly, tiresomely, toilsomely **11** strenuously, wearisomely **14** with difficulty

**labour**
◇ *anagram indicator*
**03** job, Lab **04** hard, moil, plod, roll, slog, task, toil, toss, turn, work **05** begar, birth, chore, grind, hands, pains, pangs, pitch, slave, sweat, yakka **06** drudge, duties, effort, overdo, strain, strive, suffer, throes **07** dwell on, katorga, travail, try hard, workers, workmen **08** belabour, be misled, delivery, drudgery, drudgism, exertion, go all out, hard work, struggle, work hard **09** be blinded, diligence, do to death, elaborate, employees, endeavour, hard yakka, labourers, reiterate, servitude, workforce **10** be deceived, childbirth, do your best, employment, overstress **11** flog to death, give your all, harp on about, labour pains, parturition **12** contractions, kill yourself **13** exert yourself, labor improbus, overemphasize **14** go on and on about **15** industriousness

**laboured**
◇ *anagram indicator*
**05** heavy, stiff **06** forced, leaden, worked **07** awkward, stilted, studied **08** affected, overdone, strained **09** contrived, difficult, effortful, ponderous, unnatural **10** cultivated **11** complicated, overwrought

**labourer**
**03** boy **04** hand, jack, peon **05** churl, cooly, grunt, navvy **06** bohunk, coolie, docker, drudge, hodman, Kanaka, menial, worker **07** culchie, Grecian, hobbler, pioneer, redneck, seagull, wharfie, workman **08** cottager, dataller, daytaler, farm hand, hireling **09** field hand, operative **10** hod carrier, roustabout **11** gandy dancer **12** manual worker **15** unskilled worker

**labyrinth**
**03** web **04** maze **06** enigma, jungle, puzzle, riddle, tangle, warren **07** mizmaze, network, winding **09** confusion, intricacy **10** complexity, perplexity **12** complication, entanglement

**labyrinthine**
◇ *anagram indicator*
**04** mazy **06** knotty **07** complex, tangled, winding **08** confused, involved, mazelike, puzzling, tortuous **09** Byzantine, intricate **10** convoluted, perplexing **11** complicated

**lace**
◇ *anagram indicator*
**03** net, tat, tie **04** bind, cord, do up **05** add to, blend, close, mix in, point, spike, thong, twine **06** attach, fasten, lacing, secure, string, tawdry, thrash, thread **07** crochet, flavour, fortify, latchet, netting **08** bobbinet, bootlace, filigree, mesh-work, open work, shoelace, stay tape **09** bobbin net **10** intertwine, interweave, strengthen **11** intermingle

*Lace types include:*

**04** bone, gold
**05** blond, filet, jabot, orris, point
**06** blonde, bobbin, pillow, thread, trolly
**07** footing, galloon, guipure, Honiton, Mechlin, pearlin, tatting, torchon, trolley
**08** Brussels, dentelle, duchesse, net orris, pearling
**09** Chantilly, reticella
**10** Colbertine, mignonette
**12** Valenciennes

**lacerate**
**03** cut, rip **04** claw, gash, hurt, maim, rend, rent, tear, torn **05** ganch, slash, wound **06** gaunch, harrow, injure, mangle **07** afflict, cut open, scarify, torment, torture **08** distress, mutilate **09** lancinate

**laceration**
**03** cut, rip **04** gash, maim, rent, tear **05** slash, wound **06** injury **10** mutilation

**lachrymose**
**03** sad **05** teary, weepy **06** crying, woeful **07** maudlin, sobbing, tearful, weeping **08** dolorous, mournful **10** lugubrious, melancholy

**lack**
◇ *deletion indicator*
**03** gap **04** miss, need, void, want **06** dearth, defect, penury **07** absence, not have, paucity, require, vacancy **08** scarcity, shortage **09** emptiness, privation **10** deficiency, have need of, scantiness **11** deprivation, destitution **12** be clean out of, be fresh out of **13** be deficient in, insufficiency **15** not have enough of

**lackadaisical**
**04** dull, idle, lazy, limp **05** inert **06** dreamy **07** languid **08** careless, indolent, listless, lukewarm **09** apathetic, enervated, lethargic **10** abstracted, languorous, spiritless **11** half-hearted, indifferent

**lackey**
**04** page, pawn, tool **05** gofer, guide, toady, valet **06** fawner, menial, minion, monkey, poodle, vassal, yes-man **07** doormat, equerry, footman, servant, steward **08** hanger-on, parasite, retainer **09** attendant, flatterer, sycophant **10** instrument, manservant, skip-kennel

**lacking**
◇ *deletion indicator*
**03** shy **04** poor **05** minus **06** absent, flawed, to seek, wanted **07** missing, needing, short of, wanting, without **09** defective, deficient **10** inadequate

**lacklustre**
**03** dim, dry **04** drab, dull, flat **05** vapid **06** boring, leaden **07** insipid, tedious **08** lifeless **10** spiritless, uninspired **11** commonplace **12** run-of-the-mill **13** unimaginative, uninteresting

**laconic**
**04** curt **05** blunt, brief, crisp, pithy, short, terse **06** abrupt **07** concise, spartan **08** incisive, succinct, taciturn **10** economical, to the point **12** monosyllabic

**laconically**
**07** bluntly, briefly, in a word, in brief, pithily, tersely **08** abruptly **09** concisely **10** incisively, succinctly, to the point

**lacquer**
**05** japan **07** varnish **09** hairspray **12** vernis martin **14** Coromandel work

**lacuna**
**03** gap **04** void **05** blank, break, space **06** cavity, hiatus **08** omission

**lad**
**03** boy, guy, kid, son, tad **04** boyo, chap, sort, type **05** bloke, bucko, chiel, whelp, youth **06** callan, chield, fellow, nipper **07** callant, gossoon **08** juvenile, spalpeen **09** character, schoolboy, stripling, youngster **10** individual **13** gillie-wetfoot **14** whippersnapper **15** gillie-white-foot

**ladder**
**03** run, sty **04** rank, rung, trap **05** level, point, rungs, scala, scale, steps **06** étrier, series, stairs **07** fish-way, grading, potence, ranking **08** echelons **09** companion, hierarchy **10** set of steps **12** pecking order

**laden**
**04** full **05** heavy, taxed **06** jammed, loaded, packed **07** charged, fraught, gestant, stuffed **08** burdened, hampered, pregnant, weighted **09** chock-full, oppressed **10** encumbered **11** weighed down

**la-di-da**
**04** posh **05** put-on **06** snooty **07** foppish, stuck-up **08** affected, mannered, snobbish **09** conceited **11** highfalutin, over-refined, pretentious, toffee-nosed

**ladies** *see* **toilet**

**ladle**
**03** dip **04** bail, bale, dish, lade **05** scoop, shank, spoon **06** dipper, shovel **07** divider

• **ladle out**
**07** bail out, bale out, dish out, dole out, hand out **08** disburse **10** distribute

**lady**
**01** L **04** burd, dame, miss **05** begum, lakin, siren, woman **06** damsel, duenna, female, khanum, matron, Señora **07** hidalga, ladykin, old dear, sheikha, Signora **08** countess, Señorita **09** Signorina **10** demoiselle, grande dame, noblewoman, young woman **11** gentlewoman

*See also* **girl**; **woman**

• **lady's fingers**
**04** okra **05** gumbo

• **lot of ladies**
**04** bevy

• **organized ladies**
**02** WI **15** Women's Institute

**ladylike**
**04** soft **06** modest, polite, proper **07** courtly, elegant, genteel, queenly, refined **08** cultured, decorous, delicate, matronly, polished, well-bred **09** courteous **11** respectable **12** well-mannered

**lag**
**04** drag, idle, late **05** dally, delay, steal, tardy, tarry, trail **06** arrest, dawdle, linger, loiter, lounge, retard **07** convict, saunter, shuffle **08** hang back, hindmost, imprison, straggle **10** behindhand, fall behind, retardment **11** retardation **12** drag your feet, shilly-shally **13** kick your heels **14** bring up the rear

*See also* **prisoner**

**lager** *see* **beer**

**laggard**
**05** idler, snail **06** loafer **07** dawdler, lounger **08** lingerer, loiterer, sluggard **09** saunterer, slowcoach, straggler

**lagoon**
**03** bog, fen **04** haff, lake, pond, pool **05** bayou, marsh, swamp **06** lagune, salina **08** shallows

**laid-back**
**04** calm, cool **06** at ease, casual **07** relaxed **09** easy-going, leisurely, unhurried, unworried **10** untroubled **11** free and easy, unflappable **13** imperturbable

**laid up**
**03** ill **04** sick **05** crook **07** injured **08** disabled **09** bedridden **10** housebound **11** immobilized, out of action **12** hors de combat **13** confined to bed, incapacitated, on the sick list

**lair**
**03** den, lie **04** mire **05** couch **07** retreat

*See also* **animal**

**laissez-faire**
**09** free-trade **10** free-market, permissive **14** free-enterprise, live and let live, non-interfering

**laity**
**03** lay **06** people **08** amateurs **09** lay people, outsiders **10** temporalty, unordained **12** parishioners **14** the non-ordained

**lake**
**01** L **03** dam, lac, sea **04** loch, meer, mere, pond, pool, tarn **05** basin, bayou, cowal, lough, playa, shott, water **06** lagoon, lagune, nyanza, salina **07** carmine **09** everglade, reservoir, saltchuck

*The Great Lakes:*

**04** Erie
**05** Huron
**07** Ontario
**08** Michigan, Superior

*Lakes, lochs and loughs include:*

**03** Awe, Van
**04** Abbé, Bala, Biwa, Bled, Chad, Como, Derg, Earn, Erie, Eyre, Kivu, Ness, Tana
**05** Foyle, Garda, Great, Huron, Leven, Morar, Neagh, Nyasa, Ohrid, Onega, Patos, Poopó, Tahoe, Taupo, Volta
**06** Albert, Baikal, Corrib, Crater, Finger, Geneva, Ladoga, Lomond, Louise, Malawi, Nasser, Saimaa, Taimyr, Taymyr, Vänern, Zurich
**07** Aral Sea, Balaton, Chapala, Dead Sea, Katrine, Lucerne, Ontario, Rannoch, Scutari, Torrens, Turkana
**08** Balkhash, Bodensee, Chiemsee, Issyk Kul, Lac Léman, Loch Earn, Loch Ness, Lough Awe, Maggiore, Michigan, Superior, Tiberias, Titicaca, Tonlé Sap, Victoria, Winnipeg
**09** Constance, Great Bear, Great Salt, Kammer See, Loch Leven, Loch Morar, Lough Derg, Maracaibo, Neuchâtel, Nicaragua, Ullswater, Willandra, Zeller See
**10** Caspian Sea, Great Slave, Loch Lomond, Lough Foyle, Lough Neagh, Okeechobee, Tanganyika, Windermere, Wörther See
**11** Great Bitter, Loch Katrine, Lough Corrib
**12** Derwent Water, Kielder Water
**13** Bassenthwaite, Coniston Water

**lam**
**03** hit **04** bash, beat, belt, pelt **05** clout, knock, pound, thump, whack **06** batter, escape, pummel, strike, thrash, wallop **07** leather

**lamb**
**04** cade, Elia, yean **08** yeanling

**lambast, lambaste**
**03** tan **04** beat, belt, drub, flay, flog, slag, whip **05** clout, roast, scold, thump, whack **06** batter, berate, rebuke, strike, thrash, wallop

07 censure, clobber, leather, reprove, rubbish, slag off, upbraid **08** badmouth **09** castigate, criticize, reprimand

**lambert**
**01** L

**lame**
**04** game, halt, hurt, maim, main, poor, tame, thin, weak **05** gammy **06** feeble, flimsy, maimed, mained, poorly
**07** cripple, halting, injured, limping
**08** crippled, disabled, hobbling, spavined **09** defective, hamstring, hamstrung **10** inadequate
**11** handicapped **12** unconvincing
**13** incapacitated **14** unsatisfactory
**• lame person**
**04** gimp

**lamely**
**06** feebly, tamely, weakly **07** shakily
**09** with a limp **10** hobblingly, unsteadily **12** inadequately
**14** unconvincingly

**lament**
**03** cry, sob **04** howl, keen, mean, mein, mene, moan, wail, weep
**05** dirge, dumka, elegy, groan, meane, mourn, plain, tears **06** bemoan, bewail, beweep, crying, grieve, regret, repine, sorrow, yammer **07** deplore, requiem, sobbing, ululate, wayment, weeping **08** complain, grieving, threnody **09** complaint
**11** lamentation

**lamentable**
◇ *anagram indicator*
**03** low, sad **04** mean, poor **05** lousy
**06** crying, funest, grotty, meagre, measly, tragic, woeful **07** moanful, pitiful **08** grievous, mournful, terrible, wretched **09** miserable, niggardly, sorrowful, worthless **10** deplorable, inadequate **11** distressing, regrettable, unfortunate
**12** insufficient **13** disappointing
**14** unsatisfactory

**lamentably**
**08** woefully **09** miserably, pitifully
**10** deplorably, tragically **11** regrettably
**12** inadequately **14** insufficiently
**15** disappointingly

**lamentation**
**03** cry **04** keen, moan **05** dirge, elegy, grief **06** lament, plaint, sorrow
**07** keening, sobbing, wailing, wayment, weeping **08** grieving, jeremiad, mourning, threnody
**09** ululation **11** deploration

**laminate**
**04** coat, face **05** cover, flake, layer, plate, split **06** veneer **07** foliate, overlay **08** separate, stratify
**09** exfoliate

**lamp**
**03** eye **04** bulb, Davy **05** crusy, light, torch **06** argand, crusie, Leerie, sconce
**07** cruisie, Geordie, lantern, lucigen, pendant, pendent, scamper **08** arc-light, fog light, torchier **09** light bulb, moderator, spotlight, torchière, veilleuse **10** Anglepoise®, Kleig light, Klieg light, night-light, photoflood
**11** searchlight

**lampoon**
**04** mock, skit **05** spoof, squib
**06** parody, satire, send up, send-up
**07** Pasquil, Pasquin, take off, take-off
**08** ridicule, satirize, travesty
**09** burlesque, make fun of
**10** caricature, pasquinade

**lampooner**
**07** Pasquil, Pasquin **08** parodist, satirist **09** pasquiler **10** pasquilant
**11** pasquinader **12** caricaturist

**lance**
**03** cut **04** pike, slit **05** lanch, prick, rejón, shaft, spear **06** incise, lancet, launch, pierce **07** bayonet, cut open, harpoon, javelin **08** puncture, white arm

**land**
**03** bag, get, hit, nab, net, tax, win
**04** area, deal, dock, drop, gain, give, loam, lord, moor, soil **05** acres, berth, catch, earth, end up, fetch, manor, reach, realm, state, tract **06** alight, anchor, arrive, burden, direct, domain, estate, fields, ground, lumber, nation, obtain, people, region, saddle, secure, settle, turn up, unload, whenua, wind up **07** achieve, acquire, acreage, capture, country, deliver, deplane, deposit, dry land, grounds, inflict, oppress, procure, terrain, trouble
**08** dismount, district, encumber, farmland, finish up, go ashore, property, province, take down
**09** bring down, disembark, get hold of, open space, rural area, territory, touch down, weigh down **10** administer, come to rest, fatherland, motherland, real estate, terra firma **11** countryside, terrestrial **12** come in to land, find yourself **13** bring in to land, native country
*See also* **country**; **continent**
**• amount of land**
**03** are, lot, rod, ure **04** acre, shot
**07** hectare
**• arable land**
**03** lay, lea, ley

**landing**
**04** dock, pier, quay **05** jetty, wharf
**07** arrival, greaser, harbour **08** coming in **09** alighting, belly flop, deplaning, touchdown **12** landing-place, landing-stage, three-pricker **13** putting ashore
**14** coming in to land, coming to ground, disembarkation

**landing-stair**
**04** ghat **05** ghaut

**landlady, landlord**
**04** host **05** owner **06** lessor
**07** hostess, Rachman **08** hotelier, mine host, publican, slumlord **09** innkeeper, landowner **10** freeholder, proprietor
**11** hotel-keeper **12** proprietress, restaurateur

**landmark**
**05** cairn, meith **06** beacon, crisis
**07** feature **08** boundary, milepost, monument, signpost **09** milestone, watershed **12** turning-point
*See also* **Africa**; **Asia**; **Australia**; **Canada**; **Europe**; **London**; **Middle East**; **New York**; **New Zealand**; **United Kingdom**; **United States of America**

**landscape**
**04** view **05** scene, vista **06** aspect, saikei **07** outlook, paysage, scenery
**08** panorama, prospect
**11** countryside, perspective

**landslide**
**04** slip **07** runaway **08** decisive, emphatic, landslip, rockfall
**09** avalanche, earthfall **10** éboulement
**12** overwhelming

**lane**
**02** La **03** gut, way **04** loan, loke, lone, path, wynd **05** alley, byway, entry, track
**06** avenue, boreen, byroad, ruelle, vennel **07** bikeway, channel, footway, loaning, passage, pathway, sea road, towpath, twitten **08** alleyway, driveway, footpath, twitting
**10** backstreet, passageway

**language**
**03** bat **04** cant, talk **05** argot, lingo, style **06** jargon, speech, tongue
**07** diction, wording **08** converse, parlance, phrasing, rhetoric, speaking, swearing, uttering **09** discourse, utterance **10** expression, vocabulary, vocalizing **11** phraseology, terminology, verbalizing
**12** conversation **13** communication

*Languages include:*

**02** Wu
**03** ASL, BSL, Edo, Gan, Giz, Ibo, Kru, Lao, Mam, Mon, Twi, Yue
**04** Chad, Cree, Crow, Dari, Erse, Fang, Gaul, Inca, Lapp, Manx, Maya, Moto, Nupe, Pali, Susu, Thai, Tshi, Urdu, Xosa, Zulu
**05** Attic, Aztec, Bantu, Cajun, Carib, Creek, Croat, Czech, Doric, Dutch, Farsi, Greek, Hindi, Inuit, Ionic, Iraqi, Irish, Karen, Kazak, Khmer, Latin, Malay, Maori, Masai, Norse, Osean, Punic, Saxon, Scots, Shona, Sioux, Tamil, Uzbek, Welsh, Xhosa, Yakut
**06** Arabic, Bangla, Basque, Berber, Bokmål, Celtic, Coptic, Creole, Dakota, Danish, French, Gaelic, German, Gothic, Hebrew, Lydian, Magyar, Micmac, Mohawk, Mongol, Polish, Romany, Sherpa, Slovak, Tartar
**07** Afghani, Amharic, Aramaic, Ayamará, Bengali, Bosnian, Catalan, Chinese, Chinook, Cornish, English, Euskera, Finnish, Flemish, Frisian, Guaraní, Italian, Kalmuck, Lappish, Latvian, Maltese, Mohican, Nynorsk, Punjabi, Quechua, Russian, Semitic, Siamese, Slovene, Spanish, Swahili, Swedish, Tagálog,

Turkish, Umbrian, Volapük, Walloon, Yiddish, Zapotec
**08** Albanian, Armenian, Cherokee, Croatian, Demotiki, Estonian, Etruscan, Georgian, Japanese, Malagasy, Mandarin, Moldovan, Phrygian, Pilipino, Romanian, Romansch, Sanskrit, Setswana
**09** Aborigine, Afrikaans, Algonquin, Bulgarian, Cantonese, Castilian, Dalmatian, Ethiopian, Hungarian, Icelandic, Kiswahili, Malayalam, Norwegian, Provençal, Sardinian, Ukrainian
**10** Anglo-Saxon, Babylonian, Belarusian, Hindustani, Lithuanian, Macedonian, Malayaalam, Phoenician, Portuguese, Serbo-Croat, Vietnamese
**12** ancient Greek, Katharevousa, Sign Language
**13** Middle English
**14** Lëtzebuergesch

*Invented languages include:*

**03** Ido, Neo
**06** Novial
**07** Volapük
**08** Newspeak
**09** Esperanto
**10** Occidental
**11** Interglossa, Interlingua
**12** Idiom Neutral

*Computer programming languages include:*

**01** C
**03** ADA, AWK, C++, XML
**04** HTML, Java, Perl
**05** BASIC, COBOL
**06** Delphi, Pascal, Python
**07** FORTRAN
**10** Postscript

*Language terms include:*

**02** RP
**03** ASR, NLP
**04** cant
**05** argot, idiom, lingo, slang, usage
**06** accent, brogue, creole, jargon, patois, patter, pidgin, syntax, tongue
**07** dialect, grammar
**08** buzz word, localism, Newspeak, standard
**09** etymology, phonetics, semantics
**10** journalese, vernacular, vocabulary
**11** doublespeak, linguistics, non-standard, orthography, regionalism
**12** gobbledygook, lexicography, lingua franca, vulgar tongue
**13** colloquialism

**• bad language**
**04** cuss, oath **05** curse **07** cussing **08** swearing **09** expletive, swearword

**• language unit**
**04** word **07** phoneme

**languid**
**04** dull, lazy, limp, slow, weak **05** faint, heavy, inert, slack, weary **06** feeble, pining, sickly, torpid **07** relaxed **08** drooping, flagging, inactive, listless, sluggish **09** enervated, lethargic **10** languorous, spiritless **11** debilitated, indifferent **12** uninterested **13** lackadaisical **14** unenthusiastic

**languidly**
**05** dully **06** feebly, lazily, slowly, weakly **07** heavily, inertly **08** torpidly **10** inactively, listlessly **13** lethargically

**languish**
**03** die, rot **04** fade, fail, flag, long, mope, pine, sigh, sink, want, wilt **05** brood, droop, faint, quail, waste, yearn **06** desire, grieve, hanker, hunger, sicken, sorrow, weaken, wither **07** decline **08** fall away **09** waste away **11** deteriorate

**languor**
**04** calm, lull **05** ennui, sloth **06** pining, torpor **07** fatigue, frailty, inertia, silence **08** debility, laziness, lethargy, weakness **09** faintness, heaviness, indolence, lassitude, stillness, weariness **10** affliction, dreaminess, drowsiness, enervation, feebleness, relaxation, sleepiness **12** listlessness **14** oppressiveness

**languorous**
**04** lazy, weak **05** weary **06** dreamy, feeble, sleepy, torpid **07** relaxed **08** listless **09** lethargic

**lank**
**04** lean, limp, long, slim, tall, thin **05** gaunt, lanky **06** skinny **07** flaccid, scraggy, scrawny, slender **08** drooping, lifeless, rawboned **09** emaciated, slab-sided **10** lustreless, straggling

**lanky**
**04** lean, slim, tall, thin **05** gaunt, rangy, weedy **06** gangly **07** scraggy, scrawny, slender **08** gangling

**lantern**
**04** buat, glim, lamp **05** bowat, bowet, crown, darky **06** cupola, darkey, sconce **08** bull's-eye **09** Aldis lamp, belvedere **12** stereopticon

**lanthanum**
**02** La

**Laos**
**03** LAO

**lap**
**03** leg, lip, rag, sip, sup **04** beat, dash, flap, flow, fold, lick, loop, roll, rush, slop, tour, wash, wind, wrap **05** ambit, break, cover, drink, knees, orbit, round, slosh, stage, swish, twine **06** circle, course, encase, enfold, hollow, lappet, splash, swathe, thighs **07** circuit, compass, envelop, overlap, scoop up, section, stretch, swaddle **08** distance, surround

**• lap up**
**06** absorb, relish, savour **08** listen in **09** delight in **13** accept eagerly

**lapse**
**03** end, gap **04** drop, fail, fall, go by, go on, lull, pass, sink, slip, stop, trip **05** blank, break, cease, drift, error, fault, glide, pause, slide **06** course, elapse, expire, hiatus, run out, slip by, worsen **07** blunder, decline, descent, failing, go to pot, mistake, passage, relapse, resolve, stumble **08** downturn, interval, omission, slip away, slipping **09** backslide, oversight, prescribe, terminate, worsening **10** aberration, become void, degenerate, go downhill, negligence **11** backsliding, dereliction, deteriorate, go to the dogs **12** degeneration, indiscretion, intermission, interruption **13** become invalid, deterioration, fall from grace **14** go down the tubes **15** go to rack and ruin

**lapsed**
**04** once, void **05** ended **06** former, run out **07** expired, invalid **08** finished, obsolete, outdated **09** out of date, unrenewed **11** backslidden **12** discontinued **13** non-practising

**lapwing**
**05** pewit, tewit **06** peewit, tewhit **07** teuchat **08** teru-tero

**larceny**
**05** heist, theft **06** piracy **07** robbery **08** burglary, stealing **09** pilfering **10** purloining **13** expropriation

**lard**
**04** load, saim, seam **05** enarm, seame, strew, stuff **06** fatten **07** garnish **14** interpenetrate

**larder**
**06** pantry, spence **08** scullery **09** storeroom **11** springhouse, storage room

**large**
**02** lg, OS **03** big, lge **04** full, high, huge, mega, tall, vast **05** ample, broad, bulky, giant, grand, great, heavy, jumbo, roomy **06** bumper **07** copious, diffuse, immense, liberal, mammoth, massive, monster, outsize, sizable **08** abundant, colossal, enormous, generous, gigantic, sizeable, spacious, spanking, sweeping, whopping **09** extensive, ginormous, good-sized, grandiose, humungous, king-sized, monstrous, plentiful **10** commodious, dirty great, exhaustive, monumental, prodigious, stupendous, voluminous **11** far-reaching, importantly, magnanimous, prominently, substantial, wide-ranging **12** considerable **13** comprehensive, wide-stretched **14** Brobdingnagian, ostentatiously

**• at large**
**03** out **04** free **06** abroad, mainly **07** chiefly **08** on the run **09** at liberty, generally, in general, in the main **10** by and large, on the loose, on the whole, unconfined **11** independent

**• by and large**
**06** mainly, mostly **07** as a rule **09** generally **10** on the whole **14** for the most part

**largely**
**06** mainly, mostly, widely **07** chiefly, greatly **09** generally, in the main, primarily **10** by and large, especially **11** extensively, principally **12** considerably **13** predominantly **14** for the most part, to a large extent

**largeness**
**04** bulk, size **08** vastness, wideness **09** ampleness, amplitude, broadness, grandness, greatness, heaviness, immensity **11** sizableness **12** enormousness, macrocephaly, sizeableness **13** expansiveness **14** stupendousness, voluminousness

**large-scale**
**04** epic, mega, vast, wide **05** broad **06** global **08** sweeping **09** expansive, extensive, universal, wholesale **10** nationwide **11** country-wide, far-reaching, wide-ranging **12** wide-reaching

**largesse**
**03** aid **04** alms, gift **05** grant **06** bounty **07** bequest, charity, handout, present **08** donation, kindness **09** allowance, endowment **10** generosity, liberality **11** benefaction, munificence **12** philanthropy **14** open-handedness

**lark**
◇ *anagram indicator*
**03** guy, job **04** game, play, romp, task **05** antic, caper, chore, fling, prank, revel, sport, thing **06** cavort, frolic, gambol **07** fooling, gammock, have fun, rollick, skylark **08** activity, business, escapade, mischief **09** cavorting, fool about, horseplay, mess about **10** fool around, play tricks

**larva**
**04** grub, moth, spat **05** ghost, naiad, ox-bot **06** caddis, chigoe, chigre, measle **07** budworm, chigger, hydatid, planula, pluteus, spectre, tadpole, veliger **08** army worm, bookworm, coenurus, cornworm, mealworm, wireworm, woodworm **09** auger-worm, bloodworm, doodlebug, glass-crab, joint-worm, screw-worm, sporocyst, strawworm, xylophage **10** bipinnaria, caddis-worm, cankerworm, miracidium, woolly bear **11** cabbage-worm, caterpillar, corn earworm, hellgramite **12** hellgrammite **13** leptocephalus, spruce budworm
• **larval stage**
**04** zoea **08** cercaria

**lascivious**
**04** blue, lewd **05** bawdy, crude, dirty, horny, randy, saucy **06** coarse, ribald, smutty, vulgar, wanton **07** lustful, obscene, Paphian, sensual, Sotadic **08** indecent, petulant, prurient, Sotadean, unchaste **09** lecherous, offensive, salacious **10** libidinous, licentious, scurrilous, suggestive **12** pornographic

**lash**
**03** cat, hit, tie, wag **04** beat, belt, bind, blow, dash, flog, join, rope, rush, slow, soft, stop, welt, whip, wire **05** affix, break, flail, flick, horse, pound, scold, seize, slack, slash, smash, strap, swipe, swish, thong, whack **06** attack, batter, berate, buffet, fasten, gammon, lavish, rebuke, secure, strike, stripe, stroke, swinge, switch, tether, thrash, wallop **07** bawl out, censure, insipid, lay into, reprove, scourge **08** bullwhip, make fast, squander **09** bullwhack, criticize, fulminate, horsewhip **12** tear to shreds **13** tear a strip off
• **lash out**
**04** yerk **06** thrash **07** lay into, run down **08** hit out at **09** have a go at **11** splash out on **12** tear to pieces, tear to shreds **13** tear a strip off, tear strips off **14** attack strongly **15** speak out against, spend a fortune on

**lashings**
**04** lots, tons **05** heaps, loads, piles **06** masses, oodles, stacks **11** large amount **13** great quantity

**lass**
**03** hen **04** bird, girl, miss **05** chick, filly, Jenny, popsy **06** damsel, lassie, maiden **10** schoolgirl, sweetheart, young woman **11** maid-servant

*See also* **girl**

**lassitude**
**06** apathy, torpor **07** fatigue, languor **08** dullness, lethargy, weakness **09** faintness, heaviness, tiredness, weariness **10** drowsiness, enervation, exhaustion **11** spring fever **12** listlessness, sluggishness

**lasso**
**04** lazo, rope **05** noose, reata, riata **06** lariat

**last**
◇ *tail selection indicator*
**03** end, ult **04** back, dure, go on, hind, keep, live, load, stay, take, wear **05** abide, after, cargo, close, dying, exist, final **06** behind, ending, endure, finish, hold on, keep on, latest, live on, remain, utmost, yester **07** carry on, closing, dernier, endmost, extreme, finally, hold out, persist, stand up, subsist, survive, tail-end **08** at the end, continue, farthest, furthest, hindmost, previous, rearmost, remotest, terminal, ultimate **09** at the back, at the rear, finishing **10** completion, concluding, conclusion, get through, lattermost, most recent, stick it out, ultimately **11** least likely **12** most unlikely **13** least suitable **14** coming at the end, most improbable, most unsuitable
• **at last**
◇ *tail selection indicator*
**07** finally **08** at length, in the end **10** eventually, ultimately **11** in due course **12** in conclusion
• **last word**
**04** amen, best, pick, rage **05** cream, vogue **06** latest **08** final say, ultimate **09** ultimatum **10** dernier cri, perfection **11** ne plus ultra **12** quintessence **13** final decision **14** crème de la crème, final statement **15** definite comment

**last-ditch**
**04** wild **05** final **06** all-out, heroic **07** frantic **08** frenzied, last-gasp **09** desperate, straining **10** last-chance, struggling **12** eleventh-hour

**lasting**
**05** fixed **07** abiding, durable, dureful, undying **08** enduring, external, lifelong, long-term, unending **09** ceaseless, endurable, long-lived, permanent, perpetual, surviving, unceasing **10** continuing, monumental, persisting, unchanging **11** everlasting, never-ending **12** interminable, long-standing

**lastly**
◇ *tail selection indicator*
**07** finally, to sum up **08** in the end **10** ultimately **12** in conclusion

**last-minute**
**04** late **05** hasty **06** forced, rushed **07** overdue **11** superficial **12** eleventh-hour

**latch**
**03** bar **04** bolt, hasp, hook, lock, mire **05** catch, clink, sneck **06** fasten **07** clicket **09** fastening **10** make secure
• **latch on to**
**04** twig **05** grasp, learn **06** follow **07** realize **09** apprehend **10** comprehend, understand **14** not want to leave

**late**
**03** lag, new, old **04** dead, past, slow **05** fresh, tardy **06** behind, former, latest, recent, slowly, whilom **07** current, defunct, delayed, overdue, tardily **08** backward, deceased, departed, formerly, overtime, previous, recently, sometime, umquhile, up-to-date **09** belatedly, in arrears, preceding **10** after hours, behindhand, behind time, dilatorily, last-minute, unpunctual **12** unpunctually **13** up-to-the-minute **14** behind schedule
• **of late**
**05** newly **06** lately **08** latterly, recently **10** not long ago

**lately**
**05** alate, newly **06** of late **08** latterly, recently **09** now of late **10** not long ago

**lateness**
**05** delay **09** tardiness **11** belatedness, retardation **12** dilatoriness **13** unpunctuality

**latent**
**06** hidden, secret, unseen, veiled **07** dormant, lurking, passive **08** inactive, possible **09** concealed, invisible, potential, quiescent **10** underlying, unrealized, unrevealed

11 delitescent, undeveloped, unexpressed 12 undiscovered

**later**
04 next, syne 05 after 06 latter 07 goodbye, later on 08 in a while 09 following, posterior 10 afterwards, eventually, subsequent, succeeding 11 in due course, in the future 12 at a later time, subsequently, successively 13 at a future date, at a future time, some other time 15 in the near future

**lateral**
03 lat 04 side 05 fresh 06 clever 07 oblique 08 creative, edgeways, flanking, indirect, inspired, marginal, original, sideward, sideways, slanting 09 brilliant, illogical, ingenious 10 unorthodox 11 alternative, imaginative 13 outside the box 14 unconventional

**laterally**
08 edgeways, sideways 09 obliquely 10 creatively, originally 11 illogically, ingeniously 13 imaginatively, outside the box

**latest**
02 in 03 hip, now 04 last 05 funky 06 modern, newest, trendy, with it 07 current 08 ultimate, up-to-date 10 most recent 11 fashionable 13 up-to-the-minute

**lather**
03 rub 04 flap, foam, fuss, soap, stew, suds 05 fever, froth, panic, state, sweat, tizzy 06 dither, whip up 07 anxiety, bubbles, fluster, flutter, shampoo 08 soapsuds 09 agitation

**Latin**
◇ *foreign word indicator*
01 L 03 Lat

*Latin words and expressions include:*

03 sic
04 idem, pace
05 ad hoc, circa
06 gratis, ibidem, passim
07 alumnus, a priori, de facto, erratum, floruit, in vitro, sub rosa
08 addendum, emeritus, ex gratia, gravitas, infra dig, mea culpa, nota bene, subpoena
09 ad nauseam, alma mater, carpe diem, et tu, Brute, ex officio, inter alia, ipso facto, per capita, status quo, sub judice, vox populi
10 anno Domini, ante-bellum, ex cathedra, in absentia, in extremis, magnum opus, post mortem, prima facie, quid pro quo, sine qua non, tabula rasa
11 ad infinitum, memento mori, non sequitur, tempus fugit
12 ante meridiem, caveat emptor, compos mentis, habeas corpus, post meridiem
13 camera obscura, deus ex machina, modus operandi
14 annus mirabilis, in loco parentis, pro bono publico, terra incognita
15 annus horribilis, curriculum vitae, delirium tremens, persona non grata

*See also* **day**; **month**; **number**

**latitude**
01 l 03 lat 04 play, room, span 05 field, range, reach, scope, space, sweep, width 06 extent, laxity, leeway, spread 07 breadth, freedom, liberty, licence 09 allowance, clearance 10 indulgence 11 flexibility 12 carte blanche

**latter**
03 end 04 last 05 final, later 06 modern, recent, second 07 closing, ensuing 10 concluding, succeeding, successive 13 last-mentioned

**latter-day**
06 modern, recent 07 current 10 present-day 12 contemporary

**latterly**
06 lately, of late 08 hitherto, recently 12 most recently

**lattice**
03 web 04 grid, mesh 05 grate, grill 06 grille, jacket 07 grating, network, tracery, trellis 08 espalier, fretwork, openwork 10 portcullis 11 latticework 12 reticulation

**Latvia**
02 LV 03 LVA

**laud**
04 hail 05 extol 06 admire, honour, praise 07 acclaim, applaud, approve, glorify, magnify 09 celebrate

**laudable**
06 of note, worthy 08 sterling 09 admirable, estimable, excellent, exemplary 10 creditable 11 commendable, meritorious 12 praiseworthy

**laudation**
05 glory, kudos, paean 06 eulogy, homage, praise 07 acclaim, tribute 08 accolade, blessing, devotion, encomion, encomium 09 adulation, celebrity, extolment, panegyric, reverence 10 veneration 11 acclamation 12 commendation 13 glorification

**laudatory**
06 eulogy 09 adulatory, approving 10 eulogistic, glorifying 11 acclamatory, approbatory, celebratory, encomiastic, panegyrical 12 commendatory 13 complimentary, encomiastical 14 congratulatory

**laugh**
03 fun, wag, wit, yok 04 boff, card, ha-ha, he-he, hoax, hoot, howl, jest, joke, lark, peal, peel, play, roar, yock 05 clown, comic, joker, lauch, prank, risus, snirt, sport, te-hee, trick 06 cackle, giggle, guffaw, haw-haw, hoaxer, jester, nicher, nicker, scream, tee-hee, titter 07 break up, buffoon, chortle, chuckle, snicker, snigger, snirtle 08 comedian, crease up, humorist, irrision, quipster 09 character, fall about, prankster, trickster 10 belly-laugh, cachinnate, horse laugh 11 wisecracker 12 be in stitches, cachinnation 14 practical joker, shake your sides, split your sides 15 laugh like a drain

• **laugh at**
04 jeer, mock 05 scorn, taunt 06 deride 07 scoff at 08 ridicule 09 make fun of, poke fun at 11 make a fool of 14 make jokes about

• **laugh off**
06 ignore 07 dismiss 08 belittle, minimize, pooh-pooh, shrug off 09 disregard 10 brush aside 12 make little of

**laughable**
05 comic, droll, funny 06 absurd 07 amusing, comical 08 derisive, derisory, farcical, humorous 09 diverting, hilarious, ludicrous 10 ridiculous, uproarious 11 nonsensical 12 entertaining, preposterous 13 side-splitting

**laughably**
08 absurdly 10 farcically 11 ludicrously 12 ridiculously 14 preposterously

**laughing-stock**
04 butt, dupe 05 sport 06 stooge, target, victim 08 derision, fair game 09 Aunt Sally 10 outspeckle 11 figure of fun

**laughter**
03 haw 04 glee, ha-ha 05 mirth 06 cackle, haw-haw, tee-hee 07 fou rire, hooting 08 cackling, giggling, hilarity, irrision, laughing, paroxysm 09 amusement, chortling, chuckling, guffawing, happiness, hysterics, merriment, tittering 10 risibility, sniggering 11 convulsions 12 cachinnation, cheerfulness

**launch**
04 dart, fire, hurl, open, shot 05 begin, float, found, lance, set up, shoot, start, throw 06 attack, propel 07 lancing, project, rollout, send off, unstock 08 commence, dispatch, embark on, initiate, organize 09 discharge, establish, instigate, institute, introduce, set afloat 10 inaugurate 11 set in motion 12 presentation

**launder**
◇ *anagram indicator*
04 wash 05 clean 06 trough 07 cleanse 09 washerman 11 washerwoman

**laundry**
04 wash 07 bagwash, clothes, steamie, washing 08 lavatory 10 Laundromat® 11 dry cleaner's, launderette 12 dirty clothes, dirty washing

**laurel**
03 bay 04 Stan 06 aucuba, daphne, kalmia, Laurus 08 pichurim, sweet bay

**09** sassafras, spicebush **10** greenheart, mock orange

**lava**
**04** bomb, slag **05** lahar **06** cinder, coulée, pumice, scoria **07** clinker, lapilli **08** pahoehoe **09** toadstone **10** palagonite **12** volcanic bomb **13** volcanic glass

**lavatory**
**02** WC **03** bog, can, lav, loo **04** dike, dyke, john, kazi, rear, toot **05** dunny, Elsan®, gents', heads, karsy, karzy, khazi, lavvy, privy, rears **06** carsey, karsey, ladies', lavabo, lotion, office, throne, toilet, urinal **07** cludgie, cottage, crapper, latrine **08** bathroom, dunnakin, Portaloo®, rest room, superloo, washroom **09** cloakroom, necessary **10** facilities, powder room, reredorter, thunderbox **11** convenience, earth-closet, water closet **12** smallest room **14** comfort station, little boys' room

**lavish**
**04** free, heap, lash, lush, pour, rich, wild **05** grand, spend, waste **06** bestow, deluge, expend, lordly, shower, slap-up **07** copious, fulsome, liberal, profuse **08** abundant, generous, gorgeous, princely, prodigal, prolific, splendid, squander, wasteful **09** bountiful, dissipate, excessive, expensive, exuberant, luxuriant, plentiful, profusion, sumptuous, unlimited, unsparing **10** give freely, immoderate, open-handed, profligate, thriftless, unstinting **11** extravagant, intemperate, spendthrift **12** unrestrained **13** unwithdrawing

**lavishly**
**06** freely, lushly, richly, wildly **07** grandly **09** liberally, profusely **10** abundantly, generously, splendidly **11** excessively, luxuriously, sumptuously, unsparingly **13** extravagantly, intemperately

**law**
**03** act, lay, lex **04** code, cops, pigs, rule **05** axiom, canon, edict, maxim, order, tenet **06** decree **07** charter, command, coppers, formula, lawsuit, precept, rozzers, statute, the Bill, the fuzz **08** standard, the force **09** criterion, determine, direction, directive, enactment, guideline, ordinance, principle, the police **10** boys in blue, expeditate, indulgence, litigation, regulation **11** commandment, instruction, legal action, legislation **12** constitution **13** jurisprudence, pronouncement **14** police officers, the police force

*Laws and Acts include:*

**04** DORA
**07** Riot Act, Test Act
**08** Corn Laws, Poor Laws, Stamp Act, Sugar Act
**10** Act of Union, Magna Carta, Patriot Act, Reform Acts
**11** Abortion Act, Equal Pay Act
**12** Bill of Rights, Homestead Act
**13** Act of Congress, Enclosure Acts, Parliament Act
**14** Act of Supremacy, Cat and Mouse Act, Civil Rights Act, Corporation Act, Declaratory Act, Native Title Act, Taft–Hartley Act
**15** Act of Parliament, Act of Settlement, Act of Succession, Habeas Corpus Act

*Scientific and other laws include:*

**04** Ohm's, Oral, Sod's
**05** lemon, Roman, Salic
**06** Boyle's, Hooke's, Mosaic, Snell's, Stoke's
**07** Dalton's, Hubble's, Kepler's, Murphy's, natural
**08** Charles's
**09** Avogadro's
**10** Parkinson's
**13** inverse square

• **by law**
**04** iure, jure

**law-abiding**
**04** good **06** decent, honest, lawful **07** dutiful, orderly, upright **08** obedient, virtuous **09** complying, righteous **10** honourable, upstanding **15** whiter than white

**lawbreaker**
**05** crook, felon **06** outlaw, sinner **07** convict, culprit **08** criminal, offender **09** infractor, miscreant, wrongdoer **10** delinquent, trespasser **11** perpetrator **12** transgressor

**lawcourt**
**03** bar **05** bench, court, trial **07** assizes, session **08** tribunal **09** judiciary **10** court of law

**lawful**
**04** just **05** legal, legit, licit, valid **06** proper **08** rightful **09** allowable, legalized, warranted **10** authorized, legitimate, recognized, sanctioned **11** permissible **14** constitutional

**lawfully**
**05** by law **07** legally, validly **08** by rights, properly **10** rightfully **11** permissibly **12** legitimately

**lawless**
◇ *anagram indicator*
**04** wild **05** rowdy **06** unruly **07** chaotic, illegal, riotous, rulesse **08** anarchic, criminal, mutinous, reckless, ruleless **09** insurgent, seditious, unsettled **10** anarchical, disorderly, rebellious, ungoverned, wrongdoing **11** lawbreaking **12** unrestrained **13** revolutionary, wild and woolly **15** insurrectionary

**lawlessness**
**05** chaos **06** mob law, piracy **07** anarchy, mob rule **08** disorder, rent-a-mob, lynch-law, sedition **09** mobocracy, rebellion **10** insurgency, ochlocracy, revolution **12** insurrection, racketeering

**lawman**
**03** Ohm **05** Boyle, Hooke, Mufti **09** Parkinson

**Lawrence**
**02** DH, TE

**lawrencium**
**02** Lr, Lw

**lawsuit**
**04** case, plea, suit **05** cause, trial **06** action **07** contest, dispute, process **08** argument **10** indictment, litigation **11** legal action, proceedings, prosecution

**lawyer**
**02** Av, BL **03** Att **04** Atty, silk **05** brief **06** jurist **07** counsel, mukhtar, shyster, templar **08** advocate, attorney, green-bag, Man of Law **09** lawmonger **10** legal eagle **12** legal adviser

*See also* **barrister**

*Lawyer types include:*

**02** DA, KC, QC
**05** avoué, judge
**06** avocet
**07** bencher, coroner, counsel, justice, sheriff
**08** Recorder
**09** barrister, solicitor
**11** conveyancer, crown lawyer
**12** circuit judge, jurisconsult, Lord Advocate
**13** attorney at law, Crown attorney, district judge, Queen's Counsel, sheriff depute
**14** criminal lawyer, deputy recorder, High Court judge, Lord Chancellor, public defender, Vice-Chancellor
**15** ambulance-chaser, Attorney-General

*Lawyers include:*

**04** **Hill** (Anita), **John** (Otto), **Reno** (Janet)
**05** **Booth** (Cherie), **Finch** (Atticus), **Mason** (Perry), **Mills** (Dame Barbara Jean Lyon), **Nader** (Ralph), **Slovo** (Joe), **Vance** (Cyrus R)
**06** **Bailey** (F Lee), **Butler** (Benjamin Franklin), **Carton** (Sydney), **Darrow** (Clarence), **Devlin** (Patrick, Lord), **Holmes** (Oliver Wendell), **Martin** (Richard)
**07** **Acheson** (Dean), **Clinton** (Hillary Rodham), **Haldane** (Richard, Viscount), **Kennedy** (Helena, Baroness), **Mondale** (Walter), **O'Connor** (Sandra Day)
**08** **Kunstler** (William), **Marshall** (Thurgood), **Mortimer** (Sir John)
**09** **La Guardia** (Fiorello H), **Shawcross** (Hartley William, Baron)
**10** **Birkenhead** (Frederick Edwin Smith, Earl of), **Dershowitz** (Alan)
**11** **Hore-Belisha** (Leslie, Lord)
**12** **Guicciardini** (Francesco)
**14** **Brillat-Savarin** (Anthelme)

• **lawyers**
**03** bar

**lax**
◇ *anagram indicator*
**04** wide **05** broad, loose, slack, vague **06** casual, remiss, salmon, sloppy **07** flaccid, general, inexact, lenient **08** careless, heedless, laid-back, slipshod, tolerant, wide-open **09** easy-going, imprecise, indulgent, negligent **10** inaccurate, indefinite, neglectful, permissive **11** inattentive **14** latitudinarian

**laxative**
**05** purge, salts, senna **06** ipecac, saline **07** cascara, Gregory **08** aperient, evacuant, lenitive, loosener, relaxant, solutive **09** aperitive, cathartic, purgative, taraxacum **10** eccoprotic, Epsom salts **11** health salts, ipecacuanha **14** cascara sagrada, Gregory's powder, liquid paraffin, Seidlitz powder **15** Gregory's mixture

**laxity**
**07** freedom, neglect **08** latitude, leniency, softness **09** looseness, slackness, tolerance **10** indulgence, negligence, sloppiness **11** imprecision, inexactness, nonchalance **12** carelessness, heedlessness, indifference, laissez-faire, slovenliness **14** indefiniteness, permissiveness

**lay**
**03** bet, ode, put, set **04** bear, bung, drop, laic, make, plan, poem, risk, song **05** allot, apply, beset, breed, civil, cover, embed, imbed, leave, lodge, lyric, offer, place, plant, plonk, posit, stick, wager **06** arable, assign, ballad, burden, chance, charge, design, devise, gamble, hazard, impose, impute, locate, meadow, saddle, set out, settle, submit, thrust, waylay **07** amateur, arrange, ascribe, deposit, dispose, inflict, oppress, pasture, prepare, present, produce, secular, set down, station, work out **08** encumber, engender, exorcize, madrigal, oviposit, position **09** attribute, establish, weigh down **10** make it with, put forward **11** give birth to, **12** non-qualified **13** non-specialist **15** non-professional

• **lay aside**
**04** keep, save, void **05** defer, store **06** put off, reject, shelve **07** abandon, discard, dismiss **08** postpone, put aside, set aside **09** cast aside

• **lay bare**
**04** show **05** scale, strip, unrip **06** expose, reveal, uncase, unveil **07** divulge, exhibit, explain, uncover **08** disclose, manifest

• **lay down**
**04** drop, give **05** couch, plant, plonk, state, store, yield **06** affirm, assert, depone, give up, ordain, record, submit **07** deposit, discard **09** establish, formulate, postulate, prescribe, stipulate, surrender **10** relinquish

• **lay down the law**
**07** dictate **09** crack down, dogmatize, emphasize **11** pontificate **12** rule the roost **14** read the riot act

• **lay hands on**
**03** get **04** find, grab, grip **05** bless, catch, clasp, grasp, seize, set on **06** attack, beat up, clutch, locate, obtain, ordain **07** acquire, assault, confirm, lay into, unearth **08** discover **09** get hold of, lay hold of **10** consecrate **12** bring to light

• **lay in**
**05** amass, glean, hoard, store **06** gather **07** build up, collect, stock up, store up **09** stockpile **10** accumulate

• **lay into**
**06** assail, attack **08** hit out at, let fly at, set about, tear into **09** have a go at, lash out at, pitch into

• **lay it on**
**07** flatter **08** butter up, overdo it, soft-soap **09** sweet-talk **10** exaggerate, overpraise

• **lay off**
**04** doff, drop, quit, sack, stop **05** cease, hedge, let go, let up **06** desist, give up, pay off **07** dismiss, refrain **08** leave off **09** discharge **10** leave alone **11** discontinue **13** make redundant

• **lay on**
**04** give **05** cater, pound, set up **06** impose, supply **07** furnish, inflict, provide **08** organize

• **lay out**
**03** pay **04** fell, give, plan **05** floor, spend **06** design, expend, invest, put out, set out, streek **07** arrange, display, exhibit, flatten, fork out, stretch **08** demolish, disburse, knock out, shell out, straucht, straught **09** spread out **10** contribute

• **lay up**
**04** hive, keep, save **05** amass, hoard, set by, store **07** deposit, put away, store up **08** mothball **10** accumulate

• **lay waste**
**04** rape, raze, ruin, sack **05** havoc, spoil **06** locust, ravage **07** despoil, destroy, estrepe, pillage **08** demolish, desolate **09** depredate, devastate, vandalize

**layabout**
**05** idler **06** loafer, skiver, waster **07** goof-off, laggard, lounger, shirker, wastrel **09** corner-boy, corner-man, lazybones, sundowner **10** ne'er-do-well **14** good-for-nothing

**layer**
**01** E **03** bed, hen, lie, ply, row **04** band, coat, film, seam, skin, tier, vein **05** cover, flake, plate, sheet, table **06** course, lamina, mantle, scrape **07** blanket, coating, deposit, lamella, stratum **08** covering **09** mesoblast, thickness **10** lamination **11** superficies

*See also* **atmosphere**

• **layers**
**06** strata

**layman, layperson, laywoman**
**04** laic **07** amateur, secular **08** exhorter, outsider, tertiary **11** parabolanus, parishioner, terrestrial **12** impropriator **13** local preacher, unordained man **15** non-professional, unordained woman

**lay-off**
**05** cards **06** firing, papers **07** jotters, sacking, the boot, the push, the sack **08** the elbow **09** discharge, dismissal **10** redundancy **12** unemployment

**layout**
◇ *anagram indicator*
**03** map, set **04** plan, unit **05** draft **06** design, format, outfit, sketch **07** display, outline **09** blueprint, geography **11** arrangement **12** organization **13** comprehensive

**layperson** *see* **layman, layperson, laywoman**

**laze**
**03** veg **04** idle, loaf, loll, lusk **05** chill, relax **06** bludge, lounge, unwind, veg out **08** chill out **09** bum around, lie around, sit around

**lazily**
◇ *anagram indicator*
**04** idly **06** slowly **07** slackly **10** sluggishly **13** lethargically

**laziness**
**05** sloth **07** languor **08** idleness, lethargy, slowness **09** fainéance, indolence, slackness, tardiness **10** inactivity, Oblomovism **12** dilatoriness, slothfulness, sluggishness

**lazy**
**04** idle, lusk, slow **05** inert, slack, tardy **06** laesie, lither, torpid **07** dronish, languid, luskish, work-shy **08** bone-idle, fainéant, inactive, indolent, slothful, sluggish **09** lethargic **10** languorous, slow-moving **14** good-for-nothing

**lazybones**
**04** lusk, slob, slug **05** drone, idler **06** loafer, lubber, skiver, slouch **07** goof-off, laggard, lounger, lubbard, mollusc, shirker **08** do-nought, fainéant, layabout, slowback, sluggard **09** do-nothing, sundowner **10** bedpresser, ne'er-do-well, sleepyhead **14** good-for-nothing

**leach**
**04** seep **05** drain **06** filter, osmose, strain **07** extract **08** filtrate **09** lixiviate, percolate

**lead**
◇ *head selection indicator*
**02** Pb **03** gap, tip, top, van **04** clue, cord, edge, hand, have, head, hint, hold, line, live, main, move, pass, rein, rule, shot, show, slip, star, sway **05** balls, cause, chain, chief, excel, first, guide, leash, model, outdo, pilot, plumb, prime, slugs, spend, start, steer, usher **06** convey, direct, escort, exceed, govern, induce, manage, margin, minium, outrun, prompt, sinker, string, tether, tip-off, weight **07** bring on, bullets, command,

conduct, dispose, eclipse, example, incline, leading, officer, pattern, pellets, plummet, pointer, precede, premier, primary, produce, provoke, running, surpass, undergo **08** foremost, guidance, interval, outstrip, persuade, priority, regulate, result in, star role, vanguard **09** advantage, be in front, call forth, come first, direction, extension, forefront, indicator, influence, precedent, principal, supervise, supremacy, title role, transcend **10** ammunition, bring about, experience, first place, indication, initiative, leadership, leading man, precedence, suggestion **11** be in the lead, heavy weight, leading lady, leading role, outdistance, pre-eminence, preside over, tend towards **12** be in charge of, call the shots, contribute to, starring part **13** be at the head of, principal part **15** advance position, leading position

• **lead gradually**
**04** drib

• **lead off**
**04** open **05** begin, start **07** kick off **08** commence, get going, initiate, start off **10** inaugurate

• **lead on**
**04** dupe, lure **05** tempt, trail, trick **06** draw on, entice, seduce **07** beguile, deceive, mislead **08** persuade **11** string along **12** put one over on, take for a ride **14** pull a fast one on

• **lead the way**
**04** show **05** guide **07** go first, pioneer **09** go in front, set a trend **10** be a pioneer, pave the way, show the way **11** blaze a trail **14** break new ground

• **lead up to**
**05** usher **07** prepare **08** approach **09** introduce **10** open the way, pave the way, prepare for **13** make overtures

**leaden**
**04** dull, grey, lead **05** ashen, dingy, heavy, inert, stiff **06** boring, cloudy, dismal, dreary, gloomy, sombre, wooden **07** greyish, humdrum, languid, onerous, stilted **08** laboured, lifeless, listless, overcast, plodding, sluggish **09** plumbeous **10** burdensome, cumbersome, depressing, lacklustre, oppressive, spiritless

**leader**
◇ *head selection indicator*
**02** PM **03** dux, gov, guv **04** boss, cock, head, imam **05** ariki, chief, guide, ruler, sheik, usher **06** bigwig, escort, expert, honcho, sachem, sheikh, top dog, zaddik **07** big shot, captain, coryphe, courier, founder, general, khalifa, kingpin, mahatma, manager, pioneer, skipper, tsaddik, tsaddiq, tzaddik, tzaddiq **08** big noise, caudillo, director, governor, inventor, khalifah, mocuddum, mokaddam, muqaddam, overseer, superior **09** architect, authority, big cheese, chieftain, commander, conductor, developer, editorial, innovator, liturgist, principal **10** coryphaeus, discoverer, figurehead, head honcho, pathfinder, ringleader, supervisor **11** front-runner, trailblazer **12** guiding light, leading light **13** groundbreaker **14** mover and shaker, superintendent

*See also* **governor**; **emperor**; **empress**; **king**; **leader**; **Maori**; **president**; **queen**; **Roman**; **ruler**

**leaderless**
◇ *head deletion indicator*
**08** headless **10** acephalous

**leadership**
◇ *head selection indicator*
**04** lead, rule, sway **07** command, control **08** guidance, headship, hegemony **09** authority, captaincy, direction **10** apostolate, domination, management **11** generalship, pre-eminence, premiership, supervision **12** directorship, governorship **14** administration, rangatiratanga **15** superintendency

**lead-in**
**05** debut, intro, proem, start **06** launch **07** opening, preface, prelude **08** exordium, foreword, overture, preamble, prologue **09** beginning **11** front matter **12** inauguration, introduction, presentation, prolegomenon **13** preliminaries

**leading**
◇ *head selection indicator*
**03** top **04** main, star **05** chief, first, front **06** ruling, staple **07** guiding, highest, premier, primary, supreme, top-rank **08** dominant, foremost, greatest, guidance, mistress, superior **09** directing, governing, number one, paramount, preceding, principal **10** pre-eminent **11** outstanding

**leaf**
**01** f, p **03** pad **04** flip, page, skim **05** bract, calyx, folio, frond, sepal, sheet, thumb **06** browse, folium, glance, needle, troely **07** foliole, leaflet, troelie, troolie **09** cataphyll, clinquant, cotyledon, marijuana **11** sclerophyll **12** thumb through

*Leaf parts include:*

**03** tip
**04** back, lobe, vein
**05** blade, lobus, stoma, thorn
**06** margin, midrib, sheath, stipel
**07** petiole, stipule, stomata
**08** leaf axil
**09** epidermis, leaf cells
**11** axillary bud, chloroplast

*Leaf shapes include:*

**04** oval
**05** acute, lobed, ovate
**06** cusped, entire, linear, lyrate
**07** acerose, ciliate, cordate, crenate, dentate, falcate, hastate, obovate, palmate, peltate, pinnate, ternate
**08** digitate, elliptic, reniform, subulate
**09** orbicular, runcinate, sagittate
**10** lanceolate, pinnatifid, spathulate, trifoliate
**13** doubly dentate
**15** abruptly pinnate

• **turn over a new leaf**
**05** amend, begin **06** change, reform **07** improve **10** begin again, start again **11** start afresh **12** mend your ways **14** better yourself, change your ways **15** improve yourself, make a fresh start, pull your socks up

**leaflet**
**04** bill **05** flier, flyer, pinna, tract **06** dodger, mailer **07** booklet, foliole, handout **08** brochure, circular, handbill, pamphlet

**leafy**
**05** bosky, green, shady, woody **06** bowery, leafed, leaved, shaded, wooded **07** foliose, verdant **08** frondent, frondose **11** frondescent **12** dasyphyllous

**league**
**01** l **03** cup **04** ally, band, bond, Bund, link **05** class, group, guild, Hansa, Hanse, level, union, unite **06** cartel **07** combine, compact, consort, contest **08** alliance, category, conspire, division **09** associate, coalition, co-operate, syndicate **10** amalgamate, consortium, federation, fellowship, join forces, tournament **11** affiliation, amphictyony, association, collaborate, combination, competition, confederacy, confederate, co-operative, corporation, partnership **12** band together, championship, conglomerate, Holy Alliance **13** confederation

*See also* **Australian football**; **baseball**; **football**; **rugby**

• **in league**
**06** allied, linked **08** in tandem **09** in cahoots **10** conspiring, in alliance **11** co-operating, hand in glove, in collusion **13** collaborating, in co-operation, in partnership

**leak**
**03** cut, ren, rin, run **04** blab, drip, hole, ooze, seep, tell, weep **05** break, chink, crack, exude, let in, let on, spill **06** escape, exposé, impart, let out, oozing, pass on, relate, reveal, run out, squeal **07** crevice, divulge, fissure, leakage, leaking, let slip, opening, seepage, seeping, trickle, urinate **08** disclose, exposure, give away, overflow, puncture, spillage **09** discharge, make known, make water, percolate **10** disclosure, divulgence, make public, revelation, uncovering **11** percolation **12** blow the gaffe **13** spill the beans **15** bringing to light

**leaky**
**05** holey, split **06** gizzen, porous **07** cracked, leaking **08** dripping

**09** permeable, punctured
**10** perforated, unstanched
**11** unstaunched

**lean**
**03** lie **04** abut, arid, bank, bare, bend, bony, hard, heel, lank, list, poor, prop, rest, slim, tend, thin, tilt **05** gaunt, lanky, slant, slink, slope, spare, tough **06** barren, favour, hungry, meagre, prefer, repose, scanty, skinny, slinky, sparse **07** angular, austere, haggard, incline, minceur, recline, scraggy, scrawny, slender **09** difficult, emaciated, fleshless, gravitate, rigwiddie, rigwoodie **10** inadequate, unfruitful, unpleasant **11** be at an angle **12** insufficient, unproductive, unprofitable, unsuccessful **13** uncomfortable **15** all skin and bones

• **lean on**
**04** rest **05** force **06** bank on, coerce, rely on **07** trust in **08** depend on, persuade **10** intimidate, pressurize **13** put pressure on **14** put the screws on

**leaning**
**04** bent, bias **06** liking **08** aptitude, fondness, penchant, tendency **10** attraction, partiality, preference, proclivity, propensity **11** disposition, inclination **12** predilection

**leanness**
**08** boniness, lankness, slimness, thinness **09** gauntness, lankiness **11** scragginess, scrawniness, slenderness

**lean-to**
**03** hut **04** pent, shed **05** shack **06** garage, lock-up **08** outhouse, skilling, skillion **09** penthouse

**leap**
◇ *anagram indicator*
**03** hop, lep **04** jeté, jump, lope, loup, over, rise, romp, salt, skip, soar, volt **05** bound, caper, clear, dance, fence, flier, flyer, frisk, mount, pronk, salto, sault, spang, surge, vault, volte **06** basket, bounce, breach, cavort, curvet, frolic, gambol, rocket, spring **07** échappé, falcade, soaring, upsurge, upswing **08** assemblé, cabriole, capriole, croupade, escalate, fish-dive, increase, jump over, overskip, somerset **09** elevation, entrechat, pas de chat, skyrocket **10** escalation, pigeon-wing, somersault **11** summersault

• **by leaps and bounds, in leaps and bounds**
**07** quickly, rapidly, swiftly **08** in no time **13** in no time at all

• **leap at**
**04** grab **05** seize **06** jump at, snatch **07** agree to, fall for, swallow **08** pounce on **13** accept eagerly

**learn**
**03** con, get, kon, see **04** cram, hear, larn, lear, leir, lere, read **05** conne, glean, grasp, leare, study, train **06** absorb, detect, digest, gather, get off, master, pick up, take in **07** acquire, discern, find out, gen up on, prepare, realize, receive, suss out **08** discover, memorize, remember **09** ascertain, determine, get wind of **10** assimilate, comprehend, have off pat, understand **12** get the hang of, learn by heart **13** become aware of **14** acquire skill in, commit to memory **15** gain knowledge of

**learned**
**04** cond, read, wise **06** savant, versed **07** erudite, savante **08** academic, cultured, lettered, literary, literate, pedantic, scienced, studious, well-read **09** scholarly **10** widely read **11** literatured **12** intellectual, well-educated, well-informed **13** knowledgeable

**learner**
**01** L **04** tiro, tyro **05** pupil
**06** conner, intern, novice, rookie
**07** scholar, student, trainee
**08** beginner, neophyte
**09** greenhorn **10** apprentice
**11** abecedarian

*See also* **beginner**

**learning**
**04** lear, leir, lere, lore **05** leare, study **06** wisdom **07** conning, culture, letters, tuition **08** pedantry, research **09** education, erudition, intellect, knowledge, schooling **11** edification, information, scholarship, schoolcraft

• **basic learning**
**03** RRR

**lease**
**03** let, set **04** farm, hire, loan, rent, tack **05** glean **06** let out, rental, sublet **07** chapter, charter, hire out, pasture, rent out, tenancy **08** contract **09** agreement

**leash**
**03** lym **04** bind, cord, curb, hold, lead, lime, lyam, lyme, rein, slip **05** check, trash **06** string, tether **07** control **09** restraint **10** discipline

*See also* **three**

• **strain at the leash**
**07** be dying, be eager **09** be anxious, be itching, be longing **11** be impatient

**least**
**06** fewest, lowest **07** minimum, poorest **08** smallest **09** slightest

• **at least**
**06** anyhow **07** however **09** at any rate, in any case **10** as a minimum, at the least, for all that, in any event, no less than **12** nevertheless, no matter what **14** at the very least, nothing short of **15** nothing less than, whatever happens

• **to say the least**
**13** to put it mildly **14** at the very least

**leather**
**03** taw **04** beat, butt **06** levant, spetch, thrash **08** studwork

*Leathers include:*

**03** kid
**04** buff, calf, napa, roan, shoe, wash, yuft
**05** grain, Mocha, nappa, neat's, plate, split, suede, waxed, white
**06** chrome, Nubuck, patent, Rexine®, Russia, shammy, skiver, spruce
**07** chamois, cowhide, dogskin, hogskin, kidskin, kipskin, morocco, pigskin, saffian
**08** buckskin, cabretta, calfskin, capeskin, cheverel, cheveril, cordovan, cordwain, deerskin, goatskin, lambskin, maroquin, shagreen
**09** crocodile, lacquered, sheepskin, slinkskin, snakeskin
**10** artificial
**11** aqualeather, cuir-bouilli, whitleather

**leathery**
**04** hard **05** rough, tough **06** rugged
**07** corious, durable, wizened
**08** hardened, leathern, wrinkled
**10** coriaceous

**leave**
◇ *deletion indicator*
**02** go, OK **03** let, vac **04** drop, dump, exit, jilt, levy, lose, miss, move, park, part, quit, will **05** allot, avoid, break, cause, cease, chuck, congé, ditch, endow, go off, raise, say-so, scoot, split **06** assign, commit, congee, create, day off, decamp, depart, desert, desist, devise, forget, give up, go away, hook it, lead to, mislay, resign, retire, set out, vamose **07** abandon, consent, consign, deliver, do a bunk, entrust, forsake, freedom, holiday, liberty, licence, license, produce, pull out, push off, retreat, take off, time off, vamoose, walk off, warrant **08** bequeath, choof off, clear off, come away, emigrate, farewell, furlough, generate, give over, hand down, hand over, holidays, make over, misplace, occasion, renounce, result in, run along, run out on, sanction, shove off, transmit, up sticks, vacation, withdraw **09** allowance, disappear, push along, sick leave, surrender **10** bring about, concession, give rise to, green light, hit the road, indulgence, make tracks, permission, relinquish, sabbatical **11** leave behind **12** dispensation, shoot through **13** authorization, sling your hook, take your leave **14** leave of absence, turn your back on **15** leave high and dry, take French leave

• **leave off**
**03** end **04** halt, omit, quit, stop **05** cease **06** desist, lay off **07** abstain, refrain **08** break off, give over, knock off **09** terminate **11** discontinue

• **leave out**
**03** bar, cut **04** miss, omit **06** bypass, cut out, except, ignore, reject **07** exclude, miss out, neglect **08** count out, overlook, pass over, suppress **09** cast aside, disregard, eliminate

**• leave quickly**
**08** light out

**leaven**
**04** barm, work, zyme **05** imbue, raise, swell, yeast **06** expand, puff up
**07** enliven, ferment, inspire, lighten, pervade, quicken, suffuse
**08** permeate **09** sourdough, stimulate **11** cause to rise **12** raising agent

**leaves**
**03** tea **04** atap **05** attap

**leavings**
**04** bits **05** dregs, dross, spoil, waste
**06** debris, pieces, refuse, relics, scraps
**07** remains, residue, rubbish
**08** detritus, oddments, remnants
**09** alms-drink, fragments, leftovers, remainder, sweepings **11** broken meats

**Lebanon**
**02** RL **03** LBN

**lecher**
**04** gate, goat, lech, perv, rake, roué, wolf **05** Romeo, satyr **06** wanton
**07** Don Juan, flasher, seducer
**08** Casanova, Lothario, Lovelace
**09** adulterer, debauchee, libertine, womanizer **10** fornicator, libidinist, profligate, sensualist **11** dirty old man, whoremonger

**lecherous**
**04** lewd **05** horny, pervy, randy
**06** carnal, wanton **07** codding, leering, lustful, rammish, raunchy
**08** prurient, unchaste **09** debauched, dissolute, lickerish, liquorish, salacious
**10** degenerate, dissipated, lascivious, libidinous, licentious, womanizing
**11** promiscuous **12** concupiscent

**lechery**
**04** lust **08** lewdness, salacity
**09** carnality, prurience, randiness
**10** debauchery, rakishness, sensuality, wantonness, womanizing
**11** libertinism, lustfulness, raunchiness
**13** concupiscence, lickerishness, salaciousness **14** lasciviousness, libidinousness, licentiousness

**lectern**
**04** ambo, desk **05** eagle, stand, table
**07** lettern, oratory **11** reading-desk

**lecture**
**03** act, jaw **04** read, talk **05** chide, class, scold, speak, teach **06** berate, homily, lesson, rebuke, rocket, sermon, speech **07** address, censure, chiding, expound, jawbone, prelect, reproof, reprove, tell off **08** admonish, berating, extender, harangue, instruct, reproach, scolding, travelog **09** chalk talk, discourse, give a talk, hold forth, reprimand, talking-to **10** conférence, prelection, rollicking, telling-off, travelogue, upbraiding **11** instruction, make a speech, pick holes in
**12** disquisition, dressing-down, pull to pieces, tear to pieces **13** give lessons in
**14** curtain lecture

**lecturer**
**01** L **03** don **04** lect **05** tutor
**06** docent, lector, orator, reader, talker
**07** scholar, speaker, teacher
**08** academic, preacher **09** declaimer, expounder, haranguer, pedagogue, preceptor, prelector, professor
**10** instructor, sermonizer, theologian
**11** speechifier, speechmaker
**12** conférencier, extensionist, instructress

**ledge**
**04** berm, lode, sill, step, vein **05** altar, bench, linch, ridge, shelf, stock
**06** gradin, mantel, offset, settle, shelve
**07** gradine, linchet, lynchet **08** fire-step, overhang **10** buttery-bar, firing-step, projection, scarcement
**11** mantelpiece, mantelshelf

**ledger**
**05** books **07** journal **08** accounts, register **09** inventory **10** record book
**11** account book

**lee**
**05** cover, river **06** arable, meadow, refuge **07** pasture, shelter
**09** sanctuary **10** protection

**leech**
**05** drain, toady **06** usurer **07** clinger, sponger **08** hanger-on, parasite
**09** physician, scrounger, sycophant
**10** freeloader **11** bloodsucker, extortioner

**leer**
**03** eye **04** grin, ogle, perv, wink
**05** gloat, smirk, sneer, stare, tweer, twire **06** colour, goggle, squint
**07** glad eye **10** complexion
**13** lecherous look

**leery**
**04** wary **05** chary **06** unsure
**07** careful, dubious, guarded
**08** cautious, doubting **09** sceptical, uncertain **10** suspicious **11** distrustful, on your guard

**lees**
**05** draff, dregs, grout **06** dunder, refuse **07** deposit, grounds, residue
**08** sediment **09** settlings
**11** precipitate

**leeway**
**04** play, room **05** drift, scope, slack, space **06** margin **07** freedom
**08** latitude **09** elbow-room
**11** flexibility

**left**
◇ *deletion indicator*
**01** L **03** red **04** gone, lorn, near, over, port, quit, went **06** Maoist **07** liberal, Marxist, radical **08** larboard, left-hand, left-wing, Leninist
**09** communist, sinistral, socialist, Stalinist **10** Bolshevist, Spartakist, Trotskyist, Trotskyite **11** progressive, revisionist **12** collectivist
**13** revolutionary

**• turn left**
**03** hie **04** high

**left-handed**
**06** clumsy, gauche **07** awkward, dubious, unlucky **08** southpaw
**09** ambiguous, equivocal, insincere, sinistral **10** backhanded, cack-handed, kack-handed **12** corrie-fisted, hypocritical

**left-hander**
**05** lefty **06** leftie **08** southpaw
**09** sinistral **11** cackyhander, molly-dooker

**left-over**
**04** orra **06** excess, unused
**07** oddment, settled, surplus, uneaten
**09** remaining **11** superfluous

**leftovers**
**05** dregs **06** excess, refuse, scraps
**07** remains, residue, surplus
**08** leavings, remnants **09** remainder, sweepings

**left-wing**
**04** left **06** Maoist **07** liberal, Marxist, radical **08** Leninist **09** communist, socialist, Stalinist **10** Bolshevist, Spartakist, Trotskyist, Trotskyite
**11** progressive, revisionist
**12** collectivist **13** revolutionary

**• left-winger**
**04** trot

**leg**
**02** on **03** bit, gam, lap, peg, pin
**04** crus, gamb, limb, part, prop
**05** brace, shank, stage, stump
**06** member, timber **07** pleopod, portion, section, segment, stretch, support, upright **08** swindler
**10** sheepshank **12** underpinning

**• leg it**
**03** run **04** walk **05** hurry **06** hoof it
**07** scarper **08** go by foot

**• not have a leg to stand on**
**10** be unproved **11** lack support
**12** lack an excuse **13** be unjustified

**• on its last legs**
**04** weak **06** ailing **07** failing **10** fading fast, near to ruin **11** about to fail, near to death **12** at death's door **15** about to collapse, nearing collapse

**• pull someone's leg**
**03** kid, rib **04** fool, joke **05** tease, trick
**06** have on, wind up **07** deceive
**09** make fun of **11** play a joke on
**12** take for a ride **14** pull a fast one on

**legacy**
**04** gift **06** estate **07** bequest
**08** heirloom, heritage **09** endowment, heritance, patrimony **10** bequeathal, birthright **11** inheritance

**legal**
**03** leg **05** legit, licit, right, sound, valid
**06** lawful, proper **07** allowed
**08** forensic, judicial, licensed, rightful
**09** allowable, judiciary, legalized, permitted, statutory, warranted
**10** above-board, acceptable, admissible, authorized, legitimate, sanctioned **11** permissible **12** within the law **14** constitutional
*See also* **court**; **crime**

*Legal terms include:*

**02** JP, QC
**03** bar, DPP, sue
**04** ASBO, bail, deed, dock, fine, jury, oath, plea, will, writ
**05** alibi, asset, bench, brief, by-law, claim, felon, grant, judge, juror, lease, party, proof, proxy, title, trial
**06** appeal, arrest, bigamy, charge, client, demand, equity, estate, guilty, lawyer, legacy, pardon, parole, patent, remand, repeal, the bar, waiver
**07** accused, alimony, amnesty, caution, charter, codicil, convict, coroner, custody, damages, defence, divorce, hearing, inquest, inquiry, Law Lord, lawsuit, mandate, penalty, probate, sheriff, statute, summons, tenancy, verdict, warrant, witness
**08** act of God, adultery, advocate, civil law, contract, covenant, criminal, easement, eviction, evidence, executor, freehold, hung jury, innocent, judgment, juvenile, legal aid, mortgage, offender, prisoner, receiver, reprieve, sanction, sentence, subpoena, tribunal
**09** accessory, acquittal, affidavit, agreement, annulment, barrister, common law, copyright, court case, defendant, endowment, fee simple, indemnity, intestacy, judgement, judiciary, leasehold, liability, plaintiff, precedent, probation, solicitor, testimony, trademark
**10** accomplice, allegation, confession, conveyance, decree nisi, indictment, injunction, liquidator, magistrate, settlement
**11** adjournment, arbitration, extradition, foreclosure, inheritance, local search, maintenance, plea bargain, plead guilty, proceedings, ward of court
**12** age of consent, Bill of Rights, constitution, court martial, cross-examine, Lord Advocate, misadventure, notary public
**13** King's evidence, public inquiry, Queen's Counsel, young offender
**14** decree absolute, Lord Chancellor, plead not guilty, Queen's evidence
**15** Act of Parliament, Attorney General, clerk of the court, contempt of court, power of attorney

**• legal document**
**04** deed, writ

**legality**
**08** validity **09** rightness, soundness **10** lawfulness, legitimacy **12** rightfulness **14** admissibleness, permissibility

**legalize**
**05** admit, allow **06** accept, permit, ratify **07** approve, license, warrant **08** sanction, validate **09** authorize, make legal **10** legitimize **13** decriminalize

**legally**
**05** by law **07** validly **08** by rights, lawfully, properly **10** rightfully **11** permissibly **12** legitimately

**legate**
**03** leg **05** agent, envoy **06** deputy, exarch, nuncio **08** delegate, emissary **09** messenger **10** ambassador **12** commissioner **14** representative

**legatee**
**04** heir **06** co-heir **07** devisee **08** legatary, receiver **09** co-heiress, inheritor, recipient **10** inheritrix **11** beneficiary

**legation**
**07** embassy, mission **08** ministry **09** consulate **10** commission, delegation, deputation **14** representation

**legend**
**03** key, VIP **04** myth, name, saga, star, tale **05** celeb, fable, motto, story **06** bigwig, cipher, legion, worthy **07** big name, big shot, caption, fiction, notable, romance **08** folk tale, luminary **09** celebrity, dignitary, narrative, personage, superstar, underline **11** explanation, inscription, personality **12** famous person, living legend **13** household name

*See also* **mythology**

*Arthurian legend-related terms and locations include:*

**03** Usk
**04** Bath, York
**06** Avalon, Camlan, Logres
**07** Camelot, Camlann, Carleon, Chester
**08** Caerleon, Caliburn, Lyonesse, Tintagel
**09** Badon Hill, Boscastle, Camelford, Excalibur, Holy Grail, Llyn Dinas, loadstone, Red Dragon, Roche Rock
**10** Cader Idris, Grail Table, Llyn Barfog, Round Table, Stonehenge, Tintagalon, Winchester
**11** Arthur's Seat, Cadbury Hill, Chalice Well, Craig y Dinas, Glastonbury, Merlin's Cave
**12** Alderley Edge, Arthur's Cross, Dozemary Pool, Isle of Avalon, Perilous Seat, Vale of Avalon
**13** Cadbury Castle, Questing Beast, Ship of Fairies, Siège Perilous, The Waste Lands
**14** Bamburgh Castle, Caerleon Castle, Carleon upon Usk, Dolorous Stroke, Glastonbury Tor, Island of Avalon, St Govan's Chapel, Tintagel Castle
**15** Slaughterbridge, St Michael's Mount, Sword in the Stone, The Tristan Stone, Valley of Delight

*Characters from Arthurian legend include:*

**03** Ban, Kay, Lot
**04** Bors
**05** Nimue, Uther
**06** Arthur, Elaine, Gareth (of Orkney), Gawain, Merlin, Modred
**07** Caradoc, Galahad, Gawayne, Igraine, Launfal, Mordred, Tristan
**08** Bedivere, Ironside, Lancelot, Palmerin, Parsifal, Perceval, Tristram
**09** Arondight, Guinevere
**10** Fisher King, King Arthur
**11** Morgan le Fay
**13** Lady of Shallot, Lady of the Lake
**14** Launcelot du Lac, Uther Pendragon

*See also* **knight**

*Characters from the Robin Hood legend include:*

**07** Sheriff (of Nottingham)
**08** Merry Men, Prioress (of Kirklees)
**09** Friar Tuck, Robin Hood
**10** Allan-A-Dale, Little John, Maid Marian, Prince John
**11** King Richard (the Lionheart), Will Scarlet
**13** Guy of Gisborne, Much the Miller

**legendary**
**06** fabled, famous **07** popular **08** fabulous, fanciful, glorious, honoured, immortal, mythical, renowned **09** acclaimed, fictional, storybook, well-known **10** celebrated, fictitious, remembered **11** illustrious, traditional

**legerdemain**
**05** feint **06** tricky **07** cunning **08** artifice, jugglery, juggling, trickery **09** chicanery, deception, sophistry **10** artfulness, craftiness, hocus-pocus, subterfuge **11** contrivance, logodaedaly, manoeuvring **12** manipulation **13** sleight of hand, thaumaturgics

**legibility**
**07** clarity **08** lucidity **09** clearness, lucidness, plainness, precision **10** simplicity **11** readability **12** distinctness, explicitness, readableness **15** intelligibility

**legible**
**04** neat **05** clear, lucid, plain **06** simple **07** precise **08** distinct, explicit, readable **10** easy to read **12** decipherable, intelligible **14** comprehensible

**legibly**
**06** simply **07** clearly, lucidly, plainly **08** readably **09** precisely **10** easily read, explicitly **12** intelligibly **14** comprehensibly

**legion**
**04** army, host, mass, unit **05** drove, force, horde, swarm, troop **06** cohort, legend, myriad, number, throng **07** brigade, company **08** division, numerous, regiment **09** battalion, countless, multitude **10** numberless **11** illimitable, innumerable **13** multitudinous

**• British Legion**
**03** BL

**legislate**
**05** enact, order **06** codify, decree, ordain **08** make laws, pass laws **09** authorize, establish, formulate, prescribe

**legislation**
**03** act, law, leg **04** bill, code **05** legis, rules **06** ruling **07** charter, measure, statute **09** enactment, lawmaking, ordinance **10** regulation **11** formulation **12** codification, prescription **13** authorization

**legislative**
**03** leg **05** legis **08** judicial **09** lawgiving, lawmaking **10** senatorial **12** jurisdictive **13** congressional, parliamentary

**legislator**
**02** MP **06** deputy **07** senator **08** lawgiver, lawmaker **09** nomothete **10** nomothetes **11** congressman **13** congresswoman **15** parliamentarian

**legislature**
**03** leg **05** house, legis **06** senate, states **07** chamber **08** assembly, congress **10** parliament

*See also* **parliament**

**legitimacy**
**08** fairness, legality, validity **09** rightness, soundness **10** lawfulness **11** credibility, rationality **12** plausibility, rightfulness, sensibleness **13** acceptability, admissibility **14** admissibleness, justifiability, permissibility, reasonableness

**legitimate**
**04** fair, real, true **05** legal, legit, licit, loyal, sound, valid **06** kosher, lawful, proper **07** correct, genuine, logical, natural **08** credible, rational, rightful, sensible, true-born **09** competent, justified, plausible, statutory, warranted **10** acceptable, admissible, authorized, reasonable, sanctioned **11** justifiable, well-founded **12** acknowledged

**legitimize**
**05** allow **06** permit **07** charter, entitle, license, warrant **08** legalize, sanction, validate **09** authorize **10** legitimate **13** decriminalize

**leisure**
**04** ease, rest, time **05** break, R and R, space **06** by-time **07** freedom, holiday, leasure, liberty, respite, time off, time out, vacancy **08** free time, off-hours, vacation **09** spare time **10** recreation, relaxation, retirement

- **at your leisure**

**11** unhurriedly **13** in your own time, when you want to **14** when it suits you **15** in your spare time

**leisurely**
**04** easy, lazy, slow **05** loose **06** gentle **07** relaxed, restful, unhasty **08** carefree, laid-back, tranquil **09** easy-going, unhurried **10** leisurable **11** comfortable

**lemur**
**05** indri, loris **06** aye-aye, colugo, galago, indris, macaco, sifaka **07** half-ape, meercat, meerkat, nagapie **08** mongoose, mungoose **09** babacoote, mangouste **10** angwantibo **12** Cynocephalus **13** Galeopithecus

**lend**
**03** add, sub **04** give, loan, spot **05** grant, prest **06** bestow, confer, credit, donate, impart, on-lend, supply **07** advance, furnish, provide **08** overlend, put forth **10** allow to use, contribute **11** allow to have **13** let someone use

- **lend a hand**

**03** aid **04** help **06** assist **07** help out, pitch in **09** do your bit **14** give assistance

- **lend an ear**

**04** heed **06** listen **07** give ear, hearken **10** take notice **12** pay attention

- **lend itself to**

**13** be suitable for **15** be easily used for

**length**
**01** l **04** span, term **05** piece, reach, space **06** extent, period **07** measure, portion, section, segment, stretch **08** distance, duration **09** prolixity

- **at length**

**05** fully **06** at last, in full **07** finally **10** eventually, thoroughly **11** in due course **12** exhaustively, for a long time **13** in great detail **14** after a long time **15** comprehensively

- **go to any lengths**

**10** do anything **11** try very hard **12** go to extremes

**lengthen**
**03** eik, eke **04** draw **06** eke out, expand, extend, pad out **07** draw out, prolong, spin out, stretch **08** continue, elongate, increase, protract **10** grow longer, prolongate

**lengthwise**
**05** along **07** endlong, endways, endwise **10** fore-and-aft, lengthways, vertically **12** horizontally

**lengthy**
**04** long **05** wordy **06** prolix **07** diffuse, tedious, verbose **08** drawn-out, extended, overlong, rambling **09** prolonged **10** lengthened, long-winded, protracted **12** interminable, long-drawn-out

**leniency**
**05** mercy **08** clemency, kindness, lenience, mildness, softness **09** tolerance **10** compassion, generosity, gentleness, humaneness, indulgence, moderation, tenderness **11** forbearance, forgiveness, magnanimity **14** permissiveness **15** soft-heartedness

**lenient**
**04** kind, mild **06** gentle, humane, tender **07** liberal, sparing **08** generous, merciful, moderate, soothing, tolerant **09** emollient, forgiving, indulgent, softening **10** forbearing, permissive **11** magnanimous, soft-hearted **13** compassionate

**lenitive**
**06** easing **07** calming **08** laxative, soothing **09** assuaging, relieving **10** mitigating, mollifying, palliative **11** alleviating

**lens**
**03** eye **05** glass, optic, power **06** finder, lentil, pebble, peeper **07** aplanat, contact **08** achromat, bull's-eye, eyeglass, eyepiece, meniscus **09** amplifier, condenser, magnifier, telephoto **10** anastigmat, apochromat, pantoscope **11** object-glass **12** burning-glass

**Lent**
**04** fast **06** carême, spring

**leopard**
**04** pard **05** ounce, tiger **06** pardal **07** libbard, panther, pardale **08** pardalis **12** catamountain, cat o' mountain

**leper**
**05** lazar, mesel **06** meazel, pariah **07** leprosy, outcast **11** undesirable, untouchable **13** social outcast

**leprechaun**
**03** elf, imp **04** puck **05** bogey, demon, fiend, gnome, nixie, pooka, troll **06** goblin, kelpie, kobold, red-cap, spirit, sprite **07** brownie, gremlin **09** hobgoblin

**lesbian**
**03** gay **07** Sapphic **08** sapphist **10** homosexual

**lesion**
**03** cut **04** gash, hurt, sore **05** wound **06** bruise, injury, scrape, trauma **07** scratch **08** abrasion **09** contusion **10** impairment, laceration

**Lesotho**
**02** LS **03** LSO

**less**
**03** bar **04** meno, save **05** fewer, minor, minus **06** except **07** short of, smaller, wanting, without, younger **08** inferior **09** excepting, excluding, not as many, not as much, not so many, not so much **13** smaller amount **15** to a lesser degree, to a lesser extent

**lessen**
**03** cut, dip, ebb **04** alay, bate, dull, ease, fail, flag, wane **05** abate, aleye, allay, erode, let up, lower, slack **06** absorb, deaden, go down, impair, narrow, plunge, reduce, shrink, weaken **07** abridge, curtail, decline, die down, dwindle, ease off, lighten, plummet, relieve, slacken, subside, tail off **08** belittle, come down, contract, decrease, derogate, diminish, minimize, mitigate, moderate,

nosedive, peter out, slow down, tail away **09** disparage, extenuate **10** de-escalate

**lessening**
**03** dip **05** allay, let-up **06** easing, ebbing, waning **07** cutting, decline, erosion, failure **08** batement, decrease, flagging **09** abatement, deadening, dwindling, reduction, shrinkage, weakening **10** derogation, diminution, imminution, mitigation, moderation, slackening **11** contraction, curtailment, extenuation, petering out **12** de-escalation, minimization

**lesser**
**05** lower, minor **07** smaller **08** inferior, slighter **09** secondary **11** subordinate **13** less important

**lesson**
**04** lear, leir, lere, task, text **05** class, drill, leare, model, moral, train **06** course, period, rebuke, sermon **07** example, lection, lecture, reading, seminar, warning **08** coaching, exercise, homework, instruct, liripipe, liripoop, practice, teaching, tutorial, workshop **09** deterrent, practical, scripture **10** assignment, recitation, schoolwork **11** application, instruction, master-class **12** Bible reading **13** demonstration

**lest**
**06** in case, listen **07** for fear **11** for fear that **14** in order to avoid

**let**
**02** OK **03** net **04** hire, make, rent **05** allow, cause, check, grant, lease **06** enable, hinder, let out, permit **07** agree to, hire out, prevent, rent out **08** assent to, obstacle, sanction, tolerate **09** authorize, consent to, give leave, give the OK, hindrance, restraint **10** constraint, give the nod, impediment, obstructed **11** obstruction, prohibition, restriction **12** interference **14** give permission, give the go-ahead **15** say the magic word

• **let alone**
**04** also **08** as well as **09** apart from, never mind **12** not to mention **13** not forgetting

• **let down**
**04** fail, vail **05** lower **06** betray, desert **07** abandon, depress **09** fall short **10** disappoint, disenchant, dissatisfy **11** disillusion **14** disappointment **15** leave in the lurch

• **let fly**
**03** hit **05** fling, fly at, go for, shoot **06** attack, charge, strike **07** assault, lay into **08** fall upon **09** discharge, have a go at, lash out at

• **let go**
**04** drop, free, omit, quit, sack **06** give up, unhand **07** dismiss, hang off, manumit, release, set free, slacken, unleash **08** liberate, released **10** relinquish **11** stop holding **13** make redundant

• **let in**
**04** sink **05** admit, greet **06** accept, insert, take in **07** enchase, include, receive, welcome **11** incorporate **12** allow to enter

• **let in on**
**04** tell **06** inform **07** include, let know **11** allow to know **14** allow to share in

• **let off**
**04** emit, fire **05** spare **06** acquit, excuse, exempt, ignore, pardon **07** absolve, explode, forgive, give off, release **08** detonate, liberate, reprieve **09** discharge, exonerate

• **let on**
**04** blab, tell **06** impart, pass on, relate, reveal, squeal **07** divulge, let slip **08** disclose, give away **09** make known **10** make public **13** spill the beans **15** give the game away

• **let out**
**03** job **04** blab, emit, free, leak **05** let go, utter, widen **06** betray, reveal, squeal **07** enlarge, freight, let slip, release, slacken **08** disclose **09** discharge, make known **13** spill the beans

• **let up**
**03** end **04** ease, halt, stop **05** abate, cease **06** lessen **07** die down, ease off, slacken, subside **08** decrease, diminish, moderate

**let-down**
**04** sell **07** setback, washout **08** betrayal **09** desertion **10** anticlimax **14** disappointment **15** disillusionment

**lethal**
**05** fatal, toxic **06** deadly, mortal **07** deathly, noxious, ruinous, vicious **08** venomous **09** dangerous, murderous, poisonous **10** disastrous **11** destructive, devastating **12** death-dealing

**lethally**
**07** fatally **08** mortally **09** noxiously, toxically **11** dangerously **12** disastrously **13** destructively, devastatingly

**lethargic**
**04** dull, idle, lazy, logy, slow **05** heavy, inert, weary **06** drowsy, sleepy, torpid **07** dormant, languid, passive **08** hebetant, inactive, lifeless, listless, slothful, sluggish **09** apathetic, enervated, somnolent **11** debilitated

**lethargically**
**04** idly **05** dully **06** lazily, slowly **07** heavily, inertly, wearily **08** drowsily, sleepily, torpidly **09** languidly **10** inactively, lifelessly, listlessly, slothfully, sluggishly **11** somnolently **13** apathetically

**lethargy**
**05** sloth **06** apathy, stupor, torpor **07** inertia, languor **08** dullness, idleness, inaction, laziness, slowness **09** lassitude, weariness **10** drowsiness, inactivity, sleepiness, somnolence **12** indifference, lifelessness, listlessness, sluggishness

**let-out**
**04** cure **06** escape, excuse, get-out, remedy, way out **08** loophole **09** legal flaw **11** safety valve, way of escape **12** escape clause, technicality **13** error in the law, means of escape

**letter**
**02** Ep **03** dak **04** chit, dawk, Epis, line, note, sign, sort, type **05** books, hirer, reply **06** device, figure, italic, lettre, scrawl, symbol, uncial **07** bloomer, capital, culture, epistle, message, missive, notelet, screeve, writing **08** academia, circular, dispatch, grapheme, learning, pastoral **09** character, education, epistolet, erudition, rune-stave **10** aerogramme, billet-doux, humanities, literature, round robin, semi-uncial **11** scholarship **13** belles-lettres, communication **14** correspondence **15** acknowledgement

*Letters include:*

**03** ash, edh, eth, wen, wyn
**04** aesc, ogam, wynn, yogh
**05** thorn

*See also* **alphabet**; **typeface**

• **to the letter**
**07** exactly **08** strictly **09** by the book, literally, precisely **10** accurately **11** religiously, word for word **13** in every detail, punctiliously

**lettered**
**06** versed **07** erudite, learned, studied **08** academic, cultured, educated, highbrow, informed, literary, literate, well-read **09** scholarly **10** cultivated, widely read **12** accomplished, well-educated **13** knowledgeable

**letter-opener**
**04** Dear

**letters**
**04** mail, post

**lettuce**
**07** Lactuca

*Lettuce varieties include:*

**03** cos
**04** flat
**05** lamb's, round
**06** frisée
**07** cabbage, Chinese, iceberg, romaine
**08** Batavian
**09** little gem
**10** butterhead, lollo rosso

**let-up**
**03** end **04** lull **05** break, pause **06** recess, relief **07** ceasing, respite **08** breather, interval **09** abatement, cessation, lessening, remission **10** slackening

**level**
**03** aim **04** avow, calm, even, flat, mark, rank, rase, raze, size, tell, tier, zone

**05** admit, class, drawn, equal, flush, focus, grade, guess, layer, plain, plane, plumb, point, range, stage, train **06** amount, degree, direct, even up, extent, height, on a par, open up, smooth, stable, status, steady, storey, volume **07** abreast, aligned, be frank, confess, destroy, divulge, echelon, even out, flatten, gallery, horizon, measure, regular, station, stratum, tell all, uniform **08** altitude, balanced, bulldoze, composed, constant, demolish, equalize, estimate, highness, lay waste, make flat, matching, position, pull down, quantity, standard, standing, tear down, zero in on **09** be upfront, champaign, come clean, devastate, elevation, knock down, magnitude, make level, stabilize **10** horizontal, unchanging **11** concentrate, neck and neck, unemotional, unflappable **12** level pegging, speak plainly, well-balanced **13** self-possessed **14** tell it like it is **15** keep nothing back, raze to the ground

• **on the level**
**04** fair, open **06** candid, honest **07** jannock, up-front **08** straight **10** above board, fair dinkum, straight-up **12** on the up and up **13** fair and square

**level-headed**
**04** calm, cool, sane **06** steady **07** prudent **08** balanced, composed, rational, sensible **09** practical **10** cool-headed, dependable, reasonable **11** circumspect, unflappable **12** even-tempered **13** imperturbable, self-possessed

**lever**
**03** bar, key, pry **04** lift, move, pull **05** brake, crank, force, heave, hoist, jemmy, peavy, pedal, pinch, prise, raise, shift **06** handle, peavey, switch, tiller **07** control, crowbar, treadle, treddle, trigger **08** backfall, crossbar, dislodge, joystick, knee-stop, throttle, tommy bar, water key **09** bell crank, handspike, knee-swell, rocker arm, whipstaff **10** pump-handle, tremolo arm **11** walking-beam

**leverage**
**04** grip, hold, pull, rank **05** clout, force, grasp, power, prise, prize **06** weight **08** purchase, strength **09** advantage, authority, influence **10** ascendancy

**leviathan**
**04** hulk **05** giant, Satan, Titan, whale **07** mammoth, monster **08** behemoth, colossus, gigantic **10** formidable, sea monster

**levitate**
**03** fly **04** hang, waft **05** drift, float, glide, hover **07** suspend

**levitation**
**06** flying **07** gliding, hanging, wafting **08** drifting, floating, hovering **10** suspension **11** yogic flying

**levity**
**03** fun **08** hilarity **09** flippancy, frivolity, silliness, whifflery **10** fickleness, triviality **11** glaikitness, irreverence **12** carefreeness, flippantness **13** facetiousness **15** light-mindedness, thoughtlessness

**levy**
**03** due, fee, tax **04** duty, rate, toll **05** exact, leave, raise, stent, tithe, tythe **06** charge, demand, duties, excise, gather, impose, impost, tariff **07** collect, customs, estreat, militia, precept, tallage **10** assessment, collection **12** contribution, subscription

**lewd**
**03** bad **04** bare, blue **05** bawdy, randy **06** carnal, harlot, impure, smutty, vulgar, wanton **07** Cyprian, lustful, obscene, raunchy, sensual, unclean **08** ignorant, indecent, unchaste **09** debauched, dissolute, lecherous, lubricous, salacious **10** degenerate, lascivious, libidinous, licentious, lubricious, suggestive **11** promiscuous **12** concupiscent, pornographic

**lewdly**
**07** randily **08** impurely, smuttily, vulgarly **09** lustfully, obscenely, raunchily **10** indecently **11** dissolutely, lecherously **12** degenerately **13** promiscuously

**lewdness**
**04** smut **07** crudity, lechery **08** impurity, priapism **09** bawdiness, carnality, depravity, indecency, lubricity, obscenity, randiness, vulgarity **10** debauchery, smuttiness, unchastity, wantonness **11** lustfulness, pornography **13** concupiscence, salaciousness **14** lasciviousness, licentiousness

**lexicographer**
**10** vocabulist

*Lexicographers and philologists include:*

**04** **Bopp** (Franz)
**05** **Pliny** (Gaius 'the Elder'), **Sapir** (Edward), **Skeat** (Walter William)
**06** **Bierce** (Ambrose), **Brewer** (Ebenezer Cobham), **Fowler** (Henry Watson), **Freund** (Wilhelm), **Hornby** (A S), **Murray** (Sir James Augustus Henry), **Onions** (Charles Talbut), **Trench** (Richard Chenevix)
**07** **Chomsky** (Noam), **Craigie** (Sir William Alexander), **Diderot** (Denis), **Johnson** (Samuel, 'Dr'), **Mencken** (H L), **Tolkien** (J R R), **Ventris** (Michael George Francis), **Webster** (Noah)
**08** **Chambers** (Ephraim), **Chambers** (Robert), **Chambers** (William), **Larousse** (Pierre Athanase), **Saussure** (Ferdinand de)
**09** **Furnivall** (Frederick James), **Jespersen** (Otto Harry), **Partridge** (Eric)
**10** **Amarasimha**, **Burchfield** (Robert)

**lexicon**
**03** lex, OED, TCD **08** glossary, wordbook, word-list **10** dictionary, phrase book, vocabulary **12** encyclopedia

**Leytonstone**
**03** E11

**liability**
**04** drag, dues, duty, onus **05** debit **06** burden, charge **07** arrears **08** drawback, nuisance **09** hindrance **10** impediment, obligation **11** culpability, encumbrance **12** disadvantage, indebtedness **13** answerability, inconvenience **14** accountability, responsibility **15** blameworthiness

**liable**
**03** apt **04** open **05** prone **06** likely **07** at fault, exposed, fitting, subject, tending, to blame **08** amenable, disposed, inclined, suitable **10** answerable, changeable, vulnerable **11** accountable, predisposed, responsible, susceptible

**liaise**
**07** contact, network **08** relate to **09** co-operate, interface **11** collaborate, communicate **12** work together

**liaison**
**04** link **05** agent, amour, fling, union **06** affair, broker **07** affaire, carry-on, contact, romance **08** intrigue, mediator **09** go-between, middleman, two-timing **10** arbitrator, connection, flirtation, love affair, negotiator **11** co-operation, interchange **12** bit on the side, entanglement, intermediary, relationship **13** collaboration, communication **15** working together

**liar**
**05** leear **06** falser, fibber **07** Ananias, bouncer **08** deceiver, fabulist, perjurer **09** falsifier **11** pseudologue, storyteller **12** false witness, prevaricator

**libation**
**08** oblation **09** sacrifice **13** drink offering

**libel**
**04** slur **05** abuse, smear **06** defame, malign, revile, vilify **07** calumny, slander, traduce **08** badmouth **09** aspersion, denigrate, disparage **10** calumniate, defamation, muck-raking, throw mud at **11** denigration, false report, mudslinging **12** vilification **13** disparagement **15** untrue statement

**libellous**
**05** false **06** untrue **07** abusive **09** injurious, maligning, traducing, vilifying **10** defamatory, derogatory, scurrilous, slanderous **11** denigratory, disparaging **12** calumniatory

**liberal**
◊ *anagram indicator*
**01** L **03** Lib **04** free, left, whig **05** ample, broad, frank **06** candid, giving, lavish, verlig **07** copious, leftish, lenient, profuse, radical **08** abundant, advanced, catholic, flexible, generous, handsome, left-wing, moderate, tolerant, unbiased **09** bountiful, impartial, plentiful, reformist, unsparing **10** altruistic, big-hearted, broad-based, free-handed, munificent, open-handed, open-minded **11** broad-minded, enlightened, free-hearted, libertarian, magnanimous, open-hearted, progressive, wide-ranging **12** large-hearted, unprejudiced **13** philanthropic, unwithdrawing **14** forward-looking, latitudinarian

**liberalism**
**07** leftism **10** radicalism **12** free-thinking **13** progressivism **14** libertarianism **15** humanitarianism

**liberality**
**06** bounty **07** breadth, candour, charity **08** altruism, kindness, largesse **09** tolerance **10** generosity, liberalism, toleration **11** beneficence, benevolence, catholicity, flexibility, magnanimity, munificence, prodigality **12** generousness, impartiality, magnificence, philanthropy **13** progressivism **14** free-handedness, libertarianism, open-handedness, open-mindedness, permissiveness **15** broad-mindedness, open-heartedness

**liberalize**
**04** ease **05** relax **06** loosen, reduce, soften **07** ease off, slacken **08** moderate **10** deregulate **14** lift controls on

**liberate**
**04** free **05** let go, steal **06** let out, ransom, redeem, rescue, uncage **07** deliver, manumit, release, set free, unchain **08** let loose, set loose, unfetter **09** discharge, disimmure, unshackle **10** emancipate **11** appropriate

**liberation**
**03** lib **07** freedom, freeing, liberty, loosing, release **08** uncaging **09** discharge, ransoming, releasing, unpenning **10** liberating, redemption, unchaining **11** deliverance, manumission, unfettering, unshackling **12** emancipation, risorgimento **13** franchisement **15** enfranchisement

**liberator**
**05** freer **07** rescuer, saviour **08** ransomer, redeemer **09** deliverer **10** manumitter **11** emancipator

**Liberia**
**02** LB **03** LBR

**Liber Pater**
**07** Bacchus

**libertine**
**04** rake, roué **05** Romeo **06** lecher **07** Don Juan, lustful, seducer **08** Casanova, freedman, Lothario, Lovelace, palliard **09** debauched, debauchee, dissolute, lecherous, reprobate, salacious, womanizer **10** degenerate, licentious, profligate, sensualist, voluptuary, womanizing **11** gay deceiver, promiscuous
*See also* **womanizer**

**liberty**
**03** ish **05** leave, right **07** freedom, leisure, licence, release **08** autonomy, boldness, disposal, sanction, self-rule **09** franchise, impudence, insolence, privilege **10** discretion, disrespect, indulgence, liberation, permission **11** deliverance, entitlement, familiarity, impropriety, manumission, prerogative, presumption, sovereignty **12** dispensation, emancipation, impertinence, independence **13** authorization **14** self-government **15** overfamiliarity

**• at liberty**
**04** free **05** loose **07** allowed, at large **08** entitled **09** available, permitted **10** disengaged, unhindered, unoccupied **11** not confined **12** unrestrained, unrestricted **13** unconstrained

**• take the liberty**
**08** make bold **10** be impudent **12** be so bold as to **13** be impertinent **14** show disrespect

**libidinous**
**04** lewd **05** horny, loose, randy **06** carnal, impure, wanton, wicked **07** lustful, ruttish, sensual **08** prurient, unchaste **09** debauched, lecherous, salacious **10** cupidinous, lascivious **11** promiscuous **12** concupiscent **13** whoremasterly

**libido**
**04** lust **06** ardour **07** passion, the hots **08** sex drive **09** eroticism, randiness **10** sexual urge **12** erotic desire, sexual desire **14** sexual appetite

**libra**
**01** l **02** lb

**librarian**
**03** ALA, lib

**library**
**02** BL, PL, RL **03** lib

**libretto**
**04** book, text **05** lines, words **06** lyrics, script

*Librettists include:*

**04** **Hart** (Lorenz), **Jouy** (Étienne), **Rice** (Sir Tim), **Stow** (Randolph)
**05** **Swann** (Donald)
**06** **Berlin** (Irving), **Lerner** (Alan Jay), **Malouf** (David), **Porter** (Cole)
**07** **Gilbert** (Sir W S), **Harwood** (Gwen)
**08** **Gershwin** (Ira), **Sondheim** (Stephen)
**11** **Hammerstein** (Oscar, II)

*See also* **composer**

**Libya**
**03** LAR, LBY

**licence**
**04** gale, pass **05** grant, leave, right, slang **06** excess, indult, permit, ticket **07** abandon, anarchy, charter, consent, faculty, freedom, liberty, warrant **08** approval, disorder, document, sanction, warranty **09** authority, decadence, deviation, exemption, franchise, privilege **10** creativity, debauchery, immorality, imprimatur, indulgence, permission, unruliness **11** certificate, dissipation, entitlement, impropriety, inspiration, lawlessness, libertinage, miner's right, originality, prerogative **12** carte blanche, dispensation, exaggeration, fancifulness, immoderation, independence, intemperance **13** accreditation, authorization, certification, dissoluteness, ticket of leave **14** letter-of-marque, licentiousness, self-indulgence **15** imaginativeness, letters-of-marque

**license**
**03** let **05** allow **06** permit **07** certify, consent, dismiss, empower, entitle, warrant **08** accredit, sanction **09** authorize, franchise, privilege **10** commission **14** give permission

**licentious**
**03** lax **04** lewd, wild **05** large, loose, randy **06** impure, ribald, ribaud, wanton **07** Cyprian, immoral, liberal, lustful, raunchy, rybauld **08** decadent, depraved, unchaste **09** abandoned, debauched, dissolute, lecherous, libertine **10** disorderly, dissipated, lascivious, profligate **11** promiscuous

**licentiousness**
**04** lust **07** abandon, lechery, licence, license **08** impurity, lewdness, priapism, salacity **09** prurience, randiness **10** debauchery, immorality, wantonness **11** dissipation, libertinism, lustfulness, promiscuity, raunchiness **13** dissoluteness, salaciousness **14** cupidinousness

**lichen**
**10** consortium
*See also* **alga, algae**

**licit**
**04** real **05** legal, legit **06** lawful, proper **07** correct, genuine **08** rightful **09** allowable, statutory, warranted **10** authorized, legitimate, sanctioned **12** acknowledged

**lick**
**03** bit, dab, lap, tad, wag, wet **04** beat, blow, dart, fawn, hint, spot, wash **05** brush, clean, flick, slake, smear, speck, taste, touch **06** defeat, hammer, little, ripple, sample, stroke, thrash, tongue **07** conquer, flicker, moisten, trounce **08** demolish, play over, smidgeon, vanquish **09** slaughter **13** run rings round **15** make mincemeat of

• **lick your lips**
**05** enjoy **06** relish, savour **09** drool over **10** anticipate

**licking**
**06** defeat, hiding **07** beating, lambent, tanning **08** drubbing, flogging, smacking, spanking, whipping **09** thrashing

**lid**
**03** cap, hat, top **05** cover, slide **07** scuttle, stopper **08** covering, screw cap **09** operculum

**lie**
**02** be **04** cram, keep, lair, laze, lean, rest, stay **05** abide, couch, dwell, exist, lodge, press, reach, stand **06** belong, bounce, deceit, depend, extend, invent, lounge, remain, repose **07** be found, consist, falsify, perjure, perjury, recline, romance, stretch **08** be placed, continue, tell a lie, white lie **09** be located, dissemble, fabricate, sprawl out **10** equivocate, stretch out **11** dissimulate, prevaricate **12** be positioned, make up a story, misrepresent

*Lies include:*

**03** bam, fib, gag
**04** cram, crap, flam, oner, whid
**05** fable, one-er, porky, story
**06** deceit, unfact, wunner, yanker
**07** cretism, falsity, fiction, leasing, swinger, thumper, untruth, whacker, whopper
**08** porkypie, strapper, white lie
**09** fairy tale, falsehood, half-truth, invention, mendacity, tall story
**10** concoction, fairy story, taradiddle
**11** fabrication, made-up story, out-and-outer, pseudologia, tarradiddle
**13** dissimulation, falsification, prevarication

• **give the lie to**
**05** rebut **08** disprove **10** contradict, invalidate, prove false
• **lie about**
**03** lig
• **lie in sun**
**04** bask
• **lie in wait for**
**04** lurk, trap **06** ambush, attack, waylay **08** surprise **09** ambuscade **10** lie at lurch **11** lay a trap for
• **lie low**
**04** hide, lurk **05** skulk **06** hole up **07** hide out, tappice **08** hide away, lie doggo **09** go to earth, take cover **12** go into hiding **15** conceal yourself, keep a low profile

**Liechtenstein**
**02** FL **03** LIE

**liege**
**04** king, lord **05** chief **06** master, vassal **07** subject **08** nobleman, overlord, superior **09** liege-lord **10** feudal lord

**lieutenant**
**02** DL, LL, Lt **04** loot **05** Lieut **06** deputy, guider, legate **09** assistant, number one, scavenger **11** subordinate **12** right-hand man **14** right-hand woman **15** second-in-command

**life**
**03** bio, man, pep, zip **04** élan, soul, span, time, vita, zest, zing **05** being, child, diary, fauna, flora, oomph, plant, verve, woman **06** breath, career, course, energy, entity, person, spirit, vigour **07** diaries, journal, memoirs, pizzazz, sparkle **08** activity, duration, lifespan, lifetime, vitality, vivacity **09** aliveness, animation, biography, existence, human life, life story, viability **10** animal life, enthusiasm, excitement, experience, exuberance, human being, individual, liveliness, travelling **11** continuance, high spirits **12** cheerfulness, living things **13** autobiography, effervescence, fauna and flora, meeting people **14** life expectancy, wide experience
• **come to life**
**04** rise **06** wake up **09** come alive **12** become active, become lively **14** become exciting
• **enjoy life**
**04** live
• **give your life**
**06** die for **14** give up your life **15** offer up your life
• **in present life**
**04** here
• **term of life**
**04** date

**life-and-death**
**05** vital **07** crucial, serious **08** critical **09** important **12** all-important

**lifeblood**
**04** core, soul **05** heart **06** centre, lethee, spirit **09** life-force **11** inspiration **13** essential part **15** essential factor

**lifeless**
**04** arid, bare, cold, dead, dull, flat, gone, lank, slow **05** dusty, empty, stark, stiff **06** barren, wooden **07** defunct, insipid, key-cold, passive, sterile **08** clay-cold, deceased, desolate, listless, sluggish, soulless **09** apathetic, bloodless, cauldrife, exanimate, inanimate, lethargic, stone-dead **10** colourless, insensible, lacklustre, uninspired **11** unconscious, unemotional, uninhabited, uninspiring **12** unproductive

**lifelike**
**04** real, true **05** exact, vivid **06** lively **07** ad vivum, graphic, natural **08** faithful, speaking **09** authentic, breathing, realistic **10** true-to-life

**lifelong**
**07** abiding, lasting **08** constant, enduring, lifetime **09** permanent **10** persistent **11** long-lasting **12** long-standing **14** for all your life

**lifestyle**
**04** life **08** position **09** situation, way of life **11** way of living **14** manner of living

**lifetime**
**03** day **04** days, life, span, time **06** career, course, period **08** anthesis, duration, lifespan **09** existence **10** pilgrimage

**lift**
**02** up **03** air, end, fly, run, sky **04** copy, crib, jack, move, nick, pick, ride, rise, spur, stop **05** annul, arsis, boost, clear, dig up, drive, elate, exalt, hitch, hoist, mount, press, raise, relax, shift, spout, steal **06** arrest, borrow, buoy up, cancel, convey, fillip, hold up, pick up, pull up, remove, revoke, snatch, teagle, uplift, vanish **07** airlift, elevate, heavens, relieve, rescind, root out, scatter, support, thin out, unearth, upraise **08** disperse, dissolve, elevator, hold high, increase, pick-me-up, transfer, withdraw **09** disappear, encourage, escalator, terminate, transport **10** plagiarize **11** paternoster, reassurance **12** shot in the arm **13** encouragement

*See also* **steal**

• **lift off**
**04** rear **05** climb **06** ascend, depart **07** take off **08** blast off

**lift-off**
**05** climb **06** ascent **07** take-off **08** blast-off **09** departure

**lift-shaft**
**04** well

**ligament**
**03** ACL, tie **04** bond **06** frenum **07** fraenum, urachus

**ligature**
**03** tie **04** aesc, band, bond, cord, link, rope, slur **05** strap, thong **06** string **07** bandage, binding, funicle **08** ligament **09** diphthong **10** connection, deligation, tourniquet

**light**
◇ *anagram indicator*
**03** day, eye, gay, ray, way **04** airy, beam, bulb, clue, dawn, deft, easy, fair, fine, fire, flit, glow, hint, idle, lamp, lyte, mild, pale, rest, side, soft, thin, weak **05** agile, angle, blaze, blond, cheer, faded, faint, flash, funny, glare, gleam, glint, happy, loose, match, merry, petty, put on, quick, shaft, shine, slant, small, style, sunny, taper, torch, witty **06** active, aspect, beacon, blithe, blonde, bright, candle, cheery, facile, flimsy, floaty, gentle, ignite, kindle, lively, lustre, manner, modest, nimble, pastel, porous, scanty, settle, slight, turn on **07** amusing, animate, buoyant, cheer up, cresset,crumbly, daytime, friable, glowing, insight, lantern, lenient, lighten, lighter, light up, shining, sunrise, trivial, well-lit, whitish **08** approach, bleached, brighten, carefree, cheerful, cockcrow, daybreak, daylight, delicate, dismount, feathery, graceful, humorous, lambency, luminous, moderate, pleasing, portable, radiance, switch on,

trifling, unchaste, untaxing **09** brilliant, dimension, diverting, easily dug, frivolous, irradiate, knowledge, set alight, set fire to, unheeding, worthless **10** brightness, brilliance, digestible, effortless, effulgence, first light, flashlight, floodlight, illuminate, luminosity, set burning, unexacting, weightless **11** crack of dawn, easily moved, elucidation, explanation, illuminated, lightweight, point of view, superficial, undemanding, unimportant **12** easy to digest, entertaining, illumination, light-hearted, luminescence, make cheerful **13** comprehension, enlightenment, incandescence, insubstantial, understanding **14** inconsiderable **15** inconsequential

• **bring to light**
**04** rout **06** exhume, expose, notice, reveal **07** uncover, unearth **08** disclose, discover, disinter, exhumate **09** make known

• **come to light**
**09** be exposed, be noticed, transpire **11** be made known, be uncovered **12** be discovered **13** become obvious

• **in the light of**
**08** in view of **09** because of **11** considering, remembering **13** bearing in mind, keeping in mind **14** being mindful of

• **light on, light upon**
**04** find, spot **05** hit on **06** notice **08** chance on, discover **09** encounter, stumble on **10** come across, happen upon

• **shed light on, throw light on, cast light on**
**07** clarify, enlight, explain **09** elucidate, make clear, make plain **10** illuminate

• **speck of light**
**04** peep

**lighten**
**04** calm, ease, glow, lift **05** allay, cheer, elate, shine **06** buoy up, lessen, perk up, reduce, revive, unload, uplift **07** assuage, cheer up, gladden, hearten, inspire, light up, relieve, restore **08** brighten, illumine, inspirit, levigate, mitigate **09** alleviate, encourage **10** illuminate **11** make lighter **12** make brighter

• **lighten up**
**04** cool **05** chill, relax **06** unwind **08** calm down, chill out **09** hang loose **10** take it easy **13** let yourself go, put your feet up

**lighter**
**04** pram **05** barge, praam, Zippo **07** gondola, pontoon

**light-fingered**
**03** sly **06** crafty, shifty **07** crooked, furtive **08** filching, stealing, thieving, thievish **09** dishonest, pilfering **11** shoplifting

**light-footed**
**04** deft, spry **05** agile, lithe, swift **06** active, nimble **08** graceful **09** sprightly

**light-headed**
**04** airy **05** dizzy, faint, giddy, silly, woozy **07** flighty, foolish, shallow, vacuous **08** flippant, trifling, unsteady **09** airheaded, delirious, frivolous **11** empty-headed, superficial, thoughtless, vertiginous **14** feather-brained, scatter-brained

**light-hearted**
**03** gay **04** glad, high **05** happy, jolly, merry, sunny **06** blithe, bouncy, bright, chirpy, elated, jovial, joyful **07** amusing, playful **08** carefree, cheerful **10** frolicsome, untroubled **12** entertaining, happy-go-lucky **13** inconsiderate, in good spirits, in high spirits, irresponsible

• **light-heartedness**
**06** levity

**lighthouse**
**05** fanal, phare, tower **06** beacon, pharos **12** danger signal **13** warning signal

**lightly**
**05** gaily **06** airily, easily, gently, mildly, softly, thinly **07** faintly, readily **08** breezily, casually, facilely, gingerly, slightly, sparsely **09** leniently, sparingly **10** carelessly, delicately, flippantly, heedlessly **11** frivolously, slightingly **12** effortlessly **13** thoughtlessly

**lightness**
**05** grace **06** gaiety, levity **07** agility **08** airiness, buoyancy, deftness, delicacy, mildness, porosity, thinness **09** animation, frivolity, litheness, sandiness **10** blitheness, cheeriness, fickleness, flimsiness, gentleness, liveliness, nimbleness, porousness, slightness, triviality **11** crumbliness **12** cheerfulness, delicateness, gracefulness **14** weightlessness

**lightning**
**04** fire **05** levin **08** fireball, wildfire **11** fulguration, thunderbolt, thunderclap, thunderdart **12** thunderstorm **13** ball lightning, clap of thunder, electric storm **14** chain lightning, sheet lightning **15** forked lightning, lightning strike, summer lightning, zigzag lightning

• **like lightning**
**07** a rocket, hastily, quickly, rapidly **08** speedily, wildfire **11** immediately

**lightweight**
**02** oz **04** thin **05** light, petty **06** flimsy, paltry, slight **07** trivial **08** delicate, feathery, nugatory, trifling **09** worthless **10** negligible, weightless **11** unimportant **13** insignificant, insubstantial **15** inconsequential

**likable, likeable**
**04** nice **06** genial **07** amiable, lovable, winning, winsome **08** charming, engaging, friendly, loveable, pleasant, pleasing **09** agreeable, appealing, congenial **10** attractive, personable **11** sympathetic

**like**
**02** as **03** à la, dig **04** akin, love, mate, peer, same, true, twin, want, wish **05** adore, alike, enjoy, equal, fancy, go for, match, prize, usual **06** admire, allied, choose, desire, esteem, fellow, normal, prefer, relish, select, such as, take to **07** approve, care for, cherish, of a kind, related, revel in, similar, suiting, typical, welcome **08** appeal to, be fond of, be keen on, decide on, hold dear, parallel, relating **09** analogous, befitting, delight in, identical, similar to **10** appreciate, comparable, equivalent, for example, resembling **11** counterpart, for instance, go a bundle on, much the same, would rather, would sooner **12** feel inclined, find pleasant, on the lines of, take a shine to, take kindly to **13** approximating, corresponding, find enjoyable **14** by way of example, characteristic, find attractive, in the same way as, opposite number, take pleasure in **15** along the lines of, find interesting

**likeable** *see* **likable**

**likelihood**
**06** chance **08** prospect **09** liability **10** likeliness **11** possibility, probability

**likely**
**03** apt, fit **04** fair **05** prone, right **06** liable, odds-on, proper **07** fitting, hopeful, in order, no doubt, tending **08** credible, expected, feasible, inclined, pleasing, possible, probable, probably **09** in the wind, plausible, promising **10** acceptable, believable, calculated, on the cards, presumably, reasonable **11** anticipated, appropriate, doubtlessly, foreseeable, likely as not, predictable **12** to be expected **13** as likely as not

**like-minded**
**08** agreeing, in accord **09** in harmony, in rapport, of one mind, unanimous **10** compatible, harmonious **11** in agreement **13** of the same mind

**liken**
**04** like, link **05** match **06** equate, relate **07** compare **08** parallel, similize **09** analogize, associate, correlate, juxtapose, set beside

**likeness**
**04** bust, copy, form, icon **05** guise, image, shape, study **06** effigy, sketch, statue **07** analogy, drawing, picture, replica **08** affinity, painting, portrait **09** depiction, facsimile, sculpture, semblance **10** appearance, caricature, comparison, expression, photograph, similarity, similitude, simulacrum **11** counterpart, parallelism, personation, portraiture, resemblance **12** reproduction **14** correspondence, representation

**likewise**
**02** do, so **03** als, eke, too **04** also, item **05** ditto **06** as also, to boot **07** besides,

further **08** moreover, same here **09** similarly **10** in addition **11** furthermore **12** in like manner, in the same way **14** by the same token **15** in the same manner

**liking**
**04** bent, bias, broo, brow, love **05** fancy, taste, thing **06** desire, notion, palate **07** leaning **08** affinity, fondness, penchant, soft spot, tendency, weakness **09** affection, proneness **10** attraction, partiality, preference, proclivity, propensity **11** inclination **12** appreciation, predilection, satisfaction

**lilac**
**07** laylock, syringa **08** pipe-tree

**lilt**
**03** air, hum **04** beat, lill, song, sway **05** swing **06** rhythm **07** cadence, measure **10** fingerhole **11** rise and fall

**lily**

*Lilies include:*

**03** day, may
**04** aloe, arum, pond, sego
**05** calla, camas, lotus, regal, tiger, torch, yucca
**06** camash, camass, Canada, crinum, Easter, Nuphar, scilla, smilax
**07** candock, day-lily, Madonna, may-lily, quamash, Tritoma
**08** asphodel, galtonia, gloriosa, hyacinth, martagon, nenuphar, Phormium, trillium, Turk's cap, victoria
**09** amaryllis, grass tree, herb-Paris, kniphofia, Richardia
**10** agapanthus, aspidistra, belladonna, fritillary
**11** cabbage-tree, Convallaria, Madonna-lily, red-hot poker, spatterdock
**12** Annunciation, Hemerocallis, Solomon's seal, zantedeschia
**13** butcher's broom, lily of the Nile
**15** lily of the valley, star of Bethlehem

**• lily leaf**
**03** pad

**lily-white**
**04** pure **06** chaste, virgin **08** innocent, spotless, virtuous **09** blameless, faultless, incorrupt, milk-white, uncorrupt, unsullied, untainted **11** uncorrupted, untarnished **14** irreproachable

**Lima**
**01** L

**limb**
**03** arm, leg **04** edge, fork, part, spur, wing **05** bough, spald, spall, spaul **06** border, branch, member, spalle, spauld **07** flipper, quarter, section **08** offshoot **09** appendage, extension, extremity, pterygium **10** projection

**• out on a limb**
**07** exposed **08** isolated **10** vulnerable **15** in a weak position

**limber**
**05** agile, lithe **06** lissom, pliant, supple **07** elastic, plastic, pliable **08** flexible, graceful **11** loose-limbed **12** loose-jointed

**• limber up**
**06** warm up **07** prepare, work out **08** exercise, loosen up

**limbo**

**• in limbo**
**10** in abeyance, up in the air **11** left hanging **12** left in the air **14** awaiting action **15** on the back burner

**lime**
**04** bass, bast, lind, line, teil, trap **05** leash, Tilia **06** linden, loiter, temper, viscum **07** ensnare **08** basswood

**limelight**
**04** fame **06** notice, renown **07** stardom **08** eminence **09** attention, celebrity, public eye, publicity, spotlight **10** notability, prominence **11** recognition

**limestone**
**03** cam **04** calm, calp, caum **06** kunkar, kunkur, oolite **07** coquina, scaglia **08** Coral Rag, dolomite **09** caen-stone, coral-rock, cornbrash, cornstone **10** Kentish rag, stinkstone, travertine **11** cement-stone, rottenstone, sarcophagus **12** Forest Marble, Purbeck stone **13** Purbeck marble **15** coralline oolite, Kentish ragstone, landscape-marble

**limit**
◇ *containment indicator*
◇ *tail deletion indicator*
◇ *ends selection indicator*
**03** cap, end, lid, rim, tie **04** brim, curb, edge, goal, gole, line, mete, pale, rein, roof, term **05** bound, brink, check, hem in, stint, Thule, verge **06** border, bounds, bridle, hinder, impede, margin, ration, reduce, region, tropic, utmost **07** appoint, ceiling, compass, confine, contain, control, delimit, extreme, margent, maximum, outside, specify **08** boundary, confines, deadline, division, frontier, outgoing, restrain, restrict, terminus, ultimate **09** condition, constrain, demarcate, determine, extremity, perimeter, prescribe, restraint, threshold **10** constraint, limitation, parameters **11** cut-off point, demarcation, demarkation, hold in check, keep in check, restriction, termination, ultima Thule **12** circumscribe **14** greatest amount, greatest extent **15** saturation point

**• extend beyond limit**
**03** lap

**• the limit**
**06** enough, the end, utmost **07** too much **08** the worst **11** intolerable, the final bow **12** the final blow, the last straw

**limitation**
**04** curb, snag, tail **05** block, check **06** burden, defect **07** control, reserve **08** drawback, tail male, weakness **09** condition, hindrance, inability, restraint, weak point **10** constraint, impediment, inadequacy **11** demarcation, reservation, restriction, shortcoming **12** delimitation, disadvantage, imperfection, incapability **13** qualification **15** circumscription

**limited**
◇ *ends deletion indicator*
**03** Ltd **04** tail, tyde **05** basic, borné, fixed, small **06** finite, narrow, scanty **07** checked, defined, minimal **08** confined **09** imperfect, qualified **10** controlled, inadequate, incomplete, restricted **11** constrained, determinate **12** insufficient **13** circumscribed

**limitless**
◇ *ends deletion indicator*
◇ *head deletion indicator*
◇ *tail deletion indicator*
**04** vast **06** untold **07** endless, immense **08** infinite, unending **09** boundless, countless, illimited, unbounded, undefined, unlimited **10** bottomless **11** measureless, never-ending, unspecified **12** immeasurable, incalculable, interminable **13** inexhaustible

**limp**
**03** dot, hop, lax **04** flop, gimp, halt, lank, soft, weak **05** frail, hilch, hitch, loose, slack, spent, tired, weary **06** falter, feeble, flabby, flaggy, floppy, hamble, hobble, limber, totter **07** flaccid, pliable, relaxed, shamble, shuffle, stagger, stumble, worn out **08** drooping, fatigued, flexible, lameness **09** enervated, exhausted, lethargic, out of curl **10** uneven walk **11** debilitated, out of energy **12** claudication, walk unevenly **13** walk with a limp

**limpid**
**04** pure **05** clear, lucid, plain, still **06** bright, glassy **07** flowing **08** coherent, pellucid **09** unruffled **10** untroubled **11** translucent, transparent **12** crystal-clear, intelligible **14** comprehensible

**limply**
**06** softly **07** loosely, slackly **08** flabbily, flexibly **09** flaccidly

**limpness**
**06** laxity **09** looseness, slackness **10** flabbiness, flaccidity **11** flaccidness, flexibility **12** claudication

**Lincoln**
**03** Abe

**line**
**01** l **03** bar, job, ley, pad, rew, rim, row, way **04** area, axis, back, band, bank, belt, book, card, ceil, ciel, cord, dash, draw, edge, face, file, fill, firm, flax, kind, lind, make, mark, memo, note, oche, part, path, race, rank, role, rope, rule, seam,

side, sort, talk, text, tier, type, wire, word, work **05** bound, brand, breed, cable, canon, chain, cover, e-mail, field, forte, front, hatch, inlay, limit, panel, pitch, queue, route, score, shape, skirt, slash, spiel, stock, story, strip, stuff, style, track, trade, trail, twine, verge, words **06** avenue, belief, border, career, column, course, crease, encase, family, figure, fringe, furrow, groove, letter, margin, method, parade, patter, policy, report, scheme, script, series, strain, strand, streak, string, stripe, stroke, system, thread **07** calling, channel, company, contour, descent, lineage, message, outline, pattern, profile, pursuit, scratch, variety, wrinkle **08** activity, ancestry, approach, attitude, boundary, business, defences, filament, frontier, heritage, ideology, inscribe, interest, libretto, pedigree, position, postcard, practice, province, sequence, vocation **09** crow's feet, direction, formation, front line, parentage, perimeter, periphery, procedure, reinforce, sales talk, specialty, technique, underline **10** appearance, battle zone, borderline, department, employment, extraction, firing-line, line of work, memorandum, occupation, procession, profession, silhouette, specialism, speciality, strengthen, succession, trajectory, underscore **11** battlefield, corrugation, delineation, demarcation, information **12** battleground **13** configuration, modus operandi **14** course of action, line of business, specialization **15** draughtsmanship

*See also* **poetry**; **railway**

**• curved line**
**03** tie

**• draw the line**
**05** limit **06** refuse, reject **07** exclude, rule out, say no to **08** say not to **09** stand firm **11** stop short of **15** put your foot down

**• fishing line**
**04** gimp, gymp **05** guimp

**• in line**
**03** due **06** in a row, in step, likely **08** in accord, in a queue, in series **09** in a column, in harmony **10** on the cards **11** in agreement **12** in the running **15** being considered

**• lay on the line, put on the line**
**04** risk **07** imperil **08** endanger **10** jeopardize **13** put in jeopardy

**• line up**
**05** align, array, group, lay on, order, queue, range **06** fall in, obtain, secure **07** arrange, marshal, prepare, procure, produce, queue up **08** assemble, organize, regiment **09** form ranks **10** form a queue, straighten, wait in line **11** stand in line

**• new line**
**03** zag

**• toe the line**
**07** conform **12** keep the rules **14** be conventional, follow the rules

**lineage**
**04** line, race **05** birth, breed, house, stock **06** family, parage **07** descent, lignage, progeny **08** ancestry, heredity, pedigree **09** ancestors, forebears, genealogy, offspring, whakapapa **10** descending, extraction, succession **11** descendants

**lineaments**
**04** face **05** lines **06** aspect, traits, visage **07** outline, profile **08** features, outlines **10** appearance **11** countenance, physiognomy **13** configuration

**lined**
**04** worn **05** feint, ruled **07** creased, wizened **08** furrowed, wrinkled

**linen**
**04** duck, ecru, harn, lawn, line, lint, snow **05** crash, drill, toile **06** byssus, damask, dowlas, napery, sendal, sheets, sindon, whites **07** byssine, cambric, dornick, drabbet, holland, lockram, napkins, silesia **08** bed linen, drilling, gambroon, marcella, osnaburg **09** huckaback, Moygashel®, tea towels **10** seersucker, table linen, white goods **11** pillowcases, tablecloths

**• measure of linen**
**03** lay, lea, ley

**• strip of linen**
**04** amis **05** amice

**liner**
**04** boat, ship **07** steamer **10** cruise ship

**linesman**
**04** poet **06** author, writer

**line-up**
**03** row **04** bill, cast, line, list, team **05** array, queue **09** selection **11** arrangement

**linger**
**03** lag **04** hang, hove, idle, last, lurk, stay, stop, wait **05** dally, delay, hoove, hover, tarry **06** dawdle, endure, hang on, hanker, loiter, remain, taigle **07** hold out, persist, survive **08** continue, smoulder, straggle **10** dilly-dally, hang around **11** stick around **12** take your time **13** procrastinate

**• linger on scent**
**03** tie

**lingerie**
**03** bra **04** slip **05** teddy **06** smalls, undies **07** panties **08** camisole, frillies, half-slip, knickers, scanties **09** brassiere, underwear **11** panty girdle **12** body stocking, camiknickers, underclothes **13** suspender belt, underclothing, undergarments **14** inexpressibles, unmentionables

**lingering**
**04** slow **08** dragging **09** prolonged, remaining, surviving **10** persistent, persisting, protracted **11** languishing **12** long-drawn-out

**lingo**
**03** bat **04** cant, talk **05** argot, idiom **06** jargon, patois, patter, speech, tongue **07** dialect **08** language, parlance **10** mumbo-jumbo, vernacular, vocabulary **11** terminology

**liniment**
**04** balm, wash **05** cream, salve **06** balsam, lotion **07** unguent **08** ointment **09** carron oil, emollient, opodeldoc **11** embrocation **14** camphorated oil

**lining**
◇ *insertion indicator*
**03** lag **04** cush **05** inlay, stean, steen, stein **06** casing, facing, fettle **07** backing, cushion, furring, padding, sarking, tubbing **08** brattice, brattish, brettice, doublure, steaning, steening, steining, wainscot **09** alignment, panelling **10** encasement, incasement, stiffening **11** interfacing **13** reinforcement

**link**
**03** map, tie **04** ally, bind, bond, join, knot, loop, part, ring, yoke **05** cleek, joint, merge, piece, tie-up, torch, union, unite **06** attach, bridge, couple, fasten, hook up, liaise, member, relate, swivel, team up **07** bracket, connect, element, enchain, hot line, liaison, network, shackle **08** division, identify, osculate **09** air-bridge, associate, carabiner, component, interlink, karabiner **10** amalgamate, attachment, connection, join forces **11** association, concatenate, constituent, partnership **12** relationship **13** communication, concatenation

**• link up**
**04** ally, dock, join **05** merge, unify **06** bridge, hook up, join up, meet up, team up **07** connect, network **10** amalgamate, join forces

**linkage**
**03** tie **04** bond, knot **05** joint, tie-in, tie-up, union **06** merger **07** liaison **08** alliance **09** valve gear **10** attachment, connection **11** association, partnership **12** amalgamation, relationship **13** communication

**link-up**
**05** tie-in, union **06** merger **08** alliance **10** connection **11** association, partnership **12** amalgamation, relationship

**lion**
**03** Leo **05** Aslan **12** king of beasts

**• lion's share**
**04** bulk, mass, most **08** main part, majority **09** almost all, nearly all **11** largest part **12** greatest part **13** preponderance

**lion-hearted**
**04** bold **05** brave **06** daring, heroic **07** gallant, valiant **08** fearless, intrepid, resolute, stalwart, valorous

09 dauntless, dreadless
10 courageous 12 stout-hearted

**lionize**
04 fête 05 exalt 06 honour, praise 07 acclaim, adulate, glorify, idolize, magnify 08 eulogize 09 celebrate 10 aggrandize 11 hero-worship 12 treat as a hero 14 put on a pedestal

**lip**
03 jib, lap, rim 04 brim, edge, flew, kiss, lave 05 brink, cheek, mouth, sauce, spout, verge 06 border, fipple, helmet, labium, labrum, ligula, margin, muffle 07 corolla, hare-lip 08 attitude, backchat, labellum, rudeness, underlip 09 impudence, insolence, submentum 10 effrontery 12 impertinence

**lippy**
04 pert 05 fresh, sassy, saucy 06 brazen, cheeky, lippie, mouthy 07 forward 08 impudent, insolent 09 audacious 11 impertinent 12 overfamiliar 13 disrespectful

**liquefaction**
06 fusion 07 melting, thawing 08 solation, syntexis 10 dissolving, karyolysis, liquefying 11 dissolution 13 deliquescence

**liquefy**
03 run 04 flux, fuse, melt, thaw 05 smelt 08 dissolve, fluidize, liquesce 09 liquidize 10 deliquesce

**liqueur**

*Liqueurs include:*

04 ouzo
05 Aurum®, noyau
06 Glayva, Kahlúa®, kirsch, kümmel, Malibu®, Midori®, pastis, Pernod®
07 Baileys®, curaçao, ratafia, sambuca
08 absinthe, advocaat, amaretto, Drambuie®, Galliano®, Tia Maria®
09 Cointreau®, mirabelle, Triple sec
10 Chartreuse®, limoncello, maraschino
11 Benedictine
12 cherry brandy, crème de cacao, Grand Marnier®, kirschwasser, Parfait Amour
13 crème de cassis, crème de menthe, Cuarenta y Tres
15 Southern Comfort®

*See also* **cocktail**; **spirits**

**liquid**
02 aq 03 sap, wet 04 even, pure, thin 05 clear, drink, fluid, juice, moist, runny 06 liquor, lotion, mellow, melted, molten, sloppy, smooth, steady, thawed, watery 07 aqueous, flowing, hydrous, regular, running, unfixed 08 solution, unbroken 09 liquefied, melodious 12 indisputable 13 uninterrupted

• **coloured liquid**
03 dye, ink

• **liquid for washing**
03 lye

**liquidate**
03 pay 04 kill, sell 05 clear 06 cash in, murder, pay off, remove, rub out, wind up 07 abolish, break up, destroy, disband, sell off, wipe out 08 dispatch, dissolve, massacre 09 close down, discharge, eliminate, finish off, terminate 10 annihilate, do away with, put an end to 11 assassinate, exterminate 13 convert to cash

**liquidize**
03 mix 05 blend, cream, crush, purée 07 process 10 synthesize

**liquor**
03 liq 04 bree, broo, grog, malt, vino 05 boose, booze, bouse, broth, drink, gravy, hogan, hogen, hooch, juice, plonk, sauce, stock, tinct 06 hootch, liquid, porter, rotgut, strunt, tiddly, tipple 07 alcohol, essence, extract, hokonui, shicker, spirits 08 infusion, potation 09 firewater, hard stuff, stiffener, stimulant, the bottle 10 intoxicant 11 aguardiente, jungle juice, strong drink, the creature, tickle-brain 12 Dutch courage

*See also* **drink**

• **liquor house** *see* **public house**

**liquorice**
07 nail-rod, pomfret 09 jequirity, sugarally 10 sugarallie

**lissom**
05 agile, light, lithe 06 limber, nimble, pliant, supple 07 pliable, willowy 08 flexible, graceful 09 lithesome 11 loose-limbed 12 loose-jointed

**list**
◇ *homophone indicator*
03 tip 04 bill, book, cant, file, heel, lean, leet, menu, note, roll, roon, rota, tilt 05 enrol, enter, index, slant, slate, slope, strip, table, tally 06 agenda, border, fillet, litany, recipe, record, roster, scroll, series, stripe 07 compile, incline, invoice, itemize, listing, scedule, selvage, set down 08 boundary, calendar, classify, contents, heel over, lean over, register, schedule, syllabus, tabulate 09 catalogue, checklist, directory, enumerate, inventory, programme, write down 10 tabulation 11 alphabetize, enumeration

*See also* **lean**

**listen**
◇ *homophone indicator*
04 hark, hear, heed, lest, list, mind 05 lithe 06 attend, intend 07 give ear, hearken, monitor 09 eavesdrop, lend an ear 10 auscultate, get a load of, take notice 12 pay attention 15 prick up your ears

• **listen in**
◇ *homophone indicator*
03 bug, tap 07 monitor, wiretap 08 overhear 09 eavesdrop 15 pin back your ears, prick up your ears

**listener**
03 ear

**listless**
04 dull, limp, waff 05 bored, heavy, inert 06 mopish, torpid, vacant 07 languid, passive 08 inactive, indolent, lifeless, sluggish, thowless, toneless 09 apathetic, depressed, enervated, impassive, lethargic, upsitting 10 spiritless 11 indifferent, languishing 12 uninterested 13 lackadaisical

**listlessly**
05 dully 06 limply 07 inertly 09 passively 10 inactively, lifelessly, sluggishly 11 impassively 12 spiritlessly 13 apathetically, lacking energy, lethargically

**listlessness**
05 ennui, sloth 06 acedia, apathy, torpor 07 languor, vacuity 08 lethargy 09 indolence, torpidity, upsitting 10 enervation, supineness 11 inattention, languidness 12 indifference, lifelessness, sluggishness 14 spiritlessness

**lit**
◇ *anagram indicator*
02 in 05 drunk, light, merry, tight, tipsy 06 ablaze, blotto, rested, soused 07 drunken, legless, pickled, settled, sloshed, sozzled, squiffy 09 crapulent, paralytic, plastered 10 dismounted, inebriated 11 intoxicated

**litany**
04 list 06 prayer 07 account, recital, synapte 08 devotion, irenicon, petition 09 catalogue, eirenicon 10 invocation, procession, recitation, repetition 11 enumeration 12 supplication

**literacy**
07 culture 08 learning 09 education, erudition, knowledge 10 articulacy 11 cultivation, learnedness, proficiency, scholarship 12 intelligence 13 ability to read 14 ability to write, articulateness

**literal**
03 lit 04 dull, true, typo 05 clear, close, error, exact, plain 06 actual, boring, strict, verbal 07 erratum, factual, genuine, humdrum, mistake, precise, prosaic, tedious 08 accurate, faithful, misprint, verbatim 10 colourless, uninspired 11 corrigendum, down-to-earth, undistorted, unvarnished, word-for-word 12 matter-of-fact 13 printing error, unembellished, unexaggerated, unimaginative

**literalism**
06 letter 09 biblicism, verbalism 10 textualism 13 scripturalism 14 exact rendering, fundamentalism, letter of the law

**literally**
03 lit 05 truly 06 really 07 closely, exactly, plainly 08 actually, strictly, verbatim 09 certainly, precisely 10 faithfully 11 to the letter, word for word

**literary**

**03** lit **06** formal, poetic **07** bookish, erudite, learned, refined, written **08** cultured, educated, lettered, literate, literose, well-read **09** scholarly **10** cultivated, epistolary, widely-read **12** old-fashioned

*Literary characters include:*

**02** Pi

**03** Eva (Little), Fox (Brer), Jim (Lord), Kaa, Kim, Lee (Lorelei), Pan (Peter), Pip, Roo, Tom (Uncle), Una

**04** Ahab (Captain), Bede (Adam), Bond (James), Budd (Billy), Dent (Arthur), Eyre (Jane), Finn (Huckleberry), Fogg (Phileas), Gamp (Sarah), Gray (Charlotte), Gray (Dorian), Gunn (Ben), Haze (Dolores), Heep (Uriah), Hood (Robin), Hook (Captain), Hyde (Mister), Jack, Mole, Mole (Adrian), Pooh, Pope (Giant), Ridd (John), Slop (Doctor), Tigg (Montague), Toad (Mister), Trim (Corporal), Troy (Sergeant Francis), Tuck (Friar), Wilt (Henry)

**05** Akela, Aslan, Athos, Avery (Shug), Baloo, Bates (Miss), Bloom (Leopold), Bloom (Molly), Boxer, Brown (Father), Celie, Chips (Mister), Clare (Angel), Darcy (Fitzwilliam), Darcy (Mark), Doone (Lorna), Drood (Edwin), Flint (Captain), Geste (Beau), Jones (Bridget), Jones (Tom), Kanga, Kipps (Arthur), Loman (Willy), Lucky, March (Amy), Maria (Mad), Mitty (Walter), Moore (Mrs), Mosca, Nancy, O'Hara (Kimball), O'Hara (Scarlett), Parry (Will), Piggy, Polly (Alfred), Porgy, Pozzo, Price (Fanny), Quilp (Daniel), Ralph, Ratty, Rebus (Inspector John), Remus (Uncle), Rudge (Barnaby), Satan, Sharp (Becky), Sikes (Bill), Slope (Reverend Obadiah), Sloth, Smike, Smith (Winston), Spade (Sam), Stubb, Tarka (the Otter), Titus, Topsy, Trent (Little Nell), Twist (Oliver), Wonka (Willy), Yahoo

**06** Aramis, Archer (Isabel), Arthur (King), Badger, Barkis, Belial, Bennet (Elizabeth), Bourgh (Lady Catherine de), Bovary (Emma), Brodie (Miss Jean), Brooke (Dorothea), Bucket (Charlie), Bumble (Mister), Bumppo (Natty), Bunter (Billy), Butler (Rhett), Carton (Sydney), Crusoe (Robinson), Dombey (Paul), Dorrit (Amy), Dorrit (William), Du Bois (Blanche), Eeyore, Friday (Man), Gamgee (Sam), Gatsby (Jay), Gawain, Gollum, Grimes, Hagrid (Rubeus), Hannay (Richard), Holmes (Sherlock), Jeeves (Reginald), Jekyll (Doctor Henry), Legree (Simon), Little (Vernon Gregory), Lolita, Marley (Jacob), Marner (Silas), Marple (Jane), Moreau (Doctor), Mowgli, Omnium (Duke of), Pickle (Gamaliel), Piglet, Pinkie, Pliant (Dame), Poirot (Hercule), Potter (Harry), Rabbit, Rabbit (Brer), Random (Roderick), Rob Roy, Salmon (Susie), Sawyer (Bob), Sawyer (Tom), Shandy (Tristram), Silver (Long John), Subtle, Tarzan, Tigger, Tybalt, Tyrone (James), Varden (Dolly), Wadman (Widow), Watson (Doctor John), Weller (Samuel), Wimsey (Lord Peter), Wopsle (Mister), Yahoos

**07** Andrews (Pamela), Ayeesha, Baggins (Bilbo), Baggins (Frodo), Beowulf, Biggles, Bramble (Matthew), Brer Fox, Bromden (Chief), Clinker (Humphry), Corelli (Captain Antonio), Crackit (Toby), Danvers (Mrs), Dawkins (Jack), Dedalus (Stephen), Deronda (Daniel), Despair (Giant), Don Juan, Dorigen, Dorothy, Dracula (Count), Estella, Fairfax (Jane), Gandalf, Gargery (Joe), Granger (Hermione), Grendel, Harding (Reverend Septimus), Harlowe (Clarissa), Hawkins (Jim), Higgins (Professor Henry), Hopeful, Humbert (Humbert), Ishmael, Jaggers (Mister), Jellyby (Mrs), Le Fever (Lieutenant), Maigret (Jules), Marlowe (Philip), Mellors (Oliver), Newsome (Chad), Obadiah, Orlando, Peachum (Thomas), Pierrot, Porthos, Prefect (Ford), Proudie (Doctor), Raffles, Rebecca, Scarlet (Will), Scrooge (Ebenezer), Shalott (Lady of), Shipton (Mother), Slumkey (Samuel), Squeers (Wackford), Surface (Charles), Surface (Joseph), Tiny Tim, Weasley (Ron), Wemmick (Mister), Wickham (George), William, Witches (The Three), Wooster (Bertie), Would-be (Sir Politic)

**08** Absolute (Captain), Anderson (Pastor Anthony), Backbite (Sir Benjamin), Bagheera, Bedivere (Sir), Belacqua (Lyra), Black Dog, Casaubon (Reverend Edward), Cratchit (Bob), Criseyde, Dalloway (Mrs Clarissa), Dashwood (Elinor), Dashwood (Marianne), de Winter (Max), de Winter (Rebecca), Everdene (Bathsheba), Faithful, Flanders (Moll), Flashman, Gloriana, Griselda (Patient), Gulliver (Lemuel), Havisham (Miss), Hrothgar, Jarndyce (John), Kowalski (Stanley), Kowalski (Stella), Ladislaw (Will), Lancelot (Sir), Lestrade (Inspector), MacHeath (Captain), Magwitch (Abel), Malaprop (Mrs), McMurphy (Randle Patrick), Micawber (Wilkins), Moriarty (Dean), Moriarty (Professor James), Napoleon, Nickleby (Nicholas), Paradise (Sal), Peggotty (Clara), Peterkin, Pickwick (Samuel), Queequeg, Ramotswe (Precious), Snowball, Starbuck, Svengali, Tashtego, Thatcher (Becky), The Clerk, The Friar, The Reeve, Trotwood (Betsey), Tulliver (Maggie), Twitcher (Jemmy), Vladimir

**09** Archimago, Bounderby (Josiah), Britomart, Bulstrode (Nicholas), Caulfield (Holden), Cheeryble (Charles), Christian, Churchill (Frank), Constance, D'Artagnan, Doolittle (Eliza), Fezziwigg (Mister), Golightly (Holly), Gradgrind (Thomas), Grandison (Sir Charles), Harlequin, Knightley (George), Lismahago (Obadiah), Lochinvar, Minnehaha, Pecksniff (Seth), Pendennis (Arthur), Pollyanna, Robin Hood, Rochester (Edward Fairfax), Scudamour (Sir), Shere Khan, The Knight, The Miller, The Squire, The Walrus, Tiger Lily, Trelawney (Squire), Van Winkle (Rip), Voldemort (Lord), Woodhouse (Emma), Yossarian (Captain John), Zenocrate

**10** Allan-a-Dale, Big Brother, Brer Rabbit, Challenger (Professor), Chatterley (Lady Constance), Chuzzlewit (Martin), Dumbledore (Albus), Evangelist, Fauntleroy (Little Lord), Great-heart (Mister), Heathcliff, Hornblower (Horatio), Houyhnhnms, Little John, Little Nell, Maid Marian, Quatermain (Allan), The Red King, The Tar Baby, Tinkerbell, Tweedledee, Tweedledum

**11** Copperfield (David), D'Urberville (Alec), Durbeyfield (Tess), Mickey Mouse, Mutabilitie, Pumblechook (Mister), The Dormouse, The Franklin, The Man of Law, The Merchant, The Pardoner, The Prioress, The Red Queen, The Summoner, Tiggy-Winkle (Mrs)

**12** Blatant Beast, Chaunticleer, Frankenstein (Victor), Humpty-Dumpty, Lilliputians, Osbaldistone (Francis), Rip Van Winkle, Silvertongue (Lyra), The Carpenter, The Mad Hatter, The March Hare, The Pied Piper (of Hamelin), The Red Knight, The Scarecrow

**13** The Jabberwock, The Mock Turtle, The Tin Woodman, The Wife of Bath, Winnie-the-Pooh

**14** Mephistopheles, Rikki-Tikki-Tavi, The White Rabbit, Worldly Wiseman (Mister)

**15** The Artful Dodger, The Cowardly Lion, The Three Witches, Valiant-for-Truth

*See also* **Shakespeare**

*Literary critics include:*

**04** Bell (Clive), Blum (Léon), Frye (Northrop)

**05** Hicks (Granville), Lodge (David), Stead (C K)

**06** Arnold (Matthew), Calder (Angus), Empson (Sir William), Leavis (F R),

Leavis (Q D), **Lukacs** (Georg), **Sontag** (Susan), **Wilson** (Edmund)
**07** **Ackroyd** (Peter), **Alvarez** (A), **Barthes** (Roland), **Daiches** (David), **Derrida** (Jacques), **Hoggart** (Richard), **Kermode** (Frank)
**08** **Bradbury** (Sir Malcolm), **Eagleton** (Terry), **Longinus**, **Nicolson** (Sir Harold), **Richards** (I A), **Trilling** (Lionel), **Williams** (Raymond)
**10** **Saintsbury** (George Edward Bateman)
**11** **Matthiessen** (F O), **Sainte-Beuve** (Charles Augustin)

**• literary work**
**04** book, poem **05** essay **07** article

**literate**
**07** learned **08** cultured, educated
**09** scholarly **10** able to read, proficient
**11** able to write, intelligent
**12** intellectual, well-educated
**13** knowledgeable
**• Literate in Arts**
**02** LA **03** LLA

**literati**
**06** brains **08** eggheads **09** academics, highbrows **10** illuminati, the erudite, the learned **11** cognoscenti, the studious **12** men of letters, the scholarly **13** intellectuals
**14** intelligentsia, women of letters
**15** the well-informed

**literature**
**03** lit **04** bumf, data, page **05** facts, paper **06** papers **07** hand-out, leaflet, letters **08** brochure, circular, hand-outs, leaflets, pamphlet, writings
**09** brochures, circulars, pamphlets
**11** information **12** printed works
**13** printed matter **14** published works

*Literature types include:*

**04** epic, play, saga
**05** drama, essay, novel, prose, verse
**06** comedy, parody, poetry, satire, thesis
**07** aga-saga, epistle, fantasy, fiction, lampoon, novella, polemic, tragedy, trilogy
**08** allegory, chick lit, libretto, pastiche, treatise
**09** anti-novel, biography, children's, novelette
**10** magnum opus, non-fiction, roman à clef, short story, travelogue
**11** black comedy, Gothic novel, pulp fiction
**12** bodice-ripper, crime fiction
**13** autobiography, belles-lettres, Bildungsroman, penny dreadful, travel writing
**14** science fiction
**15** epistolary novel, historical novel, picaresque novel

**lithe**
**05** agile **06** limber, lissom, listen, pliant, supple, svelte **07** lissome, pliable **08** flexible **09** lithesome
**11** loose-limbed **12** loose-jointed
**13** double-jointed

**lithium**
**02** Li

**Lithuania**
**02** LT **03** LTU **04** Lith

**litigant**
**05** party **08** claimant, opponent
**09** contender, disputant, litigator, plaintiff **10** contestant **11** complainant

**litigate**
**03** sue

**litigation**
**03** law **04** case, suit **06** action
**07** dispute, lawsuit, process **09** legal case **10** contention **11** legal action, prosecution

**litigious**
**10** disputable **11** belligerent, contentious, quarrelsome
**12** disputatious **13** argumentative

**litter**
**03** bed, hay **04** grot, junk, mess, muck, team, teme **05** brood, chaff, issue, sedan, straw, strew, trash, wagon, waste, young **06** debris, doolie, family, farrow, jumble, kindle, mahmal, mess up, refuse, shreds **07** bedding, bracken, cacolet, clutter, garbage, progeny, rubbish, scatter **08** brancard, detritus, disarray, disorder, shambles
**09** confusion, fragments, offspring, palankeen, palanquin, stretcher
**10** light couch, make untidy, untidiness
**11** make a mess of, odds and ends

**little**
**03** bit, dab, sma, wee **04** baby, curn, cute, dash, drop, hint, leet, lite, lyte, mini, nice, poco, some, spot, tine, tiny, tyne, whit **05** brief, chota, dwarf, minor, petty, pinch, scant, short, small, speck, sweet, taste, teeny, touch, trace, young **06** barely, hardly, junior, meagre, midget, minute, paltry, petite, rarely, seldom, skimpy, slight, sparse, trifle **07** faintly, modicum, nominal, not much, passing, peanuts, shortly, slender, soupçon, trickle, trivial, younger **08** exiguous, fleeting, fragment, nugatory, particle, pint-size, pleasant, scarcely, skerrick, slightly, trifling **09** ephemeral, miniature, momentary, pint-sized, transient
**10** attractive, diminutive, negligible, short-lived, smattering, transitory
**11** Lilliputian, microscopic, small amount, unimportant **12** infrequently, insufficient **13** infinitesimal, insignificant, next to nothing
**14** inconsiderable **15** a drop in the ocean

*See also* **small**

**• a little**
**03** tad **04** some
**• little by little**
**04** Eric **06** slowly **08** bit by bit, inchmeal **09** by degrees, gradually, piecemeal, poco a poco **10** step by step **13** imperceptibly, progressively
**• take a little**
**04** drib

**liturgical**
**06** formal, ritual, solemn **08** hieratic
**10** ceremonial, sacerdotal
**11** eucharistic, sacramental

**liturgy**
**04** form, rite **05** usage **06** office, ritual
**07** formula, service, worship
**08** ceremony **09** ordinance, sacrament **10** observance
**11** celebration

**livable, liveable**
**08** adequate, bearable **09** endurable, habitable, tolerable **10** acceptable, worthwhile **11** comfortable, inhabitable, supportable
**12** satisfactory
**• livable with, liveable with**
**08** bearable, passable, sociable
**09** congenial, gemütlich, tolerable
**10** compatible, harmonious
**13** companionable

**live**
**02** be **03** hot **04** hard, last, lead, pass, stay **05** abide, alert, alive, dwell, exist, lodge, spend, squat, vital, vivid
**06** active, alight, behave, bodily, endure, lively, living, public, red hot, remain, reside, urgent **07** animate, be alive, blazing, breathe, burning, charged, comport, conduct, current, dynamic, flaming, glowing, have fun, ignited, inhabit, persist, see life, subsist, survive, topical, undergo **08** continue, existent, have life, in person, live it up, personal, pressing, real-time, relevant, stirring, unstable, vigorous, volatile
**09** be settled, breathing, connected, energetic, enjoy life, explosive, important, pertinent, unwrought
**10** applicable, draw breath, experience, having life, in the flesh, unexploded, unquarried **11** electrified, not recorded **12** have your home
**13** controversial, enjoy yourself
**14** earn your living, not prerecorded, with an audience **15** support yourself
**• live it up**
**05** revel **09** celebrate, have a ball, make merry **10** go on a spree **11** make whoopee **14** push the boat out
**15** paint the town red
**• live on**
**04** feed, last **05** exist **06** rely on **07** live off, subsist **08** continue **09** subsist on
**• live wire**
**06** dynamo **08** go-getter, whizz kid
**10** ball of fire **11** eager beaver, self-starter

**liveable** *see* **livable**

**livelihood**
**03** job **04** keep, work **05** bread, crust, means, trade **06** income, living, upkeep **07** livelod, support
**08** livelood **09** existence **10** daily bread, employment, livelihead, occupation, profession, sustenance
**11** maintenance, subsistence
**13** means of living **14** bread-and-butter, means of support, source of income

**liveliness**
**04** brio, life, salt **05** oomph **06** energy, esprit, spirit, vigour **07** entrain, pizzazz **08** activity, dynamism, vitality, vivacity **09** animation, briskness, quickness, smartness **10** livelihead **11** refreshment **13** animal spirits, sprightliness, vivaciousness **14** boisterousness

**livelong**
**04** full, long **05** whole **06** entire, orpine **08** complete, enduring **10** protracted

**lively**
◇ *anagram indicator*
**03** gay **04** busy, cant, go-go, keen, pacy, racy, spry, vive, vivo, warm, wick **05** agile, alert, alive, brisk, buxom, canty, cobby, kedge, kedgy, kidge, light, ludic, merry, pacey, peart, perky, piert, quick, rapid, vital, vivid, zappy, zippy **06** active, blithe, bouncy, breezy, bright, bubbly, chirpy, crouse, frisky, heated, hectic, jaunty, living, nimble, snappy, sporty, strong, titupy, vivace **07** buckish, buoyant, buzzing, crowded, dynamic, graphic, mettled, playful, slammin', teeming, tittupy, vibrant **08** animated, brushing, bustling, cheerful, eventful, exciting, friskful, galliard, lifesome, rattling, skittish, slamming, spirited, stirring, striking, swarming, vigorous **09** colourful, energetic, lightsome, sparkling, sprightly, vivacious **10** frolicsome, mettlesome, mouvementé, refreshing **11** imaginative, interesting, stimulating **12** effervescent, enthusiastic, high-spirited, invigorating

**liven**
**04** stir **05** cheer, hot up, pep up, rouse, spice **06** buck up, jazz up, perk up, stir up **07** animate, cheer up, enliven, spice up **08** brighten, energize, vitalize **10** invigorate **11** put life into

**liverish**
**05** testy **06** crabby, crusty, grumpy, snappy, tetchy **07** crabbed, peevish **09** crotchety, irascible, irritable, splenetic **11** ill-humoured **12** disagreeable **13** quick-tempered

**livery**
**04** garb, gear, suit, togs **05** dress, get-up, habit **06** attire **07** apparel, clobber, clothes, costume, regalia, uniform **08** clothing, garments **09** irritable, vestments **11** habiliments

**livid**
**03** mad, wan **04** blae, blue, pale, waxy **05** angry, ashen, irate, pasty, white **06** fuming, leaden, pallid, purple, raging **07** bruised, enraged, furious, ghastly, greyish **08** blanched, incensed, outraged, purplish, seething **09** bloodless, indignant **10** infuriated **11** deathly pale, discoloured, exasperated, Hippocratic **12** black-and-blue

**living**
**03** job **04** life, live, true, work **05** alive, being, bread, close, crust, exact, in use, trade, vital **06** active, extant, income, lively, strong **07** animate, current, genuine, precise, support **08** animated, benefice, existing, faithful, property, vigorous **09** animation, breathing, existence, identical, lifestyle, operative, surviving, way of life **10** continuing, daily bread, livelihood, occupation, profession, sustenance **11** going strong, maintenance, subsistence **13** means of living **14** bread-and-butter, means of support, source of income

• **mode of living**
**04** diet

**living room**
**06** lounge **07** day room, parlour **09** front room **11** drawing room, sitting room **13** reception room

**lizard**

*Lizards include:*

**03** eft
**04** evet, gila, sand, seps, tegu, wall, worm
**05** blind, Draco, fence, gecko, skink
**06** agamid, dragon, flying, goanna, horned, iguana
**07** bearded, frilled, monitor, perenty
**08** basilisk, perentie, slowworm, teguexin
**09** chameleon
**10** blue-tongue, chamaeleon
**11** gila monster
**12** Komodo dragon

*See also* **animal**

**llama**
**06** alpaca **07** guanaco, huanaco

**load**
**03** arm, jag, put, tax, tod **04** a lot, cram, duty, fill, haul, heap, lade, lard, lots, onus, pack, pile, plug, seam, slot, tons **05** cargo, enter, equip, goods, heaps, miles, piles, prime, put in, scads, slide, stack, stuff, todde, worry **06** burden, charge, dozens, fill up, hordes, insert, lading, masses, oodles, scores, stacks, strain, weight **07** fraught, freight, oppress, prepare, put into, trouble **08** a million, contents, encumber, hundreds, incumber, lashings, millions, pressure, shipment **09** abundance, albatross, great deal, millstone, overwhelm, thousands, weigh down **10** commitment, obligation, oppression, overburden, saddle with **11** consignment, encumbrance, large amount, tribulation **13** prepare to fire **14** responsibility

**loaded**
◇ *anagram indicator*
**03** fap, fou **04** full, high, inky, paid, rich **05** drunk, fixed, flush, foxed, happy, inked, laden, lit up, merry, moppy, piled, set up, tight, tipsy, woozy **06** biased, blotto, bombed, canned, corked, filled, heaped, jagged, juiced, mellow, mortal, packed, rigged, ripped, soused, stewed, stinko, stoned, tiddly, wasted **07** bevvied, bonkers, bottled, charged, crocked, drunken, ebriose, fairish, half-cut, legless, maggoty, pickled, pie-eyed, sloshed, smashed, sozzled, squiffy, stacked, tiddled, trashed, wealthy, well-off, wrecked **08** affluent, bibulous, burdened, footless, in liquor, juiced up, liquored, moon-eyed, overseen, overshot, pregnant, sow-drunk, stotious, tanked up, weighted, whiffled, whistled **09** blootered, crapulent, incapable, paralytic, plastered, shickered, up the pole, well-oiled **10** blind drunk, capernoity, inebriated, in the money, obfuscated, well-heeled **11** intoxicated, made of money, rolling in it, snowed under **12** drunk as a lord, drunk as a newt, on easy street, roaring drunk **13** drunk as a piper, having had a few, under the table **14** Brahms and Liszt **15** a sheet in the wind, one over the eight, the worse for wear, under the weather

**loaf**
**03** bum, tin, veg **04** cake, cube, head, idle, laze, loll, lump, mass, mind, nous, pone, slab **05** block, brick, miche, mooch, relax, sense, slosh **06** bludge, brains, coburg, loiter, lounge, noddle, stotty, unwind, veg out **07** bloomer, brioche, challah, manchet, Panagia, stottie **08** baguette, corn pone, focaccia, gumption, Panhagia, scrapple **09** barmbrack, lie around, sit around **10** corn dodger, hang around, stand about, take it easy **11** common sense, French stick, spotted dick **12** lounge around

*See also* **bread**; **head**

• **loaf about**
**04** laze **06** lounge

**loafer**
**03** yob **04** slob **05** idler **06** bummer, skiver **07** goof-off, lounger, shirker, wastrel **08** layabout, sluggard **09** corner-boy, corner-man, lazybones, sundowner **10** ne'er-do-well **11** beachcomber

*See also* **footwear**

**loam**
**04** clay, core, lome, malm, sand, soil **05** earth **09** brickclay, malmstone **10** brick-earth

**loan**
**03** len', sub **04** lane, lend **05** allow, prest **06** credit, on-lend **07** advance, finance, imprest, lending **08** mortgage, overlend, put forth **09** allowance **12** floating debt, respondentia **13** accommodation

**loath**
**04** ugly **05** laith **06** averse **07** against, hateful, opposed **08** grudging, hesitant **09** reluctant, repulsive,

resisting, unwilling **10** indisposed **11** disinclined

**loathe**
**02** ug **04** hate **05** abhor **06** detest **07** despise, dislike **08** execrate, nauseate, not stand **09** abominate **10** recoil from **15** feel revulsion at

**loathing**
**04** hate **05** odium **06** hatred, horror, nausea **07** disgust, dislike, ill-will **08** aversion **09** antipathy, repulsion, revulsion **10** abhorrence, execration, repugnance **11** abomination, detestation

**loathsome**
**04** foul, vile **05** nasty **06** odious **07** hateful, mawkish, obscene **08** horrible, nauseous **09** abhorrent, execrable, lothefull, obnoxious, offensive, repellent, repugnant, repulsive, revolting **10** abominable, despicable, detestable, disgusting, nauseating **12** contemptible, disagreeable

**lob**
**03** shy **04** hurl, lift, loft, lout, lump, puck, toss **05** chuck, droop, fling, heave, pitch, throw **06** launch **07** lobworm, pollack

**lobby**
**04** hall, urge **05** entry, foyer, porch **06** demand **07** call for, faction, hallway, passage, promote, push for, solicit **08** anteroom, box-lobby, campaign, corridor, entrance, persuade, press for, pressure **09** influence, lobbyists, vestibule **10** passageway **11** campaign for, ginger group, waiting room **12** entrance hall **13** pressure group

**lobster**
**04** cock **08** crawfish, crayfish **09** langouste **11** langoustine

**• lobster cage**
**04** corf

**local**
◇ *foreign word indicator*
**03** bar, inn, pub **04** city, town **05** place, urban **06** boozer, narrow, native, number, parish, saloon, tavern **07** citizen, limited, topical, vicinal, village **08** district, hostelry, regional, resident **09** community, municipal, parochial, small-town **10** inhabitant, parish-pump, provincial, restricted, vernacular **11** anaesthetic, examination, public house **12** watering-hole **13** neighbourhood

*See also* **public house**

**• local worker**
**06** barman **09** bartender

**locale**
**04** area, site, spot, zone **05** locus, place, scene, venue **07** setting **08** locality, location, position **11** environment **13** neighbourhood

**locality**
**04** area, site, spot **05** locus, place, scene **06** locale, region **07** setting **08** district, position, vicinity **11** environment **12** neighborhood **13** neighbourhood **15** surrounding area

**localize**
**05** limit **06** assign **07** ascribe, confine, contain, delimit, specify **08** identify, pinpoint, restrain, restrict, zero in on **10** delimitate, narrow down **11** concentrate **12** circumscribe

**locate**
**03** fix, lay, put, set **04** find, seat, site, spot **05** build, place, plant **06** access, detect, finger, settle **07** hit upon, pick out, situate, station, uncover, unearth **08** allocate, discover, identify, pinpoint, position **09** establish, track down **10** come across, run to earth **14** lay your hands on

**• be located**
**03** sit

**location**
**04** farm, seat, site, spot **05** locus, place, point, scene, venue **06** locale, ubiety **07** setting **08** bearings, position **09** situation **11** whereabouts

**loch**
**01** L **03** dam, sea **04** lake, mere, pond, pool, tarn **05** basin, lough, water **09** reservoir

*See also* **lake**

**lock**
**03** bar, hug, jam, tag **04** curl, join, link, mesh, seal, shut, snap, trap, tuft **05** catch, clasp, grasp, latch, plait, sasse, stick, tress, unite **06** clench, clutch, engage, fasten, secure, strand **07** embrace, enclose, entwine, grapple, ringlet **08** encircle, entangle **09** certainty, fastening, interlock **12** scalping-tuft

*Locks include:*

**03** rim
**04** dead, Yale®
**05** child, Chubb®, wagon
**06** safety, spring
**07** mortice, mortise, padlock
**08** cylinder
**10** night latch
**11** combination

*Lock parts include:*

**03** bit, key, pin
**04** bolt, hasp, knob, post, rose, sash, ward
**05** latch, talon
**06** barrel, keyway, spring, staple
**07** key card, keyhole, spindle, tumbler
**08** cylinder, dead bolt, sash bolt
**09** face plate, latch bolt
**10** escutcheon, latch lever, push button
**11** mortise bolt, spindle hole, strike plate
**12** cylinder hole
**13** latch follower

**• lock out**
**03** bar **05** debar **07** exclude, keep out, shut out

**• lock up**
◇ *containment indicator*
◇ *hidden indicator*
**03** pen **04** cage, jail **06** detain, secure, shut in, shut up, wall in **07** close up, confine, put away **08** imprison **11** incarcerate **13** put behind bars

**• open lock**
**04** pick

**locker**
**07** cabinet **08** cupboard **09** container **11** compartment

**lock-up**
**03** can, jug **04** cell, gaol, jail, quod **05** choky, clink **06** chokey, cooler, garage, prison **07** slammer **09** storeroom, warehouse **10** depository, roundhouse, watch house **12** penitentiary, station house

**locomotion**
**06** action, motion, moving, travel **07** headway, walking **08** movement, progress **10** ambulation, travelling **11** progression **13** perambulation

**locus**
**04** site **05** place, point, polar, venue **06** locale, spiral **08** centrode, conchoid, envelope, locality, location, parabola, position, roulette **09** directrix, situation, wavefront **10** lemniscate **11** radical axis, whereabouts **14** director circle

**locust**
**08** devourer **10** devastator, voetganger

**locution**
**04** term **05** idiom, style **06** accent, cliché, phrase **07** diction, talking, wording **08** phrasing, speaking **10** expression, inflection, intonation **11** collocation **12** articulation, turn of phrase

**lode**
**04** reef

**lodge**
**03** box, cup, den, dig, fix, hut, inn, lay, lie, put **04** bank, club, file, host, keep, lair, live, make, nest, room, stay, stow, tent **05** board, bower, cabin, dwell, group, grove, haunt, house, imbed, infix, layer, place, put in, put up **06** billet, branch, chalet, grange, hand in, harbor, loggia, record, reside, show up, submit, teepee **07** barrack, chapter, cottage, deposit, hang out, harbour, implant, quarter, retreat, section, shelter, society, sojourn **08** campfire, get stuck, register **09** be settled, gatehouse, get caught, longhouse **10** habitation, put forward **11** accommodate, association **12** accumulation, have your home, hunting-lodge, meeting-place

**lodger**
**02** PG **05** guest **06** inmate, roomer, tenant **07** boarder **08** resident **11** paying guest

**lodgings**
**03** pad **04** digs, ferm **05** abode, board, place, rooms **06** bedsit, billet **07** flea-bag **08** dwelling, quarters
**09** bedsitter, residence
**13** accommodation, boarding house
**14** bedsitting-room

**loftily**
**07** proudly, stately **08** snootily
**09** haughtily **10** arrogantly
**12** disdainfully **14** superciliously

**lofty**
**04** high, tall **05** brent, grand, noble, proud, steep, wingy **06** aerial, lordly, raised, skyish, snooty, winged
**07** exalted, haughty, sky-high, soaring, stately, sublime **08** arrogant, elevated, esteemed, imperial, imposing, majestic, renowned, superior, towering **09** dignified **10** disdainful
**11** illustrious, patronizing, toffee-nosed **12** supercilious
**13** condescending, distinguished, high and mighty, high-stomached

**log**
**04** book, clog, file, note **05** block, chart, chock, chunk, diary, piece, stock, tally, trunk **06** billet, loggat, record, timber **07** account, daybook, journal, logbook, set down, write up
**08** register **09** logarithm

**logbook**
**03** log **05** chart, diary, tally **06** record
**07** account, daybook, journal
**08** register

**loggerheads**
**• at loggerheads**
◇ *anagram indicator*
**06** at odds **10** in conflict
**11** disagreeing, quarrelling **12** in opposition **13** like cat and dog **14** at daggers drawn

**logic**
**05** sense **06** reason **08** argument
**09** coherence, deduction, judgement, rationale, reasoning, redecraft
**10** dialectics **13** argumentation, ratiocination
*See also* **circuit**

**logical**
**04** wise **05** clear, sound, valid
**06** cogent **07** Boolean **08** coherent, rational, reasoned, relevant, sensible, thinking **09** deducible, deductive, dialectic, inductive, judicious
**10** consistent, convergent, methodical, reasonable, sequacious
**11** consecutive, dialectical, intelligent, syllogistic, well-founded **12** well-reasoned **13** well-organized **14** well-thought-out

**logically**
**07** clearly, validly **08** sensibly
**10** coherently, rationally, relevantly
**11** deductively, inductively
**12** consistently, methodically
**13** consecutively, dialectically, intelligently

**logistics**
**05** plans **07** tactics **08** planning, strategy **09** direction **10** management
**11** arrangement, engineering **12** co-ordination, organization
**13** masterminding, orchestration

**logo**
**04** mark, sign **05** badge, image
**06** device, emblem, figure, symbol
**08** insignia **09** trademark
**14** representation

**loiter**
**03** lag **04** hove, idle, lime, loaf, lurk, mike **05** dally, delay, hoove, mooch, mouch, tarry **06** dawdle, linger, lounge, taigle **07** saunter **08** lallygag, lollygag **09** hang about, waste time
**10** dilly-dally, hang around **12** take your time
**• loitering with intent**
**03** sus **04** suss

**loll**
**03** sag **04** drop, flap, flop, hang, lill, loaf
**05** droop, relax, slump **06** dangle, lounge, slouch, sprawl **07** recline

**lollop**
**03** run **04** idle, lope **05** bound
**06** canter, gallop, lounge, spring, stride

**lolly**
**05** money **06** sucker **07** lulibub **08** ice block, lollipop, Popsicle®
*See also* **money**

**London**
**03** wen **08** great wen

*London boroughs:*

**05** Brent
**06** Barnet, Bexley, Camden, Ealing, Harrow, Merton, Newham, Sutton
**07** Bromley, Croydon, Enfield, Hackney, Lambeth
**08** Haringey, Havering, Hounslow, Lewisham
**09** Greenwich, Islington, Redbridge, Southwark
**10** Hillingdon, Wandsworth
**12** Tower Hamlets
**13** Waltham Forest
**17** City of Westminster
**18** Barking and Dagenham, Kingston upon Thames, Richmond upon Thames
**20** Hammersmith and Fulham, Kensington and Chelsea

*Other districts of London include:*

**02** EC
**03** Bow, Kew, Lee
**04** Bank, Oval, Soho
**05** Acton, Angel, Erith, Hayes, Penge
**06** Arkley, Balham, Barnes, Debden, Eltham, Epping, Euston, Fulham, Hendon, Heston, Hoxton, Ilford, Kenton, Leyton, Malden, Morden, Pinner, Poplar, Purley, Putney, Temple, Waddon
**07** Aldgate, Archway, Barking, Beckton, Belmont, Borough, Brixton, Catford, Chelsea, Clapham, Cranham, Dalston, Dulwich, East End, East Ham, Edgware, Elm Park, Feltham, Hampton, Hanwell, Holborn, Hornsey, Kilburn, Mayfair, Mile End, Mitcham, Neasden, Norwood, Old Ford, Olympia, Peckham, Pimlico, Selsdon, Stepney, The City, Tooting, Wapping, Welling, Wembley, West End, West Ham, Yeading
**08** Alperton, Bankside, Barbican, Brockley, Brompton, Chiswick, Coulsdon, Crayford, Dagenham, Deptford, Edmonton, Elmstead, Finchley, Finsbury, Grays Inn, Hanworth, Hatch End, Heathrow, Highbury, Highgate, Holloway, Homerton, Hyde Park, Ickenham, Kingston, Mill Hill, Mortlake, New Cross, Nine Elms, Northolt, Osterley, Perivale, Plaistow, Richmond, Shadwell, Southall, Stanmore, Surbiton, Sydenham, Tolworth, Uxbridge, Vauxhall, Victoria, Walworth, Wanstead, Waterloo, Woodford, Woolwich
**09** Abbey Wood, Addington, Barnsbury, Battersea, Bayswater, Beckenham, Becontree, Belgravia, Blackwall, Brentford, Brimsdown, Canonbury, Chalk Farm, Chingford, Colindale, Crouch End, Docklands, Fitzrovia, Foots Cray, Gant's Hill, Gidea Park, Gipsy Hill, Goodmayes, Gospel Oak, Greenford, Green Park, Hampstead, Harefield, Harlesden, Harringay, Herne Hill, Isleworth, Kidbrooke, Kingsbury, Kingsland, Limehouse, Maida Vale, Mark's Gate, Newington, Northwood, Orpington, Park Royal, Petts Wood, Plumstead, South Bank, Southgate, Stockwell, St Pancras, Stratford, Streatham, Tottenham, Tower Hill, Tulse Hill, Upminster, Whetstone, White City, Whitehall, Willesden, Wimbledon, Wood Green
**10** Addiscombe, Albany Park, Arnos Grove, Beddington, Bellingham, Bermondsey, Blackheath, Bloomsbury, Brent Cross, Camberwell, Chase Cross, Collier Row, Creekmouth, Dollis Hill, Earls Court, Earlsfield, Embankment, Farringdon, Forest Gate, Forest Hill, Goddington, Green Lanes, Haggerston, Harlington, Harold Hill, Harold Wood, Horse Ferry, Isle of Dogs, Kennington, Kensington, King's Cross, Manor House, Marylebone, Mottingham, Paddington, Piccadilly, Queensbury, Raynes Park, Seven Dials, Seven Kings, Shad Thames, Shoreditch, Silvertown, Smithfield, Teddington, Thamesmead, Totteridge, Twickenham, Wallington, Wealdstone
**11** Bedford Park, Belsize Park, Bexleyheath, Blackfriars, Bounds Green, Brondesbury, Canada Water, Canary Wharf, Canning Town,

Chessington, Clerkenwell, Cockfosters, Cricklewood, East Dulwich, Fortis Green, Gunnersbury, Hammersmith, Highams Park, Holland Park, Kensal Green, Kentish Town, Leytonstone, Lincoln's Inn, Little Italy, Ludgate Hill, Muswell Hill, Notting Hill, Pentonville, Regent's Park, Rotherhithe, Snaresbrook, St John's Wood, Surrey Quays, Tufnell Park, Walthamstow, Westminster, Whitechapel

**12** Bethnal Green, Billingsgate, Bromley-by-Bow, Charing Cross, City of London, Colliers Wood, Covent Garden, Crossharbour, Epping Forest, Finsbury Park, Golders Green, Hatton Garden, Havering Park, London Bridge, London Fields, Palmers Green, Parsons Green, Pool of London, Primrose Hill, Seven Sisters, Sloane Square, Stamford Hill, Swiss Cottage

**13** Ardleigh Green, Chadwell Heath, Crystal Palace, Harmondsworth, Knightsbridge, Ladbroke Grove, Lancaster Gate, North Woolwich, Petticoat Lane, Shepherd's Bush, Thornton Heath, Tottenham Hale, Wanstead Flats, Winchmore Hill

**14** Angel Islington, Becontree Heath, Hackney Marshes, Stoke Newington, Tottenham Green, Wormwood Scrubs

**15** Alexandra Palace, Leicester Square, Westbourne Green

*London streets include:*

**06** Strand

**07** Aldgate, Aldwych, The Mall, Westway

**08** Kingsway, Long Acre, Millbank, Minories, Pall Mall, Park Lane, York Road

**09** Bow Street, Cheapside, Drury Lane, Haymarket, King's Road, Maida Vale, Queensway, Tower Hill, Whitehall

**10** Bond Street, Dean Street, Eaton Place, Euston Road, Fetter Lane, Fulham Road, London Wall, Onslow Road, Piccadilly, Queen's Gate, Soho Square, Vine Street

**11** Baker Street, Eaton Square, Edgware Road, Fleet Street, Goswell Road, Gower Street, High Holborn, Lambeth Road, Leather Lane, Ludgate Hill, Old Kent Road, Pimlico Road, Savoy Street, Warwick Road

**12** Albany Street, Belgrave Road, Birdcage Walk, Brompton Road, Cannon Street, Chancery Lane, Cromwell Road, Gray's Inn Road, Hatton Garden, Jermyn Street, Oxford Street, Regent Street, Sloane Square, Sloane Street, Tooley Street

**13** Bayswater Road, Bedford Square, Berwick Street, Carnaby Street, Downing Street, Garrick Street, Gerrard Street, Grosvenor Road, Knightsbridge, Lombard Street, Ludgate Circus, New Bond Street, New Fetter Lane, Newgate Street, Old Bond Street, Petticoat Lane, Portland Place, Portman Square, Russell Square, Wardour Street

**14** Belgrave Square, Berkeley Square, Coventry Street, Earl's Court Road, Earnshaw Street, Exhibition Road, Gloucester Road, Holborn Viaduct, Horseferry Road, Hyde Park Square, Kensington Road, Marylebone Road, Mayfair Gardens, Portobello Road, Stamford Street

**15** Albemarle Street, Blackfriars Road, Clerkenwell Road, Grosvenor Square, Horse Guards Road, Leicester Square, Liverpool Street, New Bridge Street, Pentonville Road, Southwark Street, St John's Wood Road, Trafalgar Square, Whitechapel Road

*London landmarks include:*

**03** V&A

**03** ICA, Kew

**04** City, Eros, Oval, Soho

**05** Barts, Lord's

**06** Big Ben, Lloyds, Temple, Thames

**07** Harrods, Mayfair, St Paul's, The City, The Mall

**08** Bow bells, Cenotaph, Gray's Inn, Hyde Park, Liberty's, Monument, St Bride's

**09** Chinatown, Cutty Sark, George Inn, Green Park, Guildhall, London Eye, London Zoo, Old Bailey, Rotten Row, Royal Mews, South Bank, Staple Inn, The Temple, Trocadero

**10** Albert Hall, Camden Lock, Cock Tavern, Earl's Court, HMS Belfast, Jewel Tower, Kew Gardens, Marble Arch, Selfridge's, Serpentine, Tate Modern, the Gherkin

**11** Apsley House, Canary Wharf, Golden Hinde, Lincoln's Inn, OXO building, Queen's House, Regent's Park, River Thames, St John's Gate, St Margaret's, St Mary-Le-Bow, Tate Britain, Tower Bridge

**12** Charterhouse, Covent Garden, Design Museum, Dickens House, Festival Hall, Globe Theatre, Guards Museum, Hatton Garden, Hay's Galleria, London Bridge, Mansion House, Spencer House, statue of Eros, St James's Park, Telecom Tower, Temple Church, Traitors' Gate

**13** Admiralty Arch, Bank of England, British Museum, Carnaby Street, Clarence House, Fortnum & Mason's, Gabriel's Wharf, Geffrye Museum, Greenwich Park, Lambeth Palace, London Dungeon, Madam Tussaud's, Nelson's Column, Petticoat Lane, Queen's Gallery, Royal Exchange, Science Museum, Somerset House, Tower of London, Wesley's Chapel

**14** Albert Memorial, Barbican Centre, British Library, Hayward Gallery, Hermitage Rooms, Lancaster House, London Aquarium, Millennium Dome, Museum of London, Portobello Road, Speakers' Corner, St Clement Danes, St James's Palace, Waterloo Bridge, Wellington Arch

**15** Bankside Gallery, Banqueting House, Brompton Oratory, Burlington House, Cabinet War Rooms, National Gallery, Royal Albert Hall, Royal Opera House, Temple of Mithras, Trafalgar Square, Westminster Hall

*London Underground lines:*

**06** Circle

**07** Central, Jubilee

**08** Bakerloo, District, Northern, Victoria

**10** East London, Piccadilly

**12** Metropolitan

**15** Waterloo and City

**18** Hammersmith and City

**21** Docklands Light Railway

*London Underground stations include:*

**04** Bank, Oval

**05** Angel

**06** Balham, Cyprus, Epping, Euston, Leyton, Morden, Pinner, Poplar, Temple

**07** Aldgate, Archway, Arsenal, Barking, Beckton, Borough, Bow Road, Brixton, Chesham, East Ham, Edgware, Holborn, Kilburn, Mile End, Neasden, Pimlico, Ruislip, St Paul's, Wapping, Watford, West Ham

**08** Amersham, Barbican, Chigwell, Hainault, Heathrow, Highgate, Lewisham, Monument, Moorgate, Mudchute, New Cross, Northolt, Perivale, Plaistow, Richmond, Royal Oak, Shadwell, Stanmore, Uxbridge, Vauxhall, Victoria, Wanstead, Waterloo

**09** Acton Town, All Saints, Bayswater, Blackwall, Bow Church, Chalk Farm, Cutty Sark, East Acton, East India, Greenford, Green Park, Greenwich, Hampstead, Harlesden, Limehouse, Maida Vale, Old Street, Park Royal, Queensway, South Quay, Southwark, Stockwell, Stratford, Tower Hill, Upton Park, West Acton, Westferry, White City, Wimbledon, Wood Green

**10** Bermondsey, Bond Street, Brent Cross, Camden Town, Devons Road, Dollis Hill, Earl's Court, East Putney, Embankment, Farringdon, Grange Hill, Hanger Lane, Heron Quays, Hillingdon, Hornchurch, Kennington, Kew Gardens, Manor House, Marble Arch, Marylebone, North Acton, Paddington, Queen's Park, Shoreditch, Tooting Bec

**11** Aldgate East, Baker Street, Barons Court, Beckton Park, Belsize Park, Blackfriars, Bounds Green, Canada

Water, Canary Wharf, Canning Town, Chorleywood, Cockfosters, Custom House, Edgware Road, Gunnersbury, Hammersmith, Holland Park, Kensal Green, Kentish Town, Kilburn Park, Latimer Road, Leytonstone, North Ealing, Northfields, Regent's Park, Rotherhithe, Royal Albert, South Ealing, Southfields, St John's Wood, Surrey Quays, Tufnell Park, Wembley Park, Westminster, Whitechapel

**12** Bethnal Green, Bromley-by-Bow, Cannon Street, Chancery Lane, Charing Cross, Chiswick Park, Clapham North, Clapham South, Colliers Wood, Covent Garden, Dagenham East, Ealing Common, East Finchley, Elverson Road, Euston Square, Finchley Road, Finsbury Park, Golders Green, Goldhawk Road, Goodge Street, Holloway Road, Lambeth North, London Bridge, Mansion House, New Cross Gate, Oxford Circus, Parsons Green, Prince Regent, Putney Bridge, Seven Sisters, Sloane Square, Stepney Green, St James's Park, Swiss Cottage, Tower Gateway, Turnham Green, Turnpike Lane, Warren Street, West Brompton

**13** Clapham Common, Gallions Reach, Hendon Central, Island Gardens, Knightsbridge, Ladbroke Grove, Lancaster Gate, Rickmansworth, Royal Victoria, Russell Square, Shepherd's Bush, Stamford Brook, Tottenham Hale, Warwick Avenue, West Hampstead, West India Quay, Wimbledon Park

**14** Blackhorse Road, Caledonian Road, Deptford Bridge, Ealing Broadway, Fulham Broadway, Gloucester Road, Hyde Park Corner, North Greenwich, South Wimbledon, Westbourne Park, West Kensington, Willesden Green

**15** Finchley Central, Harrow-on-the-Hill, Hounslow Central, Leicester Square, Liverpool Street, Notting Hill Gate, Pudding Mill Lane, Ravenscourt Park, South Kensington, Stonebridge Park, Tooting Broadway

---

**lone**

**03** one **04** lane, only, sole **05** alone **06** barren, remote, single **07** widowed **08** deserted, desolate, divorced, forsaken, isolated, secluded, separate, solitary **09** abandoned, on your own, separated, unmarried **10** by yourself, unattached **11** out-of-the-way, uninhabited **12** unfrequented **15** without a partner

**loneliness**

**08** solitude **09** aloneness, isolation, seclusion **10** desolation **12** lonesomeness, solitariness

**lonely**

**03** sad **04** lone **05** alone, unked, unket, unkid **06** barren, remote **07** outcast, unhappy **08** deserted, desolate, forsaken, isolated, lonesome, rejected, secluded, solitary, wretched **09** abandoned, destitute, miserable, reclusive **10** friendless **11** god-forsaken, out-of-the-way, uninhabited **12** solitudinous, unfrequented **13** companionless, unaccompanied

**loner**

**06** hermit **07** recluse **08** lone wolf, solitary **09** introvert **13** individualist **14** solitudinarian

**lonesome**

**03** sad **04** lone **05** alone **06** barren, lonely, remote **07** outcast, unhappy **08** deserted, desolate, forsaken, isolated, rejected, secluded, solitary, wretched **09** abandoned, destitute, miserable, reclusive **10** friendless **11** out-of-the-way, uninhabited **12** unfrequented **13** companionless, unaccompanied

**long**

**01** L **03** ake, die, far, yen **04** ache, hope, itch, lang, leng, lust, pant, pine, side, slow, tall, want, wish **05** covet, crave, dream, longa, tardy, yearn **06** desire, hanker, hunger, thirst **07** lengthy, spun out, tedious, verbose **08** expanded, extended, marathon, overlong **09** diuturnal, elongated, expansive, extensive, prolonged, spread out, stretched, sustained **10** protracted **11** far-reaching **12** interminable, long-drawn-out, stretched out

*See also* **want**

**• before long**

**04** soon **07** by and by, shortly **09** in a moment, presently **12** in a short time **14** in a minute or two **15** in the near future

**• long ago**

**03** eld **04** yore

**• Long Island**

**02** LI

**• long live**

**04** viva, vive **05** vivat **08** zindabad

**long-drawn-out**

**06** prolix **07** lengthy, spun out, tedious **08** long-spun, marathon, overlong **09** long-drawn, prolonged **10** dragging on, long-winded, protracted **12** interminable, overextended

**longer**

**04** more

**• no longer**

**02** ex

**longing**

**03** yen **04** avid, earn, erne, hope, itch, lust, urge, wish **05** brame, crave, dream, eager, greed, yearn **06** ardent, desire, hunger, hungry, pining, thirst **07** anxious, craving, wanting, wishful, wistful **08** ambition, appetent, coveting, desirous, yearning **09** breathing, cacoethes, hankering, hungering **10** aspiration, desiderium **11** languishing

**longingly**

**06** avidly, wistly **07** eagerly **08** ardently **09** anxiously, wishfully, wistfully **10** yearningly

**long-lasting**

**07** abiding, chronic **08** enduring, unfading **09** lingering, permanent, prolonged **10** continuing, protracted, unchanging **12** imperishable, long-standing

**long-lived**

**07** durable, lasting **08** enduring **09** longevous, macrobian, vivacious **11** long-lasting, macrobiotic **12** long-standing

**long-standing**

**07** abiding **08** enduring **09** long-lived **11** established, long-lasting, traditional **12** time-honoured **15** long-established, well-established

**long-suffering**

**07** patient, stoical **08** resigned, tolerant **09** easy-going, forgiving, indulgent **10** forbearant, forbearing **13** uncomplaining

**long-winded**

**05** wordy **06** prolix **07** diffuse, lengthy, tedious, verbose, voluble **08** overlong, rambling **09** garrulous, prolonged **10** discursive, protracted **11** repetitious **12** long-drawn-out

**long-windedness**

**08** longueur **09** garrulity, macrology, prolixity, verbosity, wordiness **10** volubility **11** diffuseness, lengthiness, tediousness **14** discursiveness **15** repetitiousness

**loo**

**02** WC **03** bog, lav **04** john, kazi, love, toot **05** dunny, Elsan®, gents', privy **06** ladies', throne, toilet, urinal **07** crapper, latrine **08** bathroom, lavatory, Portaloo®, rest room, superloo, washroom **09** cloakroom, lanterloo **10** facilities, powder room **11** convenience, water closet **12** smallest room **14** comfort station, little boys' room **15** little girls' room

*See also* **toilet**

**look**

**02** hi, la, lo, oi **03** air, eye, ray, see, spy **04** deek, ecce, ecco, face, gape, gawp, gaze, geek, keek, leer, mien, peek, peep, peer, quiz, scan, seem, show, view, vise, vizy **05** check, decko, dekko, focus, front, frown, glout, guise, scowl, sight, squiz, stare, study, visie, watch **06** appear, aspect, behold, blench, effect, eyeful, façade, gander, give on, glance, gledge, manner, regard, review, shufti, shufty, squint, survey, take in, vision, vizzie **07** bearing, belgard, display, examine, exhibit, eyeball, front on, glimpse, inspect, observe **08** butcher's, consider, features, give on to, look onto, once-over, overlook, scrutiny **09** eye-glance, semblance, take a look **10** appearance, be opposite, complexion, expression, get a load of, impression, inspection, scrutinize **11** contemplate, countenance, examination, observation **12** butcher's hook, take a dekko at **13** contemplation, get an eyeful of, take a gander at, take a shufti at, take a squint at **14** give a going-over **15** give the once-over, run your eyes over

**• look after**

**03** sit **04** heed, keep, mind, seek, tend **05** guard, nurse, see to, watch **06** expect **07** babysit, care for, protect **08** attend to, maintain **09** childmind, supervise, watch over **10** take care of **11** keep an eye on **12** take charge of

**• look back**

**06** recall **08** remember **09** reminisce, think back **10** retrospect

**• look down on**

**05** scorn, spurn **07** despise, disdain, sneer at **08** overpeer, pooh-pooh **09** disparage, patronize **10** talk down to **14** hold in contempt

**• look for**

**04** seek **05** await, quest **06** expect **07** hunt for, hunt out **08** scavenge **09** forage for, search for, try to find **10** fossick out

**• look forward to**

**05** await **06** expect **07** count on, hope for, long for, look for, wait for **08** envisage, envision **09** apprehend **10** anticipate

**• look into**

**03** dig **05** delve, plumb, probe, study **06** fathom, go into **07** examine, explore, inspect **08** ask about, check out, look over, research **10** scrutinize, search into **11** investigate **12** inquire about

**• look like**

**08** resemble **09** take after **11** be similar to, remind you of

**• look on, look upon**

**03** eye **04** deem, hold, view **05** count, judge, think **06** regard **07** overeye **08** consider, spectate

**• look out**

**04** mind **06** beware **07** Achtung, be alert **08** watch out **09** be careful **11** mind your eye **12** keep an eye out, pay attention **13** be on your guard, guard yourself **14** be on the qui vive

**• look over**

**04** scan, view **05** check **07** examine, inspect, monitor, surview **08** check out **09** go through **11** look through, read through **13** cast an eye over, give a once-over **15** cast your eye over

**• look to**

**05** await, besee, watch **06** expect, regard, rely on, turn to **07** count on, hope for, respect **08** consider, reckon on, resort to **10** anticipate, fall back on, think about **13** give thought to

**• look up**

**04** find, seek **05** visit **06** call on, come on, drop by, perk up, pick up, stop by **07** advance, consult, develop, hunt for, improve **08** drop in on, look in on, progress, research **09** come along, get better, search for, track down **10** ameliorate **11** make headway, pay a visit to **12** make progress

**• look up to**

**06** admire, esteem, honour, revere **07** respect **12** regard highly **13** think highly of

**lookalike**

**04** spit, twin **05** clone, image **06** double, ringer **07** replica **10** dead ringer **11** living image **12** doppelgänger **13** exact likeness, spitting image

**lookout**

**03** nit **04** huer, post, ward **05** guard, tower, watch, worry **06** affair, conder, conner, pigeon, sentry **07** concern, problem **08** business, cockatoo, prospect, sentinel, watchman, watch-out **10** speculator, watch-tower **14** responsibility **15** observation post

**• keep a lookout**

**05** watch **09** keep guard **10** be vigilant **11** remain alert **14** be on the qui vive

**loom**

**04** loon, rise, soar, tool **05** frame, mount, tower **06** appear, emerge, impend, menace **07** overtop **08** dominate, hang over, jacquard, overhang, threaten **09** implement, take shape **10** be imminent, overshadow, receptacle **13** become visible

**loony**

◇ *anagram indicator*

**03** mad, nut **04** daft, hook, wild **05** barmy, crank, crazy, loopy, nutty, potty, silly **06** crazed, insane, madman, maniac, nutter, psycho, stupid **07** berserk, bonkers, foolish, frantic, idiotic, lunatic, nutcase, oddball, strange **08** crackpot, demented, deranged, headcase, imbecile, madwoman, unhinged **09** disturbed, eccentric, fruitcake, psychotic, screwball **10** basket case, distracted, distraught, psychopath, unbalanced

*See also* **madman, madwoman**

**loop**

**01** O **03** eye, lug, tab, tie, tug **04** bend, coil, curl, fold, hank, hoop, join, kink, knop, knot, oval, purl, ring, roll, turn, wind **05** braid, curve, noose, pearl, picot, sling, snare, twirl, twist, whorl **06** becket, cannon, circle, eyelet, fasten, lasket, runner, spiral, stitch **07** connect, latchet **08** carriage, écraseur, encircle, loophole, surround **09** billabong, eye splice **10** curve round, rubber band **11** convolution, elastic band, jubilee clip

**loophole**

**04** plea **06** escape, excuse, eyelet, get-out, let-out, wicket **07** evasion, mistake, pretext **08** omission, pretence **09** ambiguity **12** escape clause

**loose**

◇ *anagram indicator*

**03** lax, off **04** ease, fast, free, lose, open, undo **05** baggy, broad, let go, losen, lowse, relax, shaky, shoot, slack, solve, unpen, untie, vague **06** detach, flabby, lessen, loosen, reduce, solute, unbind, undone, unhook, unknit, unlock, unmoor, untied, wanton, weaken, wobbly **07** at large, corrupt, escaped, flowing, general, hanging, immoral, inexact, movable, relaxed, release, sagging, set free, slacken, unbound, unclasp, unleash **08** diffused, diminish, insecure, liberate, moderate, rambling, released, unchaste, uncouple, unfasten, unlocked, unpicked, unsteady **09** abandoned, debauched, desultory, discharge, disengage, dissolute, imprecise, shapeless, uncoupled **10** degenerate, disconnect, ill-defined, inaccurate, incoherent, indefinite, indistinct, licentious, unattached, unconfined, unfastened, untethered **11** inattentive, light-heeled, promiscuous **12** disreputable, loose-fitting, unrestrained

**• at a loose end**

**04** idle **05** bored, fed up **07** aimless, off duty **09** désoeuvré **11** out of action, purposeless **14** with time to kill **15** with nothing to do

**• on the loose**

**04** free **07** at large, escaped **08** on the run **09** at liberty **10** unconfined

**loosely**

◇ *anagram indicator*

**06** freely **07** baggily, broadly, movably, slackly, vaguely **09** generally, inexactly **10** insecurely, unsteadily **11** imprecisely, shapelessly **12** inaccurately

**loosen**

**04** ease, free, undo **05** let go, loose, relax, untie **06** let out, unbind, unglue, weaken **07** deliver, release, set free, shake up, slacken, unscrew, work out **08** diminish, moderate, set loose, unfasten, unthread

**• loosen up**

**05** let up, relax **06** cool it, ease up, go easy, lessen, unwind, warm up **07** prepare, work out **08** chill out, exercise, limber up, warm down **09** hang loose

**loot**

**03** let, rob **04** haul, raid, sack, swag **05** booty, money, prize, rifle, steal **06** burgle, maraud, ravage, riches, spoils **07** despoil, pillage, plunder, ransack **08** pickings **09** steal from **10** lieutenant **11** stolen goods, stolen money

**lop**

**03** cut **04** chop, clip, crop, dock, hack, sned, trim **05** prune, sever, shrub, trash **06** cut off, detach, reduce, remove, shroud **07** curtail, shorten, take off **08** truncate **10** detruncate

**lope**
**03** run **05** bound **06** canter, gallop, lollop, spring, stride

**lopsided**
**05** askew **06** squint, uneven **07** crooked, slanted, sloping, tilting, unequal **08** one-sided **09** skew-whiff **10** off balance, unbalanced **12** asymmetrical

**loquacious**
**05** gabby, gassy, wordy **06** chatty **07** gossipy, voluble **08** babbling **09** garrulous, speechful, talkative **10** blathering, chattering **12** multiloquent, multiloquous

**loquacity**
**09** garrulity, gassiness **10** chattiness, multiloquy, volubility **12** effusiveness **13** multiloquence, talkativeness

**lord**
**01** D **02** Ld **03** Dom, God, lud **04** duke, earl, Herr, kami, king, land, losh, peer, sire, tuan **05** baron, chief, count, Maker, noble, omrah, ruler **06** bishop, Christ, Father, leader, master, prince, Yahweh **07** captain, Creator, emperor, Eternal, Holy One, Jehovah, Messiah, monarch, Saviour, the Word **08** Almighty, governor, nobleman, overlord, Redeemer, seigneur, seignior, Son of God, Son of Man, superior, suzerain, viscount **09** commander, patrician, sovereign **10** aristocrat **11** Jesus Christ, King of kings **13** grand seigneur

*See also* **nobility**

• **lord it over**
**06** act big **07** oppress, repress, swagger **08** domineer, pull rank **09** put on airs, tyrannize **10** boss around, overoffice **11** order around, queen it over **13** be overbearing

**lordliness**
**05** pride **07** disdain, majesty **09** arrogance, grandness, nobleness **11** haughtiness, imperiality **12** magnificence, splendidness **13** big-headedness, condescension, imperiousness **14** high-handedness, impressiveness, overconfidence

**lordly**
**05** grand, lofty, noble, proud **06** lavish, uppity **07** haughty, stately, stuck-up **08** arrogant, imperial, majestic, splendid **09** big-headed, dignified, grandiose, hubristic, imperious **10** disdainful, high-handed, hoity-toity, impressive, peremptory, tyrannical **11** dictatorial, domineering, magnificent, overbearing, patronizing, toffee-nosed **12** aristocratic, supercilious **13** condescending, high and mighty, overconfident

**lore**
**04** lair, lare, lear, leir, lere **05** leare, myths, thong **06** cabala, kabala, wisdom **07** beliefs, cabbala, kabbala, legends, qabalah, sayings, stories **08** folklore, kabbalah, learning, teaching **09** erudition, knowledge, mythology **10** traditions **11** scholarship **13** superstitions

**lorry**
**03** rig **04** drag **05** artic, float, truck, wagon **06** camion, pick-up, tipper **07** flatbed, trailer, vehicle **09** dump truck, Jugannath, semi-truck **10** juggernaut, removal van **11** dumper truck, semi-trailer **12** curtain-sider, double-bottom, flatbed truck, pantechnicon, trailer truck **13** drawbar outfit

**lose**
◇ *deletion indicator*
**04** drop, fail, miss, tine, tyne **05** drain, elude, evade, leese, loose, losen, spend, use up, waste **06** expend, forget, go down, ignore, mislay, outrun **07** confuse, consume, deplete, exhaust, forfeit, fritter, get lost, neglect, not find **08** be beaten, bewilder, go astray, misplace, shake off, squander, throw off **09** disregard, dissipate, fall short, stray from **10** be defeated, depart from, escape from, stop having, wander from **11** be conquered, be taken away, come to grief, fail to grasp, leave behind **12** be bereaved of, be deprived of, be divested of, come a cropper, no longer have, suffer defeat **14** be unsuccessful **15** throw in the towel

• **lose out**
**06** suffer **07** miss out **08** be beaten **14** be unsuccessful **15** be disadvantaged

• **lose yourself in something**
**11** be riveted by **12** be absorbed in, be occupied in **13** be engrossed in, be taken up with **14** be captivated by, be enthralled by, be fascinated by **15** be preoccupied in

**loser**
**04** flop **07** also-ran, failure, has-been, no-hoper, washout **08** dead loss, runner-up, write-off **10** non-starter **11** the defeated

**loss**
**04** dead, debt, harm, hurt, miss **05** traik, waste **06** damage, defeat, tinsel **07** default, deficit, missing, undoing, wastage, wounded **08** casualty, decrease, deprival, dropping, fatality **09** death toll, detriment, disprofit, mislaying, privation **10** deficiency, diminution, forfeiture, forgetting, impairment **11** bereavement, deprivation, destruction **12** disadvantage, endamagement, misplacement **13** disappearance, dispossession

• **at a loss**
**03** out **04** will, wull **07** at fault, baffled, puzzled **09** mystified, perplexed **10** bewildered, nonplussed

**lost**
◇ *anagram indicator*
**04** dead, gone, lore, lorn, past, tint **05** stray, tyned **06** astray, bygone, cursed, damned, doomed, dreamy, fallen, former, missed, ruined, wasted, way-out **07** at a loss, baffled, defunct, extinct, forlorn, mislaid, missing, puzzled, riveted, strayed, wrecked **08** absorbed, amissing, confused, occupied, vanished **09** condemned, destroyed, engrossed, misplaced, neglected, off course, perplexed **10** bewildered, captivated, demolished, enthralled, fascinated, nonplussed, spellbound, squandered **11** disappeared, disoriented, out of the way, preoccupied, taken up with, untraceable **12** absent-minded, irredeemable **13** disorientated, frittered away, long-forgotten, unrecoverable **14** gone for a Burton

• **be lost**
**04** tine, tyne

• **lost cause**
**04** flop **07** also-ran, has-been, no-hoper, washout **08** dead loss, write-off **10** non-starter **12** hopeless case **14** hopeless person

**lot, lots**
**03** cut, due, erf, set, tax **04** fall, fate, gobs, luck, many, part, plot, raft, scad, sort, tons **05** batch, bunch, cavel, crowd, group, heaps, loads, miles, piece, piles, quota, scads, share, weird **06** bundle, dozens, masses, oodles, parcel, ration, shower, stacks **07** destiny, fortune, portion **08** heritage, hundreds, jingbang, lashings, millions, quantity **09** a good deal, allotment, allowance, a quantity, gathering, shedloads, situation, sortilege, thousands **10** a great deal, assortment, collection, divination, percentage **11** bucketloads, consignment, great number, large amount, piece of land **13** circumstances, piece of ground

*See also* **fate**; **number**

• **a lot**
**04** much, scad, slew, slue **05** loads, often **06** barrel **09** any amount **10** a great deal, frequently **12** for a long time **14** to a great degree, to a great extent

• **throw in your lot with**
**06** muck in **07** pitch in **10** join forces, take part in, team up with **11** combine with **14** join forces with

**lotion**
**04** balm, wash **05** cream, salve, scrub, toner **06** balsam, tanner **07** eyewash, washing **08** aftersun, cleanser, eye-water, lavatory, liniment, ointment **09** blackwash, collyrium, emollient, sunscreen **10** aftershave, astringent, witch-hazel, yellow wash **11** arquebusade, embrocation, fomentation **12** hairdressing, retinoic acid

**lottery**
**04** draw, luck, risk **05** bingo, lotto, Tatts **06** chance, gamble, hazard, raffle

07 tombola, venture 08 art union 10 Golden Kiwi, sweepstake 11 speculation 12 gambling game

**loud**

01 f 02 ff 03 big 04 bold, high 05 brash, flash, forte, gaudy, lairy, noisy, rowdy, showy 06 brassy, brazen, flashy, garish, shrill, vulgar 07 blaring, booming, glaring, raucous, roaring 08 emphatic, gorblimy, piercing, plangent, resonant, strident, vehement 09 clamorous, deafening, gorblimey, insistent, obtrusive, tasteless 10 aggressive, flamboyant, fortissimo, resounding, stentorian, streperous, strepitant, thundering, vociferous 11 ear-piercing, full-mouthed, loud-mouthed, penetrating 12 ear-splitting, ostentatious 13 reverberating

• **very loud**

02 ff

**loudly**

01 f 02 ff 03 out 05 aloud, forte 07 lustily, noisily, shrilly 08 strongly 10 fortissimo, stridently, vehemently, vigorously 11 clamorously, deafeningly 12 resoundingly, streperously, strepitantly, uproariously, vociferously

• **very loudly**

02 ff

**loudmouth**

04 brag 06 gasbag 07 boaster, windbag 08 big mouth, blowhard, braggart 09 blusterer, swaggerer 11 braggadocio

**loud-mouthed**

04 bold 05 noisy 06 brazen, coarse, vulgar 08 boasting, bragging 10 aggressive, blustering

**loudness**

• **unit of loudness**

04 phon, sone

**loudspeaker**

06 woofer 07 tweeter 09 subwoofer

**lough** *see* **lake**

**Louisiana**

02 LA

**lounge**

04 hawm, idle, laze, loll 05 daker, relax, slump 06 dacker, daiker, lollop, repose, sprawl 07 day room, lie back, parlour, recline 08 kill time, lie about 09 front room, lie around, loll about, waste time 10 living room, take it easy 11 drawing room, sitting room 13 reception room

*See also* **laze**

**lour, lower**

04 loom 05 frown, glare, scowl 06 darken, glower, impend, menace 07 blacken 08 threaten 09 be brewing, cloud over 11 look daggers 14 give a dirty look

**louring, lowering**

04 dark, grey, grim 05 black, gurly, heavy 06 cloudy, gloomy 07 ominous 08 menacing, overcast 09 darkening, impending 10 forbidding, foreboding 11 threatening

**louse**

03 nit

*See also* **contemptible**

**lousy**

◇ *anagram indicator*

03 bad, ill, low 04 crap, poor, ropy, sick 05 awful, mingy, pants, ropey, rough, seedy 06 chatty, mouldy, no good, poorly, queasy, rotten, unwell 07 rubbish 08 below par, crawling, inferior, pathetic, terrible 09 miserable, off-colour, pedicular 10 inadequate, out of sorts, pediculous, second-rate 12 contemptible 14 unsatisfactory 15 under the weather

**lout**

03 bow, hob, lob, oaf, oik, yob 04 boor, calf, clod, coof, cuif, dolt, gawk, hick, hoon, jake, slob, swad 05 flout, loord, stoop, yahoo, yobbo 06 lubber 07 bumpkin, hallian, hallion, hallyon, lumpkin 08 bull-calf, loblolly 09 barbarian, roughneck 10 clodhopper 11 bushwhacker, chuckle-head, hobbledehoy

**loutish**

04 rude 05 crude, gawky, gruff, rough 06 coarse, oafish, rustic, vulgar 07 boorish, doltish, ill-bred, uncouth, yobbish 08 churlish, clownish, ignorant, impolite 09 unrefined 10 uneducated, unmannerly 11 clodhopping, ill-mannered, uncivilized

**lovable, loveable**

04 cute, dear 05 sweet 06 lovely, taking 07 amiable, likable, winsome 08 adorable, charming, engaging, fetching, likeable, pleasing 09 appealing, endearing 10 attractive, bewitching, delightful, enchanting 11 captivating

**love**

01 O 03 lo'e, loo, luv, nil, pet 04 amor, care, dear, doat, dote, Eros, lust, zeal, zero 05 adore, agape, amour, angel, Cupid, enjoy, fancy, honey, prize, sugar, taste 06 ardour, desire, dote on, liking, nought, poppet, regard, relish, savour, warmth 07 acushla, asthore, beloved, be mad on, care for, charity, cherish, concern, darling, dearest, dear one, delight, idolize, long for, machree, nothing, passion, rapture, sweetie, worship 08 amorance, be daft on, be fond of, be nuts on, be sold on, devotion, fondness, hold dear, intimacy, kindness, pleasure, precious, soft spot, sympathy, treasure, weakness 09 adoration, adulation, affection, be sweet on, delight in, enjoyment, favourite, Platonics, tendresse 10 appreciate, attachment, compassion, friendship, jeune amour, mavourneen, partiality, sweetheart, tenderness 11 amorousness, be devoted to, be partial to, brotherhood, inclination, infatuation, Platonicism 12 appreciation, belle passion, Frauendienst, have a crush on, like very much 13 amour courtois, be attracted to 14 have a liking for, have the hots for, take pleasure in 15 think the world of

• **fall in love with**

05 fancy 06 take to 07 fall for 09 have it bad 12 be crazy about, have a crush on, take a shine to 13 have a thing for 15 burn with passion, lose your heart to

• **in love with**

06 doting, hooked, soft on 07 charmed, smitten, stuck on, sweet on 08 besotted, mad about, mashed on 09 enamoured, nuts about, wild about 10 crazy about, infatuated, potty about 11 attracted to, enamoured of 12 have a crush on

• **love affair**

05 amour, fling 06 affair 07 carry-on, liaison, passion, romance 08 amour fou, intrigue 12 relationship 13 grande passion

• **make love**

09 philander, sleep with 11 go to bed with, have sex with 13 sleep together

**loveable** *see* **lovable**

**loveless**

03 icy 04 cold, hard 06 frigid 07 unloved 08 disliked, forsaken, unloving, unvalued 09 heartless, unfeeling 10 friendless, unfriendly 11 cold-hearted, insensitive, passionless, uncherished 12 unresponsive 13 unappreciated

**lovelorn**

06 pining 07 longing 08 desiring, lovesick, yearning 10 infatuated 11 languishing

**lovely**

04 fair 05 nasty, super, sweet 06 dreamy, pretty 07 amorous, winning 08 adorable, charming, handsome, pleasant, pleasing 09 agreeable, beautiful, enjoyable, exquisite, ravishing, wonderful 10 attractive, delightful, enchanting, marvellous 11 beautifully, good-looking 12 delightfully

**lover**

03 fan, lad 04 beau, bird, buff, date 05 fella, fiend, flame, freak, leman 06 fiancé, friend, suitor, toy boy 07 admirer, amorist, amoroso, beloved, devotee, fanatic, fiancée, partner, servant 08 amoretto, follower, lady love, loved one, mistress, other man, paramour, Platonic 09 boyfriend, man friend, philander, supporter 10 enthusiast, girlfriend, lady friend, other woman, sweetheart 11 woman friend 12 bit on the side 13 live-in partner

*Lovers include:*

04 Bess, Dido, Eros, Eyre (Jane), Hera, Hero, Ilsa, Joan, Lamb (Lady Caroline), Rick, Sand (George), Zeus

**05** Byron (Lord), Cathy, Clyde, Dante, Darby, Darcy (Mr), Harry, Helen, Laura, O'Hara (Scarlett), Paris, Porgy, Pwyll, Romeo, Sally, Tracy (Spencer)
**06** Aeneas, Antony, Bacall (Lauren), Bogart (Humphrey), Bonnie, Burton (Richard), Butler (Rhett), Caesar, Chopin, Isolde, Juliet, Marian (Maid), Nelson (Lord), Psyche, Samson, Taylor (Elizabeth), Thisbe
**07** Abelard, Barrett (Elizabeth), Bennett (Elizabeth), Delilah, Don Juan, Héloïse, Hepburn (Katharine), Leander, Louis XV, Mellors, Orlando, Orpheus, Pyramus, Rimbaud, Simpson (Mrs), Tristan, Troilus, Vronsky (Count)
**08** Beatrice, Benedick, Browning (Robert), Casanova (Giacomo Girolamo), Cressida, Eurydice, Hamilton (Lady Emma), Karenina (Anna), Lancelot, Lothario, Napoleon, Nell Gwyn, Odysseus, Penelope, Petrarch, Rhiannon, Rosalind, Verlaine
**09** Charles II, Cleopatra, Guinevere, Joséphine, Launcelot, Pompadour (Madame de), Robin Hood, Rochester (Mr), Valentino (Rudolph)
**10** Chatterley (Lady), Edward VIII, Heathcliff

**lovesick**
**06** pining **07** longing **08** desiring, lovelorn, yearning **10** infatuated **11** languishing

**love story**
**07** romance

**loving**
**04** fond, kind, warm **06** ardent, caring, doting, lovely, tender **07** adoring, amorous, devoted **08** beloving, friendly **10** passionate **11** sympathetic, warmhearted **12** affectionate

**lovingly**
**06** fondly, warmly **08** ardently, tenderly **12** passionately **14** affectionately **15** sympathetically

**low**
**03** bad, law, moo, sad **04** base, bass, blue, deep, down, dull, evil, flat, glum, hill, late, mean, meek, mild, poor, rich, sale, slow, soft **05** a snip, blaze, cheap, early, fed up, flame, hedge, lowly, muted, nadir, nasty, plain, quiet, scant, short, small, squat **06** a steal, bellow, bottom, coarse, common, gentle, gloomy, humble, humbly, hushed, junior, little, meagre, modest, paltry, ribald, ribaud, scanty, scarce, shabby, simple, smutty, sparse, sunken, vulgar, wicked **07** adverse, debased, foolish, heinous, hostile, immoral, low-born, muffled, obscene, obscure, peasant, reduced, rybauld, shallow, slashed, stunted, subdued, tumulus, unhappy **08** degraded, dejected, depraved, dog-cheap, downcast, indecent, inferior, low-lying, low point, mediocre, moderate, negative, opposing, ordinary, plebeian, resonant, sea-level, sonorous, trifling **09** dastardly, deficient, depressed, dirt-cheap, knock-down, miserable, quietened, ten a penny, whispered **10** all-time low, cheesed off, despicable, despondent, inadequate, low-pitched, low-ranking, reasonable, rock-bottom, submissive **11** downhearted, ground-level, inexpensive, lowest point, low-spirited, subordinate, unimportant **12** antagonistic, contemptible, disconsolate, disheartened, insufficient, low-watermark, unfavourable **13** below standard, dishonourable, going for a song, insignificant, unintelligent **14** down in the dumps, unsatisfactory

**low-born**
**04** poor **05** lowly **06** humble **07** obscure, peasant, plebean, villain **08** mean-born, plebeian **09** unexalted **10** low-ranking

**lowbrow**
**04** rude **05** crude **07** tabloid **08** ignorant **09** unlearned, unrefined **10** downmarket, mass-market, uncultured, uneducated, unlettered **11** unscholarly **12** uncultivated

**lowdown**
**03** gen **04** base, data, dope, info, mean, news, vile **05** facts **07** caitiff **08** shameful, wretched **09** dastardly, degrading, loathsome, reprobate, worthless **10** abominable, despicable, detestable, disgusting **11** disgraceful, information, inside story **12** contemptible, disreputable, intelligence **13** dishonourable, reprehensible

**lower**
**03** cow, cut, dip **04** drop, hush, sink, vail **05** abase, abate, couch, demit, lowly, minor, slash, stoop, under **06** bottom, debase, demean, dilute, embace, embase, humble, imbase, junior, lessen, lesser, nether, reduce, settle, submit **07** beneath, cheapen, curtail, degrade, depress, descend, let down, let fall, quieten, set down **08** belittle, bring low, decrease, diminish, disgrace, inferior, look down, low-level, move down, take down **09** bring down, dishonour, disparage, secondary, undermost **10** nethermore, underneath **11** second-class, subordinate **12** speak quietly **13** move downwards

*See also* **lour, lower**

**• lower in estimation**
**04** less

**lowering**
**03** ebb **04** dark, drop, duck, grey, grim **05** black, gurly, heavy **06** cloudy, gloomy **07** ominous, sinking **08** menacing, overcast, reducing **09** darkening, degrading, demission, impending, reduction **10** depression, forbidding, foreboding **11** degradation, letting down, threatening

*See also* **louring, lowering**

**lowest**
**03** net **04** nett

**low-grade**
**03** bad **04** naff, poor, poxy, ropy **05** awful, lousy, pants, ropey **06** crummy **07** botched, the pits, useless **08** inferior, pathetic, terrible **09** cheap-jack, third-rate **10** second-rate **11** a load of crap, poor-quality, second-class, substandard **13** below standard **14** a load of garbage, a load of rubbish, not up to scratch

**low-key**
**04** soft **05** muted, quiet **06** slight, subtle **07** relaxed, subdued **09** easy-going **10** restrained, undramatic **11** understated

**lowliness**
**07** modesty, poverty **08** humility, meekness, mildness **09** obscurity **10** commonness, simplicity **11** inferiority **12** ordinariness, unimportance **14** submissiveness **15** subordinateness

**lowly**
**04** base, mean, meek, mild, poor **05** plain **06** common, humble, junior, modest, simple **07** low-born, obscure, peasant **08** inferior, ordinary, plebeian **10** low-ranking, submissive **11** subordinate, unimportant

**low-pitched**
**03** low **04** bass, deep, rich **08** resonant, sonorous

**low-spirited**
**03** low, sad **04** down, glum **05** dowie, fed up, moody **06** gloomy **07** unhappy **08** dejected, downcast **09** depressed, miserable **10** cheesed off, despondent **11** discouraged, downhearted **12** heavy-hearted **14** down in the dumps

**loyal**
**04** feal, firm, leal, true **06** stanch, trusty **07** devoted, sincere, staunch **08** constant, faithful, reliable **09** committed, dedicated, patriotic, steadfast **10** dependable, supportive, unchanging **11** true-hearted, trustworthy **12** well-affected

**loyalty**
**06** fealty, lealty **08** devotion, fidelity **09** constancy, sincerity **10** allegiance, commitment, dedication, patriotism **11** reliability, staunchness **12** faithfulness **13** dependability, esprit de corps, steadfastness **15** trustworthiness

**lozenge**
**05** rhomb **06** cachou, jujube, rustre, tablet, troche **07** gumdrop, rhombus **08** pastille, trochisk **09** cough drop **10** trochiscus

**LSD**
**04** acid
**• LSD experience**
**04** trip

**lubber**
**03** oaf, yob **04** boor, clod, dolt, gawk, hick, lout, slob, swab **05** yahoo, yobbo
**07** bumpkin **09** barbarian
**10** clodhopper **11** hobbledehoy

**lubberly**
**05** crude, dense, gawky **06** clumsy, coarse, oafish **07** awkward, doltish, loutish, lumpish, uncouth
**08** bungling, churlish, clownish, ungainly **09** lumbering
**10** blundering **11** clodhopping, heavy-handed

**lubricant**
**03** fat, oil **04** lard, lube **06** ben-oil, grease **07** K-Y® jelly **08** oil of ben, ointment, Vaseline® **11** lubrication
**14** petroleum jelly

**lubricate**
**03** oil, wax **04** ease, help, lard, lube
**05** bribe, smear **06** assist, grease, polish, smooth **07** advance, forward, further, promote, speed up
**08** expedite **09** encourage
**10** accelerate, facilitate, make easier, make smooth **12** smooth the way

**luce**
**03** ged

**lucid**
**04** pure, sane **05** clear, plain, sober, sound **06** bright, glassy, limpid
**07** beaming, evident, obvious, radiant, shining **08** distinct, explicit, gleaming, luminous, pellucid, rational, sensible
**09** brilliant, effulgent **10** diaphanous, reasonable **11** clear-headed, crystalline, of sound mind, perspicuous, resplendent, translucent, transparent **12** compos mentis, intelligible **14** comprehensible

**lucidity**
**06** sanity **07** clarity **09** plainness, soundness **11** rationality **12** compos mentis **14** reasonableness **15** clear-headedness, intelligibility

**lucidly**
**07** clearly, plainly **09** evidently, obviously **10** explicitly **12** intelligibly
**14** comprehensibly

**luck**
**03** hap **04** fate, joss, seal, seel, seil, sele
**05** break, fluke **06** chance, hazard
**07** destiny, fortune, godsend, success
**08** accident, fortuity, good luck, the stars **10** prosperity, providence
**11** good fortune, serendipity
**14** predestination
**• bad luck**
**06** hoodoo, mishap, mozzle **07** ambs-ace, ames-ace **08** deuce-ace **09** hard lines, mischance **10** hard cheese, ill fortune **12** misadventure
**• bring bad luck**
**03** hex **04** jinx
**• good luck**
**05** sonce, sonse **06** prosit **07** wassail
**08** godspeed, waes hail **09** drink hail
**11** bonne chance
**• in luck**
**05** happy, jammy **06** timely
**08** favoured **09** fortunate, opportune
**10** advantaged, auspicious, successful
**• out of luck**
**07** hapless, unlucky **08** luckless
**11** unfortunate **12** inauspicious, unsuccessful **13** disadvantaged
**14** down on your luck

**luckily**
**07** happily **08** by chance **10** by accident, by good luck, mercifully
**11** fortunately **12** fortuitously, propitiously **14** providentially

**luckless**
**06** cursed, doomed, jinxed **07** hapless, unhappy, unlucky **08** hopeless, ill-fated **09** miserable **10** calamitous, disastrous, ill-starred **11** fortuneless, star-crossed, unfortunate
**12** catastrophic, unpropitious, unsuccessful

**lucky**
**05** canny, happy, jammy, tinny
**06** chancy, in luck, spawny, timely
**07** chancey, charmed **08** favoured
**09** departure, expedient, fortunate, opportune, promising **10** auspicious, fortuitous, just as well, propitious, prosperous, successful **12** providential
**• lucky chance**
**03** hit

**lucrative**
**07** gainful **08** well-paid **10** high-paying, productive, profitable, worthwhile **11** moneymaking
**12** advantageous, profit-making, remunerative

**lucratively**
**09** gainfully **10** profitably
**12** productively **14** advantageously, remuneratively

**lucre**
**03** pay **04** cash, dosh, gain **05** brass, bread, dough, dross, gains, lolly, money, ready **06** income, mammon, profit, riches, spoils, wealth **07** profits, readies **08** greenies, proceeds, winnings **11** spondulicks
**12** remuneration

**ludicrous**
◇ *anagram indicator*
**03** odd **04** zany **05** comic, crazy, droll, funny, silly **06** absurd
**07** amusing, comical, risible
**08** farcical, humorous, sportive
**09** burlesque, eccentric, grotesque, hilarious, laughable **10** outlandish, ridiculous **11** nonsensical
**12** preposterous
**• something ludicrous**
**04** jest

**ludicrously**
**08** absurdly **09** laughably
**11** grotesquely, hilariously
**12** outlandishly, ridiculously
**13** nonsensically **14** preposterously

**lug**
**03** ear, tow, tug **04** bear, drag, haul, hump, lift, loop, pole, pull, tote
**05** carry, heave, stick **06** handle

**luggage**
**04** gear **05** stuff, traps **06** things
**07** baggage, clobber **10** belongings
**11** impedimenta **13** paraphernalia

*Luggage includes:*

**03** bag, box
**04** case, grip
**05** chest, trunk
**06** basket, hamper, kitbag, valise
**07** holdall, satchel
**08** backpack, knapsack, rucksack, suitcase
**09** briefcase, flight bag, haversack, portfolio, travel bag
**10** vanity-case
**11** attaché case, hand-luggage, portmanteau
**12** Gladstone bag, overnight bag

**lugubrious**
**03** sad **04** glum **06** dismal, dreary, gloomy, morose, sombre, woeful
**07** baleful, doleful, serious
**08** funereal, mournful **09** sorrowful, woebegone **10** lachrymose, melancholy, sepulchral

**lugworm**
**03** lob **07** lobworm

**lukewarm**
**03** lew **04** cool **05** tepid **07** coolish, warmish **09** apathetic, impassive, Laodicean **11** half-hearted, indifferent, unconcerned **12** slightly warm, uninterested, unresponsive
**14** unenthusiastic

**lull**
**04** calm, ease, hush **05** abate, allay, let-up, pause, peace, quell, quiet, still
**06** pacify, soothe, sopite, subdue
**07** assuage, compose, silence, subside
**08** calmness **09** stillness **11** quieten down **12** tranquillity

**lullaby**
**05** baloo **07** hushaby **08** berceuse
**10** cradle song

**lumber**
**04** junk, land, load, pawn, plod, wood
**05** clump, stamp, stump, trash
**06** burden, charge, hamper, impose, jumble, prison, raffle, refuse, rumble, saddle, timber, trudge **07** clutter, rubbish, shamble, shuffle, stumble, trundle **08** encumber, imprison, pawnshop **10** flirtation **11** odds and ends **13** bits and pieces

**lumbering**
**05** heavy **06** bovine, clumsy
**07** awkward, hulking, lumpish, massive **08** bumbling, ungainly, unwieldy **09** ponderous
**10** blundering **11** elephantine, heavy-footed

**lumen**
**02** lm, lu

**luminary**
**03** VIP **04** star **05** celeb **06** bigwig, candle, expert, leader, worthy **07** big name, notable **09** authority, celebrity, dignitary, personage, superstar **12** leading light

**luminence**
**01** L
- **amount of luminence**
**03** nit

**luminescent**
**06** bright **07** glowing, radiant, shining **08** luminous **09** effulgent **10** luciferous **11** fluorescent **14** phosphorescent

**luminosity**
**04** glow **05** light **06** lustre **08** radiance **10** brightness, brilliance **12** fluorescence, illumination

**luminous**
**03** lit **05** clear, lucid **06** bright **07** glowing, lighted, radiant, shining **08** dazzling, lustrous **09** brilliant, effulgent **11** fluorescent, illuminated, illustrious, luminescent

**lump**
**03** bur, cob, dab, dad, dod, gob, lob, nub, nut, pat, wad **04** ball, bear, bees, bump, burr, cake, clat, clod, core, daud, dawd, fuse, hunk, knob, knot, knub, loaf, mass, nirl, node, pool, rock, slub, slug, take **05** blend, block, bolus, brook, bulge, bunch, chuck, chump, chunk, claut, clump, crowd, gnarl, group, hunch, knarl, lunch, piece, plook, plouk, slump, stand, thole, tuber, unite, wedge, wodge **06** bruise, bunion, dallop, dollop, endure, gather, gobbet, growth, nodule, nubble, nugget, suffer, tumour **07** cluster, collect, combine, dislike, knubble, pustule, stomach, swallow **08** bear with, coalesce, swelling, tolerate **09** carbuncle, put up with **10** concretion, protrusion, tumescence **11** consolidate, mix together, put together **12** conglomerate, protuberance

**lumpish**
**04** dull **05** gawky, gross, heavy **06** clumsy, oafish, obtuse, stolid, stupid, sullen **07** awkward, boorish, doltish, hulking **08** bungling, ungainly **09** lethargic, lumbering **10** dull-witted **11** elephantine

**lumpy**
**04** slub **05** bumpy **06** cloggy, grainy, nodose, nodous **07** bunched, clotted, curdled, grumose, grumous, knobbly **08** granular **09** congealed **10** coagulated

**Luna**
**06** Selene

**lunacy**
**05** folly, mania **06** idiocy **07** inanity, madness **08** dementia, insanity, nonsense **09** absurdity, craziness, silliness, stupidity **10** aberration, imbecility **11** derangement, foolishness, moon-madness **12** dementedness, illogicality **13** irrationality, senselessness **14** outrageousness, ridiculousness
- **fit of lunacy**
**04** lune

**lunar** *see* **Moon**

**lunatic**
◇ *anagram indicator*
**03** mad **04** daft, nuts **05** barmy, crazy, inane, loony, loopy, nutty, potty, silly **06** absurd, insane, madman, maniac, nutter, psycho, stupid **07** bonkers, foolish, idiotic, nutcase, oddball **08** crackpot, demented, deranged, headcase, imbecile, madwoman, neurotic **09** disturbed, fruitcake, illogical, psychotic, senseless **10** irrational, moonstruck, psychopath, unbalanced **11** hare-brained, nonsensical **12** insane person, moon-stricken, round the bend **13** off your rocker, round the twist

**lunch**
**04** tiff, tift **05** piece, snack **06** brunch, dinner, nacket, nocket, tiffin **07** tiffing **08** luncheon, nuncheon **10** light lunch, midday meal **11** packed lunch, Sunday lunch
- **out to lunch**
◇ *anagram indicator*
**05** crazy

**lunge**
**03** cut, hit, jab **04** dart, dash, dive, grab, leap, pass, poke, stab **05** bound, hit at **06** charge, grab at, plunge, pounce, spring, strike, thrust **08** fall upon, strike at **09** pitch into

**lungs**
- **goose lungs**
**04** soul

**lurch**
**04** list, reel, rock, roll, sway, swee, swey, veer, wait **05** filch, pitch, stoit **06** ambush, swerve, totter **07** defraud, stagger, stumble **09** forestall, overreach **11** weather roll **12** discomfiture
- **leave in the lurch**
**04** fail **06** desert **07** abandon, let down **10** disappoint **13** leave stranded **15** leave high and dry

**lure**
**03** jig **04** bait, draw, tole, toll **05** decoy, Devon, squid, stale, stool, tempt, train, troll **06** allure, carrot, entice, induce, lead on, seduce, trepan **07** attract, beguile, ensnare **08** inveigle **09** decoy-duck, honey-trap, seduction, spoonbait, spoonhook **10** allurement, attraction, enticement, inducement, temptation, trout-spoon **11** Devon minnow **12** trolling-bait **13** trolling-spoon **14** take a rise out of

**lurid**
**04** gory, loud **05** showy, vivid **06** garish, Gothic, grisly, sultry **07** ghastly, glaring, graphic, intense, macabre **08** dazzling, explicit, gruesome, horrific, shocking **09** brilliant, brimstony, revolting, startling **11** exaggerated, sensational **12** melodramatic

**luridly**
**07** vividly **08** garishly **09** intensely **10** explicitly, gruesomely, shockingly **11** brilliantly, graphically, revoltingly

**lurk**
**04** dare, hide **05** dodge, prowl, skulk, slink, sneak, snoke, snook, snoop, snowk **06** crouch, lie low, loiter **07** swindle **09** lie in wait **15** conceal yourself

**luscious**
**04** sexy **05** juicy, sweet, tasty, yummy **06** morish **07** cloying, fulsome, moreish, savoury **08** gorgeous, sensuous, smashing, stunning **09** beautiful, delicious, desirable, ravishing, succulent **10** appetizing, attractive, delectable, delightful, voluptuous **11** pleasurable, scrumptious **13** mouthwatering

**lush**
**03** sot **04** posh, rich, soak, wino **05** alkie, dense, dipso, drink, drunk, grand, green, plush, ritzy, souse, toper **06** boozer, classy, glitzy, lavish, ornate, sponge, swanky **07** alcohol, bloater, drinker, fuddler, opulent, profuse, shicker, teeming, tippler, tosspot, verdant **08** abundant, drunkard, habitual, palatial, prolific **09** alcoholic, inebriate, luxuriant, luxurious, overgrown, sumptuous **10** wine-bibber **11** dipsomaniac, extravagant, flourishing, hard drinker **12** heavy drinker

**lust**
**04** lech, will **05** greed **06** desire, hunger, libido, relish **07** avidity, craving, lechery, longing, passion, the hots **08** appetite, cupidity, lewdness, pleasure, yearning **09** horniness, prurience, randiness **10** greediness, sensuality **11** raunchiness, sexual drive **12** covetousness, sexual desire **13** concupiscence **14** lasciviousness, licentiousness
- **lust after**
**04** need, want **05** covet, crave **06** desire, lecher, slaver **07** long for **08** yearn for **09** hunger for, thirst for

**lustful**
**03** hot **04** lewd, rank **05** horny, radge, randy **06** carnal, randie, wanton **07** craving, goatish, rammish, raunchy, ruttish, sensual **08** prurient, unchaste **09** hankering, lecherous, lickerish, luxurious, salacious, venereous **10** cupidinous, lascivious, libidinous, licentious, passionate **12** concupiscent

**lustily**
**04** hard **06** loudly **07** stoutly **08** heartily, robustly, strongly **10** forcefully, powerfully, vigorously

**lustiness**
**05** power **06** energy, health, vigour **08** haleness, strength, virility **09** hardiness, stoutness, toughness **10** robustness, sturdiness **11** healthiness

**lustre**
**04** fame, gaum, glow, gorm, silk **05** glare, gleam, glint, glory, gloss, merit, sheen, shine, water **06** credit, honour, renown **07** burnish, glitter, shimmer, sparkle, varnish **08** lambency, prestige, radiance, schiller **09** lovelight, splendour **10** brightness, brilliance, refulgence **11** distinction **12** resplendence **15** illustriousness

**lustreless**
**03** mat **04** matt **05** matte

**lustrous**
**05** glacé, shiny **06** bright, glossy, sheeny **07** glowing, lambent, radiant, shining **08** dazzling, gleaming, luminous **09** brilliant, burnished, sparkling, twinkling **10** glistening, glittering, shimmering

**lusty**
**03** fit **04** hale, rank **05** beefy, bulky, frack, gutsy, stout, tough **06** hearty, lively, robust, rugged, strong, sturdy, virile **07** healthy, lustick **08** blooming, forceful, lustique, pleasant, pleasing, powerful, skelping, vigorous **09** energetic, strapping **13** hale and hearty

**lute**
**03** oud **04** pipa **06** cither **07** bandura, cithern, cittern, dichord, pandora, pandore, theorbo **08** archlute, polyphon **09** orpharion, polyphone **10** chitarrone

**lutetium**
**02** Lu

**Luxembourg**
**01** L **03** LUX

**luxuriance**
**06** excess **08** lushness, rankness, richness **09** abundance, denseness, fecundity, fertility, profusion **10** exuberance, exuberancy, lavishness, overgrowth **11** copiousness **13** sumptuousness

**luxuriant**
**04** lush, rank, rich **05** ample, dense, fancy **06** fecund, florid, lavish, ornate, rococo **07** baroque, copious, fertile, flowery, opulent, profuse, riotous, teeming **08** abundant, prolific, thriving, tropical **09** elaborate, excessive, exuberant, plenteous, plentiful, sumptuous **10** flamboyant, productive **11** extravagant, overflowing **12** overabundant **13** superabundant

**luxuriate**
**04** bask, grow **05** bloom, enjoy, revel **06** abound, frowst, relish, savour, thrive, wallow **07** burgeon, delight, indulge, prosper, relax in **08** flourish **09** have a ball **12** live in clover

**luxurious**
**04** high, lush, posh, rich **05** cushy, grand, plush, ritzy **06** costly, de luxe, glitzy, lavish, plushy, silken, swanky **07** Apician, elegant, lustful, opulent **08** affluent, delicate, feastful, pampered, splendid **09** expensive, sumptuous **10** Babylonian, mollitious **11** comfortable, magnificent **13** self-indulgent, well-appointed

**luxuriously**
**04** high **06** poshly **07** plushly **08** glitzily, lavishly, swankily **09** opulently **10** affluently **11** comfortably, deliciously, sumptuously **13** magnificently

**luxury**
**03** pie **04** luxe, Ritz **05** extra, treat **06** dainty **07** comfort **08** delicacy, delicate, grandeur, hedonism, opulence, pleasure, richness **09** affluence, grand luxe, grandness, splendour **10** costliness, indulgence, wantonness **11** lap of luxury **12** extravagance, magnificence, milk and honey, satisfaction **13** expensiveness, gratification, sumptuousness **14** self-indulgence

**lying**
**05** false **06** deceit **07** crooked, falsity, fibbing, leasing, perjury **08** two-faced **09** deceitful, dishonest, duplicity, falsehood, invention, white lies **10** dishonesty, mendacious, untruthful **11** crookedness, dissembling, fabrication, pseudologia **13** dissimulating, double-dealing, falsification **14** untruthfulness

**lynch**
**04** hang, kill **06** dewitt **07** execute **08** string up **10** put to death **13** hang by the neck

**lyre string**
**04** mese, nete **05** trite **06** hypate

**lyric**
**03** lay, ode **04** lied, pean, song **05** melic, paean **06** poetic **07** melodic, musical **08** personal **09** emotional **10** passionate, subjective

**lyrical**
**04** odic **06** poetic **07** musical **08** ecstatic, effusive, inspired, romantic **09** emotional, rapturous, rhapsodic **10** expressive, passionate **11** carried away, impassioned **12** enthusiastic

**lyrically**
**09** musically **10** effusively, poetically **11** emotionally, rapturously **12** ecstatically, expressively, passionately, romantically

**lyricist** *see* **songwriter**

**lyrics**
**04** book, text **05** words **08** libretto

# M

**M**
**02** em **04** Emma, Mike

**macabre**
◇ *anagram indicator*
**04** gory, grim, sick **05** eerie, sicko **06** Gothic, grisly, morbid **07** ghastly, ghostly, hideous **08** chilling, dreadful, gruesome, horrible, horrific, shocking **09** frightful **10** terrifying **11** frightening

**Macao**
**03** MAC

**macaroni**
**04** zite, ziti **05** dandy **06** medley **10** rockhopper

**mace**
**03** rod **04** club, maul **05** poker, staff, stick **06** cudgel

**mace-bearer**
**05** bedel **06** beadle

**Macedonia**
**02** MK **03** MKD

**macerate**
**04** mash, pulp, soak **05** blend, steep **06** soften, squash **07** liquefy, mortify **08** marinade

**Machiavellian**
**03** sly **04** foxy, wily **06** artful, astute, crafty, shrewd **07** cunning, devious **08** guileful, scheming **09** deceitful, designing, underhand **10** intriguing, perfidious **11** calculating, opportunist **12** unscrupulous **13** double-dealing

**machination**
**04** plot, ploy, ruse, wile **05** cabal, dodge, trick **06** design, device, scheme, tactic **08** artifice, intrigue **09** manoeuvre, stratagem **10** conspiracy **11** shenanigans

**machine**
**04** tool **05** motor, organ, robot **06** agency, device, engine, gadget, system, zombie **07** android, vehicle **08** catalyst, hardware, workings **09** apparatus, appliance, automaton, influence, mechanism, structure **10** instrument **11** contraption, contrivance **12** organization

**machine-gun**
**02** MG **04** Bren **05** Maxim **07** Bren gun **08** Lewis gun, Maxim-gun **12** mitrailleuse

**machinery**
**04** gear **05** tools **06** agency, system, tackle **07** channel **08** channels, gadgetry, workings **09** apparatus, equipment, mechanism, procedure, structure **11** instruments **12** organization

*Machinery includes:*

**03** Cat®, JCB®
**05** crane, dozer
**06** digger, dumper, grader, jigger
**07** dredger, grapple, gritter, skidder, tractor
**08** dragline, dustcart, fork lift, jib crane
**09** bulldozer, calfdozer, dump truck, excavator
**10** angledozer, earthmover, pile-driver, road roller, snowplough, tower crane, tracklayer, truck crane, water crane
**11** Caterpillar®, dumper truck, gantry crane, road-sweeper, wheel loader
**12** cherry picker, crawler crane, luffing crane, pick-up loader
**13** concrete mixer, floating crane, fork-lift truck, grabbing crane, platform hoist
**14** container crane, crawler tractor, tractor-scraper
**15** hydraulic shovel, luffing-jib crane, walking dragline

**machinist**
**06** worker **08** mechanic, operator **09** operative **11** factory hand

**machismo**
**08** maleness, strength, virility **09** manliness, toughness **11** masculinity

**macrocosm**
**05** world **06** cosmos, entity, planet, system **07** culture, society **08** creation, humanity, totality, universe **09** community, structure **11** solar system **12** civilization, single entity

**mad**
◇ *anagram indicator*
**03** ape, fay, fey, fie, wud **04** avid, bats, daft, fond, gyte, keen, loco, nuts, wild, wood, wowf, yond **05** angry, barmy, batty, berko, buggy, crazy, cross, daffy, dippy, dotty, flaky, gonzo, hasty, irate, livid, loony, loopy, manic, nutty, potty, queer, rabid, rapid, ratty, silly, spewy, wacko, wacky, wiggy **06** absurd, ardent, choked, crazed, cuckoo, fruity, fuming, insane, locoed, maniac, mental, raging, raving, red-mad, red-wud, screwy, stupid, troppo, whacko **07** bananas, barking, berserk, blazing, bonkers, cracked, crooked, devoted, enraged, excited, flipped, foolish, frantic, furious, hurried, idiotic, intense, lunatic, meshuga, red-wood, ropable, stroppy, uptight, violent, zealous **08** burned up, choleric, crackers, crackpot, demented, deranged, dingbats, doolally, frenetic, frenzied, hairless, in a paddy, in a strop, incensed, maniacal, meshugga, meshugge, reckless, unhinged, unstable, up in arms **09** abandoned, disturbed, energetic, fanatical, foolhardy, illogical, in a lather, infuriate, ludicrous, lymphatic, psychotic, raving mad, seeing red, ticked off, up the wall **10** aggravated, bestraught, distracted, distraught, frantic-mad, hopping mad, infatuated, infuriated, irrational, off the wall, off your nut, out to lunch, passionate, stone-crazy, unbalanced **11** disgruntled, fit to be tied, hare-brained, nonsensical, not all there, off the rails, off your head **12** crackbrained, enthusiastic, mad as a hatter, off your chump, on the warpath, preposterous, round the bend, uncontrolled, unreasonable, unrestrained **13** off your rocker, of unsound mind, out of your head, out of your mind, out of your tree, round the twist **14** off your trolley, wrong in the head **15** non compos mentis, out of your senses

**• go mad**
**04** flip **05** go ape **06** blow up, wig out **07** go crazy **09** go bananas **11** flip your lid, go ballistic **15** lose your marbles

**• like mad**
**06** avidly, wildly **07** quickly **09** furiously, hurriedly, zealously **11** fanatically, frantically **13** energetically

**Madagascar**
**02** RM **03** MDG

**madcap**
**04** cake, fury, rash, wild **05** crazy, silly **06** lively **07** flighty, hothead **08** crackpot, heedless, reckless, tearaway **09** daredevil, desperado, eccentric, firebrand, foolhardy, hotheaded, imprudent, impulsive **10** adventurer, ill-advised **11** birdbrained, hare-brained, thoughtless

**madden**
◇ *anagram indicator*
**03** bug, irk, vex **05** anger, annoy, bemad, upset **06** enrage, hassle **07** agitate, incense, inflame, provoke **08** distract, irritate **09** aggravate, drive

nuts, infuriate **10** drive crazy, exasperate **13** get on your wick, get up your nose, get your back up **14** drive up the wall **15** get on your nerves, get your dander up

**maddening**
◇ *anagram indicator*
**07** galling **08** annoying **09** upsetting, vexatious **10** disturbing, irritating **11** aggravating, infuriating, troublesome **12** exasperating

**madder**
**04** chay **05** chaya, Rubia, shaya **07** alizari **08** gardenia **10** buttonbush

**made**
• **made it**
**02** ff
• **recently made**
**03** new

**made-up**
◇ *anagram indicator*
**05** false **06** done up, unreal, untrue **07** painted **08** invented, mythical, powdered, specious **09** fairytale, fictional, imaginary, trumped-up **10** fabricated **11** make-believe **13** wearing make-up

**madhouse**
**05** Babel, chaos **06** asylum, bedlam, mayhem, uproar **07** turmoil **08** disarray, disorder, loony bin, nuthouse **09** funny farm **11** pandemonium **13** lunatic asylum **14** mental hospital

**madly**
◇ *anagram indicator*
**04** fast, very **06** wildly **07** crazily, hastily, rapidly, utterly **08** insanely **09** devotedly, excitedly, extremely, fervently, furiously, hurriedly, intensely, violently **10** completely, dementedly, frenziedly, recklessly **11** deliriously, exceedingly, frantically **12** distractedly, hysterically, irrationally, unreasonably **13** energetically, exceptionally

**madman, madwoman**
**03** nut **04** gelt, kook **05** crank, loony **06** bedlam, maniac, nutter, psycho **07** cupcake, furioso, lunatic, nutcase, oddball **08** crackpot, frenetic, headcase, imbecile **09** bedlamite, fruitcake, psychotic, screwball **10** basket case, psychopath, Tom o' Bedlam

**madness**
◇ *anagram indicator*
**03** ire **04** fury, rage, riot, zeal **05** anger, craze, folie, folly, mania, wrath **06** ardour, frenzy, lunacy, raving, uproar **07** abandon, inanity, passion **08** daftness, delusion, dementia, hysteria, insanity, keenness, nonsense, wildness **09** absurdity, agitation, craziness, furiosity, meshugaas, mishegaas, psychosis, silliness, stupidity, theomania **10** deliration, enthusiasm, excitement, fanaticism, insaneness **11** derangement, distraction, foolishness, infatuation, lycanthropy, unrestraint **12** exasperation, intoxication **13** foolhardiness, irrationality

**madrigal**
**04** fa-la

**madwoman** *see* **madman, madwoman**

**Mae**
**04** West

**maelstrom**
**04** mess **05** chaos **06** bedlam, tumult, uproar, vortex **07** turmoil **08** disorder **09** Charybdis, confusion, whirlpool **10** turbulence **11** pandemonium

**maestro**
**03** ace **06** expert, genius, master, wizard **07** prodigy **08** director, virtuoso **09** conductor

**Mafia**
**06** the Mob **10** Cosa Nostra
• **Mafia boss**
**03** don **04** capo **09** godfather
• **Mafia code**
**06** omertà
• **Mafia member**
**07** made man, pentito, soldier **09** goodfella

**magazine**
**03** mag **04** pulp, zine **05** comic, depot, e-zine, paper, slick **06** glossy, lad mag, weekly **07** arsenal, fanzine, journal, monthly **08** carousel, ordnance **09** carrousel, quarterly **10** periodical, powder room, repository, storehouse, supplement **11** fortnightly, publication **12** contemporary **14** ammunition dump

*See also* **newspaper**

**maggot**
**03** bot, fad **04** bott, mawk, whim, worm **06** gentle **09** fleshworm

**Magi** *see* **wise man** *under* **wise**

**magic**
**03** ace, art **04** cool, mega, mojo, pull **05** brill, charm, curse, goety, great, spell, wicca **06** allure, hoodoo, occult, voodoo, wicked, wonder **07** conjury, demonic, glamour, gramary, mystery, sorcery **08** black art, charming, diablery, gramarye, hermetic, illusion, magnetic, prestige, romantic, smashing, spellful, stardust, terrific, trickery, wizardry **09** conjuring, deception, diablerie, excellent, magnetism, occultism, wonderful **10** allurement, bewitching, black magic, enchanting, enticement, entrancing, marvellous, mysterious, necromancy, tremendous, witchcraft **11** captivating, enchantment, fascinating, fascination, incantation, legerdemain, thaumaturgy **12** irresistible, metaphysical, spellbinding, supernatural **13** magical powers, sleight of hand, wonder-working

**magical**
**05** magic **06** occult **07** demonic **08** charming, hermetic, spellful, stardust **09** wonderful **10** enchanting, hermetical, marvellous, mysterious **11** captivating, fascinating **12** spellbinding, supernatural

**magician**
**03** ace **05** magus, pawaw, witch **06** expert, genius, master, powwow, wizard **07** juggler, maestro, warlock, wise man **08** conjurer, conjuror, sorcerer, virtuoso **09** archimage, enchanter **11** enchantress, illusionist, necromancer, spellbinder, spellworker, thaumaturge, witch doctor **12** wonder-worker **13** miracle-worker

**magisterial**
**05** bossy **06** lordly **08** arrogant, despotic **09** assertive, imperious, masterful **10** commanding, high-handed, peremptory **11** dictatorial, domineering, overbearing **13** authoritarian, authoritative

**magistrate**
**02** JP, RM **04** beak, cadi, doge, foud, kadi, qadi **05** amman, edile, judge, jurat, mayor, prior, reeve **06** aedile, amtman, avoyer, bailie, bailli, censor, cotwal, kotwal, pretor, sharif, sherif, syndic **07** alcalde, bailiff, baillie, burgess, justice, podestà, praetor, prefect, provost, shereef, tribune **08** dictator, landdros, mittimus, praefect, quaestor **09** landamman, landdrost, Lord Mayor, novus homo, portreeve, proconsul **10** corregidor, landammann, propraetor **11** baron bailie, burgomaster, field cornet, gonfalonier, stipendiary

**magnanimity**
**05** mercy **07** charity **08** altruism, kindness, largesse, nobility **10** generosity, liberality **11** beneficence, benevolence, forgiveness, munificence **12** generousness, philanthropy, selflessness **13** bountifulness, unselfishness **14** big-heartedness, charitableness, high-mindedness, open-handedness

**magnanimous**
**03** big **04** kind **05** large, noble **06** kindly **07** liberal **08** generous, merciful, selfless **09** bountiful, forgiving, unselfish **10** altruistic, beneficent, benevolent, big-hearted, charitable, munificent, open-handed, ungrudging **11** large-minded **12** great-hearted **13** philanthropic

**magnate**
**05** baron, mogul, noble **06** bigwig, fat cat, leader, tycoon **07** big shot, notable **08** big noise, big timer **09** big cheese, executive, financier, moneybags, personage, plutocrat **12** entrepreneur **13** industrialist

*See also* **newspaper**

**magnesium**
02 Mg

**magnet**
04 bait, draw, lure 05 charm, focus 06 appeal, needle 08 solenoid 09 loadstone, lodestone 10 allurement, attraction, enticement, focal point

**magnetic**
03 mag 08 alluring, charming, engaging, gripping, hypnotic, tempting 09 absorbing, appealing, seductive 10 attractive, bewitching, enchanting, entrancing 11 captivating, charismatic, enthralling, fascinating, mesmerizing, tantalizing 12 irresistible

**magnetism**
02 it 03 mag 04 draw, grip, lure, pull 05 charm, magic, oomph, power, spell 06 allure, appeal, duende, glamor 07 glamour 08 charisma 09 hypnotism, mesmerism 10 attraction, temptation 11 captivation, enchantment, fascination 12 drawing power 13 seductiveness

**magnification**
05 boost 07 build-up 08 dilation, increase 09 deepening, expansion, extolling, extolment, hyperbole, inflation, overdoing 10 embroidery 11 enhancement, enlargement, heightening, lionization 12 augmentation, exaggeration, overemphasis 13 amplification, dramatization, embellishment, overstatement 14 aggrandizement 15 intensification

**magnificence**
04 pomp 05 glory, pride 06 luxury 07 majesty 08 grandeur, nobility, opulence, splendor 09 splendour, sublimity 10 brilliance, excellence, lavishness 11 stateliness 12 gorgeousness, resplendence 13 luxuriousness, sumptuousness 14 impressiveness

**magnificent**
04 fine, rich 05 grand, noble, royal, state 06 august, lavish, lordly, superb 07 elegant, exalted, gallant, opulent, stately, sublime 08 dazzling, glorious, gorgeous, imposing, majestic, princely, splendid, striking 09 brilliant, excellent, grandiose, luxurious, splendent, sumptuous, wonderful 10 impressive, marvellous 11 resplendent

**magnify**
05 boost 06 blow up, deepen, dilate, expand, extend, overdo 07 amplify, broaden, build up, enhance, enlarge, greaten, signify 08 heighten, increase, multiply, overplay 09 dramatize, embellish, embroider, intensify, overstate 10 exaggerate 13 overemphasize

**magniloquence**
07 bombast, fustian 08 euphuism, rhetoric 09 loftiness, pomposity, turgidity 10 orotundity 14 grandiloquence 15 pretentiousness

**magniloquent**
05 lofty 06 turgid 07 exalted, fustian, orotund, pompous, stilted 08 elevated, sonorous 09 bombastic, high-flown, overblown 10 euphuistic, rhetorical 11 declamatory, pretentious 12 high-sounding 13 grandiloquent

**magnitude**
03 mag 04 bulk, fame, mass, note, size 05 space 06 amount, extent, import, moment, volume, weight 07 expanse, measure 08 capacity, eminence, muchness, quantity, strength 09 amplitude, greatness, intensity, largeness 10 dimensions, importance 11 consequence, distinction, proportions 12 significance 13 absolute value

**magnolia**
03 bay 05 yulan 07 champac, champak 08 sweet bay 09 star anise, tulip tree 10 beaver-tree, beaver-wood 12 cucumber tree, umbrella tree

**magnum opus**
10 masterwork 11 chef d'oeuvre, masterpiece

**magpie**
03 mag, pie 04 Pica, piet, pyat, pyet, pyot 05 madge 06 maggie 09 organ-bird 10 piping crow

**mahogany**
04 toon 05 carap, khaya 06 acajou 07 Cedrela 10 chinaberry 14 chittagong wood

**maid**
03 may 04 ayah, girl, lass 05 bonne, daily, wench 06 au pair, maiden, Mrs Mop, skivvy, slavey, tweeny, virgin 07 abigail, dresser, Mrs Mopp, pucelle, servant 08 bonibell, charlady, domestic, home help, spinster, suivante, tabby cat, waitress 09 bonnibell, charwoman, housemaid, lady's maid, soubrette, tire-woman 10 bowerwoman, Cinderella, handmaiden 11 chambermaid, kitchenmaid, maidservant, serving-maid 12 cleaning lady, kitchen-wench 13 maid-of-all-work 14 femme de chambre

**maiden**
01 M 03 new 04 burd, girl, kore, lass, miss, pure, wili 05 first, nymph, popsy, unwed 06 chaste, damsel, decent, demure, female, gentle, lassie, modest, proper, seemly, vestal, virgin 07 girlish, initial 08 celibate, decorous, reserved, virginal, virtuous 09 inaugural, undefiled, unmarried, unsullied, young girl, young lady 10 initiatory, unbroached, young woman 12 bachelorette, introductory

**maidenhood**
06 honour, purity, virtue 08 chastity 10 chasteness, maidenhead

**maidenly**
04 pure 05 unwed 06 chaste, decent, demure, female, gentle, modest, proper, seemly, vestal, virgin 07 girlish 08 becoming, decorous, reserved, virginal, virtuous 09 undefiled, unmarried, unsullied 10 immaculate, unbroached

**maidservant**
03 may 04 amah, girl, maid 05 daily 06 au pair, maiden, skivvy, slavey 07 abigail, dresser, Mrs Mopp, pucelle, servant 08 charlady, domestic, suivante, waitress 09 bonnibell, charwoman, housemaid, lady's maid, soubrette 10 bowerwoman, handmaiden 11 chambermaid, kitchenmaid, parlour-maid, serving-maid 13 maid-of-all-work

**mail**
03 dak 04 dawk, post, rent, send, spam, spot 05 armor, e-mail 06 armour 07 airmail, fan mail, forward, junk fax, letters, packets, panoply, parcels, payment 08 delivery, dispatch, hate mail, junk mail, packages 09 chain mail, habergeon, halfpenny, snail mail 10 cataphract, direct mail, Post Office 11 chain armour, general post, surface mail 12 all-up service, iron-cladding, postal system, recorded mail 13 postal service 14 communications, correspondence, electronic mail, first-class mail, registered mail 15 second-class mail, special delivery

• **Royal Mail**
02 RM

**mail-coach**
04 drag

**maim**
03 mar 04 hurt, lame, main 05 wound 06 impair, injure, injury, scotch 07 cripple, cut down, disable 08 crippled, mutilate, truncate 09 disfigure 10 disability 12 incapacitate 14 put out of action

**main**
03 key, sea 04 duct, head, lame, lead, line, maim, pipe 05 cable, chief, first, grand, great, major, prime, sheer, vital 06 staple, strong 07 capital, central, channel, conduit, crucial, general, leading, pivotal, premier, primary, purpose, supreme 08 cardinal, critical, dominant, foremost, strength 09 essential, extensive, important, necessary, paramount, principal 10 pre-eminent 11 exceedingly, fundamental, outstanding, predominant 13 most important

• **in the main**
06 mostly 07 as a rule, chiefly, largely, usually 08 commonly 09 generally, in general 10 by and large, especially, on the whole 14 for the most part

**Maine**
02 ME

**mainly**
**04** much **06** mostly **07** as a rule, chiefly, largely, overall, usually **08** above all, commonly **09** generally, in general, in the main, primarily **10** by and large, especially, on the whole **11** principally **13** predominantly **14** for the most part

**mainspring**
**05** cause **06** motive, origin, reason, source **07** impulse **09** generator, incentive **10** motivation, prime mover, wellspring **11** inspiration **12** driving force, fountainhead

**mainstay**
**04** base, prop **05** basis **06** anchor, pillar **07** bulwark, support **08** backbone, buttress, linchpin **09** key player **10** foundation **11** cornerstone **12** right-hand man **14** right-hand woman **15** tower of strength

**mainstream**
**06** normal **07** average, central, general, regular, typical **08** accepted, mainline, orthodox, received, standard **11** established **12** conventional

**maintain**
**04** aver, avow, feed, hold, keep **05** carry, claim, escot, state **06** affirm, assert, avouch, defend, insist, keep up, retain, supply, uphaud, uphold **07** believe, care for, carry on, contend, declare, finance, nourish, nurture, observe, possess, profess, stand by, support, sustain **08** announce, conserve, continue, fight for, practise, preserve **09** keep going, look after **10** asseverate, perpetuate, provide for, take care of

**maintenance**
**04** care, keep **05** title **06** living, upkeep **07** aliment, alimony, defence, feeding, keeping, nurture, repairs, running, support **08** altarage, appanage **09** allowance, financing **10** carrying-on, livelihood, protection, sustenance **11** continuance, nourishment, subsistence, traineeship **12** conservation, continuation, perpetuation, preservation

**maize**
**03** Zea **04** corn, maze, samp **05** maise, mealy, mease, stamp **06** hominy, mealie **07** mealies, popcorn **09** flint corn, sweetcorn **10** Indian corn, Indian meal, masa harina **12** corn on the cob

• **maize dough**
**04** masa

• **maize loaf**
**04** pone

• **styles of maize**
**04** silk

**majestic**
**05** grand, lofty, noble, regal, royal **06** august, kingly, lordly, superb **07** awesome, exalted, pompous, queenly, stately, sublime **08** elevated, glorious, imperial, imposing, princely, splendid **09** dignified **10** impressive, marvellous, monumental **11** magnificent, resplendent **13** distinguished

**majestically**
**05** nobly **07** grandly, regally, royally, stately **08** maestoso, superbly **09** pompously, sublimely **10** gloriously, imperially, splendidly **12** impressively, marvellously **13** magnificently, resplendently

**majesty**
**04** pomp **05** glory **06** beauty, Tuanku **07** dignity, royalty **08** grandeur, nobility, regality **09** grandness, loftiness, nobleness, splendour, sublimity **11** awesomeness, exaltedness, stateliness **12** magnificence, majesticness, resplendence **14** impressiveness, majesticalness

• **Her Majesty**
**02** ER, HM **06** Brenda

• **His Majesty**
**02** HM

**major**
**03** key, Maj **04** best, main **05** chief, great, older, prime, vital **06** bigger, higher, larger, senior **07** crucial, greater, highest, keynote, largest, leading, notable, serious, supreme, weighty **08** greatest, superior **09** important, paramount, uppermost **10** pre-eminent **11** outstanding, significant

**majority**
**04** bulk, many, mass, most **07** general, manhood, the many **08** legal age, maturity **09** adulthood, nearly all, plurality, womanhood **10** generality, larger part, lion's share **11** coming of age, greater part, pre-eminence **12** age of consent, larger number, more than half **13** greater number, preponderance **15** reaching full age

**make**
◊ *anagram indicator*
**02** do **03** fix, get, mag, net, win **04** cook, earn, flow, form, gain, give, kind, maik, mark, mate, name, sort, tell, tend, turn, type, urge, vote **05** act as, add up, brand, build, cause, clear, drive, elect, equal, erect, force, frame, gross, impel, model, mould, offer, press, put up, reach, score, shape, start, state, style, total, write **06** become, coerce, come to, commit, compel, convey, create, devise, draw up, effect, impart, marque, matter, oblige, obtain, ordain, reckon, render, result, secure, select, settle, vote in, wrap up **07** achieve, acquire, add up to, appoint, arrange, attempt, bring in, chalk up, compose, compute, consort, convert, declare, deliver, dragoon, execute, fashion, install, notch up, perform, prepare, proceed, produce, promote, realize, require, serve as, shuffle, texture, think up, turn out, variety, work out **08** amount to, arrive at, assemble, bulldoze, carry out, comprise, conclude, contract, engender, estimate, generate, get ready, nominate, occasion, pressure, reckon up, set forth, take home **09** calculate, character, constrain, construct, designate, determine, discharge, establish, fabricate, formation, formulate, get down to, halfpenny, originate, pronounce, strongarm, structure, undertake **10** accomplish, bring about, constitute, contribute, function as, give rise to, perpetrate, pressurize **11** communicate, disposition, manufacture, mass-produce, prevail upon, put together **12** be to blame for **13** play the part of, play the role of **14** put the screws on **15** deliver the goods

*See also* **halfpenny**

• **make away with**
**03** nab, rid **04** do in, kill, lift, nick **05** pinch, seize, steal, swipe **06** kidnap, murder, remove, snatch **07** bump off, destroy **08** carry off, fetch off, knock off **09** slaughter **10** do away with, run off with **11** assassinate, walk off with

• **make believe**
**03** act **04** play **05** dream, enact, feign **07** imagine, play-act, pretend **09** fantasize

• **make do**
**04** cope **05** get by **06** manage **07** make out, survive **08** get along, scrape by **09** improvise **13** muddle through

• **make for**
**06** aim for, favour, lead to **07** forward, further, head for, produce, promote **09** go towards **10** facilitate **11** move towards **12** contribute to **13** be conducive to

• **make it**
**05** get on, reach **06** arrive **07** prosper, succeed, survive **11** come through, pull through **12** be successful

• **make of**
**04** rate **05** judge **06** assess, regard **07** think of, weigh up **08** consider, evaluate

• **make off**
**03** fly **04** bolt **05** brush, leave, mosey, truss **06** beat it, decamp, depart, hook it, pop off, run off **07** run away, scarper **08** clear off, up sticks **09** cut and run, shemozzle, skedaddle **12** make a getaway **15** take to your heels

• **make off with**
**03** nab **04** flog, nick, take **05** filch, pinch, steal, swipe **06** abduct, kidnap, pilfer **07** purloin **08** carry off, knock off **10** run off with **11** appropriate, walk off with

• **make out**
**03** get, see, spy **04** aver, bang, bonk, cope, espy, fare, read, scan, shag **05** claim, get by, get on, grasp, imply, prove, screw, spell **06** affirm, assert, descry, detect, divine, draw up, fathom, fill in, follow, manage **07** achieve, declare, discern, fill out, succeed, work out **08** complete, decipher, describe, discover, get along, maintain, make love, perceive,

progress, write out **09** establish, recognize **10** bear in hand, comprehend, understand **11** demonstrate, distinguish, manage to see **12** manage to hear **13** sleep together **14** get your leg over

**• make over**
**05** leave **06** assign, convey **07** dispone, dispose **08** bequeath, sign over, transfer

**• make the rounds of**
**02** do

**• make up**
◇ *anagram indicator*
**04** fill, form, meet **05** feign, frame, hatch, paint, rouge **06** create, decide, devise, doll up, invent, parcel, powder, render, repair, repent, settle, supply, tart up **07** arrange, collect, compose, concoct, dream up, perfume, provide, think up **08** complete, compound, comprise, round off **09** construct, fabricate, formulate, make peace, originate **10** constitute, shake hands, supplement **11** call it quits, put make-up on **12** be reconciled **13** Birminghamize, put on your face **14** bury the hatchet

**• make up for**
**06** offset **07** redress **08** atone for **13** compensate for, make amends for

**• make up to**
**03** eik, eke **05** court **06** chat up, cozy up, fawn on **07** toady to **08** butter up, suck up to **10** compensate, cozy up with **15** curry favour with, make overtures to

**• make way**
**06** gather **07** advance, gangway **11** allow to pass, clear the way, make room for **12** make space for, stand back for **14** allow to succeed

**make-believe**
**04** mock, sham **05** dream **06** made-up, unreal **07** charade, fantasy, feigned, pretend **08** dreaming, imagined, imitated, pretence, pretense, role-play **09** imaginary, pretended, simulated, unreality **10** fantasized, masquerade, play-acting **11** daydreaming, fabrication, imagination

**maker**
**06** author, wright **07** builder, creator, deviser **08** director, producer, repairer **09** architect **10** fabricator **11** constructor **12** manufacturer

**makeshift**
**06** cutcha, make-do **07** Band-aid®, fig leaf, stand-by, stopgap **08** pis aller **09** expedient, impromptu, temporary, timenoguy **10** improvised, substitute **11** provisional, rudimentary **13** rough and ready **14** thrown together **15** cobbled together

**make-up**
◇ *anagram indicator*
**04** form, slap **05** get-up, paint, style **06** format, nature, powder, temper **07** pancake **08** assembly, panstick, war paint **09** blackface, character, cosmetics, formation, structure, whiteface **10** foundation, maquillage **11** arrangement, composition, disposition, greasepaint, personality, temperament **12** constitution, construction, organization **13** configuration

**making**
**04** form **06** income **07** forging, profits, promise, returns, revenue, takings **08** assembly, building, capacity, creating, creation, earnings, moulding, proceeds **09** materials, modelling, potential, producing, qualities, structure **10** beginnings, capability, production **11** composition, fabrication, ingredients, manufacture **12** construction, potentiality **13** possibilities

**• in the making**
**06** coming **07** budding, nascent **08** emergent **09** incipient, potential, promising **10** burgeoning, developing **11** up and coming

**maladjusted**
◇ *anagram indicator*
**04** gaga **05** dotty **06** psycho, schizo **08** confused, neurotic, unstable **09** alienated, disturbed, estranged, screwed-up **10** disordered **12** round the bend

**maladministration**
**07** misrule **08** bungling **09** stupidity **10** blundering, corruption, dishonesty, misconduct **11** malfeasance, malpractice, misfeasance, mishandling **12** incompetence, inefficiency, malversation **13** misgovernment, mismanagement

**maladroit**
**05** inept **06** clumsy, gauche **07** awkward, unhandy **08** bungling, ill-timed, inexpert, tactless, untoward **09** graceless, ham-fisted, inelegant, unskilful **10** cack-handed **11** insensitive, thoughtless **12** undiplomatic **13** inconsiderate

**maladroitness**
**10** clumsiness, inelegance, ineptitude **11** awkwardness **12** tactlessness **13** gracelessness, insensitivity, unskilfulness **15** thoughtlessness

**malady**
**07** ailment, disease, illness, malaise **08** disorder, sickness **09** breakdown, complaint, infirmity **10** affliction **13** indisposition
*See also* **disease**

**malaise**
**05** angst **06** unease **07** anguish, anxiety, disease, illness **08** disquiet, doldrums, sickness, weakness **09** lassitude, weariness **10** depression, discomfort, discontent, enervation, melancholy, uneasiness **11** unhappiness **12** restlessness **13** indisposition

**malapropism**
**06** misuse **08** slipslop, solecism **09** wrong word **10** infelicity **11** Dogberryism **14** misapplication **15** slip of the tongue

**malapropos**
**05** inapt **07** inaptly **08** ill-timed, tactless, unseemly, untimely **10** inapposite, misapplied, tactlessly, unsuitable, unsuitably **11** inopportune, uncalled-for **12** inappositely, unseasonably **13** inappropriate, inopportunely **15** inappropriately

**malaria**
**04** ague

**Malawi**
**02** MW **03** MWI

**Malaysia**
**03** MAL, MYS

**malcontent**
**05** fed up, rebel **06** grouch, moaner, morose **07** aginner, grouser, restive, unhappy, whinger **08** agitator, grumbler **09** nit-picker, resentful **10** bellyacher, cheesed off, complainer, rebellious **11** bellyaching, disaffected, disgruntled, dissentious, ill-disposed, unsatisfied **12** discontented, dissatisfied, fault-finding, troublemaker **13** mischief-maker

**Maldives**
**03** MDV

**male**
**01** m **02** he **03** dog, man, tom **04** bull, cock, mail, stag **05** macho, manly **06** armour, boyish, virile **07** laddish, manlike **09** masculine, staminate
*See also* **animal**

**malediction**
**04** oath, wish **05** curse **07** cursing, damning, malison **08** anathema **09** damnation **10** execration **11** imprecation **12** denunciation

**malefactor**
**05** crook, felon **06** outlaw **07** convict, culprit, villain **08** criminal, evildoer, offender **09** miscreant, misfeasor, wrongdoer **10** delinquent, lawbreaker **12** transgressor

**malevolence**
**04** hate **05** spite, venom **06** hatred, malice **07** cruelty, ill-will, rancour **09** hostility, malignity **10** bitterness, fierceness, malignancy **11** viciousness **12** spitefulness, vengefulness **13** maliciousness **14** unfriendliness, vindictiveness

**malevolent**
**05** cruel **06** bitter, fierce, malign **07** baleful, hostile, vicious **08** spiteful, vengeful, venomous **09** malicious, rancorous, resentful **10** evil-minded, ill-natured, maleficent, pernicious, unfriendly, vindictive

**• malevolent being**
**04** peri

**malevolently**
**07** cruelly **08** bitterly, fiercely **09** viciously **10** spitefully, vengefully,

venomously **11** maliciously, resentfully **13** vindicatively

**malformation**
**04** warp **09** deformity **10** distortion **12** irregularity **13** disfigurement, misshapenness

**malformed**
◇ *anagram indicator*
**04** bent **06** warped **07** crooked, twisted **08** deformed **09** distorted, irregular, misshapen **10** disfigured

**malfunction**
◇ *anagram indicator*
**04** fail, flaw **05** crash, fault **06** defect, glitch, go phut, hiccup, pack up **07** conk out, failure, go kaput, go wrong **08** disorder, hiccough **09** break down, breakdown **11** stop working

**Mali**
**03** MLI, RMM

**malice**
**04** hate **05** spite, venom **06** animus, enmity, hatred, spleen **07** despite, ill-will, rancour **08** bad blood **09** animosity, hostility **10** bitchiness, bitterness, bone to pick, resentment **11** malevolence **13** maliciousness **14** vindictiveness

**malicious**
**04** evil, mean **05** snide **06** bitchy, bitter, malign **07** baleful, hostile, vicious **08** narquois, spiteful, vengeful, venomous **09** poisonous, rancorous, resentful **10** dispiteous, evil-minded, ill-natured, malevolent, pernicious **11** mischievous

**maliciously**
**08** bitterly **09** unhappily, viciously **10** spitefully, venomously **11** resentfully **12** malevolently, perniciously

**malign**
**03** bad **04** bait, evil, harm, slur **05** abuse, libel, smear **06** defame, injure, insult, vilify **07** baleful, envenom, harmful, hostile, hurtful, run down, slander, traduce **08** badmouth, sinister **09** disparage, injurious, malignant, misintend, poor-mouth **10** calumniate, malevolent **11** destructive **13** stab in the back **14** kick in the teeth

**malignancy**
**08** fatality **09** lethality, mortality, virulence **12** incurability

**malignant**
**04** evil **05** black, fatal, swart **06** deadly, lethal, malign, sullen, swarth **07** baleful, harmful, hostile, hurtful, vicious **08** cankered, Cavalier, devilish, Royalist, spiteful, venomous, viperous, virulent **09** cancerous, dangerous, incurable, injurious, malicious, poisonous, rancorous **10** malevolent, pernicious, rebellious **11** destructive, disaffected **14** uncontrollable **15** life-threatening

**malignity**
**04** gall, hate **05** spite, venom **06** animus, hatred, malice, taking **07** ill-will, rancour **08** bad blood **09** animosity, hostility, virulence **10** bitterness, deadliness, wickedness **11** balefulness, harmfulness, hurtfulness, malevolence, viciousness **12** vengefulness **13** maliciousness **14** perniciousness, vindictiveness **15** destructiveness

**malinger**
**04** loaf **05** dodge, shirk, skive, skulk, slack **07** pretend, put it on **09** gold-brick **12** swing the lead **14** pretend to be ill

**malingerer**
**06** dodger, loafer, skiver **07** shirker, slacker **11** lead-swinger

**mall**
**04** beat, maul, mell, walk **05** plaza **06** arcade **08** galleria, precinct **13** outlet village **14** shopping centre **15** shopping complex

**mallard**
**08** wild duck
• **mallard flock**
**04** sord

**malleability**
**07** pliancy **08** softness **10** compliance, plasticity, pliability, suppleness **11** ductileness, flexibility **12** adaptability **13** manageability, receptiveness, tractableness **14** susceptibility

**malleable**
◇ *anagram indicator*
**04** soft **06** pliant, supple **07** ductile, plastic, pliable **08** biddable, flexible, tractile, workable, yielding **09** adaptable, compliant, receptive, tractable **10** governable, manageable **11** persuadable, susceptible **14** impressionable

**mallow**
**04** sida

**malnourished**
**06** hungry **07** starved **08** anorexic, underfed **09** anorectic **14** undernourished

**malnutrition**
**06** hunger **08** anorexia **09** inanition **10** starvation **12** underfeeding **13** unhealthy diet **15** anorexia nervosa

**malodorous**
**04** rank **05** fetid, niffy **06** foetid, putrid, smelly **07** miasmal, miasmic, noisome, reeking **08** mephitic, miasmous, stinking **09** miasmatic, offensive **10** infragrant, miasmatous, nauseating **12** evil-smelling, foul-smelling

**malpractice**
**05** abuse **07** misdeed, offence **10** misconduct, negligence, wrongdoing **11** impropriety **12** carelessness **13** mismanagement

**malt**
**04** wort

**Malta**
**01** M **03** MLT

**maltreat**
◇ *anagram indicator*
**04** harm, hurt, maul **05** abuse, bully, hound **06** damage, injure, misuse **07** torture **08** ill-treat, mistreat **09** mishandle, victimize **10** rough-house, treat badly **11** assassinate

**maltreatment**
**04** harm, hurt **05** abuse **06** damage, ill-use, injury, misuse **07** torture **08** bullying, ill-usage **12** ill-treatment, mistreatment **13** victimization

**mammal**

*Mammals include:*

**03** ape, ass, bat, cat, cow, dog, elk, fox, gnu, pig, rat, yak
**04** bear, boar, cavy, deer, goat, hare, ibex, kudu, lion, lynx, mink, mole, paca, puma, seal, soor, tahr, vole, wolf, zebu
**05** aguti, bison, camel, civet, coney, coypu, dingo, eland, genet, hippo, horse, human, hyena, hyrax, koala, lemur, llama, loris, moose, mouse, okapi, otter, ounce, panda, potto, rhino, sheep, shrew, skunk, sloth, stoat, takin, tapir, tiger, whale, zebra
**06** aye-aye, baboon, badger, beaver, beluga, bobcat, cattle, colugo, cougar, coyote, cuscus, dassie, dugong, duiker, ermine, ferret, galago, gerbil, gibbon, gopher, hacker, impala, jackal, jaguar, jerboa, langur, marmot, marten, monkey, numbat, ocelot, possum, rabbit, racoon, reebok, rhebok, sea cow, serval, tenrec, vicuna, walrus, wapiti, weasel, wombat
**07** ant-bear, bosvark, buffalo, caracal, caribou, chamois, cheetah, dolphin, echidna, fur seal, gazelle, gerenuk, giraffe, gorilla, grampus, grizzly, guanaco, guereza, gymnura, hamster, lemming, leopard, macaque, manatee, meercat, meerkat, mole rat, muntjac, muskrat, narwhal, opossum, pack rat, panther, peccary, polecat, primate, raccoon, red deer, roe deer, sea lion, sun bear, tamarin, tarsier, wallaby, warthog, wild ass, wildcat
**08** aardvark, aardwolf, anteater, antelope, bushbaby, bushbuck, capybara, chipmunk, dormouse, duckbill, elephant, fruit bat, grey wolf, harp seal, hedgehog, house bat, kangaroo, mandrill, mangabey, marmoset, mongoose, musk deer, pacarana, pangolin, platypus, porpoise, reedbuck, reindeer, sea otter, sewer rat, squirrel, steenbok, steinbok, talapoin, wild goat
**09** Arctic fox, armadillo, bamboo rat, bandicoot, black bear, blue sheep, blue whale, brown bear, dromedary, flying fox, grey whale, grindhval, guinea pig, jungle cat,

mouse-deer, orang utan, palm civet, phalanger, polar bear, porcupine, springbok, steinbuck, thylacine, waterbuck, wolverine

**10** Barbary ape, chevrotain, chimpanzee, chinchilla, coatimundi, common seal, fallow deer, field mouse, giant panda, hartebeest, house mouse, human being, jack rabbit, kodiak bear, pilot whale, pine marten, prairie dog, rhinoceros, sperm whale, springbuck, springhare, vampire bat, white whale, wildebeest

**11** beaked whale, flying lemur, green monkey, grizzly bear, honey badger, killer whale, muntjac deer, pipistrelle, rat kangaroo, red squirrel, snow leopard

**12** Arabian camel, barbary sheep, elephant seal, grey squirrel, harvest mouse, hippopotamus, leaf-nosed bat, mountain goat, mountain lion, rhesus monkey, river dolphin, spider monkey, two-toed sloth, vervet monkey, water buffalo

**13** American bison, Bactrian camel, colobus monkey, dwarf antelope, elephant shrew, European bison, hanuman monkey, howling monkey, humpback whale, marsupial mole, mouse-eared bat, spiny anteater, Tasmanian wolf

**14** capuchin monkey, edible dormouse, flying squirrel, Indian elephant, marsupial mouse, mountain beaver, Patagonian hare, squirrel monkey, Tasmanian devil, three-toed sloth

**15** African elephant, black rhinoceros, brushtail possum, hamadryas baboon, humpbacked whale, proboscis monkey, ring-tailed lemur, Thomson's gazelle, white rhinoceros

---

*See also* **animal**; **ape**; **cat**; **cattle**; **deer**; **dog**; **horse**; **marsupial**; **monkey**; **pig**; **rodent**; **sheep**; **whale**

## mammoth

**04** huge, vast **05** giant, jumbo **06** bumper, mighty **07** immense, massive **08** colossal, enormous, gigantic, whopping **09** ginormous, herculean, leviathan **10** gargantuan, monumental, prodigious, stupendous **14** Brobdingnagian

## man

**01** b, k, m, n, p, q, r **02** bo, he, Mr, ou **03** boy, guy, IOM, lad, mun, pin **04** chap, crew, gent, hand, homo, jack, king, male, page, pawn, rook, work **05** adult, bloke, cairn, human, lover, piece, queen, staff, valet **06** bishop, castle, fellow, fiancé, geezer, helper, knight, Mister, mortal, occupy, people, person, spouse, toy boy, vassal, worker **07** chequer, draught, husband, mankind, mortals, operate, partner, servant, soldier, workman **08** employee, factotum, follower, houseboy, houseman, humanity, labourer **09** attendant, boyfriend, gentleman, humankind, human race, odd-jobman **10** human being, individual, manservant, sweetheart **11** Homo sapiens, human beings **12** be in charge of, man-of-all-work, take charge of **15** jack-of-all-trades

*See also* **boy**; **chess**

### • first man

**04** Adam

### • good man

**01** S **02** St **04** sant **05** Saint

### • old man *see* old man

### • to a man

**05** as one **07** bar none **09** one and all **11** unanimously **12** with one voice

### • wise man

**04** mage, sage **05** magus

## manacle

**03** tie **04** bind, curb **05** chain, check **06** fetter, hamper, secure **07** inhibit, shackle **08** handcuff, restrain **11** put in chains

## manacles

**05** bonds, cuffs, gyves, irons **06** chains **07** darbies, fetters, mittens, nippers **08** shackles **09** bracelets, handcuffs, snitchers, wristlets

## manage

**03** ren, rin, run, use **04** boss, cope, fare, head, keep, lead, play, rule, work **05** cut it, get by, get on, guide, shift, wield **06** direct, effect, govern, handle, head up, honcho, make do, manure, master **07** achieve, carry on, command, conduct, control, make out, operate, oversee, solicit, succeed, survive **08** be head of, bring off, contrive, deal with, engineer, get along, maneuver, navigate, organize **09** influence, manoeuvre, negotiate, supervise **10** accomplish, administer, bring about, manipulate **11** preside over, superintend **12** be in charge of

## manageable

**04** yare **05** handy **06** doable, docile, pliant, viable, wieldy **07** pliable **08** amenable, feasible, flexible, yielding **09** compliant, easy-to-use, tolerable, tractable **10** acceptable, attainable, functional, governable, reasonable, submissive **11** practicable **12** controllable **13** accommodating

## management

**04** care **05** admin, board **06** bosses, charge, owners, ruling **07** command, conduct, control, dispose, running **08** disposal, handling, managers, ordering **09** direction, directors, employers, executive, governall, governors, husbandry, stewardry, treatment **10** executives, government, intendance, intendancy, leadership, overseeing **11** directorate, proprietors, stewardship, supervision, supervisors **12** organization **14** administration **15** superintendence

## manager

**02** GM **03** guv, Mgr **04** boss, head, suit **05** agent, chair, chief **06** gaffer, honcho, serang **07** amildar, husband, planter, proctor **08** chairman, director, employer, governor, hotelier, landlady, landlord, motelier, overseer **09** conductor, contriver, directrix, executive, intendant, organizer, president, régisseur **10** chairwoman, controller, directress, head-bummer, head serang, impresario, manageress, procurator, supervisor **11** businessman, chairperson, comptroller, land-steward **12** commissioner, maître d'hôtel, manufacturer **13** administrator, businesswoman **14** chief executive, superintendent

## managerial

**09** executive **10** industrial **11** legislative, supervisory **12** departmental, governmental **14** administrative, organizational, superintendent **15** entrepreneurial

## mandate

**02** OK **03** law, let **04** okay **05** allow, edict, order **06** charge, decree, enable, permit, ratify, ruling **07** approve, bidding, command, confirm, dictate, empower, entitle, licence, precept, statute, warrant **08** legalize, sanction, validate **09** authority, authorize, consent to, direction, directive, make legal, ordinance **10** commission, injunction, king's brief **11** instruction **13** authorization **15** give authority to

## mandatory

**07** binding **08** required **09** essential, necessary, requisite **10** compulsory, imperative, obligatory

## manful

**04** bold **05** brave, hardy, manly, noble, stout **06** daring, heroic, strong **07** gallant, valiant **08** intrepid, powerful, resolute, stalwart, vigorous **09** steadfast **10** courageous, determined **11** indomitable, lion-hearted, noble-minded, unflinching **12** stout-hearted

## manfully

**04** hard **05** nobly **06** boldly **07** bravely, man-like, stoutly **08** pluckily, strongly **09** gallantly, valiantly **10** heroically, intrepidly, powerfully, resolutely, stalwartly, vigorously **11** desperately, steadfastly **12** courageously, determinedly **13** unflinchingly

## manganese

**02** Mn

### • manganese ore

**03** wad **04** wadd, wadt

## manger

**04** crib **06** cratch, feeder, trough **13** feeding trough

## mangle

◇ *anagram indicator*

**03** cut, mar **04** hack, maim, maul, rend, ruin, tear **05** botch, crush, mouth, spoil, twist, wreck **06** bungle, deform, garble, haggle, mess up **07** butcher, destroy, distort, mammock, screw up

08 calender, lacerate, mutilate
09 disfigure 11 make a hash of, make a mess of

**mangy**
04 mean, worn 05 dirty, seedy, tatty
06 filthy, scabby, shabby, shoddy
07 roynish, scruffy 08 cowardly
09 moth-eaten

**manhandle**
03 tug 04 haul, hump, maul, pull, push
05 abuse, heave, shove 06 jostle, misuse 07 rough up 08 maltreat, mistreat 10 knock about 13 handle roughly

**manhood**
08 machismo, maleness, maturity, virility 09 adulthood, manliness
10 manfulness 11 masculinity

**mania**
03 fad 04 rage, urge 05 craze, thing
06 desire, fetish, frenzy, lunacy, raving
07 craving, madness, passion
08 dementia, disorder, fixation, hysteria, insanity, wildness
09 craziness, gold-fever, obsession, psychosis, tarantism 10 aberration, compulsion, enthusiasm
11 derangement, fascination, infatuation 13 preoccupation

*Manias include:*

08 egomania
09 cynomania, demomania, ergomania, infomania, logomania, melomania, monomania, oenomania, opsomania, pyromania, theomania, tomomania, xenomania
10 anthomania, dipsomania, erotomania, hippomania, hydromania, methomania, metromania, mythomania, narcomania, necromania, nostomania
11 ablutomania, acronymania, ailuromania, bibliomania, cleptomania, demonomania, etheromania, graphomania, hedonomania, kleptomania, megalomania, nymphomania, technomania, toxicomania
12 arithmomania, balletomania, pteridomania, thanatomania, theatromania
13 flagellomania, morphinomania
14 eleutheromania

**maniac**
03 fan, nut 04 buff, kook 05 crank, fiend, freak, loony 06 madman, nutter, psycho 07 cupcake, fanatic, lunatic, nutcase, oddball 08 crackpot, headcase, madwoman 09 fruitcake, psychotic, screwball 10 enthusiast, psychopath 14 deranged person

**manic**
◇ *anagram indicator*
03 mad 04 amok, wild 05 barmy, batty, crazy, daffy, dippy, loopy 06 crazed, hectic, insane, raving 07 berserk, frantic, furious 08 demented, deranged, feverish, frenetic, frenzied
09 desperate, obsessive 10 distracted, distraught, hysterical 11 overwrought
12 uncontrolled 13 panic-stricken
14 beside yourself

**manically**
◇ *anagram indicator*
05 madly 06 wildly 09 excitedly, intensely 10 hectically 12 frenetically, hysterically

**manifest**
◇ *anagram indicator*
04 open, shew, show 05 clear, plain, prove 06 appear, attest, evince, expose, patent, reveal 07 blatant, confess, declare, display, evident, exhibit, express, glaring, obvious, present, visible 08 apparent, distinct, indicate, set forth 09 establish, extrovert, make clear, make plain, show forth 10 illustrate, noticeable
11 conspicuous, demonstrate, perceptible, transparent, unconcealed
12 be evidence of, unmistakable
13 unmistakeable

**manifestation**
◇ *anagram indicator*
04 mark, mode, show, sign 05 gleam, glory, token 06 avatar, reflex 07 display
08 Epiphany, evidence, exposure
09 theophany 10 appearance, disclosure, exhibition, exposition, expression, indication, revelation
11 angelophany, declaration, incarnation 12 illustration, presentation 13 demonstration
14 representation 15 exemplification

**manifesto**
08 platform, policies 09 programme, statement 11 declaration, publication
12 announcement, proclamation
14 pronunciamento

**manifold**
04 many 06 varied 07 copious, diverse, several, various
08 abundant, multiple, multiply, numerous 09 aggregate
12 multifarious 13 kaleidoscopic, multitudinous

**manipulate**
◇ *anagram indicator*
03 cog, ply, rig, use 04 cook, hand, milk, tong, work 05 fit up, frame, guide, knead, nurse, steer, wield
06 direct, doctor, employ, fiddle, handle, juggle, manage, wangle
07 control, exploit, falsify, finesse, massage, operate, process, shuffle, utilize 08 cash in on, engineer
09 influence, manoeuvre, negotiate
10 juggle with, tamper with, thimblerig
11 gerrymander, pull strings
12 capitalize on, wheel and deal
15 have over a barrel

**manipulation**
◇ *anagram indicator*
05 using 07 control, massage, milking, rigging, working 08 fiddling, guidance, handling, juggling, kneading, steering, wangling, wielding 09 directing, doctoring, influence, massaging, operation 11 manoeuvring, negotiation, utilization 12 exploitation, mobilization 13 falsification 14 pulling strings 15 cooking the books

**manipulative**
03 sly 04 foxy, wily 06 artful, crafty, tricky 07 cunning, devious
08 scheming, slippery 09 conniving, deceitful, designing, insidious, underhand 11 calculating, duplicitous
12 unscrupulous 13 Machiavellian

**manipulator**
04 user 05 slave 06 worker 07 handler, schemer, smoothy, wielder
08 director, engineer, operator, smart guy 09 exploiter 10 controller, influencer, manoeuvrer, negotiator, wirepuller 13 wheeler-dealer

**Manitoba**
02 MB

**mankind**
03 man 05 flesh 06 Bimana, people, public 07 mortals 08 humanity
09 humankind, human race 11 Homo sapiens, human beings

**manliness**
06 mettle, valour, vigour 07 bravery, courage, heroism, manhood
08 boldness, firmness, machismo, maleness, strength, virility
09 fortitude, hardihood
10 manfulness, resolution
11 intrepidity, masculinity
12 fearlessness, independence, resoluteness, stalwartness

**manly**
04 bold, firm, male 05 brave, macho, noble, tough 06 heroic, manful, robust, rugged, strong, sturdy, virile
08 fearless, intrepid, powerful, vigorous 09 dignified, masculine
10 courageous, determined

**man-made**
04 faux, mock 06 ersatz 09 imitation, simulated, synthetic 10 artificial
12 manufactured

**manna**
07 trehala 08 honeydew

**manner**
03 air, how, way 04 form, look, mien, mode 05 means, style 06 aspect, custom, mainor, method, stance
07 bearing, conduct, decorum, fashion, posture, process, p's and q's, routine, variety 08 approach, attitude, courtesy, good form, practice, protocol
09 behaviour, character, demeanour, etiquette, procedure, propriety, technique 10 appearance, deportment, politeness 11 formalities
12 social graces, the done thing 13 way of behaving

- **in the manner of**

02 as, of 03 à la, per

- **unconstrained manner**

04 ease

**mannered**
**05** posed, put-on **06** pseudo, thewed **07** stilted **08** affected, precious **10** artificial, euphuistic **11** pretentious

*See also* **bad-mannered**

**mannerism**
**05** habit, quirk, trait, trick **06** foible **07** feature **10** foreignism **11** peculiarity, stiltedness **12** idiosyncrasy **14** characteristic

**mannerly**
**05** civil **06** formal, polite **07** civilly, genteel, refined **08** decorous, gracious, ladylike, polished, well-bred **09** civilized, courteous **10** respectful **11** deferential, gentlemanly, well-behaved **12** well-mannered

**mannish**
**05** butch **07** laddish, mankind **09** Amazonian, masculine, tomboyish, unwomanly, viragoish **10** unfeminine, unladylike, viraginian, viraginous **11** virilescent

**mannishness**
**08** virilism **09** butchness **11** masculinity **12** unfemininity, virilescence **13** unwomanliness **14** unladylikeness

**manoeuvre**
◇ *anagram indicator*
**04** dock, ease, loop, move, pick, plan, plot, ploy, roll, ruse, turn **05** berth, cut in, dodge, drive, guide, pilot, stall, steer, trick **06** action, device, devise, direct, gambit, handle, jockey, manage, pesade, scheme, tactic, wangle **07** wheelie **08** alley-oop, artifice, contrive, engineer, exercise, intrigue, movement, navigate, snap roll, wingover **09** chandelle, checkmate, decursion, half board, negotiate, operation, stratagem **10** deployment, manipulate, subterfuge **11** machination, pull strings, skilful plan, victory roll **12** countermarch, manipulation, renversement **13** Immelmann turn

**manor**
**03** Hof **04** hall, seat, vill **05** house, villa **06** barony **07** château, Schloss **12** country house

**manpower**
**05** staff **07** workers **09** employees, personnel, workforce **14** human resources, skilled workers

**manse**
**07** deanery, rectory **08** vicarage **09** parsonage **10** glebe-house

**manservant**
**05** valet **06** butler, Jeeves **08** retainer **09** attendant

**mansion**
**04** casa, hall, home, seat **05** abode, house, manor, place, villa **06** castle **07** château, Schloss **08** dwelling **09** residence **10** habitation, manor-house

**manslaughter**
**06** murder **07** carnage, killing, slaying **08** butchery, fatality, genocide, homicide, massacre **09** bloodshed, execution, matricide, patricide, slaughter, uxoricide **10** fratricide, sororicide **11** destruction, elimination, infanticide, liquidation **13** assassination, extermination

**mantle**
**04** cape, hide, hood, mask, pall, veil, wrap **05** blush, cloak, cloud, cover, froth, layer, palla, shawl, vakas **06** bubble, capote, dolman, rochet, screen, shroud **07** blanket, conceal, envelop, obscure, pallium, pelisse, pluvial **08** covering, disguise, envelope **13** asthenosphere

**manual**
**03** ABC **05** bible, guide, human **06** by hand **07** cambist, positif **08** handbook, physical **09** companion, guidebook, portolano, vade-mecum **10** directions, mechanical, prospectus **11** book of words, enchiridion **12** encheiridion, hand-operated, instructions **13** with your hands **15** instruction book

**manually**
**06** by hand **10** physically **13** with your hands

**manufacture**
◇ *anagram indicator*
**04** form, make **05** build, forge, frame, model **06** create, devise, invent, make up, making **07** concoct, dream up, fashion, forming, process, produce, think up, turn out **08** assemble, assembly, building, creation **09** construct, fabricate, formation, modelling **10** fashioning, processing, production **11** fabrication, mass-produce, put together **12** construction **14** mass-production

**manufacturer**
**05** maker **07** builder, chemist, creator **08** producer **09** fabricant **10** paper-maker, soap boiler **11** chocolatier, constructor, tobacconist **12** factory-owner **13** industrialist

*See also* **car**

**manure**
**04** dung, hold, lime, muck, soil, tath **05** dress, guano, vraic **06** bedung, hen-pen, manage, occupy, ordure **07** compost **08** dressing **09** cultivate, droppings, fish-guano **10** composture, fertilizer **11** top-dressing **12** animal faeces, police-manure **15** animal excrement

**manuscript**
**02** MS **04** text **05** codex, paper **06** scroll, uncial, vellum **07** papyrus **08** document **09** autograph, minuscule, parchment **10** Mabinogion, palimpsest, typescript **12** opisthograph

**Manx**
◇ *tail deletion indicator*
**08** tailless

**many**
**01** C, D, K, L, M **04** a lot, lots, tons, wads **05** a mass, heaps, loads, piles, scads **06** a lot of, a wheen, hantle, lots of, masses, oodles, plenty, scores, stacks, sundry, varied **07** copious, diverse, several, umpteen, various **08** billions, hundreds, manifold, millions, multiple, numerous, zillions **09** countless, hoi polloi, thousands **10** a multitude **11** any number of, innumerable **12** a large number **13** multitudinous **14** a large number of

**Maori**

*Maori leaders include:*

**05** Ngata (Sir Apirana Turupa)
**06** Cooper (Dame Whina), Mahuta (Sir Robert), O'Regan (Sir Tipene), Pomare (Sir Maui), Ratana (Tuhupotiki Wiremu)
**07** Te Kooti (Arikirangi Te Turuki)
**09** Heke Potai (Hone Wiremu), Hongi Hika, Rua Kenana (Hepetipa)
**11** Te Rauparaha
**14** Te Heuheu Tukino (Sir Hepi)

*See also* **god, goddess**; **mythology**

**map**
**04** card, face, mark, plan, plot **05** atlas, chart, graph, inset **06** sketch **07** road-map **08** town plan **09** cartogram, delineate, gazetteer, horoscope, mappemond **10** projection, street plan **11** carte du pays, hypsography, planisphere, street guide **12** weather chart

• **map out**
**04** draw **05** draft **06** draw up, sketch **07** outline, work out

**maple**
**04** acer **05** mazer, plane **08** box elder, sycamore

**mapmakers**
**02** OS

**mar**
◇ *anagram indicator*
**04** harm, hurt, maim, ruin, scar **05** spoil, stain, sully, taint, wreck **06** damage, deface, deform, impair, injure, mangle, poison **07** blemish, tarnish **08** mutilate **09** disfigure, misguggle **10** mishguggle **11** contaminate, detract from

**maraud**
**04** loot, raid, sack **05** foray, harry **06** forage, ravage **07** despoil, pillage, plunder, raiding, ransack **08** spoliate **09** depredate **10** plundering

**marauder**
**05** rover **06** bandit, looter, mugger, outlaw, pirate, raider, robber **07** brigand, ravager, rustler **08** pillager, predator **09** buccaneer, plunderer **10** freebooter, highwayman

**marble**
**03** taw **04** ally, bool, bowl, dump, marl, onyx **05** agate, alley, bonce, touch **06** nicker, Parian **07** cipolin, knicker, paragon, plonker, plunker

08 commoney, onychite 09 cipollino, pavonazzo, scagliola 10 nero-antico 11 ophicalcite

**march**
03 Mar 04 demo, file, gait, hike, Lide, pace, step, trek, walk, yomp 05 étape, hikoi, stalk, strut, tramp, tread, troop 06 border, defile, parade, stride 07 advance, debouch, en route, forward, headway, passage, swagger 08 boundary, footslog, progress 09 evolution, paso doble 10 procession, route-march, walk-around 11 development, make headway 12 countermarch 13 demonstration

• **March 15**
04 Ides

• **section of march**
04 trio

**marches**
06 border 08 boundary, frontier, protests 10 borderland 14 border district

**mare**
04 yaud

**margarine**
04 oleo

**margin**
03 rim 04 brim, curb, edge, kerb, marg, play, rand, room, side, tail 05 bound, brink, extra, limit, marge, scope, skirt, space, verge 06 border, leeway, limits, spread 07 confine, surplus, whisker 08 boundary, confines, frontier, latitude 09 allowance, perimeter, periphery 10 difference 12 differential 15 demarcation line

**marginal**
03 low 04 marg, tiny 05 minor, small 06 minute, slight 07 minimal 08 doubtful 09 on the edge 10 borderline, negligible, peripheral 11 subordinate 13 insignificant

• **marginal note**
03 k'ri

• **of marginal value**
04 lean

**marginalization**
05 exile 08 solitude 09 aloneness, isolation, seclusion 10 alienation, detachment, loneliness, remoteness, retirement, separation, withdrawal 11 abstraction, segregation 12 dissociation, separateness, solitariness 13 disconnection, sequestration

**marginalize**
06 cut off, detach, maroon, remove, strand 07 divorce, exclude, isolate, seclude, shut out 08 abstract, alienate, separate, set apart, shut away 09 keep apart, ostracize, segregate, sequester 10 disconnect 12 cold-shoulder

**margosa**
03 nim 04 neem, nimb 05 Melia, neemb

**marijuana** *see* **cannabis**

**marina**
04 dock, port 07 harbour, mooring 12 yacht station

**marinade**
04 soak 05 imbue, souse, steep 06 infuse 07 immerse 08 marinate, permeate, saturate 09 chermoula, escabeche

**marine**
02 RM 03 sea 05 jolly, naval 06 bootee 07 aquatic, oceanic, pelagic 08 maritime, nautical, seagoing, seascape, seawater 09 saltwater, seafaring, thalassic 10 ocean-going, thalassian 11 leatherneck

**mariner**
02 AB 03 tar 04 salt 05 limey, matlo 06 matlow, sailor, sea dog, seaman 07 Jack Tar, matelot 08 deckhand, seafarer 09 navigator

*See also* **sailor**

**marital**
06 wedded 07 married, nuptial, spousal, wedding 08 conjugal, marriage 09 connubial 11 matrimonial

**maritally**
09 by wedlock, in wedlock, nuptially 10 by marriage, conjugally, in marriage 11 connubially 13 matrimonially

**maritime**
03 sea 05 naval 06 marine 07 coastal, oceanic, pelagic, seaside 08 littoral, nautical, sea-coast, seagoing, sea-trade 09 seafaring

**mark**
01 m 02 DM, mk, NB 03 aim, cut, dot, end, see, tag, tee, zit 04 blot, butt, chip, clue, dash, dent, dool, dule, flag, goal, heed, hint, keep, line, ling, logo, mind, name, nick, norm, note, scar, seal, sign, spot, stop, tatu, tick, tika, type 05 badge, brand, gauge, grade, issue, label, level, limit, model, motto, notch, patch, point, print, proof, scale, score, smear, speck, stage, stain, stamp, tally, token, trace, track 06 accent, assess, blotch, bruise, caract, denote, device, emblem, honour, listen, notice, object, picket, pimple, piquet, record, regard, smudge, smutch, stigma, symbol, target, tattoo, tattow, tittle, tracks, typify 07 blemish, correct, discern, feature, freckle, imprint, jot down, measure, observe, picquet, purpose, quality, scratch, signify, specify, symptom 08 appraise, boundary, bull's-eye, evaluate, evidence, identify, indicate, monogram, note down, remember, standard 09 attribute, birthmark, celebrate, character, criterion, designate, discolour, footprint, idiograph, intention, objective, recognize, represent, trademark, write down, yardstick 10 assessment, bear in mind, evaluation, impression, indication, percentage, take heed of, take note of 11 acknowledge, commemorate, distinguish, fingerprint, take to heart 12 characterize, fingerprints, pay tribute to 13 put your name on 14 characteristic, noteworthiness, pay attention to

• **encircling mark**
03 rim 04 ring

• **make your mark**
05 get on 06 make it 07 prosper, succeed 12 be successful, make the grade 13 hit the big time 14 make the big time

• **mark down**
03 cut 05 lower, slash 06 reduce 08 decrease

• **mark out**
03 fix 04 line 07 delimit, destine, measure 08 set apart 09 delineate, demarcate, designate, draw lines, single out, tell apart 11 distinguish 12 discriminate 13 differentiate

• **mark up**
05 put up, raise 06 hike up, jack up 08 increase

• **mark well**
02 nb 08 nota bene

• **miss mark**
03 err

• **up to the mark**
02 OK 10 acceptable, good enough 11 up to scratch 12 satisfactory

• **wide of the mark**
04 gone, wild 06 abroad, far out 09 imprecise, incorrect, off target 10 inaccurate, irrelevant 14 beside the point

**marked**
05 clear, noted, thick 06 doomed, pimply, signal, spotty, strong 07 blatant, blotchy, bruised, decided, evident, glaring, marcato, obvious, scarred, spotted, stained, watched 08 apparent, blotched, distinct, emphatic, freckled, striking 09 blemished, condemned, indicated, prominent, scratched, suspected 10 noticeable, pronounced, remarkable 11 conspicuous 12 considerable, unmistakable

**markedly**
07 clearly 08 signally 09 blatantly, decidedly, evidently, glaringly, obviously 10 distinctly, noticeably, remarkably, strikingly 11 prominently 12 considerably, emphatically, unmistakably 13 conspicuously

**marker**
03 dan, tag 04 buck, flag, goal 07 counter 08 bookmark, gybe mark, milepost, tidemark 09 milestone, stake boat

**market**
03 AIM, mkt, USM 04 call, fair, hawk, kerb, mall, mart, need, sale, sell, shop, souk, vent, want 05 agora, trade, value 06 bazaar, buying, demand, desire, outlet, peddle, retail 07 bargain, promote, selling, trading 08 business, dealings, exchange, industry, occasion, shambles 09 advertize 10 Smithfield 11 market-place, requirement 12 Billingsgate, Covent Garden, offer for sale 14 shopping centre

**• on the market**
06 on sale 07 for sale 09 available, up for sale

**marketable**
06 wanted 08 in demand, saleable, sellable, vendible 11 sought after 12 merchantable

**marketing**
04 hype 05 sales 07 pushing 08 plugging 09 promotion, publicity 11 advertising 12 distribution 13 merchandizing

**market-place**
03 suk 04 sook, souk, sukh, tron

**marksman, markswoman**
04 shot 06 sniper 07 deadeye 08 dead shot, free-shot, shootist, wing shot 09 crack shot 12 sharpshooter

**mark-up**
04 hike, leap, rise 07 upsurge 08 increase 10 escalation 13 price increase

**Marlowe**
03 Kit

**marmoset**
04 mico 07 jacchus, wistiti

**marmot**
05 bobac, bobak 08 whistler 09 woodchuck

**maroon**
05 leave 06 desert, strand 07 abandon, forsake, isolate 08 cast away 09 put ashore 11 leave behind 14 turn your back on 15 leave high and dry, leave in the lurch

**marriage**
04 link 05 match, noose, union 06 fusion, merger 07 spousal, wedding, wedlock 08 alliance, coupling, nuptials, shidduch, spousage, spousals 09 espousals, matrimony 10 connection 11 affiliation, association, combination, handfasting, partnership, unification 12 amalgamation, married state 13 confederation

*Marriage- and wedding-related terms include:*

03 vow, wed
04 ring, veil, wife
05 aisle, altar, banns, bride, dowry, elope, groom, in-law, usher, vicar
06 beenah, bigamy, digamy, favour, fiancé, garter, huppah, prenup, priest, speech, spouse
07 best man, betroth, bouquet, chuppah, consort, divorce, espouse, exogamy, fiancée, husband, Ketubah, marital, merchet, Mr Right, nuptial, page boy, propose, punalua, trigamy, wedding
08 bedright, best maid, confetti, conjugal, endogamy, hen night, jointure, levirate, maritage, minister, monogamy, monogyny, polygamy
09 annulment, coemption, common-law, communion, connubial, honeymoon, hope chest, horseshoe, hypergamy, love match, matrimony, other half, reception, registrar, stag night, trousseau
10 better half, bridesmaid, buttonhole, consortium, consummate, engagement, first dance, first night, flower girl, her indoors, him indoors, honeymonth, invitation, Lucy Stoner, maiden name, matrilocal, morganatic, patrilocal, separation, settlement, uxorilocal, wedding day
11 deuterogamy, dissolution, Gretna Green, handfasting, misalliance, morning gift, mother in-law, outmarriage, wedding cake, wedding list
12 bottom drawer, bridal shower, concubitancy, mariage blanc, open marriage, prothalamion, something new, something old, wedding dress, wedding march, wedding night
13 church service, civil marriage, hedge-marriage, holy matrimony, marriage-lines, something blue
14 matron of honour, pop the question, steal a marriage
15 chief bridesmaid, going-away outfit, marriage-licence, plight one's troth

**• promise of marriage**
04 hand

**married**
01 m 03 wed 05 wived, yoked 06 joined, united, wedded, wifely 07 hitched, marital, nuptial, spliced, spousal 08 conjugal 09 connubial, husbandly 11 matrimonial

**marrow**
03 nub 04 core, gist, like, mate, pith, soul 05 equal, heart, match, quick, stuff 06 centre, couple, kernel, spirit 07 essence, medulla, nucleus 08 zucchini 09 companion, courgette, substance 11 nitty-gritty 12 nuts and bolts, quintessence

**marry**
03 wad, wed 04 ally, fuse, join, knit, link, mate, weld, wive 05 cleek, elope, match, merge, unite 06 couple, indeed!, spouse 07 combine, connect, hitch up 08 forsooth! 09 affiliate, associate 10 amalgamate, get hitched, get married, get spliced, intermarry, take to wife, tie the knot 12 go to the world, join together 13 take the plunge 14 become espoused, lead to the altar, lead up the aisle 15 join in matrimony

**Mars**
04 Ares

**marsh**
03 bog, fen 04 mire, salt, wash 05 bayou, swamp 06 marish, morass, muskeg, salina, slough 07 corcass 08 quagmire 09 everglade, marshland 10 Everglades

**marshal**
◇ *anagram indicator*
04 lead, rank, take 05 align, array, group, guide, order, usher 06 deploy, draw up, escort, gather, line up, muster, parade 07 arrange, collect, conduct, dispose, farrier 08 assemble, organize, shepherd 09 mareschal, marischal 10 put in order 13 velt-mareschal 14 gather together

*Marshals include:*

03 Ney (Michel)
04 Earp (Wyatt), Foch (Ferdinand), Saxe (Maurice, Comte de), Tito
06 Hickok (Wild Bill), Pétain (Philippe), Tedder (Arthur, Lord), Zhukov (Georgi)
08 MacMahon (Patrice de)

*See also* **Field Marshal**

**Marshall Islands**
03 MHL

**marshy**
03 wet 04 miry 05 boggy, fenny, moory, muddy 06 quaggy, slumpy, spongy, swampy 07 fennish, moorish, paludal 08 paludine, paludose, paludous, squelchy 09 paludinal 10 paludinous 11 waterlogged

**marsupial**

*Marsupials include:*

03 roo
04 euro, tuan
05 koala, quoll
06 boodie, cuscus, glider, numbat, possum, quokka, tammar, wombat
07 bettong, dasyure, dibbler, dunnart, opossum, potoroo, wallaby
08 kangaroo, macropod, tarsiped, wallaroo
09 bandicoot, boodie-rat, koala bear, native cat, pademelon, petaurist, phalanger, thylacine, wambenger
10 native bear, Notoryctes
11 diprotodont, honey possum, rat kangaroo, rock wallaby
12 marsupial rat, pouched mouse, tree kangaroo
13 brush kangaroo, marsupial mole, Tasmanian wolf
14 marsupial mouse, Tasmanian devil, vulpine opossum
15 flying phalanger

*See also* **animal**

**mart**
04 fair, mall, souk 06 bazaar, market, outlet, staple 08 emporium, exchange 10 repository 11 market-place 14 shopping centre

**marten**
05 pekan, sable 06 fisher 07 Mustela 09 woodshock

**martial**
04 army 05 brave 06 heroic 07 hawkish, warlike 08 militant, military 09 bellicose, combative, soldierly 10 aggressive, pugnacious 11 belligerent

## martial art

*Martial arts and forms of self-defence include:*

**04** judo
**05** Iai-do, sambo, wushu
**06** aikido, karate, kung fu, t'ai chi
**07** capuera, ju-jitsu
**08** capoeira, jiu-jitsu, ninjitsu, ninjutsu, Shotokan
**09** tae kwon do
**10** kick boxing
**11** self-defence, t'ai chi ch'uan

• **martial art expert**
**03** dan

## martinet
**06** martin, tyrant **08** stickler
**09** formalist **10** taskmaster **11** slave-driver **12** taskmistress **14** disciplinarian

## Martinique
**03** MTQ

## martyr
**05** stone **06** victim **07** crucify, torment, torture **09** persecute **10** put to death
**12** give the works, put on the rack
**13** make a martyr of **14** burn at the stake **15** throw to the lions

## martyrdom
**05** agony, death, stake **06** ordeal
**07** anguish, passion, torment, torture, witness **09** suffering **11** persecution
**12** excruciation **13** baptism of fire
**14** baptism of blood

## marvel
**04** gape, gawp, gaze, marl **05** marle, stare **06** genius, goggle, wonder
**07** miracle, portent, prodigy **08** be amazed, surprise **09** eye-opener, fairy tale, not expect, sensation, spectacle
**10** fairy story, phenomenon
**12** astonishment, be astonished
**14** quite something **15** be flabbergasted

## marvellous
**03** ace, bad, def, fab, rad **04** cool, mean, mega, neat, phat **05** brill, great, magic, super **06** superb, wicked
**07** amazing, awesome, crucial, épatant, mirific, radical, wondred
**08** glorious, selcouth, splendid, terrific, wondered **09** bodacious, excellent, fantastic, mirifical, wonderful
**10** astounding, improbable, incredible, miraculous, out of sight, remarkable, stupendous, super-duper, surprising
**11** astonishing, fantabulous, magnificent, merveilleux, sensational, spectacular **12** merveilleuse, unbelievable **13** extraordinary

## marvellously
**04** very **06** highly, really **07** acutely, awfully, greatly, utterly **08** severely, terribly **09** decidedly, extremely, intensely, to a wonder, unusually
**10** dreadfully, remarkably, thoroughly, uncommonly **11** exceedingly, excessively, frightfully **12** inordinately, terrifically **13** exceptionally
**15** extraordinarily

## Maryland
**02** MD

## masculine
**01** m **02** he **03** mas **04** bold, male, masc **05** brave, butch, macho, manly
**06** heroic, robust, rugged, strong, virile
**07** gallant, manlike, mannish
**08** fearless, muscular, powerful, resolute, vigorous **09** confident, strapping **10** determined, red-blooded
**12** stout-hearted

## masculinity
**06** mettle, valour, vigour **07** bravery, courage, heroism, manhood
**08** boldness, firmness, machismo, maleness, strength, virility
**09** fortitude, hardihood, manliness
**10** manfulness, resolution
**11** intrepidity **12** fearlessness, independence, stalwartness

## mash
◇ *anagram indicator*
**03** pap **04** beat, hash, mush, pulp
**05** champ, crush, grind, paste, pound, purée, smash **06** bungle, infuse, muddle, pummel, squash **09** pulverize

## mask
**04** hide, show, veil **05** blind, cloak, cover, front, guise, matte, steep, visor, vizor **06** domino, façade, immask, infuse, masque, screen, shield, veneer, vizard **07** conceal, cover up, cover-up, goggles, inhaler, obscure, persona
**08** disguise, joncanoe, junkanoo, pretence **09** dissemble, false face, gas helmet, John Canoe, John Kanoo, semblance **10** camouflage, gorgoneion, masquerade, respirator
**11** concealment

## masquerade
◇ *anagram indicator*
**03** mum **04** mask, mumm, play, pose
**05** cloak, cover, front, guise
**06** masque **07** cover-up, dress up, pretend, profess **08** disguise, pretence
**09** deception **10** masked ball
**11** costume ball, counterfeit, dissimulate, impersonate **14** fancy dress ball **15** fancy dress party, pass yourself off

## mass
**01** m **03** lot, mob, ped, sea, sum, wad
**04** bags, ball, band, body, bulk, clod, hang, heap, herd, hunk, load, lots, lump, most, nest, pile, size, tons
**05** amass, batch, block, bolus, bunch, chaos, chunk, crowd, group, heaps, horde, loads, piece, piles, plebs, rally, stack, swarm, total, troop, whole, wodge **06** dallop, dollop, gather, huddle, medley, muster, oodles, rabble, scores, tangle, throng, weight, welter
**07** blanket, cluster, clutter, collect, general, popular **08** assemble, capacity, coagulum, entirety, indigest, majority, pandemic, quantity, riff-raff, sweeping, totality **09** abundance, aggregate, Communion, dimension, Eucharist, extensive, hoi polloi, immensity, magnitude, multitude, rotundity, universal, wholesale
**10** accumulate, assemblage, collection, concretion, congregate, large-scale, Lord's Table, widespread
**11** combination, greater part, large number, Lord's Supper, proletariat
**12** accumulation, come together, common people, draw together, lower classes, working class **13** agglutination, bring together, comprehensive, Holy Communion, preponderance
**14** across-the-board, conglomeration, indiscriminate, the rank and file, working classes

## Massachusetts
**02** MA **04** Mass

## massacre
**04** kill, slay **05** purge **06** murder, pogrom **07** butcher, carnage, killing, kill off, mow down, wipe out
**08** butchery, decimate, genocide, homicide **09** bloodbath, holocaust, liquidate, slaughter **10** annihilate, blood purge, decimation
**11** exterminate, liquidation
**12** annihilation **13** extermination
**15** ethnic cleansing

*Massacres include:*

**04** Hama, Lari
**05** Ambon, Katyn, My Lai, Paris, Sabra
**06** Bezier, Boston, Cataví, Herrin, Kanpur, Lidice, Rishon
**07** Amboyna, Babi Yar, Badajoz, Baghdad, Chatila, Glencoe, Halabja, Nanking, Tianjin
**08** Amritsar, Cawnpore, Drogheda, El Mozote, Kishinev, Novgorod, Peterloo, Tientsin
**09** Fetterman, Innocents, Jerusalem, Sand Creek, September, Trebizond
**10** Addis Ababa, Fort Pillow, Myall Creek, Paxton Boys, Sack of Rome, Srebrenica, Tlatelolco
**11** Janissaries, Sharpeville, Wounded Knee
**12** Bloody Sunday, Sabra/Chatila
**15** Oradour-sur-Glane, Sicilian Vespers, St Valentine's Day, Tiananmen Square

## massage
◇ *anagram indicator*
**03** rub **04** an mo, cook, do-in **05** alter, knead, reiki, tui na **06** doctor, fiddle, pummel **07** falsify, Jacuzzi®, rubbing, rub down, rub-down, shampoo, shiatsu, shiatzu, tripsis **08** aerotone, kneading **10** manipulate, osteopathy, percussion, petrissage, pummelling, tamper with **11** acupressure, reflexology **12** aromatherapy, manipulation, misrepresent
**13** interfere with, physiotherapy
**15** Reichian therapy, thalassotherapy

## massive
**03** big **04** bull, gang, huge, vast
**05** beamy, bulky, great, heavy, hefty, jumbo, large, solid **06** mighty
**07** hulking, immense, mammoth, popular, weighty **08** colossal, enormous, gigantic, timbered,

whopping **09** extensive, ginormous, ponderous **10** large-scale, monolithic, monumental, successful **11** substantial

**massively**
**06** vastly **07** greatly, heavily **08** very much **09** immensely **10** enormously **11** extensively **12** monumentally **13** substantially

**mast**
**03** bar, rod **04** boom, heel, nuts, pole, post, spar, yard **05** shaft, staff, stick **06** acorns, jigger **07** pannage, support, upright **10** topgallant

**master**
**01** M **02** MA, PM, RM **03** ace, Dan, guv, Mas, Mes, pro **04** baas, beak, boss, buff, curb, guru, head, Herr, lord, main, Mass, Mess, rule, sire, tame, tuan **05** adept, bwana, check, chief, grand, grasp, great, guide, learn, maven, mavin, owner, prime, quell, ruler, tutor **06** bridle, defeat, expert, gaffer, genius, govern, honcho, leader, manage, mentor, pick up, pundit, season, subdue, temper **07** acquire, captain, conquer, control, dab hand, egghead, leading, maestro, manager, skilful, skilled, skipper, teacher, wise guy **08** director, employer, foremost, governor, masterly, overcome, overlord, overseer, suppress, vanquish, virtuoso **09** commander, dexterous, overpower, pedagogue, practised, preceptor, principal, Signorino, subjugate **10** controller, instructor, past master, proficient **11** controlling, experienced, grand master, predominant, symposiarch, triumph over **12** get the hang of, professional, schoolmaster **13** most important, schoolteacher **14** schoolmistress, superintendent

**masterful**
**05** bossy, pithy **08** arrogant, despotic, powerful **09** imperious **10** autocratic, dominating, high-handed, peremptory, tyrannical **11** controlling, dictatorial, domineering, overbearing **13** authoritative

**masterly**
**03** ace **05** adept, crack **06** adroit, artful, expert, superb **07** skilful, skilled, supreme **08** polished, superior, top-notch **09** dexterous, excellent, first-rate, magistral **10** consummate **11** overbearing **12** accomplished, professional

**mastermind**
**04** mind, plan **05** forge, frame, hatch **06** brains, design, devise, direct, genius, manage **07** control, creator, dream up, inspire, manager, planner, think up **08** be behind, conceive, contrive, director, engineer, organize, virtuoso **09** architect, authority, initiator, intellect, organizer, originate **10** originator, prime mover

**masterpiece**
**05** jewel **08** creation **09** work of art **10** magnum opus, masterwork **11** chef d'oeuvre

**masterstroke**
**04** coup, feat **07** success, triumph, victory **10** attainment **11** achievement **12** coup de maître **14** accomplishment

**mastery**
**04** grip, rule **05** grasp, skill **07** ability, command, control, knowhow, prowess, triumph, victory **08** dominion **09** authority, dexterity, direction, expertise, knowledge, supremacy, upper hand **10** ascendancy, capability, domination, virtuosity **11** familiarity, proficiency, sovereignty, superiority **13** comprehension, understanding

**• strive for mastery**
**04** kemp

**masticate**
**03** eat **04** chew **05** champ, chomp, knead, munch **06** crunch **08** ruminate **09** manducate **10** chew the cud

**mastication**
**06** eating **07** chewing **08** champing, munching **10** rumination **11** manducation

**mat**
**03** rug **04** dull, felt, knot, mass, matt, taut, tawt **05** frost, matte, tatty, twist **06** carpet, felter, paunch, tangle, tatami **07** cluster, coaster, doormat, drugget **08** place mat, table mat, underlay **09** underfelt **10** interweave, lustreless

**match**
**03** fit, pit, tie, vie **04** ally, bout, copy, fuse, game, join, link, main, mate, meet, pair, peer, spar, suit, team, test, twin, yoke **05** adapt, agree, amate, blend, equal, event, fusee, fuzee, light, marry, rival, spill, tally, taper, trial, union, unite, vesta **06** accord, besort, couple, double, fellow, go with, marrow, merger, oppose, pair up, relate **07** combine, compact, compare, compete, connect, contend, contest, hitch up, Lucifer, pairing, paragon, pattern, replica **08** alliance, bonspiel, coupling, locofoco, marriage, parallel, tone with **09** accompany, companion, duplicate, encounter, harmonize, lookalike **10** competitor, complement, co-ordinate, correspond, dead ringer, equivalent, go together, keep up with, one of a pair, pit against, Promethean, tournament **11** affiliation, combination, competition, counterpart, measure up to, partnership, safety match **13** be in agreement

*See also* **game**; **sport**

**• match up to**
**04** meet **05** reach **08** approach, come up to, live up to **11** compare with, measure up to **12** make the grade

**• start of match, start the match**
**02** KO **05** break, bully **06** tee off **07** face-off, kick-off **13** break the balls

**matching**
**04** like, same, twin **06** double, in sync, paired **07** coupled, in synch, similar **08** blending, parallel **09** analogous, duplicate, identical **10** comparable, equivalent **11** correlative, harmonizing **12** co-ordinating **13** complementary, complementing, corresponding

**matchless**
**06** unique **07** perfect **08** makeless, peerless **09** nonpareil, unmatched **10** inimitable, unequalled, unexcelled, unrivalled **11** unsurpassed **12** incomparable, unparalleled, without equal **13** beyond compare

**mate**
**03** fit, pal, wed, wus **04** chum, feer, fere, join, leap, line, maik, make, nick, oppo, pair, twin, wack, wife **05** breed, buddy, china, crony, cully, equal, feare, fiere, marry, match, rival **06** baffle, buffer, cobber, co-mate, couple, deputy, fellow, friend, gender, helper, hubbie, marrow, missis, missus, mucker, pheere, spouse, subdue **07** baffled, compeer, comrade, consort, daunted, husband, Mr Right, oldster, paragon, partner **08** confound, copulate, co-worker, sidekick, workmate **09** assistant, associate, boyfriend, checkmate, colleague, companion, exhausted, other half **10** accomplice, apprentice, better half, checkmated, china plate, confounded, equivalent, girlfriend **11** counterpart, subordinate **12** fellow worker **14** opposite number

**material**
**03** gen, key **04** body, data, info, work **05** cloth, facts, gross, ideas, notes, stuff, vital **06** bodily, fabric, matter, medium **07** details, earthly, germane, low-down, numbers, serious, textile, weighty, worldly **08** apposite, concrete, evidence, palpable, physical, relevant, tangible **09** corporeal, essential, important, momentous, pertinent, substance **10** meaningful **11** information, particulars, significant, substantial **12** constituents **13** consequential, indispensable **15** facts and figures

*See also* **art**; **building**; **fabric**

**• set material in position**
**03** lay

**materialism**
**05** greed **06** hylism **08** hylicism, somatism **11** consumerism, worldliness **12** corporealism **15** acquisitiveness

**materialistic**
**07** worldly **08** banausic **09** bourgeois, mammonist, mercenary **11** acquisitive, consumerist, mammonistic **13** money-grabbing **14** bread-and-butter

**materialize**
**05** arise, occur, reify **06** appear, happen, turn up **09** take place, take shape **12** show yourself **13** become visible, come into being **14** reveal yourself

**materially**
**04** much **07** gravely, greatly
**09** basically, seriously **11** essentially
**12** considerably **13** fundamentally, significantly, substantially

**maternal**
**04** fond, kind, warm **05** mumsy
**06** caring, doting, gentle, loving, tender **08** motherly, vigilant
**09** nurturing **10** comforting, motherlike, nourishing, protective
**12** affectionate **13** understanding

**matey** *see* **maty, matey**

**mathematics**

*Branches of mathematics include:*

**06** conics
**07** algebra, applied, fluxion
**08** calculus, geometry
**09** set theory
**10** arithmetic, game theory, statistics
**11** games theory, group theory
**12** number theory, trigonometry
**13** combinatorics
**14** biomathematics
**15** metamathematics, pure mathematics

*Mathematics terms include:*

**02** pi
**03** arc, set
**04** apex, area, axes, axis, base, cube, edge, face, line, mean, mode, plus, root, side, sine, skew, unit, zero
**05** angle, chaos, chord, curve, depth, equal, graph, group, helix, locus, minus, ogive, point, ratio, solid, speed, total, width
**06** binary, chance, convex, cosine, degree, factor, height, length, linear, matrix, median, number, origin, radian, radius, sample, secant, sector, spiral, square, subset, vector, vertex, volume
**07** algebra, average, bearing, bounded, breadth, chaotic, concave, decimal, divisor, formula, fractal, integer, mapping, maximum, measure, minimum, modulus, oblique, product, segment, tangent
**08** addition, analysis, antipode, argument, bar chart, bar graph, binomial, calculus, capacity, constant, converse, cube root, diagonal, diameter, discrete, dividend, division, equation, exponent, fraction, function, geometry, gradient, identity, infinity, latitude, less than, multiple, parabola, pie chart, quadrant, quartile, quotient, rotation, symmetry, variable, variance, velocity, vertical
**09** algorithm, Cartesian, congruent, factorial, frequency, histogram, hyperbola, iteration, logarithm, longitude, numerator, odd number, operation, parameter, perimeter, remainder
**10** acute angle, arithmetic, complement, continuous, coordinate, covariance, derivative, even number, horizontal, hypotenuse, percentage, percentile, place value, proportion, protractor, Pythagoras, real number, reciprocal, reflection, regression, right-angle, square root, statistics, subtractor
**11** approximate, coefficient, combination, coordinates, correlation, denominator, determinant, enlargement, equidistant, exponential, greater than, integration, magic square, mirror image, Möbius strip, obtuse angle, permutation, plane figure, prime number, probability, Pythagorean, real numbers, reflex angle, translation, Venn diagram, whole number
**12** asymmetrical, cross section, distribution, random sample, straight line, trigonometry, universal set
**13** circumference, complex number, Mandelbrot set, mixed fraction, natural number, ordinal number, parallel lines, perpendicular, quadrilateral, scalar segment, triangulation
**14** axis of symmetry, cardinal number, common fraction, directed number, mirror symmetry, multiplication, negative number, parallel planes, positive number, rational number, transformation, vulgar fraction
**15** conjugate angles, differentiation, imaginary number, scalene triangle

*Mathematicians include:*

**03** **Dee** (John), **Lie** (Sophus)
**04** **Abel** (Niels Henrik), **Hero** (of Alexandria), **Hopf** (Heinz), **Kerr** (Roy), **Pell** (John), **Tait** (Peter Guthrie), **Thom** (René), **Venn** (John), **Weil** (André), **Weyl** (Hermann)
**05** **Bayes** (Thomas), **Boole** (George), **Dirac** (Paul), **Euler** (Leonhard), **Gauss** (Carl Friedrich), **Gödel** (Kurt), **Green** (George), **Hardy** (Godfrey), **Hoyle** (Sir Fred), **Klein** (Felix), **Monge** (Gaspard), **Peano** (Giuseppe), **Serre** (Jean-Pierre), **Snell** (Willebrod), **Vieta** (Franciscus)
**06** **Ampère** (André), **Argand** (Jean-Robert), **Bessel** (Friedrich), **Briggs** (Henry), **Cantor** (Georg), **Cauchy** (Augustin Louis, Baron), **Cayley** (Arthur), **Euclid**, **Fermat** (Pierre de), **Fields** (J C), **Fisher** (Sir Ronald), **Galois** (Évariste), **Halley** (Edmond), **Jacobi** (Carl), **Jordan** (Camille), **Kelvin** (William Thomson, Lord), **Lorenz** (Edward), **Markov** (Andrei), **Möbius** (August Ferdinand), **Moivre** (Abraham de), **Napier** (John), **Newton** (Sir Isaac), **Pappus** (of Alexandria), **Pascal** (Blaise), **Picard** (Émile), **Stokes** (Sir George), **Turing** (Alan), **Wallis** (John), **Wiener** (Norbert)
**07** **Alhazen**, **Babbage** (Charles), **Cardano** (Girolamo), **Carroll** (Lewis), **Eudoxus** (of Cnidus), **Fourier** (Joseph, Baron de), **Galileo**, **Germain** (Sophie), **Hilbert** (David), **Laplace** (Pierre, Marquis de), **Leibniz** (Gottfried), **Penrose** (Roger), **Poisson** (Siméon), **Riemann** (Bernhard), **Russell** (Bertrand, Earl), **Shannon** (Claude)
**08** **Alembert** (Jean le Rond d'), **Birkhoff** (George David), **Dedekind** (Julius), **De Morgan** (Augustus), **Guldberg** (Cato), **Hamilton** (Sir William Rowan), **Lagrange** (Joseph de, Comte), **Legendre** (Adrien-Marie), **Lovelace** (Ada, Countess of), **Mercator** (Nicolaus), **Playfair** (John), **Poincaré** (Jules)
**09** **Bernoulli** (Daniel), **Bernoulli** (Jacques), **Bronowski** (Jacob), **Descartes** (René), **Dirichlet** (Lejeune), **Fibonacci** (Leonardo), **Minkowski** (Hermann), **Whitehead** (Alfred)
**10** **Apollonius** (of Perga), **Archimedes**, **Diophantus**, **Hipparchus**, **Maupertuis** (Pierre Louis de), **Pythagoras**, **Sierpinski** (Wactaw), **Torricelli** (Evangelista), **Zeno of Elea**
**11** **al-Khwarizmi**
**12** **Eratosthenes**

**mating**
**06** fusing **07** coition, joining, pairing, uniting **08** breeding, coupling, matching, twinning **10** copulating, copulation

**matriarch**
**04** nana

**matrimonial**
**06** wedded **07** marital, married, nuptial, spousal, wedding **08** conjugal, marriage
• **matrimonial duties**
**03** bed

**matrimony**
**05** union **07** wedlock **08** marriage, nuptials, spousage **09** espousals
**12** married state

**matrix**
**03** gel, mat **04** cast, form, mold, womb
**05** array, frame, mould, plasm, table
**06** stroma **07** context, matrice
**08** analysis, chondrin, Jacobian, template **09** composite, framework, transpose **11** arrangement

**matron**
**04** dame

**matted**
**05** taggy **06** tangly **07** knotted, tangled, tousled **08** uncombed
**09** entangled **11** dishevelled **13** blood-boltered

**matter**
**02** go **03** pus **04** body, case, hyle, note
**05** count, event, issue, point, stuff, thing, topic, upset, value, worry

**06** affair, bother, import, medium, weight **07** concern, content, episode, problem, subject, trouble **08** business, distress, incident, interest, material, nuisance, question, weakness
**09** discharge, happening, make a stir, make waves, purulence, secretion, situation, substance **10** be relevant, difficulty, importance, occurrence, proceeding **11** be important, carry weight, consequence, shortcoming, suppuration **12** circumstance, cut a lot of ice, significance **13** have influence, inconvenience, mean something, momentousness
**14** be of importance **15** make a difference

**• as a matter of fact**
**05** truly **06** in fact, really **08** actually
**11** as it happens **12** in actual fact

**• matter of no importance**
**03** toy **10** triviality

**• no matter**
**09** never mind **15** it does not matter, it is unimportant

**matter-of-fact**
**03** dry **04** dull, flat **05** sober **06** thingy
**07** deadpan, prosaic **08** lifeless, positive **09** practical, pragmatic, prosaical **10** pedestrian **11** down-to-earth, emotionless, pragmatical, unemotional **13** unimaginative, unsentimental **15** straightforward

**matting**
**03** tat **04** bast

**mattress**
**03** bed **04** Lilo® **05** futon **06** airbed, pallet **07** biscuit **08** crash-mat, water bed **09** paillasse, palliasse **10** feather bed

**maturation**
**06** growth **08** fruition, ripening
**09** seasoning **11** development

**mature**
**03** age **04** bold, gray, grey, ripe, wise
**05** adult, bloom, grown, of age, ready, ripen **06** evolve, grow up, mellow, nubile, season **07** concoct, develop, fall due, grown-up, perfect, prepare, ripened **08** balanced, complete, finished, joined-up, maturate, seasoned, sensible **09** come of age, finalized, full-grown, perfected
**10** become ripe, precocious
**11** become adult, draw to a head, experienced, responsible **12** become mellow, fully fledged **13** well-developed **14** become sensible, well-thought-out

**maturity**
**03** age **06** summer, wisdom
**07** manhood, puberty **08** majority, ripeness **09** adulthood, readiness, womanhood **10** experience, full growth, mellowness, perfection
**11** coming of age **12** sensibleness
**14** responsibility **15** age of discretion

**matweed**
**04** nard

**maty, matey**
**04** kind, warm **05** close, pally, thick, tight **06** blokey, chummy, folksy, genial
**07** affable, cordial, helpful
**08** amicable, blokeish, familiar, friendly, intimate, outgoing, sociable
**09** agreeable, comradely, convivial, peaceable, receptive **10** favourable
**11** good-natured, inseparable, neighbourly, sympathetic
**12** affectionate, approachable, well-disposed **13** companionable

**maudlin**
**05** drunk, gushy, mushy, soppy, tipsy, weepy **06** sickly, sloppy, slushy
**07** fuddled, mawkish, tearful, weeping
**09** emotional, half-drunk, schmaltzy
**10** lachrymose **11** sentimental

**maul**
◇ *anagram indicator*
**03** mug, paw **04** beat, belt, claw, mall, mell **05** abuse **06** attack, batter, beat up, do over, mangle, molest, thrash, wallop **07** assault, rough up **08** ill-treat, lacerate, maltreat, mutilate
**09** manhandle **10** knock about

**maunder**
**04** ease, inch, laze, roam, rove
**05** amble, mooch, mosey, stray
**06** babble, beggar, drivel, gabble, jabber, mutter, natter, rabbit, ramble, stroll, waffle, wander, witter **07** blather, chatter, grumble, meander, prattle, shuffle **08** rabbit on

**Maureen**
**02** Mo

**Mauritania**
**03** MRT, RIM

**Mauritius**
**02** MS **03** MUS

**mausoleum**
**04** mole, tomb **05** crypt, vault
**08** catacomb, Taj Mahal **09** sepulchre
**10** undercroft **13** burial chamber

**maverick**
**05** rebel **08** agitator, outsider **09** odd one out **13** individualist, nonconformist **14** fish out of water

**maw**
**04** gulf, jaws **05** abyss, chasm, mouth
**06** gullet, throat **07** seagull, stomach
**08** appetite **11** inclination

**mawkish**
**04** flat, foul **05** gushy, mawky, mushy, soppy **06** feeble, gloopy, sickly, slushy
**07** insipid, maggoty, maudlin
**08** nauseous **09** emotional, loathsome, offensive, schmaltzy, squeamish **10** disgusting, nauseating
**11** sentimental

**mawkishly**
**06** feebly **07** mushily, soppily
**11** emotionally, loathsomely
**12** nauseatingly **13** sentimentally

**maxim**
**03** saw **04** rule **05** adage, axiom, gnome, motto **06** byword, dictum, saying **07** epigram, precept, proverb
**08** aphorism, apothegm, moralism, sentence **09** principle, sentiment, watchword **10** apophthegm, prudential

**maximize**
**05** add to, boost, breed, raise, widen
**06** bump up, deepen, expand, extend, hike up, spread, step up **07** advance, augment, broaden, build up, develop, enhance, enlarge, further, magnify, prolong, scale up **08** heighten, increase **09** intensify, propagate
**10** accumulate, strengthen

**maximum**
**03** max, top **04** acme, full, high, most, peak **06** apogee, height, summit, utmost, zenith **07** biggest, ceiling, highest, largest, supreme, topmost
**08** greatest, pinnacle, top point, ultimate **09** extremity, uttermost
**10** upper limit

**may**
**04** mote **08** hawthorn

**• may it do**
**04** dich

**maybe**
◇ *anagram indicator*
**07** could be, perhaps **08** possibly
**09** perchance **11** conceivably, possibility **12** peradventure **13** for all you know

**mayfly**
**06** day-fly **08** ephemera **09** caddis fly, ephemerid **10** green-drake
**11** Plectoptera, turkey brown

**mayhem**
◇ *anagram indicator*
**04** mess, riot **05** chaos, havoc
**06** bedlam, tumult, uproar **07** anarchy, maiming **08** disorder, madhouse
**09** confusion **10** disruption
**11** lawlessness **15** disorganization

**mayor**
**02** LM **05** maire **07** alcalde

**Mayotte**
**03** MYT

**maze**
◇ *anagram indicator*
**03** web **04** mesh **05** maise, maize, mease **06** jungle, puzzle, tangle, warren **07** complex, meander, network **09** confusion, honeycomb, intricacy, labyrinth

**me**
**02** mi, us **03** moi

**meadow**
**03** ing, lay, lea, lee, ley **04** inch, mead
**05** field, grass, green, haugh **06** leasow, saeter **07** paddock, pasture, salting
**09** grassland **11** pastureland

**meadow-grass**
**03** poa

**meagre**
**03** bar **04** arid, bony, lean, poor, puny, thin, weak **05** gaunt, mingy, small,

spare **06** barren, frugal, jejune, Lenten, maigre, measly, paltry, scanty, skimpy, skinny, slight, sparse, stingy **07** scraggy, scrawny, slender **08** exiguous, roncador, scrannel **09** deficient, emaciated, niggardly **10** inadequate, negligible, threadbare **12** insufficient **13** insubstantial

**meagreness**
**07** poverty **08** puniness **09** smallness **10** deficiency, inadequacy, measliness, scantiness, slightness, sparseness, stinginess **13** insufficiency

**meal**
**03** kai **04** fare, feed, kail, kale, meat, mess, mush **05** grout, scoff, skoff **06** farina, repast **07** meltith, surfeit **08** freeload, racahout **09** collation, raccahout, refection, scambling **12** refreshments

*Meals include:*

**03** BBQ, tea
**04** bite
**05** feast, lunch, snack
**06** barbie, brunch, buffet, dinner, nosh-up, picnic, repast, spread, supper, tiffin
**07** banquet, blow-out, high tea
**08** barbecue, cream tea, luncheon, takeaway, tea break, tea party, TV dinner
**09** breakfast, cold table, collation, elevenses
**10** fork supper, midday meal, slap-up meal
**11** dinner party, evening meal
**12** afternoon tea, safari supper
**13** harvest supper

**• before a meal**
**02** ap

**mealy-mouthed**
**04** glib, prim **07** mincing **08** indirect, reticent **09** equivocal, hestitant, plausible **10** flattering **11** euphemistic **12** overdelicate **13** over-squeamish, smooth-tongued

**mean**
**03** ace, aim, low, rad **04** base, cool, fate, fine, mega, mein, mene, mode, neat, norm, plan, poor, rare, show, vile, wish, wont **05** boffo, brill, cause, crack, cross, cruel, dirty, footy, imply, lowly, mangy, meane, mingy, nasty, prime, scall, slink, snide, tight **06** abject, aspire, common, convey, crabby, denote, design, dismal, divine, effect, entail, humble, intend, lament, lead to, mangey, matter, maungy, median, medium, middle, normal, ordain, ornery, paltry, ribald, ribaud, shabby, simple, skimpy, snotty, sordid, stingy, superb, unkind, way-out **07** appoint, average, beastly, betoken, caitiff, chintzy, connote, crucial, destine, express, grouchy, halfway, involve, mesquin, miserly, niggard, obscure, perfect, piggish, produce, propose, purport, purpose, radical, roynish, rybauld, selfish, signify, skilful, spaniel, squalid, suggest, think of **08** beggarly, complain, fabulous, grasping, heavenly, indicate, intimate, mesquine, middling, mid-point, moderate, ordinary, result in, smashing, sneaking, spiteful, splendid, stand for, stunning, terrific, top-notch, very good, whoreson, wretched **09** admirable, brilliant, crotchety, cullionly, designate, earth-bred, excellent, fantastic, first-rate, malicious, matchless, middle way, miserable, niggardly, represent, symbolize, wonderful **10** base-minded, bring about, compromise, contracted, despicable, fast-handed, first-class, give rise to, golden mean, have in mind, ill-natured, marvellous, not half bad, predestine, remarkable, surpassing, threepenny, unequalled, unfriendly, ungenerous, unpleasant **11** bad-tempered, be important, carry weight, close-fisted, close-handed, exceptional, happy medium, high-quality, magnificent, near the bone, necessitate, outstanding, sensational, superlative, tight-fisted **12** cheese-paring, disagreeable, intermediate, middle course, parsimonious, second to none, unparalleled **13** have influence, penny-pinching, uncomfortable **14** inconsiderable, out of this world **15** make a difference

**• mean time**
**02** MT

**meander**
**04** bend, ease, inch, laze, maze, roam, rove, turn, wind **05** amble, curve, mooch, mosey, snake, stray, twist **06** ramble, stroll, wander, wimple, zigzag **07** shuffle, turning, whimple **09** sinuosity **10** perplexity

**meandering**
◇ *anagram indicator*
**07** sinuous, snaking, turning, winding **08** indirect, rambling, tortuous, twisting **09** meandrous, wandering **10** circuitous, convoluted, roundabout, serpentine

**meaning**
**03** aim **04** feck, gist, goal, hang, idea, plan, wish **05** drift, point, sense, trend, value, worth **06** import, letter, object, spirit, thrust **07** essence, message, purpose **08** sentence **09** intention, objective, substance **10** aspiration, definition, expression, usefulness **11** connotation, elucidation, explanation, explication, implication **12** construction, significance **13** signification **14** interpretation

**meaningful**
**05** valid **06** useful **07** pointed, serious, telling, warning **08** eloquent, material, pregnant, relevant, speaking **09** effective, important **10** expressive, purposeful, suggestive, worthwhile **11** significant

**meaningfully**
**08** usefully **09** pointedly **10** eloquently, relevantly **11** effectively, importantly **12** expressively, purposefully, suggestively **13** significantly

**meaningless**
**04** vain **05** empty **06** absurd, futile, hollow **07** aimless, trivial, useless, vacuous **08** trifling, unsensed **09** gibberish, pointless, senseless, worthless **10** irrational, motiveless **11** nonsensical, purposeless **13** insignificant, insubstantial **14** expressionless, unintelligible

**• meaningless word, meaningless refrain**
**05** nonny **07** ducdame, mirbane **08** falderal, fal de rol, folderol, rumbelow, rum-ti-tum **09** expletive **11** rumti-iddity **12** rumpti-iddity

**meaninglessly**
**06** in vain, vainly **08** futilely **09** aimlessly, uselessly **11** pointlessly, senselessly **12** irrationally **13** purposelessly **14** unintelligibly

**meanly**
**06** poorly, slight **07** cruelly, nastily **08** beggarly, commonly, scurvily, shabbily, unkindly **09** miserably, niggardly, selfishly **10** graspingly, spitefully **12** contemptibly, ungenerously, unpleasantly

**meanness**
**09** parsimony **10** niggardise, niggardize, stinginess **11** mesquinerie, miserliness **12** illiberality **13** niggardliness, penuriousness **15** close-fistedness, close-handedness, tight-fistedness

**means**
**03** way **04** mode **05** funds, money **06** agency, assets, avenue, course, income, manner, medium, method, riches, wealth **07** capital, channel, fortune, process, vehicle **08** property **09** affluence, resources, substance **10** instrument **11** wherewithal

**• by all means**
**06** surely **08** of course **09** certainly, naturally **10** of all loves **11** à toute force **12** with pleasure

**• by means of**
**03** per, via **04** with **05** using **07** through **08** by dint of **11** as a result of **12** with the aid of **13** with the help of

**• by no means**
**04** none **05** never, no way **07** in no way **08** not at all **11** anything but **12** certainly not

**• having enough means**
**04** able

**meantime, meanwhile**
**05** among **06** for now **07** interim **12** concurrently, for the moment, in the interim **13** at the same time, in the interval, in the meantime **14** in the meanwhile, simultaneously **15** for the time being

**measly**
**04** mean, poor, puny **05** mingy, petty **06** meagre, paltry, scanty, skimpy,

spotty, stingy **07** miserly, pitiful, trivial **08** beggarly, pathetic, piddling **09** miserable, niggardly **10** ungenerous **12** contemptible

## measurable

**08** material, mensural, moderate **09** gaugeable **10** assessable, computable, fathomable, mensurable, noticeable **11** appreciable, perceptible, significant **12** determinable, quantifiable, quantitative

## measure

**02** be **03** act, cut, lot, pit **04** area, bill, bulk, deed, gage, line, mass, mete, norm, pace, part, rate, read, rule, size, step, tape, test, time, unit **05** depth, gauge, judge, level, limit, means, meter, metre, piece, plumb, quota, range, ruler, scale, scope, share, sound, units, value, weigh, width **06** action, amount, assess, course, degree, extent, fathom, height, length, method, ration, record, rhythm, size up, strain, survey, system, volume, weight **07** compute, expanse, portion, rake-off, statute **08** acid test, appraise, capacity, division, estimate, evaluate, quantify, quantity, standard, traverse **09** allotment, barometer, benchmark, calculate, criterion, determine, dimension, enactment, expedient, magnitude, procedure, restraint, treatment, yardstick **10** allocation, dimensions, litmus test, measure off, measure out, moderation, proceeding, proportion, resolution, touchstone **11** proportions

*See also* **measurement**

### • beyond measure

**08** out of cry **09** endlessly, immensely **10** extra modum, infinitely **11** excessively, inestimably, limitlessly **12** beyond belief, incalculably

### • for good measure

**06** as well **07** besides **08** as a bonus **10** in addition **11** furthermore **12** over and above

### • get the measure of, take the measure of

**04** rate **05** gauge, judge, value **06** assess, handle, reckon, size up **08** appraise, estimate, evaluate **09** calculate, determine **12** get a handle on

### • measure off

**03** fix **05** limit **07** delimit, lay down, mark out, pace out **09** demarcate, determine **10** measure out **12** circumscribe

### • measure out

**05** allot, issue **06** assign, divide **07** deal out, dole out, hand out, mete out, pour out **08** dispense, share out **09** apportion, parcel out **10** distribute, proportion

### • measure up

**02** do **07** shape up, suffice **10** fit the bill, pass muster **11** fill the bill **12** make the grade **15** come up to scratch

### • measure up to

**04** meet **05** equal, match, rival, touch **07** satisfy **08** come up to, live up to **09** match up to **11** compare with **12** make the grade

## measured

**04** slow **06** steady **07** careful, planned, precise, regular, studied **08** reasoned **09** unhurried **10** calculated, considered, deliberate, mensurable, restrained, rhythmical **12** premeditated **14** well-thought-out

## measureless

**04** vast **07** endless, immense **08** infinite **09** boundless, limitless, unbounded **10** bottomless **11** inestimable, innumerable **12** immeasurable, incalculable

## measurement

**04** area, bulk, gage, mass, size, tare, unit **05** depth, range, width **06** amount, extent, height, length, sizing, survey, volume, weight **07** expanse, gauging, reading **08** capacity, quantity, weighing **09** amplitude, appraisal, dimension, judgement, magnitude **10** assessment, estimation, evaluation, proportion **11** calculation, calibration, computation, proportions **12** appreciation **14** quantification

*Measurement units include:*

**01** f, g, k, l, m, t, y
**02** as, cg, cm, ct, dg, em, en, ft, gm, gr, hg, kg, lb, li, mg, mm, oz, pt, st, yd
**03** amp, are, bar, bel, bit, cab, cor, cup, cwt, day, ell, erg, gal, grt, hin, kat, kin, kip, kos, lay, lea, ley, log, lux, mho, mil, mna, nit, ohm, oke, pin, rem, rod, tod, ton, tun, wey
**04** acre, aune, barn, bath, baud, boll, bolt, butt, cell, cord, coss, cran, demy, dyne, epha, foot, gill, gram, hand, hour, inch, kati, khat, knot, link, mile, mill, mina, mole, muid, nail, obol, omer, peck, pica, pint, pipe, pole, pood, ream, rood, rope, seer, sone, span, tael, thou, tola, torr, vara, volt, watt, week, yard, year
**05** cable, caneh, catty, chain, cubit, ephah, farad, henry, hertz, joule, kaneh, katti, litre, lumen, metre, month, ounce, perch, point, pound, quart, stere, stone, tesla, therm, tonne, weber
**06** ampere, barrel, bushel, decade, degree, fathom, firkin, gallon, gramme, kelvin, league, minute, newton, parsec, pascal, radian, second
**07** calorie, candela, century, coulomb, decibel, fresnel, furlong, hectare, long ton, siemens, volt amp
**08** angstrom, cord foot, hogshead, kilogram, millibar, short ton
**09** becquerel, board foot, centigram, cubic foot, cubic inch, cubic yard, decimetre, foot-pound, kilolitre, kilometre, light year, metric ton, milligram, steradian
**10** atmosphere, barleycorn, centilitre, centimetre, cubic metre, fluid ounce, hectolitre, hoppus foot, horsepower, kilogramme, micrometre, millennium, millilitre, millimetre, millistere, square foot, square inch, square mile, square yard
**11** centigramme, milligramme, newton metre, square metre
**12** cable's length, nautical mile
**13** degree Celsius, hundredweight, volts per metre
**14** cubic decimetre, farads per metre, henrys per metre
**15** cubic centimetre, metres per second, newtons per metre, square decimetre, square kilometre

*See also* **measurement of pressure** *under* **pressure**; **timber**; **unit of weight** *under* **weight**; **wood**

### • Old Measurement

**02** OM

## measuring instrument

*Measuring instruments include:*

**04** rule
**05** gauge, meter
**06** octant
**07** ammeter, balance, burette, pipette, sextant
**08** luxmeter, odometer, ohmmeter, quadrant
**09** altimeter, barometer, callipers, cryometer, dosimeter, flowmeter, focimeter, hodometer, hourglass, manometer, milometer, optometer, pedometer, plumb line, pyrometer, rheometer, steelyard, stopwatch, vinometer, voltmeter, volumeter, wattmeter, wavemeter
**10** anemometer, audiometer, bathometer, clinometer, cyclometer, gravimeter, hydrometer, hyetometer, hygrometer, hypsometer, micrometer, mileometer, multimeter, ombrometer, photometer, planimeter, protractor, pulsimeter, radiosonde, tachometer, tachymeter, theodolite, vibrograph, vibrometer, viscometer
**11** calorimeter, chronometer, colorimeter, dynamometer, pluviometer, pyranometer, salinometer, seismograph, seismometer, speedometer, spherometer, tape measure, tensiometer, thermometer, vaporimeter, velocimeter, weighbridge
**12** Breathalyser®, densitometer, evaporimeter, galvanometer, inclinometer, magnetometer, psychrometer, respirometer, spectrometer, sphygmometer, trundle wheel, viscosimeter
**13** accelerometer, decelerometer, Geiger counter, saccharometer
**14** geothermometer, interferometer

*See also* **gauge**

## meat

**03** nub **04** core, crux, eats, fare, food, gist, grub, nosh, pith, tuck **05** flesh, heart, point, scran **06** kernel, marrow, tucker, viands **07** essence, nucleus, rations **08** eatables, victuals **09** substance **10** provisions, sustenance **11** comestibles, nourishment, subsistence **12** fundamentals

*Cold meats include:*

**03** ham
**04** beef, game, pâté, pork, Spam®
**06** salami, tongue, turkey
**07** biltong, chicken, chorizo, kabanos, pork pie, sausage, terrine, venison
**08** bresaola, Cervelat, cold cuts, cured ham, meat loaf, ox tongue, parma ham, pastrami, salt beef
**09** Bierwurst, glazed ham, liver paté, Mettwurst, pepperoni, rillettes, saucisson, scotch egg
**10** breaded ham, corned beef, crumbed ham, liverwurst, mortadella, prosciutto, Serrano ham
**11** sausage roll
**12** Ardennes pâté, Brunswick ham, Brussels pâté, jamón serrano, liver sausage, luncheon meat, peppered beef, Wiltshire ham
**13** chicken breast, garlic sausage, honey roast ham, Schinkenwurst, smoked sausage
**15** luncheon sausage

*Meat cuts include:*

**03** leg, rib, sey
**04** chop, clod, hand, hock, loin, neck, rack, rump, shin
**05** baron, chine, chuck, flank, hough, round, scrag, shank
**06** breast, collar, cutlet, fillet, saddle
**07** best end, brisket, buttock, knuckle, sirloin, topside
**08** escalope, forehock, noisette, popeseye, shoulder, spare rib
**09** aitchbone, médaillon
**10** silverside
**11** filet mignon, porterhouse

*Meats and meat products include:*

**03** ham, MRM, red
**04** beef, bush, duck, hare, lamb, loaf, pâté, pork, Spam®, spek, veal
**05** bacon, brawn, goose, heart, liver, mince, offal, quail, speck, steak, tripe, vifda, vivda, white
**06** brains, burger, faggot, gammon, grouse, haggis, haslet, kidney, mutton, oxtail, pigeon, polony, rabbit, tongue, turkey
**07** biltong, chicken, fatback, griskin, harslet, long pig, pemican, poultry, rissole, sausage, variety, venison
**08** bushmeat, foie gras, fricadel, luncheon, meat loaf, pemmican, pheasant, scrapple, trotters
**09** forcemeat, frikkadel, hamburger, partridge, rillettes
**10** beefburger, horseflesh, minced beef, sweetbread
**11** pig's knuckle, sausage meat
**12** black pudding, luncheon meat
**13** shield of brawn
**14** mousse de canard

**meaty**
**04** rich **05** beefy, burly, heavy, hunky, pithy, solid **06** brawny, fleshy, hearty, sturdy **08** muscular, profound **09** strapping **10** meaningful **11** interesting, significant, substantial

**mechanic**
**07** artisan **08** engineer, operator **09** artificer, grauncher, groundman, machinist, operative, repairman, tradesman **10** groundsman, millwright, technician **11** card-sharper, mechanician, tradeswoman **12** grease monkey

**mechanical**
**04** cold, dead, dull **06** manual, reflex **07** organic, routine **08** electric, habitual, lifeless, soulless **09** automated, automatic, dynamical, technical, unfeeling **10** impersonal, mechanized, unthinking **11** emotionless, instinctive, involuntary, machine-like, mechanistic, perfunctory, power-driven, unconscious, unemotional **12** matter-of-fact **14** machine-powered

**mechanically**
**09** routinely **10** as a machine, by a machine, habitually **11** intuitively, on autopilot **12** unthinkingly **13** automatically, instinctively, involuntarily, unconsciously **14** electronically

**mechanism**
**04** guts, tool **05** gears, means, motor, works **06** action, agency, device, engine, gadget, medium, method, system **07** channel, machine, process **08** gimcrack, jimcrack, movement, workings **09** apparatus, appliance, interlock, machinery, operation, procedure, propeller, structure, technique **10** components, instrument, propelment **11** contraption, contrivance, functioning, performance

**mechanize**
**07** program **08** automate **11** computerize

**medal**
**04** gold, gong **05** award, cross, model, prize **06** bronze, honour, reward, ribbon, silver, trophy **08** contorno, vernicle **09** gold medal, medallion **10** decoration, touch-piece **11** bronze medal, contorniate, silver medal

*See also* **military**

**meddle**
◇ *anagram indicator*
**03** mix, pry **04** mell, mess **05** medle, snoop **06** butt in, fiddle, kibitz, tamper, temper, tinker **07** intrude **09** interfere, intervene **10** stickybeak **12** put your oar in **14** poke your nose in, stick your oar in **15** stick your nose in

**meddlesome**
**04** nosy **05** nosey **06** prying **08** meddling, snooping **09** intruding, intrusive, pragmatic **11** interfering, mischievous, pragmatical

**mediaeval** *see* **medieval, mediaeval**

**mediate**
**06** convey, middle, settle, step in, umpire **07** referee, resolve, stickle **08** indirect, moderate, transmit **09** arbitrate, intercede, interpose, intervene, negotiate, reconcile **10** conciliate **11** intervening **12** intermediate **13** act as mediator **15** act as peacemaker

**mediation**
**11** arbitration, good offices, negotiation, peacemaking **12** conciliation, intercession, intervention **13** interposition **14** reconciliation

**mediator**
**04** mean **05** judge **06** priest, umpire **07** arbiter, referee **08** stickler **09** go-between, middleman, moderator, Ombudsman, thirdsman **10** arbitrator, interceder, intervener, negotiator, peacemaker, reconciler **11** conciliator, intercessor, interventor **12** honest broker, intermediary

**medical**
**03** med

*See also* **disease**

*Medical and surgical equipment includes:*

**03** ECG, MRI
**05** clamp, swabs
**06** canula, scales
**07** cannula, curette, dilator, forceps, inhaler, scalpel, scanner, syringe
**08** catheter, iron lung, speculum, tweezers, X-ray unit
**09** aspirator, auriscope, autoclave, CT scanner, endoscope, incubator, inhalator, nebulizer, retractor
**10** audiometer, CAT scanner, ear syringe, hypodermic, kidney dish, microscope, MRI scanner, oxygen mask, rectoscope, respirator, rhinoscope, sterilizer, ultrasound
**11** body scanner, first aid kit, laparoscope, stethoscope, stomach pump, thermometer
**12** bronchoscope, isolator tent, laryngoscope, resuscitator, surgical mask, urethroscope
**13** aural speculum, defibrillator, specimen glass
**14** oesophagoscope, operating table, ophthalmoscope, oxygen cylinder
**15** instrument table

*Medical specialists include:*

**07** dentist
**08** optician
**09** dietician, homeopath
**10** homoeopath, oncologist, orthoptist, pharmacist
**11** audiologist, chiropodist, neurologist, optometrist, pathologist, radiologist

**12** anaesthetist, cardiologist, chiropractor, embryologist, geriatrician, immunologist, obstetrician, orthodontist, orthopaedist, psychiatrist, psychologist, toxicologist
**13** dermatologist, gerontologist, gynaecologist, haematologist, paediatrician, vaccinologist
**14** bacteriologist, microbiologist, pharmacologist, rheumatologist
**15** endocrinologist, ophthalmologist, physiotherapist

*See also* **doctor**; **nurse**

- **medical man** *see* **doctor**
- **medical records**

**04** case

**medicinal**
**06** physic **07** healing, medical **08** curative, physical, remedial **11** restorative, therapeutic **12** health-giving

**medicinally**
**09** medically **10** curatively, remedially **13** restoratively **15** therapeutically

**medicine**
**03** med **04** cure, drug **05** trade **06** remedy **07** panacea **09** analeptic, physician **10** medicament, medication **12** prescription **14** pharmaceutical

*See also* **drug**

*Branches of medicine include:*

**05** ob-gyn
**07** otology, urology
**08** nosology, obs/gynae, oncology, pharmacy
**09** andrology, audiology, chiropody, dentistry, neurology, optometry, pathology, radiology
**10** cardiology, embryology, geriatrics, immunology, obstetrics, osteopathy, pediatrics, psychiatry, psychology, toxicology
**11** dermatology, diagnostics, gerontology, gynaecology, haematology, paediatrics, physiatrics
**12** anaesthetics, bacteriology, kinesiatrics, microbiology, orthodontics, orthopaedics, perinatology, pharmacology, radiotherapy, rheumatology
**13** cytopathology, endocrinology, ophthalmology, physiotherapy, psychotherapy
**14** electrotherapy, neuropathology, neuroradiology, sports medicine
**15** neuropsychiatry

*Branches of complementary medicine include:*

**04** yoga
**05** reiki
**07** massage, Pilates, Rolfing, shiatsu
**08** Ayurveda
**09** herbalism, iridology
**10** art therapy, autogenics, homeopathy, meditation, osteopathy
**11** acupressure, acupuncture, aura therapy, kinesiology, moxibustion, naturopathy, reflexology, t'ai chi ch'uan
**12** aromatherapy, Bach remedies, chiropractic, hydrotherapy, hypnotherapy, macrobiotics
**14** autosuggestion, crystal healing, herbal medicine
**15** Chinese medicine, thalassotherapy

*Medicine types include:*

**04** pill
**05** tonic
**06** arnica, emetic, gargle, tablet
**07** antacid, capsule, inhaler, linctus, lozenge, pessary, steroid
**08** diuretic, ear drops, eye drops, hypnotic, laxative, narcotic, ointment, pastille, sedative
**09** analgesic, paregoric, stimulant
**10** antibiotic, antiseptic, gripe-water, nasal spray, painkiller
**11** anaesthetic, neuroleptic, suppository
**13** antibacterial, anticoagulant, antihistamine, tranquillizer
**14** anticonvulsant, antidepressant, bronchodilator, hallucinogenic

*See also* **antibiotic**; **drug**

- **medicine box**

**04** inro

**medieval, mediaeval**
**03** med, old **07** antique, archaic **08** historic, obsolete, old-world, outmoded **09** primitive **10** antiquated **12** antediluvian, old-fashioned **13** of the Dark Ages, unenlightened **15** of the Middle Ages

**mediocre**
**04** hack, so-so **06** medium **07** average **08** adequate, inferior, middling, ordinary, passable **09** tolerable **10** not much cop, pedestrian, second-rate, uninspired **11** bog standard, commonplace, indifferent, not up to much, respectable **12** run-of-the-mill **13** insignificant, no great shakes, unexceptional **14** fair to middling **15** middle-of-the-road, undistinguished

**mediocrity**
**06** nobody **07** no-hoper, nothing **08** adequacy, dead loss, poorness **09** nonentity **10** non-starter **11** averageness, inferiority **12** indifference, ordinariness, passableness, unimportance **14** insignificance

**meditate**
**04** chew, muse, plan **05** brood, study, think **06** design, devise, intend, ponder, scheme **07** reflect **08** cogitate, consider, mull over, ruminate **09** speculate, think over **10** chew the cud, deliberate, have in mind **11** concentrate, contemplate

**meditation**
**02** TM **05** study, zazen **06** musing **07** reverie, thought **08** brooding **09** pondering **10** brown study, cogitation, reflection, ruminating, rumination **11** cerebration, mulling over, speculation **12** deliberation, excogitation **13** concentration, contemplation

**meditative**
**07** museful, pensive **08** ruminant, studious **09** prayerful **10** cogitative, reflective, ruminative, thoughtful **12** deliberative **13** contemplative

**Mediterranean**
**03** Med

**medium**
**01** m **03** med, way **04** fair, form, mean, mode, norm **05** ether, means, organ, stuff **06** agency, avenue, centre, medial, median, middle, midway, milieu **07** average, channel, element, habitat, midsize, psychic, setting, vehicle **08** ambience, material, middling, midpoint, moderate, standard **09** middle way, spiritist, substance **10** atmosphere, compromise, conditions, golden mean, influences, instrument **11** clairvoyant, environment, happy medium, necromancer **12** intermediate, middle ground, sound-carrier, spiritualist, surroundings **13** circumstances, fortune-teller **15** instrumentality, way of expressing

- **by the medium of**

**02** in

**medley**
◇ *anagram indicator*
**03** mix **04** mess, olio, olla **05** fight, mêlée **06** jumble, mingle **07** farrago, melange, mixture, variety **08** macaroni, mishmash, mixed bag, pastiche **09** confusion, macédoine, patchwork, potpourri, quodlibet **10** assortment, collection, hodgepodge, hotchpotch, miscellany, salmagundi, salmagundy **11** gallimaufry, smorgasbord **13** helter-skelter **14** conglomeration, omnium-gatherum

**meek**
**04** mild, tame, weak **05** lowly, quiet, timid **06** docile, gentle, humble, modest **07** patient **08** peaceful, resigned, yielding **09** compliant, spineless **10** forbearing, spiritless, submissive, unassuming **11** deferential **13** long-suffering, unpretentious

**meekly**
**06** gently, humbly, mildly **07** quietly **08** modestly **09** patiently **12** submissively **13** deferentially

**meekness**
**07** modesty **08** docility, humility, mildness, patience, softness, tameness, timidity, weakness **09** deference, lowliness **10** compliance, gentleness, humbleness, submission **11** forbearance, resignation,

wimpishness **12** acquiescence, peacefulness **13** long-suffering, self-abasement, spinelessness **14** self-effacement, spiritlessness, submissiveness

**meet**
◇ *juxtaposition indicator*
**03** get, pay, see **04** abut, bear, even, face, fill, game, give, hear, join, link, race, take **05** abide, cross, equal, event, greet, match, quits, rally, round, touch, unite **06** adjoin, answer, endure, fulfil, gather, handle, honour, hook up, link up, manage, muster, pay for, settle, suffer, tackle **07** balance, collect, connect, contest, convene, convoke, execute, fitting, fixture, meeting, perform, react to, receive, run into, satisfy, undergo **08** assemble, bump into, chance on, come upon, come up to, converge, cope with, deal with, listen to **09** discharge, encounter, fittingly, forgather, go through, intersect, look after, qualified, respond to, run across **10** come across, comply with, congregate, engagement, experience, foregather, happen upon, join up with, rencounter, rendezvous, tournament **11** competition, get together, measure up to **12** come together, intersection **14** get to grips with **15** make contact with
• **failure to meet**
**04** gape

**meeting**
**03** AGM, EGM, hui **04** date, meet, moot **05** rally, tryst, union, venue **07** cabinet, contact, gorsedd, session **08** abutment, assembly, camporee, concours, consulta, exercise, junction, wardmote **09** concourse, encounter, gathering, interface, interview **10** chautauqua, conference, confluence, convention, engagement, rencounter, rendezvous, watersmeet **11** appointment, assignation, conjunction, conventicle, convergence **12** intersection, introduction **13** confrontation **14** point of contact
*See also* **greeting**

**meeting-place**
**04** gild, moot, Pnyx **05** guild, house, joint, lodge, marae, venue **06** baraza, centre **07** cenacle **10** confluence, rendezvous, vestry-room **11** senate-house **12** chapterhouse

**megalomania**
**13** conceitedness **14** overestimation, self-importance **15** folie de grandeur

**meitnerium**
**02** Mt

**melancholy**
**03** low, sad **04** blue, down, glum **05** adust, blues, dumps, gloom, moody **06** dismal, gloomy, hipped, misery, rueful, somber, sombre, sorrow, spleen, woeful **07** doleful, pensive, sadness, unhappy **08** dejected, doldrums, downcast, mournful **09** allicholy, dejection, depressed, miserable, pessimism, sorrowful, splenetic, surliness, tristesse, woebegone **10** allycholly, deplorable, depression, despondent, dispirited, low spirits, lugubrious, pensieroso **11** atrabilious, despondency, downhearted, low-spirited, melancholia, melancholic, the black dog, unhappiness **12** disconsolate, heavy-hearted **13** hypochondriac, in the doldrums **14** down in the dumps
• **make melancholy**
**03** hip, hyp

**melange**
◇ *anagram indicator*
**03** mix **06** jumble, medley **07** farrago, mixture, variety **08** mishmash, mixed bag, pastiche **09** confusion, patchwork, potpourri **10** assortment, collection, hodgepodge, hotchpotch, miscellany, salmagundi **11** gallimaufry, smorgasbord **14** conglomeration, omnium-gatherum

**mêlée**
◇ *anagram indicator*
**04** fray, mess **05** brawl, broil, chaos, fight, mix-up, rally, scrum, set-to **06** affray, fracas, jumble, medley, mellay, muddle, ruckus, rumpus, tangle, tussle **07** clutter, ruction, scuffle **08** disorder, dogfight, stramash **09** confusion, scrimmage, scrummage **10** free-for-all **11** battle royal **15** disorganization

**Melia**
**03** nim **04** neem, nimb **05** neemb

**mellifluous**
**04** soft **05** sweet **06** dulcet, mellow, smooth **07** honeyed, silvery, tuneful **08** canorous, soothing **10** euphonious, harmonious **13** sweet-sounding

**mellow**
**04** full, kind, mild, rich, ripe, soft **05** happy, jolly, juicy, ripen, sweet **06** dulcet, fruity, genial, gentle, jovial, mature, placid, season, serene, smooth, soften, temper, tender **07** affable, amiable, cordial, improve, perfect, relaxed, rounded, sweeten, tuneful **08** amicable, cheerful, luscious, pleasant, resonant, tranquil **09** easy-going, melodious **10** euphonious, harmonious, pear-shaped **11** good-natured, kind-hearted **13** full-flavoured **15** make less extreme

**melodic**
**05** sweet **06** dulcet **07** musical, silvery, tuneful **09** melodious **10** euphonious, harmonious **13** sweet-sounding

**melodically**
**07** sweetly **09** musically, tunefully **11** melodiously **12** harmoniously

**melodious**
**05** sweet **06** dulcet, pretty **07** melodic, musical, Orphean, silvery, songful, tuneful **09** cantabile **10** euphonious, harmonious **13** sweet-sounding

**melodrama**
**07** tragedy **09** dramatics, high drama, staginess **10** overacting **11** histrionics, performance, tragicomedy **13** theatricality

**melodramatic**
**03** OTT **05** hammy, stagy **06** stagey **08** overdone, theatric **10** histrionic, over-the-top, theatrical **11** exaggerated, extravagant, sensational **12** histrionical, overdramatic, overstrained, transpontine **13** overemotional **15** blood-and-thunder

**melody**
**03** air **04** aria, ayre, part, song, tune **05** canto, chant, music, theme **06** cantus, rhythm, strain **07** euphony, harmony, melisma, musette, refrain **08** carillon, cavatina, part-song **09** cabaletta, cantilena, plainsong, sweetness **10** canto fermo, musicality **11** musicalness, tunefulness **12** augmentation, counterpoint **13** ranz-des-vaches **14** harmoniousness

**melon**
**04** pepo **06** casaba **07** cassaba **09** cantaloup, musk melon, Ogen melon, rock melon **10** cantaloupe, Charentais, Galia melon **11** winter melon **13** honeydew melon

**melt**
◇ *anagram indicator*
**03** ren, rin, run **04** blow, calm, flow, flux, fuse, move, thaw **05** smelt, touch **06** affect, relent, render, soften, spleen **07** defrost, liquate, liquefy, resolve **08** discandy, dissolve, moderate, unfreeze **09** discandie, uncongeal **10** colliquate, deliquesce, impregnate, make tender **12** become tender
• **melt away**
**04** fade **06** dispel, vanish **08** disperse, dissolve, evanesce, fade away **09** disappear, evaporate

**meltdown**
**06** defeat, fiasco **07** debacle, failure **08** abortion, calamity, collapse, disaster, downfall **09** breakdown **11** frustration, miscarriage **15** coming to nothing

**member**
**01** M **02** MP **03** arm, leg, MBE, Mem **04** limb, part **05** organ **06** clause, fellow **07** comrade, dumaist, element **08** adherent **09** appendage, associate, extremity, stretcher **10** subscriber **12** incorporator **14** representative

**membership**
**04** body, seat **07** fellows, members **08** comrades **09** adherence, adherents, enrolment **10** allegiance, associates, fellowship **11** affiliation, subscribers **13** participation **15** representatives

**membrane**
**03** haw, rim **04** fell, film, kell, skin, veil **05** hymen, layer, sheet, velum

**06** mucosa, septum, tissue **08** patagium **09** arachnoid, diaphragm, partition **10** integument

**memento**
**03** mem **04** Goss **05** relic, token **06** record, trophy **07** vestige **08** keepsake, memorial, reminder, souvenir **11** remembrance

**memo**
**03** fax **04** note **05** e-mail **06** letter **07** jotting, message **08** reminder **10** memorandum **11** aide-mémoire, remembrance **12** memory-jogger

**memoir**
**04** life **05** essay **06** record, report **07** account, journal **08** register **09** biography, chronicle, monograph, narrative **13** autobiography

**memoirs**
**05** diary **06** annals **07** diaries, records **08** journals, memories **09** life story **10** chronicles **11** confessions, experiences **13** autobiography, recollections, reminiscences

**memorable**
**06** catchy, unique **07** notable, special **08** eventful, historic, striking **09** important, momentous **10** impressive, noteworthy, remarkable **11** distinctive, outstanding, significant **13** consequential, distinguished, extraordinary, unforgettable

**memorandum**
**03** fax, mem **04** memo, note, slip **05** e-mail, jurat **06** letter **07** jotting, message **08** memorial, reminder **09** bordereau **11** aide-mémoire, remembrance **12** memory-jogger

**memorial**
**03** mem **05** brass, relic, stone, stupa **06** dagaba, dagoba, marker, memory, plaque, record, shrine, statue, trophy, Yizkor **07** memento, relique **08** cenotaph, ebenezer, monument, Pantheon, souvenir **09** altar-tomb, mausoleum, tombstone **10** gravestone, memorandum, monumental, remembered **11** celebratory, Norman cross, remembrance, testimonial **13** commemorative

*See also* **monument**

**memorize**
**05** learn **06** get off, record **08** remember **09** celebrate **11** learn by rote **12** learn by heart **14** commit to memory

**memory**
**03** RAM, ROM **04** mind, rote **06** honour, recall **07** tribute **09** retention, sovenance **10** observance **11** recognition, remembrance **12** recollection, reminiscence **13** commemoration **14** powers of recall

• **memory block**
**04** page

**men**
**02** OR

*See also* **man**

• **excluding men**
**03** hen

**menace**
**04** loom, lour, pain, pest, risk **05** alarm, appal, bully, daunt, peril, press, scare, shore **06** bother, coerce, danger, dismay, hazard, screws, threat **07** terrify, warning **08** big stick, browbeat, bullying, coercion, frighten, jeopardy, nuisance, pressure, threaten **09** annoyance, terrorism, terrorize **10** intimidate, pressurize **11** browbeating, frighteners, ominousness, public enemy, terrorizing **12** intimidation, troublemaker **13** tyrannization **15** thorn in your side

**menacing**
**04** grim **07** looming, louring, ominous, warning **08** alarming, minatory, sinister **09** Damoclean, dangerous, impending, minacious, threatful **10** portentous **11** frightening, threatening **12** intimidating, intimidatory

**mend**
**03** fix, sew, toe **04** beet, bete, cure, darn, heal **05** amend, clout, emend, patch, plash, refit, renew, run up, stick **06** bushel, cobble, reform, remedy, repair, revise, solder **07** correct, improve, patch up, recover, rectify, restore **08** put right, renovate, solution **09** get better, make whole **10** ameliorate, put in order, recuperate, supplement **14** mend your fences **15** put back together

• **mend your ways**
**06** reform **15** improve yourself, make a fresh start

• **on the mend**
**07** healing **08** reviving **09** improving **10** recovering **12** convalescent, convalescing, recuperating

**mendacious**
**05** false, lying **06** untrue **08** perjured **09** deceitful, deceptive, dishonest, insincere **10** fallacious, fictitious, fraudulent, perfidious, untruthful **11** duplicitous

**mendacity**
**03** lie **05** lying **06** deceit **07** perfidy, perjury, untruth **09** duplicity, falsehood **10** dishonesty, distortion, inveracity **11** fraudulence, insincerity **13** deceitfulness, falsification **14** untruthfulness

**mendelevium**
**02** Md

**mendicant**
**03** bum **04** hobo **05** fakir, frate, friar, sadhu, tramp **06** beggar, cadger, canter, craver, pauper, saddhu, toerag **07** begging, bludger, cadging, jarkman, moocher, sponger, vagrant **08** besognio, blighter, calender, vagabond, whipjack **09** scrounger **10** down-and-out, freeloader, panhandler, scrounging, supplicant **11** beachcomber, petitionary

**menial**
**03** eta, low **04** base, dull **05** lowly, slave **06** boring, drudge, humble, minion, ribald, skivvy **07** humdrum, routine, servant, servile, slavish, waister **08** dogsbody, domestic, labourer **09** attendant, degrading, demeaning, underling, unskilled **10** after-guard **11** ignominious, subservient

**menstruation**
**04** flow **06** menses, period **07** courses **08** the curse, the usual **09** monthlies **10** menorrhoea **11** monthly flow **14** menstrual cycle, time of the month

**mensuration**
**06** metage, survey **09** measuring, surveying, valuation **10** assessment, estimation, evaluation, planimetry **11** calculation, calibration, computation, measurement

**mental**
◊ *anagram indicator*
**03** ape, fey, mad **04** bats, gyte, loco, nuts, wild **05** barmy, batty, buggy, crazy, daffy, dippy, dotty, flaky, gonzo, loony, loopy, manic, nutty, potty, queer, wacko, wacky, wiggy **06** crazed, cuckoo, fruity, insane, maniac, raving, red-mad, screwy, troppo **07** bananas, barking, berserk, bonkers, cracked, frantic, lunatic, meshuga **08** abstract, cerebral, crackers, demented, deranged, dingbats, doolally, frenetic, frenzied, maniacal, rational, unhinged, unstable **09** cognitive, disturbed, lymphatic, psychotic, up the wall **10** bestraught, conceptual, distracted, distraught, frantic-mad, off the wall, off your nut, out to lunch, ridiculous, stone-crazy, unbalanced **11** not all there, off the rails, off your head, theoretical, unconscious **12** intellectual, mad as a hatter, off your chump, round the bend **13** off your rocker, of unsound mind, out of your head, out of your mind, out of your tree, round the twist **14** off your trolley, wrong in the head **15** non compos mentis, out of your senses

• **mental health workers**
**15** men in white coats

**mentality**
**04** mind **06** brains, make-up **07** faculty, mindset, outlook **08** attitude, ingenium **09** character, intellect **10** grey matter, psychology **11** disposition, frame of mind, personality, rationality **12** intelligence **13** comprehension, understanding, way of thinking **14** mental attitude **15** little grey cells

**mentally**
**07** ideally **08** inwardly **09** in the mind **10** rationally **11** emotionally **12** subjectively **14** intellectually **15** psychologically, temperamentally

**mention**
**03** say **04** cite, hint, mind, name, note, talk **05** hight, mensh, quote, speak, state **06** bename, broach, cast up, drag up, exhume, hint at, impart, notice, remark, report, reveal, speech **07** bring up, declare, divulge, let fall, refer to, speak of, specify, touch on, tribute **08** allude to, allusion, citation, disclose, instance, intimate, nominate, point out, remember **09** introduce, make known, reference, statement **10** indication, particular **11** acknowledge, communicate, observation, recognition **12** announcement, notification **14** condescend upon **15** acknowledgement

• **don't mention it**
**05** bitte **08** forget it, not at all **09** don't worry **12** it's a pleasure, it was nothing

• **not to mention**
**05** let be **06** let-a-be **07** besides **08** as well as, let alone, much less **12** not including **13** not forgetting **14** to say nothing of

**mentioned**
**05** cited **06** quoted, stated **08** foresaid, reported **09** aforesaid, fore-cited, forenamed **10** fore-quoted **13** forementioned **14** above-mentioned, aforementioned

**mentor**
**03** rav **04** guru **05** coach, guide, swami, tutor **07** adviser, advisor, teacher, trainer **09** confidant, pedagogue, therapist **10** confidante, counsellor, instructor

**menu**
**04** card, list **06** tariff **10** bill of fare **11** carte du jour

**mercantile**
**05** trade **07** salable, trading **08** saleable **09** mercenary **10** commercial, marketable **12** merchantable

**mercenary**
**04** hack, merc, paid **05** hired, venal **06** greedy, rutter, sordid **07** Hessian, pindari, Switzer **08** covetous, grasping, hired gun, hireling, huckster, pindaree **09** freelance, on the make, warmonger **10** avaricious, galloglass, lansquenet, mercantile, prostitute **11** acquisitive, condottiere, landsknecht, mammonistic **12** hired soldier, professional **13** free companion, materialistic, money-grubbing **15** money-orientated

**merchandise**
**04** ware **05** cargo, goods, stock, trade, wares **07** dealing, freight, produce **08** products, shipment **09** vendibles **11** commodities

**merchandize**
**04** hype, plug, push, sell, vend **05** carry, trade **06** deal in, market, peddle, retail, supply **07** promote **09** advertise, publicize, traffic in **10** buy and sell, distribute

**merchant**
**05** agent, bunia, trade **06** broker, bunnia, dealer, factor, jobber, seller, trader, vendor **07** Antonio **08** hoastman, retailer, salesman **09** bourgeois, négociant **10** commercial, marcantant, saleswoman, shopkeeper, supercargo, trafficker, wholesaler **11** distributor, salesperson **14** sales executive

**merciful**
**04** kind, mild **06** humane **07** clement, lenient, liberal, pitying, sparing **08** generous, gracious, tolerant **09** forgiving, merciable **10** forbearing **11** soft-hearted, sympathetic **12** humanitarian **13** compassionate, tender-hearted

**mercifully**
**06** kindly **07** luckily **10** generously, graciously, thankfully, tolerantly **11** fortunately **15** compassionately, sympathetically, tender-heartedly

**merciless**
**04** hard **05** cruel, harsh, rigid, stern **06** severe, wanton **07** callous, inhuman **08** inhumane, pitiless, ruthless **09** barbarous, heartless, unfeeling, unpitying, unsparing **10** implacable, inexorable, intolerant, relentless, unmerciful **11** hard-hearted, remorseless, unforgiving **13** unsympathetic

**mercilessly**
**07** cruelly, harshly, sternly **08** severely **09** callously **10** implacably, inexorably, pitilessly, ruthlessly **11** heartlessly **12** relentlessly **13** hard-heartedly, remorselessly

**mercurial**
**06** active, fickle, lively, mobile **07** erratic, flighty **08** spirited, unstable, variable, volatile **09** impetuous, impulsive, sprightly **10** capricious, changeable, inconstant **11** quicksilver **12** light-hearted **13** irrepressible, temperamental, unpredictable

**mercury**
**02** Hg **06** Hermes

**mercy**
**04** boon, pity **05** grace **06** favour, relief **07** godsend, quarter **08** blessing, clemency, good luck, kindness, leniency, mildness, sympathy **10** compassion, generosity, humaneness, misericord, tenderness **11** forbearance, forgiveness, misericorde **14** loving-kindness **15** humanitarianism

• **at the mercy of**
**09** exposed to, prostrate **11** at the whim of **12** in the power of, vulnerable to **14** in the control of, unarmed against

**mere**
**04** bare, lake, meer, meri, pool, poor, pure, very **05** bound, petty, plain, sheer, stark, utter **06** common, paltry, simple **07** unmixed **08** absolute, boundary, complete **10** absolutely, no more than **13** pure and simple, unadulterated

**merely**
**03** but **04** just, only **06** barely, hardly, purely, simply **08** scarcely **10** nothing but

**meretricious**
**04** bold, loud **05** cheap, flash, gaudy, jazzy, showy, tacky **06** flashy, garish, glitzy, kitsch, made up, tawdry, vulgar **09** glamorous, insincere, tasteless **10** flamboyant **11** pretentious **12** ostentatious

**merganser**
**04** smew

**merge**
**03** die, dip, mix **04** fuse, join, meet, meld, sink **05** blend, unite, verge **06** mingle, plunge, team up **07** collate, combine, run into **08** coalesce, converge, intermix, liquesce, melt into **10** amalgamate, be engulfed, join forces **11** consolidate, incorporate **12** become lost in, come together **13** bring together **15** be assimilated in, be swallowed up in

**merger**
**05** blend, union **06** fusion **08** alliance **09** coalition **11** combination, convergence **12** amalgamation, assimilation **13** confederation, consolidation, incorporation

**merit**
**03** due **04** earn, good, plus **05** asset, claim, found, value, worth **06** credit, desert, praise, reward, talent, virtue **07** be worth, deserts, deserve, justify, quality, warrant **08** goodness **09** advantage **10** be worthy of, excellence, excellency, recompense, worthiness **11** distinction, high quality, strong point **12** be entitled to, have a right to **13** justification

**merited**
**03** due **04** just **06** earned, worthy **07** condign, fitting **08** deserved, entitled, rightful **09** justified, warranted **11** appropriate **12** well-deserved

**meritorious**
**04** good **05** right **06** worthy **08** laudable, virtuous, worthful **09** admirable, deserving, estimable, excellent, exemplary, righteous **10** creditable, honourable **11** commendable **12** praiseworthy

**mermaid**
**05** siren **06** undine **07** seamaid **08** sea nymph, seawoman **11** water-spirit, water sprite

**merrily**
**06** gladly **07** happily **08** blithely, chirpily, jovially **10** cheerfully, pleasantly

**merriment**
**03** fun **05** mirth **06** frolic, gaiety **07** jollity, revelry, waggery **08** buoyance, carnival, hilarity, laughter

**09** amusement, festivity, jocundity, jolliment, joviality **10** blitheness, joyfulness, liveliness **11** high spirits **12** carefreeness, cheerfulness, conviviality, mirthfulness **13** jollification

**merry**

◇ *anagram indicator*

**03** gay **04** cant, daft, gean, glad **05** gaudy, happy, jolly, nitid, riant, tipsy, vogie **06** blithe, cheery, chirpy, frolic, jocose, jocund, jovial, joyful, lively, tiddly **07** amusing, festive, gleeful, squiffy **08** carefree, cheerful, gleesome, mirthful, pleasant, sportful, sportive **09** convivial, heartsome, hilarious **10** frolicsome **11** saturnalian **12** high-spirited, light-hearted **13** in good spirits, slightly drunk **15** one over the eight

**• make merry**

**04** gaud, rant, sing **05** dance, drink, revel **07** carouse, have fun, rejoice **09** celebrate **10** have a party **13** enjoy yourself

**merry-andrew**

**05** clown **07** buffoon **11** Jack-pudding **13** pickle-herring

**merry-go-round**

**08** carousel, galloper, joy-wheel **09** carrousel, gallopers, whirligig **10** roundabout

**merrymaking**

**03** fun **05** party, revel **06** frolic, gaiety **07** revelry **08** carousal, merimake **09** carousing, festivity, galravage, gilravage, junketing, merriment **10** galravitch, gillravage, gilravitch, rejoicings **11** celebration, gillravitch **12** conviviality **13** jollification

**mesh**

**03** net, web **04** trap **05** gauze, match, snare **06** engage, enmesh, inmesh, tangle **07** combine, connect, entwine, lattice, netting, network, tracery, trellis **08** dovetail, entangle **09** harmonize, interlock **10** co-ordinate, go together **11** fit together, latticework **12** come together, entanglement

**mesmerize**

**04** grip **06** benumb **07** enthral, stupefy **08** entrance, transfix **09** captivate, fascinate, hypnotize, magnetize, spellbind **14** hold spellbound

**mess**

◇ *anagram indicator*

**03** fix, jam, mix, mux, tip **04** dine, dirt, dump, hash, hole, meal, muck, muss, soss, spot, stew **05** botch, chaos, farce, filth, mix-up, musse, slosh **06** bungle, cock-up, course, guddle, hiccup, jumble, lash-up, litter, medley, midden, mucker, muddle, pickle, plight **07** balls-up, clutter, dilemma, failure, jackpot, pig's ear, screw-up, squalor, trouble, turmoil **08** disarray, disorder, hot water, quandary, shambles, slaister, whoopsie **09** confusion, deep water, dirtiness, praiseach, shemozzle, shimozzle, tight spot **10** difficulty, dog's dinner, filthiness, pretty pass, schemozzle, shlemozzle, untidiness **11** predicament **13** dog's breakfast, embarrassment, pig's breakfast **15** disorganization

**• make a mess of**

**04** flub, goof

**• mess about, mess around**

**04** goof, play **05** upset **06** piddle, puddle, putter **09** faff about, goof about, muck about, play about **10** faff around, fool around, goof around, play around **11** potter about **12** fiddle around

**• mess about with, mess around with**

**05** upset **06** bother **07** trouble **08** play with **10** meddle with, tamper with, treat badly **13** fool about with, inconvenience, interfere with, play about with **14** fool around with, play around with

**• mess up**

**04** foul, muff, ruin **05** bitch, bodge, botch, dirty, fluff, spoil **06** bungle, cock up, foul up, jumble, muck up, muddle, tangle, untidy **07** confuse, disrupt, louse up, screw up **08** dishevel **09** clutter up **10** disarrange **11** make a hash of, make a mess of

**message**

**03** fax **04** gist, idea, memo, news, note, task, wire, word **05** cable, drift, e-mail, moral, point, sense, telex, theme **06** errand, import, letter, notice, report, thrust **07** dépêche, epistle, essence, express, meaning, missive, purport, tidings **08** aerogram, bulletin, dispatch, irenicon, mailgram, telegram, Teletype® **09** autoreply, eirenicon, telegraph, telepheme **10** communiqué, intimation, memorandum **11** implication, marconigram, Telemessage® **12** significance **13** communication

**• end message**

**07** sign off

**• get the message**

**03** see **04** twig **05** get it, grasp **06** follow, take in **07** catch on, latch on **08** cotton on, tumble to **09** latch onto **10** comprehend, cotton on to, get the hang, get the idea, understand **11** get the point **13** catch the drift, get the picture

**messenger**

**04** page, peon, post, send **05** agent, angel, caddy, cadee, cadie, envoy **06** beadle, bearer, caddie, herald, Hermes, nuncio, runner **07** carrier, courier, express, Mercury, missive **08** dispatch, emissary, footpost **09** chaprassi, chaprassy, chuprassy, errand-boy, go-between, harbinger, woman post **10** ambassador, errand-girl, forerunner, pursuivant, shellycoat **11** internuncio **12** ambassadress, valet de place **13** gillie-wetfoot, secretary-bird **14** commissionaire **15** corbie messenger, gillie-white-foot

**messy**

◇ *anagram indicator*

**05** dirty, gungy, yucky, yukky **06** filthy, grubby, grungy, sloppy, untidy **07** chaotic, muddled, unkempt **08** bungling, confused, littered, slobbish, slovenly **09** cluttered, shambolic **10** disordered, in disarray **11** dishevelled **12** disorganized

**metal**

*Metals include:*

**01** **K** (potassium), **U** (uranium), **V** (vanadium), **W** (tungsten), **Y** (yttrium)

**02** **Ac** (actinium), **Ag** (silver), **Al** (aluminium), **Am** (americium), **Au** (gold), **Ba** (barium), **Be** (beryllium), **Bi** (bismuth), **Bk** (berkelium), **Ca** (calcium), **Cd** (cadmium), **Ce** (cerium), **Cf** (californium), **Cm** (curium), **Co** (cobalt), **Cr** (chromium), **Cs** (caesium), **Cu** (copper), **Dy** (dysprosium), **Er** (erbium), **Es** (einsteinium), **Eu** (europium), **Fe** (iron), **Fm** (fermium), **Fr** (francium), **Ga** (gallium), **Gd** (gadolinium), **Ge** (germanium), **Hf** (hafnium), **Hg** (mercury), **Ho** (holmium), **In** (indium), **Ir** (iridium), **La** (lanthanum), **Li** (lithium), **Lr** (lawrencium), **Lu** (lutetium), **Md** (mendelevium), **Mg** (magnesium), **Mn** (manganese), **Mo** (molybdenum), **Na** (sodium), **Nb** (niobium), **Nd** (neodymium), **Ni** (nickel), **No** (nobelium), **Np** (neptunium), **Os** (osmium), **Pa** (protactinium), **Pb** (lead), **Pd** (palladium), **Pm** (promethium), **Po** (polonium), **Pr** (praseodymium), **Pt** (platinum), **Pu** (plutonium), **Ra** (radium), **Rb** (rubidium), **Re** (rhenium), **Rh** (rhodium), **Ru** (ruthenium), **Sb** (antimony), **Sc** (scandium), **Sm** (samarium), **Sn** (tin), **Sr** (strontium), **Ta** (tantalum), **Tb** (terbium), **Tc** (technetium), **Th** (thorium), **Ti** (titanium), **Tl** (thallium), **Tm** (thulium), **Yb** (ytterbium), **Zn** (zinc), **Zr** (zirconium)

**03** **tin** (Sn)

**04** **gold** (Au), **iron** (Fe), **lead** (Pb), **zinc** (Zn)

**06** **barium** (Ba), **cerium** (Ce), **cobalt** (Co), **copper** (Cu), **curium** (Cm), **erbium** (Er), **indium** (In), **nickel** (Ni), **osmium** (Os), **radium** (Ra), **silver** (Ag), **sodium** (Na)

**07** **bismuth** (Bi), **cadmium** (Cd), **caesium** (Cs), **calcium** (Ca), **fermium** (Fm), **gallium** (Ga), **hafnium** (Hf), **holmium** (Ho), **iridium** (Ir), **lithium** (Li), **mercury** (Hg), **niobium** (Nb), **rhenium** (Re), **rhodium** (Rh), **terbium** (Tb), **thorium** (Th), **thulium** (Tm), **uranium** (U), **yttrium** (Y)

**08** **actinium** (Ac), **antimony** (Sb), **chromium** (Cr), **europium** (Eu),

francium (Fr), lutetium (Lu), nobelium (No), platinum (Pt), polonium (Po), rubidium (Rb), samarium (Sm), scandium (Sc), tantalum (Ta), thallium (Tl), titanium (Ti), tungsten (W), vanadium (V)
**09** aluminium (Al), americium (Am), berkelium (Bk), beryllium (Be), germanium (Ge), lanthanum (La), magnesium (Mg), manganese (Mn), neodymium (Nd), neptunium (Np), palladium (Pd), plutonium (Pu), potassium (K), ruthenium (Ru), strontium (Sr), ytterbium (Yb), zirconium (Zr)
**10** dysprosium (Dy), gadolinium (Gd), lawrencium (Lr), molybdenum (Mo), promethium (Pm), technetium (Tc)
**11** californium (Cf), einsteinium (Es), mendelevium (Md)
**12** praseodymium (Pr), protactinium (Pa)

*Metal alloys include:*

**03** pot
**04** type
**05** brass, Dutch, Invar®, Muntz, potin, steel, terne, white
**06** Alnico®, billon, bronze, latten, occamy, ormolu, oroide, pewter, solder, tambac, tombac, tombak, Y-alloy
**07** amalgam, Babbit's, chromel, Nitinol, prince's, shakudo, similor, tutania, tutenag
**08** Babbitt's, cast iron, gunmetal, Manganin®, Nichrome®, orichalc, speculum, zircaloy, Zircoloy®
**09** Britannia, Duralumin®, Dutch gold, Dutch leaf, magnalium, pinchbeck, shibuichi, white gold
**10** constantan, ferro-alloy, iridosmine, iridosmium, mischmetal, Monel metal®, mosaic gold, osmiridium, white brass
**11** chrome steel, cupro-nickel, nicrosilial, white copper
**12** German silver, nickel silver
**14** high-speed steel, phosphor-bronze, stainless steel

**• design on metal**
**04** etch
**• join metal**
**04** weld
**• metal after heating**
**04** calx
**• metal bar**
**03** zed **05** ingot
**• piece of metal**
**03** gib
**• precious metal**
**03** ore
**• thin metal**
**04** foil

## metallic
**03** tin **04** gold, iron, lead **05** harsh, rough, shiny, steel, tinny **06** copper, nickel, silver **07** grating, jarring **08** gleaming, jangling, polished **09** dissonant **10** unpleasant

## metamorphose
◇ *anagram indicator*
**05** alter **06** change, modify, mutate, remake **07** convert, remodel, reshape **09** transform, translate, transmute **11** transfigure **12** transmogrify

## metamorphosis
◇ *anagram indicator*
**06** change **07** rebirth **08** mutation **09** staminody **10** alteration, changeover, conversion, metabolism **12** modification, regeneration **13** transmutation **14** holometabolism, transformation **15** transfiguration

## metaphor
**03** met **05** image, trope **06** emblem, metaph, symbol, visual **07** analogy, picture **08** allegory **10** emblematic **12** transumption **14** figure of speech, representation

## metaphorical
**03** met **06** metaph, visual **08** symbolic **10** analogical, emblematic, figurative **11** allegorical

## metaphysical
**04** deep **05** basic, ideal **06** unreal **07** eternal, general **08** abstract, abstruse, esoteric, fanciful, profound **09** essential, high-flown, recondite, spiritual, universal **10** immaterial, impalpable, intangible, subjective **11** fundamental, incorporeal, speculative, theoretical **12** intellectual, supernatural **13** insubstantial, philosophical, unsubstantial **14** transcendental

## mete
**• mete out**
**05** allot **06** assign **07** deal out, dole out, hand out, portion **08** dispense, share out **09** apportion, divide out, ration out **10** administer, distribute, measure out

## meteor
**05** comet, drake **06** bolide **08** aerolite, aerolith, fireball **09** meteorite, meteoroid **10** exhalation **11** falling star **12** shooting star

*Meteor showers include:*

**06** Lyrids, Ursids
**07** Leonids, Taurids
**08** Geminids, Orionids, Perseids
**11** Quadrantids
**12** Eta Aquariids
**14** Alpha-Scorpiids, Delta Aquariids

## meteoric
**04** fast **05** brief, quick, rapid, swift **06** speedy, sudden **08** dazzling, flashing **09** brilliant, lightning, momentary, overnight, transient **11** spectacular **13** instantaneous

## meteorologist
**06** met man **10** weatherman **11** weathergirl, weatherlady **13** climatologist **14** weather prophet

## meteorology

*Meteorology-related terms include:*

**04** calm, eddy, flux, haar, haze, ITCZ, rime
**05** flood, front, frost, Q-code, radar, ridge, SIGWX, solar, taiga, virga
**06** arctic, el Niño, flurry, haboob, isobar, Kelvin, oxygen
**07** Celsius, chinook, climate, cyclone, drizzle, drought, graupel, mistral, monsoon, rainbow, thunder, tornado, typhoon, weather
**08** acid rain, blizzard, dewpoint, doldrums, forecast, humidity, isotherm, millibar, rainfall, windsock, wind vane
**09** advection, aerograph, altimeter, barograph, barometer, cold front, hurricane, hyetology, jet stream, lightning, Met Office, nephology, radiation, rain gauge, satellite, sub-arctic, trade wind, warm front, wind chill, wind speed
**10** aerography, air quality, anemometer, atmosphere, baroclinic, barotropic, cloud cover, conduction, convection, depression, Fahrenheit, Gulf stream, Hadley Cell, hemisphere, hyetograph, hyetometer, hygrometer, nephograph, nephoscope, nowcasting, ozone layer, rain shadow, rain shower, visibility, waterspout, wavelength
**11** air pressure, anticyclone, climatology, evaporation, ground frost, hyetography, pollen count, temperature, thermograph, thermometer, thermopause, troposphere, ultra violet, water vapour, wave cyclone
**12** cloud seeding, condensation, cyclogenesis, meteorograph, microclimate, pilot balloon, thunderstorm, weather chart, weather watch
**13** ball lightning, Beaufort scale, boundary layer, climate change, fork lightning, frontogenesis, magnetosphere, occluded front, onshore breeze, precipitation
**14** air temperature, continentality, horse latitudes, offshore breeze, prevailing wind, sheet lightning, transmissivity, weather station
**15** hyetometrograph, stationary front, weather forecast, wind-chill factor

## method
**03** art, how, way **04** form, line, mode, plan, rule **05** means, order, route, style **06** course, design, manner, scheme, system **07** fashion, pattern, process, routine **08** approach, modality, planning, practice **09** procedure, programme, structure, technique **10** regularity **11** arrangement, orderliness **12** organization **13** modus operandi **14** classification

**methodical**
**04** neat, tidy **06** formal **07** logical, ordered, orderly, planned, precise, regular **09** efficient, organized **10** deliberate, meticulous, scrupulous, structured, systematic **11** disciplined, painstaking, well-ordered **12** businesslike, systematical

**methodically**
**06** neatly, tidily **07** in place, orderly **08** formally **09** as planned, by the book, logically, precisely, regularly, to the rule, uniformly **11** efficiently **12** meticulously, scrupulously **13** painstakingly **14** systematically

**metical**
**02** Mt **03** MZM

**meticulous**
**05** exact, fussy, timid **06** strict **07** careful, precise **08** accurate, detailed, rigorous, thorough **10** fastidious, particular, scrupulous **11** overcareful, painstaking, punctilious **13** conscientious

**meticulously**
**07** exactly **08** strictly **09** carefully, precisely **10** accurately, rigorously, thoroughly **12** scrupulously **13** painstakingly, punctiliously **15** conscientiously

**métier**
**03** job **04** line **05** craft, field, forte, trade **06** sphere **07** calling, pursuit **08** business, vocation **09** specialty **10** occupation, profession, speciality **14** line of business

**metro** *see* **underground**

**metropolis**
**04** city **07** capital **08** main city **09** large city **10** cosmopolis **11** capital city, megalopolis **12** municipality **14** cultural centre

*See also* **city**

**mettle**
**04** guts, pith **05** nerve, pluck, pride, spunk **06** daring, ginger, make-up, nature, spirit, valour, vigour **07** bravery, calibre, courage, resolve, smeddum **08** backbone, boldness **09** character, endurance, fortitude, gallantry **11** disposition, intrepidity, personality, temperament **12** fearlessness **13** determination, sprightliness **14** indomitability

**mettlesome**
**04** bold **05** brave **06** ardent, daring, lively, plucky, spunky **07** gallant, valiant **08** fearless, intrepid, resolute, spirited **10** courageous **11** lion-hearted, unflinching **12** high-spirited, stout-hearted

**mew**
**04** cast, coop, gull, meow, mewl, shed **05** miaow, miaul, moult, whine **07** confine, retreat **09** caterwaul

**mewl**
**03** cry **05** whine **06** snivel, whinge **07** blubber, grizzle, whimper

**Mexican**
**03** Mex

**Mexico**
**03** MEX

**miaow**
**03** mew **04** meow, mewl **05** miaul, whine **09** caterwaul

**miasma**
**04** reek **05** fetor, odour, smell, stink **06** stench **07** malaria **08** mephitis **09** effluvium, pollution

**miasmal**
**04** foul **05** fetid **06** foetid, putrid, smelly **07** miasmic, noisome, noxious, reeking **08** mephitic, miasmous, polluted, stinking **09** miasmatic **10** malodorous, miasmatous **11** unwholesome **12** foul-smelling

**mica**
**03** mic **04** daze **07** biotite

**Michigan**
**02** MI **04** Mich

**microbe**
**03** bug **04** germ **05** virus **08** bacillus, pathogen **09** bacterium **13** micro-organism

**Micronesia**
**03** FSM

**microphone**
**03** bug

**microscope**
**03** SEM, TEM

**microscopic**
**04** tiny **06** minute **09** minuscule **10** negligible **13** imperceptible, indiscernible, infinitesimal **14** extremely small

**microscopically**
**08** minutely **09** extremely **13** imperceptibly **15** infinitesimally

**midday**
**01** m, n **04** noon **06** twelve **07** noonday **08** meridian, noontide, noontime **09** lunchtime **10** meridional, twelve noon **12** twelve o'clock

**middle**
◇ *middle selection indicator*
**03** med, mid **04** core, mean, noon **05** belly, heart, inner, midst, tummy, waist **06** centre, inside, medial, median, medium, mesial, midway, paunch **07** central, halfway, mediate, midriff, stomach **08** bull's eye, midpoint **11** bread basket, equidistant, intervening **12** halfway point, intermediate

• **in the middle of**
**05** among, while **06** during **08** busy with **09** engaged in **12** in the midst of, occupied with, surrounded by **14** in the process of

**middle-class**
**08** suburban **09** bourgeois **10** gentrified **11** white-collar **12** conventional, professional

**Middle East**

*Middle Eastern landmarks include:*

**05** Kabaa
**06** Qumran, Red Sea, Tigris
**07** Dead Sea, Ephesus
**08** Bosporus
**09** Bosphorus, Gallipoli
**10** Persepolis
**11** Grand Mosque, Hagia Sophia, River Jordan, Via Dolorosa, Wailing Wall, Western Wall
**12** Sea of Galilee
**13** Dome of the Rock
**15** Elburz Mountains

**middleman**
**05** fixer **06** broker **08** bummaree, regrater, regrator, retailer **09** go-between **10** negotiator **11** distributer, distributor **12** entrepreneur, intermediary

**Middlesex**
**02** Mx

**middling**
**02** OK **04** fair, so-so **06** fairly, medium, modest **07** average **08** adequate, mediocre, moderate, ordinary, passable **09** tolerable **10** not much cop **11** indifferent, not up to much **12** intermediate, run-of-the-mill, unremarkable **13** no great shakes, unexceptional **14** fair to middling

**midget**
**03** toy **04** baby, tiny **05** dwarf, gnome, pygmy, small, teeny **06** little, minute, pocket **07** manikin **08** mannikin, Tom Thumb **09** itsy-bitsy, miniature **10** diminutive, homunculus, teeny-weeny **11** Lilliputian, pocket-sized, small person

**midpoint**
**11** middle point **12** central point, halfway point

**midshipman**
**03** mid **04** Easy **05** middy **06** reefer, snotty **07** oldster, snottie **11** midshipmate **12** brass-bounder

**midst**
**03** hub **04** core **05** bosom, heart, thick **06** centre, depths, middle **07** nucleus **08** interior, midpoint

• **in the midst**
**04** amid **05** among **06** during **12** in the thick of, surrounded by **13** in the middle of

**midway**
**07** halfway **11** in the centre, in the middle **13** at the midpoint

**midwife**
**05** howdy **06** granny, howdie, Lucina **07** grannie **09** wise woman **10** accoucheur **11** accoucheuse

**mien**
**03** air **04** aura, look **06** allure, aspect, manner **07** bearing **08** carriage, presence **09** demeanour, semblance **10** appearance, complexion,

deportment, expression
**11** countenance

**miffed**
**04** hurt **05** irked, upset, vexed
**06** narked, peeved, piqued, put out
**07** annoyed, in a huff, nettled
**08** offended **09** aggrieved, chagrined, irritated, resentful **10** cheesed off, displeased **11** disgruntled

**might**
**04** sway **05** clout, force, power
**06** energy, muscle, valour, vigour
**07** ability, potency, prowess, stamina
**08** capacity, efficacy, strength
**09** heftiness, puissance **10** capability
**11** muscularity **12** forcefulness, powerfulness

**mightily**
**04** much, very **06** highly, hugely
**07** greatly, lustily **08** manfully, strongly, very much **09** decidedly, extremely, intensely **10** forcefully, powerfully, vigorously **11** exceedingly, strenuously
**13** energetically

**mighty**
**04** fell, huge, vast, very **05** bulky, felon, grand, great, hardy, hefty, large, lusty, stout, tough **06** highly, manful, potent, really, robust, strong **07** awfully, doughty, greatly, immense, massive, titanic, utterly, valiant **08** almighty, colossal, dominant, enormous, forceful, gigantic, mightful, muscular, powerful, puissant, stalwart, terribly, towering, vigorous **09** extremely, important, intensely, strapping, unusually, wonderful **10** dreadfully, monumental, prodigious, remarkably, stupendous, thoroughly, tremendous
**11** exceedingly, excessively, frightfully, indomitable, influential **12** terrifically, unreasonably **13** exceptionally
**15** extraordinarily

**mignonette**
**04** wald, weld **06** Reseda

**migrant**
**05** Gypsy, nomad, rover **06** roving, tinker **07** drifter, nomadic, swagger, swagman, vagrant **08** drifting, emigrant, shifting, wanderer
**09** immigrant, itinerant, migratory, transient, traveller, wandering
**10** travelling **11** peripatetic
**12** Gastarbeiter, globetrotter, transmigrant **13** globetrotting

**migrate**
**04** hike, move, roam, rove, trek **05** drift
**06** travel, voyage, wander **07** journey
**08** emigrate, relocate, resettle

**migration**
**03** ren, rin, run **04** trek **05** shift
**06** roving, travel, voyage **07** journey, passage **08** diaspora, movement
**09** walkabout, wandering
**10** emigration **12** transhumance
**15** Völkerwanderung

**migratory**
**05** Gypsy **06** roving **07** migrant, nomadic, vagrant **08** drifting, shifting
**09** immigrant, itinerant, transient, wandering **10** travelling **11** peripatetic
**13** globetrotting

**mike**
**01** M

**mild**
**04** calm, fair, kind, meek, soft, warm, weak **05** balmy, bland, faint, vague
**06** feeble, gentle, humane, mellow, modest, placid, slight, smooth, subtle, tender **07** amiable, clement, insipid, lenient, pacific **08** gall-less, mansuete, merciful, moderate, pleasant, soothing
**09** easy-going, peaceable, sensitive, tasteless, temperate **10** forbearing
**11** flavourless, good-natured, soft-hearted, sympathetic, warm-hearted
**13** compassionate, imperceptible, tender-hearted

**mildewy**
**05** fetid, fusty, mucid, musty **06** foetid, rotten **10** mucedinous

**mildly**
**06** calmly, gently, meekly, softly, subtly, warmly, weakly **07** faintly, vaguely
**08** slightly, tenderly **10** mercifully
**11** sensitively **13** imperceptibly
**15** compassionately

**mildness**
**05** mercy **06** lenity, warmth
**08** calmness, clemency, docility, kindness, leniency, meekness, softness, sympathy **09** blandness, milkiness, passivity, placidity **10** compassion, gentleness, indulgence, mellowness, moderation, smoothness, tenderness
**11** forbearance, insipidness
**12** tranquillity **13** tastelessness, temperateness

**mile**
**01** m **02** mi, ml, nm **05** n mile

**milieu**
**05** arena, scene **06** locale, medium, sphere **07** element, setting **08** location
**10** background **11** environment
**12** surroundings

**militancy**
**08** activism **09** extremism
**12** belligerence, vigorousness
**13** assertiveness **14** aggressiveness, British disease

**militant**
**07** fighter, soldier, warring, warrior
**08** activist, fighting, partisan, vigorous
**09** aggressor, assertive, combatant, combative, embattled, struggler
**10** aggressive, pugnacious
**11** belligerent, Black Muslim **12** Black Panther, militaristic

**militantly**
**10** vigorously **11** assertively
**12** aggressively **13** belligerently

**military**
**03** mil **04** army, navy **05** armed, milit
**06** forces **07** martial, militia, service, soldier, warlike **08** air force, services, soldiers, soldiery **09** soldierly
**11** armed forces, disciplined

*Military decorations include:*

**02** GC, GM, MC, MM, VC
**03** AFC, AFM, BEM, CGM, CMH, DCM, DFC, DFM, DSC, DSM, DSO
**09** Iron Cross
**10** Bronze Star, Silver Star
**11** George Cross, George Medal, Purple Heart
**13** Air Force Cross, Air Force Medal, Croix de Guerre, Legion of Merit, Military Cross, Military Medal, Victoria Cross
**14** Oak-leaf Cluster

*Military units and groups include:*

**04** file, post, wing
**05** corps, flank, fleet, group, squad, troop
**06** cohort, convoy, flight, legion, patrol, picket
**07** battery, brigade, company, echelon, militia, phalanx, platoon, section
**08** division, flotilla, garrison, regiment, squadron
**09** battalion, commandos, effective, task force
**10** detachment, flying camp, rifle-corps
**11** battle group, flying party
**12** flying column, Royal Marines
**13** guard of honour

• **military equipment**
**05** train
• **military life**
**04** camp
• **military men** *see* **soldiers** *under* **soldier**
• **military police**
**02** MP

**militate**
• **militate against**
**04** hurt **06** damage, oppose, resist
**07** contend, counter **09** go against, prejudice **10** act against, counteract, discourage **11** be harmful to, tell against, work against **12** count against, weigh against **15** be detrimental to
• **militate for**
**03** aid **04** back, help **07** advance, further, promote **08** speak for

**militia**
**02** SA, TA **04** fyrd **06** Milice **07** reserve
**08** yeomanry **09** fencibles, home guard, minutemen, trainband
**10** reservists **13** National Guard
**15** Territorial Army

**milk**
**03** tap, use **04** draw, pump, skim, whig
**05** bleed, drain, press, screw, wring
**06** rip off, siphon, stroke **07** draw off, exploit, express, extract, oppress, squeeze **08** impose on, moo-juice
**10** manipulate **11** semi-skimmed
**15** take advantage of
• **milk producer**
**03** cow **04** teat
• **not yielding milk**
**04** eild, yeld, yell

**milk-can**
**04** kirn **05** churn

**milking**
**• place for milking**
**04** loan **07** loaning

**milkman's cart**
**04** pram **05** float **09** milkfloat

**milksop**
**04** wimp, wuss **05** cissy, molly, pansy **06** coward, jessie **07** meacock **08** weakling **09** mummy's boy **10** namby-pamby

**milk-strainer**
**03** sye

**milky**
**04** soft, weak **05** white **06** chalky, cloudy, gentle, opaque **07** clouded **08** lacteous **09** milk-white, snow-white, spineless

**mill**
◇ *anagram indicator*
**03** box **04** nurl, roll, shop **05** crush, grate, grind, knurl, plant, pound, press, quern, works **06** crunch, powder, roller **07** crusher, factory, foundry, grinder **08** snuffbox, spinnery, workshop **09** comminute, pulverize **11** boxing match, molendinary **15** processing plant
**• mill around**
**05** swarm **06** stream, throng **09** move about **11** crowd around, press around

**millet**
**04** dari, dura, ragi **05** bajra, bajri, doura, durra, proso, ragee, raggy, whisk **06** bajree, dhurra, raggee **09** broom-corn **10** guinea corn

**million**
**01** m

**millstone**
**04** duty, load, onus **06** burden, ligger, runner, weight **07** trouble **09** buhrstone, burrstone **10** affliction, dead-weight, grindstone, obligation, quernstone **11** cross to bear, encumbrance
**• millstone support**
**04** rind

**millstream**
**04** lade

**Milne**
**02** AA

**mime**
**05** mimic **06** act out, signal **07** buffoon, charade, gesture, imitate, mimicry, mummery **08** dumb show, indicate, simulate **09** chironomy, pantomime, represent **11** impersonate

**mimic**
**02** do **03** ape **04** copy, echo, mime, mina, mock, myna, play **05** mynah **06** mirror, monkey, parody, parrot, send up **07** copycat, copyist, emulate, imitate, mimetic, minnick, minnock, take off **08** imitator, look like, mimicker, resemble, simulate, starling **09** mimetical, personate **10** caricature **11** impersonate **12** caricaturist, impersonator **13** impressionist

**mimicry**
**05** aping **06** parody **07** copying, mimesis, mockery, take-off **09** burlesque, imitating, imitation **10** caricature, impression, simulation **13** impersonation

**minatory**
**04** grim **07** looming, ominous, warning **08** menacing, sinister **09** impending, minacious **10** cautionary, foreboding **11** threatening **12** inauspicious, intimidatory

**mince**
◇ *anagram indicator*
**03** cut **04** chop, dice, hash, pose **05** grind, ponce **06** prance, simper **07** crumble, posture **11** strike a pose **12** attitudinize **14** walk affectedly
**• not mince your words**
**11** talk plainly **13** speak directly

**mincing**
**04** camp, nice **05** cissy, poncy **06** chi-chi, dainty, la-di-da **07** foppish, minikin **08** affected, chee-chee, precious **09** coxcombic **10** effeminate **11** coxcombical, pretentious **12** niminy-piminy

**mind**
**03** wit **04** care, head, heed, mark, note, obey, soul, tend, urge, view, will, wish, wits **05** brain, fancy, guard, sense, watch **06** attend, belief, brains, desire, expert, follow, genius, memory, notion, object, psyche, reason, recall, record, resent, sanity, spirit **07** dislike, egghead, feeling, mention, observe, opinion, outlook, purpose, respect, scholar, thinker, thought **08** academic, attend to, attitude, brainbox, listen to, remember, take care, tendency, thinking, thoughts, watch out **09** attention, intellect, intention, judgement, look after, mentality, retention, sentiment, viewpoint **10** grey matter, mastermind **11** application, disposition, inclination, keep an eye on, personality, point of view, remembrance **12** intellectual, intelligence, pay attention, recollection, subconscious **13** commemoration, comprehension, concentration, consciousness, ratiocination, understanding, way of thinking **15** little grey cells
**• bear in mind, keep in mind**
**04** note **06** retain **08** consider, remember **10** take note of **13** give thought to **15** take into account
**• be in two minds**
**05** waver **06** dither **08** be unsure, hesitate **09** vacillate **10** be hesitant, dilly-dally **11** be uncertain, be undecided **12** shilly-shally **13** sit on the fence
**• cross your mind**
**03** hit **06** come to, strike **07** occur to, think of **08** remember
**• have in mind**
**03** aim **04** plan, talk, want **06** design, intend **07** think of **11** contemplate
**• make up your mind**
**06** choose, decide, settle **07** resolve **09** determine **13** make a decision **14** reach a decision **15** come to a decision
**• mind out**
**05** watch **06** beware **07** look out **08** take care, watch out **09** be careful **12** pay attention **13** be on your guard
**• mind's eye**
**04** head **06** memory **11** imagination, remembrance **12** recollection **13** contemplation
**• never mind**
**03** too **04** also **06** skip it! **08** as well as, forget it, let alone **09** apart from, don't worry **10** nix my dolly **12** not to mention **13** not forgetting **14** not bother about, take no notice of
**• out of your mind**
**03** mad **04** nuts **05** barmy, batty, crazy, daffy, dippy, loony, loopy, manic, nutty, potty **06** crazed, cuckoo, insane, maniac, mental, raving, screwy **07** bananas, bonkers, flipped, lunatic **08** crackers, demented, deranged, doolally, frenzied, maniacal, unhinged, unstable **09** psychotic, up the wall **10** barking mad, distracted, distraught, off the wall, unbalanced **11** not all there, off the rails, off your head **12** mad as a hatter, off your chump, round the bend **13** off your rocker, of unsound mind, round the twist **14** off your trolley, wrong in the head **15** non compos mentis, out of your senses
**• put you in mind of**
**06** prompt, remind **10** call to mind **11** bring to mind **14** make you think of
**• put your mind to**
**09** persevere, take pains **10** buckle down **13** concentrate on, exert yourself
**• sharpness of mind**
**04** edge
**• speak your mind**
**11** talk plainly **14** tell it like it is
**• to my mind**
**04** heed, mark, note, obey **05** guard, watch **06** ensure, follow, I think, object, regard, resent **07** dislike, observe, respect **08** as I see it, attend to, I believe, in my view, listen to, make sure, object to, remember, take care, watch out **09** be careful, care about, look after, not forget, pay heed to, watch over **10** comply with, disapprove, personally, take care of **11** be annoyed by, in my opinion, keep an eye on, make certain, take offence **12** be bothered by, be offended by, be troubled by, have charge of, pay attention **13** concentrate on, take offence at

**mind-boggling**
**07** amazing **10** astounding, formidable, impossible, incredible, surprising **11** astonishing, exceptional, unthinkable **12** unbelievable, unimaginable **13** extraordinary, inconceivable

**mindful**
**04** wary **05** alert, alive, aware, chary **07** alive to, careful, heedful **08** inclined, sensible, watchful **09** attentive, cognizant, conscious, observant

**mindless**
**04** dull, dumb **05** dopey, thick **06** stupid **07** foolish, robotic, routine, tedious, witless **08** knee-jerk **09** automatic, illogical, negligent, senseless **10** gratuitous, irrational, mechanical **11** birdbrained, instinctive, involuntary, thoughtless **13** unintelligent

**mindlessly**
**08** stupidly **09** foolishly, routinely **11** illogically, senselessly **12** irrationally, mechanically **13** automatically, instinctively, involuntarily, thoughtlessly

**mine**
**02** my **03** dig, egg, pit, win **04** bomb, fund, lode, seam, vein, well **05** delve, dig up, hoard, shaft, stock, store, wheal **06** burrow, dig for, duffer, quarry, remove, search, source, supply, trench, tunnel, wealth **07** bonanza, coalpit, deposit, extract, reserve, unearth **08** claymore, colliery, excavate, landmine, treasury **09** coalfield, explosive, reservoir, undermine **10** excavation, repository, storehouse **11** depth charge

• **mine opening**
**03** eye **04** adit

• **mine tunnel**
**04** head

• **mining licence**
**04** gale

• **surface over a mine**
**03** day

**mine-passage**
**04** road

**miner**
**06** digger, hatter, pitman, tinner **07** collier, faceman **08** tributer **09** coalminer **10** faceworker, gold-digger, honeyeater, mineworker

**mineral**

*Minerals include:*

**03** jet
**04** alum, mica, ruby, salt, spar, talc
**05** beryl, borax, emery, flint, fluor, topaz, umber
**06** albite, blende, cerite, galena, gangue, garnet, glance, gypsum, halite, haüyne, humite, illite, jasper, kermes, lithia, maltha, natron, nosean, pyrite, quartz, rutile, silica, sphene, spinel, talcum, zircon
**07** anatase, apatite, axinite, azurite, barytes, biotite, bornite, brucite, calcite, cassite, crystal, cuprite, desmine, diamond, dysodil, epidote, jacinth, jadeite, jargoon, kandite, leucite, nacrite, olivine, pennine, peridot, pyrites, realgar, syenite, thorite, uralite, uranite, zeolite, zincite, zoisite
**08** allanite, ankerite, asbestos, autunite, blue john, boracite, brookite, calamine, calcspar, chlorite, chromite, cinnabar, corundum, crocoite, cryolite, diallage, diaspore, dolomite, dysodyle, epsomite, erionite, euxenite, feldspar, fluorite, goethite, graphite, gyrolite, hematite, hyacinth, idocrase, ilmenite, iodyrite, lazulite, lewisite, melilite, mimetite, nephrite, orpiment, plumbago, prehnite, pyroxene, rock salt, sanidine, sapphire, sardonyx, siderite, smaltite, sodalite, stannite, stibnite, stilbite, titanite, wurtzite
**09** alabaster, amphibole, anhydrite, aragonite, atacamite, bentonite, blacklead, cairngorm, celestite, cobaltite, elaterite, evaporite, fibrolite, fluorspar, fool's gold, goslarite, grossular, haematite, kaolinite, lodestone, magnesite, magnetite, malachite, marcasite, margarite, microlite, muscovite, nepholine, niccolite, olivenite, pearl spar, quartzite, saltpetre, scheelite, soapstone, sylvanite, tantalite, turquoise, uraninite, vulpinite, wavellite
**10** antimonite, aquamarine, aventurine, bloodstone, chalcedony, chrysolite, glauconite, hornblende, meerschaum, microcline, orthoclase, polyhalite, pyrolusite, samerskite, serpentine, sphalerite, tourmaline
**11** alexandrite, amphibolite, chrysoberyl, French chalk, lapis lazuli, pitchblende, sal ammoniac, smithsonite, vesuvianite
**12** chalcanthite, chalcopyrite, hemimorphite
**13** arsenopyrites
**14** hydroxyapatite, sodium chloride, yttro-columbite
**15** gooseberry-stone

**mineral water** *see* **water**

**Minerva**
**06** Athene

**mingle**
**03** mix **04** fuse, join, mell **05** alloy, blend, go out, merge, unite **06** hobnob, medley **07** combine, mixture **08** coalesce, compound, intermix **09** associate, circulate, commingle, interfuse, socialize **10** amalgamate **11** intermingle, run together **12** rub shoulders

**mingy**
**04** mean, poor, puny **05** close **06** meagre, measly, paltry, scanty, skimpy, stingy **07** miserly, pitiful, sparing, trivial **08** grudging, pathetic, piddling, ungiving **09** miserable, niggardly **10** hard-fisted, ungenerous **11** close-fisted, close-handed, tight-fisted **12** cheese-paring, parsimonious

**miniature**
**03** toy, wee **04** baby, mini, tiny **05** cameo, dwarf, small, teeny, young **06** little, midget, minute **07** diorama, reduced **08** pint-size **09** microcosm, pint-sized **10** diminutive, scaled-down, small-scale **11** microcosmic, pocket-sized, rubrication

**minimal**
**05** least, token **06** minute **07** minimum, nominal **08** littlest, smallest **09** slightest **10** negligible

**minimize**
**03** cut **05** decry, slash **06** lessen, reduce, shrink **07** curtail **08** belittle, decrease, diminish, discount, laugh off, play down **09** deprecate, disparage, soft-pedal, underrate **10** trivialize **11** make light of **12** make little of **13** underestimate

**minimum**
◇ *head selection indicator*
**03** min **05** least, nadir **06** bottom, lowest **07** minimal, tiniest **08** littlest, smallest **09** slightest **11** lowest point **12** lowest number

**minion**
**05** leech **06** drudge, fawner, lackey, menial, stooge, yes-man **07** darling, flunkey, servant **08** follower, hanger-on, henchman, hireling, parasite **09** attendant, dependant, favourite, flatterer, sycophant, underling **10** bootlicker, henchwoman **11** henchperson

**minister**
**02** PM **03** Min, Rev **04** aide, dean, tend **05** agent, dewan, diwan, elder, envoy, nurse, padre, serve, vezir, vicar, vizir **06** attend, cleric, consul, curate, deacon, divine, leader, legate, parson, pastor, priest, rector, supply, verger, visier, vizier, wait on, wizier **07** cater to, furnish, Mas-John, Mes-John, servant **08** chaplain, delegate, diplomat, emissary, Mass-John, Mess-John, official, preacher **09** churchman, clergyman, dignitary, executive, look after, presbyter **10** administer, ambassador, chancellor, politician, take care of **11** accommodate, clergywoman, Grand Vizier **12** ecclesiastic, office-holder, parish priest **13** administrator **14** representative **15** cabinet minister

*See also* **prime minister**

**ministration**
**03** aid **04** care, help **06** favour, relief **07** backing, service, succour, support **09** patronage **10** assistance **11** disposition, supervision

**ministry**
**03** Min, MOD, MOH **04** MAFF, METI **06** bureau, clergy, office **07** cabinet, service **08** the cloth **09** the church, the clergy **10** department, government, holy orders **13** the priesthood **14** administration

**Minnesota**
**02** MN **04** Minn

**minnow**
**04** pank, pink

**minor**
**03** boy, kid, son, tot **04** baby, girl, less **05** child, light, lower, petty, small **06** infant, junior, lesser, nipper, slight **07** nominal, smaller, tiny tot, toddler, trivial, unknown, younger **08** daughter, inferior, juvenile, marginal, trifling, young one **09** little one, secondary, youngster **10** negligible, peripheral, subsidiary **11** little known, second-class, subordinate, unimportant, young person **12** unclassified **13** insignificant **14** inconsiderable

**• minor item**
**02** by **03** bye

**minstrel**
**04** bard, scop **05** rimer **06** rhymer, singer **07** gleeman **08** jongleur, musician **09** hamfatter, joculator **10** troubadour

**mint**
◇ *anagram indicator*
**03** aim, nep, new, nip **04** bomb, cast, coin, fake, heap, hint, make, pile **05** as new, forge, fresh, hatch, punch, stack, stamp **06** bundle, catnep, catnip, devise, invent, make up, packet, riches, strike, unused, wealth **07** attempt, billion, concoct, falsify, fashion, fortune, million, mint-new, monarda, perfect, produce, purpose, trump up, venture **08** bergamot, billions, brand-new, millions **09** bugle-weed, construct, excellent, fabricate, megabucks, undamaged **10** first-class, immaculate, pennyroyal **11** king's ransom, loadsamoney, manufacture, unblemished

**minus**
**03** bar **04** less, save **06** except **07** short of, without **08** negative **09** excepting, excluding **10** deficiency **11** subtraction

**minuscule**
**04** fine, tiny **05** teeny **06** little, minute **09** itsy-bitsy, miniature, very small **10** diminutive, teeny-weeny **11** Lilliputian, microscopic **13** infinitesimal

**minute**
**01** m **02** mo **03** min, sec **04** note, tick, tiny **05** close, exact, flash, jiffy, minim **06** moment, second, slight, strict **07** instant, precise, trivial **08** accurate, as soon as, critical, detailed, directly, no sooner, the point, trifling **09** miniature, minuscule, short time, the moment, very small **10** diminutive, exhaustive, meticulous, negligible, the instant **11** immediately, Lilliputian, microscopic, painstaking, punctilious **13** infinitesimal, insignificant, microscopical **14** circumstantial, inconsiderable

**• in a minute**
**04** anon, soon **06** pronto **07** in a tick, shortly **08** in a flash, in a jiffy, very soon **09** in a moment **10** before long **15** in the near future

**• this minute**
**03** now **04** next, then **06** at once, pronto **07** quickly **08** as soon as, directly, promptly, right now, speedily **09** forthwith, instantly, like a shot, right away, yesterday **11** immediately, this instant **12** no sooner than, straight away, there and then, without delay **14** unhesitatingly, without more ado **15** before you know it, instantaneously, without question

**• up to the minute**
**02** in **03** now **06** latest, newest, with it **09** happening **10** all the rage, most modern, most recent **11** fashionable

**minutely**
**07** closely, exactly **08** in detail **09** precisely **10** critically **12** exhaustively, meticulously, scrupulously **13** painstakingly **14** systematically

**minutes**
**04** acta **05** notes, tapes **06** record **07** details, records **10** memorandum, transcript **11** proceedings **12** transactions

**minutiae**
**07** details, trifles **08** niceties **10** small print, subtleties **11** fine details, finer points, intricacies, particulars **12** complexities, trivialities

**miracle**
**04** sign **06** marvel, wonder **07** prodigy **10** phenomenon, wonderwork

**miraculous**
**07** amazing **09** monstrous, unnatural, wonderful **10** astounding, incredible, marvellous, monstruous, phenomenal, remarkable, superhuman, surprising, unexpected **11** astonishing **12** inexplicable, supernatural, unbelievable **13** extraordinary, unaccountable

**miraculously**
**09** amazingly **10** incredibly, remarkably **11** wonderfully **12** inexplicably, superhumanly, surprisingly, unbelievably, unexpectedly **13** unaccountably **14** supernaturally **15** extraordinarily

**mirage**
**04** loom **07** fantasy **08** illusion, phantasm **11** fata Morgana **13** hallucination **14** phantasmagoria **15** optical illusion

**mire**
**03** bog, fen, fix, jam, mud **04** dirt, hole, lair, mess, muck, ooze, quag, sink, spot, stew **05** glaur, latch, letch, marsh, slime, swamp **06** deluge, morass, pickle, slough, sludge **07** bog down, trouble **08** loblolly, quagmire **09** marshland, overwhelm **12** difficulties

**mirror**
**03** ape **04** copy, echo, show, twin **05** clone, glass, image, mimic, stone **06** depict, double, follow, parrot **07** emulate, imitate, reflect **08** busybody, likeness, speculum **09** coelostat, condenser, hand-glass, pier-glass, reflector, represent **10** dead ringer, reflection, siderostat, wing mirror **11** cheval-glass, pocket-glass, tiring-glass, toilet glass **12** keeking-glass, laryngoscope, looking-glass **13** driving-mirror, exact likeness, spitting image **14** rear-view mirror

**mirth**
**03** fun **04** glee **05** dream, sport **06** gaiety, spleen **07** delight, frolics, jollity, revelry **08** buoyancy, hilarity, laughter, pleasure **09** amusement, enjoyment, merriment, merriness **10** blitheness, jocularity **11** high spirits **12** cheerfulness

**mirthful**
**03** gay **04** glad **05** funny, happy, jolly, ludic, merry **06** amused, blithe, cheery, jocund, jovial **07** amusing, buoyant, festive, playful **08** cheerful, gladsome, laughful, laughing, sportive **09** hilarious, laughable, vivacious **10** frolicsome, uproarious **11** pleasurable **12** light-hearted **13** light-spirited

**mirthless**
**03** sad **04** glum, sour **05** gruff, moody, sulky, surly **06** gloomy, grumpy, morose, sullen **07** doleful, unhappy **08** churlish, dejected, unamused **09** depressed, miserable **10** despondent, humourless **11** crestfallen, ill-humoured, pessimistic

**miry**
**04** oozy **05** boggy, dirty, fenny, mucky, muddy, slimy **06** glaury, marshy, sludgy, swampy

**misadventure**
**06** mishap **07** bad luck, debacle, failure, ill luck, problem, reverse, setback, tragedy **08** accident, calamity, disaster, hard luck **09** cataclysm, misaunter, mischance **10** ill fortune, misfortune **11** catastrophe

**misanthrope**
**05** cynic, loner, miser, Timon **06** hermit, meanie **07** recluse **08** solitary **14** unsocial person

**misanthropic**
**05** surly **08** egoistic, inhumane **10** antisocial, malevolent, unfriendly, unsociable **13** unsympathetic

**misanthropy**
**06** egoism **08** cynicism **10** inhumanity **11** malevolence **13** antisociality **14** unsociableness

**misapply**
**05** abuse **06** misuse **07** exploit, pervert **09** misemploy **11** use unwisely **13** use unsuitably **14** misappropriate

**misapprehend**
**07** misread, mistake **11** misconceive, misconstrue **12** misinterpret **13** miscomprehend, misunderstand **15** get the wrong idea

**misapprehension**
**05** error, mix-up **07** fallacy, mistake **08** delusion **09** wrong idea **10** misreading **13** misconception **15** false impression

**misappropriate**
**03** nab, rob **04** nick **05** abuse, filch, pinch, steal **06** misuse, pilfer, pocket, thieve **07** pervert, swindle **08** embezzle, misapply, misspend, peculate **09** defalcate, knock down

**misappropriation**
**05** theft **06** misuse **07** robbing **08** stealing **09** pilfering, pocketing **10** peculation **11** defalcation **12** embezzlement **14** misapplication

**misbegotten**
**05** shady **06** stolen **07** bastard, illicit, natural **08** abortive, unlawful **09** dishonest, ill-gotten, ill-judged, imprudent, monstrous, purloined, unadvised **10** ill-advised, monstruous **11** hare-brained **12** contemptible, disreputable, ill-conceived, illegitimate

**misbehave**
◇ *anagram indicator*
**05** act up, lapse **06** be rude, offend, play up **07** carry on, disobey **08** trespass **09** be naughty, fool about, mess about, misdemean, muck about **10** fool around, transgress **11** behave badly **15** be beyond the pale, get up to mischief

**misbehaviour**
◇ *anagram indicator*
**08** mischief, misguide **10** bad manners, carrying-on, misconduct **11** impropriety, naughtiness **12** bad behaviour, disobedience, misdemeanour, mucking about **15** insubordination

**misbelief**
**05** error **06** heresy **07** fallacy, mistake **08** delusion, illusion **10** heterodoxy **11** unorthodoxy, wrong belief **13** misconception **15** misapprehension

**miscalculate**
**03** err **04** boob **06** slip up **07** blunder, go wrong, miscast **08** get wrong, miscount, misjudge **09** misreckon **12** make a mistake, overestimate **13** underestimate

**miscalculation**
**04** boob, slip **05** error, fault, gaffe, lapse **06** booboo, howler, slip-up **07** bloomer, blunder, clanger, mistake **08** miscount **09** oversight **10** aberration, inaccuracy **12** misjudgement, overestimate **13** underestimate **14** miscomputation **15** misapprehension

**miscarriage**
**05** error **06** mishap **07** failure, misdeed **08** aborting, abortion **09** breakdown, ruination **10** misconduct, perversion **13** mismanagement **14** disappointment

**miscarry**
**04** fail, flop, fold, warp **05** abort, slink **07** founder, go amiss, go wrong, misfire, miswend **10** not come off **11** bite the dust, come to grief, fall through, lose the baby **12** come a cropper **13** come to nothing

**miscellaneous**
**04** chow **05** mixed **06** motley, sundry, varied **07** diverse, jumbled, mingled, various **08** assorted, eclectic **10** variegated **11** diversified, farraginous **12** multifarious **13** heterogeneous

• **miscellaneous lot**
**04** raft

**miscellany**
**03** mix **04** olio, olla **06** jumble, medley **07** farrago, mixture, variety **08** mishmash, mixed bag, pastiche **09** anthology, diversity, patchwork, potpourri **10** assortment, collection, hotchpotch, salmagundi, salmagundy **11** collectanea, gallimaufry, miscellanea, smorgasbord **14** conglomeration, omnium-gatherum

**mischance**
**04** blow **06** mishap **07** ill luck, tragedy **08** accident, bad break, calamity, disaster **09** ill-chance **10** ill fortune, infelicity, misfortune **11** contretemps **12** misadventure

**mischief**
**03** Ate, elf, hob, imp, wag **04** bale, bane, dido, evil, harm, hurt, lark, limb, pest, puck, tyke **05** cutty, devil, gamin, rogue, scamp **06** damage, gamine, injury, monkey, nickum, pranks, rascal, terror, tricks, urchin **07** carry-on, hellion, malicho, pliskie, stirrer, trouble, varmint, villain **08** diablery, escapade, makebate, nuisance, spalpeen **09** devilment, diablerie, scallywag, vengeance **10** cockatrice, disruption, disservice, hanky-panky, impishness, shenanigan, wrongdoing **11** limb of Satan, monkey shine, naughtiness, roguishness, shenanigans **12** bad behaviour, esprit follet, misbehaviour, monkey tricks **13** barnsbreaking, funny business, jiggery-pokery **14** monkey business **15** flibbertigibbet

**mischievous**
◇ *anagram indicator*
**03** bad **04** arch, evil **05** elfin, elvan, elven, rogue **06** elfish, elvish, impish, shrewd, wicked **07** gallows, harmful, hurtful, naughty, playful, roguish, teasing, tricksy, unhappy, vicious, waggish **08** litherly, rascally, spiteful **09** ill-deedly, injurious, malicious, malignant, pestilent **10** frolicsome, pernicious, up to no good **11** destructive, detrimental, disobedient, misbehaving, troublesome **12** badly behaved

**mischievously**
◇ *anagram indicator*
**08** impishly, wickedly **09** harmfully, naughtily, playfully, roguishly, teasingly, viciously, waggishly **10** spitefully **11** injuriously, maliciously **13** destructively, disobediently

**misconceive**
**07** misread, mistake, suspect **08** misjudge **11** misconstrue **12** misapprehend, misinterpret **13** misunderstand

**misconception**
**05** error **07** fallacy, mistake **08** delusion **09** wrong idea **10** misconceit, misreading **15** false impression, misapprehension

**misconduct**
◇ *anagram indicator*
**08** adultery, misusage **10** wrongdoing **11** impropriety, malpractice, miscarriage **12** bad behaviour, misbehaviour, misdemeanour **13** mismanagement

**misconstrue**
◇ *anagram indicator*
**07** misread, mistake, pervert **08** misjudge **09** misreckon **10** misconster **11** misconceive **12** misapprehend, misinterpret, mistranslate **13** misunderstand **15** take the wrong way

**miscreant**
**05** knave, rogue, scamp **06** rascal, sinner, wicked, wretch **07** dastard, heretic, infidel, villain **08** criminal, evildoer, vagabond **09** reprobate, scallywag, scoundrel, wrongdoer **10** malefactor, profligate, villainous **11** misbeliever, scoundrelly, unbelieving **12** troublemaker **13** mischief-maker

**misdeed**
**03** sin **05** amiss, crime, error, fault, wrong **06** felony **07** offence **08** trespass, villainy **10** misconduct, peccadillo, wrongdoing **11** delinquency, miscarriage, misdemeanor, mistreading **12** misdemeanour **13** transgression

**misdemeanour**
**05** error, fault, lapse, wrong **07** misdeed, offence **08** trespass **10** misconduct, peccadillo, wrongdoing **11** malfeasance **12** indiscretion, infringement, misbehaviour **13** transgression

**misdirect**
◇ *anagram indicator*
**05** avert **06** divert, misuse **07** mislead **08** misapply, misguide **09** misinform **10** misaddress **13** give a bum steer **14** misappropriate

**miser**
**04** carl **05** hunks **06** meanie, wretch **07** niggard, save-all, Scrooge

**08** muckworm, tightwad **09** skinflint **10** cheapskate, curmudgeon, scrapegood **11** cheeseparer, scrapepenny **12** money-grubber, penny-pincher

*Misers include:*

**05** **Burns** (Montgomery)
**06** **Mammon**, **Marner** (Silas)
**07** **Scrooge** (Ebenezer)
**08** **Nickleby** (Ralph), **Trapbois**
**10** **Fardorough**, **Van Swieten** (Ghysbrecht)
**11** **Earlforward** (Henry)

### miserable
◇ *anagram indicator*
**03** low, miz, sad **04** base, blue, down, glum, mean, mizz, poor, punk, vile **05** lousy, sorry, surly **06** dismal, dreary, gloomy, grumpy, meagre, measly, mouldy, paltry, rotten, scanty, shabby, sullen **07** crushed, forlorn, grouchy, joyless, pitiful, squalid, unhappy **08** dejected, desolate, downcast, pathetic, pitiable, shameful, wretched **09** cheerless, crotchety, depressed, irritable, niggardly, sorrowful, worthless **10** deplorable, depressing, despicable, despondent, detestable, distressed, unpleasant **11** bad-tempered, disgraceful, downhearted, god-forsaken, heartbroken, ignominious, ill-tempered, low-spirited, melancholic **12** contemptible, disagreeable, disconsolate, god-forgotten, impoverished **14** down in the dumps

### miserably
◇ *anagram indicator*
**05** sadly **06** glumly, poorly **07** greatly **08** gloomily, markedly, paltrily, scantily, stingily, very much **09** niggardly, pitifully, unhappily **10** desolately **11** dangerously, desperately, sorrowfully **12** despondently, pathetically **14** disconsolately

### miserliness
**07** avarice **08** meanness **09** frugality, minginess, parsimony, tightness **10** stinginess **12** cheeseparing, covetousness **13** niggardliness, penny-pinching, penuriousness **15** close-fistedness, tight-fistedness

### miserly
**04** gare, mean **05** close, mingy, tight **06** stingy **07** chintzy, sparing **08** beggarly **09** niggardly, penurious **11** close-fisted, close-handed, tight-fisted **12** candle-paring, cheeseparing, parsimonious **13** money-grubbing, penny-pinching

### misery
**02** wo **03** miz, woe **04** bale, hell, mizz, want **05** agony, gloom, grief **06** grouch, misère, moaner, penury, sorrow, whiner **07** anguish, avarice, despair, killjoy, poverty, sadness, whinger **08** buzzkill, distress, hardship, Jeremiah, sourpuss **09** adversity, indigence, perdition, pessimist, privation, suffering, the depths **10** affliction, complainer, depression, desolation, discomfort, melancholy, misfortune, oppression, spoilsport, wet blanket **11** deprivation, destitution, living death, melancholia, unhappiness **12** wretchedness **13** prophet of doom **14** dog in the manger

### misfire
**04** fail, flop **05** abort **06** go awry **07** founder, go amiss, go wrong **08** miscarry **09** fizzle out **10** not come off **11** bite the dust, come to grief, fall through **12** come a cropper

### misfit
◇ *anagram indicator*
**04** geek **05** freak, loner **06** weirdo **07** dropout, oddball, sad sack **08** lone wolf, maverick **09** eccentric, odd one out **13** individualist, nonconformist **14** fish out of water

### misfortune
**02** wo **03** ill, woe **04** blow, evil, ruth, woes **05** trial **06** mishap, sorrow, wroath **07** bad luck, failure, ill luck, misfare, misluck, reverse, setback, tragedy, trouble **08** accident, calamity, casualty, disaster, distress, hard luck, hardship, judgment **09** adversity, judgement, mischance, mishanter **10** affliction, infelicity, mischanter **11** catastrophe, tribulation **12** misadventure

- **expression of misfortune**

**02** ah, ay, oh **03** out **04** alas, ay me, haro, waly **06** harrow **07** welaway **08** waesucks, welladay, wellaway **09** alack-a-day, wellanear **10** alas the day **12** alas the while

### misgiving
**04** fear **05** doubt, qualm, worry **06** niggle, unease **07** anxiety, scruple **08** distrust, misdoubt, mistrust **09** suspicion **10** hesitation **11** reservation, uncertainty **12** apprehension **14** second thoughts

### misguided
◇ *anagram indicator*
**04** rash **05** wrong **06** erring, misled **07** deluded, foolish, off-beam **08** mistaken **09** erroneous, ill-judged, imprudent, misplaced **10** fallacious, ill-advised **11** injudicious, misdirected, misinformed **12** misconceived **13** ill-considered

### mishandle
◇ *anagram indicator*
**04** muff **05** botch, fluff **06** bungle, fumble, mess up **07** balls up, screw up **08** maltreat, misjudge **09** mismanage **11** make a hash of, make a mess of **12** make a balls of **14** make a balls-up of, make a pig's ear of

### mishap
◇ *anagram indicator*
**04** blow **05** drere, shunt, trial **06** dreare, mucker **07** reverse, setback, trouble **08** accident, calamity, disaster, incident **09** adversity, misaunter, mischance **10** ill fortune, misfortune **11** catastrophe, disaventure, tribulation **12** disadventure, misadventure **15** stroke of bad luck

### mishit
**04** duff, thin **05** flier, flyer **06** sclaff

### mishmash
**04** hash, mess, olio, olla **05** salad **06** jumble, medley, muddle **07** farrago **08** pastiche **09** potpourri **10** hodgepodge, hotchpotch, salmagundi **11** gallimaufry **14** conglomeration

### misinform
**05** bluff **07** deceive, mislead **08** hoodwink, misguide **09** misdirect **12** take for a ride **13** give a bum steer

### misinformation
**04** dope, guff, hype, lies **05** bluff **07** baloney, eyewash **08** bum steer, nonsense **09** deception **10** misleading **12** misdirection **14** disinformation

### misinterpret
◇ *anagram indicator*
**04** warp **05** wrest **06** garble **07** distort, misread, mistake **08** misjudge **11** misconceive, misconstrue **12** misapprehend **13** misunderstand **15** take the wrong way

### misinterpretation
**10** misreading **12** misjudgement **13** misconception **14** misacceptation **15** false impression, misapprehension, misconstruction

### misjudge
**07** mistake **08** miscount **11** misconstrue **12** miscalculate, misinterpret, overestimate **13** misunderstand, underestimate

### misjudgement
**07** mistake **09** wrong idea **10** misdeeming **12** wrong opinion **14** miscalculation **15** wrong conclusion

### mislay
**04** lose, miss **07** misfile **08** misplace **11** lose sight of, lose track of **14** be unable to find

### mislead
◇ *anagram indicator*
**04** fool, snow **05** put on **06** delude **07** deceive **08** fool into, hoodwink, impose on, misguide **09** blindfold, misdirect, misinform **10** impose upon, lead astray **12** misrepresent, take for a ride **13** give a bum steer, lead into error **14** pull a fast one on, put off the scent

### misleading
◇ *anagram indicator*
**06** biased, loaded, tricky **07** evasive **08** delusive, illusive, illusory, sinister **09** ambiguous, confusing, deceiving, deceptive, equivocal **10** fallacious, unreliable

### mismanage
◇ *anagram indicator*
**03** mar **04** muff **05** botch, waste

06 bungle, foul up, mess up 07 balls up, blunder, misrule, screw up
08 misjudge, misspend 09 mishandle
11 make a hash of, make a mess of
12 make a balls of 14 make a balls-up of, make a pig's ear of

**mismanagement**
◇ *anagram indicator*
04 hash, mess 05 farce 06 bungle, cock-up, muddle 07 balls-up, failure, pig's ear 08 bungling, shambles
11 mishandling 12 misjudgement
13 pig's breakfast 14 misgovernaunce
11 lawlessness 12 indiscipline
13 misgovernment, mismanagement
15 disorganization

**mismatched**
08 clashing, mismated, unsuited
09 disparate, irregular, misallied
10 discordant, unmatching 11 ill-assorted, incongruous 12 antipathetic, incompatible 14 unreconcilable

**misogynist**
03 MCP 06 sexist 10 woman-hater
12 anti-feminist 14 male chauvinist
15 male supremacist

**misogyny**
06 sexism 12 anti-feminism 13 male supremacy 14 male chauvinism

**misplace**
◇ *anagram indicator*
04 lose, miss 06 mislay 07 misfile
08 misapply 09 misassign 11 lose sight of, lose track of 14 be unable to find

**misprint**
◇ *anagram indicator*
04 typo 05 error 07 erratum, literal, mistake 11 corrigendum 12 literal error
13 printing error

**misquote**
05 twist 06 garble, muddle 07 distort, falsify, pervert 08 misstate
09 misreport 11 misremember
12 misrepresent

**misread**
◇ *anagram indicator*
06 garble 07 distort, mistake
08 misjudge 11 misconceive, misconstrue 12 misapprehend, misinterpret 13 misunderstand 15 take the wrong way

**misrepresent**
◇ *anagram indicator*
05 abuse, belie, color, slant, twist
06 colour, garble 07 distort, falsify, pervert 08 disguise, minimize, miscolor, misquote, misstate
09 miscolour, misreport
10 exaggerate, manipulate
11 misconstrue 12 misinterpret

**misrepresentation**
◇ *anagram indicator*
08 twisting 10 distortion, perversion
12 exaggeration, manipulation, misreporting 13 falsification
15 misconstruction

**misrule**
04 riot 05 chaos 06 tumult 07 anarchy, turmoil 08 disorder, unreason
09 confusion 10 turbulence

**miss**
02 Ms 03 err 04 beat, blow, fail, flop, flub, girl, lack, lass, lose, maid, Mlle, muff, need, omit, skip, slip, trip, want, wish 05 avoid, dodge, error, evade, fault, forgo, let go, Mdlle, mourn
06 bypass, damsel, escape, fiasco, forego, kumari, lament, maiden, not see, pass up, regret 07 ache for, blunder, failure, let slip, long for, mistake, neglect, not go to, not spot, pine for 08 fräulein, leave out, miscarry, omission, overlook, pass over, Señorita, sidestep, teenager, yearn for 09 disregard, fail to get, fail to hit, grieve for, not notice, oversight, Signorina, sorrow for, young lady 10 be away from, circumvent, desiderate, not go to see, schoolgirl, young woman
11 fail to catch, fail to seize, not be part of 12 be absent from, be too late for, fail to attend, fail to notice, mademoiselle
13 feel the loss of, misunderstand, not take part in

*See also* **girl**; **woman**

**• miss out**
04 jump, omit, skip 06 bypass, ignore
07 exclude 08 leave out, pass over
09 disregard 12 dispense with

**missal**
08 breviary, mass-book, Triodion
09 formulary 10 office-book, prayerbook 11 euchologion, servicebook

**misshapen**
◇ *anagram indicator*
04 bent, ugly 06 inform, warped
07 crooked, dismayd, twisted
08 crippled, deformed 09 contorted, distorted, grotesque, malformed, monstrous 15 misproportioned

**missile**
04 bomb, dart, shot 05 arrow, shaft, shell 06 rocket, weapon 07 grenade, torpedo 10 flying bomb, projectile

*Missiles include:*

02 MX, V-2
03 AAM, ABM, AGM, ASM, ATM, SAM, SSM
04 ALCM, ASBM, ICBM, IRBM, MIRV, MRBM, Scud, SLBM, TASM
05 smart
06 AMRAAM, cruise, Exocet®, guided
07 Polaris, Trident
08 Maverick
09 ballistic, minuteman
10 sidewinder, wire-guided
11 heat-seeking
12 surface-to-air

**• missile container**
04 silo

**missing**
◇ *deletion indicator*
04 gone, lost 06 absent, astray
07 lacking, mislaid, strayed, wanting
08 awanting 09 misplaced 10 gone astray 11 disappeared 14 gone for a Burton, unaccounted-for

**mission**
02 op 03 aim, job 04 duty, goal, raid, task, work 05 chore, quest 06 action, charge, errand, office, sortie 07 calling, crusade, embassy, purpose, pursuit
08 business, campaign, exercise, legation, ministry, vocation
09 manoeuvre, operation, task force
10 assignment, commission, delegation, deputation 11 raison d'être, undertaking

**missionary**
05 envoy 07 apostle 08 champion, crusader, emissary, minister, preacher, promoter 09 converter
10 ambassador, campaigner, evangelist 12 propagandist, proselytizer

*Missionaries include:*

03 **Fox** (George), **Huc** (Evariste Régis)
04 **Luke** (St), **Mark** (St), **Paul** (St)
05 **Carey** (William), **David** (Père Armand), **Eliot** (John), **Ellis** (William), **Moody** (Dwight L), **Ricci** (Matteo), **Smith** (Eli)
06 **Damien** (Father Joseph), **Graham** (Billy), **Teresa** (Mother), **Wesley** (John)
07 **Aylward** (Gladys), **Columba** (St), **Liddell** (Eric), **ten Boom** (Corrie)
08 **Boniface** (St), **Crowther** (Samuel)
09 **McPherson** (Aimee Semple), **Southwell** (Robert)
10 **Huddleston** (Trevor), **Macpherson** (Annie), **Schweitzer** (Albert)
11 **Livingstone** (David)
13 **Francis Xavier** (St)

**Mississippi**
02 MS 04 Miss

**missive**
04 line, memo, note, sent 06 letter, report 07 epistle, message, missile
08 bulletin, dispatch 09 messenger
10 communiqué, memorandum
13 communication

**Missouri**
02 MO

**misspell**
◇ *anagram indicator*

**misspent**
04 idle 06 wasted 07 misused
08 prodigal 09 idled away
10 dissipated, misapplied, profitless, squandered, thrown away
12 unprofitable 13 frittered away

**misstate**
05 twist 06 garble 07 distort, falsify, pervert 08 misquote 09 misrelate, misreport 11 misremember
12 misrepresent

**mist**
03 dew, fog 04 drow, film, haar, haze, murk, rack, roke, smog, veil 05 cloud,

spray, steam **06** mizzle, nimbus, vapour **07** dimness, drizzle **10** exhalation **12** condensation

• **mist over, mist up**
**03** dim, fog **04** blur, veil **05** fog up, glaze **07** obscure, steam up **09** cloud over **10** become hazy **12** become cloudy **13** become blurred

## mistake
◇ *anagram indicator*
**03** err **04** bish, blue, boob, boss, flaw, flub, goof, muff, slip, take, typo **05** error, fault, fluff, gaffe, lapse, mix up, mix-up **06** booboo, cock up, domino, duff it, foul up, foul-up, goof up, howler, mess up, miscue, muddle, ricket, slip up, slip-up, stumer **07** bad move, balls up, bloomer, blooper, blunder, botch-up, clanger, clinker, confuse, erratum, fallacy, faux pas, go wrong, louse up, misread, misstep, own goal, screw up, take for **08** confound, get wrong, mesprize, misfield, misjudge, misprint, misprise, misprize, muddle up, omission, solecism **09** make a slip, oversight **10** aberration, inaccuracy, misprision, misreading **11** corrigendum, make a booboo, misconceive, misconstrue, misspelling **12** come a cropper, drop a clanger, indiscretion, misapprehend, miscalculate, misjudgement **13** misunderstand **14** miscalculation **15** misapprehension, put your foot in it, slip of the tongue

## mistaken
◇ *anagram indicator*
**03** wet **05** false, wrong **06** faulty, misled, untrue **07** at fault, deluded, in error, inexact, off base, off-beam, vicious **08** deceived, overseen **09** erroneous, ill-judged, incorrect, misguided, misprised, unfounded **10** fallacious, inaccurate, up the booay **11** inauthentic, misinformed **13** inappropriate, wide of the mark **15** got the wrong idea

## mistakenly
◇ *anagram indicator*
**07** falsely, in error, wrongly **08** unfairly, unjustly **09** by mistake **11** erroneously, incorrectly, misguidedly **12** fallaciously, inaccurately **15** inappropriately

## Mister
**02** Mr

## mistimed
**08** ill-timed, tactless, untimely **10** malapropos **11** inopportune, unfortunate **12** inconvenient, infelicitous, unseasonable **14** unsynchronized

**mistiness** *see* **mist**

## mistreat
◇ *anagram indicator*
**04** harm, hurt, maul **05** abuse, bully **06** batter, beat up, ill-use, injure, misuse, molest **08** ill-treat, maltreat, walk over **09** mishandle **10** knock about, treat badly **11** walk all over

## mistreatment
**04** harm, hurt **05** abuse **06** ill-use, injury, misuse **07** cruelty, mauling **08** bullying, ill-usage **09** battering **10** unkindness **11** manhandling, mishandling, molestation **12** ill-treatment, maltreatment **13** brutalization

## mistress
**04** amie, dame, doxy, lady, miss, wife **05** lover, tutor, wench, woman **06** ruling **07** Aspasia, herself, hetaera, leading, partner, stepney, teacher **08** goodwife, lady-love, paramour **09** belle amie, concubine, courtesan, courtezan, governess, housewife, inamorata, kept woman, principal **10** canary-bird, châtelaine, fancy woman, girlfriend, school dame **11** live-in lover **12** bit on the side **13** schoolteacher

## mistrust
**04** fear **05** doubt, qualm **06** beware **07** caution, suspect **08** be wary of, distrust, wariness **09** chariness, hesitancy, misgiving, suspicion **10** scepticism **11** uncertainty **12** apprehension, reservations **13** have no faith in **14** be suspicious of, have misgivings **15** have doubts about

## mistrustful
**03** shy **04** wary **05** chary, leery **07** cynical, dubious, fearful **08** cautious, doubtful, hesitant **09** sceptical, uncertain **10** suspicious **11** distrustful **12** apprehensive

## misty
**03** dim **04** hazy **05** foggy, fuzzy, murky, smoky, vague **06** cloudy, opaque, veiled **07** blurred, clouded, obscure, tearful, unclear **08** nebulous **10** indistinct

## misunderstand
**07** mishear, misknow, misread, mistake **08** get wrong, misjudge **11** misconstrue, misperceive **12** misapprehend, misinterpret, miss the point **13** miscomprehend **15** get the wrong idea

## misunderstanding
**03** row **04** rift, tiff **05** clash, error, mix-up **06** breach **07** discord, dispute, mistake, quarrel **08** argument, conflict, squabble **09** wrong idea **10** difference, falling-out, malentendu, misreading **12** crossed wires, disagreement, misjudgement **13** misconception **15** false impression, misapprehension, misintelligence

## misunderstood
**07** misread **08** misheard, mistaken **09** ill-judged, misjudged **12** misconstrued, unrecognized **13** unappreciated **14** misappreciated, misinterpreted, misrepresented

## misuse
◇ *anagram indicator*
**04** harm, hurt **05** abuse, waste, wrong **06** ill-use, injure, injury **07** abusion, corrupt, deceive, distort, exploit, pervert **08** ill-treat, misapply, mistreat, squander, wrong use **09** dissipate, misemploy **10** corruption, perversion, treat badly **11** mishandling, squandering **12** exploitation, ill-treatment, maltreatment, mistreatment **13** misemployment **14** malappropriate, misapplication, misappropriate

## mite
**03** bit, jot, tad **04** atom, iota, whit, worm **05** grain, ounce, scrap, spark, touch, trace **06** acarus, lepton, morsel, varroa **07** modicum, smidgen **08** berry bug **09** red spider, Sarcoptes **11** trombiculid, tyroglyphid

## mitigate
**04** calm, dull, ease, help **05** abate, allay, blunt, check, mease, quiet, remit, slake, still **06** aslake, lenify, lessen, modify, pacify, reduce, soften, soothe, subdue, temper, weaken **07** appease, assuage, lighten, mollify, placate, qualify, relieve, sweeten **08** decrease, diminish, moderate, palliate, tone down **09** alleviate, extenuate

## mitigating
**08** lenitive, mitigant **09** assuasive, modifying, tempering **10** justifying, palliative, qualifying **11** extenuating, vindicating, vindicatory

## mitigation
**06** relief **07** remorse **08** allaying, decrease, easement **09** abatement, lessening, reduction, remission, tempering **10** diminution, moderation, palliation **11** alleviation, appeasement, assuagement, extenuation **13** mollification, qualification

## mitre
**04** tiar **05** tiara

## mix
◇ *anagram indicator*
**04** card, fuse, hash, join, mash, mell, meng, mess, ming, olio, stir, suit **05** agree, alloy, blend, cross, get on, menge, merge, union, unite, whisk **06** caudle, fold in, fusion, hobnob, jumble, meddle, medley, merger, mingle, muddle **07** amalgam, combine, consort, farrago, involve, mixture, shake up, swizzle **08** coalesce, compound, confound, emulsify, get along, intermix, mingling, mishmash, pastiche **09** associate, coalition, composite, harmonize, interfuse, introduce, potpourri, socialize, synthesis **10** amalgamate, assortment, complement, fraternize, go well with, hodgepodge, homogenize, hotchpotch, infiltrate, interbreed, meet others, salmagundi, synthesize **11** combination, gallimaufry, incorporate, intermingle, interpolate, olla-podrida, put together **12** amalgamation, be compatible, conglomerate

**• mix in**
◇ *anagram indicator*
**05** add in, blend, merge **09** introduce **10** infiltrate **11** incorporate, interpolate

**• mix up**
◇ *anagram indicator*
**05** upset **06** garble, jumble, muddle, puzzle **07** confuse, disturb, involve, mistake, perplex, snarl up **08** bewilder, confound, muddle up **09** implicate **10** complicate **12** get jumbled up

**mixed**
◇ *anagram indicator*
**02** pi **03** pie, pye **04** chow, ment **05** fused, meint, meynt **06** hybrid, menged, minged, motley, united, unsure, varied **07** alloyed, blended, diverse, mingled, mongrel **08** assorted, combined, compound, confused **09** composite, crossbred, equivocal, half-caste, interbred, uncertain **10** ambivalent **11** amalgamated, conflicting, diversified, promiscuous **12** incorporated, through-other **13** contradicting, miscellaneous

**• mixed up**
◇ *anagram indicator*
**04** in on **05** upset **06** hung up **07** chaotic, muddled, puzzled **08** caught up, confused, involved, messed up **09** disturbed, embroiled, entangled, perplexed, screwed up **10** bewildered, désorienté, disordered, distracted, distraught, implicated, inculpated **11** complicated, disoriented, maladjusted **12** incriminated

**mixer**
**05** whisk **06** beater, joiner **07** blender, meddler, stirrer **08** busybody, makebate **09** disrupter, extrovert **10** interferer, liquidizer, socializer, subversive **12** troublemaker **13** food processor, mischief-maker

**mixing**
**05** cross, union **06** fusion **08** blending, mingling **09** interflow, synthesis **10** commixtion, commixture, confection, minglement **11** association, coalescence, combination, socializing **12** amalgamation **13** hybridization, interbreeding, intermingling, miscegenation **14** fraternization

**mixture**
◇ *anagram indicator*
**03** mix **04** brew, mong, olio, olla, wash **05** alloy, blend, cross, union **06** fusion, hybrid, jumble, medley, mingle **07** amalgam, compost, farrago, melange, variety **08** compound, mishmash, mixed bag, pastiche **09** composite, patchwork, potpourri, synthesis **10** assortment, composture, concoction, hodgepodge, hotchpotch, miscellany **11** coalescence, combination, olla-podrida, smorgasbord, temperature **12** amalgamation **14** conglomeration

**mix-up**
◇ *anagram indicator*
**04** mess **05** chaos, snafu **06** foul-up, jumble, muddle, tangle **07** balls-up, mistake, snarl-up **08** disorder, nonsense **09** confusion **12** complication

**moan**
**03** sob **04** beef, carp, hone, howl, mean, mein, mene, sigh, wail, weep **05** bleat, gripe, groan, meane, mourn, whine **06** bemoan, charge, grieve, grouse, lament, whinge **07** beefing, carping, censure, grumble, whimper **08** bleating, complain, grumbler **09** annoyance, bellyache, complaint, criticism, grievance, whingeing **10** accusation **11** bellyaching, kick up a fuss, lamentation **12** fault-finding **14** representation **15** dissatisfaction

**moaner**
**06** whiner **07** fusspot, grouser, niggler, whinger **08** grumbler **09** nit-picker **10** bellyacher, complainer, fussbudget **11** fault-finder

**mob**
**03** set **04** body, crew, fill, gang, herd, host, mass, pack **05** brood, crowd, drove, flock, group, horde, plebs, press, swarm, tribe, troop **06** attack, charge, jostle, masses, mobile, pester, proles, rabble, throng **07** besiege, company, king mob, overrun, set upon **08** canaille, fall upon, mobility, populace, riff-raff, surround **09** descend on, gathering, hoi polloi, multitude **10** assemblage, collection, common herd, crowd round, faex populi, rabble rout, swarm round **11** gather round, proletariat, rank and file **12** common people, ribble-rabble **13** great unwashed **15** many-headed beast

**mobile**
◇ *anagram indicator*
**04** thin **05** agile, quick **06** active, lively, motile, moving, nimble, roving, supple **07** migrant, movable, roaming **08** changing, flexible, moveable, portable **09** adaptable, energetic, itinerant, revealing, wandering **10** able to move, adjustable, ambulatory, changeable, expressive, locomotive, suggesting, travelling **11** peripatetic **12** ever-changing **13** transportable

**mobility**
**06** motion **07** agility **08** motility, motivity, vivacity **09** animation **10** locomotion, movability, suppleness **11** flexibility, movableness, portability **12** locomobility, locomotivity **14** expressiveness

**mobilization**
**08** assembly **09** mustering, summoning **10** activation **11** marshalling, preparation **12** organization

**mobilize**
◇ *anagram indicator*
**05** rally, ready **06** call up, enlist, muster, summon **07** animate, marshal, prepare **08** activate, assemble, get ready, organize **09** conscript, galvanize, make ready **14** call into action

**mob rule**
**06** mob law **08** lynch law **09** mobocracy **10** ochlocracy **13** kangaroo court, Reign of Terror

**mobster**
**04** thug **05** crook, heavy, rough, tough **06** bandit, robber **07** brigand, hoodlum, ruffian **08** criminal, gangster, hooligan, skinhead **09** bovver boy, desperado, racketeer, terrorist

**mock**
**03** ape, cod, dor, kid, rag, rib **04** fake, geck, gibe, goof, jape, jeer, rail, sham, slag **05** bogus, chaff, dummy, faked, false, fleer, flout, knock, mimic, scoff, scorn, scout, sneer, taunt, tease **06** bemock, deride, ersatz, forged, insult, parody, phoney, pseudo, send up **07** emulate, feigned, imitate, lampoon, laugh at, murgeon, pretend, slag off, take off **08** ridicule, satirize, simulate, spurious **09** burlesque, disparage, imitation, imitative, make fun of, poke fun at, pretended, simulated, synthetic **10** artificial, caricature, fraudulent, substitute **11** counterfeit, poke borak at **13** poke mullock at
*See also* **imitation**

**mocker**
**05** tease **06** critic, jeerer **07** clothes, derider, flouter, reviler, scoffer, scorner, sneerer **08** bellbird, satirist, vilifier **09** detractor, lampooner, ridiculer, tormentor **10** iconoclast, lampoonist **11** pasquinader

**mockery**
**03** dor, gab **04** jeer, quiz, sham **05** farce, fleer, scoff, scorn, serve, sneer, spoof, sport **06** banter, parody, satire, send-up **07** apology, disdain, horning, jeering, kidding, lampoon, mimicry, ragging, ribbing, sarcasm, take-off, teasing **08** contempt, derision, raillery, ridicule, scoffing, sneering, taunting, travesty **09** burlesque, charivari, contumely, emulation, imitation **10** caricature, disrespect **12** mickey-taking **13** disparagement

**mocking**
**03** wry **05** snide **07** cynical **08** derisive, derisory, illusion, impudent, irrisory, narquois, sardonic, scoffing, scornful, sneering, taunting **09** insulting, quizzical, sarcastic, satirical **10** disdainful, irreverent, wry-mouthed **12** contemptuous **13** disrespectful

**mock-up**
**04** copy **05** dummy, image, model **07** replica **09** facsimile, imitation **11** fabrication **14** representation

**mode**
**03** fad, way **04** form, kind, look, mood, plan, rage, rate **05** craze, modus, style, trend, vogue **06** custom, Dorian, lastic, Ionian, Lydian, manner, method, system **07** Aeolian, fashion, Locrian, process **08** approach, modality, Phrygian, practice **09** condition, procedure, technique **10** convention, dernier cri **11** latest thing **13** manifestation **15** fashionableness

**model**
◇ *anagram indicator*
**01** T **03** sit, toy **04** base, cast, copy, form, kind, make, mark, mode, mold, plan, pose, sort, type, wear, work **05** carve, dummy, ideal, image, medal, mould, poser, shape, sport, style **06** byword, create, design, lovely, mirror, mock-up, module, sample, sculpt, sitter **07** cutaway, display, epitome, example, exemple, fashion, paragon, pattern, perfect, reduced, replica, show off, subject, typical, variety, version **08** bozzetto, exemplar, original, paradigm, specimen, standard, template **09** archetype, dress form, exemplary, facsimile, imitation, mannequin, miniature, prototype, superwaif **10** archetypal, embodiment, small-scale, stereotype **11** guiding star **12** artist's model, fashion model, guiding light, prototypical, reproduction **14** perfect example, representation

**moderate**
**03** mod **04** calm, cool, curb, ease, fair, just, mean, mild, soft, so-so, tame **05** abate, allay, chair, check, slake, sober **06** decent, direct, gentle, lessen, medium, modest, modify, pacify, relent, soften, steady, subdue, temper **07** appease, assuage, average, chasten, control, die down, dwindle, fairish, liberal, qualify, repress, slacken, subside **08** adequate, attemper, centrist, chastise, decrease, diminish, don't know, mediocre, middling, mitigate, modulate, muscadin, ordinary, palliate, passable, play down, regulate, restrain, sensible, suppress, tone down **09** alleviate, attenuate, Menshevik, Octobrist, soft-pedal, soft-shell, supervise, temperate, tolerable, treatable **10** controlled, measurable, not much cop, reasonable, restrained **11** indifferent, keep in check, not up to much, preside over, soft-shelled **12** act as chair at, conservative, nonextremist **13** neutral person, no great shakes, well-regulated **14** fair to middling **15** act as chairman at, middle-of-the-road

**moderately**
**05** mezzo, quite **06** fairly, rather **08** passably, slightly, somewhat **10** reasonably **12** to some extent, within reason **13** within measure **14** conservatively

**moderation**
**02** ho **03** hoa, hoh **06** reason **07** caution, control, curbing, measure **08** chastity, decrease, sobriety **09** abatement, composure, lessening, reduction, restraint **10** golden mean, mitigation, regulation, relaxation, subsidence, temperance **11** alleviation, attenuation, self-control **13** self-restraint, temperateness **14** abstemiousness, reasonableness

**• in moderation**
**10** moderately **12** within bounds, within limits, within reason **15** with self-control

**modern**
**02** AD, in **03** hip, mod, new, now **04** cool, late **05** fresh, novel **06** latest, latter, modish, recent, trendy, with it **07** current, faddish, go-ahead, in style, in vogue, present, stylish, voguish **08** advanced, everyday, existing, neoteric, space-age, up-to-date **09** in fashion, inventive, latter-day, newfangle, the latest **10** all the rage, avant-garde, futuristic, innovative, neoterical, newfangled, present-day **11** commonplace, cutting edge, fashionable, modernistic, progressive, spanking new **12** contemporary **13** state-of-the-art, up-to-the-minute **14** forward-looking, hot off the press

**modernity**
**07** newness, novelty **09** freshness **10** innovation, recentness **11** originality **14** innovativeness **15** contemporaneity, fashionableness

**modernization**
**07** renewal **08** redesign, updating **09** revamping **10** renovation **11** improvement, remodelling **12** modification, regeneration **13** refurbishment **14** transformation

**modernize**
**04** do up **05** fix up, renew **06** do over, modify, reform, remake, revamp, update **07** improve, refresh, remodel **08** progress, redesign, renovate **09** get with it, refurbish, transform **10** make modern, regenerate, rejuvenate, streamline **13** bring up-to-date

**modest**
**03** coy, shy **04** fair, pure **05** lowly, plain, prude, pudic, quiet, small, timid **06** chaste, decent, demure, humble, proper, pudent, seemly, simple **07** bashful, limited, prudent **08** adequate, decorous, discreet, maidenly, moderate, ordinary, passable, reserved, retiring, verecund, virtuous **09** chastened, diffident, shamefast, tolerable **10** reasonable, shamefaced, unassuming **11** inexpensive, unobtrusive **12** satisfactory, self-effacing, unpretending **13** self-conscious, unexceptional, unpretentious **15** self-deprecating

**modestly**
**05** coyly, shyly **06** humbly, purely **07** quietly, timidly **08** chastely, decently, demurely **09** bashfully **10** adequately, discreetly, moderately, reasonably, virtuously **11** diffidently **12** unassumingly **14** satisfactorily **15** self-consciously, unpretentiously

**modesty**
**05** aidos, shame **07** coyness, decency, decorum, pudency, reserve, shyness **08** humility, pudicity, timidity **09** plainness, propriety, quietness, reticence **10** chasteness, demureness, humbleness, seemliness, simplicity **11** bashfulness **13** shamefastness **14** self-effacement, shamefacedness **15** inexpensiveness, self-deprecation

**modicum**
**03** bit, tad **04** atom, dash, drop, hint, inch, iota, mite **05** crumb, grain, ounce, pinch, scrap, shred, speck, tinge, touch, trace, woman **06** degree, little **08** fragment, molecule, particle **09** little bit **10** suggestion **11** small amount

**modification**
◇ *anagram indicator*
**05** tweak **06** change **08** mutation, revision **09** recasting, reworking, tempering, variation **10** adaptation, adjustment, alteration, limitation, moderation, modulation, refinement, remoulding **11** improvement, reformation, restriction **13** qualification **14** reorganization, transformation

**modify**
◇ *anagram indicator*
**04** dash, dull, vary **05** abate, adapt, alter, limit, touch, tweak, vowel **06** adjust, change, invert, lessen, recast, reduce, reform, revise, rework, sculpt, soften, temper, umlaut **07** convert, improve, qualify, remould, reshape **08** attemper, decrease, diminish, mitigate, moderate, overrule, redesign, retrofit, tone down, vowelize **09** diversify, transform **10** assimilate, reorganize **11** explain away **13** differentiate, trim your sails

**modish**
**02** in **03** hip, mod, now **04** chic, cool **05** jazzy, smart, vogue **06** latest, modern, tonish, trendy, with it **07** à la mode, current, stylish, tonnish, voguish **10** all the rage, avant-garde **11** fashionable, modernistic **12** contemporary **13** up-to-the-minute

**modulate**
**04** tune, vary **05** alter, lower **06** adjust, change, modify, soften, temper **07** balance, inflect **08** moderate, regulate **09** harmonize

**modulation**
**04** tone **05** shade, shift **06** accent, change, tuning **07** balance, cadence **08** lowering **09** inflexion, softening, variation **10** adjustment, alteration, inflection, intonation, moderation, regulation **12** modification **13** harmonization

**module**
**02** LM **03** bug, LEM **04** item, part, SIMM, unit **05** image, model, piece **06** factor, plug-in **07** element, section **09** component

**modus operandi**
**02** MO **03** way **04** plan, rule **06** manner, method, praxis, system **07** process **08** practice **09** operation, procedure, technique **11** rule of thumb

**mogul**
**03** VIP **05** baron, Mr Big **06** big gun, big pot, bigwig, Mughal, top dog, tycoon **07** big shot, magnate, notable, supremo **08** big noise, big wheel, padishah **09** big cheese, personage, potentate

**moist**
**03** wet **04** damp, dank, dewy **05** humid, juicy, muggy, rainy, soggy, washy **06** clammy, hydric, liquid, marshy, watery **07** drizzly, tearful, wettish **08** dripping **09** drizzling, humectant, hygrophil **12** hygrophilous

**moisten**
**03** dew, dip, wet **04** damp, lick, soak, wash **05** bathe, bedew, bewet, imbue, latch, slake, water **06** dampen, embrue, humect, humefy, humify, imbrue, madefy, sloken, sparge **07** embrewe, make wet, slocken, spairge **08** humidify, irrigate **09** humectate **10** moisturize

**moisture**
**03** dew, wet **04** damp, rain **05** humor, spray, steam, sweat, water **06** humour, liquid, vapour **07** drizzle, soaking, wetness **08** dampness, dankness, humidity **09** mugginess **10** wateriness **11** humectation, precipitate **12** condensation, perspiration **13** precipitation

**molar**
**04** wang **08** jaw-tooth **09** mill-tooth

**Moldova**
**02** MD **03** MDA

**mole**
**03** mol, spy **04** dyke, mark, pier, spot, want **05** agent, jetty, Talpa **06** blotch, groyne **07** barrier, blemish, freckle, speckle **08** causeway **09** mouldwarp, mowdiwort **10** breakwater, embankment, moudiewart, moudiewort, mowdiewart, Notoryctes **11** double agent, infiltrator, secret agent

**molest**
**03** bug, nag, vex **04** harm, hurt, rape **05** abuse, annoy, harry, hound, tease, upset, worry **06** accost, assail, attack, badger, bother, chivvy, harass, hassle, injure, needle, pester, plague, ravish **07** agitate, assault, disturb, fluster, provoke, torment, trouble **08** ill-treat, irritate, maltreat, mistreat **09** aggravate, persecute **10** exasperate **13** interfere with **15** sexually assault

**molestation**
**04** harm, rape **05** abuse **06** attack, injury **07** assault **11** disturbance, infestation **12** interference

**molester**
**06** abuser, rapist **08** attacker, ravisher **09** assaulter

**mollify**
**04** calm, ease, lull **05** abate, allay, blunt, quell, quiet, relax **06** lessen, mellow, modify, pacify, soften, soothe, temper **07** appease, assuage, compose, cushion, placate, quieten, relieve, sweeten **08** mitigate, moderate **10** conciliate, propitiate

**mollusc**

*Molluscs include:*

**03** Mya
**04** clam, slug, Unio
**05** conch, cowry, snail, spoot, squid, whelk
**06** chiton, cockle, cowrie, cuttle, dodman, limpet, loligo, mussel, nerite, oyster, winkle
**07** abalone, octopus, piddock, scallop, sea slug
**08** escargot, nautilus, sea snail, shipworm, wallfish
**09** cone shell, hodmandod, land snail, pond snail, razorclam, razorfish, tusk shell, wing shell, wing snail
**10** cuttlefish, giant squid, nudibranch, periwinkle, razor shell, Roman snail
**11** horse mussel, marine snail
**12** sea butterfly
**13** great grey slug, keyhole limpet, ramshorn snail, slipper limpet
**15** freshwater snail

*See also* **animal**; **crustacean**

**• mollusc's tongue**
**04** rasp

**mollycoddle**
**03** pet **04** baby, ruin **05** spoil **06** coddle, cosset, mother, pamper **07** indulge **08** pander to **09** spoon-feed **11** overprotect

**molten**
**05** fusil **06** fusile, melted **07** flowing **08** magmatic **09** liquefied **12** circumfusile

**molybdenum**
**02** Mo

**moment**
**02** mo **03** sec **04** hint, note, tick **05** flash, gliff, glift, jiffy, point, punto, trice, twink, value, worth **06** import, minute, puncto, second, stound, stownd, weight **07** concern, gravity, instant **08** as soon as, directly, gliffing, interest, occasion, the point, two ticks **09** short time, substance, the minute, twinkling **10** importance, the instant **11** consequence, immediately, little while, point in time, seriousness, split second, weightiness **12** significance **13** very short time **14** less than no time

**• a moment ago**
**04** enow

**momentarily**
**07** briefly **10** fleetingly, for a moment, for a second **11** temporarily **12** for an instant **13** for a short time **15** instantaneously

**momentary**
**05** brief, hasty, quick, short **07** passing **08** fleeting **09** ephemeral, momentany, spasmodic, temporary, transient **10** evanescent, short-lived, transitory **12** momentaneous **13** instantaneous

**momentous**
**05** grave, major, vital **07** crucial, fateful, pivotal, serious, weighty **08** critical, decisive, eventful, historic, pregnant **09** important **11** epoch-making, significant **12** earth-shaking, of importance **13** consequential **14** of significance **15** earth-shattering, world-shattering

**momentum**
**04** push, urge **05** drive, force, poise, power, speed **06** energy, impact, thrust **07** impetus, impulse **08** stimulus, strength, velocity **09** incentive **10** propulsion **12** driving-power

**• angular momentum**
**01** L

**Monaco**
**02** MC **03** MCO

**monarch**
**01** K, Q, R **02** ER, GR, HM, VR **03** rex, roi **04** Cole, czar, Inca, king, ksar, tsar, tzar **05** queen, ruler **06** Caesar, prince, regina **07** czarina, emperor, empress, tsarina **08** autocrat, czarevna, czaritsa, princess, the Crown, tsarevna, tsaritsa **09** cesarevna, czarevich, potentate, sovereign, tsarevich **10** cesarevich, cesarewich, czarevitch, tsesarevna, tsarevitch **11** cesarevitch, cesarewitch, crowned head, king of kings, tsesarevich, tsesarewich **12** tsesarevitch, tsesarewitch

*See also* **king**; **prince**; **princess**; **queen**

*Anglo-Saxon and English monarchs:*

**04** Cnut ('the Great'), Edwy, Grey (Lady Jane), John (Lackland), Mary (I, Tudor), Offa
**05** Edgar, Edred, Henry (I, II, III, IV, V, VI, VII, VIII), Svein (I Haraldsson, 'Fork-Beard')
**06** Alfred ('the Great'), Canute, Edmund (I, II 'Ironside'), Edward (I, II 'the Martyr', III 'the Confessor', IV, V, VI, 'the Elder'), Egbert, Harold (I Knutsson, 'Harefoot', II)
**07** Richard (I 'the Lion Heart', II, III), Stephen, William (I 'the Conqueror', II 'Rufus')
**08** Ethelred (I, II 'the Unready')
**09** Athelstan, Elizabeth (I), Ethelbald, Ethelbert, Ethelwulf

**11** Hardicanute
**13** Edgar Atheling, Knut Sveinsson

*Scottish monarchs:*

**03** Aed
**04** Dubh, Duff
**05** Bruce (Robert), Culen, David (I, II), Edgar, Giric, James (I, II, III, IV, V, VI)
**06** Baliol (Edward de), Baliol (John de), Donald (I, II, III 'Bane'), Duncan (I, II), Indulf, Lulach, Robert (I 'the Bruce', II, III)
**07** Balliol (Edward de), Balliol (John de), Kenneth (I, II, III), Macbeth, Malcolm (I, II, III 'Canmore', IV 'the Maiden'), William (I)
**08** Margaret ('Maid of Norway')
**09** Alexander (I, II, III)
**11** Constantine (I, II)
**16** Mary, Queen of Scots

*British monarchs:*

**04** Anne, Mary (II)
**05** James (VI and I), James (VII and II)
**06** Edward (VII, VIII), George (I, II, III, IV, V, VI)
**07** Charles (I, II), William (II and III of Orange, IV)
**08** Victoria
**09** Elizabeth (II)
**14** William and Mary

## monarchy
**05** realm **06** domain, empire
**07** kingdom, royalty, tyranny
**08** dominion, kingship, royalism
**09** autocracy, despotism, monocracy
**10** absolutism **11** sovereignty
**12** principality **14** sovereign state

## monastery
**03** wat **04** cell **05** abbey, gompa
**06** friary, priory, vihara **07** convent, minster, nunnery **08** cloister, lamasery
**09** coenobium, lamaserai
**12** Charterhouse

*Monasteries and convents include:*

**04** Iona
**05** Cluny
**07** Mt Athos, Shaolin
**08** Hilandar, Sénanque
**09** Melk Abbey, Tengboche
**10** Chartreuse, Douai Abbey, El Escorial, Ettal Abbey, San Lorenzo, Santa Croce, Worth Abbey
**11** Ealing Abbey, Glendalough, Lindisfarne, Parkminster, Simonopetra, Val-Duchesse, Whitby Abbey
**12** Belmont Abbey, Colwich Abbey, Monte Cassino, Mont St Michel, St John's Abbey
**13** Buckfast Abbey, Donglin Temple, Downside Abbey, Monasterboice, Rievaulx Abbey, Tyburn Convent
**14** Fountains Abbey, Stanbrook Abbey
**15** Ampleforth Abbey, Curzon Park Abbey, Portsmouth Abbey, St Cecilia's Abbey

*See also* **abbey**; **religious**

## monastic
**07** ascetic, austere, monkish, recluse
**08** celibate, eremitic, secluded, solitary **09** canonical, reclusive, withdrawn **10** anchoritic, cloistered, coenobitic, meditative **11** sequestered
**13** contemplative

*See also* **religious**

## monasticism
**07** monkery **08** monkhood
**09** austerity, eremitism, monachism, reclusion, seclusion **10** asceticism
**11** coenobitism, recluseness

## Monday
**03** Mon

## monetary
**04** cash **05** money **06** fiscal **07** capital
**08** economic **09** budgetary, financial, pecuniary

## money
**01** L, M, P **03** fat, LSD, oof, tin, utu
**04** cash, cent, coin, dibs, dosh, dust, gelt, gilt, hoot, jack, kail, kale, loot, pelf
**05** blunt, brass, bread, bucks, chink, dough, dumps, funds, gravy, lolly, means, Oscar, purse, ready, rhino, smash, sugar, wonga **06** argent, assets, greens, moolah, riches, stumpy, wealth
**07** capital, dingbat, ooftish, readies, savings, scratch, shekels **08** currency, finances, greenies **09** affluence, banknotes, megabucks, resources
**10** big bikkies, prosperity **11** legal tender, spondulicks **12** the necessary

*See also* **coin**; **currency**

### • get money from
**03** tap

### • hand over money
**03** pay

### • in the money
**04** rich **05** flush **06** loaded **07** wealthy, well-off **08** affluent, well-to-do
**10** prosperous, well-heeled **11** rolling in it **12** stinking rich

### • large amount of money
**03** wad **04** mint, pile, pots, scad

### • money collection
**03** cap **04** whip **09** whip-round

### • provide with money
**03** pay **04** fund

### • quantity of money
**03** sum

## money-box
**04** safe **05** chest **06** coffer **07** cash box, poor box **08** penny-pig **09** piggy-bank

## money-changing
**04** agio

## moneyed
**04** rich **05** flush **06** loaded **07** opulent, wealthy, well-off **08** affluent, well-to-do **10** prosperous, well-heeled
**11** comfortable, rolling in it

## money-grubbing
**07** miserly **08** grasping
**09** mammonish, mercenary
**10** quaestuary **11** acquisitive, mammonistic

## moneymaking
**06** paying **09** lucrative **10** commercial, profitable, quaestuary, successful
**12** profit-making, remunerative

## Mongolia
**03** MGL, MNG

## mongoose
**04** urva

## mongrel
◇ *anagram indicator*
**03** cur **04** kuri, mong, mutt **05** cross, mixed, pooch **06** bitser, hybrid
**07** bastard **08** half-bred **09** crossbred, half-breed, yellow dog **10** crossbreed, ill-defined, mixed breed **12** of mixed breed

## monicker
**04** name **05** alias **07** pen name
**08** nickname **09** false name, pseudonym, sobriquet, stage name
**10** soubriquet **11** assumed name

## monitor
**03** VDU **04** CCTV, note, plot, scan
**05** check, trace, track, varan, watch
**06** detect, follow, goanna, iguana, leguan, marker, record, screen, survey, worral, worrel **07** adviser, advisor, display, head boy, leguaan, observe, oversee, perenty, prefect, scanner, Varanus **08** detector, head girl, observer, overseer, perentie, recorder, watchdog **09** supervise **10** supervisor
**11** invigilator, keep an eye on, keep track of **12** dragon lizard, Komodo dragon, Komodo lizard **14** security camera

## monk
**03** Dan, Dom **04** lama **05** abbot, friar, prior **06** beguin, frater, hermit
**07** brother **08** cenobite, monastic, talapoin **09** anchorite, bullfinch, coenobite, Dalai Lama, gyrovague, mendicant, religieux, religious
**10** cloisterer, conventual, religioner
**11** abbey-lubber, religionary
**13** contemplative, possessionate

*Monks and nuns include:*

**02** Fa (Hsien), Fa (Xian)
**03** Orm
**04** Gall (St), Hume (Basil), Rule (St), Sava (St)
**05** Aidan (St), Barat (St Madeleine Sophie), Borde (Andrew), Jacob (Max), Ormin, Rancé (Armand Jean de), Sabas (St)
**06** Arnulf, Boorde (Andrew), Colman (St), Eadmer, Ernulf, Gildas (St), Gyatso (Geshe Kelsang), Gyatso (Tenzin), Merton (Thomas), Teresa (Mother), Tetzel (Johann), Turgot
**07** Adamnan (St), Adomnan (St), Arnauld (Angélique), Arnauld (Marie-Angélique), Beckett (Sister Wendy), Cabrini (St Francesca Xavier), Carpini (John of Plano), Cassian (St John), Gratian, Lydgate (John), Mortara (Edgar), Regulus (St), Schwarz (Berthold)
**08** Alacoque (St Marguerite Marie),

Bonivard (François de), **Duchesne** (St Rose Philippine), **Foucauld** (Charles de), **Houedard** (Dom Sylvester), **Pelagius**, **Rabelais** (François), **Rasputin** (Grigori)
**09** **Bonnivard** (François de), **MacKillop** (Mary), **Skobtsova** (Maria)
**10** **Bernadette** (St), **Fra Diavolo**, **Montfaucon** (Bernard de), **Torquemada** (Tomás de), **Walsingham** (Thomas), **Willibrord** (St)
**11** **Bodhidharma**, **Ponce de León** (Luis), **Scholastica** (St)
**12** **Guido d'Arezzo**
**13** **The Singing Nun**
**14** **Francis of Paola** (St), **Marianus Scotus**, **Peter the Hermit**
**15** **Bernard of Morval**

*See also* **religious**

**monkey**
**03** imp, tup **04** brat, fool, mess, muck, play, tyke **05** anger, clown, mimic, rogue, scamp, sheep **06** fiddle, fidget, footle, lackey, meddle, potter, rascal, simian, tamper, tinker, trifle, urchin **07** primate **09** interfere, scallywag **10** jackanapes **13** mischief-maker

*Monkeys include:*

**03** ape, pug, sai
**04** douc, leaf, mico, mona, saki, titi, zati
**05** Diana, drill, green, magot, night, sajou, Satan, toque
**06** baboon, bandar, bonnet, coaita, grivet, guenon, howler, langur, malmag, rhesus, sagoin, saguin, spider, tee-tee, uakari, vervet, woolly
**07** cacajou, colobus, guereza, hanuman, jacchus, macaque, sagouin, saimiri, sapajou, tamarin, tarsier, wistiti
**08** capuchin, durukuli, entellus, mandrill, mangabey, marmoset, squirrel, talapoin, wanderoo
**09** proboscis
**10** Barbary ape, moustached
**11** douroucouli, platyrrhine, white-eyelid
**13** platyrrhinian

*See also* **animal**; **ape**

• **monkey business**
**06** pranks **07** carry-on, foolery **08** clowning, mischief, trickery **09** chicanery **10** dishonesty, hanky-panky, tomfoolery **11** legerdemain, shenanigans, skulduggery **12** monkey tricks **13** funny business, jiggery-pokery, sleight-of-hand

• **monkey puzzle**
**09** araucaria, Chile pine **11** Chilean pine

**monochrome**
**05** sepia **08** monotone, unicolor **09** unicolour **10** monochroic, monotonous **11** unicolorate, unicolorous, unicoloured **13** black-and-white, monochromatic

**monocle**
**04** quiz **05** glass **08** eyeglass **13** quizzing-glass

**monogamous**
**09** monogamic **10** monandrous, monogynous

**monogamy**
**08** monandry, monogyny

**monolingual**
**08** monoglot **10** unilingual

**monolith**
**05** shaft **06** menhir, sarsen **08** megalith **13** standing stone

**monolithic**
**04** huge, vast **05** giant, rigid, solid **07** massive **08** colossal, faceless, gigantic, immobile, unmoving, unvaried **09** hidebound, immovable **10** fossilized, inflexible, monumental, unchanging **11** intractable

**monologue**
**03** rap **05** spiel **06** homily, sermon, speech **07** address, lecture, oration **09** soliloquy

**monomania**
**05** mania, thing **06** fetish **08** fixation, idée fixe, neurosis **09** fixed idea, obsession **10** fanaticism, hobby-horse **13** ruling passion **15** bee in your bonnet

**monopolize**
**03** hog **05** tie up **06** corner, occupy, take up **07** control, engross **08** dominate, take over **09** preoccupy **11** appropriate **14** have sole rights, have to yourself, keep to yourself

**monopoly**
**05** régie **06** corner **07** appalto, control **09** franchise, monopsony, privilege, sole right **10** ascendancy, domination, sole rights **14** exclusive right **15** exclusive rights

**monotonous**
**04** drab, dull, flat **05** ho-hum, samey **06** boring, deadly **07** humdrum, routine, tedious, uniform **08** plodding, tiresome, toneless, unvaried **09** unvarying, wearisome **10** all the same, colourless, mechanical, monochrome, repetitive, unchanging, uneventful, unexciting **11** repetitious **12** run-of-the-mill **13** uninteresting **14** soul-destroying

**monotony**
**06** tedium **07** boredom, humdrum, routine, taedium **08** ding-dong, dullness, flatness, sameness **10** repetition, uniformity **11** routineness **12** tiresomeness **13** wearisomeness **14** repetitiveness, uneventfulness

**monster**
**04** huge, mega, vast **05** alien, beast, brute, devil, fiend, freak, giant, jumbo **06** mutant, savage **07** immense, mammoth, massive, villain **08** colossal, colossus, enormous, gigantic, teratism, whopping **09** barbarian, ginormous, monstrous **10** tremendous **11** miscreation, monstrosity **12** malformation **13** freak of nature **14** Brobdingnagian

*Monster types include:*

**03** orc, roc
**04** cete, gila, ogre
**05** alien, gulon, harpy, lamia, phoca, troll, yowie, zombi
**06** ajatar, bunyip, dragon, gorgon, kraken, nicker, ogress, sphinx, wivern, wyvern, zombie
**07** cyclops, griffin, griffon, gryphon, prodigy, satyral, taniwha, triffid, wendigo, windigo, ziffius
**08** basilisk, behemoth, bogeyman, dinosaur, lindworm, mooncalf, mushussu, seahorse
**09** leviathan, manticore, marakihau, rosmarine, sea satyre, wasserman, whirlpool
**10** chupacabra, cockatrice, crio-sphinx, salamander, sea monster
**11** amphisbaena, hippocampus

*Monsters include:*

**02** ET
**05** Hydra, Smaug, snark
**06** Balrog, Duessa, Empusa, Fafnir, Geryon, Medusa, Nazgul, Nessie, Python, Scylla, Shelob, Sphinx, Stheno, Typhon
**07** Bathies, Caliban, Cecrops, Chimera, Cyclops, Dracula, Echidna, Euryale, Grendel
**08** Cerberus, Chimaera, Godzilla, King Kong, Minotaur, Typhoeus
**09** Charybdis
**10** Black Annis, jabberwock, Jormangund, jubjub bird, Polyphemus
**12** bandersnatch, Blatant Beast, Count Dracula, Frankenstein
**13** Cookie Monster, Hecatonchires, Questing Beast
**14** Incredible Hulk, Midgard serpent
**15** Glatysaunt Beast, Loch Ness monster

*See also* **mythical**; **mythology**

**monstrosity**
**04** evil **05** freak, teras **06** horror, mutant **07** eyesore, monster **08** atrocity, enormity, ugliness **09** carbuncle, obscenity **11** abnormality, heinousness, hellishness, hideousness, miscreation **12** dreadfulness **13** frightfulness, loathsomeness

**monstrous**
**04** evil, foul, huge, vast, vile **05** cruel, nasty **06** grisly, savage, wicked **07** heinous, hideous, immense, inhuman, mammoth, massive, vicious **08** abnormal, colossal, criminal, deformed, dreadful, enormous, freakish, gigantic, gruesome, horrible, misbegot, shocking, teratoid, terrible **09** abhorrent, atrocious, frightful,

grotesque, malformed, misshapen, unnatural **10** abominable, horrifying, miraculous, outrageous, prodigious, scandalous, tremendous
**11** disgraceful, misbegotten
**12** preposterous

## monstrously
**06** hugely, vastly **08** terribly
**09** immensely, massively **10** colossally, dreadfully, enormously, shockingly
**11** atrociously, frightfully
**12** gigantically, outrageously, scandalously, tremendously

## Montana
**02** MT **04** Mont

## month
**01** m **02** mo

*Months:*

**02** Jy
**03** Apr, Aug, Dec, Feb, Jan, Jul, Jun, Mar, May, Nov, Oct, Sep
**04** July, June, Sept
**05** April, March
**06** August
**07** January, October
**08** December, February, November
**09** September

*French month names:*

**02** Av
**03** mai
**04** août, juin, mars
**05** avril
**07** février, janvier, juillet, octobre
**08** décembre, novembre
**09** septembre

*French Revolutionary calendar month names:*

**06** Nivôse
**07** Floréal, Ventôse
**08** Brumaire, Frimaire, Germinal, Messidor, Pluviôse, Prairial
**09** Fructidor, Thermidor
**11** Vendémiaire

*German month names:*

**03** Mai
**04** Juli, Juni, März
**05** April
**06** August, Januar
**07** Februar, Oktober
**08** Dezember, November
**09** September

*Hindu calendar month names:*

**05** Magha, Pausa
**06** Asadha, Asvina
**07** Chaitra, Sravana
**08** Jyaistha, Karttika, Phalguna, Vaisakha
**10** Bhadrapada, Margasirsa
**13** Dvitiya Asadha
**14** Dvitiya Sravana

*Islamic calendar month names:*

**05** Rabi I, Rajab, Safar
**06** Rabi II, Shaban
**07** Jumada I, Ramadan, Shawwal
**08** Jumada II, Muharram
**10** Dhu al-Qadah
**11** Dhu al-Hijjah

*Italian month names:*

**05** marzo
**06** agosto, aprile, giugno, luglio, maggio
**07** gennaio, ottobre
**08** dicembre, febbraio, novembre
**09** settembre

*Jewish calendar month names:*

**02** Ab, Av
**04** Abib, Adar, Elul, Iyar
**05** Iyyar, Nisan, Sivan, Tebet, Tevet, Tisri
**06** Hesvan, Kisleu, Kislev, Shebat, Shevat, Tammuz, Tebeth, Tishri, Veadar
**07** Chislev, Heshvan
**09** Adar Sheni

*Latin month names:*

**05** Maius
**06** Julius, Junius
**07** Aprilis, Martius, October
**08** Augustus, December, November, Sextilis
**09** Januarius, Quintilis, September
**10** Februarius

*Spanish month names:*

**04** mayo
**05** abril, enero, julio, junio, marzo
**06** agosto
**07** febrero, octubre
**09** diciembre, noviembre
**10** septiembre

• **in the last month**
**03** ult **04** ulto **06** ultimo
• **the present month**
**04** inst **07** instant

## Montserrat
**03** MSR

## monument
**04** tomb **05** cairn, cross, folly, relic, token, trace **06** barrow, column, heroon, marker, pillar, record, shrine, statue **07** hogback, martyry, memento, obelisk, prodigy, pyramid, talayot, trilith, witness **08** cenotaph, evidence, memorial, reminder, sacellum
**09** headstone, mausoleum, testament, tombstone, trilithon **10** gravestone, immortelle, indication
**11** remembrance, war memorial
**13** commemoration

*Monuments and memorials include:*

**04** Eros, Homo
**05** Grant, Scott
**06** Albert, Sphinx
**07** Lincoln, Martyr's
**08** Boadicea, Cenotaph, Daibutsu, Lion Gate, Taj Mahal, Victoria
**09** Charminar, Menin Gate, Qutb Minar, Tsar's Bell
**10** Berlin Wall, Broken Ring, Ishtar Gate, Kutab Minar, London Wall, Marble Arch, Mt Rushmore, Navigators', Stonehenge, Washington
**11** Civil Rights, Eiffel Tower, Grande Arche, Great Sphinx, Machu Picchu, Madara Rider, Silbury Hill, Voortrekker
**12** Antonine Wall, Eleanor Cross, Glass Pyramid, Great Pyramid, Hadrian's Wall, Spanish Steps, Statue of Zeus, Tower of Babel
**13** Admiralty Arch, Arc de Triomphe, Great Zimbabwe, Mount Rushmore, Nelson's Column, People's Heroes, Trajan's Column, Trevi Fountain
**14** Albert Memorial, Eleanor Crosses, Gateway of India, Glastonbury Tor, Hands of Victory, Hiroshima Peace, Lenin Mausoleum, Spasskaya Tower, Stone of Destiny, Tomb of Mausolus, Wayland's Smithy, Wright Brothers
**15** Brandenburg Gate, Lincoln Memorial, Nubian monuments, Rollright Stones, Statue of Liberty, Thatta monuments

## monumental
**04** huge, vast **05** great **07** abiding, amazing, awesome, classic, immense, lasting, massive, notable **08** colossal, enduring, enormous, historic, immortal, imposing, majestic, memorial, striking
**09** important, memorable, permanent
**10** impressive, remarkable, tremendous
**11** celebratory, epoch-making, exceptional, magnificent, outstanding, significant **12** awe-inspiring, overwhelming **13** commemorative, extraordinary, unforgettable

## monumentally
**06** hugely, vastly **09** immensely, massively **10** colossally, enormously
**12** gigantically, tremendously

## mood
**03** fit, tid **04** feel, mode, sulk, tone, vein, whim **05** anger, blues, dumps, pique, tenor **06** humour, plight, spirit, temper **07** bad mood, climate, feeling, spirits **08** ambience, doldrums, optative, the sulks **09** bad temper, potential **10** atmosphere, depression, imperative, indicative, infinitive, low spirits, melancholy **11** conjunctive, disposition, frame of mind, state of mind, subjunctive
• **in the mood for**
**06** keen on, keen to **07** eager to
**08** ready for **09** willing to **10** disposed to, inclined to **11** feeling like, wanting to do **13** wanting to have

## moody
**04** glum, mopy **05** angry, faked, mopey, sulky, testy **06** broody, crabby, crusty, fickle, gloomy, morose, sullen, touchy **07** doleful, flighty, in a huff, in a mood **08** downcast, petulant, unstable, volatile **09** crotchety, impulsive, irascible, irritable, miserable, pretended **10** capricious, changeable, in a bad mood, melancholy **11** bad-tempered
**12** cantankerous **13** short-tempered, temperamental, unpredictable

**moon**
**04** idle, loaf, mope, pine **05** brood, dream, month, mooch **06** Lucina, Phoebe **08** daydream, languish **09** fantasize, satellite **13** Paddy's lantern **15** MacFarlane's buat

*Lunar seas:*

**08** Bay of Dew
**09** Moscow Sea, Sea of Cold, Smyth's Sea
**10** Bay of Heats, Central Bay, Eastern Sea, Foaming Sea, Mare Nubium, Sea of Waves, Sinus Medii, Sinus Roris
**11** Lacus Mortis, Lake of Death, Mare Crisium, Mare Humorum, Mare Imbrium, Mare Ingenii, Mare Smythii, Mare Spumans, Mare Undarum, Mare Vaporum, Marginal Sea, Palus Somnii, Sea of Clouds, Sea of Crises, Sea of Nectar, Sinus Iridum, Southern Sea
**12** Humboldt's Sea, Lake of Dreams, Mare Australe, Mare Frigoris, Mare Marginis, Mare Nectaris, Marsh of Decay, Marsh of Mists, Marsh of Sleep, Sea of Showers, Sea of Vapours, Sinus Aestuum
**13** Bay of Rainbows, Mare Orientale, Ocean of Storms, Sea of Geniuses, Sea of Moisture, Sea of Serenity
**14** Lacus Somniorum, Palus Nebularum, Sea of Fertility
**15** Mare Moscoviense, Mare Serenitatis, Palus Putredinis
**16** Mare Fecunditatis, Marsh of Epidemics, Palus Epidemiarum
**17** Mare Humboldtianum, Sea of Tranquillity
**18** Oceanus Procellarum
**19** Mare Tranquillitatis

*Moons include:*

**02** Io
**04** Moon, Rhea
**05** Ariel, Dione, Mimas, Titan
**06** Charon, Deimos, Europa, Nereid, Oberon, Phobos, Tethys, Triton
**07** Iapetus, Miranda, Proteus, Titania, Umbriel
**08** Callisto, Cruithne, Ganymede, Hyperion
**09** Enceladus

*Moon-related terms include:*

**05** lunar, phase
**06** waning, waxing
**07** far side, gibbous, new moon
**08** blue moon, crescent, dark side, full moon, half-moon, lunation, near side
**09** blood moon, moonlight, moonscape, moonshine
**11** harvest moon, hunter's moon, last quarter, quarter moon
**12** first quarter, man in the moon, synodic month, third quarter

**• once in a blue moon**
**06** seldom **08** not often **10** hardly ever, very rarely **11** almost never
**• over the moon**
**06** elated, joyful **07** fervent **08** blissful, ecstatic, euphoric, frenzied, jubilant **09** delighted, delirious, overjoyed, rapturous, rhapsodic **10** enraptured **11** high as a kite, on cloud nine, tickled pink **13** jumping for joy **15** in seventh heaven, on top of the world

**moonlike**
**05** lunar, moony **06** lunate **07** lunular, selenic **08** crescent **09** meniscoid **10** crescentic, moon-shaped

**moonshine**
**03** rot **04** bosh, bunk, crap, guff, tosh **05** hooch, month, stuff, tripe **06** bunkum, hootch, hot air, liquor, piffle, poteen **07** baloney, blather, blether, bootleg, eyewash, fantasy, hogwash, hokonui, potheen, rubbish, spirits, twaddle **08** blathers, blethers, bodiless, claptrap, nonsense, tommyrot **09** bull's wool

**moor**
**03** fix **04** bind, dock, fell, lash, muir **05** berth, heath, hitch, tie up **06** anchor, fasten, secure, upland **07** Moresco, Morisco, mudéjar, Saracen **08** make fast, moorland **09** fix firmly **10** drop anchor
**• tightly moored**
**04** girt

**moot**
**04** open, pose, stir **05** argue, plead, raise, vexed **06** broach, debate, knotty, submit **07** advance, bring up, crucial, discuss, dispute, meeting, propose, suggest **08** academic, arguable, disputed, doubtful, propound **09** debatable, difficult, insoluble, introduce, undecided, unsettled **10** discussion, disputable, put forward, unresolved **11** contestable, problematic **12** open to debate, questionable, undetermined, unresolvable **13** controversial

**mop**
**03** mat **04** mane, mass, soak, swab, wash, wipe **05** clean, dwile, shock, wiper **06** absorb, malkin, mawkin, sponge, tangle, thatch **07** grimace, swabber **08** squeegee **10** head of hair
**• mop up**
**04** swab, wash **06** absorb, secure, soak up, sponge, tidy up, wipe up **07** clean up, round up **08** deal with **09** dispose of, eliminate, finish off **10** account for, neutralize, take care of

**mope**
**04** fret, mump, peak, pine, sulk **05** boody, brood, droop, grump, moper **06** grieve, grouch, misery, moaner **07** despair, killjoy **08** languish **09** introvert, pessimist **10** depressive **11** be miserable, melancholic **12** melancholiac
**• mope about**
**04** idle, loll, moon **05** mooch **06** lounge, wander **08** languish

**moral**
**03** tag **04** good, just, pure **05** adage, maxim, noble, point, right **06** chaste, decent, dictum, honest, lesson, proper, saying, symbol **07** epigram, ethical, meaning, message, precept, proverb, upright **08** aphorism, straight, teaching, virtuous **09** blameless, certainty, emotional, righteous **10** high-minded, honourable, principled, upstanding **11** application, clean-living, encouraging **12** significance **13** incorruptible, psychological

**morale**
**04** mood **05** heart **06** spirit **07** spirits **08** optimism **10** confidence, self-esteem **11** hopefulness, state of mind **13** esprit de corps **14** self-confidence

**moralistic**
**04** smug **05** pious **08** priggish, superior **09** pietistic **10** complacent, goody-goody **11** pharisaical **12** hypocritical **13** sanctimonious, self-righteous **14** holier-than-thou

**morality**
**04** good **06** ethics, ideals, morale, morals, purity, virtue **07** conduct, decency, honesty, justice, manners **08** chastity, goodness, moralism **09** integrity, principle, propriety, rectitude, standards **10** principles **11** moral values, uprightness **12** Sittlichkeit **13** righteousness

**moralize**
**05** edify **06** preach **07** lecture **08** ethicize **09** discourse, preachify, sermonize **11** pontificate

**morally**
**05** nobly **06** justly **08** properly, socially **09** ethically **10** honourably **11** practically **13** behaviourally

**morals**
**06** ethics, habits, ideals **07** conduct, manners **08** morality, scruples **09** behaviour, integrity, moral code, standards **10** principles **11** moral values **12** Sittlichkeit **13** right and wrong
**• lax in morals**
**04** wide

**morass**
**03** bog, fen, jam **04** flow, mess, mire, moss, quag **05** chaos, marsh, mix-up, swamp **06** jumble, muddle, slough, tangle **07** clutter **08** quagmire **09** confusion, marshland, quicksand **10** can of worms

**moratorium**
**03** ban **04** halt, stay **05** delay **06** freeze **07** embargo, respite **08** stoppage **10** standstill, suspension **12** postponement

**morbid**
**04** down, grim, sick **06** ailing, gloomy, grisly, horrid, morose, sickly, sombre **07** ghastly, hideous, macabre, peccant, vicious **08** dejected, diseased, dreadful, ghoulish, gruesome, horrible **09** unhealthy **10** lugubrious, melancholy **11** pessimistic,

unwholesome **12** insalubrious **14** down in the dumps

**morbidly**
**06** grimly **08** horribly, horridly **09** hideously **10** dreadfully, ghoulishly, gruesomely

**mordant**
**04** acid, base **05** edged, harsh, sharp **06** biting, bitter **07** acerbic, caustic, cutting, mixtion, pungent, vicious, waspish **08** critical, incisive, scathing, stinging, venomous, wounding **09** sarcastic, trenchant **10** astringent, iron-liquor **11** acrimonious

**more**
**02** mo **03** mae, moe, new, più **04** root **05** added, again, extra, fresh, other, plant, spare, stump **06** better, longer, rather **07** another, further **08** moreover, repeated **09** increased **10** additional **11** alternative **13** greater number, supplementary **15** greater quantity

• **more or less**
**04** some **06** mainly, mostly **07** broadly **09** generally, in general, just about **10** by and large, on the whole, pretty much, pretty well **11** in most cases **13** predominantly **14** for the most part

• **more than**
**04** plus

• **yet more**
**03** nay

**moreover**
**03** eft **04** also **06** as well, at that, either **07** besides, further **08** likewise **10** in addition, what is more **11** furthermore **12** additionally

**mores**
**04** ways **06** custom, habits, usages **07** customs, manners **09** etiquette, practices **10** procedures, traditions, ways of life **11** conventions **14** ways of behaving

**morgue**
**08** mortuary **09** arrogance, deadhouse **11** haughtiness **12** charnel house **14** funeral parlour

**moribund**
**04** weak **05** dying **06** doomed, ebbing, fading, feeble, senile, waning **07** failing **08** comatose, expiring, lifeless, stagnant **09** crumbling, declining, dwindling **10** collapsing, in extremis, stagnating **11** obsolescent, on the way out, wasting away **14** on your last legs

**morning**
**02** am **04** dawn, morn **05** matin **07** sunrise **08** cock-crow, daybreak, daylight, forenoon **10** before noon, break of day, first light **11** crack of dawn

• **morning star**
**05** Venus **07** daystar, Lucifer **08** Phosphor **09** precursor **10** Phosphorus **11** morgenstern

**Morocco**
**02** MA **03** MAR, Mor

**moron**
**03** ass, git, mug, nit **04** berk, butt, clot, dolt, dope, dork, dupe, fool, geek, goof, jerk, kook, nerd, nerk, prat, twit **05** chump, clown, comic, dumbo, dunce, dweeb, idiot, neddy, ninny, prick, twerp, wally **06** cretin, dimwit, jester, muppet, nitwit, stooge, sucker **07** buffoon, Charlie, fat-head, halfwit, pillock, plonker, tosspot **08** dipstick, imbecile **09** birdbrain, blockhead, cloth head, ignoramus, simpleton **10** nincompoop, silly-billy **13** laughing-stock, proper Charlie

**moronic**
**03** mad **04** daft, dumb **05** barmy, batty, crazy, dotty, inane, inept, nutty, potty, silly, wacky **06** absurd, insane, simple, stupid, unwise **07** foolish, idiotic **08** gormless, ignorant **09** half-baked, ludicrous, pointless, senseless **10** half-witted, ill-advised, ridiculous **11** hare-brained, nonsensical **12** crack-brained, shortsighted, simple-minded, unreasonable **13** ill-considered, out of your mind, unintelligent **14** with a tile loose **15** with a screw loose

**morose**
**04** acid, glum, grim, grum, sour **05** gruff, moody, sulky, surly **06** crabby, gloomy, severe, sombre, sullen **07** grouchy **08** mournful, taciturn **09** depressed, saturnine **10** lugubrious **11** bad-tempered, ill-tempered, melancholic, pessimistic

**morosely**
**06** sourly **07** gruffly, moodily **08** gloomily, sullenly **10** mournfully **12** lugubriously

**morse**
**06** walrus **09** Endeavour, iddy-umpty

**morsel**
**03** bit **04** atom, bite, part **05** crumb, grain, piece, scrap, slice, taste **06** dainty, nibble, sippet, titbit **07** modicum, morceau, segment, soupçon **08** fraction, fragment, mouthful, particle **11** bonne bouche

**mortal**
◇ *anagram indicator*
**03** man **04** body, dire, Yama **05** awful, being, cruel, dying, fatal, grave, great, human, woman **06** bitter, bodily, deadly, lethal, person, severe **07** earthly, extreme, fleshly, intense, killing, worldly **08** creature, deathful, temporal, terrible, vengeful **09** corporeal, earthling, ephemeral, extremely, murderous, transient, worldling **10** human being, implacable, individual, perishable, relentless, thoroughly, unbearable **11** unrelenting **12** irremissible, unforgivable, unpardonable

• **first mortal**
**04** Adam, Yama

**mortality**
**05** death **07** carnage, killing **08** casualty, fatality, humanity **09** death rate, slaughter **10** loss of life, transience **11** earthliness, worldliness **12** ephemerality, impermanence **13** perishability

**mortally**
**07** awfully, fatally, finally, gravely, greatly **08** lethally, severely, terribly **09** extremely, intensely **12** disastrously

**mortgage**
**03** dip **04** bond, lien, loan **06** pledge, wadset **07** wadsett **08** home loan, security **09** debenture **11** hypothecate, impignorate

**mortification**
**05** shame **06** denial **07** chagrin, control **08** disgrace, ignominy, vexation **09** abasement, annoyance, dishonour, sphacelus **10** asceticism, chastening, conquering, discipline, loss of face, punishment, self-denial **11** confounding, humiliation, self-control, subjugation **12** discomfiture **13** embarrassment

**mortified**
**04** sick **06** shamed **07** ashamed, crushed, humbled **08** defeated **09** disgraced, horrified **10** confounded, gangrenous, humiliated **11** dishonoured, embarrassed

**mortify**
**03** die **04** deny, kill **05** abash, annoy, crush, shame **06** humble, offend, subdue, wither **07** affront, chagrin, chasten, conquer, control, crucify, deflate, horrify **08** bring low, chastise, confound, disgrace, gangrene, macerate, restrain, suppress **09** discomfit, dishonour, embarrass, humiliate **10** disappoint, discipline, put to shame

**mortifying**
**07** shaming **08** crushing, humbling, salutary **09** punishing, thwarting **10** chastening **11** humiliating, ignominious **12** discomfiting, embarrassing, overwhelming

**mortuary**
**06** morgue **09** deadhouse **12** charnel house **14** funeral parlour

**mosaic**
**06** musive, screen **08** terrazzo **10** pietra dura, pietre dure **11** opus musivum

**moss**
**03** hag **04** hagg **05** Musci

*Mosses include:*

**03** bog, bur, cup, fog
**04** burr, club, long, peat, tree
**05** fairy, usnea
**06** hypnum
**07** acrogen, foggage, lycopod
**08** sphagnum, staghorn
**09** wolf's claw, wolf's foot
**10** fontinalis, ground pine

• **stalk of moss capsule**
**04** seta

**most**
◇ *tail deletion indicator*
**04** bulk, mass **08** majority **09** almost all, nearly all **10** lion's share **11** largest part **12** greatest part **13** preponderance

**mostly**
◇ *deletion indicator*
**06** feckly, mainly **07** as a rule, chiefly, largely, overall, usually **08** above all **09** generally, in general, in the main **10** especially, on the whole **11** principally **13** predominantly **14** for the most part

**moth**

*Moths include:*

**01** Y
**02** lo
**03** pug, wax
**04** goat, hawk, luna, puss
**05** ghost, gypsy, tiger
**06** bogong, bugong, burnet, carpet, kitten, lackey, lappet, magpie, sphinx, turnip, winter
**07** buff-tip, clothes, emerald, emperor, hook-tip, silver-Y, six-spot, tussock
**08** cinnabar, peppered, silkworm
**10** death's-head
**11** garden tiger, pale tussock, swallowtail
**12** Kentish glory, peach blossom, red underwing
**13** processionary

*See also* **animal**; **butterfly**; **insect**

**moth-eaten**
**03** old **04** worn **05** dated, mangy, musty, seedy, stale **06** mouldy, ragged, shabby **07** ancient, archaic, decayed, outworn, worn-out **08** decrepit, moribund, obsolete, outdated, tattered **10** antiquated, threadbare **11** dilapidated **12** old-fashioned

**mother**
**02** ma **03** dam, mam, mom, mum **04** baby, base, bear, mama, rear, scum, tend **05** cause, dregs, fount, mamma, mammy, mater, mommy, mummy, mumsy, nanny, nurse, raise, roots, spoil **06** foster, matron, minnie, origin, pamper, parent, source, spring, venter **07** care for, cherish, indulge, nurture, old lady, produce **08** ancestor, fuss over, hysteria, old woman **09** look after, matriarch **10** bring forth, derivation, foundation, procreator, take care of, wellspring **11** birth mother, give birth to, overprotect **12** progenitress **13** materfamilias

*See also* **dregs**

**motherly**
**04** fond, kind, warm **06** caring, gentle, loving, tender **08** maternal, matronal **09** nurturing **10** comforting, motherlike, protective **12** affectionate

**motif**
**04** form, idea, logo **05** shape, theme, topic **06** design, device, emblem, figure **07** concept, pattern **08** ornament **10** decoration

**motion**
**03** act, bid, nod **04** flow, plan, sign, wave **05** going, offer, usher **06** action, beckon, change, direct, moving, puppet, scheme, signal, travel **07** feeling, gesture, passage, passing, project, transit **08** activity, mobility, motility, movement, progress, proposal **09** agitation, manifesto, prompting **10** indication, locomotion, suggestion, travelling **11** gesticulate, inclination, instigation, proposition **12** presentation **13** changing place, gesticulation **14** changing places, recommendation

• **in motion**
◇ *anagram indicator*
**03** off **05** about, astir, going **06** agoing, moving **07** on the go, running **08** under way **09** on the move, on the wing **10** in progress, travelling **11** functioning, operational, upon the wing

• **set in motion**
**04** move, open, stir **05** begin, found, start, steer, stire, styre **06** set off, winnow **07** actuate, kick off, promote, start up **08** activate, commence, embark on, get going, initiate, set about **09** instigate, institute, introduce **10** launch into **11** get cracking **13** begin to happen, take the plunge

**motionless**
**03** set **05** fixed, inert, rigid, still **06** at rest, frozen, halted, static **07** resting **08** becalmed, immobile, lifeless, moveless, sleeping, stagnant, standing, unmoving **09** immovable, inanimate, paralysed, unmovable **10** stationary, stock-still, transfixed **13** at a standstill

**motivate**
**04** draw, goad, lead, move, push, spur, stir, urge **05** bring, cause, drive, impel **06** arouse, excite, incite, induce, kindle, prompt, propel **07** actuate, inspire, provoke, trigger **08** activate, initiate, persuade **09** encourage, kick-start, stimulate

**motivation**
**04** push, spur, urge, wish **05** drive **06** desire, hunger, motive, reason **07** impulse **08** ambition, interest, momentum, stimulus **09** incentive, prompting **10** incitement, inducement, persuasion **11** inspiration, instigation, provocation

**motive**
**03** aim **04** goad, lure, spur, urge **05** basis, cause, motif **06** design, desire, ground, moment, object, reason **07** grounds, impulse, pretext, purpose **08** instance, occasion, sanction, stimulus, thinking **09** incentive, influence, intention, rationale **10** attraction, incitement, inducement, mainspring, motivation, persuasion, propellent **11** inspiration **13** consideration, encouragement

**motley**
**04** pied **05** mixed, tabby **06** jester, varied **07** dappled, diverse, mottled, piebald, pyebald, spotted, striped **08** assorted, brindled, many-hued, streaked **09** colourful, patchwork **10** variegated **11** diversified **12** multifarious **13** heterogeneous, miscellaneous, multicoloured, particoloured

**motor club** *see* **motoring organization**

**motorcyclists** *see* **racing**

**motoring** *see* **car**

**motoring organization**
**02** AA **03** AAA, BSM, FIA, RAC

**motor racing** *see* **racing**

**motor vehicle** *see* **car**; **vehicle**

**motorway**
**01** M **02** AB, M1 **07** freeway, thruway **08** Autobahn, turnpike **09** autopista, autoroute **10** autostrada, expressway, throughway **12** superhighway

**mottled**
**04** marl **05** chiné, jaspe, pinto, tabby **06** dapple **07** blotchy, brinded, brindle, dappled, flecked, marbled, piebald, spotted **08** blotched, brindled, freckled, speckled, splotchy, stippled, streaked **10** poikilitic, variegated

**motto**
**03** cry, mot, saw **04** posy, rule **05** adage, axiom, gnome, maxim, poesy **06** byword, device, dictum, legend, saying, slogan, truism **07** epigram, formula, ich dien, ichthys, impresa, imprese, precept, proverb **08** aphorism, epigraph **09** catchword, watchword **10** golden rule **13** e pluribus unum **15** per ardua ad astra

**mould**
◇ *anagram indicator*
**03** cut, die, mix, rot **04** cast, form, fust, kind, line, make, must, sort, type, work **05** brand, build, carve, earth, forge, frame, knead, model, plasm, print, shape, stamp, style **06** affect, blight, create, design, direct, figure, format, fungus, matrix, mildew, nature, sculpt **07** calibre, casting, chessel, control, dariole, fashion, outline, pattern, quality, ramakin, ramekin **08** meringue, ramequin, template **09** character, construct, formation, framework, influence, mustiness, sculpture, structure **10** mouldiness **11** arrangement, blister pack **12** construction **13** configuration

**moulder**
**03** rot **05** decay, waste **06** humify, perish **07** corrupt, crumble **09** decompose **10** turn to dust **12** disintegrate

**moulding**
◇ *anagram indicator*
**04** ogee, tore **05** torus

**mouldy**
◇ *anagram indicator*
**03** bad **04** fust, hoar **05** fusty, lousy, mochy, mucid, muggy, musty, stale
**06** fousty, mochie, putrid, rotten
**07** corrupt, foughty, spoiled, vinewed
**08** blighted, decaying, mildewed
**09** miserable **10** mucedinous

**moult**
**03** mew **04** cast

**mound**
**03** but, dun, hog, lot, orb, tel **04** bank, barp, butt, dike, dune, dyke, heap, hill, mote, pile, rise, tell, tump **05** agger, cairn, hoard, knoll, mogul, motte, mount, pingo, ridge, stack, store
**06** barrow, bundle, kurgan, supply, tuffet **07** hillock, hummock, rampart, tumulus **08** mine dump, mountain
**09** abundance, earthwork, elevation, monticule, stockpile, whaleback
**10** collection, embankment
**11** termitarium **12** accumulation

**mound-bird**
**05** lowan **08** megapode **09** mallee-hen **10** junglefowl, mallee-bird, mallee-fowl **11** brush turkey

**mount**
◇ *reversal down indicator*
**02** Mt **03** set, sty **04** back, base, go up, grow, lift, ride, rise, soar, stie, stye
**05** build, climb, erect, frame, get on, get up, horse, put on, raise, scale, set up, stage, stand, steed, swell, tot up
**06** accrue, ascend, jump on, launch, pile up, saddle, step up **07** arrange, backing, build up, climb on, climb up, display, exhibit, fixture, install, prepare, produce, support **08** escalade, escalate, increase, jump on to, mounting, multiply, organize, override, saddle up
**09** clamber up, climb on to, inselberg, intensify, take horse **10** accumulate, get astride **12** passe-partout

**mountain**
**03** alp, ben, lot, tor **04** berg, fell, heap, hill, mass, peak, pike, pile **05** guyot, jebel, mound, mount, stack **06** djebel, height, massif **07** backlog **08** pinnacle
**09** abundance, elevation
**12** accumulation

*Mountains and mountain ranges include:*

**02** K2
**03** Apo, Dom, Tai
**04** Alai, Alps, Blue, Cook, Etna, Fuji, Jura, Meru, Ossa, Rila, Sion, Ural
**05** Altai, Andes, Atlas, Coast, Downs, Eiger, Ghats, Halti, Huang, Kamet, Kékes, Kenya, Logan, Matra, Ozark, Qogir, Rocky, Sinai, Snowy, Table, Tatra
**06** Ararat, Cho Oyu, Deccan, Denali, Egmont, Elbert, Elbrus, Haltia, Hoggar, Lhotse, Makalu, Mourne, Musala, Pindus, Taurus, Vosges, Zagros
**07** Ahaggar, Belukha, Beskids, Everest, Fuji-san, Hua Shan, Lebanon, Manaslu, Nilgiri, Olympus, Rainier, Rhodope, Rockies, Roraima, Scafell, Skiddaw, Snowdon, Stanley, Tai Shan, Troödos
**08** Ben Nevis, Cameroon, Catskill, Caucasus, Cévennes, Damavand, Five Holy, Fujiyama, Heng Shan, Jungfrau, Kinabalu, Mauna Kea, Mauna Loa, McKinley, Pennines, Pyrenees, Rushmore, song Shan, St Helens, Taranaki
**09** Aconcagua, Allegheny, Altai Shan, Annapurna, Apennines, Blue Ridge, Broad Peak, Cotswolds, Dolomites, Grampians, Helvellyn, Himalayas, Hindu Kush, Inyangani, Karakoram, Kosciusko, Lenin Peak, Mont Blanc, Muz Tag Ata, Nanda Devi, Rakaposhi, Tirichmir, Tirol Alps, Zugspitze
**10** Adirondack, Cader Idris, Cairngorms, Cantabrian, Carpathian, Chimborazo, Dhaulagiri, Gasherbrum, Gosainthan, Great Smoky, MacDonnell, Matterhorn, Pobedy Peak, Puncak Jaya, Sagarmatha
**11** Appalachian, Arthur's Pass, Black Forest, Chomolungma, Drakensberg, Kilimanjaro, Mendip Hills, Mongo-Ma-Loba, Nanga Parbat, Pico Bolívar, Siula Grande
**12** Bavarian Alps, Cascade Range, Cheviot Hills, Darling Range, Dufourspitze, Kanchenjunga, Popocatepetl, Sierra Nevada, Southern Alps, Tibet Plateau, Ulugh Muztagh, Victoria Peak, Vinson Massif
**13** Carrantuohill, Chiltern Hills, Communism Peak, Great Dividing, Haltiatunturi, Kangchenjunga, Ojos del Salado, Stirling Range
**14** Australian Alps, Bavarian Forest, Bohemian Forest, Fichtelgebirge, Flinders Ranges, Grand St Bernard, Hamersley Range, Mackenzie Range, Musgrave Ranges, Qomolangma Feng, Thadentsonyane, Trans-Antarctic
**15** Guiana Highlands, Nevado de Illampu

*See also* **volcano**

**• mountain pass**
**04** ghat

*Mountain passes include:*

**04** Ofen
**05** Haast, Lewis, South
**06** Khyber, Lindis, Shipka
**07** Arthur's, Brenner, Oberalp, Plöcken, Simplon, Wrynose
**08** Hongshan, Yangguan
**09** Khunjerab, St Bernard
**10** St Gotthard
**12** Roncesvalles
**13** Cilician Gates, San Bernardino
**14** Grand St Bernard
**15** Little St Bernard

**• mountain peak**
**03** ben

**• mountain range**
**04** tier

**mountaineering**

*Mountaineers include:*

**04** **Hunt** (John, Lord)
**05** **Brown** (Joe), **Bruce** (C G), **Munro** (Sir Hugh), **Scott** (Doug), **Tabei** (Junko)
**06** **Haston** (Dougal), **Herzog** (Maurice), **Irvine** (Andrew), **Smythe** (Frank), **Tilman** (Bill), **Uemura** (Naomi)
**07** **Hillary** (Sir Edmund), **Mallory** (George), **Messner** (Reinhold), **Shipton** (Eric), **Simpson** (Myrtle), **Tazieff** (Haroun), **Tenzing** (Sherpa), **Whymper** (Edward)
**08** **Coolidge** (W A B), **MacInnes** (Hamish), **Whillans** (Don)
**09** **Bonington** (Sir Chris)
**10** **Hargreaves** (Alison)
**13** **Tenzing Norgay**

**mountainous**
**04** high, huge, mega, vast **05** giant, hilly, jumbo, lofty, rocky, steep
**06** alpine, craggy, upland **07** immense, mammoth, massive, soaring
**08** colossal, enormous, gigantic, highland, towering **09** ginormous, humongous

**mountebank**
**04** fake **05** antic, cheat, fraud, pseud, quack, rogue **06** antick, con man, phoney **07** anticke, antique, buffoon
**08** impostor, jongleur, swindler
**09** charlatan, pretender, trickster
**11** saltimbanco

**mourn**
**04** keen, miss, wail, weep **06** bemoan, bewail, grieve, lament, regret, sorrow
**07** deplore

**mourner**
**04** mute **06** keener, saulie, weeper
**07** griever **08** bereaved, sorrower

**mournful**
**03** sad **06** dismal, gloomy, rueful, sombre, tragic, woeful **07** dernful, doleful, elegiac, funèbre, unhappy
**08** cast-down, dearnful, dejected, desolate, downcast, funereal
**09** depressed, miserable, plaintive, sorrowful **10** lachrymose, lugubrious, melancholy **11** heartbroken, melancholic **12** disconsolate, heavy-hearted **13** broken-hearted, grief-stricken

**mournfully**
**05** sadly **08** dismally, gloomily, ruefully, sombrely **09** con dolore, dolefully, miserably, unhappily **10** desolately
**11** plaintively, sorrowfully **15** broken-heartedly

**mourning**
**05** grief **06** sorrow **07** keening, sadness, wailing, weeping **08** grieving
**09** sorrowing **10** desolation
**11** bereavement, lamentation **13** sorry business

**mouse**
**03** Mus **06** muscle, shiner **07** dunnart, Muridae, waltzer **08** black eye
**09** Zapodidae

**mousey, mousy**
**03** shy **04** drab, dull, meek **05** plain, quiet, timid **07** greyish **08** brownish, timorous **09** diffident, shrinking, withdrawn **10** colourless
**11** unassertive **12** self-effacing
**13** unforthcoming, uninteresting

**moustache**
**04** tash **05** tache **06** walrus **07** Charley, Charlie **08** whiskers **09** excrement, mustachio **10** face fungus **15** zapata moustache

**mousy** *see* **mousey, mousy**

**mouth**
◇ *head selection indicator*
**03** cry, gab, gam, gas, gob, gub, mou, mug, say **04** door, form, gall, jaws, kiss, rant, trap, vent **05** bazoo, bocca, cheek, chops, delta, hatch, inlet, nerve, sauce, stoma, utter, voice
**06** babble, cavity, hot air, kisser, oscule, outlet, portal **07** debouch, declaim, doorway, estuary, gateway, grimace, opening, orifice, speaker, whisper
**08** aperture, backchat, boasting, bragging, cakehole, entrance, idle talk, rudeness, traphole **09** brass neck, empty talk, enunciate, impudence, insolence, pronounce, utterance
**10** articulate, blustering, disrespect, effrontery, embouchure, potato trap, rattletrap **12** impertinence, laughing gear

*Mouth parts and features include:*

**03** gum, jaw, lip
**04** lips
**05** uvula
**06** tongue, tonsil
**07** hare lip
**08** lower lip, upper lip
**10** hard palate, soft palate
**11** cleft palate
**13** alveolar ridge
**15** isthmus of fauces

*See also* **teeth**

• **keep your mouth shut**
**06** clam up, shut up **07** cover up, keep mum **08** pipe down **09** keep quiet
**10** say nothing **14** hold your tongue
**15** not breathe a word

• **sew up mouth**
**04** cope

**mouthful**
**03** bit, gag, gob, sip, sup **04** bite, drop, gulp, slug **05** taste **06** gobbet, morsel, nibble, sample, titbit **07** forkful, swallow **08** spoonful **11** bonne-bouche

**mouthpiece**
**04** horn **05** agent, organ, voice
**07** journal **08** delegate **09** spokesman
**10** periodical **11** publication, spokeswoman **12** propagandist, spokesperson **14** representative

**movable**
**06** mobile **08** flexible, portable
**09** alterable, portative **10** adjustable, changeable **12** transferable
**13** transportable

**movables**
**04** gear **05** goods, stuff **06** things
**07** clobber, effects **08** chattels, property **09** furniture **10** belongings
**11** impedimenta, plenishings, possessions

**move**
◇ *anagram indicator*
**02** go **03** act, mix, wag **04** draw, lead, nose, pass, push, sell, step, stir, tack, take, urge, walk **05** bring, budge, carry, cause, drive, fetch, impel, leave, pal up, rouse, shift, shunt, swing, touch, upset **06** action, affect, arouse, change, decamp, depart, device, excite, gang up, go away, hobnob, incite, induce, mingle, motion, prompt, propel, remove, strike, submit, switch, travel **07** actuate, advance, agitate, consort, develop, disturb, gesture, hang out, impress, incline, inspire, measure, migrate, proceed, propose, provoke, quinche, removal, request, suggest **08** activity, advocate, go around, motivate, move away, movement, persuade, progress, relocate, transfer **09** associate, circulate, hang about, influence, instigate, manoeuvre, migration, move house, recommend, socialize, stimulate, stratagem, transport, transpose **10** fraternize, initiative, proceeding, put forward, relocation, take action **11** keep company, make strides, zwischenzug **12** rub shoulders
**13** gesticulation, repositioning
**15** change of address

• **get a move on**
**07** hurry up, speed up **08** step on it
**09** make haste, shake a leg **11** get cracking **12** step on the gas **15** put your foot down

• **make a move**
**02** go **05** frame, leave, split **06** depart
**07** push off **08** clear off, get going
**10** make tracks **11** do something, get cracking **13** take the plunge, take your leave

• **move aimlessly**
**04** mope

• **move around**
**04** stir **05** steer, stire, styre

• **move gradually**
**04** ease, edge

• **move in some direction**
**04** tend

• **move lightly**
**04** flit

• **move on**
**03** gee, jee **06** avaunt

• **move quickly**
**03** hop **04** tear, whid, whip, zoom

• **move round**
**04** eddy, turn

• **move sideways**
**04** crab

• **move silently**
**06** tiptoe

• **move slowly**
**03** lag **04** inch

• **move unsteadily**
**03** yaw

• **move up and down**
**03** bob **04** yo-yo

• **move violently**
**04** tear

• **on the move**
**05** astir **06** active, around, moving
**07** on the go **08** under way
**09** advancing, on the hoof, walkabout
**10** journeying, travelling **11** progressing
**13** moving forward **14** making progress

**movement**
◇ *anagram indicator*
**03** act, bit **04** fall, flow, guts, move, pace, part, play, rise, stir, wing **05** drift, drive, group, party, piece, shift, swing, tempo, trend, works **06** action, change, moving, system **07** advance, crusade, current, emotion, faction, gesture, impulse, passage, portion, section **08** activity, campaign, division, progress, shifting, stirring, tendency, transfer, workings **09** agitation, coalition, evolution, machinery, mechanism, variation **10** relocation
**11** development, improvement, progression **12** breakthrough, organization **13** gesticulation, repositioning **14** transportation

*See also* **art**, **poetry**

• **rapid eye movement**
**03** REM

• **sudden movement**
**04** dart, volt

**movie**
**04** film **05** flick, video **06** cinema, talkie **07** fleapit, picture **09** multiplex
**10** silent film **11** feature film, film theatre
**12** movie theatre, picture-house
**13** motion picture, picture-palace

*See also* **film**

**moving**
◇ *anagram indicator*
**05** astir **06** active, mobile, motile, urging **07** driving, dynamic, emotive, flowing, kinetic, leading **08** arousing, exciting, in motion, pathetic, poignant, stirring, touching, worrying
**09** affecting, emotional, inspiring, thrilling, upsetting **10** disturbing, impressive, motivating, persuasive
**11** influential, stimulating
**12** manoeuvrable **13** inspirational

**movingly**
**10** poignantly, touchingly **11** with emotion, with feeling **12** expressively, pathetically **15** inspirationally

**mow**
**03** cut, moe **04** barb, clip, crop, tass, trim **05** shear **06** scythe

• **mow down**
**04** kill **07** butcher, cut down, gun down
**08** decimate, massacre **09** shoot down, slaughter **11** cut to pieces

**mowing**
**04** math

**Mozambique**
**03** MOC, MOZ

**much**
**04** a lot, lots, many **05** ample, great, heaps, loads, molto, often, piles, scads **06** masses, mickle, muckle, oodles, plenty, stacks **07** copious, greatly **08** abundant, lashings **09** extensive, plentiful **10** a great deal, frequently, widespread **11** substantial **12** considerable, considerably **14** a great number of, to a great degree, to a great extent
• **by so much**
**03** the
• **how much**
**03** the
• **not so much**
**04** less
• **too much**
**03** OTT **04** over
• **very much**
**03** far **04** sore

**muck**
**03** mud **04** crud, dirt, dung, gold, guck, mess, mire, scum, yuck **05** filth, grime, guano, gunge, slime **06** debris, faeces, grunge, manure, ordure, rubble, scunge, sewage, sludge **09** excrement
• **muck about, muck around**
**05** upset **06** bother, meddle, mess up, potter, tamper, untidy **07** trouble **08** dishevel, disorder **09** fool about, goof about, interfere, lark about, mess about, play about **10** disarrange, fool around, goof around, lark around, mess around, play around **13** inconvenience **15** lead a merry dance, make life hell for
• **muck up**
**04** ruin **05** botch, spoil, wreck **06** bungle, cock up, mess up **07** louse up, screw up **11** make a mess of

**mucky**
**04** miry, oozy **05** dirty, grimy, gucky, messy, muddy, nasty, slimy **06** filthy, scungy, soiled, sticky **08** begrimed, mud-caked **11** bespattered

**mucous**
**05** gummy, slimy **06** snotty, viscid **07** viscous **09** glutinous **10** gelatinous **12** mucilaginous

**mud**
**03** dub **04** clay, dirt, dubs, mire, moya, ooze, silt, slab, soil **05** abuse, clart, slake, slush **06** clarts, sleech, sludge **07** clabber, slander **12** vilification
• **cover with mud**
**04** lair

**muddle**
◇ *anagram indicator*
**03** mix **04** daze, mash, mess, mull, muzz, stir **05** chaos, mix up, mix-up **06** bemuse, bungle, cock-up, fankle, guddle, jumble, mess up, pickle, puddle, puzzle, tangle **07** blunder, clutter, confuse, perplex **08** befuddle, bewilder, confound, disarray, disorder, jumble up, scramble, shambles **09** confusion **11** disorganize **12** bewilderment **15** disorganization
• **muddle through**
**04** cope **05** get by **06** make do, manage **08** get along

**muddled**
◇ *anagram indicator*
**05** addle, at sea, dazed, loose, messy, vague **06** tavert, woolly **07** chaotic, jumbled, mixed-up, taivert, tangled, unclear **08** confused **09** befuddled, perplexed, scrambled, stupefied **10** bewildered, disarrayed, disordered, incoherent **11** addle-headed, disoriented, muddy-headed **12** disorganized **13** disorientated

**muddy**
◇ *anagram indicator*
**04** dull, foul, hazy, miry, oozy, soil **05** boggy, cloud, dingy, dirty, fuzzy, grimy, mix up, mucky, murky, slimy, smear, smoky **06** bedash, bedaub, cloudy, dreggy, drumly, filthy, grouty, grubby, jumble, limous, marshy, muddle, opaque, puddle, quaggy, slabby, sloppy, sludgy, slushy, smirch, stupid, swampy, tangle, turbid **07** begrime, blurred, confuse, obscure, splashy, trouble **08** confused, jumble up, scramble **09** befuddled, bespatter, make muddy **10** indistinct **11** disorganize, make unclear, waterlogged

**muff**
◇ *anagram indicator*
**04** miss, mitt **05** botch, fluff, spoil **06** bungle, duffer, mess up, mishit **07** bungler **09** mishandle, mismanage

**muffle**
**03** gag, mob **04** dull, hush, kill, mute, wrap **05** cloak, cover, moble **06** dampen, deaden, mobble, muzzle, soften, stifle, swathe, wrap up **07** cover up, envelop, quieten, silence, smother, swaddle **08** suppress **09** blindfold

**mug**
**03** can, cup, pot, rob, sap **04** bash, bock, dupe, exam, face, fool, gull, jump, mush, phiz, swot, Toby **05** chump, clock, mouth, stein, tinny **06** attack, batter, beaker, beat up, do over, jump on, kisser, noggin, sconce, sucker, tinnie, visage, waylay **07** assault, muggins, rough up, set upon, tankard **08** features **09** simpleton, soft touch, steal from **10** knock about **11** countenance, physiognomy
*See also* **face**; **fool**
• **mug up**
**03** con **04** cram, swot **05** get up, study **06** bone up

**muggy**
**04** damp **05** close, foggy, humid, mochy, moist **06** clammy, mochie, sticky, stuffy, sultry **07** airless **10** oppressive, sweltering

**mulberry**
**04** upas **05** Morus, mvule **06** murrey **07** cowtree **08** cecropia, sycamine **10** artocarpus **11** contrayerva, Osage orange

**mule**
**04** moyl, muil **05** moyle **06** hybrid **07** slipper, sumpter **09** dziggetai

**mulish**
**05** rigid **06** wilful **07** defiant **08** perverse, stubborn **09** difficult, obstinate, pig-headed **10** headstrong, inflexible, refractory, self-willed **11** intractable, stiff-necked, wrong-headed **12** intransigent, recalcitrant, unreasonable

**mull**
• **mull over**
**05** study **06** muse on, ponder **07** examine, weigh up **08** chew over, consider, meditate, ruminate **09** reflect on, think over **10** deliberate, think about **11** contemplate

**multicoloured**
**04** pied **06** motley **07** dappled, piebald, spotted, striped **08** brindled **09** colourful **10** variegated **11** psychedelic **13** kaleidoscopic, particoloured

**multifarious**
**04** many **06** legion, sundry, varied **07** diverse **08** manifold, multiple, numerous **09** different, multiform **10** variegated **11** diversified **13** miscellaneous, multitudinous

**multiple**
**04** many **06** sundry **07** several, various **08** compound, manifold, numerous, repeated **10** collective, multiplied

**multiplicity**
**03** lot **04** host, lots, mass, tons **05** array, heaps, loads, piles **06** myriad, number, oodles, scores, stacks **07** variety **09** abundance, diversity, profusion **12** manifoldness, numerousness

**multiplied with**
**01** x **02** by

**multiply**
**04** grow **05** boost, breed **06** double, expand, extend, spread **07** augment, build up, decuple, octuple **08** centuple, increase, manifold, septuple, sextuple **09** intensify, propagate, quadruple, quintuple, reproduce **10** accumulate **11** proliferate

**multipurpose**
**05** handy **08** all-round, flexible, variable **09** adaptable, many-sided, versatile **10** adjustable, all-purpose, functional **11** resourceful **12** multifaceted **14** general-purpose

**multitude**
**03** lot, mob **04** army, herd, hive, host, lots, mass, ruck **05** crowd, horde, plebs, shoal, swarm **06** hirsel, legion, number, people, public, rabble, throng

**07** king mob **08** assembly, canaille, populace, riff-raff **09** hoi polloi **10** common herd, the million **11** rank and file **12** common people, congregation **13** great unwashed

**multitudinous**
**04** many **05** great **06** legion, myriad **07** copious, profuse, teeming, umpteen **08** abundant, infinite, manifold, numerous, swarming **09** abounding, countless **11** innumerable **12** considerable

**mum**
**02** ma **04** dumb, ma'am, mama, marm, mute **05** mummy, quiet **06** mother, silent **07** silence **08** reticent **09** secretive **10** masquerade **11** close-lipped, tight-lipped **12** close-mouthed **13** chrysanthemum, unforthcoming **15** uncommunicative

**mumble**
**04** moop, moup, mump, slur **06** fumble, murmur, mutter, rumble **07** grumble, stutter **08** splutter **11** speak softly **14** speak unclearly, talk to yourself

**mumbo-jumbo**
**04** cant, rite **05** chant, charm, magic, spell **06** humbug, jargon, ritual **07** mummery **08** claptrap, nonsense **09** gibberish, rigmarole **10** double talk, hocus-pocus **11** abracadabra, conjuration, incantation **12** gobbledygook, superstition

**mummer**
**05** actor **06** guiser, guizer **07** guisard, scudler, skudler **09** scuddaler **11** masquerader

**munch**
**03** eat **04** chew, moop, moup, mump **05** champ, chomp **06** crunch **09** masticate

**mundane**
**04** dull **05** banal, stale, trite, usual **06** boring, common, cosmic, normal **07** earthly, fleshly, humdrum, prosaic, regular, routine, secular, terrene, typical, worldly **08** everyday, ordinary, temporal, workaday **09** customary, hackneyed **11** commonplace, terrestrial

**municipal**
**04** city, town **05** civic, civil, urban **06** public **07** borough **09** community **12** metropolitan

**municipality**
**04** city, town **05** burgh **07** borough, council **08** district, precinct, township **10** department **11** département **15** local government

**munificence**
**06** bounty **08** altruism, largesse **10** generosity, liberality **11** beneficence, benevolence, hospitality **12** generousness, philanthropy **13** bounteousness, bountifulness **14** charitableness, open-handedness **15** magnanimousness

**munificent**
**04** rich **06** lavish **07** liberal **08** generous, princely **09** bounteous, bountiful **10** altruistic, beneficent, benevolent, big-hearted, charitable, free-handed, hospitable, open-handed, unstinting **11** magnanimous **15** philanthropical

**munitions**
**03** kit **04** gear, guns **05** bombs, tools **06** shells, tackle **08** armament, materiel, ordnance, supplies **09** apparatus, equipment, materials **10** provisions

**murder**
**03** hit, ice, rid **04** beat, do in, hell, kill, lick, rout, ruin, slay **05** agony, blood, botch, burke, spoil, stiff, waste, whack, wreck **06** fill in, hammer, mess up, misery, ordeal, outwit, rub out, rubout, thrash **07** anguish, bump off, butcher, clobber, destroy, execute, killing, murther, outplay, removal, slaying, take out, torment, torture, trounce, wipe out **08** blow away, butchery, dispatch, filicide, foul play, homicide, knock off, massacre, outsmart **09** bloodshed, do to death, eliminate, execution, liquidate, matricide, nightmare, overwhelm, parricide, patricide, slaughter, suffering, uxoricide **10** annihilate, fratricide, put to death, sororicide **11** assassinate, infanticide, liquidation, make a mess of **12** defeat easily, manslaughter, petty treason, wretchedness **13** assassination

*See also* **kill**

**murderer**
**04** Cain **06** killer, slayer **07** butcher **08** assassin, filicide, homicide **09** bluebeard, cut-throat, matricide, murtherer, patricide **10** man-queller **11** slaughterer **12** serial killer

*Murderers, alleged murderers and assassins include:*

**03** **Ray** (James Earl)
**04** **Aram** (Eugene), **Cain**, **Edny** (Clithero), **Hare** (William), **Kray** (Reggie), **Kray** (Ronnie), **Retz** (Gilles de Laval, Baron), **Ruby** (Jack), **Todd** (Sweeney), **West** (Fred), **West** (Rosemary)
**05** **Beane** (Sawney), **Booth** (John Wilkes), **Brady** (Ian), **Bundy** (Ted), **Burke** (William), **Craig** (Christopher), **Ellis** (Ruth), **Haigh** (John), **Havoc** (Jack), **Rudge**
**06** **Barrow** (Clyde), **Borden** (Lizzie), **Corday** (Charlotte), **Dahmer** (Jeffrey), **Lecter** (Dr Hannibal), **Manson** (Charles), **Misfit** (the), **Nilsen** (Dennis), **Oswald** (Lee Harvey), **Parker** (Bonnie), **Sirhan** (Sirhan)
**07** **Bathori** (Elizabeth), **Bentley** (Derek), **Bianchi** (Kenneth), **Chapman** (Mark), **Crippen** (Hawley Harvey), **Hindley** (Myra), **Macbeth**, **Manston** (Aeneas), **Neilson** (Donald), **Shipman** (Harold)
**08** **Barabbas**, **Christie** (John Reginald Halliday), **Claudius**, **Dominici** (Gaston), **Hanratty** (James), **Son of Sam**, **Thompson** (Edith)
**09** **Berkowitz** (David), **Bluebeard**, **Harmodius**, **McNaghten** (Daniel), **Sutcliffe** (Peter)
**10** **McNaughten** (Daniel), **McNaughton** (Daniel), **Nirdlinger** (Phyllis)
**11** **Anckarström** (Johan Jakob), **Quare Fellow** (the)
**13** **Jack the Ripper**
**14** **Moors Murderers**
**15** **Yorkshire Ripper**

**murderous**
**05** cruel, fatal **06** bloody, brutal, carnal, deadly, lethal, mortal, savage **07** arduous, killing **09** barbarous, butcherly, cut-throat, dangerous, difficult, ferocious, gruelling, homicidal, punishing, strenuous **10** exhausting, unpleasant **11** internecine, internecive **12** bloodthirsty, slaughterous

**murderously**
**06** grimly **07** fatally **09** ominously **10** alarmingly, menacingly, sinisterly **11** dangerously, homicidally **12** portentously, unpleasantly **13** threateningly **14** bloodthirstily

**murk**
**04** dark, dusk, mirk **05** gloom, night, shade **06** gloomy **07** dimness, obscure, shadows **08** darkness, twilight **09** blackness, half-light, murkiness, shadiness, tenebrity **10** cloudiness, gloominess **11** sunlessness, tenebrosity

**murky**
**03** dim, sus **04** dark, dull, grey **05** dingy, dirty, fishy, foggy, misty, muddy, rooky, shady **06** cloudy, dismal, dreary, gloomy, secret, turbid, veiled **07** obscure **08** overcast **09** cheerless, tenebrose, tenebrous **10** mysterious, suspicious, tenebrious **12** questionable

**murmur**
◇ *homophone indicator*
**03** bur, coo, hum **04** beef, burr, buzz, carp, fuss, moan, purl, purr **05** brawl, brool, bruit, drone, gripe, mourn, thrum, whine **06** babble, burble, grouse, grudge, intone, mumble, mutter, object, repine, rumble, rumour, rustle, whinge **07** beefing, carping, censure, croodle, grumble, humming, protest, purring, whisper **08** complain, rumbling, syllable **09** annoyance, bellyache, complaint, criticism, criticize, find fault, grievance, muttering, objection, undertone, whingeing **11** bellyaching **12** fault-finding **15** dissatisfaction

**murmuring**
**04** buzz, purl, purr **05** drone **06** babble, mumble, mutter, rumble **07** buzzing, droning, humming,

purring, souffle, whisper
**08** mumbling, rumbling, susurrus
**09** murmurous, muttering
**10** whispering **11** murmuration

**Murphy**
**04** spud **05** praty, tater, tatie **06** potato, pratie, tattie

**muscle**
**04** beef, thew **05** brawn, clout, force, might, power, sinew **06** mussel, tendon, weight **07** potency, stamina
**08** ligament, strength **10** sturdiness
**12** forcefulness

*Muscles include:*

**02** ab
**03** pec
**04** delt
**05** glute, psoas
**06** biceps, rectus, soleus
**07** cardiac, deltoid, gluteus, iliacus, omohyid, triceps
**08** detrusor, masseter, platysma, pronator, risorius, scalenus, splenius
**09** abdominal, complexus, eye-string, perforans, sartorius, stapedius, supinator, trapezius
**10** buccinator, quadriceps
**11** ciliary body, rhomboideus
**13** gastrocnemius
**14** xiphihumeralis
**15** latissimus dorsi, pectoralis major, pectoralis minor, peroneal muscles

• **muscle in**
**05** shove **06** butt in, jostle, push in
**09** strongarm **13** interfere with
**14** elbow your way in, force your way in, impose yourself

**muscular**
**05** beefy, burly, hefty, husky, thewy
**06** brawny, potent, robust, rugged, sinewy, strong, sturdy, thewed
**07** fibrous **08** athletic, powerful, stalwart, vigorous **09** strapping
**15** powerfully built

**muse**
**04** mews **05** brood, dream, meuse, study, think, weigh **06** ponder, review
**07** reflect **08** chew over, cogitate, consider, meditate, mull over, ruminate
**09** speculate, think over **10** deliberate
**11** contemplate **13** contemplation

*The Greek Muses:*

**04** Clio
**05** Erato
**06** Thalia, Urania
**07** Euterpe
**08** Calliope, Polymnia
**09** Melpomene
**10** Polyhymnia
**11** Terpsichore

• **the Muses**
**07** the nine

**museum**
**03** mus **07** palazzo **10** art gallery, collection, repository **14** heritage centre

*Museums and galleries include:*

**02** BM, RA
**03** ICA
**04** MoMA, MOMI, Tate
**05** Prado, Terme, V and A
**06** Correr, London, Louvre, Uffizi
**07** British, Fogg Art, Hofburg, Mankind, Pushkin, Russian, Science, Vatican
**08** Bargello, Borghese, National, Pergamum
**09** Accademia, Albertina, Arnolfini, Ashmolean, Belvedere, Cloisters, Deutsches, Hermitage, Holocaust, Modern Art, Sans Souci, Tretyakov
**10** Guggenheim, Pinakothek, Pitt-Rivers, Serpentine, Tate Modern
**11** Fitzwilliam, Imperial War, Mauritshuis, Musée d'Orsay, Pitti Palace, Rijksmuseum, Tate Britain
**12** Royal Academy, Whitworth Art
**13** Jean Paul Getty, Peace Memorial, Royal Pavilion
**14** Barbican Centre, Natural History, State Hermitage
**15** Centre Beaubourg, Frick Collection, South Bank Centre

**mush**
**03** pap **04** corn, glop, mash, pulp
**05** cream, dough, gloop, notch, paste, purée, slush, swill **07** rubbish, scallop, shmaltz **08** schmaltz, umbrella
**11** mawkishness **14** sentimentality

**mushroom**
**04** boom, grow **06** expand, spread, sprout **07** burgeon, shoot up, upstart
**08** flourish, increase, spring up, umbrella **09** luxuriate, pixy-stool
**11** proliferate

*Mushrooms and toadstools include:*

**03** cep
**04** base, ugly, wood
**05** brain, field, gypsy, horse, magic, march, morel, naked
**06** agaric, blewit, button, elf cup, ink cap, meadow, mower's, oyster, satan's, winter
**07** amanita, blewits, blusher, boletus, Caesar's, griping, parasol, porcini, truffle
**08** death cap, deceiver, hedgehog, penny bun, shiitake, sickener
**09** cramp ball, earth ball, fairy ring, fly agaric, St George's, stinkhorn
**10** champignon, false morel, lawyer's wig, liberty cap, panther cap, sweetbread, wood agaric
**11** chanterelle, clean mycena, common morel, dingy agaric, honey fungus, stout agaric, sulphur tuft, velvet shank
**12** common ink cap, dryad's saddle, false blusher, horn of plenty, larch boletus, lurid boletus, purple blewit, shaggy ink cap, slippery jack, white truffle, winter fungus, wood hedgehog
**13** buckler agaric, clouded agaric, copper trumpet, devil's boletus, emetic russula, firwood agaric, honey mushroom, Jew's ear fungus, purple boletus, satan's boletus, shaggy milk cap, shaggy parasol, summer truffle, trumpet agaric, woolly milk cap, yellow stainer
**14** common grisette, common laccaria, common puffball, fairies' bonnets, man on horseback, penny-bun fungus, saffron milk cap, yellow staining
**15** beefsteak fungus, chestnut boletus, common earthball, common stinkhorn, destroying angel, garlic marosmius, périgord truffle, stinking parasol, stinking russula, verdigris agaric

*See also* **fungus**

**mushy**
◇ *anagram indicator*
**03** wet **04** soft **05** pappy, pulpy, soppy, weepy **06** doughy, sloppy, slushy, sugary, syrupy **07** maudlin, mawkish, pulpous, squashy, squidgy **08** squelchy
**09** schmaltzy **10** saccharine
**11** sentimental

**music**
**03** fun, mus **04** note, tune **05** dream
**06** melody **07** harmony

*Music types include:*

**03** AOR, MOR, pop, rai, rap, ska
**04** folk, funk, jazz, jive, mood, raga, rock, Romo, soca, soul, zouk
**05** bebop, blues, cajun, dance, disco, house, indie, muzak, R and B, salsa, samba, sokah, swing, world
**06** atonal, ballet, choral, doo-wop, fusion, garage, gospel, grunge, hip-hop, jungle, lounge, reggae, sacred, techno, trance
**07** ambient, baroque, bhangra, Big Beat, calypso, chamber, gamelan, gangsta, karaoke, nu-metal, ragtime, skiffle, trip-hop
**08** acid jazz, ballroom, folk rock, glam rock, hardcore, hard rock, jazz-funk, jazz-rock, operatic, oratorio, punk rock, soft rock
**09** acid house, bluegrass, classical, Dixieland, honky-tonk
**10** electronic, gangsta rap, heavy metal, incidental, orchestral, twelve-tone
**11** country rock, drum and bass, rock and roll, thrash metal
**12** boogie-woogie, instrumental
**13** easy listening
**14** rhythm and blues
**15** middle-of-the-road

*See also* **jazz**; **opera**

• **compose music to**
**03** set

**musical**
**03** mus **06** dulcet, mellow **07** lyrical, melodic, tuneful **09** melodious
**10** euphonious, harmonious
**11** mellifluous **13** sweet-sounding
*See also* **instrument**; **note**

*Musicals include:*

**04** Cats, Fame, Hair, Rent
**05** Annie, Blitz, Chess, Evita, Fosse, Zorba
**06** Grease, Joseph, Kismet, Oliver!, The Wiz
**07** Cabaret, Camelot, Chicago, Company, Follies
**08** Carnival, Carousel, Fiorello!, Godspell, Mamma Mia!, Oklahoma!, Peter Pan, Show Boat
**09** Brigadoon, Funny Girl, Girl Crazy, On the Town
**10** Hello Dolly!, Kiss Me Kate, Miss Saigon, My Fair Lady
**11** A Chorus Line, Babes in Arms, Billy Elliot, Bitter Sweet, Carmen Jones, Mary Poppins, Me and My Girl, Sweeney Todd, The King and I, The Lion King, The Music Man
**12** Anything Goes, Bombay Dreams, Bye Bye Birdie, Guys and Dolls, Martin Guerre, South Pacific, The Boy Friend, The Producers
**13** Aspects of Love, Blood Brothers, Les Miserables, Man of La Mancha, The Pajama Game, West Side Story
**14** Babes in Toyland, Victor/Victoria
**15** Annie Get Your Gun, La Cage aux Folles, Mister Wonderful, Sunset Boulevard, The Sound of Music, The Woman in White

*Songs from musicals include:*

**03** One
**04** Fame
**05** Maria
**06** Do-Re-Mi, Memory, People
**07** America, Bali Ha'i, Cabaret, Camelot, Tonight
**08** Aquarius, Day by Day, Oklahoma!, Time Warp, Tomorrow
**09** Edelweiss, Evergreen, Footloose, Somewhere, Superstar, Tradition
**10** 42nd Street, Be Our Guest, Big Spender, Friendship, Hello, Dolly, I Am What I Am, I Got Rhythm, Matchmaker, Night Fever, Ol' Man River, Too Darn Hot, Willkommen
**11** 76 Trombones, All That Jazz, Luck, Be a Lady, Night and Day, Old Man River, Summer Lovin', Where is Love?, You're The Top
**12** All I Ask of You, Broadway Baby, Circle of Life, Dancing Queen, Easter Parade, Hakuna Matata, Mack the Knife, Makin' Whoopee, Rich Man's Frug, Shall We Dance?, Sound of Music, Staying Alive, Summer Nights, There She Goes, We Go Together
**13** Skimbleshanks, Sunrise, Sunset
**14** Ain't Misbehavin', Any Dream Will Do, Chim Chim Cher-ee, Close Every Door, I Dreamed a Dream, I Know Him So Well, Lonely Goatherd, Mr Mistoffelees, New York, New York, So Long, Farewell, They All Laughed, We're in the Money
**15** A Bushel and a Peck, Bells Are Ringing, Greased Lightnin', Honeysuckle Rose, I Am the Starlight, If I Were a Rich Man, Music of the Night, Put On a Happy Face, Send in the Clowns, Singin' in the Rain, Sunset Boulevard, Tell Me on a Sunday, The Lady is a Tramp, Till There Was You

*People associated with musicals include:*

**04** **Bart** (Lionel), **Hart** (Lorenz), **Kaye** (Danny), **Kern** (Jerome), **Nunn** (Trevor), **Rice** (Tim)
**05** **Black** (Don), **Donen** (Stanley), **Fosse** (Bob), **Kelly** (Gene), **Lenya** (Lotte), **Loewe** (Frederick)
**06** **Berlin** (Irving), **Coward** (Sir Noel), **Gaynor** (Mitzi), **Jolson** (Al), **Lerner** (Alan Jay), **Merman** (Ethel), **Porter** (Cole), **Prince** (Hal), **Rogers** (Ginger), **Steele** (Tommy)
**07** **Astaire** (Fred), **Burnett** (Carol), **Garland** (Judy), **Gilbert** (Sir W S), **Novello** (Ivor), **Rodgers** (Richard)
**08** **Berkeley** (Busby), **Gershwin** (George), **Gershwin** (Ira), **Minnelli** (Liza), **Robinson** (Bill 'Bojangles'), **Sondheim** (Stephen), **Ziegfeld** (Florenz, Jnr)
**09** **Bernstein** (Leonard), **Macintosh** (Cameron), **Offenbach** (Jacques)
**10** **D'Oyly Carte** (Richard)
**11** **Hammerstein** (Oscar, II), **Lloyd Webber** (Andrew, Lord)

*Musical composition types include:*

**03** jig, lay, rag
**04** aria, duet, hymn, lied, opus, raga, song, trio, tune
**05** canon, carol, étude, fugue, gigue, march, opera, piece, polka, rondo, round, suite, tango, track, waltz
**06** aubade, ballad, bolero, lieder, masque, minuet, number, pavane, shanty, sonata
**07** ballade, bourrée, cantata, fanfare, gavotte, mazurka, partita, prelude, quartet, requiem, scherzo, toccata
**08** berceuse, cavatina, chaconne, concerto, fandango, fantasia, galliard, hornpipe, madrigal, nocturne, operetta, overture, rhapsody, saraband, serenade, sonatina, symphony, zarzuela
**09** allemande, arabesque, bagatelle, cabaletta, capriccio, écossaise, farandole, impromptu, invention, pastorale, polonaise, sarabande, spiritual, voluntary
**10** barcarolle, bergamasca, concertino, humoresque, intermezzo, opera buffa, tarantella
**11** bacchanalia, ballad opera, composition, pastourelle, sinfonietta
**12** divertimento, extravaganza
**13** missa solemnis
**14** chorale fantasy, chorale prelude, concerto grosso

*See also* **song**

*Musical compositions include:*

**04** Saul
**05** Rodeo
**06** Boléro, Elijah, Études, Façade, Images
**07** Epitaph, Jephtha, Mazeppa, Messiah
**08** Ballades, Caprices, Creation, Drum Mass, Ode to Joy, Peer Gynt
**09** Capriccio, Fantaisie, Finlandia, Jerusalem, Nocturnes
**10** Arabesques, Bacchanale, Bagatelles, Concertino, Nelson Mass, The Planets, The Seasons, Water Music
**11** Curlew River, Gymnopédies, Harmony Mass, Minute Waltz, Requiem Mass, Stabat Mater, Winterreise
**12** A Sea Symphony, Danse Macabre, Golden Sonata, Karelia Suite, Kinderscenen, Linz Symphony, Piano Fantasy, Schéhérazade, Trout Quintet
**13** Alpensinfonie, Carmina Burana, Choral Fantasy, Ebony Concerto, Faust Symphony, Fêtes Galantes, German Requiem, Israel in Egypt, Metamorphoses, Missa Solemnis, On Wenlock Edge, The Art of Fugue
**14** Canticum Sacrum, Choral Symphony, Colour Symphony, Eroica Symphony, Glagolitic Mass, Prague Symphony, Rhapsody in Blue, Slavonic Dances, The Four Seasons
**15** A Child of our Time, Alexander's Feast, Children's Corner, Emperor Concerto, Haffner Symphony, Hungarian Dances, Italian Concerto, Judas Maccabaeus, Jupiter Symphony, Kossuth Overture, Manfred Symphony, Peter and the Wolf, Sicilian Vespers

*See also* **opera**; **oratorio**; **song**

*Musical terms include:*

**03** bar, bis, cue, key, tie
**04** a due, alto, arco, bass, beat, clef, coda, fine, flat, fret, hold, mode, mute, note, part, rest, root, slur, solo, tone, tune, turn
**05** ad lib, breve, buffo, chord, dolce, drone, forte, grave, largo, lento, lyric, major, metre, minim, minor, molto, pause, piano, piece, pitch, scale, score, senza, shake, sharp, staff, stave, swell, tacet, tanto, tempo, tenor, theme, triad, trill, tutti
**06** adagio, al fine, a tempo, da capo, duplet, encore, finale, legato, manual, medley, melody, octave, phrase, presto, quaver, rhythm, sempre, subito, tenuto, timbre, treble, tuning, unison, upbeat, vivace
**07** agitato, allegro, al segno, amoroso, andante, animato, attacca, bar line, cadence, con brio, concert, con moto, descant, harmony, langsam, marcato, mediant, middle C, mordent, natural, recital,

refrain, soprano, tremolo, triplet, vibrato
**08** acoustic, alto clef, arpeggio, baritone, bass clef, col canto, con fuoco, crotchet, diatonic, doloroso, dominant, downbeat, ensemble, interval, maestoso, moderato, movement, ostinato, perdendo, ritenuto, semitone, semplice, sequence, staccato, vigoroso, virtuoso
**09** alla breve, cantabile, cantilena, chromatic, contralto, crescendo, glissando, harmonics, imitation, larghetto, mezza voce, microtone, non troppo, obbligato, orchestra, pizzicato, semibreve, sextuplet, sforzando, smorzando, sostenuto, sotto voce, spiritoso, tablature, tenor clef
**10** accidental, affettuoso, allargando, allegretto, consonance, diminuendo, dissonance, dotted note, dotted rest, double flat, double stop, expression, fortissimo, intonation, ledger line, mezzo forte, modulation, pedal point, pentatonic, pianissimo, quadruplet, quintuplet, resolution, semiquaver, simple time, submediant, supertonic, tonic sol-fa, treble clef, two-two time
**11** accelerando, arrangement, decrescendo, double sharp, double trill, fingerboard, leading note, quarter tone, rallentando, rinforzando, subdominant, syncopation
**12** acciaccatura, alla cappella, appoggiatura, compound time, counterpoint, four-four time, key signature, six-eight time
**13** accompaniment, double bar line, fifth interval, improvisation, major interval, minor interval, orchestration, sixth interval, sul ponticello, third interval, three-four time, time signature, transposition
**14** cross-fingering, demisemiquaver, fourth interval, second interval
**15** perfect interval, seventh interval

## musician

*Musician types include:*

**03** duo
**04** band, bard, diva, duet, trio
**05** choir, griot, group, nonet, octet, piper, waits
**06** bugler, busker, folkie, jazzer, oboist, player, sextet, singer
**07** cellist, drummer, fiddler, harpist, maestro, Orphean, pianist, quartet, quintet, soloist
**08** clarsair, composer, ensemble, flautist, lutenist, minstrel, organist, virtuoso, vocalist
**09** balladeer, conductor, guitarist, itinerant, orchestra, performer, trumpeter, violinist
**10** one-man band, prima donna, trombonist
**11** accompanist, saxophonist
**12** backing group, clarinettist
**13** percussionist, session singer
**15** instrumentalist, session musician

*See also* **composer**; **conductor**; **libretto**; **pianist**; **singer**; **songwriter**

*Classical musicians include:*

**02** **Ax** (Emmanuel), **Ma** (Yo-Yo)
**03** **Mae** (Vanessa), **Pré** (Jacqueline du)
**04** **Bell** (Joshua), **Hahn** (Hilary), **Hess** (Dame Myra), **Lupu** (Radu), **Mork** (Truls), **Wild** (Earl)
**05** **Boehm** (Theobald), **Borge** (Victor), **Bream** (Julian), **Bülow** (Hans von), **Chung** (Kyung-Wha), **Dupré** (Marcel), **Elman** (Mischa), **Grove** (Sir George), **Isbin** (Sharon), **Ogdon** (John), **Sharp** (Cecil), **Stern** (Isaac)
**06** **Casals** (Pablo), **Czerny** (Karl), **Galway** (James), **Gitlis** (Ivry), **Kissin** (Evgeny), **Köchel** (Ludwig von) **Rizzio** (David), **Schiff** (András)
**07** **Blondel**, **Glennie** (Evelyn), **Heifetz** (Jascha), **Kennedy** (Nigel), **Menuhin** (Yehudi), **Mutter** (Anne-Sophie), **Perahia** (Murray), **Perlman** (Itzhak), **Pollini** (Maurizio), **Richter** (Sviatoslav), **Russell** (David), **Segovia** (Andrés), **Shankar** (Ravi), **Starker** (Janos)
**08** **Argerich** (Martha), **Bronfman** (Yefim), **Browning** (John), **Goossens** (Léon), **Helfgott** (David), **Holliger** (Heinz), **Horowitz** (Vladimir), **Kreisler** (Fritz), **Paganini** (Niccolò), **Sarasate** (Pablo), **Steinway** (Henry), **Vengerov** (Maxim), **Williams** (John)
**09** **Ashkenazy** (Vladimir), **Barenboim** (Daniel), **Benedetti** (Nicola), **Boulanger** (Nadia), **Broadwood** (John), **Dolmetsch** (Arnold), **Guarnieri**, **Tortelier** (Paul)
**10** **Cristofori**, **de Larrocha** (Alicia), **Paderewski** (Ignacy), **Rubinstein** (Anton), **Rubinstein** (Artur), **Stradivari** (Antonio), **Villa-Lobos** (Heitor), **Williamson** (Malcolm)
**11** **Theodorakis** (Mikis)
**12** **Guido d'Arezzo**, **Rostropovich** (Mstislav)
**14** **Jaques-Dalcroze** (Emile)

## musing

**05** study **07** reverie **08** dreaming, studying, thinking **10** brown study, cogitation, meditation, ponderment, reflection, rumination **11** abstraction, cerebration, daydreaming **13** contemplation, introspection, wool-gathering

## musk

**04** must **05** civet, moust, muist, scent **07** mimulus

## musket

**05** fusee, fusil **06** gingal, jezail, jingal **07** caliver, dragoon, gingall **08** Biscayan **09** brown Bess, queen's-arm **10** musquetoon

## musketeer

**12** mousquetaire

*Musketeers include:*

**05** Athos
**06** Aramis
**07** Porthos
**09** D'Artagnan

## Muslim

*Muslims include:*

**04** Shia
**05** Shiah, Sunni
**06** Senusi, Shiite
**07** Alawite, dervish, Mevlevi, Senussi, Sonnite, Sunnite
**08** Senoussi
**10** Karmathian
**11** Black Muslim
**15** whirling dervish

## muslin

**04** leno, mull **05** sails **06** canvas, gurrah, mulmul **07** jamdani, mulmull, organdy **08** coteline, nainsook, organdie, tarlatan **09** persienne **10** mousseline

## muss

◇ *anagram indicator*
**03** row **04** mess **06** ruffle, tousle
**08** dishevel, disorder, scramble
**09** confusion **10** disarrange, make untidy **11** disturbance, make a mess of

## mussel

**04** Unio **06** muscle, muskle
**07** Modiola, Mytilus **08** deer horn, Modiolus **09** clabby-doo, clappy-doo, date-shell

## must

◇ *anagram indicator*
**03** man, mun **04** amok, duty, maun, mote, musk, stum **05** amuck, basic, mould **06** frenzy, powder **09** essential, necessity, provision, requisite
**10** imperative, obligation, sine qua non
**11** fundamental, requirement, stipulation **12** fermentation, prerequisite

## mustard

**05** runch, senvy **08** charlock, flix-weed **09** praiseach **10** sauce-alone
**14** jack-by-the-hedge

## muster

**04** mass, meet **05** enrol, group, rally **06** call up, gather, number, parade, review, summon, throng
**07** collect, convene, convoke, display, example, hosting, marshal, meeting, round up, round-up, turnout
**08** assemble, assembly, mobilize, register, summon up **09** concourse, gathering, march past **10** assemblage, collection, congregate, convention, inspection **11** convocation **12** call together, come together, congregation, mobilization **13** bring together, demonstration **14** gather together

• **pass muster**
**07** shape up **09** measure up **10** be accepted, fit the bill **11** fill the bill **12** be

acceptable, be good enough, make the grade **15** come up to scratch

**musty**
◇ *anagram indicator*
**04** amok, damp, dank **05** amuck, frowy, funky, fusty, mucid, stale **06** fousty, frowie, mochie, mouldy, smelly, stuffy **07** airless, decayed, foughty, froughy, mildewy, vinewed **08** decaying, mildewed

**mutability**
**09** variation **11** variability **12** alterability **13** permutability **14** changeableness

**mutable**
**06** fickle **08** changing, flexible, unstable, unsteady, variable, volatile, wavering **09** adaptable, alterable, uncertain, unsettled **10** changeable, inconstant, irresolute, permutable, unreliable **11** vacillating **12** inconsistent, undependable **15** interchangeable

**mutate**
◇ *anagram indicator*
**05** alter, morph **06** change, evolve, modify, remake **07** convert, remodel, reshape **09** transform, translate, transmute **11** transfigure **12** metamorphose, transmogrify

**mutation**
◇ *anagram indicator*
**06** change **07** anomaly **09** deviation, evolution, inversion, variation **10** adaptation, alteration, revolution **11** vicissitude **12** modification **13** metamorphosis **14** transformation

**mute**
**03** mum **04** dull, dumb, stop **05** lower **06** dampen, damper, deaden, muffle, shtoom, silent, soften, stifle, subdue **07** aphasic, plosive, quieten, silence, smother, sordino **08** moderate, sourdine, suppress, taciturn, tone down, unspoken, wordless **09** noiseless, soft-pedal, voiceless **10** speechless **11** unexpressed **12** unpronounced **15** uncommunicative

**muted**
**04** dull, soft **05** faint, quiet, sorda, sordo **06** low-key, subtle **07** muffled, stifled, subdued **08** dampened, discreet, softened **10** restrained, suppressed

**mutely**
**06** dumbly **08** silently **09** in silence **10** taciturnly **11** noiselessly, voicelessly **12** speechlessly

**mutilate**
◇ *anagram indicator*
**03** cut, mar **04** hack, lame, maim, ruin **05** cut up, spoil **06** censor, damage, garble, hack up, hamble, impair, injure, mangle **07** butcher, concise, cripple, disable, distort **08** lacerate **09** disfigure, dismember **10** bowdlerize, detruncate **11** cut to pieces

**mutilation**
◇ *anagram indicator*
**06** damage **07** maiming **10** amputation **12** detruncation, dismembering **13** disfigurement

**mutinous**
◇ *anagram indicator*
**06** unruly **07** bolshie, riotous **09** insurgent, seditious **10** disorderly, rebellious, refractory, subversive **11** anarchistic, disobedient **12** contumacious, ungovernable, unsubmissive **13** insubordinate, revolutionary **14** uncontrollable

**mutiny**
**04** defy, riot **05** rebel **06** resist, revolt, rise up, rising, strife, strike, tumult **07** disobey, protest **08** defiance, uprising **09** rebellion **10** insurgence, resistance, revolution **12** disobedience, insurrection **15** insubordination

**mutt**
**03** cur, dog **04** dolt, fool, kuri **05** bitch, hound, idiot, moron, pooch **07** mongrel **08** imbecile **09** blockhead, ignoramus, thickhead **10** dunderhead

**mutter**
◇ *homophone indicator*
**04** beef, carp, fuss, mump, roin **05** gripe, royne, whine **06** grouse, mumble, murmur, object, rumble, whinge, witter **07** chunder, chunner, chunter, grumble, maunder, protest, stutter, whitter **08** chounter, complain, splutter **09** bellyache, criticize, find fault, murmuring, mussitate **14** talk to yourself, whittie-whattie

**mutton**
**02** em **05** gigot, macon, sheep, traik **07** haricot **09** Irish stew, Southdown **10** Fanny Adams **13** colonial goose

**mutual**
**05** joint **06** common, shared **09** commutual, exchanged **10** collective, commonable, reciprocal **12** interchanged **13** complementary **15** interchangeable

**muzzle**
**03** gag **04** mute **05** check, choke, snout **06** censor, fetter, stifle **07** inhibit, silence **08** gunpoint, restrain, suppress

**muzzy**
**04** hazy **05** dazed, faint, fuzzy, mused, tipsy **06** addled, groggy **07** blurred, muddled, unclear **08** confused **09** befuddled, unfocused **10** bewildered, indistinct

**my**
**01** m' **02** ha **03** cor, gad, lor **04** gosh **08** well, well

**Myanmar**
**03** BUR, MMR, MYA

**myopic**
**06** narrow, unwise **08** purblind **09** half-blind, imprudent, localized, parochial, short-term **11** near-sighted, thoughtless **12** narrow-minded, short-sighted **13** ill-considered, unadventurous, uncircumspect, unimaginative

**myriad**
**03** sea **04** army, host **05** flood, horde, swarm, toman **06** scores, throng, untold **08** millions, mountain, zillions **09** boundless, countless, limitless, multitude, thousands **10** numberless **11** innumerable **12** immeasurable, incalculable **13** multitudinous

**mysterious**
◇ *anagram indicator*
**04** dark **05** shady, weird **06** arcane, creepy, hidden, mystic, occult, secret, veiled **07** cryptic, curious, furtive, obscure, shadowy, strange **08** abstruse, baffling, esoteric, mystical, puzzling, reticent, sinister **09** enigmatic, insoluble, recondite, secretive **10** mystifying, perplexing **11** as if by magic, inscrutable **12** inexplicable, unfathomable, unsearchable **13** surreptitious

**mysteriously**
◇ *anagram indicator*
**08** arcanely, in secret, secretly **09** curiously, magically, obscurely, strangely **10** abstrusely, mystically, puzzlingly **11** cryptically, inscrutably **12** esoterically, inexplicably **13** engimatically **15** surreptitiously

**mystery**
**06** enigma, puzzle, riddle, secret **07** arcanum, problem, secrecy **08** mystique, question **09** ambiguity, conundrum, curiosity, obscurity, reticence, sacrament, weirdness **10** closed book **11** concealment, furtiveness, miracle play, strangeness **12** question mark **14** inscrutability **15** inexplicability, unfathomability

**mystic**
**04** Sofi, Sufi **05** swami **07** psychic **09** occultist, spiritist **11** allegorical, esotericist **12** spiritualist **13** metaphysicist **15** supernaturalist

**mystical**
**05** weird **06** arcane, hidden, mystic, occult **07** obscure, strange **08** abstruse, baffling, esoteric **09** recondite, spiritual **10** mysterious, paranormal **12** inexplicable, metaphysical, other-worldly, supernatural, unfathomable **13** preternatural **14** transcendental

**mysticism**
**05** deism **06** theism **07** mystery **09** occultism, spiritism **10** arcaneness **11** esotericism **12** spirituality **14** mysteriousness **15** inexplicability, supernaturalism

**mystification**
**03** awe, fog **04** daze **06** muddle **08** surprise **09** confusion **10** perplexity, puzzlement

**11** uncertainty **12** bewilderment, stupefaction **13** disconcertion **14** disorientation

**mystify**

**04** hoax **06** baffle, puzzle **07** confuse, perplex **08** bewilder, confound **09** bamboozle **10** take to town **13** metagrabolize, metagrobolize

**mystique**

**03** awe **05** charm, magic, spell **06** appeal **07** glamour, mystery, romance, secrecy **08** charisma **09** adventure **11** fascination

**myth**

**03** fib, lie **04** saga, tale **05** fable, fancy, story **06** legend **07** fallacy, fantasy, fiction, parable, untruth **08** allegory, bestiary, delusion, folk tale, pretence **09** fairy tale, invention, tall story **10** fairy story **11** fabrication **13** misconception

**• book of myths**

**04** Edda **09** Elder Edda, Prose Edda **11** Younger Edda

**mythical**

**05** put-on **06** fabled, made-up, phoney, unreal, untrue **07** fantasy, pretend **08** fabulous, fanciful, invented **09** fairytale, fantastic, imaginary, legendary, pretended **10** chimerical, fabricated, fictitious **11** make-believe, non-existent **12** mythological

*Mythical creatures and spirits include:*

**03** elf, hob, imp, orc, roc
**04** faun, fury, jinn, ogre, peri, pixy, puck, yeti
**05** afrit, demon, devil, djinn, dobby, dryad, dwarf, fairy, genie, ghost, ghoul, giant, gnome, golem, harpy, kelpy, lamia, naiad, nymph, oread, pixie, satyr, shade, Siren, sylph, troll, yowie
**06** afreet, bunyip, dobbie, dragon, dybbuk, Fafnir, Furies, Geryon, goblin, Gorgon, kelpie, kobald, kraken, Lilith, Medusa, merman, nereid, ogress, Scylla, selkie, Sphinx, sprite, wivern, yaksha
**07** banshee, Bigfoot, brownie, Cecrops, centaur, Chimera, Cyclops, Echidna, Erinyes, gremlin, Grendel, griffin, Harpies, incubus, lorelei, mermaid, Pegasus, phoenix, sandman, taniwha, unicorn, vampire, windigo
**08** basilisk, Cerberus, Gigantes, lindworm, Minotaur, seahorse, succubus, werewolf
**09** Charybdis, hamadryad, hobgoblin, mermaiden, sasquatch
**10** cockatrice, hippogriff, leprechaun, salamander, sea serpent, tooth fairy
**11** hippocampus
**15** Loch Ness monster

*See also* **bird**; **monster**

*Mythical places include:*

**03** Dis, Hel
**04** Hell, Styx
**05** Argos, Babel, Hades, Lethe, Pluto, Thule
**06** Albion, Anghar, Asgard, Avalon, Heaven, Heorot, Nedyet, Utgard
**07** Acheron, Agartha, Alfheim, Alpheus, Arcadia, Bifrost, Boeotia, Elysium, Lemuria, Nirvana, Pohjola, Tuonela
**08** Amazonia, Archeron, Atlantis, El Dorado, Niflheim, Paradise, Tir-na-nOg, Tlalocan, Valhalla, Vanaheim
**09** Cockaigne, Fairyland, Purgatory, River Styx, Yggdrasil
**10** River Lethe, Stymphalos
**11** Ultima Thule
**12** River Acheron, River Alpheus
**13** Jewel Mountain, River Archeron, The Underworld
**14** Lake Stymphalos
**15** Cloudcuckooland, The Garden of Eden, The Isle of Avalon, The Tower of Babel

*See also* **mythology**; **river**

**mythological**

**06** fabled, mythic **08** fabulous, mythical **09** fairytale, folkloric, legendary **10** fictitious **11** traditional

**mythology**

**04** lore **05** myths, tales **06** legend **07** stories **08** folklore, Pantheon **09** folk tales, tradition **10** traditions

*See also* **god, goddess**; **fate**; **fury**; **grace**; **muse**; **mythical**; **sage**

*Characters from Celtic mythology include:*

**03** Anu, Lug
**04** Badb, Bran, Danu, Lugh, Medb, Ogma
**05** Balor, Boann, Dagda, Macha, Maeve, Neman, Nuada, Oisin, Pwyll
**06** Brigit, Danaan, Deidre, Imbolc, Isolde, Ogmios, Ossian
**07** banshee, Beltane, Branwen, Brighid, Deirdre, Samhain, Tristan
**08** Manannan, Morrigan, Rhiannon, The Dagda, Tir nan-Og
**09** Bean Sidhé, Cernunnos, Conchobar
**10** Cú Chulainn, Lughnasadh
**11** Finn mac Cool
**13** Bendigeidfran, Finn mac Cumhal
**14** Bran the Blessed, Finn mac Cumhail, Tuatha dé Danaan

*Characters from Greek mythology include:*

**02** Io
**04** Ajax, Dido, Echo, Eris, Hero, Leda, Leto, Rhea
**05** Atlas, Chloe, Circe, Creon, Danae, Helen, Horae, Hydra, Irene, Ixion, Jason, Kreon, Laius, Lamia, Medea, Midas, Minos, Niobe, Orion, Paris, Priam, Rheia
**06** Aeneas, Aeolus, Alecto, Amazon, Atreus, Cadmus, Castor, Charon, Chiron, Cronus, Danaoi, Daphne, Dryads, Europa, Europe, Furies, Graiae, Hecabe, Hector, Hecuba, Hellen, Icarus, Iolaus, Kronos, Latona, Medusa, Megara, Memnon, Naiads, Nessus, Nestor, Nymphs, Oreads, Peleus, Pelops, Phoebe, Pollux, Python, Satyrs, Scylla, Semele, Sileni, Sirens, Stheno, Syrinx, Titans, Triton, Typhon
**07** Actaeon, Alcyone, Arachne, Ariadne, Calchas, Calypso, Cecrops, Cepheus, Chimera, Cyclops, Danaans, Daphnis, Diomede, Echidna, Electra, Epigoni, Erinyes, Euryale, Galatea, Gorgons, Griffin, Gryphon, Harpies, Iapetus, Jocasta, Kekrops, Laocoon, Lapiths, Leander, Maenads, Marsyas, Nereids, Oceanus, Oedipus, Orestes, Orpheus, Pandora, Pegasus, Perseus, Phaedra, Silenus, Theseus, Titania, Troilus, Ulysses
**08** Achilles, Alcestis, Alcmaeon, Anchises, Antigone, Arethusa, Atalanta, Basilisk, Centaurs, Cerberus, Chimaera, Cressida, Cyclopes, Daedalus, Diomedes, Endymion, Eteocles, Eurydice, Ganymede, Gigantes, Halcyone, Heracles, Hyperion, Iphicles, Lycurgus, Meleager, Menelaus, Minotaur, Nausicaa, Oceanids, Odysseus, Pasiphae, Penelope, Pentheus, Phaethon, Pleiades, Sarpedon, Sisyphus, Tantalus, Thyestes, Tiresias, Typhoeus
**09** Aegisthus, Agamemnon, Andromeda, Argonauts, Autolycus, Cassandra, Charybdis, Deucalion, Idomeneus, Lotophagi, Mnemosyne, Myrmidons, Narcissus, Patroclus, Polynices, Pygmalion, Semiramis, Tisiphone
**10** Amphitryon, Andromache, Cassiopeia, Cockatrice, Erechtheus, Hamadryads, Hesperides, Hippolytus, Iphigeneia, Polyneices, Polyphemus, Procrustes, Prometheus, Telemachus
**11** Bellerophon, Lotus-eaters, Neoptolemus, Philoctetes
**12** Clytemnestra, Hyperboreans, Rhadamanthus, Rhadamanthys

*Characters from Maori mythology include:*

**04** Kupe, Maui, Rona
**05** Pania
**07** Hinemoa, Mahuika
**09** Tutanekai

*Characters from Norse mythology include:*

**03** Lif
**06** Gudrun, Sigurd
**09** Berserker
**10** Lifthrasir

*Characters from Roman mythology include:*

**05** Lamia, Lares, Manes, Remus, Sibyl
**07** Danaans, Latinus, Lemures, Lucrece, Penates, Romulus, Sibylla, Tarpeia
**08** Anchises, Callisto, Hercules, Lucretia, Verginia

**09** Androcles
**10** Coriolanus, Rhea Silvia, Rhea Sylvia

*Other mythological and legendary characters include:*

**03** Qat
**04** Tell (William)
**05** Adapa, El Cid, Faust, Frost (Jack)
**06** Anansi, Arthur, Bunyan (Paul), Enkidu, George (St), Godiva (Lady), Kraken, Weland
**07** Aladdin, Ali Baba, Beowulf, Grendel, Wayland, Weiland, Weyland
**08** Baba Yaga, Brunhild, Hang Tuah, Hiawatha, Parsifal
**09** Appleseed (Johnny), Bluebeard, Lohengrin
**10** Yu the Great
**11** Old King Cole
**12** Lemminkainen, Rip Van Winkle, Scheherazade, Will-o'-the-Wisp
**14** Flying Dutchman
**15** Father Christmas

*See also* **fate**; **fury**; **god, goddess**; **grace**; **monster**; **muse**; **sage**

# N

**N**
**02** en **08** November

**nab**
**03** hat **04** bone, grab, head, nail, nick **05** catch, run in, seize **06** arrest, collar, nobble, pull in, snatch **07** capture, hilltop **09** apprehend **10** projection, promontory

**nabob**
**03** VIP **05** celeb, nawab **06** bigwig, tycoon **07** magnate **08** luminary **09** celebrity, financier, personage **11** billionaire, millionaire

**nadir**
**04** zero **06** bottom, depths **07** minimum **08** low point **10** all-time low, rock bottom **11** lowest point **12** low-watermark

**nag**
**03** bug, rip, tit, vex **04** carp, hack, jade, moan, moke, plug, yaff **05** annoy, harry, horse, scold, tease, worry **06** badger, berate, bother, grouse, harass, hassle, keep at, keffel, niggle, pester, pick on, plague, rouncy **07** earbash, henpeck, torment, trouble, upbraid **08** complain, ding-dong, irritate, keep on at **09** aggravate, Rosinante, Rozinante

**nagging**
**06** aching **07** moaning, painful **08** critical, niggling, scolding, shrewish, worrying **09** upsetting **10** continuous, irritating, nit-picking, persistent, tormenting **11** distressing

**nail**
**03** fix, nab, pin, toe **04** brad, brod, claw, grab, join, nick, stub, stud, tack, trap **05** catch, clout, rivet, screw, seize, spick, spike, sprig, talon **06** arrest, attach, collar, corner, detect, expose, fasten, hammer, nipper, nobble, pierce, pincer, reveal, secure, skewer, snatch, tingle, unguis, unmask **07** capture, clinker, pin down, toenail, uncover, unearth **08** fastener, holdfast, identify, panel pin, sparable **09** apprehend **10** fingernail, tenterhook

**• hit the nail on the head**
**10** be accurate **14** be exactly right, score a bull's eye

**naïve**
**04** naif, open **05** frank, green **06** candid, jejune, simple **07** artless, natural **08** gullible, immature, innocent, trusting, wide-eyed **09** childlike, credulous, guileless, ingenuous, primitive, simpliste, small-town, unworldly **10** simplistic, unaffected **11** unrealistic **12** having no idea, pollyannaish, unsuspecting, unsuspicious **13** born yesterday, inexperienced, unpretentious **14** bread-and-butter **15** unsophisticated

**naively**
**06** simply **08** gullibly **09** artlessly, naturally **10** immaturely, innocently **11** guilelessly, ingenuously **14** simplistically, unsuspiciously

**naivety**
**08** openness **09** credulity, frankness, innocence **10** candidness, immaturity, simplicity **11** artlessness, gullibility, naturalness **12** inexperience **13** childlikeness, guilelessness, ingenuousness

**naked**
**03** raw **04** bald, bare, nude, open, weak **05** overt, plain, stark **06** Adamic, barren, patent, simple **07** artless, blatant, denuded, evident, exposed, glaring, skyclad, unarmed **08** Adamical, disrobed, flagrant, helpless, in the raw, starkers, stripped, treeless, undraped **09** au naturel, grassless, in the buff, in the scud, powerless, unadorned, unclothed, uncovered, undressed, unguarded **10** stark-naked, start-naked, unprovided, vulnerable **11** defenceless, mother-naked, unconcealed, undisguised, unprotected, unqualified, unvarnished **12** not a stitch on **13** with nothing on **15** in the altogether

**nakedness**
**06** nature, nudity **07** the buff, undress **08** baldness, bareness, openness **09** plainness, starkness **10** barrenness, simplicity **13** the altogether

**namby-pamby**
**03** wet **04** prim, weak **05** cissy, soppy, vapid, weedy, wussy **06** feeble, prissy **07** anaemic, insipid, maudlin, mawkish, wimpish **09** spineless, white-shoe **10** colourless, wishy-washy **11** sentimental **12** pretty-pretty

**name**
**01** n **03** dub, nom, tag, VIP **04** call, cite, clan, fame, hero, nemn, note, noun, pick, star, term **05** celeb, label, state, style, title, utter **06** behalf, bigwig, choose, esteem, expert, family, famous, handle, honour, renown, repute, select **07** appoint, baptize, big name, entitle, epithet, mention, specify **08** big noise, christen, classify, cognomen, eminence, identify, luminary, monicker, nominate, prestige, somebody, standing **09** authority, celebrity, character, designate, dignitary, well-known **10** commission, denominate, give name to, popularity, prominence, reputation **11** appellation, designation, distinction **12** denomination, leading light

*Names include:*

**03** pen, pet
**04** code, full, last
**05** alias, brand, false, first, given, place, stage
**06** anonym, eponym, exonym, family, maiden, middle, proper, second
**07** agnomen, allonym, assumed, autonym, surname, toponym
**08** nickname
**09** baptismal, Christian, cryptonym, pseudonym, sobriquet, trademark
**10** diminutive, nom de plume, soubriquet
**11** nom de guerre

*See also* **boy**; **cinema**; **French**; **German**; **girl**; **Irish**; **public house**; **Scottish**; **Welsh**

**• in name only**
**07** titular

**• list of names**
**04** roll

**• name unknown**
**02** NU

**named**
**03** dit, hot **04** hote **05** cited, nempt **06** called, chosen, dubbed, picked, styled, termed, titled **07** known as **08** baptized, entitled, labelled, selected **09** appointed, mentioned, nominated, specified **10** christened, classified, designated, identified, singled out **11** by the name of, denominated **12** commissioned

**nameless**
**07** obscure, unknown, unnamed **08** untitled **09** anonymous, titleless, unheard-of **10** innominate, unlabelled **11** unspeakable, unspecified, unutterable **12** illegitimate, undesignated, unidentified **13** indescribable, inexpressible, unmentionable **15** undistinguished

**namely**
**02** ie, sc **03** viz **04** scil, sciz **05** to wit **06** famous, that is **08** scilicet **09** videlicet **10** especially **11** that is to say **12** in other words, specifically

**Namibia**
**03** NAM

**nanny**
**03** nan, pet **04** amah, ayah, baby, nana **05** nanna, nurse, spoil **06** au pair, coddle, cosset, mother, pamper **07** indulge, she-goat **08** pander to, wet-nurse **09** governess, nursemaid, spoon-feed **11** childminder, grandmother, mollycoddle, mother's help, overprotect

**nanosecond**
**02** ns

**nap**
**03** kip, nod, ziz **04** down, doze, fuzz, oose, ooze, pile, rest, shag, zizz **05** fibre, grain, seize, sleep, steal, weave **06** catnap, nod off, siesta, snooze **07** bedding, bedroll, doze off, drop off, lie down, lie-down, surface, texture **08** meridian, napoleon **09** downiness **10** forty winks, light sleep **12** sleep lightly **14** get some shut-eye, have forty winks

**napkin**
**05** doily, doyly, nappy **06** doyley **09** muckender, serviette **12** handkerchief

**nappy**
**04** oosy, oozy **05** downy, heady, jumpy, terry, tipsy, towel **06** diaper, frothy, hippen, hippin, napkin, shaggy, strong **07** hipping, nervous **09** excitable, serviette **10** disposable

**narcissism**
**06** vanity **07** conceit, egotism **08** egomania, self-love **10** self-regard **11** self-conceit **13** egocentricity, self-obsession **15** self-centredness

**narcissistic**
**04** vain **09** conceited, egotistic **10** egocentric, self-loving **11** egomaniacal, self-centred **12** self-absorbed, self-obsessed

**narcotic**
**03** hop **04** dopy, drug **05** dopey, upper **06** downer, opiate **07** anodyne, calming, dulling, numbing **08** hypnotic, sedative **09** analgesic, somnolent, soporific **10** painkiller, palliative, stupefying **11** anaesthetic, pain-dulling, painkilling **12** sleeping pill, stupefacient **13** sleep-inducing, tranquillizer **14** tranquillizing

*Narcotics include:*

**03** ava
**04** bang, benj, coca, dope, kava
**05** bhang, dagga
**06** charas, datura, pituri
**07** churrus, narceen
**08** narceine
**10** belladonna
**11** Indian berry, laurel-water
**15** cocculus indicus

*See also* **drug**

• **packet of narcotic**
**04** deck

**narked**
**05** irked, riled, vexed **06** bugged, galled, miffed, peeved, piqued **07** annoyed, in a huff, nettled **08** bothered, in a paddy, provoked **09** irritated **10** brassed off, cheesed off, got the hump **11** exasperated

**narrate**
◇ *homophone indicator*
**04** read, tell **05** state **06** detail, recite, record, relate, report, set out, unfold **07** explain, portray, recount **08** describe, rehearse, set forth **09** chronicle

**narration**
**04** tale **05** story **06** detail, report, sketch **07** account, history, reading, recital, telling **09** chronicle, portrayal, recountal, rehearsal, statement, voice-over **11** description, explanation **12** storytelling

**narrative**
**04** saga, tale **05** fable, novel, prose, récit, story **06** detail, report, sketch **07** account, history, process, reading, romance **08** allegory, anecdote, periplus, relation **09** chronicle, portrayal, statement **10** short story **11** description

**narrator**
**06** author, writer **07** relater, relator, sagaman **08** annalist, reporter **09** describer, raconteur, recounter **10** anecdotist, chronicler, tale-teller **11** commentator, storyteller **12** mythographer

**narrow**
**03** set **04** fine, keen, slim, thin, true **05** close, cramp, exact, limit, petty, rigid, scant, small, spare, taper, tight **06** biased, meagre, reduce, strait, strict **07** bigoted, confine, cramped, insular, limited, literal, precise, slender, tighten **08** confined, contract, detailed, diminish, dogmatic, exiguous, original, restrict, simplify, squeezed, straiten, tapering, thorough **09** attenuate, coarctate, constrict, hidebound, illiberal **10** attenuated, contracted, intolerant, prejudiced, restricted **11** close-minded, constricted, incapacious, reactionary, small-minded, strait-laced **12** circumscribe, conservative, incommodious, narrow-minded, parsimonious **13** circumscribed, dyed-in-the-wool

**narrowing**
**06** intake **08** stenosis, tapering, thinning **09** gathering, reduction, reductive **10** emaciation, rebatement **11** attenuation, compression, contraction, curtailment **12** constipation, constriction

**narrowly**
**04** fine, just, near **06** barely, strait **07** closely, exactly **08** only just, scarcely, straitly, strictly **09** carefully, precisely **10** by a whisker **11** attentively **12** by a short head **13** painstakingly **14** scrutinizingly

**narrow-minded**
**03** set **05** borné, petty, rigid **06** biased, warped **07** bigoted, diehard, insular, redneck, twisted **08** blimpish, verkramp **09** claustral, exclusive, hidebound, illiberal, jaundiced, parochial **10** entrenched, inflexible, intolerant, prejudiced, provincial **11** close-minded, opinionated, petty-minded, reactionary, small-minded, strait-laced **12** conservative, unreasonable **13** dyed in the wool

**narrow-mindedness**
**04** bias **07** bigotry **08** rigidity **09** prejudice **12** parochialism **13** exclusiveness, inflexibility **15** close-mindedness, petty-mindedness, small-mindedness

**narrowness**
**04** bias **07** bigotry **08** nearness, rigidity, thinness **09** closeness, pettiness, prejudice, tightness **10** insularity, limitation, meagreness **11** attenuation, intolerance, slenderness **12** conservatism, constriction, parochialism **13** exclusiveness, provincialism **14** restrictedness **15** small-mindedness

**narrows**
**05** sound **07** channel, passage, straits **08** waterway

**nascent**
**05** young **06** rising **07** budding, growing **08** evolving, naissant **09** advancing, beginning, embryonic, incipient **10** burgeoning, developing

**nastily**
◇ *anagram indicator*
**11** obnoxiously, offensively, repulsively **12** disagreeably, disgustingly, unpleasantly **13** objectionably

**nastiness**
**04** porn **05** filth, spite **06** malice **07** squalor **08** foulness, impurity, meanness **09** dirtiness, indecency, obscenity, pollution **10** defilement, filthiness, smuttiness **11** malevolence, pornography, viciousness **12** horribleness, spitefulness **13** offensiveness, repulsiveness, uncleanliness, unsavouriness **14** unpleasantness

**nasty**
◇ *anagram indicator*
**03** wet **04** blue, foul, good, mean, rank, sore, vile, wild **05** awful, crook, cruel, dirty, dodgy, foggy, grave, mucky, rainy, ribby, rough, yucky **06** filthy, grotty, horrid, lovely, odious, ribald, smutty, stormy, tricky, unkind **07** awkward, hateful, noisome, obscene, serious, squalid, vicious **08** alarming, annoying, critical, delicate, horrible, indecent, nauseous, polluted, spiteful, ticklish, worrying **09** dangerous, difficult, loathsome, malicious, obnoxious, offensive, repellent,

repugnant, repulsive, revolting, sickening **10** disgusting, ill-natured, malevolent, malodorous, unpleasant **11** bad-tempered, disquieting, distasteful, threatening **12** disagreeable, exasperating, pornographic **13** objectionable

**nation**
**04** folk, land, race, volk **05** realm, state, tribe **06** people, public, vassal **07** country, kingdom, society **08** republic **09** community **10** population

*See also* **Africa**; **America**; **Asia**; **country**; **Europe**

**national**
**01** N **03** Nat **05** civic, civil, state **06** native, public, social **07** citizen, federal, general, subject **08** domestic, internal, resident **10** inhabitant, nationwide, widespread **11** countrywide **12** governmental **13** comprehensive

*See also* **park**

**nationalism**
**07** loyalty **08** jingoism **10** allegiance, chauvinism, patriotism, xenophobia

**nationalist**
**01** N **03** Nat **07** patriot **08** jingoist, loyalist **09** flag-waver, xenophobe **10** chauvinist

**nationalistic**
**05** loyal **09** patriotic **10** jingoistic, xenophobic **12** chauvinistic **13** ethnocentrist

**nationality**
**04** clan, race **05** birth, tribe **06** nation **11** citizenship, ethnic group

*Nationalities include:*

**03** Lao
**04** Kiwi, Thai
**05** Bajan, Congo, Cuban, Czech, Dutch, Greek, Iraqi, Irish, Omani, Saudi, Swazi, Swiss, Tajik, Uzbek, Welsh
**06** Afghan, Danish, Fijian, French, German, Indian, Kenyan, Kyrgyz, Libyan, Malian, Polish, Qatari, Samoan, Somali, Syrian, Tongan, Yapese, Yemeni
**07** Angolan, Basotho, Belgian, Bosnian, British, Burmese, Chadian, Chilean, Chinese, Comoran, Cypriot, Emirati, English, Finnish, Gambian, Guinean, Haitian, Iranian, Israeli, Italian, Ivorian, Kosraen, Kuwaiti, Laotian, Latvian, Maltese, Mexican, Monacan, Mosotho, Nauruan, Palauan, Russian, Rwandan, Sahrawi, Serbian, Spanish, Swedish, Tadzhik, Turkish, Turkmen, Ugandan, Zambian
**08** Albanian, Algerian, American, Andorran, Antiguan, Armenian, Austrian, Bahamian, Bahraini, Barbudan, Batswana, Belizean, Beninese, Bolivian, Bruneian, Canadian, Chuukese, Croatian, Egyptian, Eritrean, Estonian, Filipina, Filipino, Gabonese, Georgian, Ghanaian, Grenadan, Guyanese, Honduran, Jamaican, Japanese, Lebanese, Liberian, Malagasy, Malawian, Moldovan, Moroccan, Motswana, Namibian, Nepalese, Nevisian, Nigerian, Nigerien, Peruvian, Romanian, Sahraoui, Scottish, St Lucian, Sudanese, Timorese, Togolese, Tunisian, Tuvaluan
**09** Argentine, Barbadian, Bhutanese, Brazilian, Bulgarian, Burkinabé, Burundian, Cambodian, Colombian, Congolese, Dominican, Ethiopian, Grenadian, Hungarian, Icelandic, I-Kiribati, Jordanian, Kittitian, Malaysian, Maldivian, Mauritian, Mongolian, Ni-Vanuatu, Norwegian, Pakistani, Pohnpeian, Sahrawian, Santoméan, São Toméan, Singapore, Slovakian, Slovenian, Sri Lankan, Taiwanese, Tanzanian, Ukrainian, Uruguayan
**10** Australian, Belarusian, Costa Rican, Djiboutian, Ecuadorean, Ecuadorian, Guatemalan, Indonesian, Lithuanian, Luxembourg, Macedonian, Monégasque, Mozambican, Myanmarese, New Zealand, Nicaraguan, Panamanian, Paraguayan, Philippine, Portuguese, Sahraouian, Salvadoran, Senegalese, Surinamese, Tobagonian, Venezuelan, Vietnamese, Vincentian, Zimbabwean
**11** Argentinian, Azerbaijani, Bangladeshi, Cameroonian, Cape Verdean, Kazakhstani, Marshallese, Mauritanian, Micronesian, Montenegrin, North Korean, Sammarinese, Seychellois, Singaporean, South Korean, Tajikistani, Trinidadian
**12** Luxembourger, Saudi Arabian, South African, St Vincentian
**13** Equatoguinean, Herzegovinian, Liechtenstein, Sierra Leonean
**14** Central African, Guinea-Bissauan
**15** Liechtensteiner, Papua New Guinean, Solomon Islander

**nationally**
**09** generally **10** nationwide **11** countrywide **15** comprehensively

**National Trust**
**02** NT

**nationwide**
**05** state **07** general, overall **08** national **09** extensive **10** widespread **11** countrywide **12** coast-to-coast **13** comprehensive

**native**
**03** nat, son **04** home **05** local, natal **06** inborn, inbred, innate, mother, oyster **07** built-in, citizen, connate, dweller, genuine, natural **08** domestic, home-born, home-bred, indigene, inherent, national, original, resident **09** aborigine, home-grown, ingrained, inherited, intrinsic, intuitive **10** aboriginal, autochthon, congenital, hereditary, indigenous, inhabitant, vernacular **11** instinctive **13** autochthonous, tangata whenua **15** unsophisticated

*See also* **African**; **American**; **Asian**; **European**

**nativity**
**04** putz **05** birth **06** jataka **08** delivery **09** horoscope **10** childbirth **11** parturition

**NATO**

*NATO members:*

**02** UK
**03** USA
**05** Italy, Spain
**06** Canada, France, Greece, Latvia, Norway, Poland, Turkey
**07** Belgium, Denmark, Estonia, Germany, Hungary, Iceland, Romania
**08** Bulgaria, Portugal, Slovakia, Slovenia
**09** Lithuania
**10** Luxembourg
**13** Czech Republic, United Kingdom
**14** The Netherlands
**21** United States of America

• **NATO phonetic alphabet** *see* **alphabet**

**natron**
**04** urao

**natter**
**03** gab, jaw **04** chat, talk **06** confab, gabble, gossip, jabber, rabbit, witter **07** blather, blether, chatter, chinwag, prattle **08** chit-chat, rabbit on **10** chew the fat **11** confabulate **12** conversation **14** shoot the breeze

**nattily**
**06** neatly **07** smartly **09** elegantly, stylishly **11** fashionably

**natty**
**04** chic, deft, neat, trim **05** ritzy, smart **06** clever, dapper, snazzy, spruce, swanky **07** elegant, stylish, varment, varmint **09** ingenious **11** fashionable, well-dressed

**natural**
**03** nat, raw **04** open, pure, real **05** frank, idiot, plain, usual, whole **06** candid, common, inborn, inbred, innate, kindly, native, normal, physic, simple, virgin **07** artless, built-in, connate, genuine, organic, regular, relaxed, routine, sincere, typical, unmixed **08** everyday, inherent, lifelike, ordinary, standard, unforced **09** authentic, certainty, guileless, ingenuous, ingrained, inherited, intuitive, unrefined, unstudied **10** congenital, indigenous, unaffected, unlaboured, unstrained **11** instinctive, spontaneous, unprocessed **12** additive-free, chemical-free, illegitimate, run-of-the-mill,

unregenerate **13** unpretentious **15** unsophisticated

*See also* **fool**

**• natural order**

**02** NO

**naturalist**

**08** botanist **09** biologist, Darwinist, ecologist, zoologist **11** creationist **12** evolutionist **13** life scientist **14** plant scientist

*See also* **biology**

**naturalistic**

**07** factual, graphic, natural **08** lifelike, real-life **09** realistic **10** true-to-life **12** photographic

**naturalize**

**05** adapt, adopt **06** accept **08** accustom **09** acclimate, endenizen, habituate, introduce **10** assimilate **11** acclimatize, acculturate, domesticate, enfranchise, familiarize, incorporate, nationalize

**naturally**

**05** natch **06** simply **07** clearly, frankly **08** candidly, normally, of course **09** artlessly, certainly, genuinely, logically, obviously, sincerely, typically **10** absolutely **11** ingenuously, simpliciter **13** instinctively, spontaneously

**naturalness**

**04** ease **06** purity **07** realism **08** openness, pureness **09** frankness, plainness, sincerity, wholeness **10** candidness, simpleness, simplicity **11** artlessness, genuineness, informality, spontaneity **13** ingenuousness **14** unaffectedness **15** spontaneousness

**nature**

**04** Gaia, kind, mood, sort, type **05** being, class, earth, stamp, style, world **06** cosmos, humour, make-up, temper **07** country, essence, outlook, quality, scenery, species, variety **08** category, creation, features, identity, universe **09** character, chemistry, landscape, nakedness **10** attributes, complexion, kindliness **11** countryside, description, disposition, environment, mother earth, personality, temperament **12** constitution, mother nature **14** characteristic, natural history **15** characteristics

**• according to nature**

**02** sn

**• of nature**

**04** akin

**naught**

**01** O **03** bad, ill, nil **04** evil, nowt, zero **05** zilch **06** cipher, cypher, foiled, nought, ruined **07** hurtful, immoral, nothing, sweet FA **09** worthless **10** wickedness **11** nothingness **15** sweet Fanny Adams

**naughtily**

**06** lewdly **07** bawdily **08** coarsely, vulgarly **09** defiantly, obscenely, playfully, waywardly **10** indecently, perversely **12** badly behaved **13** disobediently, mischievously

**naughtiness**

**08** defiance, lewdness, mischief **09** bawdiness, indecency, obscenity, vulgarity **10** coarseness, smuttiness **11** playfulness, waywardness **12** bad behaviour, disobedience, misbehaviour

**naughty**

◇ *anagram indicator*

**03** bad **04** blue, bold, lewd **05** bawdy **06** coarse, ribald, risqué, smutty, unruly, vulgar, wicked **07** defiant, obscene, playful, roguish, wayward **08** indecent, perverse **09** off-colour, worthless **10** refractory **11** disobedient, misbehaving, mischievous, titillating **12** badly behaved, exasperating, incorrigible **13** undisciplined

**Nauru**

**03** NAU, NRU

**nausea**

**06** hatred, puking, wamble **07** disgust, gagging **08** aversion, distaste, loathing, retching, sickness, vomiting **09** revulsion **10** queasiness, repugnance, throwing up **11** airsickness, biliousness, carsickness, detestation, seasickness **12** sick headache **14** motion sickness, travel sickness **15** morning sickness

**nauseate**

**04** turn **05** repel **06** loathe, offend, revolt, sicken **07** disgust, scunner, turn off **08** gross out, make sick **14** turn the stomach **15** turn your stomach

**nauseating**

**06** odious **08** nauseous **09** abhorrent, loathsome, offensive, repellent, repugnant, repulsive, revolting, sickening **10** chunderous, detestable, disgusting **11** distasteful **14** stomach-turning **15** stomach-churning

**nauseous**

**03** ill **04** puky, sick **05** nasty, pukey **06** queasy **07** airsick, carsick, seasick **09** loathsome, nauseated **10** disgusting, travel sick **14** about to throw up **15** under the weather

**nautical**

**05** naval **07** boating, oceanic, sailing **08** maritime, seagoing, yachting **09** seafaring

**naval**

**03** nav, sea **06** marine **08** maritime, nautical, seagoing **09** seafaring

**navel**

**03** hub **06** centre, middle **07** nombril **08** omphalos **09** umbilicus **11** belly-button, tummy-button

**navigable**

**03** nav **04** open **05** clear **08** passable, sailable **09** crossable, dirigible, unblocked **10** negotiable, voyageable **11** traversable **12** surmountable, unobstructed

**navigate**

**04** helm, plan, plot, sail **05** cross, drive, guide, pilot, steer **06** cruise, direct, handle, voyage **07** journey, skipper **09** manoeuvre, negotiate **11** plan a course

**navigation**

**03** nav **05** canal **06** voyage **07** guiding, nautics, sailing **08** cruising, guidance, pilotage, piloting, seacraft, steering, voyaging **09** directing, direction **10** seamanship **11** manoeuvring **12** helmsmanship **13** contact flight

*Navigational aids and systems include:*

**03** gee, GPS, INS, log, Vor
**05** chart, loran, pilot, radar
**07** compass, navarho, sextant
**08** bell buoy, dividers, VHF radio
**09** lightship, omnirange
**10** depth gauge, lighthouse, marker buoy
**11** chronometer, conical buoy, echo-sounder, gyrocompass
**13** nautical table, parallel ruler
**15** astronavigation, flux-gate compass, magnetic compass

**navigator**

**03** nav **05** navvy, pilot **06** master, sailor, seaman **07** mariner **08** helmsman **09** steersman

**navvy**

**06** digger, ganger, worker **07** workman **08** labourer **09** navigator **12** manual worker **14** common labourer

**navy**

**01** N **02** RN **03** RAN **05** fleet, ships **06** armada **08** flotilla, warships **10** naval fleet, naval force **12** merchant navy **15** merchant service

*See also* **rank**

**nay**

**02** no **03** nae **06** denial, indeed, in fact **07** in truth **08** actually, not at all, or rather **09** not really **11** of course not **12** certainly not **13** absolutely not, in point of fact

**near**

**02** by, nr, ny, to **03** nie, nye **04** akin, come, dear, inby, left, like, nigh **05** alike, close, ewest, forby, handy, inbye, local **06** almost, at hand, beside, come by, coming, nearby, nearly, next to, stingy **07** cling to, close by, closely, close to, looming, related, similar **08** adjacent, approach, familiar, imminent, intimate, left-hand, narrowly **09** adjoining, alongside, bordering, close in on, immediate, impending, proximate, thriftily **10** accessible, adjacent to, close-range, come closer, come nearer, comparable, contiguous, convenient, draw near to, not far away **11** approaching, bordering on, come towards, forthcoming, get closer to, in the offing, move towards, surrounding, within cooee, within range, within reach **12** contiguous to, draw nearer to, neighbouring, parsimonious

13 corresponding, within reach of 14 advance towards, closely related, parsimoniously 15 at close quarters

**• draw near**

04 come

**• near thing**

08 near miss 09 close call 10 close shave 11 nasty moment 12 narrow escape, narrow squeak

**nearby**

04 near 05 close, handy 06 beside 07 close by 08 adjacent 09 adjoining 10 accessible, convenient, not far away 11 close at hand, within cooee, within reach 12 neighbouring 13 in the vicinity 14 on your doorstep 15 at close quarters

**nearly**

◇ *deletion indicator*

◇ *tail deletion indicator*

02 ny 03 e'en, nie, nye 04 even, nigh 05 about, close 06 all but, almost, feckly, nigh on 07 closely, close on, close to, roughly 08 à peu près, as good as, nigh-hand, well-nigh 09 just about, verging on, virtually 10 intimately, more or less 11 practically 13 approximately 14 parsimoniously, scrutinizingly 15 close but no cigar

**nearness**

06 degree 08 affinity, dearness, intimacy, vicinity 09 closeness, handiness, immediacy, imminence, proximity 10 chumminess, contiguity 11 familiarity, propinquity 12 availability, neighborhood 13 accessibility, appropinquity, neighbourhood

**near-sighted**

06 myopic 08 purblind 09 half-blind 12 short-sighted

**neat**

02 ox 03 apt, cow, net 04 bull, cool, deft, dink, feat, good, mega, nett, nice, oxen, pure, smug, snod, tidy, tosh, trig, trim 05 clean, clear, crisp, dinky, genty, great, handy, jemmy, jimpy, natty, nifty, short, slick, smart, super, tight 06 adroit, cattle, clever, dainty, dapper, donsie, expert, nimble, pretty, simple, spruce, superb, wicked 07 band-box, cleanly, compact, elegant, featous, ordered, orderly, shining, skilful, unmixed 08 clean-cut, fabulous, feateous, featuous, finished, sensible, smashing, straight, terrific, well-made 09 admirable, dexterous, effective, efficient, excellent, fantastic, ingenious, organized, practised, shipshape, undiluted, wonderful 10 convenient, marvellous, tremendous 11 well-groomed, well-ordered 12 spick-and-span, undiminished, user-friendly, well-designed 13 unadulterated, well-organized 15 in apple-pie order

**neaten**

◇ *anagram indicator*

04 edge, prim, tidy, trim 05 clean, groom 06 tidy up 07 arrange, clean up, smarten 08 round off, spruce up 09 smarten up 10 square away, straighten 11 put to rights

**neatly**

04 jimp 05 aptly 06 deftly, fairly, featly, jimply, nicely, nimbly, tidily 07 adeptly, agilely, handily, smartly 08 adroitly, cleverly, daintily, expertly, prettily, sprucely 09 elegantly, precisely, skilfully, stylishly 10 accurately, feateously, gracefully 11 dexterously, efficiently 12 conveniently, effortlessly, methodically 14 systematically

**neatness**

05 grace, skill, style 06 nicety 07 agility, aptness 08 accuracy, deftness, elegance, niceness, tidiness, trimness 09 adeptness, dexterity, handiness, jemminess, precision, smartness 10 adroitness, cleverness, daintiness, efficiency, expertness, nimbleness, spruceness 11 orderliness, preciseness, skilfulness, stylishness 12 gracefulness, straightness 14 methodicalness

**Nebraska**

02 NE 04 Nebr

**nebulous**

03 dim 04 hazy 05 fuzzy, misty, vague 06 cloudy 07 obscure, shadowy, unclear 08 abstract, confused, formless, unformed 09 ambiguous, amorphous, imprecise, shapeless, uncertain 10 indefinite, indistinct 13 indeterminate

**necessarily**

04 thus 06 needly 08 no remedy, obligate, of course, perforce 09 certainly, naturally, therefore 10 inevitably, inexorably, willy-nilly 11 accordingly, ineluctably, inescapably, of necessity, unavoidably 12 by definition, compulsorily, consequently, nolens volens 13 automatically, axiomatically, indispensably

**necessary**

04 sure 05 money, needy, vital 06 needed, toilet 07 certain, crucial, needful 08 enforced, required 09 de rigueur, essential, mandatory, requisite 10 compulsory, imperative, inevitable, inexorable, obligatory 11 ineluctable, inescapable, predestined, unavoidable 13 indispensable

**necessitate**

04 mean, need, take 05 exact, force 06 compel, demand, entail, oblige 07 call for, involve, require 09 constrain 13 make necessary

**necessity**

04 fate, must, need, want 06 ananke, demand, mister, need-be, penury 07 destiny, poverty 08 exigence, exigency, extremes, hardship 09 certainty, emergency, essential, indigence, privation, requisite 10 compulsion, obligation, sine qua non 11 deprivation, desideratum, destitution, fundamental, needfulness, requirement 12 prerequisite 13 indispensable, inevitability, inexorability 14 inescapability

**• of necessity**

05 needs 08 no remedy, perforce 09 certainly 10 inevitably, inexorably 11 inescapably, unavoidably 12 by definition, compulsorily 13 automatically, indispensably

**neck**

03 col, pet 04 crag, kiss, nape, snog 05 drink, halse, hause, hawse, scrag 06 caress, cervix, scruff, smooch 08 audacity, canoodle 09 impudence

**• neck and neck**

04 even 05 drawn, equal, level 06 on a par 07 aligned, uniform 08 balanced, matching 10 nip and tuck, side by side 12 level pegging

**necklace**

04 band, torc 05 beads, chain 06 choker, corals, gorget, jewels, locket, pearls, string, torque 07 negligé, pendant, rivière, sautoir 08 carcanet, negligee 10 lavallière 11 mangalsutra

**necromancer**

05 witch 06 wizard 07 diviner, warlock 08 conjurer, magician, sorcerer 09 sorceress, spiritist 11 thaumaturge 12 spiritualist 13 thaumaturgist

**necromancy**

05 magic 06 hoodoo, voodoo 07 sorcery 08 black art, witchery, wizardry 09 spiritism 10 black magic, demonology, divination, nigromancy, witchcraft 11 conjuration, enchantment, thaumaturgy 12 spiritualism 13 magical powers, wonder-working

**necropolis**

08 cemetery, God's acre 09 graveyard 10 burial site, churchyard 11 burial place 12 burial ground, charnel house

**need**

04 call, lack, miss, must, want, wish 05 crave 06 besoin, demand, desire, egence, egency, have to, mister, rely on 07 call for, pine for, poverty, require 08 depend on, exigency, occasion, shortage, yearn for 09 cry out for, essential, necessity, neediness, requisite 10 have need of, inadequacy, obligation 11 be obliged to, be reliant on, desideratum, necessitate, requirement 12 prerequisite 13 be compelled to, be dependent on, insufficiency, justification 14 be desperate for 15 have occasion for

**• in need**

04 poor 05 needy 06 hard up 08 deprived, dirt-poor, indigent 09 destitute, penniless, penurious 11 impecunious 12 impoverished 13 disadvantaged 14 on the breadline 15 poverty-stricken, underprivileged

**needed**
**06** wanted **07** desired, lacking **08** required **09** called for, essential, necessary, requisite **10** compulsory, obligatory

**needful**
**05** needy, vital **06** needed **08** required **09** essential, necessary, requisite **10** stipulated **13** indispensable

**needle**
**03** bug, irk, nag, nib, pin, sew **04** bait, barb, gall, goad, hand, hype, hypo, miff, nark, prod, rile, spud, spur **05** annoy, arrow, briar, get at, point, prick, quill, sharp, spike, spine, sting, taunt, thorn **06** bodkin, darner, enmity, harass, heckle, marker, nettle, niggle, pester, pierce, ruffle, stylus, thread, wind up **07** bramble, bristle, dislike, obelisk, pointer, prickle, provoke, spicule, syringe, torment **08** drive mad, dry-point, irritate, splinter **09** aggravate, indicator, penetrate **10** drive crazy **11** microneedle **12** drive bananas **13** darning-needle, make sparks fly, packing-needle **14** drive up the wall, knitting needle

**needless**
**06** luxury **07** useless **08** unwanted **09** pointless, redundant, undesired **10** expendable, gratuitous **11** dispensable, purposeless, superfluous, uncalled-for, unnecessary

• **needless to say**
**06** surely **07** no doubt **08** of course **09** certainly, naturally **10** by all means, definitely **11** doubtlessly, indubitably, undoubtedly **13** without a doubt

**needlessly**
**09** uselessly **11** dispensably, pointlessly, redundantly **13** superfluously, unnecessarily

**needlework**
**06** sewing **07** tatting **08** tapestry, woolwork **09** drawn work, fancywork, hemstitch, patchwork, piqué work, plainwork, stitching, white seam **10** crocheting, embroidery **11** cross-stitch, needlepoint, seamstressy, stitchcraft, worsted-work **12** saddle stitch

**needy**
**04** poor **06** hard up, in need, strait **07** needful, wanting **08** deprived, dirt-poor, indigent **09** destitute, necessary, penniless, penurious **11** impecunious **12** impoverished **13** disadvantaged **14** on the breadline **15** poverty-stricken, underprivileged

**ne'er-do-well**
**04** spiv **05** idler **06** dodger, dosser, loafer, skelum, skiver, waster **07** bludger, goof-off, lounger, shirker, skellum, slacker, wastrel **08** layabout, schellum **09** do-nothing **10** black sheep **14** good-for-nothing

**nefarious**
**04** base, evil, foul, vile **06** odious, sinful, unholy, wicked **07** heinous, satanic, vicious **08** criminal, depraved, dreadful, horrible, infamous, infernal, shameful, terrible **09** atrocious, execrable, loathsome, monstrous **10** abominable, detestable, horrendous, iniquitous, outrageous, villainous **11** opprobrious

**negate**
**04** deny, undo, void **05** annul, quash **06** cancel, oppose, refute, reject, repeal, revoke, squash **07** explode, gainsay, nullify, rescind, retract, reverse, wipe out **08** abrogate, disprove, renounce **09** discredit, repudiate **10** contradict, invalidate, neutralize **11** countermand

**negation**
**04** veto **06** denial, repeal **07** inverse, reverse **08** contrary, converse, opposite **09** disavowal, rejection **10** abrogation, antithesis, disclaimer **12** cancellation, renunciation **13** contradiction, nullification **14** countermanding, neutralization

**negative**
**03** bad, neg **04** acid, deny, veto, weak **05** minus **06** denial, gloomy **07** adverse, counter, cynical, denying, harmful, hostile, hurtful, opposed, refusal, unlucky **08** contrary, critical, opposing, opposite, refusing, saying no **09** annulling, defeatist, injurious, rejection, spineless, unhelpful, unwilling **10** censorious, dissension, dissenting, gainsaying, neutralize, nullifying, unfriendly **11** conflicting, destructive, detrimental, obstructive, pessimistic, subtractive, uncongenial, unfortunate **12** antagonistic, inauspicious, invalidating, neutralizing, unfavourable, uninterested, unpropitious **13** contradiction, laevorotatory, unco-operative **14** unconstructive, unenthusiastic **15** disadvantageous

**negativity**
**08** cynicism **09** defeatism, pessimism **10** gloominess **12** criticalness **13** unhelpfulness, unwillingness **14** lack of interest

**neglect**
◇ *anagram indicator*
**04** fail, omit **05** abuse, scorn, shirk, skimp, spurn **06** disuse, fail in, forget, ignore, laxity, pass by, pass up, pigeon, rebuff, slight **07** abandon, default, disdain, disobey, failure, forsake **08** ignoring, incivism, infringe, leave out, let slide, omission, overlook, spurning **09** desuetude, disregard, disrepair, mislippen, oversight, slackness **10** be lax about, culpa levis, disrespect, leave alone, misprision, negligence, remissness **11** inattention, rack and ruin, shortcoming **12** carelessness, heedlessness, indifference **13** forgetfulness **14** non-performance

**neglected**
◇ *anagram indicator*
**04** waif **07** forlorn, run-down, squalid **08** derelict, deserted, forsaken, stranded, unheeded, untended, untilled, unweeded **09** abandoned, overgrown **10** uncared-for **11** dilapidated, disregarded, undervalued, unhusbanded **12** uncultivated, unmaintained **13** unappreciated

**neglectful**
**03** lax **06** remiss, sloppy **08** careless, derelict, heedless, uncaring **09** forgetful, negligent, oblivious, slighting, unmindful **11** inattentive, indifferent, thoughtless **12** disregardful

**négligé dress**
**03** mob

**negligence**
◇ *anagram indicator*
**06** laches, laxity, slight **07** default, failure, neglect **08** omission **09** culpa lata, disregard, oversight, slackness **10** remissness, sloppiness **11** inattention, shortcoming **12** carelessness, heedlessness, inadvertence, inadvertency, indifference **13** forgetfulness **15** inattentiveness, thoughtlessness

**negligent**
◇ *anagram indicator*
**03** lax **05** slack **06** casual, remiss, sloppy **07** cursory, offhand **08** careless, dilatory, heedless, uncaring **09** forgetful, unmindful **10** neglectful, neglecting, nonchalant **11** inattentive, indifferent, thoughtless

**negligible**
**04** tiny **05** minor, petty, small **06** minute, paltry **07** minimal, trivial **08** trifling **09** off the map **11** neglectable, unimportant **13** imperceptible, inappreciable, insignificant

**negotiable**
**03** neg **04** open **05** clear **08** arguable, passable **09** crossable, debatable, navigable, unblocked, undecided, unsettled **11** contestable, traversable **12** questionable, surmountable, unobstructed **14** open to question

**negotiate**
◇ *anagram indicator*
**04** deal, pass, talk **05** agree, broke, clear, cross, float, treat **06** broker, confer, debate, fulfil, haggle, manage, parley, settle **07** arrange, bargain, consult, discuss, execute, mediate, pull off, resolve, traffic, work out **08** complete, conclude, contract, get round, pass over, surmount, transact, traverse **09** arbitrate, hammer out, intercede, intervene, thrash out **11** pass through **12** wheel and deal

**negotiation**
◇ *anagram indicator*
**05** talks, treat **06** debate, parley, treaty **08** haggling, practice **09** diplomacy, mediation, parleying **10** bargaining,

conference, discussion, pulling-off
**11** arbitration, transaction
**12** hammering-out, thrashing-out

**negotiator**
**06** broker **07** haggler **08** diplomat, mediator, parleyer **09** bargainer, go-between, moderator **10** ambassador, arbitrator **11** adjudicator, intercessor
**12** intermediary **13** wheeler-dealer

**neigh**
**04** bray **05** hinny **06** nicher, nicker, whinny **07** snicker, whicker

**neighbour**
**03** bor **04** abut

**neighbourhood**
**04** area, hood, part **06** locale, region
**07** quarter **08** confines, district, environs, locality, precinct, presence, purlieus, vicinage, vicinity
**09** community, proximity, voisinage
**11** convicinity **12** surroundings
• **in the neighbourhood of**
**04** near, up to **05** about, round
**06** almost, around, nearby, next to
**07** close to, roughly **13** approximately

**neighbouring**
**04** near, next **05** local **06** nearby
**07** nearest, vicinal **08** abutting, adjacent, next-door **09** adjoining, bordering, sistering **10** connecting, contiguous, near at hand **11** close at hand, surrounding

**neighbourly**
**04** kind, warm **06** genial, social
**07** affable, amiable, cordial, helpful
**08** friendly, generous, obliging, sociable **10** hospitable **11** considerate
**13** companionable

**nemesis**
**04** fate, ruin **07** destiny **08** downfall
**09** vengeance **10** punishment
**11** destruction, retribution **14** just punishment

**neodymium**
**02** Nd

**neologism**
**07** coinage, new term, new word, novelty **09** new phrase, vogue word
**10** innovation **13** new expression

**neon**
**02** Ne

**neophyte**
**01** L **04** tiro **06** newbie, novice, rookie
**07** learner, recruit, trainee **08** beginner, newcomer **09** greenhorn, new member, noviciate, novitiate
**10** apprentice, raw recruit
**11** probationer

**Nepal**
**03** NEP, NPL

**nephrite**
**02** yu

**nepotism**
**04** bias **10** partiality **11** favouritism
**12** old school tie **13** Old Boy network
**14** jobs for the boys

**Neptune**
**08** Poseidon

**neptunium**
**02** Np

**nerd** *see* **fool**

**nerk** *see* **fool**

**nerve**
**03** lip **04** face, gall, grit, guts, neck, will
**05** brace, cheek, force, mouth, pluck, sauce, sinew, spunk, steel **06** bottle, daring, mettle, spirit, valour, vigour
**07** bolster, bravery, courage, fortify, hearten, prepare **08** audacity, boldness, chutzpah, embolden, firmness, strength, temerity
**09** bowstring, brass neck, encourage, endurance, fortitude, hardihood, impudence, insolence **10** brazenness, effrontery, invigorate, resolution, strengthen **11** intrepidity, presumption
**12** fearlessness, impertinence
**13** determination, steadfastness
**14** cool-headedness, self-confidence

*Nerves include:*

**05** optic, ulnar, vagus
**06** facial, lumbar, medial, median, radial, sacral, tibial
**07** femoral, phrenic, plantar, sciatic
**08** axillary, brachial, peroneal, thoracic
**09** cutaneous, laryngeal, occipital, olfactory
**10** splanchnic, trigeminal
**11** intercostal
**12** suboccipital
**15** lesser occipital, spinal accessory

**nerveless**
**04** calm, weak **05** inert, slack, timid
**06** afraid, feeble, flabby **07** nervous
**08** cowardly, unnerved **09** enervated, spineless **11** debilitated

**nerve-racking**
**05** tense **06** trying **07** anxious
**08** worrying **09** difficult, harrowing, maddening, stressful **10** nail-biting
**11** disquieting, distressing, frightening

**nerves**
**05** shock, worry **06** strain, stress, wobbly **07** anxiety, jitters, tension, twitter, willies **11** butterflies, fretfulness, nervousness
**12** collywobbles, crise de nerfs
**13** heebie-jeebies **14** nervous tension
• **get on someone's nerves**
**03** bug, irk, nag, vex **04** fash, gall, rile
**05** anger, annoy, tease **06** bother, harass, hassle, madden, molest, pester, plague, ruffle, wind up **07** disturb, hack off, provoke, tick off, trouble **08** brass off, irritate **09** aggravate, cheese off, displease, drive nuts **10** drive crazy, exasperate **12** drive bananas **13** make sparks fly **14** drive up the wall **15** get someone's goat, get your dander up

**nervous**
◇ *anagram indicator*
**03** shy **04** edgy, toey **05** het up, jumpy, nappy, nervy, shaky, tense, timid **06** on edge, sinewy, strong, uneasy
**07** anxious, fearful, fidgety, fretful, in a stew, jittery, keyed up, quaking, twitchy, uptight, worried, wound up
**08** agitated, in a sweat, in a tizzy, neurotic, skittish, strained, timorous, vigorous **09** excitable, flustered, perturbed, screwed-up, squirrely, tremulous **10** disquieted, squirrelly
**11** overwrought **12** all of a dither, apprehensive, highly-strung **13** having kittens, on tenterhooks

**nervous breakdown**
**06** crisis **08** neurosis **10** cracking-up, depression **11** melancholia **15** mental breakdown, nervous disorder

**nervously**
◇ *anagram indicator*
**06** edgily, on edge **07** in a stew, timidly
**08** in a sweat, in a tizzy, uneasily
**09** anxiously, fearfully, fretfully, twitchily **13** having kittens
**14** apprehensively

**nervousness**
**05** worry **06** strain, stress **07** anxiety, fluster, habdabs, tension, willies
**08** disquiet, edginess, timidity
**09** agitation **10** touchiness, uneasiness
**11** stage fright **12** excitability, perturbation, restlessness, timorousness **13** heebie-jeebies, tremulousness

**nervy**
**04** cool, edgy, high **05** het up, jumpy, shaky, tense **06** on edge, uneasy
**07** anxious, fearful, fidgety, jittery, keyed up, twitchy, uptight, worried, wound up **08** agitated, impudent, neurotic, strained **09** audacious, excitable, flustered **12** apprehensive, highly-strung **13** having kittens

**nescient**
**05** dense, thick **06** stupid, unread
**07** unaware **08** backward, clueless, ignorant, untaught **09** unlearned, untrained, unwitting **10** illiterate, innumerate, uneducated, unfamiliar, uninformed, unschooled **11** ill-informed, uninitiated **12** unacquainted
**13** inexperienced, unenlightened

**ness**
**04** naze
*See also* **headland**

**nest**
**03** den, mew, nid **04** aery, bike, bink, byke, cage, cote, dray, drey, eyry, lair, nide **05** aerie, ayrie, eyrie, haunt, lodge, nidus, perch, roost **06** refuge, settle, wurley **07** cabinet, hideout, retreat, shelter **08** hideaway, hive-nest, vespiary **09** bird-house, formicary, termitary **10** nesting-box
**11** formicarium, hiding-place, termitarium **12** accumulation, nidification **14** breeding-ground
*See also* **animal**

**nest egg**
**04** fund **05** cache, funds, store

**07** deposit, reserve, savings **08** reserves **12** bottom drawer

**nestle**
**06** cuddle, curl up, huddle, nuzzle **07** cherish, snuggle **08** cuddle up **09** snuggle up **14** huddle together

**nestling**
**04** baby **05** chick **08** suckling, weanling **09** fledgling

**net**
◇ *containment indicator*
**03** bag, end, get, let, nab, web **04** caul, drag, earn, gain, lace, leap, make, mesh, neat, nett, nick, pure, sean, take, toil, trap, trim **05** broad, catch, clean, clear, drift, final, raise, seine, snare, toils, total, trawl **06** bright, cobweb, collar, enmesh, lowest, obtain, pocket, pull in, rake in, sagene, tunnel **07** bring in, capture, dragnet, drop-net, ensnare, fishnet, general, lattice, netting, network, overall, realize, receive, tracery, trammel, unmixed, webbing **08** after tax, drift-net, entangle, filigree, meshwork, open work, seine net, take home, take-home, ultimate **09** inclusive, reticulum **10** accumulate, after taxes, conclusive, difficulty **11** latticework, take captive **15** after deductions

**nether**
**03** low **05** basal, below, lower, under **06** bottom **07** beneath, hellish, Stygian **08** inferior, infernal **09** Plutonian **10** lower-level, underworld **11** underground

**Netherlands**
**02** NL **03** NLD **04** Neth

**Netherlands Antilles**
**02** NA **03** ANT

**netherworld**
**03** pit **04** fire, hell **05** abyss, below, Hades, Sheol **06** Erebus, Tophet **07** Abaddon, Acheron, Gehenna, inferno **08** Tartarus **09** down there, Malebolge, perdition **10** other place, underworld **12** lower regions **13** bottomless pit **15** abode of the devil, infernal regions

**nettle**
**03** bug, vex **04** fret, goad, miff, nark, rami, rile **05** annoy, chafe, get at, pique, ramee, ramie, sting, tease, upset **06** harass, hassle, hen-bit, needle, ruffle, urtica, wind up **07** incense, provoke, torment **08** drive mad, irritate **09** aggravate, archangel, pellitory **10** drive crazy, exasperate **12** drive bananas **13** make sparks fly **14** artillery-plant, discountenance, drive up the wall **15** yellow archangel

**nettled**
**05** angry, cross, got at, huffy, riled, stung, vexed **06** bugged, galled, goaded, miffed, narked, peeved, piqued **07** annoyed, needled, rattled, ruffled, wound up **08** harassed, incensed, offended, provoked **09** aggrieved, driven mad, irritable, irritated **10** aggravated **11** driven crazy, exasperated **13** driven bananas **15** driven up the wall

**network**
**03** CNN, LAN, MAN, net, PCN, WAN, web **04** fret, grid, ISDN, lace, maze, mesh, PSTN, rete **05** grill, nexus **06** matrix, plexus, sagene, system, tracks **07** complex, lattice, netting, tracery, webbing **08** channels, filigree, gridiron, meshwork, open work **09** circuitry, grapevine, labyrinth, reticulum, structure **10** Eurovision **11** arrangement, convolution, latticework **12** old school tie, organization, reticulation **13** bush telegraph, Old Boy network

**neurosis**
**05** mania **06** phobia **08** disorder, fixation **09** deviation, obsession **10** affliction **11** abnormality, derangement, disturbance, instability **13** maladjustment **14** mental disorder

**neurotic**
**05** manic **06** phobic **07** anxious, deviant, nervous **08** abnormal, deranged, paranoid, unstable **09** disturbed, obsessive, unhealthy **10** compulsive, hysterical, irrational **11** maladjusted, overanxious, overwrought **14** hypersensitive

**neuter**
**01** n **03** fix, gib **04** geld, neut, spay **05** dress **06** agamic, clonal, doctor, gib-cat **07** agamous, asexual, neutral, sexless **08** caponize, castrate, conidial **09** castrated, sterilize **10** emasculate **11** monogenetic **12** intransitive

**neutral**
**04** drab, dull, fawn, gray, grey, pale **05** beige, bland, white **06** neuter, pastel **07** anaemic, anodyne, insipid **08** detached, ordinary, unbiased **09** anonymous, impartial, objective, undecided **10** colourless, even-handed, indefinite, indistinct, non-aligned, open-minded, uninvolved **11** indifferent, inoffensive, nondescript, non-partisan, unassertive, uncommitted **12** non-combatant, non-committal, unprejudiced, unremarkable **13** disinterested, dispassionate, uninteresting **14** expressionless **15** unexceptionable

**neutrality**
**10** detachment **11** disinterest **12** impartiality, non-alignment, unbiasedness **13** impartialness **14** non-involvement **15** non-intervention

**neutralize**
**04** kill, undo **05** annul **06** cancel, negate, offset **07** balance, nullify **08** negative **09** cancel out, frustrate, make up for **10** counteract, invalidate **12** incapacitate **13** compensate for **14** counterbalance

**Nevada**
**02** NV **03** Nev

**never**
**03** not **04** nary, ne'er **05** no way **07** not ever, Tib's Eve **08** at no time, not at all, Tibb's Eve **09** St Tib's Eve **10** St Tibb's Eve **11** on no account, when pigs fly **13** not for a moment, not on your life **15** not on your nellie

**never-ending**
◇ *tail deletion indicator*
**07** endless, eternal, non-stop **08** constant, infinite, unbroken, unending **09** boundless, incessant, limitless, permanent, perpetual, unceasing **10** continuous, persistent, relentless, unchanging, without end **11** everlasting, unremitting **12** interminable **13** uninterrupted

**nevertheless**
**03** but, tho, yet **05** still **06** algate, anyhow, anyway, at that, even so, howe'er, though, withal **07** algates, however **08** after all **09** in any case, quand même **10** all the same, by any means, for all that, in any event, malgré tout, not but what, regardless, still and on, tout de même **11** by some means, just the same, none but what, nonetheless, still and all **13** at the same time **15** notwithstanding

**new**
◇ *anagram indicator*
**01** N **04** mint, more, span **05** added, alien, extra, fresh, green, novel, young **06** latest, maiden, modern, modish, recent, trendy, unused, virgin, way out **07** altered, another, changed, current, further, newborn, nouveau, renewed, resumed, strange, topical, unknown, unusual **08** advanced, brand-new, creative, ignorant, improved, nouvelle, original, reformed, restored, unversed, up-to-date **09** a stranger, born-again, different, fledgling, ingenious, refreshed **10** additional, avant-garde, fledgeling, futuristic, innovative, modernized, newfangled, pioneering, present-day, redesigned, remodelled, unfamiliar **11** imaginative, regenerated, resourceful, spanking-new, ultra-modern **12** contemporary, experimental, unaccustomed, unacquainted **13** inexperienced, reinvigorated, revolutionary, state-of-the-art, supplementary, up-to-the-minute **14** ground-breaking, unconventional **15** newly discovered

**New Brunswick**
**02** NB

**newcomer**
**04** tiro **05** alien, pupil **06** blow-in, gryfon, newbie, novice, rookie **07** arrival, griffin, griffon, gryphon, incomer, learner, pilgrim, recruit, settler, trainee **08** beginner, colonist, freshman, intruder, jackaroo, jackeroo, jillaroo, neophyte, outsider, stranger **09** foreigner, greenhorn, immigrant **10** apprentice, new arrival, tenderfoot **11** probationer

**newfangled**
**03** new **05** novel **06** modern, recent,

trendy **08** gimmicky **10** futuristic **11** fashionable, modernistic, ultra-modern **12** contemporary **13** state-of-the-art

**Newfoundland and Labrador**
**02** NL

**New Hampshire**
**02** NH

**New Jersey**
**02** NJ

**newly**
◇ *anagram indicator*
**04** anew, just **05** fresh **06** afresh, lately, of late **07** freshly **08** latterly, recently

**New Mexico**
**02** NM **04** N Mex

**newness**
**06** novity, oddity **07** novelty, recency **09** freshness **10** innovation, uniqueness **11** originality, strangeness, unusualness **13** unfamiliarity

**news**
**03** gen, oil **04** data, dope, info, word **05** facts, story **06** advice, budget, exposé, gossip, latest, report, rumour **07** account, hearing, hearsay, lowdown, message, scandal, tidings **08** bulletin, dispatch, izvestia, newscast, news item **09** izvestiya, newsflash, speerings, speirings, statement **10** communiqué, disclosure, revelation **11** information **12** announcement, developments, intelligence, press release **13** advertisement, communication

*News agencies include:*

**02** AP, PA
**03** AAP, AFP, UPI
**04** NZPA, Tass
**07** Reuters
**08** ITAR-Tass
**15** Associated Press

**• piece of news**
**04** item, unco

**newspaper**
**03** rag **04** blat, post **05** blatt, daily, local, organ, paper, press, print, sheet **06** weekly **07** evening, gazette, journal, quality, tabloid, tribune **08** magazine, national, regional **09** telegraph **10** broadsheet, local paper, periodical, provincial **11** publication **12** evening paper, morning paper **13** national paper, regional paper **15** provincial paper

*Newspapers and magazines include:*

**02** FT, GQ, Ms, OK!
**03** FHM, NME, Red, She, Sun, TES, TLS, Viz
**04** Best, Chat, Chic, Elle, Heat, Judy, Life, Mail, Mind, Mizz, Mojo, More!, Real, THES, Time
**05** Bella, Bliss, Bunty, Hello!, Mandy, Maxim, Prima, Punch, Times, Vogue, Which?, Wired, Woman
**06** Forbes, Granta, Lancet, Loaded, Mirror, Nature, The Sun, War Cry
**07** Company, Esquire, Express, Fortune, Glamour, Hustler, Le Monde, Mayfair, Men Only, Newsday, Options, Playboy, Science, The Chap, The Face, The Lady, The Star, Time Out, Tribune, TV Times
**08** Campaign, Die Woche, Gay Times, Guardian, Le Figaro, Newsweek, New Woman, Scotsman, The Beano, The Dandy, The Eagle, The Field, The Month, The Oldie, The Times, USA Today
**09** Daily Mail, Daily Star, Ideal Home, Penthouse, Q Magazine, Red Pepper, Smash Hits, Telegraph, The Friend, The Grocer, The Herald, The Mirror, The People, The Tablet, The Tatler, Woman's Own
**10** Asian Times, Daily Sport, Irish Times, Private Eye, Racing Post, Radio Times, Sunday Post, Take a Break, Vanity Fair
**11** Church Times, Country Life, Daily Record, Marie Claire, Melody Maker, Morning Star, Sunday Sport, The Big Issue, The European, The Guardian, The Observer, The Universe, Woman's Realm
**12** Angling Times, Cosmopolitan, Daily Express, Family Circle, Fortean Times, History Today, Mail on Sunday, New Scientist, New Statesman, Poetry Review, Sunday Mirror, The Economist, The Pink Paper, The Spectator, Time Magazine, Woman's Weekly
**13** Catholic Times, Daltons Weekly, Farmers Weekly, Homes and Ideas, Horse and Hound, Just Seventeen, Mother and Baby, People's Friend, Reader's Digest, Sunday Express, The Bookseller, The Watchtower, Woman's Journal
**14** Caribbean Times, Catholic Herald, Financial Times, House and Garden, Literary Review, News of the World, The Boston Globe, The Independent, The New York Post, The Sunday Times, The Times Higher, Washington Post
**15** Evening Standard, Exchange and Mart, Harpers and Queen, Homes and Gardens, Sunday Telegraph, The Boston Herald, The Mail on Sunday, The New York Times

*Newspaper proprietors and magnates include:*

**04** **King** (Cecil Harmsworth), **Ochs** (Adolph Simon), **Shah** (Eddy)
**05** **Astor** (John Jacob, Lord), **Astor** (William Waldorf, Viscount), **Black** (Conrad, Lord)
**06** **Aitken** (Sir Max), **Graham** (Katherine Meyer), **Hearst** (William Randolph), **Packer** (Sir Frank), **Ridder** (Bernard H, Jnr), **Walter** (John)
**07** **Barclay** (Sir David), **Barclay** (Sir Frederick), **Camrose** (William Ewert Berry, Viscount), **Kemsley** (James Gomer Berry, Viscount), **Maxwell** (Robert), **Murdoch** (Rupert), **Pearson** (Sir Cyril Arthur), **Riddell** (George, Lord), **Scripps** (Edward Wyllis), **Thomson** (D C), **Thomson** (Roy, Lord)
**08** **Pulitzer** (Joseph)
**10** **Berlusconi** (Silvio), **Harmsworth** (Alfred, Viscount), **Harmsworth** (Harold, Viscount)
**11** **Beaverbrook** (Max, Lord)

*See also* **journalist**

**newspaperman** *see* **journalist**

**newsreader**
**06** anchor **07** newsman **08** reporter **09** anchorman, announcer, newswoman, presenter **10** journalist, newscaster **11** anchorwoman, commentator **13** correspondent

**newsworthy**
**07** notable, topical, unusual **09** arresting, important **10** noteworthy, remarkable, reportable **11** interesting, significant, stimulating

**newt**
**03** ask, eft **05** asker

**New York**
◇ *dialect indicator*
**02** NY

*New York boroughs include:*

**06** Queens
**08** Brooklyn, The Bronx
**09** Manhattan
**12** Staten Island

*Other districts of New York include:*

**04** Noho, Soho
**06** Corona, Harlem, Hollis, Inwood, Nolita, Queens
**07** Astoria, Chelsea, Clifton, Kips Bay, Midtown, Midwood, Tribeca
**08** Brooklyn, Canarsie, East Side, El Barrio, Elmhurst, Flatbush, Flatiron, Flushing, Gramercy, Rego Park, Steinway, The Bronx, West Side
**09** Briarwood, Chinatown, Flatlands, Manhattan, Ozone Park, Park Slope, Princeton, Ridgewood, The Bowery, Turtle Bay, Woodhaven, Yorkville
**10** Cobble Hill, Douglaston, Greenpoint, Ground Zero, Kew Gardens, Marble Hill, Sunset Park
**11** Borough Park, Central Park, Coney Island, East Village, Ellis Island, Forest Hills, Howard Beach, Little Italy, Little Korea, New Brighton, West Village
**12** Alphabet City, Crown Heights, Cypress Hills, Hell's Kitchen, South Jamaica, Staten Island, Williamsburg
**13** Brighton Beach, Lower East Side, Spanish Harlem, Upper East Side, Upper West Side
**14** Jackson Heights, Long Island City, Lower Manhattan, Manhattan Beach, Stuyvesant Town
**15** Brooklyn Heights, Garment District, Roosevelt Island

*New York streets include:*

**06** Bowery
**08** Broadway
**10** 14th Street, 34th Street, 42nd Street, Park Avenue, Wall Street
**11** Canal Street, Fifth Avenue, Sixth Avenue, Union Square
**13** Madison Square, Seventh Avenue
**14** East 42nd Street, West 42nd Street
**15** Central Park West, Lexington Avenue

*New York landmarks include:*

**03** JFK, Met
**04** CBGB, MoMA
**05** Macy's
**07** Barneys, Factory
**08** Broadway, Bronx Zoo, Studio 54
**09** East River, The Dakota
**10** Bronx River, Cotton Club, FAO Schwarz, Ground Zero, Rose Center, Wall Street
**11** Battery Park, Central Park, Coney Island, Ellis Island, Federal Hall, Harlem River, Hudson River, Penn Station, Shea Stadium, Times Square, Union Square
**12** Carnegie Hall, Chelsea Hotel, Hotel Chelsea, Prospect Park, The Cloisters
**13** Apollo Theater, Bloomingdale's, Lincoln Center, Lincoln Tunnel, Pan Am Building, St Paul's Church, Yankee Stadium
**14** Brooklyn Bridge, Grand Army Plaza, Waldorf Astoria, Washington Arch
**15** Flushing Meadows, Manhattan Bridge, Metlife Building, Saks Fifth Avenue, Seagram Building, Statue of Liberty, Trump World Tower

**New Zealand**
**02** NZ **03** NZL

*New Zealand cities and notable towns include:*

**06** Napier, Nelson, Timaru
**07** Dunedin, Manukau, Rotorua
**08** Auckland, Gisborne, Hamilton, Hastings, Tauranga, Wanganui
**09** Whangarei
**10** Wellington
**11** New Plymouth
**12** Christchurch, Invercargill
**15** Palmerston North

*New Zealand landmarks include:*

**05** Hawea
**06** Mt Cook, Te Anau, Wanaka
**07** Aorangi, Rotorua, Ruapehu, Waikato
**08** Mt Egmont, Wakatipu, Wanganui
**09** Fiordland, Lake Taupo
**10** Mt Victoria
**11** Rakaia Gorge
**12** Milford Sound, Southern Alps
**13** Stewart Island
**14** Otago Peninsula
**15** Mangere Mountain, Ninety Mile Beach, Whangaparaoa Bay

*See also* **electorate**; **governor**; **premier**; **prime minister**; **province**; **team**

**next**
**04** syne, then **05** along, later **06** beside **07** closest, ensuing, nearest **08** adjacent **09** adjoining, alongside, bordering, following, immediate, proximate **10** afterwards, contiguous, subsequent, succeeding, successive, tangential, thereafter **11** approximate **12** neighbouring, subsequently **13** after that time

**next-door**
**08** adjacent

**nibble**
**03** bit, eat **04** bite, gnaw, knap, moop, moup, nosh, peck, pick **05** crumb, munch, piece, snack, taste **06** morsel, pick at, titbit **07** knapple

**Nicaragua**
**03** NIC

**nice**
**03** bad, coy **04** cute, fine, good, kind **05** canny, civil, close, exact, sweet **06** dainty, decent, genial, kindly, lovely, minute, polite, strict, subtle, tickle, wanton **07** amiable, amusing, careful, likable, precise, refined, welcome **08** accurate, careless, charming, critical, delicate, friendly, likeable, pleasant, ticklish **09** agreeable, appealing, courteous, endearing, enjoyable, hazardous **10** acceptable, attractive, delectable, delightful, fastidious, meticulous, particular, satisfying, scrupulous **11** good-natured, pleasurable, respectable, sympathetic **12** entertaining, good-humoured, satisfactory, well-mannered **13** understanding **14** discriminating

**nicely**
**04** well **07** civilly **08** politely, properly **09** agreeably **10** pleasantly, pleasingly **11** courteously, pleasurably, respectably **12** attractively, delightfully **14** satisfactorily

**niceness**
**05** charm **08** kindness **10** amiability, politeness **11** likableness **12** friendliness, likeableness, pleasantness **13** agreeableness **14** attractiveness, delightfulness, respectability

**nicety**
**06** nuance **07** coyness, finesse, quiddit **08** accuracy, delicacy, quiddity, subtlety **09** exactness, fine point, precision, punctilio **10** choiceness, minuteness, perjinkity, refinement **11** distinction **14** fastidiousness, meticulousness, scrupulousness

**niche**
**04** nook, slot **05** place **06** alcove, corner, cranny, exedra, hollow, métier, mihrab, recess, shrine **07** calling, exhedra, opening **08** position, vocation **09** cubbyhole **10** fenestella, pigeonhole, tabernacle **11** columbarium **14** specialist area **15** specialized area

**nick**
**02** do **03** can, cut, jug, lag, nab, rob **04** bust, chip, dent, deny, form, jail, mark, nail, quod, scar, snip, take **05** catch, choky, clink, Devil, notch, pinch, run in, score, shape, sneck, snick, state, steal, swipe **06** arrest, collar, cooler, damage, fettle, groove, health, indent, inside, pick up, pilfer, pocket, prison, pull in, snitch **07** capture, defraud, scratch, slammer **08** knock off, porridge **09** apprehend, condition, jailhouse **11** indentation **13** police station

*See also* **prison**; **steal**

**nickel**
**02** Ni

**nickname**
**06** byname, to-name **07** epithet, moniker, pet name **08** cognomen, monicker **09** sobriquet **10** diminutive, soubriquet **12** familiar name

*See also* **Australian football**; **football**; **state**; **team**

**nifty**
**03** apt **04** chic, deft, fine, neat **05** agile, nippy, quick, sharp, slick, smart **06** adroit, clever, spruce **07** skilful, stylish **08** pleasing **09** enjoyable, excellent

**Niger**
**02** RN **03** NER

**Nigeria**
**03** NGA, NGR, WAN

**Nigerian**
**03** Ibo, Tiv **04** Efik, Igbo, Nupe **05** Hausa

**niggardliness**
**08** meanness, scarcity **09** closeness, parsimony, smallness **10** inadequacy, meagreness, paltriness, scantiness, skimpiness, stinginess **11** miserliness **12** cheeseparing, grudgingness **13** insufficiency **14** ungenerousness **15** tight-fistedness

**niggardly**
**04** hard, mean **05** close, mingy, nippy, nirly, small **06** meagre, measly, niding, nirlie, paltry, scanty, skimpy, stingy **07** miserly, nithing, sparing **08** grudging, near-gaun, nidering, ungiving **09** illiberal, miserable, niddering, niderling, penny-wise, penurious **10** hard-fisted, inadequate, near-begaun, nidderling, ungenerous **11** tight-fisted **12** cheeseparing, insufficient, parsimonious

**niggle**
**03** bug, nag **04** carp, gnaw, moan **05** annoy, cavil, query, upset, worry **06** bother, hassle, pick on, potter, trifle **07** henpeck, nit-pick, protest, quibble, trouble **08** complain, irritate, keep on at **09** complaint, criticism, criticize, objection **10** nit-picking **12** equivocation, pettifogging **13** prevarication

**night**
**04** dark, evil, nite **05** death **06** sorrow **07** evening **08** darkmans, darkness **09** ignorance, night-time, obscurity **10** affliction **11** dead of night **15** hours of darkness

**• pass the night**
**03** lie

**nightclub**
**04** club **05** disco **06** nitery **07** cabaret, hot spot, niterie **09** nightspot **11** boîte de nuit, discotheque

**nightfall**
**04** dark, dusk **06** sunset **07** evening, sundown **08** gloaming, twilight **10** crepuscule

**nightingale**
**04** Lind **06** bulbul, Progne **08** Philomel **09** Philomela, Philomene

**• sound of nightingale**
**03** jug

**nightly**
**07** at night **09** after dark, each night **10** every night **11** nocturnally **15** night after night

**nightmare**
**05** agony, trial **06** horror, ordeal **07** anguish, incubus, torment, torture **08** bad dream, calamity **09** cacodemon, cauchemar, ephialtes **10** cacodaemon **11** oneirodynia **13** hallucination **15** awful experience

**nightmarish**
**06** creepy, unreal **07** ghostly, scaring **08** alarming, dreadful, horrible, horrific **09** agonizing, harrowing **10** disturbing, terrifying **11** frightening

**night-time**
**04** dark **05** night **08** darkness **11** dead of night **15** hours of darkness

**nihilism**
**06** denial **07** anarchy, atheism, nullity **08** cynicism, disorder, negation, oblivion **09** disbelief, emptiness, pessimism, rejection, terrorism **10** abnegation, negativism, scepticism **11** agnosticism, lawlessness, nothingness, repudiation **12** non-existence, renunciation

**nihilist**
**05** cynic **07** atheist, sceptic **08** agitator, agnostic **09** anarchist, extremist, pessimist, terrorist **10** antinomian, negativist **11** disbeliever, negationist **13** revolutionary

**Nike**
**08** Victoria

**nil**
**01** O **04** duck, love, none, nowt, zero **05** zilch **06** cipher, cypher, naught, nought **07** nothing

**nimble**
**04** deft, spry, yald **05** agile, alert, brisk, fleet, light, lithe, nippy, quick, ready, smart, swack, swift, wanle, wight, yauld **06** active, clever, lissom, lively, prompt, quiver, volant, wandle, wannel, wimble **07** deliver, lissome, springe **08** flippant, graceful **09** fleet-foot, sharp-eyed, sprightly **10** sure-footed **11** light-footed, quick-moving, quick-witted, sharp-witted **13** quick-thinking

**nimbleness**
**05** grace, skill **07** agility, finesse **08** alacrity, deftness, legerity, spryness **09** alertness, dexterity, lightness, niftiness, nippiness, smartness **10** adroitness **13** sprightliness

**nimbly**
**04** fast **06** deftly, easily, spryly **07** agilely, alertly, briskly, lightly, quickly, readily, sharply, smartly, swiftly **08** actively, promptly, snappily, speedily **11** dexterously **12** proficiently **13** quick-wittedly

**nincompoop**
**04** clot, dolt, fool, nerd, poop, twit **05** chump, dunce, idiot, twerp, wally **06** dimwit, nitwit **07** plonker **08** numskull **09** blockhead, ignoramus, simpleton

**nine**
**02** IX **06** ennead **08** nonuplet, novenary, Pierides

**nineteen**
**03** XIX

**ninety**
**02** XC

**ninny** *see* **fool**

**niobium**
**02** Nb

**nip**
**02** go **03** fly, lop, nep, pop, ren, rin, run, sip **04** bite, clip, dart, dash, dock, dram, drop, grip, rush, shot, snip, tear **05** catch, chack, check, hurry, pinch, smart, sneap, steal, taste, tweak **06** arrest, nibble, snatch **07** catmint, draught, portion, squeeze, swallow **08** cutpurse, mouthful

**• nip in the bud**
**04** curb, halt, stem, stop **05** block, check **06** arrest, impede **08** obstruct **09** frustrate

**nipple**
**03** dug, pap, tit **04** teat **05** diddy, udder **06** breast **07** mamilla, papilla **08** mammilla

**nippy**
**03** icy, raw **04** cold, fast, spry **05** agile, brisk, quick, sharp **06** active, biting, chilly, frosty, nimble, speedy **07** nipping, pungent **08** piercing, stinging, waitress **09** niggardly, sprightly

**nirvana**
**03** joy **05** bliss, peace **06** heaven **07** ecstasy **08** paradise, serenity **10** exaltation **12** tranquillity **13** enlightenment

**nit-picking**
**05** fussy **07** carping, finicky **08** captious, pedantic **09** cavilling, quibbling **12** pettifogging **13** hair-splitting, hypercritical

**nitrogen**
**01** N **02** az- **03** azo-

**nitty-gritty**
**06** basics **09** key points **10** bottom line, brass tacks, essentials, main points **12** fundamentals, nuts and bolts

**nitwit**
**03** ass **04** clot, dope, fool, jerk, prat, twit **05** chump, dumbo, idiot, neddy, ninny, wally **06** dimwit, drongo **07** pillock, plonker **09** birdbrain, blockhead, simpleton **10** nincompoop, silly-billy

**Niue**
**03** NIU

**no**
◇ *deletion indicator*
**01** O **02** na **03** nae, nay, non, not **04** none, nope, uh-uh, zero **05** no way **06** aikona, denial, never a **07** refusal **08** not at all, no thanks **09** not really **11** of course not **12** certainly not, nothing doing **13** absolutely not, not on your life **14** not on your nelly, over my dead body

**nob**
**03** VIP **04** head, toff **06** bigwig, fat cat **07** big shot **09** personage **10** aristocrat

**nobble**
◇ *anagram indicator*
**02** do **03** buy, nab **04** bust, dope, drug, foil, grab, nail, nick, take **05** bribe, catch, check, get at, pinch, run in, seize, steal, swipe **06** arrest, buy off, collar, defeat, hinder, pick up, pilfer, pull in, snitch, thwart **07** disable, swindle, warn off **08** knock off, threaten **09** frustrate, hamstring, influence **10** intimidate **12** incapacitate **13** interfere with

**nobelium**
**02** No

**Nobel Prize**

*Nobel Prize winners include:*

**02** **Fo** (Dario), **Oë** (Kenzaburo)
**03** **Lee** (Tsung-Dao), **Orr** (Lord Boyd), **Paz** (Octavio), **Tum** (Rigoberta Menchú)
**04** **Belo** (Carlos), **Bohr** (Aage), **Bohr** (Niels), **Böll** (Heinrich), **Born** (Max), **Buck** (Pearl S), **Cela** (Camilo José), **Duve** (Christian de), **Gide** (André), **Hume** (John), **Hunt** (Tim), **Katz** (Sir Bernard), **King** (Martin Luther), **Koch** (Robert), **Mann** (Thomas), **Mott** (Sir Nevill F), **Nash** (John), **Rabi** (Isidor Isaac), **Rous** (Peyton), **Shaw** (George Bernard), **Tutu** (Desmond), **Urey** (Harold C)
**05** **Annan** (Kofi), **Bethe** (Hans), **Bloch** (Felix), **Bragg** (Sir Lawrence), **Bragg** (Sir William), **Bunin** (Ivan), **Camus** (Albert), **Chain** (Sir Ernst), **Crick** (Francis), **Curie** (Marie), **Curie**

(Pierre), **Debye** (Peter), **Dirac** (Paul A M), **Ebadi** (Shirin), **Eliot** (T S), **Euler** (Ulf von), **Fermi** (Enrico), **Golgi** (Camillo), **Grass** (Günter), **Haber** (Fritz), **Hesse** (Hermann), **Jerne** (Niels), **Klerk** (F W de), **Krebs** (Sir Hans), **Kroto** (Sir Harold), **Lewis** (Sinclair), **Libby** (Willard F), **Lwoff** (André), **Monod** (Jacques), **Nurse** (Sir Paul), **Pauli** (Wolfgang), **Peres** (Shimon), **Rabin** (Yitzhak), **Sachs** (Nelly), **Salam** (Abdus), **Simon** (Claude), **Soddy** (Frederick), **Stern** (Otto), **Yeats** (W B)

**06** **Arafat** (Yasser), **Baeyer** (Adolf von), **Bellow** (Saul), **Bordet** (Jules), **Calvin** (Melvin), **Carrel** (Alexis), **Cronin** (James Watson), **Debreu** (Gerard), **Enders** (John F), **Florey** (Howard, Lord), **France** (Anatole), **Frisch** (Ragnar), **Glaser** (Donald A), **Hamsun** (Knut), **Heaney** (Seamus), **Hevesy** (George von), **Hewish** (Antony), **Huxley** (Andrew F), **Lorenz** (Konrad), **Myrdal** (Gunnar), **Nernst** (Walther), **Neruda** (Pablo), **O'Neill** (Eugene), **Pavlov** (Ivan), **Perutz** (Max F), **Planck** (Max), **Porter** (George, Lord), **Sanger** (Frederick), **Sartre** (Jean-Paul), **Singer** (Isaac Bashevis), **Tagore** (Rabindranath), **Walesa** (Lech), **Watson** (James), **Wiesel** (Elie), **Wilson** (Robert)

**07** **Akerlof** (George A), **Alferov** (Zhores I), **Alvarez** (Luis), **Axelrod** (Julius), **Banting** (Sir Frederick G), **Beckett** (Samuel), **Behring** (Emil von), **Brenner** (Sydney), **Brodsky** (Joseph), **Canetti** (Elias), **Coetzee** (JM), **Dae-jung** (Kim), **Ehrlich** (Paul), **Feynman** (Richard P), **Fleming** (Sir Alexander), **Glashow** (Sheldon), **Golding** (William), **Hershey** (Alfred), **Hodgkin** (Dorothy), **Hodgkin** (Sir Alan L), **Jelinek** (Elfriede), **Jiménez** (Juan Ramón), **Kendrew** (John), **Kertész** (Imre), **Khorana** (H Gobind), **Kipling** (Rudyard), **Laxness** (Halldór), **Maathai** (Wangari), **Mahfouz** (Naguib), **Mandela** (Nelson), **Marconi** (Guglielmo), **Márquez** (Gabriel García), **Mauriac** (François), **Medawar** (Sir Peter), **Mistral** (Frédéric), **Mommsen** (Theodor), **Naipaul** (VS), **Pauling** (Linus), **Penzias** (Arno), **Röntgen** (Wilhelm Konrad), **Rotblat** (Joseph), **Russell** (Bertrand, Earl), **Seaborg** (GlenT), **Seifert** (Jaroslav), **Soyinka** (Wole), **Thomson** (J J), **Trimble** (David), **Waksman** (Selman A), **Walcott** (Derek), **Whipple** (George H), **Wilkins** (Maurice)

**08** **Appleton** (Sir Edward V), **Asturias** (Miguel Angel), **Chadwick** (Sir James), **Delbrück** (Max), **Einstein** (Albert), **Faulkner** (William), **Friedman** (Milton), **Gajdusek** (D Carleton), **Gell-Mann** (Murray), **Gordimer** (Nadine), **Hartwell** (Leland H), **Langmuir** (Irving), **Leontief** (Wassily), **Meyerhof** (Otto), **Millikan** (Robert A), **Milstein** (Cesar), **Morrison** (Toni), **Mulliken** (Robert S), **Northrop** (John H), **Sakharov** (Andrei), **Saramago** (José), **Shockley** (William B), **Tiselius** (Arne), **Tonegawa** (Susumu), **Weinberg** (Steven), **Xingjian** (Gao)

**09** **Arrhenius** (Svante), **Becquerel** (Henri), **Cherenkov** (Pavel), **Churchill** (Sir Winston), **Dalai Lama**, **Gorbachev** (Mikhail), **Hemingway** (Ernest), **Kissinger** (Henry), **Markowitz** (Harry M), **Mechnikov** (Ilya), **Michelson** (Albert A), **Nirenberg** (Marshall W), **Pasternak** (Boris), **Prudhomme** (Sully), **Rainwater** (James), **Roosevelt** (Theodore), **Sholokhov** (Mikhail), **Steinbeck** (John), **Tinbergen** (Jan), **Tinbergen** (Nikolaas)

**10** **Galsworthy** (John), **Heisenberg** (Werner), **Hofstadter** (Robert), **Lagerkvist** (Pär), **McClintock** (Barbara), **Modigliani** (Franco), **Pirandello** (Luigi), **Ramos-Horta** (José), **Rutherford** (Ernest, Lord), **Szymborska** (Wislawa)

**11** **Joliot-Curie** (Frédéric), **Joliot-Curie** (Irène), **Kantorovich** (Leonid), **Landsteiner** (Karl), **Maeterlinck** (Maurice), **Ramón y Cajal** (Santiago), **Schrödinger** (Erwin), **van der Waals** (Johannes Diderik), **Zinkernagel** (Rolf M)

**12** **Hammarskjöld** (Dag), **Mother Teresa**, **Solzhenitsyn** (Aleksandr), **Szent-Györgyi** (Albert)

**13** **Aung San Suu Kyi**, **Chandrasekhar** (Subrahmanyan), **García Márquez** (Gabriel)

**14** **Levi-Montalcini** (Rita)

## nobility

**04** nobs, rank **05** élite, glory, lords, peers, toffs **06** family, gentry, honour, nobles, virtue **07** dignity, majesty, peerage **08** eminence, grandeur, noblesse **09** grandness, integrity, nobilesse, nobleness, splendour **10** excellence, generosity, worthiness **11** aristocracy, high society, magnanimity, stateliness, superiority, uprightness **12** generousness, magnificence **14** impressiveness **15** illustriousness

*The nobility includes:*

**01** d, E, P

**02** Bt, Kt, Pr

**03** Dom, Don, Duc

**04** Bart, dame, duke, earl, jarl, lady, lord, Marq, peer

**05** baron, count, laird, liege, nawab, noble, ruler, thane

**06** daimio, Junker, knight, squire, vidame

**07** baronet, dowager, duchess, marquis, peeress, vicomte

**08** baroness, countess, governor, life peer, margrave, marquess, nobleman, seigneur, starosta, toiseach, vavasour, viscount

**09** grand duke, liege lord, magnifico, patrician

**10** aristocrat, noblewoman

**11** marchioness, viscountess

**12** grand duchess

**13** grand seigneur

## noble

**04** fine, gent, high, lady, lord, peer **05** brave, grand, great, lofty, manly **06** gentle, landed, manful, titled, vidame, worthy **07** eminent, exalted, gallant, grandee, magnate, stately **08** atheling, douzeper, elevated, generous, glorious, handsome, high-born, honoured, imposing, majestic, nobleman, splendid, virtuous **09** dignified, doucepere, excellent, patrician, unselfish, venerated **10** aristocrat, honourable, impressive, noblewoman **11** blue-blooded, high-ranking, illustrious, magnanimous, magnificent, noble-minded **12** aristocratic, great-hearted **13** distinguished **15** self-sacrificing

*See also* **nobility**

## nobly

**07** bravely **08** manfully, worthily **09** gallantly **10** generously, honourably, virtuously **11** unselfishly

## nobody

**04** Nemo **05** no one **06** cipher, menial, Pooter **07** naebody, nothing **09** nonentity **10** mediocrity **11** lightweight

## nocturnal

**05** night **09** night-time **13** active at night

## nod

**03** bow, dip, nap **04** beck, doze, sign **05** agree, sleep **06** accept, assent, beckon, drowse, nid-nod, noddle, nutate, salute, signal **07** approve, doze off, drop off, gesture, incline, support **08** greeting, indicate, say yes to **10** fall asleep, indication **11** acknowledge **15** acknowledgement

• **give the nod to**

**02** OK **03** buy **04** back, pass **05** adopt, allow, carry **06** accept, permit, ratify, second, uphold **07** agree to, approve, confirm, endorse, mandate, support **08** assent to, hold with, sanction, validate **09** authorize, consent to **11** rubber-stamp

• **nod off**

**03** nap **04** doze **05** sleep **06** drowse **07** doze off, drop off, slumber **10** fall asleep

## node

**03** bud **04** bump, knob, knot, lump **05** joint, nodus **06** growth, nodule **08** junction, swelling **09** carbuncle **11** convergence **12** protuberance

## noise

◇ *homophone indicator*

**03** cry, din, pop, row **04** bang, boom, chug, clap, coil, roar, talk, wham, zoom

**05** blare, clash, clunk, sound, whang **06** babble, bicker, clamor, hubbub, jangle, outcry, racket, report, rumble, rumour, tumult, uproar **07** brattle, clamour, clangor, clatter, discord, thunder **08** announce, clangour **09** circulate, commotion, publicize **11** pandemonium

**• amount of noise**
**02** dB **03** bel, dBA **04** phon, PNdB **07** decibel

### noiseless
**04** mute, soft **05** mousy, quiet, still **06** hushed, mousey, silent **07** catlike **09** inaudible, soundless

### noiselessly
**06** softly **07** quietly **08** silently **09** inaudibly **11** soundlessly

### noisily
**06** loudly, wallop **07** rowdily **10** fortissimo **11** deafeningly **12** boisterously, resoundingly, tumultuously, vociferously

### noisome
**03** bad **04** foul **05** fetid **06** foetid, putrid, smelly **07** harmful, hurtful, noxious, reeking **08** mephitic, stinking **09** injurious, obnoxious, offensive, poisonous, repulsive, unhealthy **10** disgusting, malodorous, nauseating, pernicious **11** deleterious, pestiferous, unwholesome **12** disagreeable, pestilential

### noisy
**01** f **02** ff **04** loud **05** roary, rowdy, vocal **06** roarie **07** blaring, blatant, booming, rackety, roaring **08** blasting, blattant, boastful, piercing, plangent, strepent **09** clamorous, deafening, turbulent **10** blusterous, boisterous, hoity-toity, strepitant, strepitoso, thundering, tumultuous, vociferous **11** rumbustious **12** ear-splitting, obstreperous

**• not too noisy**
**02** mf

### nomad
**03** San **04** Bedu **05** rover **06** Beduin, roamer, Tuareg **07** Bedouin, Bushman, migrant, rambler, Saracen, swagger, swagman, vagrant **08** Khoikhoi, vagabond, wanderer **09** Hottentot, itinerant, transient, traveller

### nomadic
**05** Gypsy **06** Beduin, roving, Tuareg **07** Bedouin, migrant, roaming, vagrant **08** drifting, Khoikhoi, Scythian **09** itinerant, migratory, unsettled, wandering **10** travelling **11** peripatetic **13** peregrinating

### nom-de-plume
**05** alias **07** pen-name **09** pseudonym **11** assumed name

### nomenclature
**06** naming **08** locution, taxonomy **10** vocabulary **11** phraseology, terminology **12** codification **14** classification

### nominal
**03** nom **04** tiny **05** nomin, small, token **06** formal, puppet **07** minimal, titular, trivial **08** so-called, supposed, symbolic, trifling **09** professed, purported **10** figurehead, in name only, ostensible, peppercorn, self-styled **11** theoretical **13** insignificant

### nominally
**08** formally **10** in name only, ostensibly **12** symbolically **13** theoretically

### nominate
**04** name, term **05** elect, put up, voice **06** assign, choose, select, submit **07** appoint, elevate, present, propose, suggest **09** designate, postulate, recommend **10** commission, substitute

### nomination
**06** choice, naming **08** election, proposal **09** selection **10** submission, suggestion **11** appointment, designation **14** recommendation

### nominative
**01** n **03** nom

### nominee
**06** runner **07** entrant **08** assignee **09** appointee, candidate **10** contestant

### nomogram
**04** abac

**non-alcoholic drink** *see* **drink**

### non-aligned
**07** neutral **09** impartial, undecided **10** uninvolved **11** independent, non-partisan, uncommitted **13** disinterested

### nonchalance
**04** calm, cool **06** aplomb **08** calmness, coolness **09** composure, sangfroid, unconcern **10** detachment, equanimity **11** insouciance **12** indifference **13** pococurantism **14** pococuranteism, self-possession

### nonchalant
**04** calm, cool **05** blasé **06** casual **07** offhand **08** careless, detached, laid-back **09** apathetic, collected, easy-going **10** insouciant **11** indifferent, pococurante, unconcerned **13** dispassionate, imperturbable **15** cool as a cucumber

### non-combatant
**06** dovish **07** conchie, neutral **08** civilian, pacifist **10** non-aligned, non-violent **11** non-fighting, peacemaking **12** conciliatory, unaggressive **14** non-belligerent **15** passive resister

### non-committal
**04** wary **05** vague **07** careful, evasive, guarded, neutral, politic, prudent, tactful **08** cautious, discreet, reserved **09** ambiguous, equivocal, tentative **10** diplomatic, indefinite **11** circumspect, unrevealing

### non compos mentis
**03** ape, fey, mad **04** bats, gyte, loco, nuts, wild **05** barmy, batty, buggy, crazy, daffy, dippy, dotty, flaky, gonzo, loony, loopy, manic, nutty, potty, queer, wacko, wacky, wiggy **06** crazed, cuckoo, fruity, insane, maniac, mental, raving, red-mad, screwy **07** bananas, barking, berserk, bonkers, cracked, frantic, lunatic, meshuga **08** crackers, demented, deranged, dingbats, doolally, frenetic, frenzied, maniacal, unhinged, unstable **09** disturbed, lymphatic, psychotic, up the wall **10** bestraught, distracted, distraught, frantic-mad, off the wall, off your nut, out to lunch, stone-crazy, unbalanced **11** not all there, off the rails, off your head **12** mad as a hatter, off your chump, round the bend **13** off your rocker, of unsound mind, out of your head, out of your mind, out of your tree, round the twist **14** off your trolley, wrong in the head **15** out of your senses

### nonconformist
**05** rebel **06** chapel **07** heretic, oddball, radical, seceder **08** maverick **09** dissenter, dissident, eccentric, heretical, protester **10** iconoclast **11** dissentient **12** secessionist **13** individualist, unco-operative **14** fish out of water

### nonconformity
**06** heresy **07** dissent **09** deviation, secession **10** heterodoxy **11** originality **12** eccentricity

### nondescript
**04** dull **05** bland, plain, vague **07** anaemic, insipid, vanilla **08** ordinary **11** commonplace, featureless, uninspiring **12** cookie-cutter, run of the mill, unattractive, unclassified, unremarkable **13** indeterminate, no great shakes, undistinctive, unexceptional, uninteresting **14** common or garden **15** undistinguished

### non-drinking
**02** TT **03** dry **10** on the wagon

### none
**01** O **02** no **03** nil **04** zero **05** no one, zilch **06** nobody, not any, not one **07** nothing **08** not a soul **10** not even one **13** not a single one

**• none the ...**
**02** no **07** not a bit **08** not at all **10** to no extent

### nonentity
**06** cipher, cypher, menial, nobody **07** nothing **08** shlepper **09** non-person, schlepper **10** mediocrity **11** lightweight

### non-essential
**08** unneeded **09** accessory, excessive, redundant **10** expendable, extraneous, peripheral **11** dispensable, inessential, superfluous, unimportant, unnecessary **13** supplementary

### nonetheless
**03** but, yet **05** still **06** anyhow, anyway, even so, though **07** however **08** after all **09** in any case **10** all the same, by

any means, for all that, in any event, regardless **11** by some means, just the same **12** nevertheless **13** at the same time **15** notwithstanding

**non-event**
**04** no-no **06** fiasco **07** let-down **08** comedown **09** damp squib **10** anticlimax **14** disappointment

**non-existence**
**05** fancy **07** absence, chimera, unbeing **08** illusion **09** unreality **11** nothingness **12** illusiveness

**non-existent**
**04** null **06** unborn, unreal **07** fancied, fantasy, missing, phantom, unbeing **08** fanciful, illusory, imagined, mythical **09** fictional, imaginary, legendary **10** chimerical, fictitious, immaterial **11** incorporeal **12** hypothetical **13** hallucinatory, insubstantial, suppositional

**non-fiction**

*Non-fiction works include:*

**06** Walden
**07** Capital, Who's Who
**08** Self-Help
**09** Kama Sutra, Leviathan, On Liberty, Table Talk, The Phaedo
**10** Das Kapital, The Annales, The Gorgias, The Poetics, The Timaeus
**11** Down the Mine, Mythologies, The Agricola, The Analects, The Germania, The Phaedrus, The Republic
**12** Novum Organum, Silent Spring, The City of God, The Second Sex, The Symposium
**13** The Story of Art
**14** A Room of One's Own, Birds of America, Eudemian Ethics, Inside the Whale, Modern Painters, Past and Present, Sartor Resartus, The Age of Reason, The Golden Bough, The Life of Jesus, The Rights of Man, The Selfish Gene
**15** Lives of the Poets, The Essays of Elia, The Female Eunuch, The Sleepwalkers

**non-flammable**
**09** fireproof **10** flameproof **12** not flammable **13** fire-resistant, incombustible, uninflammable **14** flame-resistant

**non-intervention**
**06** apathy **07** inertia **08** inaction **09** passivity **12** laissez-faire, non-alignment **14** hands-off policy, non-involvement **15** non-interference

**non-Jew**
**03** goy **07** gentile

**nonpareil**
**06** unique **09** matchless **10** inimitable, unequalled, unrivalled **12** incomparable, unparalleled, without equal **13** beyond compare

**non-partisan**
**07** neutral **08** detached, unbiased **09** impartial, objective **10** even-handed **11** independent **12** unprejudiced **13** dispassionate

**nonplus**
**04** faze, stun **05** sew up, stick, stump **06** baffle, dismay, puzzle **07** astound, confuse, flummox, mystify, perplex, stagger **08** astonish, bewilder, confound **09** discomfit, dumbfound, embarrass, take aback **10** disconcert, perplexity **11** flabbergast **14** discountenance

**nonplussed**
**05** blank, fazed **07** at a loss, baffled, floored, puzzled, stumped, stunned **08** dismayed **09** astounded, flummoxed, perplexed **10** astonished, bewildered, confounded, taken aback **11** dumbfounded, embarrassed **12** disconcerted **13** flabbergasted **14** out of your depth

**non-professional**
**03** lay **04** laic **07** amateur

**nonsense**
**03** gum, rot **04** blah, bosh, bull, bunk, cack, cock, crap, gaff, guff, jazz, junk, kack, pulp, punk, tosh **05** balls, bilge, borak, borax, folly, fudge, haver, hooey, pants, squit, stuff, trash, tripe **06** blague, bunkum, drivel, faddle, footle, gammon, havers, hoop-la, humbug, kibosh, kybosh, piffle, waffle **07** baloney, blather, blether, boloney, doggrel, eyewash, flannel, garbage, hogwash, malarky, pisheog, rhubarb, rubbish, twaddle **08** all my eye, blah-blah, blathers, blethers, bumfluff, claptrap, cobblers, doggerel, flimflam, malarkey, pishogue, tommyrot, trifling, unreason **09** absurdity, bull's wool, fandangle, gibberish, kidstakes, moonshine, mouthwash, poppycock, silliness, stupidity **10** balderdash, clamjamfry, codswallop, flapdoodle, galimatias, jabberwock, mumbo-jumbo, taradiddle, tomfoolery **11** clanjamfray, double Dutch, fiddle-de-dee, fiddlestick, foolishness, jabberwocky, tarradiddle **12** blah-blah-blah, clamjamphrie, fiddle-faddle, fiddlesticks, gobbledegook, gobbledygook **13** gas and gaiters, horsefeathers, senselessness **14** how's your father, ridiculousness
*See also* **rubbish**

**nonsensical**
◇ *anagram indicator*
**05** barmy, crazy, dotty, inane, nutty, potty, silly, wacky **06** absurd, stupid **07** fatuous, foolish **08** crackpot **09** gibberish, ludicrous, senseless **10** irrational, ridiculous **11** hare-brained, meaningless **12** preposterous **14** unintelligible

**nonsmoker**
**02** ns

**non-stop**
**07** endless, ongoing **08** constant, steadily, unbroken, unending **09** ceaseless, endlessly, incessant, unceasing **10** constantly, continuous, persistent, relentless, unbrokenly, unendingly **11** ceaselessly, incessantly, never-ending, unceasingly, unfaltering **12** continuously, interminable, interminably, relentlessly **13** round-the-clock, unfalteringly, uninterrupted, unrelentingly, unremittingly **15** uninterruptedly

**non-violent**
**06** dovish, irenic **07** passive **08** pacifist, peaceful **09** peaceable

**noodle**
**04** head, udon **05** moony, Sammy **09** blockhead, improvise, simpleton
*See also* **head**

**nook**
**03** den **04** neuk **05** angle, niche **06** alcove, cavity, corner, cranny, recess, refuge **07** hideout, opening, retreat, shelter **08** hideaway **09** cubbyhole

**noon**
**01** m, n **06** midday, middle **08** twelve pm **09** lunchtime **10** meridional, twelve noon **12** twelve o'clock

**noose**
**04** fank **05** snare **06** twitch **07** necktie **08** marriage, rope's end **12** hempen caudle

**norm**
**03** par **04** mean, rule, type **05** gauge, model, scale **07** average, measure, pattern **08** standard **09** benchmark, criterion, principle, reference, usual rule, yardstick **10** touchstone

**normal**
**05** usual **06** common **07** average, general, natural, popular, regular, routine, typical **08** accepted, everyday, habitual, ordinary, rational, standard, straight **10** accustomed, mainstream, reasonable, regulation **11** bog standard, commonplace **12** conventional, run of the mill, twenty-twenty, well-adjusted **13** perpendicular

**normality**
**06** reason **07** balance, routine **08** normalcy **09** usualness **10** adjustment, commonness, regularity, typicality **11** averageness, naturalness, rationality **12** ordinariness **14** reasonableness **15** conventionality

**normally**
**07** as a rule, as usual, usually **08** commonly **09** generally, naturally, regularly, routinely, typically **10** ordinarily **14** conventionally

**Norse**
**01** N
*See also* **god, goddess**

**north**
**01** N

**North Atlantic Treaty Organization** *see* **NATO**

**North America** *see* **America; Canada; United States of America**

**North Carolina**
**02** NC

**North Dakota**
**02** ND **04** N Dak

**north-east, north-eastern**
**02** NE

**northern**
**01** N **05** north, polar **06** Arctic, boreal **09** northerly **11** hyperborean **13** septentrional

**Northern Ireland** *see* **district; town**

**north-west, north-western**
**02** NW

**Northwest Territories**
**02** NT

**Norway**
**01** N **03** NOR

**nose**
**03** neb, pry, pug **04** beak, bill, boko, conk, ease, edge, feel, inch, push, snub **05** aroma, flair, nudge, scent, sense, smell, snoot, snout **06** hooter, nozzle, nuzzle, schnoz, snitch **08** informer, instinct **09** proboscis, schnozzle **10** move slowly, perception, projection

**• get up your nose**
**03** bug, irk, nag, vex **04** fash, gall, rile **05** anger, tease **06** bother, harass, hassle, madden, molest, pester, plague, ruffle, wind up **07** disturb, hack off, provoke, tick off, trouble **08** brass off, irritate **09** aggravate, cheese off, displease, drive nuts **10** drive crazy, exasperate **11** get your goat **12** drive bananas **13** get on your wick, get your back up, make sparks fly **14** drive up the wall, get your blood up, give you the hump **15** get on your nerves, get your dander up

**• nose around**
**03** pry **05** snoop **06** search **10** poke around, rubberneck **14** poke your nose in

**• nose out**
**06** detect, reveal **07** find out, inquire, uncover **08** discover, sniff out

**• poke your nose into**
**03** pry **05** pry in, snoop **06** butt in, fiddle, tamper **07** intrude **08** meddle in **09** interfere, intervene **10** stickybeak, tamper with **11** interfere in **12** put your oar in **14** stick your oar in

**• under your nose**
**07** clearly, plainly **09** obviously **10** plain to see **11** for all to see **12** in front of you

**nosedive**
**04** dive, drop **05** swoop **06** go down, header, plunge, purler **07** decline, plummet **08** get worse, submerge

**nosegay**
**04** posy **05** bunch, spray **07** bouquet

**nosey, nosy**
**06** prying **07** curious, probing **08** fragrant, snooping **10** meddlesome **11** inquisitive, interfering **13** eavesdropping

**• Nosey Parker**
**08** busybody

**nosh**
**03** eat, kai **04** diet, dish, eats, fare, feed, food, grub, menu, tuck **05** board, meals, scran, table **06** fodder, nibble, stores, tucker, viands **07** cooking, cuisine, rations **08** delicacy, eatables, victuals **09** nutriment, nutrition **10** bush tucker, foodstuffs, provisions, speciality, sustenance **11** comestibles, nourishment, subsistence **12** refreshments

**nosiness**
**06** prying **08** snooping **11** curiousness **12** interference **13** intrusiveness **14** meddlesomeness **15** inquisitiveness

**nostalgia**
**06** pining, regret **07** longing, regrets **08** yearning **09** mal du pays **11** remembrance, wistfulness **12** homesickness, recollection, reminiscence **13** recollections, regretfulness, reminiscences

**nostalgic**
**06** pining **07** longing, wistful **08** homesick, yearning **09** emotional, regretful **11** reminiscent, sentimental

**nostril**
**04** nare

**nostrum**
**04** cure, drug, pill **06** elixir, potion, remedy, secret **07** cure-all, panacea **08** medicine **13** universal cure **14** cure for all ills **15** universal remedy

**nosy** *see* **nosey, nosy**

**not**
◇ *anagram indicator*
◇ *deletion indicator*
**02** na, ne, no, -n't **03** non **04** nary, ne'er **05** never **06** polled

**• and not**
**03** nor

**• has not**
**03** nas **04** ain't, ha'n't

**• is not**
**03** nis, nys **04** ain't

**• not out**
**02** in, no

**notability**
**03** VIP **04** fame, note **05** celeb **06** bigwig, esteem, renown, worthy **07** big shot, magnate, notable, someone **08** big noise, eminence, luminary, somebody, top brass **09** big cheese, celebrity, dignitary, personage **10** importance **11** distinction, heavyweight **12** significance **14** impressiveness, noteworthiness, observableness

**notable**
**03** VIP **04** rare, star **05** celeb, great **06** bigwig, clever, famous, marked, signal, worthy **07** big shot, capable, eminent, serious, someone, special, unusual **08** big noise, luminary, renowned, somebody, striking, terrible, top brass, uncommon **09** big cheese, celebrity, dignitary, important, memorable, momentous, notorious, personage, well-known **10** celebrated, impressive, notability, noteworthy, noticeable, observable, particular, pre-eminent, remarkable **11** heavyweight, illustrious, outstanding, significant **12** considerable **13** distinguished, extraordinary, unforgettable

**notably**
**08** above all, markedly, signally **09** eminently **10** distinctly, especially, noticeably, remarkably, strikingly, uncommonly **12** impressively, in particular, particularly **13** conspicuously, outstandingly, significantly **15** extraordinarily

**notation**
**04** code **05** Romic, signs **06** cipher, noting, record, script, system **07** symbols **08** alphabet **09** shorthand, tablature **10** characters **11** Laban system **13** hieroglyphics, orchesography

**notch**
**01** V **03** cut, gap, jag, lip **04** dent, gash, gimp, hack, kerf, mark, mush, nick, nock, snip, step **05** cleft, crena, gouge, grade, level, score, sinus, stage, tally **06** degree, groove, indent, joggle, raffle **07** achieve, scratch, serrate, vandyke **08** incision, nail-hole, swan-mark, undercut **09** insection **11** indentation

**• notch up**
**04** gain, make **05** score **06** attain, record **07** achieve, chalk up **08** register

**notched**
**05** erose, jaggy **06** eroded, jagged, nicked, pinked **07** dentate, serrate **08** dentated, serrated **09** serrulate **10** crenellate, emarginate, serrulated **11** crenellated, denticulate **12** denticulated

**note**
**01** A, B, C, D, E, F, G, H, n **02** NB **03** log, see **04** bill, care, chit, fame, heed, item, line, long, mark, memo, mese, nete, oner, show, tone, tune **05** breve, drone, e-mail, enter, entry, fiver, gloss, large, minim, music, one-er, token **06** chitty, denote, detect, letter, minute, notice, postil, quaver, record, regard, remark, renown, signal, single, sticky, stigma, symbol, tenner, twenty, wunner **07** account, apostil, comment, element, epistle, jot down, jotting, mention, message, middle c, missive, observe, put down, receipt, refer to, touch on, voucher, witness **08** allude to, annotate, Bradbury, crotchet, eminence, footnote, indicate, perceive, prestige, register, reminder, sforzato **09** apostille, attention, greatness, non placet, semibreve, sforzando, write down **10** annotation, cognizance, commentary, fortepiano, importance, impression, indication,

inflection, intimation, marginalia, memorandum, notability, reputation, semiquaver, stigmatize
**11** consequence, distinction, explanation, explication, mindfulness, observation, pre-eminence
**12** acciaccatura, put in writing, significance **13** attentiveness, become aware of, communication, consideration **14** characteristic, demisemiquaver **15** illustriousness

*Musical notes of the sol-fa scale:*

**02** do (first), fa (fourth), la (sixth), me (third), mi (third), re (second), si (seventh), so (fifth), te (seventh), ti (seventh), ut (first)
**03** doh (first), fah (fourth), lah (sixth), ray (second), soh (fifth), sol (fifth)

*See also* **strings of a lyre** *under* **string**

**• highest note**
**03** e-la

**• of note**
**04** some

**• take note**
**02** NB **03** dig

**notebook**
**03** log **05** diary **06** cahier, jotter, record **07** daybook, journal, logbook, notepad **09** field book, table-book **10** index rerum, pocket-book **11** address book **12** exercise book

**noted**
**05** great **06** famous, marked, of note **07** eminent, notable **08** renowned **09** acclaimed, notorious, prominent, respected, well-known **10** celebrated, pre-eminent, recognized **11** illustrious **13** distinguished

**notes**
**05** draft **06** record, report, sketch **07** minutes, outline **08** jottings, synopsis **10** adversaria, commentary, personalia, transcript **11** impressions

**noteworthy**
**06** marked **07** notable, unusual **08** striking **09** important, memorable **10** impressive, particular, remarkable **11** exceptional, outstanding, significant **13** extraordinary

**nothing**
**01** O **03** nil, nix, zip **04** love, nada, nowt, void, zero **05** nihil, squat, zilch, zippo **06** cipher, cypher, menial, naught, nix-nie, nobody, nought, sod all, trifle, vacuum **07** nullity, sweet FA **08** naething, oblivion **09** emptiness, nonentity, not an iota, not a thing, worthless **10** mediocrity **11** diddly-squat, lightweight, nothingness **12** non-existence **15** sweet Fanny Adams

**• doing nothing**
**04** idle

**• for nothing**
**04** free **06** gratis, in vain **08** at no cost, futilely **09** to no avail **10** as a freebie, needlessly, on the house **12** free of charge, with no result **13** complimentary, without charge **14** unsuccessfully

**• nothing but**
**04** just, only **06** merely, simply, solely **11** exclusively

**• nothing more**
**04** mere

**nothingness**
**04** nada, void **06** vacuum **07** nullity, vacuity **08** nihilism, nihility, oblivion **09** emptiness **12** non-existence **13** worthlessness **14** insignificance

**notice**
**02** ad **03** see **04** bill, crit, espy, gaum, gorm, heed, mark, mind, news, note, sign, spot, tent **05** order **06** advert, advice, behold, detect, poster, regard, remark, review, si quis **07** comment, discern, leaflet, make out, mention, observe, thought, warning, write-up **08** apprisal, bulletin, circular, civility, critique, handbill, interest, monition, pamphlet, perceive **09** attention, awareness, criticism **10** cognizance, intimation, take heed of, take note of **11** declaration, distinguish, information, instruction, observation **12** announcement, intelligence, notification, watchfulness **13** advertisement, become aware of, communication, consideration **14** pay attention to

**• give in your notice**
**04** quit **05** leave **06** resign **07** walk out **08** step down **09** stand down **13** pack in your job **14** chuck in your job

**• give someone notice**
**03** axe **04** fire, sack, warn **05** eject **07** boot out, dismiss, kick out **08** get rid of **09** discharge

**noticeable**
**04** bold **05** clear, plain **06** marked, patent **07** evident, notable, obvious, visible **08** distinct, manifest, powerful, striking **10** detectable, impressive, measurable, observable, pronounced **11** appreciable, conspicuous, discernible, distinction, perceptible, significant **12** unmistakable **15** distinguishable

**noticeably**
**07** clearly, notably, plainly, visibly **08** markedly, patently **09** evidently, obviously **10** distinctly, strikingly **11** discernibly, perceptibly **12** unmistakably **13** conspicuously, significantly

**notification**
**05** aviso **06** advice, notice **07** message, telling, warning **09** informing, statement **10** disclosure, divulgence **11** declaration, information, publication **12** announcement, intelligence **13** communication **14** acknowledgment **15** acknowledgement

**notify**
**04** tell, warn **05** alert **06** advise, inform, reveal **07** apprise, caution, declare, divulge, placard, publish **08** acquaint, announce, disclose **09** broadcast, make known **11** communicate

**notion**
**04** idea, mind, view, whim, wish **05** fancy, vapor **06** belief, desire, liking, notice, revery, theory, vapour **07** caprice, concept, impulse, inkling, opinion, project, reverie, thought, wrinkle **08** crotchet, supposal, whim-wham **10** assumption, conception, conviction, hypothesis, impression **11** abstraction, inclination **12** anticipation, apprehension **13** understanding

**notional**
**05** ideal **06** unreal **07** fancied **08** abstract, fanciful, illusory, thematic **09** imaginary, unfounded, visionary **10** conceptual, ideational **11** speculative, theoretical **12** hypothetical **14** classificatory

**notionally**
**08** in theory **10** putatively **12** conceptually **13** conjecturally, theoretically **14** hypothetically

**notoriety**
**06** infamy **07** obloquy, scandal **08** disgrace, ignominy **09** celebrity, dishonour, disrepute, esclandre, publicity **10** opprobrium

**notorious**
**05** noted **06** arrant, notour **07** blatant, glaring **08** flagrant, ill-famed, infamous **09** egregious, well-known **10** proverbial, scandalous **11** disgraceful, ignominious, of ill repute, opprobrious **12** disreputable **13** dishonourable

**notoriously**
**06** openly **07** notably, overtly **08** arrantly, patently **09** blatantly, glaringly, obviously **10** flagrantly, infamously **11** egregiously **12** disreputably, particularly, scandalously **13** disgracefully, dishonourably, ignominiously, opprobriously, spectacularly

**notwithstanding**
**03** for, yet **05** howbe **06** even so, for all, maugre, though **07** despite, howbeit, however, maulgre **08** although, nathless, naythles **09** in spite of, natheless **10** for all that, nathelesse **11** nonetheless, non obstante **12** nevertheless, regardless of **13** at the same time

**nought**
**01** O **03** nil, nix **04** nada, nowt, null, zero **05** zilch **06** cipher, cypher, naught **07** nothing **11** nothingness

*See also* **nothing**

**noun**
**01** n **06** aptote, gerund **11** substantive

**nourish**
**03** aid **04** feed, have, help, rear, tend **05** boost, nurse **06** assist, foster, suckle **07** advance, bring up, care for, cherish, educate, forward, further, nurture, promote, support, sustain **08** attend to, maintain **09** cultivate, encourage,

stimulate **10** provide for, strengthen, take care of

**nourishing**
**04** good **06** battle **08** nutrient **09** healthful, nutritive, wholesome **10** beneficial, nutritious **11** substantial **12** alimentative, health-giving, invigorating **13** strengthening

**nourishment**
**04** diet, eats, food, grub, nosh, tuck **05** juice, scran **07** aliment, ingesta, pabulum **08** goodness **09** nouriture, nutriment, nutrition **10** nourriture, sustenance **11** subsistence

**nouveaux riches**
**08** parvenus, upstarts **10** arrivistes, the new rich

**Nova Scotia**
**02** NS

**novel**
◇ *anagram indicator*
**03** new **04** book, epic, rare, tale **05** fresh, roman, story **06** modern, unique **07** Aga saga, fiction, romance, strange, unusual **08** creative, hardback, original, uncommon **09** different, ingenious, inventive, narrative, paperback **10** innovative, pioneering, unfamiliar, unorthodox, yellowback **11** imaginative, resourceful, three-decker **12** bodice-ripper, double-decker, nouveau roman **13** Bildungsroman, unprecedented **14** ground-breaking, unconventional

*Novels and fictional works include:*

**03** Kim, She, USA
**04** Emma, Jazz, Nana, Voss
**05** Kipps, Money, Porgy, Scoop, Sybil
**06** Ben Hur, Carrie, Herzog, Lolita, Nausea, Pamela, Rob Roy, The Sea, Trilby, Utopia, Walden
**07** Babbitt, Beloved, Candide, Catch-22, Cat's Eye, Dracula, Erewhon, Euphues, Ivanhoe, Justine, Lord Jim, Orlando, Rebecca, Shirley, The Bell, The Fall, Ulysses
**08** Adam Bede, Birdsong, Clarissa, Cranford, Disgrace, Germinal, Jane Eyre, Lavengro, Lucky Jim, Moby Dick, Newcomes, Nostromo, Oroonoko, Peter Pan, Rasselas, The Idiot, The Trial, The Waves, The Years, Tom Jones, Tom Thumb, Villette, Waverley
**09** About a Boy, Amsterdam, Beau Geste, Billy Budd, Billy Liar, Dead Souls, Dubliners, Gargantua, Hard Times, Kidnapped, L'Étranger, On the Road, Rogue Male, The Devils, The Egoist, The Hobbit, The Warden, Tom Sawyer, White Fang
**10** A Man in Full, Animal Farm, Bleak House, Cancer Ward, Cannery Row, Clayhanger, Don Quixote, East of Eden, Edwin Drood, Fever Pitch, Goldfinger, Howards End, Kenilworth, Labyrinths, Lorna Doone, Persuasion, Rural Rides, The Leopard, The Rainbow, The Tin Drum, Titus Alone, Titus Groan, Uncle Remus, Vanity Fair, Westward Ho!, White Teeth
**11** A Tale of a Tub, Black Beauty, Burmese Days, Cakes and Ale, Daisy Miller, Gormenghast, Greenmantle, Little Women, Middlemarch, Mrs Dalloway, Oliver Twist, Silas Marner, Steppenwolf, The Big Sleep, The Hireling, The Outsider, The Talisman, The Third Man, War and Peace, Women in Love
**12** Anna Karenina, A Severed Head, A Suitable Boy, Barnaby Rudge, Brighton Rock, Casino Royale, Dombey and Son, Fear of Flying, Frankenstein, Little Dorrit, Madame Bovary, Moll Flanders, Of Mice and Men, Old Mortality, Rip Van Winkle, Room at the Top, The Go-Between, The Golden Ass, The Lost World, The Moonstone, The Old Devils, Volsungasaga
**13** A Kind of Loving, Arabian Nights, Brave New World, Call of the Wild, Daniel Deronda, Doctor Zhivago, Finnegans Wake, Joseph Andrews, Just So Stories, Les Misérables, Mansfield Park, Metamorphosis, New Grub Street, North and South, Schindler's Ark, Sketches By Boz, Smiley's People, Sons and Lovers, Tarka the Otter, The Awkward Age, The Bostonians, The Golden Bowl, The Jungle Book, The Last Tycoon, The Mabinogion, The Naked Lunch, The Odessa File, Thérèse Raquin, The Virginians, Under Milk Wood, Winnie-the-Pooh, Zuleika Dobson
**14** A Handful of Dust, A Room with a View, A Town Like Alice, Cider with Rosie, Death on the Nile, Decline and Fall, Fathers and Sons, Humphry Clinker, Jude the Obscure, Le Morte d'Arthur, Lord of the Flies, Lord of the Rings, Robinson Crusoe, Roderick Random, The Ambassadors, The Coral Island, The Da Vinci Code, The First Circle, The Forsyte Saga, The Great Gatsby, The Human Comedy, The Kraken Wakes, The Long Goodbye, The Lovely Bones, The Secret Agent, The Time Machine, The Water-Babies, The Woodlanders, Treasure Island, Tristram Shandy, Tropic of Cancer, Uncle Tom's Cabin, What Maisie Knew
**15** A Christmas Carol, A Farewell to Arms, A Passage to India, Cold Comfort Farm, Daphnis and Chloe, Flaubert's Parrot, Gone with the Wind, Huckleberry Finn, Le Rouge et le Noir, Northanger Abbey, Our Mutual Friend, Peregrine Pickle, Tarzan of the Apes, The African Queen, The Invisible Man, The Little Prince, The Old Wives' Tale, The Secret Garden, The Woman in White, Three Men in a Boat, To the Lighthouse, Under the Volcano, Vernon God Little, Where Eagles Dare

**novelist**
**06** author, fabler, writer **09** innovator **10** newsmonger, news-writer **11** storyteller **12** man of letters **13** fiction writer **14** creative writer, woman of letters
*See also* **author**

**novelty**
**06** bauble, gadget, trifle **07** gimmick, memento, newness, primeur, trinket **08** gimcrack, rareness, souvenir **09** curiosity, freshness **10** creativity, difference, innovation, knick-knack, uniqueness **11** originality, strangeness, unusualness **13** unfamiliarity **15** imaginativeness

**November**
**01** N **03** Nov

**novice**
**01** L **03** cub, kyu **04** tiro, tyro **05** chela, pupil **06** gryfon, newbie, rookie **07** amateur, griffin, griffon, grommet, gryphon, learner, new chum, recruit, student, trainee **08** beginner, neophyte, newcomer **09** greenhorn, noviciate, novitiate **10** apprentice, raw recruit **11** probationer

**noviciate**
**06** novice **08** training **09** novitiate, probation **10** initiation **11** trial period **13** trainee period **14** apprenticeship

**now**
**02** AD **04** next, then **05** today **06** at once **07** just now, present **08** directly, nowadays, promptly, right now **09** at present, currently, instantly, presently, right away, these days **10** at this time **11** at the moment, immediately **12** straight away, without delay **15** for the time being

• **now and then**
**07** at times **08** on and off **09** sometimes **10** on occasion **11** desultorily, now and again **12** infrequently, occasionally, once in a while, periodically, sporadically **13** spasmodically **14** from time to time, intermittently

**nowadays**
**02** AD **03** now **05** today **09** at present, currently, presently, these days **10** at this time **11** at the moment **15** in this day and age

**noxious**
**04** foul **05** toxic **06** deadly **07** harmful, nocuous, noisome, ruinous **08** damaging, menacing **09** injurious, malignant, obnoxious, poisonous, unhealthy **10** contagious, disgusting, pernicious **11** deleterious, destructive, detrimental, pestiferous, threatening, unwholesome

**nozzle**
**03** jet **04** nose, rose **05** snout, spout,

tweer, twier, twire, twyer **06** stroup, tuyère, twyere **07** ajutage, sparger, sprayer **08** adjutage **09** nosepiece, sprinkler **10** projection **13** sprinkler head

**nuance**
**04** hint **05** shade, tinge, touch, trace **06** degree, nicety **07** shading **08** overtone, subtlety **09** gradation, suspicion **10** refinement, suggestion **11** distinction **15** fine distinction

**nub**
**04** core, crux, gist, hang, knob, lump, meat, pith **05** chunk, focus, heart, pivot, point **06** centre, kernel, marrow **07** essence, gallows, nucleus **12** central point, protuberance

**nubile**
**04** sexy **05** adult **06** mature **09** desirable **10** attractive, voluptuous **12** marriageable

**nuclear**
**01** N

**nucleus**
◇ *middle selection indicator*
**03** nub **04** core, crux, meat **05** basis, focus, heart, pivot **06** centre, kernel, marrow **08** eucaryon, eukaryon, heartlet, nucellus **09** karyosome

**nude**
**03** raw **04** bare **05** naked **06** Adamic **07** denuded, exposed, skyclad **08** disrobed, in the raw, starkers, stripped, undraped **09** butt-naked, in the buff, in the scud, unclothed, uncovered, undressed **10** start-naked **11** mother-naked **12** not a stitch on **13** with nothing on **15** in the altogether
*See also* **bare**; **naked**

**nudge**
**03** dig, jab, jog **04** bump, knee, poke, prod, push **05** dunch, dunsh, elbow, shove **06** prompt

**nudity**
**04** scud **06** nudism **07** undress **08** bareness **09** nakedness **10** déshabillé, dishabille **14** state of undress **15** in the altogether

**nugatory**
**04** vain **06** futile **07** invalid, trivial, useless **08** trifling **09** valueless, worthless **10** inadequate, negligible, unavailing **11** ineffectual, inoperative, null and void **13** insignificant **15** inconsequential

**nugget**
**03** wad **04** hunk, lump, mass **05** chunk, clump, piece, wodge

**nuisance**
**04** bore, chiz, drag, hoha, hoop, hurt, pain, pest **05** chizz, trial **06** bother, burden, hoop-la, injury, plague, weight **07** problem, scunner, trouble **08** drawback, irritant, vexation **09** annoyance **10** affliction, difficulty, irritation **11** tribulation **13** inconvenience **15** thorn in your side

**null**
**04** kink, vain, void, zero **05** annul, empty, knurl **06** cipher, cypher, nought **07** invalid, nullify, revoked, useless **08** annulled **09** abrogated, cancelled, nullified, powerless, worthless **11** ineffectual, inoperative, invalidated

**nullify**
**04** kill, null, void **05** abate, annul, quash **06** cancel, negate, offset, repeal, revoke **07** abolish, rescind, reverse **08** abrogate, evacuate, renounce, set aside **10** counteract, invalidate, neutralize **11** countermand, discontinue **12** bring to an end

**nullity**
**08** voidness **10** invalidity **11** uselessness **12** non-existence **13** immateriality, powerlessness, worthlessness **14** incorporeality **15** ineffectualness

**numb**
**04** daze, dead, drug, dull, stun **05** dazed **06** benumb, deaden, freeze, frozen, torpid **07** drugged, in shock, stunned, stupefy, torpefy **08** benumbed, deadened, paralyse, sleeping **09** insensate, paralysed, stupefied, unfeeling **10** immobilize, insensible **11** immobilized, insensitive **12** anaesthetize **13** anaesthetized **14** without feeling

**number**
**01** C, D, K, L, M, n **02** no **03** act, add, num, sum **04** copy, data, item, many, song, tale, turn, unit **05** count, crowd, dance, digit, group, horde, issue, limit, local, score, tally, total, track **06** amount, cipher, figure, reckon, sketch, throng, volume **07** add up to, company, compute, decimal, delimit, edition, imprint, include, integer, numeral, ordinal, routine, several, specify **08** cardinal, estimate, fraction, printing, quantity, restrain, restrict **09** aggregate, apportion, calculate, character, enumerate, multitude **10** collection, impression, statistics **11** anaesthetic, performance **12** anaesthetist, piece of music

*Numbers include:*

**02** pi
**03** one, six, ten, two
**04** five, four, half, nine, zero
**05** eight, fifty, forty, seven, sixty, three
**06** eighty, eleven, googol, ninety, thirty, twelve, twenty
**07** billion, chiliad, fifteen, hundred, million, seventy, sixteen
**08** eighteen, fourteen, nineteen, thirteen, thousand, trillion
**09** decillion, nonillion, octillion, seventeen
**10** centillion, googolplex, one hundred, septillion, sextillion
**11** quadrillion, quintillion

*French numbers include:*

**02** un
**03** dix, six
**04** cent, cinq, deux, huit, neuf, onze, sept, zéro
**05** douze, mille, seize, trois, vingt
**06** quatre, quinze, treize, trente
**07** dix-huit, dix-neuf, dix-sept
**08** quarante, quatorze, soixante
**09** cinquante, deux mille, un million
**10** un milliard
**11** soixante-dix
**12** quatre-vingts

*German numbers include:*

**03** elf
**04** acht, drei, eins, fünf, neun, null, vier, zehn, zwei
**05** sechs, zwölf
**06** sieben
**07** achtzig, Billion, fünfzig, hundert, Million, neunzig, sechzig, siebzig, tausend, vierzig, zwanzig
**08** achtzehn, dreissig, dreizehn, fünfzehn, neunzehn, sechzehn, siebzehn, vierzehn
**09** Milliarde
**10** einhundert, eintausend

*Italian numbers include:*

**03** due, sei, tre, uno
**04** nove, otto
**05** cento, dieci, sette, venti
**06** cinque, dodici, sedici, trenta, undici
**07** novanta, ottanta, quattro, tredici
**08** diciotto, quaranta, quindici, sessanta, settanta
**09** cinquanta
**10** diciannove
**11** diciassette, quattordici

*Latin numbers include:*

**03** duo, nil, sex
**04** octo, tres, unus
**05** decem, mille, novem
**06** centum, septem
**07** quinque, sedecim, undecim, viginti
**08** duodecim, quattuor, tredecim, trigenta
**09** nonaginta, octoginta, sexaginta
**11** quadraginta, septendecim, septuaginta, undeviginti
**12** duodeviginti, quinquaginta, quinquedecim
**13** quattuordecim

*Spanish numbers include:*

**03** dos, mil, uno
**04** diez, doce, ocho, once, seis, tres
**05** cinco, nueve, siete, trece
**06** ciento, cuatro, quince, veinte
**07** catorce, noventa, ochenta, sesenta, setenta, treinta
**08** cuarenta, un millón
**09** cincuenta, dieciocho, dieciséis
**10** diecinueve, diecisiete, quinientos
**11** mil millones

• **any number**
**01** n

• **large number**
**01** n **03** lot, ten **04** army, host, raft, slew, slue
*See also* **many**

**numberless**
**04** many **06** myriad, untold **07** endless **08** infinite, unsummed **09** countless, uncounted **10** unnumbered
**11** innumerable **12** immeasurable
**13** multitudinous, without number

**numbness**
**06** stupor, torpor **08** deadness, dullness **09** paralysis **10** night-palsy
**12** stupefaction **13** insensateness, insensibility, insensitivity, unfeelingness

**numeral**
**03** num **04** unit **05** digit **06** cipher, figure, number **07** integer **09** character

*Roman numerals include:*

**01** C (hundred), D (five hundred), I (one), L (fifty), M (thousand), V (five), X (ten)
**02** II (two), IV (four), IX (nine), VI (six), XI (eleven), XV (fifteen), XX (twenty)
**03** III (three), VII (seven), XII (twelve), XIV (fourteen), XIX (nineteen), XVI (sixteen)
**04** VIII (eight), XIII (thirteen), XVII (seventeen)
**05** XVIII (eighteen)

**numerical**
**05** whole **06** graded, ranked, scalar
**07** digital, figural **08** integral
**09** identical **11** statistical
**12** hierarchical **13** computational

**numerically**
**07** in order **09** digitally **10** measurably
**12** quantifiably **13** algebraically, exponentially **14** arithmetically, mathematically

**numerous**
**04** many **05** great **06** a lot of, legion, strong, sundry, untold **07** copious, endless, profuse, several, various
**08** abundant, a good few, manifold, populous **09** countless, plentiful, quite a few **10** rhythmical **11** innumerable
**13** great in number, multitudinous

**numerousness**
**06** number **08** multeity
**09** abundance, plurality, profusion
**10** numerosity **11** copiousness
**12** manifoldness, multiplicity
**13** countlessness, plentifulness

**numinous**
**04** holy **05** deity, numen **06** divine, sacred **08** divinity, mystical
**09** religious, spiritual **10** mysterious
**12** supernatural, transcendent

**numskull**
**03** ass, git, mug, nit, sap **04** berk, clot, coot, dill, dope, dork, fool, geek, goat, goof, goop, jerk, kook, nana, nerd, nerk, nong, prat, putz, twit, yo-yo
**05** chump, dumbo, dunce, dweeb, galah, neddy, ninny, prick, schmo, twerp, wally **06** bampot, dimwit, doofus, dum-dum, josser, muppet, nig-nog, nitwit, sawney, sucker, turkey
**07** Charlie, dingbat, gubbins, jughead, pillock, plonker, saphead, tosspot, wazzock **08** boofhead, dipstick, lunkhead **09** birdbrain, blockhead, cloth head, schlemiel, simpleton
**10** headbanger, nincompoop, silly-billy
**11** chowderhead **13** proper Charlie

**nun**
**03** top **06** abbess, sister, vestal, vowess
**07** ancress, blue tit, zelator
**08** canoness, prioress, zelatrix
**09** anchoress, deaconess, zelatrice
**10** cloistress, conventual, religieuse
**14** mother superior
*See also* **monk**

**Nunavut**
**02** NU

**nuncio**
**05** envoy **06** legate **09** messenger
**10** ambassador **14** representative

**nunnery**
**05** abbey **06** priory **07** convent, nunship **08** cloister

**nuptial**
**06** bridal, wedded **07** marital, spousal, wedding **08** conjugal, hymeneal
**09** connubial **11** epithalamic, matrimonial **12** epithalamial

**nuptials**
**06** bridal **07** wedding **08** espousal, marriage, spousals **09** hymeneals, matrimony

**nurse**
◇ *containment indicator*
**03** aid **04** feed, help, keep, tend
**05** angel, boost, shark, treat **06** assist, cradle, foster, suckle **07** advance, care for, cherish, dogfish, further, harbour, nourice, nourish, nurture, promote, support, sustain **08** attend to, preserve
**09** encourage, entertain, look after
**10** breast-feed, take care of

*Nurse types include:*

**02** EN, RN
**03** aia, CNN, dry, pro, RGN, SEN, SRN, wet
**04** amah, ayah, home, maid, sick
**05** nanny, night, staff, tutor
**06** charge, dental, matron, school, sister
**07** midwife, nursery
**08** district
**09** auxiliary, children's, community, Macmillan
**10** consultant, Iain Rennie, ward sister
**11** night sister, psychiatric
**12** practitioner
**13** health visitor, State Enrolled, theatre sister
**15** locality manager, State Registered

*Nurses include:*

**05** Kenny (Elizabeth)
**06** Barton (Clara), Cavell (Edith), Rayner (Claire), Sanger (Margaret)
**07** Seacole (Mary)
**08** Pattison (Dorothy Wyndlow)
**10** Stephenson (Elsie)
**11** Nightingale (Florence)
**14** Queen Alexandra

*See also* **medical**

**nurture**
**03** aid **04** care, diet, eats, feed, food, grub, help, nosh, rear, tend, tuck
**05** boost, coach, nurse, scran, train, tutor **06** assist, cradle, foster, school
**07** advance, bring up, care for, cherish, develop, educate, feeding, further, nourish, promote, rearing, support, sustain, tending **08** boosting, instruct, training **09** cultivate, education, fostering, nouriture, nutrition, promotion, schooling, stimulate
**10** assistance, discipline, nourriture, sustenance, upbringing **11** cultivation, development, environment, furtherance, nourishment, stimulation, subsistence **13** encouragement

**nut**
**02** en **03** fan, pip **04** buff, butt, head, seed **05** crank, fiend, freak, loony, stone **06** kernel, madman, maniac, nutter, psycho, zealot **07** admirer, devotee, fanatic, lunatic, nutcase, oddball **08** crackpot, follower, headcase, madwoman **09** fruitcake, screwball, supporter **10** aficionado, basket-case, enthusiast, psychopath
**12** insane person

*Nuts include:*

**03** ben, oak, pig
**04** cola, horn, kola, pará, pili, pine, shea, wing
**05** acorn, areca, arnut, beech, betel, cedar, cream, earth, ivory, lichi, pecan, tiger
**06** almond, Brazil, cashew, castle, cobnut, cohune, corozo, ginger, hognut, illipe, lichee, litchi, lychee, monkey, oilnut, peanut, physic, poison, sleeve, souari, walnut
**07** babassu, bladder, buffalo, chesnut, coconut, filberd, filbert, gallnut, hickory, leechee, locknut, marking, palmyra, pilinut, saouari
**08** chestnut, clearing, cocoanut, cokernut, coquilla, hazelnut, quandong, sapucaia, thumbnut
**09** Barcelona, beech mast, butterfly, butternut, groundnut, macadamia, mockernut, pistachio, sassafras, scaly-bark
**10** locking-nut, Queensland, St Anthony's
**11** Molucca bean
**13** earth-chestnut, horse chestnut

*See also* **head**

**• do your nut**
**05** go mad **06** blow up, see red
**07** explode **08** boil over, freak out
**09** blow a fuse, go berserk, raise hell
**11** blow your top, flip your lid, go ballistic, go up the wall, have kittens, lose your rag **12** blow your cool, fly into a rage, lose your cool, throw a wobbly **13** hit the ceiling, throw a tantrum **14** foam at the mouth
**15** fly off the handle, go off the deep end

**nutriment**
**04** diet, eats, food, grub, nosh, tuck

**05** scran **09** nutrition **10** sustenance **11** nourishment, subsistence

**nutrition**
**04** diet, eats, food, grub, nosh, tuck **05** scran **08** eutrophy **09** nutriment **10** sustenance **11** nourishment, subsistence

**nutritious**
**04** good **09** healthful, nutritive, wholesome **10** beneficial, nourishing, sustaining **11** substantial **12** body-building, health-giving, invigorating **13** strengthening

**nuts**
◇ *anagram indicator*
**03** mad **04** avid, bats, daft, fond, keen, loco, mast, wild **05** barmy, batty, crazy, daffy, dippy, loony, loopy, nutty, potty **06** ardent, crazed, insane **07** berserk, bonkers, devoted, lunatic, smitten, zealous **08** demented, deranged, doolally, unhinged **09** disturbed, enamoured, fanatical **10** infatuated, out to lunch, passionate, unbalanced **12** enthusiastic, round the bend **13** off your rocker, out of your mind, round the twist **14** off your trolley

*See also* **mad**

**nuts and bolts**
**06** basics **07** details **10** components, essentials **11** nitty-gritty **12** fundamentals **13** bits and pieces **14** practicalities

**nutty**
**03** mad **04** nuts, wild **05** barmy, batty, crazy, daffy, dippy, loony, loopy, potty **06** crazed, insane **07** berserk, bonkers, lunatic **08** demented, deranged, doolally, unhinged **09** disturbed **10** out to lunch, unbalanced **12** round the bend **13** off your rocker, out of your mind, round the twist **14** off your trolley

**nuzzle**
**03** pet, rub **04** nose, poke, root **05** nudge, press, sniff, train **06** burrow, caress, cuddle, fondle, foster, nestle **07** bring up, snoozle, snuggle, snuzzle

**nymph**
**04** Echo, girl, lass, maid, pupa **05** dryad, houri, naiad, oread, sylph **06** damsel, maelid, maiden, nereid, sprite, Tethys, undine **07** mermaid, oceanid, rusalka **09** hamadryad

# O

**o**
**05** Oscar **06** nought **07** nothing, spangle

**oaf**
**03** auf, oik **04** boor, clod, dolt, gawk, hick, hoon, lout, ouph, slob **05** idiot, ocker, ouphe, yahoo, yobbo **06** lubber **07** bumpkin **09** barbarian, roughneck **10** changeling, clodhopper **11** hobbledehoy

**oafish**
**05** gawky, gross, ocker, rough **06** clumsy, coarse, lumpen, stolid **07** boorish, doltish, idiotic, ill-bred, loutish, lumpish, swinish, uncouth, yobbish **08** bungling, churlish, lubberly **10** unmannerly **11** clodhopping, ill-mannered

**oak**
**04** holm, ilex **05** roble **06** cerris, kermes **07** durmast, Quercus **08** corktree, flittern, wainscot **10** quercitron **13** partridge-wood **15** king of the forest

**• oak bark**
**03** tan

**oar**
**03** row **05** blade, scull, spoon, sweep **06** bow-oar, paddle, stroke **09** stroke oar

**• oar blade**
**04** peel

**oasis**
**05** haven **06** island, refuge, spring **07** hideout, retreat, sanctum **08** hideaway **09** sanctuary **12** watering-hole

**oath**
**03** vow **04** bond, cuss, word **05** curse **06** avowal, pledge **07** promise **08** cussword **09** assurance, blasphemy, curse-word, expletive, obscenity, profanity, sacrament, swear-word **11** affirmation, attestation, bad language, imprecation, malediction **12** word of honour **14** four-letter word

**• oaths and euphemisms**
**02** od **03** dod, dog, gad, gee, Gog, odd **04** drat, ecod, egad, gosh, heck,hell, igad, life, odso, oons, rats, 'slid, 'zbud **05** bedad, begad, gadso, nouns, 'sfoot, 'slife, zooks **06** cricky, crikey, 'sblood, 'sdeath, 'sheart, 'snails **07** begorra, by Jingo, crickey, jabbers, odzooks, strewth **08** begorrah, bejabers, gadzooks **09** bismillah, 'sbodikins **10** sapperment, 'sbuddikins

**obduracy**
**08** firmness, tenacity **09** obstinacy **10** doggedness, mulishness, perversity, wilfulness **11** frowardness, persistence, pertinacity **12** perseverance, resoluteness, stubbornness **13** inflexibility, intransigence, pigheadedness **14** relentlessness **15** hard-heartedness, wrongheadedness

**obdurate**
**04** firm, hard, iron **05** stony **06** dogged, flinty, wilful **07** adamant **08** hardened, stubborn **09** immovable, obstinate, pigheaded, steadfast, tenacious, unbending, unfeeling **10** determined, headstrong, implacable, inflexible, persistent, self-willed, unyielding **11** hard-hearted, intractable, stiff-necked, unrelenting **12** bloody-minded, intransigent, strong-minded

**obedience**
**04** duty **07** respect **08** docility **09** agreement, deference, obeisance, passivity, reverence **10** accordance, allegiance, compliance, observance, submission **11** amenability, dutifulness **12** acquiescence, amenableness, malleability, subservience, tractability **14** conformability, submissiveness

**obedient**
**04** bent, obdt **06** docile **07** duteous, dutiful, pliable **08** amenable, biddable, yielding **09** compliant, malleable, observant, tractable **10** bridle-wise, conforming, law-abiding, obsequious, respectful, submissive **11** acquiescent, deferential, disciplined, subservient, well-trained

**obeisance**
**03** bow **06** cringe, curtsy, homage, kowtow, salaam, salute **07** curtsey, respect **09** deference, obedience, reverence **10** salutation, submission, veneration **12** genuflection

**obelisk**
**06** column, dagger, needle, obelus, pillar **08** memorial, monument

**obese**
**03** big, fat **05** beefy, bulky, gross, heavy, hefty, large, plump, podgy, porky, round, stout, tubby **06** chubby, flabby, fleshy, portly, rotund **07** outsize, paunchy **08** roly-poly **09** corpulent, ponderous **10** overweight **11** Falstaffian, well-endowed **15** well-upholstered

**obesity**
**04** bulk **07** fatness **09** grossness, plumpness, podginess, stoutness, tubbiness **10** chubbiness, corpulence, flabbiness, overweight, portliness, rotundness

**obey**
**04** heed, keep, mind **05** bow to, defer, yield **06** comply, follow, fulfil, keep to, submit **07** abide by, act upon, conform, defer to, execute, give way, observe, perform, respect, respond **08** adhere to, carry out **09** be ruled by, consent to, discharge, surrender **10** come to heel, toe the line **11** acquiesce in, go by the book **14** do as you are told, take orders from **15** stick to the rules

**obfuscate**
◇ *anagram indicator*
**04** blur, hide, mask, veil **05** cloak, cloud, cover, shade **06** darken, muddle, shadow, shroud **07** conceal, confuse, obscure **08** bewilder, disguise **10** complicate, overshadow

**obfuscation**
**06** muddle **08** disguise **09** confusion, obscurity **11** concealment **12** complication

**obituary**
**04** obit **06** eulogy **09** necrology **11** death notice

**object**
**03** aim, end, jib **04** body, butt, goal, idea, item, sake **05** argue, cavil, demur, focus, point, rebut, thing **06** adduce, design, device, entity, gadget, impute, intent, motive, oddity, oppose, reason, recuse, refuse, resist, target, victim **07** article, exposed, opposed, present, protest, purpose **08** ambition, artefact, complain **09** challenge, intention, objective, recipient, repudiate, something, take issue, withstand **10** disapprove, interposed, phenomenon **11** beg to differ, expostulate, remonstrate **12** recalcitrate **13** interposition, take exception

**• provisional object**
**02** it

**• with the object of**
**02** to

**objection**
**02** ob **03** but **05** cavil, demur **06** boggle **07** dislike, dissent, protest, quarrel, scruple **08** argument, demurrer, question **09** challenge, complaint, exception, grievance

10 difficulty, opposition, recusation 11 disapproval 13 expostulation, recalcitrance, remonstration, unwillingness 15 dissatisfaction

**objectionable**
04 pert 05 nasty 07 hateful
09 abhorrent, loathsome, obnoxious, offensive, repellent, repugnant, repulsive, revolting, sickening
10 deplorable, despicable, detestable, nauseating, unpleasant 11 distasteful, intolerable 12 contemptible, disagreeable, unacceptable
13 exceptionable, reprehensible

**objective**
03 aim, end, obj 04 fair, goal, idea, just, mark, real, true 05 point 06 actual, design, intent, object, target, thingy
07 factual, genuine, neutral, purpose
08 ambition, clinical, detached, unbiased 09 authentic, equitable, impartial, intention 10 even-handed, impersonal, open-minded, uninvolved
12 unprejudiced 13 disinterested, dispassionate

**objectively**
06 fairly, justly 09 equitably, neutrally
11 impartially 12 even-handedly
14 with an open mind
15 disinterestedly, dispassionately

**objectivity**
07 justice 08 fairness, justness, open mind 10 detachment, thinginess
11 disinterest, outwardness, thingliness
12 impartiality 13 equitableness
14 even-handedness, open-mindedness

**objector**
05 rebel 07 opposer, striker
08 agitator, opponent 09 dissenter, dissident, protester 10 complainer
12 demonstrator

**obligate**
04 bind, make 05 force, impel, press
06 coerce, compel, oblige 07 require
08 pressure 09 constrain 10 pressurize
11 necessitate

**obligation**
03 job, tie 04 bond, cess, debt, deed, duty, must, onus, task 05 trust
06 burden, charge, demand, duress, favour 07 astrict, burthen, command
08 contract, covenant, function, pressure 09 agreement, liability
10 assignment, commitment, compulsion, incumbency
11 obstriction, requirement
12 indebtedness 14 accountability, responsibility

**obligatory**
03 set 05 usual 06 normal 07 binding, bounden, regular, routine
08 accepted, enforced, familiar, habitual, ordinary, required
09 customary, essential, incumbent, mandatory, necessary, requisite, statutory 10 compulsory, imperative
11 established, fashionable, traditional, unavoidable 12 conventional

**oblige**
03 put, tie 04 bind, help, make
05 force, impel, press, serve 06 assist, coerce, compel, please 07 gratify, require 08 astringe, obligate, pressure
09 constrain 10 pressurize
11 accommodate, necessitate 15 be given no option

**obliged**
05 bound 06 debted, forced, in debt
08 beholden, grateful, having to, indebted, in debt to, required, thankful
09 compelled, duty-bound, gratified, obligated 11 constrained, having got to, honour-bound 12 appreciative
15 under compulsion

**obliging**
04 kind 05 civil 06 polite 07 helpful, willing 08 friendly, generous, pleasant
09 agreeable, courteous, indulgent, officious 11 complaisant, considerate, co-operative, good-natured
13 accommodating

**obligingly**
07 civilly 08 politely 09 agreeably, helpfully, willingly 10 generously
11 courteously 13 considerately

**oblique**
◇ *anagram indicator*
03 obl 04 skew 05 cross, slant, slash
06 angled, squint, stroke, tilted, zigzag
07 awkward, devious, sloping, solidus, virgule, winding 08 bevelled, diagonal, inclined, indirect, rambling, sidelong, sideways, slanting, tortuous, traverse
09 divergent, skew-whiff, underhand
10 circuitous, discursive, meandering, roundabout 12 forward slash, periphrastic 14 circumlocutory, slantendicular, slantindicular

**obliquely**
05 askew 06 askant, aslant, aslope, squint 07 askance, asquint 08 sidelong
09 at an angle, evasively, slantwise, slopewise 10 diagonally, indirectly
12 circuitously

**obliterate**
04 blot 05 erase 06 deface, delete, efface, rub out 07 blot out, destroy, expunge, wipe out 08 black out, vaporize, wash away 09 eliminate, eradicate, extirpate, overscore, strike out 10 annihilate

**obliteration**
04 blot 06 rasure, razure 07 erasure
08 deletion 10 effacement, expunction 11 blotting out, destruction, elimination, eradication, extirpation 12 annihilation

**oblivion**
04 void 05 Lethe, limbo 06 disuse, pardon, stupor 07 amnesty, silence
08 darkness, deafness 09 blankness, blindness, ignorance, obscurity
11 forgiveness, nothingness
12 carelessness, non-existence
13 forgetfulness, insensibility, unmindfulness 15 inattentiveness, unconsciousness

**oblivious**
04 deaf 05 blind 07 unaware
08 careless, heedless, ignorant
09 forgetful, forgotten, negligent, unheeding, unmindful 10 insensible
11 inattentive, preoccupied, unconcerned, unconscious 12 absent-minded

**obliviousness**
07 naivety 09 greenness, ignorance, innocence, stupidity, thickness
10 illiteracy 11 unawareness
12 inexperience 13 unfamiliarity
14 unintelligence 15 unconsciousness

**obloquy**
05 abuse, blame, odium, shame
06 attack, stigma 07 calumny, censure, slander 08 bad press, disgrace, ignominy, reproach 09 aspersion, contumely, criticism, discredit, disfavour, dishonour, invective
10 defamation, detraction, opprobrium 11 humiliation
12 vilification 13 animadversion

**obnoxious**
04 vile 05 nasty 06 horrid, odious
07 exposed, hateful, hurtful, noxious
08 horrible 09 abhorrent, loathsome, offensive, repellent, repugnant, repulsive, revolting, sickening
10 deplorable, detestable, disgusting, nauseating, unpleasant 11 intolerable
12 contemptible, disagreeable, unacceptable 13 objectionable

**obscene**
03 paw 04 blue, foul, lewd, rude, sexy, vile 05 bawdy, dirty, gross, nasty
06 carnal, coarse, filthy, fruity, greasy, impure, pawpaw, risqué, sleazy, smutty, vulgar, X-rated 07 immoral, raunchy
08 hard-core, immodest, improper, indecent, prurient, shocking, unchaste
09 loathsome, off-colour, offensive, repellent, shameless 10 disgusting, licentious, lubricious, outrageous, scandalous, scurrilous, suggestive
11 disgraceful, near the bone
12 pornographic 14 near the knuckle

**obscenity**
04 cuss, dirt, evil, smut 05 curse, filth
06 sleaze 07 offence, outrage
08 atrocity, cussword, foulness, impurity, lewdness, ribaldry, ribaudry, vileness 09 bawdiness, carnality, dirtiness, eroticism, expletive, grossness, immodesty, indecency, lubricity, profanity, prurience, rybaudrye, scatology, swear-word, vulgarity 10 balderdash, coarseness, filthiness, immorality, indelicacy, wickedness 11 bad language, heinousness, imprecation, impropriety, malediction, pornography, raunchiness
12 unchasteness 13 salaciousness, shamelessness 14 four-letter word, lasciviousness, licentiousness, scurrilousness, suggestiveness

**obscure**
◇ *anagram indicator*
03 dim, fog 04 blur, dark, deep, hazy,

hide, mask, mist, veil, wrap **05** cloak, cloud, cover, dusky, faint, fuzzy, lowly, minor, misty, murky, shade, shady, vague **06** arcane, cloudy, darken, fogged, gloomy, hidden, humble, muddle, occult, opaque, remote, screen, shadow, shroud, unsung **07** blurred, complex, conceal, confuse, cryptic, eclipse, shadowy, unclear, unknown **08** abstruse, block out, darkness, disguise, doubtful, esoteric, involved, nameless, oracular, puzzling, riddling, twilight **09** concealed, confusing, enigmatic, obfuscate, oraculous, recondite, uncertain, unheard-of **10** complicate, indefinite, indistinct, mysterious, overshadow, perplexing **11** god-forsaken, little-known, out-of-the-way, unexplained, unimportant **12** impenetrable, inexplicable, unfathomable, unrecognized **13** inconspicuous, insignificant **14** indistinctness **15** undistinguished

**obscurity**
**03** fog **05** depth, night, shade **07** mystery **09** ambiguity, confusion, intricacy, lowliness, murkiness, mysticism **10** complexity, lack of fame **11** unclearness **12** abstruseness, namelessness, unimportance **13** reconditeness **14** insignificance **15** impenetrability

• **bring out of obscurity**
**04** fish

**obsequies**
**04** wake **06** burial **07** funeral **08** exequies **09** cremation, interment **10** entombment, inhumation

**obsequious**
**04** oily **06** abject, creepy, menial, smarmy **07** dutiful, fawning, fulsome, kiss-ass, servile, slavish **08** crawling, cringing, obedient, toadying, toadyish, unctuous **10** flattering, grovelling, submissive **11** bootlicking, deferential, subservient, sycophantic **12** ingratiating, knee-crooking

**observable**
**04** open **05** clear **06** patent **07** evident, notable, obvious, visible **08** apparent **09** scrutable **10** detectable, measurable, noticeable **11** appreciable, discernible, perceptible, significant **12** recognizable

**observance**
**04** Lent, puja, rite **06** custom, maying, notice, ritual **07** heeding, keeping, service, trinket, triumph **08** ceremony, festival, practice **09** adherence, attention, discharge, execution, following, formality, honouring, obedience, punctilio, reverence, sabbatism, tradition **10** compliance, fulfilment **11** celebration, performance **13** lectisternium

**observant**
**05** alert, sharp **06** seeing **07** devoted, dutiful, heedful, mindful, on guard **08** hawk-eyed, obedient, orthodox, vigilant, watchful **09** attentive, beady-eyed, committed, eagle-eyed, sharp-eyed, wide-awake **10** perceptive, percipient, practising **11** observative **12** card-carrying, on the lookout, on the qui vive

**observation**
**04** data, note **05** study **06** espial, notice, regard, remark, result, review, seeing **07** comment, finding, opinion, thought, viewing **08** eyesight, noticing, scrutiny, watching **09** attention, criticism, statement, utterance **10** annotation, cognizance, inspection, monitoring, perception, reflection **11** declaration, description, discernment, examination, information **13** consideration, pronouncement

**observatory**
**06** orrery **09** viewpoint **11** planetarium, planisphere

*Observatories include:*

**04** Keck
**05** Royal, Tower
**06** Gemini
**07** Arecibo, Palomar, Paranal
**08** Kitt Peak, Mauna Kea
**09** Greenwich
**11** Jodrell Bank, Mount Wilson
**12** Herstmonceux
**13** Tower of London
**14** Royal Greenwich

**observe**
**02** la, lo **03** eye, say, see, spy, use **04** espy, heed, hold, keep, mark, note, obey, spot, take, twig, view **05** clock, smoke, state, study, utter, watch **06** behold, detect, follow, fulfil, honour, notice, regard, remark **07** abide by, comment, declare, discern, examine, execute, inspect, look you, mention, monitor, perform, respect **08** adhere to, maintain, perceive, remember, take note **09** celebrate, conform to, discharge, recognize, speculate, surveille **10** animadvert, comply with, keep tabs on, take notice **11** commemorate, contemplate, keep an eye on, keep watch on, miss nothing **12** catch sight of **14** watch like a hawk

**observer**
**06** looker, viewer **07** watcher, witness **08** beholder, looker-on, onlooker, reporter **09** bystander, sightseer, spectator **10** eyewitness **11** commentator, speculation

**obsess**
**04** grip, rule **05** beset, eat up, haunt, hound **06** plague, prey on **07** bedevil, besiege, consume, control, engross, possess, torment **08** dominate **09** preoccupy **10** monopolize **11** have a grip on, have a hold on

**obsessed**
**05** beset **06** hipped **07** gripped, haunted, hounded, plagued **08** hung up on **09** dominated **10** bedevilled, immersed in, infatuated **11** in the grip of, preoccupied

**obsession**
**03** bug **05** mania, siege, thing **06** fetish, hang-up, phobia **07** complex **08** fixation, idée fixe, neurosis **09** monomania **10** compulsion, enthusiasm, hobby-horse **11** fascination, infatuation **12** one-track mind **13** preoccupation, ruling passion **15** bee in your bonnet

**obsessive**
**04** anal **05** fixed **08** gripping, haunting, neurotic **09** consuming, maddening **10** compulsive, tormenting **12** all-consuming, trainspotter

**obsolescence**
**06** disuse **07** failure **09** rejection, scrapping **10** redundancy **12** obsoleteness **13** disappearance

**obsolescent**
**05** aging, dated **06** ageing, fading, old hat, waning **08** dying out, moribund, outdated **09** declining, on the wane, out of date, redundant **10** on the shelf **11** on the way out, out of the ark **12** antediluvian, disappearing, old-fashioned, on the decline, past its prime

**obsolete**
**03** obs, old **04** dead **05** dated, passé **06** bygone, old hat **07** ancient, antique, disused, expired, extinct, outworn **08** in disuse, outdated, outmoded **09** discarded, out of date **10** antiquated, on the shelf **11** on the way out, out of the ark **12** antediluvian, discontinued, old-fashioned, out of fashion, past its prime **13** superannuated **14** behind the times

**obstacle**
**03** bar **04** boyg, curb, drag, gate, jump, oxer, rock, snag, stay, stop **05** catch, check, hitch, mogul **06** hazard, hiccup, hurdle, remora **07** barrier **08** blockade, blockage, drawback, handicap, stoppage, stubborn, tank trap **09** barricade, deterrent, hindrance **10** difficulty, hinderance, impediment **11** obstruction **12** Becher's Brook, entanglement, interference, interruption **14** stumbling-block

**obstinacy**
**08** firmness, obduracy, self-will, tenacity **10** doggedness, mulishness, perversity, wilfulness **11** frowardness, persistence, persistency, pertinacity **12** perseverance, resoluteness, stubbornness **13** inflexibility, intransigence, pigheadedness **14** relentlessness **15** hard-heartedness, wrongheadedness

**obstinate**
**04** dour, firm **05** rusty, stoor, stour, sture **06** cussed, dogged, kittle, mulish, stowre, sturdy, thrawn, wilful **07** adamant, bullish, diehard, hard-set,

restive, willful **08** camelish, stubborn, thraward, thrawart **09** hidebound, immovable, pigheaded, steadfast, unbending **10** bull-headed, determined, headstrong, inflexible, persistent, refractary, refractory, self-willed, stomachful, unyielding **11** hard-hearted, intractable, persevering, stiff-necked, unrelenting, wrongheaded **12** bloody-minded, contumacious, intransigent, pertinacious, pervicacious, recalcitrant, stiff-hearted, strong-minded **13** high-stomached, intransigeant

*See also* **stubborn**

**• obstinate person**
**04** mule

**obstreperous**
◇ *anagram indicator*
**04** loud, wild **05** noisy, radge, rough, rowdy **06** unruly **07** bolshie, raucous, restive, riotous, stroppy **09** clamorous, out of hand, turbulent **10** boisterous, disorderly, disruptive, refractory, rip-roaring, tumultuous, uproarious, vociferous **11** intractable, tempestuous **12** bloody-minded, uncontrolled, unmanageable **13** undisciplined

**obstruct**
◇ *containment indicator*
**03** bar **04** clog, crab, curb, foul, halt, stap, stop **05** block, brake, check, choke, cross, delay, hedge, limit, stall, stimy, stuff **06** arrest, bridle, cut off, hamper, hinder, hold up, impede, retard, stimie, stymie, thwart, waylay **07** blanket, inhibit, obscure, prevent, sandbag, shut off **08** encumber, restrict, slow down **09** barricade, frustrate, hamstring, interfere, interrupt **10** portcullis **13** interfere with

**obstruction**
**03** bar, let **04** clog, stop, veil **05** block, check, ileus, trump **07** barrier, embargo **08** blockade, blockage, obstacle, sanction, stoppage, traverse **09** barricade, body-check, deterrent, hindrance, roadblock **10** bottleneck, difficulty, filibuster, impediment, prevention **11** restriction **14** stumbling-block

**obstructive**
**07** awkward **08** blocking, delaying, negative, stalling **09** difficult, hindering, hindrance, unhelpful **10** inhibiting **11** restrictive **12** interrupting **13** unco-operative

**obtain**
**03** cop, get, pan **04** earn, gain, have, hold, make, rule, snag, take **05** exist, reach, reign, seize, stand **06** attain, come by, come to, derive, occupy, secure **07** achieve, acquire, be in use, compass, possess, prevail, procure, realize **08** hold sway **09** be in force, be the case, get hold of **11** be effective, be prevalent **14** get your hands on

**obtainable**
**05** on tap, ready **06** at hand, on call **07** to be had **09** available **10** accessible, achievable, attainable, procurable, realizable

**obtrude**
**04** sorn **05** abuse, foist **06** butt in, impose **07** break in, exploit, intrude, mislead, presume, put upon **08** encroach, protrude **13** force yourself **14** thrust yourself **15** take advantage of

**obtrusive**
**04** bold, loud, nosy **05** nosey, pushy **06** prying **07** blatant, forward, obvious **08** flagrant, meddling **09** intrusive, prominent **10** noticeable, projecting, protruding **11** conspicuous, interfering

**obtuse**
**03** dim **04** dozy, dull, dumb, slow **05** blunt, crass, dense, dopey, thick **06** stolid, stupid **09** dim-witted **10** dull-witted, slow-witted **11** insensitive **12** thick-skinned **13** unintelligent **15** slow on the uptake

**obverse**
**05** cross, heads **07** inverse, reverse **08** contrary, converse, opposite **10** antithesis **12** complemental

**obviate**
**04** save **05** avert **06** divert, remove **07** counter, prevent **08** preclude **09** forestall **10** anticipate, counteract

**obvious**
**04** bald, open, rank **05** broad, clear, plain **06** patent **07** blatant, evident, glaring, visible **08** apparent, clear-cut, distinct, manifest, palpable, pregnant **09** prominent, writ large **10** detectable, noticeable, pronounced, undeniable, well-marked **11** conspicuous, open-and-shut, perceptible, self-evident, transparent, unconcealed **12** crystal clear, recognizable, unmistakable **14** self-explaining **15** self-explanatory, straightforward

**obviously**
**03** duh **07** clearly, plainly **08** of course, patently **09** certainly, eminently, evidently **10** distinctly, manifestly, noticeably, undeniably **11** undoubtedly **12** unmistakably, without doubt

**occasion**
**02** do **04** bash, call, case, gala, hour, make, need, rise, room, time, turn **05** breed, cause, event, evoke, party, point, throw **06** affair, chance, create, effect, elicit, excuse, ground, induce, lead to, prompt, reason **07** bring on, episode, grounds, inspire, pretext, produce, provoke **08** accustom, engender, function, generate, incident, instance, juncture, persuade **09** encheason, happening, influence, originate, situation **10** bring about, experience, give rise to, occurrence **11** celebration, get-together, opportunity, requirement, social event **12** circumstance **13** justification

*See also* **event**; **party**

**occasional**
**03** odd **04** orra, rare **06** casual, daimen **08** fugitive, off and on, on and off, periodic, sometime, sporadic, uncommon **09** irregular **10** incidental, infrequent **12** intermittent

**occasionally**
**07** at times **08** casually, off and on, on and off **09** sometimes **10** now and then, once in a way, on occasion **11** at intervals, irregularly, now and again **12** every so often, infrequently, once in a while, periodically, sporadically **14** from time to time, intermittently

**occlude**
◇ *containment indicator*
**03** bar **04** clog, fill, halt, plug, seal, stop **05** block, check, choke, close, cover, dam up **06** absorb, arrest, bung up, clog up, hinder, impede, retain, stop up, thwart **08** obstruct

**occlusion**
**03** jam **04** clot **05** block **06** log jam **08** blockage, blocking, stoppage **09** hindrance **10** congestion, impediment **11** obstruction

**occult**
**03** art **04** arts **05** magic **06** arcane, hidden, secret, veiled **07** magical, obscure, unknown **08** abstruse, esoteric, mystical **09** black arts, concealed, mysticism, recondite **10** mysterious **12** metaphysical, supernatural **13** preternatural **14** transcendental **15** supernaturalism, the supernatural

*Occult- and supernatural-related terms include:*

**03** ESP, obi
**04** jinx, juju, omen, rune
**05** charm, coven, curse, relic, spell, totem, witch
**06** amulet, déjà vu, fetish, hoodoo, medium, séance, shaman, spirit, trance, vision, voodoo
**07** cabbala, diviner, evil eye, palmist, psychic, satanic, sorcery, warlock
**08** black cat, exorcism, exorcist, familiar, Satanism, Satanist, sorcerer, talisman
**09** astrology, black mass, ectoplasm, Hallowe'en, horoscope, influence, palmistry, pentagram, tarot card
**10** astrologer, black magic, broomstick, chiromancy, divination, evil spirit, hydromancy, necromancy, Ouija board®, paranormal, planchette, possession, sixth sense, white magic, witchcraft
**11** chiromancer, clairvoyant, crystal ball, divining-rod, hydromancer, incantation, necromancer, oneiromancy, poltergeist, premonition, psychometer, psychometry, second sight, witch doctor
**12** clairvoyance, oneiromancer, spiritualism, spiritualist,

supernatural, superstition, tarot reading
**13** fortune-teller, witch's sabbath
**14** Walpurgis Night

## occupancy

**03** use **04** term **06** tenure **07** holding, tenancy **09** ownership, residence **10** habitation, occupation, possession **11** inhabitancy **13** domiciliation **14** owner-occupancy

## occupant

**04** user **05** owner **06** holder, inmate, lessee, renter, tenant **08** occupier, resident, squatter **09** homeowner, incumbent **10** inhabitant **11** householder, leaseholder **13** owner-occupier

## occupation

**03** job, use **04** line, post, work **05** craft, field, trade **06** billet, career, employ, métier, tenure **07** calling, capture, control, holding, pursuit, seizure, tenancy **08** activity, business, conquest, interest, invasion, province, takeover, vocation **09** occupancy, overthrow, residence, residency **10** employment, habitation, possession, profession, walk of life **11** foreign rule, subjugation

*Occupations include:*

**02** AM, DJ, GP, MD, MP, PA
**03** MSP, nun, spy, vet
**04** aide, chef, cook, dean, dyer, hack, maid, monk, page, poet
**05** abbot, actor, agent, baker, boxer, buyer, caddy, clerk, coach, diver, envoy, friar, guide, judge, juror, mason, mayor, medic, miner, model, nanny, nurse, pilot, smith, tawer, tutor, usher, valet, vicar
**06** abbess, artist, au pair, author, banker, barber, barman, bishop, bookie, bowyer, brewer, broker, butler, cabbie, cleric, cooper, copper, coster, cowboy, critic, curate, dancer, dealer, doctor, draper, driver, editor, eggler, factor, farmer, fitter, forger, gaffer, glazer, grocer, herald, hermit, hosier, hunter, jailer, jester, jockey, joiner, lawyer, mercer, miller, ostler, packer, parson, pastor, pig-man, pirate, player, porter, potter, priest, ragman, ranger, roofer, sailor, salter, server, singer, skater, sniper, sparks, spicer, tailor, tanner, teller, tinner, trader, tycoon, typist, vendor, verger, waiter, warden, warder, weaver, welder, writer
**07** acrobat, actress, actuary, admiral, adviser, almoner, analyst, artisan, artiste, athlete, attaché, auditor, aviator, bailiff, barista, barmaid, bellboy, bellhop, bottle-o, breeder, builder, butcher, cashier, chemist, cleaner, climber, coalman, cobbler, collier, coroner, courier, cowherd, crofter, curator, cyclist, dentist, doorman, dresser, drummer, equerry, farrier, fiddler, fighter, fireman, florist, footman, foreman, frogman, general, glazier, gymnast, hangman, haulier, hostess, janitor, junkman, lace-man, lineman, lorimer, luthier, magnate, manager, marshal, masseur, midwife, milkman, oculist, officer, orderly, painter, partner, pianist, planner, plumber, poacher, popstar, postman, prefect, printer, rancher, referee, saddler, scholar, senator, servant, shearer, sheriff, showman, soldier, spinner, stapler, steward, student, surgeon, teacher, trainee, trainer, trapper, vintner, warrior, woolman, workman
**08** advocate, animator, armourer, attorney, banksman, botanist, bottle-oh, brakeman, callgirl, cardinal, chairman, chandler, chaplain, comedian, compiler, composer, conjurer, conjuror, corporal, costumer, coxswain, croupier, dairyman, deckhand, designer, diplomat, director, druggist, educator, embalmer, engineer, engraver, essayist, executor, factotum, farmhand, ferryman, film star, fishwife, forester, gangster, gardener, goatherd, governor, gunsmith, handyman, henchman, herdsman, hireling, home help, hotelier, huntsman, inventor, jeweller, labourer, landlady, landlord, lecturer, linguist, lyricist, magician, maltster, mapmaker, masseuse, mechanic, merchant, milkmaid, milliner, minister, minstrel, muleteer, musician, novelist, operator, optician, organist, pardoner, perfumer, pig-woman, polisher, preacher, producer, promoter, publican, quarrier, recorder, reporter, retailer, reviewer, salesman, sales rep, satirist, scrap-man, sculptor, seedsman, sergeant, shepherd, showgirl, smuggler, sorcerer, spaceman, spurrier, stockman, stripper, stuntman, supplier, surveyor, thatcher, upholder, waitress, watchman, wet nurse, wig-maker, woodsman, wrangler
**09** alchemist, anatomist, announcer, antiquary, architect, archivist, art critic, art dealer, assistant, associate, astronaut, attendant, barperson, barrister, biologist, bodyguard, bookmaker, brinjarry, buccaneer, bus driver, cab driver, caretaker, carpenter, charwoman, chauffeur, clergyman, coal miner, collector, columnist, commander, concierge, conductor, constable, cosmonaut, costumier, couturier, cricketer, decorator, detective, dietician, dramatist, ecologist, economist, executive, financier, fisherman, fruiterer, gas fitter, geologist, goldsmith, governess, guitarist, gutter-man, harvester, herbalist, historian, homeopath, horologer, housemaid, HR manager, hypnotist, innkeeper, inspector, ironsmith, jacksmith, landowner, launderer, laundress, librarian, lifeguard, locksmith, machinist, messenger, musketeer, navigator, newsagent, nursemaid, osteopath, outfitter, paralegal, paramedic, performer, physician, physicist, plasterer, ploughman, policeman, pop singer, poulterer, professor, publicist, publisher, puppeteer, registrar, robe maker, sailmaker, scientist, secretary, shoemaker, signaller, signalman, songsmith, spokesman, stagehand, stationer, staymaker, stevedore, subeditor, subtitler, swineherd, therapist, towncrier, tradesman, traveller, trumpeter, usherette, van driver, violinist, volunteer, whittawer, yachtsman, zookeeper, zoologist
**10** accountant, advertiser, air hostess, air steward, amanuensis, apothecary, apprentice, archbishop, astrologer, astronomer, auctioneer, baby sitter, bank teller, beautician, bellringer, bill-broker, biochemist, biographer, blacksmith, bookbinder, bookkeeper, bookseller, bricklayer, bureaucrat, campaigner, cartoonist, cartwright, chairmaker, clockmaker, coastguard, compositor, consultant, controller, copywriter, corn-dealer, corn-factor, councillor, counsellor, disc jockey, dishwasher, dramaturge, dressmaker, dry cleaner, equestrian, fellmonger, fishmonger, footballer, forecaster, frame-maker, fundraiser, gamekeeper, game warden, gatekeeper, geneticist, geochemist, geographer, glassmaker, handmaiden, headhunter, headmaster, highwayman, horologist, instructor, ironmonger, journalist, junk-dealer, keyboarder, legislator, librettist, lumberjack, magistrate, manageress, manicurist, manservant, midshipman, millwright, missionary, naturalist, negotiator, newscaster, newsmonger, nurseryman, obituarist, pallbearer, park ranger, pawnbroker, peltmonger, perruquier, pharmacist, piano tuner, playwright, podiatrist, politician, postmaster, private eye, programmer, proprietor, prospector, railwayman, removal man, researcher, ringmaster, roadmender, sales clerk, saleswoman, sempstress, shipbroker, shipwright, shopfitter, shopkeeper, signwriter, songstress, stewardess, stock agent, stockinger, stonemason, supervisor, taxi driver, technician, translator, typesetter, undertaker, unguentary,

wainwright, wharfinger, whitesmith, wholesaler, woodcarver, woodcutter
**11** accompanist, antiquarian, art director, astrologist, audio typist, bank manager, bingo caller, broadcaster, bullfighter, burn-the-wind, businessman, candlemaker, car salesman, chambermaid, cheerleader, chiropodist, clergywoman, commentator, coppersmith, delivery man, distributor, draughtsman, electrician, entertainer, estate agent, etymologist, executioner, firefighter, foot soldier, fund manager, glass blower, grave digger, greengrocer, haberdasher, hairdresser, hair stylist, head teacher, horse-dealer, illustrator, interpreter, interviewer, lifeboatman, linen-draper, lollipop man, lorry driver, metalworker, money broker, mountaineer, music-seller, neurologist, optometrist, panel beater, parlourmaid, pathologist, philatelist, philologist, philosopher, policewoman, proofreader, radiologist, relic-monger, secret agent, set designer, sociologist, sharebroker, ship builder, silversmith, steelworker, stockbroker, taxidermist, telephonist, ticket agent, tobacconist, travel agent, tree surgeon, truck driver, underwriter, upholsterer, vitraillist, wagonwright, wax-chandler, web designer, wheelwright, wool-stapler, youth worker
**12** anaesthetist, broker-dealer, cabinet maker, calligrapher, cartographer, cheesemonger, chimney sweep, chiropractor, churchwarden, civil servant, coal merchant, corn-merchant, costermonger, demonstrator, dramaturgist, entomologist, entrepreneur, event manager, fent-merchant, film director, garret-master, hotel manager, immunologist, IT consultant, longshoreman, maitre d'hotel, make-up artist, media planner, metallurgist, mineralogist, nutritionist, obstetrician, orthodontist, photographer, physiologist, ploughwright, postal worker, practitioner, PR consultant, press officer, prison warder, psychologist, radiographer, receptionist, restaurateur, sales manager, schoolmaster, screenwriter, scriptwriter, ship chandler, slink butcher, social worker, spokesperson, stage manager, statistician, stenographer, toxicologist, urban planner, veterinarian, warehouseman, wine merchant, wood engraver
**13** administrator, antique dealer, archaeologist, charity worker, choreographer, civil engineer, crane operator, criminologist, dental surgeon, food scientist, groundskeeper, gynaecologist, harbour master, health visitor, home economist, industrialist, lab technician, lexicographer, lollipop woman, mathematician, meteorologist, nightwatchman, oceanographer, old-clothesman, police officer, prison officer, rag-and-bone-man, rent collector, retail manager, scrap merchant, security guard, ship's chandler, shop assistant, sound engineer, streetcleaner, streetsweeper, support worker, traffic warden, window cleaner
**14** anthropologist, camera operator, claims assessor, draughtsperson, market gardener, marriage-broker, merchant tailor, microbiologist, music therapist, naval architect, pharmacologist, pharmacopolist, store detective, superintendent, systems analyst, tallow chandler
**15** biotechnologist, business analyst, commission agent, computer analyst, conservationist, costume designer, dental hygienist, fashion designer, flight attendant, funeral director, graphic designer, marine biologist, military officer, ophthalmologist, personal trainer, physiotherapist, police constable, refuse collector, speech therapist, stock controller, ticket collector

**occupational**
**04** work **05** trade **06** career **08** business **10** employment, job-related, vocational **12** professional

**occupied**
**04** busy, full **05** in use, taken **06** tied up **07** engaged, taken up, working **08** absorbed, employed, hard at it, immersed, tenanted **09** engrossed **11** preoccupied, unavailable

**occupier**
**04** user **06** dealer, holder, inmate, lessee, renter, tenant **08** occupant, resident, squatter **09** homeowner, incumbent **10** inhabitant **11** householder, leaseholder **13** owner-occupier

**occupy**
◇ *insertion indicator*
**03** own, use **04** busy, fill, have, hold, nest, rent, tire **05** amuse, beset, seize, trade, use up **06** absorb, divert, embusy, employ, engage, fill in, invade, live in, manure, move in, obsess, obtain, people, settle, stay in, take up, tenant **07** capture, cohabit, dwell in, engross, entreat, immerse, improve, inhabit, involve, overrun, possess **08** interest, occupate, overbusy, reside in, take over **09** entertain, preoccupy, stimulate **14** make your home in

**occur**
**03** hit **04** fall, meet **05** arise, exist **06** appear, befall, chance, crop up, dawn on, happen, obtain, result, sink in, strike, turn up **07** be found, develop, turn out **09** be present, come about, come to you, eventuate, take place, transpire **10** come to mind, come to pass **11** materialize **12** have its being, spring to mind **13** cross your mind, enter your head, present itself, suggest itself **14** manifest itself

**occurrence**
**04** case **05** event **06** action, affair **07** arising, episode **08** incident, instance **09** existence, happening, incidence **10** appearance **11** development, proceedings, springing-up **12** circumstance **13** manifestation
• **trying occurrence**
**03** cow

**ocean**
**03** sea **04** main **05** briny **07** the deep **08** high seas, millpond, profound, the drink **11** herring pond

*Oceans include:*

**06** Arctic, Indian
**07** Pacific
**08** Atlantic, Southern
**12** North Pacific, South Pacific
**13** North Atlantic, South Atlantic

*See also* **sea**

*Ocean trenches include:*

**03** Yap
**04** Java
**05** Japan, Kuril, Palau, Tonga
**06** Cayman, Ryukyu
**07** Atacama, Mariana
**08** Aleutian, Izu Bonin, Kermadec, Marianas, Mindanao, Romanche
**09** Peru-Chile
**10** Philippine, Puerto Rico
**11** Nansei Shoto
**12** Bougainville, West Caroline
**13** Middle America, South Sandwich

**ocean-going**
**05** naval **06** marine **07** sailing **08** maritime, nautical, seagoing **09** seafaring

**ochre**
**04** keel

**octave**
**04** utas

**October**
**03** Oct

**octopus**
**05** polyp, poulp **06** polype, poulpe **07** octopod **08** Octopoda **09** devilfish

**odd**
◇ *anagram indicator*
◇ *hidden alternately indicator*
**03** god, rum **04** fent, orra, rare, wild, zany **05** barmy, drôle, droll, extra, funny, kinky, queer, spare, wacky, weird **06** casual, far-out, freaky, quaint, quirky, random, single, sundry, way-out, whimsy **07** bizarre, curious, deviant, oddball, odd-like, strange,

surplus, uncanny, unusual, various, whimsey **08** abnormal, atypical, crackers, freakful, freakish, left-over, original, part-time, peculiar, periodic, seasonal, singular, uncommon, unpaired **09** different, eccentric, haphazard, irregular, remaining, temporary, unmatched, whimsical **10** additional, fortuitous, incidental, mismatched, occasional, off the wall, outlandish, remarkable **11** exceptional, superfluous **13** extraordinary, idiosyncratic, miscellaneous **14** unconventional

**• odd one out**

**04** case, cure **05** freak **06** odd bod, weirdo **07** oddball, odd fish **09** eccentric, odd man out, queer fish, tall poppy **11** odd woman out **13** nonconformist **14** fish out of water

**oddball**

◇ *anagram indicator*

**03** dag, nut, rum **04** card, case, geek, kook, loon, wack **05** crank, flake, freak **06** nutter, oddity, weirdo **07** cupcake, dingbat, odd fish, strange **08** crackpot, peculiar **09** character, eccentric, queer fish **13** nonconformist **14** fish out of water

**oddity**

**03** dag, nut, rum **04** card, case, geek, kook, loon, wack **05** flake, freak, quirk, twist **06** jimjam, misfit, nutter, object, rarity, weirdo **07** anomaly, cupcake, dingbat, oddball, odd fish **08** crackpot, queerity **09** character, curiosity, queer fish, queerness **10** phenomenon **11** abnormality, peculiarity, singularity, strangeness **12** eccentricity, idiosyncrasy **14** fish out of water

**odd-looking person**

**04** quiz

**oddly**

◇ *anagram indicator*

◇ *hidden alternately indicator*

**07** weirdly **09** curiously, strangely, unusually **10** abnormally, remarkably **11** irregularly

**oddment**

**03** bit, end **04** fent **05** patch, piece, scrap, shred **06** offcut **07** remnant, snippet **08** fragment, leftover

**odds**

**02** SP **04** edge, lead, line **05** price **06** scraps **07** chances, dispute, the line **09** advantage, supremacy **10** ascendancy, inequality, likelihood **11** probability, superiority **13** starting price

**• at odds**

**06** at outs **07** arguing **08** clashing **09** differing, out of step **10** at variance, in conflict **11** disagreeing, quarrelling **13** at loggerheads **14** in disagreement

**• ignore the odds**

◇ *hidden alternately indicator*

**• odds and ends**

**03** tat **04** bits, junk, tatt **06** debris, job-lot, litter, scraps **07** rubbish **08** cuttings, leavings, oddments, remnants, snippets **09** bric-à-brac **11** bits and bobs, odds and sods, this and that **13** bits and pieces, odd-come-shorts

**ode**

**04** awdl **06** monody, threne **07** epicede, threnos **08** Pindaric, stasimon, threnode, threnody **09** epicedium, epinicion, epinikion **12** genethliacon

**odious**

**04** foul, vile **06** horrid **07** hateful, heinous **08** horrible **09** abhorrent, execrable, loathsome, obnoxious, offensive, repugnant, repulsive, revolting **10** abominable, despicable, detestable, disgusting, unpleasant **12** contemptible, disagreeable **13** objectionable

**odium**

**05** blame, shame **06** hatred, infamy **07** censure, dislike, obloquy **08** contempt, disgrace **09** animosity, antipathy, discredit, disfavour, dishonour, disrepute **10** abhorrence, execration, opprobrium **11** detestation, disapproval, reprobation **12** condemnation **13** offensiveness **14** disapprobation

**odorous**

**05** balmy **07** pungent, scented **08** aromatic, fragrant, perfumed, redolent **11** odoriferous **13** sweet-smelling

**odour**

**02** bo **04** niff, pong, sent, waff **05** aroma, savor, scent, smell, stink, whiff **06** repute, savour, stench **07** bouquet, perfume **09** fragrance, redolence

**odourless**

**09** inodorous, unscented **10** deodorized **12** without smell **13** having no smell

**odyssey**

**04** trek **06** voyage **07** journey, travels **09** adventure, wandering **13** peregrination

**of**

**01** o' **02** de, du, on, to

**off**

◇ *anagram indicator*

**03** bad, far, ill, out **04** away, from, gone, high, kill, sick, sour **05** apart, aside, right, rough, seedy, slack, wrong **06** absent, depart!, mouldy, poorly, queasy, rancid, rotten, spoilt, turned, unwell **07** dropped, off form, shelved **08** below par, scrapped **09** abandoned, called off, cancelled, elsewhere, incorrect, off-colour, postponed **10** decomposed, indisposed, out of sorts **11** at a distance, substandard, unavailable **12** unobtainable **13** disappointing **14** unsatisfactory **15** under the weather

**offal**

**03** fry **05** gurry, heart, liver **06** kidney, refuse, tongue **07** garbage **08** entrails, lamb's fry **11** variety meat

**offbeat**

**05** kooky, wacky, weird **06** far-out, freaky, way-out **07** bizarre, oddball, strange, unusual **08** abnormal **09** eccentric **10** unorthodox **13** untraditional **14** unconventional

**off-colour**

◇ *anagram indicator*

**03** ill **04** blue, foul, lewd, rude, sexy, sick **05** crook, crude, dirty, gross, rough, seedy **06** coarse, crummy, filthy, impure, poorly, queasy, risqué, sleazy, smutty, unwell, vulgar **07** immoral, obscene, off form, run down **08** depraved, immodest, improper, indecent **09** offensive, perverted **10** degenerate, indelicate, indisposed, licentious, out of sorts, suggestive **11** peelie-wally **12** pornographic **15** under the weather

**offence**

**03** ire, sin **04** hurt, snub **05** anger, crime, fault, pique, wrong **06** injury, insult, slight **07** affront, assault, misdeed, outrage, umbrage **08** atrocity, trespass **09** annoyance, antipathy, exception, indignity, stumbling, violation **10** illegal act, infraction, resentment, wrongdoing **11** disapproval, displeasure, indignation **12** exasperation, hard feelings, infringement, misdemeanour **13** transgression **14** breach of the law

*See also* **crime**

**• take offence**

**04** huff, miff **06** be hurt, resent **07** be angry, be upset **08** be miffed, be put out, get huffy **09** be annoyed **10** be insulted, be offended, feel put out, get the hump **11** be indignant, go into a huff, take umbrage **13** be exasperated, take exception **14** take personally

**offend**

**03** err, hip, hyp, sin **04** hurt, miff, snub **05** anger, annoy, repel, upset, wound, wrong **06** injure, insult, kittle, needle, put off, put out, revolt, sicken **07** affront, disgust, do wrong, incense, outrage, provoke, umbrage, violate **08** distaste, go astray, gross out, nauseate **09** disoblige, displease **10** exasperate, transgress **11** break the law, displeasure

**offended**

**04** hurt **05** huffy, stung, upset **06** hipped, miffed, pained, piqued, put out **07** angered, annoyed, in a huff, wounded **08** incensed, outraged, smarting **09** affronted, disgusted, resentful **10** displeased **11** disgruntled, exasperated

**offender**

**07** culprit **08** criminal **09** defaulter, miscreant, wrongdoer **10** delinquent, lawbreaker, malefactor **11** guilty party, probationer **12** transgressor

**offensive**
**03** bad **04** foul, push, raid, rude, vile **05** alien, drive, grody, nasty **06** attack, charge, frowsy, frowzy, odious, sortie, thrust, wicked **07** abusive, assault, hostile, hurtful **08** annoying, impolite, indecent, insolent, invading, invasion, stinking, wounding **09** abhorrent, attacking, incursion, insulting, loathsome, obnoxious, onslaught, repellent, repugnant, revolting, sickening, unsavoury, upsetting **10** abominable, affronting, aggressive, detestable, disgusting, nauseating, outrageous, unpleasant **11** belligerent, displeasing, impertinent **12** antagonistic, disagreeable, discourteous, disrelishing, exasperating **13** disrespectful, objectionable

**offensively**
**10** detestably **12** disagreeably, disgustingly, nauseatingly, unpleasantly **13** objectionably

**offer**
**03** bid, try **04** bode, give, make, sell, show **05** essay, shore **06** afford, extend, prefer, submit, supply, tender **07** advance, attempt, bidding, express, hold out, offer up, present, proffer, propine, propose, provide, suggest, worship **08** approach, dedicate, overture, proposal, propound **09** celebrate, put in a bid, recommend, sacrifice, volunteer **10** consecrate, put forward, submission, suggestion **11** come forward, proposition, show willing **12** presentation **13** make available **14** put on the market

**offering**
**03** IPO **04** gift **05** tithe **06** ex voto, xenium **07** handout, present **08** donation, oblation **09** sacrifice **10** dedication **11** celebration **12** consecration, contribution, subscription **13** heave-shoulder

**offhand**
**04** airy, curt, rude, snap **05** ad lib, blasé, terse **06** abrupt, at once, casual **07** brusque, cursory **08** careless, cavalier, informal, laid-back **09** brevi manu, extempore, impromptu **10** cavalierly, nonchalant, off the cuff **11** free-and-easy, immediately, indifferent, perfunctory, unconcerned **12** at first blush, discourteous, happy-go-lucky, uninterested **13** unceremonious **14** currente calamo **15** at the first blush, take-it-or-leave-it, without checking

**office**
**03** aid **04** base, duty, help, hint, part, post, role, wing, word, work **05** aegis, place **06** agency, back-up, branch, bureau, charge, favour, tenure **07** backing, cockpit, section, service, support **08** advocacy, auspices, business, division, function, lavatory, position, referral, workroom **09** affiliate, mediation, patronage, situation, workplace **10** assistance, commission, department, employment, obligation, occupation, subsection, subsidiary **11** appointment, local office, subdivision **12** intercession, intervention **14** recommendation, regional office, responsibility **15** place of business

*See also* **toilet**

*Offices include:*

**02** CO, FO, PO, TO, WO
**03** box, COI, CRO, DLO, EPO, FCO, GAO, GPO, IIP, IRO, Met, NAO, OFT, OME, ONS, OPW, ORR, OSS, OST, pay, PRO, RLO, SFO, War
**04** back, BFPO, fire, HMSO, Holy, Home, land, loan, Pipe, Post
**05** Assay, Crown, front, Ofcom, Offer, Ofgas, Ofgem, Oflot, Oftel, Ofwat, paper, press, stamp
**06** Ofsted, Patent, Pat Off, police, Record, ticket
**07** booking, Foreign, sorting
**08** Chancery, Colonial, Eurostat, incident, printing, register, registry, Scottish
**09** personnel, receiving, telegraph
**10** dead-letter, employment, Quai d'Orsay, registered, Stationery
**11** general post, left-luggage, victualling
**12** Commonwealth, Serious Fraud
**13** Inland Revenue, National Audit
**14** European Patent, Meteorological, returned letter
**15** Criminal Records

*Office furniture includes:*

**04** desk, safe
**07** lectern
**08** desk lamp, fire safe
**09** partition, plan chest, stepstool, work table
**11** storage unit, swivel chair, workstation
**12** computer desk, drawing-board, fire cupboard, printer stand, typist's chair
**13** executive desk, filing cabinet, filing trolley
**14** boardroom table, display cabinet, executive chair, filing cupboard, reception chair
**15** conference table, secretarial desk

*Office equipment includes:*

**03** OHP, VDU
**05** mouse
**06** inkpad, screen, tacker
**07** cash box, monitor, planner, printer, scanner, stapler, trimmer
**08** computer, intercom, keyboard, mouse mat, plan file, shredder
**09** date-stamp, dust cover, laminator, telephone, textphone, time clock, wages book
**10** calculator, comb binder, copy holder, Dictaphone®, duplicator, fax machine, guillotine, letter tray, monitor arm, paper punch, printwheel, typewriter
**11** comb binding, hole puncher, noticeboard, photocopier, switchboard
**12** acoustic hood, letter opener, letter scales, message board, parcel scales, screen filter, telex machine, visitors' book, wire bindings
**13** data cartridge, desk organizer, microcassette, planning board, reference book, staple-remover, thermal binder, waste-paper bin, word processor
**14** adhesive binder, diskette mailer, flip-chart easel, laptop computer, slide projector, telephone index

*See also* **stationery**

• **branch office**
**02** bo

• **in office**
**02** in

• **office of bishop**
**03** see

• **office of cardinal**
**03** hat

• **out of office**
**04** late

**officer**
**03** col, off **04** lead **05** agent, envoy, polis **06** deputy, fantad, fantod, non-com, pusser, schout, varlet **07** command **08** dog's-body, official **09** appointee, dignitary, executive, inspector, messenger, subaltern **10** bureaucrat **11** board member, functionary **12** office-bearer, office-holder **13** administrator, public servant **14** representative **15** committee member

*See also* **police officer**; **rank**; **religious**; **ship**

**official**
**03** off **05** legal **06** Bumble, formal, kosher, lawful, proper, pusser, ritual, solemn **07** officer, stately **08** accepted, approved, bona fide, endorsed, licensed **09** authentic, certified, dignified, validated **10** accredited, authorized, ceremonial, legitimate, recognized, sanctioned **11** functionary **12** Jack-in-office, office-bearer, office-holder **13** authenticated, authoritative

*Officials include:*

**02** JP, MP
**05** agent, chief, clerk, druid, elder, envoy, hakim, mayor, reeve, usher
**06** atabeg, atabek, consul, Euro-MP, notary, purser, pusser
**07** bailiff, captain, coroner, equerry, manager, marshal, monitor, prefect, proctor, senator, sheriff, steward, vaivode, voivode
**08** chairman, delegate, diplomat, director, Eurocrat, executor, governor, mandarin, mayoress, minister, mud-clerk, nipcheese, overseer, provedor, providor
**09** commander, commissar, executive,

Gauleiter, inspector, ombudsman, president, principal, provedore, registrar
**10** ambassador, bureaucrat, chairwoman, chancellor, councillor, magistrate, proprietor, proveditor, railroader, supervisor
**11** chairperson, congressman, proveditore
**12** baron-officer, borough-reeve, civil servant, commissioner
**13** administrator, congresswoman, fonctionnaire
**14** representative, superintendent

**officialdom**
**04** them **08** ministry **09** mandarins, officials, the system **10** government **11** bureaucracy **12** civil service **13** administrator, civil servants **14** administration, the authorities **15** local government

**officialese**
**06** jargon **07** rubbish **08** nonsense **09** buzz words, gibberish **10** journalese **11** computerese **12** gobbledygook, psychobabble

**officially**
**08** formally, properly **09** correctly **11** on the record **12** managerially, procedurally **13** authentically **15** authoritatively

**officiate**
**03** run **05** chair **06** manage **07** conduct, oversee, preside **10** be in charge, take charge **11** superintend **12** take the chair

**officious**
**05** bossy, pushy **06** prying, spoffy **07** dutiful, forward **08** bustling, informal, meddling, obliging, overbusy, spoffish **09** diplomacy, intrusive, obtrusive **10** meddlesome **11** dictatorial, domineering, importunate, inquisitive, interfering, opinionated, over-zealous, pragmatical **13** self-important

**officiously**
**07** bossily, pushily **13** dictatorially, over-zealously **15** self-importantly, with importunity

**offing**
**• in the offing**
**04** near **06** at hand **07** in sight **08** coming up, imminent, on the way **10** coming soon, on the cards **11** close at hand **12** on the horizon **13** happening soon

**offish**
**04** cool **05** aloof **07** haughty, stuck-up **10** unsociable **11** standoffish

**off-key**
**07** jarring **09** dissonant, out of tune **10** discordant, unsuitable **11** conflicting **12** inharmonious, out of keeping **13** inappropriate

**offload**
**04** drop, dump, palm **05** chuck, shift **06** unload **07** deposit **08** get rid of, jettison, unburden **09** disburden, discharge

**off-putting**
**08** daunting **09** unnerving, upsetting **10** disturbing, formidable, unpleasant, unsettling **11** dispiriting, frightening, unappealing **12** demoralizing, discomfiting, discouraging, intimidating **13** disconcerting, disheartening

**offset**
**06** cancel **07** balance **09** cancel out, make up for **10** balance out, counteract, neutralize **11** countervail **12** counterpoise **13** compensate for **14** counterbalance

**offshoot**
**03** arm **04** limb, sien **05** bayou, plant, scion, swarm **06** branch, reform, result **07** outcome, product, spin-off **08** shoulder, sideslip **09** apophysis, appendage, billabong, by-product, outgrowth **11** consequence, development

**offspring**
**03** get, kid, son **04** baby, burd, kids, seed, sons **05** breed, brood, child, heirs, issue, spawn, young **06** babies, family, infant, nipper, source **07** infants, nippers, product, progeny **08** ancestry, children, daughter, young one **09** daughters, little one, young ones, youngster **10** generation, little ones, successors, youngsters **11** descendants

**often**
**03** oft **04** much **08** commonly, frequent, ofttimes **09** generally, many a time, many times, regularly **10** frequently, repeatedly **11** day in day out **12** time and again **13** again and again, time after time, week in week out **15** month in month out

**ogle**
**03** eye **04** leer, look **05** eliad, eye up, stare **06** eyliad, illiad **07** eyeliad, glad eye **08** oeillade **10** make eyes at

**ogre**
**03** orc **04** boyg **05** beast, bogey, brute, demon, devil, fiend, giant, troll **06** savage **07** monster, villain **08** bogeyman **09** barbarian

**Ohio**
**02** OH

**oik** *see* **cad**

**oil**
**03** fat **04** balm, news, oint **05** cream, salve, smear **06** anoint, grease, lotion **07** unguent **08** liniment, ointment **09** lubricant, lubricate **10** impregnate, make smooth **11** information

*Oils include:*

**03** ben, gas, nim, nut, til
**04** baby, cade, coal, corn, crab, derv, dika, fish, fuel, hair, neem, nimb, otto, palm, poon, rape, rock, rose, rusa, seed, tall, tung, wood, wool, zest
**05** attar, carap, crude, grass, heavy, macaw, neemb, niger, olive, ottar, poppy, pulza, rosin, salad, savin, shale, shark, snake, sperm, spike, sweet, thyme, train, whale
**06** ajowan, almond, canola, castor, chrism, cloves, cohune, diesel, illipe, jojoba, macoya, neroli, peanut, savine, Seneca, sesame
**07** arachis, cajuput, camphor, coconut, gingili, jinjili, linseed, lumbang, mineral, mirbane, mustard, myrrhol, spindle, verbena, vitriol
**08** ambrosia, bergamot, camphine, cinnamon, cod-liver, creosote, gingelly, kerosene, kerosine, lavender, macahuba, macassar, North Sea, paraffin, pristane, rapeseed, rosewood
**09** black gold, candlenut, grapeseed, neat's-foot, patchouli, patchouly, safflower, sassafras, spikenard, sunflower, vanaspati, vegetable
**10** citronella, eucalyptus, peppermint, petit grain, turpentine, ylang-ylang
**11** camphorated, chaulmoogra, wintergreen
**12** brilliantine
**15** evening primrose

**• oil platform**
**03** rig
**• oil receptacle**
**04** sump

**oily**
**03** fat **04** glib **05** fatty, slimy, suave **06** greasy, smarmy, smooth, urbane **07** buttery, servile **08** slippery, unctuous **10** flattering, obsequious, oleaginous **11** subservient **12** ingratiating **13** smooth-talking

**ointment**
**03** gel **04** balm **05** cream, salve **06** balsam, cerate, lotion, pomade **07** pomatum, unction, unguent **08** eye-salve, liniment, lipsalve, Vaseline® **09** basilicon, cold cream, collyrium, emollient, inunction, lubricant, Tiger balm® **11** embrocation, preparation
**• ointment base**
**07** lanolin

**OK**
**03** A-OK, oke, yes **04** fair, fine, good, jake, okay, pass, so-so, sure, well **05** right **06** agreed, not bad, righto **07** agree to, approve, consent, correct, go-ahead, in order, up to par **08** accurate, adequate, all right, approval, okey-doke, passable, passably, sanction, say yes to, thumbs-up, very good, very well **09** agreement, authorize, certainly, consent to, no worries, okey-dokey, permitted, tolerable, tolerably **10** acceptable, all correct, convenient, good as gold, green light, no problems, permission, reasonable, reasonably **11** approbation, endorsement, rubber-stamp, up to scratch **12** satisfactory,

she'll be right **13** authorization, Bob's your uncle, she'll be apples **14** satisfactorily

### Oklahoma
**02** OK **04** Okla

### okra
**05** gumbo **06** bhindi **11** lady's finger **12** lady's fingers

### old
◇ *archaic word indicator*
**01** O **02** ex- **03** eld, set **04** aged, auld, folk, gaga, gray, grey, oral, torn, wise, worn **05** aging, banal, corny, early, fixed, passé, stale, stock, tired, trite, usual **06** ageing, age-old, bygone, common, former, mature, past it, primal, senile, shabby **07** ancient, antique, archaic, cast-off, classic, cliché'd, decayed, earlier, elderly, lasting, one-time, quondam, routine, veteran, vintage, worn-out **08** clichéed, decaying, decrepit, earliest, enduring, habitual, historic, obsolete, original, outdated, overused, previous, primeval, pristine, sensible, sometime, time-worn **09** crumbling, customary, erstwhile, getting on, hackneyed, long-lived, out of date, primaeval, primitive, senescent, unwritten, worm-eaten **10** accustomed, antiquated, broken down, ceremonial, Dickensian, overworked, pedestrian, primordial, ramshackle, threadbare, tumbledown, uninspired, unoriginal, yawn-making **11** commonplace, established, on the way out, out of the ark, over the hill, prehistoric, stereotyped, traditional, wearing thin **12** antediluvian, cliché-ridden, conventional, long-standing, old-fashioned, run-of-the-mill, time-honoured **13** old as the hills, past your prime, platitudinous, unfashionable, unimaginative **14** behind the times, long in the tooth **15** advanced in years, long-established, no spring chicken

### old age
**03** age, eld **04** hoar, hore **05** years **06** dotage **07** oldness **08** agedness, senility **09** antiquity **10** senescence **11** elderliness, vale of years **14** advancing years, declining years **15** second childhood

### old-fashioned
◇ *archaic word indicator*
**03** old **04** dead, past **05** corny, dated, dusty, fusty, mumsy, passé, steam **06** antick, bygone, old hat, past it, Podunk, quaint, rococo, square, uncool **07** ancient, antique, archaic, arriéré, old-time **08** medieval, obsolete, outdated, outmoded, shmaltzy, vieux jeu **09** mediaeval, moth-eaten, out of date, primitive, rinky-dink, schmaltzy **10** antiquated, auld-farand, fuddy-duddy, oldfangled, written off **11** auld-farrant, Neanderthal, obsolescent, on the way out, out of the ark **12** antediluvian, out of fashion **13** unfashionable **14** behind the times

### old maid
**08** spinster

### old man
**02** pa **03** OAP **04** boss, koro **05** elder, oldie **06** bodach, father, gaffer, geezer, Nestor **07** grandad, husband, oldster **08** employer, granddad, old-timer, presbyte **09** greybeard, old codger, old stager, patriarch, pensioner **10** fuddy-duddy, golden ager, white-beard **11** grandfather **12** coffin-dodger **13** senior citizen **14** elder statesman **15** old-age pensioner

*See also* **father**; **old woman**

### old-time
**03** old **04** past **05** dated, passé **06** bygone **07** archaic **08** obsolete, outdated, outmoded **09** out of date **10** antiquated **12** old-fashioned, out of fashion **13** unfashionable **14** behind the times

### old woman
**03** bag, hag, OAP **04** aunt, kuia, trot, wife **05** biddy, crone, fagot, oldie **06** beldam, faggot, gammer, granny, grouch, mother **07** beldame, carline, fusspot, grandma, grannie, old dear **08** caillach, grumbler **09** cailleach, cailliach, grandmama, pensioner **10** complainer, golden ager, grandmamma **11** grandmother **12** coffin-dodger **13** senior citizen **15** old-age pensioner

*See also* **mother**; **old man**

### old-world
**04** past **06** bygone, quaint **07** archaic **09** auld-warld **10** antiquated, olde-worlde **11** picturesque, traditional **12** old-fashioned

### olio
**04** olla **06** medley **07** mixture **10** miscellany

### olive
**04** Olea **05** wolly **08** oleaster

### Olympics

*Olympians include:*

**03** **Coe** (Sebastian)
**04** **Clay** (Cassius), **Dean** (Christopher), **Ewry** (Ray), **Otto** (Kristin), **Papp** (Laszlo), **Todd** (Mark), **Witt** (Katarina)
**05** **Blair** (Bonnie), **Bubka** (Sergei), **Chand** (Dhyan), **Cranz** (Christl), **Curry** (John), **Henie** (Sonja), **Killy** (Jean-Claude), **Lewis** (Carl), **Lewis** (Denise), **Longo** (Jeannie), **Meade** (Richard), **Nurmi** (Paavo), **Ottey** (Merlene), **Owens** (Jesse), **Popov** (Aleksandr), **Savon** (Felix), **Spitz** (Mark), **Tomba** (Alberto)
**06** **Aamodt** (Kjetil), **Beamon** (Bob), **Bikila** (Abebe), **Biondi** (Matt), **Button** (Dick), **D'Inzeo** (Raimondo), **Fraser** (Dawn), **Heiden** (Eric), **Holmes** (Dame Kelly), **Korbut** (Olga), **Oerter** (Al), **Phelps** (Michael), **Ritola** (Ville), **Sailer** (Toni), **Thorpe** (Ian), **Thorpe** (Jim)
**07** **Ainslie** (Ben), **Boitano** (Brian), **Cousins** (Robin), **Daehlie** (Bjorn), **Edwards** (Jonathan), **Fischer** (Birgit), **Johnson** (Michael), **Klammer** (Franz), **Mathias** (Bob), **Nykänen** (Matti), **Pinsent** (Sir Matthew), **Scherbo** (Vitaly), **Schmidt** (Birgit), **Torvill** (Jayne), **Voronin** (Mikhail), **Zatopek** (Emil), **Zelezny** (Jan)
**08** **Christie** (Linford), **Comaneci** (Nadia), **Cuthbert** (Betty), **De Bruijn** (Inge), **Dityatin** (Aleksandr), **Elvstrøm** (Paul), **Gerevich** (Aladár), **Jernberg** (Sixten), **Latynina** (Larissa), **Louganis** (Greg), **Redgrave** (Sir Steve), **Stenmark** (Ingemar), **Thompson** (Daley), **Zijlaard** (Leontien)
**09** **Andrianov** (Nikolay), **Babashoff** (Shirley), **Cáslavská** (Vera), **Egerszegi** (Krisztina), **Gräfström** (Gillis), **Schneider** (Vreni), **Seizinger** (Katja), **Stevenson** (Teófilo)
**10** **Linsenhoff** (Liselott), **Moser-Proll** (Annemarie), **van Moorsel** (Leontien)
**11** **Mangiarotti** (Edouardo), **Weissmuller** (Johnny)
**12** **Blankers-Koen** (Fanny), **Gebrselassie** (Haile), **Germeshausen** (Bernhard), **Joyner-Kersee** (Jackie), **Suleymanoglu** (Naim)
**13** **Longo-Ciprelli** (Jeannie)
**14** **Griffith-Joyner** (Florence)

### Oman
**03** OMN

### omelette
**08** frittata, tortilla

### omen
**04** sign **05** freet, freit, purse, token **06** augury, boding **07** auspice, portent, presage, warning **08** bodement, dead-fire, forecast, prodrome, soothsay **09** abodement, harbinger, night-crow, prodromus, prognosis **10** foreboding, forerunner, indication, night-raven, prediction, prognostic **11** premonition, presagement **12** corpse candle, presentiment

### ominous
**07** bodeful, fateful, unlucky **08** menacing, minatory, sinister **10** foreboding, portentous **11** threatening, unpromising **12** inauspicious, unfavourable, unpropitious

### ominously
**06** grimly **10** alarmingly **11** dangerously **13** frighteningly

### omission
**03** gap, out **04** balk, lack **05** baulk **06** lacuna **07** default, elision, erasure, failure, neglect **08** deletion **09** avoidance, disregard, exception, exclusion, haplology, oversight **10** expunction, leaving-out, lipography, negligence **11** dereliction

### omit
**03** let **04** drop, fail, miss, pass, skip

05 erase 06 delete, except, forget, rub out 07 edit out, exclude, expunge, miss out, neglect 08 cross out, leave out, overlook, overskip, pass over, white out 09 disregard, eliminate, pretermit 11 leave undone 13 fail to mention

**omnibus**
09 anthology, inclusive 10 collection, compendium 11 compendious, compilation, wide-ranging 12 all-embracing, encyclopedia, encyclopedic 13 comprehensive

**omnipotence**
07 mastery 09 supremacy 10 total power 11 divine right, sovereignty 12 almightiness, plenipotence 13 absolute power, invincibility 15 all-powerfulness

**omnipotent**
07 supreme 08 almighty 10 invincible 11 all-powerful, plenipotent

**omnipresent**
08 infinite 09 limitless, pervasive, universal 10 all-present, ubiquitary, ubiquitous 12 all-pervasive

**omniscient**
07 all-wise 09 all-seeing, pansophic 10 all-knowing

**omnivorous**
10 gluttonous 12 all-devouring, pantophagous 14 eating anything, indiscriminate

**on**
◇ *anagram indicator*
◇ *juxtaposition down indicator*
01 o 02 an, by, in, of, re, to 03 leg, sur 04 atop, over, side, upon 05 about, tipsy 06 beside, tiddly 07 against, forward!, proceed!, stuck to, towards 08 feasible, touching 09 apropos of, as regards, regarding, resting on 10 acceptable, attached to, concerning, relating to 11 dealing with, practicable, referring to 12 with regard to 13 concerned with, connected with, in contact with, in the matter of, with respect to 14 on the subject of 15 with reference to

**• on and off**
08 fitfully, off and on, sporadic 09 sometimes 10 now and then, occasional, on occasion 11 at intervals, irregularly, now and again 12 every so often, intermittent, occasionally, periodically, sporadically 13 spasmodically 14 from time to time, intermittently 15 discontinuously

**• on and on**
03 e'er 04 ever 06 always 07 forever, non-stop 09 endlessly, eternally, regularly 10 all the time, constantly, frequently, habitually, repeatedly 11 ceaselessly, continually, incessantly, perpetually, recurrently 12 interminably, persistently 13 everlastingly

**once**
◇ *archaic word indicator*
04 ance, onst, when 05 after 06 former 07 firstly, long ago, on a time, one time 08 as soon as, formerly 09 at one time, in the past, upon a time 10 at one point, previously 11 in times past 12 in the old days 13 in times gone by, once upon a time, on one occasion

**• at once**
03 now, tit 04 tite, tyte 05 alike, atone, ek dum, swith, tight 06 attone, presto, pronto, statim, titely 07 at a word, attonce, attones, offhand 08 directly, promptly, right now, together 09 forthwith, hey presto, instantly, like a shot, on the spot, right away, yesterday 10 forthright 11 immediately, tout de suite 12 straightaway, without delay 13 at the same time 14 simultaneously 15 at the same moment, before you know it

**• more than once**
04 anew, over 05 again 10 repeatedly

**• once and for all**
07 finally, for good 10 decisively, positively 11 permanently 12 conclusively, definitively 14 for the last time

**• once in a while**
07 at times 08 off and on, on and off 09 sometimes 10 now and then, on occasion 11 now and again 12 infrequently, occasionally, periodically, sporadically 14 from time to time, intermittently 15 once in a blue moon

**once-over**
04 gape, gaze, look, peek, peep, test 05 audit, check, dekko, probe, stare 06 eyeful, gander, glance, shufti, squint 07 checkup, glimpse, inquiry 08 analysis, butcher's, research, scrutiny 10 inspection, monitoring 11 examination 12 confirmation, verification 13 investigation

**oncoming**
07 looming, nearing 08 approach, upcoming 09 advancing, gathering, onrushing 11 approaching

**one**
01 a, I 02 ae, us 03 ace, ane, yin 04 lone, only, sole, tane, unit 05 alike, bound, equal, fused, monad, unity, whole 06 entire, joined, single, united, wedded 07 married 08 complete, solitary 09 identical, undivided 10 harmonious, individual, like-minded

**• French one**
02 un 03 une

**• German one**
03 ein 04 eine, eins

**• Italian one, Spanish one**
03 uno

**oneness**
05 unity 07 unicity 08 identity, sameness 09 wholeness 10 singleness, uniqueness 11 consistency, homogeneity, singularity 12 completeness 13 identicalness, individuality

**onerous**
04 hard 05 heavy 06 taxing, tiring 07 arduous, exigent, weighty 08 crushing, exacting, wearying 09 demanding, difficult, fatiguing, laborious, strenuous 10 burdensome, exhausting, oppressive 11 troublesome 12 back-breaking

**oneself**

**• by oneself**
04 solo 05 alone 06 lonely, singly 07 forlorn, unaided 08 deserted, desolate, forsaken, isolated, lonesome 09 abandoned, on your own, on your tod 10 by yourself, unassisted, unattended, unescorted 11 without help 12 single-handed 13 independently, unaccompanied 15 on your Pat Malone

**one-sided**
06 biased, one-way, uneven, unfair, unjust 07 bigoted, partial, unequal 08 lopsided, partisan, separate 09 separated 10 prejudiced, unbalanced, unilateral 11 independent, inequitable 12 disconnected, narrow-minded 14 discriminatory

**one-time**
02 ex- 03 old 04 late, past 06 former 07 quondam 08 previous, sometime 09 erstwhile

**ongoing**
05 event 07 current, growing, non-stop 08 constant, evolving, unbroken, unending 09 advancing, incessant, unfolding 10 continuing, continuous, developing, in progress, unfinished 11 progressing 13 uninterrupted

**onion**
04 head, moly, ramp, sybo 05 cibol, ingan, syboe, sybow 06 chibol, shalot 07 shallot 08 scallion
*See also* **head**

**onlooker**
06 gawper, viewer 07 watcher, witness 08 beholder, looker-on, observer 09 bystander, sightseer, spectator 10 eyewitness, rubberneck

**only**
03 but, one 04 just, lone, sole 05 alone 06 anerly, at most, barely, except, merely, nobbut, purely, simply, single, singly, solely, unique 07 onliest 08 solitary 09 allenarly, exclusive 10 individual, no more than, nothing but, one and only 11 exclusively, not more than

**onrush**
04 flow, push, rush 05 flood, onset, surge, sweep 06 career, charge, stream 07 cascade 08 stampede 09 onslaught

**onset**
04 dash, fall, push, raid, rush 05 break, start 06 access, affret, attack, charge, onding, onrush, outset 07 assault, kick-off 08 outbreak, storming 09 beginning, inception, onslaught 12 commencement

**onslaught**
04 push, raid 05 blitz, drive, foray,

onset, swoop **06** attack, charge, dismay, onfall, onrush, thrust **07** assault, dead-set **08** storming **09** offensive **11** bombardment

**Ontario**
**02** ON

**onus**
**04** duty, load, task **06** burden, charge, weight **09** albatross, liability, millstone **10** obligation **11** encumbrance **14** responsibility

**onward**
**04** away

**onwards**
**02** on **05** ahead, forth **06** beyond **07** forward, in front **08** forwards

**oodles**
**04** bags, lots, tons **05** heaps, loads **06** masses **08** lashings **09** abundance

**oomph**
**02** it, SA **03** pep **04** zing **06** bounce, energy, vigour **07** pizzazz, sparkle **08** sexiness, vitality, vivacity **09** animation, sex-appeal **10** enthusiasm, exuberance, get-up-and-go

**ooze**
**03** mud, nap, sap, sew **04** drip, drop, emit, flow, leak, mire, muck, seep, silt, sipe, slob, spew, spue, sype, weep **05** bleed, drain, exude, fluff, slime **06** escape, exhale, filter, sludge **07** deposit, dribble, excrete, secrete, seepage, trickle **08** alluvium, filtrate, sediment **09** discharge, percolate, pour forth **12** overflow with

**oozy**
**04** dewy, miry **05** moist, mucky, muddy, slimy, weepy **06** sloppy, sludgy, sweaty **07** weeping **08** dripping **09** uliginose, uliginous

**opacity**
**04** body, onyx **06** nebula **07** density, leucoma **08** dullness **09** filminess, milkiness, murkiness, obscurity **10** cloudiness, opaqueness **11** obfuscation, unclearness **14** impermeability **15** impenetrability

**opal**
**07** girasol, hyalite **08** girasole **09** cacholong **10** hydrophane

**opalescence**
**05** prism **07** glitter, rainbow **08** dazzling **09** sparkling **10** glittering, shimmering **11** iridescence, multicolour **14** rainbow colours

**opalescent**
**04** shot **06** pearly **07** rainbow **08** dazzling **09** prismatic, sparkling **10** glittering, iridescent, shimmering, variegated **11** cymophanous, rainbow-like **13** multicoloured, polychromatic **15** rainbow-coloured

**opaque**
**03** dim **04** dark, dull, hazy **05** dense, dingy, misty, muddy, murky, shady, thick **06** cloudy, turbid **07** blurred, clouded, cryptic, doltish, intense, muddied, obscure, unclear **08** abstruse, baffling, esoteric, puzzling **09** confusing, difficult, enigmatic, recondite **12** as clear as mud, impenetrable, unfathomable **14** unintelligible

**OPEC**

*OPEC members:*

**04** Iran, Iraq
**05** Libya, Qatar
**06** Kuwait
**07** Algeria, Nigeria
**09** Indonesia, Venezuela
**11** Saudi Arabia
**18** United Arab Emirates

**open**
**03** dup **04** agee, airy, ajar, ajee, bare, fair, free, moot, undo, wide **05** apert, begin, blunt, broad, clear, crack, frank, holey, loose, overt, plain, split, start, unlid, unrip, untie **06** broach, candid, deploy, direct, expose, extend, flower, gaping, honest, launch, liable, ouvert, patent, porous, public, reveal, simple, spread, spring, unbolt, uncork, unfold, unfurl, unlock, unpack, unroll, unseal, unshut, vacant **07** blatant, divulge, evident, explain, exposed, general, kick off, lay bare, lidless, natural, obvious, ouverte, subject, topless, unblock, unclasp, unclose, uncover, unlatch, unscrew, upbreak, visible, yawning **08** apparent, arguable, cellular, commence, disclose, disposed, flagrant, initiate, manifest, openwork, passable, push open, separate, unbarred, unbolted, unclosed, unfasten, unfenced, unfolded, unfrozen, unhidden, unlocked, unripped, unsealed, wide open **09** available, break open, burst open, champaign, come apart, coverless, debatable, fenceless, force open, guileless, ingenuous, navigable, prise open, receptive, slide open, spread out, unblocked, uncovered, undecided, unlatched, unsettled, unstopped, well known **10** above-board, accessible, forthright, inaugurate, noticeable, obtainable, spongelike, unenclosed, unfastened, unoccupied, unreserved, unresolved, up in the air, vulnerable **11** conspicuous, get cracking, honeycombed, problematic, set in motion, susceptible, unconcealed, undisguised, unprotected, unsheltered, widely known **12** approachable, loosely woven, unobstructed, unrestricted **13** take the plunge **15** open to the risk of

**• opening words**
**06** sesame

**• open onto**
**04** face **06** lead to **08** give onto, overlook **14** command a view of

**• open up**
**03** win

**open-air**
**06** afield **07** outdoor, outside **08** alfresco, plein-air **10** out-of-doors

**open-and-shut**
**05** clear **06** simple **07** obvious **12** easily solved **13** easily decided **15** straightforward

**opener**
◇ *head selection indicator*

**open-handed**
**04** free **06** lavish **07** liberal **08** generous **09** bounteous, bountiful **10** munificent, unstinting **11** magnanimous **12** eleemosynary, large-hearted

**opening**
◇ *head selection indicator*
**02** os **03** gap, gat, job **04** adit, anus, bole, cave, dawn, gape, gate, hole, pore, port, rent, scye, slit, slot, vent, yawn **05** birth, break, chasm, chink, cleft, crack, early, first, inlet, onset, place, space, split, start, stoma, thirl **06** breach, chance, hiatus, launch, outlet, outset, window **07** crevice, fissure, foramen, initial, kick-off, orifice, ostiole, portage, primary, rupture, undoing, vacancy **08** aperture, fenestra, occasion, position, starting **09** beginning, first base, inaugural, inception, mouse hole, square one, the word go **10** commencing, fenestella, interstice **11** opportunity, possibility **12** inauguration, introductory

**openly**
**06** barely **07** bluntly, frankly, overtly, plainly, up front **08** brazenly, candidly, directly, honestly, in public, patently, publicly **09** blatantly, glaringly **10** above board, flagrantly, immodestly, in full view **11** on the square, shamelessly, unashamedly **12** forthrightly, unreservedly

**open-minded**
**04** free **05** broad **07** liberal **08** catholic, tolerant, unbiased **09** impartial, objective, receptive **10** reasonable **11** broad-minded, enlightened **12** unprejudiced **13** dispassionate **14** latitudinarian

**open-mindedness**
**06** equity **07** justice **08** equality, fairness **10** detachment, dispassion, neutrality **11** disinterest, objectivity **12** impartiality, unbiasedness **14** even-handedness **15** non-partisanship

**open-mouthed**
**06** amazed, gaping, greedy **07** shocked **08** wide-eyed **09** astounded, clamorous, expectant, surprised **10** astonished, spellbound **11** dumbfounded, widechapped **13** flabbergasted, thunderstruck

**openwork**
**04** mode

**opera**
**03** ENO **05** works **08** burletta **09** pastorale **10** music drama

13 dramma giocoso 15 dramma per musica

See also **singer**

*Operas and operettas include:*

04 Aïda
05 Faust, Manon, Norma, Tosca
06 Carmen, Otello, Salome
07 Elektra, Fidelio, Macbeth, Nabucco, Thepsis, The Ring, Werther, Wozzeck
08 Falstaff, Idomeneo, Iolanthe, La Bohème, Parsifal, Patience, Turandot
09 Billy Budd, Capriccio, Don Carlos, King Priam, Lohengrin, Rigoletto, Ruddigore, Siegfried, The Mikado, Véronique
10 Cinderella, Die Walküre, I Pagliacci, La Traviata, Oedipus Rex, Tannhäuser
11 Don Giovanni, Don Pasquale, HMS Pinafore, Il Trovatore, La Périchole, Peter Grimes, Princess Ida, The Sorceror, Trial by Jury, William Tell
12 Boris Godunov, Cosí Fan Tutte, Das Rheingold, Eugene Onegin, Manon Lescaut, Nixon in China, Porgy and Bess, The Grand Duke, The Huguenots, The Rhinegold, The Valkyries
13 Albert Herring, Der Freischütz, Dido and Aeneas, Die Fledermaus, La Belle Hélène, Moses and Aaron, Powder Her Face, The Fairy Queen, The Gondoliers, The Knot Garden, The Magic Flute, Utopia Limited
14 Le Grand Macabre, Samson et Dalila
15 Ariadne auf Naxos, Götterdämmerung, Hansel and Gretel, Le Nozze di Figaro, Madama Butterfly, Madame Butterfly, Orfeo ed Euridice, Simon Boccanegra, The Beggar's Opera, The Pearl Fishers

*Opera houses include:*

03 Met, ROH
05 Cairo, Lyric, Royal, State
06 De Munt, Sydney, the Met, Zurich
07 La Scala
08 La Fenice, San Carlo
09 La Monnaie
10 Mussorgsky, Semper Oper
11 Oper Leipzig, Teatro Liceo, Verona Arena
12 Glyndebourne, Komische Oper, Metropolitan, Opéra-Comique
13 Kennedy Center, Muziektheater, Opera Bastille, Teatro Massimo
14 Bolshoi Theatre, Estates Theatre, Hungarian State, Kungliga Operan, London Coliseum, Unter den Linden
15 Gothenburg Opera, Teatro alla Scala, Zheng Yici Peking

*Opera characters include:*

03 Eva, Liu
04 Aïda, Bess, Budd (Billy), Erda, Froh, Iago, Il Re, Loge, Luna (Il Conte di), Mime, Mimì, Pang, Pike (Florence), Ping, Pong, Tito, Vere (Captain)
05 Caius (Dr), Calaf, Falke (Dr), Faust, Freia, Gilda, Herod, Jeník, Kecal, Porgy, Rocco, Sachs (Hans), Titus, Tosca, Vasek, Wotan
06 Alcina, Alzira, Carmen, Donner, Emilia, Fafner, Fasolt, Figaro, Fricka, Gretel, Grimes (Peter), Hänsel, Isolde, Lockit (Lucy), Mantua (Duke of), Onegin (Eugene), Otello, Pamina, Pogner (Veit), Rosina, Salome, Tamino, Valery (Violetta), Wagner
07 Bartolo (Dr), Bastien, Billows, Despina, Don José, Douphol (Baron), Germont (Alfredo), Godunov (Boris), Gunther, Gutrune, Herring (Albert), Hunding, Jocasta, Leonora, Manrico, Marenka, Micaëla, Musetta, Oedipus, Peachum (Polly), Pelléas, Quickly (Mistress), Radamès, Rodolfo, Scarpia (Baron), Susanna, Tristan, Wozzeck
08 Alberich, Almaviva (Count), Almaviva (Countess), Azeucena, Claggart (John), Falstaff (Sir John), Ferrando, Herodias, Hoffmann, Lucretia, Macheath, Marcello, Mercédès, Orlofsky (Prince), Papagena, Papageno, Parsifal, Roderigo, Sarastro, Siegmund, Turandot, Valentin, Woglinde, Yamadori (Prince)
09 Angelotti (Cesare), Bastienne, Butterfly (Madame), Cherubino, Cio-Cio-San, Desdemona, Donna Anna, Dorabella, Escamillo, Esmerelda, Florestan, Guglielmo, Leporello, Lohengrin, Maddalena, Mélisande, Narraboth, Pinkerton (Lieutenant), Rigoletto, Sharpless, Siegfried, Sieglunde, Vogelsang (Kunz), Waltraute
10 Beckmesser (Sixtus), Brünnhilde, Don Alfonso, Don Basilio, Don Ottavio, Eisenstein (Gabriele von), Eisenstein (Rosalinde von), Fiordiligi, Marcellina, Monostatos, Prince Igor, Tannhäuser
11 Cavaradossi (Mario), Don Giovanni, Donna Elvira, Marschallin, Sparafucile, The Dutchman
14 Henry the Fowler, John the Baptist, Mephistopheles
15 Queen of the Night

## operate

◇ *anagram indicator*
02 go 03 act, fly, ren, rin, run, set, use 04 play, trip, work 05 drive, pilot, serve 06 direct, employ, handle, make go, manage 07 actuate, conduct, control, perform, utilize 08 function, tick over 09 manoeuvre 12 be in charge of

## operation

02 op 03 job, ure, use 04 deal, game, play, raid, task 05 using 06 action, affair, agency, attack, charge, effect, effort, motion 07 assault, control, process, running, surgery, working 08 activity, business, campaign, exercise, handling, movement 09 influence, manoeuvre, procedure 10 enterprise, management, proceeding 11 functioning, performance, transaction, undertaking, utilization 12 manipulation

• **combined operations**
02 CO

• **in operation**
02 on 04 live 05 going, valid 06 active, viable 07 in force, working 08 in action, in effect, prepared, workable 09 effective, efficient, in service 10 functional 11 functioning, operational, serviceable 12 taking effect

## operational

05 going, in use, ready 06 usable, viable 07 running, working 08 in action, prepared, workable 09 in service 10 functional 11 functioning 12 up and running 14 in working order

## operative

03 key, spy 04 dick, hand, mole 05 agent, valid, vital 06 active, shamus, sleuth, viable, worker 07 artisan, crucial, gumshoe, in force, operant, ouvrier, working, workman 08 employee, in action, in effect, labourer, mechanic, operator, ouvrière, relevant, workable 09 detective, effective, efficient, important, machinist 10 functional, private eye 11 double agent, efficacious, functioning, in operation, operational, secret agent, serviceable, significant 12 investigator

## operator

02 op 05 mover 06 dealer, driver, punter, trader, worker 07 functor, handler, manager, operant, shyster 08 director, mechanic 09 machinist, operative 10 contractor, machinator, manoeuvrer, speculator, technician 11 manipulator 12 practitioner 13 administrator, wheeler-dealer

**operetta** *see* **opera**

## opiate

04 drug, dull 06 downer 07 anodyne, bromide 08 narcotic, nepenthe, pacifier, sedative 09 soporific 10 depressant 12 stupefacient 13 tranquillizer

## opine

03 say 05 guess, judge, think 07 believe, declare, presume, suggest, suppose, surmise, suspect, venture 08 conceive, conclude 09 volunteer 10 conjecture

## opinion

03 bet 04 deem, doxy, idea, mind, view, vote 05 sense, tenet 06 belief, notion, stance, theory 07 feeling, thought 08 attitude, feelings, suffrage, thoughts 09 arrogance, judgement, sentiment, viewpoint 10 assessment, assumption, conception, conviction, estimation, impression, perception,

persuasion, reputation, standpoint **11** point of view, supposition **13** way of thinking **15** school of thought

**• in my opinion**
**03** IMO **06** I think **08** à mon avis, as I see it, I believe, in my book, in my view, me judice **10** for my money, if you ask me, personally

**• opinion tester**
**04** kite

**opinionated**
**06** biased, entêté **07** adamant, bigoted, entêtée, pompous **08** arrogant, cocksure, dogmatic, stubborn **09** obstinate, pigheaded, pragmatic **10** inflexible, pontifical, prejudiced **11** dictatorial, doctrinaire, pragmatical **12** single-minded **13** self-important **14** uncompromising

**opium**
**03** hop

**opossum**
**04** joey **05** yapok **06** yapock **07** marmose **09** phalanger **12** Didelphyidae

**opponent**
**03** foe **04** anti **05** enemy, rival **07** opposer **08** objector, opposite **09** adversary, contender, dissenter, dissident, oppugnant **10** antagonist, challenger, competitor, contestant, opposition **11** dissentient

**• opponents**
**02** NE, SW

**opportune**
**03** apt, fit **04** good **05** happy, lucky **06** proper, timely **07** fitting, in place **08** suitable **09** fortunate, pertinent, well-timed **10** auspicious, convenient, favourable, felicitous, propitious, seasonable **11** appropriate **12** advantageous, providential

**opportunism**
**07** realism **10** expediency, pragmatism **12** exploitation **15** taking advantage

**opportunity**
**03** ren, rin, run **04** hour, pick, room, roum, turn **05** break, power, scope, space **06** chance, look-in, moment **07** fitness, opening, vantage **08** occasion, overture, prospect **09** privilege **11** possibility **14** crack of the whip

**• alive to opportunity**
**04** go-go

**oppose**
**03** bar, opp **04** defy, face **05** check, fight, match **06** attack, breast, combat, hinder, impugn, offset, oppugn, repugn, resist, thwart **07** balance, compare, contest, counter, dispute, play off, prevent **08** confront, contrary, contrast, disfavor, obstruct, traverse **09** be against, challenge, disfavour, encounter, juxtapose, stand up to, withstand **10** contradict, contravene, controvert, set against **11** take against **12** argue against, disagree with, disapprove of **13** take issue with **14** counterbalance, fly in the face of

**opposed**
**03** opp **04** anti **06** averse, object **07** adverse, against, hostile **08** clashing, contrary, inimical, opposing, opposite **09** toto caelo **11** conflicting, disagreeing **12** antagonistic, incompatible, in opposition

**• as opposed to**
**01** v **02** vs **06** versus **09** as against, instead of **10** rather than **12** in contrast to

**opposing**
**05** enemy, rival **06** at odds **07** counter, hostile, opposed, warring **08** clashing, contrary, fighting, opponent, opposite **09** combatant, differing, oppugnant **10** at variance, contending **11** conflicting, contentious **12** antagonistic, antipathetic, disputatious, incompatible **14** irreconcilable

**opposite**
**02** op **03** opp **06** at odds, en face, facing, unlike **07** adverse, counter, hostile, inverse, opposed, reverse **08** clashing, contrary, converse, flip side, fronting, opponent, opposing **09** different, differing, dissident **10** antipathic, antithesis, at variance, contrasted, face to face, overthwart, poles apart **11** conflicting, over against **12** antagonistic, antithetical, inconsistent **13** contradiction, contradictory, corresponding **14** irreconcilable

**opposition**
**03** foe **05** enemy, rival **06** syzygy **07** dislike **08** clashing, contrast, distance, opponent **09** adversary, collision, hostility, other side **10** antagonism, antagonist, antithesis, reluctance, resistance **11** competition, contrariety, counter-time, counter-view, disapproval **12** colluctation, counter-stand, opposing side **13** confrontation **14** unfriendliness **15** obstructiveness

**• set in opposition**
**04** play

**oppress**
**03** vex **04** ride **05** abuse, bully, crush, grind, gripe, press, quash, quell, tread **06** burden, deject, hang on, harass, ravish, sadden, subdue, weight **07** afflict, depress, enslave, overset, repress, smother, torment, trample **08** desolate, dispirit, distress, hang over, maltreat, suppress **09** overpower, overpress, overwhelm, persecute, subjugate, suffocate, tyrannize, weigh down **10** discourage, dishearten, lie heavy on **11** walk all over **12** bear hard upon **13** treat like dirt, use as a doormat **15** bear heavily upon

**oppressed**
**06** abused **07** crushed, misused, subject **08** burdened, enslaved, harassed, troubled **09** repressed **10** maltreated, persecuted, subjugated, tyrannized **11** downtrodden **13** disadvantaged **15** underprivileged

**oppression**
**05** abuse **07** cruelty, tyranny **08** hardship **09** brutality, despotism, harshness, injustice **10** repression, subjection **11** persecution, subjugation, suppression **12** maltreatment, overpowering, overwhelming, ruthlessness

**oppressive**
**05** close, cruel, faint, harsh, heavy, muggy **06** brutal, leaden, stuffy, sultry, unjust **07** airless, inhuman, onerous, sweltry **08** crushing, despotic, pitiless, ruthless, stifling **09** burdenous, Draconian, merciless, troubling, tyrannous **10** broodiness, burdensome, iron-fisted, repressive, tyrannical **11** domineering, heavy-handed, intolerable, overbearing, suffocating **12** extortionate, overpowering, overwhelming

**oppressor**
**05** bully, tyran **06** despot, tyrant **08** autocrat, dictator, torturer **09** tormentor **10** persecutor, subjugator, taskmaster **11** intimidator, slave-driver **14** hard taskmaster

**opprobrious**
**07** abusive **08** damaging, infamous, insolent, venomous **09** insulting, invective, offensive, vitriolic **10** calumnious, defamatory, derogatory, scandalous, scurrilous **11** disgraceful, dyslogistic, reproachful **12** calumniatory, contemptuous, contumelious, vituperative

**opprobrium**
**04** slur **05** odium, shame **06** infamy, stigma **07** calumny, censure, obloquy **08** disgrace, ignominy, reproach **09** contumely, discredit, disfavour, dishonour, disrepute **10** debasement, scurrility **11** degradation

**Ops**
**04** Rhea

**opt**
**04** pick **05** elect, go for **06** choose, decide, prefer, select **08** decide on, plump for, settle on **09** single out

**optical**

*Optical instruments and devices include:*

**05** laser
**06** camera
**07** sextant
**08** spyglass
**09** endoscope, periscope, telescope
**10** binoculars, microscope, opera-glass, theodolite
**12** field-glasses, stereocamera
**13** film projector
**14** slide projector
**15** magnifying glass, photomicroscope, telescopic sight, telestereoscope

**optimism**
**05** cheer **06** morale **08** buoyancy, idealism **10** brightness, confidence, expectancy **11** hopefulness **12** cheerfulness, sanguineness **13** Leibnizianism **14** feel-good factor, Leibnitzianism

**optimistic**
**06** bright, upbeat **07** assured, bullish, buoyant, hopeful **08** cheerful, positive, sanguine **09** confident, expectant **10** idealistic, Panglossic **11** Panglossian, pollyannish **12** happy-go-lucky, pollyannaish

**optimum**
**03** opt, top **04** best **05** ideal, model **06** choice **07** highest, optimal, perfect, supreme, utopian **08** flawless **11** superlative **14** most favourable

**option**
**03** put **04** call, wish **06** choice **07** refusal **08** swaption **09** privilege, selection **10** preference **11** alternative, possibility

**optional**
**03** opt **04** free **08** elective, unforced **09** voluntary **10** permissive **11** facultative **13** discretionary

**options**
**04** menu

**opulence**
**06** luxury, plenty, riches, wealth **07** fortune **08** fullness, richness **09** abundance, affluence, profusion **10** cornucopia, easy street, lavishness, luxuriance, prosperity **11** copiousness **13** sumptuousness **14** superabundance

**opulent**
**04** posh, rich **05** plush, pluty **06** lavish **07** copious, moneyed, profuse, wealthy, well-off **08** abundant, affluent, prolific, well-to-do **09** luxuriant, luxurious, plentiful, sumptuous **10** prosperous, well-heeled **11** rolling in it **13** superabundant

**opus**
**02** op **04** work **05** piece **06** oeuvre **08** creation **10** brainchild, production **11** composition

**or**
**04** gold **05** ossia **06** before, yellow **10** conversely **13** alternatively **14** in preference to, on the other hand **15** as an alternative
*See also* **gold**

**oracle**
**04** guru, sage, seer, Urim **05** augur, sibyl **06** answer, augury, expert, mentor, pundit, vision, wizard **07** adviser, prophet, Thummin **08** forecast, prophecy **09** authority **10** divination, forecaster, high priest, mastermind, prediction, prophetess, revelation, soothsayer, specialist **13** fortune teller **14** Urim and Thummim **15** prognostication

**oracular**
**04** sage, wise **05** grave, vatic **06** arcane **07** cryptic, Delphic, obscure, ominous **08** abstruse, dogmatic, positive, two-edged **09** ambiguous, equivocal, prescient, prophetic, venerable **10** auspicious, haruspical, mysterious, portentous, predictive **11** dictatorial, significant **13** authoritative

**oral**
◇ *homophone indicator*
**04** quiz, said, viva **05** vocal **06** buccal, lively, spoken, verbal **07** uttered **08** viva voce **09** unwritten **11** nuncupative

**orally**
◇ *homophone indicator*
**07** by mouth, vocally **08** verbally, viva voce

**orange**
**11** hesperidium

*Oranges include:*

**04** gold
**05** amber, chica, chico, coral, henna, tawny, tenné, tenny
**06** anatta, anatto, aurora, chicha, kamala, kamela, kamila, roucou, salmon, tawney
**07** annatta, annatto, apricot, arnotto, jacinth, nacarat, paprika, saffron
**08** croceate, croceous, mandarin
**09** bilirubin, tangerine
**13** cadmium yellow, canthaxanthin

*Orange varieties include:*

**04** mock, Ruta, sour
**05** blood, Jaffa, navel, sweet, topaz
**06** bitter
**07** cumquat, kumquat, naartje, nartjie, satsuma, Seville
**08** bergamot, bigarade, mandarin
**09** clockwork, mandarine, tangerine
**10** clementine

• **segment of orange**
**03** pig

**orate**
**04** talk **05** speak **07** declaim, lecture **08** harangue **09** discourse, hold forth, sermonize, speechify **11** pontificate

**oration**
**05** éloge, elogy, spiel **06** eulogy, homily, korero, sermon, speech **07** address, elogium, lecture **08** eulogium, harangue **09** discourse, set speech **11** declamation

**orator**
**06** Cicero, rhetor **07** speaker, spieler **08** lecturer **09** Boanerges, declaimer, demagogue, spokesman, thunderer **10** petitioner **11** Demosthenes, rhetorician, spellbinder **12** phrasemonger, prevaricator **13** public speaker

**oratorical**
**08** eloquent, rhetoric, sonorous **09** bombastic, high-flown **10** Ciceronian, rhetorical **11** declamatory, Demosthenic **12** elocutionary, magniloquent **13** grandiloquent, silver-tongued, smooth-tongued

**oratorio**

*Oratorios include:*

**04** Saul
**06** Elijah, Esther, Joshua, Samson, Semele, St Paul
**07** Athalia, Deborah, Jephtha, Messiah, Solomon, Susanna
**08** Christus, Giuseppe, Hercules, Theodora
**09** Christmas
**10** Belshazzar, Oedipus Rex, The Seasons
**11** The Creation
**13** Israel in Egypt
**14** Alexander Balus, La Resurrezione
**15** Judas Maccabaeus

**oratory**
**04** hwyl **06** chapel, speech **07** diction **08** rhetoric **09** elocution, eloquence, proseucha, proseuche **11** chapel royal, declamation **12** speechifying, speechmaking **14** grandiloquence, public speaking

**orb**
**03** eye **04** ball, pome, ring **05** globe, mound, orbit, round, world **06** circle, sphere **07** eyeball, globule **08** bereaved, spherule

**orbit**
**03** orb **04** path **05** ambit, cycle, range, reach, scope, sweep, track **06** circle, course, domain, sphere **07** circuit, compass, revolve **08** encircle, rotation **09** eye socket, influence **10** revolution, trajectory **14** circumgyration, circumnavigate

• **point in orbit**
**04** apse **05** apsis **06** apogee **07** apolune, perigee **08** aphelion, perilune **10** perihelion **12** pericynthion, periselenium

**orchestra**

*Orchestras include:*

**03** LPO, NSO, OAE, OSM, RPO
**04** ASMF, CBSO, RLPO, RSNO
**05** Hallé
**06** Ulster
**09** Minnesota
**11** BBC Symphony, NBC Symphony
**12** Milan La Scala, Philadelphia, San Francisco
**13** Concertgebouw, Staatskapelle
**14** Boston Symphony, English Chamber, LA Philharmonic, London Symphony, Sydney Symphony, Vienna Symphony
**15** BBC Philharmonic, Chicago Symphony, Detroit Symphony, New York Symphony, Scottish Chamber, Seattle Symphony, The Philharmonia, Toronto Symphony

**orchestrate**
**03** fix **05** score **07** arrange, compose, prepare, present **08** organize **09** integrate **10** co-ordinate,

mastermind **11** put together, stage-manage

**orchestration**

**05** score **07** running, scoring, setting, version **08** planning **10** adaptation, management **11** arrangement, engineering, preparation **12** co-ordination, organization **13** harmonization, masterminding, stage-managing **14** interpretation **15** instrumentation

**orchid**

*Orchids include:*

**03** bee, bog, bug, fen, fly, man, sun
**04** blue, disa, frog, king, kite, lady, moth, musk, wasp
**05** burnt, clown, comet, ghost, giant, pansy, queen, tiger, tulip
**06** lizard, monkey, spider
**07** leopard, slipper, vanilla
**08** calanthe, cattleya, crucifix, fragrant, military, oncidium
**09** bee-orchis, birds-nest, chocolate, Christmas, coralroot, cymbidium, false musk, fly orchis, pyramidal, twayblade
**10** early marsh, epidendrum, late spider, small white
**11** cockleshell, cypripedium, dancing lady, early purple, early spider, epidendrone, green-winged, helleborine
**12** black vanilla, heath spotted, ladys' tresses, Lapland marsh, narrow-leaved, one-leaved bog, western marsh
**13** Chinese ground, common spotted, dense-flowered, elder-flowered, ladies' tresses, loose-flowered, orange blossom, southern marsh
**14** moccasin flower, violet birds-nest
**15** lesser butterfly

**ordain**

**03** fix, set **04** call, fate, rule, will **05** elect, frock, japan, order **06** anoint, assign, decree, invest, priest **07** appoint, arrange, destine, dictate, dispose, foresay, lay down, require **08** instruct, ordinate **09** destinate, establish, preordain, prescribe, pronounce **10** consecrate, foreordain, lay hands on, predestine **12** predetermine

**ordeal**

**04** pain, test **05** agony, trial **07** anguish, torment, torture, trouble **08** distress, troubles **09** bier right, gruelling, nightmare, suffering **10** affliction **11** persecution, tribulation **12** tribulations **13** baptism of fire

**order**

◇ *anagram indicator*

**02** OM **03** bid, law, OBE, ord **04** book, call, calm, chit, club, fiat, form, kind, line, nick, plan, rank, rota, rule, sect, sort, tell, type, writ **05** array, caste, class, cycle, edict, genus, grade, group, guild, level, lodge, peace, quiet, set-up, shape, state, union **06** codify, decree, degree, demand, direct, enjoin, family, fettle, kilter, lay out, layout, league, line-up, manage, method, ordain, system, tidy up **07** arrange, booking, call for, command, company, conduct, control, dictate, dispose, harmony, mandate, marshal, pattern, precept, request, require, reserve, society, sort out, species, station, summons, variety, warrant **08** apply for, classify, grouping, instruct, neatness, organize, position, practice, regulate, sequence, sorority, symmetry, tidiness **09** authorize, catalogue, community, condition, direction, directive, hierarchy, legislate, ordinance, prescribe, structure **10** commission, discipline, fellowship, fraternity, injunction, lawfulness, regularity, regulation, sisterhood, uniformity **11** application, arrangement, association, brotherhood, disposition, instruction, law and order, orderliness, requirement, requisition, reservation, send away for, stipulation, systematize, write off for **12** codification, denomination, notification, organization, pecking order, tranquillity, working order **13** secret society **14** categorization, classification

*See also* **command**; **honour**; **religious**

**• in order**

**02** OK **04** done, neat, tidy **05** right **06** lawful, likely, mended, proper **07** allowed, correct, fitting, ordered, orderly, regular, working **08** all right, arranged, suitable **09** operative, organized, permitted, shipshape **10** acceptable, classified, good as gold, in sequence, methodical, systematic **11** appropriate, categorized, functioning **13** well-organized **15** secundum ordinem

**• in order that**

**02** so

**• in order to**

**02** to **05** for to **06** so that **11** intending to, with a view to **13** with the result **14** with the purpose

**• order around**

**05** bully **07** lay down **08** browbeat, bulldoze, dominate, domineer **09** push about, tyrannize **10** boss around, order about, push around **13** lay down the law

**• out of order**

◇ *anagram indicator*

**04** bust **05** amiss, kaput, messy, wrong **06** broken, untidy **07** haywire, muddled **08** confused, gone phut, improper, unlawful, unseemly **09** conked out, incorrect, irregular, off kilter **10** broken down, disordered, not working, on the blink, on the fritz, out of sorts, out of whack, unsuitable **11** inoperative, out of course, out of kilter, uncalled-for **12** disorganized, unacceptable **13** inappropriate, out of sequence **14** not functioning **15** out of commission

**• set in order**

**02** do **03** red **04** redd, trim **05** dress, prank, right **06** betrim, fettle, pranck, snod up **07** dispone, prancke

**• special order, standing order**

**02** SO

**orderliness**

**08** neatness, tidiness, trimness **09** smartness **10** regularity, spruceness **12** organization, straightness **14** methodicalness

**orderly**

◇ *anagram indicator*

**04** neat, ruly, tidy, trim **05** quiet **06** cosmic **07** in order, ordered, regular **09** chaprassi, chaprassy, chuprassy, efficient, regularly **10** controlled, law-abiding, methodical, restrained, systematic **11** disciplined, well-behaved **12** businesslike, methodically **13** well-organized, well-regulated **15** in apple-pie order

**ordinance**

**03** law **04** fiat, rite, rule **05** canon, edict, order **06** bye-law, decree, dictum, ritual, ruling **07** command, statute **08** ceremony, planning, practice **09** directive, enactment, equipment, prescript, sacrament **10** dead-letter, injunction, observance, regulation **11** appointment, institution, preparation

**ordinarily**

**07** as a rule, usually **08** commonly, normally **09** generally, in general **10** familiarly, habitually **11** customarily **14** conventionally

**ordinary**

**01** O **03** ord **04** dull, fair **05** banal, bland, blunt, plain, usual **06** canton, common, cotise, modest, normal, simple **07** average, cottise, mundane, prosaic, quarter, regular, routine, typical, vanilla **08** everyday, familiar, habitual, mediocre, standard, workaday **09** customary, plain-Jane, quotidian **10** mainstream, pedestrian, working-day **11** bog standard, commonplace, indifferent, nondescript, unmemorable **12** conventional, run-of-the-mill, unremarkable **13** penny-farthing, unexceptional, uninteresting, unpretentious **14** bread-and-butter, common-or-garden **15** undistinguished

**• out of the ordinary**

**04** rare **05** kinky **06** unique **07** unusual **09** different, left-field, memorable **10** noteworthy, remarkable, surprising, unexpected **11** exceptional, out of the way, outstanding **13** extraordinary

**ordnance**

**03** ord **04** arms, guns **06** cannon **07** big guns, pelican, weapons **09** artillery, munitions **14** field artillery

**ordure**

**03** poo **04** crap, dirt, dung, poop

**05** filth, frass, guano, scats, stool **06** egesta, faeces **09** droppings, excrement, excretion **11** waste matter

**ore**
**03** o'er **04** over **06** tangle **07** mineral, seaweed **09** sea tangle

*Ores include:*

**03** wad
**04** wadd, wadt
**06** bog-ore, coltan, galena, rutile
**07** bauxite, bog-iron, bornite, cuprite, iron ore, oligist, schlich, uranite, wood tin
**08** beauxite, braunite, calamine, enargite, hematite, limonite, siderite, sinopite, stibnite, taconite, tenorite
**09** anglesite, blackband, coffinite, haematite, hedyphane, ironstone, kidney ore, lodestone, magnetite, malachite, manganite, minestone, morass ore, proustite, tantalite
**10** erubescite, melaconite, peacock-ore, pyrolusite, ruby silver, sphalerite, stephanite
**11** cassiterite, chloanthite, pyrargyrite, tetradymite
**12** babingtonite, chalcopyrite, pyromorphite, tetrahedrite
**13** copper pyrites, horseflesh ore
**15** stilpnosiderite

*See also* **seaweed**

**• vein of ore**
**04** rake

**Oregon**
**02** OR **04** Oreg

**organ**
**04** part, tool, unit **05** forum, paper, pedal, regal, voice **06** agency, device, medium, member **07** element, journal, process, vehicle **08** magazine, melodeon, melodion **09** component, harmonium, implement, newspaper, structure **10** instrument, mouthpiece, periodical **11** apollonicon, constituent, publication **13** kist o' whistles

*Organs include:*

**03** ear, eye
**04** lung, nose, skin
**05** bowel, brain, colon, liver, lungs, lymph, penis, vulva
**06** cervix, rectum, spleen, testes, throat, thymus, ureter, uterus, vagina
**07** bladder, kidneys, ovaries, oviduct, pharynx, scrotum, stomach, thyroid, tonsils, trachea, urethra
**08** adenoids, appendix, bronchus, clitoris, pancreas, prostate, windpipe
**09** diaphragm, pituitary, taste buds
**10** epididymis, intestines, lymph nodes, oesophagus, spinal cord
**11** gall bladder, parathyroid, vas deferens
**12** hypothalamus, thymus glands, thyroid gland
**13** adrenal glands, nervous system
**14** fallopian tubes, large intestine, small intestine
**15** ejaculatory duct, seminal vesicles

*Organ stops include:*

**04** echo, oboe, sext, tuba
**05** dolce, gamba, quint
**06** cornet, nasard, octave, tierce
**07** bombard, bourdon, clarino, clarion, fagotto, mixture, piccolo, salicet, trumpet
**08** carillon, crumhorn, diapason, diaphone, dulciana, gemshorn, krumhorn, register, waldhorn
**09** fifteenth, furniture, krummhorn, principal, pyramidon, vox humana, waldflute
**10** clarabella, fourniture, salicional
**11** superoctave, voix céleste
**12** sesquialtera
**15** corno di bassetto

**organic**
**06** biotic, GM-free, living **07** animate, natural, ordered **08** coherent **09** organized **10** biological, harmonious, mechanical, structural, structured **11** non-chemical **12** additive-free, chemical-free, instrumental **13** not artificial, pesticide-free

**organism**
**04** body, cell **05** being, biont, plant, set-up, unity, whole **06** animal, entity, system **08** creature **09** bacterium, structure **11** living thing **12** organization

*See also* **animal**; **cell**; **classification**

**organization**
◇ *anagram indicator*
**04** body, club, firm, plan **05** group, order, set-up, union, unity, whole **06** design, layout, league, method, outfit, system **07** company, concern, council, pattern, running, society **08** grouping, planning **09** authority, formation, institute, operation, structure, syndicate **10** consortium, federation, management, regulation **11** arrangement, association, composition, corporation, development, institution, methodology **12** co-ordination **13** confederation, configuration, establishment **14** administration, classification, conglomeration

**Organization of Petroleum Exporting Countries** *see* **OPEC**

**organize**
◇ *anagram indicator*
**03** ren, rin, run **04** form **05** begin, found, frame, group, mould, order, see to, set up, shape, start **06** create, embody, imbody, manage, obtain **07** arrange, develop, dispose, marshal, prepare, sort out **08** assemble, classify, regiment, tabulate **09** catalogue, construct, establish, institute, lemmatize, originate, structure **10** administer, co-ordinate, put in order **11** orchestrate, put together, rationalize, standardize, systematize **12** be in charge of

**organized**
◇ *anagram indicator*
**04** neat, tidy **07** in order, ordered, orderly, organic, planned, regular **08** arranged **09** efficient **10** methodical, structured, systematic **11** well-ordered **12** businesslike **13** well-organized, well-regulated

**orgiastic**
**04** wild **05** orgic **07** Bacchic **09** debauched, Dionysiac **12** bacchanalian

**orgy**
**04** bout, riot **05** binge, party, revel, spree **06** excess, frenzy, revels **07** debauch, revelry, splurge **08** carousal, Dionysia **09** wild party **10** indulgence, Saturnalia **11** bacchanalia

**orient**
**01** E **04** East **05** adapt, align **06** adjust, attune, rising **07** eastern, sunrise, the East **08** accustom **09** habituate, orientate **11** acclimatize, accommodate, familiarize **15** get your bearings

**oriental**
**01** E **05** Asian **07** Asiatic, Eastern **10** Far Eastern

*See also* **Asian**

**orientation**
**07** guiding, leading **08** attitude, bearings, location, position, training **09** alignment, direction, induction, placement, situation **10** adaptation, adjustment, initiation, settling-in **11** inclination, positioning **15** acclimatization, familiarization

**orifice**
**03** gap **04** hole, pore, rent, rift, slit, slot, vent **05** break, cleft, crack, inlet, mouth, space, trema **06** breach, orifex **07** crevice, fissure, opening **08** aperture, spiracle **09** micropyle **10** blastopore **11** perforation

**origin**
**04** base, dawn, germ, line, rise, root **05** basis, birth, cause, fount, roots, start, stock **06** family, launch, source, spring **07** dawning, descent, genesis, lineage **08** ancestry, creation, fountain, genetics, heritage, pedigree **09** beginning, emergence, etymology, inception, parentage, paternity, principle **10** conception, derivation, extraction, foundation, provenance, well-spring **12** commencement, fountainhead, inauguration **13** line of descent

**original**
◇ *anagram indicator*
**02** ur- **03** new **04** real, true, type **05** early, first, fresh, model, novel, prime **06** actual, innate, master, primal, unique **07** genuine, initial, opening, pattern, primary, radical, unusual

**08** creative, earliest, paradigm, primeval, pristine, standard, starting **09** archetype, authentic, embryonic, first-hand, ingenious, inventive, primaeval, primitial, primitive, prototype **10** archetypal, commencing, indigenous, innovative, pioneering, primordial, protoplast, unborrowed, unorthodox **11** imaginative, primigenial, resourceful, rudimentary **13** autochthonous **14** ground-breaking, unconventional

**originality**
**06** daring **07** newness, novelty **08** boldness **09** freshness, ingenuity **10** cleverness, creativity, innovation **11** imagination, singularity, unorthodoxy **12** creativeness, eccentricity **13** individuality, inventiveness **14** creative spirit, innovativeness **15** imaginativeness, resourcefulness
• **lacking originality**
**07** clichéd **08** clichéed **09** hackneyed

**originally**
**05** first **07** at first, by birth **08** in origin **09** initially **10** at the start **11** at the outset, to begin with **12** by derivation **14** in the beginning **15** in the first place

**originate**
**04** come, flow, form, head, rear, rise, seed, stem **05** arise, begin, found, hatch, issue, plant, set up, start **06** be born, create, derive, emerge, evolve, father, invent, launch, result, source, spring **07** develop, emanate, pioneer, proceed, produce **08** commence, conceive, discover, generate, take rise **09** establish, institute, introduce, set on foot **10** inaugurate, mastermind **11** give birth to, set in motion **13** be the father of, be the mother of

**origination**
**07** forming **08** creation **09** invention, paternity **10** conception, generation, production **11** development

**originator**
**06** author, father, mother **07** creator, founder, pioneer **08** designer, inventor **09** architect, developer, generator, initiator, innovator, the brains **10** discoverer, prime mover **11** establisher

**ornament**
**04** deck, fall, gaud, gild, knob, ouch, spar, tiki, trim **05** adorn, crown, décor, frill, gnome, jewel, mense, spray, sprig, wally **06** almond, bauble, bedeck, fallal, gewgaw, gorget, griffe, labret, relish, set-off **07** dress up, emblema, figgery, fleuron, frigger, frounce, garland, garnish, hei-tiki, lunette, netsuke, pattern, pendant, pendent, rellish, trinket, twiddle **08** barrette, bar slide, beautify, brighten, carcanet, decorate, furbelow, rocaille, sunburst, trimming **09** accessory, adornment, arabesque, dog collar, embellish, fandangle, medallion, multifoil, scalework **10** decoration, escutcheon, Japanesery, knick-knack **11** garden gnome, garnishment **12** curliewurlie, jingle-jangle **13** embellishment

**ornamental**
**05** fancy, showy **06** florid **08** adorning **10** attractive, decorative **12** embellishing, embroidering

**ornamentation**
**04** fret, seam **06** frills **07** barbola, die-work **09** adornment, fallalery, garniture, strap work **10** decoration, embroidery, enrichment, figuration, ornateness **11** barbola work, elaboration, whigmaleery **12** whigmaleerie **13** embellishment

**ornate**
◇ *anagram indicator*
**04** busy, fine **05** adorn, fancy, flash, fussy, showy **06** florid, rococo **07** baroque, elegant, flowery **08** barbaric, mandarin **09** barbarian, decorated, elaborate, grandiose, luxuriant, sumptuous **10** flamboyant, ornamented **11** embellished **12** ostentatious

**orotund**
**04** deep, full, loud, rich **05** round **06** ornate, strong **07** booming, pompous **08** imposing, powerful, sonorous, strained **09** dignified **10** resonating **11** pretentious **12** magniloquent **13** grandiloquent

**orthodox**
**04** true **05** sound, usual **06** devout, square, strict **07** canonic, correct, regular **08** accepted, catholic, faithful, official, received **09** canonical, customary, hardshell **10** conformist, recognized **11** bien pensant, established, traditional **12** conservative, conventional **13** authoritative **14** fundamentalist **15** well-established

**orthodoxy**
**05** canon, credo, creed, dogma, tenet **06** belief **07** precept **08** devotion, doctrine, teaching, trueness **09** principle, soundness **10** conformism, conformity, conviction, devoutness, properness, strictness **11** correctness **12** conservatism, faithfulness **13** inflexibility **14** fundamentalism, received wisdom, traditionalism **15** conventionality

**oscar**
**01** O

**oscillate**
**03** wag **04** hunt, sway, vary, yo-yo **05** pitch, squeg, swing, waver **06** seesaw, wigwag **07** librate, vibrate **09** fluctuate, vacillate **12** move to and fro

**oscillation**
**05** surge, swing **07** flutter **08** sine wave, swinging, wavering **09** seesawing, squegging, variation, vibration **10** swing-swang **11** fluctuation, instability, vacillation **15** shilly-shallying

**osmium**
**02** Os

**osprey**
**07** Pandion **08** fish-hawk **09** ossifrage

**ossify**
**06** harden **07** petrify **08** indurate, make hard, rigidify, solidify **09** fossilize, make fixed **10** become hard **11** become fixed

**ostensible**
**07** alleged, claimed, feigned, outward, seeming **08** apparent, presumed, so-called, specious, supposed **09** ostensive, pretended, professed, purported **11** superficial

**ostensibly**
**09** allegedly, outwardly, reputedly, seemingly **10** apparently, supposedly **11** professedly, purportedly **12** on the surface **13** superficially

**ostentation**
**03** dog **04** dash, fuss, pomp, puff, show **05** flash, pride, swank **06** ostent, parade, splash, tinsel, vanity **07** display **08** boasting, flourish, pretence, pretense, vaunting **09** flaunting, pageantry, showiness, trappings **10** flashiness, peacockery, phylactery, pretension, showing-off **11** affectation, fanfaronade, flamboyance **13** exhibitionism **14** window-dressing **15** pretentiousness

**ostentatious**
**03** OTT **04** loud **05** flash, gaudy, showy **06** flashy, garish, glitzy, kitsch, vulgar **07** splashy **08** affected, barbaric, fastuous **09** barbarian, barbarous, flaunting, obtrusive **10** flamboyant, over the top **11** conspicuous, extravagant, pretentious **13** demonstrative

**ostentatiously**
**03** OTT **05** large **06** loudly **07** showily **08** flashily, garishly **10** over the top **11** obtrusively **12** flamboyantly **13** conspicuously, extravagantly, pretentiously **15** demonstratively

**ostracism**
**04** tabu **05** exile, taboo **07** barring, boycott **09** avoidance, exclusion, expulsion, isolation, rejection **10** banishment **12** cold-shoulder, proscription **13** disfellowship **15** excommunication

**ostracize**
**03** bar, cut **04** shun, snub **05** avoid, exile, expel **06** banish, outlaw, reject **07** boycott, exclude, isolate **09** blackball, proscribe, segregate **12** cold-shoulder **13** excommunicate **14** send to Coventry

**ostrich**
**04** rhea **05** nandu **06** nandoo, nhandu **07** estrich **08** estridge, oystrige, Struthio

**OT** *see* **Bible**

**other**
◇ *anagram indicator*
**04** else, left, more **05** extra, spare **06** second, unlike **07** further, variant **08** distinct, separate **09** alternate, different, disparate, remaining **10** additional, dissimilar **11** alternative, contrasting **13** supplementary
**• all others**
**04** rest

**otherwise**
◇ *anagram indicator*
**02** or **03** aka **04** else **05** alias, if not **06** or else, unless **09** different **11** also known as, differently, failing that **12** in another way **15** in a different way, in other respects

**otherworldly**
**03** fey **04** rapt **06** dreamy **07** bemused **08** ethereal **11** preoccupied **12** absent-minded

**otiose**
**05** extra, spare **06** excess, futile **07** surplus, to spare **08** indolent, needless, unneeded, unwanted **09** excessive, redundant, remaining **10** gratuitous, unoccupied **11** superfluous, uncalled-for, unnecessary, unwarranted **12** functionless **13** supernumerary

**ottoman**
**04** pouf **05** squab

**ounce**
**02** oz **03** jot, tad **04** atom, drop, fl oz, iota, lynx, spot, tael, unce, whit **05** crumb, grain, liang, scrap, shred, speck, touch, trace **06** jaguar, morsel **07** cheetah, modicum **08** particle **11** snow leopard

**oust**
**04** fire, sack **05** eject, evict, expel **06** depose, put out, topple, unseat **07** boot out, dismiss, kick out, replace, turn out **08** dislodge, displace, drive out, force out, get rid of, supplant, throw out **09** overthrow, thrust out **10** disinherit, dispossess **13** show the door to

**out**
◇ *anagram indicator*
◇ *deletion indicator*
**02** to **03** KO'd, set **04** alas, away, bent, dead, gone **05** dated, forth, known, passé, ready **06** abroad, absent, démodé, doused, intent, old hat, public, remote, used up **07** evident, expired, exposed, in bloom, in print, out cold, outside, without **08** blooming, comatose, divulged, drawback, excluded, external, finished, forcibly, in flower, manifest, outlying, revealed, seawards **09** available, disclosed, dismissed, elsewhere, forbidden, insistent, in the open, not at home, out-of-date, published, unwelcome **10** antiquated, blossoming, completely, determined, disallowed, impossible, insensible, knocked out, not burning, not shining, obtainable, thoroughly, unsuitable **11** in full bloom, unconscious, undesirable **12** disadvantage, extinguished, inadmissible, old-fashioned, unacceptable, unreservedly **13** inappropriate, unfashionable
**• not out**
**02** no
**• out of**
**04** frae, from, hors
**• out upon it**
**04** haro **06** harrow

**out-and-out**
**04** fair, flat, rank **05** plumb, stark, total, utter **06** arrant, full-on, proper **07** perfect, regular **08** absolute, complete, outright, positive, teetotal, thorough, whole-hog **09** bald-faced, downright, right-down, up and down **10** consummate, definitely, heart-whole, inveterate **11** honest-to-God, straight-out, unmitigated, unqualified **12** unreservedly **13** dyed-in-the-wool, thoroughgoing **14** hundred-per-cent, uncompromising

**outbreak**
**04** rash **05** burst, clash, flash, storm **06** putsch **07** flare-up, upbreak, upsurge **08** epidemic, eruption, hysteria, outburst **09** explosion **10** ebullition **11** disturbance, excrescence, sudden start **13** recrudescence

**outburst**
**03** fit, rag **04** flaw, gale, gush, gust, song **05** blurt, burst, flaky, spasm, storm, surge **06** attack, escape, outcry, volley **07** boutade, flare-up, ovation, passion, seizure **08** eruption, mouthful, outbreak, paroxysm, sunburst **09** explosion **10** exuberance, exuberancy, outpouring, solar flare **11** fit of temper

**outcast**
**05** cagot, exile, leper **06** abject, outlaw, pariah, reject, wretch **07** evacuee, quarrel, refugee **08** castaway, outsider, rejected **11** untouchable **15** persona non grata

**outclass**
**03** top **04** beat **05** outdo **07** eclipse, outrank, surpass **08** outrival, outshine, outstrip **09** excel over, transcend **10** overshadow **11** outdistance **13** leave standing, put in the shade

**outcome**
**05** issue, proof **06** answer, effect, pay-off, result, sequel, upcome, upshot, wash-up **07** proceed, product **08** proceeds **09** end result, outspring **10** conclusion, dénouement **11** after-effect, consequence

**outcry**
**03** cry, row **04** fuss **05** noise **06** clamor, racket, rumour, steven, tumult, uproar, yammer **07** clamour, dissent, exclaim, protest **08** outburst **09** commotion, complaint, hue and cry, objection **10** hullabaloo, humdudgeon **11** exclamation, indignation **12** protestation, vociferation

**outdated**
**03** obs **05** dated, mumsy, passé, steam **06** démodé, old hat, past it, square, uncool **07** antique, archaic **08** obsolete, outmoded **09** out of date **10** antiquated, fuddy-duddy, oldfangled, superseded **11** obsolescent, old-fogeyish, on the way out, out of the ark **12** antediluvian, old-fashioned, out of fashion **13** unfashionable **14** behind the times

**outdistance**
**04** pass **06** outrun **07** outpace, surpass **08** outstrip, overhaul, overtake, shake off **11** leave behind, pull ahead of **13** leave standing

**outdo**
**03** cap **04** beat, best, whip **05** excel, lurch **06** defeat, exceed **07** eclipse, surpass **08** outclass, out-Herod, outshine, outstrip, overcome, superate **09** come first, transcend **10** outperform **11** outdistance **12** walk away from **13** knock spots off, put in the shade, run rings round **14** get the better of **15** go one better than, run circles round

**outdoors**
**03** out **06** abroad **07** outside **08** alfresco **10** en plein air, out-of-doors **12** in the open air

**outer**
**06** fringe, remote **07** distant, faraway, further, outside, outward, surface **08** exterior, external, outlying **09** outermost **10** peripheral **11** superficial

**outface**
**04** defy **05** beard, brave **08** confront, outbrave, outstare **09** brazen out, stand up to, stare down

**outfit**
**03** kit, rig, set **04** crew, firm, gang, garb, gear, suit, team, togs, unit, weed **05** dress, equip, fit up, get-up, group, samfu, set-up, squad, stock, tools **06** attire, clique, fit out, fit-out, kit out, layout, rig-out, samfoo, setout, supply **07** apparel, appoint, bloomer, clothes, company, costume, coterie, furnish, provide, sunsuit, turn out, turnout **08** accoutre, business, ensemble **09** apparatus, equipment, provision, separates, trappings **10** sailor suit **11** bag of tricks, corporation **12** organization **13** accoutrements, paraphernalia, shalwar-kameez

**outfitter**
**06** sartor, tailor **07** modiste **08** clothier, costumer **09** costumier, couturier **10** couturière, dressmaker **11** haberdasher

**outflow**
**03** ebb, jet **04** gush, rush **05** spout **06** efflux, spring **07** outfall, outrush

**08** drainage, effluent, effusion **09** discharge, effluence, effluvium, effluxion, emanation, emergence **10** outpouring **11** debouchment **14** disemboguement

**outflowing**
**07** emanant, gushing, leaking, rushing **08** effluent, spurting **10** debouching **11** discharging

**outfox**
**03** con, kid **04** beat, best, dupe **05** trick **06** have on, outwit **07** deceive **08** outsmart, out-think **10** outperform **12** outmanoeuvre, take for a ride **14** get the better of, pull a fast one on

**outgoing**
**02** ex- **04** last, open, past, warm **06** former, genial **07** affable, amiable, cordial, leaving **08** emissary, friendly, retiring, sociable **09** departing, easy-going, expansive, extrovert, talkative **10** gregarious, unreserved **11** expenditure, sympathetic, uninhibited **12** affectionate, approachable **13** communicative, demonstrative

**outgoings**
**04** exes **05** costs **06** outlay **08** expenses, spending **09** disbursal, overheads **11** expenditure **12** disbursement

**outgrowth**
**03** ala **04** aril, hair, horn **05** shoot **06** air-sac, effect, sprout, stolon **07** enation, product, spin-off, verruca **08** caruncle, offshoot, root hair, swelling, trichome **09** apophysis, appendage, by-product, emanation, emergence, flocculus, propagule, rostellum **10** osteophyte, pollen tube, propagulum **11** consequence, excrescence **12** appressorium, effiguration, protuberance

**outhouse**
**04** shed

**outing**
**03** out **04** hike, romp, spin, tour, trip **05** jaunt, jolly, sally **06** junket, picnic **08** ejection **09** coach tour, excursion **10** expedition **11** mystery tour **12** pleasure trip

**outlandish**
◇ *anagram indicator*
**03** odd **05** alien, wacky, weird **06** exotic, far-out, freaky, quaint, way-out **07** bizarre, curious, foreign, oddball, strange, unknown, unusual **08** peculiar **09** barbarous, eccentric, grotesque, peregrine, unheard-of, uplandish **10** unfamiliar **12** preposterous, unreasonable **13** extraordinary **14** unconventional

**outlandishness**
**07** oddness **09** queerness, weirdness **10** exoticness, quaintness **11** bizarreness, peregrinity, strangeness, unusualness **12** eccentricity **13** grotesqueness

**outlast**
**04** ride **07** outdure, outlive, outstay, survive, weather **11** come through

**outlaw**
**03** ban, bar **04** horn, Tory **05** debar, exile **06** badman, bandit, banish, forbid, pirate, robber **07** brigand, condemn, embargo, exclude, outcast **08** criminal, disallow, fugitive, marauder, prohibit **09** broken man, desperado, interdict, proscribe, Robin Hood **10** bushranger, highwayman **12** put to the horn **13** excommunicate

**outlay**
**04** cost, mise **05** price **06** charge, expend **07** expense, payment **08** expenses, spending **09** outgoings **11** expenditure **12** disbursement

**outlet**
**04** duct, exit, port, shop, vent **05** issue, store, valve **06** egress, escape, let-off, market, nozzle, sluice, way out **07** channel, conduit, culvert, opening, outfall, release, sea gate **08** débouché, emissary, femerall, retailer, supplier **10** going forth **11** safety valve **12** retail outlet **14** means of release

**outline**
**03** map **04** edge, form, plan, trim **05** braid, chart, draft, dress, shape, trace, trick **06** aperçu, design, figure, fringe, layout, précis, résumé, schema, sketch **07** balloon, contour, croquis, diagram, keyline, profile, skyline, summary, tracing **08** abstract, chalk out, contorno, esquisse, rough out, scenario, skeleton, synopsis **09** adumbrate, bare bones, bare facts, delineate, framework, lineament, programme, rough idea, sketch out, summarize, waterline **10** ground plan, main points, prospectus, silhouette **11** delineation **12** underdrawing **13** configuration **15** thumbnail sketch

**outlive**
**07** outlast, outwear, survive, weather **08** overwear **11** come through, live through

**outlook**
**04** view **05** angle, slant **06** aspect, future **07** mindset, opinion, picture **08** attitude, forecast, panorama, prospect **09** prognosis, prospects, viewpoint, world-view **10** standpoint **11** frame of mind, perspective, point of view **12** expectations **14** interpretation, Weltanschauung

**outlying**
**03** out **05** outby, outer **06** far-off, forane, outbye, remote **07** distant, far-away, outland **08** detached, far-flung, isolated **10** provincial **11** out-of-the-way **12** inaccessible

**outmanoeuvre**
**04** beat **05** outdo **06** outfox, outwit **07** sandbag **08** outflank, outsmart, outthink **10** circumvent, outgeneral **14** get the better of

**outmoded**
**05** dated, passé, steam **06** démodé, old hat, past it, square, uncool **07** archaic **08** obsolete, outdated, shmaltzy **09** out of date, schmaltzy **10** antiquated, fuddy-duddy, oldfangled, superseded **11** obsolescent, old-fogeyish, on the way out, out of the ark **12** antediluvian, old-fashioned, out of fashion **13** unfashionable **14** behind the times

**out of date**
**03** old **05** dated, passé, steam **06** démodé, old hat, passée, past it, square, uncool **07** archaic, belated, vintage **08** obsolete, outdated, outmoded, overworn **09** overdated **10** antiquated, behindhand, fuddy-duddy, oldfangled, superseded **11** obsolescent, old-fogeyish, on the way out, out of the ark, prehistoric **12** antediluvian, old-fashioned, out of fashion **13** horse-and-buggy, prehistorical, unfashionable **14** behind the times
*See also* **outdated**

**out-of-the-way**
**03** odd **04** lost **05** outer **06** far-off, hidden, lonely, remote **07** distant, far-away, obscure, unusual **08** far-flung, isolated, outlying, secluded, singular, uncommon **10** outlandish, peripheral **11** god-forsaken, little-known **12** inaccessible, unfrequented

**out of work**
**04** idle **07** jobless, laid off, resting **08** workless **09** on the dole, out of a job, redundant **10** unemployed **11** between jobs

**outpace**
**04** beat, pass **05** outdo **06** outrun **07** surpass **08** outstrip, overhaul, overtake **11** outdistance

**outpouring**
**04** flow, flux **05** blast, flood, spate, spurt **06** deluge, efflux, lavish, strain, stream **07** cascade, outflow, torrent, welling **08** effusion **09** effluence, emanation, word salad **11** debouchment **14** disemboguement

**output**
◇ *anagram indicator*
**04** gain **05** yield **06** fruits, return **07** harvest, outturn, product, turnout **10** production, throughput **11** achievement, manufacture, performance **12** productivity **14** accomplishment

**outrage**
**04** evil, fury, rage, rape **05** abuse, anger, appal, crime, shock, wrath **06** defile, enrage, horror, injure, injury, madden, offend, ravage, ravish **07** abusion, affront, assault, disgust, horrify, incense, offence, scandal, violate **08** atrocity, enormity, violence **09** barbarism, brutality, desecrate, infuriate, sacrilege, violation **10** scandalize **11** indignation

**outrageous**
◇ *anagram indicator*
**04** foul, rich, vile, wild **05** enorm, gross **06** unholy **07** furious, ghastly, heinous, obscene, ungodly, violent **08** dreadful, enormous, flagrant, gruesome, horrible, infernal, shocking, terrible **09** atrocious, egregious, excessive, monstrous, offensive, turbulent **10** abominable, diabolical, exorbitant, immoderate, inordinate, monstruous, scandalous, unbearable **11** disgraceful, extravagant, intolerable, unchristian, unspeakable **12** extortionate, insufferable, preposterous, unacceptable, unreasonable **14** unconscionable

**outrageously**
**08** horribly, terribly **09** obscenely **10** dreadfully, unbearably **11** intolerably, unspeakably **12** scandalously, unacceptably **13** disgracefully

**outré**
◇ *anagram indicator*
**03** odd **05** weird **06** far-out, freaky, way-out **07** bizarre, oddball, strange, unusual **08** shocking **09** eccentric, fantastic **10** outrageous **11** extravagant **13** extraordinary **14** unconventional

**outrider**
**05** guard **06** escort, herald **08** vanguard **09** attendant, bodyguard, precursor **12** advance guard

**outright**
**04** pure **05** clear, total, utter **06** at once, direct, openly, wholly **07** perfect, totally, utterly **08** absolute, complete, definite, directly, entirely, thorough **09** downright, instantly, out-and-out **10** absolutely, completely, explicitly, positively, thoroughly, undeniable **11** categorical, immediately, unequivocal, unmitigated, unqualified **12** straight away, there and then, unmistakable, unreservedly **13** categorically, thoroughgoing, unconditional, undisguisedly **15** instantaneously, straightforward

**outrun**
**04** beat, lose, pass **05** excel, outdo **06** exceed **07** outpace, surpass **08** outstrip, overhaul, overtake, shake off **11** leave behind, outdistance, spread-eagle **13** run faster than

**outset**
**05** onset, start **07** kick-off, opening **09** beginning, inception, threshold **12** commencement, inauguration

**outshine**
**03** top **04** beat, best **05** dwarf, excel, outdo **07** eclipse, outrank, put down, surpass, upstage **08** outclass, outstrip **09** outlustre, transcend **10** overshadow, put to shame **13** put in the shade

**outside**
◇ *anagram indicator*
◇ *containment indicator*
**03** exo- **04** ecto-, face, hors, rind, rine, slim **05** cover, extra, faint, front, outer, small, vague **06** casual, façade, remote, slight **07** distant, extreme, furth of, neutral, outdoor, outward, slender, surface, without **08** exterior, external, marginal, unbiased, unlikely, visiting **09** impartial, objective, outermost, temporary **10** appearance, consulting, extramural, extraneous, improbable, negligible **11** independent, non-resident, peripatetic, superficial **12** outer surface, self-employed **13** subcontracted

**outsider**
**05** alien **06** émigré, layman, misfit, ringer **07** outlier, roughie, visitor **08** emigrant, intruder, newcomer, stranger **09** foreigner, immigrant, non-member, odd one out, outlander **10** interloper **11** gatecrasher, non-resident

**outsize**
**02** OS **04** huge, mega, vast **05** giant, great, jumbo **07** immense, mammoth, massive, titanic, very big **08** colossal, enormous, gigantic **09** extensive, frightful, ginormous, humongous, monstrous, very large **10** gargantuan, prodigious, stupendous, tremendous

**outskirts**
**04** edge **05** edges, limit **06** margin **07** borders, fringes, suburbs **08** boundary, environs, frontier, purlieus, suburbia, vicinity **09** perimeter, periphery **13** neighbourhood

**outsmart**
**03** con, kid **04** beat, best, dupe **05** trick **06** have on, outfox, outwit **07** deceive **08** out-think **10** outperform **12** outmanoeuvre, take for a ride **14** get the better of, pull a fast one on

**outsource**
**07** farm out **08** delegate **11** contract out **12** give to others, pass to others

**outspoken**
**04** free, rude **05** bluff, blunt, broad, frank, plain, vocal **06** candid, direct **07** brusque **08** explicit, straight **10** forthright, unreserved **11** plain-spoken, Rabelaisian, unequivocal **13** unceremonious **15** straightforward

**outspokenness**
**07** freedom **08** rudeness **09** bluffness, bluntness, frankness, plainness **10** candidness, directness **11** brusqueness **14** forthrightness

**outspread**
**04** open, wide **06** flared, opened **08** expanded, extended, unfolded, unfurled, wide-open **09** fanned out, spread out, stretched **12** outstretched

**outstanding**
**03** ace, due **04** cool, some **05** brill, chief, famed, great, owing **06** famous, golden, superb, unpaid, wicked **07** eminent, notable, ongoing, payable, pending, radical, salient, special **08** left-over, renowned, smashing, striking, superior, to be done, top-notch **09** arresting, brilliant, excellent, important, memorable, prominent, remaining, unsettled, well-known **10** celebrated, impressive, noteworthy, pre-eminent, prosilient, remarkable, unfinished, unresolved **11** exceptional, superlative, uncollected **13** distinguished, extraordinary **14** extraordinaire, out of this world

**outstandingly**
**07** greatly, notably **09** amazingly, extremely **10** especially, remarkably, strikingly **12** impressively **13** exceptionally **15** extraordinarily

**outstrip**
**03** top **04** beat, cote, pass **05** outdo, outgo, strip **06** better, exceed, gain on, outrun **07** eclipse, outfoot, outpace, surpass **08** outshine, overtake **09** transcend **11** leave behind, outdistance **12** go faster than **13** leave standing

**outward**
**05** outer **06** carnal, extern, formal, public **07** evident, externe, obvious, outside, seeming, surface, visible, worldly **08** apparent, exterior, external, supposed **09** dissolute, outermost, posticous, professed **10** accidental, additional, noticeable, observable, ostensible **11** discernible, perceptible, superficial, without-door **13** superficially

**outwardly**
**07** visibly, without **09** seemingly **10** apparently, exteriorly, externally, supposedly **12** at first sight, on the outside, on the surface **13** on the face of it, superficially

**outweigh**
**06** exceed **07** surpass **08** overcome, override **09** cancel out, make up for, overpoise **10** be more than, outbalance **11** predominate, prevail over **12** be superior to, preponderate **13** be greater than, compensate for

**outwit**
**03** con, fox, kid **04** beat, best, dish, dupe **05** cheat, trick **06** better, euchre, have on, outfox **07** deceive, defraud, swindle **08** outsmart, outthink **09** crossbite, overreach **10** circumvent **12** outmanoeuvre, take for a ride **14** be cleverer than, get the better of, pull a fast one on

**outwork**
**04** moon

**outworn**
**05** stale **06** old hat, past it **07** ancient, archaic, defunct, disused **08** obsolete, outdated, outmoded, rejected

09 abandoned, exhausted, hackneyed, moth-eaten, out of date 10 antiquated 11 discredited, obsolescent 12 old-fashioned 14 behind the times

**oval**
05 ovate, ovoid 07 navette, obovate, oviform 08 elliptic 09 egg-shaped, vulviform 10 elliptical 11 ellipsoidal

**ovation**
06 bravos, cheers, praise 07 acclaim, bouquet, praises, tribute 08 accolade, applause, cheering, clapping, plaudits 09 laudation, rejoicing 11 acclamation 12 handclapping

**oven**
03 Aga, oon, umu 04 kiln, lear, leer, lehr, oast 05 hangi, micro, stove 06 calcar, cooker 07 furnace, tandoor 09 microwave 11 copper Maori 13 microwave oven

**over**
◇ *containment indicator*
◇ *juxtaposition down indicator*
◇ *reversal down indicator*
02 of, on, re, up 03 o'er, ore 04 gone, left, ower, owre, past, upon 05 about, above, aloft, along, ended, extra, upper 06 across, beyond, closed, during, excess, no more, on high, unused 07 at an end, on top of, settled, surplus 08 done with, finished, in excess, left over, more than, overhead, superior, unwanted 09 apropos of, as regards, completed, concluded, exceeding, excessive, forgotten, in the past, regarding, remaining, unclaimed 10 concerning, higher than, in addition, in charge of, in excess of, relating to, superior to, terminated, throughout 11 dealing with, in command of, referring to, superfluous 12 accomplished, with regard to 13 concerned with, connected with, in the matter of, with respect to 14 ancient history, on the subject of 15 over and done with, with reference to

• **over and above**
04 plus 06 beside 07 added to, besides, on top of 08 as well as, let alone 09 along with 12 in addition to, not to mention, together with

• **over and over**
05 often 09 ad nauseam, endlessly 10 frequently, repeatedly 11 ad infinitum, continually 12 time and again 13 again and again

**overabundance**
04 glut 06 excess 07 surfeit, surplus 08 plethora 09 profusion 10 oversupply 11 superfluity 14 superabundance 15 embarras de choix

**overact**
03 ham 04 hoke 06 overdo 07 lay it on 08 overplay, pile it on 10 exaggerate 12 lay it on thick 13 pile it on thick

**overall**
05 broad, pinny, total 06 global, pinnie 07 all-over, blanket, broadly, crawler, general, save-all, tablier 08 complete, dustcoat, out to out, pinafore, sweeping, umbrella 09 dungarees, inclusive, in general, siren suit, universal 10 altogether, boiler suit, by and large, everywhere, on the whole 12 all-embracing, all-inclusive 13 comprehensive 15 broadly speaking

**overalls**
06 jumper, pinnie 07 crawler, save-all, tablier 08 coverall, dust-coat, fatigues, pinafore, workwear 09 dungarees 10 boiler suit

**overawe**
03 awe, cow 05 abash, alarm, daunt, scare 06 dismay 07 buffalo, petrify, terrify, unnerve 08 browbeat, frighten 10 disconcert, intimidate

**overbalance**
04 slip, trip 05 upset 06 topple, tumble 07 capsize, tip over 08 fall over, keel over, overturn 10 somersault, topple over, turn turtle 15 lose your balance, lose your footing

**overbearing**
05 bossy, proud 06 la-di-da, lordly, snobby, snooty, snotty 07 haughty, stuck-up 08 arrogant, cavalier, despotic, dogmatic, masterly, smartass 09 imperious, officious, smartarse 10 autocratic, disdainful, dogmatical, high-handed, oppressive, tyrannical 11 dictatorial, domineering, toffee-nosed 12 contemptuous, presumptuous, supercilious

**overblown**
03 OTT 07 exalted 08 inflated, overdone 09 amplified, bombastic, excessive 10 burlesqued, overstated, over the top 11 caricatured, embellished, extravagant, overcharged, pretentious 13 overestimated, self-important

**overcast**
04 dark, dull, grey, hazy, whip 05 foggy, misty, shade 06 cloudy, dismal, dreary, gloomy, leaden, sombre 07 clouded, louring, recover, sunless 08 darkened 11 clouded over

**overcharge**
02 do, o/c 04 clip, rook, rush, soak 05 cheat, sting 06 diddle, extort, fleece, rip off 07 swindle 09 surcharge 11 short-change

**overcoat** *see* **coat**

**overcome**
04 beat, best, lick, rout 05 break, cover, force, fordo, moved, outdo, worst 06 broken, byword, defeat, evince, excess, expugn, hammer, master, mither, moider, outwit, subdue, thrash 07 beat off, clobber, conquer, consume, moither, outplay, overget, prevail, refrain, surplus, trounce 08 affected, choked up, convince, dead-beat, knock out, outsmart, superate, surmount, vanquish, wear down 09 exhausted, hit for six, overmatch, overpower, overthrow, overwhelm, rise above, slaughter, subjugate, underfong 10 bowled over, speechless, surmounted 11 knock for six, overpowered, overwhelmed, triumph over 12 lost for words, put on the foil 13 have the edge on 14 get the better of

**over-confident**
04 rash 05 brash, cocky 06 secure, uppish, uppity 08 arrogant, cocksure, sanguine 09 foolhardy, hubristic 10 blustering, incautious, swaggering 11 overweening, self-assured, temerarious 12 presumptuous 14 over-optimistic

**overcook**
04 burn, char 05 singe 07 blacken

**overcritical**
06 purist 07 carping, Zoilean 08 captious, over-nice, pedantic 09 cavilling 10 nit-picking, pernickety 11 persnickety 12 fault-finding, hard to please 13 hair-splitting, hypercritical 14 overparticular

**overcrowded**
06 packed 07 chocker, overrun, teeming 08 swarming 09 chock-full, congested, jam-packed, packed out 10 overloaded 11 chock-a-block, crammed full 13 overpopulated

**overdo**
05 excel 06 harass 07 fatigue, ham it up, lay it on, overact 08 camp it up, go too far, overplay, pile it on 09 overstate 10 exaggerate 11 cut it too fat, go overboard, overindulge 12 lay it on thick 13 carry to excess, pile it on thick, stretch a point

• **overdo it**
07 crack up 08 overwork 09 do too much 10 sweat blood 11 work too hard 14 strain yourself 15 burn yourself out

**overdone**
03 OTT 05 burnt, hokey, undue 07 charred, dried up, fulsome, gushing, percoct, spoiled 08 effusive, overshot 09 excessive, overbaked 10 histrionic, immoderate, inordinate, overcooked, overplayed, overstated, over the top 11 exaggerated, overwrought, unnecessary 13 overelaborate 14 burnt to a cinder 15 burnt to a frazzle

**overdose**
02 OD

**overdraft**
02 OD 04 debt 07 arrears, deficit 10 borrowings 11 liabilities 13 unpaid amounts

**overdue**
03 due 04 late, slow 05 owing, tardy 06 unpaid 07 belated, delayed, payable, pending 09 unsettled 10 behindhand, unpunctual 14 behind schedule

**overeat**
**05** binge, gorge **06** guzzle, pig out **10** eat too much, go on a binge, gormandize **11** overindulge **13** stuff yourself

**overeating**
**07** bulimia **08** bingeing, gluttony, guzzling **10** gormandise, gormandism **11** gourmandise, gourmandism, hyperphagia **14** overindulgence

**overemphasize**
**06** labour **08** belabour **10** exaggerate, overstress **13** make too much of, overdramatize

**overexert**
**• overexert yourself**
**07** fatigue **08** overdo it, overwork **11** work too hard **14** strain yourself **15** overtax yourself, wear yourself out

**overfeed**
**04** cram, glut, sate

**overflow**
**03** lip, ren, rin, run **04** ream, soak, teem **05** cover, flood, spill, surge, swamp, water **06** back-up, deluge, shower **07** overrun, redound, run over, surplus **08** brim over, flow over, inundate, outswell, pour over, spillage, submerge, surround, well over **09** discharge, overspill, spill over **10** bubble over, inundation **13** overabundance

**overflowing**
**04** full, rife **05** flush **06** filled **07** brimful, copious, crowded, profuse, teeming **08** inundant, overfull, swarming, thronged **09** abounding, bountiful, exuberant, land-flood, plenteous, plentiful, redundant **13** superabundant

**overgrown**
**04** rank

**overgrowth**
**05** naeve, nevus **06** naevus **09** gigantism **10** escalation, luxuriance, luxuriancy, rhinophyma **11** gliomatosis, hyperplasia, hypertrophy **13** overabundance **14** superabundance **15** overdevelopment

**overhang**
**03** jut **04** loom, poke **05** bulge **06** beetle, extend, impend, jut out **07** poke out, project **08** bulge out, protrude, stand out, stick out

**overhanging**
**06** beetle, shelvy **07** bulging, jutting, pendant, pendent, pensile **08** beetling, imminent **09** incumbent, pendulous, prominent **10** bulging out, jutting out, projecting, protruding **11** standing out, sticking out **14** superincumbent

**overhaul**
**03** fix **04** mend, pass **05** check **06** gain on, go over, repair, revamp, survey **07** check up, check-up, examine, inspect, outpace, rummage, service **08** outstrip, overtake, renovate **09** check over, going-over, re-examine **10** get ahead of, inspection, renovation **11** examination, investigate, outdistance, pull ahead of, recondition **14** reconditioning

**overhead**
**03** air **05** above, aloft **06** aerial, on high, raised, upward **07** average, general, up above **08** all-round, elevated **11** overhanging

**overheads**
**06** burden, oncost **07** oncosts **08** expenses **09** outgoings **10** fixed costs **11** expenditure **12** disbursement, regular costs, running costs **14** operating costs

**overheated**
**05** angry, fiery **06** roused **07** excited, flaming **08** agitated, inflamed **10** passionate **11** impassioned, overexcited, overwrought
**• overheated state**
**04** stew

**overindulge**
**03** pet **04** lush, sate **05** binge, booze, gorge, spoil **06** cosset, guzzle, pamper, pander, pig out **07** debauch, satiate **09** spoon-feed **10** eat too much, gluttonize, gormandize **11** mollycoddle **12** drink too much

**overindulgence**
**05** binge **06** excess **07** debauch, surfeit **10** overeating **12** immoderation, intemperance

**overjoyed**
**04** rapt **06** elated, joyful **08** ecstatic, euphoric, jubilant, thrilled **09** delighted, rapturous **10** enraptured, in raptures **11** high as a kite, on cloud nine, over the moon, tickled pink **14** pleased as Punch **15** in seventh heaven, on top of the world

**overlap**
**03** lap **04** ride **05** cover **07** overlay, overlie, shingle **08** coincide, flap over, override **09** imbricate

**overlay**
**04** ceil, face, line, span, whip, wrap **05** adorn, belay, cover, inlay, patch **06** spread, veneer **07** blanket, envelop, surface, varnish **08** covering, decorate, encumber, laminate, ornament

**overload**
**03** tax **04** glut **06** burden, excess, lumber, saddle, strain **07** oppress, overtax, surfeit, surplus **08** encumber, plethora **09** surcharge, weigh down **10** overburden, overcharge, oversupply **11** hypercharge, overfreight, superfluity **13** overabundance **14** superabundance

**overlook**
**04** face, miss, omit **05** leave **06** excuse, forget, ignore, pardon, pass by, slight, wink at **07** condone, forgive, let pass, let ride, neglect, oversee **08** look onto, look over, open onto, overskip, pass over **09** disregard, front onto, mislippen **11** have a view of, superintend **14** command a view of, take no notice of **15** take no account of, turn a blind eye to

**overlooked**
**07** unnoted **08** unheeded, unprized, unvalued **10** in the shade, unhonoured, unregarded, unremarked **12** unconsidered

**overly**
**03** too **04** over **06** casual, unduly **08** casually, superior **11** exceedingly, excessively **12** immoderately, inordinately, supercilious, unreasonably **13** unnecessarily **14** superciliously

**overmuch**
**06** unduly **07** too much **11** excessively **12** immoderately, inordinately, unreasonably **13** unnecessarily

**overnice**
**07** finical **08** kid glove **10** nit-picking, oversubtle, pernickety **11** overprecise, persnickety **13** oversensitive **14** overfastidious, over-meticulous, overparticular, overscrupulous

**overplay**
**06** colour, overdo, stress **07** amplify, enhance, enlarge, lay it on, magnify **08** oversell, pile it on **09** dramatize, embellish, embroider, emphasize, overstate **10** aggrandize, exaggerate, shoot a line **12** lay it on thick **13** make too much of, overdramatize, overemphasize, pile it on thick **15** stretch the truth

**overpopulated**
**06** packed **07** overrun, teeming **08** swarming **09** chock-full, congested, jam-packed, packed out **10** overloaded **11** crammed full, overcrowded

**overpower**
**04** beat, daze, move, rout **05** crush, floor, quash, quell, swelt, touch, whelm **06** dazzle, defeat, evince, master, overgo, subdew, subdue **07** confuse, conquer, perplex, stagger, swelter, trounce **08** bedazzle, bowl over, overbear, overcome, vanquish **09** dumbfound, hit for six, hypnotize, overthrow, overwhelm, subjugate, take aback **10** immobilize, overmaster **11** flabbergast, knock for six **12** affect deeply **14** affect strongly **15** gain mastery over, leave speechless

**overpowering**
**06** strong **07** extreme **08** forceful, powerful, stifling **09** sickening, tyrannous **10** compelling, nauseating, oppressive, unbearable, undeniable **11** irrefutable, suffocating **12** irresistible, overwhelming **14** uncontrollable

**over-productive**
**04** rank

**overrate**
**06** blow up **07** magnify **09** overprize, overvalue **10** overpraise
**12** overestimate **13** make too much of

**overreach**
• **overreach yourself**
**08** go too far, overdo it **14** strain yourself, try to do too much **15** burn yourself out

**override**
**05** annul, quash **06** cancel, exceed, ignore **07** nullify, overlap, rescind, reverse, surpass **08** abrogate, outweigh, overcome, overrule, overtake, set aside, vanquish
**09** disregard, supersede
**11** countermand, prevail over, trample over **12** be superior to **13** be greater than

**overriding**
**05** final, first, major, prime, prior
**06** ruling **07** pivotal, primary, supreme
**08** cardinal, dominant, ultimate
**09** essential, number one, paramount, principal **10** compelling, overruling, prevailing **11** determining, predominant **13** most important
**15** most significant

**overrule**
**05** annul **06** cancel, reject, revoke
**07** nullify, outvote, prevail, rescind, reverse **08** abrogate, disallow, overbear, override, oversway, overturn, set aside, vote down **10** invalidate
**11** countermand

**overrun**
**03** lip **05** bleed, storm, swamp
**06** attack, exceed, go over, infest, invade, occupy, ravage **07** besiege, run riot **08** inundate, overgrow, overstep, permeate **09** overreach, overshoot, overwhelm, penetrate, surge over, swarm over **10** depopulate, spread over

**overseas**
**06** abroad, exotic, remote, widely
**07** distant, faraway, foreign **08** external, outremer **10** far and wide
**11** ultramarine **13** international **14** in foreign parts, to foreign parts **15** in foreign climes, out of the country, to foreign climes

**oversee**
**03** ren, rin, run **05** guide, watch
**06** direct, manage **07** conduct, control, inspect **09** disregard, look after, supervise, watch over
**10** administer **11** keep an eye on, preside over, superintend **12** be in charge of **13** be in control of

**overseer**
**03** guv **04** baas, boss **05** chief
**06** bishop, critic, editor, gaffer, grieve, guv'nor, induna **07** captain, foreman, manager, overman, steward
**08** banksman, decurion, oversman, surveyor **09** forewoman, woodreeve
**10** foreperson, manageress, supervisor, workmaster **11** flock-master, mine-captain **12** workmistress
**14** superintendent

**overshadow**
◇ *containment indicator*
**03** dim, mar **04** veil **05** cloud, dwarf, excel, shade, spoil **06** blight, darken
**07** eclipse, obscure, protect, shelter, surpass **08** bescreen, dominate, hang over, outshine **09** adumbrate, obumbrate, rise above **10** tower above
**12** be superior to, put a damper on
**13** put in the shade **14** take the edge off

**oversight**
**04** boob, care, flub **05** error, fault, lapse
**06** charge, howler, slip-up **07** blunder, control, custody, keeping, mistake, neglect **08** handling, omission
**09** direction **10** management, parablepsy **11** dereliction, parablepsis, supervision **12** carelessness, inadvertence, inadvertency, surveillance **14** administration, responsibility **15** superintendence

**oversize**
**04** huge, mega, vast **05** giant, great, jumbo **07** immense, mammoth, massive, titanic, very big **08** colossal, enormous, gigantic **09** extensive, frightful, ginormous, humongous, monstrous, very large **10** gargantuan, monumental, prodigious, stupendous, tremendous

**overstate**
**06** colour, overdo, stress **07** amplify, enhance, enlarge, lay it on, magnify
**08** oversell, pile it on **09** dramatize, embellish, embroider, emphasize
**10** aggrandize, exaggerate, shoot a line
**12** lay it on thick **13** make too much of, overdramatize, overemphasize, pile it on thick **15** stretch the truth

**overstatement**
**06** excess, parody **08** emphasis
**09** burlesque, hyperbole **10** caricature
**11** enlargement **12** exaggeration, extravagance, overemphasis
**13** amplification, embellishment, magnification **14** overestimation
**15** pretentiousness

**overt**
**04** open **05** plain **06** patent, public
**07** evident, obvious, visible
**08** apparent, manifest **09** professed
**10** noticeable, observable
**11** conspicuous, unconcealed, undisguised

**overtake**
**03** lap **04** pass **05** catch **06** befall, engulf, gain on, go past, strike
**07** forhent, run past **08** come upon, forehent, happen to, outstrip, overhaul, ride down **09** drive past, overcatch, overwhelm **10** come up with **11** catch up with, leave behind, outdistance, pull ahead of **13** catch unawares, draw level with **14** take by surprise

**over the top** *see* **over the top** *under* **top**

**overthrow**
◇ *anagram indicator*
**03** end **04** beat, best, down, fall, oust, rout, ruin **05** crush, quash, quell, smite, spill, upset, whelm, worst **06** defeat, depose, invert, lay low, master, subdue, topple, tumble, unseat, upturn
**07** abolish, conquer, ousting, put down, run down, run over, stonker, subvert, tip over, trounce, undoing, whemmle, whomble, whommle, whummle **08** bear down, confound, dethrone, displace, downfall, keel over, overcast, overcome, overturn, ride down, supplant, turn over, vanquish
**09** bring down, confusion, knock over, overpower, overwhelm, prostrate, unseating, upsetting **10** deposition, subversion **11** destruction, humiliation, labefaction, overbalance, suppression, vanquishing **12** dethronement
**13** labefactation **14** bouleversement

**overtly**
**06** openly **07** clearly, plainly
**08** patently **09** obviously **10** in full view, manifestly, noticeably **11** for all to see **13** conspicuously

**overtone**
**04** hint **05** sense **06** nuance **07** feeling, flavour **08** harmonic, innuendo
**10** intimation, suggestion
**11** association, connotation, implication, insinuation
**12** undercurrent **13** hidden meaning

**overture**
**04** move **05** moves, offer **06** feeler, gambit, motion, signal **07** advance, feelers, opening, prelude, toccata
**08** advances, aperture, approach, proposal **09** beginning **10** invitation, suggestion **11** opening move, opportunity, proposition
**12** introduction **13** opening gambit

*Overtures include:*

**05** Cuban, Herod, Wasps
**06** Adonis, Choral, Comedy, Esther, French, Heroic, Solemn, Spring, Thalia, Tragic
**07** Aladdin, Euterpe, Festive, Holiday, Idyllic, Jubilee, Leonora, Maytime, Othello
**08** Carnival, Columbus, Coriolan, Hebrides, Hyperion, In Autumn, King Lear, Romantic, Waverley
**09** Britannia, Children's, Fairy Land, In Bohemia, Pinocchio, The Naiads
**10** Amid Nature, In the South, Salutatory
**11** East and West, Fingal's Cave, Pickwickian, Shéhérazade, The Faithful, William Tell
**12** Fair Melusina, In London Town, Rip van Winkle, Street Corner, The Rehearsal
**13** In the Highland, Shadowy Waters, The Wood-Nymphs
**14** Eighteen Twelve, Eighteen-Twelve, In Nature's Realm, In the Mountains, Romeo and Juliet
**15** Comes Autumn Time, Portsmouth Point, The Fair Melusina

**overturn**
◇ *anagram indicator*
◇ *reversal down indicator*
**03** tip **04** beat, coup, cowp, oust, veto **05** annul, crush, quash, spill, upset, whelm **06** cancel, defeat, depose, invert, repeal, revoke, topple, unseat, upturn **07** abolish, capsize, conquer, destroy, nullify, rescind, reverse, skittle, subvert, tip over, whemmle, whomble, whommle, whummle **08** abrogate, confound, dethrone, displace, keel over, overcome, override, overrule, set aside, turn over, vanquish **09** bring down, knock over, overpower, overthrow, overwhelm **11** overbalance

**overused**
**04** worn **05** stale, tired, trite **07** cliché'd **08** bromidic, clichéed **09** hackneyed, played out **10** overworked, threadbare, unoriginal **11** commonplace, stereotyped **13** platitudinous

**overview**
**05** study **06** review, survey **08** panorama, scrutiny **09** appraisal, valuation **10** assessment, inspection **11** examination, measurement **13** consideration

**overweening**
**04** vain **05** cocky, proud **06** hubris, hybris, lordly **07** haughty, pompous, swollen **08** arrogant, cavalier, cocksure, inflated, insolent, vaulting **09** conceited, excessive, hubristic, overblown, upsetting **10** high-handed, immoderate **11** egotistical, extravagant, opinionated **12** presumptuous, supercilious, vainglorious **13** outrecuidance, over-confident, self-confident

**overweight**
**03** fat **04** huge **05** ample, bulky, buxom, gross, heavy, hefty, obese, plump, podgy, stout, tubby **06** chubby, chunky, flabby, fleshy, portly **07** massive, outsize **09** corpulent **10** pot-bellied, voluptuous, well-padded **13** preponderance **15** well-upholstered

**overwhelm**
**04** beat, best, bury, daze, kill, lick, move, rout **05** amaze, crush, floor, quash, quell, swamp, touch, worst **06** defeat, deluge, engulf, hammer, ingulf, outwit, subdue, thrash **07** clobber, confuse, destroy, engulph, ingulph, oppress, outplay, overrun, prevail, stagger, trounce **08** bowl over, inundate, knock out, outsmart, overbear, overcome, submerge, vanquish **09** devastate, hit for six, overpower, overthrow, slaughter, snow under, subjugate **10** overburden **11** knock for six **12** affect deeply **13** have the edge on, knock sideways **14** affect strongly, get the better of

**overwhelming**
**04** huge, vast **05** great, large **06** strong **07** banging, extreme, immense, massive, runaway **08** crashing, enormous, forceful, powerful, stifling **09** sickening **10** compelling, formidable, foudroyant, nauseating, oppressive, unbearable, undeniable **11** irrefutable, suffocating **12** irresistible, overpowering **14** uncontrollable

**overwork**
**05** weary **06** burden, strain **07** crack up, exhaust, exploit, oppress, overtax, overuse, wear out **08** overdo it, overload **09** do too much **10** overstrain, sweat blood **11** work too hard **14** strain yourself **15** burn yourself out

**overworked**
**04** worn **05** stale, tired, trite **07** cliché'd, worn out **08** bromidic, clichéed, forswunk **09** exhausted, forswonck, hackneyed, overtaxed, played out **10** threadbare, unoriginal **11** commonplace, stereotyped, stressed out **12** overstrained **13** platitudinous

**overwrought**
**04** edgy **05** nervy, tense **06** highly, on edge, strung **07** excited, frantic, keyed up, nervous, uptight, wound up **08** agitated, worked up **10** distraught **11** overcharged, overexcited **14** beside yourself

**owe**
**10** be in debt to, be in the red, run up debts **11** be overdrawn, get into debt **12** be indebted to **13** be in arrears to

**owing**
**03** dew, due **04** owed **06** unpaid **07** overdue, payable **09** imputable, in arrears, unsettled **11** outstanding
• **owing to**
**02** of **05** due to **08** thanks to **09** because of **11** as a result of, on account of **15** in consequence of

**owl**
**04** Bubo, ruru **05** madge **06** hooter, howlet, mopoke, strich **07** boobook, dullard, smuggle **08** longhorn, mopehawk, morepork, wiseacre **09** screecher **11** glimmer-gowk

**own**
**03** ain, use **04** have, hold, keep, nain, nown **05** admit, enjoy **06** occupy, proper, retain **07** concede, confess, have got, possess, private **08** peculiar, personal **09** authentic, recognize **10** individual, monopolize, particular **11** acknowledge **12** be the owner of **13** idiosyncratic **14** have to yourself
• **on your own**
**05** alone **06** singly **07** unaided **08** isolated **09** on your tod **10** by yourself, unassisted **13** independently, off your own bat, unaccompanied
• **own up**
**05** admit **07** confess **09** come clean **11** acknowledge, plead guilty **12** tell the truth

**owner**
**05** malik, melik **06** holder, keeper, master **08** landlady, landlord, mistress **09** homeowner, possessor **10** freeholder, proprietor **11** householder, proprietary **12** proprietress

**ownership**
**04** uses **05** title **06** domain, rights **08** dominion, freehold, property **10** possession **11** proprietary **14** proprietorship

**owning**
**02** of

**ox**
**03** ure, yak **04** anoa, bull, gaur, gyal, mart, neat, urus, zebu **05** bison, bugle, gayal, steer, stirk **06** rother **07** aurochs, banteng, banting, buffalo, bullock **08** bull-beef, sapi-utan **09** sapi-outan
• **team of oxen**
**04** span

**Oxford University** *see* **college**

**oxygen**
**01** O

**oyster**
**05** plant **06** native, Ostrea **07** spondyl **08** seedling
• **oyster bed**
**04** stew

# P

**P**
**03** pee **04** papa

**pace**
**04** gait, pass, rate, step, walk **05** amble, march, pound, speed, tempo, tramp, tread **06** flight, motion, patrol, stride **07** mark out, measure, passage, running **08** celerity, movement, progress, rapidity, velocity **09** quickness, swiftness **13** walk up and down **14** rate of progress

**pacific**
**04** calm, mild **05** quiet, still **06** dovish, gentle, irenic, placid, serene, smooth **07** equable, halcyon **08** dovelike, friendly, irenical, pacifist, peaceful, tranquil **09** appeasing, peaceable, placatory, unruffled **10** diplomatic, non-violent **11** complaisant, peace-loving, peacemaking **12** conciliatory, pacificatory, propitiatory **14** nonbelligerent

**pacification**
**07** calming **08** soothing **09** placating, silencing **10** moderating, moderation, quietening **11** appeasement, peacemaking **12** conciliation, propitiation **14** quietening down

**pacifism**
**10** pacificism, satyagraha **11** non-violence, peacemaking

**pacifist**
**02** CO **04** dove **06** conchy **08** peacenik **10** pacificist, peace-lover, peacemaker **11** peace-monger

**pacify**
**04** calm, lull, tame **05** allay, crush, quell, quiet, still **06** defuse, soften, soothe, subdue **07** appease, assuage, compose, mollify, placate, put down, quieten, silence, sweeten **08** calm down, moderate **09** reconcile **10** conciliate, propitiate

**pack**
**03** bag, box, jam, mob, ram, set, tin **04** bale, band, cram, crew, fill, gang, herd, load, plot, rout, stow, swag, wrap **05** bluey, bunch, cover, crate, crowd, drove, flock, group, press, put in, stock, store, stuff, tie up, troop, truss, wedge **06** bundle, burden, carton, charge, fardel, kitbag, packet, parcel, steeve, throng, wrap up **07** compact, company, dismiss, envelop, matilda, package, prepack, squeeze **08** backpack, canister, compress, intrigue, knapsack, rucksack **09** container, haversack **10** collection **11** blister card, canisterize

**• pack in**
**03** end, jam, mob, ram **04** fill, load, stop **05** chuck, crowd, leave, press, stuff, wedge **06** charge, cram in, give up, jack in, resign, throng **07** squeeze, throw in

**• pack off**
**04** send **07** dismiss **08** dispatch **09** bundle off

**• pack round**
**04** tamp

**• pack up**
**03** end **04** fail, stop **05** crash, truss **06** bundle, finish, give up, go phut, jack in, tidy up, wrap up **07** clear up, conk out, go kaput, put away, seize up, throw in **08** empacket, tidy away **09** break camp, break down **10** call it a day **11** malfunction, stop working **12** go on the fritz **13** put things away

**package**
**03** box, lot, set **04** bale, pack, roll, unit, wrap **05** batch, group, whole **06** bundle, carton, entity, packet, pack up, parcel, wrap up **08** gift-wrap, parcel up **09** container **10** collection, shrink-wrap **11** consignment, package deal

**packaging**
**03** box **06** packet **07** packing, wrapper **08** wrappers, wrapping **09** container, wrappings **12** presentation

**• without packaging**
**03** net **04** nett

**packed**
**04** full **05** thick **06** filled, jammed **07** brimful, chocker, crammed, crowded, serried **08** thronged **09** chockfull, congested, jam-packed **10** overloaded **11** chock-a-block, overflowing

**packet**
**03** bag, box **04** a lot, bomb, case, deck, lots, mint, pack, pile, post, pots **06** bundle, carton, parcel, sachet **07** fortune, package, packing, tidy sum, wrapper **08** envelope, Jiffy bag®, wrapping **09** a bob or two, container, megabucks, padded bag **11** king's ransom, loadsamoney, pretty penny **12** small fortune **14** padded envelope

**packhorse load**
**04** seam

**packing-ring**
**04** lute

**pact**
**04** bond, deal **06** cartel, treaty **07** bargain, compact, concord, entente **08** alliance, contract, covenant **09** agreement, concordat **10** convention, settlement **11** arrangement **13** understanding

**pad**
**03** paw, ren, rin, run, wad **04** fill, flat, foot, home, line, lope, move, mute, pack, path, roll, room, sole, step, sunk, walk, wase, wrap **05** block, guard, inker, place, print, quilt, rooms, squab, stuff, tramp, tread **06** buffer, hamper, jotter, pillow, shield, tiptoe, trudge **07** blotter, bolster, bombast, bum roll, cushion, hang-out, memo pad, notepad, padding, pannier, pillion, protect, wadding **08** compress, dressing, leg-guard, notebook, quarters, stuffing **09** apartment, flip chart, footprint, penthouse **10** impregnate, protection, writing pad

**• pad out**
**06** expand **07** amplify, augment, bolster, fill out, inflate, spin out, stretch **08** flesh out, increase, lengthen, protract **09** elaborate

**padding**
**06** hot air, lining, waffle **07** bombast, filling, packing, wadding **08** crashpad, stuffing, verbiage **09** prolixity, verbosity, wordiness **10** cotton wool, cushioning, protection **11** verboseness

**paddle**
**03** oar, row **04** pull, punt, slop, wade **05** canoe, scull, steer, sweep **06** dabble, finger, plunge, propel, splash, trifle **10** lumpsucker

**paddock**
**03** pen **04** fold, frog, park, toad, yard **05** field, pound **06** corral **07** parrock **08** birdcage, compound, stockade **09** enclosure

**paddy**
**03** pet **04** bate, fury, rage, tiff **05** sawah, strop **06** taking, temper **07** passion, tantrum **08** manrider **11** fit of temper **14** manriding train

**padlock**
**03** bar **04** bolt, lock, seal, shut **05** catch, clasp, latch **06** fasten, secure **09** fastening **10** spring lock **11** mortise lock

**padre**
**05** vicar **06** cleric, curate, deacon, father, parson, pastor, priest, rector **08** chaplain, minister, reverend **09** churchman, clergyman, deaconess

**paean**
**04** hymn **05** psalm **06** anthem, eulogy

**07** ovation **08** doxology, encomium, ode to joy **09** dithyramb, panegyric **10** exultation **12** song of praise

**pagan**
**06** paynim **07** atheist, Gentile, godless, heathen, infidel, ungodly **08** idolater **09** atheistic **10** idolatrous, unbeliever **11** irreligious, nonbeliever, nullifidian, pantheistic

**page**
**01** p **02** ro, vo **03** bid, era **04** call, leaf, side **05** epoch, event, folio, phase, recto, sheet, stage, title, verso **06** ask for, period, summon **07** bellboy, bellhop, chapter, episode, footman, pageboy, send for, servant **08** announce, henchman, incident, paginate **09** attendant, messenger, tearsheet **10** henchwoman **11** henchperson

**• pages**
**02** pp

**• two pages**
**04** leaf

**pageant**
**04** play, show **05** antic, scene **06** antick, parade **07** anticke, antique, display, tableau, triumph **08** specious **09** cavalcade, spectacle **10** procession **12** extravaganza **14** representation

**pageantry**
**04** pomp, show **05** drama **06** parade **07** display, glamour, glitter **08** ceremony, flourish, grandeur **09** melodrama, showiness, spectacle, splendour **12** extravagance, magnificence **13** theatricality

**pageboy**
**04** page **07** bellboy, bellhop, footman, servant **09** attendant, messenger

**paid-up**
**05** loyal **06** active, red-hot **07** devoted, fervent, zealous **08** involved **09** committed, dedicated **11** evangelical **12** card-carrying, enthusiastic

**pail**
**03** can, kit, tub **04** bail, dixy **05** churn, dixie **06** bucket, leglan, leglen, leglin, piggin, vessel **07** pitcher, scuttle **10** slop bucket

**pain**
**02** wo **03** ake, gip, gyp, mal, woe **04** ache, bore, dole, dool, drag, hurt, pang, pest, rack, stab, sten, teen, tene **05** agony, cramp, dolor, doole, grief, gripe, shoot, smart, spasm, stend, sting, teene, thraw, throb, throe, throw, upset, worry **06** aching, be sore, bother, bummer, burden, cramps, dolour, grieve, misery, sadden, sorrow, stitch, throwe, twinge **07** afflict, agonize, ailment, anguish, anxiety, penalty, torment, torture, trouble **08** be tender, distress, headache, irritate, nuisance, smarting, soreness, vexation **09** annoyance, causalgia, heartache, suffering, throbbing **10** affliction, desolation, discomfort, heartbreak, irritation, tenderness **11** indigestion, lancination, make anxious, tribulation **12** collywobbles, wretchedness **13** make miserable, pain in the neck

**• expression of pain**
**01** O **02** oh, ow **04** argh, ouch **05** aargh

**• freedom from pain**
**04** ease

**pained**
**03** sad **04** hurt **05** stung, upset, vexed **06** piqued **07** grieved, injured, unhappy, worried, wounded **08** offended, saddened **09** aggrieved **10** distressed **11** reproachful

**painful**
**03** bad **04** achy, hard, sore **05** tough **06** aching, bitter, guilty, tender, touchy, trying **07** arduous, awkward, baleful, hurting, irksome, panging, pungent, shaming, tedious **08** exacting, grievous, inflamed, poignant, rigorous, shameful, smarting, stabbing, tortured, wretched **09** agonizing, difficult, harrowing, laborious, miserable, saddening, sensitive, strenuous, throbbing, traumatic, upsetting **10** disturbing, irritating, mortifying, unpleasant **11** disquieting, distressing, humiliating **12** disagreeable, discomfiting, embarrassing, excruciating **13** disconcerting, uncomfortable

**• be painful**
**04** tine, tyne, work

**painfully**
◇ *anagram indicator*
**04** sore **05** sadly **07** clearly **08** markedly, pitiably, terribly, woefully **09** pitifully **10** alarmingly, deplorably, dreadfully, wretchedly **11** agonizingly, excessively **13** distressingly, unfortunately **14** excruciatingly

**painkiller**
**04** bute, drug **06** remedy **07** anodyne, metopon, morphia, Nurofen® **08** lenitive, morphine, sedative **09** analgesia, analgesic **10** palliative **11** aminobutene, anaesthetic

*See also* **anaesthetic**; **analgesic**

**painless**
**04** easy **05** cushy **06** simple **08** pain-free **10** child's play, effortless **11** comfortable, trouble-free, undemanding **12** a piece of cake, plain sailing

**painlessly**
**06** easily, simply **11** comfortably **12** effortlessly **13** undemandingly

**pains**
**04** care, fash, teen, tene **05** labor, teene **06** bother, effort, labour, rheums **07** trouble **09** diligence **10** rheumatics **13** assiduousness

**• be at pains**
**06** bother **07** try hard **08** take care **09** be anxious **11** be concerned **14** put yourself out **15** make every effort

**painstaking**
**07** careful, devoted **08** diligent, sedulous, studious, thorough **09** assiduous, attentive, dedicated, searching **10** meticulous, scrupulous **11** hardworking, industrious, persevering, punctilious **13** conscientious

**paint**
**03** dye **04** bice, coat, daub, draw, fard, gaud, limn, tell, tint, wash **05** adorn, apply, brush, color, cover, evoke, smear, stain **06** bister, bistre, colour, depict, finish, sketch, tipple **07** narrate, picture, pigment, plaster, portray, priming, recount, respray, stipple, topcoat **08** colorant, decorate, depeinct, describe **09** colouring, delineate, depicture, diversify, oil colour, represent, vinyl wash **10** redecorate **11** boot-topping

*Paints include:*

**03** oil
**04** matt, oils
**05** glaze, gloss, satin, spray
**06** enamel, fabric, pastel, poster, primer
**07** acrylic, gouache, lacquer, masonry, scumble, shellac, stencil, tempera, varnish
**08** eggshell, emulsion
**09** anti-climb, distemper, undercoat, whitewash
**10** colourwash, egg tempera
**11** watercolour

**• paint the town red**
**04** rave **05** binge, go out **07** have fun, rejoice **08** live it up **09** celebrate, have a ball, whoop it up **10** have a party **11** throw a party **13** enjoy yourself, go on the razzle **14** go out on the town, push the boat out, put the flags out

**painted**
**• painted woman**
**04** pict

**painter**
**02** RA **06** artist, dauber, limner **07** Zeuxian **08** depicter **09** colourist, old master, paysagist, primitive, tactilist, vedutista **10** delineator, oil painter **11** landscapist, miniaturist, plein-airist **13** watercolorist **14** watercolourist

*Painters, printmakers and other artists include:*

**03** Arp (Jean), Dix (Otto), Ray (Man)
**04** Bell (Vanessa), Dali (Salvador), Doré (Gustave), Dufy (Raoul), Eyck (Jan van), Goya (Francisco de), Gris (Juan), Hals (Frans), Hunt (Holman), John (Augustus), John (Gwen), Kent (William), Klee (Paul), Lely (Sir Peter), Long (Richard), Marc (Franz), Miró (Joan), Nash (Paul)
**05** Bacon (Francis), Bakst (Léon), Blake (Peter), Blake (William), Bosch (Hieronymus), Brown (Ford Madox), Burra (Edward), Clark (Kenneth, Lord), Corot (Camille),

**David** (Jacques Louis), **Degas** (Edgar), **Dürer** (Albrecht), **Ernst** (Max), **Freud** (Lucian), **Gorky** (Arshile), **Greco** (El), **Grosz** (George), **Hirst** (Damien), **Homer** (Winslow), **Hooch** (Pieter de), **Johns** (Jasper), **Kahlo** (Frida), **Kitaj** (R B), **Klimt** (Gustav), **Kline** (Franz), **Léger** (Fernand), **Lewis** (Wyndham), **Lippi** (Filippino), **Lippi** (Fra Filippo), **Lowry** (L S), **Lucas** (Sarah), **Manet** (Edouard), **Monet** (Claude), **Mucha** (Alphonse), **Munch** (Edvard), **Nolan** (Sir Sidney), **Peake** (Mervyn), **Piper** (John), **Riley** (Bridget), **Sarto** (Andrea del)

**06** **Braque** (Georges), **Bratby** (John), **Cassat** (Mary), **Claude**, **Derain** (André Louis), **Escher** (Maurits Cornelis), **Fuseli** (Henri), **Giotto**, **Gordon** (Douglas), **Ingres** (Jean), **Jarman** (Derek), **Knight** (Dame Laura), **Mabuse**, **Marini** (Marino), **Martin** (John), **Massys** (Quentin), **Millet** (Jean François), **Morley** (Malcolm), **Moroni** (Giovanni Battista), **Morris** (William), **Newman** (Barnett), **O'Keefe** (Georgia), **Orozco** (José), **Palmer** (Samuel), **Peploe** (Samuel John), **Pisano** (Nicola), **Ramsay** (Allan), **Renoir** (Pierre Auguste), **Rivera** (Diego), **Rothko** (Mark), **Rubens** (Sir Peter Paul), **Scarfe** (Gerald), **Searle** (Ronald), **Seurat** (Georges), **Sisley** (Alfred), **Strong** (Sir Roy), **Stubbs** (George), **Tanguy** (Yves), **Tissot** (James), **Titian**, **Turner** (J M W), **Warhol** (Andy), **Wilkie** (Sir David), **Wright** (Joseph)

**07** **Attwell** (Mabel Lucie), **Bellini** (Giovanni), **Bonnard** (Pierre), **Boucher** (François), **Cézanne** (Paul), **Chagall** (Marc), **Chirico** (Giorgio de), **Christo**, **Cimabué**, **Courbet** (Gustave), **Cranach** (Lucas, the Elder), **Daumier** (Honoré), **Delvaux** (Paul), **Duchamp** (Marcel), **El Greco**, **Gauguin** (Paul), **Hobbema** (Meindert), **Hockney** (David), **Hodgkin** (Sir Howard), **Hogarth** (William), **Hokusai** (Katsushika), **Holbein** (Hans), **Keating** (Tom), **Martini** (Simone), **Matisse** (Henri), **Millais** (Sir John Everett), **Morisot** (Berthe), **Pevsner** (Sir Nikolaus), **Picabia** (Francis), **Picasso** (Pablo), **Pollock** (Jackson), **Poussin** (Nicolas), **Rackham** (Arthur), **Raeburn** (Sir Henry), **Raphael**, **Sargent** (John Singer), **Schiele** (Egon), **Sickert** (Walter), **Spencer** (Sir Stanley), **Tenniel** (Sir John), **Thurber** (James), **Tiepolo** (Giovanni), **Uccello** (Paolo), **Utrillo** (Maurice), **Van Eyck** (Jan), **Van Gogh** (Vincent), **Vermeer** (Jan), **Watteau** (Antoine), **Wearing** (Gillian)

**08** **Angelico** (Fra), **Annigoni** (Pietro), **Auerbach** (Frank), **Breughel** (Pieter), **Brueghel** (Pieter), **cummings** (e e), **Delaunay** (Robert), **Dubuffet** (Jean), **Goncourt** (Edmond de), **Gossaert** (Jan), **Hamilton** (Richard), **Hilliard** (Nicholas), **Landseer** (Sir Edwin), **Leonardo**, **Magritte** (René), **Malevich** (Kasimir), **Mantegna** (Andrea), **Masaccio**, **Mondrian** (Piet), **Munnings** (Sir Alfred), **Perugino**, **Piranesi** (Giambattista), **Pissarro** (Camille), **Reynolds** (Sir Joshua), **Rossetti** (Dante Gabriel), **Rousseau** (Henri, 'Le Douanier'), **Rousseau** (Théodore), **Ruisdael** (Jacob van), **Ruysdael** (Jacob van), **Topolski** (Feliks), **Vasarely** (Victor), **Veronese** (Paolo), **Vlaminck** (Maurice de), **Whistler** (James McNeill)

**09** **Beardsley** (Aubrey), **Canaletto**, **Constable** (John), **Correggio**, **De Kooning** (Willem), **Delacroix** (Eugène), **Fergusson** (John Duncan), **Fragonard** (Jean), **Friedrich** (Caspar David), **Géricault** (Théodore), **Giorgione**, **Greenaway** (Kate), **Greenaway** (Peter), **Grünewald** (Matthias), **Kandinsky** (Wasily), **Kokoschka** (Oskar), **Lancaster** (Sir Osbert), **Nicholson** (Ben), **Nollekens** (Joseph), **Pisanello**, **Rembrandt**, **Rodchenko** (Alexander), **Velázquez** (Diego)

**10** **Alma-Tadema** (Sir Lawrence), **Botticelli** (Sandro), **Burne-Jones** (Sir Edward), **Caravaggio** (Michelangelo), **Giacometti** (Alberto), **Modigliani** (Amedeo), **Motherwell** (Robert), **Parmigiano**, **Sutherland** (Graham), **Tintoretto**

**12** **Bairnsfather** (Bruce), **Fantin-Latour** (Henri), **Gainsborough** (Thomas), **Lichtenstein** (Roy), **Michelangelo**

**13** **Piero di Cosimo**

**14** **Andrea del Sarto**, **Lucas van Leyden**

**15** **Leonardo da Vinci**, **Toulouse-Lautrec** (Henri de)

## painting

**03** art, oil **04** daub, oils **08** likeness **09** cerograph, portrayal **11** delineation, scenography **13** belle peinture **14** representation

*See also* **art**

*Painting terms include:*

**04** icon, tint, tone, wash

**05** bloom, brush, easel, gesso, mural, paint, pieta, secco, tondo

**06** canvas, fresco, frieze, primer, sketch

**07** atelier, aureola, aureole, cartoon, collage, diptych, drawing, facture, gallery, gouache, impasto, limning, montage, palette, pastels, paysage, picture, pigment, scumble, sfumato, stipple, tempera

**08** abstract, aquatint, bleeding, charcoal, esquisse, fixative, frottage, hard edge, hatching, paint-box, pastoral, portrait, seascape, skyscape, thinners, triptych, vignette

**09** alla prima, aquarelle, brushwork, capriccio, encaustic, flat brush, grisaille, grotesque, landscape, mahlstick, maulstick, miniature, polyptych, scumbling, sgraffito, still life

**10** art gallery, craquelure, dead colour, figurative, hair-pencil, monochrome, paint-brush, pentimento, pochade box, round brush, sable brush, silhouette, turpentine

**11** canvas board, chiaroscuro, composition, fête galante, foreshorten, found object, illusionism, objet trouvé, oil painting, perspective, pointillism, trompe l'oeil, watercolour

**12** anamorphosis, brush strokes, camera lucida, filbert brush, illustration, palette knife, pencil sketch

**13** fête champêtre, genre painting, underpainting

**14** foreshortening

*Paintings and other artworks include:*

**04** Flag

**05** Manga, Pietà, Trees

**06** Spring

**07** Bubbles, Erasmus, Gin Lane, Olympia, Targets, The Kiss

**08** Guernica, L'Estaque, Maja Nude, Mona Lisa, The Dream

**09** Bacchanal, Black Iris, Haystacks, Henry VIII, Jerusalem, L'Escargot, Night Café, Primavera, The Scream, The Tailor

**10** Adam and Eve, Assumption, Beer Street, Blue Horses, Las Meninas, Sunflowers, The Angelus, The Hay Wain

**11** 100 Soup Cans, Arthur's Tomb, A Shrimp Girl, Crucifixion, Limp Watches, Maja Clothed, Starry Night, The Gleaners, View of Delft, Water Lilies

**12** Beata Beatrix, Black on Black, Los Caprichos, Peasant Dance, The Nightmare, The Scapegoat, The Umbrellas

**13** A Bigger Splash, Christ in Glory, Isenheim Altar, Man with a Glove, Sleeping Gypsy, The Last Supper, The Night Watch

**14** A Rake's Progress, Disasters of War, Peasant Wedding, Random Sketches, Rouen Cathedral, Sistine Madonna, The Ambassadors, The Card Players, The Four Seasons, The Rokeby Venus, The Turkish Bath, View on the Stour

**15** Absinthe Drinker, Commodore Keppel, Flight into Egypt, Madonna and Child, Madonna del Prato, Marriage à la Mode, The Annunciation, The Birth of Venus, The Charnel House, The Dance of Death, The Death of Marat, The Flagellation, The Potato Eaters, The Raft of Medusa, The Rape of Europa, Triumph of Caesar

**pair**
**02** OO, pr **03** duo, set, twa, two, wed **04** duad, duet, join, link, mate, pack, team, twae, tway, twin, yoke **05** brace, marry, match, twain, twins, unite **06** couple, geminy, join up, link up, splice, team up **07** bracket, couplet, match up, partner, twosome **10** two of a kind **11** put together **14** arrange in pairs

**paired**
**05** mated, yoked **06** double, in twos, joined, jugate, linked **07** coupled, matched, twinned **09** bracketed **10** associated

**Pakistan**
**02** PK **03** PAK

**pal**
**04** chum, mate **05** buddy, crony, cully **06** cobber, friend, winger **07** comrade, partner **08** intimate, sidekick, soul mate **09** companion, confidant **10** buddy-buddy, confidante
- **pal up**
**06** chum up, gang up, join up **11** get together, make friends **13** become friends

**palace**
**04** dome **05** court, hôtel **06** castle **07** alcázar, château, mansion, palazzo, schloss **08** basilica, seraglio **11** stately home

*Palaces include:*

**05** Pitti, Royal, Savoy
**06** Louvre, Mirror, Potala, Winter
**07** Bishop's, Crystal, People's, Sultan's, Vatican
**08** Alhambra, Blenheim, Borghese, Imperial, National, St James's, Valhalla, Walhalla
**09** Episcopal, Maharaja's, Sans Souci, Tuileries, Whitehall
**10** Buckingham, El Escorial, Fishbourne, Generalife, Kensington, Linlithgow, President's, Qusayr Amra, Quseir Amra, Schönbrunn, Versailles
**11** Archbishop's, Westminster
**13** Forbidden City, Holyrood House, Royal Pavilion, Tower of London, Windsor Castle
**14** Charlottenburg
**15** Palais de l'Elysée

**paladin**
**04** peer

**palaeontologist**

*Palaeontologists include:*

**04** Cope (Edward Drinker), Owen (Sir Richard)
**05** Gould (Stephen Jay), Marsh (O C)
**06** Dubois (Eugène), Forbes (Edward), Kurtén (Björn), Leakey (Louis), Leakey (Mary), Leakey (Richard), Osborn (Henry Fairfield), Zittel (Karl von)
**07** Colbert (Ned), Mantell (Gideon), Simpson (George Gaylord)
**08** Guettard (Jean Étienne), Johanson (Donald)

**palanquin**
**04** kago **05** palki, sedan **06** doolie, litter, palkee **07** norimon

**palatable**
**04** nice **05** tasty, yummy **06** delish, edible, morish **07** eatable, moreish, savoury, scrummy **08** pleasant, pleasing **09** agreeable, delicious, enjoyable, flavorous, succulent, toothsome **10** acceptable, appetizing, attractive, delectable **11** done to a turn, flavoursome, scrumptious **12** satisfactory **13** mouthwatering

**palate**
**04** gout **05** heart, taste, velum **06** liking, relish **07** stomach **08** appetite **09** enjoyment, taste buds **10** enthusiasm **12** appreciation, sense of taste

**palatial**
**04** posh **05** grand, plush, regal, ritzy **06** de luxe **07** opulent, stately **08** imposing, majestic, spacious, splendid **09** grandiose, luxurious, sumptuous **11** magnificent

**Palau**
**03** PLW

**palaver**
**04** flap, fuss, talk, to-do **05** hoo-ha **06** bother, bustle **07** carry-on, flatter, fluster **08** activity, business **09** commotion, kerfuffle, procedure, rigmarole **10** conference, discussion **12** song and dance

**pale**
**03** dim, wan **04** ashy, fade, gray, grey, lily, melt, pall, pole, post, thin, waxy, weak **05** appal, ashen, blank, crown, faded, faint, fence, green, light, limit, livid, lurid, mealy, muted, pasty, peaky, shaft, stain, stake, vapid, verge, waxen, white **06** blanch, bleach, chalky, column, feeble, lessen, low-key, mealie, pallid, pastel, sallow, whiten **07** anaemic, drained, dwindle, high-key, insipid, upright, whitely, whitish **08** bleached, delicate, diminish, encircle, etiolate, grow pale, maid-pale **09** bloodless, enclosure, etiolated, grow white, washed-out, whey-faced **10** colourless, pallescent, pasty-faced, restrained, wishy-washy **11** peelie-wally **12** change colour **14** complexionless
- **beyond the pale**
**08** improper, unseemly **10** unsuitable **11** intolerable **12** inadmissible, unacceptable, unreasonable **13** inappropriate

**paleness**
**04** pale **06** pallor **07** anaemia, wanness **09** pastiness, whiteness **10** sallowness **11** pallescence **14** colourlessness

**palindromic**
**07** Sotadic **08** cancrine, Sotadean

**palisade**
**05** fence **06** fraise, paling **07** barrier, bulwark, defence, stacket **08** stockade **09** barricade, enclosure **13** fortification

**pall**
**04** cloy, jade, pale, sate, tire, veil **05** cloak, cloud, daunt, gloom, weary **06** damper, mantle, shadow, shroud, sicken, weaken **07** curtain, frontal, pallium, satiate, wear off **08** corporal, covering **09** mortcloth **11** become bored, become tired, hearse-cloth
- **cast a pall over**
**03** mar **04** harm, ruin **05** spoil, upset, wreck **06** impair **07** destroy

**palladium**
**02** Pd

**palliate**
**04** ease **05** abate, allay, cloak, cover **06** excuse, lenify, lessen, soften, soothe, temper **07** assuage, conceal, lighten, mollify, relieve **08** diminish, disguise, minimize, mitigate, moderate **09** alleviate, extenuate

**palliative**
**07** anodyne, calming **08** lenitive, sedative, soothing **09** analgesic, assuasive, calmative, demulcent, paregoric **10** mitigating, mitigative, mitigatory, mollifying, painkiller **11** alleviating, alleviative, extenuative, extenuatory **13** tranquillizer

**pallid**
**03** wan **04** ashy, dull, pale, tame, waxy, weak **05** ashen, bland, lurid, pasty, tired, vapid, waxen, white **06** boring, doughy, sallow, sickly **07** anaemic, insipid, sterile, whitish **08** lifeless **09** bloodless, etiolated, whey-faced **10** colourless, pallescent, pasty-faced, spiritless, unexciting, uninspired **11** peelie-wally **13** uninteresting **14** complexionless

**pallor**
**07** anaemia, wanness **08** paleness **09** whiteness **10** chalkiness, etiolation, pallidness, sallowness **11** pallescence **13** bloodlessness

**pally**
**04** warm **05** close, thick, tight **06** chummy, folksy **08** familiar, friendly, intimate **12** affectionate

**palm**
**03** fob, paw **04** grab, hand, loof, mitt, take, vola **05** bribe **06** snatch, thenar **11** appropriate

*Palms include:*

**03** dum, ita, oil, wax
**04** atap, coco, date, doom, doum, hemp, nipa, sago
**05** areca, assai, bussu, macaw, nikau, peach, royal, Sabal, sugar, toddy
**06** buriti, cohune, corozo, Elaeis, gomuti, gru-gru, jupati, kentia, kittul, miriti, raffia, Raphia, rattan, troely
**07** babassu, cabbage, calamus, coconut, coquito, Corypha, Euterpe, moriche, palmyra,

paxiuba, pupunha, talipat, talipot, troelie, troolie
**08** carnauba, coco-tree, date-tree, groo-groo, palmetto
**10** Chamaerops
**12** chiquichiqui, Washingtonia
**15** cabbage-palmetto

**• have someone in the palm of your hand**
**13** have power over **15** have control over

**• palm off**
**05** foist **06** fob off, impose, pass on, put off, thrust, unload **07** offload, pass off, work off **08** get rid of, pass upon

**palmist**
**10** palm reader **11** clairvoyant
**13** chirographist, fortune-teller

**palmistry**
**10** chirognomy, chiromancy **11** palm reading **12** clairvoyancy **14** fortune-telling

**palmy**
**05** happy **06** golden, joyous
**07** halcyon **08** carefree, glorious, thriving **09** fortunate, luxurious
**10** prosperous, successful, triumphant
**11** flourishing

**palpable**
**04** real **05** clear, gross, plain, solid
**06** patent **07** blatant, evident, glaring, obvious, visible **08** apparent, concrete, manifest, material, tangible
**09** touchable **11** conspicuous, perceptible, substantial
**12** unmistakable **13** unmistakeable

**palpably**
**07** clearly, plainly, visibly **08** patently
**09** blatantly, evidently, glaringly, obviously **10** apparently, manifestly
**12** unmistakably **13** conspicuously, unmistakeably

**palpitate**
**04** beat, thud **05** pound, pulse, quake, shake, throb, thump **06** pit-pat, quiver, shiver **07** flutter, pitapat, pulsate, tremble, twitter, vibrate **08** pitty-pat

**palpitation**
**05** shake, throb **06** quiver, shakes
**07** flutter, shaking **08** pounding
**09** quivering, throbbing, trembling, vibration **10** fluttering

**paltry**
**03** low, tin **04** bald, bare, mean, poor, puny, vile, waff **05** cheap, minor, petty, scald, small, sorry, woful **06** jitney, meagre, measly, shabby, slight, tinpot, trashy, two-bit, vulgar, woeful
**07** foolish, miserly, pelting, pimping, piteous, trivial **08** derisory, piddling, rubbishy, trifling, wretched
**09** miserable, worthless **10** negligible, shoestring **11** unimportant
**12** contemptible, pettifogging
**13** insignificant **14** inconsiderable

**pamper**
**03** pet **04** baby **05** spoil **06** cocker, coddle, cosher, cosset, cuiter, fondle, humour, pander, pompey **07** gratify, indulge **09** spoon-feed **10** featherbed
**11** mollycoddle, overindulge

**pampered**
**06** petted, spoilt **07** coddled, high-fed, overfed **08** cosseted, indulged, spoon-fed **10** lust-dieted **12** mollycoddled

**pamphlet**
**03** pam **05** flyer, sheet, tract **06** folder, notice **07** booklet, handout, leaflet
**08** brochure, chapbook, circular
**10** mazarinade

**pan**
**03** pit, pot, wok **04** bowl, cake, cave, face, flay, hole, lead, move, scan, slag, slam, turn, well **05** basin, betel, frier, fryer, knock, ladle, roast, scale, slate, sweep, swing, track, yield **06** cavern, cavity, circle, crater, Faunus, follow, hammer, hollow, obtain, spider, vessel
**07** censure, channel, goat-god, rubbish, skillet, slag off **08** pancheon, panchion, pannikin, saucepan, traverse
**09** bed-warmer, casserole, concavity, container, criticize, frying-pan, saltworks **10** corn popper, depression, excavation **11** calefactory **12** pull to pieces **13** find fault with

**• pan out**
**05** yield **06** happen, result **07** turn out, work out **09** culminate, eventuate
**11** be exhausted, come to an end

**panacea**
**06** elixir, tutsan **07** allheal, cure-all, nostrum **10** catholicon, parkleaves
**12** panpharmacon **13** diacatholicon
**15** universal remedy

**panache**
**04** brio, dash, élan, zest **05** flair, plume, style, verve **06** energy, pazazz, pizazz, spirit, vigour **07** pazzazz, pizzazz, swagger **08** flourish **10** enthusiasm
**11** flamboyance, ostentation

**Panama**
**02** PA **03** PAN

**pancake**
**04** flam, taco **05** blini, crêpe, flamm, flawn, latke, rösti, wafer **06** blintz, flaune, fraise, froise, roesti, waffle
**07** bannock, blintze, crumpet, pikelet
**08** flapjack, omelette, tortilla **09** drop scone **10** battercake, spring roll
**11** griddle-cake **12** crêpe suzette, dropped scone

**pandemic**
**04** rife **06** common, global **07** general
**09** extensive, pervasive, prevalent, universal **10** widespread **11** far-reaching

**pandemonium**
**03** din **04** to-do **05** chaos **06** bedlam, hubbub, rumpus, tumult, uproar
**07** turmoil **08** disorder **09** commotion, confusion, hue and cry, shemozzle
**10** hullabaloo, turbulence

**pander**
**04** bawd, pimp **06** broker **07** procure
**08** procurer **11** whoremonger

**• pander to**
**06** fulfil, humour, pamper, please
**07** cater to, gratify, indulge, provide, satisfy

**pane**
**04** pean, peen, pein, pene **05** glass, panel **06** window **07** quarrel
**10** windowpane

**panegyric**
**05** éloge, elogy, paean **06** eulogy, homage, praise **07** elogium, glowing, tribute **08** accolade, citation, encomium, eulogium, praising
**09** laudation, laudatory, praiseful
**10** eulogistic, favourable, flattering
**11** encomiastic, panegyrical
**12** commendation, commendatory
**13** complimentary **14** speech of praise

**panel**
**03** orb **04** beam, jury, mola, pane, sign, slab, team, unit **05** array, board, dials, knobs, plank, plate, sheet, table
**06** coffer, levers, screen, tablet, timber
**07** buttons, console, council, inn sign, lacunar, valance, valence **08** controls, mandorla, switches, trustees
**09** cartouche, committee, dashboard, faceplate, headboard, medallion
**10** commission, focus group, patchboard **11** compartment, directorate, instruments **13** advisory group **15** instrument panel

**panelling**
**04** dado **06** coffer **07** lacunar, reredos
**08** wainscot **09** panelwork, reredorse, reredosse **11** wainscoting
**12** wainscotting

**pang**
**04** ache, cram, pain, stab **05** agony, gripe, prick, qualm, spasm, sting, stuff, thraw, throe, throw, tight **06** shower, stitch, stound, stownd, throwe, twinge
**07** anguish, crammed, crowded, scruple, stuffed **08** distress
**09** misgiving **10** discomfort, uneasiness

**pangolin**
**05** Manis **08** anteater **13** scaly anteater

**panic**
◇ *anagram indicator*
**04** fear, flap, funk **05** alarm, amaze, scare **06** dismay, frenzy, fright, horror, panick, terror **07** pannick, unnerve
**08** disquiet, flat spin, hysteria, tailspin
**09** agitation, overreact, run scared
**10** amazedness, go to pieces **11** have kittens, trepidation **12** get the shakes, lose your cool, lose your head, perturbation, sauve qui peut
**13** consternation, get the jitters, get the willies, lose your nerve **14** lose your bottle

**panic-stricken**
**06** aghast, scared **07** alarmed, frantic, panicky **08** frenzied, in a tizzy
**09** horrified, perturbed, petrified, terrified **10** frightened, hysterical **11** in a blue funk, in a flat spin, scared stiff
**12** in a cold sweat **14** terror-stricken

**pannier**
**03** pad, ped **06** dosser **07** cacolet, kajawah **09** ambulance

**panoply**
**04** garb, gear, show **05** array, dress, get-up, range **06** armour, attire **07** raiment, regalia, turn-out **08** insignia
**09** equipment, trappings

**panorama**
**04** view **05** scene, vista **06** survey
**07** scenery **08** overview, prospect, wide view **09** broad view, cyclorama, landscape, spectacle **11** perspective
**12** bird's-eye view

**panoramic**
**04** wide **05** broad **06** scenic
**07** general, overall **08** sweeping
**09** extensive, universal **10** widespread
**11** far-reaching, wide-ranging
**13** comprehensive

**pansy**
**05** pance, viola **06** kiss-me, paunce, pawnce **10** effeminate, heart's-ease, homosexual **11** herb-trinity, kiss-me-quick **14** love-in-idleness

**pant**
**03** yen **04** ache, blow, gasp, huff, long, pech, pegh, pine, puff, sigh, want
**05** covet, crave, flaff, heave, throb, yearn **06** desire, hanker, thirst, wheeze
**07** breathe **09** palpitate **11** huff and puff

**panting**
**05** eager **06** puffed, winded
**07** anxious, craving, gasping, longing, puffing **09** hankering, impatient, puffed out **10** breathless **11** out of breath, short-winded

**pantomime**
**04** mime, show **05** farce, panto
**06** masque **07** charade **08** dumbshow
**12** harlequinade

*Pantomime characters include:*

**04** Jack, Jill
**05** Giant, Wendy
**06** Beauty, Gretel, Hansel
**07** Buttons, Dandini, Emperor, King Rat
**08** Abanazer, Idle Jack, Peter Pan, The Beast
**09** Alan-a-dale, Columbine, Friar Tuck, Robin Hood
**10** Billy Goose, Cinderella, Goldilocks, Little John, Maid Marian, Maid Marion, Prince John, Tinkerbell
**11** Baron Hardup, Captain Hook, Daisy the Cow, Jack's Mother, King Richard, Mother Goose, Simple Simon, Will Scarlet
**12** Pantomime Cow, Principal Boy, Sarah the Cook, Widow Twankey, Will Scarlett, Wishee Washee
**13** Principal Girl
**14** Baroness Hardup, Fairy Godmother, Genie of the Lamp, Pantomime Horse, Prince Charming, Princess Aurora, Slave of the Ring, The Ugly Sisters
**15** Alice Fitzwarren, Princess Jasmine, Rumpelstiltskin

*Pantomimes include:*

**07** Aladdin, Ali Baba, Cinders
**08** Peter Pan, Rapunzel
**09** Pinocchio, Robin Hood, Snow White
**10** Cinderella, Goldilocks
**11** Mother Goose, Old King Cole, Puss in Boots
**12** The Pied Piper, The Snow Queen
**13** Red Riding Hood
**14** Babes in the Wood, Robinson Crusoe, Sleeping Beauty, Treasure Island
**15** Dick Whittington, Hansel and Gretel, Rumpelstiltskin, Sinbad the Sailor, The Swan Princess

**pantry**
**05** ambry, awmry **06** almery, aumbry, awmrie, larder, spence **07** butlery
**08** scullery **09** stillroom, storeroom

**pants**
**05** jeans, loons, teddy, thong **06** briefs, shorts, slacks, smalls, trunks, undies
**07** drawers, joggers, panties, rubbish, Y-fronts **08** frillies, knickers, nonsense, trousers **10** underpants **11** boxer shorts, panty girdle **12** camiknickers

**pap**
**03** goo, rot **04** crap, mash, mush, pulp
**05** purée, trash **06** breast, drivel, hot air, nipple **07** rubbish, twaddle
**08** claptrap, nonsense, soft food
**09** gibberish, poppycock **14** semi-liquid food

**papa**
**01** P
*See also* **father**

**paper**
**03** rag **04** ream, work **05** daily, essay, organ, study **06** report, thesis, weekly
**07** article, journal, tabloid **08** analysis, magazine, treatise **09** monograph, newspaper **10** broadsheet, periodical
**11** composition, examination
**12** dissertation
*See also* **newspaper**

*Paper sizes and formats include:*

**02** A0, A1, A2, A3, A4, A5
**03** pot
**04** demy, post, pott
**05** atlas, crown, folio, jésus, legal, royal
**06** letter, medium, quarto
**07** emperor, tabloid
**08** Berliner, elephant, foolscap, imperial
**09** antiquary, music-demy
**10** super-royal

*Paper types include:*

**03** art, rag
**04** bank, bond, card, note, rice, wall
**05** crêpe, graph, sugar
**06** carbon, manila, silver, tissue, toilet, vellum
**07** papyrus, tracing, writing
**08** acid-free, blotting, handmade, recycled, wrapping
**09** cardboard, cartridge, parchment
**10** pasteboard
**11** greaseproof

• **on paper**
**07** ideally **08** in theory, recorded **09** in writing, seemingly **10** officially, supposedly **11** on the record, written down **13** theoretically
**14** hypothetically, in your mind's eye
**15** in black and white

• **paper over**
**04** hide **07** conceal, cover up, obscure
**08** disguise **10** camouflage **13** put out of sight

• **paper size**
**03** pot **04** demy, pott

**papers**
**02** ID **04** bumf **05** bumph, deeds, sheaf **07** records **08** document, evidence, passbook, passport
**10** despatches, dispatches
**11** credentials **12** certificates, identity card **13** authorization, documentation
**14** driving licence, identification, qualifications

**papery**
**04** thin **05** frail, light **06** flimsy
**07** fragile **08** delicate **09** paper-thin
**10** glumaceous, membranous
**11** chartaceous, lightweight, membraneous, papyraceous, translucent **13** insubstantial, membranaceous

**Papua New Guinea**
**03** PNG

**par**
**04** mean, norm, parr **05** level, usual
**06** median, parity **07** average, balance
**08** equality, standard **09** paragraph
**10** accordance, similarity
**11** equilibrium, equivalence **12** equal footing **14** correspondence

• **below par**
**05** lousy, rough, tired **06** unwell
**08** inferior, under par **10** inadequate, not up to par, out of sorts **11** at a discount **12** below average **14** not up to scratch, unsatisfactory **15** under the weather

• **deviation from par**
**04** agio

• **on a par with**
**07** equal to **08** as good as
**12** equivalent to

• **par for the course**
**05** usual **06** normal **07** typical
**08** standard **11** predictable

• **up to par**
**02** OK **04** fine **08** adequate
**10** acceptable **11** up to scratch
**12** satisfactory

**parable**
**05** fable, story **06** lesson **07** proverb
**08** allegory **09** discourse, moral tale
**10** comparison, similitude **15** story with a moral

**parachute**
**04** pack **05** chute **06** drogue, pappus
**08** parafoil, patagium **09** aeroshell, parabrake

**parade**
**03** row **04** file, pass, shew, show **05** array, march, parry, train, vaunt **06** column, flaunt, line-up, prance, review **07** display, exhibit, pageant, process, show off, stand-to **08** brandish, ceremony, file past **09** cavalcade, decursion, motorcade, spectacle **10** appearance, exhibition, procession **11** ostentation, progression **13** demonstration

**paradigm**
**05** ideal, model **07** example, pattern **08** exemplar, original **09** archetype, framework, prototype

**paradise**
**03** joy **04** Eden **05** bliss **06** heaven, parvis, Svarga, Swarga, Swerga, utopia **07** delight, ecstasy, Elysium, rapture **08** felicity **09** afterlife, cloud nine, happiness, hereafter, home of God, next world, Shangri-La **10** life to come **12** Garden of Eden **13** Elysian Fields, seventh heaven

**paradox**
**06** enigma, oddity, puzzle, riddle **07** anomaly, mystery **09** absurdity **11** incongruity **13** contradiction, inconsistency

**paradoxical**
**06** absurd **08** baffling, puzzling **09** anomalous, enigmatic, illogical **10** impossible, improbable, mysterious **11** conflicting, incongruous **12** inconsistent **13** contradictory

**paraffin**
**07** coal oil **08** earthwax, kerosene, kerosine, photogen **09** ozocerite, ozokerite, photogene **10** mineral wax **14** petroleum jelly

**paragon**
**04** mate, rose **05** equal, ideal, match, model, pearl, rival **07** compare, epitome, paladin, pattern, phoenix, surpass **08** exemplar, standard **09** archetype, criterion, emulation, nonpareil, prototype **10** comparison **11** competition, masterpiece **12** quintessence, the bee's knees **14** crème de la crème, perfect example

**paragraph**
**03** par **04** item, para, part **05** piece **06** clause **07** article, passage, portion, section, segment **08** causerie, te igitur **10** stand first, subsection **11** subdivision

**Paraguay**
**02** PY **03** PRY

**parallel**
**03** par **04** echo, like, twin **05** agree, equal, liken, match **06** be like **07** aligned, analogy, compare, conform, similar, uniform **08** analogue, likeness, matching, resemble **09** alongside, analogous, correlate, duplicate **10** co-existing, collateral, comparable, comparison, correspond, equivalent, homologous, resembling, side by side, similarity **11** be analogous, be similar to, coextensive, correlation, counterpart, equidistant, equivalence, resemblance **12** be equivalent **13** corresponding **14** correspondence

**paralyse**
**04** dull, halt, lame, numb, stop **05** palsy, scram, shock **06** benumb, deaden, freeze **07** cripple, disable, terrify, torpefy **08** transfix **10** deactivate, debilitate, immobilize **12** anaesthetize, incapacitate

**paralysed**
**04** lame, numb **08** crippled, disabled **09** paralytic **10** paraplegic **11** immobilized **12** quadriplegic **13** incapacitated

**paralysis**
**04** halt **05** palsy, shock **07** paresis **08** deadness, diplegia, numbness, shutdown, stoppage **09** breakdown **10** Bell's palsy, hemiplegia, immobility, monoplegia, paraplegia, sideration, standstill **11** cycloplegia, paraparesis **12** debilitation, quadriplegia **13** cerebral palsy, powerlessness **15** ophthalmoplegia

**paralytic**
**04** lame, numb **05** drunk **06** blotto, canned, soused, stewed, stoned, wasted **07** legless, palsied, pie-eyed, sloshed, smashed, sozzled, wrecked **08** crippled, disabled, immobile **09** incapable, paralysed, plastered **10** hemiplegic, inebriated, monoplegic **11** immobilized, intoxicated **12** quadriplegic **13** incapacitated **15** a sheet in the wind

**parameter**
**05** limit **06** factor **08** boundary, variable **09** criterion, framework, guideline **10** indication, limitation **11** restriction **13** figure of merit, specification **14** limiting factor

**paramilitaries**
**04** sena

**paramount**
**04** main **05** chief, first, prime **07** highest, primary, supreme, topmost **08** cardinal, foremost, superior, suzerain **09** principal **10** pre-eminent **11** outstanding, predominant **13** most important

**paramour**
**04** beau **05** leman, lover, woman **07** beloved, franion, hetaera, hetaira **08** copemate, fancy man, mistress **09** concubine, copes-mate, courtesan, inamorata, inamorato, kept woman **10** bit of fluff, fancy woman **12** bit on the side

**paranoia**
**09** delusions, monomania, obsession, psychosis **11** megalomania

**paranoid**
**05** fazed **06** afraid **07** fearful **08** confused **10** bewildered, suspicious **11** distrustful

**paranormal**
◇ *anagram indicator*
**05** eerie, magic, weird **06** hidden, mystic, occult **07** ghostly, magical, phantom, psychic **08** abnormal, mystical **09** spiritual, unnatural **10** miraculous, mysterious **12** metaphysical, otherworldly, supernatural **13** preternatural

**parapet**
**03** top **04** rail, wall **05** fence, guard **06** flèche, paling, parpen **07** barrier, bastion, bulwark, defence, parpane, parpend, parpent, perpend, perpent, railing, rampart **08** barbican, bartisan, bartizan, parpoint, traverse **09** barricade **10** balustrade, battlement, embankment **13** fortification

**paraphernalia**
**04** gear **05** stuff, tools **06** tackle, things **07** baggage, effects **09** apparatus, equipment, materials, trappings **10** belongings, implements **11** accessories, odds and ends, possessions **13** accoutrements, bits and pieces

**paraphrase**
**05** gloss **06** rehash, render, reword, Targum **07** restate, version **08** rephrase **09** interpret, rendering, rewording, translate **10** rephrasing **11** restatement, translation **14** interpretation **15** put in other words

**parasite**
**03** bum, fly **05** drone, leech **06** cadger, ligger, sponge, sucker **07** bludger, epizoan, epizoon, moocher, sponger, vampire **08** endozoon, entozoon, epiphyte, hanger-on, quandang, quandong, quantong **09** endophyte, passenger, scrounger, sycophant **10** freeloader **11** bloodsucker **12** lick-trencher **14** trencher-friend, trencher-knight

*Parasites include:*

**03** bot, ked, nit
**04** bott, chat, crab, flea, kade, mite, tick
**05** fluke, louse
**06** chigoe, chigre, cootie, jigger
**07** argulus, ascarid, ascaris, Babesia, bonamia, cestode, chalcid, chigger, Giardia, pinworm
**08** hookworm, itch-mite, lungworm, nematode, sheep ked, strongyl, tapeworm, toxocara, whipworm
**09** Bilharzia, bird louse, crab louse, fish louse, fluke-worm, head louse, pediculus, roundworm, sheep tick, sporozoan, strongyle, trematode
**10** Guinea worm, Plasmodium, threadworm
**11** biting louse, sarcocystis, scabies mite, trichomonad, trypanosome
**12** echinococcus, ectoparasite, endoparasite, semiparasite
**13** hyperparasite

**parasitic**
**07** cadging, epizoan, epizoic

**08** sponging **09** biogenous, leechlike **10** scrounging **11** freeloading, parasitical **12** bloodsucking

**parasol**
**04** veil **05** shade **06** shield **07** shelter **08** marquise, sunshade, umbrella **09** en tout cas **10** protection

*See also* **umbrella**

**parcel**
**03** box, dak, lot, mob, set **04** area, band, crew, dawk, deal, gang, herd, item, pack, plot, sort, wrap **05** bunch, crowd, flock, group, patch, piece, put up, tie up, tract, troop **06** bundle, carton, make up, packet, pack up, partly, wrap up **07** company, package, portion **08** bundle up, gift-wrap, quantity **09** allotment **10** collection **11** transaction

• **parcel out**
**05** allot, whack **06** divide **07** carve up, deal out, dole out, hand out, mete out **08** allocate, dispense, share out **09** apportion, divide out **10** distribute

**parch**
**03** dry **04** bake, burn, sear **05** dry up, toast **06** scorch, wither **07** blister, shrivel, torrefy **09** dehydrate, desiccate

**parched**
**03** dry **04** arid, sear, sere **05** baked **06** burned, seared **07** dried up, gasping, thirsty **08** scorched, withered **09** blistered, waterless **10** dehydrated, desiccated, dry as a bone, shrivelled

**parchment**
**04** pell, roll **05** forel, panel **06** mezuza, scroll, vellum **07** charter, diploma, mezuzah **08** document, membrane **09** sheepskin **10** palimpsest, phylactery **11** certificate

**pardon**
**02** eh? **04** free, what? **05** bitte, grace, mercy, remit, sorry **06** acquit, excuse, let off **07** absolve, amnesty, condone, forgive, release, you what?
**08** clemency, excuse me, lenience, liberate, oblivion, overlook, reprieve, say again?, tolerate **09** acquittal, come again?, discharge, exculpate, exonerate, remission, vindicate
**10** absolution, act of grace, indulgence
**11** condonation, cry you mercy, exculpation, exoneration, forbearance, forgiveness **13** let off the hook, what did you say? **14** I beg your pardon

**pardonable**
**05** minor **06** slight, venial
**09** allowable, excusable
**10** condonable, forgivable
**11** dispensable, justifiable, permissible, warrantable **14** understandable

**pare**
**03** cut, lop **04** chip, clip, crop, dock, peel, skin, trim **05** prune, shave, shear, skive **06** reduce **07** cut back, whittle **08** clip coin, decrease

**parent**
**02** ma, pa **03** dad, dam, mam, mom, mum, pop **04** papa, rear, root, sire **05** beget, cause, daddy, folks, mamma, mammy, mommy, mummy, mumsy, raise, teach, train **06** author, create, father, foster, mother, old man, origin, source **07** bring up, creator, educate, genitor, nurture **08** begetter, generant, genetrix, genitrix, guardian, old woman, relative **09** architect, bioparent, look after, procreate, prototype **10** forerunner, originator, procreator, progenitor, solo parent, step-parent, take care of **11** birth mother, birth parent, empty-nester, progenitrix **12** foster parent, progenitress, single parent **13** be the father of, be the mother of **14** adoptive parent **15** custodial parent

**parentage**
**04** line, race **05** birth, brood, stock
**06** family, origin, source, stirps
**07** descent, lineage, origins
**08** ancestry, pedigree **09** filiation, paternity, whakapapa **10** derivation, extraction **11** affiliation

**parenthetical**
**08** inserted **09** as an aside, bracketed **10** extraneous, incidental, interposed, qualifying **11** elucidative, explanatory, intervening **13** in parenthesis

**parenthetically**
**03** btw **08** by the way **09** as an aside **11** secondarily **12** incidentally **13** as a digression

**par excellence**
**02** A1 **03** ace **04** best, cool, fine, mean, neat, rare **05** brill, great, noted, prime
**06** divine, select, superb, wicked
**07** eminent, notable, perfect, shining
**08** fabulous, flawless, heavenly, smashing, splendid, stunning, superior, terrific, top-notch, very good
**09** brilliant, excellent, exemplary, fantastic, faultless, first-rate, matchless, wonderful **10** first-class, marvellous, noteworthy, pre-eminent, remarkable, surpassing, unequalled
**11** commendable, exceptional, high-quality, magnificent, outstanding, sensational, superlative **12** praiseworthy, second to none, unparalleled
**13** distinguished **14** out of this world

**pariah**
**05** exile, leper, pi-dog **06** outlaw, pie-dog, pye-dog **07** Ishmael, outcast
**08** castaway, unperson **10** black sheep
**11** undesirable, untouchable
**15** persona non grata

**paring**
**04** peel, rind, skin **05** flake, shave, shred, slice **06** sliver **07** cutting, flaught, peeling, shaving, snippet
**08** clipping, fragment, trimming
**09** flaughter

**Paris**

*Paris districts include:*

**05** Bercy, Opéra
**06** Étoile, Louvre, Marais
**07** Pigalle
**08** Bastille, Chaillot, Left Bank, Sorbonne
**09** Chinatown, La Défense, Les Halles, Right Bank, Trocadero, Tuileries
**10** Belleville, La Villette, Montmartre, Rive Droite, Rive Gauche, Tour Eiffel
**11** Batignolles
**12** Latin Quarter, Les Invalides, Montparnasse, Place d'Italie
**13** Champs Élysées, Quartier Latin

*Paris streets include:*

**07** Pigalle
**09** Port Royal, Rue de Rome
**10** Avenue Foch, Quai d'Orsay, Rue d'Alésia
**11** Rue Dauphine, Rue de Clichy, Rue de Rennes, Rue de Rivoli, Rue de Sèvres, Rue Mazarine, Rue St-Honoré
**12** périphérique, Place d'Italie, Place Vendôme, Quai du Louvre, Quai Voltaire, Rue St-Antoine
**13** Avenue George V, Place du Tertre, Rue des Rosiers, Rue Mouffetard
**14** Place des Vosges
**15** Avenue Montaigne, Quai d'Austerlitz

*Paris landmarks include:*

**05** Seine
**06** Bourse, Louvre
**07** Pyramid
**08** Bastille, Panthéon, Pont Neuf, Sorbonne
**09** Beaubourg, Bon Marché, Invalides, la Défense, Madeleine, Notre-Dame, Orangerie, St-Sulpice, Trocadero, Tuileries
**10** Gare du Nord, Île St-Louis, Montmartre, Musée Rodin, Sacré Coeur
**11** Champ de Mars, Eiffel Tower, Grande Arche, Grand Palais, Île de la Cité, Moulin Rouge, Musée d'Orsay, Palais Royal, Pont des Arts
**12** Hôtel de Ville, Montparnasse, Opéra Garnier, Père Lachaise
**13** Arc de Triomphe, Champs-Élysées, Les catacombes, Opéra Bastille
**14** Bois de Boulogne, École Militaire, Forum des Halles, Palais du Louvre, Place de l'Étoile, Pompidou Centre, Sainte Chapelle
**15** Bois de Vincennes, Cité des Sciences, Le stade de France, Palais de Justice

**parish**
**03** par **04** fold, town **05** flock, title
**06** church, county **07** village
**08** district, parishen, parochin, peculiar, township **09** community, parischan, parochine **10** parischane
**11** churchgoers **12** congregation, denomination, parishioners

**Parisian**
◇ *foreign word indicator*

**parity**
**03** par **05** unity **07** analogy **08** affinity, equality, likeness, sameness

09 agreement, congruity, semblance 10 conformity, congruence, consonance, similarity, similitude, uniformity 11 consistency, equivalence, parallelism, resemblance 14 correspondence

**park**
01 P 02 Pk 03 put, set, zoo 04 bung, stop 05 field, leave, place, plonk, stand, walks 06 domain, draw up, pull up 07 deposit, grounds, reserve 08 paradise, position, woodland 09 grassland

*Parks include:*

04 Hyde, West
05 Green, Güell, Kings
06 Albert, Domain
07 Battery, Central, Phoenix, Regent's, Stanley
08 Gramercy, Richmond, St James's, Victoria
09 Battersea, Tuileries
10 Tiergarten
11 Champ de Mars, Vienna Woods
13 Madison Square, Tivoli Gardens
14 Bois de Boulogne
15 Bois de Vincennes

*National parks in the UK:*

06 Exmoor
08 Dartmoor
09 New Forest, Snowdonia, The Broads
10 Cairngorms
12 Lake District, Peak District
13 Brecon Beacons
14 Northumberland, North York Moors, Yorkshire Dales
18 Pembrokeshire Coast
25 Loch Lomond and the Trossachs

**parking**
01 P

**parlance**
04 cant, talk 05 argot, idiom, lingo 06 jargon, speech, tongue 07 diction 08 language, speaking 11 phraseology 12 conversation

**parley**
04 talk 05 parle, parly, speak, talks, treat 06 confab, confer, emparl, imparl, powwow 07 consult, council, discuss, meeting 08 colloquy, dialogue 09 negotiate, tête-à-tête 10 conference, deliberate, discussion, parliament 11 get together, get-together, negotiation 12 deliberation 14 parliament-cake

**parliament**
05 house, parly 06 parley 07 chamber 11 convocation, legislature

*Parliament types include:*

04 diet, duma, moot
05 boule, douma, gemot, jirga
06 majlis, senate
07 commons, council
08 assembly, congress
09 volksraad
10 consistory, lower house, upper house
12 lower chamber, upper chamber
14 Council of State
15 House of Assembly

*Parliaments and political assemblies include:*

02 EP, HK, HP
04 Dáil, Diet, Duma, Keys, Long, Pnyx, Rump, Sejm
05 boule, Forum, gemot, Lords, Porte
06 Cortes, kgotla, Majlis, Mejlis, Seanad, Senate, Senato, Soviet
07 Althing, comitia, Commons, Knesset, Lagting, Landtag, Rigsdag, Riksdag, Tynwald, zemstvo
08 Assembly, Congress, ecclesia, European, folkmoot, Imperial, Lagthing, Lok Sabha, Scottish, Sobranje, Sobranye, Stannary, Storting
09 Bundesrat, Bundestag, Directory, Eduskunta, Folketing, Landsting, Loya Jirga, Odelsting, Reichsrat, Reichstag, Skupstina, Ständerat, State Duma
10 Bundesrath, Convention, Landsthing, lower house, Odelsthing, Oireachtas, Rajya Sabha, Reichsrath, Skupshtina, St Stephen's, upper house
11 Dáil Eireann, Folketinget, House of Keys, Nationalrat, Star Chamber, Volkskammer, Westminster
12 House of Lords
13 House of States, Seanad Eireann, States General, Supreme Soviet, Welsh Assembly
14 Council of State, Estates General, House of Commons, Long Parliament, Rump Parliament, Staten-Generaal
15 Council of States, House of Assembly, People's Assembly, People's Congress

**parliamentary**
05 civil 07 elected, popular 08 decorous, official 09 lawgiving, lawmaking 10 democratic, republican, senatorial 11 legislative 12 governmental 13 congressional, legislatorial 14 representative

**parlour**
06 lounge, spence 09 front room 10 living room 11 drawing room, keeping-room, morning room, sitting room

**parlous**
04 dire 05 awful, grave 08 alarming, dreadful, horrible, perilous, shocking, terrible 09 appalling, atrocious, desperate, frightful 10 calamitous, disastrous 11 distressing 12 catastrophic

**parochial**
04 hick 05 petty 06 narrow 07 insular, limited 08 confined 09 blinkered, small-town 10 parish-pump, provincial, restricted 11 small-minded 12 narrow-minded 13 inward-looking 14 denominational

**parochialism**
09 pettiness 10 insularity, narrowness, parish pump 13 provincialism 15 small-mindedness

**parody**
03 ape 04 skit 05 mimic, spoof 06 satire, send up, send-up 07 imitate, lampoon, mimicry, take off, take-off 08 satirize, travesty 09 burlesque, imitation 10 caricature, corruption, distortion, pasquinade, perversion

**paroxysm**
03 fit 05 spasm, storm, thraw, throe, throw 06 attack, frenzy, throwe 07 flare-up, rapture, seizure 08 eruption, outbreak, outburst 09 explosion 10 convulsion

**parrot**
03 ape 04 copy, echo, Poll 05 mimic, Polly 06 repeat 07 copycat, imitate, phraser 08 imitator, popinjay, rehearse, repeater 09 reiterate

*Parrots include:*

03 fig, kea
04 grey, kaka, lory
05 galah, macaw, pygmy
06 Amazon, budgie, conure, kakapo, Nestor
07 corella, hanging, rosella
08 cockatoo, lorikeet, lovebird, parakeet, paroquet, Pesquet's, Strigops
09 cockateel, cockatiel, green leek, owl-parrot, paraquito, parrakeet, parroquet, parrotlet, Psittacus, Stringops
10 budgerigar, ring-necked
11 African grey, night-parrot, shell-parrot
13 Major Mitchell, zebra parakeet
14 shell parrakeet

**parrot-fashion**
06 by rote 10 mindlessly 12 mechanically, unthinkingly 13 automatically

**parrot-wrasse**
04 scar

**parry**
04 duck, shun, ward 05 avert, avoid, block, dodge, evade, field, put by, repel, sixte 06 parade, rebuff 07 counter, deflect, fend off, keep off, repulse, ward off 08 sidestep, stave off, tac-au-tac 09 hold at bay, keep at bay, turn aside 10 bodyswerve, circumvent 12 steer clear of

**parsimonious**
04 mean, near 05 close, mingy, tight 06 frugal, narrow, saving, scanty, stingy 07 miserly, scrimpy, sparing 08 grasping, stinting 09 niggardly, penurious 10 Aberdonian 11 close-fisted, close-handed, tight-fisted 12 candle-paring, cheeseparing 13 penny-pinching

**parsimony**
08 meanness 09 frugality, minginess, tightness 10 stinginess 11 miserliness

**12** cheeseparing **13** niggardliness, penny-pinching **15** tight-fistedness

## parson
**03** Rev **05** padre, vicar **06** cleric, curate, deacon, pastor, priest, rector **07** holy Joe **08** minister, preacher, reverend **09** churchman, clergyman, soul-curer **10** Jack-priest

## parson-bird
**03** tui

## part
◇ *hidden indicator*
◇ *hidden alternately indicator*
◇ *insertion indicator*
**02** by, pt **03** bit, bye, job **04** area, book, duty, gift, half, hand, quit, role, shed, side, some, task, tear, twin, wing, work **05** break, chore, facet, leave, organ, party, piece, scene, scrap, sever, share, skill, slice, split, twine **06** aspect, branch, charge, cleave, depart, detach, divide, factor, genius, member, module, office, region, sector, talent, volume **07** ability, break up, calibre, chapter, concern, disband, disjoin, diverge, element, episode, excerpt, extract, faculty, limited, partial, passage, persona, portion, push off, quarter, scarper, scatter, section, segment, split up, take off **08** capacity, clear off, disperse, district, division, fraction, fragment, function, get going, interest, locality, particle, separate **09** attribute, character, come apart, component, dimension, direction, dismantle, endowment, expertise, imperfect, intellect, keep apart, portrayal, push along, take apart, territory **10** capability, depart from, department, disconnect, distribute, go away from, hit the road, ingredient, instalment, make tracks, percentage, proportion, restricted, say goodbye, unfinished **11** constituent, divorce from, fragmentary, hit the trail, involvement, not complete, split up from **12** intelligence, separate from, withdraw from **13** neighbourhood, participation, take your leave **14** accomplishment, representation, responsibility **15** get divorced from, part company with

**• act the part of**
**04** come

**• assign part**
**04** cast

**• even parts**
◇ *hidden alternately indicator*

**• for the most part**
**06** mainly, mostly **07** as a rule, chiefly, largely, overall, usually **08** above all, commonly **09** generally, in general, in the main **10** by and large, especially, on the whole **11** principally **13** predominantly

**• in part**
◇ *hidden indicator*
**04** half **06** parcel, partim, partly **08** slightly, somewhat **10** up to a point **12** to some degree, to some extent

**• in the part of**
**02** as

**• odd parts**
◇ *hidden alternately indicator*

**• on the part of**
**02** by **08** caused by **10** on behalf of **12** carried out by **13** from the side of

**• part of**
◇ *hidden indicator*

**• part with**
**04** drop **05** forgo, yield **06** forego, give up **07** abandon, discard, let go of **08** jettison, renounce **09** surrender **10** relinquish

**• principal part**
**04** lead, main, mass

**• take part in**
◇ *hidden indicator*
**05** opt in **06** join in **07** go in for, partake, share in **08** assist in, engage in, help with **11** play a part in, play a role in **12** be involved in, contribute to **13** participate in

## partake
**05** enter, share **06** engage, inform **07** indulge **08** take part **10** be involved **11** participate

**• partake of**
**03** eat **04** have, show, take **05** drink, evoke, share, taste **06** evince **07** consume, receive, suggest, undergo **08** manifest **11** demonstrate

## partial
**04** half, part **06** biased, in part, unfair, unjust **07** ex parte, limited **08** affected, coloured, one-sided, partisan, twilight **09** component, imperfect **10** incomplete, prejudiced, restricted, unfinished **11** fragmentary, inequitable, predisposed, subordinate **12** preferential **14** discriminatory

**• partial to**
**06** fond of, keen on, liking, loving **08** mad about **09** taken with **10** crazy about

## partiality
**04** bias, love **05** favor **06** favour, liking **07** respect **08** fondness, inequity **09** injustice, prejudice **10** preference, proclivity, unfairness **11** inclination **12** partisanship, predilection **14** discrimination, predisposition **15** inequitableness

## partially
**05** slack **06** in part, partly **08** halflins, not fully, somewhat **09** halflings **12** fractionally, incompletely

## participant
**05** party **06** helper, member, sharer, worker **07** entrant, partner, sharing **09** associate **10** competitor, contestant, co-operator **11** contributor, shareholder **12** participator

## participate
◇ *insertion indicator*
**04** be in, help **05** enter, opt in, share **06** assist, be in it, engage, join in, muck in **07** partake **08** take part **09** co-operate, play a part, play a role **10** be involved, contribute **12** be associated

## participation
**04** part **07** sharing **09** mucking in, partaking **10** assistance **11** association, co-operation, involvement, partnership **12** contribution

## particle
**03** bit, jot, tad **04** atom, corn, curn, drop, iota, mite, spot, whit **05** crumb, grain, piece, scrap, shred, spark, speck, stime, styme, touch, trace **06** morsel, prefix, sliver, suffix, tittle **07** globule, granule, smidgen **08** fragment, molecule, ribosome **09** inclusion **11** conjunction **12** interjection

*Particles include:*

**01** W, X, Z
**03** ion, psi
**04** kaon, muon, pion
**05** anion, boson, gluon, meson, omega, quark, sigma
**06** baryon, cation, hadron, kation, lambda, lepton, parton, photon, proton
**07** neutron, nucleon, upsilon
**08** electron, neutrino, positron, thermion
**09** carbanion, gravitron, tau lepton
**10** anti-proton, gauge boson, zwitterion
**11** anti-neutron
**12** anti-neutrino

## parti-coloured
**06** motley **07** piebald **10** variegated **11** polychromic **13** polychromatic, versicoloured

## particular
**04** fact, item **05** exact, faddy, fussy, picky, point **06** choosy, detail, marked **07** certain, feature, finicky, minutia, notable, precise, respect, several, special, unusual **08** accurate, definite, detailed, distinct, especial, exacting, faithful, peculiar, specific, thorough, uncommon **09** favourite, selective **10** fastidious, individual, meticulous, noteworthy, pernickety, remarkable **11** exceptional, outstanding, painstaking, persnickety **12** circumstance **14** discriminating

**• in particular**
**07** exactly **08** in detail **09** in special, precisely, severally **10** especially, in especial **12** individually, particularly, specifically, to be specific

## particularity
**04** fact, item **05** point, quirk, trait **06** detail **07** feature **08** instance, property **10** uniqueness **11** peculiarity, singularity **12** circumstance, idiosyncrasy **13** individuality **14** characteristic **15** distinctiveness

## particularize
**06** detail **07** itemize, specify **09** enumerate, stipulate **11** individuate **13** individualize

## particularly
**07** notably **08** markedly **09** expressly, severally, unusually **10** distinctly, especially, explicitly, intimately, remarkably, uncommonly

12 individually, in particular, specifically, surprisingly
13 exceptionally 15 extraordinarily

**parting**
◇ *insertion indicator*
04 last, rift, shed 05 adieu, dying, final, going, leave, split 06 depart 07 closing, divorce, goodbye, leaving, rupture
08 breaking, division, farewell
09 departing, departure, partition, partitive 10 breaking-up, concluding, divergence, separation 11 leave-taking, valediction, valedictory 12 disseverance, disseverment 13 disseveration
*See also* **farewell**

**partisan**
03 fan 06 backer, biased, unfair, unjust, votary 07 devotee, partial
08 adherent, champion, disciple, follower, henchman, loyalist, one-sided, party man, queenite, sidesman, stalwart, upholder 09 factional, guerrilla, irregular, sectarian, supporter
10 henchwoman, prejudiced
11 henchperson, imperialist, inequitable, out-and-outer, predisposed 14 discriminatory, freedom fighter

**partisanship**
04 bias 08 interest, partyism
09 prejudice 10 partiality
12 factionalism, sectarianism

**partition**
03 bar 04 wall, with 05 panel, score, sever, share, shoji, withe 06 divide, hallan, parpen, replum, screen, septum, tabula, travis, trevis 07 barrier, break up, break-up, cloison, divider, eardrum, grating, parpane, parpend, parpent, parting, perpend, perpent, split up, treviss, wall off 08 brattice, brattish, brettice, divide up, division, fence off, parpoint, separate, traverse
09 dashboard, diaphragm, parcel out, screen off, segregate, separator, severance, splitting, subdivide
10 rood screen, separation
11 dissepiment, false bottom, room-divider, segregation, separate off, subdivision 12 dividing wall
14 dividing screen

**partly**
04 half, semi- 06 in part, parcel 07 a little 08 slightly, somewhat, to a point
09 partially 10 moderately, relatively, up to a point 12 fractionally, incompletely, to some degree, to some extent 13 in some measure

**partner**
03 man, pal, SOP 04 ally, lady, mate, oppo, pair, pard, wife 05 butty, catch, rival, woman 06 fiancé, friend, helper, lumber, sharer, spouse 07 comrade, consort, fiancée, husband, kept man, pardner 08 cavalier, copemate, co-worker, sidekick, teammate, yoke-mate 09 associate, boyfriend, cohabitee, colleague, companion, copesmate, kept woman, other half
10 accomplice, better half, co-operator, girlfriend, yoke-fellow
11 confederate, live-in lover 12 bit on the side, collaborator 13 common-law wife 14 opposite number
• **former partner**
02 ex
• **partners**
02 EW, NS

**partnership**
04 firm 05 stand, union 06 cahoot
07 company, consort, sharing, society
08 alliance 09 symbiosis, syndicate
10 fellowship, fraternity 11 affiliation, association, brotherhood, combination, co-operation, co-operative, corporation
12 conglomerate 13 collaboration, confederation, participation

**partridge**
05 quail 06 chikor, chukar, chukor
07 chikhor, flapper, tinamou
08 paitrick, percolin

**part-song**
04 glee

**party**
03 jol 04 band, body, camp, crew, fest, gang, rage, rort, rout, sect, side, team, unit 05 binge, cabal, go out, group, posse, quest, squad 06 league, parted, person, thrash 07 carouse, company, divided, faction, have fun, large it
08 alliance, function, grouping, litigant, live it up, party-goer
09 celebrate, defendant, festivity, gathering, have a ball, plaintiff, whoop it up 10 contingent, detachment, have a party, individual 11 affiliation, association, celebration, combination, get-together, have it large, throw a party 13 enjoy yourself, go on the razzle 14 go out on the town, push the boat out, put the flags out 15 paint the town red

*Parties include:*
02 do
03 hen, tea
04 bash, drum, foam, luau, orgy, rave, stag, toga, wine, wrap
05 beano, disco, hangi, house
06 at-home, beer-up, bottle, dinner, drinks, garden, grog-on, grog-up, hooley, Kneipe, picnic, pyjama, rave-up, shivoo, social, soirée, supper
07 blow-out, ceilidh, cookout, knees-up, leaving, new year, potluck, reunion, shindig, slumber
08 barbecue, birthday, bunfight, clambake, cocktail, farewell, tea fight, wingding
09 acid-house, beanfeast, Christmas, Hallowe'en, hootnanny, reception, sleepover, welcoming
10 baby shower, fancy dress, hootenanny, whist drive
11 cookie-shine, discotheque, flat-warming, muffin-fight, muffin-worry
12 bridal shower, house-warming
13 cheese and wine, coffee klatsch, fête champêtre, small-and-early

*Political parties in the UK include:*
01 L
03 BNP, Con, DUP, Lab, Lib, PUP, SNP
04 SDLP, Tory, Whig
05 Green
06 Labour
07 Liberal
08 Alliance, Sinn Féin
09 Communist
10 Democratic, Plaid Cymru, Republican, UK Unionist
11 Co-operative
12 Conservative
13 National Front, Parliamentary
14 UK Independence, Ulster Unionist
15 British National, Liberal Democrat

*Political parties worldwide include:*
02 AN, FN, PP
03 ALP, CDU, NDP, NPD, RPR
05 Green, Labor
06 Labour
07 Worker's
08 Batasuna, Democrat, Fine Gael, National, Sinn Féin
09 One Nation, Socialist
10 Fianna Fáil, Republican
12 Workers' Party
13 Bloc Québécois, Front National, National Front
14 Partido Popular

• **be a party to**
09 know about 12 be involved in
• **dancing party**
03 hop

**party-goer**
09 socialite

**parvenu**
07 climber, new rich, upstart
09 arriviste, pretender, vulgarian
12 nouveau riche 13 social climber

**pascal**
02 Pa

**pasha**
03 dey 06 bashaw

**pass**
02 go, OK 03 col, die, gap, hit, lap, nek, ren, rin, run, say, sit, tip, way 04 beat, chit, drag, emit, fill, flow, ghat, give, go by, hand, jark, kick, live, lose, make, move, okay, omit, pace, path, play, slap, turn, visa 05 adopt, allow, botte, cross, drive, enact, event, expel, ghaut, gorge, halse, hause, hawse, issue, lunge, notch, occur, outdo, poort, punto, reach, route, serve, sling, speak, spend, stand, state, swing, throw, use up, utter, voice 06 accept, assert, become, befall, be left, canyon, chalan, change, chitty, decree, defile, devote, elapse, employ, esteem, evolve, exceed, go over, go past, happen, let out, occupy, parade, permit, puncto, ratify, ravine, slip by, take up, thrust, ticket, travel 07 advance, agree to, approve, be given, challan, declare, deliver, develop, excrete, express, fade out, get over, licence, passage,

proceed, qualify, release, run past, succeed, surpass, undergo, vote for, warrant **08** advances, announce, approach, be willed, currency, go across, go beyond, graduate, outstrip, overhaul, overtake, overture, passport, proclaim, progress, sanction, slip away, transfer, transmit, traverse, validate **09** authorize, be endowed, be granted, circulate, come about, condition, disappear, discharge, disregard, drive past, get across, go through, pronounce, take place, transpire, while away **10** adjudicate, be made over, experience, fulfilment, get through, permission, protection, reputation, suggestion **11** be consigned, be inherited, go unnoticed, leave behind, make your way, outdistance, predicament, proposition, pull ahead of, sail through **12** be bequeathed, be handed down, consummation **13** authorization, be transferred, breeze through, draw level with, laissez-passer, scrape through **14** be successful in, identification, let someone have

*See also* **mountain pass** under **mountain**

• **pass as, pass for**
**10** appear to be, be taken for **12** be regarded as **13** be mistaken for

• **pass away**
**02** go **03** die **04** vade **05** forgo **06** elapse, expire, forego, pass on, peg out, pop off **07** decease **08** blow over **13** kick the bucket **14** depart this life, give up the ghost **15** breathe your last

• **pass degree**
**04** poll

• **pass off**
**04** fake **05** feign, go off, occur **06** happen, vanish **07** die down, palm off, put over, wear off **08** fade away, wear away **09** disappear, take place **11** counterfeit **12** misrepresent

• **pass out**
**03** die **04** dole, drop **05** allot, faint, swoon **07** deal out, dole out, give out, hand out **08** allocate, black out, collapse, flake out, keel over, share out, spark out **10** distribute

• **pass over**
**02** go **03** die **04** balk, miss, omit, skim **05** baulk, leave **06** forget, ignore, overgo, voyage **07** neglect **08** look over, overjump, overlook, overpass, override, overskip **09** disregard **14** take no notice of, turn a deaf ear to **15** turn a blind eye to

• **pass quickly**
**03** fly, hie, ren, rin, run

• **pass the ball to**
**04** feed

• **pass up**
**04** miss **06** ignore, refuse, reject **07** let slip, neglect **08** renounce

**passable**
**02** OK **04** fair, open, so-so **05** clear **06** decent **07** average **08** adequate, all right, mediocre, moderate, ordinary, pervious **09** allowable, navigable, tolerable, unblocked **10** acceptable, not much cop **11** practicable, presentable, respectable, traversable **12** run of the mill, satisfactory, unobstructed **13** no great shakes, unexceptional

**passably**
**05** quite **06** fairly, rather **08** somewhat **09** tolerably **10** moderately, reasonably, relatively **13** after a fashion, indifferently

**passage**
**03** cut, gap, gut, way **04** adit, coda, duct, exit, fare, flow, gate, hall, lane, lick, loan, main, neck, pace, pass, path, pend, pore, road, slap, text, tour, trek, trip **05** aisle, alley, alure, break, canal, chute, creep, cundy, entry, flume, fogou, gully, lapse, lento, lobby, locus, piano, piece, route, shaft, shoot, shute, sound, track, verse, vista **06** access, avenue, burrow, change, clause, condie, course, dromos, furrow, groove, gullet, gutter, legato, narrow, presto, screed, strait, street, throat, trance, transe, travel, trough, tunnel, voyage **07** advance, archway, cadenza, channel, conduit, doorway, episode, excerpt, extract, fistula, gallery, hallway, journey, offtake, opening, orifice, passing, prelude, running, sea lane, section, snicket, stretto, traffic, turning **08** adoption, alleyway, approval, citation, corridor, crossing, division, entrance, incident, longueur, movement, mutation, pericope, progress, ritenuto, sanction, southing, spiccato, staccato, straight, streight, thorough, transfer, waterway **09** admission, breezeway, enactment, migration, paragraph, quotation, ventiduct, vestibule **10** acceptance, occurrence, passageway, pianissimo, ritardando, scherzando, transition, tremolando, validation **11** development, safe conduct, watercourse **12** deambulatory, ratification, thoroughfare, transmission **13** authorization, metamorphosis

*Passages include:*

**04** Mona
**05** Drake, Gaspé, Umnak
**06** Akutan, Amukta, Burias, Caicos, Colvos, Mompog, Seguam, Unimak
**07** Oronsay, Palawan
**08** Amchitka, Dominica, Fenimore, Mouchoir, Saratoga, Windward
**09** Deception, Mayaguana, St Vincent
**10** Backstairs, Guadeloupe, Martinique, Mira Por Vos, Silver Bank
**11** Turks Island, Verde Island
**13** Crooked Island
**14** Jacques Cartier

**passageway**
**03** way **04** exit, hall, lane, path, port **05** aisle, alley, lobby, track **06** arcade, runway **07** gangway, hallway, passage **08** corridor, entrance **11** back passage

**passé**
**03** out **05** dated, faded **06** démodé, groovy, old hat, past it **07** outworn **08** obsolete, outdated, outmoded **09** out-of-date **10** antiquated **11** on the way out, past its best **12** old-fashioned **13** unfashionable

**passenger**
**04** fare **05** drone, rider **07** outside, shirker, voyager **08** commuter, hanger-on **09** fare-payer, traveller **10** freeloader, hitchhiker **11** strap-hanger

• **turn away passenger**
**04** bump

**passer-by**
**06** gawper **07** witness **08** looker-on, observer, onlooker **09** bystander, spectator **10** eyewitness, rubberneck

**passing**
**03** end **04** flow, loss, very **05** brief, death, hasty, march, quick, rapid, short **06** casual, course, demise, elapse, finish, slight **07** advance, cursory, decease, diadrom, passage, quietus, shallow **08** fleeting, movement **09** departure, ephemeral, momentary, perishing, temporary, transient **10** evanescent, expiration, incidental, short-lived **11** exceedingly, passing away, superficial, termination **12** transitional

• **in passing**
**07** by the by **08** by the bye, by the way **09** en passant **12** incidentally **15** parenthetically

**passion**
**03** fit, wax **04** fire, fury, heat, love, lust, pash, rage, zeal, zest **05** anger, brame, craze, mania, wrath **06** ardour, dander, desire, spirit, temper, warmth **07** avidity, craving, emotion, feeling, fervour, tantrum **08** fondness, keenness, outburst **09** adoration, affection, altitudes, eagerness, explosion, intensity, obsession, vehemence **10** enthusiasm, fanaticism **11** fascination, indignation, infatuation **12** sexual desire

• **burst of passion**
**04** gust

**passionate**
**03** hot, mad **04** avid, keen, nuts, sexy, warm, wild **05** crazy, eager, fiery, gutsy, horny, Latin, potty, randy **06** ardent, erotic, fervid, fierce, loving, stormy, strong, sultry, torrid, wilful **07** aroused, excited, fervent, intense, lustful, sensual, violent, zealous **08** choleric, frenzied, inflamed, turned on, vehement **09** emotional, excitable, fanatical, hotheaded, impetuous, impulsive, irritable, obstinate **10** headstrong, hot-blooded, self-willed **11** impassioned, tempestuous, warm-blooded **12** affectionate, enthusiastic **13** quick-tempered, waspish-headed

**passionately**
**05** hotly **06** keenly **08** ardently, fiercely, lovingly, strongly **09** con

calore, fervently, intensely, lustfully, sensually, violently, zealously
**10** erotically **11** fanatically
**14** affectionately

**passionless**
**03** icy **04** calm, cold **06** frigid, frosty **07** callous, neutral **08** detached, uncaring, unloving **09** apathetic, impartial, impassive, unfeeling, withdrawn **10** insensible, restrained, uninvolved **11** cold-blooded, cold-hearted, emotionless, indifferent, unemotional **12** unresponsive
**13** dispassionate

**passive**
**05** aloof, inert **06** docile, remote, supine **07** distant, patient, subdued, unmoved **08** detached, inactive, lifeless, resigned, yielding
**09** apathetic, compliant, lethargic, receptive, suffering **10** effortless, non-violent, submissive, uninvolved
**11** emotionless, indifferent, unassertive, unemotional, unresisting
**13** dispassionate, long-suffering
**14** unenterprising

**passively**
**09** patiently **10** lifelessly
**12** submissively **13** emotionlessly, unassertively

**passport**
**02** ID **03** key, way **04** door, pass, path, visa **05** entry, route **06** avenue, papers, permit **07** doorway **09** admission
**12** identity card **13** authorization, laissez-passer, means of access
**15** travel documents

**password**
**03** key **04** word **06** parole, signal
**07** tessera **09** watchword **10** open sesame, shibboleth **11** countersign

**past**
**02** by, pa, pt **03** ago, ygo **04** done, gone, last, late, life, near, over, ygoe, yore **05** after, agone, early, ended, forby, olden, round, since **06** behind, beside, beyond, bygone, by-past, former, gone by, latter, no more, recent, record **07** ancient, defunct, elapsed, extinct, history, long ago, one-time, worn-out **08** finished, foregone, overworn, preterit, previous, sometime **09** antiquity, completed, erstwhile, foregoing, forgotten, olden days, preceding, preterite, too old for, yesterday **10** background, bygone days, days gone by, days of yore, experience, olden times **11** bygone times, former times, good old days, track record **12** too mature for **15** over and done with

**pasta**

*Pasta types include:*

**04** orza, ziti
**05** penne, ruoti
**06** anelli, ditali, noodle, trofie
**07** fusilli, gnocchi, lasagna, lasagne, lumache, mafalde, maruzze, mezzani, noodles, pennine, ravioli
**08** bucatini, farfalle, fedelini, linguini, macaroni, rigatoni, stelline
**09** agnolotti, angel hair, casarecci, crescioni, fiochetti, manicotti, spaghetti
**10** angel's hair, bombolotti, cannelloni, conchiglie, farfalline, fettuccine, strangozzi, tagliarini, taglierini, tortellini, vermicelli
**11** cappelletti, pappardelle, tagliatelle
**12** lasagne verde
**13** elbow macaroni

**paste**
**03** fix, gum, pap **04** glue, miso, mush, pack, pâté, pulp **05** blend, purée, putty, stick **06** cement, cerate, fasten, mastic, slurry, spread, thrash **07** mixture
**08** adhesive

**pastel**
**04** pale, soft, woad **05** chalk, faint, light, muted, quiet **06** crayon, low-key, sketch, subtle **07** drawing, subdued
**08** delicate, discreet, pastille, soft-hued, vignette **11** sauce-crayon
**13** light-coloured

**pastiche**
◇ *anagram indicator*
**03** mix **04** olio **06** jumble, medley
**07** farrago, melange, mixture, variety
**08** mishmash, mixed bag **09** confusion, pasticcio, patchwork, potpourri
**10** assortment, collection, hodgepodge, hotchpotch, miscellany, salmagundi
**11** gallimaufry, olla-podrida, smorgasbord **14** conglomeration, omnium-gatherum

**pastille**
**05** sweet **06** jujube, pastel, tablet, troche **07** lozenge **09** cough drop
**10** confection, cough sweet

**pastime**
**03** fun **04** game, play **05** hobby, sport
**08** activity, pastance **09** amusement, avocation, diversion **10** abridgment, recreation, relaxation, suppliance
**11** abridgement, distraction
**12** Zeitvertreib **13** entertainment
**14** leisure pursuit **15** leisure activity

*See also* **hobby**

**past master**
**02** PM **03** ace **05** adept **06** artist, expert, wizard **07** dab hand, old hand
**08** virtuoso **10** proficient

**pastor**
**01** P **05** canon, vicar **06** cleric, deacon, divine, parson, priest, rector
**08** minister, shepherd **09** churchman, clergyman **10** prebendary
**12** ecclesiastic

**pastoral**
**03** oat **04** idyl **05** idyll, rural **06** rustic, simple **07** bucolic, country, crosier, crozier, eclogue, idyllic **08** agrarian, Arcadian, clerical, priestly, serenata
**09** bucolical, siciliano **11** ministerial, Theocritean **12** agricultural
**14** ecclesiastical

**pastry**

*Pastry types include:*

**04** filo, flan, puff
**05** choux, flaky, plain, short, sweet
**06** cheese, Danish
**07** pork-pie
**08** one-stage, piecrust
**09** rough-puff, suetcrust
**10** pâte brisée, pâte frolle, pâte sablée, pâte sucrée, shortcrust, wholewheat
**12** biscuit-crumb, pâte à savarin
**13** American crust, hot-water crust
**14** rich shortcrust

*See also* **cake**

**pasture**
**03** alp, lay, lea, lee, ley, tie, tye **04** feed, fell, food, gang, mead, raik, rake, soum, sowm, walk **05** downs, field, grass, graze, lease, leaze, range **06** leasow, meadow, saeter **07** feeding, grazing, leasowe, paddock **08** mountain, shealing, shieling **09** grassland, pasturage, sheepwalk **11** grazing land

• **pasture grass**
**04** bent **05** grama **06** fescue
**07** timothy **08** paspalum, rye grass
**09** bent grass **10** grama grass
**12** meadow fescue, sheep's fescue, timothy grass **13** dog's-tail grass, Flinders grass

**pasty**
**03** wan **04** pale, waxy **06** doughy, pallid, sallow, sickly **07** anaemic
**08** empanada **09** unhealthy **10** pasty-faced **11** oyster-patty

**pat**
**03** dab, pet, pot, tap **04** ball, burp, clap, easy, glib, lump, mass, slap, tick
**05** bepat, chunk, print, ready, slick, touch **06** caress, facile, fluent, fondle, patter, simple, smooth, stroke
**07** exactly **08** coquille, fluently
**09** perfectly, precisely **10** flawlessly, simplistic **11** faultlessly, word-for-word

• **pat someone on the back**
**06** praise **10** compliment
**12** congratulate **13** say well done to

**patch**
**03** bed, fix, lot, sew **04** area, mend, plot, snip, spot, term, time, zona
**05** botch, cloth, clout, cover, phase, piece, scrap, spell, tract **06** parcel, period, plaque, pocket, repair, shield, stitch **07** stretch **08** covering, dressing, fragment, material **09** reinforce
**10** protection

**patchwork**
**04** hash **06** jumble, medley, motley
**07** farrago, mixture **08** mishmash, pastiche **10** assortment, hotchpotch
**11** gallimaufry

**patchy**
◇ *anagram indicator*
**05** bitty **06** fitful, random, spotty, uneven **07** blotchy, erratic, macular, sketchy, varying **08** variable

09 centonate, irregular 10 incomplete 11 incongruous 12 inconsistent, inharmonious

**patent**
03 pat 04 open 05 clear, overt, plain, right 07 blatant, charter, evident, glaring, licence, obvious, visible 08 apparent, flagrant, manifest, palpable 09 copyright, expanding, ingenious, invention, privilege, spreading 10 undeniable 11 certificate, conspicuous, self-evident, transparent, unequivocal 12 crystal clear, unmistakable 13 unmistakeable 15 clear as daylight

**patently**
06 openly 07 clearly, plainly, visibly 08 palpably 09 blatantly, glaringly, obviously 10 manifestly 12 unmistakably 13 conspicuously, unequivocally, unmistakeably

**paternal**
08 fatherly, vigilant 09 concerned 10 benevolent, fatherlike, protective

**path**
02 go 03 pad, sty, way 04 berm, gate, lane, road, trod, walk, went 05 allée, orbit, route, track, trail, troad, trode 06 avenue, course, troade 07 circuit, highway, passage, pathway, slidder, towpath, walkway 08 approach, cycleway, footpath 09 bridleway, direction, footsteps 10 bridle-road, forthright

**pathetic**
◇ *anagram indicator*
03 sad 04 poor 05 sorry 06 dismal, feeble, meagre, moving, tender, woeful 07 pitiful, useless 08 derisory, pitiable, poignant, touching, wretched 09 affecting, miserable, plaintive, worthless 10 deplorable, inadequate, lamentable 11 distressing 12 contemptible, heart-rending 13 heartbreaking 14 unsatisfactory

**pathetically**
05 sadly 08 dismally, pitiably, woefully 09 miserably, pitifully 10 deplorably, lamentably, wretchedly 12 contemptibly, inadequately

**pathological**
07 chronic 08 addicted, habitual, hardened 09 confirmed, dependent, obsessive 10 compulsive, inveterate, persistent

**pathos**
06 misery 07 sadness, tragedy 08 sob stuff 09 poignancy 10 inadequacy 11 pitifulness 12 pitiableness 13 plaintiveness

**patience**
04 cool 07 bistort 08 calmness, Klondike, Klondyke, serenity, stoicism, tenacity 09 composure, diligence, endurance, fortitude, restraint, solitaire, tolerance 10 doggedness, equanimity, submission, sufferance 11 forbearance, persistence, resignation, self-control 12 monk's rhubarb, perseverance, stickability, tranquillity 13 long-suffering 14 inexcitability, unflappability

**patient**
04 calm, case, cool, kind, mild 06 client, extern, serene, tender 07 externe, invalid, lenient, stoical, subject 08 ambulant, composed, enduring, laid-back, resigned, resolute, sufferer, tolerant 09 easy-going, forgiving, indulgent, leisurely, unhurried 10 forbearant, forbearing, out-patient, persistent, restrained, submissive 11 persevering, susceptible, unflappable 12 even-tempered, patient as Job 13 accommodating, imperturbable, long-suffering, philosophical, self-possessed, uncomplaining, understanding 14 hanging in there, self-controlled

• **be patient**
04 bear

• **hospital patients**
04 ward

**patiently**
06 calmly, kindly, mildly 08 tenderly 09 leisurely 10 enduringly, resolutely, tolerantly 11 unflappably, unhurriedly 12 persistently 13 considerately, perseveringly

**patois**
04 cant 05 argot, Gumbo, lingo, slang 06 Creole, jargon, patter 07 dialect 08 Guernsey 10 vernacular 11 local speech 12 lingua franca 13 local parlance

**patriarch**
04 pope, sire 05 abuna, elder 06 father 07 founder 09 greybeard 10 Catholicos 11 grandfather, grand old man 13 paterfamilias

*Patriarchs include:*

04 Levi, Noah
05 Aaron, Abram, Enoch, Isaac, Jacob
06 Joseph
07 Abraham, Ishmael
10 Methuselah, Theophilus

**patrician**
03 nob 04 peer 05 noble 06 gentle, lordly, patron 07 grandee 08 high-born, nobleman, well-born 09 gentleman, high-class 10 aristocrat, upper-crust 11 blue-blooded 12 aristocratic, thoroughbred

**patrimony**
05 share 06 estate, legacy 07 bequest, portion, revenue 08 heritage, property 10 birthright 11 inheritance, possessions

**patriot**
05 jingo 08 jingoist, loyalist 09 flag-waver 10 chauvinist 11 nationalist

**patriotic**
05 loyal 08 loyalist 10 flag-waving, jingoistic 11 nationalist 12 chauvinistic 13 nationalistic

**patriotism**
07 loyalty 08 jingoism 10 chauvinism, flag-waving 11 nationalism

**patrol**
04 beat, tour 05 guard, round, vigil, watch 06 defend, picket, piquet, police, sentry 07 defence, inspect, monitor, picquet, protect 08 defender, policing, sentinel, sentry-go, watchman 09 milk train, patrolman 10 patrolling, protection 11 be on the beat, do the rounds, go the rounds, keep guard on, keep watch on, patrolwoman, perambulate 12 surveillance 13 keep watch over, make the rounds, night-watchman, perambulation, police officer, security guard 14 make your rounds

**patron**
05 angel, buyer, stoop, stoup, Venus 06 Apollo, backer, client, fautor, friend, helper, Hermes 07 pattern, regular, shopper, sponsor 08 advocate, champion, customer, defender, guardian, Maecenas, promoter, upholder 09 protector, purchaser, supporter 10 benefactor, frequenter, subscriber 11 sympathizer 12 benefactress 13 guardian angel 14 fairy godmother, philanthropist

**patronage**
05 aegis, trade 06 buying, custom 07 backing, funding, support 08 auspices, business, commerce, shopping 09 promotion 10 protection, purchasing 11 countenance, sponsorship 12 financial aid, subscription 13 encouragement, financial help

**patronize**
03 aid 04 back, fund, help 05 scorn 06 assist, foster, shop at 07 buy from, despise, finance, promote, protect, sponsor, support 08 champion, deal with, empatron, frequent, maintain 09 disparage, encourage 10 look down on, talk down to 12 be a regular at

**patronizing**
05 lofty 06 snooty 07 haughty, stuck up 08 scornful, snobbish, stooping, superior 10 disdainful, high-handed 11 overbearing, toffee-nosed 12 contemptuous, supercilious 13 condescending, high-and-mighty 14 holier-than-thou 15 on your high horse

**patter**
03 pat, rap, tap, yak 04 beat, drum, line, pelt, trip 05 lingo, pitch, pound, spiel 06 bicker, gabble, gammon, jabber, jargon, pit-pat, scurry, verbal 07 beating, chatter, pitapat, scuttle, tapping, verbals 08 pitty-pat 09 monologue, pattering 12 pitter-patter

**pattern**
03 key 04 copy, form, mold, norm, plan, trim, type 05 guide, ideal, match, model, motif, mould, order, shape,

style, whirl **06** design, device, dicing, figure, follow, method, sample, stripe, swatch, system **07** emulate, example, fashion, Gestalt, grecque, imitate, stencil, tracery **08** decorate, Greek key, markings, original, ornament, parallel, standard, template **09** blueprint, criterion, influence, prototype, scantling **10** craquelure, decoration **11** arrangement, instruction **13** ornamentation

**patterned**
**05** moiré **07** figured, printed, watered **09** decorated **10** ornamented

**paucity**
**04** lack, want **06** dearth, rarity **07** fewness, poverty **08** scarcity, shortage, sparsity **09** smallness **10** deficiency, meagreness, paltriness, scantiness, slightness, sparseness **11** slenderness **12** exiguousness **13** insufficiency

**paunch**
**03** gut, pod **04** kite, kyte **05** belly, rumen, tripe **07** abdomen, beer gut **08** pot-belly **09** beer belly **10** eviscerate, fat stomach **11** corporation

**paunchy**
**03** fat **05** podgy, pudgy, tubby **06** portly, rotund **07** adipose **08** stomachy **09** corpulent **10** pot-bellied

**pauper**
**06** beggar **07** have-not **08** bankrupt, indigent **09** insolvent, mendicant **10** down-and-out **11** church mouse

**pause**
**03** gap **04** halt, hold, kick, lull, rest, stay, stop, wait **05** break, cease, close, delay, demur, dwell, let up, let-up, limma **06** cesura, desist **07** adjourn, breathe, caesura, fermata, respite, sit down, time out **08** break off, breather, dieresis, hesitate, hold back, interval, stoppage, take five **09** cessation, diaeresis, interlude, interrupt, take a rest **10** hesitation, take a break **11** discontinue, freeze-frame **12** intermission, interruption **13** take a breather **14** breathing space

**pave**
**03** tar **04** flag, tile **05** cover, floor, pitch **06** cobble, tarmac **07** asphalt, surface **08** concrete **10** macadamize, tessellate **11** cobblestone

• **pave the way for**
**08** lead up to **09** introduce, take steps **10** prepare for **11** get ready for **12** make ready for, take measures **14** clear the ground

**pavement**
**03** bed, way **04** path **05** floor **07** footway, walkway **08** causeway, flagging, footpath, platform, sidewalk, trottoir **11** plainstanes, plainstones

**pavilion**
**04** flag, tent **05** kiosk **06** canopy, ensign, houdah, howdah **09** belvedere **14** jingling Johnny

**paving-block**
**03** set **04** sett

**paw**
**03** pad, pah, pud **04** foot, foul, hand, maul, poke **05** mouse, puddy, touch **06** molest, stroke **07** obscene, touch up **08** forefoot **09** manhandle, mishandle

**pawn**
**01** P **03** dip, pan, pop, toy **04** dupe, fine, hock, paan, pown, tool **05** betel, powin, spout, stake **06** impawn, lumber, pledge, puppet, stooge, wadset **07** cat's paw, deposit, gallery, peacock, wadsett **08** mortgage **09** pignerate, pignorate, plaything **10** instrument **11** impignorate, oppignerate, oppignorate **13** lay in lavender

**pawnbroker**
**05** uncle **06** lender, sheeny, usurer **07** pop-shop **08** lumberer, pawnshop **10** gombeen-man **11** money-lender, mont-de-piété **12** monte di pietà

**pay**
**02** do **03** fee **04** ante, bung, foot, give, make, pony, sold **05** atone, grant, offer, remit, repay, solde, spend, wages, yield **06** afford, answer, ante up, bestow, defray, expend, extend, income, invest, lay out, net pay, outlay, pay off, pay out, profit, rake in, refund, return, reward, salary, settle, square, suffer, supply **07** benefit, bring in, cough up, fork out, imburse, pay back, payment, produce, proffer, stipend, stump up **08** disburse, earnings, gross pay, hand over, settle up, shell out **09** discharge, indemnify, reimburse **10** be punished, commission, compensate, emoluments, honorarium, make amends, recompense, remunerate **11** foot the bill, take-home pay **12** compensation, pick up the tab, remuneration, satisfaction **13** meet the cost of, reimbursement **14** be beneficial to, be worthwhile to, let someone have

• **pay back**
**05** repay **06** pay off, punish, refund, return, settle, square **08** give back **09** reimburse, retaliate **10** recompense **11** get even with, reciprocate, take revenge **13** counter-attack **14** get your own back

• **pay for**
**04** take **05** atone, escot, prize, pryse **06** suffer **09** answer for **10** compensate, cost dearly, make amends **12** count the cost, face the music **13** be punished for **14** count the cost of, get your deserts, pay a penalty for, pay the price for

• **pay off**
**03** fix **04** fire, meet, sack, work **05** bribe, clear, repay **06** buy off, grease, honour, lay off, settle, square, suborn **07** dismiss, requite, succeed **08** amortize **09** discharge, pay in full **10** extinguish, get results, take care of **12** be successful **13** make redundant

• **pay out**
**04** veer **05** remit, spend **06** ante up, expend, lay out **07** cough up, dispend, fork out **08** disburse, hand over, part with, shell out

**payable**
**03** due **04** owed **05** owing **06** mature, unpaid **08** to be paid **09** in arrears **10** profitable **11** outstanding **13** contributable

**payload**
**04** haul, load **05** cargo, goods **06** lading **07** baggage, freight, tonnage **08** contents, shipment **11** consignment, merchandise

**payment**
**03** fee, pay, sub **04** ante, dole, fare, farm, hire, mail, rent, scot, shot, toll, wage **05** arles, modus **06** amount, hansel, outlay, payola, reward **07** advance, annuity, deposit, expense, handsel, pension, premium, primage **08** danegeld, danegelt, donation, soul-scat, soul-scot, soul-shot **09** allowance, clearance, discharge **10** instalment, prestation, punishment, quarterage, recompense, remittance, settlement **12** compensation, contribution, remuneration, satisfaction **13** consideration

• **demand payment**
**03** dun

**pay-off**
**03** fee, pay **05** bribe, wages **06** crunch, income, net pay, result, reward, salary, upshot **07** benefit, outcome, payment, stipend **08** earnings, gross pay **09** advantage, hush money, punchline, slush fund, sweetener **10** allurement, back-hander, commission, dénouement, emoluments, enticement, honorarium, inducement, recompense, settlement **11** consequence, take-home pay **12** compensation, remuneration **13** moment of truth, reimbursement **15** protection money

**PC** *see* **police officer**

**pea**
**03** dal **04** daal, dahl, dhal **05** dholl, pease **06** legume **08** kaka beak, kaka bill **09** chickling, mangetout, marrowfat, parrot-jaw, rounceval **10** parrot-beak, parrot-bill **14** chickling vetch

**peace**
**03** pax **04** calm, ease, hush, pact, rest **05** amity, frith, olive, quiet, still, truce **06** accord, repose, shalom, treaty **07** concord, harmony, silence **08** calmness, goodwill, serenity **09** agreement, armistice, ceasefire, composure, placidity, quietness, stillness **10** friendship, relaxation **11** contentment, law and order, non-violence, peace treaty, restfulness

**12** amicableness, conciliation, peacefulness, tranquillity **13** non-aggression

**peaceable**
**04** mild **05** douce **06** dovish, gentle, irenic, placid **07** cordial, pacific **08** amicable, friendly **09** easy-going, unwarlike **10** harmonious, non-violent **11** good-natured, inoffensive, peace-loving **12** conciliatory, even-tempered **13** non-aggressive

**peaceably**
**06** gently, mildly **08** amicably, placidly **09** cordially **11** pacifically **12** harmoniously **13** inoffensively

**peaceful**
**04** calm **05** quiet, still **06** gentle, irenic, placid, serene, sleepy **07** halcyon, pacific, restful **08** amicable, friendly, in repose, relaxing, tranquil **09** peaceable, reposeful, unruffled **10** harmonious, untroubled **11** undisturbed

**peacefully**
**06** calmly, gently **07** quietly **08** amicably, placidly, serenely, sleepily **09** restfully **12** harmoniously

**peacemaker**
**04** dove **06** broker **08** appeaser, mediator, pacifier, pacifist, revolver **09** make-peace **10** arbitrator **11** conciliator, intercessor, pacificator, peace-monger

**peacemaking**
**06** irenic **07** pacific **09** appeasing, mediating, mediative, mediatory **11** mediatorial **12** conciliatory, pacification

**peach**
**03** dob **06** accuse, betray, inform **07** sing out, whittle **08** quandang, quandong, quantong **09** melocoton, nectarine, victorine **10** melicotton, melocotoon **11** malakatoone

**peacock**
**03** pea **04** Pavo, pawn, pown **05** powin **06** paiock, pajock, pavone **07** paiocke, pajocke

**peak**
**02** pk **03** ben, nib, pin, tip, top **04** apex, hill, mope, peag, rise **05** crest, crise, crown, droop, mount, pique, point, prick, spike, spire, visor, vizor **06** apogee, climax, height, summer, summit, zenith **07** maximum **08** aiguille, high noon, mountain, pinnacle **09** culminate, elevation, high point **11** come to a head, culmination

**peaky**
**03** ill, wan **04** pale, sick **05** dicky, seedy **06** crummy, pallid, poorly, queasy, sickly, unwell **09** off-colour, washed-out **10** out of sorts **15** under the weather

**peal**
**04** boom, clap, howl, ring, roar, roll, toll **05** chime, clang, crash, knell **06** firing, grilse, rumble, triple **07** resound, ringing, ring out **08** carillon, resonate **10** resounding **11** reverberate **13** reverberation

**peanut**
**05** arnut **06** goober **07** arachis **08** earth-nut, earth-pea **09** goober pea, groundnut, monkey nut

**pear**
**04** tuna **05** nashi, nelis, nopal **06** Colmar, comice, nelies, pepino, seckel, seckle, warden **07** avocado, poperin **08** aguacate, bergamot, blanquet, muscadel, muscatel **09** Indian fig, poppering **10** Conference, jargonelle **11** bon chrétien, queez-maddam **12** cuisse-madame

**pearl**
**04** purl, Unio **05** nacre, union **06** barock, orient **07** barocco, baroque, granule, paragon **10** granulated

**• string of pearls**
**04** rope

**peasant**
**03** oaf **04** boor, hick, kern, lout, rude, ryot **05** churl, kerne, kisan, kulak, mujik, rural, swain, yokel **06** carlot, cottar, cotter, fellah, jungli, moujik, muzhik, raiyat, rustic **07** bumpkin, Cossack **09** campesino, contadina, contadino **10** blue-bonnet, clodhopper, provincial **13** country person **14** country bumpkin

**pebble**
**04** chip, pelt, pumy, rock **05** agate, chuck, pumie, stone **06** gallet **07** chuckie **09** pumy stone **10** dreikanter, pumie stone **12** chuckie-stane, chuckie-stone

**peccadillo**
**04** boob, slip **05** error, fault, lapse **06** slip-up **07** misdeed **10** infraction **11** delinquency **12** indiscretion, minor offence, misdemeanour

**peck**
**02** pk **03** dab, hit, jab, job, nip, rap, tap **04** bite, food, jerk, kiss, pick **05** pitch, prick **06** pickle, strike

**peculiar**
◇ *anagram indicator*
**03** ill, odd, own **04** sick **05** dizzy, droll, ferly, funny, queer, weird **06** exotic, poorly, proper, quaint, queasy, unique, unwell, way-out **07** bizarre, curious, oddball, offbeat, special, strange, unusual **08** abnormal, distinct, freakish, personal, singular, specific **09** eccentric, grotesque, preserved **10** individual, outlandish, out of sorts, particular, remarkable **11** distinctive, exceptional **12** appropriated **13** extraordinary, idiosyncratic **14** characteristic, distinguishing, unconventional **15** individualistic, under the weather

**• peculiar to**
**04** like **08** unique to **09** typical of **11** belonging to **12** indicative of **13** in keeping with

**peculiarity**
**04** mark **05** quirk, trait **06** foible, jimjam, oddity **07** feature, quality **08** hallmark, property **09** attribute, exception, mannerism, weirdness **10** shibboleth **11** abnormality, bizarreness, singularity **12** eccentricity, idiosyncrasy **13** individuality, particularity **14** characteristic **15** distinctiveness

**peculiarly**
◇ *anagram indicator*
**05** oddly **08** quaintly, uniquely **09** bizarrely, curiously, strangely, unusually **10** distinctly, remarkably, singularly **12** particularly **13** distinctively, exceptionally **15** extraordinarily

**pecuniary**
**06** fiscal **07** nummary **08** monetary **09** financial, nummulary **10** commercial

**pedagogic**
**08** academic, didactic, teaching **09** tuitional **10** scholastic **11** educational **13** instructional

**pedagogue**
**03** don **05** teach **06** master, pedant **07** dominie, teacher **08** educator, mistress **09** dogmatist, preceptor **10** instructor **12** educationist, schoolmaster **13** schoolteacher **14** educationalist, schoolmistress

**pedagogy**
**07** tuition **08** teaching, training, tutelage **09** didactics **10** pedagogics **11** instruction

**pedal**
**01** P

**pedant**
**06** purist **07** academe, casuist, egghead **08** academic, highbrow, quibbler **09** dogmatist, Dryasdust, formalist, nit-picker, pedagogue, precisian **10** literalist, scholastic, schoolmarm **11** doctrinaire, pettifogger **12** hair-splitter, intellectual, precisionist, schoolmaster **13** perfectionist

**pedantic**
**04** blue **05** exact, fussy, heavy **06** purist, stuffy **07** bookish, erudite, finical, inkhorn, pompous, precise, stilted **08** academic **09** formalist, quibbling **10** literalist, meticulous, nit-picking, particular, scholastic, scrupulous **11** pretentious, punctilious, sesquipedal **12** intellectual **13** hair-splitting, perfectionist, schoolmarmish **14** schoolmasterly, sesquipedalian

**pedantry**
**09** cavilling, dogmatism, exactness, pedantism, pomposity, quibbling **10** finicality, nit-picking, pedagogism, stuffiness **11** bookishness **12** academicness **13** hair-splitting

14 meticulousness 15 intellectualism, pedagoguishness, pretentiousness, punctiliousness

**peddle**
◇ *anagram indicator*
04 flog, hawk, push, sell, tout, vend 05 trade 06 market, smouch, trifle 07 traffic 08 huckster 12 offer for sale 14 present for sale

**pedestal**
04 base, dado, foot 05 basis, stand, trunk 06 column, pillar, plinth, podium 07 acroter, support 08 mounting, platform 09 axle-guard, stylobate 10 acroterion, acroterium, foundation 11 pillow-block

**• put on a pedestal**
05 exalt 06 admire, revere 07 adulate, idolize 08 look up to 11 hero-worship

**pedestrian**
03 ped 04 dull, flat 05 banal, hiker 06 boring, hicker, stodgy, turgid, walker 07 humdrum, mundane, prosaic 08 mediocre, ordinary, plodding 09 jaywalker 10 unexciting, uninspired, voetganger 11 commonplace, indifferent, not up to much, peripatetic 12 matter-of-fact, run-of-the-mill 13 foot-traveller, no great shakes, unimaginative

**pedigree**
03 set 04 line, race, tree 05 blood, breed, stirp, stock 06 family, series, stemma, stirps, strain 07 descent, lineage 08 ancestry, breeding, pure-bred 09 genealogy, parentage, phylogeny 10 derivation, extraction, family tree, succession 11 full-blooded 12 aristocratic, phylogenesis, thoroughbred 13 line of descent

**pediment**
07 frontal, fronton 08 frontoon 09 fastigium 12 frontispiece

**pedlar**
06 bodger, cadger, hawker, jagger, pedder, pether, seller, smouch, smouse, vendor, walker, yagger 07 camelot, chapman, packman, smouser 08 huckster 09 boxwallah, cheap-jack, gutter-man, itinerant 10 colporteur 12 street-trader 14 gutter-merchant

**pee**
01 P
*See also* **urinate**

**peek**
03 spy 04 look, peep, peer 05 blink, dekko, squiz 06 gander, glance, shufti, squint 07 glimpse, look-see 11 have a gander 12 have a look-see

**peel**
◇ *ends deletion indicator*
04 bark, pale, pare, peal, pill, rind, skin, zest 05 flake, scale, shell, shuck, stake, strip 06 grilse, remove, shovel 07 epicarp, exocarp, peeling, pillage, plunder, take off, undress 08 flake off 10 desquamate, integument 11 decorticate

**• keep your eyes peeled**
07 be alert, monitor, observe 12 watch closely 15 keep a lookout for

**peep**
03 cry, eye, pip, pry, spy 04 cook, keek, kook, look, peek, peer, pink, pipe, slit, toot, word 05 blink, cheep, chirp, dekko, issue, noise, sound, speck, tweet 06 appear, emerge, gander, glance, shufti, squeak, squint, warble 07 chatter, chirrup, glimpse, look-see, twitter 09 quick look, utterance

**peephole**
04 hole, slit 05 chink, cleft, crack, slink 07 crevice, eyehole, fissure, keyhole, opening, pinhole, spyhole 08 aperture 09 Judas hole 10 interstice 11 Judas window

**peer**
03 pry, spy 04 dick, duke, earl, gaze, lady, like, look, lord, peep, pink, scan, toot 05 baron, count, equal, match, noble, snoop, stime, styme, trier, tweer, twire 06 appear, fellow, squint, squiny 07 compeer, examine, inspect, Law Lord, marquis, peeress, squinny 08 confrère, marquess, nobleman, protrude, viscount 09 patrician 10 antagonist, aristocrat, equivalent, scrutinize 11 counterpart 12 backwoodsman
*See also* **nobility**

**peerage**
07 Debrett, red book 08 nobility 09 top drawer 10 upper crust 11 aristocracy 14 lords and ladies

**peeress**
04 dame, lady 05 noble 07 duchess 08 baroness, countess 10 aristocrat, noblewoman 11 marchioness, viscountess

**peerless**
06 unique 07 supreme 09 excellent, matchless, nonpareil, paramount, unmatched 10 incompared, unbeatable, unequalled, unexcelled, unrivalled 11 outstanding, superlative, unsurpassed 12 incomparable, second to none, unparalleled, without equal 13 beyond compare

**peeve**
03 bug, irk, vex 04 gall, rile 05 annoy 06 grouse, hassle, wind up 07 hack off, tick off 08 brass off, irritate 09 aggravate, cheese off, drive nuts, grievance 10 drive crazy, exasperate 12 drive bananas 13 make sparks fly 14 drive up the wall

**peeved**
04 sore 05 irked, riled, upset, vexed 06 bugged, galled, miffed, narked, piqued, put out, shirty 07 annoyed, hassled, in a huff, nettled, stroppy 08 in a paddy 09 irritated, ticked off 10 brassed off, cheesed off, driven nuts, got the hump 11 driven crazy, exasperated

**peevish**
03 ill 04 sour 05 cross, moody, ratty, sulky, surly, testy 06 crusty, franzy, girnie, grumpy, hipped, snappy, sullen, tetchy, touchy 07 crabbed, foolish, frabbit, frampal, fretful, grouchy, nattery, pettish, wayward 08 captious, churlish, frampold, nattered, perverse, petulant 09 crotchety, fractious, irritable, querulous, splenetic, vexatious 10 capernoity, in a bad mood 11 capernoitie, cappernoity, complaining, ill-tempered, out of temper 12 cantankerous 13 short-tempered

**peevishly**
07 crossly 08 grumpily, sullenly 09 fretfully, irritably 10 churlishly, in a bad mood, petulantly 11 fractiously

**peevishness**
03 dod, pet 05 pique 08 acrimony, fretting 09 curstness, ill-temper, petulance, testiness 10 perversity, protervity 12 captiousness, irritability 13 querulousness

**peg**
03 fix, key, leg, nog, pin, set, tap 04 brad, hook, join, knag, knob, mark, nail, plug, poke, post, step 05 dowel, limit, perch, piton, score, screw, spike, stake, theme, thole, throw 06 attach, degree, fasten, freeze, hatpeg, marker, picket, piquet, secure, spigot, target, thrust 07 control, picquet, tent pin 08 cheville, hold down, thole pin 09 soft spile, stabilize, tuning pin

**• peg away**
06 hang in 07 persist 08 keep at it, plug away, work away, work hard 09 persevere, plod along, stick at it 10 beaver away 13 apply yourself

**• take down a peg or two, bring down a peg or two**
06 humble 09 humiliate 13 cut down to size 15 bring down to size

**pejorative**
03 bad 08 negative 09 slighting 10 belittling, derogatory, unpleasant 11 deprecatory, disparaging 12 depreciating, unflattering 15 uncomplimentary

**pellet**
04 ball, drop, pill, shot, slug 05 prill 06 bullet 07 capsule, granule, lozenge 08 pithball 09 coprolite, paintball

**pell-mell**
◇ *anagram indicator*
06 rashly 07 hastily 08 disorder, headlong 09 hurriedly, posthaste 10 at full tilt, confusedly, feverishly, heedlessly, recklessly, vehemently 11 hurry-scurry, impetuously 13 helter-skelter, precipitously 14 indiscriminate

**pellucid**
04 pure 05 clear 06 bright, glassy, limpid 10 diaphanous 11 translucent, transparent

**pelt**
03 fur, hit, ren, rin, run, zip 04 beat,

belt, blow, clod, coat, dash, fell, hide, hurl, pour, race, rush, skin, tear, teem **05** hurry, scoot, speed, stone, throw **06** assail, attack, batter, bucket, career, charge, fleece, pebble, pellet, pelter, pepper, shower, sprint, squail, strike **07** bombard **08** bearskin, bepepper, coonskin, downpour, lapidate, squirrel, wolfskin **10** bucket down **15** rain cats and dogs

**pen**
◇ *containment indicator*
**03** Bic®, cub, dam, mew, nib, sty
**04** Biro®, cage, coop, fold, J-pen, note, reed, shut, stie, stye, weir **05** crawl, cruve, draft, fence, hedge, hem in, hutch, kraal, penne, pound, quill, stall, write **06** author, corral, croove, cruive, estate, shut up **07** compose, confine, dash off, enclose, felt pen, felt-tip, gladius, jot down, rastrum, writing **08** compound, note down, scribble, take down **09** ballpoint, enclosure, marker pen, sheepfold, write down **10** felt-tip pen, plantation, Rollerball®, self-filler, stylograph **11** fountain pen, highlighter, Magic Marker®
**12** ballpoint pen, penitentiary
*See also* **author**

**penal**
**08** punitive **10** corrective, vindictive
**11** retaliatory, retributive
**12** disciplinary, penitentiary

**penalize**
**04** fine **06** punish **07** correct, forfeit
**08** chastise, handicap, sanction
**09** castigate **10** discipline
**12** disadvantage

**penal servitude**
**03** lag **04** bird, time **07** katorga, stretch
**08** porridge **10** hard labour

**penalty**
**04** fine, pain, snag **05** minus, mulct
**06** amende **07** forfeit **08** downside, drawback, handicap, sentence
**09** weak point **10** punishment
**11** castigation, retribution
**12** chastisement, demerit point, disadvantage
• **pay penalty**
**03** aby **04** abye

**penance**
**06** shrift **07** penalty **08** hardship
**09** atonement, expiation, penitence
**10** punishment, reparation, repentance
**13** mortification, self-abasement
**14** self-punishment

**penchant**
**04** bent, bias **05** taste **06** foible, liking
**07** leaning **08** affinity, fondness, soft spot, tendency, weakness
**09** proneness **10** partiality, preference, proclivity, propensity **11** disposition, inclination **12** predilection
**14** predisposition

**pencil**
**03** cam **04** calm, caum **05** stump
**06** crayon **09** keelivine, keelyvine, tortillon **10** Chinagraph®

**pendant**
**03** bob **04** drop, tika, tiki **05** cross
**06** locket, luster, lustre **07** eardrop, earring, heitiki, necklet, pennant, sautoir **08** appendix, necklace, pear drop **09** girandola, girandole, lavaliere, medallion **10** lavallière, Rouen cross, stalactite

**pendent**
**06** nutant **07** hanging, pensile
**08** dangling, drooping, swinging
**09** pendulous, suspended
**11** overhanging

**pending**
**02** to **04** near, till **05** until, while
**06** before, coming, during, whilst
**07** hanging, nearing **08** awaiting, imminent, so long as **09** impending, uncertain, undecided, unsettled
**10** throughout, unresolved, up in the air **11** approaching, forthcoming, in the offing **12** in the balance

**pendulous**
**06** droopy **07** hanging, pendent, sagging, swaying **08** dangling, drooping, swinging **09** suspended
**11** overhanging

**penetrable**
**04** open **05** clear **06** porous
**08** passable, pervious **09** permeable
**10** accessible, explicable, fathomable
**12** intelligible **14** comprehensible, understandable

**penetrate**
◇ *insertion indicator*
**03** cut, see **04** bite, bore, fill, seep, sink, stab, twig **05** crack, enter, grasp, imbue, prick, probe, sease, shear, spike
**06** fathom, indent, invade, needle, pierce, rain in, sink in, strike **07** get into, make out, pervade, suffuse, suss out, work out **08** cotton on, permeate, perviate, puncture, register, saturate
**09** perforate **10** comprehend, infiltrate, understand **11** make your way

**penetrating**
◇ *insertion indicator*
**04** deep, hard, keen, loud, wise
**05** acute, clear, sharp **06** biting, shrewd, shrill **07** cutting, in-depth, ingoing, intrant, probing **08** carrying, incisive, invasive, piercing, poignant, profound, stinging, strident
**09** observant, searching **10** discerning, insightful, perceptive **14** discriminating

**penetration**
◇ *insertion indicator*
**03** wit **05** entry **06** acumen, fathom, inroad **07** insight **08** entrance, incision, invasion, keenness, piercing, pricking, stabbing **09** acuteness, pervasion, sharpness **10** astuteness, perception, permeation, puncturing, shrewdness
**11** discernment, perforation
**12** infiltration, perspicacity

**penguin**
**05** diver **06** gentoo, korora **07** pinguin
**08** macaroni **10** rockhopper, Spheniscus **11** king penguin **12** fairy penguin **13** little penguin **14** emperor penguin

**peninsula**
**03** Pen **04** cape, doab, mull **05** point
**06** tongue **10** chersonese

*Peninsulas include:*

**04** Ards, Cape, Eyre, Gyda, Huon, Kola
**05** Gaspé, Gower, Italy, Lleyn, Malay, Otago, Qatar, Sinai
**06** Alaska, Avalon, Azuero, Balkan, Carnac, Crimea, Iberia, Istria, Jaffna, Korean, Recife, Seward, Taymyr, Wirral
**07** Alaskan, Arabian, Cape Cod, Chukchi, Florida, Furness, Iberian, Jiulong, Jutland, Kintyre, Kowloon, Olympic, Yucatàn
**08** Apsheron, Cape York, Cotentin, Musandam, Pinellas, Sorrento, Yorktown
**09** Cape Verde, Gallipoli, Kamchatka, Paraguana, Peary Land
**10** Arnhem Land, Graham Land, Isle of Dogs, Nova Scotia
**11** Peloponnese
**12** Scandinavian
**14** Baja California, Isle of Portland
**15** Rinns of Galloway

*See also* **cape**

**penitence**
**05** shame **06** regret, sorrow
**07** remorse **10** contrition, repentance, ruefulness **11** compunction **12** self-reproach

**penitent**
**05** sorry **06** humble, rueful
**07** ashamed, mourner **08** contrite
**09** regretful, repentant, sorrowful
**10** apologetic, remorseful, shamefaced

**pen-name**
**06** anonym **07** allonym **09** false name, pseudonym, stage-name **10** nom de plume **11** assumed name, nom de guerre

**pennant**
**04** flag, jack **06** banner, burgee, ensign, guidon, pennon **07** colours, pendant, pendent **08** banderol, gonfalon, standard, streamer

**penniless**
**04** bust, poor **05** broke, skint, stony
**06** ruined **07** boracic **08** bankrupt, dirt-poor, indigent **09** destitute
**10** cleaned out, down and out, on the rocks, stone-broke, stony-broke
**11** impecunious **12** impoverished, on your uppers **14** on the breadline, on your beam-ends **15** poverty-stricken, strapped for cash

**Pennsylvania**
**02** PA

**penny**
**01** d, p **03** win **04** cent, wing, winn
**08** denarius, sterling

**penny-pincher**
**05** miser **06** meanie **07** niggard,

Scrooge **09** skinflint **10** cheapskate **11** cheeseparer **12** money-grubber

**penny-pinching**
**04** mean **05** close, mingy, tight **06** frugal, stingy **07** miserly **09** niggardly, scrimping **10** ungenerous **11** tight-fisted **12** cheeseparing, parsimonious

**pension**
**04** SIPP **05** board **06** corody, income **07** annuity, benefit, corrody, support, welfare **09** allowance **11** deferred pay **12** state pension **13** old-age pension **14** company pension, superannuation **15** personal pension

**pensioner**
**03** OAP **07** boarder **09** dependant **12** out-pensioner **13** retired person, senior citizen **15** gentleman-at-arms, old-age pensioner

**pensive**
**05** sober **06** dreamy, musing, solemn **07** serious, wistful **08** absorbed, thinking **09** pondering **10** cogitative, meditative, melancholy, reflective, ruminative, thoughtful **11** preoccupied **12** absent-minded **13** contemplative, lackadaisical

**pensively**
**08** dreamily **09** seriously, wistfully **12** meditatively, thoughtfully **14** absent-mindedly **15** contemplatively

**Pentateuch**
**05** Torah

**penthouse**
**03** cat **04** pent

**pent-up**
**06** curbed, held in **07** bridled, stifled **09** bottled-up, inhibited, repressed **10** restrained, suppressed

**penurious**
**04** bust, mean, poor **05** close, mingy, tight **06** hard up, scanty, stingy **07** lacking, miserly **08** beggarly, grudging, indigent **09** destitute, flat broke, niggardly, penniless **10** inadequate, ungenerous **11** close-fisted, close-handed, impecunious, tight-fisted **12** cheeseparing, impoverished, on your uppers, parsimonious **14** on your beam-ends **15** poverty-stricken

**penury**
**04** lack, need, want **06** dearth **07** beggary, poverty, straits **09** indigence, mendicity, pauperism **10** deficiency, insolvency **11** destitution **14** impoverishment

**people**
**03** men, mob **04** clan, folk, gens, land, race **05** folks, laity, ngati, plebs, tribe, tuath **06** family, hordes, humans, masses, nation, occupy, proles, public, rabble, settle, voters **07** inhabit, mankind, mortals, parents, persons, punters, society **08** citizens, colonize, humanity, populace, populate, riff-raff, servants, subjects **09** community, employees, followers, hoi polloi, humankind, relations, relatives, retainers **10** attendants, electorate, kith and kin, population **11** ethnic group, human beings, individuals, inhabitants, rank and file **12** congregation, the human race **13** general public, great unwashed

*Peoples include:*

**03** Han, Ibo, Jat, Kru, Mam, Mon, San, Tiv, Twi
**04** Ainu, Cham, Efik, Goth, Hutu, Igbo, Jute, Kroo, Lett, Moor, Motu, Nair, Nupe, Roma, Saba, Shan, Sulu, Susu, Tshi, Zulu
**05** Bajau, Bantu, Hausa, Iceni, Inuit, Karen, Khmer, Maori, Masai, Nayar, Nguni, Oriya, Saxon, Swazi, Taino, Tamil, Temne, Tonga, Tutsi, Vedda, Wolof, Yakut, Yupik
**06** Angles, Aymara, Griqua, Gurkha, Herero, Innuit, Kabyle, Kalmyk, Kikuyu, Manchu, Nyanja, Ostiak, Ostyak, Sherpa, Tswana, Tungus, Yoruba, Zyrian
**07** Barotse, Basotho, Calmuck, Cossack, Goorkha, Hittite, Kalmuck, Manchoo, Maratha, Pashtun, Quechua, Quichua, Samoyed, Swahili, Tagálog, Walloon
**08** Khoikhoi, Mahratta, Polabian, Yanomami
**09** Himyarite, Ostrogoth, Ruthenian, Sinhalese, Tocharian, Tokharian

**pep**
**02** go **03** zip **04** life, zing **05** oomph, verve **06** energy, ginger, spirit, vigour **07** pizzazz, sparkle **08** dynamism, vitality **10** ebullience, exuberance, get-up-and-go, liveliness **11** high spirits **13** effervescence

• **pep up**
**06** excite **07** animate, improve, inspire, liven up, quicken **08** energize, vitalize **09** stimulate **10** exhilarate, invigorate

**pepper**
**03** dot **04** bomb, pelt, stud **05** blitz, Piper, strew **06** assail, attack, shower **07** bombard, scatter, spatter **08** sprinkle **09** bespatter

*Pepper and peppercorns include:*

**03** ava, red
**04** bird, kava, pink
**05** black, chile, chili, green, sweet, white
**06** cherry, chilli, yellow
**07** cayenne, Jamaica, paprika, pimento
**08** allspice, capsicum, habañero, jalapeño, pimiento, piquillo
**12** Scotch bonnet

**peppermint**
**06** humbug **07** pan drop **08** bull's-eye

**peppery**
**03** hot **05** fiery, sharp, spicy, testy **06** biting, grumpy, touchy **07** caustic, piquant, pungent, waspish **08** choleric, incisive, seasoned, snappish, stinging **09** irascible, irritable, sarcastic, trenchant **10** astringent **11** hot-tempered **13** quick-tempered

**peppy**
**04** spry **05** agile, alert, alive, brisk, quick **06** active, lively, nimble **07** dynamic **08** animated, spirited, vigorous **09** energetic, sprightly, vivacious **12** enthusiastic, high-spirited

**per**
**01** a **02** by, pr **07** through

**perceive**
**03** see **04** espy, feel, hear, know, note, spot, twig, view, wind **05** grasp, learn, sense, smell, taste **06** behold, deduce, detect, gather, notice, remark, survey **07** believe, discern, glimpse, make out, observe, realize, suppose **08** conclude, discover, subitize **09** apprehend, be aware of, get wind of, recognize, undertake **10** appreciate, comprehend, understand **11** distinguish **12** catch sight of **13** be cognizant of

**perceptible**
**05** clear, plain **06** patent **07** evident, obvious, tactile, visible **08** apparent, distinct, manifest, palpable, sensible, tangible **10** detectable, noticeable, observable **11** appreciable, conspicuous, discernible, perceivable **15** distinguishable

**perception**
**04** idea, view **05** grasp, sense, taste **06** vision **07** feeling, insight, percept **09** awareness, knowledge **10** cognizance, conception, experience, impression **11** discernment, observation, recognition, sensitivity **12** appreciation, apprehension **13** consciousness, light of nature, understanding **14** discrimination, interpretation, responsiveness

• **fine perception**
**04** tact

**perceptive**
**04** deep, keen **05** acute, alert, aware, quick, sharp **06** astute, shrewd **08** delicate **09** observant, sensitive, sharp-eyed **10** discerning, insightful, percipient, responsive **11** penetrating, quick-witted **13** perspicacious, understanding **14** discriminating

**perceptively**
**06** keenly **07** sharply **08** astutely **11** observantly, sensitively **12** insightfully **15** perspicaciously

**perch**
**03** bar, lug, rod, sit **04** bass, land, perk, pole, rest, rood, ruff **05** basse, gaper, Perca, roost, ruffe **06** alight, anabas, comber, darter, fogash, sander, sauger, settle, zander, zingel **07** balance, kahawai, walleye **09** blackfish, overperch, stone bass, wreckfish **12** walleyed pike

**perchance**
**05** maybe **07** percase, perhaps **08** feasibly, possibly **11** conceivably

**percipience**
**07** insight **08** sagacity **09** acuteness, alertness, awareness, intuition, judgement **10** astuteness, perception **11** discernment, penetration, sensitivity **12** perspicacity **13** understanding

**percipient**
**05** alert, alive, aware, sharp **06** astute **07** knowing **09** judicious, observant, wide-awake **10** discerning, perceptive **11** intelligent, penetrating, quick-witted **13** perspicacious **14** discriminating

**percolate**
**03** sop **04** drip, leak, ooze, perk, seep, sift **05** drain, leach, sieve **06** filter, strain **07** pervade **08** filtrate, permeate **09** penetrate **11** pass through **13** spread through **14** trickle through

**perdition**
**04** doom, hell, loss, ruin **08** downfall, hellfire **09** confusion, damnation, ruination **11** destruction **12** annihilation, condemnation

**peregrination**
**04** tour, trek, trip **06** roving, travel, voyage **07** journey, odyssey, roaming **08** trekking **09** excursion, wandering, wayfaring **10** expedition, pilgrimage, travelling **11** exploration **13** globetrotting

**peremptory**
**04** curt **05** bossy, final, utter **06** abrupt, lordly **07** summary **08** absolute, dogmatic **09** arbitrary, assertive, imperious **10** autocratic, commanding, high-handed, imperative, tyrannical **11** dictatorial, domineering, irrefutable, overbearing **13** authoritative

**perennial**
**07** abiding, endless, eternal, lasting, undying **08** constant, enduring, immortal, unending **09** ceaseless, continual, incessant, permanent, perpetual, unceasing, unfailing **10** persistent, unchanging **11** everlasting, never-ending **12** imperishable **13** uninterrupted

**perfect**
**04** full, mint, perf, pure, true **05** exact, ideal, model, prize, right, sheer, total, utter **06** better, entire, expert, finish, fulfil, mature, polish, refine, superb, triple **07** certain, correct, improve, precise, sinless, skilful **08** absolute, accurate, complete, copybook, faithful, finished, flawless, peerless, spotless, textbook, thorough, ultimate, unmarred **09** blameless, completed, convinced, downright, elaborate, excellent, exemplary, faultless, matchless, out-and-out, wonderful **10** consummate, immaculate, impeccable, just the job, to the nines **11** experienced, superlative, unblemished **12** accomplished, incomparable

**perfection**
**04** acme, best **05** bloom, crown, ideal, model, prime **06** flower **07** paragon **08** maturity, pinnacle, ripeness, ultimate **09** polishing **10** betterment, completion, excellence, refinement **11** improvement, ne plus ultra, point-device, point-devise, realization, roundedness, superiority **12** consummation, flawlessness **13** faultlessness, impeccability, one in a million **14** immaculateness

**perfectionism**
**06** purism **08** idealism, pedantry **09** formalism **10** Utopianism

**perfectionist**
**06** pedant, purist **08** idealist, stickler **09** formalist, Free-lover **12** precisionist

**perfectly**
**04** very **05** fully, quite **06** à point, wholly **07** down pat, exactly, ideally, totally, utterly **08** entirely, superbly **09** correctly **10** absolutely, altogether, completely, flawlessly, impeccably, like a charm, thoroughly **11** faultlessly, wonderfully **12** consummately, immaculately, to perfection **14** without blemish

**perfidious**
**05** false, Punic **07** corrupt **08** disloyal, two-faced **09** deceitful, dishonest, faithless **10** traitorous, treasonous, unfaithful **11** double-faced, duplicitous, treacherous **13** double-dealing, Machiavellian, untrustworthy

**perfidy**
**06** deceit **07** falsity, treason **08** betrayal **09** duplicity, treachery **10** disloyalty, infidelity **13** double-dealing, faithlessness **14** perfidiousness, traitorousness

**perforate**
**04** bore, gore, hole, stab, tear **05** burst, drill, prick, punch, spike, split **06** pierce **07** rupture **08** puncture, trephine **09** penetrate **11** make holes in

**perforated**
**05** bored, holed **06** porous **07** drilled, ethmoid, pierced, punched **09** fenestral, punctured **10** cribriform, fenestrate, fenestrial, foraminous **11** fenestrated

**perforation**
**04** bore, hole **05** prick **06** pierce **07** foramen **08** fenestra, puncture **10** dotted line **12** fenestration

**perforce**
**10** inevitably, willy-nilly **11** necessarily, of necessity, unavoidably

**perform**
◇ *anagram indicator*
**02** do, go **03** act, cut, run **04** make, play, sing, take, work **05** dance, enact, put on, stage, throw **06** behave, effect, fulfil, recite, render **07** achieve, conduct, execute, operate, portray, present, produce, pull off, satisfy **08** appear as, atchieve, bring off, carry out, complete, despatch, dispatch, function, make good, transact **09** discharge, implement, represent **10** accomplish, bring about **12** give effect to

**performance**
**03** act **04** deed, duet, play, show, solo, spot, trio **05** doing, going, house **06** acting, action, acture, ballet, try-out **07** account, benefit, concert, conduct, recital, running, showing, working **08** hierurgy, première, set piece **09** behaviour, discharge, effecting, execution, happening, operation, portrayal, prolusion, rendering, rendition **10** appearance, completion, conducting, fulfilling, fulfilment, last hurrah, peroration, production **11** achievement, carrying-out, functioning, presentment, tour de force **12** presentation **14** accomplishment, implementation, interpretation, representation

**performer**
**04** doer, hand, moke, star, turn **05** actor, clown, comic **06** artist, author, dancer, player, singer **07** actress, artiste, old hand, ripieno, trouper **08** achiever, comedian, executor, Fancy Dan, film star, musician, operator, star turn, Thespian, topliner **09** ecdysiast, executant **10** rope-walker **11** entertainer **12** improvisator, vaudevillean, vaudevillian **15** jerry-come-tumble

**performers**
**04** cast

**perfume**
**04** balm, musk, otto, sent **05** aroma, attar, odour, ottar, scent, smell **06** chypre **07** bouquet, cologne, essence, incense **08** fumigate, opopanax **09** aromatize, fragrance, redolence, sweetness **10** frangipane, frangipani, heliotrope, Jockey Club **11** millefleurs, toilet water **12** eau-de-cologne **13** eau-de-toilette, lavender water

**perfunctorily**
**07** quickly **09** cursorily, hurriedly **10** carelessly **13** inattentively, superficially

**perfunctory**
**05** brief, quick **06** wooden **07** cursory, hurried, offhand, routine **08** careless, heedless, slipshod, slovenly **09** automatic, desultory, negligent **10** mechanical **11** inattentive, indifferent, superficial

**perhaps**
◇ *anagram indicator*
**03** say **05** haply, maybe **06** ablins, belike, happen, mayhap **07** aiblins, could be, happily, percase, yibbles **08** feasibly, possibly **09** perchance **11** conceivably **12** peradventure, you never know

**peril**
**04** risk **06** danger, hazard, menace, threat **07** apperil **08** apperill, distress, jeopardy **10** insecurity **11** uncertainty **12** endangerment

**perilous**
**04** dire **05** dicey, dodgy, hairy, risky **06** chancy, unsafe, unsure **07** exposed, parlous, perlous **08** high-risk, insecure, menacing **09** dangerous, hazardous **10** precarious, vulnerable **11** threatening

**perimeter**
**04** edge **05** limit **06** border, bounds, fringe, limits, margin **07** circuit **08** boundary, confines, frontier **09** periphery **11** outer limits **13** circumference

**period**
**03** age, end, eon, era, per **04** aeon, date, span, spin, stop, term, time, turn **05** class, cycle, epoch, phase, point, shift, space, spell, stage, stint, while, years **06** finish, lesson, menses, season **07** lecture, seminar, session, stretch **08** duration, full stop, interval, semester, the curse, tutorial **09** full point, monthlies **10** conclusion, end of story, generation **11** instruction **12** menstruation **13** menstrual flow **14** menstrual cycle, time of the month

*See also* **geological**; **historical**; **time**

**periodic**
**05** round **06** cyclic **07** regular **08** cyclical, repeated, seasonal, sporadic **09** recurrent, recurring **10** infrequent, occasional, periodical **12** intermittent, once in a while

**periodical**
**03** mag **05** organ **06** review, weekly **07** etesian, journal, monthly, regular **08** bi-weekly, bulletin, magazine **09** pictorial, quarterly, thunderer, tri-weekly **11** illustrated, publication, semi-monthly **12** trade journal

*See also* **newspaper**

**periodically**
**07** at times **08** off and on, on and off **09** sometimes **10** now and then, on occasion **11** at intervals, irregularly, now and again **12** every so often, infrequently, occasionally, once in a while, sporadically **14** from time to time, intermittently **15** every now and then

**peripatetic**
**06** mobile, roving **07** migrant, nomadic, roaming, vagrant **08** ambulant, vagabond **09** itinerant, migratory, traveling, wandering **10** ambulatory, journeying, pedestrian, travelling **12** Aristotelian

**peripheral**
**05** add-on, input, minor, outer **06** lesser, output **07** storage, surface **08** computer, marginal, outlying **09** ancillary, auxiliary, disk drive, outermost, secondary, sidelined **10** additional, borderline, incidental, irrelevant, subsidiary, tangential **11** superficial, surrounding, unimportant, unnecessary **14** beside the point, graphics tablet

**periphery**
**03** hem, rim **04** brim, edge **05** ambit, brink, skirt, verge **06** border, fringe, margin **07** circuit **08** boundary **09** outskirts, perimeter **12** outer regions **13** circumference

**periphrastic**
**07** oblique **08** indirect, rambling, tortuous **09** wandering **10** circuitous, discursive, roundabout **12** long-drawn-out **14** circumlocutory

**perish**
**02** go **03** die, rot **04** cark, exit, fail, fall, pass, ruin, tine, tyne, vade **05** choke, croak, decay, drown, go off, quell, swelt **06** depart, expire, famish, go bung, go west, pass on, peg out, pip out, pop off, starve, sterve, vanish **07** crumble, decease, destroy, die away, fall off, forfair, kick off, kiss off, snuff it, succumb **08** collapse, flatline, pass away, spark out **09** decompose, disappear, go belly up, have had it **10** hop the twig **11** bite the dust, come to an end **12** disintegrate, lose your life, pop your clogs, slip the cable **13** close your eyes, kick the bucket, meet your maker, push up daisies **14** depart this life, give up the ghost, turn up your toes **15** breathe your last, cash in your chips

**perishable**
**10** short-lived **12** decomposable, destructible **13** biodegradable

**periwinkle**
**05** vinca **06** winkle **08** Apocynum, dog-whelk **11** pennywinkle **12** strophanthus

**perjure**
**• perjure yourself**
**03** lie **12** lie under oath **13** commit perjury

**perjury**
**09** false oath, mendacity **11** crimen falsi, forswearing **12** false witness, hard swearing, oath-breaking **13** false evidence, false swearing, falsification **14** false statement, false testimony, lying under oath

**perk**
**03** tip **04** plus **05** bonus, brisk, extra, perch **07** benefit, freebie **08** dividend, gratuity **09** advantage, baksheesh, percolate **10** percolator, perquisite **13** fringe benefit **15** golden handshake
**• perk up**
**05** pep up, rally **06** buck up, cock up, look up, revive **07** cheer up, improve, liven up, recover **08** brighten **09** take heart **10** brighten up, make lively, revitalize **12** become lively

**perky**
**03** gay **04** pert **05** cocky, peppy, sunny **06** bouncy, bright, bubbly, cheery, gallus, jaunty, lively **07** buoyant, gallows **08** animated, cheerful, spirited **09** ebullient, sprightly, vivacious **12** effervescent

**permanence**
**09** constancy, endurance, fixedness, stability **10** durability, perpetuity **11** persistence **13** steadfastness **15** imperishability

**permanent**
**04** firm **05** fixed, pakka, pucka, pukka, solid **06** stable **07** abiding, durable, eternal, lasting, regular, stative **08** constant, enduring, lifelong, standing, unfading **09** immutable, indelible, perennial, perpetual, steadfast **10** invariable, unchanging **11** established, everlasting, long-lasting **12** imperishable, unchangeable **14** indestructible

**permanently**
**06** always **07** for ever, for good **08** ever more, for keeps **09** endlessly, eternally, indelibly **10** constantly, for all time, unendingly **11** ceaselessly, continually, incessantly, perpetually, unceasingly **12** in perpetuity, till doomsday **13** everlastingly, for good and all, once and for all, unremittingly **14** for ever and ever **15** till kingdom come

**permeable**
**06** porous, spongy **08** passable, pervious **09** absorbent, poromeric **10** absorptive, penetrable

**permeate**
**04** fill **05** imbue **06** leaven **07** diffuse, pervade, suffuse **08** saturate **09** penetrate, percolate **10** impregnate, infiltrate **11** impenetrate, pass through, seep through, soak through, transpierce **13** filter through, spread through

**permissible**
**02** OK **05** legal, legit **06** kosher, lawful, proper, venial **07** allowed **08** all right **09** allowable, permitted, tolerable **10** acceptable, admissible, authorized, legitimate, sanctioned

**permission**
**03** out **04** loan, pass **05** congé, exeat, leave, power **06** access, assent, congee, permit, placet, square **07** consent, freedom, go-ahead, liberty, licence, license, mandate, warrant **08** approval, pratique, sanction, thumbs-up, wayleave **09** admission, agreement, allowance, authority, clearance **10** green light, imprimatur **11** approbation, bill of sight, congé d'élire, permittance **12** dispensation **13** authorization **14** leave of absence, permis de séjour

**permissive**
**03** lax **04** free **07** lenient, liberal **08** optional, tolerant **09** easy-going, indulgent, permitted **10** forbearing **11** broad-minded **13** overindulgent **14** latitudinarian

**permit**
**03** let **04** give, pass, visa **05** admit, agree, allow, grant, smoke **06** carnet, docket, enable, suffer, ticket **07** consent, docquet, empower, indulge, licence, license, placard, warrant **08** intromit, passport, sanction, tolerate **09** authorize, green card **10** permission **11** safe-conduct **12** give the nod to **13** authorization, laissez-passer **14** permis de séjour
**• it is not permitted**
**02** nl

**permutation**
**04** perm **05** shift **06** barter, change **09** obversion, variation **10** alteration **11** commutation **13** configuration, transmutation, transposition **14** transformation

**pernicious**
**03** bad **04** evil **05** fatal, ready, swift, toxic **06** deadly, prompt, wicked **07** baneful, harmful, hurtful, noisome, noxious, ruinous **08** damaging, damnable, venomous **09** dangerous, injurious, malicious, malignant, offensive, pestilent, poisonous, unhealthy **10** maleficent, malevolent **11** deleterious, destructive, detrimental, unwholesome

**pernickety**
**04** fine, nice **05** fussy, picky **06** choosy, fiddly, tricky **07** careful, carping, finical, finicky **08** detailed, exacting **10** fastidious, nit-picking, particular **11** over-precise, painstaking, persnickety, punctilious **13** hair-splitting **14** over-particular

**peroration**
**04** talk **06** korero, speech **07** address, lecture, oration, summary **08** diatribe, pirlicue, purlicue **09** recapping, summing-up **10** conclusion **11** declamation, reiteration **14** closing remarks, recapitulation

**perpendicular**
**04** sine **05** atrip, erect, plumb, right, sheer, steep **06** abrupt, normal, offset **07** apothem, upright **08** cathetus, straight, vertical **09** downright, erectness **10** anticlinal **11** precipitous, verticality **13** at right angles

**perpetrate**
**02** do **05** wreak **06** commit, effect **07** execute, inflict, perform **08** carry out **10** accomplish, effectuate **12** be to blame for

**perpetration**
**05** doing **09** committal, execution **10** commitment **11** achievement, carrying-out, performance **14** accomplishment, implementation

**perpetrator**
**04** doer, perp **05** agent **08** executor, offender **09** committer, executant

**perpetual**
**07** abiding, endless, eternal, lasting, undying **08** constant, enduring, infinite, repeated, unbroken, unending **09** ceaseless, continual, incessant, perennial, permanent, recurrent, unceasing, unfailing, unvarying **10** continuous, persistent, persisting, unchanging **11** everlasting, never-ending, unremitting **12** interminable, intermittent **13** uninterrupted

**perpetually**
**09** endlessly, eternally **10** constantly **11** ceaselessly, continually, incessantly, permanently, unceasingly **12** interminably, persistently **13** unremittingly

**perpetuate**
**06** keep up **07** sustain **08** continue, maintain, preserve **09** keep alive, keep going **10** eternalize **11** commemorate, immortalize, memorialize

**perpetuation**
**09** extension **10** sustaining **11** lengthening, maintenance, protraction **12** continuation, keeping alive, preservation, prolongation **13** commemoration

**perpetuity**
**• in perpetuity**
**06** always **07** for ever **08** ever more **09** endlessly, eternally **10** for all time **11** perpetually **14** for ever and ever

**perplex**
◇ *anagram indicator*
**04** pose **05** beset, stump, throw **06** baffle, bother, feague, fickle, gravel, hobble, muddle, pother, pudder, puzzle, tangle, tickle **07** bumbaze, confuse, flummox, mystify, nonplus **08** bewilder, confound, entangle, throw off **09** bamboozle, dumbfound, embarrass, embrangle, imbrangle **10** complicate, difficulty, distrouble, interweave

**perplexed**
**05** spiny **07** at a loss, baffled, fuddled, muddled, puzzled, stumped, worried **08** confused **09** flummoxed, mystified, quizzical **10** bamboozled, bewildered, confounded, distraught, nonplussed, tosticated **11** embarrassed **12** disconcerted

**perplexing**
**04** hard **05** weird **06** knotty, taxing, thorny **07** amazing, complex, strange **08** baffling, involved, puzzling **09** confusing, difficult, enigmatic, intricate **10** mysterious, mystifying **11** bewildering, complicated, paradoxical **12** inexplicable, labyrinthine

**perplexity**
**05** doubt, tweak, worry **06** bother, enigma, puzzle, taking, tangle **07** dilemma, meander, mystery, nonplus, paradox **09** confusion, intricacy, labyrinth, obscurity **10** bafflement, complexity, difficulty, fickleness, puzzlement **11** distraction, disturbance, involvement, obfuscation, tostication **12** bewilderment, complication, entanglement **13** embarrassment, mystification **15** incomprehension

**perquisite**
**03** tip **04** lock, perk, plus, vail **05** bonus, extra, vales **07** apanage, benefit, freebie **08** appanage, dividend, gratuity **09** advantage, baksheesh, royal fish **10** emoluments, kitchen-fee **13** fringe benefit

**persecute**
**04** bait, hunt **05** abuse, annoy, hound, worry **06** badger, bother, harass, hassle, martyr, molest, pester, pursue **07** afflict, crucify, oppress, torment, torture **08** distress, hunt down, ill-treat, maltreat, mistreat **09** tyrannize, victimize

**persecution**
**05** abuse **07** torture, tyranny **09** martyrdom **10** dragonnade, harassment, oppression, punishment **11** crucifixion, molestation, subjugation, suppression **12** ill-treatment, maltreatment, mistreatment **13** victimization **14** discrimination

**Persephone**
**10** Proserpina

**perseverance**
**07** purpose, resolve, stamina **08** tenacity **09** assiduity, constancy, diligence, endurance **10** commitment, dedication, doggedness, resolution **11** application, persistence, persistency, pertinacity **12** stickability **13** determination, intransigence, steadfastness **14** purposefulness

**persevere**
**04** go on **05** truck **06** bash on, hang on, hold on, remain **07** carry on, persist, stick in **08** continue, plug away **09** keep going, prosecute, soldier on, stand fast, stand firm, stick at it **10** be resolute, hammer away, struggle on **11** hang in there **12** be determined, be persistent, mean business **15** stick to your guns

**Persian**
**04** Babi, Mede **05** Babee, Farsi

**persist**
**04** go on, hold, last **05** abide **06** endure, hang in, hang on, hold on, insist, keep on, linger, remain **07** carry on **08** continue, keep at it, plug away **09** hang about, keep going, persevere, soldier on, stand fast, stand firm, stick at it **10** be resolute, hang around **11** hang in there **12** be determined, be persistent

**persistence**
**04** grit **07** stamina **08** sedulity, tenacity **09** assiduity, constancy, diligence, endurance, obstinacy **10** doggedness, resolution **11** pertinacity **12** continuation, perseverance, stickability, tirelessness

13 assiduousness, determination, steadfastness

**persistent**
05 fixed 06 dogged, steady, urgent 07 endless, lasting, zealous 08 constant, diligent, enduring, obdurate, repeated, resolute, stubborn, tireless 09 assiduous, ceaseless, continual, incessant, obstinate, perpetual, steadfast, tenacious, unceasing 10 continuous, determined, persisting, purposeful, relentless, unflagging 11 importunate, intractable, never-ending, persevering, unrelenting, unremitting 12 interminable, pertinacious, stick-to-it-ive 13 indefatigable

**persistently**
10 constantly, diligently, resolutely, stubbornly, tirelessly 11 assiduously, ceaselessly, continually, incessantly, obstinately, tenaciously, unceasingly 12 continuously, interminably, relentlessly

**person**
03 bod, chi, man, per 04 body, chai, chal, fish, pers, soul, type 05 being, human, woman 06 mortal 07 someone 08 somebody 09 character 10 human being, individual

• **good person**
01 S 02 St 04 sant 05 Saint

• **individual person**
03 one

• **in person**
06 bodily, myself 08 actually 10 face to face, in the flesh, personally 13 as large as life

**persona**
04 face, mask, part, role 05 front, image 06 façade 09 character 10 public face 11 personality

**personable**
04 nice, warm 07 affable, amiable, winning 08 charming, handsome, likeable, outgoing, pleasant, pleasing 09 agreeable 10 attractive 11 good-looking, presentable

**personage**
03 VIP 04 name 05 celeb 06 bigwig, figure, worthy 07 big shot, notable 08 big noise, luminary, somebody 09 big cheese, celebrity, dignitary, headliner 11 personality 12 public figure

**personal**
03 gut, own 04 live, pers, rude 05 privy 06 bodily, secret, unique 07 abusive, hurtful, private, special 08 critical, in person, intimate, peculiar, wounding 09 exclusive, insulting, offensive, upsetting 10 derogatory, individual, in the flesh, particular, subjective 11 distinctive 12 confidential 13 disrespectful, idiosyncratic 14 characteristic

**personality**
03 VIP 04 mind, self, star 05 charm 06 figure, make-up, nature, person, psyche, temper, traits, worthy 07 notable 08 charisma, identity, selfhood, selfness 09 celebrity, character, dignitary, magnetism, personage 10 the real you 11 beastly-head, disposition, temperament 12 public figure 13 individuality

**personalize**
03 fit 04 suit 05 adapt, alter 06 adjust, modify, tailor 07 convert 09 customize, personify, transform

**personally**
05 alone 06 I think, solely 08 as I see it, I believe, in my book, in my view, in person, uniquely 09 as a slight, ourselves, privately, specially 10 for my money, if you ask me 11 exclusively, in my opinion, insultingly, offensively 12 individually, particularly, subjectively, the way I see it 13 distinctively, independently 14 confidentially

**personification**
05 image 07 epitome, essence 08 likeness 09 portrayal, semblance 10 embodiment, recreation 11 delineation, incarnation 12 quintessence 13 manifestation 14 representation

**personify**
06 embody, imbody, mirror, typify 09 epitomize, exemplify, incarnate, personize, represent, symbolize 11 hypostatize, impersonate, personalize

**personnel**
04 crew 05 staff 06 people 07 members, service, workers 08 liveware, manpower 09 employees, workforce 11 labour force 14 human resources

**perspective**
04 take, view 05 angle, scene, slant, vista 06 aspect, optics 07 balance, optical, outlook 08 attitude, peepshow, prospect, relation 09 viewpoint 10 inspection, proportion, standpoint 11 equilibrium, frame of mind, point of view 12 vantage point

**perspicacious**
04 keen 05 alert, aware, quick, sharp 06 astute, shrewd 09 judicious, observant, sagacious, sensitive, sharp-eyed 10 discerning, perceptive, percipient, responsive 11 penetrating, quick-witted 13 understanding 14 discriminating

**perspicacity**
03 wit 06 acumen, brains 07 insight 08 keenness, sagacity 09 acuteness, sharpness 10 astuteness, cleverness, shrewdness 11 discernment, penetration, percipience, perspicuity 13 sagaciousness 14 discrimination, perceptiveness

**perspicuity**
07 clarity 08 lucidity 09 clearness, limpidity, plainness, precision 10 limpidness 12 distinctness, explicitness, transparency 13 penetrability 15 intelligibility

**perspicuous**
05 clear, lucid, plain 06 limpid 07 obvious 08 apparent, distinct, explicit, manifest 11 self-evident, transparent, unambiguous 12 crystal-clear, intelligible 14 comprehensible, understandable 15 straightforward

**perspiration**
04 foam 05 sudor, suint, sweat 07 wetness 08 hidrosis, moisture 09 exudation, secretion 11 diaphoresis

**perspire**
04 drip 05 exude, sweat 06 exhale, sudate 07 secrete, swelter

**persuadable**
07 pliable 08 amenable, flexible 09 agreeable, compliant, malleable, receptive 10 susceptive 11 acquiescent, persuasible 14 impressionable

**persuade**
03 con, win 04 coax, lure, move, snow, sway, urge 05 argue, lobby, moody, plead, tempt 06 cajole, coerce, incite, induce, lead on, lean on, nobble, prompt 07 convert, prevail, satisfy, swing it, wheedle, win over 08 convince, fast-talk, get round, inveigle, lamb down, perswade, soft-soap, talk into, talk over 09 argue into, influence, sweet-talk 10 bring round 11 prevail upon, pull strings 13 bring yourself 14 put the screws on

**persuasion**
04 camp, kind, pull, sect, side, sway, view 05 clout, creed, faith, party, power 06 belief, come-on, school, urging 07 coaxing, faction, opinion, suasion 08 cajolery, coercion, pressure, soft sell 09 influence, prompting, sweet talk, viewpoint, wheedling 10 conversion, conviction, enticement, incitement, inducement, philosophy, prevailing 11 affiliation, arm-twisting, point of view, talking into, winning over 12 denomination, sweet-talking 15 school of thought

**persuasive**
05 pushy, slick, sound, valid 06 cogent, moving, potent 07 telling, weighty, winning 08 eloquent, forceful, touching 09 effective, effectual, plausible 10 compelling, convincing 11 influential 12 high-pressure, honey-tongued, smooth-spoken 13 smooth-talking, smooth-tongued

**persuasively**
08 cogently 09 plausibly 10 forcefully, powerfully 11 effectively, effectually 12 compellingly, convincingly 13 influentially

**pert**
03 gay 04 bold, coxy, flip, open 05 brash, brisk, cocky, fresh, perky,

sassy, saucy, smart, tossy **06** adroit, cheeky, cocksy, daring, jaunty, lively **07** forward **08** flippant, impudent, insolent, spirited **09** sprightly **11** flourishing, impertinent, unconcealed **12** presumptuous **13** objectionable

**pertain**
**04** long **05** apply, befit, refer **06** bear on, belong, regard, relate **07** concern **08** be part of **09** appertain, come under **10** be relevant **13** be appropriate **14** have a bearing on

**pertinacious**
**05** stiff **06** dogged, mulish, wilful **08** obdurate, perverse, resolute, stubborn **09** obstinate, tenacious **10** determined, headstrong, inflexible, persistent, purposeful, relentless, self-willed, unyielding **11** intractable, persevering **12** strong-willed **13** inquisitorial **14** uncompromising

**pertinent**
**03** apt **05** ad rem **07** apropos, fitting, germane, related **08** apposite, material, relating, relevant, suitable **10** applicable, to the point **11** appropriate

**pertness**
**04** face, sass **05** brass, cheek **08** audacity, boldness, chutzpah, rudeness **09** brashness, cockiness, freshness, impudence, insolence, sassiness, sauciness **10** brazenness, cheekiness, effrontery **11** forwardness, presumption **12** impertinence

**perturb**
◇ *anagram indicator*
**03** vex **04** faze **05** alarm, feese, feeze, phase, phese, upset, worry **06** aerate, bother, didder, dither, pheese, pheeze, rattle, ruffle **07** agitate, confuse, disturb, fluster, trouble **08** disquiet, unsettle **10** discompose, disconcert **11** make anxious **12** put the wind up

**perturbation**
**04** faze, fear, flap **05** alarm, panic, scare, shock, worry **06** didder, dismay, dither, fright, horror, terror **07** anxiety **08** disquiet, distress **10** uneasiness **11** nervousness, trepidation **12** apprehension, irregularity **13** consternation

**perturbed**
◇ *anagram indicator*
**05** upset **06** shaken, uneasy **07** alarmed, anxious, fearful, nervous, worried **08** agitated, flurried, harassed, restless, troubled **09** disturbed, flustered, unsettled **11** discomposed **12** disconcerted **13** uncomfortable

**Peru**
**02** PE **03** PER

**perusal**
**04** look, read, skim **05** check, sight, study **06** browse, glance **07** reading **08** scrutiny **10** inspection, run-through **11** examination

**peruse**
**04** read, scan, skim **05** check, study **06** browse, revise **07** examine, inspect **08** pore over **10** run through, scrutinize **11** leaf through, look through **13** glance through

**pervade**
**04** fill **05** imbue **06** affect, charge, infuse **07** diffuse, suffuse **08** permeate, saturate **09** penetrate, percolate **10** impregnate, infiltrate **11** pass through **13** spread through **14** interpenetrate

**pervasive**
**04** rife **06** common **07** diffuse, general **08** immanent **09** extensive, prevalent, universal **10** ubiquitous, widespread **11** inescapable, omnipresent

**perverse**
◇ *anagram indicator*
**03** wry **05** balky **06** cussed, donsie, thrawn, thwart, unruly, wilful **07** adverse, awkward, bolshie, crabbed, deviant, froward, peevish, stroppy, wayward **08** alarming, contrary, improper, obdurate, stubborn, worrying **09** camstairy, camsteary, difficult, incorrect, obstinate, pig-headed, senseless, unhelpful **10** camsteerie, headstrong, overthwart, rebellious, refractary, refractory, unyielding **11** disobedient, ill-tempered, intractable, obstructive, troublesome, wrong-headed **12** bloody-minded, cantankerous, cross-grained, intransigent, unmanageable, unreasonable **13** unco-operative **14** uncontrollable

**perversely**
◇ *anagram indicator*
**04** awry **09** waywardly **10** alarmingly, stubbornly, worryingly **11** obstinately, thwartingly, unhelpfully **12** cross-grained **13** obstructively **15** unco-operatively

**perversion**
◇ *anagram indicator*
**04** vice **06** misuse **08** deviance, travesty, twisting **09** depravity, deviation, kinkiness **10** aberration, corruption, debauchery, distortion, immorality, paraphilia, subversion, wickedness **11** abnormality **12** irregularity **13** exhibitionism, falsification **14** misapplication

**perversity**
◇ *anagram indicator*
**03** gee **08** obduracy **09** adversity, contumacy, obstinacy **10** cussedness, protervity, unruliness, wilfulness **11** awkwardness, frowardness, gallowsness, waywardness **12** contrariness, disobedience, stubbornness **13** intransigence, senselessness **14** rebelliousness, refractoriness **15** troublesomeness, wrong-headedness

**pervert**
◇ *anagram indicator*
**03** wry **04** perv, turn, vert, warp **05** abuse, avert, sicko, twist, wrest **06** debase, divert, garble, misuse, weirdo **07** corrupt, debauch, deflect, degrade, deprave, deviant, deviate, distort, falsify, oddball, subvert, vitiate **08** misapply **09** debauchee, misdirect, turn aside **10** degenerate, lead astray **11** misconstrue, prevaricate **12** misinterpret, misrepresent

**perverted**
◇ *anagram indicator*
**04** evil **05** kinky, pervy, sicko **06** warped, wicked **07** corrupt, debased, deviant, immoral, twisted **08** abnormal, depraved, vitiated **09** corrupted, debauched, distorted, unhealthy, unnatural

**pesky**
**06** thorny, trying, vexing **07** galling, grating, irksome, nagging **08** annoying, infernal, tiresome **09** maddening, provoking, upsetting, vexatious, worrisome **10** bothersome, confounded, disturbing, irritating **11** aggravating, displeasing, infuriating, troublesome

**pessimism**
**05** gloom **07** despair **08** cynicism, distrust, fatalism, glumness **09** defeatism, dejection, doomwatch **10** depression, gloominess, melancholy **11** despondency, Weltschmerz **12** hopelessness

**pessimist**
**05** cynic **07** doubter, killjoy, no-hoper, worrier **08** alarmist, doomsman, doomster, fatalist **09** defeatist, saturnist **10** wet blanket **11** crapehanger, crepehanger, dismal Jimmy, doomwatcher, gloom-monger, melancholic **12** doom merchant **13** prophet of doom **14** doubting Thomas

**pessimistic**
**04** glum **05** bleak, doomy **06** dismal, gloomy, morose, negate **07** cynical **08** alarmist, dejected, doubting, hopeless, negative, resigned **09** defeatist, depressed **10** depressing, despairing, despondent, fatalistic, melancholy, off-putting, suspicious **11** distrustful, downhearted **12** discouraging

**pest**
**03** bug, fly, nun **04** bane, frit, pain, pize **05** brize, curse, trial **06** blight, bother, breese, breeze, capsid, May bug, plague **07** blister, cane rat, fritfly, scourge **08** irritant, meal moth, mealy bug, nuisance, onion fly, vexation, viticide **09** annoyance, capsid bug, carrot fly, chinch bug, cornborer, May beetle, squash bug, stable fly **10** cicadellid, cockchafer, codlin moth, fowl-plague, house mouse, irritation, spider mite **11** codling moth, spermophile **13** jointed cactus, pain in the neck, red spider mite **14** American

blight, Colorado beetle, Japanese beetle **15** thorn in the flesh

**pester**
**03** bug, dun, irk, nag **04** clog, fret **05** annoy, chevy, chivy, devil, get at, hound, worry **06** badger, bother, chivvy, earwig, harass, hassle, huddle, infest, mither, moider, pick on, plague **07** besiege, disturb, moither, provoke, torment **08** doorstep, irritate **09** annoyance, beleaguer **12** rhyme to death **14** drive up the wall

**pestilence**
**04** lues **06** plague **07** cholera, disease, murrain **08** epidemic, pandemic, sickness **09** contagion, infection **11** infestation

**pestilent**
**06** deadly, vexing **07** harmful, irksome, ruinous **08** annoying, catching, diseased, infected, tiresome **09** poisonous, vexatious **10** bothersome, contagious, corrupting, infectious, irritating, pernicious **11** deleterious, destructive, detrimental, infuriating, mischievous, troublesome **12** communicable, contaminated, plague-ridden **13** disease-ridden

**pestilential**
**06** vexing **07** baneful, harmful, irksome, ruinous **08** annoying, diseased, infected, tiresome **09** pestering, poisonous **10** bothersome, contagious, detestable, infectious, irritating, pernicious **11** destructive, infuriating, troublesome **12** contaminated, plague-ridden **13** disease-ridden

**pet**
**04** cade, chou, coax, daut, dawt, dear, huff, hump, idol, kiss, neck, snog, stew, sulk, tame, tiff, tift, tout, towt **05** jewel, paddy, strop, sulks **06** caress, chosen, cosset, cuddle, dautie, dawtie, fondle, grumps, pamper, pettle, prized, smooch, stroke, temper **07** bad mood, darling, dearest, embrace, indulge, special, subdued, tantrum, the pits, trained **08** canoodle, favoured, fondling, indulged, personal, treasure **09** bad temper, cherished, favourite, preferred **10** manageable, particular **11** blue-eyed boy, teacher's pet **12** blue-eyed girl, domesticated, house-trained **14** apple of your eye

*Pets include:*

**03** cat, cow, dog, pig, rat
**04** bird, fish, goat, newt, pony
**05** goose, horse, llama, mouse, sheep
**06** alpaca, canary, donkey, ferret, gerbil, jerboa, lizard, parrot, rabbit, turtle
**07** chicken, hamster
**08** chipmunk, cyberpet, goldfish, parakeet, terrapin, tortoise
**09** guinea pig, tarantula
**10** budgerigar, chinchilla, salamander, virtual pet
**11** stick insect

*See also* **cat**; **dog**; **fish**; **horse**; **rabbit**

**peter**
**03** jar, jug **05** half-g **06** flagon

**• peter out**
**03** ebb **04** fade, fail, stop, wane **05** cease **06** go cold **07** die away, dwindle **08** diminish, taper off **09** evaporate, fizzle out **11** come to an end **13** come to nothing

**petite**
**05** bijou, dinky, small **06** dainty, little, slight **08** delicate

**petition**
**03** ask, beg, bid, sue **04** boon, plea, pray, suit, urge **05** axiom, crave, plead, press **06** adjure, appeal, prayer **07** beseech, entreat, implore, protest, request, solicit **08** call upon, entreaty **09** postulate, supplicat **10** invocation, round robin, supplicate **11** application, deprecation, memorialize **12** solicitation, supplication **14** representation

**pet name**
**03** mog, nan **04** nana **05** bunny, moggy, nanna, nanny **06** moggie **08** nickname **10** diminutive, endearment, hypocorism **11** hypocorisma

**petrel**
**05** ariel, nelly, prion **06** fulmar **07** pintado, stinker **09** stormbird **10** Cape pigeon, sea swallow **11** Procellaria

**petrified**
**04** numb **05** dazed **06** aghast, frozen **07** shocked, stunned **08** appalled, benumbed **09** horrified, stupefied, terrified **10** speechless, transfixed **11** dumbfounded, in a blue funk, scared stiff **13** having kittens, scared to death **14** horror-stricken, terror-stricken

**petrify**
**04** numb, stun **05** alarm, appal, panic, spook **06** boggle, ossify, rattle **07** horrify, stupefy, terrify **08** frighten, paralyse **09** dumbfound, fossilize **11** turn to stone **12** put the wind up

**petrol**
**03** gas, LRP **05** ethyl, juice, super **08** gasolene, gasoline

*See also* **fuel**

**petticoat**
**04** coat, slip **05** jupon, woman **06** female, kirtle **07** placket **08** balmoral, basquine, feminine **09** crinoline, wyliecoat **10** underskirt

**pettifogging**
**04** mean **05** petty **06** paltry, subtle **07** trivial **08** captious, niggling **09** casuistic, cavilling, quibbling **10** nit-picking **11** over-refined, sophistical **12** equivocating **13** hair-splitting

**pettiness**
**08** meanness **09** quibbling **10** nit-picking **12** spitefulness **15** small-mindedness

**pettish**
**05** cross, dorty, huffy, sulky **06** grumpy, tetchy, touchy **07** fretful, peevish, waspish **08** petulant, snappish **09** fractious, irritable, querulous, splenetic **11** bad-tempered, ill-humoured, thin-skinned

**petty**
**04** mean **05** minor, petit, potty, small **06** grotty, lesser, little, measly, paltry, poking, puisne, puisny, slight **07** pimping, scantle, trivial **08** grudging, niggling, picayune, piddling, piffling, spiteful, trifling **09** parochial, quibbling, scantling, secondary, small-town **10** negligible, nit-picking, parish-pump, shoestring, ungenerous **11** in a small way, inessential, small-minded, unimportant **12** contemptible, narrow-minded **13** insignificant **14** inconsiderable **15** inconsequential

**petulance**
**05** pique **06** spleen **09** bad temper, ill-humour, ill-temper, procacity, sulkiness **10** crabbiness, sullenness **11** crabbedness, peevishness, waspishness **12** irritability **13** querulousness

**petulant**
**04** sour **05** cross, mardy, moody, ratty, sulky **06** crabby, sullen, touchy, toutie, wanton **07** crabbed, forward, fretful, in a stew, peevish **08** in a paddy, snappish **09** crotchety, impatient, irritable, querulous **10** browned off, humoursome, lascivious, ungracious **11** bad-tempered, complaining, ill-humoured

**pew**
**03** box **04** seat **05** stall **08** horse box

**phalanger**
**04** tait **06** cuscus, glider, possum **07** opossum **08** Tarsipes **09** petaurist **10** honey-mouse **11** honey possum **14** flying squirrel, vulpine opossum

**phantasmagorical**
**06** unreal **07** surreal **08** ethereal, illusory **09** dreamlike, fantastic, visionary **10** chimerical, trance-like **13** hallucinatory, insubstantial, unsubstantial **14** phantasmagoric

**phantom**
**04** idol **05** ghost, spook **06** fantom, spirit, unreal, vision, wraith **07** eidolon, feature, figment, specter, spectre **08** illusion, illusory, revenant, spectral **09** imaginary **10** apparition, Scotch mist **12** Pepper's ghost **13** hallucination

**pharaoh**
**04** faro **11** river-dragon

*Pharaohs include:*

**07** Rameses
**08** Thutmose
**09** Akhenaten
**10** Hatshepsut
**11** Tut'ankhamun

**pharisaical**
**06** formal **07** preachy **09** insincere, pietistic **10** goody-goody, moralizing **12** hypocritical **13** sanctimonious, self-righteous **14** holier-than-thou

**Pharisee**
**05** fraud **06** humbug, phoney **07** pietist **09** formalist, hypocrite **10** dissembler **12** dissimulator **15** whited sepulchre

**phase**
**04** beat, faze, form, part, step, time **05** drive, morph, point, shape, spell, stage, state, worry **06** aspect, period, season **07** chapter, perturb **08** juncture, position, unsettle **09** condition **11** development

• **phase in**
**05** start **06** ease in **07** bring in **08** initiate **09** introduce **10** start using

• **phase out**
**04** stop **05** close **06** remove, wind up **07** ease off, run down **08** get rid of, taper off, wind down, withdraw **09** dispose of, eliminate, stop using, terminate

**pheasant**
**05** argus, monal **06** coucal, monaul **08** fireback, lyrebird, tragopan **09** francolin

• **brood of pheasants**
**03** eye, nid, nye **04** nide

**phenomenal**
**06** unique **07** amazing, unusual **08** singular **09** fantastic, unheard of, wonderful **10** astounding, incredible, marvellous, remarkable, stupendous **11** astonishing, exceptional, mind-blowing, sensational **12** breathtaking, mind-boggling, unbelievable, unparalleled **13** extraordinary, unprecedented **15** too good to be true

**phenomenally**
**09** amazingly **10** incredibly, remarkably **11** wonderfully **12** astoundingly, marvellously, unbelievably **13** astonishingly, exceptionally, sensationally **15** extraordinarily

**phenomenon**
**04** fact **05** event, sight **06** marvel, phenom, rarity, wonder **07** episode, miracle, prodigy **08** incident **09** curiosity, happening, sensation, spectacle **10** appearance, experience, occurrence **12** circumstance

**philander**
**05** dally, flirt, lover **08** womanize **10** fool around, play around **11** sleep around **12** have an affair, philandering, play the field

**philanderer**
**04** rake, roué, stud, wolf **05** flirt **07** dallier, Don Juan, playboy **08** Casanova **09** ladies' man, libertine, womanizer **10** lady-killer

**philanthropic**
**04** kind **06** humane **07** liberal **08** generous, selfless **09** bounteous, bountiful, unselfish **10** alms-giving, altruistic, benevolent, charitable, munificent, open-handed **11** kind-hearted **12** humanitarian **14** public-spirited

**philanthropist**
**05** donor, giver **06** backer, helper, patron **07** sponsor **08** altruist **09** alms-giver **10** benefactor **11** contributor **12** humanitarian

**philanthropy**
**04** help **06** giving **07** backing, charity **08** altruism, kindness **09** patronage **10** alms-giving, generosity, liberality **11** beneficence, benevolence, munificence, sponsorship **12** selflessness **13** bounteousness, bountifulness, social concern, unselfishness **14** open-handedness **15** humanitarianism, kind-heartedness, social awareness

**Philip**
**04** Phil

**philippic**
**05** abuse **06** attack, insult, rebuke, tirade **07** reproof **08** diatribe, harangue, reviling **09** criticism, invective, onslaught, reprimand **10** upbraiding **12** denunciation, vituperation

**Philippines**
**02** RP **03** PHL

**philistine**
**04** boor, lout **05** crass, enemy, yahoo **06** gigman, unread **07** bailiff, boorish, lowbrow **08** ignorant **09** barbarian, bourgeois, ignoramus, tasteless, unrefined, vulgarian **10** uncultured, uneducated, unlettered **12** uncultivated

**Phillip**
**04** Phil

**philologer** *see* **lexicographer**

**philosopher**
**04** guru, sage **06** expert **07** scholar, thinker **08** academic, analyser, logician, theorist **09** theorizer **12** dialectician **13** deipnosophist, metaphysicist, philosophizer **14** epistemologist

*Philosophers include:*

**04** Ayer (Sir A J), Hume (David), Joad (C E M), Kant (Immanuel), Mach (Ernst), Marx (Karl), Mill (James), Mill (John Stuart), More (Henry), Otto (Rudolf), Ryle (Gilbert), Vico (Giambattista), Weil (Simone)

**05** Bacon (Francis), Bacon (Roger), Bayle (Pierre), Benda (Julien), Bodin (Jean), Broad (Charlie Dunbar), Bruno (Giordano), Buber (Martin), Burke (Edmund), Comte (Auguste), Croce (Benedetto), Dewey (John), Dunne (John William), Frege (Gottlob), Gödel (Kurt), Hegel (Georg Wilhelm Friedrich), Hulme (T E), James (William), Locke (John), Moore (George Edward), Occam (William of), Plato, Smith (Adam), Vivés (Juan Luis)

**06** Adorno (Theodor), Anselm (St), Berlin (Sir Isaiah), Bonnet (Charles), Carnap (Rudolf), Celsus, Engels (Friedrich), Fichte (Johann Gottlieb), Goedel (Kurt), Herder (Johann Gottfried von), Hobbes (Thomas), Langer (Suzanne Knauth), Lukács (Georg), Ockham (William of), Palach (Jan), Popper (Sir Karl), Pyrrho, Sartre (Jean-Paul), Strato, Thales

**07** Aquinas (St Thomas), Bentham (Jeremy), Buridan (Jean), Derrida (Jacques), Diderot (Denis), Dilthey (Wilhelm), Edwards (Jonathan), Erasmus (Desiderius), Gentile (Giovanni), Gorgias, Haldane (Richard, Viscount), Husserl (Edmund), Hypatia, Jaspers (Karl), Leibniz (Gottfried Wilhelm), Marcuse (Herbert), Mencius, Proclus, Russell (Bertrand, Earl), Sankara, Schlick (Moritz), Spencer (Herbert), Spinoza (Baruch), Steiner (Rudolf), Tillich (Paul)

**08** Alcmaeon, Alembert (Jean le Rond d'), Averroës, Avicenna, Beauvoir (Simone de), Berkeley (Bishop George), Boethius (Anicius Manlius Severinus), Buchanan (George), Cassirer (Ernst), Cudworth (Ralph), Epicurus, Foucault (Michel), Habermas (Jürgen), Hamilton (Sir William), Hobhouse (Leonard), Longinus (Dionysius), Plotinus, Porphyry, Ram Singh, Rousseau (Jean Jacques), Sidgwick (Henry), Socrates, Spengler (Oswald)

**09** Althusser (Louis), Aristotle, Avicebrón, Bronowski (Jacob), Condorcet (Marie-Jean-Antoine-Nicolas de Caritat, Marquis de), Confucius, Descartes (René), Feuerbach (Ludwig), Heidegger (Martin), Nietzsche (Friedrich), Plekhanov (Giorgiy), Santayana (George), Schelling (Friedrich), Whitehead (Alfred North)

**10** Anaxagoras, Aristippus, Democritus, Duns Scotus (John), Empedocles, Heraclitus, Horkheimer (Max), Maimonides (Moses), Parmenides, Posidonius, Protagoras, Pythagoras, Schweitzer (Albert), Xenocrates, Xenophanes, Zeno of Elea

**11** Anaximander, Kierkegaard (Sören), Montesquieu (Charles-Louis, Baron de), Reichenbach (Hans), Shaftesbury (Anthony Ashley Cooper, Earl of), Vivekananda

**12** Merleau-Ponty (Maurice), Philo Judaeus, Schopenhauer (Arthur), Theophrastus, Wittgenstein (Ludwig), Zeno of Citium

**14** Albertus Magnus (St), Schleiermacher (Friedrich)

**15** William of Ockham

**philosophical**
**04** calm, cool, wise **05** stoic **06** placid, serene **07** erudite, learned, logical, patient, pensive, stoical **08** abstract, composed, rational, resigned **09** collected, impassive, realistic, unruffled **10** analytical, meditative, phlegmatic, reflective, thoughtful **11** theoretical, unemotional, unflappable **12** metaphysical **13** contemplative, dispassionate, imperturbable, self-possessed

*See also* **philosophy**

**philosophically**
**06** calmly **08** placidly **09** logically, patiently, stoically **10** abstractly, resignedly **11** impassively, unflappably **12** analytically **13** theoretically, unemotionally **14** metaphysically

**philosophy**
**04** view **06** reason, tenets, values, wisdom **07** beliefs, thought **08** attitude, doctrine, ideology, stoicism, thinking **09** knowledge, reasoning, viewpoint, world-view **10** principles **11** convictions, point of view

*Branches of philosophy include:*

**03** est, law
**04** mind, yoga
**05** logic, moral
**06** ethics
**07** biology, eastern, history, Sankhya, science, Vedanta
**08** axiology, language, medicine, ontology, politics, religion
**09** bioethics, economics, education, semiotics
**10** aesthetics, literature, psychology
**11** informatics, mathematics, metaphysics
**12** epistemology
**13** applied ethics, jurisprudence, phenomenology

*Philosophical schools, doctrines and theories include:*

**05** deism
**06** egoism, monism, Taoism, theism
**07** atheism, atomism, dualism, fideism, Marxism, realism, Thomism
**08** altruism, ascetism, cynicism, fatalism, feminism, hedonism, humanism, idealism, nihilism, Stoicism
**09** dogmatism, pantheism, Platonism, pluralism, solipsism
**10** absolutism, Eleaticism, empiricism, gnosticism, Kantianism, naturalism, nominalism, positivism, pragmatism, Pyrrhonism, relativism, scepticism
**11** agnosticism, determinism, Hegelianism, historicism, materialism, objectivism, rationalism, Sankhya-Yoga
**12** behaviourism, Cartesianism, Confucianism, Epicureanism, essentialism, Neoplatonism, reductionism, subjectivism
**13** antinomianism, conceptualism, descriptivism, immaterialism, neo-Kantianism, occasionalism, phenomenalism, scholasticism, structuralism
**14** existentialism, interactionism, intuitionalism, libertarianism, Nyaya-Vaisesika, prescriptivism, Pythagoreanism, sensationalism, utilitarianism, Vedanta-Mimamsa
**15** Aristotelianism, experimentalism, Frankfurt School, instrumentalism

*Philosophy terms include:*

**05** deism, logic, moral
**06** egoism, ethics, monism, theism
**07** a priori, atheism, atomism, dualism, falsafa, Marxism, realism
**08** altruism, ascetism, axiology, cynicism, fatalism, feminism, hedonism, humanism, idealism, identity, nihilism, ontology, stoicism
**09** deduction, dogmatism, induction, intuition, pantheism, Platonism, pluralism, sense data, solipsism, substance, syllogism, teleology
**10** absolutism, aesthetics, deontology, empiricism, entailment, gnosticism, Kantianism, naturalism, nominalism, positivism, pragmatism, relativism, scepticism
**11** agnosticism, a posteriori, determinism, historicism, materialism, metaphysics, objectivism, rationalism
**12** behaviourism, Confucianism, Epicureanism, epistemology, Neoplatonism, reductionism, subjectivism
**13** antinomianism, conceptualism, immaterialism, jurisprudence, neo-Kantianism, phenomenalism, phenomenology, scholasticism, structuralism
**14** existentialism, interactionism, intuitionalism, libertarianism, prescriptivism, sensationalism, utilitarianism
**15** Aristotelianism, experimentalism, instrumentalism

**phlegmatic**
**04** calm, cool **06** placid, stolid **07** stoical **08** tranquil **09** impassive, saturnine **11** indifferent, unconcerned, unemotional, unflappable **12** matter-of-fact **13** dispassionate, imperturbable **14** self-controlled

**phobia**
**04** fear **05** dread, thing **06** hang-up, hatred, horror, terror **07** anxiety, dislike **08** aversion, loathing, neurosis **09** antipathy, obsession, repulsion, revulsion **11** detestation **14** irrational fear

*Phobias include:*

**09** apiphobia, neophobia, panphobia, zoophobia
**10** acrophobia, algophobia, aquaphobia, autophobia, canophobia, cynophobia, demophobia, hodophobia, musophobia, nosophobia, pyrophobia, toxiphobia, xenophobia
**11** agoraphobia, astraphobia, cnidophobia, cyberphobia, gymnophobia, hippophobia, hydrophobia, hypnophobia, necrophobia, nyctophobia, ophiophobia, photophobia, scotophobia, tachophobia, taphephobia
**12** achluophobia, ailurophobia, belonephobia, brontophobia, entomophobia, phasmophobia, technophobia
**13** arachnophobia, arithmophobia, bacillophobia, herpetophobia
**14** anthropophobia, bacteriophobia, claustrophobia, ereuthrophobia, thalassophobia

**Phoebus**
**03** Sol, sun **05** Titan **06** Apollo, Helios

**phoenix**
**03** fum **04** fung, huma **07** paragon **12** bird of wonder

**phone**
**04** bell, buzz, call, dial, ring **06** blower, call up, mobile, ring up, tinkle **07** contact, handset **08** car phone, receiver **09** cell phone, give a bell, give a buzz, make a call, phone call, telephone **10** dog and bone, get in touch **11** give a tinkle, mobile phone **13** cordless phone

**phonetic alphabet** see **alphabet**

**phoney**
◇ *anagram indicator*
**04** fake, mock, sham **05** bogus, faker, false, fraud, hokey, pseud, put-on, quack, trick **06** ersatz, forged, humbug, pseudo, unreal **07** assumed, feigned, forgery **08** affected, impostor, spurious **09** contrived, imitation, pretender, simulated **10** fraudulent, mountebank **11** counterfeit, pretentious

**phosphorescent**
**06** bright **07** glowing, radiant **08** luminous **09** refulgent **11** luminescent, noctilucent, noctilucous

**phosphorus**
**01** P

**photocopy**
**04** copy **05** print, Xerox® **06** run off **09** duplicate, facsimile, Photostat®

**photograph**
**03** pic, pin **04** film, shot, snap, take, X-ray **05** image, Kodak®, panel, photo, piccy, print, sepia, shoot, slide, still, video **06** blow up, blow-up, record, retake **07** close-up, enlarge, montage, mug shot, picture **08** abstract, exposure, headshot, hologram, likeness, microdot, portrait, seascape, skiagram, snapshot, sun print **09** angiogram, ferrotype, karyotype,

landscape, mammogram, microgram, nephogram, photogene, photogram, radiogram, rotograph, skiagraph, visual aid, wirephoto **10** centrefold, chromatype, ferro-print, micrograph, radiograph, sun picture **11** composition, enlargement, heliochrome, platinotype, spectrogram **12** cathodograph, röntgenogram, transparency **13** capture on film, chlorobromide, daguerreotype, encephalogram **14** pyrophotograph, take a picture of **15** microphotograph, take a snapshot of

**photographer**
**07** snapper **09** cameraman, paparazzo **11** camerawoman **14** camera operator

*Photographers include:*

**03** **Ray** (Man)
**04** **Capa** (Robert), **Hill** (David Octavius), **Penn** (Irving)
**05** **Adams** (Ansel), **Arbus** (Diane), **Hardy** (Bert), **Karsh** (Yousuf), **Lange** (Dorothea), **Ritts** (Herb), **Smith** (W Eugene)
**06** **Arnold** (Eve), **Avedon** (Richard), **Bailey** (David), **Beaton** (Sir Cecil), **Brandt** (Bill), **Godwin** (Fay), **McBean** (Angus), **Miller** (Lee), **Newton** (Helmut), **Niepce** (Joseph Nicéphore), **Rankin**, **Talbot** (William Henry Fox), **Warhol** (Andy)
**07** **Brassaï**, **Cameron** (Julia Margaret), **Carroll** (Lewis), **Dodgson** (Charles Lutwidge), **Eastman** (George), **Lumière** (Auguste), **McCurry** (Steve), **Salgado** (Sebastião), **Siskind** (Aaron), **Snowdon** (Antony Armstrong-Jones, Earl of), **Waddell** (Rankin)
**08** **Daguerre** (Louis), **McCullin** (Don), **Sielmann** (Heinz), **Steichen** (Edward)
**09** **Leibovitz** (Annie), **Lichfield** (Patrick, Earl of), **Muybridge** (Eadweard James), **Rodchenko** (Alexander), **Rosenblum** (Walter), **Stieglitz** (Alfred), **Winogrand** (Garry)
**10** **Moholy-Nagy** (László)
**11** **Bourke-White** (Margaret), **Wakabayashi** (Yasuhiro)
**12** **Friese-Greene** (William)
**13** **Ducos du Hauron** (Louis)
**14** **Armstrong-Jones** (Antony), **Cartier-Bresson** (Henri)

**photographic**
**05** exact, vivid **06** filmic, minute, visual **07** graphic, natural, precise **08** accurate, detailed, faithful, lifelike **09** cinematic, pictorial, realistic, retentive **12** naturalistic

*Photographic equipment includes:*

**06** camera, tripod, viewer
**08** enlarger, light-box, stop bath
**09** camcorder, safelight
**10** fixing bath, paper drier, Vertoscope®
**11** print washer, slide viewer
**13** developer bath, enlarger timer, film projector, flash umbrella
**14** contact printer, developing tank, focus magnifier, slide projector
**15** negative carrier, print-drying rack

*Photographic accessories include:*

**04** film, lens
**06** eye-cup, filter
**07** battery, hot shoe, lens cap
**08** diffuser, disc film, flashgun, lens hood, zoom lens
**09** camera bag, flashbulb, flash card, flashcube, flash unit, macro lens, polarizer, spot meter
**10** afocal lens, lens shield, light meter, memory card, slide mount, video light, video mixer, viewfinder
**11** close-up lens, fish-eye lens, sepia filter, video editor
**12** cable release, colour filter, memory reader
**13** auxiliary lens, cartridge film, exposure meter, remote control, teleconverter, telephoto lens, wide-angle lens

**Photostat®**
**04** copy **05** print, Xerox® **06** run off **09** duplicate, facsimile, photocopy

**phrase**
**03** phr, put, say **04** cant, hook, riff, word **05** couch, frame, idiom, style, usage, utter **06** clause, cliché, mantra, remark, saying **07** comment, express, flatter, formula, mantram, present, wheedle **08** laconism, language, locution **09** catchword, formulate, pronounce, utterance **10** expression, laconicism, mondegreen **11** phraseology **12** construction, group of words, put into words **13** way of speaking **15** style of speaking

**phraseology**
**04** cant **05** argot, idiom, style **06** patois, phrase, speech, syntax **07** diction, wording, writing **08** language, parlance, phrasing **10** expression **11** terminology

**phrasing**
**05** idiom, style, words **07** diction, wordage, wording **08** language, verbiage **10** expression **11** phraseology, terminology **13** choice of words

**physical**
**04** real **05** brute, solid **06** actual, bodily, carnal, fleshy, mortal **07** earthly, fleshly, medical, somatic, spatial, visible **08** concrete, material, palpable, tangible **09** corporeal, incarnate, medicinal, wholesome **11** substantial, unspiritual **13** materialistic

**physically**
**06** bodily, really **07** visibly **08** actually, animally, tangibly **10** concretely, in your body, materially **13** substantially **15** physiologically

**physician**
**02** GP **03** doc **05** hakim, leech, medic, Paean, quack **06** doctor, healer, intern, medico **08** external, houseman, medicine **09** internist, mediciner, registrar **10** consultant, medicaster, specialist **11** physicianer **12** school doctor

*See also* **doctor**

**physics**

*Physics terms include:*

**03** gas, GUT, ion, law, QCD, QED, TOE
**04** area, atom, barn, flux, gate, heat, lens, mass, node, rule, spin, wave, WIMP, work, X-ray
**05** chaos, fermi, field, focus, force, laser, lever, light, phase, power, quark, ratio, sound, speed, SQUID, state
**06** atomic, charge, couple, energy, engine, liquid, mirror, moment, motion, optics, phonon, photon, proton, scalar, SI unit, string, theory, volume, weight
**07** circuit, density, digital, entropy, formula, gravity, inertia, neutron, nuclear, nucleus, orbital, process, statics, tension
**08** alpha ray, dynamics, electron, equation, friction, gamma ray, half-life, harmonic, infrared, molecule, momentum, neutrino, particle, polarity, pressure, rest mass, spectrum, velocity
**09** acoustics, amplitude, black body, cosmology, dimension, frequency, induction, magnetism, mechanics, Mohs scale, potential, principle, radiation, radio wave, resonance, sound wave, subatomic, substance, vibration, viscosity, white heat
**10** efficiency, elasticity, flash point, gauge boson, heavy water, Higgs boson, hydraulics, latent heat, Mach number, microwaves, reflection, refraction, relativity, resistance, separation, shear force, ultrasound, wavelength
**11** diffraction, electricity, equilibrium, evaporation, light source, oscillation, periodic law, sensitivity, temperature, ultraviolet
**12** absolute zero, acceleration, boiling point, centre of mass, critical mass, hydrostatics, interference, Kelvin effect, laws of motion, luminescence, radioisotope, spectroscopy, speed of light, standing wave, string theory, time dilation, wave property
**13** Appleton layer, beta particles, Big Bang theory, bubble-chamber, chain reaction, freezing point, hydrodynamics, incandescence, kinetic energy, kinetic theory, light emission, magnetic field, nuclear fusion, optical centre, quantum theory, radioactivity, semiconductor, supersymmetry, Thomson effect
**14** alpha particles, analogue signal,

applied physics, circuit-breaker, Coriolis effect, light intensity, nuclear fission, nuclear physics, parallel motion, states of matter, superconductor, surface tension, thermodynamics, transverse wave
**15** angular momentum, capillary action, centre of gravity, charged particle, electric current, electrodynamics, Fourier analysis, moment of inertia, perpetual motion, potential energy, specific gravity, visible spectrum

*Physicists include:*

**02** **Wu** (Chien-Shiung)
**03** **Lee** (Tsung-Dao), **Ohm** (Georg Simon)
**04** **Abbe** (Ernst), **Biot** (Jean-Baptiste), **Bohr** (Niels), **Born** (Max), **Bose** (Satyendra Nath), **Dick** (Robert Henry), **Gray** (Stephen), **Haüy** (René Just), **Hess** (Victor Francis), **Katz** (Sir Bernard), **Kerr** (John), **Land** (Edwin Herbert), **Laue** (Max Theodor Felix von), **Lenz** (Heinrich Friedrich Emil), **Mach** (Ernst), **Mott** (Sir Nevill Francis), **Néel** (Louis Eugène Félix), **Rabi** (Isidor Isaac), **Saha** (Meghnad), **Ting** (Samuel Chao Chung), **Wien** (Wilhelm), **Yang** (Chen Ning)
**05** **Aston** (Francis William), **Auger** (Pierre Victor), **Bethe** (Hans Albrecht), **Bloch** (Felix), **Bondi** (Sir Hermann), **Boyle** (Robert), **Bragg** (Sir Lawrence), **Bragg** (Sir William Henry), **Braun** (Ferdinand), **Curie** (Marie), **Curie** (Pierre), **Debye** (Peter), **Dewar** (Sir James), **Dirac** (P A M), **Dyson** (Freeman), **Esaki** (Leo), **Fermi** (Enrico), **Fuchs** (Klaus), **Gabor** (Dennis), **Gamow** (George), **Gauss** (Carl Friedrich), **Gibbs** (Josiah Willard), **Grove** (Sir William Robert), **Henry** (Joseph), **Hertz** (Heinrich Rudolf), **Higgs** (Peter), **Hooke** (Robert), **Jeans** (Sir James Hopwood), **Joule** (James Prescott), **Milne** (Edward Arthur), **Pauli** (Wolfgang), **Raman** (Sir Chandrasekhara Venkata), **Rossi** (Bruno), **Salam** (Abdus), **Segrè** (Emilio), **Stern** (Otto), **Tesla** (Nikola), **Vleck** (John Hasbrouck van), **Volta** (Alessandro Giuseppe Anastasio, Count), **Waals** (Johannes van der), **Young** (Thomas)
**06** **Ampère** (André Marie), **Bunsen** (Robert Wilhelm), **Carnot** (Sadi), **Dalton** (John), **Edison** (Thomas Alva), **Frisch** (Otto Robert), **Geiger** (Hans Wilhelm), **Glaser** (Donald Arthur), **Huxley** (Hugh Esmor), **Kelvin** (William Thomson, Lord), **Lorenz** (Ludwig Valentin), **Newton** (Sir Isaac), **Pascal** (Blaise), **Planck** (Max), **Rohrer** (Heinrich), **Stokes** (Sir George Gabriel), **Taylor** (Sir Geoffrey Ingram), **Teller** (Edward), **Wigner** (Eugene Paul), **Wilson** (Robert), **Zwicky** (Fritz)
**07** **Alferov** (Zhores I), **Alvarez** (Luis Walter), **Bednorz** (Georg), **Broglie** (Louis-Victor Pierre Raymond de), **Charles** (Jacques), **Compton** (Arthur Holly), **Coulomb** (Charles Augustin de), **Doppler** (Christian Johann), **Eastman** (George), **Faraday** (Michael), **Feynman** (Richard Phillips), **Fresnel** (Augustin Jean), **Galilei** (Galileo), **Galileo**, **Glashow** (Sheldon Lee), **Goddard** (Robert Hutchings), **Hawking** (Stephen), **Huygens** (Christiaan), **Langley** (Samuel Pierpont), **Lorentz** (Hendrik Antoon), **Marconi** (Guglielmo, Marchese), **Maxwell** (James Clerk), **Meitner** (Lise), **Oersted** (Hans Christian), **Peierls** (Sir Rudolf Ernst), **Penzias** (Arno Allan), **Poisson** (Siméon Denis), **Réaumur** (René Antoine Ferchault de), **Richter** (Burton), **Röntgen** (Wilhelm Konrad von), **Rotblat** (Sir Joseph), **Seaborg** (Glen Theodore), **Szilard** (Leo), **Thomson** (Sir J J), **Vernier** (Pierre)
**08** **Ångström** (Anders Jonas), **Appleton** (Sir Edward Victor), **Avogadro** (Amedeo), **Beaufort** (Sir Francis), **Chadwick** (Sir James), **Clausius** (Rudolf), **De Forest** (Lee), **Delbrück** (Max), **Einstein** (Albert), **Foucault** (Jean Bernard Léon), **Gell-Mann** (Murray), **Langevin** (Paul), **Lemaître** (Georges Henri), **Millikan** (Robert Andrews), **Mulliken** (Robert Sanderson), **Oliphant** (Sir Mark), **Regnault** (Henri Victor), **Sakharov** (Andrei), **Shockley** (William Bradford), **Tomonaga** (Sin-Itiro), **Van Allen** (James Alfred), **Weinberg** (Steven)
**09** **Aristotle**, **Bartholin** (Erasmus), **Becquerel** (Antoine Henri), **Birkeland** (Kristian Olaf Bernhard), **Boltzmann** (Ludwig), **Cavendish** (Henry), **Cherenkov** (Pavel), **Cockcroft** (Sir John Douglas), **Gay-Lussac** (Joseph Louis), **Heaviside** (Oliver), **Helmholtz** (Hermann von), **Michelson** (Albert Abraham)
**10** **Anaximenes**, **Fahrenheit** (Daniel), **Heisenberg** (Werner Karl), **Rutherford** (Ernest, Lord), **Torricelli** (Evangelista), **Weizsäcker** (Carl Friedrich, Baron von), **Wheatstone** (Sir Charles), **Xenocrates**
**11** **Chamberlain** (Owen), **Joliot-Curie** (Frédéric), **Joliot-Curie** (Irène), **Leeuwenhoek** (Antoni van), **Oppenheimer** (Robert), **Schrödinger** (Erwin), **Tsiolkovsky** (Konstantin), **Van de Graaff** (Robert Jemison)
**13** **Chandrasekhar** (Subrahmanyan)

## physiognomy

**03** mug **04** dial, face, look, phiz **05** clock **06** aspect, kisser, phizog, visage **07** visnomy **08** features, fisnomie, phisnomy, visnomie **09** character **11** countenance, craniognomy

## physiology

*Physiologists include:*

**04** **Best** (Charles Herbert), **Dale** (Sir Henry Hallett), **Hess** (Walter Rudolf)
**05** **Hubel** (David Hunter), **Kühne** (Wilhelm), **Lower** (Richard), **Marey** (Etienne-Jules), **Mayow** (John), **Prout** (William), **Yalow** (Rosalyn)
**06** **Adrian** (Edgar Douglas, Lord), **Bordet** (Jules), **Cannon** (Walter Bradford), **Haller** (Albrecht von), **Huxley** (Sir Andrew), **Ludwig** (Karl), **Müller** (Johannes Peter), **Pavlov** (Ivan), **Pincus** (Gregory Goodwin)
**07** **Banting** (Sir Frederick Grant), **Bayliss** (Sir William), **Beddoes** (Thomas Lovell), **Bernard** (Claude), **Borelli** (Giovanni Alfonso), **Diamond** (Jared Mason), **Galvani** (Luigi), **Haldane** (John Scott), **Helmont** (Johannes Baptista van), **Hodgkin** (Sir Alan Lloyd), **Schwann** (Theodor)
**08** **Flourens** (Pierre Jean Marie), **Magendie** (François), **Mariotte** (Edmé), **Meyerhof** (Otto Fritz), **Purkinje** (Jan Evangelista), **Starling** (Ernest Henry)
**09** **Blakemore** (Colin), **Dutrochet** (Henri), **Einthoven** (Willem), **Helmholtz** (Hermann von)
**11** **Sherrington** (Sir Charles Scott)

## physique

**04** body, form **05** build, frame, set-up, shape **06** figure, make-up **09** structure **12** constitution

## pi

**03** pie, pye **05** pious **09** confusion, religious **13** sanctimonious

## pianist

*Pianists include:*

**02** **Ax** (Emmanuel)
**04** **Bush** (Alan), **Cole** (Nat 'King'), **Hess** (Dame Myra), **John** (Sir Elton), **Lupu** (Radu), **Monk** (Thelonious Sphere), **Wild** (Earl)
**05** **Alkan**, **Arrau** (Claudio), **Basie** (Count), **Beach** (Mrs H H A), **Blake** (Eubie), **Bolet** (Jorge), **Borge** (Victor), **Bülow** (Hans), **Corea** (Chick), **Evans** (Bill), **Evans** (Gil), **Field** (John), **Friml** (Rudolf), **Gould** (Glenn), **Hallé** (Sir Charles), **Harty** (Sir Hamilton), **Henri** (Florence), **Hines** (Earl), **Joyce** (Eileen), **Lewis** (Jerry Lee), **Liszt** (Franz), **Nyman** (Michael), **Ogdon** (John Andrew Howard), **Szell** (George), **Tatum** (Art), **Tovey** (Sir Donald), **Weber** (Carl Maria von)
**06** **Albert** (Eugen d'), **Arnaud** (Yvonne), **Atwell** (Winifred), **Busoni** (Ferruccio), **Chopin** (Frédéric), **Cortot** (Alfred), **Cramer** (Johann), **Curzon** (Sir Clifford), **Czerny** (Karl), **Domino** (Fats), **Dussek** (Jan), **Garner** (Errol), **Hummel** (Johann), **Joplin** (Scott), **Kenton** (Stan), **Kissin**

(Evgeny), **Koppel** (Herman D), **Lamond** (Frederic), **Levine** (James), **Martin** (Frank), **Morton** (Jelly Roll), **Powell** (Bud), **Schiff** (András), **Serkin** (Rudolf), **Sitsky** (Larry), **Stoker** (Richard), **Taylor** (Cecil), **Tracey** (Stan), **Turina** (Joaquín), **Waller** (Fats), **Wilson** (Teddy)

**07** **Albéniz** (Isaac), **Bennett** (Sir William), **Bentzon** (Niels), **Brendel** (Alfred), **Brubeck** (Dave), **Charles** (Ray), **Goodman** (Isador), **Hancock** (Herbie), **Ibrahim** (Abdullah), **Johnson** (James P), **Kentner** (Louis), **Lipatti** (Dinu), **Malcolm** (George), **Mathias** (William), **Matthay** (Tobias), **Medtner** (Nikolai), **Perahia** (Murray), **Richter** (Svyatoslav), **Solomon**, **Sorabji** (Kaikhosru), **Taneyev** (Sergei), **Vaughan** (Sarah)

**08** **Argerich** (Martha), **Bronfman** (Yefim), **Browning** (John), **Clementi** (Muzio), **Dohnanyi** (Ernst), **Fou Ts'ong**, **Franklin** (Aretha), **Godowsky** (Leopold), **Grainger** (Percy), **Henschel** (Sir George), **Horowitz** (Vladimir), **Leighton** (Kenneth), **Lhévinne** (Josef), **Pachmann** (Vladimir de), **Peterson** (Oscar), **Richards** (Henry), **Schnabel** (Artur), **Schumann** (Clara), **Scriabin** (Aleksandr), **Skriabin** (Aleksandr), **Thalberg** (Sigismond), **Williams** (Mary Lou)

**09** **Ashkenazy** (Vladimir), **Barenboim** (Daniel), **Bernstein** (Leonard), **Butterley** (Nigel), **Ellington** (Duke), **Gieseking** (Walter), **Henderson** (Fletcher), **Landowska** (Wanda), **MacDowell** (Edward), **Moscheles** (Ignaz), **Stevenson** (Ronald), **Westbrook** (Mike)

**10** **de Larrocha** (Alicia), **Gottschalk** (Louis), **Moszkowski** (Moritz), **Paderewski** (Ignacy), **Rubinstein** (Anton), **Rubinstein** (Artur), **Scharwenka** (Xaver)

**11** **Farren-Price** (Ronald), **Mitropoulos** (Dimitri), **Reizenstein** (Franz)

**12** **Michelangeli** (Arturo), **Moiseiwitsch** (Benno), **Shostakovich** (Maxim)

**13** **Little Richard**

---

## piano

**01** p **05** grand **06** flügel, joanna **07** upright **08** music box **09** baby grand, semi-grand **12** boudoir grand, concert grand

## pick

**04** best, bite, cull, hack, open, peck, pull, wale **05** begin, cause, crack, cream, elect, élite, fix on, go for, pique, pluck, prize, start **06** choice, choose, favour, flower, gather, lead to, nibble, opt for, option, pickle, pilfer, prefer, prompt, select, take in **07** collect, harvest, mandrel, mandril, produce, provoke **08** choicest, decide on, decision, plectrum, plump for, settle on **09** break open, force open, prise open, selection, single out **10** give rise to, preference **14** crème de la crème, make up your mind

### • pick at

**04** peck **06** nibble **07** toy with **08** play with

### • pick off

**03** hit **04** kill **05** shoot, snipe **06** detach, fire at, remove, strike **07** gun down, pull off, take out **08** take away

### • pick on

**03** nag **04** bait **05** blame, bully, get at **06** needle **07** torment **09** criticize, have a go at, persecute, victimize **13** find fault with

### • pick out

**04** cull, sort, spot **05** fix on, go for **06** choose, favour, notice, opt for, prefer, select, single **07** discern, make out **08** decide on, hand-pick, perceive, separate, settle on **09** recognize, single out, tell apart **11** distinguish **12** discriminate **14** make up your mind

### • pick up

◇ *reversal down indicator*

**03** buy, get, nab **04** bust, find, gain, go on, hear, lift, nick, peck, pull, tong **05** catch, fetch, glean, grasp, hoist, learn, pinch, raise, rally, run in **06** arrest, collar, detect, gather, master, obtain, perk up, resume, take in, take up **07** acquire, call for, carry on, collect, improve, receive, recover **08** continue, contract, discover, purchase **09** apprehend, get better, get to know, give a lift, give a ride **10** begin again, chance upon, come across, cop off with, get off with, go down with, start again **11** make headway **12** make progress **13** become ill with **15** take into custody

## picket

**03** peg **04** pale, pike, post **05** guard, rebel, spike, stake, watch **06** paling, patrol, piquet, sentry **07** boycott, enclose, lookout, outpost, picquet, protest, striker, upright **08** blockade, objector, picketer, surround **09** dissident, protester, stanchion **11** demonstrate **12** demonstrator **15** go on a picket line

## pickings

**04** loot, take **05** booty, gravy, yield **06** spoils **07** plunder, profits, returns, rewards **08** earnings, proceeds

## pickle

◇ *anagram indicator*

**03** fix, jam **04** bind, cure, mess, peck, pick, salt, spot **05** achar, pinch, sauce, souse, steep **06** crisis, muddle, pilfer, plight, relish, scrape **07** chutney, dilemma, put down, straits, vinegar **08** conserve, cucumber, exigency, hot water, marinade, preserve, quandary **09** condiment, seasoning, tight spot **10** difficulty, flavouring, piccalilli **11** predicament

## pick-me-up

**05** boost, tonic **06** fillip **07** cordial **08** roborant, stimulus **09** stimulant **11** refreshment, restorative **12** shot in the arm

## pickpocket

**03** dip **04** bung, file, wire **05** diver, thief **06** dipper, nipper **07** whizzer **08** cly-faker, cutpurse, snatcher **09** pick-purse **11** bagsnatcher

## pick-up

**02** PU **03** ute, van **04** gain, rise **05** float, lorry, rally, truck, wagon **06** bakkie, growth, reform **07** advance, headway, upswing, utility **08** increase, progress, recovery, revision **09** amendment, humbucker, reception, upgrading **10** betterment, correction, rectifying **11** development, enhancement, furtherance, improvement, modernizing, reformation **12** amelioration, utility truck **13** rectification **14** rehabilitation, utility vehicle

## picky

**05** faddy, fussy **06** choosy **07** finicky **08** exacting **09** selective **10** fastidious, particular, pernickety **11** persnickety **14** discriminating

## picnic

**05** cinch, gipsy, gypsy **06** doddle, junket, outing **08** clambake, pushover, tailgate, walkover, waygoose **09** excursion, wasegoose, wayzgoose **10** child's play **11** outdoor meal, piece of cake **13** a kettle of fish, fête champêtre

## pictorial

**05** vivid **06** scenic **07** graphic **08** striking **09** schematic **10** expressive, in pictures **11** illustrated, picturesque **12** diagrammatic **13** in photographs

## picture

**03** pic, see **04** draw, film, show, tale **05** flick, movie, paint, story **06** appear, cinema, depict, flicks, movies, report **07** account, epitome, essence, imagine, outlook, portray **08** conceive, describe, envisage, envision, exemplar **09** archetype, delineate, depiction, multiplex, narrative, portrayal, represent, reproduce, semblance, situation, visualize **10** call to mind, embodiment, illustrate, impression, similitude **11** delineation, description, film theatre **12** picture-house, quintessence **13** motion picture, picture-palace **15** personification

*Pictures include:*

**04** E-fit®, icon, ikon, snap

**05** cameo, image, mural, pin-up, plate, print, slide, still, study

**06** bitmap, canvas, design, doodle, effigy, fresco, kit-cat, mosaic, sketch, veduta

**07** cartoon, collage, diptych, drawing, etching, modello, montage, mugshot, tableau, tracing, vanitas

**08** abstract, anaglyph, graffiti, graphics, kakemono, likeness,

monotype, negative, painting, panorama, Photofit®, portrait, snapshot, tapestry, transfer, triptych, vignette
**09** bricolage, engraving, identikit, landscape, miniature, old master, oleograph, still life
**10** altarpiece, caricature, photograph, silhouette
**11** oil painting, trompe l'oeil, watercolour
**12** illustration, photogravure, reproduction, self-portrait, transparency
**13** passport photo
**14** action painting, cabinet picture, representation

• **get the picture**
**03** see **05** get it, grasp **06** follow, take in **07** catch on, latch on **08** cotton on, tumble to **10** comprehend, get the idea, understand **11** get the point **13** get the message
• **put someone in the picture**
**04** tell **06** clue up, fill in, inform, notify, update **07** explain **10** keep posted **11** communicate

**pictures**
**03** pix

**picturesque**
**05** vivid **06** lovely, pretty, quaint, scenic, vulgar **07** graphic, idyllic **08** charming, pleasant, pleasing, romantic, striking **09** beautiful, colourful, depictive **10** attractive, delightful, impressive **11** descriptive

**piddling**
**03** low **04** mean, poor, puny **05** minor, petty, small, sorry **06** meagre, measly, paltry, slight **07** trivial **08** derisory, piffling, trifling, wretched **09** miserable, worthless **10** negligible **11** unimportant **12** contemptible **13** inconsiderate, insignificant

**pie**
◇ *anagram indicator*
**02** pi **03** mag, pye **04** flan, pâté, Pica, piet, pyat, pyet, pyot, tart **05** madge, pasty, patty, pirog **06** chewet, maggie, magpie, pastry **07** cobbler, floater **08** pandowdy **09** chatterer, confusion, coulibiac, croquante, vol-au-vent **10** Florentine, koulibiaca, tarte tatin **11** Banbury cake, oyster-patty
• **pie in the sky**
**05** dream **06** hot air, mirage, notion **07** fantasy, reverie, romance **08** daydream, delusion **11** jam tomorrow **13** castle in Spain **14** castle in the air

**piebald**
**04** pied **05** pinto **06** motley **07** dappled, flecked, mottled, spotted **08** brindled, skewbald, speckled **10** variegated **13** black and white, heterogeneous

**piece**
◇ *anagram indicator*
◇ *hidden indicator*
**01** b, k, n, p, q, r **03** bar, bit, cut, die, dod, écu, end, gun, man, nip, pce **04** bite, chip, daud, dawd, dice, hunk, item, king, lump, opus, part, pawn, peso, rook, slab, snip, solo, unit, work, zack **05** block, cameo, chunk, crown, crumb, dumka, flake, fleck, patch, queen, quota, scrap, shard, share, sherd, shred, slice, small, speck, stick, story, strip, study, wedge **06** bishop, bittie, castle, dollop, jitney, knight, length, lesson, morsel, offcut, report, review, sample, scliff, skliff, sliver, tidbit, titbit **07** allegro, article, combine, element, example, intrada, mammock, mummock, peeling, portion, quarter, scaling, section, segment, snippet **08** creation, division, fraction, fragment, instance, louis-d'or, mouthful, nocturne, particle, picayune, quantity, specimen, splinter **09** allotment, component, dandiprat, dandyprat, interlude, truncheon **10** allegretto, allocation, comedietta, embodiment, percentage, production, smithereen **11** composition, constituent **12** illustration **14** morceau de salon **15** exemplification
• **all in one piece**
**05** whole **06** entire, intact, unhurt **08** complete, integral, unbroken, unharmed **09** undamaged, uninjured
• **go to pieces**
**05** break **06** blow up **07** break up, crack up, go to pot **08** collapse **09** break down, fall apart **10** be overcome **11** lose control **14** have a breakdown
• **in pieces**
◇ *anagram indicator*
**05** kaput **06** broken, in bits, ruined **07** damaged, smashed **09** shattered **13** disintegrated, in smithereens
• **piece together**
**03** fit, fix **04** join, mend **05** patch, unite **06** attach, repair **07** compose, restore **08** assemble **10** rhapsodize **11** put together
• **pull to pieces, tear to pieces**
**03** nag, pan **04** slag, slam **05** blame, knock, slate, snipe **06** attack, tear up **07** censure, condemn, mammock, rubbish, run down, slag off **08** badmouth, denounce **09** criticize, dismember **10** come down on, go to town on **11** pick holes in **12** disapprove of, put the boot in, tear to shreds **13** find fault with, tear a strip off **15** do a hatchet job on

**pièce de résistance**
**05** jewel, joint, prize **09** showpiece **10** magnum opus, masterwork **11** chef-d'oeuvre, masterpiece

**piecemeal**
**06** patchy, slowly **07** partial **08** bit by bit, discrete, fitfully, in detail, sporadic **09** by degrees, dismember, partially, scattered **10** parcel-wise **11** at intervals, fragmentary, interrupted **12** intermittent, unsystematic **14** intermittently, little by little **15** in dribs and drabs

**pied**
**04** piet, pyat, pyet, pyot **06** motley **07** brindle, dappled, flecked, mottled, piebald, spotted **08** brindled, skewbald, streaked **09** irregular **10** variegated **12** varicoloured **13** multicoloured, parti-coloured

**pier**
**04** dock, mole, pile, post, quay **05** jetty, jutty, wharf **06** column, pillar **07** slipway, support, upright **08** buttress **09** Swiss roll **10** breakwater **12** landing-stage **15** clustered column

**pierce**
◇ *insertion indicator*
**03** jag, peg, ren, rin, run, tap **04** barb, bore, fill, gore, hurt, move, nail, pain, pike, pink, pith, prog, rive, slap, stab **05** drift, drill, enter, gride, gryde, lance, perce, perse, prick, probe, punch, spear, spike, spile, stake, steek, stick, sting, thirl, touch **06** broach, cleave, engore, gimlet, impale, launce, launch, needle, pearce, percen, skewer, thrill, thrust **07** bayonet, emperce, light up **08** empierce, puncture, transfix **09** lancinate, penetrate, perforate, stick into **10** run through **11** pass through, perforation, transpierce **12** burst through **13** cut to the quick, thrill through

**pierced**
**05** grypt, stung **06** pearst, pierst, pinked **07** impaled, pertuse **08** pertused **09** perforate, pertusate, punctured **10** fenestrate, foraminous, penetrated, perforated **11** fenestrated, foraminated

**piercing**
◇ *insertion indicator*
**03** raw **04** cold, keen, loud **05** acute, alert, sharp **06** Arctic, astute, biting, bitter, fierce, frosty, severe, shrewd, shrill, wintry **07** extreme, intense, numbing, painful, probing **08** freezing, perceant, shooting, stabbing **09** agonizing, searching, thrillant **10** discerning, lacerating, perceptive **11** ear-piercing, high-pitched, penetrating, penetrative, sharp-witted **12** ear-splitting, excruciating

**piercingly**
**06** keenly, loudly **07** alertly, sharply, shrilly **08** astutely, bitterly, fiercely, severely **09** extremely, intensely, numbingly, painfully **11** agonizingly **12** discerningly **13** penetratingly **14** excruciatingly

**piety**
**04** fear, pity **05** faith **07** respect **08** devotion, holiness, religion, sanctity **09** deference, fear of God, godliness, piousness, reverence **10** devoutness **11** dutifulness, saintliness **12** spirituality **13** religiousness

**piffle**
**03** rot **04** blah, bosh, bull, bunk, cock, guff, tosh **05** balls, hooey, trash, tripe **06** bunkum, drivel, trifle **07** baloney,

eyewash, hogwash, rhubarb, rubbish, twaddle **08** malarkey, nonsense, tommyrot **09** bull's wool, moonshine, poppycock **10** balderdash, codswallop **11** tarradiddle

**piffling**
**04** idle **05** empty, minor, petty, silly, small **06** paltry, slight **07** foolish, shallow, trivial **08** trifling **09** frivolous, worthless **10** inadequate, negligible **11** superficial, unimportant **12** insufficient **13** insignificant **14** inconsiderable **15** inconsequential

**pig**
**03** elt, hog, sow **04** boar, boor, cram, gilt, runt, slip, wolf, yelt **05** beast, brute, feast, gorge, piggy, scoff, shoat, shote, snarf, stuff, swine **06** animal, gobble, guffie, guzzle, piggie, piglet, porker, sucker, weaner **07** Anthony, glutton, grunter, guzzler, monster, pigling, roaster, tantony **08** gourmand, grumphie, porkling, potsherd, wild boar **09** policeman **10** greedy guts **11** earthenware, gormandizer **13** Captain Cooker

*Pigs include:*

**05** Duroc
**07** Old Spot
**08** landrace, Pietrain, Tamworth, wild boar
**09** Berkshire, Hampshire, Yorkshire
**10** Large White, potbellied, saddleback
**11** Middle White
**15** Chinese Meishian

**pigeon**
**03** nun, owl **04** barb, clay, dove, girl, gull, hoax, kuku, rock, ront, ruff, runt, spot **05** goura, homer, piper, quest, quist, ronte, squab, wonga **06** affair, culver, cushat, pouter, queest, quoist, roller, turbit, zoozoo **07** carrier, concern, cropper, fantail, jacinth, jacobin, laugher, manumea, pintado, tumbler **08** business, capuchin, horseman, ringdove, rock dove, squealer **09** archangel, solitaire, trumpeter **10** bronze-wing, Didunculus, wonga-wonga **12** mourning dove

**pigeonhole**
**03** box, tag **04** file, slot, sort **05** class, defer, label, niche, place **06** locker, put off, shelve **07** cubicle, section **08** category, classify, postpone **09** catalogue, cubby-hole **10** categorize **11** alphabetize, compartment **14** classification

**pigeon pea**
**03** dal **04** daal, dahl, dhal **05** dholl

**pig-headed**
**06** mulish, stupid, wilful **07** froward **08** contrary, perverse, stubborn **09** obstinate **10** bull-headed, headstrong, inflexible, self-willed, unyielding **11** intractable, stiff-necked, wrong-headed **12** intransigent

**piglet** *see* **pig**

**pigment**
**03** dye, hue **04** tint **05** paint, stain **06** colour, piment **08** tincture **09** colouring

*Pigments include:*

**03** hem
**04** haem, heme
**05** henna, ochre, sepia, smalt, umber
**06** bister, bistre, cobalt, cyanin, lutein, madder, sienna, zaffer, zaffre
**07** carmine, etiolin, gamboge, melanin, sinopia, turacin
**08** cinnabar, luteolin, orpiment, rose-pink, verditer, viridian
**09** anthocyan, bilirubin, colcothar, Indian red, lamp-black, lithopone, phycocyan, quercetin, zinc white
**10** Berlin blue, biliverdin, Chinese red, chlorophyl, green earth, lipochrome, madder-lake, Paris-green, pearl white, rhodophane, terre verte, vermillion
**11** anthochlore, anthocyanin, chlorophyll, King's-yellow, phycocyanin, phycophaein, phytochrome, ultramarine, Venetian red
**12** anthoxanthin, Cappagh-brown, Chinese white, chrome yellow, Naples-yellow, phaeomelanin, phycoxanthin, Prussian blue, turacoverdin, Tyrian purple, xanthopterin
**13** cadmium yellow, phycoerythrin, Scheele's green, titanium white, xanthopterine
**15** purple of Cassuis

*See also* **colour**; **dye**

**pike**
**03** gar, ged **04** jack, luce, pick, toll **05** speed **06** renege **07** garfish, walleye **08** jackfish, pickerel, turnpike **11** Lepidosteus

*Pikes include:*

**03** Esk, Red
**04** Cold, High
**05** Heron, Rispa
**06** Causey, Kidsty, Ullock
**07** Rossett, Scafell
**08** Kentmere, Langdale
**09** Angletarn, Grisedale, Sheffield
**10** Dollywagon, Nethermost

**pilaster**
**04** anta

**pile**
**03** bar, fur, jam, nap **04** a lot, beam, bing, bomb, cock, down, fuzz, hair, heap, load, lots, mass, mint, pack, post, rush, shag, tons, wool **05** amass, crowd, crush, flock, flood, fluff, heaps, hoard, loads, mound, plush, stack, store **06** bundle, charge, column, fibres, gather, heap up, masses, oodles, packet, piling, riches, stacks, stream, wealth **07** build up, collect, edifice, fortune, mansion, rouleau, squeeze, stack up, support, surface, texture, threads, upright **08** assemble, big bucks, hundreds, lashings, millions, mountain **09** arrowhead, megabucks, stockpile, thousands **10** accumulate, a great deal, assemblage, assortment, collection, foundation, quantities **11** loadsamoney, soft surface **12** accumulation **13** large building, large quantity

• **pile it on**
**06** overdo, stress **07** lay it on, magnify **08** overplay **09** dramatize, emphasize, overstate **10** exaggerate **12** lay it on thick **13** make too much of, overdramatize, overemphasize, pile it on thick

• **pile up**
**03** big **04** deck, grow, soar **07** mount up **08** escalate, increase, multiply **10** accumulate

**pile-up**
**04** bump **05** crash, prang, smash, wreck **07** smash-up **08** accident **09** collision

**pilfer**
**03** bag, lag, mag, nim, rob **04** blag, lift, mill, nick, pick, pull, smug, whip **05** boost, filch, heist, hoist, miche, mooch, mouch, pinch, sneak, steal, swipe **06** finger, nobble, pickle, snitch, thieve **07** purloin, snaffle **08** knock off, peculate, shoplift **10** run off with **12** make away with

**pilfering** *see* **theft**

**pilgrim**
**05** hadji **06** palmer **07** devotee **08** crusader, newcomer, wanderer, wayfarer **09** peregrine, traveller **10** worshipper

**pilgrimage**
**03** haj **04** hadj, hajj, tour, trip **06** wander **07** crusade, journey, mission **08** lifetime **10** expedition **13** peregrination

**pill**
**03** dex, tab **04** ball, husk, peel **05** bolus, upper **06** bomber, cachou, caplet, doctor, pellet, pilula, pilule, tablet **07** capsule, globule, lozenge, plunder **08** goofball, microdot, spansule **09** blackball **10** integument, number nine **12** multivitamin **13** pain in the neck

**pillage**
**03** rob **04** loot, peel, raid, raze, sack **05** booty, rifle, spoil, strip **06** maraud, rapine, ravage, spoils **07** despoil, plunder, ransack, robbery, seizure **08** freeboot, harrying, spoliate **09** depredate, marauding, vandalize **10** spoliation **11** depredation, devastation

**pillar**
**03** lat, man **04** goal, mast, pier, pile, pole, post, prop, rock **05** shaft, stack, stoop, stoup **06** cippus, column **07** bastion, obelisk, respond, support, telamon, trumeau, upright **08** baluster, caryatid, gendarme, lamppost, mainstay, monolith, pilaster, stalwart, standard **09** pillarbox, sandspout,

stanchion **12** lamp-standard **15** tower of strength

**pillory**
**04** cang, lash, mock **05** brand **06** attack, cangue, show up **07** laugh at, tumbrel, tumbril **08** denounce, ridicule **09** criticize **10** little-ease, stigmatize **11** cast a slur on, pour scorn on **13** hold up to shame

**pillow**
**03** bed, cod **04** rest **07** bolster, cushion **08** headrest, pulvinar

**pillowcase**
**04** bear, beer, bere, slip

**pilot**
**03** fly, run **04** crew, lead, test **05** drive, flier, flyer, guide, model, prune, steer, trial **06** airman, direct, George, handle, leader, manage, sample **07** aircrew, aviator, captain, conduct, control, hobbler, operate, shipman **08** airwoman, aviatrix, coxswain, director, governor, helmsman, lodesman, navigate **09** aviatress, commander, manoeuvre, navigator, rocketeer, steersman **10** cowcatcher, cropduster **12** experimental, first officer **14** flight engineer

**pimp**
**04** bawd, hoon, mack **05** ponce **06** broker, pandar, pander **07** hustler, procure **08** fancy man, mackerel, panderer, procurer **09** solicitor **11** fleshmonger, whoremonger

**pimpernel**
**06** burnet **09** brookweed, wincopipe, wink-a-peep **12** weather glass **14** shepherd's glass

**pimple**
**03** zit **04** boil, quat, spot **05** botch, plook, plouk, whelk **06** button, milium, papula, papule, rum-bud **07** bubukle, pustule **08** swelling **09** blackhead, carbuncle, whitehead **10** rum-blossom

**pin**
**03** fix, lay, leg, nog, peg, put **04** axle, bolt, clip, hold, join, nail, peak, stud, tack **05** affix, dowel, drift, pitch, pivot, place, preen, press, rivet, screw, spike, stage, stick, wrist **06** attach, brooch, cotter, degree, fasten, impute, pintle, secure, skewer, staple **07** ascribe, enclose, gudgeon, skittle, trenail **08** chessman, fastener, hold down, hold fast, restrain, treenail **09** attribute, constrain, thumbtack **10** immobilize

**• pin down**
**03** peg **04** make, nail **05** force, press **06** compel, define **07** specify **08** hold down, hold fast, identify, nail down, pinpoint, restrain **09** constrain, determine **10** pressurize **15** put your finger on

**pinafore**
**04** brat, tire **05** apron, pinny **06** jumper, pinner, pinnie **07** gym slip, overall, save-all **08** gym tunic

**pincers**
**06** forfex **07** forceps, nippers **08** pinchers, tweezers **10** Jaws of Life®

**pinch**
◇ *containment indicator*
**03** bag, bit, jot, nab, nip, tad **04** bite, book, bust, carp, dash, grip, hurt, lace, lift, mite, nail, nick, nirl, pook, pouk, save, shut, spot, tait, tate, whip **05** catch, chack, check, cramp, crush, filch, grasp, gripe, pleat, press, pugil, run in, seize, sneap, snuff, speck, steal, stint, swipe, taste, touch, trace, tweak, wring **06** arrest, budget, collar, crisis, detain, eke out, hamper, harass, narrow, pick up, pilfer, pincer, pull in, snatch, sneesh, stress, twinge, twitch **07** capture, confine, cut back, purloin, smidgen, soupçon, squeeze **08** compress, encroach, half-inch, hardship, knock off, peculate, pressure, restrict, sneeshan, sneeshin, souvenir **09** economize, emergency, sneeshing **10** difficulty **11** appropriate, predicament, walk off with **13** keep costs down, scrape a living, scrimp and save **14** live on the cheap **15** tighten your belt

**• at a pinch**
**11** if necessary **13** in an emergency

**• feel the pinch**
**06** be poor **12** hit a bad patch **13** have a hard time **14** be short of money, scratch a living **15** strike a bad patch, tighten your belt

**pinched**
**04** pale, thin, worn **05** drawn, gaunt, peaky **07** haggard, starved **08** careworn, narrowed, strained **12** straightened

**pine**
**04** ache, fade, fret, hone, long, sigh, wish **05** crave, dwine, mourn, yearn **06** desire, grieve, hanker, hunger, repine, thirst, weaken **08** languish **09** waste away

*Pine trees include:*

**03** nut, red
**04** blue, Huon, jack
**05** Chile, kauri, pinon, Scots, stone, sugar, white
**06** arolla, celery, cembra, Jersey, Korean, limber, Paraná, Scotch, spruce
**07** Amboina, Chilean, cluster, Mexican, radiata
**08** Japanese, Jeffrey's, knobcone, lacebark, loblolly, longleaf, mountain, Pandanus, pinaster, Scots fir, umbrella
**09** lodgepole, Scotch fir
**11** bristlecone
**12** monkey puzzle
**13** Norfolk Island

**pineapple**
**04** bomb, piña, pine **05** anana **06** ananas **07** grenade **10** tillandsia

**pining**
**04** sick

**pinion**
**03** cog, tie **04** bind, wing **05** chain, penne, truss **06** fasten, fetter, hobble, pennon **07** confine, manacle, pin down, shackle **10** immobilize

**pink**
**03** cut, top **04** acme, best, peak, peep, peer, penk, rosy, stab, wink **05** blink, knock, notch, pinky, prick, prime, punch, score, small **06** eyelet, flower, height, incise, minnow, pierce, pinkie, samlet, summit, tiptop **07** extreme, flushed, reddish, roseate, scallop, serrate **08** blinking, detonate **09** chaffinch, exquisite, perforate **10** crenellate, perfection, rose colour **12** rose-coloured

*Pinks include:*

**04** puce, rose
**05** coral, peach
**06** oyster, salmon, shrimp
**07** old rose
**08** cyclamen
**09** carnation, pompadour, shell pink
**12** mushroom pink, shocking pink

**• in the pink**
**03** fit **04** trim, well **07** healthy **08** very well **10** in good nick, in good trim, on good form **11** in good shape, right as rain **12** in fine fettle, in good health **15** in perfect health

**pinnacle**
**03** cap, top **04** acme, apex, cone, peak **05** crest, crown, spire **06** apogee, height, hoodoo, needle, pinnet, summit, turret, vertex, zenith **07** minaret, obelisk, pyramid, steeple, sublime **08** eminence **11** culmination

**pinpoint**
**04** spot **05** exact, place, right **06** define, locate **07** pin down, precise, specify **08** accurate, discover, home in on, identify, nail down, rigorous, zero in on **09** determine **10** meticulous, scrupulous **11** distinguish, punctilious **15** put your finger on

**pint**
**02** pt

**• nearly a pint**
**03** log

**pint-size**
**03** wee **04** mini, tiny **05** dinky, dwarf, pygmy, small, teeny **06** little, midget, pocket **09** miniature, pint-sized **10** diminutive, teeny-weeny **11** pocket-sized

**pioneer**
**05** begin, chips, found, set up, start **06** create, invent, launch, leader, open up **07** develop, founder, planter, settler **08** colonist, discover, explorer, initiate, inventor, labourer, way-maker **09** developer, establish, excavator, harbinger, innovator, instigate, institute, introduce, originate, spearhead **10** discoverer, lead the way, pathfinder, pave the way, sandgroper **11** bandeirante, blaze a trail, trailblazer,

voortrekker **12** First Fleeter, frontiersman **13** groundbreaker **14** break new ground, founding father, frontierswoman

*See also* **explorer**

**pious**
**02** pi **03** pia **04** good, holy, wise **05** godly, moral **06** devout **07** devoted, dutiful, saintly **08** faithful, priggish, reverent, unctuous, virtuous **09** dedicated, insincere, religious, righteous, spiritual **10** goody-goody, sanctified **12** hypocritical **13** sanctimonious, self-righteous **14** holier-than-thou

**piously**
**07** morally **08** devoutly **10** faithfully, priggishly, reverently, virtuously **11** insincerely, religiously, righteously, spiritually **14** hypocritically **15** sanctimoniously, self-righteously

**pip**
**03** die **04** hump, kill, peep, roup, seed, spot, star **05** chirp, peepe, speck, wound **06** acinus, pippin, spleen **07** ailment, disgust, offence **08** fruitlet, syphilis **09** blackball, distemper **10** grapestone

**pipe**
**03** ait, jet, oat, tap **04** clay, duct, fife, flue, hose, line, main, peep, play, pule, reed, sing, take, tube, vent, weep, worm **05** aulos, brier, bring, carry, cheep, chirp, crane, cutty, drone, flute, kelly, quill, riser, sound, tibia, trill, tweet **06** convey, dudeen, faucet, funnel, hookah, kalian, piping, shrike, shrill, siphon, supply, tubing, uptake, warble **07** calumet, channel, chanter, chibouk, chirrup, cob-pipe, conduct, conduit, dead-end, deliver, dip-pipe, nargile, nargily, passage, tweedle, twitter, whistle **08** aqueduct, bagpipes, blow pipe, claypipe, conveyor, cornpipe, cylinder, dry riser, feed-pipe, manifold, mirliton, narghile, narghily, nargileh, nargilly, overflow, pipeline, recorder, soil pipe, stopcock, tailpipe, transmit **09** blast-pipe, chibouque, drainpipe, goose-neck, narghilly, peace-pipe, pitch-pipe, standpipe, stovepipe, ventiduct, wastepipe, water pipe **10** chimney pot, gas-bracket, kill string, meerschaum **11** clyster-pipe, exhaust pipe, service pipe, tobacco-pipe **12** churchwarden, hubble-bubble, penny whistle, throttle-pipe **13** woodcock's-head **15** injection string

*See also* **tobacco**

• **pipe down**
**06** shut up **07** be quiet **11** stop talking

**pipeclay**
**03** cam **04** calm, caum

**pipe dream**
**05** dream **06** mirage, notion, vagary **07** chimera, fantasy, reverie, romance **08** daydream, delusion **09** false hope **11** pie in the sky **13** castle in Spain **14** castle in the air

**pipeline**
**04** duct, line, pipe, tube **07** channel, conduit, passage **08** conveyor

• **in the pipeline**
**07** planned **08** on the way, under way **13** in preparation **14** already started

**pipsqueak**
**05** creep, twerp **06** nobody, squirt **07** nothing, upstart **09** nonentity **11** hobbledehoy **14** whippersnapper

**piquancy**
**03** pep, zip **04** bite, edge, kick, race, salt, tang, zest **05** juice, oomph, punch, spice **06** colour, ginger, relish, spirit, vigour **07** flavour, pizzazz **08** interest, pungency, raciness, vitality **09** sharpness, spiciness **10** excitement, liveliness **11** pepperiness **13** strong flavour

**piquant**
**04** racy, tart **05** juicy, salty, sharp, spicy, tangy, zesty **06** biting, lively **07** peppery, pungent, savoury **08** poignant, seasoned, spirited, stinging **09** colourful, sparkling **10** appetizing, intriguing **11** fascinating, interesting, provocative, stimulating **14** highly seasoned

**pique**
**03** bug, get, irk, vex **04** gall, goad, huff, miff, nark, peak, rile, spur, stir, whet **05** anger, annoy, get at, peeve, point, rouse, sting, wound **06** arouse, excite, grudge, kindle, needle, nettle, offend, put out, wind up **07** affront, dudgeon, incense, mortify, offence, provoke, umbrage **08** drive mad, irritate, vexation **09** aggravate, animosity, annoyance, displease, galvanize, punctilio, stimulate **10** drive crazy, ill-feeling, irritation, resentment **11** displeasure **12** drive bananas **13** make sparks fly **14** drive up the wall

**piqued**
**03** mad **05** angry, cross, ratty, riled, vexed **06** choked, miffed, narked, peeved, put out **07** annoyed, stroppy, uptight **08** in a paddy, offended, up in arms **09** in a lather, irritated, raving mad, resentful, seeing red **10** aggravated, displeased, hopping mad **11** disgruntled, fit to be tied **12** on the warpath

**piracy**
**05** theft **06** rapine **07** robbery **08** stealing **09** hijacking, sea-roving **10** plagiarism **11** bootlegging, freebooting **12** buccaneering, infringement

• **practise piracy**
**04** rove

**piranha**
**05** perai, pirai **06** caribe, piraña, piraya **08** characid, characin

**pirate**
**04** copy, crib, lift, nick **05** pinch, poach, rover, steal **06** borrow, marque, raider, sea dog, sea rat, viking **07** brigand, corsair, sea wolf **08** algerine, knock off, marauder, picaroon, sea rover, water rat **09** buccaneer, infringer, sallee-man, sea robber **10** arch-pirate, filibuster, freebooter, plagiarist, plagiarize, water-thief **11** appropriate, plagiarizer

*Pirates include:*

**03** Tew (Thomas)
**04** Bart (Jean), Gunn (Ben), Hook (Captain), Kidd (William), Otto, Read (Mary), Smee
**05** Barth (Jean), Bones (Billy), Bonny (Anne), Bunce (Jack), Drake (Sir Francis), Every (Henry), Ewart (Nanty), Flint (Captain), Tache (Edward), Teach (Edward)
**06** Aubery (Jean-Benoit), Conrad, Jonsen (Captain), Morgan (Sir Henry), Silver (Long John), Thatch (Edward), Walker (William)
**07** Dampier (William), Lafitte (Jean), O'Malley (Grace), Rackham (John), Roberts (Bartholomew), Sparrow (Captain Jack), Trumpet (Solomon)
**08** Altamont (Frederick), Black Dog, Blackett (Nancy), Blackett (Peggy), Blind Pew, Redbeard, Ringrose (Basil)
**09** Black Bart, Cleveland (Clement)
**10** Barbarossa (Khair-ed-din), Blackbeard, Calico Jack
**14** Long John Silver

**pirouette**
**04** spin, turn **05** pivot, twirl, whirl **06** gyrate **08** gyration **15** turn on a sixpence

**pistol**
**03** dag, gat, gun, pop, rod **04** Colt®, iron **05** Luger®, piece **06** barker, heater, puffer, zip gun **07** handgun, pistole, sidearm **08** revolver, water gun **09** derringer, squirt gun **10** six-shooter **11** barking iron

*See also* **gun**

**piston**
**03** ram

**pit**
**03** bed, den, put **04** dent, gulf, hole, khud, mark, mine, play, scar, silo, sump **05** abyss, chasm, ditch, fossa, fovea, notch, stone **06** cavity, crater, dimple, hollow, indent, quarry, trench **07** blemish, depress, measure, moss hag, pothole **08** alveolus, coalmine, diggings, moss hagg, pockmark, punctule, workings **10** depression, scrobicule **11** excavations, indentation

• **pit against**
**05** match **06** oppose **07** compete **10** set against

• **the pits**
**04** crap, naff **05** awful, lousy, pants, spewy **06** cruddy, crummy **07** abysmal **08** dreadful, inferior, pathetic, terrible, very poor **09** third-rate **10** inadequate, second-rate **14** a load of rubbish, unsatisfactory

**Pitcairn Island**
**03** PCN

**pitch**
**03** aim, fix, lob, pin, pop, set, tar, yak **04** bowl, cant, cast, dive, drop, face, fall, fire, hurl, keel, line, list, mark, nets, park, peck, reel, roll, stud, sway, talk, tilt, tone, toss **05** angle, arena, chuck, cover, erect, field, fling, grade, heave, level, lurch, place, plant, point, put up, set up, slant, sling, slope, sound, spiel, throw **06** alight, bounce, degree, direct, encamp, extent, gabble, ground, height, jargon, launch, maltha, patter, plunge, settle, timbre, topple, tumble, wallow, wicket **07** asphalt, bitumen, chatter, descent, incline, plummet, set down, stadium, station **08** flounder, gradient, position, tonality **09** determine, establish, frequency, intensity, interlock, steepness **10** modulation **11** inclination, sports field **12** fall headlong, playing-field **13** move up and down

• **make a pitch for**
**05** offer, put up **06** bid for, submit, tender **07** advance, proffer, propose **08** put in for, try to get **09** try to sell **10** put forward **11** try to obtain

• **pitch in**
**04** help **06** join in, muck in **07** help out **09** co-operate, do your bit, lend a hand **10** be involved **11** participate

• **too low in pitch, too high in pitch**
**04** flat **05** sharp

**pitch-black**
**04** dark, inky **05** black, unlit **08** jet-black **09** coal-black, pitch-dark **13** unilluminated

**pitcher**
**03** can, jar, jug, urn **04** ewer, jack, sett **05** crock **06** bottle, closer, vessel **07** growler **09** container **11** screwballer **13** knuckleballer

• **pitcher plant**
**08** nepenthe **09** Nepenthes **10** Sarracenia **12** Darlingtonia

**piteous**
**03** sad **06** moving, paltry, rueful, woeful **07** pitiful, ruthful **08** mournful, pathetic, pitiable, poignant, touching, wretched **09** plaintive, sorrowful **10** lamentable **11** distressing **12** heart-rending **13** compassionate, heartbreaking

**pitfall**
**04** risk, snag, trap **05** catch, peril, snare **06** danger, hazard **08** drawback, trapfall **10** difficulty **14** stumbling-block

**pith**
**03** nub **04** core, crux, gist, meat **05** heart, point, value **06** import, kernel, marrow, matter, mettle, moment, vigour, weight **07** essence, medulla, papyrus **09** substance **10** importance **11** consequence **12** forcefulness, quintessence, salient point, significance **13** essential part

**pithead**
**04** brow

**pithily**
**07** in a word, in brief, tersely **09** compactly, concisely **10** succinctly, to the point **11** in a few words, in a nutshell **12** meaningfully

**pithy**
**05** brief, meaty, short, terse **06** cogent, strong **07** compact, concise, marrowy, pointed, summary, telling **08** forceful, forcible, incisive, lapidary, material, pregnant, succinct **09** condensed, energetic, matterful, trenchant **10** expressive, meaningful

**pitiable**
**03** sad **04** poor **05** silly, sorry **06** woeful **07** doleful, piteous, woesome **08** grievous, mournful, pathetic, wretched **09** miserable **10** distressed, lamentable **11** distressful, distressing **12** commiserable, contemptible **14** compassionable

**pitiful**
**03** low, sad **04** base, mean, poor, vile **05** lousy, seely, sorry, waefu' **06** crummy, meagre, moving, paltry, shabby, waeful, woeful **07** doleful, piteous, ruthful, the pits, waesome **08** hopeless, mournful, pathetic, pitiable, terrible, wretched **09** affecting, miserable, worthless **10** deplorable, despicable, inadequate, lamentable **11** distressing **12** contemptible, heart-rending **13** compassionate, heartbreaking, insignificant

**pitifully**
**05** sadly **08** terribly, woefully **09** miserably, piteously **10** deplorably, despicably, hopelessly, lamentably **12** contemptibly, pathetically **13** distressingly

**pitiless**
**05** cruel, harsh, stony **06** brutal, severe **07** callous, inhuman **08** inhumane, ruthless, uncaring **09** heartless, merciless, unfeeling **10** dispiteous, hard-headed, inexorable, relentless **11** cold-blooded, cold-hearted, hard-hearted, unremitting **13** unsympathetic

**pitilessly**
**07** cruelly, harshly **08** brutally **09** callously **10** ruthlessly **11** mercilessly **13** cold-bloodedly, cold-heartedly, hard-heartedly

**pittance**
**04** dole, drop **05** crumb **06** trifle **07** modicum, peanuts **11** chickenfeed **14** drop in the ocean

**pitted**
**05** holey, rough **06** dented, marked **07** foveate, notched, scarred **08** alveolar, indented, lacunose, potholed, punctate **09** alveolate, blemished, depressed, punctated **10** pockmarked

**pity**
**03** rew, rue, sin **04** ruth **05** bleed, grace, mercy, piety, shame **06** bemoan, bepity, bowels, regret, sorrow **07** bad luck, emotion, feel for, feeling, mercify, remorse, sadness, weep for **08** distress, kindness, sympathy **09** grieve for **10** compassion, condolence, have a heart, misericord, misfortune, tenderness **11** crying shame, forbearance, forgiveness, misericorde **12** feel sorry for **13** commiseration, empathize with, fellow-feeling, understanding **14** disappointment, sympathize with **15** commiserate with

• **take pity on**
**03** rue **05** spare **06** pardon **07** feel for **09** show mercy **11** have mercy on **12** feel sorry for **13** empathize with **14** emphathize with, sympathize with **15** commiserate with

**pivot**
**03** hub, lie **04** axis, axle, hang, rely, spin, turn **05** focus, heart, hinge, swing **06** centre, depend, rotate, swivel **07** fulcrum, kingpin, revolve, spindle **08** cardinal, linchpin **10** focal point **12** be contingent, central point

**pivotal**
**05** axial, focal, vital **07** central, crucial **08** critical, decisive **09** climactic, important **11** determining

**pixie**
**03** elf, imp **04** pixy **05** fairy, pisky **06** goblin, sprite **07** brownie **10** leprechaun

**pizzazz**
**04** brio, life **05** oomph **06** energy, esprit, spirit, vigour **07** entrain **08** activity, dynamism, vitality, vivacity **09** animation, briskness, quickness, smartness **10** liveliness **11** refreshment **13** sprightliness, vivaciousness **14** boisterousness

**placard**
**02** ad **04** bill, sign **05** title **06** advert, notice, poster **07** affiche, placcat, placket, sticker **13** advertisement

**placate**
**04** calm, lull **05** quiet **06** disarm, pacify, soothe **07** appease, assuage, mollify, win over **08** calm down **10** conciliate, propitiate

**placatory**
**07** calming **08** soothing **09** appeasing **10** mollifying **11** peace-making **12** conciliatory, pacificatory, propitiative, propitiatory

**place**
**01** P **02** do, Pl **03** fix, job, lay, pad, put, set **04** area, city, digs, duty, flat, home, know, lieu, park, part, pose, post, rank, rest, role, room, seat, site, sort, spot, sted, task, town **05** abode, class, grade, group, hotel, house, leave, locus, lodge, niche, order, plant, point, right, scene, space, stand, state, stead, stedd, stede, steed, topic, venue **06** assign, hamlet, induct, invest, locale, locate, region, settle, square,

status, stedde **07** appoint, arrange, concern, country, deposit, footing, install, lay down, put down, set down, setting, situate, station, village **08** allocate, building, business, classify, district, domicile, dwelling, fortress, function, identify, locality, location, pinpoint, position, property, remember, standing **09** apartment, establish, recognize, residence, situation **10** categorize, restaurant **11** appointment, battlefield, find a job for, institution, whereabouts **13** accommodation, establishment, neighbourhood **14** responsibility

*See also* **Bible**; **eating**; **entertainment**; **fictional**; **mythical**

**• all over the place**
◊ *anagram indicator*
**04** awry **05** messy **07** muddled **08** confused **09** dispersed, scattered **12** disorganized

**• at the right place**
**03** pat

**• at that place**
**05** there

**• at this place**
**04** here

**• in place**
**05** set up **07** in order, working **08** arranged **10** in position

**• in place of**
**04** lieu, vice **08** in lieu of **09** instead of **13** in exchange for

**• in the same place**
**02** ib **04** ibid **06** ibidem

**• no place**
**02** np

**• out of place**
◊ *anagram indicator*
**04** away **08** improper, out of key, tactless, unseemly **09** unfitting **10** inapposite, malapropos, unbecoming, unsuitable **12** unseasonable **13** inappropriate

**• put someone in their place**
**05** crush, shame **06** humble **07** deflate **08** bring low **09** humiliate

**• take place**
**02** be **04** fall **05** occur **06** befall, be held, betide, happen **07** come off **09** come about, transpire **10** come to pass

**• take the place of**
**06** act for **07** replace, serve as, succeed **09** supersede **10** stand in for **12** take over from **13** substitute for

**placement**
**03** job **07** placing, ranking, setting **08** locating, location, ordering **10** assignment, deployment, employment, engagement, internship, stationing **11** appointment, arrangement, disposition, emplacement, positioning **12** distribution, installation **14** classification

**placid**
**04** calm, cool, mild **05** quiet, still **06** gentle, serene **07** equable, pacific, restful, unmoved **08** composed, peaceful, tranquil **09** easy-going, peaceable, unruffled **10** untroubled **11** level-headed, undisturbed, unemotional, unexcitable, unflappable **12** even-tempered **13** imperturbable, self-possessed

**placidly**
**06** calmly, gently, mildly **08** serenely **09** restfully **10** peacefully **11** unflappably **13** imperturbably

**plagiarism**
**04** crib **05** theft **06** piracy **07** copying, lifting **08** cribbing **09** borrowing **12** infringement, reproduction **13** appropriation **14** counterfeiting

**plagiarist**
**05** thief **06** copier, pirate, robber **08** imitator **09** Autolycus

**plagiarize**
**04** copy, crib, lift, nick **05** poach, steal **06** borrow, pirate **07** imitate **09** reproduce **11** appropriate, counterfeit

**plague**
**03** bug, dog, dun, pox, vex **04** bane, blow, pest **05** annoy, curse, death, haunt, hound, swarm, tease, trial, upset, worry, wound **06** bother, hamper, harass, hassle, hinder, influx, pester **07** afflict, bedevil, cholera, disease, disturb, murrain, scourge, torment, torture, trouble **08** calamity, distress, epidemic, goodyear, invasion, irritate, nuisance, pandemic, sickness, vexation **09** aggravate, annoyance, contagion, goodyears, infection, persecute **10** affliction, Black Death, huge number, pestilence **11** infestation **13** bubonic plague, pain in the neck **15** pneumonic plague, thorn in the flesh

*The ten Biblical plagues:*

**04** lice
**05** boils, flies, frogs
**07** locusts
**08** darkness
**09** hailstorm
**18** disease of livestock
**19** death of the firstborn
**21** Nile waters turn to blood

**plain**
**04** even, flat, open, ugly **05** basic, blunt, clear, frank, level, lucid, muted, overt, prose, quite, secco, stark, utter **06** candid, direct, homely, honest, lament, modest, patent, rustic, simple, simply, **07** austere, clearly, evident, obvious, plateau, sincere, spartan, totally, unruled, utterly, visible **08** apparent, clinical, complain, flatland, home-bred, home-made, homespun, manifest, ordinary, truthful, uncurled, unlovely **09** downright, grassland, outspoken, plain-Jane, practical, tableland, unadorned **10** accessible, completely, distinctly, forthright, noticeable, restrained, thoroughly, unaffected, unassuming, uncoloured, undeniably **11** discernible, perceptible, plain-spoken, transparent, unambiguous, undecorated, unelaborate, unpatterned **12** intelligible, self-coloured, unattractive, unmistakable, unobstructed, unvariegated **13** uncomplicated, unembellished, unpretentious **14** understandable **15** clear as daylight, not much to look at, straightforward, undistinguished, unprepossessing, unsophisticated

*Plains include:*

**04** vega
**05** carse, lande, llano
**06** maidan, pampas, sabkha, steppe, tundra
**07** lowland, prairie, sabkhah, sabkhat
**08** savannah

**plain-spoken**
**04** open **05** blunt, frank, round **06** candid, direct, honest **08** explicit, outright, truthful **09** downright, outspoken **10** forthright **11** unequivocal **15** straightforward

**plaintive**
**03** sad **06** woeful **07** doleful, piteous, pitiful, unhappy, wistful **08** mournful, wretched **09** lacrimoso, lagrimoso, querulous, sorrowful **10** melancholy **11** heartbroken, high-pitched **12** disconsolate, heart-rending **13** grief-stricken

**plaintively**
**05** sadly **08** woefully **09** dolefully, lacrimoso, lagrimoso, pitifully, unhappily, wistfully **10** mournfully, wretchedly **14** disconsolately

**plait**
**04** plat **05** braid, pedal, pleat, tress **06** plight **07** frounce, leghorn **08** doubling **09** Dunstable

**plan**
◊ *anagram indicator*
**03** aim, lay, map, way **04** case, dart, hang, idea, mean, plat, plot, seek, want, wish **05** block, chart, draft, frame, means, model, shape, trace **06** design, device, devise, intend, invent, layout, map out, method, policy, schema, scheme, sketch, system **07** arrange, complot, concoct, develop, diagram, drawing, foresee, formula, outline, prepare, project, propose, purpose, resolve, think of, work out **08** conspire, contrive, envisage, organize, platform, proposal, scenario, schedule, strategy **09** architect, blueprint, formulate, intention, itinerary, procedure, programme, timetable **10** conception, mastermind, suggestion **11** arrangement, contemplate, contrivance, delineation, ichnography, premeditate, projectment, proposition **12** illustration, scale drawing **14** representation

**plane**
**03** bus, fly, jet **04** even, flat, rank, rung, sail, skim, soar, VTOL, wing **05** class,

flush, glide, jumbo, level, plain, skate, stage **06** bomber, degree, glider, planar, smooth, thrust **07** echelon, fighter, footing, jointer, regular, stratum, uniform **08** aircraft, airliner, airplane, jumbo jet, position, seaplane, sycomore, volplane **09** aeroplane, condition, fillister, swing-wing **10** buttonball, buttonwood, homaloidal, horizontal **11** flat surface **12** level surface

*See also* **aircraft**

## planet

**05** world

*Planets:*

**04** Mars
**05** Earth, Pluto, Venus
**06** Saturn, Uranus
**07** Jupiter, Mercury, Neptune

## plank

**04** beam, slab, slat **05** board, panel, sheet **06** planch, timber **08** stringer **09** washboard **12** weatherboard

## planner

**05** maker **06** author **07** creator, deviser, stylist **08** arranger, designer, inventor, producer **09** architect, contriver, developer, fashioner, organizer **10** mastermind, originator

## planning

**06** design **07** control, running **09** ordinance **10** management, projection, regulation **11** arrangement, development, preparation **12** co-ordination, organization **13** establishment **14** administration

## plant

**03** fix, put, set, sow **04** bury, gear, hide, land, mill, post, root, salt, seed, shop, slip, yard **05** found, imbed, inter, lodge, place, scion, stock, works **06** cudgel, insert, instil, locate, settle **07** conceal, cutting, factory, foundry, implant, scatter, secrete, situate, station **08** colonize, disguise, offshoot, position, workshop **09** apparatus, equipment, establish, introduce, machinery **10** transplant **11** put secretly **13** put out of sight

*See also* **flower**; **leaf**

*Plant types include:*

**03** air, pot
**04** bean, beet, bulb, bush, cane, corm, fern, herb, moss, tree, vine, weed
**05** algae, grass, house, sedge, shrub, water
**06** annual, cactus, cereal, flower, fungus, hybrid, lichen
**07** bedding, climber, foliage, sapling
**08** biennial, cultivar, epiphyte, seedling
**09** aerophyte, evergreen, perennial, succulent, vegetable
**10** herbaceous, wild flower
**11** carnivorous
**13** insectivorous

*See also* **alga, algae**; **bean**; **bulb**; **cactus**; **cereal**; **crop**; **disease**; **grass**; **herb**; **lily**; **orchid**; **palm**; **poison**; **seaweed**; **sedge**; **shrub**; **tree**; **vegetable**; **weed**

## plantation

**03** pen **04** tope **06** bosket **07** bosquet, fazenda, pinetum **08** vineyard **09** cornbrake, salicetum, shrubbery, tea garden, viticetum

## plaque

**04** sign, slab **05** badge, brass, medal, panel, plate **06** brooch, shield, tablet **07** plateau **09** cartouche, medallion, plaquette

## plaster

**03** mud **04** coat, daub, leep, teer **05** cover, gesso, grout, parge, patch, smarm, smear **06** bedaub, clatch, gypsum, laying, mortar, parget, peloid, render, screed, spread, stucco **07** bandage, Band-aid®, overlay, pugging **08** dressing, plaister, sinapism **09** beplaster, cataplasm, emplaster, Polyfilla®, rendering, roughcast **10** emplastron, emplastrum **11** Elastoplast®, plasterwork, scratchcoat **12** cover thickly, plasterboard **13** butterfly clip **14** plaster of Paris **15** sticking-plaster

## plastered

◇ *anagram indicator*

*See* **drunk**

## plastic

◇ *anagram indicator*

**04** soft **05** false **06** phoney, pliant, supple **07** ductile, man-made, pliable, shaping **08** flexible, modeller, sculptor **09** compliant, formative, malleable, mouldable, receptive, shapeable, synthetic, tractable, unnatural **10** artificial, manageable, modifiable **14** impressionable

*Plastics include:*

**03** PVC
**04** PTFE, uPVC
**05** vinyl
**06** Biopol®, Teflon®
**07** Perspex®
**08** Bakelite®, laminate, silicone
**09** celluloid®, Plexiglas®, polyester, polythene, Styrofoam®
**10** epoxy resin, plexiglass
**11** polystyrene
**12** polyethylene, polyurethane
**13** phenolic resin, polypropylene
**14** polynorbornene

## plasticity

**07** pliancy **08** softness **10** pliability, suppleness **11** flexibility, pliableness **12** malleability, tractability

## plate

**01** L, T **03** seg, tin, web **04** bowl, coat, dish, foil, gild, pane, rove, sign, slab **05** ashet, cover, layer, ortho, panel, paten, print, sheet **06** baffle, lamina, latten, muffin, plaque, remark, salver, silver, tablet, veneer **07** anodize, gravure, helping, lamella, ossicle, overlay, picture, plateau, platter, portion, serving **08** laminate, mazarine, pattress, trencher **09** galvanize, osteoderm, platinize **10** lithograph, photograph, zincograph **11** photo-relief **12** electroplate, illustration, mazarine dish

*See also* **platter**

## plateau

**04** mesa, roof **05** grade, level, plane, stage, table **06** meseta, upland **08** highland, platform **09** Altiplano, stability, tableland

## platform

**03** pad, rig, top **04** aims, bema, dais, deck, kang, plan, site **05** basis, bench, crane, dolly, floor, ideas, stage, stand, stoep, stoop, stump **06** bridge, cradle, device, flotel, gantry, machan, oil rig, pallet, perron, podium, policy, pulpit, scheme, sketch, tenets **07** balcony, decking, estrade, floatel, foretop, maintop, plateau, rostrum, soapbox, sponson, terrace, tribune **08** barbette, flooring, labellum, predella, round top, scaffold, strategy **09** crow's-nest, drillship, footplate, gangboard, manifesto, party line, programme, traverser, turntable **10** dumb waiter, intentions, objectives, principles, roundabout **11** emplacement, entablement, monkey board, paint-bridge **12** landing stage, launching-pad

## platinum

**02** Pt

## platitude

**06** cliché, truism **07** bromide, inanity **08** banality, chestnut, flatness **10** generality, stereotype **11** commonplace **15** trite expression

## platitudinous

**03** set **04** dull, flat **05** banal, corny, inane, stale, stock, tired, trite, vapid **07** cliché'd **08** clichéed, truistic, well-worn **09** hackneyed **10** overworked **11** commonplace, stereotyped

## platonic

**05** ideal **09** non-sexual, spiritual **10** idealistic **11** incorporeal, non-physical, non-romantic **12** intellectual, transcendent

## platoon

**04** team, unit **05** group, squad, troop **06** outfit, patrol, volley **07** battery, company **08** squadron

## platter

**04** dish, lanx, tray **05** graal, grail, plate **06** grayle, salver **07** charger **08** trencher

*See also* **plate**

## plaudits

**04** hand **06** praise **07** acclaim, bouquet, hurrahs, ovation **08** accolade, applause, approval, clapping **09** good press **10** rave review **11** acclamation, approbation **12** commendation, pat on the back **15** congratulations, standing ovation

## plausible

**04** fair, glib **06** cogent, likely **07** logical,

proball **08** credible, possible, probable, specious **10** acceptable, believable, colourable, convincing, imaginable, persuasive, reasonable, soft-spoken **11** conceivable, smooth-faced **12** smooth-spoken **13** silver-tongued, smooth-talking, smooth-tongued

**plausibly**
**08** possibly, probably **09** logically **10** imaginably, pleasantly, reasonably **11** commendably, conceivably **12** convincingly, persuasively

**play**
◇ *anagram indicator*
**02** do, no **03** act, fun, noh, pit, ply, toy **04** game, give, jest, laik, lake, plot, romp, room, show, work **05** caper, dance, drama, farce, flash, frisk, gleam, hobby, kicks, laugh, range, revel, rival, scope, slack, space, sport, wield **06** action, cavort, comedy, frolic, gamble, gambol, glance, join in, joking, leeway, margin, nogaku, oppose, take on, trifle **07** compete, flicker, flutter, freedom, have fun, holiday, leisure, liberty, licence, operate, pastime, perform, portray, shimmer, teasing, tragedy, twinkle, vie with **08** activity, exercise, free rein, gambling, latitude, movement **09** amusement, challenge, dalliance, diversion, enjoyment, interplay, looseness, melodrama, operation, play games, represent **10** recreation, take part in **11** flexibility, impersonate, interaction, merrymaking, move lightly, performance, transaction **12** be involved in **13** amuse yourself, enjoy yourself, entertainment, participate in, play the part of **14** compete against, divert yourself, occupy yourself

*Plays include:*

**03** RUR
**04** Loot
**05** Equus, Faust, Le Cid, Medea, Médée, Roots, Yerma
**06** Becket, Phèdre, St Joan
**07** Amadeus, Candida, Electra, Endgame, Galileo, La Ronde, Oedipus, Oleanna, Orestes, Volpone, Woyzeck
**08** Antigone, Betrayal, Everyman, Hay Fever, Huis Clos, Oresteia, Peer Gynt, Tartuffe, The Birds, The Flies, The Frogs, The Miser, The Price, The Wasps
**09** All My Sons, Happy Days, Miss Julie, Party Time, Pygmalion, Saint Joan, The Chairs, The Clouds, The Father, The Rivals, The Vortex
**10** A Dream Play, All for Love, Andromache, Andromaque, Lysistrata, Misery Guts, No Man's Land, The Bacchae, The Robbers, The Seagull, Uncle Vanya
**11** A Doll's House, Blood and Ice, Hedda Gabler, The Blue Bird, The Crucible, The Wild Duck, Trojan Women
**12** Anna Christie, Blithe Spirit, Blood Wedding, Major Barbara, Private Lives, Punch and Judy, The Alchemist, The Caretaker, The Mousetrap
**13** Arms and the Man, A Taste of Honey, Doctor Faustus, Educating Rita, Le Misanthrope, The Homecoming, The Jew of Malta, The White Devil, The Winslow Boy
**14** Can't Pay? Won't Pay!, Krapp's Last Tape, Man and Superman, Orlando Furioso, Riders to the Sea, Separate Tables, The Country Wife, The Entertainer, The Silent Woman
**15** Bartholomew Fair, Look Back in Anger, Prometheus Bound, The Beggar's Opera, The Iceman Cometh, The Three Sisters, Waiting for Godot

*See also* **Shakespeare**

**• out of play**
**04** dead

**• part of play**
**03** act

**• play around with**
◇ *anagram indicator*
**07** toy with **08** fool with **09** dally with, flirt with **10** fiddle with, fidget with, meddle with, tamper with, trifle with **12** womanize with **13** interfere with, philander with **14** mess around with

**• play at**
**06** affect **07** make out, pretend **10** put on an act **11** pretend to be

**• play down**
**08** downplay, minimize **09** gloss over, underplay **10** understate, undervalue **11** make light of **13** underestimate

**• play harshly**
**03** saw

**• play on**
**07** exploit, trade on **08** profit by **12** capitalize on **13** turn to account **15** take advantage of

**• play out**
**03** act **04** go on **05** enact **06** act out, unfold **07** carry on, exhaust, wear out **08** continue **10** be revealed

**• play the fool**
**03** fon **04** daff, fool **07** act dido, tomfool

**• play up**
**04** fool, hurt **05** annoy, boost **06** bother, stress **07** go wrong, not work, point up, trouble **09** be naughty, emphasize, highlight, misbehave, spotlight, underline **10** accentuate, exaggerate **11** give trouble, malfunction **12** be on the blink, go on the blink **13** be mischievous **15** call attention to

**• play up to**
**04** fawn **05** toady **06** cozy up **07** flatter **08** blandish, bootlick, butter up, soft-soap, suck up to **15** curry favour with

**• play with**
◇ *anagram indicator*

**play-act**
**03** act **04** fake, mime, sham **05** bluff, feign, put on **06** affect, assume **07** pretend **08** simulate **09** dissemble, fabricate **10** put on an act **11** counterfeit, impersonate **15** pass yourself off

**playboy**
**04** rake, roué **09** debauchee, ladies' man, libertine, socialite, womanizer **10** lady-killer **11** philanderer **12** man about town

**player**
**01** E, N, S, W **03** ace, ham, man **04** east, pone, star, west **05** actor, north, south **06** artist **07** actress, artiste, trifler, trouper **08** comedian, musician **09** performer, sportsman **10** all-rounder, competitor, contestant **11** accompanist, entertainer, participant, sportswoman **15** instrumentalist

*See also* **Australian football**; **baseball**; **basketball**; **chess**; **footballer**; **instrument**; **rugby**; **tennis**

**• bit player**
**05** extra

**• opposing player**
**02** it

**players**
**04** band, cast, wind **05** brass **07** strings
*See also* **football**; **orchestra**

**playful**
**03** gay, mad **05** funny, ludic **06** frisky, impish, joking, lively, toyish **07** jesting, kitteny, puckish, roguish, teasing, toysome, waggish **08** espiègle, flippant, friendly, gamesome, humorous, skittish, spirited, sportive **09** facetious, fun-loving, kittenish, piacevole **10** frolicsome, rollicking **11** mischievous **12** high-spirited, light-hearted **13** tongue-in-cheek

**playfully**
**06** in jest **08** jokingly **09** piacevole **10** humorously **11** facetiously **14** light-heartedly

**playground**
**04** park **08** play area **12** playing-field **13** amusement park **14** pleasure ground

**playmate**
**03** pal **04** chum, mate **05** buddy **06** friend **07** comrade **09** companion, neighbour **10** playfellow

**plaything**
**03** toy **04** game **05** sport **06** bauble, gewgaw, puppet, trifle **07** pastime, trinket **08** gimcrack **09** amusement

**playwright**
**06** writer **09** dramatist, tragedian **10** dramaturge **12** dramaturgist, screen writer, scriptwriter

*Playwrights and screenwriters include:*

**02** Fo (Dario)
**03** Fry (Christopher), Gay (John), Hay (Ian), Kyd (Thomas), May (Elaine)
**04** Bolt (Robert), Bond (Edward), Coen (Ethan), Coen (Joel), Dane (Clemence), Ford (John), Hare

(David), **Rowe** (Nicholas), **Shaw** (George Bernard), **Vega** (Lope de)
**05** **Albee** (Edward), **Allen** (Woody), **Arden** (John), **Bates** (Herbert Ernest), **Behan** (Brendan), **Dumas** (Alexandre), **Eliot** (T S), **Frayn** (Michael), **Friel** (Brian), **Genet** (Jean), **Gogol** (Nikolai), **Havel** (Vaclav), **Ibsen** (Henrik), **Lodge** (Thomas), **Lorca** (Federico García), **Mamet** (David), **Nashe** (Thomas), **Odets** (Clifford), **Orton** (Joe), **Otway** (Thomas), **Sachs** (Hans), **Sachs** (Nelly), **Smith** (Dodie), **Stone** (Oliver), **Synge** (John Millington), **Udall** (Nicholas), **Wilde** (Oscar), **Yeats** (W B)
**06** **Barrie** (Sir James Matthew), **Brecht** (Bertolt), **Bridie** (James), **Colman** (George), **Coward** (Sir Noël), **Dekker** (Thomas), **Dryden** (John), **Galdós** (Benito Pérez), **Goethe** (Johann Wolfgang von), **Greene** (Robert), **Herzog** (Werner), **Hilton** (James), **Huston** (John), **Jerome** (Jerome K), **Jonson** (Ben), **Kaiser** (Georg), **Lerner** (Alan Jay), **Mercer** (David), **Miller** (Arthur), **Miller** (Henry), **Musset** (Alfred de), **O'Casey** (Sean), **O'Neill** (Eugene), **Pinero** (Sir Arthur Wing), **Pinter** (Harold), **Powell** (Michael), **Racine** (Jean), **Sardou** (Victorien), **Sartre** (Jean-Paul), **Steele** (Sir Richard), **Storey** (David), **Tagore** (Rabindranath), **Wesker** (Arnold), **Wilder** (Thornton)
**07** **Anouilh** (Jean), **Arrabal** (Fernando), **Beckett** (Samuel), **Bennett** (Alan), **Büchner** (Georg), **Chapman** (George), **Chekhov** (Anton), **Cocteau** (Jean), **Coppola** (Francis Ford), **Diderot** (Denis), **Garrick** (David), **Gregory** (Lady Isabella Augusta), **Holberg** (Ludvig, Baron), **Ionesco** (Eugène), **Klinger** (Friedrich Maximilian von), **Kubrick** (Stanley), **Labiche** (Eugène), **Lardner** (Ring), **Marlowe** (Christopher), **Marston** (John), **McGough** (Roger), **Mishima** (Yukio), **Molière**, **Novello** (Ivor), **Osborne** (John), **Plautus** (Titus Maccius), **Richler** (Mordecai), **Rostand** (Edmond), **Russell** (Willy), **Shaffer** (Peter), **Shepard** (Sam), **Terence**, **Ustinov** (Sir Peter), **Vicente** (Gil), **Walcott** (Derek), **Webster** (John)
**08** **Andersen** (Hans Christian), **Banville** (Théodore de), **Beaumont** (Francis), **Björnson** (Björnstjerne), **Brentano** (Clemens), **Burgoyne** (John), **Congreve** (William), **Davenant** (Sir William), **Fielding** (Henry), **Fletcher** (John), **Hochhuth** (Rolf), **Lochhead** (Liz), **Menander**, **Mortimer** (Sir John), **Polanski** (Roman), **Rattigan** (Sir Terence), **Schiller** (Friedrich), **Shadwell** (Thomas), **Sheridan** (Richard Brinsley), **Stoppard** (Sir Tom), **Suckling** (Sir John), **Tourneur** (Cyril), **Vanbrugh** (Sir John), **Wedekind** (Frank), **Williams** (Emlyn), **Williams** (Tennessee)
**09** **Aeschylus**, **Ayckbourn** (Sir Alan), **Corneille** (Pierre), **D'Annunzio** (Gabriele), **Euripides**, **Goldsmith** (Oliver), **Hauptmann** (Gerhart), **Isherwood** (Christopher), **Mankowitz** (Wolf), **Marinetti** (Filippo Tommaso), **Middleton** (Thomas), **Poliakoff** (Stephen), **Priestley** (J B), **Rosenthal** (Jack), **Sophocles**, **Wycherley** (William)
**10** **Galsworthy** (John), **Pirandello** (Luigi), **Strindberg** (August)
**11** **Maeterlinck** (Maurice), **Shakespeare** (William)
**12** **Aristophanes**, **Beaumarchais** (Pierre-Augustin Caron de)

---

## plea

**05** alibi, claim, fains **06** appeal, excuse, fains I, placet, placit, prayer **07** defence, defense, lawsuit, pretext, request **08** demurrer, entreaty, fainites, petition, placitum, pleading **10** invocation **11** declinature, explanation, imploration, vindication **12** supplication **13** justification **14** nolo contendere

## plead

**03** ask, beg **04** moot, urge **05** argue, claim, state **06** adduce, allege, appeal, assert **07** beseech, entreat, implore, request, solicit **08** maintain, persuade, perswade, petition **09** intercede **10** put forward **12** intercede for

- **refusing to plead**

**04** mute

## pleasant

**04** cute, fine, nice **05** amene, lepid, merry, tipsy **06** genial, groovy, jocund, lekker, lovely **07** affable, amiable, amusing, likable, welcome, winsome **08** all roses, charming, cheerful, friendly, gorgeous, likeable, pleasing, savorous, sunshiny **09** agreeable, congenial, enjoyable, piacevole, toothsome **10** acceptable, delightful, gratifying, refreshing, salubrious, satisfying **11** inoffensive **12** entertaining, good-humoured **14** roses all the way

## pleasantly

**07** nice and **09** enjoyably, piacevole, plausibly **10** pleasingly **12** delightfully, refreshingly **14** entertainingly

## pleasantry

**04** jest, joke, quip **05** sally **06** banter, bon mot **08** badinage **09** enjoyment, witticism **10** jocularity **12** casual remark, pleasantness **13** polite comment **14** friendly remark

## please

**04** like, list, suit, want, will, wish **05** agree, amuse, bitte, charm, cheer, queme **06** arride, choose, desire, divert, fulfil, humour, kindly, prefer, see fit, tickle **07** aggrate, attract, cheer up, content, delight, flatter, gladden, gratify, indulge, prithee, prythee, satisfy **08** appeal to, think fit **09** captivate, entertain, make happy **11** if you please **12** je vous en prie **14** give pleasure to

- **hard to please**

**04** nice **09** difficult

## pleased

**04** glad, rapt **05** happy **06** elated **07** chuffed **08** cheerful, euphoric, grateful, gruntled, thrilled **09** contented, delighted, delirious, gratified, satisfied **10** complacent **11** on cloud nine, over the moon, tickled pink

## pleasing

**04** cute, fair, fine, good, nice **05** lusty **06** comely, liking, taking **07** amusing, savoury, winning **08** charming, engaging, pleasant **09** agreeable, desirable, enjoyable **10** acceptable, attractive, delectable, delightful, gratifying, satisfying **11** pleasurable **12** entertaining, heartwarming, honey-tongued **13** prepossessing

## pleasurable

**03** fun **04** good, nice **06** groovy, lovely **07** amusing, welcome **08** luscious, pleasant **09** agreeable, congenial, diverting, enjoyable **10** delightful, gratifying **12** entertaining

## pleasure

**03** fun, gem, joy **04** will, wish **05** glory, mirth, prize **06** choice, desire, heaven, solace, thrill **07** command, delight, elation, leisure, purpose **08** gladness, treasure **09** amusement, enjoyment, happiness, hog heaven, pleasance **10** preference, recreation, sensuality **11** complacence, complacency, contentment, dissipation, inclination **12** satisfaction **13** entertainment, gratification

- **expression of pleasure**

**03** aha, boy, oho, ooh, wow **05** good-o, oh boy, tra-la, whack, wowee, zowie **06** good-oh, gotcha, whacko **07** way to go!, whoopee **10** hubba hubba

- **it's a pleasure**

**07** any time **08** forget it, not at all **09** no problem **10** my pleasure **11** it's all right **12** it's no trouble, it was nothing, you're welcome **13** don't mention it, that's all right

- **with pleasure**

**04** fain **06** gladly **07** happily, readily **08** of course **09** willingly **11** avec plaisir

## pleasure-flight

**04** flip

## pleat

**04** fold, kilt, purl, tuck **05** braid, crimp, flute, pinch, plait, prank **06** crease, gather, goffer, pranck, pucker **07** folding, gauffer, plicate, prancke **09** plication **10** intertwine

## plebeian

**03** low **04** base, boor, mean, non-U, pleb **05** prole **06** coarse, common, vulgar, worker **07** ignoble, low-born, peasant, popular **08** commoner, roturier **09** unrefined, vulgarian **10** lower-class, uncultured **11** proletarian **12** common person, uncultivated, working-class **15** undistinguished

**plebiscite**
**04** poll, vote **06** ballot **09** straw poll **10** referendum

**pledge**
**03** vow, wad, wed **04** bail, band, bond, fine, gage, hand, oath, pass, pawn, wage, word **05** swear, vouch, wager **06** borrow, commit, engage, impawn, plight, secure, surety **07** betroth, deposit, earnest, hostage, promise, propine, warrant **08** contract, covenant, impledge, mortgage, security **09** assurance, committal, guarantee, pignorate, sacrament, undertake **10** collateral, commitment, take an oath **11** impignorate, undertaking **12** give your word, word of honour

**plenary**
**04** full, open **05** whole **06** entire **07** general **08** absolute, complete, integral, sweeping, thorough **09** unlimited **11** unqualified **12** unrestricted **13** unconditional

**plenipotentiary**
**05** envoy **06** legate, nuncio **08** absolute, diplomat, emissary, minister **09** dignitary **10** ambassador

**plenitude**
**06** bounty, excess, plenty, wealth **08** fullness, plethora **09** abundance, amplitude, profusion, repletion **10** cornucopia, entireness **11** copiousness **12** completeness **13** plenteousness, plentifulness

**plenteous**
**04** rich **05** ample **06** bumper, lavish **07** copious, fertile, liberal, profuse **08** abundant, fruitful, generous, infinite, prolific **09** abounding, bounteous, bountiful, luxuriant, plentiful **10** productive **11** overflowing **13** inexhaustible

**plentiful**
**04** easy **05** ample, routh, rowth **06** bumper, lavish **07** copious, liberal, profuse, teeming **08** abundant, fruitful, generous, infinite **09** bounteous, bountiful **10** productive **11** overflowing **13** inexhaustible

**plentifully**
**05** amply **08** lavishly **09** copiously, liberally, profusely **10** abundantly, fruitfully, generously **11** bountifully

**plenty**
**04** bags, fund, mass, mine **05** store **06** enough, foison, riches, scouth, scowth, volume, wealth **07** fortune, fulness **08** fullness, plethora, quantity **09** abundance, affluence, profusion, substance **10** abundantly, cornucopia, prosperity **11** copiousness, sufficiency, wealthiness **12** milk and honey **13** plenteousness **14** stouth and routh

• **plenty of**
**04** bags, lots, many **05** heaps, loads, piles **06** enough, masses, stacks **09** shedloads **11** large amount, large number **14** more than enough

**plethora**
**04** glut **06** excess **07** surfeit, surplus **09** abundance, profusion, repletion **11** repleteness, superfluity **12** overfullness **13** overabundance **14** superabundance

**pliability**
**08** docility **09** ductility **10** compliance, elasticity, plasticity **11** amenability, bendability, flexibility **12** adaptability, malleability **13** tractableness **14** suggestibility, susceptibility

**pliable**
**05** bendy, lithe **06** docile, pliant, supple **07** elastic, plastic **08** bendable, biddable, cheverel, cheveril, flexible, yielding **09** adaptable, compliant, malleable, receptive, tractable **10** manageable, responsive **11** persuadable, susceptible **12** superplastic **13** accommodating **14** impressionable

**pliant**
**05** bendy, lithe, swack, swank, wanle **06** docile, limber, supple, wandle, wannel, whippy **07** elastic, plastic, pliable **08** bendable, biddable, flexible, yielding **09** adaptable, compliant, malleable, receptive, tractable **10** manageable, responsive, sequacious **11** persuadable, susceptible **13** accommodating **14** impressionable

**plight**
**03** fix, jam, vow **04** case, fold, hole, mood, risk, trim **05** array, plait, point, state, swear, vouch, weave **06** enfold, engage, liking, pickle, pledge, scrape, secure, taking **07** dilemma, pliskie, promise, propose, straits, trouble **08** affiance, contract, covenant, quandary **09** condition, extremity, guarantee, situation, tight spot **10** difficulty, engagement **11** dire straits, predicament **13** circumstances

**plimsoll**
**03** dap **05** tacky **07** gym shoe **08** sandshoe

**plod**
**04** plot, slog, thud, toil **05** clump, grind, stomp, stump, tramp **06** drudge, labour, lumber, stodge, trudge **07** peg away **08** plug away **09** persevere, policeman, soldier on **11** police force, walk heavily **13** plough through

**plodder**
**03** mug, sap **06** drudge, toiler **07** dullard, slogger

**plot**
**03** bed, erf, lay, lot, map, web **04** area, brew, burn, draw, mark, pack, plan, plod, ruse **05** cabal, chart, draft, frame, hatch, patch, piece, ploat, scald, story, theme, tract **06** action, cook up, design, devise, fleece, garden, locate, map out, parcel, scheme, scorch, sketch, thread **07** collude, concoct, connive, dispose, outline, project, subject **08** conspire, contrive, intrigue, scenario **09** allotment, calculate, machinate, narrative, storyline, stratagem **10** conspiracy **11** machination

**plotter**
**06** dabble, potter **07** planner, schemer **08** dabbling, designer, paddling **09** intriguer **10** machinator **11** conspirator

**plough**
◇ *anagram indicator*
**03** ard, dig, ear, ere, pip, rib **04** beam, fail, list, plow, rive, sill, till, work **05** break, ridge, spade **06** Dipper, fallow, furrow, lister, pleuch, pleugh, rafter, ridger, thwart, turn up **07** break up, scooter, tractor, triones, wrinkle **08** the Wagon **09** Big Dipper, cultivate, Great Bear, subsoiler, Ursa Major **10** Seven Stars **11** agriculture, drill-plough, swing-plough, wheel plough **12** Charles's Wain, septentrions **13** septentriones

• **plough into**
**03** hit **06** go into **07** collide, run into **08** bump into **09** crash into, drive into, smash into

• **plough through**
**11** plod through, wade through **13** trudge through

**ploughshare**
**04** sock **05** share

**plover**
**04** dupe **06** godwit **07** dottrel, killdee, lapwing **08** dotterel, killdeer, wire bird **09** thick knee **10** Charadrius, prostitute, stone snipe

• **flock of plovers**
**04** wing

**ploy**
**04** game, move, ruse, wile **05** dodge, trick **06** device, scheme, tactic **08** artifice **09** manoeuvre, stratagem **10** subterfuge **11** contrivance

**pluck**
**03** pip, rob, tug **04** draw, fail, grit, guts, pick, plot, pook, pouk, pull, race, rase, yank **05** heart, nerve, ploat, plunk, spunk, strip, strum, thrum, twang **06** avulse, daring, evulse, finger, fleece, gather, humble, mettle, remove, rescue, snatch, spirit, take in, tweeze, twitch, valour **07** bravery, collect, courage, despoil, extract, harvest, pull off, swindle **08** audacity, backbone, boldness **09** fortitude **10** resolution **11** divellicate, intrepidity **12** fearlessness **13** determination

**pluckily**
**06** boldly **07** bravely **08** daringly **09** valiantly **10** fearlessly, heroically,

intrepidly **11** audaciously, confidently **12** courageously **13** adventurously

**plucky**
**04** bold, game, gamy **05** brave, gamey, gutsy, gutty **06** daring, feisty, gallus, gritty, heroic, spunky **07** gallows, valiant **08** fearless, intrepid, spirited **09** audacious **10** courageous, determined

**plug**
**02** ad **03** DIN, wad **04** blow, bung, cake, chew, cork, dook, fill, hype, neck, pack, puff, push, seal, stem, stop, tent, tout **05** block, blurb, choke, close, promo, punch, SCART, shoot, spile, stuff, twist **06** dossil, dottle, fipple, market, spigot, stop up, tampon **07** go-devil, mention, pessary, promote, stopper, stopple, tampion, tompion **08** good word **09** access eye, advertise, promotion, publicity, publicize **10** commercial **11** suppository **13** advertisement **14** recommendation

• **plug away**
**04** toil **06** plod on **07** peg away **08** preserve, slog away, toil away **09** persevere, soldier on **10** keep trying

**plum**
**04** best, kaki **05** cushy, prize, prune **06** choice, damson, mussel **07** bullace, quetsch **08** damaskin, prunello, victoria **09** damascene, damaskeen, damasquin, excellent, greengage, mirabelle, myrobalan, naseberry, persimmon, sapodilla **10** damasceene, first-class

**plumb**
**04** bang, dead, slap, true **05** gauge, level, probe, right, sheer, sound **06** bullet, fathom, search, spot-on **07** exactly, examine, explore, measure, plummet, utterly **08** sound out, vertical **09** delve into, out-and-out, penetrate, precisely, search out, up and down **10** straight up, vertically **11** investigate, verticality **12** straight down **13** thorough-going **15** perpendicularly

• **plumb in**
**03** fit, fix, put **05** place, put in, set up **07** install **08** position

• **plumb the depths of**
**13** reach the nadir **15** experience fully, reach rock bottom

**plumbing**

*Plumbing fittings and equipment include:*

**02** WC
**03** pan, tap, tee
**04** bath, bend, bowl, flux, hose, pipe, plug, pump, sink, tank, trap
**05** auger, basin, bidet, float, joint, P-trap, U-bend, union, valve
**06** boiler, faucet, gasket, geyser, hopper, nipple, shower, solder, toilet, urinal, washer
**07** cistern, coupler, plunger, reducer, stop end, Y-branch
**08** ballcock, cylinder, drain rod, lavatory, lever tap, mixer tap, pedestal, pipe clip, radiator, soil vent, stopcock, sump pump, valve key
**09** ball valve, blowtorch, draincock, gate valve, mains pipe, nipple key, waste pipe
**10** back boiler, bottle trap, check valve, copper pipe, copper tube, elbow joint, flare joint, header tank, pipe bender, pipe cutter, pipe wrench, programmer, septic tank, shower head, Teflon® tape, thermostat, tube cutter
**11** water closet
**12** basin spanner, ceiling joint, monkey wrench, overflow bend, pipe coupling, siphon washer
**13** deburring tool, expansion tank, lavatory chain
**14** gas water heater, Stillson® wrench
**15** immersion heater

**plume**
**04** tuft **05** crest, preen, quill **06** osprey, pappus, pinion **07** feather, marabou, panache, plumule **08** aigrette, marabout, streamer

• **plume yourself on**
**07** exult in **10** boast about **13** preen yourself, pride yourself

**plummet**
**04** dive, drop, fall, lead **05** plumb, sound **06** fathom, hurtle, plunge, tumble **07** descend **08** nose-dive **09** plumb line **11** drop rapidly, fall rapidly **15** decrease quickly

**plummy**
**01** U **04** posh **07** refined **08** affected **09** desirable, high-class **10** profitable, upper-class **12** aristocratic

**plump**
**03** fat **04** blow, bold, drop, dump, fall, flop, full, plop, sink, soss, swap, swop, tidy **05** ample, beefy, blurt, bonny, buxom, clump, dumpy, gross, jolly, large, obese, plunk, podgy, round, shoot, slump, sonsy, souse, squab, stout, swell, tubby **06** bonnie, chubby, cuddly, flabby, fleshy, plunge, portly, rotund, sonsie, strike **07** cluster, deposit, descend, put down, set down, well-fed **08** chopping, collapse, generous, matronly **09** corpulent, downright **10** cuddlesome, embonpoint, roundabout, well-liking, well-padded **11** well-covered, well-rounded **15** well-upholstered

• **plump for**
**04** back **06** choose, favour, opt for, prefer, select **07** support **08** side with

**plumpness**
**03** fat **07** fatness, obesity **09** podginess, pudginess, rotundity, stoutness, tubbiness **10** chubbiness, corpulence, fleshiness, portliness

**plunder**
**03** rob **04** loot, peel, pill, prey, raid, rape, reif, sack, swag **05** berob, booty, harry, prize, reave, reive, rifle, scoff, shave, skoff, spoil, steal, strip **06** fleece, forage, maraud, ravage, spoils, spulye **07** despoil, escheat, hership, pillage, ransack, spulyie, spulzie, stick up **08** lay waste, pickings, spoliate, spuilzie **09** depredate, devastate, herriment, herryment, sprechery **10** spreaghery **14** ill-gotten gains

**plunge**
**03** dip, jab, ram **04** bull, dash, dive, drop, duck, enew, fall, jump, mire, push, rush, sink, stab, tank, tear **05** crash, douse, dowse, drive, lunge, merge, pitch, plump, raker, shove, souse, stick, swoop, throw, whelm **06** beduck, career, charge, go down, hurtle, launch, thrust, tumble **07** demerge, demerse, descend, descent, immerge, immerse, plummet **08** bull into, dive-bomb, emplonge, implunge, nose-dive, submerge **09** immersion **10** submersion **11** drop rapidly, fall rapidly **12** enew yourself **15** decrease quickly

• **take the plunge**
**07** go for it **13** bite the bullet **14** commit yourself

**plurality**
**04** bulk, mass, most **06** galaxy, number **07** variety **08** majority **09** diversity, profusion **12** multiplicity, numerousness **13** preponderance

**plus**
**03** and **04** gain, perk, with **05** asset, bonus, extra **06** credit **07** added to, benefit, surplus **08** addition, as well as, increase, positive **09** advantage, good point **10** additional **12** advantageous, in addition to, not to mention, over and above, together with

**plush**
**04** posh, rich **05** ritzy **06** costly, de luxe, glitzy, lavish, luxury, swanky **07** opulent, stylish **08** affluent, palatial **09** luxurious, sumptuous

**Pluto**
**03** Dis **05** Hades

**plutocrat**
**05** Dives **06** fat cat, tycoon **07** Croesus, gold-bug, magnate, rich man **09** moneybags **10** capitalist **11** billionaire, millionaire

**plutonium**
**02** Pu

**ply**
◇ *anagram indicator*
**02** go **03** ren, rin, run, set, use **04** bend, birl, feed, fold, leaf, lush, play **05** apply, beset, birle, ferry, layer, sheet, trade, wield **06** assail, employ, follow, handle, harass, lavish, pursue, strand, supply, travel, work at **07** bombard, carry on, furnish, provide, utilize **08** engage in, exercise, practise **09** condition, importune, thickness **10** manipulate **13** keep supplying

**PM** *see* **prime minister**

## poach

**04** copy, lift, nick, poke, take **05** potch, steal **06** borrow, pilfer, potche, thrust **07** intrude, trample **08** encroach, infringe, trespass **11** appropriate **13** hunt illegally **14** catch illegally

## pocket

◇ *containment indicator*

**03** bag, bin, fob, pot **04** gain, lift, mini, nick, poke, take, whip **05** filch, funds, means, money, patch, pinch, pouch, purse, small, steal, touch **06** assets, budget, cavity, hollow, little, pilfer, potted **07** capital, compact, concise, placket, purloin, trouser **08** abridged, envelope, finances, fob-watch, pint-size, portable, souvenir **09** miniature, plaid-neuk, resources, small area **10** receptacle, small group **11** appropriate, compartment, wherewithal, win unfairly **12** isolated area **14** help yourself to

*See also* **steal**

## pockmark

**03** pit **04** pock, scar **07** blemish, pockpit

## pod

**03** cod **04** case, hull, husk, pipi **05** chile, chili, shell, shuck **06** chilli, legume, loment, paunch, peacod, school **07** musk-bag, peascod, silicle, siliqua, silique **08** lomentum, peasecod, silicula, silicule, strombus, sugar pea, tamarind **09** green bean, mangetout **10** cotton boll **11** pudding-pipe **12** mangetout pea

## podgy

**03** fat **05** dumpy, plump, squat, stout, tubby **06** chubby, chunky, fleshy, rotund, spuddy, stubby, stumpy **07** paunchy **08** roly-poly **09** corpulent, roll-about

## podium

**04** dais, foot, hand **05** stage, stand **07** rostrum **08** platform **09** stylobate

## poem

*Poem types include:*

**03** dit, lay, ode
**04** awdl, ditt, epic, epos, idyl, song, waka
**05** ditty, elegy, epode, haiku, idyll, lyric, rhyme, tanka, verse
**06** ballad, epopee, monody, sonnet
**07** bucolic, couplet, eclogue, epigram, georgic, pantoum, rondeau, sestina, triolet, virelay
**08** cinquain, clerihew, limerick, lipogram, madrigal, palinode, pastoral, thin poem, verselet, versicle
**09** roundelay, shape poem
**10** villanelle
**12** concrete poem, epithalamium, nursery rhyme, prothalamion

*Poems and poetry collections include:*

**02** If
**04** A Red, Crow, Days, Edda, Hope, Howl, Maud, Odes
**05** Comus, Lamia
**06** Façade, Heaven, Hellas, Marina, The Fly, Villon
**07** A Vision, Beowulf, Don Juan, Lycidas, Mariana, Marmion, Red Rose, Requiem, Rondeau, The Quip, Ulysses
**08** Bermudas, Endymion, Georgics, Gunga Din, Hiawatha, Hudibras, Hysteria, Insomnia, Kalevala, Lupercal, Queen Mab, Ramayana, The Iliad, The Night, The Pearl, The Tyger, Tithonus, To Autumn
**09** Decameron, Human Life, Jerusalem, Kubla Khan, The Aeneid, The Cantos
**10** Cherry Ripe, Christabel, Dream Songs, In Memoriam, Lalla Rookh, On an Island, The Dunciad, The Odyssey, The Poetics, The Prelude, The Village, Up in the Air, Very Old Man, View of a Pig
**11** Ars Amatoria, Empty Vessel, High Windows, Holy Sonnets, Humming-Bird, Jabberwocky, Mahabharata, Memorabilia, Remembrance, Song of my Cid, Sudden Light, Tall Nettles, Tam O'Shanter, The Eclogues, The Exstasie, The Peasants, The Retreate, The Sick Rose, The Sluggard, The Woodlark
**12** A Glass of Beer, Ash Wednesday, A Song to Celia, A Song to David, Auld Lang Syne, Bhagavad Gita, Eugene Onegin, Faith Healing, Four Quartets, Goblin Market, Hawk Roosting, Homage to Clio, Jubilate Agno, Mercian Hymns, Morte d'Arthur, Ode to Evening, Paradise Lost, Piers Plowman, The Hill-Shade, The Lucy Poems, The Troop Ship, The Visionary, The Waste Land, The Windhover
**13** Arms and the Boy, Behind the Line, Gilgamesh Epic, Leaves of Grass, Metamorphoses, Missing the Sea, Naming of Parts, Roman de la Rose, September Song, Song by Isbrand, The Book of Thel
**14** A Shropshire Lad, Divina Commedia, Leda and the Swan, Les Fleurs du Mal, Love Songs in Age, Lyrical Ballads, Orlando Furioso, Song of Hiawatha, Strange Meeting, The Divine Image, The Feel of Hands, The Garden Party, The Lotus-Eaters, The Ship of Death, Venus and Adonis
**15** Canterbury Tales, Cautionary Tales, Love without Hope, Magna est Veritas, Ode on Melancholy, Summoned by Bells, The Age of Anxiety, The Divine Comedy, The Eve of St Agnes, The Faerie Queene, The Garden of Love, The Grauballe Man, The Second Coming, The Sorrow of Love

*See also* **poetry**; **song**

## poet

**04** bard, scop **06** rhymer **07** elegist, rhymist **08** beat poet, idyllist, lyricist, minstrel **09** balladeer, poetaster, poeticule, rhymester, sonneteer, versifier **10** verse-maker **15** performance poet

*Poets include:*

**03** **Gay** (John), **Lee** (Laurie), **Paz** (Octavio), **Poe** (Edgar Allan)
**04** **Amis** (Kingsley), **Blok** (Alexander), **Cope** (Wendy), **Dunn** (Douglas), **Dyer** (Sir Edward), **Gray** (Thomas), **Gunn** (Thom), **Hill** (Geoffrey), **Hogg** (James), **Hood** (Thomas), **Hunt** (Leigh), **Lear** (Edward), **Maro** (Publius Vergilius), **Muir** (Edwin), **Nash** (Ogden), **Ovid**, **Owen** (Wilfred), **Pope** (Alexander), **Rich** (Adrienne), **Seth** (Vikram), **Vega** (Lope de)
**05** **Auden** (W H), **Basho** (Matsuo), **Benét** (Stephen Vincent), **Blake** (William), **Burns** (Robert), **Byron** (George, Lord), **Clare** (John), **Crane** (Hart), **Dante**, **Donne** (John), **Duffy** (Carol Ann), **Eliot** (T S), **Frost** (Robert), **Hardy** (Thomas), **Harte** (Brett), **Heine** (Heinrich), **Henri** (Adrian), **Hesse** (Hermann), **Homer**, **Ibsen** (Henrik), **Iqbal** (Sir Muhammad), **Keats** (John), **Keble** (John), **Lodge** (Thomas), **Lorca** (Federico García), **Marot** (Clément), **Meung** (Jean de), **Moore** (Thomas), **Myers** (Frederic William Henry), **O'Hara** (Frank), **Opitz** (Martin), **Plath** (Sylvia), **Pound** (Ezra), **Prior** (Matthew), **Pulci** (Luigi), **Raine** (Craig), **Rilke** (Rainer Maria), **Sachs** (Hans), **Sachs** (Nelly), **Scott** (Sir Walter), **Smart** (Christopher), **Smith** (Stevie), **Spark** (Dame Muriel), **Tasso** (Torquato), **Wyatt** (Sir Thomas), **Yeats** (W B)
**06** **Adcock** (Fleur), **Aragon** (Louis), **Arnold** (Matthew), **Artaud** (Antonin), **Atwood** (Margaret), **Barnes** (William), **Bellay** (Joachim du), **Belloc** (Hilaire), **Benoît**, **Binyon** (Laurence), **Bishop** (Elizabeth), **Brecht** (Bertolt), **Brontë** (Anne), **Brontë** (Emily), **Brooke** (Rupert), **Camäes** (Luís de), **Carver** (Raymond), **Cowper** (William), **Crabbe** (George), **Dunbar** (William), **Eluard** (Paul), **Empson** (Sir William), **Ennius** (Quintus), **Fuller** (Roy), **Goethe** (Johann Wolfgang von), **Graves** (Robert), **Gurney** (Ivor), **Haller** (Albrecht von), **Heaney** (Seamus), **Herder** (Johann Gottfried von), **Hesiod**, **Horace**, **Hughes** (Langston), **Jensen** (Johannes Vilhelm), **Larkin** (Philip), **Lorris** (Guillaume de), **Lowell** (Amy), **Lowell** (Robert), **Millay** (Edna St Vincent), **Milosz** (Czeslaw), **Milton** (John), **Morris** (William), **Musset** (Alfred de), **Neruda** (Pablo), **Ossian**, **Patten** (Brian), **Pindar**, **Porter** (Peter), **Racine** (Jean), **Ramsay** (Allan), **Riding** (Laura), **Sappho**, **Sidney** (Sir Philip), **Surrey**

(Henry Howard, Earl of), **Tagore** (Rabindranath), **Thomas** (Dylan), **Thomas** (Edward), **Thomas** (R S), **Valéry** (Paul), **Villon** (François), **Virgil**, **Waller** (Edmund)
**07** **Addison** (Joseph), **Akahito** (Yamabe no), **Alberti** (Leon Battista), **Aneurin**, **Angelou** (Maya), **Aretino** (Pietro), **Ariosto** (Ludovico), **Ashbery** (John), **Barbour** (John), **Beckett** (Samuel), **Beddoes** (Thomas Lovell), **Blunden** (Edmund Charles), **Boiardo** (Matteo Maria), **Brodsky** (Joseph), **Büchner** (Georg), **Caedmon**, **Campion** (Thomas), **Causley** (Charles), **Chapman** (George), **Chaucer** (Geoffrey), **Cocteau** (Jean), **Da Ponte** (Lorenzo), **Douglas** (Gawain), **Durrell** (Lawrence), **Emerson** (Ralph Waldo), **Flecker** (James Elroy), **Fröding** (Gustaf), **Gautier** (Théophile), **Herbert** (George), **Herrick** (Robert), **Holberg** (Ludvig, Baron), **Hopkins** (Gerard Manley), **Housman** (A E), **Jiménez** (Juan Ramón), **Johnson** (Samuel), **Kipling** (Rudyard), **Layamon**, **Lydgate** (John), **Macbeth** (George), **MacCaig** (Norman), **MacLean** (Sorley), **Manzoni** (Alessandro), **Martial**, **Marvell** (Andrew), **McGough** (Roger), **Mishima** (Yukio), **Mistral** (Frédéric), **Mistral** (Gabriela), **Montale** (Eugenio), **Novalis**, **Orléans** (Charles Duc d'), **Patmore** (Coventry), **Pushkin** (Alexander), **Quarles** (Francis), **Rimbaud** (Arthur), **Roethke** (Theodore), **Ronsard** (Pierre de), **Rostand** (Edmond), **Sassoon** (Siegfried), **Seferis**, **Seifert** (Jaroslav), **Shelley** (Percy Bysshe), **Sitwell** (Dame Edith), **Sitwell** (Sir Sacheverell), **Skelton** (John), **Spender** (Sir Stephen), **Spenser** (Edmund), **Stevens** (Wallace), **Terence**, **Thomson** (James), **Thoreau** (Henry David), **Vaughan** (Henry), **Vicente** (Gil), **Walcott** (Derek), **Whitman** (Walt), **Wieland** (Christoph Martin)
**08** **Anacreon**, **Andersen** (Hans Christian), **Ausonius** (Decimus Magnus), **Banville** (Théodore de), **Berryman** (John), **Brentano** (Clemens), **Brittain** (Vera), **Browning** (Elizabeth Barrett), **Browning** (Robert), **Campbell** (Roy), **Carducci** (Giosuè), **Catullus** (Gaius Valerius), **Claudian**, **Congreve** (William), **cummings** (e e), **Cynewulf**, **Davenant** (Sir William), **De La Mare** (Walter), **Drummond** (William, of Hawthornden), **Firdausi**, **Ginsberg** (Allen), **Henryson** (Robert), **Laforgue** (Jules), **Langland** (William), **Lawrence** (D H), **Leopardi** (Giacomo), **Lovelace** (Richard), **Macaulay** (Dame Rose), **Macaulay** (Thomas), **MacLeish** (Archibald), **MacNeice** (Louis), **Malherbe** (François de), **Mallarmé** (Stéphane), **Menander**, **Milligan** (Spike), **Palgrave** (Francis Turner), **Paterson** (Andrew Barton), **Petrarch**, **Robinson** (Edwin Arlington), **Rossetti** (Christina), **Rossetti** (Dante Gabriel), **Sandburg** (Carl), **Schiller** (Friedrich), **Schlegel** (August Wilhelm von), **Suckling** (Sir John), **Taliesin**, **Tibullus**, **Traherne** (Thomas), **Verlaine** (Paul), **Whittier** (John Greenleaf)
**09** **Aeschylus**, **Akhmatova** (Anna), **Bronowski** (Jacob), **Coleridge** (Samuel Taylor), **D'Annunzio** (Gabriele), **Dickinson** (Emily), **Froissart** (Jean), **Goldsmith** (Oliver), **Hölderlin** (Friedrich), **Lamartine** (Alphonse de), **Lucretius**, **Marinetti** (Filippo Tommaso), **Pasternak** (Boris), **Rochester** (John Wilmot, Earl of), **Rosenberg** (Isaac), **Santayana** (George), **Southwell** (Robert), **Swinburne** (Algernon Charles), **Ungaretti** (Giuseppe), **Zephaniah** (Benjamin)
**10** **Baudelaire** (Charles), **Bradstreet** (Anne), **Chatterton** (Thomas), **Chesterton** (G K), **Empedocles**, **FitzGerald** (Edward), **La Fontaine** (Jean de), **Lagerkvist** (Pär), **Longfellow** (Henry Wadsworth), **MacDiarmid** (Hugh), **Mayakovsky** (Vladimir), **McGonagall** (William), **Propertius** (Sextus), **Theocritus**
**11** **Apollinaire** (Guillaume), **Callimachus**, **Omar Khayyám**, **Shakespeare** (William), **Yevtushenko** (Yevegeny)
**12** **Ferlinghetti** (Lawrence)
**13** **Sackville-West** (Vita)
**14** **Dante Alighieri**, **Saint-John Perse**
**15** **Thomas the Rhymer**

• **poet laureate**
**02** PL

*Poets laureate:*

**03** **Pye** (Henry)
**04** **Rowe** (Nicholas), **Tate** (Nahum)
**06** **Austin** (Alfred), **Cibber** (Colley), **Dryden** (John), **Eusden** (Laurence), **Hughes** (Ted), **Jonson** (Ben), **Motion** (Andrew), **Warton** (Thomas)
**07** **Bridges** (Robert), **Southey** (Robert)
**08** **Betjeman** (Sir John), **Davenant** (Sir William), **Day-Lewis** (Cecil), **Shadwell** (Thomas), **Tennyson** (Alfred, Lord)
**09** **Masefield** (John), **Whitehead** (William)
**10** **Wordsworth** (William)

**poetic**
**06** moving **07** flowing, lyrical, rhyming **08** artistic, creative, graceful, metrical, poetical, symbolic **09** beautiful, sensitive **10** expressive, figurative, rhythmical **11** imaginative

**poetry**
**04** muse **05** poems, poesy, rhyme, verse **06** epopee, lyrics **07** doggrel, iambics, pennill, rhyming, versing **08** doggerel, epopoeia **09** free verse, macaronic, Parnassus, vers libre **10** macaronics **13** versification

*Poetry movements include:*

**04** Beat
**05** found, sound
**07** Acmeism, digital, epitaph, erasure, imagism
**08** concrete, medieval, pastoral, Trouvère
**09** automatic, modernism, symbolism, Troubador, Victorian
**10** Parnassian
**11** Minnesinger, objectivist, performance, Romanticism, The Movement, traditional
**12** metaphysical
**13** Black Mountain, New York School, non-conformism, post-modernism
**14** chanson de geste

*See also* **poem**

**pogrom**
**06** murder **07** carnage, killing **08** butchery, genocide, homicide, massacre **09** bloodbath, holocaust, slaughter **10** decimation **11** liquidation **12** annihilation **13** extermination **15** ethnic cleansing

**poignancy**
**04** pain **06** misery, pathos **07** emotion, feeling, sadness, tragedy **08** distress, keenness, piquancy, pungency **09** intensity, sentiment, sharpness **10** bitterness, tenderness **11** painfulness, piteousness **12** wretchedness **13** evocativeness

**poignant**
**03** sad **05** sharp **06** moving, tender, tragic **07** painful, piquant, piteous, poynant, pungent, tearful **08** haunting, pathetic, pricking, stinging, touching, wretched **09** affecting, agonizing, emotional, heartfelt, miserable, sorrowful, upsetting **11** distressing, penetrating **12** heart-rending **13** heartbreaking

**poignantly**
**05** sadly **08** movingly, tenderly **09** miserably, painfully, tearfully **10** tragically, wretchedly **11** emotionally, sorrowfully **12** pathetically

**point**
**01** E, N, S, W **02** pt **03** ace, aim, dot, end, hit, neb, nib, nub, ord, tip, top, use **04** apex, area, cape, case, core, crag, crux, cusp, fang, feat, gist, goal, head, hint, item, lace, mark, meat, ness, node, peak, pike, pith, show, site, spot, stop, time, tine, vein, whit **05** drift, facet, heart, issue, level, place, score, sense, speck, spike, stage, state, sting, taper, tenor, theme, topic, total, train, trait, value, verge **06** aspect, burden, clause, denote, detail, direct, marrow, matter, moment, motive, object, period, plight, reason, signal, thrust **07** essence, feature, heading, instant,

keynote, meaning, purpose, quality, sharpen, signify, subject, suggest **08** evidence, foreland, full stop, headland, indicate, juncture, locality, location, position, property, pungency, question, sharp end **09** attribute, condition, designate, extremity, full point, gesture at, intention, main point, north pole, objective, situation, south pole **10** conclusion, importance, particular, promontory, resolution **11** culmination **12** central point, decimal point, significance **14** characteristic, gesture towards

*See also* **compass**; **horse**

**• beside the point**
**09** unrelated **10** immaterial, irrelevant, out of place, red herring **11** unconnected

**• chief points**
**03** sum

**• in point of fact**
**03** nay **06** indeed, in fact, really **08** actually **09** in reality **15** as a matter of fact

**• lowest point**
**04** zero

**• main point**
**04** clou, gist

**• on the point of**
**07** about to, going to, ready to **10** in danger of **11** just about to, preparing to **12** on the brink of, on the verge of

**• point of view**
**03** POV **04** view **05** angle, slant **06** aspect, belief, stance **07** feeling, opinion, outlook **08** approach, attitude, position **09** judgement, sentiment, viewpoint **10** Anschauung, standpoint **11** perspective

**• point out**
**04** shew, show **05** judge **06** remind, reveal **07** bring up, mention, point to, presage, specify **08** allude to, identify, indicate **09** highlight **15** call attention to, draw attention to

**• point up**
**06** stress **09** emphasize, highlight, underline **15** call attention to

**• to the point**
**05** ad rem **07** germane, related **08** apposite, pregnant, relevant **09** connected, pertinent **10** applicable **11** appropriate

**• up to a point**
**06** partly **08** slightly, somewhat **12** to some degree, to some extent

## point-blank
**04** flat, near, open **05** blunt, frank, level, plain, reach **06** candid, direct, openly, rudely **07** bluntly, closely, close to, frankly, plainly **08** abruptly, candidly, directly, explicit, outright, straight, touching **10** explicitly, forthright, unreserved **12** at close range, forthrightly **13** unequivocally **15** straightforward

## pointed
**04** keen, urdé, urdy **05** clear, edged, sharp, spicy, urdée **06** barbed, biting, Gothic, lancet **07** cutting, mordant, obvious, precise, telling **08** acicular, aculeate, explicit, forceful, incisive, striking, tapering **09** aculeated, cuspidate, mucronate, trenchant **10** cuspidated, fastigiate, lanceolate, mucronated **11** lanceolated, near the bone, penetrating **12** epigrammatic **14** epigrammatical

## pointedly
**07** bluntly, plainly **09** defiantly, on purpose **10** explicitly **13** intentionally, provocatively

## pointer
**03** rod, tip **04** cane, clue, hand, hint, pole, sign **05** arrow, guide, index, stick, style **06** advice, fescue, needle, tongue **07** caution, warning **09** guideline, hyperlink, indicator **10** indication, suggestion **11** trafficator **13** piece of advice **14** recommendation

## pointless
◇ *tail deletion indicator*
**04** vain **05** inane **06** absurd, futile **07** aimless, foolish, useless **08** muticous **09** a mug's game, fruitless, senseless, to no avail, valueless, worthless **10** ridiculous, unavailing **11** meaningless, nonsensical **12** a waste of time, unproductive, unprofitable **13** insignificant **14** a waste of effort

## pointlessly
**06** in vain **09** aimlessly **11** senselessly **12** unprofitably **13** meaninglessly **14** unproductively

## poise
**04** bias, cool, hang **05** grace, hover, pease, peaze, peise, peize, peyse, weigh **06** aplomb, impact, ponder, steady, weight **07** balance, dignity, librate, support, suspend **08** calmness, coolness, elegance, momentum, position, serenity, suspense **09** assurance, composure **10** equanimity **11** equilibrium, self-control **13** self-assurance **14** presence of mind, self-confidence, self-possession

## poised
**03** set **04** calm, cool **05** paysd, ready, suave **06** all set, serene, urbane **07** assured, waiting **08** balanced, composed, graceful, prepared **09** collected, dignified, expectant, unruffled **11** unflappable **13** self-confident, self-possessed **14** self-controlled

## poison
**03** mar **04** warp **05** spoil, taint **06** blight, cancer, canker, defile, infect, rankle **07** corrupt, deprave, envenom, pervert, pollute **08** embitter **09** contagion, pollution **10** adulterate, corruption, envenomate, malignancy **11** contaminate **13** contamination

*Poisonous creatures include:*

**03** asp
**04** fugu, gila, seps, weta
**05** adder, cobra, viper
**06** dugite, katipo, taipan
**07** redback, sea wasp
**08** blowfish, cerastes, jararaca, jararaka, mocassin, moccasin, ringhals, rinkhals, scorpion, sea snake
**09** berg-adder, boomslang, funnel-web, globe fish, hamadryad, king cobra, puff adder, stonefish, tarantula
**10** bandy-bandy, black snake, black widow, bushmaster, copperhead, coral snake, death adder, puffer fish
**11** cottonmouth, gaboon viper, gila monster, rattlesnake
**12** box jellyfish, scorpion fish, sea porcupine, violin spider
**13** water moccasin
**15** funnel-web spider

*Poisonous plants include:*

**04** upas
**05** dwale
**06** antiar
**07** aconite, amanita, anemone, cowbane, hemlock, lantana
**08** banewort, foxglove, laburnum, mandrake, oleander, wild arum
**09** digitalis, monkshood, naked boys, naked lady, poison ivy, stinkweed, wake-robin, wolfsbane
**10** belladonna, cuckoo pint, jimson weed, stramonium, thorn apple, windflower
**12** helmet flower
**13** giant hockweed, meadow saffron
**14** castor oil plant, lords-and-ladies
**15** black nightshade

*Poisons and toxic substances include:*

**03** BHC
**04** bane, lead
**05** abrin, conin, lysol, ozone, ricin, sarin, toxin, venin, venom, VX gas
**06** arsine, curare, dioxin, G-agent, iodine, ketene, V-agent, wabain, war gas
**07** arsenic, bromine, cacodyl, coniine, cyanide, digoxin, dioxane, mercury, mineral, neurine, ouabain, stibine, tanghin
**08** antimony, atropine, chlordan, chlorine, cyanogen, cytisine, fluorine, gossypol, lobeline, melittin, nerve gas, Paraquat®, phosgene, ptomaine, ratsbane, rotenone, thebaine, urushiol
**09** aflatoxin, amygdalin, chaconine, chlordane, muscarine, mycotoxin, nux vomica, saxitoxin, white damp
**10** acrylamide, aqua Tofana, bufotenine, domoic acid, heptachlor, mustard gas, neurotoxin, oxalic acid, phosphorus, phytotoxin, picrotoxin, strychnine, tetrotoxin
**11** enterotoxin, hyoscyamine, nitric oxide, prussic acid, sugar of lead
**12** strophanthin, tetrodotoxin
**13** Scheele's green, silver nitrate

14 carbon monoxide
15 hydrogen cyanide, nitrogen dioxide

**poisoning**
03 obi 04 obia 05 obeah

*Poisoning types include:*

04 food, lead
05 algae, blood
06 iodism
07 bromism, gassing, pyaemia, sausage, toxemia
08 botulism, ergotism, plumbism, ptomaine, toxaemia
09 brominism, crotalism, fluorosis, lead colic, mephitism, sapraemia, saturnism, zinc colic
10 alcoholism, molybdosis, salicylism, salmonella, stibialism, strychnism
11 phosphorism, septicaemia
12 hydrargyrism, intoxication, strychninism
13 mycotoxicosis

**poisonous**
05 fatal, toxic, venom 06 deadly, lethal, mortal, virose 07 baneful, harmful, noxious, vicious 08 spiteful, toxicant, venomous, virulent 09 cancerous, cankerous, malicious, malignant, offensive 10 corrupting, pernicious 11 deleterious 13 contaminating

*See also* **poison**

**poke**
03 bag, dig, hit, jab, peg 04 butt, pick, pock, pote, prod, prog, push, root, rout, stab 05 elbow, goose, grope, nudge, poach, prick, proke, punch, shove, stick, stoop, wroot 06 incite, nuzzle, pocket, potter, powter, stir up, thrust 07 scuffle, snuzzle 08 itchweed, protrude

• **poke around**
04 root, rout 07 look for 09 search for 11 grope around, rake through 13 rummage around 14 look all over for

• **poke fun at**
03 cod, rag, rib 04 jeer, joke, mock, quiz 05 get at, spoof, taunt, tease 06 parody, send up 08 ridicule 09 make fun of 11 poke borak at 13 poke mullock at, take the mickey

• **poke out**
06 beetle, extend, jut out 07 extrude, project 08 overhang, protrude, stick out

**poker**

*Poker-related terms include:*

03 pat, shy
04 ante, call, flop, pair, stay, stud
05 blind, bluff, check, flush
06 kicker, suited
08 hole card, showdown, stand pat, straight
09 four-flush, full house
10 royal flush
11 busted flush, pass the buck
13 community card, straight flush

**poker-faced**
05 blank, empty 06 glazed, vacant 07 deadpan, vacuous 08 lifeless 09 apathetic, impassive 11 emotionless, indifferent, inscrutable 12 uninterested 14 expressionless, without feeling 15 uncomprehending

**poky**
04 slow, tiny 05 small, tight 06 narrow, poking 07 cramped, crowded 08 confined, powerful 10 restricted 12 incommodious

*See also* **prison**

**Poland**
02 PL 03 POL

**polar**
03 icy 04 cold 05 axial 06 arctic, frozen 07 glacial 08 freezing, opposite, Siberian 09 Antarctic 10 ambivalent 11 conflicting, dichotomous 12 antithetical 13 contradictory

**polarity**
07 duality, paradox 09 dichotomy 10 antithesis, difference, opposition, separation 11 ambivalence, contrariety 12 oppositeness 13 contradiction

**polarize**
05 split 06 divide 07 break up, split up 08 alienate, disunite, estrange, separate 09 segregate 10 drive apart 11 come between

**pole**
01 N, S 02 po 03 bar, lug, nib, oar, rod 04 bail, boom, kent, mast, post, rood, spar 05 caber, limit, perch, quant, shaft, staff, stake, stang, stick, sting 06 janker, pillar, Polack, ripeck, rypeck 07 extreme, heavens, ryepeck, support, upright 08 Polander 09 cowl-staff, extremity, stanchion 10 river horse 11 clothes-prop 12 Venetian mast

• **poles apart**
11 worlds apart 12 incompatible 14 irreconcilable

**polecat**
05 fitch, skunk 06 ferret 07 fitchet, fitchew, foumart 08 foulmart 10 prostitute

**polemic**
06 debate 07 dispute, eristic 08 argument, diatribe 09 eristical, invective, polemical 11 contentious, controversy 12 disputatious 13 argumentative, controversial

**polemicist**
06 arguer 07 debater 08 disputer, polemist 09 contender, disputant 11 logomachist

**polemics**
06 debate 07 dispute 08 argument 09 logomachy 10 contention 11 controversy, disputation 13 argumentation

**police**
◇ *anagram indicator*
04 cops, fuzz, heat, pigs, plod 05 check, filth, guard, polis, watch 06 defend, patrol, the law 07 bizzies, control, coppers, monitor, observe, Old Bill, oversee, peelers, protect, rozzers, the Bill, the fuzz 08 regulate, the force 09 keep watch, supervise 10 boys in blue 11 police force 12 constabulary, keep the peace 13 the boys in blue 14 police officers

*Police forces and branches include:*

02 AP, KP, MP, PD, SS
03 CIB, CID, KGB, Met, MGB, RMP
04 Ogpu, PSNI, RCMP, SWAT
05 cheka, Garda, Stasi
07 Europol, Gestapo, sweeney, the Yard
08 Interpol
09 Air Police, bomb squad, drug squad, porn squad, riot squad, task force, vice squad
10 riot police, Securitate, water guard
11 flying squad, gendarmerie, strike force, sweeney todd, Yardie squad
12 mobile police, Scotland Yard, secret police, Texas Rangers
13 Garda Siochana, mounted police, Schutzstaffel, Special Branch, traffic police
14 military police
15 New Scotland Yard

*Police-related terms include:*

04 ACPO, beat, book, bust, cell, nick, raid, rank, shop, tana, tank
05 ACPOS, baton, cuffs, fit-up, force, frame, go off, grass, manor, plant, pound, set-up, snout, sting, tanna, thana, tunic
06 arrest, batoon, charge, cordon, curfew, fisgig, fizgig, helmet, line-up, rumble, search, tannah, thanah, thanna, wanted
07 caution, copshop, custody, dragnet, epaulet, jemadar, manhunt, mugshot, pentito, round-up, station, stinger, stoolie, thannah, uniform, warrant
08 evidence, mouchard, panda car, precinct, prowl car, speed gun, squad car
09 blue light, centenier, handcuffs, identikit, meat wagon, on the beat, police dog, radar trap, shakedown, speed trap, truncheon
10 body armour, police cell, police trap, supergrass, tenderloin, tracker dog, watch house
11 fingerprint, flying squad, jam sandwich, Judges' Rules, stool pigeon, utility belt, warrant card
12 bertillonage, incident room, police escort, police-manure, surveillance, walkie-talkie
13 police station, rogues' gallery, search warrant, stop-and-search
14 catch red-handed, criminal record, identity parade
15 bullet-proof vest, long arm of the law, scene of the crime

## police officer

**02** DI, PC, PS, PW, SC **03** cop, pig, 'tec, WPC **04** bogy, bull, flic, gill, nark, peon, plod, slop, SOCO, trap **05** beast, bizzy, bobby, bogey, Dixon, garda, jawan, polis, sepoy, sowar, traps, wolly **06** askari, copper, escort, lawman, Mounty, peeler, redcap, rozzer, sbirro, the law **07** captain, crusher, gumshoe, John Hop, marshal, Mountie, officer, trooper, zabtieh, zaptiah, zaptieh **08** flat-foot, gendarme, sergeant, serjeant, speed-cop, walloper **09** centenier, commander, constable, detective, inspector, patrolman, policeman, woodentop **10** bluebottle, carabinero, gangbuster, lieutenant, traffic cop **11** Black and Tan, carabiniere, patrolwoman, policewoman **12** master-at-arms, peace officer, state trooper **13** beetle-crusher, branch officer **14** police sergeant, superintendent, warrant officer

*Police ranks in the UK:*

**08** Sergeant
**09** Commander, Constable, Inspector
**12** Commissioner
**14** Chief Constable, Chief Inspector, Superintendent
**18** Deputy Commissioner
**19** Chief Superintendent
**20** Deputy Chief Constable
**21** Assistant Commissioner
**23** Assistant Chief Constable
**27** Deputy Assistant Commissioner

### • police search

**04** heat **07** dragnet, manhunt
**09** shakedown

## police station

**04** nick, tana **05** tanna, thana
**06** tannah, thanah, thanna **07** copshop, thannah **08** precinct **10** watch house
**11** gendarmerie

## policy

**04** line, plan **05** rules **06** course, custom, method, scheme, stance, system **07** cunning **08** approach, position, practice, protocol, prudence, schedule, strategy **09** guideline, insurance, procedure, programme
**10** guidelines, statecraft **12** constitution
**14** code of practice, course of action

### • the best policy

**07** honesty

## polish

**03** lap, rub, wax **04** buff, bull, file, posh, sand **05** class, clean, glass, glaze, gloss, grace, poise, rub up, scour, sheen, shine, slick, style **06** finish, lustre, Polack, Poland, posh up, refine, smooth, veneer **07** beeswax, brush up, burnish, enhance, finesse, furbish, improve, perfect, planish, slicken, sparkle, touch up, varnish **08** breeding, brighten, elegance, glaciate
**09** brilliant, cultivate **10** brightness, brilliance, refinement, smoothness
**11** cultivation, rottenstone, satin finish
**13** supercalender **14** sophistication

### • polish off

**03** zap **04** bolt, do in, down, kill, wolf **05** eat up, stuff, waste **06** devour, finish, gobble, murder, rub out **07** bump off, consume, destroy, put away, take out, wipe out **08** blow away, complete, dispatch, knock off **09** dispose of, eliminate, liquidate

## polished

**05** adept, filed, shiny, suave, waxed
**06** expert, glassy, glossy, polite, sanded, smooth, snappy, urbane
**07** elegant, genteel, perfect, refined, shining, skilful **08** cultured, flawless, gleaming, graceful, lapidary, lustrous, masterly, slippery, well-bred
**09** burnished, civilized, excellent, faultless, perfected **10** consummate, cultivated, impeccable, proficient, remarkable **11** outstanding, superlative
**12** accomplished, professional, well-mannered **13** sophisticated

## polite

**05** bland, civil, suave **06** glossy, humane, urbane **07** elegant, gallant, genteel, refined, tactful **08** cultured, delicate, gracious, ladylike, obliging, polished, well-bred **09** civilized, courteous, courtlike **10** chivalrous, cultivated, diplomatic, respectful, thoughtful **11** considerate, deferential, gentlemanly, well-behaved
**12** Grandisonian, well-mannered
**13** sophisticated

## politely

**09** gallantly, tactfully **10** graciously, obligingly **11** courteously
**12** chivalrously, respectfully, thoughtfully **13** considerately
**14** diplomatically

## politeness

**04** tact **05** grace **06** polish **07** culture, manners, respect **08** civility, courtesy, elegance **09** attention, deference, diplomacy, gentility, politesse
**10** cordiality, discretion, refinement
**11** courtliness, cultivation, good manners, savoir-vivre
**12** complaisance, good breeding, graciousness, mannerliness
**14** respectfulness, thoughtfulness
**15** considerateness, gentlemanliness

## politic

**04** sage, wise **06** shrewd **07** prudent, tactful **08** discreet, sensible
**09** advisable, expedient, judicious, opportune, political, sagacious
**10** diplomatic **12** advantageous
**14** constitutional

## political

**05** civil **06** public **08** judicial
**09** executive **11** ministerial
**12** bureaucratic, governmental
**13** parliamentary **14** administrative, constitutional, party political

*See also* **parliament**; **party**

*Political ideologies include:*

**06** holism, Maoism, Nazism
**07** fascism, Marxism
**08** third way, Whiggism
**09** anarchism, communism, democracy, neo-nazism, pluralism, socialism, theocracy
**10** absolutism, Bolshevism, federalism, liberalism, neo-fascism, Trotskyism
**11** imperialism, nationalism, syndicalism, Thatcherism
**12** collectivism, conservatism
**13** individualism, republicanism, unilateralism
**14** egalitarianism, neocolonialism
**15** social democracy, totalitarianism

## politician

**02** MP **07** senator **08** minister
**09** president **13** vice president

*See also* **president**; **prime minister**

*Politicians include:*

**03** **Coe** (Sebastian, Lord), **Fox** (Charles James), **Fox** (Liam), **Fox** (Sir Marcus), **Jay** (Margaret, Lady), **Lee** (Jennie, Lady), **Lie** (Trygve), **May** (Theresa), **Pym** (John), **Wet** (Christian de), **Yeo** (Timothy)
**04** **Amos** (Valerie, Baroness), **Aziz** (Tariq), **Bell** (Martin), **Benn** (Anthony Wedgwood 'Tony'), **Benn** (Hilary), **Cato** (Marcus Porcius), **Cook** (Robin), **Debs** (Eugene Victor), **Dole** (Robert), **Foot** (Michael), **Gore** (Albert), **Haig** (Alexander), **Hain** (Peter), **Hess** (Rudolf), **Hoon** (Geoff), **Howe** (Geoffrey, Lord), **Hume** (John), **Hurd** (Douglas, Lord), **Koch** (Ed), **Kohl** (Helmut), **More** (Sir Thomas), **Nagy** (Imre), **Opik** (Lembit), **Owen** (David, Lord), **Pitt** (William, the elder), **Reid** (John), **Reno** (Janet), **Rice** (Condoleezza), **Röhm** (Ernst), **Rusk** (Dean), **Vane** (Sir Henry)
**05** **Adams** (Gerry), **Agnew** (Spiro), **Astor** (Nancy, Viscountess), **Bacon** (Francis), **Baker** (James Addison), **Baker** (Kenneth, Lord), **Bevan** (Aneurin), **Bevin** (Ernest), **Brown** (George), **Brown** (Gordon), **Burke** (Edmund), **Cecil** (William), **Cimon**, **Clark** (Alan), **Cleon**, **Davis** (David), **Dayan** (Moshe), **Dewar** (Donald), **Field** (Frank), **Freud** (Sir Clement), **Hague** (William), **Huhne** (Chris), **Kelly** (Ruth), **Kirov** (Sergey), **Krenz** (Egon), **Lenin** (Vladimir Ilyich), **Marat** (Jean Paul), **Maude** (Francis), **Nkomo** (Joshua), **Perón** (Eva), **Perón** (Isabelita), **Scott** (Sir Nicholas), **Scott** (Sir Richard), **Short** (Clare), **Smith** (Chris), **Smith** (Jacqui), **Smith** (John), **Solon**, **Steel** (David, Lord), **Straw** (Jack), **Sulla** (Lucius Cornelius), **Sully** (Maximilien de Béthune, Duc de), **Tambo** (Oliver), **Timms** (Stephen), **Vance** (Cyrus Roberts)
**06** **Abacha** (Sanni), **Abbott** (Diane), **Antony** (Mark), **Archer** (Jeffrey), **Benton** (Thomas Hart), **Blears** (Hazel), **Boyson** (Sir Rhodes), **Brandt** (Willy), **Bright** (John), **Browne** (Des), **Butler** (Richard,

Lord), **Caesar** (Julius), **Castle** (Barbara, Lady), **Cicero** (Marcus Tullius), **Clarke** (Charles), **Clarke** (Kenneth), **Cobden** (Richard), **Cripps** (Sir Stafford), **Curzon** (George, Marquis), **Danton** (Georges), **Davies** (Denzil), **Djilas** (Milovan), **Dobson** (Frank), **Dubcek** (Alexander), **Dulles** (John Foster), **Erhard** (Ludwig), **Fowler** (Sir Norman), **Gummer** (John), **Hardie** (Keir), **Harman** (Harriet), **Healey** (Denis, Lord), **Hewitt** (Patricia), **Hitler** (Adolf), **Horthy** (Miklós), **Howard** (Michael), **Hughes** (Simon), **Hutton** (John), **Irvine** (Alexander, Lord), **Jinnah** (Muhammad Ali), **Joseph** (Keith, Lord), **Jowell** (Tessa), **Kaunda** (Kenneth), **Lamont** (Norman), **Lawson** (Nigel, Lord), **Letwin** (Oliver), **Lilley** (Peter), **Mallon** (Seamus), **Marius** (Gaius), **Mellon** (Andrew William), **Mellor** (David), **Merkel** (Angela), **Mornay** (Philippe de), **Morton** (John), **Mosley** (Sir Oswald), **Mowlam** (Doctor Marjorie 'Mo'), **Nansen** (Fridtjof), **Necker** (Jacques), **Norris** (Steven), **Pandit** (Vijaya Lakshmi), **Pompey**, **Powell** (Enoch), **Prasad** (Rajendra), **Quayle** (Dan), **Roland** (Jean Mari), **Sidney** (Algernon), **Somers** (John, Lord), **Steele** (Sir Richard), **Suslov** (Mikhail), **Tebbit** (Norman, Lord), **Thorpe** (Jeremy), **Waller** (Edmund), **Walter** (Hubert), **Warren** (Earl), **Wilkes** (John), **Wolsey** (Thomas)

**07** **Acheson** (Dean), **Allende** (Salvador), **Arundel** (Thomas), **Ashdown** (Paddy), **Beckett** (Margaret), **Bedford** (John of Lancaster, Duke of), **Boateng** (Paul), **Bormann** (Martin), **Brittan** (Sir Leon), **Cameron** (David), **Canning** (George), **Cassius**, **Colbert** (Jean Baptiste), **Collins** (Michael), **Comines** (Philippe de), **Crassus** (Marcus Licinius), **Dalyell** (Tam), **Dandolo** (Enrico), **Darling** (Alistair), **De Klerk** (Frederik William), **Dorrell** (Stephen), **Fischer** (Joschka), **Fouquet** (Nicolas), **Gemayel** (Amin), **Gemayel** (Bashir), **Gemayel** (Sheikh Pierre), **Grattan** (Henry), **Grimond** (Jo, Lord), **Haldane** (Richard, Viscount), **Halifax** (Edward Frederick Lindley Wood, Earl of), **Halifax** (George Savile, Marquis of), **Harlech** (William David Ormsby Gore, Lord), **Hunyady** (János Corvinus), **Hussein** (Saddam), **Jackson** (Glenda), **Jackson** (Jesse), **Jameson** (Sir Leander Starr), **Jenkins** (Roy, Lord), **Johnson** (Alan), **Kalinin** (Mikhail), **Kaufman** (Gerald), **Kaunitz** (Wenzel Anton Fürst von), **Kennedy** (Charles), **Kennedy** (Edward M), **Kennedy** (Robert F), **Kinnock** (Neil), **Kossuth** (Lajos), **Lepidus** (Marcus Aemilius), **MacLeod** (Iain), **Malraux** (André), **Maxwell** (Robert), **Mazarin** (Jules, Cardinal), **Meacher** (Michael), **Mikoyan** (Anastas), **Milburn** (Alan), **Mondale** (Walter Frederick), **Osborne** (George), **Paisley** (Reverend Ian), **Profumo** (John), **Redmond** (John), **Redwood** (John), **Rifkind** (Sir Malcolm), **Russell** (William, Lord), **Salmond** (Alexander), **Schmidt** (Helmut), **Sithole** (Reverend Ndabaningi), **Skinner** (Dennis), **Tallien** (Jean Lambert), **Trimble** (David), **Warwick** (Richard Neville, Earl of), **William** (of Wykeham)

**08** **Adenauer** (Konrad), **Albright** (Madeleine), **Antonius** (Marcus), **Blunkett** (David), **Campbell** (Sir Menzies), **Catiline**, **Constant** (Benjamin), **Cromwell** (Oliver), **Cromwell** (Thomas), **Crossman** (Richard), **Daladier** (Edouard), **Dimitrov** (Georgi), **Dollfuss** (Engelbert), **Falconer** (Charles, Lord), **Franklin** (Benjamin), **Genscher** (Hans-Dietrich), **Goebbels** (Joseph), **Hailsham** (Quintin McGarel Hogg, Viscount), **Hamilton** (Alexander), **Harriman** (William Averell), **Honecker** (Erich), **Humphrey** (Hubert Horatio), **Ibárruri** (Dolores), **Jumblatt** (Kemal), **Karadzic** (Radovan), **Khomeini** (Ayatollah Ruhollah), **Lansbury** (George), **Lucullus** (Lucius Licinius), **Malenkov** (Giorgiy), **Marshall** (George Catlett), **Maudling** (Reginald), **McCarthy** (Eugene Joseph), **McCarthy** (Joseph Raymond), **McGovern** (George Stanley), **McNamara** (Robert Strange), **Miliband** (David), **Mirabeau** (Honoré Gabriel Riqueti, Comte de), **Montfort** (Simon de), **Morrison** (Herbert, Lord), **Pericles**, **Polignac** (Auguste Jules Armand Marie, Prince de), **Portillo** (Michael), **Prescott** (John), **Rathenau** (Walther), **Sandwich** (John Montagu, Earl of), **Schröder** (Gerhard), **Schüssel** (Wolfgang), **Shephard** (Gillian), **Shinwell** (Manny, Lord), **Stanhope** (James, Earl), **Ulbricht** (Walter), **Whitelaw** (William 'Willie', Viscount), **Williams** (Shirley, Lady), **Zinoviev** (Grigoriy)

**09** **Alexander** (Douglas), **Armstrong** (Hilary), **Boothroyd** (Betty), **Bottomley** (Virginia), **Buthelezi** (Chief Mangosuthu), **Ceausescu** (Nicolae), **Churchill** (Randolph, Lord), **Gaitskell** (Hugh), **Godolphin** (Sidney, Earl of), **Goldwater** (Barry Morris), **Heseltine** (Michael), **Kissinger** (Henry), **Kitchener** (Herbert, Earl), **Lafayette** (Marie Joseph, Marquis de), **La Guardia** (Fiorello Henry), **Luxemburg** (Rosa), **Mandelson** (Peter), **Miltiades**, **Parkinson** (Cecil, Lord), **Podgorniy** (Nikolay), **Ramaphosa** (Cyril), **Richelieu** (Armand Jean du Plessis, Cardinal and Duc de), **Robertson** (George, Lord), **Stevenson** (Adlai), **Strafford** (Thomas Wentworth, Earl of), **Streicher** (Julius), **Vyshinsky** (Andrei)

**10** **Alcibiades**, **Carrington** (Peter, Lord), **Cunningham** (Doctor Jack), **Enver Pasha**, **Hattersley** (Roy, Lord), **McGuinness** (Martin), **Metternich** (Klemens Fürst von), **Ribbentrop** (Joachim von), **Stresemann** (Gustav), **Talleyrand** (Charles Maurice de), **Waldegrave** (William), **Walsingham** (Sir Francis), **Weinberger** (Caspar), **Widdecombe** (Ann)

**11** **Beaverbrook** (Max Aitken, Lord), **Bolingbroke** (Henry St John, Viscount), **Castlereagh** (Robert Stewart, Viscount), **Chamberlain** (Joseph), **Chamberlain** (Sir Austen), **Cincinnatus** (Lucius Quinctius), **Demosthenes**, **George-Brown** (Lord), **Hore-Belisha** (Leslie, Lord), **Livingstone** (Ken), **Machiavelli** (Niccolò), **Mountbatten** (Louis, Earl), **Shaftesbury** (Anthony Ashley Cooper, Earl of), **Wilberforce** (William)

**12** **Boutros-Ghali** (Boutros), **Hammarskjöld** (Dag), **Themistocles**

**13** **Chateaubriand** (François Auguste René, Viscount of), **Fabius Maximus** (Quintus)

**14** **Heathcoat-Amory** (David)

## politics

**05** state **06** civics **09** diplomacy, power game **10** government, statecraft **11** machination, manoeuvring, Weltpolitik **12** machinations, Machtpolitik, manipulation **13** party politics, power politics, power struggle, public affairs, statesmanship **14** affairs of state, haute politique, political views, wheeler-dealing **15** local government

## poll

**03** cut, dod, get, net, pow, win **04** clip, gain, head, trim, vote **05** count, shear, tally **06** ballot, census, obtain, parrot, return, sample, survey, voting **07** canvass, dishorn, pollard, receive, returns, solicit, sondage **08** campaign, question, register, sampling **09** ballot-box, head count, interview, straw poll, straw vote **10** Gallup poll, individual, plebiscite, referendum **11** electioneer, opinion poll, show of hands **14** market research

## pollack

**03** lob **05** coley, lythe **06** saithe **08** coalfish **09** sea salmon

## polled

**03** not **04** nott

## pollen

**06** farina **08** bee-bread **09** witchmeal

**pollute**
◇ *anagram indicator*
**03** mar **04** file, foul, soil, warp
**05** blend, dirty, spoil, stain, sully, taint
**06** befoul, canker, debase, defile, infect, poison **07** besmear, blacken, corrupt, defiled, deprave, profane, tarnish, vitiate **09** make dirty
**10** adulterate **11** contaminate

**pollution**
◇ *anagram indicator*
**03** fug **04** smog **05** stain, taint
**07** fouling, soilure **08** foulness, impurity, staining, sullying
**09** depravity, dirtiness, infection, muckiness **10** blackening, corruption, debasement, defilement, filthiness, tarnishing **12** adulteration
**13** contamination

**polonium**
**02** Po

**polychromatic**
**06** motley **07** mottled, rainbow
**08** many-hued **10** polychrome, variegated **12** many-coloured, varicoloured **13** kaleidoscopic, multicoloured, parti-coloured

**polyglot**
**08** linguist **11** multiracial, polyglottal, polyglottic **12** cosmopolitan, multilingual **13** international, multilinguist

**polymath**
**06** oracle **07** know-all **10** all-rounder, pansophist, polyhistor

**pomp**
**04** show **05** glory, state **06** parade, ritual, vanity **07** display, glitter, majesty, triumph **08** ceremony, flourish, grandeur **09** formality, pageantry, solemnity, spectacle, splendour
**10** brilliance, ceremonial, procession
**11** ostentation **12** magnificence **14** self-importance **15** ceremoniousness

**pomposity**
**04** airs **05** pride **06** vanity **07** bombast, fustian **08** euphuism, rhetoric
**09** arrogance, loftiness, turgidity
**10** pretension, stuffiness **11** affectation, haughtiness, preachiness, presumption
**13** condescension, imperiousness, magniloquence **14** grandiloquence, self-importance **15** pretentiousness

**pompous**
**03** big **04** vain **05** budge, grant, heavy, lofty, proud, state, windy **06** la-di-da, snooty, solemn, stuffy, turgid
**07** flowery, fustian, haughty, orotund, preachy, stately, stilted **08** affected, arrogant, inflated, magnific
**09** bombastic, conceited, elaborate, grandiose, high-flown, imperious, important, ororotund, overblown
**10** aldermanly, euphuistic, magnifical, portentous **11** highfalutin, magisterial, magnificent, overbearing, patronizing, pretentious **12** aldermanlike, highfaluting, high-sounding, magniloquent, ostentatious, presumptuous, supercilious
**13** condescending, self-important

**pond**
**04** lake, mere, pool, rink, stew, tank, tarn **05** flash, pound, viver **06** puddle
**07** piscary, piscina, piscine **08** Atlantic, fish-stew, turlough **09** waterhole
**10** oceanarium, seaquarium
**12** watering-hole

**ponder**
**04** mull, muse, pore **05** brood, poise, study, think, volve, weigh **06** muse on, reason **07** analyse, examine, reflect, revolve **08** cogitate, consider, incubate, meditate, mull over, pore over, turn over **09** cerebrate, ponderate **10** deliberate, excogitate, puzzle over **11** contemplate, ratiocinate **12** ruminate over **13** give thought to

**ponderous**
**04** dull, huge **05** bulky, heavy, hefty
**06** clumsy, dreary, prolix, stodgy, stolid
**07** awkward, massive, serious, stilted, tedious, verbose, weighty
**08** laboured, lifeless, pedantic, plodding, unwieldy **09** graceless, laborious, lumbering **10** cumbersome, flat-footed, humourless, long-winded, pedestrian, slow-moving
**11** elephantine, heavy-footed, heavy-handed

**ponderously**
**06** slowly **07** heavily **08** clumsily, stodgily **09** awkwardly, seriously, tediously, verbosely **11** gracelessly, laboriously **12** cumbersomely, pedantically

**ponderousness**
**06** tedium **08** gravitas **09** heaviness, stolidity **10** stodginess **11** seriousness, weightiness **13** laboriousness
**14** humourlessness

**pong** *see* **smell**

**pontifical**
**05** papal **06** snooty **07** Aaronic, pompous, preachy **08** didactic, dogmatic, prelatic, splendid
**09** Aaronical, apostolic, imperious
**10** portentous **11** magisterial, overbearing, pretentious, sermonizing
**13** condescending, self-important
**14** ecclesiastical

**pontificate**
**05** spiel **06** preach **07** declaim, expound, lecture **08** harangue, moralize, perorate, sound off
**09** dogmatize, hold forth, pronounce, sermonize **13** lay down the law

**pontoon**
**05** float **07** caisson, vingt-un
**09** blackjack, twenty-one, vingt-et-un

**pony** *see* **horse**

**pooh-pooh**
**04** pish **05** scoff, scorn, sneer, spurn
**06** deride, reject, slight **07** disdain, dismiss, sniff at **08** belittle, minimize, play down, ridicule **09** disparage, disregard **10** brush aside **12** make little of **15** laugh out of court

**pool**
**03** dub, hag, lin, pot, spa **04** ante, bank, bath, dump, flow, fund, hagg, lake, lido, linn, meer, mere, pond, ring, sump, tank, tarn, team **05** flash, group, kitty, merge, plash, plesh, purse, share, stank
**06** cartel, chip in, lasher, muck in, puddle, supply **07** combine, jackpot, Jacuzzi®, piscina, piscine, reserve
**08** Bethesda **09** backwater, composite, syndicate, waterhole
**10** accumulate, amalgamate, collective, consortium, contribute, natatorium **11** put together
**12** accumulation, paddling-pool, swimming-bath, swimming-pool, watering-hole **13** swimming-baths

**poor**
◇ *anagram indicator*
**03** bad, low, sad **04** bare, duff, mean, mere, naff, puir, ropy, thin, weak
**05** broke, cronk, crook, jerry, lowly, needy, pants, ropey, skint, sober, sorry, stony **06** barren, cruddy, crummy, faulty, feeble, hard-up, humble, hungry, ill off, in need, meagre, measly, ornery, paltry, rotten, scanty, shoddy, skimpy, sparse **07** hapless, lacking, low-rent, obolary, pitiful, reduced, rubbish, unhappy, unlucky, useless, wanting
**08** badly off, bankrupt, beggared, beggarly, below par, depleted, deprived, dirt-poor, exiguous, ill-fated, indigent, inferior, low-grade, luckless, mediocre, one-horse, pathetic, pitiable, shameful, strapped, waterish, wretched **09** defective, deficient, destitute, exhausted, flat broke, fruitless, imperfect, miserable, penniless, penurious, third-rate, worthless **10** cleaned-out, distressed, ill-starred, inadequate, low-quality, second-rate, spiritless, stony-broke, straitened, threadbare
**11** impecunious, near the bone, necessitous, substandard, unfortunate
**12** impoverished, insufficient, on your uppers, unproductive, without means
**13** below standard, disadvantaged, in Queer Street **14** on the breadline, on your beam ends, unsatisfactory
**15** poverty-stricken, strapped for cash, underprivileged

**poorly**
◇ *anagram indicator*
**03** ill **04** sick **05** badly, seedy **06** ailing, feebly, groggy, meanly, rotten, sickly, unwell **08** below par, faultily, rottenly, shabbily, shoddily **09** off colour
**10** indisposed, inexpertly, inferiorly, out of sorts **12** inadequately
**13** incompetently **14** insufficiently, unsuccessfully **15** under the weather

**pop**
◇ *anagram indicator*
**03** nip, put **04** bang, boom, cola, dash, drop, papa, pawn, push, rush, shot, slip, snap, soda **05** burst, crack, go off,

hurry, poppa, shoot, shove, slide **06** insert, pistol, poppet, report, thrust **07** darling, explode, popular, propose **08** protrude, suddenly **09** explosion, go quickly **10** fizzy drink **12** leave quickly **13** fizzy lemonade **15** go for a short time

*See also* **father**; **pawn**; **singer**; **song**

**• pop off**
**03** die **06** pass on, peg out **07** snuff it **08** flatline, pass away **09** have had it **13** kick the bucket

**• pop up**
**05** occur **06** appear, crop up, show up, turn up **09** come along **11** materialize

**pope**
**03** SSD **04** ruff **05** ruffe **06** Il Papa **07** pontiff **10** Holy Father **11** His Holiness **12** Bishop of Rome **13** Vicar of Christ

*Popes:*

**03** Leo
**04** Cono, Joan, John, Mark, Paul, Pius
**05** Caius, Donus, Felix, Lando, Linus, Peter, Soter, Urban
**06** Adrian, Agatho, Albert, Fabian, Julius, Lucius, Martin, Philip, Sixtus, Victor
**07** Anterus, Clement, Damasus, Gregory, Hadrian, Hilarus, Hyginus, Marinus, Paschal, Pontian, Romanus, Sergius, Stephen, Ursinus, Zosimus
**08** Agapetus, Anicetus, Benedict, Boniface, Calixtus, Eugenius, Eulalius, Eusebius, Formosus, Gelasius, Honorius, Innocent, John Paul, Liberius, Nicholas, Novatian, Pelagius, Siricius, Theodore, Vigilius, Vitalian
**09** Adeodatus, Alexander, Anacletus, Callistus, Celestine, Cornelius, Deusdedit, Dionysius, Dioscorus, Evaristus, Hormisdas, Marcellus, Miltiades, Severinus, Silverius, Sisinnius, Sylvester, Symmachus, Theodoric, Valentine, Zacharias
**10** Anastasius, Hippolytus, Laurentius, Sabinianus, Simplicius, Zephyrinus
**11** Christopher, Constantine, Eleutherius, Eutychianus, Marcellinus, Telesphorus

**popinjay**
**03** fop **04** beau, dude, toff **05** dandy, pansy, swell **06** parrot **07** coxcomb, peacock

**poplar**
**03** asp **05** abele, aspen **06** aspine **09** tacamahac, tacmahack, tulip tree **10** cottonwood

**poppy**
**07** Papaver, ponceau **08** argemone **09** bloodroot **10** coquelicot **12** eschscholzia **13** eschscholtzia

**poppycock**
**03** rot **04** blah, bosh, bull, bunk, crap, guff, tosh **05** balls, bilge, folly, hooey, trash, tripe **06** drivel, humbug, piffle, waffle **07** baloney, blether, flannel, hogwash, rhubarb, rubbish, twaddle **08** blathers, claptrap, cobblers, nonsense, tommyrot **09** gibberish, silliness, stupidity **10** balderdash, codswallop **11** foolishness **12** gobbledygook

**populace**
**03** mob **04** folk, herd **05** crowd, plebs **06** masses, people, proles, public, rabble **07** natives, punters, society **08** canaille, citizens, riff-raff **09** community, hoi polloi, multitude, occupants, residents **10** common herd, multitudes **11** inhabitants, proletariat, rank and file, third estate **12** common people **13** general public, great unwashed

**popular**
**02** in **03** big, hip, lay, now, pop **04** cool, laic **05** famed, liked, noted, stock, usual **06** common, famous, modish, simple, trendy, vulgar, wanted **07** admired, amateur, current, demotic, desired, general, massive **08** accepted, approved, exoteric, favoured, idolized, in demand, in favour, ordinary, plebeian, renowned, standard **09** acclaimed, customary, favourite, household, prevalent, universal, well-known, well-liked **10** accessible, all the rage, celebrated, democratic, mass-market, prevailing, simplified, well-graced, widespread **11** fashionable, sought-after **12** conventional, non-technical **13** non-specialist **14** understandable

**popularity**
**04** fame **05** glory, kudos, vogue **06** esteem, favour, regard, renown, repute **07** acclaim, worship **08** approval, currency **09** adoration, adulation **10** acceptance, mass appeal, reputation **11** approbation, idolization, lionization, recognition

**popularize**
**06** spread **08** simplify **09** propagate, vulgarize **10** generalize **11** democratize, familiarize **12** universalize **14** give currency to, make accessible

**popularly**
**03** pop **05** vulgo **06** widely **07** usually **08** commonly **09** generally, regularly **10** ordinarily **11** customarily, universally **13** traditionally **14** conventionally, non-technically

**populate**
**05** dwell **06** live in, occupy, people, settle **07** inhabit, overrun, peopled **08** colonize **09** devastate, inhabited

**population**
**03** pop **04** folk **06** people **07** natives, society **08** citizens, populace **09** community, occupants, residents, stabilate **11** inhabitants

**populous**
**06** packed **07** crowded, teeming **08** crawling, numerous, swarming **11** overpeopled **13** overpopulated

**porcelain**

*Porcelain makes include:*

**03** Bow
**04** Ming, Noke, Wade
**05** Arita, Delft, Derby, Spode
**06** Minton, Sèvres, Vienna
**07** Belleek, Bristol, Chelsea, Dresden, Limoges, Meissen, Nanking, Satsuma
**08** Caughley, Coalport, Copeland, Wedgwood
**09** Chantilly, Davenport, Worcester
**10** Cookworthy, Crown Derby, Rockingham
**12** Royal Doulton
**14** Royal Worcester

*Porcelain types include:*

**04** bisk, frit
**05** Hizen, Imari, ivory, Kraak
**06** bamboo, bisque, Canton, jasper, Parian, tender
**07** biscuit, crackle, faience, nankeen
**08** eggshell, Kakiemon, Yingqing
**09** bone china, copper red, hard-paste, soft-paste
**10** jasperware, saltglazed
**11** Capodimonte, chinoiserie, clair de lune, famille rose
**12** blanc-de-Chine, blue and white, famille jaune, famille verte
**14** soapstone paste

*See also* **pottery**

**porch**
**04** hall, stoa **05** foyer, lobby, stoep, stoop **07** galilee, hallway, portico, veranda **09** colonnade, vestibule **12** entrance-hall

**porcupine**
**05** urson **10** porpentine

**pore**
**04** hole, vent **05** stoma **06** outlet, stigma **07** foramen, opening, orifice **08** aperture, lenticel **09** micropore **11** perforation

**• pore over**
**03** con, kon **04** read, scan **05** brood, conne, study **06** go over, peruse, ponder **07** dwell on, examine **10** scrutinize **11** contemplate **14** examine closely, study intensely

**porgy**
**04** scup **06** braise, braize **08** scuppaug

**porker** *see* **pig**

**pornographic**
**04** blue, lewd, pink, porn **05** adult, bawdy, dirty, gross, nasty, porno **06** coarse, erotic, filthy, risqué, X-rated **07** obscene **08** indecent, prurient **09** off-colour, salacious **11** titillating

**pornography**
**04** dirt, porn, smut **05** filth, nasty, porno **07** curiosa, erotica **08** facetiae, peep-show **09** bawdiness, grossness, indecency, obscenity, skinflick, snuff film **10** snuff movie, snuff video, video nasty **13** sexploitation **15** girlie magazines

## porous

**04** airy, open **05** holey **06** spongy **07** foveate **08** cellular, pervious **09** absorbent, permeable **10** cancellate, cancellous, foraminous, penetrable, spongelike **11** cancellated, cavernulous, foraminated, honeycombed

## porpoise

**06** seahog, sea-pig **07** dolphin, pellach, pellack, pellock, porpess **08** Phocaena, porpesse, sea swine **09** mere swine, porcpisce

## porridge

**04** gaol, jail, samp, stir **05** kasha, sadza **06** hominy, supawn **07** brochan, polenta, pottage, suppawn **08** parritch, sentence **09** mealie pap, praiseach, stirabout **12** hasty pudding

## port

**01** L **02** pt **03** bag **04** dock, gate, left, ruby **05** carry, haven, hithe, jetty, roads **06** convey **07** bearing, borough, harbour, retinue, seaport **08** dockland, larboard, porthole, suitcase **09** anchorage, demeanour, docklands, roadstead **10** deportment, harbourage

*Ports include:*

**03** Gao, Lae, Rio, Vac
**04** Aden, Apia, Baku, Bari, Caen, Cebu, Ciba, Cork, Deal, Doha, Elat, Faro, Hull, Kiel, Kobe, Linz, Lomé, Lüda, Nice, Oban, Omsk, Oran, Oslo, Oulu, Pula, Riga, Safi, Sfax, Suez, Suva, Tyre, Vigo, Wick
**05** Accra, Agana, Aqaba, Arica, Basle, Basra, Beira, Belém, Blyth, Brest, Busan, Colón, Dakar, Davao, Dover, Dubai, Emden, Galle, Gavle, Genoa, Ghent, Gijon, Haifa, Ibiza, Izmir, Kayes, Kazan, Koper, Lagos, Larne, Leith, Liège, Macao, Malmo, Masan, Miami, Nampo, Natal, Omaha, Osaka, Ostia, Palma, Paris, Poole, Praia, Pusan, Rouen, Sakai, Salem, Ségou, Sitra, Skien, Split, Surat, Tampa, Tanga, Tokyo, Tomsk, Torun, Tulsa, Tunis, Turku, Ulsan, Vaasa, Varna, Worms, Wuhan
**06** Aarhus, Abadan, Agadir, Ancona, Annaba, Ashdod, Avarua, Aveira, Aviles, Balboa, Bamako, Banjul, Bastia, Batumi, Beirut, Bergen, Bissau, Bombay, Boston, Bremen, Bruges, Calais, Callao, Camden, Cannes, Cochin, Dalian, Dammam, Darwin, Denver, Dieppe, Douala, Dublin, Duluth, Dundee, Durban, Durres, El Paso, Galway, Gdansk, Gdynia, Grodno, Hamina, Havana, Hobart, Huelva, Inchon, Jarrow, Jeddah, Juneau, Kalgar, Kandla, Kaunas, Khulna, Lisbon, Lobito, London, Luanda, Lübeck, Madras, Malabo, Malaga, Manama, Manaus, Manila, Maputo, Matrah, Mersin, Mobile, Muscat, Nacala, Nagoya, Nantes, Napier, Naples, Narvik, Nassau, Nelson, Newark, Niamey, Ningbo, Nouméa, Nyborg, Odense, Odessa, Oporto, Ostend, Penang, Phuket, Quebec, Recife, Rijeka, Rimini, Samara, Samsun, Santos, Sasebo, Sittwe, Sousse, St John, St-Malo, St Paul, Sydney, Szeged, Tacoma, Thurso, Timaru, Toledo, Toulon, Toyama, Treves, Vannes, Velsen, Venice, Warsaw, Whitby, Xiamen, Yangon
**07** Aalborg, Abidjan, Ajaccio, Alcudia, Algiers, Almeria, Antibes, Antwerp, Bangkok, Belfast, Berbera, Bizerta, Bourgas, Bristol, Buffalo, Cabinda, Calabar, Caldera, Calicut, Cardiff, Catania, Cayenne, Chicago, Cologne, Colombo, Conakry, Corinth, Corinto, Cotonou, Dampier, Detroit, Douglas, Dunedin, Dunkirk, Esbjerg, Fukuoka, Funchal, Geelong, Glasgow, Grimsby, Halifax, Hamburg, Harstad, Harwich, Hodeida, Honiara, Honiari, Houston, Ipswich, Iquique, Jakarta, Karachi, Kowloon, Kuching, Kushiro, La Plata, Larnaca, La Union, Le Havre, Livorno, Marsala, Melilla, Memphis, Messina, Mindelo, Mombasa, Newport, New Ross, Niigata, Niterói, Oakland, Okayama, Palermo, Papeete, Paradip, Pasajes, Piraeus, Portree, Rangoon, Ravenna, Rosaria, Rosario, Rostock, Salerno, San José, San Juan, San Remo, Santa Fe, Sao Tomé, Saratov, Seattle, Seville, Shimizu, Stanley, St John's, St Louis, Swansea, Tallinn, Tampico, Tangier, Taranto, Tel Aviv, Tianjin, Tilbury, Toronto, Trieste, Tripoli, Vitebsk, Vitoria, Wroclaw, Xingang, Zhdanov
**08** Aberdeen, Abu Dhabi, Acajutla, Acapulco, Adelaide, Alicante, Arbroath, Asunción, Auckland, Benghazi, Bordeaux, Boulogne, Brindisi, Brisbane, Cagliari, Calcutta, Cape Town, Castries, Changsha, Chimbote, Djibouti, Dortmund, Duisburg, Dunleary, Falmouth, Flushing, Freeport, Freetown, Gisborne, Godthaab, Greenock, Guyaquil, Hakodate, Halmstad, Hamilton, Hay Point, Helsinki, Holyhead, Honolulu, Istanbul, Kawasaki, Keflavik, Kingston, Kinshasa, Kirkaldy, Kirkwall, Kismaayo, Klaipeda, La Coruna, La Guaira, La Spezia, Lattakia, Limassol, Limerick, Mandalay, Mannheim, Marbella, Matanzas, Mazatlan, Monrovia, Montreal, Montrose, Mormugao, Moulmein, Mulhouse, Murmansk, Nagasaki, New Haven, Newhaven, Pago Pago, Plymouth, Portland, Port Said, Port-Vila, Ramsgate, Richmond, Roskilde, Rosslare, Salonica, Salvador, San Diego, San Pedro, Santarém, Savannah, Semarang, Shanghai, Simbirsk, Smolensk, St Helier, Stockton, St-Tropez, Surabaya, Syracuse, Szczecin, Takoradi, Tauranga, Torshavn, Ullapool, Valencia, Valletta, Veracruz, Voronezh, Weymouth, Yokohama, Zanzibar
**09** Algeciras, Amsterdam, Anchorage, Archangel, Astrakhan, Baltimore, Barcelona, Bujumbura, Cartagena, Cherbourg, Cleveland, Constance, Constanta, Dordrecht, Dubrovnik, Esztergom, Europoort, Famagusta, Fleetwood, Flensburg, Fortaleza, Frankfurt, Fremantle, Galveston, Gateshead, Gibraltar, Gravesend, Heraklion, Hiroshima, Immingham, Kagoshima, Kaohsiung, Karlsruhe, King's Lynn, Kingstown, Kozhikode, Langesund, Las Palmas, Launceton, Liverpool, Long Beach, Lowestoft, Magdeburg, Mahajanga, Maracaibo, Mariehamn, Melbourne, Milwaukee, Mizushima, Mogadishu, Nashville, Newcastle, Nuku'alofa, Palembang, Palm Beach, Paranagua, Peterhead, Phnom Penh, Port Limon, Port Louis, Port Natal, Port Sudan, Reykjavík, Rio Grande, Rochester, Rotterdam, Santander, Sassandra, Sheerness, Singapore, Stavanger, St-Nazaire, Stockholm, Stornoway, Stralsund, Stranraer, Sundsvall, Takamatsu, Tarragona, Toamasina, Trebizond, Trondheim, Tuticorin, Vancouver, Vicksburg, Vientiane, Volgograd, Walvis Bay, Yaroslavl, Zeebrugge, Zhenjiang, Zrenjanin
**10** Alexandria, Basseterre, Baton Rouge, Belize City, Bratislava, Bridgeport, Bridgetown, Cap Haitian, Casablanca, Charleston, Chittagong, Cienfuegos, Copenhagen, East London, Felixstowe, Folkestone, Fray Bentos, Fredericia, George Town, Georgetown, Gothenburg, Hartlepool, Hildesheim, Iskenderun, Kansas City, Kitakyushu, Kompong Som, Kuwait City, Leeuwarden, Libreville, Little Rock, Los Angeles, Louisville, Manchester, Manzanillo, Marseilles, Mina Qaboos, Mina Sulman, Montego Bay, Montevideo, Mostaganem, New Orleans, Nouadhibou, Nouakchott, Oranjestad, Paramaribo, Pittsburgh, Port Gentil, Portishead, Portsmouth, Port Talbot, Providence, Sacramento, Salina Cruz, San Lorenzo, Santa Marta, Sebastopol, Sevastopol, Strasbourg, Sunderland, Talcahuano, Thunder Bay, Townsville, Valparaiso, Wellington, Willemstad, Wilmington, Workington, Zaporozhye
**11** Antofagasta, Bahia Blanca, Bandar Abbas, Brazzaville, Bremerhaven, Bridlington, Brownsville, Buenos Aires, Charlestown, Chattanooga, Dar es Salaam, Fraserburgh, Grangemouth, Helsingborg,

Krasnoyarsk, Livingstone, Lossiemouth, Mar del Plata, Minneapolis, Narayanganj, New Plymouth, New York City, Novosibirsk, Panama Canal, Pasir Gudang, Point-a-Pitre, Pointe-Noire, Pondicherry, Port Cartier, Port Moresby, Porto Alegre, Port of Spain, Punta Arenas, Qinhuangdao, Richards Bay, Rostov-on-Don, Southampton, Three Rivers, Vladivostok

**12** Barranquilla, Buenaventura, Fort de France, Frederikstad, Jacksonville, Kota Kinabalu, Kristiansand, Ludwigshafen, New Amsterdam, New Mangalore, Novorossiysk, Philadelphia, Ponta Delgada, Port Adelaide, Port-au-Prince, Port Harcourt, Port Victoria, Puerto Cortes, Rio de Janeiro, Saint George's, San Francisco, San Sebastian, Santo Domingo, St Petersburg, Tel Aviv-Jaffa, Ujung Pandang, Villahermosa

**13** Ellesmere Port, Frederikshavn, Great Yarmouth, Ho Chi Minh City, Hook of Holland, Middlesbrough, Port Elizabeth, Semipalatinsk, Sihanoukville

**14** Dnepropetrovsk, Port Georgetown, Santiago de Cuba

**15** Barrow-in-Furness, Charlotte Amalie, Frankfurt am Main, Nizhniy Novgorod

---

**• port authority**
**03** PLA

**portability**
**09** handiness **10** movability
**11** compactness, convenience
**13** manageability

**portable**
**05** handy **07** compact, movable
**08** luggable **09** endurable, portatile
**10** convenient, conveyable, manageable **11** lightweight
**13** transportable

**portal**
**04** door, gate **05** way in **06** access
**07** doorway, gateway, opening
**08** entrance

**portend**
**04** bode, omen **05** augur **06** herald, import, warn of **07** bespeak, betoken, point to, predict, presage, promise, purport, signify **08** announce, forebode, forecast, foreshow, foretell, forewarn, indicate, threaten
**09** adumbrate, be a sign of, foretoken, harbinger **10** foreshadow
**13** prognosticate

**portent**
**04** omen, sign **05** augur, token
**06** augury, boding, marvel, ostent, threat **07** presage, prodigy, warning
**08** forecast, prodrome **09** harbinger, precursor **10** foreboding, forerunner, indication, prognostic **11** forewarning, ominousness, premonition
**12** presentiment **13** foreshadowing, prefiguration, signification
**15** prognostication

**portentous**
**04** dire, vain **05** proud **06** snooty, solemn **07** amazing, crucial, fateful, haughty, ominous, pompous
**08** affected, arrogant, menacing, sinister **09** conceited, grandiose, imperious, important, momentous
**10** astounding, foreboding, impressive, miraculous, prodigious, remarkable
**11** epoch-making, magisterial, overbearing, patronizing, pretentious, significant, threatening **12** awe-inspiring, earth-shaking, ostentatious, presumptuous, supercilious
**13** condescending, extraordinary, self-important

**portentously**
**08** snootily **09** haughtily, pompously
**10** arrogantly **11** conceitedly
**13** patronizingly **14** superciliously
**15** condescendingly, self-importantly

**porter**
**04** page **05** caddy, cadee, cadie, hamal
**06** bearer, caddie, entire, hammal, humper, redcap **07** bell-boy, bellhop, carrier, doorman, dvornik, janitor
**08** bummaree, doorsman
**09** caretaker, concierge, out-porter
**10** door-keeper, gatekeeper
**11** double-stout, night-porter **12** ticket-porter **13** door attendant **14** baggage-carrier, baggage-handler, commissionaire

**portico**
**04** stoa **05** porch **06** exedra, parvis, xystus **07** distyle, exhedra, narthex, parvise, veranda **08** prostyle, verandah
**09** colonnade, decastyle, hexastyle, octastyle, octostyle **10** pentastyle, tetrastyle **11** dodecastyle

**portion**
**02** go **03** bit, cut, dot, lot, rag **04** deal, dole, dose, fate, luck, meed, mite, part, tait, tate, what **05** allot, dowry, grist, order, piece, quota, ratio, share, slice, small, space, taste, wedge, whack, wodge **06** assign, chance, divide, kismet, morsel, parcel, ration, region
**07** carve up, destiny, dole out, fortune, helping, kenning, measure, rake-off, scantle, section, segment, serving, slice up, tranche **08** allocate, division, fraction, fragment, particle, pittance, quantity, share out **09** allotment, allowance, apportion, partition, scantling, something **10** allocation, distribute, percentage, proportion

**portliness**
**07** fatness, obesity **08** fullness
**09** ampleness, beefiness, dumpiness, heaviness, plumpness, rotundity, roundness, stoutness, tubbiness
**10** chubbiness, corpulence, fleshiness
**11** paunchiness

**portly**
**03** fat **05** ample, gaucy, gawcy, gawsy, heavy, large, obese, plump, round, stout **06** gaucie, rotund, stocky
**08** matronly **09** corpulent
**10** aldermanly, overweight
**12** aldermanlike

**portrait**
**04** icon **05** image, pin-up, story, study
**06** Kit-Cat, sketch **07** account, drawing, picture, profile, retrate
**08** likeness, painting, pourtray, retraitt, vignette **09** composite, depiction, miniature, portrayal **10** caricature, full-length, half-length, photograph, pourtraict **11** description, whole-length **12** carte-de-viste, self-portrait
**14** representation **15** thumbnail sketch

**portray**
**03** act **04** draw, play, take **05** evoke, image, paint **06** depict, sketch
**07** perform, picture, present
**08** describe, portrait, pourtray
**09** pantomime, personify, represent
**10** illustrate **11** impersonate **12** act the part of, characterize **13** play the part of

**portrayal**
**05** study **06** acting, sketch **07** drawing, picture **08** painting **09** depiction, evocation, rendering **11** delineation, description, performance
**12** presentation **14** interpretation, representation

**Portugal**
**01** P **02** Pg **03** PRT

**Portuguese**
**02** Pg

**pose**
**03** act, air, ask, put, set, sit **04** airs, role, sham **05** cause, claim, feign, front, model, posit **06** affect, assert, create, façade, lead to, puzzle, stance, submit
**07** advance, arrange, bearing, posture, present, pretend, produce, propose, suggest **08** attitude, carriage, position, pretence, propound, result in
**09** postulate, put on airs **10** constitute, deportment, give rise to, masquerade, put forward, put on an act
**11** affectation, impersonate
**12** attitudinize, contrapposto **15** pass yourself off

**Poseidon**
**07** Neptune

**poser**
**04** sham **05** pseud **06** enigma, phoney, poseur, puzzle, riddle, sitter
**07** dilemma, mystery, poseuse, problem, show-off, sticker
**08** impostor, posturer **09** charlatan, conundrum, play-actor **10** mind-bender **11** brainteaser **12** brain-twister
**13** attitudinizer, exhibitionist, vexed question

**poseur**
**04** sham **05** poser, pseud **06** phoney
**07** poseuse, show-off **08** impostor, posturer **09** charlatan, play-actor
**13** attitudinizer, exhibitionist

**posh**
**01** U **04** rich, swag **05** dandy, fancy,

grand, money, plush, pluty, smart, swish **06** classy, de-luxe, la-di-da, lavish, luxury, select, snazzy, superb, swanky **07** elegant, opulent, stylish **08** top-class, up-market **09** exclusive, expensive, halfpenny, high-class, luxurious, sumptuous **10** upper-class **11** fashionable

**posit**
**03** set **04** pose **05** state **06** assert, assume, submit **07** advance, dispose, presume **08** propound **09** postulate, predicate **10** put forward

**position**
**03** fix, job, lie, pos, put, set **04** area, case, duty, pose, post, rank, role, site, spot, view **05** array, grade, level, place, point, pozzy, scene, stand, state **06** belief, deploy, factor, lay out, locate, office, orient, plight, possie, settle, stance, status **07** arrange, bearing, dispose, factors, install, opinion, outlook, posture, ranking, setting, situate, station **08** attitude, capacity, function, locality, location, prestige, standing **09** condition, establish, influence, postulate, situation, viewpoint **10** background, employment, occupation, standpoint **11** appointment, arrangement, disposition, point of view, predicament, whereabouts **13** circumstances **14** state of affairs

• **in fixed position**
**02** to

**positive**
**01** p **03** pos **04** firm, good, plus, rank, real, sure **05** basic, clear, sheer, utter **06** actual, direct, upbeat, useful **07** assured, certain, express, helpful, hopeful, perfect, positif, precise, reality **08** absolute, cheerful, clear-cut, complete, concrete, decisive, definite, emphatic, explicit, material, outright, thorough **09** assertive, categoric, confident, convinced, downright, out-and-out, practical, promising, veritable **10** conclusive, consummate, convincing, definitive, encouraged, favourable, optimistic, productive, undeniable **11** affirmative, categorical, encouraging, irrefutable, unequivocal, unmitigated **12** constructive, indisputable, matter-of-fact, unmistakable **13** incontestable **14** dextrorotatory

**positively**
**06** firmly, surely **07** finally **09** assuredly, certainly, expressly **10** absolutely, decisively, definitely, undeniably **12** conclusively, emphatically, indisputably, unmistakably **13** categorically, incontestably, unequivocally **14** unquestionably

**possess**
◇ *containment indicator*
**03** get, own **04** gain, have, hold, take **05** boast, enjoy, haunt, imbue, seize, wield **06** attain, inform, obsess, obtain, occupy **07** acquire, bedevil, bewitch, control, enchant, inhabit, inherit, overget **08** acquaint, demonize, dominate, maintain, take over **09** infatuate, influence **12** be gifted with **13** be blessed with, be endowed with, take control of

**possessed**
**03** mad **06** crazed, cursed, raving **07** berserk, haunted **08** besotted, consumed, demented, frenzied, maddened, obsessed, spirited **09** bewitched, demonized, dominated, enchanted, hag-ridden **10** bedevilled, controlled, infatuated, mesmerized

**possession**
**03** fee **04** grip, hand, hold **05** craze, thing, title **06** having, tenure **07** control, custody, holding, tenancy **08** haunting **09** obsession, occupance, occupancy, ownership **10** domination, occupation **11** infatuation **14** proprietorship

• **in possession**
◇ *containment indicator*

**possessions**
**03** all, ana **04** aver, gear, good **05** goods, stuff, worth **06** assets, estate, riches, things, wealth **07** baggage, clobber, effects, luggage **08** chattels, movables, outsight, property **09** sprechery, territory **10** belongings, spreaghery **12** temporalties **13** accoutrements, paraphernalia, temporalities, worldly wealth **15** personal effects

**possessive**
**06** greedy **07** jealous, selfish **08** clinging, covetous, genitive, grasping **10** dominating **11** acquisitive, controlling, domineering **14** overprotective

**possessiveness**
**05** greed **08** jealousy **11** selfishness **12** covetousness **13** exclusiveness **15** acquisitiveness

**possibility**
**04** fear, hope, odds, risk **05** maybe, posse **06** chance, choice, danger, hazard, option, talent **07** promise **08** prospect, recourse **09** off-chance, potential, prospects **10** advantages, likelihood, preference **11** alternative, contingency, feasibility, probability, proposition **12** capabilities, expectations, potentiality **13** attainability **14** conceivability, practicability

**possible**
◇ *anagram indicator*
**06** doable, likely, odds-on, viable **07** tenable **08** credible, feasible, probable, workable **09** potential, promising **10** achievable, attainable, imaginable, on the cards, realizable **11** conceivable, practicable **13** that can be done **14** accomplishable

**possibly**
◇ *anagram indicator*
**03** e'er **04** ever, well **05** at all, maybe **07** in posse, perhaps **09** hopefully **10** by any means **11** by any chance, conceivably **12** peradventure

**possum**
**04** tait **07** opossum **08** Tarsipes **09** phalanger **10** honey-mouse **11** sugar glider

**post**
**03** dak, job, leg, pin, put **04** beat, bitt, jamb, mail, move, pale, pole, prop, send **05** affix, e-mail, haste, newel, pin up, place, put up, shaft, stake, strut **06** assign, attach, column, locate, office, picket, pillar, report, second **07** airmail, appoint, display, forward, letters, packets, parcels, publish, situate, station, stick up, support, upright, vacancy **08** announce, baluster, banister, delivery, dispatch, junk mail, packages, palisade, position, standard, transfer, transmit **09** advertise, broadcast, circulate, mail-coach, make known, publicize, put on duty, situation, snail mail, stanchion **10** assignment, direct mail, employment, packet-boat, Post Office **11** appointment, surface mail **12** all-up service, postal system, recorded mail **13** postal service **14** communications, correspondence, electronic mail, first-class mail, registered mail **15** second-class mail, special delivery

• **keep someone posted**
**06** fill in, inform **12** keep informed, keep up to date **13** keep in the loop

**postal order**
**02** PO

**postcard**
**02** pc

**poster**
**02** ad **04** bill, sign **05** solus **06** advert, notice **07** placard, sticker **08** bulletin, play bill, show bill **12** announcement **13** advertisement

**posterior**
**03** ass, bum **04** back, butt, hind, rear, rump, seat, tail **05** after, later **06** behind, bottom, dorsal, hinder, jacksy, latter **07** ensuing, jacksie **08** backside, buttocks, haunches, rearward **09** following, hinder end, posterity, posticous **10** subsequent, succeeding **12** hindquarters

**posterity**
**04** seed **05** heirs, issue **07** progeny **08** children, mokopuna **09** offspring, posterior **10** succession, successors **11** descendants

**posthaste**
**06** at once, pronto, speedy **07** hastily, quickly, swiftly **08** directly, full tilt, promptly, speedily **09** immediate **11** double-quick, immediately **12** straightaway, with all speed

**postman, postwoman**
**04** post **06** postie **07** courier, mailman **11** mail-carrier, mail handler **12** postal

worker **13** letter-carrier **15** delivery officer

**post-mortem**
**02** PM **06** review **07** autopsy **08** analysis, autopsia, necropsy **10** dissection, necroscopy **11** examination

**Post Office**
**02** PO **03** GPO **04** BFPO

**postpone**
**04** stay, wait **05** defer, delay, frist, refer, table, waive **06** freeze, put off, retard, shelve **07** adjourn, do later, prolong, put back, rejourn, sleep on, suspend **08** hold over, mothball, postpose, prorogue, protract, put on ice, withhold **09** carry over, sleep on it, stand over **10** pigeonhole, reschedule **11** subordinate **13** procrastinate

**postponed**
**05** on ice **06** frozen, put off **07** shelved **08** deferred, held over **09** adjourned, suspended **10** in abeyance, protracted **11** carried over, pigeonholed **15** on the back burner

**postponement**
**04** stay **05** delay **06** freeze, put-off **07** respite **08** deferral **09** deferment **10** moratorium, suspension **11** adjournment, prorogation **13** backwardation

**postscript**
**02** PS **03** PPS **07** codicil **08** addendum, addition, appendix, epilogue **09** afterword **10** supplement **12** afterthought

**postulate**
**05** axiom, claim, posit **06** assume **07** advance, lay down, presume, propose, suppose **08** nominate, petition, theorize **09** stipulate **10** assumption, postulatum, presuppose, put forward **11** hypothesize, stipulation

**posture**
**03** set **04** pike, pose, site, view **05** guard, mudra, stand, strut **06** affect, belief, motion, sprawl, stance **07** bearing, gesture, opinion, outlook, show off **08** attitude, carriage, position **09** arabesque, decubitus, defensive, offensive, put on airs, viewpoint **10** decumbence, decumbency, deportment, standpoint **11** counter-view, disposition, point of view **12** attitudinize **15** strike attitudes

**postwoman** *see* **postman, postwoman**

**posy**
**05** motto, poesy, spray **07** bouquet, corsage, nosegay **08** affected **09** sentiment **10** buttonhole **12** tussie mussie

**pot**
**02** po **03** box, can, cup, jar, pan, pat, tea, urn **04** bank, bowl, fund, lota, olla, pool, stew, test, vase **05** basin, crewe, crock, cruse, kitty, lotah, purse **06** aludel, bowpot, caster, chatti, chatty, pipkin, pocket, pottle, tajine, teapot, tipple, trivet, trophy, vessel **07** marmite, pitcher, planter, pothole, reserve **08** boughpot, cauldron, crucible, gallipot, plantpot, pot-au-feu **09** casserole, coffee pot, flowerpot **10** chamberpot, receptacle **11** earthenware, manufacture **13** potentiometer
*See also* **cannabis**

**potable**
**04** safe **05** clean **08** beverage **09** drinkable **10** fit to drink

**potassium**
**01** K

**potato**
**03** alu, yam **04** aloo, chat, spud **05** boxty, early, tater, tatie **06** batata, camote, murphy, pratie, tattie **07** scallop, scollop

*Potatoes include:*

**04** Cara, chat, seed, ware
**05** praty, Sante, Saxon, sweet
**06** camote, Estima, kidney, kumara
**07** Desiree
**09** Charlotte, Kerr's Pink, Maris Peer
**10** Duke of York, King Edward, Maris Piper
**12** Golden Wonder
**15** Pentland Javelin

**pot-bellied**
**03** fat **05** kedge, kedgy, kidge, obese, tubby **06** portly **07** bloated, paunchy **09** corpulent, distended **10** abdominous, gor-bellied, overweight

**pot-belly**
**03** gut, pot **05** belly **06** paunch **08** tunbelly **09** beer belly, bow window, spare tyre **11** corporation

**potency**
**04** kick, sway **05** force, might, power, punch **06** energy, muscle, vigour **07** cogency, control **08** capacity, efficacy, strength **09** authority, headiness, influence, potentate, potential, puissance **12** potentiality, powerfulness **13** effectiveness **14** persuasiveness **15** efficaciousness

**potent**
**06** active, cogent, mighty, prince, strong, virile **07** dynamic, pungent **08** dominant, eloquent, forceful, powerful, puissant, vigorous **09** effective, energetic, potentate **10** commanding, compelling, convincing, impressive, persuasive **11** efficacious, influential **12** intoxicating, overpowering **13** authoritative

**potentate**
**04** czar, king, tsar, tzar **05** chief, mogul, queen, ruler **06** despot, dynast, huzoor, leader, prince, tyrant **07** emperor, empress, monarch **08** autocrat, dictator, overlord **09** chieftain, sovereign **10** panjandrum **11** head of state

**potential**
◇ *anagram indicator*
**04** gift **05** flair **06** future, hidden, latent, likely, powers, talent **07** ability, budding, dormant, promise, virtual, would-be **08** aptitude, aspiring, capacity, implicit, inherent, possible, powerful, probable **09** concealed, embryonic, promising, resources **10** capability, developing, unrealized **11** efficacious, possibility, prospective, undeveloped

**potentiality**
**05** power **07** ability, potence, potency, promise **08** aptitude, capacity, prospect **09** potential **10** capability, likelihood, virtuality **13** possibilities

**potentially**
◇ *anagram indicator*
**07** in posse **08** latently, possibly, probably **09** dormantly, virtually **10** implicitly, inherently, in potentia **15** in all likelihood

**potion**
**04** brew, dose **05** drink, tonic **06** elixir **07** draught, mixture, philtre **08** beverage, medicine, potation **10** concoction

**potpourri**
**04** olio **06** jumble, medley **07** melange, mixture **08** mishmash, pastiche **09** confusion, patchwork, selection **10** assortment, collection, hodgepodge, hotchpotch, miscellany **11** gallimaufry, olla-podrida, smorgasbord

**potter**
**04** muck, poke **05** amble, daker **06** dacker, daidle, daiker, dawdle, dodder, fettle, footle, loiter, niggle, pootle, putter, tiddle, tinker, toddle **07** plotter, plouter, plowter **09** mess about **10** dilly-dally
• **potter about**
**05** truck **06** humbug, muddle **09** fart about, fool about, mess about, muck about, play about **10** fart around, fool around, mess around, muck around, play around **11** fiddle about, tinker about **12** fiddle around, tinker around **13** do nothing much

**pottery**
**04** bank

*Pottery includes:*

**04** Ming, Tang, Wade
**05** Bizen, china, Crown, Delft, Poole
**06** basalt, bisque, Dunoon, flambé, Hummel, Jasper, Parian, Sèvres
**07** biscuit, ceramic, Dresden, faience, Meissen, redware
**08** ceramics, Coalport, crockery, maiolica, majolica, rakuware, Rookwood, slipware
**09** agateware, bone china, creamware, Davenport, delftware, hard-paste, ironstone, Jackfield, pearlware,

porcelain, red figure, saltglaze, soft-paste, stoneware, tin-glazed, Worcester
**10** Jasper ware, lead-glazed, lustre ware, Parian ware, Queen's ware, terra cotta, Wemyss ware
**11** black figure, earthenware, Florian ware, pâte-sur-pâte, Portmeirion, soufflé ware, spatter ware
**12** Royal Doulton, transfer ware, Wedgwood ware
**13** Claremont ware, Hazledene ware, Staffordshire, tortoiseshell, willow pattern
**14** ironstone china
**15** cauliflower ware, Royal Crown Derby, Wedgwood pottery

*Pottery makers include:*

**03** **Fry** (Laura), **Rie** (Dame Lucie)
**04** **Boyd** (Arthur), **Boyd** (Merric), **Vyse** (Charles), **Wood** (Aaron), **Wood** (Enoch), **Wood** (John), **Wood** (Ralph), **Wood** (Ralph, Jnr), **Wyse** (Henry Taylor)
**05** **Adams** (Truda), **Adams** (William), **Amour** (Elizabeth), **Cliff** (Clarice), **Coper** (Hans), **Finch** (Alfred William), **Korin** (Ogata), **Leach** (Bernard), **Mason** (Miles), **Moore** (Bernard), **Perry** (Grayson)
**06** **Cardew** (Michael), **Carter** (Truda), **Dwight** (John), **Hamada** (Shoji), **Kenzan** (Ogata), **Murray** (William Staite), **Taylor** (William Howson)
**07** **Astbury** (John), **Britton** (Alison), **Doulton** (Sir Henry), **Execias**, **Exekias**, **Forsyth** (Gordon), **Fritsch** (Elizabeth), **Gardner** (Peter), **Grotell** (Maija), **Palissy** (Bernard), **Twyford** (Joshua)
**08** **Fujiwara** (Kei), **Robineau** (Adelaide), **Wedgwood** (Josiah), **Whieldon** (Thomas), **Yamamoto** (Toshu)
**09** **Kaneshige** (Toyo), **Moorcroft** (William)
**10** **Euphronios**

*Pottery terms include:*

**04** kiln, raku, slip
**05** delft, glaze, model
**06** basalt, enamel, figure, firing, flambé, ground, jasper, lustre, sagger
**07** celadon, ceramic, crazing, faience, fairing
**08** armorial, bronzing, flatback, maiolica, majolica, monogram, slip-cast
**09** china clay, cloisonné, creamware, grotesque, ironstone, overglaze, porcelain, sgraffito, stoneware
**10** art pottery, maker's mark, spongeware, terracotta, underglaze
**11** crackleware, earthenware, scratch blue
**12** blanc-de-chine
**13** Staffordshire, Willow pattern
**15** mandarin palette

*See also* **porcelain**

## potty

◇ *anagram indicator*
**03** ape, fey, mad **04** avid, bats, daft, fond, gyte, keen, loco, nuts, wild **05** barmy, batty, buggy, crazy, daffy, dippy, dotty, flaky, gonzo, loony, loopy, manic, nutty, petty, queer, silly, wacko, wacky, wiggy **06** ardent, crazed, cuckoo, fruity, insane, maniac, mental, raving, red-mad, screwy **07** bananas, barking, berserk, bonkers, cracked, devoted, frantic, lunatic, meshuga, zealous **08** crackers, demented, deranged, dingbats, doolally, frenetic, frenzied, gazunder, maniacal, trifling, unhinged, unstable **09** disturbed, fanatical, lymphatic, psychotic, up the wall **10** bestraught, chamberpot, distracted, distraught, frantic-mad, infatuated, off the wall, off your nut, out to lunch, passionate, stone-crazy, unbalanced **11** not all there, off the rails, off your head **12** enthusiastic, mad as a hatter, off your chump, round the bend **13** off your rocker, of unsound mind, out of your head, out of your mind, out of your tree, round the twist **14** off your trolley, wrong in the head **15** non compos mentis, out of your senses

## pouch

**03** bag, sac, tip **04** poke, sack, spur
**05** bursa, cecum, purse, scrip
**06** caecum, ovisac, pocket, wallet
**07** papoose, sporran **08** codpiece, pappoose, reticule **09** container, marsupium, spleuchan **10** receptacle
**11** gaberlunzie **12** diverticulum

## poultry

*Poultry and game birds include:*

**03** hen
**04** duck, teal
**05** goose, quail, snipe
**06** grouse, pigeon, turkey, wigeon
**07** chicken, ostrich, pochard
**08** pheasant, woodcock
**09** partridge, ptarmigan
**10** guinea fowl, woodpigeon

*See also* **chicken**; **duck**; **game**

## pounce

**04** dart, dive, drop, fall, grab, jump, leap, pink **05** bound, lunge, punch, swoop **06** ambush, attack, dive on, fall on, jump on, powder, snatch, spring, strike, thrust **07** assault, descend, swoop on **08** puncture, sandarac, sprinkle **09** descend on, sandarach
**10** cuttle-bone **12** take unawares
**13** catch off guard, catch unawares
**14** take by surprise

## pound

**01** L **02** as, lb **03** bar, pen, pun, sov
**04** bang, bash, beat, bray, drum, fold, mash, pace, pelt, plod, pond, punt, quid, thud, walk, yard **05** crush, grind, lay on, libra, nevel, oncer, pownd, smash, squid, stamp, stomp, throb, thump, tramp, tread **06** batter, bruise, corral, hammer, nicker, pestle, powder, pummel, shower, strike, trudge
**07** balance, confine, contund, contuse, enclose, iron man, penfold, pinfold, pulsate, smacker **08** compound, levigate **09** comminute, enclosure, granulate, palpitate, pound coin, pulverize, smackeroo, sovereign, triturate **12** jimmy-o'goblin **13** pound sterling

## pour

**03** jet, ren, rin, run, tip **04** emit, flow, gush, hush, leak, ooze, rain, rush, spew, teem **05** crowd, drain, flood, issue, serve, spill, spout, spurt, swarm
**06** course, decant, stream, throng
**07** cascade, come out, let flow, pour out **08** disgorge, make flow, pelt down, sprinkle, teem down **09** discharge
**10** bucket down, disembogue **15** rain cats and dogs

• **pour forth**
**04** gush, vent, well
• **pour out**
**04** lave

## pout

**03** bib **04** lour, mope, moue, poot, sulk, tout, towt **05** blain, boody, poult, scowl **06** brassy, glower **07** grimace
**08** long face, make a lip **09** make a moue, pull a face

## poverty

**04** lack, need, want **06** dearth, penury
**07** beggary, paucity **08** distress, hardship, poorness, poortith, scarcity, shortage **09** depletion, indigence, necessity, privation **10** bankruptcy, deficiency, inadequacy, insolvency, meagreness, shabbiness
**11** deprivation, destitution, locust-years
**13** impecuniosity, insufficiency, pennilessness **14** impoverishment

## poverty-stricken

**04** poor **05** broke, needy, skint, stony
**07** obolary, squalid **08** bankrupt, beggared, dirt-poor, indigent, strapped **09** destitute, flat broke, penniless, penurious **10** cleaned-out, distressed, stony-broke
**11** impecunious **12** impoverished, on your uppers **13** in Queer Street **14** on your beam-ends

## powder

**04** beat, blue, bran, bray, dust, kohl, mash, must, pulv, salt, seed, talc
**05** cover, crush, grind, moust, muist, smalt, smash, strew **06** farina, grains, pestle, pounce, pulvil, saline
**07** alcohol, araroba, scatter, smeddum
**08** amberite, coal dust, levigate, magnesia, pemoline, pulvilio, pulville, sprinkle, woodmeal **09** comminute, granulate, pulverize, pulvillio, triturate, wood flour **10** icing sugar, ivory-black, thimerosal **11** mould-facing, washing-blue **13** efflorescence, platinum black

## powdered

**04** semé **05** semée **06** seméed

## powdery

**03** dry **04** ashy, fine **05** dusty, loose, mealy, sandy **06** chalky, floury, grainy, ground, mealie **07** crumbly, friable **08** granular, levigate, powdered **09** pulverous **10** granulated, pulverized **11** pulverulent **12** efflorescent

**power**
**01** P **03** arm, eon, say, vis **04** aeon, mana, pull, rule, sway, watt **05** clout, force, index, juice, might, oomph, right, state, teeth **06** energy, muscle, nation, people, vigour **07** ability, command, control, country, faculty, licence, mastery, potency, warrant **08** capacity, clutches, dominion, exponent, strength **09** authority, influence, intensity, potential, privilege, supremacy **10** ascendancy, capability, competence, domination, superpower **11** prerogative, sovereignty **12** forcefulness, potentiality, powerfulness **13** authorization, effectiveness

*Power stations include:*

**06** Huntly
**07** Benmore
**08** Bankside, Dounreay, Sizewell, Yallourn
**09** Battersea, Chernobyl, Dungeness, Manapouri, Windscale
**10** Sellafield
**11** Wallerawang
**12** Marsden Point
**14** Snowy Mountains
**15** Three Mile Island

• **have sufficient power**
**03** can
• **having enough power**
**04** able
• **the powers that be**
**04** them **09** the system **14** the authorities

**powerful**
**03** hot **04** high **05** burly, gutty, hardy, tough **06** brawny, cogent, mighty, potent, punchy, robust, strong, studly **07** intense, leading, telling, winning **08** dominant, forceful, forcible, mightful, muscular, puissant **09** effective, energetic, knock-down, prevalent, strapping **10** commanding, compelling, convincing, impressive, noticeable, persuasive, prevailing **11** all-powerful, efficacious, exceedingly, high-powered, influential **12** overwhelming **13** authoritative

**powerfully**
**04** hard, high **06** highly, strong **08** cogently, forcibly, mightily, potently, strongly **09** tellingly **10** forcefully, vigorously **12** convincingly, impressively, persuasively

**powerless**
**04** numb, weak **05** frail, unfit **06** feeble, infirm, unable **07** unarmed **08** benumbed, disabled, helpless, impotent **09** castrated, hamstrung, incapable, paralysed, toothless **10** impuissant, vulnerable, weak-handed **11** debilitated, defenceless, ineffective, ineffectual **13** incapacitated

**practicability**
**03** use **05** value **07** utility **09** handiness, viability **10** usefulness **11** feasibility, operability, possibility, workability **12** practicality, workableness

**practicable**
**02** on **06** doable, viable **08** feasible, operable, passable, possible, workable **09** practical, realistic **10** achievable, attainable **11** functioning, performable

**practical**
**04** real **05** handy **06** active, actual, strong, useful **07** applied, hands on, skilled, trained, virtual, working **08** everyday, feasible, in effect, ordinary, sensible, suitable, workable, workaday **09** effective, efficient, essential, hard-nosed, pragmatic, qualified, realistic **10** functional, hard-boiled, hard-headed, proficient **11** applicative, commonsense, down-to-earth, experienced, practicable, pragmatical, serviceable, utilitarian **12** accomplished, businesslike, matter-of-fact **14** bread-and-butter
• **practical joke**
**03** gag **04** feat, hoax, jape, joke, scam **05** antic, caper, prank, stunt, trick **06** frolic **07** fast one, frame-up, leg-pull **09** booby trap **11** apple-pie bed

**practicality**
**05** sense **06** basics **07** realism, utility **08** practice **09** soundness **10** experience, pragmatism, usefulness **11** common sense, feasibility, nitty-gritty, workability **12** nuts and bolts **13** practicalness **14** practicability, serviceability

**practically**
**06** all but, almost, nearly **07** morally **08** in effect, sensibly, well-nigh **09** just about, virtually **10** pretty much, pretty well, rationally, reasonably **11** essentially, in principle **13** fundamentally, pragmatically, realistically **14** matter-of-factly

**practice**
**03** ism, job, net, ure, use, way **04** firm, wont, work **05** drill, habit, study, trade, usage **06** action, career, custom, dry run, effect, method, policy, system, try-out, warm-up **07** company, pursuit, reality, routine, work-out **08** business, dummy run, exercise, plotting, scheming, training, trickery **09** actuality, following, operation, procedure, rehearsal, tradition **10** convention, employment, experience, occupation, profession, run-through **11** application, partnership, performance, preparation **13** establishment
• **out of practice**
**05** rusty **07** disused **10** out of habit **11** unpractised **13** disaccustomed, out of the habit
• **put into practice**
**03** use **05** apply **07** perform **08** exercise, put to use **09** make use of **13** put into action, put into effect

**practise**
**02** do **03** use **04** plot **05** apply, drill, study, train **06** effect, follow, go over, polish, pursue, refine, repeat, tamper, work at, work on **07** execute, observe, perfect, perform, prepare **08** carry out, engage in, exercise, frequent, maintain, rehearse **09** go through, implement, prosecute, undertake **10** run through **15** put into practice

**practised**
**03** old **04** able **05** adept **06** expert, traded, versed **07** knowing, skilful, skilled, trained, veteran **08** finished, masterly, seasoned **09** prevalent, qualified **10** consummate, proficient **11** experienced **12** accomplished, experimented **13** knowledgeable

**practitioner**
**03** ace, pro **04** buff, doer **05** crack **06** expert, master, pundit **07** dab hand, maestro, old hand **08** virtuoso **09** authority **10** practician, proficient, specialist **12** professional

**pragmatic**
**05** edict **08** busybody, sensible **09** efficient, hard-nosed, practical, realistic **10** hard-headed, meddlesome **11** opinionated, utilitarian **12** businesslike, matter-of-fact **13** unsentimental

**pragmatism**
**07** realism **08** ad hocery, humanism **10** unidealism **11** opportunism **12** practicalism, practicality **14** hard-headedness, utilitarianism **15** instrumentalism

**pragmatist**
**07** realist **08** humanist **11** opportunist, utilitarian **12** practicalist

**praise**
**03** los, rap **04** hail, hery, laud, loos, puff, rave, sell, tout, wrap **05** adore, bless, blurb, carol, cheer, cry up, exalt, extol, glory, herry, herye, roose **06** admire, eulogy, homage, honour, talk up, thanks **07** acclaim, applaud, bouquet, build up, commend, crack up, flatter, glorify, hosanna, magnify, ovation, promote, tribute, worship **08** accolade, applause, appraise, approval, bouquets, cheering, devotion, emblazon, encomium, eulogium, eulogize, flattery, plaudits, rave over, set forth **09** adoration, adulation, laudation, panegyric, recognize **10** admiration, compliment, hallelujah, wax lyrical **11** acknowledge, approbation, recognition, speak well of, testimonial **12** commendation, congratulate, pay tribute to, thanksgiving **13** glorification, speak highly of **14** congratulation
• **expression of praise**
**07** hosanna **08** alleluia **10** halleluiah, hallelujah

**praiseworthy**
**04** fine **06** worthy **08** laudable, sterling **09** admirable, deserving, estimable,

excellent, exemplary, reputable **10** creditable, honourable **11** commendable

**praising**
**09** adulatory, approving, laudative, laudatory, panegyric **10** eulogistic, favourable, flattering, plauditory, worshipful **11** approbatory, encomiastic, promotional **12** commendatory **13** complimentary **14** congratulatory, recommendatory

**pram**
**05** buggy, praam **08** bassinet, stroller **09** Baby Buggy®, pushchair **12** baby carriage, perambulator

**prance**
◇ *anagram indicator*
**04** jump, leap, romp, skip **05** bound, brank, caper, dance, frisk, prank, stalk, strut, swank, titup, vault **06** canary, cavort, curvet, frolic, gambol, jaunce, jaunse, parade, spring, tittup **07** caracol, prankle, show off, swagger, trounce **08** caracole

**prank**
**03** jig, rig **04** fold, gaud, joke, lark, reak, reik **05** antic, caper, pleat, stunt, trick **06** escape, frolic, prance, pranck, vagary, wedgie **07** prancke **08** capering, escapade, fredaine, prancing **11** monkey shine **13** practical joke

**prankster**
**05** joker, rogue **06** hoaxer, jester **07** funster **08** quipster **09** trickster **14** practical joker

**praseodymium**
**02** Pr

**prat**
**03** ass, mug, nit, oaf **04** berk, clot, dope, dork, fool, geek, jerk, nerd, twit **05** chump, clown, dumbo, dunce, idiot, ninny, pratt, prick, twerp, wally **06** cretin, dimwit, dum-dum, muppet, nitwit, sucker **07** fat-head, halfwit, pillock, plonker **08** buttocks, imbecile, innocent, numskull **09** birdbrain, ignoramus, lamebrain, simpleton, thickhead **10** nincompoop **11** knucklehead
*See also* **bottom**

**prattle**
**03** gab, gup, jaw, yap **04** chat, talk **06** babble, drivel, gabble, gossip, hot air, jabber, patter, rattle, tattle, witter **07** blabber, blather, blether, chatter, gabnash, nashgab, prating, twaddle, twattle, twitter **08** chitchat, nonsense **09** bavardage, gibberish **11** foolishness

**prattler**
**06** gossip, magpie, rattle, talker, tatler **07** babbler, blether, gabbler, tattler, windbag **09** chatterer, loudmouth **10** chatterbox **12** blabbermouth

**pray**
**03** ask, beg, bid, say **05** adore, crave, daven, plead, thank **06** call on, invoke, praise, talk to **07** beseech, beseeke, confess, entreat, implore, prithee, prythee, request, solicit, speak to, worship **08** petition **09** imprecate **10** be at prayer, say a prayer, supplicate **11** commune with **14** say your prayers, wrestle with God

**prayer**
**03** act, ave, cry **04** bead, bede, bene, plea **06** appeal, litany, mantra, novena, orison, praise **07** collect, request, worship **08** devotion, doxology, entreaty, petition, suffrage **09** adoration, communion **10** confession, fellowship, invocation **11** imprecation **12** intercession, supplication, thanksgiving

*Prayers include:*

**02** Om
**03** act
**05** adhan, Ardas, grace, salat, Shema
**06** Amidah, Gloria, Rosary, Yizkor
**07** Angelus, khotbah, khutbah
**08** Agnus Dei, Ave Maria, Habdalah, Hail Mary, Havdalah, Kaddhish, Kol Nidre, shahadah
**09** Confiteor, Our Father
**10** Benedictus, Lychnapsia, Magnificat, requiescat
**11** Lord's Prayer, Paternoster, Sursum Corda
**12** Divine Office, Kyrie eleison, Nunc Dimittis
**15** act of contrition

**• call to prayer**
**04** azan

**prayer-book**
**06** mahzor, missal, primer, siddur **07** liturgy, machzor, ordinal, primmer **08** breviary, Triodion **09** euchology, formulary **11** euchologion, service-book

**preach**
**04** urge **05** teach **06** advise, exhort, sermon **07** address, deliver, lecture **08** admonish, advocate, harangue, moralize, proclaim, prophesy **09** inculcate, preachify, predicate, recommend, sermonize **10** apostolize, evangelize **11** give a sermon, pontificate **15** spread the gospel

**preacher**
**05** molla **06** mollah, moolah, mullah, parson, ranter **07** apostle, holy Joe, martext, prophet **08** homilist, minister, pulpiter, sermoner, spintext **09** Boanerges, clergyman, gospeller, itinerant, moralizer, predicant, predikant, pulpiteer, sermoneer **10** ecclesiast, evangelist, Holy Roller, licentiate, missionary, revivalist, sermonizer, tub-thumper **11** Bible-basher, devil-dodger, lay preacher, probationer **12** Bible-pounder, Bible-thumper, circuit rider, pontificater, tent preacher **13** field preacher, local preacher, televangelist **15** open-air preacher

**preaching**
**05** dogma **06** gospel, pulpit **07** evangel, kerygma, message, sermons **08** doctrine, homilies, precepts, prophecy, teaching **09** predicant **10** evangelism, homiletics **11** exhortation, instruction, sermonizing, tub-thumping **12** Bible-bashing **13** pontificating, tent preaching

**preachy**
**02** pi **05** pious **08** didactic, dogmatic, edifying **09** homiletic, hortatory, pharisaic, pietistic, religiose **10** moralistic, moralizing, pontifical **11** exhortatory, sermonizing **13** pontificating, sanctimonious, self-righteous **14** holier-than-thou

**preamble**
**05** proem **06** lead-in **07** preface, prelude **08** exordium, foreword, overture, prologue **11** preparation **12** introduction, prolegomenon **13** preliminaries

**prearrange**
**07** diarize, prepare, pre-plan **08** organize, schedule **09** plan ahead **12** predetermine

**prearranged**
**03** set

**precarious**
◇ *anagram indicator*
**04** iffy **05** dicey, dicky, dodgy, hairy, risky, shaky **06** chancy, unsafe, unsure, wobbly **07** dubious, trickle **08** doubtful, insecure, ticklish, unstable, unsteady **09** dangerous, hazardous, uncertain, unsettled **10** touch and go, unreliable, vulnerable **11** treacherous **12** supplicating, undependable **13** unpredictable

**precariously**
◇ *anagram indicator*
**07** riskily, shakily **08** unsafely, unstably **10** insecurely, unreliably, unsteadily **11** dangerously, hazardously **13** unpredictably

**precaution**
**04** care **07** caution **08** forewarn, prudence, security **09** foresight, insurance, provision, safeguard **10** protection, providence, safety belt **11** forethought, preparation **12** anticipation **13** attentiveness **14** circumspection, farsightedness

**precautionary**
**06** safety **07** prudent **08** cautious **09** judicious, provident **10** far-sighted, preventive, protective **11** preliminary, preparatory **12** preventative

**precede**
**04** head, lead **06** forego, herald **07** forerun, preface, prelude, prevene, prevent, usher in **08** antecede, antedate, go before **09** come first, go ahead of, harbinger, introduce **10** anticipate, come before **14** take precedence

**precedence**
**03** pas **04** lead, rank **05** place **08** eminence, priority **09** seniority,

supremacy **10** ascendancy, first place, preference, right of way **11** preaudience, pre-eminence, superiority **12** pride of place

• **take precedence over**

**09** take place **10** come before, take rank of

## precedent
**04** case, lead **05** model, token **07** example, pattern **08** exemplar, instance, paradigm, parallel, standard **09** criterion, yardstick

## preceding
**04** past **05** above, prior, supra **06** former **07** earlier, leading **08** anterior, previous **09** aforesaid, foregoing, precedent **10** antecedent, precursive, prevenient **11** preliminary **14** aforementioned

## precept
**03** law **04** rule **05** axiom, canon, maxim, motto, order **06** charge, decree, dictum, rubric, saying **07** command, mandate, statute **08** doctrine, sentence **09** direction, directive, guideline, institute, ordinance, principle **10** convention, injunction, regulation **11** commandment, instruction

## precinct
**04** area, land, mall, zone **05** bound, close, court, lands, limit, verge **06** milieu, sector, vihara **07** confine, quarter, section, temenos **08** boundary, building, district, division, environs, galleria, locality, purlieus, vicinity **09** buildings, enclosure, food court, peribolos, peribolus, surrounds **13** neighbourhood **14** shopping centre

## preciosity
**06** chichi **08** tweeness **11** affectation, floweriness, marivaudage **13** artificiality **14** over-refinement **15** pretentiousness

## precious
**04** dear, fine, nice, rare, twee **05** ditsy, ditzy, grand, loved, tatty **06** adored, chichi, choice, costly, dainty, prized, valued **07** beloved, darling, dearest, flowery, revered **08** affected, idolized, mannered, valuable **09** cherished, contrived, egregious, expensive, extremely, favourite, priceless, simulated, treasured **10** artificial, dearbought, fastidious, high-priced **11** inestimable, overrefined, pretentious **12** confoundedly

• **precious stone** *see* **gem**

## precipice
**04** crag, drop **05** bluff, brink, cliff, krans, kranz, scarp, steep **06** escarp, height, krantz **08** precepit **09** cliff face, sheer drop **10** escarpment

## precipitate
**04** hurl, rash **05** brief, cause, fling, flock, hasty, heave, hurry, quick, rapid, shoot, speed, swift, throw **06** abrupt, flocks, hasten, induce, plunge, sludge, speedy, sudden, thrust **07** advance, bring on, frantic, further, hurried, quicken, speed up, trigger, violent **08** expedite, headlong, heedless, occasion, reckless **09** breakneck, hot-headed, impatient, impetuous, impulsive, magistery **10** accelerate, bring about, indiscreet, unexpected **11** precipitant, precipitous

## precipitately
**06** rashly **07** hastily, quickly, rapidly **08** abruptly, headlong, suddenly **09** violently **10** recklessly **11** frantically, impetuously, impulsively **12** unexpectedly

## precipitation

*Precipitation includes:*

**03** dew, fog
**04** hail, mist, rain, snow
**05** sleet
**06** shower
**07** drizzle
**08** downpour, rainfall, snowfall
**09** rainstorm, snowflake

*See also* **ice**; **snow**; **weather**

## precipitous
**04** high **05** sharp, sheer, steep **06** abrupt, sudden **07** steepup **08** headlong, steepeup, vertical **10** steepdowne **11** steepedowne **13** perpendicular

## précis
**05** sum up, table **06** digest, résumé, sketch **07** abridge, epitome, outline, run-down, shorten, summary **08** abstract, compress, condense, contract, synopsis **09** epitomize, summarize, synopsize **10** abbreviate, compendium, conspectus **11** abridgement, contraction, encapsulate **12** abbreviation, condensation **13** encapsulation

## precise
**03** dry **04** nice, prim, very **05** exact, fixed, razor, right, rigid, tight **06** actual, formal, minute, narrow, strict **07** buckram, careful, correct, express, factual, finical, literal, pointed, starchy **08** accurate, clear-cut, definite, detailed, distinct, explicit, faithful, preceese, priggish, punctual, rigorous, specific, succinct, surgical **09** authentic, identical **10** blow-by-blow, fastidious, meticulous, particular, scrupulous **11** ceremonious, punctilious, puritanical, unambiguous, unequivocal, word-for-word **13** conscientious

## precisely
**03** yes **04** just, slap, to a T, true **05** plumb, quite, right, sharp, smack **06** agreed, bang on, dead on, indeed, just so, spot-on **07** clearly, exactly **08** minutely, of course, on the dot, strictly, verbatim, you got it **09** certainly, correctly, literally **10** absolutely, accurately, distinctly, that's right **11** by the squire, on the button, word for word

## precision
**04** care **06** detail, rigour **08** accuracy, neatness **09** exactness **10** exactitude **11** correctness, preciseness, reliability **12** distinctness, explicitness, faithfulness **13** particularity **14** fastidiousness, meticulousness, scrupulousness **15** punctiliousness

## preclude
**03** bar **04** stop **05** avoid, check, debar, estop **06** hinder **07** exclude, inhibit, obviate, prevent, rule out **08** prohibit, restrain **09** eliminate, foreclose, forestall

## precocious
**04** fast **05** ahead, early, quick, smart **06** bright, clever, farand, gifted, mature **07** farrand, farrant, forward **08** advanced, far ahead, talented **09** brilliant, developed, premature **11** auld-farrant **13** old for your age

## preconceive
**06** assume, expect, ideate **07** imagine, picture, presume, project **08** conceive, envisage **09** visualize **10** anticipate, presuppose **12** predetermine

## preconception
**04** bias, idea **06** notion **09** prejudice, prenotion **10** assumption, conjecture **11** expectation, presumption **12** anticipation, prejudgement **14** predisposition, presupposition

## precondition
**04** must **09** condition, essential, necessity **10** sine qua non **11** requirement, stipulation **12** prerequisite

## precursor
**04** sign **05** usher **06** herald **07** pioneer, prelude **08** ancestor, forebear, way-maker **09** harbinger, messenger **10** antecedent, forerunner, indication, progenitor **11** morning star, predecessor, trailblazer **13** curtain-raiser

## precursory
**05** prior **07** warning **08** anterior, previous **09** preceding, prefatory, preludial, prelusive, prodromal **10** antecedent, precursive, prevenient **11** preliminary, preparatory **12** introductory **13** preambulatory

**predator** *see* **bird**; **cat**; **spider**

## predatory
**06** greedy, lupine **07** hunting, preying, wolfish **08** covetous, ravaging, thieving **09** marauding, pillaging, predative, rapacious, raptorial, voracious, vulturine, vulturous **10** avaricious, despoiling, plundering, predaceous, predacious **11** acquisitive, carnivorous, deleterious, destructive, raptatorial

## predecessor
**08** ancestor, forebear **09** precursor **10** antecedent, antecessor, forefather, forerunner, progenitor

**predestination**
**03** lot **04** doom, fate **07** destiny
**11** reprobation **14** foreordination

**predestine**
**04** doom, fate, mean **06** intend
**07** destine **08** foredoom, pre-elect
**09** preordain **10** foreordain
**12** predestinate, predetermine

**predetermined**
**03** set **05** fated, fixed **06** agreed, doomed **07** settled **08** arranged, destined, ordained **11** prearranged, predestined **12** foreordained

**predicament**
**03** box, fix, jam **04** cart, hole, mess, pass, spot, stew **06** crisis, hiccup, pickle, plight, scrape, taking
**07** dilemma, impasse, trouble
**08** chancery, hot water, how-d'ye-do, quandary **09** deep water, emergency, situation, tight spot **10** praemunire
**12** kettle of fish

**predicate**
**04** aver, avow, base, rest **05** build, found, imply, posit, state **06** affirm, assert, avouch, ground, preach
**07** contend, declare, premise
**08** maintain, proclaim **09** establish, postulate **11** be dependent

**predict**
**03** bet **04** cast **05** augur **06** divine
**07** foresay, foresee, portend, presage, project, warrant **08** forecast, foreshew, foreshow, foretell, prophesy
**09** auspicate, forespeak **10** vaticinate
**11** second-guess **13** prognosticate

**predictable**
**04** sure **05** trite, usual **06** likely, odds-on **07** certain **08** expected, foregone, foreseen, knee-jerk, probable, reliable
**09** customary **10** dependable, imaginable, on the cards, unoriginal
**11** anticipated, foreseeable
**12** unsurprising

**prediction**
**03** bet **06** augury **07** fortune
**08** forecast, prophecy, soothsay
**09** horoscope, prognosis
**10** divination, prognostic
**11** auspication, soothsaying
**14** fortune-telling **15** prognostication

**predictive**
**07** augural **09** prophetic **10** diagnostic, divinatory, prognostic **11** foretelling
**12** anticipating

**predilection**
**04** bent, bias, love **05** fancy, taste
**06** liking **07** leaning **08** affinity, fondness, penchant, soft spot, tendency, weakness **09** affection
**10** enthusiasm, partiality, preference, proclivity, propensity **11** inclination
**14** predisposition

**predispose**
**04** bias, make, move, sway **06** affect, induce, prompt **07** dispose, incline
**08** persuade **09** influence, prejudice
**10** make liable

**predisposed**
**05** prone, ready **06** biased, liable, minded **07** subject, willing
**08** amenable, disposed, inclined, prepared **09** agreeable **10** favourable, prejudiced **11** susceptible **12** not unwilling, well-disposed

**predisposition**
**04** bent, bias **07** leaning **08** penchant, tendency **09** liability, prejudice, proneness **10** likelihood, preference, proclivity, propensity **11** disposition, inclination, willingness **12** potentiality, predilection **13** vulnerability
**14** susceptibility

**predominance**
**04** edge, hold, rain, sway **05** power, raine, reign **06** weight **07** control, mastery, numbers **08** dominion, hegemony **09** dominance, influence, supremacy, upper hand
**10** ascendancy, leadership, prepotence, prepotency, prevalence
**11** paramountcy, prepollence, prepollency, superiority
**13** preponderance

**predominant**
**04** main **05** chief, prime **06** master, potent, ruling, strong **07** capital, leading, primary, supreme
**08** dominant, forceful, powerful
**09** ascendant, ascendent, important, in control, paramount, principal, sovereign **10** prevailing **11** controlling, influential, most obvious
**12** preponderant **13** most important
**14** most noticeable, preponderating
**15** in the ascendancy

**predominantly**
**06** mainly, mostly **07** as a rule, chiefly, largely, overall, usually **08** above all, commonly **09** generally, in general, in the main, primarily **10** by and large, especially, on the whole **11** principally
**14** for the most part

**predominate**
**04** rule, tell **05** reign **06** obtain
**07** prevail **08** dominate, outweigh, override, overrule **09** outnumber, transcend **10** overshadow
**12** preponderate, rule the roast **15** be in the majority

**pre-eminence**
**04** fame, palm **06** renown, repute
**08** majority, prestige **09** supremacy
**10** excellence, prominence
**11** distinction, paramountcy, sovereignty, superiority **12** peerlessness, predominance **13** matchlessness, transcendence **15** incomparability

**pre-eminent**
**03** gun **04** arch, star **05** chief, first, grand, great **06** famous, unique
**07** eminent, extreme, leading, palmary, supreme, topping **08** foremost, renowned, singular, superior
**09** excellent, first-rate, matchless, palmarian, prominent, unmatched
**10** inimitable, unequalled, unrivalled
**11** exceptional, outstanding, superlative, unsurpassed
**12** incomparable, transcendent
**13** distinguished, most important

**pre-eminently**
**04** only **07** notably **08** paravant, signally **09** eminently, paravaunt, primarily, supremely **10** especially, inimitably, peerlessly, singularly, strikingly **11** exclusively, matchlessly, principally **12** emphatically, incomparably, particularly, surpassingly **13** conspicuously, exceptionally, par excellence, superlatively

**pre-empt**
**05** seize, usurp **06** assume, secure, thwart **07** acquire, prevent, replace
**08** arrogate, supplant **09** forestall
**10** anticipate **11** appropriate

**preen**
**03** pin **04** bask, deck, do up, trim, whet
**05** adorn, array, clean, exult, gloat, groom, pique, plume, pride, primp, prink, proin, proyn, prune, slick **06** doll up, proign, proine, proyne, smooth, tart up **07** dress up, trick up **08** beautify, prettify, spruce up, trick out
**12** congratulate

**preface**
**04** open **05** begin, index, proem, start
**06** launch, prefix, prolog **07** epistle, precede, prelims, prelude
**08** exordium, foreword, lead up to, preamble, prologue **09** introduce
**11** avant-propos, frontmatter
**12** introduction, prolegomenon
**13** preliminaries

**prefatory**
**07** opening **08** exordial, proemial
**09** preludial, prelusive, prelusory
**10** antecedent, precursory
**11** explanatory, prefatorial, preliminary, preparatory **12** introductory, prolegomenal **13** preambulatory

**prefect**
**05** grave **07** monitor **08** praefect
**09** commander, prepostor
**10** magistrate, praepostor, prepositor, supervisor **13** administrator

**prefer**
**03** opt **04** back, file, pick, want, wish
**05** adopt, bring, elect, exalt, fancy, go for, lodge, place, press, raise
**06** choose, desire, favour, honour, move up, opt for, select **07** advance, elevate, pick out, present, promote, support **08** advocate, plump for
**09** recommend, single out
**10** aggrandize, like better **11** be partial to, would rather, would sooner

**preferable**
**05** nicer **06** better, chosen
**08** favoured, superior **09** advisable, desirable, preferred **11** more desired, recommended **12** advantageous

**preferably**
**05** first **06** rather, sooner **07** ideally

09 for choice 10 from choice, if possible, much rather, much sooner 12 by preference 13 for preference

**preference**
03 fad 04 bent, bias, kink, mark, pick, will, wish 05 fancy 06 choice, desire, liking, option 07 leaning 08 cup of tea, druthers, forehand, priority
09 favourite, selection 10 partiality, precedence 11 favouritism, first choice, inclination, pre-election
12 predilection 14 discrimination
**• in preference to**
06 before 08 by choice 09 for choice, in place of, instead of 10 from choice, rather than

**preferential**
06 better, biased 07 partial, special
08 favoured, partisan, superior
10 favourable, privileged
12 advantageous

**preferment**
04 rise 06 step up 07 dignity
09 elevation, prelation, promotion, upgrading 10 betterment, exaltation
11 advancement, furtherance, improvement 14 aggrandizement

**preferred**
03 pet 06 choice, chosen 07 desired
08 approved, favorite, favoured, selected 09 favourite, predilect
10 authorized, sanctioned
11 recommended

**prefigure**
04 bode, mean, type 05 augur
06 signal 07 portend, predict, presage, promise, signify, suggest 08 indicate, prophesy 10 foreshadow
13 prognosticate

**pregnancy**
06 cyesis 09 family way, gestation, gravidity 10 conception 11 parturition
12 child-bearing, impregnation
13 fertilization 14 being with child

**pregnant**
04 full, gone, rich 05 clear, great, heavy, in pig, in pup, pithy, quick, witty
06 cogent, filled, gravid, in calf, in foal, loaded 07 charged, fertile, fraught, obvious, pointed, replete, teeming, telling, weighty 08 eloquent, enceinte, fruitful, preggers, swelling, with calf, with foal 09 expectant, expecting, in the club, in trouble, inventive, momentous, up the duff, up the pole, with child, with young 10 big-bellied, convincing, expressive, fertilized, meaningful, parturient, productive, suggestive, up the spout, up the stick
11 impregnated, significant 12 great-bellied 14 in the family way

**prehistoric**
03 old 05 early 06 Minoan 07 ancient, archaic, Ogygian 08 earliest, obsolete, outmoded, Pelasgic, primeval 09 out-of-date, primaeval, primitive
10 antiquated, primordial 11 out of the ark 12 antediluvian 14 before the flood

**prejudge**
06 assume 07 presume 09 forejudge, prejudice 10 anticipate, presuppose
11 prejudicate 12 predetermine

**prejudice**
03 mar 04 bias, harm, hurt, load, loss, ruin, sway 05 slant, spoil, wreck
06 ageism, colour, damage, hinder, impair, injure, injury, racism, sexism, weight 07 bigotry, distort, incline
08 classism, endanger, jaundice, misogyny 09 condition, detriment, influence, injustice, preoccupy, undermine 10 chauvinism, impairment, partiality, predispose, preference, prepossess, unfairness, xenophobia 11 intolerance, misanthropy, prejudicate
12 anticipation, anti-Semitism, disadvantage, one-sidedness, partisanship, prejudgement
13 preoccupation 14 discrimination
15 be detrimental to

**prejudiced**
06 ageist, biased, loaded, racist, sexist, unfair, unjust, warped 07 bigoted, ex parte, insular, partial, slanted 08 one-sided, partisan, weighted 09 blinkered, distorted, illiberal, jaundiced, parochial
10 chauvinist, influenced, intolerant, subjective, xenophobic 11 anti-Semitic, conditioned, predisposed, prejudicial 12 chauvinistic, narrow-minded, prepossessed
14 discriminatory

**prejudicial**
07 harmful, hurtful, noxious
08 damaging, inimical 09 injurious
11 deleterious, detrimental
12 unfavourable 15 disadvantageous

**preliminary**
04 test 05 early, first, pilot, prior, proem, start, trial 06 basics
07 advance, initial, opening, preface, prelude, primary 08 earliest, exordial, exordium, foreword, preamble, prodrome 09 beginning, inaugural, prefatory, rudiments 10 groundwork, precursory, qualifying 11 exploratory, formalities, foundations, preparation, preparative, preparatory
12 experimental, introduction, introductory, prolegomenon

**prelude**
05 proem, start 06 entrée, herald, opener, verset 07 intrada, opening, preface 08 exordium, foreword, overture, preamble, prodrome, prologue 09 beginning, harbinger, induction, praeamble, precursor
10 forerunner, praeludium
11 preliminary, preparation
12 commencement, introduction, prolegomenon 13 curtain-raiser

**premature**
04 prem, rash, soon 05 early, hasty
07 preemie, too soon 08 ill-timed, previous, timeless, too early, untimely
09 impetuous, impulsive, precocial
10 praecocial 11 inopportune, precipitate 13 ill-considered, jumping the gun

**prematurely**
05 early 06 rashly 07 hastily, too soon
08 too early, untimely 11 impetuously, impulsively 12 incompletely

**premeditated**
06 wilful 07 planned 08 intended, prepense, propense 09 conscious, contrived 10 calculated, considered, deliberate, preplanned 11 cold-blooded, intentional, prearranged
12 aforethought 13 predetermined

**premeditation**
06 design 07 purpose 08 planning, plotting, scheming 09 intention
11 forethought 12 aforethought, deliberation 13 determination
14 deliberateness, prearrangement

**premier**
03 top 04 head, main 05 chief, first, prime 07 highest, initial, leading, primary, supreme 08 cardinal, earliest, foremost, original 09 paramount, principal 10 chancellor, pre-eminent
13 chief minister, first minister, prime minister

*Premiers of New Zealand:*

03 **Fox** (William)
04 **Grey** (Sir George), **Hall** (John), **Weld** (Frederick Aloysius)
05 **Stout** (Sir Robert), **Vogel** (Sir Julius)
06 **Domett** (Alfred), **Pollen** (Daniel), **Seddon** (Richard John), **Sewell** (Henry)
08 **Atkinson** (Sir Harry Albert), **Ballance** (John), **Stafford** (Edward William), **Whitaker** (Frederick)
10 **Waterhouse** (George Marsden)

*See also* **prime minister**

**première**
05 debut 07 opening 10 first night
12 first showing, opening night

**premise**
05 basis, lemma, posit, state 06 assert, assume, prefix, reason, thesis 07 lay down 08 argument 09 assertion, postulate, predicate, statement, stipulate 10 assumption, hypothesis, presuppose, take as true
11 hypothesize, proposition, supposition 14 presupposition

**premises**
04 site 05 place 06 estate, office
07 grounds 08 building, property
13 establishment

**premium**
02 ap, pm 05 bonus, prize 06 bounty, reward 07 grassum 08 extra sum, interest, key money 09 insurance, surcharge 10 instalment 11 extra charge 12 an arm and a leg, overcharging 14 regular payment
15 daylight robbery
**• at a premium**
04 rare 06 scarce 08 above par
12 hard to come by, like gold dust 13 in great demand, in short supply

**• put a premium on**
**06** favour **08** hold dear, treasure **10** appreciate **12** regard highly, value greatly **15** set great store by

**premonition**
**04** fear, idea, omen, sign **05** hunch, worry **07** anxiety, feeling, portent, presage, specter, spectre, warning **09** intuition, misgiving, suspicion **10** foreboding, gut feeling, prevention, sixth sense **11** forewarning **12** apprehension, funny feeling, presentiment

**preoccupation**
**05** thing **06** hang-up **07** concern, reverie **08** fixation, interest, oblivion **09** obsession, prejudice **10** absorption, enthusiasm, hobby-horse **11** abstraction, daydreaming, distraction, engrossment, pensiveness **12** heedlessness, one-track mind **13** obliviousness, prepossession, wool-gathering **15** bee in your bonnet, inattentiveness

**preoccupied**
**06** intent **07** engaged, faraway, fixated, pensive, taken up **08** absorbed, distrait, heedless, immersed, involved, obsessed **09** engrossed, oblivious, wrapped up **10** abstracted, distracted **11** daydreaming **12** absent-minded **13** deep in thought

**preoccupy**
**03** eat **04** bias **05** eat up **06** absorb, engage, fixate, obsess, occupy, take up **07** involve **09** prejudice **10** prepossess

**preordain**
**04** doom, fate **07** destine **10** foreordain, prearrange, predestine **12** predestinate, predetermine

**preparation**
◇ *anagram indicator*
**04** plan, prep **05** study **06** basics, lotion, potion, supply **07** address, mixture **08** assembly, coaching, compound, cosmetic, homework, medicine, planning, practice, revision, training **09** equipping, provision, readiness, rudiments, spadework **10** concoction, foundation, groundwork, production **11** application, arrangement, composition, development, mise en place **12** construction, organization **13** preliminaries

**preparatory**
**05** basic **07** initial, opening, primary **09** prefatory **10** antecedent, elementary, precursory **11** fundamental, preliminary, rudimentary **12** introductory

**• preparatory to**
**06** before **07** prior to **10** previous to **11** in advance of **15** in expectation of

**prepare**
◇ *anagram indicator*
**02** do **03** fix, mix **04** boun, busk, cock, edit, make, plan **05** bowne, coach, draft, dress, equip, prime, set up, study, teach, tee up, train **06** adjust, attire, cooper, devise, digest, draw up, fit out, gear up, rig out, supply, warm up **07** arrange, compose, concoct, fashion, produce, provide, psych up **08** assemble, contrive, exercise, get ready, instruct, organize, practise **09** construct, make ready **10** pave the way **11** put together **12** get into shape **13** throw together **14** set the scene for

**• prepare yourself**
**12** gird yourself **13** brace yourself, steel yourself **15** fortify yourself, gird up your loins

**prepared**
◇ *anagram indicator*
**03** fit, set **04** yare **05** fixed, ready **07** in order, planned, waiting, willing **08** arranged, disposed, inclined **09** organized **11** predisposed

**• prepared with**
**03** à la

**preparedness**
**05** order **07** fitness **08** procinct **09** alertness, readiness **10** expectancy **11** preparation **12** anticipation

**preponderance**
**04** bulk, mass, sway **05** force, power **06** weight **08** dominion, majority **09** dominance, supremacy **10** ascendancy, domination, lion's share, overweight, prevalence **11** superiority **12** predominance **13** extensiveness, greater number

**preponderant**
**06** larger **07** greater **08** dominant, foremost, superior **09** important **10** overriding, overruling, prevailing **11** controlling, predominant, significant

**preponderate**
**04** rule, tell **07** prevail **08** dominate, outweigh, override, overrule **09** outnumber, weigh with **11** predominate **13** turn the scales **14** turn the balance **15** be in the majority

**prepossessing**
**04** fair **06** taking **07** amiable, lovable, winning, winsome **08** alluring, charming, engaging, fetching, handsome, inviting, likeable, loveable, magnetic, pleasing, striking **09** appealing, beautiful **10** attractive, bewitching, delightful, enchanting **11** captivating, fascinating, good-looking

**preposterous**
◇ *anagram indicator*
◇ *reversal indicator*
**05** crazy **06** absurd **07** asinine, foolish **08** farcical, shocking **09** ludicrous, monstrous, senseless **10** impossible, incredible, irrational, monstruous, outrageous, ridiculous **11** intolerable, nonsensical, unthinkable **12** unbelievable, unreasonable

**preposterously**
**08** absurdly **10** incredibly, shockingly **11** intolerably, ludicrously **12** outrageously, ridiculously, unbelievably, unreasonably

**prerequisite**
**04** must **05** basic, vital **06** needed **07** needful, proviso **08** required **09** condition, essential, mandatory, necessary, necessity, requisite **10** imperative, obligatory, sine qua non **11** fundamental, requirement **12** precondition **13** indispensable, qualification

**prerogative**
**03** due **05** claim, droit, right **06** choice, purvey **07** liberty, licence, royalty **08** immunity, sanction **09** advantage, authority, exemption, privilege **10** birthright **11** entitlement **12** carte blanche

**presage**
**04** bode, omen, sign **05** abode, augur **06** augury, herald, reveal, threat, warn of **07** bespeak, betoken, point to, portend, portent, predict, promise, signify, warning, warrant **08** announce, forebode, forecast, foretell, forewarn, indicate, threaten **09** adumbrate, be a sign of, foretoken, harbinger, precursor **10** foreboding, forerunner, foreshadow, indication, prognostic **11** forewarning, premonition **12** presentiment **13** foreshadowing, prefiguration, prognosticate, signification **15** prognostication

**Presbyterian**
**04** Whig

**prescience**
**08** prophecy **09** foresight, prevision **11** second sight **12** clairvoyance, precognition **13** foreknowledge, propheticness **14** far-sightedness

**prescient**
**06** divine **07** psychic **08** divining **09** far-seeing, prescious, prophetic **10** discerning, divinatory, far-sighted, perceptive **11** clairvoyant, foreknowing, foresighted, previsional

**prescribe**
**03** act, fix, set **04** rule **05** lapse, limit, order **06** advise, decree, define, direct, enjoin, impose, ordain **07** appoint, command, confine, dictate, lay down, require, specify **09** stipulate

**prescribed**
**03** set **07** decreed **08** assigned, laid down, ordained **09** formulary, prescript, specified, statutory **10** regulation, statutable, stipulated

**prescription**
**04** drug **05** scrip **06** advice, recipe, remedy, script **07** formula, mixture **08** leechdom, medicine **09** direction, guideline, optometry, treatment **10** concoction, guidelines **11** instruction, preparation **14** recommendation

**prescriptive**
**05** rigid **08** didactic, dogmatic

**09** customary, normative
**10** preceptive **11** dictatorial, legislating, prescribing **13** authoritarian

**presence**
**03** air **04** aura, face **05** being, ghost, poise **06** appeal, person, shadow, spirit **07** bearing, company, dignity, phantom, spectre **08** assembly, carriage, charisma, nearness, Shekinah, vicinity, visitant
**09** closeness, demeanour, existence, magnetism, occupancy, proximity, residence, Shechinah **10** apparition, appearance, attendance, attraction
**11** personality, propinquity
**13** companionship, neighbourhood, self-assurance **14** self-confidence

• **in the presence of**
**02** by

• **presence of mind**
**04** cool **05** poise **06** aplomb
**08** calmness, coolness **09** alertness, composure, sangfroid **10** equanimity
**11** self-command **13** self-assurance
**14** self-possession, unflappability
**15** level-headedness

**present**
**02** pr **03** box, gie, now, tip **04** gift, give, here, host, near, perk, pres, show
**05** apply, award, being, endow, grant, mount, offer, put on, ready, stage, there
**06** at hand, bestow, bounty, cadeau, confer, convey, depict, donate, extend, favour, moment, nearby, prefer, submit, tender, to hand **07** compère, current, deliver, display, douceur, entrust, exhibit, freebie, handout, hold out, instant, perform, picture, porrect, portray, pressie, prezzie, proffer, propine **08** announce, describe, donation, existent, existing, gratuity, hand over, largesse, offering, organize
**09** attending, available, delineate, endowment, immediate, introduce, make known, represent, sweetener
**10** present-day, put forward
**11** benefaction, close at hand, demonstrate **12** bring forward, characterize, contemporary, contribution, in attendance, put on display

• **at present**
**03** now **05** today **06** the now **07** just now **09** currently **10** at this time **11** at the moment

• **for the present**
**03** now **06** for now, pro tem **12** for the moment **13** in the meantime **15** for the time being

• **present yourself**
**05** arise, occur, pop up **06** appear, arrive, attend, crop up, emerge, happen, show up, turn up **11** come to light, materialize

• **the present day**
**03** now **05** today **08** nowadays
**09** currently **10** at this time, here and now

**presentable**
**04** neat, tidy **05** clean, smart
**06** decent, spruce **08** passable
**09** quite good, tolerable **10** acceptable
**11** respectable **12** satisfactory
**14** smartly dressed

**presentation**
**04** form, show, talk **05** award
**06** format, launch, layout, object, speech, system **07** address, display, lecture, program, recital, seminar, showing, staging **08** awarding, bestowal, donating, exterior, granting, mounting **09** collation, conferral, packaging, programme, rendition, structure, unveiling **10** appearance, exhibition, presenting, production
**11** arrangement, investiture, making known, performance **12** disquisition, introduction, organization
**13** demonstration, poster session
**14** representation

**present-day**
**02** AD **06** latest, living, modern
**07** current, present **08** existing, up-to-date **11** fashionable **12** contemporary

**presenter**
**02** MC **04** host **05** emcee **06** anchor
**07** compère **08** frontman
**09** anchorman, announcer
**10** postulator **11** anchorwoman, sportcaster **12** sportscaster
*See also* **radio**; **television**

**presentiment**
**04** fear **05** hunch **07** feeling, presage
**08** bad vibes, bodement, forecast
**09** intuition, misgiving **10** foreboding, presension **11** expectation, forethought, premonition
**12** anticipation, apprehension, forebodement

**presently**
**03** now **04** enow, soon **05** in a mo
**06** pronto, the now **07** by and by, in a tick, shortly **08** directly, in a jiffy **09** at present, currently, in a minute, in a moment, in a second, ipso facto, these days **10** before long, inevitably **11** at the moment, immediately, necessarily
**12** in a short time **13** in a short while

**preservation**
**06** repair, safety, upkeep **07** defence, keeping, storage, support
**08** guarding, security **09** retention, upholding **10** protection **11** cold storage, maintenance, reservation, safekeeping **12** conservation, continuation, freeze-drying, perpetuation, safeguarding
**13** refrigeration

**preserve**
**03** can, dry, jam, tin **04** area, corn, cure, hain, keep, salt, save **05** candy, chase, chill, field, guard, jelly, lay up, realm, salve, smoke, store **06** bottle, cocoon, defend, domain, embalm, forest, freeze, keep up, kipper, konfyt, pickle, retain, season, secure, shield, sphere, uphold **07** care for, confect, kyanize, protect, put down, reserve, shelter, sustain **08** chow-chow, conserve, continue, creosote, maintain
**09** desiccate, freeze-dry, look after, marmalade, powellize, safeguard, sanctuary **10** perpetuate, safari park, speciality, take care of
**11** commemorate, game reserve, quick-freeze, reservation **13** nature reserve

**preside**
**03** run **04** head, lead, rule **05** chair
**06** direct, govern, head up, manage
**07** conduct, control **08** moderate
**09** hold court, officiate **10** administer
**12** be in charge of, be in the chair, be the chair of, call the shots, take the chair **15** be the chairman of

**president**
**01** P **04** boss, dean, head, Pres, prex
**05** chief, prexy, ruler **06** leader, preses
**07** manager, praeses, speaker
**08** director, governor **09** commodore, moderator, principal **10** chancellor, chief-baron, controller **11** chief barker, Earl Marshal, head of state **13** Dean of Faculty, Earl Marischal **15** Grand Pensionary

*Presidents include:*

**03** **Moi** (Daniel arap), **Rau** (Johannes), **Zia** (Muhammad)
**04** **Amin** (Idi), **Díaz** (Porfirio), **Khan** (Ayub), **Ozal** (Turgut), **René** (France-Albert), **Rhee** (Syngman), **Tito** (Josip Broz)
**05** **Ahmed** (Shehabuddin), **Assad** (Hafez al-), **Banda** (Hastings), **Botha** (P W), **Havel** (Vaclav), **Heuss** (Theodor), **Klerk** (F W de), **Mbeki** (Thabo), **Menem** (Carlos), **Obote** (Milton), **Perón** (Juan), **Perón** (Martínez de), **Putin** (Vladimir), **Ramos** (Fidel), **Sadat** (Anwar el-)
**06** **Aideed** (Mohammed), **Aquino** (Corazon), **Banana** (Canaan), **Bao Dai**, **Bhutto** (Zulfikar Ali), **Biswas** (Abdur Rahman), **Calles** (Plutarco Elías), **Castro** (Fidel), **Chirac** (Jacques), **Ciampi** (Carlo Azeglio), **Gaulle** (Charles de), **Geisel** (Ernesto), **Herzog** (Chaim), **Juárez** (Benito), **Kruger** (Paul), **Kuchma** (Leonid), **Lahoud** (Émile), **Marcos** (Ferdinand), **Mobutu**, **Mugabe** (Robert), **Nasser** (Gamal Abdel), **Nathan** (Sellapan Ramanathan), **Ortega** (Daniel), **Pierce** (Franklin), **Préval** (René), **Rahman** (Ziaur), **Renner** (Karl), **Santos** (José Eduardo dos), **Somoza** (Anastasio), **Somoza** (Luis), **Valera** (Éamon de), **Vargas** (Getúlio), **Walesa** (Lech)
**07** **Atatürk** (Mustapha Kemal), **Batista** (Fulgencio), **Bolívar** (Simón), **Cardoso** (Fernando Henrique), **Demirel** (Süleyman), **Estrada** (Joseph Ejercito), **Gaddafi** (Muammar), **Gemayel** (Amin), **Gromyko** (Andrei), **Habibie** (Jusuf), **Hussein** (Saddam), **Iliescu** (Ion), **Khatami** (Sayed Ayatollah Mohammad), **Mancham** (James), **Mandela** (Nelson), **Masaryk** (Thomás), **Mubarak** (Hosni),

**Nkrumah** (Kwame), **Parnell** (Charles Stewart), **Sampaio** (Jorge), **Suharto** (Thojib N J), **Sukarno** (Ahmed), **Tudjman** (Franjo), **Weizman** (Ezer), **Yanayev** (Gennady), **Yeltsin** (Boris), **Zhivkov** (Todor)
**08** **Andropov** (Yuri), **Aristide** (Jean-Bertrand), **Bani-Sadr** (Abolhassan), **Brezhnev** (Leonid), **Chamorro** (Violeta), **Childers** (Erskine), **Cosgrave** (William Thomas), **Duvalier** (François 'Papa Doc'), **Duvalier** (Jean-Claude 'Baby Doc'), **Fujimori** (Alberto), **Galtieri** (Leopoldo), **Griffith** (Arthur), **Karadzic** (Radovan), **Kenyatta** (Jomo), **Khamenei** (Sayed Ali), **Kravchuk** (Leonid), **MacMahon** (Patrice de), **Makarios** (Cyprus Enosis), **McAleese** (Mary), **Mengistu** (Haile Mariam), **Museveni** (Yoweri), **Napoleon**, **Pinochet** (Augusto), **Poincaré** (Raymond), **Pompidou** (Georges), **Rawlings** (Jerry), **Robinson** (Mary), **Waldheim** (Kurt), **Weizmann** (Chaim), **Zia Ul-Haq** (Muhammad)
**09** **Ceausescu** (Nicolae), **Chernenko** (Konstantin), **Gorbachev** (Mikhail), **Ho Chi Minh**, **Kim Il-sung**, **Kim Jong Il**, **Mao Zedong**, **Milosevic** (Slobodan), **Narayanan** (Kocheril Raman), **Pilsudski** (Józef), **Sun Yat-Sen**
**10** **Alessandri** (Arturo), **Betancourt** (Rómulo), **Hindenburg** (Paul von), **Jaruzelski** (Wojciech), **Jiang Zemin**, **Khrushchev** (Nikita), **Kubitschek** (Juscelino), **Mannerheim** (Carl Gustav, Baron von), **Mitterrand** (François), **Najibullah** (Mohammad), **Rafsanjani** (Ali Akbar Hashemi), **Stroessner** (Alfredo), **Voroshilov** (Kliment)
**13** **Paz Estenssoro** (Víctor)
**14** **Mobutu Seze Seko**
**15** **Giscard d'Estaing** (Valéry)

*Presidents of the United States of America:*

**03** **Abe**, **Ike**, **Ron**
**04** **Bill**, **Bush** (George), **Bush** (George W), **Ford** (Gerald R), **Polk** (James K), **Taft** (William H)
**05** **Adams** (John), **Adams** (John Quincy), **Buren** (Martin van), **Grant** (Ulysses S), **Hayes** (Rutherford B), **Nixon** (Richard M), **Tyler** (John)
**06** **Arthur** (Chester A), **Carter** (Jimmy), **Hoover** (Herbert), **Monroe** (James), **Pierce** (Franklin), **Reagan** (Ronald), **Taylor** (Zachary), **Truman** (Harry S), **Wilson** (Woodrow)
**07** **Clinton** (Bill), **Harding** (Warren G), **Jackson** (Andrew), **Johnson** (Andrew), **Johnson** (Lyndon B), **Kennedy** (John F), **Lincoln** (Abraham), **Madison** (James)
**08** **Buchanan** (James), **Coolidge** (Calvin), **Fillmore** (Millard), **Garfield** (James A), **Harrison** (Benjamin), **Harrison** (William Henry), **McKinley** (William)
**09** **Cleveland** (Grover), **Jefferson** (Thomas), **Roosevelt** (Franklin D), **Roosevelt** (Theodore)
**10** **Eisenhower** (Dwight D), **Washington** (George)

## press

**02** AP, UP **03** AAP, CUP, hug, jam, lie, mob, OUP, sit, vex **04** airn, bear, cram, iron, mash, pack, push, roll, urge **05** beset, clasp, crowd, crush, flock, force, grasp, hacks, horde, hurry, knead, pinch, plead, print, stamp, stuff, surge, swarm, troop, worry, wring **06** caress, closet, coerce, compel, cuddle, demand, enfold, exhort, harass, lean on, nuzzle, papers, praise, smooth, squash, strain, stress, strive, throng, thrust **07** afflict, besiege, call for, depress, embrace, entreat, express, flatten, implore, imprint, oppress, push for, reports, reviews, squeeze, swing it, thrutch, trample, trouble, urgency **08** articles, bookcase, campaign, compress, coverage, expedite, fast-talk, insist on, petition, pressmen, pressure, push down, soft-soap, the media **09** constrain, criticism, hold close, importune, multitude, news media, paparazzi, reporters, smooth out, sweet-talk, treatment **10** journalism, newspapers, pressurize, presswomen, supplicate **11** Fleet Street, journalists, pull strings, push forward, rotary press **12** fourth estate, newspapermen **13** photographers, printing press, put pressure on **14** correspondents, newspaperwomen, put the screws on **15** printing-machine, the fourth estate, turn the screws on

*See also* **news**

• **press close**
**04** serr **05** serre

• **press forward**
**04** push, spur, urge **05** drive

• **member of the press** *see* **journalist**

• **press on**
**04** go on, toil **05** crowd **06** plod on **07** carry on, go ahead, peg away, proceed **08** continue, plug away, slog away, toil away **09** keep going, persevere, soldier on, stick at it **10** keep trying, press ahead

## pressed

**04** laid, lain **06** forced, pushed, rushed **07** bullied, coerced, hard-run, hurried, lacking, short of **08** harassed **09** pressured **10** bludgeoned, browbeaten, railroaded **11** constrained, deficient in, pressurized **15** having too little, not having enough

## pressing

**03** key **05** acute, vital **06** urgent **07** burning, crucial, exigent, serious **08** critical, crowding **09** demanding, essential, important **10** imperative **11** importunate **12** high-priority

**pressman** *see* **journalist**

## pressure

**01** P **04** heat, load, push **05** aggro, bully, drive, force, power, press, stamp **06** burden, coerce, compel, demand, duress, hassle, lean on, oblige, strain, stress, weight **07** dragoon, problem, swing it, tension, trouble, urgency **08** bludgeon, browbeat, bulldoze, bullying, coercion, crushing, fast-talk, railroad, soft-soap **09** adversity, constrain, heaviness, squeezing, sweet-talk **10** compulsion, constraint, difficulty, harassment, impression, obligation, pressurize **11** compression, constraints, pull strings **13** put pressure on **14** put the screws on

• **blood pressure**
**02** BP **03** ABP

• **extreme/high/low pressure**
**02** EP, HP, LP

• **measurement of pressure**
**02** mb, Pa **03** atm, bar, psi **04** torr **05** barye **06** pascal **07** megabar **08** microbar, millibar **10** atmosphere

## pressurize

**05** bully, drive, force, press **06** coerce, compel, lean on, oblige **07** dragoon, swing it **08** bludgeon, browbeat, bulldoze, fast-talk, pressure, railroad, soft-soap **09** constrain, sweet-talk **11** pull strings **12** put the acid on **13** put pressure on **14** put the screws on

## prestige

**04** fame, mana **05** charm, izzat, kudos, magic **06** credit, esteem, honour, regard, renown, status **07** glamour, stature **08** eminence, standing **09** authority, influence **10** ascendancy, importance, reputation **11** distinction

## prestigious

**05** great **06** famous **07** eminent, exalted **08** blue-chip, esteemed, imposing, juggling, renowned, up-market **09** deceitful, important, prominent, reputable, respected, well-known **10** celebrated, impressive **11** high-ranking, illustrious, influential **13** distinguished

## presumably

**06** I guess **07** no doubt **08** I presume, probably **09** doubtless, seemingly **10** apparently, most likely, very likely **11** doubtlessly **15** in all likelihood

## presume

**04** dare **05** infer, think **06** assume, deduce, take it **07** believe, go so far, imagine, suppose, surmise, venture **09** undertake **10** make so bold, presuppose, take as read **11** hypothesize **14** take for granted, take the liberty **15** have the audacity

• **presume on**
**05** trust **06** bank on, rely on **07** count on, exploit **08** depend on **15** take advantage of

## presumption

**03** lip **04** gall, neck **05** cheek, guess, mouth, nerve, sauce **06** belief

07 opinion, surmise 08 assuming, audacity, boldness, chutzpah, temerity 09 arrogance, assurance, brass neck, deduction, impudence, inference, insolence, upsetting 10 assumption, conjecture, effrontery, hypothesis, likelihood 11 forwardness, probability, supposition 12 impertinence 13 outrecuidance 14 presupposition

**presumptive**
06 likely 07 assumed 08 believed, credible, expected, inferred, possible, probable, supposed 09 designate, plausible 10 believable, reasonable, understood 11 conceivable, conjectural, prospective 12 hypothetical

**presumptuous**
04 bold 05 cocky, fresh, lippy, pushy, saucy 06 cheeky, mouthy 07 forward 08 arrogant, cocksure, impudent, insolent 09 audacious, bigheaded, conceited 11 impertinent 12 over-familiar 13 over-confident

**presuppose**
05 imply, posit 06 accept, assume 07 premise, presume, suppose 08 consider 09 postulate 11 necessitate 14 take for granted

**presupposition**
06 belief, theory 07 premise, premiss 10 assumption, hypothesis 11 presumption, supposition 13 preconception

**pretence**
03 act, lie 04 mask, ruse, sham, show, veil, wile 05 bluff, cloak, cover, feint, front, guise 06 acting, deceit, excuse, façade, faking, humbug, posing, veneer 07 charade, daubery, display, pretext 08 feigning, trickery 09 deception, falsehood, false show, hypocrisy, invention, posturing, semblance, showiness 10 appearance, masquerade, play-acting, pretension, profession, simulation 11 affectation, dissembling, fabrication, make-believe, ostentation 12 false colours 13 dissimulation 15 pretentiousness

**pretend**
03 act, kid 04 fake, mime, play, sham 05 bluff, claim, feign, frame, kiddy, let on, offer, put on 06 affect, allege, assume, semble 07 imagine, play-act, profess, purport, purpose, put it on, suppose 08 indicate, simulate 09 dissemble, fabricate, imaginary 10 put on an act 11 counterfeit, impersonate, make believe 15 pass yourself off

**pretended**
04 fake, sham 05 bogus, false, moody, put on 06 avowed, phoney, pseudo 07 alleged, assumed, feigned, pretend 08 affected, so-called, specious, spurious, supposed, vizarded 09 imaginary, professed, purported, soi-disant 10 artificial, fictitious, ostensible, self-styled 11 counterfect, counterfeit 14 supposititious

**pretender**
06 suitor 07 claimer, would-be 08 aspirant, claimant 09 candidate

**pretension**
04 airs, show 05 claim 06 demand, vanity 07 conceit, pretext 08 ambition, pretence 09 hypocrisy, pomposity, showiness 10 aspiration, profession, purporting 11 affectation, floweriness, ostentation 12 snobbishness 13 dissimulation, magniloquence 14 self-importance 15 pretentiousness

**pretentious**
03 big, OTT 04 fine, twee 05 false, large, pseud, showy 06 chichi, phoney, pseudo, shoddy, uppish 07 kitschy, pompous, tinhorn 08 affected, fantoosh, immodest, inflated, mannered, pseudish, snobbish 09 ambitious, bombastic, conceited, elaborate, flaunting, grandiose 10 artificial, flamboyant, over-the-top 11 exaggerated, extravagant 12 high-sounding, magniloquent, ostentatious, vainglorious 13 overambitious, self-important

**pretentiously**
07 showily 08 uppishly 09 pompously 10 snobbishly 12 artificially, flamboyantly 14 ostentatiously 15 self-importantly

**pretentiousness**
04 show, side 05 swank 06 chichi, kitsch, posing 08 flummery, grandeur, paraffle, pretence, pretense, pseudery 09 posturing 10 flatulence, flatulency, floridness, pretension, uppishness 11 flamboyance, floweriness, ostentation 13 ambitiousness, theatricality 14 attitudinizing

**preternatural**
07 no'canny, unusual 08 abnormal 11 exceptional 12 supernatural 13 extraordinary

**pretext**
04 hook, mask, plea, ploy, ruse, sham, show, veil 05 cloak, cloke, color, cover, guise, salvo, stale 06 colour, excuse 07 off-come, umbrage 08 occasion, pretence, pretense 09 semblance 10 appearance, pretension, red herring 13 alleged reason

**prettify**
04 deck, do up, gild, trim 05 adorn 06 bedeck, doll up, tart up 07 deck out, garnish, trick up 08 beautify, decorate, ornament, trick out 09 embellish, smarten up

**prettily**
06 neatly, nicely 08 daintily 09 elegantly, winsomely 10 charmingly, engagingly, gracefully, pleasantly, pleasingly 11 beautifully 12 attractively, delightfully

**pretty**
04 cute, fair, fine, neat, nice, twee, very 05 bonny, grand, purty, quite 06 bonnie, clever, comely, dainty, fairly, incony, lovely, rather, tricky 07 elegant, fairway, inconie, not half, winsome 08 charming, delicate, engaging, graceful, handsome, keepsake, keepsaky, pleasant, pleasing, somewhat, stalwart 09 appealing, beautiful, extremely, ingenious, tolerably 10 attractive, decorative, delightful, knick-knack, moderately, personable, reasonably 11 commendable, good-looking, substantial 12 chocolate-box, considerable 13 prepossessing

**prevail**
03 win 04 ring, rule 05 avail, occur, reign 06 abound, have it, obtain, win out 07 conquer, succeed, triumph 08 be common, be normal, hold sway, overcome, override, overrule, persuade, perswade 09 be current, be present 10 be accepted, win through 11 be customary, carry the day, gain mastery, predominate 12 be victorious, preponderate 14 gain ascendancy

• **prevail upon**
03 win 04 rule, sway, urge 06 induce, lean on, prompt 07 incline, win over 08 convince, persuade, pressure, soft-soap, talk into 09 influence, sweet-talk 10 bring round, pressurize 11 pull strings

**prevailing**
03 set 04 main 05 chief, usual 06 common, ruling 07 average, current, general, in style, in vogue, popular, supreme 08 accepted, dominant, powerful, reigning 09 ascendant, customary, effective, in fashion, most usual, prepotent, prevalent, principal 10 compelling, mainstream, most common, widespread 11 controlling, established, fashionable, influential, predominant 12 preponderant

**prevalence**
03 ren, rin, run 04 hold, rule, sway 07 mastery, primacy 08 currency, ubiquity 09 frequency, profusion 10 acceptance, ascendancy, commonness, popularity, regularity 11 commonality 12 omnipresence, predominance, universality 13 order of the day, pervasiveness, preponderance

**prevalent**
03 set 04 rife 05 usual 06 common, vulgar 07 current, endemic, general, popular, rampant, regnant 08 accepted, dominant, enzootic, epidemic, everyday, frequent, powerful 09 customary, extensive, pervasive, universal 10 prevailing, ubiquitous, victorious, widespread 11 established

**prevaricate**
03 lie 05 cavil, dodge, evade, hedge, mudge, shift 06 waffle 07 deceive, deviate, pervert, quibble, shuffle, whiffle 09 be evasive, pussyfoot, stonewall 10 equivocate, transgress

**12** shilly-shally, tergiversate **13** sit on the fence

**prevarication**
**03** fib, lie **04** fibs **06** deceit **07** evasion, fibbing, untruth **08** pretence **09** cavilling, deception, falsehood, half-truth, quibbling **12** equivocation, pussyfooting **13** falsification **14** tergiversation **15** shilly-shallying

**prevaricator**
**04** liar **06** dodger, evader, fibber, Jesuit **07** casuist, sophist **08** caviller, deceiver, quibbler **09** hypocrite **10** dissembler **11** equivocator, pettifogger

**prevent**
**02** sa' **03** bar, let **04** balk, foil, halt, help, keep, save, stop **05** avert, avoid, block, check, debar, deter, stimy **06** arrest, hamper, hinder, impede, stimie, stymie, thwart **07** fend off, head off, inhibit, obviate, precede, ward off **08** hold back, keep from, obstruct, preclude, prohibit, restrain, stave off **09** foreclose, forestall, frustrate, intercept **10** anticipate **11** hold in check

**prevention**
**03** bar **05** check **07** balking, empeach, foiling, halting, impeach **08** obstacle **09** arresting, avoidance, exclusion, hampering, hindrance, obviation, safeguard **10** deterrence, fending off, heading off, hinderance, impediment, precaution, preclusion, staving off, warding off **11** elimination, frustration, obstruction, premonition, prophylaxis **12** anticipation **13** contraception

**preventive**
**05** block **06** remedy, shield **08** obstacle **09** deterrent, hindrance, safeguard **10** impediment, inhibitory, pre-emptive, prevenient, prevention, protection, protective **11** neutralizer, obstruction, obstructive **12** anticipatory, preventative, prophylactic **13** counteractive, precautionary

**previous**
**02** ex- **04** past **05** prior **06** before, former **07** earlier, one-time, quondam **08** sometime **09** erstwhile, foregoing, preceding, premature **10** antecedent

**previously**
**04** erst, fore, once **05** afore **06** before **07** already, earlier **08** formerly, hitherto, until now **09** at one time, earlier on, erstwhile, in the past **10** beforehand, heretofore

**prey**
**03** mug **04** game, kill **05** booty, ravin, soyle **06** quarry, rapine, target, victim **07** afflict, fall guy, plunder, spreagh **08** distress **11** depredation

**• prey on**
**03** con, eat **04** hunt, kill **05** bleed, catch, haunt, prowl, seize, worry **06** burden, devour, feed on, fleece, plague **07** exploit, live off, moth-eat, oppress, predate, raven on, torment, trouble, vampire **08** distress, hang over, pounce on **09** depredate, weigh down **15** take advantage of

**price**
**02** pr **03** fee, sum **04** bill, cost, fare, levy, rate, toll **05** prise, prize, value, worth **06** amount, assess, charge, figure, outlay, result, reward **07** expense, forfeit, payment, penalty **08** appraise, estimate, evaluate, expenses, valorize **09** quotation, sacrifice, valuation **10** assessment **11** consequence, expenditure **12** consequences, preciousness **13** fix the price at, set the price at

**• at any price**
**09** at any cost, à tout prix **15** whatever it takes, whatever the cost

**• at a price**
**04** dear **09** expensive **11** at a high cost **12** at a high price

**• fix price**
**03** peg

**priceless**
**04** dear, rare, rich **05** comic, funny **06** costly, prized **07** amusing, a scream, killing, riotous **08** precious, unvalued, valuable **09** cherished, expensive, hilarious, treasured **10** invaluable **11** inestimable **12** incalculable, incomparable **13** inappreciable, irreplaceable, side-splitting

**pricey**
**04** dear **05** steep **06** costly **07** sky-high **09** excessive, expensive **10** exorbitant, high-priced **11** over the odds **12** costing a bomb, extortionate **15** costing the earth, daylight robbery

**prick**
**03** dot, jab, jag, pin **04** acme, bite, bore, brod, brog, cloy, gash, hole, itch, mark, nick, pain, pang, peak, prod, prog, slit, stab **05** harry, point, punch, rowel, smart, spike, sting, thorn, worry, wound **06** accloy, gnaw at, harass, incite, pierce, plague, prey on, target, tingle, twinge **07** pinhole, prickle, torment, trouble **08** distress, puncture, smarting **09** perforate **11** perforation

**• prick up your ears**
**06** attend **09** lend an ear **10** take note of **12** pay attention, take notice of **13** listen eagerly **15** listen carefully, pin back your ears

**prickle**
**03** nip **04** barb, itch, pang, spur, tine **05** point, prick, prong, smart, spike, spine, sting, thorn **06** needle, tingle, twinge **07** acantha, aculeus, itching, spicula **08** smarting, stinging **09** sensation **11** formication **12** paraesthesia **14** pins and needles

**prickly**
**04** edgy, hard **05** armed, jaggy, ratty, rough, spiky, spiny, tough **06** barbed, crabby, grumpy, on edge, shirty, spiked, thorny, touchy, tricky **07** bearded, brambly, bristly, grouchy, pronged, stroppy **08** aculeate, delicate, echinate, scratchy **09** aculeated, crotchety, difficult, echinated, irritable, sensitive **10** acanaceous **11** bad-tempered, complicated, problematic, thin-skinned, troublesome **12** acanthaceous **13** problematical, short-tempered

**prickly pear**
**04** tuna **05** nopal **07** opuntia **09** Indian fig

**pride**
**03** ego, joy **05** prime **06** flower, honour, mettle, vanity **07** conceit, delight, dignity, disdain, egotism, elation, stomach **08** pleasure, smugness, snobbery **09** arrogance, proudness, self-image, self-worth, splendour **10** exuberance, self-esteem **11** haughtiness, ostentation, presumption, self-conceit, self-respect **12** boastfulness, magnificence, satisfaction, triumphalism **13** bigheadedness, gratification **14** self-importance **15** pretentiousness

**• pride and joy**
**03** joy **04** best, pick **05** élite, glory **06** finest, flower **07** darling, delight **10** choice part, select part **14** apple of your eye, crème de la crème, pick of the bunch

**• pride yourself on**
**05** vaunt **07** exult in, glory in, revel in **09** brag about, crow about **10** boast about **11** take pride in **13** plume yourself, preen yourself **15** flatter yourself

**priest**
**01** P **02** Pr **03** Eli **05** Aaron, clerk, Zadok **06** cleric, Elijah, Elisha, father, orator **07** prelate, secular **08** man of God **09** churchman, clergyman **10** hierophant, woman of God **11** churchwoman, clergywoman **12** ecclesiastic **13** man of the cloth **15** woman of the cloth

*Priests include:*

**02** HP, PP
**04** abbé, arch, curé, high, lama, papa, pope
**05** bonze, druid, magus, mambo, padre, rabbi, vicar
**06** deacon, flamen, Levite, lucumo, parish, parson, pastor, shaman, zymite
**07** Brahman, patrico, pontiff, Pythian, tohunga
**08** bacchant, corybant, hierarch, minister, neophyte, seminary, Syriarch
**09** bacchanal, confessor, deaconess, lack-Latin, oratorian, patercove, presbyter
**10** arch-flamen, masspriest, seminarian, seminarist
**11** hedge-parson, hedge-priest
**12** concelebrant, Redemptorist

**priestess**
**03** nun **05** mambo **06** abbess, Pythia, sister, vestal **07** beguine, Pythian

**08** canoness, prioress **09** bacchante, deaconess, Pythoness, religious **11** clergywoman

**priesthood**
**08** the cloth **09** the church **10** full orders, hierocracy, holy orders, priestship **11** the ministry **12** the pastorate **13** sacerdotalism

**priestly**
**07** Aaronic **08** clerical, hieratic, pastoral **09** Aaronical, canonical **10** priestlike, sacerdotal **14** ecclesiastical

**prig**
**05** filch, prude, thief **06** haggle, tinker **07** coxcomb, entreat, holy Joe, killjoy, old maid, puritan **09** importune, Mrs Grundy, precisian **10** goody-goody, holy Willie

**priggish**
**04** prim, smug **05** prude **06** stuffy **07** prudish, starchy **10** goody-goody **11** puritanical, strait-laced **12** narrow-minded **13** sanctimonious, self-righteous **14** holier-than-thou

**prim**
**03** mim **04** smug **05** fussy, mimsy **06** demure, formal, mimsey, neaten, prissy, proper, quaint, stuffy **07** perjink, precise, primsie, prudish, starchy **08** priggish **10** fastidious, fuddy-duddy, governessy, old-maidish, particular **11** puritanical, strait-laced **12** primigravida **13** schoolmarmish

**primacy**
**07** command **08** dominion **09** dominance, seniority, supremacy **10** ascendancy, leadership, paramouncy **11** pre-eminence, sovereignty, superiority

**prima donna**
**04** diva **10** female lead **11** leading lady, moody person **14** leading soprano

**primaeval** *see* **primeval, primaeval**

**primal**
**04** main **05** basic, chief, first, major, prime **07** central, highest, initial, primary **08** earliest, greatest, original, primeval **09** paramount, primaeval, primitive, principal **10** primordial **11** fundamental, primigenial, primogenial

**primarily**
◇ *head selection indicator*
**05** first **06** mainly, mostly **07** chiefly, firstly **09** basically, in essence, in the main **10** especially **11** essentially, principally **12** nothing if not, particularly **13** fundamentally, predominantly **15** in the first place

**primary**
**04** main **05** basic, chief, first, prime **06** direct, simple **07** capital, highest, initial, leading, opening, radical, supreme **08** cardinal, dominant, earliest, foremost, greatest, original, primeval, ultimate **09** beginning, elemental, essential, first-hand, paramount, primaeval, primitive, principal **10** elementary, idiopathic, primordial **11** fundamental, predominant, rudimentary **12** introductory

**primate**
**06** bishop **07** Bigfoot **10** archbishop

*Primates include:*

**03** ape
**04** mico
**05** chimp, drill, human, indri, jocko, lemur, loris, orang, pigmy, pongo, pygmy, satyr
**06** aye-aye, baboon, bonobo, chacma, colugo, dog-ape, galago, gelada, gibbon, indris, macaco, malmag, monkey, sifaka, wou-wou, wow-wow
**07** gorilla, hoolock, jacchus, macaque, meercat, meerkat, nagapie, siamang, tarsier, wistiti
**08** bushbaby, great ape, hylobate, mandrill, marmoset, mongoose, night-ape
**09** babacoote, catarhine, hamadryad, orang-utan, prosimian
**10** angwantibo, catarrhine, chimpanzee, protohuman, silverback
**11** homo sapiens, orang-outang
**12** Cynocephalus, ourang-outang, paranthropus
**13** Galeopithecus, Kenyapithecus
**15** pygmy chimpanzee

*See also* **ape**; **monkey**

**prime**
**03** top **04** acme, best, fang, fill, main, peak **05** bloom, brief, chief, coach, equip, gen up, phang, pride, train **06** charge, choice, clue up, fill in, flower, gear up, height, heyday, inform, notify, select, zenith **07** blossom, classic, highest, leading, premier, prepare, primary, quality, supreme, typical **08** best part, foremost, get ready, maturity, original, pinnacle, standard, top-grade **09** excellent, first-rate, make ready, principal **10** first-class, perfection, pre-eminent **11** culmination, predominant **12** paradigmatic, prototypical **14** characteristic, quintessential

**prime minister**
**02** PM **05** dewan, diwan **07** premier **08** quisling **09** Taoiseach **10** chancellor **11** Grand Vizier **13** chief minister, first minister

*Prime Ministers of Australia:*

**04** **Cook** (Joseph), **Holt** (Harold), **Page** (Earle), **Reid** (George)
**05** **Bruce** (Stanley), **Forde** (Francis Michael), **Hawke** (Bob), **Lyons** (Joseph)
**06** **Barton** (Edmund), **Curtin** (John), **Deakin** (Alfred), **Fadden** (Arthur), **Fisher** (Andrew), **Fraser** (Malcolm), **Gorton** (John), **Howard** (John), **Hughes** (Billy), **McEwen** (John), **Watson** (Chris)
**07** **Chifley** (Ben), **Keating** (Paul), **McMahon** (William), **Menzies** (Robert), **Scullin** (James), **Whitlam** (Gough)

*Prime Ministers of Canada:*

**04** **King** (William Lyon Mackenzie)
**05** **Abbot** (John J C), **Clark** (Joseph)
**06** **Borden** (Robert), **Bowell** (Mackenzie), **Tupper** (Charles), **Turner** (John)
**07** **Bennett** (R B), **Laurier** (Wilfrid), **Meighen** (Arthur), **Pearson** (Lester B), **Trudeau** (Pierre)
**08** **Campbell** (Kim), **Chrétien** (Jean), **Mulroney** (Brian), **Thompson** (John S D)
**09** **Macdonald** (John A), **Mackenzie** (Alexander), **St Laurent** (Louis)
**11** **Diefenbaker** (John G)

*Prime Ministers of New Zealand:*

**04** **Bell** (Francis), **Kirk** (Norman Eric), **Nash** (Walter), **Ward** (Joseph)
**05** **Clark** (Helen), **Lange** (David), **Moore** (Mike)
**06** **Bolger** (James), **Coates** (Gordon), **Forbes** (George William), **Fraser** (Peter), **Massey** (William), **Palmer** (Geoffrey), **Savage** (Michael Joseph), **Seddon** (Richard)
**07** **Holland** (Sidney), **Muldoon** (Robert), **Rowling** (Wallace), **Shipley** (Jenny)
**08** **Holyoake** (Keith), **Marshall** (John Ross)
**09** **Hall-Jones** (William), **Mackenzie** (Thomas)

*See also* **premier**

*Prime Ministers of the United Kingdom:*

**04** **Bute** (John Stuart, Earl), **Eden** (Sir Anthony), **Grey** (Charles Grey, Earl), **Home** (Alec Douglas-Home, Earl), **Peel** (Robert), **Pitt** (William)
**05** **Blair** (Tony), **Cecil** (Robert), **Derby** (Edward Stanley, Earl), **Heath** (Ted), **Major** (John), **North** (Frederick North, Lord)
**06** **Attlee** (Clement), **Pelham** (Henry), **Wilson** (Harold)
**07** **Asquith** (Herbert), **Baldwin** (Stanley), **Balfour** (Arthur), **Canning** (George), **Grafton** (Augustus Henry Fitzroy, Duke), **Russell** (John, Lord), **Walpole** (Robert)
**08** **Aberdeen** (George Hamilton-Gordon, Lord), **Bonar Law** (Andrew), **Disraeli** (Benjamin), **Goderich** (Frederick John Robinson, Viscount), **Perceval** (Spencer), **Portland** (William Henry Cavendish Bentinck, Duke), **Rosebery** (Archibald Philip Primrose, Earl), **Thatcher** (Margaret, Lady)
**09** **Addington** (Henry), **Callaghan** (James, Lord), **Churchill** (Sir Winston), **Gladstone** (William), **Grenville** (George), **Grenville** (William Wyndham, Lord),

**Liverpool** (Robert Jenkinson, Earl), **MacDonald** (Ramsay), **Macmillan** (Harold), **Melbourne** (William Lamb, Viscount), **Newcastle** (Thomas Pelham-Holles, Duke), **Salisbury** (Robert Gascoyne-Cecil, Marquess), **Shelburne** (William Petty-Fitzmaurice, Earl)
**10** **Devonshire** (William Cavendish, Duke), **Palmerston** (Henry John Temple, Viscount), **Rockingham** (Charles Watson Wentworth, Marquess), **Wellington** (Arthur Wellesley, Duke), **Wilmington** (Spencer Compton, Earl)
**11** **Chamberlain** (Neville), **Douglas-Home** (Alec), **Lloyd George** (David)
**17** **Campbell-Bannerman** (Henry)

*Prime Ministers of other countries include:*

**02** **Nu** (U)
**03** **Ito** (Hirobumi)
**04** **Meir** (Golda), **Moro** (Aldo), **Tojo** (Hideki)
**05** **Ahern** (Bertie), **Assad** (Hafez al-), **Azaña** (Manuel), **Aznar** (José María), **Banda** (Hastings Kamuzu), **Barak** (Ehud), **Barre** (Raymond), **Begin** (Menachem), **Botha** (Louis), **Botha** (P W), **Craxi** (Bettino), **Desai** (Morarji), **Faure** (Edgar), **Hoxha** (Enver), **Juppé** (Alain), **Khama** (Sir Seretse), **Laval** (Pierre), **Lynch** (Jack), **Malan** (Daniel), **Nehru** (Jawaharlal), **Obote** (Milton), **Pasic** (Nikola), **Peres** (Shimon), **Prodi** (Romano), **Putin** (Vladimir), **Rabin** (Yitzhak), **Sadat** (Anwar el-), **Singh** (Manmohan), **Smith** (Ian), **Smuts** (Jan), **Spaak** (Paul Henri)
**06** **Bhutto** (Benazir), **Bhutto** (Zulfikar Ali), **Briand** (Aristide), **Bruton** (John), **Castro** (Fidel), **Chirac** (Jacques), **Fabius** (Laurent), **Gandhi** (Indira), **Gandhi** (Rajiv), **Gaulle** (Charles de), **Hun Sen**, **Jospin** (Lionel), **Li Peng**, **Manley** (Michael), **Mugabe** (Robert), **Neguib** (Mohammed), **O'Neill** (Terence, Lord), **Pétain** (Philippe), **Pol Pot**, **Pombal** (Sebastião de Carvalho, Marquês de), **Rahman** (Sheikh Mujibur), **Rhodes** (Cecil), **Shamir** (Yitzhak), **Sharif** (Nawaz), **Sharon** (Ariel), **Thiers** (Adolphe)
**07** **Berisha** (Sali), **Cresson** (Édith), **Gasperi** (Alcide de), **Halifax** (Charles Montagu, Earl of), **Haughey** (Charles), **Hertzog** (J B M), **Kosygin** (Alexei), **Lubbers** (Ruud), **Molotov** (Vyacheslav), **Nkrumah** (Kwame), **Nyerere** (Julius), **Vorster** (John), **Yeltsin** (Boris)
**08** **Ben Bella** (Ahmed), **Bismarck** (Otto, Fürst von), **Bulganin** (Nikolai), **Daladier** (Édouard), **de Valera** (Éamon), **González** (Felipe), **Kenyatta** (Jomo), **Mahathir** (bin Mohamad), **Nakasone** (Yasuhiro), **Poincaré** (Raymond), **Pompidou** (Georges), **Quisling** (Vidkun), **Reynolds** (Albert), **Vajpayee** (Atal Bihari), **Verwoerd** (Hendrik), **Zapatero** (José Luis Rodríguez)
**09** **Andreotti** (Giulio), **Ben-Gurion** (David), **Hashimoto** (Ryutaro), **Kim Il-sung**, **Kim Jong Il**, **Mussolini** (Benito), **Netanyahu** (Binyamin), **Stanishev** (Sergei)
**10** **Balkenende** (Jan Peter), **Berlusconi** (Silvio), **Clemenceau** (Georges), **Fitzgerald** (Garrett), **Jaruzelski** (Wojciech), **Lee Kuan Yew**
**11** **Verhofstadt** (Guy)
**12** **Bandaranaike** (S W R D), **Chernomyrdin** (Viktor)
**13** **Brookeborough** (Basil Brooke, Viscount)

## primer
**05** Donat, Donet **06** manual **08** prodrome, textbook **09** absey-book, detonator, prodromus **12** introduction

## primeval, primaeval
**03** old **05** basic, early, first **06** inborn, innate, primal **07** ancient, natural, Ogygian **08** earliest, inherent, original **09** intuitive, primitial, primitive **10** primordial **11** instinctive, prehistoric **12** autochthonal

## primitive
**02** ur- **03** pro- **04** wild **05** crude, early, first, naive, rough **06** primal, savage, simple **07** ancient, natural, primary, radical **08** backveld, earliest, original, primeval **09** barbarian, primaeval **10** aboriginal, antiquated, elementary, primordial, uncultured **11** fundamental, rudimentary, uncivilized, undeveloped **12** antediluvian, old-fashioned, protomorphic **15** unsophisticated

## primly
**07** fussily **08** prissily, stuffily **09** prudishly

## primordial
**03** old **05** early, first **07** ancient **08** earliest, original, primeval **09** primaeval, primitive **11** instinctive, prehistoric, rudimentary **12** autochthonal, protomorphic

## primp
**04** tidy **05** groom, preen **06** doll up, tart up **07** brush up, dress up, smarten **08** beautify, spruce up, titivate

## prince
**01** P **02** Pr **03** mir, ras **04** amir, duke, khan, king, lord, raja, rana **05** ameer, chief, Mirza, nawab, nizam, queen, rajah, ruler, Tunku **06** leader, lucumo, potent, sharif, sherif, Tengku **07** infante, monarch, shereef **08** archduke, atheling, gospodar, hospodar, maharaja, tetrarch **09** Beelzebub, maharajah, potentate, princekin, princelet, royal duke, sovereign **10** princeling, Upper Roger **13** prince consort **14** porphyrogenite

*Princes include:*

**03** **Hal**
**04** **Igor**, **Ivan**, **John** (of Gaunt)
**05** **Edgar** (the Atheling), **Harry**, **Henry** (the Navigator), **James**
**06** **Albert**, **Andrew**, **Arthur**, **Edward**, **Edward** (the Black Prince), **Philip**
**07** **Charles**, **Michael** (of Kent), **Rainier**, **Richard**, **William**
**08** **Llywelyn**, **Vladimir**
**09** **Ferdinand**
**11** **James Stuart**
**15** **Alexander Nevski**, **Bernhard Leopold**

## Prince Edward Island
**02** PE

## princely
**04** huge, vast **05** grand, noble, regal, royal **06** lavish, superb **07** immense, liberal, mammoth, massive, prenzie, stately **08** colossal, enormous, en prince, generous, glorious, handsome, imperial, imposing, majestic, splendid **09** bounteous, sovereign, sumptuous **10** impressive, large-scale, stupendous, tremendous **11** magnanimous, magnificent **12** considerable

## princess
**04** lady, rani **05** begum, ruler **07** infanta, monarch **09** potentate, sovereign **11** archduchess **13** crown princess

*Princesses include:*

**02** Di
**03** Ida
**04** Anne
**05** Alice, Diana, Fiona, Grace, Regan
**06** Salome
**07** Eudocia, Eugenie, Goneril, Jezebel, Matilda
**08** Beatrice, Caroline, Cordelia, Margaret
**09** Alexandra, Charlotte, Elizabeth, Stephanie
**10** Pocahontas
**11** Anna Comnena

## principal
**03** key **04** arch, boss, head, main **05** chief, first, major, money, prime, ruler **06** assets, leader, rector **07** capital, central, decuman, highest, leading, manager, primary, supreme, truncal **08** cardinal, director, dominant, especial, foremost, in charge, mistress **09** essential, paramount **10** capital sum, controller, headmaster, pre-eminent **11** controlling, head teacher **12** capital funds, headmistress **13** most important **14** superintendent

## principality
**05** duchy, realm, Wales **06** empire, Monaco, Orange **07** Andorra, dukedom, earldom, kingdom, Muscovy **08** dominion, Walachia **09** archduchy, princedom, sultanate, Wallachia **10** dependency, federation, grand duchy, palatinate, principate **11** archdukedom **12** protectorate **13** confederation, Liechtenstein

**principally**
**06** mainly, mostly **07** chiefly **08** above all **09** capitally, in the main, primarily **10** especially **12** particularly **13** predominantly **14** for the most part

**principle**
**03** key, law **04** code, germ, idea, root, rule, seed, soul **05** axiom, basis, canon, creed, dogma, geist, maxim, Sakti, tenet, truth **06** dictum, ethics, honour, morals, origin, reason, Shakti, source, spirit, theory, virtue **07** brocard, decency, element, formula, precept, probity, theorem **08** doctrine, morality, rudiment, scruples, standard **09** beginning, component, criterion, essential, headstone, institute, integrity, postulate, rationale, rectitude, standards **10** classicism, conscience, golden rule, groundwork, primordial, principium, seminality **11** fundamental, proposition, uprightness **12** classicalism

• **in principle**
**07** ideally **08** in theory **09** in essence **10** en principe **13** theoretically

**principled**
**04** just **05** moral **06** decent **07** ethical, upright **08** virtuous **09** righteous **10** high-minded, honourable, scrupulous **11** respectable, right-minded **13** conscientious

**print**
**04** copy, etch, font, lith, mark, oleo, snap, type **05** fount, issue, mould, photo, stamp **06** design, record, run off, strike **07** bromide, edition, engrave, impress, imprint, letters, picture, publish, replica **08** aquatint, put to bed, register, snapshot, typeface **09** aquatinta, engraving, facsimile, footprint, lettering, newspaper, oleograph, reproduce, strike off **10** characters, exactitude, impression, lithograph, photograph, typescript **11** fingerprint **12** reproduction

*See also* **painter**

• **in print**
**07** in stock **09** available, published **10** obtainable **13** in circulation

• **out of print**
**02** op **07** sold out **10** out of stock **11** unavailable **12** off the market, unobtainable

**printer**
• **instruction to printer**
**04** dele, hash, stet **05** caret

**printing**

*Printing methods include:*

**03** CTP
**05** laser, litho
**06** ink-jet, offset, screen
**07** etching, gravure
**08** intaglio
**09** bubble-jet, collotype, engraving
**10** silk-screen, xerography
**11** die-stamping, duplicating, flexography, letterpress, lithography, rotary press, stencilling, twin-etching
**12** lino blocking, thermography
**13** colour-process, electrostatic
**14** photoengraving
**15** computer-to-plate, copper engraving

*Printing and publishing terms include:*

**02** em, en
**03** CTP, TLS, TPS
**04** bulk, case, CMYK, copy, demi, font, kern, laid, logo, sewn, stet, text, tint, trim, type, typo
**05** bleed, caret, chase, cloth, cover, flong, forme, litho, moiré, press, proof, quoin, roman, widow, zinco
**06** galley, gutter, indent, italic, jacket, mackle, margin, matrix, octavo, orphan, Ozalid®, quarto, take in, unsewn, web-fed
**07** bromide, carding, cast-off, compose, dot gain, end even, foiling, leaders, leading, literal, opacity, Pantone®, reprint, strip in, woodcut
**08** bad break, bold face, Linotype®, logotype, misprint, Monotype®, mottling, offprint, spoilage, strike-on, take over, typeface, type spec
**09** backing-up, catchword, condensed, duodecimo, finishing, Intertype®, letterset, lower-case, makeready, newsprint, overprint, run-around, sans serif, signature, trim marks, type scale, upper-case, web offset
**10** back margin, collograph, column inch, compositor, dot-etching, dustjacket, feathering, first proof, hard hyphen, imposition, impression, large print, manuscript, perfecting, ragged left, see-through, soft hyphen, stereotype, typescript
**11** drum printer, electrotype, initial caps, line printer, ragged right, running head, running text, typesetting, typographer
**12** author's proof, character set, expanded type, flat-bed press, inking roller, machine proof, registration, specimen page
**13** composing room, cylinder press, image printing, justification, printing press, small capitals, wood engraving
**14** relief printing, thermal printer
**15** camera-ready copy

*See also* **typeface**

**printmaker** *see* **painter**

**prior**
**05** elder **06** former **07** earlier **08** previous **09** foregoing, preceding **10** antecedent, magistrate

• **prior to**
**03** pre **04** till, up to **05** until **06** before **09** preceding **11** earlier than, in advance of

**priority**
**04** rank **07** the lead **09** essential, main thing, seniority, supremacy **10** first place, paramouncy, precedence, preference, right of way **11** pre-eminence, requirement, superiority **12** first concern, highest place, pole position, primary issue, top of the tree **13** supreme matter

**priory**
**05** abbey **06** friary **07** convent, nunnery **08** cloister, priorate **09** béguinage, monastery **14** religious house

**prise**
**03** pry **04** lift, move **05** force, hoist, jemmy, lever, raise, shift **06** winkle **08** dislodge, leverage, purchase

**prison**
**03** bin, can, HMP, jug, pen, pit **04** bird, brig, cage, cell, coop, gaol, jail, nick, quad, quod, stir, tank **05** choky, clink, gulag, kitty, limbo **06** bagnio, chokey, cooler, inside, lock-up, lumber **07** bull pen, confine, custody, dungeon, enclose, hoosgow, slammer **08** bastille, big house, hoosegow, porridge, restrain, the hulks, the joint **09** bridewell, calaboose, detention, jailhouse, Lob's pound, massymore **10** guardhouse **11** confinement **12** imprisonment, penitentiary **15** detention centre

*Prisons include:*

**04** Maze
**05** Fleet, Pozzi
**06** Albany, Attica, Folsom
**07** Brixton, Feltham, Newgate
**08** Alcatraz, Bastille, Belmarsh, Dartmoor, Holloway, Long Kesh, Lubyanka, Sing Sing
**09** Fremantle, Parkhurst, the Scrubs
**10** San Quentin, Wandsworth
**11** Hanoi Hilton, Pentonville, Strangeways
**12** Devil's Island, Rikers Island, Robben Island
**13** Tower of London
**14** Wormwood scrubs

**prisoner**
**03** con, lag, POW **05** lifer, trust **06** détenu, inmate, old lag, trusty **07** captive, convict, culprit, détenue, hostage, passman **08** detainee, internee, jailbird, yardbird **10** recidivist **13** prisoner of war, state prisoner

**prissily**
**06** primly **07** fussily **08** stuffily **09** prudishly

**prissy**
**04** prim **05** fussy **06** demure, formal, proper, stuffy **07** finicky, po-faced, precise, prudish, starchy **08** priggish **09** squeamish **10** effeminate, fastidious, old-maidish, particular **11** puritanical, strait-laced **13** schoolmarmish

**pristine**
**04** pure **05** clean, first, fresh **06** former, primal, unused, virgin **07** initial,

primary **08** earliest, original, primeval, unspoilt **09** primaeval, primitive, unchanged, undefiled, unspoiled, unsullied, untouched **10** immaculate, primordial **11** primigenial, uncorrupted

**privacy**
**07** private, privity, retreat, secrecy **08** solitude **09** isolation, quietness, seclusion **10** retirement **11** concealment, privateness **12** independence **13** sequestration **15** confidentiality

**private**
**03** own, Pte, Pvt **04** swad **05** alone, aside, close, privy, quiet, Tommy **06** closed, closet, gunner, hidden, remote, secret, swaddy **07** postern, privacy, soldier, special, squaddy **08** domestic, familiar, homefelt, hush-hush, intimate, isolated, personal, reserved, retiring, secluded, separate, singular, solitary, squaddie **09** concealed, exclusive, innermost, top secret, withdrawn **10** classified, commercial, free-market, individual, particular, privatized, privileged, unofficial **11** clandestine, enlisted man, independent, introverted, out-of-the-way, sequestered, Tommy Atkins, undisturbed **12** confidential, off the record **13** intraparietal, self-contained, self-governing, single soldier **14** denationalized, free-enterprise, private soldier **15** non-governmental, self-determining

• **in private**
**07** sub rosa **08** in camera, in secret, secretly **09** privately **12** in confidence **14** confidentially **15** behind the scenes

• **private detective** *see* **detective**

**privateer**
**06** marque, pirate **07** brigand, corsair, cruiser, sea wolf **09** buccaneer, sea robber **10** filibuster, freebooter

**private eye** *see* **detective**

**privately**
**05** aside **06** inside, within **07** at heart, privily, sub rosa **08** deep down, in camera, in secret, inwardly, secretly **09** in private **10** personally, to yourself **12** in confidence, under the rose **13** deep inside you **14** confidentially

**privation**
**04** lack, loss, need, want **06** misery, penury **07** poverty **08** distress, hardship **09** austerity, indigence, neediness, suffering **10** affliction **11** deprivation, destitution

**privilege**
**03** due **05** honor, prise, right, title **06** honour, octroi, patent **07** benefit, faculty, freedom, liberty, licence **08** immunity, priority, sanction **09** advantage, authority, commodity, exemption, franchise **10** birthright, concession, seignorage **11** entitlement, prerogative, seigniorage **12** dispensation, status symbol

**privileged**
**04** rich **05** élite **06** exempt, immune, ruling, secret **07** private, special, wealthy **08** excepted, favoured, honoured, hush-hush, powerful **09** chartered, indulgent, top secret **10** advantaged, authorized, classified, sanctioned, unofficial **12** confidential, off the record

**privy**
**02** WC **03** bog, can, lav, loo **04** Ajax, kazi **05** dunny, gents', heads, jakes, siege **06** cloaca, closet, ladies', secret, toilet, urinal **07** cottage, crapper, draught, latrine, private **08** familiar, intimate, lavatory, rest room, washroom **09** cloakroom, garderobe **10** powder room, thunderbox **11** water closet **12** draught-house, smallest room **14** comfort station

• **privy to**
**04** in on **06** wise to **07** aware of **09** clued up on **10** apprised of, genned up on **11** cognizant of **13** informed about **14** in the know about

**prize**
**03** aim, cup, lot, pie, top **04** best, gain, goal, gree, hope, loot, love, palm, plum, tern **05** award, booty, great, honor, match, medal, plate, price, purse, stake, value **06** desire, esteem, honour, revere, reward, spoils, stakes, trophy **07** capture, cherish, jackpot, laurels, pennant, perfect, pillage, plunder, premium, seizure, winning **08** accolade, champion, hold dear, leverage, pickings, purchase, smashing, terrific, top-notch, treasure, winnings **09** excellent, first-rate, treasured **10** appreciate **11** outstanding, wooden spoon **12** award-winning, prize-winning **13** think highly of **14** out of this world **15** set great store by

*See also* **award**

**prize-winner**
**03** dux **05** champ **06** winner **08** champion, prizeman **09** cup-winner, medallist **10** prizewoman

*See also* **Nobel Prize**

**pro**
**03** ace, aye, for **06** expert, master, wizard **07** backing, dab hand, old hand **08** virtuoso **09** authority **10** consultant, in favour of, past master, prostitute, specialist, supporting **12** practitioner, probationary, professional

*See also* **prostitute**

**probability**
**04** odds **06** chance **07** chances **08** prospect **10** likelihood, likeliness **11** expectation, possibility

**probable**
**06** likely, odds-on **07** seeming **08** a fair bet, apparent, credible, expected, feasible, possible **09** plausible **10** believable, forseeable, on the cards **11** anticipated, predictable **12** to be expected

**probably**
**04** like **05** maybe **06** belike, likely **07** perhaps **08** a fair bet, arguably, possibly **09** doubtless, like as not **10** most likely, presumably **11** as like as not, it looks like **13** as likely as not, the chances are **15** in all likelihood

**probation**
**04** test **05** proof, trial **07** testing **09** noviciate **10** test period **11** supervision, trial period **14** apprenticeship

**probationer**
**04** tiro **05** pupil **06** novice, rookie **07** amateur, learner, recruit, student, trainee **08** beginner, neophyte, newcomer, stibbler **09** greenhorn, noviciate **10** apprentice, raw recruit

**probe**
**04** bore, feel, poke, prod, sift, tent, test **05** check, drill, plumb, sound, study, style **06** device, go into, pierce, search, stilet, stylet, tracer **07** analyse, examine, explore, inquest, inquire, inquiry **08** analysis, look into, research, scrutiny, searcher **09** penetrate **10** instrument, scrutinize **11** examination, exploration, investigate **13** investigation **14** scrutinization

*Space probes include:*

**04** Luna
**06** Viking
**07** Galileo, Mariner, Pioneer, Voyager
**09** Messenger
**10** Deep Impact
**14** Cassini–Huygens

**probity**
**05** worth **06** equity, honour, virtue **07** honesty, justice **08** fairness, fidelity, goodness, morality **09** integrity, rectitude, sincerity **11** uprightness **12** truthfulness **13** righteousness **14** honourableness **15** trustworthiness

**problem**
◇ *anagram indicator*
**02** BO **03** fix, sum **04** bore, boyg, drag, hole, knot, mess, pain, pest, prob, snag **05** facer, issue, poser, thing, worry **06** bother, enigma, hassle, indaba, matter, pickle, plight, puzzle, riddle, unruly **07** dilemma, toughie, trouble, wrinkle **08** irritant, nuisance, quandary, question, vexation **09** annoyance, conundrum, dichotomy, difficult, tight spot **10** conclusion, delinquent, difficulty, irritation, mind-bender **11** brainteaser, dire straits, disobedient, predicament, troublesome **12** brain-twister, complication, intransigent, recalcitrant, unmanageable **13** Chinese puzzle, inconvenience, pain in the neck **14** no-win situation, uncontrollable **15** thorn in your side

*See also* **economics**; **environment**

**problematic**
◇ *anagram indicator*
**04** hard, moot **06** thorny, tricky **07** awkward, dubious **08** doubtful, involved, puzzling **09** debatable, difficult, enigmatic, intricate, uncertain **10** a minefield, perplexing **11** a can of worms, troublesome **12** questionable **13** problematical

**procedure**
**02** op **03** way **04** move, play, step **05** drill, means **06** action, course, custom, fetich, fetish, method, policy, scheme, system **07** conduct, fetiche, formula, measure, process, routine, tactics **08** practice, strategy, technics **09** mechanics, operation, technique **11** advisedness, methodology, performance **12** plan of action **13** modus operandi **14** course of action

**proceed**
**02** go, on **03** put **04** come, fand, flow, fond, go on, make, pass, rake, stem, sway, yead, yede, yeed **05** arise, begin, ensue, get on, issue, start, trace **06** come on, derive, follow, happen, move on, pass on, result, spring **07** advance, carry on, emanate, go ahead, press on, prosper **08** continue, progress **09** go forward, originate, prosecute, take steps **10** make a start **11** get under way, make your way, set in motion

**• proceed with difficulty**
**04** limp

**proceedings**
**04** acta, case, diet **05** deeds, moves, steps, trial **06** action, annals, doings, events, report **07** account, affairs, lawsuit, matters, minutes, process, records, reports **08** archives, business, dealings, measures, ongoings **10** activities, happenings, litigation, manoeuvres, operations, procedures **12** transactions **14** course of action

**proceeds**
**04** gain **05** motza, yield **06** avails, income, motser, profit, return **07** produce, profits, returns, revenue, takings **08** earnings, receipts **12** intromission

**process**
◇ *anagram indicator*
**03** way **04** mode, sort, step **05** alter, edict, means, stage, train, treat **06** action, change, course, growth, handle, manner, method, refine, system **07** advance, changes, convert, prepare **08** attend to, deal with, movement, practice, progress **09** evolution, formation, narrative, operation, procedure, technique, transform **10** proceeding **11** development, progression

**• in the process of**
**05** being **11** in the making **13** in preparation, in the course of, in the middle of

**procession**
**03** run **04** demo, file, pomp, walk **05** corso, march, train **06** column, course, exequy, parade, series, stream **07** cortège, funeral, pageant, triumph **08** Moharram, Muharram, Muharrem, progress, sequence **09** cavalcade, motorcade **10** succession **11** hunger march **13** demonstration, manifestation

**proclaim**
**03** ask, bid, cry **04** ring, show, sing **05** knell, sound **06** affirm, blazon, herald, notify, out-ask, preach, summon **07** declare, enounce, give out, profess, protest, publish, testify, trumpet **08** announce, denounce, indicate **09** advertise, broadcast, circulate, make known, preconize, pronounce, show forth **10** annunciate, annuntiate, apostolize, promulgate **11** blaze abroad

**proclamation**
**03** ban **04** oyes, oyez, rule **05** banns, edict, order **06** decree, notice **07** command, kerygma, placard **08** proclaim **09** broadcast, hue and cry, indiction, manifesto, preaching **11** affirmation, circulation, declaration, publication **12** announcement, annunciation, notification, promulgation, proscription **13** advertisement, order of the day, pronouncement **14** pronunciamento

**proclivity**
**04** bent, bias **07** leaning **08** penchant, tendency, weakness **09** liability, proneness **10** liableness, propensity **11** disposition, inclination **12** predilection **14** predisposition

**procrastinate**
**05** dally, defer, delay, stall **06** put off, retard **07** prolong **08** postpone, protract **09** temporize **10** dilly-dally **11** play for time **12** drag your feet

**procrastination**
**08** deferral, delaying, stalling **10** cunctation **11** temporizing **12** dilatoriness **13** dilly-dallying **15** delaying tactics

**procreate**
**04** sire **05** beget, breed, spawn **06** father, mother **07** produce **08** conceive, engender, generate, multiply **09** propagate, reproduce

**proctor**
**04** prog **08** proggins

**procure**
**03** buy, get, win **04** earn, find, gain, hire, hook, pimp, sort **05** ponce **06** come by, hustle, induce, obtain, pander, pick up, secure **07** acquire, provide, solicit **08** purchase **09** get hold of, importune **10** lay hands on **11** appropriate, requisition

**procurer**
**04** bawd, hoon, mack, pimp **05** madam, ponce **06** broker, pander **07** hustler **08** fancy man, mackerel, panderer **09** procuress, solicitor **11** fleshmonger, whoremonger

**prod**
**03** awl, dig, jab, job **04** brod, butt, goad, move, poke, push, spur, stir, urge **05** egg on, elbow, goose, nudge, prick, probe, punch, shove **06** incite, prompt, skewer, thrust **08** motivate, reminder, stimulus **09** encourage, prompting, stimulate **10** motivation **13** encouragement

**prodigal**
**06** lavish, wanton, waster **07** copious, profuse, wastrel **08** profuser, reckless, spendall, unthrift, wasteful **09** bounteous, bountiful, excessive, exuberant, luxuriant, sumptuous, unsparing, unthrifty **10** big spender, immoderate, profligate, squanderer **11** extravagant, improvident, intemperate, spendthrift, squandering

**prodigality**
**05** waste **06** excess, plenty, wastry **07** abandon, wastery **08** richness **09** abundance, amplitude, profusion **10** exuberance, lavishness, luxuriance, profligacy, wantonness **11** copiousness, dissipation, squandering **12** extravagance, immoderation, intemperance, recklessness, wastefulness **13** bounteousness, plenteousness, sumptuousness, unthriftiness

**prodigious**
**04** huge, vast **05** giant **07** amazing, immense, mammoth, massive, unusual **08** abnormal, colossal, enormous, fabulous, gigantic, striking, terrific **09** fantastic, monstrous, startling, wonderful **10** astounding, gargantuan, impressive, inordinate, marvellous, miraculous, monumental, phenomenal, portentous, remarkable, staggering, stupendous, tremendous **11** exceptional, spectacular **12** immeasurable **13** extraordinary **14** flabbergasting

**prodigiously**
**06** vastly **09** amazingly, immensely, massively, unusually **10** remarkably **11** wonderfully **12** astoundingly, impressively, phenomenally, staggeringly **13** exceptionally, fantastically, spectacularly

**prodigy**
**05** freak **06** genius, marvel, phenom, rarity, wonder **07** miracle, monster, portent **08** moniment, monument, virtuoso, whizz kid **09** curiosity, sensation **10** mastermind, phenomenon, wonderwork, wunderkind **11** child genius, gifted child, phaenomenon, wonder child

**produce**
◇ *anagram indicator*
**04** bear, crop, eggs, food, give, grow, kind, make, show **05** beget, breed, build, cause, crops, dig up, evoke, fruit,

issue, mount, offer, put on, raise, stage, stuff, throw, wheel, yield **06** create, direct, effect, extend, get out, invent, manage, output, put out, supply, upcome **07** advance, arrange, compose, deliver, develop, execute, exhibit, fashion, furnish, harvest, perform, prepare, present, product, proffer, provide, provoke **08** assemble, bring out, engender, generate, increase, knock out, occasion, organize, proceeds, products, put forth, result in **09** construct, fabricate, originate **10** bring about, bring forth, come up with, foodstuffs, give rise to, put forward, vegetables
**11** commodities, demonstrate, give birth to, manufacture, put together
**12** bring forward **13** dairy products

**producer**
**04** hand **05** maker **06** farmer, grower
**07** manager **08** director, generant
**09** generator, presenter, régisseur
**10** impresario, undertaker
**12** manufacturer
*See also* **director**

**product**
**04** item, work **05** fruit, goods, issue, wares, yield **06** effect, legacy, output, result, return, upshot **07** article, outcome, produce, spin-off
**08** artefact, creation, offshoot **09** by-product, commodity, invention, offspring, outgrowth **10** end-product, production **11** consequence, merchandise, producement

**production**
◇ *anagram indicator*
**04** film, play, show, work **05** drama, fruit, opera, revue, yield **06** fruits, making, output, return **07** concert, harvest, musical, returns, staging
**08** assembly, building, creation, mounting **09** direction, extension, formation, producing **10** management
**11** achievement, composition, development, fabrication, manufacture, origination, performance, preparation
**12** construction, organization, presentation, productivity
**13** manufacturing

**productive**
**04** busy, rich **06** fecund, useful
**07** fertile, gainful, teeming **08** creative, fructive, fruitful, pregnant, prolific, valuable, vigorous **09** effective, efficient, energetic, inventive, rewarding **10** beneficial, generative, profitable, worthwhile **11** increaseful, procreative **12** constructive, fructiferous, high-yielding

**productivity**
**05** yield **06** output **08** capacity, work rate **10** efficiency, production
**12** fruitfulness **14** productiveness

**profanation**
**05** abuse **06** misuse **08** violence
**09** blasphemy, sacrilege, violation
**10** debasement, defilement, perversion **11** desecration
**12** dishonouring

**profane**
**03** lay **04** foul **05** abuse, crude
**06** coarse, debase, defile, filthy, misuse, unholy, vulgar **07** abusive, godless, impious, pervert, pollute, secular, unclean, ungodly, violate, worldly **08** temporal **09** desecrate, misemploy **10** foul-spoken, idolatrous, irreverent, unhallowed
**11** blasphemous, contaminate, foul-mouthed, irreligious **12** sacrilegious, unsanctified **13** disrespectful, unconsecrated

**profanity**
**04** oath **05** abuse, curse **07** cursing, impiety **08** swearing **09** blasphemy, expletive, obscenity, sacrilege, swear-word **10** execration **11** imprecation, irreverence, malediction, profaneness
**14** four-letter word

**profess**
**03** own **04** aver, avow **05** admit, claim, state **06** affirm, allege, assert **07** certify, confess, confirm, declare, make out, pretend, purport **08** announce, maintain, proclaim **09** dissemble
**10** lay claim to **11** acknowledge

**professed**
**06** avowed **07** alleged, would-be
**08** apparent, declared, so-called, supposed **09** certified, confirmed, pretended, purported, soi-disant
**10** ostensible, proclaimed, self-styled
**12** acknowledged **13** self-confessed

**profession**
**03** job **04** line, post **05** claim, craft, trade **06** avowal, career, métier, office
**07** calling **08** averment, business, position, pretence, vocation
**09** admission, assertion, situation, statement, testimony **10** confession, employment, line of work, occupation, walk of life **11** affirmation, appointment, declaration
**12** announcement
**15** acknowledgement

**professional**
**03** ace, pro **04** able **05** adept, buppy, maven, mavin, whizz, yuppy
**06** expert, master, wizard, yuppie
**07** dab hand, maestro, old hand, regular, skilful, skilled, trained
**08** educated, licensed, masterly, virtuoso **09** authority, competent, dexterous, efficient, practised, qualified **10** consultant, past master, proficient, specialist **11** experienced
**12** accomplished, businesslike, practitioner **13** knowledgeable

**professor**
**02** RP **03** don, STP **04** dean, prof
**05** chair, hodja, khoja **06** fellow, khodja, reader, regent **07** adjoint, provost **08** academic, emeritus, lecturer **09** principal **12** intellectual
**13** head of faculty **14** vice chancellor

**proffer**
**04** hand **05** offer **06** extend, submit, tender **07** advance, hold out, present, propose, suggest **09** volunteer

**proficiency**
**05** knack, skill **06** talent **07** ability, aptness, finesse, mastery **08** aptitude
**09** adeptness, dexterity, expertise, technique **10** capability, competence, experience **11** skilfulness
**14** accomplishment
• **level of proficiency**
**03** dan **05** grade

**proficient**
**03** apt **04** able, wise **05** adept
**06** clever, expert, gifted, useful
**07** capable, skilful, skilled, trained
**08** masterly, talented **09** competent, effective, efficient, qualified **10** past master **11** experienced
**12** accomplished, passed master

**profile**
**02** CV **04** biog, form, line, vita
**05** cameo, chart, graph, lines, shape, study **06** figure, purfle, résumé, review, sketch, survey, talweg **07** contour, diagram, drawing, outline, thalweg
**08** analysis, half-face, portrait, side view, template, vignette **09** biography, half-cheek **10** silhouette
**11** description, examination
**15** curriculum vitae, thumbnail sketch
• **high profile**
**08** exposure **10** prominence, visibility
**12** the limelight, the spotlight **15** public attention
• **keep a low profile**
**06** lie low **12** escape notice, hide yourself **14** avoid publicity

**profit**
**03** pay, use **04** boot, gain, gelt, perk, vail **05** avail, bonus, bunce, gravy, gross, serve, value, worth, yield
**06** excess, income, margin, return
**07** benefit, bestead, improve, killing, rake-off, revenue, surplus, takings, vantage **08** dividend, earnings, fast buck, increase, interest, proceeds, receipts, winnings **09** advantage, commodity, make money **10** bottom line, percentage, perquisite, usefulness
**11** improvement **13** make megabucks
**15** line your pockets, make loadsamoney
• **profit by, profit from**
**03** use **04** milk **07** exploit, utilize
**08** cash in on **12** capitalize on, put to good use **15** take advantage of, turn to advantage
• **share of profit**
**03** lay

**profitable**
**03** fat **05** juicy, utile **06** paying, plummy, useful **07** gainful, helpful, payable **08** behovely, economic, fruitful, valuable **09** available, expedient, lucrative, rewarding
**10** beneficial, commercial, in the black, productive, successful, worthwhile
**11** moneymaking **12** advantageous,

remunerative **13** advantageable, cost-effective

**profitably**
**08** usefully, valuably **10** fruitfully **12** beneficially, commercially, economically, productively, successfully

**profiteer**
**06** extort, fleece **07** exploit **09** exploiter, racketeer **10** overcharge **11** extortioner **12** extortionist **13** make a fast buck **14** make a quick buck

**profiteering**
**09** extortion **10** Rachmanism **12** exploitation, racketeering

**profitless**
**04** idle, vain **06** futile **07** useless **08** gainless, wasteful **09** fruitless, pointless, thankless, to no avail, worthless **10** unavailing **11** ineffective, ineffectual, to no purpose **12** unproductive, unprofitable **14** unremunerative

**profligacy**
**05** waste **06** excess **09** abundance, depravity, profusion **10** corruption, debauchery, degeneracy, immorality, lavishness, wantonness **11** dissipation, libertinism, prodigality, promiscuity, squandering, unrestraint **12** extravagance, improvidence, recklessness, wastefulness **13** dissoluteness, unthriftiness **14** licentiousness

**profligate**
**04** rake, roué **05** loose **06** wanton, waster, wicked **07** corrupt, Don Juan, immoral, wastrel **08** defeated, depraved, prodigal, reckless, wasteful **09** abandoned, debauched, debauchee, dissolute, excessive, libertine, reprobate **10** Corinthian, degenerate, dissipated, immoderate, iniquitous, licentious, overthrown, squanderer **11** extravagant, improvident, promiscuous, spendthrift, squandering **12** unprincipled

**profound**
**03** sea **04** deep, wise **05** abyss, great, ocean **06** marked **07** erudite, extreme, intense, learned, radical, serious, sincere, weighty **08** absolute, abstruse, complete, esoteric, thorough **09** extensive, heartfelt, recondite, sagacious **10** deep-seated, discerning, exhaustive, thoughtful **11** far-reaching, penetrating **12** impenetrable **13** philosophical, thoroughgoing

**profoundly**
**04** deep **06** deeply, keenly **07** acutely, greatly **08** heartily **09** extremely, intensely, seriously, sincerely **10** thoroughly

**profundity**
**05** depth **06** acumen, wisdom **07** insight **08** learning, sagacity, severity, strength **09** erudition, extremity, intensity **11** penetration, perspicuity, seriousness **12** abstruseness, intelligence, perspicacity, profoundness **14** perceptiveness

**profuse**
**04** rich **05** ample **06** lavish **07** copious, fulsome, liberal **08** abundant, generous **09** excessive, luxuriant, plentiful, unsparing **10** immoderate, inordinate, over the top, unstinting **11** extravagant, large-handed, overflowing **12** colliquative, overabundant **13** superabundant

**profusely**
**08** lavishly **09** copiously, liberally **10** abundantly **11** unsparingly **12** immoderately, unstintingly **13** extravagantly

**profusion**
**04** glut, lots, riot, tons **05** heaps, loads, waste **06** excess, lavish, plenty, wealth **07** surplus **08** plethora **09** abundance, multitude, plenitude **10** profligacy **11** copiousness, prodigality, superfluity **12** extravagance **13** unsparingness **14** superabundance

**progenitor**
**05** stock **06** father, mother, parent, source, tupuna **07** founder **08** ancestor, begetter, forebear **09** precursor **10** antecedent, forefather, forerunner, instigator, originator, procreator **11** predecessor **12** primogenitor

**progeny**
**04** burd, race, seed **05** breed, issue, stock, young **06** family, scions **07** lineage **08** children, increase, mokopuna **09** offspring, posterity, quiverful **10** generation **11** descendants

**prognosis**
**07** outlook, surmise **08** forecast, prospect **09** diagnosis **10** assessment, evaluation, prediction, projection **11** expectation, forecasting, speculation **15** prognostication

**prognosticate**
**05** augur **06** divine, herald **07** betoken, portend, predict, presage **08** forebode, forecast, foretell, indicate, prophesy, soothsay **09** harbinger **10** foreshadow

**prognostication**
**04** omen **07** surmise **08** forecast, precurse, prophecy **09** horoscope, prejudice, prejudize, prognosis **10** prediction, projection **11** expectation, speculation

**programme**
**04** book, list, plan, show **05** lay on **06** agenda, course, design, line up, line-up, map out, scheme **07** arrange, episode, itemize, listing, project, work out **08** calendar, schedule, syllabus **09** broadcast, formulate, simulcast, timetable **10** curriculum, prearrange, production, prospectus **11** performance **12** plan of action, presentation, transmission **13** order of events

*See also* **radio**; **television**

**programming** *see* **language**

**progress**
**02** go **03** ren, rin, run, way **04** gain, go on, grow, sail **05** bloom, going **06** better, career, come on, course, growth, mature, thrive **07** advance, blossom, circuit, develop, headway, improve, journey, onwards, passage, proceed, prosper, recover, shape up, success **08** continue, distance, flourish, increase, movement, traverse **09** come along, evolution, go forward, promotion, upgrading **10** betterment, forge ahead, periegesis, proceeding, procession **11** advancement, development, improvement, make headway, make strides, make your way, move forward, progression, step forward **12** breakthrough, continuation, make progress, steps forward **14** be getting there **15** forward movement

**• in progress**
**02** on **06** on foot **07** en train, going on, in train, on-going **08** on the way, under way **09** happening, occurring **10** continuing, proceeding **11** not finished, on the stocks **12** not completed **13** in preparation, in the pipeline

**• make progress**
**04** roll

**progression**
**05** chain, cycle, order, train **06** course, motion, series, stream, string **07** advance, headway, passage, process **08** movement, progress, pub-crawl, sequence **10** paraphonia, precession, resolution, succession **11** advancement, development **12** direct motion **15** forward movement

**progressive**
**04** left, prog **06** modern **07** creator, deviser, dynamic, go-ahead, gradual, growing, liberal, pioneer, radical **08** advanced, left-wing, reformer **09** advancing, developer, innovator, reformist **10** avant-garde, continuing, developing, escalating, increasing, innovative, modernizer, originator **11** enlightened, trailblazer, up-and-coming **12** accelerating, enterprising, fresh thinker, intensifying **13** revolutionary **14** forward-looking **15** forward-thinking

**progressively**
**07** forward **08** bit by bit, by stages, forwards, in stages **09** by degrees, gradually, piecemeal **10** step by step **12** hand over hand, increasingly **14** little by little

**prohibit**
**03** ban, bar **04** stop, veto **06** defend,

enjoin, forbid, hamper, hinder, impede, outlaw **07** exclude, injunct, prevent, rule out **08** obstruct, preclude, restrict **09** interdict, proscribe

**prohibited**
**05** taboo **06** banned, barred, vetoed **07** illegal **08** verboten **09** embargoed, forbidden, off-limits **10** contraband, disallowed, proscribed **11** interdicted

**prohibition**
**03** ban, bar **04** tabu, veto **07** embargo, forbode **08** negation **09** exclusion, forbiddal, interdict **10** constraint, forbidding, injunction, prevention **11** forbiddance, obstruction, restriction **12** disallowance, interdiction, proscription

**prohibitionist**
**03** dry **09** pussyfoot **11** teetotaller **12** abolitionist

**prohibitive**
**05** steep **07** sky-high **09** excessive **10** exorbitant, forbidding, impossible, repressive **11** prohibiting, prohibitory, restraining, restrictive, suppressive **12** extortionate, preposterous, proscriptive

**project**
**03** job, jut **04** cast, hurl, idea, kick, plan, sail, task, work **05** bulge, chuck, fling, gauge, jetty, throw **06** beetle, design, devise, expect, extend, intend, jut out, launch, map out, notion, propel, reckon, reflex, scheme, screen **07** obtrude, predict, propose, venture **08** activity, campaign, contract, estimate, exercise, forecast, outstand, overhang, proposal, protrude, stand out, stick out, workshop **09** calculate, discharge, programme **10** assignment, conception, enterprise, occupation **11** externalize, extrapolate, undertaking **12** predetermine

**projectile**
**04** ball, bomb, shot **05** shell **06** bullet, mortar, rocket, tracer **07** grenade, missile **08** case-shot, fireball **09** ballistic, impelling **13** guided missile

**projecting**
**05** proud **08** beetling, exserted **09** exsertile, extrusive, extrusory, obtrusive, prominent **10** protrudent, protruding, protrusive **11** overhanging, sticking out

• **projecting part**
**03** arm, ear, fin **04** nose, tang

**projection**
**03** cam, cog, jut, lug, nab, out, rag **04** beak, nose, peak, plan, sail, sill, spur, tusk **05** bulge, ledge, prong, ridge, sally, scrag, shelf, snout, spike, strap, tooth **06** calcar, corner, design, nozzle, outjet, outjut, relief, tongue **07** jutting, process **08** estimate, forecast, overhang, oversail, planning **09** dentation, reckoning **10** estimation, prediction, prominence, promontory **11** calculation, computation, excrescence, expectation, orthography **12** protuberance **13** extrapolation

**proletarian**
**06** common **08** ordinary, plebeian **12** working-class

**proletariat**
**03** mob **04** herd **05** plebs **06** lumpen, masses, proles, rabble **08** canaille, riff-raff **09** commoners, hoi polloi **10** commonalty **11** rank and file, third estate **12** common people, lower classes, working class **13** great unwashed

**proliferate**
**05** breed **06** expand, extend, rocket, spread, thrive **07** build up, burgeon **08** escalate, flourish, increase, multiply, mushroom, snowball **09** intensify, reproduce **11** grow quickly **15** increase rapidly

**proliferation**
**06** spread **07** build-up **08** increase **09** expansion, extension, rocketing **10** escalation **11** duplication, ecblastesis, mushrooming, snowballing **13** concentration, rapid increase **14** multiplication **15** intensification

**prolific**
**04** rank **06** broody, fecund **07** copious, fertile, profuse **08** abundant, fruitful **09** luxuriant, plentiful **10** productive **11** fertilizing **12** reproductive

**prolix**
**04** long **05** prosy, wordy **07** diffuse, lengthy, tedious, verbose **08** rambling, tiresome **09** prolonged, rigmarole **10** digressive, discursive, long-winded, pleonastic, protracted

**prolixity**
**06** length **08** longueur, pleonasm, rambling, verbiage **09** prosiness, verbosity, wandering, wordiness **10** boringness **11** diffuseness, tediousness, verboseness **13** copia verborum **14** discursiveness, long-windedness

**prologue**
**05** index, proem **07** preface, prelude **08** exordium, foreword, preamble **09** introduce, prooemion, prooemium **11** preliminary, prolegomena **12** introduction

**prolong**
**05** delay **06** extend, linger **07** drag out, draw out, respite, spin out, stretch, sustain **08** continue, elongate, lengthen, postpone, prorogue, protract **10** perpetuate, stretch out

**prolongation**
**04** tail **08** appendix, urostyle **09** extension, gonophore **10** androphore, carpophore, stretching, trichogyne **11** lengthening, protraction **12** continuation, perpetuation

**promenade**
**04** pier, prom, turn, walk **05** front, mosey, paseo, strut **06** airing, parade, stroll **07** saunter, swagger, terrace, walkway **08** breather, seafront **09** boulevard, esplanade, polonaise, walkabout **10** sally forth **11** perambulate **14** constitutional

**promethium**
**02** Pm

**prominence**
**03** rib **04** boss, bump, crag, cusp, fame, hump, lump, name, note, rank, rise **05** bulge, cliff, crest, mound, torus **06** height, renown, rising, tragus, weight **07** jutting, mastoid, process, stature **08** eminence, emphasis, headland, pinnacle, prestige, standing, swelling **09** celebrity, elevation, greatness **10** antitragus, colliculus, embossment, importance, projection, prominency, promontory, protruding, reputation, top billing **11** distinction, pre-eminence **12** pride of place, protuberance **15** conspicuousness, illustriousness

• **into prominence**
**02** up

**prominent**
**03** top **04** main **05** A-list, chief, noted **06** famous, goggle, marked **07** bulging, eminent, jutting, leading, notable, obvious, popular, salient **08** beetling, foremost, renowned, striking **09** acclaimed, egregious, important, obtrusive, respected, to the fore, well-known **10** celebrated, jutting out, noticeable, pre-eminent, projecting, protrudent, protruding, protrusive **11** conspicuous, eye-catching, high-profile, illustrious, outstanding, protuberant, standing out, sticking out **12** unmistakable **13** distinguished, unmistakeable

**promiscuity**
**06** laxity **09** depravity, looseness **10** debauchery, immorality, profligacy, protervity, wantonness **11** dissipation **13** dissoluteness **14** licentiousness, permissiveness, sleeping around

**promiscuous**
◇ *anagram indicator*
**04** fast **05** loose, mixed, slack **06** casual, random, wanton **07** immoral **08** sluttish, swinging **09** abandoned, debauched, dissolute, haphazard **10** accidental, dissipated, licentious, profligate **12** of easy virtue **14** indiscriminate, sleeping around

**promise**
**03** vow **04** avow, bond, hand, hete, hint, oath, sign, word **05** augur, flair, hecht, hight, swear, vouch **06** assure, behote, commit, denote, engage, hint at, pledge, plight, talent **07** ability, behight, betoken, betroth, compact, presage, signify, suggest, warrant **08** aptitude, contract, covenant, evidence, indicate, look like **09** assurance, be a sign of, committal,

guarantee, potential, undertake **10** capability, commitment, engagement, indication, suggestion, take an oath **11** expectation, undertaking **12** give your word, word of honour **13** pollicitation **15** give an assurance

• **promised land**

**04** Zion **06** Canaan, heaven, Utopia **07** Elysium **08** El Dorado, paradise **09** Shangri-la **13** Elysian fields

*See also* **heaven**

**promising**

**04** able, rosy **06** bright, gifted, likely **07** budding, hopeful **08** talented, towardly **09** favorable **10** auspicious, favourable, optimistic, propitious **11** encouraging, up-and-coming

**promissory note**

**02** pn **03** IOU

**promontory**

**03** hoe, nab **04** bill, cape, head, mull, naze, ness, spur **05** bluff, cliff, point, ridge **08** eminence, foreland, headland **09** peninsula, precipice **10** projection, prominence

**promote**

**03** aid, ren, rin, run **04** back, help, hype, make, plug, push, sell, urge **05** boost, exalt, raise **06** assist, foster, honour, market, move up, peddle, prefer, puff up **07** advance, elevate, endorse, espouse, forward, further, nurture, sponsor, support, upgrade **08** advocate, champion **09** advertise, encourage, publicize, recommend, stimulate **10** aggrandize, popularize **11** merchandize **12** contribute to, kick upstairs

**promoter**

**07** pleader, speaker, sponsor **08** advocate, champion, exponent, upholder **09** furtherer, projector, proponent, spokesman, supporter **10** campaigner, evangelist, vindicator **11** spokeswoman **12** spokesperson

**promotion**

**02** ad **04** hype, puff, rise **05** promo **06** advert, move-up, payola, remove, urging **07** backing, puffery, pushing, support, venture **08** advocacy, boosting, campaign, espousal, plugging, speeding **09** elevation, fostering, marketing, prelation, publicity, upgrading **10** exaltation, preferment, propaganda **11** advancement, advertising, development, furtherance **12** contribution **13** advertisement, encouragement **14** aggrandizement, recommendation

**prompt**

**02** OP **03** cue **04** help, hint, jolt, lead, make, move, prod, spur, urge **05** alert, cause, eager, early, frack, impel, quick, rapid, ready, sharp, swift **06** bang on, dead on, direct, elicit, incite, induce, on time, remind, speedy, spot-on, sudden, timely **07** exactly, inspire, instant, premove, produce, provoke, willing **08** expedite, motivate, occasion, on the dot, promptly, punctual, reminder, result in, stimulus **09** call forth, encourage, immediate, instigate, refresher, stimulate **10** give rise to, pernicious, punctually, responsive **11** expeditious, to the minute **12** unhesitating **13** encouragement, instantaneous

**prompting**

**04** hint, urge **06** advice, motion, urging **07** jogging, pushing **08** pressing, pressure, prodding, reminder **09** influence, reminding **10** admonition, assistance, incitement, persuasion, protreptic, suggestion **13** encouragement

**promptly**

**03** pdq, tit **04** asap, tite, tyte **05** sharp, tight **06** bang on, dead on, on time, pronto, spot-on, titely, yarely **07** exactly, lightly, quickly, smartly, swiftly **08** chop-chop, directly, on target, on the dot, speedily **09** forthwith, instantly, like a shot, posthaste, yesterday **10** punctually **11** immediately, to the minute **12** in short order **14** unhesitatingly, without more ado **15** before you know it, pretty damn quick

**promptness**

**05** haste, speed **08** alacrity, dispatch **09** alertness, briskness, eagerness, quickness, readiness, swiftness **10** expedition **11** promptitude, punctuality, willingness

**promulgate**

**05** issue **06** decree, notify, spread **07** declare, promote, publish **08** announce, proclaim **09** advertise, broadcast, circulate, make known, publicize **10** make public **11** communicate, disseminate

**promulgation**

**08** issuance **11** declaration, publication, publicizing **12** announcement, proclamation, promulgating **13** communication, dissemination

**prone**

**03** apt **04** bent, flat **05** eager, given, ready **06** homily, liable, likely **07** subject, tending, willing **08** disposed, face down, inclined, proclive **09** prostrate, recumbent, stretched **10** full-length, horizontal, procumbent, vulnerable **11** predisposed, susceptible

**proneness**

**04** bent, bias **07** aptness, leaning **08** penchant, tendency, weakness **09** liability **10** proclivity, propensity **11** disposition, inclination **14** susceptibility

**prong**

**03** tip **04** fang, fork, spur, tang, tine **05** grain, point, spike, tooth **10** projection

**pronounce**

◇ *homophone indicator*

**03** say **04** give, pass, vote **05** judge, mouth, sound, speak, utter, voice **06** affirm, assert, decree, stress, tongue **07** bring in, declare, deliver, express **08** announce, proclaim, vocalize **09** enunciate **10** adjudicate, articulate

**pronounceable**

**07** sayable, vocable **09** speakable, utterable **10** enunciable **11** articulable, expressible

**pronounced**

◇ *homophone indicator*

**05** broad, clear, thick **06** marked, strong **07** decided, evident, obvious **08** definite, distinct, positive, striking, terrible **10** noticeable **11** conspicuous **12** unmistakable **13** unmistakeable

**pronouncement**

**05** edict **06** decree, dictum **09** assertion, ipse dixit, judgement, manifesto, statement **11** declaration **12** announcement, notification, proclamation, promulgation **14** pronunciamento

**pronunciation**

**06** accent, saying, speech, stress **07** diction, voicing **08** delivery, orthoepy, uttering **09** elocution, phonetics **10** inflection, intonation, modulation **11** enunciation **12** articulation, vocalization

**proof**

**02** ap **04** pull, slip, test **05** assay, issue, prief, repro, tight **06** galley, priefe, strong, upshot **07** outcome, proofed, testing, treated, warrant, witness **08** argument, evidence **09** bombproof, fireproof, foolproof, leakproof, probation, rainproof, repellent, resistant, testimony, windproof **10** argumentum, childproof, experience, impervious, smoking gun, soundproof, validation, waterproof **11** attestation, bulletproof, tamperproof **12** confirmation, impenetrable, invulnerable, verification, weatherproof **13** certification, corroboration, demonstration, documentation **14** authentication, substantiation **15** impenetrability, invulnerability

• **adduce as proof**

**04** cite

**prop**

**03** leg, set **04** lean, post, rest, stay **05** brace, punch, rance, shaft, shore, sprag, staff, stand, stick, stilt, stoop, stoup, strut, stull, truss **06** anchor, brooch, column, crutch, hold up, pillar, steady, tiepin, uphold **07** balance, bolster, bunting, fulcrum, shore up, studdle, support, sustain, upright **08** buttress, mainstay, maintain, property, underpin, underset, upholder **09** bolster up, crippling, propeller, stanchion, supporter **10** underwrite **11** clothes-pole, point d'appui, proposition **14** flying buttress

**propaganda**
**04** hype **08** Agitprop, ballyhoo **09** promotion, publicity **11** advertising, information **12** brainwashing **14** disinformation, indoctrination

**propagandist**
**07** plugger **08** advocate, promoter **09** canvasser, proponent, publicist **10** evangelist **11** pamphleteer **12** hot gospeller, proselytizer **13** indoctrinator

**propagandize**
**06** preach, uphold **07** promote, win over **08** advocate, argue for, champion, persuade, press for, talk into **09** brainwash, re-educate **10** pressurize **11** campaign for **12** indoctrinate

**propagate**
**04** grow, pipe **05** beget, breed, layer, spawn **06** spread **07** diffuse, produce, promote, propage, provine, publish, traduce **08** generate, increase, multiply, proclaim, seminate, transmit **09** broadcast, circulate, procreate, publicize, reproduce **10** distribute, promulgate **11** communicate, disseminate, proliferate

**propagation**
**06** spread **08** breeding, increase, spawning **09** diffusion, promotion, spreading **10** generation **11** circulation, procreation **12** distribution, promulgation, reproduction, transmission **13** communication, dissemination, proliferation **14** multiplication

**propel**
**02** ca' **03** caa', leg, oar, row **04** loft, move, pole, pump, punt, push, sail, send, swim, waft **05** drive, force, impel, power, scull, shoot, shove, wheel **06** launch, paddle, thrust **07** project **09** frogmarch **11** push forward

**propeller**
**03** fan **04** prop, vane **05** helix, rotor, screw **06** pusher **07** tractor **08** airscrew, thruster **09** tail rotor, tilt-rotor

**propensity**
**04** bent, bias **06** foible **07** aptness, leaning **08** penchant, tendency, weakness **09** liability, proneness, readiness **10** proclivity **11** disposition, inclination **14** predisposition, susceptibility

**proper**
**01** U **03** ain, due, own **04** prim, real, true, very **05** exact, right **06** actual, comely, decent, dueful, formal, goodly, kosher, polite, seemly, strict **07** correct, dewfull, fitting, genteel, genuine, gradely, precise, prudish, refined **08** accepted, accurate, decorous, graithly, ladylike, orthodox, peculiar, singular, suitable, thorough **09** befitting, out-and-out, shipshape **10** acceptable **11** appropriate, comme il faut, established, exceedingly, gentlemanly, respectable **12** conventional, well-becoming

**properly**
**04** duly **05** right **07** exactly, gradely, rightly **08** actually, entirely, graithly, strictly, suitably **09** correctly, extremely, fittingly, precisely **10** acceptably, accurately, flawlessly, unerringly **11** faultlessly, respectably **13** appropriately **14** conventionally

**• properly so called**
**04** true

**property**
**03** fee **04** gear, land, mark, prop **05** acres, fonds, goods, house, means, quirk, trait **06** assets, estate, houses, living, riches, things, wealth **07** capital, clobber, effects, feature, fitness, holding, quality **08** chattels, holdings, premises **09** affection, attribute, buildings, ownership, propriety, resources, substance **10** belongings, real estate **11** appropriate, peculiarity, possessions **12** idiosyncrasy **13** individuality, paraphernalia **14** characteristic

**prophecy**
**06** augury **07** message **08** forecast **09** preaching, prognosis **10** divination, prediction **11** second sight, soothsaying **12** vaticination **14** fortune-telling **15** prognostication

**prophesy**
**05** augur **06** preach **07** foresee, predict **08** forecast, foretell, forewarn **10** vaticinate **13** prognosticate

**prophet, prophetess**
**04** seer **05** sibyl **06** oracle **07** tipster, völuspa **10** forecaster, foreteller, soothsayer **11** clairvoyant, vaticinator **13** fortune-teller **14** prognosticator

*Prophets and prophetesses include:*

**02** Is
**03** Dan, Hag, Hos, Isa, Jer, Jon, Mic, Nah, Sam
**04** Amos, Ezek, Joel, Obad, Zeph
**05** Hosea, Jonah, Micah, Moses, Nahum
**06** Barton (Elizabeth), Daniel, Elijah, Elisha, Haggai, Isaiah, Nathan, Samuel, St John
**07** Ezekiel, Malachi, Obadiah
**08** Jeremiah, Mohammed, Muhammad, Nehemiah
**09** al-Mokanna, Zephaniah, Zoroaster
**11** Zarathustra
**12** the Nun of Kent
**13** the Maid of Kent
**14** John the Baptist

**• prophet of doom**
**08** doomster, Jeremiah **09** Cassandra, doomsayer, pessimist **11** doomwatcher **12** doom merchant

**prophetic**
**03** fey **05** vatic **06** mantic **07** augural, fateful **08** oracular **09** fatidical, oraculous, presaging, prescient, sibylline, vaticidal **10** divinatory, predictive, prognostic **11** apocalyptic, forecasting **13** foreshadowing

**prophylactic**
**04** safe **06** condom, rubber, sheath **07** Femidom®, johnnie, scumbag, treacle **09** deterrent **10** inhibitory, precaution, pre-emptive, preventive, protective **11** obstructive **12** anticipatory, female condom, French letter, immunization, preservative, preventative **13** contraceptive, counteractive, precautionary, viper's bugloss

**propinquity**
**03** tie **05** blood **07** kinship **08** affinity, nearness, relation, vicinity **09** adjacency, closeness, proximity **10** connection, contiguity **11** affiliation, kindredness, kindredship **12** relationship **13** consanguinity, neighbourhood

**propitiate**
**06** pacify, soothe **07** appease, mollify, placate, satisfy **09** reconcile **10** conciliate

**propitiation**
**09** atonement, pacifying, placation **11** appeasement, peacemaking **12** conciliation, pacification **13** mollification **14** reconciliation

**propitiatory**
**08** soothing **09** appeasing, assuaging, expiatory, pacifying, placative, placatory **10** mollifying **11** peacemaking **12** conciliatory, pacificatory, propitiative **14** reconciliatory

**propitious**
**04** rosy **05** happy, lucky **06** benign, bright, kindly, timely **08** friendly, gracious **09** favorable, fortunate, opportune, promising, wholesome **10** auspicious, beneficial, benevolent, favourable, prosperous, reassuring **11** encouraging **12** advantageous, well-disposed

**proponent**
**06** backer, friend, patron **08** advocate, champion, defender, exponent, favourer, partisan, proposer, upholder **09** apologist, proposing, supporter **10** enthusiast, propounder, subscriber, vindicator

**proportion**
**03** cut **04** bulk, mass, part, size **05** depth, quota, ratio, scale, share, split, whack, width **06** amount, extent, height, length, volume **07** analogy, balance, breadth, measure, portion, segment **08** capacity, division, fraction, graduate, quotient, symmetry **09** magnitude **10** dimensions, percentage **11** temperature **12** distribution, measurements, relationship **14** correspondence, slice of the cake

**proportional**
**04** even **08** logistic, relative, relevant **09** analogous, equitable **10** comparable, consistent, equivalent, logistical **12** commensurate **13** corresponding, proportionate

**proportionally**
**06** evenly **07** pro rata **10** comparably, relatively **14** commensurately
**15** correspondingly, proportionately

**proposal**
**03** bid **04** plan **05** offer, terms
**06** design, motion, scheme, tender
**07** project **08** overture, supposal
**09** manifesto, programme
**10** resolution, suggestion
**11** proposition **12** presentation
**14** recommendation

**propose**
**03** aim, bid, pop **04** face, mean, moot, move, name, plan, talk, vote **05** offer, place, put up, slate, table **06** design, intend, motion, submit, tender
**07** advance, bethink, bring up, imagine, present, proffer, propone, purpose, suggest, suppose **08** advocate, converse, nominate, propound, put forth **09** discourse, enunciate, introduce, recommend **10** ask to marry, have in mind, put forward
**14** pop the question **15** plight your troth

**proposition**
**03** job **04** pass, plan, prop, task **05** offer
**06** accost, come-on, motion, scheme, tender, theory **07** advance, premise, project, solicit, theorem, venture
**08** activity, approach, disjunct, overture, proposal **09** alternant, manifesto, programme, universal
**10** hypothesis, suggestion **11** make a pass at, subcontrary, undertaking
**14** recommendation

**propound**
**03** put, set **04** move, pose **06** submit
**07** advance, contend, lay down, present, propone, propose, purpose, suggest **08** advocate, set forth
**09** postulate **10** put forward

**proprietary**
**03** pty

**proprietor, proprietress**
**04** lord **05** owner **06** patron
**07** esquire **08** landlady, landlord, zemindar **09** landowner, possessor, publisher **10** deed holder, freeholder, landholder **11** leaseholder, proprietrix, title-holder **12** entrepreneur
*See also* **newspaper**

**propriety**
**05** mense **07** aptness, decency, decorum, fitness, manners, modesty, p's and q's, quality **08** breeding, civility, courtesy, delicacy, elegance, elegancy, property, protocol, standard
**09** character, etiquette, ownership, punctilio, rectitude, rightness
**10** bienséance, convention, politeness, refinement, seemliness **11** correctness, good manners **12** becomingness, ladylikeness, social graces, suitableness, the done thing
**14** respectability, social niceties
**15** appropriateness, gentlemanliness

**propulsion**
**04** push **05** drive, power **06** thrust
**07** impetus, impulse **08** momentum, pressure, traction **09** impulsion
**10** propelment **11** motive force
**12** driving force

**pro rata**
**06** evenly **10** comparably, relatively
**14** commensurately, proportionally
**15** correspondingly, proportionately

**prosaic**
**03** dry **04** dull, flat, tame **05** banal, bland, stale, trite, vapid **06** boring
**07** humdrum, mundane, routine, vacuous **08** everyday, ordinary, workaday **09** hackneyed
**10** monotonous, pedestrian, uninspired, unpoetical
**11** commonplace, uninspiring
**12** matter-of-fact **13** unimaginative

**prosaically**
**05** dully **07** blandly **09** mundanely
**10** ordinarily **12** monotonously
**13** uninspiringly **15** unimaginatively

**proscribe**
**03** ban, bar **04** damn, doom **05** black, exile, expel **06** banish, deport, forbid, outlaw, reject **07** boycott, censure, condemn, embargo, exclude
**08** denounce, disallow, prohibit
**09** blackball, interdict, ostracize
**10** expatriate **13** excommunicate

**proscription**
**03** ban, bar **05** exile **07** barring, boycott, censure, damning, embargo
**08** ejection, eviction, outlawry
**09** exclusion, expulsion, interdict, ostracism, rejection **10** banishment
**11** deportation, prohibition
**12** condemnation, denunciation, expatriation, proclamation
**15** excommunication

**prosecute**
**02** do **03** sue, try **05** chase **06** accuse, charge, indict, pursue, summon
**07** arraign, proceed, process **08** litigate
**10** put on trial **11** take to court **12** bring charges **13** prefer charges

**prosecution**
**05** trial **08** charging **10** accusation, indictment, litigation **11** impeachment
**13** taking to court **15** bringing charges

**prosecutor**
**02** DA, PF **06** fiscal **08** quaestor
**10** avvogadore **11** prosecutrix **12** Lord Advocate **13** judge advocate
**14** advocate-depute

**proselyte**
**07** convert, recruit **08** neophyte
**09** new person **10** catechumen **11** new believer **13** changed person

**proselytize**
**07** convert, win over **08** persuade
**10** bring to God, evangelize **12** make converts, propagandize **15** spread the gospel

**Proserpina**
**10** Persephone

**prosody**

*Prosody terms include:*

**04** foot, iamb
**05** canto, envoy, epode, ictus, Ionic, metre, paeon
**06** choree, dactyl, dipody, dizain, laisse, miurus, rondel, sonnet
**07** ballade, caesura, couplet, distich, elision, pantoum, pyrrhic, rondeau, Sapphic, spondee, strophe, triolet, tripody, triseme, trochee, virelay
**08** anapaest, choriamb, cinquain, eye rhyme, Pindaric, quatrain, tribrach, trimeter
**09** anacrusis, assonance, catalexis, dispondee, ditrochee, free verse, half-rhyme, hexameter, macaronic, monometer, monorhyme, rime riche, tetrapody
**10** amphibrach, amphimacer, blank verse, consonance, enjambment, galliambic, heptameter, pentameter, rhyme royal, tetrameter, villanelle
**11** Alcaic verse, alexandrine, broken rhyme, linked verse, long-measure, septenarius
**12** alliteration, antibacchius, Leonine rhyme, Pythian verse, sprung rhythm
**13** abstract verse, feminine rhyme, heroic couplet, hypermetrical, internal rhyme
**14** feminine ending, masculine rhyme, rime suffisante
**15** feminine caesura, masculine ending, poulters' measure

**prospect**
**04** face, hope, nose, odds, seek, view
**05** quest, scene, sight, vista, visto
**06** aspect, chance, future, search, survey **07** chances, examine, explore, fossick, inspect, look for, lookout, opening, outlook, promise **08** belle vue, likeness, panorama **09** landscape, spectacle, viewpoint **10** likelihood
**11** expectation, opportunity, perspective, possibility, probability
**12** anticipation

**prospective**
**04** -to-be **06** coming, future, likely
**07** awaited, would-be **08** aspiring, destined, expected, hoped-for, imminent, intended, possible, probable **09** designate, potential
**11** anticipated, approaching, forthcoming

**prospectus**
**04** list, plan **06** scheme **07** leaflet, outline **08** brochure, pamphlet, syllabus, synopsis **09** catalogue, manifesto, programme **10** conspectus, literature **11** description
**12** announcement

**prosper**
**04** boom, thee **05** bloom, get on **06** do well, flower, thrive **07** advance, blossom, burgeon, proceed, succeed
**08** flourish, get ahead, grow rich, progress **09** get on well **11** turn out well

**12** be successful, make progress, make your pile **13** hit the big time, hit the jackpot **14** go up in the world **15** get on in the world

**prosperity**
**04** boom, good **06** clover, luxury, plenty, riches, thrift, wealth **07** fortune, success, welfare **08** sunshine **09** affluence, wellbeing **10** bed of roses, easy street **11** good fortune, lap of luxury, the good life **14** the life of Riley

**• spell of prosperity**
**02** up **04** boom

**prosperous**
**04** fair, rich **05** blest, lucky, sleek **06** well in **07** blessed, bonanza, booming, opulent, thrifty, wealthy, well-off **08** affluent, blooming, thriving, well-to-do **09** fortunate **10** burgeoning, felicitous, successful, well-heeled, well-to-live **11** flourishing, rolling in it

**prostitute**
**03** pro, pug, tom **04** bawd, dell, drab, moll, punk, road, stew, tart **05** brass, broad, poule, quail, quiff, stale, tramp, trull, wench, whore **06** betray, bulker, callet, debase, demean, floosy, floozy, geisha, harlot, hooker, misuse, mutton, plover **07** cheapen, cocotte, degrade, devalue, floosie, floozie, hetaera, hetaira, hostess, hustler, lorette, pervert, polecat, profane, rent-boy, trollop, venture **08** bona-roba, call-girl, dolly-mop, magdalen, misapply, strumpet **09** courtesan, courtezan, hackneyed, hierodule, loose fish, mercenary, sacrifice, sex worker **10** cockatrice, convertite, fancy woman, loose woman, rough trade, vizard-mask **11** fallen woman, fille de joie, laced mutton, night-walker, poule de luxe, public woman, working girl **12** fille des rues, scarlet woman, street-walker **13** grande cocotte **14** lady of the night, woman of the town

**prostitution**
**04** vice **07** the game, whoring **08** harlotry, whoredom **10** social evil **13** street-walking

**prostrate**
**03** sap **04** fell, flat, laid, ruin, tire **05** all-in, crush, drain, level, prone **06** bushed, fallen, lay low, pooped **07** crushed, exhaust, fatigue, flatten, laid low, wear out, whacked, worn out **08** dead beat, flatling, flatlong, helpless, overcome, tired out, trailing **09** exhausted, flatlings, knock down, lying down, lying flat, overthrow, overwhelm, paralysed, pooped out, powerless **10** devastated, horizontal, procumbent **11** defenceless, overwhelmed, tuckered out

**• prostrate yourself**
**05** kneel **06** cringe, grovel, kowtow, submit **07** bow down **13** abase yourself

**prostration**
**03** bow **05** grief **06** kowtow **07** despair **08** collapse, kneeling, weakness **09** abasement, dejection, obeisance, paralysis, weariness **10** depression, desolation, exhaustion, submission **11** despondency **12** genuflection, helplessness **15** slough of despond

**protactinium**
**02** Pa

**protagonist**
**04** hero, lead **06** banker, leader **07** heroine **08** adherent, advocate, champion, exponent, mainstay **09** principal, proponent, supporter, title role **10** prime mover **12** moving spirit **13** leading figure, leading player, main character **14** chief character, standard-bearer

**protean**
◇ *anagram indicator*
**07** amoebic, mutable **08** variable, volatile **09** many-sided, mercurial, multiform, versatile **10** changeable, inconstant **11** polymorphic **12** ever-changing, polymorphous

**protect**
◇ *containment indicator*
**04** keep, save **05** cover, guard **06** defend, escort, screen, secure, shield **07** buckler, care for, harbour, shelter, support, warrant **08** bestride, conserve, enshield, keep safe, preserve, savegard **09** look after, ring-fence, safeguard, watch over **10** overshadow, strengthen, take care of

**protected**
**06** immune

**protection**
**03** lee **04** care, egis, ward, wing **05** aegis, bield, cover, guard **06** armour, asylum, buffer, charge, refuge, safety, screen, shield **07** barrier, buckler, bulwark, custody, defence, defense, shelter **08** security, umbrella, wardship **09** insurance, patronage, safeguard **11** concubinage, defensative, maintenance, safekeeping **12** conservation, entrenchment, guardianship, intrenchment, preservation

**• in protection from**
**04** agin **07** against

**protective**
**04** wary **06** condom **07** careful **08** armoured, covering, fatherly, maternal, motherly, paternal, vigilant, watchful **09** defensive, fireproof, shielding, windproof **10** insulating, possessive, sheltering, waterproof **14** over-protective

**protector**
**03** pad **04** faun **05** guard **06** buffer, father, keeper, minder, patron, regent, screen, shield **07** bolster, buckler, counsel, cushion, gardant **08** advocate, champion, Cromwell, defender, guardant, guardian, pectoral **09** bodyguard, safeguard **10** benefactor, protectrix **11** patron saint, protectress **12** father-figure

**protégé, protégée**
**04** ward **05** pupil **06** charge **07** student **08** disciple, follower **09** dependant, discovery **11** blue-eyed boy **14** white-headed boy

**protein**

*Proteins include:*

**03** TSP, TVP
**04** zein
**05** abrin, actin, opsin, prion, renin
**06** avidin, casein, cyclin, enzyme, fibrin, globin, gluten, kinase, lectin, leptin, myosin, papain, pepsin, rennin
**07** albumen, albumin, elastin, gliadin, histone, hordein, insulin, plasmin, sericin, trypsin, tubulin
**08** aleurone, amandine, collagen, cytokine, ferritin, gliadine, globulin, glutelin, integrin, lysozyme, protease, thrombin
**09** apoenzyme, fibrillin, invertase, isomerase, luciferin, myoglobin, phaseolin, prolamine, protamine, sclerotin
**10** calmodulin, complement, conchiolin, dystrophin, factor VIII, fibronogen, interferon
**11** angiostatin, angiotensin, haemoglobin, interleukin, lipoprotein, plasminogen, transferrin, tropomyosin
**12** immunoglobin, neurotrophin, proteoglycan
**13** ceruloplasmin, lactoglobulin

**protest**
**03** vow **04** avow, demo, fuss, riot **05** abhor, argue, demur, gripe, hikoi, march, sit in, sit-in **06** affirm, appeal, assert, attest, avowal, insist, object, obtest, oppose, outcry, picket, reject, squawk, strike, whinge, work-in **07** boycott, contend, declare, dissent, profess, reclaim, scruple, testify **08** announce, complain, demurral, disagree, insist on, maintain, proclaim, speak out **09** assertion, complaint, deprecate, down tools, exception, objection, take issue **10** contention, disapprove, go on strike, opposition, work to rule, work-to-rule **11** affirmation, attestation, declaration, demonstrate, disapproval, kick up a fuss, mass meeting, remonstrate **12** announcement, disagreement, hunger strike, proclamation, protestation, remonstrance **13** demonstration, remonstration, take exception

**• expression of protest**
**01** O **02** oh **03** say, why **04** come, I say!, what **07** come now **08** come come

**protestation**
**03** vow **04** oath **06** avowal, outcry, pledge **07** dissent, protest

**09** assurance, complaint, objection, statement, testimony **10** profession **11** affirmation, declaration **12** asseveration, disagreement, remonstrance **13** expostulation, remonstration

**protester**
**05** rebel **06** picket **07** opposer, striker **08** agitator, mutineer, objector, opponent **09** dissenter, dissident **10** complainer **11** Remonstrant **12** demonstrator

**protocol**
**02** IP **03** FTP, TCP, WAP **04** HTTP, IMAP, kawa, MIDI **05** TCP/IP **06** custom **07** decorum, manners, p's and q's **08** good form **09** etiquette, procedure, propriety **10** civilities, convention **11** formalities **15** code of behaviour

**prototype**
**04** type **05** model **06** mock-up **07** example, pattern **08** exemplar, original, paradigm, standard **09** archetype, precedent

**protract**
**06** extend, linger **07** drag out, draw out, prolong, spin out, sustain **08** continue, lengthen, postpone, protrude **09** keep going **10** make longer, stretch out

**protracted**
**04** long **07** endless, lengthy, spun out **08** drawn-out, extended, livelong, overlong **09** postponed, prolonged **12** interminable, long-drawn-out, stretched out

**protrude**
**03** jut, pop **04** peer, poke, pout **05** bulge, stick, strut **06** beetle, exsert, extend, goggle, jut out, strout **07** extrude, obtrude, poke out, project **08** protract, stand out, stick out **11** come through

**protruding**
**05** goofy, proud **06** astrut **07** jutting **09** exsertive, extrusive, extrusory, obtrusive, prominent, underhung **10** jutting out, protrudent, protrusive **11** protuberant, sticking out

**protrusion**
**03** jag, jut **04** bump, knob, lump **05** bulge **06** hernia **07** pedicle, process **08** shoulder, swelling **09** obtrusion, outgrowth **10** projection, staphyloma **11** cephalocele, eventration, meningocele **12** exophthalmia, exophthalmos, exophthalmus, protuberance **13** encephalocele

**protuberance**
**03** bud, nub **04** ball, boss, bulb, bump, hump, knap, knob, lump, nurl, teat, wame, wart, welt **05** bulge, caput, ergot, gemma, inion, knurl, mount, nodus, tuber, whelk **06** casque, nipple, paunch, pimple, tumour, venter, wallet **07** condyle, crankle, mamelon, mamilla, papilla, process **08** mammilla, pot-belly, swelling, tubercle **09** apophysis, beer belly, outgrowth **10** bulging-out, projection, prominence, protrusion **11** excrescence

**protuberant**
**04** full **05** proud **06** astrut, rotund **07** bottled, bulbous, bulging, bunched, gibbous, jutting, popping, swollen **08** beetling, swelling **09** exsertive, extrusive, extrusory, prominent **10** protrudent, protruding, protrusive

**proud**
**04** brag, glad, smug, vain **05** cocky, dicty, grand, happy, noble, stout **06** dickty, lordly, snooty, superb, worthy **07** content, haughty, jutting, notable, pleased, pompous, stately, stuck-up, sublime **08** arrogant, boastful, fearless, glorious, honoured, imposing, jumped-up, misproud, pleasing, proudful, puffed up, scornful, snobbish, splendid, swelling, thrilled, top-proud **09** bigheaded, cockhorse, conceited, contented, delighted, dignified, gratified, hubristic, imperious, memorable, prominent, red-letter, satisfied, untamable, wonderful **10** complacent, gratifying, high-handed, honourable, jutting out, marvellous, projecting, satisfying **11** egotistical, magnificent, outstanding, overbearing, overweening, protuberant, sticking out, toffee-nosed, walking tall **12** high-spirited, presumptuous, supercilious **13** high and mighty, self-important, self-satisfied **14** full of yourself, self-respecting

**proudly**
**04** brag **06** smugly, vainly **08** snootily **09** haughtily **10** arrogantly, boastfully **11** bigheadedly, conceitedly, contentedly, delightedly, with delight **14** appreciatively

**provable**
**08** testable **09** evincible **10** attestable, verifiable **11** confirmable **12** corroborable, demonstrable **13** establishable

**prove**
**03** try **04** shew, show, test, trie **05** argue, check **06** attest, pan out, prieve, suffer, try out, verify **07** analyse, bear out, certify, confirm, darrain, darrayn, deraign, examine, justify, make out, qualify, stand up, turn out **08** darraign, darraine, document, evidence, validate **09** ascertain, be the case, bring home, come about, darraigne, determine, establish, eventuate, transpire **10** experience **11** corroborate, demonstrate **12** authenticate, substantiate **13** bear witness to

**proven**
**05** tried, valid **06** proved, tested **07** checked **08** accepted, attested, definite, reliable, verified **09** authentic, certified, confirmed, undoubted **10** dependable **11** established, trustworthy **12** corroborated

**provenance**
**06** origin, source, spring **10** birthplace, derivation **11** provenience

**provender**
**03** kai **04** chow, eats, fare, feed, food, grub, nosh, tuck **05** scoff **06** fodder, forage, stores, tucker, viands **07** aliment, edibles, pabulum, pasture, provand, provend, rations **08** eatables, proviant, supplies, victuals **09** groceries, repasture **10** foodstuffs, provisions, sustenance **11** comestibles

**proverb**
**03** saw **05** adage, axiom, gnome, maxim, motto **06** byword, dictum, saying **07** parable, precept **08** aphorism, paroemia **10** apophthegm, whakatauki

**proverbial**
**05** famed **06** famous **07** typical **08** accepted, infamous, renowned **09** axiomatic, customary, legendary, notorious, well-known **10** archetypal **11** traditional **12** acknowledged, conventional, time-honoured

**provide**
◇ *anagram indicator*
**02** do **03** add **04** give, lend, suit **05** allow, besee, bring, cater, equip, lay on, offer, put on, serve, state, stock, yield **06** afford, fit out, impart, kit out, outfit, purvey, supply **07** compare, furnish, lay down, plan for, prepare, present, require, specify **09** stipulate, take steps **10** anticipate, arrange for, contribute, prepare for **11** accommodate **12** make plans for, take measures **13** make provision **15** take precautions

• **provide for**
**04** fend, keep **05** besee, cover, do for, endow **07** support, sustain **08** maintain **09** look after **10** take care of

**provided**
**02** so **05** given **06** sobeit **08** as long as, assuming, so long as **09** presuming **10** in the event **11** on condition **14** with the proviso

**providence**
**04** care, fate, luck **06** thrift, wisdom **07** caution, destiny, economy, fortune **08** disaster, God's will, prudence, sagacity **09** foresight, judgement **11** forethought **13** judiciousness **14** circumspection, far-sightedness

**provident**
**06** frugal **07** careful, prudent, thrifty **08** cautious **09** judicious, sagacious **10** economical, far-sighted **11** circumspect

**providential**
**05** happy, lucky **06** timely **07** welcome **09** fortunate, opportune **10** convenient, fortuitous, heaven-sent

**providentially**
**07** happily, luckily **11** coveniently, fortunately, opportunely **12** fortuitously

**provider**
**05** angel, donor, giver **06** earner, funder, patron, source **07** sponsor **08** mainstay, supplier **09** supporter **10** benefactor, wage-earner **11** breadwinner

**providing**
**02** if **05** given **08** as long as, assuming, provided **09** presuming **10** in the event **11** on condition **14** with the proviso

**province**
**04** area, dorp, duty, line, nome, role, zone **05** field, realm, reame, shire, state **06** charge, circar, colony, county, domain, office, pigeon, region, sircar, sirkar, sphere **07** concern, eparchy, mudiria, rectory, satrapy, vilayet **08** business, district, function, mudirieh **09** backwater, backwoods, eparchate, territory, the sticks **10** department, dependency, the boonies **12** patriarchate, the boondocks **14** responsibility **15** middle of nowhere

*Canadian provinces and territories:*

**05** Yukon
**06** Quebec
**07** Alberta, Nunavut, Ontario
**08** Labrador, Manitoba
**10** Nova Scotia
**12** New Brunswick, Newfoundland, Saskatchewan
**14** Yukon Territory
**15** British Columbia
**18** Prince Edward Island
**20** Northwest Territories
**23** Newfoundland and Labrador

*Ireland's ancient provinces:*

**06** Ulster
**07** Munster
**08** Connacht, Leinster

*New Zealand provinces:*

**05** Otago
**06** Nelson
**08** Auckland, Taranaki, Westland
**09** Fiordland, Hawke's Bay, Northland, Southland
**10** Canterbury, Wellington
**11** Marlborough

*South African provinces:*

**07** Gauteng, Limpopo
**09** Free State, North West
**10** Mpumalanga
**11** Eastern Cape, Western Cape
**12** KwaZulu-Natal, Northern Cape

**provincial**
**04** hick **05** local, naive, rural, yokel **06** narrow, rustic **07** country, hayseed, insular, limited, peasant **08** mofussil, outlying, regional, suburban **09** hillbilly, home-grown, parochial, presidial, small-town **10** intolerant, parish-pump, unpolished **11** small-minded **12** narrow-minded **13** inward-looking **14** country bumpkin **15** unsophisticated

**provincialism**
**08** localism **10** insularity, Patavinity **11** regionalism **12** parochialism, sectionalism **13** provinciality

**provision**
**04** food, plan, step, term **05** rider, stock, store, stuff **06** clause, giving, stocks, stores, supply, viands **07** measure, proviso, rations, service **08** eatables, services, supplies, victuals **09** allowance, amenities, condition, equipping, foodstuff, groceries, resources, stouthrie **10** concession, facilities, furnishing, outfitting, precaution, stoutherie, sustenance **11** arrangement, contingency, preparation, requirement, stipulation **12** contribution **13** qualification, specification

**provisional**
**05** Provo **06** pro tem **07** interim, stopgap **09** makeshift, temporary, tentative **11** conditional, pencilled in **12** transitional

**provisionally**
**06** pro tem **07** interim **09** meanwhile **11** temporarily, tentatively **15** for the time being

**proviso**
**04** term **05** rider **06** clause **07** strings **09** condition, provision **10** limitation **11** requirement, reservation, restriction, stipulation **13** qualification

**provocation**
**04** dare **05** cause, taunt **06** injury, insult, motive, reason **07** affront, grounds, offence **08** angering, enraging, stimulus, vexation **09** annoyance, challenge, eliciting, grievance **10** generation, incitement, inducement, irritation, motivation, production **11** aggravation, inspiration, instigation, stimulation **12** exasperation **13** justification

**provocative**
**04** sexy **05** tarty **06** erotic **07** abusive, galling, piquant, teasing **08** alluring, annoying, arousing, exciting, inviting, tempting **09** insulting, in-yer-face, offensive, seductive **10** in-your-face, irritating, outrageous, suggestive **11** aggravating, challenging, infuriating, stimulating, tantalizing, titillating **12** exasperating

**provocatively**
**06** sexily **08** sexually **10** alluringly, annoyingly, erotically, invitingly, temptingly **11** offensively, seductively **12** outrageously, suggestively **13** infuriatingly **14** exasperatingly

**provoke**
**03** bug, vex **04** goad, miff, move, nark, prod, rile, spur, stir **05** anger, annoy, cause, egg on, evoke, get at, pique, rouse, sound, taunt, tease **06** appeal, elicit, enrage, entice, excite, harass, hassle, incite, induce, insult, kindle, madden, needle, nettle, offend, prompt, summon, wind up **07** incense, inflame, inspire, produce, promote **08** drive mad, engender, generate, irritate, motivate, occasion **09** aggravate, call forth, challenge, infuriate, instigate, stimulate, tantalize **10** drive crazy, exacerbate, exasperate, give rise to **12** drive bananas **13** make sparks fly **14** drive up the wall

**provoking**
**06** irking, vexing **07** agaçant, galling, irksome **08** agaçante, annoying, tiresome **09** maddening, offensive, vexatious **10** irritating **11** aggravating, infuriating, obstructive, stimulating **12** exasperating

**prow**
**03** bow **04** bows, fore, head, nose, ship, stem **05** front, prore **07** valiant **08** cut-water, forepart

**prowess**
**04** grit, guts **05** nerve, pluck, skill, spunk **06** bottle, daring, genius, talent, valour **07** ability, bravery, command, courage, heroism, mastery **08** aptitude, audacity, facility **09** adeptness, dexterity, expertise, gallantry, vassalage **10** adroitness, attainment, capability **11** intrepidity, proficiency, skilfulness **12** fearlessness **13** dauntlessness **14** accomplishment

**prowl**
**04** hunt, lurk, nose, roam, rove **05** creep, lurch, mouse, prole, proll, proul, range, ratch, skulk, slink, sneak, snoke, snook, snoop, snowk, stalk, steal **06** cruise, patrol, search **08** scavenge **14** move stealthily

**prowler**
**06** patrol, proler, roamer **07** proller, prouler, stalker **08** tenebrio **09** nighthawk, scavenger

**proximity**
**08** nearness, vicinity **09** adjacency, closeness **10** contiguity **11** propinquity **13** juxtaposition, neighbourhood

**proxy**
**05** agent **06** deputy, factor **07** stand-in **08** attorney, delegate **09** surrogate **10** substitute **14** representative
• **by proxy**
**02** pp

**prude**
**04** prig **07** old maid, puritan **09** Mrs Grundy **10** goody-goody, schoolmarm

**prudence**
**04** care **05** Metis **06** policy, saving, thrift, wisdom **07** caution, economy **08** planning, sagacity, wariness **09** canniness, foresight, frugality, good sense, husbandry, judgement, vigilance **10** discretion, precaution, providence **11** advisedness, common sense, forethought, happy medium,

heedfulness, penny-wisdom
**12** cautiousness, preparedness
**13** judiciousness **14** circumspection, far-sightedness **15** circumspectness

**prudent**
**04** ware, wary, wise **06** frugal, shrewd
**07** careful, politic, thrifty **08** cautious, discreet, sensible, vigilant **09** judicious, provident, sagacious **10** discerning, economical, far-sighted
**11** circumspect, ware and wise, well-advised, wise-hearted
**13** considerative

**prudently**
**06** warily, wisely **08** sensibly, shrewdly
**09** advisedly, carefully **10** discreetly, vigilantly **11** providently
**12** economically, far-sightedly

**prudery**
**08** primness **09** Grundyism
**10** prissiness, puritanism, strictness, stuffiness **11** overmodesty, starchiness
**12** priggishness **13** squeamishness
**14** old-maidishness

**prudish**
**04** prim **05** mimsy **06** demure, mimsey, prissy, proper, stuffy **07** po-faced, starchy **08** overnice, priggish, pudibund **09** squeamish, Victorian
**10** goody-goody, old-maidish, overmodest **11** puritanical, strait-laced
**12** narrow-minded **13** schoolmarmish, ultra-virtuous

**prune**
**03** cut, lop **04** clip, dock, pare, plum, sned, snip, spur, trim **05** preen, proin, proyn, shape, shred **06** cut off, dehorn, prewyn, proign, proine, proyne, pruine, reduce, reform, switch **07** cut back, shorten **08** prunello **10** French plum

**prurient**
**04** blue, lewd **05** dirty **06** erotic, smutty **07** itching, lustful, obscene
**08** desirous, indecent **09** lecherous, salacious **10** cupidinous, lascivious, libidinous **11** voyeuristic
**12** concupiscent, pornographic

**pry**
**03** dig **04** nose, peep, peer, poke, toot
**05** delve, prise, snoop **06** ferret, meddle **07** gumshoe, intrude
**08** prodnose **09** interfere
**10** stickybeak **12** put your oar in
**14** poke your nose in **15** stick your nose in

**prying**
**04** nosy **05** nosey, peery **06** snoopy, spying **07** curious, peering
**08** meddling, snooping **09** intrusive
**10** meddlesome **11** inquisitive, interfering

**psalm**
**02** Ps **03** Psa **04** hymn, poem, song
**05** chant, paean, tract **06** choral, prayer, proper, venite **07** cantate, chorale, introit, tractus **08** canticle, Jubilate, Miserere **09** neckverse
**10** paraphrase

**psalm tune**
**04** tone

**pseud**
**04** sham **05** false, fraud, poser
**06** humbug, phoney, poseur, trendy
**11** pretentious

**pseudo**
**04** fake, mock, sham **05** bogus, false, pseud, quasi- **06** ersatz, phoney
**08** spurious **09** imitation, pretended, ungenuine **10** artificial **11** counterfeit, pretentious

**pseudonym**
**05** alias **06** anonym **07** allonym, pen-name **09** false name, incognito, stage name **10** nom de plume **11** assumed name, nom de guerre

*Pseudonyms include:*

**03** **Day** (Doris), **Pop** (Iggy), **Tey** (Josephine)
**04** **Alda** (Alan), **Bell** (Acton), **Bell** (Currer), **Bell** (Ellis), **Cage** (Nicolas), **Dors** (Diana), **Ford** (Ford Madox), **Gish** (Lillian Diana), **Hite** (Shere), **Holm** (Sir Ian), **John** (Sir Elton), **Lulu**, **Lynn** (Dame Vera), **Piaf** (Edith), **Reed** (Lou), **Rhys** (Jean), **Ross** (Diana), **Saki**, **Sand** (George), **West** (Dame Rebecca), **West** (Nathanael), **Wood** (Natalie), **York** (Susannah)
**05** **Allen** (Woody), **Bizet** (Georges), **Black** (Cilla), **Bowie** (David), **Caine** (Sir Michael), **Clark** (Petula), **Cline** (Patsy), **Dylan** (Bob), **Eliot** (George), **Flynn** (Errol), **Garbo** (Greta), **Gorky** (Maxim), **Grant** (Cary), **Grant** (Richard E), **Hardy** (Oliver), **Henry** (O), **Holly** (Buddy), **Jason** (David), **Keith** (Penelope), **Lanza** (Mario), **Leigh** (Vivien), **Loren** (Sophia), **Moore** (Demi), **Moore** (Julianne), **Niven** (David), **Queen** (Ellery), **Ryder** (Winona), **Scott** (Ronnie), **Seuss** (Dr), **Smith** (Stevie), **Solti** (Sir Georg), **Stern** (Daniel), **Sting**, **Twain** (Mark), **Wayne** (John), **Welch** (Raquel)
**06** **Bacall** (Lauren), **Bardot** (Brigitte), **Berlin** (Irving), **Brooks** (Mel), **Burton** (Richard), **Conrad** (Joseph), **Crosby** (Bing), **Curtis** (Tony), **Fields** (Dame Gracie), **Foster** (Jodie), **France** (Anatole), **Gibbon** (Lewis Grassic), **Harlow** (Jean), **Heston** (Charlton), **Irving** (Sir Henry), **Jolson** (Al), **Keaton** (Diane), **Laurel** (Stan), **London** (Jack), **Lugosi** (Bela), **McBain** (Ed), **Mirren** (Helen), **Monroe** (Marilyn), **Morton** (Jelly Roll), **Neeson** (Liam), **Orwell** (George), **Peters** (Ellis), **Rogers** (Ginger), **Salten** (Felix), **Sapper**, **Scales** (Prunella), **Simone** (Nina), **Spacey** (Kevin), **Steele** (Tommy), **Turner** (Lana), **Turner** (Tina), **Waters** (Muddy), **Weldon** (Fay), **Wesley** (Mary), **Wonder** (Stevie)
**07** **Andrews** (Dame Julie), **Bachman** (Richard), **Bennett** (Tony), **Bogarde** (Sir Dirk), **Bronson** (Charles), **Carroll** (Lewis), **Deneuve** (Catherine), **Dinesen** (Isak), **Douglas** (Kirk), **Gardner** (Ava), **Garland** (Judy), **Hepburn** (Audrey), **Higgins** (Jack), **Holiday** (Billie), **Jacques** (Hattie), **Karloff** (Boris), **Kincaid** (Jamaica), **Le Carré** (John), **Lindsay** (Robert), **Lombard** (Carole), **Matthau** (Walter), **Mercury** (Freddie), **Michael** (George), **Miranda** (Carmen), **Molière**, **Montand** (Yves), **Novello** (Ivor), **Richard** (Sir Cliff), **Robbins** (Harold), **Russell** (Lillian), **Shepard** (Sam), **Swanson** (Gloria), **Wyndham** (John), **Wynette** (Tammy)
**08** **Bancroft** (Anne), **Coltrane** (Robbie), **Coolidge** (Susan), **Costello** (Elvis), **Crawford** (Joan), **Dietrich** (Marlene), **Gershwin** (George), **Gershwin** (Ira), **Goldberg** (Whoopi), **Hayworth** (Rita), **Kingsley** (Ben), **MacLaine** (Shirley), **Ma Rainey**, **Pickford** (Mary), **Robinson** (Edward G), **Sly Stone**, **Stanwyck** (Barbara), **Stoppard** (Tom), **Voltaire**, **Williams** (Tennessee)
**09** **Bernhardt** (Sarah), **Bo Diddley**, **Charteris** (Leslie), **Fairbanks** (Douglas), **Lancaster** (Burt), **Leadbelly**, **Offenbach** (Jacques), **Streisand** (Barbra), **Valentino** (Rudolph)
**10** **Howlin' Wolf**, **Washington** (Dinah), **Westmacott** (Mary)
**11** **Springfield** (Dusty)

**pshaw**
**03** och

**psych**
• **psych out**
**03** cow **05** alarm, appal, bully, daunt, get to, scare, throw, upset **06** coerce, compel, dismay, lean on, menace, rattle
**07** overawe, terrify, warn off
**08** browbeat, bulldoze, domineer, frighten, pressure, unsettle
**09** terrorize, tyrannize **10** intimidate, pressurize **13** put off balance, turn the heat on **14** put the screws on
• **psych yourself up**
**13** brace yourself, nerve yourself, steel yourself **14** gear yourself up, pluck up courage, work yourself up

**psyche**
**04** mind, self, soul **05** anima
**06** pneuma, spirit **09** awareness, inner self, intellect **10** inmost self
**11** personality **12** intelligence, subconscious **13** consciousness, heart of hearts, individuality, innermost self, understanding **15** deepest feelings

**psychiatrist**
**06** shrink **07** analyst **08** alienist
**09** therapist **10** head doctor, psychiater
**12** headshrinker, psychologist, trick cyclist **13** psychoanalyst
**14** psychoanalyser **15** man in a white coat, psychotherapist

*Psychiatrists and psychoanalysts include:*

**04** **Beck** (Aaron), **Jung** (Carl), **Rank** (Otto)
**05** **Adler** (Alfred), **Clare** (Anthony), **Freud** (Anna), **Freud** (Sigmund), **Fromm** (Erich), **Jones** (Ernest), **Klein** (Melanie), **Lacan** (Jacques), **Laing** (Ronald David), **Meyer** (Adolf), **Reich** (Wilhelm), **Szasz** (Thomas)
**06** **Berger** (Hans), **Bowlby** (John), **Hitzig** (Julius), **Snyder** (Solomon)
**07** **Bleuler** (Eugen), **Erikson** (Erik), **Persaud** (Raj)
**08** **Maudsley** (Henry), **Sullivan** (Harry Stack), **Wernicke** (Carl)
**09** **Alexander** (Franz), **Alzheimer** (Alois), **Kraepelin** (Emil), **Menninger** (Karl), **Rorschach** (Hermann)
**11** **Krafft-Ebing** (Richard, von)
**13** **Wagner-Jauregg** (Julius)

*See also* **psychology**

## psychic

**04** seer **05** augur **06** medium, mental, mystic, occult, oracle **07** diviner, prophet **08** mystical, telepath **09** cognitive, emotional, spiritual, visionary **10** mind-reader, prophetess, soothsayer, telepathic **11** clairvoyant, telekinetic **12** extrasensory, intellectual, supernatural **13** fortune-teller, psychological **14** spiritualistic

**psychoanalyst** *see* **psychiatrist**

## psychological

**06** mental, unreal **08** cerebral
**09** cognitive, emotional, imaginary
**10** conceptual, irrational, subjective
**11** theoretical, unconscious **12** all in the mind, intellectual, subconscious
**13** psychosomatic

## psychologically

**08** mentally **11** cognitively, emotionally
**12** conceptually, subjectively
**13** theoretically, unconsciously
**14** intellectually

## psychology

**04** mind **06** habits, make-up
**07** mindset, motives **08** conation, hedonics, psychics **09** attitudes
**10** child-study, gestaltism
**12** pneumatology **14** metapsychology, study of the mind **15** mental chemistry

*Branches of psychology include:*

**03** bio
**04** para
**05** child, depth, neuro, sport
**06** health, social
**07** abnormal, clinical, criminal, forensic
**08** hedonics
**09** cognitive, narrative
**10** industrial, structural
**11** educational
**12** evolutionary, experimental, occupational
**13** developmental, environmental, psychobiology, psychometrics, transpersonal
**14** organizational, psychoanalysis
**15** psychopathology

*Psychology theories include:*

**07** atomism, Gestalt, Jungian
**08** Adlerian, Freudian, Jamesian, Lacanian
**09** cognitive, Pavlovian
**10** functional, humanistic, Skinnerian, structural
**11** behavioural, personality
**13** connectionism, functionalism, structuralism
**14** associationism, psychoanalytic

*Psychological conditions and disorders include:*

**06** autism, manias
**07** agnosia, bulimia, phobias
**08** dementia, neurosis, paranoia
**09** addiction, anhedonia, Asperger's, psychosis, Tourette's
**10** abreaction, Alzheimer's, blindsight, depression, dysmorphia, Munchausen, sociopathy
**11** kleptomania, psychopathy
**12** hypochondria
**13** acatamathesia, battle fatigue, schizophrenia
**15** anorexia nervosa, bipolar disorder

*Psychological therapies include:*

**03** art
**05** drama, group, hypno
**06** colour, psycho
**07** Gestalt
**08** aversion
**09** cognitive
**10** regression
**11** behavioural, counselling
**12** electroshock
**13** interpersonal, person-centred, psychodynamic

*Psychologists include:*

**04** **Bain** (Alexander)
**05** **Binet** (Alfred), **James** (William), **Pratt** (Joseph Gaither), **Rhine** (Joseph Banks)
**06** **De Bono** (Edward), **Kinsey** (Alfred Charles), **Morris** (Robert Lyle), **Murphy** (Gardner), **Piaget** (Jean), **Pinker** (Steven), **Terman** (Lewis Madison)
**07** **Cattell** (Raymond Bernard), **Eysenck** (Hans Jürgen), **Skinner** (Burrhus Frederic)
**09** **Thorndike** (Edward Lee)
**10** **Wertheimer** (Max)

*See also* **psychiatrist**

## psychopath

**06** madman, maniac, psycho
**07** lunatic **08** madwoman **09** mad person, psychotic, sociopath

## psychopathic

**03** mad **06** insane, psycho **07** lunatic
**08** demented, deranged, maniacal
**09** psychotic **10** unbalanced

## psychosomatic

**06** unreal **09** imaginary **10** irrational, subjective **12** all in the mind
**13** psychological

## psychotic

**03** fey **04** bats, gyte, loco, nuts, wild **05** barmy, batty, buggy, crazy, daffy, dippy, dotty, flaky, gonzo, loony, loopy, manic, nutty, potty, queer, wacko, wacky, wiggy **06** crazed, cuckoo, fruity, insane, maniac, mental, raving, red-mad, screwy **07** bananas, barking, berserk, bonkers, cracked, frantic, lunatic, meshuga **08** crackers, demented, deranged, dingbats, doolally, frenetic, frenzied, maniacal, unhinged, unstable **09** disturbed, lymphatic, up the wall **10** bestraught, distracted, distraught, frantic-mad, off the wall, off your nut, out to lunch, stone-crazy, unbalanced **11** not all there, off the rails, off your head **12** mad as a hatter, off your chump, round the bend **13** off your rocker, of unsound mind, out of your head, out of your mind, out of your tree, round the twist **14** off your trolley, wrong in the head **15** non compos mentis, out of your senses

## ptarmigan

**04** rype

**pub** *see* **public house**

## puberty

**05** teens, youth **08** maturity
**09** growing up **10** pubescence
**11** adolescence **12** teenage years
**14** young adulthood

## public

**03** out **04** fans, open **05** civic, civil, crowd, known, overt, plain, state **06** buyers, common, famous, masses, nation, people, social, tavern, voters **07** country, eminent, exposed, federal, general, obvious, patrons, popular, society **08** audience, citizens, communal, everyone, national, official, populace **09** available, clientèle, community, consumers, customers, followers, important, multitude, prominent, published, respected, universal, well-known **10** accessible, celebrated, collective, electorate, government, population, recognized, spectators, supporters, widespread **11** illustrious, influential, unconcealed **12** acknowledged, nationalized, unrestricted **13** international

• **in public**

**06** openly **08** publicly **09** in the open **10** in full view **11** for all to see

## public house

**02** PH **03** bar, inn, pub **04** houf, howf **05** grill, hotel, houff, house, howff, local, table **06** boozer, lounge, saloon, shanty, tavern **07** brewpub, canteen, counter, potshop, shebeen, taproom, wine bar **08** ale house, bona fide, groggery, hostelry **09** brasserie, free house, gin palace, jerry-shop, lounge bar, lush-house **12** watering-hole

*Public house names include:*

**04** Bell, Bull, Ship, Swan
**05** Crown, Globe

06 Anchor, Castle, George, New Inn, Plough
07 Railway, Red Lion
08 Green Man, Nags Head, Royal Oak, Victoria
09 Black Bull, Cross Keys, King's Arms, King's Head, White Hart, White Lion, White Swan
10 Black Horse, Golden Lion, Queen's Head, Wheatsheaf, White Horse
12 Fox and Hounds, Rose and Crown
13 Hare and Hounds, Prince of Wales
14 Coach and Horses
15 George and Dragon

**publican**
**04** host **06** barman **07** barmaid, tapster **08** hotelier, landlady, landlord, mine host, taverner **09** barperson, bartender, innkeeper, tax farmer **11** hotel-keeper **12** saloon-keeper, tax collector

**publication**
**04** book, buik, buke **05** daily, forum, issue, title **06** serial, volume, weekly **07** booklet, fanzine, journal, leaflet, monthly, release **08** brochure, handbill, hardback, magazine, pamphlet, printing **09** newspaper, paperback, quarterly, reporting **10** disclosure, half-yearly, newsletter, periodical, production, publishing **11** circulation, declaration, festschrift **12** announcement, broadcasting, distribution, notification, proclamation
• **prepare for publication**
**04** edit

**publicity**
**03** air **04** hype, plug, puff **05** boost **06** splash **07** acclaim, build-up, réclame **08** ballyhoo **09** attention, limelight, marketing, notoriety, promotion **10** propaganda **11** advertising
• **publicity agent**
**02** PA

**publicize**
**04** hype, plug, push **05** blaze **06** market **07** promote **08** announce, headline **09** advertise, broadcast, make known, spotlight **10** make public, promulgate **11** disseminate

**public-spirited**
**08** generous **09** unselfish **10** altruistic, charitable **12** humanitarian **13** conscientious, philanthropic **15** community-minded

**public transport** *see* **transport**

**publish**
**03** run **04** vent **05** carry, issue, print, sound **06** delate, import, notice, notify, pirate, poster, put out, report, reveal, spread **07** declare, diffuse, divulge, gazette, placard, produce, release **08** announce, bring out, disclose, evulgate, proclaim, put about, put forth, set forth **09** advertise, broadcast, celebrate, circulate, divulgate, fulminate, give forth, make known, paperback, paragraph, publicize, serialize, syndicate **10** distribute, make public, promulgate **11** communicate, disseminate
*See also* **printing**

*Publishers and imprints include:*

02 DK
03 CUP, OUP, Pan
04 Reed
05 Corgi, Letts, Orion
06 Europa, Puffin, Viking, Virago
07 A&C Black, Berlitz, Cassell, Collins, Longman, Merriam, Methuen, Pearson, Picador, Pimlico, Usborne
08 BBC Books, Chambers, Everyman, Flamingo, Gollancz, Ladybird, Larousse, Michelin, Palgrave
09 Allen Lane, Black Swan, Blackwell, Doubleday, Harlequin, Heinemann, Macmillan, Routledge
10 Allen & Unwin, Bloomsbury, Bodley Head, Faber & Faber, Hutchinson, McGraw-Hill, Paul Hamlyn, Scholastic, Times Books, Transworld
11 Bantam Press, Bertelsmann, Fodor Guides, Rand McNally, Random House, Rough Guides
12 André Deutsch, Butterworths, Chatto & Windus, Edward Arnold, Fourth Estate, Jonathan Cape, Lonely Planet, Mills and Boon, Penguin Books, Reed Elsevier, Sweet & Maxwell, Thames & Hudson
13 AOL/Time Warner, Atlantic Books, Hachette Livre, HarperCollins, Reader's Digest, Little, Brown & Co, Secker & Warburg, Simon & Schuster
14 Canongate Books, Chambers Harrap, Chrysalis Books, Hodder Headline, Springer-Verlag
15 Houghton Mifflin, Mitchell Beazley

**pucker**
**04** fold, ruck, shir **05** pleat, purse, shirr **06** cockle, crease, furrow, gather, ruckle, ruffle **07** crinkle, crumple, screw up, shrivel, wrinkle **08** compress, contract **09** agitation, confusion **11** corrugation

**puckered**
**05** pursy **06** plissé, rucked **07** bullate, creased, ruckled **08** gathered, wrinkled

**puckering**
**04** shir **05** shirr

**puckish**
**03** sly **06** impish **07** naughty, playful, roguish, teasing, waggish **08** sportive **09** whimsical **10** frolicsome **11** mischievous

**pudding**
**03** pie, pud **04** tart **05** sweet **06** afters, pastry **07** dessert
*See also* **cake**; **dessert**

**puddle**
**03** dub, sop **04** pant, pool, slop, soss, sump **05** flush, plash, plesh **06** muddle **07** muddler, plashet

**puddock**
**04** frog, toad

**puerile**
**05** inane, silly **07** babyish, foolish, trivial **08** childish, immature, juvenile, trifling **09** infantile **10** adolescent **13** irresponsible

**Puerto Rico**
**03** PRI

**puff**
**02** ad **04** blow, drag, draw, fuff, gasp, gulp, gust, huff, pant, plug, pull, push, suck, toke, waff, waft, waif **05** blast, extol, flaff, pluff, skiff, smoke, swell, whiff, whift **06** breath, expand, flatus, flurry, market, praise, wheeze **07** breathe, commend, draught, inflate, promote **09** advertise, marketing, promotion, publicity, publicize **10** homosexual **11** ostentation **12** commendation **13** advertisement
• **puff out**
**03** bag, sag **04** bulb, hump **05** belly, bloat, bulge, heave, swell **06** bepuff, billow, blouse, dilate, expand **07** balloon, distend, enlarge, project **08** protrude

**puffed**
**06** done in, winded **07** gasping, panting **08** inflated **09** distended, exhausted **10** breathless **11** out of breath
• **puffed up**
**05** bloat, elate, proud **06** pluffy **07** swollen, ventose **08** arrogant, prideful **09** bigheaded **13** high and mighty, self-important, swollen-headed **14** full of yourself

**puffin**
**08** rock-bird, Tom-noddy **09** sea parrot **10** Fratercula **11** Tammie Norie

**puffy**
**05** pursy **07** bloated, dilated, swollen **08** engorged, enlarged, inflated, puffed up **09** bombastic, distended **10** oedematous

**pugilism**
**04** ring **06** boxing **07** the ring **08** fighting, fistiana, the fancy **11** the noble art **12** the prize-ring **13** prize-fighting **15** the noble science

**pugilist**
**03** ham, pug **05** boxer **07** bruiser, fighter **12** prize-fighter

**pugnacious**
**07** hostile **09** bellicose, combative **10** aggressive **11** bad-tempered, belligerent, contentious, hot-tempered, quarrelsome **12** antagonistic, disputatious **13** argumentative

**puke**
**03** cat **04** barf, boke, honk, sick, spew **05** heave, retch, vomit **06** emesis, emetic, sick up **07** bring up, chuck up, chunder, fetch up, throw up, upchuck **08** disgorge, parbreak, retching **10** egurgitate **11** regurgitate

**pull**
**03** lug, rip, row, tow, tug **04** drag, draw, fire, haul, jerk, lure, raid, sole, sowl, suck, sway, tear, turn, yank **05** charm, clout, heave, pluck, power, proof, soole, sowle, steal, tempt, trail, tweak **06** allure, arrest, damage, entice, muscle, pull in, pull up, remove, snatch, sprain, strain, twitch, uproot, weight, wrench **07** attract, bring in, draught, draw out, extract, pull out, root out, stretch, take out **08** exertion, withdraw **09** advantage, dislocate, influence, magnetism, magnetize **10** allurement, attraction, resistance **12** drawing power, forcefulness

**• pull apart**
**03** pan **04** part, pick, slam **05** slate **06** attack **07** run down **08** demolish, distrain, separate **09** criticize, dismantle, dismember, take apart, tear apart **11** pick holes in **12** pick to pieces, pull to pieces, take to pieces, tear to shreds **15** do a hatchet job on

**• pull back**
**04** draw **06** retire **07** back out, retreat **08** draw back, fall back, withdraw **09** disengage

**• pull down**
**07** destroy, unbuild **08** bulldoze, demolish, take down **09** dismantle, knock down **10** dilapidate **15** raze to the ground

**• pull in**
**03** nab **04** book, bust, draw, earn, halt, lure, make, nick, park, stop **05** clear, run in, seize **06** allure, arrest, arrive, be paid, collar, detain, draw in, entice, pull up, rake in **07** attract, bring in, capture, collect, receive **08** take home **09** apprehend **15** take into custody

**• pull off**
**05** pluck **06** detach, fulfil, manage, remove, rip off **07** achieve, succeed, take off, tear off **08** bring off, carry off, carry out, separate **10** accomplish

**• pull out**
**04** quit **05** leave **06** depart, desert **07** abandon, back out, draw out, move out, pluck up, retreat **08** evacuate, withdraw

**• pull through**
**05** rally **07** improve, recover, survive, weather **09** get better **10** recuperate **11** come through **12** get well again

**• pull together**
**04** draw **05** rally **06** team up **09** co-operate **11** collaborate **12** work together

**• pull up**
**04** balk, halt, park, stop **05** baulk, blame, brake, chide, scold **06** arrest, berate, carpet, draw up, pull in, rebuke, uproot, uptear **07** censure, lecture, reprove, tell off, tick off **08** admonish, draw rein, pull over **09** castigate, criticize, eradicate, reprimand **10** take to task **11** come to a halt **14** read the riot act

**• pull yourself together**
**11** snap out of it **15** buck up your ideas, control yourself

**pulled up**
**02** pu

**pulley**
**04** swig

**pullover**
**03** top **06** jersey, jumper, woolly **07** sweater, tank top **10** sweatshirt **11** windcheater

**pulp**
**03** pap **04** beat, gush, mash, mush, must, pith **05** chyme, cream, crush, flesh, gloop, paste, pound, purée, shred, slush **06** bathos, marrow, pomace, squash **07** furnish **08** nonsense, schmaltz **09** corniness, liquidize, nostalgia, pulverize, triturate **10** sloppiness, tenderness **11** mawkishness, romanticism **12** chemical wood, emotionalism **14** sentimentalism, sentimentality

**pulpit**
**03** tub **04** ambo, dais, desk, tent, wood **05** stand **06** mimbar, minbar, podium **07** lectern, rostrum, soapbox **08** platform **11** three-decker

**pulpy**
**04** soft **05** mushy, pappy **06** fleshy, sloppy **07** baccate, crushed, squashy **09** succulent

**pulsate**
**04** beat, drum, thud **05** pound, pulse, throb, thump **06** hammer, quiver **07** vibrate **09** oscillate, palpitate

**pulsating**
**07** pulsing **09** pulsatile, pulsative, pulsatory, vibratile, vibrating, vibrative **11** oscillating, palpitating

**pulsation**
**04** beat **05** ictus, throb **07** beating **09** heartbeat, throbbing, vibration **11** oscillation, palpitation **12** vibratiuncle

**pulse**
**03** dal, pea **04** bean, beat, daal, dahl, dhal, drum, gram, thud, tick **05** pound, throb, thump **06** legume, rhythm, stroke, thrill **07** beating, flutter, pulsate, vibrate **08** drumming, pounding, sphygmus, thudding, thumping **09** calavance, caravance, pulsation, throbbing, vibration **11** oscillation

*See also* **bean**

**pulverize**
◇ *anagram indicator*
**04** mill, pulp **05** crush, grind, pound, smash **06** bruise, defeat, hammer, powder, squash, thrash **07** crumble, destroy **08** demolish, vanquish **09** comminute, triturate **10** annihilate **12** contriturate

**puma**
**05** tiger **06** cougar **07** couguar, panther **09** catamount **12** mountain lion

**pummel**
◇ *anagram indicator*
**03** fib, hit **04** bang, beat, soak **05** knock, pound, punch, thump **06** batter, hammer, pommel, strike

**pump**
**03** jet **04** draw, gush, push, quiz, send **05** drain, drive, force, grill, spout, spurt, surge **06** bowser, inject, siphon **08** inflater, inflator **09** grease gun, hydropult **11** interrogate **12** cross-examine **13** cross-question **14** put the screws on

*See also* **footwear**

**• pump out**
**05** drain, empty **06** siphon **07** bail out, draw off **08** force out

**• pump up**
**04** fill **06** blow up, puff up **07** inflate **08** increase

**pumpkin**
**06** cashaw, cushaw **07** pompion, pumpion **12** Jack-o'-lantern **14** Queensland blue **15** vegetable marrow

**pun**
**03** ram **04** quip **05** pound **06** clinch **07** quibble **08** equivoke **09** calembour, equivoque, jeu de mots, witticism **10** pundigrion **11** paronomasia, play on words **13** double meaning, play upon words **14** double entendre

**punch**
**03** bop, box, cut, die, fib, hit, jab, job, mat, zap **04** bash, biff, bite, blow, boff, bore, bust, clip, cuff, dong, hole, kick, plug, poke, prod, slug, sock, wind **05** black, check, clout, drill, drive, force, knock, power, prick, rumbo, stamp, thump, verve **06** energy, impact, pierce, pounce, pummel, stingo, strike, thwack, vigour, wallop, whammy **07** king hit, panache, pizzazz **08** keypunch, puncture, strength **09** bolo punch, perforate **10** roundhouse **11** coup de poing, make a hole in, sucker-punch **12** bunch of fives, counter-punch, forcefulness, fourpenny one **13** effectiveness **15** knuckle sandwich

**punch-drunk**
**05** dazed, dizzy, woozy **06** groggy **07** reeling **08** confused, unsteady **09** befuddled, slap-happy, stupefied **10** staggering

**punch-up**
**03** row **05** brawl, fight, scrap, set-to **06** dust-up, fracas, ruckus, shindy **07** scuffle **08** argument, ding-dong **10** free-for-all **12** stand-up fight

**punchy**
**05** dazed, zappy **06** lively, strong **07** dynamic **08** forceful, incisive, powerful, spirited, vigorous **09** effective **10** aggressive

**punctilio**
**05** pique, punto **06** detail, nicety, puncto **08** ceremony, delicacy **09** exactness, fine point, formality, precision **10** convention, exactitude,

particular, refinement, strictness **11** distinction, finickiness, preciseness **13** particularity **14** meticulousness, scrupulousness **15** punctiliousness

**punctilious**
**04** prim **05** exact, fussy, picky **06** choosy, formal, picked, proper, strict **07** careful, finicky, precise **08** punctual **10** meticulous, nit-picking, particular, pernickety, scrupulous **11** ceremonious, persnickety **13** conscientious

**punctiliously**
**07** exactly **09** carefully, precisely **12** meticulously, scrupulously **15** conscientiously

**punctual**
**05** early, exact, on cue **06** on time, prompt **07** precise **08** on the dot, up to time **09** well-timed **10** bang on time, dead on time, in good time **11** punctilious

**punctuality**
**09** readiness **10** promptness, regularity, strictness **11** promptitude

**punctually**
**05** sharp **06** bang on, dead on, on time, prompt, spot-on **07** exactly **08** on the dot, promptly, up to time **09** precisely **11** on the button, on the stroke, to the minute **13** on the stroke of

**punctuate**
**04** stop **05** break, point **06** pepper **07** break up **08** sprinkle **09** emphasize, interject, interrupt **10** accentuate **11** intersperse

**punctuation**

*Punctuation marks include:*

**04** dash, star
**05** colon, comma
**06** hyphen, period, quotes
**07** solidus
**08** asterisk, brackets, ellipsis, full stop
**09** backslash, semicolon
**10** apostrophe
**11** parentheses, speech marks
**12** question mark
**13** oblique stroke
**14** inverted commas, quotation marks, square brackets
**15** exclamation mark

**puncture**
◇ *insertion indicator*
**03** cut **04** bite, bore, flat, hole, leak, nick, slit **05** burst, prick, spike **06** holing, pierce, pounce **07** blow-out, deflate, flatten, let down, put down, rupture **08** centesis, flat tyre, piercing **09** humiliate, penetrate, perforate, spinal tap **11** make a hole in, perforation

**pundit**
**04** buff, guru, sage **05** maven, mavin **06** expert, gooroo, master, savant **07** adviser, maestro, teacher **09** authority

**pungency**
**03** nip **04** bite, kick, tang **05** oomph, point, power, sting **07** pizzazz, sarcasm **08** mordancy, strength **09** sharpness, spiciness **10** causticity, trenchancy **11** pepperiness **12** incisiveness **13** strong flavour

**pungent**
**03** hot **04** acid, fell, keen, racy, salt, sour, tart **05** acrid, acute, fiery, nippy, sharp, spicy, tangy **06** biting, bitter, strong **07** burning, caustic, cutting, mordant, painful, peppery, piquant, pointed **08** aromatic, incisive, piercing, poignant, powerful, scathing, stinging **09** sarcastic, trenchant **11** penetrating

**punish**
◇ *anagram indicator*
**03** log **04** beat, cane, fine, flog, gate, hang, harm, lash, slap, sort, whip **05** abuse, scold, scour, shend, smack, spank, visit, wreak **06** amerce, batter, damage, defeat, ground, hammer, misuse, pay out, strafe, straff, thrash **07** chasten, correct, crucify, justify, knee-cap, rough up, scourge, sort out, trounce **08** chastise, decimate, imprison, keelhaul, maltreat, masthead, penalize, serve out **09** castigate, strappado **10** come down on, discipline **11** bring to book **12** come down upon, give it laldie **14** bring to justice, make someone pay, throw the book at **15** give someone hell, make an example of

**• be punished**
**03** pay

**punishable**
**07** illegal **08** criminal, culpable, unlawful **10** chargeable, indictable **11** blameworthy, convictable

**punishing**
**04** hard **05** cruel, harsh **06** severe, taxing, tiring **07** arduous, testing **08** crushing, grinding, grueling, wearying **09** crippling, demanding, fatiguing, gruelling, strenuous **10** burdensome, exhausting **12** backbreaking

**punishment**
**04** harm, pine, toco, toko **05** force, impot **06** damage, ill-use, injury **07** deserts, penalty, revenge **08** ferocity, sentence **10** correction, discipline, imposition, storminess, turbulence **11** retribution **12** chastisement, maltreatment **13** rough handling **15** short sharp shock

*Punishments include:*

**04** cane, fine, gaol, jail, rope
**05** exile, lines, strap
**06** gating, hiding, prison
**07** beating, belting, borstal, capital, flaying, hitting, jankers, lashing, the cane, the rack, the rope
**08** corporal, demotion, flogging, slapping, smacking, solitary, spanking, the birch, whipping
**09** chain gang, detention, exclusion, execution, expulsion, grounding, larruping, probation, scourging, strappado, the stocks, thrashing, torturing
**10** banishment, cashiering, decimation, defrocking, internment, leathering, suspension, the slipper, unfrocking
**11** confinement, deportation, house arrest, keelhauling, knee-capping, mastheading, penal colony
**12** confiscation, dressing-down, imprisonment
**13** horsewhipping, incarceration, sequestration
**14** transportation
**15** excommunication, walking the plank

**• place of punishment**
**04** cang, gaol, Hell, jail, tron **05** Hades, trone **06** cangue, prison, sin bin **07** borstal, dungeon, gallows, pillory, tumbrel, tumbril **08** scaffold, solitary, Tartarus **09** black hole, cart's-tail, the stocks **10** little-ease **11** penal colony **12** cucking stool, whipping-post

*See also* **prison**

**punitive**
**04** hard **05** cruel, harsh, penal, stiff **06** severe **08** crushing **09** crippling, demanding, gruelling, punishing **10** burdensome, chastising, corrective, vindictive **11** castigatory, retaliatory, retributive, vindicatory **12** disciplinary

**punter**
**03** guy **04** chap **05** bloke **06** backer, better, client, fellow, person **07** gambler, wagerer **08** consumer, customer **10** individual **11** handicapper

**puny**
**04** tiny, weak **05** frail, minor, petty, scram, small, weary **06** feeble, little, measly, puisne, puisny, sickly **07** pimping, shilpit, stunted, trivial **08** piddling, reckling, trifling **10** diminutive, undersized **11** undeveloped **13** inexperienced, insignificant **14** underdeveloped **15** inconsequential

**pupil**
**01** L **04** coed, prep, ward **05** cadet **06** alumna, bursar, day-boy, grader, junior, novice, old boy, preppy, senior **07** alumnus, ashrama, boarder, day-girl, learner, monitor, old girl, prefect, protégé, scholar, student **08** beginner, bluecoat, disciple, grey-coat, praefect, protégée, schoolie **09** classmate, schoolboy, St Trinian **10** abiturient, academical, apprentice, charity-boy, day-boarder, day-scholar, gymnasiast, schoolgirl, Wykehamist **11** charity-girl, class-fellow, Westminster **12** pupil teacher **13** apple of the eye, kindergärtner **14** kindergartener, parlour-boarder

**• former pupil**
**02** OB **06** alumna, old boy
**07** alumnus, old girl

**puppet**
**04** doll, dupe, gull, Judy, pawn, tool **05** Punch, puppy **06** mammet, maumet, mawmet, mommet, motion, poppet, stooge **07** cat's-paw, Guignol **08** creature, quisling **09** dependant, fantoccio, rod puppet **10** fantoccino, figurehead, hand puppet, instrument, Jack of Lent, marionette, mouthpiece **11** glove puppet, Punchinello **12** finger puppet

**puppy**
**03** pup **05** whelp **06** lapdog **08** young dog

**purchase**
**03** buy, get, win **04** deal, earn, gain, grip, hold **05** asset, booty, goods, grasp, price, prise, prize **06** assets, obtain, pay for, pick up, secure, snap up, strive **07** acquire, bargain, emption, procure, seizure, shop for **08** foothold, holdings, invest in, leverage, property **09** advantage **10** go shopping, investment, possession **11** acquisition, possessions, splash out on

**purchaser**
**05** buyer, hirer **06** client, emptor, patron, vendee **07** shopper **08** consumer, customer **11** perquisitor

**pure**
**03** net, pur **04** fair, fine, free, good, holy, meer, mere, neat, nett, puer, real, true **05** clean, clear, fresh, moral, noble, sheer, snowy, solid, total, utter, white **06** chaste, decent, honest, kosher, modest, purity, refine, simple, virgin, worthy **07** aseptic, cleanly, cleanse, genuine, natural, perfect, sincere, sterile, unmixed, upright, utterly **08** absolute, abstract, academic, complete, flawless, germ-free, heavenly, hygienic, innocent, pristine, sanitary, spotless, straight, thorough, undrossy, unsoiled, virginal, virginly, virtuous **09** authentic, blameless, downright, essential, excellent, incorrupt, righteous, Saturnian, snow-white, spiritous, stainless, unalloyed, undefiled, undiluted, unsullied **10** antiseptic, completely, homozygous, honourable, immaculate, intemerate, sterilized, uninfected, unpolluted **11** conjectural, disinfected, speculative, theoretical, unblemished, unmitigated, unqualified **12** unadulterate **13** unadulterated **14** heavenly-minded, uncontaminated

**pure-bred**
**07** blooded **08** pedigree, true-born, true-bred **09** pedigreed, pure-blood **11** full-blooded, pure-blooded **12** thoroughbred

**purée**
**03** dal **04** fool **06** coulis, hummus, kissel, humous **07** houmous **08** hoummous **10** baba ganouj **11** baba ganoush **12** baba ghanouzh

**purely**
**04** just, only **06** merely, simply, solely, wholly **07** totally, utterly **08** chastely, entirely **09** unmixedly **10** absolutely, completely, thoroughly **11** exclusively, wonderfully **15** unconditionally

**purgative**
**05** aloes, enema, jalap, purge, salts, yapon, yupon **06** cacoon, emetic, ipecac, yaupon **07** calomel, drastic, jalapin, purging, rhubarb **08** aperient, elaterin, evacuant, laxative, lenitive **09** cathartic, cleansing, colocynth, croton oil, physic nut **10** abstersive, cholagogue, depurative, eccoprotic, Epsom salts, hiera-picra, higry-pigry, number nine **11** bitter aloes, cathartical, chrysarobin, ipecacuanha **12** black draught **13** diacatholicon **14** hickery-pickery

**purgatory**
**04** hell **05** agony, swamp **06** misery, ordeal, ravine **07** anguish, purging, torment, torture **09** cleansing, expiatory **12** hopelessness, wretchedness

**purge**
**03** rid **04** kill, oust, soil, work **05** clear, eject, expel, scour **06** depose, purify, remove **07** absolve, clarify, cleanse, dismiss, expiate, ousting, removal, root out, wipe out **08** absterge, clean out, clear out, disposal, ejection, get rid of **09** catharize, cleansing, eradicate, expulsion, expurgate, purgative, witch hunt **10** rooting-out **11** eradication, exterminate **13** extermination

**purification**
**05** purge **06** lustre **07** elution, lustrum **08** cleaning **09** catharsis, cleansing, epuration, purgation **10** absolution, depuration, filtration, fumigation, lustration, redemption, refinement **11** sublimation **12** desalination, disinfection, sanitization, zone refining **13** deodorization **14** reverse osmosis, sanctification **15** decontamination

**purify**
**03** try **04** clay, fine **05** clean, purge, scrub **06** distil, filter, redeem, refine, retort, shrive **07** absolve, chasten, clarify, cleanse, epurate, expurge, freshen, furbish, mundify, rectify, sublime **08** chastise, defecate, depurate, filtrate, fumigate, lustrate, sanctify, sanitize **09** catharize, deodorize, disinfect, expurgate, sterilize, sublimate, sublimize **10** circumcise **13** decontaminate

**purifying**
**06** fining **07** lustral, purging **08** refining **09** cathartic, cleansing, purgative **10** depurative, lustration **11** cathartical, expurgation **12** purificatory **13** mundificative

**purism**
**08** Atticism, pedantry **09** austerity, formalism, fussiness, orthodoxy, restraint **10** classicism, strictness **13** over-precision **14** fastidiousness

**purist**
**05** fussy **06** pedant, strict **07** finicky **08** captious, pedantic, puristic, quibbler, stickler **09** dogmatist, formalist, nit-picker, over-exact, quibbling **10** fastidious, literalist, nit-picking **11** over-precise **12** precisionist **13** hypercritical **14** over-fastidious, over-meticulous, over-particular, uncompromising

**puritan**
**04** prig **05** prude **06** zealot **07** fanatic, killjoy, pietist **08** Cromwell, Ironside, moralist, rigorist **09** Ironsides, precisian, Roundhead **10** goody-goody, spoilsport **14** disciplinarian

**puritanical**
**04** prim **05** rigid, stern, stiff **06** proper, severe, strict, stuffy **07** ascetic, austere, bigoted, precise, prudish, puritan, zealous **09** fanatical **10** abstemious, goody-goody, moralistic **11** round-headed, strait-laced **12** disapproving, narrow-minded **14** disciplinarian

**puritanism**
**07** bigotry **08** primness, rigidity, severity, zealotry **09** austerity, propriety, sternness, stiffness **10** abstinence, asceticism, fanaticism, narrowness, self-denial, strictness **11** prudishness **12** priggishness, rigorousness **14** abstemiousness, self-discipline

**purity**
**04** pure **05** truth **06** candor, honour, orient, virtue **07** candour, clarity, decency, honesty **08** chastity, goodness, morality, nobility, pureness, sanctity **09** chiarezza, cleanness, clearness, freshness, innocence, integrity, rectitude, sincerity, virginity **10** perfection, simplicity, worthiness **11** cleanliness, genuineness, uprightness **12** authenticity, flawlessness, virtuousness **13** blamelessness, untaintedness, wholesomeness

• **person of purity**
**04** lily

**purlieus**
**06** bounds, limits **07** borders, fringes, suburbs **08** confines, environs, vicinity **09** outskirts, perimeter, periphery, precincts **12** surroundings **13** neighbourhood

**purloin**
**03** bag, rob **04** lift, nick, take, whip **05** annex, filch, pinch, steal, swipe **06** finger, nobble, pilfer, pocket, remove, rip off, snitch, thieve **07** cabbage, snaffle **08** abstract, scrounge, souvenir **10** run off with **11** appropriate **12** make away with

**purple**

*Purples include:*

**04** anil, plum, puce, puke
**05** lilac, mauve, pansy, prune
**06** cerise, damson, indigo, maroon, violet
**07** fuchsia, fuschia, heather, magenta, purpure

08 amethyst, burgundy, hyacinth, lavender, mulberry
09 aubergine
11 royal purple

**purport**
04 bear, gist, idea, mean, seem, show 05 claim, drift, imply, point, sense, tenor, theme 06 allege, assert, convey, denote, import, intend, pose as, spirit, thrust 07 bearing, betoken, declare, express, meaning, portend, pretend, profess, purpose, signify, suggest 08 indicate, maintain, proclaim, tendency 09 direction, substance 11 implication 12 significance

**purportedly**
09 allegedly, dubiously 10 apparently, doubtfully, ostensibly, putatively, reportedly, supposedly 13 by all accounts

**purpose**
03 aim, end, use 04 gain, goal, good, hope, idea, mean, plan, talk, wish, zeal 05 basis, drive, point, teleo-, telos, value 06 aspire, decide, design, desire, effect, intend, motive, object, reason, result, settle, target, vision 07 benefit, outcome, propose, purport, resolve 08 ambition, backbone, converse, devotion, firmness, function, meditate, tenacity 09 advantage, constancy, determine, intention, objective, principle, rationale 10 aspiration, dedication, doggedness, motivation, resolution, usefulness 11 application, contemplate, persistence 12 conversation, perseverance 13 determination, justification, steadfastness

• **on purpose**
08 à dessein, by design, wilfully 09 knowingly, purposely, wittingly 11 consciously 12 deliberately 13 intentionally 14 premeditatedly

**purposeful**
04 firm 06 dogged 07 decided 08 constant, positive, purposed, resolute, resolved 09 steadfast, tenacious 10 deliberate, determined, persistent, unwavering 11 persevering, unfaltering 12 single-minded, strong-willed

**purposefully**
10 resolutely 11 steadfastly, tenaciously 12 persistently, unwaveringly 13 perseveringly, unfalteringly 14 single-mindedly

**purposeless**
04 vain 05 empty 06 wanton 07 aimless, useless, vacuous 08 goalless, needless 09 pointless, senseless, shapeless, unmeaning 10 gratuitous, motiveless, objectless, unasked-for 11 nonsensical, thoughtless, uncalled-for, unnecessary

**purposely**
08 by design, wilfully 09 expressly, knowingly, on purpose 10 designedly 11 consciously 12 calculatedly, deliberately, specifically 13 intentionally 14 premeditatedly

**purse**
◇ *containment indicator*
04 bung, fisc, fisk, gift, prim 05 award, burse, close, funds, means, money, pouch, prize 06 pocket, pucker, reward, wallet 07 coffers, present, tighten, wrinkle 08 compress, contract, crumenal, finances, money-bag, treasury 09 exchequer, resources, spleuchan 10 pocketbook 12 draw together, porte-monnaie 13 press together

**pursuance**
07 pursuit 08 pursuing 09 discharge, effecting, execution, following 10 completion, fulfilment 11 achievement, performance, prosecution 12 effectuation 14 accomplishment

**pursue**
03 dog, sew, sue 04 hunt, seek, tail 05 chace, chase, harry, hound, stalk, track, trail 06 aim for, follow, harass, hold to, keep on, keep up, persue, pursew, shadow, try for 07 carry on, conduct, go after, perform, poursew, poursue, run down 08 aspire to, continue, engage in, follow up, hunt down, maintain, practise, run after 09 give chase, make after, persecute, persist in, prosecute, search for, strive for 10 whore after 11 inquire into, investigate, persevere in, work towards 12 have your goal 15 apply yourself to

**pursuit**
03 aim 04 goal, hunt, line, suit 05 caper, chase, chevy, chivy, craft, hobby, quest, trade, trail 06 attain, chivvy, search 07 hot trod, hunting, pastime, pursual, tailing 08 activity, interest, poursuit, pursuing, stalking, tracking, vocation 09 endeavour, following, hue and cry, poursuitt, pursuance, shadowing, specialty 10 aspiration, employment, occupation, speciality 11 continuance, persistence, wildfowling 12 perseverance 13 investigation

**purvey**
04 sell 05 cater, stock 06 deal in, pass on, retail, spread, supply 07 furnish, provide, publish, trade in, victual 08 put about, transmit 09 propagate, provision, publicize 11 communicate, disseminate

**purveyor**
06 dealer, seller, trader, vendor 08 manciple, provedor, provider, providor, provisor, retailer, stockist, supplier 09 provedore 10 propagator, proveditor, victualler 11 proveditore, transmitter 12 communicator, disseminator

**pus**
06 matter 07 quitter, quittor, seropus 09 diapyesis, discharge 11 suppuration

**push**
02 go 03 jog, put, ram 04 birr, bunt, butt, cram, goad, horn, hype, jolt, plug, poke, pole, prod, raid, spur, urge 05 boost, bully, drive, dunch, dunsh, egg on, elbow, foray, force, impel, knock, nudge, onset, press, shove 06 charge, coerce, effort, energy, firing, hustle, incite, jostle, market, notice, papers, peddle, plunge, propel, ramrod, squash, the axe, thrust, vigour 07 advance, assault, company, depress, impulse, promote, sacking, squeeze, the boot, the chop 08 ambition, dynamism, invasion, persuade, press for, pressure, the elbow, vitality 09 advertise, constrain, discharge, dismissal, encourage, incursion, influence, manhandle, offensive, onslaught, publicize, your cards 10 enterprise, get-up-and-go, initiative, pressurize 12 forcefulness 13 determination 14 marching orders, put the screws on

• **push around**
05 bully 06 pick on 07 torment 09 terrorize, victimize 10 intimidate

• **push off**
04 move, scat 05 leave, scram 06 beat it, depart, go away 07 buzz off, scarper 08 clear off, clear out, run along, shove off 09 make a move, push along 10 make tracks

• **push on**
04 go on, toil, urge 06 plod on 07 advance, carry on, go ahead, peg away, press on, proceed 08 continue, plug away, slog away, toil away 09 keep going, persevere, soldier on, stick at it 10 keep trying

**pushed**
06 hard-up, rushed 07 harried, hurried, pinched, pressed, short of 08 harassed, strapped 09 stretched 11 hard-pressed 13 under pressure 14 in difficulties

**pushover**
03 mug 04 dupe, gull 05 cinch 06 doddle, picnic, stooge, sucker 07 fall guy 08 duck soup, walkover, weakling 09 easy touch, soft touch 10 child's play 11 piece of cake, sitting duck 13 sitting target

**pushy**
04 bold 05 bossy, brash 07 forward 08 arrogant, assuming, forceful 09 ambitious, assertive 10 aggressive 11 impertinent 12 presumptuous 13 over-confident, self-assertive

**pusillanimity**
08 timidity, weakness 10 cravenness, feebleness 11 fearfulness, gutlessness, poltroonery 12 cowardliness, timorousness 13 spinelessness

**pusillanimous**
04 weak 05 timid 06 craven, feeble, scared, yellow 07 chicken, fearful, gutless, wimpish 08 cowardly, timorous 09 spineless, weak-kneed 11 lily-livered 12 faint-hearted, mean-spirited 14 chicken-hearted

**pussyfoot**
**03** pad **05** creep, hedge, prowl, slink, steal **06** tiptoe **09** mess about **10** equivocate **11** prevaricate **12** tergiversate **14** prohibitionist

**pustule**
**04** boil, pock **05** ulcer **06** blotch, fester, papule, pimple **07** abscess, blister, whitlow **08** eruption **09** carbuncle, whitehead **10** uredosorus

**put**
**02** do **03** add, bet, fix, lay, pin, pit, say, set **04** cast, dump, flow, give, have, hurl, levy, park, post, push, rank, rest, risk, sink, sort, turn, word **05** affix, apply, class, couch, drive, exact, force, frame, gauge, grade, group, guess, impel, offer, place, plonk, speak, spend, stake, stand, state, throw, utter, voice **06** append, assert, assign, attach, call on, chance, charge, commit, convey, demand, devote, gamble, impose, impute, incite, invest, locate, oblige, phrase, reckon, reduce, render, repose, set out, settle, submit, tender, thrust **07** arrange, ascribe, bumpkin, connect, convert, deposit, dispose, express, inflict, lay down, present, proceed, proffer, propose, require, set down, situate, station, subject, suggest, venture, work out **08** classify, dedicate, estimate, position, propound, set forth **09** attribute, constrain, establish, formulate, greenhorn, lay before, pronounce, set before, translate, transport **10** categorize, contribute, transcribe **11** guesstimate **12** bring forward

• **put about**
**04** tell **06** spread **07** publish **08** announce, distress **09** circulate, make known **11** disseminate

• **put across**
**06** convey **07** clarify, explain, express, get over, put over **08** bring off, spell out **09** get across, make clear **11** bring home to, communicate **12** get through to **14** make understood

• **put aside**
**04** keep, save, stow **05** hoard, lay by, put by, set by, stash, store **06** retain, shelve **07** reserve **08** lay aside, salt away, set apart, set aside **09** stockpile **12** put to one side **13** keep in reserve

• **put away**
**03** eat **04** down, jail, keep, kill, save, stow, wolf **05** drink, eat up, lay by, put by, scoff, snarf, store, waive **06** bang up, commit, devour, guzzle, lock up, pack up, retain, tuck in **07** cashier, certify, confine, consume, divorce, reserve, swallow **08** imprison, lay aside, put aside, renounce, send down, set aside **09** polish off, stockpile **11** incarcerate **13** keep in reserve

• **put back**
**05** defer, delay, remit **06** freeze, return, shelve, tidy up **07** adjourn, clear up, replace, repulse, restore, suspend **08** postpone, put on ice, tidy away **09** clear away, reinstate **10** reschedule **13** procrastinate **14** take a raincheck

• **put down**
**03** fix, lay, log **04** alay, drop, kill, laid, list, snub, stop **05** abase, aleye, allay, blame, crush, enter, lower, plonk, quash, quell, shame, sneap **06** attach, charge, defeat, humble, reckon, record, slight, squash **07** ascribe, confute, deflate, degrade, destroy, jot down, mortify, repress, set down, silence, squelch, surpass **08** belittle, note down, outshine, register, stamp out, suppress, underlay **09** attribute, deprecate, disparage, humiliate, write down **10** put to sleep, transcribe **12** take down a peg

• **put forward**
**03** lay, run **04** move, pose, urge **05** offer, table **06** assign, obtend, prefer, submit, tender **07** advance, present, proffer, propone, propose, suggest **08** nominate **09** hold forth, introduce, recommend

• **put in**
◇ *insertion indicator*
**03** fit **05** enter, input **06** insert, submit **07** install, present **09** introduce

• **put in for**
**05** order **06** ask for **07** request **08** apply for **11** requisition, write off for **14** fill in a form for

• **put off**
**03** fob, fub **04** daff, doff **05** daunt, defer, delay, deter, lay by, shift **06** dismay, divert, shelve, sicken **07** adjourn, confuse, deflect, dismiss, respite, suspend **08** dissuade, distract, nauseate, postpone, put on ice, turn away **09** sidetrack, talk out of, turn aside **10** demoralize, disconcert, discourage, dishearten, intimidate, reschedule **13** procrastinate **14** take a raincheck

• **put on**
**02** do **03** add, don **04** fake, give, robe, sham, wear **05** affix, apply, feign, lay on, mount, place, stage, try on **06** affect, assume, attach, impose, plug in, supply, turn on **07** connect, dress in, get into, perform, present, pretend, produce, provide, start up, throw on **08** activate, organize, simulate, slip into, switch on **10** change into **11** make believe **12** get dressed in **13** get dolled up in

• **put out**
**03** irk **04** dout, faze, hurt **05** anger, annoy, douse, dowse, issue, snuff, upset, utter **06** bother, offend, quench **07** dismiss, disturb, extinct, perturb, provoke, publish, smother, trouble **08** announce, bring out, disclose, impose on, irritate, stamp out, unsettle **09** broadcast, circulate, infuriate, make known **10** discommode, disconcert, exasperate, extinguish, mistrysted **13** inconvenience

• **put through**
**06** manage **07** achieve, execute, process **08** bring off, complete, conclude, finalize **10** accomplish

• **put together**
**04** join **05** build, frame, marry **06** cobble, made up, make up **07** compile, concoct **08** assemble **09** carpenter, construct **11** fit together **13** piece together

• **put up**
◇ *reversal down indicator*
**03** inn, pay **04** give **05** build, erect, float, house, lodge, offer, raise, sling, stake **06** bump up, choose, hike up, invest, jack up, pledge, supply **07** advance, propose, provide, sheathe, shelter, suggest **08** assemble, compound, escalate, increase, nominate **09** construct, recommend **10** put forward **11** accommodate, give a room to

• **put upon**
**07** exploit **08** impose on **13** inconvenience, take liberties **14** take for granted **15** take advantage of

• **put up to**
**04** goad, urge **05** egg on **06** incite, prompt **08** persuade **09** encourage

• **put up with**
**04** bear, lump, take, wear **05** abide, allow, brook, stand **06** accept, endure, suffer **07** stomach, swallow **08** stand for, tolerate **13** take lying down

**putative**
**07** alleged, assumed, reputed **08** presumed, reported, supposed **10** reputative **11** conjectural, theoretical **12** hypothetical, suppositious **13** suppositional

**put-down**
**03** dig **04** gibe, snub **05** sneer **06** insult, rebuff, slight **07** affront, sarcasm **11** humiliation **13** disparagement, slap in the face

**put-off**
**04** curb **06** damper, excuse **07** evasion **08** obstacle **09** deterrent, hindrance, restraint **10** constraint **12** disincentive, postponement **14** discouragement

**putrefaction**
**03** rot **05** decay, mould **06** fungus, mildew, sepsis **07** rotting **08** going bad **09** perishing, putridity **11** putrescence **13** decomposition

**putrefy**
**03** rot **05** addle, decay, go bad, mould, spoil, stink, taint **06** fester, perish **07** corrupt **08** gangrene **09** decompose **11** deteriorate

**putrescent**
**07** rotting **08** decaying, mephitic, stinking **09** festering, perishing **10** putrefying **11** decomposing

**putrid**
**03** bad, off **04** foul, rank **05** addle, fetid **06** addled, foetid, mouldy, rancid, rotten, turned **07** corrupt, decayed, tainted **08** decaying, polluted, stinking **10** decomposed, disgusting **11** decomposing **12** contaminated

**put-upon**
**04** used **06** abused **09** exploited, imposed on **10** maltreated, persecuted **14** inconvenienced

**puzzle**
◇ *anagram indicator*
**04** beat, crux, pose **05** brood, floor, poser, stump, think **06** baffle, bemuse, enigma, fickle, figure, gravel, kittle, ponder **07** bumbaze, confuse, dilemma, flummox, mystery, mystify, nonplus, paradox, perplex, problem, stagger, tickler **08** bewilder, confound, consider, entangle, intrigue, meditate, mull over, muse over, question **09** bamboozle, fascinate **10** complicate, deliberate, mind-bender, perplexity **11** brainteaser **12** bewilderment, brain-twister **13** metagrobolize **14** beat your brains, rack your brains, think hard about

*Puzzles include:*

**04** maze, quiz
**05** logic, rebus
**06** hanjie, jigsaw, kakuro, riddle, sudoku
**07** anagram, hangman, sorites, tangram
**08** acrostic, wordgame
**09** crossword, conundrum
**10** alphametic, cryptogram, Rubik's Cube®, wordsearch
**12** magic pyramid

• **puzzle out**
**03** get **04** suss **05** crack, solve **06** decode **07** clear up, resolve, sort out, suss out, unravel, work out **08** decipher, think out, untangle **09** figure out **13** metagrabolize, metagrobolize, piece together **15** find the answer to

**puzzled**
**04** lost **05** at sea **06** beaten **07** at a loss, baffled, floored, in a haze, stumped **08** confused **09** flummoxed, mystified, perplexed **10** bamboozled, bewildered, confounded, nonplussed

**puzzlement**
**05** doubt **06** wonder **08** surprise **09** confusion **10** bafflement, perplexity **11** incertitude, uncertainty **12** astonishment, bewilderment, doubtfulness **13** bamboozlement, mystification **14** disorientation

• **expression of puzzlement**
**02** ha **03** hah, hey, huh **04** anan, anon **05** heigh **06** indeed

**puzzling**
**05** queer, trick **06** arcane, knotty, posing **07** bizarre, cryptic, curious, strange, unclear **08** abstruse, baffling, involved, mystical, peculiar, riddling, tortuous **09** ambiguous, confusing, damnedest, enigmatic, equivocal, intricate **10** misleading, mysterious, mystifying, perplexing, Sphynx-like **11** bewildering, enigmatical, mind-bending **12** impenetrable, inexplicable, labyrinthine, mind-boggling, unfathomable **13** unaccountable

**pygmy**
**03** elf, toy, wee **04** baby, tiny **05** atomy, dwarf, elfin, small **06** midget, minute, pocket **07** manikin, Negrito, stunted **08** dwarfish, half-pint, Tom Thumb **09** miniature, minuscule, pint-sized, thumbling **10** diminutive, fingerling, homunculus, undersized **11** hop-o'-my-thumb, Lilliputian

**pyramid**
**05** stack **08** teocalli, ziggurat, zikkurat

**pyromaniac**
**04** pyro **07** firebug **08** arsonist **10** fire-raiser, incendiary

# Q

**Q**
**03** cue **06** Quebec **13** trichosanthin

**Qatar**
**01** Q **02** QA **03** QAT

**quack**
**04** fake, sham **05** bogus, false, fraud, pseud **06** cowboy, crocus, doctor, humbug, phoney **07** empiric **08** impostor, so-called, spurious, supposed, swindler **09** charlatan, pretended, pretender, trickster **10** fraudulent, medicaster, mountebank **11** counterfeit, masquerader, quacksalver, saltimbanco, unqualified

**quackery**
**04** sham **05** fraud **06** humbug **09** imposture, phoniness **10** empiricism **11** fraudulence **12** charlatanism **13** mountebankery, mountebankism

**quadrangle**
**04** quad **05** court, plaza **06** piazza, square **08** cloister **09** courtyard, enclosure, esplanade

**quaff**
**04** down, gulp, swig **05** booze, drain, drink, swill **06** guzzle, imbibe, quaich, tipple **07** carouse, draught, swallow, toss off **08** drink off **09** crush a cup, knock back

**quagmire**
**03** bog, fen, fix **04** hole, mess, mire, quag **05** marsh, swamp **06** morass, pickle, slough **07** dilemma, problem **08** entangle, hot water, quandary, wagmoire **09** deep water, quicksand, tight spot **10** perplexity

**quail**
**05** colin, cower, daunt, quake, shake, whore **06** blench, caille, cringe, falter, flinch, recoil, shiver, shrink, subdue **07** decline, shudder, shy away, slacken, tremble **08** back away, bobwhite, draw back, hemipode, languish, percolin, pull back **09** partridge

**quaint**
◇ *anagram indicator*
**03** odd **04** fine, twee **05** droll, funky, queer, sweet **06** queint, whimsy **07** bizarre, cunning, curious, skilful, strange, unusual, whimsey **08** charming, fanciful, old-world **09** ingenious, whimsical **10** antiquated, attractive, auld-farand, olde-worlde **11** picturesque **12** old-fashioned

**quaintly**
**05** oddly **09** curiously, strangely, unusually **10** charmingly **11** whimsically **12** attractively **13** picturesquely

**quaintness**
**05** charm **11** unusualness **13** whimsicalness **14** attractiveness **15** picturesqueness

**quake**
◇ *anagram indicator*
**04** move, rock, sway **05** heave, quail, shake, throb **06** didder, dither, quiver, shiver, tremor, wamble, wobble **07** pulsate, shudder, tremble, vibrate **08** convulse

**qualification**
**05** rider, skill **06** caveat, degree **07** ability, diploma, fitness, proviso **08** aptitude, capacity, training **09** allowance, condition, exception, exemption, provision **10** adaptation, adjustment, capability, competence, limitation **11** certificate, eligibility, proficiency, reservation, restriction, stipulation, suitability **12** modification **13** certification **14** accomplishment

*Qualifications include:*

**02** AB, AM, AS, BA, BD, BE, BL, BM, BS, DC, DD, DS, IB, MA, MB, MD, MS
**03** BAI, BAS, BCh, BCL, BDS, BEd, BRE, BSc, ChB, ChM, CSE, DCh, DCL, DDS, DEd, DPh, DSc, DTh, EdB, EdD, FPC, LHD, LLB, LLD, LLM, MBA, MCh, MDS, MEd, MSc, NVQ, ONC, OND, PhD, ScB, ScD, SCE, SVQ, ThD, VMD
**04** BAgr, BCom, BEng, B ès L, B ès S, BLit, BMus, BTEC, BVM&S, DEng, DIng, DLit, DMus, GCSE, GNVQ, LitB, LitD, MBSc, MCom, MDSc, MMus, MusB, MusD
**05** BArch, BComm, BLitt, BPhil, DLitt, DPhil, LittB, LittD, Lower, MEcon, MLitt, MPhil, MTech
**06** A level, BAgric, BPharm, degree, DTheol, Higher, MPharm, O grade, O level
**07** AS level
**10** eleven-plus, Lower grade, School Cert
**11** Higher grade, Legum doctor
**12** Doctor of Laws, Master of Arts, Master of Laws
**13** Advanced level, Bachelor of Law, Doctor of Music, Legum magister, Master of Music, Ordinary grade, Ordinary level, Standard grade
**14** Advanced Higher, Artium Magister, Bachelor of Arts, Bachelor of Laws, Magister Artium
**15** Bachelor of Music, Doctor of Letters, Doctor of Science, Doctor of Surgery, Master of Letters, Master of Science, Master of Surgery, Medicinae Doctor

**qualified**
**03** fit **04** able, meet **05** adept **06** expert, fitted **07** bounded, capable, guarded, limited, skilful, skilled, trained **08** cautious, eligible, equipped, licensed, modified, prepared, reserved, talented **09** certified, chartered, competent, efficient, equivocal, practised **10** contingent, proficient, restricted **11** conditional, experienced, provisional **12** accomplished, professional **13** circumscribed, knowledgeable

**qualify**
**03** fit **04** ease, pass, vary **05** abate, allow, alloy, coach, equip, limit, prove, teach, train **06** adjust, define, ground, lessen, modify, permit, reduce, soften, temper, weaken **07** appease, certify, confirm, delimit, empower, entitle, license, prepare, warrant **08** classify, diminish, graduate, instruct, mitigate, moderate, restrain, restrict, sanction **09** alleviate, authorize, be allowed, contemper, make ready **10** be eligible, capacitate, habilitate **12** characterize **15** make conditional

**quality**
**01** Q **02** it **04** cast, kind, make, mark, rank, sort, type **05** class, grade, level, merit, skill, trait, value, worth **06** aspect, make-up, manner, nature, status, timbre **07** calibre, feature, variety **08** eminence, property, standard **09** attribute, character, condition **10** excellence, profession, refinement **11** distinction, peculiarity, pre-eminence, superiority **14** accomplishment, characteristic

• **quality assurance**
**02** QA

**qualm**
**04** fear **05** doubt, worry **07** anxiety, concern, scruple **08** disquiet **09** hesitancy, misgiving **10** hesitation, reluctance, uneasiness **11** compunction, uncertainty **12** apprehension **14** disinclination

**quandary**
**03** fix, jam **04** hole, mess **06** muddle, pickle **07** dilemma, impasse, problem

09 confusion, tight spot 10 difficulty, perplexity 11 predicament
12 bewilderment

**quantify**
05 count, weigh 06 number
07 measure, specify 08 evaluate
09 calculate, calibrate, determine, enumerate

**quantity**
02 qt 03 lot, qty, sum 04 area, bulk, deal, dose, lots, many, mass, much, part, size, tons 05 heaps, loads, quota, reams, scrap, share, total 06 amount, extent, length, masses, number, oodles, stacks, volume, weight
07 breadth, content, expanse, measure, portion 08 capacity, fragment 09 aggregate, allotment, extension, magnitude 10 proportion

*See also* **measurement**

- **in equal quantities**

01 ā 02 āā 03 ana

- **small quantity**

04 curn, drib, lock

- **unknown quantity**

01 X, Y, Z

**quarantine**
09 detention, isolation, lazaretto, quarenden, quarender 10 quarrender
11 quarrington, segregation

**quarrel**
03 jar, row, wap 04 beef, feud, miff, slam, spat, tiff, tift, whid 05 argue, brawl, broil, cavil, chide, clash, fault, fight, flite, flyte, knock, run-in, scrap, set-to, slate 06 barney, bicker, breach, breeze, bust-up, charge, differ, dust-up, fracas, fratch, jangle, quar'le, quarry, ruffle, rumble, schism, square, strife
07 brattle, cast out, censure, contend, dispute, dissent, fall out, outcast, outfall, punch-up, wrangle
08 argument, conflict, disagree, squabble, vendetta 09 caterwaul, complaint, criticize, have words, objection 10 contention, difference, differency, difficulty, dissension, falling-out 11 altercation, controversy, disputation, pick holes in 12 be at variance, disagreement, pull to pieces
13 exchange blows, exchange words, find fault with, part brass rags, shouting match, slanging match 15 be at loggerheads

**quarrelling**
06 at odds, rowing, strife 07 discord, feuding, warring 08 fighting, variance
09 bickering, scrapping, wrangling
10 at variance, contending, contention, discordant, disharmony, dissension, squabbling 11 altercation, disputation, dissentient 12 argy-bargying
13 argumentation, at loggerheads
14 vitilitigation

**quarrelsome**
06 chippy 07 scrappy, stroppy
09 bellicose, camstairy, camsteary, debateful, irascible, irritable
10 camsteerie, pugnacious
11 belligerent, contentious, hot-tempered, ill-tempered
12 cantankerous, disputatious
13 argumentative 14 ready for a fight

**quarry**
04 game, goal, kill, mark, prey
05 chase, curry, prize, spoil 06 currie, object, target, victim 07 quarrel
08 stone pit 09 glory hole, slaughter

**quarter**
01 E, N, q, S, W 02 qr, qu 03 pad 04 airt, area, digs, east, hand, part, pity, post, side, spot, west, zone 05 board, grace, house, lodge, mercy, north, place, point, put up, quart, rooms, south
06 billet, favour, fourth, ghetto, medina, pardon, region, sector
07 Moorery, section, shelter, station, two bits 08 barracks, clemency, district, division, domicile, dwelling, leniency, locality, lodgings, province, quartern, vicinity 09 direction, residence, territory 10 compassion, habitation, indulgence
11 accommodate, forgiveness
13 accommodation, neighbourhood

*See also* **compass**

**quarterly**
02 qu 04 quar 12 three-monthly

**quarters**
04 camp 05 house 06 ghetto
07 lodging

*See also* **accommodation**

**quartz**
04 jasp 05 flint, prase 06 jasper, morion 07 crystal 08 amethyst, tiger eye 09 buhrstone, burrstone, cacholong, cairngorm, carnelian, cornelian, goldstone, tiger's eye
10 avanturine, aventurine, chalcedony
11 rock crystal 12 Bohemian ruby, Spanish topaz 14 Bristol-diamond, cairngorm-stone 15 occidental topaz

**quash**
04 void 05 annul, crush, quell
06 cancel, defeat, repeal, revoke, scotch, squash, subdue 07 nullify, rescind, reverse 08 abrogate, override, overrule, overturn, set aside, suppress
09 overthrow 10 invalidate, put an end to 11 countermand

**quaver**
03 sob 05 break, quake, shake, throb, trill, waver 06 quiver, tremor, warble, wobble 07 flicker, flutter, pulsate, shudder, tremble, tremolo, vibrate, vibrato 09 oscillate, trembling, vibration 10 eighth note 11 quaveriness

**quay**
03 kay, key 04 dock, pier 05 jetty, levee, wharf 07 harbour

**queasiness**
06 nausea 07 gagging 08 retching, sickness, vomiting 11 airsickness, biliousness, carsickness, seasickness
12 sick headache 14 motion sickness, travel sickness 15 morning sickness

**queasy**
03 ill 04 sick 05 dizzy, faint, giddy, green, queer, rough 06 groggy, uneasy, unwell 07 bilious 08 nauseous, sickened 09 hazardous, nauseated, squeamish, unsettled 10 fastidious, out of sorts, scrupulous 15 under the weather

**Quebec**
01 Q 02 QC

**queen**
01 Q, R 02 ER, FD, HM, Qu, VR 03 VIR
04 idol, rani 05 belle, charm, ranee, ruler, Venus 06 beauty, prince, Brenda, regina 07 consort, empress, majesty, monarch 08 princess 09 sovereign
11 head of state

*Queens include:*

03 Mab
04 Anne, Anne (of Cleves), Emma, Grey (Jane, Lady), Joan (of Navarre), Mary, Mary (Queen of Scots), Mary (of Teck), Parr (Catherine)
05 Maeve, Maria, Marie (de Médici), Sheba
06 Boleyn (Anne), Esther, Hearts, Himiko, Howard (Catherine), Louisa, Nzinga, Salote, Silvia, Soraya
07 Beatrix, Eleanor (of Aquitaine), Eleanor (of Castile), Juliana, Macbeth (Lady), Seymour (Jane), Titania, Zenobia
08 Adelaide, Berenice, Boadicea, Boudicca, Caroline (of Ansbach), Caroline (of Brunswick), Clotilda (St), Gloriana, Isabella (of Castile), Kristina, Margaret (St), Margaret (of Anjou), Philippa (of Hainault), Victoria
09 Alexandra, Artemisia, Brunhilde, Catherine (de Médici), Catherine (of Aragon), Catherine (of Braganza), Christina, Cleopatra, Elizabeth, Fredegond, Margrethe, Mary Tudor, Nefertiti, Semiramis, Woodville (Elizabeth)
10 Hatshepsut, Lakshmi Bai, Wilhelmina
13 Margaret Tudor
14 Henrietta Maria
15 Charlotte Sophia, Marie Antoinette

**queenly**
05 grand, noble, regal, royal 06 august
07 reginal, stately, sublime 08 gracious, imperial, majestic, splendid
09 dignified, imperious, sovereign
11 monarchical

**queer**
◇ *anagram indicator*
03 gay, ill, mar, odd, rum 04 camp, foil, harm, iffy, ruin, sick 05 botch, butch, cheat, dizzy, faint, fishy, funny, giddy, quare, rough, shady, spoil, upset, weird, wreck 06 Fifish, impair, quaint, queasy, shifty, stymie, thwart, unwell
07 bizarre, curious, deviant, dubious, lesbian, strange, suspect, unusual
08 abnormal, bisexual, doubtful,

endanger, peculiar, puzzling, ridicule, singular, uncommon **09** eccentric, frustrate, irregular, unnatural **10** homosexual, jeopardize, mysterious, outlandish, out of sorts, remarkable, suspicious, unorthodox **11** counterfeit, light-headed **13** extraordinary, funny peculiar **14** unconventional **15** under the weather

**queerness**
**06** oddity **11** abnormality, bizarreness, curiousness, peculiarity, singularity, strangeness, unorthodoxy, unusualness **12** eccentricity, irregularity, uncommonness **13** anomalousness, unnaturalness

**quell**
**03** die **04** alay, calm, hush, kill, rout, stay **05** abash, abate, aleye, allay, crush, quash, quiet **06** defeat, pacify, perish, soothe, squash, stifle, subdue **07** appease, conquer, put down, silence, slaying, subside **08** mitigate, moderate, overcome, suppress, vanquish **09** alleviate, overpower **10** disconcert, extinguish, put an end to, spiflicate **11** spifflicate

**quench**
**04** cool, sate, stop **05** douse, slake **06** put out, sloken, stanch, stifle **07** destroy, satiate, satisfy, slocken, smother, staunch **08** snuff out, stamp out **10** extinguish

**querulous**
**04** sour **05** cross, fussy, ratty, testy **06** shirty **07** carping, fretful, grouchy, peevish **08** captious, critical, petulant **09** fractious, grumbling, irascible, irritable, plaintive **11** complaining **12** cantankerous, discontented, dissatisfied, fault-finding

**query**
**01** Q **02** qy **03** ask **05** doubt, qualm **06** quaere, qualms **07** dispute, inquire, inquiry, problem, quibble, suspect **08** distrust, mistrust, question **09** challenge, suspicion **10** disbelieve, hesitation, scepticism, uneasiness **11** quarrel with, reservation, uncertainty **12** question mark **13** be sceptical of, throw doubts on

**quest**
**03** aim **04** bark, goal, hunt, yelp **06** search, voyage **07** crusade, inquiry, journey, mission, purpose, pursuit, seeking, venture **08** ringdove **09** adventure **10** enterprise, expedition, pilgrimage, wood pigeon **11** exploration, undertaking **13** investigation

• **in quest of**
**03** for, out **06** out for **08** questing **10** hunting for **11** in pursuit of **12** harking after, searching for, seeking after, trying to find **14** trying to obtain

**question**
**01** Q **02** Qu **03** ask **04** chin, poll, pose, pump, quiz **05** demur, doubt, grill, issue, point, poser, probe, query, theme, topic **06** debate, matter, motion, quaere, riddle, teaser **07** debrief, discuss, dispute, enquiry, erotema, eroteme, examine, inquire, inquiry, problem, scruple, subject **08** argument, converse, erotesis, proposal **09** backspeer, backspeir, catechize, challenge, conundrum, interview, objection **10** difficulty, disbelieve, discussion **11** controversy, interrogate, investigate, proposition, uncertainty **12** conversation, cross-examine, peradventure, point at issue **13** cross-question, interrogation, interrogatory **15** have doubts about, have qualms about

• **in question**
**07** at issue **09** concerned **14** being discussed **15** under discussion

• **out of the question**
**06** absurd **10** impossible, ridiculous **11** unthinkable **12** unacceptable, unbelievable

• **without question**
**07** on trust **11** immediately **14** unhesitatingly, unquestionably, without arguing

**questionable**
◇ *anagram indicator*
**04** iffy **05** fishy, shady, vexed **07** dubious, immoral, suspect **08** arguable, doubtful, improper, unproven **09** debatable, equivocal, uncertain, unsettled **10** at question, disputable, suspicious **11** problematic **12** undetermined **13** controversial, problematical

**questioner**
**07** doubter, sceptic **08** agnostic, examiner, inquirer **09** catechist **10** catechizer, inquisitor, quizmaster **11** disbeliever, interrogant, interviewer **12** interlocutor, interrogator, investigator **14** question-master

**questionnaire**
**04** form, quiz, test **06** survey **11** opinion poll **14** market research

**queue**
**03** row **04** file, line, tail **05** chain, order, train **06** back up, column, fall in, in line, line up, series, string **07** pigtail **08** sequence, tailback **09** breadline, crocodile, form a line **10** form a queue, procession, succession, wait in line **11** stand in line **13** concatenation

**quibble**
**03** pun **04** carp, quip **05** cavil, dodge, query, quirk **06** haggle, niggle, peck at, snatch **07** brabble, nit-pick, protest, quiblin, quiddit, quillet **08** equivoke, pettifog, quiddity **09** complaint, criticism, equivoque, objection **10** equivocate, nit-picking, split hairs **11** prevaricate **12** carriwitchet, equivocation, pettifogging **13** avoid the issue, find fault with, prevarication

**quibbler**
**07** casuist, niggler, sophist **08** caviller, chicaner **09** nit-picker **11** equivocator, pettifogger **12** hair-splitter

**quibbling**
**07** carping, evasive **08** captious, critical, niggling, overnice **09** ambiguous, casuistic, cavilling, chicanery, chicaning **10** nit-picking **12** equivocating, pettifogging **13** hair-splitting, logic-chopping, word-splitting

**quick**
**03** hot, pdq **04** fast, keen, rath, soon, yare **05** agile, alive, brief, brisk, flash, hasty, nifty, nippy, rapid, rathe, ready, sharp, smart, swift, zippy **06** astute, clever, dapper, living, mobile, nimble, presto, prompt, shrewd, speedy, sudden **07** cursory, express, flutter, hurried, instant, rapidly, schnell **08** expedite, fleeting, pregnant, shifting **09** immediate, receptive, sensitive, sprightly **10** discerning, perceptive, responsive **11** expeditious, intelligent, perfunctory, quick-witted, sharp-witted **12** without delay **13** instantaneous **15** pretty damn quick, quick off the mark

**quicken**
**04** stir, whet **05** couch, hurry, rouse, speed **06** arouse, excite, hasten, incite, kindle, revive, stir up **07** advance, animate, enliven, hurry up, inspire, refresh, speed up **08** activate, dispatch, energize, expedite, revivify **09** galvanize, instigate, stimulate **10** accelerate, couch grass, invigorate, reactivate, revitalize, strengthen **11** precipitate **12** reinvigorate

**quickly**
**04** cito, fast, soon, vite **05** apace, quick, slick, swith **06** presto, pronto **07** briskly, express, hastily, rapidly, readily, smartly, swiftly **08** abruptly, promptly, smartish, speedily **09** cursorily, hurriedly, instantly, like a shot, like smoke, overnight, posthaste **11** at the double, immediately, prestissimo **12** a mile a minute, lickety-split, with dispatch **13** expeditiously, perfunctorily **14** at a rate of knots, hell for leather, unhesitatingly **15** instantaneously, like the clappers

**quickness**
**05** speed **06** acumen **07** agility **08** celerity, keenness, rapidity **09** acuteness, alertness, briskness, hastiness, immediacy, nimblesse, readiness, sharpness, swiftness **10** astuteness, expedition, nimbleness, promptness, shrewdness, speediness, suddenness **11** penetration, promptitude **12** intelligence **13** precipitation **15** quick-wittedness

**quick-tempered**
**05** fiery, testy **06** snappy, touchy **07** waspish **08** choleric, petulant, shrewish, volcanic **09** excitable, explosive, impatient, impulsive, irascible, irritable, splenetic **11** hot-tempered, quarrelsome **13** temperamental

**quick-witted**
**04** keen **05** acute, alert, sharp, smart, witty **06** astute, bright, clever, crafty, shrewd **09** ingenious, wide-awake **10** perceptive **11** intelligent, penetrating, ready-witted, resourceful **12** nimble-witted **15** quick off the mark

**quid**
**01** L **03** sov **04** chew, oner **05** libra, pound, squid **06** guinea, nicker **07** smacker **09** sovereign, substance **12** jimmy-o'goblin **13** pound sterling
*See also* **pound**

**quid pro quo**
**04** swap **07** damages **08** exchange, trade-off **09** mutuality, tit for tat **10** equivalent **11** co-operation, equivalence, give-and-take, reciprocity **12** compensation, remuneration **13** reciprocation

**quiescent**
**04** calm **05** inert, quiet, still **06** asleep, at rest, latent, placid, serene, silent **07** dormant, passive, resting **08** inactive, peaceful, sleeping, tranquil **09** reposeful **10** in abeyance, motionless, untroubled **11** undisturbed

**quiet**
**01** p **02** QT, sh **03** dry, low, shy **04** calm, ease, hush, loun, lown, lull, meek, mild, pale, rest, soft **05** doggo, faint, lound, lownd, muted, peace, shtum, sober, still, stoic, stumm **06** gentle, hushed, lonely, low-key, pastel, placid, repose, secret, serene, settle, shtoom, shtumm, silent, sleepy, stilly, subtle **07** appease, easeful, muffled, orderly, private, schtoom, silence, subdued **08** composed, discreet, isolated, man-to-man, peaceful, personal, reserved, reticent, retiring, secluded, serenity, taciturn, tranquil **09** inaudible, introvert, noiseless, quietness, soundless, stillness, withdrawn **10** indistinct, phlegmatic, restrained, thoughtful, untroubled **11** inoffensive, sequestered, undisturbed, unexcitable, unflappable **12** confidential, off-the-record, peacefulness, tranquillity, unfrequented, woman-to-woman **13** imperturbable, noiselessness, soundlessness, unforthcoming, without a sound **15** uncommunicative, undemonstrative
*See also* **silence**

**quieten**
**04** calm, dull, hush, mute **05** lower, quell, quiet, shush, sober, still **06** deaden, muffle, pacify, reduce, shut up, smooth, soften, soothe, stifle, subdew, subdue **07** compose, silence **08** calm down, diminish **12** tranquillize

**quietly**
**01** p **04** loun, lown, soft **05** lound, lownd, still **06** calmly, gently, meekly, mildly, mutely, softly **08** modestly, placidly, secretly, silently **09** inaudibly, privately **10** peacefully, tranquilly **11** noiselessly, soundlessly **12** deliberately **13** unobtrusively **15** surreptitiously

**quietness**
**04** calm, hush, lull **05** peace, quiet, still **06** repose **07** inertia, silence **08** calmness, dullness, quietude, serenity **09** composure, placidity, stillness **10** inactivity, quiescence **12** peacefulness, tranquillity **14** uneventfulness

**quietude**
**04** calm, hush, rest **05** peace, quiet **06** repose **07** ataraxy, silence **08** ataraxia, calmness, coolness, serenity **09** composure, placidity, quietness, stillness **10** equanimity, sedateness **11** restfulness **12** peacefulness, tranquillity

**quietus**
**03** end **05** death **06** demise **07** decease, release **08** dispatch, quashing **09** death-blow, discharge, silencing **10** extinction **11** acquittance, coup de grâce, death-stroke, elimination **15** finishing stroke

**quilt**
**05** doona, duvet, twilt **06** downie, kantha, thrash **07** comfort **08** bedcover, coverlet **09** bedspread, comforter, eiderdown **11** counterpane **12** counterpoint **14** patchwork quilt

**quince**
**03** bel **04** bael, bhel **06** feijoa **08** japonica **11** chaenomeles, queene-apple

**quinine**
**04** kina **05** china, quina **08** cinchona, kinakina **09** quinquina **10** chinachina, quinaquina

**quinsy**
**06** angina **08** cynanche, prunella **09** squinancy **11** tonsillitis

**quintessence**
**04** core, gist, pith, soul **05** heart **06** elixir, kernel, marrow, spirit **07** essence, extract, pattern **08** exemplar, quiddity **10** embodiment **12** distillation **15** personification, sum and substance

**quintessential**
**05** ideal **06** entire **07** perfect, typical **08** complete, ultimate **09** essential **10** consummate, definitive **12** archetypical, prototypical

**quip**
**03** gag **04** gibe, jest, joke **05** crack, quirk **06** retort, zinger **07** epigram, quibble, riposte **08** one-liner **09** wisecrack, witticism **10** knick-knack, pleasantry **12** carriwitchet

**quirk**
**03** way **04** kink, quip, turn, whim **05** fluke, freak, habit, knack, thing, trait, trick, twist **06** foible, hang-up, oddity, vagary **07** caprice, feature, quibble **09** curiosity, mannerism, obsession **11** peculiarity **12** eccentricity, idiosyncrasy **14** characteristic

**quirkiness**
**06** oddity **07** anomaly **08** zaniness **09** wackiness, weirdness **10** aberration, freakiness **11** abnormality, bizarreness, peculiarity, singularity, strangeness, unorthodoxy **12** eccentricity, freakishness, idiosyncrasy **13** nonconformity **14** capriciousness

**quirky**
◇ *anagram indicator*
**03** odd **04** wild, zany **05** barmy, drôle, droll, funky, funny, kinky, queer, wacky, weird **06** far-out, freaky, way-out, whimsy **07** bizarre, curious, deviant, oddball, strange, uncanny, unusual **08** aberrant, abnormal, atypical, crackers, freakish, original, peculiar, singular, uncommon **09** different, eccentric, irregular, whimsical **10** capricious, off the wall, outlandish, remarkable **11** exceptional **13** extraordinary, idiosyncratic **14** unconventional

**quisling**
**05** Judas **06** puppet **07** traitor **08** betrayer, renegade, turncoat **12** collaborator **14** fifth columnist

**quit**
**02** go **03** end, rid **04** drop, exit, free, part, stop, void **05** avoid, cease, clear, leave, quite, quyte, repay, shift, stash **06** acquit, decamp, depart, desert, desist, give up, go away, pack in, quight, resign, retire, vacate **07** abandon, abstain, forsake, requite **08** leave off, renounce, withdraw **09** surrender **10** chicken out, relinquish **11** discontinue

**quite**
**03** all, yes **04** full, just, real, tout, very **05** clean, clear, fully, right, sheer **06** depart, enough, fairly, indeed, quight, rather, really, resign, wholly **07** absolve, exactly, totally, utterly **08** actually, entirely, every bit, somewhat **09** every whit, perfectly, precisely **10** absolutely, completely, moderately, reasonably, relatively **12** to some degree, to some extent **13** comparatively

• **not quite**
◇ *tail deletion indicator*
**06** almost, nearly

**quits**
**04** even, meet **05** equal, evens, level **06** square

• **call it quits**
**04** stop **05** cease **08** break off **09** make peace **10** call it a day **11** discontinue **12** stop fighting **14** bury the hatchet **15** lay down your arms

**quitter**
**03** pus, rat **06** skiver **07** shirker **08** apostate, defector, deserter, recreant, renegade **10** delinquent

**quiver**
◇ *anagram indicator*
**05** quake, shake, throb **06** active, bicker, nimble, quaver, shiver, thrill, tingle, tremor, wobble **07** feather, flicker, flutter, pulsate, shudder, tremble, twinkle, vibrate **08** flichter **09** oscillate, palpitate, pulsation, vibration **11** oscillation, palpitation

**quixotic**
**06** errant **07** Utopian **08** fanciful, romantic **09** impetuous, impulsive, unworldly, visionary **10** chivalrous, idealistic, starry-eyed **11** extravagant, fantastical, unrealistic **13** impracticable

**quiz**
**03** eye **04** hoax, pump, test, yo-yo **05** grill, smoke, trail **07** examine, monocle **08** question **09** bandalore **11** competition, examination, interrogate, questioning **12** cross-examine **13** cross-question, interrogation, questionnaire

*Radio and television quiz shows include:*

**02** QI
**03** 3–2–1
**05** 15 to 1
**08** Bullseye, Eggheads
**09** Countdown, Odd One Out, Small Talk
**10** Mastermind, Masterteam, Screen Test
**11** Call My Bluff, Catchphrase, Give Us a Clue, Just a Minute, Spot the Tune, The Food Quiz, The News Quiz, What's My Line?
**12** Ask the Family, Blockbusters, Bognor or Bust, Face the Music, Fifteen to One, Going for Gold, Lucky Numbers, Name That Tune, Strike It Rich, Take Your Pick, Telly Addicts, Winning Lines
**13** Blankety Blank, Bob's Full House, Going for a Song, Strike It Lucky
**14** Brain of Britain, Family Fortunes, The Weakest Link, Wheel of Fortune, Winner Takes All
**15** Double Your Money, The Price Is Right

**quizzical**
**06** amused **07** amusing, baffled, comical, curious, mocking, puzzled, teasing **08** humorous, sardonic **09** inquiring, mystified, perplexed, satirical, sceptical **11** questioning

**quizzically**
**06** askant **07** askance **09** curiously, mockingly **11** inquiringly, sceptically **13** questioningly

**quoit**
**04** coit, disc, disk, ring
*See also* **buttocks**

**• target in quoits**
**03** hub, pin, tee

**quota**
**03** cut **04** part **05** share, slice, whack **06** quotum, ration **07** portion **09** allowance **10** allocation, assignment, contingent, percentage, proportion **11** slice of cake **14** numerus clausus

**quotation**
**03** bid, tag **04** cost, line, rate **05** piece, price, quote **06** charge, figure, tender **07** cutting, excerpt, extract, listing, passage, remnant **08** allusion, citation, estimate **09** reference, selection **14** locus classicus

**quote**
**04** cite, coat, cote, echo, name **05** coate **06** adduce, allege, drag up, recall, recite, repeat **07** examine, mention, refer to **08** allude to **09** recollect, reproduce **10** scrutinize

**quoted**
**05** cited **06** stated **08** reported **09** instanced **10** referred to, reproduced **13** forementioned **14** above-mentioned

**quotidian**
**05** daily **06** common, normal **07** diurnal, regular, routine **08** day-to-day, everyday, habitual, ordinary, repeated, workaday **09** customary, recurrent **11** bog-standard, commonplace **12** run-of-the-mill

# R

**R**
**02** ar **05** Romeo

**rabbi**

*Chief Rabbis include:*

**04** **Hart** (Aaron), **Lyon** (Hart)
**05** **Adler** (Hermann), **Adler** (Nathan), **Hertz** (J H), **Sacks** (Jonathan)
**06** **Brodie** (Israel)
**09** **Hirschell** (Solomon)
**10** **Jakobovits** (Immanuel, Lord)
**12** **Tevele Schiff** (David)

**rabbit**
**03** bun, doe **04** buck, cony, go on, talk **05** bunny, coney, daman, drone, hyrax **06** dassie, dodder, wander, wibble **07** go-devil, maunder **08** confound **09** give forth **11** bunny rabbit

*Rabbits and hares include:*

**03** fox, lop, Rex, tan
**04** jack, pika, rock, sage
**05** brown, Dutch, hotot, sable, satin, swamp, water
**06** Alaska, Angora, Arctic, Havana, oar-lap, Polish, silver, tapeti, Vienna
**07** Argente, Belgian, Flemish
**08** European, riverine, snowshoe
**09** Harlequin, Himalayan
**10** chinchilla, cottontail, New Zealand, Van Beveren
**11** black silver, English spot, Rhinelander

• **rabbit on**
**03** gab, yap **04** go on **06** babble, natter, waffle, witter **07** blather, blether, chatter, maunder **08** witter on **09** go on and on, maunder on

**rabble**
**03** mob, tag **04** herd, rout **05** crowd, horde, meiny, plebs **06** gabble, masses, meiney, meinie, menyie, proles, raffle, ragtag, rascal, tagrag, throng **07** doggery **08** canaille, populace, riff-raff, varletry **09** colluvies, hoi polloi, rascaille, rascality **10** clamjamfry **11** clanjamfray, proletariat, rank and file **12** clamjamphrie, common people, raggle-taggle **13** great unwashed

**rabble-rouser**
**08** agitator **09** demagogue, firebrand **10** incendiary, ringleader, tub-thumper **12** troublemaker

**rabble-rousing**
**10** stirring up **11** tub-thumping **13** troublemaking

**Rabelaisian**
**04** lewd, racy **05** bawdy, gross **06** coarse, earthy, ribald, risqué, vulgar **08** indecent **09** exuberant, satirical **11** extravagant, uninhibited **12** unrestrained

**rabid**
**03** mad **04** wild **06** ardent, crazed, raging **07** berserk, bigoted, burning, extreme, fervent, frantic, furious, violent, zealous **08** frenzied, maniacal **09** fanatical, ferocious, obsessive **10** hysterical, intolerant, irrational **11** hydrophobic, overzealous, unreasoning **12** narrow-minded

**rabies**
**05** lyssa **08** rabidity **09** rabidness **11** hydrophobia

**race**
**03** cut, fly, ren, rin, run, sex, zap, zip **04** bolt, clan, dart, kind, line, rach, rase, raze, rush, seed, slit, tear, zoom **05** blood, breed, chase, erase, genus, house, hurry, pluck, quest, ratch, scoot, slash, speed, stock, trial, tribe **06** career, colour, family, gallop, ginger, hasten, nation, people, snatch, stirps, strain **07** contest, dynasty, kindred, lineage, rivalry, scratch, species **08** ancestry, go all out, piquancy **09** parentage **10** accelerate, contention, extraction, get a move on **11** competition, ethnic group, get cracking, racial group, run like hell **15** take part in a race

*Races include:*

**02** TT
**04** Oaks
**05** Derby, Leger
**06** Le Mans
**07** St Leger
**08** Boat Race, Milk Race, RAC Rally
**09** Grand Prix
**11** Admiral's Cup, America's Cup, Breeder's Cup, Giro d'Italia, the Classics
**12** Melbourne Cup, Tour de France
**13** Diamond Sculls, Grand National, Kentucky Derby, Tourist Trophy
**14** Greyhound Derby, London Marathon
**15** Indianapolis 500, Monte Carlo rally, New York Marathon

*Race types include:*

**03** ski
**04** arms, dash, road, sack
**05** cycle, horse, motor, relay, space, yacht
**06** keirin, rowing, slalom, sprint
**07** harness, hurdles, pancake, pursuit, regatta, walking
**08** downhill, marathon, scramble, speedway, stock car, swimming, trotting
**09** Grand Prix, greyhound, motocross, motor-race, time trial, walkathon
**10** cyclo-cross, Formula One, motorcycle, track event
**11** donkey derby, egg-and-spoon, three-legged, wheelbarrow
**12** cross-country, steeplechase

**racecourse**
**03** lap **04** turf **05** track **06** course, dromos **07** circuit **08** speedway **09** racetrack **10** hippodrome

*Racecourses include:*

**03** Ayr
**04** York
**05** Ascot, Epsom
**07** Aintree, Chester, Newbury, Sandown, Warwick
**08** Goodwood, Wetherby
**09** Doncaster, Leicester, Newcastle, Newmarket, Towcester
**10** Cheltenham, Epsom Downs, Flemington, Longchamps, Pontefract
**11** Haydock Park, Kempton Park, Musselburgh, Sandown Park, Thistledown
**12** Hamilton Park

**racehorse**
**05** neddy, stiff **06** mudder, novice **07** no-hoper **08** cocktail, outsider, yearling **12** morning glory, thoroughbred

*See also* **horse**

**racial**
**04** folk **06** ethnic, tribal **07** genetic **08** national **09** ancestral, inherited **12** ethnological, genealogical

**raciness**
**03** pep **04** zest **06** energy **07** pizzazz **08** dynamism, lewdness, ribaldry **09** animation, bawdiness, crudeness, freshness, indecency, vulgarity **10** coarseness, ebullience, indelicacy, liveliness, smuttiness **11** naughtiness, zestfulness **12** exhilaration **14** suggestiveness

**racing**

*Horse racing-related terms include:*

**03** dam
**04** colt, firm, foal, form, good, hard, head, mare, nose, odds, sire, soft, stud, tote, trip, turf, yard

**05** evens, fence, field, filly, going, heavy, owner, place, silks, stake **06** chaser, faller, jockey, length, maiden, novice, odds-on, pull up, sprint, stable, stayer, tic-tac, weight **07** classic, furlong, gelding, meeting, tipster, trainer **08** blinkers, handicap, hurdling, juvenile, outsider, racecard, stallion, standard, stewards, yearling, yielding **09** ante-poste, bookmaker, favourite, group race, non-runner, pacemaker, short head **10** all-weather, bumper race, flat racing, listed race, parade ring, stakes race **11** accumulator, connections, handicapper, hunter chase, pattern race, photo finish, Triple Crown, winning post **12** handicap race, National Hunt, starting gate, steeplechase, thoroughbred, weighing room **14** conditions race **15** stewards' enquiry

*Formula One Grand Prix circuits include:*

**05** Imola, Monza **06** Sakhir, Sepang, Suzuka **07** Bahrain **08** Istanbul, Shanghai **10** Albert Park, Hockenheim, Interlagos, Magny-Cours, Monte Carlo **11** Hungaroring, Nurburgring, Silverstone **12** Indianapolis **13** Francorchamps

*Formula One motor racing teams include:*

**05** Honda **06** Toyota **07** Ferrari, McLaren, Midland, Red Bull, Renault **08** Williams **09** BMW Sauber, Toro Rosso **10** Super Aguri **13** Red Bull Racing

*Motor racing drivers, motorcyclists and associated figures include:*

**04** **Foyt** (A J), **Hill** (Damon), **Hill** (Graham), **Hunt** (James), **Ickx** (Jacky), **Moss** (Stirling) **05** **Alesi** (Jean), **Clark** (Jim), **Clark** (Roger), **Hulme** (Denny), **Lauda** (Niki), **McRae** (Colin), **Olsen** (Ole), **Petty** (Richard), **Prost** (Alain), **Rossi** (Valentino), **Sainz** (Carlos), **Senna** (Ayrton), **Unser** (Al), **Unser** (Bobby) **06** **Ascari** (Alberto), **Berger** (Gerhard), **Briggs** (Barry), **Button** (Jensen), **Doohan** (Michael), **Dunlop** (Joey), **Fangio** (Juan), **Irvine** (Eddie), **Lawson** (Eddie), **Mauger** (Ivan), **Piquet** (Nelson), **Sheene** (Barry), **Walker** (Murray) **07** **Brabham** (Sir Jack), **Brundle** (Martin), **Ferrari** (Enzo), **Fogarty** (Carl), **Guthrie** (Janet), **Mäkinen** (Tommi), **Mansell** (Nigel), **McLaren** (Bruce), **Mikkola** (Hannu), **Roberts** (Kenny), **Rosberg** (Keke), **Rosberg** (Nico), **Segrave** (Sir Henry), **Stewart** (Sir Jackie), **Surtees** (John) **08** **Agostini** (Giacomo), **Andretti** (Mario), **Campbell** (Donald), **Campbell** (Sir Malcolm), **Hailwood** (Mike), **Häkkinen** (Mika), **Oldfield** (Barney), **Williams** (Sir Frank) **09** **Blomqvist** (Stig), **Chevrolet** (Louis), **Coulthard** (David), **Earnhardt** (Dale), **Hawthorne** (Mike), **Kankkunen** (Juha) **10** **Fittipaldi** (Emerson), **Schumacher** (Michael), **Schumacher** (Ralf), **Villeneuve** (Jacques) **12** **Rickenbacker** (Eddie)

*Motor racing-related terms include:*

**03** lap, pit **04** apex, grid, oval, pits, pole, T-car **05** apron, shunt **06** out lap, slicks **07** chicane, cockpit, hairpin, marshal, pace car, paddock, pit lane, pit stop, stagger, steward **08** dirty air, drafting, fishtail, lollipop, outbrake, pit board, straight **09** Brickyard, parade lap, parc fermé, safety car, telemetry **10** back marker, gravel trap, qualifying, racing line, run-off area, slipstream, team orders **11** braking zone, pit straight, victory lane **12** formation lap, pole position **13** launch control, scrutineering, start straight, stop-go penalty, superspeedway **14** finish straight

## racism

**04** bias **08** jingoism **09** apartheid, prejudice, racialism **10** chauvinism, xenophobia **14** discrimination **15** racial prejudice

## racist

**04** Nazi **05** bigot **07** bigoted **09** racialist **10** chauvinist, intolerant **13** discriminator **14** discriminatory

## rack

**04** bink, hack, haik, hake, heck, pain, tear **05** agony, crash, creel, drift, drive, flake, frame, pangs, shake, shelf, stand, touse, touze, towse, towze, track, wrack, wrest, wring **06** extort, harass, harrow, holder, misery, strain, stress, wrench **07** afflict, agonize, anguish, crucify, distort, oppress, remnant, stretch, support, torment, torture, trestle **08** convulse, distress, lacerate, vertebra **09** framework, structure, suffering, vengeance **10** affliction, excruciate, overstrain, punishment **11** destruction, devastation, persecution, portmanteau **13** umbrella stand

• **on the rack**

**06** in pain **07** in agony **09** in trouble, suffering **10** in distress **11** under stress **13** under pressure **14** in difficulties

• **rack your brains**

**05** study **09** think hard **11** concentrate, think deeply **13** put your mind to

## racket

**03** bat, con, din, job, row **04** fuss, game, rort, scam **05** dodge, fraud, noise, trick **06** fiddle, hubbub, outcry, rattle, scheme, tumult, uproar **07** clamour, swindle, yelling **08** business, shouting, snowshoe **09** commotion, deception, gold brick **10** hullabaloo, hurly-burly, occupation **11** dissipation, disturbance, pandemonium **14** responsibility

## racketeering

**05** fraud **08** cheating, fiddling, fleecing, stealing, stinging **09** extortion, swindling **10** chiselling, defrauding, ripping off **12** overcharging **14** taking for a ride **15** cooking the books

## raconteur

**07** relater **08** narrator, reporter **09** describer **10** anecdotist, chronicler **11** commentator, storyteller

**racquet** *see* **racket**

## racy

**04** blue, rude **05** bawdy, crude, dirty, peppy, salty, spicy, witty, zippy **06** coarse, lively, ribald, risqué, smutty, vulgar **07** buoyant, dynamic, naughty, piquant, pungent, zestful **08** animated, indecent, spirited, vigorous **09** ebullient, energetic, off-colour, sparkling, vivacious **10** boisterous, fast-moving, indelicate, suggestive **12** enthusiastic

## radar

• **radar image**

**04** blip

• **radar signal**

**04** echo **05** angel

## raddled

◇ *anagram indicator*

**05** drawn, gaunt **06** wasted **07** haggard, in a mess, unkempt, worn out **11** dishevelled **15** the worse for wear

## radiance

**03** joy **04** glow **05** bliss, gleam, light, sheen, shine **06** lustre **07** delight, ecstasy, elation, glitter, rapture **08** pleasure **09** beaminess, happiness, radiation, splendour **10** brightness, brilliance, effulgence, luminosity, refulgence **12** resplendence **13** incandescence

## radiant

**05** beamy, happy, lit up **06** bright, elated, joyful **07** beaming, beamish, glowing, lambent, pleased, shining **08** blissful, ecstatic, gleaming, glorious, luminous, splendid **09** brilliant, delighted, effulgent, refulgent, sparkling **10** glittering, in raptures, profulgent **11** illuminated, magnificent, on cloud nine, over the moon, resplendent **12** incandescent **15** in seventh heaven, on top of the world

**radiate**
**03** ray **04** beam, emit, glow, pour, shed **05** gleam, issue, shine **06** branch, spread **07** diffuse, diverge, emanate, give off, scatter, send out **08** disperse **09** oscillate, send forth, spread out **10** divaricate **11** disseminate

**radiation**
**04** rays **05** waves **08** emission **09** emanation **12** transmission

*Radiation includes:*

**02** ir, UV
**03** UVA, UVB, UVC, UVR
**04** beta, hard, heat, soft
**05** alpha, gamma, light, X-rays
**06** cosmic
**07** Hawking, visible
**08** Cerenkov, gamma ray, infrared, ionizing
**09** black body
**10** background, black light, insolation, microwaves, radio waves, synchroton
**11** ultraviolet
**12** beta particle
**13** alpha particle
**14** bremsstrahlung
**15** electromagnetic

**• radiation unit**
**03** rad, rem, rep

**radical**
**03** rad, red **04** amyl, aryl, dyad, root **05** allyl, basic, butyl, cetyl, group, hexad, hexyl, monad, rebel, total, triad, utter, vinyl, yippy **06** acetyl, benzal, benzil, benzyl, entire, heptad, innate, ligand, methyl, native, pentad, phenyl, propyl, tetrad, yippie **07** benzoyl, carbene, drastic, extreme, fanatic, Jacobin, natural, oxonium, primary, radicle **08** absolute, ammonium, carbonyl, carboxyl, complete, glyceryl, glycosyl, hydroxyl, inherent, left-wing, militant, original, profound, reformer, sweeping, thorough **09** elemental, essential, extremist, fanatical, intrinsic, isopropyl, primitive, reformist **10** deep-seated, elementary, exhaustive, nitro-group, rebellious, vinylidene **11** benzylidine, far-reaching, fundamental, methyl group, phosphonium, rudimentary **13** comprehensive, ferricyanogen, ferrocyanogen, revolutionary, thoroughgoing **14** fundamentalist

**radio**
**08** wireless

*Radio stations include:*

**03** LBC, XFM
**04** Kiss
**06** Jazz FM, Kiss FM, Radio 1, Radio 2, Radio 3, Radio 4
**08** Five Live
**09** BBC London, Capital FM, Classic FM, Radio Five, Talksport
**11** Virgin Radio
**12** World Service
**13** Radio Caroline, Radio Scotland
**15** Radio Luxembourg

*Radio programmes include:*

**02** PM
**04** ITMA
**05** Today
**10** Home Truths, The Archers, Woman's Hour
**11** Just a Minute, You and Yours
**12** Any Questions?, Poetry Please, Start the Week
**13** Book at Bedtime, Pick of the Week, Round the Horne, The World at One
**14** Brain of Britain
**15** It's That Man Again

*See also* **quiz**

**• on the radio**
◇ *homophone indicator*
**02** DJ **10** disc jockey

**• radio presenter**
**02** DJ **10** disc jockey

*Radio presenters include:*

**04** **Mayo** (Simon), **Peel** (John), **Ross** (Jonathan), **Tong** (Pete)
**05** **Cooke** (Alistair), **Evans** (Chris), **Stern** (Howard), **Vance** (Tommy), **Wogan** (Terry), **Young** (Sir Jimmy)
**06** **Harris** (Bob), **Jensen** (Kid), **Lamacq** (Steve), **Lamarr** (Mark), **Lawley** (Sue), **Moyles** (Chris), **Murray** (Jenni), **Savile** (Sir Jimmy), **Travis** (Dave Lee), **Walker** (Johnnie), **Whiley** (Jo), **Wright** (Steve)
**07** **Edmonds** (Noel), **Everett** (Kenny), **Freeman** (Alan 'Fluff'), **Keillor** (Garrison), **Kershaw** (Andy), **Pickles** (Wilfred), **Plomley** (Roy), **Redhead** (Brian), **Tarrant** (Chris)
**08** **Anderson** (Marjorie), **Campbell** (Nicky), **Humphrys** (John), **Metcalfe** (Jean), **Westwood** (Tim)
**09** **Blackburn** (Tony), **MacGregor** (Sue), **Radcliffe** (Mark)
**10** **Gambaccini** (Paul), **Hardcastle** (William)
**11** **Nightingale** (Annie)

**radioactive**
**03** hot

**radish**
**05** mooli, runch **06** daikon **08** Raphanus

**radium**
**02** Ra

**radon**
**02** Rn

**raffish**
**04** loud **05** cheap, gaudy, gross, showy **06** casual, coarse, flashy, garish, jaunty, rakish, sporty, tawdry, trashy, vulgar **07** dashing, uncouth **08** bohemian, careless, improper **09** dissolute, tasteless **10** dissipated, flamboyant **12** devil-may-care, disreputable, meretricious

**raffle**
**04** draw **05** notch, sweep **06** jumble, lumber, rabble, tangle **07** crumple, lottery, rubbish, tombola **08** riff-raff **10** sweepstake

**raft**
**04** heap **05** balsa, crowd, float **09** catamaran **11** Carley float

**rag**
◇ *anagram indicator*
**03** kid, lap, rib, row, tat **04** bait, duds, flag, fray, goof, haze, jeer, mock, sail, slut, tatt **05** argue, cloth, clout, lapje, scold, scrap, shred, taunt, tease, towel **06** badger, banter, duster, lappie, tagrag, tatter, wallop **07** duddery, flannel, garment, remnant, torment, wrangle **08** farthing, ridicule **09** newspaper, schmutter **10** floorcloth, paper money, raggedness **12** handkerchief

*See also* **newspaper**

**• bunch of rags**
**03** mop

**ragamuffin**
**04** waif **05** gamin, ragga **06** urchin **11** guttersnipe **14** tatterdemalion **15** tatterdemallion

**ragbag**
**03** mix **04** olio **05** salad **06** jumble, medley **07** mixture **08** mishmash, pastiche, slattern **09** confusion, potpourri **10** assemblage, assortment, hodgepodge, hotchpotch, miscellany **11** olla-podrida **14** omnium-gatherum

**rage**
◇ *anagram indicator*
**03** ire **04** bait, bate, bayt, fume, fury, ramp, rant, rave, tear **05** anger, craze, flame, flood, go mad, mania, paddy, party, radge, storm, vogue, wrath **06** ardour, frenzy, raving, see red, seethe, temper, tumult **07** bluster, explode, madness, passion, rampage, tantrum, thunder, violent **08** boil over, paroxysm, violence **09** blow a fuse, do your nut, raise hell, spit blood **10** hit the roof, paddy-whack **11** blow a gasket, blow your top, flip your lid, go up the wall, lose your rag **12** blow your cool, lose your cool, spit feathers **14** foam at the mouth **15** fly off the handle, go off the deep end

**• all the rage**
**02** in **03** now **04** cool **06** trendy **07** in vogue, popular, stylish **08** the craze **10** the in thing **11** fashionable

**ragged**
◇ *anagram indicator*
**04** poor, rag'd, rent, torn **05** duddy, holey, ragde, rough, tatty **06** duddie, frayed, jagged, raguly, ripped, rugged, shabby, shaggy, tagrag, uneven, untidy **07** erratic, in holes, notched, scruffy, tattery, unkempt, worn-out **08** indented, indigent, serrated, tattered **09** destitute, in tatters, irregular **10** down and out, down-at-heel, fragmented, straggling, threadbare **12** disorganized

14 tatterdemalion 15 falling to pieces, tatterdemallion

**raging**
03 mad 04 amok, wild 05 amuck, angry, irate, rabid 06 fuming, ireful, raving, stormy 07 enraged, furious, violent 08 flagrant, frenzied, furibund, incensed, seething, wrathful
09 turbulent 10 infuriated, tumultuous
11 fulminating

**raid**
02 do 04 bust, loot, pull, road, rode, rush, sack 05 blitz, foray, onset, rifle, sally, storm, swoop 06 assail, attack, bodrag, charge, forage, hold-up, inroad, invade, maraud, sortie, strike 07 air raid, assault, break-in, descent, pillage, plunder, ram-raid, ransack, robbery, set upon, spreagh 08 dawn raid, invasion 09 break into, descend on, excursion, incursion, onslaught, sneak-raid 12 Baedeker raid

**raider**
05 crook, shark, thief 06 looter, pirate, robber, viking 07 brigand, invader, villain 08 attacker, criminal, marauder, pillager 09 plunderer, ransacker

**rail**
03 bar 04 flow, gush, jeer, mock, rung, sora, spar 05 abuse, cloak, decry, raile, rayle, scoff 06 attack, banter, Rallus, revile 07 arraign, censure, garment, inveigh, protest, upbraid 08 denounce, reviling, ridicule 09 castigate, criticize, fulminate 10 slang-whang, vituperate, vociferate 11 neckerchief

**railing**
04 rail 05 fence, rails 06 paling, pulpit
07 barrier, fencing, manrope, parapet, pushpit 08 parclose, raillery
09 fireguard 10 balustrade

**raillery**
04 joke 05 chaff, irony, sport 06 banter, joking, satire 07 jeering, jesting, kidding, mockery, ragging, railing, ribbing, teasing 08 badinage, diatribe, dicacity, repartee, ridicule
09 chiacking, invective 10 persiflage, pleasantry

**railway**
02 Ry 03 rly, Rwy 04 line, rail 05 rails, track 08 railroad

*Railways include:*

01 L
02 el
03 cog, ell
04 rack, ship, tube
05 cable, light, metro, model
06 garden, scenic, siding, subway
07 cutting, express, freight, tramway
08 cable-car, electric, elevated, main line, monorail, mountain
09 funicular, goods line, InterCity®, trunk line
10 branch line, broad gauge, feeder line
11 crémaillère, narrow gauge, underground
12 rapid transit
13 high-speed line, passenger line, rack-and-pinion, standard gauge

*Railway-related terms include:*

02 CN
03 ABC, ATC, ATP, bay, cab, car, CPR, EWS, GWR, lie, LMS, LNE, lye, RMT, rod, RPC, SRA, Sta, tie, TOC, van
04 APEX, bank, crew, dock, dome, frog, halt, LNER, RUCC, slot, SPAD, spur, stay, TPWS
05 aisle, berth, bogey, bogie, brake, brute, coach, coupé, crank, depot, diner, grate, guard, local, Mogul, shunt, T-rail, train, wagon
06 banker, boiler, branch, buffer, coaler, diesel, gricer, hopper, piston, points, porter, reefer, saloon, siding, stoker, target, tender, tunnel, up-line, waggon, Y-track
07 ballast, banking, bay-line, buckeye, bulgine, butcher, caboose, cocopan, cutting, drag-bar, drawbar, entrain, fettler, firebox, fireman, hostler, lineman, locoman, network, off-peak, Pullman, railage, railbed, railbus, railcar, railman, roadbed, signals, sleeper, station, tank car, turnout, viaduct, whistle, yardman
08 box-wagon, Bradshaw, brakeman, brake van, bullgine, cant-rail, carriage, catenary, choo-choo, corridor, coupling, crosstie, down-line, draw-gear, firehole, fire-tube, fly-under, horse box, junction, live-rail, loop-line, main line, manrider, motorail, motorman, overpass, pilotman, platform, puff-puff, rack rail, railcard, railhead, roomette, side-line, smokebox, subgrade, terminus, trackage, trackbed, wagon-lit
09 brakesman, buffet car, checkrail, concourse, conductor, couchette, crossover, cross-sill, day return, dining-car, drag-chain, fishplate, footboard, footplate, funicular, goods line, goods yard, guardrail, guard's van, interrail, iron horse, jerkwater, lengthman, overshoot, palace-car, parlor car, plate rail, pointsman, rail-borne, rail-motor, railwoman, second man, sidetrack, signal box, signalman, slip-coach, steam pipe, tank wagon, third rail, train mile, trunk line, turntable, vestibule, wheelbase
10 baggage-car, brake block, branch line, broad-gauge, centre-rail, draught-bar, embankment, Eurotunnel, feeder line, griddle car, home-signal, lengthsman, locomotive, luggage-van, parlour car, platelayer, Pullman car, railroader, railwayman, smokestack, steam brake, supersaver, surfaceman, switchback, tank engine, zone-ticket
11 compartment, gandy dancer, goods engine, left-luggage, people mover, pilot engine, rack railway, railroad car, ship railway, side cutting, sleeping car, strap-hanger, throatplate, track-walker, underbridge, underground, vacuum brake, whistle stop
12 double-header, driving wheel, engine-driver, euroterminal, footplateman, loading gauge, rolling stock, running board, shunting yard, station house, trainspotter
13 conductor rail, dead man's pedal, level crossing, sleeping coach, standard gauge, stationmaster, through-ticket
14 dead man's handle, shuttle service, superelevation
15 marshalling yard

*See also* **train**

• **railway station**

*Railway stations include:*

05 Crewe
06 Euston
08 Victoria, Waterloo, Waverley
09 St Pancras
10 Gare de Lyon, Gare du Nord, Kings Cross, Marylebone, Paddington, Piccadilly
11 Penn Station
12 Charing Cross, Gare St Lazare, Grand Central, Hauptbahnhof, Montparnasse
15 Clapham Junction, Gare d'Austerlitz, Liverpool Street

*See also* **London**

**rain**
03 wet 04 pelt, pour, roke, sile, smir, smur, spet, spit, teem, weep 05 blash, brash, raine, reign, smirr, storm, water
06 bucket, deluge, mizzle, shower, squall, volley 07 drizzle, skiffle, torrent
08 down-come, downfall, downpour, pour down, rainfall, sprinkle
09 raindrops, rainstorm, sunshower
10 bucket down, cloudburst, Scotch mist, tipple down 12 thunderstorm
13 precipitation, the clouds open
15 rain cats and dogs

**rainbow**
03 arc, bow 04 arch, iris 05 prism
06 bruise, dew-bow, fog-bow, irised, sunbow 07 moon-bow 08 irisated, spectral, spectrum 09 arc-en-ciel, prismatic, steelhead, water gall
10 iridescent, opalescent, variegated, weather gaw 11 rainbow-like, weather gall 13 kaleidoscopic

*Colours of the rainbow:*

03 red
04 blue
05 green
06 indigo, orange, violet, yellow

**raincoat**
03 mac 04 mack, mino 08 Burberry®
09 macintosh 10 mackintosh

**rainy**
03 wet 04 damp, soft 05 moist

06 hyetal, watery **07** drizzly, pluvial, showery **08** pluviose, pluvious **09** inclement

**raise**
◇ *reversal indicator*
**02** up **03** get **04** buoy, grow, jack, levy, lift, moot, rear, rise, stir **05** amass, boost, breed, build, cairn, cause, elate, erect, evoke, exalt, extol, hoist, leave, mount, put up, rally, rouse, set up, utter, weigh **06** araise, arayse, arouse, broach, bump up, create, excite, gather, hike up, hold up, jack up, lift up, muster, obtain, push up, step up, stir up, take up, uplift **07** advance, amplify, augment, bring up, collect, develop, educate, elevate, enhance, heave up, magnify, nurture, present, produce, provoke, recruit, suggest, upgrade **08** activate, assemble, escalate, heighten, increase, purchase **09** construct, cultivate, establish, institute, intensify, introduce, propagate **10** accumulate, give rise to, put forward, strengthen **11** get together

**raised**
◇ *reversal down indicator*
**05** cameo **06** relief **07** applied, relievo **08** appliqué, elevated, embossed

**rake**
**03** hoe **04** comb, hunt, roam, roué **05** amass, graze, level, rifle, scour, slope, track **06** gather, gay dog, harrow, lecher, scrape, search, smooth, strafe, straff, string, wanton **07** collect, incline, journey, pasture, playboy, ransack, rummage, scratch, swinger **08** buckrake, hedonist, Lothario, muck-rake, prodigal, rakehell **09** debauchee, dissolute, horse rake, libertine **10** accumulate, degenerate, profligate, sensualist **11** spendthrift, stubble rake **14** pleasure-seeker

**• rake in**
**03** net **04** earn, make, reap **05** fetch, gross **06** haul in, pull in **07** bring in, get paid, receive

**• rake up**
**05** dig up, raise **06** drag up, remind, revive **07** bring up, mention **08** dredge up **09** introduce

**rake-off**
**03** cut **04** part **05** share, slice **07** portion **10** percentage, proportion

**rakish**
**05** loose, natty, sharp, smart **06** breezy, casual, dapper, flashy, jaunty, sinful, snazzy, sporty **07** dashing, immoral, raffish, stylish **08** debonair, depraved, prodigal **09** abandoned, debauched, dissolute, lecherous, libertine **10** degenerate, dissipated, flamboyant, licentious, nonchalant, profligate **11** adventurous **12** devil-may-care

**rally**
**04** demo, rely **05** group, march, unite **06** banter, gather, morcha, muster, perk up, pick up, really, reform, revive, summon **07** collect, convene, get well, improve, marshal, meeting, recover, regroup, renewal, reunion, revival, round up **08** assemble, assembly, comeback, jamboree, mobilize, organize, recovery **09** gathering, get better, re-enforce **10** assemblage, bounce back, conference, congregate, convention, reassemble, recuperate, reorganize, resurgence **11** be on the mend, convocation, get together, improvement, mass meeting, pull through **12** band together, come together, gain strength, recuperation **13** bring together, demonstration

**ram**
**03** hit, jam, pun, tup **04** beat, bump, butt, cram, dash, drum, pack, slam, stem, tamp **05** Aries, crash, crowd, drive, force, pound, smash, stuff, wedge **06** corvus, hammer, punner, strike, thrust, wether **07** block up, squeeze **08** compress

**ramble**
◇ *anagram indicator*
**03** gas, jaw **04** hike, roam, rove, tour, trek, trip, walk, wind **05** amble, drift, jaunt, range, stray, tramp, troll **06** babble, dodder, natter, rabbit, stroll, waffle, wander, wanton, witter, zigzag **07** blather, blether, chatter, digress, diverge, meander, saunter, traipse **08** bushwalk, rabbit on, straggle, witter on **09** excursion, expatiate **15** go off at a tangent

**rambler**
**05** hiker, rover **06** roamer, walker **07** drifter **08** stroller, wanderer, wayfarer **09** saunterer, traveller **10** bushwalker

**rambling**
◇ *anagram indicator*
**05** wordy **06** errant, vagary **07** verbose **08** errantry, trailing **09** desultory, excursive, sprawling, spreading, wandering **10** circuitous, digressive, disjointed, incoherent, long-winded, roundabout, straggling **12** disconnected, long-drawn-out, periphrastic **14** skimble-skamble

**rami**
**04** rhea **10** China grass, grass cloth

**ramification**
**04** limb **06** branch, effect, result, sequel, upshot **07** outcome **08** offshoot **09** branching, outgrowth **11** consequence, development, implication **12** complication, divarication

**ramp**
**03** rob **04** rage, rise, romp **05** climb, grade, slope **06** ramson, snatch, tomboy **07** incline, swindle **08** gradient **09** acclivity, declivity

**rampage**
◇ *anagram indicator*
**04** fury, rage, rant, rave, rush, tear **05** storm **06** charge, frenzy, furore, mayhem, uproar **07** run amok, run riot, run wild, turmoil **08** violence **09** go berserk **10** rush wildly **11** destruction **13** rush violently

**• on the rampage**
◇ *anagram indicator*
**04** amok, wild **06** wildly **07** berserk, violent **08** frenzied **09** in a frenzy, violently **12** out of control

**rampant**
◇ *anagram indicator*
◇ *reversal indicator*
**04** rank, rife, wild **06** fierce, raging, wanton **07** profuse, rearing, riotous, violent **08** epidemic, pandemic **09** excessive, out of hand, prevalent, unbridled, unchecked **10** widespread **12** high-spirited, out of control, uncontrolled, unrestrained

**rampart**
**04** bank, fort, ring, wall **05** fence, guard **06** abatis, vallum **07** abattis, bastion, bulwark, defence, parapet, rampire **08** security **09** barricade, earthwork **10** breastwork, embankment, stronghold **13** fortification

**ramshackle**
◇ *anagram indicator*
**05** shaky **06** flimsy, ruined, unsafe **07** rickety, run-down **08** decrepit, derelict, unsteady **09** crumbling, neglected, tottering **10** broken-down, jerry-built, tumbledown **11** dilapidated

**ranch**
**04** farm, tear **05** range **06** estate, spread **07** fazenda, station **08** estancia, hacienda, property **09** dude ranch **10** plantation **12** sheep station **13** cattle station

**rancid**
**03** bad, off **04** foul, high, rank, sour **05** fetid, frowy, musty, stale **06** foetid, frowie, putrid, rotten, turned **07** froughy, noisome, noxious **08** overripe **10** malodorous, unpleasant

**rancorous**
**06** bitter **07** acerbic, hostile **08** spiteful, vengeful, venomous, virulent **09** malignant, resentful, splenetic **10** implacable, malevolent, vindictive **11** acrimonious

**rancour**
**04** hate **05** spite, venom **06** animus, enmity, grudge, hatred, malice, spleen **07** ill-will **08** acrimony, sourness **09** animosity, antipathy, hostility, malignity, virulence **10** bitterness, ill-feeling, resentment **11** malevolence **13** resentfulness **14** vindictiveness

**rand**
**01** R

**random**
◇ *anagram indicator*
**04** spot, wild **05** stray **06** casual, chance **07** aimless, freedom **08** sporadic **09** arbitrary, desultory, haphazard, hit-or-miss, irregular, unplanned **10** accidental, at a venture, fortuitous, hit-and-miss, hitty-missy, incidental, stochastic, unarranged **11** purposeless, scattershot

**12** uncontrolled, unmethodical, unsystematic **13** serendipitous **14** indiscriminate

• **at random**

◇ *anagram indicator*

**06** hobnob **07** at large **08** at rovers, randomly **09** aimlessly, haphazard **11** arbitrarily, haphazardly, irregularly **12** fortuitously, incidentally, sporadically **13** purposelessly **14** unmethodically **15** à tort et à travers

**randomly**

◇ *anagram indicator*

**08** at random **09** aimlessly **11** arbitrarily, haphazardly, irregularly **12** incidentally, sporadically **13** purposelessly **14** unmethodically

**randy**

**03** hot **04** sexy **05** horny, rudas **06** virago **07** amorous, aroused, goatish, lustful, raunchy, satyric **08** turned-on **09** lecherous **10** boisterous, lascivious **12** concupiscent

**range**

**02** go **03** ren, rin, row, run **04** area, file, kind, line, oven, raik, rank, roam, rove, sort, span, type, vary **05** align, amble, array, carry, chain, class, cover, drift, field, gamut, genus, grade, grass, group, level, orbit, order, reach, ridge, scale, scope, stove, stray, sweep **06** bounds, cooker, domain, draw up, extend, extent, limits, line up, meadow, radius, ramble, series, sierra, sphere, spread, string, stroll, wander **07** arrange, compass, dispose, earshot, grazing, paddock, pasture, purview, species, stretch, variety **08** classify, confines, distance, latitude, province, spectrum **09** amplitude, catalogue, diversity, fluctuate, grassland, pasturage, selection **10** assortment, categorize, cordillera, parameters, pigeonhole, straighten **11** grazing land **12** distribution

*See also* **mountain**

• **range over**

**04** scur, sker **05** skirr **06** squirr

**rangy**

**05** lanky, leggy, roomy, weedy **06** skinny **08** gangling, rawboned **10** long-legged, long-limbed **11** mountainous

**rank**

**03** row **04** état, file, foul, gree, line, lush, mark, nobs, rate, sort, tier, type, vile **05** acrid, align, caste, class, dense, élite, fetid, grade, gross, group, level, lords, lusty, order, peers, place, range, sheer, stale, toffs, total, utter **06** arrant, coarse, column, degree, draw up, estate, family, foetid, gentry, line up, nobles, putrid, rancid, series, status, string, strong **07** arrange, blatant, dispose, echelon, glaring, peerage, profuse, pungent, station, stratum, swollen, utterly, violent **08** absolute, abundant, classify, complete, division, flagrant, mephitic, nobility, organize, position, shocking, standing, stinking, thorough, vigorous **09** condition, downright, formation, luxuriant, offensive, out-and-out, overgrown, repulsive, revolting, violently **10** categorize, disgusting, graveolent, malodorous, outrageous, unpleasant **11** aristocracy, high society, unmitigated, unqualified **12** disagreeable, evil-smelling **14** classification

*Air force ranks:*

**05** major
**07** captain, colonel, general
**08** corporal, sergeant
**10** air marshal
**11** aircraftman
**12** air commodore, aircraftsman, group captain, major general, pilot officer
**13** aircraftwoman, flying officer, wing commander
**14** aircraftswoman, air vice-marshal, flight sergeant, squadron leader, warrant officer
**15** air chief marshal, first lieutenant
**16** brigadier general, flight lieutenant, second lieutenant
**17** lieutenant colonel, lieutenant general
**19** leading aircraftsman
**20** general of the air force
**21** leading aircraftswoman
**25** marshal of the Royal Air Force

*Army ranks:*

**05** major
**07** captain, colonel, general, marshal, private
**08** corporal, sergeant
**09** brigadier
**10** bombardier, lieutenant
**12** field marshal, major general
**13** lance-corporal, staff sergeant
**14** warrant officer
**15** first-lieutenant, lance-bombardier
**16** brigadier-general, general of the army, second-lieutenant
**17** lieutenant colonel, lieutenant-general

*Naval ranks:*

**06** ensign, rating, seaman
**07** admiral, captain
**09** captain RN, commander, commodore
**10** able seaman, lieutenant, midshipman
**11** rear admiral, vice-admiral
**12** fleet admiral, petty officer
**13** leading seaman, sublieutenant
**14** warrant officer
**16** commodore admiral
**17** admiral of the fleet, chief petty officer
**19** lieutenant-commander
**21** lieutenant junior grade

*See also* **nobility**; **police**

• **other ranks**

**02** OR

• **rank and file**

**03** mob **04** herd **05** crowd, plebs **06** masses, proles, rabble **08** populace, riff-raff, soldiers **09** hoi polloi **10** grass-roots **11** ordinary men, proletariat **12** common people **15** private soldiers

**rankle**

**03** bug, irk, vex **04** gall, rile **05** anger, annoy, peeve **06** fester, nettle, poison **08** embitter, irritate **11** get your goat **13** get on your wick, get up your nose, get your back up **14** get your blood up **15** get on your nerves

**rank-smelling**

**04** olid

**ransack**

**04** comb, fish, hunt, loot, raid, rake, ripe, sack **05** harry, rifle, scour, strip **06** maraud, ravage, search **07** despoil, pillage, plunder, rummage **09** depredate, devastate, go through, ranshakle **10** ranshackle **13** turn inside out **14** rummage through, turn upside down

**ransom**

**04** free **05** atone, money, price **06** buy off, pay-off, redeem, rescue **07** deliver, freedom, payment, release, set free **08** liberate **09** atonement **10** liberation, redemption **11** deliverance, restoration, setting free **15** buy the freedom of

**rant**

**03** cry **04** rand, rave, roar, yell **05** mouth, shout, storm **06** bellow, crying, tirade **07** bluster, bombast, declaim, oration, roaring, yelling **08** diatribe, harangue, rhetoric, shouting, tear a cat, tub-thump **09** hold forth, philippic **10** slang-whang, tear the cat, vociferate **11** declamation, rant and rave **12** vociferation

**rap**

**03** hit, pan, tap **04** bang, blow, clip, cuff, flak, grab, knap, rail, slam, whit, wrap **05** blame, boost, clout, crime, flick, flirt, knock, ragga, scold, slate, stick, swear, thump, whack **06** batter, hammer, hip-hop, patter, punish, rattle, rebuke, snatch, strike, yanker **07** censure, commend, gangsta, reprove, run down, slating, testify **08** knocking, slamming **09** castigate, criticize, reprimand **10** come down on, punishment **11** acclamation, castigation, pick holes in **12** pull to pieces, tear to pieces, tear to shreds

• **take the rap**

**08** pay for it **10** be punished **12** face the music, take the blame **14** get it in the neck

**rapacious**

**06** greedy **07** preying, wolfish, wolvish **08** esurient, grasping, ravening, ravenous, uncaring, usurious **09** marauding, predatory, voracious, vulturine, vulturish, vulturous

**10** avaricious, insatiable, plundering **12** extortionate

• **rapacious person**

**04** kite

**rapacity**

**05** greed, usury **07** avarice, avidity **08** voracity **09** esurience, esuriency, vulturism **10** greediness **11** wolfishness **12** graspingness, ravenousness **13** predatoriness, rapaciousness, shark's manners, voraciousness **14** insatiableness

**rape**

**03** rob **04** loot, raid, sack **05** abuse, navew, strip **06** defile, rapine, ravage, ravish **07** assault, despoil, looting, outrage, pillage, plunder, ransack, sacking, seizure, violate, vitiate **08** coleseed, date rape, deflower, gang rape, gang-rape, maltreat, ravaging, spoliate, violence **09** depredate, devastate, stripping, transport, violation **10** defilement, plundering, ransacking, ravishment, spoliation **11** depredation, devastation **12** despoliation, maltreatment **13** sexual assault, statutory rape **15** assault sexually

**rapid**

**03** pdq **04** fast **05** brisk, chute, hasty, nifty, quick, shoot, shute, swift, zippy **06** lively, prompt, speedy **07** express, hurried, stickle **08** headlong **09** splitting **11** expeditious, precipitate **13** like lightning **15** pretty damn quick

**rapidity**

**04** rush **05** haste, hurry, speed **08** alacrity, celerity, dispatch, velocity **09** briskness, fleetness, quickness, swiftness **10** expedition, promptness, speediness **11** promptitude **15** expeditiousness, precipitateness

**rapidly**

**04** fast **05** quick **06** pronto **07** briskly, hastily, like fun, quickly, swiftly **08** promptly, speedily **09** hurriedly **11** at the double, like winking **12** a mile a minute, lickety-split **13** expeditiously, precipitately **14** at a rate of knots, hell for leather **15** like the clappers

**rapine**

**04** prey, rage, raid, rape **05** raven, ravin **06** ravine **07** looting, sacking, seizure **08** ravaging **09** stripping, transport, violation **10** defilement, plundering, ransacking, ravishment, spoliation **11** depredation, devastation **12** despoliation

**rapport**

**04** bond, link **07** empathy, harmony **08** affinity, relation, sympathy **10** connection **12** relationship **13** understanding

**rapprochement**

**07** détente, reunion **09** agreement, softening **13** harmonization, reconcilement **14** reconciliation

**rapt**

**06** intent, way-out **07** charmed, gripped **08** abducted, absorbed, ecstatic, ravished, snatched, thrilled **09** bewitched, delighted, enchanted, engrossed, entranced **10** captivated, enraptured, enthralled, fascinated, spellbound **11** preoccupied, rhapsodical, transported **12** concentrated

**rapture**

**03** joy **05** bliss **07** delight, ecstasy, elation **08** euphoria, felicity, paroxysm **09** cloud nine, happiness, transport **10** enragement, exaltation **11** delectation, enchantment **12** exhilaration **13** seventh heaven, top of the world

• **go into raptures**

**04** fire, gush, rave **05** drool **06** excite, praise **07** enthuse, inspire **08** motivate **10** bubble over, effervesce, wax lyrical

**rapturous**

**05** happy **06** joyful, joyous **07** exalted **08** blissful, ecstatic, euphoric, ravished **09** delighted, entranced, overjoyed, rhapsodic **11** dithyrambic, on cloud nine, over the moon, tickled pink, transported **12** enthusiastic **15** in seventh heaven, on top of the world

**rare**

◇ *anagram indicator*

**04** seld, thin **05** early **06** choice, geason, scarce, sparse, superb **07** curious, unusual **08** precious, sporadic, superior, uncommon **09** excellent, exquisite, matchless, recherché, underdone **10** far between, infrequent, remarkable **11** exceptional, outstanding, superlative **12** incomparable, like gold dust, unparalleled **13** extraordinary, one in a million **15** thin on the ground

**rarefied**

**04** high, thin **05** noble **06** select, subtle **07** private, refined, special, sublime, tenuous **08** esoteric, tenuious **09** exclusive **10** attenuated

**rarely**

**04** seld **06** hardly, little, seldom **08** choicely, scarcely **10** hardly ever, once in a way **12** infrequently, occasionally, once in a while, scarcely ever, sporadically **13** spasmodically **14** intermittently **15** once in a blue moon

**raring**

**04** keen **05** eager, ready **07** itching, longing, willing **09** desperate, impatient **12** enthusiastic

**rarity**

**03** gem **04** find **05** curio, pearl **06** marvel, wonder **08** scarcity, shortage, thinness, treasure **09** curiosity, nonpareil **10** sparseness **11** infrequency, strangeness, unusualness **12** uncommonness **14** collector's item

**rascal**

**03** imp **04** loon, lown **05** devil, lorel, losel, lowne, rogue, scamp, skelm, smaik **06** lozell, rabble, schelm, skelum, tinker, toerag, varlet **07** a bad hat, cullion, hallian, hallion, hallyon, knavish, lorrell, skellum, villain, wastrel **08** scalawag, schellum, spalpeen, vagabond, wretched **09** rascaille, scallawag, scallywag, scoundrel, skeesicks, son of a gun **10** ne'er-do-well, rascallion, scapegrace **11** rapscallion **13** mischief-maker **14** good-for-nothing, two-for-his-heels

**rascally**

**03** bad, low **04** base, evil, mean **06** arrant, wicked **07** crooked, hangman, knavish, roguish, vicious **09** dishonest, reprobate **10** villainous **11** furciferous, mischievous, scoundrelly **12** disreputable, unscrupulous **14** good-for-nothing

**rash**

◇ *anagram indicator*

**03** run **04** dash, drag, fast, itch, rush, tear, wave **05** flood, hasty, heady, hives, slash, spate, stick **06** deluge, madcap, plague, series, unwary **07** rosacea, roseola, torrent **08** careless, epidemic, eruption, headlong, heat rash, heedless, madbrain, outbreak, reckless, temerous **09** audacious, dare-devil, foolhardy, hot-headed, impetuous, imprudent, impulsive, over-hasty, pompholyx, premature, unguarded, urticaria **10** headstrong, ill-advised, indiscreet, irritation, madbrained, nettlerash, unthinking **11** adventurous, furthersome, hare-brained, harum-scarum, hasty-witted, precipitate, temerarious **13** ill-considered, inconsiderate

**rashly**

**07** hastily **08** headlong, unwarily **09** on impulse **10** carelessly, heedlessly, recklessly **11** audaciously, impetuously, imprudently, impulsively, over-hastily **12** indiscreetly **15** without thinking

**rashness**

**08** audacity, hazardry, temerity **09** brashness, hastiness, incaution **10** imprudence **12** carelessness, heedlessness, indiscretion, precipitance, precipitancy, recklessness **13** foolhardiness, impulsiveness, precipitation **14** incautiousness **15** adventurousness, thoughtlessness

**rasp**

**03** bug, jar, rub **04** file, risp, sand **05** croak, grate, grind, peeve, scour **06** abrade, cackle, scrape, squawk **07** grating, scratch, screech **08** grinding, irritate **09** excoriate, harshness, raspberry **10** hoarseness **15** get on your nerves

**rasping**

**05** gruff, harsh, husky, raspy, rough **06** croaky, filing, hoarse **07** grating, jarring, raucous **08** creaking, croaking, gravelly, scratchy **10** stridulant

**rat**
**03** rot, spy **04** blab, blow, fink, mole, nark, nose, shop, sing, stag, vole **05** dob on, grass, hutia, Judas, peach, puppy, sneak, snout, split **06** agouta, betray, canary, finger, fizgig, gopher, inform, ratton, rumble, snitch, squeal, tell on **07** peacher, stoolie, traitor **08** approver, Arvicola, betrayer, denounce, informer, musk-cavy, promoter, renegade, sand mole, snitcher, squeaker, squealer, tell-tale, turncoat **09** bandicoot, informant, sycophant, water vole, whisperer **10** discoverer, supergrass **11** incriminate, stool pigeon **12** cutting grass **13** strike-breaker, whistle-blower

**rate**
**03** fee, MPH, pay, ret, sum, tax **04** cess, cost, deem, duty, hire, mode, pace, rank, time, toll **05** allot, basis, chide, class, count, grade, judge, merit, price, prize, ratio, scale, scold, speed, sum up, tempo, value, weigh, worth **06** admire, amount, assess, charge, degree, esteem, extent, figure, manner, rating, reckon, regard, tariff **07** adjudge, deserve, justify, measure, payment, reprove, respect, tallage, warrant, weigh up **08** appraise, classify, consider, estimate, evaluate, relation, standard, velocity **09** calculate **10** be worthy of, categorize, estimation, percentage, proportion **12** be entitled to, have a right to

*See also* **scold**

• **at any rate**
**05** at all **06** anyhow, anyway **07** at least **09** in any case **10** at the least, in any event, regardless **12** nevertheless

**rather**
**03** gay, gey, yes **04** a bit, more, some, very **05** quite **06** a bit of, fairly, indeed, pretty, sooner, sort of **07** a little, instead **08** by choice, slightly, somewhat **09** for choice **10** from choice, moderately, much rather, much sooner, noticeably, preferably, relatively **12** by preference, to some degree, to some extent **13** for preference, significantly

**ratification**
**08** approval **10** validation
**11** affirmation, endorsement
**12** confirmation **13** authorization, certification, corroboration
**14** authentication, seal of approval
**15** stamp of approval

**ratify**
**02** OK **04** amen, seal, sign **06** affirm, strike, uphold **07** agree to, approve, certify, confirm, endorse, warrant
**08** legalize, sanction, validate
**09** authorize, establish, preconize
**10** homologate **11** corroborate, countersign **12** authenticate

**rating**
**02** AB **04** mark, rank **05** class, grade, order, score **06** degree, status
**07** grading, placing, ranking, set-down
**08** category, position, standing
**09** adjudging, appraisal
**10** assessment, evaluation
**14** classification

**ratio**
**04** rate **05** index **07** balance, portion
**08** fraction, quotient, relation, symmetry **09** allowance
**10** percentage, proportion
**11** correlation **12** relationship
**14** correspondence

**ration**
**03** lot **04** food, part, save **05** allot, issue, limit, point, quota, share
**06** amount, budget, stores, supply, viands **07** control, deal out, dole out, hand out, helping, measure, mete out, portion **08** allocate, conserve, dispense, restrict, supplies, victuals
**09** allotment, allowance, apportion, divide out **10** allocation, distribute, foodstuffs, iron ration, measure out, percentage, proportion, provisions
**11** compo ration

**rational**
**04** sane, wice, wise **05** lucid, sober, sound **06** normal **07** logical, prudent
**08** balanced, cerebral, grounded, sensible, thinking **09** cognitive, judicious, realistic, reasoning, sagacious **10** Apollonian, discursive, reasonable **11** circumspect, clear-headed, enlightened, intelligent, well-founded **12** intellectual
**13** philosophical, ratiocinative **15** in your right mind

**rationale**
**05** basis, logic **06** motive, reason, theory, thesis **07** grounds, purpose, reasons **09** principle, reasoning
**10** hypothesis, motivation, philosophy
**11** explanation, raison d'être

**rationalization**
**06** excuse **08** excusing, updating
**11** explanation, vindication
**12** streamlining **13** justification, modernization **14** reorganization

**rationalize**
**04** trim **06** excuse, update **07** explain, justify **09** cut back on, modernize, vindicate **10** account for, pragmatize, reorganize, streamline **11** cut out waste, explain away

**rationally**
**06** sanely **07** lucidly **08** sensibly
**09** logically, prudently **10** reasonably, thinkingly **11** judiciously, sagaciously, without bias **13** intelligently
**15** philosophically

**rattle**
◇ *anagram indicator*
**03** jar, rap **04** bang, bump, faze, jolt, reel, tirl **05** alarm, clang, clank, clink, knock, shake, upset **06** bounce, hurtle, jangle, jingle, put off, put out, racket, ruckle **07** clapper, clatter, confuse, disturb, fluster, jarring, jolting, shaking, sistrum, unnerve, vibrate **08** clanking, clinking, irritate, unsettle **09** crepitate, vibration **10** disconcert
**13** tintinnabulum **15** throw off balance

• **rattle off**
**04** list **06** recite, repeat **07** reel off
**10** run through **11** list quickly

• **rattle on**
**03** gab **04** yack **05** prate **06** cackle, gabble, jabber, natter, witter
**07** blether, chatter, chunter, prattle
**08** rabbit on

**ratty**
**05** angry, cross, short, testy **06** peeved, snappy, touchy, untidy **07** annoyed, crabbed, grouchy, unkempt
**08** wretched **09** impatient, irritable
**13** short-tempered

**raucous**
**04** loud **05** harsh, husky, noisy, rough, rusty, sharp **06** hoarse, raucid, shrill
**07** grating, jarring, rasping **08** piercing, strident **10** discordant, scratching, screeching **11** ear-piercing

**raunchy**
**04** lewd, sexy **05** bawdy **06** earthy, erotic, nubile, shabby, slinky
**07** sensual **08** alluring, arousing, inviting **09** desirable, provoking, salacious, seductive **10** attractive, suggestive, voluptuous **11** flirtatious, provocative, stimulating, titillating
**12** pornographic

**ravage**
◇ *anagram indicator*
**04** loot, raze, ruin, sack **05** harry, havoc, level, spoil, wreck **06** damage, maraud **07** despoil, destroy, looting, pillage, plunder **08** demolish, lay waste, wreckage **09** depredate, devastate, ruination **10** desolation, ransacking, spoliation **11** depredation, destruction, devastation
**12** despoliation, leave in ruins

**ravaged**
◇ *anagram indicator*
**06** spoilt **07** war-torn, war-worn, wrecked **08** desolate **09** destroyed, ransacked, shattered, war-wasted
**10** battle-torn, devastated

**rave**
◇ *anagram indicator*
**02** do **03** cry **04** bash, fume, hail, orgy, rage, rant, roar, yell **05** crazy, disco, extol, go ape, go mad, party, shout, storm, taver **06** babble, bellow, blow up, jabber, ramble, rave-up, see red, seethe, sizzle, taiver **07** acclaim, blow-out, enthuse, explode, knees-up, thunder **08** boil over, carousal, ecstatic, freak out, praising **09** blow a fuse, do your nut, excellent, go bananas, go berserk, laudatory, raise hell, rapturous, wonderful **10** be mad about, favourable, hit the roof, talk wildly, wax lyrical **11** blow a gasket, blow your top, celebration, flip your lid, go up the wall, have kittens, infatuation, lose your rag, rant and rave **12** blow your cool, enthusiastic, fly into a rage, lose your cool, throw a wobbly
**13** throw a tantrum **14** acid-house

party, foam at the mouth, go into raptures, lose your temper **15** fly off the handle, get all steamed up, go off the deep end

**raven**
**03** jet **04** Grip, inky, prey **05** black, crake, dusky, ebony, ravin, sable **06** corbie, rapine **07** preying **08** jet-black **09** coal-black

**ravenous**
**06** greedy, hungry **07** starved, wolfish, wolvish **08** famished, starving **09** rapacious, voracious **10** insatiable, plundering, very hungry

**rave-up**
**02** do **04** bash, orgy **05** party **06** thrash **07** blow-out, debauch, shindig **08** carousal **11** celebration

**ravine**
**03** gap, lin **04** gill, khor, khud, linn, nala, pass, prey **05** abyss, cañon, chine, flume, ghyll, gorge, goyle, grike, gryke, gulch, gully, heuch, heugh, kloof, nalla, nulla **06** arroyo, canyon, clough, coulée, gullet, gulley, nallah, nullah, rapine **07** preying **09** purgatory

*See also* **gorge**

**raving**
◇ *anagram indicator*
**03** mad **04** wild **05** barmy, batty, crazy, loony, loopy **06** insane, maniac, mental **07** berserk, furious **08** demented, deranged, frenzied **09** delirious **10** barking mad, frantic-mad, hysterical, irrational, unbalanced **12** round the bend **13** out of your mind, round the twist

**ravings**
**06** drivel, yammer **07** prattle, rubbish, twaddle **08** nonsense **09** gibberish **10** balderdash, mumbo-jumbo **12** gobbledygook

**ravish**
**04** rape **05** abuse, charm, force **06** abduct, defile **07** assault, bewitch, delight, enchant, enthral, oppress, outrage, overjoy, violate **08** entrance, maltreat, stuprate, suppress **09** captivate, enrapture, fascinate, spellbind **11** constuprate **15** assault sexually, force yourself on

**ravishing**
**06** lovely, raping **07** radiant **08** alluring, charming, dazzling, gorgeous, stunning **09** beautiful, seductive **10** bewitching, delightful, enchanting **11** enthralling **12** transporting

**raw**
**03** new, red, wet **04** bare, cold, damp, hard, open, sore **05** basic, bleak, blunt, chill, crude, crudy, cruel, frank, fresh, green, harsh, naive, naked, nippy, plain, rough, wersh **06** biting, bitter, bloody, brutal, callow, candid, chafed, chilly, grazed, strong, tender **07** abraded, exposed, intense, natural, scraped, tartare **08** freezing, ignorant, immature, piercing, uncooked, ungenial **09** outspoken, realistic, scratched, sensitive, unrefined, unskilled, untrained, untreated, untutored, unwrought **10** excoriated, forthright, true-to-life, unfinished, unprepared **11** unpractised, unprocessed **13** inexperienced

**ray**
**02** re **04** beam, hint, look **05** array, dirty, dress, flash, gleam, glint, manta, roker, shaft, skate, spark, trace **06** defile, glance, streak, stream **07** flicker, glimmer, homelyn, radiate, torpedo, twinkle **09** cramp-fish, thornback **10** indication, sea vampire, suggestion

**raze**
**04** fell, race, rase, ruin **05** erase, graze, level, wreck **06** scrape, slight **07** destroy, flatten **08** bulldoze, demolish, pull down, tear down **09** dismantle, knock down

**razor**
**04** keen **05** sharp **06** shaver **07** precise **09** cut-throat **11** cutting edge

**re**
**03** are, ray **05** about **09** regarding **10** concerning **12** with regard to **14** on the subject of **15** with reference to

**reach**
**03** bay, fax, hit, rax, win **04** call, come, deal, gain, hand, hent, hold, make, pass, ring, shot, span, take **05** ambit, get at, get to, grasp, phone, power, range, retch, scope, seize, touch **06** amount, arrive, attain, come at, come to, extend, extent, go up to, snatch, spread, strike **07** achieve, command, compass, contact, control, get onto, project, speak to, stretch, write to **08** amount to, arrive at, artifice, come up to, continue, distance, go down to, latitude, make it to **09** authority, extension, get hold of, go as far as, influence, telephone **10** come down to, stretch out **12** get through to, jurisdiction **14** get in touch with **15** communicate with

*See also* **retch**

• **reach down**
**03** dip

• **reach out**
**04** push

**react**
◇ *anagram indicator*
**03** act **04** defy **05** rebel, reply **06** answer, behave, oppose, resist, rise up **07** dissent, respond **08** kick back, retroact **09** retaliate **11** acknowledge, reciprocate

**reaction**
**05** reply, stink **06** answer, recoil, reflex **08** backlash, backwash, feedback, kickback, response, reversal **09** reversion, swing-back **11** retaliation **12** repercussion **13** counteraction, reciprocation **14** antiperistasis, counterbalance **15** acknowledgement

**reactionary**
◇ *anagram indicator*
◇ *reversal indicator*
**06** Junker **07** Bourbon, diehard, redneck **08** mandarin, rightist, Sadducee **09** right-wing, young fogy **10** Neandertal, young fogey **11** Neanderthal, right-winger, traditional **12** conservative, Neandertaler **13** Neanderthaler **14** Neanderthal man, traditionalist **15** backward-looking

**read**
**03** maw, rad **04** look, name, scan, show, skim **05** solve, speak, study, teach, utter **06** advise, browse, decode, glance, look at, peruse, recite, record, saying **07** counsel, declaim, declare, deliver, dip into, display, examine, expound, learned, measure, perusal **08** abomasum, browsing, construe, decipher, indicate, pore over, register, scanning, scrutiny, skimming **09** interpret **10** comprehend, scrutinize, understand **11** leaf through **12** flick through, thumb through **13** browse through **14** interpretation

• **read aloud**
◇ *homophone indicator*

• **read into**
**05** infer **06** deduce, reason **08** construe **09** interpret **12** misinterpret

**readable**
**05** clear **07** legible **08** gripping **09** enjoyable **10** easy to read **11** captivating, enthralling, interesting, stimulating **12** decipherable, entertaining, intelligible, worth reading **13** unputdownable **14** comprehensible, understandable

**reader**
**06** hearer, lector, taster **08** audience, bookworm, epistler, lectress, lecturer, listener **09** addressee, epistoler, prelector **10** pocketbook **13** bibliophagist

**readership**
**08** audience, regulars **09** following **11** subscribers

**readily**
**04** soon **06** easily, freely, gladly **07** eagerly, happily, lightly, quickly, rapidly, swiftly **08** promptly, smoothly, speedily, with ease **09** willingly **12** effortlessly **14** unhesitatingly

**readiness**
**04** ease **05** alert, skill **07** fitness **08** alacrity, aptitude, facility, gameness, keenness, rapidity **09** eagerness, handiness, quickness **10** promptness **11** inclination, preparation, promptitude, willingness **12** availability, preparedness

• **in readiness**
**05** ready **06** on call **07** at point **08** at a point, at points, prepared **09** available, on standby **10** standing by **11** at all points, on full alert **13** in preparation

**reading**
**04** scan, text **05** piece, study **06** figure, lesson, record **07** display, edition, lection, passage, perusal, recital, section, version **08** browsing, decoding, register, scrutiny
**09** rendering, rendition **10** indication, inspection, recitation **11** deciphering, examination, measurement
**13** understanding **14** interpretation
**• variant reading**
**02** vl

**reading-desk**
**04** ambo **07** lectern

**ready**
**02** go **03** apt, fit, set **04** boun, cash, easy, free, game, keen, near, ripe, yare
**05** alert, bound, bowne, close, eager, equip, handy, happy, order, prest, prime, prone, quick, rapid, sharp, swift
**06** all set, astute, at hand, clever, direct, on hand, prompt, speedy, to hand
**07** about to, addrest, ad manum, arrange, attired, dressed, forward, pleased, prepare, present, scratch, waiting, willing **08** arranged, disposed, equipped, finished, geared up, hard cash, inclined, liable to, likely to, organize, pregnant, prepared
**09** addressed, available, completed, dexterous, fitted out, immediate, organized, psyched up, rigged out
**10** accessible, convenient, discerning, perceptive, pernicious, ready money, the needful **11** predisposed, resourceful, within reach
**12** enthusiastic, on the point of, on the verge of, unhesitating **14** argent comptant
**• at the ready**
**03** set **06** all set, poised **08** prepared
**09** mobilized

**real**
**04** rial, ryal, sure, trew, true **05** quite, right, royal, truly, utter, valid **06** actual, dinkum, honest, proper, really, thingy
**07** certain, dinki-di, dinky-di, factual, fervent, genuine, sincere **08** absolute, bona fide, complete, concrete, dinky-die, existing, material, official, physical, positive, rightful, tangible, thorough, truthful, unfabled **09** authentic, heartfelt, immovable, occurring, simon-pure, unfeigned, veritable
**10** fair dinkum, legitimate, sure-enough, unaffected **11** substantial, substantive **12** from the heart

**realign**
◇ *anagram indicator*
**09** reshuffle **10** straighten

**realism**
**06** sanity **08** saneness **09** actuality
**10** naturalism, pragmatism, televérité
**11** genuineness, naturalness, rationality
**12** authenticity, cinéma vérité, faithfulness, lifelikeness, practicality, sensibleness, truthfulness

**realistic**
**04** real, true **05** close, vivid
**07** genuine, graphic, logical, natural
**08** detached, faithful, lifelike, rational, real-life, sensible, truthful
**09** authentic, hard-nosed, objective, practical, pragmatic **10** figurative, hard-boiled, hard-headed, true-to-life, unromantic **11** commonsense, down-to-earth, level-headed **12** businesslike, clear-sighted, matter-of-fact
**13** unsentimental

**realistically**
**05** truly **07** vividly **08** sensibly
**09** genuinely, logically **10** faithfully, rationally, truthfully **11** graphically, objectively, practically **12** figuratively
**13** authentically, pragmatically
**14** unromantically **15** unsentimentally

**reality**
**04** fact **05** truth **06** effect, verity
**07** realism **08** positive, real life, validity
**09** actuality, certainty, existence, real world, thingness **10** thinginess
**11** genuineness, materiality, tangibility, thingliness **12** authenticity, corporeality **14** substantiality
**• in reality**
**05** truly **06** indeed, in fact, really **07** for real, in truth **08** actually **09** in earnest
**10** in practice **12** in actual fact, in all but name **13** in point of fact **15** as a matter of fact

**realization**
**04** gain **05** grasp **06** making
**07** earning, selling **08** clearing, fetching **09** awareness **10** acceptance, cognizance, completion, fulfilment, perception **11** achievement, discernment, performance, recognition **12** appreciation, apprehension, consummation
**13** actualization, comprehension, consciousness, understanding
**14** accomplishment, implementation
**• expression of realization**
**03** why

**realize**
**03** get, net, see **04** earn, gain, make, twig **05** clear, fetch, glean, grasp, learn
**06** accept, effect, encash, fulfil, obtain, take in **07** achieve, bring in, catch on, discern, perform, produce, sell for
**08** complete, cotton on, discover, perceive, register, tumble to
**09** actualize, apprehend, ascertain, implement, recognize **10** accomplish, appreciate, articulate, bring about, comprehend, concretize, consummate, effectuate, understand
**11** see the light **13** become aware of

**really**
**03** way **04** very **05** quite, rally, truly
**06** highly, indeed, in fact, quight, simply, surely, verily **08** actually, honestly, in effect, severely
**09** certainly, extremely, genuinely, intensely, sincerely **10** absolutely, positively, remarkably, straight up, thoroughly **11** undoubtedly **13** as large as life, categorically, exceptionally

**realm**
**04** area, land **05** field, orbit, reame, reign, state, world **06** domain, empire, region, sphere **07** country, kingdom, royalty **08** monarchy, province, queendom **09** territory **10** department
**12** principality

**reap**
**03** cut, get, mow, win **04** crop, gain, swap, swop **05** shear **06** derive, garner, gather, obtain, secure **07** acquire, collect, harvest, realize, receive

**rear**
◇ *reversal indicator*
◇ *tail selection indicator*
**03** end **04** back, grow, hind, last, lift, loom, rise, rump, soar, tail **05** breed, erect, hoist, nurse, raise, rouse, set up, stern, tower, train **06** behind, bottom, foster, hinder, hold up, lift up, parent, rise up, stir up, take up **07** bring up, build up, care for, educate, elevate, nurture, tail-end **08** backside, buttocks, hindmost, instruct, lavatory, rearmost **09** cultivate, look after, originate, posterior
*See also* **toilet**

**rearrange**
◇ *anagram indicator*
**04** vary **05** alter, rejig, shift **06** adjust, change **07** reorder **08** rejigger
**09** reshuffle **10** reposition, reschedule
**11** consolidate

**reason**
**03** aim, end, wit **04** case, goal, mind, nous **05** argue, basis, brain, cause, color, infer, logic, sense, solve, think
**06** colour, debate, deduce, excuse, ground, induce, motive, object, reckon, remark, sanity, wisdom
**07** defence, discuss, examine, grounds, impetus, premise, pretext, purpose, resolve, thought, warrant, work out
**08** argument, cogitate, conclude, converse, gumption, occasion, think out **09** cerebrate, discourse, encheason, incentive, intellect, intention, judgement, rationale, reasoning, syllogize **10** inducement, moderation, motivation, proportion
**11** common sense, explanation, raison d'être, ratiocinate, rationality
**12** intelligence, use your brain
**13** comprehension, consideration, justification, ratiocination, understanding **15** intellectuality
**• reason with**
**04** coax, move, urge **08** persuade
**09** argue with, plead with **10** debate with **11** discuss with, expostulate
**15** remonstrate with
**• within reason**
**10** moderately **12** in moderation, within bounds, within limits **15** with self-control

**reasonable**
**02** OK **03** low **04** fair, just, okay, sane, wise **05** sound **06** modest, viable
**07** average, logical **08** credible, moderate, possible, rational, reasoned, sensible **09** judicious, plausible, practical, sagacious, tolerable,

wholesome **10** acceptable **11** competitive, inexpensive, intelligent, justifiable, well-advised **12** satisfactory **13** no great shakes **14** understandable, well-thought-out

**reasonably**

**02** OK **04** okay **05** quite **06** fairly, rather, wisely **08** passably, sensibly, somewhat **09** plausibly, tolerably **10** adequately, moderately, rationally **13** intelligently

**reasoned**

**05** clear, sound **07** logical **08** rational, sensible **09** judicious, organized **10** methodical, systematic **14** well-thought-out

**reasoning**

**04** case **05** logic, proof **07** ijtihad, thought **08** analysis, argument, thinking **09** casuistry, deduction, induction, rationale, syllogism, synthesis **10** hypothesis, philosophy **11** cerebration, supposition **13** argumentation, ratiocination **14** interpretation **15** rationalization

**reassemble**

◇ *anagram indicator*

**05** rally **07** rebuild **09** re-enforce **11** reconstruct

**reassurance**

**05** cheer **06** urging **07** coaxing, comfort, succour **08** cheering **10** heartening, incitement, motivation, persuasion **11** consolation, exhortation, inspiration, stimulation **13** encouragement

*See also* **encouragement**

**reassure**

**05** brace, cheer, nerve, rally **06** buoy up, stroke **07** bolster, cheer up, comfort, confirm, hearten, inspire **08** inspirit, reinsure **09** cosy along, encourage

**rebate**

**04** dull **05** abate, blunt **06** rabbet, reduce, refund **08** decrease, discount **09** allowance, deduction, reduction, repayment

**rebel**

◇ *anagram indicator*

**04** defy, riot **06** flinch, mutine, mutiny, oppose, recoil, resist, revolt, rise up, shrink **07** aginner, beatnik, defiant, disobey, dissent, heretic, run riot, shy away **08** agitator, apostate, mutineer, mutinous, pull back, recusant, revolter **09** dissenter, guerrilla, insurgent **10** malcontent, rebellious, schismatic **11** disobedient, turn against **12** malcontented, paramilitary **13** insubordinate, nonconformist, revolutionary **14** freedom fighter **15** insurrectionary

*Rebels include:*

**04** **Aske** (Robert), **Ball** (John), **Cade** (Jack), **Kett** (Robert)
**05** **Lalor** (Peter)
**06** **Fawkes** (Guy)
**09** **Glendower** (Owen)
**10** **Engelbrekt**

*See also* **revolutionary**

**rebellion**

**04** coup, riot **06** heresy, mutine, mutiny, revolt, rising **07** dissent, treason **08** defiance, uprising **09** coup d'état **10** insurgence, insurgency, opposition, resistance, revolution **12** disobedience, insurrection **15** insubordination

*Rebellions include:*

**03** Rum
**07** Fifteen, Whiskey
**08** Jacobite
**09** Forty-Five
**10** the Fifteen
**12** Easter Rising, the Forty-Five
**14** Eureka Stockade

**rebellious**

◇ *anagram indicator*

◇ *reversal indicator*

**06** unruly **07** defiant, rioting **08** mutinous **09** insurgent, malignant, obstinate, rebelling, resistant, seditious **10** disorderly, refractory **11** disobedient, intractable **12** contumacious, recalcitrant, ungovernable, unmanageable **13** insubordinate, revolutionary **15** insurrectionary

**rebirth**

**07** renewal, revival **11** reawakening, renaissance, restoration **12** regeneration, rejuvenation, resurrection, risorgimento **13** reincarnation **14** revitalization

**rebound**

**04** fail **05** carom **06** bounce, double, recoil, re-echo, resile, result, return, spring **07** bricole, redound **08** backfire, ricochet **09** boomerang, carambole, reflexion, throw back **10** backfiring, bounce back, reflection, spring back **11** reverberate **12** defeat itself, repercussion **13** reverberation **14** score an own goal **15** be self-defeating, come home to roost

**rebuff**

**03** cut **04** snub **05** check, noser, spurn **06** refuse, reject, rubber, slight **07** decline, put down, put-down, refusal, repulse, set-down, squelch **08** brush-off, spurning, turn down **09** knock back, rejection, repudiate **10** discourage **11** counterbuff, one in the eye, repudiation **12** cold shoulder, cold-shoulder **13** slap in the face **14** a flea in your ear, discouragement, kick in the teeth

**rebuild**

◇ *anagram indicator*

**06** reform, remake **07** re-edify, remodel, restore **08** renovate **09** reaedifye, refashion **10** reassemble **11** reconstruct **12** haussmannize, rehabilitate

**rebuke**

**04** rate, slap, snub, trim **05** blame, check, chide, sauce, scold, score, stick **06** carpet, earful, lesson, talk to, threap, threep **07** censure, lecture, reproof, reprove, rollick, speak to, tell off, tick off, trounce, upbraid **08** admonish, call down, keelhaul, reproach, restrain, scolding, trimming **09** carpeting, castigate, dress down, go crook at, go crook on, objurgate, pitch into, raspberry, reprimand **10** admonition, go to town on, rollicking, telling-off, ticking-off **11** castigation, comeuppance, remonstrate **12** countercheck, dressing-down, give an earful **13** remonstration, tear off a strip **14** throw the book at **15** give someone hell

**rebut**

**05** elide, quash, repel **06** defeat, negate, recoil, refute **07** confute, explode **08** disprove, overturn **09** discredit **10** invalidate **12** give the lie to

**rebuttal**

**06** defeat **08** disproof, negation **09** overthrow **10** refutation **11** confutation **12** invalidation

**recalcitrance**

**08** defiance **09** obstinacy **10** wilfulness **11** waywardness **12** disobedience, stubbornness **13** unwillingness **14** refractoriness **15** insubordination

**recalcitrant**

**06** unruly, wilful **07** defiant, wayward **08** contrary, renitent, stubborn **09** obstinate, unwilling **10** refractory **11** disobedient, intractable **12** contumacious, ungovernable, unmanageable, unsubmissive **13** insubordinate, unco-operative **14** uncontrollable

**recall**

◇ *reversal indicator*

**05** annul, evoke **06** call up, cancel, go over, memory, repeal, revoke, summon **07** nullify, reclaim, rescind, retract, retreat, think of, unswear **08** abrogate, call back, dredge up, recision, remember, summon up, withdraw **09** annulment, bring back, order back, recollect, reminisce **10** abrogation, call to mind, retraction, revocation, summon back, withdrawal **11** countermand, remembrance, think back to **12** cancellation, recollection **13** nullification, order to return **14** countermanding

**recant**

**04** deny **05** unsay **06** abjure, disown, recall, revoke **07** disavow, rescind, retract **08** abrogate, disclaim, forswear, renounce, unpreach, withdraw **09** repudiate **10** apostatize

**recantation**

**06** denial, revoke **08** apostasy, palinode, palinody **09** disavowal **10** abjuration, disclaimer, disownment, revocation, withdrawal **11** repudiation **12** renunciation, retractation

**recapitulate**
**05** recap, sum up **06** go over, repeat, review **07** recount, restate, run over **09** reiterate, summarize

**recapitulation**
**06** review **07** summary **08** epanodos **09** summing-up **10** repetition **11** reiteration, restatement, summarizing

**recast**
◇ *anagram indicator*
**05** alter **06** modify, revamp, revise, rework **07** rewrite **08** rephrase, revision

**recce**
**04** case, scan **05** probe **06** patrol, search, spy out, survey **07** examine, explore, inspect, observe **08** check out, scouting, scrutiny **10** expedition, inspection, scrutinize **11** examination, exploration, investigate, observation, reconnoitre **13** investigation, reconnoitring **14** reconnaissance

**recede**
◇ *reversal indicator*
**03** ebb **04** drop, fade, sink, wane **05** abate **06** go back, lessen, retire, return, shrink **07** decline, dwindle, fall off, regress, retreat, slacken, subside **08** decrease, diminish, move away, withdraw **10** retrograde

**receipt**
**03** pay, rec **04** chit, note, rept, slip, stub **05** gains, paper, recpt, tally **06** chitty, docket, income, recipe, return, ticket **07** gaining, getting, profits, returns, takings, voucher, warrant **08** capacity, delivery, deriving, earnings, proceeds, turnover **09** obtaining, quittance, receiving, reception **10** acceptance **11** acquittance, counterfoil, dock-warrant **13** money received **14** deposit-receipt **15** acknowledgement, proof of purchase

**receive**
◇ *containment indicator*
**03** get **04** bear, draw, gain, hear, hold, take **05** admit, fence, greet, latch, let in **06** accept, come by, derive, gather, obtain, pick up, suffer, take up **07** acquire, be given, collect, contain, embrace, harbour, inherit, react to, sustain, undergo, welcome **08** meet with, perceive **09** apprehend, encounter, entertain, entertake, go through, respond to **10** experience, learn about **11** accommodate, take on board **12** be informed of, find out about

**receiver**
**03** tap **05** donee, fence, radio, tuner **07** catcher, grantee, handset, legatee **08** assignee, receptor, wireless **09** apparatus, recipient, televisor **10** radiopager **11** beneficiary **13** satellite dish **14** stamp collector **15** direction-finder, superheterodyne

**recent**
**03** low, new **04** late **05** fresh, novel, young **06** latest, latter, modern **07** current **08** ci devant, neoteric, up-to-date **09** latter-day **10** neoterical, present-day **11** Post-Glacial **12** contemporary **13** up-to-the-minute

**recently**
**04** late **05** newly **06** lately, of late **07** freshly **09** yesterday **10** not long ago **13** a short time ago

**receptacle**
**04** bath, sink **05** bosom, purse **06** holder, vessel **09** container, reservoir **10** repository **11** conceptacle, reservatory **12** receptaculum

**reception**
**02** do **04** bash **05** beano, levee, party **06** accoil, at-home, durbar, pick-up, rave-up, ruelle, social **07** ovation, receipt, reunion, shindig, welcome **08** assembly, function, greeting, occasion, reaction, response **09** admission, gathering, treatment **10** acceptance, assumption, bel-accoyle, bon accueil, recipience, recipiency **11** get-together, recognition **12** entertaining **13** entertainment **15** acknowledgement

**receptive**
**04** open **05** quick **07** willing **08** amenable, flexible, friendly, pregnant **09** recipient, sensitive, welcoming **10** accessible, favourable, hospitable, interested, open-minded, responsive **11** suggestible, susceptible, sympathetic **12** approachable, open to reason **13** accommodating

**recess**
◇ *reversal indicator*
**03** bay, cwm **04** apse, bole, bunk, cove, ingo, nook, rest **05** ambry, awmry, bower, break, heart, hitch, niche, oriel, press, sinus **06** alcove, almery, aumbry, awmrie, bowels, bunker, cavity, cirque, closet, corner, corrie, depths, exedra, hollow, indent, locule **07** adjourn, exhedra, holiday, innards, loculus, mortice, mortise, outshot, reaches, respite, time off, time out **08** cupboard, interior, interval, playtime, vacation **09** blank door, breaktime, embrasure, embrazure, seclusion, sepulcher, sepulchre **10** depression, penetralia, retirement **11** blank window, columbarium, indentation **12** confessional, intermission

**recession**
**05** crash, slide, slump **06** trough **07** decline, failure **08** collapse, downturn, shake-out **10** depression, withdrawal **15** economic decline

**recherché**
**04** rare **06** arcane, choice, exotic, select **07** obscure, refined, tenuous **08** abstruse, esoteric **10** far-fetched

**recipe**
**01** r **03** rec, way **04** dish, take **05** guide, means **06** method, system **07** formula, process, receipt **09** procedure, technique **10** directions **11** ingredients **12** instructions, prescription

**recipient**
**05** donee **06** vessel **07** grantee, legatee **08** assignee, donatory, receiver **09** receiving, receptive **10** suscipient **11** beneficiary

**reciprocal**
**05** joint **06** mutual, reflex, shared **07** inverse **08** requited, returned **09** commutual, exchanged, reflexive **10** equivalent, quid pro quo **11** alternating, correlative, give-and-take **13** complementary, corresponding **14** interdependent **15** interchangeable

**reciprocate**
**04** swap **05** equal, match, repay, reply, trade **06** return **07** requite, respond **08** exchange **09** alternate, do the same **10** correspond **11** interchange **12** give in return

**reciprocity**
**08** exchange **09** isopolity, mutuality **11** alternation, equivalence, give-and-take **14** correspondence **15** interdependence

**recital**
**04** show **06** report **07** account, concert, reading, telling **08** relation **09** narration, rendering, rendition **10** recitation, repetition **11** commination, declamation, description, enumeration, performance, solmization **14** interpretation

**recitation**
**03** ave **04** poem, tale **05** piece, story, verse **07** passage, reading, recital, telling **09** monologue, narration, rendering **10** party piece **11** incantation, performance

**recite**
**04** scan, tell **05** chant, chime, daven, speak **06** chaunt, relate, repeat **07** declaim, deliver, itemize, narrate, perform, recount, reel off **08** say aloud **09** enumerate, improvise, rattle off **10** articulate, rhapsodize **11** improvisate

**reckless**
◇ *anagram indicator*
**04** rash, wild **05** brash, hasty, perdu, ton-up **06** madcap, perdue **07** wildcat **08** careless, heedless, kamikaze, mindless, tearaway **09** blindfold, daredevil, desperate, foolhardy, imprudent, negligent, rantipole, rechlesse, retchless **10** ill-advised, incautious, indiscreet **11** harum-scarum, inattentive, precipitate, temerarious, thoughtless **12** devil-may-care **13** irresponsible

**recklessly**
◇ *anagram indicator*
**06** rashly **07** hastily **09** full fling, like water **10** carelessly, mindlessly

11 desperately, negligently
13 irresponsibly, thoughtlessly

**recklessness**
06 Bayard 07 madness 08 rashness
09 incaution 10 imprudence, negligence 11 desperation, gallowsness, inattention
12 carelessness, heedlessness, mindlessness 13 foolhardiness
15 thoughtlessness

**reckon**
03 sum 04 call, deem, make, rate
05 add up, class, count, fancy, gauge, guess, judge, place, sum up, tally, think, total, value, vogue 06 assess, assume, esteem, expect, figure, impute, number, regard 07 account, believe, compute, imagine, put down, suppose, surmise, think of, work out 08 appraise, consider, estimate, evaluate, look upon
09 calculate, designate, enumerate, figure out 10 conjecture

• **reckon on**
04 face 06 bank on, expect, rely on
07 count on, foresee, hope for, plan for, trade on, trust in 08 depend on, figure on 10 anticipate, bargain for 14 take for granted 15 take into account

• **reckon with**
04 cope, deal, face 05 treat 06 expect, handle 07 foresee, plan for
08 consider 10 anticipate, bargain for
15 take into account

• **reckon without**
06 ignore 08 overlook 09 disregard, not expect, not notice 13 fail to think of

• **to be reckoned with**
05 great 06 mighty, strong 07 weighty
08 forceful, powerful 09 important
10 formidable 11 influential, significant
12 considerable

**reckoning**
03 due, tab 04 bill, doom, tale, time
05 count, datal, lawin, score, tally, total
06 charge, lawing, number, paying
07 account, daytale, opinion, payment
08 addition, counting, estimate
09 appraisal, damnation, judgement
10 assessment, estimation, evaluation, fellowship, imputation, punishment, settlement, working-out
11 calculation, computation, enumeration, retribution

**reclaim**
04 tame 05 waste 06 appeal, assart, polder, recall, redeem, regain, rescue
07 get back, recover, restore, salvage
08 civilize, retrieve, take back, wildness 09 claim back, recapture, reinstate 10 regenerate, submersion

**reclamation**
06 rescue 07 salvage 08 recovery
09 regaining, retrieval 11 restoration
12 regeneration 13 reinstatement

**recline**
03 lie 04 bend, loll, rest 06 lounge, repose, sprawl 07 incline, lie down
08 lean back 09 recumbent 10 stretch out

**recluse**
04 monk 05 loner 06 anchor, hermit
07 ascetic, eremite, stylite
08 anchoret, enclosed, monastic, retiring, secluded, solitary
09 anchoress, anchorite, solitaire
10 monastical, solitarian
11 monasterial

**reclusive**
07 ascetic, recluse 08 eremitic, isolated, monastic, retiring, secluded, solitary 09 withdrawn 10 anchoritic, cloistered, hermitical 11 sequestered

**recognition**
06 honour, recall, reward, salute, thanks 07 grating, knowing, placing, respect 08 allowing, approval, sanction, spotting 09 admission, awareness, detection, discovery, gratitude, knowledge 10 acceptance, admittance, cognizance, confession, perception, validation
11 endorsement, realization, remembrance 12 appreciation, recognizance, recollection, thankfulness 13 consciousness, understanding 14 identification
15 acknowledgement

**recognize**
03 ken, own, see, wit 04 know, nose, spot, tell 05 admit, adopt, allow, grant, place 06 accept, acknow, honour, notice, recall, reward, salute
07 approve, concede, confess, discern, endorse, not miss, pick out, realize, respect 08 identify, perceive, remember, sanction, validate
09 apprehend, be aware of, recollect
10 appreciate, call to mind, legitimate, not mistake, understand
11 acknowledge, know by sight 13 be conscious of, be thankful for

**recoil**
◇ *reversal indicator*
03 shy 04 kick 05 quail, react, rebut
06 falter, flinch, recule, resile, revert, shrink, spring 07 misfire, rebound, recoyle, recuile, redound, retreat, shy away 08 backfire, backlash, draw back, jump back, kickback, move back, reaction, requoyle, undertow, withdraw 09 boomerang
10 degenerate, resilience, resiliency, spring back 11 reverberate
12 repercussion 15 come home to roost

**recollect**
◇ *anagram indicator*
◇ *reversal indicator*
05 think 06 recall 07 bethink
08 récollet, remember, summon up
09 reminisce 10 call to mind

**recollection**
◇ *anagram indicator*
06 memory, recall 08 souvenir
09 anamnesis 10 impression
11 remembrance 12 reminiscence

**recommend**
04 move, plug, tout, urge, wish
05 guide 06 advise, commit, exhort, inform, praise, preach 07 advance, approve, commend, consign, counsel, endorse, propose, suggest
08 advocate, set forth, vouch for 10 put forward

**recommendation**
03 tip 04 plug 06 advice, coupon, praise, urging 07 counsel 08 advocacy, approval, blessing, good word, guidance, proposal, sanction
09 reference 10 suggestion
11 endorsement, testimonial
12 commendation, exhortations
14 special mention

**recompense**
03 fee, pay 05 repay, wages
06 amends, answer, return, reward
07 damages, guerdon, payment, redress, requite, satisfy 08 requital
09 indemnify, make up for, reimburse, repayment 10 compensate, remunerate, reparation 11 restitution
12 compensation, remuneration, remuneratory, satisfaction
13 consideration, gratification
15 indemnification

**reconcile**
04 mend, wean 05 agree, atone
06 accept, accord, adjust, attone, make up, pacify, regain, remedy, settle, square, submit, upknit 07 appease, compose, mollify, patch up, placate, rectify, resolve, reunite 08 face up to, put right 09 harmonize, make peace
10 conciliate, propitiate, shake hands
11 accommodate 12 come to accept, reconsecrate 13 bring together, make your peace 14 bury the hatchet

**reconciliation**
05 peace 06 accord 07 détente, harmony, reunion 08 squaring
09 agreement, atonement
10 adjustment, compromise, resolution, settlement, syncretism
11 appeasement, explanation, harmonizing 12 conciliation, pacification, propitiation
13 accommodation, mollification, rapprochement

**recondite**
04 dark, deep 06 arcane, hidden, secret 07 obscure, retired 08 abstruse, esoteric, involved, mystical, profound
09 concealed, difficult, intricate
10 mysterious 11 complicated

**recondition**
◇ *anagram indicator*
03 fix 05 refit, renew 06 repair, revamp
07 remodel, restore 08 overhaul, renovate 09 refurbish

**reconfigure**
◇ *anagram indicator*

**reconnaissance**
04 scan 05 probe, recce, recco, reccy
06 patrol, search, survey 08 scouting, scrutiny 09 discovery 10 expedition, inspection 11 examination, exploration, observation
13 investigation, reconnoitring

**reconnoitre**
**04** case, scan **05** probe, recce, scout **06** patrol, spy out, survey **07** examine, explore, inspect, observe **08** check out, remember **10** scrutinize **11** investigate

**reconsider**
**06** modify, review, revise **07** rethink **08** reassess **09** re-examine, think over **10** think twice **13** think better of

**reconsideration**
**06** review **07** rethink **09** fresh look **12** reassessment **13** re-examination **14** second thoughts

**reconstitute**
◇ *anagram indicator*

**reconstruct**
◇ *anagram indicator*
**04** redo **06** recast, reform, remake, revamp **07** rebuild, remodel, restore **08** make over, recreate, renovate **09** refashion, reproduce **10** reassemble, regenerate, reorganize **11** recondition, re-establish

**record**
**02** CD, EP, LP **03** can, cut, log, rec **04** best, burn, case, data, disc, disk, edit, file, -gram, keep, list, make, mark, mono, note, read, show, tape **05** album, chart, diary, elpee, enrol, enter, entry, notes, score, trace, video, vinyl **06** annals, career, enroll, manage, memoir, memory, minute, obtain, report, single **07** account, achieve, chalk up, display, dossier, express, fastest, history, journal, lay down, logbook, minutes, myogram, narrate, notch up, produce, put down, release, set down, supreme, swinger, tracing, witness **08** aerogram, annalize, archives, best ever, calendar, cassette, complete, document, evidence, indicate, inscribe, kymogram, memorial, MiniDisc®, preserve, protocol, rap sheet, register, reminder, take down **09** anemogram, catalogue, celebrate, chronicle, documents, recording, testimony, videotape, write down **10** accomplish, background, enregister, instrument, memorandum, seismogram, tape-record, top-ranking, transcribe, unequalled **11** compact disc, fastest time, meteorogram, photography, put on record, remembrance, sphygmogram, superlative, track record, unsurpassed, world record **12** personal best, unparalleled, without equal, world-beating **13** documentation **14** autoradiograph, record-breaking **15** best performance, curriculum vitae
*See also* **recording**

• **off the record**
**07** private, sub rosa **09** privately **10** unofficial **12** confidential, unofficially **14** confidentially

• **on record**
**04** ever **05** noted **06** on file **10** documented **11** written down **13** publicly known

**recorder**
**03** VCR, VTR **05** clerk, video **06** marker, scorer, scribe **07** diarist, Walkman® **08** annalist, black box, CD burner **09** archivist, DVD burner, flûte-à-bec, historian, registrar, secretary **10** chronicler, Dictaphone® **11** chronologer, fipple flute, score-keeper, tape machine **12** English flute, remembrancer, stenographer, tape recorder **13** video recorder **14** cassette-player

**recording**

*Recordings include:*

**02** 45, 78, CD, EP, LP
**03** DAT, DVD, MP3, vid
**04** disc, mono, tape, tele
**05** album, video, vinyl
**06** record, single, stereo
**08** cassette, MiniDisc®
**09** audiotape, phonogram, video disc, videotape
**11** compact disc, compact disk, long-playing
**12** extended play, magnetic tape
**13** microcassette, video cassette

**recount**
**04** tell **05** refer **06** depict, detail, impart, recite, relate, repeat, report, run off, unfold **07** account, narrate, portray **08** describe, rehearse **09** reminisce **11** communicate

**recoup**
**05** repay **06** refund, regain **07** get back, recover, recruit, win back **08** claw back, make good, retrieve **09** indemnify, reimburse, repossess **10** compensate, recompense

**recourse**
**04** flow **06** access, appeal, choice, option, refuge, remedy, resort, return, way out **09** turning to **10** recurrence, withdrawal **11** alternative, possibility

• **have recourse to**
**03** use **04** take **06** betake, employ, turn to **07** utilize **08** exercise, resort to **09** make use of **10** fall back on **15** avail yourself of

**recover**
◇ *anagram indicator*
**04** cure, heal, mend **05** amend, rally **06** attain, pick up, recoup, recure, redeem, regain, rescue, retake, revive **07** fetch up, get back, get over, get well, improve, reclaim, recoure, recower, recruit, recycle, replevy, restore, salvage, win back **08** overcast, replevin, retrieve **09** come round, get better, recapture, repossess **10** ameliorate, bounce back, convalesce, feel better, recuperate **11** be on the mend, get stronger, pull through, revendicate **12** gain strength **13** turn the corner

**recovered**
**04** over

**recovery**
**05** rally **06** pick-up, recure, regain, rescue, upturn **07** healing, mending, recover, revival, salvage, upswing **08** comeback, rallying **09** recapture, recouping, recycling, regaining, retrieval **10** second wind **11** improvement, reclamation, restoration **12** amelioration, recuperation, regeneration, repossession **13** convalescence, convalescency, dead-cat bounce **14** electrowinning, rehabilitation **15** reconvalescence

**recreate**
◇ *anagram indicator*
**05** amuse, renew **07** refresh **09** replicate, reproduce **11** reconstruct **12** reinvigorate

**recreation**
**03** fun, rec **04** game, play **05** hobby, sport **07** leisure, pastime **08** pleasure **09** amusement, diversion, enjoyment **10** relaxation **11** distraction, refreshment **12** intermission **13** entertainment **14** leisure pursuit **15** leisure activity

**recrimination**
**06** retort **07** quarrel **08** comeback, reprisal **09** bickering **10** accusation **11** retaliation **13** counter-attack, countercharge

**recruit**
**02** AR **03** yob **04** levy, tiro **05** draft, enrol, raise, rooky, sprog **06** engage, enlist, gather, muster, nig-nog, novice, nozzer, obtain, rookie, sign up, swabby, take on **07** acquire, convert, draftee, learner, procure, renewal, restore, trainee **08** assemble, beginner, headhunt, initiate, mobilize, newcomer, unionize, yardbird **09** conscript, greenhorn, reinforce, replenish **10** apprentice, new entrant, talent-spot **11** put together, restoration **12** reinvigorate **13** reinforcement

**recruitment**
**05** press **08** drafting, engaging **09** enlisting, enrolment, signing-up **10** engagement **12** conscription, mobilization

**rectification**
**09** amendment **10** adjustment, correction, making good **11** improvement, reformation **12** putting right, setting right

**rectify**
**03** fix **04** cure, mend **05** amend, emend, right **06** adjust, better, reform, remedy, repair **07** correct, improve, redress **08** make good, put right, set right **10** ameliorate **11** dephlegmate

**rectitude**
**06** honour, virtue **07** decency, honesty, justice, probity **08** goodness, morality **09** exactness, integrity, rightness **11** correctness, uprightness **12** straightness **13** righteousness **14** scrupulousness

**recto**
02 ro

**rector**
01 R 04 Rect 06 parson

**recumbent**
04 flat 05 lying, prone 06 supine
07 leaning, recline, resting
08 lounging, reclined 09 lying down, prostrate, reclining, sprawling
10 horizontal

**recuperate**
04 mend 05 rally 06 pick up, revive
07 get well, improve, recover 09 get better 10 bounce back, convalesce
11 be on the mend, get stronger, pull through 13 turn the corner

**recuperation**
05 rally 06 recure, upturn 07 healing, mending, revival 08 rallying, recovery
11 improvement, restoration
12 amelioration 13 convalescence, convalescency 14 rehabilitation
15 reconvalescence

**recur**
03 ren, rin, run 05 prime 06 repeat, return, revert 07 persist 08 reappear
09 come round 11 happen again, perseverate 12 repeat itself 14 come round again

**recurrence**
06 return, rhythm 08 paroxysm, recourse 09 flashback, reversion
10 appearance, regularity, repetition, restenosis, revolution 11 persistence
12 alliteration, continuation, reminiscence 14 redintegration

**recurrent**
◇ *reversal indicator*
07 chronic, regular 08 cyclical, frequent, habitual, periodic, repeated
09 continual, recurring 10 persistent, repetitive 12 intermittent

**recycle**
◇ *anagram indicator*
04 save 05 re-use 07 reclaim, recover, salvage 09 reprocess

**red**
◇ *anagram indicator*
01 c 04 cent, comb, redd, rede, rosy
06 florid, refuse, rubric 07 clear up, flaming, flushed, glowing, leftist, reddish, rubbish, vacated 08 blushing, inflamed, rubicund 09 bloodshot, Bolshevik, communist, rubescent, rufescent, socialist 10 erubescent, shamefaced, testaceous
11 carbuncular, disentangle, embarrassed, incarnadine, lateritious, sanguineous 12 Cain-coloured
13 revolutionary

*Reds include:*

04 guly, pink, rose, ruby, rust, wine
05 brick, gules, henna, ruddy
06 auburn, cerise, cherry, claret, damask, ginger, maroon, minium, modena, murrey, rufous, russet, Titian, tomato, Tyrian
07 carmine, carroty, cramesy, crimson, fuschia, lobster, nacarat, scarlet, stammel, vermeil
08 beetroot, blood-red, brick-red, burgundy, cardinal, chestnut, cinnabar, cramoisy, sanguine
09 carnation, solferino, vermilion
10 Chinese red, coccineous, coquelicot, terracotta
11 burnt sienna, incarnadine, sang-de-boeuf

---

**• in the red**
04 bust 05 broke 06 in debt
08 bankrupt 09 in arrears, insolvent, overdrawn, penniless 10 on the rocks, owing money 12 impoverished, on your uppers 13 gone to the wall 14 on your beam ends

**• red and inflamed**
03 raw

**• see red**
05 go mad 07 explode 08 boil over
09 do your nut 10 hit the roof
11 become angry, blow your top, lose your rag 12 blow your cool, fly into a rage, lose your cool 14 lose your temper 15 fly off the handle

**red-blooded**
05 lusty, manly 06 hearty, lively, robust, strong, virile 08 vigorous
09 masculine

**redcap**
02 MP

**redden**
03 rud 04 gild, rosy, ruby 05 blush, flush, go red 06 colour, rubefy
07 crimson, scarlet, suffuse

**reddish**
03 red 04 pink, rosy 05 ruddy, sandy
06 flushy, ginger, rufous, russet
08 pyrrhous, rubicund 09 bloodshot, gingerous, rufescent

**• reddish brown**
03 bay 04 rust, sore 06 russet

**redecorate**
04 do up, redo 09 refurbish

**redeem**
03 buy 04 cash, free, save 05 lowse, trade 06 acquit, cash in, change, offset, ransom, recoup, regain, rescue
07 absolve, buy back, convert, deliver, expiate, get back, reclaim, recover, release, reprive, repryve, salvage, set free, trade in 08 atone for, exchange, liberate, outweigh, repreeve, reprieve, retrieve 09 discharge, make up for, repossess 10 emancipate, recuperate, repurchase 13 compensate for 14 give in exchange 15 remove guilt from

**redemption**
06 ransom, rescue 07 freedom, release, trade-in 08 exchange, recovery 09 atonement, expiation, retrieval, salvation 10 fulfilment, liberation, reparation, repurchase
11 deliverance, reclamation
12 compensation, emancipation, repossession 13 reinstatement

**redeploy**
◇ *anagram indicator*

**redevelop**
◇ *anagram indicator*

**redevelopment**
◇ *anagram indicator*

**red-handed**
07 napping 08 in the act, off-guard, on the hop, unawares 10 by surprise 12 in the very act

**redistribute**
◇ *anagram indicator*

**redistribution**
◇ *anagram indicator*

**redness**
03 rud 04 glow, heat 05 flush

**redolent**
07 odorous, scented 08 aromatic, fragrant, perfumed 09 evocative, remindful 10 suggestive 11 reminiscent
13 sweet-smelling

**redoubtable**
05 awful 06 mighty, strong 07 fearful, valiant 08 dreadful, fearsome, powerful, resolute, terrible
10 formidable

**redound**
04 cast, tend 05 ensue, surge
06 effect, result, return 07 conduce, rebound, reflect 08 overflow
10 contribute

**redraft**
◇ *anagram indicator*
06 revise, rework 07 rewrite

**redress**
03 aid 04 help 05 amend, right
06 adjust, avenge, reform, relief, remead, remede, remedy, remeid
07 balance, correct, justice, payment, rectify, requite, restore 08 put right, readjust, regulate, requital
09 atonement 10 assistance, compensate, correction, recompense, reparation 11 restitution
12 compensation, satisfaction
15 indemnification

**reduce**
◇ *tail deletion indicator*
02 ax 03 axe, cut, put 04 alay, clip, diet, dock, ruin, slim, trim 05 abate, adapt, aleye, allay, annul, drive, force, halve, lower, scant, slake, slash 06 absorb, adjust, deduct, demote, dilute, draw in, humble, impair, lessen, master, rebate, shrink, subdue, weaken 07 conquer, curtail, cut back, cut down, deflate, degrade, deplete, devalue, disband, shorten, thicken 08 beat down, come down, condense, contract, decrease, diminish, discount, downsize, make less, minimize, mitigate, moderate, overcome, restrict, separate, step down, take down, vanquish, wear down, wind down 09 bring down, comminute, deoxidate, deoxidize, downgrade, go on a diet, humiliate, knock down, overpower, translate,

water down **10** abbreviate, de-escalate, impoverish, lose weight **11** make smaller, weight-watch **12** disintegrate **13** whittle away at **14** take the edge off

**reduction**
◇ *tail deletion indicator*
**03** cut **04** drop, fall, loss, wear **06** rebate **07** cutback, decline **08** batement, clipping, decrease, discount, drawdown **09** allowance, deduction, lessening, narrowing, shrinkage, weakening **10** concession, correction, diminution, downsizing, hatchet job, limitation, moderation, rebatement, shortening **11** compression, contraction, curtailment, devaluation, discounting, restriction, subjugation, subtraction **12** abbreviation, condensation, depreciation, minimization

**redundancy**
**04** boot, push, sack **05** cards, elbow **06** excess, firing, notice, papers **07** jotters, removal, sacking, surplus **08** cheville, pleonasm **09** discharge, dismissal, expulsion, laying-off, prolixity, tautology, verbosity, wordiness **10** downsizing, exuberance, exuberancy, repetition **11** superfluity, uselessness **12** outplacement **14** marching-orders

**redundant**
**05** extra, fired, wordy **06** excess, otiose, padded, sacked **07** copious, jobless, laid off, surging, surplus, verbose **08** unneeded, unwanted **09** dismissed, excessive, out of work **10** pleonastic, unemployed **11** inessential, overflowing, repetitious, superfluous, unnecessary **12** periphrastic, tautological **13** supernumerary

**redwood**
**07** big tree, sequoia

**re-edit**
◇ *anagram indicator*

**reef**
**03** cay, key **04** bank, motu, scar **05** ridge, scaur, shoal **06** skerry **07** bombora, sandbar **08** sandbank **10** square knot
• **reefer**
**05** coral
*See also* **cannabis**

**reek**
**03** hum **04** fume, honk, ming, niff, pong **05** fetor, fumes, odour, reech, smell, smoke, stink, whiff **06** exhale, stench, vapour **08** malodour, mephitis **09** effluvium **10** exhalation

**reel**
◇ *anagram indicator*
**03** din **04** pirn, rock, roll, spin, sway, swim **05** fling, lurch, pitch, spool, swift, swirl, twirl, waver, wheel, whirl, wince, winch **06** bobbin, falter, gyrate, rattle, totter, wobble **07** revolve, stagger, stumble **08** hoolican **09** eightsome, hoolachan **10** multiplier
• **reel off**
**04** list **06** recite, repeat **09** rattle off **10** run through **11** list quickly

**refashion**
◇ *anagram indicator*
**06** adjust, reform, rehash **07** convert, rebuild **11** reconstruct

**refer**
**04** cite, mean, send **05** apply, guide, point, quote, remit **06** advert, allude, appeal, assign, belong, commit, direct, hand on, hint at, look at, look up, pass on, permit, relate, turn to **07** bring up, concern, consult, deliver, mention, pertain, put over, speak of, touch on **08** describe, indicate, relegate, resort to, transfer **09** recommend, represent, reproduce **10** be relevant
• **refer to**
**03** see

**referee**
**03** ref, ump **05** judge, zebra **06** umpire **07** arbiter, mediate **08** linesman, mediator **09** arbitrate, intercede **10** adjudicate, arbitrator **11** adjudicator, commissaire, referendary

**reference**
**03** ref **04** hint, note **05** mensh **06** regard, remark, source, squint **07** bearing, mention, respect **08** allusion, citation, footnote, innuendo, instance, relation **09** authority, character, quotation **10** connection, pertinence, retrospect **11** credentials, endorsement, testimonial **12** illustration **13** applicability **14** recommendation
• **with reference to**
**02** re **05** about **07** apropos **09** as regards, regarding **10** concerning, relating to, relevant to, respecting **11** referring to **12** with regard to **13** in the matter of, with respect to **14** on the subject of

**referendum**
**04** poll, vote **06** survey, voting **10** plebiscite

**referral**
**07** sending **08** handover, pointing, transfer **09** direction, handing on, passing on

**refine**
◇ *anagram indicator*
**03** try **04** fine, hone, pure, sift, test **05** clear, exalt, treat **06** distil, filter, polish, purify, rarefy, repure, strain **07** chasten, clarify, cleanse, elevate, improve, perfect, process **08** chastise, civilize, freebase, repurify **09** cultivate, elaborate, sublimize, subtilize **11** cut and carve **12** spiritualize

*Products and byproducts of refining include:*

**03** tar
**05** sugar
**07** asphalt, bitumen, treacle
**08** molasses
**11** golden syrup

*See also* **fuel**; **hydrocarbon**; **sugar**

**refined**
**04** fine, pure **05** Attic, civil, clear, couth, exact, horsy **06** gentle, horsey, inland, picked, polite, subtle, urbane **07** classic, courtly, elegant, foppish, genteel, precise, stylish, treated **08** Augustan, cultured, cutglass, delicate, educated, filtered, gracious, ladylike, polished, precious, purified, rarefied, well-bred **09** civilized, distilled, processed, sensitive, spiritual **10** cultivated **11** gentlemanly **12** well-mannered **13** gentlewomanly, sophisticated **14** discriminating

**refinement**
**05** grace, style, taste **06** nicety, polish **07** culture, exility, finesse **08** addition, breeding, chastity, civility, delicacy, elegance, elegancy, subtlety, urbanity **09** amendment, gentility, technique **10** alteration, subtleness **11** cultivation, elaboration, good manners, improvement **12** amelioration, modification **14** discrimination, sophistication

**refit**
◇ *anagram indicator*
**04** mend **05** renew **06** repair, revamp **07** furbish **08** facelift, renovate **09** refurbish **10** renovation

**reflect**
◇ *reversal indicator*
**04** cast, chew, echo, mull, muse, shed, show **05** brood, dwell, glass, glint, image, shine, study, think **06** advise, depict, mirror, ponder, reveal **07** bespeak, display, exhibit, express, imitate, portray, redound, scatter, tarnish **08** cogitate, consider, disgrace, indicate, manifest, meditate, mull over, ruminate, send back **09** bounce off, cerebrate, discredit, repercuss, reproduce, speculate, throw back **10** chew the cud, deliberate **11** communicate, contemplate, demonstrate, reverberate **14** give a bad name to, put in a bad light

**reflection**
◇ *reversal indicator*
**04** baby, echo, idea, life, slur, view **05** blame, image, shame, study **06** belief, musing, reflex **07** censure, display, eidolon, feeling, opinion, rebound, thought **08** disgrace, feelings, likeness, reproach, thinking **09** aspersion, criticism, discredit, disrepute, portrayal, snowblink, viewpoint **10** cogitation, epiphonema, expression, impression, indication, meditation, rumination **11** cerebration, mirror image, observation **12** deliberation, repercussion **13** consideration, contemplation, demonstration, manifestation

**reflective**
**06** dreamy **07** pensive **08** absorbed

**09** pondering, reasoning
**10** cogitating, meditative, ruminative, thoughtful **12** deliberative
**13** contemplative

**reflex**
**06** direct **07** natural, project
**08** autotomy, knee-jerk, unwilled
**09** automatic, re-entrant
**10** expression, mechanical, reciprocal, re-entering **11** instinctive, involuntary, spontaneous **13** manifestation
**14** Babinski effect, uncontrollable
**15** without thinking

**reform**
◇ *anagram indicator*
**04** mend **05** amend, prune, purge
**06** anneal, better, change, repair, revamp, revise **07** correct, disband, dismiss, improve, rebuild, rectify, redress, remodel, restore, shake up, shake-up **08** chastise, renovate, revision **09** amendment, refashion, transform **10** ameliorate, betterment, correction, rebuilding, regenerate, renovation, reorganize
**11** improvement, reconstruct, remodelling, restoration
**12** reconstitute, rehabilitate
**13** rectification, revolutionize
**14** reconstruction, rehabilitation, reorganization

**reformat**
◇ *anagram indicator*

**reformation**
◇ *anagram indicator*
**08** progress, revision **09** amendment
**10** renovation **11** improvement, restoration **12** amelioration, palingenesis, regeneration
**13** rectification **14** rehabilitation

**reformer**
**03** rad **06** mucker **07** Hussite, liberal, Lollard, Owenite, radical **08** do-gooder, Lutheran **09** Calvinist, reformado, Wyclifite, Zwinglian
**10** Wycliffite **11** progressive
**12** Pestalozzian **13** bleeding heart, revolutionary, whistle-blower

*Reformers include:*

**03** Hus (Jan)
**04** Huss (John), Knox (John), Mill (John Stuart), Owen (Robert)
**05** Perón (Evita)
**06** Calvin (John), Luther (Martin), Wiclif (John), Wyclif (John)
**07** Stanton (Elizabeth Cady), Wycliff (John), Zwingli (Huldreich), Zwingli (Ulrich)
**08** Wicliffe (John), Wycliffe (John)
**10** Pestalozzi (Johann)
**11** Wilberforce (William)

**refractory**
**05** balky, surly, tough **06** mulish, sturdy, unruly, wilful **07** defiant, naughty, restive **08** perverse, stubborn
**09** difficult, obstinate, resistant
**10** headstrong, rebellious
**11** contentious, disobedient, intractable **12** cantankerous, contumacious, disputatious, recalcitrant, unmanageable **13** fire-resistant, unco-operative
**14** uncontrollable

**refrain**
**03** bob, tag **04** curb, fa la, juba, keep, quit, song, stop, tune **05** avoid, cease, forgo, spare, wheel **06** burden, chorus, desist, eschew, fading, fa la la, forego, give up, melody, strain **07** abstain, burthen, ducdame, forbear, hold off
**08** faburden, falderal, leave off, overcome, overture, renounce, repetend, response, restrain, rum-ti-tum, surcease, withhold **09** do without, hemistich, supersede, tirra-lyra, turnagain, undersong
**10** epistrophe, ritornello, tirra-lirra
**11** rumti-iddity **12** rumpti-iddity

**refresh**
**03** jog **04** cool, prod, stir **05** brace, renew, slake **06** arouse, prompt, refect, remind, repair, repose, revive
**07** enliven, fortify, freshen, restore
**08** activate, energize, recreate, revivify
**09** reanimate, recomfort, stimulate
**10** exhilarate, invigorate, rejuvenate, revitalize **11** refocillate **12** reinvigorate

**refreshing**
**03** new **04** cool **05** fresh, novel
**06** caller **07** bracing, welcome
**08** original, reviving **09** different, inspiring **10** energizing, freshening, not another, unexpected **11** inspiriting, refrigerant, stimulating **12** exhilarating, invigorating **15** thirst-quenching

**refreshment**
**03** tea **04** bait, food **05** drink, snack
**06** drinks, repast **07** elevens, renewal, revival **09** elevenses, four-hours, refection, twalhours **10** freshening, recreation, sustenance **11** reanimation, restoration, stimulation, water of life
**12** food and drink, invigoration
**14** reinvigoration, revitalization

**refreshments**
**04** eats, food, grub, nosh **06** drinks, snacks, tucker **07** aliment, titbits
**08** eatables **09** elevenses **10** provisions, sustenance **12** food and drink

**refrigerate**
**03** ice **04** cool **05** chill **06** freeze
**08** keep cold

**refuge**
**04** dive, hole, holt, home **05** haven
**06** asylum, burrow, harbor, island, resort **07** harbour, hideout, hospice, retreat, shelter **08** bolthole, funkhole, hideaway, security **09** sanctuary
**10** protection, stronghold, subterfuge
**11** sheet anchor **13** place of safety

**refugee**
**05** exile, reffo **06** émigré **07** escapee, runaway **08** fugitive **10** contraband
**12** asylum seeker **15** displaced person, stateless person

**refulgent**
**06** bright **07** beaming, lambent, radiant, shining **08** gleaming, lustrous
**09** brilliant, irradiant **10** glistening, glittering **11** resplendent

**refund**
**05** repay **06** rebate, return **07** imburse, pay back, restore **08** give back
**09** reimburse, repayment
**10** redisburse **13** reimbursement

**refurbish**
◇ *anagram indicator*
**04** do up, mend **05** refit **06** repair, revamp **07** re-equip, remodel, restore
**08** overhaul, renovate **10** redecorate
**11** recondition

**refurbishment**
◇ *anagram indicator*
**07** doing-up **09** refitting, repairing, revamping **10** renovation
**11** recondition, restoration
**12** redecoration

**refusal**
**02** no **04** veto **06** denial, nay-say, rebuff **07** repulse **08** negation, spurning **09** knock-back, raspberry, rejection **11** repudiation, turning-down, withholding **12** incompliance, non-admission, nothing doing **13** non-acceptance **14** nolo episcopari

• **first refusal**
**06** choice, option **11** opportunity
**13** consideration **15** right of purchase

**refuse**
◇ *anagram indicator*
**03** jib, red **04** bran, deny, junk, marc, nill, rape, redd, scum **05** draff, dregs, dross, flock, husks, offal, repel, say no, spurn, trash, waste **06** debris, litter, naysay, pass up, rebuff, reject, resist, scoria, sewage **07** decline, garbage, offscum, rubbish, sullage **08** leavings, renounce, tailings, turn down, withhold **09** knock back, repudiate, riddlings, throw back **11** offscouring
**12** kitchen-stuff, offscourings, rejectamenta **13** draw the line at, shake your head **14** dig your heels in

**refutation**
**08** disproof, elenchus, negation, rebuttal **09** overthrow **11** confutation

**refute**
**04** deny, meet **05** rebut, refel
**06** negate **07** confute, counter, reprove, silence **08** disprove, redargue
**09** discredit, overthrow **12** deny strongly, give the lie to

**regain**
**04** find **06** recoup, retake **07** get back, reclaim, recover, win back **08** recovery, retrieve, return to, take back
**09** recapture, reconcile, repossess

**regal**
**05** noble, royal **06** kingly, lordly
**07** queenly, stately **08** imperial, majestic, princely, sceptred
**09** sceptered, sovereign **11** magnificent

**regale**
**03** ply **05** amuse, feast, serve
**06** divert, junket **07** delight, gratify,

kitchen, refresh **09** captivate, entertain, fascinate

**regard**

**03** eye, see **04** care, deem, gaum, gorm, heed, look, love, mark, note, rate, view **05** gauge, judge, point, think, value, watch **06** aspect, behold, detail, esteem, follow, gaze at, hold of, honour, look at, look on, matter, notice, repute, tender **07** believe, concern, imagine, observe, respect, set down, subject, suppose, weigh up **08** appraise, approval, consider, estimate, listen to, look upon, relation, respects, sympathy **09** affection, attention, deference, greetings, intention, reference **10** admiration, advertence, advertency, bear in mind, best wishes, estimation, good wishes, particular, retrospect, scrutinize **11** approbation, compliments, contemplate, observation, salutations **12** take notice of **13** consideration **14** loving kindness, pay attention to **15** give the once-over, take into account

• **with regard to, in regard to**

**02** re **04** as to **05** about, anent **07** apropos, vis-à-vis **09** as regards, in terms of **10** as concerns, concerning **12** in relation to **13** with respect to **14** on the subject of **15** with reference to

**regardful**

**05** aware **07** careful, dutiful, heedful, mindful **08** noticing, watchful **09** attentive, observant **10** respectful, respective, thoughtful **11** circumspect, considerate

**regarding**

**02** re **04** as to **05** about **07** apropos, vis-à-vis **09** as regards **10** concerning, in regard to **12** in relation to, with regard to **13** when it comes to, with respect to **14** on the subject of **15** with reference to

**regardless**

◇ *deletion indicator*

**06** anyhow, anyway **08** careless, heedless **09** at any cost, negligent, unmindful **10** at any price, neglectful **11** come what may, inattentive, indifferent, nonetheless, respectless, unconcerned **12** disregarding, irregardless, nevertheless, no matter what **13** inconsiderate

**regenerate**

◇ *anagram indicator*

**05** renew **06** change, revive, uplift **07** refresh, renewed, restore **08** inspirit, reawaken, rekindle, renovate, revivify **09** reproduce, twice-born **10** invigorate, rejuvenate, revitalize **11** reconstruct, re-establish **12** reconstitute, reinvigorate

**regenerated**

◇ *anagram indicator*

**03** new

**regeneration**

**07** renewal **10** neogenesis, renovation **11** reformation, restoration **12** morphallaxis, palingenesis, rejuvenation, reproduction **13** homomorphosis **14** reconstitution, reconstruction, reinvigoration **15** re-establishment

**regime**

**03** way **04** diet, fast, rule **05** order, reign **06** method, system **07** command, control, formula, pattern, regimen, routine **08** practice, schedule, tyrannis **09** direction, procedure, programme **10** abstinence, government, leadership, management **11** kleptocracy **13** establishment **14** administration **15** short sharp shock

**regiment**

**04** army, band, body, crew, gang **05** group **06** cohort, pultun, tercio **07** battery, brigade, company, platoon **08** squadron

*Army regiments include:*

**02** RA, RE, TA
**03** SAS
**04** REME
**05** Kings, Paras
**06** London
**07** Gurkhas, Lowland
**08** Cheshire
**09** Fusiliers, Parachute, Royal Tank
**10** Black Watch, Life Guards, Royal Irish, Royal Scots, Royal Welsh
**11** Highlanders, Horse Guards, Irish Guards, Scots Guards, Welsh Guards
**12** Army Air Corps, Close Support, Green Howards, Green Jackets, Gurkha Rifles, Rifle Brigade, Royal Anglian, Royal Hussars, Royal Lancers, Royal of Wales
**13** Artists' Rifles, Light Dragoons, Light Infantry, Staffordshire
**14** General Support, Royal Artillery, Royal Engineers
**15** Grenadier Guards, Rifle Volunteers, Territorial Army

**regimented**

**06** strict **07** ordered **09** organized, regulated **10** controlled, methodical, systematic **11** disciplined **12** standardized, systematized

**region**

**01** E **03** end **04** area, belt, high, land, part, wild, zona, zone **05** ambit, bundu, burgh, duchy, field, manor, orbit, place, range, realm, reame, scope, shire, state, tract, waste, wilds, world **06** county, domain, empire, estate, garden, ghetto, parish, riding, sector, sphere **07** borough, climate, country, diocese, emirate, expanse, granary, heavens, hundred, kingdom, mission, quarter, section, suburbs, terrain **08** autonomy, badlands, district, division, dominion, foreland, interior, province, time zone **09** backwoods, bailiwick, climature, continent, goldfield, heartland, inner city, outskirts, periphery, territory **10** borderland, hemisphere, playground, wilderness **11** breadbasket, God's country, reservation, terra ignota **12** municipality, principality, subcontinent **13** catchment area, neighbourhood **14** God's own country, postal district, terra incognita

*Regions include:*

**03** Zug
**04** Jura, León, Midi, Ruhr, Vaud
**05** Angus, Dixie, Gower, Lazio, Liège, Loire, Marne, Namur, Norte, Otago, Rhine, Rhône, Rioja, Somme, Taupo, Tyrol, Urals
**06** Acadia, Alsace, Apulia, Aragón, Argyll, Azores, Bayern, Beiras, Burgos, Centro, Crimea, Hessen, Iberia, Latium, Lisboa, Molise, Mt Cook, Murcia, Nelson, Ozarks, Puglia, Savoie, Saxony, Sicily, Top End, Umbria, Valais, Veneto, Vosges, Wanaka
**07** Abruzzo, Algarve, Almería, Ardenne, Bavaria, Bohemia, Borders, Brabant, Castile, Corsica, Drenthe, Galicia, Hainaut, Jutland, La Loire, La Rioja, Liguria, Limburg, Lucerne, Madeira, Marches, Midwest, Moselle, Navarra, Navarre, Picardy, Riviera, Rotorua, Ruapehu, Shannon, Siberia, Silesia, Thurgau, Tuscany, Utrecht, Venetia, Waikato, Zeeland
**08** Alentejo, Alicante, Ardennes, Asturias, Auvergne, Bretagne, Brittany, Burgundy, Calabria, Calvados, Campania, Canaries, Cataluña, Caucasus, Charente, Chechnya, Dalmatia, Dordogne, Eastland, Flanders, Grampian, Hebrides, Holstein, Lappland, Limousin, Lombardy, Lorraine, Manawatu, Normandy, Picardie, Piedmont, Provence, Pyrenees, Rust Belt, Saarland, Sardinia, Taranaki, Trentino, Val d'Oise, Valencia, Wallonia, Wanganui
**09** Andalucía, Andalusia, Aquitaine, Bible Belt, Bourgogne, Cantabria, Carinthia, Castellón, Catalonia, Champagne, Charentes, Côte d'Azur, Deep South, Fiordland, Flevoland, Friesland, Groningen, Gulf Coast, Hawkes Bay, Highlands, Languedoc, Maritimes, Neuchâtel, Northland, Pomerania, Red Centre, Rhineland, Schleswig, Snowdonia, Southland, Southwest, The Burren, Thuringia, Trossachs, Wairarapa, West Coast
**10** Appalachia, Basilicata, Canterbury, Coromandel, Costa Brava, Gelderland, Graubünden, Great Lakes, Horowhenua, New England, Overijssel, Palatinate, Westphalia
**11** Bay of Plenty, Black Forest, Brandenburg, Central Belt, Costa Blanca, Costa del Sol, Costa Dorada, Extremadura, Great Plains, Île-de-France, Marlborough, Mid-Atlantic, Zuid-Holland
**12** American West, Bay of Islands,

Noord-Brabant, Noord-Holland, The Kimberley
**13** Barossa Valley, Basque Country, Brecon Beacons, Canary Islands, Emilia-Romagna, Middle America, Pays-de-la-Loire
**14** Castile and Leon, Channel Islands, Snowy Mountains
**15** Balearic Islands, Bernese Oberland, Eastern Seaboard

*See also* **council**; **county**; **department**; **district**; **electorate**; **geography**; **province**; **state**

**• in the region of**
**03** odd **04** near, some **05** about, circa **06** around, nearly **07** close to, loosely, roughly **09** just about, not far off, rounded up **10** give or take, more or less, round about **11** approaching, rounded down **13** approximately, or thereabouts, something like **14** in round numbers **15** in the vicinity of

**regional**
**05** local, zonal **08** district **09** localized, parochial, sectional **10** provincial

**register**
**03** log, say, tax **04** cast, file, list, mark, note, poll, read, roll, show, tone **05** album, clock, diary, enrol, enter, files, index, notes, range, voice **06** annals, betray, book in, docket, enlist, enroll, ledger, lidger, muster, record, regest, reveal, roster, sign on, turn in **07** almanac, check in, diptych, display, exhibit, express, journal, listing, notitia, put down, set down, terrier **08** archives, cadastre, indicate, inscribe, manifest, menology, obituary, schedule, take down **09** cartulary, catalogue, chronicle, directory, enrolment, matricula, registrar **10** enregister, enrollment **11** demonstrate, matriculate, patent-rolls **12** put in writing, transfer book

**registrar**
**05** clerk **07** actuary **08** annalist, greffier, official, recorder, register **09** archivist, secretary **10** cataloguer, chronicler **11** protocolist, protonotary **12** prothonotary, sheriff clerk **13** administrator

**registration**
**04** list, rego **05** reggo **06** noting, record **07** logging **08** entering, register **09** enrolment, recording, signing-on **10** checking-in **11** inscription

**regress**
◇ *reversal indicator*
**03** ebb **04** wane **05** lapse **06** recede, return, revert **07** re-entry, relapse, retreat **09** backslide, retrocede, reversion **10** degenerate, retrogress **11** deteriorate

**regret**
**03** rew, rue **04** weep **05** grief, mourn, shame **06** bemoan, desire, grieve, lament, relent, repent, sorrow **07** be sorry, deplore, remorse **08** had-I-wist **09** deprecate, feel sorry, penitence **10** bitterness, contrition, repentance **11** compunction **12** be distressed, feel bad about, self-reproach **14** be disappointed, disappointment

**• expression of regret**
**02** ay **03** ach, och **04** alas **05** alack, ewhow **06** if only **07** out upon **09** alack-a-day

**regretful**
**03** sad **05** sorry **06** rueful **07** ashamed **08** contrite, penitent **09** repentant, sorrowful **10** apologetic, remorseful **12** disappointed

**regrettable**
**03** sad **05** sorry, wrong **06** too bad **07** unhappy, unlucky **08** shameful **09** upsetting **10** deplorable, ill-advised, lamentable **11** disgraceful, distressing, unfortunate **13** disappointing, reprehensible

**regrettably**
**04** alas **05** sadly **08** sad to say **09** unhappily, unluckily, worse luck **11** sad to relate **13** unfortunately

**regular**
**03** set **04** even, flat **05** daily, fixed, level, loyal, swell, usual **06** common, giusto, hourly, normal, proper, smooth, stated, steady, strict, weekly, yearly **07** average, canonic, certain, classic, correct, monthly, orderly, private, routine, typical, uniform **08** approved, balanced, constant, everyday, frequent, habitual, official, ordinary, orthodox, periodic, rhythmic, standard, standing, thorough **09** canonical, customary, out-and-out, permanent, recurring, unvarying, veritable **10** consistent, methodical, periodical, systematic, unchanging **11** commonplace, established, symmetrical **12** conventional, evenly spread, professional, time-honoured **13** well-organized

**regularly**
◇ *hidden alternately indicator*
**05** often **10** frequently **13** like clockwork

**regulate**
◇ *anagram indicator*
**03** run, set **04** rule, tune **05** align, aline, guide, order **06** adjust, baffle, direct, govern, handle, manage, settle, square **07** arrange, balance, conduct, control, monitor, oversee **08** moderate, modulate, organize **09** supervise **10** administer **11** superintend, synchronize

**regulation**
**02** AR **03** act, law, set **04** code, rule **05** by-law, edict, fixed, order, usual **06** bye-law, curfew, decree, dictum, dosage, normal, pusser, ruling **07** command, control, dictate, precept, statute **08** accepted, guidance, official, orthodox, required, standard **09** customary, direction, directive, mandatory, ordinance, principle, procedure, statutory **10** management, obligatory, prescribed **11** commandment, requirement, supervision **12** dispensation **13** pronouncement **14** administration **15** superintendence

**regurgitate**
**04** puke, spew **05** heave, retch, vomit **06** posset, repeat, sick up, spit up **07** bring up, fetch up, regorge, restate, throw up **08** disgorge, ruminate, say again **09** reiterate, tell again **12** recapitulate

**rehabilitate**
**04** mend, save **05** clear, rehab, renew **06** adjust, redeem, reform **07** convert, rebuild, restore **08** renovate **09** normalize, reinstate **11** recondition, reconstruct, re-establish, reintegrate **12** reconstitute, reinvigorate

**rehash**
◇ *anagram indicator*
**05** alter, rejig **06** change, rework **07** restate, rewrite **08** rejigger **09** rearrange, refashion, rejigging, reshuffle, reworking **11** restatement **13** rearrangement

**rehearsal**
**05** drill **06** dry run **07** hersall, reading, recital **08** band-call, dummy run, exercise, practice, trial run, woodshed **09** narration **10** repetition, run-through **11** enumeration, preparation, read-through, walk-through

**rehearse**
**05** block, drill, train **06** go over, recite, relate, repeat, try out **07** narrate, pour out, prepare, recount **08** block out, practise **09** enumerate, pour forth **10** run through

**reign**
**04** rain, ring, rule, sway **05** exist, occur, power, raine, rayne, realm **06** be king, domain, empire, govern, obtain **07** be queen, command, control, kingdom, prevail **08** dominion, hold sway, monarchy **09** be in power, be present, influence, Silver Age, supremacy **10** ascendancy, be in charge, government **11** be in command, be in control, pontificate, predominate, sovereignty **12** predominance **14** be in government, sit on the throne

**reigning**
**05** world **06** ruling **07** current, in power, present, regnant **09** governing, in command, in control, incumbent, presiding **10** victorious

**reimburse**
**05** repay **06** refund, return **07** pay back, restore **08** give back **09** indemnify **10** compensate, recompense, remunerate

**reimbursement**
**06** refund **09** indemnity, repayment **10** recompense **12** compensation

**rein**
**04** curb, halt, hold, stop **05** brake, check, limit **06** answer, arrest, bridle

07 control, harness 08 hold back, reindeer, restrain, restrict
09 overcheck, restraint 11 restriction

**• free rein**

07 freedom, liberty 08 free hand
10 free-for-all 11 blank cheque, open slather 12 carte blanche, laissez-faire

**reincarnation**

07 rebirth, samsara 12 palingenesis
14 metempsychosis

**reindeer**

04 deer, rein 06 tarand 07 caribou

*Father Christmas's reindeer:*

05 Comet, Cupid, Vixen
06 Dancer, Dasher, Donner
07 Blitzen, Prancer, Rudolph

**reinforce**

◇ *containment indicator*
04 line, prop, stay 05 brace, shore, steel
06 beef up, harden, stress, supply
07 augment, enforce, fortify, recruit, stiffen, support, toughen 08 buttress, increase, renforce 09 emphasize, re-enforce, underline 10 strengthen, supplement 11 consolidate

**reinforcement**

04 help, prop, stay 05 brace, shore
06 back-up 07 recruit, support
08 addition, buttress, emphasis, increase, reserves 09 hardening
10 supplement 11 auxiliaries, enlargement 12 augmentation
13 amplification, fortification, re-enforcement, strengthening
15 supplementaries

**reinstate**

06 recall, return 07 replace, reseize, restore 08 give back 09 reappoint, reinstall 11 re-establish 12 rehabilitate

**reinstatement**

06 recall, return 10 giving-back, reposition 11 replacement, restoration
15 re-establishment

**reiterate**

04 ding 05 recap, resay 06 repeat, retell, stress 07 iterate, restate
08 rehearse 09 emphasize
10 ingeminate 12 recapitulate

**reject**

◇ *reversal indicator*
03 bin, nix, pip 04 cast, deny, dice, jilt, kill, spin, veto 05 repel, scrap, spurn, trash 06 rebuff, recuse, refuse, second
07 cast off, cast-off, condemn, decline, despise, discard, dismiss, exclude, failure, forsake, outcast, repulse, say no to 08 athetize, brush off, disallow, disclaim, jettison, renounce, set aside, throw out, turn away, turn down
09 eliminate, knock back, reprobate, repudiate, throw away 10 disapprove
11 give the push 13 kick into touch
14 throw overboard, turn your back on
15 wash your hands of

**rejection**

04 push, veto 05 spurn 06 denial, rebuff
07 heave-ho, refusal 08 brush-off, turn-down 09 athetesis, declining, dismissal, exclusion, knock-back
10 discarding 11 elimination, jettisoning, reprobation, repudiation, turning-down 12 cold shoulder, renunciation 14 Dear John letter

**rejig**

◇ *anagram indicator*
07 re-equip, shake up 09 modernize, rearrange 10 reorganize, streamline
11 rationalize, restructure

**rejoice**

03 joy 05 exult, glory, revel 07 be happy, delight, gladden, triumph 08 be joyful, jubilate 09 be pleased, celebrate, make merry, whoop it up
10 jump for joy 11 be delighted 12 take pleasure

**rejoicing**

03 joy 05 glory 07 delight, elation, ovation, revelry, triumph 08 euphoria, gladness, jubilant, pleasure 09 festivity, happiness 10 exaltation, exultation, jubilation 11 celebration, merrymaking

**rejoin**

◇ *anagram indicator*
04 quip 05 reply 06 answer, retort
07 respond, riposte 08 repartee

**rejoinder**

04 quip 05 reply 06 answer, retort
07 riposte 08 comeback, repartee, response

**rejuvenate**

05 renew 06 revive 07 refresh, restore
08 recharge, rekindle, revivify
09 freshen up, reanimate
10 regenerate, revitalize
12 reinvigorate

**rejuvenation**

07 renewal, revival 11 restoration, shunamitism 12 regeneration
14 reinvigoration, revitalization

**relapse**

04 fail, sink, weed, weid 05 lapse
06 revert, weaken, worsen 07 decline, regress, setback 08 fall away
09 backslide, reversion, weakening, worsening 10 degenerate, recurrence, regression, retrogress 11 backsliding, deteriorate, hypostrophe
13 deterioration, retrogression

**relate**

04 ally, join, link, rede, tell 05 apply, fable, refer, story 06 couple, detail, empart, impart, recite, report
07 compare, concern, connect, feel for, narrate, pertain, present, recount, respect 08 describe, hit it off, identify
09 appertain, associate, bring back, correlate, delineate, discourse, empathize, get on with, make known
10 be relevant, sympathize, understand 11 communicate 12 have a rapport 13 get on well with 14 have a bearing on

**related**

03 kin, rel 04 akin 05 joint, of kin
06 affine, agnate, allied, kinred, linked, mutual 07 affined, cognate, kindred
08 narrated, referred, relevant
09 connected, pertinent 10 affiliated, associated, correlated 11 concomitant
12 accompanying, interrelated
14 consanguineous, interconnected
15 of the same family

**relation**

03 kin, rel, sib 04 bond, link, term
05 ratio 06 affine, family, regard, rellie
07 bearing, kindred, kinsman, linking, rapport, recital, respect 08 alliance, kinsfolk, relative 09 connexion, kinswoman, narrative, reference, relevance, statement 10 collateral, comparison, connection, pertinence, similarity 11 affiliation, application, correlation, information
12 relationship 13 interrelation
14 correspondence, correspondency
15 interconnection, interdependence
*See also* **narrative**; **relative**

**relations**

03 kin, sex 05 folks, terms, union
06 coitus, family 07 affairs, coition, contact, kindred, kinsman, liaison, quarter, rapport, rellies 08 contacts, dealings, intimacy, kinsfolk
09 kinswoman, relatives 10 copulation, love-making 11 connections, interaction, intercourse
12 associations, consummation, relationship 14 communications
15 carnal knowledge

**relationship**

03 kin, tie 04 bond, link, ties 05 blood, fling, ratio, thing, tie-up 06 affair
07 account, kinship, liaison, rapport, romance, sibship 08 affinity, alliance, intimacy, parallel 09 chemistry, closeness 10 connection, flirtation, friendship, love affair, proportion, similarity 11 association, correlation

**• end relationship**

04 dump, jilt 07 break up, divorce, split up

**relative**

03 kin, rel 06 family, rellie 07 germane, kindred, kinsman, related 08 apposite, kinsfolk, moderate, parallel, relation, relevant 09 connected, connexion, dependant, dependent, kinswoman, pertinent 10 applicable, comparable, connection, reciprocal, respective
11 appropriate, comparative, correlative 12 commensurate, interrelated, proportional
13 corresponding, proportionate

*Relatives include:*

02 ex
03 bro, dad, mom, mum, sis, son
04 aunt, gran, heir, nana, twin, wife
05 aunty, daddy, mummy, nanna, nanny, niece, uncle
06 auntie, cousin, ex-wife, father, german, godson, grampa, granny, mother, nephew, parent, sister, spouse
07 brother, grandad, husband, partner, sibling, stepdad, stepmum, stepson

**08** daughter, godchild, grandson
**09** ex-husband, godfather, godmother, stepchild
**10** grandchild, half-sister, stepfather, stepmother, step-parent, stepsister, twin-sister
**11** first cousin, foster-child, god-daughter, grandfather, grandmother, grandparent, half-brother, stepbrother, twin-brother
**12** foster-parent, second cousin, stepdaughter
**13** grand-daughter

**relatively**
**05** quite **06** fairly, rather **08** somewhat **12** by comparison, in comparison **13** comparatively

**relax**
◇ *anagram indicator*
**03** veg **04** calm, ease, fall, rest **05** abate, chill, loose, lower, remit, slump **06** cool it, lessen, loosen, reduce, relent, sedate, soften, unbend, unknit, unrein, unwind, veg out, weaken **07** ease off, mollify, resolve, slacken, unbrace, unclasp, unpurse **08** calm down, chill out, de-stress, diminish, kick back, loosen up, moderate, wind down **09** hang loose, lighten up **10** liberalize, take it easy **12** tranquillize **13** let yourself go, put your feet up **14** take things easy **15** let your hair down

**relaxation**
**03** fun **04** rest **05** let-up **06** easing, repose **07** détente, leisure, relâche **08** chill-out, pleasure **09** abatement, amusement, enjoyment, lessening, loosening, reduction, softening, unwinding, weakening **10** autogenics, meditation, misericord, moderation, recreation, slackening **11** délassement, distraction, loosening up, misericorde, refreshment **13** entertainment

**relaxed**
◇ *anagram indicator*
**04** calm, cool, easy **05** loose **06** at ease, atonic, casual, comodo, unbent **07** commodo, languid, restful **08** carefree, composed, downbeat, informal, laid-back, toneless, unbraced, unstrung **09** collected, easy-going, graspless, leisurely, unhurried **11** comfortable, uninhibited **12** happy-go-lucky

**relay**
◇ *anagram indicator*
**04** send, time, turn **05** carry, shift, spell, stint **06** hand on, pass on, period, spread, supply **07** message **08** dispatch, transmit **09** broadcast, circulate, programme **11** communicate **12** transmission **13** communication

**release**
**04** free, undo **05** exeem, exeme, issue, let go, loose, remit, untie **06** acquit, convey, excuse, exempt, launch, let off, let-off, loosen, reveal, unbind, unlock, unveil **07** absolve, acquite, deliver, divulge, freedom, liberty, present, publish, relieve, set free, slacken, unchain, unclasp, unleash, unloose **08** acquight, announce, bulletin, disclose, liberate, uncouple, unfasten **09** acquittal, circulate, discharge, disengage, exemption, exonerate, make known, quitclaim, quittance, remission, surrender, unshackle **10** absolution, disclosure, distribute, emancipate, liberation, make public, publishing, relinquish, revelation **11** acquittance, declaration, deliverance, enlargement, exoneration, manumission, publication **12** announcement, emancipation, proclamation **13** make available

**relegate**
**05** eject, exile, expel, refer **06** assign, banish, demote, deport, reduce **07** consign, degrade, entrust **08** delegate, dispatch, sideline, transfer **09** downgrade **10** expatriate **12** Stellenbosch

**relent**
**04** ease, melt **05** abate, allow, let up, relax, yield **06** give in, regret, repent, soften, unbend, weaken **07** die down, ease off, give way, melting, slacken, slowing **08** moderate **09** come round **10** capitulate **14** change your mind

**relentless**
**04** grim, hard **05** cruel, harsh, stern **06** fierce **08** pitiless, ruthless **09** cut-throat, incessant, merciless, punishing, unceasing **10** implacable, inexorable, inflexible, persistent, unflagging, unyielding **11** cold-hearted, hard-hearted, remorseless, unforgiving, unrelenting, unremitting **14** uncompromising

**relevance**
**07** aptness, bearing **10** pertinence **11** suitability **12** appositeness, significance **13** applicability **15** appropriateness

**relevant**
**03** apt **04** live **06** german, proper **07** apropos, fitting, germane, related **08** apposite, material, relative, suitable **09** congruous, pertinent **10** admissible, applicable, to the point **11** appropriate, significant **12** proportional, to the purpose

**reliability**
**07** honesty **09** certainty, constancy, integrity, precision **10** steadiness **12** faithfulness **13** dependability **14** responsibility **15** trustworthiness

**reliable**
**04** safe, sure, true **05** solid, sound, white **06** honest, stable, tested, trusty **07** certain, devoted, dutiful, regular, staunch **08** bankable, constant, credible, faithful **09** unfailing **10** dependable **11** predictable, responsible, trustworthy, well-founded **12** well-grounded **13** authoritative, conscientious **14** copper-bottomed

**reliance**
**05** faith, trust **06** belief, credit **09** assurance **10** confidence, conviction, dependance, dependence

**relic**
**05** scrap, shell, token, trace **06** corpse, fossil, relict **07** antique, memento, relique, remains, remanié, remnant, vestige **08** artefact, fragment, heirloom, holdover, keepsake, moniment, monument, reminder, souvenir, survival **09** antiquity **11** remembrance

**relief**
**03** aid **04** alms, cure, help, rest **05** break, let-up, locum, proxy **06** back-up, easing, remedy, repose, rescue, saving, succor, supply **07** comfort, redress, release, relievo, reserve, respite, rilievo, stand-by, stand-in, succour, support **08** allaying, breather, calmness, easement, soothing **09** abatement, assuaging, diversion, happiness, lessening, reduction, remission, surrogate **10** assistance, mitigation, palliation, relaxation, substitute, sustenance, understudy **11** alleviation, consolation, deliverance, reassurance, refreshment, replacement **12** interruption

• **expression of relief**
**04** phew, whew **06** wheugh **08** thank God **12** thank heavens **13** thank goodness

**relieve**
**03** aid **04** beet, bete, cure, ease, feed, free, heal, help, save, stop **05** abate, allay, break, expel, pause, spare, spell **06** assist, excuse, exempt, lessen, reduce, remove, rescue, soften, soothe, succor **07** assuage, bestead, break up, comfort, console, deliver, dismiss, release, replace, set free, slacken, succour, support, sustain **08** liberate, mitigate, palliate, reassure, unburden **09** alleviate, discharge, interrupt, punctuate **10** stand in for, substitute **11** discontinue **12** bring to an end, take over from **14** take the place of

**relieved**
**04** glad **05** eased, happy **07** cheered, pleased **08** thankful **09** refreshed **10** encouraged

**religion**
**04** code **05** creed, dogma, faith **07** beliefs **08** doctrine **12** belief system

*Religions include:*

**03** Bon, Zen
**04** Shi'a
**05** Amish, Baha'i, Druze, Islam, Sunni
**06** Sufism, Taoism, voodoo
**07** animism, Baha'ism, Essenes, Jainism, Jesuits, Judaism, Lamaism, Moonies, Opus Dei, Orphism, Quakers, Saivism, Saktism, Sikhism
**08** Baptists, Buddhism, Druidism, Hasidism, Hinduism, paganism, Tantrism, Wahhabis
**09** Ahmadiyya, Cabbalism, Calvinism,

Methodism, Mithraism, Mormonism, occultism, Parseeism, shamanism, Shintoism, Vedantism, Waldenses
**10** Adventists, Brahmanism, Evangelism, Gnosticism, Iconoclasm, Puritanism, Soka Gakkai
**11** Anabaptists, Anglicanism, Catholicism, Creationism, Freemasonry, Hare Krishna, Lutheranism, Manichaeism, Scientology, Zen Buddhism
**12** Albigensians, Christianity, Confucianism, Nestorianism, Unitarianism
**13** Church in Wales, Protestantism, Reform Judaism, Salvation Army
**14** Fundamentalism, Oxford Movement, Pentecostalism, Rastafarianism, Rosicrucianism, Society of Jesus, Ultramontanism, Zoroastrianism
**15** ancestor-worship, Church of England, Presbyterianism

## religious

**02** pi **03** pia **04** holy **05** godly, pious **06** devout, divine, sacred, strict **07** serious **08** reverent, rigorous **09** believing, committed, doctrinal, righteous, spiritual **10** devotional, God-fearing, meticulous, practising, scriptural, scrupulous **11** church-going, theological **13** conscientious

*See also* **Bible**; **festival**; **scripture**; **service**; **symbol**

*Religious buildings include:*

**04** Kaba
**05** Ka'aba
**06** Kasbah
**07** Abu Mena, al-Azhar
**08** Pantheon
**09** Abu Simbel, Acropolis, Borobudur, Eye Temple, Kinkakuji, Parthenon, Propylaea, Sacred Way, Sun Temple, Temple Bar
**10** Blue Mosque, Erechtheum, Harimandir, Sacré Coeur
**11** Ajanta caves, Ellora caves, Erechtheion, Great Sphinx, Hagia Sophia, Temple Mount, Wailing Wall, Western Wall, York Minster
**12** Boyana Church, Ely Cathedral, Golden Temple, Great Pyramid, Monte Cassino, Norton Priory, Pagan temples, Temple of Hera, Temple of Isis, Watton Priory
**13** Cordoba Mosque, Dome of the Rock, Horyuji Temple, Kailasa Temple, Muhammad's Tomb, Rila Monastery, Vézelay Church
**14** Belém Monastery, Dilwara temples, Golden Pavilion, Kazan Cathedral, Mahamuni Pagoda, My Son Sanctuary, Reims Cathedral, Ripon Cathedral, Sagrada Familia, Suleiman Mosque, Temple of Amon-Ra, Temple of Apollo, Temple of Athena, Temple of Heaven, Ummayyad Mosque, Wells Cathedral
**15** Aachen Cathedral, Amiens Cathedral, Chavín de Huantar, Durham Cathedral, Exeter Cathedral, Ggantija temples, Pyramid of Cheops, Pyramid of the Sun, Shwe Dagon Pagoda, Shwezigon Pagoda, Speyer Cathedral, Temple of Artemis, Temple of Hathoor, Temple of Solomon, Temple of Somnath

*See also* **abbey**; **cathedral**; **worship**

*Religious figures include:*

**03** **Fry** (Elizabeth), **Hus** (Jan), **Roy** (Ram Mohan)
**04** **Bede** (St, 'the Venerable'), **Eddy** (Mary), **Huss** (John), **John** (of Leyden), **King** (Martin Luther), **Knox** (John), **Penn** (William), **Pire** (Dominique), **Shaw** (Anna Howard), **Tutu** (Desmond), **Weil** (Simone)
**05** **Amman** (Jacob), **Booth** (William), **Condé** (Louis Prince de), **Farel** (Guillaume), **Grove** (Sir George), **Jesus**, **Keble** (John), **Lao Zi**, **Lewis** (Clive Staples), **Mahdi** (El), **Paley** (William), **Paris** (Matthew), **Smith** (Joseph), **Soper** (Donald, Lord), **Waite** (Terry), **Young** (Brigham)
**06** **Arnold** (of Brescia), **Baxter** (Richard), **Becket** (St Thomas à), **Besant** (Annie), **Boehme** (Jakob), **Borgia**, **Browne** (Robert), **Browne** (Sir Thomas), **Buddha**, **Bunyan** (John), **Calvin** (John), **Christ**, **Gandhi** (Mohandas), **Garvey** (Marcus), **Graham** (Billy), **Hillel**, **Hutter** (Leonhard), **Jowett** (Benjamin), **Julian** (of Norwich), **Kempis** (Thomas à), **Lao-tzu**, **Luther** (Martin), **Mather** (Cotton), **Mesmer** (Franz Anton), **Olcott** (Colonel Henry Steel), **Pilate** (Pontius), **Raikes** (Robert), **Ridley** (Nicholas), **Rogers** (John), **Sieyès** (Emmanuel Joseph Comte), **Tetzel** (Johann), **Wesley** (John)
**07** **Aga Khan**, **al-Banna** (Hassan), **Ayeshah**, **Buchman** (Frank), **Coligny** (Gaspard de), **Cranmer** (Thomas), **Crowley** (Aleister), **Erasmus** (Desiderius), **Falwell** (Jerry), **Fénelon** (François), **Hubbard** (L Ron), **Jackson** (Jesse), **Latimer** (Hugh), **Mahatma**, **Müntzer** (Thomas), **Paisley** (Reverend Ian), **Photius**, **Russell** (Charles Taze), **Russell** (Jack), **Sithole** (Reverend Ndabaningi), **Spooner** (William Archibald), **Steiner** (Rudolf), **Tyndale** (William), **William** (of Malmesbury), **William** (of Ockham), **William** (of Tyre), **Wishart** (George), **Zwingli** (Huldreich)
**08** **Agricola** (Johann), **Andrewes** (Lancelot), **Barabbas**, **Buchanan** (George), **Caiaphas**, **Khomeini** (Ayatollah Ruhollah), **Mahavira** (Vardhamana), **Mohammed**, **Muhammad**, **Pelagius**, **Rasputin** (Grigoriy), **Selassie** (Emperor Haile), **Williams** (Roger), **Wycliffe** (John)
**09** **Akhenaten**, **Bar Kokhba** (Simon), **Blavatsky** (Madame Helena), **Confucius**, **Dalai Lama**, **Guru Nanak**, **Joan of Arc** (St), **McPherson** (Aimee Semple), **Niemöller** (Martin), **Zoroaster**
**10** **Belshazzar**, **Fateh Singh** (Sant), **Huntingdon** (Selina Hastings, Countess of), **Manichaeus**, **Savonarola** (Girolamo), **Swedenborg** (Emmanuel), **Torquemada** (Tomás de), **Whitefield** (George)
**11** **Bodhidharma**, **Jesus Christ**, **Prester John**, **Ramakrishna**, **Wilberforce** (William)
**12** **Krishnamurti** (Jiddu)
**13** **Judas Iscariot**
**15** **Francis of Assisi (St)**

*Religious officers include:*

**03** nun
**04** dean, guru, imam, monk, pope
**05** abbot, canon, elder, friar, imaum, kohen, padre, prior, rabbi, rebbe, swami, vicar
**06** abbess, bishop, clergy, curate, deacon, father, mullah, parson, pastor, priest, rector
**07** muezzin, prelate, proctor
**08** cardinal, chaplain, minister, preacher
**09** ayatollah, clergyman, Dalai Lama, deaconess, Monsignor, Tashi Lama
**10** archbishop, archdeacon, arch-priest, chancellor
**11** clergywoman, Panchen Lama
**14** mother superior

*See also* **archbishop**; **cardinal**; **missionary**; **pope**; **theologian**

*Religious orders include:*

**04** IBVM, Sufi
**05** Taizé
**06** Culdee, Essene, Jesuit, Loreto, Marist
**07** Jesuits, Marists, Rifaite
**08** Buddhist, Capuchin, Grey nuns, Minorite, Trappist, Ursuline
**09** Barnabite, Capuchins, Carmelite, Dominican, Marianist, Mawlawite, mendicant, Salesians, Trappists, Ursulines
**10** Bernardine, Carmelites, Carthusian, Celestines, Cistercian, Conventual, Dominicans, Franciscan, Gilbertine, Grey friars, Norbertine, Oratorians, Poor Clares
**11** Augustinian, Benedictine, Black friars, Camaldolite, Carthusians, Cistercians, Franciscans, Ignorantine, Sylvestrine, White friars
**12** Augustinians, Austin friars, Benedictines
**13** Society of Mary
**14** Knights Templar, Sisters of Mercy, Society of Jesus

*See also* **monastery**; **sect**

• **religious education**

**02** RE, RI

**religiously**
**08** strictly **10** rigorously **11** doctrinally, spiritually **12** meticulously, scrupulously **13** theologically **15** conscientiously

**relinquish**
**04** cede, drop, part, quit **05** cease, demit, forgo, let go, waive, yield **06** desert, desist, forego, give up, resign **07** abandon, abstain, discard, forsake, give out, release, retreat **08** abdicate, hand over, part with, renounce **09** repudiate, surrender **11** discontinue

**reliquary**
**04** chef, tope **09** encolpion **10** tabernacle

**relish**
**03** sar **04** gout, gust, like, love, lust, tang, zest **05** adore, charm, enjoy, gusto, sauce, savor, smack, spice, taste, tooth **06** bumalo, degust, flavor, palate, pickle, savour, vigour **07** botargo, bummalo, chutney, delight, flavour, garnish, kitchen, rellish, revel in, stomach **08** appetite, bumaloti, caponata, opsonium, piquancy, pleasure, vivacity **09** appetizer, bummaloti, condiment, delight in, enjoyment, seasoning **10** appreciate, Bombay duck, experience, flavouring, liveliness **12** appreciation, satisfaction
**• lose relish**
**04** pall

**relocate**
**02** go **04** move **05** leave **06** go away, remove **08** move away, transfer, up sticks **09** move house **13** change address

**reluctance**
**07** dislike **08** aversion, distaste, loathing **09** hesitancy, renitency **10** hesitation, opposition, repugnance, resistance **12** backwardness **13** indisposition, recalcitrance, unwillingness **14** disinclination

**reluctant**
**03** shy **04** loth, slow **05** loath **06** averse **08** backward, grudging, hesitant, loathful, renitent **09** resisting, squeamish, unwilling **10** indisposed, struggling **11** disinclined **14** unenthusiastic

**rely**
**04** bank, lean, rest **05** count, trust **06** be sure, depend, reckon **07** swear by

**remain**
**02** be **03** lie **04** bide, keep, last, rest, stay, wait **05** abide, abode, await, dwell, leave, stand, stick, tarry **06** endure, linger, stay on **07** climate, persist, prevail, subsist, survive **08** continue, outstand **09** hang about, stand good **10** be left over, hang around, stay behind **11** stick around

**remainder**
**04** lave, rest **06** excess **07** balance, remains, remanet, remnant, residue, surplus **08** remanent, residuum, vestiges **09** carry-over, leftovers **11** superfluity

**remaining**
**03** odd **04** last, left, over **05** other, spare **06** unused **07** abiding, lasting, remnant, unspent **08** left over, remanent, residual **09** lingering, surviving **10** persisting, unfinished **11** outstanding

**remains**
**03** ash **04** body, dust, rest, ruin **05** ashes, bones, dregs, ruins **06** corpse, crumbs, debris, relics, scraps, traces **07** cadaver, carcase, residue **08** dead body, detritus, leavings, oddments, remnants, vestiges **09** fragments, leftovers, reliquiae, remainder, reversion **11** odds and ends

**remake**
◇ *anagram indicator*
**06** mutate **07** rebuild **09** modernize, reproduce, transmute **11** reconstruct **12** metamorphose

**remark**
**03** hit, say **04** barb, jeer, note, quip, shot **05** ad-lib, sally, state **06** assert, insult, notice, reason **07** clanger, comment, declare, mention, observe, opinion **08** brickbat, cynicism, intimacy, one-liner, remarque **09** assertion, gallantry, pronounce, reference, statement, stricture, utterance, witticism **10** commentary, reflection, trivialism **11** commonplace, declaration, discourtesy, non sequitur, observation **12** obiter dictum **13** pronouncement **14** noteworthiness **15** acknowledgement

**remarkable**
◇ *anagram indicator*
**03** odd **04** fine, rare, some, tall, unco **06** signal **07** amazing, notable, strange, unusual **08** singular, striking, uncommon **09** damnedest, important, memorable, momentous, prominent **10** hellacious, impressive, inimitable, miraculous, noteworthy, phenomenal, pre-eminent, surpassing, surprising **11** conspicuous, exceptional, outstanding, significant **12** considerable, unbelievable **13** distinguished, extraordinary
**• remarkable thing**
**04** lulu

**remarkably**
**04** unco **08** signally, uncommon **09** unusually **10** uncommonly **12** considerably, surprisingly **13** exceptionally, outstandingly, significantly **15** extraordinarily

**remedy**
◇ *anagram indicator*
**03** fix **04** cure, ease, heal, help, mend, sort **05** azoth, dinic, salve, solve, tonga, treat **06** answer, bicarb, nosode, physic, posset, recure, relief, remead, remede, remeid, repair, soothe **07** arcanum, control, correct, nostrum, panacea, plaster, rectify, redress, relieve, restore, sort out, therapy **08** antidote, cephalic, corn-cure, leechdom, lungwort, medicine, mitigate, pilewort, put right, solution, specific **09** echinacea, eyebright, Galenical, hoarhound, horehound, magistery, prescript, salvarsan, treatment **10** catholicon, corrective, counteract, medicament, medication, reparation, simillimum, tarantella **11** oil of cloves, restorative **12** panpharmacon **13** antiscorbutic, antispasmodic, viper's bugloss **14** countermeasure, white horehound

**remember**
**03** mem **04** keep, mark, mind **05** evoke, learn, place, think **06** honour, recall, record, remind, retain **07** mention, think of **08** hark back, look back, memorize, summon up **09** celebrate, recognize, recollect, reminisce, think back **10** bear in mind, call to mind **11** commemorate, hold against, reconnoitre **12** learn by heart, pay tribute to **13** send greetings **14** commit to memory, send best wishes, send good wishes **15** send your regards

**remembrance**
**04** mind **05** relic, token **06** memory, recall, record **07** memento, thought **08** keepsake, memorial, monument, reminder, souvenir **09** nostalgia, sovenance **10** memorandum, retrospect **11** recognition, recordation, testimonial **12** recollection, reminiscence **13** commemoration

**remind**
**04** hint **05** evoke, nudge **06** call up, prompt **08** remember, take back **10** call to mind **11** bring to mind **13** jog your memory **14** make you think of, put you in mind of

**reminder**
**04** hint, memo, note, prod **05** nudge, token **06** prompt **07** memento **08** keepsake, souvenir **09** red letter **10** memorandum, phylactery, prompt-note, suggestion, verbal note **11** aide-mémoire, remembrance **12** reality check

**reminisce**
**06** recall, review **08** hark back, look back, remember **09** recollect, think back **10** retrospect

**reminiscence**
**06** memoir, memory, recall, review **08** anecdote **10** reflection **11** remembrance **12** recollection **13** retrospection
**• collection of reminiscences**
**03** ana

**reminiscent**
**08** redolent **09** evocative, nostalgic, remindful **10** suggestive

**remiss**
**03** lax **04** slow **05** slack, tardy **06** casual, sloppy **07** wayward

08 careless, culpable, dilatory, heedless, slipshod 09 forgetful, negligent, unmindful 10 neglectful 11 inattentive, indifferent, slack-handed, thoughtless 13 lackadaisical

**remission**
03 ebb 04 lull 05 let-up 06 excuse, pardon, repeal 07 amnesty, release, respite 08 decrease, remittal, reprieve 09 abatement, acquittal, annulment, discharge, exemption, lessening, reduction, remitment, weakening 10 abrogation, absolution, diminution, indulgence, indulgency, moderation, relaxation, rescinding, revocation, slackening, suspension 11 alleviation, exoneration, forgiveness 12 cancellation 13 acceptilation

**remit**
03 pay 04 mail, post, send 05 abate, brief, refer, relax, scope, untax 06 cancel, desist, direct, give up, orders, pardon, pass on, repeal, revoke, settle 07 forward, release, rescind, suspend 08 abrogate, dispatch, hold over, set aside, transfer, transmit 10 guidelines, overslaugh 12 instructions 13 authorization 14 responsibility

**remittance**
03 fee 07 payment, sending 08 dispatch 09 allowance, remitment 13 consideration

**remnant**
03 bit, end, tag 04 butt, fent, rump 05 piece, scrap, shred, trace, wrack 06 offcut 07 balance, oddment, outlier, remains, residue, vestige, witness 08 fragment, leftover, remanent 09 quotation, remainder, remaining 12 odd-come-short

**remodel**
◇ *anagram indicator*
04 turn 05 adapt, alter, renew, shape 06 adjust, change, mutate, reform 07 convert, furbish, rebuild 08 renovate 09 modernize, refurbish, transform 11 recondition, reconstruct 12 metamorphose

**remonstrance**
07 protest, reproof 08 petition 09 complaint, exception, grievance, objection, reprimand 10 opposition 12 protestation 13 expostulation 14 representation

**remonstrate**
05 argue, gripe 06 object, oppose 07 dispute, dissent, protest 08 complain 09 challenge 11 demonstrate, expostulate 13 take issue with 15 take exception to

**remorse**
03 rew, rue 04 bite, pity, ruth, worm 05 grief, guilt, shame 06 regret, sorrow 08 ayenbite, had-I-wist 09 penitence 10 contrition, mitigation, repentance, ruefulness 11 compunction 12 contriteness, self-reproach 13 bad conscience

**remorseful**
03 sad 05 sorry 06 guilty, rueful 07 ashamed 08 contrite, penitent 09 chastened, regretful, repentant, sorrowful 10 apologetic 11 guilt-ridden 12 compunctious, on a guilt trip 13 compassionate

**remorseless**
04 hard 05 cruel, harsh, stern 06 savage 07 callous 08 inhumane, pitiless, ruthless 09 merciless 10 implacable, inexorable, relentless, unmerciful 11 hard-hearted, undeviating, unforgiving, unrelenting, unremitting, unstoppable 12 unremorseful

**remorselessly**
07 cruelly, harshly 08 savagely 09 callously 10 implacably, inexorably, ruthlessly 11 mercilessly 12 relentlessly 13 unremittingly

**remote**
03 far, out 04 back, long, poor, slim 05 aloof, faint, inapt, small 06 far-off, lonely, meagre, slight, upland 07 devious, distant, dubious, faraway, outback, outside, removed, slender 08 backveld, detached, doubtful, isolated, outlying, reserved, secluded, unlikely 09 not matter, ungermane, unrelated, up the bush, withdrawn 10 extraneous, immaterial, improbable, inapposite, in the mulga, irrelative, irrelevant, negligible, out of place, peripheral, tangential, uninvolved, up the mulga 11 back-country, god-forsaken, in the sticks, off the point, out-of-the-way, standoffish, unconcerned, unconnected, unimportant, up the Boohai 12 inaccessible, inapplicable, inconsequent, long-distance 13 beside the mark, inappropriate, insignificant 14 beside the point, inconsiderable, unapproachable 15 having no bearing, not coming into it, uncommunicative

**removable**
07 movable 09 separable 10 detachable, eradicable 12 transferable

**removal**
04 boot, move, push, sack 05 elbow, shift 06 firing, murder 07 ousting, purging, sacking 08 ablation, deletion, disposal, ejection, eviction, riddance, shifting 09 abolition, clearance, departure, discharge, dismissal, expulsion, taking-off, uprooting 10 conveyance, deposition, detachment, displacing, evacuation, extraction, relegation, relocation, taking away, withdrawal 11 subtraction, transferral 12 dislodgement, obliteration, transference, transporting 14 transportation

**remove**
03 nip, rid 04 dele, doff, fire, flit, lift, move, oust, pick, sack, shed, take, void, weed 05 amove, carry, eject, eloin, erase, evict, expel, purge, raise, shift, strip 06 ablate, convey, cut off, cut out, delete, depose, detach, efface, eloign, excise, extort, get out, go away, lop off, remble, rub out, unseat 07 abolish, absence, boot out, cart off, cashier, cast out, collect, destroy, dismiss, edge out, expurge, extract, pull off, pull out, put away, removal, take off, take out, tear off 08 amputate, cross out, dislodge, disloign, displace, estrange, get rid of, relegate, relocate, separate, subtract, take away, throw out, transfer, withdraw 09 discharge, eliminate, go off with, strike out, translate, transport 10 blue-pencil, obliterate 11 deaccession

**remunerate**
03 pay 05 repay 06 reward 07 redress 09 indemnify, reimburse 10 compensate, recompense

**remuneration**
03 fee, pay 04 sold 05 solde, wages 06 income, profit, reward, salary 07 payment, stipend 08 earnings, retainer 09 emolument, indemnity, repayment 10 honorarium, recompense, remittance 12 compensation 13 reimbursement

**remunerative**
04 rich 06 paying 07 gainful 08 fruitful 09 lucrative, rewarding 10 profitable, worthwhile 11 moneymaking

**renaissance**
07 new dawn, rebirth, renewal, revival 08 new birth 09 awakening 10 renascence, resurgence 11 reawakening, re-emergence, restoration 12 reappearance, regeneration, rejuvenation, resurrection, Risorgimento 13 recrudescence

**renascent**
06 reborn 07 renewed, revived 09 born again, redivivus, resurgent 10 reanimated, reawakened, re-emergent 11 resurrected

**rend**
03 rip 04 rent, rive, stab, tear 05 break, burst, sever, smash, split, wring 06 cleave, divide, pierce, to-rend 07 rupture, shatter 08 fracture, lacerate, separate, splinter 09 tear apart 10 dilacerate

**render**
◇ *anagram indicator*
02 do 03 gie, pay, put, try 04 give, make, melt, play, show, sing, turn 05 leave, yield 06 change, depict, give up, make up, return, submit, supply, tender 07 clarify, deliver, display, exhibit, explain, furnish, perform, present, proffer, provide 08 describe, give back, hand over, manifest 09 cause to be, interpret, represent, reproduce, surrender, translate 10 contribute, transcribe

**rendering**
04 crib, show 05 gloss 06 acting

**07** reading, version **09** portrayal, rendition, rewording **10** appearance, paraphrase, production, rephrasing **11** explanation, metaphrasis, performance, translation **12** presentation **13** transcription **14** interpretation, representation, simplification **15** transliteration

**rendezvous**
**02** RV **04** date, meet **05** haunt, rally, tryst, venue **06** gather, muster, resort **07** collect, convene, meeting **08** assemble, converge **10** engagement **11** appointment, assignation **12** come together, meeting-place **13** trysting-place

**rendition**
**05** gloss **07** reading, version **08** delivery **09** depiction, execution, portrayal, rendering, rewording, surrender **10** paraphrase, rephrasing **11** arrangement, explanation, performance, translation **12** construction, presentation **13** transcription **14** interpretation, simplification **15** transliteration

**renegade**
◇ *anagram indicator*
**03** rat **05** rebel **06** outlaw **07** runaway, traitor **08** apostate, betrayer, defector, deserter, disloyal, mutineer, mutinous, recreant, runagate, turncoat **09** dissident **10** backslider, perfidious, rebellious, traitorous, unfaithful **11** backsliding, treacherous **13** tergiversator

**renege**
**04** deny, pike **05** renig, welsh **06** refuse **07** default, renague, renegue **08** renounce **09** backslide, repudiate **10** apostatize **13** cross the floor

**renegotiate**
◇ *anagram indicator*

**renew**
◇ *anagram indicator*
**03** new **04** mend, stum **05** boost, refit **06** extend, reform, reline, repair, repeat, reseat, resume, revive **07** brush up, prolong, refresh, remodel, replace, reprise, reprize, restart, restate, restock, restore, retrace **08** continue, innovate, overhaul, reaffirm, recreate, renforce, renovate **09** modernize, refurbish, reiterate, replenish, transform **10** invigorate, recommence, regenerate, rejuvenate, revitalize **11** recondition, re-establish, resuscitate **12** reconstitute, reinvigorate

**renewal**
**05** flush **06** repair **07** rebirth, recruit, revival **08** new birth, nidation **09** recruital **10** kiss of life, re-creation, renovation, repetition, resumption **11** continuance, reiteration, restatement **12** instauration, regeneration, rejuvenation, resurrection **13** reaffirmation, refurbishment, replenishment, resuscitation **14** recommencement, reconditioning, reconstitution, reconstruction, reinvigoration, revitalization, revivification

**renounce**
**03** cut **04** deny, reny, shun **05** forgo, renay, reney, renig, spurn, waive **06** abjure, desist, disown, eschew, forego, forsay, give up, pass up, recant, recede, refuse, reject, renege, resign, revolt **07** abandon, abstain, discard, disgown, foresay, forsake, put away, renague, renegue **08** abdicate, abnegate, disclaim, forswear, sign away, swear off **09** repudiate, surrender **10** declare off, disinherit, disprofess, relinquish **14** forisfamiliate **15** wash your hands of

**renovate**
◇ *anagram indicator*
**04** do up **05** refit, renew **06** reform, repair, revamp **07** furbish, improve, remodel, restore **08** overhaul **09** modernize, refurbish, translate **10** redecorate, regenerate **11** recondition **12** rehabilitate **13** give a facelift

**renovation**
**05** refit **06** repair **07** renewal **08** facelift **11** improvement, restoration **13** modernization, refurbishment **14** reconditioning

**renown**
**04** bays, fame, , mana, mark, note **05** glory, kudos, rumor **06** esteem, honour, luster, lustre, repute, rumour **07** acclaim, stardom **08** eminence, prestige **09** celebrate, celebrity **10** prominence, reputation **11** distinction, pre-eminence **15** illustriousness

**renowned**
**05** famed, noted **06** fabled, famous **07** eminent, notable **08** of repute **09** acclaimed, prominent, splendent, well-known **10** celebrated, illustrate, pre-eminent **11** illustrious, prestigious **13** distinguished

**rent**
◇ *anagram indicator*
**03** fee, let, rip **04** cost, farm, gale, hire, mail, rate, ript, take, tare, tear, tore, torn **05** cuddy, gavel, lease, riven, split **06** let out, rental, ripped, screed, sublet **07** charter, divided, fissure, hire out, payment, rent out, revenue, severed **08** lacerate, purchase, ruptured **09** lacerated, torn apart **11** ripped apart

**renunciation**
**06** denial **07** kenosis, waiving **08** giving up, shunning, spurning **09** disowning, forsaking, rejection, surrender **10** abdication, abnegation, abstinence, desistance, discarding, disclaimer **11** abandonment, disclaiming, recantation, repudiation **13** disinheriting **14** relinquishment, self-abnegation

**reorder**
◇ *anagram indicator*
**04** edit **09** rearrange, transpose

**reorganize**
◇ *anagram indicator*
**05** rejig **07** shake up **09** modernize, rearrange **10** streamline **11** rationalize, restructure **12** reconstitute

**repackage**
◇ *anagram indicator*

**repair**
◇ *anagram indicator*
**02** go **03** fix, sew **04** darn, form, heal, mend, move, nick, turn **05** order, patch, refit, renew, shape, state **06** adjust, doctor, fettle, kilter, make up, remead, remede, remedy, remeid, remove, resort, retire, return, tinker **07** mending, patch up, rectify, redress, refresh, restore, service **08** maintain, make good, overhaul, put right, renovate, revivify, stitch up, withdraw **09** concourse, condition **10** adjustment, reparation **11** improvement, maintenance, restoration, wend your way **12** preservation, working order

**reparable**
**07** curable, savable **10** corrigible, remediable, restorable **11** recoverable, rectifiable, retrievable, salvageable

**reparation**
**04** boot **06** amends, remead, remede, remedy, remeid, repair **07** damages, redress, renewal **08** requital, solatium **09** atonement, indemnity **10** assythment, recompense **11** restitution **12** compensation, propitiation, satisfaction

**repartee**
**03** wit **06** banter, retort **07** jesting, riposte **08** backchat, badinage, wordplay **09** bantering, cross-talk, witticism **11** give and take

**repast**
**04** feed, food, meal **05** board, lunch, snack, table **06** spread **08** victuals **09** collation, refection **11** nourishment
*See also* **meal**

**repatriate**
**04** oust **05** exile, expel **06** banish, deport **09** extradite, ostracize, transport

**repay**
**03** pay **04** apay, quit **05** appay, quite, quyte, yield **06** avenge, quight, rebate, refund, return, reward, settle, square **07** pay back, requite, revenge **09** get back at, quittance, reimburse, retaliate **10** compensate, recompense, remunerate **11** get even with, reciprocate **12** settle up with **14** settle the score

**repayment**
**06** amends, rebate, refund, reward **07** payment, redress, revenge **08** requital **09** tit for tat, vengeance **10** recompense, reparation **11** eye for an eye, restitution, retaliation, retribution **12** compensation, remuneration **13** reciprocation, reimbursement

**repeal**
**04** lift, void **05** annul, quash, unlaw **06** abjure, cancel, recall, recant, revoke **07** abolish, nullify, repress, rescind, retract, reverse **08** abrogate, quashing, reversal, set aside, withdraw **09** abolition, annulment **10** abrogation, invalidate, rescinding, rescission, revocation, withdrawal **11** countermand, rescindment **12** cancellation, invalidation **13** nullification

**repeat**
◇ *repetition indicator*
**03** rep, rpt **04** copy, echo, redo **05** ditto, labor, quote, recap, recur, renew, rerun, thrum **06** do over, go over, labour, parrot, patter, recite, record, re-echo, relate, replay, reshow, retail, retell, reword, run off, screed **07** confirm, divulge, iterate, persist, recount, replica, reprise, reprize, restate **08** redouble, rehearse, remurmur, say again **09** celebrate, circulate, do to death, duplicate, reiterate, replicate, reproduce, reshowing **10** repetition **11** duplication, perseverate, rebroadcast, reduplicate, restatement **12** recapitulate, reproduction **14** recapitulation

**repeated**
◇ *repetition indicator*
**07** regular **08** constant, frequent, multiple, periodic **09** continual, recurrent, recurring **10** persistent, reiterated, rhythmical **12** repercussive

**repeatedly**
◇ *repetition indicator*
**05** often **10** frequently **11** over and over **12** time and again **13** again and again, time after time

**repel**
◇ *reversal indicator*
**05** check, fight, parry, rebut, spurn **06** offend, oppose, rebuff, refuse, reject, resist, revolt, sicken **07** beat off, decline, disgust, hold off, repulse, turn off, ward off **08** beat back, drive off, fight off, nauseate, push back **09** drive back, force back, keep at bay, repudiate **11** make you sick **13** be repugnant to **15** turn your stomach

**repellent**
**04** foul, grim, vile **05** nasty **06** horrid **07** hateful, obscene **08** shocking **09** abhorrent, loathsome, obnoxious, offensive, repugnant, repulsive, revolting, sickening **10** abominable, despicable, disgusting, nauseating, off-putting, unpleasant **11** distasteful, rebarbative **12** contemptible, disagreeable **13** objectionable

• **insect repellent**
**04** deet **07** camphor

**repent**
**03** rue **04** turn **06** lament, recant, regret, relent, sorrow **07** be sorry, confess, deplore, reptant **08** do a U-turn **09** be ashamed **10** be contrite **11** be converted, feel remorse, see the light **14** beat your breast

**repentance**
**03** rue **05** grief, guilt, ruing, shame, U-turn **06** regret, rueing, sorrow **07** penance, remorse **08** metanoia **09** penitence **10** confession, contrition, conversion **11** compunction, recantation

**repentant**
**05** sorry **06** guilty, rueful **07** ashamed, attrite **08** contrite, penitent **09** chastened, regretful, sorrowful **10** apologetic, remorseful

**repercussion**
**04** echo **06** effect, recoil, result, ripple **07** rebound, spin-off **08** backlash, backwash **09** shock wave **10** reflection, side-effect **11** consequence **13** reverberation

**repertoire**
**04** list **05** range, stock, store **06** supply **07** reserve **09** repertory, reservoir **10** collection, repository

**repetition**
◇ *repetition indicator*
**04** echo, rote **05** troll **06** answer, repeat, return **07** copying, echoing, quoting, reprise **08** iterance **09** echolalia, iteration, rehearsal, replicate, tautology **10** recurrence, redundancy **11** duplication, epanalepsis, reiteration, restatement, superfluity **12** reappearance **14** recapitulation

**repetitious**
**04** dull **05** windy, wordy **06** boring, prolix **07** tedious, verbose **08** unvaried **09** redundant **10** long-winded, monotonous, pleonastic, unchanging **12** pleonastical, tautological

**repetitive**
**04** dull **05** samey **06** boring **07** tedious **08** unvaried **09** automatic, iterative, recurrent **10** mechanical, monotonous, unchanging **14** soul-destroying

**rephrase**
**06** recast, reword **07** rewrite **10** paraphrase **13** put another way **14** ask differently, say differently **15** put in other words

**repine**
**04** beef, fret, moan, mope, pine, sulk **05** brood **06** grieve, grouch, grouse, grudge, lament, murmur **07** grumble **08** complain, languish

**replace**
◇ *anagram indicator*
**04** oust **06** act for, change, follow, hang up, refund, return **07** pre-empt, put back, relieve, replant, restore, succeed **08** deputize, displace, exchange, make good, supplant **09** come after, fill in for, reinstate, supersede **10** stand in for, substitute **11** re-establish **14** take the place of

**replaceable**
**09** throwaway **10** disposable, expendable **12** exchangeable **13** biodegradable, non-returnable, substitutable **15** interchangeable

**replacement**
**05** proxy **06** fill-in, supply **07** bionics, reserve, stand-in **09** spare part, successor, surrogate **10** jury-rudder, substitute, understudy **12** arthroplasty, substitution

**replenish**
**04** fill **05** renew, stock, top up **06** fill up, make up, people, refill, reload, supply **07** furnish, provide, recruit, refresh, replace, restock, restore **08** recharge

**replenishment**
**06** supply **07** filling, renewal **09** provision, refilling **10** recharging, restocking, supplyment **11** replacement, restoration

**replete**
**04** full **05** sated **06** filled, full up, gorged, jammed **07** brimful, charged, chocker, crammed, glutted, implete, stuffed, teeming, well-fed **08** brimming, satiated **09** abounding, chock-full, jam-packed **11** chock-a-block, well-stocked **12** well-provided

**repletion**
**04** glut **07** satiety **08** fullness, plethora **09** plenitude, satiation **11** superfluity **12** completeness, overfullness **14** superabundance

**replica**
**04** copy, spit **05** clone, dummy, model **06** repeat **08** gold disc, gold disk **09** duplicate, facsimile, imitation **10** immortelle **12** reproduction

**replicate**
**03** ape **04** copy **05** clone, mimic, reply **06** follow, repeat **08** recreate **09** duplicate, reproduce **10** repetition **11** reduplicate

**reply**
**04** echo **05** duply, react **06** answer, come in, rejoin, retort, return, triply **07** counter, respond, riposte **08** come back, comeback, reaction, rebutter, repartee, response, surrebut, talk back **09** drink-hail, quadruply, rejoinder, replicate, retaliate, surrejoin, write back **11** acknowledge, reciprocate, replication, retaliation, surrebutter **12** surrejoinder, triplication **13** countersignal **15** acknowledgement

**report**
◇ *homophone indicator*
**03** air, cry, rat, rpt **04** bang, boom, buzz, fame, file, item, name, news, note, rept, shop, shot, tale, talk, tell, word **05** blast, brief, bruit, cover, crack, crash, grass, noise, piece, relay, split, state, story, voice **06** cahier, convey, credit, detail, esteem, furphy, gossip, honour, notify, pass on, record, relate, renown, repute, return, rumour, squeal, tell on, update **07** account, article,

declare, divulge, dossier, give out, hearsay, message, minutes, narrate, opinion, publish, recount, stature, stool on, whisper, write-up **08** announce, blue book, bulletin, complain, describe, disclose, document, inform on, proclaim, register, relation, set forth, standing **09** appraisal, broadcast, celebrity, character, chronicle, circulate, delineate, explosion, judgement, narrative, statement, testimony **10** assessment, communiqué, evaluation, inspection, reputation, stenograph **11** communicate, compte rendu, declaration, delineation, description, distinction, examination, information **12** announcement, press release, procès-verbal **13** communication, reverberation

**reportedly**
◇ *homophone indicator*
**09** allegedly **10** apparently, ostensibly, putatively, supposedly **13** by all accounts

**reporter**
**03** cub **04** hack **05** press **06** leg-man **07** fireman, Jenkins **08** leg-woman, newshawk, pressman **09** announcer, columnist, newshound, roundsman **10** journalist, newscaster, news-writer, presswoman, tripehound **11** commentator **12** newspaperman **13** correspondent **14** newspaperwoman

**repose**
**03** kef, kif, lay, lie, put, set **04** affy, calm, ease, kaif, laze, lean, rest **05** lodge, peace, place, poise, quiet, relax, sleep, store **06** aplomb, invest **07** confide, deposit, dignity, entrust, recline, respite, slumber **08** calmness, quietude, serenity **09** composure, night-rest, quietness, stillness **10** equanimity, inactivity, relaxation **11** restfulness **12** tranquillity **14** self-possession

**reposition**
◇ *anagram indicator*
**05** shift **09** rearrange

**repository**
**03** urn **04** bank, mart, safe, tomb **05** depot, store, vault **06** museum **07** archive, dustbin, spicery **08** magazine, treasury **09** confidant, container, repertory, salvatory, sepulchre, warehouse **10** collection, depository, promptuary, receptacle, storehouse

**reprehensible**
**03** bad, ill **04** base **06** errant, erring, remiss **07** ignoble **08** blamable, culpable, shameful, unworthy **10** censurable, delinquent, deplorable **11** blameworthy, condemnable, disgraceful, opprobrious **13** discreditable, objectionable

**represent**
◇ *anagram indicator*
**02** be **03** act, set **04** draw, mark, mean, show **05** act as, enact, evoke, refer **06** act for, allege, denote, depict, embody, figure, render, sketch, typify **07** display, exhibit, express, perform, picture, portray, present **08** amount to, appear as, describe, speak for, stand for **09** appear for, character, depicture, designate, epitomize, exemplify, personify, sculpture, symbolize **10** constitute, illustrate **11** deputize for **12** characterize, correspond to **13** act on behalf of **14** act in the name of, be equivalent to **15** speak on behalf of

**representation**
◇ *anagram indicator*
**02** MP **04** bust, icon, ikon, play, show **05** envoy, image, model, proxy, stage **06** deputy, reflex, report, shadow, sketch, statue **07** account, drawing, picture, protest, request, showing, stand-in **08** delegate, likeness, petition, portrait, prospect **09** complaint, depiction, depicture, pictogram, portrayal, spectacle, spokesman, statement, tablature **10** allegation, ambassador, councillor, delegation, deputation, mouthpiece, production, thermoform **11** Congressman, delineation, description, explanation, performance, presentment, restoration, spokeswoman **12** cross-section, illustration, presentation, remonstrance, reproduction, spokesperson **13** Congresswoman, expostulation, tableau vivant **14** reconstruction, representative

**representative**
**02** MP **03** rep **05** agent, envoy, proxy, rider, usual, vakil **06** bagman, chosen, deputy, exarch, normal, sample, vakeel **07** drummer, elected, stand-in, typical **08** delegate, devolved, elective, salesman, specimen, symbolic **09** appointed, delegated, exemplary, nominated, spokesman, traveller **10** ambassador, archetypal, authorized, councillor, delegation, deputation, emblematic, exhibitive, indicative, mouthpiece, saleswoman **11** congressman, salesperson, spokeswoman **12** ambassadress, commissioned, commissioner, illustrative, representant, spokesperson **13** decentralized, heir-portioner **14** characteristic **15** knight of the road

**repress**
◇ *containment indicator*
**04** cork, curb **05** check, crush, quash, quell, sit on, sneap **06** cork up, master, muffle, repeal, stifle, subdue **07** control, inhibit, oppress, put down, reprime, silence, sit upon, smother, swallow **08** bottle up, dominate, domineer, hold back, keep back, keep down, overcome, restrain, suppress, vanquish **09** overpower, subjugate **11** bite your lip

**repressed**
**06** hung-up, pent-up **07** uptight **09** inhibited, withdrawn **10** frustrated **11** introverted **14** self-restrained

**repression**
**07** control, gagging, tyranny **08** coercion, crushing, muffling, quashing, quelling, stifling **09** despotism, restraint **10** censorship, constraint, domination, inhibition, oppression, smothering **11** holding-back, subjugation, suffocation, suppression **12** dictatorship

**repressive**
**05** cruel, harsh, tough **06** severe, strict **08** absolute, coercive, despotic **10** autocratic, dominating, oppressive, tyrannical **11** dictatorial **12** totalitarian **13** authoritarian

**reprieve**
**05** let-up, spare **06** acquit, let off, pardon, redeem, relief, rescue **07** amnesty, forgive, relieve, reprive, reprove, respite **08** abeyance, repreeve, show pity **09** abatement, deferment, remission, show mercy **10** suspension **12** postponement **13** let off the hook **15** stay of execution

**reprimand**
**04** jobe, lace **05** blame, check, chide, scold, slate, targe **06** berate, bounce, carpet, earful, rebuke, rocket, see off **07** bawl out, catch it, censure, chew out, go off at, lambast, lecture, reproof, reprove, rouse on, tell off, tick off, wigging **08** admonish, lace into, lambaste, reproach **09** carpeting, castigate, criticize, dress down, pull apart, schooling, take apart, talking-to **10** admonition, telling-off, ticking-off, upbraiding **11** castigation **12** dressing-down **13** call to account, tongue-lashing **14** bring to account, slap on the wrist **15** smack on the wrist

**reprisal**
**05** prize **06** ultion **07** redress, reprise, reprize, revenge **08** requital **09** recaption, recapture, tit for tat, vengeance **11** eye for an eye, retaliation, retribution **12** compensation **13** counter-attack, recrimination

**reprise**
**03** act **04** play, sing **05** prize, put on, renew **06** relate, repeat **07** copying, echoing, narrate, perform, quoting, reissue **08** iterance, reprisal **09** iteration, recapture, rehearsal **10** repetition **11** reiteration, restatement **12** compensation **14** recapitulation

**reproach**
**04** blot, slur, twit, wite, wyte **05** blame, braid, chide, scold, scorn, shame, shend, slate, smear, stain, taunt, touch, wight **06** bounce, carpet, defame, earful, rebuke, rocket, see off, stigma, upcast **07** bawl out, blemish, catch it, censure, chew out, condemn, nayword, obloquy, reproof, reprove,

tell off, tick off, upbraid, wigging
**08** admonish, contempt, disgrace, dishonor, ignominy, repriefe, scolding
**09** carpeting, criticism, criticize, discredit, dishonour, disparage, dispraise, disrepute, dress down, mispraise, pull apart, reprehend, reprimand, take apart, talking-to
**10** admonition, cri de coeur, disrespect, imputation, opprobrium, reflection, telling-off, ticking-off
**11** degradation, disapproval
**12** condemnation, dressing-down
**13** find fault with **14** slap on the wrist
**15** smack on the wrist

**• term of reproach**
**03** gib **04** runt **05** besom, bisom, madam **06** ronyon, truant **07** Cataian, Catayan, runnion **09** rigwiddie, rigwoodie

**reproachful**
**08** critical, scolding, scornful
**09** reproving **10** censorious, upbraiding **11** castigating, disgraceful, disparaging, opprobrious
**12** disappointed, disapproving, fault-finding

**reprobate**
**03** bad, rep **04** base, rake, roué, vile
**05** knave, rogue, scamp **06** damned, disown, rascal, reject, sinful, sinner, wicked, wretch **07** censure, corrupt, dastard, immoral, villain **08** criminal, depraved, evildoer, hardened, vagabond **09** abandoned, dissolute, miscreant, scallywag, scoundrel, shameless, wrongdoer **10** degenerate, ne'er-do-well, profligate
**11** reprobative, reprobatory
**12** condemnatory, incorrigible, troublemaker, unprincipled
**13** mischief-maker

**reprocess**
◇ *anagram indicator*
**07** recycle

**reproduce**
◇ *anagram indicator*
**03** ape **04** copy, echo, redo **05** breed, cline, clone, match, mimic, print, refer, spawn, Xerox® **06** follow, mirror, pirate, remake, render, repeat
**07** emulate, enlarge, express, gemmate, imitate, reflect **08** autotype, generate, multiply, recreate, refigure, simulate **09** bear young, duplicate, facsimile, give birth, photocopy, Photostat®, phototype, procreate, propagate, replicate **10** hectograph, regenerate, transcribe **11** proliferate, reconstruct

**reproduction**
**04** copy, hi-fi, mono **05** clone, print, repro, Xerox® **06** ectype, piracy
**07** edition, picture, replica
**08** breeding, monogeny, monogony
**09** duplicate, facsimile, imitation, photocopy, Photostat®
**10** amphimixis, generation, viviparism
**11** gamogenesis, monogenesis, procreation, propagation, replication
**12** regeneration **14** multiplication, representation

**reproductive**
**03** sex **06** sexual **07** genital **08** prolific
**10** generative **11** procreative, progenitive, propagative

**reproof**
**04** rate **05** shame, sloan **06** earful, lesson, rebuke, rocket, sermon
**07** censure, jarring, lecture, upbraid, wigging **08** berating, disgrace, disproof, repriefe, reproach, reproval, scolding **09** carpeting, criticism, reprimand, reproving, schooling, talking-to **10** admonition, correption, telling-off, ticking-off, upbraiding
**11** castigation **12** condemnation, dressing-down, reprehension
**14** curtain lecture, disapprobation, slap on the wrist **15** smack on the wrist

**• expression of reproof**
**03** now, tut **04** come, toot, tuts
**05** toots **06** tut-tut **07** come now, now then **08** come come

**reprove**
**03** rap **04** rate **05** chide, scold, slate
**06** berate, bounce, carpet, rebuke, refute, see off, take up **07** bawl out, catch it, censure, chew out, condemn, lecture, rouse on, tell off, tick off, upbraid **08** admonish, call down, disprove, reprieve, reproach
**09** castigate, criticize, dress down, pull apart, reprehend, reprimand, take apart **10** take to task

**reptile**

*Reptiles include:*

**04** croc, tegu
**05** gator
**06** caiman, cayman, garial, gavial, mugger, turtle
**07** gharial, hicatee, snapper, tuatara
**08** aligarta, galapago, hiccatee, matamata, stinkpot, teguexin, terrapin, tortoise
**09** alligarta, alligator, crocodile, hawksbill, mud turtle, sea turtle
**10** loggerhead, musk turtle
**11** green turtle, leatherback
**13** giant tortoise, water tortoise
**14** leathery turtle, snapping turtle
**15** hawksbill turtle

*See also* **animal**; **dinosaur**; **lizard**; **snake**

**republic**

*Republics include:*

**03** USA
**04** Chad, Cuba, Fiji, Iran, Iraq, Laos, Mali, Peru, Togo
**05** Benin, Burma, Chile, China, Congo, Egypt, Gabon, Ghana, Haiti, India, Italy, Kenya, Malta, Nauru, Niger, Palau, Sudan, Syria, Yemen
**06** Angola, Brazil, Cyprus, France, Greece, Guinea, Guyana, Israel, Latvia, Malawi, Mexico, Panama, Poland, Russia, Rwanda, Taiwan, Turkey, Uganda, Zambia
**07** Albania, Algeria, Armenia, Austria, Belarus, Bolivia, Burundi, Croatia, Ecuador, Estonia, Finland, Georgia, Germany, Hungary, Iceland, Ireland, Lebanon, Liberia, Moldova, Myanmar, Namibia, Nigeria, Romania, Senegal, Somalia, Tunisia, Ukraine, Uruguay, Vanuatu, Vietnam
**08** Botswana, Bulgaria, Cameroon, Colombia, Djibouti, Ethiopia, Honduras, Kiribati, Maldives, Mongolia, Pakistan, Paraguay, Portugal, Slovakia, Slovenia, Sri Lanka, Suriname, Tanzania, Zimbabwe
**09** Argentina, Cape Verde, Costa Rica, East Timor, Guatemala, Indonesia, Lithuania, Macedonia, Mauritius, Nicaragua, San Marino, Singapore, The Gambia, Venezuela
**10** Azerbaijan, Bangladesh, El Salvador, Kazakhstan, Kyrgyzstan, Madagascar, Mauritania, Mozambique, North Korea, Seychelles, South Korea, Tajikistan, Uzbekistan
**11** Burkina Faso, Côte d'Ivoire, Philippines, Sierra Leone, South Africa, Switzerland
**12** Guinea-Bissau, Turkmenistan
**13** Czech Republic, Western Sahara
**15** Marshall Islands

*See also* **country**

**repudiate**
**04** deny **05** repel **06** abjure, desert, disown, nochel, reject, revoke
**07** abandon, cast off, disavow, discard, divorce, forsake, notchel, rescind, retract, reverse **08** denounce, disclaim, renounce **09** disaffirm
**10** disprofess **14** turn your back on

**repudiation**
**06** denial **09** disavowal, disowning, rejection **10** abjuration, disclaimer, retraction **11** recantation
**12** renunciation **13** disaffirmance
**14** disaffirmation

**repugnance**
**05** odium **06** hatred, horror, nausea, revolt **07** allergy, disgust, dislike
**08** aversion, distaste, loathing
**09** abhorring, antipathy, repulsion, revulsion **10** abhorrence, reluctance, repugnancy **11** reluctation
**13** inconsistency

*See also* **disgust**; **distaste**

**repugnant**
**04** foul, vile **05** alien **06** averse, horrid, odious **07** adverse, hateful, hostile, noisome, opposed **08** inimical
**09** abhorrent, loathsome, obnoxious, offensive, repellent, resisting, revolting, sickening, unwilling
**10** abominable, disgusting, nauseating
**11** distasteful **12** antagonistic, antipathetic, incompatible, inconsistent, unacceptable
**13** contradictory, objectionable

**repulse**
**04** foil, snub **05** check, refel, repel,

spurn **06** defeat, rebuff, refuse, reject **07** beat off, disdain, failure, put back, refusal, reverse **08** spurning **09** disregard, drive back, rejection **11** repudiation **14** disappointment

**repulsion**
**06** action, effect, hatred **07** disgust **08** aversion, distaste, loathing **09** disrelish, revulsion **10** abhorrence, repellence, repellency, repugnance **11** detestation, raison d'être

**repulsive**
**04** cold, foul, icky, loth, ugly, vile **05** gross, loath, nasty **06** horrid, odious **07** hateful, heinous, hideous, squalid **08** reserved, shocking **09** abhorrent, loathsome, obnoxious, offensive, repellent, repelling, repugnant, revolting, sickening **10** abominable, despicable, disgusting, forbidding, nauseating, off-putting, unpleasant **11** distasteful **12** contemptible, disagreeable, evil-favoured, unattractive **13** objectionable, reprehensible

**repulsively**
**10** abominably, despicably, shockingly **11** obnoxiously **12** disagreeably, disgustingly, nauseatingly, unpleasantly **13** objectionably

**reputable**
**04** good, gude, guid **06** honest, worthy **07** upright **08** esteemed, reliable, virtuous **09** admirable, estimable, excellent, respected **10** creditable, dependable, honourable **11** respectable, trustworthy **12** of good repute, of high repute **13** well-thought-of **14** irreproachable

**reputation**
**03** los, rep **04** fame, loos, name, note, pass, rank **05** image, izzat, voice **06** credit, esteem, honour, infamy, renown, repute, status **07** opinion, respect, stature **08** estimate, good name, position, prestige, standing **09** celebrity, character, notoriety **10** estimation **11** distinction **12** good standing **14** respectability

**repute**
**04** fame, name, odor **05** odour, rumor, savor, stock **06** esteem, regard, renown, report, rumour, savour **07** stature **08** good name, standing **09** celebrity **10** estimation, reputation **11** distinction

• **of doubtful repute**
**03** shy

**reputed**
**03** dit **04** held, said **06** judged **07** alleged, assumed, seeming, thought **08** apparent, believed, presumed, putative, reckoned, regarded, rumoured, supposed **09** estimated **10** considered, ostensible, reputative

**reputedly**
**09** allegedly, seemingly **10** apparently, ostensibly, supposedly **12** reputatively **13** by all accounts

**request**
**03** ask, beg, hit **04** boon, call, plea, seek, suit, wish **05** apply, order **06** adjure, appeal, ask for, behest, demand, desire, invite, prayer **07** beseech, bespeak, call for, call out, entreat, require, send for, solicit **08** apply for, entreaty, petition, pleading, put in for **09** impetrate **10** invitation, supplicate, write in for **11** application, imploration, petitioning, requisition, write off for **12** solicitation, supplication

**require**
**03** ask **04** draw, lack, make, miss, need, take, want, will, wish **05** crave, exact, force, order **06** call on, compel, demand, desire, direct, enjoin, entail, govern, oblige **07** call for, command, involve, requere, request, solicit **08** insist on, instruct **09** be short of, constrain, stipulate **11** necessitate **13** be deficient in

**required**
**03** set **05** vital **06** needed **07** advised **08** demanded **09** essential, mandatory, necessary, requisite **10** compulsory, obligatory, prescribed, stipulated **11** recommended, unavoidable

**requirement**
**04** fike, lack, must, need, term, want **06** demand **07** proviso **08** occasion **09** condition, essential, necessity, provision, requisite **10** obligation, sine qua non **11** desideratum, stipulation **12** precondition, prerequisite **13** qualification, specification

**requisite**
**03** due, set **04** must, need **05** vital **06** needed **07** needful **08** required **09** condition, essential, implement, mandatory, necessary, necessity **10** compulsory, obligatory, prescribed, sine qua non **11** desideratum, requirement, stipulation **12** desiderative, precondition, prerequisite **13** indispensable, qualification, specification

**requisition**
**03** use **04** call, take **05** order, press, seize **06** demand, indent, occupy **07** request, seizure, summons **08** put in for, take over, takeover **10** commandeer, confiscate, occupation **11** application, appropriate **12** confiscation **13** appropriation, commandeering

**requital**
**06** amends, pay-off, return **07** payment, quittal, redress **09** indemnity, quittance, repayment **10** recompence, recompense, reparation **11** restitution, retribution **12** compensation, satisfaction **15** indemnification

**requite**
**03** pay **04** apay, quit **05** repay **06** avenge, pay off, return, reward **07** redress, respond, satisfy **08** even up on, requight **09** reimburse, retaliate **10** compensate, recompense, remunerate **11** reciprocate **14** counterbalance

**rescind**
**04** void **05** annul, quash **06** cancel, negate, recall, repeal, revoke **07** cut away, nullify, retract, reverse **08** abrogate, overturn, set aside **10** invalidate **11** countermand

**rescission**
**06** recall, repeal **08** negation, reversal, voidance **09** annulment **10** abrogation, retraction, revocation **11** rescindment **12** cancellation, invalidation **13** nullification

**rescue**
**04** free, save **05** pluck **06** ransom, redeem, relief, reskew, reskue, saving **07** deliver, freeing, recover, release, relieve, reprive, repryve, salvage, set free **08** bring off, liberate, recovery, repreeve, reprieve, retrieve **09** extricate, salvation **10** emancipate, liberation, redemption **11** deliverance **12** emancipation

**research**
**03** res **04** test **05** probe, study, tests **06** assess, review, search **07** analyse, examine, explore, inquiry, inspect, postdoc, testing **08** analysis, look into, scrutiny **10** assessment, experiment, groundwork, inspection, scrutinize **11** examination, exploration, fact-finding, investigate **13** investigation **15** experimentation

**researcher**
**06** boffin **07** analyst, student **08** inquirer **09** inspector **11** field worker **12** investigator

**resemblance**
**04** like **05** image, match **06** parity **07** analogy **08** affinity, likeness, nearness, parallel, sameness **09** agreement, assonance, closeness, congruity, facsimile, homophyly **10** appearance, comparison, conformity, likelihood, similarity, similitude, uniformity **11** parallelism **13** comparability **14** correspondence

**resemble**
**04** echo **05** favor, mimic **06** be like, depict, favour, mirror **07** compare **08** approach, look like, parallel **09** duplicate, take after **11** be similar to

**resent**
**04** envy **06** grudge **07** dislike, stomach **08** begrudge, object to **09** be angry at, grumble at, take amiss **12** have a derry on **13** take offence at, take umbrage at **15** feel aggrieved at, feel bitter about, take exception to

**resentful**
**04** hurt **05** angry, irked **06** bitter, ireful, miffed, peeved, piqued, put out **07** envious, jealous, wounded **08** grudging, incensed, offended, spiteful **09** aggrieved, indignant,

irritated, malicious **10** embittered, stomachful, stomachous, vindictive **13** in high dudgeon

**resentment**
**03** ire **04** envy, hurt, miff **05** anger, derry, pique, snuff, spite **06** grudge, malice **07** dudgeon, ill-will, offence, umbrage **08** bad blood, ill blood, jealousy, vexation **09** animosity, annoyance, hostility **10** bad feeling, bitterness, ill-feeling, irritation **11** displeasure, high dudgeon, indignation **12** hard feelings **14** vindictiveness

**reservation**
**03** res, rez **04** park **05** demur, doubt, order, qualm, salvo, tract **06** doubts, qualms, safety, saving, upkeep **07** booking, defence, enclave, keeping, proviso, reserve, scruple, storage, support **08** guarding, homeland, preserve, scruples, security **09** condition, hesitancy, misgiving, retention, sanctuary, upholding **10** engagement, hesitation, limitation, misgivings, protection, scepticism **11** appointment, arrangement, maintenance, safekeeping, stipulation **12** conservation, continuation, perpetuation, preservation, safeguarding **13** arrière-pensée, qualification **14** advance booking, prearrangement, second thoughts

• **without reservation**
**07** utterly **08** entirely, outright **09** gloves-off **10** completely **11** boots and all **12** unreservedly **14** unhesitatingly, wholeheartedly

**reserve**
**02** TA **03** AVR, ice, MNR, res, RNR **04** area, bank, book, fund, help, hold, keep, park, pool, RNVR, save **05** cache, defer, delay, extra, hoard, order, proxy, spare, stock, store, tract **06** backup, engage, fill-in, put off, retain, secure, shelve, supply **07** adjourn, backlog, earmark, enclave, modesty, savings, shyness, stand-in, support, suspend **08** coldness, coolness, distance, hold back, hold over, keep back, Landwehr, lay aside, postpone, preserve, set apart, set aside, Wavy Navy **09** aloofness, auxiliary, reservoir, restraint, reticence, ring-fence, sanctuary, secondary, stockpile, successor, surrogate **10** accumulate, additional, arrange for, arrière-ban, detachment, limitation, prearrange, remoteness, substitute, understudy **11** alternative, auxiliaries, replacement, reservation, restriction **12** accumulation, put on one side, put to one side **13** secretiveness, self-restraint **14** reinforcements **15** supplementaries

• **in reserve**
**02** by **05** spare **06** in hand, stored, to hand, unused **07** in petto, in store **08** set aside **09** available, in pectore

**reserved**
**03** shy **04** cold, cool, held, kept **05** aloof, close, meant, saved, taken **06** booked, modest, remote, silent **07** distant, engaged, on appro, ordered, private, retired, strange **08** arranged, backward, cautious, destined, intended, retained, reticent, retiring, set aside, taciturn **09** diffident, earmarked, repulsive, secretive, spoken for, withdrawn **10** designated, restrained, unsociable **11** introverted, prearranged, standoffish **12** unresponsive **13** self-contained, unforthcoming **14** unapproachable **15** uncommunicative

**reservoir**
**03** vat **04** bank, fund, lake, loch, pond, pool, sump, tank, well **05** basin, stock, store **06** gilgai, header, holder, source, supply **07** cistern, gas tank, ghilgai, hot well, urinary **08** fountain, reserves **09** container, inkholder, stockpile, wind chest **10** header tank, receptacle, repository, steam chest **11** reservatory **12** accumulation

**resettle**
◇ *anagram indicator*
**07** migrate **08** emigrate **09** immigrate **10** transplant

**reshape**
◇ *anagram indicator*
**05** alter **06** adjust, modify, mutate **07** convert **12** metamorphose

**reshuffle**
◇ *anagram indicator*
**05** shift **06** change, revise **07** realign, regroup, shake up, shake-up, shuffle **08** revision, upheaval **09** rearrange **10** regrouping, reorganize **11** interchange, realignment, restructure **12** redistribute **13** rearrangement, restructuring **14** redistribution, reorganization

**reside**
**03** lie, sit **04** hive, keep, live, rest, stay **05** abide, board, dwell, exist, house, lodge **06** inhere, occupy, remain, settle **07** hang out, inhabit, sojourn **09** be present **10** be inherent **11** be contained

**residence**
**03** pad, res **04** digs, flat, hall, home, nest, seat, stay **05** abode, house, lodge, manor, place, villa **06** des res, palace **07** cottage, domicil, lodging, mansion, sojourn **08** domicile, dwelling, lodgings, mansonry, quarters **09** apartment, residency **10** habitation, mansionary, praetorium, presidency, second home **11** country seat, inhabitance, inhabitancy, squarsonage, summerhouse **12** country house **13** dwelling-place **14** winter quarters

**resident**
**05** guest, local **06** client, inmate, ledger, leiger, lieger, live-in, lodger, tenant **07** citizen, dweller, en poste, gremial, leidger, patient, resiant, resider, settled **08** dwelling, inherent, living-in, occupant, occupier **09** commorant, permanent, sojourner, transient **10** inhabitant, inhabiting, stationary **11** householder **13** neighbourhood

**residential**
**07** exurban **08** commuter, suburban **09** dormitory

**residual**
**03** net **06** excess, unused **07** surplus **08** left-over **09** reliquary, remaining **10** unconsumed

**residue**
**04** coke, gunk, lees, rest **05** dregs, extra, mazut, pitch, scrap, snuff **06** excess, mazout, pomace, slurry **07** asphalt, astatki, balance, clinker, remains, remnant, surplus, tankage, vinasse **08** charcoal, mine dump, overflow, residuum **09** asphaltum, carry-over, leftovers, remainder **10** difference, racemation, terra rossa **11** apiezon oils **12** caput mortuum

**resign**
**04** quit **05** demit, forgo, leave, waive, yield **06** forego, give up, retire, submit, vacate **07** abandon, entrust, forsake, throw up **08** abdicate, forelend, renounce, step down **09** stand down, surrender **10** relinquish

• **resign yourself**
**03** bow **05** yield **06** accept, comply, submit **09** acquiesce **11** come to terms

**resignation**
**06** notice **07** waiving **08** giving-up, patience, stoicism, yielding **09** defeatism, demission, departure, passivity, surrender **10** abdication, acceptance, compliance, retirement, submission **12** acquiescence, renunciation, standing-down, stepping-down **13** non-resistance **14** reconciliation, relinquishment

• **expression of resignation**
**04** well **05** ho-hum **07** heigh-ho

**resigned**
**07** passive, patient, stoical **08** yielding **09** defeatist **10** reconciled, submissive **11** acquiescent, unresisting **12** unprotesting **13** long-suffering, philosophical, uncomplaining

**resignedly**
**09** patiently, stoically **12** submissively **15** philosophically, uncomplainingly

**resilience**
**04** give, kick **06** bounce, recoil, spring **07** granite **08** buoyance, buoyancy, strength **09** hardiness, toughness **10** bounciness, elasticity, plasticity, pliability, suppleness **11** flexibility, springiness **12** adaptability **14** unshockability

**resilient**
**05** hardy, tough **06** bouncy, strong, supple **07** buoyant, elastic, plastic, pliable, rubbery, springy **08** flexible **09** adaptable, recoiling, springing **10** rebounding **11** unshockable **13** irrepressible

**resin**
**03** lac **04** aloe, hing, kino **05** alkyd, aloes, amber, animé, copal, damar, elemi, epoxy, pitch, rosin, Saran®, vinyl **06** balsam, conima, dammar, dammer, guaiac, mastic, storax **07** acrylic, caranna, carauna, copaiba, copaiva, gamboge, hashish, jalapin, ladanum, mastich, Perspex®, shellac, xylenol **08** Araldite®, Bakelite®, cannabin, galbanum, guaiacum, hasheesh, kauri gum, olibanum, opopanax, propolis, retinite, sandarac, scammony, sweet gum **09** asafetida, courbaril, elaterite, sagapenum, sandarach, tacamahac, tacmahack **10** asafoetida, assafetida, euphorbium, turpentine **11** assafoetida, gum ammoniac, podophyllin **12** Canada balsam, frankincense, gum sandarach **13** Burgundy pitch, spirit varnish, thermoplastic

**resist**
**04** buck, curb, defy, face, fend, halt, stem, stop, wear **05** avoid, check, fight, repel **06** battle, combat, defend, hinder, impede, jack up, oppose, refuse, thwart **07** contend, counter, deforce, prevent, weather **08** confront, fight off, obstruct, restrain, stick out, struggle **09** stand up to, withstand **10** counteract, gainstrive **12** stand against **14** hold out against

**resistance**
**01** R **04** drag, kick, pull **05** fight, stand **06** battle, combat **07** refusal **08** defiance, fighting, struggle **09** avoidance, contumacy, hindrance, impedance, repulsion, restraint, thwarting **10** contention, impediment, opposition, prevention **11** contumacity, counter-time, obstruction **12** counter-stand, withstanding **13** confrontation, counteraction, intransigence **14** antiperistasis

• **passive resistance**
**09** passivism **10** satyagraha **11** vis inertiae

**resistant**
**04** anti- **05** proof, stiff, tough **06** immune, strong **07** defiant, opposed, viscous **08** renitent **09** unwilling, windproof **10** impervious, shellproof, shockproof, unaffected, unyielding, waterproof **12** antagonistic, intransigent, invulnerable **13** unsusceptible

**resolute**
**03** set **04** bold, firm **05** fixed, hardy, stout, tough **06** dogged, intent, steady, strong, sturdy **07** adamant, decided, diehard, earnest, granite, serious, staunch **08** constant, obdurate, resolved, stalwart, stubborn **09** dauntless, dedicated, obstinate, steadfast, tenacious, unbending, undaunted **10** determined, flat-footed, inflexible, relentless, unswerving, unwavering, unyielding **11** persevering, unflinching **12** single-minded, strong-willed

**resolutely**
**06** firmly **08** steadily, strongly **09** adamantly, earnestly, seriously, staunchly **10** inflexibly, resolvedly, stubbornly **11** dauntlessly, obstinately, steadfastly **12** relentlessly, unswervingly, unwaveringly **13** unflinchingly **14** single-mindedly

**resolution**
◇ *anagram indicator*
**03** res **04** rede, zeal **05** point **06** answer, decree, motion, result **07** courage, finding, granite, melting, resolve, solving, thought, verdict **08** analysis, boldness, decision, devotion, firmness, solution, tenacity **09** constancy, judgement, willpower **10** abreaction, commitment, dedication, doggedness, intentness, sorting out, working out **11** declaration, earnestness, persistence, proposition, seriousness, unravelling **12** perseverance **13** determination, disentangling, inflexibility, steadfastness

**resolve**
◇ *anagram indicator*
**03** fix, vow **04** melt, zeal **05** lapse, patch, relax, solve, untie **06** answer, assure, bottle, decide, detail, divide, inform, pecker, reduce, settle **07** analyse, analyze, break up, convert, courage, itemize, sort out, sublate, talk out, unravel, work out **08** boldness, conclude, devotion, dissolve, firmness, separate, settle on, tenacity **09** anatomize, break down, constancy, decompose, determine, dissipate, factorize, transform, willpower **10** commitment, dedication, doggedness, intentness **11** disentangle, earnestness, persistence, seriousness **12** disintegrate, perseverance **13** determination, inflexibility, steadfastness, straighten out **14** make up your mind, sense of purpose

**resonance**
**05** depth **08** fullness, richness, sonority, strength, vibrancy **09** plangency **10** mesomerism, resounding **12** canorousness **13** reverberation

**resonant**
**04** deep, full, rich **06** fruity, plummy, strong **07** booming, echoing, ringing, vibrant **08** canorous, plangent, sonorous **10** pear-shaped, resounding **11** reverberant **13** reverberating

**resonate**
**04** boom, echo, ring **05** sound **06** re-echo **07** resound, thunder **11** reverberate

**resort**
◇ *anagram indicator*
**02** go **03** spa, use **04** dive, draw, seek, spot, step **05** apply, frame, haunt, trade, visit **06** appeal, center, centre, chance, course, lounge, museum, option, refuge, repair, revert **07** doggery, measure **08** frequent, recourse **09** concourse, dude ranch, frequency, patronize, thronging **10** rendezvous, sanatorium, sanitarium **11** alternative, night-cellar, possibility **12** health resort **13** holiday centre **14** course of action, stamping-ground

*Resorts include:*

**04** Nice, Rhyl
**05** Aspen, Davos
**06** Cairns, Cannes, St Ives, St-Malo, Whitby
**07** Funchal, Margate, Newquay, Torquay, Ventnor, Zermatt
**08** Alicante, Aviemore, Benidorm, Biarritz, Chamonix, Honolulu, Klosters, Marbella, Montreux, Penzance, Skegness, St Helier, St Moritz, St-Tropez, Weymouth
**09** Albufeira, Blackpool, Galveston, Gold Coast, Kitzbühel, Lanzarote, Morecambe, Nantucket
**10** Baden Baden, Bondi Beach, Costa Brava, Eastbourne, Lake Placid, Long Island, Miami Beach, Monte Carlo, Windermere
**11** Bognor Regis, Bournemouth, Bridlington, Cleethorpes, Coney Island, Costa Blanca, Costa del Sol, Costa Dorada, Gran Canaria, Grand Bahama, Palm Springs, Scarborough
**12** San Sebastian, Santa Barbara, Waikiki Beach
**13** Great Yarmouth, Southend-on-Sea
**15** Martha's Vineyard, Weston-super-Mare

*See also* **spa**

• **in the last resort**
**06** at last **07** finally **08** after all, in the end **10** eventually, ultimately **13** fundamentally, sooner or later

• **resort to**
**03** use **04** seek **06** employ, invoke, turn to **07** utilize **08** exercise, frequent **09** make use of **10** fall back on **14** have recourse to **15** avail yourself of

**resound**
**04** boom, echo, ring **05** sound **06** re-echo **07** thunder, vibrate **08** resonate **11** reverberate

**resounding**
**04** full, loud, rich **05** great, vocal **07** booming, echoing, notable, reboant, ringing, roaring, vibrant **08** decisive, emphatic, plangent, resonant, rumorous, sonorous, striking, thorough **09** memorable, resonance **10** conclusive, impressive, remarkable, resonating, thunderous **11** outstanding **13** reverberating

**resource**
**03** wit **04** fund, pool **05** funds, means, money, power, store **06** assets, course, device, fodder, resort, riches, source, supply, talent, wealth **07** ability, capital, reserve **08** artifice, holdings, property, reserves, supplies **09** expedient, ingenuity, materials, stockpile **10** capability, chevisance, enterprise, initiative **11** contrivance, imagination,

wherewithal **12** accumulation **13** inventiveness **15** resourcefulness

**resourceful**
**04** able **05** fendy, sharp, witty **06** adroit, bright, clever **07** capable **08** creative, original, talented **09** ingenious, inventive, versatile **10** innovative **11** imaginative, quick-witted **12** enterprising

**resourceless**
**06** feeble **07** useless **08** feckless, helpless, hopeless **09** shiftless **10** inadequate

**respect**
**03** way **04** duty, face, heed, obey **05** facet, honor, point, sense, value **06** admire, aspect, detail, esteem, follow, fulfil, homage, honour, matter, notice, praise, regard, revere **07** bearing, devoirs, feature, observe, regards, worship **08** adhere to, consider, courtesy, relation, venerate **09** approve of, attention, deference, greetings, obeisance, reference, reverence **10** admiration, appreciate, best wishes, cognizance, comply with, connection, good wishes, high regard, particular, politeness, veneration **11** approbation, compliments, high opinion, recognition, salutations **12** appreciation **13** attentiveness, consideration, show regard for, think highly of **14** characteristic, pay attention to, thoughtfulness **15** set great store by, take into account

**• title of respect, word of respect**
**01** U **03** Esq, oom, sir **04** Esqr, tuan **05** hodja, honor, khoja, molla **06** father, gaffer, honour, khodja, kumari, mollah, moolah, mullah **07** Bahadur, effendi, esquire **08** holiness, talapoin **10** burra sahib, worshipful

**• with respect to**
**02** of, on, re **03** for, wrt **04** as to **05** about **07** apropos **09** as regards **10** concerning, in regard to **12** in relation to, with regard to **14** on the subject of **15** with reference to

**respectability**
**07** decency, honesty **09** gentility, integrity **10** worthiness **11** uprightness **15** trustworthiness

**respectable**
**02** OK **04** fair, good, neat, nice, tidy **05** clean **06** decent, honest, not bad, seemly, worthy **07** savoury, upright **08** adequate, all right, clean-cut, decorous, mediocre, menseful, passable, superior **09** dignified, reputable, respected, sponsible, tolerable **10** above-board, acceptable, fairly good, honourable, reasonable, salubrious **11** appreciable, clean-living, presentable, trustworthy **12** considerable

**respected**
**06** valued **07** admired **08** esteemed **12** highly valued **14** highly esteemed, highly regarded **15** thought highly of

**respectful**
**05** civil **06** humble, polite **07** courtly, dutiful **08** reverent **09** courteous, regardful **11** deferential, reverential, subservient **12** well-mannered

**respectfully**
**07** civilly **08** mannerly, politely **10** reverently **11** courteously **13** deferentially, reverentially

**respecting**
**05** about **07** vis-à-vis **09** regarding **10** concerning **11** considering, in respect of **12** with regard to **13** with respect to

**respective**
**03** own **07** heedful, several, special, various **08** personal, relative, relevant, separate, specific **09** regardful **10** individual, particular **11** considerate **13** corresponding **14** discriminating

**respectively**
**06** in turn **08** one by one **09** severally, specially **12** individually, particularly, specifically **15** correspondingly, in the order given

**respite**
**03** gap **04** halt, lull, rest, stay **05** break, delay, frist, let-up, pause, truce **06** give up, hiatus, put off, recess, relief **07** leisure, prolong **08** breather, interval, reprieve **09** abatement, breathing, cessation, deferment, remission **10** moratorium, relaxation, suspension **11** adjournment **12** intermission, interruption, postponement **14** breathing space

**resplendent**
**06** bright **07** beaming, fulgent, radiant, shining **08** dazzling, gleaming, glorious, luminous, lustrous, splendid **09** brilliant, effulgent, irradiant, refulgent **10** glittering **11** magnificent **13** splendiferous

**respond**
**04** rise **05** react, reply **06** answer, behave, rejoin, retort, return **07** counter **10** answer back **11** acknowledge, reciprocate

**response**
**03** tic **04** echo, rise **05** reply, touch **06** answer, retort, return **07** riposte **08** comeback, feedback, reaction **09** rejoinder **10** phototaxis **11** respondence **15** acknowledgement

**responsibility**
**04** baby, care, duty, onus, role, task **05** blame, fault, guilt, power, trust **06** affair, burden, charge, pidgin, racket **07** concern, honesty **08** business, maturity **09** adulthood, authority, soundness, stability **10** obligation **11** culpability, reliability **13** answerability, dependability **14** accountability **15** trustworthiness

**responsible**
**04** sane **05** adult, sober, sound **06** guilty, honest, liable, mature, stable, steady **07** at fault, leading, to blame **08** culpable, managing, powerful, rational, reliable, sensible, solidary **09** executive, high-level, important **10** answerable, dependable, in charge of, reasonable **11** accountable, blameworthy, controlling, in control of, level-headed, trustworthy **13** authoritative, conscientious, correspondent **14** decision-making

**responsibly**
**08** honestly, reliably, sensibly, steadily **10** dependably, rationally, reasonably **15** conscientiously

**responsive**
**04** open **05** alert, alive, awake, aware, quick, sharp **06** with it **08** amenable, reactive, sentient, swinging **09** answering, excitable, on the ball, receptive, sensitive, teachable **10** perceptive, respondent, stimulable, switched on **11** forthcoming, susceptible, sympathetic **12** responsorial **13** correspondent **14** impressionable

**responsiveness**
**05** mouth **08** openness **09** alertness, awareness **11** sensitivity **13** receptiveness **14** susceptibility

**rest**
**03** alt, lie, nap, sit, veg **04** base, calm, doze, ease, halt, hang, last, laze, lean, lull, noon, prop, rely, stay, stop **05** break, cease, hinge, light, pause, quiet, relax, sleep, smoko, spell, stand **06** alight, anchor, bottom, cradle, depend, endure, excess, feutre, fewter, holder, lounge, others, recess, remain, repose, settle, siesta, snooze, steady, veg out **07** balance, be based, breathe, holiday, leisure, lie down, lie-down, persist, recline, relâche, remains, remnant, residue, respite, sit down, slumber, support, surplus, time off **08** breather, continue, idleness, interval, quietude, remnants, residuum, vacation **09** anchorage, cessation, interlude, leftovers, remainder, sabbatism, stillness **10** inactivity, quiescence, quiescency, relaxation, standstill, take breath, take it easy **12** intermission, tranquillity **13** put your feet up **14** breathing space, motionlessness

**• and the rest**
**07** and so on **08** et cetera, et ceteri **10** and so forth

**• lay to rest**
**04** bury **05** inter

**• rest upon**
**04** ride

**restaurant**

*Restaurant types include:*

**04** café, caff
**05** diner, grill, NAAFI
**06** bistro, buffet, chippy, pull-in
**07** canteen, carvery, chipper, milk bar, taverna, tea room, tea shop
**08** creperie, mess room, pizzeria, snack-bar, sushi bar, taqueria, teahouse

09 brasserie, burger bar, cafeteria, coffee bar, dining-car, grill room, refectory, trattoria
10 dining room, health food, rotisserie, steakhouse
11 eating-house, greasy spoon, sandwich bar, self-service
12 drivethrough, Internet café, luncheonette, motorway café
13 transport café
15 fish-and-chip shop, ice-cream parlour

*Restaurants include:*

06 The Ivy
07 El Bulli
09 L'Escargot
10 Paul Bocuse, Savoy Grill, The Fat Duck
11 The Wolseley
12 Gordon Ramsay, Heinz Winkler, The River Café, Waterside Inn
15 Les Pres d'Eugenie, Patrick Guilbaud

*Fast food restaurant chains include:*

03 KFC
06 Wendy's
08 Pizza Hut, Taco Bell
09 Harvester, McDonald's
10 Burger King, Dairy Queen, Little Chef
12 Domino's Pizza, Dunkin' Donuts, Hard Rock Café, Pizza Express
13 Baskin-Robbins, Harry Ramsden's
14 Subway Sandwich

**restaurateur** *see* **chef**

**restful**
**04** calm **05** quiet, still **06** placid, serene **07** calming, languid, relaxed **08** peaceful, relaxing, soothing, tranquil **09** leisurely, unhurried **11** comfortable, undisturbed

**restitution**
**06** amends, refund, return **07** damages, redress, restore **08** requital **09** indemnity, repayment, restoring **10** recompense, reparation **11** restoration **12** compensation, remuneration, satisfaction **13** reimbursement **15** indemnification

**restive**
**04** edgy **05** inert, jumpy, resty, tense **06** on edge, uneasy, unruly, wilful **07** anxious, fidgety, fretful, nervous, restiff, uptight, wayward **08** agitated, restless **09** fidgeting, impatient, obstinate, turbulent, unsettled **10** hot-mouthed, refractory **12** recalcitrant, unmanageable **13** undisciplined **14** uncontrollable

**restiveness**
**10** turbulence, unruliness, wilfulness **11** waywardness **12** restlessness

**restless**
◇ *anagram indicator*
**04** edgy, toey **05** jumpy **06** broken, on edge, uneasy, unruly **07** agitato, anxious, fidgety, fretful, jittery, nervous, restive, unquiet, uptight, worried **08** agitated, disquiet, troubled **09** disturbed, fidgeting, impatient, sleepless, turbulent, unsettled **10** changeable, wanrestful **13** uncomfortable

**restlessly**
**09** anxiously, fretfully, nervously **11** impatiently, turbulently

**restlessness**
**04** fike **05** hurry **06** bustle, fidget, unrest **07** anxiety, jitters, turmoil **08** activity, disquiet, dynamism, edginess, insomnia, movement **09** agitation, dysphoria, gate fever, jumpiness **10** fitfulness, inquietude, transience, turbulence, uneasiness **11** disturbance, fretfulness, inconstancy, instability, jactitation, nervousness, restiveness, spring fever, worriedness **12** fermentation **13** heebie-jeebies, unsettledness

**restoration**
◇ *anagram indicator*
**06** repair, return **07** recruit, renewal, revival **08** recovery **09** recruital **10** kiss of life, rebuilding, renovation **11** refreshment, replacement, restitution **12** instauration, refurbishing, rejuvenation **13** reinstatement **14** reconstitution, reconstruction, rehabilitation, reinstallation, revitalization **15** re-establishment

**restore**
◇ *anagram indicator*
**03** fix **04** do up, heal, mend, stet **05** renew **06** reform, repair, return, revamp, revive **07** build up, rebuild, recover, recruit, redress, refresh, replace, retouch **08** give back, hand back, refigure, re-impose, renovate, retrieve, revivify, undelete **09** reanimate, redeliver, re-enforce, refurbish, reinstate, restitute **10** bring round, redecorate, rejuvenate, revitalize, strengthen **11** recondition, reconstruct, re-establish, reintegrate, reintroduce, restitution **12** reconstitute, redintegrate, rehabilitate, reinvigorate

**restrain**
◇ *containment indicator*
**03** bit, dam, tie **04** bank, bind, curb, heft, hold, jail, keep, rein, stay, stop **05** bound, chain, check, still, stint, trash **06** arrest, behold, bridle, coerce, detain, fetter, forbid, govern, hinder, hold in, hopple, impede, keep in, prison, rebuke, strain, subdue, tether **07** abstain, chasten, cohibit, confine, contain, control, impound, inhibit, injunct, manacle, prevent, refrain, repress, tighten **08** bottle up, chastise, compesce, conclude, hold back, hold down, imprison, keep back, keep down, obstruct, regulate, restrict, suppress, withhold **09** immanacle, temperate **10** hamshackle **11** hold captive, hold in check, keep in check

**restrained**
**03** dry **04** calm, cold, cool, mild, soft **05** aloof, muted, quiet, sober **06** chaste, formal, low-key, modest, severe, steady, subtle **07** captive, classic, ordered, refined, relaxed, subdued **08** discreet, measured, moderate, reserved, ritenuto, tasteful **09** forbidden, temperate **10** abstemious, controlled **11** unemotional, unobtrusive **14** self-controlled, self-restrained **15** uncommunicative

**restraint**
**03** dam, lid, tie **04** curb, grip, hold, rein, stay **05** block, bonds, check, cramp, limit, stint, trash **06** bridle, chains, duress, limits **07** barrier, bondage, control, fetters, measure, reserve **08** coercion, prudence **09** captivity, hindrance **10** constraint, inhibition, limitation, moderation, prevention **11** confinement, restriction, self-control, suppression **12** countercheck, imprisonment, restrictions, straitjacket **13** judiciousness **14** self-discipline

**restrict**
◇ *containment indicator*
**03** tie **04** bind, curb, fast, hold **05** bound, cramp, hem in, limit, pinch, scant, stint, thirl **06** go slow, hamper, hinder, impede, ration **07** astrict, combine, confine, contain, control, curtail, inhibit, peg down, tighten **08** handicap, localize, regulate, restrain, straiten, strangle **09** condition, constrain, constrict, demarcate **15** draw in your horns, pull in your horns

**restricted**
**05** close, small, tight **06** closed, narrow, secret, strict **07** bounded, cramped, limited, private **08** confined **09** exclusive, parochial, regulated **10** controlled **11** constricted

**restriction**
**03** ban **04** curb, rule **05** bound, check, limit, stint **06** burden, chains, ration **07** confine, control, embargo, proviso, reserve **08** handicap **09** condition, restraint, stricture **10** constraint, limitation, regulation **11** stipulation **13** qualification

**restructure**
**05** rejig **07** shake up **09** modernize, rearrange **10** reorganize, streamline **11** rationalize

**result**
**03** end, sum, win **04** flow, make, mark, stem, turn **05** arise, ensue, event, fruit, grade, issue, occur, score **06** answer, derive, effect, emerge, evolve, finish, follow, fruits, happen, pan out, pay-off, revert, sequel, spring, upshot **07** develop, emanate, outcome, proceed, product, rebound, spin-off, verdict **08** decision, reaction **09** by-product, come out of, corollary, culminate, eventuate, judgement,

terminate **10** conclusion, end-product, resolution, side effect **11** consequence, implication, termination
**12** repercussion

**resultant**
**07** ensuing **09** following, resulting
**10** consequent, subsequent

**resume**
**04** go on **06** reopen, take up **07** carry on, proceed, restart **08** continue, re-occupy, take back **09** reconvene, summarize **10** begin again, recommence, start again
**11** rejuvenesce, take up again

**résumé**
**02** CV **05** recap **06** digest, précis, review, sketch, wrap-up **07** epitome, outline, run-down, summary
**08** abstract, overview, pirlicue, purlicue, synopsis **09** breakdown
**14** recapitulation **15** curriculum vitae

**resumption**
**06** sequel **07** re-entry, renewal, reprise, restart **09** reopening
**10** proceeding, resurgence
**11** epanalepsis **12** continuation
**14** recommencement
**15** re-establishment

**resurgence**
**06** return **07** rebirth, revival
**10** renascence, resumption
**11** re-emergence, renaissance
**12** re-appearance, resurrection, risorgimento **13** recrudescence
**14** revivification

**resurrect**
**05** renew **06** revive **07** restore
**08** disinter **09** bring back, re-install
**10** reactivate, revitalize **11** re-establish, reintroduce, resuscitate **13** restore to life **15** bring back to life

**resurrection**
**06** return **07** rebirth, renewal, revival
**08** comeback **09** anastasis
**10** resurgence **11** renaissance, restoration **12** reappearance
**13** resuscitation **14** revitalization
**15** re-establishment

**resuscitate**
**04** save **05** renew **06** rescue, revive
**07** quicken, restore **08** revivify
**09** reanimate, resurrect **10** bring round, revitalize **12** reinvigorate

**resuscitated**
**07** revived **08** restored **09** redivivus
**11** resurrected **12** redintegrate
**13** redintegrated

**resuscitation**
**03** CPR **07** renewal, revival
**10** quickening **11** restoration
**12** resurrection, revitalizing
**14** reinvigoration, revivification

**retain**
◇ *containment indicator*
**03** pay, ret **04** grip, heft, hire, hold, keep, save **05** brief, grasp **06** employ, engage, keep on, keep up, recall
**07** contain, occlude, reserve
**08** conserve, continue, contract, hang on to, hold back, maintain, memorize, preserve, remember **09** recollect
**10** bear in mind, call to mind, commission, hold fast to, keep hold of, keep in mind

**retainer**
**03** fee **05** valet **06** lackey, menial, vassal **07** advance, deposit, footman, jackman, samurai, servant
**08** domestic, follower **09** attendant, dependant, supporter **10** galloglass
**11** gallowglass **12** retaining fee

**retaliate**
**06** avenge **07** hit back, pay home
**09** fight back, get back at **10** strike back
**11** get even with, reciprocate, take revenge **13** counter-attack **14** get your own back, pay someone back

**retaliation**
**06** retort, talion, ultion **07** revenge
**08** reprisal **09** retorsion, retortion, tit for tat, vengeance **10** quid pro quo
**11** eye for an eye, lex talionis, like for like, retribution **13** an eye for an eye, counter-attack, reciprocation

**retard**
**03** lag **04** curb, slow **05** brake, check, delay, tardy **06** belate, hinder, hold up, impede **07** slacken **08** handicap, obstruct, postpone, restrict, slow down **10** decelerate **11** put a brake on
**12** incapacitate **13** put the brake on

**retardation**
**03** lag **05** delay **07** slowing
**08** dullness, impeding, slowness
**09** hindering, hindrance **10** deficiency, hysteresis, incapacity, inhibition, retardment **11** obstruction
**12** incapability **14** mental handicap

**retch**
**03** gag **04** barf, boak, bock, boke, keck, puke, reck, spew **05** heave, reach, vomit **06** sick up, strain
**07** chuck up, fetch up, throw up
**08** disgorge **11** regurgitate **13** heave the gorge

**retching**
**04** heft, keck **06** nausea, puking
**07** gagging, spewing **08** reaching, vomiting **12** vomiturition

**retention**
**05** gripe **06** saving **07** custody, holding, keeping **09** hanging-on, holding on **11** continuance, keeping hold, maintenance **12** preservation

**rethink**
**06** modify, review, revise **08** forthink, reassess **09** re-examine, think over
**10** reconsider, think twice **13** think better of

**reticence**
**07** reserve, silence **08** muteness
**09** quietness, restraint **10** diffidence
**11** taciturnity **13** secretiveness

**reticent**
**03** shy **05** quiet **06** silent **08** boutonné, reserved, taciturn **09** boutonnée, diffident, inhibited, secretive
**10** restrained **11** close-lipped, tight-lipped **12** close-mouthed, close-tongued **13** unforthcoming
**15** uncommunicative

**reticule** *see* **bag**

**retinue**
**04** many, port, tail **05** aides, meiny, staff, suite, train **06** escort, meiney, meinie, menyie **07** cortège, sowarry
**08** equipage, servants, sowarree
**09** comitatus, entourage, followers, following, personnel **10** attendancy, attendants

**retire**
◇ *reversal indicator*
**02** go **03** den **04** move, step **05** leave
**06** bow out, decamp, depart, go away, recede, resign, return **07** go aside, retreat, scratch **08** draw back, step down, stop work, withdraw **09** leave work **10** give up work, retirement
**11** stop working **14** lick your wounds

**retired**
◇ *reversal indicator*
**02** ex- **03** ret, rtd **04** past, retd
**06** former **07** private **08** emeritus, secluded, solitary **09** recondite, withdrawn **11** sequestered

**retirement**
**04** exit **06** recess **07** bedtime, privacy, retreat **08** solitude **09** departure, obscurity, seclusion **10** loneliness, withdrawal **11** recluseness, resignation

**retiring**
◇ *reversal indicator*
**03** coy, shy **05** quiet, timid **06** humble, modest **07** bashful, recluse
**08** reserved, reticent **09** diffident, shrinking **10** retreating, unassuming
**11** unassertive, unobtrusive **12** self-effacing

**retort**
**04** quip **05** reply, sally **06** answer, clinch, rejoin, return, zinger
**07** counter, floorer, respond, riposte, squelch **08** backword, comeback, outfling, repartee, response, turn upon
**09** rejoinder, retaliate, squelcher, throw back, wisecrack **11** retaliation

**retract**
◇ *reversal indicator*
**04** deny **05** unsay **06** abjure, cancel, disown, draw in, move in, recant, renege, repeal, revoke **07** disavow, rescind, reverse, unspeak, unswear
**08** abrogate, disclaim, draw back, move back, pull back, renounce, take back, withdraw **09** repudiate

**retreat**
◇ *reversal indicator*
**03** den, mew **04** flee, lair, nest, neuk, nook, quit, rout **05** arbor, haven, leave, lodge, tower **06** alcove, arbour, ashram, asylum, bug out, decamp,

depart, flight, recede, recoil, recule, reduit, refuge, retire, shrink **07** back off, give way, harbour, hideout, privacy, recoyle, recuile, redoubt, retrait, retrate, shelter **08** crawfish, draw back, fall back, funkhole, growlery, hideaway, pull back, pull-back, retraict, retraite, solitude, turn back, turn tail, withdraw **09** back-pedal, climb down, climb-down, departure, hermitage, katabasis, sanctuary, seclusion **10** disadvance, evacuation, give ground, ivory tower, retirement, withdrawal **11** drawing-back, falling-back, pulling-back **12** beat a retreat, hibernaculum, interglacial, interstadial

**retrench**
**03** cut **04** pare, save, trim **05** limit, prune **06** lessen, reduce **07** curtail, cut back, husband **08** decrease, diminish, slim down **09** economize **15** tighten your belt

**retrenchment**
**03** cut **07** cutback, economy, pruning, run-down **09** reduction, shrinkage **11** contraction, cost-cutting, curtailment, cutting back

**retribution**
**03** utu **05** karma **06** reward, talion **07** justice, Nemesis, payment, redress, revenge **08** reprisal, requital **09** reckoning, repayment, vengeance, vengement **10** punishment, recompense **11** just deserts, retaliation **12** compensation, satisfaction

**retrieve**
**04** mend, read, save **05** fetch **06** access, recoup, redeem, regain, remedy, repair, rescue, return **07** get back, read out, reclaim, recover, restore, salvage **08** make good **09** bring back, recapture, repossess **11** put to rights

**retro**
**03** old **04** past **05** passé **06** bygone, former, period **07** antique, old-time **10** olde-worlde **12** old-fashioned **13** in period style

**retrograde**
◇ *reversal indicator*
**06** recede **07** inverse, regrede, reverse **08** backward, contrary, downward, negative **09** declining, reverting, worsening **10** retrogress **11** deteriorate **12** degenerating **13** deteriorating, retrogressive

**retrogress**
◇ *reversal indicator*
**03** ebb **04** drop, fall, sink, wane **06** recede, retire, return, revert, worsen **07** decline, regress, relapse, retreat **08** withdraw **09** backslide **10** degenerate, retrograde **11** deteriorate **12** degeneration

**retrogression**
**03** ebb **04** drop, fall **06** return **07** decline, regress, relapse **09** worsening **10** recidivism, regression **13** deterioration **14** retrogradation

**retrospect**
**06** regard, review, survey **08** look back **09** hindsight **10** reflection **11** remembrance **12** afterthought, recollection, thinking back **13** re-examination

**• in retrospect**
◇ *reversal indicator*
**11** looking back **12** on reflection, thinking back **13** retroactively, with hindsight **15** retrospectively

**retrospective**
◇ *reversal indicator*
**11** ex post facto, retro-active **14** retro-operative **15** backward-looking

**retrospectively**
**11** ex post facto, looking back **12** in retrospect, on reflection, thinking back **13** retroactively, with hindsight

**return**
◇ *reversal indicator*
**03** ret **04** data, form, gain, turn **05** equal, match, recur, remit, repay, reply, yield **06** answer, go back, income, profit, record, refund, rejoin, render, report, retort, retour, revert, reward **07** account, benefit, bring in, counter, declare, deliver, get back, pay back, put back, redound, regress, replace, requite, respond, restore, revenue, riposte, takings **08** announce, come back, comeback, come home, delivery, document, exchange, give back, hand back, hand down, interest, proceeds, reappear, recourse, requital, send back, take back, turn away, turn back **09** advantage, backtrack, come again, do the same, pronounce, recursion, reimburse, reinstate, repayment, reversion, round-trip, statement **10** correspond, giving-back, home-coming, recompense, recurrence, taking-back **11** handing-back, happen again, reciprocate, replacement, restoration **12** reappearance **13** reciprocation, reinstatement

**• in return**
◇ *reversal indicator*
**08** mutually **10** in exchange, in response **12** equivalently, reciprocally

**• point of no return**
**07** Rubicon

**Réunion**
**03** REU

**re-use**
◇ *anagram indicator*
**07** recycle **12** reconstitute

**revamp**
◇ *anagram indicator*
**04** do up **05** refit **06** recast, repair, revise **07** rebuild, restore **08** overhaul, renovate **09** modernize, refurbish **11** recondition, reconstruct **12** rehabilitate

**reveal**
◇ *anagram indicator*
**04** ingo, leak, show, tell **05** let on **06** betray, bewray, descry, expose, impart, let out, unfold, unmask, unveil **07** confess, display, divulge, exhibit, express, ingoing, lay bare, let slip, presage, publish, throw up, unbosom, uncover, unearth, unshale **08** announce, decipher, disbosom, disclose, discover, give away, manifest, proclaim, unshadow **09** broadcast, make aware, make known, publicize, undeceive **10** make public **11** communicate **12** blow the lid on, bring to light, expose to view, lift the lid on **15** take the wraps off

**revealing**
**05** sheer **06** daring, low-cut **08** giveaway, telltale **10** diaphanous, indicative, revelatory, see-through **11** significant

**revel**
◇ *anagram indicator*
**02** do **03** fug, joy **04** bask, crow, gala, orgy, rave, riot, wake **05** comus, enjoy, gloat, glory, lap up, party, roist, spree **06** rave-up, relish, savour, shivoo, thrive, wallow **07** carouse, debauch, delight, indulge, knees-up, large it, rejoice, roister, royster **08** carousal, live it up **09** bacchanal, celebrate, festivity, luxuriate, make merry, night-rule, whoop it up **10** have a party, saturnalia **11** celebration, have it large, merrymaking, take delight **12** raise the roof, take pleasure **13** jollification **14** push the boat out **15** paint the town red

**revelation**
**04** fact, leak, news, show **06** detail, vision **07** display **08** betrayal, epiphany, exposure, giveaway **09** admission, eye-opener, unmasking, unveiling **10** apocalypse, confession, disclosure, divulgence, exhibition, expression, revealment, uncovering, unearthing **11** information, publication **12** announcement, broadcasting, proclamation **13** communication, manifestation

**reveller**
**05** raver **07** roister, royster **08** bacchant, carouser, corybant **09** bacchanal, party-goer, roisterer, wassailer **10** celebrator, goodfellow, merrymaker, roaring boy **12** bacchanalian **14** pleasure-seeker

**revelry**
**03** fun **04** riot **05** party, reels **07** jollity, wassail **08** carousal **09** festivity **10** debauchery **11** celebration, festivities, merrymaking **12** celebrations **13** jollification

**revenge**
**03** get, utu **05** repay **06** avenge, pay off, ultion **07** hit back, redress, wreak of **08** avenging, reprisal, requital, revanche, serve out, vendetta **09** fight back, get back at, retaliate, tit for tat, vengeance **10** avengement, punishment **11** eye for an eye, get even with, retaliation, retribution **12** satisfaction, settle a score **14** get

your own back, pay someone back **15** take vengeance on

**revengeful**
**06** bitter **08** pitiless, spiteful, vengeful, wreakful **09** malicious, malignant, merciless, resentful, vengeable **10** implacable, malevolent, unmerciful, vindictive **11** unforgiving, vindicative

**revenue**
**04** fisc, fisk, gain, rent **05** yield **06** income, profit, return **07** profits, rewards, takings **08** incoming, interest, proceeds, receipts **09** patrimony, primitiae

**reverberate**
**04** boom, echo, ring **06** recoil, re-echo **07** rebound, reflect, resound, vibrate **08** resonate **09** repercuss

**reverberation**
**04** echo, wave **06** effect, recoil, result, ripple **07** rebound, ringing **09** re-echoing, resonance, shock wave, vibration **10** reflection, resounding **11** consequence, replication **12** repercussion

**revere**
**04** fear **05** adore, exalt **06** admire, esteem, honour **07** idolize, respect, worship **08** look up to, venerate **09** reverence **11** pay homage to **13** think highly of

**reverence**
**03** awe **04** fear **05** adore, dread **06** admire, esteem, hallow, homage, honour, revere **07** idolism, overawe, respect, worship **08** devotion, venerate **09** adoration, deference, obeisance **10** admiration, exaltation, high esteem, necrolatry, veneration **11** acknowledge, bibliolatry **13** ecclesiolatry

**reverent**
**04** awed **05** pious **06** devout, humble, loving, solemn **07** adoring, devoted, dutiful **08** admiring, obeisant **10** respectful **11** deferential, reverential, worshipping

**reverie**
**05** study **06** musing, trance **08** daydream **10** brown study **11** abstraction, daydreaming, inattention **13** preoccupation, woolgathering

**reversal**
◇ *reversal indicator*
**02** un- **04** blow, swap **05** check, delay, knock, trial, upset, U-turn **06** defeat, mishap, repeal **07** failure, problem, reverse, setback, turning, undoing **08** exchange, hardship, negation **09** about face, adversity, annulment, inversion, revulsion, turnabout, turnround, volte-face **10** affliction, difficulty, misfortune, rescinding, revocation, turnaround **12** cancellation, misadventure **13** nullification **14** countermanding, disappointment

**reverse**
◇ *reversal indicator*
**04** back, blow, pile, rear, swap, turn, undo **05** alter, annul, check, delay, quash, tails, trial, up-end, upset, verso, woman **06** cancel, change, defeat, invert, mishap, negate, repeal, return, revert, revoke, stroke **07** backset, counter, failure, inverse, problem, regress, rescind, retract, retreat, setback, transit **08** backward, contrary, converse, exchange, flip-flop, flipside, hardship, inverted, opposite, overrule, overturn, renverse, reversal, set aside, withdraw **09** adversity, back-pedal, backtrack, disaffirm, other side, overthrow, transpose, turn round, underside **10** affliction, antithesis, backhanded, difficulty, invalidate, misfortune, transverse, turn around **11** change round, countermand, vicissitude **12** misadventure **13** move backwards **14** disappointment, drive backwards, put back to front, turn upside-down

**reversion**
◇ *reversal indicator*
**06** return **07** atavism, escheat, regress **09** puerilism, throwback **10** giving-back, regression, taking-back **11** handing-back, hypostrophe, restoration **13** reinstatement, retrogression

**revert**
◇ *reversal indicator*
**04** fall **05** lapse, recur **06** a tempo, fall in, go back, recoil, resort, result, resume, return **07** cut back, regress, relapse, reverse, run wild, try back **08** fail safe **09** throw back, turn again **10** retrogress

**review**
◇ *anagram indicator*
◇ *reversal indicator*
**03** pan **04** crit, view **05** judge, slate, study, weigh **06** appeal, assess, go over, notice, rating, report, revise, size up, survey **07** analyse, discuss, examine, inspect, journal, rethink, weigh up, write up, write-up **08** analysis, appraise, critique, evaluate, magazine, reassess, reviewal, revision, scrutiny **09** appraisal, comment on, criticism, criticize, judgement, recension, re-examine, summing-up **10** assessment, commentary, evaluation, periodical, reconsider, re-evaluate, retrospect, scrutinize **11** examination, take stock of **12** reassessment, recapitulate, re-evaluation, tour d'horizon **13** re-examination **14** recapitulation **15** reconsideration

**reviewer**
**05** judge **06** critic **07** arbiter **08** essayist, observer **11** commentator, connoisseur

**revile**
**04** hate, rail **05** abuse, libel, scorn, smear **06** defame, malign, missay, vilify **07** despise, inveigh, miscall, slander, traduce **08** reproach **09** denigrate **10** blackguard, calumniate, vituperate

**revise**
◇ *anagram indicator*
**03** Rev **04** cram, edit **05** alter, amend, emend, learn, mug up, study **06** change, go over, modify, peruse, recast, revamp, review, reword, rework, swot up, update **07** correct, recense, redraft, rewrite **08** bone up on, memorize, optimize **09** expurgate, re-examine **10** reconsider **13** think better of

**revision**
**03** Rev **06** change, recast, review **07** editing **08** homework, learning, studying, swotting, updating **09** amendment, recasting, recension, rereading, reworking, rewriting **10** alteration, correction, diorthosis, emendation, memorizing **12** modification **13** re-examination **14** reconstruction

**revitalize**
**05** renew **06** revive **07** refresh, restore **08** revivify **09** reanimate, resurrect **10** reactivate, rejuvenate **12** reinvigorate

**revival**
**04** Romo **06** upturn **07** Odinism, rebirth, renewal, upsurge **08** comeback, wakening **09** awakening, lightning **10** quickening, resurgence **11** neopaganism, reawakening, renaissance, restoration **12** resurrection, risorgimento **13** resuscitation, the kiss of life **14** reintroduction, revitalization **15** re-establishment

**revive**
**04** wake **05** rally, renew, rouse **06** awaken, rake up, relive **07** animate, cheer up, comfort, quicken, recover, refresh, restore **08** reawaken, rekindle, revivify **09** reanimate, resurrect **10** bring round, invigorate, reactivate, revitalize **11** re-establish, reintroduce, resuscitate **12** reinvigorate
• **revivers**
**10** Epsom salts

**revivify**
**05** renew **06** repair, revive **07** refresh, restore **08** inspirit **09** reanimate **10** invigorate, reactivate, revitalize **11** resuscitate

**reviving**
**05** tonic **07** bracing, cordial **11** reanimating, revivescent, revivifying, reviviscent, stimulating **12** enheartening, exhilarating, invigorating, refreshening, regenerating **13** resuscitative **14** reinvigorating

**revocation**
**06** repeal, revoke **08** negation, quashing, reversal, revoking **09** abolition, annulment, repealing

**10** rescinding, rescission, retraction, revokement, withdrawal **11** countermand, repudiation **12** cancellation, invalidation, retractation **13** nullification **14** countermanding

**revoke**
**04** lift **05** annul, check, quash, recal, renig **06** cancel, negate, recall, recant, renege, repeal, unpray **07** abolish, nullify, renague, renegue, rescind, retract, reverse, unshoot, unshout **08** abrogate, withdraw **09** unpredict **10** invalidate, revocation **11** countermand

**revolt**
◇ *anagram indicator*
**04** coup, riot, rise **05** rebel, repel, shock **06** defect, mutiny, offend, putsch, resist, rise up, rising, sicken **07** disgust, dissent, fall off, outrage **08** apostasy, fall away, futurism, nauseate, uprising **09** breakaway, coup d'état, defection, Jacquerie, rebellion, revulsion, secession **10** revolution, scandalize, take up arms **12** insurrection **13** expressionism **15** Romantic Revival, the Paris Commune, turn your stomach

**revolting**
◇ *anagram indicator*
**02** up **04** foul, vile **05** grody, nasty **07** hateful, heinous **08** horrible, shocking **09** abhorrent, appalling, insurgent, loathsome, obnoxious, offensive, repellent, repugnant, repulsive, sickening **10** abominable, disgusting, nauseating, off-putting **11** distasteful **13** reprehensible

**revolution**
◇ *anagram indicator*
◇ *reversal indicator*
**04** coup, roll, spin, turn **05** cycle, orbit, round, wheel, whirl **06** change, circle, mutiny, putsch, revolt, rising **07** circuit, inqilab, revolve **08** gyration, mutation, rotation, upheaval, uprising **09** cataclysm, coup d'état, rebellion, sex change **10** innovation, insurgence, revolvency **11** reformation **12** insurrection **13** metamorphosis **14** transformation

*Revolutions include:*

**04** July
**06** French
**07** October, Russian
**08** American, Cultural, February, Glorious
**10** Industrial
**12** Agricultural

**revolutionary**
◇ *anagram indicator*
◇ *reversal indicator*
**03** new, red **04** trot **05** novel, rebel **07** drastic, radical **08** complete, Leninist, mutineer, mutinous **09** anarchist, Bolshevik, different, extremist, insurgent, Menshevik, seditious **10** avant-garde, filibuster, innovative, rebellious, Sandinista, subversive, Trotskyist, Trotskyite **11** anarchistic, progressive, sansculotte **12** experimental **13** revolutionist, thoroughgoing **14** ground-breaking **15** insurrectionary, insurrectionist

*Revolutionaries include:*

**03** Che
**04** Biko (Steve), Cade (Jack), Kett (Robert), Marx (Karl)
**05** Allen (Ethan), Fanon (Frantz), Gorky (Maxim), Henry (Patrick), Kirov (Sergey), Lenin (Vladimir Ilyich), Marat (Jean Paul), Paine (Tom), Radek (Karl), Rykov (Alexey), Sands (Bobby), Sucre (Antonio José de), Tyler (Wat), Villa (Pancho)
**06** Arafat (Yasser), Baader (Andreas), Barras (Paul François Jean Nicolas, Comte de), Castro (Fidel), Corday (Charlotte), Danton (Georges), Fawkes (Guy), Fuller (Margaret), Hébert (Jacques René), Kassem (Abdul Karim), Madero (Francisco), Moreno (Mariano), Qassim (Abd al-Krim), Stalin (Joseph), Zapata (Emiliano)
**07** Bakunin (Mikhail), Barnave (Antoine), Blanqui (Auguste), Bolívar (Simón), Catesby (Robert), Goldman (Emma), Guevara (Che), Mandela (Nelson), Meinhof (Ulrike Marie), Princip (Gavrilo), Sandino (Augusto César), Savimbi (Jonas), Tallien (Jean Lambert), Trotsky (Leon), Wallace (William)
**08** Abu Nidal, Bin Laden (Osama), Bukharin (Nikolay), Hereward (the Wake), Kerensky (Alexander), Lilburne (John), Mirabeau (Honoré Gabriel Riqueti, Comte de), Proudhon (Pierre Joseph), Santerre (Antoine Joseph), Zinoviev (Grigoriy)
**09** Christian (Fletcher), Garibaldi (Giuseppe), Guillotin (Joseph), Kropotkin (Knyaz Peter), Luxemburg (Rosa), Mao Zedong, Nana Sahib, Plekhanov (Georgi), Saint-Just (Louis de), Spartacus, Sun Yat-Sen
**10** Delescluze (Charles), Desmoulins (Camille)
**11** Jiang Jieshi, Robespierre (Maximilien de)
**13** Chiang Kai-Shek, Paz Estenssoro (Víctor)

**revolutionize**
**06** reform **09** transform **10** reorganize **11** restructure, transfigure **14** turn upside-down

**revolve**
**02** go **03** ren, rev, rin, run **04** move, spin, turn **05** orbit, pivot, think, twist, wheel, whirl **06** circle, gyrate, hang on, ponder, return, rotate, swivel, turn on **07** focus on, hinge on, turning **08** centre on, roll back **10** circumduct, revolution **11** circumvolve **13** concentrate on

**revolver**
**03** gat, gun, rod **04** Colt®, iron **05** rifle **06** airgun, pistol **07** bulldog, firearm, handgun, shooter, shotgun **10** peacemaker, six-shooter **12** shooting iron

**revolving**
**07** turning **08** gyrating, gyratory, rotating, spinning, whirling **12** peristrephic

**revulsion**
**04** hate **06** hatred, nausea, recoil, revolt **07** disgust, dislike **08** aversion, distaste, loathing **09** repulsion **10** abhorrence, repugnance, withdrawal **11** abomination, detestation
*See also* **disgust**; **distaste**

**reward**
**03** pay **04** gain, meed, wage **05** bonus, medal, merit, prise, prize, repay, wages, yield **06** bounty, desert, honour, pay-off, profit, quarry, return **07** benefit, guerdon, payment, premium, present, requite, salvage, testern, warison **08** consider, decorate, requital, sanction, warrison **09** head money, recognize, reguerdon, repayment **10** compensate, decoration, punishment, recompense, remunerate **11** just deserts, retribution **12** compensation, remuneration

**rewarding**
**08** edifying, fruitful, pleasing, valuable **09** enriching, lucrative **10** beneficial, fulfilling, gratifying, productive, profitable, satisfying, worthwhile **11** retributive **12** advantageous, remunerative

**rewording**
**04** edit **08** revision **09** rewriting **10** metaphrase, paraphrase, rephrasing **11** metaphrasis

**rework**
◇ *anagram indicator*
**04** edit **05** alter, amend, emend **06** change, go over, modify, peruse, recast, revamp, review, revise, reword, update **07** correct, recense, redraft, rewrite **09** expurgate, re-examine, refashion **10** reconsider **13** think better of

**rewrite**
◇ *anagram indicator*
**04** edit **05** emend, tweak **06** recast, revise, reword, rework **07** correct, redraft, rescore **08** inscribe, rescript

**Rex**
**01** R

**rhea**
**03** Ops **04** rami **05** nandu, ramee, ramie **06** nandoo, nhandu

**rhenium**
**02** Re

**rhesus**
**02** Rh

**rhetoric**
**07** bombast, fustian, oratory, periods

09 eloquence, hyperbole, pomposity, prolixity, verbosity, wordiness
10 oratorical 11 speechcraft
13 magniloquence 14 grandiloquence, long-windedness

**rhetorical**
05 grand, showy, wordy 06 florid, prolix 07 aureate, flowery, pompous, verbose 09 bombastic, high-flown, insincere, stylistic 10 artificial, flamboyant, long-winded, oratorical
11 declamatory, pretentious
12 Churchillian, high-sounding, magniloquent 13 grandiloquent

*Rhetorical devices include:*

03 pun
05 irony, trope
06 aporia, bathos, climax, simile, zeugma
07 auxesis, epigram, erotema, litotes, meiosis, paradox
08 anaphora, chiasmus, diallage, diegesis, ellipsis, epanodos, erotetic, innuendo, metaphor, metonymy, oxymoron, parabole, symploce
09 asyndeton, cataphora, dissimile, epizeuxis, euphemism, hendiadys, hypallage, hyperbole, increment, prolepsis, syllepsis, tautology
10 abscission, anastrophe, anticlimax, antithesis, apostrophe, dysphemism, enantiosis, epanaphora, epiphonema, epistrophe, metalepsis, synchrysis, synecdoche
11 anacoluthon, anadiplosis, antiphrasis, antonomasia, catachresis, enumeration, epanalepsis, hypostrophe, hypotyposis, paraleipsis, parenthesis
12 alliteration, antimetabole, epanorthosis, onomatopoeia
13 amplification, dramatic irony, epanadiplosis, mixed metaphor, vicious circle
14 antimetathesis, double entendre, figure of speech
15 pathetic fallacy, personification

**rheumatoid arthritis**
02 RA

**rhino** *see* **money**

**Rhode Island**
02 RI

**rhodium**
02 Rh

**rhubarb**
03 rot, row 05 Rheum 06 rumpus
08 nonsense, pie-plant, squabble
09 rhapontic

**rhyme**
03 ode 04 poem, rime, song, tink
05 chime, ditty, rhime, verse
06 crambo, jingle, poetry, rhythm, verses 07 couplet 08 limerick
09 harmonize 13 versification

*Rhymes include:*

03 end, eye
04 half, head, male, near, rich, tail
05 slant, vowel
06 female, riding, tailed
08 feminine, internal
09 assonance, identical, masculine, pararhyme, rime riche
10 apocopated, cynghanedd, rhyme royal
13 rime suffisant

**rhythm**
04 beat, flow, lilt, stot, time 05 metre, pulse, rhyme, swing, tempo, throb
06 accent 07 cadence, cadency, harmony, measure, numbers, pattern
08 movement 09 voltinism

**rhythmic**
04 go-go 06 metric, steady
07 flowing, lilting, pulsing, regular
08 metrical, periodic, repeated
09 pulsating, throbbing 10 rhythmical
• **rhythmic pattern**
04 raga, tala 05 talea

**rib**
03 bar 04 band, bone, cord, gill, vein, wale, welt, wife 05 costa, groin, nerve, ogive, ridge, shaft, tease 06 cutlet, lierne, purlin 07 feather, futtock, nervure, ribbing, support
08 moulding, pork-chop, ridicule
09 tierceron 10 mutton chop 13 cross-springer 14 pleurapophysis

**ribald**
03 low 04 base, blue, lewd, mean, racy, rude 05 bawdy, gross 06 coarse, earthy, filthy, ribaud, risqué, smutty, vulgar 07 jeering, mocking, naughty, obscene, rybauld 08 derisive, indecent 09 off-colour, satirical
10 irreverent, licentious, scurrilous
11 foul-mouthed, Rabelaisian
13 disrespectful

**ribaldry**
04 smut 05 filth 07 jeering, lowness, mockery 08 baseness, derision, raciness, ribaudry, rudeness
09 bawdiness, grossness, indecency, obscenity, rybaudrye, vulgarity
10 coarseness, earthiness, scurrility, smuttiness 11 naughtiness
14 licentiousness

**ribbing**
06 banter 07 baiting, goading, kidding, mocking, ragging, teasing
08 annoying, ridicule, taunting
09 badgering 11 provocation

**ribbon**
03 jag, pad, tie 04 band, cord, line, pads, sash, tape 05 braid, cloth, flash, shred, strip, tenia 06 caddis, cordon, ferret, fillet, radula, riband, streak, stripe, taenia, tassel, tatter 07 caddice, caddyss, elastic, hatband, ribband, tieback 08 hair-band, headband, quilling, streamer 09 petersham, sword knot 10 cordon bleu, ticker tape
11 multistrike, watchspring

**rice**
04 reis, twig 05 paddy 07 arborio, zizania 09 brushwood

**rich**
03 fat 04 busy, deep, fine, full, high, lush, oily, oofy, warm 05 ample, fatty, flush, grand, heavy, juicy, ritzy, spicy, sweet, tasty, vivid 06 absurd, active, bright, costly, creamy, fecund, fruity, ironic, lavish, lively, loaded, mellow, monied, ornate, packed, strong
07 copious, fertile, intense, moneyed, opulent, profuse, replete, rolling, savoury, steeped, vibrant, wealthy, well-off 08 abundant, affluent, eventful, exciting, fruitful, gorgeous, luscious, palatial, precious, prolific, resonant, sonorous, splendid, valuable, well-to-do 09 abounding, brilliant, delicious, elaborate, expensive, laughable, luxurious, pecunious, plenteous, plentiful, priceless, sumptuous 10 filthy rich, full-bodied, in the money, outrageous, productive, prosperous, ridiculous, well-heeled
11 made of money, magnificent, mellifluous, overflowing, rolling in it
12 preposterous, rhinocerical, stinking rich, unreasonable, well-provided, well-supplied 13 full-flavoured 15 with money to burn

**riches**
04 dosh, gold, loot, pelf 05 brass, bread, dough, gravy, lolly, lucre, means, money, ready, smash 06 assets, greens, mammon, moolah, stumpy, wealth
07 fortune, readies, scratch, shekels
08 greenies, opulence, property, treasure 09 affluence, megabucks, resources, substance 10 prosperity
11 filthy lucre, spondulicks 12 the necessary

**richly**
04 well 05 fully 08 floridly, lavishly, properly, strongly, suitably
09 elegantly, opulently 10 completely, gorgeously, palatially, splendidly, thoroughly 11 elaborately, expensively, exquisitely, luxuriously, sumptuously
13 appropriately

**richness**
05 depth, taste 07 fatness 08 business, elegance, fullness, loudness, oiliness
09 abundance, fattiness, fertility, heaviness, intensity, juiciness, provision, resonance, splendour
10 creaminess, excitement, lavishness, liveliness, luxuriance, mellowness
12 eventfulness, magnificence
13 exquisiteness, luxuriousness, plentifulness, sumptuousness

**rickety**
◇ *anagram indicator*
05 crazy, shaky 06 feeble, flimsy, wobbly 07 tottery 08 decrepit, derelict, insecure, unstable, unsteady
10 broken-down, jerry-built, ramshackle 11 dilapidated

**ricochet**
03 bob, dap 04 jump, leap, stot
05 bound, carom, stoit, throw
06 bounce, recoil, spring 07 rebound
10 bounce back, spring back

**rid**
**04** free, quit **05** clear, expel, purge, shift **06** purify, remove **07** cleanse, deliver, relieve **08** unburden **11** disencumber

• **get rid of**
**04** cast, dump, junk **05** chuck, ditch, eject, expel, scrap, shake, shunt **06** remove, see off, unload **07** abolish, deep-six, discard **08** choke off, chuck out, clear off, clear out, down with, jettison, railroad, shake off, shrug off, throw out **09** dispose of, eliminate, eradicate, get shot of, throw away **10** do away with, put an end to **12** dispense with, make away with

**riddance**
**06** relief **07** freedom, release, removal **08** disposal, ejection **09** clearance, expulsion, purgation **11** deliverance, elimination **13** extermination

**riddle**
**03** mar **04** fill, koan, sift **05** guess, poser, sieve, solve **06** enigma, filter, infest, pepper, pierce, puzzle, strain, teaser, winnow **07** charade, cribble, mystery, pervade, problem **08** permeate, puncture **09** conundrum, logogriph, perforate **10** conclusion, mind-bender **11** brainteaser **12** brain-twister

**ride**
**02** go **03** sit **04** burn, lift, move, road, rode, spin, surf, trip, trot **05** cycle, drive, jaunt, pedal, steer **06** gallop, handle, manage, outing, saddle, travel **07** bobsled, control, journey, overlap **08** bestride, dominate, progress **09** bobsleigh, promenade **12** steeplechase

**rider**
**02** PS **05** biker, bikie **06** hussar, jockey, knight **07** dragoon, eventer **08** horseman, reinsman **09** corollary **10** cavalryman, equestrian, horsewoman, showjumper **11** mosstrooper **12** equestrienne, horse soldier

**ridge**
**02** ås **03** bur, hoe, rib, rig **04** balk, band, bank, burr, drum, edge, hill, kame, keel, list, lump, nurl, rand, reef, wale, welt **05** arête, baulk, costa, crest, esker, halse, hause, hawse, knurl, ledge, linch, raphe, torus **06** crista, ripple, saddle **07** corn rig, crinkle, drumlin, hogback, hummock, linchet, lynchet, wrinkle, yardang **08** eminence, hog's back, sastruga **09** knife-edge, razorback **10** escarpment, promontory **12** superciliary, thank-you-ma'am

**ridicule**
**03** guy, kid, rag, rib **04** gibe, goof, jeer, jest, josh, mock **05** chaff, irony, mimic, queer, scoff, scorn, smoke, sneer, taunt, tease **06** banter, deride, parody, poo-poo, satire, send up **07** crucify, jeering, lampoon, laugh at, mockery, pillory, reticle, sarcasm, teasing **08** badinage, derision, laughter, pooh-pooh, reticule, satirize, taunting **09** absurdity, burlesque, humiliate, make fun of, poke fun at **10** caricature, make game of **11** make a game of **12** depreciation **13** have a game with, poke mullock at

**ridiculous**
◇ *anagram indicator*
**04** rich **05** crazy, droll, funny, silly **06** absurd, mental, stupid **07** comical, damfool, foolish, risible **08** derisory, farcical, humorous, shocking **09** facetious, hilarious, laughable, ludicrous **10** cockamamie, incredible, outrageous **11** nonsensical **12** contemptible, preposterous, unbelievable

**ridiculously**
◇ *anagram indicator*
**08** absurdly **09** laughably **10** incredibly, shockingly **11** ludicrously **12** outrageously, surprisingly, unbelievably, unreasonably **14** preposterously

**rife**
**06** common, raging **07** current, general, rampant, teeming **08** abundant, epidemic, frequent, swarming **09** abounding, extensive, prevalent **10** ubiquitous, widespread **11** overflowing, predominant

**riff-raff**
**03** mob **04** raff, scum **05** dregs, scaff **06** rabble, raffle **07** rubbish **08** canaille, rent-a-mob **09** hoi polloi, scaff-raff **12** undesirables

**rifle**
◇ *anagram indicator*
**02** M1 **03** gun, gut, rob, SLR **04** loot, pick, sack **05** fusil, strip **06** burgle, injure, maraud, Mauser, musket, search, weapon **07** bandook, bundook, carabin, carbine, despoil, express, firearm, Martini, pillage, plunder, ransack, rummage, shotgun **08** Armalite®, carabine, disarray, firelock, petronel **09** chassepot, flintlock **10** Lee Enfield, Winchester® **11** elephant gun **12** Martini-Henry

**rift**
**03** gap, row **04** feud, hole, slit **05** belch, break, chink, cleft, crack, fault, fight, space, split **06** breach, cavity, cleave, cranny, schism **07** crevice, fissure, opening **08** argument, conflict, division, fracture **10** alienation, difference, separation **11** altercation **12** disagreement, estrangement

**rig**
◇ *anagram indicator*
**03** kit **04** cook, fake, garb, gear **05** dress, equip, fit up, forge, prank, ridge, set up, trick, twist **06** clothe, doctor, fiddle, fit out, frolic, gunter, jack-up, outfit, tackle **07** distort, falsify, massage, pervert, swindle **08** fittings, fixtures **09** apparatus, equipment, machinery, structure **10** manipulate, tamper with **12** misrepresent **13** accoutrements

• **rig out**
**03** fit **04** garb, robe, trim, wear **05** array, dress, equip, get up, put on **06** attire, clothe, fit out, kit out, outfit, supply **07** dress up, furnish, get into, provide, trick up, turn out **08** accoutre, trick out **09** make ready

• **rig up**
**05** build, dress, equip, erect, fit up, fix up **07** arrange, knock up **08** assemble **09** construct, improvise **11** put together **13** throw together **14** cobble together

**right**
**01** r **02** OK, rt **03** due, fit, fix, oke **04** fair, good, just, lien, okay, real, Tory, true, user, well **05** claim, droit, exact, legal, moral, power, quite, sound, truth, utter, valid **06** actual, avenge, bang-on, direct, equity, ethics, fairly, honest, honour, justly, lawful, pronto, proper, repair, seemly, settle, spot on, virtue, wholly **07** charter, correct, ethical, exactly, factual, fitting, freedom, genuine, honesty, justice, licence, precise, rectify, redress, stand up, totally, upright, utterly, warrant **08** absolute, accepted, accurate, approved, becoming, business, complete, directly, entirely, fairness, goodness, legality, morality, properly, put right, sanction, slap bang, straight, suitable, thorough, true-blue, virtuous **09** all the way, authentic, authority, by the book, correctly, desirable, equitable, factually, impartial, integrity, like a shot, opportune, precisely, privilege, propriety, rectitude, righteous, rightness, right-wing, territory, title deed, veritable, vindicate, yesterday **10** absolutely, acceptable, accurately, admissible, auspicious, birthright, completely, convenient, favourable, favourably, honourable, lawfulness, permission, preferable, principled, propitious, put in order, reasonable, straighten **11** appropriate, entitlement, immediately, opportunity, prerogative, reactionary, straightway, uprightness **12** advantageous, conservative, impartiality, satisfactory, the done thing, truthfulness, without delay **13** perpendicular, righteousness, straighten out **14** as the crow flies, characteristic, satisfactorily **15** before you know it, in a straight line

• **by rights**
**06** de jure, justly **07** legally, rightly **08** lawfully, properly **09** correctly **10** in fairness, rightfully **11** justifiably **12** legitimately

• **in the right**
**09** justified, warranted **10** vindicated

• **put to rights, set to rights**
**03** fix **04** sort **05** fix up **06** remedy, settle **07** correct, rectify **10** put in order, straighten **13** straighten out

• **right away**
**03** now **04** ASAP **06** at once, pronto **08** directly, in a jiffy, promptly

09 forthwith, instantly, like a shot, yesterday 11 immediately 12 straight away, without delay 13 from the word go 15 before you know it

• **right-hand man, right-hand woman**

02 PA 04 aide 06 deputy, helper 08 henchman 09 assistant, man Friday, number two, secretary 10 girl Friday, henchwoman, lieutenant, understudy 11 backroom boy, helping hand, henchperson, subordinate 12 backroom girl 15 second-in-command

• **right of way**

04 lead, rank 08 eminence, priority 09 seniority, supremacy 10 first place, precedence, preference 11 pre-eminence, superiority

• **within your rights**

07 allowed 08 entitled 09 justified, permitted 10 reasonable

**righteous**

04 fair, good, just, pure 05 legal, moral, valid 06 honest, lawful, proper, worthy 07 ethical, saintly, sinless, upright 08 virtuous 09 blameless, equitable, excellent, excusable, guiltless, incorrupt, justified, warranted 10 acceptable, defensible, God-fearing, honourable, law-abiding, legitimate, reasonable 11 explainable, justifiable, supportable, well-founded 14 irreproachable

**righteousness**

06 dharma, equity, honour, purity, virtue 07 honesty, justice, probity 08 goodness, holiness, morality 09 integrity, rectitude 11 ethicalness, uprightness 12 faithfulness 13 blamelessness 14 sanctification

**rightful**

03 due 04 just, real, true 05 legal, valid 06 de jure, lawful, proper 07 correct, genuine 08 bona fide, suitable 10 authorized, legitimate

**rightfully**

06 de jure, justly 07 legally, rightly 08 by rights, lawfully, properly 09 correctly 11 justifiably 12 legitimately

**rightly**

04 well 06 fairly, justly 07 legally, morally 08 by rights, lawfully, properly 09 correctly, equitably, fittingly 10 reasonably 11 justifiably 12 legitimately 13 appropriately

**rigid**

03 set 04 firm, hard 05 fixed, harsh, stern, stiff, stony, tense 06 ramrod, severe, starch, strict 07 austere, hard-set, spartan 08 cast-iron, rigorous, stubborn 09 inelastic, stringent, tramlined, unbending 10 inflexible, invariable, unyielding 11 unalterable, unrelenting 12 intransigent 14 uncompromising

**rigidity**

06 fixity 08 hardness, obduracy 09 obstinacy, stiffness 10 stringency 12 immovability, immutability, inelasticity, stubbornness, unsuppleness 13 immutableness, inflexibility, intransigence 14 intractability

**rigmarole**

04 fuss, to-do 06 bother, hassle, jargon, ragman 07 carry-on, palaver, process, ragment, twaddle 08 nonsense 09 gibberish 11 performance, riddle-me-ree

**rigorous**

04 firm, hard 05 close, exact, harsh, rigid, stern, tough 06 severe, strait, strict 07 ascetic, austere, precise, spartan, violent 08 accurate, exacting, straight, streight, thorough 09 laborious, stringent, unsparing 10 meticulous, scrupulous 11 painstaking, punctilious 12 intransigent 13 barrack square, conscientious 14 uncompromising

**rigorously**

06 strait 07 exactly 08 straight, streight 09 precisely 10 accurately, thoroughly 12 meticulously, scrupulously 13 painstakingly, punctiliously

**rigour**

05 trial 06 ordeal 08 accuracy, firmness, hardness, hardship, rigidity, severity 09 austerity, exactness, harshness, precision, privation, sternness, stiffness, suffering, toughness 10 strictness, stringency 11 preciseness 12 thoroughness 13 inflexibility, intransigence 14 meticulousness 15 punctiliousness

**rig-out**

03 kit 04 garb, gear, togs 05 dress, get-up, habit 06 livery, outfit, things 07 apparel, clobber, clothes, costume, raiment, uniform 08 clothing, garments

**rile**

◇ *anagram indicator*

03 bug, irk, vex 04 roil 05 anger, annoy, peeve, pique, upset 06 hassle, nettle, put out, wind up 07 agitate, hack off, tick off 08 brass off, irritate 09 aggravate, cheese off, drive nuts 10 drive crazy, exasperate 11 get your goat 12 drive bananas 13 get on your wick, get up your nose, get your back up, make sparks fly 14 drive up the wall, get your blood up, give you the hump 15 get on your nerves, get your dander up

**rill** *see* **brook**

**rim**

03 lip 04 brim, edge, ring, shoe, wood 05 apron, bezel, brink, chimb, chime, chine, felly, helix, rymme, skirt, velum, verge 06 border, felloe, fiddle, girdle, margin, strake 08 membrane 10 peritoneum 13 circumference

**rind**

04 bark, husk, peel, rine, rynd, skin, zest 05 crust, gourd, shell 06 citron 07 epicarp, outside 09 crackling 10 integument, orange peel

**ring**

01 O 03 mob, rim 04 area, band, bell, belt, buzz, call, cell, club, crew, dial, ding, disc, disk, echo, gang, gird, halo, hoop, link, loop, peal, sing, tang, ting, toll, tore 05 arena, atoll, chime, clang, clink, group, hem in, knell, phone, reach, reign, round, sound, torus 06 cage in, call up, cartel, circle, clique, collar, girdle, jingle, keeper, league, re-echo, ring up, signet, terret, territ, tingle, tinkle, torret, turret 07 annulet, annulus, circlet, circuit, combine, coterie, enclose, resound, society, vibrate 08 alliance, ding-dong, encircle, proclaim, pugilism, resonate, sorority, surround 09 enclosure, encompass, gathering, give a bell, give a buzz, phone call, syndicate, telephone 10 fraternity 11 association, give a tinkle, reverberate, wedding band 12 circumscribe, organization 14 tintinnabulate

• **prize ring**

02 PR

• **ring of wagons**

04 laer 06 corral, laager

**ringleader**

05 chief 06 brains, leader 08 fugleman 09 spokesman 10 bell-wether, mouthpiece 11 spokeswoman 12 spokesperson

**ringlet**

04 curl, lock

**rinse**

03 dip, wet 04 sind, synd, wash 05 bathe, clean, flush, swill 06 sloosh 07 cleanse, wash out 09 flush away, wash clean

**riot**

◇ *anagram indicator*

03 row 04 fray, hoot, orgy, rage, rant, rave, rout, show, tear 05 brawl, fight, laugh, mêlée, rebel, revel, storm 06 affray, charge, fracas, hubbub, mutiny, rave-up, revolt, rise up, rising, scream, strife, tumult, uproar 07 anarchy, display, quarrel, rampage, revelry, run amok, run riot, run wild, turmoil, whoobub 08 disorder, feasting, flourish, hubbuboo, partying, race riot, uprising 09 commotion, confusion, go berserk, rebellion 10 debauchery, exhibition, indulgence, insurgence, rush wildly, turbulence 11 disturbance, lawlessness, merrymaking 12 extravaganza, insurrection 14 go on the rampage

• **run riot**

◇ *anagram indicator*

04 rage, rant, rave, tear 05 storm 06 charge 07 rampage, run amok, run wild 09 go berserk 10 rush wildly 14 go on the rampage

**riotous**

◇ *anagram indicator*

04 loud, wild 05 noisy, rowdy 06 unruly, wanton 07 lawless, roaring,

violent **08** mutinous **10** boisterous, disorderly, ragmatical, rebellious, tumultuous, uproarious
**12** ungovernable, unrestrained
**13** insubordinate **14** uncontrollable
**15** insurrectionary

**riotously**
◇ *anagram indicator*
**05** ariot **06** loudly, wildly **07** noisily
**12** tumultuously **14** uncontrollably

**rip**
◇ *anagram indicator*
**03** cut **04** coop, gash, hack, hole, rend, rent, ripp, slit, tear **05** burst, shred, slash, split **06** ladder **07** handful, rupture **08** cleavage, lacerate, separate
• **rip off**
**02** do **03** con, rob **04** dupe **05** cheat, steal, sting, trick **06** diddle, fleece
**07** defraud, exploit, swindle **09** gold-brick **10** overcharge

**ripe**
**03** fit **05** grope, grown, ready, right
**06** mature, mellow, search, timely
**07** forward, perfect, ransack, ripened
**08** complete, drop-ripe, finished, in season, rare-ripe, seasoned, spoiling, suitable, thorough **09** developed, excellent, excessive, opportune, premature, ratheripe, under-ripe
**10** auspicious, favourable, fully grown, propitious **11** spoiling for
**12** advantageous **14** fully developed

**ripen**
**03** age **06** mature, mellow, season
**07** develop **13** gather to a head
**14** come to maturity **15** bring to maturity

**rip-off**
**03** con **04** scam, swiz **05** cheat, fraud, sting, theft **06** diddle **07** robbery, swindle **08** cheating, con trick, stealing
**09** gold brick **12** exploitation
**15** daylight robbery

**riposte**
**04** quip **05** reply, sally **06** answer, rejoin, retort, return **07** respond
**08** comeback, repartee, response
**09** rejoinder **11** reciprocate

**ripple**
◇ *anagram indicator*
**04** curl, eddy, flow, fret, pirl, purl, ring, wave **06** babble, burble, crease, effect, gurgle, jabble, pucker, result, riffle, ruffle, wimple **07** crumple, lapping, ripplet, wavelet, whimple, wrinkle
**08** undulate **09** shock wave
**10** crispation, undulation
**11** consequence, disturbance
**12** repercussion **13** reverberation

**rise**
◇ *reversal down indicator*
**02** up **03** sty, try **04** buoy, flow, go up, grow, head, hill, leap, lift, loom, riot, soar, stie, stye **05** arise, begin, climb, get up, issue, mount, pluff, prove, raise, rebel, slope, start, swell, tower
**06** appear, ascend, ascent, come in, defect, emerge, growth, harden, jump up, leap up, mutiny, origin, resist, revolt, rising, rocket, source, spring, upturn, volume **07** advance, attempt, climb up, dissent, emanate, improve, incline, prosper, react to, respond, slope up, soaring, stand up, upsurge
**08** approach, commence, escalate, increase, occasion, overgrow, progress, response, spring up, surmount, towering **09** acclivity, ascendant, ascendent, elevation, get higher, increment, intensify, originate, promotion **10** be promoted, do your best, escalation, take up arms
**11** advancement, get out of bed, improvement, move upwards, upward slope **12** amelioration, make progress
**13** exert yourself, get to your feet
**14** aggrandizement
• **give rise to**
◇ *reversal down indicator*
**04** make **05** cause, evoke, raise, spawn
**06** create, effect, elicit, induce, lead to, prompt **07** bring on, inspire, produce, provoke **08** engender, generate, persuade **09** influence, originate
**10** bring about

**risible**
**05** comic, droll, funny **06** absurd
**07** amusing, comical **08** farcical, humorous **09** hilarious, laughable, ludicrous **10** ridiculous **11** rib-tickling
**13** side-splitting

**rising**
◇ *reversal down indicator*
**04** bull, hill, riot, rise **06** émeute, origin, revolt, uprest, uprise, uprist
**07** growing, soaring **08** emerging, mounting, naissant, swelling, uprising
**09** advancing, ascendant, ascendent, ascending, assurgent, insurgent
**10** increasing, prominence, revolution
**11** approaching **12** insurrection, intensifying

**risk**
**04** dare, dice, fear **05** flier, peril, stake, throw **06** chance, danger, gamble, hazard, impawn, threat **07** imperil, venture **08** chance it, endanger, jeopardy **09** adventure **10** go for broke, jeopardize, self-danger
**11** possibility, speculation, take a chance, uncertainty **12** lay on the line, play with fire, put on the line **13** put in jeopardy
• **against all risks**
**03** aar
• **at the risk of**
**02** on

**risky**
**04** iffy **05** dicey, dodgy, hairy
**06** chancy, risqué, touchy, tricky, unsafe
**07** chancey **08** high-risk, perilous
**09** dangerous, hazardous, uncertain
**10** precarious, touch-and-go
**11** venturesome

**risqué**
**04** blue, racy, rude **05** adult, bawdy, crude, dirty, risky, saucy, spicy
**06** coarse, earthy, fruity, ribald, smutty
**07** naughty **08** immodest, improper, indecent **09** off-colour **10** indelicate, suggestive **14** near the knuckle

**rite**
**03** act **04** bora, form, orgy **05** pawaw, right, usage **06** custom, office, powwow, ritual, symbol **07** dry Mass, liturgy, service, worship **08** ceremony, practice **09** formality, ordinance, procedure, sacrament **10** ceremonial, commixtion, commixture, dry service, initiatory, observance **11** subincision
**12** confirmation, superstition

**ritual**
**03** act, set **04** form, rite, wont **05** habit, usage **06** Agadah, cultus, custom, fetich, fetish, formal, lavabo **07** fetiche, Haggada, liturgy, routine, sacring, service **08** ceremony, habitual, Haggadah, lavatory, practice, trumpery **09** customary, custumary, formality, formulary, ordinance, procedure, sacrament, solemnity, tradition **10** ceremonial, consuetude, convention, mumbo-jumbo, observance, prescribed, procedural
**11** apotropaism, celebration, traditional
**12** conventional, prescription
**14** consuetudinary

**ritualistic**
**06** formal, ritual, solemn **07** festive, stately **08** official **09** customary, dignified, formulaic, formulary
**10** ceremonial **11** traditional

**ritzy**
**04** posh, rich **05** cushy, grand, plush
**06** costly, de luxe, glitzy, lavish, swanky
**07** elegant, opulent, stylish **08** affluent, pampered, splendid **09** expensive, luxurious, sumptuous **11** comfortable, magnificent **13** self-indulgent, well-appointed

**rival**
**03** vie **04** mate, peer, vier **05** equal, match, touch **06** fellow, oppose
**07** emulate, nemesis, opposed, paragon, partner, vie with **08** corrival, opponent, opposing, parallel
**09** adversary, competing, contender
**10** antagonist, challenger, collateral, competitor, contestant, in conflict, opposition **11** compare with, compete with, competitive, conflicting, contend with, measure up to **12** in opposition
**13** in competition

**rivalry**
**05** vying **06** strife **07** contest
**08** conflict, rivality, struggle
**09** emulation **10** antagonism, contention, corrivalry, in-fighting, opposition **11** competition
**12** corrivalship **15** competitiveness

**riven**
**04** rent **05** split **07** divided, severed
**08** ruptured **09** torn apart **11** ripped apart

**river**
**01** R **03** lee, rio **05** flood
**11** watercourse

*River and watercourse types include:*

**02** ea
**03** cut, pow, sny
**04** beck, burn, flow, khor, kill, lake, lane, nala, rill, snye, wadi, wady
**05** bourn, brook, canal, creek, delta, ditch, drain, firth, flume, fresh, frith, inlet, mouth, nalla, nulla, rhine, shott, whelm
**06** arroyo, broads, influx, nallah, nullah, rapids, rillet, runnel, source, spruit, stream
**07** channel, estuary, freshet, riveret, rivulet, torrent
**08** affluent, brooklet, effluent, influent, waterway
**09** anabranch, backwater, billabong, confluent, headwater, streamlet, tributary
**10** confluence, head-stream, millstream, streamling
**11** trout stream, water splash
**12** distributary, embranchment, water-channel
**14** mountain stream

*Rivers include:*

**02** Ob, Po
**03** Ain, Axe, Bug, Cam, Dee, Don, Ems, Esk, Exe, Fal, Fly, Han, Ill, Inn, Lea, Lee, Lim, Lot, Mun, Nid, Our, Red, San, Tay, Taz, Ure, Usk, Váh, Wye
**04** Aare, Adur, Aire, Amur, Arno, Avon, Bann, Cher, Coco, Dart, East, Ebro, Eden, Elbe, Gail, Hong, Isis, Kemi, Lena, Nene, Neva, Nile, Oder, Ohio, Ouse, Oxus, Ping, Ravi, Ruhr, Saar, Spey, Swan, Taff, Tees, Test, Towy, Tyne, Ural, Vaal, Wear, Yalu, Yare
**05** Adige, Argun, Benue, Boyne, Cauca, Chari, Clyde, Congo, Donau, Douro, Fleet, Forth, Glåma, Indus, Jumna, Loire, Marne, Meuse, Mosel, Neath, Negro, Neman, Niger, Peace, Pearl, Pecos, Plata, Plate, Rhine, Rhône, Saône, Seine, Snake, Somme, Tagus, Tamar, Teifi, Tiber, Tisza, Trent, Tweed, Volga, Volta, Weser, Yukon, Zaire
**06** Amazon, Angara, Brazos, Chenab, Clutha, Danube, Dnestr, Escaut, Fraser, Gambia, Ganges, Grande, Hudson, Humber, Irtysh, Jhelum, Jordan, Kagera, Kistna, Kolyma, Liffey, Mekong, Mersey, Murray, Orange, Ottawa, Pahang, Paraná, Ribble, Salado, Severn, Seyhan, Sutlej, Thames, Tigris, Tornio, Ubangi, Vltava, Wabash, Yamuna, Yellow
**07** Alpheus, Darling, Dnieper, Garonne, Glommen, Helmand, Huang He, Huang Ho, Lachlan, Limpopo, Lualaba, Madeira, Marañón, Maritsa, Narmada, Orinoco, Pechora, Potomac, Salween, Schelde, Selenga, Sénégal, Shannon, Tarim He, Ucayali, Uruguay, Vistula, Waikato, Yangtze, Yenisei, Zambezi
**08** Arkansas, Blue Nile, Canadian, Colorado, Columbia, Delaware, Dniester, Dordogne, Missouri, Okavango, Paraguay, Tunguska, Wanganui, Zhu Jiang
**09** Churchill, Crocodile, Euphrates, Great Ouse, Irrawaddy, Mackenzie, Rio Grande, Tennessee, White Nile
**10** Albert Nile, Bass Strait, Des Plaines, Sacramento, San Joaquin, Shenandoah, St Lawrence, Walla Walla
**11** Mississippi, Shatt al-Arab
**12** Murrumbidgee, Saskatchewan, Victoria Nile

*Mythical rivers include:*

**04** Alph, Styx
**05** Lethe
**07** Acheron, Alpheus, Cocytus, Oceanus
**08** Achelous, Eridanos
**10** Phlegethon

• **river valley**
**04** wadi, wady **05** water **07** wind gap

**rivet**
**04** grip **05** clink **06** absorb, arrest, clinch, excite **07** engross, enthral **08** intrigue **09** captivate, fascinate
• **fix rivet**
**04** pane, pean, peen, pein, pene

**riveting**
**08** exciting, gripping, hypnotic, magnetic **09** absorbing, arresting **10** engrossing **11** captivating, enthralling, fascinating, interesting **12** spellbinding

**road**
**03** via **04** raid, ride, rode, tour **06** course **07** railway, roadway **09** dismissal, incursion **10** journeying, prostitute, travelling

*Road types include:*

**01** A, B, C, E
**02** Rd, St
**03** Ave, way
**04** drag, high, lane, mews, pass, ring, side, slip, toll
**05** alley, byway, close, gated, Roman, route, strip, track, trunk
**06** avenue, bypass, parade, rat run, relief, strand, street, subway
**07** beltway, dead end, flyover, freeway, highway, off ramp, parkway, private, through
**08** alleyway, autobahn, causeway, clearway, crescent, cul-de-sac, metalled, motorway, overpass, red route, short cut, speedway, trackway, turnpike
**09** autoroute, boulevard, bridleway, cart track, dirt track, esplanade, green lane, promenade, underpass
**10** autostrada, bridlepath, cloverleaf, expressway, interstate, unmetalled
**11** gravel track, scenic route, single track
**12** mountain pass, superhighway, thoroughfare, unclassified
**14** gyratory system
**15** dual-carriageway

*Roads include:*

**02** A1, M1, M2, M3, M4, M5, M6, M8, M9
**03** M25, M40, M62
**07** Route 66, Westway
**08** Fosse Way, Highway 1, Silk Road
**09** Appian Way, Burma Road, Highway 61
**10** Cassian Way, Dere Street, Khyber Pass
**12** El Camino Real, King's Highway, Périphérique, Sturt Highway
**13** North Circular, South Circular, Stuart Highway, Watling Street
**14** Great Ocean Road, Great River Road, Le Périphérique, Pacific Highway

**roadhouse** *see* **public house**

**roam**
**04** rake, rove, trek, walk **05** amble, drift, prowl, range, raven, stray, tramp, wheel **06** ramble, stroam, stroll, travel, wander **07** meander **08** ambulate, squander, traverse **09** wandering **11** perambulate, peregrinate

**roar**
**03** cry **04** bawl, bell, boom, hoot, howl, roin, rore, rote, rout, yell **05** blare, crash, laugh, royne, shout **06** bellow, guffaw, holler, rumble, scream, shriek **07** break up, thunder **08** crease up **09** fall about **14** split your sides **15** laugh like a drain

**roaring**
**04** full, loud, rich **05** great **07** bluster, booming, echoing, notable, ringing, riotous, vibrant **08** decisive, emphatic, resonant, sonorous, striking, thorough **09** memorable **10** conclusive, impressive, remarkable, resonating, resounding, thunderous **11** outstanding **13** reverberating

**roast**
**04** bake, rost **05** brown, parch, swale, swayl, sweal, sweel **06** banter **07** torrefy **08** barbecue **11** decrepitate

**rob**
**02** do **03** mug, pad, rub **04** blag, fake, loot, mill, nick, raid, ramp, roll, sack **05** berob, bunco, bunko, cheat, flimp, heist, pluck, reave, reive, rifle, screw, stiff, sting **06** burgle, do over, hijack, hold up, pirate, rip off **07** bereave, defraud, deprive, despoil, pillage, plunder, ransack, stick up, swindle **08** highjack, knock off, turn over **09** depredate, steal from

**robber**
**04** Tory **05** cheat, fraud, rover, thief **06** bandit, con man, dacoit, dakoit, latron, looter, mugger, pirate, raider **07** brigand, burglar, cateran, ladrone, pandoor, pandour, stealer **08** hijacker, swindler **09** embezzler, plunderer **10** highjacker, highwayman, land-pirate, roberdsman, robertsman **11** motor-bandit
*See also* **thief**

**robbery**
**04** blag, raid, toby **05** fraud, heist, theft **06** hold-up, piracy, rip-off, snatch **07** break-in, dacoity, dakoiti, larceny, low toby, mugging, pillage, plunder, stick-up, swindle **08** burglary, high toby, stealing **09** dacoitage, latrociny, pilferage **10** plundering **11** latrocinium **12** embezzlement, smash-and-grab **13** housebreaking

**robe**
**04** garb, gown, vest, wrap **05** camis, camus, drape, dress, habit, talar **06** attire, chimer, clothe, dolman, khalat, khilat, killut, kimono, peplos, peplus, purple **07** apparel, cassock, chimere, chrisom, costume, kellaut, wrapper **08** bathrobe, christom, parament, peignoir, vestment, wardrobe **09** housecoat, nightgown **10** palliament **12** chrisom-cloth, dressing-gown

**Robert**
**03** Bob, Rob **05** Bobby **06** Bobbie, Rabbie, Robbie

**Robin Hood** *see* **legend**

**robot**
**05** golem **06** cyborg, zombie **07** android, machine, nanobot **08** telechir **09** automaton

**robust**
**03** fit, raw **04** hale, iron, rude, well **05** crude, hardy, sonsy, stout, tough **06** coarse, direct, earthy, hearty, ribald, risqué, rugged, sonsie, strong, sturdy **07** healthy, sthenic **08** athletic, forceful, muscular, powerful, stalwart, thickset, vigorous **09** energetic, strapping, well-built **10** able-bodied, no-nonsense **11** down-to-earth **15** straightforward, tough as old boots

**rock**
◇ *anagram indicator*
**03** AOR, jow, tip **04** cill, coin, crag, daze, reef, reel, roll, sill, stun, sway, tilt, toss, trap, tuff, whin **05** crack, lurch, pitch, shake, shock, stone, swing **06** danger, pebble, totter, wobble **07** astound, boulder, diamond, distaff, outcrop, shoggle, stagger, startle **08** astonish, bewilder, hard core, obstacle, surprise, take back, undulate **09** dumbfound, oscillate **12** move to and fro

*See also* **singer**

*Rocks include:*

**02** aa
**03** ore
**04** coal, lava, marl
**05** chalk, chert, flint, shale, slate
**06** basalt, gabbro, gneiss, gravel, marble, schist
**07** breccia, granite
**08** dolerite, hornfels, obsidian, porphyry
**09** argillite, greywacke, limestone, sandstone, soapstone
**10** greenstone, serpentine
**11** pumice stone
**12** conglomerate

**• on the rocks**
**06** doomed, failed, in a fix, in a jam **07** failing, in a hole, in a mess **08** hopeless, in pieces, in shreds, slipping, unstable **09** in a bad way, in a scrape, penniless **11** at an impasse **12** in difficulty **14** in difficulties

**rocket**
**02** V-1, V-2 **04** soar, wald, weld **05** onion, retro, tower **06** rucola **07** arugula, missile, shoot up **08** Congreve, escalate, roquette, thruster **09** reprimand **10** flying bomb, projectile **13** guided missile, launch vehicle **15** increase quickly, St Barbara's cress

**rocky**
◇ *anagram indicator*
**04** hard, weak **05** rough, shaky, stony, tipsy **06** craggy, flinty, pebbly, rugged, wobbly **08** unstable, unsteady, wobbling **09** difficult, tottering, uncertain **10** staggering, unpleasant, unreliable **14** unsatisfactory

**rococo**
**04** bold **05** showy **06** florid, ornate **07** baroque, flowery **08** fanciful, rocaille, vigorous **09** decorated, elaborate, exuberant, fantastic, grotesque, whimsical **10** convoluted, flamboyant **11** embellished, extravagant, overwrought **13** overdecorated, overelaborate **15** churrigueresque

**rod**
**03** bar, cue, lug **04** calm, came, cane, mace, pole, reed, rood, spit, twig, vare, wand **05** baton, shaft, staff, stave, stick, strut, swits **06** pistol, switch **07** ellwand, probang, sceptre, scollop, tringle **08** caduceus, metewand, meteyard, revolver, stanchel, stancher **09** metestick, stanchion

*See also* **gun**

**rodent**

*Rodents include:*

**03** rat
**04** cavy, cony, hare, paca, pika, vole
**05** aguti, coypu, mouse
**06** agouti, beaver, ferret, gerbil, gopher, hog-rat, jerboa, marmot, rabbit
**07** cane rat, hamster, lemming, meerkat, muskrat, ondatra, potoroo
**08** black rat, brown rat, capybara, chipmunk, dormouse, hampster, hedgehog, musquash, sewer rat, squirrel, tucutuco, viscacha, water rat
**09** bandicoot, groundhog, guinea pig, porcupine, water vole, woodchuck
**10** chinchilla, fieldmouse, prairie dog, springhaas, springhase
**11** kangaroo rat, red squirrel, spermophile
**12** grey squirrel, harvest mouse

**roe**
**04** melt, milt, raun, rawn **06** caviar, cavier **07** caviare **08** caviarie

**roentgenium**
**02** Rg

**rogue**
◇ *anagram indicator*
**05** cheat, crook, drôle, fraud, gipsy, Greek, gypsy, hempy, knave, scamp **06** con man, donder, limmer, rascal, scally, terror, varlet **07** skellum, vagrant, villain, wastrel, wrong 'un **08** deceiver, dummerer, palliard, swindler **09** fraudster, miscreant, prankster, reprobate, scallywag, scoundrel, son of a gun **10** disruptive, ne'er-do-well, rascallion, slip-string **11** mischievous, rapscallion **12** hedge-creeper **14** good-for-nothing

**roguish**
**04** arch **05** hempy, shady **06** cheeky, impish, wicked **07** crooked, knavish, playful, waggish **08** criminal, espiègle, rascally **09** deceitful, deceiving, dishonest, swindling **10** confounded, coquettish, fraudulent, frolicsome, rascal-like, slip-string, villainous **11** mischievous **12** unprincipled, unscrupulous

**roister**
**04** brag, romp **05** boast, revel, strut **06** frolic **07** bluster, carouse, large it, rollick, swagger **09** blusterer, celebrate, make merry, whoop it up **11** have it large **15** paint the town red

**roisterer**
**06** buster, ranter **07** boaster, roister **08** braggart, carouser, reveller **09** blusterer, swaggerer

**roisterous**
**04** loud, wild **05** noisy, rowdy **09** clamorous, exuberant **10** boisterous, disorderly, uproarious **12** obstreperous

**role**
**03** bit, fat, job **04** duty, lead, part, post, task **05** cameo, place, stead **08** capacity, function, name part, position **09** cameo-part, character, portrayal, situation **11** comprimario **12** principal boy, spear carrier **13** character part, impersonation **14** representation

**roll**
◇ *anagram indicator*
**02** go **03** bap, bun, ren, rin, rob, run, wad **04** bind, boom, bowl, coil, curl, drum, echo, file, flow, fold, furl, list, move, pass, peal, reel, roar, rock, spin, sway, toss, turn, waul, wawl, wind, wrap **05** crush, cycle, dandy, index, level, lurch, pitch, press, spool, start, swell, swing, trill, twirl, twist, wheel, whirl **06** annals, billow, bobbin, census, elapse, enfold, enwrap, gyrate, rafale, record, rental, roller, roster, rotate, rumble, scroll, smooth, tumble, volley, volume, volute, wallow, wander, welter **07** envelop, flatten, go round, grumble,

notitia, reeling, resound, revolve, rocking, rouleau, stagger, swagger, terrier, thunder, tossing, trindle, trundle **08** crescent, cylinder, gyration, pitching, register, rotation, schedule, undulate **09** billowing, catalogue, chronicle, directory, inventory, press down, resonance, turn round **10** muster-file, revolution, undulation **11** reverberate **13** reverberation

*See also* **bread**

**• roll in**

**04** come **06** appear, arrive, blow in, come in, flow in, pour in, rush in, show up, turn up **07** flood in **09** be present **10** be received

**• rolling in it**

**04** rich **05** flush **06** loaded **07** moneyed, wealthy, well-off **08** affluent, well-to-do **10** filthy rich, in the money, prosperous, well-heeled **11** made of money **12** stinking rich **15** with money to burn

**• roll up**

**04** furl **06** arrive, gather **07** convene **08** assemble **10** congregate, intervolve

**roller**

**02** RR **07** trundle **10** Rolls-Royce®

**rollicking**

◇ *anagram indicator*

**05** merry, noisy **06** banzai, frisky, hearty, jaunty, jovial, joyous, lively, rebuke, rocket **07** censure, chiding, lecture, playful, reproof, romping **08** berating, carefree, harangue, reproach, roisting, scolding, spirited, sportive **09** cavorting, exuberant, reprimand, sprightly, talking-to **10** boisterous, frolicsome, rip-roaring, roisterous, telling-off, upbraiding **12** devil-may-care, dressing-down, light-hearted **13** swashbuckling

**rolling**

◇ *anagram indicator*

**06** goggle, waving **07** heaving, surging **08** rippling, undulant **10** undulating, volutation

**roll-on roll-off**

**04** ro-ro

**roly-poly**

**03** fat **05** buxom, plump, podgy, pudgy, round, tubby **06** barrel, chubby, rotund **07** rounded **10** butterball, overweight

**Roman**

*Roman emperors:*

**03** Leo
**04** Geta, Nero, Otho, Zeno
**05** Carus, Gaius, Galba, Nerva, Titus
**06** Avitus, Decius, Gallus, Julian, Philip, Probus, Trajan, Valens
**07** Carinus, Florian, Gordian, Gratian, Hadrian, Marcian, Maximin, Maximus, Severus, Tacitus
**08** Aemilian, Arcadius, Augustus, Aurelian, Balbinus, Caligula, Claudius, Commodus, Constans, Domitian, Galerius, Honorius, Licinius, Macrinus, Majorian, Maximian, Numerian, Olybrius, Pertinax, Tiberius, Valerian
**09** Anthemius, Caracalla, Gallienus, Hostilian, Maxentius, Procopius, Vespasian, Vitellius
**10** Diocletian, Elagabalus, Magnentius, Quintillus, Theodosius
**11** Constantine, Constantius, Julius Nepos, Lucius Verus, Valentinian
**13** Antoninus Pius, Libius Severus
**14** Didius Julianus, Marcus Aurelius
**15** Romulus Augustus
**16** Alexander Severus, Petronius Maximus, Septemius Severus

*Roman kings:*

**07** Romulus
**12** Ancus Marcius
**13** Numa Pompilius
**14** Servius Tullius
**15** Tullus Hostilius
**17** Tarquinius Priscus
**18** Tarquinius Superbus

*Romans include:*

**04** **Cato, Livy, Ovid**
**05** **Lucan, Pliny**
**06** **Antony** (Mark), **Brutus, Cicero** (Marcus Tullius), **Horace, Pilate** (Pontius), **Pompey, Seneca, Vergil, Virgil**
**07** **Atticus** (Titus Pomponius), **Cassius, Juvenal, Martial, Plautus** (Titus Maccius), **Roscius, Tacitus, Terence**
**08** **Agricola** (Gnaeus Julius), **Catilina** (Lucius Sergius), **Catiline, Catullus** (Gaius Valerius), **Claudian, Gracchus** (Tiberius Sempronius), **Lucretia**
**09** **Agrippina, Lucretius, Spartacus, Suetonius**
**10** **Coriolanus** (Gaius), **Quintilian**
**14** **Marcus Antonius**

*See also* **god, goddess; mythology; numeral**

**romance**

**03** lie, see, woo **04** date, gest, tale **05** amour, charm, chase, court, fling, geste, idyll, novel, story, thing **06** affair, colour, legend, whimsy **07** crusade, fantasy, fiction, glamour, liaison, mystery, passion, Romanic, romaunt **08** intrigue **09** adventure, fairytale, fantasize, go out with, love story, melodrama, overstate, sentiment **10** attachment, exaggerate, excitement, fairy story, love affair **11** fascination **12** bodice-ripper, go steady with, relationship **15** romantic fiction

**Romania**

**02** RO **03** ROU

**romantic**

**04** fond, wild **05** soppy **06** dreamy, Gothic, loving, sloppy, tender **07** amorous, dreamer, idyllic, utopian **08** exciting, fanciful, idealist, quixotic, stardust, unlikely **09** fairytale, fantastic, imaginary, legendary, visionary **10** fictitious, idealistic, improbable, lovey-dovey, mysterious, optimistic, passionate, starry-eyed **11** extravagant, fascinating, impractical, sentimental, unrealistic **14** sentimentalist

**romantically**

**06** fondly **08** lovingly, tenderly **09** amorously **10** excitingly, fancifully **12** mysteriously, passionately **13** extravagantly, impractically, sentimentally **14** idealistically, optimistically **15** unrealistically

**Rome** *see* **hill**

**Romeo**

**01** R **05** lover **06** gigolo **07** Don Juan **08** Casanova, Lothario **09** ladies' man **10** lady-killer

**romp**

**03** rig **04** lark, play, ramp, skip **05** caper, frisk, hempy, revel, sport, spree **06** cavort, frolic, gambol, hoiden, hoyden, tomboy **07** roister, rollick

**rondo**

**04** rota

**roof**

**05** vault **06** canopy **07** ceiling, rigging, shelter **08** covering, dwelling **11** culmination

*Roof types include:*

**03** hip
**04** bell, dome, flat, helm, ogee, span
**05** gable
**06** cupola, French, lean-to, saddle
**07** gambrel, mansard, monitor, pitched
**08** flat roof, imperial, pavilion, sawtooth, thatched
**09** onion dome
**10** imbricated, saucer dome
**12** geodesic dome, sloped turret
**13** conical broach
**14** gable-and-valley, pendentive dome

**• hit the roof**

**05** go mad **06** blow up, see red **07** explode **08** boil over, freak out **09** do your nut **11** blow your top, flip your lid, go up the wall, lose your rag **12** blow your cool, lose your cool **15** fly off the handle, go off the deep end

**roof-gutter**

**04** roan, rone **05** rhone **08** roanpipe, ronepipe

**rook**

**01** R **02** do **03** con **04** bilk, crow **05** cheat, squab, sting **06** castle, diddle, fleece, rip off **07** defraud, swindle **09** card-sharp, gold-brick, simpleton **10** overcharge **12** take for a ride

**room**

**02** rm **03** ben, but, end, oda **04** area, seat **05** range, scope, space, stead **06** chance, extent, leeway, margin, volume **07** expanse, legroom **08** capacity, headroom, latitude, occasion **09** allowance, elbow-room **10** Lebensraum **11** appointment, compartment, opportunity

*Rooms include:*

**02** WC
**03** bed, box, day, den, loo
**04** ante, bath, cell, dark, hall, loft, play, rest, sick, tack, wash, work
**05** attic, board, cabin, class, cloak, court, foyer, front, games, green, guard, guest, lobby, music, porch, salon, spare, staff, state, stock, store, study
**06** cellar, common, dining, engine, family, larder, living, locker, lounge, lumber, office, pantry, rumpus, saddle, strong, studio, toilet
**07** boudoir, buttery, chamber, control, cubicle, drawing, fitting, kitchen, landing, laundry, lecture, library, meeting, morning, nursery, parlour, reading, seminar, sitting, smoking, utility, waiting
**08** assembly, basement, chambers, changing, dressing, lavatory, scullery, workshop
**09** breakfast, dormitory, mezzanine, reception, sun lounge
**10** consulting, laboratory, recreation
**11** kitchenette, lounge-diner
**12** conservatory, kitchen-diner
**15** en suite bathroom

**• have room for**
**04** stow

**roomy**
**04** wide **05** ample, broad, large, rangy **07** sizable **08** generous, sizeable, spacious **09** capacious, extensive **10** commodious, voluminous

**root**
**03** fix, nub, rad, set, tap, yam **04** axis, base, core, germ, grub, hail, home, moor, more, pull, seat, seed, spur, stem **05** basis, cause, cheer, embed, fount, heart, radix, shout, stick, tuber **06** anchor, bottom, etymon, family, fasten, ground, kernel, nuzzle, origin, radish, reason, sinker, source **07** applaud, calamus, cheer on, essence, ginseng, implant, nucleus, origins, parsnep, parsnip, radical, radicle, rhizome, rummage, snuzzle, support, turbith, turpeth, vetiver **08** entrench, heritage, radicate, scammony **09** beginning, encourage, establish, principle **10** background, beginnings, birthplace, derivation, foundation **11** fundamental **12** fountainhead, sarsaparilla **13** starting point
**• put down roots**
**09** set up home **10** settle down **12** make your home
**• root and branch**
**06** wholly **07** finally, totally, utterly **08** complete, entirely, thorough **09** radically **10** completely, thoroughly
**• root around**
**03** dig, pry **04** hunt, nose, poke **05** delve **06** burrow, ferret, forage **07** rummage
**• root out**
**06** dig out, remove, uproot **07** abolish, destroy, outweed, uncover, unearth **08** discover, get rid of **09** clear away, eliminate, eradicate, extirpate **10** put an end to **11** exterminate
**• take root**
**08** take hold **11** become fixed **15** establish itself

**rooted**
**04** deep, felt, firm **05** fixed, rigid **06** deeply **07** radical **08** radicate **09** confirmed, ingrained, radicated **10** deep-seated, entrenched **11** established

**rootless**
**04** free **06** moving **07** nomadic **08** carefree, drifting, floating, homeless **09** itinerant, transient, unsettled, wandering **14** of no fixed abode

**rootstock**
**04** race **05** orris

**rope**
**03** tie **04** bind, jeff, lash, moor, stay **05** hitch, lasso **06** fasten

*Rope types include:*

**03** guy, tow
**04** cord, drag, fall, head, line, seal, stay, tack, vang, warp
**05** brace, cable, lasso, noose, widdy
**06** bridle, halter, hawser, hobble, lariat, runner, strand, string, tackle, tether
**07** bobstay, bowline, cordage, cringle, halyard, lanyard, lashing, marline, mooring, outhaul, painter, ratline
**08** buntline, clew-line, dockline, downhaul, dragline, gantline
**09** hackamore

**• know the ropes**
**05** learn **06** master **12** know the drill, know the score **13** know what's what
**• rope in**
**06** engage, enlist **07** involve **08** inveigle, persuade, talk into

**ropy, ropey**
**04** duff, poor **05** rough **06** unwell **07** stringy **08** below par, inferior **09** deficient, glutinous, off colour **10** inadequate **11** substandard **14** not up to scratch, unsatisfactory

**rose**
**03** riz **04** geum, Jack, moss **05** avens, brere, briar, brier **07** Bourbon, monthly, paragon, rosette **08** noisette, primrose **09** crampbark, eglantine, perpetual, remontant **10** erysipelas, floribunda, water elder **12** snowball tree **13** cranberry bush, cranberry tree
**• rose fruit**
**03** hep, hip

**rosette**
**04** chou, rose **06** rosace, rosula **07** cockade **13** wedding favour **14** provincial rose

**rosin**
**05** resin, roset, rosit, rozet, rozit **09** colophony

**roster**
**04** list, roll, rota **05** index **07** listing **08** register, schedule **09** directory

**rostrum**
**04** beak, bema, dais **05** stage **06** podium **08** platform

**rosy**
**03** red **04** pink, rose **05** fresh, ruddy, sunny **06** bright, florid **07** auroral, flushed, glowing, hopeful, reddish, roseate, rose-red **08** aurorean, blooming, blushing, cheerful, inflamed, rose-hued, roselike, rose-pink, rubicund **09** bloodshot, promising **10** auspicious, favourable, optimistic, reassuring **11** encouraging, rose-scented **12** rose-coloured **14** healthy-looking

**rot**
◇ *anagram indicator*
**03** rat, ret **04** blah, bosh, bunk, halt, joke, rait, rate, rust, tosh **05** decay, go bad, go off, hooey, mould, spoil, taint, tease **06** bluing, bunkum, drivel, fester, go sour, humbug, kibosh, kybosh, perish, piffle **07** baloney, blueing, corrode, corrupt, crumble, garbage, hogwash, putrefy, rhubarb, rubbish **08** claptrap, cobblers, collapse, malarkey, Merulius, nonsense **09** corrosion, decompose, moonshine, poppycock **10** codswallop, corruption, degenerate **11** deteriorate **12** disintegrate, putrefaction **13** decomposition, deterioration **14** disintegration

**rota**
**04** list, roll **05** canon, index, rondo, round **06** course, roster **07** listing, routine **08** register, schedule **09** directory

**rotary**
**07** turning **08** gyrating, gyratory, rotating, spinning, whirling **09** revolving **10** roundabout

**rotate**
◇ *reversal indicator*
**04** reel, roll, spin, turn **05** pivot, rabat, whirl **06** gyrate, swivel **07** go round, rabatte, revolve, twiddle **09** alternate, move round, spin round, turn about, turn round **10** change face **11** interchange, reciprocate, take in turns **13** take it in turns

**rotation**
**04** spin, turn **05** cycle, orbit, round, whirl **06** swivel **07** turning **08** gyration, sequence, spinning, whirling **10** revolution, succession, swivelling **11** alternation

**rote**
**• learn by rote**
**08** memorize **11** learn off pat **14** commit to memory **15** learn from memory, learn off by heart

**rotten**
◇ *anagram indicator*
**03** bad, ill, off, rat **04** evil, foul, mean, poor, poxy, punk, rank, ropy, sick, sour **05** awful, dirty, fetid, lousy, manky, nasty, putid, ropey, rough **06** addled, bloody, crummy, damned, darned,

dashed, foetid, grotty, guilty, mouldy, poorly, putrid, spoilt, unwell, wicked **07** beastly, blasted, corrupt, decayed, flaming, gone off, immoral, rotting, tainted, unsound **08** blinking, blooming, decaying, dratting, dreadful, flipping, horrible, inferior, infernal, low-grade, stinking, terrible, wretched **09** dishonest, off colour, putrefied **10** confounded, decomposed, despicable, inadequate, mouldering, putrescent, unpleasant **12** contemptible, unprincipled **13** dishonourable **14** disintegrating

## rotter

**03** cad, cur, pig, rat **04** fink, heel **05** beast, louse, rogue, swine **07** bounder, dastard, stinker **08** blighter **09** scoundrel **10** blackguard

## rotund

**03** fat **04** full, rich **05** heavy, obese, plump, podgy, round, stout, tubby **06** chubby, fleshy, portly **07** bulbous, orotund, rounded, spheral, spheric **08** globular, resonant, roly-poly, sonorous **09** corpulent, orbicular, rotundate, spherical, spherular **10** impressive **12** magniloquent **13** grandiloquent

## roué

**04** rake **06** lecher, wanton **08** rakehell **09** debauchee, libertine **10** profligate, sensualist

## rough

◇ *anagram indicator*

**03** ill, ned, row, yob **04** curt, hard, hazy, rude, sick, thug, wild **05** asper, basic, blunt, bully, bumpy, crude, cruel, dirty, draft, gruff, gurly, hairy, harsh, hasty, husky, lousy, lumpy, model, nasty, noisy, plain, quick, raggy, raspy, rocky, rowdy, ruggy, rusty, scaly, sharp, stern, stony, tough, tousy, touzy, towsy, towzy, vague, yobbo **06** brutal, choppy, coarse, craggy, grotty, hoarse, jagged, lively, mock-up, poorly, raucle, rotten, ruffle, rugged, severe, shaggy, sketch, stormy, uneven, unkind, unwell, vulgar **07** bristly, bruiser, brusque, brutish, cursory, drastic, extreme, general, gnarled, grained, hirsute, inexact, of a sort, of sorts, outline, prickly, rasping, raucous, ruffian, sketchy, throaty, unkempt, unshorn, violent **08** agitated, aspirate, below par, croaking, forceful, gravelly, guttural, hooligan, impolite, muricate, scabrous, scratchy, strident, unbroken, ungentle, unshaven **09** difficult, energetic, estimated, harrowing, imprecise, iron-sided, irregular, merciless, muricated, off colour, primitive, roughneck, turbulent, unfeeling, unhealthy, unrefined **10** aggressive, astringent, boisterous, broadbrush, discordant, disorderly, hard-handed, incomplete, unfinished, unpleasant, unpolished **11** approximate, belligerent, insensitive, ramgunshoch, rudimentary, tempestuous, uncivilized **12** tiger country, unelaborated **15** under the weather

### • rough out

**05** draft **06** mock up, sketch **07** outline **11** draw in rough **14** give a summary of

### • rough up

**03** mug **04** bash, do in **06** beat up **08** maltreat, mistreat **09** manhandle **10** knock about

## rough-and-ready

**05** basic, crude, plain **06** bodgie, make-do, simple **07** hurried, sketchy, stop-gap **09** makeshift, unrefined **10** unpolished **11** approximate, provisional

## rough-and-tumble

**05** brawl, fight, mêlée, scrap **06** affray, dust-up, fracas, rumpus **07** punch-up, scuffle **08** struggle

## roughen

◇ *anagram indicator*

**04** chap, hack, rasp, stab **05** chafe, graze, rough, scuff, spray **06** abrade, ruffle **07** coarsen, harshen, spreaze, spreeze **08** asperate, spreathe, spreethe, unsmooth **09** granulate

## roughly

◇ *anagram indicator*

**01** c **02** ca **03** cir **04** circ **05** about, circa **06** around, nearly, wildly **07** close to, cruelly, harshly, loosely, noisily, rowdily, toughly **08** brutally, unkindly **09** just about, not far off, rounded up, violently **10** forcefully, give or take, more or less, round about **11** approaching, mercilessly, rounded down **12** boisterously **13** approximately, energetically, insensitively, in the region of, or thereabouts, something like **14** in round figures, in round numbers **15** in the vicinity of

## roughneck

**04** lout, thug **05** rough, rowdy, tough, yobbo **06** keelie **07** bruiser, ruffian **08** bully boy, hooligan, larrikin

## roulade

**03** run **05** trill

## round

◇ *anagram indicator*

◇ *containment indicator*

◇ *reversal indicator*

**01** O **03** fat, lap, orb **04** ball, band, beat, bend, bout, coil, disc, disk, full, game, heat, hoop, past, path, ring, rota, tour, walk **05** about, ample, cycle, flank, globe, globy, level, plump, rough, route, scope, skirt, stage, stout **06** around, beyond, bypass, candid, chubby, circle, course, curved, honest, patrol, period, portly, rotund, series, sphere, sphery **07** all over, circlet, circuit, discoid, globate, go round, rounded, routine, session, whisper **08** circular, cylinder, disclike, framed by, globular, hooplike, milk-walk, move past, sequence, sonorous, spheroid, to and fro, vigorous **09** corpulent, discoidal, enclosing, estimated, finish off, full-orbed, globelike, imprecise, orbicular, spherical, unsparing **10** ball-shaped, disc-shaped, encircling, enveloping, everywhere, indirectly, on all sides, ring-shaped, succession, throughout, to all parts **11** approximate, cylindrical, on every side, plain-spoken, surrounding, travel round, unqualified **12** circuitously, encompassing, everywhere in, here and there, on all sides of, to all parts of **13** on every side of **15** in all directions

### • round about

**01** c **02** ca **03** cir **04** circ **05** about, circa **06** around, nearly **07** close to, loosely, roughly **09** just about, not far off, rounded up **10** give or take, more or less **11** approaching, rounded down **13** approximately, in the region of, or thereabouts, something like **14** in round numbers **15** in the vicinity of

### • round off

**03** cap, end **04** turn **05** close, crown **06** finish, parcel, top off **08** complete, conclude **09** finish off

### • round on

**05** abuse **06** attack, turn on **07** lay into, set upon

### • round up

**04** herd **05** group, rally **06** gather, muster **07** collect, marshal **08** assemble **13** bring together

## roundabout

**05** plump **06** rotary **07** devious, evasive, oblique, waltzer, winding **08** indirect, tortuous, twisting **10** circuitous, meandering **12** merry-go-round, periphrastic **13** traffic circle **14** circumlocutory **15** circumambagious

## roundly

**06** openly **07** bluntly, frankly, sharply **08** fiercely, severely **09** intensely, violently **10** completely, forcefully, rigorously, thoroughly, vehemently **11** outspokenly

## round-up

**05** rally, rodeo **06** muster, précis, survey **07** herding, summary **08** assembly, overview **09** collation, gathering **10** collection **11** marshalling **14** bang-tail muster

## rouse

◇ *anagram indicator*

**04** call, fire, firk, move, rear, send, stir, wake, yerk **05** abray, amove, anger, awake, evoke, flush, get up, impel, raise, roust, set up, shake, start, steer, stire, styre, unbed, waken **06** abrade, abraid, arouse, awaken, bumper, call up, excite, incite, induce, kindle, ruffle, stir up, summon, turn on, wake up, whip up, work up **07** agitate, disturb, inflame, knock up, provoke, shake up **08** carousal, enkindle, irritate, reveille **09** galvanize, instigate, look alive, stimulate, suscitate

## rousing

**05** brisk, great **06** lively, moving **07** beating, violent, wakeful

**08** exciting, spirited, stirring, vigorous **09** awakening, inspiring **10** incitation **11** stimulating **12** electrifying, exhilarating **13** heart-stirring **14** spirit-stirring

## rout

**04** beat, fuss, grub, herd, lick, pack, riot, roar, rowt **05** brawl, chase, crush, flock, snore **06** bellow, defeat, dispel, flight, grub up, hammer, rabble, thrash, turn up **07** beating, clamour, clobber, conquer, retreat, scatter, trounce, turn out **08** conquest, drubbing, stampede, vanquish **09** discomfit, hurricane, overthrow, shoot down, slaughter, subjugate, thrashing, trouncing **11** disturbance, put to flight, subjugation, walk all over

## route

**03** run, way **04** beat, line, path, road, send, tail, walk **05** round, trail **06** avenue, bypass, convey, course, direct **07** airline, circuit, forward, journey, passage, transit **08** delivery, despatch, dispatch, main line, sideline **09** direction, itinerary, milk round **10** flight path, navigation **11** long paddock **12** wallaby track

## routine

**03** act, run, rut, way, yak **04** dull, rota, wont **05** banal, chain, chore, drill, habit, heigh, ho-hum, lines, order, piece, round, spiel, usage, usual **06** boring, common, custom, groove, method, normal, patter, regime, schtik, shtick, system, wonted **07** formula, heigh-ho, humdrum, jogtrot, milk run, mundane, pattern, schtick, tedious, typical **08** day-to-day, everyday, familiar, habitual, heich-how, ordinary, practice, schedule, standard, tiresome, workaday **09** customary, hackneyed, mechanics, procedure, programme, treadmill, unvarying **10** monotonous, unoriginal **11** journey-work, performance, perfunctory, predictable **12** conventional, run-of-the-mill **13** institutional **14** bread-and-butter

## routinely

**07** usually **08** commonly, normally **09** regularly, typically **10** habitually **11** customarily **14** conventionally

## rove

◇ *anagram indicator*

**04** roam **05** drift, range, stray **06** cruise, ramble, stroll, wander **07** meander, traipse **08** stravaig **09** gallivant, wandering **11** go walkabout

## rover

**05** Gypsy, nomad **06** nomade, pirate, ranger, robber **07** drifter, rambler, seacock, vagrant **08** gadabout, wanderer **09** itinerant, transient, traveller **10** stravaiger

## row

**03** din, oar, rag **04** bank, deen, file, line, pull, rank, roll, tier, tiff **05** argue, brawl, chain, fight, noise, queue, rammy, range, rough, scold, scrap, set-to **06** assail, bicker, column, dust-up, fracas, hubbub, racket, rumpus, series, shindy, splore, string, stroke, tumult, uproar **07** bobbery, clamour, dispute, quarrel, ruction, shindig, wrangle **08** argument, conflict, rebuking, remigate, scolding, sequence, squabble **09** commotion **10** falling-out **11** altercation, arrangement, controversy, disturbance **12** disagreement **13** slanging match

### • in a row

**04** arew, arow **06** in turn, serial **09** on the trot **10** back to back **12** continuously, sequentially, successively **13** consecutively **15** uninterruptedly

## rowan

**04** sorb

## rowdy

**03** yob **04** loud, lout, wild **05** money, noisy, rorty, rough, tough, yahoo, yobbo **06** apache, blowsy, blowzy, keelie, unruly **07** brawler, hoodlum, lawless, riotous, ruffian, stroppy **08** hooligan, larrikin, tearaway **09** bovver boy **10** boisterous, brat packer, disorderly **12** obstreperous, unrestrained

## rower

**03** oar **06** stroke **07** oarsman, sculler **09** oarswoman, stroke oar

## rowing

*Rowing-related terms include:*

- **03** bow, cox, rig
- **04** crew, easy, four, gate, keel, loom, pair, quad, rate, skeg, span, wash
- **05** blade, catch, coxed, drive, eight, pitch, scull, shell, stern
- **06** boatie, button, collar, gunnel, length, puddle, rating, rigger, skying, stroke
- **07** bowside, coxless, gunwale, regatta, row over, sculler
- **08** coxswain, paddling, rowlocks
- **09** ergometer, head races, outrigger, slide seat, stretcher
- **10** catch a crab, feathering, pivot point, strokeside
- **11** double scull, single scull, the Boat Race
- **13** getting spoons
- **15** jumping the slide

### • rowing boat

**04** four, pair **05** eight

## royal

**04** king, real, rial, ryal **05** grand, queen, regal **06** august, kingly, prince, regius, superb **07** queenly, stately **08** imperial, imposing, kinglike, majestic, princely, princess, splendid **09** basilical, queenlike, sovereign **10** impressive **11** magnificent, monarchical

## royally

**07** grandly, greatly **08** superbly **10** splendidly **11** wonderfully **12** impressively, tremendously **13** magnificently

## royalty

**08** residual

## rub

◇ *anagram indicator*

**03** dub, pat, rob, wax **04** buff, faze, fret, snag, soap, wipe **05** apply, catch, chafe, clean, curry, emery, grate, grind, hitch, knead, pinch, put on, rosin, scour, scrub, shine, smear, stone, towel **06** abrade, buff up, caress, fondle, fridge, impede, liquor, nuzzle, polish, rubber, scrape, smooth, spread, stroke, work in **07** burnish, flannel, furbish, massage, problem, rub-down, scratch, snuzzle, trouble **08** drawback, irritate, kneading, obstacle, soft-soap **09** embrocate, hindrance, triturate **10** difficulty, impediment

### • rub along

**04** cope **05** get by, get on **06** manage **08** get along

### • rub down

**03** dry **04** wash, wisp **05** clean, curry **06** smooth, sponge **07** massage **08** wash down

### • rub in

**06** harp on, stress **08** insist on **09** emphasize, highlight, underline **10** make much of

### • rub off on

**05** alter **06** affect, change **09** influence, transform **14** have an effect on

### • rub out

**04** do in, kill **05** erase **06** cancel, delete, efface, murder **07** bump off **09** eliminate, finish off, liquidate **10** do away with, obliterate, put to death **11** assassinate

### • rub up the wrong way

**03** bug, get, irk, vex **05** anger, annoy, get to, peeve **06** needle, niggle, wind up **08** irritate **11** get your goat **13** get up your nose

## rubber

*Rubber types and trees include:*

- **03** ule
- **04** buna, cold, foam, hard, hule, pará, root
- **05** butyl, crêpe, hevea, India, Lagos, sorbo
- **06** sponge
- **07** ebonite, guayule, seringa
- **08** Funtumia, neoprene, Silastic®
- **09** camelback, vulcanite
- **10** caoutchouc, gum elastic, mangabeira
- **14** high-hysteresis

## rubberneck

**04** gape, gawk, gawp, view **05** stare, watch **06** goggle, look at **07** tourist

## rubbish

◇ *anagram indicator*

**03** red, rot, tat **04** blah, bosh, bull, bunk, cack, crap, dirt, gash, grot, guff, junk, kack, mush, redd, tosh **05** balls, bilge, brock, chaff, culch, dreck, dross, garbo, hokum, hooey, pants, scrap, stuff, trade, trash, tripe, truck, waste **06** bunkum, cultch, debris, drivel, litter,

piffle, raffle, refuse, rubble **07** baloney, eyewash, garbage, gubbins, hogwash, mullock, rhubarb, twaddle
**08** bulldust, claptrap, cobblers, detritus, malarkey, nonsense, riff-raff, tommyrot, trashery, trumpery **09** bull's wool, gibberish, moonshine, mouthwash, poppycock, sweepings
**10** balderdash, clamjamfry, codswallop, excrementa, tomfoolery
**11** clanjamfray **12** clamjamphrie, gobbledegook, gobbledygook

### rubbish heap
**03** tip **04** coup, cowp, dump, toom
**06** midden **08** laystall **09** scrapheap
**13** kitchen midden

### rubbishy
**05** cheap, junky, petty, tatty, tripy
**06** cruddy, crummy, grotty, paltry, shoddy, tawdry, tinpot, trashy, tripey
**08** gimcrack, inferior, riff-raff **09** third-rate, throw-away, valueless, worthless
**10** low-quality, second-rate
**14** unsatisfactory

### rubble
**04** muck **05** ruins, waste, wreck
**06** debris **07** moellon, remains, rubbish **08** hard core, wreckage
**09** fragments

### rubidium
**02** Rb

### ruby
**05** agate, balas, blood **06** redden
**09** starstone **12** pigeon's-blood

### ruction
**03** din, row **04** fuss, rout, to-do
**05** brawl, noise, scrap, storm **06** fracas, racket, ruffle, rumpus, uproar **07** carry-on, dispute, protest, quarrel, rookery, trouble **09** commotion, hue and cry, kerfuffle **11** altercation, disturbance

### ruddy
**03** red **04** rosy **05** fresh **06** bloody, blowsy, blowzy, bright, cherry, darned, dashed, florid, rubric **07** blasted, crimson, flushed, glowing, healthy, reddish, rubious, scarlet **08** annoying, blooming, blushing, flipping, infernal, rubicund, sanguine, sunburnt
**10** confounded **11** carnationed, flammulated **12** apple-cheeked, high-coloured

### rude
◇ *anagram indicator*
**04** blue, curt, lewd **05** basic, bawdy, crude, dirty, gross, harsh, nasty, rough, sharp, short **06** abrupt, cheeky, coarse, filthy, ribald, risqué, robust, rugged, simple, smutty, sudden, vulgar
**07** abusive, bestial, boorish, brusque, ill-bred, naughty, obscene, peasant, uncivil, uncouth, violent **08** barbaric, churlish, ignorant, impolite, improper, impudent, indecent, insolent
**09** barbarian, giant rude, goustrous, insulting, makeshift, offensive, primitive, salacious, startling, unrefined, unskilled, untutored, unwrought **10** heathenish, illiterate, indelicate, uncultured, uneducated, unexpected, unpleasant, unpolished
**11** bad-mannered, bad-tempered, ill-mannered, impertinent, near the bone, rudimentary, uncivilized, undeveloped
**12** disagreeable, discourteous
**13** disrespectful, rough-and-ready
**14** near the knuckle

### rudely
**06** curtly **07** harshly **08** abruptly, suddenly **09** abusively, brusquely
**10** impolitely, impudently, insolently
**12** disagreeably, unexpectedly, unpleasantly **14** discourteously
**15** disrespectfully

### rudeness
**05** abuse **09** barbarism, Gothicism, impudence, insolence, rusticity **10** bad manners, disrespect, ill manners, incivility **11** discourtesy, grossièreté, uncouthness **12** impertinence, impoliteness **14** unpleasantness

### rudimentary
**03** pro- **05** basic, crude, rough
**06** simple **07** initial, primary, reduced, seminal **08** inchoate **09** embryonic, embryotic, essential, imperfect, makeshift, primitive, remaining, surviving, vestigial **10** elementary, incomplete, primordial
**11** abecedarian, fundamental, undeveloped **12** functionless, introductory **13** rough-and-ready
**15** unsophisticated

### rudiments
**03** ABC **05** abcee, absey **06** basics
**08** elements **10** beginnings, essentials, principles **11** foundations
**12** fundamentals **15** first principles

### rue
**03** rew **04** pity, Ruta **05** mourn
**06** bemoan, bewail, grieve, lament, regret, repent, sorrow **07** be sorry, deplore, harmala **09** herb-grace
**10** repentance, thalictrum **11** be regretful, herb-of-grace **14** feel remorse for

### rueful
**03** sad **05** sorry **06** dismal, woeful
**07** doleful, piteous, pitiful **08** contrite, grievous, mournful, penitent, pitiable
**09** plaintive, regretful, repentant, sorrowful, woebegone **10** apologetic, deplorable, lugubrious, melancholy, remorseful **15** self-reproachful

### ruff
**03** ree **04** band, pope, slam **05** frill, reeve, rough, trump **06** fraise, ruffle, tippet **07** applaud, elation, partlet
**08** applause **09** blackfish
**10** excitement

### ruffian
**03** ned, yob **04** hoon, lout, thug
**05** brute, bully, rogue, rough, rowdy, tough, yobbo **06** Apache, brutal, rascal, thuggo, toerag **07** bruiser, hoodlum, sweater, villain, violent
**08** bully-boy, hooligan, larrikin, plug-ugly **09** bovver boy, bully-rook, cut-throat, desperado, lager lout, miscreant, roughneck, ruffianly, scoundrel **10** highbinder **11** trailbaston

### ruffle
◇ *anagram indicator*
**03** bug, irk, vex **04** fold, line, rile, ruff, tuck **05** anger, annoy, frill, pleat, rough, rouse, upset **06** bustle, crease, fringe, furrow, gather, hassle, nettle, pucker, put out, rattle, ripple, rumple, snatch, tangle, tousle, tumult, wind up
**07** agitate, bluster, confuse, crinkle, crumple, falbala, flounce, fluster, flutter, perturb, quarrel, swagger, trouble, valance, wrinkle **08** brass off, dishevel, disorder, irritate, struggle, trimming **09** aggravate, agitation, annoyance, cheese off, drive nuts, encounter, pantalets **10** disarrange, discompose, drive crazy, exasperate
**11** pantalettes **12** drive bananas
**13** make sparks fly **14** drive up the wall

### rug
**03** mat, rya, tug, wig **04** felt, haul, kali, snug **05** kelim, kilim, pilch, share, throw **06** carpet, khilim, Kirman, numdah, secure, toupee, toupet
**07** bergama, doormat, flokati, matting
**08** bergamot, covering, underlay
**09** hairpiece, prayer mat, underfelt
**11** buffalo robe **13** floor-covering, Persian carpet

*See also* **carpet**

### rugby
**02** RL, RU

*Rugby League teams and nicknames include:*

**04** Eels, Reds
**05** Bears, Bulls, Kiwis, Lions, Storm
**06** Eagles, Giants, Hull FC, Kumuls, Rhinos, Sharks, Tigers, Wolves
**07** Blue Sox, Broncos, Cowboys, Dragons, Knights, Raiders
**08** Bulldogs, Panthers, Roosters, Warriors, Wildcats
**09** Kangaroos, Rabbitohs, Tomahawks
**10** Lionhearts
**11** Bravehearts, Leeds Rhinos, St Helens RFC
**13** Bradford Bulls, London Broncos, Widnes Vikings, Wigan Warriors
**15** Irish Wolfhounds, Leigh Centurions, Les Chanticleers, Salford City Reds

*Rugby League-related terms include:*

**02** RL
**03** try
**04** back, feed, lock, pack, prop, punt
**05** dummy, put-in, scrum
**06** centre, hooker, in-goal, tackle, winger
**07** dropout, forward, hand-off, knock on, offload, offside, penalty, try line
**08** blood bin, drop goal, free-kick, front row, full-back, gain line, goal line, half-back, handover, open side, scissors, sidestep, stand-off, turnover
**09** blind side, dummy half, field goal,

place kick, scrum-half
**10** charge down, conversion, five-eighth, penalty try, up and under, zero tackle
**11** forward pass, grubber kick, play-the-ball, sixth tackle, touch-in-goal
**12** dead-ball line, loose forward, three-quarter
**13** loose-head prop
**14** acting half-back
**15** twenty-metre line

*Rugby players include:*

**03** **Fox** (Neil)
**04** **Hare** (William Henry 'Dusty'), **Hill** (Richard), **John** (Barry), **Lomu** (Jonah), **Sole** (David), **Tait** (Alan), **Wood** (Keith)
**05** **Batty** (Grant), **Bevan** (Brian), **Botha** (Naas), **Ellis** (William Webb), **Lydon** (Joe), **Meads** (Colin), **Price** (Graham), **Rives** (Jean-Pierre), **Sella** (Philippe)
**06** **Andrew** (Rob), **Blanco** (Serge), **Boston** (Billy), **Brooke** (Zinzan), **Calder** (Finlay), **Cotton** (Fran), **Craven** (Danie), **Davies** (Jonathan), **Gibson** (Mike), **Irvine** (Andy), **Kirwan** (John)
**07** **Bennett** (Phil), **Campese** (David), **Carling** (Will), **Duckham** (David), **Edwards** (Gareth Owen), **Edwards** (Shaun), **Farrell** (Andy), **Gregory** (Andy), **Guscott** (Jeremy), **Jenkins** (Neil), **Laidlaw** (Roy), **McBride** (Willie John), **Meninga** (Mal), **O'Reilly** (Tony)
**08** **Beaumont** (Bill), **Hastings** (Gavin), **Millward** (Roger), **Scotland** (Ken), **Slattery** (Fergus), **Sullivan** (Jim), **Williams** (John Peter Rhys 'JPR'), **Williams** (John 'JJ'), **Woodward** (Sir Clive)
**09** **Dallaglio** (Lawrence), **Farr-Jones** (Nick), **McGeechan** (Ian), **Underwood** (Rory), **Wilkinson** (Jonny)
**10** **Rutherford** (John)
**11** **Fitzpatrick** (Sean)
**12** **Starmer-Smith** (Nigel)

*Rugby Union teams and nicknames include:*

**04** Oaks, Reds
**05** Lelos, Lions, Pumas, Wasps
**06** Eagles
**07** Canucks, Dragons
**08** Brumbies, Les Bleus, Los Teros, Saracens, Waratahs
**09** All Blacks, Bath Rugby, Wallabies
**10** Gli Azzurri, Gloucester, Harlequins, Leeds Tykes, Sale Sharks, Springboks
**11** London Irish
**14** Cherry Blossoms
**15** Leicester Tigers

*Rugby Union-related terms include:*

**02** RU
**03** gas, tee, try
**04** back, cite, feed, hack, lock, mark, maul, pack, ping, prop, ruck
**05** clear, drive, dummy, phase, put-in, scrum, touch, wheel
**06** centre, hooker, in-goal, jumper, sevens, tackle, uglies, winger
**07** back row, binding, box kick, dropout, flanker, fly hack, fly-half, forward, hand-off, knock on, lifting, line-out, offload, offside, recycle, restart, try line
**08** blood bin, crossing, drop goal, free-kick, front row, full back, gain line, goal line, half-back, miss move, open side, scissors, scrum cap, set piece, sidestep, standoff, turnover
**09** back three, blind side, breakdown, crash ball, front five, grand slam, place kick, scrum-half, second row, tap tackle, third half, tight five, touchline, twenty-two
**10** charge down, conversion, pack leader, penalty try, tap penalty, touch judge, up and under
**11** cover tackle, forward pass, grubber kick, number eight, outside half, pushover try, ten-man rugby, triple crown, up the jumper, wing forward
**12** dead-ball line, inside centre, loose forward, three-quarter
**13** dummy scissors, loose-head prop, outside centre, tight-head prop
**14** against the head
**15** truck and trailer

## rugged

**04** firm, rude, wild **05** bumpy, burly, hardy, rocky, rough, stark, stony, tough **06** craggy, jagged, knaggy, knotty, robust, shaggy, sinewy, stormy, strong, sturdy, uneven **07** gnarled, uncouth **08** furrowed, muscular, resolute, stalwart, vigorous **09** iron-bound, irregular, tenacious, well-built **10** determined, unwavering **11** unflinching **13** weather-beaten

## ruggedly

**07** rockily, roughly, starkly, toughly **08** strongly, unevenly **10** muscularly, vigorously **11** irregularly

## ruin

◇ *anagram indicator*

**03** mar **04** cook, dish, do in, doom, fall, harm, heap, Hell, loss, raze, sink **05** botch, break, chaos, crash, crush, decay, do for, folly, fordo, havoc, smash, spoil, whelm, wreck **06** banjax, damage, debris, defeat, injure, jigger, mess up, penury, perish, ravage, relics, rubble, traces, unmake **07** carcase, carcass, cripple, destroy, failure, remains, screw up, scupper, scuttle, shatter, subvert, undoing **08** bankrupt, collapse, demolish, detritus, disaster, down-come, downfall, lay waste, remnants, shambles, vestiges, wreckage **09** breakdown, devastate, disrepair, fragments, indigence, overthrow, overwhelm, perdition, ruination, seduction, shipwreck **10** bankruptcy, demolition, impoverish, insolvency, subversion, wreak havoc **11** destruction, devastation **12** do violence to, make bankrupt **13** make insolvent **14** bouleversement, disintegration

**• in ruins**

**04** sunk **06** ruined **07** damaged, ruinate, wrecked **08** decrepit **09** destroyed **10** broken-down, devastated, ramshackle, tumbledown **11** dilapidated **12** falling apart

## ruination

**04** fall **05** decay, havoc **06** damage, defeat **07** failure, undoing **08** collapse, downfall, wreckage **09** breakdown, disrepair, overthrow **11** destruction, devastation **14** disintegration

## ruined

◇ *anagram indicator*

*See* **bankrupt**

## ruinous

**05** waste **06** ruined **07** damaged, decayed, in ruins, wrecked **08** decrepit, tottered **09** crippling, destroyed, excessive, shattered **10** broken-down, calamitous, devastated, disastrous, exorbitant, immoderate, ramshackle **11** cataclysmic, devastating, dilapidated **12** catastrophic, extortionate, unreasonable

## ruinously

**11** excessively **12** exorbitantly, immoderately, unreasonably **14** extortionately

## rule

**01** r **03** law, raj **04** dash, find, form, lead, line, norm, rain, ring, sway, wont **05** axiom, canon, guide, habit, judge, maxim, norma, order, power, raine, reign, sutra, tenet, truth **06** custom, decide, decree, direct, govern, manage, method, regime, rubric, ruling, settle, squier, squire, truism **07** command, conduct, control, dictate, formula, lay down, mastery, ordinar, plummet, precept, prevail, resolve, routine, royalty, statute **08** dominate, dominion, kingship, ordinary, practice, protocol, regulate, standard, thearchy **09** authority, criterion, determine, direction, establish, guideline, gynocracy, hagiarchy, influence, mobocracy, officiate, ordinance, prescript, principle, procedure, pronounce, queenship, supremacy **10** adjudicate, administer, convention, corrective, government, leadership, mastership, ochlocracy, prevalence, regulation **11** be in control, commandment, gubernation, instruction, preside over, restriction, sovereignty, stratocracy, tridominium **12** call the shots, jurisdiction **14** administration

**• as a rule**

**06** mainly **07** usually **08** normally **09** generally, in general, in the main **10** by and large, on the whole, ordinarily **14** for the most part

**• collection of rules**

**03** pie, pye **04** code

**• rule out**
**03** ban **06** forbid, reject **07** dismiss, exclude, prevent **08** disallow, preclude, prohibit **09** eliminate

**ruler**

*Rulers include:*

**03** aga, mir, oba
**04** amir, czar, duce, emir, head, jarl, kaid, khan, king, ksar, lord, meer, naik, raja, rana, rani, ratu, shah, tsar, tzar
**05** begum, mpret, nawab, nizam, queen, rajah, ratoo
**06** atabeg, atabek, caesar, caliph, consul, Führer, gerent, kaiser, leader, mikado, prince, regent, satrap, sheikh, shogun, sultan
**07** czarina, emperor, empress, monarch, pharaoh, sultana, toparch, tsarina, viceroy
**08** governor, maharani, overlord, padishah, princess, suzerain
**09** commander, maharajah, potentate, president, sovereign
**10** controller
**11** gouvernante, head of state
**15** governor-general

*See also* **emperor**; **empress**; **king**; **monarch**; **president**; **prime minister**; **queen**

**ruling**
**04** main **05** chief **06** decree **07** finding, leading, supreme, verdict **08** decision, dominant, in charge, judgment, reigning **09** governing, in control, judgement, principal, sovereign **10** commanding, resolution **11** controlling, on the throne, predominant **12** adjudication **13** pronouncement **15** most influential

**rum**
◇ *anagram indicator*
**03** odd **04** good **05** droll, funny, queer, tafia, weird **06** taffia **07** Bacardi®, bizarre, cachaça, curious, strange, suspect, unusual **08** abnormal, demerara, freakish, peculiar, singular **10** suspicious **13** funny-peculiar

**rumble**
**04** boom, roar, roll **05** grasp, groan **06** lumber, mutter **07** grumble, quarrel, thunder **11** disturbance, reverberate **13** reverberation

**rumbustious**
**04** loud, wild **05** noisy, rough, rowdy **06** robust, unruly, wilful **07** wayward **08** roisting **09** clamorous, exuberant **10** boisterous, disorderly, refractory, roisterous, uproarious **12** obstreperous, unmanageable

**ruminant**
**10** meditative

*Ruminants include:*

**02** ox
**03** cow
**04** goat
**05** camel, sheep
**06** musk ox
**07** giraffe
**08** antelope, cavicorn
**09** pronghorn

*See also* **cattle**; **antelope**

*Stomachs of ruminants include:*

**05** bible, rumen
**06** bonnet, fardel, paunch
**09** king's-hood, manyplies, rennet-bag, reticulum

**ruminate**
**04** muse **05** brood, think **06** ponder **07** reflect **08** chew over, cogitate, consider, meditate, mull over **10** chew the cud, deliberate **11** contemplate

**rummage**
**03** tat **04** fish, hunt, junk, root, stir **05** delve, rifle, touse, touze, towse, towze, wroot **06** ferret, forage, jumble, powter, search **07** examine, explore, fossick, ransack **08** overhaul, turn over, upheaval **09** bric-à-brac, commotion **10** poke around, root around **11** odds and ends **13** search through

**rumour**
**03** cry, say **04** buzz, fame, goss, hint, kite, news, talk, tell, word **05** bruit, noise, on-dit, say-so, sough, story, voice **06** breeze, canard, furphy, gossip, murmur, outcry, renown, report, repute, speech **07** clamour, hearsay, publish, scandal, tidings, whisper **08** put about **09** circulate, grapevine **10** bruit about **11** bruit abroad, fama clamosa, information, noise abroad, scuttlebutt, speculation, underbreath **12** tittle-tattle **13** bush telegraph

**rump**
**03** ass, bum, can **04** butt, coit, dock, duff, prat, rear, seat, tail, tush **05** booty, croup, fanny, nache, natch, podex, quoit, stern, trace **06** behind, bottom, breech, croupe, haunch, heinie **07** keister, remains, remnant, residue, vestige **08** backside, buttocks, derrière, haunches **09** fundament, leftovers, posterior, remainder, uropygium **12** hindquarters

**rumple**
**04** fold **05** crush, touse, touze, towse, towze **06** crease, pucker, ruffle, tousle, tumble **07** crinkle, crumple, derange, scrunch, wrinkle **08** dishevel, disorder

**rumpus**
**03** row **04** fuss, rout **05** brawl, noise **06** fracas, furore, ruckus, shindy, tumult, uproar **07** bagarre, rhubarb, ruction **08** brouhaha **09** commotion, confusion, kerfuffle, shemozzle, shimozzle **10** disruption, schemozzle, shlemozzle **11** disturbance

**run**
◇ *anagram indicator*
**01** r **02** do, go **03** cut, hit, jet, jog, own, pen, ply, ren, rin, rip, set, sty, use, way **04** bolt, call, coop, dart, dash, drip, emit, flee, flow, fold, fuse, gash, goal, go on, gush, hare, have, head, hole, hunt, keep, kind, last, lauf, lead, leak, line, lope, mark, melt, move, need, pass, pour, race, ride, road, roll, romp, rush, show, slip, slit, snag, sort, spew, spin, take, tear, tend, trip, trot, type, work, yard **05** bleed, brush, carry, chain, chase, class, corso, cross, cycle, drive, enter, glide, hurry, incur, issue, jaunt, point, pound, print, range, reach, round, route, scoot, score, shoal, slash, slide, speed, spell, split, spurt, stand, track, trill **06** become, career, chance, charge, convey, course, curdle, demand, direct, elapse, extend, follow, fulfil, gallop, hasten, ladder, manage, outing, period, pierce, schuss, scurry, series, spread, sprint, stream, string, thrust, travel **07** average, be valid, carry on, cascade, clamour, compete, conduct, contend, control, execute, feature, include, journey, operate, oversee, paddock, passage, perform, possess, proceed, promote, publish, revolve, roulade, run away, scamper, scarper, scutter, scuttle, shuttle, smuggle, stretch, trickle, variety **08** be played, be staged, carry out, category, continue, distance, function, maintain, organize, overflow, pressure, progress, regulate, sequence, step on it, traverse **09** be mounted, broadcast, challenge, coagulate, discharge, enclosure, excursion, free use of, give a lift, give a ride, implement, supervise, transport, undertake **10** administer, be in effect, be produced, co-ordinate, flight path, prevalence, succession, take part in **11** be performed, be presented, communicate, opportunity, superintend **12** be in charge of **13** be in control of, be in operation **15** travel regularly

**• in the long run**
**06** at last **08** in the end **10** eventually, ultimately

**• on the run**
**04** free **07** at large, escaped, pursued **08** on the lam **09** at liberty **10** on the loose, unconfined **11** running away **14** trying to escape

**• run across**
**04** meet **07** run into **08** bump into **09** encounter **10** chance upon, come across **12** meet by chance

**• run after**
**04** tail **05** chase **06** follow, pursue

**• run along**
**04** scat **05** be off, leave **06** go away **07** buzz off, scarper **08** clear off, off you go **09** on your way **10** off with you **11** away with you

**• run along the ground**
**04** taxi

**• run away**
**03** cut **04** bolt, bunk, flee, lift, nick **05** avoid, dodge, elope, evade, filch, leave, pinch, scapa, steal **06** beat it, decamp, desert, escape, ignore, pocket, run off, scarpa **07** abscond, make off, neglect, nick off, purloin, scarper, vamoose **08** cheese it, clear off, overlook **09** coast home,

disregard, do a runner, skedaddle, win easily **10** brush aside **11** appropriate, make off with, walk off with **12** win hands down **13** make a run for it **14** shut your eyes to, take no notice of, turn your back on

- **run down**

**03** cut, hit, pan **04** bust, drop, slag, slam, tire, trim **05** knock, slate, weary **06** attack, defame, pooped, reduce, strike, weaken **07** curtail, exhaust, rubbish, run over, slag off, whacked **08** belittle, decrease, denounce, lose time **09** criticize, cut back on, denigrate, disparage, knackered, knock down, knock over **12** pull to pieces, tear to pieces

- **run for it**

**03** fly **04** bolt, flee **05** scram **06** escape **07** do a bunk, make off, retreat, scarper, vamoose **09** skedaddle **11** give leg bail

- **run in**

**03** nab **04** bust, jail, lift, nail, nick **05** pinch **06** arrest, collar, pick up **09** apprehend

- **run into**

**03** hit, ram **04** face, meet **05** crash, equal **06** come to, strike **07** add up to **08** amount to, bump into **09** encounter, run across **10** chance upon, come across, experience **11** collide with **12** meet by chance **13** come up against

- **run off**

**04** bolt, copy **05** elope, print, Xerox® **06** decamp, escape, repeat **07** abscond, make off, produce, recount, run away, scarper **09** duplicate, photocopy, Photostat®, skedaddle

- **run off with**

**04** lift, nick **05** filch, pinch, steal **06** pocket **07** purloin **08** take away **09** elope with **11** appropriate, make off with, run away with, walk off with **12** make away with

- **run on**

**04** go on, last **05** reach **06** extend **07** carry on **08** continue

- **run out**

**02** ro **03** end **04** fail, leak **05** cease, close, dry up **06** elapse, expire, finish **07** exhaust, give out **08** be used up **09** terminate **10** be finished **11** be exhausted

- **run out on**

**04** dump, jilt **05** chuck, ditch, leave **06** desert, maroon, strand **07** abandon, forsake **09** walk out on **15** leave in the lurch

- **run over**

**03** hit **04** flow, heat **05** recap **06** go over, repeat, review, strike, survey **07** run down **08** overflow, practise, rehearse **09** knock down, overthrow, reiterate **10** run through **12** recapitulate

- **run through**

**04** read **05** spend, waste **06** review, survey **07** examine, exhaust, run over **08** practise, rehearse, squander **09** dissipate, go through **11** fritter away, read through

- **run to**

**05** equal, total **06** afford, come to **07** add up to **08** amount to **12** have enough of

- **run together**

**03** mix **04** fuse, join **05** blend, merge, unite **06** concur, mingle **07** combine **08** coalesce **09** commingle **10** amalgamate

**runaway**

**04** wild **05** fugie, loose **06** flight, truant **07** escaped, escapee, escaper, refugee **08** deserter, fugitive **09** absconder **11** loup-the-dyke **12** out of control, uncontrolled

**run-down**

**03** cut, ill **04** drop, weak **05** dingy, peaky, recap, seedy, tired, weary **06** grotty, résumé, review, shabby, sketch, unwell **07** cutback, decline, drained, outline, summary, worn-out **08** analysis, briefing, decrease, decrepit, fatigued, synopsis **09** enervated, exhausted, neglected, reduction, unhealthy **10** broken-down, ramshackle, run-through, tumble-down, uncared-for **11** curtailment, debilitated, dilapidated

**rune**

**03** ash, wen, wyn **04** aesc, wynn

**run-in**

**05** brush, fight, set-to **06** dust-up, tussle **07** dispute, quarrel, wrangle **08** approach, argument, skirmish **11** altercation, contretemps **13** confrontation

**runnel** *see* **brook**

**runner**

**03** ski **04** scud, skid, slip, stem, tout **05** agent, blade, miler, racer, shoot, slide, slipe, sprig **06** bearer, jogger, sprout, stolon **07** athlete, courier, courser, harrier, slipper, tendril **08** fugitive, offshoot, smuggler, sprinter **09** flagellum, lampadist, messenger, racehorse, sarmentum **10** competitor **11** participant **13** dispatch rider

- **do a runner**

**02** go **04** exit, quit **05** scoot **06** decamp, depart, go away, hook it, set out **07** do a bunk, pull out, push off, take off, vamoose **08** clear off, shove off, up sticks **09** disappear, push along **10** make tracks **13** sling your hook, take your leave **15** take French leave

- **runners**

**05** field

**running**

◇ *anagram indicator*

**04** easy **05** hasty **06** charge, in a row, moving, racing **07** conduct, contest, control, current, cursive, flowing, jogging, ongoing, rushing, working **08** constant, unbroken **09** candidacy, ceaseless, direction, incessant, itinerant, on the trot, operation, perpetual, shortlist, sprinting, stampede, unceasing **10** contention, continuous, leadership, management, regulation, successive **11** competition, consecutive, controlling, discharging, functioning, performance, supervision **12** co-ordination, in succession, organization **13** uninterrupted **14** administration **15** superintendency

**runny**

◇ *anagram indicator*

**05** fluid **06** liquid, melted, molten, watery **07** diluted, flowing **09** liquefied

**run-of-the-mill**

**02** OK **04** fair, so-so **06** common, normal **07** average **08** everyday, mediocre, middling, ordinary **09** tolerable **11** bog standard, not up to much **12** unimpressive, unremarkable **13** no great shakes, unexceptional **14** common-or-garden **15** undistinguished

**rupture**

◇ *anagram indicator*

**04** rend, rent, rift, tear **05** break, burst, crack, sever, split **06** breach, bust-up, cut off, divide, hernia, rhexis, schism **07** quarrel **08** breaking, bursting, division, fracture, puncture, scissure, separate **09** amniotomy **10** falling-out, separation **12** disagreement, estrangement

**rural**

**04** hick **06** forane, rustic, sylvan, upland **07** bucolic, country, peasant, predial **08** agrarian, agrestic, mofussil, pastoral, praedial **09** bucolical, uplandish **11** countryside **12** agricultural **13** cracker-barrel

**ruse**

**04** hoax, plan, plot, ploy, sham, wile **05** blind, dodge, stall, trick **06** device, scheme, tactic **08** artifice **09** deception, imposture, manoeuvre, stratagem **10** subterfuge

**rush**

**03** fly, ren, rin, rip, run **04** belt, bolt, bomb, call, dart, dash, fall, flaw, flow, gush, lash, leap, need, pelt, push, race, raid, rash, star, stir, tear **05** fling, flood, haste, hurry, onset, press, run at, scour, shoot, spate, speat, speed, starr, storm, surge **06** attack, bustle, career, charge, demand, flurry, gallop, hasten, random, sprint, streak, stream, strike **07** assault, cariere, clamour, defraud, quicken, speed up, tantivy, urgency, viretot **08** activity, despatch, dispatch, pressure, rapidity, scramble, stampede **09** commotion, make haste, onslaught, star grass, swiftness **10** accelerate, excitement, get a move on, hurly-burly, overcharge, shave-grass, spring tide, starr grass **11** run like hell **13** precipitation **14** hive of activity **15** hustle and bustle

**rushed**

**04** busy, fast **05** brisk, hasty, quick, rapid, swift **06** hectic, prompt, urgent

07 cursory, hurried 08 careless
09 emergency 11 expeditious, superficial

**Russia**
03 RUS

*Russian cities and notable towns include:*

04 Omsk
05 Kazan
06 Moscow, Moskva, Samara
07 Irkutsk
08 Novgorod
09 Archangel, Volgograd
11 Archangelsk, Chelyabinsk, Novosibirsk, Rostov-on-Don, Vladivostok
12 Ekaterinburg, St Petersburg
13 Yekaterinburg
15 Nizhniy Novgorod

**Russian**
04 czar, tsar, tzar 05 Lenin, Putin, Raisa
07 czarina, Trotsky, tsarina, Yeltsin
08 czaritsa, Rasputin, tsaritsa
09 Gorbachev

*Russians include:*

05 Khant
06 Buryat, Ostyak
07 Bashkir, Cossack
08 Siberian
09 Muscovite
10 Volga Tatar

**rust**
03 rot 05 decay, dross, stain, uredo
07 corrode, decline, ferrugo, oxidize, tarnish 09 corrosion, oxidation, verdigris 11 deteriorate

**rust-coloured**
03 red 05 brown, rusty, sandy, tawny
06 auburn, copper, ginger, russet, titian
07 coppery, gingery, reddish
08 chestnut 10 rubiginose, rubiginous
11 ferruginous 12 ferrugineous, reddish-brown

**rustic**
◇ *anagram indicator*
03 hob, oaf 04 boor, carl, clod, hick, hind, rude 05 bacon, borel, churl, clown, crude, Hodge, plain, rough, rural, swain, yokel 06 borrel, clumsy, coarse, forest, hodden, oafish, russet, simple, sylvan 07 artless, awkward, boorish, borrell, bucolic, bumpkin, Corydon, country, culchie, hayseed, peasant, uncouth, woollen
08 backveld, clownish, homespun, pastoral, Strephon 09 bucolical, chawbacon, graceless, hillbilly, Hobbinoll, ingenuous, maladroit, unrefined, uplandish 10 bogtrotter, clodhopper, countryman, indelicate, provincial, uncultured 11 clodhopping, countrified, countryside
12 countrywoman 13 country cousin, cracker-barrel 15 unsophisticated

**rustle**
◇ *anagram indicator*
04 raid, sigh 05 steal, swish 06 bustle, fissle, hustle, whoosh 07 crackle, whisper 08 crepitus, rustling, susurrus
09 crinkling, susurrate 10 whispering
11 crepitation, susurration

• **rustle up**
04 make 07 scare up 10 get quickly
11 get together, put together
14 prepare quickly, provide quickly

**rusty**
03 red 04 dull, poor, weak 05 brown, dated, rough, sandy, stale, stiff, tawny
06 auburn, copper, ginger, russet, rusted, titian 07 coppery, gingery, raucous, reddish 08 chestnut, corroded, creaking, impaired, outmoded, oxidized, time-worn
09 deficient, obstinate, tarnished
10 aeruginous, antiquated, rubiginose, rubiginous 11 discoloured, ferruginous, rust-covered, unpractised
12 ferrugineous, old-fashioned, reddish-brown, rust-coloured 13 out of practice

**rut**
05 ditch, gouge, grind, habit, track
06 furrow, groove, gutter, system, trough 07 channel, humdrum, pattern, pothole, routine 09 treadmill, wheelmark 10 daily grind, wheel track
11 indentation 12 same old place, same old round

**ruthenium**
02 Ru

**rutherfordium**
02 Rf

**ruthless**
04 fell, grim, hard 05 cruel, harsh, stern
06 brutal, fierce, savage, severe
07 callous, inhuman, vicious
08 felonous, pitiless 09 barbarous, cut-throat, dog-eat-dog, Draconian, ferocious, heartless, merciless, unfeeling, unsparing 10 hard-bitten, implacable, inexorable, relentless, unmerciful 11 hard-hearted, remorseless, third-degree, unforgiving, unrelenting

**ruthlessly**
06 grimly 07 cruelly, harshly
08 brutally, fiercely, savagely, severely
09 callously 10 inexorably, pitilessly
11 mercilessly, unfeelingly
12 unmercifully 13 hard-heartedly, remorselessly

**Rwanda**
03 RWA

# S

**S**
**02** es **03** ess **06** sierra
**• S-shape**
**04** ogee **08** swan neck

**Sabbath**
**01** S **03** Sat, Sun **06** Sunday **07** Shabbat **08** Saturday

**sable**
**03** jet **04** dark, inky **05** black, dusky, ebony, raven **06** darken, pitchy, sombre **08** midnight, zibeline **09** coal-black, pitch-dark, zibelline **10** pitch-black

**sabotage**
◇ *anagram indicator*
**03** mar **04** ruin **05** spoil, wreck **06** damage, impair, ratten, thwart, weaken **07** cripple, destroy, disable, disrupt, scupper **08** spoiling, wrecking **09** crippling, disabling, rattening, undermine, vandalism, vandalize, weakening **10** disruption, impairment **11** destruction **12** incapacitate

**sac**
**03** bag, pod **04** cyst **05** bursa, pouch, theca **06** ink-bag, pocket, vesica **07** bladder, capsule, saccule, vesicle **08** aerostat, cisterna, follicle, tympanum, vesicula **09** lithocyst, spore case **10** air-bladder, nematocyst, sporangium, vitellicle **11** gall bladder, pericardium **12** diverticulum

**saccharine**
**05** gushy, mushy, soppy, sweet **06** sickly, sloppy, sugary, syrupy **07** cloying, dulcite, dulcose, honeyed, maudlin, mawkish **08** dulcitol **09** oversweet, schmaltzy **10** nauseating **11** sentimental, sickly-sweet

**sachet**
**03** bag **04** pack **06** packet **07** musk-bag, package **08** envelope, musk-ball, scent bag, wrapping **09** container **12** bouquet garni

**sack**
◇ *anagram indicator*
◇ *deletion indicator*
**03** axe, bag, bed, can, mat, rob **04** fire, loot, muid, pack, raid, rape, raze, ruin **05** cards, gunny, level, pouch, rifle, spoil, strip, waste **06** budget, firing, lay off, maraud, notice, papers, pocket, rapine, ravage, razing, remove, the axe **07** boot out, despoil, destroy, dismiss, dust bag, jotters, looting, pillage, plunder, sacking, satchel, the boot, the chop, the push **08** demolish, earth-bag, lay waste, the elbow **09** depredate, desecrate, devastate, discharge, dismissal, hop-pocket, levelling, marauding, select out **10** give notice, plundering, the heave-ho **11** depredation, desecration, destruction, devastation, send packing **12** despoliation **13** make redundant **14** marching orders

**sacrament**
**04** rite **05** order **06** ritual **07** mystery, nagmaal, penance **08** ceremony, practice **09** communion, Eucharist, ordinance **10** holy orders, observance **11** institution **13** Holy Communion **14** extreme unction

**sacred**
**04** holy **05** godly **06** divine, secure **07** blessed, devoted, revered, sainted, saintly **08** accursed, defended, hallowed, heavenly, priestly **09** dedicated, protected, religious, respected, spiritual, venerable **10** devotional, inviolable, sacrosanct, sanctified **11** consecrated, impregnable, untouchable **14** ecclesiastical

**sacredness**
**08** divinity, holiness, sanctity **09** godliness, solemnity **11** saintliness **13** inviolability, sacrosanctity **15** invulnerability

**sacrifice**
◇ *deletion indicator*
**04** loss **05** forgo, let go, offer **06** forego, gambit, give up, victim **07** abandon, forfeit, offer up, sacrify **08** giving-up, hecatomb, immolate, lustrate, oblation, offering, renounce **09** holocaust, martyrize, molochize, sacrifide, slaughter, surrender **10** immolation, juggernaut, lustration, relinquish **11** abandonment, destruction, sin-offering, taurobolium **12** propitiation, renunciation **13** acceptilation, burnt-offering, heave-offering, heave-shoulder, suovetaurilia **14** blood-sacrifice

**sacrificial**
**06** votive **07** atoning **08** oblatory, piacular **09** expiatory **10** reparative **12** propitiatory

**sacrilege**
**06** heresy **07** impiety, mockery, outrage **09** blasphemy, profanity, violation **10** disrespect, irreligion **11** desecration, irreverence, profanation

**sacrilegious**
**06** unholy **07** godless, impious, profane, ungodly **09** heretical **10** irreverent **11** blasphemous, desecrating, irreligious, profanatory **13** disrespectful

**sacrosanct**
**06** sacred, secure **08** hallowed **09** protected, respected **10** inviolable **11** impregnable, untouchable

**sad**
◇ *anagram indicator*
**02** wo **03** low, woe **04** blue, down, dull, glum **05** dowie, dusky, fed up, grave, heavy, mesto, sated, sober, sorry, staid, stiff, upset **06** dismal, doughy, gloomy, sedate, tragic **07** doleful, earnest, joyless, painful, pitiful, serious, tearful, unhappy, wistful **08** constant, dejected, downcast, grievous, lovesick, mournful, pathetic, pitiable, poignant, shameful, subtrist, touching, tragical, wretched **09** depressed, heart-sore, long-faced, miserable, sorrowful, sportless, steadfast, upsetting, woebegone **10** calamitous, deplorable, depressing, despondent, disastrous, distressed, lamentable, melancholy, rock bottom **11** crestfallen, disgraceful, distressing, downhearted, low-spirited, regrettable, unfortunate **12** at rock bottom, disconsolate, heart-rending, heavy-hearted, in low spirits **13** grief-stricken, heartbreaking **14** down in the dumps

**Sadat**
**05** Anwar

**sadden**
**05** upset **06** deject, dismay, grieve **07** attrist, depress **08** cast down, contrist, dispirit, distress **09** bring down **10** discourage, dishearten **14** break your heart, drive to despair, get someone down

**saddle**
**03** col, pad, tax **04** land, load, seat, sell **05** panel, pilch, selle **06** burden, charge, impose, lumber **07** kajawah, pigskin, pillion **08** encumber

**sadism**
**05** spite **07** cruelty **08** savagery **09** barbarity, brutality **10** bestiality, inhumanity **11** callousness, malevolence, viciousness **12** ruthlessness **13** heartlessness, sado-masochism, schadenfreude, unnaturalness

**sadist**
**05** brute **06** abuser, savage, terror **07** monster **08** molester, torturer **09** barbarian

**sadistic**
**05** cruel **06** brutal, savage **07** bestial, inhuman, vicious **08** pitiless **09** barbarous, merciless, perverted, unnatural

**sadly**
◇ *anagram indicator*
**04** alas **08** dismally, gloomily, sad to say **09** miserably, tearfully, unhappily, unluckily, weepingly, worse luck **10** dejectedly **11** regrettably, sad to relate, sorrowfully **12** despondently **13** unfortunately **14** heavy heartedly

**sadness**
**03** woe **04** pain **05** grief **06** dismay, misery, pathos, regret, sorrow **07** tragedy, waeness **08** distress, glumness **09** bleakness, dejection, heartache, poignancy **10** depression, desolation, dismalness, gloominess, low spirits, melancholy, misfortune, sombreness **11** despondency, dolefulness, joylessness, tearfulness, unhappiness, Weltschmerz **12** mournfulness, wretchedness **13** cheerlessness, contristation, sorrowfulness **14** lugubriousness

**safe**
**04** fine, good, hunk, sure **05** ambry, awmry, chest, peter, sound, timid, tried, vault **06** almery, aumbry, awmrie, coffer, condom, honest, immune, intact, proven, secure, tested, unhurt **07** cash box, certain, guarded, keister, prudent, upright **08** all right, cautious, defended, harmless, non-toxic, reliable, unharmed **09** innocuous, protected, sheltered, strongbox, undamaged, uninjured, unscathed **10** dependable, deposit box, depository, home and dry, honourable, repository **11** circumspect, impregnable, in good hands, out of danger, responsible, trustworthy **12** conservative, invulnerable, non-poisonous, safe and sound, safe as houses, unassailable **13** out of harm's way, unadventurous, with whole skin **14** copper-bottomed, uncontaminated, unenterprising

**safe-conduct**
**04** jark, pass **06** convoy, permit **07** licence, warrant **08** passport **09** safeguard **13** authorization, laissez-passer

**safeguard**
**05** cover, guard **06** defend, screen, secure, shield, surety **07** defence, protect, shelter **08** preserve, security **09** assurance, guarantee, insurance, look after, palladium **10** precaution, preventive, protection, take care of **11** safe-conduct **12** preservative, preventative

**safekeeping**
**04** care, ward **05** trust **06** charge **07** custody, keeping **08** wardship **10** protection **11** supervision **12** guardianship, surveillance

**safely**
**06** surely **08** securely **11** impregnably, out of danger, without harm, without risk **13** out of harm's way, without injury

**safety**
**05** cover **06** refuge **07** shelter, welfare **08** fail-safe, immunity, safeness, security **09** safeguard, sanctuary, soundness **10** preventive, protection, protective **11** reliability **12** harmlessness, preventative **13** dependability, precautionary **14** impregnability **15** trustworthiness

**sag**
**03** bag, dip, low **04** bend, drop, fail, fall, flag, flop, give, hang, sink, slip, swag, wilt **05** droop, slide, slump **06** falter, weaken **07** decline, spinach, subside **08** downturn, low point **09** dwindling, reduction **10** depression **11** hang loosely

**saga**
**04** Edda, epic, epos, tale, yarn **05** story **06** epopee **07** history, romance **08** epopoeia **09** adventure, chronicle, narrative, soap opera **11** roman fleuve

**sagacious**
**03** fly **04** able, sage, wary, wily, wise **05** acute, canny, quick, sharp, smart **06** astute, shrewd **07** knowing, prudent, sapient **09** judicious, wide-awake **10** discerning, far-sighted, insightful, long-headed, perceptive, percipient **11** intelligent, long-sighted, penetrating **13** perspicacious

**sagacity**
**05** sense **06** acumen, wisdom **07** insight **08** judgment, prudence, sapience, wariness, wiliness **09** acuteness, canniness, foresight, judgement, sharpness **10** astuteness, shrewdness **11** discernment, knowingness, penetration, percipience **12** perspicacity **13** judiciousness, understanding

**sage**
**04** guru, wise **05** canny, clary, elder, hakam, orval, rishi **06** astute, expert, master, Nestor, oracle, pundit, salvia, saulge, savant, tohunga **07** knowing, learned, mahatma, politic, prudent, sapient, Solomon, teacher, wise man **08** sensible, wiseacre **09** authority, judicious, maharishi, sagacious, wise woman **10** discerning, wise person **11** intelligent, philosopher **13** knowledgeable, perspicacious

*The Seven Sages:*

**04** **Bias** (of Priene in Caria)
**05** **Solon** (of Athens)
**06** **Chilon** (of Sparta), **Thales** (of Miletus)
**08** **Pittacus** (of Mitylene)
**09** **Cleobulus** (tyrant of Lindus in Rhodes), **Periander** (tyrant of Corinth)

**sagely**
**04** ably **06** wisely **07** acutely, quickly, sharply **08** astutely, shrewdly **09** knowingly, prudently **11** judiciously **12** discerningly, perceptively **13** intelligently **15** perspicaciously

**saggy**
**03** lax **04** limp, weak **05** loose, slack **06** droopy, feeble, floppy **07** falling, sagging **08** drooping, dropping

**said**
◇ *homophone indicator*
**03** quo', sed **04** quod **05** quoth

**sail**
**03** fan, fly, ply, rag, van **04** boat, scud, ship, skim, soar, Vela, waft, wing **05** coast, float, glide, pilot, plane, steer, sweep, yacht **06** cruise, embark, put off, voyage **07** captain, go by sea, sea wing, set sail, skipper **08** navigate, put to sea **09** leave port **11** travel by sea, weigh anchor

*Sails include:*

**03** jib, lug, rig, sky, top, try
**04** fore, gaff, head, kite, main, moon, stay, stun
**05** drift, genoa, royal, smoke, sprit, storm
**06** bonnet, canvas, course, jigger, lateen, mizzen, square, stuns'l
**07** foretop, gaff-top, jury rig, maintop, spanker, spencer
**08** forestay, gennaker, storm try, studding
**09** crossjack, foreroyal, moonraker, spinnaker, stargazer
**10** Bermuda rig, fore-and-aft, main course, skyscraper, topgallant
**13** fore-and-aft rig
**14** fore-topgallant

• **part of a sail**
**04** bunt, luff, nock, reef **05** belly **06** bonnet

• **sail into**
**05** shoal **06** attack, let fly, turn on **07** assault, lay into **08** set about, tear into

• **sail through**
**10** pass easily **11** romp through **15** succeed in easily

**sailing**
**07** boating **08** yachting

*Sailing-related terms include:*

**04** beat, gybe, helm, jibe, port
**05** abaft, fetch, lay up
**06** astern, course, leeway, upwind, yawing
**07** backing, bearing, beating, heeling, lee helm, running, tacking
**08** downwind, port tack, reaching, under way, windward
**09** alongside, laying off, letting go, starboard
**10** broad reach, casting off, close

reach, going about, ready about!
**11** close-hauled, coming about, goose-winged, steerage way
**12** sail trimming, spilling wind
**13** across the wind, hard on the wind, starboard tack
**15** fixing a position, stepping the mast, taking soundings

## sailor

*Sailor types include:*

**02** AB, OS, PO
**03** cox, gob, mid, tar
**04** hand, jack, mate, salt, tarp, Wren
**05** bosun, janty, limey, matlo, middy, pilot, rower
**06** bargee, hearty, jaunty, lascar, marine, master, matlow, pirate, purser, rating, sea boy, seadog, seaman, swabby, topman, Triton
**07** boatman, captain, crewman, Jack tar, jauntie, mariner, matelot, oarsman, old salt, sculler, shipman, skipper, waister
**08** Argonaut, cabin boy, coxswain, deck hand, helmsman, leadsman, seafarer, shipmate, water dog, water rat
**09** boatswain, buccaneer, fisherman, galiongee, greenhand, navigator, sailor-man, sea lawyer, shellback, steersman, tarpaulin, yachtsman
**10** able rating, able seaman, bluejacket, liberty-man, midshipman, tarpauling
**11** foremastman, leatherneck, tarry-breeks, yachtswoman
**12** able seawoman
**13** canvas-climber

*Sailors include:*

**04** **Ahab** (Captain), **Byng** (George), **Byng** (John), **Cook** (James), **Diaz** (Bartolomeu), **Gama** (Vasco da), **Hood** (Samuel, Viscount), **Howe** (Richard, Earl), **Kidd** (William), **Ross** (Horatio), **Ross** (Sir James Clark), **Ross** (Sir John), **Spee** (Count Maximilian von)
**05** **Adams** (Will), **Blake** (Robert), **Bligh** (William), **Cabot** (John), **Cabot** (Sebastian), **Doria** (Andrea), **Drake** (Sir Francis), **Hawke** (Edward, Lord), **Henry** (the Navigator), **Jones** (Paul), **Peary** (Robert Edwin), **Tromp** (Maarten)
**06** **Baffin** (William), **Beatty** (David, Earl), **Benbow** (John), **Bering** (Vitus), **Dönitz** (Karl), **Fisher** (John, Lord), **Hudson** (Henry), **Nelson** (Horatio, Viscount), **Nimitz** (Chester), **Ruyter** (Michiel Adriaanzoon de), **Tasman** (Abel Janszoon), **Vernon** (Edward)
**07** **Barentz** (William), **Decatur** (Stephen), **Fitzroy** (Robert), **Hawkins** (Sir John), **Hawkyns** (Sir John), **Kolchak** (Alexander), **Lord Jim**, **Marryat** (Captain Frederick), **Pytheas**, **Raleigh** (Sir Walter), **Selkirk** (Alexander), **Tirpitz** (Alfred von), **Weddell** (James)
**08** **Beaufort** (Sir Francis), **Columbus** (Christopher), **Cousteau** (Jacques Yves), **Elvström** (Paul), **Jellicoe** (John Rushworth, Earl), **Magellan** (Ferdinand), **Pitcairn** (Robert), **Sandwich** (Edward Montagu, Earl of), **Vespucci** (Amerigo)
**09** **Christian** (Fletcher), **Frobisher** (Sir Martin), **Grenville** (Sir Richard), **MacArthur** (Dame Ellen), **St Vincent** (John Jervis, Earl of), **Vancouver** (George)
**10** **Chichester** (Sir Francis), **Erik the Red**, **Villeneuve** (Pierre de)
**11** **Collingwood** (Cuthbert, Lord), **Elphinstone** (George Keith, Viscount Keith), **Mountbatten** (Louis, Earl)
**12** **Bougainville** (Louis Antoine, Comte de), **Knox-Johnston** (Sir Robin), **Themistocles**

*See also* **admiral**; **pirate**; **ship**

• **sailors**
**02** MN, RM, RN **03** RAN, RFA, RYA, RYS **04** navy

## saint

**01** S **02** St **03** Ste **04** hagi-, holy, sant **05** angel, hagio-, saunt **06** hallow, patron, santon **07** tutelar **08** tutelary **11** patron saint **13** guardian saint

*Saints include:*

**03** **Ivo**, **Leo**
**04** **Adam**, **Anne**, **Bede**, **Gall**, **Joan** (of Arc), **John**, **John** (Chrysostom), **John** (of the Cross), **John** (the Baptist), **Jude**, **Lucy**, **Luke**, **Mark**, **Mary**, **Mary** (Magdalene), **Paul**, **Zita**
**05** **Agnes**, **Aidan**, **Alban**, **Amand**, **Basil** (the Great), **Bruno** (of Cologne), **Clare**, **Cyril**, **Cyril** (of Alexandria), **David**, **Denis**, **Edwin**, **Giles**, **James**, **Louis**, **Paula**, **Peter**, **Titus**, **Vitus**
**06** **Albert** (the Great), **Andrew**, **Anselm**, **Antony**, **Antony** (of Padua), **Aquila**, **Cosmas**, **Damian**, **Dismas**, **Edmund**, **Edmund** (Campion), **Edward** (the Martyr), **Fiacre**, **George**, **Helena**, **Hilary** (of Poitiers), **Jerome**, **Joseph**, **Joseph** (of Arimathea), **Justin**, **Martha**, **Martin**, **Monica**, **Oliver**, **Oliver** (Plunket), **Oswald**, **Philip**, **Prisca**, **Robert**, **Simeon**, **Teresa** (of Avila), **Thomas**, **Thomas** (Aquinas), **Thomas** (Becket), **Thomas** (More), **Thomas** (à Becket), **Ursula**
**07** **Adamnan**, **Ambrose**, **Anthony**, **Anthony** (of Padua), **Barbara**, **Bernard** (of Clairvaux), **Bernard** (of Menthon), **Bridget**, **Cecilia**, **Clement**, **Columba**, **Crispin**, **Cyprian**, **Dominic**, **Dorothy**, **Dunstan**, **Erasmus**, **Francis** (Romulus), **Francis** (Xavier), **Francis** (of Assisi), **Francis** (of Sales), **Gabriel**, **Gregory** (of Nazianzus), **Gregory** (of Tours), **Gregory** (the Great), **Isidore** (of Seville), **Leonard**, **Matthew**, **Michael**, **Pancras**, **Patrick**, **Stephen**, **Swithin**, **Theresa** (of Lisieux), **Timothy**, **Vincent** (de Paul), **Wilfrid**
**08** **Albertus** (Magnus), **Angelico**, **Barnabas**, **Benedict** (of Nursia), **Boniface**, **Cuthbert**, **Genesius**, **Ignatius** (of Loyola), **Irenaeus**, **Lawrence**, **Margaret**, **Matthias**, **Nicholas**, **Polycarp**, **Veronica**, **Vladimir**, **Walpurga**
**09** **Alexander**, **Alexander** (Nevsky), **Augustine** (of Canterbury), **Augustine** (of Hippo), **Catherine**, **Genevieve**, **Homobonus**, **Honoratus**, **John Bosco**, **John of God**, **Kentigern**, **Ladislaus**, **Methodius**, **Sebastian**, **Valentine**, **Wenceslas**
**10** **Appollonia**, **Athanasius**, **Bernadette**, **Crispinian**, **John Fisher**, **Stanislaus**, **Thomas More**, **Wenceslaus**
**11** **Bonaventure**, **Christopher**
**12** **Justin Martyr**
**13** **Martin of Tours**, **Thomas Apostle**, **Thomas Aquinas**
**14** **Albert the Great**, **Francis de Sales**, **Francis of Paola**
**15** **Aquila and Prisca**, **Cosmas and Damian**, **Francis of Assisi**, **Gregory the Great**, **Our Lady of Loreto**, **Raymond Nonnatus**

## St Helena

**03** SHN

## St Kitts and Nevis

**03** KNA, SCN

## saintliness

**05** faith, piety **06** purity, virtue **08** chastity, goodness, holiness, morality, sanctity **09** godliness, innocence **10** asceticism, devoutness, sanctitude, self-denial **11** blessedness, sinlessness, uprightness **12** selflessness, spirituality, spotlessness **13** blamelessness, righteousness, self-sacrifice, unselfishness

## St Lucia

**02** WL **03** LCA

## saintly

**04** good, holy, pure **05** godly, moral, pious **06** devout, worthy **07** angelic, blessed, ethical, sinless, upright **08** innocent, spotless, virtuous **09** believing, blameless, religious, righteous, saintlike, spiritual **10** God-fearing

## St Vincent and the Grenadines

**02** WV **03** VCT

## sake

**03** aim **04** gain, goal, good, saki **05** cause **06** behalf, object, profit, reason, regard **07** account, benefit, purpose, respect, welfare **08** interest **09** advantage, objective, wellbeing **13** consideration

## salacious

**04** blue, lewd, salt **05** bawdy, horny, randy **06** carnal, coarse, erotic, fruity,

ribald, smutty, steamy, wanton
**07** lustful, obscene, raunchy, ruttish
**08** improper, indecent, prurient
**09** lecherous **10** lascivious, libidinous, lubricious, scurrilous **12** concupiscent, pornographic

**salaciousness**
**08** lewdness **09** bawdiness, indecency, obscenity, prurience **10** smuttiness, steaminess **11** lustfulness, pornography
**13** concupiscence, lecherousness
**14** lasciviousness

**salad**
◇ *anagram indicator*

*Salads include:*

**04** herb, rice, slaw
**05** fruit, Greek, green, pasta
**06** Caesar, potato, tomato
**07** mesclum, mesclun, niçoise, Russian, seafood, tabouli, Waldorf
**08** coleslaw, couscous
**09** mixed leaf, tabbouleh, three bean
**11** bulgar wheat
**15** mustard and cress

*Salad ingredients include:*

**03** egg, ham, nut
**04** meat, tuna
**05** bacon, chard, cress, olive
**06** borage, carrot, celery, endive, lovage, potato, rocket, tomato
**07** anchovy, arugula, chicken, chicory, crouton
**08** bacon bit, beetroot, cold meat, coleslaw, cucumber
**09** boiled egg, corn-salad, green bean, new potato, radicchio, sweetcorn
**10** cos lettuce, lollo rosso, mayonnaise, salad cream, watercress
**11** salad burnet, spring onion
**12** cherry tomato, lamb's lettuce, round lettuce
**13** hard-boiled egg, roasted pepper, salad dressing
**14** iceberg lettuce, sundried tomato

*See also* **lettuce**

*Salad dressings include:*

**06** Caesar, French
**07** Italian, Russian
**10** blue cheese, mayonnaise, salad cream
**11** vinaigrette
**14** Thousand Island

**salamander**
**03** olm **07** axolotl **08** mudpuppy
**10** hellbender **12** springkeeper

**salaried**
**04** paid **05** waged **11** emolumental, remunerated, stipendiary
**12** emolumentary

**salary**
**03** fee, pay **05** screw, wages
**06** income **07** stipend **08** earnings
**09** allowance, emolument
**10** honorarium **12** remuneration

**sale**
**04** deal, seal, vend, vent **05** trade
**06** wicker, willow **07** selling, traffic, vending **08** disposal **09** marketing
**10** bargaining **11** transaction

*Sales include:*

**04** boot, fair, work
**06** autumn, bazaar, forced, garage, jumble, market, online, public, spring, summer, winter
**07** auction, car-boot, charity, January, private, rummage, warrant
**08** bazumble, clearing, cold call, e-auction, tabletop
**09** clearance, end-of-line, mail order, mid-season, pre-season, remainder, telesales, trade show
**10** exhibition, exposition, fleamarket, open market, second-hand
**11** bring-and-buy, closing-down, end-of-season, on-promotion, stocktaking
**12** bargain offer, church bazaar, grand opening, of the century, special offer
**13** online auction
**14** pyramid selling
**15** of bankrupt stock

• **for sale**
**06** on sale, to sell **07** in stock
**09** available, up for sale **10** in the shops, obtainable, up for grabs **11** for purchase, on the market **12** wanted to sell

• **sale or return**
**03** SOR

**saleable**
**08** vendible **09** desirable
**10** marketable **11** sought-after
**12** merchantable

**salesperson**
**03** rep **05** clerk **07** shop-boy
**08** salesman, shop-girl **09** salesgirl, saleslady **10** salesclerk, saleswoman, shopkeeper **13** sales engineer, shop assistant **14** representative, sales assistant

**salient**
**04** main **05** bulge, chief **06** signal
**07** leaping, obvious, saltant **08** striking
**09** arresting, important, principal, prominent, springing **10** noticeable, pronounced, remarkable
**11** conspicuous, outstanding, significant

**saliva**
**04** foam, spit **05** drool, spawl, water
**06** phlegm, slaver, sputum **07** dribble, spittle **13** expectoration

**sallow**
**03** wan **04** pale, sale, seal **05** adust, ashen, pasty, sally, sauch, saugh, waxen
**06** pallid, sickly, willow, yellow
**07** anaemic **09** jaundiced, unhealthy, yellowish **10** colourless, goat-willow

**sally**
**04** dash, jest, joke, quip, raid, rock, rush, sway, trip **05** amble, bound, crack, drive, erupt, foray, issue, jaunt, mosey, surge **06** attack, bon mot, breeze, charge, escape, frolic, outing, retort, sallee, sallow, sortie, stroll, thrust, wander **07** assault, outrush, riposte, saunter, venture **08** escapade
**09** excursion, incursion, offensive, promenade, wisecrack, witticism
**10** jeu d'esprit, projection **11** snatch squad

**salmon**
**03** fry, lax, lox **04** chum, cock, coho, kelt, keta, masu, mort, parr **05** cohoe, nerka, smolt, sprod **06** baggit, dorado, grilse, kipper, ligger, samlet
**07** bluecap, gravlax, kokanee, quinnat, redfish, salamon, shedder, skegger, sockeye **08** blueback, humpback, rockfish, springer **09** blackfish, brandling, bull trout, gravadlax
**10** fingerling, ouananiche
**12** Oncorhynchus

**salt**
**02** AB **03** sal, tar, wit, zip **04** corn, cure, dear, leap, saut, zest **05** briny, punch, rapid, salty, sault, smack, taste
**06** marine, rating, relish, sailor, saline, salted, savour, seaman, vigour
**07** flavour, mariner, pungent, saltish, sea-salt **08** brackish, interest, merum sal, mordancy, piquancy, pungency, seafarer **09** expensive, salacious, seasoning, waterfall **10** liveliness, trenchancy **11** acclimatize **14** sodium chloride

*Salts include:*

**05** azide
**06** aurate, borate, folate, halite, iodate, iodide, malate, oleate
**07** bay salt, caprate, citrate, cyanate, ferrate, formate, lactate, maleate, nitrate, nitrite, oxalate, sorbate, tannate, toluate, viscose
**08** arsenite, benzoate, butyrate, caproate, chlorate, chloride, chromate, plumbate, pyruvate, rock salt, silicate, stearate, sulphate, sulphide, sulphite, tartrate, vanadate, xanthate
**09** ascorbate, bath salts, carbamate, carbonate, glutamate, manganate, molybdate, periodate, phosphate, phthalate, solar salt, succinate, table salt
**10** antimonite, bichromate, dichromate, Epsom salts, liver salts, salicylate
**11** bicarbonate, health salts, persulphate, sal volatile
**12** borosilicate, permanganate, Rochelle-salt
**13** smelling salts

• **salt away**
**04** bank, hide, save **05** amass, cache, hoard, stash **07** collect, put away, store up **08** put aside, set aside **09** stockpile
**10** accumulate

• **take with a pinch of salt, take with a grain of salt**
**08** hesitate, question **10** disbelieve
**14** have misgivings **15** have hesitations, not fully believe

**salty**
**04** racy, salt **05** briny, spicy, tangy, witty **06** lively, saline, salted **07** mordant, piquant, savoury **08** animated, brackish, exciting, vigorous **09** trenchant **11** salsuginous, stimulating

**salubrious**
**06** benign, decent **07** healthy **08** hygienic, pleasant, salutary, sanitary **09** healthful, wholesome **10** beneficial, refreshing **11** respectable **12** health-giving, invigorating

**salutary**
**04** good **06** timely, useful **07** healthy, helpful **08** hygienic, sanitary, valuable **09** practical, wholesome **10** beneficial, profitable, refreshing **12** advantageous, health-giving, invigorating

**salutation**
**03** ave, hat **04** g'day, hail, skol **05** jambo, skoal **06** homage, prosit, salaam, salute **07** address, all-hail, ave Mary, good-day, good-den, good-e'en, wassail, welcome **08** ave Maria, good-even, greeting, Hail Mary, regreets, respects **09** goodnight, obeisance, reverence, time of day **10** excitement, good-morrow **11** good-evening, good-morning **13** good afternoon
*See also* **greeting**

**salute**
**03** bow, cap, nod **04** hail, mark, move, wave **05** coupé, greet, halse, salue, salvo **06** banzai, coupee, homage, honour **07** address, gesture, half-cap, present, tribute, welcome **08** greeting, Sieg Heil **09** celebrate, handshake, recognize, reverence **11** acknowledge, celebration, present arms, recognition **12** pay tribute to **15** acknowledgement, make your manners

**salvage**
**04** save **05** salve **06** redeem, repair, rescue, retain, savage, saving **07** get back, raising, reclaim, recover, restore **08** conserve, preserve, recovery, retrieve **09** regaining, retrieval **10** recuperate **11** reclamation, restoration **12** regeneration **13** reinstatement

**salvation**
**06** rescue, saving **08** lifeline **10** liberation, redemption **11** deliverance, reclamation, soteriology **12** preservation

**salve**
**03** saw **04** balm, calm, ease, hail, heal **05** cream, smear **06** anoint, lotion, remedy, soothe **07** clear up, comfort, explain, lighten, relieve, salvage **08** greeting, liniment, ointment **09** harmonize, vindicate **10** medication **11** application, embrocation, preparation

**salver**
**04** dish, tray **05** plate **06** server, waiter **07** charger, platter **08** trencher

**samarium**
**02** Sm

**same**
**02** ae, do, id **03** ilk, one **04** idem, like, self, twin, very, ylke **05** alike, ditto, equal, samey, thick, thilk **06** all one, as much, mutual, thicky **07** similar, uniform **08** matching, selfsame, unvaried **09** duplicate, identical, unchanged, unvarying **10** carbon copy, changeless, comparable, consistent, equiparate, equivalent, reciprocal, synonymous, unchanging, unvariable **11** the very same **12** the aforesaid **13** corresponding, one and the same, substitutable, the above-named **15** interchangeable
• **all the same**
**03** but, yet **05** still **06** anyhow, anyway, even so **07** however **09** in any case **10** by any means, for all that, in any event, not but what, regardless, tout de même **11** by some means, nonetheless **12** nevertheless **15** birds of a feather, notwithstanding
• **the same as**
**02** iq **08** idem quod

**sameness**
**06** déjà vu, tedium **07** oneness **08** ding-dong, equality, identity, likeness, monotone, monotony **09** dead-level, mannerism **10** repetition, similarity, uniformity **11** consistency, duplication, resemblance **13** identicalness, indistinction, invariability **14** changelessness, predictability **15** standardization

**samey**
**04** same **05** alike **07** similar, tedious, uniform **09** identical **10** monotonous, unchanging **11** predictable **12** cookie-cutter

**Samoa**
**02** WS **03** WSM

**sample**
◇ *hidden indicator*
**03** sip, try **04** blad, cast, core, sign, test, type **05** dummy, match, model, piece, pilot, taste, toile, trial **06** muster, swatch, taster, try out **07** examine, example, inspect, pattern, typical **08** instance, prospect, sampling, specimen, transect **09** breakbeat, foretaste, scantling **10** assay-piece, experience, indication **12** cross-section, illustration, illustrative **13** demonstration, demonstrative **14** representative **15** depleted uranium

**sanatorium**
**03** san **06** clinic **07** sick bay **08** hospital **09** infirmary **10** health farm, sanitarium **12** health centre, health resort **13** medical centre

**sanctification**
**05** piety **06** purity **08** devotion, holiness **09** godliness **10** sacredness **11** blessedness **12** spirituality **13** righteousness

**sanctify**
**04** back, wash **05** allow, bless, exalt **06** anoint, hallow, permit, purify, ratify **07** absolve, approve, cleanse, confirm, endorse, license, support, warrant **08** accredit, canonize, dedicate, make holy, sanction, set apart **09** authorize **10** consecrate, legitimize, make sacred, underwrite

**sanctimonious**
**02** pi **04** holy, smug **05** pious **08** priggish, superior, unctuous **09** pietistic **10** goody-goody, moralizing **11** pharisaical **12** hypocritical **13** self-righteous **14** holier-than-thou

**sanctimoniousness**
**04** cant **06** humbug **07** pietism **08** saintism, smugness **09** hypocrisy **10** moralizing, pharisaism **11** complacency, preachiness **12** priggishness, unctuousness **13** righteousness

**sanction**
**02** OK **03** ban, oke **04** back, fiat, okay **05** allow **06** permit, ratify **07** approof, approve, backing, boycott, confirm, embargo, endorse, go-ahead, licence, license, penalty, support, sustain, warrant **08** accredit, approval, royalize, sanctify, sentence, suffrage, thumbs-up **09** agreement, authority, authorize, deterrent **10** green light, legitimize, permission, punishment, underwrite **11** approbation, countenance, endorsement, prohibition, restriction **12** confirmation, ratification, subscription **13** accreditation, authorization

**sanctity**
**05** grace, piety **06** purity, virtue **08** devotion, goodness, holiness **09** godliness, saintship **10** sacredness **11** blessedness, saintliness **12** spirituality **13** inviolability, religiousness, righteousness, sacrosanctity **14** sanctification

**sanctuary**
**04** area, park **05** altar, frith, girth, grith, haven, tract **06** asylum, church, oracle, refuge, safety, shrine, temple **07** Alsatia, chancel, enclave, hideout, reserve, retreat, sanctum, shelter **08** delubrum, hideaway, immunity, preserve, security **09** holy place, nymphaeum, privilege, sacrarium, safeguard **10** frithsoken, protection, tabernacle **11** reservation **12** holy of holies **14** place of worship

**sanctum**
**03** den **05** study **06** refuge, shrine **07** hideout, retreat **08** hideaway **09** cubbyhole, holy place, sanctuary **12** holy of holies

**sand**
**04** grit, rock **05** beach, sands, shore **06** desert, strand **08** seashore **10** wilderness
• **sand dune, sand dunes**
**03** erg **04** areg, dene, down, seif

**06** barkan **07** barchan, barkhan
**08** barchane

**sandal**
**04** geta, zori **05** jelly, thong **06** galosh, golosh, Jandal® **07** chappal, galoche, talaria **08** flip-flap, flip-flop, huarache, slipslop **09** alpargata **12** calceamentum

**sandalwood**
**05** algum, almug **06** santal **07** sanders
**08** quandang, quandong, quantong
**10** buffalo-nut **11** sanderswood
**13** Barbados pride

**sandarac**
**04** arar

**sandbank**
**02** ås **03** bar, key **04** dune, kaim, kame, reef **05** esker, hurst, shelf, shoal
**07** sand bar, yardang **08** sandhill
**10** harbour-bar
**• opening between sandbanks**
**03** gat

**sand-eel**
**04** grig, lant **05** lance **06** launce

**Sandhurst**
**03** RMA **04** RMAS

**sandpiper**
**03** ree **04** knot, ruff **05** reeve, terek
**06** dunlin, ox-bird, willet **07** sea lark
**08** peetweet, redshank, sand-lark, sand-peep, sea snipe **10** greenshank, sanderling, yellowlegs

**sandstone**
**04** grit **05** fakes **06** arkose, dogger, faikes, Flysch, kingle **07** hassock
**08** sand-flag **09** bluestone, firestone, greensand, gritstone, holystone, quartzite, tile stone **10** brownstone
**13** millstone grit

**sandwich**
◇ *containment indicator*
**03** bap, BLT, wad **04** roti, wrap **05** butty, piece, round **06** burger, hoagie, sarney, sarnie **07** toastie **09** submarine
**10** jeely piece **11** intercalate, three-decker **12** double-decker **14** croque-monsieur

**sandy**
◇ *dialect indicator*
**03** red **04** Scot **05** light, rusty, tawny
**06** auburn, ginger, gritty, Titian, yellow
**07** coppery, gingery, reddish, yellowy
**08** sabulose, sabulous **09** gingerous, psammitic, yellowish **10** arenaceous
**13** reddish-yellow

**sane**
**04** wice, wise **05** lucid, sober, sound
**06** formal, normal, stable **07** herself, himself **08** all there, balanced, moderate, rational, sensible, yourself
**09** judicious **10** reasonable **11** level-headed, of sound mind, responsible, right-minded **12** compos mentis, well-balanced **15** in your right mind

**sangfroid**
**04** cool **05** nerve, poise **06** aplomb, phlegm **08** calmness, coolness
**09** assurance, composure
**10** dispassion, equanimity
**11** nonchalance, self-control
**12** indifference **14** cool-headedness, self-possession, unflappability

**sanguinary**
**04** gory, grim **05** cruel **06** bloody, brutal, savage **08** bloodied, pitiless, ruthless **09** merciless, murderous
**12** bloodthirsty

**sanguine**
**03** red **04** gory, pink, rosy **05** fresh, ruddy **06** ardent, bloody, florid, lively
**07** assured, buoyant, flushed, hopeful, roseate, unbowed **08** animated, blood-red, cheerful, rubicund, spirited
**09** confident, expectant, unabashed
**10** optimistic **13** over-confident
**14** over-optimistic

**sanitary**
**04** pure **05** clean **07** aseptic, healthy, sterile **08** germ-free, hygienic
**09** wholesome **10** antiseptic, salubrious, unpolluted **11** disinfected
**14** uncontaminated

**sanitize**
**05** clean **06** filter, purify, refine
**07** cleanse, clean up, freshen
**08** fumigate **09** deodorize, disinfect, expurgate, sterilize **13** decontaminate, make palatable **14** make acceptable
**15** make presentable

**sanity**
**04** mind **05** sense **06** health, reason, wisdom **08** lucidity, prudence
**09** good sense, normality, soundness, stability **11** common sense, rationality
**13** balance of mind, judiciousness
**14** responsibility **15** level-headedness, right-mindedness, soundness of mind

**San Marino**
**03** RSM, SMR

**Santa Claus**
**06** St Nick **10** St Nicholas **11** Kris Kringle **12** Kriss Kringle **15** Father Christmas

**São Tomé and Príncipe**
**02** ST **03** STP

**sap**
**03** box, git, mug, nit **04** clot, fink, fool, jerk, ooze, prat, sura, twit **05** bleed, drain, erode, idiot, juice, moron, toddy
**06** energy, impair, nitwit, reduce, trench, vigour, weaken **07** deplete, essence, exhaust **08** diminish, enervate, enfeeble, imbecile, palm wine, vitality, wear away, wear down
**09** lifeblood, palm-honey, undermine
**10** debilitate, karyolymph, plant fluid, vital fluid

**sapi-utan**
**04** anoa

**sapling**
**05** plant **06** tellar, teller, tiller **08** ash-plant, flittern **09** ground-ash, ground oak

**sapper**
**02** RE

**sarcasm**
**04** jibe, wipe **05** irony, scorn **06** gibing, satire **07** acidity, mockery
**08** acrimony, contempt, cynicism, derision, mordancy, ridicule, scoffing, sneering **09** invective **10** bitterness, resentment, trenchancy
**12** spitefulness
**• expression of sarcasm**
**03** gee

**sarcastic**
**04** acid **05** sarky, sharp, snide, witty
**06** biting **07** acerbic, caustic, cutting, cynical, jeering, mocking, mordant, pungent, satiric **08** derisive, derisory, incisive, ironical, sardonic, scathing, scoffing, scornful, sneering, taunting
**09** invective, satirical **10** back-handed, Juvenalian, Voltairian **11** disparaging
**12** sharp-tongued

**sarcastically**
**09** cynically, jeeringly **10** ironically, scathingly, scornfully, tauntingly
**11** satirically

**sardonic**
**03** dry, wry **05** cruel **06** biting, bitter
**07** acerbic, cynical, jeering, mocking, mordant **08** derisive, scornful, sneering **09** heartless, malicious, sarcastic **11** acrimonious
**12** contemptuous

**sash**
**03** obi **04** belt **05** lungi, scarf, shash
**06** girdle **07** baldric, burdash, chassis
**08** baldrick, cincture **09** waistband
**10** cummerbund

**Saskatchewan**
**02** SK

**sassy**
**04** pert **05** fresh, lippy, saucy
**06** brazen, cheeky, mouthy **07** forward
**08** impudent, insolent **09** audacious
**11** impertinent **12** overfamiliar
**13** disrespectful

**Satan**
**05** devil **06** Belial **07** Abaddon, arch-foe, Lucifer, Old Nick, Shaitan
**08** Apollyon, the Devil, the Enemy
**09** arch-enemy, arch-felon, arch-fiend, Beelzebub, leviathan **10** the Evil One, the serpent, the Tempter **12** the Adversary **13** the old serpent
**14** Mephistopheles

**satanic**
**04** dark, evil **05** black **06** damned, sinful, wicked **07** demonic, hellish, inhuman **08** accursed, devilish, diabolic, fiendish, infernal **09** satanical
**10** abominable, diabolical, iniquitous, malevolent, sulphurous

**sate**
**04** cloy, fill, glut **05** gorge, satay, slake
**06** accloy, sicken, stodge **07** gratify, satiate, satisfy, surfeit **08** overfill, saturate

**sated**
**03** sad

**satellite**
**04** aide, moon **06** colony, lackey, minion, planet, puppet, vassal **07** moonlet **08** adherent, disciple, dominion, follower, hanger-on, parasite, province, retainer, sidekick, smallsat **09** attendant, dependant, spaceship, sycophant **10** dependency, spacecraft **11** subordinate **12** orbiting body, protectorate, space station

*Satellites include:*

**03** CAT
**04** ECHO
**05** Astra, TIROS
**06** Oshumi, Rohini
**07** Asterix, Horizon, Sputnik, Transit
**08** Explorer, INMARSAT, Intelsat, Prospero
**09** Early Bird, Long March
**11** Black Knight

*See also* **moon**

**satiate**
**04** cloy, fill, glut, jade, sate **05** gorge, slake, stuff **07** engorge, glutted, satisfy, surfeit **08** nauseate, overfeed, overfill

**satiety**
**07** surfeit **08** cloyment, fullness **09** repletion, satiation **10** saturation **11** repleteness **12** over-fullness, satisfaction **13** gratification **14** overindulgence

**satire**
**03** wit **04** jeer, skit **05** irony, satyr, spoof, squib **06** glance, parody, send-up, taxing **07** lampoon, Pasquil, Pasquin, sarcasm, Sotadic, take-off **08** raillery, ridicule, Sotadean, travesty **09** burlesque, invective **10** caricature, mazarinade **12** mickey-taking **15** comedy of manners

**satirical**
**06** biting, bitter **07** abusive, acerbic, caustic, cutting, cynical, mocking, mordant **08** derisive, incisive, ironical, sardonic, Swiftian, taunting **09** invective, sarcastic, trenchant **10** irreverent, ridiculing **12** Archilochian

**satirist**
**05** satyr **06** mocker, satire **07** Pasquil, Pasquin **08** parodist **09** lampooner, pasquiler, ridiculer **10** cartoonist, lampoonist, pasquilant **11** pasquinader **12** caricaturist

*Satirists include:*

**03** **Loy** (Myrna)
**04** **Cech** (Svatopluk), **Isla** (José Francisco de), **Pope** (Alexander)
**05** **Börne** (Ludwig), **Brown** (Thomas), **Cooke** (Ebenezer), **Ellis** (George), **Larra** (Mariano José de), **Meung** (Jean de), **Nashe** (Thomas), **Nesin** (Aziz), **Swift** (Jonathan)
**06** **Butler** (Samuel), **Giusti** (Giuseppe), **Horace**, **Lucian**, **Murner** (Thomas), **Pindar** (Peter), **Wolcot** (John)
**07** **Barclay** (John), **Juvenal**, **Marston** (John), **Mencken** (Henry Louis), **Persius**, **Régnier** (Mathurin), **Thurber** (James)
**08** **Apuleius** (Lucius), **Beerbohm** (Max), **Fischart** (Johann), **Lucilius** (Gaius), **Rabelais** (François)
**09** **Churchill** (Charles), **Delavigne** (Casimir), **Junqueiro** (Ablio Manuel Guerra), **Petronius** (Arbiter), **Whitehead** (Paul)
**10** **Mandeville** (Bernard)
**12** **Konstantinov** (Aleko)

*See also* **comedian**

**satirize**
**04** mock **06** deride, parody, send up **07** lampoon, Pasquil, Pasquin, take off **08** ridicule **09** burlesque, criticize, make fun of, poke fun at **10** caricature

**satisfaction**
**03** pay **04** ease **05** pride **06** amends, change, liking **07** comfort, content, damages, delight, payment, redress **08** pleasure, requital **09** atonement, enjoyment, happiness, indemnity, quittance, wellbeing **10** conviction, fulfilment, recompense, reparation, settlement, suffisance **11** complacence, complacency, contentment, restitution, vindication **12** compensation **13** gratification, reimbursement **15** indemnification

**satisfactorily**
**06** nicely **08** passably **10** acceptably, adequately, favourably **11** competently **12** sufficiently

**satisfactory**
**02** OK **03** A-OK, oke **04** fair, fine, nice, okay, well **05** sweet **06** cushty, proper **07** atoning, average **08** adequate, all right, passable, suitable **09** competent, copacetic, copasetic, favorable, kopasetic **10** acceptable, convincing, favourable, sufficient, tickety-boo **11** tickettyboo, up to scratch, up to the mark

**satisfied**
**04** full, paid, smug, sure **05** happy, sated **07** certain, content, pleased, replete **08** pacified, positive, satiated **09** contented, convinced, persuaded, reassured **13** self-satisfied

**satisfy**
**03** pay **04** apay, fill, meet, sate, stay **05** agree, appay, serve, slake **06** answer, assure, defray, fulfil, please, quench, settle, supply **07** appease, assuage, content, delight, gratify, indulge, placate, qualify, requite, satiate, suffice, surfeit **08** convince, live up to, persuade, reassure **09** discharge, indemnify **10** comply with **13** be adequate for, compensate for **15** be sufficient for

**satisfying**
**04** cool **06** enough, far-out, square, way-out **07** filling **08** cheering, pleasing **10** convincing, fulfilling, gratifying, harmonious, persuasive, refreshing **11** pleasurable **12** satisfactory

**saturate**
**03** wet **04** fill, glut, sate, soak **05** flood, imbue, souse, steep **06** drench **07** pervade, suffuse, surfeit **08** overfill, permeate, waterlog **09** surcharge **10** impregnate **14** make wet through

**saturated**
**05** drunk **06** imbued, soaked, sodden, soused **07** flooded, soaking, sopping, steeped **08** drenched, dripping, suffused, wringing **09** permeated **11** impregnated, waterlogged

**saturation**
**06** sating **07** filling, soaking **08** flooding, glutting **09** pervading, satiation, suffusion **10** permeation

**Saturday**
**03** Sat

**Saturn**
**06** Cronus

**saturnine**
**04** dour, dull, glum **05** grave, heavy, moody, stern **06** dismal, gloomy, morose, severe, sombre **07** austere **08** taciturn **09** withdrawn **10** melancholy, phlegmatic, unfriendly **15** uncommunicative

**satyr**
**05** silen **06** satire **07** silenus **08** satirist, woodwose **09** orang-utan, woodhouse

**sauce**
**03** dip, lip **04** sass **05** brass, cheek, mouth, nerve **06** rebuke, relish **08** audacity, backchat, belabour, dressing, pertness, rudeness **09** condiment, flippancy, freshness, impudence, insolence, sauciness **10** brazenness, cheekiness, disrespect, flavouring **11** irreverence, presumption **12** impertinence, malapertness

*Sauces include:*

**02** HP®
**03** jus, red, soy
**04** fish, hard, mint, mole, soja, soya, wine
**05** apple, bread, brown, caper, cream, curry, fudge, garum, gravy, melba, pesto, salsa, satay, shoyu, white
**06** catsup, cheese, chilli, coulis, fondue, fu yung, hoisin, mornay, nam pla, oxymel, oyster, panada, reform, tamari, tartar, tomato, tommy K
**07** catchup, custard, Daddies®, harissa, ketchup, nuoc mam, passata, rouille, sabayon, soubise, supreme, Tabasco®, tartare, velouté
**08** barbecue, béchamel, bigarade, chasseur, marinara, piri-piri, salpicon, yakitori
**09** béarnaise, black bean, bolognese, carbonara, chocolate, cranberry, demi-glace, espagnole, Marie Rose, remoulade, Worcester
**10** avgolemono, chaudfroid,

Cumberland, mayonnaise, mousseline, napoletana, puttanesca, salad cream, salsa verde, stroganoff
11 bourguignon, buerre blanc, hollandaise, horseradish, vinaigrette
12 brandy butter, sweet-and-sour
13 crème anglaise, salad dressing
14 Worcestershire

**saucepan**
**03** pan, pot, wok **05** fryer **06** chafer, goblet, vessel **07** milk pan, skillet **08** pancheon **09** casserole, container, frying-pan **12** double boiler

**saucy**
**04** pert, rude **05** fresh, lippy, peart, piert, sassy **06** brazen, cheeky, fruity, gallus **07** forward, gallows **08** flippant, impudent, insolent, malapert **10** disdainful, irreverent, lascivious **11** impertinent **12** presumptuous **13** disrespectful

**Saudi Arabia**
**02** SA **03** SAU

**saunter**
**04** walk **05** amble, daker, mooch, mosey, shool, shule **06** dacker, daiker, dander, dauner, dawdle, dawner, ramble, shoole, stroll, toddle, wander **07** daunder, meander **09** promenade **10** knock about **11** knock around **14** constitutional

**sausage**

*Sausages include:*

**04** beef, lamb, lola, pork
**05** blood, liver, Lorne, Lyons, snags, weeny, wurst
**06** banger, bumbar, garlic, hot dog, kishke, lolita, mumbar, polony, salami, summer, weenie, Wiener, wienie
**07** abruzzo, baloney, Bologna, boloney, cabanos, chorizo, corn dog, kabanos, klobasa, merguez, saveloy, zampone
**08** cervelat, chaurice, chourico, cocktail, drisheen, kielbasa, linguica, peperoni, Toulouse
**09** andouille, bierwurst, blutwurst, boerewors, bratwurst, chipolata, cotechino, lap cheong, loukanika, pepperoni, saucisson
**10** bauerwurst, boudin noir, cervellata, Cumberland, knackwurst, knockwurst, liverwurst, mortadella
**11** boudin blanc, boudin rouge, frankfurter, Wienerwurst
**12** andouillette, black pudding, Lincolnshire

**savage**
**04** bite, boor, claw, fell, grim, maul, slam, tear, wild **05** beast, brute, churl, cruel, feral, harsh, slate **06** attack, bloody, brutal, fierce, immane, mangle **07** beastly, furious, inhuman, monster, rubbish, run down, salvage, untamed, vicious, wild man **08** barbaric, denounce, lacerate, pitiless, ruthless, sadistic, terrible, warrigal **09** barbarian, barbarous, cut-throat, dog-eat-dog, ferocious, merciless, murderous, primitive, wild woman **10** go to town on, wild person **11** pick holes in, uncivilized **12** bloodthirsty, catamountain, cat o' mountain, pull to pieces, pull to shreds, tear to pieces, tear to shreds **14** undomesticated **15** do a hatchet job on

**savagely**
**07** cruelly, harshly **08** brutally, fiercely **09** viciously **10** pitilessly, ruthlessly **11** barbarously, ferociously, mercilessly **12** barbarically

**savagery**
**06** ferity, sadism **07** cruelty **08** ferocity, wildness **09** barbarism, barbarity, brutality, roughness **10** bestiality, fierceness, inhumanity **11** brutishness, viciousness **12** pitilessness, ruthlessness **13** mercilessness, murderousness, primitiveness

**savant**
**04** guru, sage **06** master, pundit **07** learned, scholar **09** authority **10** mastermind **11** philosopher **12** accomplished, intellectual, man of letters **14** woman of letters

**save**
**02** sa' **04** free, hain, hold, keep, safe **05** guard, hoard, lay up, put by, spare, stash, store **06** budget, but for, except, export, gather, hinder, redeem, rescue, retain, screen, shield, snudge, unless **07** bail out, collect, cut back, deliver, obviate, prevent, protect, reclaim, recover, release, reserve, salvage, set free, use less **08** conserve, cut costs, excepted, keep safe, liberate, preserve, put aside, retrieve, set aside, sock away **09** apart from, aside from, be thrifty, economize, except for, excluding, safeguard, stockpile **10** buy cheaply **11** not counting **13** scrimp and save **14** live on the cheap **15** get someone out of, tighten your belt

**saving**
**03** cut **04** fund **05** store **06** frugal, thrift **07** bargain, capital, careful, economy, nest egg, sparing, thrifty **08** discount, reserves **09** excepting, redeeming, reduction, resources, salvatory **10** economical, mitigating, preserving, protecting, qualifying **11** extenuating, investments, reservation **12** compensating, compensatory, conservation, preservation

**saviour**
**04** Jesu **05** Jesus **06** Christ **07** Messiah, rescuer **08** champion, defender, Emmanuel, guardian, Mediator, redeemer **09** deliverer, Lamb of God, liberator, protector **11** emancipator

**savoir-faire**
**04** tact **05** poise **07** ability, finesse, knowhow **08** urbanity **09** assurance, diplomacy, expertise **10** capability, confidence, discretion **11** social grace **12** social graces **14** accomplishment

**savour**
**03** sar **04** hint, like, odor, sair, salt, tang, zest **05** aroma, enjoy, odour, scent, smack, smell, speak, spice, taste, touch, trace **06** relish, repute, resent, season **07** bouquet, flavour, perfume, revel in, suggest **08** piquancy, seem like **09** delight in, fragrance **10** appreciate, smattering, suggestion **14** enjoy to the full, take pleasure in, taste to the full

**savoury**
**04** tapa **05** gusty, salty, sapid, snack, spicy, tangy, tapas, tasty, yummy **06** canapé, gustie, nibble, samosa, spiced **07** gustful, piquant, scrummy **08** aigrette, aromatic, fragrant, luscious **09** appetizer, delicious, palatable **10** appetizing **11** amuse-bouche, amuse-gueule, bonne-bouche, flavoursome, hors d'oeuvre, respectable, scrumptious **13** mouthwatering

**savvy**
**03** sly **04** keen, know, wily **05** acute, alert, canny, sharp, skill, smart **06** artful, astute, callid, clever, crafty, shrewd **07** cunning, know-how, knowing **09** judicious, observant, sagacious **10** calculated, discerning, far-sighted, perceptive, understand **11** calculating, intelligent, well-advised **13** knowledgeable, perspicacious **14** discriminating

**saw**
**03** mot, say, sow **05** adage, axiom, gnome, maxim, salve **06** byword, decree, dictum, saying **07** epigram, proverb **08** aphorism **10** apophthegm **11** commonplace

*Saws include:*

**03** jig, rip
**04** band, fret, hack, hand
**05** bench, chain, panel, tenon
**06** coping, rabbet, scroll
**07** compass, pruning
**08** circular, crosscut
**09** radial-arm
**11** power-driven

**say**
◇ *homophone indicator*
**02** eg **03** add, put, saw **04** read, sway, tell, vote, word **05** assay, claim, clout, drawl, grunt, guess, imply, judge, orate, order, power, reply, speak, state, utter, voice **06** affirm, allege, answer, assert, assume, convey, mutter, phrase, recite, reckon, rejoin, remark, render, repeat, report, retort, reveal, rumour, speech, weight **07** comment, declare, deliver, divulge, exclaim, express, imagine, mention, observe, opinion, perform, presume, respond, signify, suggest, suppose, surmise **08** announce, disclose, estimate, indicate, instruct, intimate, maintain, rehearse **09** authority, ejaculate, enunciate, influence, pronounce **10** articulate, for

example **11** come out with, communicate, turn to speak **12** put into words **13** approximately, chance to speak

**• that is to say**
**02** ie, sc **03** viz **05** id est, to wit **06** namely, that is **09** c'est-à-dire, videlicet **12** in other words

**saying**
◇ *homophone indicator*
**03** mot, saw **04** cant, dict, read, rede, reed, word **05** adage, axiom, gnome, maxim, motto, reede **06** bon mot, byword, cliché, dictum, phrase, remark, slogan, wisdom **07** diction, epigram, fadaise, precept, proverb **08** aphorism, apothegm, overword **09** platitude, quotation, rusticism, statement **10** apophthegm, expression **11** catch phrase **12** word of wisdom **13** household word, pearl of wisdom

**say-so**
**02** OK **04** word **06** dictum, rumour **07** backing, consent, go-ahead, hearsay **08** approval, sanction, thumbs-up **09** agreement, assertion, assurance, authority, guarantee **10** green light, permission **11** affirmation **12** asseveration, ratification **13** authorization

**scab**
**03** rat **08** blackleg **13** strike-breaker

**scabies**
**04** itch **05** psora

**scaffold**
**05** stage, tower **06** gantry, gibbet **07** catasta, gallows, hanging, sustain, the rope **08** platform **09** framework **11** scaffolding

**scald**
**04** burn, leep, plot, poet, sear **05** brand, ploat, scaud, skald **06** paltry, scabby, scorch, scurfy **07** blister **09** cauterize

**scalding**
**07** boiling, burning **08** steaming **09** piping hot **10** blistering **12** extremely hot

**scale**
**04** coat, film, go up, leaf, scan **05** climb, crust, flake, gamme, gamut, layer, level, Libra, mount, order, palea, plate, range, ratio, reach, scope, scurf, shell, skail, weigh **06** ascend, degree, extent, furfur, gunter, ladder, lamina, plaque, series, shin up, spread, squama, tartar **07** clamber, coating, compass, conquer, deposit, measure, ranking **08** escalade, register, scramble, sequence, spectrum, surmount **09** hierarchy, limescale **10** graduation, proportion **11** calibration, progression **12** encrustation, pecking order, relative size **15** measuring system

**• scale down**
**04** drop **06** lessen, reduce, shrink **07** cut back, cut down **08** contract, decrease, make less

**• scale up**
**05** boost, raise **06** bump up, expand, hike up, step up **07** augment, build up, develop, enhance, further, improve **08** increase **09** intensify **10** accumulate, strengthen

**scaliness**
**06** furfur **08** dandruff **09** flakiness, leprosity **10** scurfiness, squamation, squamosity **12** scabrousness

**scallop**
**03** dag **04** clam, gimp, mush **05** grill **06** pecten **07** queenie **08** coquille

**scaly**
**05** flaky, rough **06** branny, scabby, scurfy, shabby **07** leprose, leprous **08** lepidote, scabrous, scarious, squamate, squamose, squamous **09** furfurous **10** squamulose **12** desquamative, desquamatory, furfuraceous

**scam**
**03** con **04** game **05** dodge, fraud, trick **06** fiddle, racket, rip-off, scheme **07** swindle **08** business **09** deception, gold brick

**scamp**
**03** imp **05** devil, losel, rogue **06** fripon, monkey, rascal, skelum, wretch **07** skellum **08** blighter, scalawag, schellum, spalpeen, vagabond **09** reprobate, scallawag, scallywag **10** highwayman **12** troublemaker **13** mischief-maker **14** good-for-nothing, whippersnapper

**scamper**
**03** fly, ren, rin, run **04** dart, dash, lamp, race, romp, rush **05** hurry, scoot, scoup, scowp **06** decamp, frolic, gambol, hasten, scurry, sprint **07** scuttle, skitter **08** scramble

**scan**
**03** con, kon **04** read, skim, test **05** check, climb, conne, judge, probe, scale, spell, study, sweep **06** go over, review, search, survey **07** CAT scan, examine, inspect, run over **08** glance at, scrutiny **09** interpret, screening **10** inspection, run through, scrutinize, sector scan **11** examination, flip through, investigate, leaf through **12** flick through, thumb through **13** browse through, investigation, scintilliscan **14** run your eye over

**scandal**
**04** blot, dirt, -gate, pity, slur **05** libel, shame, shock, smear, stain **06** defame, furore, gossip, outcry, uproar **07** calumny, obloquy, offence, outrage, rumours, slander **08** disgrace, ignominy, reproach **09** black mark, discredit, dishonour **10** defamation, dirty linen, opprobrium **11** crying shame **12** dirty laundry, dirty washing **13** embarrassment

**scandalize**
**05** appal, repel, shock **06** dismay, insult, offend, revolt **07** affront, disgust, horrify, outrage, slander **08** disgrace

**scandalmonger**
**06** gossip, tattle **07** defamer, tattler **08** busybody, quidnunc, traducer **09** muck-raker **10** talebearer **11** calumniator, Nosey Parker, sweetie-wife **12** gossip-monger

**scandalous**
**05** gamey, juicy **06** untrue **07** blatant **08** flagrant, improper, infamous, shameful, shocking, unseemly **09** appalling, atrocious, libellous, malicious, monstrous **10** abominable, defamatory, outrageous, scurrilous, slanderous **11** disgraceful, opprobrious, sensational, unspeakable **12** disreputable **13** dishonourable

**Scandinavian**
**05** Norse

*Scandinavians include:*

**04** Dane, Finn
**05** Swede
**06** Norman, viking
**08** Norseman
**09** Icelander, Norwegian, Varangian

**scandium**
**02** Sc

**scanner**

*Scanners include:*

**02** CT
**03** CAT, PET
**04** body, SPET
**07** barcode, flatbed
**10** Emi-Scanner®

**scant**
**04** bare, jimp **05** short, stint **06** barely, jimply, little, measly, reduce, slight, sparse **07** limited, minimal, sparing **08** exiguous, restrict, scantily, scarcity **09** deficient, hardly any **10** inadequate, little or no **12** insufficient

**scantily**
**06** barely, poorly **08** meagrely, scarcely, skimpily, sparsely **11** deficiently **12** inadequately **14** insufficiently

**scanty**
**03** low, shy **04** bare, hard, poor, thin **05** brief, light, scant, short, skimp, spare **06** little, meagre, narrow, scrimp, skimpy, sparse **07** limited, scrimpy **08** exiguous **09** deficient, penurious **10** inadequate, restricted **12** insufficient **13** insubstantial

**scapegoat**
**05** bunny, patsy **06** stooge, sucker, victim **07** fall guy **11** whipping-boy

**scar**
**04** mark, wipe **05** brand, cliff, hilum, scare, scaur, shock, spoil, wound **06** blotch, damage, deface, injure, injury, keloid, lesion, stigma, trauma, ulosis **07** blemish, desmoid, pockpit **08** cicatrix, pockmark, sword-cut **09** cicatrice, cicatrize, discolour, disfigure **10** cicatricle, defacement, stigmatize, traumatize **11** cicatricula, leaf-cushion **12** cicatrichule, parrot-wrasse **13** disfigurement **14** discolouration

**scarce**
**03** few **04** dear, rare **05** scant, tight **06** meagre, scanty, sparse **07** lacking, sparing, unusual **08** uncommon **09** deficient, not enough, too little **10** inadequate, infrequent **12** insufficient, like gold dust **13** in short supply

**• make yourself scarce**
**05** scoot **06** go fast **07** dash off **08** run for it, rush away **10** make tracks **12** leave quickly **15** take to your heels

**scarcely**
**03** not **05** uneth **06** barely, hardly, uneath **08** no sooner, not at all, only just, scantily, scrimply, uneathes, unnethes **12** certainly not **13** definitely not

**scarcity**
**04** lack, want **05** scant **06** dearth, famine, rarity **07** paucity **08** exiguity, rareness, shortage **09** scantness **10** deficiency, scantiness, sparseness **11** infrequency **12** uncommonness **13** insufficiency, niggardliness

**scare**
**04** scar, scat, shoo **05** alarm, appal, daunt, gally, gliff, glift, panic, scaur, shock, skear, skeer, start **06** affray, dismay, fright, horror, menace, rattle, scarre, terror **07** perturb, petrify, startle, terrify, unnerve **08** frighten, hysteria, threaten **09** terrorize **10** intimidate, make afraid, scare silly **11** fearfulness **12** put the wind up **14** make frightened

**scarecrow**
**04** bogy **05** bogle, sewel **06** boggle, malkin, mawkin, shewel **07** boggard, boggart **09** galli-crow, gally-crow **10** crow-keeper **11** galli-bagger, galli-beggar, gally-bagger, gally-beggar, potato bogle, tattiebogle

**scared**
**03** rad **05** cowed **06** afraid, shaken **07** alarmed, anxious, chicken, fearful, jittery, nervous, panicky, quivery, worried **08** startled, unnerved **09** petrified, terrified **10** frightened, terrorized **11** in a blue funk **13** having kittens, panic-stricken, scared to death **14** terror-stricken

**scaremonger**
**08** alarmist **09** Cassandra, jitterbug, pessimist **11** doomwatcher **13** prophet of doom

**scarf**
**10** chaplaincy

*Scarfs, veils and other head cloths include:*

**04** caul, doek, haik, hyke, rail, sash, veil
**05** curch, fichu, haick, hejab, hijab, pagri, shawl, stole, volet, whisk
**06** chadar, chador, cravat, haique, kiss-me, madras, rebozo, screen, tippet, turban, weeper, wimple
**07** belcher, chaddar, chaddor, chuddah, chuddar, dopatta, dupatta, foulard, kufiyah, modesty, muffler, necktie, orarium, puggery, puggree, whimple, yashmak
**08** babushka, chrismal, kaffiyeh, kalyptra, keffiyeh, kerchief, mantilla, neckatee, puggaree, vexillum
**09** comforter, headcloth, headscarf, muffettee
**10** fascinator, headsquare, lambrequin
**11** kiss-me-quick, neckerchief, nightingale

**scarlet**
**03** red **06** redden, vermil **07** vermeil, vermell, vermily **08** cardinal **09** vermeille, vermilion

**scarper**
**02** go **04** bolt, flee, flit **05** leave, scram **06** beat it, decamp, depart, escape, vanish **07** abscond, bunk off, do a bunk, run away, vamoose **08** clear off, run for it **09** disappear, skedaddle **10** hightail it **13** make a run for it

**scary**
**05** eerie, hairy **06** creepy, skeary, skeery, spooky **08** alarming, chilling, daunting, fearsome, shocking, timorous **10** disturbing, forbidding, formidable, horrifying, petrifying, terrifying **11** frightening, hair-raising **12** intimidating, white-knuckle **13** bloodcurdling, spine-chilling

**scathing**
**04** acid **05** harsh **06** biting, bitter, brutal, fierce, savage, severe **07** caustic, cutting, mordant **08** critical, scornful, stinging **09** ferocious, sarcastic, trenchant, unsparing, vitriolic, withering **11** detrimental, devastating

**scatter**
◇ *anagram indicator*
**03** dot, sow **05** blind, fling, flurr, scail, scale, shake, skail, strew **06** berley, burley, dispel, divide, litter, shower, spread **07** break up, diffuse, disband, disject, scamble, shatter, spatter **08** disperse, disunite, separate, splutter, sprinkle, squander **09** bescatter, broadcast, dissipate **10** dispersion, scattering, sprinkling **11** backscatter, disseminate, intersperse **12** disintegrate **14** cast to the winds **15** fling to the winds, throw to the winds

**scatterbrained**
**05** ditsy, ditzy, dizzy **06** scatty **08** carefree, careless **09** airheaded, forgetful, frivolous, impulsive, slaphappy **10** unreliable **11** empty-headed, hare-brained, inattentive, thoughtless **12** absent-minded **13** irresponsible, wool-gathering **14** feather-brained

**scattering**
**03** few **07** break-up, handful, poor-oot, pour-out **10** dispersion, smattering, sprinkling **12** disgregation

**scatty**
◇ *anagram indicator*
**10** abstracted **11** empty-headed, hare-brained, harum-scarum **12** absent-minded **14** scatterbrained

**scavenge**
**04** hunt, rake **06** forage, search **07** cleanse, look for, rummage **08** scrounge

**scavenger**
**04** dieb, hyen **05** hyena, raker **06** hyaena, jackal **07** forager, gorcrow, scaffie, vulture **08** caracara, night-man, rummager, scavager **09** scrounger **13** lion's provider

**scenario**
**04** plan, plot **05** scene, state **06** résumé, scheme, script **07** outline, summary **08** sequence, synopsis **09** programme, situation, storyline **10** continuity, projection, screenplay **13** circumstances **14** state of affairs

**scene**
**03** act, set **04** area, clip, fuss, part, show, site, spot, to-do, veil, view **05** arena, drama, field, place, scena, sight, stage, vista **06** circus, furore, locale, milieu, screen **07** context, curtain, display, episode, outlook, pageant, picture, scenery, setting, tableau, tantrum **08** backdrop, division, incident, locality, location, outburst, panorama, position, prospect **09** commotion, induction, kerfuffle, landscape, situation, spectacle **10** background, exhibition, proceeding, speciality **11** environment, performance, streetscape, whereabouts **13** tableau vivant **14** area of activity, area of interest **15** three-ring circus

**• behind the scenes**
**06** within **08** secretly **09** backstage, in private, privately **10** on the quiet, out of sight **11** not in public **15** surreptitiously

**• scenes**
**04** play

**scenery**
**03** set **04** view **05** décor, scene, vista **07** film set, outlook, scenary, setting, terrain **08** backdrop, panorama, prospect **09** landscape **10** background **11** mise-en-scène **12** surroundings

**scenic**
**05** grand **06** pretty **08** striking **09** beautiful, panoramic **10** attractive, impressive **11** picturesque, spectacular **12** awe-inspiring, breathtaking

**scent**
**04** nose, odor, sent, vent, waft **05** aroma, fumet, odour, sense, smell, sniff, spoor, trace, track, trail **06** detect **07** bouquet, cologne, discern, essence, fumette, nose out, perfume **08** perceive, sniff out **09** fragrance, recognize, redolence **11** toilet water **12** eau-de-cologne **13** become aware of, eau-de-toilette

**scented**
**04** rank **07** roseate **08** aromatic, fragrant, perfumed **13** sweet-smelling

**sceptic**
**05** cynic **07** atheist, doubter, scoffer **08** agnostic **10** questioner, unbeliever **11** disbeliever, rationalist **14** doubting Thomas

**sceptical**
**07** cynical, dubious, infidel **08** academic, doubtful, doubting, hesitant, scoffing **10** hesitating, suspicious, Voltairian **11** distrustful, incredulous, mistrustful, pessimistic, questioning, unbelieving, unconvinced **12** disbelieving

**scepticism**
**05** doubt **07** atheism, dubiety **08** cynicism, distrust, nihilism, unbelief **09** disbelief, hesitancy, pessimism, Sadducism, suspicion **10** Pyrrhonism **11** agnosticism, incredulity, rationalism, Sadduceeism **12** doubtfulness

• **expression of scepticism**
**02** ha **04** umph **09** away you go! **11** away with you! **12** pigs might fly

**sceptre**
**03** rod **05** baton, staff **06** bauble

**schedule**
**04** book, form, list, plan, time **05** diary, slate, table **06** agenda, assign, scheme **07** appoint, arrange **08** calendar, organize, syllabus **09** catalogue, inventory, itinerary, programme, timetable **10** enschedule

• **behind schedule**
**04** late **07** overdue **10** behindhand, behind time **11** running late

• **on schedule**
**05** on tap **06** on time **07** on track **08** on course, on target **15** according to plan

• **place in schedule**
**04** slot **06** window

**schema**
**03** map **04** form, plan **05** chart, shape **06** design, figure, layout, scheme, sketch **07** diagram, outline, profile, tracing **09** lineament **11** delineation **13** configuration

**schematic**
**07** graphic **08** symbolic **10** simplified **12** diagrammatic, illustrative

**scheme**
◇ *anagram indicator*
**03** gin, key, map **04** dart, game, idea, plan, plat, plot, ploy, ruse **05** angle, chart, draft, frame, shape, shift, table **06** bubble, design, device, devise, layout, method, schema, sketch, system, tactic **07** collude, connive, diagram, nostrum, outline, pattern, project, tactics, work out **08** conspire, contrive, escapade, intrigue, pedigree, platform, practice, practise, proposal, schedule, strategy **09** blueprint, machinate, manoeuvre, procedure, programme, stratagem, underplot **10** conspiracy, manipulate, mastermind, suggestion **11** arrangement, delineation, disposition, proposition, pull strings **12** machinations **13** configuration **14** course of action

**schemer**
**03** fox **07** plotter, wangler **08** conniver, deceiver **09** contriver, intrigant, intriguer **10** intrigante, intriguant, machinator, mastermind, politician, wire-puller **11** intriguante, Machiavelli **13** éminence grise, Machiavellian, wheeler-dealer

**scheming**
**03** sly **04** foxy, wily **06** artful, crafty, tricky **07** cunning, devious **08** practice, slippery **09** conniving, deceitful, designing, insidious, underhand **11** calculating, duplicitous **12** manipulative, unscrupulous **13** Machiavellian

**schism**
**04** rift, sect **05** break, group, split **06** breach **07** discord, faction, rupture **08** disunion, division, scission, splinter **09** severance **10** detachment, separation **12** estrangement

**schismatic**
**05** rebel **08** apostate, renegade, seceding **09** breakaway, heretical **10** dissenting, separatist **12** secessionist

**schmaltz**
**04** glop, gush, mush, pulp **05** slush **09** soppiness **10** sloppiness **11** mawkishness, romanticism **12** emotionalism **14** sentimentality

**scholar**
**01** L **02** BA, MA **05** clerk, pupil **06** day-boy, expert, pundit, savant **07** artsman, bookman, Dantist, day-girl, egghead, Grecian, learner, Maulana, Pauline, savante, student **08** academic, bookworm, boursier, disciple, Saxonist, schoolie, Semitist, taberdar **09** authority, Gothicist, schoolboy, schoolman, Talmudist **10** Carthusian, day-scholar, mastermind, postmaster, scholastic, schoolgirl **11** philosopher, schoolchild **12** intellectual, man of letters **14** woman of letters **15** person of letters

**scholarly**
**06** school **07** bookish, clerkly, erudite, learned **08** academic, highbrow, lettered, literate, studious, well-read **09** clerklike **10** analytical, scholastic, scientific **12** intellectual **13** conscientious, knowledgeable

**scholarship**
**05** award, burse, grant **06** wisdom **07** bursary **08** learning **09** education, endowment, erudition, knowledge, schooling **10** exhibition, fellowship **11** learnedness, Orientalism

**scholastic**
**06** subtle **07** bookish, learned, precise, teacher **08** academic, lettered, literary, pedantic **09** pedagogic, scholarly, schoolman **10** analytical **11** educational

**school**
**02** GS **03** gam, pod, Sch, set **04** club, coed, high, prep, scul, sect **05** class, coach, drill, flock, group, guild, prime, scull, shoal, teach, train, troop, tutor, verse **06** circle, clique, infant, junior, league, pupils, sculle **07** academy, college, company, coterie, educate, faction, faculty, madrasa, prepare, primary, society, yeshiva **08** admonish, division, instruct, madrasah, madrassa, seminary, students, yeshivah **09** institute, madrassah, medresseh, palaestra, secondary **10** assemblage, department, discipline, foundation, kohanga reo, university **11** association, institution, pedagoguery **12** indoctrinate

*Schools include:*

**03** LSE
**04** Eton
**05** Rugby, Slade
**06** Ascham, Fettes, Harrow, Te Aute
**07** Loretto, Roedean, St Paul's
**08** Bluecoat, Hogwarts
**09** Cranbrook
**10** Ampleforth, Grange Hill, Greyfriars, Shrewsbury, Stonyhurst, St Trinian's, The Friends, Winchester
**11** Abbotsleigh, Giggleswick, Gordonstoun, Marlborough, Perth Modern, Westminster
**12** Chalet School, Charterhouse, Linbury Court, Malory Towers, Marcia Blaine
**13** Dotheboys Hall, James Ruse High, Queen Victoria
**14** Fort Street High, Geelong Grammar, The Kings School
**15** Merchant Taylors'

*See also* **art**; **educational**

**schoolboy, schoolgirl** *see* **pupil**

**schooling**
**05** drill **07** reproof, tuition **08** coaching, guidance, learning, teaching, training **09** education, grounding, reprimand **10** discipline **11** instruction, preparation **12** book-learning **14** indoctrination

**schoolteacher**
**06** master **07** dominie, teacher **08** educator, mistress, schoolie **09** pedagogue **10** instructor, schoolmarm **12** schoolmaster **14** schoolmistress

**schooner**
**04** tern **12** fore-and-after

**science**
**03** art, sci **05** skill **09** dexterity, expertise, knowledge, technique **10** discipline, technology **11** proficiency **14** specialization

*Sciences include:*

**04** agri, food, life
**05** earth
**06** botany

07 anatomy, biology, ecology, geology, medical, natural, physics, zoology
08 chemurgy, computer, domestic, dynamics, genetics, robotics
09 acoustics, astronomy, chemistry, dietetics, economics, materials, mechanics, pathology, political, sociology
10 biophysics, entomology, geophysics, graphology, hydraulics, metallurgy, mineralogy, morphology, physiology, psychology, toxicology, veterinary
11 aeronautics, archaeology, behavioural, climatology, cybernetics, diagnostics, electronics, engineering, linguistics, mathematics, meteorology, ornithology, ultrasonics
12 aerodynamics, agricultural, anthropology, astrophysics, biochemistry, geochemistry, geographical, macrobiotics, microbiology, pharmacology
13 environmental
14 geoarchaeology, nuclear physics, radiochemistry, thermodynamics
15 electrodynamics, space technology

*See also* **science fiction** *under* **fiction**

**scientific**
05 exact 07 orderly, precise
08 accurate, thorough 09 regulated, scholarly 10 analytical, controlled, methodical, systematic
12 mathematical 13 demonstrative
*See also* **law**

*Scientific concepts include:*

04 area, heat, mass, time, work
05 force, power
06 energy, length, stress, torque, volume
07 density
08 enthalpy, momentum, pressure, velocity
09 frequency, impedance, reactance, viscosity
10 admittance, plane angle, solid angle
11 capacitance, conductance, power factor, susceptance, temperature
12 acceleration, electric flux, illumination, luminous flux, magnetic flux, permeability, permittivity
13 electric force, kinetic energy, moment of force
14 electric charge, mass rate of flow, self inductance, surface tension
15 angular momentum, electric current, moment of inertia, potential energy, velocity of light

*Scientific instruments include:*

06 strobe
07 coherer, vernier
08 barostat, cryostat, rheocord, rheostat
09 decoherer, heliostat, hodoscope, hydrostat, hygrostat, image tube, microtome, slide rule, telemeter, tesla coil, thyratron, zymoscope
10 centrifuge, collimator, eudiometer, heliograph, humidistat, hydrophone, hydroscope, hygrograph, iconoscope, microscope, nephograph, pantograph, radarscope, radiosonde, tachograph, teinoscope, thermostat
11 chronograph, fluoroscope, stactometer, stauroscope, stroboscope, transformer, transponder, tunnel diode
12 dephlegmator, electrosonde, oscillograph, oscilloscope, spectroscope
13 Geiger counter, phonendoscope, tachistoscope
14 absorptiometer, image converter, interferometer, torsion balance
15 electromyograph, telethermoscope

**scientist**
05 brain 06 boffin, doctor, expert, genius 07 analyst, ologist, planner, thinker 08 designer, engineer, inventor 09 intellect, magnetist 10 alchemist, mastermind, researcher 11 backroom-boy 12 entomologist, experimenter, intellectual, investigator, technologist
14 explorationist, research worker
*See also* **anatomy**; **anthropology**; **archaeology**; **astronomer**; **bacteriology**; **biochemistry**; **biology**; **botany**; **chemist**; **computer**; **economist**; **engineer**; **genetics**; **geography**; **inventor**; **mathematics**; **palaeontologist**; **physics**; **physiology**; **psychology**; **zoology**

**scintilla**
03 bit, jot 04 atom, hint, iota, mite, spot, whit 05 grain, piece, scrap, shred, spark, speck, trace 07 modicum, remnant, snippet 08 fragment, particle, skerrick

**scintillate**
04 wink 05 blaze, flash, gleam, glint, shine, spark 07 glisten, glitter, sparkle, twinkle 09 coruscate

**scintillating**
05 witty 06 bright, lively 07 shining
08 animated, dazzling, exciting, flashing 09 brilliant, ebullient, sparkling, twinkling, vivacious
10 glittering 11 stimulating
12 exhilarating, invigorating

**scion**
03 imp 04 cion, heir, sien, syen, twig
05 child, graft, plant, seyen, shoot, sient, sprig 06 branch, sprout
08 offshoot 09 offspring, successor
10 descendant 11 engraftment

**scissors**
06 cizers, forfex, shears 13 pinking shears

**scoff**
03 dor, eat, rib 04 bolt, chow, eats, food, gall, geck, gibe, grub, gulp, jeer, jibe, meal, mock, nosh, rail, tuck, wolf
05 binge, knock, scaff, scorn, scran, snarf, sneer, taunt, tease 06 deride, devour, gall at, geck at, gobble, guzzle, nosh-up, revile 07 consume, despise, laugh at, mockery, plunder, poke fun, put away 08 belittle, eatables, pooh-pooh, ridicule 09 disparage, finish off, nutriment, nutrition 10 foodstuffs, provisions, sustenance 11 comestibles, nourishment, subsistence
12 refreshments

**scoffing**
07 cynical, mocking 08 derisive, derisory, fiendish, scathing, sneering, taunting 09 sarcastic 11 disparaging
14 Mephistophelic
15 Mephistophelean, Mephistophelian

**scold**
03 jaw, nag, rag, row, wig, yap 04 Fury, rage, rant, rate, yaff 05 blame, brawl, chide, flite, flyte, go off, shrew, slang, vixen 06 berate, blow up, callet, dragon, rattle, rebuke, virago, yankie
07 censure, earbash, go off at, jawbone, lambast, lecture, reprove, rouse on, speak to, start on, tell off, tick off, trimmer, upbraid 08 admonish, harridan, reproach, spitfire, tear into, Xantippe 09 brimstone, castigate, go crook at, henpecker, objurgate, reprimand, start in on, take apart, termagant 10 take to task
11 clapperclaw 15 give it to someone

**scolding**
03 row 05 doing 06 dirdam, dirdum, earful, rating, rebuke 07 chiding, hearing, lecture, reproof, rollick, wigging 08 jobation, sasarara, siserary, slanging 09 carpeting, jawbation, reprimand, sassarara, sisserary, talking-to, termagant 10 earbashing, earwigging, telling-off, ticking-off, upbraiding 11 castigation, throughgaun 12 dressing-down, through-going

**scombroid fish**
04 seer, seir

**scoop**
03 dig, dip, lap 04 bail, coup, grab, lade, pale 05 empty, gouge, ladle, spoon 06 bailer, bucket, dipper, exposé, hollow, latest, remove, scrape, shovel 07 helping, portion
08 excavate, ladleful, spoonful
09 exclusive, sensation 10 revelation
11 inside story

**scoot**
03 run, zip 04 belt, bolt, dart, dash, rush, scud, tear 05 hurry, scout, shoot
06 beat it, career, scurry, sprint, squirt, tootle 07 scarper, scuttle, vamoose
09 skedaddle

**scope**
03 aim, VDU, way 04 area, play, room, span, wale 05 ambit, field, orbit, range, reach, realm, remit, round, space, sweep, swing, verge 06 cinema, domain, extent, leeway, limits, scouth, scowth, sphere 07 breadth, compass,

display, freedom, liberty, monitor, purpose, purview **08** capacity, confines, coverage, latitude
**09** dimension, elbow-room
**11** opportunity **12** spaciousness

**scorch**
**03** fry **04** burn, char, plot, sear
**05** adust, blast, dry up, parch, ploat, roast, scald, scath, singe, slash, swale, swayl, sweal, sweel **06** birsle, scaith, scathe, sizzle, skaith, wither
**07** blacken, frizzle, scowder, shrivel, torrefy **08** scouther, scowther
**09** discolour

**scorching**
**05** blast **06** baking, red-hot, torrid
**07** boiling, burning, searing
**08** roasting, sizzling, tropical
**09** withering **10** blistering, scowdering, sweltering **11** scouthering
**12** extremely hot

**score**
**02** XX **03** cut, get, law, net, rit, run, set, sum, win **04** case, earn, gain, gash, hail, hits, line, lots, make, mark, nick, ritt, runs, slit **05** adapt, basis, count, facts, goals, gouge, graze, hosts, issue, marks, notch, put on, slash, tally, total, truth, write **06** aspect, attain, crowds, droves, groove, grudge, incise, indent, masses, matter, points, reason, record, result, scotch, scrape, shoals, swarms, target, the gen, twenty **07** account, achieve, arrange, be one up, chalk up, concern, dispute, engrave, grounds, legions, motives, myriads, notch up, outcome, quarrel, scratch, subject
**08** argument, hundreds, incision, millions, question, register
**09** complaint, enumerate, grievance, reckoning, situation, thousands, what's what **10** instrument, keep a tally, multitudes, the picture **11** explanation, have the edge, orchestrate **12** be successful **13** hit the jackpot **14** state of affairs **15** the whole picture

• **even the score**
**06** avenge **07** get back **09** retaliate
**14** settle the score

• **score off**
**09** humiliate **11** have the edge **12** get one over on

• **score out**
**05** erase **06** cancel, delete, efface, remove **07** expunge **08** cross out
**09** strike out **10** obliterate

**scorn**
**04** geck, mock, shun, spit, zing
**05** blurt, spurn **06** deride, rebuff, refuse, reject, scorch, slight **07** crucify, despise, disdain, disgust, dismiss, laugh at, mockery, sarcasm, scoff at, sneer at, sniff at **08** contempt, derision, mesprise, mesprize, misprise, misprize, ridicule, sneering **09** contumely, disparage **10** look down on
**11** haughtiness **12** scornfulness
**13** disparagement

**scornful**
**07** haughty, jeering, mocking
**08** arrogant, derisive, sardonic, scathing, scoffing, sneering
**09** insulting, sarcastic, slighting
**10** disdainful, dismissive **11** disparaging
**12** contemptuous, supercilious

**scornfully**
**09** haughtily **10** arrogantly, derisively, scathingly, sneeringly **11** slightingly, witheringly **12** disdainfully, dismissively
**13** disparagingly **14** contemptuously, superciliously

**scorpion**
**07** Scorpio **08** ballista, pedipalp
**11** Eurypterida

**Scot**
◇ *dialect indicator*
**03** Mac **04** Gael
*See also* **Scottish**

**scotch**
**04** gash, halt, maim, ruin, stop
**05** block, quash, score, strut, wedge, wreck **07** scupper, scuttle **09** frustrate
**10** put an end to, put a stop to **11** put the lid on **12** bring to an end **13** pull the plug on

**scot-free**
**04** safe **05** clear **06** unhurt **07** untaxed
**08** shot-free, unharmed
**09** undamaged, uninjured, unrebuked, unscathed **10** unpunished
**12** unreproached **13** unreprimanded
**15** without a scratch

**Scotland** *see* **council**; **town**

**Scotsman** *see* **Scot**; **Scottish**

**Scottish**
◇ *dialect word indicator*
*See also* **monarch**

*Scottish first names include:*

**03** Ian, Rab, Rae
**04** Doug, Euan, Ewan, Ewen, Greg, Iain, Iona, Isla, Jess, Jock
**05** Ailsa, Angus, Arran, Blair, Calum, Clyde, Colin, Craig, Isbel, Logan, Lorna, Lorne, Sandy
**06** Aileen, Callum, Dougie, Elspet, Gordon, Gregor, Hamish, Kelvin, Lilias, Mhàiri, Rabbie, Ranald, Vanora
**07** Cameron, Douglas, Elspeth, Malcolm
**08** Campbell, Catriona

*Scottish clans include:*

**04** Ross
**05** Baird, Bruce, Grant, Innes, Munro, Scott
**06** Brodie, Buchan, Dunbar, Duncan, Dundas, Eliott, Elliot, Forbes, Fraser, Gordon, Graeme, Graham, Irvine, Irving, Lennox, Mackay, Macnab, Macrae, Moffat, Monroe, Murray, Napier, Ogilvy, Ramsay, Stuart
**07** Balfour, Cameron, Douglas, Macduff, Maclean, Macleod, Macneil, Malcolm, Ogilvie, Stewart, Wallace
**08** Anderson, Campbell, Drummond, Ferguson, Hamilton, Macaulay, MacInnes, Macneill, Oliphant, Sinclair, Stirling, Urquhart
**09** Armstrong, Colquhoun, Fergusson, Henderson, Johnstone, MacAlpine, MacAndrew, MacArthur, MacCallum, Macdonald, Macgregor, Macintosh, Macintyre, Mackenzie, Mackinnon, Macmillan, Nicholson, Robertson
**10** Macdonnell, Macdougall, Mackintosh, Macpherson, Sutherland
**11** MacAllister, MacLauchlan, MacLaughlan, Macnaughton

**scoundrel**
**03** cur, dog, rat **04** scab **05** cheat, hound, louse, rogue, scamp, swine
**06** donder, louser, rascal, rotter, scally
**07** bounder, dastard, ruffian, stinker, villain **08** blighter, spalpeen, vagabond
**09** miscreant, reprobate, scallywag
**10** blackguard, hounds-foot, ne'er-do-well **14** good-for-nothing

**scour**
◇ *anagram indicator*
**03** rub **04** comb, drag, full, hunt, rake, scur, sker, wash, wipe **05** clean, flush, purge, scout, scrub, skirr, skirt
**06** abrade, forage, polish, punish, scrape, search, squirr **07** burnish, cleanse, ransack, rummage **08** clear out **14** turn upside-down

**scourge**
**04** bane, beat, cane, evil, flog, lash, whip **05** birch, curse, flail, strap, trial
**06** burden, menace, plague, punish, switch, terror, thrash **07** afflict, penalty, torment, torture **08** chastise, nuisance, scorpion **09** devastate, flagellum
**10** affliction, discipline, misfortune, punishment **13** cat-o'-nine-tails
**14** disciplinarium **15** thorn in your side

**scout**
**03** cub, spy **04** case, hunt, look, mock, seek **05** flout, probe, recce, rover, scoot, sixer, snoop, spial, watch
**06** beaver, escort, person, search, spying, spy out, survey **07** explore, inspect, look for, lookout, observe, pickeer, scourer, spotter, wolf cub
**08** check out, outrider, scurrier, vanguard **09** recruiter, scurriour
**10** discoverer, tenderfoot
**11** investigate, reconnoitre, voortrekker
**12** advance guard **13** talent spotter

**scowl**
**04** lour, pout **05** frown, glare, gloom, lower **06** glower **07** grimace **09** black look, dirty look, overgloom **13** look daggers at

**scrabble**
◇ *anagram indicator*
**03** dig, paw **04** claw, grub, root
**05** grope **06** scrape, scrawl
**07** clamber, scratch **08** scramble

**scraggy**
◇ *anagram indicator*
**04** bony, lean, thin **05** gaunt, lanky
**06** skinny, wasted **07** angular, scrawny,

unkempt **08** raw-boned
**09** emaciated, irregular **10** straggling
**14** undernourished

**scram**
**04** bolt, flee, puny, quit, scat **05** leave, scoot **06** beat it, depart, get out, go away **07** buzz off, do a bunk, scarper, vamoose **08** clear off, clear out, shove off, withered **09** disappear, skedaddle
**15** take to your heels

**scramble**
◇ *anagram indicator*
**03** mix, ren, rin, run, vie **04** dash, muss, push, race, rush **05** climb, crawl, grope, hurry, mêlée, mix up, musse, scale, vying **06** battle, bustle, hasten, hustle, infuse, jockey, jostle, jumble, muddle, scurry, strive, swerve, tussle
**07** clamber, compete, contend, disturb, grabble, rat race, scaling, scamble, shuffle **08** scrabble, sprattle, stampede, struggle **09** commotion, confusion **10** free-for-all
**11** competition, disorganize

**scrap**
**03** axe, bit, ort, rag, row **04** atom, bite, bits, drop, dump, glim, iota, junk, mite, part, shed, snap, tiff **05** argue, brawl, crumb, crust, ditch, fight, grain, patch, piece, scrip, set-to, shard, sherd, shred, trace, waste **06** battle, bicker, bundle, cancel, dust-up, fracas, morsel, sliver, splore, stitch, tatter, verset **07** abandon, break up, discard, dispute, fall out, punch-up, quarrel, remains, remnant, residue, scissel, scissil, scuffle, snippet, vestige, wrangle **08** argument, chuck out, demolish, disagree, fraction, fragment, get rid of, jettison, leavings, leftover, mouthful, particle, quantity, skerrick, squabble, write off
**09** leftovers, scrapings, throw away
**11** odds and ends, odds and sods
**12** disagreement **13** bits and pieces
• **on the scrap heap**
**06** dumped **07** ditched **08** rejected
**09** discarded, forgotten, redundant
**10** jettisoned, written off

**scrape**
**03** cut, fix, hoe, paw, rub **04** bark, clat, claw, file, hole, mess, rake, rase, rasp, raze, skin **05** claut, clean, curet, erase, flesh, grate, graze, grind, scalp, scart, scour, scrab, scuff, shave, shred
**06** abrade, hobble, pickle, plight, remove, splore **07** curette, descale, dilemma, scratch, snapper, trouble
**08** abrasion, distress, scrabble, wrong box **09** curettage, shemozzle, shimozzle, tight spot **10** difficulty, praemunire, schemozzle, shlemozzle
**11** predicament
• **scrape by**
**05** get by, skimp **06** eke out, scrimp
**13** muddle through
• **scrape through**
**08** just pass **09** barely win **11** only just win **13** just succeed in
• **scrape together**
**07** round up, scuffle **11** get together
**12** pool together **15** just manage to get

**scrappy**
◇ *anagram indicator*
**05** bitty **06** untidy **07** sketchy
**08** slapdash, slipshod **09** piecemeal
**10** disjointed, incomplete
**11** belligerent, fragmentary, quarrelsome, superficial
**12** disconnected, disorganized

**scraps**
**04** odds **05** brock, trash **08** dog's-meat

**scratch**
◇ *anagram indicator*
◇ *deletion indicator*
**03** cut, rit, rub **04** cash, clat, claw, etch, gash, line, mark, nick, race, rase, ritt, skin, tear **05** claut, curry, Devil, fluke, gouge, graze, rough, scart, score, scrab, scram, scrat, scuff, tease, wound
**06** abrade, casual, incise, scramb, scrape, scrawm, streak **07** engrave
**08** abrasion, lacerate, scrabble
**09** haphazard, impromptu
**10** improvised, laceration, ready money **11** clapperclaw, unrehearsed
**13** rough-and-ready
• **up to scratch**
**02** OK **08** adequate **09** competent, tolerable, up to snuff **10** acceptable, good enough, reasonable **11** up to the mark **12** satisfactory

**scrawl**
**03** jot, pen **06** doodle **07** dash off, jot down, scratch, writing **08** scrabble, scribble, squiggle **10** cacography
**11** handwriting **12** write quickly **14** bad handwriting

**scrawny**
**04** bony, lean, thin **05** lanky
**06** meagre, skinny, sparse **07** angular, scraggy, scranny **08** raw-boned, underfed **09** emaciated
**14** undernourished

**scream**
**03** cry, eek, wit **04** bawl, hoot, howl, riot, roar, wail, yawp, yell, yelp
**05** comic, joker, laugh, shout **06** holler, shriek, squawk, squeal **07** screech
**08** comedian **09** character **13** cry blue murder **15** shout blue murder

**screech**
**03** cry **04** howl, yell, yelp **06** screak, scream, shriek, squawk, squeal
**07** scraich, scraigh, screich, screigh, scriech, scritch, shriech, shritch, skreigh, skriech, skriegh, ululate

**screen**
**03** net, VDU, vet **04** grid, hide, mask, mesh, scan, show, sift, sort, test, veil
**05** blind, check, chick, cloak, cover, front, gauge, grade, grill, guard, scope, shade, sieve **06** awning, canopy, defend, façade, filter, grille, purdah, riddle, sconce, shield, shroud
**07** conceal, cribble, curtain, divider, examine, monitor, netting, picture, present, process, protect, reredos, shelter **08** abat-jour, disguise, evaluate, parclose, traverse **09** broadcast, dashboard, faceplate, partition, reredorse, reredosse, safeguard
**10** camouflage, protection
**11** concealment, investigate, room-divider **12** clothes-horse
• **screen off**
**04** hide **06** divide **07** conceal, protect
**08** fence off, separate **09** divide off, partition **11** separate off **12** partition off

**screenwriter** *see* **playwright**

**screw**
◇ *anagram indicator*
**03** fix, pay, pin, rob **04** bolt, brad, milk, nail, tack, turn, wind **05** bleed, cheat, clamp, force, rivet, twist, wages, wrest, wring **06** adjust, burgle, extort, fasten, pucker, salary **07** defraud, distort, extract, squeeze, tighten, wrinkle
**08** compress, contract, fastener, pressure **09** constrain, skinflint
**10** pressurize **12** extortionist
• **put the screws on**
**05** force **06** coerce, compel, lean on
**07** dragoon **09** constrain, strongarm
**10** pressurize
• **screwed up**
**05** upset **06** hung up **07** mixed up, muddled, puzzled **08** confused, messed up **09** disturbed, perplexed
**10** bewildered, disordered, distracted, distraught **11** disoriented, maladjusted
• **screw up**
**04** knot, ruin **05** botch, spoil, twist
**06** bungle, cock up, mess up, pucker
**07** contort, crumple, disrupt, distort, louse up, squinch, stuff up, tighten, wrinkle **08** contract, summon up
**09** mishandle, mismanage **11** make a hash of

**screwy**
◇ *anagram indicator*
**03** mad, odd **04** daft **05** batty, crazy, dotty, nutty, queer, tipsy, weird
**08** crackers **09** eccentric **12** round the bend **13** round the twist

**scribble**
**03** jot, pen **05** write **06** doodle, scrawl
**07** dash off, jot down, scratch, writing
**08** bescrawl, scrabble, squiggle
**10** bescribble, cacography
**11** handwriting **14** bad handwriting

**scribbler**
**04** hack **06** writer **09** ink-jerker, pen-pusher, pot-boiler **10** ink-slinger
**11** inkhorn-mate, verse-monger
**12** paper-stainer

**scribe**
**04** hack **05** clerk, write **06** author, incise, mallam, penman, writer
**07** copyist **08** recorder, reporter
**09** pen-pusher, scrivener, secretary
**10** amanuensis **11** transcriber
**12** calligrapher, hierographer

**scrimmage**
**03** row **04** fray, riot **05** brawl, bully, fight, mêlée, rouge, scrap, scrum, set-to **06** affray, bovver, dust-up, shindy
**07** scuffle **08** skirmish, squabble, struggle **10** free-for-all **11** disturbance

**scrimp**
**04** save **05** limit, pinch, skimp, stint **06** barely, reduce, scanty, scrape **07** curtail, shorten, stinted **08** restrict **09** cut back on, economize **15** tighten your belt

**script**
**02** MS **04** book, copy, hand, Jawi, text **05** Cufic, Kufic, lines, ronde, words **06** Arabic, nagari **07** letters, linear A, linear B, writing **08** dialogue, Gurmukhi, libretto, longhand, nastalik, nasta'liq, Sumerian **09** minuscule **10** devanagari, manuscript, screenplay **11** calligraphy, Cypro-Minoan, handwriting, running-hand **14** rustic capitals, shooting script
- **insert into script**

**03** cue

**scripture**
**02** RE, RI

*Religious writings include:*

**02** NT, OT
**05** Bayan, Bible, Koran, Qur'an, sutra, Torah, Vedas, Zohar
**06** Gemara, gospel, Granth, Hadith, I Ching, Kojiki, Mishna, Talmud, Tantra
**07** epistle, Li Ching, Puranas, Shari'ah
**08** Haft Wadi, Halakhah, Ramayana, Shu Ching
**09** Adi Granth, Apocrypha, Chuang-tzu, Chu'un Ch'iu, Decalogue, Digambara, Hexateuch, scripture, Shih Ching, Tripitaka
**10** Heptateuch, Lotus Sutra, Nohon Shoki, Pentateuch, Svetambara, Tao-te-ching, Upanishads, Zend-Avesta
**11** Bardo Thodol, Mahabharata
**12** Bhagavad Gita, Kitab al-Aqdas, Milindapanha, New Testament, Old Testament
**14** Dead Sea Scrolls, Mahayana Sutras, Revised Version
**15** Ten Commandments

*See also* **Bible**

**scroll**
**04** curl, list, roll **05** draft, paper, scrow, Sefer, Torah **06** mezuza, scrowl, stemma, Thorah, volume, volute **07** mezuzah, scrowle **08** cartouch, makimono, megillah, rocaille, schedule **09** cartouche, inventory, parchment **10** monkey tail, phylactery, Sefer Torah

**Scrooge**
**05** crowd, miser **06** meanie **07** niggard, squeeze **08** tightwad **09** skinflint **10** cheapskate **12** money-grubber, penny-pincher

**scrounge**
**03** beg, bum **04** blag **05** cadge **06** bludge, borrow, scunge, sponge **07** purloin

**scrounger**
**03** bum **05** mooch, mouch **06** beggar, cadger, scunge **07** bludger, moocher, sponger **08** borrower, parasite **10** freeloader

**scrub**
◇ *deletion indicator*
**03** axe, rub **04** bush, drop, wash, wipe **05** brush, clean, scour, shrub **06** cancel, delete, drudge, forget, give up, purify **07** abandon, abolish, cleanse, garigue, thicket **08** garrigue **09** backwoods, brushwood, exfoliate, holystone, scrubland **10** improvised, undersized **11** discontinue, undergrowth **13** insignificant

**scruff**
**04** nape **05** scuff, scuft

**scruffy**
◇ *anagram indicator*
**05** daggy, dirty, messy, seedy **06** grotty, ragged, scurvy, shabby, sloppy, untidy **07** run-down, squalid, unkempt, worn-out **08** dog-eared, slovenly, sluttish, tattered **09** ungroomed **10** bedraggled, down-at-heel, slatternly **11** dishevelled **12** disreputable
- **scruffy person**

**03** dag **04** slob **06** scruff

**scrum**
**04** ruck

**scrumptious**
**05** tasty, yummy **06** morish **07** moreish, scrummy **08** gorgeous, luscious **09** delicious, exquisite, succulent **10** appetizing, delectable, delightful **11** magnificent **13** mouthwatering

**scrunch**
**04** chew, mash **05** champ, crush, grate, grind, screw, twist **06** crunch, squash **07** crumple, screw up **09** crumple up

**scruple**
**03** scr **04** balk **05** demur, doubt, qualm, stick **06** boggle, ethics, morals, shrink **07** protest, stickle **08** hesitate, hold back, question **09** disbelief, misgiving, objection, standards, vacillate **10** difficulty, hesitation, perplexity, principles, reluctance, think twice, uneasiness **11** be reluctant, compunction, reservation, vacillation **13** point of honour **14** second thoughts

**scrupulous**
**04** nice **05** exact, moral **06** honest, minute, queasy, queazy, spiced, strict, tender **07** careful, ethical, precise, upright **08** captious, rigorous, thorough **09** religious **10** fastidious, honourable, meticulous, principled **11** painstaking, punctilious **13** conscientious **14** high-principled

**scrutinize**
**04** coat, cote, scan, sift **05** coate, probe, quote, study **06** go over, peruse, search **07** analyse, canvass, examine, explore, inspect, run over **08** look over **09** go through **10** run through **11** investigate, look through

**scrutiny**
**05** probe, study **06** search **07** canvass, check-up, close-up, inquiry, perusal **08** analysis, docimasy **10** inspection **11** examination, exploration **13** investigation

**scud**
**03** fly **04** blow, dart, East, gust, race, sail, skim, slap **05** shoot, speed, spoom, spoon

**scuff**
**03** rub **04** cuff, drag **05** brush, graze, scuft **06** abrade, scrape, scruff **07** scratch

**scuffle**
◇ *anagram indicator*
**03** hoe, row **04** fray **05** brawl, clash, fight, scrap, set-to **06** affray, cuffle, dust-up, rumpus, tussle **07** bagarre, contend, grapple, punch-up, quarrel, scarify, shuffle **08** pull caps, struggle **09** commotion **11** come to blows, disturbance **14** rough-and-tumble

**sculpt**
◇ *anagram indicator*
**03** cut, hew **04** cast, form **05** carve, model, mould, shape **06** chisel **07** fashion **09** represent, sculpture
- **he/she sculpted**

**02** sc **08** sculpsit

**sculptor**
**05** hewer, mason **06** artist, carver, caster **07** moulder, plastic **08** figurist, modeller **09** chiseller, craftsman **10** sculptress **11** craftswoman, stone-carver

*Sculptors include:*

**03** **Arp** (Hans), **Ray** (Man)
**04** **Bell** (John), **Bone** (Phyllis), **Caro** (Sir Anthony), **Gabo** (Naum), **Gill** (Eric), **King** (Philip), **Mach** (David), **Rude** (François)
**05** **Andre** (Carl), **Bacon** (John), **Beuys** (Joseph), **Cragg** (Tony), **Davey** (Grenville), **Frink** (Dame Elisabeth), **Johns** (Jasper), **Koons** (Jeff), **Manzú** (Giacomo), **Moore** (Henry), **Myron**, **Rodin** (Auguste), **Smith** (David Roland), **Story** (William)
**06** **Calder** (Alexander), **Canova** (Antonio), **Cousin** (Jean), **Deacon** (Richard), **Hatoum** (Mona), **Kapoor** (Anish), **Marini** (Marino), **Pisano** (Andrea), **Pisano** (Giovanni), **Robbia** (Luca della), **Scopas**, **Walker** (Dame Ethel)
**07** **Bernini** (Gianlorenzo), **Cellini** (Benvenuto), **Christo**, **Duchamp** (Marcel), **Epstein** (Sir Jacob), **Gormley** (Antony), **Klinger** (Max), **Longman** (Evelyn), **Millett** (Kate), **Phidias**, **Samaras** (Lucas)
**08** **Boccioni** (Umberto), **Brancusi** (Constantin), **Chadwick** (Lynn), **Ghiberti** (Lorenzo), **Hepworth** (Dame Barbara), **Landseer** (Sir Edwin), **Paolozzi** (Eduardo Luigi), **Pheidias**, **Tinguely** (Jean)
**09** **Borromini** (Francesco), **Bourgeois** (Louise), **Donatello**, **Oldenburg** (Claes), **Roubiliac** (Louis François), **Whiteread** (Rachel)

**10** Giacometti (Alberto), Polyclitus, Praxiteles, Schwitters (Kurt), Verrocchio (Andrea del)
**11** Della Robbia (Luca), Goldsworthy (Andy)
**12** Jeanne-Claude, Michelangelo
**14** Gaudier-Brzeska (Henri)
**15** Leonardo da Vinci

**sculpture**
◇ *anagram indicator*

*Sculpture types include:*

**04** bust, cast, head, herm, kore
**05** group
**06** bronze, effigy, figure, kouros, marble, relief, statue
**07** carving, kinetic, telamon, waxwork
**08** caryatid, Daibutsu, figurine, maquette, moulding
**09** bas-relief, statuette
**10** high-relief
**11** plaster cast

*Sculptures and statues include:*

**04** Adam, Kore, Zeus
**05** Angel, Cupid, David, House, Medea, Moses, Pietà, Torso
**06** Balzac
**07** Bacchus, Genesis, Liberty, Lincoln, Mercury, Merzbau, Spiders, The Kiss, The Wall
**08** Cantoria, Ecce Homo, Eggboard, Have Pity!, Mahamuni, Piscator
**09** A Universe, Seated Man, Slate Cone
**10** Discobolus, Doryphorus, Double Talk, Ledge Piece, Orange Bath, Running Man, Single Form, The Thinker
**11** Gomateswara, Kiss and Tell, Pierced Form, Spear Bearer, Venus de Milo
**12** Cactus People, Elgin Marbles, Feast of Herod
**13** Discus Thrower, Fallen Warrior, People in a Wind, Veduggio Sound
**14** Cosimo de' Medici, Fontana Magiore, Horse Lying Down, Japanese War God, Sailing Tonight, The Age of Bronze, The Gates of Hell, The Three Graces
**15** Angel of the North, Athena Promachos, Buddhas of Bamian, Christ in Majesty, Figure and Clouds, Giant Clothespin, Madonna and Child, Recumbent Figure

**scum**
**04** dirt, film, foam, slag **05** dregs, dross, froth, layer, plebs, spume, trash **06** mantle, mother, rabble **07** rubbish, sullage **08** covering, pellicle, riff-raff, sandiver **09** epistasis, glass-gall **10** impurities **12** undesirables **13** great unwashed **14** dregs of society, lowest of the low

**scupper**
**03** axe **04** foil, kill, ruin, sink **05** do for, wreck **06** cock up, defeat, mess up **07** destroy, disable, louse up, screw up, scuttle, torpedo **08** demolish, submerge **09** overthrow, overwhelm

**scurf**
**05** scald, scale **06** furfur, scruff **07** furfair **08** dandriff, dandruff **09** flakiness, scaliness **12** scabrousness

**scurfy**
**05** flaky, lepra, scald, scaly **06** scabby, scurvy **07** leprose, leprous, scabrid **08** lepidote, scabrous, scarious **09** furfurous **11** scaberulous **12** furfuraceous

**scurrility**
**05** abuse **07** obloquy **08** foulness, rudeness **09** grossness, indecency, invective, nastiness, obscenity, vulgarity **10** coarseness **11** abusiveness **12** vituperation **13** offensiveness **14** scurrilousness

**scurrilous**
**04** foul, rude **06** coarse, vulgar **07** abusive, obscene, Sotadic **08** indecent, Sotadean **09** insulting, libellous, offensive, salacious **10** defamatory, Fescennine, scandalous, slanderous **11** disparaging **12** vituperative

**scurry**
**03** fly, ren, rin, run **04** dart, dash, race, rush, scud, scur, sker, skim, trot **05** hurry, scoot, scour, skirr, whirl **06** beetle, bustle, flurry, hasten, skurry, sprint, squirr **07** scamper, scutter, scuttle, skelter **08** bustling, scramble **09** beetle off **10** scampering **15** hustle and bustle

**scurvy**
**03** bad, low **04** base, mean, vile, yaws **05** dirty, scall, sorry **06** abject, rotten, scurfy, shabby **07** ignoble, low-down, pitiful, roynish, scruffy **08** whoreson **09** worthless **10** despicable **12** contemptible **13** dishonourable

**scuttle**
◇ *anagram indicator*
**03** hod, ren, rin, run **04** rush, scud **05** hurry **06** bustle, hasten, scurry **07** scamper, scuddle, scutter, skuttle **08** scramble, scrattle **09** purdonium

**scythe**
**03** mow **11** bushwhacker
- **part of scythe**

**04** sned **05** snath, snead **06** snathe, sneath

**sea**
**03** mer **04** deep, host, main, mass, salt, tide **05** briny, ocean, swell, waves **06** afloat, marine **07** aquatic, expanse, oceanic **08** maritime **09** abundance, multitude, profusion, roughness, saltwater, seafaring **11** large number

*Seas include:*

**03** Med, Red
**04** Aral, Azov, Dead, East, Java, Kara, Ross, Sulu
**05** Banda, Black, Coral, Crete, Irish, Japan, North, Timor, White
**06** Aegean, Baltic, Bering, Celtic, Flores, Inland, Ionian, Laptev, Nan Hai, Scotia, Tasman, Yellow
**07** Andaman, Arabian, Arafura, Barents, Caspian, Celebes, Dong Hai, Galilee, Marmara, Okhotsk, Solomon, Weddell
**08** Adriatic, Amundsen, Beaufort, Bismarck, Hebrides, Huang Hai, Labrador, Ligurian, McKinley, Sargasso
**09** Caribbean, East China, Greenland, Norwegian
**10** Philippine, Setonaikai, South China, Tyrrhenian
**11** Yam Kinneret
**12** East Siberian
**13** Mediterranean
**14** Bellingshausen

*See also* **moon**; **ocean**
- **at sea**

◇ *anagram indicator*
**04** lost **06** adrift, afloat **07** baffled, puzzled **08** confused **09** mystified, perplexed **10** bewildered **11** disoriented **12** disorganized **13** disorientated

**seabird** *see* **bird**

**seaborgium**
**02** Sg

**sea bream**
**03** sar, tai **05** porgy, sargo **06** braise, braize, porgie, sargos, sargus **07** old wife **08** tarwhine

**seafaring**
**05** naval **06** marine **07** oceanic, sailing **08** maritime, nautical, sea-going **10** ocean-going

**seafood**

*Seafood and seafood dishes include:*

**04** bisk, clam, crab
**05** prawn, squid, sushi, whelk
**06** bisque, cockle, mussel, oyster, paella, scampi, shrimp, winkle
**07** abalone, lobster, octopus, risotto, scallop, tempura, toheroa
**08** calamari, coquille, crawfish, crevette, marinara, zarzuela
**09** jambalaya, king prawn, surf'n'turf
**10** tiger prawn
**11** clam-chowder, Dublin prawn, fritto misto, fruits de mer, langoustine, tiger shrimp
**13** bouillabaisse, Norway lobster, prawn cocktail
**14** Dublin Bay prawn

*See also* **crustacean**; **fish**; **mollusc**

**seahorse**
**06** tangie, walrus **08** pipefish **09** hippodame, sea dragon **11** hippocampus, lophobranch

**seal**
**04** chop, cork, jark, lute, plug, seel, shut, stop **05** bulla, close, O-ring, plumb, puppy, sigil, stamp, tie up **06** cachet, clinch, enseal, fasten, obsign, ratify, secure, settle, signet, stop up, wicker, willow **07** close up, confirm, consign, enclose, stopper, tar-seal, tighten, ziplock **08** bachelor,

conclude, finalize, insignia, set apart **09** assurance, footprint, obsignate **10** impression, imprimatur, shake hands, waterproof **11** attestation, counterseal **12** confirmation, make airtight, ratification **14** authentication, make watertight

*Seals include:*

**03** fur
**04** grey, hair, harp, monk
**05** otary, phoca, silky
**06** common, hooded, ribbon, sea dog, sealch, sealgh, selkie, silkie
**07** harbour, sea bear, sea calf, sea lion, Weddell
**08** Atlantic, elephant, seecatch
**09** crab-eater, Greenland, whitecoat
**10** saddleback, sea leopard
**11** sea elephant

**• in the place of the seal**
**02** LS **11** loco sigilli
**• seal off**
**03** cap **06** cut off, fasten **07** block up, isolate, shut off **08** close off, fence off **09** cordon off, segregate **10** quarantine

**sealed**
**04** shut **06** closed, corked **07** plugged **08** hermetic **09** sigillate **10** hermetical, watertight **12** draught-proof

**seam**
**04** fell, join, line, lode, saim, vein, weld **05** joint, layer, quilt, raphe, seame **06** grease, suture, thread **07** closure, joining, stratum, wrinkle **08** cartload, edge coal, junction, wayboard **09** stitching **10** weighboard **12** dorsal suture **15** middle-stitching

**seaman**
**02** AB **03** Kru, tar **04** Kroo **06** merman, sailor **07** killick, killock
*See also* **sailor**

**sea-mist**
**04** haar

**sea-monster**
**03** orc **04** cete **05** Phoca **06** kraken **07** ziffius **08** seahorse **09** leviathan, rosmarine, sea satyre, wasserman, whirlpool **11** hippocampus
*See also* **monster**

**seamy**
**03** low **04** dark **05** nasty, rough **06** sleazy, sordid **07** squalid **09** unsavoury **10** unpleasant **12** disreputable

**sear**
**03** dry, fry **04** burn, char, seal, sere, wilt **05** brand, brown, dry up, parch, seare, singe **06** scorch, sizzle, wither **07** burning, shrivel **08** withered **09** cauterize

**search**
**03** pry **04** comb, fish, hunt, rake, ripe, scur, seek, sift, sker **05** check, frisk, grope, probe, quest, rifle, scour, sieve, skirr, sweep **06** ferret, forage, squirr, survey **07** enquire, enquiry, examine, explore, fossick, inquire, inquiry, inspect, look for, pursuit, ransack, rifling, rummage **08** prospect, research, scrutiny **09** cast about, go through, ranshakle **10** inspection, ransacking, ranshackle, scrutinize **11** examination, exploration, investigate, look through **12** perquisition **13** investigation, perscrutation, turn inside-out **14** turn upside-down
**• in search of**
**07** seeking **09** in quest of **10** looking for **11** in pursuit of **12** searching for **15** on the lookout for
**• search me**
**05** dunno **09** I don't know, it beats me, I've no idea **12** ask me another **15** I haven't got a clue, you've got me there
**• search out**
**04** scan **06** ferret **07** explore **08** indigate **10** run to earth **11** run to ground

**searching**
**04** home, keen **05** alert, close, quest, sharp **06** intent, minute, trying **07** probing **08** piercing, thorough **09** observant **10** discerning **11** penetrating, prospecting **13** inquisitional **14** strand-scouring

**searing**
**05** cruel **06** brutal, fierce, savage, severe **07** blazing, burning, extreme, intense, mordant **08** scathing **09** ferocious, scorching, trenchant, vitriolic **10** unbearable **11** devastating **12** insufferable

**seaside**
**05** beach, coast, sands, shore **06** strand **08** seashore

**season**
**03** age **04** fall, salt, seal, seel, seil, sele, span, term, tide, time **05** inure, pep up, phase, prime, ripen, savor, spell, spice, train, treat **06** harden, haysel, master, mature, mellow, period, savour, temper **07** flavour, prepare, toughen **08** festival, interval, moderate, tone down **09** condiment, condition **10** add herbs to, add sauce to, fence month, summertide, summertime **11** add pepper to, add relish to **13** add flavouring

*Seasons include:*

**03** dry, wet
**04** high, open
**05** close, rainy, silly
**06** autumn, closed, spring, summer, winter
**07** festive, holiday, monsoon
**08** breeding, shooting
**12** Indian summer

**• in season**
**02** in **07** growing **09** available **10** obtainable **11** on the market

**seasonable**
**04** tidy **06** timely, timous **07** fitting, timeous, welcome **08** suitable **09** opportune, well-timed **10** convenient, forehanded, tempestive **11** appropriate **12** providential

**seasoned**
**03** old **04** salt **06** mature, spiced **07** veteran **08** cayenned, hardened **09** practised, toughened, weathered **10** habituated, well-versed **11** conditioned, established, experienced, long-serving **12** acclimatized **13** battle-scarred, weather-beaten

**seasoning**
**04** salt **05** herbs, salad, sauce, spice **06** pepper, relish, spices **07** salting **08** dressing, duxelles **09** condiment **10** celery salt, flavouring, weathering **11** fines herbes
*See also* **herb**

**seat**
**03** fit, fix, hub, pew, put, see, set, sit **04** axis, base, form, hold, home, pouf, sell, site, sofa, sunk, take **05** abode, bench, cause, chair, heart, house, perch, place, sedes, selle, siege, slide, stall, stool, swing, villa **06** bottom, centre, dukery, ground, humpty, locate, origin, pouffe, reason, saddle, settle, source, throne **07** capital, contain, deposit, footing, install, mansion, pillion, sitting, station **08** location, position, sociable, tribunal **09** faldstool, residence, situation **10** foundation, metropolis, strapontin **11** accommodate, have room for, reservation, stately home **12** confessional, headquarters, rumble-tumble
*See also* **chair**

**seating**
**04** room **05** seats **06** chairs, places **13** accommodation

**sea trout**
**04** peal, peel **05** sewen, sewin **06** finnac **07** finnack, finnock, herling, hirling

**seaweed**

*Seaweeds include:*

**03** ore, red
**04** agar, alga, kelp, kilp, nori, tang, ulva, ware
**05** arame, domoi, dulse, fucus, kombu, laver, varec, vraic, wrack
**06** fucoid, tangle, varech, wakame
**07** oarweed, oreweed, redware, sea lace, sea moss, seaware
**08** agar-agar, bull kelp, gulfweed, porphyra, rockweed, sargasso, seawrack, whipcord
**09** carrageen, coralline, coral weed, driftweed, Irish moss, Laminaria, nullipore, sargassum, seabottle, sea girdle, sea tangle, thongweed
**10** badderlock, carragheen, Ceylon moss, green laver, sea lettuce, see whistle, tangleweed
**11** purple laver, sea furbelow
**12** bladderwrack, peacock's tail, phaeophyceae, Rhodophyceae

*See also* **alga, algae**

**secede**
04 quit 05 break, leave 06 resign, retire 08 separate, split off, withdraw 09 break away 10 apostatize 12 disaffiliate 14 turn your back on

**seceders**
04 cave

**secession**
05 break, split 06 revolt, schism 08 apostasy, seceding 09 breakaway, defection 10 withdrawal 14 disaffiliation

**secluded**
03 shy 05 close 06 cut off, hidden, lonely, remote, secret 07 private, recluse, retired, shadowy 08 in purdah, isolated, purdahed, shut away, solitary, umbratic 09 claustral, cloistral, concealed, sheltered, withdrawn 10 cloistered 11 out-of-the-way, sequestered, umbratilous 12 unfrequented

**seclusion**
04 nook 06 bypath, hiding, purdah, recess 07 byplace, privacy, retreat, secrecy, shelter 08 bolt hole, retiracy, solitude 09 hermitage, isolation, reclusion, sequester 10 remoteness, retirement, withdrawal 11 concealment, recluseness 13 sequestration

**second**
01 s 02 mo 03 aid, sec 04 back, beta, help, jiff, move, next, send, tick, twin 05 extra, flash, jiffy, lower, other, shift, spare, trice, vouch 06 assign, assist, backer, back up, back-up, change, deputy, double, helper, lesser, minute, moment 07 advance, another, approve, endorse, forward, further, helpful, instant, promote, support 08 inferior, relocate, repeated, transfer 09 agree with, alternate, assistant, attendant, duplicate, encourage, favouring, following, secondary, supporter, twinkling 10 additional, subsequent, succeeding, supporting 11 alternative, split second, subordinate 12 right-hand man 13 supplementary 14 right-hand woman 15 second-in-command

• **second to none**
04 best 06 superb 07 supreme 08 peerless 09 brilliant, matchless, nonpareil, paramount 10 inimitable, unrivalled 11 superlative, unsurpassed 12 incomparable, without equal 13 beyond compare, nulli secundus 15 without parallel

**secondary**
05 extra, lower, minor, spare 06 back-up, deputy, feeder, lesser, relief, second 07 derived, reserve 08 delegate, indirect, inferior, Mesozoic 09 ancillary, auxiliary, resulting 10 derivative, subsidiary, supporting 11 alternative, subordinate, unimportant 12 non-essential

**second-class**
01 B 08 inferior, mediocre 10 second-best, second-rate, uninspired 11 indifferent, unimportant, uninspiring 15 undistinguished

**second-hand**
03 old 04 used, worn 08 borrowed, indirect, pre-owned 09 nearly-new, obliquely, secondary, vicarious 10 derivative, hand-me-down, indirectly 11 reach-me-down 12 incidentally, tralaticious, tralatitious 13 formerly owned 14 on the grapevine

**second-in-command**
06 backer, deputy, helper 09 assistant, attendant, number two, supporter 12 right-hand man 14 right-hand woman

**secondly**
03 too 04 also, next 06 as well 07 besides, further 08 moreover 09 what's more 10 in addition 11 furthermore 12 additionally 14 into the bargain

**second-rate**
04 poor, ropy 05 cheap, crook, lousy, ropey, tacky 06 grotty, lesser, shoddy, tawdry, tinpot 08 inferior, low-grade, mediocre 10 second-best, uninspired 11 second-class, substandard, unimportant, uninspiring 15 undistinguished

**secrecy**
04 dern 05 dearn, wraps 07 hidling, hidlins, mystery, privacy, privity, silence, stealth 08 disguise, hidlings 09 seclusion 10 camouflage, confidence, covertness 11 concealment, furtiveness 12 hugger-mugger, stealthiness 15 confidentiality

**secret**
03 key, sly 04 code, dark, deep, dern, rune 05 close, dearn, hushy, privy 06 answer, arcane, closet, covert, cut off, enigma, hidden, inward, lonely, mystic, occult, recipe, remote, unseen 07 arcanum, covered, cryptic, formula, furtive, hidling, hidlins, mystery, nostrum, private, retired, unknown 08 abstruse, back-door, discreet, esoteric, hidlings, hush-hush, isolated, secluded, shrouded, shut away, sneaking, solitary, solution, stealthy 09 concealed, disguised, recondite, sensitive, sheltered, tête-à-tête, top secret, underhand 10 backstairs, classified, cloistered, confidence, mysterious, restricted, undercover, unrevealed 11 camouflaged, clandestine, inside story, know-nothing, out-of-the-way, sequestered, underground, undisclosed, unpublished 12 confidential, hugger-mugger, Naples yellow, unfrequented, unidentified 13 hole-and-corner, private matter, surreptitious 14 cloak-and-dagger 15 between you and me, under-the-counter

• **in secret**
07 in petto, on the qt, privily, quietly 08 covertly, in camera, on the sly, secretly 09 furtively, in pectore, in private, privately 10 on the quiet, stealthily, under cover, unobserved 12 hugger-mugger, in confidence, subterranean 13 clandestinely 14 confidentially 15 surreptitiously

• **secret agent**
03 spy 04 Bond, mole 05 scout 07 snooper 10 enemy agent 11 double agent 12 foreign agent 14 fifth columnist 15 undercover agent

**secretary**
02 PA 03 Sec 04 Secy, temp 05 clerk 06 munshi, scribe, typist 07 famulus 08 moonshee 09 assistant, man Friday, town clerk 10 amanuensis, chancellor, girl Friday, secretaire 11 protonotary 12 person Friday, prothonotary, stenographer

**secrete**
04 bury, emit, hide, leak, ooze, take, veil 05 cache, cover, exude, leach, water 06 screen, secern, shroud 07 conceal, cover up, emanate, excrete, give off, lactate, produce, release, send out 08 disguise, salivate 09 discharge, sequester, stash away 11 appropriate

**secretion**
04 lerp 05 sebum, slime 06 liquor, oozing, pruina, smegma, succus 07 cerumen, hormone, leakage, osmosis, release 08 autacoid, emission, honeydew 09 discharge, emanation, exudation, incretion, lactation, recrement 10 osmidrosis, production, royal jelly, secernment 12 lachrymation

**secretive**
03 sly 04 cagy, deep 05 cagey, close, quiet 06 intent 07 cryptic 08 reserved, reticent, taciturn 09 enigmatic, withdrawn 11 tight-lipped 13 unforthcoming 15 uncommunicative

**secretively**
07 quietly 08 silently 10 reticently, taciturnly 13 enigmatically

**secretly**
05 close 06 dernly 07 dearnly, on the qt, privily, quietly 08 covertly, in camera, in secret, on the sly 09 furtively, in private, privately 10 on the quiet, stealthily, under-board, under cover, unobserved 11 underground 12 in confidence 13 clandestinely 14 confidentially 15 surreptitiously

**sect**
03 sex 04 camp, clan, cult, wing 05 group, order, party 06 church, school 07 cutting, faction 08 division 09 tradition 11 subdivision 12 denomination 13 splinter group

*Religious sects include:*

05 Amish
07 Ahmadis, Cathars, Moonies, Shakers, Zealots

**09** Ahmadiyya, Lubavitch
**10** Mennonites
**11** Hare Krishna, Therapeutae

*See also* **sectarian**

**sectarian**
**04** Babi **05** Amish, Babee, bigot, Cynic, hodja, khoja, rigid, Saiva, Yezdi **06** Berean, Cathar, Dunker, khodja, Marist, Moonie, Mormon, Mucker, narrow, Ophite, ranter, Sabian, Seeker, Senusi, Shaiva, Shiite, Tunker, Wahabi, Yezidi, Zabian, zealot **07** Adamite, Alawite, Baptist, bigoted, Cainite, Dunkard, extreme, fanatic, hillmen, insular, Ismaili, Karaite, limited, Senussi, Tsabian, Wahabee, Wahhabi, Yezidee, Zezidee **08** Calixtin, cliquish, Darbyite, dogmatic, Donatist, Dukhobor, Familist, hillfolk, Mandaean, Maronite, Mendaite, partisan, Pharisee, Senoussi, Stundist **09** Calixtine, dogmatist, Doukhobor, Encratite, exclusive, extremist, factional, fanatical, Harmonist, Harmonite, Hesychast, hidebound, Israelite, Mennonite, Nasoraean, parochial, Paulician **10** anabaptist, Holy Roller, Karmathian, prejudiced, separatist **11** abecedarian, Albigensian, Black Muslim, Campbellite, doctrinaire, Hare Krishna, Lubavitcher, Plymouthist, Plymouthite, Sandemanian **12** denomination, Muggletonian, narrow-minded **13** convulsionary, fractionalist, Hemerobaptist, Perfectionist, Philadelphian, Schwenkfelder **14** denominational, Schwenkfeldian **15** Christadelphian, Plymouth Brother

**section**
**01** s **03** bit **04** area, part, sect, unit, wing, zone **05** conic, piece, share, slice **06** branch, region, sector **07** article, chapter, passage, portion, segment **08** campfire, district, division, fraction, fragment **09** Caesarean, Caesarian, component, induction, paragraph **10** department, instalment **11** subdivision
• **all sections**
**02** AS

**sectional**
**05** class, local **06** racial **07** divided, partial **08** regional, separate **09** exclusive, factional, localized, sectarian **10** individual, separatist

**sector**
**04** area, gore, part, zone **05** field **06** branch, octant, region **07** quarter, section, sextant **08** category, district, division, precinct, quadrant **11** subdivision

**secular**
**03** lay **05** civil, state **06** age-old, layman **07** agelong, earthly, profane, worldly **08** temporal **12** non-religious, non-spiritual

**secure**
◇ *containment indicator*
**03** bag, bar, fix, get, pin, pot, rug, tie, win **04** bolt, bond, fast, firm, gain, hunk, land, lash, lock, moor, nail, safe, shut, sure, take, vest **05** chain, close, cover, fixed, guard, happy, quoin, rivet, solid, tie up, tight **06** anchor, assure, attach, closed, come by, defend, ensure, fasten, immune, line up, locked, lock up, obtain, screen, sealed, shield, stable, steady, sturdy, take up **07** acquire, assured, certain, confirm, endorse, padlock, procure, protect, relaxed, settled, sponsor, warrant **08** careless, definite, fastened, make fast, make safe, reliable, shielded, unharmed **09** confident, contented, establish, fortified, get hold of, guarantee, immovable, protected, reassured, safeguard, sheltered, steadfast, undamaged **10** batten down, conclusive, dependable, home and dry, strengthen, underwrite **11** comfortable, established, impregnable, make certain, self-assured, well-founded **13** make certain of, out of harm's way, self-confident

**securely**
**06** firmly, safely, stably **07** tightly **08** robustly, steadily, strongly, sturdily **09** immovably **11** impregnably, out of danger, steadfastly

**security**
**03** wad, wed **04** care, ease, gage, gilt, lock **05** cover **06** anchor, asylum, pledge, refuge, safety, surety **07** caution, custody, defence **08** guaranty, immunity, warranty **09** assurance, certainty, guarantee, insurance, safeguard, sanctuary **10** collateral, confidence, conviction, precaution, protection, safeguards **11** peace of mind, precautions, safe-keeping **12** carelessness, positiveness, preservation, surveillance **14** over-confidence **15** invulnerability

**sedan**
**05** chair **06** jampan, litter **09** palanquin

**sedate**
**03** sad **04** calm, cool, dull **05** douce, grave, noble, quiet, relax, sober, staid, stiff **06** demure, pacify, proper, seemly, serene, solemn, soothe, worthy **07** earnest, serious **08** calm down, composed, decorous, tranquil **09** collected, dignified, unruffled **10** deliberate, slow-moving, unexciting **11** quieten down, unflappable **12** tranquillize **13** imperturbable

**sedately**
**05** nobly **06** calmly **07** quietly, soberly **08** demurely, serenely, worthily **09** earnestly, seriously **10** decorously **11** with dignity **12** deliberately **13** imperturbably

**sedative**
**06** downer, opiate **07** anodyne, calming **08** lenitive, narcotic, quietive, relaxing, soothing **09** calmative, composing, soporific **10** depressant **11** barbiturate **12** sleeping-pill **13** tranquillizer **14** tranquillizing

*Sedatives and tranquillizers include:*

**06** Amytal®, Ativan®, Valium®
**07** codeine, Librium®, lupulin
**08** diazepam, Nembutal®, Rohypnol®, tetronal, thridace
**09** barbitone, clozapine, lorazepam, Temazepam
**10** clonazepam
**11** amobarbital, deserpidine, laurel-water, scopalamine, thalidomide
**12** meprobramate, methaqualone, promethazine
**14** chloral hydrate, cyclobarbitone, pentobarbitone, phenobarbitone

**sedentary**
**05** still **06** seated **07** sessile, sitting **08** immobile, inactive, unmoving **09** desk-bound **10** stationary

**sedge**

*Sedges include:*

**04** star
**05** Carex, chufa, starr
**07** bulrush, papyrus
**08** clubrush, sawgrass, tiger nut
**09** deergrass
**13** umbrella plant, water chestnut

**sediment**
**03** lee **04** lees, silt, warp **05** crust, dregs, feces, grout, varve **06** bottom, faeces, fecula **07** bottoms, deposit, grounds, residue **08** residuum **09** turbidite **10** deposition, hypostasis **11** precipitate **13** coffee grounds

**sedition**
**06** mutiny, revolt **07** treason **09** agitation, rebellion, treachery **10** disloyalty, subversion **11** fomentation **12** insurrection **13** rabble-rousing **15** insubordination

**seditious**
**08** disloyal, factious, inciting, mutinous **09** agitating, dissident, fomenting **10** rebellious, refractory, subversive, traitorous **13** insubordinate, rabble-rousing, revolutionary **15** insurrectionist

**seduce**
◇ *insertion indicator*
**04** jape, lure, pull, ruin, undo, vamp **05** charm, tempt, wrong **06** allure, betray, chat up, entice **07** attract, beguile, corrupt, debauch, deceive, deprave, ensnare, mislead **08** bejesuit, dishonor, inveigle **09** dishonour **10** get into bed, lead astray **12** make a play for **15** take advantage of

**seducer**
**04** goat, rake, wolf **05** flirt, Romeo **06** undoer **07** charmer, Don Juan **08** betrayer, Casanova, deceiver, lady's man, Lothario **09** ladies' man, libertine, womanizer **11** philanderer

**seduction**
**04** lure, ruin **05** charm **06** allure, appeal, come-on **09** deception **10** allurement, attraction, corruption,

enticement, misleading, temptation **11** beguilement

**seductive**
**04** sexy **06** honied, luring, sultry **07** honeyed **08** alluring, arousing, charming, enticing, inviting, tempting **09** appealing, beguiling, deceiving **10** attractive, bewitching, come-hither, misleading **11** captivating, flirtatious, provocative, tantalizing, temptatious **12** honey-tongued, irresistible

**seductress**
**04** vamp **05** Circe, siren **07** Delilah, Lorelei **09** temptress **11** femme fatale

**sedulous**
**04** busy **08** constant, diligent, resolved, tireless, untiring **09** assiduous, laborious **10** determined, persistent, unflagging **11** industrious, painstaking, persevering, unremitting **13** conscientious

**see**
**01** C, v **02** la, lo **03** ask, Ely, get **04** date, deek, deem, ecce, espy, know, lead, look, mark, meet, note, seat, show, spot, take, vide, view **05** court, get it, grasp, judge, learn, sight, think, usher, visit, voilà, watch **06** behold, decide, escort, fathom, follow, go with, look at, notice, regard, take in **07** consult, diocese, discern, find out, foresee, glimpse, imagine, inquire, make out, observe, picture, predict, realize, reflect, run into, speak to, take out, witness **08** bump into, consider, discover, envisage, forecast, identify, perceive **09** accompany, apprehend, ascertain, determine, encounter, go out with, interview, latch onto, lay eyes on, recognize, set eyes on, visualize **10** anticipate, appreciate, chance upon, clap eyes on, come across, comprehend, confer with, cotton onto, experience, get a look at, understand **11** distinguish, investigate **12** catch sight of **15** keep company with
*See also* **diocese**

**• see about**
**02** do **03** fix **06** manage, repair **07** arrange, sort out **08** attend to, consider, deal with, organize **09** look after **10** take care of

**• see around**
◇ *containment indicator*

**• see through**
**06** fathom, hang in, rumble **07** persist, realize, support, sustain **08** continue, stick out **09** encourage, get wise to, keep going, not give up, penetrate, persevere **10** get through, understand **14** not be taken in by **15** not be deceived by

**• see to**
**02** do **03** fix **04** mind **06** ensure, manage, repair **07** arrange, sort out **08** attend to, deal with, make sure, organize **09** look after **10** take care of **11** make certain

**seed**
**03** egg, nut, pea, pip, pit, sow, urd **04** bean, corn, dust, germ, moit, mote, ovum, race, root **05** argan, carvy, cause, child, grain, heirs, lupin, ovule, piñon, semen, spawn, sperm, start, stone, young **06** bonduc, embryo, family, kernel, lentil, lupine, origin, powder, reason, source **07** genesis, nucleus, reasons **08** chickpea, children, peaberry, sprinkle, young one **09** beginning, fruit body, jequirity, offspring, sword-bean, young ones **10** successors **11** descendants **12** fruiting body, spermatozoon **13** jequirity bean, water chestnut

**• go to seed, run to seed**
**04** bolt **05** decay **07** decline, go to pot **08** get worse, go to hell **10** degenerate, go downhill **11** deteriorate, go to the dogs **14** go down the tubes

**• seed covering**
**03** bur, ear **04** aril, burr, husk

**seediness**
**05** decay, scuzz **09** dirtiness **10** shabbiness, untidiness **11** squalidness **12** dilapidation

**seedy**
◇ *anagram indicator*
**03** ill **04** sick **05** dirty, mangy, ribby, rough, tatty **06** ailing, chippy, crummy, groggy, grotty, mangey, maungy, poorly, shabby, sleazy, untidy, unwell **07** run-down, scruffy, squalid **08** decaying **09** off-colour **10** out of sorts **11** dilapidated **15** under the weather

**seek**
**03** aim, ask, beg, try **04** cast, hunt, want **05** chase, court **06** aspire, desire, follow, gun for, invite, lay out, pursue, resort, search, strive **07** attempt, enquire, entreat, examine, hunt for, inquire, look for, mole out, request, solicit **08** petition, prospect **09** endeavour, look after, search for, try to find

**seeker**
**05** chela, hound **06** novice **07** student, zetetic **08** disciple, enquirer, inquirer, searcher

**seem**
**04** feel, look **05** befit, sound **06** appear, semble **08** look like **11** pretend to be, show signs of, strike you as **12** come across as **13** have the look of

**seeming**
**05** quasi- **06** pseudo **07** assumed, outward, surface **08** apparent, external, semblant, specious, supposed **09** pretended **10** ostensible, semblative **11** superficial

**seemingly**
**09** allegedly, outwardly **10** apparently, ostensibly **12** on the surface **13** on the face of it, superficially

**seemly**
**03** fit **04** meet, nice **06** comely, decent, honest, proper, suited **07** fitting **08** becoming, decorous, handsome, maidenly, suitable **09** befitting **10** attractive **11** appropriate, comme il faut, respectable

**seep**
**04** drip, leak, oose, ooze, sipe, soak, sype, well **05** drain, exude **07** dribble, trickle **08** permeate **09** percolate

**seepage**
**04** leak **06** oozing **07** leakage, osmosis **08** dripping **09** exudation **11** percolation

**seer**
**04** seir **05** augur, sibyl **07** prophet, seeress, spaeman, wise man **08** spaewife **10** prophetess, soothsayer

**seesaw**
**04** yo-yo **05** pitch, swing **06** teeter **08** wild mare **09** alternate, fluctuate, oscillate

**seethe**
◇ *anagram indicator*
**04** boil, fizz, foam, fume, rage, rise, teem **05** froth, go ape, storm, surge, swarm, swell **06** blow up, bubble, buller, see red, simmer **07** be angry, be livid, explode, ferment **08** boil over, smoulder **09** be furious, blow a fuse **10** be incensed, be outraged, effervesce **11** blow a gasket, go ballistic **12** blow your cool, lose your cool **14** foam at the mouth **15** fly off the handle, go off the deep end

**see-through**
**05** filmy, gauzy, sheer **06** flimsy **08** gossamer **09** gossamery **11** translucent, transparent

**segment**
**03** bit, pig **04** exon, link, lith, part, ring **05** cut up, femur, halve, joint, piece, slice, split, urite, wedge **06** divide, scliff, skliff, somite, telson **07** article, isomere, overlay, portion, section, uromere **08** division, metamere, separate **09** anatomize, propodeon, prothorax, sternebra **10** arthromere, metathorax, proglottid, proglottis, trochanter **11** compartment **12** articulation

**segregate**
**06** cut off **07** exclude, isolate, seclude **08** separate, set apart **09** keep apart, ostracize, sequester **10** dissociate, quarantine

**segregation**
**09** apartheid, isolation **10** quarantine, separation **12** dissociation, setting apart **13** sequestration **14** discrimination

**seize**
◇ *containment indicator*
**03** bag, cly, nab, nap **04** bone, grab, grip, hend, hold, nail, snap, take **05** annex, catch, ceaze, cleek, grasp, latch, reach, sease, seaze, seise, usurp

**06** abduct, areach, arrest, attach, attain, clutch, collar, graple, hijack, kidnap, nobble, ravish, snatch, tackle **07** capture, forhent, grapple, impound, possess, prehend **08** forehent **09** apprehend, deprehend, get hold of, lay hold of, lay hold on, penetrate **10** commandeer, confiscate, grab hold of, lay hands on, take hold of **11** appropriate, catch hold of, requisition, sequestrate

**• seize on**
**04** grab **07** exploit **08** fasten on **12** grasp eagerly

**• seize up**
**03** jam **04** stop **06** go phut, pack up **07** conk out **09** break down **11** malfunction, stop working

**seizure**
**03** fit **04** grab, rape **05** catch, prise, prize, spasm **06** arrest, attack, extent, hijack, rapine, taking **07** capture, seysure **08** paroxysm, purchase, reprisal, wingding **09** abduction, distraint, snatching **10** annexation, attachment, convulsion, pre-emption **12** apprehension, confiscation **13** appropriation, commandeering, sequestration

**seldom**
**04** rare **06** rarely **07** unoften **10** hardly ever, infrequent **12** infrequently, occasionally, scarcely ever **15** once in a blue moon

**select**
**03** top **04** best, cull, pick, posh, sort **05** elect, élite, prime **06** choice, choose, favour, finest, invite, opt for, prefer **07** appoint, extract, limited, special, supreme **08** decide on, selected, settle on, superior **09** excellent, exclusive, first-rate, single out **10** cherry-pick, first-class, hand-picked, privileged **11** high-quality **12** make choice of

**selection**
**04** blad, pick **05** blaud, range **06** choice, dim sum, line-up, medley, option **07** Auslese, palette, variety **09** anthology, cold table, potpourri **10** assortment, collection, miscellany, preference **11** smörgåsbord

**selective**
**05** fussy, picky **06** choosy **07** careful, finicky **10** discerning, fastidious, particular, pernickety **11** persnickety **14** discriminating

**selectively**
**08** by choice **09** carefully **12** discerningly, particularly **14** differentially, preferentially

**Selene**
**04** Luna

**selenium**
**02** Se

**self**
**01** I **03** ego, own, sel **04** same, sell, soul, very **05** atman, seity **06** person **08** identity **09** identical, number one, the real me **10** inner being, yours truly **11** body and soul, personality **13** heart of hearts

**self-assembly**
**03** DIY **07** kit-form **08** flat-pack **13** prefabricated

**self-assertive**
**05** bossy, perky, pushy **07** pushing **08** forceful, immodest **10** aggressive, commanding, high-handed, peremptory **11** dictatorial, domineering, heavy-handed, overbearing, overweening **13** authoritarian

**self-assurance**
**06** aplomb **09** assurance, cockiness **10** confidence **11** assuredness **12** cocksureness, positiveness **14** overconfidence, self-confidence, self-possession

**self-assured**
**05** cocky **07** assured **08** cocksure **09** confident **13** overconfident, self-collected, self-confident, self-possessed **14** sure of yourself

**self-centred**
**07** selfish **09** egotistic **10** egocentric **11** egotistical, self-seeking, self-serving **12** narcissistic, self-absorbed **14** self-interested

**self-confidence**
**03** ego **05** poise **06** aplomb **07** opinion **09** assurance, composure **10** confidence **12** positiveness, self-reliance **13** self-assurance

**self-confident**
**04** bold, cool **07** assured **08** cocksure, composed, fearless, positive **09** confident, unabashed **11** self-assured, self-reliant **13** self-possessed

**self-conscious**
**03** coy, shy **05** timid **07** awkward, bashful, nervous **08** blushing, insecure, retiring, sheepish, timorous **09** diffident, ill at ease, shrinking **10** shamefaced **11** embarrassed **12** self-effacing **13** uncomfortable

**self-contained**
**02** s/c **05** quiet **07** private **08** discrete, reserved, separate **09** secretive **11** independent, self-reliant **12** free-standing **14** self-sufficient

**self-control**
**04** cool **06** temper **07** dignity, encraty **08** calmness, patience **09** composure, restraint, willpower **10** self-denial, temperance **11** self-mastery **13** self-restraint **14** self-discipline

**• lose self-control**
**04** flip, snap **05** break

**self-defence** *see* **martial art**

**self-denial**
**10** asceticism, moderation, temperance **12** selflessness **13** self-sacrifice, unselfishness **14** abstemiousness, self-abnegation

**self-discipline**
**07** resolve **09** willpower **11** persistence, self-control, self-mastery **13** determination

**self-employed**
**06** casual **08** part-time **09** freelance, temporary **10** consultant, out-of-house **11** independent

**self-esteem**
**03** ego **05** pride **07** conceit, dignity **09** self-image, self-pride **10** self-regard **11** amour-propre, self-respect **13** self-assurance **14** self-confidence

**self-evident**
**05** clear, plain **07** obvious **08** manifest **09** axiomatic **10** undeniable **11** inescapable **14** unquestionable

**self-explanatory**
**05** clear, plain **07** obvious **10** accessible, easy-to-read **11** self-evident **12** approachable, easy-to-follow, intelligible **14** comprehensible, understandable

**self-glorification**
**07** egotism **09** egotheism **14** self-admiration, self-exaltation

**self-governing**
**04** free **09** autonomic, sovereign **10** autonomous **11** independent **15** self-determining

**self-government**
**06** swaraj **08** autarchy, autonomy, home rule **09** democracy **11** sovereignty **12** independence **15** self-sovereignty

**self-importance**
**04** pomp **06** vanity **07** conceit, donnism **09** arrogance, cockiness, pomposity, pushiness **10** pretension **11** pompousness, self-opinion **13** bigheadedness, bumptiousness, conceitedness **15** self-consequence

**self-important**
**04** coxy, vain **05** cocky, proud, pushy **06** chesty, cocksy **07** pompous **08** arrogant, egoistic **09** bigheaded, bumptious, conceited, egotistic, strutting **10** portentous, swaggering **11** egotistical, overbearing, pragmatical, pretentious, swell-headed **13** consequential, swollen-headed **14** self-consequent

**self-indulgence**
**06** excess **08** hedonism **10** high living, profligacy, sensualism **11** dissipation **12** extravagance, intemperance **13** dissoluteness

**self-indulgent**
**06** wanton **09** dissolute **10** dissipated, hedonistic, immoderate, profligate **11** extravagant, intemperate **15** pleasure-seeking

**self-interest**
**04** self **08** self-love **10** expediency, self-regard **11** selfishness, self-serving

**selfish**
**04** mean **06** greedy **07** miserly **08** covetous **09** egotistic, mercenary **10** egocentric **11** calculating, egotistical, self-centred, self-seeking, self-serving **13** inconsiderate **14** self-interested

**selfishly**
**08** greedily **12** ungenerously **13** egotistically **14** egocentrically **15** inconsiderately, only for yourself

**selfishness**
**05** greed **06** egoism **07** egotism **08** meanness, self-love **10** self-regard **11** self-seeking, self-serving **12** self-interest **15** self-centredness

**selfless**
**08** generous **09** unselfish **10** altruistic **11** magnanimous, self-denying **13** philanthropic **15** self-sacrificing

**selflessness**
**08** altruism **10** generosity, self-denial **11** magnanimity **12** philanthropy **13** self-sacrifice, unselfishness

**self-possessed**
**04** calm, cool **06** poised **07** assured **08** composed, together **09** collected, confident, unruffled **11** self-assured, unflappable **13** self-collected

**self-possession**
**04** cool, head **05** nerve, poise **06** aplomb **08** calmness, coolness **09** assurance, composure, sangfroid **10** confidence **11** self-command **13** collectedness, self-assurance **14** self-confidence, unflappability

**self-reliance**
**07** autarky **11** self-support **12** independence **14** self-sustenance **15** self-sufficiency, self-sustainment

**self-reliant**
**08** autarkic **10** autarkical **11** independent **14** self-sufficient, self-supporting, self-sustaining

**self-respect**
**05** pride **07** dignity **10** self-esteem, self-regard **11** amour-propre **13** self-assurance **14** self-confidence

**self-restraint**
**07** encraty **08** patience **09** willpower **10** continence, continency, moderation, self-denial, temperance **11** forbearance, self-command, self-control **14** abstemiousness, self-discipline, self-government

**self-righteous**
**02** pi **04** smug **05** pious **08** priggish, superior **09** pietistic **10** complacent, goody-goody, moralistic **11** pharisaical **12** hypocritical **13** sanctimonious **14** holier-than-thou

**self-righteousness**
**09** goodiness, piousness **10** pharisaism **12** priggishness **14** goody-goodiness **15** pharisaicalness

**self-sacrifice**
**08** altruism **10** generosity, self-denial **12** selflessness **13** unselfishness **14** self-abnegation

**self-satisfaction**
**05** pride **08** smugness **11** complacency, contentment **12** self-approval **15** self-approbation

**self-satisfied**
**04** smug **05** proud **08** puffed up **10** complacent **13** self-righteous

**self-seeking**
**07** selfish **09** careerist, mercenary, on the make **10** self-loving **11** acquisitive, calculating, gold-digging, self-serving **12** self-endeared **13** opportunistic **14** fortune-hunting, self-interested

**self-styled**
**07** would-be **08** so-called **09** pretended, professed, soi-disant **10** self-titled **13** self-appointed

**self-sufficient**
**11** independent, self-reliant **13** self-contained **14** self-supporting, self-sustaining

**self-supporting**
**11** independent, self-reliant **13** self-financing **14** self-sufficient, self-sustaining

**self-willed**
**05** elvan, elven **06** cussed, elfish, elvish, wilful **07** froward, willful **08** perverse, stubborn **09** obstinate, pig-headed **10** headstrong, refractory **11** intractable, opinionated, stiff-necked **12** bloody-minded, ungovernable **15** self-opinionated

**sell**
**04** flog, hawk, hype, mart, push, seat, self, tout, vend, vent **05** carry, cry up, go for, selle, shift, stock, trade, trick **06** barter, betray, deal in, export, handle, import, market, peddle, praise, retail, saddle, smouch **07** auction, chaffer, let-down, promote, trade in, win over **08** exchange, persuade, retail at **09** advertise, deception, dispose of, traffic in **10** be priced at, bring round **11** merchandize **13** get support for **14** disappointment, get approval for
• **sell out**
**04** fail **05** rat on **06** betray, fink on **07** stool on **08** run out of **11** be exhausted, double-cross **12** be out of stock, have none left **13** stab in the back

**seller**
**06** trader, vendor **08** huckster, merchant, stockist, supplier
• **seller's opinion**
**02** so

**selling**
**07** dealing, trading, traffic, vending **09** marketing, promotion, vendition **11** trafficking **12** salesmanship, transactions **13** merchandizing

**selvage**
**04** list, roon, rund **05** royne

**semblance**
**03** air **04** copy, garb, idol, life, look, mask, show, sign **05** front, ghost, guise, image **06** aspect, façade, veneer **07** seeming **08** likeness, pretence, pretense **10** apparition, appearance, likelihood, similarity, similitude, simulacrum **11** resemblance

**semen**
**03** cum **04** come, gism, jism, jizz, seed **05** sperm, spoof, spunk **06** jissom **09** ejaculate **12** seminal fluid

**semi-liquid**
**04** slab **05** slimy **06** blashy, globby

**seminal**
**05** major **08** creative, germinal, original, seminary **09** formative, important **10** generative, innovative, productive **11** imaginative, influential, rudimentary

**seminar**
**05** class, forum **07** lecture, meeting, session **08** colloquy, tutorial, workshop **09** symposium **10** colloquium, conference, convention, discussion, study group

**seminary**
**03** Sem **06** school **07** academy, college, nursery, yeshiva **08** yeshivah **09** institute **10** theologate **11** institution **15** training college

**send**
**04** beam, cast, emit, fire, hurl, mail, make, move, post, turn **05** drive, fling, grant, radio, relay, remit, shoot, swash, throw **06** arouse, commit, convey, direct, excite, get off, launch, propel, thrill, turn on **07** address, consign, deliver, forward, project **08** despatch, dispatch, redirect, televise, transmit **09** broadcast, cause to be, discharge, give a buzz, give a kick, messenger, stimulate **11** communicate **12** put in the mail, put in the post **14** give pleasure to
• **send away**
**04** hunt, pack, void **05** drive **07** dismiss, pack off **08** despatch, dispatch
• **send for**
**05** get in, order **06** summon **07** call for, command, request
• **send forth**
**04** beam, pour **05** fling, shoot, speed **08** expedite **09** discharge
• **send off**
**04** ship **06** let fly, set off **08** despatch, dispatch, order off **12** order to leave
• **send up**
◇ *reversal down indicator*
**04** mock **05** mimic **06** parody **07** imitate, take off **08** ridicule, satirize

**send-off**
**05** start **07** goodbye, push-off **08** farewell **09** departure **11** leave-taking

**send-up**
**04** skit **05** spoof **06** parody, satire **07** mockery, take-off **09** burlesque, imitation **10** mickey-take

**Senegal**
**02** SN **03** SEN

**senile**
**03** old **04** aged, gaga **06** doited, doitit **07** failing **08** confused, decrepit **09** doddering, senescent

**senility**
**03** eld **04** eild **06** dotage, old age **07** anility, paracme **08** caducity **09** infirmity **10** senescence **11** decrepitude **14** senile dementia **15** second childhood

**senior**
**02** Sr **03** Sen, Snr **04** aîné, sire **05** aînée, chief, doyen, elder, first, major, older **06** higher **07** ancient, doyenne **08** superior **11** high-ranking

• **senior citizen**
**03** OAP **09** pensioner **10** golden ager **12** coffin-dodger **13** retired person **15** old-age pensioner

**seniority**
**03** age **04** rank **06** status **08** priority, standing **09** ancientry, antiquity, signeurie **10** importance, precedence **11** superiority

**sensation**
**03** hit, wow **04** aura, itch, stir **05** sense, vibes **06** furore, pit-pat, splash, thrill, tingle, winner **07** emotion, feeling, outrage, pitapat, prickle, scandal, success, symptom, triumph **08** goneness, pitty-pat **09** agitation, awareness, commotion **10** Empfindung, excitement, impression, perception **13** consciousness

**sensational**
**04** gamy, pulp **05** gamey, juicy, lurid, shock **06** superb, yellow **07** amazing **08** dramatic, drop-dead, exciting, fabulous, galvanic, gorgeous, shocking, smashing, stirring, terrific **09** excellent, fantastic, revealing, startling, thrilling, wonderful **10** astounding, horrifying, impressive, incredible, marvellous, scandalous, staggering **11** exceptional, spectacular **12** breathtaking, electrifying, melodramatic **15** blood-and-thunder

**sense**
**03** wit **04** feel, gist, mind, nous, wits **05** brain, drift, grasp, logic, point, savvy, tenor **06** brains, detect, divine, import, intuit, notice, nuance, pick up, reason, wisdom **07** ability, discern, faculty, feeling, meaning, observe, opinion, purport, purpose, realize, suspect **08** gumption, judgment, perceive, prudence **09** awareness, be aware of, direction, intuition, judgement, recognize, sensation, substance **10** appreciate, cleverness, comprehend, definition, denotation, experience, impression, perception, understand **11** common sense, discernment, implication, sensibility **12** appreciation, apprehension, intelligence, significance **13** be conscious of, comprehension, consciousness, judiciousness, understanding **14** interpretation, reasonableness

• **in this sense**
**02** hs **08** hoc sensu

• **make sense of**
**05** grasp **06** fathom **07** make out **09** figure out **10** comprehend, make much of, understand

**senseless**
**03** mad, out **04** daft, numb, surd **05** batty, crazy, dotty, inane, silly **06** absurd, futile, insane, stupid, unwise **07** fatuous, foolish, idiotic, moronic, out cold, stunned **08** deadened, mindless **09** illogical, insensate, ludicrous, pointless, unfeeling **10** insensible, irrational, ridiculous **11** meaningless, nonsensical, purposeless, unconscious **12** unreasonable **13** anaesthetized, load of rubbish **14** load of nonsense

**sense-organ**
**03** ear, eye **04** nose, palp **06** tongue **09** sensillum **15** mechanoreceptor

**sensibility**
**05** taste **07** feeling, insight **08** delicacy, emotions, feelings **09** awareness, intuition, sentiment **10** sentiments **11** discernment, sensitivity **12** appreciation **13** sensitiveness, sensitivities **14** perceptiveness, responsiveness, sentimentality, susceptibility

**sensible**
**04** sane, wise **05** aware, sharp, sober, solid, sound, tough, witty **06** clever, mature, shrewd, strong **07** evident, logical, prudent, working **08** everyday, ordinary, rational, wise-like **09** judicious, practical, realistic, sagacious, sensitive, wholesome **10** discerning, far-sighted, functional, no-nonsense, perceptive, reasonable, responsive, vulnerable **11** appreciable, clear-headed, commonsense, down-to-earth, hard-wearing, intelligent, level-headed, perceptible, serviceable, susceptible, well-advised **14** commonsensical

• **sensible of**
**07** alive to, aware of **09** mindful of **11** cognizant of, conscious of, convinced of, observant of, sensitive to **13** understanding **14** acquainted with

**sensibly**
**06** wisely **07** handily **08** cleverly, shrewdly, strongly, suitably, usefully **09** logically, prudently **10** rationally, reasonably **11** judiciously, practically, sagaciously, serviceably **12** functionally **13** realistically

**sensitive**
**04** fine, soft **05** aware, exact, quick **06** kittly, tender, touchy, tricky **07** awkward, brittle, careful, fragile, precise, tactful **08** delicate, discreet, reactive, sentient **09** cold-short, difficult, emotional, irritable **10** diplomatic, discerning, perceptive, responsive, sensitized, vulnerable **11** considerate, problematic, susceptible, sympathetic, thin-skinned **12** appreciative, highly strung **13** controversial, hyperesthetic, temperamental **14** hyperaesthesic, hyperaesthetic, impressionable, well-thought-out

**sensitivity**
**07** algesia **08** delicacy, esthesia, fineness, softness, sympathy **09** aesthesia, aesthesis, awareness, fragility **11** discernment **12** appreciation, radiesthesia, reactiveness **13** receptiveness, vulnerability **14** perceptiveness, responsiveness, susceptibility

**sensual**
**04** lewd, sexy **05** brute, gross, horny, randy **06** animal, bodily, brutal, carnal, erotic, sexual, sultry **07** fleshly, lustful, swinish, worldly **08** embodied, physical **09** lecherous, pandemian **10** licentious, voluptuary, voluptuous **12** encarnalized **13** self-indulgent

**sensuality**
**08** lewdness, pleasure, sexiness **09** animalism, carnality, eroticism, prurience **10** debauchery, profligacy **11** gourmandize, libertinism, lustfulness **13** lecherousness, salaciousness **14** lasciviousness, licentiousness, voluptuousness

**sensuous**
**04** lush, rich **08** pleasant, pleasing **09** aesthetic, luxurious, sumptuous **10** gratifying, voluptuous **11** pleasurable

**sensuously**
**06** lushly, richly **11** luxuriously, pleasurably, sumptuously **12** gratifyingly, voluptuously

**sentence**
**03** swy **04** bird, doom, time **05** curse, judge, lifer, maxim, order **06** decree, period, punish, ruling **07** condemn, opinion, verdict **08** aphorism, decision, judgment, penalize, porridge **09** judgement **10** adjudgment, punishment **11** adjudgement **12** condemnation **13** pronouncement **15** pass judgement on

**sententious**
**05** brief, pithy, short, terse **06** gnomic **07** canting, compact, concise, laconic, pointed, pompous, preachy **08** succinct **09** axiomatic **10** aphoristic, moralistic, moralizing **11** judgemental **12** epigrammatic **13** sanctimonious

**sentient**
**04** live **05** aware **06** living **07** feeling, sensile **08** reactive **09** conscious, sensitive **10** responsive

**sentiment**
**04** idea, posy, view **05** maxim, slops **06** belief, hobnob, pledge **07** emotion,

feeling, opinion, romance, thought **08** attitude, judgment, softness **09** judgement **10** persuasion, tenderness **11** mawkishness, point of view, romanticism, sensibility **14** sentimentality **15** soft-heartedness

**sentimental**
**05** corny, gooey, gucky, gushy, hokey, mushy, soppy, weepy, yucky, yukky **06** gloopy, loving, sickly, sloppy, slushy, sugary, tender, too-too **07** boy-girl, gushing, maudlin, mawkish, missish, treacly **08** cornball, pathetic, romantic, rose-pink, shmaltzy, touching **09** emotional, nostalgic, rosewater, schmaltzy **10** lovey-dovey, Wertherian **11** soft-hearted, tear-jerking **12** affectionate, chocolate-box **13** lackadaisical

**sentimentality**
**03** goo, yuk **04** gush, mush, pulp, yuck **05** gloop, slush **06** bathos **07** feeling, shmaltz, treacle **08** schmaltz **09** corniness, nostalgia, sentiment **10** sloppiness, tenderness **11** mawkishness, romanticism, sensibility **12** emotionalism **14** sentimentalism

**sentry**
**05** guard, watch **06** centry, picket **07** lookout, vedette **08** sentinel, watchman **09** out-sentry

**separable**
**08** distinct, dividant, dividual, partible **09** different, divisible, removable **10** detachable, particular **11** independent **15** distinguishable

**separate**
**03** red, sep, try **04** comb, part, redd, shed, sort, twin **05** alone, apart, break, sever, shear, split, twine **06** cut off, demark, depart, detach, divide, reduce, remove, secede, single, sunder, sundry, winnow **07** break up, discerp, disjoin, dislink, dispart, diverge, divided, divorce, isolate, seclude, several, sort out, split up **08** abstract, break off, detached, discreet, discrete, disperse, dissever, distinct, distract, disunite, divorced, isolated, offprint, prescind, set apart, solitary, uncouple, withdraw **09** come apart, demarcate, different, disengage, dismantle, disparate, disunited, intervene, keep apart, partition, segregate, single out, take apart, uncombine, unrelated **10** autonomous, disconnect, disjointed, dissociate, individual, particular, segregated, unattached **11** disentangle, independent, part company, unconnected **12** disaffiliate, disconnected **15** become estranged

**separated**
**05** apart **06** parted, remote **07** divided, split up **08** isolated, separate, sundered **09** disunited **10** dissociate, poles apart, segregated **12** disconnected, poles asunder **13** disassociated, discontinuous

**separately**
**05** alone, apart **06** singly **07** asunder, divisim **08** one by one **09** in several, severally **10** absolutely, discretely, personally **12** individually **13** independently **14** discriminately

**separating**
**07** parting, sifting **08** abducent, dividing, divisive **09** isolating, precisive **10** discretive **11** intervening, segregating **12** partitioning **13** disengagement

**separation**
**03** gap **04** gulf, rift **05** split **06** schism, wrench **07** break-up, divorce, freedom, parting, split-up **08** avulsion, dialysis, disunion, dividing, division, farewell, interval, solution **09** apartheid, isolation, severance **10** detachment, divergence, uncoupling **11** demarcation, demarkation, disjunction, distinction, leave-taking, segregation **12** disgregation, disseverment, dissociation, estrangement **13** disconnection, disengagement **14** centrifugation

**separatist**
**05** rebel **08** apostate, renegade, seceding **09** breakaway, dissenter, heretical **10** dissenting, schismatic **11** Independent **12** secessionist

**separatists**
**03** ETA

**September**
**03** Sep **04** Sept

**septic**
**06** putrid **08** infected, poisoned **09** festering **10** putrefying **11** suppurating **12** putrefactive

**sepulchral**
**03** sad **04** deep **05** grave **06** dismal, gloomy, hollow, morbid, solemn, sombre, woeful **07** charnel **08** funereal, mournful **09** cheerless **10** lugubrious, melancholy **11** sepulchrous

**sepulchre**
**04** tomb **05** grave, vault **06** burial, entomb **09** mausoleum **10** repository **11** burial place

**sequel**
**03** end **05** issue, suite **06** pay-off, result, upshot **07** outcome **08** follow-up, sequence **09** after-clap, followers **10** conclusion, successors **11** consequence, development **12** consequences, continuation

**sequence**
**03** run, set **04** line, suit **05** chain, cycle, order, track, train **06** course, series, string **10** procession, succession **11** arrangement, consequence, progression

**sequester**
**04** take **05** seize **06** detach, remove **07** impound, isolate, seclude, shut off **08** alienate, insulate, set apart, set aside, shut away **09** seclusion **10** commandeer, confiscate **11** appropriate, sequestrate

**sequestered**
**05** quiet **06** lonely, remote **07** outback, private, retired **08** isolated, secluded **10** cloistered **11** out-of-the-way **12** unfrequented

**sequestrate**
**04** take **05** seize **07** impound **09** sequester **10** commandeer, confiscate **11** appropriate

**seraphic**
**04** holy, pure **06** divine, serene **07** angelic, saintly, sublime **08** beatific, blissful, heavenly, innocent **09** celestial **10** seraphical

**Serbia and Montenegro**
**03** SCG, YUG

**serenade**
**04** wake **07** horning **08** chivaree, shivaree **09** charivari

**serendipitous**
**05** happy, lucky **06** chance **09** fortunate **10** accidental, fortuitous, unexpected

**serendipity**
**04** luck **06** chance **07** fortune **08** accident, fortuity **11** coincidence, good fortune

**serene**
**04** calm, cool **05** clear, quiet, still **06** placid, serein **07** halcyon **08** composed, peaceful, seraphic, tranquil **09** unclouded, unruffled **10** seraphical, untroubled **11** undisturbed, unflappable **12** tranquillize **13** imperturbable

**serenely**
**06** calmly **07** quietly **08** placidly **10** peacefully, tranquilly **13** imperturbably

**serenity**
**04** calm, cool **05** peace **06** repose **08** calmness, quietude **09** composure, placidity, quietness, stillness **12** peacefulness, tranquillity **14** unflappability

**serf**
**05** helot, slave, thete, thirl **06** thrall **07** bondman, servant, villein **08** adscript, bondmaid, bondsman **09** bond-slave, bondwoman **10** bondswoman **11** bondservant

**sergeant**
**02** PS **03** NCO, Sgt **04** Cuff, Serg, Troy **05** Bilko, chips, sarge, Sergt **06** Buzfuz **08** havildar

**series**
**03** row, run, ser, set **04** line **05** chain, cycle, early, order, train **06** catena, course, stream, string **07** library **08** bead-roll, pedigree, sequence **10** succession **11** arrangement, progression **13** concatenation

**• new series**
**02** NS

**serious**
**03** bad, big, sad **04** deep, dour, grim, tidy **05** acute, ample, grave, great, heavy, large, quiet, sober, staid, stern **06** honest, lavish, no joke, severe, solemn, somber, sombre, urgent **07** crucial, earnest, genuine, pensive, sincere, sizable, weighty **08** abundant, critical, generous, grievous, perilous, pressing, sizeable, worrying **09** dangerous, difficult, important, long-faced, momentous, plentiful, unsmiling **10** humourless, precarious, thoughtful, unlaughing **11** far-reaching, preoccupied, significant, substantial **12** considerable, life-and-death **13** consequential, of consequence

**seriously**
**04** very **05** badly, jolly **06** highly, really, sorely **07** acutely, awfully, for real, gravely, greatly, utterly **08** severely, solemnly, terribly **09** au sérieux, decidedly, earnestly, extremely, intensely, sincerely, unusually **10** critically, dreadfully, grievously, remarkably, thoroughly, uncommonly **11** dangerously, exceedingly, excessively, frightfully, joking apart, joking aside **12** immoderately, inordinately, terrifically, thoughtfully, unreasonably **13** distressingly, exceptionally **15** extraordinarily

**seriousness**
**06** moment, weight **07** gravity, urgency **08** gravitas, sobriety **09** solemnity, staidness, sternness **10** importance, sedateness **11** earnestness **12** significance **14** humourlessness

**sermon**
**03** ser **04** talk **06** homily, preach **07** address, karakia, khotbah, khotbeh, khutbah, lecture, message, oration, reproof **08** harangue **09** discourse, talking-to **10** preachment **11** declamation, exhortation

**serow**
**04** thar

**serpent**
**05** lamia, snake **06** ellops **08** basilisk, sea snake **09** ouroboros **10** cockatrice
*See also* **snake**

**serpentine**
**05** snaky **06** ophite **07** coiling, crooked, sinuous, snaking, winding **08** asbestos, tortuous, twisting **09** ophiolite, snakelike **10** chrysotile, meandering, retinalite **12** serpentiform

**serrated**
**06** jagged, pinked **07** notched, sawlike, toothed **08** indented, saw-edged **09** crenulate **10** crenulated, saw-toothed, serrulated **11** serratulate **12** diprionidian **14** monoprionidian

**serried**
**05** close, dense **06** massed **07** compact, crowded **08** close-set **13** close together

**servant**
**03** boy, man **04** drug, help, jack **06** drudge, helper **07** subject **08** hireling **09** ancillary, assistant, attendant **10** ministrant

*Servants include:*

**03** fag, gip, gyp
**04** char, chef, cook, hind, maid, page
**05** boots, carer, daily, groom, nanny, slave, valet, wench
**06** au pair, barman, batman, butler, chokra, garçon, haiduk, lackey, menial, ostler, skivvy, tweeny, waiter
**07** barmaid, bellboy, bellhop, cleaner, equerry, flunkey, footman, gossoon, pageboy, steward, tapsman
**08** charlady, coachman, dogsbody, domestic, factotum, handmaid, henchman, home help, house boy, retainer, scullion, servitor, turnspit, waitress, wet nurse
**09** chauffeur, errand boy, governess, housemaid, lady's maid, seneschal
**10** chauffeuse, handmaiden, henchwoman, manservant, stewardess
**11** body servant, boot-catcher, chambermaid, henchperson, housekeeper, kitchen-maid, parlour-maid
**12** domestic help, scullery maid
**13** care assistant, lady-in-waiting, livery-servant
**14** commissionaire

**serve**
◇ *anagram indicator*
**02** do, ka **03** ace, act, aid, kae, let **04** deal, help, sair, wait **05** avail, valet **06** answer, assist, attend, dish up, fulfil, lackey, supply, wait on **07** benefit, deliver, dish out, dole out, further, give out, lacquey, perform, present, provide, satisfy, succour, suffice, support, undergo, work for, work out, worship **08** carry out, complete, function, wait upon **09** be of use to, discharge, go through **10** distribute, minister to, take care of **11** do the work of **12** be employed by **13** be of benefit to, be of service to, do a good turn to

**• serve up**
◇ *reversal down indicator*

**service**
**02** RN **03** ace, fee, job, let, RAF, use **04** army, duty, help, navy, rite, sorb, tune, turn, work **05** check, usage **06** course, duties, forces, go over, labour, repair, ritual **07** amenity, benefit, repairs, utility, worship **08** activity, air force, business, ceremony, disposal, facility, function, maintain, military, overhaul, resource **09** advantage, ordinance, sacrament, servicing **10** assistance, employment, expediting, observance, usefulness **11** maintenance, performance, recondition **12** availability

*Religious services include:*

**04** Mass
**06** matins
**07** baptism, evening, funeral, morning, wedding
**08** compline, evensong, High Mass, marriage, memorial
**09** communion, Eucharist
**10** bar mitzvah, bat mitzvah, dedication
**11** christening, Christingle, Lord's Supper, nuptial Mass, remembrance, Requiem Mass
**12** confirmation, Midnight Mass, thanksgiving
**13** Holy Communion, Holy Matrimony
**14** First Communion, morning prayers
**15** harvest festival

**• in service**
**05** in use **07** working **09** operative **10** functional **11** in operation **12** in regular use **14** in working order

**• of service**
**06** useful **07** helpful **09** of benefit **10** beneficial, profitable **12** advantageous

**• on active service**
**03** oas

**• out of service**
**04** phut **05** kaput **06** broken, faulty, kaputt **08** out of use, packed up **09** conked out, defective **10** not working, on the blink, on the fritz, out of order

**serviceable**
**04** good **05** plain, tough **06** simple, strong, usable, useful **07** durable, helpful **08** availful, sensible **09** effective, efficient, practical, unadorned **10** beneficial, commodious, convenient, dependable, functional, profitable **11** hard-wearing, utilitarian **12** advantageous

**serviceman** *see* **aircraftsman**; **sailor**; **soldier**

**servicemen** *see* **air force**; **army**; **navy**

**servile**
**03** low **04** base, mean **05** lowly, slimy **06** abject, humble, menial, vassal **07** fawning, slavish, subject **08** cringing, toadying, unctuous **09** groveling **10** controlled, grovelling, obsequious, submissive **11** bootlicking, subservient, sycophantic

**servility**
**05** slime **07** fawning **08** baseness, meanness, toadyism **09** abjection **10** abjectness, grovelling, sycophancy **11** bootlicking, slavishness **12** subservience, unctuousness **13** self-abasement **14** obsequiousness, submissiveness

**serving**
**05** share **06** amount, ration **07** bowlful, helping, portion **08** plateful, spoonful **11** ministering

**servitude**
**05** bonds **06** chains, thrall **07** bondage, peonage, peonism, serfdom, slavery **08** thirlage, thraldom **09** obedience, vassalage **10** stillicide, subjection, villeinage **11** enslavement, subjugation

**sesame**
**03** til **04** beni, teel **05** benne, benni **06** semsem **07** gingili, jinjili **08** gingelly

**session**
**04** bevy, sesh, Sess, term, time, year **05** bevvy, drill, shoot, spell **06** clinic, grog-on, grog-up, period, séance **07** hearing, meeting, sitting, stretch **08** assembly, semester **09** scrimmage, talkathon **10** conference, discussion **11** church court, down-sitting

*See also* **term**

**• be in session**
**03** set, sit

**• close a session**
**04** rise

**set**
◇ *anagram indicator*
**02** TV **03** dip, dot, fix, gel, kit, lay, lot, pit, ply, put **04** band, bulb, cake, club, dump, firm, gang, give, jell, knit, look, name, park, plan, rate, rest, sink, stud, turn **05** adapt, apply, array, batch, befit, begin, cause, class, crowd, embed, fixed, frame, grant, group, jelly, lodge, mount, pitch, place, plant, plonk, posit, radio, ready, rigid, scene, score, set up, stage, stake, start, stick, stock, telly, usual, value, wings, write **06** adjust, agreed, all set, assign, become, choose, circle, clique, create, decide, devise, direct, formal, go down, harden, impose, incite, insert, lead to, locate, ordain, outfit, prompt, select, series, set off, set out, settle, strict, vanish **07** agree on, appoint, arrange, bearing, compose, confirm, congeal, consign, coterie, decided, decline, deposit, dispose, faction, install, lay down, posture, prepare, produce, provide, regular, resolve, routine, scenery, setting, settled, sharpen, situate, specify, station, stiffen, subside, thicken, trigger **08** allocate, arranged, backdrop, category, conclude, delegate, equipped, everyday, finished, get ready, habitual, occasion, ordained, organize, position, prepared, propound, put right, regulate, result in, schedule, sequence, solidify, sprinkle, standard **09** appointed, coagulate, completed, customary, designate, determine, direction, disappear, establish, harmonize, ingrained, make ready, organized, prescribe, scheduled, specified, stipulate, variegate **10** assemblage, assortment, background, become firm, become hard, bring about, collection, compendium, complement, co-ordinate, deliberate, determined, entrenched, expression, give rise to, inaugurate, inflexible, prescribed, television, trigger off **11** crystallize, established, inclination, intentional, mise-en-scène, orchestrate, prearranged, stereotyped, synchronize, traditional **12** conventional **13** predetermined **14** bring into being

**• set about**
**05** begin, frame, start **06** attack, tackle **08** commence, embark on **09** get down to, undertake

**• set against**
**05** weigh **06** assail, divide, oppose **07** balance, compare **08** alienate, contrast, disunite, estrange **09** juxtapose

**• set apart**
**04** seal **06** divide, ordain **07** mark off, reserve **08** put aside, separate **09** segregate, sequester **11** distinguish, peculiarize **12** put on one side, put to one side **13** differentiate, make different

**• set aside**
**04** keep, save **05** allot, annul, break, lay by, put by **06** cancel, ignore, reject, repeal, revoke, select **07** discard, earmark, put away, reserve, reverse **08** abrogate, discount, keep back, lay aside, mothball, overrule, overturn, put aside, separate, set apart **09** sequester, slight off, stash away, supersede **10** give over to **13** keep in reserve

**• set back**
◇ *reversal indicator*
**04** cost, slow **05** check, delay **06** hinder, hold up, impede, retard, thwart **07** reverse **08** surprise

**• set down**
**03** lay **04** drop, land, note, snub, take **05** judge, pitch, state **06** affirm, assert, depose, encamp, esteem, record, regard **07** ascribe, deposit, lay down **08** note down **09** attribute, discharge, establish, formulate, prescribe, stipulate, subscribe, write down **12** put in writing

**• set forth**
**03** say **04** shew, show **05** leave, state **06** depart, praise, record, set off, set out **07** clarify, declare, display, exhibit, explain, expound, present, publish **08** describe, start out **09** delineate, elucidate, explicate, recommend

**• set in**
◇ *insertion indicator*
**04** come **05** begin, inset, start **06** arrive **08** commence

**• set off**
**05** begin, leave, light, start **06** blow up, depart, ignite, prompt, set out **07** commend, display, enhance, explode, show off, trigger **08** activate, contrast, detonate, heighten, initiate, set forth, start out, touch off **09** encourage, intensify **10** trigger off **11** set in motion, take the road **14** counterbalance **15** throw into relief

**• set on**
**03** mug, out, sic, tar **04** bent, firm, sick, sool **05** fixed, go for, tarre **06** attack, beat up, dogged, intent, strong, turn on **07** assault, dead set, decided, lay into, set upon **08** fall upon, hell-bent, resolute, resolved, stubborn **09** insistent, steadfast, tenacious **10** determined, persistent, purposeful, unwavering **11** persevering, unflinching **12** single-minded, strong-minded, strong-willed **14** uncompromising

**• set out**
◇ *anagram indicator*
**03** put **04** boun, laid **05** adorn, begin, bowne, leave, start **06** depart, lay out, set off, strike **07** arrange, display, exhibit, explain, expound, present, take off **08** describe, start out

**• set up**
◇ *reversal down indicator*
**02** up **03** rig **04** form, rear, trap **05** array, begin, build, erect, fit up, found, frame, pitch, raise, sport, start **06** create, settle **07** arrange, compose, dispose, elevate, mounted, prepare **08** assemble, initiate, organize **09** construct, establish, institute, introduce **10** constitute, inaugurate **11** incriminate **13** accuse falsely **14** bring into being

**setback**
◇ *reversal indicator*
**04** blip, blow, snag **05** check, delay, hitch, knock, upset **06** blight, defeat, hiccup, hold-up, rebuff, whammy **07** problem, relapse, reverse **08** body blow, hiccough, reversal **09** hindrance, throwback **10** difficulty, impediment, misfortune **11** obstruction **14** disappointment, stumbling-block

**settee**
**04** sofa **05** couch, futon, squab **06** canapé, day-bed, lounge **07** bergère, dos-à-dos, sofa bed **09** bed-settee, davenport, tête-à-tête **12** chesterfield

**setter**
**01** I **02** me **03** spy **07** dropper

**• setter's**
**04** mine

*See also* **crossword**

**setting**
**04** site, vail **05** frame, scene **06** chaton, locale, milieu, period **07** context, framing, monture, scenery **08** fixation, location, mounting, position **09** placement **10** background **11** environment, mise-en-scène, perspective **12** surroundings

**setting-up**
**05** start **08** creation, founding **09** inception **10** foundation, initiation **11** institution **12** inauguration, introduction **13** establishment

**settle**
**03** fix, pay **04** drop, fall, foot, kill, land, lite, live, nest, perk, rest, sink, stun **05** agree, bench, clear, fix up, ledge, light, lodge, lower, order, perch, pitch, plant, quiet, solve, state **06** accept, adjust, alight, ante up, choose, clinch, decide, defray, go down, occupy, people, repose, reside, square **07** agree on, appoint, arrange,

compact, compose, confirm, cough up, descend, discuss, dispose, fork out, inhabit, install, patch up, resolve, subside **08** colonize, come down, complete, conclude, decide on, organize, populate, regulate, settle up, square up **09** determine, discharge, establish, light upon, reconcile **10** compromise, put in order **12** make your home, put down roots **13** do the business

**• settle down**

**05** still **06** shut in, soothe **07** compose, quieten **08** calm down **09** buy a house, get down to, gravitate **10** get married **12** buckle down to, put down roots, start a family **13** concentrate on, knuckle down to **15** apply yourself to, make comfortable

**settlement**

◇ *anagram indicator*

**02** pa **03** pah, utu **04** camp, fine, post **05** truce **06** bustee, colony, hamlet **07** kibbutz, manyata, outpost, payment, sinking, village **08** clearing, contract, decision, defrayal, manyatta, ordering, presidio **09** agreement, Ausgleich, bandobast, Botany Bay, bundobust, clearance, community, discharge, rancherie **10** completion, conclusion, encampment, occupation, patching up, plantation, population, resolution, subsidence **11** arrangement, down-sitting, liquidation, termination **12** colonization, lake dwelling, organization, satisfaction **13** accommodation, establishment **14** reconciliation

**settler**

**07** bushman, incomer, new chum, pilgrim, pioneer, planter **08** colonist, newcomer, shagroon, squatter **09** colonizer, immigrant, inhabiter, Varangian **10** pure Merino **11** beachcomber, Cromwellian **12** frontiersman **14** frontierswoman

**set-to**

**03** row **04** bout, spat **05** brush, fight, scrap **06** barney, bust-up, dust-up, fracas **07** contest, quarrel, wrangle **08** argument, conflict, exchange, squabble **09** argy-bargy **11** altercation **12** disagreement **13** slanging-match

**set-up**

◇ *reversal down indicator*

**06** format, system **08** business **09** framework, structure **10** conditions **11** arrangement, composition, disposition **12** organization **13** circumstances

**seven**

**01** S **03** VII **06** heptad, Pleiad **08** hebdomad **09** septenary

**Seven Against Thebes**

*The Seven Greek champions who attacked Thebes:*

**06** Tydeus
**08** Adrastus, Capaneus
**09** Polynices
**10** Amphiaraus, Hippomedon
**13** Parthenopaeus

**Seven Deadly Sins** *see* **sin**

**seven hills of Rome** *see* **hill**

**Seven Sisters colleges** *see* **university**

**seventeen**

**04** XVII

**seventy**

**03** LXX

**Seven Wonders of the World** *see* **wonder**

**sever**

**03** cut, end, hew, nip **04** chop, hack, part, pith, rend **05** break, cease, split **06** cleave, cut off, detach, divide, lop off, nip off **07** chop off, disjoin, divorce, tear off **08** alienate, amputate, break off, dissever, dissolve, disunite, estrange, separate **09** disbranch, terminate **10** disconnect, dissociate **13** cut the painter

**several**

**04** a few, many, some **06** divers, sundry **07** diverse, various **08** assorted, distinct, separate **09** a number of, different, disparate, quite a few **10** individual, particular

**severally**

**06** apiece, singly **08** seriatim **10** discretely, separately **12** individually, in particular, particularly, respectively, specifically

**severe**

**03** bad, ill **04** cold, dour, grim, hard **05** acute, cruel, eager, grave, harsh, penal, plain, rigid, sharp, snell, sober, stark, stern, tough **06** fierce, modest, morose, shrewd, simple, strict, strong, taxing, trying **07** arduous, ascetic, austere, caustic, drastic, extreme, intense, serious, spartan, violent **08** Catonian, critical, Draconic, exacting, forceful, grievous, grinding, perilous, pitiless, powerful, rigorous, ruthless **09** agonizing, dangerous, demanding, difficult, Draconian, Dracontic, inclement, merciless, punishing, splitting, stringent, swingeing, unadorned, unbending, unsmiling, unsparing **10** astringent, burdensome, forbidding, functional, hard-handed, inexorable, iron-fisted, iron-handed, relentless, tyrannical, unbearable **11** strait-laced, undecorated **12** businesslike, disapproving, excruciating **13** Rhadamanthine, unembellished, unsympathetic

**severely**

**04** hard, sore **05** badly **06** coldly, dourly, grimly, hardly, sorely **07** acutely, gravely, harshly, sharply, sternly **08** bitterly, strictly **09** extremely, intensely **10** critically, rigorously **11** dangerously **14** disapprovingly

**severity**

**05** wrath **06** rigour **07** gravity **08** bareness, coldness, grimness, hardness, strength **09** acuteness, austerity, extremity, harshness, intensity, plainness, sharpness, sternness, toughness **10** asceticism, fierceness, severeness, simplicity, spartanism, strictness, stringency **11** seriousness **12** forcefulness, pitilessness, ruthlessness, ungentleness **13** mercilessness

**sew**

**03** hem, run, sue **04** bind, darn, mend, ooze, seam, tack, whip, work **05** baste, drain **06** needle, stitch **08** overcast, overhand **09** embroider **10** buttonhole, whipstitch **12** saddle-stitch

**sewage**

**04** soil **07** sullage

**sewer**

**04** sure **05** drain, shore, sough **06** cloaca, needle, tailor

**sex**

**01** f, m **04** male **05** union **06** allure, coitus, female, gender, libido **07** coition, glamour **08** congress, embraces, intimacy, sexiness **09** magnetism, sex appeal, sexuality **10** commixtion, copulation, lovemaking, sensuality **11** fornication, intercourse **12** consummation, desirability, reproduction, **13** seductiveness **14** voluptuousness **15** carnal knowledge, sexual relations

**sex appeal**

**02** it, SA **05** oomph

**sexless**

**01** n **06** neuter **07** asexual, unsexed **08** unsexual **10** undersexed, unfeminine **11** unmasculine **15** parthenogenetic

**sexton**

**06** fossor, verger **09** caretaker, sacristan **10** grave-maker **11** grave-digger

**sexual**

**03** sex **05** gamic **06** carnal, coital, erotic **07** genital, raunchy, sensual **08** venereal **11** procreative **12** reproductive

**sexuality**

**04** lust **06** desire **08** sexiness, virility **09** carnality, eroticism **10** sensuality, sexual urge **12** sexual desire **14** voluptuousness **15** sexual instincts

**sexy**

**04** phat **06** erotic, nubile, slinky, steamy **07** raunchy, sensual **08** alluring, arousing, beddable, exciting, inviting, tempting **09** desirable, provoking, salacious, seductive **10** attractive, suggestive, voluptuous **11** fascinating, flirtatious, provocative, stimulating, titillating **12** pornographic

**Seychelles**
**02** SY **03** SYC

**shabbily**
**08** rottenly, unfairly **09** scruffily **10** despicably, shamefully **11** inelegantly **12** contemptibly, disreputably, unacceptably **13** dishonourably, unfashionably

**shabby**
**03** low **04** mean, poky, worn **05** cheap, dingy, dirty, dowdy, faded, mangy, oorie, ourie, owrie, pokey, scaly, seedy, tacky, tatty **06** frayed, mangey, maungy, paltry, poking, ragged, rotten, scurvy, shoddy, unfair **07** raunchy, run-down, scruffy, squalid, worn-out **08** dog-eared, low-lived, shameful, tattered, unworthy **09** moth-eaten, out at heel **10** broken-down, despicable, down-at-heel, flea-bitten, ramshackle, threadbare, tumbledown **11** dilapidated, in disrepair **12** contemptible, disreputable, unacceptable **13** discreditable, dishonourable

**shack**
**03** hut **04** dump, hole, shed **05** cabin, hovel, hutch **06** lean-to, shanty

**shackle**
**03** tie **04** bind, bond, gyve, iron, rope **05** chain, limit **06** couple, fetter, hamper, hobble, impede, secure, tether, thwart **07** darbies, inhibit, manacle, trammel **08** encumber, handcuff, handicap, obstruct, restrain, restrict **09** bracelets, constrain, hamstring, hindrance, restraint **10** constraint, fetterlock, hamshackle **11** encumbrance, obstruction, restriction

**shad**
**05** allis **06** allice, twaite

**shade**
**03** dim, hue, tad **04** cast, dash, dusk, hide, hint, part, tint, tone, ugly, veil **05** blind, cloud, color, cover, ghost, gloom, swale, tinge, touch, trace, umbra, visor, vizor **06** amount, awning, canopy, colour, darken, degree, memory, nuance, screen, shadow, shield, shroud, spirit **07** conceal, curtain, dimness, obscure, parasol, phantom, protect, shadows, shelter, spectre, umbrage, variety **08** bongrace, covering, darkness, gloaming, overcast, reminder, sunblind, sunshade, tincture, twilight, umbrella **09** gradation, inumbrate, murkiness, obscurity, represent, semblance, shadiness, suspicion **10** apparition, difference, gloominess, overshadow, protection, suggestion **12** semi-darkness **14** block light from

*See also* **black**; **blue**; **colour**; **dye**; **green**; **grey**; **orange**; **pigment**; **pink**; **purple**; **rainbow**; **red**; **white**; **yellow**

**• a shade**
**04** a bit **06** a touch, a trace, rather **07** a little, a trifle **08** slightly

**• put in the shade**
**03** top **04** beat **05** dwarf, excel **07** eclipse, outrank, surpass **08** outclass, outshine

**• shade off**
**04** melt, pass **05** blend **07** gradate **10** intergrade

**shadow**
**03** dog, pal **04** dusk, hide, hint, pall, scog, scug, skug, stag, tail **05** cloud, cover, ghost, gloom, image, scoog, scoug, shade, shape, stalk, trace, trail, umbra, watch **06** blight, darken, follow, screen, shield, sleuth, spirit, typify, unreal **07** dimness, feigned, obscure, outline, remnant, sadness, shelter, trouble, umbrage, vestige **08** darkness, follower, gloaming, overhang, penumbra, sidekick, twilight **09** companion, detective, obscurity, remainder, suspicion **10** foreboding, overshadow, protection, silhouette, suggestion **11** tenebrosity **12** semi-darkness **14** Brocken spectre, representation

**• a shadow of your former self**
**07** apology, remnant, vestige **13** poor imitation, weaker version

**• without a shadow of a doubt**
**05** truly **06** surely **07** clearly, no doubt **08** of course **09** assuredly, certainly, doubtless **10** most likely **11** indubitably, undoubtedly **12** indisputably, without doubt **14** unquestionably

**shadowy**
**03** dim **04** dark, hazy **05** faint, murky, shady, vague **06** gloomy, unreal **07** ghostly, obscure, phantom, unclear **08** ethereal, illusory, nebulous, secluded, spectral, symbolic **09** dreamlike, imaginary, tenebrose, tenebrous **10** ill-defined, indistinct, intangible, mysterious, tenebrious **11** crepuscular, umbratilous **13** indeterminate, unsubstantial

**shady**
**03** dim **04** cool, dark, iffy **05** bosky, fishy, leafy **06** bowery, louche, opaque, shaded, shifty, veiled **07** clouded, covered, crooked, dubious, obscure, shadowy, suspect, umbrose, umbrous **08** screened, shielded, shrouded, sinister, slippery **09** dishonest, protected, tenebrose, tenebrous, umbratile, underhand, unethical **10** caliginous, mysterious, suspicious, tenebrious, umbrageous, unreliable **11** umbratilous, umbriferous **12** disreputable, questionable, unscrupulous **13** untrustworthy

**shaft**
**03** ash, bar, fil, pit, ray, rod **04** beam, butt, dart, duct, dupe, fill, flue, fust, hilt, pole, sink, stem, tige, well **05** arbor, arrow, scape, shank, stale, stalk, stave, steal, steel, steil, stele, stick, stock, stulm, winze **06** handle, pencil, pillar, rachis, scapus, steale, tunnel **07** missile, passage, swindle, upright, winning **08** hoistway **09** truncheon

**shaggy**
**04** rag'd **05** bushy, hairy, nappy, ragde, tousy, touzy, towsy, towzy **06** horrid, ragged, woolly **07** crinose, hirsute, unkempt, unshorn **09** mop-headed **10** long-haired **11** dishevelled

**shake**
◇ *anagram indicator*
**03** jog, wag, wap **04** bump, faze, jerk, jolt, pump, rock, roll, shog, stir, sway, wave **05** alarm, alert, crack, heave, lower, quake, rouse, shock, split, swing, throb, trill, upset, waver, wield, wring **06** bounce, didder, dindle, dinnle, dismay, dodder, happen, hustle, jigger, jiggle, joggle, jostle, judder, justle, lessen, moment, quiver, rattle, reduce, shiver, summon, totter, trillo, twitch, weaken, wobble **07** agitate, concuss, disturb, fissure, perturb, quaking, rocking, shake up, shoggle, shoogle, shudder, tremble, unnerve, vibrate **08** brandish, convulse, diminish, distress, flourish, frighten, unsettle **09** oscillate, shivering, throbbing, trembling, undermine, vibration **10** convulsion, discompose, intimidate, shuddering, unsettling **11** disturbance, oscillation

**• shake a leg**
**05** hurry **07** hurry up **08** step on it **10** get a move on, look lively **11** get cracking **15** get your skates on

**• shake off**
**04** heal, lose, mend **05** elude, rally **06** escape, pick up, revive **07** get away, get over, get well, improve **08** dislodge, get rid of, outstrip, shrug off **09** get better **10** bounce back, convalesce, feel better, recuperate **11** be on the mend, get away from, give the slip, leave behind, outdistance, pull through, recover from **12** gain strength **13** turn the corner

**• shake up**
**03** mix **05** alarm, rouse, shock, upset **06** jumble, rattle **07** disturb, succuss, unnerve, upbraid **08** distress, unsettle **09** rearrange, reshuffle **10** reorganize **11** restructure

**Shakespeare**
**02** WS **07** the Bard **13** The Swan of Avon

*Shakespeare's characters include:*

**03** **Hal** (Prince), **Nym**, **Sly** (Christopher)
**04** **Ajax**, **Anne** (Lady), **Dull**, **Fool** (The), **Ford** (Mistress), **Hero**, **Iago**, **John** (Don), **John** (King), **Kate**, **Kent** (Earl of), **Lear** (King), **Moth**, **Page** (Mistress), **Puck**, **Snug**
**05** **Ariel**, **Bagot**, **Belch** (Sir Toby), **Bushy**, **Celia**, **Diana**, **Edgar**, **Feste**, **Flute**, **Gobbo** (Launcelot), **Green**, **Julia**, **Maria**, **Nurse**, **Paris** (Count), **Pedro** (Don), **Regan**, **Romeo**, **Snout**, **Speed**, **Timon**, **Titus**, **Viola**
**06** **Alonso**, **Angelo**, **Antony** (Mark), **Armado** (Don Adriano de), **Audrey**, **Banquo**, **Bianca**, **Bottom** (Nick), **Brutus**, **Cassio**, **Cloten**, **Cobweb**, **Dromio**, **Duncan** (King), **Edmund**,

Emilia, Fabian, Hamlet, Hecate, Hector, Helena, Henry V (King), Hermia, Imogen, Jaques, Juliet, Launce, Marina, Oberon, Oliver (de Bois), Olivia, Orsino, Oswald, Pistol, Pompey, Porter, Portia, Quince, Silvia, Thisbe, Ursula, Verges, Yorick
**07** Adriana, Antonio, Berowne, Bertram (Count of Rousillon), Caliban, Capulet, Cesario, Claudio, Costard, Fleance, Goneril, Gonzalo, Henry IV (King), Henry VI (King), Horatio, Hotspur, Iachimo, Jessica, Laertes, Lavinia, Leontes, Lepidus, Lorenzo, Luciana, Macbeth, Macbeth (Lady), Macduff, Malcolm, Mariana, Martext (Sir Oliver), Miranda, Nerissa, Octavia, Ophelia, Orlando, Othello, Paulina, Perdita, Proteus, Pyramus, Quickly (Mistress), Shallow, Shylock, Sycorax, Theseus, Titania, Troilus
**08** Bardolph, Bassanio, Beatrice, Benedick, Benvolio, Charmian, Claudius, Cordelia, Cressida, Dogberry, Falstaff (Sir John), Florizel, Fluellen, Ganymede, Gertrude, Hermione, Isabella, Laurence (Friar), Lucretia, Lysander, Malvolio, Mercutio, Montague, Pandarus, Parolles, Pericles, Polonius, Prospero, Rosalind, Rosaline, Stephano, Trinculo
**09** Aguecheek (Sir Andrew), Antigonus, Cleopatra, Collatine, Cornelius, Cymbeline, Demetrius, Desdemona, Enobarbus, Ferdinand, Ferdinand (King of Navarre), Frederick (Duke), Henry VIII (King), Hippolyta, Hortensio, Katharina, Katharine (Princess of France), Nathaniel (Sir), Petruchio, Polixenes, Richard II, Sebastian, Valentine, Vincentio (Duke)
**10** Antipholus (of Ephesus), Antipholus (of Syracuse), Collatinus, Coriolanus, Fortinbras, Gloucester (Earl of), Holofernes, Jaquenetta, Richard III, Starveling, Tarquinius, Touchstone
**11** Mustard-seed, Peasblossom, Rosencrantz
**12** Guildenstern, Julius Caesar, Three Witches
**15** Robin Goodfellow, Titus Andronicus

*Shakespeare's plays:*

**06** Hamlet, Henry V
**07** Macbeth, Othello
**08** King John, King Lear, Pericles
**09** Cymbeline, Henry VIII, Richard II
**10** Coriolanus, Richard III, The Tempest
**11** As You Like It
**12** Julius Caesar, Twelfth Night
**13** Timon of Athens
**14** Henry IV Part One, Henry IV Part Two, Henry VI Part One, Henry VI Part Two, Romeo and Juliet, The Winter's Tale
**15** Titus Andronicus
**16** Henry VI Part Three, Love's Labours Lost
**17** Measure for Measure, The Comedy of Errors
**18** Antony and Cleopatra, Troilus and Cressida
**19** Much Ado About Nothing, The Merchant of Venice, The Taming of the Shrew
**20** All's Well That Ends Well
**21** A Midsummer Night's Dream, Hamlet, Prince of Denmark
**22** The Merry Wives of Windsor
**23** The Two Gentlemen of Verona

**shake-up**
**08** upheaval **09** reshuffle **11** disturbance **13** rearrangement, restructuring **14** reorganization

**shaky**
◇ *anagram indicator*
**04** weak **05** dicky, loose, quaky, rocky, wonky **06** coggly, cranky, dickey, flimsy, wobbly **07** dubious, quavery, rickety, suspect, tottery, unsound **08** insecure, unstable, unsteady, wavering **09** doddering, faltering, quivering, tentative, tottering, trembling, tremulous, uncertain, unfounded **10** precarious, staggering, ungrounded, unreliable **11** unsupported **12** questionable **13** untrustworthy

**shale**
**04** husk, till **05** blaes, fakes, shell **06** blaise, blaize, faikes **09** torbanite **12** porcellanite **14** Kupferschiefer

**shall**
**02** 'll

**shallow**
**03** ebb **04** bank, flat, flew, flue, idle **05** empty, fleet, petty, shoal **06** flimsy, shoaly, simple, slight, spread **07** foolish, surface, trivial **08** ignorant, skin-deep, trifling **09** frivolous, insincere **11** meaningless, superficial, unscholarly **13** rattle-brained **14** one-dimensional

**sham**
◇ *anagram indicator*
**03** cod **04** copy, fake, hoax, idol, mock **05** bogus, cheat, dummy, false, feign, fraud, mimic, pseud, put on, put-on, snide **06** affect, con man, humbug, phoney, pseudo, shoddy, stumer **07** feigned, forgery, imitate, pretend **08** deceiver, fakement, feigning, imposter, impostor, pretence, pretense, simulate, spurious, swindler **09** brummagem, charlatan, dissemble, gold brick, imitation, imposture, pinchbeck, pretended, pretender, simulated, synthetic **10** artificial, pasteboard, simulation **11** counterfeit, make believe, make-believe, mock-modesty, synthetical **12** impersonator

**shaman**
**05** pawaw **06** healer, powwow **07** angekok, tohunga **08** angekkok, magician, sorcerer **11** medicine man, witch doctor **13** medicine woman

**shamble**
**04** drag, limp **06** doddle, falter, hobble, scrape, toddle **07** bauchle, scamble, shuffle

**shambles**
**04** mess **05** chaos, havoc, wreck **06** bedlam, muddle, pigsty **07** anarchy **08** abattoir, butchery, disarray, disorder, madhouse **09** confusion **10** slaughtery **14** slaughterhouse **15** disorganization

**shambling**
**05** loose **06** clumsy **07** awkward **08** lurching, ungainly, unsteady **09** lumbering, shuffling **10** disjointed **13** unco-ordinated

**shambolic**
**05** messy **07** chaotic, muddled **08** confused **10** in disarray **12** disorganized **14** all over the shop

**shame**
**03** fie, fye, out, sin **04** alas, pity **05** abash, aidos, guilt, pudor, shend, stain, sully, taint **06** ashame, debase, humble, infamy, rebuke, show up, stigma, too bad **07** bad luck, beshame, degrade, modesty, mortify, remorse, reproof, scandal **08** confound, disgrace, dishonor, ignominy, repriefe, reproach, ridicule **09** confusion, discredit, dishonour, disrepute, embarrass, humiliate **10** misfortune, opprobrium, put to shame **11** bashfulness, compunction, degradation, humiliation **13** embarrassment, mortification **14** disappointment, shamefacedness
• **put to shame**
**05** shend **06** humble, rebuke, show up **07** eclipse, mortify, surpass, upstage **08** disgrace, outclass, outshine, outstrip **09** embarrass, humiliate

**shamefaced**
**05** sorry **06** guilty **07** abashed, ashamed **08** blushing, contrite, penitent, pudibund, red-faced, sheepish **09** mortified, regretful **10** apologetic, humiliated, remorseful **11** embarrassed **13** uncomfortable

**shameful**
**03** low **04** base, foul, mean, poor, vile **06** wicked **07** heinous, ignoble, shaming **08** indecent, shocking, unworthy **09** atrocious, pudendous **10** abominable, inglorious, mortifying, outrageous, scandalous **11** disgraceful, humiliating, ignominious **12** contemptible, embarrassing **13** discreditable, dishonourable, reprehensible

**shamefully**
**10** shockingly **11** atrociously **12** confoundedly, outrageously, scandalously **13** disgracefully, ignominiously, reprehensibly **14** embarrassingly

**shameless**
**05** brash **06** brazen, wanton **07** blatant, corrupt, defiant **08** blattant, browless, depraved, flagrant,

hardened, immodest, improper, impudent, indecent, insolent, unseemly, unshamed **09** abashless, audacious, bald-faced, barefaced, dissolute, frontless, unabashed, unashamed, unbashful **10** brass-faced, impenitent, indecorous, unbecoming, unblushing **11** ithyphallic, unregretful, unrepentant **12** incorrigible, unprincipled

**shamelessly**
**09** blatantly, defiantly **10** immodestly, improperly, indecently
**11** unashamedly **12** incorrigibly

**shanty**
**03** hut **04** shed **05** bothy, cabin, hovel, hutch, shack **06** chanty, lean-to
**07** chantey, chantie, shantey
**• shanty town**
**06** favela **10** bidonville

**shape**
◇ *anagram indicator*
**03** air, cut, hew **04** cast, form, look, make, plan, trim, turn **05** adapt, alter, block, build, carve, forge, frame, guide, guise, image, lines, model, mould, state **06** adjust, aspect, create, define, design, devise, direct, embody, fettle, figure, format, health, kilter, modify, sculpt **07** conduce, develop, fashion, outline, pattern, prepare, produce, profile, purpose, remodel, whittle
**08** contours, likeness, organize, physique, regulate **09** character, condition, construct, determine, influence, sculpture, semblance, structure **10** apparition, appearance, silhouette **11** accommodate
**13** configuration
*See also* **circle**; **figure**; **triangle**
**• shape up**
**06** come on **07** develop, improve
**08** flourish, progress **09** take shape
**11** make headway, move forward
**12** make progress
**• take shape**
**03** gel **04** form **06** inform **11** become clear, materialize **12** come together
**14** become definite

**shapeless**
◇ *anagram indicator*
**05** dumpy **07** chaotic **08** deformed, formless, indigest, nebulous, unformed, unframed **09** amorphous, irregular, misshapen **11** purposeless, undeveloped, unfashioned
**12** unstructured **13** unfashionable
**15** ill-proportioned

**shapely**
**04** neat, tidy, trig, trim **06** comely, gainly, pretty **07** elegant, featous
**08** feateous, featuous, graceful **09** well-set-up **10** attractive, curvaceous, forehanded, voluptuous, well-formed, well-turned **11** clean-limbed

**shard**
**03** bit, gap **04** chip, part **05** piece, scrap, sherd **06** shiver, sliver
**08** fragment, particle, splinter

**share**
**03** cut, due, lot, rug **04** divi, part, snap, snip, sock **05** allot, divvy, halve, quota, snack, split, whack **06** assign, common, divide, finger, ration
**07** carve up, deal out, dole out, give out, go Dutch, hand out, partake, portion, rake-off, section **08** allocate, dividend, division, go halves, interest, ordinary, share out **09** allotment, allottery, allowance, apportion, bank-stock, co-portion **10** allocation, contingent, distribute, percentage, plough-iron, proportion **11** go halvesies, participate **12** compare notes, contribution, go fifty-fifty, have a share in **14** slice of the cake
**• share out**
**05** allot, split **06** assign **07** divvy up, give out, hand out, mete out **08** divide up **09** apportion, parcel out
**10** distribute
**• shareholder**
**09** ploughman

**shark**
**05** crook **07** fleecer, sharper, slicker, sponger **08** man-eater, operator, parasite, swindler **11** extortioner
**12** extortionist **13** wheeler-dealer

*Sharks include:*

**03** cat, fox, saw
**04** blue, bull, mako
**05** blind, dusky, ghost, lemon, night, nurse, sagre, swell, tiger, whale, zebra
**06** beagle, carpet, goblin, salmon, school, sea cat
**07** basking, bramble, dogfish, leopard, requiem, sleeper, soupfin
**08** blacktip, grey reef, mackerel, thresher, whitetip
**09** angelfish, epaulette, Greenland, man-eating, porbeagle, sand tiger, sevengill, sharpnose, wobbegong
**10** Colclough's, great white, hammerhead, Portuguese, shovelhead
**11** ragged-tooth, smooth-hound

**sharp**
**03** fit, sly **04** able, acid, cold, curt, edgy, fine, gleg, keen, neat, sour, tart, tidy, wily **05** acidy, acrid, acute, alert, brisk, clear, crisp, cruel, eager, edged, harsh, natty, nifty, quick, rapid, razor, smart, snell, spiky, stark, tangy, tight
**06** abrupt, acidic, artful, astute, barbed, biting, bitter, bright, clever, crafty, fierce, hungry, jagged, marked, severe, shrewd, snappy, strong, sudden
**07** acerbic, brusque, burning, caustic, cunning, cutting, elegant, exactly, extreme, hairpin, hurtful, intense, nipping, piquant, pointed, pungent, stylish, varment, varmint, violent
**08** abruptly, all there, clear-cut, definite, distinct, freezing, incisive, on the dot, peracute, piercing, poignant, promptly, sardonic, scathing, serrated, shooting, stabbing, stinging, suddenly, venomous, vinegary **09** deceptive, dishonest, malicious, observant, on the ball, precisely, sarcastic, trenchant, vitriolic, voiceless **10** astringent, discerning, knife-edged, needle-like, perceptive, punctually, razor-edged, razor-sharp, unexpected
**11** acrimonious, fashionable, intelligent, penetrating, quick-witted, well-defined **12** twenty-twenty, unexpectedly

**sharpen**
**03** set **04** edge, file, hone, keen, whet
**05** frost, grind, point, stone, strop
**09** acuminate

**sharp-eyed**
**08** hawk-eyed, noticing **09** eagle-eyed, observant **10** perceptive
**11** keen-sighted **12** eagle-sighted

**sharply**
**05** smack **06** curtly **07** acutely, clearly, harshly, quickly, rapidly, starkly, tightly
**08** abruptly, bitterly, fiercely, markedly, suddenly **09** brusquely **10** definitely, distinctly, venomously
**12** unexpectedly **13** acrimoniously, sarcastically, vitriolically

**sharpness**
**04** edge, whet **05** venom **06** acuity, acumen **07** clarity, cruelty, sarcasm, vitriol **08** keenness, severity
**09** acuteness, crispness, eagerness, harshness, intensity, precision
**10** astuteness, definition, fierceness, shrewdness **11** brusqueness, discernment, observation, penetration
**12** incisiveness **14** perceptiveness

**shatter**
◇ *anagram indicator*
**04** bust, dash, ruin, star **05** blast, break, burst, crack, craze, crush, smash, split, upset, wreck **06** shiver **07** destroy, explode, scatter **08** demolish, fragment, overturn, splinter
**09** devastate, overwhelm, pulverize
**10** disappoint, smithereen **14** break your heart

**shattered**
◇ *anagram indicator*
**05** all in, weary **06** broken, done in, pooped, zonked **07** crushed, worn out
**08** dead beat, dog-tired, tired out
**09** exhausted, fagged out, knackered, plastered, pooped out **10** devastated
**11** overwhelmed, ready to drop, tuckered out

**shattering**
**06** severe **08** crushing, damaging, smashing **10** paralysing **11** devastating
**12** overwhelming

**shave**
**03** cut **04** barb, crop, pare, trim
**05** brush, graze, plane, shear, touch
**06** barber, fleece, paring, scrape
**07** plunder
**• close shave**
**09** close call, near touch **10** close thing, narrow miss **11** lucky escape
**12** narrow escape

**Shaw**
**03** GBS

**shawl**
**04** wrap **05** scarf, stole, tozie **06** afghan, tonnag, zephyr **07** blanket, dopatta, dupatta, tallith, whittle **08** pashmina, shatoosh, turnover **09** shahtoosh **10** India shawl **11** prayer shawl **12** Kashmir shawl, Paisley shawl

**she**
**01** a **03** her **04** elle
*See also* **girl**

**sheaf**
**04** gait, garb **05** bunch, garbe, gerbe, truss **06** armful, bundle **07** dorlach

**shear**
**03** cut **04** clip, crop, trim **05** shave, strip **06** barber, fleece **07** scissor, tonsure **08** clipping, separate **09** penetrate

**sheath**
**04** case **05** ocrea, shard, shell, theca, volva **06** casing, cocoon, condom, ochrea, rubber, sleeve, vagina **07** johnnie, root cap, velamen **08** covering, envelope, scabbard, urceolus, vaginula, vaginule, wrapping **09** epidermis **10** caddis-case, coleoptile, endodermis, neurilemma, neurolemma, rhinotheca, thumbstall, zoothecium **11** perineurium **12** French letter, perichaetium, prophylactic, rhamphotheca

**shed**
◇ *deletion indicator*
**03** hut, mew, sow **04** cast, drop, emit, give, molt, part, pour, skeo, skio **05** hovel, linny, moult, shack, shine, spend, spill, spilt, throw **06** impart, lean-to, linhay, linney, remove, shower, slough **07** cast off, diffuse, discard, emitted, fall off, let fall, parting, radiate, scatter, send out, shippen, shippon **08** building, disperse, get rid of, give away, outhouse, separate, skillion **10** besprinkle

- **shed tears**

**03** sob **04** bawl, howl, wail, weep **05** whine **06** snivel **07** blubber, whimper **09** be in tears **14** burst into tears, cry your eyes out

**sheen**
**05** gleam, gloss, shine, water **06** bright, luster, lustre, patina, polish **07** burnish, shimmer, shining, sparkle, varnish **08** radiance **09** beautiful, shininess **10** brightness, brilliance

**sheep**
**03** ewe, hog, joe, keb, mug, ram, teg, tup, yeo, yow **04** fold, hogg, lamb, tegg, yowe **05** crone, flock, yowie **06** bident, gimmer, hidder, hirsel, hogget, lamber, theave, wether, woolly **07** jumbuck, twinter **08** hoggerel **09** shearling **10** bell-wether, woollyback

*Sheep include:*

**03** Rya
**04** Dala, Gute, Soay
**05** ammon, ancon, aodad, Jacob, Lleyn, Lonck, Masai, Rygja, Texel, Tunis, urial
**06** aoudad, Arcott, argali, Awassi, Balwen, Beltex, bharal, burhel, burrel, Dorper, Galway, Masham, merino, muflon, Romney
**07** Barbary, bighorn, burrell, burrhel, caracul, Cheviot, Colbred, Gotland, karakul, Karaman, Lincoln, Loghtan, Loghtyn, mouflon, Romanov, Roussin, Ryeland, St Croix, Steigar, Suffolk, Tibetan, Vendeen
**08** Columbia, Cotswold, herdwick, Katahdin, Loaghtan, Meatlinc, moufflon, Ouessant, Peliquey, Portland, Shetland, thinhorn, troender
**09** blackface, Charolais, Costentin, Leicester, Marco Polo, Southdown, Teeswater
**10** Charollais
**11** Wensleydale
**15** Border Leicester

- **flock of sheep**

**04** fold, trip

**sheepish**
**05** silly **07** abashed, ashamed, foolish **09** chastened, mortified **10** shamefaced **11** embarrassed **13** self-conscious, uncomfortable

**sheepskin**
**04** napa, roan **05** basan, Mocha, nappa **06** mouton, shammy, skiver **07** chamois, morocco **11** wash leather **13** shammy leather

- **sheepskin coat**

**07** posteen, zamarra, zamarro **08** poshteen **10** Afghan coat

**sheer**
**04** bend, fine, flat, full, main, mere, pure, rank, thin, turn, veer **05** blank, clear, drift, gauzy, light, plumb, quite, sharp, shift, stark, steep, swing, total, utter **06** abrupt, bright, flimsy, simple, swerve **07** deflect, deviate, diverge, perfect **08** absolute, complete, delicate, gossamer, thorough, unbroken, vertical **09** deviation, downright, out-and-out, unmingled, veritable **10** diaphanous, see-through, vertically **11** precipitous, translucent, transparent, unmitigated, unqualified **12** unadulterate **13** perpendicular, thoroughgoing, unadulterated, unconditional

**sheet**
**03** cel, sht, web **04** cell, coat, film, leaf, page, pane, sail, sill, skin, slab **05** cover, folio, layer, panel, piece, plate, reach, sweep **06** lamina, shroud, veneer **07** blanket, blotter, coating, expanse, overlay, stratum, stretch, surface **08** bed linen, covering, membrane, pamphlet **09** Celluloid®, newspaper **10** broadsheet

**shelf**
**03** bar **04** bank, bink, rack, reef, sill, step **05** bench, ledge, shoal, stage **06** shelve, shrine **07** bracket, counter, retable, sand bar, terrace **08** credence, credenza, informer, sandbank, shelving **11** mantelpiece, mantelshelf **12** chimney piece

- **on the shelf**

**06** single **09** on your own, unmarried **10** spouseless, unattached **15** without a partner

**shell**
◇ *anagram indicator*
◇ *ends deletion indicator*
**03** pod **04** body, bomb, case, clam, hull, husk, mail, rind, shot **05** blitz, chank, conch, cowry, crust, frame, ormer, shale, shard, sheal, sheel, shiel, shill, shuck, testa **06** attack, bullet, casing, cockle, cowrie, fire on, mussel, pellet, sea pen **07** admiral, barrage, bombard, carcase, carcass, chassis, cochlea, grenade, limacel, missile, scallop, scollop **08** carapace, covering, sea acorn, skeleton, univalve **09** explosive, framework, Midas's ear, structure, turbinate **10** integument, projectile **11** globigerina **12** pelican's-foot

- **shell money**

**04** peag, peak **06** wakiki, wampum **10** wampumpeag

- **shell out**

**04** ante, give **05** pay up, spend **06** ante up, donate, expend, lay out, pay out **07** cough up, fork out **08** disburse **10** contribute

**shellfish**

- **young shellfish**

**04** spat
*See also* **fish**; **mollusc**; **seafood**

**shelter**
◇ *containment indicator*
**03** cot, lee **04** cote, hide, loun, lown, roof, scog, scug, skug, tent **05** bield, bivvy, bothy, cover, guard, haven, house, hovel, lound, lownd, put up, scoog, scoug, shade **06** asylum, bunker, covert, defend, dugout, harbor, maimai, refuge, safety, sconce, screen, shadow, shield, shroud, wiltja **07** conceal, defence, embower, harbour, imbower, lodging, protect, retreat, roofing **08** security, snow-hole **09** coverture, safeguard, sanctuary, screening **10** overshadow, protection **11** accommodate, cold harbour, weather-fend **13** accommodation

**sheltered**
**03** lee **04** cosy, loun, lown, snug, warm **05** lound, lownd, quiet, shady **06** shaded **07** covered, retired, sharded **08** isolated, screened, secluded, shielded **09** protected, reclusive, unworldly, withdrawn **10** cloistered, in the shade

**shelve**
**04** halt **05** defer, ledge, shelf, shunt, slope **06** put off **07** incline, suspend **08** lay aside, mothball, postpone, put aside, put on ice **09** sidetrack **10** pigeonhole

**shepherd**
**04** Acis, herd, lead **05** guide, steer, swain, usher **06** convoy, escort, feeder, pastor, tar-box **07** conduct, herdboy, herdess, marshal **08** guardian, herdsman **09** herd-groom, protector **11** flockmaster, shepherd boy, shepherdess **12** shepherdling

**sheriff**
**06** grieve, lawman, shirra **07** bailiff **08** landdros, shireman, viscount **09** landdrost **10** shire-reeve

**sherry**
**04** fino **05** Xeres **06** doctor **07** amoroso, oloroso, sherris **08** Montilla **10** manzanilla **11** amontillado, Bristol-milk

• **sherry glass**
**06** copita **08** schooner

**shield**
**05** cover, fence, guard, pelta, shade, targe **06** buckle, defend, screen, shadow **07** buckler, bulwark, defence, forfend, mantlet, protect, rampart, shelter, support, ward off **08** keep safe, mantelet, plastron **09** protector, safeguard **10** escutcheon, protection

**shift**
◇ *anagram indicator*
**03** rid **04** core, move, post, quit, sell, slip, span, tack, time, tour, turn, vary, veer, warp, work **05** alter, budge, carry, cimar, cymar, evade, relay, smock, spell, stint, swing, U-turn **06** adjust, change, fidget, go away, hirsle, manage, modify, period, put off, remove, swerve, switch, wrench **07** chemise, consume, removal, stretch, swallow **08** artifice, dislodge, displace, get rid of, movement, pis aller, relocate, transfer **09** cutty-sark, expedient, fluctuate, rearrange, transpose, variation **10** alteration, relocation, reposition **11** contrivance, fluctuation, lodging turn, prevaricate **12** displacement, modification, tergiversate **13** rearrangement, transposition

**shiftless**
**04** idle, lazy **05** inept **07** aimless **08** feckless, goalless, indolent, slothful **11** incompetent, ineffectual, inefficient, unambitious **12** resourceless **13** directionless, irresponsible, lackadaisical **14** good-for-nothing, unenterprising

**shifty**
◇ *anagram indicator*
**04** iffy, wily **05** shady **06** crafty, louche, tricky **07** cunning, devious, dubious, evasive, furtive **08** scheming, slippery **09** deceitful, dishonest, underhand **10** contriving **11** duplicitous **13** untrustworthy

**shilling**
**01** s **03** bob, hog **06** deaner, teston **09** twalpenny **11** shovelboard, twalpennies, twelve-penny **12** shuffleboard

**shilly-shally**
**05** waver **06** dither, falter, seesaw, teeter **08** hesitate, hum and ha **09** fluctuate, hem and haw, mess about, vacillate **10** dilly-dally **11** prevaricate, vacillation **12** be indecisive, indecisively **13** sit on the fence **14** whittie-whattie

**shimmer**
◇ *anagram indicator*
**04** glow, haze, play **05** gleam, glint **06** lustre **07** flicker, glimmer, glisten, glitter, sparkle, twinkle **10** glistening **11** iridescence, scintillate

**shimmering**
◇ *anagram indicator*
**05** shiny **07** glowing, shining **08** gleaming, luminous, lustrous **09** chatoyant **10** avanturine, aventurine, glistening, glittering, iridescent **12** incandescent

**shin**
**03** sin **04** soar **05** climb, mount, scale, shoot, skink, swarm **06** ascend, shinny **07** clamber **08** scrabble, scramble

**shine**
**03** rub, wax **04** beam, buff, dash, emit, glow, lamp, leam, leme, star **05** brush, excel, flash, glare, glaze, gleam, glint, gloss, light, party, rub up, sheen, skyre **06** beacon, come up, dazzle, lustre, patina, polish, shindy **07** burnish, effulge, flicker, give off, glimmer, glisten, glitter, radiate, shimmer, sparkle, twinkle **08** lambency, radiance, resplend, stand out **09** irradiate **10** brightness, effulgence, incandesce **11** be brilliant, be excellent **12** be pre-eminent, luminescence, phosphoresce **13** be outstanding, incandescence

**shingle**
**06** chesel, chisel

**shingles**
**04** zona **06** zoster **12** herpes zoster

**shininess**
**05** gleam, sheen, shine **06** lustre, polish **07** burnish, glitter **10** brightness, effulgence, glossiness

**shining**
**04** glow, neat **05** beamy, glary, light, lucid, moony, nitid, sheen **06** bright, candid, glossy, golden, lucent, marble, starry **07** aeneous, beaming, eminent, fulgent, glowing, lamping, leading, perfect, radiant **08** flashing, gleaming, glinting, glooming, glorious, luminous, lustrous, relucent, rutilant, splendid **09** brilliant, effulgent, excellent, sparkling, splendent, twinkling **10** celebrated, flickering, glistening, glittering, pre-eminent, profulgent, shimmering **11** conspicuous, illustrious, magnificent, outstanding, resplendent **12** incandescent **13** distinguished **14** phosphorescent

**shiny**
**05** raven, silky, sleek **06** bright, glossy, sheeny **07** shining **08** gleaming, lustrous, polished **09** burnished **10** glistening, shimmering

**ship**
**04** boat, post, send **05** craft **06** embark, vessel **07** send off **08** aircraft

*Ship and boat types include:*

**01** E, Q, U
**02** el, mv, NS, SS, TB
**03** air, ark, bum, cat, cog, cot, day, dow, fly, gig, gun, HMS, hoy, ice, jet, kit, man, MTB, mud, pig, RMS, row, sub, tow, tub, tug, USS, war
**04** bark, brig, buss, cock, cott, dhow, dory, falt, fire, flag, flat, fold, four, grab, HMAS, HMCS, hulk, hush, junk, keel, koff, life, long, mail, maxi, pair, pink, pont, post, pram, prau, proa, prow, punt, ro-ro, saic, scow, show, snow, surf, tall, tern, tilt, Turk, waka, well, wind, yawl, zulu
**05** aviso, barca, barge, botel, butty, cabin, canal, canoe, casco, coble, coper, crare, dandy, dingy, drake, ferry, funny, guard, gulet, hatch, horse, house, jolly, kayak, ketch, laker, light, liner, motor, oiler, peter, pilot, plate, power, praam, prahu, prore, razee, river, rotor, saick, scout, scull, seine, shell, shore, skiff, slave, sloop, smack, speed, stake, steam, store, swamp, tanka, track, tramp, troop, umiak, wager, waist, whale, whiff, xebec, yacht, zabra
**06** advice, argosy, banker, barque, bateau, battle, bethel, bireme, caique, carvel, castle, coaler, cobble, cockle, codder, coffin, convoy, cooper, crayer, cutter, dingey, dinghy, dogger, dragon, droger, dromon, drover, dugout, flying, galiot, galley, gay-you, hooker, hopper, jigger, lateen, launch, lorcha, lugger, masula, monkey, mother, narrow, nuggar, oomiac, oomiak, packet, paddle, pedalo, pirate, prison, puffer, pulwar, puteli, randan, reefer, rowing, runner, sailer, saique, sampan, sandal, sanpan, school, schuit, schuyt, settee, slaver, tanker, tartan, torpid, trader, turret, wangan, wangun, wherry
**07** assault, Berthon, birlinn, budgero, capital, caravel, clipper, coaster, collier, consort, coracle, corsair, cruiser, currach, curragh, dredger, drifter, drogher, dromond, factory, felucca, four-oar, frigate, gabbard, gabbart, galleon, galliot, Geordie, gondola, landing, liberty, lighter, lymphad, man-o'-war, mistico, mudscow, mystery, nacelle, oomiack, pair-oar, passage, patamar, pearler, pinnace, piragua, pirogue, polacca, pontoon, sailing, scooter, shallop, sharpie, sponger, steamer, tartane, torpedo, trawler, trireme, vedette, victory, wanigan, warship, weather

**08** bilander, billyboy, budgerow, car ferry, corocore, corocoro, corvette, dahabieh, dispatch, eight-oar, galleass, galliass, gallivat, hospital, hoveller, Indiaman, ironclad, log-canoe, longship, mackinaw, man-of-war, masoolah, massoola, merchant, monohull, montaria, periagua, pleasure, repeater, row barge, runabout, sally-man, schooner, skipjack, smuggler, Spaniard, training, trimaran, water bus, woodskin
**09** bomb-ketch, Bucentaur, catamaran, commodore, container, dahabeeah, dahabiyah, dahabiyeh, daysailer, daysailor, destroyer, firefloat, flying jib, freighter, herringer, Hollander, hydrofoil, klondiker, klondyker, lapstrake, lapstreak, leviathan, long-liner, minelayer, monoxylon, motoscafo, multihull, Norwegian, oil-burner, oil tanker, outrigger, privateer, randan gig, receiving, sallee-man, speedster, steamship, store ship, submarine, surf canoe, transport, two-decker, two-master, vaporetto, well smack
**10** armour-clad, bomb-vessel, brigantine, free-trader, hovercraft, icebreaker, minehunter, quadrireme, seal-fisher, tea clipper, trekschuit, triaconter, victualler, windjammer
**11** bulk carrier, cockleshell, dreadnought, galley-foist, merchantman, minesweeper, motor launch, penteconter, purse-seiner, quinquereme, sallee-rover, salmon coble, side-wheeler, steam launch, steam packet, steam vessel, submersible, three-decker, three-master, victualling, wooden horse
**12** cabin cruiser, deepwaterman, double-decker, East-Indiaman, line-of-battle, screw steamer, single-decker, square-rigger, stern-wheeler, tangle-netter, tramp steamer, troop carrier
**13** Canadian canoe, paddle steamer, revenue cutter, roll-on roll-off
**14** Flying Dutchman, ocean-greyhound, turbine steamer
**15** aircraft-carrier, floating battery, logistics vessel

*Ships include:*

**03** QE2
**04** Ajax, Argo, Hood, Nina
**05** Argus, Maine, Pinta
**06** Beagle, Bounty, Cathay, Oriana, Pequod, Renown
**07** Alabama, Amistad, Belfast, Blücher, Olympic, Pelican, Potomac, Repulse, Tirpitz, Titanic, Victory
**08** Ark Royal, Bismarck, Canberra, Fearless, Graf Spee, Intrepid, Iron Duke, Mary Rose, Royal Oak
**09** Adventure, Aquitania, Britannia, Britannic, Carinthia, Cutty Sark, Discovery, Endeavour, Gipsy Moth, Gneisenau, Lexington, Lusitania, Mayflower, Normandie, Queen Mary, Sheffield, Téméraire, Terranova
**10** Golden Hind, Hispaniola, Invincible, Mauretania, Prinz Eugen, Resolution, Santa Maria, Washington
**11** Dawn Treader, Dreadnought, Illustrious, Scharnhorst
**12** African Queen, Great Britain, Great Eastern, Great Western, Marie Celeste
**13** Prince of Wales
**14** Flying Dutchman, Queen Elizabeth
**15** Admiral Graf Spee, General Belgrano, Queen Elizabeth 2

*Ship parts include:*

**03** bow, box, oar, rig
**04** beam, brig, brow, bunk, cant, deck, head, hold, hull, keel, mast, poop, port, prow, sail
**05** berth, bilge, cabin, cable, cleat, davit, hatch, hawse, stern, wheel, winch
**06** anchor, bridge, fender, fo'c'sle, funnel, galley, gunnel, hawser, rigger, rudder, tiller
**07** bollard, bulwark, caboose, capstan, counter, gangway, gun deck, gunwale, hammock, landing, quarter, rowlock, top deck, transom
**08** binnacle, boat deck, bulkhead, hatchway, main deck, poop deck, porthole, wardroom
**09** afterdeck, chart room, crosstree, crow's nest, forecabin, gangplank, lower deck, radio room, stanchion, starboard, stateroom, waterline
**10** boiler room, engine room, figurehead, flight deck, forecastle, pilot house, stabilizer
**11** chain locker, paddle wheel, quarter deck
**12** companion way, Plimsoll line
**13** promenade deck
**14** superstructure
**15** companion ladder

*Ships' crewmen and officers include:*

**02** AB
**04** mate
**06** master, purser
**07** captain, steward
**08** cabin-boy, ship's boy
**09** first mate
**10** able rating, able seaman

*See also* **sailor**

## shipping

*Shipping forecast areas:*

**04** Sole, Tyne
**05** Dover, Forth, Lundy, Malin, Wight
**06** Bailey, Biscay, Dogger, Faroes, Fisher, Humber, Thames, Viking
**07** Fastnet, FitzRoy, Forties, Rockall, Shannon
**08** Cromarty, Fair Isle, Hebrides, Irish Sea, Plymouth, Portland
**09** Trafalgar
**10** Finisterre
**11** German Bight, North Utsire, South Utsire
**16** South-East Iceland

### • shipping order

**02** so

## shipshape

**04** neat, tidy, trig, trim **06** proper, spruce **07** orderly **11** well-planned **12** businesslike, spick and span **13** well-organized, well-regulated

## shirk

**04** balk, duck, funk, shun **05** avoid, baulk, dodge, evade, skive, slack **06** bludge **07** goof off, soldier **08** get out of **09** duck out of, duckshove, gold-brick **10** play truant, shrink from **12** wriggle out of

## shirker

**05** idler, piker, poler, shirk **06** dodger, loafer, skiver, truant **07** bludger, goof-off, quitter, slacker, sneak-up, soldier **08** absentee, embusqué, layabout **09** gold brick **10** duckshover, malingerer **12** carpet-knight

## shirt

**01** T **04** sark, serk **05** kurta, parka **06** caftan, camese, camise, kaftan, khurta **07** dasheki, dashiki, partlet **08** guernsey, subucula

## shiver

◇ *anagram indicator*

**03** bit **04** chip, grew, grue **05** break, crack, flake, piece, quake, shake, shard, shred, shrug, smash, split, start **06** didder, dither, quiver, sliver, tremor, twitch **07** chitter, flutter, frisson, shatter, shaving, shudder, tremble, vibrate **08** cold sore, fragment, splinter **09** disshiver, palpitate, vibration **10** smithereen **11** smithereens

## shivery

**04** cold **05** ourie **06** chilly **07** brittle, chilled, nervous, quaking, quivery, shaking, trembly **08** fluttery, shuddery **09** trembling

## shoal

**03** bar, mob, ren, rin, run **04** bank, mass, reef **05** flock, group, horde, shelf, swarm **06** school, throng **07** schoole, shallow **08** sandbank **09** multitude **10** assemblage

## shock

◇ *anagram indicator*

**03** jar, mat, mop **04** blow, daze, head, jerk, jolt, mane, mass, numb, shog, stun, turn **05** amaze, appal, crash, knock, repel, shake, shook, sixty, start, stook, upset **06** dismay, fright, horror, impact, offend, poodle, revolt, sicken, stound, stownd, tangle, thatch, trauma, whammy **07** agitate, astound, disgust, horrify, jarring, outrage, perturb, scandal, stagger, startle, stupefy, unnerve **08** astonish, bewilder, bowl over, confound, disquiet, distress, gross out, nauseate, paralyse, surprise, unsettle **09** bombshell, collision, dumbfound, knock back, take aback **10** scandalize, traumatize **11** thunderbolt **12** perturbation **13** consternation, rude awakening **15** bolt from the blue

• **shock absorber**
**04** oleo **07** oleo leg, snubber

• **shock treatment**
**03** ECT, EST

• **shocked**
**06** aghast

**shocking**
**04** foul, vile **05** awful **06** daring **07** épatant, ghastly, hideous **08** dreadful, horrible, horrific, terrible **09** abhorrent, appalling, atrocious, execrable, frightful, loathsome, monstrous, offensive, repugnant, repulsive, revolting, sickening **10** abominable, deplorable, detestable, diabolical, disgusting, horrifying, nauseating, outrageous, perturbing, scandalous, unbearable, unsettling **11** disgraceful, disquieting, distressing, intolerable, unspeakable

**shockingly**
**08** terribly **10** abominably, deplorably, dreadfully, unbearably **11** appallingly, atrociously, frightfully, repulsively, revoltingly, sickeningly **12** disgustingly, outrageously, scandalously **13** disgracefully

**shoddy**
◇ *anagram indicator*
**04** poor, ropy, sham **05** cheap, crook, ropey, tacky, tatty **06** tawdry, trashy **07** rag-wool, rubbish **08** careless, gimcrack, inferior, jimcrack, rubbishy, slapdash, slipshod **09** cheapjack, third-rate **10** devil's dust, second-rate **11** poor-quality

**shoe** *see* **footwear**

**shoemaker**
**04** snab, snob **05** sutor **06** cosier, cozier, soutar, souter, sowter **07** cobbler, crispin **08** cordiner **09** bootmaker **10** cordwainer

**shoemaking**
**08** cobblery, cobbling **10** bootmaking **14** the gentle craft

**shoot**
**03** aim, bud, fly, gun, hit, imp, lob, pop, pot, rod, tip, zap, zip **04** belt, bolt, cast, chit, cyme, dart, dash, dump, film, fire, germ, grow, hurl, kick, kill, plug, poot, pout, race, rush, slip, snap, tear, twig, wand, whip, whiz **05** blast, chute, fling, graft, hurry, loose, pluff, rapid, scion, scoot, shell, slide, spear, speed, spire, spray, sprig, start, throw, tower, video, whisk, wound **06** branch, charge, direct, hurtle, injure, launch, let fly, let off, propel, sprint, sprout, streak, strike, sucker **07** bombard, burgeon, cutting, gun down, mow down, pick off, project, shoot up, snipe at, stretch, tendron **08** detonate, go all out, offshoot, open fire **09** bring down, discharge, germinate, spindling **10** get a move on, photograph **11** crystallize, precipitate

**shooter** *see* **gun**; **gunman**

**shop**
**03** buy, get, rat **05** grass, split, store **06** betray, pick up, prison, squeal, tell on **07** stool on **08** emporium, imprison, inform on, purchase **09** buy things, stock up on **10** go shopping **11** tell tales on **12** retail outlet **13** do the shopping

*Shop types include:*

**01** e
**02** op, PX
**03** toy
**04** book, chip, deli, farm, grog, shoe, tuck
**05** baker, dairy, dress, offie, phone, stall, sweet, video
**06** barber, bazaar, bookie, bottle, chippy, corner, draper, grocer, market, online, record, tailor
**07** betting, butcher, charity, chemist, chipper, clothes, florist, saddler
**08** boutique, hardware, jeweller, milliner, pharmacy, takeaway
**09** bookmaker, drugstore, newsagent, outfitter, stationer, superette
**10** candy store, chain store, electrical, fishmonger, health-food, ironmonger, mini-market, off-licence, pawnbroker, post office, radio and TV, second-hand, superstore
**11** bottle store, fish and chip, five-and-dime, greengrocer, haberdasher, hairdresser, hypermarket, launderette, online store, opportunity, supermarket, tobacconist
**12** cash-and-carry, confectioner, delicatessen, general store, indoor market
**13** computer store, farmers' market
**15** department store

*French shops include:*

**05** tabac
**08** boutique, épicerie
**09** boucherie, librairie
**10** bijouterie, confiserie, fromagerie, parfumerie, pâtisserie, rôtisserie
**11** boulangerie, charcuterie
**12** chocolaterie, grand magasin, poissonnerie

*Shops include:*

**03** BHV
**04** Tati
**05** Macy's
**07** Hamleys, Harrods, Jenners, Liberty
**08** Tiffany's
**09** Century 21, Printemps
**10** FAO Schwarz, Selfridge's
**11** Le Bon Marché
**13** Bloomingdale's, Harvey Nichols, La Samaritaine
**15** Bergdorf Goodman, Fortnum and Mason, Saks Fifth Avenue

**shopkeeper**
**05** owner **06** dealer, trader **07** manager **08** merchant, retailer, salesman, stockist **09** bourgeois, boxwallah, tradesman **10** proprietor, saleswoman **11** storekeeper, tradeswoman **13** counter-jumper **14** counter-skipper

**shopper**
**05** buyer **06** client **08** consumer, customer **09** purchaser

**shore**
**04** bank, hold, prop, sand, stay, warn **05** beach, brace, coast, drain, front, offer, rance, sands, sewer **06** hold up, menace, prop up, rivage, strand **07** seaside, shingle, support **08** buttress, lakeside, littoral, seaboard, seashore, threaten, underpin **09** foreshore, promenade, reinforce, waterside **10** strengthen, waterfront **11** threatening

**shorebird**
**04** knot **06** dunlin, ox-bird **07** sea lark **08** sand-lark, surfbird
*See also* **bird**

**shorn**
**03** cut **04** bald **06** polled, shaved, shaven **07** crew-cut, cropped **08** deprived, stripped **09** beardless

**short**
◇ *tail deletion indicator*
**03** low, shy, wee **04** curt, neat, poor, rude **05** blunt, brief, crisp, dumpy, gruff, hasty, pithy, quick, scant, sharp, small, squat, swift, teeny, terse, tight **06** abrupt, curtly, direct, little, meagre, petite, scanty, scarce, slight, snappy, sparse, stubby, teensy **07** briefly, brittle, brusque, compact, concise, cursory, lacking, limited, passing, summary, uncivil, wanting **08** abridged, abruptly, fleeting, impolite, pint-size, snappish, succinct, suddenly **09** condensed, curtailed, deficient, ephemeral, fugacious, minuscule, momentary, pint-sized, shortened, temporary, transient, truncated **10** aphoristic, compressed, diminutive, evanescent, inadequate, short-lived, summarized, to the point, transitory **11** abbreviated, Lilliputian **12** abbreviation, discourteous, insufficient, unexpectedly

• **fall short**
**05** fault, under **09** be lacking **12** be inadequate **14** be insufficient

• **in short**
**04** once **05** in sum **06** in fine **07** at a word, briefly, in a word, in brief, to sum up **09** concisely, in one word **11** in a few words, in a nutshell, summarizing **12** in conclusion

• **little short of**
**02** on **07** towards

• **short of**
**03** bar, but **04** save **05** low on, under **06** but for **07** barring, besides, lacking, missing, short on, wanting **08** less than, omitting **09** apart from, aside from,

except for, excepting, excluding, other than, pushed for **10** leaving out, this side of **11** deficient in, not counting

**shortage**
**04** lack, need, shtg, want **06** dearth, drouth **07** absence, deficit, drought, paucity, poverty, wantage **08** scarcity **09** shortfall, skills gap **10** deficience, deficiency, inadequacy **13** insufficiency

**shortcoming**
**03** sin **04** flaw **05** fault **06** defect, foible **07** failing, frailty **08** drawback, weakness **09** weak point **12** imperfection

**shorten**
◇ *tail deletion indicator*
**03** cut **04** clip, crop, dock, pare, trim **05** check, prune, sum up **06** lessen, reduce, take up **07** abridge, curtail, cut down, scantle **08** compress, condense, contract, decrease, diminish, pare down, truncate **09** epitomize, telescope **10** abbreviate **11** make shorter **13** become shorter

**shortened**
◇ *tail deletion indicator*
**03** cut **06** curtal **07** curtate **08** abridged **09** condensed **10** abbreviate, abstracted, contracted, summarized **11** abbreviated **12** abbreviatory

**shortfall**
**04** lack, loss **07** arrears, default, deficit **08** shortage **10** deficiency

**shorthand**
**02** s/h **11** phonography, stenography, tachygraphy **12** Speedwriting®

**short-lived**
**05** brief, short **07** passing **08** caducous, fleeting, volatile **09** ephemeral, fugacious, momentary, temporary, transient **10** evanescent, transitory **11** impermanent

**shortly**
◇ *tail deletion indicator*
**04** soon **06** curtly, rudely **07** bluntly, briefly, by and by, gruffly, sharply, tersely **08** abruptly, directly, in a while **09** brusquely, presently, uncivilly **10** before long, impolitely **14** discourteously, in a little while

**shorts**
**07** baggies, cut-offs **08** Bermudas, hot pants

**short-sighted**
**04** rash **05** hasty **06** myopic, unwise **08** careless, heedless **09** impolitic, imprudent **10** ill-advised, unthinking **11** improvident, injudicious, near-sighted, thoughtless **13** ill-considered, uncircumspect

**short-staffed**
**11** shorthanded **12** understaffed **13** below strength

**short-tempered**
**05** fiery, ratty, testy **06** crusty, touchy **07** grouchy **08** choleric **09** crotchety, impatient, irascible, irritable **10** crotcheted **11** bad-tempered, hot-tempered **13** quick-tempered

**short-winded**
**05** puffy, pursy **07** gasping, panting, puffing, purfled **10** breathless

**shot**
◇ *anagram indicator*
**02** go **03** ace, aim, fix, get, hit, jab, lob, peg, pop, pot, shy, try **04** ball, bang, bash, burl, dink, dose, dram, kick, putt, scot, slug, snap, stab, turn **05** blast, crack, fling, guess, image, moiré, photo, pluff, print, range, reach, set-up, shoat, shote, slide, snipe, spell, throw, whack **06** bullet, corner, effort, gunner, header, hunter, jumper, pellet, ruined, shotte, sitter, sniper, strike, stroke **07** attempt, gunfire, missile, mottled, payment, pelican, penalty, picture, shooter, watered **08** advanced, marksman, moon-ball, snapshot **09** discharge, endeavour, explosion, injection, mitraille **10** ammunition, cannonball, iridescent, markswoman, photograph, point-blank, projectile, variegated **11** inoculation, vaccination **12** contribution, immunization, transparency

**• call the shots**
**04** head, lead **06** direct, head up, manage **07** command **09** give a lead, supervise **10** be in charge **15** wear the trousers

**• good shot**
**07** deadeye

**• like a shot**
**06** at once **07** eagerly, quickly **09** instantly, willingly **11** immediately **12** without delay **14** unhesitatingly

**• not by a long shot**
**04** ne'er **05** never, no way **07** in no way **08** not at all **09** by no means **12** certainly not **13** not in the least

**• shot in the arm**
**04** lift **05** boost **06** fillip, uplift **07** impetus **08** stimulus **11** fresh talent **13** encouragement

**• shot in the dark**
**05** guess **09** guesswork, wild guess **10** blind guess, conjecture **11** speculation

**shoulder**
**04** bear, hump, push **05** carry, elbow, force, press, shove, spald, spall, spaul **06** accept, assume, jostle, spalle, spauld, take on, thrust **07** support, sustain **09** undertake **10** coathanger **13** heave-offering

**• give someone the cold shoulder**
**03** cut **04** shun, snub **05** blank, shame, spurn **06** humble, ignore, insult, rebuff, rebuke, slight, squash **07** mortify, put down **08** brush off **09** disregard, humiliate **13** slap in the face **14** kick in the teeth

**• rub shoulders with**
**07** mix with **08** meet with **10** hobnob with **13** associate with, hang about with, socialize with **14** fraternize with, hang around with, knock about with **15** knock around with

**• shoulder to shoulder**
**06** united **07** closely **08** together **10** hand in hand, in alliance, side by side **13** co-operatively **15** working together

**shout**
**03** bay, cry **04** bawl, call, howl, roar, rort, yawp, yell **05** cheer, claim, clame, jodel, round, stand, treat, yodel, yodle **06** bellow, cry out, heckle, holler, scream, shriek, squawk **07** barrack, call out, exclaim, glory be, sing out **11** acclamation, rant and rave, stand a round **12** buy drinks for, conclamation **14** raise your voice

*Shouts and cries include:*

**02** io
**03** hup, nix
**04** euoi, evoe, fall, fore, haro, I-spy, rivo, shoo, sola
**05** chevy, chivy, evhoe, evohe, havoc, heigh, holla, hollo, hooch, huzza
**06** banzai, chivvy, eureka, halloa, halloo, harrow, hoicks, yoicks
**07** glory be, heureka, kamerad, tally-ho, tantivy
**08** alleluia, gardyloo, Geronimo, harambee
**09** scaldings, stop thief!
**10** halleluiah, hallelujah, view-halloo, westward ho!

*See also* **war cry** *under* **war**

**shouting**
**03** hue

**shove**
**04** bump, bung, jolt, push **05** barge, crowd, drive, elbow, force, press **06** jostle, propel, thrust **07** thrutch **08** shoulder

**• shove off**
**04** scat **05** hop it, leave, scoot, scram **06** beat it, depart, go away **07** buzz off, do a bunk, get lost, push off, rack off, scarper, vamoose **08** choof off, clear off, clear out, run for it **09** skedaddle

**shovel**
**03** dig, van **04** heap, main, move, peel **05** clear, scoop, shift, shool, spade **06** bucket, dredge **07** backhoe, dust-pan **08** excavate **09** excavator **13** backhoe loader

**show**
◇ *hidden indicator*
**03** air, con **04** come, expo, fair, give, lead, mean, pose, shew, sign, take, wear **05** array, front, guide, guise, offer, prove, sight, steer, teach, usher **06** affair, appear, arrive, attend, chance, depict, direct, escort, expose, façade, parade, record, reveal, set out, turn up **07** clarify, conduct, display, divulge, exhibit, explain, expound, express, panache, pizzazz, portray, present, produce, showing, signify, staging, suggest, uncover **08** disclose, evidence, illusion, indicate, instruct, manifest, point out, pretence, register

**09** accompany, elucidate, exemplify, make clear, make known, make plain, operation, programme, semblance, showiness, spectacle **10** appearance, be evidence, exhibition, exposition, illustrate, impression, indication, play-acting, production, profession **11** affectation, arrangement, demonstrate, flamboyance, make it clear, make visible, materialize, opportunity, ostentation, performance, proceedings, undertaking **12** extravaganza, organization, plausibility, presentation **13** bear witness to, demonstration, entertainment, exhibitionism, manifestation **14** representation, window dressing

• **show off**

◇ *anagram indicator*

**04** brag **05** boast, pronk, strut, swank, vapor **06** flaunt, hot-dog, parade, set off, vapour **07** display, enhance, exhibit, swagger **08** brandish, flourish **09** advertise **10** grandstand, put on an act **11** demonstrate **15** show to advantage

• **show up**

**04** come **05** lodge, shame **06** appear, arrive, bewray, expose, hand in, reveal, turn up, unmask **07** lay bare, let down, mortify, uncloak **08** disgrace, pinpoint **09** embarrass, highlight, humiliate **10** put to shame **11** make visible, materialize

**showdown**

**05** clash **06** climax, crisis **07** face-off **10** dénouement **11** culmination **13** confrontation, moment of truth

**shower**

◇ *anagram indicator*

**04** fall, hail, heap, load, pang, pelt, play, pour, rain, scat, scud, skit **05** drift, pound, skatt, spray, water **06** attack, deluge, lavish, pelter, pepper, stream, volley **07** barrage, scowder, torrent **08** inundate, rainfall, scouther, scowther, sprinkle **09** aspersion, avalanche, drizzling, overwhelm **10** kitchen tea, sprinkling **13** thunder-shower

*See also* **meteor**

**showiness**

**05** glitz, swank **07** glitter, pizzazz, varnish **09** ritziness **10** flashiness, razzmatazz **11** flamboyance, ostentation **12** razzle-dazzle **15** pretentiousness

**showing**

**04** expo, show **06** record **07** account, display, staging **08** evidence, symbolic **09** endeictic, ostensive, statement **10** appearance, exhibition, impression, indicative, revelatory **11** descriptive, elucidative, explanatory, explicatory, performance, significant, track record **12** illustrative, presentation **13** demonstrative **14** representation, representative **15** past performance

**showing-off**

**05** swank **07** egotism, swagger **08** boasting, bragging **09** vainglory **10** peacockery **11** braggadocio **13** exhibitionism

**showjumper** *see* **equestrian**

**showman**

**07** show-off **09** performer, publicist **10** impresario, ring-master **11** entertainer **14** self-advertiser

**show-off**

**05** poser **06** poseur **07** boaster, egotist, know-all, peacock, swanker **08** braggart **09** swaggerer **13** exhibitionist

**showy**

**03** gay **04** fine, loud **05** brave, fancy, flash, flory, gaudy, ritzy, spicy, viewy **06** branky, brassy, dressy, flashy, flossy, garish, glitzy, ornate, swanky, tawdry **07** buckeye, dashing, pompous, splashy, stylish **08** fantoosh, gorgeous, sparkish, specious, tinselly **10** bling-bling, flamboyant, glittering **11** conspicuous, pretentious **12** ostentatious

**shred**

**03** bit, cut, jot, rag, rip, tag **04** atom, chop, iota, mite, snip, spot, tear, whit, wisp **05** cut up, grain, grate, piece, prune, rip up, scrap, slice, speck, taver, trace **06** agnail, cut off, paring, ribbon, screed, sliver, taiver, tatter, tear up **07** frazzle, mammock, modicum, mummock, peeling, remnant, snippet, vestige **08** clipping, fragment, hangnail, julienne, particle

**shrew**

**03** nag **04** Fury, Kate, tana **05** bitch, curse, scold, shrow, sorex, vixen **06** dragon, Tupaia, virago **07** muskrat, sondeli **08** banxring, harridan, spitfire **09** bangsring, henpecker, Katharina, termagant, Xanthippe **10** petrodrome

**shrewd**

**03** sly **04** arch, evil, hard, keen, wily, wise **05** acute, alert, canny, savey, savvy, sharp, smart **06** argute, artful, astute, biting, callid, clever, crafty, keenly, savvey, severe, shrowd **07** cunning, gnostic, hurtful, knowing, prudent **08** piercing, shrewish, spiteful, vixenish **09** judicious, observant, sagacious **10** calculated, discerning, far-sighted, formidable, hard-headed, ill-natured, long-headed, perceptive **11** calculating, intelligent, mischievous, well-advised **12** cut-and-thrust, sharp-sighted **13** perspicacious **14** discriminating, ill-conditioned

**shrewdly**

**05** slyly **06** wisely **07** cannily **08** argutely, artfully, astutely, cleverly, craftily **09** knowingly, unhappily **11** judiciously, sagaciously **12** far-sightedly, perceptively **15** perspicaciously

**shrewdness**

**05** grasp **06** acumen, wisdom **08** astucity, gumption, prudence, sagacity **09** acuteness, callidity, canniness, judgement, sharpness, smartness **10** astuteness **11** discernment, knowingness, penetration **12** intelligence, perspicacity **14** perceptiveness

**shrewish**

**06** shrewd **07** nagging, peevish **08** captious, petulant, scolding, vixenish **09** querulous, termagant **10** henpecking, ill-natured, wasp-tongu'd **11** bad-tempered, complaining, ill-humoured, ill-tempered, quarrelsome **12** discontented, fault-finding, sharp-tongued

**shriek**

**03** cry **04** howl, wail, yell, yelp **05** pling, shout, skirl **06** cry out, scream, scrike, shreek, shreik, shrike, squawk, squeal **07** screech, screich, screigh, scriech, shright, shritch, skreigh, skriech, skriegh **08** screamer **09** caterwaul **11** exclamation **15** exclamation mark

**shrill**

**04** high, keen **05** acute, sharp **06** argute, treble **08** piercing, screechy, strident **09** screaming **10** screeching **11** ear-piercing, high-pitched, penetrating **12** ear-splitting

**shrimp**

**05** krill, prawn **06** squill **07** squilla **08** crevette **09** Euphausia, schizopod **10** stomatopod

**shrine**

**04** dome, fane, tope **05** chest, darga, image, stupa **06** chapel, church, dagaba, dagoba, pagoda, scrine, scryne, temple, vimana **07** cabinet, martyry **08** delubrum, feretory, marabout **09** holy place, sanctuary **10** tabernacle **11** sacred place

**shrink**

**04** balk, dare, nirl, shun **05** cling, cower, crine, quail, shrug, wince **06** blench, cringe, flinch, gizzen, lessen, narrow, recoil, reduce, retire, shy off, swerve, wither **07** atrophy, drop off, dwindle, fall off, give way, retreat, shorten, shrivel, shy away, wrinkle **08** back away, contract, decrease, diminish, draw back, withdraw **09** cower away, start back **10** constringe, withdrawal **11** contraction, grow smaller **12** psychiatrist **13** become smaller **15** have qualms about

**shrivel**

**03** dry **04** burn, nirl, sear, welk, wilt **05** cling, crine, dry up, parch **06** blight, gizzen, pucker, scorch, shrink, wither **07** dwindle, frizzle, wrinkle **08** pucker up **09** dehydrate, desiccate

**shrivelled**

**03** dry **04** sere **06** gizzen, shrunk **07** dried up, wizened **08** puckered, shrunken, withered, wrinkled, writhled **09** emaciated **10** desiccated

**shroud**
**03** fog, lop **04** hide, pall, veil, wrap
**05** cloak, cloth, cloud, cover, shade
**06** branch, mantle, screen, sindon, swathe **07** blanket, clothes, conceal, envelop, garment, shelter
**08** cerement, covering, enshroud, loppings **09** cerecloth
**12** graveclothes, winding-sheet

**shrouded**
**06** hidden, veiled **07** cloaked, clouded, covered, swathed, wrapped
**09** blanketed, concealed, enveloped
**10** enshrouded

**shrub**
**04** bush **07** arboret

*Shrubs include:*

**03** box, ivy, til
**04** coca, hebe, nabk, Rosa, rose
**05** brere, briar, brier, broom, buaze, buchu, bucku, bwazi, holly, lilac, nebek, peony, yucca
**06** azalea, daphne, laurel, mallow, mimosa, nebbuk, nebeck, privet, sesame
**07** arbutus, Banksia, boronia, bramble, dogwood, fuchsia, heather, jasmine, phlomis, rhatany, spiraea, weigela
**08** barberry, berberis, bilberry, buddleia, camellia, clematis, euonymus, gardenia, japonica, krameria, laburnum, lavender, magnolia, musk rose, viburnum, wistaria, wisteria
**09** beach plum, bean caper, eucryphia, firethorn, forsythia, hydrangea
**10** bitter-king, buffalo-nut, buttonbush, mock orange, witch hazel
**11** calycanthus, cotoneaster, honeysuckle
**12** blackcurrant, buffalo-berry, rhododendron
**13** Barbados pride, butcher's broom, mountain avens

*See also* **plant**

**shrug**
**• shrug off**
**06** ignore **07** dismiss, neglect **08** brush off **09** disregard **14** take no notice of

**shrunken**
**05** gaunt **06** shrunk, wasted
**07** reduced **09** emaciated
**10** cadaverous, contracted, shrivelled, sphacelate **11** sphacelated

**shudder**
**04** grew, grue **05** creep, grise, heave, quake, shake, shrug, spasm **06** judder, quiver, shiver, tremor **07** frisson, tremble, vibrate **08** convulse
**10** convulsion

**shuffle**
◇ *anagram indicator*
**03** mix **04** drag, limp, make, pack
**05** dodge, hedge, mix up, scuff, stack
**06** doddle, falter, hobble, jumble, riffle, scrape, switch, toddle **07** confuse, evasion, patch up, scuffle, shamble
**08** artifice, disorder, intermix, jumble up, scramble, shauchle **09** rearrange, reshuffle **10** move around, reorganize
**11** shift around **12** tergiversate

**shun**
◇ *deletion indicator*
**03** shy **04** snub **05** avoid, elude, evade, evite, spurn **06** eschew, ignore
**09** attention, ostracize **11** shy away from **12** cold-shoulder, keep away from, steer clear of

**shunt**
**04** move, take **05** bring, budge, carry, crash, fetch, shift, swing **06** bypass, mishap, shelve, switch **08** relocate, transfer **09** sidetrack, transport, transpose

**shut**
**02** to **03** bar **04** bolt, jail, lock, seal, slam, spar, tine **05** close, latch, put to, shoot, steek **06** cage in, closed, coop up, fasten, immure, intern, lock up, secure **07** confine **08** imprison
**11** incarcerate, put the lid on
**• shut down**
**04** halt, stop **05** cease, close, scram
**07** suspend **09** close down, switch off, terminate **10** inactivate **11** discontinue
**• shut in**
**04** cage **05** box in, embar, hem in, imbar **06** cage in, empale, immure, impale, keep in **07** confine, enclose, fence in, inclose, occlude **08** imprison, restrain **10** encloister
**• shut off**
**06** cut off **07** exclude, isolate, occlude, seclude **08** obstruct, separate
**09** segregate, switch off
**• shut out**
**03** bar **04** fend, hide, mask, veil
**05** cover, debar, exile **06** banish, outlaw, screen **07** conceal, cover up, exclude, lock out **08** block out
**09** ostracize
**• shut up**
**03** gag, pen **04** hush, jail, lock, pent
**05** cabin, close, frank, quiet **06** bang up, cage in, clam up, closet, coop up, encage, hush up, immure, incage, intern, lock up **07** confine, keep mum, quieten, silence **08** imprison, pipe down **09** endungeon **11** incarcerate
**14** hold your tongue

**shutter**
**05** blind, shade **06** douser, louver, louvre, screen **07** scuttle **08** abat-jour, jalousie

**shuttle**
**03** ply, run **05** flute, shunt **06** seesaw, travel **07** commute, shottle
**09** alternate **10** go to and fro
**11** shuttlecock **13** netting-needle

**shy**
**03** coy, jib **04** cagy, gibe, shot, shun, toss, wild **05** cagey, chary, fling, mousy, squab, throw, timid **06** demure, modest, mousey, scanty, skeigh
**07** attempt, bashful, indrawn, nervous, startle, strange **08** backward, cautious, farouche, hesitant, reserved, reticent, retiring, secluded, timorous, willyard, willyart **09** diffident, inhibited, shrinking, withdrawn **10** suspicious
**11** embarrassed, introverted **12** self-effacing, unproductive **13** self-conscious
**• fight shy of**
**04** shun **05** avoid, spurn **06** eschew
**12** steer clear of
**• shy away**
**03** jib **04** balk, buck, rear **05** avoid, quail, spook, start, wince **06** flinch, recoil, shrink, swerve **07** startle
**08** back away

**shyly**
**05** coyly **06** cagily **07** charily, timidly
**09** bashfully **10** cautiously, hesitantly, reticently **11** diffidently **15** self-consciously

**shyness**
**07** coyness, modesty **08** caginess, timidity **09** chariness, hesitancy, mousiness, reticence, timidness
**10** constraint, diffidence, inhibition
**11** bashfulness, nervousness
**12** timorousness **13** embarrassment

**SI**

*SI prefixes include:*

**03** exa
**04** atto, deca, deci, giga, kilo, mega, nano, peta, pico, tera
**05** centi, femto, hecto, micro, milli, yocto, yotta, zepto, zetta

**sibling**
**04** twin **06** german, sister **07** brother

**sibyl**
**04** seer **06** oracle, Pythia **07** seeress, völuspa **09** pythoness, sorceress, wise woman **10** prophetess

**sick**
◇ *anagram indicator*
**03** ill **04** weak **05** angry, black, bored, chase, crook, cruel, fed up, gross, rough, seedy, tired, weary **06** ailing, feeble, groggy, laid up, pining, poorly, puking, queasy, sickly, unwell, vulgar
**07** airsick, annoyed, bilious, carsick, enraged, heaving, macabre, seasick, set upon **08** diseased, gruesome, nauseous, retching, vomiting
**09** disgusted, hacked off, mortified, nauseated, off colour, spewing up, tasteless, uncle Dick **10** browned off, cheesed off, in bad taste, indisposed, out of sorts, throwing up, travel-sick
**11** disgruntled **12** disappointed, sick and tired **15** under the weather
**• be sick**
**03** ail, gag **04** barf, puke, spew, spue
**05** heave, retch, vomit **07** fetch up, throw up **10** feel queasy **12** feel nauseous

**sicken**
**03** ail, get **05** appal, catch, repel
**06** pick up, put off, revolt **07** develop, disgust, turn off **08** contract, nauseate

**09** become ill, succumb to **10** go down with **12** come down with **13** become ill with **15** turn your stomach

**sickening**
**04** foul, vile **08** nauseous, shocking **09** appalling, loathsome, offensive, repellent, repulsive, revolting **10** chunderous, disgusting, nauseating, off-putting **11** distasteful **12** cringe-making, cringeworthy **14** stomach-turning

**sickly**
**03** wan **04** pale, puly, sick, weak **05** faint, frail, gushy, mushy, soppy, sweet, wersh **06** ailing, donsie, feeble, infirm, morbid, pallid, slushy, sugary, syrupy, weakly **07** anaemic, bilious, cloying, insipid, languid, mawkish, pimping, queachy, queechy **08** delicate **09** revolting, schmaltzy, unhealthy, washed out **10** indisposed, nauseating **14** valetudinarian

**sickness**
**03** bug, mal **04** dwam, puna **05** dwalm, dwaum, qualm, virus **06** malady, nausea, puking **07** ailment, disease, heaving, illness, soroche, surfeit **08** disorder, retching, vomiting **09** complaint, ill-health, infirmity, spewing up **10** affliction, queasiness, throwing up **11** airsickness, biliousness, carsickness, seasickness **13** indisposition **14** motion sickness, travel sickness **15** morning sickness

**side**
◇ *ends selection indicator*
**01** L, R **02** 11, XI, XV **03** end, rim **04** area, bank, camp, edge, face, hand, jamb, left, long, page, sect, team, teme, view, wing, zone **05** angle, brink, cause, facet, flank, limit, minor, party, right, shore, slant, verge **06** aspect, border, eleven, fringe, lesser, margin, region, sector **07** faction, fifteen, lateral, oblique, profile, quarter, section, surface **08** boundary, district, division, flanking, interest, marginal, sidelong, sideward, sideways **09** arrogance, direction, periphery, secondary, viewpoint **10** department, incidental, standpoint, subsidiary **11** point of view, subordinate **13** neighbourhood, splinter group

*See also* **football**

- **at the side of**

**02** by

- **both sides**

◇ *ends selection indicator*

- **change sides**

**06** defect **08** come over

- **from side to side**

**04** over **06** across

- **side by side**

**06** jugate **07** abreast **10** collateral **11** cheek by jowl, neck and neck **14** heads and thraws **15** next to each other

- **side-effect**

**04** echo **06** effect, recoil, result, ripple **07** outcome, rebound, spin-off **08** backwash **09** aftermath, by-product **11** consequence **12** repercussion **13** reverberation

- **side with**

**04** back **06** favour, prefer **07** support, vote for **08** join with **09** agree with **10** team up with **13** be on the side of **15** give your backing, give your support

- **take someone's side**

**04** back, help **06** favour, prefer **07** support, vote for **08** join with, motivate **09** encourage **13** be on the side of **14** sympathize with

**sideline**
**04** game, omit **05** eject, exile, expel, hobby, sport **06** banish, demote, deport **07** degrade, exclude, pastime, pursuit **08** interest, relegate, transfer **09** amusement, diversion, downgrade, second job **10** expatriate, recreation, relaxation **13** entertainment **14** divertissement, leisure pursuit **15** leisure activity

**sidelong**
**06** covert, secret, tilted **07** oblique, sloping **08** indirect, sideward, sideways **13** surreptitious

**side-splitting**
**05** funny **07** amusing, a scream, comical, killing, riotous **08** farcical, humorous **09** hilarious, laughable **10** hysterical, uproarious

**sidestep**
**04** duck **05** avoid, dodge, elude, evade, shirk, skirt **06** bypass **09** give a miss **10** circumvent **14** find a way around

**sidetrack**
**05** shunt **06** divert **07** deflect, head off **08** distract **12** lead away from

**sideways**
**04** side **07** askance, athwart, lateral, oblique, slanted **08** crabwise, edgeways, edgewise, indirect, sidelong, sideward **09** laterally, obliquely, sidewards, to the side **14** from side to side

**siding**
**03** lie, lye **04** spur **07** turnout **09** sidetrack

**sidle**
**04** edge, inch **05** creep, slink, sneak

**siege**
**04** dung, rank, seat **05** class, privy, sedge **06** throne **07** leaguer **08** blockade **09** obsession, offensive **11** besiegement, distinction **12** encirclement **13** beleaguerment

*Sieges include:*

**04** Acre, Metz, Troy, Waco
**05** Alamo, Derry, Kuito, Paris, Rouen
**06** Janina, London, Quebec, Toulon, Vienna
**07** Antioch, Bristol, Granada, Lucknow, Orléans
**08** Damascus, Drogheda, Limerick, Mafeking, Roxburgh, Sarajevo, Syracuse, The Alamo
**09** Barcelona, Jerusalem, Kimberley, Ladysmith, Leningrad, Silistria, Singapore, Vicksburg
**10** Charleston, Kut al-amara, Montevideo, Sevastopol
**12** Tenochtitlán
**14** Balcombe Street, Constantinople, Entebbe Airport, Iranian Embassy, Munich Olympics, Spaghetti House

**sierra**
**01** S

**Sierra Leone**
**03** SLE, WAL

**siesta**
**03** nap **04** doze, rest **05** sleep **06** catnap, repose, snooze **10** forty winks, relaxation **12** afternoon nap

**sieve**
**03** sye **04** sift, sort, tems **05** temse **06** bolter, filter, girdle, remove, riddle, screen, searce, search, sifter, strain, winnow **07** boulter, cribble, griddle, trommel **08** colander, separate, strainer

**sift**
**03** try **04** bolt, sort, tems **05** boult, probe, sieve, study, temse **06** filter, garble, review, riddle, screen, searce, search, strain, winnow **07** analyse, cribble, discuss, examine **08** pore over, separate **10** scrutinize **11** investigate

**sigh**
**04** moan **05** heave, sithe, sough, swish **06** besigh, exhale, grieve, lament, rustle **07** breathe, crackle, suspire, whisper **08** complain **09** susurrate

- **sigh for**

**03** cry **04** long, pine, weep **05** mourn, yearn **06** grieve, lament **08** languish **13** cry for the moon

**sight**
**03** eye, see **04** bead, espy, look, show, spot, vane, view **05** range, scene, skill, visor **06** beauty, behold, fright, glance, marvel, seeing, vision, wonder **07** amenity, discern, display, eyesore, feature, glimpse, insight, make out, observe, perusal **08** eyesight, judgment, landmark, perceive, prospect **09** beholding, curiosity, judgement, spectacle, splendour **10** appearance, estimation, exhibition, perception, visibility **11** distinguish, monstrosity, observation **12** ability to see, conspectuity, sense of sight **13** field of vision, range of vision **14** faculty of sight **15** place of interest

*Ways of describing sight impairment include:*

**06** myopic
**08** purblind
**09** amaurotic, cataracts, half-blind, sand-blind, snow-blind
**10** astigmatic, far-sighted, night-blind, nyctalopic, presbyopic, stone-blind

**11** blind as a bat, colour-blind, hemeralopic, long-sighted, near-sighted
**12** glaucomatous, short-sighted, trachomatous
**13** hypermetropic

---

**• catch sight of**
**03** see, spy **04** espy, mark, note, spot, view **05** watch **06** look at, notice
**07** discern, glimpse, make out
**08** identify, perceive **09** recognize, set eyes on **10** clap eyes on
**• lose sight of**
**04** omit **06** forget, ignore **07** neglect
**08** overlook, put aside **09** disregard
**12** slip your mind **14** fail to remember
**• set your sights on**
**05** aim at **06** seek to **07** plan for
**08** intend to **09** strive for **11** work towards **13** aspire towards

**sightless**
**05** blind **07** eyeless **08** unseeing
**09** invisible, unsighted, unsightly
**10** visionless

**sightseer**
**07** tourist, tripper, visitor
**10** rubberneck **12** excursionist, holidaymaker

**sign**
**01** V **03** act, nod, tag **04** bode, clue, code, hint, levy, logo, mark, omen, shew, show, wave, wink, word
**05** badge, board, draft, enrol, frank, proof, raise, sigil, stamp, token, trace, write **06** action, attest, augury, banner, beckon, caract, cipher, effigy, emblem, engage, enlist, ensign, figure, gather, marker, motion, muster, notice, obelus, obtain, poster, ratify, signal, sign up, symbol, take on **07** acquire, ale-bush, ale-pole, betoken, bus stop, earnest, endorse, express, gesture, glimmer, initial, insigne, placard, pointer, portent, presage, promise, recruit, symptom, witness **08** ale-stake, assemble, evidence, headhunt, ideogram, indicate, inscribe, insignia, mobilize, movement, signpost **09** autograph, character, conscript, harbinger, ideograph, indicator, sacrament, subscribe **10** death-token, denotement, foreboding, indication, suggestion, talent-spot, three balls **11** barber's pole, communicate, countersign, forewarning, gesticulate, phraseogram, put together, recognition, significant **12** shilling mark
**13** gesticulation, manifestation
**14** representation **15** prognostication

*See also* **zodiac**

**• from the sign**
**02** DS **08** dal segno
**• sign over**
**06** convey **07** consign, deliver, entrust
**08** make over, transfer, turn over
**09** surrender
**• sign up**
**04** hire, join **05** enrol **06** employ, engage, enlist, join up, sign on, take on
**07** recruit **08** register **09** volunteer
**15** join the services

**signal**
◇ *anagram indicator*
**04** clue, hint, mark, show, sign, toll, waff, waft **05** alert, recal, token
**06** beckon, convey, famous, gryfon, maroon, motion, recall, target, tip-off
**07** eminent, express, gesture, griffin, griffon, gryphon, message, notable, pointer, signify, symptom, warning
**08** evidence, glorious, indicate, intimate, striking **09** important, memorable, momentous, telegraph
**10** impressive, indication, intimation, noteworthy, remarkable
**11** communicate, conspicuous, exceptional, gesticulate, outstanding, significant **13** distinguished, extraordinary

*Signals and warnings include:*

**03** cue, gun, nod, pip, SOS
**04** bell, buoy, fire, flag, gong, home, honk, horn, pips, taps, toot, wave, wink
**05** alarm, bugle, flare, knell, larum, light, pager, robot, shout, siren, vigia
**06** beacon, buzzer, hooter, klaxon, mayday, rocket, tattoo, tocsin, war cry, winker
**07** bleeper, car horn, foghorn, go-ahead, red card, red flag, torpedo, whistle
**08** car alarm, diaphone, drumbeat, high sign, password, red alert, red light, reveille
**09** alarm-bell, detonator, fire alarm, indicator, larum-bell, Morse code, signal box, storm cone, Very light, watch fire, watchword, white flag
**10** alarm clock, amber light, Bengal fire, curfew bell, green light, hand signal, heliograph, lighthouse, Lutine bell, smoke alarm, time signal, yellow card, yellow flag
**11** Bengal light, bicycle bell, gale warning, smoke signal, starter's gun, storm signal, trafficator, trumpet call, warning shot
**12** burglar alarm, final warning, storm warning, warning light
**13** Belisha beacon, flashing light, personal alarm, police whistle, security alarm, signal letters, traffic lights
**14** distress signal
**15** semaphore signal

---

**signature**
**01** X **03** sig, tag **04** hand, mark, name
**05** cross, frank, sheet **08** initials
**09** autograph, theme song, theme tune
**10** criss-cross, sign-manual
**11** endorsement, inscription, John Hancock **12** subscription

**significance**
**04** gist, pith **05** ethos, force, point, sense **06** import, matter, slight, weight
**07** essence, meaning, message, purport **08** interest **09** magnitude, relevance, solemnity **10** importance, inwardness **11** consequence, implication, seriousness
**12** implications **13** consideration

**significant**
**03** big, key **04** sign **05** vital **06** cosmic, marked, of note **07** crucial, fateful, meaning, ominous, serious, telling, weighty **08** critical, eloquent, material, pregnant, relevant, senseful, symbolic
**09** important, memorable, momentous **10** expressive, indicative, meaningful, noteworthy, suggestive
**11** appreciable, symptomatic
**12** considerable **13** consequential

**significantly**
**07** notably, vitally **09** crucially, knowingly, meaningly **10** critically, eloquently, materially, noticeably, remarkably **11** appreciably, perceptibly
**12** considerably, expressively, meaningfully, suggestively

**signify**
**04** mark, mean, show **05** count, imply, skill, spell **06** bemean, convey, denote, import, matter, signal **07** betoken, connote, declare, exhibit, express, magnify, portend, suggest **08** indicate, intimate, proclaim, stand for, transmit
**09** be a sign of, importune, make waves, represent, symbolize **10** be relevant **11** be important, carry weight, communicate **13** have influence **14** be of importance **15** be of consequence

**signpost**
**04** clue, sign **06** marker **07** placard, pointer, waypost **08** handpost
**09** guidepost, indicator **10** fingerpost, indication

**silence**
**03** gag **04** calm, hush, lull, mute
**05** abate, burke, peace, quell, quiet, still **06** deaden, muffle, muzzle, stifle, subdue **07** clamour, infancy, put down, quieten, reserve, secrecy **08** calmness, cut short, dumbness, muteness, oblivion, suppress **09** cough down, dumbfound, quietness, reticence, stillness **10** quiescence, strike dumb
**11** taciturnity **12** peacefulness, tranquillity, wordlessness
**13** noiselessness, secretiveness, soundlessness, voicelessness **14** altum silentium, speechlessness
**• expressions invoking silence**
**02** sh, st **03** mum, shh **04** hist, hush, tace **05** dry up, peace, quiet, shush, whish, whist **06** belt up, shut up, wheesh, whisht, wrap up **07** wheesht
**08** button it, give over, pack it in, pipe down **09** say no more **10** enough said, keep shtoom, stay shtoom **11** give it a rest **12** cut the cackle, put a sock in it, shut your face **13** hold your peace, shut your mouth **14** hold your tongue, not another word

*See also* **quiet**

**silent**
**03** mum **04** calm, dumb, hush, mute
**05** dummy, muted, quiet, shtum, still, stumm, tacit, whist **06** hushed,

shtoom, shtumm, sullen, whisht **07** implied, schtoom, sulking, wheesht **08** implicit, peaceful, reserved, reticent, taciturn, tuneless, unspoken, unvoiced, wordless **09** conticent, inaudible, mumchance, noiseless, quiescent, secretive, soundless, voiceless **10** creepmouse, dumbstruck, speechless, tongue-tied, understood **11** inoperative, obmutescent, tight-lipped, unexpressed **12** languageless

**silently**
**06** calmly, dumbly, mutely, stilly **07** quietly, tacitly, unheard **08** ex tacito **09** inaudibly **10** wordlessly **11** noiselessly, quiescently, soundlessly **12** speechlessly, without a word

**silhouette**
**04** form **05** shape **06** shadow **07** contour, outline, profile, skyline **08** stand out **09** configure, delineate **11** configurate, delineation **12** shadow figure **13** configuration

**silicon**
**02** Si

**silk**
**02** KC, QC **03** bur **04** burr **05** crape, moire, satin, surah, tulle **06** crepon, faille, pongee, sendal **07** alamode, challie, challis, marabou, organza, ottoman, taffeta **08** boulting, marabout, prunella, prunelle, prunello, taffetas **09** barrister, filoselle, grenadine **10** peau de soie **11** Canton crepe **12** bolting cloth, King's Counsel, moire antique **13** Queen's Counsel

• **silk yarn**
**04** tram **08** chenille **09** organzine

**silky**
**04** fine, seal, soft **05** sleek **06** glossy, satiny, selkie, silken, silkie, smooth **07** velvety **08** lustrous **09** sericeous **10** diaphanous

**silliness**
◇ *anagram indicator*
**05** folly **06** idiocy **08** daftness, rashness **09** absurdity, barminess, frivolity, inaneness, looniness, loopiness, pottiness, stupidity **10** immaturity **11** fatuousness, foolishness **12** childishness, recklessness **13** foolhardiness, frivolousness, irrationality, ludicrousness, pointlessness, senselessness **14** ridiculousness **15** meaninglessness

**silly**
◇ *anagram indicator*
**03** nit **04** berk, clot, daft, dope, dumb, fool, rash, soft, twit **05** apish, barmy, bunny, dazed, dilly, dizzy, dotty, dumbo, goose, idiot, inane, inept, loopy, ninny, nutty, potty, seely, wally **06** absurd, cuckoo, dotish, drippy, duffer, feeble, humble, nitwit, simple, spoony, stupid, unwise **07** fatuous, foolish, halfwit, idiotic, missish, puerile, spooney, strange, stunned **08** childish, harmless, immature, pitiable, reckless **09** airheaded, brainless, foolhardy, frivolous, hen-witted, ignoramus, illogical, imprudent, ludicrous, pointless, senseless, simpleton **10** irrational, nincompoop, ridiculous, silly-billy **11** defenceless, hair-brained, hare-brained, injudicious, meaningless, nonsensical, thoughtless **12** feeble-minded, preposterous, unreasonable **13** irresponsible, unintelligent **14** feather-brained, scatterbrained

**silt**
**03** mud **04** ooze **06** sludge **07** deposit, residue, sullage **08** alluvium, illuvium, sediment **10** brick-earth

• **silt up**
**03** dam **04** clog **05** block, choke **06** clog up **07** block up, congest

**silvan**
**05** leafy **06** forest, wooded **08** arcadian, forestal, forested, woodland **09** arboreous, forestine **11** tree-covered

**silver**
**02** Ag **05** plate, snowy **06** albata, argent, siller **07** bonanza, cutlery **08** pale grey **11** whitish-grey **12** British plate, greyish-white

**similar**
**04** akin, like **05** alike, close, samey **07** related, uniform **08** such like **09** analogous, semblable **10** coincident, comparable, equivalent, homologous, resembling **11** homogeneous, much the same **13** corresponding

**similarity**
**06** kinred **07** analogy, kindred, kinship **08** affinity, homogeny, likeness, relation, sameness **09** agreement, closeness **10** conformity, congruence, similitude, uniformity **11** concordance, equivalence, homogeneity, isomorphism, parallelism, resemblance **13** comparability, compatibility **14** correspondence

**similarly**
**08** likewise **09** by analogy, uniformly **12** in the same way **14** by the same token **15** correspondingly

**similitude**
**07** analogy, parable **08** affinity, likeness, relation, sameness **09** agreement, closeness, semblance **10** comparison, congruence, likelihood, similarity, uniformity **11** equivalence, parallelism, resemblance **13** comparability, compatibility **14** correspondence

**simmer**
**04** boil, burn, fume, rage, stew **06** bubble, seethe **08** smoulder **10** boil gently, cook gently

• **simmer down**
**06** lessen **07** subside **08** calm down, cool down **15** become less angry, collect yourself, control yourself

**simpering**
**03** coy **05** silly **06** smirky **07** missish **08** affected, giggling **13** schoolgirlish, self-conscious

**simple**
**04** bald, easy, mean, mere, open, slow **05** afald, basic, blunt, clear, crude, cushy, green, lucid, naive, naked, plain, seely, sheer, silly, sorry, stark **06** a cinch, aefald, afawld, candid, direct, honest, semple, soigné, stupid **07** a doddle, aefauld, artless, austere, classic, foolish, gullish, idiotic, low-tech, natural, onefold, sincere, soignée, spartan, unfussy **08** Arcadian, backward, homespun, innocent, inornate, no-frills, ordinary, retarded, semplice **09** a cakewalk, a pushover, a walkover, boastless, credulous, easy as pie, easy-peasy, Galenical, guileless, ingenuous, primitive, Saturnian, unadorned, unlearned, unskilled **10** effortless, elementary, half-witted, unaffected, uninvolved **11** incomposite, inelaborate, Mickey Mouse, open-and-shut, rudimentary, unambiguous, undecorated **12** a piece of cake, feeble-minded, inartificial, simple-minded, unsuspecting **13** low technology, rough and ready, uncomplicated, unembellished, unpretentious **14** comprehensible, understandable, unsophisticate **15** straightforward, unsophisticated

**simple-minded**
**03** twp **05** dopey, goofy, idiot **06** simple, stupid **07** artless, foolish, idiotic, moronic, natural **08** backward, imbecile, innocent, retarded **09** brainless, cretinous, dim-witted **12** addle-brained, feeble-minded **14** not the full quid **15** unsophisticated

**simpleton**
**03** daw, mug **04** clot, dolt, dope, dupe, flat, fool, gaby, loon, poop, rook, simp, tony, twit, zany **05** booby, bunny, cokes, dunce, goose, idiot, moron, ninny, noddy, patsy, spoon, sumph, twerp **06** gander, Johnny, nincom, nincum, nitwit, noodle, simple, stupid **07** dawcock, dullard, gomeral, gomeril, jackass, Johnnie, juggins, mafflin **08** Abderite, flathead, imbecile, maffling, numskull, shot-clog, softhead, wiseacre, woodcock **09** blockhead, Gothamist, Gothamite, greenhorn, nicompoop **10** green goose, hoddy-doddy, nickumpoop, nincompoop **11** ninny-hammer

*See also* **fool**

**simplicity**
**04** ease **06** purity **07** candour, clarity, honesty, naiveté, naivety **08** easiness, facility, lucidity, openness, simplism **09** frankness, gracility, innocence, niaiserie, plainness, restraint, rusticity, simplesse, sincerity, starkness **10** clean lines, directness, simpleness

11 artlessness, naturalness
13 guilelessness 14 elementariness
15 intelligibility

**simplification**
09 reduction 10 paraphrase
11 abridgement, explanation
13 clarification 14 interpretation, popularization

**simplify**
06 reduce 07 abridge, clarify, explain, sort out, unravel 08 decipher, make easy, untangle 09 interpret 10 make easier, paraphrase, popularize, streamline 11 disentangle 14 make accessible

**simplistic**
03 pat 04 naif 05 naive 06 facile, simple 07 shallow 08 sweeping
10 oversimple 11 superficial
14 oversimplified

**simplistically**
06 simply 07 naively 08 facilely
09 shallowly 13 superficially

**simply**
04 just, only 05 quite, truly 06 easily, merely, purely, really, solely, wholly
07 clearly, lucidly, plainly, totally, utterly
08 directly, semplice 09 naturally, obviously, shallowly, tout court
10 absolutely, altogether, completely, positively, undeniably 11 simpliciter
12 intelligibly, unreservedly, without doubt 14 unquestionably
15 unconditionally

**Simpson**
02 OJ 04 Bart, Lisa 05 Homer, Marge
06 Maggie, Wallis

**simulate**
03 act 04 copy, echo, fain, fake, mock, sham 05 faine, fayne, feign, mimic, put on 06 affect, assume, parrot
07 feigned, imitate, pretend, reflect
08 parallel 09 duplicate, reproduce
11 counterfeit, make believe

**simulated**
04 fake, faux, mock, sham 05 bogus, put-on 06 phoney, pseudo
07 assumed, feigned, man-made
08 spurious 09 imitation, insincere, pretended, synthetic 10 artificial, substitute 11 inauthentic, make-believe

**simultaneous**
05 simul 08 parallel 10 coexistent, coinciding, concurrent, synchronic
11 concomitant, synchronous
15 coinstantaneous, contemporaneous

**simultaneously**
06 at once 07 at one go 08 in unison, together 09 all at once, at one time
10 in parallel 11 all together 13 at the same time, synchronously
14 synchronically

**sin**
03 err 04 debt, evil, fall, pity, shin, sine
05 crime, error, fault, folly, guilt, lapse, shame, since, stray, wrong 06 offend
07 badness, do wrong, go wrong, impiety, misdeed, offence, offense
08 go astray, iniquity, trespass
09 misbehave 10 commit a sin, immorality, sinfulness, transgress, wickedness, wrongdoing
11 ungodliness 12 misdemeanour
13 fall from grace, transgression
15 irreligiousness, unrighteousness

*The Seven Deadly Sins:*

04 envy, lust
05 anger, greed, pride, sloth, wrath
06 acedia
07 accidie, avarice
08 gluttony
12 covetousness

**since**
02 as 03 ago, sin 04 past, sens, sine, sith, syne, ygoe 05 after, agone, being, until 06 seeing, sithen 07 because, owing to, sithens, through 08 sithence, until now 09 following 10 inasmuch as, seeing that 11 as a result of, on account of 12 from that time, subsequent to 13 from the time of
15 considering that, from the time that

**sincere**
04 open, pure, real, true 05 afald, frank
06 aefald, afawld, candid, dinkum, direct, hearty, honest, simple, single
07 aefauld, artless, cordial, dinki-di, earnest, fervent, genuine, natural, serious, unmixed, up front 08 bona fide, truthful 09 guileless, heartfelt, ingenuous, unfeigned 10 above board, fair dinkum, heart-whole, no-nonsense, unaffected 11 plain-spoken, true-hearted, trustworthy, undesigning
12 plain-hearted, wholehearted
13 simple-hearted, single-hearted, unadulterated 15 straightforward

**sincerely**
05 truly 06 entire, really, simply
08 honestly 09 earnestly, genuinely, in earnest, seriously 10 truthfully
11 unfeignedly 12 unaffectedly
14 wholeheartedly

**sincerity**
05 truth 06 candor, honour, purity
07 candour, honesty, probity, realtie
08 openness 09 frankness, integrity
10 directness 11 artlessness, earnestness, genuineness, seriousness, uprightness 12 truthfulness
13 guilelessness, ingenuousness
15 trustworthiness

**sinecure**
05 cinch 06 doddle, picnic 07 plum job 08 cushy job 10 gravy train, soft option 11 money for jam 15 money for old rope

**sinewy**
04 wiry 05 burly 06 brawny, robust, strong, sturdy 07 nervous, stringy
08 athletic, muscular, stalwart, vigorous 09 strapping

**sinful**
03 bad 04 evil 05 wrong 06 erring, fallen, guilty, unholy, wicked
07 corrupt, immoral, impious, ungodly
08 criminal, depraved, wrongful
10 iniquitous 11 irreligious, unrighteous

**sinfulness**
03 sin 05 guilt 07 impiety 08 iniquity, peccancy 09 depravity 10 corruption, immorality, wickedness 11 peccability, ungodliness 13 transgression
15 unrighteousness

**sing**
03 hum 04 lilt, pipe, rant, ring, scat, slur 05 carol, chant, chirp, croon, jodel, trill, yodel, yodle 06 chaunt, chorus, intone, quaver, record, second, squall, squeal, strain, warble 07 confess, measure, perform, whistle
08 serenade, vocalize 09 celebrate
13 burst into song

• **sing out**
03 cry 04 bawl, call, yell 05 cooee, peach, shout 06 bellow, cry out, holler, inform

**Singapore**
03 SGP

**singe**
04 burn, char, sear 05 swale, swayl, sweal, sweel 06 scorch, swinge
07 blacken, scowder 08 scouther, scowther

**singer**

*Singer types include:*

03 pop
04 alto, bard, bass, diva, folk, wait
05 carol, mezzo, opera, tenor
06 chorus, treble
07 crooner, pop star, soloist, soprano, warbler
08 baritone, barytone, castrato, choirboy, falsetto, minstrel, songster, vocalist
09 balladeer, chanteuse, choirgirl, chorister, contralto, precentor, sopranist
10 prima donna, songstress, troubadour
11 Heldentenor
12 counter-tenor, mezzo-soprano
13 basso profondo, basso profundo

*See also* **bird**

*Singers include:*

03 **Day** (Doris)
04 **Cole** (Nat 'King'), **Lynn** (Dame Vera), **Piaf** (Edith)
05 **Lloyd** (Marie), **Paige** (Elaine)
06 **Atwell** (Winifred), **Bassey** (Dame Shirley), **Church** (Charlotte), **Crosby** (Bing), **Fields** (Dame Gracie), **Jolson** (Al), **Lauder** (Sir Harry), **Lillie** (Beatrice), **Steele** (Tommy)
07 **Andrews** (Dame Julie), **Garland** (Judy), **Miranda** (Carmen), **Robeson** (Paul), **Secombe** (Sir Harry), **Sinatra** (Frank)

08 **Bygraves** (Max), **Liberace**
09 **Belafonte** (Harry), **Chevalier** (Albert)

*Classical singers include:*

04 **Butt** (Dame Clara), **Lind** (Jenny), **Popp** (Lucia), **Tear** (Robert)
05 **Baker** (Dame Janet), **Craig** (Charles), **Evans** (Sir Geraint), **Ewing** (Maria), **Field** (Helen), **Gigli** (Beniamino), **Lanza** (Mario), **Lenya** (Lotte), **Melba** (Dame Nellie), **Patti** (Adelina), **Pears** (Sir Peter)
06 **Bowman** (James), **Callas** (Maria), **Caruso** (Enrico), **Davies** (Ryland), **Deller** (Alfred), **Kirkby** (Emma), **Norman** (Jessye), **Terfel** (Bryn), **Turner** (Dame Eva), **Van Dam** (José)
07 **Baillie** (Dame Isobel), **Bartoli** (Cecilia), **Caballé** (Montserrat), **Domingo** (Plácido), **Ferrier** (Kathleen), **Garrett** (Lesley), **Hammond** (Dame Joan), **Lehmann** (Lotte), **Nilsson** (Birgit), **Vickers** (Jon)
08 **Carreras** (José), **Flagstad** (Kirsten), **Te Kanawa** (Dame Kiri)
09 **Chaliapin** (Fyodor), **Forrester** (Maureen), **McCormack** (John), **Pavarotti** (Luciano)
10 **Söderström** (Elisabeth), **Sutherland** (Dame Joan)
11 **Schwarzkopf** (Dame Elisabeth)
12 **De Los Angeles** (Victoria)

*Folk singers, musicians and bands include:*

03 **Gow** (Niel)
04 **Baez** (Joan), **Bain** (Aly), **Reid** (Robert)
05 **Sharp** (Cecil James), **Simon** (Paul)
06 **Browne** (Ronnie), **Fisher** (Archie), **Foster** (Stephen Collins), **Fraser** (Marjory Kennedy), **Mackay** (Charles), **Martyn** (John), **Nairne** (Carolina), **Pogues**, **Runrig**, **Seeger** (Pete)
07 **Burgess** (John Davey), **Cassidy** (Eva), **Clannad**, **Donegan** (Lonnie), **Donovan**, **Gaughan** (Dick), **Guthrie** (Woody), **MacColl** (Ewan), **Robeson** (Paul), **Skinner** (James Scott), **Thomson** (George)
08 **Marshall** (William), **Morrison** (Van), **O'Donnell** (Daniel), **Rafferty** (Gerry)
09 **Dubliners**, **Henderson** (Hamish), **Leadbelly**, **Robertson** (Jeannie), **The Pogues**
10 **Williamson** (Roy)

*Jazz singers and musicians include:*

03 **Guy** (Buddy), **Ory** (Kid)
04 **Cole** (Nat 'King'), **Getz** (Stan), **Kidd** (Carole), **King** (B B), **Monk** (Thelonius), **Pine** (Courtney), **Shaw** (Artie)
05 **Baker** (Chet), **Basie** (Count), **Corea** (Chick), **Davis** (Miles), **Evans** (Gil), **Hines** (Earl), **Jones** (Quincy), **Krupa** (Gene), **Laine** (Dame Cleo), **Roach** (Max), **Scott** (Ronnie), **Smith** (Bessie), **Smith** (Tommy), **Sun Ra**, **Tatum** (Art), **Young** (Lester)
06 **Barber** (Chris), **Bechet** (Sidney), **Blakey** (Art), **Domino** (Fats), **Dorsey** (Tommy), **Garner** (Errol), **Gordon** (Dexter), **Herman** (Woody), **Hodges** (Johnny), **Hooker** (John Lee), **Joplin** (Scott), **Kenton** (Stan), **Miller** (Glenn), **Mingus** (Charles), **Morton** (Jelly Roll), **Oliver** (King), **Parker** (Charlie), **Powell** (Bud), **Simone** (Nina), **Tracey** (Stan), **Walker** (T-Bone), **Waller** (Thomas 'Fats'), **Waters** (Muddy)
07 **Bennett** (Tony), **Broonzy** (Big Bill), **Brubeck** (Dave), **Charles** (Ray), **Coleman** (Ornette), **Goodman** (Benny), **Hampton** (Lionel 'Hamp'), **Hancock** (Herbie), **Hawkins** (Coleman), **Holiday** (Billie 'Lady Day'), **Hot Five**, **Ibrahim** (Abdullah), **Jackson** (Milt), **Jarrett** (Keith), **Johnson** (James Price), **Metheny** (Pat), **Mezzrow** (Mezz), **Rollins** (Sonny), **Shorter** (Wayne), **Vaughan** (Sarah)
08 **Adderley** (Cannonball), **All Stars**, **Calloway** (Cab), **Coltrane** (John), **Eldridge** (Roy), **Franklin** (Aretha), **Gershwin** (George), **Hot Seven**, **Marsalis** (Wynton), **Mulligan** (Gerry), **Peterson** (Oscar)
09 **Armstrong** (Louis 'Satchmo'), **Christian** (Charlie), **Dankworth** (Sir John), **Ellington** (Duke), **Gillespie** (Dizzy), **Grappelli** (Stephane), **Henderson** (Fletcher), **Leadbelly**, **Lunceford** (Jimmie), **Lyttelton** (Humphrey), **Reinhardt** (Django), **Teagarden** (Jack)
10 **Fitzgerald** (Ella), **McLaughlin** (John), **Thielemans** (Toots), **Washington** (Dinah)
11 **Beiderbecke** (Bix), **Howling Wolf**
12 **Jazz Warriors**

*Opera singers include:*

03 **Mei** (Lanfang)
04 **Lind** (Jenny), **Pons** (Lily), **Popp** (Lucia), **Tear** (Robert), **Ward** (David)
05 **Allen** (Sir Thomas), **Baker** (Dame Janet), **Evans** (Sir Geraint), **Ewing** (Maria), **Freni** (Mirella), **Gedda** (Nicolai), **Gigli** (Beniamino), **Gobbi** (Tito), **Horne** (Marilyn), **Jones** (Dame Gwyneth), **Kollo** (René), **Kraus** (Alfredo), **Lanza** (Mario), **Luxon** (Benjamin), **Melba** (Dame Nellie), **Patti** (Adelina), **Pears** (Sir Peter), **Pinza** (Ezio), **Price** (Leontyne), **Siepi** (Cesare), **Sills** (Beverly), **Teyte** (Dame Maggie)
06 **Bowman** (James), **Callas** (Maria), **Caruso** (Enrico), **Davies** (Ryland), **Dawson** (Peter), **Deller** (Alfred), **de Luca** (Giuseppe), **Farrar** (Geraldine), **García** (Manuel), **Garden** (Mary), **Harper** (Heather), **Hotter** (Hans), **Ludwig** (Christa), **Minton** (Yvonne), **Norman** (Jessye), **Reszke** (Jean de), **Scotto** (Renata), **Studer** (Cheryl), **Tauber** (Richard), **Terfel** (Bryn), **Turner** (Dame Eva), **Van Dam** (José)
07 **Barstow** (Dame Josephine), **Bartoli** (Cecilia), **Caballé** (Montserrat), **Domingo** (Placido), **Farrell** (Eileen), **Ferrier** (Kathleen), **Garrett** (Lesley), **Jurinac** (Sena), **Lehmann** (Lilli), **Lehmann** (Lotte), **Migenes** (Julia), **Milanov** (Zinka), **Nilsson** (Birgit), **Stratas** (Teresa), **Tebaldi** (Renata), **Tibbett** (Lawrence), **Traubel** (Helen), **Vickers** (Jon)
08 **Anderson** (Marian), **Berganza** (Teresa), **Bergonzi** (Carlo), **Björling** (Jussi), **Carreras** (José), **Dernesch** (Helga), **Flagstad** (Kirsten), **Lawrence** (Marjorie), **Melchior** (Lauritz), **Piccaver** (Alfred), **Ponselle** (Rosa), **Schumann** (Elisabeth), **Seefried** (Irmgard), **Te Kanawa** (Dame Kiri)
09 **Berberian** (Cathy), **Brannigan** (Owen), **Chaliapin** (Feodor), **Christoff** (Boris), **Della Casa** (Lisa), **Del Monaco** (Mario), **Forrester** (Maureen), **Hendricks** (Barbara), **McCormack** (John), **McCracken** (James), **Pavarotti** (Luciano)
10 **Galli-Curci** (Amelita), **Los Angeles** (Victoria de), **Martinelli** (Giovanni), **Söderström** (Elisabeth), **Sutherland** (Dame Joan), **Tetrazzini** (Luisa)
11 **Schwarzkopf** (Dame Elisabeth)
12 **de los Angeles** (Victoria), **Shirley-Quirk** (John)
14 **Fischer-Dieskau** (Dietrich)

*Pop and rock singers, musicians and bands include:*

02 **U2**
03 **ELO**, **Eno** (Brian), **Jam**, **Lee** (Peggy), **Pop** (Iggy), **REM**, **Yes**
04 **Abba**, **AC/DC**, **B52s**, **Baez** (Joan), **Blur**, **Bush** (Kate), **Cash** (Johnny), **Cher**, **Cray** (Robert), **Crow** (Sheryl), **Cure**, **Devo**, **Dion** (Celine), **Dury** (Ian), **Gaye** (Marvin), **Joel** (Billy), **John** (Sir Elton), **Khan** (Chaka), **King** (Carole), **Kiss**, **Lulu**, **Piaf** (Edith), **Pulp**, **Reed** (Lou), **Ross** (Diana), **Rush**, **Sade**, **Shaw** (Sandie), **UB40**, **Vega** (Suzanne), **Wham!**
05 **Adams** (Bryan), **Berry** (Chuck), **Black** (Cilla), **Bolan** (Marc), **Bowie** (David), **Brown** (James), **Byrds**, **Byrne** (David), **Carey** (Mariah), **Clash**, **Cohen** (Leonard), **Davis** (Sammy, Junior), **Doors**, **Dylan** (Bob), **Ferry** (Bryan), **Flack** (Roberta), **Haley** (Bill, and the Comets), **Jarre** (Jean-Michel), **Jones** (Grace), **Jones** (Tom), **Kinks**, **Lewis** (Jerry Lee), **Melua** (Katie), **Moyet** (Alison), **Oasis**, **Queen**, **Simon** (Carly), **Simon** (Paul), **Smith** (Patti), **Starr** (Ringo), **Twain** (Shaniah), **Verve**, **Waits** (Tom), **White** (Barry), **Wings**, **Young** (Neil), **Zappa** (Frank), **ZZ Top**
06 **Atwell** (Winifred), **Bassey** (Shirley), **Cocker** (Joe), **Cooper** (Alice), **Crosby** (Bing), **Damned**, **Denver** (John), **Domino** (Fats), **Eagles**,

Easton (Sheena), Fields (Dame Gracie), Jolson (Al), Joplin (Janis), Knight (Gladys, and the Pips), Lauper (Cyndi), Lennon (John), Lennox (Annie), Marley (Bob), Midler (Bette), Newman (Randy), Palmer (Robert), Pitney (Gene), Pogues, Police, Prince, Richie (Lionel), Sedaka (Neil), Simone (Nina), Smiths, Summer (Donna), Taylor (James), The Who, Turner (Tina), Wonder (Stevie)

**07** Animals, Beatles, Bee Gees, Blondie, Bon Jovi, Charles (Ray), Clapton (Eric), Cochran (Eddie), Collins (Phil), Diamond (Neil), Diddley (Bo), Donovan, Gabriel (Peter), Garland (Judy), Genesis, Hendrix (Jimi), Hollies, Houston (Whitney), Jackson (Janet), Jackson (Michael), Madonna, Mercury (Freddie), Michael (George), Minogue (Kylie), Monkees, Orbison (Roy), Osmonds, Pickett (Wilson), Presley (Elvis), Redding (Otis), Richard (Sir Cliff), Santana (Carlos), Shadows, Sinatra (Frank), Squeeze, Stevens (Cat), Stewart (Rod), Vincent (Gene), Warwick (Dionne)

**08** Coldplay, Costello (Elvis), Franklin (Aretha), Green Day, Harrison (George), Liberace, Mitchell (Joni), Morrison (Van), New Order, Oldfield (Mike), Robinson (Smokey), Vandross (Luther), Van Halen, Williams (Robbie)

**09** Aerosmith, Beach Boys, Chevalier (Albert), Garfunkel (Art), Kraftwerk, McCartney (Paul), Motorhead, Pink Floyd, Radiohead, Roxy Music, Simply Red, Status Quo, Steely Dan, Streisand (Barbra), The Pogues, Thin Lizzy

**10** Carpenters, Deep Purple, Def Leppard, Duran Duran, Eurythmics, Guns 'n' Roses, Iron Maiden, Moody Blues, Portishead, Pretenders, Sex Pistols, Shangri-las, Spice Girls, Stranglers

**11** Armatrading (Joan), Culture Club, Cypress Hill, Dire Straits, Human League, Joy Division, Judas Priest, Led Zeppelin, Public Enemy, Simple Minds, Springfield (Dusty), Springsteen (Bruce), Temptations

**12** Black Sabbath, Dead Kennedys, Fleetwood Mac, Grateful Dead, Talking Heads

**13** Little Richard, Rolling Stones, Spandau Ballet

**14** Everly Brothers, Pointer Sisters, Public Image Ltd

**15** Neville Brothers

---

## single

**03** ane, one **04** free, lone, only, poor, sole, solo, thin, unit, weak **05** afald, alone, small, unwed **06** aefald, afawld, honest, one run, simple, slight, unique, versal **07** aefauld, one-fold, simplex, sincere **08** by itself, celibate, distinct, isolated, man-to-man, one-to-one, separate, singular, solitary, unbroken, unshared **09** available, exclusive, on your own, undivided, unmarried **10** by yourself, determined, individual, one and only, particular, unattached, uncombined **12** woman-to-woman **14** person-to-person

• **single out**

**04** pick **05** hit on **06** choose, pick on, select **07** hit upon, isolate **08** decide on, hand-pick, identify, pinpoint, separate, set apart **09** highlight, victimize **11** distinguish, separate out

## single-handed

**04** solo **05** alone **07** unaided **09** on your own **10** by yourself, unassisted **11** independent, without help **13** independently, unaccompanied

## single-minded

**03** set **05** afald, fixed **06** aefald, afawld, dogged **07** aefauld, devoted, onefold **08** resolute, tireless **09** committed, dedicated, ingenuous, obsessive, steadfast **10** determined, unswerving, unwavering **11** persevering, undeviating **12** monomaniacal

## singly

**04** only **05** alone **06** solely **08** one by one **10** distinctly, one at a time, on their own, separately, singularly **12** individually **13** independently

## singular

**01** s **03** odd **04** sing **05** queer **06** proper, single, unique **07** curious, eminent, private, strange, unusual **08** atypical, peculiar, uncommon **09** eccentric **10** noteworthy, pre-eminent, remarkable **11** conspicuous, exceptional, out-of-the-way, outstanding **12** unparalleled **13** extraordinary

## singularity

**05** quirk, twist **06** oddity **07** oddness, oneness **09** queerness **10** uniqueness **11** abnormality, curiousness, peculiarity, strangeness **12** eccentricity, idiosyncrasy, irregularity **13** individuality, particularity

## singularly

**06** singly **07** notably **08** signally **09** bizarrely, strangely, unusually **10** especially, peculiarly, remarkably, uncommonly **12** particularly, pre-eminently, prodigiously, surprisingly **13** conspicuously, exceptionally, outstandingly **15** extraordinarily

## sinister

**01** L **02** lh **04** dark, evil, left **05** cruel, shady **06** Gothic, louche, malign, wicked **07** harmful, ominous, unlucky, vicious **08** menacing **09** underhand **10** disturbing, forbidding, malevolent, misleading, portentous, terrifying **11** disquieting, frightening, threatening **12** inauspicious

## sink

◇ *anagram indicator*

**03** bog, dig, dip, ebb, lay, pay, pot, sag, set **04** bore, damn, dive, drop, fade, fail, fall, flag, foil, fund, mire, risk, ruin, slip **05** abate, basin, bason, decay, drill, drive, droop, drown, embed, lapse, let in, lower, merge, put in, shaft, slump, stoop, wreck **06** cloaca, devall, engulf, fall in, go down, insert, invest, jawbox, lay out, lessen, plough, plunge, settle, vanish, weaken, worsen **07** abandon, abolish, capsize, conceal, decline, degrade, descend, destroy, dwindle, founder, go lower, go to pot, go under, immerse, plummet, put down, scupper, scuttle, subside, succumb, venture **08** cesspool, collapse, decrease, demolish, diminish, excavate, submerge, suppress **09** devastate, disappear, gravitate, penetrate **10** degenerate, go downhill **12** draught-house

## sinless

**04** pure **08** innocent, virtuous **09** faultless, guiltless, undefiled, unspotted, unsullied **10** immaculate, impeccable **11** unblemished, uncorrupted

## sinner

**08** criminal, evil-doer, offender **09** miscreant, reprobate, wrongdoer **10** backslider, impenitent, malefactor, trespasser **12** transgressor

## sinuous

**04** ogee, wavy **05** lithe **06** curved, slinky **07** bending, coiling, curling, curving, sinuate, turning, weaving, winding, wriggly **08** tortuous, twisting **10** meandering, serpentine, undulating

## sip

**03** sup **04** drop, sowp, tiff, tift **05** drink, taste **06** sample, sipple **08** delibate, mouthful, spoonful **11** drink slowly

## sir

**02** Sr **03** Dan, Don **04** baas, Herr, stir, tuan **05** bwana, sahib, Señor **06** Mister, Signor, sirrah, stirra **07** lording, mynheer, Signior, Signore, stirrah **08** Monsieur

## siren

**04** vamp **05** alarm, Circe, syren **06** hooter, tocsin **07** charmer, Delilah, foghorn, Lorelei, mermaid **08** car alarm **09** fire alarm, temptress **10** seductress **11** femme fatale **12** burglar alarm **13** moaning minnie, personal alarm, security alarm

**sissy** *see* **cissy**

## sister

**02** Sr **03** nun, sib, sis **04** siss **05** titty **06** abbess, fellow, friend, german, vowess **07** comrade, partner, sibling **08** prioress, relation, relative **09** associate, colleague, companion **10** full sister, half-sister, twin-sister **11** blood-sister

## sit

**02** do **03** fit, lie, put **04** bear, hang, hold, meet, pass, pose, rest, seat, take **05** befit, brood, clock, model, perch, place, press, roost, serve, squat, stand, weigh **06** gather, locate, reside, settle **07** consult, contain, convene, deposit, sit down, situate **08** assemble, be seated, position, study for, take part **09** be a member, squat down **10** deliberate, take part in **11** accommodate, be a member of, be in session, have room for **12** have space for, take your seat

**• sit back**
**05** relax **09** do nothing **15** not be involved in

**• sit in on**
**04** join **05** watch **06** attend **07** observe **11** be present at

**• sit on**
**04** ride **05** brood, cover

**• sit upright**
**04** perk

**site**
**03** lot, put, set **04** area, plot, seat, spot **05** place, scene, venue **06** ground, locate **07** install, posture, setting, situate, station, website **08** locality, location, platform, position **09** situation

**sitting**
**04** seat **05** spell **06** assize, clutch, period, seated, sejant **07** hearing, meeting, sejeant, session **08** assembly, brooding, sederunt **12** consultation

**sitting room**
**06** lounge, parlor, sitter **07** day room, parlour **08** anteroom **09** front room **10** living room **11** drawing room **13** reception room

**situate**
**03** put, set **04** site **05** place **06** locate **07** install, station **08** position **12** circumstance

**situation**
**03** job, lie **04** case, post, rank, seat, site, spot **05** place, score, set-up, state **06** locale, milieu, office, status **07** affairs, climate, picture, setting, station **08** juncture, locality, location, position, scenario **09** condition **10** conditions, employment **11** appointment, environment, predicament, state of play **12** lie of the land, what's going on **13** circumstances **14** state of affairs

**six**
**02** VI **04** sice, size **05** hexad **06** senary, sestet **07** sestett **08** sestette **09** half-dozen **10** half-a-dozen

**six-footer** *see* **insect**

**sixpence**
**04** kick, zack **05** tizzy **06** bender, tanner, tester, teston **07** testern, testril **08** testrill

**sixteen**
**03** XVI

**sixty**
**02** LX

**sizable, sizeable**
**05** hefty **06** decent, goodly **07** biggish, largish **08** generous **11** fairly large, respectable, substantial **12** considerable

**size**
**04** area, bulk, mass **05** range, scale **06** amount, assize, extent, height, length, volume **07** bigness, expanse, measure **08** quantity, vastness **09** allowance, dimension, greatness, immensity, largeness, magnitude **10** dimensions **11** measurement, proportions **12** measurements

**• size up**
**04** rate **05** gauge, judge **06** assess **07** measure, suss out, weigh up **08** appraise, estimate, evaluate

**sizeable** *see* **sizable, sizeable**

**sizzle**
**03** fry **04** hiss, sear, spit **06** scorch **07** crackle, frizzle, sputter

**skate**
**03** ray **04** rink **06** rocker
*See also* **ice skating**

**skeletal**
**05** drawn, gaunt **06** wasted **07** haggard **08** shrunken **09** emaciated, fleshless, unfleshed **10** cadaverous **11** skin-and-bone **13** hollow-cheeked

**skeleton**
**04** plan **05** atomy, basic, bones, draft, frame **06** lowest, sketch **07** anatomy, minimum, outline, reduced, support **08** corallum, smallest **09** bare bones, blueprint, framework, polyzoary, structure, tentorium **10** coenosteum **11** polyzoarium **12** endoskeleton

**sketch**
**03** act **04** draw, line, plan, skit, turn **05** draft, paint, rough, scene, skiff, spoof, trick **06** aperçu, depict, design, memoir, parody, pencil, précis, résumé, satire, send-up, visual **07** cartoon, croquis, diagram, draught, drawing, ébauche, modello, outline, portray, profile, summary, take-off **08** abstract, block out, bozzetto, esquisse, platform, rough out, scenario, skeleton, synopsis, vignette **09** bare bones, bare facts, burlesque, delineate, framework, programme, represent, rough idea, thumbnail **10** caricature, designment, main points, pencilling, prospectus **11** delineation, description **12** mickey-taking **13** prosopography **14** representation **15** thumbnail sketch

**sketchily**
**07** hastily, roughly, vaguely **08** patchily **09** cursorily **11** imperfectly **12** inadequately, incompletely **13** perfunctorily

**sketchy**
◇ *anagram indicator*
**05** bitty, crude, hasty, rough, vague **06** meagre, patchy, slight **07** cursory, scrappy **09** defective, deficient, imperfect **10** inadequate, incomplete, unfinished, unpolished **11** perfunctory, provisional, superficial **12** insufficient

**skew**
**04** awry, bias **05** slant, twist, weigh **06** biased, colour **07** distort, falsify, oblique **09** obliquity **12** asymmetrical, misrepresent

**skewer**
**04** prod **05** kebab **06** skiver **09** brochette

**skier**

*Skiers include:*

**04** **Hess** (Erika)
**05** **Cranz** (Christl), **Killy** (Jean Claude), **Maier** (Hermann), **Tomba** (Alberto)
**06** **Dahlie** (Björn), **Figini** (Michela), **Sailer** (Toni), **Wenzel** (Hanni)
**07** **Edwards** (Eddie 'The Eagle'), **Klammer** (Franz), **Nykänen** (Matti), **Simpson** (Myrtle)
**08** **Kostelic** (Janica), **Nykaenen** (Matti), **Stenmark** (Ingemar), **Walliser** (Maria)
**09** **Schneider** (Vreni), **Smetanina** (Raisa)
**10** **Girardelli** (Marc), **Moser-Pröll** (Annemarie), **Zurbriggen** (Pirmin)

**skiing**

*Skiing events include:*

**05** grass, mogul, relay, speed
**06** aerial, alpine, nordic, slalom, sprint, super-g
**07** jumping, pursuit
**08** combined, downhill, halfpipe
**09** classical, dual mogul, freestyle, snowboard
**11** giant slalom
**12** cross-country

*Skiing-related terms include:*

**04** gate
**05** daffy, glide, inrun, piste, split
**06** basket, big air, edging, kicker, k point, outrun, p point, schuss
**07** grip wax, hairpin, harries, kick wax, takeoff
**08** glide wax, table top, Telemark
**09** freestyle, large hill, mass start, Steilhang, V-position
**10** Hahnenkamm, helicopter, normal hill
**11** egg position, scramble leg, spread eagle
**12** starting gate, tuck position, vertical gate
**13** backscratcher, critical point, herringboning

**skilful**
**03** hot, sly **04** able, deft, good, hend, mean, wise **05** adept, canny, handy, smart **06** adroit, artful, clever, expert, gifted, quaint, skeely, versed **07** capable, cunning, knowing, learned, skilled, trained **08** dextrous, masterly, tactical, talented, well-seen **09** competent, dexterous, efficient, ingenious, practised **10** diplomatic, proficient, well-versed **11** experienced, industrious, workmanlike **12** accomplished,

diplomatical, professional **14** nimble-fingered

**skilfully**
**04** ably, well **06** deftly, yarely **07** capably, handily **08** cleverly, expertly **11** competently **12** proficiently

**skill**
**03** art **04** chic, feat, hand **05** craft, knack, power, savey, savvy, sight, touch **06** matter, reason, savvey, talent **07** ability, cunning, finesse, know-how, mastery, quality, science, signify **08** aptitude, artifice, deftness, facility, training **09** adeptness, expertise, handiness, knowledge, smartness, technique **10** adroitness, cleverness, competence, efficiency, experience, expertness **11** proficiency, skilfulness **12** intelligence **14** accomplishment, discrimination **15** professionalism

**skilled**
**04** able, good **05** adept **06** expert, gifted **07** capable, skilful, trained **08** complete, masterly, schooled, talented **09** competent, efficient, practised, qualified **10** consummate, proficient **11** experienced **12** accomplished, professional

**skim**
**03** fly **04** ream, sail, scan, skip **05** brush, cream, float, glide, graze, plane, skate, skiff, touch **06** bounce **07** run over, skitter, take off **08** glance at, separate **09** despumate **10** hydroplane, run through **11** flip through, leaf through, look through, read quickly **12** flick through, thumb through **13** browse through

**skimp**
**05** pinch, spare, stint **06** scanty, scrimp **08** withhold **09** cut back on, economize **10** be mean with, cut corners **12** be economical **15** tighten your belt

**skimpy**
**04** mean, thin **05** brief, short, small, tight **06** meagre, measly, scanty, sparse, stingy **07** miserly, sketchy **08** beggarly, exiguous **09** niggardly **10** inadequate **12** insufficient **13** insubstantial

**skin**
**03** pod **04** drum, fell, film, flay, hide, hull, husk, peel, pelt, rind, rine **05** cover, crust, graze, layer, strip **06** casing, fleece, scrape **07** coating, outside, surface, swindle **08** covering, membrane, tegument **10** complexion, integument

*Skin parts include:*

**04** derm, hair, hide, pore
**05** cutis, derma
**06** corium, dermis
**07** cuticle, papilla
**09** epidermis
**10** sweat gland
**11** lower dermis
**12** hair follicle
**14** sebaceous gland

*Skin diseases and conditions include:*

**02** EB, XP
**04** acne, boba, buba, rash, yaws
**05** favus, tinea, warts
**06** eczema, herpes, ulcers
**07** anthrax, gum rash, leprosy, scabies
**08** dandruff, melanoma, ringworm
**09** keratosis, psoriasis
**10** dermatitis, dermatosis, framboesia
**11** prickly heat
**12** athlete's foot, button scurvy

**• by the skin of your teeth**
**06** barely **08** narrowly, only just **10** a near thing, by a whisker **11** a close thing

**skin-deep**
**05** empty **07** outward, shallow, surface **08** external **10** artificial **11** meaningless, superficial **13** superficially

**skinflint**
**05** miser, screw **06** meanie **07** niggard, Scrooge **08** tightwad **09** flay-flint **11** cheeseparer **12** penny-pincher

**skinny**
**04** lean, thin **07** scraggy, scrawny **08** skeletal, underfed **09** emaciated **11** skin-and-bone **12** tight-fitting **14** undernourished

**skip**
◇ *anagram indicator*
◇ *deletion indicator*
**03** bob, cut, hop **04** dart, jump, leap, miss, omit, pass, race, rush, tear **05** bound, caper, dance, dodge, flisk, frisk, slipe **06** bounce, cavort, gambol, prance, spring, tittup **07** captain, miss out, scamper, skipper, trounce **08** dumpster, leave out, overleap, overskip, ricochet **10** bottle bank **11** move quickly

**skirmish**
**05** argue, brawl, brush, clash, fight, mêlée, scrap, set-to **06** affray, battle, combat, dust-up, fracas, tussle **07** contend, dispute, fall out, pickeer, punch-up, quarrel, scuffle, wrangle **08** argument, conflict, scarmoge **09** encounter **10** engagement, velitation **11** altercation, escarmouche **13** confrontation, running battle

**skirt**
**03** hug, rim **04** coat, edge, gore, kilt, maxi, mini, tutu **05** avoid, evade, flank, woman, women **06** border, bypass, circle, margin, piupiu **07** go round, midriff **08** lava-lava, wrapover **09** move round, petticoat **10** circumvent, wraparound **13** find a way round **14** circumnavigate

**skit**
**03** act **04** hoax, turn **05** scene, spoof **06** parody, satire, send-up, sketch **07** take-off **09** burlesque **10** caricature **12** mickey-taking

**skittish**
**03** coy **05** jumpy **06** fickle, frisky, lively, skeigh, wanton **07** fidgety, kitteny, nervous, playful, restive **08** startish, unsteady, volatile **09** excitable, frivolous, kittenish **10** changeable **11** light-headed **12** highly-strung

**skittles**
**04** pins **05** bowls, kails **07** tenpins **08** ninepins **10** kettle-pins, kittle-pins **11** skittle-pins **13** tenpin bowling

**skive**
**04** idle, laze **05** dodge, evade, shirk, skulk, slack **07** bunk off, goof off **08** malinger **09** avoid work **12** swing the lead

**skiver**
**05** idler **06** dodger, loafer, skewer **07** goof-off, shirker, slacker **09** do-nothing **10** malingerer

**skivvy** *see* **servant**

**skulduggery**
**08** trickery **09** chicanery, duplicity, swindling **10** hanky-panky **11** fraudulence, shenanigans **12** machinations **13** double-dealing, jiggery-pokery **15** underhandedness

**skulk**
**03** pad **04** hide, lurk, lusk **05** creep, miche, mooch, mouch, prowl, shool, shule, slide, slink, sneak, steal **06** loiter, shoole **08** malinger **09** lie in wait, pussyfoot

**skunk**
**04** atoc, atok **05** zoril **06** zorino **07** polecat, zorilla, zorille, zorillo

**sky**
**03** air **04** blue, lift **05** azure, carry, space **06** welkin **07** ambient, heavens, the blue, weather **08** empyrean **09** firmament **10** atmosphere **12** upper regions **13** vault of heaven

**skyscraper**
**10** tower block **14** sliver building

**slab**
**03** mud, tab **04** blad, hawk, hunk, lump, pane, slat, tile, turf **05** blaud, block, board, brick, chunk, dalle, piece, plate, slate, slice, stela, stele, table, wedge, wodge **06** bunker, ice pan, ledger, lidger, marble, marver, metope, mihrab, peever, planch, plaque, quarry, sheave, tablet **07** briquet, portion, viscous **08** capstone **09** briquette **10** altar-stone, superaltar **11** paving-stone **12** drawing board, Moabite stone, plasterboard

**slack**
◇ *anagram indicator*
**03** lax **04** ease, give, idle, lash, lazy, limp, play, room, slow, veer **05** baggy, dodge, loose, quiet, shirk, skive, surge, tardy **06** excess, flabby, leeway, lessen, reduce, remiss, sloppy, softly **07** flaccid, get less, hanging, languid, neglect, relaxed, sagging, slacken

**08** careless, decrease, diminish, flapping, flexible, inactive, malinger, moderate, slapdash, slow down, sluggish **09** easy-going, looseness, negligent, nerveless, partially **10** neglectful, permissive **11** inattentive, promiscuous **12** become slower **13** spare capacity **14** insufficiently

**slacken**

**• slacken off**

**04** ease, slow **05** abate, relax **06** lessen, loosen, reduce **07** ease off, get less, release **08** decrease, diminish, forslack, moderate, slow down **10** take it easy **12** become slower

**slacker**

**05** idler **06** loafer, skiver **07** dawdler, shirker **08** embusqué, layabout **10** malingerer **12** clock-watcher **14** good-for-nothing

**slag**

**• slag off**

**04** mock, slam **05** abuse, knock, slate **06** berate, deride, insult, malign **07** lambast, run down **08** lambaste **09** criticize

**slake**

**03** mud **04** daub, lick, sate **05** abate, allay, slime, smear **06** deaden, quench, reduce, sloken **07** assuage, gratify, hydrate, moisten, mudflat, satiate, satisfy, slacken, slocken, subside **08** mitigate, moderate **10** extinguish

**slam**

**03** pan **04** bang, clap, dash, hurl, ruff, slag, slap, swap, swop **05** clash, crash, fling, slate, smash, throw, thump, trump **06** attack **07** censure, rubbish, run down, slag off **08** denounce **09** criticize **12** pull to pieces, tear to pieces, tear to shreds **13** find fault with **15** do a hatchet job on

**slander**

**03** mud **04** slur **05** libel, smear **06** defame, malign, missay, vilify **07** asperse, calumny, obloquy, scandal, traduce **08** backbite, badmouth, vilipend **09** aspersion, denigrate, disparage, sclaunder **10** backbiting, calumniate, defamation, detraction, fling mud at, muck-raking, scandalize, sling mud at, throw mud at **11** denigration, mudslinging, speak evil of, traducement **12** evil-speaking, vilification **13** disparagement, smear campaign **14** cast aspersions

**slanderous**

**05** false **06** untrue **07** abusive **08** damaging **09** aspersive, aspersory, insulting, libellous, malicious **10** backbiting, calumnious, defamatory **12** calumniatory, venom'd-mouth'd

**slang**

**04** cant **05** argot, chain, lingo, scold **06** jargon, patois, patter **07** cockney **09** vulgarism **10** mumbo-jumbo, vituperate, watch chain **11** criminalese, doublespeak **12** gobbledygook **13** colloquialism

**slanging match**

**03** row **04** spat **05** set-to **06** barney **07** dispute, quarrel **08** argument **09** argy-bargy **11** altercation **13** shouting match

**slant**

**03** dip **04** bend, bias, jibe, lean, list, ramp, skew, spin, tilt, view, warp **05** angle, bevel, pitch, slash, slope, splay, twist **06** camber, chance, colour, glance, shelve, sklent, weight **07** be askew, distort, incline, leaning, oblique, opinion, sloping **08** attitude, diagonal, emphasis, gradient **09** embrasure, embrazure, obliquity, prejudice, viewpoint **10** distortion **11** inclination, point of view **12** forward slash, one-sidedness

**slanting**

**05** askew, bevel, slope **06** aslant, tilted **07** asklent, dipping, leaning, listing, oblique, sloping, tilting **08** at a slant, diagonal **09** inclining **11** on an incline

**slap**

**03** hit, set **04** bang, biff, blow, clap, cuff, daub, dead, scud, slam, snub, sock, spat, swap, yank **05** apply, clout, pandy, plonk, plumb, plump, punch, right, skelp, smack, spank, stick, thump, twank, whack **06** breach, buffet, clatch, make-up, pierce, rebuke, sclaff, spread, strike, wallop **07** clobber, exactly, plaster, put down, set down **08** directly, slap-bang, straight, suddenly **09** precisely, violently **10** paddy-whack **11** strike hands

**• slap in the face**

**04** blow, snub **06** insult, rebuff, rebuke **07** affront, put-down, repulse **09** indignity, rejection **11** humiliation

**• slap on the wrist**

**04** flak **05** blame, stick **06** earful, rebuke **07** censure, slating **08** knocking, slamming **09** carpeting, reprimand **10** punishment, rollicking, telling-off, ticking-off **11** castigation, comeuppance **12** dressing-down

**slapdash**

◇ *anagram indicator*

**04** rash **05** hasty, messy **06** clumsy, sloppy, untidy **07** hurried, offhand **08** careless, slipshod, slovenly **09** haphazard, negligent, roughcast **10** disorderly, last-minute **11** perfunctory, thoughtless **14** thrown-together

**slap-happy**

**05** dazed, giddy, woozy **06** casual **07** reeling **08** reckless, slapdash **09** haphazard, hit-or-miss **10** boisterous, nonchalant, punch-drunk **12** happy-go-lucky **13** irresponsible

**slapstick**

**05** farce **06** comedy **09** horseplay, low comedy **10** buffoonery, custard pie, knockabout, tomfoolery

**slap-up**

**06** lavish, superb **08** princely, splendid **09** elaborate, excellent, first-rate, luxurious, sumptuous **10** first-class **11** magnificent, superlative

**slash**

**03** axe, cut, jag, rip **04** curb, gash, hack, race, rase, rash, raze, rend, rent, slit, snip, tear **05** knife, prune, score, slant, slice **06** reduce, scorch, stroke **07** curtail, oblique, solidus, urinate, virgule **08** decrease, diagonal, incision, lacerate **09** carbonado **10** laceration, separatrix **12** forward slash

*See also* **urinate**

**slate**

**03** cam, pan, rag **04** calm, caum, ragg, slag, slam, slat **05** abuse, blame, knock, scold, set on **06** berate, killas, rebuke, sklate **07** censure, propose, rubbish, run down, slag off **08** schedule, tomahawk **09** alum-shale, criticize, pull apart, reprimand, spilosite **10** black chalk, tabula rasa **11** sclate-stane **12** pull to pieces, tear to pieces, tear to shreds **14** Knotenschiefer **15** do a hatchet job on

**• size of roofing slate**

**04** lady **05** peggy, queen, small **06** double **07** duchess **08** countess, princess **09** small lady **11** marchioness, viscountess

**slatternly**

**05** dirty, dowdy **06** frowzy, frumpy, sleazy, sloppy, untidy **07** unclean, unkempt **08** frumpish, slipshod, slovenly, sluttish **10** bedraggled

**slaughter**

**04** beat, best, drub, kill, lick, rout, slay **05** halal, worst **06** battue, defeat, hallal, hammer, murder, outwit, subdue, thrash **07** butcher, carnage, clobber, conquer, killing, murther, outplay, trounce **08** butchery, massacre, outsmart, overcome, vanquish **09** bloodbath, bloodshed, holocaust, liquidate, mactation, overpower, overwhelm, sacrifice, subjugate **10** annihilate, put to death **11** exterminate, liquidation, meat packing **12** annihilation **13** extermination, have the edge on **14** get the better of, putting to death

**slaughtered**

◇ *anagram indicator*

*See* **drunk**

**slaughterhouse**

**08** abattoir, butchery, shambles

**Slav**

**04** Serb, Sorb, Wend **05** Sclav **06** bohunk

*See also* **European**

**slave**

**03** boy **04** esne, serf, slog, toil **05** grind, sweat, theow **06** abject, addict, drudge, labour, lackey, maroon, menial, sclave, skivvy, thrall, vassal **07** bondman, captive, odalisk, predial, servant, villein **08** bondmaid, bondsman, Mameluke, odalique, praedial **09** bond-slave, bondwoman, Gibeonite, odalisque **10** bondswoman, contraband **11** bondservant, galley slave **15** work your guts out

**slave-driver**
**05** bully **06** despot, tyrant **08** autocrat, dictator, martinet **09** oppressor **10** taskmaster

**slaver**
**05** drool, spawl **06** drivel **07** dribble, slobber, spittle **08** salivate **09** beslobber

**slavery**
**04** yoke **06** thrall **07** bondage, serfdom **08** drudgery, nativity, slabbery, thraldom **09** captivity, servitude, thralldom, vassalage **11** bond-service, enslavement, enthralment, subjugation **12** enthrallment

**slavish**
**03** low **04** mean, meek **06** abject, menial, strict **07** fawning, literal, servile **08** cringing **09** imitative, laborious **10** grovelling, obsequious, submissive, uninspired, unoriginal **11** deferential, subservient, sycophantic **13** unimaginative

**slavishly**
**06** meekly **08** strictly **12** submissively, unoriginally **13** unresistingly **15** unimaginatively

**slay**
**04** kill **06** murder, rub out **07** butcher, destroy, execute **08** despatch, dispatch, massacre **09** eliminate, slaughter **10** annihilate **11** assassinate, exterminate

**slaying**
**05** quell **06** murder **07** killing **08** butchery, despatch, dispatch, massacre **09** mactation, slaughter **11** destruction, elimination **12** annihilation **13** assassination, extermination

**sleazy**
**03** low **05** grody, seedy, tacky **06** crummy, sleezy, sordid **07** corrupt, squalid **10** slatternly **12** disreputable

**sledge**
**03** bob **04** dray, luge, pulk, sled **05** pulka, slide, slipe, train **06** hurdle, pulkha, Ski-doo®, sleigh **07** bobsled, dogsled, kibitka, travois **08** toboggan **09** bobsleigh **10** fore-hammer **11** hurly-hacket, skeleton bob **12** sledgehammer

**sleek**
**04** calm, smug, soft **05** glide, shiny, silky, slick, smalm, smarm **06** glossy, oilily, silken, smooth, soothe **07** stylish **08** lustrous, smoothly, thriving **10** prosperous **11** insinuating, well-groomed

**sleep**
**03** kip, nap, ziz **04** bunk, doss, doze, rest, zizz **05** death, dover, go off **06** catnap, drowse, nod off, repose, siesta, snooze **07** bye-byes, drop off, shut-eye, slumber **08** be asleep, crash out, dormancy, doss down, drift off, flake out, REM sleep **09** hibernate **10** fall asleep, forty winks **11** have a snooze, hibernation **12** get some sleep **13** sleep like a log **14** have forty winks **15** go out like a light

**• go to sleep**
**03** kip **04** dove, doze **05** go off **06** catnap, nod off, snooze **07** doze off, drop off **08** crash out, drift off, fall over **10** fall asleep **14** have forty winks

**• put to sleep**
**06** sopite **07** destroy, put down

**sleepily**
**06** slowly **07** heavily, quietly, wearily **08** drowsily, torpidly **09** languidly **10** inactively, sluggishly **13** lethargically

**sleepiness**
**06** torpor **07** languor **08** doziness, lethargy **09** drowsihed, heaviness, oscitancy **10** drowsihead, drowsiness, oscitation, somnolence, somnolency

**sleeping**
**04** idle **06** asleep **07** dormant, passive, unaware **08** abeyance, becalmed, dormient, inactive, off guard **10** slumbering **11** daydreaming, hibernating, inattentive **12** spine-bashing

**sleepless**
**05** alert, awake **07** wakeful **08** restless, vigilant, watchful **09** disturbed, insomniac, wide-awake **10** unsleeping

**sleeplessness**
**08** insomnia **11** wakefulness **12** insomnolence

**sleepwalker**
**10** somnambule **11** night-walker **12** noctambulist, somnambulist

**sleepwalking**
**12** noctambulism, somnambulism **13** somnambulance **14** noctambulation, somnambulation

**sleepy**
**04** dull, slow **05** heavy, quiet, still, tired, weary **06** drowsy, lonely, torpid **07** languid, slumbry **08** comatose, hypnotic, inactive, isolated, peaceful, sleepery, sluggish, slumbery, soporose, soporous, tranquil **09** lethargic, slumbrous, somnolent, soporific **10** languorous, slumberous **11** lethargical, sequestered, undisturbed **12** unfrequented

**sleeve**
**03** arm **04** bush **05** brass, gigot, gland, liner **06** drogue, manche **08** wind cone

**sleigh**
**04** dray, luge **05** pulka, slide, slipe, train **06** Ski-doo®, sledge **07** bobsled, dogsled, kibitka, travois **08** toboggan **09** bobsleigh **10** snowmobile **11** hurly-hacket, skeleton bob

**sleight of hand**
**05** magic, skill **08** artifice, trickery **09** deception, dexterity **10** adroitness **11** legerdemain **12** manipulation

**slender**
**04** fine, jimp, lean, slim, thin, trim **05** faint, scant, small, swank **06** feeble, flimsy, little, meagre, narrow, remote, scanty, slight, svelte **07** gracile, tenuous, thready, willowy **08** exiguous, graceful, tenuious **09** deficient, sylphlike, willowish **10** inadequate **12** insufficient **14** inconsiderable

**sleuth**
**04** dick, tail **05** track, trail **06** shadow **07** gumshoe, tracker **09** detective, Pinkerton **10** bloodhound, private eye
*See also* **detective**

**slice**
◇ *hidden indicator*
**03** cut **04** chip, chop, fade, hunk, part, slab **05** carve, chunk, crisp, cut up, lunch, piece, round, sever, share, shive, slash, swipe, wafer, wedge, whack, whang **06** cantle, collop, croûte, divide, rasher, runner, sheave, sliver **07** frustum, helping, portion, scallop, scollop, section, segment, shaving, tranche **08** doorstep, separate **09** allotment **10** allocation **14** slice of the cake

**slick**
**04** deft, easy, glib, trim **05** quick, sharp, sheen, shiny, sleek, smart, suave **06** adroit, deftly, glibly, glossy, polish, smarmy, smooth, tidy up, urbane **07** quickly, skilful **08** masterly, polished, smoothly, unctuous **09** dexterous, efficient, insincere, plausible, well-oiled **10** altogether, persuasive, simplistic **11** streamlined **12** professional **13** smooth-talking, smooth-tongued, sophisticated, well-organized **14** smooth-speaking

**slide**
◇ *anagram indicator*
**03** ski **04** drop, fall, skid, skim, slip **05** chute, coast, glide, lapse, mount, plane, shoot, skate **06** decamp, hirsle, ice run, lessen, plunge, runner, sledge, worsen **07** decline, descend, descent, falling, plummet, relapse, slidder, slither **08** decrease, get worse, glissade, landslip, toboggan **10** depreciate, go smoothly **11** deteriorate, diapositive **12** depreciation, move smoothly, transparency **13** helter-skelter

**slight**
**03** cut, pet **04** raze, slim, slur, snub, thin **05** elfin, frail, light, minor, petty, scant, scorn, small, spurn, wispy **06** dainty, flimsy, ignore, insult, little, meanly, minute, modest, offend, paltry, petite, rebuff, single, smooth, subtle **07** affront, despise, disdain, fragile,

neglect, sketchy, sleight, slender, tenuous, trivial **08** brush-off, contempt, delicate, misprise, misprize, overlook, rudeness, tenuious, trifling **09** disparage, disregard **10** diminutive, disrespect, negligence, negligible **11** discourtesy, unimportant **12** cold shoulder, cold-shoulder, indifference **13** imperceptible, inappreciable, insignificant, insubstantial, slap in the face **14** inconsiderable, kick in the teeth **15** inconsequential

**slighting**
**07** abusive **08** mesprise, mesprize, misprise, misprize, scornful **09** insulting, offensive **10** belittling, defamatory, derogatory, disdainful, neglectful, slanderous **11** disparaging **12** supercilious **13** disrespectful **15** uncomplimentary

**slightly**
**04** a bit **05** quite **06** rather **07** a little, a trifle, halfway, lightly **08** somewhat **12** to some degree, to some extent

**slim**
**03** axe **04** diet, lean, poor, thin, trim **05** faint, leggy, lower, scant, small **06** crafty, flimsy, lessen, little, meagre, reduce, remote, scanty, shrink, slight, svelte, weaken **07** curtail, cut back, cut down, slender, tenuous, willowy **08** contract, decrease, downsize, graceful, make less, minimize, moderate, restrict, sylphine, sylphish, wind down **09** bring down, go on a diet, sylphlike, willowish **10** inadequate, lose weight **11** make smaller **12** insufficient **14** inconsiderable

**slime**
**03** goo, mud **04** gunk, mess, muck, ooze, yuck **05** slake **06** matter, sludge **07** bitumen

**slimy**
**04** miry, oily, oozy **05** gucky, muddy **06** glairy, greasy, limous, mucous, sludgy, smarmy, sticky **07** servile, viscous **08** creeping, glareous, slippery, toadying, unctuous **09** glaireous, uliginose, uliginous **10** disgusting, grovelling, obsequious **11** sycophantic **12** ingratiating

**sling**
**03** lob, shy **04** band, give, hang, hurl, loop, pass, toss **05** bribe, chuck, fling, heave, pitch, put up, scarf, strap, sweep, swing, throw **06** dangle, prusik **07** bandage, support, suspend **08** ballista, catapult, selvagee **09** parbuckle

**slink**
**04** lean, lurk, mean, slip **05** creep, droop, miche, prowl, sidle, skulk, sneak, steal **07** starved

**slinky**
**04** lean **05** sleek, tight **07** sinuous **08** clinging **09** skin-tight **12** close-fitting, tight-fitting **13** figure-hugging

**slip**
◇ *anagram indicator*
**03** don, err, ren, rin, run **04** boob, cast, chit, drop, fall, flub, goof, note, shim, sink, skid, skip, trip, wear **05** creep, error, fault, glide, jupon, lapse, leash, paper, piece, plant, put on, scape, scrap, skate, slide, slink, slive, slump, sneak, steal, strip **06** booboo, cave in, cock-up, coupon, escape, howler, kirtle, lapsus, piping, plunge, pull on, runner, sledge, slip-up, worsen **07** bloomer, blunder, clanger, cutting, decline, failure, get into, go to pot, incline, mistake, plummet, scedule, slidder, slither, stumble, take off, voucher **08** decrease, get worse, omission, quickset, schedule **09** disengage, landslide, oversight, petticoat **10** change into, descendant, underskirt **11** certificate, change out of, deteriorate, galley proof, go to the dogs **12** get dressed in, indiscretion, lapsus calami **13** lapsus linguae **14** go down the tubes, lapsus memoriae **15** lose your balance, lose your footing

**• a slip of a**
**04** slim, thin **05** small, young **06** slight **07** fragile, slender **08** delicate

**• give someone the slip**
**04** duck **05** dodge **08** flee from, shake off **10** escape from **11** get away from, run away from **14** break loose from

**• let slip**
**04** balk, blab, leak, miss, tell **05** baulk **06** betray, let out, reveal, squeal **07** divulge **08** disclose, give away, overslip **13** spill the beans **15** give the game away

**• slip away**
**05** evade **06** elapse

**• slip up**
**03** err **04** boob, fail, goof **05** botch, fluff **06** bungle, cock up, goof up **07** blunder, deceive, go wrong, screw up, stumble **08** get wrong **10** disappoint **12** make a mistake, miscalculate

**slipper**
**04** muil, mule, pump **06** loafer, panton, sandal **07** baboosh, babuche **08** babouche, flip-flop, mocassin, moccasin, pabouche, pantable, pantofle, slip-shoe **09** houseshoe, pantoffle, pantoufle **13** carpet-slipper

**slippery**
◇ *anagram indicator*
**03** icy, wet **04** foxy, glib, glid, oily **05** false, slime, slimy **06** clever, crafty, glassy, greasy, shifty, skiddy, slippy, smarmy, smooth **07** cunning, devious, elusive, evasive, glidder, slither **08** glibbery, gliddery, perilous, sliddery, slithery, two-faced, unstable **09** dangerous, deceitful, dishonest, lubricous, uncertain **10** lubricious, perfidious, unreliable **11** duplicitous, treacherous **13** unpredictable, untrustworthy

**slipshod**
◇ *anagram indicator*
**03** lax **06** casual, sloppy, untidy **08** careless, slapdash, slovenly **09** negligent **12** disorganized

**slip-up**
**04** boob, flub, goof, slip **05** error, fault **06** booboo, cock-up, howler **07** bloomer, blunder, clanger, failure, mistake **08** omission **09** oversight **12** indiscretion

**slit**
**03** cut, rip, rit **04** fent, gash, loop, loup, peep, race, rend, rent, ritt, sipe, slot, snip, tear, vent **05** knife, lance, slash, slice, spare, speld, split **06** pierce **07** fissure, opening, pertuse **08** aperture, incision, loophole, pertused **09** pertusate, pertusion **10** buttonhole **11** placket-hole

**slither**
**04** skid, slip, worm **05** creep, glide, slide, slink, snake **08** slippery

**sliver**
**03** bit **04** chip, rove **05** flake, piece, scrap, shard, shred, slice, wafer **06** paring, shiver **07** shaving **08** fragment, splinter

**slob**
**03** mud, oaf, yob **04** boor, lout, ooze **05** churl **06** sloven, sludge **07** mud-flat **08** layabout **10** philistine **14** good-for-nothing

**slobber**
**04** slop **05** drool **06** drivel, slaver **07** dribble **08** salivate **14** foam at the mouth

**slog**
**03** hit **04** bash, belt, hike, plod, slug, sock, toil, trek, work **05** clout, graft, grind, slave, slosh, smite, sweat, thump, tramp **06** effort, labour, strike, trudge, wallop **08** exertion, struggle, work hard **09** peg away at, persevere **10** plug away at, sweat blood **13** plough through **15** work till you drop

**slogan**
**03** cry **04** logo **05** chant, motto **06** jingle, splash, war cry **07** tag line **08** slughorn **09** battle-cry, catchword, slughorne, watchword **10** shibboleth **11** catch phrase, rallying cry **12** back to basics

**sloop**
**03** hoy **05** dandy, smack **06** cutter

**slop**
**05** slosh, slush, spill **06** puddle, splash **07** slather, slobber, spatter **08** overflow, slattern, splatter, wash away **09** policeman

**slope**
**03** bow, dip, lie, tip **04** bank, brae, cant, drop, fall, heel, kant, lean, rake, ramp, rise, tilt **05** pitch, slant, splay, verge **06** ascent, aslant, breast, decamp, escarp, glacis, shelve **07** decline, descent, incline, upgrade **08** fall away, shelving, slanting **09** acclivity, disappear, downgrade, watershed **11** inclination

**• slope off**
**06** decamp, go away **08** slip away, sneak off **09** steal away **12** leave quietly

**sloping**
**03** dip **05** askew, slant **06** angled, canted, supine **07** canting, leaning, oblique, tilting **08** at a slant, bevelled, inclined, shelving, sidelong, slanting **09** acclivous, declivous, inclining **11** acclivitous, declivitous

**sloppily**
**07** hastily, messily **08** untidily **09** hurriedly **10** carelessly **11** haphazardly **15** lackadaisically

**sloppy**
◇ *anagram indicator*
**03** wet **05** baggy, corny, gooey, gucky, gushy, hasty, messy, muddy, mushy, runny, slack, soggy, soppy **06** clumsy, liquid, sickly, slushy, sozzly, untidy, watery **07** gushing, hurried, maudlin, mawkish, splashy **08** careless, romantic, slapdash, slattery, slipshod, slovenly **09** haphazard, hit-or-miss, schmaltzy **10** amateurish, wishy-washy **11** sentimental **12** disorganized **13** lackadaisical

**slosh**
◇ *anagram indicator*
**03** hit **04** bash, beat, biff, pour, slap, slog, slop, slug, sock, wade **05** clout, punch, spray, swash, swipe, thump **06** shower, splash, strike, thwack, wallop **08** flounder

**slot**
**03** bar, fit, gap, put **04** bolt, hole, slit, spot, time, vent **05** crack, niche, notch, place, space, track **06** assign, groove, insert, tracks, window **07** channel, install, opening, vacancy **08** aperture, position **10** pigeonhole

**sloth**
**02** ai **04** unau **06** acedia, torpor **07** accidie, inertia, mylodon **08** idleness, laziness, mylodont **09** fainéance, indolence, slackness **10** inactivity **12** listlessness, slothfulness, sluggishness

**slothful**
**04** idle, lazy **05** inert, slack, sweer, sweir **06** sweert, sweirt, torpid **07** skiving, sweered, workshy **08** fainéant, inactive, indolent, listless, sluggish **09** do-nothing

**slouch**
**04** bend, loll **05** droop, hunch, mooch, slump, stoop **06** lounge **07** shamble, shuffle **08** drooping

**Slovakia**
**02** SK **03** SVK

**Slovenia**
**03** SLO, SVN

**slovenly**
◇ *anagram indicator*
**05** dirty, messy **06** sloppy, untidy **07** scruffy, unclean, unkempt **08** careless, slattery, slipshod, sluttish **09** slammakin **10** slammerkin, slatternly **12** disorganized

**slow**
**03** dim, twp **04** daft, dead, dull, dumb, lash, late, lazy, poky **05** delay, dense, dopey, gross, largo, lento, loath, pokey, quiet, slack, tardy, thick, unapt **06** adagio, averse, boring, obtuse, retard, sleepy, stupid **07** andante, delayed, glacial, gradual, lagging, slacken, slack up, tedious **08** creeping, dawdling, dilatory, hesitant, measured, plodding, retarded, sluggish, stagnant, tiresome **09** larghetto, leisurely, lingering, loitering, ponderous, prolonged, reluctant, slacken up, unhurried, unwilling, wearisome **10** deliberate, dull-witted, indisposed, lentissimo, protracted, slow-motion, slow-moving, slow-witted, uneventful **11** disinclined **12** long-drawn-out **13** at a snail's pace, time-consuming, unintelligent, uninteresting **14** slow off the mark **15** slow on the uptake

**• slow down**
**04** curb, stem **05** brake, check, delay, relax **06** detain, do less, ease up, hold up, relent, retard, wait up **08** calm down, chill out, handicap, hold back, keep back, restrict **09** hang loose **10** decelerate, take it easy **11** reduce speed **12** throttle back, throttle down **14** put the brakes on

**• slowing down**
**03** rit **04** rall **08** ritenuto **10** ritardando **11** rallentando

**• slow up**
**04** rein

**slowly**
**05** largo, lento **06** adagio, lazily **08** steadily **09** by degrees, gradually, larghetto, leisurely **10** lentissimo, ploddingly, sluggishly **11** ponderously, unhurriedly **13** at a snail's pace **14** little by little **15** slowly but surely

**sludge**
**03** mud **04** gunk, mire, muck, ooze, silt, slag, slob, slop **05** dregs, gunge, mudge, slime, slush, swill **07** residue **08** sediment

**slug**
**04** bash, boff, gulp, oner, swat **05** douse, dowse, limax, one-er, slosh, souse, swash **06** bullet, lander, wallop, wunner **07** lounder, swallow **08** Linotype®, sea lemon **10** bêche-de-mer

**sluggish**
**04** dull, idle, lazy, slow **05** heavy, inert, resty, tardy **06** jacent, torpid **07** languid **08** inactive, indolent, lifeless, listless, slothful **09** apathetic, lethargic, somnolent **10** languorous, phlegmatic, slow-moving **12** unresponsive

**sluggishness**
**05** sloth **06** apathy, lentor, phlegm, torpor **07** inertia, languor **08** dullness, lethargy, slowness **09** fainéance, heaviness, indolence, lassitude **10** drowsiness, somnolence, stagnation **12** listlessness, slothfulness

**sluice**
**04** wash **05** drain, flush, inlet, koker, sasse, slosh, sluse, slush, swill **06** drench, outlet **07** channel, cleanse, conduit, passage **08** irrigate, lock gate, penstock **09** floodgate, water gate

**slum**
**05** hovel **06** favela, ghetto **07** rookery **10** shanty town **11** cabbagetown **15** across the tracks

**slumber**
**03** kip, nap **04** doze, rest **05** sleep, sloom **06** drowse, repose, snooze **07** shut-eye **08** lethargy **10** forty winks

**slummy**
**05** dirty, seedy **06** sleazy, sordid **07** decayed, run-down, squalid **08** wretched **10** ramshackle **11** overcrowded

**slump**
**03** low, sag **04** bend, drop, fail, fall, flop, loll, sink **05** crash, droop, flump, plump, slide, stoop **06** go down, lounge, plunge, slouch, trough, worsen **07** decline, failure, plummet, subside **08** collapse, decrease, downturn, lowering, nosedive **09** downswing, recession, worsening **10** depression, go downhill, stagnation **11** deteriorate, devaluation **13** deterioration

**slur**
**04** blot, blur **05** cheat, libel, smear, stain **06** insult, mumble, slight, stigma **07** affront, calumny, slander, stumble **08** besmirch, disgrace, innuendo, ligature, reproach, splutter **09** aspersion, discredit, disparage **11** insinuation **13** disparagement **14** speak unclearly

**slush**
**04** gush, mush, pulp, slop, snow **05** slosh, sposh, swash **06** lapper, lopper **07** wet snow **08** schmaltz **09** soppiness **10** sloppiness **11** mawkishness, melting snow, romanticism **12** emotionalism **14** sentimentality

**slut**
**04** drab, slag, tart **05** bitch, hussy **06** clatch, drazel, hooker, pussel, puzzle, sloven **07** floozie, pucelle, trollop **08** dolly-mop, scrubber, slattern, slummock **09** dratchell **10** loose woman, prostitute **11** draggle-tail

*See also* **prostitute**

**sly**
**03** fly **04** foxy, leer, slee, wily **05** canny, carny, peery, smart **06** artful, astute, carney, clever, covert, crafty, expert, impish, secret, shifty, shrewd, sleeky, sneaky, subtle, tricky **07** cunning, devious, furtive, illicit, knowing, roguish, sleekit **08** guileful, scheming, stealthy, weaselly **09** conniving, insidious, secretive, underhand

11 clandestine, mischievous
13 surreptitious
**• on the sly**
07 on the qt 08 covertly, in secret, secretly 09 furtively, in private, privately 10 stealthily, under cover
13 clandestinely, underhandedly
15 surreptitiously
**• sly person**
03 tod 04 coon 06 weasel

**slyly**
◇ *anagram indicator*
07 cannily 08 artfully, covertly, shrewdly 09 cunningly, deviously, furtively 10 stealthily
13 underhandedly 15 surreptitiously

**smack**
03 box, hit, pat, tap 04 bang, belt, biff, blow, clap, cuff, dash, hint, kiss, like, slap, sock, tack, tang, thud, zest
05 clout, crack, crash, enjoy, evoke, plumb, punch, right, smell, spank, speck, spice, taste, thump, tinge, touch, trace, twang, whack, whiff
06 bawley, flavor, heroin, hint at, hooker, nuance, relish, savour, smatch, smouch, strike, thwack, wallop
07 clobber, coaster, exactly, flavour, revel in, sharply, smacker, suggest
08 directly, intimate, piquancy, savour of, slap-bang, straight 09 delight in, precisely 10 absolutely, appreciate, impression, intimation, paddy-whack, suggestion 11 bring to mind, remind you of 13 give a hiding to 14 take pleasure in 15 put over your knee

*See also* **hit**; **kiss**

**• smack your lips**
05 enjoy 06 relish, savour 09 delight in, drool over 10 anticipate

**smacker** *see* **kiss**

**small**
◇ *deletion indicator*
01 S 03 low, sma, wee 04 mean, mini, pink, poky, puny, tiny 05 bitsy, diddy, dwarf, minor, petty, pinky, short, teeny, tiddy, totty, young 06 broken, dilute, humble, little, meagre, minute, narrow, paltry, peerie, peewee, petite, pinkie, pocket, scanty, single, slight, stupid, teensy, tottie 07 ashamed, compact, cramped, crushed, foolish, ignoble, limited, slender, trivial 08 confined, deflated, degraded, delicate, dwarfish, pint-size, trifling 09 disgraced, miniature, minuscule, pint-sized
10 diminutive, humiliated, inadequate, negligible, ungenerous, unimposing
11 embarrassed, microscopic, pocket-sized, unimportant 12 insufficient, teensy-weensy 13 inappreciable, infinitesimal, insignificant
14 inconsiderable

**small-minded**
04 mean 05 petty, rigid 06 biased, little
07 bigoted, insular 09 cat-witted, hidebound, illiberal, parochial
10 intolerant, prejudiced, ungenerous
12 narrow-minded

**smallness**
07 exility, fewness, paucity 08 tininess
09 small size 10 littleness, minuteness, slightness 11 compactness, parvanimity 12 microcephaly
14 diminutiveness

**small-time**
05 minor, petty 08 piddling 09 no-account 10 small-scale 11 unimportant
13 insignificant 15 inconsequential

**smarminess**
07 suavity 08 oiliness, toadying
09 servility 10 sycophancy, unctuosity
12 unctuousness 14 obsequiousness

**smarmy**
04 oily 05 suave 06 smooth
07 fawning, servile 08 crawling, toadying, unctuous 10 obsequious
11 bootlicking, sycophantic
12 ingratiating

**smart**
01 U 03 nip 04 ache, bite, burn, chic, cool, fine, flip, hurt, neat, pacy, pert, posh, smug, tidy, trim 05 acute, brisk, dandy, gemmy, janty, jemmy, kooky, natty, nifty, nobby, pacey, prick, ritzy, saucy, sharp, slick, smoke, spiff, sting, swank, sweat, swish, throb, tippy, witty
06 astute, brainy, bright, clever, dapper, glitzy, jaunty, kookie, larney, modish, pusser, shrewd, snappy, snazzy, spiffy, spruce, swanky, tiddly, tingle, twinge
07 crabbit, elegant, stylish, swagger, tiddley 08 all there, rattling, sprauncy
09 expensive, on the ball, vivacious
11 fashionable, intelligent, presentable, well-dressed, well-groomed 13 well-turned-out
**• smart alec**
07 know-all, wise guy 08 wiseacre
09 smartarse 10 clever dick 11 clever clogs, smartyboots, smartypants

**smarten**
04 tidy 05 clean, groom, primp, prink
06 neaten, polish, spruce, tidy up
08 beautify, make neat, make tidy, spruce up

**smartly**
06 neatly, tidily 07 briskly, hastily, nattily, quickly, rapidly, readily, swiftly 08 abruptly, directly, promptly, snazzily, speedily 09 elegantly, hurriedly, instantly, stylishly
11 fashionably, immediately, presentably 14 unhesitatingly
15 instantaneously

**smash**
◇ *anagram indicator*
02 go 03 hit, run, wow 04 bang, bash, bump, cash, dash, ruin 05 break, crack, crash, crush, drive, knock, prang, thump, wreck 06 bingle, defeat, pile-up, plough, shiver, strike, winner
07 collide, destroy, shatter, smash-up, success, triumph 08 accident, demolish, knockout, smash hit, splinter, squabash, stramash
09 collision, pulverize, sensation
12 disintegrate

**smashing**
05 great, super 06 superb 07 dashing
08 crushing, fabulous, terrific
09 excellent, fantastic, first-rate, wonderful 10 first-class, marvellous, shattering, stupendous, tremendous
11 magnificent, sensational, superlative
12 exhilarating

**smattering**
03 bit 04 dash 06 basics, smatch
07 modicum 08 elements
09 rudiments 10 sprinkling

**smear**
03 dab, gum, oil, pay, rub, tar, wax
04 blot, blur, coat, daub, gaum, gild, gorm, lard, lick, mark, slap, slur, soot, spot 05 blood, cover, libel, patch, pitch, salve, slake, slime, smalm, smarm, stain, sully, taint 06 anoint, bedaub, blotch, defame, grease, malign, slairg, smudge, spread, streak, vilify 07 blacken, obloquy, plaster, slander, slather, slubber, splodge, splotch, tarnish, treacle 08 badmouth
09 aspersion 10 calumniate, defamation, muck-raking, turpentine
11 false report, mudslinging
12 vilification

**smell**
03 fug, hum 04 funk, fust, gale, guff, ming, must, niff, nose, odor, pong, ponk, reek 05 aroma, fetor, odour, scent, sniff, snuff, stink, trace, whiff
06 miasma, savour, stench 07 bouquet
08 malodour, mephitis, pungency
09 fragrance, redolence

*Particular smells include:*

02 BO
04 feet, musk, rose
05 basil, booze, ozone, smoke, spice
06 cheese, coffee, garlic, nutmeg, pepper
07 alcohol, camphor, incense, menthol, perfume, vanilla
08 bergamot, lavender
09 body odour, patchouli, pot pourri, woodsmoke
10 eucalyptus, peppermint
11 wintergreen

**smelly**
03 bad, off 04 foul, high, nosy, olid, rank, ripe 05 fetid, nosey, olent, pongy
06 foetid, mingin, putrid 07 honking, humming, noisome, reeking
08 mephitic, stinking 10 malodorous
12 foul-smelling 14 strong-smelling

**smile**
04 beam, grin, leer 05 drink, laugh, smirk, sneer, treat 06 favour, giggle, simper, smoile, smoyle, titter
07 chuckle, snigger 11 be all smiles

**smirk**
04 grin, leer, trim 05 sneer 06 simper, spruce 07 grimace, snigger

**smitten**
05 beset, épris 06 éprise, in love, struck 07 charmed, hard-hit, plagued
08 beguiled, burdened, obsessed,

troubled **09** afflicted, attracted, bewitched, enamoured **10** bowled over, captivated, infatuated **12** enthusiastic

**smock**
**04** slop **05** frock, shift **07** chemise, smicket

• **lady's smock**
**05** spink **09** cardamine **12** cuckoo flower

**smog**
**03** fog **04** haze, mist **05** fumes, smoke **06** vapour **07** exhaust **09** pea-souper, pollution

**smoke**
**03** dry, fog, gas **04** cure, draw, fume, lunt, mist, puff, quiz, reek, roke, smog **05** fumes, reast, reest, reist, smart, smoor **06** draw on, puff on, smudge, suffer, thrash, vapour **07** exhaust, light up, smother, tear gas **08** preserve, ridicule, smoulder **09** London ivy

*See also* **cigarette**; **tobacco**

**smoky**
**04** dark, grey, hazy **05** black, foggy, fuggy, grimy, murky, peaty, reeky, sooty **06** cloudy, rechie, reechy, reekie, smoggy, smudgy **07** reechie **10** suspicious

**smooch**
**03** hug, pet **04** hold, kiss, neck, snog **05** clasp, nurse **06** caress, cuddle, enfold, fondle, nestle **07** embrace, snuggle **08** canoodle

**smooth**
**03** aid, dub **04** calm, ease, easy, even, file, flat, glib, help, iron, mild, rich, roll, sand, smug, snod, soft, trim **05** allay, bland, brent, dress, filed, float, flush, grind, level, plane, press, shiny, silky, sleek, slick, sooth, still, suave, sweet, terse, thick **06** assist, classy, creamy, fluent, glassy, glossy, legato, mature, mellow, pacify, polish, serene, silken, simple, sleeky, smarmy, soothe, steady, urbane **07** appease, assuage, elegant, equable, even out, fawning, flatten, flatter, flowing, mollify, plaster, regular, rub down, sleekit, slicken, uniform, velvety, worsted **08** blandish, calm down, charming, crawling, glabrate, glabrous, hairless, levigate, mitigate, palliate, peaceful, polished, rhythmic, slippery, tranquil, unbroken, unctuous **09** agreeable, alleviate, burnished, encourage, plausible, press down, unruffled **10** continuous, effortless, facilitate, horizontal, make easier, persuasive, unwrinkled **11** legatissimo, like a mirror, mellifluent, mellifluous, plaster down, problem-free, trouble-free, undisturbed **12** ingratiating, plain sailing **13** full-flavoured, over-confident, smooth-talking, sophisticated, uninterrupted **14** clear the way for **15** straightforward

**smoothly**
**06** calmly, easily, evenly, legato, mildly **07** cleanly, equably, sleekly, slickly, voluble **08** fluently, serenely, steadily **10** peacefully, pleasantly, soothingly, swimmingly, tranquilly **11** legatissimo **12** effortlessly

**smoothness**
**04** ease, flow **05** shine **06** finish, polish, rhythm **07** fluency **08** calmness, evenness, facility, flatness, serenity, softness **09** levelness, lubricity, silkiness, sleekness, stillness **10** efficiency, glassiness, regularity, steadiness **11** velvetiness **12** unbrokenness **14** effortlessness

**smooth-talking**
**04** glib **05** bland, slick, suave **06** facile, smooth **09** plausible **10** flattering, persuasive **12** conciliatory **13** silver-tongued

**smother**
**04** damp, hide, wrap **05** choke, cover, smoke, smoor, smore, snuff **06** cocoon, dampen, muffle, put out, shroud, stifle, welter **07** conceal, envelop, oppress, overlie, repress **08** damp down, inundate, keep back, smoulder, strangle, suppress, surround, throttle **09** overwhelm, suffocate **10** asphyxiate, extinguish **11** suffocation

**smoulder**
**04** boil, burn, foam, fume, rage **05** smoke **06** fester, seethe, simmer **07** smother

**smudge**
**04** blot, blur, daub, mark, soil, spot **05** dirty, smear, stain **06** blotch, offset, smouch, smutch, streak **07** blacken, blemish **08** besmirch **09** dirty mark, make dirty

**smug**
**04** neat, prim **05** sleek, steal **06** hush up, smooth, spruce **08** priggish, smirking, superior, unctuous **09** conceited **10** complacent **13** self-righteous, self-satisfied **14** holier-than-thou

**smuggle**
**03** owl, ren, rin, run **05** steal **07** bootleg

**smuggler**
**04** mule **05** owler **06** runner **07** courier **10** bootlegger, drug-runner, free-trader, moonshiner **13** contrabandist

**smutty**
**04** blue, lewd, racy, rude **05** bawdy, crude, dirty, gross **06** coarse, filthy, fruity, ribald, risqué, sleazy, vulgar **07** obscene, raunchy **08** improper, indecent, prurient **09** off colour, salacious **10** indelicate, suggestive **12** pornographic

**snack**
**04** bite, gorp, meze, snap, tapa, wrap **05** bever, butty, chack, fours, lunch, share, tapas, taste **06** buffet, crisps, nacket, nibble, nocket, snatch, supper, tidbit, titbit **07** bar meal, elevens, fourses, nibbles, zakuska **08** bar lunch, pick-me-up, sandwich, scroggin, trail mix **09** appetizer, bite to eat, Bombay mix, elevenses, light meal **11** amuse-bouche, hors d'oeuvre, refreshment **12** potato crisps, refreshments **15** pork scratchings

**snaffle**
**03** bag, nab, win **04** gain, grab, grip, nail, pull, take **05** grasp, pluck, seize, steal, swipe, wrest **06** arrest, clutch, collar, secure, wrench **07** bridoon, capture, purloin, snabble **08** pounce on **09** get hold of **10** take hold of **11** make off with

**snag**
**03** bug, jag, nog, rip **04** hole, sneb, snub, tear **05** catch, hitch, stump **06** banger, ladder, obtain, secure, snubbe **07** problem, sausage, setback **08** drawback, obstacle **10** difficulty **12** complication, disadvantage **13** inconvenience **14** stumbling-block

**snail**
**05** crawl, helix **06** dodman, nerite **08** escargot, wallfish **09** hodmandod, wing shell

**snake**
**04** bend, drag, loop, naga, wind, worm **05** creep, curve, twine **06** drudge, ramble, spiral, wretch, zigzag **07** deviate, meander, serpent **08** Joe Blake, ophidian

*Snakes include:*

- **03** asp, boa, rat, sea
- **04** boma, bull, corn, file, hoop, king, milk, naga, Naia, Naja, pine, pipe, ring, rock, sand, seps, tree, whip, worm
- **05** adder, black, blind, brown, cobra, coral, Elaps, grass, green, krait, mamba, racer, tiger, viper, water
- **06** carpet, dipsas, dugite, ellops, flying, gaboon, garter, gopher, indigo, karait, python, ribbon, smooth, taipan
- **08** anaconda, cerastes, colubrid, cylinder, jararaca, jararaka, mocassin, moccasin, pit viper, ringhals, rinkhals, sucurujú
- **09** berg-adder, boomslang, coachwhip, hamadryad, hamadryas, king cobra, puff adder, river-jack
- **10** bandy-bandy, bushmaster, copperhead, death adder, dendrophis, fer-de-lance, Gabon viper, massasauga, sidewinder
- **11** constrictor, cottonmouth, diamondback, gaboon viper, horned viper, massasauger, rattlesnake
- **12** carpet python
- **13** diamond python, water moccasin
- **14** boa constrictor, river-jack viper

**snap**
**03** nip, pic **04** bark, bite, chop, film, grip, knap, shot, snip, span, take, tick, time, whit **05** break, catch, cheat, click,

clink, crack, flick, gnash, grasp, growl, hanch, photo, print, scrap, seize, share, shoot, snack, snarl, snick, spell, split, still, stint **06** abrupt, bark at, fillip, period, record, retort, snatch, sudden **07** crackle, earring, give way, growl at, instant, offhand, picture, sharper, snarl at, stretch **08** collapse, fracture, separate, snapshot, splinter **09** crepitate, immediate, lash out at, on-the-spot **10** photograph, unexpected **14** speak angrily to, speak sharply to

• **snap up**
**03** nab **04** grab **05** grasp, pluck, seize **06** pick up, snatch **08** pounce on **10** buy quickly

**snappy**
**04** chic, edgy **05** brisk, cross, hasty, natty, quick, ratty, smart, testy **06** crabby, crusty, lively, modish, snazzy, touchy, trendy **07** brusque, crabbed, elegant, grouchy, stroppy, stylish **08** polished, up-to-date **09** crotchety, energetic, irascible, irritable **10** ill-natured **11** bad-tempered, fashionable, ill-tempered **13** instantaneous, quick-tempered, short-tempered, up-to-the-minute

• **make it snappy**
**05** hurry **06** buck up **07** hurry up **08** go all out, jump to it, step on it **09** come along, look sharp, shake a leg **10** look lively **11** get cracking **15** get your skates on

**snare**
◇ *containment indicator*
**03** gin, net, web **04** grin, hook, toil, trap, weel, wire **05** catch, fraud, noose, seize, toils **06** cobweb, engine, entrap, spring, trepan **07** capture, ensnare, pitfall, springe **08** lime-twig **09** spider web **10** allurement, temptation **12** entanglement

**snarl**
◇ *anagram indicator*
**04** bark, girn, gnar, gurn, howl, knar, knot, snap, snar, yelp **05** gnarl, gnarr, growl, ravel, twist **06** enmesh, jumble, muddle, tangle **07** confuse, embroil, ensnare, entwine, grumble **08** complain, entangle **09** lash out at **10** complicate **13** show your teeth

**snarl-up**
**04** mess **05** mix-up **06** jumble, muddle, tangle **08** gridlock **09** confusion **10** traffic jam **12** entanglement

**snatch**
**03** bag, bit, nab, nip, rap, win **04** gain, glom, grab, grip, nail, part, pull, race, ramp, rase, snap, snip, take **05** catch, grasp, piece, pluck, reach, seize, snack, spell, steal, swipe, whift, wrest **06** abduct, clutch, collar, gobble, kidnap, ruffle, secure, twitch, wrench **07** claucht, claught, quibble, robbery, section, segment, snippet **08** fraction, fragment, pounce on **09** get hold of **10** kidnapping, smattering, take hold of **11** make off with **13** take as hostage

**snazzy**
**05** jazzy, ritzy, showy, smart **06** flashy, snappy, sporty, with it **07** dashing, raffish, stylish **08** swinging **10** attractive, flamboyant **11** fashionable **13** sophisticated

**sneak**
**03** pad, rat **04** lurk, mole, peak, shop, slip **05** creep, grass, prowl, quick, sidle, skulk, slide, slink, snoke, snook, snowk, split, steal **06** covert, cringe, secret, snitch, spirit, squeal **07** furtive, grass on, smuggle, stoolie, stool on **08** informer, inform on, squealer, stealthy, surprise, tell-tale **09** tell tales **11** clandestine, stool pigeon **13** surreptitious, whistle-blower

**sneaking**
**04** mean **06** hidden, secret **07** furtive, lurking, nagging, private, sleekit **08** grudging, niggling, unvoiced, worrying **09** crouching, intuitive, underhand **10** persistent, suppressed **11** sheep-biting, unexpressed **13** surreptitious, uncomfortable

**sneaky**
**03** low, sly **04** base, mean **05** nasty, shady, snide **06** shifty **07** cunning, devious, furtive, low-down **08** cowardly, guileful, slippery **09** deceitful, dishonest, malicious, unethical **10** unreliable **12** contemptible, disingenuous, unscrupulous **13** double-dealing, untrustworthy

**sneer**
**04** gibe, grin, jeer, mock **05** laugh, scoff, scorn, smirk, taunt **06** deride, insult, slight, twitch **07** disdain, mockery, snicker, snigger **08** derision, ridicule **10** look down on **12** curl your lips

**sneeze**
**05** neese, neeze **07** atishoo

**sneezing**
**12** sternutation

**snicker**
**05** laugh, neigh, sneer **06** giggle, nicker, titter **07** chortle, chuckle, snigger, snirtle

**snide**
**04** base, mean, sham **05** nasty **06** biting, unkind **07** caustic, cynical, hurtful, jeering, mocking **08** derisive, scathing, scoffing, scornful, sneering, spiteful, taunting **09** dishonest, malicious, sarcastic **10** derogatory, ill-natured **11** counterfeit, disparaging

**sniff**
**04** hint, nose, sent, vent **05** aroma, scent, shmek, smell, snift, snuff, trace, whiff **06** inhale, nuzzle, snivel **07** breathe, schmeck, sniffle, snifter, snuffle **10** impression, intimation, suggestion **11** get a whiff of

• **sniff at**
**04** mock, shun, vent **05** scorn, spurn **06** deride, refuse, reject, slight **07** disdain, dismiss, laugh at, scoff at, smell at, sneer at **08** overlook **09** disparage, disregard **10** look down on

**sniffy**
**06** snobby **07** haughty **08** scoffing, scornful, sneering, snobbish, superior **10** disdainful **12** contemptuous, supercilious **13** condescending

**snifter** *see* **dram**

**snigger**
**05** laugh, smirk, sneer **06** giggle, nicher, nicker, titter **07** chortle, chuckle, snicker, whicker

**snip**
**03** bit, cut **04** clip, crop, dock, nick, slit, snap, trim **05** notch, piece, prune, scrap, share, shred, slash, sneck, snick, steal **06** incise, snatch, tailor **07** bargain, good buy, snippet **08** clipping, discount, fragment, giveaway **09** certainty, reduction **12** special offer **13** value for money

**snipe**
**04** fool, walk, wisp **05** scape **06** attack **09** criticism, criticize **12** heather-bleat **14** heather-bleater, heather-bluiter, heather-blutter

**sniper**
**06** haiduk **08** partisan **09** guerrilla, irregular, terrorist **11** bushwhacker, franc-tireur, guerrillero **14** freedom fighter

**snippet**
**03** bit **04** part, snip **05** piece, scrap, shred **06** snatch **07** cutting, portion, section, segment **08** clipping, fragment, particle

**snivel**
**03** cry, sob **04** bawl, blub, cant, moan, weep **05** sniff, snift, whine **06** whinge **07** blubber, grizzle, sniffle, snuffle, whimper

**snivelling**
**06** crying **07** moaning, weeping, whining **09** grizzling, sniffling, snuffling, whingeing **10** blubbering, whimpering

**snob**
**04** scab **05** swank **07** bighead, cobbler, élitist, high-hat, parvenu **08** blackleg, townsman **09** shoemaker **13** social climber

**snobbery**
**04** airs, side **05** pride **07** disdain **09** arrogance, loftiness **10** pretension, snootiness, uppishness **11** haughtiness, superiority **12** snobbishness **13** airs and graces, condescension **15** pretentiousness

**snobbish**
**05** dicty, lofty, proud **06** dickty, snobby, snooty, uppish, uppity **07** haughty, stuck-up **08** affected, arrogant, jumped-up, superior **10** disdainful, hoity-toity, toffee-nose **11** patronizing, pretentious, toffee-nosed

**12** supercilious **13** condescending, high and mighty

**snog**
**03** hug, pet **04** hold, kiss, neck **05** clasp, nurse **06** caress, cuddle, enfold, fondle, nestle, smooch **07** embrace, snuggle **08** canoodle

**snoop**
**03** pry, spy **04** nose **05** sneak **06** meddle **07** gumshoe, meddler, Paul Pry, snooper **08** busybody, meddling **09** interfere **11** Nosey Parker **12** interference, put your oar in **14** poke your nose in, stick your oar in **15** stick your nose in

**snooper**
**03** pry, spy **05** snoop **07** meddler, Paul Pry **08** busybody **11** Nosey Parker **12** eavesdropper

**snooty**
**05** lofty, proud **06** snobby, uppity **07** haughty, stuck-up **08** affected, arrogant, jumped-up, snobbish, superior **10** disdainful, hoity-toity **11** patronizing, pretentious, toffee-nosed **12** supercilious **13** condescending, high and mighty

**snooze**
**03** kip, nap **04** calk, doze **05** caulk, dover, sleep **06** catnap, nod off, repose, siesta **07** drop off, shut-eye, slumber **10** forty winks **14** have forty winks

**snout**
**03** neb **04** beak, nose **05** sword, trunk **06** muzzle, nozzle, snitch **07** gruntle, tobacco **08** informer **09** cigarette, proboscis, schnozzle

*See also* **nose**

**snow**
**03** ice **05** linen **06** heroin, whiten, winter **07** cocaine **08** blizzard, morphine, snowfall **09** snowdrift, snowstorm **10** snowflakes **12** snow flurries

*Snow types and formations include:*

**03** red
**04** corn, crud, firn, névé
**05** drift, flake, sleet, slush
**06** powder, sludge, yellow
**07** cornice, flaught
**08** sastruga
**09** avalanche, spindrift

*See also* **ice**

**snowman**
**04** yeti **06** frosty

**snub**
**03** cut **04** knob, shun, slap, snag, sneb, snib, stop, stub **05** blank, check, frump, shame, sloan, sneap, snool, spurn **06** humble, ignore, insult, rebuff, rebuke, slight, squash **07** affront, heave-ho, mortify, put down, put-down, set-down, squelch **08** brush off, brush-off **09** disregard, humiliate **11** down-setting, humiliation **12** cold shoulder, cold-shoulder **13** slap in the face **14** give the heave-ho, kick in the teeth

**snuff**
**04** stop, vent **06** pulvil, rappee, sneesh

• **snuff out**
**03** end **04** kill **05** choke, crush, douse, erase **06** put out, quench, remove, stifle **07** abolish, blow out, destroy, smother **08** suppress **09** eliminate, eradicate **10** dampen down

**snug**
**03** rug **04** cosh, cosy, cozy, snod, warm **05** comfy, tight **06** couthy, homely, secure **07** compact, couthie **08** friendly, intimate **09** sheltered, skintight **11** comfortable **12** close-fitting **13** figure-hugging

**snuggle**
**03** hug **04** cose **06** cozy up, cuddle, curl up, nestle, nuzzle **07** croodle, embrace

**snugly**
**06** cosily, warmly **07** tightly **08** securely **11** comfortably

**so**
**02** as **03** sae, sic, soh, sol **04** ergo, thus, well **05** hence **06** soever **08** insomuch, likewise, provided **09** therefore, thereupon **10** thereafter **11** accordingly

**soak**
**03** mop, ret, sog, sop, wet **04** beat, buck, rait, rate, sipe, sype **05** bathe, imbue, souse, steep **06** drench, embrue, guzzle, imbrue, infuse, pummel, seethe, sodden, sponge **07** embrewe, immerse **08** macerate, marinate, permeate, saturate, submerge **09** drenching, penetrate **10** overcharge

*See also* **drunkard**

**soaking**
**03** sop **05** steep **06** sluicy, soaked, sodden **07** sopping **08** drenched, dripping, wringing **09** saturated, streaming **10** sopping wet, wet through **11** waterlogged **15** soaked to the skin

**soap**
**04** ball, cake, curd **05** money **06** sudser, tablet **07** flannel, flatter **08** flattery, washball **09** soap opera **12** shaving-stick

*Soaps include:*

**03** Lux®
**04** Dove®, hard, soft
**05** glass, Pears®, sugar
**06** liquid, marine, saddle, toilet, yellow
**07** Castile, coal-tar, shaving, Spanish, Windsor
**08** carbolic, mountain, olive-oil
**09** Palmolive®
**10** coconut-oil

*Soap operas include:*

**06** Dallas
**07** Dynasty, The Bill
**08** Casualty
**09** Brookside, Emmerdale, Holby City, Hollyoaks, River City
**10** EastEnders, Neighbours, The Archers
**11** Home and Away

**soar**
**03** fly **04** rise, sore, wing, zoom **05** climb, fly up, glide, mount, plane, soare, tower **06** ascend, rocket, sorrel, spiral **07** take off **08** escalate **09** skyrocket **15** increase quickly

**sob**
**03** cry, sab **04** bawl, blub, howl, weep, yoop **06** boohoo, snivel **07** blubber, singult, snotter **09** shed tears

**sober**
**02** TT **03** dry, sad **04** calm, cool, dark, drab, dull, poor, sane **05** douce, grave, plain, quiet, staid **06** demure, feeble, sedate, serene, severe, solemn, sombre, steady **07** austere, earnest, serious, subdued **08** composed, moderate, rational, teetotal **09** abstinent, dignified, drying out, practical, realistic, temperate, unexcited, unruffled **10** abstemious, on the wagon, reasonable, restrained, thoughtful, unliquored **11** clear-headed, level-headed, unconcerned **12** off the bottle **13** dispassionate, sober as a judge **14** self-controlled, stone-cold sober

• **sober up**
**06** dry out **10** sleep it off **13** clear your head

**sobriety**
**07** gravity **08** calmness, coolness **09** composure, restraint, soberness, solemnity, staidness **10** abstinence, moderation, sedateness, steadiness, temperance **11** seriousness, teetotalism **13** self-restraint **14** abstemiousness **15** level-headedness

**sobriquet, soubriquet**
**03** tag **04** name, term **05** label, style, title **06** handle **07** epithet **08** cognomen, monicker, nickname **11** appellation, designation **12** denomination

**so-called**
**07** alleged, nominal, would-be **08** supposed **09** pretended, professed, purported, soi-disant **10** ostensible, self-styled

**soccer** *see* **football**

**sociability**
**10** affability, chumminess, cordiality **12** congeniality, conviviality, friendliness **14** gregariousness **15** neighbourliness

**sociable**
**04** maty, warm **05** matey **06** chummy, clubby, folksy, genial, social **07** affable, cordial **08** clubable, familiar, friendly, outgoing **09** clubbable, convivial, extrovert **10** accessible, gregarious,

hospitable **11** companiable, conversable, neighbourly **12** approachable **13** companionable

**social**
**02** do **04** bash **05** civic, dance, group, party **06** at-home, common, public, rave-up, thrash **07** blow-out, general, knees-up, leisure **08** communal, function, sociable, societal **09** amusement, community, convivial, gathering, organized **10** collective, gregarious, neighborly, sociologic **11** get-together, neighbourly, sympathetic **12** recreational, sociological **13** entertainment

**• social insect**
**03** ant **05** queen

**• social standing**
**04** rank **05** class **11** consequence

**socialism**
**07** leftism, Marxism **08** Leninism **09** communism, Stalinism, welfarism **10** Trotskyism **12** collectivism

**socialist**
**03** red, Soc **04** pink, Trot **05** pinko **06** commie, leftie **07** leftist **08** hard-left, left-wing **09** Bolshevik, communist, Menshevik, welfarist **10** left-winger, Trotskyist, Trotskyite **11** parlour pink

**socialize**
**03** mix **05** go out **06** hobnob, mingle **08** converse **09** entertain **10** be sociable, fraternize, meet people **11** get together **12** meet socially

**society**
**01** S **03** Soc **04** band, body, club, nobs, tong **05** élite, group, guild, toffs, union **06** circle, gentry, league, nation, people, public, swells **07** company, culture, mankind **08** alliance, humanity, nobility, sorority **09** community, humankind, human race, top drawer **10** federation, fellowship, fraternity, friendship, population, sisterhood **11** aristocracy, association, brotherhood, camaraderie, corporation, high society, the smart set **12** civilization, organization, upper classes **13** companionship, polite society, Sloane Rangers, the upper crust

*Societies include:*

**03** BCS, BPS, CSP, ENS
**04** BNES, BRCS
**05** ASLEF, Royal
**06** burial, choral, Dorcas
**07** benefit, Camorra
**08** affluent, building, friendly, Red Cross

**sock**
**04** drub, hose, tabi **06** argyle, Argyll, thrash **08** half-hose, knee-high **11** ploughshare

**socket**
**03** pod **04** hose, jack, ouch, port **05** hosel, point **06** budget, eye-pit, keeper **07** eyehole, hot shoe, torulus **08** alveolus **10** lampholder, power point, tabernacle

**sod**
**04** delf, fail, turf **05** delph, divot, scraw, sward **06** ground

**sodden**
**03** wet **04** miry **05** boggy, soggy **06** boiled, doughy, marshy, poachy, soaked **07** drookit, soaking, sopping **08** drenched **09** saturated **11** waterlogged

**sodium**
**02** Na

**sofa**

*Sofas include:*

**05** couch, divan, futon, squab
**06** canapé, day bed, litter, lounge, settee, sunbed
**07** bergère, casting, dos-à-dos, lounger, sofa bed
**09** banquette, bed-settee, davenport, tête-à-tête, twoseater
**10** sun lounger
**11** studio couch
**12** chaise-longue, chesterfield

**soft**
**01** B, p **02** mp, pp **03** dim, lax, low **04** easy, fool, hold, kind, lash, mild, pale, waxy, weak **05** bland, cushy, downy, faint, fuffy, furry, light, milky, mulch, mulsh, mushy, muted, piano, pulpy, quiet, rainy, silky, sweet **06** crumby, doughy, dulcet, fleecy, gentle, gently, hushed, low-key, mellow, pastel, pliant, shaded, silken, smooth, sonant, spongy, supple, tender, voiced **07** cottony, diffuse, ductile, elastic, flowing, fungous, lenient, liberal, pillowy, plastic, pliable, quietly, springy, squashy, squishy, subdued, unsized, velvety **08** cushiony, delicate, diffused, flexible, generous, merciful, pleasant, soothing, squelchy, tolerant, yielding **09** easy-going, forgiving, indulgent, luxurious, malleable, melodious, sensitive, spineless, whispered **10** bituminous, effeminate, forbearing, mezzo-piano, permissive, pianissimo, prosperous, restrained, successful, unarmoured **11** a bed of roses, comfortable, mellifluous, soft-hearted, sympathetic, unprotected **12** affectionate, dough-kneaded

**• soft in the head**
**04** daft **05** barmy, dotty, loopy, nutty, potty **06** stupid, unwise **07** foolish, puerile **08** childish, immature **09** senseless **13** irresponsible, unintelligent

**• soft spot**
**06** liking **08** fondness, penchant, weakness **10** fontanelle, partiality, proclivity

**soften**
**03** pad, ret **04** blet, calm, cree, ease, melt, rait, rate, soak **05** abate, lower, malax, quell, relax, still, water **06** digest, lessen, mellow, muffle, reduce, relent, soothe, subdue, temper **07** appease, assuage, cushion, lighten, liquefy, mollify, quicken, unsteel **08** calm down, diminish, dissolve, humanize, macerate, malaxate, mitigate, moderate, modulate, palliate, tone down **09** alleviate, emolliate **10** intenerate

**• soften up**
**04** melt **06** disarm, weaken **07** win over **08** butter up, persuade, soft-soap **10** conciliate

**soft-hearted**
**04** kind **06** gentle, tender **08** generous **10** benevolent, charitable **11** sentimental, sympathetic, warm-hearted **12** affectionate **13** compassionate, tender-hearted

**softly-softly**
**06** low-key **07** careful, patient **08** cautious, delicate, indirect **09** tentative **10** diplomatic, restrained **11** circumspect

**soft-pedal**
**06** go easy, subdue **08** minimize, moderate, play down, tone down

**soggy**
**03** wet **04** damp **05** boggy, heavy, moist, pulpy, soppy **06** marshy, soaked, sodden, spongy, sultry, swampy **07** soaking, sopping **08** drenched, dripping **09** saturated **10** sopping wet, spiritless **11** waterlogged

**soil**
**04** clay, dirt, dung, dust, foul, lair, land, loam, mire, smut, spot, tash **05** black, dirty, earth, filth, humus, mould, muddy, smear, solum, stain, sully **06** befoul, damage, defile, fatten, ground, region, sewage, smudge **07** begrime, country, pollute, slubber, tarnish **08** besmirch **09** territory **10** terra firma

**soiled**
**05** dingy, dirty, grimy, manky, tarry **06** grubby **07** spotted, stained, sullied **08** maculate, polluted **09** tarnished

**sojourn**
**04** rest, stay, stop **05** abide, dwell, lodge, tarry, visit **06** reside **08** stopover **09** tarriance **10** tabernacle **13** peregrination

**Sol**
**06** Helios

**solace**
**05** allay, cheer **06** relief, soften, soothe **07** comfort, console, succour, support **08** mitigate, pleasure **09** alleviate, amusement **10** condolence **11** alleviation, consolation

**soldier**
**03** ant, Joe, man, vet **04** swad **05** shirk **06** swaddy **07** shirker, veteran **10** red herring

*Soldier types include:*

**02** GI
**03** NCO

**04** merc, para, peon
**05** cadet, poilu, tommy
**06** ensign, gunner, hussar, lancer, marine, sapper, sentry, sniper, troops
**07** dragoon, fighter, officer, orderly, private, recruit, regular, terrier, trooper, warrior
**08** commando, fusilier, partisan, rifleman
**09** centurion, conscript, guardsman, guerrilla, irregular, mercenary, minuteman
**10** cavalryman, serviceman
**11** infantryman, legionnaire, paratrooper, Territorial
**12** sharpshooter

*Soldiers include:*

**02** **Li** (Hongzhang)
**03** **Cid** (El), **Lee** (Robert E), **Ney** (Michel), **Wet** (Christian de), **Zia** (Muhammad)
**04** **Alba** (Ferdinand Alvarez de Toledo, Duke of), **Alva** (Ferdinand Alvarez de Toledo, Duke of), **Cade** (Jack), **Foch** (Ferdinand), **Haig** (Alexander), **Haig** (Douglas, Earl), **Jodl** (Alfred), **John** (Don), **Khan** (Ayub), **Röhm** (Ernst), **Tojo** (Hideki)
**05** **Allen** (Ethan), **Bader** (Sir Douglas), **Barak** (Ehud), **Botha** (Louis), **Bowie** (James), **Bruce** (Robert), **Cimon**, **Clive** (Robert, Lord), **Dayan** (Moshe), **Essex** (Robert Devereux, Earl of), **Gates** (Horatio), **Grant** (Ulysses S), **Inönü** (Ismet), **Monck** (George), **Murat** (Joachim), **Perón** (Juan), **Pride** (Sir Thomas), **Rabin** (Yitzhak), **Smuts** (Jan), **Sucre** (Antonio José de), **Sully** (Maximilien de Béthune, Duc de), **Timur**, **Zhu De**
**06** **Anders** (Wladyslaw), **Antony** (Mark), **Arnold** (Benedict), **Blamey** (Sir Thomas Albert), **Brutus** (Marcus Junius), **Butler** (Benjamin Franklin), **Caesar** (Julius), **Cortés** (Hernán), **Custer** (George Armstrong), **Dundee** (John Graham, Viscount of), **Dunois** (Jean d'Orléans Comte), **Edward** (the Black Prince), **Egmont** (Graaf van Gavre), **Ershad** (Hossain Muhammad), **Eugene** (of Savoy), **Franco** (Francisco), **Gaulle** (Charles de), **Gordon** (Charles George), **Granby** (John Manners, Marquis of), **Greene** (Nathanael), **Ireton** (Henry), **Keitel** (Wilhelm), **Marius** (Gaius), **Moltke** (Helmuth, Graf von), **Napier** (Robert, Lord), **Nasser** (Gamal Abd al-), **Neguib** (Mohammed), **Patton** (George), **Pétain** (Philippe), **Pompey**, **Prokop** (the Bald), **Raglan** (Fitzroy James Henry Somerset, Lord), **Rahman** (Ziaur), **Revere** (Paul), **Rommel** (Erwin), **Rupert** (Prince), **Scipio** (Publius Cornelius), **Vauban** (Sebastien le Prestre de), **Wavell** (Archibald, Earl), **Zhukov** (Giorgiy)
**07** **Agrippa** (Marcus Vipsanius), **Allenby** (Edmund, Viscount), **Almagro** (Diego de), **Artigas** (José Gervasio), **Atatürk** (Mustapha Kemal), **Baldwin**, **Bazaine** (Achille), **Bedford** (John of Lancaster, Duke of), **Blücher** (Gebbard Leberecht von Fürst von), **Bourbon** (Charles), **Boycott** (Charles Cunningham), **Bradley** (Omar Nelson), **Cadogan** (William, Earl), **Cassius**, **Coligny** (Gaspard de), **Dreyfus** (Alfred), **Fairfax** (Thomas, Lord), **Farnese** (Alessandro), **Gaddafi** (Muammar), **Gemayel** (Bashir), **Hunyady** (János Corvinus), **Jackson** (Thomas Jonathan), **Kolchak** (Alexander), **Kutuzov** (Mikhail, Knyaz), **Lambert** (John), **Masséna** (André), **Maurice** (Prince), **Metaxas** (Ioannis), **Mortier** (Edouard Adolphe Casimir Joseph), **Pizarro** (Francisco), **Ptolemy**, **Roberts** (Frederick, Earl), **Sherman** (William Tecumseh), **St Leger** (Barry), **Tancred**, **Turenne** (Henri de la Tour d'Auvergne, Vicomte de), **Vendôme** (Louis Joseph Duc de), **Warwick** (Richard Neville, Earl of), **William** (Prince of Orange), **Wrangel** (Pyotr, Lord)
**08** **Agricola** (Gnaeus Julius), **Alvarado** (Pedro de), **Anglesey** (Henry William Paget, Marquis of), **Antonius** (Marcus), **Arminius**, **Badoglio** (Pietro), **Bentinck** (William, Lord), **Boadicea**, **Burgoyne** (John), **Burnside** (Ambrose Everett), **Campbell** (Sir Colin), **Cardigan** (James Thomas Brudenell, Earl of), **Cromwell** (Oliver), **Eichmann** (Adolf), **Ginckell** (Godert de), **Guiscard** (Robert), **Hamilton** (James, Duke of), **Harrison** (William Henry), **Hereward** (the Wake), **Horrocks** (Sir Brian), **Ironside** (William, Lord), **Itúrbide** (Agustín de), **Lawrence** (Thomas Edward), **Lucullus** (Lucius Licinius), **MacMahon** (Marie Edme Patrice Maurice de), **Marshall** (George Catlett), **Mengistu** (Haile Mariam), **Montfort** (Simon de), **Montrose** (James Graham, Marquis of), **Napoleon**, **Nobunaga** (Oda), **Pershing** (John Joseph), **Potemkin** (Grigoriy), **Pugachev** (Emelyan), **Seleucus**, **Sheridan** (Philip Henry), **Sikorski** (Wladyslaw), **Skorzeny** (Otto), **Stanhope** (James, Earl), **Tokugawa** (Ieyasu), **Valdivia** (Pedro de), **Wolseley** (Garnet, Viscount), **Xenophon**, **Yamagata** (Prince Aritomo), **Zia Ul-Haq** (Muhammad)
**09** **Alexander** (Harold, Earl), **Antonescu** (Ion), **Bonaparte** (Jérôme), **Carausius** (Marcus Aurelius Mausaeus), **Cavendish** (William), **Garibaldi** (Giuseppe), **Gneisenau** (August, Graf Neithardt von), **Hasdrubal**, **Hideyoshi** (Toyotomi), **Kim Il-sung**, **Kitchener** (Herbert, Earl), **Lafayette** (Marie Joseph, Marquis de), **MacArthur** (Douglas), **Miltiades**, **Spartacus**
**10** **Abercromby** (Sir Ralph), **Alanbrooke** (Alan Francis Brooke, Viscount), **Alcibiades**, **Auchinleck** (Sir Claude), **Belisarius**, **Clausewitz** (Karl von), **Cornwallis** (Charles, Marquis), **Cumberland** (William, Duke of), **Eisenhower** (Dwight D), **Germanicus**, **Hindenburg** (Paul von), **Karageorge**, **Montgomery** (Bernard, Viscount), **Schlieffen** (Alfred, Graf von), **Stroessner** (Alfredo), **Voroshilov** (Kliment), **Washington** (George), **Wellington** (Arthur Wellesley, Duke of)
**11** **Baden-Powell** (Robert, Lord), **Black Prince**, **Genghis Khan**, **Marlborough** (John Churchill, Duke of), **Mohammed Ali**, **Münchhausen** (Baron von)
**12** **Ptolemy Soter**, **Stauffenburg** (Claus, Graf von)
**13** **Fabius Maximus** (Quintus), **Rouget de Lisle** (Claude Joseph)
**14** **Pinochet Ugarte** (Augusto)
**15** **Scipio Africanus** (Publius Cornelius), **Seleucus Nicator**

• **soldier on**
**06** hang on, hold on, keep on, remain
**08** continue, keep at it, plug away
**09** keep going, persevere, stick at it
**11** hang in there

• **soldiers**
**02** OR, RE, TA **03** GIs **04** army
**06** legion **08** garrison

## sole

**03** one **04** lone, only, palm, pull, sill, slip, sowl **05** alone, capon, clump, mered, soole, sowle **06** meered, single, thenar, unique **07** uniform **08** singular, solitary **09** exclusive, scaldfish **10** individual

## solecism

**04** boob **05** error, gaffe, lapse **06** booboo, howler **07** blunder, faux pas, mistake **08** cacology **09** absurdity, gaucherie, indecorum **11** anacoluthon, impropriety, incongruity

## solely

**04** just, only **05** alone **06** merely, simply, singly **08** entirely, uniquely **09** allenarly **10** completely **11** exclusively **14** single-handedly

## solemn

**02** po **04** awed, glum **05** grand, grave, pious, sober, state **06** august, devout, formal, honest, owlish, ritual, sedate, sombre **07** earnest, genuine, po-faced, pompous, serious, sincere, stately **08** imposing, majestic **09** committed, dignified, momentous, venerable **10** ceremonial, impressive, portentous, thoughtful **11** ceremonious, reverential **12** awe-inspiring, wholehearted

## solemnity

**04** rite **06** ritual **07** dignity, gravity **08** ceremony, grandeur, sanctity **09** formality **10** ceremonial, observance, sacredness **11** celebration, earnestness, proceedings, seriousness, stateliness **13** momentousness **14** impressiveness, portentousness

**solemnize**
**04** keep **06** honour **07** dignify, observe, perform **09** celebrate **11** commemorate

**solemnly**
**07** gravely, soberly **08** formally **09** earnestly, seriously **10** faithfully

**sol-fa** *see* **note**

**solicit**
**03** ask, beg, sue, woo **04** bash, drum, pray, seek, tout **05** apply, court, crave, plead **06** accost, ask for, hustle, incite, manage **07** accoast, beseech, canvass, conduct, entreat, implore, request, require **08** apply for, petition **09** importune **10** supplicate **11** proposition

**solicitor**
**02** QC, SL, WS **03** Att, Sol, SSC **04** Atty, Solr, tout **06** lawyer **08** advocate, attorney, law agent, recorder **09** barrister, canvasser **10** crown agent

**solicitous**
**05** eager **06** caring, uneasy **07** anxious, careful, earnest, jealous, worried, zealous **08** troubled **09** attentive, concerned **11** considerate **12** apprehensive

**solicitude**
**04** care, cark, fear **05** worry **06** regard **07** anxiety, concern, trouble **08** disquiet **10** uneasiness **13** attentiveness, consideration **15** considerateness

**solid**
**04** firm, hard, pure, real **05** cubic, dense, gross, sober, sound, thick, valid **06** cogent, decent, square, stable, strong, sturdy, trusty, worthy **07** compact, cubical, durable, genuine, serious, unmixed, upright, wealthy, weighty **08** concrete, reliable, sensible, tangible, unbroken, unvaried **09** steadfast, unalloyed, unanimous, undivided, well-built **10** compressed, continuous, dependable, holosteric, unshakable, upstanding **11** level-headed, long-lasting, respectable, substantial, trustworthy, unshakeable, well-founded **12** well-grounded **13** authoritative, unadulterated, uninterrupted

**solidarity**
**05** unity **06** accord **07** concord, harmony **08** cohesion **09** agreement, consensus, soundness, stability, unanimity **10** team spirit **11** camaraderie **13** esprit de corps **14** like-mindedness

**solidify**
**03** gel, set **04** cake, clot, jell **06** go hard, harden **07** congeal **09** coagulate, corporify **10** become hard **11** crystallize

**soliloquy**
**06** homily, sermon, speech **07** address, lecture, monolog, oration **09** monologue

**solitary**
**03** one **04** lone, monk, sole **05** alone, loner **06** hermit, lonely, remote, single **07** ancress, ascetic, dernful, eremite, recluse, retired, stylite **08** dearnful, desolate, isolated, lonesome, lone wolf, monastic, secluded, separate **09** anchoress, anchorite, reclusive, untrodden, unvisited, withdrawn **10** by yourself, cloistered, friendless, hermitical, monastical, unsociable **11** introverted, monasterial, out-of-the-way, sequestered **12** inaccessible, Jimmy Woodser, unfrequented **13** companionless, individualist

**solitude**
**07** privacy **09** aloneness, isolation, seclusion **10** desolation, loneliness, remoteness, retirement, singleness **12** introversion, lonesomeness **13** reclusiveness, unsociability **14** friendlessness

**solo**
**04** aria, ayre, lone **05** alone, break, récit **06** single **07** cadenza **09** on your own **10** by yourself, unattended, unescorted **12** single-handed **13** unaccompanied

**Solomon Islands**
**03** SLB

**solution**
◇ *anagram indicator*
**02** aq **03** fix, gel, key, lye, mix, sol **05** blend, brine **06** answer, liquid, liquor, remedy, result, saline, way out **07** cure-all, formula, mixture, panacea, solvent **08** compound, emulsion, quick fix **09** rationale, unfolding **10** resolution, suspension **11** elucidation, explanation, unravelling **12** decipherment **13** clarification **15** disentanglement

**solve**
◇ *anagram indicator*
**04** read, undo, work **05** crack, guess, loose, untie **06** answer, assoil, fathom, puzzle, remedy, riddle, settle, unbind, unfold **07** clarify, clear up, explain, expound, rectify, resolve, unravel, work out **08** decipher, put right, solution, think out, unriddle **09** figure out, interpret, puzzle out **11** disentangle **12** think through

**solvent**
**04** DMSO **05** ether, sound **06** dioxan, toluol **07** benzine, dioxane, toluene **08** alcahest, alkahest, methanol, terebene **09** able to pay, banana oil, detergent, financial, menstruum, out of debt **10** chloroform, extractant, in the black, in the clear, unindebted **11** cyclohexane **12** banana liquid, creditworthy, ethyl acetate, nitromethane, salt of sorrel **14** banana solution, petroleum ether **15** propylene glycol, trichloroethane

**solver**
**11** solutionist
• **solvers**
**02** ye **03** you

**Somalia**
**02** SO **03** SOM

**sombre**
**03** dim, sad **04** dark, drab, dull **05** dingy, grave, morne, shady, sober **06** dismal, gloomy, morose, solemn **07** doleful, joyless, obscure, serious, shadowy, subfusc, subfusk **08** funereal, mournful **09** depressed **10** lugubrious, melancholy

**some**
◇ *hidden indicator*
**03** any, few, one **04** they **07** certain, several **10** remarkable **11** outstanding, such-and-such **12** considerable

**somebody**
**03** one, VIP **04** name, star **05** mogul, nabob **06** bigwig, quidam **07** big shot, magnate, notable, someone **08** big noise, big wheel, luminary **09** celebrity, dignitary, personage, superstar **10** panjandrum **11** heavyweight **13** household name

**someday**
**05** later **06** one day **07** by and by, later on **08** sometime **10** eventually, ultimately **11** in due course **13** sooner or later **14** one of these days

**somehow**
◇ *anagram indicator*
**06** in a way **11** by some means, come what may **15** by hook or by crook, one way or another

**someone** *see* **somebody**

**somersault**
◇ *anagram indicator*

**sometime**
**02** ex **04** late, then **06** former, one day **07** earlier, one-time, quondam, retired, someday **08** emeritus, formerly, previous **09** erstwhile, in the past **10** occasional, previously **11** another time

**sometimes**
**07** at times **08** off and on, on and off **09** somewhile **10** now and then, on occasion, otherwhile, somewhiles **11** now and again, on occasions, otherwhiles **12** every so often, occasionally, once in a while **14** from time to time

**somewhat**
**04** a bit **05** kinda, quite **06** a bit of, fairly, kind of, pretty, rather, sort of **07** a little **08** slightly **10** moderately, relatively **12** to some degree, to some extent

**somnolent**
**04** dozy **06** drowsy, sleepy, torpid **08** comatose, oscitant **09** half-awake, heavy-eyed, soporific

**Somnus**
**06** Hypnos

**son**
**01** s **03** boy, lad **04** fils **05** child, lewis **06** epigon, filius, laddie, native **07** epigone **08** disciple **09** offspring **10** descendant, inhabitant

*Sons include:*

**04** **Abel**, **Amis** (Martin), **Bush** (George W), **Cain**, **Esau**, **Pitt** (William)
**05** **Dumas** (Alexandre), **Groan** (Titus), **Harry** (Prince), **Isaac**, **Jacob**, **Milne** (Christopher Robin), **Morel** (Paul), **Waugh** (Auberon)
**06** **Andrew** (Prince), **Edward** (Prince), **Gandhi** (Rajiv), **Hamlet**, **Joseph**
**07** **Absalom**, **Charles** (Prince), **Douglas** (Michael), **Hotspur**, **Laertes**, **Oedipus**, **Simpson** (Bart), **William** (Prince)
**08** **Benjamin**, **Dimbleby** (David), **Dimbleby** (Jonathan), **Florizel**, **Pontifex** (Ernest)
**09** **Dumas fils**
**10** **Duke of York**
**11** **Jesus Christ**
**13** **Prince of Wales**
**14** **Pitt the Younger** (William)

• **son of**
**01** M', O' **02** Mc **03** Mac

**song**

*Songs include:*

**03** air, art, fit, lay, oat, ode, pop, pub, war
**04** aria, bird, duet, folk, glee, hymn, lied, lilt, love, pean, rock, rune, tune
**05** blues, carol, catch, chant, dirge, ditty, elegy, lyric, paean, plain, psalm, torch, yodel
**06** amoret, anthem, ballad, chorus, gospel, jingle, lieder, lyrics, melody, number, shanty
**07** calypso, cantata, canzone, chanson, descant, lullaby, refrain, requiem, wassail
**08** bird call, canticle, canzonet, madrigal, serenade, threnody
**09** barcarole, cantilena, dithyramb, epinikion, roundelay, spiritual
**10** plainchant, recitative
**11** bothy ballad, chansonette, rock and roll
**12** epithalamium, nursery rhyme

*See also* **poem**

*Pop songs include:*

**03** Bad
**04** 1999, Gold, Help!, True
**05** Clair, Diana, Faith, Layla, My Way, Relax, Shout
**06** Apache, Atomic, The End, Vienna, Volare
**07** Delilah, D.I.V.O.R.C.E., Hey Jude, Holiday, Imagine, Jamming, Let It Be, Rat Trap, Respect, Sailing, Starman
**08** Answer Me, Antmusic, At the Hop, Baby Love, Downtown, Love Me Do, Mamma Mia, Our House, Parklife, Peggy Sue, The Boxer, The Model, Thriller, Wannabee, Waterloo
**09** Albatross, Dance Away, I Feel Love, Maggie May, Metal Guru, Penny Lane, Praise You, Release Me, Something, Stand By Me, Wild Thing, Yesterday
**10** All Shook Up, Annie's Song, Band of Gold, Billie Jean, Blue Monday, Bye Bye Baby, House of Fun, King Creole, Lazy Sunday, Living Doll, Millennium, Moving On Up, Night Fever, Perfect Day, Purple Haze, Reet Petite, Ring of Fire, Wonderwall
**11** All Right Now, American Pie, Back for Good, Baker Street, Cathy's Clown, Firestarter, From Me to You, Glad All Over, Golden Brown, I Got You Babe, I'm Not in Love, Light My Fire, Like a Virgin, Lily the Pink, Mrs Robinson, Oliver's Army, Space Oddity, Tainted Love, Voodoo Chile
**12** All or Nothing, Bat Out of Hell, Born in the USA, Born to be Wild, Come on Eileen, Common People, Dancing Queen, Eleanor Rigby, God Only Knows, Material Girl, No Woman No Cry, The Birdy Song, West End Girls
**13** Blueberry Hill, Brass in Pocket, Design for Life, Don't You Want Me, Into the Groove, It's Not Unusual, It's Now or Never, Jailhouse Rock, Last Christmas, Long Tall Sally, Mary's Boy Child, Mull of Kintyre, Oh, Pretty Woman, Only the Lonely, Pinball Wizard, Summer Holiday, Tears in Heaven
**14** 20th Century Boy, A Hard Day's Night, Blue Suede Shoes, Good Vibrations, Karma Chameleon, Stand By Your Man, Sunny Afternoon, That'll Be the Day, The Power of Love, Waterloo Sunset, White Christmas, Wonderful World
**15** Baby One More Time, Begin the Beguine, Blowin' in the Wind, Candle in the Wind, Careless Whisper, Congratulations, God Save the Queen, Heartbreak Hotel, Hotel California, I Shot the Sheriff, Jumpin' Jack Flash, Killing me Softly, Love is all Around, Paperback Writer, Puppet on a String, Rivers of Babylon, Unchained Melody, When I Fall In Love, Yellow Submarine

*See also* **musical**

• **song and dance**
**03** ado **04** flap, fuss, stir, to-do **05** hoo-ha, tizzy **06** bother, furore, pother, tumult **09** commotion, kerfuffle **11** performance

**songster**
**06** singer **07** crooner, soloist, warbler **08** minstrel, vocalist **09** balladeer, chanteuse, chorister **10** troubadour

**songwriter**

*Songwriters and lyricists include:*

**03** **Pop** (Iggy)
**04** **Bart** (Lionel), **Cahn** (Sammy), **Cash** (Johnny), **Hart** (Lorenz), **John** (Sir Elton), **Kern** (Jerome), **Reed** (Lou), **Rice** (Sir Tim)
**05** **Berry** (Chuck), **Brown** (James), **Cohan** (George Michael), **Davis** (Miles), **Dylan** (Bob), **Holly** (Buddy), **Loewe** (Frederick), **Simon** (Paul), **Smith** (Tommy), **Sousa** (John Philip), **Swann** (Donald), **Weill** (Kurt)
**06** **Berlin** (Irving), **Coward** (Sir Noël), **Fields** (Dorothy), **Joplin** (Scott), **Lennon** (John), **Lerner** (Alan Jay), **Marley** (Bob), **Mercer** (Johnny H), **Morton** (Jelly Roll), **Oliver** (King), **Parker** (Charlie), **Porter** (Cole), **Seeger** (Pete), **Waller** (Thomas 'Fats'), **Warren** (Harry)
**07** **Collins** (Phil), **Dickson** (Barbara), **Donovan**, **Gilbert** (Sir Wiliam), **Guthrie** (Woody), **Hendrix** (Jimi), **Loesser** (Frank), **MacColl** (Ewan), **Mancini** (Henry), **Novello** (Ivor), **Orbison** (Roy), **Rodgers** (Richard), **Romberg** (Sigmund)
**08** **Coltrane** (John), **Costello** (Elvis), **Gershwin** (George), **Mitchell** (Joni), **Morrison** (Van), **Sondheim** (Stephen)
**09** **Bernstein** (Leonard), **Ellington** (Duke), **Faithfull** (Marianne), **Gillespie** (Dizzy), **McCartney** (Sir Paul)
**10** **Carmichael** (Hoagy)
**11** **Armatrading** (Joan), **Hammerstein** (Oscar), **Lloyd Webber** (Andrew, Lord), **Springsteen** (Bruce)

**sonorous**
**04** full, loud, rich **05** round **07** orotund, ringing, rounded **08** plangent, resonant, sounding **09** high-flown, ororotund **10** full-voiced, resounding **11** full-mouthed **12** full-throated, high-sounding **13** grandiloquent

**soon**
**04** anon **05** early, quick **06** pronto, timely **07** betimes, ere long, in a tick, just now, readily, shortly **08** in a hurry, in a jiffy, in no time **09** any minute, in a minute, in a moment, presently, willingly **10** before long **12** any minute now, in a short time, without delay **13** in no time at all **14** in a little while, in a moment or two, round the corner **15** in the near future

• **as soon as**
**04** once, when **07** whene'er **08** directly, eftsoons, whenever **10** right after **11** immediately, in the wake of **13** directly after

**sooner**
**06** before, rather **07** earlier, instead **08** by choice **09** for choice, in advance **10** beforehand, from choice, much rather, preferably **12** by preference **13** for preference

• **no sooner than**
**06** barely, hardly **08** only just, scarcely

• **sooner or later**
**06** at last **07** finally **08** after all, at length, in the end **10** eventually, ultimately **11** in due course **12** in the long run, subsequently

**soot**
**04** coom, smut **05** colly **06** smutch **08** gas black **09** lampblack

**soothe**
**04** balm, calm, coax, ease, hush, lull **05** accoy, allay, quiet, salve, sleek, still **06** augury, back up, cajole, pacify, settle, smooth, soften, temper **07** appease, assuage, comfort, compose, confirm, flatter, mollify, quieten, relieve, support **08** blandish, calm down, mitigate, palliate **09** alleviate **10** settle down **11** quieten down **12** foretokening, tranquillize

**soothing**
**04** soft **05** balmy **06** anetic, gentle **07** anodyne, calming, easeful, lenient, restful **08** balsamic, lenitive, relaxing **09** assuasive, demulcent, emollient, paregoric **10** palliative

**soothsayer**
**04** seer **05** augur, sibyl **07** Chaldee, diviner, prophet **08** Chaldaic, haruspex **10** foreteller, prophetess **14** prognosticator

**sophisticated**
**04** cool, gold **05** couth, slick, suave **06** hi-tech, inland, subtle, urbane **07** complex, elegant, refined, stylish, worldly **08** advanced, cultured, delicate, high-tech, joined-up, polished, seasoned, space-age **09** civilized, elaborate, executive, expensive, falsified, intricate **10** cultivated **11** adulterated, complicated, experienced, worldly wise **12** cosmopolitan **13** state-of-the-art **15** highly developed

**sophistication**
**05** poise **07** culture, finesse **08** elegance, urbanity **10** experience **11** savoir-faire, savoir-vivre, worldliness

**sophistry**
**07** fallacy, quibble, sophism **08** elenchus **09** casuistry, choplogic **10** paralogism **14** false reasoning

**soporific**
**06** hypnic, opiate, sleepy **07** poppied, Seconal® **08** hypnotic, narcotic, sedative **09** dormitive, somnolent **10** poppy water **11** anaesthetic **12** sleeping pill **13** sleep-inducing, tranquillizer **14** benzodiazepine, sleeping tablet, tranquillizing

**soppy**
**03** wet **04** daft, soft, wild **05** corny, crazy, gooey, mushy, silly, soggy, weepy **06** cheesy, gloopy, sloppy, slushy **07** cloying, maudlin, mawkish, wimpish **08** drenched **09** schmaltzy **10** lovey-dovey **11** sentimental **13** overemotional

**soprano**
**01** S **03** sop **05** mezzo **06** treble **08** castrato

**sorcerer**
**04** mage **05** magus, witch **06** magian, voodoo, wizard **07** angekok, warlock **08** angekkok, magician **09** enchanter, sorceress **10** reim-kennar **11** enchantress, necromancer **13** thaumaturgist

**sorcery**
**05** charm, magic, spell, wicca **06** voodoo **07** pisheog **08** diablery, malefice, pishogue, witching, wizardry **09** diablerie, warlockry **10** black magic, necromancy, witchcraft **11** enchantment, incantation, thaumaturgy

**sordid**
**03** low **04** base, foul, mean, vile **05** dirty, grimy, mucky, seamy, seedy **06** filthy, scungy, shabby, sleazy, soiled, tawdry **07** corrupt, debased, immoral, miserly, squalid, stained, unclean **08** degraded, grasping, shameful, wretched **09** abhorrent, debauched, dishonest, mercenary, niggardly **10** degenerate, despicable **11** ignominious, self-seeking **12** disreputable **13** dishonourable

**sore**
**03** cut, raw, red **04** bite, boil, gall, hard, hurt, sair **05** angry, blain, botch, chafe, felon, graze, grief, nasty, nerve, ulcer, upset, vexed, wound **06** aching, bitter, chafed, fester, lesion, miffed, peeved, scrape, shiver, sorrel, tender, the raw, touchy **07** abscess, annoyed, anthrax, bruised, burning, eagerly, hurting, injured, painful, quittor, wounded **08** abrasion, grievous, inflamed, offended, reddened, severely, smarting, stinging, swelling **09** afflicted, aggrieved, irritable, irritated, painfully, resentful, sensitive **10** affliction, cheesed off, distressed, grievously, laceration **12** inflammation **13** distressingly

**sorely**
**04** much **06** highly **07** greatly, notably **08** markedly, very much **09** extremely **10** noticeably, powerfully, remarkably **11** exceedingly **13** significantly, substantially

**sorrel**
**03** oca **04** soar, sore **05** soare, sorel **06** oxalis, sorell **07** bilimbi, sourock **08** shamrock, sourwood **09** carambola, sour-gourd

**sorrow**
**03** rew, rue, woe **04** moan, pain, pine, pity, ruth, weep **05** be sad, grief, mourn, night, sorra, trial, worry **06** bemoan, bewail, dolour, grieve, lament, misery, regret, repent **07** agonize, anguish, feel sad, remorse, sadness, trouble **08** distress, hardship, mourning **09** dejection, heartache, suffering, tristesse **10** affliction, compassion, contrition, heartbreak, misfortune **11** be miserable, lamentation, tribulation, unhappiness, Weltschmerz **12** wretchedness **13** feel miserable

*See also* **grief**

**sorrowful**
**02** wo **03** sad, wae, woe **05** sorry, trist, woful **06** dismal, rueful, triste, woeful **07** baleful, careful, doleful, painful, piteous, ruthful, tearful, unhappy, wailful **08** dejected, grievous, mournful, wretched **09** afflicted, depressed, miserable, woebegone **10** lamentable, lugubrious, melancholy **11** distressing, heartbroken **12** disconsolate, heart-rending, heavy-hearted

**sorry**
◇ *anagram indicator*
**02** wo **03** bad, sad, woe **04** mean, poor **05** moved, upset **06** dismal, rueful, simple **07** ashamed, pitiful, pitying, unhappy **08** contrite, grievous, pathetic, penitent, shameful, wretched **09** concerned, miserable, regretful, repentant, worthless **10** apologetic, distressed, remorseful, shamefaced **11** distressing, guilt-ridden, sympathetic, unfortunate **12** contemptible, heart-rending **13** compassionate, understanding

• **be sorry for**
**03** rew, rue **06** repent **08** forthink

**sort**
◇ *anagram indicator*
**03** fit, ilk, lot, set **04** beat, geld, kind, make, race, rank, sift, type **05** agree, allot, befit, brand, breed, class, genre, genus, grade, group, order, stamp, style, woman **06** accord, adjust, assign, divide, family, kidney, manner, nature, parcel, person, punish, screen, select **07** arrange, company, consort, dispose, fashion, procure, provide, quality, species, variety **08** category, classify, organize, separate **09** catalogue, character, segregate **10** categorize, collection, distribute, put in order **11** description, systematize **12** denomination

• **out of sorts**
◇ *anagram indicator*
**03** ill **04** mean, sick, weak **05** crook, cross, dicky, frail, narky, nohow, ratty, rough, seedy **06** ailing, crabby, crummy, feeble, groggy, grumpy, infirm, laid up, poorly, queasy, rotten, shirty, snappy, unwell **07** crabbed, grouchy, in a huff, in a mood, in a sulk, run down, run-down, stroppy **08** below par, choleric, diseased, nohowish **09** bedridden, crotchety, fractious, impatient, in a bad way, irritable, off-colour, unhealthy **10** in a bad mood **11** bad-tempered **13** mops and brooms, quick-tempered **14** down in the dumps, down in the mouth **15** under the weather

• **sort of**
◇ *anagram indicator*
**04** a bit **05** kinda, quite **06** fairly, kind of, pretty, rather **07** a little **08** slightly, somewhat **10** moderately, relatively **12** to some degree, to some extent

• **sort out**
**04** rank **05** class, grade, group, order,

solve **06** choose, divide, select **07** arrange, clear up, resolve, work out **08** classify, organize, put right, separate **09** segregate **10** categorize, put in order

**sortie**
**04** raid, rush **05** foray, sally, swoop **06** attack, charge **07** assault, outfall **08** invasion **09** offensive

**so-so**
**02** OK **04** fair **06** not bad **07** average, neutral **08** adequate, mediocre, middling, moderate, ordinary, passable **09** tolerable **11** indifferent, respectable **12** run-of-the-mill **13** no great shakes, unexceptional **14** comme ci comme ça, fair to middling **15** undistinguished

**soubriquet** *see* **sobriquet, soubriquet**

**sought-after**
**02** in **03** big, hip, hot, now **04** cool **05** liked **06** modish, trendy, wanted **07** admired, desired, popular **08** approved, favoured, in demand, in favour **09** favourite, well-liked **10** all the rage **11** fashionable **13** in great demand

**soul**
**02** ba, ka **03** âme, ego, man **04** alma, life, mind **05** anima, model, shade, woman **06** person, pneuma, psyche, reason, spirit **07** element, epitome, essence, example, feeling, passion **08** creature, humanity, inner man, sympathy **09** character, inner self, intellect **10** compassion, embodiment, human being, individual, inner being, inner woman, tenderness, vital force **11** inspiration, sensitivity **12** appreciation **13** heart of hearts, understanding **15** personification

**soulful**
**06** moving **08** eloquent, mournful, profound **09** emotional, heartfelt, sensitive **10** expressive, meaningful

**soulless**
**04** cold, dead, mean **05** bleak, cruel, empty **06** unkind **07** callous, ignoble, inhuman **08** lifeless **09** unfeeling **10** mechanical, spiritless **11** dehumanized **12** mean-spirited **13** characterless, uninteresting, unsympathetic **14** soul-destroying

**sound**
◇ *homophone indicator*
**03** din, fit, say, voe **04** deep, firm, goad, good, hale, look, mean, safe, sane, seem, tend, test, toll, tone, trig, true, vibe, well **05** firth, fiord, fjord, gauge, go off, inlet, noise, plumb, probe, radio, right, sense, solid, swoon, tease, tenor, utter, valid, voice, whole **06** appear, cogent, deeply, fathom, intact, notion, proven, robust, secure, severe, strait, strong, sturdy, timbre, unhurt **07** channel, declare, earshot, estuary, examine, express, extreme, feeling, greatly, healthy, inspect, intense, logical, measure, passage, perfect, provoke, publish, resound, serious, weighty **08** announce, complete, orthodox, proclaim, profound, rational, reliable, resonate, severely, thorough, unbroken, very much, vigorous **09** enunciate, excellent, extremely, intensely, judicious, pronounce, resonance, seriously, undamaged, uninjured, very great, wholesome **10** articulate, completely, dependable, impression, profoundly, reasonable, thoroughly, unimpaired, vigorously **11** disease-free, implication, in good shape, investigate, reverberate, substantial, trustworthy, well-founded **12** in fine fettle, in good health, sound as a bell, well-grounded **13** authoritative, reverberation **15** in good condition

*Sounds include:*

**03** cry, hum, pip, pop, sob, tap
**04** bang, beep, boom, buzz, chug, clap, echo, fizz, hiss, honk, hoot, moan, peal, ping, plop, ring, roar, sigh, slam, snap, thud, tick, ting, toot, wail, whiz, yell, yoop
**05** blare, blast, bleep, chime, chink, chirm, clack, clang, clank, clash, click, clink, clunk, crack, crash, creak, drone, grate, groan, knock, plonk, skirl, slurp, smack, sniff, snore, snort, swish, throb, thump, twang, vroom, whine, whirr, whish, whizz, whoop
**06** bubble, crunch, gabble, gollar, goller, gurgle, hiccup, jangle, jingle, murmur, patter, rattle, report, rumble, rustle, scrape, scream, sizzle, splash, squeak, squeal, tinkle, whoosh
**07** brattle, chatter, clatter, crackle, explode, graunch, grizzle, pitapat, screech, squelch, thunder, whimper, whistle
**08** splutter
**11** taratantara

*Animal sounds include:*

**03** baa, bay, caw, coo, kaw, low, mew, moo, wee, yap
**04** bark, bell, blat, bray, bump, crow, hiss, honk, hoot, howl, purr, roar, woof, yawp, yelp, yowl
**05** bleat, cheep, chirp, cluck, crake, croak, groin, growl, grunt, miaow, neigh, pewit, quack, scape, snarl, tweet
**06** bellow, cackle, gobble, heehaw, peewit, squawk, squeak, warble, whinny
**07** chirrup, gruntle, looning, screech, trumpet, twitter, whicker
**09** caterwaul

*Geographical sounds include:*

**03** Hoy, Rum
**04** Bute, Calf, Crow, Deer, Eigg, Holm, Iona, Jura, King, Mull, Papa, Rock, Yell
**05** Barra, Canna, Cross, Exuma, Gigha, Inner, Islay, Luing, Puget, Sanda, Shuna, Sleat
**06** Breton, Harris, Norton, Pabbay, Raasay, Ramsey, Sanday, Shiant, Turner
**07** Arisaig, Bardsey, Caswell, Cuillin, Gairsay, McMurdo, Milford, Pamlico, St Mary's
**08** Auskerry, Bluemull, Breaksea, Colgrave, Doubtful, Kotzebue, Taransay
**09** Albemarle, Casiguran, Currituck, Eynhallow, Lancaster, Shapinsay
**10** Chandeleur, Cumberland, Kilbrannan, King George, Long Island, New Georgia, Possession
**11** Mississippi, Roes Welcome
**12** Prince Albert
**13** Prince William

• **by the sound of it**
◇ *homophone indicator*

• **sound measure/unit**
**02** dB **03** bel **04** phon, sone **07** decibel, phoneme, segment **09** kilohertz

• **sound out**
**03** ask **04** pump **05** probe **06** survey **07** canvass, examine, suss out **08** question, research **11** investigate

**soundly**
**04** fast **05** fully, quite, tight **06** deeply **07** greatly, solidly, totally, utterly, validly **08** entirely, securely, severely, very much **09** downright, extremely, intensely, logically, perfectly, seriously **10** absolutely, completely, dependably, profoundly, reasonably, thoroughly, vigorously **15** authoritatively

**soundtrack**
**10** theme music

**soup**
◇ *anagram indicator*

*Soups include:*

**03** dal, pea, pho
**04** cawl, crab, dhal, game, miso
**05** adrak, blaff, broth, egusi, gumbo, locro, misua, rasam, snert, stock
**06** ajiaco, asapao, barley, birria, bisque, borsch, cocido, congee, fennel, guacho, harira, lentil, noodle, oxtail, pazole, posole, potage, potato, reuben, sambar, tomato, turtle, won ton
**07** borscht, chicken, chowder, tarator, turbana
**08** borschch, broccoli, callaloo, chirmole, consommé, ful nabed, gazpacho, halászlé, julienne, mondongo, mushroom, okroshka, sancocho, solianka, split pea
**09** asparagus, bird's nest, cacciucco, Clanallen, escabeche, fasolatha, pea and ham, pepperpot, picadillo, quimbombo, royal game, rozsolnyk, shark's fin, tom kha gai, white foam
**10** avgolemono, caldo verde, minestrone, mock turtle, mole de olla, sauerkraut, superkanja, watercress
**11** clam chowder, cock-a-leekie, cullen skink, French onion, gaeng

som kai, gaeng som pla, Scotch broth, tom yam goong, vichyssoise
12 bouneschlupp, brown Windsor, cockieleekie, guriltai shul, mulligatawny
13 bouillabaisse, chicken noodle, cream of tomato, potato and leek, stracciatella
14 lentil and bacon
15 Queen Anne's broth

**sour**
**03** bad, off **04** acid, rank, tart, tiff, tift, turn **05** acerb, acidy, aygre, eager, heavy, nasty, ratty, sharp, spoil, surly, tangy, wersh **06** acetic, bitter, canker, crusty, morose, rancid, shirty, strong, turned **07** acerbic, acetous, austere, crabbed, curdled, envenom, grouchy, peevish, pungent, subacid **08** alienate, churlish, embitter, verjuice, vinegary **09** acidulent, acidulous, resentful **10** disenchant, embittered, exacerbate, exasperate, make bitter, unpleasant **11** acrimonious, bad-tempered, ill-tempered **12** disagreeable, inharmonious, unsuccessful

**source**
**03** urn **04** font, head, mine, rise, root, well, ylem **05** cause, fount, radix, start, stock **06** author, origin, sourse, spring, supply, whence **07** surging **08** wellhead **09** authority, beginning, generator, good hands, informant, principle, rootstock, water head **10** derivation, originator, primordium, provenance, springhead, wellspring **11** fons et origo **12** commencement, fountainhead

**sourpuss**
**04** crab **05** grump, shrew **06** grouse, kvetch, misery, whiner **07** killjoy, whinger **08** buzzkill, grumbler **10** crosspatch **14** dog in the manger

**souse**
**03** dip, ear, sou **04** dash, duck, dunk, sink, soak, wash **05** douse, plump, smite, souce, sowce, sowse, steep, thump **06** drench, impact, pickle, plunge, sowsse, strike **07** ducking, immerse, impinge **08** drunkard, marinade, marinate, saturate, submerge, suddenly **09** drenching

**south**
◇ *tail selection down indicator*
**01** S **02** So **03** Sth **04** Midi

**South Africa**
**02** SA, ZA **03** RSA, ZAF **04** S Afr

**South African**
**02** SA **04** S Afr

**South America** *see* **America**; **god, goddess**

**South Carolina**
**02** SC

**South Dakota**
**02** SD **04** S Dak

**south-east, south-eastern**
**02** SE

**southern**
**01** S **05** south **07** austral **09** southerly **10** meridional

**south-west, south-western**
**02** SW

**souvenir**
**05** relic, steal, token **06** trophy **07** memento, purloin, relique **08** keepsake, reminder **11** remembrance

**sovereign**
**01** K, L, Q **02** ER, HM **03** bar, sov **04** king, quid, tsar **05** chief, crown, pound, queen, royal, ruler, squid **06** canary, couter, kingly, nicker, prince, ruling, shiner, sovran, utmost **07** emperor, empress, extreme, monarch, queenly, smacker, supreme, thick'un **08** absolute, autocrat, dominant, imperial, majestic, princely **09** paramount, potentate, principal, unlimited **10** autonomous, self-ruling, unequalled, unrivalled **11** independent, outstanding, predominant **12** jimmy-o'goblin **13** pound sterling, self-governing

*See also* **king**; **queen**

**sovereignty**
**03** raj **04** sway **07** primacy, royalty **08** autonomy, chiefdom, dominion, imperium, kingship, regality, synarchy **09** chiefship, princedom, queenship, supremacy **10** ascendancy, domination, suzerainty **11** condominium, pre-eminence **12** independence **13** thalassocracy, thalattocracy **14** rangatiratanga, self-government

**sow**
**03** elt, saw **04** gilt, seed, yelt **05** drill, lodge, plant, strew **06** spread **07** bestrew, implant, scatter **08** disperse, seminate **09** broadcast **10** distribute, inseminate **11** disseminate

*See also* **pig**

**sozzled**
◇ *anagram indicator*
**05** happy, merry, tight, tipsy **06** blotto, tiddly **07** drunken, pickled, squiffy, tiddley **09** crapulent, plastered **10** inebriated **11** intoxicated

**spa**
**06** spring **07** Kurhaus

*Spas include:*

**03** Dax
**04** Bath
**05** Baden, Baños, Epsom, Sochi, Vichy
**06** Aachen, Boston, Buxton, Ilkley, Trebon
**07** Lourdes, Malvern, Matlock
**08** Carlsbad, Shearsby, Woodhall
**09** Bad Elster, Droitwich, Harrogate, Marienbad, Velingrad
**10** Baden Baden, Cheltenham, Leamington
**11** Bad Dürrheim, Scarborough
**12** Strathpeffer
**13** Aix-la-Chapelle, Knaresborough
**14** Tunbridge Wells

**space**
**02** em, en **03** gap **04** area, lung, play, room, seat, span, time, void **05** array, blank, break, chasm, order, place, range, scope, shift, spell, stint, sweep **06** cosmos, extent, galaxy, lacuna, leeway, margin, period, volume **07** arrange, be apart, dispose, expanse, opening, stretch **08** capacity, interval, latitude, omission, set apart, space out, universe **09** amplitude, clearance, deep space, elbow-room, expansion, string out **10** empty space, interstice, Lebensraum, outer space, put in order, stretch out **11** the Milky Way **12** intermission **13** accommodation

*Space travel-related terms include:*

**03** bus, ELV, ESA, ISS, LOX, LRV, MCC
**04** NASA
**05** abort, flyby, orbit
**06** CAPCOM, drogue, G force, hydyne, launch, module, rocket
**07** booster, coolant, docking, lift-off, mission, payload, re-entry, shuttle, vidicon
**08** attitude, blast-off, free-fall, fuel cell, fuel tank, lunanaut, moonwalk, nose cone, sloshing
**09** astronaut, cosmonaut, hydrazine, launch pad, light year, lunarnaut, spaceship, space suit
**10** heat shield, pogo effect, propellant, rendezvous, spacecraft, space probe, trajectory
**11** lunar module, solar system, zero gravity
**12** ascent module, launch window, lunar landing, man on the moon, microgravity, space station
**13** command module, descent module, jet propulsion, launch vehicle, space sickness
**14** escape velocity, mission control, weightlessness
**15** re-entry corridor

*Spacecraft include:*

**02** LM
**03** ISS, LEM, Mir
**06** Skylab, Tardis
**07** Gemini 4, Vostok 1, Vostok 5, Vostok 6
**08** Apollo 11, Apollo 13, Apollo 17, Columbia, Freedom 7, Nostromo, Red Dwarf, Sputnik 1, Sputnik 2, Voskhod 1, Voskhod 2
**09** Discovery, Endeavour, Liberator, Pioneer 10, Shenzhou V
**10** Challenger, USS Voyager
**11** Fireball XL5, Heart of Gold
**12** SS Discovery 1, Thunderbird 3, Thunderbird 5
**13** Moonbase Alpha, USS Enterprise

*See also* **probe**

**spaceman, spacewoman** *see* **astronaut**

**spacious**
**03** big **04** huge, open, vast, wide **05** ample, broad, large, roomy **07** immense, sizable **08** palatial, sizeable **09** capacious, expansive, extensive, uncrowded **10** commodious

**spade**
**01** S **03** loy **04** pick, spay, spit **05** graft, slane, spado, spayd **06** paddle, pattle, pettle, spayad, tuskar, tusker **07** cas crom, tushkar, tushker, twiscar **08** caschrom **09** flaughter **11** paddle-staff **12** breastplough
• **spades**
**01** S

**spadework**
**06** labour **08** drudgery, homework **10** donkey-work, foundation, groundwork **11** preparation **15** preliminary work

**Spain**
**01** E **03** ESP **06** España
• **in Spain**
◇ *foreign word indicator*

**span**
**04** arch, last, link, term, time, yoke **05** cover, cross, fresh, piece, range, reach, scope, spell, vault **06** bridge, extend, extent, length, period, spread, wind up **07** compass, include, measure, overlay, stretch **08** bestride, distance, duration, interval, traverse **09** encompass **10** overbridge

**spangle**
**01** O **06** sequin **07** glitter **09** paillette

**Spaniard**
**03** don

**spaniel**
**04** mean **07** fawning

*Spaniels include:*

**03** toy
**04** land
**05** field, water
**06** cocker, Sussex
**07** clumber
**08** Blenheim, papillon, springer
**10** Irish water, Maltese dog
**11** King Charles

**Spanish** *see* **day**; **month**; **number**

**spank**
**03** tan **04** cane, slap **05** smack, whack **06** paddle, strike, thrash, thwack, wallop **07** slipper **15** put over your knee

**spanking**
**04** fast, fine, very **05** brand, brisk, quick, scuds, smart, swift **06** lively, snappy, speedy **07** exactly, totally, utterly **08** gleaming, spirited, striking, vigorous **09** energetic **10** absolutely, completely, paddy-whack, positively, strikingly **12** invigorating

**spanner**
**03** key **06** wrench **12** monkey wrench

**spar**
**03** bar, box **04** gaff, pole, rail, shut, spat, tiff **05** argue, scrap, sprit **06** barite, bicker, fasten, rafter, ricker, steeve **07** barytes, contend, contest, dispute, fall out, quarrel, wrangle, wrestle **08** bowsprit, cryolite, mainboom, skirmish, squabble **09** outrigger **10** martingale **11** torpedo boom **12** swinging-boom, wollastonite **13** rhodochrosite

**spare**
**04** bony, free, gash, give, hain, lank, lean, over, save, slim, thin **05** allow, avoid, extra, gaunt, grant, guard, hoard, scant, skimp, stint **06** afford, defend, frugal, let off, meagre, modest, pardon, scanty, secure, skimpy, skinny, unused **07** forbear, forgive, leisure, not harm, protect, provide, refrain, release, reserve, scraggy, scrawny, slender, sparing, surplus **08** buckshee, leftover, part with, reprieve, unwanted, withhold **09** auxiliary, do without, emergency, remaining, safeguard, subsecive **10** additional, subsidiary, take care of, unoccupied **11** show mercy to, superfluous **12** dispense with **13** manage without, supernumerary, supplementary **15** all skin and bones
• **to spare**
**05** extra **06** unused **07** surplus **08** left over **09** in reserve, remaining
• **with little to spare**
**04** fine **06** narrow

**sparing**
**05** canny, mingy, scant **06** frugal, meagre, scarce, stingy, strait **07** careful, miserly, prudent, thrifty **09** penurious **10** economical **11** close-fisted, tight-fisted

**sparingly**
**06** nighly **08** frugally, meagrely, scrimply, stingily **09** carefully, prudently **12** economically

**spark**
**03** bit, jot **04** atom, beau, funk, hint, iota **05** flake, flame, flare, flash, gleam, glint, lover, scrap, spunk, touch, trace **06** kindle **07** animate, bluette, flaught, flicker, glimmer, sparkle, vestige **08** skerrick **09** scintilla **10** suggestion **11** electrician
• **spark off**
**04** stir **05** cause, start **06** excite, incite, kindle, prompt, set off **07** inspire, provoke, trigger **08** occasion, start off, touch off **09** stimulate **10** give rise to, trigger off **11** precipitate

**sparkle**
**03** vim **04** beam, brio, dash, fire, fizz, glow, life, zest **05** flash, gleam, glint, shine, spark **06** bubble, dazzle, energy, spirit **07** be witty, emicate, flicker, glimmer, glisten, glister, glitter, pizzazz, shimmer, twinkle **08** be bubbly, be lively, radiance, vitality, vivacity **09** animation, coruscate, emication **10** be animated, be spirited, brilliance, ebullience, effervesce, enthusiasm, get-up-and-go, liveliness **11** be ebullient, be vivacious, coruscation, scintillate **13** scintillation **14** be effervescent, be enthusiastic

**sparkling**
**05** fizzy, witty **06** bubbly, lively **07** emicant **08** aglitter, animated, flashing, gleaming, spritzig **09** brilliant, frizzante, pétillant, twinkling **10** carbonated, glistening, glittering **11** coruscating, scintillant **12** effervescent **13** scintillating
• **make sparkling**
**09** carbonate

**sparrow**
**04** tody **05** sprug **06** mossie **07** dunnock, pinnock, spadger, titling **08** accentor, prunella, ricebird **09** paddy-bird **11** whitethroat **13** hedge-accentor

**sparse**
**04** rare, thin **06** meagre, scanty, scarce, slight **07** scrawny **08** scattery, sporadic **09** scattered **10** infrequent

**sparsely**
**08** meagrely, scantily, scarcely, slightly **12** sporadically

**spartan**
**05** bleak, hardy, harsh, plain **06** frugal, severe, simple, strict **07** ascetic, austere, harmost, joyless, laconic **08** rigorous **09** stringent, temperate **10** abstemious **11** disciplined, self-denying **12** militaristic

**spasm**
**03** fit, tic **04** bout, grip, jerk **05** burst, cramp, crick, gripe, spell, start, thraw, throe, throw, tonus **06** access, attack, clonus, frenzy, hippus, throwe, twitch **07** seizure, trismus **08** eruption, outburst, paroxysm **10** blepharism, convulsion, tonic spasm **11** clonic spasm, contraction, laryngismus **12** childcrowing

**spasmodic**
◇ *anagram indicator*
**05** jerky **06** fitful **07** erratic, spastic **08** periodic, sporadic **09** irregular **10** convulsive, occasional **12** intermittent

**spasmodically**
**08** off and on, on and off **11** now and again **12** occasionally, periodically, sporadically **14** intermittently

**spate**
**04** flow, rush **05** flood, speat **06** deluge, series **07** torrent **10** outpouring

**spatter**
◇ *anagram indicator*
**03** jap **04** daub, jaup, soil **05** dirty, spray **06** bedaub, dabble, shower, splash **07** bestrew, scatter, speckle, splodge **08** splatter, sprinkle **09** bespatter **10** besprinkle

**spawn**
**03** fry, roe **04** blot, make, redd, seed, spat, spit, teem **05** brood, cause, culch,

sperm **06** create, cultch, lead to **07** bring on, produce **08** engender, generate **09** offspring, originate **10** bring about, give rise to

**spay**
**03** fix **04** geld **05** spade, spayd **06** doctor, neuter, spayad **08** castrate **09** sterilize **10** emasculate

**speak**
◇ *homophone indicator*
**03** gab, say, yak **04** chat, mang, pipe, talk, tell, word **05** argue, sound, state, utter, voice **06** witter **07** address, chatter, declaim, declare, discuss, expound, express, lecture, mention **08** converse, describe, harangue, platform **09** enunciate, hold forth, pronounce **10** articulate **11** communicate **13** have a word with

• **speak angrily**
**04** pelt

• **speak for**
**06** act for **08** stand for **09** represent **15** speak on behalf of

• **speak of**
**05** voice **07** discuss, mention, refer to **13** make mention of **15** make reference to

• **speak out**
**03** ope **04** open **06** defend **07** protest, support **11** say publicly, speak openly

• **speak tediously**
**05** prose

• **speak to**
**04** warn **05** scold **06** accost, attest, bounce, carpet, rebuke **07** address, bawl out, discuss, lecture, rouse on, tell off, tick off, upbraid **08** admonish **09** dress down, go crook at, pull apart, reprimand, take apart **10** go to town on **11** bring to book **13** have a word with **14** throw the book at **15** give someone hell

• **speak up**
**06** defend **07** protest, support **10** talk loudly **11** say publicly, speak openly **14** raise your voice, talk more loudly

**speaker**
**05** mouth **06** orator, talker, woofer **07** tweeter **08** lecturer, top tweet **09** spokesman, subwoofer **10** mouthpiece, prolocutor **11** first person, spokeswoman **12** spokesperson

**spear**
**03** ash, gad, gig **04** dart, gade, gaid, pike, pile, reed **05** lance, pilum, spire, stick **06** glaive, gleave, waster **07** assagai, assegai, harpoon, javelin, leister, trident **08** assegaai, gavelock, lancegay **09** boar-spear, demi-lance, fish-spear, handstaff, truncheon **12** burn the water

**spearhead**
**03** van **04** head, lead **05** front, guide **06** launch, leader **07** pioneer **08** initiate, overseer, vanguard **09** front line **11** cutting edge, trailblazer **15** leading position

**special**
◇ *anagram indicator*
**01** S **02** sp **05** exact, major **06** choice, select, unique **07** notable, precise, unusual **08** detailed, intimate, peculiar, singular, specific **09** different, dividuous, exclusive, important, memorable, momentous, red-letter **10** individual, noteworthy, particular, remarkable **11** distinctive, exceptional, outstanding, significant **13** distinguished, extraordinary **14** characteristic

**specialist**
**06** brains, expert, master **07** attaché **08** boutique **09** authority **10** consultant **11** connoisseur **12** professional

*Specialists include:*

**03** vet
**07** Arabist, biblist, cambist, chemist
**08** alienist, apiarist, aquarist, arborist, botanist, canonist
**09** archivist, biblicist, biologist, Braillist, campanist, Celticist
**10** aerologist, aeronomist, agrologist, agronomist, algebraist, algologist, batologist, biochemist, bryologist
**11** carpologist
**12** apiculturist, bibliopolist, biophysicist, bioscientist, cerographist, choreologist
**13** acupuncturist, agrobiologist, anagrammatist, arachnologist, archaeologist, calligraphist, campanologist, carcinologist, chirographist
**14** aerodynamicist, anthropologist, bacteriologist, chalcographist
**15** agriculturalist, arboriculturist, biopsychologist, biotechnologist

*See also* **medical**

**speciality**
**03** bag **04** gift **05** field, forte **06** talent **07** feature **08** strength **09** specialty **11** area of study **12** field of study

**specialization**
**05** focus **12** special study **13** concentration **14** special subject **15** special interest

**specialize**
**05** major, study **06** follow **07** focus on, major in, specify **13** concentrate on, differentiate

**specially**
◇ *anagram indicator*
**07** express **08** uniquely **09** expressly **10** distinctly, explicitly **11** exclusively **12** in particular, particularly, specifically

**species**
**02** sp **03** spp **04** kind, sort, type **05** breed, class, genus, group **07** variety **08** category **10** collection **11** description

**specific**
**03** set **05** exact, fixed **07** express, limited, precise, special, trivial **08** clear-cut, concrete, definite, detailed, explicit **10** determined, particular **11** unambiguous, unequivocal, well-defined

**specifically**
**07** clearly, exactly, plainly **09** expressly, specially **10** definitely, distinctly **11** exclusively **12** in particular, particularly **13** unambiguously

**specification**
**04** item, spec **06** detail, naming **07** listing **09** condition, statement **10** particular **11** delineation, description, designation, instruction, requirement, stipulation **13** qualification

**specify**
**04** cite, list, name **05** limit, state **06** assign, define, detail, set out **07** frutify, itemize, mention **08** describe, indicate, spell out **09** delineate, designate, enumerate, stipulate **10** condescend, specialize **13** particularize **14** condescend upon

**specimen**
**04** copy, sort, swab, type **05** assay, model, piece **06** person, sample **07** example, exhibit, pattern **08** exemplar, instance, paradigm **12** illustration **14** representative

**specious**
**04** fair **05** false, showy **06** untrue **07** pageant, unsound **08** imposing **09** beautiful, casuistic, deceptive, fair-faced, plausible, sophistic **10** fallacious, misleading **11** sophistical

**speck**
**03** bit, dot, fat, jot, pip **04** atom, blot, flaw, iota, mark, mite, mote, peep, spek, spot, whit **05** bacon, fault, fleck, grain, peepe, shred, stain, trace **06** defect, sheave, tittle **07** blemish, floater, spangle, speckle **08** particle

**speckled**
**03** gay **05** mealy **06** dotted, mealie, spotty, ticked **07** brinded, brindle, dappled, flecked, mottled, spotted **08** brindled, freckled, stippled **09** fleckered, sprinkled **11** lentiginous **13** trout-coloured

**spectacle**
**04** shew, show **05** scene, sight **06** marvel, object, parade, wonder **07** display, pageant, picture **09** bullfight, curiosity, pageantry, raree-show **10** exhibition, outspeckle, phenomenon **11** performance **12** extravaganza, son et lumière

**spectacles**
**02** OO **05** specs **06** specks **07** glasses, goggles, lorgnon **08** bifocals, cheaters, gig-lamps, horn-rims **09** barnacles, glass eyes, lorgnette, preserves, trifocals **10** eyeglasses, sunglasses, varifocals **13** granny glasses, pebble-glasses **14** National Health, pinhole glasses

**spectacular**
**04** show **05** grand **06** daring
**07** amazing, display, opulent, pageant
**08** dazzling, dramatic, glorious, splendid, striking, stunning
**09** colourful, spectacle **10** exhibition, flamboyant, impressive, remarkable, staggering **11** astonishing, eye-catching, magnificent, outstanding, resplendent, sensational
**12** breathtaking, extravaganza, ostentatious **13** extraordinary

**spectacularly**
**09** amazingly **10** gloriously, remarkably, strikingly, stunningly
**12** impressively, staggeringly
**13** astonishingly, magnificently, outstandingly, sensationally
**15** extraordinarily

**spectator**
**06** viewer **07** watcher, witness
**08** beholder, looker-on, observer, onlooker, passer-by **09** bystander, ringsider **10** eyewitness, groundling, rubberneck, supervisor, wallflower

**spectral**
**05** eerie, weird **06** spooky **07** ghostly, phantom, shadowy, uncanny
**08** eldritch **09** phantosme, unearthly
**11** disembodied, incorporeal
**12** supernatural **13** insubstantial

**spectre**
**04** fear **05** bogle, dread, ghost, larva, shade, spook **06** bodach, Empusa, menace, shadow, spirit, threat, vision, wraith **07** phantom **08** phantasm, presence, revenant, visitant
**09** phantosme **10** apparition

**spectrum**
**05** gamme, prism, range **07** rainbow
**10** after-image

**speculate**
**04** muse, risk, view **05** guess
**06** gamble, hazard, wonder
**07** examine, imagine, observe, reflect, suppose, surmise, venture **08** cogitate, consider, meditate, theorize
**10** conjecture, deliberate
**11** contemplate, hypothesize

**speculation**
**04** risk, spec **05** flier, flyer, guess
**06** gamble, hazard, theory, vision, wisdom **07** flutter, surmise, theoric, venture, viewing **08** gambling, ideology, observer **09** adventure, guesswork, theorique **10** conjecture, hypothesis, theorizing **11** imagination, supposition **12** deliberation
**13** consideration, contemplation, flight of fancy **14** a shot in the dark

**speculative**
**04** iffy **05** dicey, risky, vague **06** chancy
**08** abstract, academic, notional, unproven **09** hazardous, tentative, theoretic, uncertain **10** indefinite
**11** conjectural, theoretical
**12** hypothetical, transcendent
**13** suppositional, unpredictable

**speculator**
**04** bear, bull **05** piker **07** gambler, lookout **08** boursier, watchman
**09** pinhooker **10** adventurer, land-jobber **11** adventuress, speculatist, speculatrix, stockjobber **12** money-spinner

**speech**
◇ *anagram indicator*
◇ *homophone indicator*
**03** say **04** rant, talk **05** lingo, spiel, voice **06** accent, homily, jargon, korero, parole, patter, rumour, saying, sermon, tirade, tongue **07** address, dialect, diction, lecture, mention, message, oration **08** colloquy, delivery, dialogue, diatribe, harangue, language, parlance **09** discourse, elocution, monologue, philippic, soliloquy, utterance **11** enunciation
**12** articulation, conversation
**13** communication, pronunciation

*Parts of speech include:*

**01** a, n, v
**02** vb, vi, vt
**03** adj, adv, art
**04** noun, prep, verb
**06** adnoun, adverb, gerund, plural, prefix, suffix
**07** article, pronoun
**08** singular
**09** adjective, gerundive
**10** common noun, connective, copulative, participle, proper noun
**11** conjunction, phrasal verb, preposition
**12** abbreviation, interjection
**13** auxiliary verb
**14** transitive verb
**15** definite article, relative pronoun

• **speech defect**
**04** lisp **07** stammer, stutter
**10** impediment

**speechless**
**03** mum **04** dumb, mute **06** aghast, amazed, silent **07** shocked
**08** unworded **09** astounded, voiceless
**10** dumbstruck, struck dumb, tongue-tied **11** dumbfounded, obmutescent
**12** inarticulate, languageless, lost for words **13** thunderstruck

**speed**
**01** v **02** AS **03** bat, mph **04** belt, clip, dash, fare, knot, pace, pelt, race, rate, rush, tear, zoom **05** haste, hurry, tempo, whisk **06** career, cruise, gallop, hasten, hurtle, sprint **07** quicken, succeed, success **08** alacrity, celerity, despatch, dispatch, momentum, rapidity, step on it, velocity **09** bowl along, quickness, swiftness
**10** accelerate, promptness
**11** amphetamine **12** acceleration, step on the gas **14** step on the juice
**15** expeditiousness, put your foot down

• **increase speed**
**03** gun **10** accelerate, give the gun

• **speed up**
**05** hurry **06** hasten, open up, spur on, step up **07** advance, forward, further, promote, quicken **08** expedite, go faster, step on it **09** stimulate
**10** accelerate, facilitate **11** drive faster, gather speed, pick up speed, precipitate, put on a spurt **12** gain momentum, step on the gas **14** step on the juice **15** put your foot down

**speedily**
**04** fast, post **06** pronto **07** betimes, hastily, on wings, quickly, rapidly, swiftly **08** in a hurry, promptly
**09** hurriedly, posthaste **11** at the double
**12** a mile a minute, lickety-split
**13** expeditiously **14** at a rate of knots, hell for leather **15** like the clappers

**speedwell**
**06** hen-bit **08** bird's-eye, fluellin, neckweed, veronica **09** brooklime

**speedy**
**03** pdq **04** fast **05** hasty, nippy, quick, rapid, swift, zappy, zippy **06** nimble, prompt **07** cursory, express, hurried, summary **09** immediate, posthaste
**11** expeditious, precipitate **15** pretty damn quick

**spell**
**02** go **03** fit, hex, jag, ren, rin, run
**04** bout, mean, mojo, pull, rest, rune, rung, scan, scat, span, tack, term, time, turn **05** augur, charm, imply, magic, patch, shift, skatt, spurt, stint, trick, weird **06** allure, course, extent, grigri, herald, lead to, lesson, period, season, signal, snatch, trance, whammy
**07** cantrip, enchant, glamour, innings, portend, presage, promise, relieve, session, signify, sorcery, stretch, suggest **08** amount to, greegree, grisgris, indicate, interval, splinter, witchery **09** discourse, influence, magnetism **10** attraction, open sesame
**11** abracadabra, bewitchment, conjuration, contemplate, enchantment, fascination, incantation, paternoster **12** drawing power, entrancement, supplication

• **cast a spell on**
**05** charm **07** attract, bewitch, enchant, encharm, enthral **09** captivate, fascinate, mesmerize

• **spell out**
**06** detail **07** clarify, explain, specify
**09** elucidate, emphasize, make clear, stipulate

**spellbinding**
**08** gripping, riveting **10** bewitching, enchanting, entrancing **11** captivating, enthralling, fascinating, mesmerizing

**spellbound**
**04** rapt **07** charmed, gripped, riveted
**09** bewitched, enchanted, entranced
**10** captivated, enraptured, enthralled, fascinated, hypnotized, mesmerized, transfixed **11** transported

**spelling**
**02** sp **11** orthography

**spend**
**02** do **03** use **04** blow, fill, kill, live,

pass, shed, ware **05** apply, put in, use up, waste **06** devote, employ, expend, finish, invest, lay out, occupy, pay out, take up **07** consume, cough up, exhaust, fork out, fritter, outwear, stump up **08** contrive, disburse, shell out, squander **09** splash out, while away **14** spend like water

**spendthrift**
**06** waster **07** wastrel **08** prodigal, profuser, unthrift, wasteful **10** high-roller, profligate, squanderer
**11** extravagant, improvident, scattergood, squandering

**spent**
**04** gone, used **05** all in, weary
**06** bushed, done in, effete, fagged, pooped, used up, zonked **07** drained, wearied, whacked, worn out **08** burnt out, consumed, dead beat, dog-tired, expended, finished, jiggered, overworn, tired out, weakened
**09** exhausted, fagged out, knackered, pooped out, shattered **11** debilitated, tuckered out

**sperm**
**04** eggs **05** brood, semen, spawn
**06** gamete **07** sex cell **08** germ cell
**09** offspring **10** spermaceti
**11** spermatozoa **12** seminal fluid, spermatozoon

**spew**
**04** barf, emit, gush, puke **05** belch, issue, retch, spurt, vomit **06** sick up
**07** bring up, chuck up, chunder, fetch up, spit out, throw up **08** disgorge
**11** regurgitate

**sphere**
**03** orb, set **04** area, ball, band, rank
**05** class, crowd, field, globe, group, orbit, range, realm, round, scope, world **06** circle, clique, domain, extent, planet **07** compass, globule
**08** capacity, function, province, universe **09** territory **10** department, discipline, speciality

**spherical**
**05** round **06** global, rotund **07** globate, globoid, globose **08** globular
**09** orbicular **10** ball-shaped **11** globe-shaped

**spice**
**03** pep, zap, zip **04** kick, life, mull, stir, tang, vary, zest **05** gusto, hot up, liven, pep up, rouse, touch **06** buck up, colour, jazz up, perk up, relish, savour, stacte, stir up **07** animate, enliven, liven up **08** brighten, energize, ginger up, piquancy, tincture, vitalize
**09** diversify, seasoning **10** excitement, flavouring, invigorate, sweetmeats
**11** put life into

*See also* **herb**

**spick and span**
**04** neat, tidy, trim **05** clean **06** spruce
**08** polished, scrubbed, spotless, well-kept **09** shipshape **10** immaculate
**11** uncluttered

**spicy**
**03** hot **04** blue, racy, tart **05** adult, juicy, sharp, showy, tangy **06** ribald, risqué
**07** peppery, picante, piquant, pointed, pungent, raunchy **08** aromatic, fragrant, improper, indecent, seasoned, unseemly **09** flavoured
**10** indecorous, indelicate, scandalous, suggestive **11** flavoursome, near the bone, sensational **12** well-seasoned
**14** near the knuckle

**spider**
**07** beastie, spinner

*Spiders and arachnids include:*

**03** red
**04** bird, mite, tick, wolf
**05** bolas, money, water, zebra
**06** diadem, epeira, katipo, mygale, violin
**07** araneid, harvest, hunting, jumping, limulus, redback
**08** huntsman, scorpion, trapdoor
**09** funnel-web, harvester, phalangid, tarantula
**10** black widow, cheesemite, harvestman, saltigrade
**11** harvest mite, harvest tick
**12** book-scorpion, whip scorpion
**13** horseshoe crab

---

**spiel**
**04** line **05** pitch **06** patter, speech
**07** oration, recital **11** sales patter

**spies** *see* **spy**

**spignel**
**03** meu **09** baldmoney

**spike**
**03** add, ear, gad, nib **04** barb, brod, cloy, drug, lace, nail, spit, tang, tine
**05** beard, chape, mix in, point, prick, prong, rowel, spear, spick, spine, spire, stake, stick **06** catkin, impale, reject, skewer, spadix **07** bayonet, pricket
**09** dosshouse, frustrate, strobilus
**10** filopodium, projection
**11** contaminate **13** Anglo-Catholic

**spill**
**03** ren, rin, run, tip **04** drip, fall, flow, kill, leak, pour, shed, slop, well **05** scail, scale, skail, spile, taper, throw, upset, waste **06** escape, oozing, run out, tumble **07** cropper, destroy, fidibus, leakage, leaking, run over, scatter, seepage, seeping, slatter, swatter
**08** accident, disgorge, overflow, overturn, spillage, spilling
**09** discharge, pipe-light **11** lamplighter, percolation, pipe-lighter **13** candle-lighter

• **spill the beans**
**03** rat **04** blab, tell **05** grass, split
**06** inform, squeal, tell on **07** tell all
**11** blow the gaff **15** give the game away

**spin**
◇ *anagram indicator*
**03** cut, run **04** flap, play, reel, ride, tell, tizz, trip, turn **05** drive, jaunt, panic, spirt, state, swirl, tizzy, twirl, twist, wheel, whirl, whirr **06** circle, dither, gyrate, hurtle, invent, make up, outing, relate, rotate, swivel **07** draw out, dream up, fluster, go round, journey, narrate, revolve, twizzle **08** gyration, rotation **09** agitation, commotion, fabricate, pirouette, turn about, turn round **10** revolution

• **spin doctor**
**03** pro **07** spinner

• **spin out**
**06** extend, pad out **07** amplify, prolong
**08** lengthen, protract, wiredraw
**09** keep going

• **spin round**
**04** gyre, purl

**spindle**
**03** pin, rod **04** axis, axle, spit **05** arbor, fusee, fuzee, pivot, staff, verge

**spindly**
**04** long, thin **05** lanky, weedy
**06** gangly, skinny **07** spidery
**08** fusiform, gangling, skeletal
**09** attenuate **10** attenuated **14** spindle-shanked

**spine**
**04** barb, grit, guts **05** chine, pluck, quill, spike, spunk, thorn **06** bottle, dorsum, mettle, needle, rachis, spirit
**07** bravery, bristle, courage, prickle, rhachis, spinule **08** backbone, spiculum, strength **09** fortitude, Jew's-stone, ridge bone, vertebrae
**10** resolution **12** spinal column
**13** determination **15** ichthyodorulite, ichthyodorylite, vertebral column

**spine-chilling**
**05** eerie, scary **06** spooky
**10** horrifying, terrifying **11** frightening, hair-raising **13** bloodcurdling

**spineless**
**03** wet **04** soft, weak **05** cissy, milky, timid, wussy **06** feeble, yellow
**07** chicken, wimpish **08** boneless, cowardly, muticous, timorous
**09** weak-kneed **10** indecisive, irresolute, spiritless, submissive
**11** ineffective, lily-livered, vacillating
**12** faint-hearted, invertebrate

**spin-off**
**06** effect, result **10** side effect
**11** consequence **12** repercussion
**13** reverberation

**spinster**
**07** old maid

**spiny**
**05** spiky **06** briery, thorny **07** prickly, spinose, spinous, thistly **08** spicular
**09** acanthoid, acanthous, perplexed, spiculate **11** spiniferous, spinigerous, troublesome **12** acanthaceous

**spiral**
**04** coil, dive, go up, gyre, rise, soar, wind **05** climb, helix, screw, spire, twist, whorl **06** circle, coiled, gyrate, plunge, rocket, volute, wreath
**07** cochlea, helical, plummet, voluted, whorled, winding, wreathe **08** circular, cochlear, curlicue, dive-bomb,

escalate, gyroidal, increase, nosedive, scrolled, tailspin, twisting, volution **09** cochleate, corkscrew, skyrocket **10** cochleated **11** convolution, drop rapidly, fall rapidly **15** decrease quickly

**spire**
**03** tip, top **04** coil, cone, peak, reed **05** crest, crown, point, shoot, spear, spike, spyre, stalk, tower **06** belfry, broach, flèche, spiral, sprout, summit, turret **07** shoot up, steeple **08** pinnacle

**spirit**
**02** ka **03** air, div, fay, imp, nix, pep, zip **04** atua, brio, deev, deva, fire, gist, grit, guts, jinn, kick, life, mind, mood, nixy, soul, zeal, zest **05** angel, anima, cheer, demon, devil, drift, fairy, fiend, force, genie, ghost, jinni, monad, nixie, pluck, sense, shade, spook, spunk, tenor, verve **06** ardour, bottle, breath, djinni, energy, humour, jinnee, kidnap, make-up, mettle, morale, psyche, shadow, sprite, temper, vigour, wraith **07** bravery, courage, essence, feeling, meaning, mindset, outlook, phantom, pizzazz, purport, quality, sparkle, spectre **08** attitude, backbone, feelings, presence, revenant, tendency, visitant, vivacity **09** animation, breathing, character, élan vital, elemental, encourage, inner self, kidnapper, principle, substance, willpower **10** apparition, atmosphere, complexion, enterprise, enthusiasm, inner being, liveliness, motivation, resolution, vital force **11** disposition, frame of mind, implication, state of mind, temperament **13** dauntlessness, determination **14** characteristic

*See also* **mythical**

**• spirit away**
**05** carry, seize, steal, whisk **06** abduct, convey, kidnap, remove **07** capture, purloin, snaffle **08** abstract

**spirited**
**04** bold, gamy, racy **05** fiery, gamey, gutty **06** active, ardent, feisty, gallus, lively, plucky, spunky **07** dashing, gallows, valiant, zealous **08** animated, resolute, spanking, stomachy, valorous, vigorous **09** confident, energetic, sparkling, vivacious **10** courageous, determined, mettlesome, passionate, sprightful, stomachful, stomachous **12** high-spirited

**spiritless**
**03** low **04** cold, dead, dowf, dull, poor, tame, weak **05** amort, soggy **06** craven, droopy, jejune, mopish, torpid **07** anaemic, hilding, languid, unmoved **08** dejected, enervate, lifeless, listless **09** apathetic, bloodless, depressed, exanimate, inanimate **10** despondent, dispirited, lacklustre, melancholy, wishy-washy **11** sprightless **12** faint-hearted, muddy-mettled **14** unenthusiastic

**spirit-level**
**04** vial

**spirits**
**04** ginn, jinn, mood **05** djinn, hooch **06** humour, liquor, temper **07** alcohol **08** attitude, emotions, feelings **09** firewater, moonshine **11** strong drink, temperament **12** strong liquor, the hard stuff

*Spirits include:*

**03** gin, kir, rum, rye
**04** feni, grog, ouzo, raki, sake
**05** fenny, Pimm's®, vodka
**06** brandy, cognac, eggnog, geneva, grappa, kirsch, mescal, mezcal, pastis, Pernod®, poteen, Scotch, whisky
**07** aquavit, Bacardi®, bitters, bourbon, Campari, dark rum, genever, pink gin, sloe gin, tequila, whiskey
**08** Armagnac, Calvados, eau de vie, Hollands, hot toddy, sambucca, schnapps, vermouth, white rum, witblits
**09** apple-jack, aqua vitae, framboise, golden rum, mirabelle, slivovitz, spiced rum
**10** malt whisky, usquebaugh
**11** gold tequila, Hollands gin, peach brandy
**12** añejo tequila
**13** peach schnapps, silver tequila
**15** reposado tequila

*See also* **cocktail**; **liqueur**

**spiritual**
**04** aery, holy **05** aerie, witty **06** clever, divine, sacred **07** psychic **08** ethereal, heavenly **09** pneumatic, psychical, religious, unfleshly, unworldly **10** devotional, immaterial, intangible **11** incorporeal **12** metaphysical, otherworldly, supernatural, transcendent **14** ecclesiastical

**spit**
**03** dig, gob, yex **04** fuff, hawk, hiss, hook, jack, rasp, slag, spet, yesk **05** drool, eject, issue, spade, spawl, spawn, spume, sword **06** bespit, broach, phlegm, saliva, skewer, slaver, sputum **07** dribble, replica, spittle, sputter **08** broacher, emptysis, spadeful, splutter, turnspit **09** brochette, discharge, smoke-jack **10** rotisserie **11** expectorate **13** expectoration

**• spitting image**
**04** twin **05** clone **06** double, ringer **07** picture, replica **08** dead spit, likeness **09** lookalike **10** dead ringer **13** exact likeness

**spite**
**03** irk, vex **04** evil, gall, hate, hurt **05** annoy, upset, venom, wound **06** grudge, hatred, injure, malice, maugre, offend, put out, rancor, spight, thwart **07** ill-will, maulgre, provoke, rancour **08** irritate **09** animosity, hostility, ill nature, malignity, vengeance **10** bitterness, ill-feeling, resentment **11** malevolence **12** hard feelings, spitefulness **13** maliciousness **14** vindictiveness

**• in spite of**
**03** for **04** with **06** malgré, maugre **07** against, defying, despite, maulgre **08** after all, malgrado **11** in the face of **12** nevertheless, regardless of, undeterred by **13** be that as it may **15** notwithstanding

**spiteful**
**05** catty, cruel, nasty, petty, snide **06** barbed, bitchy, bitter, shrewd, wicked **07** cattish, hostile, vicious, waspish **08** vengeful, venomous, viperish **09** cat-witted, malicious, malignant, rancorous, resentful **10** ill-natured, malevolent, vindictive **11** ill-disposed **12** evil-tempered

**spitefully**
**07** cruelly **08** bitchily, bitterly **10** venomously **11** maliciously, resentfully **12** malevolently, vindictively

**spitting image** *see* **spit**

**splash**
◇ *anagram indicator*
**03** jap, lap, wet **04** beat, dash, daub, jaup, plop, show, slop, soss, spat, spot, stir, wade, wash **05** bathe, blash, blaze, break, burst, patch, plash, slosh, slush, smack, spray, stain, surge, swash, touch **06** batter, bedash, blazon, buffet, dabble, effect, flaunt, flouse, floush, impact, jabble, paddle, plunge, shower, sozzle, splish, splosh, spread, squirt, streak, strike, wallow **07** beating, display, exhibit, plaster, scatter, slatter, spatter, splatch, splodge, splotch, splurge, swatter, trumpet **08** splatter, sprinkle, squatter **09** publicity, publicize, sensation **10** excitement, impression **11** ostentation

**• splash out**
**05** spend **07** lash out, splurge **08** invest in **13** be extravagant **14** push the boat out

**spleen**
**03** pip **04** bile, gall, lien, melt, milt **05** anger, miltz, mirth, pique, spite, venom, wrath **06** animus, hatred, malice **07** boredom, caprice, ill-will, impulse, rancour, stomach **08** acrimony **09** animosity, bad temper, hostility, ill-humour, malignity **10** bitterness, melancholy, resentment **11** biliousness, malevolence, peevishness **12** spitefulness **14** vindictiveness

**splendid**
**04** braw, fine, rich **05** bonny, grand, great, jolly, super **06** bonnie, bright, divine, lavish, superb **07** gallant, glowing, opulent, radiant, stately, sublime, supreme **08** dazzling, fabulous, glorious, gorgeous, imposing, lustrous, pontific, renowned, terrific **09** admirable, brilliant, effulgent, excellent, luxurious, refulgent, sumptuous, wonderful **10** celebrated, first-class, glittering, impressive, marvellous, pontifical,

remarkable **11** exceptional, illustrious, magnificent, outstanding, resplendent **13** distinguished

**splendidly**
**07** grandly **08** superbly **09** admirably **10** remarkably **11** brilliantly, wonderfully **12** impressively, marvellously **13** exceptionally, magnificently, outstandingly

**splendour**
**04** glow, pomp, show **05** éclat, gleam, glory, pride **06** dazzle, finery, fulgor, luster, lustre, luxury **07** display, fulgour, majesty, panache
**08** ceremony, flourish, grandeur, opulence, radiance, richness
**09** solemnity, spectacle **10** brightness, brilliance **12** magnificence, resplendence **13** sumptuousness
**15** illustriousness

**splenetic**
**04** acid, sour **05** angry, cross, ratty, testy **06** bitchy, crabby, morose, sullen, touchy **07** bilious, crabbed, fretful, peevish **08** choleric, churlish, petulant, spiteful **09** envenomed, irascible, irritable, irritated, rancorous
**10** melancholy **11** atrabilious, bad-tempered

**splice**
◇ *anagram indicator*
**03** tie **04** bind, join, knit, mesh
**05** braid, graft, marry, plait, unite
**06** fasten **07** connect, entwine
**09** interlace **10** intertwine, interweave
• **get spliced**
**03** wed **10** get hitched, get married, tie the knot **13** take the plunge **15** plight your troth

**splinter**
**03** bit **04** chip, flaw **05** break, flake, piece, shard, shred, skelf, smash, spale, spall, spalt, speel, spelk, spell, split
**06** cleave, paring, shiver, sliver, splint
**07** crumble, flinder, shatter, shaving, spicula, spicule **08** flinders, fracture, fragment **11** smithereens
**12** disintegrate **15** break into pieces

**split**
◇ *insertion indicator*
**03** cut, gap, rat, rip **04** chop, dual, open, part, rend, rent, rift, rive, shop, slit, tear **05** allot, break, burst, cleft, crack, grass, halve, leave, peach, sever, shake, share, slash, spall, spalt, wreck
**06** betray, bisect, breach, broken, cleave, cloven, divide, rumble, schism, shiver, sliver, spring, sprung, squeal, stitch, tell on **07** break up, break-up, carve up, cracked, crevice, disband, discord, disrupt, divided, divorce, divulge, dole out, fissure, hand out, rupture, spalted, stool on, twofold
**08** allocate, bisected, cleavage, crevasse, disunion, disunite, division, inform on, ruptured, separate, set apart, share-out, splinter
**09** apportion, fractured, parcel out, partition **10** alienation, difference, dissension, distribute, divergence, separation **11** incriminate, part company **12** estrangement
**14** dissociate from **15** become alienated, become estranged
• **split up**
**04** part **06** divide **07** break up, disband, divorce **08** separate **11** get divorced, part company

**split-up**
**07** break-up, divorce, parting
**10** alienation, separation
**12** estrangement

**spoil**
◇ *anagram indicator*
**03** end, gum, mar, mux, pie, ret, rot
**04** baby, cook, foul, game, harm, hurt, kill, rait, rate, ruin, sour, turn **05** bitch, blunk, bodge, booty, botch, bribe, decay, go bad, go off, gum up, louse, queer, strip, taint, upset, wreck, wrong
**06** boodle, coddle, cosset, curdle, damage, deface, deform, foul up, go sour, impair, injure, mangle, mess up, murder, pamper, poison, prizes, quarry, wash up **07** bauchle, bitch up, blemish, butcher, corrupt, deprive, despoil, destroy, distort, indulge, louse up, pillage, plunder, pollute, screw up, tarnish, viciate, vitiate **08** distaste, go rotten, mutilate **09** decompose, disfigure, spoon-feed, vulgarize
**10** impairment, obliterate, spoliation
**11** contaminate, deteriorate, mollycoddle, overindulge, prejudicate
**12** acquisitions, become rotten, put a damper on **15** cast a shadow over, pour cold water on
• **spoil for**
**07** long for **08** be keen on, yearn for
**10** be eager for, be intent on

**spoils**
**04** gain, haul, loot, swag **05** booty, bribe **06** boodle, damage, prizes, profit, trophy **07** benefit, pillage, plunder, spulzie, the game
**08** pickings, winnings **10** impairment, spoliation **11** spolia opima
**12** acquisitions, despoliation

**spoilsport**
**04** nark **06** damper, misery, wowser
**07** killjoy, meddler **08** buzzkill **10** wet blanket **11** party-pooper **14** dog in the manger

**spoke**
**04** rung **06** radius

**spoken**
◇ *homophone indicator*
**03** sed **04** oral, said, told **06** stated, verbal, voiced **07** uttered **08** declared, phonetic, viva voce **09** expressed, unwritten

**spokesman, spokeswoman**
**05** agent, mouth, voice **06** broker, orator **07** foreman **08** delegate, mediator **09** forewoman, go-between
**10** arbitrator, foreperson, mouthpiece, negotiator, prolocutor **12** intermediary, propagandist, spokesperson
**14** representative

**sponge**
**03** beg, bum, mop **04** mump, swab, wash, wipe **05** cadge, clean, mooch, mouch, shool, shule **06** bludge, borrow, loofah, shoole, spunge, sucker
**07** monaxon, zimocca **08** bedeguar, drunkard, freeload, hanger-on, parasite, quandang, quandong, quantong, scrounge, victoria **09** glass-rope, hyalonema, sea orange
**13** mermaid's glove, sulphur sponge
*See also* **drunkard**
• **sponge cake**
**06** coburg, trifle **09** lamington, madeleine, Swiss roll **11** lady's finger
**12** lady's fingers **14** charlotte russe
• **sponge spicule**
**06** hexact, sclere, tylote **07** monaxon, pentact, rhabdus, tetract, triaxon
**08** polyaxon, tetraxon, triaxial
**09** polyaxial, spiraster

**sponger**
**03** bum **06** beggar, bummer, cadger
**07** bludger, moocher **08** borrower, hanger-on, parasite, scambler
**09** scrounger **10** freeloader, smell-feast

**spongy**
◇ *anagram indicator*
**04** fozy, soft **05** light **06** poachy, porous **07** drunken, elastic, fungous, springy, squashy **08** cushiony, yielding
**09** absorbent, cushioned, resilient
**10** absorptive, cancellate, cancellous
**11** cancellated

**sponsor**
**04** back, fund **05** angel, vouch
**06** backer, friend, gossip, patron, surety
**07** finance, promise, promote, support
**08** bankroll, promoter, stand for
**09** godfather, godmother, guarantee, guarantor, patronize, subsidize, supporter, susceptor **10** subsidizer, undertaker, underwrite **11** be a patron of, underwriter

**sponsorship**
**03** aid **05** funds, grant **07** backing, finance, subsidy, support
**09** patronage, promotion **10** assistance
**11** endorsement **12** financial aid

**spontaneity**
**07** impulse **08** instinct **11** naturalness
**13** improvisation **15** extemporization, instinctiveness

**spontaneous**
**04** free **06** reflex **07** natural, willing
**08** free-will, knee-jerk, unbidden, unforced, untaught **09** automatic, autonomic, extempore, impromptu, impulsive, unplanned, unstudied, voluntary **10** ultroneous, unprompted
**11** instinctive, uncompelled, unrehearsed **12** unhesitating
**14** unpremeditated **15** spur of the moment

**spontaneously**
**05** ad-lib **06** freely **09** extempore, impromptu, on impulse, unplanned, willingly **10** off the cuff, unprompted

**11** impulsively, voluntarily
**13** instinctively **15** of your own accord

**spoof**
**03** con **04** fake, game, hoax, joke
**05** bluff, prank, trick **06** parody, satire, send-up **07** lampoon, leg-pull, mockery, take-off **08** travesty
**09** burlesque, deception **10** caricature

**spooky**
**05** eerie, scary, weird **06** creepy
**07** ghostly, macabre, uncanny
**08** chilling **09** unearthly **10** mysterious
**11** frightening, hair-raising
**12** supernatural **13** spine-chilling

**spool**
**04** pirn, reel **06** bobbin **07** trundle

**spoon**
**05** court, labis, ladle, scoop **07** spatula
**08** cochlear **09** cochleare, courtship, simpleton

**spoon-feed**
**04** baby **05** spoil **06** cosset, pamper
**07** indulge **10** featherbed
**11** mollycoddle, overindulge

**sporadic**
**06** random, uneven **07** erratic
**08** episodic, isolated **09** irregular, scattered, spasmodic **10** episodical, infrequent, occasional **12** intermittent

**sporadically**
**08** off and on, on and off **10** now and then **11** now and again **12** occasionally, periodically **13** spasmodically
**14** intermittently

**sport**
◇ *anagram indicator*
**03** fun, gig **04** game, jest, joke, laik, lake, play, wear **05** amuse, mirth, wager
**06** banter, frolic, humour, joking, trifle
**07** display, exhibit, jesting, kidding, mockery, pastime, show off, teasing
**08** activity, exercise, pleasure, ridicule, sneering, squander **09** amusement, dalliance, diversion, plaything
**10** recreation **13** entertainment

*See also* **athletics**; **American football**; **Australian football**; **baseball**; **boxing**; **competition**; **cricket**; **football**; **golf**; **gymnastics**; **ice hockey**; **race**; **rugby**; **stadium**; **tennis**

*Sports include:*

**04** golf, judo, polo, pool
**05** bowls, darts, fives, rugby
**06** boules, boxing, discus, diving, futsal, hockey, karate, kung fu, luging, Nascar®, pelota, quoits, rowing, shinty, skiing, slalom, soccer, squash, tennis
**07** angling, aquafit, archery, camogie, cricket, croquet, curling, fencing, fishing, gliding, hunting, hurling, jogging, jujitsu, keep-fit, netball, putting, running, sailing, shot put, snooker, surfing, walking
**08** aerobics, baseball, biathlon, canoeing, climbing, football, handball, high-jump, hurdling, lacrosse, long-jump, pétanque, ping-pong, rounders, shooting, swimming, trotting, yachting
**09** athletics, badminton, billiards, bobsleigh, decathlon, go-karting, ice-hockey, pole vault, pot-holing, sky-diving, tae kwon do, triathlon, water polo, wrestling
**10** basketball, drag-racing, gymnastics, ice-skating, pentathlon, real tennis, skin-diving, triple-jump, volleyball
**11** cycle racing, horse-racing, motor racing, show-jumping, table-tennis, tobogganing, water-skiing, windsurfing
**12** aqua aerobics, cross-country, orienteering, pitch and putt, rock-climbing, snowboarding, speed skating, trampolining
**13** bungee jumping, coarse fishing, roller-skating, tenpin bowling, weightlifting
**14** downhill skiing, Gaelic football, mountaineering, speedway racing, stock-car racing
**15** greyhound-racing

*Sports equipment includes:*

**03** bow, cue, fly, jig, mat, net, oar, ski, tee
**04** bail, bait, beam, bolt, bowl, épée, foil, gaff, hook, jack, lure, mask, mitt, nets, pins, puck, rack, reel, rest, rope, shot, wood
**05** arrow, boule, brush, caman, chalk, float, rings, sabre, stump, table, trace
**06** bridge, discus, fly rod, hammer, hurley, priest, spider, wicket
**07** cue ball, fly reel, javelin, keep-net, netball, snorkel
**08** aqualung, baseball, crossbow, football, gang-hook, golfball, golf club, ice-skate, punch-bag, ski stick, toboggan, water-ski
**09** disgorger, face-guard, gum shield, punch-ball, rugby ball, sailboard, snow board, surfboard
**10** basketball, cricket bat, fishing-rod, hockey ball, roller boot, skateboard, speed skate, tennis ball, trampoline, volleyball
**11** balance beam, baseball bat, bowling ball, boxing glove, cricket ball, fishing-line, hockey skate, hockey stick, in-line skate, paternoster, pommel horse, racket press, rollerblade, roller-skate, shuttlecock, snooker ball, spinning rod, springboard
**12** billiard ball, curling stone, golfing glove, isometric bar, parallel-bars, tennis racket
**13** catcher's glove, horizontal bar, vaulting horse
**14** ice-hockey stick
**15** badminton racket

*Sports positions include:*

**04** lock, slip, wing
**05** cover, gully, mid-on, point, rover
**06** batter, centre, goalie, hooker, libero, long on, mid-off, setter, winger
**07** batsman, catcher, fine leg, flanker, fly-half, fly slip, forward, leg slip, long leg, long off, number 8, pitcher, ruckman, sweeper, torpedo
**08** attacker, backstop, defender, fullback, halfback, left back, left wing, long stop, short leg, split end, third man, tight end, wing back
**09** deep cover, deep point, first base, first slip, left field, left guard, leg gulley, mid-wicket, right back, right wing, ruck rover, scrum-half, short stop, square leg, third base, third slip
**10** back pocket, cover point, defenceman, extra cover, goal attack, goalkeeper, goaltender, inside left, left tackle, midfielder, point guard, right field, right guard, second base, second slip, silly mid-on, silly point, wing attack
**11** centre field, deep fine leg, full-forward, goal defence, goal shooter, inside right, left forward, prop forward, quarterback, right tackle, silly mid-off, wing defence
**12** left half-back, power forward, right forward, short fine leg, small forward, stand-off half, wicketkeeper
**13** backward point, centre-forward, deep mid-wicket, deep square leg, forward pocket, half-back flank, loosehead prop, right half-back, shooting guard, tighthead prop
**14** centre half-back, deep extra cover, left corner-back, short mid-wicket
**15** left half-forward, right corner-back, short extra cover

**sporting**
◇ *anagram indicator*
**04** fair, just **06** decent, modest
**08** ladylike **10** honourable, reasonable
**11** considerate, gentlemanly, respectable **13** sportsmanlike

**sportive**
**03** gay **05** ludic, merry **06** frisky, jaunty, lively, wanton **07** amorous, coltish, playful, toysome **08** gamesome, prankish, skittish **09** kittenish, ludicrous, sprightly, vivacious
**10** frolicsome, rollicking

**sportsperson**
**04** blue, jock

*Sportspeople include:*

**04** **Bird** (Larry), **Dean** (Christopher), **Khan** (Jahangir), **Lowe** (John), **Nudd** (Bob), **Witt** (Katerina)
**05** **Curry** (John), **Davis** (Fred), **Davis** (Joe), **Davis** (Steve), **Ender** (Kornelia), **Kelly** (Sean), **O'Neal** (Shaquille), **Spitz** (Mark), **White** (Jimmy)
**06** **Briggs** (Karen), **Bryant** (David), **Davies** (Sharron), **Fraser** (Dawn), **Hendry** (Stephen), **Jordan** (Michael), **LeMond** (Greg), **Malone** (Karl), **Merckx** (Eddy), **Pulman** (John), **Wilkie** (David), **Wilson** (Jocky)

**07** **Allcock** (Tony), **Bristow** (Eric), **Cousins** (Robin), **Gretzky** (Wayne), **Harding** (Tonya), **Higgins** (Alex 'Hurricane'), **Hinault** (Bernard), **Johnson** (Earvin 'Magic'), **O'Reilly** (Wilfred), **Reardon** (Ray), **Rodnina** (Irina), **Torvill** (Jayne), **Zaitsev** (Aleksandr)
**08** **Boardman** (Chris), **Indurain** (Miguel), **Kerrigan** (Nancy), **Redgrave** (Sir Steve), **Williams** (Rex)
**09** **Cipollini** (Mario), **Hazelwood** (Mike)
**10** **Barrington** (Jonah)
**11** **Abdul-Jabbar** (Kareem), **Chamberlain** (Wilt 'the Stilt'), **Weissmuller** (Johnny)

*See also* **athlete**; **Australian football**; **baseball**; **boxer**; **chess**; **cricket**; **footballer**; **golfer**; **gymnastics**; **horseman, horsewoman**; **motor**; **mountaineering**; **rugby**; **skier**; **tennis**

## sporty

**03** fit **04** loud **05** natty, showy **06** casual, flashy, jaunty, lively, snazzy, trendy **07** outdoor, stylish **08** athletic, informal **09** energetic

## spot

**03** bit, dot, eye, fix, jam, pin, pip, see, zit **04** area, bite, blob, blot, blur, boil, daub, drop, espy, flaw, fret, give, hole, lend, mail, mark, meal, mess, moil, mold, mole, peep, plot, pock, show, site, slot, smut, soil, some, sore, time, turn **05** cloud, fleck, freak, hilum, naeve, nerve, nevus, niche, patch, peepe, place, plook, plouk, point, pupil, scene, speck, stain, sully, swale, taint **06** blotch, descry, detect, garden, little, locale, locate, macula, morsel, naevus, notice, papula, papule, pickle, pimple, plight, recess, scrape, smudge, splash, stigma **07** airtime, blemish, discern, flecker, freckle, lentigo, make out, observe, ocellus, opening, pick out, pustule, setting, spangle, speckle, splodge, splotch, tarnish, trouble **08** fenestra, identify, locality, location, maculate, position, quandary **09** birthmark, blackhead, freckling, programme, recognize, reprehend, situation **10** cicatricle, death-token, difficulty, maculation **11** cicatricula, performance, predicament, small amount **12** catch sight of, cicatrichule **13** discoloration

**• on the spot**

**02** in **04** down, next **05** alert **06** at once, pronto **07** quickly **08** directly, in a jiffy, promptly, right now, speedily, sur place **09** forthwith, instantly, like a shot, right away **10** this minute **11** immediately, this instant **12** straight away, there and then, without delay **13** straightforth, with a siserary **14** unhesitatingly, without more ado **15** before you know it, instantaneously, without question

**• spot-on**

**04** true **05** close, exact, right **06** bang on, dead-on, strict **07** correct, factual, precise **08** accurate, definite, detailed, explicit, flawless, specific, unerring **09** excellent, faultless, on the nail **10** on the money **11** on the button

## spotless

**04** pure **05** clean, white **06** chaste, virgin **07** shining **08** gleaming, innocent, unmarked, virginal **09** blameless, faultless, snow-white, unstained, unsullied, untainted, untouched **10** immaculate **11** unblemished **12** spick and span **14** irreproachable

## spotlight

**04** baby, fame, spot **05** brute **06** stress **07** feature, focus on, point up **08** emphasis, interest **09** attention, emphasize, highlight, limelight, notoriety, public eye, underline **10** accentuate, foreground, illuminate **15** draw attention to, public attention, throw into relief

## spotted

**03** gay **04** pied **06** dotted, macled, parded, spotty **07** brindle, dappled, flecked, guttate, macular, mottled, piebald **08** brindled, guttated, maculose, polka-dot, speckled

## spotty

**04** pied, poxy **05** acned, bitty **06** dotted, measly, patchy, pimply, uneven **07** blotchy, dappled, erratic, flecked, mottled, piebald, pimpled, spotted, varying **08** speckled **12** inconsistent

## spouse

**04** feer, fere, mate, wife **05** feare, fiere, hubby **06** missus, pheere **07** consort, husband, partner **09** companion, other half **10** better half

## spout

**03** jet **04** blow, emit, flow, go on, gush, pawn, pour, rant, rose, spew **05** chute, erupt, mouth, orate, shoot, spiel, spray, spurt, surge **06** geyser, nozzle, outlet, squirt, stream, stroup, waffle, witter **07** bespout, declaim **08** disgorge, fountain, gargoyle, pawnshop, rabbit on, spout off, witter on **09** discharge, expatiate, hold forth, sermonize **10** spout forth, waterspout **11** pontificate

## sprain

**03** hip **04** pull, rick, turn **05** crick, stave, twist, wrest, wrick **06** injure, wrench **09** dislocate **12** shoulder slip

## sprat

**04** brit, Jack **06** garvie **07** garvock **08** brisling

## sprawl

**04** flop, loll **05** slump, trail **06** lounge, ramble, repose, slouch, spread **07** recline, scamble, stretch **08** sprangle, straggle

## spray

◇ *anagram indicator*

**03** jet, wet **04** Alar®, foam, gush, Mace®, mist, posy, scud, twig **05** froth, shoot, spout, sprig, spume, swish **06** branch, drench, mister, shower, spritz, squirt, wreath **07** aerosol, bouquet, corsage, diffuse, drizzle, garland, nosegay, scatter, spatter, sprayer **08** aigrette, atomizer, disperse, moisture, mothball, nebulize, spray gun, sprinkle, vaporize **09** aspersion, nebulizer, spindrift, sprinkler, squirt gun, vaporizer **10** golden rose, propellant, spoondrift, waterspout **11** disseminate **13** water-sprinkle

## spread

◇ *anagram indicator*

**03** air, lay, ren, rin, run, set, sow, ted **04** coat, grow, laid, open, span, teer, walk **05** apply, cover, feast, flare, layer, order, party, put on, ranch, reach, scale, smear, spray, strew, sweep, swell, treat, widen **06** dilate, dinner, effuse, expand, extend, extent, fan out, lay out, mantle, repast, slairg, smooth, sprawl, unfold, unfurl, unroll **07** advance, arrange, banquet, blow-out, broaden, compass, develop, diffuse, enlarge, expanse, go round, open out, overlay, publish, radiate, scatter, stretch **08** disperse, escalate, extended, get round, increase, mushroom, swelling, transmit **09** advertise, broadcast, circulate, diffusion, displayed, expansion, large meal, make known, percolate, propagate, publicize, spill over **10** dispersion, distribute, escalation, gain ground, grow bigger, make public, promulgate **11** communicate, development, dinner party, disseminate, mushrooming, proliferate, propagation **12** become bigger, broadcasting, distribution, transmission **13** communication, dissemination, proliferation

*Spreads include:*

**03** jam
**04** marg, oleo, pâté
**05** honey, marge
**06** butter
**07** Marmite®, Nutella®
**08** dripping, Vegemite®
**09** butterine, lemon curd, margarine, marmalade
**11** lemon cheese
**12** peanut butter
**13** oleomargarine

## spree

**03** bat, bum, jag **04** bout, bust, orgy, tear **05** binge, blind, fling, revel, skite, skyte **06** bender, junket, randan, razzle, splore **07** blinder, carouse, debauch, splurge **08** jamboree **12** razzle-dazzle

## sprig

**04** brad, stem, twig **05** bough, scion, shoot, spray **06** branch

## sprightly

**04** airy, spry **05** agile, brisk, perky **06** active, blithe, gallus, hearty, jaunty, lively, nimble, sprack **07** gallows, ghostly, playful **08** animated, cheerful, spirited **09** energetic, mercurial, vivacious **10** frolicsome, spirituous **12** light-hearted

**spring**
◇ *anagram indicator*
**03** eye, gin, hop, lep, spa **04** bend, bolt, come, dawn, give, grow, hair, jump, leap, Lent, open, rise, root, skip, stem, stot, voar, ware, warp, well **05** arise, basis, bound, burst, cause, copse, crack, dance, issue, prime, shoot, spang, split, start, vault, youth **06** appear, bounce, derive, emerge, energy, geyser, origin, pounce, recoil, salina, source, spirit, sprout, strain **07** descend, develop, emanate, explode, proceed, rebound **08** balneary, brine-pan, brine-pit, buoyancy, wellhead **09** animation, beginning, briskness, originate **10** bounciness, elasticity, liveliness, resilience, wellspring **11** black smoker, flexibility, springiness, undergrowth **12** cheerfulness, fountainhead **14** reveal suddenly
• **spring up**
**04** grow, rise **05** start **06** upblow **07** develop, shoot up **08** fountain, mushroom, sprout up **11** proliferate **13** come into being **14** appear suddenly

**springtime** *see* **spring**

**springy**
**05** crisp, lofty **06** bouncy, spongy **07** buoyant, elastic, rubbery, squidgy, tensile **08** flexible, stretchy, tensible **09** resilient

**sprinkle**
◇ *anagram indicator*
**03** dot, set **04** drop, dust, salt, sand, seed, sift **05** flake, flour, spang, spray, strew, sugar **06** dredge, pepper, pounce, powder, shower, sparge, splash **07** asperge, sawdust, scatter, spairge, spatter, trickle **08** beflower, disponge, dispunge, lavender, strinkle **09** bespatter, diversify **10** scowdering **11** aspersorium, scouthering

**sprinkling**
**03** few **04** dash **05** touch, trace **07** baptism, dusting, handful, scatter, sifting, trickle **08** sprinkle **09** admixture, aspersion **10** scattering, smattering

**sprint**
**03** fly, run, zip **04** belt, dart, dash, race, tear **05** scoot, shoot **06** career, scurry

**sprite**
**03** elf, imp, pug **04** bogy, puck **05** bogle, dryad, fairy, gnome, kelpy, naiad, nymph, pixie, pouke, sylph **06** goblin, kelpie, spirit **07** apsaras, brownie, spright **10** apparition, leprechaun **11** water spirit

**sprout**
**03** bud **04** chit, germ, grow **05** scion, shoot, spire, spirt **06** come up, spring **07** develop, tendron **08** put forth, spring up **09** germinate, pullulate, turnip top **10** descendant

**spruce**
**04** chic, cool, neat, smug, trim **05** brisk, natty, nifty, Picea, sleek, smart, smirk, spiff, Tsuga **06** dapper, snazzy, spiffy, sprush **07** band-box, elegant, finical, hemlock, smarten **11** well-dressed, well-groomed **13** well-turned-out
• **spruce up**
**04** tidy **05** groom, preen, primp **06** neaten, tart up, tidy up **08** titivate **09** smarten up

**spry**
**05** agile, alert, brisk, nippy, peppy, quick, ready **06** active, nimble, supple **09** energetic, sprightly

**spud** *see* **potato**

**spume**
**04** fizz, foam, head, scum, spit, suds **05** froth, yeast **06** lather **07** bubbles **13** effervescence

**spunk**
**04** grit, guts **05** heart, match, nerve, pluck, spark **06** bottle, fire up, mettle, spirit, tinder **07** courage **08** backbone, chutzpah, gameness **09** touchwood, toughness **10** resolution

**spur**
**04** goad, heel, limb, poke, prod, stud, urge **05** drive, ergot, impel, prick, prong, rowel, spica, spike, strut **06** branch, calcar, fillip, hasten, incite, induce, motive, offset, prompt, propel, Rippon, siding, spurne **07** impetus **08** motivate, stimulus **09** encourage, incentive, star wheel, stimulant, stimulate **10** incitement, inducement, motivation, projection, protrusion **12** embranchment, protuberance **13** encouragement
• **on the spur of the moment**
**08** suddenly **09** extempore, impromptu, on impulse, on the spot **10** upon the gad **11** impetuously, impulsively **12** unexpectedly **13** spontaneously, thoughtlessly **15** without planning

**spurious**
◇ *anagram indicator*
**03** bad, dog **04** fake, mock, sham **05** bogus, cronk, false **06** forged, phoney, pseudo **07** bastard, feigned **08** pseudish **09** contrived, deceitful, imitation, pretended, simulated, trumped-up **10** adulterate, adulterine, apocryphal, artificial, fraudulent **11** counterfeit, make-believe **12** illegitimate **14** supposititious

**spurn**
**04** kick, snub, trip **05** scorn, tread **06** ignore, rebuff, reject, slight **07** condemn, despise, disdain, repulse, say no to **08** turn away, turn down **09** disregard, repudiate **10** look down on **12** cold-shoulder

**spurt**
**03** fit, jet **04** boak, bock, boke, gush, kick, pour, pump, rush, spin, well **05** burst, erupt, issue, shoot, spate, spray, start, surge **06** access, skoosh, squirt, stream **07** welling **08** eruption, increase **10** outpouring

**spy**
**03** eye, see **04** espy, look, mole, nark, spie, spot, tout, wait **05** agent, plant, scout, spial, spook, spyal **06** beagle, descry, notice, setter, shadow, survey **07** discern, glimpse, make out, observe, sleeper, snooper **08** discover, emissary, mouchard **10** enemy agent **11** double agent, secret agent, under-espial **12** catch sight of, foreign agent **13** intelligencer **14** fifth columnist **15** undercover agent

*Spies include:*

**03** **Pym** (Magnus)
**04** **Bond** (James), **Hale** (Nathan), **Hiss** (Alger)
**05** **André** (John), **Blake** (George), **Blunt** (Anthony Frederick), **Fuchs** (Klaus Emil Julius), **Karla**, **Szabo** (Violette), **Wynne** (Greville)
**06** **Howell** (James), **Philby** (Kim), **Smiley** (George), **Tubman** (Harriet), **Vidocq** (Eugène François), **Werner** (Ruth)
**07** **Burgess** (Guy Francis de Moncy), **Maclean** (Donald)
**08** **Lonsdale** (Gordon Arnold), **Mata Hari**
**09** **Carstares** (William), **Rosenberg** (Ethel), **Rosenberg** (Julius)
**10** **Cairncross** (John)

• **spies**
**02** MI **03** CIA, KGB, MI5, MI6 **05** Stasi **06** Mossad
• **spy on**
**04** tout **05** watch **07** observe **10** keep tabs on **11** keep an eye on **14** observe closely

**spymaster**
**01** M

**squabble**
**03** row **04** spat, tiff, tift **05** argue, brawl, clash, fight, scrap, set to, set-to **06** barney, bicker **07** dispute, quarrel, rhubarb, wrangle **08** argument **09** have words **12** disagreement

**squad**
**03** set **04** band, crew, gang, team, unit **05** force, group, troop **06** outfit **07** brigade, company, platoon

**squadron**
**03** red, RYS, sqn **04** blue **10** escadrille

**squalid**
**03** low **04** foul, mean, vile **05** dingy, dirty, grimy, mucky, nasty, ribby, seedy **06** filthy, grotty, grubby, sleazy, slummy, sordid, untidy **07** obscene, run-down, unclean, unkempt **08** improper, shameful, slovenly, wretched **09** neglected, offensive, repulsive **10** broken-down, Dickensian, disgusting, ramshackle, uncared-for, unpleasant **11** dilapidated, disgraceful

**squall**
**03** cry **04** blow, drow, gale, gust, howl,

moan, wail, wind, yell, yowl **05** groan, storm **06** flurry **07** sumatra, tempest **08** williwaw **09** hurricane, windstorm

**squally**
**04** wild **05** blowy, gusty, rough, windy **06** stormy **07** gustful **08** blustery **09** turbulent **10** blustering **11** tempestuous

**squalor**
**04** dirt, slum **05** decay, filth, grime **07** neglect, skid row **08** dung-heap, dung-hill, foulness, meanness, skid road **09** dinginess, dirtiness, griminess, muckiness **10** filthiness, grubbiness, sleaziness **11** squalidness, uncleanness **12** wretchedness

**squander**
**04** blow, blue, lash, muck, roam **05** spend, sport, waste **06** bezzle, expend, gamble, lavish, misuse, mucker, plunge, wander **07** consume, fritter, scamble, scatter, slather, splurge **08** disperse, fool away, misspend, straggle **09** dissipate, sport away, throw away **10** muddle away **11** fritter away, splash out on

**square**
**01** S,T **02** sq **03** fit, pay **04** even, fair, full, just, quad, rule, suit, true **05** adapt, agree, align, bribe, canon, exact, fogey, level, match, order, plaza, scarf, solid, tally **06** accord, adjust, dinkum, equity, evenly, fairly, honest, settle, tailor **07** balance, conform, diehard, ethical, fitting, genuine, honesty, quarrel, resolve, solidly, swagger, upright **08** complete, directly, fairness, honestly, old fogey, put right, regulate, set right, settle up, standard, straight, suitable, thick-set **09** conformer, criterion, equitable, harmonize, headscarf, make equal, reconcile **10** above-board, conformist, correspond, dissension, fuddy-duddy, honourable, on the level, quadrangle, satisfying, straighten, town square **11** marketplace, rectangular, right-angled, strait-laced, unequivocal **12** buttoned-down, conservative, market square, old-fashioned **13** perpendicular, quadrilateral, stick-in-the-mud **14** traditionalist **15** be congruous with, conventionalist

*Squares include:*

**03** Red
**05** Times
**06** Sloane
**07** Central, Madison, People's
**08** Berkeley, Victoria
**09** Leicester, Tiananmen, Trafalgar
**10** Bloomsbury, Washington
**12** Covent Garden

**squarely**
**04** bang, dead, just **05** plumb, right, smack **07** exactly **08** directly, straight **09** precisely **12** unswervingly

**squash**
**03** jam **04** mash, pack, pulp, snub **05** crowd, crush, grind, pound, press, quash, quell, smash, stamp **07** distort, flatten, put down, silence, squeeze, squelch, squidge, trample **08** compress, macerate, suppress **09** dilutable, humiliate, pulverize, squeezing **10** annihilate

**squashy**
**04** soft **05** mushy, pappy, pulpy **06** spongy **07** sopping, springy, squidgy, squishy **08** squelchy, yielding **10** squelching

**squat**
**03** sit **04** bend, ruck **05** croup, dumpy, fubby, fubsy, hunch, kneel, podgy, pudgy, short, stoop **06** chunky, crouch, croupe, hunker, pyknic, stocky, stubby **07** squabby **08** thickset **09** crouching **10** hunker down **12** absquatulate, Humpty-dumpty

**squawk**
**03** cry, nag **04** beef, carp, crow, fuss, hoot, moan, yelp **05** bitch, bleat, croak, gripe, groan, growl, grump, whine **06** cackle, grouch, grouse, object, scream, shriek, squeal, whinge **07** carry on, grumble, protest, scrauch, scraugh, screech **08** complain **09** bellyache, criticize, find fault **11** kick up a fuss, raise a stink **15** have a bone to pick

**squeak**
**03** eek **04** peep, pipe **05** cheep, chirk, creak, whine **06** inform, squeal **07** confess

**squeal**
**03** cry, rat, wee **04** howl, shop, sing, tell, wail, yell, yelp **05** grass, shout, sneak, split, stool **06** betray, inform, scream, shriek, snitch, squawk **07** screech, sell out **08** complain **09** tell tales

**squeamish**
**03** coy **04** sick **06** queasy, queazy **07** finicky, mawkish, missish, prudish **08** delicate, nauseous **09** nauseated **10** fastidious, particular, scrupulous **11** punctilious, strait-laced **12** mealy mouthed

**squeeze**
◇ *containment indicator*
**03** hug, jam, nip, ram **04** cram, grip, hold, mash, milk, pack, pulp, push, shoe, suck **05** bleed, chirt, clasp, crowd, crush, force, grasp, gripe, juice, pinch, press, shove, stuff, sweat, twist, wedge, wrest, wring **06** clutch, cuddle, enfold, extort, fleece, jostle, lean on, mangle, scruze, squash, strain, thrust **07** embrace, extract, rubbing, scrooge, scrouge, squidge, thrutch, tighten **08** compress, pressure, sandwich, scrowdge, shoehorn, wring out **09** boyfriend, hold tight **10** congestion, girlfriend, pressurize **14** put the screws on

**squid**
**01** L **04** quid **05** pound **06** loligo, nicker **07** ink-fish, smacker **08** calamari, calamary **10** sleeve fish

**squiffy**
◇ *anagram indicator*
**05** happy, merry, tight, tipsy **06** blotto, tiddly **07** drunken, pickled, sozzled, tiddley **09** crapulent, plastered **10** inebriated **11** intoxicated

**squint**
**03** aim **04** awry, cast, gaze, glee, gley, hint, peep, peer, pink, scan **05** askew, blink, twire **06** aslant, glance, gledge, gleyed, skelly, squiny **07** crooked, glimpse, oblique, skellie, squinny **08** cockeyed, cross-eye, indirect, strabism, tendency, walleyed **09** obliquely, off-centre, skew-whiff **10** hagioscope, side-glance, strabismic, strabismus **11** look askance **12** sideways look

**squire**
**04** rule **05** canon **06** attend, donzel, escort, Junker, squier **08** scutiger, squarson **12** armour-bearer

**squirm**
◇ *anagram indicator*
**04** move, worm **05** shift, twist **06** fidget, wiggle, writhe **07** agonize, wriggle **08** flounder, squiggle

**squirrel**
**03** bun **04** skug, vair **05** hoard **06** gopher, suslik, taguan **07** meercat, meerkat **08** chipmuck, chipmunk **09** chickaree **10** prairie dog **11** flickertail, spermophile

• **squirrel away**
**04** hide, save **05** hoard, lay in, lay up, put by, store **06** save up **07** conceal, put away, stock up **08** salt away, set aside **09** stash away, stockpile

• **squirrel's nest**
**04** cage, dray, drey

**squirt**
**03** jet **04** emit, gush, pour, spew, well **05** chirt, eject, expel, issue, scoot, shoot, spirt, spout, spray, spurt, surge **06** scoosh, skoosh, stream **07** spew out **09** discharge, ejaculate

• **sea squirt**
**08** ascidian, cunjevoi

**Sri Lanka**
**02** CL **03** LKA

**stab**
**02** go **03** cut, jab, try **04** ache, bash, dirk, fork, gash, gore, kris, pain, pang, pink, push, shot **05** crack, essay, knife, prick, prong, slash, spasm, spear, stick, throb, whirl, wound **06** injure, injury, pierce, skewer, thrust, twinge **07** attempt, bayonet, poniard, venture **08** incision, puncture, stiletto, transfix **09** endeavour

• **stab in the back**
**06** betray **07** deceive, let down, sell out, slander **08** inform on **11** double-cross

**stabbing**
**05** acute, sharp **07** knifing, painful **08** piercing, shooting, stinging **09** throbbing

**stability**
**06** fixity, fixure **07** balance
**08** firmness, solidity **09** constancy, soundness **10** durability, regularity, secureness, steadiness, sturdiness, uniformity **11** reliability
**15** unchangeability

**stabilize**
**03** fix, peg **06** firm up, freeze, secure, steady **07** balance, support
**08** equalize, valorize **09** establish
**10** keep steady, make stable **11** make uniform

**stable**
**04** barn, fast, firm, sure **05** fixed, solid, sound, stall **06** secure, static, steady, strong, sturdy **07** abiding, durable, lasting, regular, uniform **08** balanced, constant, enduring, reliable, together
**09** permanent **10** deep-rooted, dependable, invariable, unchanging, unswerving, unwavering
**11** established, long-lasting, substantial, well-founded
**12** unchangeable **13** self-balancing
• **stablehand**
**06** ostler

**stack**
**03** lot **04** fill, flue, heap, load, many, mass, pile, rick, ruck, save, tons, vent
**05** amass, clamp, heaps, hoard, loads, mound, piles, shaft, stash, stock, store
**06** funnel, gather, granum, masses, oodles **07** chimney **08** assemble **09** a good deal, stockpile **10** accumulate, a great deal, collection **12** accumulation, a large amount, great numbers

**stadium**
**04** bowl, park, ring **05** arena, field, pitch, track, venue **06** ground
08 coliseum **09** colosseum, velodrome **11** sports field
**12** amphitheatre, sports ground

*Sports stadia and venues include:*

**04** Oval
**05** Ascot, Epsom, Ibrox, Imola, Lords, Monza, Troon
**06** Henley, Le Mans
**07** Aintree, Anfield, Daytona, Olympia, San Siro, The Oval
**08** Highbury, Sandwich
**09** Cresta Run, Edgbaston, Longchamp, Muirfield, Newmarket, St Andrews, The Belfry, Turnberry, Villa Park, Wimbledon
**10** Brooklands, Carnoustie, Celtic Park, Cheltenham, Elland Road, Fairyhouse, Headingley, Hockenheim, Interlagos, Meadowbank, Millennium, Monte Carlo, Twickenham
**11** Belmont Park, Brands Hatch, Hampden Park, Murrayfield, Old Trafford, Royal Lytham, Sandown Park, Silverstone, The Crucible, The Rose Bowl, Trent Bridge, Windsor Park
**12** Goodison Park, Texas Stadium, Wembley Arena
**13** Azteca Stadium, Caesar's Palace, Crystal Palace, Heysel Stadium, Royal Birkdale, The Albert Hall, White Hart Lane
**14** Anaheim Stadium, Churchill Downs, Stamford Bridge, Wembley Stadium
**15** Bernabeu Stadium, Cardiff Arms Park, Flushing Meadows, Maracana Stadium

**staff**
**03** man, rod **04** cane, crew, mace, pike, pole, prop, team, wand, work
**05** baton, crook, cross, equip, stave, stick **06** burden, crutch, cudgel, occupy, stanza, supply, taiaha, warder
**07** bourdon, crosier, crozier, operate, provide, scepter, sceptre, support, workers **08** arbalest, ash-plant, manpower, officers, pastoral, teachers
**09** employees, personnel, truncheon, workforce **10** alpenstock **11** secretariat
**12** secretariate **13** establishment
**14** human resources

**stag**
**03** dog **04** colt, male **05** royal, staig
**06** follow, humble, hummel, shadow
**07** brocket, knobber **08** imperial, informer, stallion **10** ten-pointer

**stage**
**02** do **03** lap, leg, pin **04** dais, give, step, tier, time, trek **05** apron, arena, field, floor, lay on, level, mount, phase, point, put on, realm, scene, shelf, stand
**06** direct, length, period, podium, sphere, storey **07** arrange, perform, present, produce, rostrum, setting, soapbox **08** backdrop, division, engineer, juncture, organize, platform, scaffold **10** background **11** orchestrate, put together, stage-manage
• **the stage**
**03** rep **05** drama **07** theatre, the play
**09** dramatics, theatrics, the boards
**11** Thespian art **12** show business
**13** the footlights

**stagecoach**
**03** fly **05** dilly **09** diligence

**stagger**
◇ *anagram indicator*
**04** reel, rock, roll, step, stot, stun, sway
**05** amaze, lurch, pitch, shake, shock, stoit, waver **06** bumble, daidle, falter, recoil, recule, teeter, totter, wintle, wobble **07** astound, blunder, nonplus, recoyle, recuile, stoiter, stotter, stupefy
**08** astonish, bowl over, confound, hesitate, keel over, surprise, titubate, wavering **09** dumbfound, overwhelm
**11** flabbergast

**staggered**
◇ *anagram indicator*
**05** dazed **06** amazed **07** shocked, stunned **08** open-eyed, startled
**09** astounded, surprised
**10** astonished, bewildered, bowled over, confounded, gobsmacked, taken aback **11** dumbfounded **12** lost for words **13** flabbergasted, knocked for six

**staggering**
◇ *anagram indicator*
**06** groggy **07** amazing, rolling
**08** dramatic, shocking, stunning
**09** titubancy **10** astounding, stupefying, surprising, titubation, unexpected, unforeseen
**11** astonishing **12** mind-boggling

**stagnant**
**04** dull, foul, slow **05** dirty, dying, inert, quiet, stale, still **06** filthy, smelly, torpid
**08** brackish, inactive, moribund, sluggish, standing **09** lethargic, unflowing, unhealthy **10** motionless

**stagnate**
**03** rot **04** idle, rust **05** decay **06** fester
**07** decline, putrefy **08** languish, vegetate **09** do nothing **10** degenerate
**11** deteriorate **14** become stagnant

**staid**
**03** sad **04** calm, prim **05** grave, quiet, sober, stiff **06** demure, formal, proper, sedate, solemn, sombre, steady
**07** serious, starchy **08** composed, decorous **09** permanent **12** buttoned-down **13** serious-minded

**stain**
**03** dye **04** blot, mail, mark, meal, mote, slur, smit, soil, spot, tint **05** bedye, black, chica, chico, cloud, color, dirty, henna, paint, shame, smear, sully, taint, tinge **06** blotch, chicha, colour, damage, embrue, imbrue, injure, injury, marble, smirch, smudge, smutch
**07** attaint, blacken, blemish, corrupt, embrewe, inkspot, soilure, splodge, splotch, tarnish, varnish **08** besmirch, Congo red, discolor, disgrace, maculate, sanguine **09** discolour, dishonour, osmic acid, pollution, soiliness **10** ensanguine, trypan blue
**11** contaminate **12** methyl violet, picrocarmine **13** Coomassie Blue®, discoloration **14** discolouration

**stair, stairs**
**04** ghat, pair, trap, vice **05** ghaut, grece, scale, sweep **06** perron, stayre
**07** caracol **08** caracole, escalier, turnpike **09** escalator, forestair
**10** backstairs, scale stair **11** common stair **12** companionway, winding stair
**13** scale and platt, turnpike stair
**14** apples and pears, escalier dérobé, scale staircase **15** companion ladder, moving staircase, spiral staircase

**stake**
**02** go **03** bet, peg, pot, put, rod, set, tie, vie **04** ante, gage, hold, mise, pale, pawn, pile, play, pole, post, prop, race, rest, risk, stob **05** brace, claim, prize, put in, put on, put up, share, spike, spile, stang, state, stick, tie up, wager
**06** assert, chance, demand, fasten, gamble, hazard, hold up, loggat, paling, picket, pierce, piquet, pledge, prop up, secure, tether **07** concern, contest, declare, picquet, support, venture **08** interest, standard, winnings
**09** establish **10** investment, lay claim to
**11** competition, involvement, requisition

• **stake out**
**05** watch **06** define, survey **07** delimit, mark off, mark out, outline, reserve **08** stake off **09** demarcate **11** keep an eye on

**stakes**
**03** bet **04** pool

• **row of stakes**
**04** wear, weir **05** orgue **06** paling, zareba, zariba, zereba, zeriba **07** zareeba **08** estacade, palisade, stockade **09** worm fence

**stale**
**03** dry, off, old **04** flat, hard, lure, sour **05** banal, blown, corny, fusty, jaded, musty, shaft, stalk, stock, tired, trite, urine **06** handle, mouldy **07** gone off, insipid, pretext, tainted, urinate, worn-out **08** clichéed, hardened, overused **09** hackneyed, tasteless, worthless **10** uninspired, unoriginal **11** commonplace, stereotyped **12** cliché-ridden, overfamiliar, run-of-the-mill **13** platitudinous

**stalemate**
**03** tie **04** draw, halt **07** impasse **08** blockade, deadlock, stand-off, zugzwang **10** standstill **15** Mexican standoff

**stalk**
**03** bun, kex **04** haft, hunt, keck, pace, rush, seta, stem, step, tail, twig, walk **05** chase, haunt, kecks, march, quill, shaft, shoot, spire, stale, stipe, strig, track, trail, trunk **06** bennet, branch, follow, kecksy, keksye, pursue, shadow, stride **07** pedicel, pedicle, petiole **08** peduncle **09** creep up on, give chase, track down **10** sporophore

*See also* **stem**

**stall**
**03** bay, pen, pew **04** bulk, coop, crib, ruse, slow, staw, trap **05** booth, decoy, defer, delay, dwell, hedge, kiosk, place, stand, table, trick **06** corral, hold up, induct, put off, stable, travis, trevis **07** counter, cowshed, cubicle, install, shamble, surface, surfeit, sutlery, treviss, tribune **08** fauteuil, flypitch, horse box, obstruct, platform, postpone, put on ice, slow down **09** enclosure, news-stand, stasidion, stonewall, temporize **10** equivocate, standstill **11** compartment, play for time **12** drag your feet

**stallion**
**04** stag **05** staig **06** cooser, cusser, entire **07** cuisser, kestrel, staniel, stannel, stanyel **09** courtesan, stud horse **10** stonehorse

**stalwart**
**05** burly, hardy, loyal, stout **06** brawny, daring, pretty, robust, rugged, steady, strong, sturdy, trusty **07** buirdly, devoted, staunch, valiant **08** athletic, faithful, intrepid, muscular, reliable, resolute, vigorous **09** committed, stalworth, steadfast, strapping **10** dependable, determined **11** indomitable

**stamina**
**04** grit, guts **05** fiber, fibre, force, power **06** bottom, energy, vigour **07** stamens **08** strength **09** endurance, fortitude **10** resilience, resistance **12** staying power

**stammer**
**03** hum **04** lisp **06** babble, falter, gibber, mumble **07** stumble, stutter **08** hesitate, splutter **12** speech defect

**stamp**
**03** cut, die, fix, tag **04** beat, cast, coin, form, kind, mark, mash, mint, pulp, seal, sort, type **05** brand, breed, crush, grind, label, mould, pound, press, print, punch, tread **06** cachet, emboss, enface, incuse, preace, prease, signet, squash, stramp, strike **07** engrave, fashion, impress, imprint, mintage, preasse, quality, trample, variety **08** hallmark, identify, inscribe **09** character, designate, signature **10** categorize, definitive, impression, tripudiate **11** attestation, description **12** characterize **13** authorization

*Famous and rare stamps include:*

**08** Bull's eye, Penny Red
**09** Basel dove, Penny Blue
**10** Mount Athos, Penny Black, Red Mercury, Scinde Dawk, VR official
**11** Jenny invert, St Louis bear
**12** Inverted swan
**13** Black Honduras, Inverted Jenny, Uganda Cowries

• **stamp out**
**03** end **04** curb, kill **05** crush, quash, quell **06** quench, scotch **07** destroy, put down **08** suppress **09** eliminate, eradicate, extirpate **10** extinguish, put an end to

**stampede**
**03** fly, ren, rin, run **04** dash, flee, race, rout, rush, tear **05** shoot **06** charge, flight, gallop, onrush, sprint **07** debacle, scatter **09** breakaway **10** scattering **12** sauve qui peut

**stance**
**04** line **05** angle, slant, stand **06** policy, stanza **07** bearing, opinion, posture, stretch **08** attitude, carriage, position **09** viewpoint **10** deportment, standpoint **11** point of view

**stanch**
**03** dam **04** halt, plug, stay, stem, stop **05** allay, block, check, loyal **06** arrest, hearty, quench, trusty **07** styptic, zealous **08** constant **09** floodgate, seaworthy **10** watertight

**stand**
**02** be **03** bin, nef, put, set **04** base, bear, bier, case, dais, desk, hold, line, park, post, rack, rise, wait **05** abide, allow, angle, bipod, booth, brook, erect, exist, frame, get up, place, plant, shelf, slant, stage, stall, stool, table, up-end **06** cradle, endure, locate, obtain, policy, remain, stance, suffer, tripod **07** be erect, be valid, counter, dumpbin, monopod, opinion, prevail, stand up, station, stomach, support, sustain, swallow, tribune, undergo, weather **08** attitude, cope with, guéridon, live with, monopode, pedestal, platform, position, stillage, stilling, stillion, stoppage, tolerate **09** be in force, be upright, put up with, viewpoint, withstand **10** be in effect, experience, resistance, standpoint **11** point of view **12** be on your feet, straighten up **13** get on your feet, get to your feet **14** rise to your feet

• **stand by**
**04** back **06** affirm, defend, hold to, uphold **07** stick by, support **08** adhere to, champion, side with **10** stand up for, stick up for

• **stand down**
**04** quit **06** give up, resign, retire **08** abdicate, step down, withdraw

• **stand for**
**04** bear, mean **05** allow, brook **06** denote, endure **07** betoken, signify, stomach **08** indicate, tolerate **09** put up with, represent, symbolize

• **stand in for**
**07** replace **08** cover for **10** understudy **11** deputize for **13** substitute for **14** hold the fort for, take the place of

• **stand out**
**04** show **06** extend, jut out, strout **07** jump out, poke out, project **08** stick out **09** be obvious **11** catch the eye **12** be noticeable **13** be conspicuous, stick out a mile

• **stand up**
**04** jilt, rise, wash **05** get up **06** cohere, hold up **07** let down, upstare **09** hold water **10** fail to meet **11** remain valid **12** straighten up **13** get to your feet **14** rise to your feet

• **stand up for**
**06** adhere, defend, uphold **07** protect, stand by, support **08** champion, fight for, side with **10** stick up for **13** remain loyal to

• **stand up to**
**04** defy, face **05** brave **06** endure, oppose, resist **08** confront, face up to **09** challenge, withstand

**standard**
**03** par, set, std **04** base, code, flag, mark, norm, rate, rule, type **05** basic, color, ethic, fixed, gauge, grade, guide, ideal, level, model, moral, norma, stock, usual **06** banner, colors, colour, ensign, normal, pennon, sample, square, staple **07** average, classic, colours, example, labarum, measure, pattern, pennant, popular, quality, regular, routine, scruple, typical **08** accepted, approved, exemplar, gonfalon, habitual, official, ordinary, orthodox, paradigm, streamer, vexillum **09** archetype, benchmark, criterion, customary, guideline, horsetail, principle, yardstick **10** definitive, prevailing, recognized, touchstone **11** established, Lesbian

rule, requirement **12** conventional **13** authoritative, specification

**standard-bearer**
**06** cornet, ensign **07** alférez, ancient **08** standard **09** vexillary **11** gonfalonier

**standardize**
**08** equalize, regiment **09** normalize **10** homogenize, regularize, stereotype **11** mass-produce, systematize

**stand-in**
**03** sub **04** temp **05** locum, proxy **06** deputy, second **08** delegate, stuntman **09** surrogate **10** stuntwoman, substitute, understudy **11** pinch-hitter **14** representative **15** second-in-command

**standing**
**04** foul, rank **05** dirty, erect, fixed, stale, still **06** filthy, repute, smelly, status **07** footing, lasting, rampant, regular, settled, station, up-ended, upright **08** brackish, duration, eminence, position, repeated, stagnant, vertical **09** existence, permanent, perpetual, seniority, unflowing, unhealthy **10** experience, motionless, on your feet, reputation **11** continuance, established **13** perpendicular

**stand-off**
**03** tie **04** draw, halt **07** impasse **08** blockade, deadlock **10** five-eighth, standstill

**standoffish**
**04** cold, cool **05** aloof **06** remote **07** distant **08** detached, reserved **09** withdrawn **10** unfriendly, unsociable **14** unapproachable **15** uncommunicative

**standpoint**
**05** angle, slant **06** stance **07** station **08** position **09** viewpoint **11** perspective, point of view **12** vantage point

**standstill**
**03** jam, jib **04** halt, lull, rest, stop **05** pause, stall, stand, tie-up **06** hold-up, log jam **07** dead-set, impasse **08** deadlock, dead stop, gridlock, stoppage, unmoving **09** cessation, stalemate **10** dead-finish, stationary, still-stand

• **to a standstill**
**02** up **04** down

**staple**
**03** key **04** main **05** basic, chief, major, sadza, vital **06** matoke **07** leading, matooke, primary, stapple, stopple **08** foremost, plantain, standard **09** essential, fastening, important, necessary, principal **11** fundamental, ship biscuit **13** indispensable

**star**
**03** orb, sun **04** idol, lead, moon, nova **05** celeb, major, shine **06** bigwig, famous, planet, shiner, sphere **07** big name, big shot, leading **08** asterisk, asteroid, luminary, talented **09** bespangle, brilliant, celebrity, paramount, personage, principal, prominent, satellite, superstar, well-known **10** celebrated, leading man, pre-eminent **11** illustrious, leading lady **12** heavenly body, leading light **13** celestial body, household name

*Stars include:*

**03** Dog, sun
**04** Mira, nova, Pole, Vega
**05** Deneb, Dubhe, Merak, North, Rigel, Spica
**06** meteor, Pollux, pulsar, quasar, Sirius
**07** Alphard, Antares, Canopus, Capella, falling, neutron, Polaris, Procyon
**08** Achernar, Arcturus, Barnard's, red dwarf, red giant, shooting
**09** Aldebaran, Alderamin, Fomalhaut, supernova
**10** Beta Crucis, Betelgeuse, brown dwarf, supergiant, white dwarf
**11** Alpha Boötis, Alpha Crucis, Delta Cephei
**12** Alpha Doradus
**13** Alpha Centauri
**15** Proxima Centauri

*See also* **constellation**

**starboard**
**01** R **05** right

**starchy**
**04** prim **05** staid, stiff **06** formal, stuffy **07** precise **11** ceremonious, punctilious, strait-laced **12** conventional

**stare**
**04** dare, gape, gawk, gawp, gaze, gorp, look, ogle **05** glare, watch **06** glower, goggle **07** fisheye, outface **08** starling **10** rubberneck

• **be staring you in the face**
**09** be blatant **13** be conspicuous, be very obvious, stick out a mile

**starfish**
**07** asterid **08** asteroid **09** stellerid **10** asteridian, bipinnaria, fivefinger **11** fivefingers, stelleridan **13** crown of thorns

**stark**
**04** bald, bare, grim, pure **05** bleak, blunt, clean, clear, empty, harsh, plain, quite, sharp, sheer, stern, stiff, total, utter **06** arrant, barren, dreary, gloomy, severe, simple, wholly **07** austere, obvious, totally, utterly **08** absolute, clear-cut, complete, desolate, distinct, entirely, flagrant, forsaken, starkers, thorough **09** downright, out-and-out, unadorned **10** absolutely, altogether, completely, consummate, depressing, stark-naked, start-naked **11** undecorated, unmitigated, unqualified **13** unembellished

**stark-naked**
**04** nude **05** naked, stark **06** unclad **08** en cuerpo, in the raw, starkers, stripped **09** in the buff, in the nude, undressed **15** in the altogether

**start**
◇ *head selection indicator*
**03** bug, fit, gin, law, off, set **04** dart, dawn, fire, jerk, jump, leap, make, open, roll **05** abray, arise, begin, birth, braid, break, burst, debut, found, get-go, go-off, issue, leave, onset, rouse, set up, shoot, spasm, spurt, wince **06** abrade, abraid, appear, boggle, create, depart, flinch, kick in, launch, origin, outset, recoil, set off, set out, shrink, spring, turn on, twitch **07** combust, getaway, jump-off, kick off, kick-off, opening, pioneer, trigger **08** activate, commence, conceive, embark on, fire away, get going, initiate, outburst **09** beginning, emergence, establish, inception, instigate, institute, introduce, originate, set on foot **10** convulsion, embark upon, foundation, inaugurate, initiation, trigger off **11** get cracking, get under way, institution, origination **12** commencement, inauguration, introduction **13** come into being **14** bring into being **15** get things moving

• **did not start, fail to start**
◇ *head deletion indicator*

**starter**
◇ *head selection indicator*
**04** meze, whet **05** tapas **06** bhajee, canapé, entrée, relish **08** antepast, apéritif, cocktail **09** appetizer **11** first course, hors d'oeuvre **13** prawn cocktail

**starting point**
**03** tee **04** base **06** origin **07** scratch **08** terminus **11** springboard

**startle**
**03** shy **04** rock **05** alarm, amaze, scare, shock, spook, start, upset **06** affray **07** agitate, astound, disturb, perturb **08** astonish, frighten, surprise, unsettle **11** make you jump

**startling**
**06** sudden **07** épatant **08** alarming, dramatic, galvanic, shocking **10** astounding, staggering, surprising, unexpected, unforeseen **11** astonishing **12** electrifying **13** extraordinary

**starvation**
**04** pine **05** death **06** famine, hunger **07** fasting **10** famishment **12** malnutrition **13** extreme hunger

**starve**
**03** die **04** clem, deny, diet, fast, pine **05** faint **06** famish, hunger, perish, sterve **07** atrophy, deprive **11** deteriorate

**starving**
**05** dying, faint **06** hungry **08** famished, ravenous, underfed **10** very hungry **14** undernourished

**stash**
**04** fund, heap, hide, mass, pile, quit, stop, stow **05** cache, hoard, lay up, store **06** closet, desist, save up **07** conceal, reserve, secrete **08** salt

away **09** reservoir, stockpile **10** collection **12** accumulation, squirrel away

**state**

◇ *homophone indicator*

**03** put, say **04** aver, case, état, flap, land, name, pomp, tell **05** endow, glory, panic, phase, realm, shape, stage, tizzy, utter, voice **06** affirm, assert, bother, canopy, dither, estate, formal, nation, plight, public, report, reveal, set out, settle, status, tizwas **07** council, country, declare, dignity, display, divulge, express, fluster, install, kingdom, majesty, pompous, present, specify, stately **08** announce, ceremony, disclose, grandeur, national, official, position, proclaim, property, republic **09** condition, establish, formulate, make known, situation, splendour, statement, territory **10** articulate, ceremonial, federation, government, parliament, promulgate **11** authorities, communicate, magnificent, predicament **12** governmental **13** circumstances, Establishment, parliamentary **14** administration

*See also* **province**

*Australian states and territories:*

**02** NT, SA, WA
**03** ACT, NSW, QLD, TAS, VIC
**08** Tasmania (TAS), Victoria (VIC)
**10** Queensland (QLD)
**13** New South Wales (NSW)
**14** South Australia (SA)
**16** Western Australia (WA)
**17** Northern Territory (NT)
**26** Australian Capital Territory (ACT)

*Australian state residents' nicknames:*

**08** Top Ender
**09** cornstalk, Croweater, gumsucker, Taswegian
**10** sandgroper
**11** Territorian, Vandemonian
**12** bananabender
**13** Apple Islander
**14** Cabbage Patcher
**15** Cabbage Gardener

*Indian states and union territories:*

**03** Goa
**05** Assam, Bihar, Delhi
**06** Kerala, Orissa, Punjab, Sikkim
**07** Gujarat, Haryana, Manipur, Mizoram, Tripura
**08** Nagaland
**09** Jharkhand, Karnataka, Meghalaya, Rajasthan, Tamil Nadu
**10** Chandigarh, West Bengal
**11** Daman and Diu, Lakshadweep, Maharashtra, Pondicherry, Uttaranchal
**12** Chhattisgarh, Uttar Pradesh
**13** Andhra Pradesh, Madhya Pradesh
**15** Himachal Pradesh, Jammu and Kashmir
**16** Arunachal Pradesh
**17** Andaman and Nicobar
**19** Dadra and Nagar Haveli

*US states:*

**04** Iowa, Ohio, Utah
**05** Idaho, Maine, Texas
**06** Alaska, Hawaii, Kansas, Nevada, Oregon
**07** Alabama, Arizona, Florida, Georgia, Indiana, Montana, New York, Vermont, Wyoming
**08** Arkansas, Colorado, Delaware, Illinois, Kentucky, Maryland, Michigan, Missouri, Nebraska, Oklahoma, Virginia
**09** Louisiana, Minnesota, New Jersey, New Mexico, Tennessee, Wisconsin
**10** California, Washington
**11** Connecticut, Mississippi, North Dakota, Rhode Island, South Dakota
**12** New Hampshire, Pennsylvania, West Virginia
**13** Massachusetts, North Carolina, South Carolina
**18** District of Columbia

*US state abbreviations and zip codes:*

**02** **AK** (Alaska), **AL** (Alabama), **AR** (Arkansas), **AZ** (Arizona), **CA** (California), **CO** (Colorado), **CT** (Connecticut), **DC** (District of Columbia), **DE** (Delaware), **FL** (Florida), **GA** (Georgia), **HI** (Hawaii), **IA** (Iowa), **ID** (Idaho), **IL** (Illinois), **IN** (Indiana), **KS** (Kansas), **KY** (Kentucky), **LA** (Louisiana), **MA** (Massachusetts), **MD** (Maryland), **ME** (Maine), **MI** (Michigan), **MN** (Minnesota), **MO** (Missouri), **MS** (Mississippi), **MT** (Montana), **NC** (North Carolina), **ND** (North Dakota), **NE** (Nebraska), **NH** (New Hampshire), **NJ** (New Jersey), **NM** (New Mexico), **NV** (Nevada), **NY** (New York), **OH** (Ohio), **OK** (Oklahoma), **OR** (Oregon), **PA** (Pennsylvania), **RI** (Rhode Island), **SC** (South Carolina), **SD** (South Dakota), **TN** (Tennessee), **TX** (Texas), **UT** (Utah), **VA** (Virginia), **VT** (Vermont), **WA** (Washington), **WI** (Wisconsin), **WV** (West Virginia), **WY** (Wyoming)
**03** **Ala** (Alabama), **Ark** (Arkansas), **Del** (Delaware), **Fla** (Florida), **Ill** (Illinois), **Ind** (Indiana), **Nev** (Nevada), **Tex** (Texas), **Wis** (Wisconsin), **W Va** (West Virginia), **Wyo** (Wyoming)
**04** **Ariz** (Arizona), **Colo** (Colorado), **Conn** (Connecticut), **Kans** (Kansas), **Mass** (Massachusetts), **Mich** (Michigan), **Minn** (Minnesota), **Miss** (Mississippi), **Mont** (Montana), **N Dak** (North Dakota), **Nebr** (Nebraska), **N Mex** (New Mexico), **Okla** (Oklahoma), **Oreg** (Oregon), **S Dak** (South Dakota), **Tenn** (Tennessee), **Wash** (Washington)
**05** **Calif** (California)

*US state nicknames:*

**08** **Bay State** (Massachusetts), **Gem State** (Idaho)
**09** **Beef State** (Nebraska), **Corn State** (Iowa), **Free State** (Maryland), **Old Colony** (Massachusetts)
**10** **Aloha State** (Hawaii), **First State** (Delaware), **Peach State** (Georgia), **Sioux State** (North Dakota)
**11** **Beaver State** (Oregon), **Coyote State** (South Dakota), **Creole State** (Louisiana), **Empire State** (New York), **Garden State** (New Jersey), **Golden State** (California), **Gopher State** (Minnesota), **Little Rhody** (Rhode Island), **Nutmeg State** (Connecticut), **Show Me State** (Missouri), **Silver State** (Nevada), **Sooner State** (Oklahoma), **Sunset State** (Oklahoma)
**12** **Beehive State** (Utah), **Buckeye State** (Ohio), **Bullion State** (Missouri), **Chinook State** (Washington), **Diamond State** (Delaware), **Granite State** (New Hampshire), **Hawkeye State** (Indiana), **Heart of Dixie** (Alabama), **Hoosier State** (Indiana), **Old Line State** (Maryland), **Prairie State** (Illinois), **Tar Heel State** (North Carolina)
**13** **Big Sky Country** (Montana), **Camellia State** (Alabama), **Equality State** (Wyoming), **Keystone State** (Pennsylvania), **Land of Lincoln** (Illinois), **Lone Star State** (Texas), **Magnolia State** (Mississippi), **Mainland State** (Alaska), **Mountain State** (West Virginia), **Old North State** (North Carolina), **Palmetto State** (South Carolina), **Pine Tree State** (Maine), **Sunshine State** (Florida, New Mexico, South Carolina), **Treasure State** (Montana)
**14** **Bluegrass State** (Kentucky), **Evergreen State** (Washington), **Great Lake State** (Michigan), **Jayhawker State** (Kansas), **North Star State** (Minnesota), **Panhandle State** (West Virginia), **Sagebrush State** (Nevada), **Volunteer State** (Tennessee), **Wolverine State** (Michigan)
**15** **Centennial State** (Colorado), **Plantation State** (Rhode Island), **The Last Frontier** (Alaska)
**16** **Flickertail State** (North Dakota), **Grand Canyon State** (Arizona), **Peace Garden State** (North Dakota)
**17** **America's Dairyland** (Wisconsin), **Constitution State** (Connecticut), **Land of Enchantment** (New Mexico), **Land of Opportunity** (Arkansas)
**18** **Green Mountain State** (Vermont), **Mother of Presidents** (Virginia)

• **in a state**

**05** het up, upset **07** anxious, hassled, in a stew, ruffled, worried **08** agitated, in a tizzy, troubled, worked up **09** flustered **10** distressed **13** panic-stricken

• **state of affairs**

**03** job **04** case **05** scene **06** crisis, plight, status **07** posture **08** juncture, position **09** condition, situation **11** predicament **12** kettle of fish, lie of the land **13** circumstances

**stately**

**05** grand, lofty, noble, proud, regal, royal **06** august, solemn **07** courtly, elegant, pompous **08** glorious, graceful, imperial, imposing, majestic, measured, splendid **09** dignified, mausolean **10** ceremonial, deliberate, impressive, majestical **11** ceremonious, magnificent

**statement**

**04** note **05** state, story, table **06** exposé, report, verbal **07** account, preface **08** averment, bulletin, manifest, relation **09** assertion, testimony, utterance **10** communiqué, disclosure, divulgence, revelation, white paper **11** affirmation, declaration, enunciation, presentment **12** announcement, constatation, presentation, press release, procès-verbal, proclamation, promulgation **13** communication **14** representation

**state-of-the-art**

**02** in **03** hip, new **04** cool **05** fresh, novel **06** hi-tech, latest, modern, modish, recent, trendy, with it **07** complex, go-ahead, in vogue, present **08** advanced, high-tech, space-age, up-to-date **09** inventive, the latest **10** futuristic, innovative, newfangled, present-day **11** complicated, cutting edge, modernistic, progressive **12** contemporary **13** up-to-the-minute **14** forward-looking **15** highly developed

**statesman, stateswoman**

**03** GOM **06** leader **08** diplomat, wealsman **10** homme d'état, politician **11** grand old man **14** elder statesman

*See also* **politician**

**static**

**05** fixed, inert, still **06** stable, steady **07** resting **08** constant, immobile, unmoving **09** unvarying **10** changeless, motionless, stationary, unchanging **11** undeviating **13** at a standstill, Maginot-minded

**station**

**03** lay, set, Sta **04** base, camp, farm, halt, post, rank, seat, send, site, stop **05** class, depot, grade, level, place, plant, point, rowme, stand **06** assign, centre, locate, office, status **07** appoint, channel, habitat, install, quarter **08** exchange, garrison, location, position, standing, terminus **09** establish, fare-stage **10** wavelength **11** park-and-ride, place of duty, whistle stop **12** headquarters **13** establishment, stopping-place

*See also* **London; police station; power; radio; railway station** *under* **railway**

**stationary**

**05** fixed, inert, still **06** at rest, ledger, lidger, moored, parked, static **07** resting, sessile, settled **08** constant, immobile, standing, unmoving **09** sedentary **10** motionless, standstill **13** at a standstill

**stationery**

*Stationery items include:*

**03** ink, pen, pin
**04** file
**05** diary, label, ruler, toner
**06** eraser, folder, marker, pencil, rubber, staple, Tipp-Ex®
**07** blotter, Blu-Tack®, divider, file tab, Filofax®, memo pad
**08** calendar, cash book, envelope, Jiffy bag®, notebook, scissors, stamp pad
**09** card index, clipboard, desk diary, flip chart, index card, notepaper, paper clip, Sellotape®, wall chart
**10** calculator, drawing pin, filing tray, floppy disk, graph paper, paper knife, Post-it note®, ring binder, rubber band
**11** account book, address book, bulldog clip, carbon paper, elastic band, rubber stamp, treasury tag
**12** adhesive tape, computer disk, copying paper, pocket folder, printer label, printer paper, writing paper
**13** expanding file, lever arch file, paper fastener, printer ribbon, tape dispenser
**14** document folder, document wallet, manila envelope, spiral notebook, suspension file, window envelope
**15** cartridge ribbon, correcting paper, correction fluid, headed notepaper, pencil-sharpener

**statue**

**02** ka **04** bust, head, idol, kore, tiki **05** gnome, image, torso **06** bronze, effigy, figure, kouros, xoanon **07** carving, stookie **08** acrolith, colossus, figurine, monument **09** sculpture, statuette **10** polychrome **11** garden gnome, whole-length **14** representation

*See also* **sculpture**

**statuesque**

**04** tall **05** regal **07** stately **08** handsome, imposing, majestic **09** dignified **10** impressive

**stature**

**04** fame, rank, size **06** height, inches, renown, weight **08** attitude, eminence, prestige, standing, tallness **09** elevation, loftiness **10** importance, prominence, reputation **11** consequence

**status**

**04** rank **05** class, grade, level, state **06** degree, weight **07** quality, station **08** eminence, position, prestige, standing **09** character, condition **10** importance, reputation **11** consequence, distinction **14** territoriality

**statute**

**03** act, law **04** rule **05** edict, ukase **06** assize, decree **07** Riot Act **09** capitular, enactment, ordinance **10** lex scripta, regulation, written law **13** interlocution, Septennial Act **15** act of parliament

**staunch**

**04** firm, halt, plug, stay, stem, stop, sure, true **05** allay, block, check, loyal, sound, stout **06** arrest, hearty, quench, stanch, strong, trusty **07** devoted, styptic, zealous **08** constant, faithful, reliable, resolute, yeomanly **09** committed, floodgate, seaworthy, steadfast **10** dependable, watertight **11** trustworthy

**staunchly**

**06** firmly **08** yeomanly **10** implacably, resolutely **11** steadfastly **12** unswervingly **13** unfalteringly, unflinchingly

**stave**

**03** bar, lag, rod **05** break, shaft, staff **06** sprain, stanza **07** break up

• **stave off**

**04** foil **05** avert, avoid, parry, repel **07** deflect, fend off, prevent, repulse, ward off **08** keep back **09** keep at bay, turn aside

**stay**

**04** curb, halt, hold, keep, last, live, prop, rest, sist, stop, wait, wire **05** abide, abode, allay, await, block, board, brace, cease, check, defer, delay, dwell, lodge, pause, put up, quell, strut, tarry, visit **06** arrest, desist, detain, endure, hinder, linger, put off, remain, reside, settle **07** adjourn, appease, control, holiday, persist, prevent, satisfy, shoring, sojourn, stay put, support, suspend **08** buttress, continue, obstacle, obstruct, postpone, prorogue, put on ice, reprieve, restrain, stopover, suppress, vacation **09** deferment, endurance, hang about, remission, restraint, stanchion **10** hang around, suspension **11** continuance, discontinue, take a room at **12** postponement **13** reinforcement

**staying power**

**04** grit, guts **05** fibre, force, power, steel **06** bottom, energy, vigour **07** stamina **08** strength **09** endurance, fortitude **10** resilience, resistance

**steadfast**

**03** sad **04** fast, firm **05** fixed, loyal **06** intent, manful, stable, steady, strong, sturdy **07** staunch **08** constant, faithful, reliable, resolute **09** dedicated, immovable **10** dependable, implacable,

unswerving, unwavering
**11** established, perseverant, persevering, unfaltering, unflinching
**12** single-minded, stout-hearted

**steadily**
**06** calmly, evenly **07** soberly
**08** sensibly **09** regularly, seriously
**10** constantly, rationally **12** all year round, on an even keel **13** round the clock **15** uninterruptedly

**steady**
**03** fix **04** calm, even, firm, rest
**05** brace, check, fixed, relax, sober, staid, still, usual **06** poised, secure, soothe, stable, subdue **07** balance, compose, control, regular, serious, settled, support, uniform **08** balanced, constant, habitual, reliable, resolute, restrain, sensible, unbroken, unmoving
**09** boyfriend, ceaseless, customary, immovable, incessant, perpetual, rock-solid, stabilize, steadfast, unexcited, unvarying **10** consistent, controlled, dependable, girlfriend, motionless, persistent, unchanging, unvariable, unwavering **11** consistence, consistency, established, industrious, unexcitable, unfaltering, unflappable, unremitting **12** on an even keel, tranquillize, well-balanced
**13** imperturbable, uninterrupted
**14** self-controlled

**steak**
**05** T-bone **08** pope's eye **09** entrecôte
**11** porterhouse **13** Chateaubriand

**steal**
**03** bag, cly, dip, lag, mag, nap, nim, nip, rob **04** blag, bone, crib, duff, glom, knap, lift, magg, mill, nick, pick, pull, slip, smug, snip, take, whip **05** annex, boost, bribe, creep, filch, heist, hoist, miche, mooch, mouch, pinch, poach, purse, shaft, shank, slide, slink, sneak, steel, steil, stele, swipe, theft
**06** abduct, burgle, convey, finger, handle, hijack, kidnap, nobble, pickle, pilfer, pocket, rip off, rustle, scrump, skrimp, skrump, snatch, snitch, steale, thieve, tiptoe, twitch **07** bargain, break in, cabbage, good buy, knock up, purloin, slither, smuggle, snaffle
**08** abstract, discount, embezzle, giveaway, half-inch, high-jack, knock off, liberate, peculate, scrounge, shoplift, souvenir **09** condiddle, duckshove, go off with, reduction, relieve of **10** burglarize, plagiarize, run off with **11** appropriate, make off with, pick a pocket, walk off with **12** make away with, special offer **13** value for money **14** help yourself to, misappropriate

**stealing**
**05** swipe, theft **06** piracy, snatch
**07** break-in, larceny, mugging, nicking, robbery, stick-up **08** burglary, filching, pinching, poaching, thievery, thieving
**09** pilferage, pilfering, sprechery
**10** peculation, plagiarism, purloining, spreaghery **11** shoplifting
**12** embezzlement, smash-and-grab
**13** appropriation

**stealth**
**05** theft **07** secrecy, slyness
**10** covertness, sneakiness
**11** furtiveness **12** stealthiness
**15** unobtrusiveness
- **by stealth**

**08** stowlins **09** stownlins **10** à la dérobée, stolenwise

**stealthily**
**05** slyly **08** covertly, secretly **09** by stealth, cunningly, furtively, stownlins
**10** à la dérobée, stolenwise
**15** surreptitiously

**stealthy**
**03** sly **05** mousy, quiet **06** covert, mousey, secret, sneaky **07** catlike, cunning, furtive **09** secretive, underhand **11** clandestine, unobtrusive
**13** surreptitious

**steam**
**04** haze, mist, roke **05** force **06** energy, exhale, spirit, vapour, vigour
**07** stamina **08** activity, dampness, moisture, momentum, outdated
**09** eagerness **10** enthusiasm, exhalation, liveliness **11** water vapour
**12** condensation, old-fashioned
- **get steamed up**

**07** explode **08** boil over, get angry, get het up **09** blow a fuse, do your nut
**10** get annoyed, get excited, hit the roof
**11** have kittens, lose your rag **12** blow your cool, fly into a rage, get flustered, lose your cool **15** fly off the handle
- **let off steam**

**08** sound off **13** let yourself go **15** air your feelings
- **steam up**

**05** fog up **06** mist up
- **under your own steam**

**05** alone **07** unaided **10** by yourself
**11** without help **13** independently

**steamer**
**02** SS **03** str, USS **06** packet, puffer
**09** propeller, steamboat, steamship, vaporetto, whaleback **10** packet-boat, packet-ship, paddle-boat **11** side-wheeler, steam-packet, steam vessel
**12** screw steamer **13** paddle steamer
**14** ocean-greyhound

**steaming**
◇ *anagram indicator*
*See* **drunk**

**steamy**
**03** hot **04** blue, damp, hazy, sexy
**05** close, humid, misty, muggy, stewy
**06** erotic, sticky, sultry, sweaty
**07** amorous, gaseous, lustful, raunchy, sensual, vapoury **08** steaming, vaporous **09** seductive, vapourish
**10** lubricious, passionate, sweltering, vaporiform

**steed**
**03** nag **04** hack, jade, sted **05** horse, mount, stedd, stede **06** stedde
**07** charger **09** Rosinante

**steel**
**05** brace, nerve, psych, shaft, shank, steal, steil, stele, sword **06** handle, harden, steale **07** fortify, prepare, toughen **15** trustworthiness

**steely**
**04** firm, grey, hard **05** harsh **06** strong
**08** blue-grey, pitiless, resolute
**09** merciless, steel-blue
**10** determined, inflexible, unyielding
**13** steel-coloured

**steep**
**03** sop **04** bold, buck, damp, dear, fill, high, mask, plot, soak, stey **05** bathe, bluff, brent, brine, embay, imbue, lofty, sharp, sheer, souse, stiff **06** abrupt, costly, drench, imbrue, infuse, pickle, rennet, seethe, steepy, sudden
**07** arduous, cragged, ensteep, extreme, immerse, moisten, pervade, stickle, suffuse **08** headlong, macerate, marinate, permeate, saturate, submerge, vertical
**09** difficult, excessive, expensive
**10** exorbitant, incredible, inordinate, overpriced, over the top, precipiced
**11** acclivitous, declivitous, exaggerated, exponential, high-pitched, precipitous, uncalled-for
**12** extortionate, unreasonable
**13** perpendicular

**steeple**
**05** spire, tower **06** belfry, turret
**11** rood-steeple **12** spire-steeple

**steeply**
**07** rapidly, sharply **08** abruptly, suddenly

**steer**
**03** con, cox **04** beef, cann, conn, helm, lead, stir, stot, tack **05** drive, guide, pilot, usher **06** direct, govern, steare
**07** conduct, control **08** navigate
- **steer clear of**

**04** shun **05** avoid, dodge, evade, skirt
**06** bypass, escape, eschew
**10** circumvent **12** keep away from

**stem**
**03** dam, pin, ram **04** axis, beam, bine, cane, come, corm, culm, curb, flow, halm, halt, plug, race, runt, stop, tail, tamp **05** arise, block, check, haulm, issue, shaft, shank, shoot, stalk, stock, trunk **06** arrest, bamboo, branch, breast, derive, family, oppose, resist, spring, stanch **07** contain, develop, emanate, hop-vine, staunch **08** kail-runt, peduncle, restrain **09** originate
**11** pipe-stapple, pipe-stopple **14** have its origins

**stench**
**04** niff, pong, reek **05** odour, smell, stink, whiff **06** miasma **08** mephitis

**stentorian**
**04** full, loud **06** strong **07** booming, ringing, vibrant **08** carrying, powerful, resonant, sonorous, strident
**10** thundering, thunderous
**13** reverberating

**step**
**03** act, fix, pas, peg **04** deed, gait, gree, gris, move, pace, rank, rung, trip, walk **05** glide, grade, grece, grees, grese, grice, grise, grize, level, notch, phase, point, print, stage, stair, stamp, stile, titup, trace, track, tramp, tread **06** action, degree, effort, gradin, greece, greese, griece, pit-pat, remove, stride, tittup **07** advance, gradine, grecian, measure, pitapat, process, shuffle, stempel, stemple, twinkle **08** démarche, footfall, footstep, greesing, gressing, halfpace, movement, pitty-pat, progress **09** expedient, footprint, gradation, manoeuvre, procedure **10** impression, proceeding **11** development, pas de basque, progression **14** course of action

*See also* **dance**

• **in step**
**08** in accord, in unison, together **09** in harmony **11** in agreement

• **out of step**
**06** at odds **09** not in step **13** at loggerheads **14** in disagreement

• **step by step**
**06** slowly **08** bit by bit, gradatim **09** gradually **13** progressively **14** little by little, one step at a time

• **step down**
**04** quit **05** leave **06** resign, retire **08** abdicate, withdraw **09** stand down **14** give up your post

• **step in**
**07** intrude, mediate **09** arbitrate, intercede, interfere, interrupt, intervene

• **step up**
**05** boost, raise **07** augment, build up, speed up **08** escalate, increase **09** intensify **10** accelerate

• **watch your step**
**07** look out **08** take care, watch out **09** be careful **11** be attentive **12** mind how you go

**stereotype**
**03** tag **04** cast **05** label, model, mould **06** cliché, stereo **07** formula, pattern **08** typecast **09** formalize **10** categorize, convention, pigeonhole **11** mass-produce, standardize **15** conventionalize, fixed set of ideas

**stereotyped**
**05** banal, corny, fixed, stale, stock, tired, trite **07** cliché'd **08** clichéed, overused, standard **09** hackneyed **10** threadbare, unoriginal **12** cliché-ridden, conventional, mass-produced, standardized, unchangeable **13** platitudinous, stereotypical

**sterile**
**03** dry **04** arid, bare, pure, vain **05** clean, moory, stale **06** barren, futile **07** aseptic, moorish, useless **08** abortive, acarpous, germ-free, germless, infecund, lifeless **09** fruitless, infertile, pointless **10** antiseptic, sterilized, unfruitful, uninfected, uninspired, unyielding **11** disinfected, ineffectual **12** unproductive, unprofitable **13** unimaginative **14** uncontaminated

**sterility**
**06** atocia, purity **07** asepsis **08** futility **09** cleanness, impotence **10** barrenness, inefficacy **11** infertility, unfecundity, uselessness **12** disinfection **13** fruitlessness, pointlessness **14** unfruitfulness **15** ineffectiveness

**sterilize**
**04** geld, spay **05** clean **06** doctor, neuter, purify, retort **07** cleanse **08** castrate, fumigate **09** autoclave, disinfect **13** make infertile

**sterling**
**03** ace, stg **04** mean, neat, pure, real, ster, true **05** brill, great, sound **06** worthy **07** genuine **08** smashing, standard, starling, terrific, top-notch **09** authentic, excellent **10** first-class **11** superlative **12** second to none **14** out of this world

**stern**
**04** back, grim, hard, helm, iron, poop, rear, rump, star, tail **05** cruel, harsh, rigid, stark, starn, tough **06** ramrod, severe, sombre, strict **07** austere, tail end **08** exacting, rigorous **09** demanding, Draconian, stringent, unsmiling, unsparing **10** forbidding, inflexible, relentless, tyrannical, unyielding **11** unrelenting **13** authoritarian

**sternly**
**06** grimly **07** cruelly, harshly **08** severely, sombrely, strictly **10** inflexibly **12** forbiddingly, relentlessly

**Stevenson**
**03** RLS

**stew**
◇ *anagram indicator*
**03** fix, jug **04** boil, cook, fret, fuss, hash, hole **05** daube, salmi, stove, sweat, tizzy, worry **06** bother, braise, burgoo, paella, pother, ragout, salmis, scouse, simmer, tajine, tizwas **07** agonize, cholent, chowder, fluster, goulash, haricot, navarin, stovies, swelter, tzimmes **08** matelote, mulligan, pot-au-feu, zarzuela **09** agitation, carbonade, carbonado, casserole, cassoulet, Irish stew, lobscouse, potpourri, succotash **10** carbonnade, lob's course, maconochie, prostitute **11** olla-podrida, ratatouille, slumgullion **13** bouillabaisse

**steward**
**05** dewan, diwan, reeve **06** bailie, butler, commis, factor, waiter **07** bailiff, baillie, foreman, maître d', marshal, mormaor **08** khansama, manciple, official, overseer, waitress **09** attendant, caretaker, custodian, khansamah, major-domo, seneschal, sommelier **10** air hostess, stewardess, supervisor **11** chamberlain **12** maître d'hôtel **14** homme d'affaires **15** flight attendant

**stick**
**03** fix, gad, gum, jab, jam, jut, lay, pin, put, set **04** bear, bind, bond, clog, drop, flak, fuse, glue, grip, hang, hold, join, last, poke, push, rest, site, stab, stay, stop, tack, tape, trap, twig, weld, yard **05** abide, abuse, affix, blame, cling, dwell, paste, place, prick, spear, stand, tally **06** adhere, attach, branch, cement, clog up, endure, fasten, impale, insert, linger, locate, pierce, remain, rocket, secure, solder, switch, thrust **07** carry on, confine, deposit, install, persist, reproof, scruple, set down, stomach, swallow **08** continue, position, protrude, puncture, tolerate, transfix **09** criticism, hostility, penetrate, put up with **10** punishment **11** come to a halt **12** dressing-down **13** get bogged down

*Sticks include:*

**02** ko
**03** bat, lug, rod
**04** cane, club, cosh, pike, pole, post, wand, whip
**05** baton, billy, birch, crook, lathi, staff, stake, waddy
**06** alpeen, crutch, cudgel, hockey, kierie, tripod
**07** sceptre, walking, woomera
**08** bludgeon, cocktail
**09** truncheon
**10** alpenstock, knobkerrie, shillelagh

• **stick at**
**04** balk **05** demur, doubt, pause **06** keep at, recoil, stop at **07** persist, scruple **08** continue, hesitate, plug away **09** persevere **10** shrink from **13** draw the line at

• **stick by**
**04** back **06** defend, hold to, uphold **07** stand by, support **08** adhere to, champion, side with **10** stand up for, stick up for

• **stick it out**
**07** persist **08** continue, keep at it, plug away **09** persevere **11** hang in there **13** grin and bear it

• **stick out**
**04** perk **05** bulge **06** extend, jut out, tongue **07** poke out, project **08** protrude **09** be obvious **12** be noticeable **13** be conspicuous

• **stick to**
**04** obey **06** accept, follow, fulfil, hold to, keep to, uphold **07** abide by, agree to, observe, respect, stand by **08** adhere to, carry out, submit to **09** conform to, discharge **10** comply with, toe the line **11** go along with, go by the book

• **stick up for**
**06** defend, uphold **07** protect, stand by, support **08** champion, fight for **10** speak up for, stand up for **13** take the part of, take the side of

• **the sticks**
**04** bush, wops **05** scrub **07** boonies,

hickdom, outback, wop-wops
**08** backveld, yokeldom
**09** backwoods, boondocks **10** back-blocks **11** remote areas, up the Boohai
**13** end of the earth **15** middle of nowhere

**sticker**
**03** bur **04** tine

**stickiness**
**03** goo **04** gaum, gorm, tack
**09** glueyness, gooeyness, gumminess, tackiness, viscidity **10** syrupiness
**12** adhesiveness **13** glutinousness

**stick-in-the-mud**
**05** fogey **06** fossil, square **08** fogeyish, old fogey, outmoded **09** Victorian
**10** antiquated, back number, fossilized, fuddy-duddy **12** antediluvian, buttoned-down, conservative
**13** unadventurous

**stickler**
**03** nut **06** backer, maniac, pedant, purist, second, umpire **07** fanatic, fusspot **08** mediator **09** regulator
**10** fussbudget **12** precisianist
**13** perfectionist, quarterdecker

**sticky**
**04** limy **05** chewy, close, dauby, gluey, gooey, goopy, gummy, humid, jammy, muggy, tacky, tough **06** claggy, clammy, clarty, clingy, cloggy, gummed, smeary, stodgy, sultry, sweaty, thorny, tricky, viscid
**07** awkward, viscous **08** adhesive, delicate, ticklish **09** difficult, glutinous, sensitive, tenacious **10** oppressive, sweltering, unpleasant
**12** embarrassing
• **sticky substance**
**03** goo, gum **04** glit, goop, gunk, lime
**05** gunge **06** viscin **08** mucilage, propolis

**stiff**
**03** rob **04** cold, dead, firm, hard, prim, taut, very **05** brisk, cheat, dense, fresh, harsh, large, rigid, solid, stark, stoor, stour, sture, tense, thick, tight, tough, windy **06** aching, chilly, corpse, formal, murder, potent, severe, stowre, strict, strong, tiring **07** arduous, austere, awkward, certain, drastic, extreme, pompous, stilted, unlucky, viscous
**08** decorous, exacting, forceful, hardened, priggish, reserved, rigorous, stubborn, vigorous **09** alcoholic, arthritic, demanding, difficult, Draconian, excessive, extremely, inelastic, laborious, resistant, rheumatic, stringent, unbending
**10** ceremonial, formidable, inflexible, solidified, unyielding **11** ceremonious, challenging, constrained, rheumaticky, standoffish **12** intoxicating, pertinacious

**stiffen**
**03** gel, set **04** jell **05** brace, stark, steel, tense **06** harden, starch **07** congeal, fortify, tense up, thicken, tighten
**08** ankylose, solidify **09** anchylose, bandoline, coagulate, reinforce, Trubenise, Trubenize® **10** strengthen

**stiff-necked**
**05** proud **06** formal **07** haughty
**08** arrogant, stubborn **09** obstinate, pig-headed, unnatural **11** opinionated
**12** contumacious **14** uncompromising

**stifle**
**04** curb, funk, hush **05** check, choke, crush, quash, quell, stive **06** dampen, deaden, hush up, keep in, muffle, subdue **07** repress, silence, smother, swallow **08** gulp back, gulp down, hold back, restrain, scomfish, strangle, suppress **09** constrain, suffocate
**10** asphyxiate, extinguish

**stigma**
**04** blot, mark, note, pore, scar, slur, spot **05** brand, shame, stain, taint
**07** blemish **08** disgrace, spiracle
**09** dishonour

**stigmatize**
**04** mark, note **05** brand, label, shame, stain **06** vilify **07** blemish, condemn
**08** demonize, denounce, disgrace, vilipend **09** discredit

**still**
**03** but, e'en, ene, yet **04** calm, deep, even, hush, kill, mild **05** abate, accoy, allay, inert, peace, quiet **06** always, distil, even so, hushed, pacify, serene, settle, silent, smooth, soothe, static, subdue, though **07** appease, assuage, however, quieten, quietly, restful, silence **08** although, constant, immobile, inactive, lifeless, moderate, peaceful, restrain, serenity, stagnant, tranquil, unmoving, until now
**09** continual, noiseless, quiescent, quietness, sedentary, stillness, unruffled **10** constantly, for all that, inactively, motionless, stationary, stock-still, unstirring **11** nonetheless, undisturbed **12** nevertheless, peacefulness, tranquillity, tranquillize, up to this time **13** in spite of that, in spite of this, noiselessness
**15** notwithstanding
• **be still**
**03** lie **04** hush, rest **06** remain, repose

**stillness**
**04** calm, hush, rest **05** peace, quiet
**06** repose **07** silence **08** calmness, coolness, quietude, serenity
**09** composure, placidity, quietness
**10** equanimity, sedateness
**11** restfulness **12** peacefulness, tranquillity

**stilted**
**05** stiff **06** forced, wooden
**08** laboured, mannered **09** unnatural
**10** artificial **11** constrained

**stimulant**
**01** E **03** kat, qat **04** khat **05** betel, chile, chili, tonic, upper **06** chilli, cinder
**07** caffein, cardiac, digoxin, ecstasy, guaraná, pep pill, reviver **08** caffeine, coramine, doxapram, excitant, incitant, lobeline, pemoline, pick-me-up
**09** analeptic, cantharis, dance drug, digitalin, nux vomica, sassafras, whetstone **11** nikethamide, purple heart, restorative, winter's bark
**13** dexamfetamine, smelling salts
**14** dexamphetamine
**15** methamphetamine

**stimulate**
**03** fan, jog **04** fire, goad, hype, spur, urge **05** gee up, hop up, impel, rouse
**06** arouse, buck up, excite, fillip, hype up, incite, induce, kindle, prompt, whip up **07** animate, hearten, inflame, inspire, provoke, quicken, trigger
**08** activate, irritate, motivate
**09** challenge, encourage, instigate
**10** potentiate, trigger off

**stimulating**
**07** bracing, piquant, rousing
**08** excitant, exciting, galvanic, stirring
**09** inspiring, provoking, stimulant
**10** intriguing, suggestive **11** interesting, provocative **12** exhilarating

**stimulation**
**06** ginger **07** arousal **08** kindling
**09** animation, prompting
**10** excitement, incitement, irritation, motivation, quickening **11** inspiration, instigation, provocation
**13** encouragement

**stimulus**
**03** jog **04** goad, jolt, kick, prod, push, spur, whet **05** drive, sting **06** fillip
**07** impetus **09** incentive
**10** incitement, inducement
**11** provocation **12** shot in the arm
**13** encouragement

**sting**
**02** do **03** con, nip, rob **04** barb, bite, burn, edge, goad, hurt, lurk, pain, pole, scam, tang **05** annoy, cheat, fraud, point, prick, smart, spite, stang, trick, upset, wound **06** diddle, fiddle, fleece, grieve, injure, injury, malice, needle, nettle, offend, racket, rip off, rip-off, tingle **07** aculeus, deceive, defraud, incense, piercer, provoke, sarcasm, swindle, torment **08** distress, irritate, pungency, stimulus, trickery, urticate
**09** deception, gold brick, gold-brick, heartache, sharpness **10** causticity, exasperate, incitement, irritation
**11** causticness, viciousness
**12** incisiveness, take for a ride
**13** double-dealing, sharp practice

**stinging**
**05** smart, urent **07** burning, hurtful, piquant **08** aculeate, poignant, smarting, tingling, urticant, wounding
**09** aculeated, injurious, offensive
**10** irritating **11** distressing

**stingy**
**04** hard, mean, near **05** close, mingy, tight **06** hungry, skimpy, snippy
**07** costive, miserly, niggard, save-all
**09** niggardly, penurious **11** bad-tempered, tight-fisted **12** candle-paring, cheeseparing, parsimonious
**13** penny-pinching

**stink**
**03** hum, row **04** flap, fuss, guff, honk, ming, niff, pong, reek, stir, suck **05** be bad, hoo-ha, odour, smell **06** bother, furore, hassle, stench **07** be awful, be nasty, fluster, trouble **08** bad smell, malodour, mephitis **09** commotion, foul smell **12** be despicable, be unpleasant, song and dance

**stinker**
**03** cur, dog, rat **04** scab **05** cheat, hound, louse, rogue, scamp, swine **06** fulmar, horror, louser, petrel, plight, rascal, rotter **07** bounder, dastard, problem, ruffian, shocker, villain **08** blighter, stinkard, vagabond **09** miscreant, reprobate, scallywag, scoundrel **10** blackguard, difficulty, impediment, ne'er-do-well **11** predicament **14** good-for-nothing

**stinking**
**03** bad **04** foul, vile **05** awful, fetid, nasty, niffy, pongy **06** foetid, mingin', rotten **07** humming, minging, stenchy **08** terrible **10** disgusting, unpleasant **12** contemptible

**stint**
**03** bit **04** bout, save, stop, time, turn **05** allot, cease, check, limit, pinch, quota, scant, share, shift, skimp, spare, spell, stent **06** period, scrimp **07** scantle, skimp on, stretch **08** begrudge, restrain, restrict, withhold **09** allowance, apportion, economize, restraint **11** restriction

**stipend**
**03** ann **05** annat, grant **06** income, salary **07** alimony, annuity, benefit, payment, pension **08** expenses **09** allowance **10** assistance **11** maintenance **12** contribution

**stipulate**
**06** demand **07** article, lay down, provide, require, set down, specify **08** covenant, insist on **09** guarantee

**stipulation**
**05** point, rider **06** clause, demand **07** proviso **08** contract **09** condition, postulate, provision **11** requirement **12** precondition, prerequisite **13** specification

**stir**
◇ *anagram indicator*
**03** ado, jee, jog, mix, wag **04** beat, flap, fuss, moot, move, to-do, turn, whip **05** blend, budge, churn, hoo-ha, pique, quich, raise, rouse, shake, shift, steer, stire, tizzy, touch **06** affect, bustle, excite, flurry, muddle, prison, puddle, quatch, quetch, quitch, quiver, racket, riffle, rustle, thrill, tumult, twitch, uproar **07** agitate, clutter, disturb, ferment, flutter, inspire, provoke, quinche, rummage, tempest, torment, tremble **08** activity, disorder, movement **09** agitation, commotion, kerfuffle, sensation **10** excitement **11** disturbance **12** song and dance
*See also* **prison**

• **stir up**
**03** jog **04** fire, poke, rear, spur, wake **05** amove, awake, drive, impel, poach, raise, rouse, roust, waken **06** arouse, awaken, excite, incite, kindle, prompt, racket, rustle **07** agitate, animate, disturb, inflame, inspire, provoke, quicken, rummage **08** motivate **09** electrify, encourage, galvanize, instigate, stimulate

**stirring**
◇ *anagram indicator*
**04** live **05** heady **06** lively, moving **07** emotive, rousing, working **08** dramatic, exciting, spirited **09** animating, inspiring, thrilling **11** impassioned, stimulating **12** exhilarating, intoxicating

**stitch**
**03** hem, sew **04** darn, mend, seam, tack **06** repair **09** embroider
*See also* **embroidery**

• **stitch up**
**03** con **04** shop, trap **05** fit up, grass, plant, set up **06** rumble, suture **07** swindle **11** double-cross, incriminate **13** stab in the back

**stock**
**03** box, log, set **04** cows, fund, heap, keep, line, name, pack, pigs, pile, post, race, sell, team **05** banal, basic, block, blood, bonds, breed, cache, carry, equip, fumet, funds, goods, herds, hoard, money, plant, range, sheep, store, stump, talon, tired, trite, trunk, usual, wares **06** assets, cattle, common, credit, deal in, family, flocks, handle, horses, kit out, market, repute, shares, source, strain, supply, trough **07** animals, average, capital, descent, fumette, furnish, holding, kindred, lineage, opinion, plenish, provide, regular, reserve, routine, species, stretch, trade in, variety, worn-out **08** accoutre, ancestry, clichéed, equities, good name, ordinary, overused, pedigree, pressure, quantity, standard, standing, stoccado **09** amassment, customary, equipment, essential, genealogy, hackneyed, inventory, livestock, parentage, portfolio, provision, relatives, reservoir, selection, stockpile, traffic in **10** assortment, background, collection, estimation, extraction, investment, repertoire, reputation, securities **11** commodities, farm animals, merchandise, merchandize, stereotyped, traditional **12** accumulation, conventional, run-of-the-mill

• **in stock**
**06** on sale **07** for sale **09** available **11** on the market **12** on the shelves

• **stock up**
**03** buy **04** fill, heap, load, save **05** amass, buy up, hoard, lay in, store **06** fill up, gather, heap up, pile up **07** put away, stack up, store up **08** put aside, salt away **09** provision, replenish, stash away, stockpile **10** accumulate

• **take stock**
**06** assess, review, size up, survey **07** weigh up **08** appraise, estimate, evaluate, reassess **09** re-examine **10** re-evaluate

**stockade**
**06** zareba, zariba, zereba, zeriba **07** zareeba

**stocking**
**05** nylon, stock **06** hogger, moggan **07** popsock, spattee **08** boothose, knee-high **10** understock **11** netherstock
*See also* **sock**

**stockings**
**04** hose **07** hold-ups, legwear **11** netherlings

**stockpile**
**04** fund, heap, keep, pile, save **05** amass, cache, hoard, stock, store **06** gather, heap up, pile up **07** put away, reserve, store up **08** put aside **09** amassment, reservoir **10** accumulate **12** accumulation

**stock-still**
**05** inert, still **06** static **08** immobile, inactive, unmoving **10** motionless, stationary, unstirring

**stocky**
**05** broad, dumpy, short, solid, squat **06** blocky, chunky, stubby, stumpy, sturdy **07** nuggety **08** thickset **11** mesomorphic

**stodgy**
**04** dull **05** heavy, solid, staid **06** boring, formal, leaden, solemn, stuffy, turgid **07** filling, starchy, tedious **08** laboured **10** fuddy-duddy, spiritless, unexciting, uninspired **11** substantial **12** indigestible **13** unimaginative **14** unenterprising

**stoical**
**04** calm, cool **07** patient **08** resigned **09** accepting, impassive **10** forbearing, phlegmatic **11** indifferent, unemotional, unexcitable **13** dispassionate, imperturbable, long-suffering, philosophical, uncomplaining **14** self-controlled **15** self-disciplined

**stoicism**
**07** ataraxy **08** ataraxia, calmness, fatalism, patience **09** fortitude, stolidity **10** acceptance, dispassion, philosophy **11** forbearance, impassivity, resignation **12** indifference **13** long-suffering **14** unexcitability

**stoke**
**04** tend **09** add coal to, add fuel to, add wood to **11** keep burning **12** feed with fuel

**stokes**
**01** S

**stolen**
**03** hot **04** bent **05** taken **06** nicked, swiped **07** nobbled, punched

**08** pilfered **09** ill-gotten, purloined, ripped off **10** knocked off

**• stolen goods**
**03** tom **04** crib, loot, soup, waif **05** cheat, theft **07** stealth **08** tweedler **09** stouthrie **10** stoutherie, tomfoolery

**stolid**
**02** po **04** dull, slow **05** beefy, heavy **06** bovine, solemn, wooden **07** lumpish, po-faced **08** blockish **09** apathetic, impassive **10** phlegmatic **11** indifferent, unemotional, uninspiring **13** unimaginative

**stomach**
**03** gut, maw, tum **04** bear, craw, guts, puku, read, take, vell, zest **05** abide, belly, bible, bingy, brook, gorge, pride, rumen, stand, taste, tummy **06** bonnet, desire, digest, endure, fardel, hunger, inside, liking, omasum, paunch, relish, rennet, resent, spirit, spleen, suffer, tum-tum, venter **07** abdomen, courage, gizzard, insides, passion **08** abomasum, appetite, pot-belly, submit to, tolerate **09** approve of, king's-hood, manyplies, put up with, rennet-bag, reticulum **10** little Mary, psalterium **11** bread basket, corporation, disposition, inclination **13** determination

*See also* **ruminant**

**• without stomach**
◇ *middle deletion indicator*

**stomach ache**
**05** colic **06** gripes, gut rot **09** bellyache, dyspepsia, tummy ache **12** hypochondria **13** grass staggers **15** stomach staggers

**stone**
**02** st **03** gem, pip, pit, rag, set **04** flag, hone, plum, rock, seed, sett, slab **05** jewel, lapis **06** cobble, gibber, gonnie, goolie, kernel, mirror, pebble, yonnie **07** boondie, boulder, brinnie **08** endocarp, gemstone, sardonyx, testicle **09** flagstone, headstone, tombstone **10** concretion, gravestone

*See also* **birth**; **gem**; **rock**

**stoned** *see* **drunk**

**stonewall**
**03** lie **05** dodge, evade, hedge, shift **06** waffle **07** deceive, quibble, shuffle **09** be evasive, pussy-foot **10** equivocate **11** prevaricate **12** shilly-shally **13** sit on the fence

**stony**
**03** icy **04** cold, hard **05** blank, rigid, rocky, stern **06** chilly, frigid, frosty, gritty, pebbly, severe, steely **07** adamant, callous, deadpan, hostile, petrous, shingly **08** gravelly, obdurate, pitiless **09** heartless, lapideous, merciless, unfeeling **10** inexorable, petrifying, poker-faced, unfriendly **11** indifferent, unforgiving **12** unresponsive **14** expressionless

**stooge**
**04** butt, dupe, feed, foil, pawn **06** drudge, lackey, puppet **07** cat's paw, fall guy **08** henchman **09** scapegoat **11** subordinate

**stool**
**05** coppy, stand **06** buffet, sunkie, tripod **07** creepie, cricket, taboret, tumbrel, tumbril **08** stillage, tabouret

**stoop**
**03** bow, sag **04** bend, curb, duck, lean, lout, lowt, poke, post, prop, sink **05** courb, deign, droop, hunch, kneel, lower, porch, slump, squat, steep, stoep, stope, stoup, swoop **06** bucket, cringe, crouch, patron, resort, slouch, stoope, submit **07** bending, decline, descend, descent, ducking, incline **08** hunching, lowering, verandah **09** go so far as, go so low as, supporter, vouchsafe **10** condescend **11** inclination **13** condescension, lower yourself

**stop**
**03** bar, can, dit, end **04** bung, cork, halt, hold, kick, kill, live, plug, poop, quit, rein, rest, seal, sist, snub, stap, stay, stem **05** block, board, break, cease, check, choke, close, cover, dwell, embar, imbar, lodge, media, pause, put up, snuff, sprag, stage, stall, stash, stimy, tarry, visit **06** anchor, arrest, cut off, desist, detain, devall, draw up, finish, hinder, impede, keep up, pack in, pack up, rein in, reside, scotch, settle, stanch, stimie, stop up, stymie, thwart, wind up **07** abandon, bus stop, chuck it, close up, occlude, prevent, refrain, sojourn, station, staunch, suspend **08** conclude, draw rein, give over, hold hard, knock off, leave off, obstacle, obstruct, pack it in, pack it up, restrain, stopover, stoppage, suppress, terminus, withhold **09** cessation, diaphragm, fare stage, foreclose, frustrate, hindrance, intercept, interrupt, obstruent, punctuate, terminate **10** conclusion, standstill **11** come to an end, come to a rest, destination, discontinue, termination **12** bring to an end, bring to a rest, interruption **13** stopping-place **14** discontinuance **15** discontinuation

*See also* **organ**

**• expressions ordering a stop**
**02** ha, ho, wo **03** hoa, hoh **04** easy, proo, pruh, toho, whoa **05** avast

**stopgap**
**05** shift **06** resort **09** emergency, expedient, impromptu, makeshift, temporary **10** improvised, substitute **11** provisional **12** expediential **13** improvisation, rough-and-ready

**stopover**
**04** rest, stop **05** break, visit **07** layover, sojourn, stop-off **13** overnight stay

**stoppage**
**03** cut, jam **04** blin, halt, stop **05** check, choke, hitch, sit-in, stand, stick **06** arrest, freeze, hartal, hold-up, outage, pull-up, strike **07** closure, embargo, removal, shut-off, walk-out **08** asphyxia, blackout, blockage, decrease, discount, obstacle, shutdown, stayaway **09** allowance, breakdown, cessation, deduction, hindrance, occlusion, reduction, taking off **10** inhibition, standstill, taking away, withdrawal **11** haemostasis, obstruction, subtraction, suppression, termination **12** heart failure, interruption **14** discontinuance **15** discontinuation

**stopper**
**03** tap **04** bung, cork, plug, seal **06** spigot **07** stopple **08** screwtop

**storage**
**• computer storage**
**03** RAM, ROM

**store**
**03** lot **04** bank, barn, fund, heap, keep, load, mine, pack, save, shop, stow **05** cache, hoard, house, lay by, lay in, lay up, stash, stock, stuff, value **06** coffer, esteem, garner, gather, larder, panary, plenty, supply, vintry **07** buttery, collect, deposit, furnish, keeping, lay down, put down, reserve **08** cupboard, minimart, multiple, put aside, quantity, salt away, treasury **09** abundance, amassment, livestock, provision, reservoir, stockpile, storeroom, warehouse **10** accumulate, chain store, corner shop, depository, groceteria, repository, storehouse **11** hypermarket, stock up with, sufficiency, supermarket **12** accumulation, retail outlet, squirrel away **15** department store

**• set store by, lay store by**
**05** value **06** admire, esteem **13** think highly of **14** consider highly

**storehouse**
**04** barn, fund, hold, silo **05** depot, étape, vault **06** cellar, garner, larder, pantry, pataka, wealth **07** armoury, arsenal, buttery, granary **08** dene-hole, elevator, entrepot, magazine, treasury **09** repertory, thesaurus, warehouse **10** depository, repository **12** conservatory

**storey**
**04** deck, flat, tier **05** attic, étage, floor, level, stage **06** flight **07** stratum **08** basement, bel étage, entresol **09** triforium **10** clearstory, clerestory, downstairs, first floor **11** ground floor

**stork**
**06** argala, jabiru **08** adjutant, shoebill **09** whale-head **10** saddlebill

**storm**
◇ *anagram indicator*
**03** row **04** fume, rage, rand, rant, rave, roar, rush, stir, tear, to-do **05** shout, stamp **06** assail, attack, charge, furore, outcry, rumpus, seethe, tumult, uproar **07** assault, clamour, explode, flounce, turmoil **08** brouhaha, outbreak, outburst, paroxysm **09** agitation, commotion, kerfuffle, offensive,

onslaught **10** hit the roof
**11** disturbance **12** lose your cool
**14** foam at the mouth

*Storms include:*

**03** ice, sea, sun
**04** dust, gale, hail, line, rain, sand, snow
**05** buran, devil
**06** baguio, calima, haboob, meteor, pelter, squall
**07** cyclone, monsoon, Shaitan, tempest, thunder, tornado, typhoon, violent
**08** blizzard, downpour, magnetic
**09** bourasque, dust devil, hurricane, whirlwind
**10** cloudburst, electrical

**stormy**
◇ *anagram indicator*
**04** foul, wild **05** dirty, gusty, rainy, rough, windy, wroth **06** choppy, raging, rugged, unruly, wintry
**07** gustful, squally, wintery **08** blustery, oragious, stormful **09** inclement, turbulent **10** boisterous, passionate
**11** tempestuous

**story**
**03** bar, fib, gag, lie, rib **04** baur, bawr, epic, idyl, item, joke, myth, plot, saga, tale, tier, yarn **05** fable, floor, idyll, novel, rumor, theme **06** legend, record, relate, report, rumour, serial, storey **07** account, article, episode, fantasy, feature, fiction, history, recital, romance, shocker, untruth
**08** anecdote, jeremiad, nouvelle, oratorio, phantasy, relation, thriller
**09** chronicle, falsehood, narrative, statement, storyline **10** allegation, Munchausen, rib-tickler **11** fabrication, historiette, Munchhausen **12** old wives' tale, spine-chiller

*See also* **novel**; **tale**

**storyteller**
**04** bard, liar **06** author, writer
**08** narrator, novelist, romancer, tell-tale
**09** raconteur **10** anecdotist, chronicler, raconteuse

**stout**
**03** big, fat **04** bold, tall **05** beefy, brave, bulky, burly, cobby, gutsy, hardy, heavy, lusty, obese, plump, proud, solid, thick, tough, tubby **06** brawny, entire, fierce, fleshy, gritty, heroic, manful, plucky, portly, robust, spunky, stanch, stocky, strong, stuffy, stuggy, sturdy
**07** durable, gallant, hulking, staunch, valiant **08** arrogant, athletic, chopping, enduring, fearless, forceful, intrepid, muscular, resolute, stalwart, stubborn, thickset, valorous, vigorous
**09** corpulent, dauntless
**10** courageous, determined, embonpoint, overweight, unyielding
**11** substantial

**stoutly**
**06** boldly **07** toughly **08** fiercely, strongly **09** staunchly **10** fearlessly, resolutely

**stove**
**03** Aga **04** kiln, oven, stew **05** grill, range **06** cockle, cooker, heater, Primus® **07** caboose, chaufer, furnace
**08** chauffer, hothouse, pot-belly
**09** gas cooker, kitchener **10** base-burner, calefactor, salamander
**12** cooking-range

**stow**
◇ *containment indicator*
**04** cram, crop, load, pack **05** place, stash, store, stuff **06** bundle
**07** deposit, put away **11** flemish down
• **stow away**
**04** hide, snug, tuck **05** put up **07** put away **14** travel secretly **15** conceal yourself

**straggle**
**03** gad, lag **04** roam, rove, tail
**05** amble, drift, range, stray, trail
**06** loiter, ramble, sprawl, spread, wander **07** scatter, vagrant
**08** sprangle, squander **09** string out
**10** dilly-dally

**straggly**
**05** loose **06** random, untidy **07** aimless
**08** drifting, rambling, straying
**09** irregular, spreading, strung out
**10** straggling **12** disorganized

**straight**
**03** het, str **04** even, fair, flat, gain, just, neat, pure, slap, tidy, true **05** blunt, frank, level, right, smack, spang **06** at once, candid, decent, direct, honest, normal, pronto, square, unbent
**07** aligned, bluntly, clearly, frankly, in order, orderly, plainly, settled, sincere, unmixed, upright **08** accurate, arranged, balanced, candidly, directly, faithful, honestly, promptly, reliable, slap-bang, unbroken, uncurved, vertical **09** downright, instantly, on the trot, organized, outspoken, right away, shipshape, tramlined, unbending, uncurving, undiluted **10** consistent, continuous, forthright, honourable, horizontal, law-abiding, point-blank, successive, unswerving, upstanding
**11** consecutive, immediately, outspokenly, rectilineal, rectilinear, respectable, trustworthy, undeviating
**12** continuously, conventional, forthrightly, heterosexual, orthotropous, successively, without delay **13** consecutively, unadulterated, uninterrupted **14** as the crow flies
**15** straightforward, uninterruptedly
• **off the straight**
**04** agee, ajee **08** cockeyed
• **straight away**
**03** now **06** at once, pronto **08** directly, like that **09** instantly, right away
**11** immediately, incontinent **12** just like that, there and then, without delay
**13** incontinently

**straighten**
◇ *anagram indicator*
**04** tidy, yelm **05** align, dress, order, range, yealm **06** adjust, neaten, tidy up, unbend **07** arrange, stretch **08** put right **10** put in order **12** make straight
**14** become straight
• **straighten out**
**06** extend, settle, tidy up **07** clear up, correct, realign, rectify, resolve, sort out, untwist **08** put right **10** put in order, regularize **11** disentangle
• **straighten up**
**05** stand **07** stand up **10** stand erect
**12** stand upright

**straightforward**
**04** easy, even, open **05** clear, frank, pakka, plain, pucka, pukka **06** candid, direct, honest, simple **07** genuine, jannock, sincere, up-front **08** no frills, truthful **09** outspoken **10** child's play, elementary, forthright, on the level, penny-plain, point-blank, unexacting
**11** undemanding, undesigning **12** a piece of cake **13** plain-speaking, uncomplicated, without frills

**strain**
**03** air, fit, rax, sye, tax, try, tug, way
**04** aria, fitt, hurt, kind, play, pull, race, rack, rick, seil, sift, sile, sing, song, sort, tear, tire, tune, type, vein, work
**05** blood, breed, drain, drive, exert, fitte, force, fytte, heave, labor, music, point, press, retch, shear, sieve, sound, stock, theme, trace, trait, twist, worry, wrick, wring **06** burden, demand, duress, effort, extend, family, filter, goggle, injure, injury, labour, melody, purify, riddle, screen, sprain, spring, streak, stress, stripe, strive, tauten, weaken, wrench **07** anxiety, descent, distend, element, embrace, express, fatigue, lineage, measure, overtax, quality, squeeze, stretch, tension, tighten, variety **08** ancestry, compress, elongate, exertion, go all out, overwork, pedigree, pressure, restrain, separate, struggle, tendency
**09** endeavour, offspring, percolate, suspicion, tiredness, weariness
**10** exhaustion, extraction, proclivity, suggestion **11** disposition **12** do your utmost **14** beyond the limit, characteristic, push to the limit
**15** make every effort

**strained**
**05** drawn, false, heavy, stiff, tense
**06** forced, sprung, uneasy, wooden
**07** awkward, intense **08** laboured
**09** intensive, unnatural, unrelaxed
**10** artificial, non-natural
**11** constrained, embarrassed **13** self-conscious, uncomfortable

**strainer**
**03** sye **04** seil, sile, tems **05** sieve, siler, tammy, temse **06** filter, milsey, riddle, screen, sifter **08** colander **09** cullender

**strait**
**02** St **03** fix, gat, gut, jam **04** belt, hole, kyle, mess **05** close, inlet, needy, sound, tight **06** crisis, narrow, pickle, plight, strict **07** channel, closely, dilemma, narrows, poverty, tighten, tightly **08** distress, hardship, narrowly, rigorous, straight, streight, strictly

**09** emergency, extremity **10** difficulty, perplexity, rigorously **11** hard-pressed, predicament **13** embarrassment

*Straits include:*

**03** Rae
**04** Adak, Bass, Cook, Haro, Irbe, Kara, Palk, Pitt, Soya
**05** Banks, Bohai, Cabot, Canso, Davis, Dease, Dover, Kerch, Korea, Luzon, Menai, Osumi, Sunda, Tatar
**06** Bering, Dundas, Etolin, Fisher, Hecate, Hormuz, Hudson, Lombok, Solent, Sunday, Tablas, Taiwan, Tokara, Torres, Vitiaz
**07** Balabac, Chatham, Dampier, Denmark, Florida, Formosa, Foveaux, Georgia, Le Maire, Makasar, Malacca, McClure, Messina, Mindoro, Otranto, Polillo, Rosario, Tsugaru
**08** Bosporus, Clarence, Karimata, Kattegat, Mackinac, Magellan, Makassar, Shelikof, Tsushima, Victoria
**09** Belle Isle, Bonifacio, Bosphorus, Gibraltar, Great Belt, La Pérouse, Linapacan, Van Diemen
**10** Juan de Fuca, Little Belt
**11** Dardanelles
**12** Bougainville, Investigator
**13** San Bernardino
**14** Northumberland, Queen Charlotte
**15** Dolphin and Union

**straitened**
**04** poor **07** limited, reduced
**09** difficult **10** distressed, restricted
**11** embarrassed **12** impoverished

**strait-laced**
**04** prim **06** narrow, proper, strict, stuffy
**07** prudish, starchy, uptight
**08** priggish, unstuffy **09** tight-lace
**10** moralistic, tight-laced **11** puritanical
**12** narrow-minded **13** prim and proper

**strand**
**03** ply **04** kemp, lock, sand, wire, wisp
**05** beach, fibre, front, piece, sands, shore, tress, twist **06** bundle, factor, gutter, length, maroon, sliver, string, strond, thread **07** element, feature, monofil, rivulet **08** filament, multifil, seashore **09** component, foreshore
**10** ingredient, waterfront
**11** homopolymer **12** optical fibre
**13** multifilament **14** vascular bundle

**stranded**
**07** aground, beached, wrecked
**08** forsaken, grounded, helpless, marooned **09** abandoned, penniless
**10** high and dry, in the lurch
**11** shipwrecked **14** left in the lurch

**strange**
◇ *anagram indicator*
**03** new, odd, rum, shy **04** unco
**05** alien, crazy, fraim, fremd, funny, kinky, novel, queer, silly, unked, unket, unkid, wacky, weird **06** exotic, freaky, fremit, stupid, unreal **07** bizarre, curious, foreign, oddball, offbeat, surreal, uncanny, uncouth, unknown, untried, unusual **08** abnormal, peculiar, selcouth, singular, straunge, uncommon, unversed, wondrous
**09** eccentric, estranged, fantastic, irregular, unheard-of, wonderful, wonderous **10** mysterious, mystifying, off the wall, outlandish, perplexing, remarkable, surprising, unexpected, unfamiliar **11** exceptional, unexplained **12** inexplicable, unaccustomed, unacquainted
**13** extraordinary

**strangely**
◇ *anagram indicator*
**05** oddly **07** weirdly **08** wondrous
**09** bizarrely, curiously, unusually, wonderous **10** abnormally, peculiarly, remarkably, singularly, uncommonly
**12** inexplicably, unexpectedly
**13** exceptionally

**strangeness**
**01** S **06** oddity **07** oddness **08** eeriness
**09** queerness **10** exoticness
**11** abnormality, bizarreness, peculiarity, singularity, uncanniness
**12** eccentricity, irregularity

**stranger**
**04** unco **05** alien, fraim, fremd, guest
**06** fremit, frenne **07** incomer, pilgrim, visitor **08** newcomer, outsider
**09** foreigner, non-member **10** new arrival

• **a stranger to**
**10** unversed in **14** unaccustomed to, unfamiliar with **15** inexperienced in

**strangle**
**03** gag **04** kill **05** check, choke
**06** impede, keep in, stifle **07** garotte, garrote, inhibit, repress, smother
**08** garrotte, hold back, restrain, suppress, thrapple, thropple, throttle
**09** bowstring, constrict, suffocate
**10** asphyxiate **11** strangulate

**strap**
**03** tab, tie **04** band, beat, belt, bind, cord, flog, hang, jess, lash, rein, taws, whip **05** leash, sling, strop, tawse, thong, truss **06** barber, credit, fasten, muzzle, secure **07** bandage, leather, scourge **08** backband, selvagee
**10** watchguard

**strapping**
**03** big **05** beefy, burly, hefty, hunky, husky **06** brawny, robust, strong, sturdy **07** hulking **08** chopping, swanking **09** thrashing, two-handed, well-built

**stratagem**
**04** coup, plan, plot, ploy, ruse, wile
**05** dodge, fetch, guile, guyle, trick
**06** device, feeler, scheme, tactic
**08** artifice, intrigue, maneuver, trickery
**09** deception, malengine, manoeuvre
**10** subterfuge **11** counter-plot, machination **12** ruse de guerre

**strategic**
**03** key **05** vital **07** crucial, planned, politic **08** critical, decisive, tactical
**09** essential, important **10** calculated, commanding, deliberate, diplomatic
**11** strategical

**strategy**
**03** ESS **04** plan **06** design, policy, scheme **07** maximin, minimax, tactics
**08** approach, game plan, planning, schedule **09** blueprint, procedure, programme **11** generalship, geostrategy **12** plan of action **14** shark repellent

**stratification**
**07** bedding, ranking, sorting
**08** division, layering **09** gradation, hierarchy **10** graduation
**14** categorization, classification

**stratum**
**03** bed **04** lode, post, rank, seam, tier, vein **05** caste, class, grade, group, layer, level, table **06** region **07** bracket, cap rock, coal-bed, day-coal, station
**08** category, wayboard **09** Corallian
**10** weighboard **14** stratification

**straw**
**04** halm, wase **05** chaff, haulm, strae
**06** buntal, litter, thatch **07** stubble
**08** strammel, strummel

• **bundle of straw, bundles of straw**
**04** wisp, yelm **05** truss, yealm
**06** kemple

• **straw hat**
**04** hive **06** basher, boater **07** leghorn
**09** coolie hat, Dunstable **10** balibuntal

**stray**
◇ *anagram indicator*
**03** err, odd, tag **04** lost, roam, rove, waff, waif **05** amble, drift, freak, range, traik **06** casual, chance, common, estray, ramble, random, wander, wilder
**07** deviate, digress, diverge, erratic, get lost, go wrong, meander, roaming, saunter **08** alleycat, drifting, go astray, homeless, isolated, maverick, straggle, stravaig, stray cat, stray dog
**09** abandoned, forwander, scattered, straggler, wandering, wander off
**10** accidental, exorbitate, occasional
**15** go off at a tangent, go off the subject

**streak**
**03** fly **04** band, belt, dart, dash, daub, lace, line, mark, race, rach, roll, rush, tear, time, vein, waif, wake, wale, wave, weal, zoom **05** flash, fleck, freak, layer, ratch, smear, speed, spell, stint, stria, strip, sweep, touch, trace, vibex, whizz
**06** beat it, gallop, hurtle, period, ribbon, scurry, smudge, sprint, strain, strake, stripe, stroke **07** element, scarper, scratch, stretch, striate, vamoose, whistle **09** skedaddle

**streaked**
**05** lined **06** banded, barred, hawked, hawkit, veined **07** brinded, brindle, flecked, streaky, striate, striped
**08** brindled **09** fleckered **11** tear-stained

**stream**
**03** fly, jet, pow, ren, rin, run **04** beck, burn, flap, flow, gush, kill, lake, lane,

nala, pour, rill, rush, shed, tide, well **05** brook, burst, creek, crowd, drift, float, flood, issue, nalla, nulla, river, spill, spout, surge, trail **06** course, deluge, efflux, gutter, nallah, nullah, rillet, streel, volley **07** cascade, current, flutter, rivulet, torrent **08** affluent, influent, tendency **09** tributary **10** outpouring, succession **11** watercourse

**streamer**
**04** flag, vane **05** plume **06** banner, ensign, fallal, pennon, pinnet, ribbon **07** bandrol, pennant **08** banderol, bannerol, gonfalon, standard, vexillum **09** banderole, bannerall

**streamlined**
**05** sleek, slick **06** smooth **07** well-run **08** graceful **09** efficient, organized **10** modernized, time-saving **11** aerodynamic **12** rationalized **13** smooth-running, up-to-the-minute

**street**
**02** St **03** rue, way **04** gate, lane, road **06** avenue **12** thoroughfare

*See also* **London**; **New York**; **Paris**; **road**

**• man in the street, woman in the street**
**07** Joe Blow **09** Joe Bloggs, Joe Public, Mr Average **10** Joe Sixpack, Mrs Average **13** average person, average punter **14** ordinary person **15** ordinary citizen

**streetwalker** *see* **prostitute**

**strength**
**04** bant, bent, gift, grit, guts, iron, main, thew **05** asset, brawn, clout, depth, force, forte, might, nerve, point, power, sinew, thing, truth, vigor **06** ardour, energy, fizzen, foison, fusion, health, métier, muscle, spirit, talent, vigour, weight **07** ability, bravery, cogency, courage, fitness, fushion, passion, potence, potency, stamina, urgency **08** aptitude, fervency, firmness, keenness, pungency, solidity, validity **09** advantage, fortitude, hardiness, influence, intensity, sharpness, solidness, soundness, specialty, stoutness, toughness, vehemence, vividness **10** brute force, complement, durability, resilience, resistance, resolution, robustness, speciality, sturdiness **11** athleticism, graphicness, persistence, strong point **12** forcefulness, might and main **13** assertiveness, determination, effectiveness **14** impregnability, persuasiveness

**• lose strength**
**04** fade, pall **05** faint, waste **08** wind down

**• on the strength of**
**07** based on **09** because of **10** by virtue of **11** on account of **12** on the basis of

**strengthen**
**03** arm, man **04** fish, line, stay **05** brace, cleat, edify, force, rally, serve, sinew, steel, wharf **06** anneal, back up, beef up, harden, munite, picket, piquet, prop up, turn up **07** afforce, bolster, build up, confirm, fortify, hearten, nourish, picquet, protect, refresh, restore, shore up, stiffen, support, toughen **08** buttress, heighten, increase **09** encourage, intensify, reinforce **10** invigorate, work-harden **11** consolidate, corroborate **12** substantiate

**strenuous**
**04** bold, hard, keen, warm **05** eager, heavy, tough **06** active, taxing, tiring, uphill, urgent **07** arduous, earnest, weighty, zealous **08** forceful, resolute, spirited, tireless, vigorous **09** demanding, difficult, energetic, gruelling, laborious, tenacious **10** blistering, determined, exhausting **13** indefatigable

**strenuously**
**06** boldly **08** actively **10** forcefully, resolutely, tirelessly, vigorously **11** tenaciously

**stress**
◇ *anagram indicator*
**04** beat, birr, rack **05** brunt, force, ictus, shear, value, worry **06** accent, burden, hassle, repeat, strain, trauma, weight **07** anxiety, point up, straits, tension, trouble **08** distress, emphasis, hardship, pressure, priority **09** distraint, emphasize, highlight, spotlight, underline **10** accentuate, difficulty, exaggerate, importance, underscore, uneasiness **12** accentuation, apprehension, significance, thermal shock

**stressed**
**04** edgy **05** jumpy, tense **06** on edge, strong, uneasy **07** anxious, fidgety, jittery, keyed up, nervous, uptight, worried **08** emphatic, restless, strained **09** screwed up **10** distraught, emphatical **11** overwrought, stressed out **12** apprehensive **13** under pressure

**stressful**
**05** tense **06** uneasy **07** charged, fraught **08** strained, worrying **10** nail-biting **12** high-pressure, nerve-racking

**stretch**
**03** rax, ren, rin, run, tax, try **04** area, last, line, pull, push, rack, span, term, test, time **05** offer, perch, range, reach, space, spell, stint, sweep, tract, widen **06** bouncy, expand, extend, extent, go up to, lay out, length, period, pliant, return, spread, strain, streek, supple, tauten, unfold, unroll **07** broaden, buoyant, draw out, elastic, expanse, hold out, plastic, pliable, present, proffer, project, prolong, rubbery, springy, tighten **08** come up to, continue, distance, elongate, flexible, go down to, lengthen, protract, reach out, straucht, straught, stretchy, yielding **09** challenge, extension, go as far as, make wider, resilient, spread out, stimulate **10** come down to, exaggerate, make longer, straighten **11** become wider, elasticated, stretchable **12** become longer, exaggeration, put demands on **13** extensibility

**• stretch out**
**05** crane, reach, relax **06** extend, intend, put out, sprawl, string **07** hold out, lie down, recline

**• stretch your legs**
**06** stroll **08** exercise **09** move about, promenade, take a walk **10** go for a walk, take the air **13** take a breather

**stretcher**
**04** rack **06** gurney, litter

**strew**
**03** sow **04** lard, rush, snow, toss **05** level, straw, strow **06** litter, spread **07** bestrew, scatter **08** bespread, disperse, sprinkle **10** besprinkle

**stricken**
**03** hit **06** struck **07** injured, smitten, wounded **08** affected **09** afflicted

**strict**
**04** firm, hard, true **05** clear, close, exact, harsh, rigid, stern, tight, total, tough, utter **06** giusto, narrow, proper, severe, strait **07** austere, literal, precise, regular **08** absolute, accurate, clear-cut, complete, faithful, intimate, orthodox, rigorous, straight, streight **09** Draconian, religious, stringent **10** inflexible, iron-fisted, iron-handed, meticulous, no-nonsense, particular, restricted, scrupulous **11** hard and fast **13** authoritarian, barrack square, conscientious, thoroughgoing **14** disciplinarian, uncompromising

**strictly**
**04** only **06** firmly, purely, strait, wholly **07** sternly, totally **08** narrowly, properly, severely, straight, straitly, streight, uniquely **10** absolutely, completely, definitely, in every way, inflexibly, positively, rigorously **11** exclusively **13** categorically, unambiguously, unequivocally **14** in every respect, unquestionably

**• strictly speaking**
**07** exactly **09** literally, precisely **11** to the letter

**strictness**
**06** rigour **08** accuracy, firmness, rigidity, rigorism, severity **09** austerity, exactness, harshness, precision, rigidness, sternness **10** stringency **12** rigorousness **13** barrack square, stringentness **14** meticulousness, scrupulousness

**stricture**
**04** flak **05** blame, bound, limit **06** rebuke **07** binding, censure, closure, confine, control, reproof **09** criticism, restraint, tightness **10** constraint, strictness **11** restriction **13** animadversion

**stride**
**04** lamp, lope, pace, sten, step, walk

**05** stalk, stend, tread **06** stroam **07** advance, galumph **08** bestride, gallumph, movement, progress, straddle **10** overstride **11** progression

**• take something in your stride**
**11** do blindfold, make light of **14** cope with easily, deal with easily, think nothing of

**strident**
**04** loud **05** harsh, rough **06** shrill, urgent **07** booming, grating, jarring, rasping, raucous, roaring **08** clashing, jangling **09** clamorous, unmusical **10** discordant, screeching, stentorian, stridulant, thundering, vociferous

**strife**
**03** row **04** bate, feud **05** sturt **06** barrat, battle, brigue, combat, debate, hassle, mutiny **07** bargain, conteck, contest, discord, dispute, ill-will, quarrel, rivalry, trouble, warfare **08** argument, conflict, fighting, friction, striving, struggle, variance **09** animosity, bickering, hostility, wrangling **10** contention, dissension, ill-feeling **11** controversy, quarrelling **12** colluctation, contestation, disagreement

**strike**
**03** bop, box, cob, fix, hit, lam, pat, ram, rap, tip, wap, zap **04** bang, beat, belt, biff, blad, blow, buff, chap, chip, clap, coin, cuff, dart, deal, draw, feel, find, fist, flog, gowf, hook, knee, look, neck, pane, pash, pean, peck, peen, pein, pene, pole, raid, rush, seem, slam, slap, slat, sock, swap, swop, take, toll, tonk, trap, yerk **05** adopt, bandh, blast, blaud, catch, chime, clout, crash, douse, dowse, fight, impel, knock, lower, plump, pound, prang, print, punch, reach, shoot, sit-in, slant, smack, smite, sound, souse, spank, stamp, storm, swipe, thump, touch, whack **06** affect, affrap, alight, ambush, appear, assail, assume, attack, batter, blight, broach, buffet, cancel, charge, clinch, come to, dawn on, delete, go-slow, hammer, hit out, mutiny, paddle, poleax, ratify, revolt, sclaff, set out, settle, smooth, stroke, take on, thrash, thwack, wallop **07** achieve, afflict, agree on, assault, bewitch, clobber, come out, compute, deliver, embrace, impinge, impress, inflict, occur to, percuss, poleaxe, protest, torpedo, uncover, unearth, walk out, walk-out **08** arrive at, come upon, describe, discover, estimate, look like, pounce on, register, set about, settle on, siderate, stayaway, stoppage, stop work, storming, strickle **09** dismantle, down tools, encounter, événement, interpose, penetrate, surrender **10** bird impact, chance upon, come to mind, constitute, happen upon, work to rule, work-to-rule **11** collide with **13** have the look of

**• on strike**
**03** out

**• strike back**
**07** hit back **09** fight back, get back at, retaliate **11** get even with, reciprocate **14** get your own back, pay someone back

**• strike down**
**04** fell, kill, ruin, slay **05** smite **06** murder **07** afflict, destroy **11** assassinate

**• strike out**
**03** paw **05** erase **06** cancel, delete, efface, remove, rub out **08** cross out **09** strike off **10** obliterate **13** strike through

**• strike up**
**05** begin, start **07** kick off **08** commence, initiate **09** establish, instigate, introduce

**strike-breaker** *see* **scab**

**striking**
**04** bold, dash, fine **06** pretty, strike **07** beating, evident, obvious, salient, visible **08** dazzling, distinct, frappant, gorgeous, sizzling, spanking, stunning **09** arresting, beautiful, distingué, glamorous, memorable **10** attractive, distinguée, impressive, incidental, noticeable, percussion, percutient, photogenic, remarkable **11** astonishing, conspicuous, eye-catching, good-looking, outstanding **13** extraordinary

**string**
**01** G **03** row, tie **04** cord, file, hang, hoax, lace, line, link, loop, nete, rake, rope, yarn **05** cable, chain, chord, drove, fibre, leash, queue, quint, sling, strap, tie up, train, twine **06** column, fasten, humbug, number, series, strand, stream, thairm, thread **07** connect, elastic, festoon, suspend **08** lichanos, nicky-tam, paramese, paranete, sequence, shoelace **10** procession, succession

**• string along**
**04** dupe, fool, hoax **05** bluff **06** humbug **07** deceive, mislead **09** co-operate, play false **12** put one over on, take for a ride

**• string out**
**06** extend, fan out, wander **08** disperse, lengthen, protract, space out, straggle **09** spread out **10** stretch out

**• strings of a lyre**
**04** mese, nete **05** trite **06** hypate **08** lichanos, paramese, paranete **09** parhypate

**• string up**
**03** top **04** hang, kill, kilt **05** lynch, run up, truss **15** send to the gibbet

**• with no strings attached**
**13** unconditional

**stringency**
**06** rigour **07** demands **08** firmness **09** exactness, toughness **10** strictness **12** rigorousness **13** inflexibility

**stringent**
**04** firm, hard **05** harsh, rigid, tight, tough **06** severe, strict **07** binding, extreme **08** exacting, rigorous **09** demanding **10** inflexible **14** uncompromising

**stringy**
**04** ropy, wiry **05** chewy, ropey, tough **06** sinewy **07** fibrous, gristly **08** leathery

**strip**
**03** bar, bit, gut, jib, rig **04** area, band, bare, bark, belt, bend, doff, flay, gear, husk, lath, list, loot, peel, pull, rand, roon, rund, sash, skin, slat, slip, tack, tirl, tirr, togs, welt, zona, zone **05** clear, empty, get-up, ledge, linch, piece, pluck, press, royne, ruler, shear, shred, shuck, spoil, strap, thong, tract, unrip **06** denude, devest, divest, expose, extent, lardon, outfit, peeler, ribbon, rig-out, screed, splent, spline, splint, straik, strake, stripe, stroke, swathe, things, uncase, unload **07** clobber, clothes, colours, deprive, despoil, disrobe, expanse, feather, flaught, flitter, fumetto, lardoon, lay bare, parking, peeling, pillage, plunder, ransack, stretch, tear off, uncover, undress **08** airstrip, clean out, clothing, degrease, flake off, separate, unclothe **09** dismantle, excoriate, pull apart, take apart **10** disfurnish, dispossess, striptease **11** disassemble **12** straightedge, take to pieces **13** swaddling-band

**stripe**
**03** bar **04** band, belt, blow, lash, line, list, pale, snip, zone **05** flash, fleck, guard, slash, strip, vitta, whelk **06** ribbon, straik, strain, strake, streak **07** chevron, endorse **09** laticlave, pin-stripe

**striped**
**06** banded, barred, pirnie, pirnit, stripy **07** bausond, guarded, streaky, vittate **08** endorsed, streaked, striated **10** variegated **11** finch-backed

**stripling**
**03** boy, lad **05** youth **07** young 'un **08** teenager **09** fledgling, youngster **10** adolescent **11** hobbledehoy

**strive**
**03** try, tug, vie **04** toil, work **05** bandy, fight, force, heave, press **06** aspire, battle, combat, engage, follow, labour, pingle, preace, prease, resist, strain **07** attempt, bargain, compete, contend, contest, enforce, preasse, try hard, wrestle **08** campaign, do battle, endeavor, purchase, struggle **09** endeavour, persevere **10** do your best **11** give your all **12** do your utmost **13** exert yourself

**stroke**
**03** cut, hit, pat, pet, rub **04** beat, bell, belt, biff, blow, coup, dash, dint, hand, jole, joll, jowl, line, milk, move, push, shot, slap, touk, tuck, whet **05** boast, chuck, cross, ictus, joule, knock, pulse, scoop, shock, smack, spasm, strip, sweep, swipe, thump, touch, trait,

whack **06** action, attack, buffet, caress, fondle, glance, motion, stound, stownd, strike, struck, thwack, tittle, wallop **07** clobber, flatter, massage, nobbler, outlash, reverse, reverso, seizure, solidus, strooke, upright, whample **08** collapse, flourish, movement **09** encourage, grand coup **10** back-hander, coup d'éclat, pile-driver, sideration, thrombosis **11** achievement **12** punto reverso, punto riverso, repercussion **14** accomplishment

*See also* **swimming**

**stroll**
**04** turn, walk **05** amble, troll **06** bummel, dander, dauner, dawdle, dawner, lounge, ramble, toddle, wander **07** daunder, meander, saunter **08** ambulate **10** go for a walk **14** constitutional **15** stretch your legs

**stroller**
**06** walker **07** dawdler, flâneur, rambler, vagrant **08** wanderer **09** itinerant, pushchair, saunterer

**strong**
**01** f **03** fit, hot, str **04** able, bull, deep, firm, full, hale, keen, rank, sour, very, well, yald **05** beefy, brave, burly, clear, eager, great, gross, gutsy, hardy, heady, heavy, lusty, nappy, pithy, sharp, solid, sound, spicy, stiff, stout, thewy, tough, valid, vivid, wight, yauld **06** active, ardent, biting, brawny, cogent, fierce, marked, mighty, potent, robust, rugged, secure, severe, sinewy, sturdy, trusty, urgent **07** devoted, doughty, durable, evident, fervent, graphic, healthy, intense, marrowy, obvious, piquant, pollent, pungent, telling, violent, weighty **08** athletic, cast-iron, clear-cut, decisive, definite, forceful, forcible, grievous, muscular, numerous, positive, powerful, profound, resolute, stalwart, stressed, vehement, vigorous **09** assertive, committed, competent, confident, effective, efficient, excelling, heavy-duty, plausible, resilient, resistant, steadfast, strapping, undiluted, well-built **10** aggressive, compelling, convincing, courageous, determined, emphasized, fast-moving, formidable, hogen-mogen, passionate, persistent, persuasive, pronounced, reinforced, remarkable **11** efficacious, hard-wearing, long-lasting, substantial **12** concentrated, enthusiastic, single-minded, strong-minded, strong-willed **13** well-protected **14** highly seasoned **15** highly flavoured

• **strong point**
**04** bent, gift **05** asset, forte, thing **06** métier, talent **08** aptitude, strength **09** advantage, specialty **10** speciality

**strongarm**
**06** terror **07** violent **08** bully-boy, bullying, coercive, forceful, physical, thuggish **10** aggressive, oppressive **11** threatening **12** intimidatory

**strongbox**
**04** safe **05** chest, vault **06** coffer **07** cash box **10** deposit box, depository, repository

**stronghold**
**04** aery, eyry, fort, hold, holt, keep **05** aerie, ayrie, eyrie, tower **06** castle, center, centre, refuge **07** bastion, citadel, outpost **08** fastness, fortress, hill-fort

**strongly**
**06** deeply, firmly **07** durably, solidly, toughly **08** markedly **09** intensely **10** definitely, forcefully, muscularly, positively, powerfully, resolutely **11** resiliently **12** athletically **13** substantially

**strong-minded**
**04** firm **08** resolute **09** steadfast, tenacious, unbending **10** determined, iron-willed, unwavering **11** independent **12** strong-willed **14** uncompromising

**strong-willed**
**06** wilful **07** wayward **08** obdurate, stubborn **09** obstinate **10** inflexible, refractory, self-willed **11** intractable **12** intransigent, recalcitrant

**strontium**
**02** Sr

**stroppy**
**05** ratty, rowdy **06** shirty **07** awkward, bolshie **08** perverse **09** difficult, unhelpful **10** refractory **11** bad-tempered, quarrelsome **12** bloody minded, cantankerous, obstreperous **13** unco-operative

**structural**
**06** design **07** organic **08** tectonic **09** edificial **11** formational **14** constructional, organizational **15** configurational

**structure**
◇ *anagram indicator*
**04** form, make **05** build, frame, set-up, shape **06** design, fabric, make-up, system **07** arrange, build up, chassis, edifice **08** assemble, building, erection, organize **09** construct, formation, framework **10** contexture **11** arrangement, composition **12** architecture, conformation, constitution, construction, organization **13** configuration

**struggle**
◇ *anagram indicator*
**03** tug, vie, war **04** agon, camp, toil, work **05** agony, brawl, clash, fight, pains, scrum **06** battle, combat, effort, engage, hassle, labour, ruffle, strain, strife, strift, strive, tussle **07** agonize, compete, contend, contest, grapple, problem, scuffle, trouble, try hard, tuilyie, tuilzie, warfare, wrestle **08** conflict, exertion, flounder, skirmish, slugfest, sprangle **09** encounter, handgrips, luctation, scrimmage, scrummage **10** difficulty, do your best **11** competition, give your all, hostilities **12** do your utmost **13** exert yourself, passage of arms

**strumpet** *see* **prostitute**

**strut**
**03** jet **04** cock, prop, spur **05** brank, bulge, dwang, glory, major, pronk, raker, stalk, swank **06** flaunt, parade, prance, scotch, strout, strunt **07** nervure, peacock, swagger **08** protrude, stanchel, stancher, tail boom **09** stanchion

**stub**
**03** end **04** butt, grub, snub, stob **05** stump **06** dog-end, fag end, snubbe **07** remnant **11** counterfoil

**stubborn**
**05** rigid, stiff, stoor, stour, stout, sture **06** dogged, mulish, ornery, stowre, thrawn, wilful **07** adamant **08** obdurate, obstacle, perverse **09** difficult, hidebound, obstinate, opinioned, pig-headed, rigwiddie, rigwoodie, tenacious, unbending **10** headstrong, inflexible, inveterate, persistent, refractory, self-willed, unyielding **11** intractable, opinionated, stiff-necked **12** cantankerous, contumacious, intransigent, opinionative, pertinacious, recalcitrant, stiff-hearted, strong-willed, unmanageable **14** overdetermined, uncompromising **15** not open to reason, stubborn as a mule

*See also* **obstinate**

**stubbornly**
**08** doggedly, wilfully **10** inflexibly, perversely **11** obstinately, pig-headedly, tenaciously **12** persistently **14** intransigently

**stubby**
**05** dumpy, short, squat **06** chunky, stumpy **08** thickset

**stuck**
**04** fast, firm **05** fixed, glued **06** beaten, jammed, joined, rooted **07** at a loss, baffled, stalled, stumped **08** cemented, embedded, fastened, immobile **09** perplexed, unmovable **10** bogged down, nonplussed **13** at your wits' end

• **get stuck into**
**05** begin, start **06** tackle **08** embark on, set about **09** get down to

• **stuck on**
**05** mad on **06** fond of, keen on, nuts on **07** sweet on **09** wild about **10** crazy about, dotty about **12** obsessed with **14** infatuated with

**stuck-up**
**05** proud **06** snooty, uppish **07** haughty **08** arrogant, snobbish, toplofty **09** bigheaded, conceited **10** hoity-toity **11** patronizing, toffee-nosed, toploftical **12** supercilious **13** condescending, high and mighty

**stud**
**03** seg, set **04** boss, knob, nail, race, spur, stop, tack **05** pitch, prick, rivet, stump **06** popper **07** clinker
**08** doornail **11** pop-fastener **12** clip-fastener, snap-fastener **13** press fastener

**studded**
**03** set **06** dotted **07** flecked, spotted, starred **08** mamillar, spangled, speckled **09** mamillary, scattered, sprinkled **10** bejewelled, bespangled, icy-pearled, ornamented **12** star-spangled

**student**
**01** L **04** semi, soph **05** bejan, pupil, semie, softa, welly **06** bejant, bursar, medico, premed, tosher, wellie
**07** alumnus, bookman, fresher, grinder, learner, scarfie, scholar, Templar, trainee **08** disciple, freshman, premedic **09** collegian, schoolboy, semi-bajan, sophomore
**10** apprentice, green welly, schoolgirl
**11** collegianer, probationer
**12** extensionist, postgraduate
**13** undergraduate
• **student group**
**03** NUS

**studied**
**05** voulu **06** forced, versed, wilful
**07** planned **08** affected, designed, well-read **09** conscious, contrived, unnatural **10** artificial, calculated, deliberate, purposeful **11** intentional
**12** premeditated **13** over-elaborate

**studio**
**06** school **07** atelier, bottega, gallery
**08** workroom, workshop

**studious**
**05** eager **07** bookish, careful, earnest, serious **08** academic, diligent, sedulous, thorough **09** assiduous, attentive, scholarly **10** deliberate, meticulous, reflective, thoughtful
**11** hard-working, industrious
**12** intellectual

**study**
**03** con, den, dig, kon **04** cram, muse, plod, read, scan, swot, work, zeal
**05** conne, essay, learn, mug up, paper, train **06** bone up, devise, digest, office, peruse, ponder, read up, report, review, revise, studio, survey, thesis
**07** analyse, article, examine, inquiry, library, major in, perusal, reading, reflect, reverie, subject, thought
**08** analysis, bone up on, consider, cramming, critique, homework, instruct, interest, learning, meditate, pore over, research, revision, scrutiny, swotting, workroom **09** attention, monograph, workplace **10** deliberate, inspection, scrutinize **11** contemplate, examination, inclination, investigate, lucubration, preparation, prolegomena, scholarship
**12** propaedeutic **13** consideration, contemplation, investigation

*Subjects of study include:*

**02** D&T, IT
**03** art, ICT, law, PSE
**04** PHSE
**05** craft, dance, drama, music, sport
**06** botany, design
**07** anatomy, biology, driving, ecology, fashion, fitness, geology, history, physics, pottery, science, zoology
**08** commerce, eugenics, genetics, heraldry, medicine, penology, politics, theology
**09** astrology, astronomy, chemistry, cosmology, economics, education, erotology, ethnology, forensics, geography, languages, logistics, marketing, mechanics, mythology, pathology, shorthand, sociology, surveying, web design
**10** humanities, journalism, literature, metallurgy, philosophy, physiology, psychology, publishing, statistics, technology, visual arts
**11** accountancy, agriculture, archaeology, calligraphy, citizenship, dressmaking, electronics, engineering, linguistics, mathematics, metaphysics, meteorology, ornithology, photography, the Classics, typewriting
**12** anthropology, architecture, horticulture, lexicography, media studies, oceanography, pharmacology
**13** gender studies, home economics, librarianship, marine studies, women's studies
**14** food technology, leisure studies, natural history, social sciences, word processing
**15** building studies, business studies, computer studies, creative writing, hotel management

**stuff**
**03** jam, kit, pad, ram, wad **04** clog, cram, crap, fill, gear, hoax, lard, line, load, pack, pang, push, sate, stap, stow, trig, tuck **05** binge, blash, block, cloth, crowd, farce, force, fudge, goods, gorge, items, money, press, shove, squab, store, wedge **06** bung up, fabric, gobble, guzzle, liquor, matter, pig out, steeve, stodge, tackle, things, thrust
**07** bombast, clobber, essence, filling, furnish, luggage, objects, rubbish, satiate, squeeze, woollen **08** articles, compress, garrison, gross out, material, nonsense, obstruct, stuffing
**09** equipment, furniture, materials, provision, substance **10** belongings, gormandize **11** overindulge, possessions **13** paraphernalia

**stuffing**
◇ *containment indicator*
◇ *hidden indicator*
**05** farce, kapok **07** bombast, farcing, filling, packing, padding, pudding, wadding **08** dressing, quilting, stopping **09** deafening, forcemeat, taxidermy

**stuffy**
**04** dull, prim **05** close, fuggy, fusty, heavy, muggy, musty, staid, stale, stiff, stivy, stout, sulky **06** dreary, frowsy, frowzy, poking, stodgy, sturdy, sultry
**07** airless, pompous, starchy **08** stifling
**10** fuddy-duddy, oppressive **11** strait-laced, suffocating **12** buttoned-down, conventional, old-fashioned, unventilated **13** uninteresting

**stultify**
**04** dull, numb **05** blunt **06** negate, stifle, thwart **07** nullify, smother, stupefy **08** hebetate, suppress
**10** invalidate

**stumble**
◇ *anagram indicator*
**03** err **04** fall, peck, reel, slip, trip
**05** lapse, lurch, stoit **06** falter, hamble
**07** blunder, founder, snapper, stagger, stammer, stotter, stutter **08** flounder, hesitate, titubate **09** false step
**10** disconcert **15** lose your balance
• **stumble across, stumble on**
**04** find **08** discover **09** encounter
**10** chance upon, come across, happen upon

**stumbling-block**
**03** bar **04** snag **06** hurdle **07** barrier, scandal **08** obstacle **09** hindrance
**10** difficulty, impediment
**11** obstruction **12** Becher's Brook

**stump**
**03** end, leg, nog, peg **04** butt, dare, foil, more, runt, snag, stob, stub, stud
**05** floor, scrag, stock, stool, trunk
**06** baffle, defeat, dog-end, fag end, outwit, puzzle, wicket **07** confuse, flummox, mystify, nonplus, perplex, remains, remnant, staddle, stubble
**08** bewilder, confound **09** bamboozle, challenge, dumbfound, tortillon
• **stump up**
**03** pay **05** pay up **06** ante up, chip in, donate, pay out **07** cough up, fork out
**08** hand over, shell out **10** contribute

**stumped**
**02** st **05** stuck **07** baffled, floored, stymied **09** flummoxed, perplexed
**10** bamboozled, nonplussed

**stumpy**
**04** cash **05** dumpy, heavy, nirly, short, squat, thick **06** chunky, nirlie, stocky, stubby **07** stubbed **08** thickset

**stun**
**02** KO **04** daze, kayo **05** amaze, devel, dover, knock, shock, stonn, stoun, Taser® **06** abrade, bruise, deafen, devvel, settle, stonne, stound
**07** astound, confuse, stagger, stupefy
**08** astonish, bedeafen, bewilder, bowl over, confound, knock out, overcome
**09** dumbfound, overpower
**11** flabbergast, knock for six

**stunned**
**04** numb **05** dazed, silly **06** aghast, amazed, stupid **07** floored, in a daze, shocked **09** astounded, staggered, stupefied **10** astonished, devastated,

gobsmacked **11** dumbfounded **13** flabbergasted

**stunner**
**02** KO **03** wow **05** peach, siren **06** beauty, looker, lovely **07** charmer, cracker, dazzler, smasher **08** knockout **09** sensation **10** eye-catcher, good-looker, heart-throb **11** femme fatale

**stunning**
**05** great **06** dazing, lovely **07** amazing **08** dazzling, drop-dead, fabulous, gorgeous, smashing, striking **09** beautiful, brilliant, ravishing, wonderful **10** impressive, incredible, marvellous, remarkable, staggering, stupefying **11** sensational, spectacular **12** stupefaction **13** extraordinary

**stunningly**
**09** amazingly **10** fabulously, gorgeously, remarkably, strikingly **11** beautifully, brilliantly, wonderfully **12** impressively, marvellously, staggeringly **13** spectacularly **15** extraordinarily

**stunt**
**03** act **04** curb, deed, feat, hype, nirl, ramp, slow, stop, turn **05** check, dwarf, stock, trick **06** action, arrest, hamper, hinder, impede, retard, wheeze **07** exploit, inhibit **08** restrict **10** enterprise **11** performance

**stunted**
**04** puny, tiny **05** nirly, small **06** little, nirlie **07** dwarfed, scroggy, scrubby **08** dwarfish, scroggie, scrubbed, withered **10** diminutive, undersized, wanthriven

**stupefaction**
**04** daze **06** wonder **08** blackout, numbness, stunning **09** amazement **10** amazedness, bafflement **12** astonishment, bewilderment, state of shock **13** senselessness

**stupefy**
**04** daze, drug, dull, mull, numb, stun **05** amaze, dozen, hocus, shock **06** bemuse, benumb, drowse, fuddle, mither, moider **07** astound, moither, stagger **08** bowl over, etherize, knock out, somniate **09** devastate, dumbfound **11** knock for six

**stupendous**
**04** huge, vast **06** killer, superb **07** amazing, immense **08** colossal, enormous, fabulous, gigantic, stunning **09** fantastic, wonderful **10** astounding, marvellous, phenomenal, prodigious, staggering, tremendous **12** breathtaking, overwhelming **13** extraordinary

**stupid**
◇ *anagram indicator*
**03** dim, jay, mad, twp **04** dopy, dull, dumb, rash, slow **05** barmy, brute, crass, crazy, dazed, dense, divvy, dopey, doted, dovie, dunny, flaky, foggy, goofy, gross, inane, looby, loony, loopy, muddy, potty, silly, stupe, thick **06** absurd, boring, bovine, donsie, facile, futile, groggy, lumpen, owlish, tavert, wooden **07** damfool, doltish, donnard, donnart, donnerd, donnert, fatuous, foolish, glaiket, glaikit, idiotic, insulse, lunatic, moronic, puerile, stunned, taivert, witless **08** anserine, backward, besotted, blockish, Boeotian, boobyish, clueless, donnered, gaumless, gormless, mindless, sluggish **09** brainless, fat-witted, foolhardy, half-assed, imbecilic, laughable, ludicrous, pointless, senseless, stupefied **10** beef-witted, dull-witted, fatbrained, half-witted, ill-advised, indiscreet, insensible **11** beef-brained, blunt-witted, clay-brained, conceitless, hair-brained, hare-brained, heavy-headed, injudicious, meaningless, nonsensical, not all there, thickheaded, unconscious **12** feeble-minded, hammer-headed, muttonheaded, simple-minded, sodden-witted, thick-skulled, woodenheaded **13** chuckle-headed, irresponsible, pudding-headed, semiconscious, thick as a plank **15** slow on the uptake

**stupidity**
**05** folly **06** bêtise, idiocy, lunacy, torpor **07** dimness, duncery, fatuity, goosery, inanity, madness, naivety **08** dopiness, doziness, dullness, dumbness, futility, insanity, rashness, slowness **09** absurdity, asininity, bruteness, crassness, denseness, insulsity, oscitancy, puerility, silliness, thickness **10** crassitude, imbecility, ineptitude, obtuseness **11** fatuousness, foolishness, glaikitness **12** indiscretion **13** brainlessness, foolhardiness, ludicrousness, pointlessness, senselessness **14** impracticality

**• expression of stupidity**
**03** doh, duh

**stupidly**
◇ *anagram indicator*
**07** inanely, sillily **08** absurdly **09** fatuously, foolishly **10** mindlessly **12** unthinkingly **13** irresponsibly

**stupor**
**04** coma, daze **06** torpor, trance **07** inertia **08** blackout, lethargy, numbness, oblivion **12** state of shock, stupefaction **13** insensibility **15** unconsciousness

**sturdy**
**03** gid **04** dunt, firm **05** burly, giddy, hardy, husky, rough, solid, stout **06** hearty, mighty, robust, rugged, steeve, stieve, stocky, strong, stuffy **07** durable, staunch, violent **08** athletic, lubberly, muscular, powerful, resolute, stalwart, turnsick, vigorous, well-made **09** impetuous, obstinate, steadfast, tenacious, well-built **10** determined, refractory **11** flourishing, substantial

**sturgeon**
**04** huso **05** elops **06** beluga, ellops **07** osseter, sevruga, sterlet **10** shovelnose

**stutter**
**04** lisp **06** falter, mumble **07** sputter, stammer, stumble **08** hesitate, splutter **12** speech defect

**style**
◇ *anagram indicator*
**03** cut, dub, pen, tag, way **04** call, chic, dash, form, hand, kind, make, mode, name, sort, term, tone, type, vein **05** adapt, flair, genre, index, label, shape, taste, tenor, title, trend, vogue **06** custom, design, gnomon, luxury, manner, method, phrase, polish, tailor, wealth **07** address, comfort, diction, entitle, fashion, panache, pattern, pointel, pointer, produce, variety, wording **08** approach, category, elegance, grandeur, language, phrasing, urbanity **09** affluence, designate, smartness, suaveness, technique **10** appearance, denominate, dressiness, expression, refinement **11** flamboyance, methodology, stylishness **14** sophistication

**• in the style of**
**03** à la **05** after, -esque

**stylish**
**03** fly **04** chic, posh **05** janty, natty, nifty, ritzy, sharp, showy, smart, swish **06** chichi, classy, dressy, jaunty, modish, snappy, snazzy, sporty, trendy, urbane **07** à la mode, dashing, elegant, in vogue, refined, voguish **08** polished **11** fashionable **13** sophisticated

**stylus**
**03** gad, pen **04** hand **05** index, probe, style **06** needle **07** pointer **08** graphium

**stymie**
**04** balk, foil **05** stump **06** baffle, defeat, hamper, hinder, hogtie, impede, puzzle, thwart **07** flummox, mystify, nonplus, snooker **08** confound **09** bamboozle, frustrate, interfere

**styptic**
**06** amadou, matico, stanch **07** staunch **10** astringent **11** haemostatic

**suave**
**04** glib **05** bland, civil **06** polite, smooth, urbane **07** affable, refined, worldly **08** charming, debonair, polished, unctuous **09** agreeable, civilized, courteous **10** soft-spoken **13** sophisticated

**suavity**
**05** charm **08** civility, courtesy, urbanity **09** blandness **10** politeness, refinement, smoothness **11** worldliness **12** agreeability, unctuousness **14** sophistication

**sub**
**04** dues, gift, lend, temp **05** agent, locum, proxy, U-boat **06** deputy, fill-in, relief, supply **07** advance, payment, reserve, stand-by, stand-in, stopgap

**08** donation, offering **09** makeshift, surrogate **10** substitute, understudy **11** locum tenens, pinch-hitter, replacement **12** contribution, subscription **13** membership fee

**subaquatic**
**07** subaqua **08** demersal, undersea **09** submarine, submersed **10** subaqueous, underwater

**subatomic particle** *see* **particle**

**subconscious**
**02** id **03** ego **04** deep, mind **05** inner **06** hidden, latent, psyche **08** super-ego **09** innermost, inner self, intuitive, repressed **10** inner being, subliminal, suppressed, underlying **11** instinctive, unconscious **15** unconscious self

**subcontract**
**07** farm out **08** delegate **09** outsource **11** contract out **12** give to others, pass to others

**subdue**
**03** cow **04** adaw, damp, mate, tame **05** accoy, allay, break, charm, check, crush, daunt, quail, quash, quell **06** defeat, do down, humble, master, mellow, pacify, reduce, soften, starve, step on, stifle, subact, subdew, take in **07** achieve, chasten, conquer, control, crucify, daunton, mortify, overrun, quieten, repress, subject **08** chastise, moderate, overcome, restrain, suppress, vanquish **09** overpower, soft-pedal, subjugate **10** bring under, discipline **12** put a damper on **14** get the better of **15** gain mastery over

**subdued**
**03** dim, sad **04** soft **05** grave, muted, quiet, sober, still **06** abated, hushed, low-key, pastel, shaded, silent, solemn, sombre, subtle **07** captive, passive, serious, submiss **08** dejected, delicate, downcast, lifeless, softened **09** depressed, noiseless, toned-down, unexcited **10** restrained **11** crestfallen, unobtrusive **13** irrepressible **14** down in the dumps

**subject**
**03** apt, put, sub **04** case, open, subj **05** bound, field, issue, liege, motif, point, prone, theme, thirl, topic **06** affair, aspect, client, expose, ground, liable, likely, matter, native, subdew, subdue, submit, vassal, victim **07** caitive, captive, citizen, exposed, hanging, lay open, patient, resting, servant, servile **08** amenable, business, disposed, inferior, liegeman, national, obedient, question, resident **09** dependant, dependent, depending, guinea pig, subjugate, substance, underling **10** answerable, cognizable, contingent, discipline, inhabitant, subjugated, submissive, underlying, vulnerable **11** accountable, area of study, conditional, constrained, participant, subordinate, subservient, susceptible **12** field of study

*See also* **study**

**subjection**
**06** chains, defeat **07** bondage, mastery, slavery **08** exposure, question, shackles **09** captivity, servitude, vassalage **10** discipline, domination, oppression **11** enslavement, subjugation

**subjective**
**06** biased **07** bigoted **08** personal **09** emotional, intuitive **10** individual, nominative, prejudiced **11** instinctive **13** idiosyncratic, introspective

**subjugate**
**04** tame **05** crush, quell **06** defeat, master, reduce, subdue, thrall **07** conquer, enslave, oppress **08** overcome, suppress, vanquish **09** overpower, overthrow **14** get the better of **15** gain mastery over

**sublimate**
**04** turn **05** exalt **06** divert, purify, refine **07** alcohol, channel, elevate, flowers **08** heighten, redirect, transfer **09** transmute

**sublime**
**04** high **05** exalt, grand, great, lofty, noble, utter **06** august, winged **07** Dantean, exalted, extreme, intense, supreme **08** complete, elevated, empyreal, glorious, heavenly, imposing, majestic **09** celestial, Dantesque, spiritual **10** majestical **11** magnificent **12** transcendent

**subliminal**
**06** hidden **09** concealed **11** unconscious **12** subconscious, subthreshold

**submarine**
**03** sub **05** U-boat **06** hoagie, X-craft **07** pigboat

**submerge**
**03** dip **04** bury, dive, duck, dunk, sink, take **05** drown, flood, swamp, whelm **06** deluge, engulf, go down, plunge **07** conceal, immerse, plummet **08** implunge, indrench, inundate, overflow, submerse, suppress **09** overwhelm **12** go under water **13** put under water

**submerged**
**04** sunk **06** hidden, sunken, unseen, veiled **07** cloaked, drowned, swamped **08** immersed, obscured **09** concealed, inundated, submersed **10** underwater

**submission**
**05** entry **06** assent, tender **07** tabling **08** averment, giving in, meekness, offering, proposal **09** agreement, assertion, deference, obedience, passivity, statement, surrender, tendering **10** compliance, confession, suggestion **11** resignation **12** acquiescence, capitulation, contribution, introduction, presentation, resignedness, subscription **13** subordination **14** submissiveness

**submissive**
**04** meek, weak **06** docile, humble, supine **07** passive, patient, servile, subdued **08** biddable, obedient, resigned, yielding **09** compliant, malleable **10** weak-willed **11** acquiescent, deferential, downtrodden, reverential, subordinate, subservient, unresisting **12** ingratiating, self-effacing **13** accommodating, uncomplaining

**submissively**
**06** humbly, meekly, weakly **09** cap in hand, passively, patiently **10** obediently **13** deferentially, subserviently **15** uncomplainingly

**submit**
**03** bow, put **04** aver, bend, move **05** agree, argue, claim, defer, lower, offer, posit, refer, state, stoop, table, yield **06** accede, assert, comply, expose, give in, permit, prefer, render, resign, send in, tender **07** consent, give way, lay down, passage, present, proffer, propose, subject, succumb, suggest, violate **08** propound **09** acquiesce, introduce, lay before, subscribe, surrender **10** bow the knee, capitulate, come to heel, kiss the rod, put forward **11** bend the knee, come to terms, subordinate **12** knuckle under **13** bite the bullet **15** lay down your arms

**subnormal**
**03** low **04** slow **08** backward, inferior, retarded **11** below normal **12** below average, feeble-minded

**subordinate**
◇ *juxtaposition down indicator*
**04** aide **05** lower, lowly, minor, under **06** deputy, junior, lesser, menial, second, skivvy, stooge, submit, vassal **07** subject **08** dogsbody, inferior, marginal, offsider, servient, sidekick **09** ancillary, assistant, attendant, auxiliary, dependant, dependent, secondary, subaltern, underling **10** submissive, subsidiary, underlying **11** lower in rank, subservient **12** lower-ranking, second fiddle **14** understrapping

**subordination**
**09** servitude **10** dependence, subjection, submission **11** inferiority **12** subservience

**subscribe**
**04** back, give, sign, take **05** agree **06** answer, assent, chip in, donate, pledge, submit **07** approve, endorse, fork out, support **08** advocate, shell out, sign up to **10** contribute, underwrite **12** buy regularly **13** take regularly **15** pay for regularly

**subscriber**
**06** member **08** customer **13** regular reader

**subscription**
**04** dues, gift **06** assent **07** payment **08** donation, offering, sanction

**09** signature **10** abonnement, submission **11** endorsement **12** contribution **13** membership fee

**subsequent**
**04** next **05** later **06** future **07** ensuing **09** following, resulting **10** consequent, succeeding **12** postliminary

**subsequently**
**05** after, later **09** afterward **10** afterwards **12** consequently

**subservience**
**08** humility **09** deference, obedience, servility, servitude **10** subjection **11** dutifulness **12** acquiescence **13** subordination **14** submissiveness

**subservient**
**05** lower, minor **06** junior, lesser **07** fawning, servile, slavish, subject **08** inferior, toadying, unctuous **09** ancillary, auxiliary, dependent, secondary **10** obsequious, submissive, subserving, subsidiary **11** bootlicking, deferential, subordinate, sycophantic **12** ingratiating, instrumental, subalternate **13** less important

**subside**
**03** ebb **04** adaw, drop, ease, fall, lull, sink, wane **05** abate, let up, lower, quell, slake, sound, swoon, swoun **06** cave in, lessen, quench, recede, settle, swound **07** assuage, decline, descend, die down, dwindle, founder, quieten, slacken **08** collapse, decrease, diminish, dissolve, get lower, moderate, peter out, pipe down

**subsidence**
**03** ebb, sag **04** swag **07** decline, descent, sinking **08** collapse, decrease, settling **09** abatement, lessening **10** diminution, settlement, slackening **12** de-escalation, detumescence

**subsidiary**
**02** by **03** bye **04** part, side, wing **05** minor **06** aiding, branch, feeder, lesser **07** section **08** division, offshoot **09** accessory, adjective, affiliate, ancillary, assistant, auxiliary, secondary, succursal **10** additional, collateral, supporting **11** subordinate, subservient **12** contributory **13** supplementary

**subsidize**
**03** aid **04** back, fund **07** endorse, finance, promote, sponsor, support **08** invest in **10** underwrite **12** contribute to **14** give a subsidy to

**subsidy**
**03** aid **04** help **05** grant **07** backing, finance, funding, headage, support **09** allowance **10** assistance, investment, subvention **11** endorsement, sponsorship **12** contribution, underwriting

**subsist**
**04** last, live **05** exist **06** endure, remain **07** consist, hold out, survive **08** continue

**subsistence**
**04** food, keep **06** living **07** aliment, rations, support **08** survival **09** existence **10** livelihood, provisions, sustenance **11** continuance, maintenance, nourishment

**substance**
**03** sum **04** body, gist, mass, meat, pith, quid, text **05** basis, being, force, means, money, power, stuff, theme, topic, truth **06** amount, assets, burden, entity, fabric, ground, import, matter, medium, riches, wealth, weight **07** essence, fortune, meaning, reality, subject **08** material, property, solidity, validity **09** actuality, affluence, influence, marijuana, resources **10** foundation, prosperity **11** consistence, consistency, materiality, tangibility **12** concreteness, corporeality, significance **13** subject matter **14** meaningfulness

**substandard**
**04** poor **05** crook **06** shoddy **07** damaged **08** below par, inferior **09** imperfect **10** inadequate, second-rate **12** unacceptable **14** not up to scratch

**substantial**
**03** big **04** firm, hard, main, real, rich, tidy, true **05** ample, basic, bulky, great, large, solid, sound, stout, tough **06** actual, hearty, pretty, stable, strong, sturdy **07** central, durable, filling, notable, primary, sizable, wealthy, weighty **08** affluent, cast-iron, concrete, enduring, existing, generous, inherent, material, powerful, sizeable, tangible, valuable, well-to-do **09** corporeal, essential, heavy-duty, important, intrinsic, principal, well-built **10** meaningful, measurable, prosperous, remarkable, successful, worthwhile **11** fundamental, influential, significant **12** considerable

**substantially**
**06** mainly **07** at heart, largely **08** in effect **09** in the main **10** materially **11** essentially **12** considerably **13** fundamentally, significantly **14** to a great extent

**substantiate**
**05** prove **06** back up, embody, uphold, verify **07** bear out, confirm, support **08** validate **11** corroborate **12** authenticate

**substantive**
**02** sb **04** noun, real **05** solid, subst, valid **07** factual **08** concrete, material **09** intrinsic **11** fundamental, substantial

**substitute**
**03** sub **04** -ette, heir, lieu, swap, temp **05** agent, cover, locum, proxy, vicar **06** acting, change, deputy, double, ersatz, fill in, fill-in, relief, supply, switch **07** commute, fig leaf, relieve, replace, reserve, stand-by, stand in, stand-in, stopgap **08** deputize, exchange, replacer, take over **09** alternate, makeshift, prorector, subrogate, surrogate, temporary **10** changeling, proproctor, understudy, use instead **11** alternative, interchange, locum tenens, pinch-hitter, replacement **12** act instead of **14** take the place of

**substitution**
**04** swap **06** change, switch **08** exchange, novation, swapping **09** switching **10** delegation, innovation, resolution **11** interchange, replacement

**subsume**
**03** add **04** hold **05** add in, admit, cover, enter, put in **06** embody, insert, take in **07** contain, count in, embrace, enclose, include, swallow **08** comprise, take over **09** encompass, introduce **10** comprehend **11** incorporate

**subterfuge**
**04** hole, ploy, ruse, wile **05** dodge, trick **06** excuse, refuge, scheme **07** evasion, off-come, pretext **08** artifice, intrigue, pretence **09** creep-hole, deception, duplicity, expedient, manoeuvre, stratagem **11** deviousness, machination

**subtle**
◇ *anagram indicator*
**03** sly **04** deep, fine, mild, nice, wily **05** faint **06** artful, astute, clever, crafty, low-key, minute, shrewd, slight, subtil, suttle, tricky **07** complex, cunning, devious, elusive, implied, refined, tactful, tenuous **08** abstruse, delicate, dextrous, discreet, indirect, profound, rarefied, ticklish **09** dexterous, insidious, intricate, sophistic, strategic, toned-down **10** impalpable, indefinite, indistinct, scholastic **11** overrefined, sophistical, understated **13** sophisticated **14** discriminating

**subtlety**
**05** guile, skill **06** acumen, nicety, nuance **07** cunning, finesse, quillet, slyness **08** delicacy, sagacity, wiliness **09** acuteness, faintness, intricacy, mutedness, suttletie **10** artfulness, astuteness, cleverness, craftiness, refinement **11** deviousness, discernment **14** discrimination, indefiniteness, indistinctness, sophistication

**subtly**
◇ *anagram indicator*
**05** slyly **06** mildly, suttly **07** faintly **08** artfully, astutely, cleverly **09** cunningly, deviously, tenuously **10** indirectly **11** deceitfully **12** indefinitely, indistinctly

**subtract**
**04** dock, take **05** debit **06** deduct, remove **07** detract **08** diminish, take away, withdraw, withhold

**suburb**
**04** burb **08** banlieue, faubourg, purlieus, suburbia **09** dormitory, outskirts **12** commuter belt

13 bedroom suburb, dormitory town
15 dormitory suburb, residential area

**suburban**
04 dull 06 narrow 07 insular
08 commuter 09 bourgeois, parochial
10 provincial 11 middle-class, residential 12 conventional, narrow-minded 13 unimaginative
14 common-or-garden

**subversive**
07 riotous, traitor 08 quisling
09 dissident, seditious, terrorist, weakening 10 disruptive, incendiary, traitorous, treasonous 11 destructive, seditionist, treacherous, undermining
12 discrediting, inflammatory, troublemaker 13 revolutionary, troublemaking 14 fifth columnist, freedom fighter

**subvert**
04 raze, ruin 05 upset, wreck
06 debase, poison 07 corrupt, deprave, destroy, disrupt, pervert, vitiate 08 confound, demolish, overturn, sabotage 09 overthrow, undermine 10 demoralize, invalidate
11 contaminate

**subway**
04 dive, tube 05 metro 06 tunnel
09 underpass 11 underground

**succeed**
04 fare, work 05 cut it, ensue, fadge, get on, reach, speed 06 answer, attain, come on, do well, follow, fulfil, make it, manage, result, thrive, walk it, win out
07 achieve, crack it, devolve, inherit, make out, prevail, prosper, pull off, realize, replace, triumph, turn out, work out 08 approach, bring off, carry out, complete, flourish, get there, go places, make good, take over 09 come after, win the day 10 accomplish, get results, strike gold, take effect, win through 11 come through, squeeze home 12 be successful, make the grade, steal the show, turn up trumps
13 hit the jackpot 14 fall on your feet, land on your feet, take the place of
• **succeed to**
06 accede, assume 07 inherit, replace
08 come into, take over 09 enter upon, supersede

**succeeding**
04 next 05 later 06 coming, to come
07 ensuing 09 following 10 hereditary, subsequent, successive

**success**
02 go, up 03 hit, VIP, win, wow
04 fame, luck, riot, star 05 celeb, fluke, smash 06 bigwig, upshot, winner
07 big name, big shot, fortune, sell-out, triumph, victory 08 eminence, sequence, smash hit, somebody, speeding 09 celebrity, happiness, sensation 10 attainment, bestseller, completion, fulfilment, prosperity, succession 11 achievement, realization
12 box-office hit 13 coup de théâtre, flash in the pan, flying colours
14 accomplishment, positive result
• **expression of success**
03 Jai 05 bingo 06 eureka, hurrah
07 heureka, hey pass 09 hey presto

**successful**
03 top 05 boffo, lucky, socko
06 famous 07 booming, leading, popular, thriven, wealthy, winning
08 affluent, fruitful, thriving, unbeaten
09 fortunate, lucrative, rewarding, well-known 10 home and dry, productive, profitable, prosperous, riding high, satisfying, triumphant, victorious 11 bestselling, flourishing, moneymaking 12 chart-busting

**successfully**
04 fine, well 05 great 08 famously
09 feliciter 10 swimmingly
11 beautifully 12 victoriously

**succession**
03 run 04 flow, line 05 chain, cycle, order, train 06 course, series, string
08 pedigree, sequence 09 accession, attaining, elevation, posterity
10 assumption, procession, survivance
11 continuance, inheritance, progression 12 continuation
• **in succession**
06 in a row, in turn 07 by-and-by, en suite, running 08 seriatim, straight
09 on the trot 12 sequentially, successively 13 consecutively
15 uninterruptedly

**successive**
06 serial 07 running, sequent
09 following 10 hereditary, sequential, succeeding 11 consecutive

**successively**
07 running 09 on the trot 12 in succession, sequentially
13 consecutively 15 uninterruptedly

**successor**
04 heir 05 coarb 06 co-heir, comarb, epigon, relief 07 epigone, khalifa
08 khalifah 09 inheritor, succeeder
10 descendant, next in line, substitute
11 beneficiary, replacement

**succinct**
05 brief, crisp, pithy, short, terse
07 compact, concise, in a word, summary 08 Laconian 09 condensed
10 to the point 12 close-fitting

**succinctly**
07 briefly, crisply, in a word, in brief, pithily, tersely 09 compactly, concisely
10 to the point

**succour**
03 aid 04 help 05 nurse 06 assist, foster, relief 07 comfort, help out, relieve, support 08 befriend
09 encourage 10 assistance, minister to 11 helping hand 13 ministrations

**succulent**
04 lush, rich 05 juicy, moist, sappy, tasty 06 cactus, fleshy, mellow 08 ice plant, luscious, spekboom, stapelia
09 echeveria, kalanchoe
11 sempervivum 13 mouthwatering

**succumb**
03 die 04 fall 05 catch, die of, yield
06 give in, pick up, submit 07 die from, give way 08 collapse, contract
09 surrender 10 capitulate, go down with 12 knuckle under

**suck**
04 draw, pull 05 drain 06 absorb, blot up, draw in, hoover, imbibe, soak up, sponge, suckle 07 exhaust, extract, suction
• **suck up to**
04 fawn 05 creep, toady 06 grovel
07 flatter, truckle 10 ingratiate 11 curry favour

**sucker**
03 mug, sap 04 butt, dupe, fool
05 graft, leech, patsy, sweet, toady
06 sponge, stooge, tellar, teller, tiller, victim 07 cat's-paw, muggins, osculum
08 lollipop, parasite, pushover, surculus 10 acetabulum

**suckle**
04 feed 05 nurse 07 nourish 08 wet-nurse 10 breastfeed

**suction**
07 sucking 08 draining 09 absorbing, drawing-in 10 extraction

**Sudan**
03 SDN, SUD

**sudden**
04 fast, rash, snap 05 ferly, flash, hasty, quick, rapid, sharp, swift 06 abrupt, prompt, speedy 07 hurried, quantum
08 dramatic, meteoric 09 extempore, immediate, impetuous, impulsive, overnight, startling 10 improvised, surprising, unexpected, unforeseen
11 subitaneous 13 instantaneous, unanticipated 15 spur-of-the-moment

**suddenly**
03 pop 04 slap, swap, swop 05 souse
06 astart, subito 07 asudden, at a blow, quickly, sharply 08 abruptly, unwarely
09 all at once, extempore
11 immediately 12 à l'improviste, all of a sudden, out of the blue, unexpectedly 13 with a siserary 14 at one fell swoop, in one fell swoop, without warning 15 instantaneously

**suddenness**
05 haste 09 hastiness 10 abruptness
11 hurriedness 13 impulsiveness
14 unexpectedness

**suds**
04 beer, foam 05 froth 06 lather
07 bubbles 09 soapiness

**sue**
03 beg 05 court, plead 06 appeal, charge, follow, indict, pursue, summon
07 beseech, entreat, implead, process, solicit 08 petition 09 prosecute 11 beg for a fool, take to court 12 bring to trial

**suffer**
◇ *anagram indicator*
03 die, let, pay 04 ache, bear, feel,

have, hurt **05** abide, allow, gripe, incur, prove, stand, thole **06** endure, grieve, permit, sorrow **07** agonize, support, sustain, undergo **08** be in pain, meet with, tolerate **09** go through, put up with **10** experience **11** be afflicted

**suffering**
◇ *anagram indicator*
**04** hurt, pain, pine **05** agony, trial **06** misery, ordeal, plight **07** anguish, hurting, passion, torment, torture **08** distress, hardship **09** adversity, afflicted, endurance **10** affliction, discomfort **12** wretchedness

**suffice**
**02** do **05** serve **06** answer **07** content, satisfy **08** be enough **09** measure up **10** be adequate, fit the bill **11** fill the bill **12** be sufficient

**sufficiency**
**05** store **06** enough, plenty **07** satiety **08** adequacy, bellyful **09** abundance **10** competence, competency **11** sufficience **12** adequateness

**sufficient**
**04** enow, good **05** ample **06** decent, enough, plenty **08** adequate **09** competent, effective **12** satisfactory

• **a sufficient quantity**
**02** qs **15** quantum sufficit

**suffocate**
**05** choke, smoke, smoor, smore, stive **06** stifle **07** oppress, smother **08** strangle, throttle **10** asphyxiate **12** be breathless **14** make breathless

**suffrage**
**04** vote **06** prayer **08** sanction **09** franchise **11** right to vote **15** enfranchisement

**suffuse**
**03** dip **04** gild **05** bathe, cover, flood, imbue, steep, tinge **06** colour, infuse, mantle, redden, spread **07** pervade **08** permeate **09** transfuse

**sugar**
**03** LSD **05** money, sweet **06** heroin **08** flattery

*Sugars include:*

**03** gur
**04** beet, cane, date, goor, loaf, lump, milk, palm, spun, wood
**05** brown, fruit, grape, icing, maple, syrup, white
**06** aldose, barley, caster, castor, golden, hexose, invert, ketose, xylose
**07** glucose, glycose, jaggery, lactose, maltose, mannose, pentose, refined, sucrose, treacle
**08** demerara, dextrose, fructose, levulose, molasses, powdered
**09** arabinose, galactose, laevulose, raffinose, trehalose, unrefined
**10** granulated, saccharose
**12** crystallized
**13** confectioner's

**sugary**
**05** corny, gushy, mushy, soppy, sweet **06** sickly, sloppy, slushy, syrupy **07** gushing, maudlin, mawkish, sugared **08** touching **09** emotional, schmaltzy, sweetened **10** lovey-dovey, saccharine **11** sentimental

**suggest**
**04** hint, move, vote **05** evoke, float, imply, smack, smell, table, tempt **06** advise, allude, hint at, prompt, savour, submit **07** connote, counsel, present, propose, smack of, smell of **08** advocate, envisage, indicate, intimate, nominate **09** insinuate, recommend **10** come up with, put forward **11** bring to mind **12** bring forward

**suggestion**
**04** hint, idea, kite, note, plan, ring, wind **05** smack, touch, trace, twang, whiff **06** motion **07** pointer, wrinkle **08** allusion, innuendo, proposal **09** prompting, prompture, suspicion **10** incitement, indication, intimation, submission, temptation **11** implication, insinuation, proposition **12** aesthesiogen **13** piece of advice **14** recommendation

**suggestive**
**04** blue, lewd **05** bawdy, dirty **06** ribald, risqué, sexual, smutty **07** meaning **08** immodest, improper, indecent, redolent **09** evocative, off-colour **10** expressive, indelicate, indicative **11** provocative, reminiscent, stimulating, titillating

**suicide**
**06** suttee **07** seppuku **08** felo de se, hara-kiri, hari-kari **10** self-murder **11** ending it all, parasuicide **12** self-violence **13** happy dispatch, self-slaughter **14** self-immolation **15** killing yourself, self-destruction, topping yourself

• **commit suicide**
**08** end it all **11** top yourself **12** do yourself in, kill yourself, take your life **14** commit hari-kari **15** take your own life

**suit**
**03** fit, gee, hit, set **04** case, meet **05** agree, apply, befit, besit, cause, clubs, do for, match, queme, suite, trial **06** action, answer, attire, become, drapes, effeir, effere, hearts, outfit, please, series, spades, square **07** contest, costume, crawler, dispute, fashion, flatter, furnish, gratify, lawsuit, overall, process, provide, pursuit, satisfy, suffice **08** argument, clothing, diamonds, ensemble, petition, sequence, tailleur **09** agree with, courtship, plus fours, tally with **10** complement, fit the bill, go well with, litigation, look good on, qualify for **11** fill the bill, proceedings, prosecution **12** set of clothes **13** be suitable for, harmonize with **14** be acceptable to, be applicable to **15** be convenient for

*Suits include:*

**01** g
**03** cat, dry, Mao, NBC, sun, wet
**04** body, Eton, jump, play, swim, zoot
**05** drape, dress, noddy, pants, shell, siren, sleep, space, sweat, track, union
**06** boiler, diving, flying, lounge, monkey, riding, safari, sailor, tsotsi
**07** bathing, leisure, penguin, trouser
**08** birthday, business, pressure, skeleton, sleeping

**suitability**
**07** aptness, fitness **09** congruity, rightness **10** competence, competency, congruence, congruency, timeliness **11** convenience, fittingness **12** appositeness **13** opportuneness **14** correspondence, correspondency **15** appropriateness

**suitable**
**03** apt, due, fit **04** able, good **05** right **06** giusto, liable, proper, seemly, suited **07** fitting **08** adequate, agreeing, all right, apposite, becoming, decorous, relevant **09** agreeable, befitting, competent, congruent, consonant, in keeping, opportune, pertinent **10** acceptable, applicable, compatible, convenient, well-suited **11** appropriate, well-matched **12** satisfactory

**suitably**
**05** fitly, quite **06** as well **08** properly **09** fittingly **10** acceptably **11** accordingly **13** appropriately

**suitcase**
**03** bag **04** case, port **05** trunk **06** valise **07** holdall **09** flight bag, portfolio, travel bag **10** vanity-case **11** attaché case, hand-luggage, portmanteau **12** overnight-bag

**suite**
**03** set **04** flat, tail **05** court, rooms, train **06** ballet, escort, sequel, series **07** partita, retinue **08** chambers, sequence, servants **09** apartment, cassation, entourage, followers, furniture, household, retainers **10** attendants, collection, set of rooms **11** hospitality **12** divertimento

**suitor**
**04** beau **05** lover, swain, wooer **07** admirer **08** follower, young man **09** boyfriend, pretender **10** petitioner, pretendant, pretendent **11** detrimental

**sulk**
**03** dod, pet **04** dort, huff, miff, mood, mope, mump, pout **05** boody, brood, grump, pique **06** grouse, temper **07** bad mood **08** be miffed **09** bad temper, be in a huff **13** pull a long face

• **the sulks**
**03** pet **04** dods, hump, tout, towt **05** glout, grump **06** glumps, strunt **07** strunts

**sulkily**
**07** crossly, moodily **08** morosely, sullenly **10** grudgingly **11** resentfully

**sulky**
**05** aloof, cross, huffy, humpy, moody, pouty, ratty **06** glumpy, grouty, grumpy, jinker, miffed, moping, morose, put out, stuffy, sullen **07** pettish
**08** brooding, grudging, stunkard
**09** resentful **10** out of sorts, unsociable
**11** bad-tempered, disgruntled
**13** gumple-foisted

**sullen**
**04** dark, dour, dull, glum, grim, sour
**05** black, cross, heavy, moody, sulky, surly **06** broody, dismal, dogged, gloomy, leaden, morose, silent, solein, sombre **07** lumpish, mumpish
**08** churlish, farouche, perverse, stubborn, stunkard **09** cheerless, obstinate, resentful, simpleton
**11** black-browed **15** uncommunicative

**sullenly**
**06** glumly, sourly **07** crossly, moodily, sulkily **08** gloomily, morosely
**10** churlishly, stubbornly **11** obstinately, resentfully

**sullenness**
**05** gloom **08** brooding, glumness, sourness **09** glowering, heaviness, moodiness, sulkiness, surliness
**10** moroseness

**sully**
**03** mar **04** soil, spot **05** dirty, spoil, stain, taint **06** assoil, befoul, damage, darken, defile, smirch, smutch
**07** blemish, distain, pollute, tarnish
**08** besmirch, disgrace **09** dishonour
**11** contaminate

**sulphur**
**01** S **09** brimstone

**sultan, sultana**
**06** despot, fiddle, raisin, sharif, sherif, soldan **07** shereef **08** padishah
**09** Grand Turk **12** Grand Signior
**13** Grand Seignior

**sultanate**
**04** Oman **06** Brunei

**sultry**
**03** hot **04** sexy **05** close, humid, lurid, muggy, soggy **06** sticky, stuffy
**07** airless, sensual, sweltry **08** alluring, stifling, tempting **09** seductive
**10** attractive, indelicate, oppressive, passionate, sweltering, voluptuous
**11** provocative, suffocating

**sum**
**03** add **05** penny, score, tally, total, whole **06** amount, answer, height, number, result **07** summary
**08** entirety, quantity, sum total
**09** abatement, aggregate, carry-over, exemplify, reckoning, summarize, summation **10** completion, remittance
**11** culmination

• **large sum**
**04** pots **11** golden hello **12** a king's ransom, a pretty penny **15** golden handshake

• **small sum**
**04** dime **05** groat, penny **08** pittance

• **sum up**
**03** add **04** foot, wind **05** close, compt, count, gauge, recap **06** assess, embody, review, size up, upknit
**08** conclude, consider, evaluate
**09** epitomize, exemplify, inventory, summarize **11** encapsulate
**12** recapitulate **14** put in a nutshell

**summarily**
**07** hastily, swiftly **08** abruptly, promptly, speedily **09** forthwith
**11** arbitrarily, immediately
**12** peremptorily, without delay
**13** expeditiously

**summarize**
**03** pot, sum **05** recap, sum up
**06** docket, minute, précis, resume, review, sketch **07** abridge, outline, shorten **08** abstract, condense, pirlicue, purlicue **09** epitomize, synopsize **10** abbreviate
**11** encapsulate

**summary**
**02** CV **04** curt, plan **05** brief, creed, hasty, recap, short, summa, swift
**06** aperçu, digest, direct, docket, précis, prompt, résumé, review, speedy, summar, wrap-up **07** cursory, docquet, epitome, instant, minutes, offhand, outline, rundown, sylloge, tabloid **08** abstract, argument, overview, succinct, synopsis
**09** arbitrary, condensed, immediate, summation, summing-up
**10** compendium, conspectus, Hitopadesa, main points, memorandum, peremptory
**11** abridgement, aide-mémoire, compendious **12** balance-sheet, condensation, without delay **13** bank statement, instantaneous, unceremonious **14** recapitulation
**15** abstract of title, curriculum vitae

**summerhouse**
**06** gazebo **08** pavilion **09** belvedere, root house **11** garden-house

**summit**
◇ *head selection indicator*
**03** top **04** acme, acro-, apex, head, peak, pike **05** crest, crown, glory, point, spire, talks **06** apogee, climax, height, vertex, zenith **07** hilltop, meeting **08** pinnacle **09** sublimity
**10** conference, discussion
**11** culmination, negotiation
**12** altaltissimo, consultation

**summon**
**03** bid **04** buzz, call, cite, gong, hail, hist, hoop, page, ring, sist, toll, warn
**05** knell, order, rally, rouse, shake, whoop **06** accite, arouse, beckon, call up, demand, drum up, gather, invite, muster, ring up, work up **07** call out, conjure, convene, convent, convoke, history, pluck up, provoke, screw up, send for, trumpet, whistle
**08** assemble, mobilize, muster up
**09** challenge, preconize, recollect

• **summon up**
**05** evoke, rally, rouse **06** arouse, gather, muster, revive, work up
**07** convene, pluck up, screw up
**08** assemble, mobilize **09** recollect
**10** call to mind

**summons**
**04** call, writ **05** bluey, cital, order, rouse
**06** gather, what ho, wo ha ho
**07** warning, war note, whistle
**08** citation, monition, reveille, subpoena **09** challenge **10** arrière-ban, injunction, invocation **11** clarion call, curtain call **12** gathering-cry
**13** parking ticket **14** interpellation

**sumptuous**
**04** dear, rich **05** grand, plush **06** costly, de luxe, lavish, slap-up, superb
**07** opulent **08** gorgeous, palatial, princely, splendid **09** expensive, luxurious **11** extravagant, magnificent

**sun**
**01** S **03** day, tan **04** bake, bask, star, year **05** brown, light **07** daystar
**08** daylight, eye of day, insolate, sunbathe, sunlight, sunshine

• **sun god**
**02** Ra, Re **03** Sol **05** Horus, Surya
**06** Apollo, Helios, Tammuz
**07** Phoebus

**sunbathe**
**03** sun, tan **04** bake, bask **05** brown
**07** sunbake **08** insolate

**sunburnt**
**03** red **05** brown, burnt **07** peeling
**08** inflamed **09** blistered **10** blistering
**13** weather-beaten

**Sunday**
**01** S **03** Sun

**sunder**
**03** cut **04** chop, part **05** sever, split
**06** cleave, divide, sundra, sundri
**07** disally, sundari **08** dissever, disunite, separate **09** dissunder

**sundry**
**04** a few, some **06** divers, varied
**07** diverse, several, various
**08** assorted, separate **09** different
**13** miscellaneous

**sunk**
◇ *anagram indicator*
**03** pad **04** bank, deep, lost
**06** doomed, failed, in a fix, in a jam, ruined **07** done for **08** finished, knee-deep **09** submerged **10** up the creek, up the spout

**sunken**
**05** drawn, laigh, lower **06** buried, hollow **07** concave, haggard, lowered
**08** hollowed, recessed **09** cellarous, depressed, submerged

**sunless**
**04** dark, grey, hazy **05** bleak **06** cloudy, dismal, dreary, gloomy, sombre
**08** overcast **09** cheerless
**10** depressing

**sunlight**
**03** sun **05** light **08** daylight, sun's rays
**12** natural light

**sunny**
**04** fine, glad **05** clear, happy, merry **06** blithe, bouncy, bright, bubbly, cheery, genial, joyful, sunlit **07** beaming, buoyant, hopeful, radiant, smiling, summery **08** cheerful, pleasant, sunshiny **09** brilliant, cloudless, unclouded **10** optimistic **12** light-hearted

**sunrise**
**04** dawn **05** sun-up **06** aurora, orient **07** morning **08** cock-crow, daybreak, daylight **10** break of day, first light **11** crack of dawn

**sunset**
**04** dusk **07** evening, sundown **08** gloaming, twilight **09** nightfall **10** close of day

**sup** *see* **eat**; **dine**

**super**
**03** ace **04** cool, good!, mega, neat **05** brill, great **06** lovely!, superb, wicked **08** glorious, peerless, smashing, terrific, top-notch **09** excellent, matchless, wonderful **10** delightful, marvellous **11** magnificent, outstanding, sensational **12** incomparable

**superannuated**
**03** old **04** aged **06** past it, senile **07** elderly, retired **08** decrepit, moribund, obsolete **10** antiquated **12** pensioned off **13** put out to grass

**superb**
**03** ace **04** fine, neat, posh **05** brill, grand, great, proud **06** choice, lavish **07** haughty **08** clipping, dazzling, fabulous, gorgeous, jim-dandy, smashing, splendid, superior, terrific **09** admirable, brilliant, excellent, exquisite, first-rate, wonderful **10** first-class, impressive, marvellous, remarkable, unrivalled **11** fantabulous, magnificent, outstanding, superlative, unsurpassed **12** breathtaking

**supercilious**
**05** lofty, proud **06** lordly, overly, snooty, snotty, snouty, uppish, uppity **07** haughty, stuck-up **08** arrogant, cavalier, insolent, jumped-up, scornful, superior **09** imperious **10** disdainful, hoity-toity, toffee-nose **11** high-sighted, overbearing, patronizing, toffee-nosed **12** contemptuous, vainglorious **13** condescending

**superficial**
◇ *containment indicator*
**05** hasty, outer **06** casual, facile, slight **07** alleged, cursory, hurried, outside, outward, passing, seeming, shallow, sketchy, surface, trivial **08** apparent, careless, cosmetic, exterior, external, skin-deep, slapdash **09** frivolous, surficial **10** ostensible, peripheral **11** lightweight, perfunctory **13** insignificant **14** one-dimensional

**superficiality**
**09** lightness **10** simplicity, slightness, triviality **11** externality, shallowness **13** frivolousness, worthlessness

**superficially**
**07** outward **08** casually, skin-deep **09** hurriedly, outwardly, seemingly **10** apparently, carelessly, externally, ostensibly **12** on the surface

**superfine**
**03** sup **04** supe **05** super **09** rosewater

**superfluity**
**04** glut **05** extra **06** excess **07** surfeit, surplus **08** pleonasm, plethora **09** overflush, superflux **10** exuberance, overgrowth, redundancy, surplusage **13** excessiveness **14** superabundance

**superfluous**
**05** extra, spare, waste **06** de trop, excess, frilly, otiose **07** surplus, to spare **08** needless, unneeded, unwanted **09** excessive, redundant, remaining **10** excrescent, fifth-wheel, gratuitous, prolixious **11** at a discount, uncalled-for, unnecessary, unwarranted **13** supernumerary

**superhuman**
**03** god **04** hero **05** great **06** bionic, divine, heroic **07** goddess, immense **09** herculean **10** paranormal, phenomenal, prodigious, stupendous **12** supernatural **13** extraordinary, preternatural

**superimpose**
**03** add **05** lay on, put on **07** lay over, overlay **08** transfer **10** overstrike

**superintend**
**03** run **05** steer **06** direct, handle, manage **07** control, inspect, oversee **08** overlook **09** supervise **10** administer **12** be in charge of **13** be in control of

**superintendence**
**04** care **06** charge, survey **07** control, running **08** episcopy, guidance **09** direction, oversight **10** government, inspection, management **11** supervision **12** surveillance **14** administration

**superintendent**
**04** boss, Supt **05** chief, super **06** gaffer, viewer, warden **07** curator, manager **08** curatrix, director, governor, overseer **09** conductor, inspector, intendant **10** controller, provincial, supervisor **13** administrator

**superior**
**03** sup **04** boss, fine, over **05** chief, elder, fancy, lofty, prime, prize, upper **06** better, choice, de luxe, higher, la-di-da, lordly, select, senior, snooty, uppish, uppity **07** foreman, generic, greater, haughty, manager, premium, quality, stuck-up, upstage **08** director, jumped-up, lah-di-dah, overlord, snobbish, top-notch **09** admirable, excellent, exclusive, first-rate, high-class, high-grade, high-toned, paramount, preferred, principal, top-drawer, top-flight, top-sawyer **10** disdainful, first-class, supervisor, unrivalled **11** exceptional, good-quality, high-quality, outstanding, patronizing, pretentious, toffee-nosed **12** higher in rank, supercilious, transcendent **13** condescending, distinguished, par excellence

• **without superior**
**04** odal, udal **07** alodial, topless **08** allodial

**superiority**
**04** edge, gree, lead **07** numbers **08** eminence **09** advantage, dominance, supremacy **10** ascendancy, mastership **11** pre-eminence **12** predominance

**superlative**
**03** ace, -est, sup **04** best **05** brill **06** superl **07** highest, supreme **08** greatest, peerless, unbeaten **09** brilliant, excellent, first-rate, matchless **10** consummate, first-class, unbeatable, unrivalled **11** magnificent, outstanding, unsurpassed **12** transcendent, unparalleled

**supermarket**
**08** minimart **09** superette **10** superstore **11** hypermarket **12** cash-and-carry

**supernatural**
**03** fay, fey, fie **05** eerie, magic, weird **06** hidden, mystic, occult **07** ghostly, magical, phantom, psychic, uncanny **08** abnormal, daemonic, daimonic, eldritch, mystical **09** spiritual, unnatural, witchlike **10** miraculous, mysterious, paranormal **12** metaphysical, otherworldly **13** hyperphysical, preternatural **14** transcendental
*See also* **occult**

**supernumerary**
**04** orra **05** extra, spare **06** excess **07** surplus **09** excessive, redundant **11** superfluous **13** extraordinary

**supersede**
**04** oust **05** usurp **06** desist, remove **07** discard, refrain, replace, succeed **08** displace, override, set aside, supplant **12** Stellenbosch, take over from **14** take the place of

**supersonic transport**
**03** AST, SST

**superstition**
**04** myth **05** magic **07** fallacy **08** delusion, illusion **10** Aberglaube **11** apotropaism **12** old wives' tale

**superstitious**
**05** false **06** freety, freity **08** delusive, illusory, mythical **10** fallacious, groundless, irrational

**supervise**
**03** run **04** edit **05** guide, nanny, targe, watch **06** direct, handle, manage, umpire **07** conduct, control, inspect, monitor, oversee **08** bear-lead **09** look after, watch over **10** administer,

invigilate **11** keep an eye on, preside over, superintend **12** be in charge of **13** be in control of

**supervision**
**04** care, duty **06** charge **07** control, running **08** guidance **09** direction, oversight **10** inspection, management **11** instruction **12** surveillance **14** administration **15** superintendence

**supervisor**
**04** boss **05** chief **06** umpire, warden **07** foreman, manager, monitor, proctor, steward **08** director, governor, overseer **09** forewoman, inspector, roundsman, spectator **10** brewmaster, foreperson, sheep-biter, toolpusher **11** floorwalker, invigilator **12** floor manager **13** administrator **14** superintendent

**supervisory**
**09** executive **10** managerial, overseeing **11** directorial **14** administrative, superintendent

**supine**
**03** sup **04** flat, idle, lazy, weak **05** bored, inert **06** torpid **07** languid, passive, sloping, upright **08** careless, heedless, inactive, inclined, indolent, listless, resigned, slothful, sluggish **09** apathetic, lethargic, negligent, prostrate, recumbent, spineless **10** horizontal, spiritless **11** indifferent, unresisting **12** uninterested

**supper**
**03** tea **04** mass **05** snack **06** dinner, hawkey, hockey, horkey **07** nagmaal **10** rere-supper **11** aftersupper, evening meal

**supplant**
**04** oust **05** usurp **06** cut out, remove, topple, unseat, uproot **07** pre-empt, replace **08** displace **09** overthrow, supersede **12** take over from **14** take the place of

**supple**
**05** agile, leish, lithe, lofty, wanle **06** limber, pliant, souple, wandle, wannel, whippy **07** bending, elastic, fawning, plastic, pliable, sinuous **08** flexible, graceful, yielding **09** willowish **10** stretching **11** loose-limbed **12** loose-jointed **13** double-jointed

**supplement**
**02** PS **03** eik, eke, SCP, sup, TES, TLS **04** mend, supp **05** add-on, add to, annex, boost, extra, relay, rider, suppl, top up **06** eke out, extend, fill up, insert, make up, sequel, supply **07** augment, codicil, help out, pull-out **08** addendum, addition, additive, appendix, increase, salt lick, schedule **09** Beta fibre, reinforce, sooterkin **10** Beres drops, complement, Incaparina, postscript, suppletion

**supplementary**
**05** added, extra **06** bolt-on, second **07** ripieno **08** attached **09** ancillary, auxiliary, corollary, expletory, secondary, suppliant **10** additional **12** accompanying **13** complementary

**suppliant**
**07** begging, craving **09** imploring **10** beseeching, entreating **11** importunate, reinforcing **12** supplicating **13** supplementary

**supplicant**
**06** suitor **07** pleader **09** applicant, postulant, suppliant **10** petitioner

**supplicate**
**04** pray **05** plead **06** appeal, invoke **07** beseech, entreat, request, solicit **08** petition

**supplication**
**04** plea, suit **06** appeal, orison, prayer **07** request **08** entreaty, petition, pleading, rogation **10** invocation **11** conjuration, imploration, obsecration **12** solicitation

**supplicatory**
**06** humble **07** begging **09** imploring, precative, precatory **10** beseeching **11** imprecatory, petitioning, postulatory **12** supplicating

**supplier**
**05** donor **06** dealer, seller, vendor **08** provider, retailer **09** connexion, outfitter **10** connection, wholesaler **11** contributor

**supply**
◇ *anagram indicator*
**03** due, fit, gas **04** bank, crop, feed, fill, find, food, fund, give, heap, help, lend, load, mass, pile, sell, temp, wood **05** cache, endew, endow, endue, equip, grant, grist, hoard, indew, indue, labor, plumb, serve, stake, stock, store, yield **06** amount, donate, fit out, labour, occupy, outfit, output, plenty, purvey, source, stores **07** furnish, plenish, produce, proffer, provide, rations, reserve, satisfy, service, victual **08** minister, quantity **09** equipment, materials, reinforce, replenish, reservoir, stockpile **10** contribute, cornucopia, provisions, substitute, supplement **11** necessities **15** cut and come again

**support**
◇ *juxtaposition down indicator*
**03** aid, arm, bra, cup, leg, tee **04** abet, axle, back, base, bear, care, feed, food, fund, help, keep, pier, pole, post, prop, raft, rest, root, skid, stay **05** brace, carry, grant, truss **06** assist, back up, be with, corset, crutch, defend, endure, foster, hold up, pillar, prop up, ratify, relief, second, uphold, verify **07** backing, bear out, bolster, capital, care for, comfort, confirm, defence, endorse, espouse, finance, funding, further, loyalty, nourish, promote, run with, shore up, sponsor, subsidy, sustain, trestle **08** advocate, approval, be behind, befriend, be kind to, buttress, champion, document, donation, espousal, evidence, maintain, motivate, skeleton, strength, sympathy, underpin, validate **09** bolster up, encourage, look after, patronage, provision, reinforce, subsidize **10** allegiance, assistance, foundation, friendship, motivation, protection, provide for, rally round, strengthen, sustenance, take care of, underwrite, validation **11** corroborate, foundations, maintenance, sponsorship, subsistence **12** authenticate, be in favour of, confirmation, contribute to, contribution, moral support, ratification, substantiate, substructure, underpinning, verification **13** encouragement **14** authentication, be supportive to, give strength to, substantiation, sympathize with **15** give a donation to, take the weight of, tower of strength

• **be supported**
**04** live, rest **05** float

• **expression of support**
**03** olé

**supporter**
◇ *juxtaposition down indicator*
**03** bra, fan, leg **04** ally, beam, belt, foot, prop **05** angel, donor, stoop, voter **06** braces, friend, helper, patron, pillar, second **07** apostle, booster, partner, sponsor **08** adherent, advocate, champion, co-worker, defender, follower, henchman, janizary, militant, promoter, seconder, upholder **09** apologist, crossbeam **10** ideologist, well-wisher **11** contributor, sympathizer **12** bottle-holder, understander

**supporting**
**03** pro- **06** behind

**supportive**
**06** caring **07** helpful **08** positive **09** attentive, sensitive **10** comforting, reassuring **11** affirmative, encouraging, sympathetic **13** understanding **14** on someone's side

**suppose**
**02** if **03** say **04** take **05** fancy, guess, imply, infer, judge, opine, posit, sepad, think **06** assume, devise, expect, reckon, uphold **07** believe, dare say, imagine, presume, propose, put case, require, surmise, warrant **08** conceive, conclude, consider, perceive **09** calculate, postulate **10** conjecture, presuppose, put the case **11** expectation, hypothesize **14** take for granted

**supposed**
**07** alleged, assumed, feigned, reputed **08** believed, imagined, presumed, putative, reported, rumoured, so-called **11** conjectured **12** hypothetical **14** supposititious

• **supposed to**
**07** meant to **09** obliged to **10** expected to, intended to, required to

**supposedly**
**09** allegedly **10** apparently, ostensibly,

putatively, reportedly **13** by all accounts

**supposing that**
**02** if

**supposition**
**02** if **04** idea **05** guess **06** notion, theory **07** fiction, opinion, surmise **10** assumption, conjecture, hypothesis **11** postulation, presumption, speculation **14** presupposition

**suppress**
**04** kill, sink, stay, stop **05** burke, check, choke, crush, elide, mince, quash, quell, sit on **06** cancel, censor, hold in, hush up, ravish, squash, stifle, subdue **07** conceal, contain, control, cushion, inhibit, put down, repress, silence, sit upon, smother, squelch **08** black out, blank out, block out, gulp back, gulp down, hold back, moderate, restrain, stamp out, strangle, submerge, throttle, vanquish, vote down, withhold **09** choke back, choke down **10** put an end to **11** clamp down on, crack down on, keep in check, strangulate **14** knock on the head, put the tin hat on, put the tin lid on

**suppression**
**05** check **07** cover-up, elision **08** blackout, crushing, ischuria, quashing, quelling, stoppage **09** clampdown, crackdown, epistasis **10** censorship, ecthlipsis, extinction, inhibition, smothering **11** comstockery, concealment, dissolution, elimination, prohibition, termination

**suppurate**
**04** ooze, weep **06** fester, gather **08** maturate **09** discharge

**suppuration**
**03** pus **09** diapyesis, festering, mattering, pyorrhoea

**supremacy**
**04** rule, sway **05** power **07** control, mastery, primacy **08** dominion, hegemony, lordship, regalism **09** dominance **10** ascendancy, domination **11** paramountcy, pre-eminence, sovereignty **12** predominance

**supreme**
**03** sup, top **04** best, head, last, Supr **05** chief, final, first, grand, prime **06** sudder, utmost **07** extreme, highest, leading, sublime **08** crowning, foremost, greatest, imperial, peerless, ultimate **09** excellent, first-rate, matchless, paramount, principal, sovereign **10** consummate, first-class, pre-eminent, prevailing **11** culminating, predominant, superlative, unsurpassed **12** incomparable, second-to-none, transcendent, world-beating

**supremely**
**04** very **06** highly, really **07** acutely, greatly, utterly **08** severely **09** decidedly, extremely, intensely, unusually **10** remarkably, thoroughly, uncommonly **11** exceedingly, excessively, sovereignly **12** inordinately, terrifically **13** exceptionally **15** extraordinarily

**sure**
**02** OK **03** yes **04** fast, fine, firm, okay, safe **05** bound, clear, loyal, pakka, pucka, pukka, right, sewer, solid **06** agreed, indeed, secure, siccar, sicker, stable, steady, tested **07** assured, certain, decided, precise **08** accurate, all right, definite, faithful, of course, positive, reliable, sure-fire, unerring, very well **09** certainly, confident, convinced, effective, foolproof, steadfast, undoubted, unfailing **10** dependable, guaranteed, home and dry, inevitable, infallible, sure-footed, undeniable, unwavering **11** efficacious, irrevocable, trustworthy, undoubtedly, unfaltering **12** indisputable, never-failing, safe as houses, unmistakable **14** unquestionable

• **for sure**
**06** indeed **07** clearly, plainly **09** certainly, obviously **10** absolutely, definitely, for certain, positively, undeniably **11** indubitably, undoubtedly **12** unmistakably, without doubt **13** categorically **14** unquestionably **15** without question

• **make sure**
**04** look **05** check **06** assure, ensure, insure, secure, verify **07** betroth, confirm **09** ascertain, guarantee **11** make certain

• **make sure of having**
**03** see

**surely**
**05** syker **06** firmly, safely, siccar, sicker **07** no doubt **09** assuredly, certainly **10** definitely, inevitably, inexorably **11** confidently, doubtlessly, indubitably, undoubtedly **12** without doubt **14** unquestionably

**surety**
**04** bail, bond **06** borrow, pledge, safety **07** caution, deposit, hostage, sponsor, warrant **08** bondsman, security, warranty **09** assurance, cautioner, certainty, frithborh, guarantee, guarantor, indemnity, insurance, mortgagor, safeguard **10** undertaker

**surface**
**03** top **04** area, face, rise, side, skin **05** arise, outer, plane **06** appear, come up, emerge, façade, veneer **07** outside, outward **08** aerofoil, apparent, covering, exterior, external, reappear **11** come to light, materialize, superficial

• **on the surface**
**04** upon **09** seemingly **10** apparently, externally, ostensibly **13** at first glance, superficially

**surfeit**
**04** cram, fill, glut, staw **05** gorge, stall, stuff **06** excess, gutful **07** gorging, satiate, satiety, surplus **08** bellyful, cloyment, gluttony, overcloy, overfeed, overfill, plethora **09** repletion, satiation **11** overfulness, repleteness, superfluity **14** overindulgence, superabundance

**surge**
**03** jaw **04** eddy, flow, gush, jerk, pour, rise, roll, rush, wave **05** break, heave, spike, sweep, swell, swirl, waves, whelm **06** billow, efflux, roller, seethe, stream, upgush, uprush, wallow, welter **07** breaker, pouring, redound, upsurge, upswing **08** escalate, increase **09** transient **10** escalation **15** intensification

**surgeon**
**02** BS, ch, CM, DS, MS **03** BCh, ChB, ChM, DCh, LCh, MCh, vet **04** surg **05** LChir **06** doctor, extern, intern **07** externe, interne **08** orthopod, sawbones **09** trephiner **10** chirurgeon **11** lithotomist **12** lithotritist **13** lithotriptist **14** lithontriptist

*Surgeons include:*

**04** **Bell** (Sir Charles), **Mayo** (Charles Horace), **Reed** (Walter)
**05** **Broca** (Paul Pierre), **Paget** (Sir James)
**06** **Carrel** (Alexis), **Cooper** (Sir Astley), **Hunter** (John), **Lister** (Joseph, Lord), **Treves** (Sir Frederick), **Yacoub** (Sir Magdi)
**07** **Barnard** (Christiaan), **Burkitt** (Denis Parsons), **Cushing** (Harvey Williams), **MacEwen** (Sir William), **McIndoe** (Sir Archibald)
**08** **Beaumont** (William), **Billroth** (Theodor), **Charnley** (Sir John)

*See also* **doctor**; **medical**

• **sea surgeon**
**04** tang **06** doctor **10** doctor-fish

**surgery**
**03** ops

*Surgery types include:*

**06** biopsy
**07** keyhole, nose job, plastic
**08** cosmetic, elective, facelift, lobotomy
**09** Caesarean, colostomy, open-heart, sex change, skin graft, spare-part, tummy tuck
**10** autoplasty, cordectomy, iridectomy, laparotomy, lumpectomy, mastectomy, nip and tuck, phlebotomy, thymectomy, transplant, varicotomy
**11** angioplasty, cryosurgery, enterostomy, gastrectomy, laparoscopy, mammoplasty, rhinoplasty, splenectomy, tracheotomy, trepanation
**12** appendectomy, circumcision, corneal graft, hysterectomy, laryngectomy, microsurgery, neurosurgery, tonsilectomy, tracheostomy, trephination
**13** adenoidectomy, prostatectomy, psychosurgery, stomatoplasty,

thyroidectomy, tonsillectomy
**14** appendicectomy, coronary bypass, pancreatectomy, reconstructive
**15** cholecystectomy, thoracocentesis

*Surgery-related terms include:*

**02** op
**04** CABG, seam
**05** couch, curet, donor, graft, stoma, taxis, truss
**06** canula, domino, dossil, garrot, hobday, lancet, post-op, reduce, stitch, trepan, trocar
**07** cannula, catling, curette, forceps, garotte, myotome, operate, scalpel, section, theatre, torsion
**08** ablation, adhesion, bistoury, cannular, capeline, centesis, clinical, compress, cosmesis, crow-bill, curarine, écraseur, garrotte, incision, incisure, invasive, trephine
**09** abduction, autograft, cannulate, capelline, collodion, crow's-bill, curettage, depressor, dermatome, diastasis, enucleate, operation, osteotome, piggyback, resection, retractor, tamponade, tamponage, tenaculum
**10** deligation, diorthosis, discussion, guillotine, lithotrite, lithotrity, osteoclast
**11** anaesthetic, arthrodesis, autoplastic, cannulation, curettement, decapsulate, exteriorize, incarnation, laparoscope, lithotripsy, lithotritor, prosthetics
**12** fenestration, lithotripter, lithotriptor, lunar caustic, paracentesis, scarificator, short circuit, tissue-typing
**13** cyclodialysis, decompression, herniorrhaphy, operating room, post-operative, premedication, under the knife
**14** embryo transfer, operating table

**surgical** *see* **medical**

**Suriname**
**03** SME, SUR

**surly**
**04** grum **05** bluff, cross, cynic, gruff, gurly, stoor, stour, sture, sulky, testy **06** crusty, grumpy, morose, stowre, sullen **07** brusque, crabbed, cynical, grouchy, haughty, uncivil **08** churlish **09** crotchety, irascible **10** ill-natured, refractory, ungracious **11** bad-tempered **12** cantankerous

**surmise**
**04** idea **05** fancy, guess, infer, opine **06** assume, deduce, notion **07** imagine, opinion, presume, suppose, suspect, thought **08** conclude, consider **09** deduction, inference, speculate, suspicion **10** allegation, assumption, conclusion, conjecture, hypothesis **11** possibility, presumption, speculation, supposition

**surmount**
**03** top **04** rise, rush **05** crest **06** breast, exceed, master **07** conquer, get over, surpass **08** overcome, superate, vanquish **09** transcend **11** prevail over, triumph over

**surpass**
**03** cap, top **04** bang, beat, ding, pass, whap, whop **05** excel, outdo, outgo **06** better, exceed, overgo **07** eclipse, outbrag, outpeer, overtop, paragon, put down **08** go beyond, outclass, outrival, outshine, outstrip, surmount, underlay **09** transcend **10** overshadow, tower above **12** beat to sticks, leave for dead **13** knock spots off

**surpassing**
**04** rare **07** corking, supreme, topping **08** frabjous **09** bettering, exceeding, matchless **10** inimitable, phenomenal, unrivalled **11** exceptional, outstanding, unsurpassed **12** incomparable, transcendent **13** extraordinary

**surplice**
**04** sark **05** cotta, ephod, stole **06** rochet

**surplus**
**04** glut, over, plus **05** extra, spare **06** excess, unused **07** balance, o'ercome, overage, residue, surfeit **08** left over, overcome, overplus, owrecome, wine lake **09** carry-over, leftovers, redundant, remainder, remaining **11** superfluity, superfluous

**surprise**
**03** wow **04** drop, find, stun **05** alert, amaze, seize, shock, start **06** dismay, expose, unmask, wonder **07** astound, confuse, find out, nonplus, stagger, startle **08** astonish, bewilder, blow away, bowl over **09** amazement, bombshell, burst in on, curveball, surprisal, take aback **10** disconcert, revelation, wonderment **11** flabbergast, incredulity, knock for six, thunderbolt **12** astonishment, bewilderment **13** catch in the act, catch unawares **14** catch red-handed **15** bolt from the blue

• **expression of surprise**
**01** O **02** ah, eh, ha, ho, my, oh **03** aha, coo, cor, gee, god, hah, hoa, hoh, law, lor, man, oho, ooh, ook, say, wow **04** dear, egad, gosh, hech, igad, I say, Jeez, lawk, lord, losh, odso, phew, well, what, whew, yike **05** arrah, blimy, fancy, gadso, glory, godso, golly, hallo, hello, hullo, Jeeze, Jesus, lawks, lordy, lumme, lummy, ma foi, mercy, musha, my God, my hat, never, wowee, yikes, zowie **06** blimey, by Jove, Christ, cricky, crikey, cripes, crumbs, dear me, gemini, geminy, gemony, heaven, indeed, jiminy, my word, oh dear, wheugh, whoops, zounds **07** bless me, brother, caramba, cravens, crickey, crimine, crimini, crivens, deary me, gee whiz, glory be, good-now, heavens, jeepers, stone me, too much **08** crivvens, dearie me, good-lack, goodness, gorblimy, gracious, I declare, man alive, stroll on, well well **09** blood oath, cor blimey, fancy that, good grief, gorblimey, I never did, Jesus wept, mercy on us, son of a gun **10** conscience, gracious me, Great Scott, hell's bells, hell's teeth, hoity-toity, upon my soul, upon my word, well I never **11** bless my soul, good heavens, to think of it **12** good gracious, heavens above, my conscience, strike a light, well I declare **13** Gordon Bennett, just think of it, stone the crows **14** it's a small world **15** jeepers creepers

**surprised**
**05** agape **06** amazed **07** shocked, stunned **08** jiggered, startled **09** astounded, staggered **10** astonished, gobsmacked, nonplussed, speechless **11** dumbfounded, open-mouthed **12** lost for words **13** flabbergasted, thunderstruck

**surprising**
◇ *anagram indicator*
**05** funny **07** amazing, strange **08** shocking, stunning **09** obreption, startling, wonderful **10** astounding, incredible, remarkable, staggering, unexpected, unforeseen **11** astonishing, jaw-dropping, unlooked-for **13** extraordinary

**surprisingly**
◇ *anagram indicator*
**07** funnily **09** amazingly, strangely **10** incredibly, remarkably, stunningly **11** wonderfully **12** staggeringly, unexpectedly **13** astonishingly **15** extraordinarily

**surrender**
**04** cede, quit **05** forgo, waive, yield **06** bail up, forego, give in, give up, remise, render, resign, strike, submit, turn in **07** abandon, cession, concede, enfeoff, kamerad, let go of, release, succumb, waiving **08** abdicate, renounce, yielding **09** rendition, sacrifice, surrendry **10** abdication, capitulate, relinquish, submission **11** abandonment, leave behind, resignation **12** capitulation, lower the flag, renunciation **13** cessio bonorum, strike the flag **14** relinquishment **15** lay down your arms, throw in the towel, throw in your hand

**surreptitious**
**03** fly, sly **06** covert, hidden, secret, sneaky, veiled **07** furtive **08** stealthy **09** underhand **10** behind-door, subreptive **11** clandestine **12** unauthorized

**surrogate**
**05** proxy **06** deputy **07** stand-in **10** substitute **11** replacement **14** representative

**surround**
◇ *containment indicator*
**03** lap, orb, rim **04** brim, edge, gird, halo, moat, pack, ring, zone **05** beset, bound, brink, hedge, hem in, limit,

round, verge, water **06** begird, border, bounds, edging, empale, encase, enhalo, fringe, garter, girdle, impale, incase, invest, margin, picket, piquet **07** besiege, compass, confine, embosom, enclave, enclose, enround, envelop, environ, fence in, go round, imbosom, inclose, picquet, rampart, setting **08** cincture, confines, encircle, overflow, palisade, stockade **09** encompass, perimeter, periphery **10** circumvent, water about **11** close in upon **13** circumference, circumvallate

**surrounding**
◇ *containment indicator*
**06** gherao, nearby **07** ambient **08** adjacent **09** adjoining, bordering **10** encircling **12** encompassing, neighbouring

**surroundings**
**05** scene **06** milieu **07** context, element, habitat, setting **08** ambience, environs, locality, vicinity **10** background **11** environment, mise en scène **12** circumstance **13** neighbourhood

**surveillance**
**04** care **05** check, watch **06** charge, spying **07** control **08** scrutiny **09** direction, vigilance **10** inspection, monitoring, regulation **11** observation, stewardship, supervision **12** guardianship, suicide watch **15** superintendence

**survey**
**03** map, spy **04** form, plan, plot, poll, quiz, scan, test, view **05** chart, level, probe, recce, study, sweep **06** assess, look at, review, size up **07** examine, inspect, measure, observe, overeye, surview **08** appraise, consider, episcopy, estimate, evaluate, look over, once-over, overview, perceive, prospect, research, scrutiny, traverse **09** appraisal, summing-up, supervise, valuation **10** assessment, conspectus, inspection, plane-table, scrutinize **11** contemplate, examination, measurement, opinion poll, reconnoitre, triangulate **12** Domesday book, Doomsday book, tour d'horizon **13** consideration, perambulation, questionnaire, triangulation **14** market research, reconnaissance **15** superintendence

**surveyor**
**02** CS **08** assessor, examiner, overseer **09** geodesist, inspector

**survival**
**06** coping **08** hangover, leftover, managing **09** endurance, existence **10** will to live **11** continuance, persistence, withholding **12** perseverance, staying power

**survive**
**04** cope, last, live, stay **05** exist, rally **06** endure, live on, make it, manage, remain **07** die hard, hold out, live out, outlast, outlive, persist, recover, weather **08** be extant, continue **09** withstand **10** get through **11** come through, live through, pull through

**susceptibility**
**07** feeling **08** openness, tendency, weakness **09** liability, proneness **10** proclivity, propensity **11** gullibility, sensitivity **13** sensibilities, vulnerability **14** predisposition, responsiveness, suggestibility **15** defencelessness

**susceptible**
**04** open, weak **05** given, prone **06** at risk, liable, tender **07** capable, patient, subject **08** disposed, gullible, inclined **09** credulous, easily led, receptive, sensitive **10** responsive, vulnerable **11** defenceless, impressible, predisposed, suggestible **14** impressionable

**suspect**
◇ *anagram indicator*
**03** sus **04** fear, feel, iffy, suss **05** dodgy, doubt, fancy, fishy, guess, infer, smoke, sniff, snuff **07** believe, dubious, jalouse, misdeem, suppose, surmise **08** be wary of, conclude, consider, distrust, doubtful, jealouse, misdoubt, mistrust **09** debatable, mislippen, smell a rat, speculate, suspicion **10** conjecture, have a hunch, inadequate, suspicious, unreliable **11** misconceive **12** insufficient, questionable **13** be uneasy about **15** have doubts about, have qualms about

**suspend**
**04** hang, hold, side, stay **05** cease, debar, defer, delay, expel, swing **06** arrest, dangle, ground, hang up, put off, recess, remove, shelve **07** adjourn, dismiss, entrain, exclude, keep out, shut out, unfrock **08** disperse, postpone, prorogue, put on ice, sideline, stand off **09** interrupt **10** pigeonhole **11** discontinue **13** put in abeyance

**suspended**
**06** put off **07** delayed, hanging, pendent, pending, pensile, shelved **08** dangling, deferred, put on ice **09** postponed **10** underslung

**suspense**
**05** doubt, poise **07** anxiety, tension **09** cessation, deferring **10** excitement, expectancy, indecision, insecurity **11** expectation, nervousness, uncertainty **12** anticipation, apprehension, doubtfulness, intermission

**• in suspense**
**06** on edge **07** eagerly, keyed up **09** anxiously **11** expectantly **13** on tenterhooks **15** with bated breath

**suspension**
**03** sol **04** foam, mist, stay **05** break, delay **07** removal, respite **08** abeyance, abeyancy, deferral **09** cessation, debarment, deferment, dismissal, exclusion, expulsion, grounding, remission **10** inhibition, moratorium, unfrocking **11** adjournment, standing-off **12** intermission, interruption, postponement **14** pseudosolution

**suspicion**
**03** sus **04** dash, hint, idea, suss **05** doubt, hunch, qualm, shade, sniff, tinge, touch, trace **06** belief, breath, notion, qualms, shadow **07** caution, feeling, glimmer, inkling, opinion, soupçon, surmise, suspect, umbrage **08** distrust, misdoubt, mistrust, paranoea, paranoia, wariness **09** chariness, intuition, misgiving, scintilla **10** conjecture, intimation, misdeeming, misgivings, scepticism, sixth sense, suggestion **12** apprehension, funny feeling

**suspicious**
◇ *anagram indicator*
**03** odd **04** iffy, suss, wary **05** chary, dodgy, fishy, funny, queer, shady, smoky **06** guilty, shifty, uneasy, unsure **07** dubious, strange, suspect **08** doubtful, peculiar **09** dishonest, equivocal, irregular, sceptical **10** misdeeming, suspectful, suspecting **11** distrustful, mistrustful, unbelieving **12** apprehensive, disbelieving, questionable

**suspiciously**
**05** oddly **06** warily **07** shadily **09** dubiously, strangely **10** doubtfully **11** dishonestly, sceptically **12** questionably **13** distrustfully, mistrustfully, unbelievingly **14** apprehensively, disbelievingly

**Sussex**
**• division of Sussex**
**04** rape

**sustain**
**03** aid **04** bear, buoy, face, feed, help, hold, prop, ride **05** abide, carry, stand **06** assist, buoy up, endure, foster, hold up, keep up, prop up, suffer, upbear, uphold, upstay **07** aliment, carry on, comfort, endorse, nourish, nurture, prolong, receive, relieve, ride out, support, suspend, undergo **08** continue, happen to, maintain, protract, sanction, scaffold **09** encourage, go through, keep going, underbear **10** experience, provide for, sustentate **14** give strength to

**sustained**
**06** steady, tenuto **07** ongoing **08** constant **09** perpetual, prolonged, sostenuto **10** continuing, continuous, protracted **11** unremitting **12** long-drawn-out

**sustenance**
**04** fare, food, grub, nosh **05** scoff **06** viands **07** aliment, support **08** victuals **09** autophagy, provender, refection **10** autophagia, livelihood, provisions **11** comestibles, maintenance, nourishment, subsistence, sufficience

**svelte**
**04** slim **05** lithe **06** lissom, urbane **07** elegant, shapely, slender, willowy **08** graceful, polished **09** sylphlike **13** sophisticated

**swag**
**03** sag **04** drum, sway **05** bluey **07** bed roll, festoon, matilda, plunder **10** depression, subsidence

**swagger**
**04** brag, cock, crow, roll, show **05** boast, brank, pronk, smart, strut, swank, vapor **06** parade, prance, ruffle, square, vapour **07** bluster, panache, roister, royster, show off **08** parading, prancing, tigerism **09** arrogance **11** ostentation **12** go over the top

**swallow**
◇ *containment indicator*
**03** buy, eat, pop **04** bear, bolt, down, gulp, slug, swig, take **05** abide, abyss, ariel, drink, gorge, gulch, quaff, scoff, shift, stand, thole, trust **06** accept, devour, endure, englut, gobble, guzzle, ingest, martin, Progne, stifle, take in, throat, up with **07** believe, consume, contain, fall for, martlet, repress, smother, stomach, subsume, take off **08** down with, gobble up, gulp down, hold back, martinet, suppress, tolerate **09** knock back, polish off, put up with, worry down **11** be certain of, house martin
• **swallow hole**
**04** sink **06** dolina, doline **07** swallet **08** sinkhole
• **swallow up**
**06** absorb, enfold, engulf **07** engulph, envelop, ingulph, overrun **08** take over **09** overwhelm **10** assimilate **11** ingurgitate

**swamp**
**03** bog, fen, mud, vly **04** mire, quag, sink, vlei **05** beset, cowal, flood, Lerna, Lerne, marsh **06** deluge, Dismal, drench, engulf, morass, muskeg, slough **07** besiege, bog down, Dismals, wash out **08** inundate, loblolly, overload, quagmire, saturate, submerge, waterlog **09** overwhelm, purgatory, quicksand, swampland, weigh down

**swampy**
**03** wet **04** miry **05** boggy, fenny, soggy **06** marshy, quaggy **07** paludal **08** squelchy **09** uliginose, uliginous **11** waterlogged

**swan**
**03** cob, pen **04** Leda **06** cygnet, Cygnus

*Swans include:*

**04** mute
**05** black
**07** Bewick's, whooper
**08** whooping
**09** trumpeter, whistling

**swank**
**04** brag, show, swot **05** agile, boast, pronk, smart, strut **06** parade, pliant **07** conceit, display, posture, show off, slender, swagger **08** bragging **09** vainglory **10** showing-off **11** ostentation **12** attitudinize, boastfulness **13** conceitedness, preen yourself **15** pretentiousness

**swanky**
**04** posh, rich **05** fancy, flash, grand, plush, ritzy, showy, smart, swish **06** de luxe, flashy, lavish, plushy **07** stylish **09** exclusive, expensive, glamorous, luxurious, sumptuous **11** fashionable, pretentious **12** ostentatious

**swap, swop**
◇ *anagram indicator*
**03** hit **04** blow, flop, slam **05** bandy, plump, smite, trade **06** barter, strike, stroke, switch **07** traffic **08** exchange, suddenly, trade-off **09** transpose **10** substitute **11** interchange **12** substitution **13** transposition

**sward**
**03** sod **04** turf

**swarm**
**03** fry, mob **04** army, bike, body, byke, cast, herd, host, mass, nest, pack, shin, teem **05** crowd, drove, flock, flood, horde, shoal, surge, troop **06** abound, colony, hotter, myriad, stream, swerve, throng **08** offshoot **09** multitude **10** congregate
• **be swarming with**
**08** abound in **13** be crowded with, be overrun with, be teeming with **14** be crawling with, be hotching with, be thronged with **15** be bristling with

**swarthy**
**04** dark **05** black, brown, dusky **06** tanned **08** blackish **11** black-a-vised, dark-skinned

**swashbuckling**
**04** bold **06** daring, robust **07** dashing, gallant **08** exciting, spirited **09** dare-devil **10** courageous, flamboyant, swaggering **11** adventurous

**swat**
**03** hit **04** biff **05** lunge, swipe, whack **06** strike, wallop **07** fly-flap, lash out

**swathe**
**03** lap **04** bind, fold, furl, wind, wrap **05** cloak, drape **06** enwrap, shroud **07** bandage, envelop, sheathe, swaddle **08** enshroud, wrapping

**sway**
**04** bend, lean, reel, rock, roll, rule, shog, swag, swee, swey, veer, wave **05** clout, hoist, lurch, power, sally, shake, swale, swing, thraw, wield **06** affect, direct, divert, govern, induce, swerve, swinge, teeter, titter, totter, waddle, wobble **07** command, control, convert, incline, proceed, reeling, rocking, shoogie, shoogle, stagger, win over **08** convince, dominate, dominion, hegemony, overrule, persuade, rotation **09** authority, dominance, fluctuate, influence, oscillate, supremacy, vacillate **10** ascendancy, bring round, government, leadership **11** fluctuation, oscillation, prevail upon, sovereignty **12** jurisdiction, predominance **13** preponderance
• **hold sway**
**04** rule **05** reign **07** prevail **09** have power **10** wield power **13** exercise power, have authority, have influence, lay down the law

**Swaziland**
**02** SD **03** SWZ

**swear**
**03** eff, rap, vow **04** aver, avow, cuss, damn, oath **05** abuse, blind, curse **06** abjure, adjure, affirm, assert, attest, depose, insist, invoke, objure, pledge **07** declare, promise, testify **08** be on oath, forswear, maledict **09** blaspheme, imprecate, overswear **10** asseverate, take an oath **11** be under oath, eff and blind, take the oath **12** damn and blast **14** abjure the realm, pledge yourself, turn the air blue, use bad language **15** promise solemnly
• **swear by**
**06** rely on **07** trust in **08** depend on **09** believe in **11** have faith in **14** put your faith in

**swearing**
**07** cursing, cussing **08** language **09** blasphemy, profanity **10** coprolalia, expletives **11** bad language **12** foul language, imprecations, maledictions **14** strong language

**swear-word**
**04** cuss, oath **05** curse **08** cussword, swearing **09** blasphemy, expletive, obscenity, profanity **11** bad language, imprecation **12** foul language **14** four-letter word

**sweat**
**04** drip, flap, fuss, toil **05** chore, exude, panic, smart, sudor, tizzy, worry **06** dither, effort, labour, lather, sudate, tizwas **07** anxiety, fluster, secrete, soldier, swelter **08** drudgery, hidrosis, moisture, perspire, sudation **09** agitation, cold sweat, death-damp, mucksweat **10** osmidrosis, perspirate, stickiness **11** bloody-sweat, diaphoresis **12** perspiration, sweat buckets **13** sweat like a pig

**sweaty**
**04** damp **05** moist **06** clammy, sticky **08** forswatt, sudorous, sweating **10** perspiring

**Sweden**
**01** S **03** SWE

**sweep**
**03** arc, fly **04** bend, drag, dust, lash, move, pass, poke, push, race, roll, sail, scud, skim, soop, span, sway, tear, wash, whip, wipe **05** besom, broom, brush, clean, clear, curve, drive, elbow, force, glide, range, scoop, scope, shove, sling, surge, swath, swing, swipe, swoop, vista, whisk **06** action,

extent, glance, hurtle, jostle, onrush, remove, search, stroke, swathe, thrust, vacuum **07** clean up, clear up, compass, ensweep, expanse, gesture, impetus, stretch **08** besom out, movement, overrake, snowball, vastness **09** besom away, clearance, curvature, immensity, sooterkin **10** blackguard, pump-handle **11** move quickly **13** spread quickly

**• sweep under the carpet**
**04** hide **06** hush up **07** conceal, cover up **08** suppress **09** gloss over, paper over

**sweeper**
**05** broom **06** libero

**sweeping**
**04** sway, wide **05** broad, swing **06** global **07** blanket, general, radical, rubbish **08** thorough **09** extensive, universal, wholesale **10** simplistic **11** far-reaching, wide-ranging **12** all-embracing, all-inclusive **13** comprehensive, thoroughgoing **14** across-the-board, indiscriminate, oversimplified

**sweepstake**
**04** draw **05** sweep, Tatts **07** lottery **08** gambling **11** sweepstakes, Tattersall's

**sweet**
**03** pud **04** cute, dear, easy, icky, kind, mild, pure, ripe, soft, soot, twee **05** balmy, candy, clean, clear, dolce, fresh, glacé **06** afters, benign, dulcet, gentle, kindly, lovely, mellow, pretty, sickly, sugary, syrupy, tender **07** amiable, beloved, candied, darling, dessert, honeyed, lovable, musical, odorous, pudding, sweetie, tuneful, winning, winsome **08** adorable, all right, aromatic, charming, engaging, fragrant, gracious, likeable, loveable, luscious, perfumed, pleasant, pleasing, precious, redolent **09** agreeable, ambrosial, appealing, beautiful, cherished, delicious, melodious, sweetened, sweetmeat, treasured, wholesome **10** attractive, confection, delightful, euphonious, harmonious, saccharine **11** mellifluous, odoriferous, sickly sweet **12** affectionate, ingratiating, satisfactory, sweet-scented **13** confectionery, sweet-sounding

*Sweets include:*

**03** gum, ice
**04** jube, Mars®, mint, rock
**05** fudge, halva, jelly
**06** bonbon, confit, humbug, jujube, nougat, tablet, toffee
**07** alcorza, caramel, fondant, gumdrop, lozenge, pomfret, praline, truffle, wine gum
**08** acid drop, bull's eye, confetti, lollipop, marzipan, noisette, pastille, pear drop
**09** chocolate, jelly baby, jelly bean, lemon drop, liquorice
**10** candyfloss, chewing-gum, gobstopper, peppermint
**11** aniseed ball, barley sugar, marshmallow, toffee apple
**12** butterscotch, dolly mixture
**13** Edinburgh rock, fruit pastille
**14** pineapple chunk, Turkish delight

*See also* **cake**; **dessert**

**• sweet on**
**06** fond of, keen on, liking **08** mad about **09** far gone on **10** crazy about **12** ravished with **14** infatuated with

**sweetbread**
**03** bur **04** burr

**sweeten**
**04** ease **05** honey, sugar **06** mellow, pacify, soften, soothe, temper **07** appease, cushion, mollify, relieve **08** mitigate **09** alleviate **10** add sugar to, edulcorate

**sweetheart**
**02** jo **03** joe **04** beau, dear, dona, duck, girl, lass, love **05** bonny, donah, flame, leman, lover, Romeo, swain, toots **06** amoret, bonnie, steady, suitor, sweety, tootsy **07** admirer, beloved, darling, sweetie **08** Dulcinea, follower, lady-love, truelove, young man **09** betrothed, boyfriend, inamorata, inamorato, valentine, young lady **10** girlfriend

**sweetly**
**04** soot **05** dolce, soote **06** easily, evenly, in tune, kindly, softly **08** lovingly, mellowly, smoothly, steadily, tenderly **09** tunefully, winsomely **10** charmingly, dolcemente, pleasantly **11** melodiously **12** delightfully, effortlessly, euphoniously, harmoniously **14** affectionately

**sweetness**
**04** love **05** aroma, charm, sirup, syrup **07** douceur, euphony, harmony **08** kindness **09** balminess, dulcitude, fragrance, freshness, saccharin **10** amiability, loveliness, mellowness, saccharine, succulence, sugariness, tenderness **11** sweet temper, winsomeness **12** lusciousness, mellifluence, pleasantness

**sweet-smelling**
**05** balmy **07** odorous **08** aromatic, fragrant, perfumed, redolent **09** ambrosial **11** odoriferous **12** sweet-scented

**swell**
**03** bag, don, fop, sea **04** beau, blab, boll, bulb, bulk, dude, grow, hove, huff, lord, plim, posh, puff, rise, toff, wave **05** adept, belly, berry, blast, bloat, bulge, bunch, dandy, elate, farce, grand, great, heave, mount, plump, raise, ritzy, smart, surge **06** bigwig, billow, blow up, de luxe, dilate, expand, extend, fatten, flashy, louden, puff up, step up, strout, swanky, tumefy, volume, wallow **07** augment, balloon, distend, enlarge, ferment, heaving, incline, inflate, stylish, tumesce **08** belly out, escalate, heighten, increase, mushroom, outswell, snowball **09** backwater, cockscomb, excellent, exclusive, intensify, intumesce, loudening, roughness, skyrocket, wonderful **10** accelerate, distension, grow larger, undulation **11** enlargement, fashionable, proliferate

**swelling**
**03** sty **04** boil, boll, bulb, bump, gall, knob, knot, lump, node, stye **05** bulge, heave, mouse, nodus, proud, tuber, tumor **06** bruise, nodule, pimple, rising, torose, torous, tumour, venter **07** blister, chancre, pillowy, tympany, vesicle **08** nodosity, pulvinus, scirrhus, tubercle **09** chilblain, gathering, puffiness **10** distension, tumescence, turgescent **11** enlargement, tumefaction **12** inflammation, intumescence, protuberance

**sweltering**
**03** hot **05** humid, muggy, stewy **06** baking, clammy, steamy, sticky, sultry, torrid **07** airless, boiling **08** roasting, sizzling, stifling, tropical **09** scorching **10** oppressive **11** suffocating

**swerve**
**03** wry **04** bend, lean, skew, sway, swee, swey, turn, veer, warp **05** faint, sheer, shift, stray, swarm, swing, twist **06** shrink, wander **07** deflect, deviate, diverge, incline, inswing **08** outswing, scramble **09** deviation **10** deflection

**swift**
**04** fast **05** agile, brief, brisk, fleet, hasty, nippy, quick, rapid, ready, short, wight **06** abrupt, flying, lively, nimble, prompt, speedy, sudden, winged **07** express, flighty, hurried **09** feathered, immediate, screecher **10** pernicious **11** dispatchful, expeditious, tiger-footed **13** screech-martin

**swiftly**
**04** fast **05** apace **07** express, hotfoot, quickly, rapidly **08** promptly, speedily **09** hurriedly, instantly, posthaste **10** at full tilt **11** double-quick **13** expeditiously

**swiftness**
**05** speed **08** alacrity, celerity, despatch, dispatch, rapidity, velocity **09** fleetness, immediacy, quickness, readiness **10** expedition, promptness, speediness, suddenness **13** immediateness, instantaneity

**swill**
◇ *anagram indicator*
**04** gulp, swig, wash **05** drain, drink, quaff, rinse, slops, waste **06** gargle, guzzle, imbibe, refuse, sluice **07** consume, hogwash, pigwash, swallow, toss off **08** pig's-wash, pigswill **09** knock back, scourings

**• swill out**
**05** clean, flush, rinse **06** drench, sluice **07** cleanse, wash out **08** wash down

**swim**
◇ *anagram indicator*
**03** bob, dip, fin, ren, rin, run **04** soom, swan, whim **05** bathe, crawl, float **06** paddle **07** snorkel **08** take a dip **09** strike out **10** tread water

**swimmer** *see* **fish**

**swimming**
◇ *anagram indicator*

*Swimming strokes include:*

**03** fly
**05** crawl
**07** trudgen
**09** back crawl, butterfly, dog-paddle, freestyle
**10** backstroke, front crawl, sidestroke
**11** doggy-paddle
**12** breaststroke
**15** Australian crawl

*Swimming- and diving-related terms include:*

**02** IM
**03** fly, rip
**04** pike, tuck
**05** block, boost, entry, scull, split
**06** inward, layout, length, medley
**07** forward, reverse
**08** armstand, backward, flamingo
**09** ballet leg, eggbeater, elevation
**10** tumble turn
**11** dolphin kick, flutter kick, rocket split
**12** combined spin
**13** negative split
**14** continuous spin
**15** backstroke flags

*Swimmers and divers include:*

**04** **Klim** (Michael), **Otto** (Kristin), **Rose** (Murray), **Webb** (Matthew)
**05** **Crapp** (Lorraine), **Curry** (Lisa), **Ender** (Kornelia), **Evans** (Janet), **Gould** (Shane), **Gross** (Michael), **Lewis** (Hayley), **Riley** (Samantha), **Spitz** (Mark)
**06** **Biondi** (Matt), **Davies** (Sharron), **Durack** (Fanny), **Ederle** (Gertrude), **Fraser** (Dawn), **Loader** (Danyon), **O'Neill** (Susie), **Phelps** (Michael), **Thorpe** (Ian), **Wilkie** (David)
**07** **Goodhew** (Duncan), **Hackett** (Grant), **Perkins** (Kieren), **Wickham** (Tracey)
**08** **Champion** (Malcolm), **Charlton** (Boy), **De Bruijn** (Inge), **Louganis** (Greg), **Streeter** (Alison), **Van Wisse** (Tammy), **Williams** (Esther)
**09** **Armstrong** (Duncan), **Kellerman** (Annette)
**11** **Beaurepaire** (Sir Frank), **Weissmuller** (Johnny)

**• swimming organ**
**03** oar **05** ctene

**swimming costume** *see* **swimsuit**

**swimmingly**
**06** easily **08** smoothly, very well **12** successfully **13** like clockwork, without a hitch

**swimming-pool**
**04** lido **05** baths **10** natatorium **11** leisure pool **12** swimming-bath, swimming-pond **13** swimming-baths

**swimsuit**
**03** tog **04** togs **05** tanga, thong **06** bikini, cossie, trunks **07** bathers, maillot, tankini **08** monokini, one-piece **11** bathing suit **12** bathing dress **14** bathing costume **15** swimming costume

**swindle**
**02** do **03** con, gyp, rig **04** beat, chiz, dupe, fake, have, lurk, ramp, rook, scam, skin, take **05** bunco, bunko, cheat, chizz, fraud, gouge, grift, let in, mulct, pluck, shaft, sting, trick, twist **06** bucket, chouse, diddle, fiddle, fleece, hustle, nobble, racket, rip off, rip-off **07** con game, deceive, defraud, exploit, skelder, tweedle **08** clean-out, con trick, fakement, sell a pup, stitch up, trickery **09** bamboozle, deception, financier, gold brick, gold-brick, sell smoke **10** overcharge **12** put one over on, take for a ride **13** double-dealing, sharp practice

**swindler**
**03** con, leg **04** hood, rook **05** cheat, crook, fraud, rogue, shark **06** chouse, con man, escroc, rascal **07** fiddler, grifter, hoodlum, hustler, magsman, slicker, spieler **08** blackleg, con woman, impostor **09** charlatan, chiseller, con artist, fraudster, trickster **10** mountebank **12** bunko-steerer

**swine**
**03** hog, pig **04** boar, boor **05** beast, brute, rogue **06** rascal **09** scoundrel **14** good-for-nothing

**• bit of a swine**
**03** ham **05** bacon

**swing**
◇ *anagram indicator*
**03** fix, get **04** bend, hang, hurl, jive, lean, make, move, rock, shog, spin, sway, swee, swey, turn, vary, veer, wave, wind **05** curve, fix up, pivot, scope, set up, shift, sling, sweep, twist, wheel, whirl **06** change, dangle, excite, motion, rhythm, rotate, stroke, swerve, waving **07** achieve, arrange, attract, control, impetus, incline, shoogie, vibrate **08** brandish, fishtail, movement, organize, sweeping **09** fluctuate, oscillate, pendulate, variation, vibration **11** fluctuation, oscillating, oscillation

**swingeing**
**04** huge **05** great, harsh, heavy **06** severe **07** drastic, extreme, serious **08** thumping **09** Draconian, excessive, punishing, stringent **10** exorbitant, oppressive **11** devastating **12** extortionate

**swinging**
◇ *anagram indicator*
**03** hip **06** lively, modern, trendy, with it **07** dynamic, hanging, stylish, swaying, turning **08** exciting, up-to-date **10** jet-setting **11** fashionable, oscillatory **12** contemporary **13** up-to-the-minute

**swipe**
**03** hit **04** biff, blow, gulp, lift, nick, slap, sock, swat, whip, wipe **05** clout, filch, lunge, pinch, slice, smack, steal, swath, whack **06** pilfer, strike, stroke, wallop **07** lash out, purloin

**swirl**
◇ *anagram indicator*
**04** curl, eddy, purl, spin, wind **05** churn, twirl, twist, wheel, whirl **07** agitate, revolve, swizzle **09** circulate **10** tourbillon **11** tourbillion

**swish**
**04** cane, flog, lash, posh, wave, whip **05** birch, flash, grand, plush, ritzy, smart, swell, swing, swirl, twirl, whirl, whisk, whizz **06** de luxe, rustle, swanky, swoosh, thrash, whoosh **07** elegant, stylish, whistle **08** brandish, flourish **09** exclusive, sumptuous **11** fashionable

**switch**
◇ *anagram indicator*
◇ *reversal indicator*
**03** put, rod **04** beat, cane, jerk, lash, swap, turn, twig, veer, whip **05** birch, lever, prune, relay, shift, shoot, shunt, thong, trade, tress, whisk **06** barter, beat up, branch, button, change, divert, gain-up, scutch, toggle, twitch **07** control, convert, deflect, deviate, replace **08** cryotron, exchange, reversal **09** about-turn, rearrange, transpose **10** alteration, changeover, substitute **11** interchange, on-off device, replacement **12** substitution **13** chop and change **14** circuit-breaker

**• switch off**
**03** cut **07** shut off, turn off, turn out **08** flick off **09** close down **11** stop working

**• switch on**
**05** put on **06** set off, turn on **07** flick on, operate **08** activate **10** trigger off

**Switzerland**
**02** CH **03** CHE

**swivel**
**04** spin, turn **05** pivot, twirl, wheel **06** gyrate, rotate **07** revolve **09** pirouette

**swollen**
**04** rank **05** bloat, puffy, tumid **06** bolled, bollen, gourdy, turgid **07** blabber, bloated, bulbous, bulging, dilated, distent, gibbose, gibbous **08** blubbery, engorged, enlarged, expanded, hydropic, inflamed, inflated, puffed up **09** blubbered, distended, tumescent **11** incrassated

**swoop**
**04** dive, drop, fall, rush **05** lunge, souse,

stoop **06** attack, plunge, pounce **07** descend, descent **09** onslaught

- **at one fell swoop**

**07** in one go **08** suddenly **09** all at once, at one time, by one blow **13** on one occasion **15** by a single action

**swop** *see* **swap, swop**

**sword**
**03** war **04** spit

*Swords include:*

**03** fox
**04** back, épée, foil, simi
**05** bilbo, blade, brand, broad, court, estoc, kukri, saber, sabre, short, skean, skene, small, steel
**06** espada, glaive, hanger, katana, kirpan, rapier, sweard, Toledo, waster
**07** curtana, curtaxe, gladius, hunting, Morglay, shabble, spurtle, whinger, yatagan
**08** claymore, curtalax, damaskin, falchion, schläger, scimitar, spadroon, whiniard, whinyard, white arm, yataghan
**09** curtalaxe, damascene, damaskeen, damasquin, Excalibur
**10** damasceene
**12** spurtle-blade, toasting fork, toasting iron

*See also* **dagger**; **knife**

- **cross swords**

**05** argue, fight **06** bicker **07** contend, contest, dispute, quarrel, wrangle **08** be at odds, disagree **15** be at loggerheads

**sworn**
**07** devoted, eternal **08** attested **09** confirmed **10** implacable, inveterate, relentless

**swot**
**03** mug **04** cram, work **05** learn, mug up, study, swank **06** bone up, revise **08** memorize

**sybarite**
**07** epicure, playboy **08** hedonist, parasite **09** bon vivant, epicurean, pleasurer **10** sensualist, voluptuary **14** pleasure-seeker

**sybaritic**
**04** easy **07** sensual **09** epicurean, luxurious, parasitic **10** hedonistic, voluptuous **13** self-indulgent **14** pleasure-loving **15** pleasure-seeking

**sycophancy**
**07** fawning **08** cringing, flattery, toadyism **09** adulation, kowtowing, servility, truckling **10** grovelling, toad-eating **11** bootlicking, slavishness **14** backscratching, obsequiousness, oleaginousness

**sycophant**
**05** slave, toady **06** fawner, yes-man **07** crawler, cringer, placebo, sponger **08** claqueur, hanger-on, parasite, truckler **09** flatterer, groveller, toad-eater **10** bootlicker **12** cookie-pusher **13** apple polisher, backscratcher

**sycophantic**
**05** slimy **06** smarmy **07** fawning, servile, slavish **08** cringing, toadying, unctuous **09** truckling **10** flattering, grovelling, obsequious, oleaginous, toad-eating **11** bootlicking, parasitical, time-serving **12** ingratiating **13** sycophantical **14** backscratching

**syllabus**
**03** syl **04** plan **05** table **06** course **07** outline **08** schedule **09** programme **10** curriculum

**syllogism**
**08** argument **09** abduction, deduction, enthymeme **11** epicheirema, proposition

**sylph-like**
**04** slim **05** lithe **06** slight, svelte **07** elegant, slender, willowy **08** graceful **11** streamlined

**sylvan** *see* **silvan**

**symbiotic**
**07** epizoan, epizoic **09** commensal, epizootic **10** endophytic, synergetic **11** co-operative, interactive **14** interdependent

**symbol**
**04** mark, rune, sign, type **05** creed, image **06** figure **09** character, ideograph **14** representation

*Symbols include:*

**01** A, Å, @, B, C, ©, D, e, F, g, H, I, J, K, L, M, N, O, P, Q, R, ®, S, T, U, V, W, X, Y, Z
**02** Ac, Ag, Al, Am, Ar, As, At, Au, Ba, BB, Be, Bh, Bi, Bk, Bq, Br, Ca, Cd, Ce, Cf, Cl, Cm, Co, CQ, Cr, Cs, Cu, Db, Ds, Dy, Er, Es, Eu, Fe, ff, Fm, Fr, Ga, Gd, Ge, Gy, Ha, He, Hf, Hg, HH, Ho, Hs, Hz, In, Ir, kg, Kr, La, Li, lm, Lr, Lu, Lw, lx, Md, Mg, Mn, Mo, Mt, MV, Na, Nb, Nd, Ne, Ni, No, Np, Oe, Os, Pa, Pb, Pd, Pm, Po, Pr, Pt, Pu, Ra, Rb, Re, Rf, Rg, Rh, Rn, Ru, Sb, Sc, Se, Sg, Si, Sm, Sn, Sr, Sv, Ta, Tb, Tc, Te, Th, Ti, Tl, Tm, Wb, Xe, Yb, Zn, Zr
**03** BBB, dBA, kat, LXX, mol, rad
**04** icon, ikon, logo
**05** badge, brand, crest, motif, token, totem
**06** cipher, emblem, smiley, uraeus
**08** caduceus, ideogram, insignia, logogram, monogram, swastika
**09** pentagram, trademark, watermark
**10** coat of arms, hieroglyph, pictograph
**12** yellow ribbon

*Religious symbols include:*

**02** Om
**03** IHC, IHS
**04** ankh, fish, yoni
**05** cross, linga
**06** chakra, filfot, fylfot, lingam
**07** Ik Onkar, mandala, menorah, yin-yang
**08** crescent, swastika
**11** Christingle, star of David

*See also* **element**

**symbolic**
**05** token **07** shadowy, typical **10** emblematic, figurative, meaningful, symbolical **11** allegorical, significant **12** illustrative, metaphorical **14** representative

**symbolically**
**07** as a sign **09** as a symbol **10** as an emblem **11** by this token **12** figuratively **14** emblematically

**symbolize**
**04** mean, type **05** agree **06** denote, emblem, figure, symbol, typify **07** betoken, combine, express, present, signify **08** stand for **09** epitomize, exemplify, personate, personify, represent

**symmetrical**
**03** sym **04** even **07** dimeric, regular, uniform **08** balanced, parallel **10** consistent, harmonious **11** well-rounded, zygopleural **12** isobilateral, proportional, right-and-left **13** actinomorphic, corresponding

**symmetry**
**07** balance, harmony **08** evenness **09** agreement, congruity **10** proportion, regularity, uniformity **11** consistency, parallelism, proportions **14** correspondence

**sympathetic**
**04** kind, soft, warm **06** caring, genial, kindly, social, tender **07** feeling, pitying **08** friendly, likeable, pleasant, sociable, tolerant **09** agreeable, concerned, congenial, consoling, simpatico **10** comforting, compatible, favourable, interested, like-minded, solicitous, supportive **11** considerate, encouraging, kind-hearted, neighbourly, warm-hearted **12** affectionate, appreciative, well-disposed **13** commiserating, commiserative, companionable, compassionate, sympathetical, understanding

**sympathetically**
**06** kindly, warmly **09** feelingly, pityingly **11** consolingly, sensitively **12** comfortingly, responsively, supportively **13** warm-heartedly **14** appreciatively **15** compassionately, understandingly

**sympathize**
**03** rap **04** pity **07** care for, comfort, condole, console, feel for **09** empathize, encourage, respond to **10** appreciate, correspond, understand **11** commiserate, show concern **12** be supportive, feel sorry for, identify with, show interest

**sympathizer**
**03** fan **06** backer **07** admirer **08** adherent, condoler, partisan **09** supporter **10** copperhead, well-wisher **15** fellow-traveller

**sympathy**
**04** pity **05** aroha **06** accord, solace, warmth **07** comfort, empathy, harmony, rapport, support **08** affinity, approval, kindness **09** agreement, closeness **10** compassion, tenderness **11** approbation, condolences, consolation, correlation, Weltschmerz **12** appreciation **13** commiseration, consideration, encouragement, fellow-feeling, understanding **14** correspondence, thoughtfulness **15** warm-heartedness

**• expression of sympathy**
**02** ah, aw **04** dear **05** shame, sorry, there **06** dear me, oh dear, too bad **07** deary me **08** dearie me, good-lack **09** hard lines, tough luck **10** hard cheese

**symptom**
**03** sym **04** mark, note, sign **05** fever, hives, rigor, token **06** signal **07** anxiety, display, feature, hard pad, warning **08** evidence, merycism, necrosis, prodrome **09** ketonuria, prodromus, rosetting **10** diagnostic, expression, indication, nettle rash, prognostic **11** hydrophobia, proteinuria **13** demonstration, epiphenomenon, malabsorption, manifestation **14** characteristic

*See also* **disease**

**symptomatic**
**07** typical **10** associated, indicative, suggesting, suggestive **14** characteristic

**synagogue**
**04** shul **06** temple

**synchronize**
**04** sync, tune **05** synch

**syndicate**
**04** bloc, ring **05** group, judge **06** cartel **07** censure, combine, council **08** alliance **11** association, combination

**synonymous**
**07** similar, the same **09** identical **10** comparable, equivalent, tantamount **13** corresponding, substitutable **15** interchangeable

**synopsis**
**05** recap **06** digest, précis, résumé, review, schema, sketch **07** outline, run-down, summary **08** abstract **09** summation **10** abridgment, compendium, conspectus, tabulation **11** abridgement **12** condensation **14** recapitulation

**synthesis**
**05** alloy, blend, union **06** fusion **07** amalgam, welding **08** compound, pastiche **09** anabolism, composite **11** coalescence, combination, integration, pantheology, unification **12** amalgamation, glycogenesis **13** individuation

**synthesize**
**04** fuse, weld **05** alloy, blend, merge, unify, unite **07** combine **08** coalesce, compound **09** integrate **10** amalgamate

**synthetic**
◇ *anagram indicator*
**03** syn **04** fake, faux, mock, sham **05** bogus **06** ersatz, pseudo **07** man-made, plastic **09** imitation, simulated **10** artificial **12** manufactured

**Syria**
**03** SYR

**syrup**
**03** rob **05** sirup **06** orgeat **07** glucose, linctus, treacle **08** quiddany **09** cocky's joy, diacodion, diacodium, grenadine, moskonfyt **10** capillaire, maple syrup

**syrupy**
**05** corny, gushy, mushy, soppy, sweet, weepy **06** loving, sickly, sloppy, slushy, sugary **07** gushing, honeyed, maudlin, mawkish **08** pathetic, romantic **09** emotional, oversweet, schmaltzy, sweetened **10** lovey-dovey, saccharine **11** sentimental, sickly sweet, tear-jerking **12** affectionate

**system**
**03** way **04** mode, plan, rule, them **05** logic, means, order, set-up, usage **06** method, scheme **07** network, process, routine **08** approach, practice **09** apparatus, framework, mechanism, procedure, structure, technique **11** arrangement, methodology, orderliness **12** co-ordination, organization **13** modus operandi, the government **14** classification, the authorities **15** systematization, the powers that be

**systematic**
**07** logical, ordered, orderly, planned **08** habitual, methodic **09** efficient, organized **10** methodical, scientific, structured **11** intentional, well-ordered, well-planned **12** businesslike, standardized, systematized **13** well-organized

**systematize**
**04** plan **05** order **06** codify **07** arrange, dispose **08** classify, organize, regiment, regulate, tabulate **09** methodize, structure **10** schematize **11** make uniform, rationalize, standardize

# T

**T**
**03** tee, toc **04** tock **05** tango

**TA**
**10** volunteers **15** Territorial Army

**tab**
**03** fob, tag **04** bill, cost, drug, flap, pill **05** check, label, strap, tally **06** marker, tablet, ticket **07** Ecstasy, sticker, trimmer **08** ring pull, tabulate **09** cigarette, tabulator

• **keep tabs on**
**07** observe **11** keep an eye on **12** watch closely

**tabby**
**04** girl, wavy **05** woman **06** banded, stripy **07** brindle, mottled, striped **08** brindled, streaked **10** variegated

**table**
**03** bar **04** chow, diet, dish, fare, food, grub, list, menu, move, nosh, plan, slab, tuck **05** bench, chart, graph, index, layer, panel, stand **06** figure, record, submit **07** diagram, picture, propose, suggest, worktop **08** register, schedule, syllabus, tabulate **09** catalogue, committee, inventory, programme, timetable **10** put forward, speciality, tabulation **12** string-course **13** entertainment

*Tables include:*

**03** bed, loo, tea, top
**04** bird, card, desk, draw, drum, high, pier, pool, sand, side, sofa, work
**05** altar, board, lunch, night
**06** bureau, coffee, dining, dinner, dolmen, gaming, inking, lowboy, picnic, teapoy, toilet, vanity
**07** capstan, console, counter, cricket, drawing, draw-top, dresser, gateleg, snooker, trestle, writing
**08** billiard, credence, credenza, draw-leaf, dressing, drop-leaf, guéridon, mahogany, pembroke, piecrust
**09** breakfast, communion, operating, refectory
**10** dissecting, gate-legged, greencloth, occasional
**12** council-board
**13** bonheur-du-jour

*Tableware includes:*

**03** cup, jug, mug
**04** bowl
**05** ashet, cruet, plate
**06** goblet, saucer, teacup, teapot, tureen
**07** creamer, milk jug, platter, tumbler
**08** cream jug, flatware, mazarine, rice bowl, salt mill
**09** coffee cup, coffee pot, gravy boat, pasta bowl, pasta dish, pepper pot, salad bowl, sauceboat, side plate, soup plate, sugar bowl, toast rack, wineglass
**10** bread plate, butter dish, cereal bowl, cruet-stand, pepper mill, salt shaker, soup tureen
**11** butter plate, cheese plate, dessert bowl, dessert dish, espresso cup, serving bowl, serving dish
**12** dessert plate, mazarine dish, pudding-plate
**13** mazarine plate
**14** serving platter

• **inner table**
**04** home

**tableau**
**05** scene **07** diorama, picture **08** vignette **09** portrayal, spectacle **13** tableau vivant **14** representation

**tableland**
**04** mesa, puna **05** Karoo **06** Karroo **07** plateau

**tablet**
**01** E **03** pad, tab **04** ball, dove, pill, slab **05** album, benny, bolus, panel, plate, stela, stele **06** abacus, caplet, marker, pellet, plaque, Roofie, tabula, troche **07** capsule, diptych, lozenge, sleeper, surface **08** monument, triglyph **09** medallion, tablature, wobbly egg **10** osculatory, tabula rasa **11** purple heart **12** disco biscuit, Rosetta stone

**tabletalk**
**03** ana

**tabloid** *see* **newspaper**

**taboo**
**03** ban **04** tabu, tapu, veto **05** curse **06** banned, vetoed **08** anathema, ruled out **09** exclusion, forbidden, interdict, ostracism, restraint **10** prohibited, proscribed, sacrosanct **11** prohibition, restriction, unthinkable **12** interdiction, proscription, unacceptable **13** unmentionable

**tabulate**
**03** tab **04** list, sort **05** chart, index, order, range, table **06** codify **07** arrange **08** classify **09** catalogue **10** categorize, tabularize **11** systematize

**tabulation**
**07** listing, sorting, tabling **08** indexing, ordering **11** arrangement, cataloguing **14** categorization, classification

**tacit**
**06** silent **07** implied **08** implicit, inferred, unspoken, unstated, unvoiced, wordless **10** understood **11** unexpressed

**taciturn**
**04** cold, dumb, mute **05** aloof, quiet **06** silent **07** distant **08** detached, reserved, reticent **09** withdrawn **10** of few words **11** tight-lipped, untalkative **12** close-mouthed **13** unforthcoming **15** uncommunicative

**tack**
**03** add, fix, pin, sew, tag, way **04** line, nail, path, plan, take, turn, veer **05** affix, annex, baste, catch, lease, smack, spell **06** append, attach, attack, course, fasten, method, policy, sleaze, staple, stitch, swerve, tactic, tenure, tingle, zigzag **07** bearing, go about, heading, process, tintack **08** approach, club-haul, strategy **09** come about, direction, procedure, technique, thumbtack **10** drawing-pin, stickiness **12** change course, line of action **14** course of action **15** change direction

*See also* **horse**

**tackle**
◇ *containment indicator*
**03** cat, rig, try **04** chin, foul, gear, grab, halt, sack, stop, take, whip **05** begin, block, catch, grasp, hoist, seize, stuff, tools **06** attack, burton, garnet, handle, jigger, outfit, pulley, take on, things **07** address, attempt, clobber, deflect, go about, harness, have a go, rigging, weapons **08** attend to, confront, deal with, embark on, face up to, obstruct, set about, wade into **09** apparatus, challenge, encounter, equipment, get down to, intercept, trappings, undertake **10** clew-garnet, get to grips, ground-hold, implements, take hold of **11** come to grips, grapple with, topping lift **12** interception, intervention **13** accoutrements, paraphernalia **14** get to grips with **15** apply yourself to, come to grips with

**tacky**
**03** wet **04** naff **05** dingy, gaudy, gluey, gooey, gummy, messy, tatty **06** flashy, grotty, ragged, shabby, shoddy, sleazy, sloppy, sticky, tawdry, untidy, vulgar **07** kitschy, scruffy **08** adhesive, plimsoll, tattered **09** tasteless **10** threadbare

**tact**
**05** skill **07** finesse **08** delicacy,

judgment, prudence, subtlety
**09** dexterity, diplomacy, judgement
**10** adroitness, discretion, perception
**11** discernment, savoir-faire, sensitivity, tactfulness **13** consideration, judiciousness, understanding
**14** thoughtfulness

**tactful**
**06** adroit, polite, subtle, tender
**07** careful, politic, prudent, skilful
**08** delicate, discreet, kid-glove
**09** judicious, sensitive **10** diplomatic, discerning, perceptive, thoughtful
**11** considerate **12** diplomatical
**13** understanding

**tactfully**
**08** politely, tenderly **09** carefully, prudently, skilfully **10** delicately, discreetly **11** judiciously, sensitively
**12** thoughtfully **14** diplomatically

**tactic**
**03** way **04** move, plan, ploy, ruse
**05** means, moves, shift, trick
**06** course, device, method, policy, scheme **07** audible **08** approach, campaign, game plan, hardball, soft sell, strategy **09** expedient, manoeuvre, procedure, stratagem
**10** manoeuvres, subterfuge **12** line of attack **14** course of action, full-court press

**tactical**
**05** smart **06** adroit, artful, clever, shrewd **07** cunning, planned, politic, prudent, skilful **09** judicious, strategic
**10** calculated

**tactician**
**05** brain **07** planner **08** diplomat, director **10** campaigner, mastermind, politician, strategist **11** co-ordinator
**12** orchestrator

**tactless**
**04** rude **05** crass, rough **06** clumsy, gauche, unkind **07** awkward, hurtful
**08** careless, impolite, unsubtle
**09** impolitic, imprudent, maladroit, unfeeling **10** blundering, indelicate, indiscreet **11** injudicious, insensitive, thoughtless **12** discourteous, undiplomatic **13** inappropriate, inconsiderate

**tactlessness**
**08** rudeness **09** bad timing, gaucherie
**10** clumsiness, crassitude, indelicacy, ineptitude, maladdress **11** boorishness, discourtesy **12** impoliteness, indiscretion **13** insensitivity, maladroitness **15** thoughtlessness

**tadpole**
**08** polliwig, polliwog, pollywig, pollywog **09** porwiggle

**tag**
**03** add, dag, dub, tab, tig **04** call, flap, mark, name, note, slip, tack, term
**05** affix, aglet, annex, badge, label, maxim, moral, motto, quote, shred, strap, style, tally, title **06** adjoin, aiglet, anklet, append, attach, cliché, dictum, docket, fasten, phrase, rabble, saying, ticket **07** entitle, epithet, kabaddi, proverb, refrain, remnant, sticker
**08** allusion, bracelet, christen, identify, nickname **09** designate, quotation
**10** aglet babie, expression, Kimball tag
**11** aiguillette, description, stock phrase, treasury tag **12** identity disc
**14** identification

• **tag along**
**04** tail **05** trail **06** follow, shadow
**09** accompany

**tail**
◇ *tail selection indicator*
**03** dog, end, fan, fud, uro- **04** back, flag, herd, rear, rump, scut **05** brush, queue, stalk, stern, suite, track, trail, train **06** behind, bottom, follow, pursue, shadow, shamus, sleuth
**07** gumshoe, limited, rear end, retinue
**08** backside, buttocks, cynosure, straggle **09** appendage, detective, extremity, posterior **10** conclusion, private eye **11** termination
**12** investigator

• **part of tail**
**03** fin **04** dock

• **tail back**
**03** jam **04** line **05** queue **06** back up

• **tail off**
**03** die **04** drop, fade, wane **06** die out
**07** decline, drop off, dwindle
**08** decrease, fall away, peter out, taper off

• **turn tail**
**04** bolt, flee **06** beat it, decamp, escape **07** abscond, run away, scarper
**09** skedaddle

**tailback**
**03** row **04** file, line, tail **05** queue, train
**06** backup, column **09** crocodile
**10** procession

**tailor**
◇ *anagram indicator*
**03** cut, fit **04** dung, snip, suit, trim
**05** adapt, alter, darzi, flint, mould, shape, style **06** adjust, cutter, modify, sartor, teller **07** convert, fashion, modiste, whipcat **08** clothier, costumer, seamster **09** costumier, couturier, customize, outfitter
**10** dressmaker, prick-louse, seamstress, whipstitch **11** accommodate, personalize **13** prick-the-louse

**tailor-made**
**05** ideal, right **06** fitted, suited
**07** bespoke, perfect **08** tailored
**11** custom-built **13** made-to-measure

**taint**
◇ *anagram indicator*
**04** blot, flaw, harm, ruin, soil, spot, wilt
**05** dirty, fault, muddy, shame, smear, smoke, spoil, stain, sully, tinge
**06** befoul, blight, damage, defect, defile, infect, injure, mildew, poison, stigma, weaken, wither **07** blacken, blemish, corrupt, deprave, envenom, pollute, tarnish **08** disgrace
**09** attainder, contagion, dishonour, infection, pollution **10** adulterate, corruption **11** contaminate
**12** adulteration **13** contamination

**Taiwan**
**02** RC **03** TWN

**Tajikistan**
**02** TJ **03** TJK

**take**
◇ *containment indicator*
**01** r **02** do **03** bag, buy, eat, fet, get, nim, rec, use, win **04** bear, bite, book, deem, draw, fall, fett, gain, gate, give, grab, grip, haul, have, help, hent, hire, hold, last, lead, lift, need, nick, note, pick, read, rent, seat, show, twig, view, work **05** abide, admit, adopt, angle, begin, bring, carry, catch, charm, cheat, drink, drive, ferry, fetch, filch, grasp, guide, learn, lease, pinch, scoff, seize, slant, stand, steal, study, teach, think, use up, usher, visit, whisk, yield
**06** abduct, accept, aspect, assume, attain, become, betake, blight, choose, clutch, come by, convey, decide, deduct, demand, derive, detect, devour, endure, engage, escort, fathom, follow, freeze, gather, guzzle, handle, imbibe, income, ingest, inhale, kidnap, obtain, occupy, pay for, profit, pursue, recipe, reckon, regard, remove, return, secure, select, snatch, strike, suffer, tuck in **07** achieve, acquire, be given, believe, bewitch, call for, capture, conduct, conquer, consume, contain, deceive, deliver, detract, examine, execute, extract, find out, go along, major in, measure, mistake, observe, perform, portray, presume, procure, profits, purloin, react to, receive, require, returns, revenue, set down, stomach, succeed, suppose, swallow, swindle, takings, undergo
**08** attitude, be taught, carry off, consider, cope with, cotton on, deal with, discover, look upon, proceeds, purchase, receipts, remember, research, settle on, shepherd, submerge, subtract, surprise, take away, tolerate, vanquish
**09** accompany, apprehend, ascertain, captivate, determine, eliminate, establish, fathom out, gate-money, get hold of, lay hold of, put up with, respond to, transport, undertake, viewpoint, withstand **10** bear in mind, comprehend, confiscate, drive along, experience, photograph, standpoint, take effect, understand
**11** accommodate, acknowledge, appropriate, be effective, frame of mind, have room for, necessitate, perspective, point of view, subscribe to, travel along **12** have space for, vantage point **13** be efficacious
**14** interpretation, produce results
**15** have a capacity of

• **let him/her take**
**03** cap

• **take after**
**04** echo **06** be like, favour, mirror
**08** look like, resemble, surprise **11** be similar to

**• take against**
**06** oppose **07** despise, dislike **08** object to **12** disapprove of

**• take apart**
**03** nag, pan **04** carp, slag, slam **05** blame, knock, slate, snipe **06** attack **07** analyse, censure, condemn, nit-pick, rubbish, run down, slag off **08** badmouth, denounce, separate **09** criticize, dismantle, disparage **10** come down on, go to town on **11** disassemble, pick holes in **12** disapprove of, pull to pieces, put the boot in, take to pieces, tear to shreds **13** find fault with, tear a strip off **15** do a hatchet job on, pass judgement on

**• take back**
**04** deny **05** evoke **06** call up, recant, regain, remind, resume, retake, return **07** get back, reclaim, replace, restore, retract **08** disclaim, give back, hand back, renounce, send back, withdraw **09** repossess, repudiate **12** eat your words **14** make you think of, put you in mind of

**• take down**
**04** note, raze **05** level, lower **06** record, reduce, remove **07** demount, get down, put down, set down **08** demolish, pull down **09** dismantle, write down **10** put on paper, transcribe **11** disassemble, make a note of

**• take in**
◇ *containment indicator*
**03** con, lap **04** dupe, fool **05** admit, cheat, cover, grasp, trick **06** absorb, digest **07** contain, deceive, embrace, include, mislead, realize, receive, shelter, swindle, welcome **08** comprise, hoodwink **09** bamboozle, encompass **10** appreciate, assimilate, comprehend, understand **11** accommodate, incorporate

**• take off**
◇ *deletion indicator*
**02** go **03** ape, fly **04** bolt, doff, drop, flee, mock, rise, shed, soar, work **05** climb, leave, mimic, mount, strip **06** ascend, decamp, deduct, depart, detach, divest, do well, make it, parody, remove, send up **07** abscond, bunk off, catch on, discard, imitate, lift off, prosper, pull off, run away, scarper, succeed, tear off, undress **08** discount, flourish, go places, satirize, subtract, take away, throw off **09** disappear, do a runner, skedaddle **10** caricature, strike gold **11** impersonate **12** get undressed **13** become popular, hit the jackpot **14** become airborne

**• take on**
◇ *containment indicator*
◇ *juxtaposition indicator*
**04** copy, face, hire, kill **05** enrol, fight **06** accept, assume, defeat, employ, engage, enlist, escort, oppose, retain, tackle **07** acquire, destroy, extract, recruit, vie with **08** get angry, get upset **09** entertain, make a fuss, undertake **11** compete with, contend with

**• take out**
**03** fix, see, zap **04** dele, do in, draw, kill **05** set up, shoot, waste **06** be lent, borrow, cut out, defeat, delete, detach, escort, except, excise, get out, go with, murder, remove, rub out **07** arrange, bump off, butcher, destroy, execute, extract, pull out, wipe out, work out **08** blow away, despatch, dispatch, knock off, massacre, organize, settle on **09** accompany, eliminate, finish off, go out with, have a loan, liquidate, polish off **10** do away with, put to death **11** assassinate, exterminate **14** use temporarily

**• take over**
**05** adopt **06** buy out **07** subsume **10** run the show **12** take charge of **13** gain control of

**• take to**
**04** like **05** begin, start **08** commence, set about **09** undertake **10** appreciate, launch into **12** become keen on, find pleasant **14** find attractive

**• take up**
◇ *insertion indicator*
◇ *reversal down indicator*
**03** use **04** fill, lift, rear **05** adopt, begin, raise, start, use up **06** absorb, accept, assume, engage, occupy, pick up, pursue, resume **07** agree to, carry on, consume, engross **08** commence, continue, embark on **10** monopolize **13** hang about with **14** knock about with **15** get involved with

**take-off**
**05** spoof **06** ascent, flight, flying, parody, send-up **07** lift-off, mimicry **08** climbing, drawback, scramble, travesty **09** departure, imitation **10** caricature **13** impersonation

**takeover**
**04** coup **06** buyout, merger **09** coalition **11** combination **12** amalgamation **13** incorporation

**taking**
**04** gain, gate **05** yield **06** income, plight **07** profits, returns, revenue, winning, winsome **08** alluring, catching, charming, earnings, engaging, fetching, pickings, pleasing, proceeds, receipts, winnings **09** agitation, appealing, beguiling, gate-money **10** attractive, compelling, delightful, enchanting, infectious, intriguing, perplexity **11** bewitchment, captivating, fascinating **13** prepossessing

**tale**
**03** bam, fib, lie, toy **04** epic, gest, hoax, myth, rede, reed, saga, talk, yarn **05** blood, fable, geste, novel, porky, reede, roman, spiel, story, total, weird **06** legend, number, report, rumour **07** account, fabliau, Märchen, mystery, novella, odyssey, parable, romance, untruth, whopper **08** allegory, anecdote, jeremiad, sob story **09** discourse, fairytale, falsehood, folk story, narrative, reckoning, storiette, storyette, tall story, tradition **10** fairy story, hair-raiser **11** fabrication **12** old wives' tale, superstition **14** traveller's tale

**talent**
**04** bent, feel, gift, nous **05** flair, forte, knack, power, skill, talon **06** genius **07** ability, aptness, faculty **08** aptitude, capacity, facility, ingenium, long suit, new blood, strength **09** endowment **11** disposition, showmanship, strong point **12** shot in the arm

**talented**
**04** able, deft **05** adept **06** adroit, clever, gifted **07** capable, skilful **08** artistic **09** brilliant, versatile **10** proficient **11** well-endowed **12** accomplished

**talisman**
**04** idol, ju-ju **05** charm, totem **06** amulet, fetish, mascot, symbol, telesm **07** abraxas, periapt **10** phylactery

**talk**
**03** gab, gas, jaw, rap, say, yak **04** blab, bull, cant, chat, tell, yack **05** grass, haver, lingo, moody, mouth, noise, noyes, orate, parle, slang, speak, spiel, utter, voice, words **06** babble, confab, confer, debate, devise, gossip, haggle, havers, jabber, jargon, jaw-jaw, korero, natter, parley, rabbit, report, rumour, sermon, speech, squeal, yabber **07** address, baloney, bargain, blether, boloney, chatter, chinwag, clatter, confess, dialect, discuss, earbash, express, hearsay, lecture, malarky, meeting, oration, palaver, prattle, seminar, twaddle **08** badinage, chitchat, conclave, converse, dialogue, flimflam, haggling, idiolect, inform on, language, malarkey **09** discourse, gibberish, interview, negotiate, symposium, tell tales, tête-à-tête, utterance **10** articulate, balderdash, bargaining, conference, discursion, discussion, namby-pamby **11** communicate, negotiation **12** consultation, conversation, disquisition, tittle-tattle **13** rabbit and pork, spill the beans, spread rumours **15** give the game away

**• foolish talk**
**04** bosh **05** haver **06** havers

**• impudent talk**
**03** lip **08** slack jaw

**• talk back**
**06** retort **07** riposte **09** retaliate **10** answer back, be cheeky to **12** answer rudely

**• talk big**
**04** brag, crow **05** boast, swank, vaunt **07** bluster, show off **10** exaggerate

**• talk down to**
**07** despise **09** patronize **10** look down on

**• talk into**
**04** coax, sway **07** win over **08** convince, persuade **09** encourage **10** bring round

**• talk nonsense**
**03** gum, rot **04** jive **05** bleat, haver **06** havers

**• talk out of**
**04** stop **05** deter **06** put off **07** prevent **08** dissuade **10** discourage

**talkative**
**04** gash **05** gabby, gassy, talky, vocal, wordy **06** chatty, mouthy **07** gossipy, verbose, voluble **09** expansive, garrulous **10** long-winded, loquacious, unreserved **11** forthcoming, long-tongued **13** communicative

**talker**
**05** prose **06** orator, tatler **07** speaker, tattler, twaddle **08** lecturer **09** chatterer **10** chatterbox, motormouth **11** speechmaker **12** blatherskite, bletherskate, communicator **14** bletheranskate

**talking-to**
**06** rebuke, rocket **07** lecture, reproof, wigging **08** reproach, scolding **09** carpeting, criticism, reprimand **10** telling-off, ticking-off **12** dressing-down

**tall**
**03** big **04** hard, high, long **05** giant, great, lanky, lofty, stout, taunt **06** absurd, taxing, towery, trying **07** doughty, dubious, sky-high, soaring **08** elevated, exacting, gigantic, towering, unlikely **09** bombastic, demanding, difficult, overblown **10** far-fetched, improbable, incredible, remarkable **11** challenging, exaggerated, implausible **12** preposterous, unbelievable

**tallness**
**06** height **07** stature **08** altitude **09** loftiness, procerity

**tally**
**03** add, fit, sum, tab, tag **04** list, nick, roll, stub, suit, tick **05** adapt, add up, agree, count, label, match, score, stick, stock, tie in, total **06** accord, concur, credit, figure, reckon, record, square, ticket **07** account, conform **08** coincide, register **09** calculate, duplicate, harmonize, nickstick, reckoning **10** correspond **11** counterfoil, counterpart, enumeration

**tame**
**03** pet **04** calm, curb, dull, flat, lame, mail, meek, weak **05** bland, break, quell, train, vapid **06** boring, bridle, docile, entame, feeble, gentle, humble, master, mellow, pacify, soften, subdue, temper, wonted **07** amenage, break in, conquer, humdrum, insipid, reclaim, repress, subdued, tedious, trained **08** amenable, biddable, broken in, domestic, lifeless, mansuete, obedient, overcome, suppress **09** kids' stuff, subjugate, tractable, wearisome **10** accustomed, cultivated, discipline, house-train, manageable, spiritless, submissive, unexciting, uninspired **11** bring to heel, disciplined, domesticate, uninspiring, unresisting **12** domesticated **13** unadventurous, uninteresting **14** unenterprising

**tamper**
**03** fix, rig **04** work **05** alter **06** bishop, damage, doctor, fiddle, juggle, meddle, monkey, temper, tinker **07** falsify **08** contrive, medicate, practise **09** interfere, mess about, muck about, undermine **10** manipulate **11** interpolate **12** put your oar in **14** poke your nose in, stick your oar in **15** stick your nose in

**tan**
**04** bark, beat, belt, cane, flay, flog, lash, whip **05** beige, birch, brown, clout, spank, strap, tawny, whack **06** bronze, thrash, wallop **07** go brown, tangent **09** turn brown **10** light brown, make darker **12** become darker **14** yellowish brown

**tang**
**03** pep **04** barb, bite, edge, hint, kick, ring **05** aroma, point, prong, punch, scent, smack, smell, spice, spike, sting, taste, tinge, touch, trace, whiff **06** savour **07** flavour **08** overtone, piquancy, pungency **09** sharpness **10** sea-surgeon, suggestion

**tangible**
**04** hard, real **05** solid **06** actual **07** evident, tactile, visible **08** concrete, definite, manifest, material, palpable, physical, positive **09** corporeal, touchable **11** discernible, perceptible, substantial, well-defined **12** unmistakable

**tangle**
◇ *anagram indicator*
**03** mat, ore, web **04** coil, fank, knot, maze, mesh, mess, nest, taut, tawt, trap **05** catch, mix-up, ravel, skein, snarl, twist **06** burble, enmesh, entrap, fankle, hamper, icicle, jumble, muddle, raffle **07** confuse, embroil, ensnare, involve, perplex, snarl-up **08** argument, conflict, convolve, entangle, mess with **09** confusion, drift-weed, embroglio, imbroglio, implicate, interlace, labyrinth, Laminaria **10** intertwine, intertwist, interweave, perplexity, wilderness **11** convolution, embroilment, intertangle **12** complication, entanglement

**tangled**
◇ *anagram indicator*
**05** messy **06** knotty, matted **07** complex, haywire, jumbled, knotted, mixed up, muddled, snarled, tousled, twisted **08** confused, involved, tortuous **09** entangled, intricate **10** convoluted **11** complicated, dishevelled

**tango**
**01** T

**tangy**
**04** acid, tart **05** fresh, sharp, spicy **06** biting, strong **07** piquant, pungent

**tank**
**03** vat **04** pond, pool, stew **05** basin **06** defeat, header, panzer, refuel, thrash **07** cistern, sponson, whippet **08** aquarium, flush-box, sponsing **09** baptistry, container, gasholder, gasometer, reservoir, Valentine **10** baptistery, receptacle, septic tank, shield pond **11** armoured car **12** precipitator **13** shielding pond **15** armoured vehicle

**tanning material**
**04** puer, pure **07** valonea, valonia **08** vallonia

**tantalize**
**04** bait, balk, mock **05** taunt, tease, tempt **06** allure, entice, lead on, thwart **07** beguile, provoke, torment, torture **09** frustrate, titillate **10** disappoint

**tantalum**
**02** Ta

**tantamount**
**05** equal **08** as good as **09** the same as **10** equivalent, synonymous **12** commensurate

**tantrum**
**03** fit, pet **04** fury, rage **05** paddy, scene, storm **06** blow-up, temper, wobbly **07** flare-up **08** hissy fit, outburst, paroxysm, tirrivee, tirrivie **10** conniption **11** fit of temper

**Tanzania**
**03** EAT, TZA

**tap**
**03** bob, bug, hit, pat, rap, tat, tip, tit, top, use **04** beat, blip, bung, cock, drum, milk, mine, plug, tack, tick, touk, tuck **05** bleed, chuck, drain, knock, spout, touch, valve **06** broach, draw on, faucet, pierce, pirate, pit-pat, quarry, siphon, spigot, strike, stroup **07** bibcock, draw off, exploit, monitor, percuss, petcock, pitapat, stopper, utilize, wiretap **08** draw upon, listen to, pitty-pat, receiver, stopcock **09** light blow, make use of **10** listen in on **11** eavesdrop on **15** listening device, take advantage of

**• on tap**
**05** handy, ready **06** at hand, on hand **09** available **10** accessible

**tape**
**03** tie **04** band, bind, seal **05** stick, strip, video **06** fasten, record, ribbon, secure, string **07** binding **08** cassette **09** audiotape, recording, Sellotape®, videotape **10** gaffer tape, Scotch tape®, sticky tape, tape-record **11** masking tape, video-record **12** adhesive tape, magnetic tape, passe-partout **13** audio cassette, tape-recording, video cassette **14** video recording

**taper**
**04** fade, nose, slim, thin, wane, wick **05** spill **06** acumen, candle, die off, lessen, narrow, reduce **07** die away, dwindle, tail off, thin out **08** decrease,

diminish, make thin, peter out, wax light **09** attenuate **10** become thin, make narrow **12** become narrow

**tapir**
**04** anta **07** sladang **08** seladang

**tar**
**05** set on **06** maltha, sailor
**11** pissasphalt
*See also* **sailor**

• **smear with tar**
**03** pay

• **tar derivative**
**05** furan, indol, pitch **06** cresol, furane, indene, indole, phenol, picene, retene, xylene **07** acridin, aniline, benzene, indulin, naphtha, picamar, skatole, styrene **08** acridine, cerulein, creasote, creosote, heavy oil, induline, nigrosin, pyridine, safranin **09** carbazole, coumarone, nigrosine, primuline, safranine **10** anthracene, benzpyrene **11** creosote oil, naphthalene, phenanthene

**tardily**
**04** late **06** slowly **09** belatedly
**10** sluggishly **12** late in the day, unpunctually **13** not before time **15** at the last minute

**tardiness**
**05** delay **08** dawdling, lateness, slowness **11** belatedness
**12** dilatoriness, sluggishness
**13** unpunctuality **15** procrastination

**tardy**
**03** lag **04** late, slow **05** slack **06** retard
**07** belated, delayed, overdue
**08** backward, dawdling, dilatory, retarded, sluggish **09** loitering
**10** behindhand, last-minute, unpunctual **12** eleventh-hour
**15** procrastinating

**tare**
**01** t **04** tine, weed **05** vetch **06** darnel

**target**
**03** aim, end **04** butt, game, goal, mark, prey, seek **05** aim at **06** aim for, object, quarry, try for, victim **07** purpose
**08** ambition, bull's eye **09** intention, objective **11** destination **14** have as your goal

• **centre of target**
**03** pin **04** bull **06** carton **08** bull's-eye

• **on target**
**05** exact **06** bang on, on time, spot-on
**07** precise **08** accurate, on course
**10** on schedule **15** according to plan

**tariff**
**03** tax **04** duty, levy, menu, rate, toll
**06** excise, zabeta **07** charges, customs
**08** schedule **09** price list **10** bill of fare
**13** list of charges

**tarnish**
**03** dim, mar **04** blot, dull, film, rust, soil, spot **05** spoil, stain, sully, taint
**06** befoul, darken, impair, patina
**07** blacken, blemish, corrode
**08** besmirch **09** discolour
**10** blackening **13** discoloration

**taro**
**04** coco, eddo **05** cocco **07** dasheen

**tarry**
**03** lag **04** bide, leng, rest, stay, stop, wait **05** abide, await, dally, delay, pause
**06** dawdle, linger, loiter, remain, stay on
**07** sojourn

**tart**
**03** pie, pro, tom **04** acid, bawd, drab, flan, moll, slut, sour **05** brass, broad, patty, quiff, sharp, tangy, tramp, wench, whore **06** biting, bitter, geisha, harlot, hooker, pastry, quiche **07** acerbic, caustic, cocotte, cutting, floozie, hetaera, hostess, hustler, lorette, piquant, pungent, rent-boy, strudel, tartlet, trollop **08** call girl, incisive, magdalen, mirliton, sardonic, scathing, scrubber, strumpet, vinegary
**09** acidulous, charlotte, courtesan, croquante, hierodule, loose fish, sarcastic, trenchant **10** astringent, fancy woman, loose woman, prostitute, rough trade, vizard-mask
**11** fallen woman, fille de joie, night-walker, poule de luxe, working girl
**12** fille des rues, scarlet woman, street-walker **13** grande cocotte **14** lady of the night, woman of the town

• **tart up**
**06** doll up **07** dress up, smarten
**08** decorate, renovate **09** embellish, smarten up **10** redecorate

**tartar**
**05** scale, Tatar **08** beeswing, calculus

**task**
**03** job, tax **04** darg, duty, pain, snap, toil, work **05** chore, grind, stint
**06** burden, charge, errand, killer, labour, pensum **07** mission, stretch
**08** activity, business, exercise, hard time, trauchle **09** challenge, job of work, soft thing **10** assignment, commission, employment, engagement, enterprise, imposition, occupation **11** piece of work, undertaking

• **take to task**
**04** slam **05** blame, knock, scold, slate
**06** attask, pull up, rebuke **07** censure, chapter, lecture, reprove, tell off, tick off, upbraid **08** reproach **09** criticize, reprimand

**Tasmania**
**03** Tas **06** Tassie

**taste**
**03** bit, eat, sar, sip, try **04** bent, bite, dash, drop, feel, gout, know, meet, pree, tang, test **05** enjoy, fancy, grace, piece, smack, style **06** choice, desire, hunger, liking, morsel, nibble, polish, relish, sample, savour, thirst, titbit
**07** culture, decorum, discern, finesse, flavour, leaning, make out, soupçon, undergo **08** appetite, breeding, elegance, fondness, judgment, mouthful, penchant, perceive
**09** encounter, etiquette, hankering, judgement, propriety **10** experience, partiality, perception, preference, refinement **11** cultivation, discernment, distinguish, inclination, sensitivity, stylishness **12** appreciation, predilection, tastefulness
**13** differentiate **14** discrimination

*Tastes include:*

**03** hot
**04** acid, sour, tart
**05** acrid, bland, fishy, meaty, nutty, salty, sapid, sharp, spicy, sweet, tangy
**06** acidic, bitter, citrus, creamy, fruity, sugary
**07** insipid, peppery, piquant, pungent, savoury
**08** vinegary
**11** bittersweet

**tasteful**
**05** smart, tasty **06** dainty, pretty
**07** correct, elegant, refined, stylish
**08** artistic, charming, cultured, delicate, graceful, gracious, pleasing, polished **09** aesthetic, beautiful, exquisite, judicious **10** cultivated, fastidious, harmonious, restrained, well-judged **14** discriminating

**tastefully**
**07** smartly **09** elegantly, stylishly
**10** charmingly, delicately, graciously
**11** beautifully, exquisitely, judiciously
**12** artistically, harmoniously

**tasteless**
**04** dull, flat, loud, mild, naff, rude, thin, weak **05** bland, cheap, crass, crude, gaudy, plain, showy, stale, tacky, vapid, wersh **06** boring, flashy, garish, kitsch, tawdry, vulgar, watery **07** insipid, insulse, uncouth, wearish **08** improper, tactless, unseemly **09** graceless, inelegant, unfitting, unsavoury
**10** indiscreet **11** flavourless, watered-down **13** uninteresting

**tasting**
**05** assay, smack, trial **07** testing
**08** sampling **09** gustation
**10** assessment

**tasty**
**04** nice **05** spicy, sweet, tangy, yummy
**06** morish **07** gustful, moreish, piquant, savoury **08** luscious, tasteful
**09** delicious, flavorous, palatable, succulent, toothsome **10** appetizing, attractive, delectable **11** flavoursome, interesting, scrumptious
**13** mouthwatering

**tatter**

• **in tatters**
**03** rag **06** broken, in bits, in rags, ragged, ruined **07** in ruins, wrecked
**08** in pieces, in shreds **09** destroyed, in ribbons, shattered **10** devastated

**tattered**
◇ *anagram indicator*
**04** torn **05** tatty **06** frayed, ragged, ripped, shabby **07** scruffy
**10** threadbare **14** tatterdemalion
**15** tatterdemallion

**tattie** *see* **potato**

**tattler**
**04** blab **06** gossip **08** busybody, tell-tale **09** chatterer **10** newsmonger, talebearer, tale-teller **12** rumour-monger **13** scandalmonger

**tattoo**
**03** tat **04** moko, tatu **06** tattow
**08** drumming

**taunt**
**03** dig, rib **04** bait, barb, gibe, gird, goad, jeer, jest, jibe, jive, mock, twit **05** fling, sneer, tease **06** deride, insult, revile **07** catcall, censure, mockery, provoke, sarcasm, teasing, torment **08** brickbat, derision, reproach, ridicule, taunting **09** make fun of, poke fun at **11** provocation

**taut**
**03** mat **05** rigid, stiff, tense, tight **06** tangle, tensed **07** anxious, fraught, worried **08** strained **09** stretched, tightened, unrelaxed **10** contracted

**tautological**
**05** wordy **07** verbose **09** redundant
**10** pleonastic, repetitive
**11** superfluous

**tautology**
**08** pleonasm **09** iteration, verbosity
**10** redundancy, repetition
**11** duplication, perissology, superfluity
**14** repetitiveness

**tavern**
**03** bar, inn, pub **04** bush, dive **05** fonda, joint, local **06** boozer, Kneipe, public **08** alehouse, hostelry, tap-house **09** roadhouse **10** night-house, trust-house **11** night-cellar, public house

**taw**
**03** tew **04** ally, flog, whip **05** alley, thong

**tawdry**
**05** cheap, fancy, gaudy, showy, tacky, tatty **06** cheapo, flashy, garish, vulgar
**07** chintzy **08** tinselly, trumpery
**09** tasteless **10** glittering
**11** gingerbread

**tawny**
**03** tan **04** fawn **05** khaki, sandy
**06** fulvid, golden, yellow **07** fulvous
**08** xanthous **11** golden brown

**tax**
**03** aid, lot, sap, try **04** cess, duty, levy, load, rate, scot, sess, soak, test, tire **05** drain, exact, stent, weary, weigh **06** assess, burden, charge, demand, impose, impost, strain, stress, tariff, weaken, weight **07** exhaust, stretch, wear out **08** encumber, enervate, overload, pressure **09** agistment, weigh down **10** accusation, assessment, imposition
**12** contribution **13** make demands on

*Taxes include:*

**02** PT
**03** GST, sur, VAT
**04** geld, gelt, PAYE, poll, scat, skat, toll
**05** rates, scatt, tithe
**06** excise, income
**07** airport, council, customs, gabelle
**08** property, Rome-scot
**09** death duty, head money, insurance
**10** capitation, estate duty, value added
**11** corporation, inheritance, Peters' pence
**12** capital gains, pay as you earn
**15** capital transfer, community charge

• **tax collectors**
**02** IR **03** IRS

**taxi**
**03** cab **06** fiacre, samlor **07** Joe Baxi, minicab, taxicab **09** hansom-cab
**10** hackney cab **12** hackney coach
**15** hackney carriage

**taxing**
**04** hard **05** heavy, tough **06** satire, tiring, trying **07** censure, onerous, testing, wearing **08** draining, exacting, wearying **09** demanding, punishing, stressful, wearisome **10** burdensome, enervating, exhausting

**taxman**
**02** IR **03** IRS

**tea**
**03** cha, tay **04** char **05** cuppa **06** tisane
**07** Rosy Lee **08** infusion, Rosie Lee, stroupan **09** stroupach

*See also* **cannabis**

*Teas and herbal teas include:*

**03** ice, kat, qat
**04** beef, bush, chai, herb, iced, khat, mate, mint, sage
**05** Assam, black, bohea, brick, caper, China, congo, fruit, green, hyson, lemon, pekoe, senna, yerba
**06** Ceylon, congou, herbal, oolong, oulong
**07** cambric, instant, jasmine, lapsang, redbush, rooibos, rosehip, Russian, twankay
**08** camomile, Earl Grey, Lady Grey, souchong, switchel
**09** breakfast, chamomile, gunpowder
**10** Darjeeling
**11** orange pekoe
**13** decaffeinated
**15** lapsang souchong

**teach**
**03** con, kon **04** cram, larn, lear, leir, lere, read, show, take **05** coach, conne, din in, drill, edify, guide, leare, learn, train, tutor, verse **06** advise, direct, ground, impart, inform, parrot, preach, school
**07** counsel, din into, educate, lecture, perfect **08** accustom, disciple, hammer in, instruct **09** brainwash, condition, enlighten, foreteach, inculcate, pedagogue **10** discipline, hammer into, potty-train
**11** demonstrate, give lessons
**12** indoctrinate

**teacher**
**03** rav **04** Miss **05** guide **07** dominie, prophet **08** educator, schoolie
**09** pedagogue, schoolman
**10** instructor, scholastic
**12** demonstrator, instructress
**13** gerund-grinder

*Teacher types include:*

**03** AST, don
**04** dean, form, guru, head
**05** barbe, coach, molla, rabbi, rebbe, tutor, usher
**06** docent, doctor, duenna, fellow, gooroo, mallam, master, mentor, mollah, moolah, mullah, munshi, pedant, pundit, reader, school, supply
**07** acharya, adviser, crammer, starets, staretz, student, trainer
**08** lecturer, mistress, moonshee, sol-faist
**09** governess, maharishi, mnemonist, pedagogue, preceptor, principal, professor, rebbetzin, reception
**10** counsellor, deputy head, headmaster, head of year, instructor, paedotribe, schoolmarm
**11** housemaster, preceptress, upper school
**12** demonstrator, headmistress, mademoiselle, middle school, pastoral head, posture-maker, private tutor, schoolmaster
**13** housemistress, nursery school, posture-master, primary school
**14** schoolmistress, senior lecturer
**15** college lecturer, secondary school

*Teachers include:*

**04** **Beck** (Madame), **Eyre** (Jane), **Hart** (Sheba), **King** (Anna), **Lamb** (Michael), **Nunn** (Sir Percy), **Wilt** (Henry)
**05** **Brill** (Miss), **Chips** (Mr), **Crane** (Edwina), **Crick** (Tom), **Dixon** (Jim), **Doyle** (Patrick), **Handy** (Charles Brian), **Henri** (Frances), **Levin** (Sam), **Odili**, **Snape** (Severus)
**06** **Alcott** (Bronson), **Angelo** (Albert), **Arnold** (Thomas), **Brodie** (Miss Jean), **Coppin** (Fanny Marion Jackson), **Cotton** (George Edward Lynch), **Covett** (Barbara), **Graham** (Martha), **Grimes** (Captain), **Gyatso** (Geshe Kelsang), **Hagrid** (Rubeus), **Harris** (Crocker), **Hillel**, **Hornby** (A S), **Ramsay** (Dunstan), **Solent** (Wolf)
**07** **Darling** (Sir James Ralph), **Eckhart** (Miss), **Enketei** (Mira), **Fischer** (Marcus), **Keating** (John), **Krishna**, **Lowther** (Gordon), **Matthay** (Tobias), **Mr Chips**, **Mulcahy** (Henry), **Peecher** (Emma), **Porpora** (Nicola), **Saville** (Colin), **Squeers** (Wackford), **Vaughan** (Barbara), **Wackles** (Sophy)
**08** **Bridgman** (Laura Dewey), **Caldwell** (George), **Chipping** (Mr), **Doubloon** (Maggie), **Lewisham** (George), **Prodicus**, **Sullivan** (Anne)
**09** **Batchelor** (Barbie), **Bellgrove** (Professor), **Braidwood** (Thomas), **Hartright** (Walter), **Headstone** (Bradley), **Strasberg** (Lee)
**10** **Dumbledore** (Albus), **Leadbetter**

(David), Madame Beck, Madam Hooch, McGonagall (Minerva), Protagoras
12 Pennyfeather (Paul), Stanislavsky
13 M'Choakumchild (Mr)

**• teachers**
03 ATL, NUT 06 NASUWT

**teaching**
04 lair, lare, lore, TEFL, TESL 05 dogma, tenet, TESOL 06 loring, wisdom 07 precept, tuition 08 doctrine, pedagogy 09 didactics, education, principle, tradition 10 pedagogism 11 instruction, instructive, pedagoguism

**team**
02 11, XI, XV 03 set 04 band, crew, gang, pair, side, yoke 05 brood, bunch, chain, group, shift, squad 06 équipe, line-up, litter, outfit, pick-up, stable, troupe 07 company, offence, offense, turn-out 08 equipage

*National team nicknames in Australia and New Zealand include:*

05 Opals
07 Boomers, Olyroos
08 Matildas
09 All Blacks, All Whites, Kangaroos, Socceroos, Wallabies
10 Hockeyroos
11 Kookaburras, Silver Ferns

*See also* **Australian football**; **baseball**; **basketball**; **cricket**; **football**; **racing**; **rugby**

**• team up**
04 join, yoke 05 match, unite 06 couple 07 combine 09 co-operate 10 join forces 11 collaborate 12 band together, come together, work together

**teamwork**
10 fellowship, team spirit 11 co-operation, joint effort 12 co-ordination 13 collaboration, esprit de corps

**tear**
03 fly, nip, rag, ren, rin, rip, run, zap, zip 04 bead, belt, blob, bolt, bomb, claw, dart, dash, gash, grab, hole, plow, pull, race, rage, rash, rend, rent, rive, rush, slip, slit, snag, tire, yank, zing, zoom 05 hurry, pluck, ranch, scoot, seize, sever, shoot, shred, slash, speed, split, spree, vroom, whizz, wound, wrest 06 career, charge, divide, gallop, injure, injury, ladder, mangle, plough, screed, snatch, sprint, sunder, tatter, unroot 07 eye-drop, mammock, rupture, scratch 08 lacerate, mutilate, step on it 09 pull apart, water drop 10 break apart, laceration, mutilation

**• in tears**
03 sad 05 upset, weepy 06 crying
07 sobbing, tearful, wailing, weeping
09 emotional, sorrowful
10 blubbering, distressed, whimpering

**• tear down**
07 destroy 08 demolish, pull down
09 dismantle, knock down

**tearaway**
05 rough, rowdy, tough 06 madcap, rascal 07 hoodlum, hothead, ruffian 08 hooligan, reckless 09 daredevil, impetuous, roughneck 10 delinquent 14 good-for-nothing

**tearful**
03 sad, wet 05 misty, moist, upset, weepy 06 crying 07 doleful, in tears, sobbing, weeping 08 mournful 09 emotional, sorrowful, upsetting 10 blubbering, distressed, lachrymose, whimpering 11 distressing

**tease**
◇ *anagram indicator*
03 kid, mag, rag, rib, rot, vex 04 bait, chip, gibe, goad, goof, grig, josh, mock, nark, tose, toze 05 annoy, chaff, kiddy, sound, taunt, teaze, toaze, touse, touze, towse, towze, worry 06 badger, banter, bother, chiack, chyack, needle, pester, plague, wind up 07 mamaguy, perplex, provoke, torment 08 back-comb, irritate, ridicule 09 aggravate, have a go at, make fun of, poke fun at, tantalize

**technetium**
02 Tc

**technical**
06 expert 07 applied 09 practical 10 artificial, electronic, industrial, mechanical, scientific, specialist 11 specialized 12 computerized, professional 13 technological

**technically**
11 practically 12 mechanically 14 electronically, professionally, scientifically 15 technologically

**technician**
06 fitter 08 engineer, mechanic, operator 09 machinist, operative, rocketeer 11 mechanician, vision mixer 12 phlebotomist, radiographer

**technique**
03 art, way 04 mode 05 craft, ELISA, knack, means, skill, style, touch, trick 06 course, manner, method, system 07 ability, fashion, knowhow, mastery, technic 08 approach, artistry, delivery, facility, technics 09 animation, dexterity, execution, expertise, procedure, serialism 10 capability, holography, millefiori, rag-rolling 11 performance, proficiency, skilfulness 12 oil immersion 13 craftsmanship, modus operandi

**technology**

**• appropriate technology, alternative technology**
02 AT

**• information technology**
02 IT 08 infotech 11 informatics

**tedious**
04 drab, dull, flat, long 05 a drag, banal, prosy, samey, weary 06 boring, draggy, dreary, dreich, tiring 07 humdrum, irksome, operose, prosaic, routine 08 lifeless, long-spun, tiresome, unvaried, wearying 09 laborious, wearisome 10 dragsville, long-winded, monotonous, unexciting, uninspired 11 balls-aching 12 long-drawn-out, run-of-the-mill 13 uninteresting

**• tedious person**
04 bore 06 foozle

**tedium**
03 rut 05 ennui 07 boredom, routine 08 banality, drabness, dullness, monotony, sameness, vapidity 09 prosiness 10 dreariness 11 irksomeness, tediousness 12 lifelessness 14 monotonousness

**tee**
01 T

**teem**
04 bear, brim, pour, rain 05 burst, crawl, empty, spawn, swarm 06 abound, be full 07 bristle, produce 08 increase, multiply, overflow, pelt down 09 pullulate 10 bucket down 11 chuck it down, proliferate 15 rain cats and dogs

**teeming**
04 full 05 alive, great, thick 06 packed 07 copious, crowded, replete 08 abundant, brimming, bursting, childing, crawling, fruitful, numerous, pregnant, seething, swarming 09 bristling, chock-full, plentiful 11 chock-a-block, overflowing, pullulating

**teenage**
05 young 08 immature, juvenile, teenaged, youthful 10 adolescent

**teenager**
03 boy, Mod, yob 04 girl, teen 05 minor, youth 06 rocker 07 sharpie 08 juvenile 09 rangatahi 10 adolescent, bobbysoxer, junior miss, young adult 11 teeny-bopper, young person 13 emerging adult

**teeny**
03 wee 04 tiny 06 minute, teensy, teenty, titchy 07 teentsy 09 miniature, minuscule 10 diminutive, teeny-weeny 11 microscopic 12 teensy-weensy

**teeter**
◇ *anagram indicator*
04 reel, rock, roll, sway 05 lurch, pitch, pivot, shake, waver 06 seesaw, totter, wobble 07 balance, stagger, tremble 08 hesitate 09 vacillate

**teeth**

*Teeth include:*

03 cap, dog, egg, eye, gag, gam, jaw
04 baby, back, buck, fang, fore, gold, milk, mill, tush, tusk, wang, wolf
05 cheek, colt's, crown, false, first, molar, plate, store, sweet, upper
06 bridge, canine, chisel, corner, cuspid, wisdom
07 denture, grinder, incisor, scissor, snaggle
08 bicuspid, dentures, impacted, premolar

**09** milk-molar, permanent, sectorial, serration
**10** carnassial, first molar, masticator, molendinar, third molar
**11** multicuspid, second molar
**12** snaggletooth
**13** first premolar
**14** central incisor, lateral incisor, second premolar

### teetotal

**02** TT **05** sober **06** tee-tee **08** complete **09** abstinent, out-and-out, temperate **10** abstemious, on the wagon

### teetotaller

**02** TT **06** tee-tee, wowser **09** abstainer, nephalist, Rechabite **10** non-drinker **12** water-drinker

### telegram

**03** fax **04** wire **05** cable, telex **09** cablegram, radiogram, telegraph **11** night letter, Telemessage®

### telegraph

**04** send, wire **05** cable, telex **06** signal **08** telegram, transmit **10** radiograph **11** teleprinter **12** Telautograph® **14** radiotelegraph

• **telegraph office**

**02** TO

### telepathy

**03** ESP **10** sixth sense **11** mind-reading, second sight **12** clairvoyance

### telephone

**03** tel **04** buzz, call, dial, ring, tele- **05** phone **06** blower, call up, ring in, ring up **07** contact, handset, hot line **08** receiver **09** give a bell, give a buzz, make a call **10** get in touch **11** give a tinkle

• **on the telephone**

◇ *homophone indicator*

### telescope

**03** cut **04** trim, tube **05** crush, optic, scope **06** reduce, shrink, squash **07** abridge, compact, curtail, shorten, squeeze **08** compress, condense, contract, spyglass, truncate **09** binocular, optic tube, reflector, refractor **10** abbreviate, binoculars, concertina, equatorial **11** perspective **13** prospect-glass

### televise

**03** air **04** beam, show **05** cable, put on, relay **06** screen **08** transmit **09** broadcast

### television

**02** TV **03** box, set **04** tele, tube **05** cable, telly **06** the box **07** the tube **08** boob tube, idiot box, receiver **09** goggle-box **11** cablevision, small screen **13** narrowcasting

*Television programme types include:*

**04** news, soap
**05** anime, drama
**06** repeat, sitcom
**07** cartoon, phone-in, reality
**08** bulletin, chat show, docusoap, game show, quiz show
**09** panel game, soap opera
**11** documentary
**12** makeover show

*Television channels include:*

**02** E4
**03** ABC, CNN, Fox, HBO, MTV, NBC, QVC, S4C, VH1
**04** BBC1, BBC2, BBC3, BBC4, CBBC, CNBC, Five, ITV1, ITV2, ITV3
**06** Sky One
**07** Fox News, History, Sky News
**08** BBC World, Cbeebies, Channel 4, FilmFour, Living TV
**09** al-Jazeera, BBC News 24, Bloomberg, Discovery, Eurosport, Sky Movies, Sky Sports
**11** Nickelodeon

*Television programmes include:*

**02** ER, QI
**03** CSI, QED
**04** GMTV, M*A*S*H
**05** Arena, Bread, Kojak, LA Law, Shaft
**06** Batman, Bottom, Cheers, Dallas, Hi-De-Hi, Lassie, Minder, Mr Bean, Quincy, Sharpe, Tiswas
**07** Bagpuss, Blake's 7, Columbo, Dynasty, Frasier, Friends, Holiday, Horizon, Lovejoy, Maigret, Mr Magoo, Omnibus, Poldark, Pop Idol, Rainbow, Rawhide, Spender, Taggart, The Bill, The Word, Tonight, Top Gear
**08** 'Allo 'Allo, Baywatch, Bergerac, Casualty, Dad's Army, Eldorado, Faking It, NYPD Blue, Panorama, Porridge, Red Dwarf, Roseanne, Seinfeld, Sgt Bilko, Star Trek, Stingray, The Saint, Time Team, Trumpton, Watchdog, Wife Swap
**09** Andy Pandy, Blind Date, Blue Peter, Brookside, Countdown, Doctor Who, Dr Kildare, Emmerdale, Father Ted, Happy Days, Heartbeat, Holby City, Hollyoaks, I Love Lucy, Jackanory, Miami Vice, News at Ten, Newsnight, Newsround, Parkinson, South Park, That's Life, The X Files, Twin Peaks, Up Pompeii!
**10** Ally McBeal, Big Brother, Blackadder, Crossroads, Deputy Dawg, EastEnders, Gladiators, Grandstand, Grange Hill, Howards' Way, Jim'll Fix It, Kavanagh QC, Masterchef, Mastermind, Miss Marple, Neighbours, On the Buses, Pebble Mill, Perry Mason, Play School, Postman Pat, Quatermass, Rising Damp, The Goodies, The Monkees, The Sweeney, The Waltons, The Wombles, The X-Factor, Wacky Races
**11** Animal Magic, Call My Bluff, Catchphrase, Come Dancing, Crackerjack, Fame Academy, Give Us a Clue, Ground Force, Hawaii Five-O, Home and Away, Juke Box Jury, Life on Earth, Teletubbies, The Avengers, The Fast Show, The Fugitive, The Good Life, The Prisoner, The Simpsons, Tom and Jerry, What's My Line?, Yes, Minister
**12** As Time Goes By, Blockbusters, Candid Camera, Citizen Smith, Fawlty Towers, Fifteen to One, It's a Knockout, Knots Landing, Melrose Place, Moonlighting, Mork and Mindy, Open All Hours, Peak Practice, Points of View, Question Time, Sesame Street, Terry and June, The Young Ones, Thunderbirds, Top of the Pops
**13** A Touch of Frost, Blankety Blank, Bob the Builder, Breakfast Time, Emmerdale Farm, Hamish Macbeth, Ivor the Engine, Little Britain, Match of the Day, May to December, Muffin the Mule, Pinky and Perky, Ready, Steady, Go, Sex and the City, Songs of Praise, Spitting Image, Steptoe and Son, The Likely Lads, The Liver Birds, The Lone Ranger, The Muppet Show, The Sky at Night, The Two Ronnies, The World at War, Whicker's World
**14** Animal Hospital, Ballykissangel, Cagney and Lacey, Captain Pugwash, Charlie's Angels, Family Fortunes, Gardener's World, Inspector Morse, Murder, She Wrote, My Friend Flicka, Record Breakers, The Flintstones, The Frost Report, The Weakest Link, This Is Your Life, Tomorrow's World, To the Manor Born, Wheel of Fortune, Worzel Gummidge
**15** Birds of a Feather, Camberwick Green, Hill Street Blues, Midsomer Murders, One Man and His Dog, Ready Steady Cook, Remington Steele, Starsky and Hutch, The Addams Family, The Big Breakfast, The Man from UNCLE, The New Statesman, The Price is Right, The Twilight Zone, Watch with Mother, You've Been Framed

*See also* **quiz**

*Television presenters include:*

**03** **Ant** (Anthony McPartlin), **Dec** (Declan Donnelly)
**04** **Muir** (Frank), **Ross** (Jonathan)
**05** **Aspel** (Michael), **Black** (Cilla), **Bragg** (Melvyn, Lord), **Evans** (Chris), **Frost** (Sir David), **James** (Clive), **Moore** (Sir Patrick), **Negus** (Arthur), **Wogan** (Terry)
**06** **Carson** (Johnny), **Norden** (Denis), **Norman** (Barry), **Paxman** (Jeremy), **Rayner** (Claire), **Savile** (Sir Jimmy)
**07** **Andrews** (Eamon), **Bellamy** (David), **Edmonds** (Noel), **Forsyth** (Bruce), **Kennedy** (Sir Ludovic), **Madeley** (Richard), **Rantzen** (Esther), **Starkey** (David), **Tarrant** (Chris), **Wheldon** (Sir Huw), **Whicker** (Alan), **Winfrey** (Oprah)
**08** **Bakewell** (Joan), **Campbell** (Nicky), **Finnigan** (Judy), **Stoppard** (Miriam), **Sullivan** (Ed)
**09** **Ant and Dec** (Anthony McPartlin/Declan Donnelly), **Magnusson** (Magnus), **Parkinson** (Michael)

**10** Titchmarsh (Alan)
**12** Attenborough (Sir David)
**14** Richard and Judy (Richard Madeley/Judy Finnigan)

• **television system**
**03** PAL **10** flat-screen **13** closed circuit

**tell**
**03** bid, rat, say, see **04** blab, shop, show, talk **05** alter, brief, count, drain, grass, order, speak, state, story, utter
**06** advise, affect, assure, betray, change, charge, decree, direct, gossip, impart, inform, notify, recite, relate, report, reveal, sketch, squeal, tattle, unfold **07** apprise, command, confess, declare, dictate, discern, divulge, exhaust, explain, let know, make out, mention, narrate, portray, recount, require, versify **08** acquaint, announce, count out, denounce, describe, disclose, discover, identify, inform on, instruct, perceive, proclaim
**09** authorize, broadcast, delineate, elucidate, make known, recognize, tell apart, tell tales, transform
**10** comprehend, understand **11** blow the gaff, communicate, distinguish
**12** discriminate **13** differentiate, spill the beans, take its toll of **14** give the low-down, have an effect on **15** give the game away

• **tell off**
**04** slam **05** chide, knock, scold, slate
**06** berate, bounce, carpet, rebuke, see off **07** bawl out, catch it, censure, chew out, lecture, reprove, tick off, upbraid
**08** reproach **09** dress down, pull apart, reprimand, take apart **14** give a talking-to

**teller**
**05** clerk, griot **06** banker, tailor, tellar, tiller **07** cashier, sapling **09** bank clerk, raconteur, treasurer **10** Munchausen, raconteuse **11** Munchhausen

**telling**
**06** cogent, marked **07** pointed
**08** powerful **09** effective, narration, narrative, numbering, revealing
**10** convincing, impressive, meaningful, persuasive **11** instruction, significant

**telling-off**
**03** row **06** earful, rebuke, rocket
**07** chiding, lecture, reproof, wigging
**08** reproach, scolding **09** carpeting, reprimand, talking-to **10** bawling-out, ticking-off, upbraiding **11** castigation
**12** dressing-down **14** kick in the pants, slap on the wrist **15** smack on the wrist

**tell-tale**
**03** spy **05** clype, grass, sneak
**06** buzzer, snitch **07** stoolie, tattler
**08** blabbing, give-away, informer, snitcher, squealer **09** betraying, revealing **10** indicating, meaningful, noticeable, revelatory, suggestive, tale-teller, tattle-tale **11** perceptible, secret agent **12** unmistakable **15** snake in the grass

**tellurium**
**02** Te

**telly** *see* **television**

**temerity**
**04** gall **05** cheek, nerve **06** daring
**08** audacity, boldness, rashness
**09** impudence **10** effrontery
**11** presumption **12** impertinence, recklessness **13** impulsiveness

**temper**
**03** wax **04** alay, calm, cool, fury, mood, rage, tone, trim, tune **05** aleye, allay, alloy, anger, assay, blood, delay, paddy, radge, scene, storm **06** adjust, anneal, attune, harden, humour, lessen, master, meddle, modify, nature, reduce, season, soften, soothe, tamper, weaken **07** assuage, bad mood, chasten, flare-up, fortify, passion, roughen, tantrum, toughen
**08** attitude, calmness, comeddle, mitigate, moderate, palliate, tone down **09** alleviate, annoyance, character, composure, condition, fireworks, ill-humour, petulance
**10** resentment, strengthen
**11** disposition, fit of temper, frame of mind, self-control, state of mind, temperament **12** constitution, irritability, pyrotechnics, tranquillity
*See also* **bad-tempered**

• **lose your temper**
**05** go mad **06** see red **07** explode
**08** boil over, freak out, get angry
**09** blow a fuse, do your nut, go bananas, go up a wall, raise hell **10** hit the roof **11** blow a gasket, blow your top, flip your lid, get up in arms, go up the wall, lose your rag **12** blow your cool, fly into a rage, lose your cool, throw a wobbly **13** get aggravated, have a hissy fit, hit the ceiling, throw a tantrum **14** foam at the mouth **15** fly off the handle, get all steamed up, go off the deep end

**temperament**
**04** bent, mood, soul **05** blood, humor
**06** humour, kidney, make-up, mettle, nature, phlegm, spirit, temper
**07** climate, outlook **08** attitude, tendency **09** character, composure, fieriness, moodiness, tempering
**10** complexion, compromise, impatience, touchiness, volatility
**11** disposition, frame of mind, personality, sensitivity, state of mind
**12** constitution, excitability, idiosyncrasy, irritability
**13** explosiveness, hot-headedness, red-headedness

**temperamental**
**05** fiery, moody **06** inborn, innate, touchy **07** natural **08** artistic, inherent, neurotic, petulant, volatile
**09** emotional, excitable, explosive, hot-headed, impatient, ingrained, irritable, mercurial, sensitive **10** capricious, congenital, hot-blooded, passionate, unreliable **12** highly strung **13** over-emotional, over-sensitive, unpredictable **14** constitutional, hypersensitive

**temperamentally**
**08** innately **09** basically, naturally
**10** inherently **13** fundamentally

**temperance**
**08** sobriety **09** austerity, restraint
**10** abstinence, continence, moderation, self-denial **11** prohibition, self-control, teetotalism **13** self-restraint **14** abstemiousness, self-discipline

**temperate**
**04** calm, fair, mild **05** balmy, sober
**06** gentle, stable **07** clement, equable
**08** balanced, composed, moderate, pleasant, sensible, teetotal
**09** abstinent, agreeable, continent
**10** abstemious, controlled, reasonable, restrained **11** self-denying **12** even-tempered **14** self-controlled, self-restrained

**temperature**
**01** t **04** temp **05** fever **07** mixture
**10** proportion **12** constitution

**tempest**
**04** gale **05** storm **06** furore, squall, tumult, uproar **07** cyclone, ferment, tornado, turmoil, typhoon
**08** upheaval **09** bourasque, commotion, hurricane **11** disturbance

**tempestuous**
**04** high, wild **05** gusty, rough, windy
**06** fierce, heated, raging, stormy, wrathy **07** furious, intense, squally, violent **08** blustery, feverish
**09** turbulent **10** boisterous, passionate, tumultuous **11** impassioned
**12** uncontrolled

**template**
**03** jig **04** form, mold **05** frame, model, mould **06** master, matrix **07** pattern, profile **08** strickle **09** blueprint, prototype **10** master page, stylesheet
**12** cookie-cutter

**temple**
**03** wat **04** fane, naos **06** church, haffet, haffit, mandir, mosque, pagoda, shrine
**07** mandira **08** teocalli **09** joss house, sanctuary, synagogue **10** tabernacle
**14** place of worship
*See also* **religious**; **worship**

**tempo**
**04** beat, pace, rate, time **05** agoge, metre, pulse, speed, throb **06** rhythm
**07** cadence, measure **08** movement, velocity

**temporal**
**04** good **05** civil **06** carnal, mortal, timely **07** earthly, fleshly, profane, secular, worldly **08** material
**11** terrestrial **12** temporaneous

**temporarily**
**06** for now, pro tem **07** briefly **08** for a time **10** fleetingly **11** momentarily, transiently **12** in the interim, transitorily
**15** for the time being

**temporary**
**05** brief **06** fill-in, pro tem **07** Band-aid®, interim, passing, stopgap **08** fleeting, temporal **09** ephemeral, fugacious, makeshift, momentary, provisory, short-term, transient **10** evanescent, short-lived, transitory **11** impermanent, provisional **12** temporaneous **14** extemporaneous

**temporize**
**05** delay, pause, stall **08** hang back **09** hum and haw **10** equivocate **11** play for time **12** tergiversate **13** procrastinate

**tempt**
**03** woo **04** bait, bayt, coax, draw, lure, tice **05** assay, educe, egg on **06** allure, cajole, entice, incite, induce, invite **07** attempt, attract, dispose, incline, provoke, suggest **08** inveigle, persuade **09** tantalize

**temptation**
**04** bait, draw, lure, pull **05** snare, trial **06** allure, appeal, urging **07** attempt, coaxing **08** cajolery **09** influence, seduction, tentation **10** allurement, attraction, cloven hoof, enticement, incitement, inducement, invitation, invitement, persuasion, suggestion

**tempting**
**04** sexy **08** alluring, enticing, inviting **09** lickerish, liquorish, seductive **10** appetizing, attractive **11** tantalizing **13** mouthwatering

**temptress**
**04** vamp **05** Circe, flirt, siren **06** Dalila **07** Dalilah, Delilah, Lorelei **08** coquette **09** sorceress **10** seductress **11** enchantress, femme fatale

**ten**
**01** X **02** 10 **05** decad **06** decade, dectet, denary

**tenable**
**05** sound **06** viable **08** arguable, credible, feasible, rational **09** plausible **10** believable, defendable, defensible, reasonable **11** justifiable, supportable **12** maintainable

**tenacious**
**04** fast, firm **05** tight, tough **06** claggy, dogged, grippy, secure, sticky **07** adamant **08** adhesive, clinging, cohesive, obdurate, resolute, stubborn **09** obstinate, retentive, steadfast **10** determined, persistent, purposeful, relentless, unshakable, unswerving, unyielding **11** persevering, unshakeable **12** intransigent, single-minded

**tenacity**
**04** guts, hold **05** force, power **07** resolve **08** fastness, firmness, obduracy, solidity, strength **09** diligence, obstinacy, solidness, toughness **10** doggedness, resolution **11** application, persistence, pertinacity, staunchness **12** forcefulness, perseverance, resoluteness, stubbornness **13** determination, inflexibility, intransigence, steadfastness **14** indomitability

**tenancy**
**05** lease **06** tenure **07** holding, renting **09** leasehold, occupancy, residence **10** incumbency, occupation, possession

**tenant**
**04** ryot **05** baron, dwell, gebur, thane **06** farmer, lessee, mailer, occupy, raiyat, renter, socman **07** cottier, métayer, socager, sokeman **08** gavelman, occupant, occupier, resident, suckener **09** incumbent, pendicler **10** inhabitant, landholder **11** householder, leaseholder

**• be a tenant**
**03** sit

**tend**
**02** go **03** aim, ren, rin, run **04** bear, bend, grow, head, herd, keep, lamb, lead, lean, make, mind, move, wait **05** dress, groom, guard, nurse, offer, point, see to, serve, sound, verge, watch **06** affect, attend, escort, handle, invite, manage, wait on **07** care for, conduce, hearken, incline, nurture, protect **08** attend to, be liable, maintain, wait upon **09** cultivate, gravitate, look after, watch over **10** be inclined, minister to, take care of **11** keep an eye on **13** show a tendency

**tendency**
**03** set **04** bent, bias, turn **05** drift, trend **06** course, genius, levity **07** aptness, bearing, conatus, heading, leaning **08** movement **09** direction, liability, proneness, readiness **10** partiality, proclivity, propensity **11** disposition, inclination **14** predisposition, susceptibility

**tendentious**
**06** biased **07** at issue **08** disputed, doubtful **09** debatable, polemical **10** disputable **11** contentious **12** questionable **13** controversial

**tender**
**03** bid, new, raw, red **04** care, fond, give, kind, nesh, plan, pram, sair, soft, sore, warm, weak **05** chary, coins, early, frail, green, juicy, money, offer, praam, price, value, young **06** aching, callow, caring, dainty, extend, feeble, fleshy, gentle, humane, kindly, loving, regard, render, submit **07** advance, amoroso, amorous, beloved, bruised, cherish, concern, fragile, painful, pinnace, present, proffer, propose, suggest **08** currency, delicate, estimate, fondness, footsore, generous, immature, inflamed, merciful, pathetic, proposal, romantic, smarting, youthful **09** banknotes, easy to cut, emotional, evocative, quotation, sensitive, soft-paste, succulent, throbbing, volunteer **10** affettuoso, benevolent, easy to chew, scrupulous, submission, suggestion, vulnerable **11** considerate, proposition, sentimental, soft-hearted, sympathetic **12** affectionate **13** compassionate, inexperienced, tender-hearted **14** impressionable

**tender-hearted**
**04** fond, kind, mild, warm **06** benign, caring, gentle, humane, kindly, loving **07** feeling, pitying **08** merciful **09** sensitive **10** benevolent, responsive **11** considerate, kind-hearted, sentimental, soft-hearted, sympathetic, warm-hearted **12** affectionate **13** compassionate

**tenderly**
**06** fondly, gently, warmly **08** lovingly **10** affettuoso, generously **11** emotionally, sensitively **12** benevolently, romantically **13** considerately, sentimentally **14** affectionately **15** compassionately, sympathetically

**tenderness**
**04** ache, care, love, pain, pity **05** mercy, youth **06** aching, liking, warmth **07** feeling, rawness **08** bruising, delicacy, devotion, fondness, humanity, kindness, softness, soreness, sympathy, weakness **09** affection, fragility, frailness, greenness, juiciness, sweetness **10** attachment, callowness, compassion, feebleness, gentleness, humaneness, immaturity, irritation, succulence **11** amorousness, benevolence, painfulness, sensitivity **12** delicateness, inexperience, inflammation, youthfulness **13** consideration, sensitiveness, vulnerability **14** loving-kindness, sentimentality **15** soft-heartedness, warm-heartedness

**tendon**
**05** sinew **06** leader, paxwax **09** hamstring **11** aponeurosis, heart-string

**tenet**
**04** rule, view **05** canon, credo, creed, dogma, maxim **06** belief, thesis **07** opinion, precept **08** doctrine, teaching **09** principle **10** adiaphoron, conviction **11** presumption **14** article of faith

**Tennessee**
**02** TN **04** Tenn

**tennis**
**10** jeu de paume **12** sphairistike

*Tennis players include:*

**04** **Ashe** (Arthur), **Borg** (Björn), **Cash** (Pat), **Graf** (Steffi), **Hoad** (Lew), **King** (Billie Jean), **Ryan** (Elizabeth), **Wade** (Virginia)

**05** **Budge** (Don), **Bueno** (Maria), **Court** (Margaret), **Evert** (Chris), **Jones** (Ann), **Laver** (Rod), **Lendl** (Ivan), **Lloyd** (Chris), **Perry** (Fred), **Roche** (Tony), **Seles** (Monica), **Stich** (Michael), **Vilas** (Guillermo), **Wills** (Helen)

**06** **Agassi** (Andre), **Austin** (Tracy), **Barker** (Sue), **Becker** (Boris), **Cawley** (Evonne), **Drobny** (Jaroslav), **DuPont** (Margaret), **Edberg** (Stefan), **Gibson** (Althea), **Henman** (Tim), **Hewitt** (Lleyton), **Hingis** (Martina), **Hopman** (Harry), **Kramer** (Jack), **Murray** (Andy), **Rafter** (Pat), **Tilden** (Bill)
**07** **Borotra** (Jean), **Brookes** (Sir Norman Everard), **Connors** (Jimmy), **Emerson** (Roy), **Federer** (Roger), **Godfree** (Kitty), **Lacoste** (Rene), **Lenglen** (Suzanne), **Maskell** (Dan), **McEnroe** (John), **Nastase** (Ilie), **Novotna** (Jana), **Renshaw** (Willie), **Sampras** (Pete), **Sedgman** (Frank), **Shriver** (Pam)
**08** **Capriati** (Jennifer), **Connolly** (Maureen 'Little Mo'), **Gonzales** (Pancho), **Krajicek** (Richard), **Newcombe** (John), **Rosewall** (Ken), **Rusedski** (Greg), **Sabatini** (Gabriela), **Williams** (Serena), **Williams** (Venus)
**09** **Davenport** (Lindsay), **Goolagong** (Evonne), **Sharapova** (Maria), **Woodforde** (Mark)
**10** **Ivanisevic** (Goran), **Kafelnikov** (Yevgeny), **Kournikova** (Anna), **Wills Moody** (Helen), **Woodbridge** (Todd)
**11** **Navratilova** (Martina)
**15** **Goolagong Cawley** (Evonne)

*Tennis-related terms include:*

**03** ace, ATP, let, lob, LTA, set, WTA
**04** love, pass
**05** AELTC, break, deuce, drive, fault, rally, serve, slice, smash
**06** return, umpire, volley, winner
**07** ballboy, net cord, runback
**08** backhand, ballgirl, baseline, drop shot, forehand, line call, love game, midcourt, net judge, overhead, overrule, set point, tie-break, wood shot
**09** advantage, backcourt, baseliner, break back, foot fault, forecourt, hold serve, line judge, mini-break, sweet spot, tramlines, two-handed
**10** break point, cross court, deuce court, match point
**11** block volley, double fault, service game, service line
**12** approach shot, ground stroke, mixed doubles, service court
**13** second service
**14** advantage court, serve and volley

**tenor**
**01** T **03** aim, way **04** feck, gist, path **05** drift, point, sense, theme, trend, Trial **06** burden, course, intent, spirit **07** essence, meaning, purport, purpose, texture **08** tendency **09** direction, substance

**tense**
**01** t **04** edgy, taut, work **05** brace, drawn, heavy, jumpy, rigid, stiff, tight **06** narrow, on edge, strain, taught, uneasy **07** anxious, charged, fidgety, fraught, jittery, keyed up, nervous, stiffen, stretch, tighten, uptight, worried **08** contract, exciting, restless, strained, worrying **09** inflexion, screwed up, stressful, stretched **10** distraught, inflection, nail-biting **11** overwrought, stressed out **12** apprehensive, nerve-racking **13** under pressure

*Grammatical tenses include:*

**02** pt
**03** pat
**04** past
**06** aorist, future
**07** perfect, present
**08** preterit
**09** imperfect, preterite
**10** pluperfect
**11** conditional, past perfect
**12** gnomic aorist, past historic
**13** future perfect
**14** present perfect
**15** paragogic future

**tensely**
**08** in a state, uneasily **09** anxiously, nervously, worriedly **10** restlessly **11** stressed out **14** apprehensively

**tension**
**04** feud **05** clash, worry **06** nerves, strain, stress, strife, unrest, wobbly **07** anxiety, discord, dispute, ill-will, jitters, quarrel, willies **08** conflict, disquiet, distress, edginess, friction, pressure, rigidity, suspense, tautness, variance **09** agitation, antipathy, hostility, stiffness, straining, tightness **10** antagonism, contention, dissension, opposition, stretching, uneasiness **11** butterflies, nervousness **12** apprehension, collywobbles, disagreement, hypertension, restlessness **13** confrontation, heebie-jeebies
• **equal tension**
**08** isotonic
• **high tension**
**02** HT
• **low tension**
**02** LT
• **premenstrual tension**
**03** PMT
• **surface tension**
**01** T

**tent**
**04** camp, heed **05** probe

*Tents include:*

**03** box, ger, gur, mat
**04** bell, dome, kata, tilt, tipi, yurt
**05** bivvy, black, frame, lodge, ridge, tepee, tupik, yourt
**06** big top, canopy, canvas, teepee, tunnel, wigwam
**07** conical, marquee, touring, trailer, yaranga
**10** single hoop, tabernacle
**11** hooped bivvy
**12** sloping ridge, sloping wedge
**13** barrel-vaulted, crossover pole

• **tent village**
**04** duar **05** douar, dowar

**tentacle**
**03** arm **04** horn **06** feeler **12** hectocotylus

**tentative**
**04** test **05** pilot, timid, trial **06** unsure **08** cautious, doubtful, hesitant, unproven, wavering **09** diffident, faltering, peirastic, uncertain, undecided **10** indefinite **11** conjectural, exploratory, provisional, speculative, unconfirmed **12** experimental **13** to be confirmed

**tentatively**
**06** on spec **07** timidly **08** gingerly **10** cautiously, doubtfully, hesitantly **12** indefinitely **13** peirastically, provisionally, speculatively **14** experimentally

**tenterhooks**
• **on tenterhooks**
**05** eager **07** anxious, excited, keyed up, nervous, waiting **08** watchful **09** expectant, impatient **10** in suspense **15** with bated breath

**tenuous**
**04** fine, hazy, slim, thin, weak **05** shaky, vague **06** flimsy, slight, subtle **07** dubious, fragile, slender **08** delicate, doubtful, rarefied **09** recherché **10** indefinite **12** questionable **13** insubstantial

**tenure**
**03** fee, feu **04** tack, term, time **05** lease, tenor **06** papacy, socage **07** burgage, fee-farm, holding, popedom, soccage, tenancy **08** frank-fee, steelbow, vavasory, venville **09** commendam, gavelkind, leasehold, occupancy, pastorate, priorship, rabbinate, residence, sokemanry, villenage **10** archontate, cottierism, government, habitation, incumbency, occupation, possession, villeinage **12** frankalmoign **13** knight service **14** proprietorship, subinfeudation

**tepee**
**04** tent, tipi

**tepid**
**03** lew **04** cool **07** warmish **08** lukewarm **09** apathetic **11** half-hearted, indifferent **14** unenthusiastic

**terbium**
**02** Tb

**term**
**03** dub, end, tag **04** call, fees, name, span, time, word **05** bound, close, costs, label, limit, point, rates, space, spell, style, title **06** clause, course, detail, finish, period, phrase, prices, season, tariff **07** charges, entitle, epithet, footing, proviso, session, stretch **08** boundary, duration, fruition, interval, locution, position, semester, standing, terminus **09** condition, designate, provision, relations, trimester **10** conclusion, denominate, expression, particular **11** appellation, culmination, designation, restriction,

stipulation **12** denomination, relationship **13** qualification, specification

*Terms and sessions include:*

**04** Lent
**06** Easter, Hilary
**07** Trinity
**10** Michaelmas

**• come to terms**
**06** accept, submit **08** compound **10** articulate **11** accommodate **12** come to accept **14** resign yourself

**• in terms of**
**09** as regards **10** in regard to **12** in relation to, with regard to **13** with respect to

**• on good terms**
**02** in

**terminal**
◇ *tail selection indicator*
**03** end, VDU **04** last, pole, POST, RJET **05** acute, depot, dying, fatal, final, limit **06** deadly, ending, garage, lethal, mortal, utmost **07** console, extreme, killing, monitor, station **08** boundary, desinent, keyboard, last stop, limiting, railhead, terminus, ultimate **09** confining, extremity, incurable **10** concluding **11** desinential, termination, untreatable, workstation **12** end of the line

**• terminal part**
**03** cap **06** cloaca, rectum **12** sigmoid colon **14** sigmoid flexure

**terminally**
**07** fatally **08** lethally, mortally **09** incurably **11** malignantly

**terminate**
**03** end **04** fall, stop **05** abort, cease, close, issue, lapse **06** cut off, expire, finish, result, run out, wind up **07** dismiss **08** complete, conclude, dissolve, leave off **10** put an end to **11** come to an end, discontinue **12** bring to an end

**termination**
**03** end **05** close, finis, issue **06** demise, effect, ending, expiry, finale, finish, result **07** success **08** abortion, boundary, naricorn **09** cessation **10** completion, conclusion, dénouement **11** consequence **15** discontinuation

**terminology**
**05** terms, words **06** jargon **08** language **10** glossology, vocabulary **11** expressions, phraseology **12** nomenclature

**terminus**
◇ *tail selection indicator*
**03** end **04** goal **05** close, depot, limit **06** garage, target **07** station **08** boundary, terminal **09** extremity **11** air terminal, destination, termination **12** end of the line **13** starting-point

**termite**
**03** ant **07** duck-ant, royalty, wood ant **08** white ant **09** woodlouse

**Terra**
**04** Gaia

**terrace**
**03** Ter **04** Terr **05** beach, bench, linch, shelf **06** offset, perron, tarras **07** balcony, sun deck, veranda **08** barbette, crescent, platform, verandah **09** promenade **10** undercliff

**terrain**
**04** land **06** ground **07** country, terrane, terrene **09** landscape, territory **10** topography **11** countryside

**terrapin**
**04** emys **06** slider **08** redbelly **11** diamondback **13** water tortoise

**terrestrial**
**04** land **06** global, layman **07** earthly, mundane, terrene, worldly **09** subastral, tellurian

**terrible**
◇ *anagram indicator*
**03** bad, big, ill **04** foul, grim, naff, poor, poxy, ropy, sick, vile, weak **05** awful, great, large, lousy, nasty, pants, ropey, sorry **06** aching, crappy, crummy, faulty, gloomy, guilty, horrid, in pain, poorly, severe, unwell **07** ashamed, extreme, fearful, hateful, hideous, intense, notable, painful, serious, tearing, the pits, unhappy, useless **08** contrite, diseased, dreadful, gruesome, hopeless, horrible, horrific, inferior, mediocre, pathetic, pokerish, shocking **09** abhorrent, appalling, defective, deficient, frightful, harrowing, imperfect, monstrous, obnoxious, offensive, repulsive, revolting, third-rate **10** abortional, apologetic, despondent, disgusting, hellacious, inadequate, indisposed, outrageous, pronounced, remorseful, second-rate, shamefaced, unpleasant **11** a load of crap, distressing, exceptional, incompetent, ineffective, substandard, unspeakable **12** unacceptable **14** a load of garbage, a load of rubbish, unsatisfactory **15** under the weather

**terribly**
◇ *anagram indicator*
**04** evil, much, very **06** evilly **07** awfully, greatly **09** decidedly, extremely, seriously **10** thoroughly **11** desperately, exceedingly, frightfully

**terrier**
**04** roll **08** register, rent-roll **09** inventory **11** territorial

*Terriers include:*

**03** fox
**04** bull, Skye
**05** cairn, foxie, Irish, Welsh
**06** Border, Boston, Scotch, Scotty, Westie, Yorkie
**07** pit bull, Scottie, Tibetan
**08** Aberdeen, Airedale, Doberman, Scottish, Sealyham, wire-hair
**09** Kerry blue, schnauzer, Yorkshire
**10** Australian, Bedlington, Manchester, wire-haired
**11** Jack Russell
**12** West Highland
**13** Dandie Dinmont
**15** American pit bull

**terriers**
**02** TA

**terrific**
**03** ace **04** cool, huge, mega, neat, wild **05** brill, crack, great, large, super, triff **06** superb, wicked **07** amazing, awesome, crucial, extreme, hell of a, intense **08** dreadful, enormous, fabulous, gigantic, smashing **09** brilliant, excellent, excessive, fantastic, wonderful **10** marvellous, prodigious, remarkable, stupendous, terrifying, tremendous **11** frightening, magnificent, outstanding, sensational **12** breathtaking **13** extraordinary **14** out of this world

**terrifically**
**04** very **05** jolly **06** highly, really **07** acutely, awfully, greatly, utterly **08** severely, terribly **09** decidedly, extremely, intensely, unusually **10** dreadfully, remarkably, thoroughly, uncommonly **11** exceedingly, excessively, frightfully **12** immoderately, inordinately, unreasonably **13** exceptionally **15** extraordinarily

**terrified**
**04** awed **06** aghast, scared **07** alarmed **08** appalled, dismayed **09** horrified, petrified **10** frightened **11** in a blue funk, intimidated, scared stiff **12** horror-struck **13** having kittens, panic-stricken, scared to death

**terrify**
**04** fear, gast, numb **05** alarm, appal, ghast, grise, panic, scare, shock **06** agrise, agrize, agryze, dismay, rattle **07** horrify, petrify **08** affright, frighten, paralyse **09** terrorize **10** intimidate, scare stiff **12** put the wind up

**territorial**
**04** area **05** zonal **08** district, domainal, regional **09** localized, sectional **11** topographic **12** geographical

**territorials**
**02** TA

**territory**
**03** Ter **04** area, land, mark, Terr, turf, zone **05** field, state, tract **06** county, domain, region, sector **07** abthane, apanage, country, outland, terrain **08** appanage, backyard, district, outlands, preserve, province, sheikdom, toparchy, township **09** khedivate, sheikhdom **10** dependency, home ground, khediviate, possession, Reichsland **11** trusteeship **12** jurisdiction
*See also* **province**; **state**

**terror**
**03** bug **04** bogy, fear **05** alarm, bogle, demon, devil, dread, fiend, panic, poker, rogue, shock **06** dismay, fright,

horror, rascal **07** bugbear, monster **08** affright, blue funk, tearaway **09** cold sweat, scarecrow, terrorism **10** amazedness **11** trepidation **12** intimidation **13** consternation

**terrorist**
**06** bomber, gunman, player **07** butcher **08** agitator, assassin, attacker, militant **09** aggressor, anarchist, assailant, guerrilla **11** seditionist **13** revolutionary **14** freedom fighter, fundamentalist, urban guerrilla

• **terrorist militia**
**02** SA

**terrorize**
**04** prey **05** alarm, bully, scare, shock **06** coerce, menace **07** horrify, oppress, petrify, terrify **08** browbeat, frighten, threaten **09** strongarm **10** intimidate **12** put the wind up

**terse**
**04** curt **05** blunt, brief, crisp, pithy, short **06** abrupt, gnomic, smooth, snappy **07** brusque, compact, concise, laconic **08** clean-cut, incisive, succinct **09** condensed **10** elliptical, to the point **12** epigrammatic, monosyllabic

**test**
**03** MOT, pix, pyx, sap, SAT, try, van **04** Esda, exam, load, pass, quiz, tire **05** assay, check, drain, exact, probe, proof, prove, study, testa, touch, trial, trier, weary **06** assess, burden, dry run, impose, ordeal, prieve, sample, screen, strain, try out, try-out, verify, weaken **07** analyse, check-up, examine, exhaust, inspect, reagent, scratch, stretch, wear out **08** analysis, appraise, audition, check out, crucible, encumber, enervate, evaluate, overload, prospect, sounding, trial run **09** challenge, criterion, probation, questions, testimony, time trial **10** assessment, evaluation, experience, experiment, inspection, pilot study, scrutinize, shibboleth **11** examination, exploration, investigate **13** investigation, make demands on, questionnaire **14** scrutinization

*See also* **examination**

• **stand the test**
**04** wash

**testament**
**02** NT, OT **04** Test, will **05** proof **07** earnest, tribute, witness **08** covenant, evidence **09** testimony **11** attestation **13** demonstration **15** exemplification

**testicles**
**04** nuts **05** balls, groin **07** cojones, doucets, dowsets, gooleys, goolies **08** cobblers, knackers, lamb's fry **12** family jewels

**testify**
**03** rap **04** avow, show **05** state, swear, vouch **06** affirm, assert, attest, back up, depone, verify **07** certify, confirm, declare, endorse, speak to, support **08** proclaim **09** establish **11** bear witness, corroborate, demonstrate **12** give evidence, substantiate

**testimonial**
**04** chit **06** chitty **07** tribute **09** character, reference **10** credential **11** certificate, endorsement **12** commendation **14** recommendation

**testimony**
**05** proof **06** attest, report **07** support, tribute, witness **08** evidence **09** affidavit, assertion, statement **10** deposition, indication, profession, submission **11** affirmation, attestation, declaration **12** confirmation, verification **13** corroboration, demonstration, manifestation

**testy**
**05** cross, ratty **06** crusty, grumpy, shirty, snappy, sullen, tetchy, touchy **07** crabbed, fretful, peevish, stroppy, waspish **08** captious, petulant, snappish **09** crotchety, impatient, irascible, irritable, splenetic **11** bad-tempered, quarrelsome **12** cantankerous **13** quick-tempered, short-tempered

**tetchy**
**05** ratty **06** crusty, grumpy, shirty, touchy **07** grouchy, peevish, teachie **08** scratchy, snappish **09** crotchety, irascible, irritable **11** bad-tempered **13** short-tempered

**tête-à-tête**
**03** jaw **04** chat, talk **06** confab, natter, secret **07** twasome, twosome **08** chitchat, dialogue **10** face to face **12** a quattr'occhi, confidential, conversation, heart-to-heart

**tether**
**03** tie **04** bind, bond, cord, lash, lead, line, rope **05** chain, hitch, leash, tie up **06** fasten, fetter, picket, piquet, secure **07** manacle, picquet, shackle **08** restrain **09** fastening, restraint

**Teutonic**
**03** Ger **04** Teut **05** Dutch **06** German **08** Germanic

**Texas**
**02** TX **03** Tex

**text**
**04** body, book **05** Bible, issue, point, theme, topic, verse, words **06** matter, source **07** chapter, content, passage, reading, set book, subject, wording **08** libretto, sentence, textbook **09** paragraph **10** main matter **11** boilerplate **13** subject matter

**texture**
**03** web **04** feel, wale, woof **05** grain, touch, weave **06** fabric, finish, tissue **07** quality, surface, weftage **09** character, structure, texturize **10** appearance **11** composition, consistency **12** constitution

**Thailand**
**01** T **03** THA

**thallium**
**02** Tl

**thank**
**03** owe **06** credit **07** aggrate, remercy **09** recognize **10** appreciate, be grateful **11** acknowledge **13** say thank you to

**thankful**
**07** obliged, pleased **08** beholden, grateful, indebted, relieved **09** contented **12** appreciative

**thankfulness**
**09** gratitude **10** obligation **12** appreciation, indebtedness

**thankless**
**07** useless **09** fruitless **10** ungrateful, unrequited, unrewarded **11** unrewarding **12** unprofitable, unrecognized **13** unappreciated **14** unacknowledged

**thanks, thank you**
**02** ta **05** mercy **06** cheers, credit **08** bless you, gramercy, thank you **09** gratitude **10** many thanks **11** much obliged, recognition **12** appreciation, gratefulness, thanksgiving **13** thank-offering **14** acknowledgment **15** acknowledgement

• **thanks to**
**05** due to **07** owing to, through **09** because of **11** as a result of, on account of

**that**
**02** as, so, yt **03** how, yon **04** such **05** which **07** because

• **that French**
**03** que, qui

• **that is, that's**
**02** dh, ie **05** id est **09** das heisst

**thatching**
**04** atap, reed **05** attap

**thaw**
**04** melt, warm **05** de-ice, fresh, relax **06** heat up, soften **07** defrost, liquefy **08** defreeze, dissolve, loosen up, unfreeze **09** uncongeal

**the**
**01** t' **02** ye

• **the French**
**02** la, le **03** les

• **the German**
**03** das, der, die

• **the Italian**
**01** i **02** il, la, le

• **the Spanish**
**02** el, la **03** las, los

**theatre**
**04** hall, shop **05** drama **06** cinema **08** the stage **09** dramatics, playhouse, theatrics, the boards **10** opera house **11** Thespian art **12** amphitheatre, show business **13** the footlights

*See also* **cinema**

*Theatres include:*

**03** Pit
**04** Rose, Swan
**05** Abbey, Globe, Lyric, Savoy

**06** Albery, Apollo, Donmar, Lyceum, Old Vic, Palace, Queen's
**07** Adelphi, Aldwych, Almeida, Garrick, Gielgud, Mermaid, Olivier, Phoenix
**08** Barbican, Broadway, Coliseum, Crucible, Dominion, Festival, National, Young Vic, Ziegfeld
**09** Cottesloe, Criterion, Drury Lane, Haymarket, Lyttelton, Palladium, Playhouse
**10** Royal Court
**11** Comedy Store, Duke of York's, Her Majesty's, Moulin Rouge, Royal Lyceum, Shaftesbury
**12** Covent Garden, Sadler's Wells, Theatre Royal, Winter Garden
**13** Folies Bergère, Prince of Wales, The Other Place, The Roundhouse
**14** Barbican Centre
**15** Donmar Warehouse, London Palladium

*Theatre parts include:*

**03** box, pit, set
**04** area, drop, flat, grid, loge
**05** apron, decor, flies, house, logum, spots, stage, wings
**06** border, bridge, circle, floats, floods, lights, loggia, scruto, stalls
**07** balcony, catwalk, curtain, cut drop, gallery, leg drop, rostrum, the gods, upstage
**08** backdrop, coulisse, trapdoor
**09** backstage, cyclorama, downstage, forestage, green room, mezzanine, open stage, tormentor
**10** auditorium, footlights, fourth wall, ghost light, prompt side, proscenium
**11** drop-curtain, house lights, upper circle
**12** orchestra pit
**13** safety curtain
**14** opposite prompt, proscenium arch, revolving stage
**15** proscenium doors

*Theatre-related terms include:*

**02** BS, LX, OB, OP, PS
**03** act, cue, fée, fly, gel, rep, run, vis, yok
**04** call, cast, flat, grid, juve, loge, plot, pong, rake, tabs, wash, yock
**05** actor, ad lib, angel, aside, derig, dry up, fit-up, genre, get-in, lines, lodge, props, re-rig, scene, spike, usher
**06** baffle, chorus, corpse, critic, double, dry ice, Equity, flyman, fringe, get-out, make-up, miscue, places, prompt, review, script, walk-on
**07** actress, costume, curtain, dresser, matinee, pittite, preview, project, rhubarb, rigging, scenery, tableau, upstage, West End
**08** audience, audition, blackout, block out, Broadway, business, coulisse, dialogue, director, duologue, entr'acte, interval, libretto, overture, pass door, play-goer, producer, ring down, thespian, wardrobe, white out
**09** backlight, backstage, beginners, box office, break a leg, chaperone, curtain up, cyclorama, double act, downstage, footlight, full house, limelight, monologue, periaktos, programme, rehearsal, repertory, soliloquy, soubrette, spotlight, stage crew, stage door, stage hand, stage left, usherette, visual cue
**10** book-holder, dénouement, first night, followspot, fourth wall, get the bird, in the wings, prompt book, prompt copy, prompt desk, prompt side, stagecraft, stage right, understudy, walk-around
**11** bastard side, centre stage, curtain call, curtain time, die the death, greasepaint, house lights, iron curtain, leading lady, off-Broadway, quick change, read-through, stage fright, top one's part, wind machine
**12** breeches part, breeches role, first-nighter, front of house, intermission, jeune premier, juvenile lead, monstre sacré, principal boy, prompt corner, prompt script, stage manager, travesty role
**13** bastard prompt, curtain-raiser, curtain speech, grande vedette, jeune première, safety curtain
**14** dress rehearsal, opposite prompt, special effects
**15** genteel business, opposite bastard

*See also* **director**

## • theatre award
**04** Tony

## theatrical
◇ *anagram indicator*
**03** OTT **04** camp **05** showy, stagy **06** forced, scenic, unreal **07** actorly, pompous **08** actorish, actressy, affected, dramatic, mannered, overdone, thespian **09** emotional **10** artificial, histrionic, over the top **11** exaggerated, extravagant **12** histrionical, melodramatic, ostentatious

*Theatrical forms include:*

**03** Noh
**04** mime, play
**05** farce, opera, revue
**06** Absurd, ballet, circus, comedy, fringe, kabuki, masque, puppet, street
**07** cabaret, Cruelty, mummery, musical, pageant, tableau, tragedy
**08** duologue, operetta
**09** burlesque, melodrama, monologue, music hall, pantomime
**10** in-the-round
**11** black comedy, kitchen-sink, miracle play, mystery play
**12** Grand Guignol, morality play, Punch and Judy
**13** fringe theatre, musical comedy, puppet theatre, street theatre
**14** comedy of menace
**15** comedy of humours, comedy of manners, legitimate drama

**Thebes** *see* **Seven Against Thebes**

## theft
**03** job **04** blag, crib **05** fraud, heist, steal, sting, swipe, touch **06** mainor, rip-off, stouth, walk-in **07** larceny, lifting, mugging, nicking, pilfery, robbery, stealth, stick-up, swiping **08** burglary, filching, nobbling, pinching, plagiary, rustling, stealing, thieving **09** autocrime, pilferage, pilfering, stouthrie, swindling **10** purloining, stoutherie, stouthrief **11** kleptomania, shoplifting **12** embezzlement, smash-and-grab

## them
**02** 'em **03** hem **04** some

## thematic
**08** notional **09** taxonomic **10** conceptual **14** classificatory

## theme
**03** peg **04** gist, idea, song, talk, text, tune **05** essay, lemma, motif, paper, story, topic, topos **06** burden, matter, melody, mythos, mythus, thesis, thread **07** burthen, essence, keynote, o'ercome, subject, subtext **08** argument, overcome, owrecome **09** leitmotif, leitmotiv **11** composition **12** dissertation **13** subject matter

## then
**03** now, tho, too **04** also, next, soon, syne, thus **05** after, and so **06** as well **07** besides, further **08** moreover **09** as a result, therefore, whereupon **10** afterwards, at that time, by that time, in addition **11** accordingly, at that point, furthermore, in those days **12** additionally, at a later date, at that moment, consequently, subsequently

## theocracy
**04** Zion **08** thearchy

## theologian
**02** DD **03** ThD **06** divine **09** schoolman

*Theologians include:*

**03** **Eck** (Johann), **Ela** (Jean-Marc)
**04** **Baur** (Ferdinand Christian), **Bede** ('the Venerable', St), **John** (of Damascus, St), **More** (Henry), **Otto** (Rudolf), **Paul** (St)
**05** **Arius**, **Barth** (Karl), **Buber** (Martin), **Colet** (John), **Cyril** (of Alexandria, St), **Llull** (Ramón), **Mbiti** (John S), **Paley** (William), **Pusey** (Edward Bouverie), **Young** (Thomas)
**06** **Alcuin**, **Anselm** (St), **Butler** (Joseph), **Calvin** (John), **Hooker** (Richard), **Jansen** (Cornelius), **Jerome** (St), **Mather** (Increase), **Newman** (John Henry, Cardinal), **Ockham** (William of), **Origen**, **Pascal** (Blaise), **Rahner** (Karl)
**07** **Abelard** (Peter), **Aquinas** (St Thomas), **Arnauld** (Antoine), **Bernard** (of Clairvaux, St), **Clement** (of Alexandria), **Cyprian** (St), **Eckhart** (Johannes), **Edwards** (Jonathan), **Gregory** (of Nazianzus,

St), **Gregory** (of Nyssa), **Grotius** (Hugo), **Lombard** (Peter), **Sankara**, **Spinoza** (Baruch), **Tillich** (Paul Johannes), **William** (of Ockham)
**08** **Arminius** (Jacobus), **Berengar** (of Tours), **Bultmann** (Rudolf Karl), **Chalmers** (Thomas), **Cudworth** (Ralph), **Eusebius**, **Ignatius** (of Loyola, St), **Irenaeus** (St), **Sprenger** (Jacob)
**09** **Augustine** (St), **Bessarion** (John), **Nagarjuna**, **Söderblom** (Nathan)
**10** **Athanasius** (St), **Bellarmine** (St Robert), **Bonhoeffer** (Dietrich), **Duns Scotus** (John), **Macquarrie** (John), **Rosenzweig** (Franz), **Schweitzer** (Albert), **Swedenborg** (Emanuel), **Tertullian**, **Weizsäcker** (Karl Heinrich)
**11** **Bonaventure** (St), **Kierkegaard** (Sören Aabye)
**12** **Justin Martyr** (St)
**14** **Schleiermacher** (Friedrich)

**theological**
**06** divine **09** doctrinal, religious
**10** scriptural **12** hierological
**14** ecclesiastical

**theology**
**08** divinity **09** dogmatics **14** school-divinity

**theorem**
**04** rule **06** dictum **07** formula
**09** deduction, postulate, principle, statement **10** hypothesis
**11** proposition

**theoretical**
**04** pure **05** ideal **07** a priori, on paper
**08** abstract, academic, armchair, notional **10** conceptual **11** conjectural, doctrinaire, speculative
**12** hypothetical **13** suppositional

**theoretically**
**07** a priori, ideally, on paper **08** in theory **09** nominally, seemingly
**10** notionally **11** in principle
**12** conceptually **14** hypothetically

**theorize**
**05** guess **07** suppose **08** propound
**09** formulate, postulate, speculate
**10** conjecture **11** hypothesize

**theory**
**03** ism, law **04** idea, plan, view
**05** guess **06** notion, scheme, system, thesis **07** opinion, surmise **08** proposal
**09** principle, rationale **10** assumption, conjecture, hypothesis, philosophy
**11** abstraction, postulation, presumption, speculation, supposition

*Theories include:*

**03** GUT, TOE
**04** game
**05** chaos
**06** atomic, number, string
**07** Big Bang, quantum
**09** collision, Darwinism, evolution
**10** panspermia, relativity
**11** catastrophe
**12** Grand Unified, Milankovitch
**14** plate tectonics
**15** butterfly effect

**• in theory**
**07** a priori, ideally, on paper
**09** seemingly **10** notionally **11** in principle **12** conceptually **13** in the abstract, theoretically
**14** hypothetically

**therapeutic**
**04** good **05** tonic **06** curing **07** healing
**08** curative, remedial, salutary, sanative
**09** medicinal **10** beneficial, corrective
**11** restorative **12** advantageous, ameliorative, health-giving

**therapy**
**04** cure **05** tonic **06** remedy
**07** healing **09** treatment
**12** therapeutics

*Therapies include:*

**02** OT
**03** art, CST, HRT, LDT, ORT, sex
**04** drug, play, zone
**05** aroma, chemo, drama, group, hydro, hypno, music, photo, radio, reiki
**06** beauty, family, physio, primal, psycho, retail, speech
**07** electro, Gestalt, Rolfing, shiatsu
**08** aversion
**09** behaviour, cognitive, herbalism
**10** homeopathy, osteopathy, regression, ultrasound
**11** acupressure, acupuncture, biofeedback, homoeopathy, irradiation, moxibustion, naturopathy, reflexology
**12** chiropractic, craniosacral, electroshock, faith healing, horticulture, occupational, reminiscence
**13** confrontation, dream analysis, heat treatment

*See also* **psychological**

**there**
**04** ecco **06** yonder

**thereabouts**
**05** about **07** roughly **12** near that date
**13** approximately **14** near that number

**thereafter**
**02** so **04** next, upon **09** after that
**10** afterwards **11** accordingly
**12** subsequently **13** after that time

**therefore**
**02** so **04** ergo, then, thus **05** and so, argal **06** forthy, so then **09** as a result
**11** accordingly **12** consequently **13** for that reason

**thereupon**
**02** so **06** withal **08** with that, with this
**11** immediately

**thesaurus**
**05** Roget **07** lexicon **08** synonymy, treasury, wordbook **10** dictionary, repository, storehouse, vocabulary, wordfinder **12** encyclopedia

**these**
**04** thir

**thesis**
**04** idea, view **05** essay, paper, theme, topic **06** theory **07** opinion, premise, subject **08** argument, position, proposal, treatise **09** monograph, statement **10** contention, hypothesis
**11** composition, proposition
**12** disquisition, dissertation

**thick**
**03** big, fat, hub **04** daft, deep, dull, dumb, fast, full, slow, this, warm, wide
**05** broad, bulky, close, dense, dippy, dopey, focus, foggy, gross, gruff, heart, heavy, husky, lumpy, midst, murky, rough, solid, soupy, stiff, stout **06** centre, chunky, creamy, croaky, filled, grouty, hoarse, marked, middle, opaque, packed, simple, smoggy, strong, stupid, turbid, unfair **07** chocker, closely, clotted, compact, crowded, foolish, muffled, obvious, rasping, teeming, thicket, thickly, throaty, unclear, viscous, woollen **08** abundant, brimming, bursting, close-set, crawling, croaking, definite, frequent, gormless, gravelly, guttural, intimate, numerous, striking, swarming **09** abounding, brainless, bristling, condensed, dim-witted, excessive, semi-solid, squabbish
**10** coagulated, frequently, indistinct, noticeable, pronounced **11** chock-a-block, overflowing, substantial
**12** concentrated, impenetrable
**13** thick as a plank, unintelligent

**thicken**
**03** gel, set **04** cake, clot, curd, jell, meal
**05** upset **06** curdle, reduce
**07** congeal, stiffen **08** condense, solidify **09** coagulate **10** incrassate, inspissate **13** make more solid
**15** become more solid

**thickening**
**04** roux **08** clubbing **09** callosity
**14** hyperkeratosis **15** atherosclerosis, middle-age spread, primitive streak

**thicket**
**04** bosk, wood **05** brake, brush, copse, cover, grove, shola **06** bosket, greave, maquis, queach **07** bosquet, coppice, spinney **08** chamisal, fernshaw, reed-rand, reed-rond **09** canebrake, chaparral, salicetum **10** dead-finish
**11** bramble-bush

**thickhead**
**03** git, oaf **04** berk, clot, dope, dork, fool, geek, prat, twit **05** chump, dummy, dunce, idiot, moron, ninny, twerp **06** dimwit, nitwit **07** buffoon, fathead, halfwit, pinhead **08** imbecile, numskull **09** blockhead
**10** nincompoop

**thick-headed**
**04** dumb, slow **05** barmy, dense, dopey, loony, loopy, potty, thick
**06** obtuse, stupid **07** asinine, doltish, foolish, idiotic, moronic **08** gormless
**09** brainless, dim-witted, imbecilic
**10** dull-witted, slow-witted
**11** blockheaded, not all there **13** thick as a plank **15** slow on the uptake

**thickness**
**03** bed, ply **04** band, body, bulk, coat, film, loft, seam, vein **05** layer, sheet, width **06** extent, lamina **07** breadth, density, deposit, stratum **08** diameter **09** bulkiness, closeness, solidness, viscosity **11** consistency, pachydermia **14** third dimension

**thickset**
**05** beefy, bulky, burly, dense, heavy, solid, squat **06** brawny, robust, stocky, strong, sturdy **07** nuggety, squabby **08** muscular, powerful **09** well-built **12** heavily built

**thick-skinned**
**05** tough **06** inured **07** callous **08** hardened **09** hard-nosed, unfeeling **10** hard-boiled, impervious **11** insensitive **12** case-hardened, invulnerable **14** pachydermatous **15** tough as old boots

**thief**
**05** crook **06** magpie, nicker **07** filcher, stealer, tea leaf **08** larcener, pilferer **09** Autolycus, larcenist, plunderer **12** kleptomaniac

*Thieves and robbers include:*

**03** dip, pad
**04** bung, coon, file, prig, Tory, wire, yegg
**05** diver, fraud, heist, kiddy, rover, sneak
**06** bandit, bulker, chummy, con man, dacoit, dakoit, dipper, hotter, ice man, latron, lifter, limmer, looter, mugger, nipper, pirate, raider, robber
**07** abactor, blagger, booster, brigand, burglar, cateran, cosh boy, footpad, hoister, ladrone, land-rat, nobbler, nut-hook, pandoor, pandour, poacher, prigger, rustler, twoccer, whizzer, yeggman
**08** cly-faker, cutpurse, hijacker, huaquero, rapparee, river-rat, swindler
**09** area-sneak, cracksman, embezzler, fraudster, pick-purse, ram-raider, sea robber
**10** cat-burglar, gully-raker, highjacker, highwayman, horse-thief, land-pirate, man-stealer, pickpocket, roberdsman, robertsman, shoplifter, sneak thief, water thief
**11** motor-bandit, poddy-dodger, safe-breaker, safe-cracker, snatch-purse, snow-dropper, stair-dancer
**12** appropriator, baby-snatcher, cattle duffer, cattle-lifter, housebreaker, sheep-stealer, snow-gatherer
**13** highway robber
**15** resurrectionist, resurrection man

**thieve**
**03** bag, lag, rob **04** blag, lift, nick, pull, whip **05** cheat, filch, heist, hoist, pinch, poach, steal, swipe **06** burgle, nobble, pilfer, rip off **07** plunder, purloin, snaffle, swindle **08** abstract, embezzle, knock off, peculate **10** run off with **11** make off with **14** misappropriate

**thieving**
**05** theft **06** piracy **07** crooked, larceny, lifting, mugging, nicking, pugging, robbery **08** banditry, burglary, filching, stealing, thievery **09** dishonest, furacious, larcenous, pilferage, pilfering, predatory, rapacious **10** fraudulent, peculation, plundering, ripping off **11** crookedness, knocking off, sheep-biting, shoplifting **12** embezzlement **13** light-fingered **14** sticky-fingered

**thievish**
**07** crooked, furtive **08** thieving **09** dishonest, furacious, larcenous, predatory, rapacious, theftuous **10** fraudulent **13** light-fingered, tarry-fingered **14** nimble-fingered, sticky-fingered

**thin**
**04** bony, fine, lame, lank, lean, poor, rare, slim, soft, trim, weak **05** faint, filmy, gaunt, gauzy, lanky, light, quiet, runny, scant, sheer, spare, wispy **06** dilute, feeble, flimsy, lessen, meagre, narrow, paltry, rarefy, reduce, refine, scanty, scarce, single, skimpy, skinny, slight, sparse, svelte, wasted, watery, weaken **07** diluted, dwindle, scraggy, scrawny, slender, spindly, tenuous, weed out **08** anorexic, decrease, delicate, diminish, gossamer, rarefied, scrannel, shrunken, skeletal, straggly, tenuious, tinkling **09** attenuate, defective, deficient, emaciated, paper-thin, scattered, untenable, wafer-thin, water down **10** attenuated, diaphanous, inadequate, see-through, wishy-washy **11** high-pitched, implausible, lightweight, thin as a rake, translucent, transparent, underweight **12** inconclusive, unconvincing **13** insubstantial **14** make more watery, undernourished

• **on thin ice**
**06** at risk, unsafe **08** insecure **10** in jeopardy, precarious, vulnerable **12** open to attack

**thing**
**02** it **03** act, aim, bag, job **04** baby, bent, bias, body, deed, fact, fear, feat, gear, idea, item, love, task, togs, tool **05** chore, court, event, fancy, gismo, goods, mania, point, stuff, taste, tools, trait, waldo **06** action, affair, aspect, attire, desire, detail, device, dinges, doodah, entity, factor, fetish, gadget, hang-up, horror, liking, matter, notion, object, phobia, tackle, thingy **07** apparel, article, baggage, clobber, clothes, concept, council, dislike, effects, element, episode, exploit, feature, leaning, luggage, machine, problem, quality, thought, whatsit **08** activity, affinity, assembly, aversion, clothing, creature, cup of tea, fixation, fondness, garments, idée fixe, incident, oddments, penchant, property, soft spot, tendency, thingamy, weakness **09** affection, apparatus, attribute, condition, equipment, happening, implement, mechanism, obsession, proneness, situation, substance, thingummy **10** attraction, belongings, instrument, occurrence, parliament, partiality, particular, phenomenon, possession, preference, proceeding, proclivity, propensity, speciality **11** arrangement, bits and bobs, contrivance, eventuality, inclination, odds and ends, possessions, undertaking, what you like **12** appreciation, circumstance, one-track mind, predilection, thingummybob, thingummyjig, what's-its-name **13** bits and pieces, paraphernalia, preoccupation **14** characteristic, responsibility, what-d'you-call-it, what turns you on

• **the thing**
**03** hip **04** cool **06** latest, modish, trendy **07** current, in vogue, popular **09** in fashion, the latest **10** all the rage **11** fashionable

**think**
**04** deem, feel, hold, muse, seem **05** brood, cense, guess, judge, opine **06** design, esteem, expect, figure, intend, look on, ponder, reason, recall, reckon, regard, review **07** believe, conceit, foresee, imagine, presume, purpose, reflect, suppose, surmise, thought, weigh up **08** chew over, cogitate, conceive, conclude, consider, envisage, estimate, meditate, mull over, remember, ruminate **09** calculate, cerebrate, determine, recollect, sleep on it, take stock, visualize **10** anticipate, assessment, cogitation, conjecture, deliberate, evaluation, meditation, reflection **11** concentrate, contemplate **12** deliberation **13** consideration, contemplation

• **think better of**
**06** revise **07** rethink **10** reconsider, think again, think twice **11** get cold feet **13** decide not to do

• **think much of**
**04** rate **05** prize, value **06** admire, esteem, reckon **07** respect **10** set store by **13** think highly of

• **think nothing of**
**13** consider usual **14** consider normal

• **think over**
**06** digest, ponder **07** weigh up **08** chew over, consider, meditate, mull over, ruminate **11** contemplate, reflect upon

• **think up**
**06** create, design, devise, invent **07** concoct, dream up, imagine **08** conceive, contrive **09** visualize

**thinkable**
**06** likely **08** feasible, possible **09** cogitable **10** imaginable, reasonable, supposable **11** conceivable

**thinker**
**04** sage **05** brain **07** scholar **08** theorist **09** intellect **10** ideologist, mastermind, philosophe **11** philosopher **12** theoretician

**thinking**
**04** idea, view **06** theory **07** logical, opinion, outlook, thought **08** cultured, judgment, position, rational, sensible, thoughts **09** appraisal, judgement, reasoning **10** analytical, assessment, conclusion, evaluation, meditative, philosophy, reflective, thoughtful **11** conclusions, intelligent **12** excogitation, intellectual **13** contemplative, philosophical, sophisticated

**thin-skinned**
**04** soft **06** tender, touchy **07** prickly **08** snappish **09** irritable, sensitive **10** vulnerable **11** easily upset, susceptible **14** hypersensitive

**third-rate**
**03** bad **04** naff, poor, poxy, ropy **05** awful, lousy, pants, ropey **06** crappy, crummy, shoddy **07** botched, the pits, useless **08** inferior, low-grade, mediocre, pathetic, slipshod, terrible **10** low-quality **11** a load of crap, indifferent, poor-quality, substandard **13** cheap and nasty **14** a load of garbage, a load of rubbish, not up to scratch, unsatisfactory

**thirst**
**03** yen **04** long, lust, want **05** crave, yearn **06** desire, drouth, hanker, hunger, thrist, thrust **07** aridity, craving, drought, dryness, longing, passion **08** appetite, keenness, yearning **09** eagerness, hankering **11** drouthiness, have a yen for, parchedness, thirstiness

**thirsty**
**03** dry **04** adry, arid, avid, keen **05** dying, eager **06** greedy, hungry **07** athirst, burning, craving, drouthy, gasping, itching, longing, parched, thristy **08** desirous, droughty, hydropic, yearning **09** hankering, thirsting **10** dehydrated

**thirteen**
**04** XIII

**thirty**
**03** XXX

**this**
**03** hic, hoc

**Thomas**
**03** Tom

**thong**
**03** taw **04** band, belt, cord, lash, lore, riem **05** strap, strip, whang **06** Jandal® **07** latchet **08** flip-flop **11** shoe latchet

**thorium**
**02** Th

**thorn**
**04** barb **05** doorn, point, prick, spike, spine **06** needle **07** acantha, aculeus, bristle, prickle

**thorny**
**05** armed, dicey, sharp, spiky, spiny, tough, vexed **06** barbed, briery, knotty, sticky, tricky, trying **07** awkward, bristly, complex, irksome, pointed, prickly, spinose, spinous **08** delicate, ticklish, worrying **09** acanthous, difficult, harassing, intricate, upsetting **10** convoluted **11** problematic, troublesome

**thorough**
**04** deep, full, good, pure **05** close, pakka, pucka, pukka, sheer, sound, total, utter **06** damned, entire, narrow, proper **07** careful, in-depth, ingoing, perfect, radical, regular, through **08** absolute, complete, rigorous, sweeping **09** downright, efficient, extensive, intensive, out-and-out, searching **10** exhaustive, methodical, meticulous, resounding, scrupulous, widespread **11** down-the-line, painstaking, unmitigated, unqualified **12** all-embracing, all-inclusive **13** comprehensive, conscientious, thoroughgoing

**thoroughbred**
**07** blooded, pur sang **08** pedigree, pure-bred **09** pedigreed, pure-blood **11** full-blooded, pure-blooded **12** high-spirited

**thoroughfare**
**03** way **04** road **05** corso **06** access, avenue, street **07** highway, passage, roadway **08** broadway, motorway, turnpike **09** boulevard, concourse **10** passageway **12** king's highway

**thoroughgoing**
**04** deep, full, pure **05** sheer, total, utter **06** entire, strict **07** careful, in-depth, perfect **08** absolute, complete, deep-dyed, outright, rigorous, sweeping **09** downright, extensive, intensive, out-and-out **10** exhaustive, methodical, meticulous, scrupulous, widespread **11** painstaking, unmitigated, unqualified **12** all-embracing, all-inclusive **13** comprehensive **14** uncompromising

**thoroughly**
**02** up **03** out **04** well **05** à fond, fully, good-o, quite **06** good-oh, mortal **07** soundly, totally, utterly **08** entirely, even-down **09** carefully, downright, every inch, inside out, perfectly, throughly **10** absolutely, completely, sweepingly **11** assiduously, back to front, efficiently, intensively **12** exhaustively, meticulously, scrupulously, well and truly **13** painstakingly, root and branch **15** comprehensively, conscientiously

**those**
**03** tho **04** thae, them, they

**though**
**02** if **03** but, yet **05** still, while **06** even if, even so **07** granted, however **08** allowing, although **09** admitting **10** all the same, for all that **11** nonetheless **12** nevertheless **15** notwithstanding

**thought**
**03** aim **04** care, heed, hint, hope, idea, idée, mind, muse, plan, view **05** dream, fancy, grief, study, think, touch, trace **06** belief, design, musing, notion, pensée, reason, regard, theory **07** anxiety, conceit, concept, concern, feeling, gesture, opinion, purpose **08** judgment, kindness, prospect, scrutiny, sympathy, thinking **09** appraisal, attention, intention, judgement, pondering, reasoning **10** aspiration, assessment, cogitation, compassion, conception, conclusion, conviction, estimation, meditation, reflection, resolution, rumination, solicitude, tenderness **11** cerebration, expectation, point of view **12** anticipation, deliberation **13** consciousness, consideration, contemplation, introspection **14** thoughtfulness **15** considerateness

**thoughtful**
**04** deep, kind, wary **05** quiet **06** caring, dreamy, solemn, tender **07** careful, heedful, helpful, mindful, pensive, prudent, serious, wistful **08** absorbed, cautious, profound, sobering, studious, thinking **09** attentive, unselfish **10** abstracted, cogitative, conceitful, methodical, pensieroso, reflective, solicitous **11** considerate, sympathetic **13** compassionate, considerative, contemplative, in a brown study, introspective, lost in thought

**thoughtfully**
**06** deeply **07** quietly **08** dreamily **09** carefully, helpfully, mindfully, pensively, seriously, wistfully **10** cautiously, profoundly **11** unselfishly **12** methodically, reflectively **13** considerately **15** compassionately, contemplatively, introspectively, sympathetically

**thoughtless**
**04** rash, rude, vain **05** hasty, silly **06** remiss, stupid, unkind, unwise **07** étourdi, foolish, selfish **08** carefree, careless, étourdie, heedless, impolite, mindless, reckless, tactless, uncaring **09** blindfold, frivolous, imprudent, negligent, unfeeling **10** ill-advised, incogitant, indiscreet, unthinking, unweighing **11** giddy-headed, improvident, inattentive, insensitive, light-headed, precipitate **12** absent-minded, undiplomatic **13** ill-considered, inconsiderate

**thoughtlessly**
**06** rashly, rudely **08** stupidly **09** foolishly **10** carelessly, impolitely, recklessly, tactlessly **11** unfeelingly **12** indiscreetly **13** inattentively, insensitively **15** inconsiderately

**thousand**
**01** G, K, M **04** thou **05** grand, mille **07** chiliad **09** millenary

**thrall**
**04** grip, serf **05** hands, power, slave

**07** bondage, control, enslave, serfdom, slavery **08** clutches, enslaved, thraldom **09** servitude, vassalage **10** subjection **11** enslavement, subjugation

**thrash**
**02** do **03** hit, lam, pay, tan **04** beat, belt, cane, drub, flog, jerk, lace, lash, lick, rout, rush, sock, tank, toss, trim, whap, whip, whop **05** bless, cream, crush, dress, flail, party, paste, pound, quilt, smoke, spank, swish, targe, towel, whack, whale **06** beat up, defeat, donder, hammer, larrup, lather, punish, raddle, thresh, wallop, writhe **07** clobber, lambast, lay into, leather, scourge, swaddle, trounce **08** beat up on, demolish, lambaste, vanquish, work over **09** dress down, horsewhip, marmelize, overwhelm, pulverize, slaughter, surcingle **11** walk all over **13** have the edge on

• **thrash out**
**06** debate, settle **07** discuss, hash out, resolve **09** hammer out, negotiate **11** clear the air

**thrashing**
**04** rout **05** doing, laldy **06** caning, defeat, hiding, laldie, wiping **07** beating, belting, lamming, lashing, licking, pasting, tanking, tanning, whaling **08** crushing, dressing, drubbing, flogging, quilting, strap-oil, whacking, whipping, whopping **09** hammering, strapping, towelling, trouncing, walloping **10** clobbering, leathering, punishment **12** chastisement, dressing-down

**thread**
**03** end **04** ease, inch, line, move, pass, plot, push, silk, wind, yarn **05** braid, drift, fibre, Lurex®, motif, seton, shoot, strip, tenor, theme, thrid, thrum, twine, twist, weave **06** course, lingel, lingle, needle, strand, streak, string, suture **07** meander, subject, worsted **08** filament **09** direction, storyline **14** train of thought

**threadbare**
**03** old **04** bare, poor, worn **05** corny, stale, stock, tatty, tired, trite **06** frayed, meagre, ragged, shabby **07** napless, scruffy, worn-out **08** overused, overworn, tattered, well-worn **09** hackneyed, moth-eaten **11** commonplace, stereotyped **12** cliché-ridden

**threat**
**04** omen, risk **05** peril, stick **06** danger, hazard, menace **07** portent, presage, war drum, warning **08** big stick **09** blackmail, ultimatum **10** foreboding **11** commination **12** brutum fulmen, denunciation **14** enemy at the door

**threaten**
**03** cow, vow **04** burn, loom, mint, warn **05** augur, bully, flank, shore **06** extort, impend, lean on, loom up, menace, scorch **07** imperil, portend, presage, scowder, warn off **08** approach, browbeat, endanger, forebode, hang over, look like, scouther, scowther **09** blackmail, comminate, terrorize **10** be imminent, foreshadow, intimidate, jeopardize, pressurize, push around **11** lift a hand to **13** be in the offing **14** lift your hand to, put the screws on

**threatening**
**04** grim, ugly **05** lurid, nasty, shore **07** bravado, looming, ominous, warning **08** frowning, imminent, menacing, minatory, sinister **09** impending, minacious **10** broodiness, cautionary, forbidding, foreboding **11** commination, comminative **12** denunciatory, inauspicious, intimidatory

• **threatening character**
**04** omen

**three**
**03** III, ter-, tri- **04** tern, tray, trey, trio **05** leash, prial, triad **06** parial **07** pairial, triplet **09** pair-royal

• **Three Wise Men** *see* **wise man** *under* **wise**

**threesome**
**04** trio **05** triad **06** triple, triune, troika **07** trilogy, trinity, triplet **08** triptych **11** triumvirate

**thresh**
**03** hit **04** flog, jerk, rush, toss **05** flail, swish **06** thrash, writhe

**threshold**
**04** cill, dawn, door, sill **05** brink, entry, limen, start, verge **06** outset **07** doorway, opening **08** door-sill, doorstep, entrance **09** beginning, inception **12** commencement **13** starting-point

**thrice** *see* **three**

**thrift**
**04** gain **06** saving **07** economy, savings, sea pink **08** prudence, sea grass **09** frugality, husbandry, parsimony **10** prosperity, providence **11** carefulness **12** conservation **14** sea gillyflower

**thriftless**
**06** lavish **08** prodigal, wasteful **09** imprudent, unthrifty **10** profligate **11** dissipative, extravagant, improvident, spendthrift

**thrifty**
**04** wary **05** fendy **06** frugal, saving **07** careful, prudent, sparing **09** husbandly, provident **10** conserving, economical, prosperous **12** parsimonious

**thrill**
**03** gas, joy **04** bang, buzz, dirl, glow, kick, move, stir **05** flush, pulse, rouse, shake, thirl, throb **06** arouse, charge, dindle, dinnle, excite, pierce, quiver, shiver, tingle, tremor **07** delight, feeling, flutter, frisson, pulsate, shudder, tremble, vibrate **08** pleasure **09** adventure, electrify, galvanize, sensation, stimulate, vibration **10** excitement, exhilarate, the shivers **11** give a buzz to, give a kick to, stimulation

**thrilling**
**07** quaking, rousing, shaking, vibrant **08** electric, exciting, gripping, riveting, stirring, tinglish **09** shivering, trembling, vibrating **10** rip-roaring, shuddering **11** hair-raising, sensational, stimulating **12** action-packed, electrifying, exhilarating, soul-stirring **13** heart-stirring

**thrive**
**02** do **04** boom, gain, grow, thee **05** bloom **06** come on, do well, profit **07** advance, blossom, burgeon, develop, prosper, succeed **08** flourish, increase **11** make headway **12** make progress

**thriving**
**04** well **07** booming, growing, healthy, wealthy **08** affluent, blooming **10** blossoming, burgeoning, developing, prosperous, successful **11** comfortable, flourishing

**throat**
**04** crag, craw **05** gorge, halse, hause, hawse **06** fauces, gullet **07** pharynx, swallow, trachea, weasand **08** prunella, thrapple, thropple, throttle, windpipe **10** oesophagus, the Red Lane

• **part of throat**
**04** gula

**throaty**
**03** low **04** deep **05** gruff, husky, thick **06** hoarse **07** rasping, raucous **08** croaking, guttural **12** full-throated

**throb**
◇ *anagram indicator*
**04** beat, drum, jump, pant, quop **05** pound, pulse, thump **06** stound, stownd, tingle **07** pulsate, vibrate **08** drumming, pounding, thumping **09** heartbeat, palpitate, pulsation, vibration **11** palpitation

**throe**
**03** fit **04** pain, pang, stab **05** agony, spasm, thraw **07** anguish, seizure, torture, travail **08** distress, paroxysm **09** deid-thraw, suffering **10** convulsion

• **in the throes of**
**08** busy with **12** in the midst of **13** in the middle of, wrestling with **14** in the process of, struggling with **15** preoccupied with

**thrombosis**
**03** DVT **08** apoplexy, coronary **09** blood clot **11** heart attack

**throne**
**03** see **04** gadi, seat **05** exalt, siege, stool **07** tribune **08** cathedra, enthrone, kingship, lavatory **09** mercy-seat **12** bed of justice
*See also* **toilet**

**throng**
**03** jam, mob **04** bevy, busy, cram, fill,

herd, host, mass, pack **05** bunch, crowd, crush, flock, horde, press, swarm **06** jostle, preace, prease, thrang **07** besiege, crowded, preasse **08** converge, crowding, intimate **09** multitude **10** assemblage, congregate, mill around **12** congregation, grex venalium

**throttle**
**03** gag, gun **05** check, choke, scrag **06** keep in, stifle **07** inhibit, silence, smother **08** hold back, restrain, strangle, suppress, thrapple, thropple, wiredraw **09** suffocate **10** asphyxiate **11** accelerator, strangulate

**through**
**02** by, in **03** per, tra-, via **04** done, yond, yont **05** among, clear, due to, ended, fully, using **06** across, direct, during **07** between, by way of, clear of, express, non-stop, owing to, totally **08** entirely, finished, thanks to **09** because of, by means of, completed, connected, throughly **10** by virtue of, completely, terminated, thoroughly, throughout, to the end of **11** as a result of, on account of **12** continuously **13** until the end of, with the help of **15** all the way across, uninterruptedly, without a break in

• **through and through**
**05** fully **06** wholly **07** totally, utterly **08** entirely, to pieces **09** to the core **10** altogether, completely, thoroughly **11** all to pieces **12** unreservedly **13** to the backbone **14** in every respect **15** from top to bottom

**throughout**
**04** over **05** along **06** during, widely **07** all over **08** all round **09** up and down **10** all through, completely, everywhere, in all parts **11** extensively, in every part **12** in the whole of, ubiquitously **13** in every part of, in the course of

**throughput**
**05** yield **06** fruits, output, return **07** harvest, outturn, product, turnout **10** production **11** manufacture **12** productivity

**throw**
◇ *anagram indicator*
**02** go **03** hip, lob, peg, put, shy, wap **04** blow, bung, cast, dash, emit, faze, fell, flip, give, host, hurl, lose, puck, putt, scat, send, shed, shot, toss, turn, whap, whop, work, yerk **05** chuck, ditch, fling, floor, force, heave, lay on, pitch, put on, skatt, sling, spang, spasm, spill, upset, whang, while **06** baffle, bemuse, direct, launch, propel, purler, put out, rattle, unseat, upcast, wheech, wuther **07** arrange, confuse, disturb, execute, give off, operate, perform, perplex, produce, project, radiate, unhorse, whither **08** astonish, catapult, confound, dislodge, jaculate, occasion, organize, overturn, paroxysm, surprise, switch on, unsaddle **09** bring down, discomfit, dumbfound, prostrate **10** disconcert **11** cause to fall, move quickly

*See also* **wrestling**

• **throw away**
**04** blow, dump, lose **05** ditch, scrap, waste **06** reject **07** discard **08** chuck out, get rid of, jettison, squander, throw out **09** chuck away, dispose of **11** fritter away **12** dispense with

• **throw headlong**
**04** purl

• **throw off**
**04** cast, drop, shed **05** elude **06** divest **07** abandon, cast off, discard, discuss **08** get rid of, jettison, shake off **10** escape from

• **throw out**
**04** cast, dump, emit **05** ditch, eject, evict, expel, exude, fling, scrap **06** reject, unseat **07** bring up, diffuse, discard, dismiss, emanate, give off, mention, produce, project, radiate, refer to, send out, turf out, turn out **08** distance, distract, jettison, point out, turn down **09** introduce, throw away **10** disconcert, speak about **12** dispense with

• **throw over**
**04** drop, jilt, quit **05** chuck, leave **06** desert, reject **07** abandon, discard, forsake **10** finish with

• **throw up**
**03** gag **04** barf, jack, puke, quit, spew, toss **05** heave, leave, retch, vomit **06** cast up, give up, jack in, pack in, resign, reveal, sick up **07** abandon, bring up, chuck in, chuck up, chunder, fetch up, upchuck **08** disgorge, renounce **10** relinquish **11** regurgitate

**throwaway**
**05** cheap **06** casual **07** offhand, passing **08** careless **10** disposable, expendable, undramatic, unemphatic **13** biodegradable, non-returnable

**throwback**
**06** return **07** setback **09** reversion **10** taking back **11** restoration **13** reinstatement, retrogression

**thrush**
**04** chat **05** mavis, sprue, veery **06** missel, sylvia, Turdus **07** antbird, redwing, wagtail **08** throstle **09** fieldfare, olive-back, ring ouzel, solitaire, stormcock **10** bush-shrike, missel-bird **12** throstle-cock

**thrust**
**03** dig, jab, jam, pop, put, ram, ren, rin, run **04** bear, butt, chop, dash, foin, gist, poke, pote, prod, prog, push, rash, side, sock, stab, stap, stop, tilt, urge **05** crowd, drift, drive, foist, force, impel, lunge, pitch, poach, point, power, press, shove, stick, stuck, tenor, theme, wedge **06** burden, impose, motive, muscle, muzzle, pierce, plunge, potche, propel, saddle, thirst **07** aventre, essence, impetus, impulse, inflict, intrude, message, thrutch **08** encumber, momentum, pressure, protrude **09** have-at-him, penetrate, substance **10** imbroccata **11** pertinacity **13** determination

**thrustplane**
**04** sole

**thud**
**04** bang, bash, beat, dump, plod, wham **05** clonk, clump, clunk, crash, flump, knock, smack, thump **06** bounce, wallop **07** thunder

**thug**
**04** goon **05** rough, tough, yobbo **06** bandit, goonda, killer, mugger, robber, thuggo, tsotsi **07** cosh boy, gorilla, hoodlum, ruffian, villain **08** assassin, gangster, hooligan, murderer, plug-ugly **09** cut-throat, phansigar, roughneck

**thuggery**
**05** abuse **06** murder **07** killing **08** atrocity, butchery, foul play, violence **09** brutality, vandalism **10** inhumanity **11** hooliganism, viciousness

**thulium**
**02** Tm

**thumb**
**04** inch **06** pollex

• **thumb through**
**04** scan, skim **06** peruse **08** glance at **11** flip through, leaf through **12** flick through **13** browse through

**thumbnail**
**05** brief, pithy, quick, short, small **07** compact, concise **08** succinct **09** miniature

**thumbs-down**
**02** no **06** rebuff **07** refusal **08** negation, turn down **09** rejection **11** disapproval

**thumbs-up**
**02** OK **03** yes **07** go-ahead **08** approval, sanction **10** acceptance, green light **11** affirmation **13** encouragement

**thump**
**03** box, cob, dad, dod, hit, rap **04** bang, beat, blow, bonk, bump, cuff, daud, dawd, ding, dong, dump, dunt, paik, slap, thud, tund, whap, whop **05** clout, clunk, crash, knock, pound, punch, smack, souse, throb, whack **06** batter, hammer, pummel, strike, thrash, thwack, wallop **07** bethump, pulsate, trounce **09** palpitate

**thumping**
**03** big **04** huge, mega, very **05** great **06** highly, really, severe **07** extreme, greatly, immense, intense, mammoth, massive, titanic **08** colossal, enormous, gigantic, severely, terrific, towering, whopping **09** excessive, extremely, intensely, seriously, swingeing, unusually **10** exorbitant, gargantuan, impressive, monumental, remarkably, thundering, tremendous **12** tremendously

**thunder**
**03** cry **04** bang, bawl, boom, clap, howl, peal, roar, roll, yell **05** blast, crack, crash, shout **06** bellow, holler, rumble, scream, shriek **07** clamour, foulder, resound **08** crashing, intonate, outburst **09** explosion, fulminate, upthunder **11** reverberate **13** reverberation **14** raise your voice

**thundering**
**04** very **05** great **06** really, tonant **07** greatly **08** enormous, severely **09** excessive, extremely, intensely, unusually **10** altitonant, foudroyant, monumental, remarkable, tremendous **11** unmitigated

**thunderous**
**04** loud **05** noisy **07** booming, roaring **08** rumbling **09** deafening **10** resounding, tumultuous **12** ear-splitting **13** reverberating

**thunderstruck**
**05** agape, dazed **06** aghast, amazed **07** floored, shocked, stunned **09** astounded, flummoxed, paralysed, petrified, staggered **10** astonished, bowled over, nonplussed **11** dumbfounded, open-mouthed **12** wonder-struck **13** flabbergasted, knocked for six **14** wonder-stricken

**Thursday**
**02** Th **03** Thu **04** Thur **05** Thurs

**thus**
**02** so **04** ergo, then **05** hence **08** like this **09** as follows, in this way, therefore **11** accordingly **12** consequently, frankincense
• **thus far**
**05** so far **07** up to now **08** until now **09** up till now **13** up to this point **14** up to the present

**thwack**
**03** hit **04** bash, beat, blow, cuff, flog, slap **05** clout, smack, thump, whack **06** buffet, strike, wallop

**thwart**
**03** pip **04** balk, foil, stop **05** baulk, block, check, crimp, cross, spite, stimy, thraw **06** across, baffle, banjax, defeat, hamper, hinder, hogtie, impede, nobble, oppose, stimie, stymie **07** adverse, athwart, pre-empt, prevent, snooker, stonker **08** conflict, obstruct, perverse, traverse **09** crosswise, forestall, frustrate, hindrance **10** transverse **11** frustration **12** cross-grained **13** put the skids on

**tic**
**04** jerk **05** spasm **06** twitch **13** tic douloureux

**tick**
**02** mo **03** dot, jar, pat, sec, tap **04** beat, line, mark, tock, work, worm **05** check, click, flash, jiffy, tally, trice, trust **06** choose, credit, minute, moment, second, select, stroke, whimsy **07** instant **08** indicate, tick-tock **09** twinkling **10** crib-biting
• **tick off**
**04** mark, pick **05** check, chide, prick, scold **06** bounce, carpet, rebuke, see off, select **07** bawl out, catch it, chew out, reprove, rollick, rouse on, tell off, upbraid **08** call down, check off, indicate, reproach **09** dress down, go crook at, go crook on, pull apart, reprimand, take apart **10** go to town on **13** tear off a strip **14** throw the book at **15** give someone hell, put a tick against

**ticker**
**05** clock, heart, watch **08** examiner

**ticket**
**03** tag **04** card, pass, slip, stub **05** carte, check, label, token **06** ballot, coupon, docket, permit, return **07** licence, sticker, voucher, warrant **09** pass-check **11** certificate, counterfoil **12** lunch voucher **13** authorization **15** luncheon voucher
• **ticket seller**
**04** tout

**tickle**
**04** beat, nice **05** amuse, touch **06** divert, excite, kittle, please, stroke, thrill, tingle **07** delight, gratify, perplex **08** insecure, interest, ticklish, unstable **09** entertain, stimulate, titillate

**ticklish**
**04** nice **05** dodgy, risky **06** kittly, knotty, subtle, thorny, touchy, tricky **07** awkward, trickle **08** critical, delicate, unchancy, unstable **09** difficult, hazardous, sensitive **10** precarious **11** problematic

**tiddly** *see* **drunk**

**tide**
**03** ebb, ren, rin, run, sea **04** flow, flux, neap, tied, time **05** drift, flood, tenor, trend, water **06** course, happen, season, spring, stream **07** current **08** festival, movement, sea-water, tendency **09** direction **10** rising tide **11** opportunity
• **sudden rise of tide**
**04** bore, eger **05** eagre
• **tide over**
**03** aid **04** help **06** assist **07** help out, sustain **09** keep going **10** see through **11** help through

**tidily**
**06** just so, neatly **07** in order, in place, orderly, smartly **12** immaculately, methodically **14** systematically

**tidings**
**03** gen **04** dope, news, word **06** advice, report **07** message **08** bulletin **09** greetings **11** information **12** intelligence **13** communication

**tidy**
◇ *anagram indicator*
**02** do **03** red **04** fair, good, neat, redd, trim **05** ample, clean, groom, kempt, large, order, plump, primp, slick, smart, spick **06** comely, fettle, neaten, redd up, spruce **07** arrange, band-box, brush up, clean up, clear up, in order, ordered, orderly, shapely, sizable, smarten, tiddley **08** clear out, generous, sizeable, spruce up, well-kept **09** declutter, efficient, organized, shipshape **10** immaculate, methodical, seasonable, square away, straighten, systematic **11** respectable, substantial, uncluttered, well-groomed, well-ordered **12** businesslike, considerable, spick-and-span, straighten up **13** clear the decks, straighten out

**tie**
**03** fix **04** band, bind, bond, clip, curb, draw, duty, join, knot, lace, lash, link, moor, rope, tape **05** chain, cramp, limit, strap, unite **06** attach, be even, copula, couple, fasten, hamper, hinder, impede, oblige, ribbon, secure, tether **07** be equal, confine, confirm, connect, kinship, liaison, necktie, shackle **08** dead heat, deadlock, ligature, restrain, restrict **09** constrain, fastening, hindrance, restraint, stalemate **10** allegiance, commitment, connection, constraint, friendship, limitation, obligation **11** affiliation, be all square, restriction **12** relationship **13** be neck and neck

*Ties include:*

**03** bow
**04** bolo, neck
**05** ascot, dicky, stock
**06** clip-on, cravat, dickey, dickie, kipper, string
**07** overlay, owrelay, soubise
**08** bootlace, kerchief
**09** neckcloth, solitaire, steenkirk, waterfall
**10** tawdry lace
**11** neckerchief

• **tie down**
**03** fix **05** limit **06** hamper, hinder **07** confine **08** restrain, restrict **09** constrain
• **tied up**
**04** busy
• **tie in with**
**08** relate to **09** agree with, fit in with **13** correlate with **15** be connected with
• **tie together**
**04** knit **05** fagot **06** faggot
• **tie up**
**04** bind, do up, lash, moor, rope, seal **05** cable, chain, truss **06** attach, bail up, commit, engage, fasten, invest, ligate, occupy, secure, settle, string, tether, wind up, wrap up **07** connect, engross, Gordian, reserve **08** conclude, finalize, keep busy, restrain **09** terminate **11** spread-eagle **15** make unavailable

**tie-in**
**04** link **05** tie-up **06** hook-up **07** liaison **08** relation **10** connection **11** affiliation, association **12** co-ordination, relationship

**tier**
**03** row **04** band, bank, belt, deck, line, rank, tire, zone **05** floor, layer, level, stage, story **06** gradin, storey

**07** echelon, gradine, stratum **09** bleachers

## tie-up

**04** bond, link **05** tie-in **07** analogy, mooring **08** alliance, parallel, relation **09** reference **10** connection, stand-still **11** association, correlation **12** entanglement, relationship **13** interrelation **14** correspondence

## tiff

**03** pet, row, sip **04** dram, huff, miff, sour, spat, sulk **05** dress, drink, lunch, scrap, set-to, stale, words **06** barney, dust-up, temper **07** dispute, quarrel, tantrum **08** squabble, trick out **09** ill-humour **10** difference, falling-out **12** disagreement

## tiger

**04** puma **06** jaguar **07** leopard, stripes **08** man-eater **11** Machaerodus, Machairodus

## tight

◇ *anagram indicator*

**04** even, fast, firm, hard, mean, near, neat, pang, snug, taut, trig, trim **05** close, dodgy, drunk, fixed, harsh, merry, rigid, stiff, tense, tipsy, tough **06** at once, narrow, scanty, scarce, sealed, secure, severe, stingy, stoned, strict, tiddly, tricky **07** awkward, compact, concise, cramped, legless, limited, miserly, precise, sloshed, smashed, soundly, sozzled **08** airtight, clenched, delicate, hermetic, promptly, rigorous, strained, tanked up **09** competent, dangerous, difficult, niggardly, not enough, plastered, skin-tight, stretched, stringent, too little, well-oiled **10** compressed, hard-fought, impervious, inadequate, inflexible, restricted, soundproof, watertight **11** constricted, intoxicated, neck and neck, problematic, tight-fisted, well-matched **12** close-fitting, impenetrable, insufficient, parsimonious **13** evenly matched, figure-hugging, in short supply, penny-pinching

## tighten

**03** fix **04** swig **05** brace, cinch, close, cramp, crush, screw, swift, tense **06** beef up, fasten, firm up, narrow, pull up, secure, strait, take in, tauten, wind up **07** squeeze, stiffen, stretch **08** heighten, increase, make fast, restrain, rigidify, straiten **09** constrict, pull tight, toughen up **10** constringe, strengthen **12** make stricter

## tight-fisted

**04** mean **05** mingy, tight **06** stingy **07** miserly, sparing **08** grasping **09** niggardly **10** fast-handed **12** parsimonious **13** penny-pinching

## tight-lipped

**03** mum **04** mute **05** quiet **06** silent **08** reserved, reticent, taciturn **09** secretive **11** close-lipped **12** close-mouthed **13** unforthcoming **15** uncommunicative

## till

**02** to **03** dig, ear, ere, set **04** EPOS, farm, up to, work **05** peter, shale, until **06** plough **07** cash box, through, towards **08** checkout, rotavate, rotovate **09** cultivate **10** all through, cash drawer **11** boulder clay **12** cash register **13** up to the time of

## tilt

**03** hut, tip **04** bank, cant, cock, duel, heel, just, kant, lean, list, peak, ride, rock, rush, spar, tent, toss, trip **05** angle, clash, cover, fight, joust, pitch, slant, slope **06** attack, awning, camber, careen, charge, combat, jostle, justle, thrust **07** contend, contest, dispute, incline **08** attitude, heel over, tilt yard **09** encounter, pas d'armes **10** tournament **11** inclination

### • at full tilt

**06** all out **07** flat out **08** very fast **10** at full pelt, at top speed **11** at full blast, at full speed, very quickly **13** with full force

## timber

**03** log, rib **04** balk, beam, lath, pole, rung, spar, tree, wale, wood **05** baulk, board, build, karri, maple, plank, trees **06** forest, lumber, wooden **07** bunting, chesnut, templet **08** chestnut, stumpage, template, woodland **09** beechwood, sapodilla, unmusical **10** afrormosia, swing-stock **11** palmyra wood

*See also* **tree**; **wood**

### • measurement of timber *see* measurement of wood *under* wood

### • timber carrier

**04** gill, jill

## timbre

**04** ring, tone **05** clang, color, klang, sound **06** colour, tamber **07** quality **08** tonality **09** resonance **10** klangfarbe, tone colour **12** voice quality

## time

**01** t **03** fix, set **04** aeon, beat, date, life, mora, peak, sith, span, term, tide **05** clock, count, meter, metre, point, space, spell, stage, tempo, while **06** adjust, heyday, rhythm **07** arrange, control, measure, session, stretch **08** duration, instance, interval, juncture, lifespan, occasion, regulate, schedule **09** calculate, programme, timetable **15** fourth dimension

*Times and periods of time include:*

**02** am, pm
**03** age, day, eon, era, min
**04** dawn, dusk, fall, hour, morn, noon, week, year
**05** epoch, month, night, sun-up, today
**06** autumn, decade, midday, minute, moment, morrow, period, season, second, spring, summer, sunset, winter
**07** bedtime, century, chiliad, daytime, evening, instant, midweek, morning, quarter, sunrise, teatime, tonight, weekday, weekend
**08** eternity, high noon, lifetime, tomorrow, twilight
**09** afternoon, decennium, fortnight, light-year, midsummer, nightfall, night-time
**10** generation, millennium, nanosecond, yesteryear
**11** long-weekend, microsecond, millisecond
**12** quinquennium
**13** the early hours, wee small hours

*Time zones include:*

**02** AT, CT, ET, MT, PT
**03** AST, BST, CET, CST, EET, EST, GMT, HST, MST, PST, WET
**04** AKST, CYST, HAST, WAST, WEST
**08** zulu time
**10** Alaska Time
**11** Central Time, Eastern Time, Pacific Time
**12** Atlantic Time, Mountain Time
**13** Greenwich Time

*See also* **geology**

### • after expected time

**04** late

### • ahead of time

**05** ahead, early **06** sooner **07** earlier, in front, up front **09** in advance **10** beforehand, previously

### • ahead of your time

**03** new **05** novel **07** radical **10** avant-garde, innovative **11** progressive **12** experimental **13** revolutionary

### • all the time

**05** among **06** always **07** forever, nonstop **08** all along **10** constantly **11** continually, incessantly, perpetually **12** continuously, interminably **15** twenty-four-seven

### • at all times

**03** e'er **04** ever **12** early and late

### • at any time

**03** e'er **04** ever, once, onst **07** anytime

### • at one time

**04** once **07** long ago **08** formerly **10** at one point, previously **11** in times past **14** simultaneously

### • at the proper time

**04** duly

### • at the right time

**03** pat

### • at the same time

**03** but, yet **04** then **05** still **06** anyway, at once, even so **07** however **08** meantime, together **09** meanwhile **10** for all that, in parallel **11** all together, nonetheless **12** concurrently, nevertheless **14** simultaneously **15** in the same breath, notwithstanding

### • at times

**06** whiles **08** off and on, on and off **09** sometimes **10** now and then **11** now and again, on occasions **12** every so often, occasionally **14** from time to time

### • behind the times

**03** old **04** past **05** dated **06** old hat **08** obsolete **09** out of date **10** fuddy-duddy, oldfangled **11** god-forsaken **12** god-forgotten, old-fashioned, out of fashion **13** unfashionable

**• behind time**
**04** late **05** tardy **06** behind **07** delayed, overdue **10** unpunctual **14** behind schedule
**• brief space of time**
**02** mo **03** bit, sec, wee
**• common time**
**01** C
**• fit time**
**03** tid
**• former times**
**03** eld **04** yore
**• for the time being**
**06** for now, pro tem **07** just now **08** meantime, right now **09** at present, meanwhile, presently **10** pro tempore **11** at the moment, temporarily **12** for the moment **13** for the present, in the meantime
**• from time to time**
**07** at times **09** sometimes **10** now and then, on occasion **11** ever and anon, now and again, still and end **12** every so often, occasionally, once in a while, periodically, sporadically, still and anon **13** spasmodically **14** intermittently **15** every now and then
**• in good time**
**05** early **06** indeed, on time, timely, timous **07** betimes, timeous **08** timously **09** timeously **10** punctually **11** ahead of time **14** bright and early **15** ahead of schedule, with time to spare
**• in time**
**06** on time **10** eventually, not too late, punctually **11** early enough
**• on time**
**05** sharp **06** bang on, dead on, spot on, spot-on **07** exactly **08** on the dot, promptly, punctual **09** precisely **10** on schedule, punctually
**• opportune time**
**04** seal, seel, seil, sele
**• play for time**
**05** delay, stall **08** hang fire, hesitate **09** stonewall, temporize **10** filibuster **12** drag your feet **13** procrastinate
**• taking extra time**
**04** lean
**• time after time**
**05** often **09** many times **10** frequently, repeatedly **11** recurrently **12** time and again **13** again and again **15** on many occasions

**time-honoured**
**03** old **05** fixed, usual **06** age-old **07** ancient **08** historic **09** customary, venerable **10** accustomed **11** established, traditional **12** conventional **15** long-established

**timeless**
**07** abiding, ageless, endless, eternal, lasting **08** enduring, ill-timed, immortal, unending, untimely **09** deathless, immutable, permanent, premature **10** changeless, unchanging **11** everlasting **12** imperishable **14** indestructible

**timely**
**04** soon **05** early **06** prompt **08** punctual, suitable, temporal **09** opportune, well-timed **10** convenient, felicitous, propitious, seasonable, tempestive **11** appropriate **14** at the right time

**times**
**01** X

**timetable**
**03** fix, set **04** list, rota **05** diary, set up **06** agenda, roster **07** arrange, diarize, listing **08** calendar, schedule **09** programme **10** curriculum

**time-worn**
**03** old **04** aged, worn **05** dated, hoary, lined, passé, rusty, stale, stock, tired, trite **06** ragged, ruined, shabby **07** ancient, cliché'd, outworn, run-down, worn out **08** bromidic, clichéed, decrepit, dog-eared, well-worn, wrinkled **09** hackneyed, out of date, weathered **10** broken-down, threadbare

**timid**
**03** shy **05** cissy, pavid, wimpy **06** afraid, modest, mousey, scared, yellow **07** bashful, chicken, fearful, gutless, nervous, wimpish **08** cowardly, retiring, timorous **09** shrinking, spineless **10** frightened, hen-hearted, irresolute, meticulous **11** lily-livered **12** apprehensive, faint-hearted **13** pigeon-hearted, pusillanimous **14** chicken-hearted, chicken-livered

**timidity**
**04** fear **07** shyness **09** cowardice **11** bashfulness, fearfulness **13** pusillanimity

**timorous**
**03** coy, shy **04** eery **05** aspen, eerie, mousy, scary, timid **06** afraid, aspine, modest, mousey, scared, scarey **07** bashful, fearful, meacock, nervous **08** cowardly, retiring **09** diffident, shrinking, tentative, trembling, tremulous **10** frightened, irresolute **12** apprehensive, faint-hearted **13** pusillanimous, unadventurous

**tin**
**02** Sn **03** can **05** money **06** paltry **09** argentine, Dutch oven
*See also* **money**

**tincture**
**02** or **03** dye, fur, hue, Sol **04** bufo, dash, hint, tint **05** aroma, imbue, metal, scent, shade, smack, spice, stain, tinge, touch, trace **06** arnica, colour, elixir, infuse, season, smatch **07** flavour, sericon, suffuse **08** laudanum, permeate **09** seasoning **10** suggestion **12** friar's balsam

**tine**
**03** bay, bez **04** lose, shut, snag, tare, teen, tiny, tray, trey, trez **05** point, prong, royal, spike, spire **06** kindle, perish **07** bay-tine, enclose **08** brow-tine, surroyal, trey-tine **09** bay-antler **10** affliction, brow-antler, trey-antler **11** crown antler

**tinge**
**03** bit, dye, eye **04** cast, dash, drop, hint, tang, tint, wash **05** imbue, pinch, shade, smack, stain, taint, tinct, touch, trace **06** colour **07** flavour, suffuse **08** encolour, tincture **09** encrimson **10** smattering, sprinkling, suggestion

**tingle**
**04** glow, itch, ring **05** prick, sting, thirl, throb **06** dindle, dinnle, quiver, shiver, thrill, tickle, tinkle, tremor **07** itching, prickle, tremble, vibrate **08** stinging, tickling **09** prickling **10** gooseflesh **12** goosepimples **14** pins and needles

**tingling**
**04** dirl **05** sting **06** dindle, dinnle **07** prickly

**tinker**
**03** toy **04** play, prig, tink **05** caird, fixer, Gypsy **06** dabble, fiddle, hawker, meddle, mender, pedlar, potter, rascal, repair, tamper, trifle **07** botcher, bungler, didakai, didakei, didicoi, didicoy, tinkler **08** diddicoy **09** fool about, itinerant, mess about **10** fool around, mess around

**tinkle**
**04** bell, buzz, call, ding, peal, ring **05** chime, chink, clink **06** jangle, jingle, tingle **07** urinate **09** phone call

**tinny**
**04** thin **05** cheap, harsh, lucky **06** flimsy, jingly **07** jarring **08** jangling, metallic **09** cheapjack **11** high-pitched, poor-quality **13** insubstantial

**tinpot**
**03** bad **04** poor, ropy **05** awful, ropey **06** crummy, paltry, shoddy **07** useless **08** inferior, mediocre, pathetic, rubbishy, slipshod **09** defective, imperfect **10** low-quality, second-rate **11** incompetent, substandard **13** insignificant **14** unsatisfactory

**tinsel**
**04** loss, sham, show **05** cheap, gaudy, showy **06** flashy, tawdry, trashy **07** display, glitter, spangle **08** frippery, gimcrack, specious **09** clinquant, gaudiness **10** garishness, pretension, triviality **11** flamboyance, ostentation, superficial **12** meretricious, ostentatious **13** artificiality, worthlessness **14** insignificance **15** meaninglessness

**tint**
**03** dye, hew, hue **04** cast, tone, wash **05** color, rinse, shade, stain, taint, tinct, tinge, touch, trace **06** affect, colour, streak **08** tincture

**tinware**
**04** tole

**tiny**
**03** wee **04** mini **05** diddy, small, teeny, weeny **06** little, midget, minute, petite, pocket, slight, teensy **08** dwarfish, trifling **09** itsy-bitsy, itty-bitty, miniature, minuscule, pint-sized **10** diminutive, fractional, negligible,

teeny-weeny **11** Lilliputian, microscopic **13** infinitesimal, insignificant **14** circumstantial

**tip**

◇ *head selection indicator*

**03** cap, end, nap, nib, tap, top **04** acme, apex, bung, cant, clue, dump, gift, give, hand, head, hint, horn, lean, list, noop, pass, peak, perk, pour, tell, tilt, toom, toss, vail, warn **05** bonus, crown, dodge, empty, point, pouch, shoot, slant, spill, trick, upset, vales **06** advice, advise, convey, gryfon, inform, midden, reward, summit, tip off, tip-off, topple, unload **07** capsize, caution, cumshaw, douceur, griffin, griffon, gryphon, incline, pointer, pour out, present, propine, slender, staithe, suggest, warning, wrinkle **08** bonamano, forecast, forewarn, gratuity, overturn, pinnacle, slag heap, surmount **09** backshish, bakhshish, baksheesh, buonamano, extremity, pourboire **10** backsheesh, perquisite, refuse-heap, remunerate, suggestion, topple over **11** information, rubbish-heap **13** gratification **14** recommendation

**tip-off**

◇ *head deletion indicator*

**04** clue, hint, wire **07** pointer, warning **10** suggestion **11** information

**tipple**

**03** bib, pot **04** down, dram, swig **05** booze, drink, paint, quaff, usual **06** imbibe, liquor, poison **07** alcohol, indulge **09** knock back **12** regular drink **14** favourite drink

**tippler**

**03** sot **04** lush, soak, wino **05** alkie, dipso, drunk, toper **06** bibber, boozer, sponge **07** drinker, tosspot, winebag **08** drunkard, maltworm **09** inebriate **11** dipsomaniac, hard drinker

**tipsy**

◇ *anagram indicator*

**03** wet **04** awry **05** askew, bosky, drunk, happy, lushy, merry, moony, muzzy, nappy, oiled, rocky, tight, totty, woozy **06** mellow, screwy, slewed, sprung, squiff, tiddly **07** a pip out, screwed, squiffy, tiddled **08** cockeyed, glorious, pleasant, top-heavy **09** a peepe out, well-oiled **10** a peg too low **15** the worse for wear

**tirade**

**04** rant **05** abuse **06** laisse **07** lecture **08** diatribe, harangue, outburst **09** invective, monorhyme, philippic **11** fulmination **12** admonishment, denunciation

**tire**

**03** tax **04** bore, cook, drop, flag, tyre **05** drain, dress, sew up, train, use up, weary **06** attire, bejade, strain, tucker, volley **07** apparel, breathe, exhaust, fatigue, tire out, wear out **08** enervate, outweary, pinafore **09** broadside, equipment, furniture, headdress

**tired**

**03** old **04** beat, jack, sick **05** all in, blown, bored, corny, fed up, jaded, rough, stale, trite, weary **06** bushed, drowsy, pooped, sleepy, wabbit, zonked **07** cliché'd, drained, shagged, wappend, wearied, whacked, worn-out **08** clichéed, dead-beat, dog-tired, dog-weary, fatigate, fatigued, flagging, outspent **09** enervated, exhausted, fagged out, forjaskit, forjeskit, hackneyed, knackered, pooped out, shattered, washed-out **10** clapped-out, shagged out, war-wearied, world-weary **11** ready to drop, tuckered out **12** sick and tired, world-wearied

**tireless**

**08** diligent, resolute, untiring, vigorous **09** energetic, unwearied **10** determined, unflagging **11** industrious **13** indefatigable, inexhaustible

**tirelessly**

**10** diligently, resolutely, untiringly, vigorously **13** energetically, indefatigably

**tiresome**

**04** dull **05** weary **06** boring, gallus, tiring, trying **07** gallows, humdrum, irksome, routine, tedious **08** annoying **09** fatiguing, laborious, vexatious, wearisome **10** irritating, monotonous, prolixious, unexciting **11** troublesome **12** exasperating **13** uninteresting

**tiring**

**04** hard **05** stiff, tough **06** taxing **07** arduous **08** draining, exacting, wearying **09** demanding, difficult, fatiguing, laborious, strenuous, wearisome **10** enervating, exhausting

**tiro, tyro**

**05** pupil **06** novice **07** learner, starter, student, trainee **08** beginner, freshman, initiate, neophyte **09** greenhorn, novitiate **10** apprentice, catechumen, tenderfoot

**tissue**

**03** web **04** mesh, suet, tela **05** gauze, stuff, weave **06** fabric, matter **07** Kleenex®, network, texture **08** gossamer, material **09** structure, substance, variegate **10** aerenchyma, interweave, mesenchyme **11** toilet paper **12** facial tissue, sclerenchyma, toilet tissue

**titan**

**05** Atlas, giant **06** Helios **08** colossus, Hercules, Hyperion, superman **09** leviathan **10** Prometheus

**titanic**

**04** huge, vast **05** giant, jumbo **06** mighty **07** immense, mammoth, massive **08** colossal, enormous, gigantic, towering **09** cyclopean, herculean, monstrous **10** monumental, prodigious, stupendous **11** mountainous

**titanium**

**02** Ti

**titbit**

**05** scrap, snack, treat **06** dainty, morsel **08** delicacy **09** appetizer **11** bonne-bouche

**tit for tat**

**03** hat **06** in kind, titfer **07** revenge **08** reprisal, requital **10** quid pro quo **11** blow for blow, counterblow, counterbuff, lex talionis, like for like, retaliation **13** an eye for an eye, countercharge

**tithe**

**03** pay, tax **04** duty, give, levy, rate, rent, toll **05** disme, teind, tenth **06** assess, charge, impost, take in, tariff **07** tribute **08** decimate, hand over **10** assessment

**titillate**

**05** tease **06** arouse, excite, thrill, tickle, turn on **07** provoke **08** interest, intrigue **09** stimulate, tantalize

**titillating**

**04** lewd, sexy **05** lurid **06** erotic **07** naughty, teasing **08** arousing, exciting **09** seductive, thrilling **10** intriguing, suggestive **11** captivating, interesting, provocative, sensational, stimulating

**titivate**

**05** groom, preen, primp, prink **06** doll up, make up, tart up **07** touch up **09** refurbish, smarten up

**title**

**03** dub, tag **04** book, call, game, head, name, rank, term, work **05** claim, crown, deeds, label, match, prize, right, style **06** credit, eponym, handle, legend, office, stakes, status, trophy **07** caption, contest, credits, dukedom, entitle, epithet, heading, laurels **08** headline, monicker, nickname, position, subtitle **09** designate, honorific, ownership, privilege, pseudonym, sobriquet **10** nom-de-plume, soubriquet **11** appellation, competition, designation, entitlement, inscription, prerogative, publication **12** championship, denomination **13** form of address **14** proprietorship

*Titles include:*

**01** M, U
**02** Dr, Mr, Ms
**03** bey, Dan, Dom, Don, Mrs, Pir, Rav, Reb, Rex, san, Sir, Sri, Ven
**04** amir, Aunt, babu, bhai, Capt, Dame, Devi, Doña, emir, Frau, Herr, Imam, Lady, Lord, Ma'am, Miss, Prof, sama, Sant, Shri, tuan
**05** baboo, begum, ghazi, hodja, khoja, Madam, Mirza, molla, padre, pasha, Rebbe, Señor, Swami, Uncle
**06** Doctor, Father, khodja, kumari, Madame, Master, Mister, mollah, moolah, Mother, mullah, Regina, Señora, Signor, Sister, Tuanku
**07** Bahadur, Brother, Captain, Colonel,

effendi, esquire, Signior, Signora , Signore
08 Fräulein, Highness, memsahib, Mistress, Monsieur, Señorita, Viscount
09 Monsignor, Professor, Signorina, Signorino, Your Grace
10 burra sahib
11 Monseigneur, Your Majesty, Your Worship
12 Mademoiselle
15 Right Honourable

**titter**
04 mock, sway 05 laugh, te-hee
06 cackle, giggle, tee-hee, totter
07 chortle, chuckle, snicker, snigger, whicker

**tittle-tattle**
03 jaw, yak 04 chat, idle, yack
06 babble, cackle, gossip, natter, rumour, witter 07 blather, blether, chatter, hearsay, prattle, twaddle
08 chitchat, rabbit on, yack-yack 09 tell tales 10 yackety-yak

**titular**
05 token 06 formal, puppet
07 nominal 08 honorary, official, putative, so-called 10 in name only, self-styled

**to**
01 t' 02 at, au, of, on 03 à la, aux, for, tae 04 near, till, unto 05 until
06 before, beside 07 against, as far as, forward, towards

**toad**
04 bufo, pipa 07 paddock, puddock
10 natterjack

**toadstool** *see* **mushroom**

**toady**
04 fawn, sook, zany 05 crawl, creep
06 cringe, fawner, grovel, jackal, kowtow, lackey, minion, sucker, suck up, yes-man 07 crawler, flatter, flunkey, Jenkins, truckle 08 bootlick, butter up, hanger-on, parasite, suck-hole, toadfish, truckler 09 flatterer, groveller, sycophant 10 bootlicker, tuft-hunter
11 curry favour, kiss the feet, lick-platter, lickspittle 12 bow and scrape

**to and fro**
◇ *palindrome indicator*

**toast**
04 bake, heat, warm 05 brown, crisp, drink, grill, roast 06 birsle, heat up, honour, pledge, salute, scorch, warm up 07 drink to, tribute 08 barbecue, brindisi, scouther 09 sentiment 10 best wishes, compliment, salutation
11 compliments

*See also* **cheers**

**tobacco**
04 burn, chaw, chew, pipe, plug, quid, weed 05 bacco, baccy 07 the weed

*Tobacco and tobacco preparations include:*

04 capa, shag
05 régie, snout, snuff, snush, twist
06 burley, dottle, rappee, return, sneesh
07 caporal, chewing, Latakia, nail-rod, perique, pigtail
08 bird's-eye, canaster, honeydew, short-cut, Virginia
09 broad-leaf, cavendish, flue-cured, mundungus, strip-leaf

*Tobacco pipes include:*

03 cob
04 bong, clay
05 briar, brier, cutty, hooka, peace, water
06 dudeen, hookah, kalian
07 calumet, chibouk, chillum, corncob, dudheen, nargile, nargily
08 calabash, narghile, narghily, nargileh, nargilly
09 chibouque, narghilly
10 meerschaum
12 churchwarden, hubble-bubble
13 woodcock's-head

**toboggan**
04 dray, luge 05 pulka, slide, slipe, train
06 Ski-doo®, sledge, sleigh
07 bobsled, dogsled, kibitka, travois
09 bobsleigh 11 hurly-hacket, skeleton bob

**today**
03 now 06 the day 07 just now, this day 08 nowadays, right now 09 these days 11 this evening, this morning, this very day 12 at this moment 13 the present day, this afternoon 14 the present time

**toddle**
04 reel, rock, sway 05 lurch, shake, waver 06 falter, teeter, totter, waddle, wobble 07 saunter, stagger, stumble
14 move unsteadily, walk unsteadily

**toddler**
04 trot

**to-do**
03 ado 04 flap, fuss, stew, stir 05 hoo-ha 06 bother, bustle, flurry, furore, rumpus, tumult, unrest, uproar
07 quarrel, ruction, turmoil
08 brouhaha, razmataz 09 agitation, commotion 10 excitement, hullabaloo, razzmatazz 11 disturbance, performance, razzamatazz

**toe**
04 kick 05 digit 06 hallux, tootsy
07 dewclaw, tootsie 09 prehallux
12 tootsy-wootsy

**together**
03 cum 04 calm, cool 05 as one, atone, on end 06 attone, in a row, stable, united 07 as a team, jointly
08 composed, in unison, mutually, sensible 09 all at once, at one time, in company, in concert, on the trot, organized, pari passu 10 back to back, hand in hand, side by side 11 down-to-earth, level-headed, unflappable
12 collectively, concurrently, continuously, in succession, successively, well-adjusted, well-balanced 13 at the same time, consecutively, in conjunction, well-organized, without a break 14 as a partnership, commonsensical, simultaneously 15 in collaboration, working together

• **come together**
03 gel 04 jell, meet 05 close, rally
07 collect, convene 10 amalgamate

**Togo**
02 TG 03 TGO

**toil**
03 net, tew, tug 04 grub, moil, slog, trap, work 05 graft, grind, labor, slave, snare, sweat, swink, yakka 06 drudge, effort, labour, murder, strive, yacker, yakker 07 fatigue, murther, slaving, travail, turmoil 08 drudgery, drudgism, exertion, hard work, industry, plug away, struggle 09 persevere
10 contention, donkey-work
11 application, elbow grease 12 push yourself 14 Hercules' choice 15 work like a Trojan

**toiler**
05 navvy, slave 06 drudge, menial, worker 07 grafter, slogger 08 labourer
09 struggler, workhorse 10 workaholic

**toilet**
02 WC 03 APC, bog, can, lat, lav, loo
04 dike, head, john, kazi, toot, tout
05 dunny, Elsan®, heads, jacks, lavvy, potty 06 lavabo, throne, urinal
07 cludgie, cottage, crapper, latrine
08 bathroom, lavatory, outhouse, Portaloo®, rest room, superloo, the gents', washroom 09 cloakroom, necessary, the ladies' 10 facilities, powder room, reredorter, throne room, thunderbox 11 convenience, earth-closet, water closet 12 dressing-room, smallest room 14 comfort station, little boys' room, necessary house, necessary place 15 Parliament House

**toilsome**
04 hard 05 tough 06 severe, taxing, uphill 07 arduous, painful, tedious, toiling, toylsom 08 tiresome
09 difficult, fatiguing, herculean, laborious, strenuous, toylesome, wearisome 10 burdensome
12 backbreaking

**token**
04 clue, disc, mark, seal, sign, slug
05 check, index, jeton, proof, scrip, staff 06 coupon, emblem, hollow, jetton, pledge, signal, slight, symbol
07 counter, memento, minimal, nominal, portent, tessera, voucher, warning 08 cosmetic, evidence, keepsake, memorial, moniment, monument, reminder, souvenir, symbolic 09 insincere, precedent, sacrament, triumphal 10 abbey-piece, emblematic, expression, indication, plague-spot 11 perfunctory, recognition, remembrance, superficial
12 abbey-counter, recognizance
13 demonstration, manifestation
14 representation

**told**
◇ *homophone indicator*

**tolerable**
**02** OK **04** fair, so-so **06** not bad **07** average **08** adequate, all right, bearable, mediocre, middling, ordinary, passable **09** endurable, tollolish **10** acceptable, fairly good, not much cop, reasonable, sufferable **11** indifferent **12** run-of-the-mill, satisfactory **13** no great shakes, unexceptional

**tolerably**
**06** enough, fairly **08** bearably **10** acceptably, adequately, ordinarily, reasonably **12** sufficiently **13** indifferently

**tolerance**
**04** give, play **05** swing **06** lenity **07** laxness, stamina **08** leniency, patience, sympathy **09** allowance, clearance, endurance, fortitude, toughness, variation **10** good-humour, indulgence, liberalism, resilience, resistance, toleration **11** fluctuation, forbearance, magnanimity **13** understanding **14** open-mindedness, permissiveness **15** broad-mindedness

**tolerant**
**03** lax **04** fair, soft **06** decent **07** lenient, liberal, patient **08** catholic, enduring, mellowed **09** compliant, easy-going, forgiving, indulgent **10** charitable, forbearing, open-minded, permissive **11** broad-minded, free and easy, kind-hearted, magnanimous, sympathetic **12** unprejudiced **13** long-suffering, understanding

**tolerate**
**04** bear, have, take, wear **05** abear, abide, admit, allow, stand, thole **06** accept, endure, pardon, permit, suffer **07** condone, indulge, receive, stomach, swallow, warrant **08** sanction **09** put up with **11** countenance

**toleration**
**06** lenity **07** laxness, stamina **08** leniency, patience, sanction, sympathy **09** allowance, endurance, fortitude, toughness **10** acceptance, indulgence, liberalism, resilience, resistance, sufferance **11** forbearance, magnanimity **13** understanding **14** open-mindedness, permissiveness **15** broad-mindedness

**toll**
**03** bar, due, fee, jow, tax **04** call, cost, duty, harm, jole, joll, jowl, levy, loss, lure, peal, pike, rate, ring, warn **05** chime, clang, death, decoy, joule, knell, price, sound **06** charge, damage, demand, herald, injury, octroi, signal, strike, tariff **07** payment, penalty, pierage, pontage, scavage, tallage, tollage **08** announce, hardship **09** streetage, suffering **13** adverse effect

**tomb**
**04** bury, cist **05** crypt, death, grave, speos, vault **06** burial, dolmen, entomb, heroon, marble, shrine, tholus **07** funeral, mastaba, reposit **08** catacomb, cenotaph, hypogeum, monument, sacellum **09** hypogaeum, mausoleum, sepulcher, sepulchre, sepulture **10** repository **11** burial-place, sarcophagus **13** Holy Sepulchre

**tomboy**
**04** ramp, romp **05** hempy **06** hoiden, hoyden

**tombstone**
**05** stone **06** marble **08** memorial, monument **09** headstone **10** gravestone **12** through-stane, through-stone **13** memorial stone

**tomcat**
**03** gib

**tome**
**03** tom **04** book, opus, work **06** volume

**tomfoolery**
**03** tom **05** hooey, larks **06** idiocy **07** inanity, rubbish, trifles **08** clowning, mischief, nonsense **09** horseplay, jewellery, ornaments, silliness, stupidity **10** buffoonery, carrying on, skylarking **11** foolishness, shenanigans **12** childishness, larking about, messing about

**ton**
**01** t **03** tun **07** fashion

**tone**
**03** air, hue **04** cast, feel, mood, note, suit, tint, tune, vein **05** blend, drift, force, match, pitch, shade, sound, style, tenor, tinge, twang **06** accent, colour, effect, go with, humour, manner, spirit, stress, temper, timbre, volume **07** quality **08** attitude, emphasis, strength, tincture, tonality **09** character, harmonize **10** co-ordinate, expression, go well with, inflection, intonation, modulation **12** accentuation

• **high tone**
**03** alt

• **tone down**
**03** dim **06** dampen, reduce, soften, subdew, subdue, temper **07** assuage, lighten **08** mitigate, moderate, play down, restrain **09** alleviate, soft-pedal

• **tone up**
**04** buck, trim **05** brace **06** buck up, tune up **07** freshen, shape up, touch up **08** brighten, limber up **09** sharpen up **10** invigorate

**toneless**
**03** dim **04** dull, grey **05** faded **07** neutral, relaxed **08** listless, tuneless **09** soundless, unmusical **10** colourless **11** unmelodious **12** unexpressive **14** expressionless

**Tonga**
**03** TON

**tongue**
**04** cant, doab, lick, rasp, spit, talk, vote **05** argot, clack, idiom, lingo, slang, utter, voice **06** glossa, jargon, lingua, patois, radula, red rag, speech **07** clapper, dialect **08** language, parlance **09** discourse, pronounce, utterance **10** articulate, vernacular **12** articulation

*See also* **language**

**tongue-tied**
**04** dumb, mute **06** silent **08** wordless **09** voiceless **10** dumbstruck, speechless **11** mush-mouthed **12** inarticulate, lost for words, tongue-tacked

**tonic**
**01** t **05** boost, final **06** bracer, fillip, saloop **07** cordial, home key, keynote **08** pick-me-up, roborant **09** analeptic, refresher, stimulant **11** restorative **12** shot in the arm **15** fundamental note

*See also* **note**

**too**
**03** tae **04** also, over, very **06** as well, overly, unduly **07** besides **08** likewise, moreover **09** extremely **10** in addition **11** excessively, furthermore **12** inordinately, ridiculously, unreasonably

**tool**
**03** cut **04** dupe, over, pawn, work, yoke **05** agent, chase, gismo, means, shape, tanto **06** agency, device, gadget, medium, minion, puppet, stooge, troppo, weapon **07** cat's-paw, fashion, flunkey, machine, utensil, vehicle **08** artefact, decorate, hireling, ornament **09** apparatus, appliance, implement **10** instrument, over-the-top **11** contraption, contrivance **12** intermediary

*Tools include:*

**02** ax
**03** awl, axe, gad, hod, hoe, loy, saw, sax, van
**04** adze, burr, card, celt, file, fork, froe, goad, hawk, jack, mace, mall, maul, peel, pick, plow, prod, prog, rake, rasp, risp, rule, snap, spud, vice
**05** auger, bevel, clamp, dolly, drill, level, plane, punch, snips, spade, steel, tongs
**06** bodkin, chaser, chisel, dibber, dibble, fuller, gimlet, hammer, jigsaw, mallet, mortar, needle, pestle, pliers, plough, sander, scutch, scythe, shears, shovel, sickle, trowel, wrench
**07** bolster, bradawl, chopper, cleaver, crowbar, forceps, fretsaw, hacksaw, handsaw, hay fork, jointer, mattock, nail gun, pick-axe, pincers, scalpel, scriber, stapler, swingle, T-square
**08** billhook, chainsaw, dividers, penknife, scissors, spraygun, tenon-saw, thresher, tommy bar, tweezers
**09** grass-rake, jack-plane, pitchfork, plumb-line, secateurs, set-square
**10** jackhammer, paper-knife, protractor

**11** brace and bit, crochet hook, paper-cutter, pocket-knife, screwdriver, spirit level
**12** angle grinder, caulking-iron, digging stick, pruning-knife, sledgehammer, socket-wrench, wirestripper
**13** pinking-shears, pruning-shears, soldering-iron

*See also* **gardening**; **saw**

**tooth**
**03** cog, jag **05** crena, prong, taste **06** dentil, joggle, relish **08** appetite, denticle **09** interlock, serration **10** serrations **13** denticulation
*See also* **teeth**

**toothsome**
**04** nice **05** sweet, tasty, yummy **06** dainty, morish **07** moreish, savoury, scrummy **08** luscious, pleasant, tempting **09** agreeable, delicious, palatable **10** appetizing, attractive, delectable **11** flavoursome, scrumptious **13** mouthwatering

**top**
◇ *head selection indicator*
**02** up **03** cap, cop, lid, nun, tip **04** acme, apex, beat, best, comb, cork, head, kill, lead, main, peak, roof, rule, tuft **05** chief, cover, crest, crown, excel, first, outdo, prime, ridge, shirt, smock, upper **06** apogee, better, blouse, climax, coppin, exceed, finest, finish, height, jersey, jumper, ruling, summit, T-shirt, upmost, upward, utmost, vertex, zenith **07** cacumen, command, eclipse, garnish, highest, leading, maximum, premier, premium, spinner, stopper, supreme, surpass, sweater, tank top, topmost, topsail, topspin **08** crowning, decorate, dominant, foremost, greatest, outshine, outstrip, pinnacle, pullover, superior, surmount, tee shirt, very good **09** be first in, finish off, paramount, principal, sovereign, transcend, uppermost **10** pre-eminent, sweatshirt **11** culminating, culmination **12** highest point
*See also* **cut**

• **over the top**
**03** OTT **05** undue **06** lavish **07** extreme, too much **08** a bit much **09** excessive **10** exorbitant, immoderate, inordinate **11** extravagant, uncalled-for **12** unreasonable

• **top and tail**
◇ *ends deletion indicator*

• **top off**
◇ *head deletion indicator*

• **top up**
**05** add to, boost **06** fill up, refill, reload **07** augment **08** increase, recharge **09** replenish **10** supplement

**topi**
**03** hat **04** sola **05** solah **07** sola hat **10** sola helmet

**topic**
**04** head, text **05** issue, place, point, theme, topos **06** matter, thesis **07** subject **08** argument, question **09** hot button **10** hobby-horse, touch-me-not **11** commonplace, hardy annual, old chestnut **12** talking point **13** subject matter

**topical**
**05** local **06** recent **07** current, popular **08** familiar, relevant, up-to-date **10** newsworthy **12** contemporary **13** up-to-the-minute

**topless**
◇ *head deletion indicator*

**topmost**
**03** top **05** first, upper **06** apical **07** highest, leading, maximum, supreme **08** dominant, foremost, loftiest, supernal **09** paramount, principal, uppermost

**top-notch**
**02** A1 **03** ace, top **04** cool, fine, mega **05** crack, prime, super **06** superb, way-out, wicked **07** leading, premier, radical, supreme **08** peerless, splendid, superior **09** admirable, excellent, first-rate, matchless, top-flight **10** first-class **11** exceptional, outstanding, superlative **12** second-to-none **14** out of this world

**topping**
◇ *juxtaposition down indicator*
**05** crust **07** tipping **08** arrogant **09** excellent, wonderful

**topple**
◇ *anagram indicator*
**03** tip **04** fall, oust **05** upset **06** totter, tumble, unseat **07** capsize, dismast, tip over **08** collapse, dethrone, displace, fall over, keel over, overturn **09** bring down, knock down, knock over, overthrow **11** overbalance

**top-secret**
**06** secret **07** private **08** hush-hush, intimate, personal **09** sensitive **10** classified, restricted **12** confidential, off-the-record

**topsy-turvy**
◇ *anagram indicator*
**05** messy **06** untidy **07** chaotic, jumbled, mixed-up **08** confused **09** confusion, inside out **10** disorderly, in disorder, upside down **11** disarranged, in confusion **12** disorganized, looking-glass, tapsalteerie, tapsieteerie

**torch**
**04** burn, link, tead, wisp **05** brand, flare, light, teade **06** ignite, lampad **07** cresset, roughie **08** arsonist, flambeau, splinter **09** firebrand, set alight, set fire to, set on fire **10** flashlight **11** put a match to

**torment**
◇ *anagram indicator*
**03** vex **04** bane, pain, pest, pine **05** agony, annoy, curse, grill, hound, tease, worry, wrack **06** badger, bother, harass, harrow, misery, ordeal, pester, plague **07** afflict, agitate, anguish, bedevil, crucify, furnace, Gehenna, provoke, scourge, torture, trouble **08** distress, irritate, nuisance, vexation **09** annoyance, martyrdom, persecute, suffering, tantalize **10** affliction, harassment, irritation **11** persecution, provocation **13** pain in the neck **15** thorn in the flesh

**torn**
◇ *anagram indicator*
**03** cut **04** rent, slit **05** split **06** ragged, ribbon, ripped, unsure **07** divided, enriven **08** lacerate, wavering **09** dithering, lacerated, uncertain, undecided **10** in two minds, irresolute **11** vacillating

**tornado**
**04** gale **05** storm **06** squall **07** cyclone, monsoon, tempest, twister, typhoon **09** hurricane, whirlwind **10** waterspout

**torpedo**
**03** ray **05** wreck **07** tin fish **09** cramp-fish **11** electric ray

**torpid**
**04** dead, dull, lazy, numb, slow **05** inert **06** drowsy, sleepy, supine **07** dormant, passive **08** deadened, inactive, indolent, lifeless, listless, sluggish **09** apathetic, lethargic, nerveless, somnolent **10** insensible, languorous **11** lethargical

**torpor**
**05** sloth **06** acedia, apathy, stupor **07** inertia, languor **08** dullness, hebetude, laziness, lethargy, numbness, slowness **09** indolence, inertness, passivity, stupidity, torpidity **10** drowsiness, inactivity, sleepiness, somnolence **12** lifelessness, listlessness, sluggishness

**torrent**
**04** gush, rush **05** flood, spate, storm **06** deluge, stream, volley **07** barrage, blatter, cascade **08** downpour, outburst **10** inundation

**torrential**
**05** heavy **07** driving, pelting, teeming **10** inundating, persistent **11** pouring down **13** bucketing down

**torrid**
**03** hot **04** arid, sexy **06** desert, erotic, red-hot, steamy **07** amorous, blazing, boiling, parched **08** scorched, sizzling, stifling, tropical **09** scorching, waterless **10** blistering, passionate, sweltering

**torsk**
**04** cusk

**tortoise**
**06** gopher **07** hicatee, testudo **08** galapago, hiccatee, terrapin

**tortuous**
◇ *anagram indicator*
**06** zigzag **07** curving, devious,

sinuous, winding **08** indirect, involved, twisting **09** ambagious, Byzantine **10** circuitous, convoluted, meandering, roundabout, serpentine **11** complicated

**torture**

◇ *anagram indicator*

**03** fry, gip, gyp **04** pain, pine **05** abuse, agony, worry, wrack **06** harrow, martyr, misery, murder, plague, punish **07** afflict, agonize, anguish, crucify, murther, trouble **08** distress, ill-treat, mistreat **09** martyrdom, persecute, suffering, tantalize **10** affliction, excruciate, punishment **11** forcipation, persecution **12** excruciation, ill-treatment, mistreatment

*Torture forms and instruments include:*

**03** gin, saw
**04** boot, cage, pear, rack
**05** brank, gadge, irons, jougs, screw, wheel
**06** carcan, engine, harrow, picana, shabeh, spider, stocks, turcas
**07** bilboes, boiling, cat's paw, hooding, picquet, pillory, pincers, scourge, stoning, torment
**08** bootikin, branding, garrotte, knotting, pendulum, pressing, shin vice, trip-hook
**09** bastinado, gauntlets, gridirons, picketing, scarpines, strappado, treadmill
**10** brazen bull, cattle prod, impalement, iron collar, iron maiden, Judas scale, pilliwinks, spiked hare, starvation, suspension, thumbscrew, treadwheel
**11** cave of roses, forcipation, German chair, head crusher, Judas cradle, keelhauling, knee-capping, squassation, thumbscrews, wooden horse
**12** ball and chain, ducking-stool, flesh tearers, scold's bridle, shrew's fiddle, skull crusher, Spanish chair, water torture
**13** cat-o'-nine-tails, electric shock, heretic's forks, Spanish mantle
**14** Austrian ladder, devil-on-the-neck, disembowelment, drunkard's cloak
**15** confession chair

**Tory**

**01** C **03** Con **04** blue **07** tantivy **08** Abhorrer **12** Conservative

**toss**

◇ *anagram indicator*

**03** bum, lob, shy, tip **04** birl, cant, cast, flip, hurl, jerk, jolt, loft, perk, puck, rock, roll, sway **05** bandy, brank, chuck, drink, fling, heave, lurch, pitch, shake, sling, throw **06** bridle, dandle, slight, sprawl, squirm, thrash, tumble, welter, writhe **07** agitate, blanket, canvass, flutter, wriggle **09** commotion, confusion

**tot**

**03** dop, nip, sum **04** baby, dram, mite, shot, slug, swig **05** bairn, child **06** finger, infant **07** measure, swallow, toddler

*See also* **add**; **baby**; **drink**

**• tot up**

**03** add, sum **05** add up, count, mount, tally, total **06** reckon **07** compute, count up, mount up **09** calculate

**total**

**03** add, all, lot, sum, tot **04** full, make, mass, rank **05** add up, count, gross, reach, sheer, sum up, tot up, utter, whole **06** all-out, amount, come to, entire, reckon **07** count up, full-out, perfect, pur sang **08** absolute, amount to, complete, entirety, integral, outright, subtotal, thorough, totality **09** aggregate, downright, out-and-out **10** consummate, grand total, undisputed **11** unmitigated, unqualified **13** comprehensive, thoroughgoing, unconditional

**totalitarian**

**08** despotic, one-party **09** tyrannous **10** monocratic, monolithic, omnipotent, oppressive **11** dictatorial **12** undemocratic **13** authoritarian

**totality**

**03** all, sum **05** total, whole **06** cosmos **07** pleroma **08** entirety, fullness, universe **09** aggregate, wholeness **10** entireness, everything **12** completeness

**totally**

**05** fully, quite **06** wholly **07** utterly **08** entirely, outright **09** perfectly **10** absolutely, completely, thoroughly **11** boots and all, undividedly **12** consummately, undisputedly **13** unmitigatedly **14** wholeheartedly **15** comprehensively, unconditionally

**totter**

◇ *anagram indicator*

**04** reel, rock, roll, sway **05** lurch, shake, waver **06** daddle, dodder, falter, hotter, quiver, teeter, titter, topple, waddle, wobble **07** be shaky, stagger, stumble, tremble **10** be insecure, be unstable, be unsteady **12** be precarious **14** move unsteadily

**touch**

**03** art, bit, dab, eat, hit, jot, nie, pat, pet, tap, tat, tig, use, way **04** abut, blow, dash, draw, feel, hand, harm, hint, hold, kiss, make, meet, move, nigh, nose, palm, palp, skim, spot, stir, take **05** bribe, brush, cheat, cover, drink, equal, flair, grain, graze, knack, match, pinch, point, reach, rival, skiff, skill, smack, speck, spice, stamp, style, taste, theft, tinge, trace, trait, upset, verge, weave, whiff, wound **06** adjoin, affect, aspect, attain, better, border, broach, caress, come to, detail, devour, finger, finish, fondle, handle, injure, little, manner, method, molest, muzzle, nicety, pierce, pocket, regard, sadden, smatch, strike, stroke, tickle **07** ability, concern, consume, contact, disturb, feature, impinge, impress, inspire, involve, knuckle, mention, minutia, rapport, receive, refer to, soupçon, speak of, surface, taction, texture, touch up **08** addition, allude to, approach, come near, deal with, fineness, remark on **09** dexterity, direction, influence, suspicion, tactility, technique **10** connection, suggestion, touchstone **11** association **12** lay a finger on, put a finger on **13** communication, craftsmanship, hold a candle to **14** be contiguous to, correspondence, have an effect on, have an impact on **15** come into contact

**• touch down**

**04** land **05** rouge **06** come in **11** come to earth **12** come in to land

**• touch off**

**04** fire **05** begin, cause, light
**06** arouse, foment, ignite, set off
**07** actuate, inflame, provoke, trigger
**08** detonate, initiate, spark off
**10** trigger off

**• touch up**

**03** tat **04** tatt **06** revamp **07** brush up, enhance, improve, patch up, perfect, retouch **08** polish up, renovate, round off **09** finish off

**touch-and-go**

**04** dire, near **05** close, dodgy, hairy, risky **06** sticky, tricky **07** offhand, parlous **08** critical, perilous **09** dangerous, hazardous, uncertain **10** precarious **12** nerve-racking

**touchdown**

**07** arrival, landing **08** coming in **14** coming in to land

**touched**

**03** mad **04** daft **05** barmy, batty, crazy, dotty, loopy, moved, nutty, upset **06** insane **07** bonkers, stirred **08** affected, deranged, inspired **09** disturbed, eccentric, impressed **10** influenced, unbalanced

**touchiness**

**09** bad temper, petulance, surliness, testiness **10** grumpiness, tetchiness **11** crabbedness, grouchiness, peevishness, pettishness **12** captiousness, irascibility, irritability

**touching**

**03** sad **05** hongi **06** libant, moving, tender **07** attaint, darshan, piteous, pitiful, tangent **08** handball, pathetic, pitiable, poignant, stirring, tangency **09** affecting, emotional, fingering, upsetting **10** concerning, contiguous, disturbing, impressive **11** cloud-topped **12** cloud-kissing, heart-rending **13** heartbreaking

**touchstone**

**04** norm, test **05** gauge, guide, model, proof **07** measure, pattern **08** standard, template **09** benchmark, criterion, yardstick **11** Lydian stone

**touchwood**

**04** funk, monk, punk **05** spunk **09** matchwood

**touchy**
**04** edgy, sore **05** cross, huffy, miffy, mifty, risky **06** badass, chippy, feisty, grumpy, ornery, snuffy, tricky
**07** awkward, crabbed, grouchy, huffish, peevish, prickly **08** badassed, captious, delicate **09** difficult, irascible, irritable, sensitive **11** bad-tempered, problematic, thin-skinned
**13** controversial, over-sensitive, quick-tempered

**tough**
**03** fit, nut, yob **04** firm, grim, hard, lout, thug **05** brute, bully, burly, butch, chewy, hardy, harsh, rigid, rough, rowdy, solid, stern, stiff, teuch, teugh, yobbo **06** badass, ballsy, keelie, knotty, robust, rugged, severe, sticky, strict, strong, sturdy, taxing, thorny, uphill
**07** adamant, arduous, callous, durable, fibrous, gristly, rubbery, ruffian, unlucky, vicious, violent, viscous
**08** badassed, baffling, criminal, exacting, hardened, hooligan, leathery, muscular, plug-ugly, puzzling, resolute, stalwart, vigorous **09** bovver boy, cut-throat, difficult, hardnosed, laborious, lager lout, obstinate, resilient, resistant, roughneck, strenuous, tenacious, violently, well-built **10** determined, disorderly, inflexible, perplexing, refractory, unpleasant, unyielding
**11** distressing, intractable, troublesome, unfortunate
**12** aggressively **13** uncomfortable
**14** tough as leather, uncompromising

**toughen**
**04** neal **05** brace **06** anneal, harden
**07** fortify, stiffen **09** reinforce
**10** strengthen **12** make stricter, substantiate

**toughness**
**04** grit, guts **08** firmness, obduracy, strength, tenacity **09** hardiness
**10** resilience, resistance, ruggedness, sturdiness **13** determination, inflexibility

**toupee**
**03** jiz, rug, wig **04** gizz **05** caxon, jasey, major **06** bagwig, bobwig, Brutus, peruke, tie-wig **07** buzz-wig, periwig, Ramilie, spencer **08** postiche
**09** hairpiece **10** scratch-wig
**14** transformation

**tour**
◇ *anagram indicator*
**02** do **03** van **04** hike, ride, road, rode, trip **05** drive, jaunt, round, tramp, visit
**06** course, outing **07** circuit, explore, go round, journey **08** roadshow, sightsee **09** barnstorm, excursion, walkabout **10** expedition, inspection
**11** travel round **12** drive through
**13** peregrination **14** journey through

**tourist**
**05** emmet **06** tourer **07** grockle, tripper, visitor, voyager **09** sightseer, sojourner, traveller **10** day-tripper, rubberneck **12** excursionist, globetrotter, holidaymaker

• **tourist attraction** *see* **Africa**; **America**; **Asia**; **Australia**; **Canada**; **Europe**; **London**; **Middle East**; **New York**; **New Zealand**; **Paris**

**tournament**
**04** meet, seed **05** basho, event, jerid, joust, match **06** jereed, series
**07** contest, meeting, tourney
**08** carousel **09** carrousel **10** round robin **11** bridge-drive, competition
**12** championship

**tousled**
**06** untidy **07** ruffled, rumpled, tangled, tumbled, unkempt **08** messed up
**10** disordered, in disarray
**11** disarranged, dishevelled

**tout**
**03** all, ask, pet **04** hawk, hype, plug, pout, push, seek, sell **05** blast, every, plier, trade, watch, whole **06** appeal, barker, inhale, market, peddle, praise, runner, toilet **07** commend, endorse, promote, solicit **08** petition
**09** advertise **11** workwatcher

**tow**
**03** lug, tug **04** drag, draw, haul, pull, rope **05** track, trail **09** transport

• **in tow**
**08** in convoy **10** by your side
**12** accompanying

**towards**
**02** to **03** for **04** near **05** about, anent, -wards **06** almost, nearly **07** close to, nearing **09** regarding **10** concerning, on the way to **11** approaching **12** to help pay for, with regard to **13** with respect to

**tower**
**03** cap, top **04** loom, rear, rise, sail, soar
**05** excel, mount, shoot **06** ascend, exceed **07** eclipse, surpass **08** dominate, overlook **09** transcend **10** overshadow
*See also* **tug**

*Tower types include:*

**04** bell, fort, gate, keep, mill, peel, rood, shot
**05** block, broch, clock, ivory, minar, pagod, round, spire, Texas, watch, water
**06** belfry, castle, church, column, donjon, gopura, nurhag, pagoda, turret
**07** bastion, citadel, conning, control, cooling, lookout, minaret, mirador, nuraghe, steeple
**08** barbican, bastille, brattice, fortress, hill-fort, martello, scaffold
**09** belvedere, campanile, smock mill, tower mill
**10** skyscraper, stronghold
**11** demi-bastion
**13** fortification

*Towers include:*

**02** CN
**03** AMP, Sky
**04** Pisa
**05** Babel, Clock, Macau, Sears, Seoul, Tokyo
**06** Big Ben, Dragon, Eiffel, Kiev TV, London, Riga TV, Tahoto
**07** Alma-Ata, Leaning, Olympic, Praha TV, Yueyang
**08** Tallin TV, Tashkent, Tengwang
**09** Blackpool, Donauturm, Ostankino, Tianjin TV
**10** Collserola, Liberation
**11** Fernsehturm, The Euromast, Yellow Crane
**12** Petronas Twin, Stratosphere
**15** Oriental Pearl TV

• **tower of strength**
**04** prop **06** pillar **07** support
**08** mainstay **09** supporter **12** friend in need

**towering**
**04** high, tall **05** great, lofty **07** extreme, soaring, sublime, supreme **08** colossal, elevated, gigantic, imposing
**10** impressive, inordinate, monumental, surpassing, unrivalled
**11** magnificent, outstanding
**12** incomparable, overpowering
**13** extraordinary

**town**
**04** burg, city, dorp, toun **05** borgo, bourg, burgh, urban **06** favela, Podunk, pueblo **07** borough, new town, suburbs, village **08** township
**09** enclosure, outskirts, urban area
**10** county town, market town, metropolis, settlement **11** conurbation
**12** municipality **13** urban district

*County towns include:*

**03** Ayr
**04** Mold, Wick, York
**05** Banff, Cupar, Derry, Elgin, Lewes, Nairn, Omagh, Perth, Truro
**06** Armagh, Brecon, Durham, Exeter, Forfar, Lanark, London, Oakham, Oxford
**07** Appleby, Bedford, Belfast, Bristol, Cardiff, Chester, Denbigh, Dornoch, Ipswich, Kinross, Lerwick, Lincoln, Matlock, Morpeth, Newport, Norwich, Peebles, Preston, Reading, Renfrew, Selkirk, Taunton, Warwick, Wigtown
**08** Aberdeen, Barnsley, Beverley, Cardigan, Carlisle, Cromarty, Dingwall, Dumfries, Greenlaw, Hereford, Hertford, Jedburgh, Kingston, Kirkwall, Monmouth, Pembroke, Rothesay, Stafford, Stirling
**09** Aylesbury, Beaumaris, Cambridge, Dolgellau, Dumbarton, Newcastle
**10** Haddington, Huntingdon, Linlithgow, Manchester, Montgomery, Nottingham, Presteigne, Shrewsbury, Stonehaven, Trowbridge, Winchester
**11** Clackmannan, Downpatrick, Enniskillen, Northampton
**12** Kircudbright
**13** Middlesbrough, Northallerton

*English towns include:*

**03** Ely
**04** Bath, Bury, Hove, Hull, York
**05** Ascot, Corby, Cowes, Crewe, Derby, Dover, Epsom, Ewell, Hythe, Leeds, Lewes, Luton, Otley, Poole, Ripon, Rugby, Truro, Wells, Wigan
**06** Barnet, Bexley, Bodmin, Bolton, Bootle, Boston, Buxton, Darwen, Dudley, Durham, Exeter, Harlow, Harrow, Ilkley, Jarrow, Kendal, London, Ludlow, Oakham, Oldham, Oundle, Oxford, Slough, St Ives, Stroud, Torbay, Warley, Whitby, Widnes, Wirral, Woking, Yeovil
**07** Andover, Arundel, Ashford, Bedford, Berwick, Bristol, Brixham, Burnley, Chatham, Cheddar, Chester, Crawley, Croydon, Dorking, Evesham, Exmouth, Gosport, Grimsby, Halifax, Harwich, Haworth, Helston, Horsham, Ipswich, Keswick, Lincoln, Malvern, Margate, Matlock, Morpeth, Newport, Norwich, Padstow, Preston, Reading, Redruth, Reigate, Royston, Runcorn, Salford, Stilton, Sudbury, Swindon, Taunton, Telford, Tilbury, Torquay, Ventnor, Walsall, Wantage, Warwick, Watford, Windsor
**08** Abingdon, Barnsley, Basildon, Beverley, Bradford, Brighton, Carlisle, Coventry, Dartford, Falmouth, Grantham, Hastings, Hatfield, Hereford, Hertford, Kingston, Knowsley, Minehead, Newhaven, Nuneaton, Penzance, Plymouth, Ramsgate, Redditch, Richmond, Rochdale, Sandwell, Solihull, Spalding, Stafford, St Albans, Stamford, St Helens, Thetford, Westbury, Weymouth, Worthing
**09** Aldeburgh, Aldershot, Ambleside, Ashbourne, Axminster, Aylesbury, Blackburn, Blackpool, Bletchley, Bracknell, Cambridge, Dartmouth, Doncaster, Gateshead, Gravesend, Greenwich, Guildford, Harrogate, King's Lynn, Lancaster, Leicester, Lichfield, Liverpool, Lowestoft, Lyme Regis, Maidstone, Morecambe, Newcastle, Newmarket, Rochester, Rotherham, Salisbury, Sheerness, Sheffield, Sherborne, Southport, Southwold, St Austell, Stevenage, Stockport, Stratford, Wakefield, Worcester
**10** Birkenhead, Birmingham, Bridgwater, Bromsgrove, Buckingham, Canterbury, Chelmsford, Cheltenham, Chichester, Colchester, Darlington, Dorchester, Eastbourne, Felixstowe, Folkestone, Gillingham, Gloucester, Hartlepool, Huntingdon, Kenilworth, Kensington, Launceston, Letchworth, Maidenhead, Manchester, Nottingham, Pontefract, Portsmouth, Scunthorpe, Shrewsbury, Sunderland, Tewkesbury, Warrington, Washington, Whitehaven, Winchester
**11** Bognor Regis, Bournemouth, Cirencester, Cleethorpes, Farnborough, Glastonbury, High Wycombe, Northampton, Scarborough, Shaftesbury, Southampton
**12** Chesterfield, Clacton-on-Sea, Great Malvern, Huddersfield, Loughborough, Macclesfield, Milton Keynes, North Shields, Peterborough, South Shields, Stoke-on-Trent, West Bromwich
**13** Bury St Edmunds, Ellesmere Port, Great Yarmouth, Kidderminster, Leamington Spa, Littlehampton, Lytham St Anne's, Middlesbrough, Saffron Walden, Southend-on-Sea, West Bridgford, Wolverhampton
**14** Ashby-de-la-Zouch, Bishop Auckland, Chipping Norton, Hemel Hempstead, Henley-on-Thames, Stockton-on-Tees, Tunbridge Wells
**15** Ashton-under-Lyne, Barrow-in-Furness, Burton upon Trent, Sutton Coldfield, Weston-Super-Mare

*Northern Irish towns include:*

**05** Derry, Larne, Newry, Omagh
**06** Antrim, Armagh, Bangor, Lurgan
**07** Belfast, Lifford, Lisburn
**08** Limavady, Portrush, Strabane
**09** Ballymena, Banbridge, Coleraine, Cookstown, Dungannon, Portadown
**10** Ballyclare, Ballymoney
**11** Downpatrick, Enniskillen, Londonderry, Magherafelt, Newtownards, Portstewart
**13** Carrickfergus

*Scottish towns include:*

**03** Ayr
**04** Oban, Tain, Wick
**05** Alloa, Banff, Elgin, Keith, Kelso, Nairn, Perth, Scone, Troon
**06** Alness, Dunbar, Dundee, Dunoon, Forfar, Girvan, Glamis, Hawick, Huntly, Irvine, Lanark, Thurso
**07** Airdrie, Alloway, Braemar, Dornoch, Falkirk, Glasgow, Golspie, Gourock, Lerwick, Mallaig, Paisley, Peebles, Portree, Selkirk
**08** Aberdeen, Arbroath, Banchory, Dalkeith, Dingwall, Dumfries, Dunblane, Fortrose, Giffnock, Greenock, Hamilton, Jedburgh, Kirkwall, Montrose, Stirling, Ullapool
**09** Ardrossan, Callander, Clydebank, Dumbarton, Edinburgh, Inverness, Inverurie, Kingussie, Kirkcaldy, Lockerbie, Peterhead, Pitlochry, Prestwick, St Andrews, Stornoway, Stranraer
**10** Coatbridge, Dalbeattie, Galashiels, Glenrothes, Kilmarnock, Kincardine, Linlithgow, Livingston, Motherwell, Newtonmore, Stonehaven
**11** Blairgowrie, Campbeltown, Cowdenbeath, Crianlarich, Cumbernauld, Dunfermline, Fort William, Fraserburgh, Grangemouth, Gretna Green, Invergordon, John o'Groats, Port Glasgow
**12** Auchterarder, East Kilbride, Lochgilphead
**13** Castle Douglas, Kirkcudbright, Kirkintilloch
**14** Grantown-on-Spey

*Welsh towns include:*

**04** Bala, Mold, Rhyl
**05** Barry, Conwy, Tenby, Tywyn
**06** Bangor, Brecon, Ruthin
**07** Cardiff, Cwmbrân, Denbigh, Harlech, Newport, Newtown, Swansea, Wrexham
**08** Aberdare, Barmouth, Bridgend, Cardigan, Chepstow, Ebbw Vale, Hay-on-Wye, Holyhead, Lampeter, Llanelli, Monmouth, Pembroke, Pwllheli, Rhayader, St David's, Treorchy
**09** Aberaeron, Carnarvon, Colwyn Bay, Dolgellau, Fishguard, Llandudno, Llangefni, Pontypool, Prestatyn, Welshpool
**10** Caernarfon, Caerphilly, Carmarthen, Llandovery, Llangollen, Pontypridd, Porthmadog, Port Talbot
**11** Abergavenny, Abertillery, Aberystwyth, Builth Wells, Machynlleth
**12** Milford Haven
**13** Haverfordwest, Merthyr Tydfil

*See also* **city**; **United Kingdom**

• **mushroom town**
**04** camp

• **open space in town**
**04** lung

**town-dweller**
**03** cit **05** towny **07** burgher, citizen, oppidan **08** townsman, urbanite **10** townswoman

**township**
**02** tp **04** deme, vill **06** parish **07** village **09** community

**toxic**
**06** deadly, lethal **07** baneful, harmful, noxious **08** poisoned **09** dangerous, poisonous, unhealthy

*See also* **poison**

**toy**
**04** jest, play, whim **05** dally, flirt, knack, model, sport, trick **06** bauble, beaker, fiddle, gewgaw, paddle, tinker, trifle **07** reduced, replica, trinket **08** crotchet **09** automaton, mess about, miniature, plaything **10** knick-knack, mess around, small-scale **12** reproduction

*Toys include:*

**03** ark, gun, top
**04** ball, bike, dart, doll, farm, fort, game, gonk, kite, Lego®, Sega®, XBox®, yo-yo

05 coral, Dinky®, slide, swing, teddy, trike
06 cap-gun, garage, go-kart, guitar, paints, pop-gun, puzzle, rattle, rocker, seesaw, tea set
07 balloon, bicycle, box-kite, crayons, Digimon®, dreidel, drum set, Frisbee®, Game Boy®, marbles, Meccano®, ocarina, Play-Doh®, Pokémon®, rag doll, sandpit, scooter, shoofly, soft-toy, tumbler, Turtles®
08 catapult, doll's cot, football, GameCube®, golliwog, hula-hoop, Matchbox®, mirliton, model car, model kit, Nintendo®, Noah's ark, pedal-car, pinwheel, skipjack, squeaker, Subbuteo®, train set, tricycle, windmill
09 Action Man®, aeroplane, bandalore, Care Bears, doll's pram, gyroscope, playhouse, pogo stick, Sindy doll®, swingball, teddy bear, video game, whirligig
10 baby-walker, Barbie doll®, doll's buggy, doll's house, fivestones, hobby-horse, kewpie doll, musical box, pantograph, peashooter, Plasticene®, Rubik's Cube®, Scalextric®, skateboard, Steiff bear, Super Mario®, tin soldier, toy soldier, trampoline, typewriter, weather box, Wendy house
11 baby-bouncer, glove puppet, PlayStation®, shape-sorter, spacehopper, spinning top, stroboscope, Tantalus cup, thaumatrope, tiddly winks, water pistol, wheel of life
12 action figure, boxing-gloves, computer game, executive toy, jack-in-the-box, jigsaw puzzle, kaleidoscope, model railway, mountain bike, My Little Pony, paddling-pool, Power Rangers®, praxinoscope, rocking-horse, skipping-rope, walkie-talkie, weather house
13 Bob the Builder®, building block, climbing-frame, modelling clay, Newton's cradle, sewing machine, Space Invaders®, Tiny-Tears doll®
14 activity centre, bucket and spade, building-blocks, building-bricks, Cartesian devil, Cartesian diver, electronic game, Paddington Bear, Powerpuff Girls®

---

**trace**
**03** bit, dog, jot, map, way **04** calk, copy, dash, draw, dreg, drop, find, hint, hunt, mark, move, plan, scar, seek, show, sign, spot, walk **05** chart, dig up, draft, pinch, relic, savor, scent, smack, spoor, stalk, tinge, token, touch, track, tract, trail, whiff, write **06** course, depict, derive, detect, engram, follow, fossil, pursue, record, savour, shadow, sketch **07** analyse, mark out, outline, proceed, remains, remnant, run down, soupçon, thought, uncover, unearth, vestige **08** chalk out, describe, discover, engramma, evidence, footmark, generate, moniment, monument, traverse **09** delineate, footprint, scintilla, suspicion, track down **10** hide or hair, impression, indication, suggestion **11** counterdraw, hide nor hair

**track**
**03** dog, pug, ren, rin, run, way **04** beat, hunt, line, loke, mark, path, race, rack, rail, rake, road, sent, sign, slot, tail, tram, trod, wake **05** chase, drift, orbit, piste, route, scent, spoor, stalk, trace, tract, trade, trail, tread, troad, trode
**06** course, follow, groove, ground, inside, pursue, riding, runway, shadow, sleuth, troade **07** circuit, footing, monitor, portage, tramway
**08** argument, cycleway, footmark, footstep, sequence, sideline, speedway, traverse **09** cyclepath, footprint **10** serpentine, trajectory

*See also* **athletics**

**• keep track of**
**04** plot **05** check, grasp, trace, watch
**06** follow, record **07** monitor, observe, oversee **10** keep up with, understand
**11** keep an eye on
**• lose track of**
**04** miss **06** forget **08** misplace **13** lose touch with **15** lose contact with
**• make tracks**
**02** go **04** dash **05** leave, scram **06** beat it, depart **07** dash off, make off
**09** disappear **10** hit the road **15** leave footprints
**• off the beaten track**
**06** remote **07** private **08** isolated, outlying, secluded **11** god-forsaken, in the sticks, out-of-the-way
**12** unfrequented
**• on track**
**06** on time **08** on course, on target
**10** on schedule
**• track down**
**04** find **05** catch, dig up, trace
**06** detect, expose, turn up **07** capture, nose out, run down, uncover, unearth
**08** discover, hunt down, sniff out
**09** ferret out **10** run to earth **11** run to ground
**• tracks**
**02** Ry

**tract**
**03** lot **04** area, dene, plot, vast, zone
**05** clime, essay, monte, trace, track
**06** desert, extent, homily, region, sermon **07** booklet, expanse, leaflet, quarter, stretch, terrain **08** brochure, district, pamphlet, tractate, treatise
**09** discourse, monograph, territory
**12** disquisition, dissertation

**tractable**
**04** tame **05** tawie **06** docile, pliant
**07** pliable, willing **08** amenable, biddable, obedient, towardly, tractile, workable, yielding **09** compliant, malleable, treatable **10** governable, manageable, submissive
**11** complaisant, persuadable
**12** controllable

**traction**
**04** drag, grip, pull **07** draught, drawing, haulage, pulling **08** adhesion, friction
**09** telferage **10** propulsion, telpherage

**tractor**
**03** cat **07** backhoe, pedrail, skidder
**09** bulldozer **13** backhoe loader
**14** traction engine

**trade**
**02** go **03** art, buy, job, ply, ren, rin, run, way **04** deal, line, mart, sell, swap, work **05** craft, skill, track, trail, tread
**06** barter, buying, career, course, custom, market, métier, mister, occupy, peddle, resort, switch **07** bargain, calling, dealing, rubbish, selling, traffic
**08** business, commerce, exchange, medicine, merchant, peddling, practice, sideline, transact, treading, vocation **09** carpentry, clientele, customers, marketing **10** contraband, do business, employment, line of work, occupation, profession
**11** commodities, merchandize, shopkeeping, trafficking
**12** transactions

**trademark**
**04** logo, mark, name, sign **05** badge, brand, crest, label, quirk, stamp
**06** emblem, symbol **07** feature
**08** hallmark, insignia **09** attribute, brand name, idiograph, tradename
**10** brand label, speciality **11** peculiarity
**12** idiosyncrasy **14** characteristic, typical quality **15** proprietary name

**tradename**
**02** TN **05** brand, label

**trader**
**05** bania, buyer, plier **06** banian, banyan, broker, dealer, seller, vendor
**07** higgler, peddler **08** marketer, merchant, pitchman, retailer, supplier
**09** barrow boy, marketeer, tradesman
**10** easterling, shopkeeper, trafficker, wholesaler **11** tradeswoman

**tradesman, tradeswoman**
**05** buyer **06** dealer, seller, trader, vendor, worker **07** artisan
**08** mechanic, merchant, retailer
**09** craftsman **10** journeyman, shopkeeper **11** craftswoman

**tradition**
**03** way **04** rite **05** habit, usage
**06** belief, cabala, custom, kabala, legend, praxis, ritual **07** cabbala, kabbala, qabalah, routine
**08** ceremony, folklore, kabbalah, practice **10** convention, observance
**11** institution

**traditional**
**03** old, set **04** folk, oral **05** fixed, usual
**06** age-old **07** old-line, pompier, routine **08** habitual, historic
**09** customary, traditive, unwritten
**10** accustomed, ceremonial
**11** established **12** conservative, conventional, time-honoured, tralaticious, tralatitious **15** long-established

**traditionalist**
**07** diehard **08** old fogey, old guard, old-liner **09** formalist **11** reactionary **12** conservative **13** stick-in-the-mud **15** conventionalist

**traduce**
**04** slag **05** abuse, decry, knock, smear **06** defame, insult, malign, revile, vilify **07** asperse, blacken, detract, run down, slag off, slander **08** transmit **09** denigrate, deprecate, disparage, propagate, translate **10** calumniate, depreciate **12** misrepresent

**traducer**
**06** abuser **07** defamer, knocker, smearer **08** asperser, vilifier **09** detractor, slanderer **10** denigrator, deprecator, disparager, mud-slinger **11** calumniator

**traffic**
**03** buy **04** cars, deal, sell **05** queue, trade, truck **06** barter, hold-up, peddle **07** bargain, contact, dealing, freight, trade in, trading **08** business, commerce, dealings, exchange, gridlock, intrigue, peddling, shipping, tailback, vehicles **09** negotiate, relations, transport **10** congestion, do business, passengers, traffic jam **11** commodities, intercourse, trafficking **13** communication **14** transportation

**trafficker**
**05** agent **06** broker, dealer, monger, seller, trader **07** peddler **08** marketer, merchant, supplier **11** distributor **12** merchandizer

**tragedy**
**04** blow **06** buskin **08** calamity, disaster **09** adversity **10** affliction, misfortune **11** catastrophe, unhappiness

**tragic**
◇ *anagram indicator*
**03** sad **04** dire **05** awful, fatal **06** deadly **07** unhappy, unlucky **08** buskined, dreadful, ill-fated, pathetic, pitiable, shocking, terrible, Thespian, wretched **09** appalling, miserable, sorrowful **10** calamitous, deplorable, disastrous **11** unfortunate **12** catastrophic **13** heartbreaking

**tragically**
**07** awfully **08** terribly **10** dreadfully, shockingly, wretchedly **11** appallingly

**trail**
◇ *juxtaposition indicator*
**03** dog, lag, tow, way **04** drag, draw, fall, hang, haul, hunt, path, pull, road, sign, tail, wake **05** chase, droop, marks, piste, reach, route, scent, spoor, stalk, sweep, trace, track, trade, train **06** dangle, dawdle, extend, follow, linger, loiter, pursue, ramble, runway, shadow, sleuth, stream, streel, trapes **07** abature, draggle, traipse **08** footpath, straggle, tag along, trauchle **09** footmarks **10** footprints

**• destroy trail**
**04** foil

**• trail away**
**04** fade, sink **06** lessen, shrink, weaken **07** die away, dwindle, subside, tail off **08** decrease, diminish, fade away, fall away, melt away, peter out, taper off, trail off **09** disappear

**trailblazer**
**06** leader **07** founder, pioneer **09** developer, innovator **10** discoverer, pathfinder **13** ground-breaker

**train**
◇ *anagram indicator*
**03** aim, set **04** drag, file, line, lure, path, sack, tail, tire **05** breed, chain, coach, court, drill, flier, flyer, focus, groom, learn, level, local, longe, lunge, order, point, staff, study, suite, teach, track, trail, tutor **06** allure, cafila, column, convoy, direct, ground, kafila, lesson, nuzzle, school, series, sledge, stream, string **07** bring up, caffila, caravan, cortège, educate, improve, prepare, process, retinue, work out **08** be taught, choo-choo, exercise, instruct, practise, puff-puff, rehearse, sequence **09** be trained, entourage, followers, following, household, inculcate **10** attendants, be prepared, discipline, procession, succession **11** progression **12** indoctrinate **13** concatenation

*Train types include:*

**01** Q
**02** up
**03** APT, HST, owl, TGV, way
**04** boat, down, loco, mail, milk
**05** goods, hover, mixed, paddy, steam
**06** bullet, diesel, Maglev
**07** baggage, express, freight, through
**08** cable-car, corridor, monorail, push-pull
**09** aerotrain, excursion, high-speed, Intercity®, manriding
**10** locomotive
**12** Freightliner®
**13** accommodation
**14** shuttle service
**15** steam locomotive

*Trains include:*

**06** Rocket, Thomas
**07** Mallard, The Ghan
**09** The A-Train
**13** Indian Pacific, Orient Express, Trans-Siberian
**14** Flying Scotsman
**15** Hogwarts Express

**trained**
**03** fit **08** schooled **10** discerning **11** experienced

**trainee**
**01** L **02** AT, ET **04** tiro **05** cadet, pupil **06** intern, novice **07** interne, learner, student **08** beginner **10** apprentice **11** probationer

**trainer**
**02** PT **05** coach, tutor **06** mentor **07** handler, teacher **08** educator **10** instructor
*See also* **footwear**; **horseman, horsewoman**

**training**
◇ *anagram indicator*
**02** PT **03** CAT, CBT **05** drill **07** lessons, nurture, tuition, workout **08** coaching, exercise, learning, pedagogy, practice, teaching, tutoring **09** education, grounding, schooling **10** bringing up, discipline, tirocinium, upbringing, working-out **11** instruction, preparation **14** apprenticeship

**• out of training**
**04** soft

**• youth in training**
**04** page

**traipse**
**03** gad **04** plod, slog, trek **05** trail, tramp, trape **06** slouch, trudge **08** slattern

**trait**
**04** thew **05** quirk, touch, trick **06** stroke **07** feature, quality **08** property **09** attribute **11** peculiarity **12** idiosyncrasy **14** characteristic

**traitor**
**03** dog **05** Judas, kulak **07** nithing **08** betrayer, deceiver, defector, deserter, informer, proditor, quisling, renegade, traditor, treacher, turncoat, two-timer **09** traitress, treachour **11** backstabber, treachetour **12** collaborator, double-dealer **13** double-crosser **14** fifth columnist

**traitorous**
**05** false **06** untrue **08** apostate, disloyal, renegade **09** faithless, seditious **10** perfidious, unfaithful **11** treacherous, treasonable **13** dishonourable, double-dealing **14** double-crossing

**trajectory**
**04** line, path **05** orbit, route, track, trail **06** course, flight **10** flight path

**trammel**
◇ *anagram indicator*
**03** bar, net, tie **04** bond, clog, curb, rein **05** block, catch, chain, check **06** enmesh, entrap, fetter, hamper, hinder, hobble, impede **07** capture, confine, ensnare, inhibit, shackle **08** entangle, handicap, obstacle, restrain, restrict **09** hindrance, restraint **10** impediment **14** stumbling-block

**tramp**
**03** bum **04** hike, hobo, plod, roam, rove, slag, slut, step, tart, trek, walk **05** caird, jakey, march, piker, rogue, stamp, stomp, stump, trail, tread, tromp, wench, whore **06** dosser, hooker, ramble, sloven, toerag, truant, trudge, vagrom, walker, whaler **07** dingbat, floater, floozie, gangrel, swagger, swagman, tinkler, traipse, trample, trollop, vagrant **08** clochard, cursitor, derelict, footslog, scrubber, slattern, straggle, stroller, vagabond

09 landloper, sundowner, toeragger 10 down-and-out, loose woman, prostitute 11 rinthereout, scatterling, Weary Willie 12 hallan-shaker 15 knight of the road

**trample**
04 foil 05 crush, poach, potch, stamp, tramp, tread, tromp 06 insult, squash, stramp 07 flatten, hobnail 08 override, ride down

**trance**
04 daze 05 dream, spell 06 stupor, transe 07 ecstasy, rapture, reverie 08 entrance 09 catalepsy 12 somnambulism 15 unconsciousness

**tranche**
03 cut 04 part 05 block, piece, slice, wedge 06 length 07 portion, section, segment 10 instalment

**tranquil**
04 calm, cool, easy 05 quiet, still 06 hushed, placid, sedate, serene, silent 07 pacific, relaxed, restful 08 composed, laid-back, peaceful 09 reposeful, unexcited 10 untroubled 11 undisturbed, unflappable 12 even-tempered 13 imperturbable, unimpassioned 14 disimpassioned

**tranquillity**
03 lee 04 calm, hush, rest 05 peace, quiet 06 repose 07 ataraxy, silence 08 ataraxia, calmness, coolness, quietism, quietude, serenity 09 composure, placidity, quietness, stillness 10 equanimity, sedateness 11 restfulness 12 peacefulness

**tranquillize**
04 calm, lull 05 quell, quiet, relax 06 opiate, pacify, sedate, serene, soothe 07 compose 09 narcotize

**tranquillizer**
06 downer, opiate 07 bromide 08 narcotic, quietive, sedative 09 calmative 10 depressant 11 barbiturate 12 sleeping pill
*See also* **sedative**

**transact**
02 do 05 enact 06 handle, manage, settle 07 carry on, conduct, execute, perform 08 carry out, conclude, despatch, dispatch 09 discharge, negotiate, prosecute 10 accomplish

**transaction**
03 job 04 deal, deed 06 action, affair, annals, doings, gamble, matter, record 07 affairs, bargain, minutes, passage, reports 08 business, concerns, debt swap, goings-on, handling, straddle 09 agreement, discharge, enactment, execution 10 enterprise, proceeding, put-through, settlement, swap option 11 arrangement, negotiation, proceedings, undertaking 12 control event, part-exchange, publications

**transactions**
02 tr 07 affairs, dealing, journal, memoirs

**transcend**
04 beat 05 excel, outdo 06 exceed 07 eclipse, surpass 08 go beyond, outshine, outstrip, overstep, surmount 09 rise above 11 leave behind

**transcendence**
09 greatness, sublimity, supremacy 10 ascendancy, excellence, paramouncy 11 paramountcy, pre-eminence, superiority 12 predominance 13 matchlessness, transcendency 15 incomparability

**transcendent**
07 sublime, supreme 08 numinous, peerless 09 excellent, excelling, ineffable, matchless, spiritual 10 superhuman, surpassing 11 magnificent, superlative 12 incomparable, supernatural, transcending, unparalleled 13 unsurpassable

**transcendental**
05 vague 08 mystical 09 excelling, spiritual 10 mysterious 12 metaphysical, otherworldly, supereminent, supernatural, transcending 13 preternatural

**transcribe**
04 copy, note 06 copy up, record, render 07 Braille, copy out, rewrite, write up 08 take down, write out 09 reproduce, translate 13 transliterate

**transcript**
04 copy, note 05 tenor 06 record, tenour 07 version 09 duplicate 10 manuscript 11 translation 12 reproduction 13 transcription 15 exemplification, transliteration

**transcription**
07 version 10 writing-out 11 translation 12 reproduction, transumption 15 transliteration

**transfer**
◇ *anagram indicator*
02 ET 03 EFT, PET, PMT 04 deed, flit, GIFT, hand, move, pass, take, turn, ZIFT 05 carry, grant, ladle, remit, shift 06 assign, change, convey, pounce, remove 07 consign, pipette, removal 08 alienate, give over, hand over, handover, movement, relocate, sign away, sign over, transmit 09 negotiate, transhume, transport, transpose 10 assignment, changeover, conveyance, relocation, transplant 12 displacement, transduction, transference, transmission 13 transposition

**transfigure**
◇ *anagram indicator*
05 alter, exalt, morph 06 change 07 convert, glorify 08 idealize 09 transform, translate, transmute 11 apotheosize 12 metamorphose

**transfix**
04 hold, spit, stun 05 rivet, spear, spike, stick 06 empale, impale, pierce, skewer 07 bestick, engross, petrify 08 paralyse 09 fascinate, hypnotize, mesmerize, spellbind 10 run through

**transform**
◇ *anagram indicator*
04 turn 05 adapt, alter, morph, renew 06 absorb, change, mutate, reform 07 commute, convert, lithify, rebuild, receive, remodel, resolve 08 disclose 09 sovietize, translate, transmute, transpose 10 trans-shape, transverse 11 reconstruct, transfigure 12 decentralize, metamorphose, transmogrify 13 revolutionize 15 unprotestantize

**transformation**
◇ *anagram indicator*
03 wig 06 change, reform 07 turning 08 dilation, mutation, petalody, phyllody, reaction, rotation, sepalody 09 reflexion, sea change, variation 10 alteration, conversion, dilatation, metaplasia, metastasis, reflection, revolution 11 reformation, translation 13 metamorphosis, transmutation 15 theriomorphosis, transfiguration

**transfuse**
05 imbue 06 instil 07 pervade, suffuse 08 permeate, transfer

**transgress**
03 err, sin 04 defy 05 break, lapse 06 breach, exceed, offend 07 disobey, violate 08 encroach, infringe, overstep, trespass 09 misbehave 10 contravene 11 prevaricate

**transgression**
03 sin 04 debt, slip 05 crime, error, fault, lapse, scape, wrong 06 breach, escape 07 misdeed, offence, offense 08 iniquity, peccancy, trespass 09 overgoing, violation 10 infraction, peccadillo, wrongdoing 12 disobedience, encroachment, infringement, misbehaviour, misdemeanour, overstepping 13 contravention

**transgressor**
05 felon 06 debtor, sinner 07 culprit, villain 08 criminal, evil-doer, offender 09 miscreant, wrongdoer 10 delinquent, lawbreaker, malefactor, trespasser

**transience**
07 brevity 08 caducity, fugacity 09 briefness, shortness 11 evanescence 12 ephemerality, fleetingness, fugitiveness, impermanence 13 deciduousness, temporariness 14 transitoriness

**transient**
05 brief, fleet, short 06 bubble, flying 07 passing 08 fleeting, volatile 09 ephemeral, fugacious, momentary, short-term, temporary 10 evanescent, short-lived, transitory 11 impermanent 13 summer-seeming

**transistor**
03 FET

**transit**
**05** route **06** travel **07** haulage, journey, passage, reverse **08** carriage, crossing, movement, shipment, transfer **10** conveyance, journeying, pass across **11** culmination **14** transportation

**• in transit**
**05** by air, by sea **06** by rail, by road **07** en route **08** on the way **10** travelling

**transition**
**04** flux, leap, move **05** shift **06** change, switch **07** passage, passing **08** movement, progress **09** evolution, metabasis **10** alteration, changeover, conversion, metastasis, unbecoming **11** composition, development, progression **12** transitional **13** metamorphosis, rite of passage, transmutation **14** transformation

**transitional**
**05** fluid **07** interim, passing **08** changing, twilight **09** temporary, unsettled **11** provisional **12** evolutionary, intermediate **13** developmental

**transitory**
**05** brief, fleet, short **06** flying **07** passing **08** fleeting **09** deciduous, ephemeral, fugacious, momentary, short-term, temporary, transient **10** evanescent, fly-by-night, short-lived **11** impermanent

**translate**
◇ *anagram indicator*
◇ *foreign word indicator*
**03** put **04** move, turn **05** alter, shift **06** change, decode, encode, reduce, render, reword **07** conster, convert, English, explain, improve, traduce **08** construe, decipher, relocate, renovate, simplify, transfer **09** enrapture, interpret, transform, transmute, transport **10** metaphrase, paraphrase, transcribe **12** transmogrify **13** transliterate

**translation**
◇ *anagram indicator*
**03** key **04** crib, move, pony **05** gloss, horse, shift **06** change, motion **07** version **08** transfer **09** rendering, rendition, rewording **10** alteration, conversion, metaphrase, paraphrase, rephrasing, traduction **11** explanation, metaphrasis **12** transumption **13** metamorphosis, transcription, transmutation **14** interpretation, simplification, transformation **15** transliteration

**translator**
**02** tr **03** CLT **07** exegete, glosser, Rhemist **08** dragoman, linguist, polyglot **09** Englisher, exegetist, glossator **10** glossarist, metaphrast, paraphrast **11** interpreter, paraphraser

**translucent**
**05** clear **06** limpid **08** lancelet, pellucid **10** diaphanous, membranous, see-through, translucid **11** membraneous, transparent **13** membranaceous

**transmigration**
**07** rebirth **13** reincarnation **14** metempsychosis, Pythagoreanism, transformation

**transmission**
**04** show **06** entail, signal, spread **07** beaming, episode, message, passage, sending **08** carriage, despatch, dispatch, relaying, shipment, transfer **09** broadcast, diffusion, imparting, programme, simulcast, transport **10** convection, conveyance, production, trajection **11** consignment, performance **12** broadcasting, presentation, transference **13** communication, dissemination, transmittance

**• end of transmission**
**04** over **10** over and out

**transmit**
**03** fax **04** beam, bear, buzz, pass, pipe, send **05** carry, modem, radio, relay, remit **06** convey, hand on, impart, pass on, report, send on, spread **07** conduct, consign, diffuse, forward, mediate, message, network, radiate, send out, traduce, traject **08** despatch, dispatch, hand down, telecast, televise, transfer **09** broadcast, propagate, satellite, transport **11** communicate, disseminate, interrogate

**transmute**
◇ *anagram indicator*
**05** alter **06** change, remake **07** convert, permute, sublime **08** transmew **09** alchemize, permutate, sublimate, transform, translate, transmove **10** transverse **11** transfigure **12** metamorphose, transmogrify

**transparency**
**05** photo, slide, water **07** clarity, picture **08** openness, overhead **09** clearness, filminess, frankness, gauziness, limpidity, plainness, sheerness **10** candidness, directness, limpidness, patentness, photograph **11** obviousness, pellucidity **12** apparentness, distinctness, explicitness, pellucidness, translucence, translucency **13** translucidity **14** diaphanousness, forthrightness **15** perspicuousness, unambiguousness

**transparent**
**04** open **05** clear, filmy, gauzy, lucid, plain, sheer, white **06** candid, direct, limpid, patent, watery **07** evident, hyaline, hyaloid, obvious, tiffany, visible **08** apparent, distinct, explicit, manifest, pellucid **10** colourless, diaphanous, forthright, noticeable, see-through **11** discernible, perceptible, translucent, unambiguous, undisguised, unequivocal **12** semipellucid, transpicuous, unmistakable **15** straightforward

**transparently**
**07** clearly, plainly **08** patently **09** evidently, obviously **10** distinctly, explicitly, noticeably **11** discernibly, perceptibly **12** unmistakably **13** unambiguously, unequivocally

**transpire**
**05** arise, ensue, occur, prove **06** appear, befall, exhale, happen **07** come out, turn out **09** come about, take place **10** come to pass **11** become known, be disclosed, come to light **14** become apparent

**transplant**
**04** move **05** graft, repot, shift **06** remove, uproot **07** replant **08** displace, plant out, relocate, resettle, transfer **12** cluster graft

**transport**
◇ *anagram indicator*
**02** MT **03** AST, fit, lag, put, ren, rin, run, SST **04** bear, haul, move, rail, rape, rush, ship, take, waft **05** bliss, bring, carry, cycle, exile, fetch, shift, witch **06** convey, deport, frenzy, ravish, remove, thrill **07** delight, ecstasy, elation, freight, haulage, medevac, overjoy, rapture, removal, traject, transit, vehicle **08** carriage, entrance, euphoria, shipment, shipping, transfer **09** captivate, carry away, electrify, enrapture, spellbind, translate **10** conveyance **12** exhilaration **13** seventh heaven, transportance **14** transportation

*See also* **travel**; **vehicle**

*Public transport includes:*

**03** bus, cab
**04** taxi, tram, tube
**05** ferry, metro, train
**07** omnibus, railway, trolley
**10** stage-coach, trolleybus
**11** park-and-ride, underground
**12** light railway

**transportation**
**07** airlift, freight, haulage, railage, removal, traffic, transit, waftage **08** carriage, shipment, shipping, transfer **09** fishyback **10** conveyance

**transported**
◇ *anagram indicator*
**04** rapt **05** piped **08** traveled **09** rhapsodic, travelled

**transpose**
◇ *anagram indicator*
**02** tr **04** move, swap, turn **05** alter, shift **06** change, invert, switch **07** convert, reorder **08** exchange, flip-flop, transfer **09** rearrange, transform **10** substitute **11** interchange, metathesize **13** anagrammatize

**transverse**
**05** cross **06** thwart **07** oblique, reverse **08** diagonal **09** crossways, crosswise, transform **10** overthwart **11** transversal

**trap**
◇ *containment indicator*
**03** gin, gob, net, pit, pot **04** drop, dupe,

fall, grin, hook, lime, lock, lure, mesh, ploy, ruse, take, toil, weel, wile **05** bazoo, catch, creel, decoy, fault, mouth, noose, plant, snare, spell, sting, toils, trick **06** ambush, bunker, corner, danger, device, enmesh, entrap, hazard, tangle **07** beguile, capture, confine, deceive, ensnare, flytrap, gin trap, mantrap, mist-net, pin down, pitfall, putcher, rat-trap, springe **08** artifice, cakehole, catch-pit, deadfall, fall-trap, inveigle, putcheon, trapdoor, traphole, trickery **09** booby-trap, deception, mouse-trap, snaphance, stratagem **10** catch-basin, dig a pit for, potato trap, snaphaunce, snaphaunch, subterfuge

*See also* **carriage**

**trapped**
◇ *insertion indicator*
**05** duped, stuck **06** caught, netted, snared **07** tricked **08** ambushed, beguiled, cornered, deceived, ensnared **09** inveigled **10** surrounded **11** in by the week

**trapper**
**06** hunter **08** covering, huntsman, voyageur **12** backwoodsman, frontiersman

**trappings**
**04** gear **05** dress **06** finery, livery, things **07** clothes, panoply, raiment **08** fittings, fixtures, housings **09** equipment, furniture, ornaments, trimmings **10** adornments, fripperies **11** accessories, decorations, furnishings **13** accoutrements, paraphernalia **14** accompaniments

**trash**
◇ *anagram indicator*
**03** mar, pan, rot **04** blah, bosh, bull, bunk, carp, dust, guff, junk, ruin, scum, sink, slam **05** balls, blame, break, check, decry, dreck, dregs, hooey, knock, leash, slate, smash, snipe, spoil, tripe, waste, wreck **06** attack, drivel, grunge, harass, kitsch, litter, rabble, ravage, refuse, scraps, trudge **07** baloney, censure, condemn, destroy, eyewash, garbage, hogwash, rhubarb, rubbish, run down, shatter, torpedo, wear out **08** badmouth, canaille, demolish, denounce, malarkey, nonsense, riff-raff, trashery, write off **09** criticize, denigrate, devastate, disparage, excoriate, gibberish, moonshine, sweepings, trashtrie, vandalize **10** balderdash, come down on, go to town on, vituperate **11** pick holes in **12** disapprove of, gobbledygook, offscourings, pull to pieces, put the boot in, tear to shreds, undesirables **13** find fault with, play havoc with, tear a strip off **15** do a hatchet job on, pass judgement on

**trashy**
**04** naff **05** cheap **06** crappy, flimsy, kitsch, paltry, shabby, shoddy, tawdry, tinsel **07** kitschy **08** inferior, rubbishy **09** cheap-jack, third-rate, worthless **12** meretricious

**trauma**
**04** hurt, jolt, pain **05** agony, grief, shock, upset, wound **06** damage, injury, lesion, ordeal, strain, stress **07** anguish, torture **08** disorder, distress, upheaval **09** suffering **11** disturbance

**traumatic**
**07** harmful, hurtful, painful **08** shocking, wounding **09** agonizing, injurious, stressful, upsetting **10** disturbing, unpleasant **11** distressing, frightening

**traumatize**
**04** daze, hurt, numb, stun **05** amaze, appal, shock, upset **06** dismay, grieve, offend **07** astound, horrify, outrage, stagger, startle, stupefy **08** distress, paralyse

**travail**
**04** slog, toil **05** grind, sweat, tears **06** effort, labour, strain, stress, throes, travel **07** travois, trouble **08** distress, drudgery, exertion, hardship **09** suffering **10** birth-pangs, childbirth **11** labour pains, tribulation

**travel**
**02** go **03** ren, rin, run **04** meve, move, pass, ride, roam, rove, tour, trip, tube, walk, wend, wing **05** cover, cross, vroom, wagon, wheel **06** ramble, troupe, voyage, waggon, wander **07** advance, conduct, explore, impetus, journey, passage, proceed, touring, tourism, travail, trolley, wayfare **08** go abroad, progress, traverse **09** excursion, make a trip **10** expedition, go overseas, journeying, travelling, wanderings **11** make your way, see the world, sightseeing **13** globetrotting

*See also* **space**

***Travel methods and forms include:***

**03** bus, fly, row, ski
**04** bike, hike, punt, ride, sail, tour, trek, trip, walk
**05** cycle, drive, jaunt, march, motor, pilot, skate, steam, visit
**06** aviate, cruise, flight, outing, paddle, ramble, safari, voyage
**07** commute, holiday, journey, mission, shuttle
**09** excursion, freewheel, hitch-hike, migration, orienteer
**10** expedition, pilgrimage
**11** exploration

**traveller**
**03** rep **05** agent, Gypsy, hiker, nomad, rider, tramp **06** bagman, spacer, tinker, tourer, viator **07** aviator, bushman, drifter, drummer, migrant, rambler, tourist, tripper, vagrant, voyager **08** aviatrix, commuter, explorer, roadster, salesman, seafarer, spaceman, wanderer, wayfarer **09** itinerant, passenger, peregrine, sightseer **10** commercial, saleswoman, spacewoman **11** salesperson **12** excursionist, globetrotter, holidaymaker **14** representative **15** knight of the road

**travelling**
◇ *anagram indicator*
**04** road, rode **06** mobile, moving, roving **07** migrant, nomadic, roaming, sailing, touring, vagrant **08** homeless **09** itinerant, itinerary, migrating, migratory, on the move, on the road, unsettled, wandering, wayfaring **11** peripatetic

**travel-worn**
**05** tired, weary **07** seasick, waygone, wayworn **08** footsore **09** jet-lagged **10** saddle-sore **11** travel-weary

**traverse**
**03** lap, ply, ren, rin, run **04** deny, ford, pace, plod, race, ride, roam, span, walk, wear, wind, wing **05** cover, cross, motor, range, stump, trace, track, tramp **06** bridge, denial, oppose, overgo, parade, screen, thwart, voyage, wander **07** barrier, curtain, descend, dispute, examine, measure, oblique, parapet **08** consider, crossing, go across, pass over, progress, walk over **09** adversity, go through, negotiate, partition **10** contradict, crosspiece **11** obstruction, pass through, peregrinate **12** travel across **13** contradiction, travel through

**travesty**
**04** sham **05** farce, spoof **06** parody, send-up, wind-up **07** apology, mockery, take-off **08** disguise **09** black mass, burlesque, tall story **10** caricature, corruption, distortion, perversion

**trawl**
**04** comb, hunt, sift, wade **06** search **07** look for **11** investigate

**treacherous**
**03** icy **05** dirty, false, Punic, risky, snaky **06** guiled, trappy, unsafe, untrue **08** disloyal, perilous, slippery **09** dangerous, deceitful, faithless, hazardous, two-timing **10** perfidious, precarious, traitorous, unfaithful, unreliable **11** duplicitous **12** backstabbing, false-hearted **13** double-hearted, hollow-hearted, untrustworthy **14** double-crossing

**treacherously**
**07** falsely **08** mala fide **10** disloyally **11** deceitfully, faithlessly **12** perfidiously

**treachery**
**07** treason **08** bad faith, betrayal, sabotage, trahison **09** duplicity, falseness, Judas kiss, perfidity, two-timing **10** disloyalty, hollowness, infidelity, Punic faith **11** fides Punica, traitorhood **12** backstabbing **13** deceitfulness, double-dealing, faithlessness **14** double-crossing, unfaithfulness

**tread**
**02** go **04** beat, form, gait, hike, pace, plod, step, trek, walk **05** clamp, clump, crush, dance, march, press, spurn, stamp, trace, track, trade, tramp **06** squash, stramp, stride, trudge, walk on **07** chalaza, flatten, footing, oppress, trample **08** business, copulate, footfall, footmark, footstep **09** footprint, press down **11** cicatricula

• **tread on someone's toes**
**03** irk, vex **04** hurt **05** annoy, upset **06** bruise, injure, offend **07** affront **08** infringe **10** discommode, disgruntle **13** inconvenience

**treason**
**06** mutiny **07** perfidy **08** sedition, trahison **09** duplicity, rebellion, treachery **10** disloyalty, subversion **11** lese-majesty, leze-majesté, leze-majesty, perduellion, traitorhood **12** disaffection **14** traitorousness

**treasonable**
**05** false **08** disloyal, mutinous **09** faithless, seditious **10** perfidious, rebellious, subversive, traitorous, unfaithful

**treasure**
**03** gem **04** cash, gems, gold, love **05** adore, cache, guard, hoard, money, prize, value **06** dote on, esteem, jewels, revere, riches, taonga, wealth **07** cherish, darling, fortune, idolize, worship **08** hold dear, preserve **09** valuables **11** masterpiece, pride and joy **13** think highly of **14** crème de la crème

**treasurer**
**06** bursar, fiscal, purser **07** cashier, steward **08** quaestor **10** camerlengo, camerlingo, cash-keeper **11** purse-bearer

**treasury**
**04** bank, fisc, fisk **05** cache, chest, funds, hoard, money, store, vault **06** assets, camera, corpus **07** bursary, capital, coffers **08** finances, revenues **09** exchequer, resources, thesaurus **10** repository, storehouse

**treat**
◇ *anagram indicator*
**02** do **03** buy, fun, rub, tar, tub, use, vat, vet, wax **04** cure, gift, give, heal, tend, view, wine, worm **05** amuse, apply, besee, cover, dress, feast, lay on, nurse, paint, party, prime, put on, serve, smear, stand, study, waste, wheel **06** doctor, handle, manage, outing, parley, pay for, regale, regard, review, thrill **07** banquet, care for, delight, discuss, present, provide, take out **08** attend to, consider, deal with, medicate, pleasure, spread on, surprise **09** amusement, cover with, enjoyment, entertain, excursion, look after, negotiate, poeticize, tartarize **10** indulgence, minister to, pay the bill **11** celebration, foot the bill, negotiation **13** behave towards, entertainment, gratification

**treatable**
**07** curable **08** moderate, operable **09** medicable, reparable, tractable **10** reformable, remediable **11** rectifiable

**treatise**
**05** essay, ethic, paper, study, summa, tract **06** Cybele, system, thesis **07** pandect **08** Almagest, lapidary, pamphlet, prodrome, tractate **09** cosmology, discourse, festilogy, festology, monograph **10** arithmetic, dendrology, exposition, halieutics **11** gnomonology **12** disquisition, dissertation

**treatment**
◇ *anagram indicator*
**03** EST, use **04** care, cure, deal **05** doing, usage **06** action, demean, notice, reason, remedy **07** affront, conduct, dealing, demaine, demayne, demeane, healing, measure, nursing, quarter, regimen, surgery, therapy **08** cosmesis, coverage, dealings, handling **09** behaviour, discursus, going-over **10** asepticism, discussion, management, medicament, medication, observance **12** manipulation, therapeutics **13** antisepticism **14** discountenance

**treaty**
**04** bond, deal, pact **05** peace **06** pledge **07** bargain, compact, concord **08** alliance, assiento, contract, covenant, entreaty, protocol **09** agreement, concordat **10** convention, engagement **11** negotiation **12** pacification

*Treaties and agreements include:*

**03** Edo (Treaty of)
**04** Jay's (Treaty), Rome (Treaty of), SALT
**05** Baden, Dover (Treaty of), Ghent (Treaty of), Kyoto (accord), Lyons (Treaty of), Paris (Treaties of), Union
**06** Amiens (Treaty of), Berlin (Treaty of), London (Treaties of), Madrid (Treaty of), Passau (Treaty of), Poland (Partitions of), Tilsit (Treaties of), Vienna (Treaties of)
**07** Barrier (Treaties), Dresden (Treaty of), Nanjing (Treaty of), Nystadt (Treaty of), Tianjin (Treaty of), Utrecht (Peace of)
**08** Brussels (Treaty of), Kanagawa (Treaty of), Lausanne (Treaty of), Pyrenees (Treaty of the), Tientsin (Treaty of)
**09** Bucharest (Treaties of), Hay-Herrán (Treaty), Karlowitz (Treaty of), Pressburg (Treaty of), St Germain (Treaty of)
**10** Adrianople (Treaty of), Anglo-Iraqi (Treaty), Maastricht (Treaty), Magna Carta, Paris Pacts, San Stefano (Treaty of), Versailles (Treaty of), Warsaw Pact, Washington (Treaty of), Westphalia (Peace of)
**11** Fort Stanwix (Treaties of), Locarno Pact, Vereeniging (Peace of), Westminster (Treaty of)
**12** Brest-Litovsk (Treaty of), Lateran Pacts
**13** North Atlantic (Treaty), Social Chapter, Triple Entente
**14** Hague Agreement, Hoare-Laval Pact
**15** Entente Cordiale, Munich Agreement

**treble**
**04** high **05** sharp **06** piping, shrill, triple **07** soprano **09** threefold **11** high-pitched

**tree**
**04** bush, limb, spar **05** shrub **06** corner, wooden **07** gallows **08** pedigree

*See also* **palm**; **pine**; **rubber**

*Tree types include:*

**03** nut
**04** palm
**05** covin, fruit
**06** bonsai, citron, citrus, forest, timber
**07** conifer, dwarfed
**08** hardwood, softwood
**09** broad-leaf, Christmas, deciduous, evergreen
**10** ornamental

*Trees include:*

**02** bo, ti
**03** ash, asp, bay, bel, box, elm, fig, fir, gum, ita, jak, koa, may, nim, oak, sal, tea, ule, yew
**04** acer, akee, arar, atap, bito, coco, cola, dali, dhak, dika, dita, eugh, gean, holm, hule, ilex, jack, kola, lime, lind, mate, mowa, neem, nipa, olea, ombu, palm, pear, pine, plum, poon, rata, rimu, shea, sorb, teak, teil, toon, upas, yang
**05** ackee, afara, alder, apple, aspen, assai, balsa, beech, birch, cacao, carob, cedar, china, ebony, elder, fruit, guava, hazel, holly, karri, kauri, larch, lemon, lilac, lotus, mango, maple, morus, olive, papaw, peach, pecan, piñon, pipal, plane, rowan, salix, thorn, tulip, yucca
**06** acacia, almond, bamboo, banana, banyan, baobab, bonsai, cashew, cassia, cherry, damson, gingko, jarrah, laurel, linden, papaya, pawpaw, poplar, prunus, quince, rubber, sapele, spruce, walnut, willow
**07** apricot, Banksia, blue gum, conifer, cork oak, cypress, dogwood, hickory, quassia, redwood, sequoia, wych elm
**08** chestnut, date palm, Dutch elm, ghost gum, hardwood, hawthorn, hornbeam, mahogany, mandarin, mangrove, mulberry, oleaster, softwood, sycamore, tamarisk
**09** araucaria, blackwood, Chile pine, crab apple, deciduous, evergreen, jacaranda, kauri-pine, leylandii, melaleuca, paperbark, persimmon, Scots pine, stone pine,

whitebeam, wych-hazel
- **10** blackthorn, breadfruit, cottonwood, Douglas fir, eucalyptus, ornamental, sandalwood, witch hazel
- **11** bottle brush, bristlecone, coconut palm, copper beech, false acacia, golden larch, London plane, mountain ash, pussy willow, silver birch, silver maple
- **12** monkey puzzle, Monterey pine, Wellingtonia
- **13** angel's trumpet, horse chestnut, Japanese maple, sweet chestnut, weeping willow
- **14** cedar of Lebanon, Lombardy poplar
- **15** bristlecone pine

**• abounding in trees**
**04** elmy, oaky, piny
**• clump of trees**
**03** mot **04** mott **05** bluff, copse, motte, plump **06** spinny **07** spinney
**• embedded tree**
**04** snag
**• isolated tree**
**04** ombu
**• tree stump**
**04** runt
**• tree trunk**
**03** log **04** bole, butt, stud **06** ricker

**tree-planted walk**
**04** xyst **06** xystos, xystus

**trek**
**04** drag, hike, plod, roam, rove, slog, trip, walk, yomp **05** march, stage, tramp **06** ramble, safari, trudge **07** journey, migrate, odyssey, traipse **09** migration **10** expedition

**trellis**
**03** net **04** grid, mesh **05** grate **06** grille **07** grating, lattice, network, treille **08** espalier **09** framework **11** latticework **12** reticulation

**tremble**
◇ *anagram indicator*
**04** rock **05** quake, shake **06** dither, dodder, hotter, judder, quaver, quiver, shiver, tremor, wobble, wuther **07** shudder, vibrate, whither **09** vibration **13** tremulousness

**trembling**
◇ *anagram indicator*
**04** yips **06** quaver, shakes **07** quaking, rocking, shaking **09** juddering, quavering, quivering, shivering, tremulous, vibration **10** heart-quake, shuddering **11** oscillation, trepidation

**tremendous**
**04** huge, vast **05** great **06** wicked **07** amazing, corking, howling, immense, massive **08** colossal, dreadful, enormous, gigantic, smashing, terrific, towering **09** wonderful **10** formidable, impressive, incredible, marvellous, prodigious, remarkable, stupendous, thundering **11** exceptional, sensational, spectacular **13** extraordinary **14** out of this world

**tremendously**
**04** very **06** highly, really **07** acutely, awfully, greatly, utterly **08** severely **09** decidedly, extremely, intensely, unusually **10** remarkably, thoroughly, uncommonly **11** exceedingly, excessively, frightfully **12** immoderately, inordinately, terrifically, unreasonably **13** exceptionally **15** extraordinarily

**tremor**
**05** quake, shake, shock **06** dindle, dinnle, quaver, quiver, shiver, thrill, wobble **07** shudder, temblor, tremble **09** agitation, foreshock, marsquake, moonquake, quavering, trembling, vibration **10** earthquake, titubation

**tremulous**
◇ *anagram indicator*
**05** aspen, jumpy, shaky, timid **06** afraid, aspine, scared **07** anxious, excited, fearful, jittery, nervous, quivery, shaking, trembly **08** agitated, timorous, unsteady, wavering **09** quavering, quivering, shivering, trembling, vibrating **10** frightened

**trench**
**03** cut, fur, pit, sap **04** dike, dyke, foss, furr, grip, leat, leet, line, moat, rill **05** boyau, ditch, drain, fosse, gripe, verge **06** border, furrow, gullet, gutter, trough **07** channel, cunette, slidder **08** encroach, entrench, parallel, waterway **09** earthwork **10** excavation **12** entrenchment
*See also* **ocean**

**trenchant**
**05** acute, blunt, clear, sharp, terse **06** astute, biting **07** acerbic, caustic, cutting, mordant, pungent **08** clear-cut, distinct, emphatic, forceful, incisive, scathing, vigorous **09** effective **10** forthright, no-nonsense, perceptive **11** penetrating, unequivocal **13** perspicacious

**trend**
**03** fad **04** bend, bent, flow, look, mode, rage, tide, turn, wind **05** craze, drift, style, vogue **06** course, downer, latest **07** bearing, current, fashion, leaning **08** downturn, tendency **09** bandwagon, consensus, direction, downswing **10** mainstream, rising tide **11** inclination, radical chic **13** name of the game

**trendsetter**
**05** model **06** leader, new man **07** pioneer **08** new woman **09** innovator, modernist, modern man **11** modern woman, trailblazer **12** avant-gardist **13** avant-gardiste, groundbreaker

**trendy**
**02** in **03** hip, now **04** cool **05** funky, natty **06** groovy, latest, modish, snazzy, with it **07** right-on, stylish, voguish **10** all the rage **11** fashionable **13** up-to-the-minute

**trepidation**
**04** fear **05** alarm, dread, worry **06** dismay, fright, nerves, qualms, tremor, unease **07** anxiety, emotion, jitters, shaking **08** disquiet **09** agitation, cold sweat, quivering, trembling **10** excitement, misgivings, uneasiness **11** butterflies, nervousness, palpitation **12** apprehension, perturbation **13** consternation

**trespass**
**03** sin **05** poach, wrong **06** invade, offend **07** impinge, intrude, offence, violate **08** encroach, infringe, invasion, obdurate, poaching **09** intrusion, violation **10** transgress, wrongdoing **12** encroachment, infringement, misdemeanour **13** contravention, transgression

**trespasser**
**06** sinner **07** burglar, poacher **08** criminal, evil-doer, intruder, offender **10** delinquent, encroacher **12** transgressor

**tress**
**04** curl, hair, lock, tail **05** braid, bunch, plait, swits **06** strand, switch **07** pigtail, ringlet **08** trammels

**trial**
**03** try **04** bane, case, exam, pest, test **05** assay, check, cross, dummy, grief, pilot, probe, study **06** appeal, assess, assize, bother, burden, dry run, hassle, misery, ordeal, sample, screen, trinal, try out, try-out **07** analyse, approof, attempt, contest, examine, hearing, inquiry, lawsuit, retrial, scratch, testing, test run, trouble **08** appraise, audition, distress, dummy run, endeavor, evaluate, hardship, nuisance, practice, tribunal, vexation **09** adventure, adversity, annoyance, endeavour, probation, rehearsal, selection, suffering, threefold **10** affliction, experiment, litigation, temptation **11** approbation, competition, cross to bear, examination, exploratory, investigate, provisional, tribulation **12** cause célèbre, experimental, probationary **13** pain in the neck **14** experiment with **15** thorn in the flesh

**triangle**

*Triangles include:*

- **05** right
- **07** Bermuda, eternal, Pascal's, scalene, similar, warning
- **09** cocked hat, congruent, isosceles, spherical
- **11** acute-angled, equilateral, right-angled
- **12** obtuse-angled

**triangular**
**08** trigonal, trigonic **09** trigonous **10** three-sided, trilateral, triquetral **11** triquetrous **13** three-cornered **14** triangle-shaped
**• triangular piece**
**04** gair, gare, gore **05** fichu, godet

**tribal**
**05** class, group **06** ethnic, family, native **08** gentilic **09** sectional **10** indigenous

**tribe**
**03** iwi, rod **04** clan, hapu, race, sept **05** blood, breed, caste, class, group, house, ngati, stock **06** branch, family, nation, people **07** dynasty **08** division **11** ethnic group

*Tribes of Israel:*

**03** Dan, Gad
**05** Asher, Judah
**06** Reuben, Simeon
**07** Ephraim, Zebulun
**08** Benjamin, Issachar, Manasseh, Naphtali

*See also* **Aboriginal**; **African**; **American**; **Asian**; **European**

**tribulation**
**03** woe **04** blow, care, pain **05** curse, grief, trial, worry **06** burden, misery, ordeal, sorrow **07** anxiety, reverse, travail, trouble **08** distress, hardship, vexation **09** adversity, heartache, suffering **10** affliction, misfortune **11** unhappiness **12** wretchedness

**tribunal**
**03** bar, EAT **04** rota **05** bench, court, trial **07** hearing **09** Areopagus, committee **11** examination, inquisition **12** confessional **13** kangaroo court

**tribune**
**04** bema

**tributary**
**04** fork **05** bogan, river **06** branch, feeder, stream **08** influent **09** confluent **10** head-stream **12** contributing

**tribute**
**03** due, fee, tax **04** cain, duty, gift, kain, levy, scat, skat, toll **05** gavel, paean, proof, scatt **06** charge, credit, eulogy, homage, honour, praise, tariff **07** payment, pension, present, respect **08** accolade, applause, encomium, evidence, good word, offering, Rome-scot **09** drift-land, gratitude, panegyric, Rome-penny **10** compliment, dedication **11** good opinion, high opinion, Peter's pence, recognition, testimonial **12** commendation, contribution **15** acknowledgement

**trice**
**02** mo **03** sec **04** haul, tick **05** flash, jiffy, shake **06** minute, moment, pulley, second **07** instant **09** twinkling

**trichosanthin**
**01** Q

**trick**
◇ *anagram indicator*
**02** do **03** art, con, fix, fob, fun, gag, kid, rig, tip, toy **04** dupe, fake, feat, flam, fool, gift, gull, hang, have, hoax, jape, joke, mock, pass, pawk, ploy, rook, ruse, scam, sell, sham, trap, trim, turn, vice, wile **05** antic, bluff, bogus, caper, cheat, cozen, dodge, false, flair, fraud, glaik, gleek, knack, plant, prank, quirk, skill, skite, skyte, spell, stall, stunt, watch **06** adroit, antick, begunk, chouse, deceit, delude, device, diddle, double, ersatz, forged, frolic, genius, have on, illude, juggle, lead on, mirage, outwit, palter, rip-off, secret, shavie, take in, talent **07** ability, anticke, antique, beguile, chicane, deceive, defraud, faculty, fantasy, fast one, feigned, frame-up, knowhow, leg-pull, mislead, pliskie, roughie, skylark, slinter, swindle, trinket, wrinkle **08** artifice, capacity, doubling, facility, flimflam, gimcrack, hoodwink, illusion, jimcrack, prestige, skin game, subtlety **09** deception, defective, expedient, gold brick, imitation, manoeuvre, mousetrap, stratagem, technique, underplot **10** apparition, artificial, capability, hocus-pocus, pleasantry, subterfuge, subtleness, under-craft, unreliable **11** conjuration, counter-cast, counterfeit, galliardise, hornswoggle, legerdemain, monkey shine, pull one over **12** starting hole, take for a ride, trick of light **13** double-shuffle, practical joke, sleight of hand **14** pull a fast one on, three-card monte

• **number of tricks**
**03** nap **04** book, slam

• **trick out**
**04** do up, fard, tiff **05** adorn, array **06** attire, bedeck, doll up, tart up **07** dress up, trick up **08** decorate, ornament, spruce up

**trickery**
**04** trap **05** fraud, guile **06** deceit, ropery, slight **07** cantrip, cunning, dodgery, jookery, joukery, sleight **08** artifice, cheating, illusion, jugglery, practice, pretence, wiliness **09** chicanery, deception, duplicity, imposture, stratagem, swindling **10** conveyance, dishonesty, hanky-panky, hocus-pocus, imposition, shenanigan, subterfuge **11** contrivance, legerdemain, shenanigans, skulduggery **12** skullduggery **13** double-dealing, funny business, jiggery-pokery, sleight of hand **14** joukery-pawkery, monkey business **15** smoke and mirrors

**trickle**
**03** ren, rin, run **04** drib, drip, drop, leak, ooze, seep **05** exude **06** filter, gutter **07** dribble, driblet, drizzle, dropple, seepage **08** dribblet, ticklish **09** percolate **10** flow slowly, precarious

**trickster**
**04** hood, rook **05** cheat, fraud, joker, rogue, shark **06** con man, dodger, hoaxer, rascal **07** cozener, diddler, hoodlum, hustler, tricker **08** con woman, deceiver, impostor, swindler **09** artificer, charlatan, con artist, fraudster, pretender, tregetour **10** dissembler, mountebank **11** illy whacker

**tricky**
◇ *anagram indicator*
**03** sly **04** foxy, wily **05** dicey, dodgy, elvan, elven, nasty **06** artful, crafty, elfish, elvish, knotty, pretty, shifty, subtle, thorny **07** awkward, cunning, devious, finicky **08** delicate, scheming, slippery, ticklish **09** deceitful, difficult, sensitive **11** complicated, legerdemain, problematic

**tried**
**06** proved, proven, tested **07** trusted **08** reliable **10** dependable **11** established, trustworthy

**trifle**
**03** bit, fig, toy **04** dash, doit, drop, fool, iota, play, song, spot **05** dally, flirt, sport, straw, touch, trace, wally **06** bauble, dabble, daidle, faddle, fiddle, fisgig, fizgig, frivol, geegaw, gewgaw, little, meddle, niggle, paddle, palter, peddle, piffle, pingle, potter, tiddle, trivia, wanton **07** flamfew, fribble, nothing, old song, quiddle, trinket **08** falderal, fal de rol, flea-bite, folderol, niffnaff, whim-wham **09** bagatelle, mess about, plaything **10** dilly-dally, knick-knack, mess around, triviality **11** fiddlestick, inessential, small amount **12** fiddle-faddle **13** play the wanton

**trifling**
**04** idle **05** empty, minor, petty, potty, seely, silly, small **06** faddle, fallal, futile, paltry, slight **07** fooling, foolish, puerile, shallow, trivial **08** baubling, boy's play, childish, fiddling, frippery, immoment, nonsense, nugatory, piddling, piffling **09** dalliance, desipient, fribbling, fribblish, frivolous, whifflery, worthless **10** negligible **11** superficial, unimportant **12** fiddle-faddle **13** insignificant **14** inconsiderable **15** inconsequential

**trigger**
**04** spur **05** catch, cause, lever, start **06** elicit, prompt, set off, switch **07** produce, provoke **08** activate, generate, initiate, spark off, stimulus, touch off **09** day-length **10** bring about **11** set in action, set in motion

**trill**
**04** lilt, pipe, roll, sing **05** flute, shake, twirl **06** quaver, warble **07** trundle

**trim**
◇ *head deletion indicator*
◇ *tail deletion indicator*
**03** cut, dub, fit, fur, lop, net, way **04** barb, chop, clip, cool, crop, dink, dock, edge, face, form, lace, neat, nett, pare, slim, snip, snod, tidy, tosh, trig **05** adorn, array, braid, cheat, dress, frill, guard, natty, order, prune, roach, ruche, shape, shave, shear, slick, smart, smirk, state, tight, trick **06** adjust, border, dapper, donsie, edging, fettle, fit out, fringe, health, humour, neaten, plight, reduce, smooth, snazzy, spruce, svelte, temper, thrash, tidy up, trimly

07 arrange, balance, compact, curtail, cut down, festoon, fitness, garnish, orderly, slender **08** clean-cut, contract, decorate, decrease, diminish, fittings, ornament, trimming, well-kept **09** condition, cut back on, embellish, scale down, shipshape, underbear **10** decoration **11** clean-limbed, disposition, in good order, presentable, streamlined, well-dressed, well-groomed **12** spick-and-span **13** well-turned-out

**trimming**
**03** end **04** gimp, gymp, trim **05** braid, extra, frill, guard, guimp, robin **06** border, edging, fringe, paring, piping, robing **07** cascade, cutting, falbala, garnish, macramé, macrami, marabou **08** clipping, frou-frou, furbelow, marabout **09** accessory, adornment, balancing, garniture, passement **10** decoration **11** fimbriation **13** accompaniment, embellishment, ornamentation, passementerie

**Trinidad and Tobago**
**02** TT **03** TTO

**trinket**
**04** seal **05** bijou, charm, jewel, trick **06** bauble, doodad, doodah, geegaw, gewgaw, trifle **07** flamfew, trankum **08** delicacy, gimcrack, kickshaw, ornament, whim-wham **09** bagatelle, kickshaws **10** knick-knack **11** whigmaleery **12** whigmaleerie

**trio**
**05** triad **06** triune, troika **07** musette, trilogy, trinity, triplet **08** terzetto, triunity **09** threesome **10** triplicity **11** triumvirate

*See also* **three**; **threesome**

**trip**
◇ *anagram indicator*
**03** hop, ren, rin, run **04** buzz, fall, flip, high, hurl, kilt, link, ride, sail, skip, slip, spin, tilt, tour **05** caper, dance, dream, drive, error, flock, foray, gaffe, jaunt, jolly, lapse, slide, spurn, waltz, whirl **06** booboo, bummer, gambol, howler, outing, sortie, spring, tiptoe, tootle, totter, tumble, vision, voyage **07** bloomer, blunder, clanger, fantasy, faux pas, journey, mistake, stagger, stumble **08** freak-out, illusion **09** excursion, false step **10** apparition, expedition, experience, inaccuracy **13** hallucination **15** lose your footing

• **trip up**
**04** trap **05** catch, snare, trick **06** ambush, outwit, waylay **07** ensnare **08** catch out, fall over, outsmart, surprise **09** wrongfoot **10** disconcert **15** throw off balance

**tripe**
**03** rot **04** blah, bosh, guff, tosh **05** balls, hooey, trash **06** bunkum, drivel **07** baloney, eyewash, garbage, hogwash, inanity, rhubarb, rubbish, twaddle **08** claptrap, entrails, malarkey, nonsense, tommyrot **09** bullswool, moonshine, poppycock **10** balderdash

**triple**
**04** trio **05** third, triad **06** treble, triune, troika **07** perfect, trilogy, trinity, triplet **08** three-ply, three-way, triunity **09** threefold, threesome **10** sdrucciola, three times, tripartite, triplicate, triplicity **11** triumvirate

**tripod**
**03** cat, pod **06** trivet **08** triangle **09** brand-iron

**tripper**
**07** grockle, tourist, voyager **09** sightseer, traveller **12** excursionist, holidaymaker

**trite**
**04** dull, worn **05** banal, corny, stale, stock, tired **06** beaten, common **07** cliché'd, routine, worn-out **08** clichéed, cornball, ordinary, overdone, overused, overworn, tritical, truistic, well-worn **09** hackneyed, rinky-dink **10** threadbare, uninspired, unoriginal **11** commonplace, Mickey Mouse, novelettish, predictable, stereotyped, well-trodden **12** run-of-the-mill **13** platitudinous

**tritium**
**01** T **13** heavy hydrogen

**triton**
**03** eft **04** evet, newt

**triumph**
**03** hit, joy, win **04** beat, coup, crow, feat, pomp **05** exult, gloat, glory, paean, revel, trump **06** defeat, insult **07** conquer, elation, mastery, pageant, prevail, prosper, rejoice, succeed, success, swagger, victory **08** conquest, dominate, jubilate, overcome, overcrow, vanquish, walkover **09** celebrate, exultance, exultancy, festivity, happiness, overwhelm, rejoicing, sensation, win the day **10** attainment, exultation, jubilation, observance **11** achievement, celebration, gain mastery **12** masterstroke **13** flying colours **14** accomplishment

• **expression of triumph**
**02** ha, ho, io **03** aha, hah, hey, hoa, hoh, Jai, oho, olé **04** ha-ha **05** heigh, there **06** yippee **07** so there

**triumphant**
**05** proud **06** elated, joyful **07** crowing, winning **08** boastful, exultant, gloating, glorious, jubilant **09** cock-a-hoop, rejoicing, triumphal **10** conquering, successful, swaggering, victorious **11** celebratory **12** prize-winning

**trivia**
**03** pap **06** Hecate **07** details, trifles **08** minutiae **12** trivialities **13** irrelevancies **14** technicalities

**trivial**
**04** bald **05** banal, dinky, minor, petty, small, trite **06** flimsy, frothy, little, measly, paltry **08** everyday, gimcrack, piddling, piffling, snippety, trifling **09** frivolous, quibbling, rinky-dink, small beer, worthless **10** incidental, negligible, peppercorn, vernacular **11** commonplace, meaningless, unimportant **12** cutting no ice, pettifogging **13** insignificant, no great shakes **14** inconsiderable **15** inconsequential, of no consequence

**triviality**
**06** detail, trifle **07** nothing **08** banality, frippery, nonsense, pretence **09** frivolity, pettiness, puerility, smallness **10** nothingism **11** foolishness **12** technicality, unimportance **13** worthlessness **14** insignificance **15** meaninglessness

**trivialize**
**07** devalue, scoff at **08** belittle, minimize, play down **09** underplay **10** depreciate, undervalue **12** Hollywoodize **13** underestimate

**troglodyte**
**04** wren **11** cave-dweller

**troll**
**03** elf **04** drow, harl, jinn, roll, rove, spin, trow **05** dwarf, gnome, pooka **06** allure, goblin, ramble, stroll **07** trundle **08** trolling **09** circulate **10** repetition

**trolley**
**04** corf **05** bogey, bogie, brute, dolly, truck **07** tramcar **09** caddie car **10** caddie cart, traymobile **11** dinner-wagon

**trollop**
**03** pro, pug, tom **04** bawd, dell, drab, moll, punk, road, stew, tart **05** brass, broad, quail, quiff, stale, tramp, trull, wench, whore **06** bulker, callet, geisha, harlot, hooker, mutton, plover **07** cocotte, floozie, hetaera, hostess, hustler, lorette, polecat, rent-boy, venture **08** bona-roba, callgirl, dolly-mop, magdalen, strumpet **09** courtesan, hierodule, loose fish **10** cockatrice, convertite, fancy woman, loose woman, prostitute, rough trade, vizard-mask **11** fallen woman, fille de joie, laced mutton, night-walker, poule de luxe, public woman, working girl **12** fille des rues, painted woman, scarlet woman, street-walker **13** grande cocotte **14** lady of the night, woman of the town

**troop**
**02** go, tp **03** mob **04** army, band, body, crew, gang, herd, kern, pack, team, turm, unit, walk **05** bunch, crowd, flock, group, horde, kerne, march, squad, swarm, turme **06** parade, school, stream, throng, troupe, trudge **07** cavalry, company, consort, convoys, gunners, militia, traipse **08** assemble, brigades, division, fighters, military, platoons, soldiers, squadron **09** commandos, fusiliers, gathering,

multitude, regiments, squadrons **10** assemblage, contingent, paratroops, servicemen **11** armed forces, infantrymen **12** paratroopers, servicewomen

**trophy**

**03** cup, pot **05** award, prize **06** spoils **07** laurels, memento **08** souvenir **10** silverware

*Trophies include:*

**02** TT
**05** FA Cup
**06** Fed Cup
**07** Auld Mug, Gold Cup, Grey Cup, Uber Cup
**08** Davis Cup, Ryder Cup, The Ashes, World Cup
**09** Aresti Cup, Curtis Cup, Thomas Cup, Walker Cup
**10** Masters Cup, Solheim Cup, Stanley Cup, Winston Cup
**11** Admiral's Cup, America's Cup, Eschborn Cup, Kinnaird Cup, McCarthy Cup
**12** Camanachd Cup, Lugano Trophy
**13** Heisman trophy, Leonard Trophy, Sam Maguire Cup
**14** Continental Cup, Jesters' Club Cup
**15** Champions Trophy, Lilienthal Medal, Louis Vuitton Cup, Nascar Nextel Cup, Scotch Whisky Cup

*See also* **award**

**tropical**

**03** hot **05** humid **06** steamy, sultry, torrid **07** boiling, very hot **08** stifling **09** luxuriant **10** boiling hot, figurative, sweltering

**trot**

**03** jog, ren, rin, run **04** crib, pace **05** crone **06** bustle, canter, scurry **07** dogtrot, heigh-ho, jogtrot, passage, scamper, scuttle, tripple **08** heich-how

**• on the trot**

**04** busy **06** in a row, in turn **10** back to back **12** continuously, sequentially, successively **13** consecutively **15** uninterruptedly

**• trot out**

**06** adduce, drag up, recite, relate, repeat **07** bring up, exhibit **08** bring out, rehearse **09** reiterate **12** bring forward

**troubadour**

**04** poet **06** singer **08** jongleur, mariachi, minstrel, trouvère, trouveur **09** balladeer, cantabank **11** Minnesinger

**trouble**

◇ *anagram indicator*

**03** ado, ail, dog, fix, jam, noy, vex, woe **04** care, fash, fuss, gram, heat, mess, moil, pain, rile, work **05** annoy, grame, grief, kaugh, muddy, pains, sturt, trial, upset, visit, weigh, worry **06** barrat, bother, burden, corner, cumber, defect, effort, harass, hassle, hatter, kiaugh, molest, pickle, put out, sadden, scrape, shadow, shtook, shtuck, strife, tsuris, tumult, unease, unrest **07** afflict, agitate, ailment, anxiety, concern, disease, disturb, failure, illness, mismake, perplex, perturb, problem, schtook, schtuck, thought, torment, travail, tsouris **08** disorder, disquiet, distress, exercise, exertion, fighting, hardship, headache, hot water, irritate, nuisance, problems, shutdown, stalling, stopping, struggle, upheaval, vexation **09** adversity, agitation, annoyance, attention, breakdown, commotion, complaint, heartache, packing-up, suffering, tight spot, weigh down **10** affliction, conking-out, cutting-out, difficulty, disability, discommode, disconcert, irritation, misfortune, solicitude, uneasiness **11** botheration, disturbance, malfunction, tribulation **13** inconvenience, make the effort **14** solicitousness, thoughtfulness

**troubled**

◇ *anagram indicator*

**05** tense, upset **06** afraid, on edge, uneasy **07** anxious, fearful, fretful, nervous, uptight, worried **08** agonized, bothered, dismayed, strained **09** concerned, disturbed, ill at ease, perturbed **10** disquieted, distracted, distraught, distressed, frightened **11** overwrought **12** apprehensive **14** hot and bothered

**troublemaker**

**05** mixer **07** inciter, stirrer **08** agitator **09** bovver boy **10** incendiary, instigator, ringleader **12** rabble-rouser **13** mischief-maker

**troublesome**

◇ *anagram indicator*

**04** hard **05** pesky, rowdy, spiny **06** infest, plaguy, taxing, thorny, tricky, trying, unruly **07** awkward, brickle, irksome, plaguey, testing **08** annoying, exacting, fashious, tiresome **09** demanding, difficult, laborious, turbulent, vexatious, wearisome, worrisome **10** bothersome, disturbing, irritating, perturbing, plaguesome, rebellious **11** importunate, mischievous **12** incommodious, inconvenient **13** insubordinate, unco-operative

**trough**

**03** gum, hod, tie, tye **04** crib, duct **05** chute, ditch, drain, flame, gully, hutch, shoot, shute, stock, trunk **06** backet, feeder, furrow, groove, gutter, hollow, hopper, manger, sluice, straik, strake, trench, valley **07** channel, conduit, launder **08** sheep-dip **09** sand table **10** depression **12** seasoning-tub **13** feeding trough **14** watering-trough

**trounce**

**04** beat, best, drub, lick, rout **05** crush, paste, thump **06** defeat, hammer, harass, indict, punish, rebuke, thrash, wallop **07** clobber, shellac **09** overwhelm, slaughter

**troupe**

**03** set **04** band, cast **05** group, troop **06** ballet **07** company

**trouper**

**05** actor **06** player **07** artiste, old hand, veteran **08** thespian **09** performer **10** theatrical **11** entertainer

**trousers**

**04** bags, daks, keks **05** cords, jeans, kecks, Levis®, longs, pants, trews **06** Capris, chinos, denims, shorts, slacks, trouse **07** gauchos, nankins, trouses **08** bloomers, breeches, bumsters, flannels, nankeens, overalls, trossers, trowsers **09** corduroys, dungarees, moleskins, strossers **10** Capri pants, cargo pants, drainpipes, Oxford bags, spongebags **12** innominables, reach-me-downs **14** indescribables, inexpressibles

**• part of trousers**

**03** fly

**trout**

**04** peal, peel **05** sewen, sewin **06** finnac **07** finnack, finnock, herling, hirling, rainbow **08** gillaroo, whitling **09** steelhead **10** fingerling, squeteague

**Troy**

**01** t **05** Ilium

**truancy**

**07** absence, jigging, skiving, wagging **08** shirking **11** absenteeism, French leave, malingering

**truant**

**03** jig, kip, wag **04** bunk **05** dodge, hooky, idler, miche, mitch, mooch, shirk, skive **06** absent, desert, dodger, hookey, skiver **07** goof off, missing, runaway, shirker, vagrant **08** absentee, deserter, malinger, skive off **09** play hooky **10** malingerer, play the wag, play truant

**truce**

**03** pax **04** lull, rest, stay **05** break, fains, let-up, peace **06** barley, fains I **07** respite, treague **08** fainites, interval **09** armistice, ceasefire, cessation **10** moratorium, suspension **12** intermission, pacification

**truck**

**02** PU **03** HGV, ute, van **04** skip, tram **05** bogey, bogie, chore, dolly, float, lorry, trade, wagon **06** bakkie, barter, crummy, dumper, pick-up, tipper, waggon **07** bargain, contact, rubbish, traffic, trolley, trundle, utility **08** business, commerce, dealings, exchange **09** honey-cart, persevere, relations **10** connection, honey-wagon, juggernaut **11** association, honey-waggon, intercourse **12** curtain-sider, utility truck **13** communication **14** utility vehicle

**truculence**

**08** defiance, rudeness, violence **09** hostility, pugnacity **11** bellicosity **12** belligerence, disobedience

**14** aggressiveness **15** bad-temperedness, quarrelsomeness

**truculent**
**04** rude **05** cross, cruel **06** fierce, savage, sullen **07** defiant, hostile, violent **09** bellicose, combative **10** aggressive, pugnacious **11** bad-tempered, belligerent, contentious, disobedient, ill-tempered, quarrelsome **12** antagonistic, discourteous, obstreperous **13** argumentative, disrespectful

**trudge**
**03** pad **04** haul, hike, plod, slog, toil, trek, vamp, walk **05** clump, march, stump, tramp, trash **06** labour, lumber, stodge, taigle, trapes **07** shuffle, splodge, splotch, traipse, trudger **10** pad the hoof

**true**
**04** fast, firm, flat, just, leal, real, trew, very **05** close, exact, loyal, plumb, right, sooth, truly, truth, valid **06** actual, dinkum, honest, proper, trusty, truthy **07** correct, devoted, dinki-di, exactly, factual, genuine, precise, rightly, sincere, staunch, typical **08** absolute, accurate, constant, faithful, honestly, properly, reliable, rightful, straight, truthful, unerring **09** authentic, corrected, correctly, dedicated, perfectly, precisely, steadfast, veracious, veritable, veritably **10** accurately, dependable, fair dinkum, faithfully, honourable, legitimate, truthfully, undeniable, unerringly **11** conformable, true-hearted, trustworthy, veraciously
- **hold true**
**02** go

**true-blue**
**04** true **05** loyal **06** trusty **07** devoted, diehard, staunch **08** constant, faithful, orthodox **09** committed, confirmed, dedicated **10** unwavering **12** card-carrying **13** dyed-in-the-wool **14** uncompromising

**truism**
**05** axiom, truth **06** cliché **07** bromide **09** platitude **11** commonplace

**truly**
**04** fegs, full, real, true, very **05** quite **06** certes, indeed, in fact, really, simply, surely, verily **07** exactly, greatly, in truth, rightly, soothly **08** actually, honestly, of a truth, on my word, properly **09** certainly, correctly, extremely, genuinely, in reality, precisely, sincerely, soothlich, veritable **10** constantly, definitely, on my honour, truthfully, undeniably **11** indubitably, steadfastly, undoubtedly **13** exceptionally, o' my conscience, without a doubt **14** upon conscience

**trump**
**03** cap, top **04** ruff **05** blast, outdo **06** allege **07** deceive, eclipse, surpass, triumph, trumpet, upstage **08** Jew's-harp, outshine **13** knock spots off
- **trump up**
**04** fake **06** cook up, create, devise, invent, make up **07** concoct, falsify **08** contrive **09** fabricate

**trumped-up**
**04** fake **05** bogus, faked, false **06** made-up, phoney, untrue **08** cooked-up, invented, spurious **09** concocted, contrived, falsified **10** fabricated

**trumpery**
**05** cheap, nasty, showy **06** flashy, shabby, shoddy, tawdry, trashy **07** mockado, rubbish, useless **08** rubbishy, trifling **09** valueless, worthless **10** pasteboard **12** meretricious

**trumpet**
**03** bay, cry, lur **04** call, horn, lure, parp, roar, toot, tuba **05** blare, blast, bugle, chide, clang, conch, shell, shout, sound, trump **06** bellow, cornet, corona, herald, lituus, sennet, summon, tucket **07** alchemy, alchymy, buccina, clarino, clarion, corolla, salpinx, tantara **08** announce, denounce, proclaim, ram's horn, trombone **09** advertise, broadcast, celebrate, last trump **11** taratantara **12** watering-call
- **blow your own trumpet**
**04** brag, crow **05** boast, skite, swank **07** show off, talk big **09** loudmouth **15** blow your own horn

**trumps**
- **ace of trumps**
**03** tib
- **no trumps**
**02** NT

**truncate**
**03** cut, lop **04** clip, crop, dock, maim, pare, trim **05** prune **06** reduce **07** curtail, shorten **08** cut short, diminish **10** abbreviate

**truncheon**
**04** club, cosh **05** baton, billy, carve, staff, stick **06** batoon, billie, cudgel **09** shillalah **10** billystick, knobkerrie, nightstick, shillelagh

**trundle**
**04** bowl, chug, hoop, roll, spin **05** trill, troll, truck, twirl **06** castor, cruise, roller **07** trindle **09** freewheel

**trunk**
**03** box, leg, log **04** body, bole, bulk, butt, case, nose, runt, stem, tube **05** chest, crate, frame, shaft, snout, stalk, stick, stock, torso **06** coffer **08** Saratoga, sea chest, suitcase **09** proboscis, telescope **10** pea-shooter **11** portmanteau

**truss**
**03** pad, tie **04** bind, hang, pack, prop, stay, wrap **05** brace, joist, shore, strap, strut **06** bundle, corbel, fasten, lace up, pack up, pinion, secure, tether, tuck up **07** bandage, binding, dorlach, make off, support **08** bundle up, buttress, muffle up, string up **09** principal

**trust**
**03** EZT, VCT **04** affy, care, duty, give, hope, tick, trow **05** faith **06** assign, assume, bank on, belief, charge, commit, credit, expect, rely on **07** believe, combine, confide, consign, count on, custody, entrust, imagine, presume, suppose, surmise, swear by **08** be sure of, credence, delegate, depend on, fidelity, reliance, turn over **09** assurance, believe in, certainty **10** commitment, confidence, conviction, dependance, dependence, obligation, protection, street cred **11** expectation, safekeeping, trusteeship **12** guardianship **14** put your trust in, responsibility

**trustee**
**02** tr **05** agent **06** keeper **08** assignee, executor, guardian **09** custodian, executrix, fiduciary **10** depositary **13** administrator

**trusting**
**05** naive **06** unwary **08** gullible, innocent, trustful **09** confiding, credulous, ingenuous, unguarded **12** unsuspecting **13** unquestioning

**trustworthiness**
**05** steel **07** honesty, loyalty **08** devotion **09** integrity, stability **10** commitment **11** reliability **12** faithfulness, sensibleness **13** dependability, steadfastness **14** honourableness, responsibility **15** faithworthiness, level-headedness

**trustworthy**
**04** safe, true **05** loyal, sound **06** honest, stable, trusty **07** devoted, ethical, staunch, upright **08** faithful, reliable, sensible **09** authentic, committed, steadfast **10** creditable, dependable, honourable, principled **11** level-headed, responsible **14** good as your word

**trusty**
**04** firm, true **05** loyal, solid **06** honest, stanch, steady, strong **07** staunch, upright **08** faithful, reliable **09** greatcoat **10** dependable, supportive **11** responsible, trustworthy **15** straightforward

**truth**
**04** fact, true **05** axiom, facts, maxim, right, sooth **06** honour, truism, verity **07** candour, honesty, loyalty, realism, reality **08** accuracy, fidelity, validity, veracity **09** actualité, actuality, constancy, exactness, frankness, home truth, integrity, knowledge, precision, principle, rightness, sincerity **10** cold turkey, legitimacy **11** correctness, genuineness, historicity, uprightness **12** authenticity, faithfulness, truthfulness **14** honourableness, the gospel truth
- **in truth**
**05** sooth, troth, truly **06** indeed, in fact,

really, surely, troggs **07** insooth, soothly **08** actually, en vérité, forsooth, honestly, in effect **09** assuredly, in reality, soothlich **10** to be honest **11** truth to tell **12** in actual fact **13** if truth be told, in point of fact **15** as a matter of fact

**truthful**
**04** open, true **05** exact, frank, right, sooth, valid **06** candid, honest **07** correct, factual, precise, sincere **08** accurate, faithful, reliable, soothful, straight **09** realistic, soothfast, veracious, veridical, veritable **10** forthright, veridicous **11** trustworthy

**truthfully**
**05** truly **06** openly **08** honestly, reliably **09** correctly, factually, precisely, sincerely **10** accurately, faithfully

**truthfulness**
**06** verity **07** candour, honesty **08** openness, veracity **09** frankness, sincerity **11** uprightness **12** straightness **13** righteousness

**try**
**02** go **03** aim, sap, tax **04** bash, fand, fond, hear, pree, pull, seek, shot, sift, stab, test, tire **05** annoy, assay, crack, drain, essay, fling, judge, prove, taste, tempt, trial, weary, whirl **06** choice, effort, purify, refine, render, sample, strain, stress, strive, try out, weaken **07** afflict, attempt, examine, exhaust, extract, have a go, inspect, stretch, turn out, undergo, venture, wear out **08** appraise, evaluate, irritate, purified **09** appraisal, endeavour, give it a go, have a bash, have a shot, have a stab, undertake **10** evaluation, experience, experiment, have a crack **11** investigate **13** make demands on

• **try out**
**04** test **05** taste, try on **06** sample **07** inspect **08** appraise, check out, evaluate **10** have a pop at, take a pop at

**trying**
**04** hard **05** tough, trial **06** severe, taxing **07** arduous, testing **08** annoying, tiresome **09** demanding, difficult, searching, stressful, vexatious, wearisome **10** bothersome, irritating **11** aggravating, distressing, troublesome **12** exasperating

• **trying situation**
**03** cow

**tub**
**03** dan, keg, kid, kit, tun, vat **04** back, bath, butt, cask, cowl, kier **05** basin, keeve, kieve, stand **06** barrel, bucket, pulpit **07** bathtub, bran-pie, bran tub, salt-fat, washtub **08** ash-leach, hogshead, lucky dip, salt-foot, swill-tub **09** container

**tubby**
**03** fat **05** buxom, obese, plump, podgy, pudgy, stout **06** chubby, portly, rotund **07** paunchy **08** roly-poly **09** corpulent **10** overweight **15** well-upholstered

**tube**
**03** CRT, vas **04** duct, hose, pipe, vein **05** inlet, shaft, spout, trunk **06** outlet, tubing **07** channel, conduit, snorkel **08** aircraft, cylinder **09** capillary **13** television set, umbilical cord
*See also* **London**

**tuber**
**03** set **04** coco, eddo **05** cocco **06** jicama, mashua, potato, yautia **08** earth-nut **10** seed potato **11** sweet potato **13** water chestnut

**tuberculosis**
**02** TB **05** lupus **08** phthisis, scrofula **11** consumption **12** pearl disease

**tubular**
**04** pipy **05** piped, tubal, tubar **06** tubate **07** quilled **08** pipelike, tubelike, tubiform, tubulate, tubulous, vasiform

**tuck**
**03** tap **04** beat, chow, cram, ease, eats, fold, food, grub, kilt, nosh, push **05** meals, pleat, scoff, scrab, snack, stuff **06** crease, gather, hamper, insert, pucker, rapier, ruffle, snacks, stroke, thrust **08** eatables **11** comestibles **12** gird yourself

• **tuck away**
**04** hide, save **05** hoard, store **06** save up **07** conceal **09** stash away

• **tuck in, tuck into**
◇ *insertion indicator*
**03** eat, sup **04** dine **05** eat up, feast, gorge, scoff **06** devour, gobble **08** wolf down **11** eat heartily

• **tuck in, tuck up**
**04** kilt **05** truss **06** fold in, wrap up **07** cover up **08** make snug, put to bed **09** fold under **15** make comfortable

**Tuesday**
**02** Tu **03** Tue **04** Tues

**tuft**
**03** dag, top **04** coma, hank, knop, knot, lock, tait, tate, tuzz, wisp **05** beard, brush, bunch, clump, crest, flock, plume, quiff, scopa, swits, truss, tuffe, whisk **06** dallop, dollop, goatee, pencil, pompom, pompon, switch, tassel, toorie, tourie, tuffet **07** cluster, cowlick, daglock, fetlock, flaught, floccus, hassock, pompoon, scopula, topknot, tussock **08** aigrette, corn silk, dislodge, fascicle, imperial, plumelet **09** fascicule, flocculus, scalp lock **10** fasciculus **12** witches' broom

**tug**
**03** lug, pug, rug, tit, tow **04** drag, draw, haul, jerk, pull, rive, tire, toil, yank **05** heave, pluck **06** jigger, strain, strive, wrench **07** saccade, tow boat, tracker

**tuition**
**05** grind **07** lessons **08** coaching, guidance, teaching, training, tutelage **09** education, schooling **11** instruction **12** guardianship

**tumble**
◇ *anagram indicator*
**04** dive, drop, fall, flop, reel, roll, sway, toss, trip **05** heave, lurch, pitch, slide, touse, touze, towse, towze **06** jumble, plunge, rumple, topple, tousle, touzle, trip up, unseat, welter **07** decline, plummet, stumble **08** collapse, decrease, dishevel, disorder, fall over, nosedive **09** knock down, overthrow, tumble-dry **10** disarrange, somersault, throw about **12** fall headlong

• **tumble to**
**03** get **04** suss, twig **05** grasp, savvy **07** realize **08** perceive **09** latch on to **10** comprehend, cotton on to, understand **13** become aware of, get the picture

**tumbledown**
◇ *anagram indicator*
**05** shaky **06** ruined, unsafe **07** crumbly, rickety, ruinous **08** decrepit, unstable, unsteady **09** crumbling, tottering **10** broken-down, ramshackle **11** dilapidated **14** disintegrating

**tumbler**
**03** cup, mug **05** glass **06** beaker, goblet **07** acrobat, gymnast, tumbrel **10** water glass **13** contortionist, drinking-glass **15** jerry-come-tumble

**tumid**
**06** turgid **07** bloated, bulbous, bulging, flowery, fulsome, pompous, stilted, swollen **08** affected, enlarged, inflated, puffed up **09** bombastic, distended, grandiose, high-flown, overblown, tumescent **10** euphuistic **11** pretentious, protuberant **12** magniloquent **13** grandiloquent

**tummy**
**03** gut **05** belly **06** inside, paunch **07** abdomen, insides, stomach **08** pot-belly **11** bread basket, corporation

**tumour**
**03** -oma **04** lump, onco- **06** cancer, growth **08** neoplasm, swelling **09** turgidity **10** malignancy

*Tumours include:*

**05** gumma, myoma, Wilm's
**06** epulis, glioma, lipoma, myxoma
**07** adenoma, angioma, fibroma, myeloma, sarcoma
**08** lymphoma, melanoma, teratoma, xanthoma
**09** carcinoma, papilloma, syphiloma
**10** meningioma
**11** astrocytoma, rodent ulcer
**12** glioblastoma, mesothelioma, osteosarcoma
**13** neuroblastoma
**14** retinoblastoma

**tumult**
◇ *anagram indicator*
**03** din, row **04** coil, riot, rore, rout, stir **05** babel, brawl, chaos, deray, hurly, noise, stoor, stour, surge, whirl **06** affray, bedlam, bustle, fracas, hubbub, mutiny, racket, romage, ruffle, rumpus, stowre, strife, unrest, uproar **07** brattle, clamour, ferment, turmoil **08** disarray, disorder, shouting,

stramash, upheaval, williwaw **09** agitation, commotion, confusion, hurricane **10** hullabaloo, hurly-burly, rabblement **11** disturbance, pandemonium **12** pandaemonium

**tumultuous**
**04** loud, wild **05** noisy, rowdy **06** fierce, hectic, raging, stormy, unruly **07** excited, fervent, riotous, violent **08** agitated, frenzied, restless, troubled, vehement **09** clamorous, deafening, disturbed, troublous, turbulent **10** boisterous, disorderly, hurly-burly, tumultuary **12** uncontrolled

**tumulus**
**03** how, low **04** howe, mote **05** motte **06** barrow

**tune**
**03** air, set, toy **04** ayre, dump, lilt, note, port, rant, song, tone, toon **05** adapt, dance, ditty, loure, motif, pitch, round, theme, utter **06** adjust, attune, choral, chorus, jingle, maggot, melody, spring, strain, temper **07** express, hunt's-up, melisma, ragtime **08** folk-tune, regulate, saraband, serenade **09** harmonize, sarabande, siciliano, signature, theme song, theme tune **10** light-o'-love **11** schottische, synchronize **13** melodiousness, signature tune

• **change your tune**
**14** change your mind

• **in tune with**
**04** true **07** d'accord **12** agreeing with, in accord with **13** in harmony with **14** in sympathy with **15** in agreement with

• **out of tune**
**04** ajar **05** false **06** at odds, off-key **07** jarring, untuned **08** distuned, mistuned, out of key, scordato **11** disagreeing

**tuneful**
**04** tuny **06** catchy, mellow **07** melodic, musical, tunable **08** pleasant, sonorous, tuneable **09** agreeable, melodious **10** euphonious, harmonious **11** mellifluous

**tuneless**
**05** harsh **06** atonal, silent **08** clashing **09** dissonant, unmelodic, unmusical **10** discordant, unpleasant **11** cacophonous, horrisonant, unmelodious **12** disagreeable

**tungsten**
**01** W

**tunic**
**05** ao dai, kurta **06** blouse, camese, camise, chiton, kabaya, kameez, khurta, kirtle, tabard, taberd **07** choroid, tunicle **08** chorioid **09** laticlave **12** chorioid coat

**tuning device**
**03** peg **08** magic eye

**Tunisia**
**02** TN **03** TUN

**tunnel**
**03** dig, sap **04** bore, flue, head, hole, mine **05** cundy, drift, qanat, shaft **06** burrow, condie, subway, syrinx **07** chimney, gallery, incline, passage **08** excavate, wormhole **09** penetrate, undermine, underpass **10** passageway

*Tunnels include:*

**03** Aki, Box
**05** Keijo, Rokko
**06** FATIMA, Fréjus, Fucino, Haruna, Hoosac, Kanmon, Mersey, Moffat, Seikan, Thames
**07** Arlberg, Cascade, Channel, Chunnel, Holland, Laerdal, Øresund, Simplon, Vereina
**08** Apennine, Flathead, Hokuriku, Hyperion, Lierasen, Nakayama, Posilipo, Tronquoy
**09** Dayaoshan, Eupalinus, Furka Base, Mont Blanc
**10** Chesbrough, Dai-shimizu, Gorigamine, Lotschberg, Qinling I-II, Rogers Pass, St Gotthard
**11** Kilsby Ridge, Mt MacDonald, Shin shimizu, Tower Subway
**12** Detroit River, Moscow subway
**13** Great Apennine, Iwate Ichinohe, Severomuyskiy
**14** NEAT St Gotthard, Romeriksporten
**15** Monte Santomarco, Orange-Fish River

**tunny**
**04** tuna **13** horse mackerel

**turban**
**05** mitre, pagri, toque **06** tulban **07** puggery, puggree, turband, turbant, turbond **08** puggaree, tulipant **09** turribant

**turbid**
**03** dim **04** foul, hazy **05** dense, foggy, fuzzy, muddy, murky, riley, roily, thick **06** cloudy, drumly, impure, opaque **07** clouded, muddled, unclear **08** confused, feculent **09** turbulent, unsettled **10** disordered, incoherent

**turbulence**
◇ *anagram indicator*
**05** chaos, storm **06** buller, tumult, unrest **07** boiling, turmoil **08** disorder, upheaval **09** agitation, commotion, confusion, roughness **10** disruption **11** instability, pandemonium

**turbulent**
◇ *anagram indicator*
**04** wild **05** noisy, rough, rowdy **06** choppy, raging, stormy, unruly **07** foaming, furious, riotous, violent **08** agitated, blustery, confused, factious, mutinous, unstable **09** in turmoil, unbridled, unsettled **10** boisterous, disordered, disorderly, outrageous, rebellious, tumultuous **11** combustious, tempestuous **12** obstreperous **13** insubordinate, undisciplined

**turf**
**03** sod **04** clod, fail, feal, lawn, terf **05** divot, gazon, glebe, grass, green, patch, scraw, sward, terfe **06** gazoon **07** flaught **09** territory **12** putting green

• **turf out**
**04** fire, oust, sack **05** eject, elbow, evict, expel **06** banish, remove **07** dismiss, kick out, turn out **08** chuck out, fling out, throw out **09** discharge **10** dispossess **14** give the elbow to

**turgid**
**07** dilated, flowery, fulsome, pompous, stilted, swollen, turgent **08** affected, inflated **09** bombastic, grandiose, high-flown, overblown **11** extravagant, pretentious **12** magniloquent, ostentatious **13** grandiloquent

**Turkey**
**02** TR **03** TUR

**Turkmenistan**
**02** TM **03** TKM

**Turks and Caicos Islands**
**03** TCA

**turmoil**
◇ *anagram indicator*
**03** din, row **04** dust, moil, stir, toil **05** chaos, noise, stoor, stour **06** bedlam, bustle, flurry, hubbub, pother, pudder, stowre, tumult, uproar **07** ferment, trouble **08** disarray, disorder, disquiet, upheaval **09** agitation, commotion, confusion **10** turbulence **11** disturbance, pandemonium, tracasserie **12** pandaemonium **13** Sturm und Drang **14** the devil and all

• **place of turmoil**
**04** hell **11** Pandemonium **12** Pandaemonium

**turn**
◇ *anagram indicator*
◇ *reversal indicator*
**01** U **02** go **03** act, aim, fit, jar, lot, rev, say, set, uey **04** bash, bend, bent, bias, bout, cast, form, grow, loop, make, move, pass, reel, roll, send, shot, slew, slue, sour, spin, stab, time, veer, wind **05** adapt, alter, apply, crack, curve, cycle, drift, drive, focus, go bad, go off, hinge, issue, mould, pivot, point, round, scare, shape, shift, shock, spell, spoil, start, stint, swing, trend, trick, twirl, twist, whirl **06** adjust, appeal, attend, become, chance, change, circle, corner, crisis, curdle, depend, direct, divert, do a uey, favour, fright, gyrate, invert, manner, modify, mutate, period, render, resort, return, rotate, spiral, swerve, swivel, take up **07** benefit, convert, deflect, develop, deviate, fashion, go round, heading, illness, leaning, remodel, reverse, revolve, routine, service, winding **08** aptitude, come to be, courtesy, exigency, give back, good deed, gyration, hand over, kindness, nauseate, occasion, reversal, rotation, round off, surprise, tendency, transfer **09** chuck a uey, deviation, direction, faintness, infatuate, performer, transform, translate, transmute,

variation **10** alteration, appearance, difference, divergence, make rancid, propensity, revolution **11** culmination, inclination, nervousness, opportunity, performance, vicissitude **12** become rancid, have recourse, metamorphose **13** act of kindness **15** go round and round

• **to a turn**

**07** exactly **09** correctly, perfectly, precisely **12** to perfection

• **turn against**

**07** dislike **08** distrust **12** disapprove of **13** make hostile to **15** become hostile to

• **turn aside**

**04** daff **05** avert, parry, swits, twist **06** depart, divert, put off, swerve, switch **07** askance, deflect, deviate, diverge, diverse, fend off, reverse, ward off **08** withdraw **09** sidetrack

• **turn away**

**05** avert **06** depart, refuse, reject, return **07** decline, deflect, deviate **08** move away, send away **09** discharge **12** cold shoulder, cold-shoulder

• **turn back**

◇ *reversal indicator*

**05** clock, repel **06** go back, return, revert, revolt **07** reflect, retreat **09** drive back, force back, retrovert

• **turn down**

**04** bend, mute, veto **05** lower, spurn **06** double, invert, lessen, muffle, rebuff, reduce, refuse, reject, soften **07** decline, quieten **08** decrease **09** knock back, repudiate **11** make quieter

• **turn in**

**04** sell, shop **05** dob in, enter, grass, rat on **06** betray, give in, give up, hand in, invert, retire, return, rumble, submit, tell on, tender **07** deliver, go to bed, let down, sack out, sell out, split on, stool on **08** denounce, give back, go back on, hand over, inform on, register, renege on, squeal on **09** hit the hay, surrender, walk out on **10** hit the sack **11** double-cross, turn traitor **12** be disloyal to **13** stab in the back **14** be unfaithful to, break faith with

• **turn of events**

**06** affair, result **07** outcome **08** incident **09** happening **10** occurrence, phenomenon

• **turn off**

**04** bore, hang, kill, quit, stop **05** leave, repel **06** divert, offend, put off, sicken, unplug **07** deviate, disgust, dismiss, pull off, shut off, turn out **08** alienate, complete, nauseate, shut down **09** branch off, displease, switch off **10** depart from, disconnect, discourage, disenchant **11** turn against

• **turn of phrase**

**05** idiom, style **06** saying **07** diction **08** locution, metaphor **10** expression, foreignism **11** phraseology

• **turn on**

**04** plug **05** put on, start **06** arouse, attack, excite, fall on, hang on, please, plug in, rest on, ride on, thrill **07** attract, connect, hinge on, lay into, round on, set upon, start on, start up **08** activate, depend on, switch on **09** start in on, stimulate **14** be contingent on

• **turn out**

**02** go **03** try **04** come, fire, make, rout, sack, sort, trie **05** clear, dress, eject, empty, end up, ensue, evict, expel, fadge, issue, prove **06** appear, arrive, attend, banish, become, bounce, clothe, deport, emerge, happen, muster, pan out, result, show up, turn up, unplug **07** develop, dismiss, drum out, fall out, kick out, present, produce, succeed, turf out, turn off **08** assemble, chuck out, churn out, clean out, clear out, throw out **09** be present, come about, discharge, eventuate, fabricate, switch off, transpire **10** disconnect **11** manufacture

• **turn over**

◇ *reversal down indicator*

**02** TO **03** rob **04** flip, mill, mull, roll **05** upend, upset, volve **06** assign, invert, pass on, ponder, tumble **07** capsize, consign, deliver, examine, reverse, start up **08** consider, hand over, keel over, meditate, mull over, overturn, roll over, ruminate, transfer **09** reflect on, surrender, think over **10** deliberate, think about, turn turtle **11** contemplate

• **turn up**

◇ *reversal down indicator*

**02** go **03** act, dig **04** bash, bend, bias, cock, come, find, loop, plow, root, rout, shew, show, spin, stab, time **05** crack, curve, cycle, dig up, drift, raise, round, scare, shift, shock, spell, stint, trend, twirl, twist, whirl, wroot **06** appear, arrive, attend, cast up, chance, change, circle, corner, expose, fright, grub up, invert, look up, period, plough, reveal, show up, swivel **07** amplify, disgust, disturb, illness, leaning, routine, subsoil, turn out, uncover, unearth **08** disclose, discover, gyration, increase, occasion, reversal, rotation, tendency **09** be present, deviation, direction, faintness, intensify, performer, variation **10** alteration, appearance, difference, divergence, make louder, propensity, revolution, strengthen **11** inclination, materialize, nervousness, opportunity, performance **12** bring to light

**turncoat**

**03** rat **04** fink, scab **07** seceder, traitor **08** apostate, blackleg, defector, deserter, renegade, renegate **10** backslider **11** Vicar of Bray **13** tergiversator

**turned**

◇ *reversal indicator*

**03** off **04** sour **06** soured **08** reversed **09** fashioned **10** upside down

**turning**

◇ *anagram indicator*

◇ *reversal indicator*

**04** bend, fork, turn **05** curve **07** shaping, turn-off, winding **08** junction, reversal, rotation **09** deviation **10** conversion, crossroads **14** transformation

**turning-point**

**04** crux, turn **06** crisis, moment, tropic **08** solstice **09** watershed **10** crossroads **13** moment of truth **14** critical moment, decisive moment

**turnip**

**04** neep **05** navew, swede **07** tumshie **09** breadroot **10** dunderhead

**turnout**

**04** gate, gear, team, togs **05** array, crowd, dress, get-up **06** attire, muster, number, outfit, output, siding, strike, things **07** clobber, clothes, display, striker **08** assembly, audience **09** gathering **10** appearance, assemblage, attendance **12** congregation

**turnover**

◇ *reversal indicator*

**04** flow **05** yield **06** bridie, change, income, output, volume **07** outturn, profits, revenue **08** business, movement **10** production **11** replacement **12** productivity, transference

**turpitude**

**04** evil **07** badness **08** baseness, foulness, iniquity, vileness, villainy **09** depravity **10** corruption, degeneracy, immorality, sinfulness, wickedness **11** corruptness, criminality, viciousness **13** nefariousness **14** flagitiousness

**tusk**

**03** gam **04** tush **05** torsk

**tussle**

**03** vie **04** bout, fray **05** brawl, fight, mêlée, scrap, scrum, set-to, touse, touze, towse, towze **06** battle, dust-up, fracas, tousle, touzle **07** compete, contend, contest, grapple, punch-up, scuffle, tuilyie, tuilzie, wrestle **08** conflict, scramble, struggle **09** scrimmage **10** contention **11** competition

**tutelage**

**03** eye **04** care **05** aegis **06** charge **07** custody, tuition **08** guidance, teaching, wardship **09** education, patronage, schooling, vigilance **10** protection **11** instruction, preparation **12** guardianship

**tutor**

**04** abbé, guru **05** coach, drill, guide, teach, train **06** direct, mentor, school **07** control, dominie, educate, lecture, teacher **08** educator, governor, guardian, instruct, lecturer **09** governess, preceptor, supervise **10** discipline, instructor, répétiteur, supervisor **11** preceptress **12** schoolmaster

**tutorial**

**05** class **06** lesson **07** guiding, seminar, teach-in **08** coaching, didactic, teaching **09** educative, educatory **13** instructional

**Tuvalu**
**03** TUV

**TV** *see* **television**

**twaddle**
**03** rot **04** blah, bosh, bunk, guff, tosh **05** balls, hooey, stuff, trash **06** bunkum, drivel, gabble, gossip, hot air, piffle, tattle, waffle **07** baloney, eyewash, fadaise, garbage, hogwash, inanity, rhubarb, rubbish, twattle **08** blathers, blethers, claptrap, malarkey, nonsense, slipslop, tommyrot **09** bullswool, moonshine, poppycock **10** balderdash **12** gobbledygook

**tweak**
◇ *anagram indicator*
**03** fit, nip, tug **04** jerk, pull, suit **05** adapt, pinch, twist **06** adjust, change, modify, tuning, twinge, twitch **07** fitting, shaping, squeeze **08** fine-tune, revision **09** agitation, amendment, arranging **10** adaptation, adjustment, alteration, conversion, fine-tuning, perplexity **11** accommodate, rearranging, remodelling **12** modification **13** accommodation, rearrangement **15** make adjustments

**twee**
**04** cute **05** sweet **06** cutesy, dainty, pretty, quaint **08** affected, precious **11** sentimental

**twelve**
**02** dz **03** doz, XII **05** dozen **06** zodiac

**Twelve Days of Christmas** *see* **Christmas**

**twenty**
**02** XX

**twice**
◇ *repetition indicator*
**02** bi-, di- **03** bin-, bis **06** doubly

**twiddle**
◇ *anagram indicator*
**04** turn **05** twirl, twist **06** adjust, fiddle, finger, rotate, swivel, wiggle **07** twitter **08** ornament
• **twiddle your thumbs**
**08** kill time **13** kick your heels **15** have nothing to do

**twig**
**03** get, see **04** reis, rice, whip, with **05** birch, grasp, shoot, spray, sprig, stick, swits, twist, withe, withy **06** branch, fathom, fettle, rumble, switch, wattle, wicker **07** catch on, fashion, observe, ramulus, realize, sarment **08** cotton on, offshoot, perceive, tumble to **10** comprehend, understand
*See also* **understand**

**twilight**
**03** dim, ebb **04** dusk, last **05** dying, final, gloom **06** ebbing, sunset **07** decline, dimness, evening, obscure, partial, shadowy **08** cockshut, demi-jour, evenfall, gloaming, glooming, owl-light **09** crepuscle, darkening, declining, half-light **10** crepuscule, indefinite **11** crepuscular **12** transitional **15** Götterdämmerung

**twin**
**04** dual, join, link, mate, pair, part, yoke **05** clone, gemel, match **06** couple, double, fellow, paired, ringer **07** combine, couplet, deprive, matched, twofold **08** didymous, likeness, matching, parallel, separate **09** corollary, duplicate, identical, lookalike **10** complement, dead ringer, equivalent **11** counterpart, symmetrical **13** corresponding

*Twins include:*

**04** Esau, Gibb (Maurice), Gibb (Robin), Kray (Reggie), Kray (Ronnie)
**05** Diana, Jacob, Remus, Viola, Waugh (Mark), Waugh (Steve)
**06** Apollo, Bunker (Chang), Bunker (Eng), Castor, Dromio (of Ephesus), Dromio (of Syracuse), Pollux
**07** Artemis, Piccard (Auguste), Piccard (Jean-Felix), Romulus, Stanley (Francis), Stanley (Freelon), Weasley (Fred), Weasley (George)
**08** Hercules, Iphicles, Louis XIV, Philippe
**09** O'Sullivan (Isabel), O'Sullivan (Pat), Sebastian
**10** Antipholus (of Ephesus), Antipholus (of Syracuse), Tweedledee, Tweedledum

**twine**
**04** bend, coil, cord, curl, knit, loop, part, wind, wrap, yarn **05** braid, plait, twist, weave **06** spiral, string, tangle, thread **07** deprive, entwine, wreathe, wriggle **08** encircle, separate, surround, whipping **09** intorsion, intortion **10** intertwine

**twinge**
**04** ache, grip, pain, pang, stab **05** cramp, pinch, prick, spasm, throb, throe, twang, tweak **06** stitch, twitch **08** shooting

**twinkle**
◇ *anagram indicator*
**04** wink **05** blink, flash, gleam, glint, light, shine, twink **06** quiver **07** flicker, glimmer, glisten, glitter, shimmer, shining, sparkle, vibrate **09** coruscate, twinkling **11** coruscation, scintillate **13** scintillation

**twinkling**
◇ *anagram indicator*
**02** mo **03** sec **04** jiff, tick, wink **05** flash, jiffy, nitid, shake, trice, twink **06** bright, minute, moment, no time, second **07** instant, shining, winking **08** blinking, flashing, gleaming, polished **09** short time, sparkling **10** flickering, glimmering, glistening, glittering, shimmering **11** coruscating **13** scintillating, scintillation

**twirl**
◇ *anagram indicator*
**04** coil, curl, spin, turn, wind **05** pivot, trill, twist, wheel, whirl, whorl **06** gyrate, rotate, spiral, swivel **07** revolve, trundle, twiddle, twizzle **08** gyration, rotation **09** pirouette **10** revolution **11** convolution **12** tirlie-wirlie

**twirling**
◇ *anagram indicator*
**05** gyral **07** pivotal **08** gyratory, pivoting, rotating, rotatory, spinning, whirling **09** revolving **10** swivelling **11** pirouetting

**twist**
◇ *anagram indicator*
**03** arc, cue **04** bend, coil, cord, curl, flaw, kink, loop, rick, roll, rove, skew, slew, slue, spin, turn, twig, warp, whim, wind **05** alter, angle, braid, break, curve, freak, plait, quirk, screw, slant, twine, twirl, weave, wrest, wrick, wring **06** change, defect, deform, foible, garble, oddity, rotate, spiral, sprain, squirm, strain, strand, swivel, tangle, thread, wamble, wigwag, wimple, wreath, wrench, writhe, zigzag **07** contort, distort, entwine, falsify, pervert, revolve, swindle, torsion, twizzle, whimple, wreathe, wriggle **08** entangle, misquote, misshape, squiggle, surprise, wresting **09** misreport, turnabout, variation **10** aberration, contortion, distortion, intertwine, perversion **11** convolution, peculiarity **12** idiosyncrasy, imperfection, misrepresent
• **twist someone's arm**
**05** bully, force **06** coerce, lean on **07** dragoon **08** bulldoze, persuade **10** intimidate, pressurize **14** put the screws on

**twisted**
◇ *anagram indicator*
**03** odd **04** wavy **05** kinky, thraw **06** thrawn, thrown, warped **07** deviant, sinuous, strange, tortile, winding **08** peculiar, squiggly **09** contorted, perverted, unnatural

**twister**
**04** gale **05** cheat, crook, fraud, rogue, storm **06** con man, phoney, squall **07** cyclone, monsoon, tempest, tornado, typhoon **08** con woman, deceiver, swindler **09** con artist, hurricane, scoundrel, trickster, whirlwind **10** blackguard

**twisty**
**06** zigzag **07** curving, sinuous, winding **08** indirect, tortuous **10** circuitous, meandering, roundabout, serpentine

**twit**
**03** ass, git **04** berk, clot, dope, dork, fool, geek, goop, nerd, nerk, prat **05** chump, clown, dweeb, idiot, ninny, twerp **06** nig-nog, nitwit **07** airhead, halfwit, plonker, saphead, twitter **08** imbecile **09** blockhead, simpleton **10** nincompoop **11** knuckle-head **13** proper Charlie

**twitch**
◇ *anagram indicator*
**03** tic, tig, tit, tug **04** jerk, jump, pull, yips **05** blink, pluck, shake, spasm, start, tweak **06** quiver, shiver, snatch, tremor **07** flutter, the yips, tremble **09** vellicate **10** convulsion

**twitchy**
**04** edgy **05** het up, jerky, jumpy, nervy, shaky, tense **06** on edge, uneasy **07** anxious, fidgety, in a stew, jittery, keyed up, nervous, panicky, restive, uptight, wound up **08** agitated, in a sweat, in a tizzy **12** apprehensive

**twitter**
**03** cry, gab **04** chat, sing, song **05** cheep, chirp, tweet **06** babble, gabble, gossip, jabber, jargon, warble, witter **07** blather, blether, chatter, chirrup, chitter, prattle, twaddle, whistle **08** chirping, tweeting **09** palpitate **10** chirruping

**two**
**02** II **04** pair **05** deuce, twain **06** couple
• **the two**
**04** both

**two-faced**
**05** false, lying **07** devious **09** deceitful, insincere **10** Janus-faced, perfidious **11** dissembling, duplicitous, treacherous **12** hypocritical **13** double-dealing, untrustworthy

**twofold**
**04** dual, twin **05** duple **06** bifold, binary, double, duplex **07** twafald, twifold, twyfold **09** duplicate

**two-master**
**04** buss

**twosome**
**03** duo **04** duet, pair **06** couple **09** tête-à-tête

**two-up**
**03** swy **05** swy-up **07** swy game

**two-wheeler**
**04** cart

**Tyche**
**07** Fortuna

**tycoon**
**05** baron, mogul **06** fat cat **07** magnate, supremo **08** big noise **09** big cheese, financier, moneybags **10** capitalist **12** entrepreneur, moneyspinner **13** industrialist

**Tyler**
**03** Wat

**Tyneside**
**02** NE

**type**
◇ *anagram indicator*
**03** ilk, key, set **04** face, font, form, hair, kind, make, mark, norm, sort **05** brand, breed, class, fount, genre, genus, group, model, order, print, stamp, style **06** emblem, letter, number, strain, symbol **07** epitome, example, letters, numbers, pattern, species, symbols, variety **08** category, exemplar, insignia, original, printing, specimen, standard, typeface **09** archetype, character, exemplify, lettering, prefigure, prototype, symbolize, typewrite **10** characters, embodiment, foreshadow **11** description, designation, subdivision **12** anticipation, quintessence **13** foreshadowing **14** classification
• **confused type**
**02** pi **03** pie, pye
• **type size**
**03** gem **04** body, pica **05** canon **06** minion **07** brevier, English **09** bourgeois, Columbian, nonpareil **10** longprimer **11** emerald type, Great Primer

**typeface**

*Typefaces include:*

**05** Arial
**06** Bell MT, Impact, Lucida, Modern, Tahoma
**07** Courier, Curlz MT, Marlett, MS Serif, Verdana
**08** Garamond, Jokerman, MS Gothic, MS Mincho, Playbill, Rockwell, Webdings
**09** Colonna MT, Wide Latin, Wingdings
**10** Arial Black, Courier New, Lucida Sans
**11** Baskerville, Book Antiqua, Comic Sans MS, MS Sans Serif, Poor Richard, Trebuchet MS
**13** Century Gothic, Lucida Console, Times New Roman
**14** Franklin Gothic
**15** Bookman Old Style

**typhoon**
**05** storm **06** squall, typhon **07** cyclone, tempest, tornado, twister **09** hurricane, whirlwind

**typical**
**04** trew, true **05** model, stock, typal, typic, usual **06** normal, Podunk **07** average, classic **08** ordinary, orthodox, standard, true-bred **10** archetypal, emblematic, figurative, indicative, stereotype **11** distinctive **12** conventional, illustrative, run-of-the-mill **13** typographical **14** characteristic, quintessential, representative

**typically**
**07** as a rule, usually **08** normally **09** routinely **10** habitually, ordinarily **11** classically, customarily

**typify**
**05** image **06** embody, imbody, shadow **08** indicate **09** epitomize, exemplify, personify, represent, symbolize **10** foreshadow, illustrate **11** encapsulate, foresignify **12** characterize

**tyrannical**
**05** cruel, harsh **06** lordly, severe, strict, unjust **08** absolute, despotic, Neronian, ruthless, satrapal, tyrannic **09** arbitrary, imperious **10** autocratic, despotical, high-handed, oppressive, peremptory, repressive **11** dictatorial, domineering, magisterial, overbearing **12** overpowering, totalitarian, unreasonable **13** authoritarian

**tyrannize**
**04** lord **05** bully, crush **06** coerce **07** dictate, enslave, oppress, repress **08** browbeat, domineer, suppress **09** subjugate, terrorize **10** intimidate, lord it over

**tyranny**
**07** cruelty, liberty **08** severity **09** autocracy, despotism, harshness, injustice **10** absolutism, domination, oppression, strictness **12** dictatorship, ruthlessness **13** imperiousness **14** high-handedness

**tyrant**
**05** bully, pewee **06** despot, peewee **08** autocrat, dictator, martinet **09** oppressor, tyranness **10** absolutist, taskmaster **11** slave-driver **13** authoritarian

*See also* **despot**

**tyro** *see* **tiro, tyro**

# U

**U**
**07** uniform **10** upper-class

**ubiquitous**
**06** common, global **08** frequent
**09** pervasive, universal
**10** everywhere, ubiquarian, wall-to-wall **11** ever-present, omnipresent

**ubiquity**
**09** frequency **10** commonness, popularity, prevalence
**12** omnipresence, universality
**13** pervasiveness

**Uganda**
**03** EAU, UGA

**ugliness**
**04** evil **06** danger, horror, menace
**08** disgrace, enormity, vileness
**09** deformity, nastiness, plainness
**10** homeliness, horridness
**11** heinousness, hideousness, monstrosity **12** unloveliness
**13** frightfulness, offensiveness, repulsiveness, unsightliness
**14** unpleasantness

**ugly**
◇ *anagram indicator*
**04** evil, foul, loth, vile **05** grave, loath, nasty, plain **06** gorgon, grotty, homely, horrid, oughly, ouglie, unfair
**07** hideous, hostile, ogreish
**08** alarming, deformed, horrible, ill-faced, ill-faste, ill-faurd, plug-ugly, shocking, sinister, terrible, unlovely
**09** dangerous, frightful, grotesque, loathsome, misshapen, monstrous, obnoxious, offensive, repulsive, revolting, ugly as sin, unsightly
**10** disgusting, ill-looking, ill-natured, unpleasant **11** disquieting, ill-favoured, threatening **12** disagreeable, evil-favoured, unattractive
**13** objectionable **15** unprepossessing

**UK** *see* **United Kingdom**

**Ukraine**
**02** UA **03** UKR

**ulcer**
**04** boil, noma, sore **05** issue, rupia
**06** aphtha, canker, fester **07** abscess, bedsore, fistula, sycosis **08** open sore
**09** impostume **10** plague-sore, ulceration **11** peptic ulcer **13** varicose ulcer **14** decubitus ulcer

**ulster**
**02** NI **04** coat

**ulterior**
**06** covert, hidden, secret **07** private, remoter, selfish **08** personal
**09** concealed, secondary
**10** underlying, unrevealed
**11** undisclosed, unexpressed

**ultimate**
◇ *tail selection indicator*
**03** end, ult **04** best, last, peak **05** basic, final, ideal **06** height, summit, utmost
**07** closing, epitome, extreme, highest, maximum, perfect, primary, radical, supreme, topmost **08** eventual, furthest, greatest, last word, limiting, remotest, terminal **09** elemental
**10** concluding, perfection, the mostest
**11** chef d'oeuvre, culmination, fundamental, masterpiece, summum bonum, superlative **12** consummation
**14** daddy of them all

**ultimately**
◇ *tail selection indicator*
**03** ult **06** at last **07** finally **08** after all, in the end **09** basically, primarily
**10** eventually **13** fundamentally, sooner or later **15** in the last resort

**ultra-**
**05** extra **09** extremely, unusually
**10** especially, remarkably **11** excessively
**13** exceptionally **15** extraordinarily

**ultraviolet**
**02** UV

**ululate**
**03** cry, sob **04** hoot, howl, keen, moan, wail, weep **05** mourn **06** holler, lament, scream **07** screech

**umbrage**
• **take umbrage**
**06** be hurt, resent **07** be angry, be upset **08** be miffed, be put out, get huffy **09** be annoyed **10** be insulted, be offended, feel put out **11** take offence
**13** be exasperated, take exception
**14** take personally

**umbrella**
**05** aegis, cover, **06** agency **08** auspices
**09** en tout cas **10** protection

*Umbrellas and parasols include:*

**04** gamp, mush
**05** dumpy
**06** brolly, chatta
**07** gingham
**08** marquise, mushroom, ombrella, sunshade, umbrello
**09** en tout cas
**11** bumbershoot

**umpire**
**03** ref, ump **05** judge **06** odd-man
**07** arbiter, control, daysman, mediate, oddsman, referee **08** linesman, mediator, moderate, oversman, stickler
**09** arbitrate, birlieman, byrlaw-man, moderator **10** adjudicate, arbitrator
**11** adjudicator
*See also* **cricket**

**umpteen**
**06** plenty **08** millions, numerous, very many **09** a good many, countless, thousands **11** innumerable

**UN** *see* **United Nations**

**unabashed**
**04** bold **06** brazen **07** blatant
**09** abashless, confident, unashamed, undaunted **10** undismayed **11** bold as brass, unconcerned **13** in countenance, unembarrassed

**unable**
**04** weak **05** unfit **06** cannot
**08** impotent **09** incapable, powerless
**10** inadequate, unequipped
**11** incompetent, ineffectual, unqualified

**unabridged**
**04** full **05** uncut, whole **06** entire
**08** complete **10** full-length
**11** uncondensed, unshortened
**12** unexpurgated

**unacceptable**
**04** non-U **05** wrong **07** a bit off
**09** obnoxious, offensive, unwelcome
**10** unpleasant, unsuitable
**11** intolerable, undesirable
**12** disagreeable, inadmissible
**13** beyond the pale, disappointing, objectionable **14** unsatisfactory

**unaccommodating**
**05** rigid **08** perverse, stubborn
**09** obstinate, unbending **10** inflexible, unyielding **11** disobliging
**12** intransigent **13** uncomplaisant, unco-operative **14** uncompromising

**unaccompanied**
**04** lone, solo **05** alone, secco
**06** lonely, silent, single **09** on your own
**10** by yourself, unattended, unescorted **12** single-handed

**unaccountable**
**03** odd **04** free **05** queer **06** immune
**07** bizarre, curious, strange, unusual
**08** baffling, peculiar, puzzling, singular, uncommon **09** insoluble, unheard-of
**10** mysterious **11** astonishing
**12** impenetrable, inexplicable, unfathomable **13** extraordinary, not answerable, unexplainable **14** not responsible

**unaccountably**
**09** strangely **10** bafflingly, incredibly, puzzlingly **12** inexplicably, miraculously, mysteriously, mystifyingly **13** unexplainably

**unaccustomed**
**03** new **06** unused, unwont **07** strange, unusual **08** uncommon, unwonted, wontless **09** different, inusitate **10** remarkable, surprising, unexpected, unfamiliar **11** unpractised **12** unacquainted **13** extraordinary, inexperienced, unprecedented

**unacquainted**
**06** unused **07** strange, unknown, unusual **08** ignorant **10** unfamiliar, uninformed **12** unaccustomed **13** inexperienced

**unadorned**
**04** bald, bare **05** plain, stark **06** severe, simple **07** undight **08** homespun **10** restrained **11** undecorated, unvarnished **12** unornamented **13** unembellished **15** straightforward

**unadulterated**
**04** neat, pure, real, true **05** sheer, solid, total, utter **06** simple **07** genuine, natural, perfect, sincere, unmixed **08** absolute, complete, flawless, straight, thorough **09** authentic, downright, unalloyed, undiluted **11** unmitigated, unqualified **14** unsophisticate **15** unsophisticated

**unaffected**
**04** real, true **05** naive, plain **06** candid, honest, immune, simple **07** artless, genuine, natural, sincere, unmoved **08** unspoilt **09** guileless, ingenuous, unaltered, unchanged, untouched **10** impervious, unassuming **11** indifferent, unconcerned **13** unpretentious **15** straightforward, unsophisticated

**unafraid**
**05** brave **06** daring **08** fearless, intrepid, unfeared **09** confident, dauntless, undaunted **10** courageous, unshakable **11** unshakeable **13** imperturbable

**unalterable**
**05** final, fixed, rigid **09** immovable, immutable, permanent **10** inflexible, invariable, unchanging, unyielding **11** hard and fast, reverseless **12** unchangeable

**unaltered**
**04** as is **09** invariant

**unanimity**
**05** unity **06** accord, unison **07** concert, concord, harmony **09** agreement, consensus **10** congruence **11** concurrence, consistency **14** like-mindedness

**unanimous**
**05** as one, joint, solid **06** common, united **08** in accord **09** concerted **10** concordant, consistent, harmonious, like-minded **11** in agreement **12** single-minded

**unanimously**
**05** as one **06** nem con **08** as one man **09** in concert, of one mind, unopposed **10** conjointly **12** with one voice **15** by common consent

**unannounced**
**06** abrupt, chance, sudden **07** amazing, unusual **09** startling **10** accidental, fortuitous, surprising, unexpected, unforeseen **11** astonishing, unlooked-for **13** unanticipated, unpredictable

**unanswerable**
**05** final **08** absolute **10** conclusive, unarguable, undeniable **11** irrefutable **12** indisputable, irrefragable **13** incontestable

**unanswered**
**04** open **05** vexed **07** in doubt **09** undecided, unsettled **10** unrequited, unresolved, up in the air

**unappetizing**
**07** insipid **09** tasteless, unsavoury **10** off-putting, unexciting, uninviting, unpleasant **11** distasteful, unappealing, unpalatable **12** disagreeable, unattractive **13** uninteresting

**unapproachable**
**04** cold, cool **05** aloof **06** remote **07** distant **08** reserved **09** withdrawn **10** forbidding, unfriendly, unsociable **11** standoffish **12** inaccessible, unresponsive **15** uncommunicative

**unapt**
**04** slow **05** inapt, unfit **08** unfitted, unsuited, untimely **10** inapposite, malapropos, unsuitable **12** inapplicable, unseasonable **13** inappropriate

**unarmed**
**04** bare, open, weak **05** inerm, naked **07** exposed **08** helpless **10** unweaponed, vulnerable **11** defenceless, unprotected

**unashamed**
**04** open **06** direct, honest **07** blatant **08** bashless **09** shameless, unabashed **10** impenitent **11** unconcealed, undisguised, unrepentant

**unasked**
**08** unbidden, unsought, unwanted **09** uninvited, voluntary **10** unrequired **11** spontaneous, unannounced, unrequested, unsolicited

**unassailable**
**05** sound **06** proven, secure **08** absolute, positive **09** well-armed **10** conclusive, invincible, inviolable, undeniable **11** impregnable, irrefutable **12** indisputable, inexpugnable, invulnerable **13** incontestable, well-fortified

**unassertive**
**03** shy **04** meek **05** mousy, quiet, timid **06** mousey **07** bashful **08** backward, retiring, timorous **09** diffident **10** unassuming **12** self-effacing

**unassuming**
**03** shy **04** meek **05** quiet **06** demure, humble, modest, simple **07** natural **08** reticent, retiring **10** restrained **11** unassertive, unobtrusive **12** self-effacing, underbearing **13** unpretentious

**unattached**
**04** free **05** loose **06** single **08** detached **09** available, fancy-free, footloose, on your own, unengaged, unmarried **10** by yourself, with no ties **11** independent, uncommitted **12** unaffiliated

**unattended**
**05** alone **07** ignored **08** forsaken **09** abandoned, forgotten, neglected, unguarded, unwatched **10** unescorted **11** disregarded **12** unsupervised **13** unaccompanied

**unattractive**
**04** ugly **05** plain, warby **06** grungy, homely, skanky **08** ill-faurd, uncomely, unlovely **09** offensive, repellent, unsavoury, unsightly, unwelcome **10** disgusting, off-putting, unexciting, uninviting, unpleasant **11** distasteful, ill-favoured, unappealing, undesirable, unpalatable **12** disagreeable, unappetizing **13** no oil painting, objectionable **15** not much to look at, unprepossessing

**unauthorized**
**07** illegal, illicit **08** unlawful **09** forbidden, irregular **10** prohibited, unapproved, unlicensed, unofficial **11** unchartered, unwarranted **12** illegitimate, unsanctioned

**unavailing**
**04** vain **06** beaten, failed, futile, losing **07** sterile, unlucky, useless **08** abortive, defeated, luckless, nugatory, thwarted **09** fruitless **10** frustrated **11** ineffective, unfortunate **12** unprevailing, unproductive, unprofitable, unsuccessful

**unavoidable**
**04** sure **05** fatal, fated **07** certain **08** destined, required **09** mandatory, necessary **10** compulsory, inevitable, inexorable, obligatory **11** ineluctable, inescapable, predestined

**unaware**
**04** deaf **05** blind **07** witless **08** heedless, ignorant, wareless **09** in the dark, oblivious, unknowing, unmindful, unwitting **10** insentient, uninformed, with no idea **11** incognizant, unconscious **12** unsuspecting **13** unenlightened

**unawares**
**05** aback **07** unwares **08** abruptly, off guard, on the hop, suddenly **09** in the dark, red-handed **10** by surprise, mistakenly, unprepared **11** insidiously, unknowingly, unwittingly

12 accidentally, à l'improviste, unexpectedly, unthinkingly
13 inadvertently, unconsciously
15 unintentionally

**unbalanced**
◇ *anagram indicator*
03 mad 05 barmy, crazy 06 biased, insane, mental, uneven, unfair, unjust 07 erratic, lunatic, unequal, unsound 08 crackers, demented, deranged, doolally, lopsided, one-sided, partisan, unstable, unsteady 09 disturbed, stir-crazy 10 irrational, prejudiced 11 dysharmonic, inequitable, mentally ill 12 asymmetrical, round the bend 13 round the twist 14 wrong in the head

**unbearable**
06 too bad 07 too much 08 the limit 10 importable 11 intolerable, unendurable 12 excruciating, insufferable, the last straw, unacceptable 13 insupportable

**unbeatable**
04 best 07 supreme 09 excellent, matchless, rock-solid 10 invincible 11 indomitable, unstoppable 13 unconquerable, unsurpassable

**unbeaten**
07 supreme, unbowed, winning 09 unsubdued 10 triumphant, undefeated, victorious 11 unconquered, unsurpassed 12 unvanquished

**unbecoming**
08 improper, indecent, infra dig, unseemly, unworthy 09 unfitting, unseeming, unsightly 10 indecorous, indelicate, misseeming, unladylike, unsuitable 11 unbefitting 12 ill-beseeming, unattractive
13 inappropriate, ungentlemanly
15 infra dignitatem

**unbeknown**
• **unbeknown to**
07 unknown 09 unheard of
10 unrealized 11 unperceived
13 unbeknownst to

**unbelief**
05 doubt 07 atheism 09 disbelief
10 scepticism 11 agnosticism, incredulity

**unbelievable**
06 unreal 07 amazing 08 unlikely
10 far-fetched, impossible, improbable, incredible, outlandish, remarkable, staggering 11 astonishing, implausible, incredulous, unthinkable
12 preposterous, unconvincing, unimaginable 13 extraordinary, inconceivable

**unbelievably**
09 amazingly 10 incredibly
12 outlandishly, unimaginably
13 inconceivably 15 extraordinarily

**unbeliever**
06 zendik 07 atheist, doubter, infidel, sceptic 08 agnostic 11 disbeliever, nullifidian 14 doubting Thomas

**unbelieving**
07 dubious, infidel 08 doubtful, doubting 09 miscreant, sceptical
10 suspicious 11 distrustful, incredulous, nullifidian, unconvinced, unpersuaded 12 disbelieving

**unbend**
04 thaw, undo 05 relax 06 uncoil, uncurl 08 loosen up, unbuckle, unbutton, unfasten, unfreeze
10 straighten

**unbending**
04 firm 05 aloof, rigid, stern, stiff, tough
06 formal, severe, strict 07 distant
08 Catonian, hardline, relaxing, reserved, resolute, stubborn
10 forbidding, formidable, inflexible, unyielding 12 intransigent
14 uncompromising

**unbiased**
04 fair, just 06 candid 07 neutral
08 balanced 09 equitable, impartial, objective 10 even-handed, fair-minded, open-minded, uncoloured
11 independent 12 uninfluenced, unprejudiced 13 disinterested, dispassionate

**unbidden**
04 free 07 unasked, willing
08 unforced, unwanted 09 uninvited, unwelcome, voluntary 10 unprompted
11 spontaneous, unsolicited

**unbind**
04 free, undo 05 loose, solve, untie
06 loosen, unyoke 07 release, set free, unchain, unloose 08 liberate, unfasten, unfetter, unloosen 09 unshackle

**unblemished**
04 pure 05 clear, white 07 perfect
08 flawless, spotless, unflawed
09 unspotted, unstained, unsullied, untainted 10 immaculate
11 untarnished 13 unimpeachable
14 irreproachable

**unblinking**
04 calm, cool 06 steady 07 assured
08 composed, fearless, unafraid
09 impassive 10 unwavering
11 emotionless, unemotional, unfaltering, unflinching, unshrinking
13 imperturbable

**unblushing**
04 bold 06 amoral, brazen 07 blatant
08 immodest, impudent 09 shameless, unabashed, unashamed
13 unembarrassed 15 conscience-proof

**unborn**
06 coming, future, to-come
07 awaited, in utero 08 expected, unyeaned 09 embryonic
10 subsequent, succeeding 11 non-existent

**unbosom**
04 bare, tell 05 admit 06 let out, reveal
07 confess, confide, divulge, lay bare, pour out, tell all, uncover 08 disclose, unburden

**unbounded**
04 vast 07 endless 08 infinite
09 boundless, limitless, unbridled, unchecked, unlimited
12 immeasurable, unconfinable, uncontrolled, unrestrained, unrestricted

**unbreakable**
05 solid, tough 06 rugged, strong
07 durable 09 resistant, toughened
10 adamantine 11 infrangible
12 shatterproof 14 indestructible

**unbridled**
04 wild 07 rampant, riotous
08 unbitted, uncurbed 09 excessive, unchecked 10 immoderate, licentious, profligate, ungoverned 11 intemperate
12 uncontrolled, unrestrained
13 unconstrained

**unbroken**
04 wild 05 rough, sheer, solid, whole
06 entire, in a row, intact, single
07 endless, non-stop, unbroke, untamed 08 complete, constant, seamless, unbeaten 09 ceaseless, incessant, perpetual, unceasing, undivided, unmatched 10 continuate, continuous, successive, unequalled, unrivalled 11 progressive, unremitting, unsurpassed 13 uninterrupted
14 undomesticated

**unburden**
04 bare, tell 05 admit 06 let out, reveal
07 cast off, confess, confide, divulge, lay bare, offload, pour out, tell all, uncover 08 disclose 09 discharge

**unbutton**
04 undo

**uncalled-for**
07 unasked 08 needless, unsought
09 unwelcome 10 gratuitous, undeserved, unprompted, unprovoked
11 unjustified, unnecessary, unsolicited, unwarranted

**uncannily**
05 oddly 08 spookily 09 bizarrely, strangely 10 incredibly, remarkably
11 unnaturally 12 mysteriously
14 supernaturally 15 extraordinarily

**uncanny**
03 odd 05 eerie, queer, weird
06 creepy, spooky, unsafe 07 bizarre, strange 08 eldritch, pokerish
09 fantastic, unearthly, unnatural, wanchancy 10 incredible, mysterious, remarkable, wanchancie
11 exceptional 12 supernatural
13 extraordinary, preternatural, unaccountable

**uncared-for**
07 run-down, squalid 08 derelict, deserted, forsaken, stranded, untended, untilled, unweeded
09 abandoned, neglected, overgrown
11 dilapidated, disregarded, undervalued, unhusbanded
12 uncultivated, unmaintained
13 unappreciated

**uncaring**
**04** cold **07** callous, unmoved **09** unfeeling **11** indifferent, unconcerned **12** uninterested **13** inconsiderate, marble-hearted, unsympathetic **14** marble-breasted

**unceasing**
**07** endless, non-stop, undying **08** constant, unbroken, unending **09** ceaseless, continual, continued, incessant, perpetual **10** continuous, persistent, relentless **11** everlasting, never-ending, unrelenting, unremitting

**unceremonious**
**04** rude **06** abrupt, casual, direct, sudden **07** off-hand, relaxed **08** familiar, impolite, informal, laid-back, sans gêne **09** easy-going **10** unofficial **11** undignified **12** discourteous **13** disrespectful

**uncertain**
◇ *anagram indicator*
**04** iffy, open **05** dicey, dodgy, risky, shaky, vague **06** chancy, fitful, slippy, unsure **07** chancey, dubious, erratic, unclear, unknown, vagrant, various **08** doubtful, hesitant, insecure, slippery, unsteady, variable, wavering **09** hazardous, irregular, undecided, unsettled **10** ambivalent, changeable, inconstant, indefinite, in two minds, of two minds, precarious, touch-and-go, unreliable, unresolved, up in the air **11** speculative, unconfirmed, unconvinced, vacillating **12** equivocating, in the balance, questionable, undetermined **13** indeterminate, unforeseeable, unpredictable

**uncertainly**
**05** shyly **06** warily **07** timidly **09** dubiously, haltingly **10** delayingly, doubtfully, hesitantly, in two minds, waveringly **11** reluctantly, sceptically, tentatively, unwillingly **12** indecisively, irresolutely, stammeringly, stutteringly **13** half-heartedly, vacillatingly

**uncertainty**
**02** if **05** doubt, qualm **06** qualms **07** dilemma **09** ambiguity, confusion, misgiving, riskiness, vagueness **10** hesitation, insecurity, perplexity, puzzlement, scepticism, uneasiness **11** ambivalence, contingency **12** bewilderment, irresolution, peradventure **13** unreliability

**unchallengeable**
**05** final **07** sacless **08** absolute **10** conclusive **11** impregnable, irrefutable **12** inappellable, indisputable, irrefragable **13** incontestable

**unchangeable**
**05** final, fixed **07** eternal **08** constant **09** immutable, permanent **10** changeless, invariable, unchanging **11** stereotyped **12** irreversible **14** intransmutable

**unchanging**
**04** same **06** steady **07** abiding, eternal, lasting **08** constant, enduring **09** permanent, perpetual, phaseless, steadfast, unvarying **10** changeless, invariable

**uncharitable**
**04** hard, mean **05** cruel, harsh, stern **06** severe, unkind **07** callous **09** unfeeling **10** unfriendly, ungenerous **11** hard-hearted, insensitive, unchristian, unforgiving **13** unsympathetic **15** uncompassionate

**uncharted**
**03** new **05** alien **06** virgin **07** foreign, strange, unknown **09** unplumbed **10** unexplored, unfamiliar, unsurveyed **12** undiscovered

**unchaste**
**04** lewd **05** frail, light, loose **06** fallen, impure, wanton **07** defiled, immoral, wappend **08** depraved, immodest **09** dishonest, dissolute **10** licentious **11** light-heeled, promiscuous

**unchecked**
**03** raw **04** wild **06** unruly **07** rampant, riotous, violent **08** uncurbed, unreined **09** unbridled **10** boisterous, unhindered **12** uncontrolled, unrestrained **13** undisciplined

**uncivil**
**04** curt, rude **05** gruff, surly **06** abrupt, coarse **07** bearish, boorish, brusque, ill-bred, uncouth **08** churlish, impolite, unseemly **09** menseless **10** ungracious, unmannerly **11** bad-mannered, ill-mannered **12** discourteous **13** disrespectful

**uncivilized**
**04** wild **05** rough **06** savage **07** boorish, brutish, heathen, salvage, uncouth, untamed **08** barbaric, impolite **09** barbarian, barbarous, primitive, unrefined **10** antisocial, heathenish, illiterate, tramontane, uncultured, uneducated **13** unenlightened **15** unsophisticated

**unclassifiable**
**05** vague **07** elusive **08** doubtful **09** uncertain **10** ill-defined, indefinite, indistinct **11** indefinable, undefinable **13** indescribable, indeterminate **14** unidentifiable

**unclassified**
**05** basic, known **06** lowest, public **07** general, minimal, minimum **08** official, revealed, ungraded **09** disclosed, published **11** on the record **12** unrestricted **14** for publication

**uncle**
**03** eme, oom **10** pawnbroker

*Uncles include:*

**03** Bob, Joe, Pio, Sam, Tom
**05** Henry, Lynch (Andrew), Remus, Silas, Vanya
**06** Domkin (George), Fester, Jasper (John), Julius, Shandy (Toby), Wilson (Arthur)
**07** Flowers (Philip), Forsyte (Old Jolyon), Trotter (Albert), Quentin
**08** Bulgaria, Claudius, McCaslin (Buck), McCaslin (Buddy)
**09** Cobbleigh (Tom), Old Jolyon
**10** Richard III
**11** Pumblechook
**15** Richard the Third

**unclean**
**03** bad **04** evil, foul, lewd **05** dirty, grimy **06** filthy, grubby, impure, soiled, wicked **07** corrupt, defiled, profane, sullied, tainted **08** ordurous, polluted **10** unhygienic **11** adulterated, unwholesome **12** contaminated

**unclear**
**03** dim **04** hazy, iffy **05** foggy, vague **06** unsure **07** dubious, obscure **08** doubtful **09** ambiguous, equivocal, non liquet, uncertain, unsettled **10** convoluted, indefinite, indistinct **12** undetermined

**unclothed**
**04** bare, nude **05** naked **06** unclad **08** disrobed, in the raw, starkers, stripped **09** in the buff, undressed **10** stark-naked **15** in the altogether

**uncomfortable**
**04** cold, hard, mean **05** tense, unked, unket, unkid **06** on edge, uneasy **07** anxious, awkward, cramped, nervous, painful, worried **08** troubled **09** disturbed, ill at ease **10** disquieted, distressed, ill-fitting, irritating **11** discomfited, embarrassed **12** disagreeable **13** self-conscious

**uncommitted**
**04** free **07** neutral **08** floating **09** available, fancy-free, footloose, undecided **10** non-aligned, unattached, uninvolved **11** non-partisan **12** free-floating

**uncommon**
◇ *anagram indicator*
**03** odd **04** rare, seld, very **05** queer **06** scarce **07** bizarre, curious, notable, special, strange, unusual **08** abnormal, atypical, peculiar, singular, striking **10** infrequent, remarkable, remarkably, unfamiliar **11** distinctive, exceptional, out of the way, outstanding **12** like gold dust **13** extraordinary **15** thin on the ground

**uncommonly**
◇ *anagram indicator*
**04** seld, very **06** rarely, seldom **09** extremely, strangely, unusually **10** abnormally, peculiarly, remarkably, singularly **12** infrequently, occasionally, particularly **13** exceptionally, outstandingly

**uncommunicative**
**03** shy **04** curt **05** aloof, brief, close, quiet **06** silent **08** reserved, reticent,

retiring, taciturn **09** diffident, secretive, withdrawn **10** buttoned-up, unsociable **11** tight-lipped **12** unresponsive **13** unforthcoming

**uncomplicated**
◇ *anagram indicator*
**04** easy **05** clear **06** direct, simple **10** uninvolved **11** undemanding **15** straightforward

**uncompromising**
**04** firm **05** rigid, stiff, tough **06** gritty, strict **07** diehard **08** hardline, obdurate, stubborn **09** hard-faced, hardshell, immovable, obstinate, out-and-out, unbending **10** inexorable, inflexible, unyielding **12** intransigent **15** unaccommodating

**unconcealable**
**05** clear, plain **07** obvious **08** manifest **09** insistent **13** irrepressible **14** insuppressible, uncontrollable

**unconcealed**
**04** open, pert **05** frank, naked, overt **06** patent, public **07** blatant, evident, obvious, visible **08** admitted, apparent, manifest, unveiled **09** unashamed **10** noticeable **11** conspicuous **12** ill-concealed, undissembled **13** self-confessed **15** undistinguished

**unconcern**
**06** apathy **09** aloofness **10** detachment, negligence, remoteness **11** callousness, disinterest, insouciance, nonchalance **12** indifference **13** pococurantism

**unconcerned**
**04** cool **05** aloof, sober **06** casual, remote **07** callous, distant, relaxed, unmoved **08** carefree, careless, composed, detached, not fussy, uncaring **09** apathetic, impartial, not fussed, oblivious, unruffled, unworried **10** complacent, insouciant, nonchalant, uninvolved, untroubled **11** indifferent, pococurante, unperturbed **12** uninterested **13** disinterested, dispassionate, unsympathetic

**unconditional**
**04** full, pure **05** total, utter **06** entire **07** plenary **08** absolute, complete, definite, outright, positive, termless **09** categoric, downright, out-and-out, unlimited **10** conclusive, unreserved **11** categorical, unequivocal, unqualified **12** unrestricted, wholehearted **13** thoroughgoing

**unconditionally**
**05** fully **06** purely **07** totally **08** entirely **10** absolutely, completely **11** simpliciter **12** unreservedly **13** categorically, unequivocally **14** wholeheartedly

**unconfirmed**
**08** ignorant, unproved, unproven **10** unratified, unverified **14** uncorroborated **15** unauthenticated, unsubstantiated

**unconformity**
**12** irregularity **13** disconformity, discontinuity

**uncongenial**
**08** unsuited **09** unsavoury **10** discordant, unfriendly, uninviting, unpleasant **11** displeasing, distasteful, unappealing **12** antagonistic, antipathetic, disagreeable, incompatible, unattractive **13** unsympathetic

**unconnected**
**07** foreign **08** confused, detached, separate **09** illogical, unrelated **10** disjointed, incoherent, irrational, irrelevant, unattached **11** independent, off the point **12** disconnected **13** inappropriate, unco-ordinated **14** beside the point

**unconquerable**
**08** enduring **09** ingrained **10** inveterate, invincible, unbeatable, unyielding **11** indomitable, insuperable **12** irresistible, overpowering, undefeatable **13** irrepressible **14** insurmountable

**unconscionable**
**06** amoral, unholy **07** extreme, ungodly **08** criminal **09** excessive, unearthly, unethical **10** exorbitant, immoderate, inordinate, outrageous **11** extravagant **12** preposterous, unpardonable, unprincipled, unreasonable, unscrupulous **13** unjustifiable, unwarrantable

**unconscious**
**03** out **04** deaf **05** blind, dazed **06** asleep, innate, latent, put out, reflex, zonked **07** drugged, fainted, in a coma, out cold, stunned, unaware, witless **08** comatose, heedless, ignorant, knee-jerk, lifeless **09** automatic, collapsed, concussed, impulsive, oblivious, passed out, repressed, senseless, unmindful, unwitting **10** accidental, blacked out, insensible, knocked out, subliminal, suppressed, unthinking **11** inadvertent, incognizant, inconscient, inconscious, instinctive, involuntary **12** subconscious **13** unintentional **14** dead to the world, out for the count

• **render unconscious**
**04** stun **06** lay out, put out **07** garotte, garrote **08** garrotte, knock out

**unconsciously**
**10** heedlessly, insensibly **11** impulsively, obliviously, unmindfully, unwittingly **12** accidentally, subliminally, unthinkingly **13** automatically, inadvertently, instinctively, involuntarily **15** unintentionally

**unconsciousness**
**04** coma, doze **05** faint, sleep **06** snooze, torpor, trance **08** blackout, daydream, narcosis, numbness **12** inconscience, stupefaction **13** insensibility

**unconstraint**
**07** abandon, freedom **08** openness **09** unreserve **10** liberality, relaxation **11** unrestraint **12** laissez-faire

**uncontrollable**
**03** mad **04** wild **06** strong, unruly **07** furious, violent **08** absolute **10** disorderly **11** intractable **12** indisputable, out of control, ungovernable, unmanageable **13** irrepressible

**uncontrolled**
◇ *anagram indicator*
**04** wild **06** random, randon, unruly **07** rampant, riotous, runaway, violent **08** uncurbed **09** unbridled, unchecked **10** boisterous, unhindered, unmastered **12** unrestrained **13** undisciplined

**unconventional**
◇ *anagram indicator*
**03** odd **04** rare, zany **05** gipsy, gypsy, spacy, wacky, weird **06** far-out, freaky, fringe, spacey, way-out **07** bizarre, oddball, offbeat, radical, unusual **08** abnormal, bohemian, freakish, original, uncommon **09** different, eccentric, irregular, left-field **10** avant-garde, individual, long-haired, unorthodox **11** alternative, uncustomary **12** experimental **13** idiosyncratic

**unconvincing**
**04** lame, weak **05** fishy **06** farfet, feeble, flimsy **07** dubious, suspect **08** doubtful, unlikely **10** far-fetched, improbable **11** implausible **12** questionable

**uncooked**
**03** raw **09** au naturel

**unco-operative**
**04** rude **07** awkward, cubbish, stroppy **08** stubborn **09** obstinate, unhelpful **10** unpleasant **12** bloody-minded

**unco-ordinated**
◇ *anagram indicator*
**05** inept **06** clumsy **07** awkward **08** bumbling, bungling, ungainly **09** maladroit **10** disjointed, ungraceful **11** clodhopping

**uncork**
**04** open, undo **05** clear, crack **06** broach, expose, unseal **07** uncover **08** push open **09** break open, burst open, force open, prise open, slide open

**uncouth**
◇ *anagram indicator*
**04** rude **05** crude, rough **06** clumsy, coarse, gauche, rugged, rustic, unrude, vulgar **07** awkward, boorish, loutish, unknown **08** impolite, improper, ungainly, unseemly **09** graceless, rough-hewn, unrefined **10** uncultured, unfamiliar, ungraceful **11** bad-mannered, ill-mannered, uncivilized **12** uncultivated **15** unsophisticated

**uncover**
**04** bare, leak, open, peel, rake, show

**05** dig up, strip, unlid **06** detect, exhume, expose, reveal, unheal, unhele, unmask, unrake, unveil, unwrap **07** dismask, divulge, lay bare, lay open, unearth **08** disclose, discover, unbonnet, unshroud **09** make known, unsheathe **12** bring to light **13** blow the lid off, lift the lid off, take the lid off

**uncritical**
**05** naive **07** unfussy **08** gullible, trusting **09** accepting, credulous, incurious **11** superficial, unselective **12** undiscerning **13** unquestioning **14** non-judgemental

**unctuous**
**04** glib, oily **05** slick, suave **06** creamy, greasy, smarmy, smooth **07** fawning, gushing, servile **09** insincere, pietistic, plausible **10** obsequious **11** sycophantic **12** ingratiating **13** sanctimonious

**uncultivated**
**03** new **04** wild **05** feral, rough, waste **06** desert, fallow, incult **07** natural, wilding **11** unhusbanded

**uncultured**
**04** hick, rude **05** crude, ocker, rough **06** coarse, incult, rustic **07** boorish, ill-bred, uncouth **09** barbarous, unrefined **10** philistine **11** uncivilized **12** uncultivated **14** unintellectual **15** unsophisticated

**undaunted**
**04** bold **05** brave **07** impavid, unbowed **08** fearless, intrepid, resolute, unafraid **09** dauntless, steadfast, unalarmed **10** courageous, undeterred, undismayed, unflagging **11** indomitable **13** undiscouraged

**undecided**
**04** moot, open **05** vague **06** unsure **07** dubious, in doubt, unknown **08** doubtful, hesitant, wavering **09** debatable, dithering, uncertain, unsettled **10** ambivalent, indecisive, indefinite, in two minds, irresolute, of two minds, unresolved, up in the air **11** uncommitted **12** equivocating, in the balance **13** unestablished

**undecorated**
**05** plain, stark **06** severe, simple **07** austere **08** inornate **09** classical, unadorned **10** functional **12** unornamented **13** unembellished

**undefeated**
**07** supreme, unbowed, winning **08** unbeaten **09** unsubdued **10** triumphant, victorious **11** unconquered, unsurpassed **12** unvanquished

**undefended**
**04** open **05** naked **07** exposed, unarmed **09** pregnable, unguarded **10** vulnerable **11** defenceless, unfortified, unprotected

**undefiled**
**04** pure **05** clean, clear **06** chaste, intact, virgin **07** sinless **08** flawless, spotless, unsoiled, virginal **09** inviolate, unspotted, unstained, unsullied **10** immaculate, intemerate **11** unblemished

**undefined**
**04** hazy **05** vague **06** woolly **07** inexact, shadowy, tenuous, unclear **08** formless, nebulous **09** imprecise **10** ill-defined, indefinite, indistinct **11** unexplained, unspecified **13** indeterminate

**undemonstrative**
**04** cold, cool **05** aloof, stiff **06** formal, remote **07** distant **08** reserved, reticent **09** impassive, withdrawn **10** phlegmatic, restrained **11** unemotional **12** unresponsive **15** uncommunicative

**undeniable**
**04** sure **05** clear **06** patent, proven **07** certain, evident, obvious **08** definite, manifest, positive **09** excellent, hard facts, undoubted **11** beyond doubt, indubitable, irrefutable **12** indisputable, unmistakable **13** incontestable **14** beyond question, unquestionable **15** unexceptionable

**undeniably**
**09** certainly **10** definitely, positively **11** beyond doubt, indubitably, undoubtedly **12** indisputably, unmistakably **14** beyond question, unquestionably

**undependable**
**06** fickle **07** erratic **08** unstable, variable **09** mercurial, uncertain **10** capricious, changeable, inconstant, unreliable **11** fair-weather, treacherous **12** inconsistent **13** irresponsible, unpredictable, untrustworthy

**under**
◇ *juxtaposition down indicator*
**04** down, less **05** below, lower **06** within **07** beneath **08** downward, junior to, less than, under par **09** lower than **10** inferior to, underneath **11** secondary to, subordinate **13** subordinate to, subservient to

**underclothes** *see* **underwear**

**undercover**
**03** sly **06** covert, hidden, secret **07** furtive, private **08** hush-hush, stealthy **09** concealed **11** clandestine, underground **12** confidential, intelligence **13** surreptitious

**undercurrent**
**04** aura, hint **05** drift, sense, tinge, trend **07** feeling, flavour **08** movement, overtone, tendency, underset, undertow **09** underflow, undertone **10** atmosphere, suggestion

**undercut**
**04** mine **05** filet **08** excavate, gouge out, scoop out, underbid **09** hollow out, undermine, undersell **10** tenderloin, underprice **11** undercharge **14** charge less than

**underdog**
**04** prey **05** loser **06** victim **07** outcast **08** outsider **09** little man **11** unfortunate, weaker party **12** the exploited

**underdone**
**04** rare **09** half-baked

**underestimate**
**07** dismiss **08** belittle, minimize, misjudge, play down **09** disparage, sell short, underrate **10** look down on, trivialize, undervalue **12** miscalculate

**undergarment** *see* **underwear**

**undergo**
**04** bear **05** enjoy, stand **06** endure, suffer **07** sustain, weather **08** submit to, tolerate, underlie **09** go through, put up with, withstand **10** experience **11** pass through

**underground**
**04** tube **05** metro **06** buried, covert, hidden, secret, subway, sunken **07** covered, furtive, illegal, radical **08** secretly **09** concealed, hypogeous **10** avant-garde, hypogaeous, subversive, undercover, unofficial, unorthodox **11** alternative, below ground, clandestine **12** experimental, subterranean **13** revolutionary, surreptitious **15** below the surface

*Underground and metro transport systems include:*

**01** T
**04** BART, DART
**07** the Tube
**09** Chicago El, Rome Metro
**10** City Circle, Paris Métro
**11** Berlin S-Bahn, Berlin U-Bahn, Madrid Metro, Munich S-Bahn, Munich U-Bahn
**13** New York Subway
**15** Clockwork Orange, Washington Metro

*See also* **London**

**undergrowth**
**05** brush, scrub **06** briars, bushes, shrubs, spring **07** bracken, thicket **08** brambles **09** brushwood, shrubbery, underwood **10** vegetation **11** ground cover

**underhand**
**03** sly **05** shady **06** crafty, secret, shonky, sneaky **07** crooked, devious, furtive, immoral, oblique **08** improper, scheming, sinister, sneaking, stealthy **09** deceitful, deceptive, dishonest, unethical **10** backstairs, fraudulent **11** clandestine, unobtrusive **12** unscrupulous **13** hole-and-corner, surreptitious

**underline**
**04** mark **06** stress **07** point up **09** emphasize, highlight, italicize **10** accentuate, foreground, underscore **15** draw attention to

**underling**
**05** slave **06** lackey, menial, minion, nobody **07** flunkey, servant
**08** hireling, inferior, munchkin, weakling **09** nonentity **11** subordinate

**underlying**
**04** root **05** basal, basic **06** hidden, latent, veiled **07** lurking, primary, subject
**08** inherent **09** concealed, essential, intrinsic, subjacent **10** elementary
**11** fundamental, subordinate

**undermine**
**03** dig, mar, sap **04** mine **05** erode
**06** damage, impair, injure, tunnel, weaken **07** cripple, destroy, handbag, subvert, vitiate **08** excavate, sabotage, undercut, wear away **09** underwork
**14** make less secure

**undernourished**
**06** hungry **07** starved **08** anorexic, underfed **09** anorectic
**12** malnourished

**underprivileged**
**04** poor **05** needy **06** in need, in want
**08** deprived **09** destitute, oppressed
**10** in distress **11** impecunious
**12** impoverished **13** disadvantaged

**underrate**
**07** dismiss **08** belittle, inferior
**09** disparage, downgrade, extenuate, sell short **10** depreciate, look down on, undervalue **13** underestimate

**under-secretary**
**02** US

**undersell**
**03** cut **05** slash **06** reduce **08** mark down, play down, undercut
**09** disparage, sell short **10** depreciate, understate **11** undercharge

**undershirt**
**04** vest **06** semmit **07** singlet, surcoat

**undersized**
**03** wee **04** puny, tiny **05** dwarf, pygmy, scrub, small, teeny **06** little, minute, teensy **07** runtish, stunted **08** pint-size
**09** atrophied, miniature, pint-sized
**11** underweight **14** underdeveloped
**15** achondroplastic

**understand**
**03** dig, get, see **04** gaum, gorm, hear, know, read, take, twig **05** catch, click, get it, grasp, imply, learn, savey, savvy, think **06** accept, assume, fathom, follow, gather, make of, rumble, savvey, take in **07** believe, comfort, discern, elusive, feel for, get wise, make out, presume, realize, support, suppose, suss out **08** conceive, conclude, contrive, cotton on, perceive, tumble to **09** apprehend, empathize, enter into, figure out, interpret, latch onto, penetrate, recognize **10** appreciate, comprehend, sympathize
**11** commiserate, make sense of **12** feel sorry for, get a handle on, get the hang of, identify with, know the ropes **13** get the message, get the picture, the penny drops

**• failure to understand**
**04** anan, anon

**understandable**
**05** clear, lucid, plain **06** direct
**07** natural **08** expected **10** acceptable, accessible, admissible, penetrable, reasonable **11** transparent, unambiguous **12** intelligible, unsurprising **14** comprehensible, self-explaining **15** self-explanatory, straightforward

**understanding**
**03** ken **04** gaum, gorm, head, idea, kind, pact, view, with **05** grasp, sense, trust **06** accord, belief, loving, notion, tender, uptake, wisdom **07** bargain, comfort, command, compact, conceit, empathy, entente, feeling, harmony, insight, lenient, opinion, patient, support **08** sympathy, tolerant
**09** agreement, awareness, forgiving, hindsight, intellect, judgement, knowledge, sensitive **10** compassion, discerning, forbearing, impression, perception, supportive, thoughtful
**11** arrangement, considerate, consolation, discernment, intelligent, sympathetic **12** appreciation, apprehension, intelligence
**13** commiseration, compassionate, comprehension **14** interpretation

**understate**
**07** dismiss **08** belittle, minimize, play down **09** soft-pedal, underplay
**11** make light of

**understated**
**04** mild **05** faint **06** low-key, subtle
**07** implied **08** indirect **09** toned-down
**10** indefinite, indistinct

**understatement**
**07** litotes, meiosis **09** dismissal, restraint **12** minimization, underplaying

**understood**
**05** tacit **07** assumed, implied
**08** accepted, familiar, implicit, inferred, presumed, unspoken, unstated
**09** unwritten **11** transparent

**understudy**
**05** locum **06** deputy, double, fill-in, relief **07** reserve, stand-in **10** substitute
**11** replacement

**undersurface**
**03** pad **04** sole **05** belly **08** intrados, pavilion **09** gastraeum

**undertake**
**03** try **05** agree, begin **06** accept, assume, pledge, tackle, take on
**07** attempt, promise, receive
**08** commence, contract, covenant, deal with, embark on, perceive, set about, shoulder **09** endeavour, get down to, guarantee, set in hand, underfong **10** enterprise, take in hand
**13** put your hand to, set your hand to
**14** commit yourself, get to grips with, grasp the nettle, turn your hand to
**15** apply yourself to

**undertaker**
**06** editor, surety **07** sponsor
**08** compiler, upholder **09** mortician, projector, publisher **10** contractor
**12** entrepreneur **15** funeral director

**undertaking**
**03** job, vow **04** call, plan, task, word
**06** affair, effort, pledge, scheme
**07** attempt, emprise, project, promise, venture, warrant **08** business, campaign, contract, warranty
**09** assurance, challenge, endeavour, guarantee, operation **10** commitment, enterprise **12** enterprising

**undertone**
**04** aura, hint **05** tinge, touch, trace
**06** murmur **07** feeling, flavour, whisper
**09** undernote, undersong
**10** atmosphere, intimation, suggestion
**11** connotation **12** undercurrent

**undervalue**
**07** disable, dismiss **08** disprize, minimize, misjudge, misprise, misprize
**09** disparage, sell short, underrate
**10** depreciate, look down on
**13** underestimate

**underwater**
**06** sunken **08** demersal, demersed, immersed, undersea, undertow
**09** submarine, submerged
**10** subaquatic, subaqueous

**underwear**
**06** smalls, undies **08** grundies, lingerie, scanties, skivvies, underset
**09** innerwear **10** underlinen
**11** underthings **12** underclothes
**13** underclothing, undergarments
**14** unmentionables

*Underwear includes:*

**03** bra
**04** body, coms, jump, slip, vest
**05** bania, cimar, combs, cymar, jupon, pants, shift, tanga, teddy, thong, tunic
**06** banian, banyan, basque, briefs, corset, garter, girdle, knicks, semmit, skivvy, teddie, trunks
**07** chemise, drawers, G-string, hosiery, linings, panties, singlet, spencer, Y-fronts
**08** bloomers, camisole, chuddies, frillies, knickers, subucula, thermals
**09** brassière, crinoline, jockstrap, long johns, petticoat, stockings, union suit, wyliecoat
**10** suspenders, underdress, underpants, undershirt, underskirt
**11** boxer shorts, directoires, undershorts
**12** body stocking, camiknickers, combinations
**13** liberty bodice, suspender-belt
**14** French knickers

**underweight**
**04** thin **08** underfed **10** undersized
**11** half-starved **14** undernourished

**underworld**
**03** Dis, pit **04** Ades, fire, hell **05** abyss,

below, Hades, Sheol **06** Erebus, the mob, Tophet **07** Abaddon, Acheron, Gehenna, inferno **08** gangland, Tartarus **09** down there, Malebolge, perdition **10** other place, subterrene **11** nether world, underground **12** lower regions **13** bottomless pit, criminal world **14** organized crime **15** abode of the devil, infernal regions

**underwrite**
**04** back, fund, sign **05** write **06** insure **07** approve, confirm, endorse, finance, initial, sponsor, support **08** sanction **09** authorize, guarantee, subscribe, subsidize **11** countersign

**undesirable**
**04** foul **05** nasty **08** disliked, riff-raff, unwanted **09** obnoxious, offensive, repugnant, unwelcome **10** unpleasant, unsuitable **11** distasteful, unwished-for **12** disagreeable, unacceptable **13** objectionable

**undeveloped**
**04** rude **06** latent, neuter **07** dwarfed, stunted **08** immature, inchoate, unformed **09** embryonic, infantile, potential, unfledged **10** developing, primordial, Third World **12** less advanced **14** underdeveloped

**undignified**
**06** clumsy **07** foolish **08** improper, ungainly, unseemly **09** inelegant **10** indecorous, unbecoming, unsuitable **13** inappropriate

**undiluted**
**04** neat, pure **05** heady, sheer, utter **06** strong **07** unmixed **08** straight, unspoilt **09** unalloyed, unblended **11** unmitigated, unqualified **12** concentrated

**undisciplined**
◇ *anagram indicator*
**04** wild **06** unruly, wanton, wilful **07** wayward **08** unsteady **09** untrained **10** unreliable, unschooled **11** disobedient **12** disorganized, obstreperous, uncontrolled, unrestrained, unsystematic **13** unpredictable

**undisguised**
**04** bald, open **05** frank, naked, overt, stark, utter **06** patent **07** blatant, evident, genuine, obvious **08** apparent, explicit, manifest, outright, unmasked, unveiled **09** unadorned **11** transparent, unconcealed **12** undissembled **13** thoroughgoing

**undisguisedly**
**06** openly **07** frankly, overtly **08** outright, patently **09** blatantly, obviously **12** unreservedly **13** transparently

**undisputed**
**04** fact, sure **07** certain **08** accepted, unargued **09** undoubted **10** conclusive, recognized, undeniable **11** indubitable, irrefutable, uncontested **12** acknowledged, indisputable, unchallenged, unquestioned

**undistinguished**
**04** so-so **05** banal, plain **06** common **07** ordinar, plebean **08** everyday, inferior, mediocre, nameless, ordinary, plebeian **10** not much cop, pedestrian **11** indifferent, not up to much **12** run-of-the-mill, unimpressive, unremarkable **13** no great shakes, unexceptional

**undisturbed**
**04** calm, even **05** quiet **06** placid, serene **07** equable **08** composed, tranquil, wakeless **09** collected, quietsome, unruffled, untouched **10** motionless, unaffected, untroubled **11** unconcerned, unperturbed **13** uninterrupted

**undivided**
**03** one **04** full **05** solid, total, whole **06** entire, intact, single, united **07** serious, sincere **08** combined, complete, unbroken **09** dedicated, exclusive, unanimous **10** individual, unreserved **11** individuate, pro indiviso, unqualified **12** concentrated, wholehearted

**undo**
◇ *anagram indicator*
**03** dup, mar **04** free, open, poop, ruin **05** annul, crush, loose, poupe, quash, solve, spoil, untie, unzip, upset, wreck **06** cancel, defeat, loosen, offset, repeal, revoke, seduce, unbend, unclew, unhook, unlace, unlock, unwind, unwork, unwrap **07** destroy, nullify, release, retract, reverse, shatter, subvert, undight, unravel, unshape **08** overturn, separate, set aside, unbuckle, unbutton, unfasten **09** disanoint, undermine **10** invalidate, neutralize, obliterate **11** disentangle

**undoing**
◇ *anagram indicator*
**04** ruin **05** shame **06** defeat **07** opening **08** collapse, disgrace, downfall, reversal, weakness **09** defeature, overthrow, ruination **10** defeasance **11** destruction, unfastening

**undomesticated**
**04** wild **05** feral **06** savage **07** natural, untamed **11** uncivilized **12** ferae naturae

**undone**
◇ *anagram indicator*
**04** left, lost, open **05** loose **06** adrift, opened, ruined, untied **07** ignored, omitted, seduced, unlaced **08** annulled, betrayed, unlocked **09** destroyed, forgotten, neglected, unwrought **10** incomplete, passed over, unbuttoned, unfastened, unfinished **11** outstanding, uncompleted, unfulfilled **14** unaccomplished
• **come undone**
**03** run

**undoubted**
**04** sure **06** patent **07** certain, obvious **08** definite **10** undisputed **11** indubitable, irrefutable, uncontested, undesirable **12** acknowledged, indisputable, unchallenged, unquestioned **14** unquestionable

**undoubtedly**
**04** sure **06** surely **07** no doubt **08** of course **09** assuredly, certainly, doubtless **10** definitely, manifestly, no question, undeniably **11** beyond doubt, indubitably **12** unmistakably, without doubt **14** unquestionably

**undreamed-of**
**07** amazing **08** undreamt **09** unheard-of **10** incredible, miraculous, unexpected, unforeseen, unhoped-for, unimagined **11** astonishing, unsuspected **13** inconceivable

**undress**
**04** peel, shed **05** strip **06** devest, divest, nudity, remove, streak, uncase, unrobe **07** discase, disrobe, peel off, take off **08** disarray, unclothe **09** disattire, nakedness **10** déshabillé, dishabille **11** make unready **13** get your kit off

**undressed**
**04** nude **05** naked **08** disrobed, en cuerpo, in the raw, starkers, stripped, untented **09** in the buff, self-faced, unclothed **10** stark-naked **12** not a stitch on **15** in the altogether

**undue**
**07** extreme **08** improper, needless **09** excessive, obtrusive **10** immoderate, inordinate, undeserved **11** exaggerated, extravagant, superfluous, uncalled-for, unjustified, unnecessary, unwarranted **12** unreasonable **13** inappropriate

**undulate**
**04** roll, wave, wavy **05** heave, surge, swell **06** billow, ripple **07** vibrate **11** rise and fall

**undulating**
**04** wavy **05** waved **06** undate **07** rolling, sinuous **08** flexuose, flexuous, rippling, undulant, undulose, undulous **09** billowing, up-and-down **10** undulatory

**unduly**
◇ *anagram indicator*
**03** too **04** over **08** overmuch **10** wrongfully **11** excessively, obtrusively **12** immoderately, inordinately, unreasonably **13** exaggeratedly, unjustifiably, unnecessarily

**undutiful**
**05** slack **06** remiss **08** careless, disloyal, unfilial **09** negligent **10** defaulting, delinquent, neglectful

**undying**
**07** abiding, eternal, lasting **08** constant, immortal, infinite,

unending, unfading **09** deathless, perennial, permanent, perpetual, unceasing **10** continuing **11** everlasting, sempiternal **12** imperishable, undiminished **14** indestructible

**unearth**
**04** find **05** dig up **06** detect, dig out, exhume, expose, reveal **07** uncover **08** discover, disinter, excavate **12** bring to light

**unearthly**
**05** eerie, weird **06** absurd, creepy, unholy **07** ghostly, phantom, strange, uncanny, ungodly **08** eldritch **09** appalling, celestial, unheard-of **10** horrendous, outrageous **12** otherworldly, preposterous, supernatural, unreasonable **13** preternatural, spine-chilling **14** unconscionable

**unease**
**05** alarm, doubt, worry **06** qualms **07** anxiety, dis-ease **08** disquiet **09** agitation, misgiving, suspicion **10** discomfort, inquietude, uneasiness **11** nervousness **12** apprehension, perturbation

**uneasily**
**04** hard

**uneasiness**
**05** alarm, doubt, qualm, worry **06** qualms, unease **07** anxiety, dis-ease, malaise, misease, trouble **08** disquiet **09** agitation, dysphoria, misgiving, suspicion **10** discomfort, inquietude, solicitude **11** nervousness **12** apprehension, perturbation **14** distemperature, solicitousness **15** dissatisfaction

**uneasy**
◇ *anagram indicator*
**04** edgy **05** nervy, shaky, tense, upset **06** on edge, queasy, queazy, unsure **07** alarmed, anxious, fidgety, jittery, keyed up, nervous, restive, twitchy, unquiet, worried, wound up **08** agitated, disquiet, insecure, restless, strained, troubled, worrying **09** disturbed, ill at ease, impatient, perturbed, troubling, unnerving, unrestful, unsettled **10** disquieted, disturbing, perturbing, unsettling **11** disquieting **12** apprehensive **13** disconcerting, uncomfortable

**uneconomic**
**10** loss-making **12** uncommercial, unprofitable **15** non-profit-making

**unedifying**
**04** idle

**uneducated**
**06** unread **08** ignorant, untaught **09** benighted, lack-Latin, unlearned **10** illiterate, philistine, uncultured, uninformed, unschooled **12** uncultivated

**unemotional**
**04** cold, cool **05** bland **06** stolid **08** detached, reserved **09** apathetic, bloodless, impassive, objective, unfeeling **10** phlegmatic **11** indifferent, passionless, unexcitable **12** phlegmatical, unresponsive **13** dispassionate **15** undemonstrative

**unemphatic**
**08** downbeat **10** played-down **11** underplayed, understated, unobtrusive **12** soft-pedalled **14** unostentatious

**unemployed**
**04** idle **07** jobless, laid off, unwaged **08** workless **09** on the dole, out of work, redundant **10** unoccupied

**unending**
**07** endless, eternal, undated, undying **08** constant **09** ceaseless, continual, incessant, perpetual, unceasing **10** continuous **11** everlasting, never-ending, unremitting **12** interminable **13** thorough-going, uninterrupted

**unendurable**
**10** shattering, unbearable **11** intolerable **12** insufferable, overwhelming **13** insupportable

**unenthusiastic**
**04** cool, damp **05** blasé, bored **07** neutral, unmoved **08** lukewarm **09** apathetic, Laodicean **10** nonchalant **11** half-hearted, indifferent, unimpressed **12** uninterested, unresponsive

**unenviable**
**09** dangerous, difficult, thankless **10** unpleasant **11** uncongenial, undesirable **12** disagreeable **13** uncomfortable

**unequal**
**06** biased, uneven, unfair, unjust, unlike **07** not up to, varying **08** lopsided, unfitted, unsuited **09** different, disparate, excessive, incapable, irregular, unmatched **10** dissimilar, inadequate, unbalanced **11** incompetent, inequitable, unqualified **12** asymmetrical, not cut out for **14** discriminatory

**unequalled**
**06** unique **07** supreme **08** peerless, unbeaten, unpeered **09** matchless, nonpareil, paramount, unmatched **10** inimitable, pre-eminent, surpassing, unrivalled **11** exceptional, unpatterned, unsurpassed **12** incomparable, transcendent, unparalleled

**unequivocal**
**05** clear, plain **06** direct, square **07** evident, express **08** absolute, definite, distinct, explicit, outright, positive, straight **10** unreserved **11** categorical, unambiguous, unqualified **12** unmistakable **15** straightforward

**unequivocally**
**06** firmly **07** clearly **08** directly **10** definitely, distinctly, explicitly, positively **12** unmistakably **13** unambiguously **14** unquestionably

**unerring**
**04** dead, sure **05** clean, exact **07** certain, perfect, uncanny **08** accurate, inerrant **09** faultless, unfailing **10** impeccable, infallible

**unerringly**
**04** bang, dead **10** accurately, infallibly **11** unfailingly

**unethical**
**04** evil **05** shady, wrong **06** wicked **07** illegal, illicit, immoral **08** improper **09** dishonest, underhand **12** disreputable, unprincipled, unscrupulous **13** dishonourable **14** unprofessional

**uneven**
◇ *anagram indicator*
**03** odd **05** bumpy, jerky, lumpy, rough, ruggy, stony **06** coarse, craggy, fitful, jagged, patchy, rugged, spotty, unfair **07** crooked, erratic, ruffled, rumpled, streaky, unequal **08** lopsided, one-sided, scratchy, unsteady, variable **09** inequable, irregular, spasmodic **10** accidented, changeable, ill-matched, unbalanced **11** fluctuating, inequitable **12** asymmetrical, inconsistent, intermittent

**uneventful**
**04** dull **05** quiet **06** boring **07** humdrum, routine, tedious **08** everyday, ordinary, unvaried **10** monotonous, unexciting **11** commonplace, unmemorable **12** run-of-the-mill, unremarkable **13** unexceptional, uninteresting

**unexampled**
**05** novel **06** unique **09** unheard-of, unmatched **10** unequalled **11** unpatterned **12** incomparable, unparalleled **13** unprecedented **15** never before seen

**unexceptionable**
**04** mild, safe **05** bland **08** harmless, innocent **09** excellent, innocuous, peaceable **10** undeniable **11** inoffensive **15** unobjectionable

**unexceptional**
**04** so-so **05** usual **06** common, normal **07** average, typical **08** everyday, mediocre, ordinary **10** not much cop **11** indifferent, not up to much, unmemorable **12** run-of-the-mill, unimpressive, unremarkable **13** no great shakes **15** undistinguished

**unexcitable**
**04** calm, cool **06** serene **07** relaxed **08** composed, laid-back **09** contained, easy-going, impassive **10** phlegmatic **11** passionless **13** dispassionate, imperturbable, self-possessed, unimpassioned

**unexpected**
◇ *anagram indicator*
**04** snap **05** shock **06** abrupt, chance, sudden, unware, unwary, wonder

07 amazing, unhoped, unusual, unwarie 08 emergent, unweened 09 inopinate, startling 10 accidental, fortuitous, surprising, unforeseen 11 astonishing, unlooked-for 13 unanticipated, unpredictable

**unexpectedly**
◇ *anagram indicator*
06 unware 08 abruptly, by chance, suddenly, unawares, unwarely 11 ex improviso 12 accidentally, à l'improviste, fortuitously, out of the blue, phenomenally, refreshingly, surprisingly 13 unpredictably 14 without warning

**unexpressive**
05 blank 06 vacant 07 deadpan 08 immobile 09 impassive 11 emotionless, inscrutable 12 inexpressive 13 inexpressible 14 expressionless

**unfading**
04 fast 07 abiding, durable, lasting, undying 08 constant, enduring, fadeless 09 evergreen, unfailing 12 imperishable 13 immarcescible

**unfailing**
04 sure, true 05 loyal 06 steady 07 certain, staunch, undying 08 constant, faithful, reliable, unerring, unfading 09 steadfast 10 dependable, infallible 12 indefectible, inexhaustive 13 inexhaustible

**unfair**
◇ *anagram indicator*
04 bent, foul, ugly 05 crook, shady, thick 06 biased, unjust 07 a bit off, bigoted, crooked, partial, slanted 08 one-sided, partisan, weighted, wrongful 09 arbitrary, deceitful, dishonest, unethical, unmerited 10 prejudiced, unbalanced, undeserved 11 inequitable, uncalled-for, unwarranted 12 below the belt, over the score, unprincipled, unreasonable, unscrupulous 14 discriminatory

**unfairly**
◇ *anagram indicator*
04 foul 07 wrongly 08 biasedly, unjustly 09 illegally, partially 10 improperly, unlawfully 11 dishonestly, inequitably 12 unreasonably

**unfairness**
04 bias 05 cross 07 bigotry, unright 08 inequity, misusage 09 injustice, prejudice 10 partiality 12 one-sidedness, partisanship 14 discrimination 15 inequitableness

**unfaithful**
05 false 06 fickle, unleal, untrue 07 godless 08 cheating, disloyal 09 deceitful, dishonest, faithless, insincere, two-timing 10 adulterous, inconstant, perfidious, unreliable 11 duplicitous, treacherous, unbelieving 13 double-dealing, untrustworthy

**unfaltering**
04 firm 05 fixed 06 steady 08 constant, resolute, tireless, untiring 09 steadfast, unfailing 10 unflagging, unswerving, unwavering, unyielding 11 unflinching 12 pertinacious 13 indefatigable

**unfamiliar**
◇ *anagram indicator*
03 new 05 alien, novel 07 curious, foreign, strange, uncouth, unknown, unusual 08 selcouth, uncommon, unversed 09 different, uncharted, unskilled 10 unexplored, uninformed 11 unpractised 12 unaccustomed, unacquainted, unconversant 13 inexperienced

**unfashionable**
03 out 04 lame 05 daggy, dated, dowdy, passé 06 démodé, old hat, square 08 obsolete, outmoded, unmodish 09 out of date, shapeless, unpopular 10 antiquated 12 old-fashioned, out of fashion

**unfasten**
04 open, undo 05 loose, unbar, unfix, unpin, untie, unzip 06 detach, loosen, unbend, unhasp, unlock, unwrap 07 unclasp, unloose, untruss 08 separate, unbuckle, uncouple, unloosen 10 disconnect

**unfathomable**
04 deep 06 hidden 07 abysmal 08 abstruse, baffling, esoteric, profound 09 unplumbed, unsounded 10 bottomless, fathomless, mysterious, unknowable 11 inscrutable, unsoundable 12 immeasurable, impenetrable, inexplicable 14 indecipherable

**unfavourable**
03 bad, ill 04 foul, poor 07 adverse, hostile, ominous, unlucky 08 contrary, critical, inimical, negative, untimely, untoward 09 ill-suited 10 prejudiced, unfriendly 11 in a bad light, inopportune, threatening, unfortunate, unpromising 12 discouraging, inauspicious, unseasonable 15 disadvantageous, uncomplimentary

**unfavourably**
03 ill 05 badly 06 poorly 09 adversely, in bad part, in ill part, unhappily 10 negatively 13 unfortunately, unpromisingly

**unfeeling**
04 cold, hard 05 cruel, harsh, stony 06 brutal 07 callous, inhuman 08 hardened, pitiless, uncaring 09 heartless, merciless 10 impassible, iron-headed, iron-witted 11 hard-hearted, insensitive, iron-hearted 13 unsympathetic

**unfeigned**
04 pure, real 05 frank 07 genuine, natural, sincere 08 unforced 09 heartfelt 10 unaffected 11 spontaneous 12 undissembled, wholehearted

**unfettered**
04 free 09 chainless, unbridled, unchecked 10 unconfined, unhampered, unhindered, unshackled 11 uninhibited 12 unrestrained, untrammelled 13 unconstrained

**unfinished**
◇ *tail deletion indicator*
05 crude, rough 06 undone 07 lacking, sketchy, wanting 08 half-done, inchoate 09 deficient, imperfect, incondite 10 incomplete 11 uncompleted, unfulfilled 14 unaccomplished

**unfit**
◇ *anagram indicator*
04 weak 05 inapt 06 feeble, flabby, impair, unable, unmeet 07 unequal, useless 08 decrepit, disabled, improper, unsuited 09 condemned, incapable, unhealthy, untrained 10 inadequate, ineligible, out of shape, unprepared, unsuitable 11 debilitated, ill-equipped, incompetent, ineffective, unqualified 12 disqualified 13 inappropriate, incapacitated 14 out of condition

**unflagging**
05 fixed 06 steady 07 staunch 08 constant, tireless, untiring 09 assiduous, unceasing, unfailing 10 persistent, unswerving 11 persevering, undeviating, unfaltering, unremitting 12 never-failing, single-minded 13 indefatigable

**unflappable**
04 calm, cool 07 equable 08 composed, laid-back 09 collected, easy-going, impassive, supercool, unruffled, unworried 10 phlegmatic 11 level-headed, unexcitable 13 imperturbable, self-possessed

**unflattering**
05 blunt 06 candid, honest 08 critical 09 outspoken 10 unbecoming 12 unattractive, unfavourable 15 uncomplimentary, unprepossessing

**unflinching**
04 bold, firm, sure 05 fixed 06 steady 07 staunch 08 constant, resolute, stalwart, unshaken 09 steadfast 10 determined, unblenched, unblinking, unswerving, unwavering 11 unblenching, unfaltering, unshrinking

**unflinchingly**
04 fast 06 boldly, firmly 08 steadily 09 staunchly 10 resolutely 11 steadfastly 12 unswervingly, unwaveringly 13 unfalteringly, unshrinkingly

**unfold**
04 grow, open, show, tell, undo 06 deploy, emerge, evolve, extend, relate, result, reveal, spread, unclew, uncoil, unfurl, unroll, untuck, unwrap 07 clarify, develop, display, explain, flatten, narrate, open out, present, uncover, unravel, work out

08 describe, disclose, shake out, undouble 09 come about, elaborate, explicate, interpret, make known, spread out 10 disenvelop, disinvolve, illustrate, straighten, stretch out 13 straighten out

**unforeseen**
06 casual, sudden 07 amazing, unusual 09 startling 10 surprising, unexpected 11 astonishing, unavoidable, unlooked-for, unpredicted 13 unanticipated, unpredictable

**unforgettable**
07 notable, special 08 historic, striking 09 important, indelible, memorable, momentous 10 impressive, noteworthy, remarkable 11 distinctive, exceptional, significant 13 extraordinary

**unforgivable**
08 shameful 10 deplorable, outrageous 11 disgraceful, inexcusable, intolerable 12 contemptible, indefensible, unpardonable 13 reprehensible, unjustifiable

**unforgiven**
10 unabsolved, unredeemed 11 unrepentant 12 unregenerate

**unfortunate**
◇ *anagram indicator*
03 ill 04 evil, poor 05 tough 06 doomed 07 adverse, hapless, ruinous, unhappy, unlucky 08 hopeless, ill-fated, ill-timed, luckless, untimely, untoward, wretched 09 ill-omened 10 calamitous, deplorable, disastrous, ill-advised, lamentable, unpleasant, unsuitable 11 evil-starred, injudicious, inopportune, misfortuned, regrettable 12 disaventrous, unfavourable, unsuccessful 13 inappropriate, misadventured 14 disadventurous 15 disadvantageous

**unfortunately**
◇ *anagram indicator*
04 alas 05 sadly 08 sad to say 09 unhappily, unluckily, worse luck 11 regrettably, sad to relate 13 I am sorry to say

**unfounded**
04 idle 05 false 08 baseless, spurious, unproven 09 trumped-up 10 bottomless, fabricated, groundless 11 conjectural, unjustified, unsupported 14 uncorroborated 15 unsubstantiated

**unfrequented**
04 lone 06 lonely, remote, untrod 08 deserted, desolate, isolated, secluded, solitary, untraded, wasteful 09 untrodden, unvisited 11 god-forsaken, sequestered, uninhabited

**unfriendly**
04 cold, cool, sour 05 aloof, chill, fraim, fremd, surly 06 chilly, fremit, frosty, frozen, unkind, wintry 07 distant, hostile, wintery 08 inimical, strained, unkindly 10 aggressive, unpleasant, unsociable 11 ill-disposed, quarrelsome, standoffish, uncongenial, unwelcoming 12 antagonistic, disagreeable, inauspicious, inhospitable, inimicitious 13 unneighbourly 14 unapproachable

**unfrock**
06 demote, depose, ungown 07 degrade, dismiss, suspend

**unfruitful**
04 arid 06 barren 07 sterile 08 infecund 09 exhausted, fruitless, infertile 10 unprolific 11 infructuous, unrewarding 12 impoverished, unproductive, unprofitable

**unfurl**
04 grow, open, undo 05 break 06 emerge, evolve, extend, result, spread, uncoil, unfold, unroll, unwrap 07 develop, display, flatten, open out, uncover, unravel, work out 09 come about, spread out 10 straighten, stretch out 13 straighten out

**ungainly**
◇ *anagram indicator*
05 gawky 06 clumsy, gauche, ungain 07 awkward, loutish, uncouth 08 gangling, unwieldy 09 awkwardly, inelegant, lumbering, maladroit 10 ungraceful 13 unco-ordinated

**ungodly**
05 world 06 sinful, wicked 07 corrupt, godless, immoral, impious, profane 08 depraved, unsocial 09 unearthly 10 horrendous, iniquitous, outrageous 11 blasphemous, intolerable, irreligious 12 preposterous, unreasonable 14 unconscionable

**ungovernable**
04 wild 06 unruly 10 disorderly, masterless, rebellious, refractory, ungoverned 12 unmanageable 14 uncontrollable, unrestrainable

**ungracious**
04 rude 07 boorish, ill-bred, mesquin, offhand, uncivil 08 churlish, impolite, mesquine 09 graceless 10 ungraceful, unhandsome, unmannerly 11 bad-mannered, disgracious 12 discourteous 13 disrespectful

**ungrateful**
04 rude 07 ingrate, irksome, selfish, uncivil 08 heedless, impolite 09 thankless 10 ungracious, unthankful 11 ill-mannered 12 disagreeable 14 unappreciative

**unguarded**
04 rash 06 unwary 07 exposed, foolish 08 careless, heedless, off guard 09 foolhardy, impolitic, imprudent, lippening, unweighed 10 incautious, indiscreet, undefended, unscreened, unthinking, vulnerable 11 defenceless, inadvertent, inattentive, thoughtless, unpatrolled, unprotected 12 undiplomatic 13 ill-considered, uncircumspect

**ungulate**
03 cow 04 deer 05 horse, takin, tapir 06 hoofed 09 Dinoceras 10 Deinoceras, mesohippus, rhinoceros, rhinocerot 11 rhinocerote 12 hippopotamus, Uintatherium 13 Palaeotherium, Titanotherium

**unhappily**
◇ *anagram indicator*
04 alas 05 sadly 08 sad to say, shrewdly 09 unluckily, worse luck 11 maliciously, regrettably, sad to relate 12 unfavourably 13 unfortunately 14 unsuccessfully

**unhappy**
◇ *anagram indicator*
03 low, sad 04 blue, down, glum 05 fed up, inapt, upset 06 clumsy, gloomy 07 awkward, hapless, unlucky 08 dejected, downcast, ill-fated, luckless, mournful, tactless 09 depressed, ill-chosen, long-faced, miserable, sorrowful, woebegone 10 despondent, dispirited, ill-advised, ill-starred, melancholy, unsuitable 11 crestfallen, injudicious, mischievous, unfortunate 12 disconsolate, infelicitous 13 inappropriate 14 down in the dumps

**unharmed**
04 safe 05 sound, whole 06 intact, unhurt 09 undamaged, uninjured, unscathed, untouched

**unhealthy**
03 ill 04 sick, weak 05 crook, frail, pasty 06 ailing, feeble, infirm, morbid, poorly, sickly, unwell 07 harmful, invalid, noxious, unsound 08 diseased, epinosic 09 dangerous, injurious, unnatural 10 indisposed, insalutary, insanitary, unhygienic, unsanitary 11 debilitated, detrimental, unwholesome 12 insalubrious

**unheard-of**
03 new 06 unsung 07 obscure, unknown, unusual 08 shocking 09 offensive 10 outrageous, unfamiliar, unheralded 11 exceptional, undreamed-of, unthinkable 12 preposterous, unacceptable, unbelievable, undiscovered, unimaginable 13 extraordinary, inconceivable, unprecedented

**unheeded**
07 ignored, unnoted 08 unminded, untented 09 disobeyed, forgotten, neglected, unnoticed 10 overlooked, unobserved, unremarked 11 disregarded

**unhelpful**
04 rude 06 rustic, touchy 07 awkward, boorish, cubbish, loutish, prickly, stroppy 08 stubborn 09 irritable, obstinate 10 unpleasant 11 disobliging, obstructive, troublesome 12 bloody-minded 13 oversensitive, unco-operative 15 unaccommodating

**unheralded**
**06** unsung **08** surprise **09** unnoticed **10** unexpected, unforeseen **11** unannounced **12** unadvertised, unproclaimed, unpublicized, unrecognized

**unhesitating**
**05** ready **06** prompt **07** instant **08** implicit **09** automatic, confident, immediate **10** unwavering **11** spontaneous, unfaltering **12** wholehearted **13** instantaneous, unquestioning

**unhinge**
**05** craze, upset **06** madden **07** confuse, derange, unnerve **08** disorder, distract, drive mad, unsettle **09** unbalance

**unhinged**
**03** mad **04** nuts **05** barmy, crazy, loony, loopy, nutty, potty **06** insane **07** berserk, bonkers, frantic, lunatic **08** confused, demented, deranged **09** delirious, disturbed, unsettled **10** disordered, distraught, irrational, out to lunch, unbalanced **11** not all there **12** round the bend **13** off your rocker, of unsound mind, out of your mind, round the twist **15** non compos mentis

**unholy**
◇ *anagram indicator*
**04** evil **06** sinful, wicked **07** corrupt, godless, immoral, impious, ungodly **08** depraved, dreadful, shocking, terrible **09** unearthly, unnatural **10** horrendous, iniquitous, outrageous **11** blasphemous, irreligious **12** unreasonable **14** unconscionable

**unhook**
**04** free, undo **05** loose, untie **06** loosen **07** release **08** unfasten

**unhoped-for**
**10** incredible, surprising, unexpected, unforeseen **11** undreamed-of, unlooked-for **12** unbelievable, unimaginable **13** unanticipated

**unhurried**
**04** calm, easy, slow **06** sedate **07** relaxed **08** laid-back **09** easy-going, leisurely **10** deliberate

**unhurt**
**02** OK **04** okay, safe **05** sound, whole **06** intact **08** all right, unharmed **09** uninjured, unscathed, untouched **12** whole-skinned

**unhygienic**
**04** foul **05** dirty **06** filthy, impure **07** dirtied, noisome, noxious, unclean **08** feculent, infected, infested, polluted **09** unhealthy **10** insanitary **11** unhealthful, unsanitized **12** contaminated, insalubrious **13** disease-ridden

**unidentified**
**06** secret **07** obscure, strange, unknown, unnamed **08** nameless, unmarked **09** anonymous, incognito **10** mysterious, unfamiliar **12** unclassified, unrecognized

**unification**
**05** union **06** enosis, fusion, merger **07** uniting **08** alliance **09** coalition **10** federation **11** coalescence, combination, integration **12** amalgamation **13** confederation, incorporation

**uniform**
**01** U **03** rig **04** even, flat, garb, like, same, sole, suit **05** alike, dress, equal, habit, level, robes **06** livery, outfit, smooth, stable, steady **07** costume, equable, regalia, regular, similar **08** constant, insignia, of a piece, unbroken **09** identical, unvarying **10** consistent, invariable, monotonous, throughout, unchanging **11** homogeneous, regimentals, undeviating

**uniformity**
**06** tedium **08** drabness, dullness, evenness, flatness, monotony, sameness **09** constancy **10** regularity, similarity, similitude **11** homogeneity **12** homomorphism **13** invariability

**unify**
**03** mix **04** bind, fuse, join, weld **05** blend, merge, unite **07** combine **08** coalesce **09** integrate **10** amalgamate **11** consolidate **12** come together **13** bring together

**unifying**
**06** unific **07** henotic, uniting **11** combinatory, esemplastic, reconciling **13** consolidative

**unimaginable**
**07** amazing **08** unlikely **09** fantastic, unheard-of **10** far-fetched, impossible, incredible, outlandish, staggering **11** astonishing, implausible, undreamed-of, unthinkable **12** mind-boggling, preposterous, unbelievable, unconvincing **13** extraordinary, inconceivable

**unimaginative**
**03** dry **04** dull, tame **05** banal, samey, stale, usual **06** barren, boring **07** mundane, prosaic, routine **08** lifeless, ordinary **09** hackneyed **10** flat-footed, pedestrian, unexciting, uninspired, unoriginal **11** predictable **12** matter-of-fact

**unimpaired**
**05** sound **06** entire, intact **08** integral
• **remain unimpaired**
**04** last

**unimpeachable**
**07** perfect **08** reliable, spotless **09** blameless, faultless **10** dependable, immaculate, impeccable **11** unblemished **12** unassailable **14** irreproachable, unquestionable **15** unchallengeable

**unimpeded**
**04** free, open **05** clear **08** all-round **09** unblocked, unchecked **10** unhampered, unhindered **11** uninhibited **12** unrestrained, untrammelled **13** unconstrained

**unimportant**
**04** idle **05** light, minor, petty **06** slight **07** trivial **08** marginal, nugatory, peddling, trifling **09** minuscule, no big deal, secondary, small-time, worthless **10** immaterial, incidental, irrelevant, negligible, peripheral **11** down-the-line, Mickey Mouse **12** inconsequent **13** insignificant, insubstantial, no great shakes **14** inconsiderable **15** inconsequential, of no consequence

**unimpressive**
**04** dull **06** common **07** average **08** mediocre, ordinary **10** unexciting, unimposing **11** commonplace, indifferent **12** unremarkable **13** unexceptional, uninteresting, unspectacular **15** undistinguished

**uninhabited**
**04** lone **05** empty **06** desert, lonely, vacant **08** deserted, desolate, wasteful **09** abandoned, unpeopled, unsettled **10** unoccupied **11** unpopulated

**uninhibited**
**04** free, open **05** frank **06** candid, rave-up **07** natural, relaxed **08** informal **09** abandoned, liberated, outspoken **10** unreserved **11** spontaneous **12** uncontrolled, unrestrained, unrestricted **13** unconstrained **15** unself-conscious

**uninspired**
**04** dull **05** samey, stale, stock, trite **06** boring **07** humdrum, pompier, prosaic **08** ordinary **10** flat-footed, pedestrian, unexciting, unoriginal **11** commonplace, indifferent, uninspiring **13** unexceptional, unimaginative, uninteresting **15** undistinguished

**uninspiring**
**03** dry **04** dull, flat, tame **05** ho-hum, samey, stale, trite **06** boring, dreary, jejune, tiring **07** humdrum, insipid, prosaic, routine, tedious **08** tiresome, unvaried **10** long-winded, monotonous, uneventful, unexciting **11** commonplace, repetitious, stultifying **13** institutional, unimaginative, uninteresting **14** soul-destroying

**unintelligent**
**04** dull, dumb, slow **05** dense, silly, thick **06** obtuse, stupid **07** fatuous, foolish, witless **08** gormless **09** brainless **10** half-witted, unthinking **11** empty-headed, unreasoning

**unintelligible**
**07** complex, garbled, jumbled, muddled, obscure **08** involved, puzzling **09** illegible, scrambled **10** incoherent, mysterious, unreadable **11** complicated, double Dutch **12** impenetrable, inarticulate, unfathomable **14** indecipherable

**unintentional**
**08** careless **09** unplanned, unwilling, unwitting **10** accidental, fortuitous, unintended **11** inadvertent, involuntary, unconscious
**12** uncalculated **14** unpremeditated

**uninterested**
**05** blasé, bored **07** distant **08** listless
**09** apathetic, impassive, incurious
**10** uninvolved **11** indifferent, pococurante, unconcerned
**12** unresponsive **14** not giving a damn, not giving a hoot, not giving a toss, unenthusiastic

**uninteresting**
**03** dry **04** drab, dull, flat, tame
**05** samey, stale **06** boring, dreary
**07** humdrum, prosaic, tedious
**08** tiresome **09** incurious, wearisome
**10** monotonous, pedestrian, uneventful, unexciting **11** indifferent, uninspiring **12** unimpressive

**uninterrupted**
**06** steady **07** endless, non-stop
**08** constant, peaceful, straight, unbroken, unending **09** ceaseless, continual, continued, incessant, sustained, unceasing **10** continuous
**11** undisturbed, unremitting

**uninvited**
**07** unasked **08** unbidden, unsought, unwanted **09** unwelcome
**11** unsolicited

**uninviting**
**09** offensive, repellent, repulsive, unsavoury **10** forbidding, off-putting, unpleasant **11** distasteful, unappealing, undesirable, unwelcoming
**12** disagreeable, unappetizing, unattractive

**uninvolved**
**04** free **06** dégagé **09** fancy-free, footloose, unengaged **10** unattached, unhampered, unhindered
**11** independent, uncommitted
**12** untrammelled

**union**
**01** U **04** club, yoke **05** blend, close, unity **06** accord, cement, fusion, league, merger **07** harmony, joining, mixture, uniting, wedding, wedlock
**08** alliance, juncture, marriage, nuptials, spousage **09** agreement, coalition, espousals, matrimony, synthesis, unanimity **10** consortium, couplement, federation, trade union, Zollverein **11** association, cementation, coadunation, coalescence, combination, concurrence, confederacy, conjugation, conjunction, unification
**12** amalgamation **13** confederation, consolidation **14** conglutination

*See also* **rugby**

*Unions include:*

**02** AU, CU, EU
**03** AUT, CDU, CGT, CWU, EIS, EMU, FBU, GMB, ITU, NFU, NUJ, NUM, NUS, NUT, RFU, RMT
**04** BIFU, CCCP, TGWU, UEFA, USSR, ZANU, ZAPU
**05** BECTU, T and G
**06** Amicus, Soviet, UNISON
**07** African
**08** European

**unionist**
**01** U **02** UU

**unique**
**03** one **04** lone, only, sole **05** alone
**06** one-off, single **07** unusual
**08** peerless, singular, solitary
**09** matchless, nonpareil, unmatched
**10** inimitable, one and only, one of a kind, pre-eminent, sui generis, unequalled, unrivalled **11** idiographic
**12** incomparable, unparalleled
**13** unprecedented

**uniquely**
**04** only **06** singly, solely **08** by itself, markedly **09** specially **10** inimitably, peculiarly, peerlessly, remarkably, singularly **11** in its own way, matchlessly
**12** incomparably **13** distinctively

**unison**
**05** unity **06** accord **07** concert, concord, harmony **09** agreement, unanimity **11** co-operation

• **in unison**
**08** in chorus **09** in harmony
**10** homophonic **11** in agreement **13** at the same time, in co-operation
**14** simultaneously **15** at the same moment

**unit**
**03** ace, one **04** item, part **05** corps, force, piece, squad, whole **06** entity, module, patrol, system **07** brigade, element, portion, section, segment
**08** assembly **09** component, task force **10** detachment, individual
**11** constituent

*See also* **measurement**; **military**; **measurement of pressure** *under* **pressure**; **unit of weight** *under* **weight**

**unite**
**03** fay, lap, tie, wad, wed **04** ally, band, fuse, join, knit, knot, link, lock, meng, ming, pool, weld **05** blend, clasp, close, joint, marry, menge, merge, twist, unify **06** cement, cleave, couple, embody, imbody, splice **07** accrete, combine, conjoin, connect, consort
**08** coalesce, copulate, federate
**09** associate, coadunate, conjugate, co-operate, synoecize
**10** amalgamate, close ranks, join forces
**11** confederate, consolidate, incorporate **12** concorporate, conglutinate, pull together
**15** consubstantiate, make common cause

**united**
**01** U **03** one **04** ment **05** meint, meynt
**06** agreed, allied, menged, minged, pooled **07** unified **08** combined, conjoint, in accord **09** concerted, conjoined, corporate, unanimous
**10** affiliated, collective, like-minded
**11** amalgamated, conjunctive, co-operative, in agreement
**12** incorporated **13** concorporated

**United Arab Emirates**
**03** ARE, UAE

**United Kingdom**
**02** UK

*See also* **prime minister**

*UK cities include:*

**03** Ely
**04** Bath, York
**05** Derby, Leeds, Newry, Ripon, Truro, Wells
**06** Armagh, Bangor, Dundee, Durham, Exeter, London, Oxford
**07** Belfast, Bristol, Cardiff, Chester, Glasgow, Lincoln, Lisburn, Newport, Norwich, Preston, Salford, Swansea
**08** Aberdeen, Bradford, Carlisle, Coventry, Hereford, Kingston, Plymouth, St Albans, St David's, Stirling
**09** Cambridge, Edinburgh, Inverness, Lancaster, Leicester, Lichfield, Liverpool, Newcastle, Salisbury, Sheffield, Wakefield, Worcester
**10** Birmingham, Canterbury, Chichester, Gloucester, Manchester, Nottingham, Portsmouth, Sunderland, Winchester
**11** Londonderry, Southampton, Westminster
**12** Brighton
**13** Wolverhampton

*UK landmarks include:*

**04** Fens, Tyne
**06** Big Ben, Exmoor, Mersey, Severn, Thames
**07** Avebury, Glencoe, Needles, Snowdon
**08** Balmoral, Bass Rock, Ben Nevis, Dartmoor, Land's End, Loch Ness
**09** Cape Wrath, Chilterns, Cotswolds, Helvellyn, London Eye, New Forest, Offa's Dyke, Royal Mile, Snowdonia, Tay Bridge
**10** Beachy Head, Cader Idris, Holy Island, Ironbridge, Kew Gardens, Loch Lomond, Lough Earne, Lough Neagh, Stonehenge, The Gherkin, Windermere
**11** Arthur's Seat, Canary Wharf, Forth Bridge, Hever Castle, Isle of Wight, John O'Groats, Leeds Castle, Lizard Point, Menai Bridge, Old Man of Hoy, Scafell Pike, York Minster
**12** Antonine Wall, Brighton Pier, Castle Howard, Cheddar Gorge, Forest of Dean, Hadrian's Wall, Hampton Court, Humber Bridge, Lake District, Peak District, Seven Sisters, Severn Bridge
**13** Arundel Castle, Blue John Caves, Brecon Beacons, Bridge of Sighs, Hatfield House, Liver Building,

Norfolk Broads, Robin Hood's Bay, Royal Pavilion, Tower of London, Warwick Castle, Windsor Castle
**14** Blackpool Tower, Blenheim Palace, Giant's Causeway, Holyrood Palace, Inverary Castle, Isle of Anglesey, Sherwood Forest, Stirling Castle, Wells Cathedral
**15** Angel of the North, Bodleian Library, Caledonian Canal, Cerne Abbas Giant, Chatsworth House, Edinburgh Castle, Flamborough Head, Grand Union Canal, Post Office Tower, St Michael's Mount

*See also* **town**

**United Nations**

*United Nations members:*

**04** Chad, Cuba, Fiji, Iran, Iraq, Laos, Mali, Oman, Peru, Togo
**05** Benin, Chile, China, Congo, Egypt, Gabon, Ghana, Haiti, India, Italy, Japan, Kenya, Libya, Malta, Nauru, Nepal, Niger, Palau, Qatar, Samoa, Spain, Sudan, Syria, Tonga, Yemen
**06** Angola, Belize, Bhutan, Brazil, Canada, Cyprus, France, Greece, Guinea, Guyana, Israel, Jordan, Kuwait, Latvia, Malawi, Mexico, Monaco, Norway, Panama, Poland, Russia, Rwanda, Sweden, Turkey, Tuvalu, Uganda, Zambia
**07** Albania, Algeria, Andorra, Armenia, Austria, Bahrain, Belarus, Belgium, Bolivia, Burundi, Comoros, Croatia, Denmark, Ecuador, Eritrea, Estonia, Finland, Georgia, Germany, Grenada, Hungary, Iceland, Ireland, Jamaica, Lebanon, Lesotho, Liberia, Moldova, Morocco, Myanmar, Namibia, Nigeria, Romania, Senegal, Somalia, St Lucia, Tunisia, Ukraine, Uruguay, Vanuatu, Vietnam
**08** Barbados, Botswana, Bulgaria, Cambodia, Cameroon, Colombia, Djibouti, Dominica, Ethiopia, Honduras, Kiribati, Malaysia, Maldives, Mongolia, Pakistan, Paraguay, Portugal, Slovakia, Slovenia, Sri Lanka, Suriname, Tanzania, Thailand, Zimbabwe
**09** Argentina, Australia, Cape Verde, Costa Rica, East Timor, Guatemala, Indonesia, Lithuania, Macedonia, Mauritius, Nicaragua, San Marino, Singapore, Swaziland, The Gambia, Venezuela
**10** Azerbaijan, Bangladesh, El Salvador, Kazakhstan, Kyrgyzstan, Luxembourg, Madagascar, Mauritania, Mozambique, New Zealand, North Korea, Seychelles, South Korea, Tajikistan, The Bahamas, Uzbekistan
**11** Afghanistan, Burkina Faso, Côte d'Ivoire, Philippines, Saudi Arabia, Sierra Leone, South Africa, Switzerland
**12** Guinea-Bissau, Turkmenistan
**13** Czech Republic, Liechtenstein, United Kingdom
**14** Papua New Guinea, Solomon Islands, The Netherlands
**15** Marshall Islands, St Kitts and Nevis
**16** Brunei Darussalam, Equatorial Guinea
**17** Antigua and Barbuda, Dominican Republic, Trinidad and Tobago
**18** São Tomé and Príncipe, United Arab Emirates
**19** Serbia and Montenegro
**20** Bosnia and Herzegovina
**21** United States of America
**22** Central African Republic
**25** St Vincent and the Grenadines
**27** Federated States of Micronesia
**28** Democratic Republic of the Congo

**United States of America**
**02** US **03** USA

*See also* **president**

*US cities include:*

**02** LA, NY
**03** NYC
**05** Boise, Dover, Miami, Salem
**06** Albany, Austin, Boston, Dallas, Denver, Helena, Juneau, Pierre, St Paul, Topeka
**07** Atlanta, Augusta, Chicago, Concord, Detroit, Houston, Jackson, Lansing, Lincoln, Madison, Memphis, New York, Olympia, Phoenix, Raleigh, Santa Fe, Seattle, Trenton
**08** Bismarck, Cheyenne, Columbia, Columbus, Hartford, Honolulu, Las Vegas, Portland, Richmond, San Diego
**09** Annapolis, Baltimore, Des Moines, Frankfort, Milwaukee, Nashville
**10** Baton Rouge, Carson City, Charleston, Harrisburg, Little Rock, Los Angeles, Montgomery, Montpelier, New Orleans, Pittsburgh, Providence, Sacramento, San Antonio, Washington
**11** New York City, Springfield, Tallahassee
**12** Indianapolis, Oklahoma City, Philadelphia, Salt Lake City, San Francisco, Washington DC
**13** Jefferson City

*US landmarks include:*

**05** Yukon
**07** Capitol, Rockies
**08** Colorado, Lake Erie, Missouri, Mt Elbert, Mt Vernon, Pentagon, Yosemite
**09** Graceland, Hollywood, Hoover Dam, Lake Huron, Milwaukee, Mt Rainier
**10** Everglades, Great Lakes, Joshua Tree, Mt McKinley, Mt Rushmore, Mt St Helens, Sears Tower, White House
**11** Grand Canyon, Lake Ontario, Liberty Bell, Mississippi, Pearl Harbor, Space Needle, Yellowstone
**12** Appalachians, Carnegie Hall, Lake Michigan, Lake Superior, Niagara Falls
**13** Great Salt Lake
**14** Brooklyn Bridge, Monument Valley, Rocky Mountains
**15** Lincoln Memorial, Statue of Liberty

*See also* **president**; **state**

**unity**
**03** one **05** peace, union **06** accord **07** concert, concord, harmony, oneness **09** agreement, consensus, integrity, unanimity, wholeness **10** solidarity **11** unification **12** amalgamation, togetherness

**universal**
**01** U **03** all **05** total, whole **06** common, cosmic, entire, global, varsal, versal **07** general **08** all-round, catholic, ecumenic **09** unlimited, worldwide **10** ecumenical, ubiquitous **11** omnipresent **12** all-embracing, all-inclusive **13** comprehensive **14** across-the-board

**universality**
**08** entirety, totality, ubiquity **10** commonness, generality, prevalence **11** catholicity **12** completeness, predominance **14** generalization

**universally**
**06** always **09** uniformly **10** everywhere, invariably **12** ubiquitously

**universe**
**03** all **05** world **06** cosmos, nature **07** heavens **08** creation, everyone **09** firmament, macrocosm **14** the sum of things

**university**
**01** U **03** uni **07** academy, college, varsity **08** academia **09** institute **11** polytechnic

*Ivy League universities:*

**04** Yale
**05** Brown
**07** Cornell, Harvard
**08** Columbia
**09** Dartmouth, Princeton
**12** Pennsylvania

*Seven Sisters colleges:*

**05** Smith
**06** Vassar
**07** Barnard
**08** Bryn Mawr
**09** Radcliffe, Wellesley
**12** Mount Holyoke

*Universities include:*

**02** OU
**03** LSE, MIT, UCL
**04** City, Open, UCLA
**05** Aston, Keele, UMIST
**06** Brunel, Durham, Leiden, Napier, Oxford
**07** Caltech, Warwick
**08** Ann Arbor, Berkeley, Sorbonne, Stanford
**09** Cambridge, St Andrews
**10** De Montfort, Heriot-Watt

12 Robert Gordon, Thames Valley
13 Royal Holloway
14 Trinity College
15 California State, Imperial College, Juilliard School

*See also* **college**

**• at university**
02 up

**unjust**
05 wrong 06 biased, unfair, wanton 07 partial, unequal 08 one-sided, partisan, wrongful, wrongous 10 iniquitous, prejudiced, undeserved 11 inequitable, unjustified, unrighteous 12 unreasonable

**unjustifiable**
05 undue 09 excessive 10 immoderate, outrageous 11 inexcusable, uncalled-for, unwarranted 12 indefensible, unacceptable, unforgivable, unpardonable, unreasonable

**unkempt**
◇ *anagram indicator*
05 messy, ratty, rough, tousy, touzy, towsy, towzy 06 frowsy, frowzy, scungy, shabby, sloppy, untidy 07 rumpled, scraggy, scruffy, squalid, tousled 08 scraggly, slobbish, slovenly, uncombed 09 mal soigné, shambolic, ungroomed 10 disordered, scraggling, unpolished 11 dishevelled

**unkind**
04 mean 05 cruel, harsh, nasty, snide 06 bitchy, shabby 07 callous, inhuman, vicious 08 inhumane, pitiless, ruthless, spiteful, uncaring, unkindly 09 heartless, malicious, unfeeling 10 malevolent, unfriendly 11 cold-hearted, disobliging, hard-hearted, insensitive, thoughtless 12 uncharitable 13 inconsiderate, unsympathetic

**unkindness**
05 spite 07 cruelty 08 meanness 09 harshness 10 ill-feeling, inhumanity 11 callousness 13 insensitivity, maliciousness 14 unfriendliness 15 hard-heartedness

**unknowable**
06 untold 08 infinite 12 incalculable, unfathomable, unimaginable 13 unconditioned, unforeseeable, unpredictable 15 unascertainable

**unknowing**
06 chance, unwist 07 unaware 08 ignorant 09 unplanned, unwitting 10 accidental, unintended, unthinking 11 inadvertent, involuntary, unconscious 12 unsuspecting 13 unintentional

**unknown**
01 X, Y, Z 03 ign, new 04 dark 05 alien 06 hidden, occult, secret, unkent, untold 07 foreign, obscure, strange, unnamed 08 nameless, unkenned 09 anonymous, concealed, incognito, uncharted, unheard-of 10 mysterious, substance x, undivulged, unexplored, unfamiliar, unrevealed 11 undisclosed 12 undiscovered, unidentified

**unlawful**
06 banned 07 illegal, illicit, vicious 08 criminal, non licet, outlawed, wrongful 09 forbidden 10 prohibited, unlicensed 12 illegitimate, unauthorized, unsanctioned 13 against the law

**unleash**
04 free 05 let go, loose, untie 07 deliver, release, set free, unloose 08 let loose, untether

**unless**
03 but 04 less, nisi, save 06 except 07 without

**unlettered**
08 ignorant, untaught 09 unlearned, untutored 10 illiterate, uneducated, unlessoned, unschooled

**unlike**
06 unlich 07 difform, diverse, opposed, unequal, various 08 distinct, opposite 09 as against, different, disparate, divergent, unconform, unrelated 10 contrasted, dissimilar, ill-matched 11 as opposed to 12 dissimilar to, incompatible, in contrast to 13 different from, heterogeneous 14 out of character

**unlikely**
◇ *anagram indicator*
04 last, slim 05 faint, fishy, small 06 farfet, remote, slight, unlike 07 distant, dubious, outside, suspect 08 doubtful 09 fictional 10 far-fetched, improbable, improbably, incredible, suspicious, unexpected, unsuitable 11 implausible, unpromising 12 questionable, unbelievable, unconvincing, unimaginable 13 inconceivable 14 inconsiderable 15 unprepossessing

**unlimited**
◇ *ends deletion indicator*
04 full, vast 05 great, total 06 untold 07 endless, immense 08 absolute, complete, infinite 09 boundless, countless, extensive, limitless, shoreless, unbounded, unchecked, unimpeded, universal 10 indefinite, unconfined, unhampered 11 confineless, illimitable, unqualified 12 immeasurable, incalculable, uncontrolled, unrestricted 13 inexhaustible, unconditional, unconstrained 15 all-encompassing

**unload**
04 dump 05 empty, strip 06 remove, unlade, unpack, unship, vacate 07 disload, offload, relieve 08 unburden, uncharge 09 disburden, discharge, unfraught 10 disburthen

**unlock**
04 free, open, undo 05 unbar 06 unbolt 07 release, unlatch 08 disclose, unfasten

**unlooked-for**
05 lucky 06 chance 08 surprise 09 fortunate 10 fortuitous, surprising, unexpected, unforeseen, unhoped-for 11 undreamed-of, unpredicted, unthought-of 13 unanticipated

**unloved**
05 hated 06 dumped 07 spurned 08 detested, disliked, forsaken, loveless, rejected, unwanted 09 neglected, unpopular 10 uncared-for

**unluckily**
04 alas 05 sadly 08 sad to say 09 unhappily, worse luck 11 regrettably, sad to relate 13 I am sorry to say, unfortunately

**unlucky**
04 poor 05 black, stiff, tough 06 cursed, donsie, doomed, jinxed, wicked 07 adverse, hapless, infaust, ominous, unhappy 08 ill-fated, luckless, sinister, unchancy, untoward, wretched 09 ill-omened, mischancy, miserable, wanchancy 10 calamitous, disastrous, ill-starred, left-handed, unpleasant, wanchancie 11 star-crossed, unfortunate, unpromising 12 catastrophic, inauspicious, unfavourable, unpropitious, unsuccessful 14 down on your luck 15 disadvantageous

**unmanageable**
04 wild 05 bulky 06 gallus, unruly, wanton 07 awkward, gallows, ropable, unhandy, unweldy 08 ropeable, unwieldy 09 difficult, wieldless 10 cumbersome, disorderly, refractary, refractory, weeldlesse 11 intractable, troublesome 12 incommodious, inconvenient, obstreperous, recalcitrant, ungovernable 13 impracticable 14 uncontrollable

**unmanly**
03 wet 04 base, soft, weak 05 cissy, weedy, wussy 06 craven, effete, feeble, yellow 07 wimpish 08 cowardly, womanish 09 weak-kneed 10 effeminate, namby-pamby 11 lily-livered 13 dishonourable 14 chicken-hearted

**unmannerly**
04 rude 07 boorish, ill-bred, low-bred, uncivil, uncouth 08 impolite 09 graceless, misleared 10 ungracious 11 bad-mannered, ill-mannered 12 badly-behaved, discourteous 13 disrespectful

**unmarried**
04 free, lone 05 unwed 06 maiden, single 08 celibate, divorced 09 available, on your own, separated 10 unattached 11 partnerless

**unmask**
04 bare, show 06 detect, expose, reveal, show up, unveil 07 uncloak, uncover, unvisor 08 disclose, discover, unvizard

**unmatched**
**03** odd **04** orra **06** unique **07** supreme **08** peerless **09** matchless, nonpareil, paramount **10** consummate, unequalled, unexampled, unfellowed, unrivalled **11** unparagoned, unsurpassed **12** incomparable, unparalleled **13** beyond compare

**unmentionable**
**05** taboo **08** immodest, indecent, shameful, shocking **09** forbidden **10** abominable, scandalous, unpleasant **11** disgraceful, unspeakable, unutterable **12** embarrassing

**unmerciful**
**04** hard **05** cruel **06** brutal **07** callous **08** pitiless, ruthless, sadistic, uncaring **09** heartless, merciless, spareless, unfeeling, unsparing **10** implacable, relentless **11** remorseless, unrelenting

**unmethodical**
**06** random **07** muddled **08** confused **09** desultory, haphazard, illogical, irregular **10** disorderly **11** unorganized **12** unsystematic **13** unco-ordinated

**unmindful**
**03** lax **04** deaf **05** blind, slack **06** remiss **07** unaware **08** careless, heedless **09** forgetful, negligent, oblivious, unheeding **10** neglectful, regardless **11** inattentive, indifferent, unconscious

**unmistakable**
**04** sure **05** clear, frank, plain **06** patent **07** blatant, certain, decided, evident, glaring, obvious **08** clear-cut, definite, distinct, explicit, manifest, positive, striking, univocal **10** pronounced, undeniable **11** conspicuous, indubitable, unambiguous, unequivocal, well-defined **12** indisputable **14** beyond question, unquestionable

**unmistakably**
**06** surely **07** clearly, plainly **08** proclaim **09** blatantly, certainly, evidently, obviously **10** definitely, distinctly, manifestly, undeniably **11** doubtlessly, indubitably **12** indisputably, without doubt **13** conspicuously, unambiguously, unequivocally **14** unquestionably **15** without question

**unmitigated**
**04** grim, pure, rank **05** harsh, sheer, utter **06** arrant **07** intense, perfect **08** absolute, complete, outright, thorough, unabated, unbroken **09** downright, out-and-out **10** consummate, persistent, relentless, unmodified, unredeemed, unrelieved **11** unqualified, unrelenting, unremitting **12** unalleviated, undiminished **13** thoroughgoing

**unmixed**
**03** net, raw **04** mere, neat, nett, pure **07** sincere **09** unallayed **12** unadulterate, uncompounded **13** unadulterated

**unmoved**
**04** calm, cold, firm **06** steady **07** adamant, dry-eyed **08** resolute, resolved, unshaken **09** impassive, unbending, unchanged, unfeeling, unstirred, untouched **10** determined, inflexible, unaffected, unwavering **11** indifferent, unconcerned, undeviating, unimpressed **12** unresponsive **13** dispassionate

**unnamed**
**04** anon **05** house **09** anonymous

**unnatural**
◇ *anagram indicator*
**03** odd **05** false, queer, stiff **06** farfet, forced, formal, staged, unholy, wooden **07** bizarre, feigned, fustian, heinous, inhuman, pompous, stilted, strange, uncanny, unusual **08** abnormal, absonant, affected, freakish, kindless, laboured, peculiar, strained, uncommon, unkindly **09** anomalous, contrived, insincere, irregular, monstrous, perverted **10** artificial, disnatured, far-fetched, forcedness, monstruous **11** constrained, stiff-necked **12** cataphysical, supernatural **13** against nature, extraordinary, self-conscious, unspontaneous

**unnaturally**
◇ *anagram indicator*
**05** oddly **08** unkindly **09** strangely, unusually **10** abnormally, peculiarly, uncommonly **11** irregularly **15** extraordinarily

**unnecessarily**
**10** needlessly **11** excessively **12** immoderately **13** superfluously

**unnecessary**
**06** wasted **08** needless, unneeded, unwanted **09** excessive, redundant **10** expendable, gratuitous, unrequired **11** dispensable, inessential, superfluous, uncalled-for **12** non-essential, tautological

**unnerve**
**05** alarm, daunt, scare, shake, unman, upset, worry **06** deject, dismay, put out, rattle, weaken **07** fluster, perturb, shake up **08** confound, disquiet, frighten, unsettle **10** demoralize, disconcert, discourage, dishearten, intimidate

**unnoticed**
**06** unseen **07** ignored **08** unheeded **09** neglected **10** overlooked, unobserved, unremarked **11** disregarded **12** undiscovered, unrecognized

**unobstructed**
**04** fair, open **05** plain

**unobtrusive**
**05** quiet **06** humble, low-key, modest **07** subdued **08** retiring **09** underhand **10** restrained, unassuming **11** unassertive **12** self-effacing, unaggressive, unnoticeable **13** inconspicuous, unpretentious **14** unostentatious

**unobtrusively**
**06** humbly **07** on the QT, quietly **08** modestly **10** on the quiet **15** inconspicuously, surreptitiously, unpretentiously

**unoccupied**
**04** free, idle, room, void **05** empty, waste **06** otiose, vacant **07** jobless **08** deserted, forsaken, inactive, workless **09** at liberty, désoeuvré **10** disengaged, unemployed **11** uninhabited, unpopulated

**unofficial**
**04** curb, kerb **05** black **06** fringe **07** illegal, private **08** informal, personal **10** undeclared, unratified **11** alternative, unconfirmed **12** confidential, off-the-record, unauthorized **15** unauthenticated

**unoriginal**
**05** stale, trite **06** copied **07** cribbed, derived, slavish **09** hackneyed, ready-made **10** derivative, second-hand, uninspired **11** predictable **12** cliché-ridden **13** unimaginative

**unorthodox**
◇ *anagram indicator*
**03** new **04** cult, zany **05** fresh, novel **06** fringe, way-out **07** unusual **08** abnormal, creative **09** eccentric, heterodox, irregular, left-field **10** innovative, off the wall **11** alternative **13** nonconformist **14** unconventional

**unpaid**
**03** due **04** free **05** owing **06** unfeed **07** overdue, payable, pending, pro bono, unwaged **08** honorary **09** remaining, unsettled, voluntary **10** unsalaried **11** outstanding, uncollected **14** pro bono publico, unremunerative

**unpalatable**
**05** nasty **06** bitter **07** insipid **08** inedible **09** offensive, repellent, repugnant, uneatable, unsavoury **10** disgusting, unpleasant **11** distasteful **12** disagreeable, unappetizing, unattractive

**unparalleled**
**04** rare **06** unique **07** supreme **08** peerless **09** matchless, unmatched **10** unequalled, unrivalled **11** exceptional, superlative, unsurpassed **12** incomparable, without equal **13** beyond compare, unprecedented

**unpardonable**
**08** shameful, shocking **10** deplorable, outrageous, scandalous **11** disgraceful, inexcusable **12** indefensible, irremissible, unforgivable **13** reprehensible, unjustifiable **14** unconscionable

**unperturbed**
**04** calm, cool **06** placid, poised,

serene **08** composed, tranquil **09** collected, impassive, unexcited, unruffled, unworried **10** untroubled **11** undisturbed, unflappable, unflinching, unflustered **13** self-possessed

**unpleasant**
**03** bad **04** foul, grim, mean, rude, sour **05** awful, crook, nasty, surly **06** filthy, mingin', stinky, ungain, unkind **07** drastic, hostile, minging, noisome **08** impolite **09** offensive, repugnant, repulsive, traumatic **10** aggressive, disgusting, ill-natured, unfriendly **11** bad-tempered, distasteful, quarrelsome, troublesome, undesirable, unpalatable **12** disagreeable, discourteous, unappetizing, unattractive **13** objectionable

**unpleasantness**
**04** fuss **05** upset **06** bother, furore **07** scandal, trouble **08** bad blood **09** annoyance, esclandre, nastiness **10** bad feeling, ill-feeling **13** embarrassment

**unpolished**
**04** bare, rude **05** crude, rough **06** coarse, vulgar **07** sketchy, uncouth, unfiled, unkempt **08** agrestic, home-bred, unpolite, unworked **09** unrefined **10** provincial, uncultured, unfinished **11** uncivilized, unfashioned **12** uncultivated **13** rough and ready, wild and woolly **15** unsophisticated

**unpopular**
**05** hated **07** avoided, ignored, shunned, unloved **08** detested, disliked, rejected, unwanted **09** neglected, unwelcome **10** friendless **11** undesirable **12** unattractive **13** unfashionable, unsought-after

**unprecedented**
**03** new **07** unheard, unknown, unusual **08** abnormal, freakish, original, uncommon **09** unheard-of **10** remarkable, unequalled, unexampled, unrivalled **11** exceptional **12** unparalleled **13** extraordinary, revolutionary

**unpredictable**
◇ *anagram indicator*
**06** chance, fickle, random, slippy **07** erratic **08** slippery, unstable, variable, volatile **09** mercurial **10** capricious, changeable, inconstant, unexpected, unreliable **12** incalculable **13** unforeseeable

**unprejudiced**
**04** fair, just **08** balanced, detached, unbiased **09** impartial, objective **10** even-handed, fair-minded, open-minded, uncoloured **11** enlightened, non-partisan, unpossessed **12** cosmopolitan **13** dispassionate

**unpremeditated**
**07** offhand **09** extempore, impromptu, impulsive, unplanned **10** fortuitous, off-the-cuff, unprepared **11** spontaneous, unmeditated, unrehearsed **13** unintentional **15** spur-of-the-moment

**unprepared**
**03** raw **05** ad-lib, crude **07** napping, unready **09** half-baked, surprised, unplanned, unwilling **10** flat-footed, improvised, incomplete, off-the-cuff, unfinished, unpurvaide, unpurveyed **11** ill-equipped, spontaneous, unrehearsed **12** unsuspecting **14** on the wrong foot

**unprepossessing**
**04** ugly **05** plain **06** homely **08** ordinary, unlikely, unlovely **10** forbidding, unexciting, unpleasing **11** indifferent, unappealing **12** unattractive, unremarkable **13** unexceptional, uninteresting **15** undistinguished

**unpretentious**
**05** plain **06** homely, honest, humble, modest, simple **07** natural **08** discreet, ordinary **10** penny-plain, unaffected, unassuming **11** unobtrusive **14** unostentatious **15** straightforward

**unprincipled**
**07** corrupt, crooked, devious, immoral **09** deceitful, dishonest, reprobate, underhand, unethical **10** profligate **12** uninstructed, unscrupulous **13** discreditable, dishonourable **14** unprofessional

**unproductive**
**03** dry, shy **04** arid, dead, idle, lean, poor, vain, yeld, yell **05** blank, waste **06** barren, futile, otiose **07** sterile, useless **09** fruitless, infertile, worthless **10** unfruitful **11** ineffective, unrewarding **12** unprofitable **13** inefficacious **14** unremunerative

**unprofessional**
**03** lax **06** casual, sloppy **08** improper, inexpert, unseemly **09** negligent, unethical, unskilled, untrained **10** amateurish, indecorous **11** incompetent, inefficient **12** inadmissible, unacceptable, unprincipled, unscrupulous **13** inexperienced

**unprofitable**
**04** lean **08** bootless

**unpromising**
**06** gloomy **07** adverse, ominous **08** doubtful, unlikely **10** depressing **11** dispiriting **12** discouraging, inauspicious, unfavourable, unpropitious

**unprotected**
**04** open, soft **05** naked **06** liable **07** exposed, unarmed **08** helpless **09** uncovered, unguarded **10** unattended, undefended, unshielded, vulnerable **11** defenceless, unfortified, unsheltered

**unprovable**
**12** unverifiable **14** indemonstrable, indeterminable, undemonstrable **15** unascertainable

**unqualified**
**05** inapt, round, total, unfit, utter **07** amateur, perfect, plenary **08** absolute, complete, outright, positive, thorough **09** downright, incapable, out-and-out, unallayed, untrained **10** consummate, ineligible, unlicensed, unprepared, unreserved, unsuitable **11** categorical, ill-equipped, incompetent, unequivocal, unmitigated **12** unrestricted, wholehearted **13** inexperienced, unconditional

**unquestionable**
**04** sure **05** clear **06** patent **07** certain, obvious **08** absolute, definite, flawless, manifest **09** faultless **10** conclusive, undeniable **11** indubitable, irrefutable, self-evident, unequivocal **12** indisputable, unchallenged, unmistakable **13** incontestable **14** beyond question

**unquestionably**
**06** firmly **07** clearly **08** directly **09** certainly **10** definitely, distinctly, explicitly, manifestly, positively **11** indubitably, irrefutably **12** unmistakably **13** unambiguously, unequivocally

**unquestioning**
**08** implicit **11** unqualified **12** questionless, unhesitating, wholehearted **13** unconditional

**unravel**
◇ *anagram indicator*
**04** fray, free, undo **05** solve **06** evolve, unknit, unknot, unwind **07** clear up, explain, resolve, sort out, work out **08** separate, untangle **09** extricate, figure out, interpret, penetrate, puzzle out **11** disentangle **13** straighten out

**unreadable**
**07** complex, garbled, jumbled, muddled, obscure **08** involved, puzzling **09** illegible, scrambled **10** incoherent, mysterious **11** complicated, double Dutch **12** impenetrable, inarticulate, unfathomable **14** indecipherable, unintelligible

**unreal**
**04** fake, faux, mock, sham **05** false, phony **06** aerial, ersatz, hollow, made-up, phoney, shadow, untrue **07** amazing, bizarre, phantom, pretend **08** aeriform, fanciful, illusive, illusory, mythical, nebulous, notional **09** fairytale, fantastic, imaginary, legendary, moonshiny, phantosme, storybook, synthetic, visionary, whimsical **10** artificial, chimerical, fictitious, immaterial, incredible, ungrounded **11** Disneyesque, make-believe, non-existent **12** hypothetical, unbelievable **13** insubstantial

**unrealistic**
**08** quixotic, romantic, wild-eyed

10 idealistic, impossible, unworkable
11 impractical, theoretical
12 unreasonable 13 impracticable
14 over-optimistic

**unreality**
09 irreality, phoniness 10 hollowness, phoneyness 11 bizarreness, make-believe 12 fancifulness, illusoriness, nebulousness, non-existence
13 artificiality, imaginariness

**unreasonable**
03 mad, OTT 05 silly, steep, undue
06 absurd, biased, stupid, unfair, unjust
07 foolish, froward, obscene 08 a bit much, exacting, perverse 09 arbitrary, excessive, expensive, illogical, ludicrous, senseless 10 exorbitant, far-fetched, headstrong, immoderate, iniquitous, irrational, outrageous, over the top, scandalous 11 extravagant, nonsensical, opinionated, uncalled-for, unchristian, unjustified, unrealistic, unwarranted 12 extortionate, inconsistent, preposterous, unacceptable 13 unco-operative, unjustifiable

**unreasoning**
04 wild 05 brute, crazy, silly 06 absurd, unwise 07 brutish, foolish, invalid, unsound 09 arbitrary, beastlike, illogical, senseless 10 groundless, irrational, ridiculous 11 implausible, nonsensical 12 inconsistent, unreasonable 14 beside yourself

**unrecognizable**
07 altered, changed 09 disguised, incognito 10 unknowable
12 incognizable 14 unidentifiable

**unrecognized**
06 unseen 07 ignored 08 unheeded
09 neglected, unnoticed 10 overlooked, unobserved, unremarked
11 disregarded 12 undiscovered

**unrefined**
03 raw 05 blunt, crude, rough
06 coarse, earthy, rustic, vulgar
07 bestial 09 rough-hewn, untreated
10 uncultured, unfinished, unpolished, unpurified 11 unprocessed
12 uncultivated 15 unsophisticated

**unregenerate**
06 sinful, wicked 07 natural
08 hardened, obdurate, stubborn
09 abandoned, obstinate, shameless
10 impenitent, persistent, refractory, unreformed 11 intractable, unconverted, unrepentant
12 incorrigible, recalcitrant

**unrelated**
06 unlike 07 foreign 08 distinct, separate 09 different, disparate
10 dissimilar, extraneous, irrelevant
11 independent, off the point, unconnected 12 inconsequent, relationless, unassociated 14 beside the point

**unrelenting**
05 cruel, stern 06 steady 07 endless
08 constant, pitiless, ruthless, unabated, unbroken 09 ceaseless, continual, incessant, merciless, perpetual, unceasing, unsparing
10 continuous, implacable, inexorable, relentless, unmerciful
11 remorseless, unforgiving, unremitting 12 intransigent
14 uncompromising

**unreliable**
◇ *anagram indicator*
04 iffy 05 dodgy, false, trick 06 fickle, shonky 07 unsound 08 doubtful, fallible, in-and-out, mistaken, slippery, unstable 09 deceptive, erroneous, sieve-like, uncertain 10 fly-by-night, inaccurate 11 implausible
12 disreputable, questionable, unconvincing, undependable
13 irresponsible, temperamental, untrustworthy

**unremitting**
08 constant, tireless, unabated, unbroken 09 assiduous, ceaseless, continual, continued, incessant, intensive, perpetual, unceasing
10 continuous, relentless
11 irremissive, remorseless, unrelenting
13 indefatigable

**unrepentant**
07 callous 08 hardened, obdurate
09 confirmed, shameless, unabashed, unashamed 10 impenitent
12 incorrigible, unapologetic, unregenerate

**unrequited**
07 ignored, snubbed, spurned
08 rejected 09 discarded, neglected
10 unanswered 11 not returned
12 unrecognized 14 unacknowledged, unreciprocated

**unreserved**
04 free, full, open 05 frank, total
06 candid, direct, entire 08 absolute, complete, explicit, outgoing, unbooked 09 extrovert, outspoken, talkative, unlimited 10 forthright
11 uninhibited, unqualified, whole-footed 12 heart-to-heart, unhesitating, unrestrained, unrestricted, wholehearted 13 communicative, demonstrative, unconditional

**unreservedly**
03 out 05 fully 07 totally, utterly
08 entirely, outright 09 out-and-out
10 absolutely, completely
14 unhesitatingly, wholeheartedly
15 unconditionally

**unresisting**
04 meek 06 docile 07 passive
08 obedient 09 unsisting
10 submissive

**unresolved**
04 moot 05 vague, vexed 07 pending
08 doubtful, unsolved 09 undecided, unsettled 10 indefinite, irresolute, unanswered, up in the air
12 undetermined 13 problematical

**unresponsive**
04 cool 05 aloof 06 frigid 07 unmoved
08 echoless 09 apathetic, withdrawn
10 unaffected 11 indifferent
12 uninterested 13 unsympathetic

**unrest**
◇ *anagram indicator*
05 worry 06 unease 07 discord, protest, turmoil 08 disorder, disquiet
09 agitation, commotion, rebellion
10 discontent, dissension, uneasiness
11 disturbance 12 disaffection, perturbation, restlessness
15 dissatisfaction

**unrestrained**
◇ *anagram indicator*
04 free, wild 05 frank, loose 06 hearty, lavish, wanton 07 natural, rampant, unyoked 08 impotent 09 abandoned, libertine, unbounded, unbridled, unchecked 10 boisterous, immoderate, inordinate, unbuttoned, unfettered, unhindered, unlaboured, unreserved 11 extravagant, full-frontal, intemperate, uninhibited, unrepressed
12 uncontrolled 13 irrepressible, unconstrained, wild and woolly

**unrestricted**
◇ *anagram indicator*
04 free, open 05 clear 06 public
08 absolute, open door 09 chainless, unbounded, unimpeded, unlimited, unopposed 10 free-for-all, unhindered, unreserved
12 discretional, unobstructed
13 discretionary, unconditional

**unripe**
05 green 07 unready 08 immature
09 unripened 11 out of season, undeveloped

**unrivalled**
07 supreme 08 peerless 09 matchless, nonpareil, unmatched, untouched
10 inimitable, unequalled
11 superlative, unsurpassed
12 incomparable, unparalleled, without equal 13 beyond compare

**unruffled**
04 calm, cool, even 05 level 06 serene, smooth 08 composed, peaceful, tranquil 09 collected 10 untroubled
11 undisturbed, unperturbed
13 imperturbable

**unruly**
◇ *anagram indicator*
04 rag'd, wild 05 ragde, rowdy
06 stormy, wanton, wilful 07 lawless, riotous, rulesse, wayward
08 mutinous, ruleless, torn-down
09 camstairy, camsteary, turbulent
10 camsteerie, disorderly, disruptive, headstrong, rebellious, refractary, refractory 11 disobedient, intractable
12 obstreperous, recalcitrant, ungovernable, unmanageable
13 insubordinate, undisciplined
14 uncontrollable

**unsafe**
05 dicey, fishy, hairy, risky 06 chancy

07 exposed, uncanny, unsound 08 high-risk, insecure, perilous, unstable 09 dangerous, hazardous, uncertain 10 precarious, unreliable, vulnerable 11 defenceless, treacherous

**unsaid**
08 unspoken, unstated, unvoiced 09 unuttered 10 undeclared 11 unexpressed, unmentioned 12 unpronounced

**unsatisfactory**
04 lame, poor, ropy, tame, weak 05 empty, lousy, rocky, ropey, wrong 06 faulty 08 inferior, mediocre 09 defective, deficient, imperfect, off-colour 10 inadequate, unsuitable 11 displeasing, frustrating 12 insufficient, unacceptable, unsatisfying 13 disappointing, dissatisfying

**unsavoury**
05 nasty 06 sordid 07 squalid 09 obnoxious, offensive, on the nose, repellent, repugnant, repulsive, revolting, sickening, tasteless 10 disgusting, nauseating, unpleasant 11 distasteful, undesirable, unpalatable 12 disagreeable, disreputable, unappetizing, unattractive 13 objectionable

**unscathed**
04 safe 05 sound, whole 06 intact, unhurt 08 unharmed 09 undamaged, uninjured, untouched 13 with whole skin

**unscramble**
◇ *anagram indicator*
06 decode 08 decipher

**unscrupulous**
07 corrupt, crooked, immoral 08 improper, ruthless 09 dishonest, shameless, unethical 10 Rottweiler, unscrupled, villainous 12 unprincipled 13 dishonourable 14 unconscionable

**unseasonable**
08 ill-timed, mistimed, untimely 10 malapropos, out of place, seasonable, unsuitable 11 inopportune 12 intempestive 13 inappropriate

**unseasoned**
05 green 08 unprimed 09 unmatured, untreated 10 unprepared, untempered

**unseat**
04 oust 05 throw 06 depose, remove, topple, unship 07 dismiss, unhorse 08 dethrone, dishorse, dismount, displace, unsaddle 09 discharge, overthrow

**unseemly**
◇ *anagram indicator*
05 undue 06 indign 07 uncivil 08 improper, uncomely, unhonest 09 unrefined 10 ill-looking, indecorous, indelicate, unbecoming, unhandsome, unsuitable 11 unbefitting, undignified 12 disreputable 13 discreditable, inappropriate

**unseen**
06 hidden, uneyed, veiled 07 cryptic, lurking, obscure 09 concealed, invisible, unnoticed 10 unbeholden, undetected, unobserved 11 unobtrusive 13 inexperienced

**unselfish**
04 kind 05 noble 07 liberal 08 generous, selfless 10 altruistic, charitable, open-handed, single-eyed 11 magnanimous, self-denying 12 humanitarian 13 disinterested, philanthropic 14 public-spirited, self-forgetting 15 self-sacrificing

**unsentimental**
05 tough 09 hard-faced, hardnosed, practical, pragmatic, realistic, unfeeling 10 hard-headed, iron-headed, unromantic 11 hard as nails, level-headed, unemotional

**unserviceable**
02 U/S

**unsettle**
◇ *anagram indicator*
04 faze 05 feese, feeze, phase, phese, shake, throw, unfix, upset 06 bother, pheese, pheeze, rattle, ruffle 07 agitate, confuse, disturb, fluster, perturb, trouble 09 discomfit, unbalance 10 discompose, disconcert 11 destabilize

**unsettled**
◇ *anagram indicator*
04 edgy, open 05 fazed, owing, shaky, tense, upset 06 futile, on edge, queasy, queazy, roving, shaken, uneasy, unpaid 07 aimless, anxious, fidgety, lawless, overdue, payable, vagrant 08 agitated, confused, deserted, desolate, doubtful, drifting, goalless, insecure, rambling, restless, troubled, unguided, unnerved, unstable, unsteady, vagabond, variable 09 abandoned, disturbed, flustered, in arrears, pointless, turbulent, uncertain, undecided, unpeopled, wandering 10 changeable, inconstant, irresolute, undirected, unoccupied, unresolved, up in the air 11 disoriented, outstanding, purposeless, to be decided, undiscussed, uninhabited, unmotivated, unpopulated 12 indetermined, in the balance, undetermined 13 directionless, unpredictable 14 in a state of flux

**unshakable, unshakeable**
04 firm, sure 05 fixed 06 stable 07 staunch 08 constant, resolute 09 immovable, steadfast 10 determined, unswerving, unwavering 11 well-founded 12 unassailable

**unsightly**
04 ugly 07 hideous 09 repugnant, repulsive, revolting 10 off-putting, unpleasant 11 carbuncular 12 disagreeable, unattractive 15 unprepossessing

**unskilful**
03 bad 05 inept 06 clumsy, gauche 07 awkward 08 bungling, fumbling, inexpert, unartful, untaught 09 maladroit, unskilled, untrained 10 amateurish, uneducated, unhandsome, untalented 11 incompetent, unpractised, unqualified 13 inexperienced 14 unprofessional

**unskilled**
04 rude 06 simple, ungain 07 unwitty 08 inexpert 09 unperfect, untrained 10 amateurish 11 incompetent, unpractised, unqualified 13 inexperienced 14 unprofessional

**unsociable**
04 cold, cool 05 aloof 06 chilly 07 distant, hostile 08 reserved, retiring, solitary, taciturn 09 reclusive, withdrawn 10 insociable, unfriendly 11 introverted, standoffish, uncongenial 12 inhospitable 13 unforthcoming, unneighbourly 15 uncommunicative, uncompanionable

**unsoiled** *see* **unsullied**

**unsolicited**
07 unasked 08 unsought, unwanted 09 sponte sua, uninvited, unwelcome, voluntary 10 gratuitous, unasked-for 11 spontaneous, uncalled-for, unrequested

**unsophisticated**
03 jay 04 naif 05 basic, crude, naive, plain 06 direct, native, simple 07 artless, genuine, natural, verdant 08 cornball, corn-pone, innocent 09 childlike, guileless, ingenuous, small-town, unrefined, unworldly 10 provincial, unaffected, uninvolved 11 rudimentary, undeveloped 13 inexperienced, unadulterated, uncomplicated, unpretentious 15 straightforward

**unsound**
◇ *anagram indicator*
03 ill 04 weak 05 false, frail, shaky, wonky 06 ailing, broken, faulty, flawed, hollow, rotten, unsafe, unwell, wobbly 07 damaged, injured, invalid, rickety 08 delicate, deranged, diseased, insecure, unhinged, unstable, unsteady 09 dangerous, defective, erroneous, illogical, unfounded, unhealthy, untenable 10 disordered, fallacious, ill-founded, unbalanced, unreliable 11 unwholesome

**unsparing**
04 hard 05 harsh, round, stern 06 lavish, severe 07 drastic, liberal, profuse 08 abundant, generous, rigorous, ruthless, slashing 09 bountiful, merciless, plenteous 10 implacable, munificent, open-handed, relentless, ungrudging, unmerciful, unstinting 11 unforgiving 14 uncompromising

**unspeakable**
05 awful 08 dreadful, horrible,

nameless, shocking, terrible
**09** appalling, execrable, frightful, monstrous, nefandous **10** horrendous
**11** unthinkable, unutterable
**12** unbelievable, unimaginable
**13** inconceivable, indescribable, inexpressible, unmentionable

**unspeakably**
**07** awfully **08** terribly **11** appallingly, frightfully, unthinkably, unutterably
**12** horrendously, unbelievably, unimaginably **13** inconceivably, indescribably, inexpressibly

**unspecified**
**05** vague **07** obscure, unknown, unnamed **09** uncertain, undecided, undefined **10** indefinite, mysterious
**12** undetermined, unidentified

**unspectacular**
**04** dull **06** boring, common **07** average
**08** mediocre, ordinary, plodding
**10** unexciting **12** unimpressive, unremarkable **13** uninteresting

**unspoilt**
**07** natural, perfect **08** pristine, unharmed **09** preserved, unchanged, undamaged, untouched
**10** unaffected, unimpaired
**11** unblemished **15** unsophisticated

**unspoken**
**04** mute **05** tacit **06** silent, unsaid
**07** assumed, implied **08** implicit, inferred, unstated, wordless
**09** unuttered, voiceless **10** undeclared, understood **11** unexpressed

**unstable**
◇ *anagram indicator*
**03** mad **04** nuts, weak **05** barmy, batty, crazy, daffy, dippy, dodgy, loony, loopy, moody, nutty, risky, shaky **06** fitful, infirm, insane, labile, mental, slippy, tickle, unsafe, wankle, wobbly
**07** bananas, bonkers, brittle, bruckle, erratic, flighty, meshuga, rickety, unsound **08** crackers, deranged, insecure, instable, ricketty, shifting, slippery, ticklish, unhinged, unstayed, unsteady, variable, volatile, wavering
**09** disturbed, mercurial, tottering, unsettled **10** capricious, changeable, inconstant, off balance, off the wall, out to lunch, precarious, unbalanced, unreliable **11** fluctuating, light-minded, off your head, unballasted, vacillating
**12** inconsistent, round the bend **13** off your rocker, round the twist, unpredictable, untrustworthy **14** off your trolley, wrong in the head

**unsteady**
◇ *anagram indicator*
**05** dotty, giddy, shaky, totty, warby
**06** cranky, groggy, titupy, unsafe, wambly, wavery, wobbly **07** doddery, rickety, tittupy **08** insecure, skittish, unstable, variable, waverous
**09** irregular, tottering, versatile
**10** flickering, inconstant, precarious, unreliable **11** light-headed, treacherous, unballasted

• **be unsteady**
**04** flit **05** waver **06** coggle, wobble
**09** vacillate

**unstinting**
**04** full **05** ample, large **06** lavish
**07** liberal, profuse **08** abundant, generous, prodigal **09** abounding, bountiful, plentiful, unsparing
**10** munificent, ungrudging

**unstoppable**
**07** undying **08** unending **09** unceasing
**10** inevitable **11** unavoidable, unrelenting, unremitting **13** without a let-up

**unsubstantial**
**04** airy **07** shadowy **10** cloud-built

**unsubstantiated**
**07** dubious **08** unproved, unproven
**09** debatable **10** disputable, unattested, unverified
**11** unconfirmed, unsupported
**12** questionable **13** unestablished
**14** uncorroborated

**unsuccessful**
**04** lost, sour, vain **06** beaten, failed, futile, losing **07** bungled, fumbled, sterile, unlucky, useless **08** abortive, defeated, luckless, thwarted, washed-up **09** fruitless **10** frustrated, miscarried, trade-falne, unavailing
**11** ineffective, ineffectual, trade-fallen, unfortunate **12** unproductive, unprofitable

**unsuitable**
**05** amiss, inapt, inept, unapt, unfit
**08** improper, unlikely, unseemly, unsorted, unsuited **09** unfitting
**10** inapposite, ineligible, malapropos, out of place, unbecoming
**11** incongruent, incongruous
**12** incompatible, inconvenient, infelicitous, unacceptable
**13** inappropriate

**unsullied**
**04** pure **05** clean **06** intact **07** perfect
**08** pristine, spotless, unsoiled
**09** stainless, undefiled, unspoiled, unspotted, unstained, untainted, untouched **10** immaculate
**11** unblackened, unblemished, uncorrupted, untarnished

**unsung**
**07** obscure, unknown **08** unhailed
**09** anonymous, forgotten, neglected, unpraised **10** overlooked, unhonoured
**11** disregarded, unacclaimed
**12** uncelebrated, unrecognized
**14** unacknowledged

**unsure**
**05** vague **07** dubious, unknown
**08** doubtful, hesitant, insecure, wavering **09** dithering, sceptical, tentative, uncertain, undecided
**10** ambivalent, indefinite, in two minds, irresolute, precarious, suspicious **11** uncommitted, unconvinced, unpersuaded
**12** equivocating **13** untrustworthy

**unsurpassed**
**07** supreme **08** unbeaten **09** matchless, unmatched **10** surpassing, unequalled, unexcelled, unrivalled **11** exceptional, superlative **12** incomparable, second-to-none, transcendent, unparalleled
**13** state-of-the-art

**unsurprising**
**08** expected, forecast, foreseen, hoped-for, promised **09** looked-for, predicted, wished-for **10** forseeable
**11** anticipated, predictable

**unsuspecting**
**05** naive **06** simple, unwary
**07** unaware **08** gullible, innocent, off guard, trustful, trusting **09** credulous, ingenuous **11** unconscious
**12** unsuspicious

**unswerving**
**04** firm, sure, true **05** fixed **06** direct, steady **07** devoted, staunch
**08** constant, resolute, untiring
**09** dedicated, immovable, steadfast
**10** unflagging, unwavering
**11** undeviating, unfaltering **12** single-minded

**unsympathetic**
**04** cold, hard **05** cruel, harsh, stony
**06** unkind **07** callous, hostile, inhuman, unmoved **08** pitiless, soulless, uncaring **09** hard-faced, heartless, unfeeling, unpitying **11** hard as nails, hard-hearted, ill-disposed, indifferent, insensitive, unconcerned
**12** antagonistic, unresponsive

**unsystematic**
**06** random, sloppy, untidy **07** chaotic, jumbled, muddled **08** confused, slapdash **09** haphazard, illogical, irregular, shambolic, unplanned
**10** disorderly **11** unorganized
**12** disorganized, unmethodical, unstructured **13** unco-ordinated
**14** indiscriminate

**untamed**
**04** wild **05** feral **06** fierce, savage
**07** haggard, salvage **08** unmanned
**09** barbarous **10** unmellowed, untameable **14** undomesticated

**untangle**
**04** undo **05** solve **07** resolve, unravel, work out **09** extricate **11** disentangle
**13** straighten out

**untarnished**
**04** pure **05** clean **06** bright, intact
**07** glowing, shining **08** polished, pristine, spotless, unsoiled, unspoilt
**09** burnished, stainless, unbraided, unspotted, unstained, unsullied
**10** immaculate, impeccable
**11** unblemished **13** unimpeachable

**untenable**
**05** rocky, shaky **06** flawed **07** unsound
**09** illogical, intenable **10** fallacious
**11** inexcusable **12** indefensible, unreasonable **13** insupportable, unjustifiable, unsustainable
**14** unmaintainable

**unthinkable**
**06** absurd **08** shocking, unlikely **09** illogical, unheard-of **10** impossible, improbable, incredible, outrageous, staggering **11** implausible, incogitable **12** preposterous, unbelievable, unimaginable, unreasonable **13** inconceivable

**unthinking**
**04** rash, rude **06** unkind, vacant **08** careless, heedless, impolite, knee-jerk, tactless **09** automatic, impulsive, negligent, Pavlovian **10** incogitant, indiscreet, mechanical **11** insensitive, instinctive, involuntary, thoughtless, unconscious **12** undiplomatic, unrespective **13** inconsiderate

**unthinkingly**
**06** rashly, rudely **08** stupidly **09** foolishly **10** carelessly, impolitely, recklessly, tactlessly **11** unfeelingly **12** indiscreetly **13** inattentively, insensitively, thoughtlessly **15** inconsiderately

**untidily**
**07** dirtily, messily **08** sloppily **09** scruffily **10** disorderly, sluttishly **11** chaotically **12** topsy-turvily **13** shambolically **15** like a dog's dinner

**untidy**
◇ *anagram indicator*
**04** foul **05** dirty, messy, ratty, tatty **06** sloppy **07** chaotic, haywire, jumbled, muddled, raunchy, rumpled, scruffy, unkempt **08** slipshod, slovenly, sluttish **09** cluttered, shambolic **10** bedraggled, disorderly, slatternly, topsy-turvy **11** dishevelled **12** disorganized, unsystematic

**untie**
**04** free, undo **05** loose, solve **06** loosen, unbind, unknit, unknot, unwrap **07** release, resolve, unhitch, untruss **08** unfasten

**until**
**02** to **04** till, unto, up to **05** hasta, prior, while **06** before, up till **07** prior to **08** as late as **11** earlier than, up to the time

**untimely**
**05** early **07** awkward **08** ill-timed, immature, timeless **09** importune, premature **10** malapropos, unsuitable **11** inopportune, prematurely, unfortunate **12** inauspicious, inconvenient, infelicitous, intempestive, unseasonable, unseasonably **13** inappropriate, inopportunely

**untiring**
**06** dogged, steady **07** devoted, staunch **08** constant, resolute, tireless **09** dedicated, incessant, tenacious, unceasing, unfailing **10** determined, persistent, unflagging **11** persevering, unfaltering, unremitting **13** indefatigable

**untold**
**08** infinite **09** boundless, countless, uncounted **10** unnumbered, unreckoned **11** innumerable, measureless, uncountable, undreamed-of, unutterable **12** immeasurable, incalculable, unimaginable **13** inconceivable, indescribable, inexhaustible, inexpressible

**untouched**
**04** safe **06** intact, unhurt, virgin **08** pristine, unharmed **09** unaltered, unchanged, undamaged, uninjured, unscathed, unstirred **10** unaffected, unimpaired, unrivalled **11** unimpressed

**untoward**
**05** amiss **07** adverse, awkward, froward, ominous, unlucky **08** annoying, contrary, ill-timed, improper, unseemly, untimely, worrying **09** unfitting, vexatious **10** disastrous, indecorous, irritating, unbecoming, unexpected, unsuitable **11** inopportune, troublesome, unfortunate **12** inauspicious, inconvenient, unfavourable, unpropitious **13** inappropriate

**untrained**
**03** raw **06** unbred **07** amateur **08** inexpert, untaught **09** unskilled **10** uneducated, unschooled **11** incompetent, unpractised, unqualified **13** inexperienced, undisciplined **14** unprofessional

**untried**
**03** new **05** novel **08** unproved, untested **10** innovative, innovatory **11** exploratory **12** experimental **13** unestablished

**untroubled**
**04** calm, cool **06** placid, serene, steady **08** composed, peaceful, tranquil **09** impassive, unexcited, unruffled, unstirred, unworried **11** unconcerned, undisturbed, unflappable, unflustered, unperturbed **14** inapprehensive

**untrue**
◇ *anagram indicator*
**05** false, wrong **06** made-up, mythic **07** inexact, untruly **08** disloyal, mistaken, mythical, two-faced **09** deceitful, deceptive, dishonest, erroneous, incorrect, legendary, trumped-up, two-timing **10** fabricated, fallacious, fraudulent, inaccurate, misleading, perfidious, unfaithful, unofficial, untruthful **11** inauthentic **12** untruthfully **13** untrustworthy

**untrustworthy**
**05** false **06** fickle, sleeky, slippy, unsure, untrue **08** disloyal, slippery, two-faced, untrusty **09** deceitful, dishonest, faithless **10** capricious, fly-by-night, unfaithful, unreliable, untruthful **11** duplicitous, treacherous **12** disreputable **13** dishonourable

**untruth**
**03** fib, lie **04** crap, tale **05** false, lying, porky, story **06** deceit **07** falsity, fiction, perjury, whopper **09** falsehood, falseness, invention, tall story **10** inveracity **11** fabrication, made-up story **14** unfaithfulness, untruthfulness

**untruthful**
**05** false, lying **06** untrue **07** crooked **08** invented, two-faced **09** deceitful, dishonest, erroneous, fictional, insincere **10** fabricated, fallacious, mendacious **11** unveracious **12** hypocritical

**untutored**
**06** simple **07** artless **08** ignorant, inexpert, unversed **09** unlearned, unrefined, untrained **10** illiterate, uneducated, unlessoned, unschooled **11** unpractised **12** uninstructed **13** inexperienced **15** unsophisticated

**untwine**
**06** uncoil, unwind **07** unravel, untwist **10** disentwine

**untwist**
**05** ravel, unlay **06** detort, uncoil, unwind **07** unravel, untwine

**unused**
**03** new **04** idle **05** blank, clean, extra, fresh, spare **06** maiden **07** surplus, unusual **08** left over, pristine, untapped, unwonted **09** available, remaining, untouched **10** unemployed, unfamiliar **11** unexploited, unpractised **12** unaccustomed, unacquainted **13** inexperienced

**unusual**
◇ *anagram indicator*
**03** odd **04** rare, unco **05** freak, kinky, queer, weird **06** exotic, freaky, unwont **07** bizarre, curious, offbeat, special, strange **08** abnormal, atypical, freakish, peculiar, singular, uncommon, unwonted **09** anomalous, different, eccentric, irregular **10** phenomenal, remarkable, surprising, unexpected, unfamiliar, unorthodox **11** exceptional, out of the way **12** unacquainted **13** extraordinary, unprecedented **14** unconventional

*See also* **strange**

**unusually**
◇ *anagram indicator*
**04** very **05** oddly **08** devilish **09** bizarrely, curiously, extremely **10** especially, peculiarly, remarkably, singularly **11** exceedingly **12** particularly, prodigiously, tremendously **13** exceptionally **15** extraordinarily

**unutterable**
**07** extreme **09** egregious, ineffable, nefandous **11** unspeakable **12** overwhelming, unimaginable **13** indescribable, inexpressible

**unvarnished**
**04** bare, pure **05** frank, naked, plain, sheer, stark **06** candid, honest, simple **07** sincere **09** unadorned **11** undisguised **13** unembellished **15** straightforward

**unveil**
**04** bare **06** betray, expose, reveal, unmask **07** divulge, lay bare, lay open, uncover **08** disclose, discover **09** make known **11** disenshroud **12** bring to light **13** take the lid off

**unwanted**
**05** extra **06** otiose **07** outcast, surplus, useless **08** rejected, unneeded **09** discarded, redundant, undesired, uninvited, unwelcome **10** unrequired **11** superfluous, unnecessary, unsolicited

**unwarranted**
**05** wrong **06** unjust **10** gratuitous, groundless, undeserved, unprovoked **11** inexcusable, uncalled-for, unjustified, unnecessary **12** indefensible, unreasonable **13** unjustifiable

**unwary**
**04** rash **05** hasty **08** careless, heedless, off guard, reckless **09** imprudent, unguarded **10** incautious, indiscreet, unthinking **11** thoughtless

**unwashed**
**04** dark, dull, foul, miry **05** black, dirty, dusty, grimy, manky, messy, mucky, muddy, slimy, sooty, yucky **06** chatty, clarty, cloudy, cruddy, filthy, greasy, grotty, grubby, grungy, scungy, shabby, soiled **07** clouded, defiled, grufted, scruffy, squalid, stained, sullied, unclean **08** polluted, unsoaped **09** tarnished **10** flea-bitten, insanitary, unhygienic

• **the great unwashed**
**05** plebs **06** the mob **07** the herd **08** riff-raff, the crowd **09** the crowds, the masses, the rabble **12** the hoi polloi **13** the lower class **14** the proletariat, the rank and file **15** the common people, the lower classes, the working class

**unwavering**
**06** steady, sturdy **07** staunch **08** resolute, unshaken, untiring **09** dedicated, rock-solid, steadfast, tenacious **10** consistent, determined, unflagging, unshakable, unswerving **11** down-the-line, undeviating, unfaltering, unshakeable **12** single-minded **13** unquestioning

**unwelcome**
**08** excluded, rejected, unwanted, worrying **09** uninvited, unpopular, upsetting **10** unpleasant **11** distasteful, undesirable, unpalatable **12** disagreeable, unacceptable

**unwell**
**03** bad, ill **04** ropy, sick **05** badly, crook, dicky, queer, ropey, rough, unfit, warby **06** ailing, groggy, poorly, sickly **07** run down **09** in a bad way, off-colour, unhealthy **10** indisposed, out of sorts **15** under the weather

**unwholesome**
**03** bad, wan **04** evil, junk, pale **05** pasty **06** morbid, pallid, sickly, wicked **07** anaemic, harmful, immoral, noxious, tainted, unsound **08** epinosic **09** degrading, depraving, poisonous, unhealthy **10** corrupting, insalutary, insanitary, perverting, unhygienic **12** demoralizing, innutritious, insalubrious

**unwieldy**
**05** bulky, hefty **06** clumsy **07** awkward, hulking, massive, weighty **08** cumbrous, ungainly **09** ponderous **10** cumbersome **12** incommodious, inconvenient, unmanageable

**unwilling**
**04** loth, slow **05** loath **06** averse **07** opposed **08** backward, grudging, hesitant, loathful **09** reluctant, repugnant, resistant **10** indisposed **11** disinclined **13** unintentional **14** not having any of, unenthusiastic

**unwillingness**
**08** nolition, slowness **09** hesitancy, objection **10** reluctance **12** backwardness, loathfulness **13** indisposition **14** disinclination

**unwind**
◇ *anagram indicator*
**03** veg **04** undo **05** chill, relax **06** cool it, unclew, uncoil, unreel, unroll, unwrap, veg out **07** slacken, unravel, unreave, untwist **08** calm down, chill out, wind down **09** hang loose **10** take it easy **11** disentangle **13** let yourself go, put your feet up **14** take things easy **15** let your hair down

**unwise**
◇ *anagram indicator*
**04** rash **05** silly **06** insane, stupid, unredy **07** foolish, unready **08** reckless **09** foolhardy, ill-judged, impolitic, imprudent, senseless **10** ill-advised, indiscreet **11** improvident, inadvisable, inexpedient, injudicious, thoughtless **12** short-sighted **13** ill-considered, irresponsible

**unwitting**
**06** chance **07** unaware **09** unknowing, unplanned, unweeting **10** accidental, unintended, unthinking **11** inadvertent, involuntary, unconscious **12** unsuspecting **13** unintentional

**unwonted**
**04** rare **07** strange, unusual **08** atypical, peculiar, singular, uncommon **09** unheard-of **10** infrequent, unexpected, unfamiliar **11** exceptional, uncustomary **12** unaccustomed **13** extraordinary

**unworldly**
**05** green, naive **08** gullible, innocent **09** ingenuous, spiritual, visionary **10** idealistic **11** impractical **12** metaphysical, otherworldly **13** inexperienced **14** transcendental **15** unsophisticated

**unworried**
**08** composed, downbeat **09** collected, unabashed, unruffled **10** undismayed, untroubled **11** unperturbed

**unworthy**
**04** base **06** indign, shabby **07** ignoble **08** improper, inferior, shameful, unseemly, wanwordy **09** unfitting, worthless **10** despicable, ineligible, unbecoming, undeserved, unsuitable **11** disgraceful, incongruous, unbefitting, undeserving **12** contemptible, disreputable **13** discreditable, dishonourable, inappropriate **14** unprofessional

**unwritten**
**04** oral **05** tacit **06** verbal **08** accepted, implicit, unpenned **09** customary **10** recognized, understood, unrecorded **11** traditional, word-of-mouth **12** conventional

**unwrought**
**03** raw **04** live, rude

**unyielding**
**04** firm, grim, hard **05** rigid, solid, stern, stiff, stout, tough **06** marble **07** adamant, granite, staunch **08** hardline, obdurate, resolute, stubborn **09** immovable, inelastic, iron-bound, obstinate, steadfast, unbending **10** determined, implacable, inexorable, inflexible, relentless, rock-ribbed, unwavering **11** intractable, unrelenting **12** intransigent, pertinacious **14** uncompromising

**unzip**
**04** free, open, undo **06** detach, loosen, unhook, unpack, unwind **07** release **08** separate **10** decompress

**up**
◇ *reversal down indicator*

**up-and-coming**
**05** eager **07** pushing **09** ambitious, assertive, go-getting, promising **12** enterprising

**up and down**
◇ *palindrome indicator*

**upbeat**
**04** rosy **06** bright, cheery **07** bullish, buoyant, hopeful **08** cheerful, positive **09** promising **10** favourable, heartening, optimistic **11** encouraging **14** forward-looking

**upbraid**
**04** twit **05** chide, scold, storm **06** berate, rebuke, upbray **07** censure, reproof, reprove, shake up **08** admonish, reproach **09** castigate, criticize, go crook at, go crook on, reprimand **10** exprobrate

**upbringing**
**04** care **07** nurture, raising, rearing,

tending **08** breeding, teaching, training **09** education, parenting **10** bringing-up **11** cultivation, instruction

**upcoming**
**04** near **05** close **06** at hand, coming **07** looming **08** imminent, in the air, on the way **09** impending **11** approaching, forthcoming, in the offing **12** on the horizon **13** about to happen, almost upon you **14** round the corner **15** fast approaching

**update**
**05** amend, renew **06** revamp, revise **07** correct, upgrade **08** renovate **09** modernize

**up-front**
**04** free, open **05** bluff, blunt, early, first, frank, plain **06** candid, direct, honest, sooner **07** advance, earlier, genuine, initial, primary, sincere **08** explicit, straight, truthful **09** downright, in advance, initially, outspoken **10** beforehand, forthright **11** hard-hitting, plain-spoken **12** introductory **15** straightforward

**upgrade**
**05** raise **06** better, uphill, uprate **07** advance, elevate, enhance, improve, promote **09** modernize **10** ameliorate, make better

**upheaval**
**05** chaos, upset **06** romage, uplift, upturn **07** rummage, shake-up, turmoil, upthrow **08** disorder, shake-out **09** confusion, overthrow **10** disruption, earthquake, revolution **11** disturbance

**uphill**
**04** hard **05** tough **06** ascent, taxing, tiring **07** arduous, onerous, upgrade **09** ascending, difficult, gruelling, laborious, punishing, strenuous, wearisome **10** burdensome, exhausting

**uphold**
**04** back, keep **06** defend, hold to **07** confirm, endorse, fortify, justify, promote, stand by, stand to, support, sustain, warrant **08** advocate, champion, maintain **09** vindicate **10** strengthen **11** countenance

**upkeep**
**04** care, keep **06** outlay, repair **07** oncosts, running, support **08** expenses **09** overheads **10** sustenance **11** expenditure, maintenance, subsistence **12** conservation, preservation, running costs **14** operating costs

**uplift**
◇ *reversal down indicator*
**04** draw, lift **05** boost, edify, elate, exalt, heave, hoist, raise **06** better, lift up, mark-up, refine **07** advance, collect, elevate, improve, inspire, raising, upgrade, upthrow **08** civilize, increase, upheaval **09** cultivate, elevation, enlighten **10** ameliorate, betterment, enrichment, refinement **11** advancement, cultivation, edification, enhancement, improvement **13** enlightenment

**upmarket**
**04** fine, high **05** prime, prize **06** choice, de luxe, select **07** quality, upscale **08** prestige, superior, top-notch **09** admirable, excellent, exclusive, expensive, first-rate, high-class, reputable, top-flight **10** first-class, respectful, unrivalled **11** exceptional, good-quality, prestigious **13** distinguished, par excellence

**upper**
**03** top **04** high, over **06** higher, senior **07** eminent, exalted, greater, loftier, topmost **08** elevated, superior **09** important, uppermost

• **upper hand**
**04** edge, sway **07** control, mastery **08** dominion, eminence, forehand **09** advantage, dominance, supremacy **10** ascendancy, domination **11** superiority

**upper-class**
**01** U **04** posh **05** élite, noble **06** plummy, swanky **07** toffish **08** cutglass, high-born, well-born, well-bred **09** exclusive, high-class, patrician, top-drawer **11** blue-blooded **12** aristocratic

**uppermost**
**03** top **04** main **05** chief, first, major **07** highest, leading, primary, supreme, topmost **08** dominant, foremost, greatest, loftiest **09** paramount, principal **10** pre-eminent **11** predominant

**uppity**
**05** cocky **06** swanky **07** stuck-up **08** affected, arrogant, assuming, snobbish **09** bigheaded, bumptious, conceited **10** hoity-toity **11** impertinent, overweening, toffee-nosed **12** presumptuous, supercilious **13** self-important

**upright**
**04** good, just **05** erect, moral, noble, sheer, steep, white **06** decent, honest, supine, worthy **07** ethical **08** straight, vertical, virtuous **09** elevation, reputable, righteous **10** high-minded, honourable, principled, upstanding **11** respectable, trustworthy, verticality **13** at right angles, incorruptible, perpendicular

• **set upright**
**04** cock, rear **05** erect **10** straighten

**uprising**
◇ *reversal down indicator*
**06** mutiny, putsch, revolt, rising **08** intifada **09** coup d'état, overthrow, rebellion **10** insurgence, revolution **12** insurrection

**uproar**
**03** din **04** flaw, hell, riot **05** noise, raird, rammy, reird **06** bedlam, clamor, dirdam, dirdum, émeute, fracas, furore, hubbub, mayhem, outcry, racket, randan, rumpus, tumult **07** clamour, garboil, ruction, turmoil, whoobub **08** brouhaha, disorder, hubbuboo **09** commotion, confusion, imbroglio **10** hullabaloo, rough music, turbulence **11** pandemonium **12** insurrection, katzenjammer, Pandaemonium **13** collieshangie

**uproarious**
**04** loud, wild **05** noisy, rowdy **07** killing, riotous **08** confused **09** clamorous, deafening, hilarious **10** boisterous, hysterical, rip-roaring, rollicking, rowdy-dowdy **11** rib-tickling **12** unrestrained **13** side-splitting

**uproot**
**04** weed **05** rip up **06** pull up, remove **07** destroy, root out, weed out, wipe out **08** displace, supplant **09** eradicate **11** averruncate

**upset**
◇ *anagram indicator*
◇ *reversal down indicator*
**03** bug, eat, tip **04** coup, cowp, hurt, purl **05** het up, shake, shock, spill, worry **06** bother, chew up, choked, dismay, grieve, gutrot, gutted, jangle, malady, put out, ruffle, sadden, shaken, take on, tip out, topple, upcast **07** agitate, ailment, annoyed, anxious, break up, capsize, confuse, disrupt, disturb, fluster, grieved, illness, jealous, overset, perturb, reverse, shake up, shake-up, trouble, unhappy, unnerve, uptight, worried **08** agitated, bothered, confused, dismayed, disorder, disquiet, distress, in a state, irritate, overturn, renverse, sickness, surprise, troubled, unsteady, upheaval, worked up **09** aggrieved, agitation, complaint, disturbed, flustered, in a bad way, knock over, mess about, overthrow, perturbed, shattered, unsettled **10** discompose, disconcert, disruption, distressed, mess around, traumatize, tumble over **11** coup the cran, destabilize, discomposed, disorganize, disturbance **12** disconcerted, perturbation, play hell with **13** play havoc with **14** discomboberate, discombobulate

**upsetting**
◇ *anagram indicator*
**08** alarming, assuming, worrying **09** conceited, overthrow, startling **10** disturbing, off-putting, perturbing, unsettling **11** distressing, frightening, overturning, presumption **13** disconcerting

**upshot**
**03** aim, end **05** issue, loose, proof **06** finish, pay-off, result, sequel **07** outcome, success **10** conclusion, dénouement **11** consequence, culmination

**upside down**
◇ *reversal down indicator*
**05** upset **06** turned **07** chaotic,

inverse, jumbled, muddled, up-ended **08** confused, inverted, messed up, upturned **10** disordered, in disarray, overturned, resupinate, topsy-turvy, wrong way up **11** wrong side up **13** heels o'er gowdy, heels over head

**• turn upside down**
**05** up-end, upset **06** invert, mess up **07** disturb, whemmle, whomble, whommle, whummle **08** demolish **09** overthrow **10** make untidy, topsy-turvy **11** disorganize **13** turn inside out

**upstage**
**03** top **04** beat, best **05** dwarf, excel, outdo **07** eclipse, outrank, surpass **08** outclass, outshine, outstrip, superior **09** transcend **10** overshadow, put to shame **11** stand-offish **13** put in the shade

**upstanding**
**04** firm, good, true **05** erect, moral **06** honest, strong **07** ethical, upright **08** virtuous **10** four-square, honourable, principled **11** trustworthy **13** incorruptible

**upstart**
**06** nobody **07** parvenu **08** jumped-up, mushroom **09** arriviste **10** new-fangled **12** nouveau riche **13** social climber

**upsurge**
**04** gain, hike, rise **05** boost, surge **06** growth, spread, step-up, upturn **07** advance, build-up **08** addition, increase **09** expansion, extension, increment, rocketing **10** escalation **11** development, enlargement, heightening, mushrooming, snowballing **12** augmentation, skyrocketing **13** proliferation **15** intensification

**uptight**
**04** edgy **05** angry, nervy, tense **06** hung-up, on edge, uneasy **07** anxious, prickly **09** irritated **11** strait-laced **12** conventional

**up-to-date**
**02** in **03** hip, new, now, rad **04** cool, gear **06** groovy, latest, modern, recent, trendy, with it **07** à la page, current **08** space-age, swinging **09** in fashion, prevalent **10** all the rage, present-day **11** fashionable, in the groove **12** contemporary **13** state-of-the-art, up to the minute

**• bring up-to-date**
**09** modernize

**upturn**
◇ *anagram indicator*
◇ *reversal down indicator*
**04** rise **05** boost **07** revival, upsurge, upswing **08** increase, recovery, upheaval **10** betterment **11** disturbance, improvement **12** amelioration

**upward, upwards**
◇ *reversal down indicator*
**03** top **06** rising, uphill **07** going up **08** moving up **09** ascending

**• upwards of**
**04** over **05** above **08** more than **09** exceeding **10** higher than, in excess of

**uranium**
**01** U

**urban**
**04** city, town **05** civic **07** built-up, oppidan **09** inner-city, municipal **12** metropolitan **13** megalopolitan

**urbane**
**05** civil, suave **06** smooth **07** elegant, refined **08** cultured, debonair, mannerly, polished, well-bred **09** civilized, courteous **10** cultivated **12** well-mannered **13** sophisticated

**urbanity**
**04** ease **05** charm, grace **06** polish **07** culture, suavity **08** civility, courtesy, elegance **10** eutrapelia, refinement, smoothness **11** cultivation, worldliness **12** mannerliness **14** sophistication

**urchin**
**03** elf, imp, kid **04** brat, waif **05** child, gamin, rogue **06** rascal **07** mudlark **08** hedgehog, hurcheon, townskip **09** hunchback **10** ragamuffin **11** guttersnipe

**urge**
**03** beg, hie, nag, yen **04** goad, hist, itch, need, prod, push, spur, wish **05** chevy, chirp, chivy, drive, egg on, fancy, force, impel, plead, press **06** advise, appeal, chivvy, compel, desire, excite, exhort, hasten, incite, induce, libido, threap, threep **07** beseech, counsel, enforce, entreat, impetus, implore, impulse, incense, longing, procure **08** advocate, persuade, perswade, yearning **09** cacoethes, constrain, eagerness, encourage, instigate, prompting, recommend, stimulate **10** compulsion **11** inclination

**• urge on**
**02** ca' **03** caa', egg, hie **04** edge, mush, spur **05** whoop, yoick **06** compel, giddap, giddup, halloa, halloo, hoicks, whet on, yoicks **07** giddy-up **09** instigate **11** whet forward

**urgency**
**04** need **05** haste, hurry, press **06** preace, prease, stress **07** gravity, preasse **08** clamancy, exigency, instance, instancy, pressure, priority **09** extremity, necessity **10** importance **11** importunity, seriousness **14** imperativeness

**urgent**
**04** dire **05** acute, eager, grave, prior, vital **07** crucial, earnest, exigent, instant, serious **08** critical, emergent, pressing, strident **09** emergency, essential, immediate, important, importune, insistent, necessary, strenuous **10** compelling, imperative, persistent, persuasive **11** top-priority

**urinate**
**02** go **03** pee, wee, wet **04** leak, whiz **05** slash, stale, urine, whizz **06** pee-pee, piddle, tiddle, tinkle, wee-wee, widdle **07** relieve **09** make water, micturate, pass water, take a leak **11** spend a penny **12** be taken short, ease yourself **13** be caught short **15** relieve yourself

**urn**
**04** olla **07** kitchen, ossuary, samovar **08** the Ashes **09** ballot box

**Uruguay**
**01** U **03** ROU, Uru, URY

**US**
◇ *dialect word indicator*

**usable**
**05** valid **07** current, working **08** fit to use **09** available, practical **10** functional **11** exploitable, operational, serviceable

**usage**
**03** law, use, way **04** form, mode, rule **05** habit, idiom, style **06** custom, method, usance **07** control, meaning, practic, routine, running **08** handling, parlance, practice **09** etiquette, formalism, modernism, operation, procedure, tradition, treatment **10** consuetude, convention, employment, expression, management, regulation **11** application, institution, phraseology, terminology **12** way of writing **13** way of speaking

**use**
◇ *anagram indicator*
**02** do **03** end, ply, try, ure **04** call, good, help, milk, need, work **05** abuse, apply, avail, bleed, cause, enjoy, point, right, spend, treat, usage, value, waste, wield, worth **06** custom, demand, draw on, employ, expend, follow, handle, misuse, object, profit, resort **07** ability, benefit, consume, exhaust, exploit, observe, operate, purpose, service, utilize **08** accustom, cash in on, deal with, exercise, impose on, occasion, practise, put to use, resort to **09** advantage, go through, habituate, make use of, manoeuvre, necessity, operation, privilege, regularly **10** employment, get through, imposition, manipulate, permission, usefulness **11** application, utilization **12** exploitation, manipulation, mistreatment **13** bring into play **15** take advantage of

**• used to**
**06** wont to **07** given to, prone to **08** inured to **10** adjusted to, at home with **11** practised in **12** accustomed to, familiar with, habituated to, in the habit of, no stranger to **14** acclimatized to

**• use up**
◇ *reversal down indicator*
**03** sap **04** burn, take **05** drain, spend, waste **06** absorb, devour, finish, peruse, work up **07** consume, deplete,

eat into, exhaust, fritter, tire out
**08** squander **09** go through

**used**
◇ *anagram indicator*
**04** wont, worn **05** usual **06** expert, soiled **07** cast-off **08** dog-eared, pre-owned **09** customary, nearly-new
**10** hand-me-down, second-hand
**11** experienced

**useful**
**04** able **05** handy, nifty **06** expert
**07** helpful, skilful, skilled **08** behovely, fruitful, valuable **09** competent, effective, practical, practised, rewarding **10** all-purpose, beneficial, convenient, functional, productive, proficient, profitable, worthwhile
**11** experienced, serviceable
**12** advantageous **14** general-purpose

**usefulness**
**03** use **04** good, help **05** avail, value, worth **06** profit **07** benefit, fitness, service, utility **08** efficacy
**09** advantage **10** efficiency
**11** convenience **12** practicality
**13** functionality **15** serviceableness

**useless**
◇ *anagram indicator*
**03** bad, dud **04** bung, idle, poor, ropy, vain, void, weak **05** awful, kaput, lousy, ropey **06** futile, grotty, no good
**07** botched **08** bootless, frippery, hopeless, pathetic, terrible, unusable
**09** fruitless, half-assed, incapable, pointless, to no avail, unhelpful, worthless **10** broken-down, clapped-out, effectless, unavailing, unworkable
**11** impractical, incompetent, ineffective, ineffectual, inefficient
**12** unproductive, unprofitable
**13** inefficacious **14** a load of garbage, a load of rubbish, good-for-nothing

**uselessness**
**08** futility, idleness **09** inutility
**10** ineptitude **12** hopelessness, incompetence **14** impracticality, ineffectuality **15** ineffectiveness

**usher**
**04** lead, show **05** guide, macer, pilot, steer **06** direct, escort **07** chobdar, conduct, marshal **08** Black Rod, huissier **09** accompany, assistant, attendant, introduce, usherette
**10** doorkeeper

• **usher in**
**06** herald, launch, ring in **07** precede
**08** announce, initiate **09** introduce
**10** inaugurate **13** pave the way for
**14** mark the start of

**usual**
**05** stock **06** common, normal, wonted
**07** average, general, ordinar, regular, routine, typical **08** accepted, customed, everyday, expected, familiar, habitual, ordinary, orthodox, standard **09** customary
**10** accustomed, exceptless, recognized, regulation
**11** commonplace, established, predictable, traditional
**12** conventional **13** unexceptional

**usually**
**03** usu **06** mainly, mostly **07** as a rule, chiefly **08** commonly, normally
**09** generally, in the main, on average, regularly, routinely, typically **10** by and large, habitually, on the whole, ordinarily **13** traditionally **14** for the most part

**usurer**
**05** gripe **07** Shylock **09** loan-shark
**10** gombeen-man, note-shaver
**11** money-lender **12** extortionist

**usurp**
**04** take **05** annex, seize, steal
**06** assume **08** arrogate, supplant, take over **10** commandeer **11** appropriate

**usury**
**06** excess **07** gombeen **08** interest
**09** extortion **12** money-lending

**Utah**
**02** UT

**utensil**
**04** tool **06** device, gadget
**09** apparatus, appliance, implement
**10** instrument **11** contrivance

*Kitchen utensils include:*

**03** bin, pan, wok
**04** etna, fork
**05** corer, ladle, mouli, sieve, tongs, whisk
**06** baster, bun tin, grater, juicer, karahi, mincer, peeler, shears, sifter, skewer, stoner, tureen, zester
**07** blender, cake tin, cleaver, cocotte, flan tin, grinder, loaf tin, milk pan, ramekin, skillet, skimmer, spatula, steamer, terrine
**08** blini pan, breadbin, colander, crêpe pan, cruet set, egg-timer, grill pan, ham stand, herb mill, mandolin, pie plate, saucepan, scissors, stockpot, tea caddy, teaspoon, wine rack
**09** bain marie, blowtorch, brochette, can-opener, casserole, corkscrew, dough hook, egg slicer, fish slice, fondue set, frying pan, gravy boat, mezzaluna, muffin tin, paella pan, pie funnel, punch bowl, sharpener, spice rack, tin-opener, toast rack
**10** breadboard, breadknife, butter dish, cook's knife, egg coddler, egg poacher, fish kettle, jelly mould, knife block, liquidizer, mixing bowl, nutcracker, pasta ladle, pasta maker, pepper mill, quiche dish, rice cooker, rolling pin, slow cooker, steak knife, storage jar, table knife, tea infuser, waffle iron, wine cooler
**11** baking sheet, boning knife, butter knife, cheese board, cheese knife, cooling rack, garlic press, melon baller, omelette pan, oyster knife, pastry board, pastry brush, potato ricer, roasting pan, sandwich tin, soufflé dish, tea strainer, thermometer, wooden spoon
**12** bottle opener, butter curler, carving knife, cheese slicer, deep-fat fryer, dessert spoon, egg separator, flour dredger, icing syringe, measuring jug, nutmeg grater, palette knife, pastry cutter, potato masher, pudding basin, pudding mould, salad spinner, serving spoon, yoghurt maker
**13** butcher's block, chopping-board, draining spoon, food processor, ice-cream scoop, kitchen scales, lemon squeezer, preserving pan
**14** measuring spoon, pressure cooker, straining spoon, vegetable knife
**15** grapefruit knife, meat thermometer, mortar and pestle

**utilitarian**
**05** lowly **06** useful **08** sensible
**09** effective, efficient, practical, pragmatic **10** convenient, functional
**11** down-to-earth, serviceable
**13** unpretentious

**utility**
**03** use, ute **04** good, help, tool **05** avail, value, worth **06** profit **07** benefit, fitness, service **08** efficacy
**09** advantage **10** efficiency, usefulness
**11** convenience **12** practicality
**15** serviceableness

**utilize**
**03** use **05** adapt **06** employ **07** exploit
**08** put to use, resort to **09** make use of
**13** turn to account **15** take advantage of

**utmost**
**03** end, top **04** best, last, most, peak
**05** final **07** extreme, hardest, highest, maximum, supreme **08** farthest, furthest, greatest, remotest, ultimate
**09** outermost, paramount
**11** furthermost

**Utopia**
**04** Eden **05** bliss **06** heaven **07** Elysium
**08** paradise **09** Shangri-la **12** Garden of Eden **13** heaven on earth, seventh heaven

**Utopian**
**04** airy **05** dream, ideal **07** Elysian, perfect, wishful **08** fanciful, illusory, romantic **09** fantastic, imaginary, visionary **10** chimerical, idealistic, unworkable **11** impractical

**utter**
◇ *homophone indicator*
**03** say **04** dead, emit, pass, pure, rank, talk, tell, vend, vent **05** outer, plain, sheer, sound, speak, stark, state, total, voice **06** accent, arrant, entire, goddam, put out, reveal, tongue
**07** declaim, declare, deliver, divulge, express, extreme, goddamn, perfect
**08** absolute, announce, complete, monotone, outright, positive, proclaim, thorough, vocalize
**09** downright, enunciate, goddamned, out-and-out, pronounce, verbalize
**10** articulate, consummate
**11** categorical, come out with, unmitigated, unqualified **12** put into words **13** thoroughgoing

**utterance**
**03** cry **04** talk, word **05** drawl, mouth, voice **06** remark, speech, tongue **07** comment, inanity, opinion **08** delivery, prophecy **09** outgiving, prolation, speech act, statement **10** expression, outpouring **11** declaration, enunciation **12** announcement, articulation, proclamation **13** pronouncement

**utterly**
**03** dog **04** dead, pure, rank **05** fully, plumb, stark **06** goddam, wholly **07** goddamn, totally **08** entirely **09** downright, goddamned, perfectly, to the wide **10** absolutely, completely, thoroughly **13** categorically

**U-turn**
**03** uey **07** wheelie **08** reversal **09** about-turn, backtrack, volte-face

**Uzbekistan**
**02** UZ **03** UZB

# V

**V**
**03** vee **06** victor

**vacancy**
**03** gap, job **04** hole, post, room **05** blank, place **07** inanity, leisure, opening, vacuity **08** idleness, position **09** blankness, emptiness, situation **10** inactivity **11** opportunity

**vacant**
**04** free, void **05** blank, empty, inane **06** absent, dreamy, unused **07** deadpan, vacuous **08** deserted, gaumless, gormless, not in use, unfilled **09** abandoned, available **10** unoccupied, unthinking **11** inattentive, uninhabited **12** absent-minded **14** expressionless

**vacate**
**04** quit **05** annul, leave, waive **06** unload **07** abandon **08** evacuate, withdraw

**vacated**
**03** red **04** redd

**vacation**
**03** vac **04** hols, long, rest, trip **05** break, leave **06** recess **07** holiday, leisure, non-term, time off, vacance, voiding **08** furlough, holidays **12** intermission

**vaccinate**
**03** jab, jag **07** protect, syringe **08** immunize **09** inoculate

**vaccination**
**03** jab **04** dose, shot **09** injection **11** inoculation **12** immunization

**vacillate**
◇ *anagram indicator*
**04** halt, sway, wave **05** haver, waver **06** didder, dither, teeter, waffle, wobble **07** whiffle **08** hesitate **09** fluctuate, oscillate, temporize **11** back and fill **12** shilly-shally, tergiversate **14** blow hot and cold, go back and forth

**vacillating**
◇ *anagram indicator*
**06** feeble **08** hesitant, waffling, wavering **09** spineless, uncertain **10** indecisive, irresolute, unresolved, willy-nilly **11** oscillating **15** shilly-shallying

**vacillation**
◇ *anagram indicator*
**06** waffle **08** wavering, wobbling **09** dithering, hesitancy **10** hesitation, indecision **11** fluctuation, inconstancy **12** irresolution, shilly-shally **13** temporization **14** indecisiveness, tergiversation **15** shilly-shallying

**vacuity**
**04** void **05** space **06** apathy, hollow, vacuum **07** inanity **08** idleness **09** blankness, emptiness **11** nothingness, vacuousness **12** listlessness

**vacuous**
**04** idle, void **05** blank, empty, inane **06** stupid, vacant **07** foolish **08** unfilled **09** apathetic **11** empty-headed **14** expressionless

**vacuum**
**03** gap, vac **04** void **05** chasm, space **06** Hoover®, lacuna **07** vacuity **09** emptiness **11** nothingness

• **vacuum flask**
**05** dewar **07** Thermos®

**vagabond**
**03** bum **04** hobo **05** caird, nomad, piker, rogue, rover, scamp, tramp **06** beggar, dosser, rascal, roving **07** dingbat, floater, gadling, gangrel, migrant, outcast, vagrant **08** clochard, cursitor, palliard, runabout, runagate, straggle, wanderer **09** itinerant, landloper, súndowner, unsettled **10** down-and-out, land-louper **11** rinthereout, scatterling, Weary Willie **12** hallan-shaker **15** knight of the road

**vagary**
**04** whim **05** fancy, prank, quirk **06** fegary, humour, megrim, whimsy **07** caprice **08** crotchet, rambling **10** digression

**vagrancy**
**08** nomadism **09** wandering **10** itinerancy, travelling **12** homelessness, rootlessness

**vagrant**
◇ *anagram indicator*
**03** bum **04** hobo **05** caird, derro, rogue, scamp, tramp **06** beggar, dosser, rascal, roving, truant, vagrom, walker **07** drifter, erratic, floater, gangrel, nomadic, roaming, tinkler **08** cursitor, homeless, rootless, straggle, stroller, vagabond, wanderer **09** itinerant, landloper, shiftless, uncertain, unsettled, wandering **10** inconstant, land-louper, travelling **11** rinthereout, scatterling **12** gang-there-out, hallan-shaker, rolling stone **14** circumforanean **15** circumforaneous

**vague**
◇ *anagram indicator*
**03** dim, lax **04** hazy **05** faint, foggy, fuzzy, loose, misty, rough, woozy **06** unsure, wander, woolly **07** blurred, evasive, general, inexact, obscure, of a sort, of sorts, shadowy, sketchy, unclear **08** nebulous, yonderly **09** ambiguous, amorphous, imprecise, uncertain, undefined, unfocused **10** ill-defined, indefinite, indistinct, out of focus, unspecific **11** approximate, generalized **12** undetermined, woolly-minded **13** indeterminate **14** transcendental

**vaguely**
◇ *anagram indicator*
**05** dimly **07** faintly **08** slightly, vacantly **09** distantly, inexactly, obscurely **11** imprecisely **14** absent-mindedly

**vagueness**
**07** dimness **08** haziness **09** ambiguity, faintness, fuzziness, looseness, obscurity **10** generality, impression, woolliness **11** imprecision, uncertainty **12** inexactitude

**vain**
**04** idle **05** empty, proud, vogie, waste **06** devoid, futile, hollow, snooty **07** foppish, haughty, stuck-up, useless **08** abortive, affected, arrogant, nugatory, vaporous, wasteful **09** bigheaded, conceited, coxcombic, fruitless, pointless, worthless **10** coxcomical, groundless, peacockish, sleeveless, swaggering, unavailing **11** coxcombical, egotistical, empty-headed, pretentious, swell-headed, thoughtless **12** narcissistic, ostentatious, unproductive, unprofitable **13** high and mighty, self-important, swollen-headed

• **in vain**
**04** no go **06** vainly **07** in waste **09** fruitless, to no avail, uselessly **10** for nothing **11** fruitlessly **13** ineffectually **14** unsuccessfully

**vainglorious**
**04** vain **05** cocky, proud **06** swanky **07** crowing **08** arrogant, boastful, bragging, puffed up **09** bigheaded, conceited **10** swaggering **11** egotistical **13** swollen-headed **14** self-flattering

**vainly**
**04** no go **07** for vain, to no end **09** to no avail, uselessly **10** for nothing **11** fruitlessly **13** ineffectually **14** unsuccessfully

**vale** *see* **farewell**; **valley**

**valediction**
**05** adieu, aloha **06** shalom, so long **07** goodbye, send-off **08** farewell **11** leave-taking **14** shalom aleichem

**valedictory**
**04** last **05** final **07** parting **08** farewell **10** apopemptic

**valet**
**03** man **06** Jeeves, lackey **07** lacquey **10** manservant **11** body servant **14** valet de chambre

**valetudinarian**
**04** weak **05** frail **06** feeble, infirm, sickly, weakly **07** invalid **08** delicate, neurotic **13** hypochondriac

**valiant**
**04** bold, prow **05** brave **06** heroic, mighty, plucky, strong **07** gallant, staunch **08** fearless, intrepid, valorous **09** audacious, dauntless **10** courageous, determined **11** indomitable, lion-hearted, redoubtable **12** stout-hearted

**valiantly**
**06** boldly **07** bravely **08** pluckily **09** gallantly, staunchly **10** fearlessly, heroically, intrepidly **11** audaciously, dauntlessly, indomitably **12** courageously **14** stout-heartedly

**valid**
**04** good, just **05** legal, sound **06** cogent, lawful, proper, strong **07** binding, genuine, logical, weighty **08** bona fide, credible, licensed, official **09** authentic, available, effectual **10** accredited, applicable, approbated, legitimate, meaningful, reasonable **11** justifiable, substantial, well-founded **12** acknowledged, well-grounded

**validate**
**06** attest, ratify, verify **07** certify, confirm, endorse **08** accredit, legalize **09** authorize, formalize **10** underwrite **11** corroborate **12** authenticate, substantiate

**validation**
**11** attestation, endorsement **12** confirmation, ratification **13** accreditation, authorization, corroboration, formalization **14** authentication

**validity**
**05** force, logic, point, vigor **06** vigour, weight **07** cogency, grounds **08** legality, strength **09** authority, soundness, substance **10** lawfulness, legitimacy **14** justifiability

**valley**
**03** cwm, den, ria **04** comb, dale, dean, dell, dene, gill, glen, park, vale, wadi, wady **05** combe, coomb, griff, grike, gryke, gulch, heuch, heugh, slade, Tempe, water **06** clough, coombe, dingle, graben, griffe, hollow, strath, Tophet, trough **07** Gehenna, wind gap **09** re-entrant

**valorous**
**04** bold **05** brave **06** heroic, plucky **07** doughty, gallant, valiant **08** fearless, intrepid, stalwart **09** dauntless **10** courageous, mettlesome **11** lion-hearted **12** stout-hearted

**valour**
**05** value, worth **06** mettle, spirit, virtue **07** bravery, courage, heroism, prowess **08** boldness, valiance, valiancy, war-proof **09** fortitude, gallantry **11** doughtiness, intrepidity **12** fearlessness **15** lion-heartedness

**valuable**
**04** dear **05** noble **06** costly, golden, prized, useful, valued, worthy **07** helpful **08** fruitful, precious **09** cherished, deserving, expensive, important, priceless, treasured **10** beneficial, invaluable, profitable, worthwhile **12** advantageous, constructive

**valuation**
**05** price, prise, prize, stent, value **06** extent, survey **08** estimate **09** appraisal, expertise **10** assessment, evaluation **11** stocktaking **12** appraisement

**value**
**03** use **04** cost, gain, good, prys, rate **05** merit, price, prize, worth **06** admire, assess, esteem, ethics, morals, profit, survey **07** benefit, cherish, respect, revere, utility **08** appraise, efficacy, estimate, evaluate, hold dear, treasure **09** advantage, standards **10** appreciate, excellence, importance, principles, usefulness **11** put a price on **12** desirability, significance **15** set great store by

- **of little value**
**03** low **05** cheap **06** common

- **something of little value**
**04** damn **06** button, trifle **10** boondoggle

**valued**
**04** dear **05** loved **06** priced, prized **07** beloved **08** esteemed **09** cherished, respected, treasured **14** highly regarded

**valueless**
**04** naff, poor **05** cheap **06** futile, paltry, trashy **07** trivial, useless **08** nugatory, rubbishy, trifling, unusable **09** pointless, worthless **10** unavailing **11** ineffectual, meaningless, unimportant **13** insignificant

**valve**

*Valves include:*

**04** ball, blow, gate, side, tube
**05** bleed, choke, clack, diode, heart, slide
**06** escape, mitral, mixing, needle, poppet, puppet, safety, triode, ventil
**07** exhaust, petcock, seacock, snifter, tetrode
**08** bicuspid, bistable, cylinder, dynatron, snifting, throttle, turncock
**09** air-intake, butterfly, induction, injection, magnetron, non-return, semilunar, thyratron
**10** Eustachian, thermionic

**vamp**
**05** Circe, flirt, siren **06** trudge **07** charmer, Delilah, Lorelei, patch up **08** coquette **09** temptress **10** seductress **11** enchantress, femme fatale

**van**
**02** RV **03** ute **04** wing **05** lorry, truck, wagon **06** camper, pick-up, waggon **07** caravan, minivan, trailer, utility **08** carriage, vanguard **09** advantage, Dormobile®, meat wagon, motor home, Winnebago® **10** baggage-car, black Maria, freight-car, mobile home, panel truck **11** patrol-wagon, railroad car **12** pantechnicon, utility truck **14** utility vehicle

**vanadium**
**01** V

**vandal**
**03** yob **04** lout, thug **05** rough, rowdy, tough **06** locust, mugger **07** hoodlum, mobster, ravager, ruffian, wrecker **08** hooligan **09** bovver boy, desolater, despoiler, ransacker **10** delinquent, demolisher **11** annihilator

**vandalize**
◇ *anagram indicator*
**04** ruin, sink **05** break, smash, trash, wreck **06** ravage **07** destroy, shatter, torpedo **08** demolish, write off **09** devastate

**vane**
**03** fan, web **04** fane, wing **05** blade, plume **07** dogvane **08** windsail **11** weathercock

**vanguard**
**03** van **04** fore, lead **05** front **09** forefront, front line, spearhead **10** firing line

**vanish**
**04** exit, fade **05** faint, ghost, leave **06** depart, die out, exhale **07** emanate, evanish, fade out **08** disperse, dissolve, evanesce, fade away, melt away, peter out **09** disappear, evaporate, fizzle out **11** go up in smoke **12** end up in smoke **13** dematerialize

**vanity**
**04** airs, pomp **05** folly, pride **07** conceit, egotism, foppery **08** futility, idleness, self-love, vainesse, vainness **09** arrogance **10** narcissism, pretension, snootiness, triviality **11** affectation, haughtiness, ostentation, self-conceit **12** extravagance **13** bigheadedness, conceitedness, dressing-table

**vanquish**
**04** beat, drub, lick, rout **05** crush, paste, quell, smash, thump **06** defeat,

hammer, humble, master, subdue, thrash **07** clobber, conquer, repress, trounce **08** confound, overcome **09** overpower, overwhelm, subjugate **10** annihilate **11** triumph over **15** make mincemeat of

**Vanuatu**
**03** VUT

**vapid**
**04** dull, flat, limp, weak **05** banal, bland, stale, trite **06** boring, flashy, jejune, watery **07** insipid, tedious, vacuous **08** lifeless, tiresome **10** colourless, wishy-washy **11** uninspiring

**vaporous**
**04** fumy, vain **05** foggy, misty **06** flimsy, fumous, steamy **07** gaseous **08** fanciful, halitous **10** chimerical **13** insubstantial

**vapour**
**03** fog **04** brag, damp, fume, haze, mist, reek, roke **05** boast, fumes, smoke, steam **06** breath **07** halitus, show off, swagger **09** evaporate **10** exhalation

**variable**
**01** X, Y, Z **03** var **04** Mira **05** Algol **06** factor, fickle, fitful, uneven **07** moonish, mutable, Protean **08** flexible, shifting, unstable, unsteady, wavering **09** fluxional, irregular, parameter **10** changeable, fluxionary, inconstant **11** chameleonic, fluctuating, vacillating **13** pulsating star, temperamental, unpredictable

**variance**
**04** odds **06** strife **07** discord, dispute, dissent **08** conflict, division **09** deviation, dichotomy, variation **10** alteration, difference, dissension, divergence **11** discrepancy **12** disagreement **13** inconsistency

• **at variance**
**03** odd **06** at odds, at outs **07** arguing **08** clashing **09** differing, out of step **10** in conflict **11** conflicting, disagreeing, quarrelling **13** at loggerheads **14** in disagreement

**variant**
◇ *anagram indicator*
**03** var **05** rogue **07** derived, deviant, variate, varying, version **08** modified **09** changeful, character, different, divergent, variation **11** alternative, diversified

**variation**
◇ *anagram indicator*
**05** pulse **06** change **07** fluxion, novelty, variant, variety, varying **08** variance **09** departure, deviation, diversity, saltation **10** alteration, alternance, difference, inflection, modulation **11** discrepancy, fluctuation **12** orthogenesis

**varied**
◇ *anagram indicator*
**05** dedal, mixed **06** daedal, motley, sundry **07** diverse, various **08** assorted **09** different **10** accidented **11** wide-ranging **12** multifarious **13** heterogeneous, miscellaneous

**variegated**
◇ *anagram indicator*
**04** pied **05** jaspe, paned, vairé **06** broken, motley, veined **07** brocked, brockit, clouded, dappled, marbled, mottled, various **08** distinct, speckled, streaked **09** checkered, chequered, dapple-bay, harlequin, proud-pied **10** poikilitic **12** varicoloured **13** multicoloured, parti-coloured, party-coloured

**variety**
◇ *anagram indicator*
**03** var **04** brew, kind, make, sort, type **05** brand, breed, class, color, range **06** change, colour, medley, strain **07** mixture, species **08** category **09** diversity, pot-pourri, variation **10** assortment, collection, difference, miscellany, subspecies **11** versatility **12** multiplicity **13** dissimilarity **14** classification

**various**
◇ *anagram indicator*
**04** many **05** mixed **06** motley, sundry, unlike, varied **07** diverse, several, varying **08** assorted, distinct **09** different, differing, disparate, uncertain **10** changeable, dissimilar, variegated **11** diversified **13** heterogeneous, miscellaneous

**varnish**
**03** lac **04** coat, dope **05** glair, glaze, gloss, japan, resin **06** dammar, dammer, enamel, lacker, mastic, polish, veneer **07** coating, lacquer, mastich, shellac **08** kauri gum, shell-lac **10** lacquering, nail enamel, nail polish **12** French polish, Japan lacquer, vernis martin **13** etching ground

**vary**
◇ *anagram indicator*
**04** hunt **05** alter, clash, range, spice, waver **06** change, depart, differ, modify **07** deviate, diverge, inflect, qualify, variate **08** be at odds, disagree, modulate **09** alternate, diversify, embellish, fluctuate, oscillate, permutate, transform **12** metamorphose

**vase**
**03** jar, jug, urn **04** ewer **05** diota, flask **06** hydria, luster, lustre, vessel **07** amphora, Canopus, pitcher, potiche **09** moon flask **10** Canopic jar, Canopic urn, cornucopia

**vassal**
**03** man **04** serf **05** liege, slave **06** client, thrall **07** bondman, servile, subject, villein **08** bondsman, liegeman, retainer **09** dependant **11** bondservant, subordinate

**vassalage**
**03** fee **04** fief **07** bondage, prowess, serfdom, slavery **08** thraldom **09** servitude **10** dependence, subjection, villeinage **11** subjugation

**vast**
**04** huge **05** great **07** immense, massive **08** colossal, cyclopic, enormous, far-flung, gigantic, infinite, sweeping **09** boundless, cyclopean, cyclopian, extensive, limitless, monstrous, unlimited **10** monumental, tremendous **11** appreciable, never-ending **12** considerable, immeasurable

**vastly**
**06** hugely **07** greatly **09** immensely, massively **10** enormously, infinitely **11** boundlessly, extensively, limitlessly **12** immeasurably **13** without limits

**vat**
**03** fat, tub **04** back, case, keir, kier, tank **05** cuvée, keeve, stand **06** barrel, girnel, tan-pit **07** wine fat **08** pressfat

**Vatican City**
**01** V **03** VAT

**vault**
◇ *anagram indicator*
**04** arch, dome, jump, leap, over, roof, span, tomb, vaut **05** bound, clear, crypt, embow, vaute, vawte **06** cavern, cellar, cupola, heaven, hurdle, spring **07** concave **08** leap-frog **09** cul-de-four, mausoleum, wagon roof **10** depository, repository, strongroom, undercroft, wine-cellar **11** safe-deposit **13** safety-deposit

**vaunt**
**03** gab **04** brag, crow **05** boast, swank **06** flaunt, parade **07** exult in, show off, trumpet **08** vanguard **15** blow your own horn

**veer**
**04** cast, tack, turn, wind **05** sheer, shift, slack, swing, wheel **06** broach, change, pay out, swerve, wester **07** box-haul, deviate, diverge, norther, peel off, souther, whiffle **09** come round

**vegetable**

*Vegetables include:*

**03** oca, pea, yam
**04** bean, cole, eddo, kale, leek, neep, okra, sium, spud, taro, wort
**05** chard, choko, cress, gumbo, laver, mooli, onion, swede
**06** bhindi, carrot, celery, chives, chocho, daikon, endive, fennel, garlic, lentil, manioc, marrow, pepper, potato, radish, rocket, sorrel, squash, tomato, turnip
**07** avocado, bok choy, cabbage, cardoon, cassava, chayote, chicory, lettuce, pak choi, parsnip, pumpkin, salsify, shallot, skirret, spinach, tapioca
**08** baby corn, beetroot, borecole, broccoli, capsicum, celeriac, cucumber, eggplant, finochio, kohlrabi, leaf beet, mushroom, red onion, soya bean, zucchini
**09** artichoke, asparagus, aubergine,

bean shoot, broad bean, calabrese, courgette, finocchio, mange tout, petit pois, red pepper, Romanesco, sweetcorn
**10** bean sprout, butter bean, French bean, lollo rosso, red cabbage, runner bean, swiss chard, watercress
**11** cauliflower, Chinese leaf, green pepper, lady's finger, spring onion, sweet potato
**12** marrow-squash, savoy cabbage, summer squash, turnip greens, winter squash, yellow pepper
**13** ladies' fingers
**14** Brussels sprout, Chinese cabbage, globe artichoke
**15** vegetable marrow

*See also* **bean**

**vegetarian**
**05** vegan, vegie **06** veggie **08** ovo-lacto **09** lactarian **11** Pythagorean

**vegetate**
**04** idle **07** moulder **08** go to seed, languish, stagnate **09** do nothing, rusticate **10** degenerate **11** deteriorate

**vegetation**
**04** sudd **05** flora, plant, trees **06** plants **07** flowers, herbage, verdure, vesture **08** greenery, savagery

**vehemence**
**04** fire, heat, zeal **05** force, power, verve **06** ardour, energy, fervor, vigour, warmth **07** fervour, passion, urgency **08** emphasis, fervency, strength, violence **09** animation, intensity **10** enthusiasm **12** forcefulness

**vehement**
**03** hot **04** keen, warm **05** eager **06** ardent, fervid, fierce, heated, strong, urgent **07** earnest, fervent, intense, violent, zealous **08** animated, emphatic, forceful, forcible, powerful, spirited, vigorous **10** passionate, thunderous **11** impassioned **12** enthusiastic

**vehicle**
**05** means, organ **06** agency, medium **07** channel **09** mechanism, transport **10** conveyance, instrument

*Vehicles include:*

**03** bus, cab, car, cat, fly, gig, HGV, tip, ute, van
**04** arba, biga, bike, boat, cart, drag, dray, duck, ekka, hack, Jeep®, kago, kart, scow, ship, sled, solo, tank, taxi, tram, trap, tube, wain
**05** araba, coach, cycle, lorry, plane, stage, sulky, train, truck, Vespa®, wagon
**06** bakkie, camper, hansom, hearse, Humvee®, jalopy, jinker, landau, litter, Maglev, sidecar, sledge, sleigh, surrey, tandem, troika, tuk tuk
**07** bicycle, caravan, dog-cart, minibus, minivan, omnibus, phaeton, Pullman, ricksha, scooter, sleeper, tractor, trailer, Transit®, trishaw
**08** barouche, brougham, Cape cart, golf cart, monorail, rickshaw, toboggan, tricycle, wagon-lit
**09** bobsleigh, buck-wagon, charabanc, motorbike
**10** boneshaker, four-in-hand, jinricksha, jinrikisha, juggernaut, motorcycle, post-chaise, Scotch cart, sedan-chair, service car, stagecoach, trolleybus
**11** caravanette, jinrickshaw, steam-roller
**12** double-decker, pantechnicon
**13** fork-lift truck, penny-farthing
**15** hackney-carriage

*See also* **aircraft**; **bicycle**; **car**; **carriage**; **ship**

*International Vehicle Registration codes include:*

**01** A (Austria), B (Belgium), C (Cuba), D (Germany), E (Spain), F (France), G (Gabon), H (Hungary), I (Italy), J (Japan), K (Cambodia), L (Luxembourg), M (Malta), N (Norway), P (Portugal), Q (Qatar), S (Sweden), T (Thailand), V (Vatican City), Z (Zambia)
**02** AL (Albania), AM (Armenia), AZ (Azerbaijan), BD (Bangladesh), BF (Burkina Faso), BG (Bulgaria), BH (Belize), BR (Brazil), BS (The Bahamas), BW (Botswana), BY (Belarus), BZ (Belize), CH (Switzerland), CI (Côte d'Ivoire), CL (Sri Lanka), CO (Colombia), CR (Costa Rica), CU (Cuba), CY (Cyprus), CZ (Czech Republic), DK (Denmark), DY (Benin), DZ (Algeria), EC (Ecuador), ES (El Salvador), ET (Egypt), FL (Liechtenstein), FR (Faroe Islands), GB (Great Britain), GE (Georgia), GH (Ghana), GR (Greece), HK (Hong Kong), HR (Croatia), IL (Israel), IR (Iran), IS (Iceland), JA (Jamaica), KS (Kyrgyzstan), KZ (Kazakhzstan), LB (Liberia), LS (Lesotho), LT (Lithuania), LV (Latvia), MA (Morocco), MC (Monaco), MD (Moldova), MK (Macedonia), MS (Mauritius), MW (Malawi), NA (Netherlands Antilles), NL (Netherlands), NZ (New Zealand), PA (Panama), PE (Peru), PK (Pakistan), PL (Poland), PY (Paraguay), QA (Qatar), RA (Argentina), RB (Benin), RC (Taiwan), RG (Guinea), RH (Haiti), RI (Indonesia), RL (Lebanon), RM (Madagascar), RN (Niger), RO (Romania), RP (Philippines), RU (Burundi), SA (Saudi Arabia), SD (Swaziland), SK (Slovakia), SN (Senegal), SO (Somalia), SU (Belarus), SY (Seychelles), TG (Togo), TJ (Tajikistan), TM (Turkmenistan), TN (Tunisia), TR (Turkey), TT (Trinidad and Tobago), UA (Ukraine), UZ (Uzbekistan), VN (Vietnam), WD (Dominica), WG (Grenada), WL (St Lucia), WS (Samoa), WV (St Vincent and the Grenadines), YV (Venezuela), ZA (South Africa), ZW (Zimbabwe)
**03** AFG (Afghanistan), AND (Andorra), ARM (Armenia), AUS (Australia), BDS (Barbados), BIH (Bosnia and Herzegovina), BOL (Bolivia), BRN (Bahrain), BRU (Brunei), BUR (Myanmar), CAM (Cameroon), CDN (Canada), DOM (Dominican Republic), EAK (Kenya), EAT (Tanzania), EAU (Uganda), EAZ (Tanzania), EST (Estonia), ETH (Ethiopia), FIN (Finland), FJI (Fiji), GAB (Gabon), GBA (Alderney), GBG (Guernsey), GBJ (Jersey), GBM (Isle of Man), GBZ (Gibraltar), GCA (Guatemala), GUY (Guyana), HKJ (Jordan), IND (India), IRL (Ireland), IRQ (Iraq), KWT (Kuwait), LAO (Laos), LAR (Libya), MAL (Malaysia), MEX (Mexico), MGL (Mongolia), MOC (Mozambique), NAM (Namibia), NAU (Nauru), NEP (Nepal), NGR (Nigeria), NIC (Nicaragua), PNG (Papua New Guinea), RCA (Central African Republic), RCB (Republic of Congo), RCH (Chile), RGB (Guinea-Bissau), RIM (Mauritania), RMM (Mali), ROK (South Korea), ROU (Uruguay), RSM (San Marino), RUS (Russia), RWA (Rwanda), SCG (Serbia and Montenegro), SGP (Singapore), SLO (Slovenia), SME (Suriname), SUD (Sudan), SVN (Slovenia), SYR (Syria), TCH (Chad), USA (United States of America), WAG (The Gambia), WAL (Sierra Leone), WAN (Nigeria), YAR (Yemen), ZRE (Democratic Republic of the Congo)

**veil**
**04** caul, film, hide, mask, mist, vail, vele **05** blind, burka, burqa, cloak, cover, scarf, scene, shade, veale, velum, volet **06** boorka, canopy, chadar, chador, kiss-me, mantle, purdah, shroud, sudary, weeper, wimple **07** bourkha, chaddar, chaddor, chuddah, chuddar, conceal, cover up, curtain, humeral, modesty, obscure, veiling, whimple, yashmak **08** chrismal, covering, disguise, kalyptra, mantilla, sudarium **09** encurtain **10** camouflage, lambrequin **11** concealment, kiss-me-quick

*See also* **scarf**

**veiled**
**06** covert, hidden, masked, secret **07** cloaked, covered, obscure **08** indirect, shrouded **09** concealed, disguised **13** surreptitious

**vein**
**03** rib **04** lode, mode, mood, seam, tone, vena **05** costa, nerve, style, tenor, varix **06** cavity, humour, marble, strain, streak, stripe **07** fissure, nervure, stratum **08** stringer **11** blood vessel, disposition, inclination, temperament

*Veins and arteries include:*

**05** aorta, iliac, renal, ulnar
**06** portal, radial, thread, tibial
**07** basilic, carotid, coeliac, femoral, frontal, gastric, hepatic, jugular, organic, precava, saphena, splenic
**08** axillary, brachial, coronary, postcava, praecava, superior, temporal, varicose, vena cava
**09** popliteal, pulmonary, spermatic
**10** innominate, mesenteric, subclavian
**11** common iliac
**14** anterior tibial
**15** brachiocephalic, posterior tibial

**veined**
**05** jaspe **06** venose, venous
**07** marbled **08** streaked **10** reticulate, variegated

**velocity**
**01** v **04** pace, rate **05** speed
**08** celerity, rapidity **09** fleetness, quickness, swiftness
**• velocity constant**
**01** k

**velvet**
**05** gains, panne **06** dévoré, vellet, velour, velure **07** mockado, velours
**08** chenille, suedette, winnings
**09** three-pile

**venal**
**04** bent **06** venous **07** buyable, corrupt
**08** bribable, grafting **09** mercenary
**10** simoniacal **11** corruptible

**vendetta**
**04** feud **06** enmity **07** quarrel, rivalry
**08** bad blood **09** blood-feud

**vendor**
**06** seller, trader **07** butcher, camelot
**08** merchant, salesman, stockist, supplier

**veneer**
**04** mask, show **05** front, gloss, guise, layer **06** façade, fineer, finish
**07** coating, display, surface
**08** covering, pretence **09** grass-moth
**10** appearance, lamination

**venerable**
**03** Ven **04** aged, Bede, wise **06** august
**07** revered **08** esteemed, honoured
**09** dignified, respected, venerated
**10** worshipped

**venerate**
**04** fear **05** adore **06** esteem, honour, revere **07** iconize, respect, worship
**09** reverence

**veneration**
**03** awe **05** dulia, honor **06** esteem, honour, latria **07** douleia, respect, worship **08** devotion **09** adoration, aniconism, reverence, sublimity
**10** hyperdulia, Mariolatry, Maryolatry
**12** symbololatry

**Venezuela**
**02** YV **03** VEN

**vengeance**
**03** utu **04** harm **05** curse, wrack, wreak **07** revenge **08** mischief, reprisal, requital **09** extremely, vengement **10** avengement
**11** exceedingly, retaliation, retribution
**• with a vengeance**
**05** fully **07** flat out, greatly **09** furiously, like crazy, to the full, violently
**10** forcefully, powerfully, thoroughly, vigorously **11** exceedingly, to the utmost, with a wanion **12** with a witness **13** energetically **14** to a great degree, to a great extent **15** with a wild wanion

**vengeful**
**08** avenging, punitive, spiteful
**09** rancorous **10** implacable, revengeful, vindictive **11** retaliatory, retributive

**venial**
**05** minor **06** slight **07** trivial **08** trifling
**09** excusable **10** forgivable, negligible, pardonable **11** permissible
**13** insignificant

**venom**
**04** hate **05** spite, toxin, virus **06** enmity, malice, poison **07** envenom, ill-will, rancour, swelter **08** acrimony
**09** animosity, hostility, poisonous, virulence **11** malevolence

**venomous**
**05** fatal, toxic **06** bitter, deadly, lethal
**07** baleful, baneful, noxious, vicious
**08** spiteful, viperish, viperous, virulent **09** malicious, malignant, poisonous, rancorous **10** malevolent, vindictive

**vent**
**03** air, gap **04** duct, emit, flue, hole, pipe, sale **05** salse, scent, sniff, snuff, utter, voice, wreak **06** crenel, escape, let out, market, outlet, smoker
**07** airhole, chimney, express, opening, orifice, passage, pour out, publish, release **08** aperture, blowhole, breather, emission, spiracle, vomitory
**09** discharge, solfatara **10** mud volcano **11** black smoker, let off steam, take it out on **14** counter-opening

**ventilate**
**03** air, fan **04** cool **06** aerate, debate, winnow **07** discuss, express, freshen

**ventilation**
**06** airing **07** cooling **08** aeration
**10** freshening

**venture**
**03** put **04** dare, jump, luck, mint, risk, sink **05** assay, fling, foray, stake, throw, wager **06** chance, gamble, hazard, venter, ventre **07** advance, exploit, imperil, presume, pretend, project, suggest **08** be so bold, endanger, make bold **09** adventure, endeavour, operation, promotion, speculate, volunteer **10** enterprise, prostitute, put forward **11** speculation, undertaking
**14** take the liberty

**venturesome**
**04** bold **05** brave, risky **06** daring, plucky **07** doughty **08** fearless, intrepid, spirited **09** audacious, daredevil, dauntless **10** courageous
**11** adventurous **12** enterprising

**venue** *see* **stadium**

**venus**
**04** clam **05** cohog **06** copper, Hesper, quahog, venery, vesper **07** Lucifer, quahaug **08** Hesperus **09** Aphrodite, round clam **11** evening star, morning star

**veracious**
**04** true **05** exact, frank **06** honest
**07** factual, genuine **08** accurate, credible, faithful, truthful

**veracity**
**05** truth **07** candour, honesty, probity
**08** accuracy **09** frankness, integrity, rectitude **10** exactitude **12** truthfulness

**veranda**
**05** lanai, porch, stoep, stoop **06** piazza
**07** decking, gallery, terrace, viranda, virando

**verbal**
◇ *homophone indicator*
**04** oral, said **05** abuse, vocal **06** insult, spoken **07** literal, uttered, voluble
**09** invective **10** articulate, linguistic
**11** word-of-mouth

**verbalize**
**03** say **04** tell, word **05** speak, state, utter, voice **06** assert, convey, report
**07** declare, get over, put over
**08** announce, point out **09** enunciate, formulate, pronounce, put across
**10** articulate, put in words
**11** communicate, give voice to **12** put into words

**verbatim**
**07** closely, exactly **09** literally, precisely
**11** to the letter, word for word

**verbiage**
**06** waffle **07** wordage, wording
**08** pleonasm **09** prolixity, verbosity
**10** repetition **11** periphrasis, perissology **14** circumlocution

**verbose**
**05** gassy, windy, wordy **06** prolix
**07** diffuse, voluble, wordish
**09** garrulous **10** long-winded, loquacious, pleonastic **12** periphrastic
**14** circumlocutory

**verbosity**
**08** verbiage **09** garrulity, loquacity, prolixity, windiness, wordiness
**10** logorrhoea, multiloquy **14** long-windedness, loquaciousness

**verdant**
**04** lush **05** fresh, green, leafy, virid
**06** virent **11** viridescent

**verdict**
**05** vardy **06** ruling, verdit **07** finding, opinion **08** decision, judgment, recovery, sentence **09** judgement
**10** assessment, conclusion
**12** adjudication, rough justice

**verdure**
**05** grass **07** foliage, greenth, herbage, leafage **08** greenery, verdancy, viridity **09** freshness, greenness **12** viridescence

**verge**
**03** rim, rod **04** brim, edge, pale, tend **05** brink, limit, merge, point, range, scope, slope, touch, virge **06** border, edging, margin, trench **07** horizon, incline **08** boundary, precinct **09** threshold **11** long paddock **12** jurisdiction

• **verge on**
**04** near **08** approach, border on **11** come close to, tend towards

**verification**
**05** audit, proof **08** checking **10** validation **11** attestation **12** ascertaining, confirmation, constatation **13** corroboration **14** authentication, substantiation

**verify**
**05** audit, check, prove **06** attest **07** bear out, confirm, support **08** accredit, validate **09** ascertain **11** corroborate **12** authenticate, substantiate

**verisimilitude**
**07** realism **09** semblance **10** likeliness **11** credibility, resemblance, ring of truth **12** authenticity, plausibility **13** vraisemblance

**veritable**
**04** fair, rank, real, true **05** right, sheer, utter **06** actual **07** genuine, perfect, regular **08** absolute, complete, outright, positive, thorough **09** out-and-out **10** consummate **11** unmitigated

**verity**
**05** sooth, truth **07** reality **08** validity, veracity **09** actuality, soundness **12** authenticity, truthfulness

**vermin**

*Vermin include:*

**03** rat
**04** lice, mice, moth
**05** louse, mouse
**06** pigeon, weevil
**09** cockroach

*See also* **rodent**

**Vermont**
**02** VT

**vermouth**
**02** It **06** French **07** Cinzano®, Martini®

**vernacular**
**05** idiom, lingo, local **06** common, jargon, native, speech, tongue, vulgar **07** dialect, endemic, popular, trivial **08** informal, language, parlance **09** idioticon **10** colloquial, indigenous **12** vulgar tongue

**Veronica**
**04** Hebe **09** speedwell

**versatile**
◇ *anagram indicator*
**05** handy **07** Protean **08** all-round, flexible, unsteady, variable **09** adaptable, many-sided **10** adjustable, all-purpose, changeable **12** multifaceted, multipurpose

**verse**
**01** v **04** line, rime, sijo, vers **05** haiku, Ionic, meter, metre, rhyme **06** heroic, jingle, poetry, riddle, stanza **07** doggrel, elegiac, iambics, Leonine, pennill, stichos, strophe, versify **08** doggerel, elegiacs, glyconic, singsong, trochaic, versicle **09** amphigory, vers libre **11** acatalectic, septenarius **12** Archilochian, nursery rhyme **13** vers de société, vers d'occasion, versification

**versed**
**02** up **04** deep, read **06** strong, traded, turned **07** learned, perfect, skilled, studied, versant **08** deep-read, familiar, overseen, reversed, scienced, seasoned **09** competent, practised **10** conversant, proficient **11** experienced **13** knowledgeable

**versifier**
**04** poet **06** rhymer, verser **07** poetess, rhymist **09** metrifier, poetaster, poeticule, rhymester **10** verse-maker, verse-smith **11** verse-monger **12** versificator

**version**
◇ *anagram indicator*
**02** EV, NV, RV **04** form, kind, sort, type **05** cover, Itala, model, style **06** design, report, Rev Ver, Targum, update **07** account, edition, reading, turning, variant **08** rough cut **09** microcosm, portrayal, rendering **10** adaptation, paraphrase **11** translation **14** interpretation, King James Bible

**versus**
**01** v **02** vs **06** facing **07** against, playing **08** opposing **09** as against, instead of **10** rather than **11** as opposed to **12** in contrast to **14** in opposition to

**vertex**
**03** top **04** acme, apex, peak **05** crown **06** apogee, height, summit, zenith **08** pinnacle **09** extremity **12** highest point

**vertical**
**05** apeak, apeek, erect, on end, plumb, sheer **07** upright **10** straight up, upstanding **13** perpendicular

**vertigo**
**06** megrim **09** dizziness, giddiness, wooziness **15** light-headedness

**verve**
**03** zip **04** brio, dash, élan, life **05** force, gusto **06** energy, relish, spirit, vigour, whammo **07** fervour, passion, pizzazz, sparkle **08** vitality, vivacity **09** animation **10** enthusiasm, liveliness

**very**
**01** v **02** ae **03** e'er, way **04** ever, fell, mega, mere, pure, real, same, self, très, true, unco **05** assai, awful, dooms, exact, hefty, ideal, jolly, molto, plain, quite, sheer, stiff, truly, utter **06** actual, as hell, damned, deeply, dogged, ever so, highly, mighty, pretty, proper, really, simple **07** acutely, all that, awfully, genuine, good and, gradely, greatly, hell of a, hellova, helluva, majorly, only too, passing, perfect, precise **08** bitching, devilish, graithly, selfsame, spanking, stinking, suitable, terribly, uncommon **09** eminently, extremely, identical, unusually **10** absolutely, abundantly, incredibly, not a little, remarkably, uncommonly **11** exceedingly, excessively **12** particularly, unbelievably

**vessel**
**03** ark, jar, jug, pot, tun, vat **04** boat, bowl, ewer, ship **05** craft, plate **06** barque, holder **07** airship, pitcher, vassail, vessail **09** container **10** receptacle

*See also* **container**; **ship**

**vest**
**03** bib **04** garb, robe **05** drape, dress, endow, grant, lodge **06** bestow, clothe, confer, invest, semmit, supply **07** descend, devolve, empower, entrust, garment, singlet **08** sanction, vestment **09** authorize, waistcoat **10** undershirt **11** sequestrate

**Vesta**
**06** Hestia

**vestibule**
**04** hall **05** entry, foyer, lobby, porch **06** atrium, exedra **07** exhedra, hallway, narthex, portico, pronaos, tambour **08** anteroom, entrance **09** forecourt **11** oeil-de-boeuf **12** entrance hall

**vestige**
**04** hint, mark, sign **05** print, scrap, shred, token, touch, trace, track, whiff **06** relics **07** glimmer, inkling, remains, remnant, residue **09** footprint, remainder, suspicion **10** impression, indication

**vestigial**
**07** reduced **09** remaining, surviving **10** incomplete **11** rudimentary, undeveloped

**vestment**
**04** vest **09** vestiment

*Clerical vestments include:*

**03** alb
**04** cope, cowl, hood
**05** amice, cotta, ephod, frock, habit, mitre, scarf, stole
**06** mantle, rochet, saccos, sakkos, tippet, wimple
**07** biretta, cassock, chimere, humeral, maniple, pallium, soutane, tallith, tunicle
**08** chasuble, dalmatic, mozzetta, rational, scapular, skullcap, surplice, yarmulka
**09** dog-collar, phelonion

10 Geneva gown, omophorion, phaelonion, sticharion
11 Geneva bands, humeral veil
12 superhumeral
14 clerical collar

**vet**
**04** scan **05** audit, check **06** review, screen, survey **07** examine, inspect **08** appraise, check out **10** scrutinize **11** investigate

**vetch**
**03** ers **04** tare, tine **05** fitch

**veteran**
**03** old, pro **05** adept **06** expert, master **07** old hand, warrior **08** old-timer, seasoned **09** old stager, practised **10** campaigner, pastmaster, proficient **11** experienced, long-serving **13** battle-scarred, old campaigner

**veto**
**03** ban, nix **05** block **06** forbid, negate, reject **07** embargo, rule out **08** disallow, negative, prohibit, turn down **09** blackball, interdict, proscribe **10** thumbs-down **11** prohibition **12** proscription

**vex**
**03** bug, noy **04** fret, haze, hump, rile **05** annoy, grief, spite, upset, worry **06** bother, enrage, excess, grieve, harass, hassle, molest, needle, pester, put out, rankle, wind up **07** afflict, agitate, chagrin, discuss, disturb, hack off, perturb, provoke, tick off, torment, trouble **08** bepester, brass off, distress, irritate **09** aggravate, cheese off **10** exasperate

**vexation**
**03** noy **04** bind, bore, fury, pain **05** anger, pique, upset, worry **06** bother, plague **07** chagrin **08** headache, irritant, nuisance **09** annoyance **11** aggravation, frustration **12** exasperation **14** disappointment

*See also* **annoyance**

**vexatious**
**05** pesky **06** noyous, plaguy, trying, vexing **07** irksome, nagging, nimious, peevish, plaguey, teasing **08** annoying, fashious, worrying **09** pestilent, provoking, upsetting, worrisome **10** bothersome, burdensome, irritating, tormenting **11** aggravating, infuriating, pestiferous, troublesome **12** exasperating

**vexed**
**04** moot, sore **05** irate, riled, tough, upset **06** knotty, miffed, narked, peeved, put out, tricky **07** annoyed, awkward, debated, hassled, nettled, ruffled, worried **08** agitated, bothered, confused, disputed, harassed, provoked, troubled **09** contested, difficult, disturbed, flustered, in dispute, irritated, perplexed **10** aggravated, displeased, infuriated **11** exasperated

**viability**
**10** expedience **11** feasibility, possibility, workability **12** practicality **13** achievability **14** practicability, reasonableness

**viable**
**05** sound **08** feasible, operable, possible, workable **10** achievable, commercial **11** practicable, sustainable

**vibes**
**04** aura, feel **08** ambience, emotions, feelings **10** atmosphere, vibrations

**vibrancy**
**02** go **04** life, zest **05** oomph **06** energy, spirit, vigour **07** pizzazz, sparkle, stamina **08** strength, vitality, vivacity **09** animation **10** exuberance, get-up-and-go, liveliness

**vibrant**
**05** vivid **06** bright, lively **07** dynamic **08** animated, electric, resonant, spirited, striking, vigorous **09** brilliant, colourful, energetic, sparkling, thrilling, vibrating, vivacious **12** electrifying

**vibrate**
◇ *anagram indicator*
**03** jar **04** dirl, ring, sway **05** quake, shake, swing, thirl **06** dindle, dinnle, hotter, judder, quiver, shimmy, shiver, thrill, tingle **07** flutter, pulsate, resound, shudder, tremble, twinkle **08** brandish, resonate, undulate **09** oscillate, pendulate **11** reverberate

**vibration**
**03** jar **04** dirl **05** pulse, quake, throb **06** dindle, dinnle, hotter, judder, quiver, shimmy, thrill, tremor **07** diadrom, flutter, frisson, shaking **08** fremitus **09** juddering, pulsation, resonance, trembling **10** resounding **11** oscillation, seismic wave **12** seismic shock **13** reverberation, tremulousness

**vicar**
**03** Rev, Vic **06** cleric, curate, deputy, parson, pastor, priest, rector **08** chaplain, minister, preacher, reverend **09** clergyman **10** arch-priest, substitute **11** clergywoman **15** perpetual curate

**vicarious**
**06** acting **08** indirect **09** surrogate **10** empathetic, second-hand **11** substituted

**vice**
**03** sin **04** evil, flaw, grip, tool **05** fault, screw **06** defect, foible **07** blemish, buffoon, failing **08** bad habit, iniquity, weakness **09** depravity, evil-doing **10** bestiality, degeneracy, immorality, profligacy, wickedness, wrongdoing **12** besetting sin, imperfection **13** transgression

**vice versa**
**02** vv **09** inversely **10** conversely, oppositely **12** contrariwise, reciprocally

**vicinity**
**04** area **08** district, environs, locality, nearness **09** precincts, proximity **11** propinquity **12** surroundings **13** neighbourhood

**vicious**
**03** bad **04** foul, mean, vile **05** catty, cruel, nasty **06** bitchy, brutal, faulty, fierce, impure, lethal, morbid, savage, wicked **07** heinous, immoral, violent **08** depraved, impaired, mistaken, spiteful, unlawful, venomous, virulent **09** barbarous, dangerous, ferocious, malicious, malignant **10** malevolent, vindictive **11** bad-tempered

**viciously**
**06** wildly **07** cruelly **08** brutally, fiercely, lethally, savagely **09** violently

**viciousness**
**05** spite, venom **06** malice **07** cruelty, rancour **08** ferocity, savagery **09** brutality, depravity, viciosity, virulence, vitiosity **10** bitchiness, wickedness **11** malevolence **12** spitefulness

**vicissitude**
**04** turn **05** shift, twist **06** change **07** weather **08** mutation **09** deviation, variation **10** alteration, revolution **11** alternation, fluctuation

**victim**
**04** butt, dupe, fool, host, mark, prey **05** patsy **06** martyr, muggee, nebish, quarry, sucker, target **07** fall guy, nebbich, nebbish **08** casualty, fatality, murderee, paranoic, soft mark, sufferer **09** paranoeic, paranoiac, sacrifice, scapegoat **11** sitting duck **13** sitting target

• **fall victim to**
**05** catch **07** develop, fall for **08** contract **09** succumb to **10** fall prey to **11** be taken in by **12** be attacked by, be deceived by, be overcome by **14** be stricken with **15** become a target of

**victimize**
**03** con **04** dupe, fool, rook **05** bully, cheat, frame, shaft, sting, trick **06** fleece, pick on, prey on, rip off **07** deceive, defraud, exploit, swindle **08** hoodwink, stitch up **09** bamboozle, persecute **11** have it in for

**victor**
**01** V **05** champ, first **06** top dog, winner **08** bangster, champion **09** conqueror **10** vanquisher **11** pancratiast, prize-winner **13** victor ludorum

**Victoria**
**02** VR **03** Vic **04** Nike

**victorious**
**03** top **05** first **07** winning **08** champion, unbeaten **09** prevalent **10** conquering, successful, triumphant **11** vanquishing **12** prize-winning

**victory**
**01** V **02** VE, VJ **03** Jai, win **04** gree, Nike **07** mastery, success, triumph, winning

**08** conquest, squeaker, walk-away, walkover **09** checkmate, landslide **11** subjugation, superiority, triple crown

**• sign of victory**
**01** V

**victuals**
**04** chow, eats, food, grub, nosh, tuck **05** bread, scran **06** stores, viands **07** aliment, edibles, rations, vittles **08** eatables, supplies **10** provisions, sustenance **11** comestibles

**vie**
**03** bid **05** fight, rival, stake **06** strive **07** compare, compete, contend, contest, declare **08** corrival, struggle **09** challenge

**Vietnam**
**02** VN **03** VNM

**view**
**02** Vw **03** see **04** espy, idea, look, scan **05** angle, judge, range, scene, sight, study, vista, watch **06** aspect, belief, descry, gaze at, look at, notion, regard, review, sketch, survey, vision **07** account, examine, feeling, glimpse, inspect, observe, opinion, outlook, picture, purpose, thought, witness **08** attitude, consider, eyesight, panorama, perceive, portrait, prospect, scrutiny **09** intention, judgement, landscape, portrayal, sentiment, spectacle **10** appearance, assessment, conviction, estimation, impression, inspection, perception, scrutinize **11** contemplate, examination, expectation, observation, perspective **13** contemplation, range of vision

**• in view of**
**07** whereas **11** considering **13** bearing in mind

**• on view**
**05** shown **06** on show **07** showing **09** displayed, exhibited, on display, presented **10** made public

**viewer**
**07** goggler, watcher **08** observer, onlooker **09** inspector, spectator

**viewpoint**
**05** angle, slant **06** stance **07** feeling, opinion **08** attitude, position, prospect **10** standpoint **11** observatory, perspective, point of view

**vigil**
**04** wake **05** watch **07** lookout **08** stake-out, watching **10** deathwatch **11** wakefulness **12** pernoctation

**vigilance**
**05** guard, watch **07** caution **09** alertness **11** carefulness, guardedness, observation, wakefulness **12** watch and ward, watchfulness **13** attentiveness **14** circumspection

**vigilant**
**05** alert, awake, aware **07** careful, jealous, wakeful **08** cautious, wakerife, watchful **09** Argus-eyed, attentive, observant, wide-awake **10** on the watch, unsleeping **11** circumspect, on your guard **12** on the lookout, on the qui vive

**vigilante**
**05** guard, watch **07** lookout **08** sentinel, watchman **10** armed guard **11** watchperson **13** Guardian Angel, security guard

**vignette**
**03** act **04** plan, turn **05** cameo, draft, scene **06** design, sketch **07** diagram, drawing, outline **08** abstract, skeleton **14** representation

**vigorous**
◇ *anagram indicator*
**04** go-go, hard, rank **05** alive, brisk, green, hefty, lusty, round, sound, stout, tough, vital, vivid, young **06** active, bouncy, lively, manful, punchy, raucle, robust, rugged, sprack, strong, vegete **07** dynamic, healthy, intense, lustick, nervous **08** animated, athletic, forceful, forcible, lustique, muscular, powerful, spirited, swanking, youthful **09** energetic, gymnastic, strenuous **11** flourishing, full-blooded, gymnastical

**vigorously**
◇ *anagram indicator*
**04** hard **06** lively **07** briskly, eagerly, lustily **08** heartily, strongly **09** in a big way **10** forcefully, like billy-o, powerfully **11** like billy-oh, strenuously **12** like old boots **13** energetically

**vigour**
**03** pep, vim, zip **04** bant, birr, brio, dash, élan, fire, pith **05** flush, force, gusto, heart, might, moxie, oomph, power, verve **06** energy, health, spirit, stingo **07** pizzazz, potency, stamina **08** activity, dynamism, strength, virility, vitality, vivacity **09** animation, toughness **10** liveliness, robustness **12** forcefulness **13** vivaciousness

**vile**
◇ *anagram indicator*
**03** bad, low **04** base, evil, foul, mean, vild **05** nasty, vilde **06** horrid, impure, paltry, scurvy, sinful, wicked **07** beastly, corrupt, debased, earthly, noxious, scabbed, vicious **08** depraved, horrible, infamous, wretched **09** appalling, degrading, loathsome, miserable, obnoxious, offensive, repugnant, repulsive, revolting, sickening, villanous, worthless **10** degenerate, despicable, detestable, disgusting, iniquitous, nauseating, scandalous, unpleasant, villainous **11** disgraceful, distasteful **12** contemptible, disagreeable

**vileness**
**04** evil **06** infamy **07** outrage **08** baseness, foulness, meanness, ugliness **09** depravity, nastiness, profanity, turpitude **10** corruption, degeneracy, wickedness **11** noxiousness **13** offensiveness

**vilification**
**03** mud **05** abuse **07** calumny **09** aspersion, contumely, criticism, invective **10** defamation, revilement, scurrility **11** denigration, mud-slinging **12** calumniation, vituperation **13** disparagement

**vilify**
**04** slag, slam **05** abuse, decry, knock, slate, smear, snipe **06** berate, debase, defame, malign, revile **07** asperse, rubbish, run down, slag off, slander, traduce **08** badmouth, denounce, vilipend **09** denigrate, disparage **10** calumniate, stigmatize, vituperate

**village**
**03** vil **04** dorp, duar, gram, vill, wick **05** aldea, douar, dowar, kraal, thorp **06** hamlet, kainga, thorpe **07** clachan, endship, kampong, kirkton, outport **08** kirk town, township **09** borghetto, community, rancheria **10** Chautauqua, settlement

**villain**
**04** base **05** baddy, bravo, devil, heavy, knave, rogue **06** baddie, rascal, wretch **07** low-born, villein **08** criminal, escapado, evildoer, scelerat **09** miscreant, reprobate, scelerate, scoundrel, wrongdoer **10** malefactor

*Villains include:*

**04** Case, Cass (Dunstan), Hyde (Mr), Iago
**05** Bates (Norman), Doone (Carver), Queeg (Captain), Regan
**06** Lecter (Dr Hannibal), Oswald, Silver (Long John)
**07** Antonio, Bateman (Patrick), Blofeld (Ernst), Goneril
**08** Cornwall (Duke of), Injun Joe
**09** Voldemort (Lord)
**10** Darth Vader, Goldfinger (Auric), Richard III
**12** Aaron the Moor
**14** Bonnie and Clyde, Sauron the Great

**villainous**
**03** bad **04** evil, vile **05** cruel **06** gallus, sinful, wicked **07** debased, gallows, heinous, inhuman, roguish, vicious **08** criminal, depraved, fiendish, terrible **09** miscreant, nefarious, notorious **10** degenerate, detestable, iniquitous **11** disgraceful, opprobrious

**villainy**
**03** sin **04** vice **05** crime **07** badness, knavery, roguery **08** atrocity, baseness, disgrace, iniquity **09** depravity, rascality, turpitude **10** wickedness **11** criminality, delinquency

**vindicate**
**04** free **05** clear, right, salve **06** acquit, assert, avenge, uphold, verify **07** absolve, darrain, darrayn, deraign, justify, warrant **08** advocate, champion, darraign, darraine, maintain **09** darraigne, exculpate, exonerate **11** corroborate

**vindication**
**07** apology, defence, defense, support **08** apologia, theodicy **09** assertion **10** apologetic **11** exculpation, exoneration, extenuation **12** compurgation, verification **13** justification **14** substantiation

**vindictive**
**08** punitive, spiteful, vengeful, venomous **09** malicious, rancorous **10** implacable, malevolent, revengeful **11** retributive, unforgiving, vindicative

**vine**
**06** muscat **08** grape ivy, heartpea, muscadel, muscatel **09** ayahuasco, heartseed **10** wonga-wonga **12** winter cherry

**vinegar**
**05** eisel **06** alegar, eisell, energy, vigour **07** souring **08** wood acid **10** acetic acid

**vintage**
**03** cru, era, old **04** best, crop, fine, ripe, time, wine, year **05** epoch, prime **06** choice, gather, mature, origin, period, select **07** classic, harvest, quality, supreme, veteran **08** enduring, superior **09** gathering **11** high-quality

**viol**
**02** gu **03** gju, gue **05** quint, rebec **06** quinte, rebeck

**viola**
**04** alto **05** gamba, pance, pansy **06** paunce, pawnce, violet

**violate**
◇ *anagram indicator*
**04** rape **05** abuse, break, flout, fract, wreck **06** breach, defile, invade, molest, offend, ravish **07** debauch, defiled, despoil, disobey, disrupt, disturb, infract, outrage, profane, vitiate **08** infringe, stuprate **09** desecrate, dishonour **10** contravene, transgress **13** interfere with

**violation**
◇ *anagram indicator*
**04** rape **05** abuse, crime **06** breach, mopery **07** offence, outrage **08** invasion, trespass **09** injustice, sacrilege, vitiation **10** defilement, disruption, infraction, spoliation, stupration **11** desecration, profanation **12** infringement, private wrong **13** breach of trust, contravention, transgression

**violence**
**04** fury, rage, rape **05** force, might, power, wrath **06** frenzy, injury, tumult **07** cruelty, outrage, passion **08** ferocity, fighting, foul play, savagery, severity, strength, wildness **09** bloodshed, brutality, intensity, roughness, vehemence **10** aggression, fierceness, turbulence **11** hostilities, profanation **12** forcefulness

**violent**
◇ *anagram indicator*
**03** het, hot **04** high, rage, rank, rude, wild **05** acute, cruel, fiery, force, great, harsh, heady, hefty, rough, sharp, tough **06** brutal, fierce, savage, severe, stormy, strong, sturdy **07** drastic, extreme, flaming, furious, intense, riotous, rousing, ruffian, vicious **08** dramatic, forceful, forcible, maddened, powerful, slap-bang, towering, vehement **09** ferocious, hot-headed, impetuous, murderous, turbulent **10** aggressive, headstrong, outrageous, passionate, tumultuous **11** destructive, devastating **12** bloodthirsty, excruciating, ungovernable, unrestrained **15** blood-and-thunder

**violently**
◇ *anagram indicator*
**04** rank, slap **05** amain, tough **06** wildly **07** cruelly, greatly, sharply **08** brutally, fiercely, savagely, severely, slap-bang, strongly **09** extremely, intensely, viciously **10** powerfully **11** ferociously, hot-headedly, impetuously **12** aggressively, dramatically **14** uncontrollably, with a vengeance

**violin**
**02** gu **03** gju, gue, kit **05** Amati, strad **06** catgut, fiddle, leader **07** chikara **10** Stradivari **12** Stradivarius

• **violin part**
**03** nut, rib **04** back, neck, soul **05** belly, f-hole, table **06** bridge, button **07** bass-bar **08** purfling **09** sound post **11** fingerboard

**VIP**
**03** nib, pot **04** lion, star **06** bigwig, top dog **07** big name, big shot, magnate, notable **08** big noise, luminary, somebody **09** big cheese, celebrity, dignitary, personage **11** heavyweight

**viper**
**03** asp **05** adder **08** cerastes, mocassin, moccasin **09** berg-adder, river-jack **10** fer-de-lance **11** rattlesnake

**virago**
**04** fury **05** randy, scold, shrew, vixen **06** amazon, dragon, gorgon, randie, tartar **08** harridan **09** battle-axe, brimstone, termagant, Xanthippe

**virgin**
**03** new **04** girl, maid, pure **05** fresh, Virgo **06** chaste, intact, maiden, modest, vestal **07** Madonna, pucelle **08** celibate, maidenly, spotless, unspoilt, virginal **09** stainless, undefiled, unsullied, untainted, untouched **10** immaculate, unattained **11** unblemished, unexploited

**virginal**
**04** pure **05** fresh, snowy, white **06** chaste, vestal, virgin **08** celibate, maidenly, pristine, spotless **09** stainless, undefiled, untouched **10** immaculate **11** uncorrupted, undisturbed **15** parthenogenetic

**Virginia**
**02** VA

**Virgin Islands**
**02** VI **03** BVI, VGB, VIR

**virginity**
**05** honor **06** cherry, honour, purity, virtue **08** chastity, pucelage **09** innocence **10** chasteness, maidenhead, maidenhood

**virile**
**05** lusty, macho, manly **06** potent, robust, rugged, strong **08** forceful, muscular, vigorous **09** masculine, strapping **10** red-blooded

**virility**
**06** energy, vigour **07** manhood, potency **08** machismo **09** manliness **10** ruggedness **11** masculinity

**virtual**
**07** implied **08** implicit, in effect, virtuous **09** effective, essential, potential, practical **11** prospective **12** in all but name

**virtually**
**06** almost, nearly **08** as good as, in effect **09** in essence **10** more or less **11** effectively, practically **12** in all but name, to all intents

**virtue**
**04** good, plus **05** asset, merit, vertu, worth **06** credit, dharma, honour, valour, vertue **07** benefit, honesty, probity, quality **08** efficacy, goodness, morality, strength **09** advantage, attribute, rectitude, virginity **10** excellence, worthiness **11** saving grace **14** accomplishment, high-mindedness

*The seven virtues:*

**04** hope
**05** faith
**07** charity, justice
**08** prudence
**09** fortitude
**10** temperance

• **by virtue of**
**07** by way of, owing to **08** by dint of, thanks to **09** because of, by means of **11** on account of **13** with the help of

**virtuosity**
**05** éclat, flair, skill **06** finish, polish **07** bravura, finesse, mastery, panache **08** artistry, wizardry **09** expertise **10** brilliance

**virtuoso**
**06** expert, genius, master **07** maestro, prodigy, skilful **08** dazzling, masterly **09** brilliant, excellent

**virtuous**
**04** good **05** moral **06** chaste, decent, graced, honest, worthy **07** angelic, ethical, upright, virtual **08** innocent **09** blameless, continent, exemplary, righteous **10** honourable, upstanding **11** clean-living, respectable **12** squeaky-clean **13** incorruptible, unimpeachable **14** above suspicion, high-principled, irreproachable **15** beyond suspicion

**virulence**
**05** spite, venom **06** hatred, malice, poison, rancor, spleen **07** rancour, vitriol **08** acrimony, toxicity
**09** hostility, malignity **10** antagonism, bitterness, malignancy
**11** malevolence, viciousness
**14** vindictiveness

**virulent**
**05** fatal, toxic **06** bitter, deadly, lethal, severe **07** extreme, hostile, intense, vicious, waspish **08** spiteful, venomous
**09** injurious, malicious, malignant, poisonous, rancorous, vitriolic
**10** blistering, malevolent, pernicious, vindictive **11** acrimonious

**virus**

*Viruses include:*

**03** CDV, DNA, EBV, flu, FLV, HIV, HPV, pox, pro, RNA
**04** arbo, cold, ECHO, filo, HTLV, myxo, rota
**05** Ebola, flavi, hanta, irido, lenti, parvo, phage, retro, rhino
**06** baculo, calici, cowpox, herpes, papova
**07** oncorna, picorna, polyoma, variola
**08** morbilli, Vaccinia
**09** Coxsackie, influenza, papilloma
**10** hepatitis A, hepatitis B, hepatitis C, Lassa fever, leaf mosaic
**11** Epstein-Barr
**13** bacteriophage, parainfluenza
**14** human papilloma
**15** canine distemper

**visa**
**04** pass, visé **06** carnet, docket, permit
**07** licence, warrant **08** passport, sanction **09** green card **10** permission
**11** endorsement, safe-conduct
**13** authorization, laissez-passer
**14** permis de séjour

**vis-à-vis**
**06** facing **08** opposite **09** as regards
**10** face-to-face **11** over against **12** in relation to

**viscera**
**04** guts **06** bowels, vitals **07** giblets, innards, insides **08** entrails, gralloch, harigals **09** harigalds **10** intestines

**viscous**
**04** slab **05** gluey, gooey, gummy, stiff, tacky, thick, tough **06** glairy, mucous, sticky, viscid **07** treacly, viscose
**08** glareous **09** glaireous, glutinous, resistant **10** gelatinous
**12** mucilaginous

**Vishnu** *see* **incarnation**

**visible**
**04** open **05** clear, overt, plain
**06** patent, visual **07** evident, exposed, in sight, obvious, showing
**08** apparent, manifest, palpable
**10** aspectable, in evidence, noticeable, observable **11** conspicuous, discernible, perceivable, perceptible, unconcealed, undisguised
**12** recognizable **15** distinguishable

**visibly**
**06** openly **07** clearly, overtly, plainly
**08** patently **09** evidently, obviously
**10** manifestly, noticeably
**11** perceptibly **13** conspicuously

**vision**
**04** idea, look, view **05** dream, ghost, ideal, image, sight **06** glance, mirage, seeing, wraith **07** aisling, chimera, fantasy, imagine, insight, phantom, picture, spectre **08** daydream, delusion, eyesight, illusion, phantasm
**09** foresight, intuition, phantosme
**10** apparition, conception, perception, revelation **11** fata Morgana, imagination, mental image
**13** hallucination, mental picture **14** far-sightedness **15** optical illusion

**visionary**
**04** aery, seer **05** aerie **06** dreamy, mystic, unreal **07** dreamer, prophet, utopian **08** airdrawn, fanciful, idealist, illusory, quixotic, romantic, theorist
**09** fantasist, imaginary, moonshiny, prophetic **10** daydreamer, Don Quixote, far-sighted, idealistic, ideologist, ivory-tower, perceptive **11** impractical, translunary, unpractical, unrealistic
**13** impracticable, rainbow-chaser

**visit**
**03** gam, see **04** call, chat, mump, stay, stop, take **05** curse, haunt, pop in, smite **06** call by, call in, call on, come by, drop by, look in, look up, plague, punish, stop by, stop in, take in, wait on
**07** afflict, examine, inflict, inspect, sojourn, stop off, trouble **08** call in on, drop in on, frequent, go and see, go over to, stay with, stop in at, stop over, wait upon **09** call round, come round, excursion, first-foot, go round to, house call, stop off at **10** salutation, stop over at **13** spend time with

**visitation**
**05** trial, visit **06** blight, ordeal
**08** calamity, disaster, haunting
**10** appearance, infliction, inspection, punishment **11** catastrophe, examination **13** manifestation

**visitor**
**05** guest **06** caller **07** company, tourist
**08** manuhiri, stranger **09** traveller
**12** holidaymaker **13** bird of passage

**visor**
**05** sight **06** mesail, mezail, umbrel, umbril **07** umbrere **08** umbriere

**vista**
**04** view **05** scene **06** avenue, vision
**07** outlook **08** enfilade, panorama, prospect **11** perspective

**visual**
**05** optic **06** ocular, visive **07** optical, visible **08** specular **10** observable

**visualize**
**03** see **07** imagine, picture
**08** conceive, envisage, envision

**vital**
**03** key **05** alive, basic **06** lively, living, urgent, zoetic **07** animate, crucial, dynamic, vibrant **08** animated, critical, decisive, forceful, spirited, vigorous
**09** energetic, essential, important, necessary, requisite, vivacious
**10** imperative, life-giving, quickening
**11** fundamental, significant
**12** invigorating, life-and-death
**13** indispensable

**vitality**
**02** go **03** sap, zap **04** life, zest, zing
**05** juice, oomph **06** bounce, energy, fizzen, foison, spirit, vigour **07** fushion, pizzazz, sparkle, stamina, vivency
**08** strength, vivacity **09** animation
**10** exuberance, get-up-and-go, liveliness **13** vivaciousness

**vitally**
**08** urgently **09** crucially **10** critically, decisively **11** essentially, importantly
**13** fundamentally, significantly

**vitamin**

*Vitamins include:*

**01** A, B, C, D, E, G, H, K, P
**06** biotin, citrin, niacin
**07** adermin, aneurin, retinol, thiamin
**08** carotene, thiamine
**09** folic acid, menadione
**10** calciferol, pyridoxine, riboflavin, tocopherol
**11** menaquinone, pteroic acid
**12** ascorbic acid, bioflavonoid, linoleic acid
**13** linolenic acid, nicotinic acid, phylloquinone
**14** cyanocobalamin, dehydroretinol, ergocalciferol, phytomenadione
**15** cholecalciferol, pantothenic acid, vitamin B complex

**vitiate**
**03** mar **04** harm, rape, ruin **05** blend, spoil, sully, taint **06** blight, debase, defile, impair, injure, mucker, weaken
**07** blemish, corrupt, debauch, deprave, devalue, nullify, pervert, pollute, violate **09** undermine
**10** adulterate, invalidate
**11** contaminate

**vitriolic**
**06** biting, bitter **07** abusive, acerbic, caustic, mordant, vicious **08** sardonic, scathing, venomous, virulent
**09** malicious, trenchant
**11** acrimonious, destructive
**12** vituperative

**vituperate**
**03** nag **04** slag, slam **05** abuse, blame, knock, slang, slate **06** berate, rebuke, revile, vilify **07** censure, rubbish, run down, slag off, upbraid
**08** denounce, reproach **09** castigate
**10** blackguard

**vituperation**
**04** flak **05** abuse, blame, stick
**07** censure, obloquy **08** diatribe, knocking, reproach **09** contumely, invective, philippic, reprimand
**10** revilement, rubbishing, scurrility

**11** castigation, objurgation, slagging-off **12** vilification

**vituperative**
**05** harsh **07** abusive **08** sardonic, scornful **09** insulting, withering **10** belittling, censorious, derogatory, scurrilous **11** fulminatory, opprobrious **12** calumniatory, denunciatory

**vivacious**
**05** jolly, merry, smart **06** bright, bubbly, chirpy, lively **08** animated, cheerful, spirited, sportive **09** ebullient, in spirits, long-lived, sparkling, sprightly **12** effervescent, high-spirited, light-hearted

**vivacity**
**02** go **03** fiz, zap **04** brio, élan, fizz, life, zing **05** oomph **06** energy, spirit, vigour **07** pizzazz, sparkle, spirits **08** activity, dynamism, vitality **09** animation, merriness **10** ebullience, liveliness **13** effervescence

**vivid**
**04** live, rich, vive **05** clear, lurid, sharp **06** bright, lively, strong **07** dynamic, eidetic, glaring, glowing, graphic, intense, vibrant **08** animated, dazzling, distinct, dramatic, lifelike, powerful, spirited, striking, vigorous **09** brilliant, colourful, graphical, memorable, pictorial, realistic **11** picturesque

**vividly**
**06** richly **07** clearly **08** brightly, strongly **09** intensely, memorably, vibrantly **10** distinctly, powerfully **11** brilliantly, graphically **12** dramatically, flamboyantly

**vividness**
**04** glow, life **05** color **06** colour **07** clarity, realism **08** lucidity, radiance, strength **09** intensity, sharpness **10** brightness, brilliancy, refulgence

**viz**
**02** ie, sc **04** scil, sciz **05** to wit **06** namely, that is **08** scilicet **09** videlicet **11** that is to say **12** in other words, specifically

**vocabulary**
**04** cant **05** idiom, lexis, vocab, words **07** lexicon **08** glossary, language, wordbook **09** idioticon, thesaurus **10** dictionary **11** nomenclator **12** Basic English, nomenclature

**vocal**
◇ *homophone indicator*
**04** oral, said, sung **05** blunt, frank, noisy **06** phonal, shrill, spoken, voiced **07** uttered **08** eloquent, strident **09** expressed, outspoken, talkative **10** articulate, expressive, forthright, resounding, vociferous

**vocalize**
**03** air, say **04** sing, tell, vent, word **05** speak, state, utter, voice **06** assert, convey, report **07** declare, express, get over, put over **08** announce, intimate, point out **09** enunciate, formulate, pronounce, put across, ventilate, verbalize **10** articulate **11** communicate, give voice to **12** put into words

**vocally**
**10** eloquently, stridently **12** articulately, expressively, forthrightly

**vocation**
**03** job **04** line, post, role, work **05** craft, trade **06** career, métier, office **07** calling, mission, pursuit **08** business **10** employment, occupation, profession

**vociferous**
**04** loud **05** blunt, frank, noisy, vocal **08** shouting, strident, vehement **09** clamorous, outspoken **10** forthright, thundering **12** obstreperous

**vociferously**
**06** loudly **07** bluntly, frankly, noisily, vocally **10** stridently, vehemently **11** outspokenly

**vogue**
**03** fad **04** mode, rage **05** craze, style, taste, trend **06** custom **07** fashion, the rage **08** the thing **09** the latest **10** popularity **11** fashionable

**• in vogue**
**02** in **06** modish, trendy, with it **07** current, popular, stylish, voguish **09** prevalent **11** fashionable **13** up-to-the-minute

**voice**
**03** air, say, vox **04** alto, bass, cast, pipe, tone, view, vote, will, wish **05** elect, mezzo, mouth, organ, sound, taish, tenor, utter, words **06** airing, assert, convey, medium, report, rumour, singer, speech, taisch, talk of, throat, tongue, treble **07** acclaim, appoint, declare, divulge, express, mention, opinion, soprano, speak of **08** approval, castrato, decision, disclose, falsetto, language, nominate **09** contralto, enunciate, utterance, verbalize **10** articulate, expression, give tongue, inflection, instrument, intonation, mouthpiece, reputation **11** contra-tenor, Heldentenor **12** articulation, counter-tenor, mezzo-soprano

**void**
**03** gap **04** emit, lack, null, vain, want **05** abyss, annul, avoid, belch, blank, chasm, clear, drain, eject, empty, inane, inept, space **06** cancel, cavity, devoid, hollow, lacuna, remove, vacant, vacuum **07** dismiss, drained, emptied, invalid, lacking, nullify, opening, rescind, send out, useless, vacuity **08** abnegate, annulled, defecate, deserted, evacuate, nugatory, send away, unfilled **09** blankness, cancelled, clear away, discharge, emptiness, nullified, worthless **10** invalidate, unoccupied, unutilized **11** ineffectual

**volatile**
◇ *anagram indicator*
**05** giddy, Latin **06** fickle, fitful, lively **07** erratic, flighty **08** fleeting, restless, skittish, unstable, unsteady, variable, volcanic **09** explosive, irregular, mercurial, transient, unsettled, up and down **10** capricious, changeable, inconstant, short-lived **11** light-winged **13** temperamental, unpredictable

**volatility**
**09** shakiness **10** fickleness, fitfulness, insecurity **11** flightiness, fluctuation, inconstancy, instability, uncertainty, variability **12** irresolution, unsteadiness **13** unreliability **14** capriciousness, changeableness, precariousness

**volcano**
**05** salse **08** spitfire **15** burning mountain

*Volcanoes include:*

**03** Apo, Awu, Usu
**04** Etna, Fuji, Laki, Taal
**05** Hekla, Kenya, Mayon, Pelée, Thera, Thira, Unzen
**06** Ararat, Erebus, Hudson, Katmai, Sangay
**07** Jurullo, Kilauea, Rainier, Ruapehu, Surtsey, Tambora, Vulcano
**08** Cotopaxi, Krakatoa, Mauna Kea, Mauna Loa, Pinatubo, St Helens, Tarawera, Vesuvius
**09** Aconcagua, Coseguina, El Chichon, Helgafell, Karisimbi, Lamington, Paricutín, Pichincha, Santorini, Stromboli, Tongariro
**10** Bezymianny, Chimborazo, Galunggung, La Soufrire, Lassen Peak, Tungurahua
**11** Kilimanjaro, Nyamuragira
**12** Citlaltépetl, Ixtaccihuatl, Klyuchevskoy, Popocatèpetl
**13** Nevado del Ruiz, Ojos del Salado, Soufrire Hills, Volcán El Misti
**14** Cerro Incahuasi
**15** Haleakala Crater

**vole**
**08** Arvicola, water dog, water rat **10** water mouse **11** meadow mouse

**volition**
**04** will **06** choice, option **07** purpose **08** choosing, election, free will, velleity **10** preference, resolution **13** determination

**• of your own volition**
**06** freely **08** by choice **09** purposely, willingly **11** consciously, voluntarily **12** deliberately **13** intentionally, spontaneously **15** of your own accord

**volley**
**04** hail, tire **05** blast, burst, round, salvo **06** flight, shower **07** barrage, platoon **08** cannonry **09** cannonade, discharge, fusillade **11** bombardment

**volte-face**
◇ *reversal indicator*
**05** U-turn **08** reversal **09** about-face, about-turn, turnabout **13** enantiodromia

**voluble**
**06** chatty, fluent, verbal **07** twining,

verbose **09** garrulous, talkative **10** articulate, changeable, loquacious **11** forthcoming

**volume**
**01** v **03** tom, vol **04** body, book, bulk, code, mass, rise, roll, size, tome **05** codex, noise, sound, space, swell **06** amount, scroll **07** omnibus **08** capacity, decibels, loudness, quantity, solidity **09** aggregate, amplitude **10** dimensions **11** publication

**voluminous**
**03** big **04** full, huge, vast **05** ample, bulky, large, roomy **08** spacious **09** billowing, capacious

**voluntarily**
**06** freely **08** by choice, by my will **09** purposely, willingly **12** deliberately **13** intentionally **15** of your own accord

**voluntary**
**03** vol **04** free **06** unpaid, votive, willed **07** willing **08** designed, free-will, optional, postlude, unforced **09** volunteer **10** deliberate, gratuitous, purposeful, ultroneous, unsalaried, without pay **11** intentional, spontaneous, unsolicited

**volunteer**
**03** vol **05** offer **06** tender **07** advance, proffer, propose, suggest **08** activist, do-gooder, fencible **09** home guard, reformado, voluntary **10** put forward **11** come forward, helping hand, step forward **15** voluntary worker
• **volunteers**
**02** TA **03** AVR, CDV, UVF, VAD **04** RNVR

**voluptuary**
**07** playboy **08** hedonist, sybarite **09** bon vivant, bon viveur, debauchee, epicurean, libertine **10** profligate, sensualist **14** pleasure-seeker

**voluptuous**
**05** buxom **06** sultry **07** opulent, sensual, shapely **08** enticing, luscious, sensuous **09** luxurious, seductive **10** curvaceous, effeminate, goloptious, goluptious, hedonistic **11** full-figured **13** self-indulgent

**vomit**
**03** cat **04** barf, boak, bock, boke, honk, puke, sick, spew, spue **05** heave, retch **06** be sick, emetic, sick up **07** bring up, chuck up, chunder, fetch up, throw up, upchuck **08** disgorge, parbreak **10** egurgitate **11** regurgitate

**vomiting**
**04** puke, sick **06** emesis, puking **07** barfing, spewing **08** ejection, parbreak, retching, sickness **10** chundering, sick as a dog **11** hyperemesis **12** anacatharsis, haematemesis **13** regurgitation **15** morning sickness

**voracious**
**04** avid **06** greedy, hungry **07** swinish **08** edacious, gourmand, ravening, ravenous **09** devouring, rapacious **10** gluttonous, insatiable, omnivorous, prodigious, voraginous

**voracity**
**05** greed **06** hunger **07** avidity, edacity **08** rapacity **12** ravenousness

**vortex**
**04** eddy **05** whirl **09** maelstrom, whirlpool, whirlwind **10** tourbillon **11** tourbillion

**votary**
**06** addict **07** devotee, Paphian, sectary **08** adherent, bacchant, believer, disciple, follower **10** worshipper

**vote**
**01** X **02** no **03** aye, nay, yea, yes **04** poll **05** elect, go for, put in, voice **06** ballot, choose, opt for, return **07** declare, propose, re-elect, suggest, write-in **08** division, election, plump for, suffrage **09** franchise **10** plebiscite, referendum **11** ballot paper, show of hands **12** go to the polls **15** enfranchisement
• **vote in**
**04** pick **05** adopt, co-opt, elect, voice **06** choose, opt for, prefer, return, select **07** appoint, vote for **08** decide on, plump for **09** designate, determine
• **vote out**
**04** oust **06** demote, remove, topple, unseat **07** boot out, dismiss, turf out **08** dethrone, displace **09** overthrow

**voter**
**02** no **03** nay, yea, yes **04** vote **05** fagot **06** faggot **07** burgher, citizen **08** balloter, colonist, outvoter **10** franchiser, free person, ten-pounder **11** constituent **13** floating voter

**vouch**
• **vouch for**
**04** back **06** affirm, assert, assure, avouch, uphold, verify **07** certify, confirm, endorse, support, swear to, warrant **08** attest to, speak for **09** answer for, guarantee **10** asseverate

**voucher**
**02** LV **04** chit, note **05** paper, token **06** chitty, coupon, ticket **07** warrant **08** document **09** book token, gift token **11** youth credit

**vouchsafe**
**04** cede, give **05** deign, grant, vouch, yield **06** accord, bestow, beteem, confer, impart **07** beteeme **09** guarantee **10** condescend

**vow**
**03** vum **04** avow, hest, hete, oath **05** heast, hecht, hight, swear **06** affirm, behote, bename, devote, heaste, pledge **07** behight, profess, promise, protest **08** dedicate **09** nuncupate, undertake **11** nuncupation **12** give your word

**vowel**
**01** a, e, i, o, u
• **vowel sound**
**05** schwa

**voyage**
**04** sail, tour, trip **06** course, cruise, safari, travel **07** journey, odyssey, passage, traffic, travels **08** crossing, put to sea, shipping, traverse **10** enterprise, expedition, navigation **12** rough passage **13** middle passage

**Vulcan**
**10** Hephaestus

**vulgar**
**03** low **04** lewd, loud, naff, rude, vulg **05** bawdy, broad, cheap, crude, dirty, flash, gaudy, rough, showy, tacky, tarty, usual **06** coarse, common, filthy, flashy, garish, glitzy, kitsch, public, ribald, risqué, tawdry **07** boorish, general, ill-bred, obscene, plebean, popular, uncouth, upstart **08** banausic, gorblimy, impolite, improper, indecent, low-lived, ordinary, plebeian **09** customary, gorblimey, hoi polloi, low-minded, off-colour, offensive, pandemian, prevalent, tasteless, unrefined **10** indecorous, indelicate, suggestive, threepenny, uncultured, vernacular **11** commonplace, distasteful, near the bone, picturesque **12** ostentatious **13** cheap and nasty **15** unsophisticated

**vulgarian**
**04** pleb, snob **05** tiger **07** plebean, tigress **08** plebeian

**vulgarity**
**07** crudity **08** ribaldry, rudeness **09** crudeness, gaudiness, indecency **10** coarseness, garishness, tawdriness **11** ostentation

**vulnerable**
◇ *anagram indicator*
**04** open, weak **06** tender **07** exposed **08** helpless, high-risk, in danger, insecure, wide open **09** powerless, pregnable, sensitive, unguarded **11** defenceless, susceptible, unprotected **12** open to attack **15** exposed to danger

**vulture**
**05** gripe, grype, urubu **06** condor **08** aasvogel, zopilote **09** gallinazo, gier-eagle, ossifrage **11** carrion crow, lammergeier, lammergeyer **13** turkey buzzard

# W

**W**
**07** double-u, whiskey **09** double-you

**wacky**
◇ *anagram indicator*
**03** odd **04** daft, wild, zany **05** crazy, goofy, loony, loopy, nutty, silly **06** screwy **07** bonkers, erratic, offbeat **09** eccentric **10** irrational **13** unpredictable

**wad**
**03** bun, pad **04** ball, cake, hunk, lump, mass, plug, roll **05** block, chunk, marry, wodge **06** bundle, dossil, pledge **07** pledget **08** sandwich, security

**wadding**
**06** filler, lining **07** batting, filling, packing, padding **08** stuffing **10** cotton wool **14** quilting-cotton

**waddle**
**04** rock, sway **06** clumsy, daidle, hoddle, toddle, totter, wobble **07** shuffle

**wade**
**02** go **04** ford, roll **05** cross, lurch **06** paddle, splash, wallow, welter **08** flounder, traverse

• **wade in**
**05** set to **06** tear in **07** pitch in **08** launch in **10** get stuck in **11** wade through **12** trawl through **13** plough through

**wader, wading bird** *see* **bird**

**wafer**
**04** host, seal **05** matza, matzo **06** matzah, matzoh

**waffle**
**04** guff, wave **05** gofer, waver **06** babble, gaufer, gaufre, gopher, hot air, jabber **07** blather, blether, padding, prattle **08** blathers, blethers, nonsense, rabbit on, witter on **09** vacillate, verbosity, wittering, wordiness **10** cotton wool **11** vacillation **12** gobbledygook

**waft**
**04** blow, puff, turn, wave, wing **05** carry, drift, float, glide, scent, whiff **06** beckon, breath, breeze, winnow **07** current, draught **08** transmit **09** transport

**wag**
◇ *anagram indicator*
**03** bob, nod, wit **04** fool, lick, move, rock, stir, sway, walk, wave **05** clown, comic, droll, joker, shake, swing, troll **06** fellow, gagman, jester, quiver, truant, waggle, wiggle, wobble **07** flutter, vibrate **08** banterer, brandish, comedian, humorist **09** oscillate

**wage**
**03** fee, pay, war **04** gage, hire, levy, meed **05** bribe, screw **06** battle, hazard, pledge, pursue, reward, salary **07** carry on, conduct, contend, execute, imprest, payment, pension, returns, stipend **08** earnings, engage in, penny-fee, pittance, practise **09** allowance, emolument, undertake **10** recompense, wage-packet **12** compensation, remuneration

**wager**
**03** bet, lay, wad, wed **04** gage, punt, risk **05** put on, sport, stake **06** chance, gamble, hazard, pledge **07** flutter, lay odds, venture **09** speculate **11** speculation **14** gaming contract

**waggish**
**04** arch **05** droll, funny, merry, witty **06** facete, impish, jocose **07** amusing, comical, jesting, jocular, playful, puckish, risible, roguish **08** humorous, sportive **09** bantering, facetious **10** frolicsome **11** mischievous

**waggle**
◇ *anagram indicator*
**03** wag **04** wave **05** shake **06** bobble, jiggle, wiggle, wobble **07** flutter **09** oscillate **12** niddle-noddle

**wagon**
**03** car, van **04** cart, corf, drag, dray, wain **05** buggy, float, gambo, hutch, lorry, train, truck **06** boxcar, camion, hopper, telega **07** caisson, chariot, cocopan, flatcar, fourgon, gondola, kibitka, tank car, tartana **08** carriage, democrat, schooner **09** low-loader **10** freight-car, luggage-van **15** prairie schooner

• **on the wagon**
**02** TT **06** tee-tee **08** teetotal

**waif**
**04** puff, weft **05** stray, wefte **06** orphan, streak, urchin **07** wasting **09** foundling, neglected, wandering **10** ragamuffin

**wail**
**02** io **03** cry, sob **04** howl, keen, moan, weep, yowl **05** groan **06** bemoan, lament, yammer **07** ululate, vagitus, weeping **08** complain **09** complaint, ululation

**waistcoat**
**04** vest **05** gilet **06** bodice, bolero, jerkin **07** surcoat

**wait**
**03** spy **04** bide, halt, hold, rest, stay, tend **05** abide, await, delay, lurch, pause, stand, tarry, watch **06** ambush, attend, escort, expect, hang in, hang on, hold-up, linger, remain, sit out, taihoa **07** stand by **08** hang fire, hesitate, hold back, interval, sentinel, watchman **09** bide tryst, hang about **10** hang around, hesitation **12** bide your time **13** lick your chops

• **wait on**
**03** see **04** tend **05** serve **06** attend **07** work for **08** attend to **09** look after **10** minister to, take care of

**waiter, waitress**
**04** host, tray **05** Nippy **06** busboy, butler, carhop, commis, garçon, mousmé, Nippie, salver, server **07** busgirl, hostess, maître d', mousmee, pannier, steward, waitron **08** watchman **09** attendant, sommelier **10** stewardess **12** maître d'hôtel

**waive**
**04** cede **05** avoid, defer, evade, forgo, yield **06** forego, give up, ignore, reject, resign, vacate **07** abandon, forsake, put away **08** postpone, renounce, set aside **09** do without, surrender **10** relinquish **12** dispense with, strain a point

**waiver**
**08** deferral **09** remission, surrender **10** abdication, disclaimer **11** abandonment, resignation **12** postponement, renunciation **14** relinquishment

**wake**
**04** fire, goad, path, prod, rear, rise, stir, warn, wash, whet **05** alert, arise, awake, egg on, get up, rouse, track, trail, train, vigil, waken, watch, waves **06** arouse, awaken, come to, excite, notify, revive, signal, stir up **07** animate, funeral **08** activate, backwash, festival, lichwake, lykewake, serenade **09** aftermath, galvanize, reanimate, stimulate **10** bring round, death-watch **11** make aware of **13** become aware of **15** make conscious of

**wakeful**
**04** wary **05** alert **06** waking **07** heedful, rousing **08** restless, vigilant, wakerife, watchful, waukrife **09** attentive, awakening, insomniac, observant, sleepless **10** unsleeping

**wakefulness**
**05** vigil **08** insomnia **09** vigilance

12 restlessness, watchfulness
13 attentiveness, sleeplessness

**waken**
04 fire, rise, stir, wake, whet 05 awake, evoke, get up, rouse 06 arouse, awaken, excite, ignite, kindle, stir up, waking 07 animate, enliven, quicken 08 activate 09 galvanize, stimulate

**Wales** *see* **council**; **town**

**walk**
03 lag, leg, pad, wag, way 04 beat, foot, gait, hike, hump, lane, lead, limp, mall, move, pace, path, pawn, plod, step, trek, trog, turn, xyst, yomp 05 allée, alley, amble, drive, flock, guide, march, paseo, round, route, steps, stump, track, trail, tramp, tread, usher 06 avenue, behave, depart, escort, foot it, hoof it, pasear, ramble, rounds, sashay, spread, stride, stroll, trapes, trudge, xystos, xystus 07 alameda, berceau, circuit, conduct, gallery, passage, pathway, saunter, terrace, traipse, walkway 08 ambulate, carriage, footpath, frescade, go on foot, pavement, shepherd, sidewalk, traverse, withdraw 09 accompany, boulevard, circulate, disappear, esplanade, promenade 10 ambulatory, pad the hoof, pipe-opener 11 perambulate 13 hunting-ground, pedestrianize 15 stretch your legs

- **walk off with, walk away with**

03 bag, nip 04 lift, nick, whip 05 filch, pinch, steal, swipe 06 nobble, pocket 07 knock up, snaffle 08 knock off, liberate, souvenir 09 duckshove, go off with, relieve of 10 run off with 11 make off with 14 help yourself to

- **walk of life**

04 area, line 05 arena, field, trade 06 career, course, métier, sphere 07 calling, pursuit 08 activity, vocation 10 background, occupation, profession

- **walk out**

05 leave 06 mutiny, revolt, strike 07 protest 08 stop work 09 down tools 10 go on strike

- **walk out on**

04 dump, jilt 06 desert 07 abandon, forsake 08 run out on 15 leave high and dry, leave in the lurch

- **walk over**

05 abuse, cross 06 misuse 07 oppress 08 ill-treat, impose on, traverse 09 profiteer, trample on 10 manipulate 12 take for a ride 13 take liberties 14 play off against, pull a fast one on 15 take advantage of

- **walk unsteadily**

04 halt, stot 06 daddle, hobble, paddle, totter 07 shamble, stumble

**walker**
03 ped 05 hiker 06 fuller, ganger 07 rambler, vagrant 08 forester 09 ambulator 10 colporteur, pedestrian 11 stick insect

**walking-stick**
04 cane 05 waddy 06 kebbie, waddie 07 hickory 08 ash-plant 10 blackthorn 11 Malacca-cane 12 Penang-lawyer
*See also* **stick**

**walk-out**
06 revolt, strike 07 protest 08 stoppage 09 rebellion

**walkover**
02 WO 05 cinch 06 doddle 07 easy win, laugher 08 cakewalk, pushover 10 child's play 11 easy victory, piece of cake

**walkway**
04 lane, path, road 07 passage, pathway 08 footpath, pavement, sidewalk 09 esplanade, promenade

**wall**
02 wa' 04 mure

*Wall types include:*

03 dam, sea
04 dike, dyke
05 block, brick, death, fence, hedge, inner, mural, party
06 bailey, cavity, garden, paling, screen, shield
07 barrier, bulwark, curtain, divider, parapet, rampart, sea-wall
08 abutment, bulkhead, buttress, dry-stone, obstacle, palisade, stockade
09 barricade, enclosure, partition, retaining
10 embankment
11 breeze-block, load-bearing, outer bailey
13 fortification, stud partition
14 flying buttress

*Walls include:*

05 Great
06 Berlin
07 Wailing, Western
08 Antonine, Hadrian's

- **go to the wall**

04 fail, flop, fold 05 slump 06 finish, go bust 07 founder, go under 08 collapse 09 break down 11 come to an end, fall through 12 disintegrate 13 come to nothing

- **wall in**

03 pen 04 cage, hold, ring, wrap 05 bound, fence, frame, hedge, hem in 06 circle, corral, shut in 07 close in, confine, enclose, envelop 08 encircle, surround 09 encompass 10 circummure 12 circumscribe

**wallaby**
06 quokka, tammar 13 brush kangaroo

**wallet**
04 case 05 pouch, purse 06 folder, holder 08 bill-fold, notecase, pochette 10 pocketbook

**wallop**
03 hit, lam 04 bash, beat, beer, belt, blow, bonk, drub, kick, lick, rout, swat, whop 05 clout, crush, paste, pound, punch, smack, swipe, thump, whack 06 batter, buffet, defeat, gallop, hammer, pummel, strike, thrash, thwack 07 clobber, heavily, noisily, trounce 08 flounder, vanquish
*See also* **beer**; **blow**

**wallow**
03 lie 04 bask, blow, loll, roll, wade 05 enjoy, glory, heave, lurch, revel, surge 06 muddle, relish, splash, tumble, well up, welter 07 delight, indulge, slubber 08 flounder 09 luxuriate

**walrus**
05 morse 06 sea cow 08 seahorse 09 rosmarine

**wan**
04 dark, pale, took, weak 05 ashen, bleak, faint, lurid, pasty, waxen, weary, white 06 feeble, gained, gloomy, pallid, sickly 07 anaemic, ghastly 08 mournful 09 washed out, whey-faced 10 colourless 11 discoloured

**wand**
03 rod 04 mace, twig, vare 05 baton, sprig, staff, stick 06 batoon 07 sceptre, thyrsus 08 caduceus 09 goldstick

**wander**
◇ *anagram indicator*
03 err, gad 04 moon, rave, roam, roll, rove, veer, wend 05 amble, drift, mooch, mouch, prowl, range, ratch, stray, taver, vague, wheel 06 babble, cruise, depart, gibber, maraud, mither, moider, ramble, streel, stroam, stroll, swerve, taiver, wilder 07 deviate, digress, diverge, maunder, meander, moither, pilgrim, saunter, swan off, traipse 08 aberrate, bewilder, divagate, go astray, squander, straggle, stravaig, traverse, turn away 09 bat around, excursion, expatiate, forwander, kick about, moon about 10 kick around, moon around, pilgrimage, ratch about 11 extravagate, lose your way, peregrinate, vagabondize 12 stooge around, talk nonsense 14 walk the streets

**wanderer**
04 waif 05 Gypsy, nomad, rover, stray 06 nomade, ranger 07 drifter, erratic, pilgrim, rambler, vagrant, voyager 08 prodigal, stroller, vagabond, wayfarer 09 itinerant, straggler, traveller 12 rolling stone

**wandering**
03 gad 04 roam, rove, waff, waif 05 drift, error 06 errant, erring, flight, roving 07 erratic, journey, meander, nomadic, odyssey, strayed, travels, vagrant 08 aberrant, drifting, errantry, homeless, rambling, rootless, vagabond, voyaging 09 departure, deviation, erroneous, evagation, excursion, itinerant, migratory, strolling, unsettled, walkabout, wayfaring 10 aberration, digression, divergence, journeying, meandering, solivagant, travelling 11 extravagant, noctivagant, peripatetic

**13** peregrination, peregrinatory
**14** circumforanean
**15** circumforaneous

**wane**
**03** dim, ebb **04** drop, fade, fail, fall, sink, welk **05** abate, decay, droop, welke **06** fading, lessen, shrink, vanish, weaken, wither **07** atrophy, decline, dwindle, failure, sinking, subside **08** contract, decrease, diminish, fade away, peter out, taper off **09** abatement, dwindling, lessening, weakening **10** diminution, subsidence **11** contraction, tapering off **12** degeneration

**• on the wane**
**06** ebbing, fading **08** dropping, moribund **09** declining, dwindling, lessening, subsiding, weakening, withering **11** obsolescent, on the way out, tapering off **12** degenerating, on the decline **13** deteriorating, on its last legs

**wangle**
**03** fix **04** work **06** fiddle, manage, scheme **07** arrange, falsify, finagle, pull off **08** contrive, engineer **09** manoeuvre **10** manipulate **12** wheel and deal

**want**
**04** lack, like, lust, miss, mole, need, pine, will, wish **05** covet, crave, fancy **06** besoin, dearth, defect, demand, desire, hunger, penury, pining, thirst **07** absence, blemish, call for, craving, hope for, long for, longing, paucity, pine for, poverty, require **08** appetite, coveting, feel like, scarcity, shortage, yearn for, yearning **09** be without, hunger for, indigence, privation, thirst for **10** deficiency, desiderate, feebleness, inadequacy, scantiness **11** destitution, requirement **13** be deficient in, insufficiency

**wanting**
**03** for **04** less, poor **05** needy, short **06** absent, faulty **07** lacking, missing, without **08** amissing, desirous **09** defective, deficient, imperfect **10** inadequate **11** substandard **12** insufficient, unacceptable **13** disappointing **14** not up to scratch, unsatisfactory

**wanton**
◇ *anagram indicator*
**03** gay, rig **04** idle, lewd, nice, rake, rash, roué, slut, tart, wild **05** cadgy, whore **06** frisky, frolic, harlot, impure, jovial, kidgie, lecher, toyish, trifle, unjust, unruly **07** amorous, Don Juan, immoral, riggish, smicker, toysome, trifler, trollop, twigger **08** arrogant, Casanova, immodest, insolent, petulant, prodigal, reckless, skittish, sportive, strumpet **09** abandoned, arbitrary, debauchee, dissipate, dissolute, lecherous, libertine, malicious, merciless, pointless, shameless **10** capricious, cork-heeled, dissipated, gratuitous, groundless, lascivious, malevolent, prostitute, unprovoked, voluptuary **11** extravagant, promiscuous **12** unmanageable, unrestrained **13** self-indulgent, undisciplined, unjustifiable

**war**
**04** army **05** clash, excel, fight, worse, worst **06** combat, defeat, enmity, stoush, strife, strive **07** contend, contest, ill-will, make war, wage war, warfare **08** campaign, conflict, fighting **09** bloodshed **10** antagonism, contention, take up arms **11** cross swords, hostilities **13** confrontation

*War types include:*

**03** hot
**04** cold, germ, holy
**05** blitz, civil, jihad, total, trade, world
**06** ambush, attack, battle, jungle, nerves, trench
**07** assault, limited, nuclear, private
**08** chemical, intifada, invasion, skirmish, struggle
**09** attrition, guerrilla
**10** asymmetric, biological, blitzkrieg, engagement, manoeuvres, resistance
**11** bombardment
**12** asymmetrical, state of siege
**13** armed conflict, counter-attack

*Wars include:*

**03** Cod
**04** 1812, Boer, Gulf, Iraq, Sikh, Zulu
**05** Chaco, Dutch, Great, Maori, Opium, Punic, Roses, World
**06** Afghan, Balkan, Barons', Gallic, Indian, Korean, Six-Day, Trojan, Vendée, Winter
**07** Bishops', Crimean, Italian, Mexican, Pacific, Persian, Servile, Vietnam
**08** Crusades, Football, Iran-Iraq, Peasants', Religion, Ten Years'
**09** Black Hawk, Falklands, Yom Kippur
**10** Devolution, Jenkins' Ear, Napoleonic, Peninsular, Queen Anne's, Seven Years', Suez Crisis
**11** Arab-Israeli, Eighty Years', Indian Civil, King Philip's, Thirty Years'
**12** English Civil, Hundred Years', Independence, King William's, Russian Civil, Russo-Finnish, Russo-Turkish, Spanish Civil
**13** American Civil, Grand Alliance, Russo-Japanese
**14** Boxer Rebellion, Franco-Prussian, Indian Uprising, July Revolution, Triple Alliance
**15** Easter Rebellion

*See also* **battle**

**• war cry**
**04** hoop, word **05** havoc, whoop **06** banzai, slogan **07** war song **08** Geronimo **09** alalagmos, battle-cry, watchword **11** rallying-cry

**• war god**
**03** Tiu, Tiw, Tyr **04** Mars **08** Quirinus

**warble**
**03** cry **04** call, sing, song **05** carol, chirl, chirp, trill, yodel **06** quaver, record, relish **07** chirrup, rellish, twitter

**ward**
**04** area, care, fend, room, unit, zone **05** guard, minor, parry, pupil, spike, watch **06** charge **07** cubicle, custody, lookout, protégé, quarter **08** district, division, precinct, protégée **09** apartment, dependant, maternity **10** protection, sanatorium, sanitarium **11** compartment **12** guardianship

**• ward off**
**04** fend, wear, weir **05** avert, avoid, block, dodge, evade, parry, repel **06** defend, shield, thwart **07** beat off, deflect, fend off, forfend **08** stave off, turn away **09** drive back, forestall, turn aside **11** averruncate

**warden**
**06** keeper, ranger, regent, warder **07** curator, janitor, steward **08** bearward, guardian, meter man, overseer, sentinel, watchman **09** caretaker, concierge, constable, custodian, meter maid, protector **10** gatekeeper, supervisor **11** housekeeper, lollipop man **12** lollipop lady **13** administrator, lollipop woman **14** superintendent

**warder**
**05** guard, screw **06** jailer, keeper, warden **08** wardress **09** beefeater, custodian **13** prison officer

**wardrobe**
**04** robe **06** attire, closet, locker, outfit **07** almirah, apparel, armoire, cabinet, clothes **08** cupboard, garments **09** garderobe

**warehouse**
**04** hong, shed **05** depot, store **06** bodega, godown, lock-up **07** store up **08** entrepot **09** goods shed, stockroom **10** depository, repository, storehouse **11** freight shed

**wares**
**05** goods, stock, stuff **07** brokery, pedlary, produce **08** ironware, products **11** charcuterie, commodities, merchandise

**warfare**
**03** war **04** arms **05** blows **06** battle, combat, strife **07** contest, discord, feuding **08** campaign, conflict, fighting, struggle **10** contention **11** hostilities **13** confrontation, passage of arms

**warily**
**06** cagily **07** charily **08** gingerly, uneasily, with care **09** carefully, guardedly **10** cautiously, hesitantly, vigilantly, watchfully **12** suspiciously **13** circumspectly, distrustfully **14** apprehensively

**wariness**
**04** care **06** cautel, unease **07** caution **08** caginess, distrust, prudence, wariment **09** alertness, attention,

foresight, hesitancy, suspicion, vigilance **10** discretion **11** carefulness, heedfulness, mindfulness **12** apprehension, watchfulness **14** circumspection

**warlike**
**07** hawkish, hostile, martial **08** cavalier, militant, military **09** bellicose, combative **10** aggressive, battailous, pugnacious, unfriendly **11** belligerent **12** antagonistic, bloodthirsty, militaristic, warmongering

**warlock**
**05** demon, witch **06** wizard **08** conjurer, magician, sorcerer **09** enchanter **11** necromancer

**warm**
**03** het, hot, lew, sun **04** beat, fine, heat, kind, luke, melt, rich, stir, thaw **05** angry, balmy, calid, close, eager, fresh, rouse, sunny, tepid, toast **06** ardent, caring, excite, genial, hearty, heated, heat up, kindly, lively, loving, mellow, please, reheat, tender, toasty **07** affable, amiable, amorous, animate, beating, cheer up, cordial, delight, earnest, enliven, excited, fervent, glowing, intense, liven up, sincere, thermal, zealous **08** cheerful, friendly, interest, lukewarm, make warm, relaxing, vehement, well-to-do **09** harassing, heartfelt, stimulate, strenuous, temperate **10** hospitable, indelicate, passionate **11** comfortable, kind-hearted, sympathetic **12** affectionate, enthusiastic **15** put some life into

• **warm to**
**11** begin to like

• **warm up**
**04** heat **07** prepare **08** exercise, limber up, loosen up

**warm-blooded**
**04** rash **06** ardent, lively **07** earnest, fervent **08** spirited **09** emotional, excitable, impetuous, vivacious **10** hot-blooded, passionate **11** endothermic, homothermal, homothermic **12** enthusiastic, homothermous, idiothermous

**warm-hearted**
**04** kind **06** ardent, genial, hearty, kindly, loving, tender **07** cordial **08** generous **11** kind-hearted, sympathetic **12** affectionate **13** compassionate, tender-hearted

**warmonger**
**04** hawk **09** aggressor **10** militarist **12** sabre-rattler

**warmth**
**04** care, fire, glow, heat, love, zeal **05** ardor, flame **06** ardour **07** fervour, hotness, passion, unction **08** fervency, kindness, sympathy, warmness **09** affection, eagerness, intensity, sincerity, vehemence **10** compassion, cordiality, enthusiasm, kindliness, tenderness **11** hospitality **12** friendliness

**warn**
**03** vor **04** tell, urge **05** alert, awarn, shore **06** advise, exhort, forbid, inform, notify, rebuke, summon, tip off **07** caution, command, counsel, let know, portend, presage, reprove, warrant **08** admonish, forewarn, instruct **09** factorize, premonish, reprimand **10** give notice **13** sound the alarm **14** put on your guard

**warning**
**04** call, hint, omen, sign, wire **05** alarm, alert **06** advice, augury, caveat, lesson, notice, signal, threat, tip-off **07** caution, counsel, example, ominous, portent, presage, summons **08** monition, monitory **10** admonition, admonitory, cautionary, wake-up call, yellow card **11** information, premonition, premonitory, threatening **12** notification **13** advance notice

*See also* **signal**

• **expression of warning**
**03** nix, now **04** cave, fore, gang, mind **06** timber **07** Achtung, you wait! **08** gardyloo **09** scaldings

**warp**
◇ *anagram indicator*
**04** bend, bent, bias, cast, kink, turn **05** kedge, quirk, throw, twist **06** buckle, defect, deform, spring, swerve **07** contort, corrupt, deviate, distort, entwine, pervert **08** miscarry, misshape **09** deviation **10** contortion, distortion, perversion **11** deformation **12** irregularity

**warrant**
**04** able, back, fiat, keep, warn **05** allow, proof, sepad, swear **06** affirm, assure, avouch, behote, defend, excuse, pardon, permit, pledge, uphaud, uphold **07** approve, behight, call for, caption, certify, consent, declare, defence, deserve, empower, endorse, entitle, justify, licence, license, precept, predict, presage, promise, protect, require, support, voucher **08** defender, detainer, guaranty, mittimus, sanction, security, transire, vouch for, warranty **09** answer for, assurance, authority, authorize, consent to, diligence, execution, guarantee, underclay, vouchsafe **10** commission, permission, underwrite, validation **11** necessitate **12** bench-warrant, death warrant, fugie-warrant, peace-warrant **13** authorization, justification, search warrant **14** lettre de cachet

• **warrant officer**
**02** WO **03** CSM, RSM **04** bos'n **05** bosun **09** boatswain

**warrantable**
**05** legal, right **06** lawful, proper **09** allowable, estimable, excusable, necessary **10** defensible, reasonable **11** accountable, justifiable, permissible

**warranty**
**04** bond **06** pledge **08** contract, covenant, evidence **09** assurance, guarantee **11** certificate **13** authorization, justification

**warring**
◇ *anagram indicator*
**05** at war **07** hostile, opposed **08** fighting, opposing **09** combatant, embattled **10** contending **11** belligerent, conflicting **14** at daggers drawn

**warrior**
**05** brave, ghazi **06** Amazon, haiduk, wardog, warman **07** berserk, fighter, heyduck, soldier, warlock, warwolf **08** champion, warhorse **09** berserker, combatant **11** fighting man

**warship**
**03** cog, ram **06** galley **07** cruiser, man-o'-war **08** man-of-war **09** blockship, destroyer, first-rate **10** battleship, turret ship **11** capital ship, dreadnaught, dreadnought, torpedo boat **13** battle-cruiser

**wart**
**03** wen **04** lump **06** anbury, growth **07** verruca **09** keratosis, papilloma **10** angleberry **11** excrescence **12** protuberance

**wary**
**04** cagy, ware **05** alert, aware, cagey, chary, leery, tenty **06** tentie **07** careful, guarded, heedful, prudent, thrifty **08** cautious, vigilant, watchful **09** attentive, wide-awake **10** on the alert, suspicious **11** circumspect, distrustful, on your guard **12** on the lookout **14** circumspective

**wash**
**03** fen, lap, lip, mop, wet **04** bath, beat, coat, dash, flow, hold, lave, lick, roll, sind, slop, soak, synd, wave, wipe **05** bathe, clean, layer, marsh, rinse, scrub, souse, stain, stick, sujee, surge, sweep, swell, swill **06** douche, lotion, shower, sloosh, soogee, soogie, soojey, splash, sponge, stream **07** cleanse, coating, launder, laundry, moisten, shampoo, stand up, washing **08** cleaning, swab down **09** cleansing, freshen up, have a bath, have a wash, hold water **10** be accepted, laundering, pass muster **11** be plausible, carry weight, have a shower **12** bear scrutiny, be believable, be convincing, get cleaned up **15** bear examination

• **wash your hands of**
**07** abandon **08** give up on

**washed-out**
**03** wan **04** flat, pale **05** all in, ashen, drawn, faded, spent, weary **06** pallid **07** anaemic, drained, haggard, worn-out **08** blanched, bleached, dog-tired, fatigued, tired-out **09** exhausted, knackered **10** colourless, lacklustre **14** dead on your feet

**Washington**
**02** WA **04** Wash

**washout**
**04** flop, mess **06** fiasco **07** debacle,

failure **08** disaster **11** lead balloon **14** disappointment

**wasp**
**05** vespa **06** hornet **07** gallfly **08** ruby-tail **09** cuckoo fly, mud dauber, velvet ant **12** yellow jacket

**waspish**
**05** cross, testy **06** bitchy, crabby, grumpy, touchy **07** crabbed, grouchy, peevish, prickly **08** captious, critical, petulant, snappish, spiteful, virulent **09** crotchety, irascible, irritable **11** bad-tempered, ill-tempered **12** cantankerous

**wastage**
**04** loss **05** decay **07** atrophy **08** draining, marasmus **10** emaciation, exhausting **11** dissipation, squandering **12** degeneration **14** frittering away

**waste**
◇ *anagram indicator*
**03** nub **04** bare, blow, crud, gash, kill, knub, lose, loss, pass, pine, rape, raze, ruin, sack, slag, vain, wild **05** abuse, bleak, drain, dregs, dross, empty, erode, extra, husks, offal, scrap, slops, spend, spill, spoil, trash **06** barren, debris, desert, dismal, dreary, expend, injure, lavish, litter, misuse, ravage, refuse, shrink, slurry, unused, wither **07** atrophy, consume, despoil, destroy, exhaust, garbage, neglect, pillage, rubbish, ruinous, shrivel, splurge, useless **08** cast away, desolate, effluent, emaciate, lay waste, left-over, misspend, rejected, squander, unwanted **09** depredate, devastate, dissipate, go through, leftovers, profusion, recrement, throw away, worthless **10** desolation, devastated, dilapidate, get through, impoverish, unoccupied **11** consumption, destruction, dissipation, expenditure, fritter away, offscouring, prodigality, prodigalize, squandering, superfluous, uninhabited **12** extravagance, offscourings, uncultivated, unproductive, unprofitable, wastefulness **13** supernumerary **14** misapplication **15** become emaciated
*See also* **kill**

**wasted**
◇ *anagram indicator*
**04** high, lost, weak **05** drunk, gaunt, spent **07** useless, war-worn, worn-out **08** ill-spent, needless, shrunken, weakened, withered **09** atrophied, emaciated, exhausted, washed-out **10** shrivelled, squandered, unrequired **11** unexploited, unnecessary **12** down the drain

**wasteful**
**04** vain **06** lavish **07** ruinous **08** desolate, prodigal, wastfull, wastrife **09** unthrifty, wasterife **10** profitless, profligate, thriftless **11** extravagant, improvident, spendthrift, uninhabited **12** uneconomical, unfrequented

**wasteland**
**04** fell, void, wild **05** waste, wilds **06** desert **07** thwaite **08** badlands **09** emptiness **10** barrenness, wilderness

**wasting**
**05** tabes **07** atrophy **08** marasmic, marasmus, phthisis, syntexis **09** cirrhosis, consuming, symptosis **10** colliquant, destroying, emaciating, enfeebling, tabescence **11** colliquable, consumption, consumptive, devastating, tabefaction **12** colliquative, contabescent

**wastrel**
**04** waif **05** idler, waste **06** feeble, loafer, refuse, skiver **07** goof-off, lounger, shirker **08** layabout **09** lazybones **10** malingerer, ne'er-do-well, profligate **11** spendthrift **14** good-for-nothing

**watch**
**03** eye, nit, see, spy **04** espy, heed, keep, mark, mind, nark, note, scan, tend, tout, view, wait, wake, ward **05** await, clock, flock, guard, scout, spial, vigil **06** follow, gape at, gaze at, look at, look on, look to, notice, peer at, regard, shadow, survey, ticker **07** inspect, look out, lookout, monitor, observe, outlook, overeye, protect, stare at **08** repeater, sentinel, take care, take heed, tick-tick **09** alertness, attention, be careful, look after, timepiece, vigilance **10** inspection, keep tabs on, stemwinder, take care of, wristwatch **11** chronometer, contemplate, keep an eye on, observation, superintend, supervision **12** pay attention, pernoctation, surveillance, watchfulness
*See also* **clock**

**• watch out**
**04** mind **06** notice **07** keep nit, look out **08** cockatoo, stand nit **10** be vigilant **12** keep a lookout **13** stand cockatoo

**• watch over**
**04** mind, tend, ward **05** guard **06** defend, shield **07** protect, shelter **08** preserve, sentinel, shepherd **09** look after, supervise **10** take care of **11** keep an eye on **14** stand guard over

**watchdog**
**07** monitor **08** guard dog, guardian, house-dog **09** custodian, inspector, ombudsman, protector, regulator, vigilante **10** scrutineer **11** housekeeper

**watcher**
**03** spy **05** Argus **06** viewer **07** lookout, witness **08** audience, looker-on, observer, onlooker **09** spectator **10** eyewitness, televiewer

**watchful**
**04** wary **05** alert, chary **07** guarded, heedful **08** cautious, open-eyed, vigilant, wakerife, waukrife **09** adviceful, attentive, avizefull, observant, wide awake **10** suspicious **11** circumspect, on your guard **12** on the lookout, on the qui vive

**watchfulness**
**07** caution **08** wariness **09** alertness, attention, dragonism, suspicion, vigilance **10** observance **11** heedfulness **12** cautiousness **13** attentiveness **14** circumspection, suspiciousness

**watchman**
**04** wait **05** guard **06** waiter **07** Charley, Charlie, rug gown, wakeman **08** chokidar, night-man **09** caretaker, chowkidar, custodian **10** speculator **13** security guard

**watchword**
**03** cry **05** maxim, motto **06** byword, signal, slogan **07** nayword, tag line **08** buzz word, password **09** battle-cry, catchword, magic word, principle **10** shibboleth **11** catchphrase, rallying-cry

**water**
**02** aq, ea **03** eau, sea, wet **04** aqua, hose, lake, rain, soak **05** class, douse, drink, flood, ocean, river, spray **06** dampen, drench, lustre, saliva, stream **07** current, moisten, quality, torrent **08** flooding, irrigate, moisture, saturate, sprinkle, surround **09** Adam's wine **10** excellence **12** transparency
*See also* **lake**; **river**; **sea**

*Mineral water brands include:*

**05** Evian®
**06** Buxton®, Ty Nant®, Vittel®, Volvic®
**07** Perrier®
**08** Aqua Pura®
**10** Strathmore®
**13** Pennine Spring®, San Pellegrino®
**14** Highland Spring®

**• hold water**
**04** hold, wash, work **05** stand, stick **06** cohere, hold up **07** stand up **08** convince, ring true **09** make sense **10** be accepted **11** be plausible, carry weight, pass the test, remain valid **12** bear scrutiny, be believable, be convincing **15** bear examination

**• water carrier**
**06** bhisti **07** bheesty, bhistee **08** Aquarius, bheestie

**• water down**
**03** mix **04** thin **06** dilute, soften, weaken **07** qualify **08** mitigate, moderate, play down, tone down **09** attenuate, soft-pedal **10** adulterate

**watercourse**
**04** burn, khor, lead, nala, rean, reen, wadi **05** brook, canal, ditch, drain, nalla, nulla, rhine, rhyne, river, shott, whelm **06** arroyo, nallah, nullah, spruit, stream **07** channel **09** sunk fence **12** water-channel
*See also* **river**

**waterfall**
**03** lin **04** drop, fall, foss, linn, salt **05** chute, falls, force, rapid, sault, shoot, shute, spout **06** lasher, rapids

**07** cascade, chignon, necktie, torrent **08** cataract, overfall **10** salmon leap

*Waterfalls include:*

**05** Angel, Della, Glass, Pilao, Tysse
**06** Boyoma, Iguaçu, Krimml, Ormeli, Ribbon, Tugela
**07** Mtarazi, Niagara, Stanley, Thukela
**08** Cuquenán, Gavarnie, Gullfoss, Itatinga, Kaieteur, Takkakaw, Victoria, Wallaman, Yosemite
**09** Churchill, Dettifoss, Giessbach, Multnomah, Staubbach
**10** Cleve-Garth, Sutherland, Wollomombi
**11** Reichenbach, Trummelbach
**12** Cusiana River, Paulo Alfonso, Silver Strand
**13** Mardalsfossen, Tyssetrengane, Upper Yosemite, Vestre Mardola

**waterproof, waterproof material**
**03** mac **04** mack **05** loden **06** anorak, arctic, cagoul, camlet, coated, kagool, kagoul, poncho **07** Barbour®, cagoule, camelot, jaconet, kagoule, oilskin, proofed, slicker, tanking **09** damp-proof, macintosh, sou'wester, tarpaulin **10** impervious, mackintosh, rubberized, tarpauling, trench coat, watertight **11** Barbour® coat, gutta-percha, impermeable **12** antigropelos **13** antigropeloes, Barbour® jacket **14** water-repellent, water-resistant

**watertight**
**04** firm **05** sound **06** sealed, stanch **07** staunch **08** airtight, flawless, hermetic **09** foolproof **10** waterproof **11** impregnable **12** indisputable, unassailable

**watery**
**03** wet **04** damp, thin, weak **05** blear, eager, fluid, moist, runny, soggy, vapid, washy **06** bleary, liquid, serous, sloppy **07** aqueous, diluted, hydrous, insipid, shilpit **08** hydatoid, skinking, squelchy **09** tasteless **10** wishy-washy **11** adulterated, flavourless, transparent, watered-down

**wave**
◇ *anagram indicator*
**03** sea, waw **04** curl, flap, flow, foam, rash, rush, sign, stir, surf, sway, waff, waft, wawe **05** crimp, drift, float, flood, flote, froth, hover, shake, surge, sweep, swell, swing, trend, waver **06** beckon, billow, comber, direct, quiver, ripple, roller, signal, stream, waffle **07** breaker, current, decuman, feather, flutter, gesture, impulse, soliton, tide rip, upsurge, wavelet **08** backwash, brandish, flourish, increase, indicate, movement, outbreak, tendency, undulate, whitecap **09** tidal wave, vacillate **10** crispation, supersonic, undulation, white horse **11** beachcomber, gesticulate, ground swell

• **make waves**
**12** cause trouble **13** disturb things, stir up trouble

• **wave aside**
**05** spurn **06** reject, shelve **07** dismiss **08** set aside **09** disregard **10** brush aside **15** pour cold water on

• **wave down**
**06** summon **08** flag down **12** signal to stop

**waver**
◇ *anagram indicator*
**04** reel, rock, sway, vary, wave **05** haver, shake **06** change, didder, dither, falter, seesaw, teeter, totter, waffle, wobble **07** give way, stagger, tremble **08** hesitate **09** fluctuate, hum and haw, oscillate, vacillate **10** equivocate **11** be undecided **12** shilly-shally

**waverer**
**07** doubter, haverer, wobbler **08** ditherer **14** shilly-shallier

**wavering**
◇ *anagram indicator*
**04** wavy **05** shaky **07** dithery, stagger **08** doubtful, doubting, firmless, havering, hesitant **09** ambiguous, dithering, hesitance, hesitancy **10** hesitation, indecision, in two minds, of two minds **11** vacillatory **12** double-minded **15** shilly-shallying

**wavy**
**04** undé **05** curly, curvy, oundy, undee **06** nebulé, nebuly, repand, ridged, undate, wiggly, zigzag **07** curling, curving, rippled, sinuate, sinuous, undated, winding **08** sinuated, undulate, wavering **09** snow goose **10** flamboyant, undulating, undulatory **11** fluctuating

**wax**
**03** say **04** cere, grow, kiss, pela, rise, seal, talk, tell **05** mount, speak, state, swell, utter, voice, widen **06** become, expand, extend, spread **07** address, broaden, cerumen, declaim, declare, develop, enlarge, express, fill out, magnify, passion **08** converse, increase, paraffin **09** enunciate, get bigger, hold forth, pronounce **10** articulate **11** communicate

**waxen**
**03** wan **04** pale **05** ashen, livid, white **06** pallid **07** anaemic, ghastly, whitish **09** bloodless **10** colourless

**waxy**
**04** soft **05** irate, pasty, waxen **06** pallid **07** cereous **08** incensed **09** ceraceous **11** impressible **14** impressionable

**way**
◇ *anagram indicator*
**01** E, N, S, W **02** Rd, St, Wy **03** far, via **04** gate, lane, mode, path, plan, road, rode, room, tool, very, will, wise, wont **05** habit, lines, means, route, scope, state, style, track, trait, usage, weigh **06** access, avenue, course, custom, esteem, manner, method, nature, really, street, system, temper **07** channel, conduct, fashion, highway, journey, passage, pathway, process, respect, roadway **08** approach, district, position, practice, progress, strategy **09** behaviour, condition, direction, mannerism, procedure, technique **10** instrument **11** disposition, peculiarity, personality, temperament **12** idiosyncrasy, thoroughfare **14** characteristic, course of action **15** instrumentality

• **all the way**
**02** up **04** thro, thru **07** through **08** straight

• **by the way**
**02** ob **03** BTW **06** obiter **07** apropos **09** en passant, in passing **11** secondarily **12** incidentally **14** by the same token **15** à propos de bottes, parenthetically

• **either way**
◇ *palindrome indicator*

• **give way**
**02** go **03** sag **04** bend, cede, sink **05** break, burst, crack, yield **06** cave in, fall in, give in, relent, shrink, spring, submit, swerve **07** concede, subside, succumb **08** collapse, fall back, withdraw **09** give place, surrender **10** capitulate, give ground **12** disintegrate

• **make your way**
**04** wend **06** travel **07** journey

• **on the way**
**07** en route **09** in transit

• **quickest way**
**07** beeline

• **under way**
**05** afoot, begun, going **06** moving **07** started **08** in motion **10** in progress **11** in operation, progressing **12** off the ground

• **way of life**
**04** life **05** world **08** position **09** lifestyle, situation **12** modus vivendi

• **ways and means**
**04** cash **05** funds, tools **07** capital, methods **08** capacity, reserves **09** procedure, resources **10** capability **11** wherewithal

• **whichever way you look at it**
◇ *palindrome indicator*

**wayfarer**
**05** Gypsy, nomad, rover **06** viator, walker **07** pilgrim, swagger, swagman, trekker, voyager **08** traveler, wanderer **09** itinerant, journeyer, piepowder, traveller **12** globetrotter

**wayfaring**
**06** roving **07** nomadic, walking **08** drifting, rambling, voyaging **09** itinerant, wandering **10** journeying, travelling **11** peripatetic

**waylay**
**03** lay **05** belay, catch, seize **06** accost, ambush, attack, hold up **07** set upon, stick up **08** obstruct, surprise **09** intercept **10** buttonhole **12** lie in wait for

**way-out**
**04** lost, rapt, wild **05** crazy, wacky, weird **06** exotic, far-out, freaky **07** bizarre, off-beat, unusual **09** eccentric, excellent, fantastic, left-field **10** avant-garde, outlandish,

unorthodox **11** exceptional, progressive **12** experimental **14** unconventional

**wayward**
**06** fickle, unruly, wilful **07** peevish **08** contrary, obdurate, perverse, stubborn **09** irregular, obstinate **10** capricious, changeable, headstrong, rebellious, refractory, self-willed **11** disobedient, intractable, loup-the-dyke **12** contumacious, incorrigible, ungovernable, unmanageable **13** insubordinate, unpredictable

**waywardness**
**08** obduracy **09** contumacy, obstinacy **10** perversity, unruliness, wilfulness **12** contrariness, disobedience, perverseness, stubbornness **14** rebelliousness **15** insubordination

**weak**
**01** W **03** dim, low **04** dull, fade, gone, lame, poor, puny, soft, thin **05** cissy, faint, frail, milky, runny, shaky, weedy **06** debile, facile, faulty, feeble, flimsy, infirm, meagre, pallid, sickly, single, slight, unable, watery **07** brickle, diluted, exposed, fragile, insipid, lacking, muffled, stifled, unsound, useless, worn out **08** cowardly, delicate, fatigued, impotent **09** defective, deficient, enervated, exhausted, forceless, imperfect, powerless, spineless, strung out, tasteless, unguarded, unhealthy, untenable **10** effeminate, fizzenless, foisonless, fusionless, inadequate, indecisive, indistinct, irresolute, unstressed, vulnerable **11** adulterated, debilitated, defenceless, fushionless, impressible, ineffectual, unprotected **12** inconclusive, invertebrate, unconvincing **13** imperceptible **14** inconsiderable, valetudinarian

**weaken**
**03** sap **04** fade, fail, flag, kill, pall, thin, tire **05** abate, appal, craze, delay, droop, lower, taint **06** deduct, dilute, ease up, impair, lessen, reduce, soften, temper **07** cripple, disable, dwindle, exhaust, give way, unnerve **08** diminish, enervate, enfeeble, entender, intender, mitigate, moderate, paralyse, soften up **09** extenuate, undermine, water down **10** debilitate, disconcert, effeminate, effeminize **12** incapacitate **13** disinvigorate **14** take the edge off

**weakening**
**06** easing, fading, waning **07** failing **08** dilution, flagging, lowering **09** abatement, dwindling, lessening, reduction **10** enervation, impairment, moderation **11** extenuation, frontolysis, undermining **12** debilitation, diminishment, enfeeblement

**weakling**
**03** wet **04** drip, tonk, weed, wimp, wuss **05** cissy, mouse, wally **06** coward **07** dilling, doormat, milksop **08** softling, underdog **09** underling **10** namby-pamby

**weakly**
**06** feebly, lamely **07** faintly, frailly **08** slightly **09** tenuously **10** helplessly **11** implausibly, powerlessly **12** dispiritedly, indecisively, pathetically **13** ineffectively

**weak-minded**
**04** daft **07** pliable **09** compliant, spineless, weak-kneed **10** irresolute, submissive **11** complaisant, persuadable, persuasible **12** faint-hearted **13** pusillanimous

**weakness**
**04** flaw **05** doubt, fault, folly **06** defect, dotage, foible, liking **07** acrasia, apepsia, blemish, cachexy, failing, frailty, languor, passion **08** azoturia, cachexia, debility, delicacy, fondness, frailtee, penchant, soft spot, trembles **09** frailness, impotence, infirmity, lassitude, weak point **10** deficiency, effeminacy, enervation, feebleness, flimsiness, incapacity, myasthenia, proclivity **11** dubiousness, inclination, paraparesis, shortcoming, tenuousness, uncertainty, unsoundness **12** Achilles' heel, delicateness, doubtfulness, enfeeblement, imperfection, phonasthenia, predilection, unlikelihood, unlikeliness **13** improbability, powerlessness, vulnerability **14** far-fetchedness, implausibility, predisposition **15** ineffectiveness, second childhood

**weal**
**04** mark, scar, wale, welt **05** bends, ridge, wheal, wound **06** streak, stripe **07** welfare **08** cicatrix **09** cicatrice, contusion **12** commonwealth **14** the sum of things

**wealth**
**04** cash, ease, mass, pelf **05** funds, goods, lucre, means, money, store **06** assets, bounty, estate, mammon, plenty, riches **07** capital, finance, fortune, fulness, tallent, warison **08** fullness, opulence, property, richesse, treasure, treasury, warrison **09** abundance, affluence, plenitude, profusion, resources, substance, wellbeing **10** cornucopia, prosperity **11** copiousness, loadsamoney, possessions

**wealthy**
**04** oofy, posh, rich **05** flush, pluty, solid **06** fat-cat, loaded **07** moneyed, opulent, well-off **08** affluent, well-to-do **10** filthy rich, prosperous, well-heeled **11** comfortable, made of money, rolling in it, substantial **12** stinking rich

**weapon**
**03** arm

*Weapons include:*

**03** bow, gas, gun, Uzi
**04** bomb, Colt®, cosh, dirk, épée, foil, ICBM, Mace®, mine, pike, Scud
**05** arrow, billy, bolas, CS gas, H-bomb, knife, lance, Luger®, panga, rifle, sabre, sling, spear, sword, Taser®, vouge
**06** airgun, cannon, cudgel, dagger, Exocet®, glaive, jambok, magnum, Mauser, mortar, musket, pistol, rapier, rocket, six-gun, taiaha, tomboc
**07** assegai, balista, bayonet, bazooka, bomblet, Bren gun, caltrop, halberd, harpoon, longbow, machete, pole-axe, poniard, sjambok, sten gun, stun gun, tear-gas, torpedo
**08** air rifle, atom bomb, ballista, blowpipe, calthrop, catapult, chemical, claymore, crossbow, field gun, howitzer, landmine, nail bomb, nerve gas, nunchaku, oerlikon, partisan, revolver, scimitar, shuriken, stiletto, threshel, time-bomb, tomahawk, tommy gun
**09** automatic, battleaxe, boomerang, Mills bomb, smart bomb, truncheon, turret-gun
**10** bowie knife, broadsword, flick-knife, gatling gun, machine-gun, mustard gas, napalm bomb, peashooter, shillelagh, six-shooter
**11** Agent Orange, blunderbuss, bow and arrow, cluster-bomb, daisy-cutter, depth-charge, hand grenade, kalashnikov, neutron bomb, submunition, water pistol
**12** bunker buster, flame-thrower, hydrogen bomb, quarterstaff
**13** Cruise missile, knuckleduster, submachine-gun
**14** incendiary bomb, rocket-launcher
**15** thermobaric bomb, Winchester® rifle

*See also* **dagger**; **gun**; **knife**; **missile**; **sword**

**wear**
◇ *insertion indicator*
**03** air, don, fly, rub, use **04** bear, edge, fray, have, pack, pass, show, stub **05** carry, dress, erode, grind, guide, mount, put on, spend, sport, waste, weary **06** abrade, accept, affect, assume, attire, become, damage, endure, have on, outfit **07** believe, clothes, conduct, consume, corrode, costume, display, dress in, erosion, exhaust, exhibit, fashion, service, utility **08** abrasion, clothing, friction, garments, tolerate, traverse **09** corrosion **10** durability, employment, usefulness **11** be clothed in, be dressed in, deteriorate, wear and tear **12** become weaker **13** become thinner, deterioration **14** fray at the edges

• **wear down**
**05** erode, grind **06** abrade, impair, lessen, reduce **07** attrite, consume, corrode, degrade, rub away

**08** diminish, macerate, overcome, soften up **09** grind down, undermine **10** chip away at

**• wear off**

**03** ebb **04** fade, fray, wane **05** abate **06** lessen, weaken **07** dwindle, subside **08** decrease, diminish, peter out **09** disappear

**• wear on**

**04** go by, go on, pass **06** elapse

**• wear out**

**03** sap **04** fray, mush, tire **05** break, drain, erode, trash, use up, waste **06** harass, impair, peruse, strain, stress **07** consume, exhaust, fatigue, frazzle, knacker, knock up, tire out **08** enervate, forspend, overteem **09** forespend **11** deteriorate, wear through

### wearily

**07** tiredly **08** drowsily, sleepily **10** listlessly **11** unexcitedly **13** lethargically

### weariness

**05** ennui **07** fatigue, languor **08** lethargy **09** lassitude, tiredness **10** drowsiness, enervation, exhaustion, sleepiness **11** prostration, Weltschmerz **12** listlessness, taedium vitae

**• expression of weariness**

**04** hech **07** heigh-ho

### wearing

◇ *containment indicator*

**02** in **06** taxing, tiring, trying **07** erosive, irksome **08** tiresome **09** consuming, fatiguing, wearisome **10** durability, exhausting, oppressive **12** exasperating

### wearisome

**04** dull **06** boring, dreary, trying **07** humdrum, irksome, tedious, wearing **08** annoying, tiresome, weariful **09** fatiguing, vexatious **10** bothersome, burdensome, exhausting, monotonous **11** troublesome **12** exasperating

### weary

**03** bug, fag, irk, sap, tax **04** bore, cloy, fade, fail, jade, puny, tire **05** all in, annoy, bored, drain, ennui, jaded, tired **06** aweary, betoil, burden, bushed, done in, drowsy, harass, pooped, sicken, sleepy, zonked **07** drained, exhaust, fatigue, tedious, tire out, wear out, whacked, worn out **08** awearied, dead beat, dog-tired, dog-weary, enervate, fatigued, forweary, half-dead, irritate, tiresome, toil-worn, trauchle, wiped out **09** exhausted, fagged out, knackered, overweary, pooped out, ramfeezle, think long, unexcited **10** brassed off, browned off, cheesed off, debilitate, exasperate **11** tuckered out **12** bored to tears, sick and tired, uninterested **14** unenthusiastic

### wearying

**06** taxing, tiring, trying **07** wearing **08** draining **09** fatiguing, wearisome **10** exhausting

### weasel

**04** mink **05** stoat, taira, tayra **06** grison, marten **07** whitret **08** whittret **09** delundung, wolverene, wolverine **10** whitterick

### weather

**03** dry, set, sky **04** gain, pass **05** brave, slope, stand **06** endure, expose, harden, resist, season, suffer **07** climate, dryness, outlook, ride out, survive, toughen **08** forecast, humidity, overcome, stick out, surmount, windward **09** rise above, sunniness, windiness, withstand **10** cloudiness, conditions, get through **11** come through, live through, pull through, temperature

*Weather phenomena include:*

**03** fog, ice
**04** gale, hail, haze, mist, rain, smog, snow, thaw, wind
**05** cloud, frost, sleet, slush, storm
**06** breeze, deluge, shower, squall
**07** chinook, cyclone, drizzle, drought, mistral, monsoon, rainbow, tempest, thunder, tornado, twister, typhoon
**08** black ice, downpour, heatwave, sunshine
**09** hoar frost, hurricane, lightning, snowstorm, whirlwind

*See also* **cloud**; **ice**; **precipitation**; **snow**; **storm**; **wind**

**• under the weather**

**03** ill **04** ropy, sick **05** crook, drunk, lousy, queer, ropey, rough, seedy **06** ailing, groggy, grotty, poorly **08** below par, hung over, nauseous **09** off-colour, squeamish **10** indisposed, out of sorts **15** the worse for wear

### weave

◇ *anagram indicator*

**03** rya, web **04** cane, fuse, knit, lace, spin, wind **05** braid, merge, plait, tweel, twill, twist, unite **06** create, damask, make up, plight, tissue, zigzag **07** compose, entwine, inweave, texture **08** contrive **09** construct, fabricate, interlace, interwork **10** criss-cross, intercross, intertwine, interweave **11** put together

### weaver

**04** loom

### weaver bird

**04** taha **06** bishop, ox-bird, quelea **09** grenadier **10** zebra finch **11** Java sparrow

### web

**03** mat, net **04** knot, mesh, plot, tela, trap, vane, weft **05** skein, snare **06** tangle **07** complex, lattice, netting, network, texture, webbing **08** intrigue, lacework, mesh-work, vexillum **11** fabrication, interlacing, latticework

### wed

**03** wad **04** ally, fuse, join, link, yoke **05** blend, marry, merge, unify, unite, wager **06** pledge, splice **07** combine, espouse **08** coalesce, security **09** commingle **10** get hitched, get married, get spliced, interweave, take to wife, tie the knot **13** take the plunge **14** lead to the altar, lead up the aisle

### wedded

**06** joined, wifely **07** marital, married, nuptial, spousal **08** conjugal **09** connubial, husbandly **11** matrimonial

### wedding

**05** union **06** bridal, huppah, mating **07** chuppah, nuptial, wedlock **08** espousal, hymeneal, hymenean, marriage, nuptials, spousage **09** espousals, matrimony **11** epithalamic, matrimonial **15** marriage service

*See also* **anniversary**; **marriage**

### wedge

**03** fit, gad, gib, jam, key, ram **04** cram, lump, pack, push, trig **05** block, chock, chunk, cleat, crowd, force, lodge, piece, quoin, stuff, wodge **06** cotter, scotch, thrust **07** blaster, feather, squeeze **08** doorstop, triangle **09** space band, whipstock

### wedlock

**05** union **08** marriage **09** matrimony **13** holy matrimony

### Wednesday

**03** Wed **04** Weds

### wee

**03** pee, sma **04** leak, tiny **05** small, teeny, urine, weeny **06** little, midget, minute, teensy **07** urinate **09** itsy-bitsy, miniature, minuscule **10** diminutive, negligible, teeny-weeny **11** Lilliputian, microscopic **13** insignificant

### weed

**03** hoe **04** tare

*Weeds include:*

**03** ers
**04** dock, moss
**05** daisy, vetch
**06** fat hen, oxalis, spurge, yarrow
**07** bracken, ragweed, ribwort
**08** bindweed, duckweed, knapweed, self-heal
**09** chickweed, coltsfoot, dandelion, ground ivy, groundsel, horsetail, knotgrass, liverwort, pearlwort, snakeweed, speedwell, sun spurge
**10** cinquefoil, common reed, couch grass, curled dock, deadnettle, sow thistle, thale cress
**11** ground elder, meadow grass, petty spurge, salad burnet, white clover
**12** annual nettle, rough hawkbit, sheep's sorrel
**13** common burdock, field wood rush, large bindweed, pineapple weed, small bindweed
**14** common plantain, shepherd's purse
**15** broad-leaved dock, burnet saxifrage, common chickweed, creeping thistle, greater plantain,

lesser celandine, perennial nettle, stemless thistle

*See also* **cannabis**; **seaweed**; **tobacco**

**• weed out**
**05** purge **06** remove **07** isolate, root out **08** get rid of **09** eliminate, eradicate, extirpate

**weedkiller**
**06** diquat **08** atrazine, Paraquat®, simazine **09** herbicide, weedicide **10** glyphosate **11** glufosinate, graminicide **14** sodium chlorate

**weedy**
**03** wet **04** puny, thin, weak **05** frail, lanky, wussy **06** feeble, skinny **07** insipid, scrawny, wimpish **08** gangling **09** weak-kneed **10** undersized

**week**
**01** w **03** ouk **04** oulk

**weekly**
**09** by the week, every week, once a week **10** hebdomadal **11** hebdomadary **12** hebdomadally

**weep**
**03** cry, sob **04** bawl, blub, drip, leak, moan, ooze, pipe, rain, seep, wail **05** droop, exude, greet, mourn, whine **06** beweep, boo-hoo, greete, grieve, lament, snivel **07** blubber, outweep, whimper **09** be in tears, shed tears **11** pipe your eye

**weepy**
**04** oozy **05** teary **06** crying, labile **07** sobbing, tearful, weeping **08** greeting, sob-stuff **09** melodrama **10** blubbering, lachrymose, tear-jerker **11** sentimental

**weigh**
**03** sit, way **04** ride **05** loose, poise, raise, scale, worry **06** burden, ponder **07** afflict, balance, depress, examine, get down, oppress, perpend, trouble **08** bear down, consider, evaluate, mull over, unanchor **09** disanchor, ponderate, reflect on, think over **10** deliberate, meditate on **11** contemplate **13** have a weight of **14** tip the scales at

**• weigh down**
**04** load **05** pease, peaze, peise, peize, peyse, poise, worry **06** burden **07** afflict, depress, get down, oppress, trouble **08** bear down, outweigh, overload **09** press down, weigh upon

**• weigh up**
**05** scale **06** assess, ponder, size up **07** balance, compare, discuss, examine **08** chew over, consider, evaluate, mull over **09** think over **10** deliberate **11** contemplate

**weighing machine**
**04** tron **05** trone **06** bismar **09** steelyard

**weight**
**01** w **02** wt **03** agw, gvw **04** bias, bulk, duty, gr wt, last, lead, load, mark, mass, nt wt, onus, pith, sway, tare **05** angle, clout, flesh, force, pease, peaze, peise, peize, peyse, poise, power, slang, slant, twist, value, wecht, worry **06** burden, impact, moment, scales, slight, strain **07** ballast, gravity, oppress, plummet, tonnage, trouble **08** gravitas, handicap, live load, poundage, pressure, quantity **09** authority, heaviness, influence, prejudice, substance, unbalance, weigh down **10** importance, importancy, ponderance, ponderancy **11** avoirdupois, consequence, encumbrance **12** significance **13** consideration, preponderance **14** impressiveness, responsibility

*See also* **boxing**

**• unit of weight**
**01** g, k, l, t **02** as, cg, ct, dg, gm, gr, hg, kg, lb, mg, oz, st **03** cwt, grt, kat, kin, kip, mna, oke, tod, ton, wey **04** boll, gram, kati, khat, kilo, mina, obol, pood, rotl, seer, tola, unce **05** candy, carat, catty, kandy, katti, liang, maneh, maund, ounce, picul, pikul, pound, stone, tical, todde, tonne **06** candie, carrat, cental, denier, dirhem, fother, gramme, kantar, shekel, talent **07** centner, lispund, scruple **08** decigram, lispound **09** centigram, milligram **10** decigramme **11** centigramme, milligramme

**weightless**
**04** airy **05** light **11** imponderous **13** insubstantial

**weighty**
**05** bulky, grave, great, heavy, hefty, solid, vital **06** severe, solemn, taxing **07** crucial, massive, onerous, pesante, serious **08** critical, exacting, pregnant, worrying **09** demanding, difficult, important, momentous, ponderous **10** burdensome **11** influential, significant, substantial **13** authoritative, consequential

**weir**
**03** pen **04** wear **05** cauld, garth, guard **06** lasher **07** ward off **09** fish-garth

**weird**
◇ *anagram indicator*
**03** odd, rum **04** doom, eery, fate **05** charm, eerie, queer, spell, witch **06** creepy, far-out, spooky, way-out, weyard **07** bizarre, destine, ghostly, strange, uncanny, weyward **08** eldritch, forewarn, freakish, peculiar, witching **09** grotesque, happening, left-field, unearthly, unnatural **10** mysterious **12** supernatural **13** preternatural

**weirdly**
**06** eerily **08** spookily **09** bizarrely, strangely **11** unnaturally **12** mysteriously **14** supernaturally

**weirdo**
**03** dag, nut **04** card, case, cure, geek, kook, loon, wack **05** crank, flake, freak, loony **06** nutter **07** cupcake, dingbat, nutcase, oddball, odd fish **08** crackpot **09** character, eccentric, fruitcake, queer fish **14** fish out of water

**welcome**
◇ *containment indicator*
**04** free, hail, meet **05** greet **06** accept, salute **07** acclaim, embrace, karanga, popular, powhiri, proface, receive **08** glad hand, greeting, haeremai, pleasant, pleasing **09** agreeable, approve of, ben venuto, desirable, gratulate, reception, red carpet **10** acceptable, acceptance, delightful, gratifying, refreshing, salutation, salutatory **11** acclamation, appreciated, hospitality **13** be pleased with **15** be satisfied with

**welcoming**
**04** cosy, warm **06** genial, hearty **07** affable, cordial, earnest **08** amicable, cheerful, friendly, homelike, pleasant, relaxing, sociable **09** agreeable, gemütlich, heartfelt, open-armed **10** hospitable **11** comfortable, stimulating, warm-hearted **12** affectionate, invigorating, wholehearted

**weld**
**04** bind, bond, fuse, join, link, pile, seal, seam, wald **05** braze, joint, seize, unite, wield **06** cement, solder **07** connect **09** dyer's-weed **10** mignonette, yellow-weed **11** dyer's rocket **15** dyer's-yellowweed

**welfare**
**04** good, heal, weal **05** hayle, state **06** health, income, profit **07** benefit, comfort, fortune, payment, pension, sick pay, success **08** interest, security **09** advantage, allowance, happiness, soundness, wellbeing **10** commonweal, prosperity **14** social security

**well**
**02** my, OK, so **03** eye, far, fit, jet, lor, sae, spa **04** ably, bien, eddy, fine, flow, font, good, gush, ooze, pool, pour, rise, rush, seep, weel **05** aweel, fitly, flood, fount, fully, good-o, issue, lucky, right, sound, spout, spurt, surge, swell, wally **06** atweel, cavity, deeply, easily, fairly, geyser, good-oh, highly, kindly, proper, robust, source, spring, stream, strong, supply, warmly **07** adeptly, clearly, closely, cockpit, fortune, greatly, happily, healthy, luckily, Mickery, rightly, spouter, trickle **08** all right, brim over, decently, expertly, fountain, genially, pleasing, probably, properly, suitably, thriving, very much, wellhead **09** advisable, agreeable, agreeably, carefully, certainly, correctly, fittingly, fortunate, glowingly, reservoir, skilfully, to a wonder, water hole **10** able-bodied, abundantly, adequately, admiringly, completely, favourably, generously, hospitably, intimately, pleasantly, profoundly, rigorously, splendidly, thoroughly, very likely, wellspring **11** approvingly, comfortable, comfortably,

competently, conceivably, effectively, efficiently, excellently, flourishing, fortunately, intensively **12** considerably, conveniently, in good health, proficiently, prosperously, satisfactory, successfully, sufficiently, watering hole **13** hale and hearty, industriously, quite possibly, substantially, weeping spring **14** satisfactorily, to a great extent **15** comprehensively

- **as well**

**03** als, and, tae, too **04** also, both **06** to boot **07** besides **08** moreover **10** in addition **11** furthermore **14** into the bargain

- **as well as**

**09** along with, including **12** in addition to, not to mention, over and above, together with **14** to say nothing of

- **well done**

**04** euge **05** bravo **06** encore, hurrah **08** congrats, good show **13** à la bonne heure **15** congratulations

**well-advised**

**04** wise **05** sound **06** shrewd **07** politic, prudent **08** sensible **09** judicious, sagacious **10** far-sighted, reasonable **11** circumspect, long-sighted

**well-balanced**

**04** even, sane **05** level, sober, sound **06** sorted, stable **08** balanced, rational, sensible, together **10** harmonious, reasonable **11** level-headed, symmetrical, well-ordered **12** well-adjusted

**well-behaved**

**04** good **06** polite, orderly **08** mannerly, obedient **09** compliant **10** good as gold, respectful **11** considerate, co-operative **12** under control, well-mannered

**wellbeing**

**04** good **06** health, wealth **07** comfort, welfare **09** eudaemony, happiness **10** eudaemonia, good health

**well-bred**

**05** civil **06** polite, urbane **07** gallant, genteel, refined **08** cultured, ladylike, mannerly **09** courteous **10** cultivated, upper-crust **11** blue-blooded, comme il faut, gentlemanly **12** aristocratic, well-mannered **13** well-brought-up

**well-built**

**05** beefy, burly, stout **06** brawny, strong, sturdy **08** muscular **09** strapping

**well-deserved**

**03** due **04** just, meet **07** condign, merited **08** deserved, rightful **09** justified **11** appropriate

**well-disposed**

**06** toward **07** healthy **08** amicable, friendly, towardly **09** agreeable, well-aimed **10** benevolent, favourable, well-minded, well-placed **11** sympathetic **12** well-arranged

**well-dressed**

**04** chic, neat, tidy, trim **05** natty, smart **06** dapper, spruce **07** elegant, stylish **11** fashionable, well-groomed

**well-founded**

**03** fit **05** right, sound, valid **06** proper **08** sensible **09** plausible, warranted **10** acceptable, reasonable **11** justifiable, sustainable

**well-groomed**

**04** neat, tidy, trim **05** smart **06** dapper, soigné, spruce **07** soignée **11** well-dressed **13** well-turned-out

**well-heeled**

**04** oofy, posh, rich **05** flush, solid **06** fat-cat, loaded **07** moneyed, opulent, wealthy, well-off **08** affluent, well-to-do **10** filthy rich, prosperous **11** comfortable, made of money, rolling in it, substantial **12** stinking rich

**well-informed**

**02** up **06** au fait, sussed **07** clued-up **09** au courant

**well-known**

**04** name **05** famed, noted, usual **06** common, famous, notour, of note **07** eminent, notable **08** familiar, renowned **09** notorious **10** celebrated, proverbial **11** illustrious, widely-known

**well-mannered**

**05** civil **06** polite, urbane **07** gallant, genteel, refined **08** cultured, ladylike, mannerly, well-bred **09** bien élevé, courteous **10** cultivated, upper-crust **11** blue-blooded, gentlemanly **12** aristocratic, house-trained **13** well-brought-up

**well-nigh**

**05** welly **06** all but, almost, nearly **09** just about, virtually **11** practically

**well-off**

**04** bein, bien, rich **05** flush, lucky **06** loaded, monied **07** moneyed, wealthy **08** affluent, thriving, well-to-do **09** fortunate **10** filthy rich, forehanded, in the money, prosperous, successful, well-heeled **11** comfortable, made of money, rolling in it **12** stinking rich **15** with money to burn

**well-read**

**07** studied **08** cultured, educated, lettered, literate **12** well-informed **13** knowledgeable

**Wells**

**02** HG

**well-spoken**

**05** clear **06** fluent **08** coherent, eloquent **10** articulate **13** well-expressed

**well-thought-of**

**07** admired, revered **08** esteemed, honoured **09** respected, venerated **10** looked up to **14** highly regarded

**well-to-do**

**04** oofy, posh, rich, warm **05** flush **06** fat-cat, loaded **07** moneyed, wealthy, well-off **08** affluent **10** filthy rich, prosperous **11** comfortable, made of money, rolling in it, substantial **12** stinking rich

**well-versed**

**02** up **06** au fait **07** trained **08** deep-read, familiar **10** acquainted, conversant **11** experienced **13** knowledgeable

**well-wisher**

**03** fan **06** friend **09** supporter **10** well-willer **11** sympathizer

**well-worn**

**04** worn **05** corny, stale, stock, tired, trite **06** frayed, ragged, shabby **07** cliché'd, scruffy, worn-out **08** clichéed, overused, timeworn **09** hackneyed **10** threadbare, unoriginal **11** commonplace, stereotyped **13** battle-scarred

**welsh**

**01** W **02** do **05** cheat **06** diddle **07** defraud, swindle

*Welsh first names include:*

**03** Dai, Huw, Nye, Wyn
**04** Aled, Alun, Ceri, Dewi, Enid, Eryl, Evan, Glyn, Gwen, Gwyn, Ifor, Ioan, Owen, Rees, Rhys, Siôn
**05** Carys, Cerys, Dilys, Dylan, Elwyn, Emlyn, Emrys, Ffion, Gavin, Haydn, Howel, Hywel, Idris, Ieuan, Lloyd, Madoc, Megan, Nerys, Olwen, Olwin, Olwyn, Rhian, Tudor
**06** Dafydd, Delyth, Dilwyn, Eirian, Eirlys, Eluned, Gareth, Gaynor, Gladys, Glenda, Glenys, Glynis, Gwenda, Gwilym, Howell, Mervyn, Morgan, Olwyne
**07** Aneirin, Aneurin, Bronwen, Brynmor, Eiluned, Geraint, Gwenyth, Gwillym, Gwyneth, Myfanwy, Myrddin, Peredur, Vaughan
**08** Angharad, Llewelyn, Meredith, Morwenna, Rhiannon
**09** Gwendolen, Gwenllian

*See also* **county**; **town**

**welt**

**03** dry **04** beat, blow, lash, mark, scar, weal **05** ridge, world, wound **06** streak, stripe, wither **08** cicatrix **09** cicatrice, contusion

**welter**

**03** web **04** mess, roll, toss, wade **05** heave, lurch, pitch **06** jumble, muddle, splash, tangle, wallow **07** smother **08** flounder, mish-mash **09** confusion **10** hotchpotch

**wend** *see* **Slav**

- **wend your way**

**02** go **04** hike, move, plod, walk **05** amble **06** travel, trudge, wander **07** meander, proceed **08** progress **11** make your way

**west**

**01** W **03** Mae **08** New World, Occident **10** Occidental

**• go west**
◇ *reversal indicator*
**03** die **06** perish **11** be destroyed **12** be dissipated

**western**
**01** W **06** ponent **07** westlin
**10** occidental

**Western Sahara**
**03** ESH

**West Virginia**
**02** WV **03** W Va

**wet**
**03** dip, wat **04** damp, dank, dram, drip, fool, jerk, moil, nerd, rain, soak, soft, sour, wash, weak, weed, weet, wimp, wuss **05** bewet, cissy, douse, flood, humid, idiot, imbue, madid, moist, muggy, rainy, softy, soggy, soppy, spray, steep, swamp, sweat, tipsy, wally, water, weedy **06** beweep, clammy, daggle, dampen, drench, drippy, effete, embrue, feeble, imbrue, liquid, madefy, slippy, sloppy, sluice, soaked, sodden, soused, splash, spongy, watery **07** debauch, draggle, drizzle, embrewe, milksop, moisten, pouring, raining, showery, soaking, sopping, squidgy, tearful, teeming, wetness, wimpish **08** bedabble, bedrench, dampness, drenched, dripping, humidity, irrigate, moisture, pathetic, saturate, slippery, sprinkle, timorous, weakling, wringing **09** drizzling, irriguous, moistness, saturated, spineless **10** clamminess, imbruement, irresolute, namby-pamby, sopping wet
**11** ineffective, ineffectual, madefaction, waterlogged
**12** condensation

**• wet behind the ears**
**03** new, raw **05** green, naive **06** callow
**08** gullible, immature, innocent
**09** untrained **13** inexperienced

**• wet patch** *see* **sea**

**wetness**
**03** wet **04** damp **05** water **06** liquid
**08** dampness, dankness, humidity, moisture **09** sogginess **10** clamminess, rising damp, soddenness
**12** condensation

**whack**
**03** box, cut, hit, lot, rap **04** bang, bash, beat, belt, biff, blow, cuff, part, slap, sock **05** clout, quota, share, smack, stint, thump **06** buffet, murder, strike, stroke, thrash, wallop **07** attempt, clobber, portion, rake-off **08** division
**09** allowance, parcel out **10** allocation, percentage, proportion **14** slice of the cake

**whacking**
**04** huge, mega, vast **05** giant, gross, jumbo **07** beating, immense, mammoth, massive, socking, Titanic, whaling **08** almighty, colossal, enormous, gigantic, great big, plonking, whopping **09** ginormous, humongous, monstrous, thrashing, walloping **10** astronomic, gargantuan, large-scale, prodigious, stupendous, tremendous **11** God-almighty
**12** considerable

**whale**
**05** Cetus **06** thrash

*Whales include:*

**03** fin, orc, sei
**04** blue, grey, orca
**05** black, minke, pigmy, piked, pilot, right, sperm, white
**06** baleen, beaked, beluga, caa'ing, finner, killer
**07** bowhead, dolphin, finback, grampus, Layard's, narwhal, rorqual, toothed
**08** humpback, porpoise
**09** Greenland, grindhval, razorback, whalebone
**10** bottlenose, humpbacked
**11** bottle-nosed, false killer
**12** river dolphin, strap-toothed
**13** common rorqual, Risso's dolphin, sulphur-bottom
**15** gangetic dolphin, harbour porpoise

**wharf**
**03** kay, key **04** dock, pier, quay **05** jetty
**06** marina, staith **07** staithe
**08** dockyard, quayside **12** landing-stage

**what**
**02** eh, my

**what's-its-name**
**05** gismo, thing **06** doings, doodad, doodah, doofus, jigger, thingy
**07** doobrey, doobrie, whatnot, whatsit
**08** thingamy **09** doohickey, jigamaree, jiggumbob, thingummy, timenoguy
**12** thingummybob, thingummyjig
**14** what-d'you-call-it
**15** whatchamacallit

**wheat**
**04** corn **05** durum, emmer, fitch, rivet, spelt **06** bulgur, sharps **07** bulghur, einkorn **08** amelcorn, semolina, Triticum

**wheedle**
**03** cog **04** blag, coax, draw **05** carny, charm, court **06** cajole, carney, cozy up, cuiter, entice, induce, phrase, whilly
**07** beguile, flatter, tweedle, win over
**08** butter up, inveigle, persuade, soft-soap, talk into **09** sweet-talk, whillywha **10** whillywhaw

**wheel**
◇ *reversal indicator*
**04** disc, hoop, reel, ring, roam, roll, spin, turn **05** dolly, orbit, pivot, ratch, rhomb, snail, swing, truck, twirl, whirl
**06** circle, dollar, gyrate, roller, rotate, sheave, swivel, wander **07** bicycle, go round, refrain, revolve, trindle, trochus, trolley, truckle **08** encircle, gyration, rotation, tricycle **10** revolution

*Wheels include:*

**03** big, cog, fly
**04** buff, cart, gear, idle, mill, worm
**05** bedel, bevel, crown, drive, idler, sakia, wagon, water
**06** castor, charka, escape, Ferris, paddle, prayer, sakieh
**07** balance, driving, fortune, potter's, ratchet, sakiyeh
**08** roulette, spinning, sprocket, spur gear, steering
**09** Catherine
**13** spinning jenny, throwing table, whirling-table

**• at the wheel**
**07** driving, turning **08** in charge, steering **09** at the helm, directing, heading up, in command, in control
**11** responsible **14** behind the wheel

**wheeze**
**03** gag **04** gasp, hiss, idea, joke, pant, plan, ploy, rasp, ruse **05** antic, cough, crack, prank, story, stunt, trick, whiss
**06** scheme **07** whaisle, whaizle, whistle, wrinkle **08** anecdote, chestnut, one-liner **11** catchphrase
**13** practical joke

**whelp**
**03** cub, pup **05** puppy **07** brachet
**08** bratchet

**whereabouts**
**04** site **05** place **08** location, position, vicinity **09** situation

**wherewithal**
**04** cash, dosh, loot **05** brass, bread, dough, funds, gravy, lolly, means, money, ready, smash **06** greens, moolah, stumpy **07** capital, readies, scratch, shekels **08** greenies, supplies
**09** megabucks, necessary, resources
**11** spondulicks

**whet**
**04** edge, file, hone, stir **05** grind, preen, rouse **06** arouse, awaken, excite, incite, kindle, stroke **07** provoke, quicken, sharpen **08** appetize, increase
**09** stimulate, titillate **11** scythe-stone

**whiff**
**04** gust, hint, puff, reek **05** aroma, blast, cigar, jiffy, odour, scent, smell, sniff, stink, touch, trace **06** breath, inhale, stench **07** draught, glimpse, soupçon **09** cigarette, suspicion
**10** suggestion

**while**
**02** as **04** span, time, when **05** spell, throw, until **06** period, season
**07** stretch, whereas **08** although, interval **09** the whilst **13** in the middle of

**• while away**
**03** use **04** pass **05** spend, use up
**06** devote, occupy

**whim**
**03** fad, toy **04** flam, idea, kink, swim, urge **05** crank, craze, fancy, flisk, freak, quirk **06** humour, maggot, megrim, notion, vagary, whimsy **07** caprice, conceit, impulse, passion, whimsey
**08** crotchet **11** whigmaleery
**12** whigmaleerie

**whimper**
**03** cry, sob **04** mewl, moan, pule, weep **05** groan, whine **06** snivel, whinge **07** grizzle, sniffle

**whimsical**
**03** fay, fey, fie, odd **05** dotty, droll, fairy, funny, queer, weird **06** quaint, quirky, whimsy **07** baroque, curious, playful, toysome, unusual **08** fanciful, peculiar **09** crotchety, eccentric, fantastic, impulsive **10** capricious, crotcheted **11** Disneyesque, fantastical, mischievous **13** unpredictable

**whimsy**
**03** odd **04** tick, whim **05** droll, funny, weird **06** fisgig, fizgig, quaint, quirky **07** curious, playful, unusual **08** fanciful, peculiar **09** eccentric, whimsical **10** changeable **13** unpredictable

**whine**
**03** cry, sob **04** beef, carp, moan, pule, wail **05** bleat, gripe, groan **06** grouch, grouse, kvetch, peenge, whinge, yammer **07** grizzle, grumble, wheenge, whimper **08** complain **09** bellyache, complaint

**whinge**
**04** beef, carp, moan **05** greet, gripe, groan, winge **06** grouse, peenge **07** grumble, wheenge **08** complain **09** bellyache, complaint

**whip**
◇ *anagram indicator*
**03** cat, fly, mix, tan, tat, taw **04** beat, belt, cane, crop, dart, dash, firk, flay, flit, flog, goad, hide, jerk, lash, prod, pull, push, rush, spur, stir, tear, urge, whap, whop, yank **05** birch, braid, drive, flash, knout, outdo, quirt, rouse, steal, strap, swish, thong, whack, whang, whisk **06** beat up, breech, defeat, driver, feague, incite, larrup, prompt, punish, snatch, switch, thrash, wallop **07** agitate, chabouk, cowhide, instant, kurbash, overlay, provoke, rawhide, scourge, sjambok **08** ash-plant, bullwhip, chastise, coachman, kourbash, overcast, vapulate **09** bullwhack, castigate, coachwhip, flagellum, horsewhip, instigate, longe whip, lunge whip, stock whip **10** black snake, discipline, flagellate, riding-crop **11** hunting-crop, hunting-whip, lunging whip, overcasting **13** cat-o'-nine-tails

• **whip up**
◇ *anagram indicator*
**04** beat **06** arouse, excite, foment, incite, kindle, stir up, work up **07** agitate, inflame, provoke, psych up **09** instigate, stimulate

**whippersnapper**
**03** imp **05** scamp **06** nipper, rascal **07** upstart, whiffet **08** whipster **09** pipsqueak, scallywag **11** hobbledehoy **14** snipper-snapper

**whipping**
**05** knout **06** caning, defeat, hiding, laldie **07** beating, belting, lashing, tanning **08** birching, flogging, spanking **09** scourging, thrashing, walloping **10** punishment **11** castigation, overcasting **12** flagellation

**whirl**
◇ *anagram indicator*
**04** daze, eddy, reel, roll, spin, tirl, turn **05** pivot, round, swing, swirl, twirl, twist, waltz, wheel **06** bustle, circle, flurry, gyrate, hubbub, jumble, muddle, rotate, series, swivel, tumult, uproar **07** revolve **08** gyration, rotation **09** agitation, commotion, confusion, giddiness, pirouette, turn round **10** hurly-burly, revolution, succession **12** circumgyrate, merry-go-round

• **give something a whirl**
**03** try **06** strive **07** attempt, have a go, venture **09** endeavour, have a bash, have a lash, have a shot, have a stab **10** have a crack **11** give it a burl

**whirlpool**
**04** eddy, gulf, weal, weel, weil, wiel **05** gurge **06** vortex **08** sea purse, swelchie **09** Charybdis, maelstrom

**whirlwind**
**04** eddy, rash **05** babel, chaos, hasty, noise, quick, rapid, swift **06** bedlam, furore, hubbub, speedy, tumult, typhon, uproar, vortex **07** anarchy, clamour, cyclone, tornado, turmoil, typhoon **08** headlong, madhouse **09** commotion, confusion, impetuous, impulsive, lightning, sand-devil **10** hullabaloo, tourbillon **11** pandemonium, tourbillion, white squall

**whisk**
◇ *anagram indicator*
**03** fly, mix, zip **04** beat, belt, bolt, bomb, dart, dash, dive, lash, pelt, race, rush, stir, tear, tuft, whid, whip, wipe **05** brush, flick, hurry, scoot, shoot, speed, sweep, swish, whist **06** beater, chowri, chowry, hasten, switch, twitch **07** panicle **09** egg beater **12** swizzle-stick

**whiskey**
**01** W

**whisky**
**04** dram, half **05** hooch **06** hootch **08** the grain **09** aqua vitae, good stuff, the cratur **10** barley-bree, barley-broo, usquebaugh **11** barley-broth, mountain dew, the Auld Kirk, water of life

*Whiskies include:*

**03** rye
**04** malt
**06** poteen, red-eye, Scotch
**07** blended, Bourbon, potheen, spunkie
**08** peat-reek, sour mash
**09** moonshine
**10** cornbrandy, corn whisky, single malt, tanglefoot
**12** the real McCoy
**13** the real Mackay
**14** chain lightning, tarantula juice

**whisper**
**03** bur **04** burr, buzz, hark, hint, hiss, sigh **05** round, sough, tinge, trace, whiff **06** breath, gossip, mumble, murmur, mutter, report, rumour, rustle, tittle, whisht **07** breathe, divulge, soupçon, wheesht **08** innuendo, intimate, low voice, susurrus **09** insinuate, soft voice, suspicion, susurrate, undertone **10** quiet voice, say quietly, suggestion **11** insinuation, pig's whisper **12** speak quietly, stage whisper **14** whittie-whattie

**whistle**
**04** call, ping, pipe, sing, song, sowf **05** cheep, chirp, siren, sowff, sowth, whiss **06** hooter, siffle, throat, warble **07** catcall, summons, tweedle, warbler, wheeple **09** quail-call, quail-pipe

**whit**
**03** bit, jot, rap **04** atom, dash, drop, fico, haet, ha'it, hate, hoot, iota, mite, snap, spot **05** aught, crumb, grain, piece, pinch, point, scrap, shred, speck, straw, trace **06** little **07** modicum, red cent **08** fragment, particle

**white**
**03** wan **04** hoar, leuc-, leuk-, pale, pure **05** ashen, hoary, leuco-, leuko-, light, moral, pasty, waxen **06** albino, bright, honest, pallid **07** albumen, anaemic, niveous, upright **08** innocent, reliable, spotless, virtuous **09** blameless, bloodless, burnished, stainless, undefiled **10** auspicious, colourless, favourable, honourable, immaculate **11** transparent, unblemished, unburnished **12** light-skinned

*Whites include:*

**04** ecru, grey, lily, opal, whey
**05** cream, ivory, milky, snowy
**06** argent, creamy, pearly, silver
**08** magnolia
**09** champagne, lily-white, snow-white
**11** silver-white

**white-collar**
**06** office **08** clerical, salaried **09** executive, non-manual **12** professional

**whiten**
**03** cam **04** calm, caum, fade, pale, snow **06** blanch, bleach **08** dealbate, etiolate, pipeclay **09** whitewash

**whitewash**
**04** beat, best, drub, -gate, hide, lick **05** crush, paste **06** granny, hammer, thrash **07** clobber, conceal, cover up, cover-up, grannie, trounce **08** suppress **09** calcimine, deception, gloss over, Kalsomine® **10** camouflage **11** concealment, make light of **13** defeat utterly

**whittle**
**03** cut, hew, use **04** fret, pare, trim **05** carve, erode, peach, shape, shave, use up **06** reduce, scrape **07** blanket, consume, eat away **08** diminish, wear away **09** undermine

**whole**
**03** all, fit, lot, sum **04** full, hale, mint, unit, well **05** piece, sound, total, uncut **06** entire, entity, healed, intact, strong, unhurt **07** healthy, perfect
**08** complete, ensemble, entirety, fullness, integral, sum total, totality, unbroken, unedited, unharmed
**09** aggregate, inviolate, undamaged, undivided, uninjured **10** altogether, completely, everything, in one piece, unabridged **11** full-blooded
• **on the whole**
**06** mostly **07** as a rule **08** all in all
**09** generally, in general, in the main
**10** by and large **13** predominantly
**14** for the most part

**wholehearted**
**04** real, true, warm **06** hearty
**07** devoted, earnest, genuine, sincere, zealous **08** complete, emphatic
**09** committed, dedicated, heartfelt, unfeigned **10** passionate, unreserved, unstinting **11** boots and all, unqualified
**12** enthusiastic

**wholeheartedly**
**06** warmly **08** heartily **09** genuinely, sincerely **10** completely
**12** emphatically, passionately, unreservedly

**wholesale**
**04** mass **05** broad, great, total **06** en bloc **07** in gross, massive, totally
**08** outright, sweeping **09** extensive, massively **11** extensively, far-reaching, wide-ranging **12** all-inclusive
**13** comprehensive **14** indiscriminate
**15** comprehensively

**wholesome**
**04** good, pure **05** clean, moral, sound, sweet **06** decent, proper **07** bracing, ethical, healthy, helpful, holesom
**08** edifying, healsome, holesome, hygienic, physical, remedial, salutary, sanitary, sensible, virtuous
**09** healthful, improving, righteous, uplifting **10** beneficial, healthsome, honourable, nourishing, nutritious, propitious, reasonable, refreshing, salubrious **11** respectable
**12** invigorating, squeaky-clean

**wholly**
**03** all **04** only **05** clear, fully, quite **06** in toto, purely **07** sheerly, totally, utterly
**08** entirely **09** perfectly, tout à fait
**10** absolutely, altogether, completely, thoroughly **11** exclusively **14** in every respect **15** comprehensively

**whoop**
**02** ho! **03** cry **04** hoop, hoot, roar, yell
**05** cheer, shout **06** holler, hurrah, scream, shriek

**whopper**
**03** fib, lie **05** fable, giant, whale
**07** cracker, mammoth, monster, plumper, slapper, stonker, swapper, swinger, swopper, untruth
**08** colossus, scrouger **09** falsehood, leviathan, tall story **10** fairy story, socdolager, sogdolager **11** fabrication, sockdolager, sockdoliger, sockdologer
**12** hippopotamus, slockdolager
*See also* **lie**

**whopping**
**03** big **04** huge, mega, vast **05** giant, great, jumbo, large **07** immense, mammoth, massive, whaling
**08** almighty, enormous, gigantic, great big, plonking, slapping, whacking
**09** ginormous, humongous, thrashing, walloping **10** monumental, prodigious, staggering, tremendous **11** God-almighty **13** extraordinary

**whore**
**03** pro, pug, tom **04** bawd, dell, drab, hoor, moll, punk, road, stew, tart
**05** brass, broad, quail, quiff, stale, tramp, trull, wench **06** bulker, callet, geisha, harlot, hooker, mutton, plover
**07** cocotte, floozie, hetaera, hostess, hustler, lorette, Paphian, pinnace, polecat, rent-boy, trollop, venture
**08** bona-roba, callgirl, dolly-mop, magdalen, strumpet **09** courtesan, hierodule, loose fish **10** cockatrice, convertite, fancy woman, loose woman, prostitute, rough trade, vizard-mask **11** fallen woman, fille de joie, laced mutton, night-walker, poule de luxe, public woman, working girl
**12** fille des rues, scarlet woman, street-walker **13** grande cocotte **14** lady of the night, woman of the town
*See also* **prostitute**

**whorehouse**
**03** kip **04** crib, stew **06** bagnio, bordel
**07** brothel, Corinth **08** bordello, cathouse, hothouse, red light
**10** bawdy-house, flash-house
**12** knocking-shop, leaping-house
**13** sporting house, vaulting-house
**14** house of ill fame **15** disorderly house

**whorl**
**04** coil, loop, turn **05** helix, twirl, twist
**06** spiral, volute, vortex **07** calicle, calycle, corolla **08** calycule, gyration, verticil, volution **09** corkscrew
**11** convolution

**wicked**
◇ *anagram indicator*
**03** ace, bad, def, fab, ill, rad **04** cool, evil, foul, mean, mega, neat, vile, wick
**05** awful, boffo, brill, cruel, felon, nasty, wrong **06** divine, fierce, groovy, guilty, impish, severe, sinful, unholy, unkind, way-out **07** amazing, corrupt, crucial, debased, harmful, heinous, immoral, intense, naughty, radical, roguish, ungodly, unlucky, vicious **08** clinking, depraved, devilish, dreadful, fabulous, heavenly, perverse, rascally, shameful, spiteful, stonking, terrible, terrific **09** abandoned, admirable, atrocious, brilliant, difficult, dissolute, egregious, excellent, fantastic, felonious, high-viced, injurious, miscreant, nefarious, offensive, scelerate, worthless **10** abominable, evil-minded, facinorous, flagitious, iniquitous, not half bad, scandalous, unpleasant, villainous **11** distressing, facinerious, mischievous, sensational, the business, troublesome, unrighteous **12** black-hearted, second to none, unprincipled **14** out of this world

**wickedness**
**03** ill, sin **04** evil **06** naught **07** impiety, pravity, villany **08** atrocity, enormity, evilness, foulness, iniquity, vileness, villainy **09** amorality, depravity, reprobacy **10** corruption, immorality, sinfulness **11** abomination, corruptness, heinousness
**12** devilishness, fiendishness, shamefulness **13** dissoluteness
**15** unrighteousness

**wickerwork**
**05** ratan **06** rattan, wattle, wicker
**10** basket-work, wattle-work

**wide**
**01** w **04** full, vast, wily **05** ample, baggy, broad, fully, great, loose, roomy
**06** astray, astute, remote **07** dilated, distant, general, immense
**08** expanded, extended, spacious
**09** all the way, capacious, extensive, off course, off target **10** completely, off the mark **11** far-reaching, wide-ranging
**12** latitudinous **13** comprehensive
**15** to the full extent

**wide-awake**
**04** keen, wary **05** alert, aware, sharp
**06** astute, roused **07** heedful, wakened
**08** vigilant, watchful **09** conscious, observant, on the ball **10** fully awake, on the alert, on your toes **11** quick-witted **12** on the qui vive

**wide-eyed**
**04** open **05** dazed, frank, fresh, naive
**06** amazed, simple **07** angelic, artless, natural, shocked, stunned **08** dewy-eyed, gullible, innocent, open-eyed, startled, trustful, trusting
**09** astounded, childlike, credulous, guileless, ingenuous, staggered, surprised, unworldly **10** astonished, bewildered, bowled over, confounded, gobsmacked, taken aback
**11** dumbfounded, open-mouthed
**12** lost for words, unsuspecting
**13** flabbergasted, inexperienced, knocked for six, thunderstruck
**15** unsophisticated

**widely**
**07** broadly **09** generally **11** extensively
**15** comprehensively

**widen**
**06** dilate, expand, extend, flanch, let out, spread **07** broaden, distend, enlarge, flaunch, stretch **08** increase

**wide-open**
**04** open, wide **06** gaping, spread
**07** exposed **09** outspread
**10** vulnerable **11** defenceless, susceptible, unfortified, unprotected
**12** outstretched

**wide-ranging**
**05** broad **08** sweeping, thorough **09** extensive, important, momentous, universal **10** widespread **11** far-reaching, scattershot, significant **13** comprehensive, thoroughgoing

**widespread**
**04** rife **05** broad **06** common, global **07** general, prolate **08** far-flung, sweeping **09** extensive, pervasive, prevalent, universal, unlimited, wholesale **10** wall-to-wall **11** far-reaching

**widow**
**04** sati **05** widdy **06** relict, suttee **07** bereave, dowager **08** feme sole, war widow **10** grass widow **11** hempen widow **12** queen dowager

**width**
**01** w **04** beam, span **05** girth, range, reach, scope **06** extent **07** breadth, compass, measure **08** diameter, latitude, wideness **09** amplitude, broadness, largeness, thickness **13** extensiveness

**wield**
**03** ply, use **04** gain, have, hold, play, rule, sway, wave, weld, wild, wind **05** apply, enjoy, exert, shake, sownd, swing **06** employ, handle, manage **07** command, control, possess, utilize **08** brandish, exercise, flourish, maintain **10** manipulate

**wife**
**01** w **02** ux **03** rib **04** dame, frau, lady, mate **05** bride, dutch, femme, queen, woman **06** missis, missus, spouse, vahine, wahine **07** consort, hostess, old lady, partner **08** helpmate, helpmeet, princess **09** child-wife, companion, concubine, first lady, other half **10** better half, her indoors, stepmother **11** little woman, sister-in-law **12** kickie-wickie, married woman **13** daughter-in-law **14** the little woman

**wig**
**03** jiz, tie **04** gizz, jasy, jazy **05** caxon, Irish, jasey, major, scold, syrup **06** bagwig, bobwig, Brutus, peruke, tie-wig, toupee, toupet **07** buzz-wig, periwig, Ramilie, scratch, spencer **08** perruque, postiche, Ramilies, Ramillie **09** hairpiece, Ramillies **10** full-bottom, scratch-wig **14** transformation

**wiggle**
**03** wag **04** jerk **05** shake, twist **06** jiggle, squirm, twitch, waggle, writhe **07** wriggle

**wild**
◇ *anagram indicator*
**03** mad, shy **04** bush, daft, keen, nuts, rash **05** angry, crazy, feral, livid, messy, myall, nutty, potty, rough, rowdy, waste, weald, wield **06** absurd, barren, casual, chance, choppy, desert, ferine, fierce, fuming, gallus, raging, random, rugged, savage, stormy, unruly, untame, untidy, unwise **07** agitato, aimless, bananas, berserk, blazing, bonkers, brutish, enraged, excited, fervent, foolish, frantic, furious, gallows, lawless, natural, rampant, riotous, ropable, salvage, tousled, uncouth, unkempt, untamed, violent, wayward **08** agitated, agrestal, blustery, chimeric, demented, desolate, fanciful, forsaken, frenzied, incensed, reckless, romantic, ropeable, terrific, unbroken, uncombed, vehement, warragal, warragle, warragul, warrigal **09** agrestial, arbitrary, barbarous, enjoyable, fanatical, fantastic, ferocious, foolhardy, haphazard, hit-or-miss, imprudent, impulsive, irregular, primitive, turbulent, unsettled **10** accidental, boisterous, chimerical, disordered, disorderly, distracted, distraught, fortuitous, hopping mad, incidental, infuriated, irrational, licentious, outrageous, passionate, ridiculous **11** approximate, dishevelled, extravagant, fantastical, impractical, purposeless, tempestuous, uncivilized, uninhabited, unpopulated **12** enthusiastic, ferae naturae, inhospitable, out of control, preposterous, unconsidered, uncontrolled, uncultivated, ungovernable, unmanageable, unrestrained **13** impracticable, serendipitous, undisciplined, uninhabitable **14** beside yourself, indiscriminate, skimble-skamble, uncontrollable, undomesticated

• **run wild**
◇ *anagram indicator*
**04** lamp, riot **05** feral **07** rampage

**wild animal** *see* **animal**

**wilderness**
**05** waste, wilds **06** desert, jungle **09** wasteland

**wild flower** *see* **flower**

**wildlife**
**05** fauna **07** animals

**wildly**
◇ *anagram indicator*
**07** angrily, noisily **08** absurdly, casually **09** aimlessly, defiantly, foolishly, furiously, riotously **10** recklessly **11** arbitrarily, chaotically, haphazardly **12** anarchically, boisterously, outrageously, rebelliously, ridiculously **13** extravagantly, fantastically, irresponsibly **14** preposterously, uncontrollably, unmethodically, unrestrainedly

**wilds**
**06** desert **07** outback **09** the sticks, wasteland **10** the boonies, wilderness **11** remote areas **12** the boondocks **15** the back of beyond

**wiles**
**05** fraud, guile, ploys, ruses **06** deceit, dodges, tricks **07** cunning, devices **08** cheating, trickery **09** chicanery, deception **10** artfulness, craftiness, manoeuvres, stratagems, subterfuge **12** contrivances

**wilful**
**06** dogged, mulish **07** planned, wayward, willing **08** contrary, obdurate, perverse, stubborn, willyard, willyart **09** conscious, obstinate, pig-headed, voluntary **10** calculated, deliberate, determined, headstrong, inflexible, refractory, self-willed, unyielding **11** intentional, intractable **12** intransigent, premeditated **14** uncompromising

**will**
**02** 'll **03** aim, way **04** lust, mind, Self, want, wish **05** fancy, leave, order **06** astray, choice, choose, compel, confer, decree, desire, devise, direct, intend, option, ordain, pass on **07** at a loss, command, feeling, purpose, require, resolve **08** attitude, bequeath, decision, hand down, pass down, pleasure, transfer, volition **09** dispose of, intention, testament, willpower **10** bewildered, discretion, preference, resolution **11** disposition, inclination, prerogative **13** determination **14** purposefulness

**William**
**02** Wm **04** Bill, Will **05** Billy, Willy

**willing**
**02** on **04** game, glad, keen **05** eager, happy, prone, ready **06** chosen **07** content, pleased, up for it **08** amenable, biddable, disposed, inclined, prepared, so-minded **09** agreeable, compliant, volitient, voluntary **10** consenting, favourable **11** co-operative, intentional **12** enthusiastic, well-disposed

**willingly**
**04** leve, lief, soon **05** lieve **06** freely, gladly **07** eagerly, happily, readily **08** by choice, in a hurry **09** like a shot **10** cheerfully **11** voluntarily **12** nothing loath **14** unhesitatingly

**willingness**
**04** will, wish **06** desire, favour **07** consent **08** volition **09** agreement, readiness **10** compliance, enthusiasm **11** disposition, inclination **12** complaisance **13** agreeableness

**will-o'-the-wisp**
**06** min min **07** fen-fire, spunkie **08** wildfire **09** nightfire **11** fatuous fire, ignis fatuus **12** Jack-o'-lantern **13** friar's lantern

**willow**
**04** sale, seal **05** osier, salix, sauch, saugh, withy **06** sallow

**willowy**
**04** slim, tall **05** lithe **06** limber, lissom, supple, svelte **07** slender **08** flexible, graceful **09** lithesome, sylph-like

**willpower**
**04** grit, will **05** drive **07** resolve **10** commitment, doggedness,

resolution **11** persistence, self-command, self-control, self-mastery **13** determination **14** self-discipline, strength of will

**willy-nilly**
**08** by chance, perforce, randomly **10** carelessly **11** arbitrarily, haphazardly, irregularly, necessarily, of necessity **12** compulsorily, nolens volens **14** unmethodically

**wilt**
**03** ebb, sag, wot **04** fade, fail, flag, flop, sink, wane, woot **05** droop, faint, taint **06** lessen, weaken, wither **07** dwindle, shrivel **08** diminish, grow less, languish

**wily**
**03** fly, sly **04** foxy, wide **05** sharp **06** artful, astute, crafty, shifty, shrewd, tricky **07** crooked, cunning, versute **08** cheating, guileful, scheming **09** deceitful, deceptive, designing, underhand **10** intriguing, streetwise

**wimp**
**03** wet **04** clot, drip, fool, jerk, nerd, tonk, weed, wuss **05** clown, softy, wally **07** milksop **10** namby-pamby

**wimpish**
**03** wet **04** soft, weak **05** cissy, weedy, wussy **06** drippy, effete, feeble **08** pathetic, timorous **09** spineless **10** irresolute, namby-pamby **11** ineffective, ineffectual

**win**
**03** get, net, pot **04** earn, gain, mine **05** carry, catch, penny, reach **06** allure, attain, effect, obtain, open up, result, secure **07** achieve, acquire, collect, conquer, mastery, prevail, procure, receive, succeed, success, triumph, victory **08** atchieve, carry off, conquest, overcome, persuade **09** come first, win the day **10** accomplish, strike gold **11** come in first, finish first, squeeze home **12** be victorious, come out on top, turn up trumps, win hands down **13** hit the jackpot, squeak through **14** achieve success

**• win over**
**04** sway **05** bribe, charm **06** allure, engage, nobble **07** attract, buy over, convert **08** convince, persuade, win round **09** influence, talk round **10** bring round, conciliate **11** prevail upon

**wince**
**04** jerk, jump, kick, reel **05** cower, quail, start **06** blench, cringe, flinch, recoil, roller, shrink **08** draw back **09** pull a face

**wind**
◇ *anagram indicator*
**02** go **03** air **04** bend, burp, coil, curl, furl, gale, gust, haul, hint, loop, puff, reel, roll, turn, veer, wrap **05** blast, curve, hoist, snake, twine, twist, weave, wield **06** breath, breeze, enfold, ramble, spiral, writhe, zigzag **07** bluster, conceit, current, deviate, draught, meander, turning, wreathe, wriggle **08** encircle **10** air-current, flatulence, suggestion **12** twist and turn

*Winds include:*

**04** berg, bise, bora, east, föhn, helm
**05** Eurus, north, Notus, trade, zonda
**06** Auster, Boreas, buster, doctor, El Niño, levant, samiel, simoom, zephyr
**07** Aquilon, austral, chinook, cyclone, etesian, gregale, khamsin, meltemi, mistral, monsoon, pampero, sirocco, tornado, twister
**08** Argestes, Favonian, Favonius, libeccio, westerly, williwaw
**09** harmattan, hurricane, nor'wester, snow eater, southerly
**10** Cape doctor, Euroclydon, prevailing, tramontana, wet chinook, willy-willy
**11** anticyclone
**15** southerly buster

**• get wind of**
**07** learn of **08** discover **09** hear about **12** find out about **13** become aware of

**• in the wind**
**06** likely **08** expected, probable **10** on the cards **13** about to happen

**• put the wind up**
**05** alarm, daunt, panic, scare, spook **06** boggle, rattle **07** agitate, perturb, startle, unnerve **08** frighten **10** discourage **13** sound the alarm

**• wind down**
**04** slow, stop **05** chill, relax **06** cool it, ease up, lessen, reduce, unwind **07** decline, dwindle, subside **08** calm down, chill out, diminish, slow down **09** hang loose, lighten up **10** slacken off, take it easy **11** come to an end, quieten down **12** bring to an end **13** let yourself go, put your feet up **14** take things easy **15** let your hair down

**• wind up**
**03** end, kid, rib **04** fool, furl, goof, span, stop **05** anger, annoy, close, end up, hoist, tease, trick, uptie **06** excite, finish, settle **07** agitate, tighten **08** conclude, finalize, finish up, irritate **09** close down, liquidate, make fun of, terminate **10** disconcert **12** bring to an end, find yourself **13** bring to a close **15** pull someone's leg

**windbag**
**04** bore **06** gasbag, gossip **07** blether, boaster **08** bigmouth, braggart

**winded**
**06** puffed **07** panting **09** out of puff, puffed out **10** breathless **11** out of breath

**windfall**
**04** find **05** manna **06** caduac **07** bonanza, godsend, jackpot **12** stroke of luck **13** treasure-trove

**winding**
◇ *anagram indicator*
**04** mazy, turn **06** creeky, spiral **07** bending, coiling, crankle, crooked, curving, devious, sinuate, sinuous, turning, twining **08** flexuose, flexuous, indirect, sinuated, tortuous, twisting **09** meandrian, meandrous **10** circuitous, convoluted, meandering, roundabout, serpentine **11** anfractuous **12** serpentinous **14** crinkle-crankle

**window**
**05** light **07** opening

*Windows include:*

**03** bay, bow
**04** pane, rose, sash, shop
**05** oriel
**06** dormer, French, lancet, louvre, Norman, screen, ticket
**07** compass, lucarne, sliding
**08** astragal, bull's eye, casement, fanlight, porthole, skylight
**09** decorated, mullioned, patio door
**10** windscreen
**11** oeil-de-boeuf
**12** double-glazed, early English, quarterlight, stained glass
**13** double-glazing, perpendicular
**14** Catherine wheel
**15** secondary-glazed

**windpipe**
**05** pipes **06** larynx, throat **07** pharynx, trachea, weasand **08** thrapple, thropple, throttle **11** weasand-pipe

**windswept**
**04** open **05** bleak, blowy, messy, windy **06** barren, untidy **07** exposed, in a mess, ruffled, tousled, unkempt **08** desolate **09** windblown **10** disordered **11** dishevelled, unprotected, unsheltered

**windward**
**04** luff **07** weather

**• beat to windward**
**04** turn, work **06** laveer

**• to windward**
**02** up **05** aloof **08** a-weather

**windy**
**04** wild **05** blowy, gusty, nervy, timid, wordy **06** afraid, breezy, on edge, prolix, scared, stormy, turgid, uneasy **07** anxious, chicken, nervous, pompous, squally, ventose, verbose **08** blustery, rambling, stressed **09** bombastic, garrulous, windswept **10** frightened, long-winded **11** tempestuous

**wine**
**02** en- **03** eno-, oen-, oin-, vin **04** oeno-, oino-, vino

*Wines include:*

**03** Dão, dry, red, sec
**04** Asti, brut, Cava, fino, hock, port, rosé, sack, Sekt, Tent
**05** blush, bombo, Douro, Fitou, Gamay, house, Mâcon, Médoc, plonk, Rioja, Soave, straw, sweet, Syrah, table, Tavel, Tokay, tonic, white
**06** Alsace, Barolo, Barsac, Beaune, canary, claret, grappa, Graves, Malaga, Malbec, Merlot, mulled, Muscat, Pontac, sherry, Shiraz
**07** alicant, Amarone, Auslese, Barbera,

Bunyuls, Chablis, Chianti, Cinsaut, demi-sec, Madeira, Margaux, Marsala, moselle, oloroso, Orvieto, retsina, sangria, vintage, Vouvray
**08** Alicante, Bordeaux, Brunello, bucellas, Burgundy, Carignan, Cinsault, Dolcetto, Frascati, Garnacha, Glühwein, Grenache, house red, jerepigo, Kabinett, Malvasia, Marsanne, Montilla, Muscadet, muscatel, Nebbiolo, New World, Palomino, Pauillac, Pinotage, Pornerol, Riesling, Rousanne, ruby port, Sancerre, Sauterne, Sémillon, Spätlese, Spumante, St Julien, Vermouth
**09** Bardolino, Carignane, champagne, Colombard, dry sherry, fortified, Frizzante, Hermitage, Lambrusco, Langue d'Oc, Minervois, Pinot Gris, Pinot Noir, Sauternes, sparkling, St-Émilion, Tarragona, tawny port, Trebbiano, Ugni Blanc, white port, Zinfandel
**10** Barbaresco, Beaujolais, Chambertin, Chardonnay, Constantia, Grignolino, house white, Manzanilla, Mateus Rosé, Monastrell, Muscadelle, Piesporter, Pinot Blanc, Sangiovese, Verdicchio, vinho verde
**11** alcohol-free, amontillado, Chenin Blanc, Niersteiner, Pinot Grigio, Pouilly-Fumé, Rüdesheimer, Steinberger, sweet sherry, Tempranillo, vintage port
**12** Blanc de Noirs, Côtes du Rhône, Johannisberg, medium sherry, Pedro Ximénez, Ruby Cabernet, Tinta Barroca, Valpolicella
**13** Blanc de Blancs, Cabernet Franc, Château Lafite, Liebfraumilch, Montepulciano, Pouilly-Fuissé
**14** Crémant d'Alsace, Crémant de Loire, Lacrima Christi, Sauvignon Blanc
**15** Crozes-Hermitage, Gewürztraminer, lachryma Christi

*Wine-bottle sizes include:*

**06** flagon, magnum
**08** jeroboam, rehoboam
**09** balthazar
**10** methuselah, salmanazar
**11** Marie-Jeanne
**14** nebuchadnezzar

*See also* **bottle**

• **wine-grower**
**05** viner **08** vigneron

**wine glass**
**05** flute, glass **06** goblet **07** balloon **08** schooner **09** straw-stem

**wing**
**02** el **03** ala, arm, fan, fly, set, van **04** flit, move, part, pass, race, sail, side, soar, vane, waft, zoom **05** alula, flank, flock, glide, group, hurry, penny, pinna, right, speed **06** annexe, branch, circle, flight, hasten, pinion, travel **07** adjunct, coterie, faction, section, segment **08** grouping **09** extension, liverwing **10** attachment **11** parascenium

• **wing it**
**04** vamp **05** ad-lib **06** busk it **09** play by ear **11** extemporize **15** speak off the cuff

**wingless**
◇ *ends deletion indicator*

**wink**
**04** pink **05** blink, eliad, flash, gleam, glint **06** eyliad, illiad, moment, second **07** connive, eyeliad, flicker, flutter, glimmer, glitter, instant, nictate, sparkle, twinkle **08** oeillade **09** nictation, nictitate **10** glimmering **11** nictitation, split second

• **wink at**
**06** ignore **07** condone, neglect **08** overlook, pass over **09** disregard **14** take no notice of **15** turn a blind eye to

**winkle**
**04** pupu, worm **05** flush, force, prise **07** draw out, extract **09** extricate

**winner**
**03** ace, dux **05** champ **06** top dog, victor **08** champion, prizeman **09** conqueror, medallist **10** prizewoman, vanquisher **11** prizewinner, title-holder, world-beater **13** Nobel laureate

**winning**
**02** up **05** sweet **06** lovely **07** amiable, winsome **08** alluring, charming, engaging, fetching, pleasing, unbeaten **09** beguiling, endearing **10** attractive, bewitching, conquering, delightful, enchanting, persuasive, successful, triumphant, undefeated, victorious **11** captivating, vanquishing **13** prepossessing

**winnings**
**05** booty, gains, prize **06** prizes, spoils, velvet **07** jackpot, profits, takings **08** proceeds **10** prize money

**winnow**
**03** fan, fly, van **04** comb, cull, flap, part, sift, sort, waft **06** divide, screen, select **07** diffuse, flutter **08** separate **09** ventilate

**winsome**
**05** sweet **06** comely, lovely, pretty **07** amiable **08** alluring, charming, cheerful, engaging, fetching, pleasant, pleasing **09** appealing, beguiling, endearing **10** attractive, bewitching, delectable, delightful, enchanting **11** captivating **13** prepossessing

**wintry**
**03** icy, raw **04** cold, cool **05** bleak, harsh, snowy **06** arctic, biting, chilly, dismal, frosty, frozen, hiemal, stormy **07** brumous, glacial, hostile **08** desolate, freezing, hibernal, piercing **09** cheerless **10** Decemberly, unfriendly **11** Decemberish

**wipe**
**03** dab, dry, mop, rub **04** blow, dust, jibe, null, scar, swab **05** brand, brush, clean, clear, dicht, dight, erase, purge, scrub, sweep, swipe **06** cancel, forget, reject, remove, sponge, strike **07** cleanse, deterge, expunct, expunge, sarcasm, take off **08** absterge, get rid of, take away **09** eliminate, eradicate **12** handkerchief

• **wipe out**
**03** zap **04** kill, null, raze **05** erase, purge, sweep, waste **06** efface, murder, rub out, sponge **07** abolish, blot out, destroy, expunct, expunge **08** blow away, decimate, demolish, massacre **09** eliminate, eradicate, extirpate, liquidate, polish off **10** annihilate, obliterate **11** exterminate

**wire**
**04** bind, coil **05** cable, snare **06** aerial, needle, tip-off **07** connect, protect, support, warning **08** telegram **09** telegraph, telephone **10** pickpocket **11** information **13** finishing line

**wire-pulling**
**04** pull **05** clout **08** intrigue, plotting, scheming **09** influence **10** conspiring **12** manipulation

**wiry**
**04** lean, wavy **05** rough, tough **06** coarse, sinewy, strong **08** muscular

**Wisconsin**
**02** WI **03** Wis

**wisdom**
**05** sense **06** genius, reason, sanity **07** insight **08** learning, prudence, sagacity, sapience **09** erudition, foresight, judgement, knowledge **10** astuteness, experience **11** common sense, discernment, penetration, skilfulness, speculation **12** intelligence **13** comprehension, enlightenment, judiciousness, understanding **14** circumspection

**wise**
**03** way **04** sage, wice **05** aware, godly, pious, sound, weise, weize, witty **06** astute, clever, manner, owlish, shrewd **07** erudite, knowing, learned, politic, prudent, sapient, skilful **08** discreet, educated, informed, rational, sensible **09** judicious, sagacious **10** discerning, far-sighted, perceptive, proficient, reasonable **11** circumspect, common-sense, enlightened, experienced, intelligent, long-sighted, well-advised **12** well-informed **13** knowledgeable, sophisticated, understanding

• **put wise**
**04** tell, warn **05** alert **06** clue in, fill in, inform, notify, tip off, wise up **07** apprise **10** intimate to **15** put in the picture

• **wise man**

*The Three Wise Men:*

**06** Caspar
**08** Melchior
**09** Balthasar

*See also* **sage**

**wiseacre**
**03** owl **05** Solon **07** wise guy **08** wiseling **09** Gothamite, smart alec **10** clever dick **11** smartypants

**wisecrack**
**03** gag, pun **04** barb, gibe, jest, joke, quip **05** funny **06** in-joke **08** one-liner **09** witticism

**wisely**
**06** sagely **07** clearly, soundly **08** sensibly, shrewdly **09** advisedly, knowingly **10** rationally **11** sagaciously **12** perceptively **13** intelligently

**wish**
**03** ask, bid, wis, yen **04** hope, know, long, lust, need, pine, urge, want, whim, will, wist **05** covet, crave, fancy, order, yearn **06** aspire, desire, direct, hanker, hunger, liking, prefer, thirst **07** believe, bewitch, bidding, command, craving, longing, request, require **08** fondness, instruct, yearning **09** hankering, recommend **10** aspiration, preference **11** inclination, instruction, malediction

• **best wishes**
**04** best **08** mazeltov, well-wish **09** good-speed

**wishy-washy**
**04** flat, pale, thin, weak **05** bland, vapid **06** feeble, sloppy, watery **07** diluted, insipid, vanilla **09** tasteless **10** namby-pamby **11** ineffective, ineffectual, watered-down **12** milk-and-water

**wisp**
**04** lock, tuft, wase **05** flock, piece, plume, shred, twist **06** strand, thread

**wispy**
**04** fine, thin **05** faint, frail, light **06** flimsy, slight **07** fragile **08** delicate, ethereal, gossamer, straggly **10** attenuated **13** insubstantial

**wistful**
**03** sad **06** dreamy, intent, musing **07** earnest, forlorn, longing, pensive, wishful **08** dreaming, mournful, yearning **09** regretful **10** meditative, melancholy, reflective, thoughtful **12** disconsolate **13** contemplative

**wistfully**
**05** sadly **09** forlornly, longingly, pensively **10** mournfully **11** plaintively **12** thoughtfully

**wit**
**03** wag **04** know, mind, nous, salt **05** comic, joker, sense **06** banter, brains, esprit, gagman, humour, levity, reason, wisdom **07** discern, insight, marbles, sparkle **08** badinage, comedian, concetto, drollery, gumption, humorist, merum sal, repartee, sagacity, satirist **09** Attic salt, bel esprit, eutrapely, faculties, funniness, ingenuity, intellect, invention, judgement, mother wit, recognize, wittiness **10** astuteness, cleverness, eutrapelia, jocularity, liveliness, shrewdness **11** common sense, imagination, information, waggishness **12** homme d'esprit, intelligence **13** facetiousness, understanding

**witch**
**04** mage, wich, wych **05** crone, magus **08** magician

*Witches, witch doctors and wizards include:*

**03** hag, hex
**05** Hecat, lamia, sibyl, weird
**06** Hecate, magian, mganga, shaman, voodoo, wisard, zendik
**07** angekok, carline, sangoma, warlock, wise man
**08** angekkok, conjurer, marabout, night-hag
**09** enchanter, galdragon, occultist, pythoness, sorceress, wise woman, witch-wife
**10** besom-rider, craigfluke, reim-kennar
**11** enchantress, gyre-carline, medicine man, necromancer, thaumaturge
**12** Weird Sisters
**13** thaumaturgist

*Witch- and wizard-related terms include:*

**03** hex
**04** mojo, muti, wart
**05** charm, coven, goety, magic, spell, wicca
**06** cackle, potion, Sabbat, voodoo, voudou
**07** cantrip, gramary, hag-seed, pricker, Sabbath, sorcery
**08** black art, black cat, cauldron, diablery, familiar, gramarye, pishogue, wizardry
**09** diablerie, enchanted, occultism, the occult, witch's hat
**10** black magic, broomstick, divination, necromancy, witchcraft
**11** apotropaism, conjuration, enchantment, incantation, thaumaturgy, the black art, witch-finder
**12** witching hour
**14** Walpurgis night

**witchcraft**
**03** obi **04** obia **05** magic, obeah, spell, wicca **06** makatu, voodoo **07** myalism, sorcery **08** wizardry **09** occultism, the occult **10** black magic, divination, necromancy **11** conjuration, enchantment, incantation, the black art

**witch doctor**
**06** mganga, shaman **07** angekok, sangoma **08** magician, marabout **11** medicine man **13** medicine woman

**witch hunt**
**08** hounding **09** hue and cry **11** McCarthyism

**with**
◇ *juxtaposition indicator*
**01** w **02** by, in, of **03** cum, mit **04** avec **05** among, using **06** beside, having **08** together **09** including **10** containing, possessing **13** accompanied by **14** in the company of

**withdraw**
◇ *deletion indicator*
**02** go **04** pull, walk **05** annul, leave, unsay **06** abjure, call in, cancel, cry off, depart, detach, go away, opt out, recall, recant, recede, recoil, remove, repair, retire, revoke, secede, shrink **07** abolish, back out, call off, deflect, draw out, drop out, extract, give way, go aside, inshell, nullify, pull out, rescind, retract, retreat, scratch, subduce, subduct, take out **08** disclaim, draw back, evacuate, fall back, pull away, pull back, separate, step down, subtract, take away, take back **09** turn aside **10** declare off, shrink back **11** contract out, discontinue **14** absent yourself

**withdrawal**
**03** tap **04** exit **06** exodus, recall, shrink **07** Dunkirk, removal, retiral, retreat **08** backword, delivery, pullback, recourse **09** breakaway, departure, disavowal, recession, revulsion, secession **10** abjuration, disclaimer, drawing out, evacuation, extraction, retirement, revocation, subduction, taking away **11** abstraction, drawing back, falling back, pulling back, recantation, repudiation, subtraction **13** disengagement

**withdrawn**
**03** shy **05** aloof, quiet **06** hidden, remote, silent **07** distant, private, retired **08** alienate, detached, isolated, reserved, retiring, secluded, solitary, taciturn **09** introvert, shrinking **10** unsociable **11** introverted, out-of-the-way **12** unresponsive **13** unforthcoming **15** uncommunicative

**wither**
**03** die, dry **04** fade, sear, sere, wane, welk, welt, wilt **05** arefy, blast, decay, droop, dry up, taint, waste **06** blight, die off, gizzen, perish, scorch, shrink, weaken **07** decline, destroy, dwindle, miff off, mortify, shrivel **08** fade away, languish **09** disappear, humiliate **12** disintegrate

**withering**
**06** deadly, fading **08** autumnal, blasting, scathing, scornful, snubbing, wounding **09** blighting, scorching **10** marcescent, mortifying **11** destructive, devastating, humiliating **12** contemptuous, death-dealing

**withhold**
◇ *deletion indicator*
**04** curb, hide, keep, stop **05** check **06** deduct, detain, refuse, retain **07** conceal, control, decline, forbear, repress, reserve **08** hold back, keep back, postpone, restrain, subtract, suppress **11** keep in check

**within**
◇ *hidden indicator*
◇ *insertion indicator*
**02** in **04** into **05** intra **06** entire, herein, inside **07** indoors, not over **08** inside of, inwardly **09** in reach of **10** enclosed by **12** surrounded by

**with it**
**02** in **03** hep, hip **04** cool **05** funky, natty, ritzy, vogue **06** glitzy, groovy, modern, modish, snazzy, trendy
**08** up-to-date **10** all the rage
**11** fashionable, progressive
**12** contemporary **13** up-to-the-minute

**without**
◇ *containment indicator*
**01** a-, x **02** an-, ex, w/o **03** sen **04** less, sans, sine **06** beyond, except, unless **07** lacking, needing, outside, wanting **08** free from, in need of **09** not having, outwardly **10** deprived of

**withstand**
**04** bear, defy, face **05** brave, fight, stand **06** endure, hinder, oppose, resist, take on, thwart **07** hold off, hold out, last out, survive, weather
**08** confront, cope with, tolerate, tough out **09** put up with, stand fast, stand firm, stand up to **10** tough it out **14** hold your ground **15** stand your ground

**witless**
**04** daft, dull, nuts **05** barmy, crazy, inane, loony, loopy, nutty, potty, silly
**06** cuckoo, mental, raving, stupid
**07** bonkers, foolish, idiotic, moronic, unaware **08** doolally, gaumless, gormless, mindless **09** cretinous, imbecilic, senseless, up the wall
**10** half-witted **11** empty-headed, off the rails, unconscious **12** mad as a hatter, off your chump **13** off your rocker, unintelligent **14** wrong in the head

**witness**
**03** see **04** mark, note, show, sign, view **05** prove, see in, teste, watch **06** affirm, attest, depose, evince, expert, look on, notice, obtest, record, verify, viewer
**07** bear out, confirm, endorse, observe, support, testify, vouchee, watcher **08** deponent, evidence, looker-on, observer, onlooker, perceive, speak for, validate
**09** attestant, authority, bystander, spectator, testifier, testimony
**10** eyewitness, man of skill **11** bear witness, compurgator, corroborate, countersign **12** be evidence of, give evidence

• **bear witness**
**04** aver, show **05** prove **06** adjure, affirm, assert, attest, evince, record, verify **07** certify, confirm, declare, display, endorse, testify **08** evidence, manifest, vouch for **10** asseverate
**11** corroborate, demonstrate

**witter**
**04** chat **06** babble, drivel, gabble, gossip, jabber, patter, rattle **07** blather, blether, chatter, twaddle, twattle, twitter

**witticism**
**03** hit, pun **04** jibe, joke, quip **06** bon mot **07** epigram, riposte **08** one-liner, repartee **09** impromptu, wisecrack
**10** jeu d'esprit, pleasantry **11** play on words
*See also* **joke**

**wittingly**
**08** by design, wilfully **09** knowingly, on purpose, purposely, studiedly, willingly
**10** designedly **11** consciously
**12** calculatedly, deliberately
**13** intentionally

**witty**
**04** wise **05** comic, droll, funny, light, salty, smart **06** clever, lively
**07** amusing, jocular, lambent, waggish
**08** discreet, fanciful, humorous, original, pregnant, sensible **09** brilliant, conceited, facetious, ingenious, sarcastic, sparkling, spiritual, spirituel, whimsical **11** coruscating, sharp-witted, spirituelle

**wizard**
**03** ace, hex **04** good, star, whiz
**05** adept, great, super, witch
**06** expert, genius, master, superb, wisard **07** hotshot, maestro, prodigy, warlock, wise man **08** conjurer, magician, smashing, sorcerer, terrific, virtuoso **09** brilliant, enchanter, enjoyable, fantastic, occultist, wonderful **10** delightful, marvellous, tremendous **11** necromancer, sensational, thaumaturge
*See also* **witch**

**wizened**
**04** thin, worn **05** lined **07** dried up, gnarled **08** shrunken, withered, wrinkled **10** shrivelled

**wobble**
◇ *anagram indicator*
**04** rock, sway **05** quake, shake, waver
**06** coggle, dither, dodder, quaver, quiver, seesaw, teeter, totter, tremor, wabble **07** precess, quaking, shoggle, stagger, tremble, vibrate **08** hesitate
**09** fluctuate, oscillate, vacillate, vibration **11** oscillation **12** shilly-shally, unsteadiness, wibble-wobble

**wobbly**
◇ *anagram indicator*
**05** shaky, wonky **06** uneven, unsafe
**07** doddery, rickety **08** unstable, unsteady **09** doddering, quavering, teetering, tottering, trembling
**10** unbalanced

**Wodehouse**
**02** PG

**woe**
**02** wo **03** sad, wae **04** bale, dool, dule, pain **05** agony, curse, doole, gloom, grief, sorry, tears, trial **06** burden, misery, sorrow, tsuris **07** anguish, sadness, trouble, tsouris **08** calamity, disaster, distress, hardship, wretched
**09** adversity, dejection, heartache, suffering **10** affliction, depression, heartbreak, melancholy, misfortune
**11** tribulation, unhappiness
**12** wretchedness

**woebegone**
**03** sad **04** blue **06** gloomy **07** doleful, forlorn, tearful **08** dejected, downcast, mournful, troubled, wretched **09** long-faced, miserable, sorrowful
**10** dispirited, lugubrious **11** crestfallen, downhearted, tear-stained
**12** disconsolate **13** grief-stricken
**14** down in the mouth

**woeful**
◇ *anagram indicator*
**03** bad, sad **04** mean, poor **05** awful, cruel, lousy, sorry, waefu' **06** feeble, gloomy, paltry, rotten, tragic, waeful
**07** doleful, unhappy, waesome
**08** dreadful, grieving, grievous, hopeless, mournful, pathetic, pitiable, shocking, terrible, wretched
**09** afflicted, appalling, miserable, sorrowful **10** calamitous, deplorable, disastrous, inadequate, lamentable
**11** disgraceful, distressing
**12** catastrophic, disconsolate, heart-rending **13** disappointing, heartbreaking

**woefully**
**05** sadly **07** awfully, lousily
**08** gloomily, pitiably, terribly
**09** dolefully, forlornly, miserably, unhappily **10** deplorably, dreadfully, hopelessly, lamentably, mournfully, shockingly, tragically, wretchedly
**11** appallingly **12** disastrously, pathetically **13** disgracefully
**14** disconsolately

**wolf**
**04** lobo **05** Romeo **06** coyote, lecher
**07** Don Juan, Isegrim, seducer
**08** Casanova, Isengrim **09** ladies' man, thylacine, womanizer **10** lady-killer
**11** philanderer

• **wolf down**
**04** bolt, cram, gulp **05** gorge, scoff, stuff **06** devour, gobble **07** put away
**08** pack away

**woman**
**01** w **03** bit, chi, gin, hag, hen, her, she, Tib, tit **04** baby, bint, bird, chai, doll, fair, feme, frau, girl, jane, Judy, lady, lass, maid, Mary, minx, mort, peat, puss, sort, tart, wife **05** belle, biddy, broad, chick, cutie, cutty, dolly, femme, fille, filly, flirt, hussy, lover, madam, peach, popsy, quean, randy, wench **06** au pair, blowze, cummer, damsel, female, geisha, gillet, jillet, kimmer, lassie, maiden, moppet, number, ogress, sheila, shiksa, tomboy, tottie, wahine
**07** bag lady, fiancée, mystery, nymphet, partner, reverse **08** mistress, princess
**09** charwoman, dolly bird, plain Jane
**10** bit of stuff, Cinderella, girlfriend, sweetheart **11** beauty queen
**12** bachelorette, bobby-dazzler
*See also* **girl**

**• first woman**
**03** Eve **07** Pandora
**• good woman**
**01** S **02** St **04** sant **05** Saint

**womanhood**
**05** woman **08** maturity **09** adulthood, womankind, womenfolk, womenkind **10** muliebrity, womenfolks

**womanizer**

*Womanizers and libertines include:*

**04** goat, lech, rake, roué, wolf
**05** letch, Romeo
**06** gay dog, lecher
**07** Don Juan, seducer, wastrel
**08** Casanova, Lothario, Lovelace, palliard, rakehell
**09** debauchee, ladies' man, libertine, reprobate, voluptary
**10** Corinthian, lady-killer, profligate, sensualist
**11** gay deceiver, philanderer

**womanly**
**04** kind, warm **06** female, tender **07** shapely **08** feminine, ladylike, motherly, womanish **10** effeminate, well-formed

**women**
**• excluding women**
**04** stag
**• Women's Institute**
**02** WI

*See also* **woman**

**wonder**
**03** awe **04** gape, marl, muse **05** doubt, ferly, marle, query, sight, think **06** admire, marvel, ponder, puzzle, rarity **07** cruller, inquire, miracle, prodigy, reflect **08** be amazed, meditate, pleasure, question, surprise **09** amazement, curiosity, nonpareil, spectacle, speculate **10** admiration, conjecture, phenomenon, stand in awe, wonderment **11** ask yourself, be astounded, be surprised, fascination **12** astonishment, be astonished, bewilderment **13** be dumbfounded **14** be lost for words

*The Seven Wonders of the World:*

**15** Pyramids of Egypt
**16** Colossus of Rhodes
**18** Pharos of Alexandria
**21** Statue of Zeus at Olympia
**23** Hanging Gardens of Babylon
**24** Mausoleum of Halicarnassus, Temple of Artemis at Ephesus

**• expression of wonder**
**01** O **02** oh **03** god, wow **04** gosh, whew **05** wowee **06** heyday, wheugh **07** good-now **08** gracious **09** Jesus wept **13** stone the crows

**wonderful**
**03** ace, def, fab, old, rad **04** boss, cool, keen, mean, mega, neat **05** beaut, boffo, brill, bully, crack, dicty, dilly, great, hunky, jammy, lummy, socko, super, triff **06** castor, divine, famous, far-out, geason, groovy, mighty, peachy, superb, way-out, wicked, wizard **07** amazing, awesome, capital, classic, crucial, elegant, épatant, magical, mirable, radical, ripping, stellar, strange, tipping, topping, triffic, trimmer **08** champion, clinking, fabulous, glorious, heavenly, jim-dandy, knockout, smashing, spiffing, splendid, stonking, stunning, terrific, top-notch **09** admirable, brilliant, copacetic, excellent, fantastic, righteous, startling **10** astounding, delightful, incredible, marvellous, not half bad, phenomenal, remarkable, staggering, stupendous, surprising, tremendous **11** astonishing, fantabulous, magnificent, outstanding, sensational **12** second to none **13** extraordinary **14** out of this world

**wonderfully**
**06** purely **09** amazingly, extremely **10** incredibly **12** phenomenally, terrifically, tremendously, unbelievably **13** fantastically

**wonky**
**04** awry, weak **05** amiss, askew, shaky, wrong **06** wobbly **07** crooked, unsound **08** unsteady **09** skew-whiff

**wont**
**03** use, way **04** fain, rule, used **05** given, habit **06** custom **07** routine **08** inclined, practice **10** accustomed, habituated

**wonted**
**04** tame **05** daily, usual **06** common, normal **07** regular, routine **08** familiar, frequent, habitual **09** customary **10** accustomed, habituated **12** conventional

**woo**
**03** wow **04** seek **05** chase, court **06** pursue **07** address, attract, look for, romance **09** cultivate, encourage **10** make love to, pay court to **13** seek the hand of

**wood**
**03** mad, wud **04** bowl, hyle, shaw, tree **05** copse, cross, grove, hurst, trees, woods, xylem **06** fierce, forest, planks, pulpit **07** coppice, furious, spinney, thicket **08** woodland **10** plantation

*See also* **forest**; **golf club**; **timber**

*Woods include:*

**03** ash, box, cam, elm, fir, nut, oak, ply, red, sap, yew
**04** bass, cord, cork, deal, ebon, fire, hard, iron, lana, lime, pine, pink, pulp, rose, sasa, soft, teak
**05** alder, apple, balsa, beech, black, brush, cedar, drift, ebony, green, hazel, heart, larch, maple, match, olive, peach, plane, ramin, satin, tiger, torch, tulip, utile, white, zebra
**06** acacia, bamboo, bitter, brazil, candle, cherry, cotton, linden, lumber, obeche, orange, padauk, pedauk, poplar, rubber, sandal, sapele, spruce, timber, veneer, walnut, willow
**07** Amboina, bubinga, hickory, palmyra, quassia
**08** amaranth, chestnut, cocobolo, hornbeam, kindling, mahogany, red lauan, seasoned, silky oak, sycamore
**09** chipboard, hardboard, jacaranda, quebracho
**10** afrormosia, Douglas fir, paper birch
**11** black cherry, lignum vitae, purple heart, tulip poplar, white walnut, yellow birch
**13** sweet chestnut

**• measurement of wood**
**04** cord **05** stere **06** fathom, square **08** standard **09** board-foot, decastere, decistere **10** hoppus foot **15** hoppus cubic foot
**• out of the woods**
**04** safe **06** secure **10** home and dry, in the clear **11** out of danger **12** safe and sound **15** out of difficulty
**• piece of wood**
**03** cat, log **04** beam, chip, lath, slat **05** block, board, dwang, plank, split, staff, wedge **06** batten, billet, fillet, flitch, loggat, planch, timber, tipcat **07** bunting **08** splinter **09** four-by-two, scantling, two-by-four

**wooded**
**05** woody **06** sylvan **08** forested, nemorous, timbered **09** arboreous **11** arboraceous, tree-covered

**wooden**
**04** dull, hard, slow, tree **05** blank, empty, heavy, rigid, stiff, treen, woody **06** clumsy, leaden, stodgy, stupid, timber, vacant **07** awkward, deadpan, stilted, vacuous **08** lifeless, ligneous **09** graceless, impassive, inhibited, unnatural **10** insensible, spiritless **11** emotionless, unemotional **12** unresponsive **14** expressionless

**woodland**
**04** bush, wood **05** copse, grove, trees, woods **06** forest, miombo, timber **07** boscage, boskage, coppice, spinney, thicket **10** plantation

**woodpecker**
**05** Picus **06** yaffle, yucker **07** awlbird, flicker, piculet, witwall **08** hickwall, rainbird **10** yaffingale

**wood sorrel**
**03** oca **06** oxalis **08** shamrock

**woody**
**05** bosky **06** sylvan, wooded, wooden, xyloid **08** forested, ligneous **11** tree-covered

**wool**
**02** oo **03** ket **04** coat, down, hair, kemp, noil, yarn **05** flock, llama, noils **06** Angora, botany, fleece, jersey, pelage, staple, two-ply, vicuña **07** floccus, morling **08** cashmere, mortling, shatoosh **09** shahtoosh, strouding **13** linsey-woolsey
**• pull the wool over someone's eyes**
**03** con **04** dupe, fool **05** trick

06 delude, take in 07 deceive 08 hoodwink 09 bamboozle 12 pull a swiftie, put one over on 14 pull a fast one on

**wool-gathering**
06 dreamy 11 day-dreaming, distraction, inattention 12 absent-minded 13 forgetfulness, preoccupation

**woollen fabric** *see* **fabric**

**woolly**
04 hazy 05 downy, foggy, fuzzy, hairy, sheep, vague, woozy 06 cloudy, fleecy, fluffy, frizzy, jersey, jumper, lanate, lanose, shaggy 07 blurred, muddled, sweater, unclear, woollen 08 cardigan, confused, floccose, nebulous, pullover 10 flocculent, ill-defined, indefinite, indistinct 12 woolly-haired

**woozy**
05 dazed, dizzy, rocky, tipsy, vague 06 wobbly, woolly 07 bemused, blurred, fuddled 08 confused, unsteady 09 befuddled, nauseated 11 light-headed

**word**
03 gen, mot, put, say, vow 04 book, chat, dope, hint, info, name, news, oath, sign, talk, term, text, will 05 couch, order, speak, state, write 06 advice, decree, gossip, honour, lyrics, notice, phrase, pledge, remark, report, rumour, saying, script, signal, war cry 07 account, command, comment, explain, express, flatter, go-ahead, hearsay, low-down, mandate, message, palabra, promise, scandal, tidings, vocable, warning, whisper 08 bulletin, dispatch, libretto, password, thumbs-up 09 assertion, assurance, guarantee, statement, tête-à-tête, utterance, watchword 10 communiqué, discussion, expression, green light 11 commandment, declaration, designation, information, instruction, speculation, undertaking 12 consultation, conversation, intelligence 13 communication

*See also* **speech**

**• have words**
03 row 05 argue 06 bicker 07 dispute, quarrel 08 disagree, squabble

**• in a word**
07 briefly, in brief, in short, to sum up 09 concisely, to be brief 10 succinctly 11 in a nutshell, summarizing 14 to put it briefly

**• in other words**
02 ie 05 id est 06 that is

**• word for word**
06 verbal 07 closely, exactly, literal 08 ad verbum, verbatim 09 literally, precisely 10 accurately

**wordiness**
06 waffle 07 wordage 08 verbiage 09 garrulity, loquacity, prolixity, verbosity 10 logorrhoea 11 diffuseness, perissology, verboseness 13 garrulousness 14 long-windedness 15 verbal diarrhoea

**wording**
04 text 05 style, tenor, words 07 diction, wordage 08 language, phrasing, speaking, verbiage 09 subtitles, utterance, verbalism 10 expression 11 phraseology, terminology 13 choice of words

**word-perfect**
05 exact 06 spot-on 08 accurate, faithful 13 letter-perfect

**wordplay**
03 pun, wit 04 puns 07 punning 08 repartee 10 witticisms 11 paronomasia

**wordy**
05 windy 06 phrasy, prolix 07 diffuse, verbose 08 rambling 09 garrulous 10 discursive, long-winded, loquacious

**work**
◇ *anagram indicator*
02 do, go, op 03 art, dig, fag, fix, hat, job, ply, ren, rin, run, sew, tut, use 04 ache, acts, book, char, deed, duty, edge, farm, form, fuss, guts, line, make, mill, move, opus, plan, play, poem, shop, slog, take, task, tick, till, toil 05 cause, chore, craft, drive, field, graft, guide, knead, model, mould, parts, piece, plant, purge, shape, shift, skill, slave, study, trade, trick 06 action, cajole, career, charge, create, doings, drudge, effect, effort, fiddle, go well, handle, labour, manage, métier, oeuvre, strain, wangle 07 achieve, actions, arrange, calling, control, execute, factory, fashion, ferment, foundry, innards, mission, operate, peg away, perform, process, prosper, pull off, pursuit, squeeze, succeed, travail, trouble, writing 08 business, contrive, creation, drudgery, engineer, exercise, exertion, function, have a job, industry, movement, painting, plug away, treatise, vocation, workings, workshop 09 cultivate, embroider, influence, machinery, manoeuvre, mechanism, penetrate 10 accomplish, assignment, be employed, bring about, commission, embroidery, employment, livelihood, manipulate, occupation, production, profession 11 achievement, be effective, composition, elbow grease, pull strings, undertaking, workmanship 12 be successful, working parts 13 exert yourself, installations 14 accomplishment, be satisfactory, earn your living, line of business, responsibility 15 slog your guts out

**• bit of work**
01 J 03 erg 05 joule 08 therblig

**• day's work**
04 darg 05 stent, stint 06 man-day 07 journey

**• the works**
06 the lot 10 everything 11 the whole lot 15 the whole shebang

**• work out**
04 dope, plan, toil 05 drill, serve, solve, total, train 06 come to, deduce, devise, evolve, finish, go well, invent, pan out, warm up 07 add up to, arrange, clear up, come out, develop, dope out, exhaust, expiate, keep fit, prosper, resolve, sort out, succeed, turn out 08 amount to, contrive, exercise, organize, practise 09 calculate, construct, elaborate, figure out, formulate, puzzle out 10 understand 11 be effective, put together

**• work up**
03 tew 04 meng, ming, move, spur, whet 05 menge, reach, rouse, use up 06 arouse, excite, expand, incite, kindle, stir up, subact 07 achieve, agitate, animate, build up, ferment, inflame 08 generate, summon up 09 elaborate, instigate, stimulate

**workable**
06 doable, viable 08 feasible, possible 09 practical, realistic 11 practicable

**workaday**
04 dull 06 common 07 average, humdrum, mundane, prosaic, routine, toiling, work-day, working 08 everyday, familiar, ordinary 09 labouring, practical 11 commonplace 12 run-of-the-mill

**worker**
03 ant, bee 04 hand, peon, temp 06 coater, Indian, key man, legger, toiler 07 artisan, grinder, ouvrier, workman 08 employee, grisette, labourer, mechanic, ouvrière, strapper, stuccoer 09 craftsman, midinette, operative, salaryman, tradesman, workhorse, workwoman 10 mechanical, painstaker, railroader, wage-earner, workaholic, working man 11 breadwinner, craftswoman, proletarian, tradeswoman 12 Gastarbeiter, willing horse, working woman 13 member of staff

**workforce**
03 men 05 hands, staff 06 labour 07 workers 08 manpower, skeleton 09 employees, personnel, shop floor 10 workpeople 11 labour force 14 human resources

**working**
◇ *anagram indicator*
02 on 03 pit 04 guts, live, mine 05 going, parts, shaft, waste, works 06 action, active, in a job, in work, manner, method, quarry, system 07 innards, process, routine, running 08 diggings, employed, movement 09 endeavour, labouring, machinery, mechanism, operating, operation, operative 10 in business 11 excavations, functioning, operational 12 up and running, working parts 13 installations 14 in working order

**workman, workwoman**
04 hand, hobo 05 hunky, navvy 06 beamer, glazer, master, worker

**07** artisan **08** apron-man, employee, gunsmith, labourer, mechanic
**09** artificer, craftsman, operative, prud'homme, stage hand
**10** journeyman, surfaceman
**11** craftswoman **12** manual worker, tradesperson

**workmanlike**
**05** adept **06** expert **07** careful, skilful, skilled **08** masterly, thorough
**09** competent, efficient **10** proficient
**11** painstaking **12** businesslike, professional, satisfactory

**workmanship**
**03** art **04** work **05** craft, skill **06** finish
**07** facture, tooling **08** artifice, artistry
**09** execution, expertise, handiwork, technique **10** handicraft
**11** manufacture **13** craftsmanship

**workmate**
**03** lad **08** co-worker **09** associate, colleague **10** work-fellow, yoke-fellow
**12** fellow-worker

**workout**
**05** drill **06** warm-up **08** aerobics, exercise, practice, training
**10** gymnastics, isometrics
**11** eurhythmics, limbering up
**13** callisthenics

**workshop**
**03** lab **04** mill, shop **05** class, forge, plant, works **06** garage, smithy, studio
**07** atelier, factory, seminar
**08** plumbery, smithery, workroom
**09** cooperage, symposium
**10** laboratory, study group **11** machine-shop, rigging-loft **15** discussion group

**work-shy**
**04** idle, lazy, lusk, slow **05** inert, slack, tardy **06** laesie, lither, torpid
**07** languid, luskish **08** bone-idle, fainéant, inactive, indolent, slothful, sluggish **09** lethargic **10** languorous, slow-moving **14** good-for-nothing

**workwoman** *see* **workman, workwoman**

**world**
**03** age, era, man, orb **04** area, days, life, star, vale **05** class, earth, epoch, field, globe, group, realm, times **06** cosmos, domain, nature, people, period, planet, public, sphere, system **07** kingdom, mankind, reality, section, society
**08** creation, division, everyone, humanity, province, universe
**09** everybody, existence, humankind, human race, situation, way of life
**10** department, experience, population **11** environment
**12** heavenly body

*World heritage sites include:*

**03** Bam, Omo, Taï
**04** Agra, Bath, Graz, Lima, Manú, Pisa, Riga, San'a, Troy, Tyre
**05** Aksum, Awash, Berne, Bosra, Copán, Cuzco, Delos, Galle, Hatra, Kandy, Lyons, Ohrid, Paris, Petra, Quito, Siena, Sucre, Uluru
**06** Abomey, Aleppo, Amazon, Assisi, Bassae, Byblos, Cyrene, Darién, Delphi, Durham, Göreme, Kakadu, Naples, Oporto, Orkney, Paphos, Potosí, Puebla, Sangay, Sousse, Thebes, Toledo, Treves, Venice, Verona, Vienna, Warsaw
**07** Abu Mena, Avebury, Avignon, Baalbek, Caracas, Djemila, Garamba, Gwynedd, Holy See, Olympia, San Juan, Segovia, St Kilda, Vicenza, Virunga
**08** Agra Fort, Alhambra, Altamira, Carthage, Chartres, Damascas, Durmitor, Florence, Ghadamès, Hattusas, Mount Tai, Palenque, Pyramids, Pyrénées, Sabratha, Salvador, Salzburg, Shark Bay, Sigiriya, Stari Ras, Taj Mahal, Timbuktu, Valletta, Würzburg
**09** Abu Simbel, Auschwitz, Ayutthaya, Dubrovnik, Edinburgh, Epidaurus, Greenwich, Gros Morne, Huascarán, Jerusalem, Mesa Verde, Nemrut Dag, Parthenon, Serengeti
**10** El Escorial, Everglades, Generalife, Hierapolis, Hildesheim, Ironbridge, Monte Albán, Monticello, Persepolis, Pont du Gard, Stonehenge, Versailles
**11** Ajanta caves, Danube Delta, Ellora caves, Gorée Island, Hagia Sophia, Leptis Magna, Machu Picchu, Madara Rider, Mohenjo-daro, Quedlinburg, Teotihuacán, Vatican City, Western Wall, Westminster, Yellowstone
**12** Altamira Cave, Ancient Kyoto, Fraser Island, Hadrian's Wall, Koguryo Tombs, Mont-St-Michel, Santo Domingo, The Great Wall
**13** Fontainebleau, Fontenay Abbey, Great Zimbabwe, Rila Monastery, Tower of London
**14** Aldabra Islands, Blenheim Palace, Elephanta caves, Fountains Abbey, Giant's Causeway, Heraion of Samos, Imperial Palace
**15** Aachen Cathedral, Amiens Cathedral, Ironbridge Gorge, Kasbah of Algiers, Kathmandu Valley, Nubian monuments, Speyer Cathedral, Statue of Liberty

**• on top of the world**
**05** happy **06** elated, joyful **08** ecstatic, euphoric, exultant, jubilant, thrilled
**09** delighted, exuberant, overjoyed, rapturous **10** enraptured, in raptures
**11** exhilarated, high as a kite, on cloud nine, over the moon, tickled pink
**14** pleased as Punch **15** in seventh heaven

**• out of this world**
**02** ET **03** ace, rad **04** cool, mean, mega, neat **05** brill, great **06** divine, superb, way-out, wicked **07** crucial, radical **08** fabulous, heavenly, smashing, stonking, stunning, terrific
**09** excellent, fantastic, wonderful
**10** delightful, incredible, marvellous, phenomenal, remarkable
**11** sensational **12** second to none, unbelievable **13** indescribable

**worldly**
**06** carnal, greedy, mortal, urbane
**07** earthly, knowing, mondain, mundane, outward, profane, secular, selfish, terrene **08** covetous, grasping, material, mondaine, physical, temporal
**09** ambitious, corporeal **10** avaricious, streetwise **11** experienced, terrestrial, unspiritual, worldly-wise
**12** cosmopolitan **13** materialistic, sophisticated

**worldly-wise**
**06** shrewd, urbane **07** cynical, knowing, worldly **10** cultivated, perceptive, streetwise **11** experienced
**12** cosmopolitan **13** sophisticated

**worldwide**
**06** global **07** general, mondial
**08** catholic **09** universal **10** ubiquitous
**11** transglobal **13** international

**worm**
**04** grub **05** snake **06** dragon, maggot, squirm **07** remorse

*Worms include:*

**03** eel, lug, pin, rag
**04** flat, hook, tape
**05** arrow, earth, fluke, leech, round
**06** peanut, ribbon, thread
**07** annelid, bristle
**08** sea mouse
**10** blood fluke, liver fluke

**worn**
**03** old **04** bare, used **05** all in, drawn, jaded, spent, tatty, tired, trite, weary
**06** bushed, done in, frayed, ragged, shabby **07** haggard, thumbed, worn-out **08** careworn, dog-tired, fatigued, strained, tattered **09** exhausted, hackneyed, in tatters, knackered
**10** threadbare **13** weather-bitten

**• worn out**
**03** old **04** beat, gone, past, used **05** all in, banal, corny, rough, seedy, stale, stock, tacky, tatty, tired, trite, warby, weary **06** bushed, common, done in, épuisé, failed, frayed, pooped, ragged, shabby, wasted, zonked **07** cliché'd, épuisée, to-worne, traikit, useless, wearied, whacked, worn-out
**08** clichéed, dead-beat, decrepit, dog-tired, dog-weary, forfairn, overused, tattered, time-worn, tired out
**09** bedridden, disjaskit, exhausted, geriatric, hackneyed, knackered, moth-eaten, pooped out, shattered, washed-out, worm-eaten **10** broken-down, clapped-out, overworked, pedestrian, shagged out, threadbare, uninspired, unoriginal, yawn-making
**11** commonplace, ready to drop, stereotyped, tuckered out, wearing thin **12** cliché-ridden, journey-bated, overscutched, run-of-the-mill **13** on its last legs, platitudinous, unimaginative

**worried**
◇ *anagram indicator*
**04** worn **05** het up, tense, upset, wired

**06** afraid, on edge, uneasy **07** anxious, fearful, fretful, haunted, in a stew, jittery, nervous, uptight **08** agonized, bothered, dismayed, in a tizzy, strained, troubled **09** concerned, disturbed, ill at ease, perturbed **10** disquieted, distracted, distraught, distressed, frightened **11** overwrought **12** apprehensive **14** beside yourself, hot and bothered **15** a bundle of nerves

**worrisome**

**05** hairy, scary **06** vexing **07** irksome **08** insecure, worrying **09** agonizing, upsetting, vexatious **10** bothersome, disturbing, nail-biting, perturbing **11** disquieting, distressing, frightening, troublesome

**worry**

◇ *anagram indicator*

**03** bug, dog, eat, nag, tew, tiz, vex **04** bite, care, faze, fear, frab, fret, gnaw, pest, stew **05** annoy, choke, deave, deeve, devil, eat up, feese, feeze, go for, harry, phase, phese, sweat, tease, tizzy, touse, touze, towse, towze, trial, upset **06** attack, badger, bother, burden, hang-up, harass, hassle, misery, niggle, pester, pheese, pheeze, pingle, plague, savage, strain, stress, tear at, unease, worrit **07** agitate, agonize, anguish, anxiety, concern, disturb, perturb, problem, tension, torment, trouble **08** disquiet, distress, headache, irritate, nuisance, unsettle, vexation **09** aggravate, agitation, annoyance, be anxious, misgiving **10** be troubled, irritation, perplexity **11** disturbance, fearfulness **12** apprehension, be distressed, perturbation **13** consternation **14** responsibility

• **expression of worry**

**04** uh-oh, yike **05** yikes **06** cripes

**worrying**

**05** hairy, scary **06** trying, uneasy **07** anxious, weighty **08** alarming, niggling **09** agonizing, harassing, upsetting, worrisome **10** disturbing, nail-biting, perturbing, unsettling **11** disquieting, distressing, troublesome

**worsen**

**04** sink, slip **06** weaken **07** decline, go to pot **08** get worse, heighten, increase **09** aggravate, intensify **10** degenerate, exacerbate, go downhill **11** deteriorate **13** go down the tube **14** go down the tubes

**worsening**

**05** decay **07** decline **10** pejoration **12** degeneration, exacerbation **13** deterioration, retrogression

**worship**

**02** Wp **04** laud, love, puja **05** adore, deify, exalt, extol, glory **06** admire, homage, honour, Ibadat, praise, prayer, pray to, regard, revere **07** adulate, dignity, glorify, idolize, opus Dei, prayers, respect **08** adultery, devotion, geolatry, idolatry, naturism, religion, satanism, venerate **09** adoration, adulation, aniconism, devotions, diabolism, laudation, pyrolatry, reverence, snake cult **10** astrolatry, bardolatry, exaltation, eye-service, heliolatry, iconolatry, litholatry, ophiolatry, reputation, veneration **11** angelolatry, be devoted to, deification, idolization, physiolatry, theriolatry **13** anthropolatry, glorification, thaumatolatry

*Places of worship include:*

**03** wat
**04** fane, kirk, shul
**05** abbey, gompa
**06** bethel, chapel, church, mandir, masjid, mosque, pagoda, shrine, temple, vihara
**07** chantry, convent, minster
**08** gurdwara
**09** cathedral, monastery, synagogue
**10** tabernacle
**12** meeting-house

*See also* **abbey**; **religious**

**worshipful**

**02** Wp **04** awed, Wpfl **05** pious **06** devout, humble, loving, solemn **07** adoring, devoted, dutiful **08** admiring, obeisant **10** respectful **11** deferential, reverential

**worshipper** *see* **believer**

**worst**

**03** war **04** beat, best, drub, lick **05** crush, paste, smash, thump **06** damage, defeat, hammer, master, subdue, thrash **07** clobber, conquer, trounce **08** overcome, pessimal, pessimum, vanquish **09** devastate, overpower, overthrow, slaughter, subjugate, whitewash **10** annihilate **13** run rings round **14** get the better of **15** make mincemeat of

**worth**

**02** be **03** use **04** cost, gain, good, help, rate **05** avail, carat, merit, price, value, virtu **06** become, carrat, credit, desert, happen, profit, virtue **07** benefit, deserts, quality, service, utility **08** eminence, meriting, repaying, valuable **09** advantage, deserving, substance **10** assistance, excellence, excellency, importance, justifying, usefulness, warranting, worthiness **11** possessions **12** significance

**worthily**

**04** well **08** laudably, reliably, valuably **09** admirably **10** creditably, honourably **11** commendably

**worthless**

**03** bad, bum, low **04** base, junk, naff, orra, poor, punk, raca, vile, waff **05** blown, cheap, junky, light, sorry, tripy **06** abject, cruddy, crummy, draffy, drossy, futile, naught, no good, ornery, paltry, trashy, tripey **07** corrupt, drunken, ignoble, mauvais, nothing, shotten, trivial, useless **08** beggarly, castaway, draffish, gimcrack, jimcrack, mauvaise, nugatory, rubbishy, sixpenny, trifling, twopenny, unusable, unworthy, wanwordy, wretched **09** brummagem, cheap-jack, no-account, pointless, valueless **10** despicable, unavailing, unprizable **11** ineffectual, littleworth, meaningless, stramineous, unimportant **12** contemptible **13** insignificant **14** good-for-nothing, not worth shucks

• **worthless thing**

**03** mud **04** dirt, grot **05** nyaff **06** fag end **10** catchpenny

**worthlessness**

**07** ambs-ace, ames-ace **08** futility **09** cheapness **11** lack of worth, nothingness, unusability, uselessness **13** pointlessness **15** ineffectualness, meaninglessness

**worthwhile**

**04** good **05** tanti **06** useful, worthy **07** gainful, helpful, of value **08** valuable **09** estimable, rewarding **10** beneficial, productive, profitable **11** justifiable **12** advantageous, constructive

**worthy**

**03** fit, VIP **04** good, name **05** moral, noble **06** big gun, bigwig, decent, honest, honour, top dog **07** big shot, notable, upright **08** big noise, laudable, luminary, reliable, somebody, top brass, valuable, virtuous **09** admirable, big cheese, deserving, dignitary, estimable, excellent, personage, reputable, righteous **10** creditable, excellence, honourable, notability, worthwhile **11** appropriate, commendable, meritorious, respectable, trustworthy **12** praiseworthy

**would**

**01** 'd

**would-be**

**04** keen **05** eager **07** budding, hopeful, longing, wannabe, wishful **08** aspiring, striving **09** ambitious, soi-disant **10** optimistic **12** endeavouring, enterprising

**wound**

◇ *anagram indicator*

**03** cut, hit, pip **04** ache, bite, blow, dunt, gash, harm, hurt, pain, scar, sore, stab, tear, vuln, win't **05** bless, graze, grief, saber, sabre, shock, shoot, slash, touch, upset **06** damage, grieve, injure, injury, insult, lesion, offend, pierce, slight, trauma **07** anguish, mortify, scratch, torment **08** distress, lacerate, puncture, sword-cut **09** vulnerate **10** heartbreak, laceration, traumatism, traumatize

**wow**

**03** boy, cor

**wrack**

◇ *anagram indicator*

**05** wreck **07** remnant, seaweed, torment, torture **08** wreckage **09** vengeance **10** punishment **11** destruction, devastation

**wraith**
**05** ghost, shade, spook **06** double, spirit **07** phantom, spectre **08** revenant **10** apparition, astral body **12** doppelgänger

**wrangle**
**03** rag, row **04** herd, spar, spat, tiff **05** argue, clash, fight, scrap, set-to **06** argufy, barney, bicker, cample, cangle, debate, dust-up, hassle, jangle, tussle **07** brabble, brangle, contend, contest, dispute, fall out, punch-up, quarrel, wrestle **08** argument, disagree, ergotize, squabble **09** altercate, argy-bargy, bickering, have it out, have words **10** digladiate **11** altercation, controversy, cross swords **12** disagreement **13** have it out with, slanging match **15** be at loggerheads, have a bone to pick

**wrap**
◇ *containment indicator*
**03** hap, lap, rug, wap **04** bind, cape, fold, hide, mail, pack, robe, roll, snug, wind **05** amice, boost, cloak, cover, scarf, shawl, sheet, stole, throw **06** clothe, cocoon, emboss, encase, enfold, mantle, muffle, parcel, roll up, shroud, swathe, wimple **07** commend, embrace, enclose, envelop, flannel, immerse, involve, obscure, package, snuggle, swaddle, whimple **08** bemuffle, bundle up, enswathe, entangle, gift-wrap, inswathe, parcel up, surround **09** clingfilm, night-rail **11** acclamation

• **wrap up**
**03** end, hap **04** mail **05** dry up **06** belt up, bundle, enfold, infold, pack up, parcel, shut up, wind up **07** be quiet, package **08** complete, conclude, gift-wrap, muffle up, parcel up, pipe down, round off **09** finish off, terminate **11** dress warmly, give it a rest **12** put a sock in it **13** bring to a close, shut your mouth **14** hold your tongue **15** wear warm clothes

**wrapper**
**04** case **05** cover, folio, paper **06** casing, jacket, sheath, sleeve **08** covering, envelope, Jiffy bag®, wrapping **09** packaging **10** dust jacket

**wrapping**
**04** case, foil **05** paper **06** carton, swathe **07** tinfoil, wrapper **08** envelope, Jiffy bag® **09** packaging **10** bubble pack, Cellophane® **11** blister card, blister pack, envelopment, silver paper

**wrapt** *see* **rapt**

**wrath**
**03** ire **04** fury, rage **05** anger, angry **06** ardour, choler, spleen, temper **07** passion **09** annoyance **10** bitterness, irritation, resentment **11** displeasure, indignation **12** exasperation

**wrathful**
**03** mad **05** angry, cross, irate, ratty, spewy, wroth **06** bitter, choked, ireful, raging **07** crooked, enraged, furious, ropable, stroppy, uptight **08** burned up, furibund, hairless, in a paddy, incensed, up in arms **09** in a lather, indignant, raving mad, seeing red, ticked off **10** aggravated, displeased, hopping mad, infuriated **11** disgruntled, fit to be tied **12** on the warpath

**wreak**
**04** harm, vent **05** cause **06** avenge, bestow, create, damage, effect, punish **07** execute, express, inflict, unleash **08** carry out, drive out, exercise **09** vengeance **10** bring about, perpetrate, punishment

**wreath**
**03** lei **04** band, loop, ring **05** crown, torse **06** anadem, circle **07** chaplet, circlet, coronet, festoon, garland **09** snowdrift **10** civic crown

**wreathe**
**04** coil, turn, wind, wrap **05** adorn, crown, twine, twist, wring **06** enfold, enwrap, shroud **07** contort, entwine, envelop, festoon **08** decorate, encircle, surround **10** intertwine, interweave

**wreck**
◇ *anagram indicator*
**03** gum, mar **04** crab, loss, mess, ruin, sink **05** break, gum up, mouse, smash, split, spoil, trash, wrack **06** cast up, debris, pieces, ravage, rubble **07** chicken, destroy, disable, flotsam, handbag, remains, shatter, torpedo, undoing **08** breaking, cast away, demolish, derelict, disaster, neurotic, smashing, stramash, write off, write-off **09** devastate, fragments, ruination, shipwreck **10** basket-case, demolition, disruption, shattering **11** bag of nerves, destruction, devastation **13** play havoc with **14** bundle of nerves

**wreckage**
◇ *anagram indicator*
**04** ruin **05** lagan, ligan, wrack **06** debris, pieces, rubble **07** flotsam, remains **08** detritus **09** fragments

**wrench**
**03** fit, rip, tug **04** ache, blow, jerk, pain, pang, pull, rick, tear, yank **05** force, shock, twist, wrest, wring **06** sorrow, sprain, strain **07** distort, sadness, spanner **08** upheaval **09** uprooting

**wrest**
**03** win **04** pull, rack, take, turn **05** force, screw, seize, thraw, twist, wring **06** sprain, strain, wrench **07** distort, extract, pervert **10** distortion **12** misinterpret

**wrestle**
**03** vie **05** argue, fight **06** battle, combat, debate, strive, tussle, wraxle, writhe **07** bulldog, contend, contest, dispute, grapple, scuffle, wrangle, wriggle **08** struggle

**wrestling**
◇ *anagram indicator*

*Wrestling holds and throws include:*

**03** hug
**04** lock
**06** grovet, nelson, souple, suplex
**07** bear hug, buttock, hip-lock
**08** arm throw, body lock, headlock, scissors
**09** ankle lace, body throw
**10** Boston crab, full nelson, hammerlock
**11** backbreaker, scissor hold
**12** cross-buttock, scissors hold, stranglehold
**14** grand amplitude

*Wrestling-related terms include:*

**03** hug, mat, pin
**04** bout, fall, hold, open, sumo
**05** judge
**06** action, bridge, souple
**07** default, referee
**08** arm throw, body lock, chairman, exposing, reversal, takedown
**09** ankle lace, body throw, bridge out, freestyle, grapevine, gut wrench, passivity
**10** arm control, Greco-Roman
**13** central circle, cross-body ride, passivity zone
**14** danger position, grand amplitude, protection area
**15** double-leg tackle, single leg tackle, technical points

**wretch**
**03** rat **04** worm **05** being, devil, exile, miser, rogue, snake, swine **06** insect, rascal, vassal **07** cullion, outcast, ruffian, scroyle, villain **08** blighter, creature, recreant, vagabond **09** miscreant, miserable, rakeshame, scoundrel **10** peelgarlic, pilgarlick, rascallion **11** rapscallion **14** good-for-nothing

**wretched**
◇ *anagram indicator*
**02** wo **03** bad, low, sad, woe **04** base, mean, poor, vile **05** awful, ratty, seely, sorry, woful **06** abject, bloody, cursed, damned, darned, dashed, effing, gloomy, odious, paltry, rascal, woeful, wretch **07** blasted, doleful, flaming, forlorn, hapless, hateful, piteous, pitiful, unhappy, unlucky **08** annoying, blinking, blooming, dejected, downcast, dratting, dreadful, fiendish, flipping, hopeless, horrible, inferior, infernal, pathetic, pitiable, shameful, shocking, terrible **09** appalling, atrocious, depressed, life-weary, loathsome, miserable, worthless **10** confounded, deplorable, despicable, detestable, distraught, distressed, melancholy, outrageous, unpleasant **11** crestfallen, unfortunate **12** contemptible, disconsolate **13** broken-hearted

**wretchedly**
**05** sadly **07** awfully, lousily

**08** gloomily, pitiably, terribly, woefully **09** dolefully, forlornly, miserably, unhappily **10** deplorably, dreadfully, hopelessly, lamentably, mournfully, shockingly, tragically **11** appallingly **12** disastrously, pathetically **13** disgracefully **14** disconsolately

**wriggle**
**04** bend, duck, edge, jerk, shun, turn, wind, worm **05** crawl, dodge, elude, evade, hedge, shirk, sidle, slink, snake, twine, twist **06** escape, eschew, jiggle, squirm, twitch, waggle, wamble, wiggle, writhe, zigzag **07** forbear, wrestle **08** get out of, get round, scriggle, sidestep, squiggle **09** extricate, give a miss, manoeuvre **10** body-swerve, circumvent **11** abstain from, refrain from, run away from **12** keep away from, stay away from, steer clear of

**wring**
**04** coil, hurt, pain, rack, rend, stab, tear **05** exact, force, pinch, screw, thraw, twist, wound, wrest **06** coerce, extort, harrow, injure, mangle, pierce, wrench, writhe **07** distort, extract, squeeze, torture, wreathe **08** distress, lacerate

**wrinkle**
**03** tip **04** fold, idea, line, lirk, plow, ruck, seam **05** frown, ridge, rivel, whelk **06** crease, furrow, gather, notion, plough, pucker, ruckle, ruck up, ruffle, rumple, runkle, trench, wimple **07** crankle, crimple, crinkle, crumple, frounce, frumple, shrivel, whimple **08** unsmooth **09** corrugate **10** suggestion, unevenness **11** corrugation

**wrinkled**
**04** ropy **05** crêpy, ropey **06** crepey, crimpy, ridged, rucked, rugate, rugose, rugous **07** creased, crinkly, furrowy, puckery, ruffled, rumpled, wizened, wrinkly, wrizled **08** crankled, crinkled, crumpled, frounced, furrowed, puckered, rivelled, writhled **09** chamfered **10** corrugated

**wrist**
**06** carpus **11** shackle-bone

**writ**
**04** tolt **05** brief, sci fa **06** capias, decree, elegit, extent, venire **07** dedimus, latitat, precept, process, summons, warrant **08** mandamus, mittimus, noverint, replevin, subpoena **09** nisi prius **10** certiorari, court order, devastavit, distringas, inhibition, injunction, law-burrows, praemunire **11** fieri facias, jury-process, quo warranto, scire facias, supersedeas, supplicavit **12** habeas corpus, quare impedit, venire facias **13** ad inquirendum, audita querela

**write**
**03** pen **04** copy, note **05** carve, chalk, draft, print, trace **06** create, decree, draw up, indite, pencil, record, scrawl, scribe, scrive **07** compose, dash off, engrave, jot down, put down, screeve, scrieve, set down **08** foretell, inscribe, note down, register, scribble, sling ink, take down **09** character, poeticize, transpose **10** correspond, transcribe, underwrite **11** communicate, make a note of

• **write off**
**05** annul, crash, smash, wreck **06** cancel, delete **07** destroy, nullify, smash up, wipe out **08** amortize, cross out, demolish **09** disregard **11** forget about

**writer**
**03** pen **06** author **12** man of letters **14** woman of letters

*Writers include:*

**04** bard, hack, poet
**05** clerk
**06** author, editor, fabler, penman, pen-pal, rhymer, scribe
**07** copyist, diarist
**08** annalist, composer, essayist, lyricist, novelist, penwoman, reporter, satirist
**09** columnist, dramatist, historian, pen-friend, penpusher, scribbler, sonneteer, web author
**10** biographer, chronicler, copywriter, journalist, librettist, playwright
**11** contributor, ghost writer, storyteller
**12** leader-writer, poet laureate, scriptwriter, stenographer
**13** calligraphist, correspondent, court reporter, fiction writer, lexicographer
**14** autobiographer
**15** technical author, technical writer

*See also* **author**; **biography**; **chef**; **diary**; **essay**; **fable**; **historian**; **journalist**; **lexicographer**; **literary**; **playwright**; **poet**; **satirist**

• **the writer**
**02** me

• **this writer**
**01** I

**write-up**
**05** study **06** rating, report, review, survey **08** analysis, critique, scrutiny **09** appraisal, criticism, judgement, recension, summing-up **10** assessment, commentary, evaluation **11** examination

**writhe**
◇ *anagram indicator*
**03** wry **04** coil, curl, jerk, toss, wind **05** thraw, twist, wring **06** squirm, thrash, thresh, wiggle **07** contort, distort, wrestle, wriggle **08** scriggle, struggle **10** intertwine **12** twist and turn

**writing**
**02** MS **03** pen **04** dite, fist, hand, opus, text, work **05** entry, print, prose, words **06** scrawl, script, volume **08** document, scribble **10** manuscript, penmanship **11** calligraphy, composition, handwriting, publication

*Writing instruments include:*

**03** nib, pen
**04** Biro®, reed
**05** quill
**06** crayon, dip pen, pencil, stylus
**07** cane pen
**08** brailler, CD marker, steel pen
**09** ballpoint, eraser pen, ink pencil, marker pen
**10** felt-tip pen, lead-pencil, rollerball, typewriter
**11** board marker, fountain pen, highlighter
**12** cartridge pen, writing brush
**13** laundry marker, Roman metal pen, word-processor
**14** calligraphy pen, coloured pencil
**15** permanent marker

*Writings include:*

**04** blog, book, news, poem, tale
**05** diary, drama, essay, lyric, paper, story, study
**06** annals, letter, memoir, record, report, review, satire, script, sketch, sonnet, thesis, weblog
**07** account, apology, article, epistle, feature, history, journal, parable, profile
**08** apologia, critique, treatise, yearbook
**09** biography, chronicle, criticism, discourse, editorial, life story, monograph, narrative, statement, technical
**10** commentary, literature, propaganda, scientific, travelogue
**11** confessions, copywriting, documentary
**12** dissertation
**13** autobiography, legal document
**14** correspondence
**15** advertising copy, curriculum vitae, newspaper column

*See also* **alphabet**; **scripture**

**written**
**06** penned **07** drawn up, set down **08** recorded **09** pen-and-ink **10** documental, documented **11** documentary, transcribed

**wrong**
◇ *anagram indicator*
**01** X **03** bad, bum, sin **04** awry, back, bent, evil, harm, tort **05** abuse, amiss, badly, crime, crook, error, false, inapt, spoil **06** astray, curved, damage, delict, faulty, guilty, impair, injure, injury, inside, seduce, sinful, unfair, unjust, wicked **07** abusion, abusive, crooked, defraud, illegal, illicit, immoral, in error, inverse, misdeed, off base, off beam, offence, reverse, to blame, twisted, unright, wrongly **08** contrary, criminal, faultily, improper, inequity, iniquity, inverted, mistaken, opposite, trespass, unlawful, unseemly **09** defective, dishonest, dishonour, erroneous, felonious, grievance, imprecise, incorrect, inexactly, injustice, off target, unethical, unfitting **10** fallacious, immorality, improperly, inaccurate,

inapposite, indecorous, iniquitous, malapropos, mistakenly, out of order, sinfulness, unfairness, unsuitable, up the spout, wickedness, wrongdoing **11** blameworthy, erroneously, imprecisely, incongruous, incorrectly, misinformed, unjustified
**12** inaccurately, infelicitous, infringement, unlawfulness
**13** dishonourable, hardly the time, inappropriate, reprehensible, transgression, wide of the mark
**14** hardly the place, unconventional, unsatisfactory

**• go wrong**
**04** fail, miss **05** stray **06** go phut, pack up **07** conk out, pervert, seize up **08** backfire, collapse, go astray, walk awry **09** break down, not make it
**11** come to grief, come unglued, come unstuck, malfunction, stop working
**12** come a cropper, go on the blink, go on the fritz **13** become unstuck, come to nothing **14** be unsuccessful

**• in the wrong**
**04** harm, hurt **05** abuse, cheat
**06** guilty, ill-use, injure, malign **07** at fault, in error, oppress, to blame **08** ill-treat, maltreat, mistaken, mistreat
**09** discredit, dishonour
**11** blameworthy **12** misrepresent

**wrongdoer**
**05** felon **06** sinner **07** culprit
**08** criminal, evildoer, offender
**09** miscreant **10** delinquent, lawbreaker, malefactor, trespasser
**12** transgressor

**wrongdoing**
**03** sin **04** evil, miss **05** crime, error, fault **06** felony **07** misdeed, offence **08** iniquity, mischief
**09** misfaring **10** immorality, maleficent, maleficial, sinfulness, wickedness
**11** delinquency, lawbreaking, maleficence, malfeasance
**13** transgression

**wrongful**
**04** evil **05** wrong **06** unfair, unjust, wicked **07** illegal, illicit, immoral
**08** criminal, improper, tortious, unlawful **09** dishonest, injurious, unethical **11** blameworthy, unjustified, unwarranted **12** illegitimate
**13** dishonourable, reprehensible

**wrongfully**
**03** ill **06** unduly **08** unfairly, unjustly
**09** illegally, illicitly, immorally
**10** criminally, improperly
**11** dishonestly, unethically **13** against the law **14** illegitimately

**wrongly**
◇ *anagram indicator*
**05** amiss, badly **07** athwart, in error
**09** by mistake **10** mistakenly
**11** erroneously, incorrectly
**12** inaccurately

**wrought**
◇ *anagram indicator*
**04** made **06** beaten, formed, ornate, shaped **08** hammered **09** decorated, fashioned **10** decorative, ornamental, ornamented **12** manufactured

**• wrought up**
**05** upset **07** anxious, nervous, ruffled, worried **08** agitated, in a tizzy, troubled, unnerved **09** disturbed, flustered, in a lather, unsettled
**10** distraught **12** disconcerted

**wry**
**03** dry **05** askew, canny, cross, droll, pawky, thraw, witty **06** bitter, ironic, swerve, thrawn, uneven, warped, writhe **07** contort, crooked, mocking, pervert, twisted **08** deformed, perverse, sardonic, scoffing
**09** contorted, distorted, sarcastic
**10** distortion, ill-natured

**Wyoming**
**02** WY **03** Wyo

# X

**X**
**02** ex **03** chi, ten **04** xray

**xenon**
**02** Xe

**xenophobia**
**06** racism **09** racialism, xenophoby **13** ethnocentrism **15** ethnocentricity

**xenophobic**
**06** racist **09** parochial, racialist **12** ethnocentric **13** ethnocentrist

**Xerox®**
**04** copy **05** print **06** run off **09** duplicate, facsimile, photocopy, Photostat®, reproduce

**xylophone**
**07** gamelan, marimba **08** sticcado, sticcato **09** xylorimba **12** metallophone

**Xmas**
**02** Xm **04** Noel, Yule **05** Nowel **06** Crimbo, Nowell **08** Chrissie, Nativity, Yuletide **09** Christmas **13** Christmas-tide, Christmas-time

**X-ray, xray**
**01** X **08** skiagram **09** angiogram, mammogram, pyelogram, radiogram, sialogram, skiagraph, X-ray image **10** mammograph, radiograph, röntgen ray **11** shadowgraph **13** encephalogram **14** encephalograph, X-ray photograph

# Y

**Y**
**03** wye **06** yankee

**yacht**
**02** MY **04** maxi, scow **06** dragon **07** cruiser **08** keelboat **10** knockabout

**yack**
**03** gab, jaw, yap **04** blah, chat, rant **06** babble, confab, gossip, harp on, hot air, jabber, tattle **07** blather, chatter, chinwag, prattle, twattle **08** witter on, yack-yack **11** yackety-yack

**yam**
**06** camote **09** breadroot, Dioscorea **11** sweet potato

**yank**
◇ *anagram indicator*
**03** tug **04** blow, haul, jerk, pull, slap **05** heave **06** snatch, wrench

**yankee**
**01** y

**yap**
**03** cur, gab, jaw **04** bark, fool, yelp **05** mouth, nyaff, scold **06** babble, jabber, natter, yatter **07** bumpkin, chatter, prattle **08** witter on

**yard**
**01** y **02** yd **03** Hof, ree **04** mews, quad, reed **05** court, garth, meuse **06** garden **08** knackery **09** courtyard **10** quadrangle, rick-barton **13** barrack square, cloister-garth

**yardstick**
**05** gauge, scale **07** measure **08** standard **09** benchmark, criterion, guideline **10** comparison, touchstone

**yarn**
**03** abb **04** gimp, gymp, line, tale, tram, wool **05** fable, fibre, guimp, lisle, story, twist **06** Angora, bouclé, cotton, crewel, mohair, saxony, strand, thread, two-ply, zephyr **07** four-ply, genappe, textile, worsted **08** anecdote, chenille, wheeling **09** Crimplene®, fibroline, fingering, organzine, tall story **10** water twist **11** fabrication

**yawn**
**04** gant, gape **08** oscitate

**yawning**
**04** huge, vast, wide **06** drowsy, gaping **08** wide-open **09** cavernous, oscitancy **10** oscitation

**yaws**
**04** boba, buba **10** framboesia **12** button scurvy

**yea** *see* **yes**

**year**
**01** a, y **02** yr **03** sun **11** twelvemonth **12** calendar year

*Years include:*

**03** gap
**04** leap
**05** great, lunar, solar
**06** fiscal, Hebrew, Julian, Sothic
**07** natural, perfect, tropica
**08** academic, Platonic, sidereal
**09** canicular, financial
**10** sabbatical
**11** anomalistic, equinoctial
**12** astronomical
**14** ecclesiastical

*See also* **animal**

**• many years**
**03** age, eon, era **04** aeon **05** calpa, decad, kalpa, yonks **06** decade, lustre, pentad **07** century, chiliad, lustrum **08** triennia **09** centenary, decennary, decennium, great year, millenary, millennia, septennia, triennial, triennium **10** centennial, millennium, quadrennia, septennium **11** bimillenary, quadrennium, quinquennia **12** donkey's years, quinquennium

**• in the year**
**01** a **02** an **04** anno

**• in this year**
**02** ha **07** hoc anno

**• year in, year out**
**09** endlessly, regularly **10** repeatedly **11** continually **12** monotonously, persistently, time and again **13** again and again

**yearbook**
**06** annual

**yearling**
**03** hog **05** stirk

**yearly**
**02** pa **05** per an **06** annual **07** per year **08** annually, per annum **09** every year, once a year, perennial **11** perennially

**yearn**
**03** yen **04** ache, earn, erne, itch, long, pant, pine, sigh, want, wish **05** covet, crave, fancy, green, grein **06** desire, hanker, hunger, thirst **08** languish **09** think long

**yearning**
◇ *anagram indicator*
**03** yen **04** wish **05** fancy **06** desire, hanker, hunger, pining, rennet, thirst **07** craving, longing, panting, wistful **09** hankering **11** nympholepsy

**yeast**
**04** barm, bees, cell, yest **06** leaven, torula **13** Saccharomyces

**yell**
**03** cry **04** bawl, howl, roar, yeld, yelp, yowl **05** shout, tiger, whoop **06** barren, bellow, cry out, holler, scream, shriek, squall, squeal **07** screech, yelloch **08** skelloch **12** unproductive

**yellow**
**04** nesh, soft, weak, yolk **05** faint, mangy, timid **06** coward, cowish, craven, flaxen, fulvid, sallow, scared **07** chicken, citrine, fearful, fulvous, gutless, jittery, luteous, meacock, nithing, unmanly, wimpish, xanthic **08** clay-bank, cowardly, icterine, timorous, unheroic, xanthous **09** dastardly, spineless, vitellary, vitelline, weak-kneed **10** flavescent, spiritless **11** icteritious, lily-livered, milk-livered, sensational, sulphureous **12** faint-hearted, weak-spirited, white-livered, xanthochroic **13** pusillanimous, yellow-bellied **14** chicken-hearted, chicken-livered

*Yellows include:*

**02** or
**04** buff, gold, sand
**05** amber, khaki, lemon, maize, ochre, peach, tawny, topaz
**06** auburn, canary, fallow, golden, sienna, sulfur
**07** mustard, saffron, sulphur
**08** daffodil, primrose
**10** chartreuse, light-brown
**11** straw-colour

**yellowhammer**
**04** yite **08** yeldring, yeldrock, yoldring

**yelp**
**03** bay, cry, yap, yip **04** bark, yawp, yell, yowl **05** boast, nyaff, quest **06** squeal

**Yemen**
**03** YAR, YEM

**yen**
**01** Y **02** Yn **04** itch, lust, urge **05** thing, yearn **06** desire, hunger **07** craving, longing, passion **08** yearning **09** hankering

**yeoman**
**04** exon **07** goodman **09** beefeater

**yes**
**01** I **02** ay, OK **03** aye, yah, yea, yep **04** okay, ou ay, sure, yeah **05** jokol, quite, right, uh-huh, yokul **06** agreed, and how, indeed, ja wohl, rather

07 quite so 08 all right, of course, very well 09 certainly 10 absolutely, by all means, definitely 11 affirmative

**yes-man**
05 toady 06 lackey, minion 07 crawler 09 sycophant, toad-eater 10 bootlicker

**yet**
03 but, now, too 04 also, even 05 as yet, by now, howbe, so far, still 06 anyway, by then, even so 07 already, besides, further, howbeit, however, thus far 08 hitherto, moreover, until now 09 up till now 10 all the same, for all that, heretofore, in addition, up till then 11 furthermore, just the same, nonetheless 12 nevertheless, up to this time 14 into the bargain 15 notwithstanding

**• as yet**
05 so far 07 thus far, till now, up to now 08 hitherto 13 up to this point

**yield**
◇ *anagram indicator*
03 bow, net, pan, pay, sag 04 bear, bend, cede, crop, duck, earn, fall, give, haul, meal, vail 05 admit, agree, allow, defer, fetch, forgo, grant, gross, repay 06 accede, accord, afford, cave in, comply, forego, give in, give up, income, output, permit, profit, render, resign, return, reward, submit, supply 07 abandon, bring in, concede, consent, deliver, furnish, give out, give way, harvest, produce, product, provide, revenue, succumb, takings 08 abdicate, earnings, fructify, generate, give over, part with, proceeds, renounce 09 acquiesce, fructuate, give place, surrender 10 bring forth, capitulate, give ground, knock under, relinquish 11 admit defeat, go along with 12 knuckle under 14 resign yourself 15 throw in the towel

**yielding**
◇ *anagram indicator*
04 easy, give, soft 05 buxom 06 facile, flabby, pliant, quaggy, spongy, supple 07 ductile, elastic, pliable, springy 08 amenable, biddable, flexible, obedient, obliging 09 compliant, complying, resilient, tractable 10 compliance, submissive 11 acquiescent, complaisant, unresisting 13 accommodating

**yob, yobbo**
03 hob, lob, oaf, oik 04 boor, calf, clod, coof, cuif, dolt, gawk, hick, hoon, jake, lout, slob, swad 05 yahoo, yobbo 06 lubber 07 bumpkin, hallion, lumpkin 08 bull-calf, loblolly 09 barbarian, lager lout, roughneck 10 clodhopper 11 chuckle-head, hobbledehoy

**yobbish**
04 rude 05 crude, gawky, gruff, rough 06 coarse, oafish, rustic, vulgar 07 boorish, doltish, ill-bred, loutish, uncouth 08 bungling, churlish, ignorant, impolite 09 unrefined 10 uneducated, unmannerly 11 clodhopping, ill-mannered, uncivilized

**yobbo** *see* **yob, yobbo**

**yoke**
03 bow, tie 04 bond, join, link, span, team, tool 05 hitch, thing, union, unite 06 burden, couple, halter, inspan, object, square 07 bondage, bracket, connect, enslave, harness, slavery, tyranny 08 coupling 09 servility, servitude 10 oppression 11 enslavement, subjugation

**yokel**
04 boor, hick, jake, Jock, rube 06 joskin, rustic 07 bucolic, hayseed, peasant 09 hillbilly 10 clodhopper 13 country cousin 14 country bumpkin

**you**
01 U 02 du, tu 03 Sie 04 thee, vous

**• you and me**
02 us, we

**young**
03 fry, kid, new 04 baby 05 brood, early, green, issue, jeune, small 06 babies, family, infant, junior, litter, little, recent, youthy 07 ageless, growing, progeny, teenage, youthly 08 childish, children, immature, juvenile, under age, vigorous, youthful 09 beardless, childlike, fledgling, miniature, offspring, unfledged 10 adolescent, fledgeling, little ones 11 undeveloped 13 inexperienced 15 in the first flush

*See also* **animal**

**younger**
02 yr 04 less 05 chota 06 junior 10 latter-born

**youngster**
03 boy, cub, kid, lad, tot 04 brat, girl, gyte, lass, teen, tyke, wean 05 bairn, bimbo, child, smout, sprog, youth 06 nipper, rug rat, shaver 07 hellion, protegé, subteen, tiny tot, toddler, young 'un 08 teenager, young man 10 adolescent, ankle-biter, knave-bairn, young adult, young woman 11 young person

**your**
02 yr 03 thy

**• yours**
05 thine

**• yours truly**
02 me 06 myself 09 tout à vous

**youth**
03 boy, kid, lad 04 colt, lout, lowt, page, teen, yoof 05 child, prime, teens 06 Adonis, childe, chylde, gunsel, infant, keelie, kipper, spring 07 boyhood, homeboy, juvenal, May-lord 08 calf-time, girlhood, homegirl, juvenile, springal, teenager, the young, young man 09 childhood, freshness, greenhorn, hot-rodder, lager lout, salad days, springald, stripling, youngster 10 adolescent, immaturity, recentness, young adult 11 adolescence, hobbledehoy, leaping-time, teeny-bopper, young people 12 inexperience, teenage years

**youthful**
04 spry 05 fresh, young 06 active, boyish, lively, tender, vernal 07 buoyant, girlish 08 blooming, childish, immature, juvenile, vigorous 09 sprightly, youngling, youngthly 13 inexperienced, well-preserved 14 bread-and-butter 15 in the first flush

**youthfulness**
06 vigour 08 spryness, vivacity 09 freshness 10 juvenility, liveliness 12 juvenileness 13 sprightliness, vivaciousness

**yowl**
03 bay, cry 04 bawl, howl, wail, yawl, yell, yelp 06 squall 07 screech, ululate 09 caterwaul

**ytterbium**
02 Yb

**yttrium**
01 Y

**yuck**
02 fy 03 yuk 04 itch, yech

**yucky**
04 foul 05 dirty, gross, itchy, messy, mucky 06 filthy, grotty, grungy, sickly 08 horrible 09 revolting 10 disgusting, unpleasant

**Yukon Territory**
02 YT

# Z

**Z**
**03** zed, zee **04** Zulu **06** izzard

**Zambia**
**01** Z **03** RNR, ZMB

**zany**
◇ *anagram indicator*
**03** odd **04** daft **05** crazy, droll, funny, kooky, toady, wacky **06** absurd
**07** amusing, bizarre, comical
**08** clownish, merryman **09** eccentric, screwball, simpleton **10** ridiculous

**Zanzibar**
**03** EAZ

**zap**
**03** hit **04** do in, kill **05** erase, force, shoot **06** rub out, strike **07** bump off, correct, destroy, wipe out **08** vitality
**09** finish off

**zeal**
**04** fire, zest **05** gusto, study, verve
**06** ardour, energy, fervor, spirit, vigour, warmth **07** bigotry, fervour, passion
**08** devotion, keenness **09** eagerness, intensity, vehemence, zelotypia
**10** commitment, dedication, enthusiasm, fanaticism **11** earnestness
**12** propagandism

**zealot**
**05** bigot **07** fanatic, radical, zealant
**08** militant, partisan **09** extremist
**10** enthusiast **11** eager beaver

**zealous**
**04** keen, warm **05** eager, fiery
**06** ardent, fervid, gung-ho, stanch
**07** bigoted, burning, devoted, diehard, earnest, fervent, intense, staunch
**08** militant, spirited **09** committed, dedicated, fanatical, strenuous
**10** passionate **11** impassioned, true-devoted **12** enthusiastic, wholehearted **14** enthusiastical

**zealously**
**06** keenly **07** eagerly **08** ardently
**09** earnestly, fervently, instantly, staunchly **11** fanatically
**12** passionately

**zenith**
**01** z **03** top **04** acme, apex, peak
**06** apogee, climax, height, summit, vertex **07** optimum **08** meridian, pinnacle **09** high point **11** culmination
**12** highest point

**zero**
**01** O, z **03** nil, zip **04** blob, duck, love, null **05** nadir, zilch, zippo **06** bottom, cipher, cypher, naught, nought
**07** nothing **08** duck's egg, goose-egg
**12** absolute zero

• **zero in on**
**05** fix on **06** aim for **07** focus on, head for, level at, train on **08** centre on, direct at, home in on, pinpoint
**10** converge on **13** concentrate on

**zest**
**04** husk, peel, rind, rine, skin, tang, zeal, zing **05** crust, gusto, shell, spice, taste **06** relish, savour, vigour **07** epicarp, flavour **08** appetite, interest, keenness, piquancy **09** eagerness, enjoyment
**10** enthusiasm, exuberance, integument, liveliness **11** joie de vivre

**Zeus**
**07** Jupiter

**zigzag**
**03** yaw **04** tack, wind **05** curve, snake, twist **07** crooked, meander, sinuous, vandyke, winding **08** indented, traverse, twisting **10** meandering, serpentine **14** crinkle-crankle

**Zimbabwe**
**02** ZW **03** ZWE

**zinc**
**02** Zn

**zing**
**02** go **03** pep, zip **04** brio, dash, élan, life, zest **05** oomph, punch, scorn
**06** energy, spirit, vigour **07** pizzazz, sparkle **08** vitality **09** animation, criticize **10** enthusiasm, get-up-and-go, liveliness **11** joie de vivre

**zip**
**01** O **02** go **03** fly, pep **04** belt, dash, élan, life, pelt, race, rush, tear, whiz, zero, zest, zing, zoom **05** drive, flash, gusto, hurry, oomph, punch, scoot, shoot, speed, verve, vroom, whisk, whizz **06** energy, spirit, vigour, whoosh **07** nothing, pizzazz, sparkle
**08** vitality **10** enthusiasm, get-up-and-go, liveliness **13** slide fastener

*See also* **United States of America**

**zirconium**
**02** Zr

**zither**
**06** cither **07** cithern, cittern, kantela, kantele **08** autoharp

**zodiac**
**04** year **07** baldric **08** baldrick
**09** baudricke

*Zodiac signs:*

**03** Leo, Ram
**04** Bull, Crab, Fish, Goat, Lion
**05** Aries, Libra, Twins, Virgo
**06** Archer, Cancer, Gemini, Pisces, Scales, Taurus, Virgin
**07** Balance, Scorpio
**08** Aquarius, Scorpion
**09** Capricorn
**11** Sagittarius, Water-bearer
**12** Water-carrier

**zone**
**01** z **04** area, belt, zona **05** tract **06** girdle, region, sector, sphere **07** section, stratum **08** district, province **09** territory

**zoo**
**06** aviary **08** aquarium **09** menagerie
**10** animal park, safari park
**14** zoological park

**zoology**

*Branches of zoology include:*

**07** ecology, zoonomy, zootaxy
**08** cetology, oecology
**09** acarology, hippology, mammalogy, ophiology, therology
**10** autecology, conchology, embryology, entomology, limacology, malacology, morphology, nematology
**11** arachnology, herpetology, ichthyology, insectology, myrmecology, ornithology
**12** gnotobiology, parasitology, protozoology, zoopathology
**13** helminthology, neuroethology, palaeozoology, zoophysiology
**14** archaeozoology
**15** lepidopterology

*Zoologists include:*

**03** **Pye** (John David)
**04** **Beer** (Sir Gavin Rylands de), **Mayr** (Ernst Walter), **Owen** (Savi)
**05** **Fabre** (Jean Henri), **Hubel** (David Hunter), **Krebs** (Sir John), **Krogh** (August), **Kühne** (Wilhelm)
**06** **Darwin** (Charles), **Flower** (Sir William Henry), **Frisch** (Karl von), **Kinsey** (Alfred), **Lorenz** (Konrad Zacharias), **Morris** (Desmond John), **Müller** (Johannes Peter), **Newton** (Alfred), **Pavlov** (Ivan)
**07** **Agassiz** (Louis), **Audubon** (John James), **Dawkins** (Richard), **Durrell** (Gerald), **Galvani** (Luigi), **Hodgkin** (Sir Alan Lloyd), **Mantell** (Gideon Algernon), **Medawar** (Sir Peter Brian), **Wallace** (Alfred Russel)
**08** **Hamilton** (William Donald), **Linnaeus** (Carolus)
**09** **Aristotle**, **Schaudinn** (Fritz

Richard), **Tinbergen** (Nikolaas)
**10** **Kettlewell** (Henry Bernard David)
**11** **Sherrington** (Sir Charles Scott)
**12** **Wigglesworth** (Sir Vincent Brian), **Wynne-Edwards** (Vero Copner)

**zoom**

**03** fly, zap, zip **04** belt, buzz, dash, dive, pelt, race, rush, soar, tear, whiz **05** flash, shoot, speed, vroom, whirl **06** hurtle, streak **08** go all out

**zulu**

**01** Z

• **Zulu warriors**

**04** impi